REFERENCE MATERIAL

D1107454

Cottage Grove Public Library
700 E Gibbs Ave
Cottage Grove OR 97424

THE
MOTION PICTURE
GUIDE

THE MOTION PICTURE GUIDE

L - M

1927-1983

Jay Robert Nash
Stanley Ralph Ross

CINEBOOKS, INC.
Chicago, 1986
Publishers of THE COMPLETE FILM RESOURCE CENTER

Ref
791.43
Motion
v.5

Publishers: Jay Robert Nash, Stanley Ralph Ross; **Editor-in-Chief:** Jay Robert Nash; **Executive Editor:** Stanley Ralph Ross; **Associate Publisher and Director of Development:** Kenneth H. Petchenik; **Senior Editor-in-Charge:** Jim McCormick; **Senior Editors:** David Tardy, Robert B. Connelly; **Production Editor:** William Leahy; **Associate Editors:** Oksana Lydia Creighton, Jeffrey H. Wallenfeldt, Edie McCormick, Michaela Tuohy, Jeannette Hori, Tom Legge; **Contributing Editors:** James J. Mulay (Chief Contributing Editor), Daniel Curran, Michael Theobald, Arnie Bernstein, Phil Pantone, Brian Brock; **Assistant Editors:** Debra Schwieder, Susan Fisher, Donna Roth, Marla Kruglik, Kristina Marcy, Sarah von Fremd, Wendy Anderson; **Art Production and Book Design:** Cathy Anetsberger; **Research Staff:** Shelby Payne (Associate Editor and Chief Researcher), William C. Clogston, Tobi Elliott, Carol Pappas, Rosalyn Mathis, Millicent Mathis, Andrea Nash; **Business/Legal:** Judy Anetsberger.

Associate Publishers: Howard Grafman, Lynn Christian, James and Monica Vrettos, Antoinette Mailliard, Brent H. Nettle, Michael Callie, Constance Shea, Barbara Browne Cramer.

Editorial and Sales Offices: CINEBOOKS, 6135 N. Sheridan Road, Chicago, Illinois 60660.

Copyright © 1986, CINEBOOKS, INC.

All rights reserved; no part of this book or subsequent volumes of THE MOTION PICTURE GUIDE may be reproduced or utilized in any form or by any means, electronic or mechanical, including photocopying, recording or by any information storage and retrieval system, without permission in writing from the Publisher. Inquiries should be addressed to CINEBOOKS, INC., 6135 N. Sheridan Road, Chicago, Illinois 60660.

Library of Congress Catalog Card Number: 85-071145
ISBN: 0-933997-00-0 THE MOTION PICTURE GUIDE (10 Vols.)
      0-933997-05-1 THE MOTION PICTURE GUIDE, Vol V (L-M)

Printed in the United States
First Edition
This volume contains 4,331 entries.

1 2 3 4 5 6 7 8 9 10

JUL 20 '88

THIS VOLUME IS DEDICATED TO
FRANK CAPRA
MICHAEL CURTIZ
HOWARD HAWKS
ALFRED HITCHCOCK
JOHN HUSTON
FRITZ LANG
LEWIS MILESTONE
KING VIDOR
RAOUL WALSH
WILLIAM WELLMAN
ORSON WELLES
WILLIAM WYLER

HOW TO USE INFORMATION IN THIS GUIDE

ALPHABETICAL ORDER

All entries have been arranged alphabetically throughout this and all subsequent volumes. In establishing alphabetical order, all articles (A, An, The) appear after the main title (AFFAIR TO REMEMBER, AN). In the case of foreign films the article precedes the main title (LES MISERABLES appears in the letter L) which makes, we feel, for easier access and uniformity. Contractions are grouped together and these will be followed by non-apostrophized words of the same letters. B.F.'s DAUGHTER is at the beginning of the letter B, not under BF.

TITLES

It is important to know what title you are seeking; use the *complete* title of the film. The film ADVENTURES OF ROBIN HOOD, THE, cannot be found under merely ROBIN HOOD. Many films are known under different titles and we have taken great pains to cross-reference these titles. (AKA, also known as) as well as alternate titles used in Great Britain (GB). In addition to the cross-reference title only entries, AKAs and alternate titles in Great Britain can be found in the title line for each entry. An alphabetically arranged comprehensive list of title changes appears in the Index volume (Vol. X).

RATINGS

We have rated each and every film at critical levels that include acting, directing, script, and technical achievement (or the sad lack of it). We have a *five-star* rating, unlike all other rating systems, to signify a film superbly made on every level, in short, a masterpiece. At the lowest end of the scale is *zero* and we mean it. The ratings are as follows: *zero* (not worth a glance), *(poor), **(fair), ***(good), ****(excellent), *****(masterpiece, and these are few and far between). Half-marks mean almost there but not quite.

YEAR OF RELEASE

We have used in all applicable instances the year of United States release. This sometimes means that a film released abroad may have a different date elsewhere than in these volumes but this is generally the date released in foreign countries, not in the U.S.

FOREIGN COUNTRY PRODUCTION

When possible, we have listed abbreviated names of the foreign countries originating the production of a film. This information will be found within the parenthesis containing the year of release. If no country is listed in this space, it is a U.S. production.

RUNNING TIME

A hotly debated category, we have opted to list the running time a film ran at the time of its initial U.S. release but we will usually mention in the text if the film was drastically cut and give the reasons why. We have attempted to be as accurate as possible by consulting the most reliable sources.

PRODUCING AND DISTRIBUTING COMPANIES

The producing and/or distributing company of every film is listed in abbreviated entries next to the running time in the title line (see abbreviations; for all those firms not abbreviated, the entire firm's name will be present).

COLOR OR BLACK-AND-WHITE

The use of color or black-and-white availability appears as c or bw following the producing/releasing company entry.

CASTS

Whenever possible, we give *the complete cast and the roles played* for each film and this is the case in 95% of all entries, the only encyclopedia to ever offer such comprehensive information in covering the entire field. The names of actors and actresses are in Roman lettering, the names of the roles each played in Italic inside parentheses.

SYNOPSIS

The in-depth synopsis for each entry (when such applies) offers the plot of each film, critical evaluation, anecdotal information on the production and its personnel, awards won when applicable and additional information dealing with the production's impact upon the public, its success or failure at the box office, its social significance, if any. Acting methods, technical innovations, script originality are detailed. We also cite other productions involving an entry's personnel for critical comparisons and to establish the style or genre of expertise of directors, writers, actors and technical people.

REMAKES AND SEQUELS

Information regarding films that have sequels, sequels themselves or direct remakes of films can be found at the very end of each synopsis.

DUBBING AND SUBTITLES

We will generally point out in the synopsis when a foreign film is dubbed in English, mostly when the dubbing is poor. When voices are dubbed, particularly when singers render vocals on songs mimed by stars, we generally point out these facts either in the cast/role listing or inside the synopsis. If a film is in a foreign language and subtitled, we signify the fact in a parenthetical statement at the end of each entry (In Italian, English subtitles).

CREDITS

The credits for the creative and technical personnel of a film are extensive and they include: p (producer, often executive producer); d (director); w (screenwriter, followed by adaptation, if any, and creator of original story, if any, and other sources such as authors for plays, articles, short stories, novels and non-fiction books); ph (cinematographer, followed by camera system and color process when applicable, i.e., Panavision, Technicolor); m (composer of musical score); ed (film editor); md (music director); art d (art director); set d (set decoration); cos (costumes); spec eff (special effects); ch (choreography); m/l (music and lyrics); stunts, makeup, and other credits when merited. When someone receives two or more credits in a single film the credits may be combined (p&d, John Ford) or the last name repeated in subsequent credits shared with another (d, John Ford; w. Ford, Dudley Nichols).

GENRES/SUBJECT

Each film is categorized for easy identification as to genre and/or subject and themes at the left-hand bottom of each entry. (Western, Prison Drama, Spy Drama, Romance, Musical, Comedy, War, Horror, Science-Fiction, Adventure, Biography, Historical Drama, Children's Film, Animated Feature, etc.) More specific subject and theme breakdowns will be found in the Index (Vol. X).

PR AND MPAA RATINGS

The Parental Recommendation provides parents having no knowledge of the style and content of each film with a guide; if a film has excessive violence, sex, strong language, it is so indicated. Otherwise, films specifically designed for young children are also indicated. The Parental Recommendation (**PR**) is to be found at the right-hand bottom of each entry, followed, when applicable, by the **MPAA** rating. The PR ratings are as follows: **AAA** (must for children); **AA** (good for children); **A** (acceptable for children); **C** (cautionary, some objectionable scenes); **O** (completely objectionable for children).

KEY TO ABBREVIATIONS

Foreign Countries:

Arg.	Argentina
Aus.	Australia
Aust.	Austria
Bel.	Belgium
Braz.	Brazil
Brit.	Great Britain (GB when used for alternate title)
Can.	Canada
Chi.	China
Czech.	Czechoslovakia
Den.	Denmark
E. Ger.	East Germany
Fin.	Finland
Fr.	France
Ger.	Germany (includes W. Germany)
Gr.	Greece
Hung.	Hungary
Ital.	Italy
Jap.	Japan
Mex.	Mexico
Neth.	Netherlands
Phil.	Philippines
Pol.	Poland
Rum.	Rumania
S.K.	South Korea
Span.	Spain
Swed.	Sweden

Key to Abbreviations (continued)

Switz.	Switzerland
Thai.	Thailand
USSR	Union of Soviet Socialist Republics
Yugo.	Yugoslavia

Production Companies, Studios and Distributors (U.S. and British)

AA	ALLIED ARTISTS
ABF	Associated British Films
AE	Avco Embassy
AEX	Associated Exhibitors
AH	Anglo-Hollandia
AIP	American International Pictures
AM	American
ANCH	Anchor Film Distributors
ANE	American National Enterprises
AP	Associated Producers
AP&D	Associated Producers & Distributors
ARC	Associated Releasing Corp.
Argosy	Argosy Productions
Arrow	Arrow Films
ART	Artcraft
Astra	Astra Films
AY	Aywon
BA	British Actors
B&C	British and Colonial Kinematograph Co.
BAN	Banner Films
BI	British Instructional
BIFD	B.I.F.D. Films
BIP	British International Pictures
BJP	Buck Jones Productions
BL	British Lion
Blackpool	Blackpool Productions
BLUE	Bluebird
BN	British National
BNF	British and Foreign Film
Boulting	Boulting Brothers (Brit.)
BP	British Photoplay Production
BPP	B.P. Productions
BRIT	Britannia Films
BRO	Broadwest
Bryanston	Bryantston Films (Brit.)
BS	Blue Streak
BUS	Bushey (Brit.)
BUT	Butchers Film Service
BV	Buena Vista (Walt Disney)
CAP	Capital Films
CC	Christie Comedy
CD	Continental Distributing
CHAD	Chadwick Pictures Corporation
CHES	Chesterfield
Cineguild	Cineguild
CL	Clarendon
CLIN	Clinton
COL	COLUMBIA
Colony	Colony Pictures
COM	Commonwealth
COMM	Commodore Pictures
COS	Cosmopolitan (Hearst)
DE	Dependable Exchange
DGP	Dorothy Gish Productions
Disney	Walt Disney Productions
DIST	Distinctive
DM	DeMille Productions
DOUB	Doubleday
EAL	Ealing Studios (Brit.)
ECF	East Coast Films
ECL	Eclectic
ED	Eldorado
EF	Eagle Films
EFF & EFF	E.F.F. & E.F.F. Comedy
EFI	English Films Inc.
EIFC	Export and Import Film Corp.
EL	Eagle-Lion
EM	Embassy Pictures Corp.

EMI	EMI Productions
EP	Enterprise Pictures
EPC	Equity Pictures Corp.
EQ	Equitable
EXCEL	Excellent
FA	Fine Arts
FC	Film Classics
FD	First Division
FN	First National
FOX	20TH CENTURY FOX (and Fox Productions)
FP	Famous Players (and Famous Players Lasky)
FRP	Frontroom Productions
Gainsborough	Gainsborough Productions
GAU	Gaumont (Brit.)
GEN	General
GFD	General Films Distributors
Goldwyn	Samuel Goldwyn Productions
GN	Grand National
GOTH	Gotham
Grafton	Grafton Films (Brit.)
H	Harma
HAE	Harma Associated Distributors
Hammer	Hammer Films (Brit.)
HD	Hagen and Double
HM	Hi Mark
HR	Hal Roach
IA	International Artists
ID	Ideal
IF	Independent Film Distributors (Brit.)
Imperator	Imperator Films (Brit.)
IP	Independent Pictures Corp.
IN	Invincible Films
INSP	Inspirational Pictures (Richard Barthelmess)
IV	Ivan Film
Javelin	Javelin Film Productions (Brit.)
JUR	Jury
KC	Kinema Club
KCB	Kay C. Booking
Knightsbridge	Knightsbridge Productions (Brit.)
Korda	Alexander Korda Productions (Brit.)
Ladd	Ladd Company Productions
LAS	Lasky Productions (Jesse L. Lasky)
LFP	London Films
LIP	London Independent Producers
Lorimar	Lorimar Productions
LUM	Lumis
Majestic	Majestic Films
Mascot	Mascot Films
Mayflowers	Mayflowers Productions (Brit.)
Metro	Metro
MFC	Mission Film Corporation
MG	Metro-Goldwyn
MGM	METRO-GOLDWYN-MAYER
MON	Monogram
MOR	Morante
MS	Mack Sennett
MUT	Mutual
N	National
NG	National General
NGP	National General Pictures (Alexander Korda, Brit.)
NW	New World
Orion	Orion Productions
Ortus	Ortus Productions (Brit.)
PAR	PARAMOUNT
Pascal	Gabriel Pascal Productions (Brit.)
PDC	Producers Distributors Corp.

Key to Abbreviations (continued)

PEER	Peerless	Beta	Beta Films (Ger.)
PWN	Peninsula Studios	CA	Cine-Alliance (Fr.)
PFC	Pacific Film Company	Caddy	Caddy Films (Fr.)
PG	Playgoers	CCFC	Compagnie Commerciale Francais Einematographique (Fr.)
PI	Pacific International	CDD	Cino Del Duca (Ital.)
PIO	Pioneer Film Corp.	CEN	Les Films de Centaur (Fr.)
PM	Pall Mall	CFD	Czecheslovak Film Productions
PP	Pro Patria	CHAM	Champion (Ital.)
PRC	Producers Releasing Corporation	Cinegay	Cinegay Films (Ital.)
PRE	Preferred	Cines	Cines Films (Ital.)
		Cineriz	Cinerez Films (Ital.)
QDC	Quality Distributing Corp.	Citel	Citel Films (Switz.)
		Como	Como Films (Fr.)
RAY	Rayart	CON	Concordia (Fr.)
RAD	Radio Pictures	Corona	Corona Films (Fr.)
RANK	J. Arthur Rank (Brit.)		
RBP	Rex Beach Pictures	D	Documento Films (Ital.)
REA	Real Art	DD	Dino De Laurentiis (Ital.)
REG	Regional Films	Dear	Dear Films (Ital.)
REN	Renown	DIF	Discina International Films (Fr.)
REP	Republic	DPR	Films du Palais-Royal (Fr.)
RF	Regal Films		
RFD	R.F.D. Productions (Brit.)	EX	Excelsa Films (Ital.)
RKO	RKO RADIO PICTURES		
Rogell	Rogell	FDP	Films du Pantheon (Fr.)
Romulus	Romulus Films (Brit.)	Fono	Fono Roma (Ital.)
Royal	Royal	FS	Filmsonor Productions (Fr.)
SB	Samuel Bronston	Gala	Fala Films (Ital.)
SCHUL	B.P. Schulberg Productions	Galatea	Galatea Productions (Ital.)
SEL	Select	Gamma	Gamma Films (Fr.)
SELZ	Selznick International (David O. Selznick)	Gemma	Gemma Cinematografica (Ital.)
SF	Selznick Films	GFD	General Film Distributors, Ltd. (Can.)
SL	Sol Lesser	GP	General Productions (Fr.)
SONO	Sonofilms	Gray	(Gray Films (Fr.)
SP	Seven Pines Productions (Brit.)		
SRP	St. Regis Pictures	IFD	Intercontinental Film Distributors
STER	Sterling		
STOLL	Stoll	Janus	Janus Films (Ger.)
SUN	Sunset	JMR	Macques Mage Releasing (Fr.)
SYN	Syndicate Releasing Co.		
SZ	Sam Zimbalist	LF	Les Louvre Films (Fr.)
		LFM	Les Films Moliere (Fr.)
TC	Two Cities (Brit.)	Lux	Lux Productions (Ital.)
T/C	Trem-Carr		
THI	Thomas H. Ince	Melville	Melville Productions (Fr.)
TIF	Tiffany	Midega	Midega Films (Span.)
TRA	Transatlantic Pictures		
TRU	Truart	NEF	N.E.F. La Nouvelle Edition Francaise (Fr.)
TS	Tiffany/Stahl	NFD	N.F.D. Productions (Ger.)
UA	UNITED ARTISTS	ONCIC	Office National pour le Commerce et L'Industrie Cinematographique (Fr.)
UNIV	UNIVERSAL (AND UNIVERSAL INTERNATIONAL)	Ortus	Ortus Films (Can.)
Venture	Venture Distributors	PAC	Production Artistique Cinematographique (Fr.)
VIT	Vitagraph	Pagnol	Marcel Pagnol Productions (Fr.)
		Parc	Parc Films (Fr.)
WAL	Waldorf	Paris	Paris Films (Fr.)
WB	WARNER BROTHERS (AND WARNER BROTHERS-SEVEN ARTS)	Pathe	Pathe Films (Fr.)
		PECF	Productions et Editions Cinematographique Francais (Fr.)
WEST	Westminster	PF	Parafrench Releasing Co. (Fr.)
WF	Woodfall Productions (Brit.)	PIC	Produzione International Cinematografica (Ital.)
WI	Wisteria	Ponti	Carlo Ponti Productions (Ital.)
WORLD	World		
WSHP	William S. Hart Productions	RAC	Realisation d'Art Cinematographique (Fr.)
		Regina	Regina Films (Fr.)
ZUKOR	Adolph Zukor Productions	Renn	Renn Productions (Fr.)
		SDFS	Societe des Films Sonores Tobis (Fr.)
Foreign		SEDIF	Societe d'Exploitation ed de Distribution de Films (Fr.)
ABSF	AB Svensk Film Industries (Swed.)	SFP	Societe Francais de Production (Fr.)
Action	Action Films (Fr.)	Sigma	Sigma Productions (Fr.)
ADP	Agnes Delahaie Productions (Fr.)	SNE	Societe Nouvelle des Establishments (Fr.)
Agata	Agata Films (Span.)		
Alter	Alter Films (Fr.)	Titanus	Titanus Productions (Ital.)
Arch	Archway Film Distributors	TRC	Transcontinental Films (Fr.)
Argos	Argos Films (Fr.)		
Argui	Argui Films (Fr.)	UDIF	U.D.I.F. Productions (Fr.)
Ariane	Les Films Ariane (Fr.)	UFA	Deutsche Universum-Film AG (Ger.)
Athos	Athos Films (Fr.)	UGC	Union Generale Cinematographique (Fr.)
		Union	Union Films (Ger.)
Belga	Belga Films (Bel.)		
		Vera	Vera Productions (Fr.)

L

L-SHAPED ROOM, THE****

(1962, Brit.) 142m Romulus/Davis-Royal-COL bw

Leslie Caron (Jane Fosset), Anthony Booth (Youth in Street), Avis Bunnage (Doris), Patricia Phoenix (Sonia), Verity Edmett (Jane II), Tom Bell (Toby), Cicely Courtneidge (Mavis), Harry Locke (News Agent), Ellen Dryden (Girl in News Agent's), Emlyn Williams (Dr. Weaver), Jenny White (Monica), Brock Peters (Johnny), Gerry Duggan (Bert), Joan Ingram (Woman in Park), Mark Eden (Terry), Stanley Morgan (Waiter in Club), Gerald Sim (Doctor In Hospital), Pamela Sholto, Ruth Burns, Diane Clare (Nurses), Arthur White (Milkman), Bernard Lee (Charlie), Nanette Newman (Girl at End), Kay Walsh (Prostitute).

An excellent, albeit talky, drama with enough comedy to leaven the heaviness. Caron is a late-twenties-aged French woman who departs her home in the provinces and moves to London. She spends a sexual weekend and gets pregnant. Rather than have an abortion, she decides to have the baby after meeting a money-hungry gynecologist in London's famed Harley Street (Williams). By this time, she's moved to a sleazy boarding house in Notting Hill Gate and occupies the small L-shaped room of the title. The house is filled with characters and she soon falls for Bell, an out-of-work writer. Since everyone in the small hotel knows everyone else, Caron's and Bell's affair is the main topic of conversation and the tenants are thrilled by what's transpiring. The other people who live there, actresses, hookers, et al, are sentimental about the love that's flourishing but Bell's best friend, Peters, is incensed. He's a jazz musician with a conservative streak and when he learns that Caron is pregnant (not by Bell), he tells Bell in an attempt to split the two. Bell is angered and leaves Caron, who responds by taking some "abortion pills" given to her by Courtneidge, an aging actress who occupies a room below Caron's. The pills fail to work and Caron is actually relieved. Bell returns but cannot accept the fact that Caron is having a baby by someone else. Caron goes to the hospital to have the child and Bell arrives with a copy of a story he's written about their situation. It's called "The L-Shaped Room." Caron returns to France and leaves the story in Bell's room with a note attached to it saying that "it's a lovely story but it has no end." That's basically what's wrong with the movie. What's right with the film is that we are made to care deeply about Caron and Bell and all the others, and for that alone, we want them to succeed. It's a character piece with many sidetracks and incidents and no singular thrust to the story, but Forbes and company do it so well that we must believe the ancient adage "If you like the people, you'll like the movie." In treatment, this film is very much like a British version of a Chayefsky story, MARTY or THE BACHELOR PARTY or MIDDLE OF THE NIGHT. Forbes has seldom done better work. All secondary roles are well cast, particularly Lee (who was M in all the Bond movies) and Bunnage, as the landlady in the boarding house. Music includes "Piano Concerto No. 1" by Johannes Brahms, performed by Peter Katin.

p, James Woolf, Richard Attenborough; d&w, Bryan Forbes (based on the novel The L-Shaped Room by Lynne Reid Banks); ph, Douglas Slocombe; m, John Barry; ed, Anthony Harvey; art d, Ray Simm; cos, Beatrice Dawson; makeup, Harry Frampton.

Drama   (PR:C   MPAA:NR)

LA BABY SITTER**

(1975, Fr./Ital./Ger.) 110m Cite-Champion-TIT/SNC c (AKA: BABYSITTER)

Maria Schneider (Michele), Sydne Rome (Ann), Robert Vaughn (Star), Vic Morrow (Stunt Man), Nadja Tiller (Lotte), Carl Mohner (Franklin), John Whittington (Boots), Renato Pozzetto (Gianni).

Maria Schneider costars with Rome as a pair involved in the kidnaping of the child of Rome's wealthy ex-lover. Most of the picture is pretty one-dimensional, though Schneider does give a riveting performance as she did in Michelangelo Antonioni's THE PASSENGER (1975), released the same year. This picture also shares the same screenwriter (Peploe) and producer (Ponti) as THE PASSENGER.

p, Carlo Ponti; d, Rene Clement; w, Clement, Mark Peploe, Luciano Vincenzano, Nicolas Badalucca; ph, Alberto Spagnoli (Eastmancolor); m, Francis Lai; ed, C. Lack.

Crime/Drama   (PR:O   MPAA:NR)

LA BAI DES ANGES   (SEE: BAY OF ANGELS, 1964, Fr.)

LA BALANCE**½

(1983, Fr.) 102m Les Films Ariane-Films A2-Spectrafilm/Gala c (AKA: THE NARK)

Nathalie Baye (Nicole), Philippe Leotard (Dede), Richard Berry (Palouzi), Christophe Malavoy (Tintin), Jean-Paul Connart (Le Belge), Bernard Freyd (Le Capitaine), Albert Dray (Carlini), Florent Pagny (Simoni), Jean-Daniel Laval (Arnaud), Luc-Antoine Diquero (Picard), Maurice Ronet (Massina), Tcheky Karyo (Petrovic), Anne-Claude Salimo (Sabrina), Michel Anphoux (Guy), Raouf Ben Yaghlane (Djerbi), Robert Atlan (Ayouche), Guy Dhers (Calemard), Francois Berleand (Inspecteur Mondaine), Sam Karmann (Paulo), Galia Dujardin, Andrey Laxinni, Fiorella de Gennaro, Claude Villers, Mostefa, Zerguine, Marc Ballis, Patrick Guillaume.

American director Bob Swaim brought the gangster style with an authentic touch to France and gave Parisians just what they wanted. It's a power game played by one-time mobster Leotard and prostitute Baye, and the cops who try to pressure them into informing. There are some nice moments—a colorful opening sequence and an unlikely traffic jam shootout which results in someone getting a bullet in the Walkman—but it just adds up to some Saturday night entertainment without much

thought. The Parisians' love for this picture came in the form of numerous Cesars, including one for Best Picture. (In French; English subtitles.)

p, Georges Dancigers, Alexandre Mnouchkine; d, Bob Swaim; w, Swaim, M. Fabiani; ph, Bernard Zitzermann (Eastmancolor); m, Roland Bocquet; ed, Francoise Javet; art d, Eric Moulard; cos, Catherine Meurisse; m/l, Bocquet, Boris Bergman.

Crime Drama   Cas.   (PR:O   MPAA:R)

LA BATAILLE DU RAIL   (SEE: BATTLE OF THE RAILS, 1949, Fr.)

LA BEAUTE DU DIABLE   (SEE: BEAUTY AND THE DEVIL, 1952, Fr.)

LA BELLA MUGNAIA   (SEE: MILLER'S WIFE, THE, 1955, Ital.)

LA BELLE AMERICAINE***

(1961, Fr.) 100m Film D'Art-Panorama-Corflor/CD bw (AKA: AMERICAN BEAUTY, THE)

Robert Dhery (Marcel), Colette Brosset (Paulette), Alfred Adam (Alfred), Louis De Funes (Viralot/Police Station Chief), Bernard Lavalette (Minister Of Commerce), Christian Marin (Pierrot), Catherine Sola (Isabelle Zoutin), Robert Rollis (Maurice), Jacques Fabbri (Fatso), Jacques Legras (Riri), Michel Serrault (Chauveau), Annie Ducaux (Mme. Lucanzas), Elaine D'Almeida (Simone), Helene Dieudonne (Granny), Jean Carmet (Tramp), Jacques Charrier (Obliging Motorist), Roger Pierre (Snob In Sports Car), Jean Marc Thibault (Effeminate Young Man), Gilberte Geniat (Mme. Zoutin), Pierre Dac, Robert Burnier, Didier Daix, Robert Destain, Bernard Dheran, Max Favalelli, Maurice Gardett, Jean Richard, Pierre Tchernia, Pepere the dog.

A jovial comedy about a French worker, Dhery (who also wrote and directed), who gets the chance to buy a "beautiful American" Cadillac for $100. The car becomes the envy of his neighbors and employers, the latter of which fire him in their jealousy. The acquisition of the auto leads to a number of comic instances involving the Minister of Commerce, who takes a liking to the car, as well as an occasion in which Dhery and his wife Brosset get locked in the trunk. (In French; English subtitles.)

p, Henri Diamant-Berger, Arthur Lesser; d, Robert Dhery; w, Dhery, Pierre Tchernia, Alfred Adam; ph, Ghislain Cloquet; m, Gerard Calvi; ed, Albert Jurgenson; English subtitles, Herman G. Weinberg.

Comedy   (PR:A   MPAA:NR)

LA BELLE CAPTIVE   (SEE: BEAUTIFUL PRISONER, THE, 1983, Fr.)

LA BELLE EQUIPE   (SEE: THEY WERE FIVE, 1936, Fr.)

LA BELLE ET LA BETE   (SEE: BEAUTY AND THE BEAST, 1947, Fr.)

LA BELLE ET LE CAVALIER

(SEE: MORE THAN A MIRACLE, 1967, Ital./Fr.)

LA BETE HUMAINE***½

(1938, Fr.) 105m Paris/Juno bw (AKA: THE HUMAN BEAST)

Jean Gabin (Jacques Lantier), Simone Simon (Severine), Fernand Ledoux (Roubaud, Severine's husband), Julien Carette (Pecqueux), Blanchette Brunoy (Flore), Jean Renoir (Cabuche, the Poacher), Gerard Landry (Dauvergne's Son), Jenny Helia (Philomene), Colette Regis (Victoire), Jacques Berlioz (Grand-Morin), Leon Larive (Grand-Morin's servant), Georges Spanelly (Camy-Lamothe), Emile Genevois, Jacques B. Brunius (Farmhands), Marcel Perez (Lampmaker), Claire Gerard (Traveler), Tony Corteggiani (Supervisor), Guy Decomble (Gate Keeper), Georges Peclet (Railway Worker), Charlotte Clasis (Aunt Phasie), Marceau (Mechanic).

Train engineer Gabin is infatuated with Simon, who is already married. Her husband, Ledoux, fearful that he may be fired, has her plea to his powerful superior and she secures Ledoux's job by offering her body to the man. Ledoux, insane with jealousy, plots to kill his superior, an act witnessed by Gabin. Ledoux then sends Simon to Gabin as a means of ensuring the engineer's silence. Again, Simon's convincing ways lie in her bedroom prowess, resulting in a romance between the pair. Simon tries to persuade Gabin to kill Ledoux, who has not been the same since the murder. Gabin is torn, and in a fit of insanity strangles Simon. He then jumps off a speeding train to his death. Based on the novel by Emile Zola (whose book Nana was also adapted by Renoir in 1926), Renoir took great pains to film the script in a realistic manner. Avoiding the use of sets and rear-screen projection, he secured a short section of train track on which they were allowed to shoot. They attached the lights and camera to the front of the locomotive and behind that had one additional car which served as a dressing room for the actors. At one point, as the train was to pass through a tunnel, cameraman Courant attached the camera to a platform on the side of the locomotive. The train went through the tunnel, knocking the camera into the wall. Considered by some to be Gabin's best performance, he most definitely displays a motivation lacking in Zola's characterization. The cat-like Simon is perfect as the persuasive beauty who drives both Gabin and Ledoux to their destructive deeds. This picture was remade by Fritz Lang as HUMAN DESIRE, which was Lang's second remake of a Renoir film. His first was SCARLET STREET, a remake of LA CHIENNE. Includes the song, "Le P'tit Coeur de Ninon," anonymous Italian song from 1920.

p, Robert Hakim, Raymond Hakim; d&w, Jean Renoir (based on the novel by

Emile Zola); ph, Curt Courant; m, Joseph Kosma; ed, Marguerite Renoir, Suzanne de Troeye; set d, Eugene Lourie.

Drama **Cas.** **(PR:A MPAA:NR)**

LA BISBETICA DOMATA

(SEE: TAMING OF THE SHREW, THE, 1967, U.S./Ital.)

LA BOHEME*½** (1965, Ital.) 107m Cosmotel/WB c

Gianni Raimondi *(Rodolfo)*, Mirella Freni *(Mimi)*, Rolando Panerai *(Marcello)*, Gianni Maffeo *(Schnaunard)*, Ivo Vinco *(Colline)*, Adriana Martino *(Musetta)*, Carlo Badioli *(Benoit)*, Virgilio Carbonari *(Alcindoro)*, Franco Ricciardi *(Parpignol)*, Giuseppe Morresi *(Sergeant)*, Carlo Forti *(Customs Official)*, Angelo Mercuriali *(Salesman)*, Orchestra and Chorus of La Scala, Milan.

Zeffirelli more than successfully brings his stage production of Giacomo Puccini's famed opera to the screen. This picture has everything—beautiful photography, awesome sets, and a genius score. Often called one of the best filmings of opera ever made. The La Scala Orchestra of Milan was conducted by celebrated composer Herbert von Karajan.

p, Herbert von Karajan; d, Franco Zeffirelli (based on the novel *Scenes De La Vie De Boheme* by Henri Murger, and from the opera by Giuseppe Giacosa and Lugi Illica); ph, Werner Krein (Technicolor); m, Giacomo Puccini; ed, Alice Seedorf; prod d, Zeffirelli; cos, Marcel Escoffier.

Opera **(PR:A MPAA:NR)**

LA BONNE SOUPE**

(1964, Fr./Ital.) 97m Belstar Productions-Les Films du Siecle-Dear Film/International Classics bw (AKA: CARELESS LOVE; THE GOOD SOUP)

Annie Girardot *(Young Marie-Paule)*, Marie Bell *(Older Marie-Paule)*, Gerard Blain *(Painter)*, Bernard Blier *(Monsieur Joseph)*, Jean-Claude Brialy *(Jacquot)*, Blanchette Brunoy *(Angele)*, Claude Dauphin *(Monsieur Oscar)*, Sacha Distel *(Roger)*, Daniel Gelin *(Raymond)*, Denise Grey *(Madame Boudard)*, Jane Marken *(Madame Alphonse)*, Christian Marquand *(Lucien Volard)*, Felix Marten *(Odilon)*, Raymond Pellegrin *(Armand)*, Franchot Tone *(Montasi, Jr.)*, Danielle Volle *(Janine)*.

Bell plays a middle-aged woman gambler who relates her life story to a casino croupier during a lapse in the action. Quickly switching to Girardot playing Bell at a younger age, she goes from one situation to another, all a result of her romantic endeavors with a variety of men. In only one affair does she genuinely fall in love, this being with Brialy, a bartender whose life ends in tragedy when he is shot during an attempted robbery of the bar. Girardot/Bell eventually does settle down to a long and devoted marriage that produces a daughter. But this also ends as a result of Bell's succumbing to the seductiveness of the man (Marquand) who was to marry her daughter. LA BONNE SOUPE ends on a rather upbeat note with Bell leaving the gambling casino with millionaire Tone, continuing in the adventurous, romantic ways she had long followed. Episodic treatment hurts the pacing, but the capable performances, particularly of the various men popping in and out, manage to keep the happily hedonistic story interesting.

p, Andre Hakim; d&w, Robert Thomas (based on the play by Felicien Marceau); ph, Roger Hubert; m, Raymond Le Senechal; ed, Henri Taverna; md, Jacques Metehen; art d, Jacques Saulnier; set d, Charles Merangel; cos, Maurice Albray; spec eff, Jean Fouchet; makeup, Lina Gallet.

Drama **(PR:C MPAA:NR)**

LA BOUM½** (1983, Fr.) 108m Triumph c

Claude Brasseur *(Francois)*, Brigitte Fossey *(Francoise)*, Sophie Marceau *(Vic)*, Denise Grey *(Poupette)*, Dominque Lavanant *(Vanessa)*, Bernard Giraudeau *(Eric)*.

Marceau is a 13-year-old French girl who is trying to make it through adolescence despite the shaky relationship of her parents Brasseur and Fossey. Marceau is a pretty, thoroughly watchable young girl but the film's innocent charm gives way to predictable situations. It's overwhelmingly favorable box-office reception led to LA BOUM 2 (released in 1982, a year after LA BOUM's French release), one of only a handful of French sequels. (In French; English subtitles.)

p, Alain Poire; d, Claude Pinoteau; w, Daniele Thompson, Pinoteau; ph, Edmond Sechan; m, Vladimir Cosma; ed, Marie-Joseph Yoyotte; art d, Jacques Bufnoir.

Drama **Cas.** **(PR:A MPAA:PG)**

LA CAGE** (1975, Fr.) 90m Lira-UGC-Parma c

Lino Ventura *(Julien)*, Ingrid Thulin *(Helene)*.

An odd picture to either love or hate about a spiteful but loving ex-wife (Thulin) who is visited by the husband she divorced years earlier (Ventura). Ventura attempts to buy the country house Thulin got as part of the settlement, but is promptly locked in a cage in the cellar. She then confesses her love for him, to which Ventura responds that it was her possessiveness that sent him packing. She obviously hasn't changed much over the years and the audience can't build up much sympathy. It comes as a pleasant surprise when Thulin lets gas fill the house and is inadvertently blown up when a postman (who happens to be carrying her alimony check) drops buy and rings the doorbell. Played, in part, as a comedy, it still leaves much to be desired.

d, Pierre Granier-Deferre; w, Pascal Jardin, Granier-Deferre (based on the play by Jack Jacquine); ph, Walter Wottitz (Eastmancolor); ed, Jean Ravel.

Comedy/Drama **(PR:C MPAA:NR)**

LA CAGE AUX FOLLES****

(1979, Fr./Ital.) 103m Les Productions Artistes Associes-DaMa Produzione SPA/UA c (AKA: THE MAD CAGE; BIRDS OF A FEATHER)

Ugo Tognazzi *(Renato)*, Michel Serrault *(Albin/"Zaza")*, Michel Galabru *(Charrier)*, Claire Maurier *(Simone)*, Remy Laurent *(Laurent)*, Benny Luke *(Jacob)*, Carmen Scarpitta *(Madame Charrier)*, Luisa Maneri *(Andrea)*.

Under less sure hands, this could have wound up as a disaster but Molinaro was able to accurately lens the long-running play (more than seven years) and wring every drop of humor from it. Tognazzi and Serrault have been lovers for more than 20 years. Serrault stars as the lead "drag queen" at La Cage Aux Folles, a Saint Tropez nightclub, and Tognazzi, the more masculine of the two, runs the day-to-day operations of the *boite*. Many years before, Tognazzi took some time off from being gay to father Laurent in a one-night stand. Since then, the two men have raised the boy and he is now coming home from college with the news that he is engaged to marry Maneri, whose father, Galabru, is the secretary of the blue-nosed Union of Moral Order. Therefore, Laurent has lied about his parentage and told Galabru that his father is a cultural attache and that his mother has six children. Galabru is worried that his own reputation may suffer when he learns that the president of the Union has died in bed with an under-age prostitute. His wife, Scarpitta, says that the marriage of their daughter into such as illustrious family as Laurent's will remove any taint of scandal. The apartment where Tognazzi and Serrault live is a riot of colors, very wild, with all sorts of pornographic statuary. When Laurent invites his prospective in-laws to dine at the apartment, the two men hurriedly alter the nature of their abode until it resembles the interior of a monastery. They also put their black and very effeminate male maid, Luke, on his best behavior. Tognazzi calls upon Laurent's mother, Maurier, a woman he hasn't seen in more than two decades. He asks her to come to the apartment to see her son and she agrees. Then she tries to seduce him the way she did so many years before. Serrault walks in on the attempted seduction, is hurt by what he sees, and leaves Tognazzi. Later, at the train station where Serrault is planning to leave Saint Tropez, Tognazzi catches up with him and convinces Serrault that he loves him and him alone and that the other thing was a large mistake. When Galabru, Scarpitta, and Maneri arrive, Serrault is now totally dressed in drag and pretending to be Laurent's mother. Tognazzi attempts to keep the real mother from entering, but can't locate her. The dinner is a shambles. Luke gets hysterical at seeing Serrault and, in the course of events, Serrault's wig is knocked to the side moments before Maurier arrives. Galabru realizes he is in a den of homosexuals and fears being caught there. The members of the La Cage Aux Folles cast enter to fete Tognazzi and Serrault on their 20th anniversary as a committed couple. Galabru would like to flee but there are many reporters waiting outside, so Galabru must dress in full drag in order to get away, which he does successfully. Laurent and Maneri are finally wed and Serrault gets a trifle jealous because Maurier is at the church. After all, that woman had nothing to do with the raising of Laurent, and now *she's* getting the motherly glory. Tognazzi takes Serrault's hand tenderly and assures him that it's just for propriety; Laurent knows that his *real maman* is Serrault. Neither of the two leads is gay in real life and both manage to carry off the deception well. The humor is often predictable but it is so good-natured that we don't mind. The funniest sequence is when Tognazzi attempts to teach Serrault how to be "butch" while stirring his tea and buttering his toast. It's almost like the scene in MY FAIR LADY when Higgins attempts to school Eliza in ladylike manners. The movie earned more than $40 million, and spawned a dreadful sequel and a fabulously successful musical on the stage. Serrault won the French "Cesar" award as Best Actor and the Academy of Motion Picture Arts and Sciences nominated it for Direction, Screenplay and Costume Design. Despite the apparent risk in making a movie where two gay men are the lead roles, it was basically an old-fashioned bedroom farce, and tamer than most, at that. In a sentence, it's "Boy Meets Boy, Boy Loses Boy, Boy Gets Boy." Serrault starred on the stage in the same role he played in the film and Tognazzi is a veteran Italian comic actor who has distinguished himself in such movies as THE CONJUGAL BED, THE APE WOMAN, and VIVA ITALIA among many others since his film career began in 1950. The funniest single line in the film is spoken by Galabru when they are dressing him in a woman's clothes in order to escape the prying press. He looks at himself in the mirror and sadly exclaims: "White makes me look fat."

p, Marcello Danon; d, Edouard Molinaro; w, Danon, Molinaro, Francis Veber, Jean Poiret (based on the play by Poiret); ph, Armando Mannuzzi (Eastmancolor); m, Ennio Morricone; ed, Robert Isnardon, Monique Isnardon; art d, Mario Garbuglia; cos, Piero Tosi, Ambra Danon.

Comedy **Cas.** **(PR:O MPAA:R)**

LA CAGE AUX FOLLES II** (1981, Ital./Fr.) 100m DaMa/UA c

Ugo Tognazzi *(Renato Baldi)*, Michel Serrault *(Albin Mougeotte/Zaza Napoli)*, Gianni Frisoni *(Barman at Cabaret)*, Mark Bodin *(Caramel)*, Benny Luke *(Jacob)*, Gianrico Tondinelli *(Walter)*, Philippe Cronenberver *(Waiter/Negresco)*, Francis Missana *(Handsome Young Man)*, Marie-Claude Douquet *(Pretty Girl)*, Ricardo Berlingeri *(Desk Clerk-Hotel de Lys)*, Piero Morgia *(Killer in Hotel)*, Marcel Bozzuffi *(Broca)*, Michel Galabru *(Simon Charrier)*, Giovanni Vettorazzo *(Milan)*, Pierre Desmet *(Proprietor Le Roi du Bleu)*, Tom Felleghy *(Andrew Manderstam)*, Danilo Recanatesi *(Dr. Boquillon)*, Nello Pazzafini *(Mangin)*, Renato Basso *(Rouget)*, Antonio Francioni *(Michaux)*, Nazareno Natale *(Demis)*, Stelio Candelli *(Hans)*, Giorgio Cerioni *(Gunther)*, Roberto Bisacco *(Ralph)*, Roberto Caporali *(Terrorist Accomplice)*, Paola Borboni *(Signora Baldi)*, Glauco Onorato *(Luigi)*.

Spurred by the huge success of the original, the producers rushed this sequel into the works and came up short in every way. Whereas the first film had lots of heart, this is just another spy picture with the added twist of the two heroes being heroines with baritone voices. Serrault thinks that Tognazzi no longer finds him attractive so he seeks to make Tognazzi jealous, dresses up in drag, and is picked up in a cafe by a spy who is escaping enemy agents. The spy uses Serrault as his getaway cover and soon enough, as you might expect, Serrault now has the precious microfilm in his possession. The French attempt to use Serrault as bait to catch the bad guys and the two men go to Italy where Tognazzi introduces Serrault (still in drag) as his wife. Tognazzi's mother, Borboni, is shocked by this "woman's" appearance and says she'd hoped her son would marry someone prettier. In the end, everyone shows up to get the film, the villains are defeated, and the two men are reunited. Luke reprises his role as the maid, as does Galabru as their son's father-in-law. Whatever comedy is in the picture is provided by Serrault as he sings, tries to be macho (a repeat from the first film), faces down the villains, etc. Tognazzi doesn't have much to do and the picture just sort of lies there. Despite the "R" rating, this is as family a film as a Dean Martin and Jerry Lewis movie but not nearly as funny. The producers had planned to make a few more of these but this was such a dud that only one more shot was fired in 1986, thankfully.

p, Marcello Danon; d, Edouard Molinaro; w, Francis Veber (based on a story by Danon, Veber, Jean Poiret); ph, Armando Nannuzzi (Technicolor); m, Ennio Morricone; ed, Robert Isnardon; prod d, Luigi Scaccianoce; art d, Francesco Saverio Chianese; cos, Ambra Danon; makeup, Piero Antonio Mecacci.

Comedy **Cas.** **(PR:C-O MPAA:R)**

LA CASSE (SEE: BURGLARS, THE, 1972, Ital./Fr.)

LA CHAMBRE VERTE (SEE: GREEN ROOM, THE, 1979, Fr.)

LA CHASSE A L'HOMME (SEE: MALE HUNT, 1965, Fr./Ital.)

LA CHIENNE* 1/2**

(1975, Fr.) 100m Films Jean Renoir-Braunberger-Richebe/Ajay bw (AKA: ISN'T LIFE A BITCH?; THE BITCH)

Michel Simon *(Maurice Legrand)*, Janie Mareze *(Lulu Pelletier)*, Georges Flament *(Andre Jaugin, "DeDe")*, Magdelaine Berubet *(Mme. Adele Legrand)*, Gaillard *(Sgt. Alexis Godard)*, Jean Gehret *(Mons. Dagodet)*, Alexandre Rignault *(Langelard, The Art Critic)*, Lucien Mancini *(Walstein, The Art Dealer)*, Courme *(The Colonel)*, Max Dalban *(Bonnard, A Colleague of M. Legrand)*, Romain Bouquet *(M. Henriot, Legrand's Boss)*, Henri Guisol *(Amedee, The Waiter At The Cafe)*, Pierre Destys *(Gustave, A Pal Of Dede)*, Jane Pierson *(The Concierge)*, Argentin *(The Magistrator)*, Mlle. Doryans *(Yvonne)*, Sylvain Itkine *(Dede's Lawyer)*, Colette Borelli *(Lily, Lulu's Friend)*.

Released in France in 1931, LA CHIENNE was Renoir's second sound film and the first to gain him the recognition which would soon become legendary. After his ON PURGE BEBE (a rarely seen short feature from the same year), Renoir prepared this adaptation of Fouchardiere's novel with his eye on his wife Catherine Hessling for the title role. The studio, however, insisted on Mareze and Renoir reluctantly agreed—a decision which led to a divorce shortly afterwards. Mareze (who died soon after the filming in a car crash on the Riviera) took the role of Lulu, a lovable but manipulative prostitute whom businessman and weekend painter Simon falls in love with. He courts her and throws his money at her even though she is quite attached (in a motherly sort of way) to her pimp, Flament. In the meantime, Flament sells Simon's paintings under the guise of a mysterious American named Clara Wood. "Clara's" career skyrockets and eventually Simon learns that it is Mareze that is selling the paintings. He willingly forgives her and gives in to her "requests" for more money. Still unaware that she is a prostitute, it is not until he catches Mareze in bed with Flament that he finally realizes who, in the broadest sense, she really is. He still fails to learn his lesson and, the next morning, returns to Mareze sympathizing with what he believes to be her terrible situation. He is awakened by her insistence that she is not in love with him and that she enjoys Flament's company. Simon promptly lashes out and strikes her dead. Justice takes a strangely poetic turn as Flament is the one accused and sent to death, while Simon goes free. In one of Renoir's most startling and perfect endings, Simon is seen as a doorman for an art gallery which sells his own paintings. An often-overlooked highlight of Renoir's momentous career which was well worth the 44-year wait. In the meantime, however, Fritz Lang remade LA CHIENNE as SCARLET STREET (1945), with Edward G. Robinson—a more than commendable remake.

p, Charles David; d, Jean Renoir; w, Renoir, Andre Girard (based on a novel by Georges de la Fouchardiere); ph, Theodore Sparkuhl; ed, Denise Batcheff-Tual, Marguerite Renoir, Jean Renoir; art d, Gabriel Scognamillo; m/l, "Sois Bonne, O Ma Belle Inconnue," Eugenie Buffet (Toselli); "Malbrough S'en Va-t-en Guerre," Buffet (Michel Simon).

Drama **(PR:C-O MPAA:NR)**

LA CHINOISE***

(1967, Fr.) 95m Gueville-Parc-Athos-Simar-Anouchka c (LA CHINOISE, OU PLUTOT A LA CHINOISE: UN FILM EN TRAIN DE SE FAIRE)

Anne Wiazemski *(Veronique)*, Jean-Pierre Leaud *(Guillaume)*, Michel Semeniako *(Henry)*, Lex de Bruijn *(Kirilov)*, Juliet Berto *(Yvonne)*, Omar Diop *(Comrade X)*, Francis Jeanson *(Himself)*, Blandine Jeanson.

A heavily political picture which, in typical Godardian fashion, favors the distancing practices of Bertolt Brecht and an interest in contemporary culture over narrative expectations. What little story there is has Wiazemski, the leader of a revolutionary student quintet, planning and ultimately bungling an assassination attempt by mistaking apartment number 23 for 32, thereby killing the wrong man. More important, however, is Godard's acute examination of the political climate of the period. While the politics are in the forefront of LA CHINOISE, what is commonly overlooked is Godard's superior sense of humor, most notably in a sequence which has one of the young rebels trying on a variety of strangely political eyeglasses. The film's end sheds some light on the revolutionaries by revealing that they are guests in the bourgeois vacation home of a friend's parents, readying themselves for a return to college for fall classes. Godard demonstrates his foresight by ending the film with the title card: "End of a beginning." In less than a year Paris was nearly shut down because of student revolts—revolts which were fueled at the Faculte de Nanterre, the very university that Wiazemski's character attended.

d&w, Jean-Luc Godard; ph, Raoul Coutard (Eastmancolor); m, Karl-Heinz Stockhausen; ed, Agnes Guillemot, Delphine Desfons.

Drama **(PR:C-O MPAA:NR)**

LA CINTURA DI CASTITA

(SEE: ON MY WAY TO THE CRUSADES, I MET A GIRL WHO . . . , 1969, U.S./Ital.)

LA CITTA PRIGIONIERA (SEE: CONQUERED CITY, 1966, Ital.)

LA CITTA SI DIFENDE (SEE: FOUR WAYS OUT, 1954, Ital.)

LA COLLECTIONNEUSE***

(1971, Fr.) 88m Les Films Du Losange-Rome Paris/Pathe c

Patrick Bauchau *(Adrien)*, Haydee Politoff *(Haydee)*, Daniel Pommereulle *(Daniel)*, Alain Jouffroy *(Writer)*, Mijanou Bardot *(Carole)*, Seymour Hertzberg [Eugene Archer] *(Sam)*, Annik Morice *(Carole's Friend)*, Denis Berry *(Charlie)*, Brian Belshaw *(Haydee's Lover)*, Donald Cammell *(Boy At St. Tropez)*, Alfred De Graff *(Lost Tourist)*, Pierre Richard Bre, Patrice de Bailliencourt *(Men in Car)*.

The third in a series of six films by Rohmer grouped under the heading "The Moral Tales" was originally made in 1967 but not released in the U.S. until Rohmer's MY NIGHT AT MAUD'S received such widely acclaimed success. As in the other films, LA COLLECTIONNEUSE is filled with talk, the characters attempting to achieve a unified whole via their moral and philosophical stances. Bauchau is the handsome young man faced with the problem of whether to sleep with Politoff, the pretty temptress who is staying at the same boarding house during his vacation in St. Tropez. Listening to her carry on with a number of different men, he sits back and reads haughty books in a quest to purify himself, something which also requires staying clear of sex and normal materialistic pursuits. But this girl proves to be a direct antagonist to his desired goals and the perfect ploy by which Rohmer can question the notions people have stuck in the back of their heads about what is morally correct. Bauchau undertakes an analysis of the situation, taking a pretty grim perspective toward the girl's antics. What he actually does is talk himself into inactivity; when he finally gets a chance to sleep with Politoff, he runs away, convinced that he has done the right thing in remaining faithful to higher ideals. But he wanted to have an affair with her all along and was just searching for a way to suppress contact. The narrative structure follows a pattern that resembles Rohmer's other films, a presentation of a threatened moral stance. As always the male opts out of taking chances for a more secure existence. Bauchau could be criticized for being much too haughty and self-possessed to be very likable, but is otherwise a perfect subject for Rohmer's experiment. The beautiful temptress played by Politoff is not really required to do much beyond looking nice, allowing the camera to do all the work. Almendros captures the beauty of Politoff and the scenery with an acute sense of detail. (In French; English subtitles.)

p, Georges Beauregard, Barbet Schroeder; d, Eric Rohmer; w, Rohmer, Patrick Bauchau, Haydee Politoff, Daniel Pommereulle; ph, Nestor Almendros (Eastmancolor); m, Blossom Toes, Giorgio Gomelsky; ed, Jacquie Raynal.

Drama **(PR:C-O MPAA:NR)**

LA CONGA NIGHTS* 1/2 (1940) 59m UNIV bw

Hugh Herbert *(Henry I. Dibble, Jr./Faith Dibble/Hope Dibble/Charity Dibble/Prudence Dibble/Mrs. Henry I. Dibble, Sr.)*, Dennis O'Keefe *(Steve Collins)*, Constance Moore *(Helen Curtiss)*, Ferike Boros *(Mama O'Brien)*, Joe Brown, Jr., *(Delancey O'Brien)*, Sally Payne *(Lucy Endover)*, Frank Orth *(Dennis O'Brien)*, Barnett Parker *(Hammond)*, Eddie Quillan *(Titus Endover)*, Armida *(Carlotta De Vera)*.

Long before Alec Guinness attempted several roles in KIND HEARTS AND CORONETS and Peter Sellers tried it in DR. STRANGELOVE, the unlikely Hugh Herbert attempted to portray six different characters in this film, five of them women. Now if he'd only had F. Hugh Herbert, the screenwriter, around to write him a good script, it might have wound up better than it did. Herbert is a music aficionado who has made a fortune in real estate and is slightly dotty. O'Keefe is a cab driver/performer who picks up Moore as she is fleeing the rent on her last boarding house. She's a singer who is out of work and can't afford a place to stay. O'Keefe takes her to his boarding house where everybody is an entertainer. The tenants are due to be evicted because of non-payment on the rent and they all get together to stage a show to make enough money to save their dwelling. They start a nightclub in the place and it's about to be shut down when Herbert arrives, likes what he hears, and is surprised to find that he actually owns the place. He makes a gift of it to O'Keefe and Moore. Herbert does well as Herbert, but when it comes to playing his mother and his four sisters, it's a bad joke. A few songs include the traditional "La Cucaracha," arranged by Harold Potter, and "Chance Of A Lifetime," "Carmenita McCoy," and "Havana." Silent actor Eddie Quillan, whose career in films spanned more than 60 years, is effective as Payne's husband. They play a pair of battling honeymooners who can't agree on anything, least of all why they made this movie. The only thing to recommend this film is the mercifully short length.

p, Ken Goldsmith; d, Lew Landers; w, Jay Dratler, Harry Clork, Paul Gerard Smith (based on the story by Dratler, Clork, and Smith); ph, Elwood Bredell; ed, Ted Kent; md, Charles Previn; art d, Jack Otterson; m/l, Sam Lerner, Frank Skinner.

Comedy **(PR:A MPAA:NR)**

LA CONGIUNTURA (SEE: ONE MILLION DOLLARS, 1965, Ital.)

LA CROIX DES VIVANTS (SEE: CROSS OF THE LIVING, 1963, Fr.)

LA CUCARACHA* 1/2

(1961, Mex.) 90m Azteca c (AKA: THE SOLDIERS OF PANCHO VILLA)

Maria Felix *(La Cucaracha)*, Emilio Fernandez *(Col. Zeta)*, Dolores Del Rio

(Chabela), Pedro Armendariz *(Razo)*, Antonio Aguilar *(Capt. Ventura)*, Ignacio Lopez Tarso, Flor Silvestre [Guillermina Jimenez], Cuco Sanchez, Lupe Carriles, Miguel Manzano, Alicia del Lago.

Felix plays the part of a woman who raises the enthusiasm of a troop of soldiers fighting on the side of Pancho Villa. The officer in charge is in love with Del Rio, but is loved by Felix. Eventually the officer is killed, leaving behind a pregnant Felix who then joins up with the Mexican forces. Released in Mexico in 1958.

p&d, Ismael Rodriguez; w, Rodriguez, Jose Bolanos Prado, Jose Luis Celis, Ricardo Garibay; ph, Gabriel Figueroa (Eastmancolor); m, Raul Lavista; ed, Fernando Martinez; art d, Edward Fitzgerald.

War Drama **(PR:A MPAA:NR)**

LA DECADE PRODIGIEUSE (SEE: TEN DAYS' WONDER, 1972, Fr.)

LA DENTELLIERE (SEE: LACEMAKER, THE, 1977, Fr.)

LA DOLCE VITA***** (1961, Ital./Fr.) 180m Riama-Pathe-Gray/Astor-AIP bw

Marcello Mastroianni *(Marcello Rubini)*, Anita Ekberg *(Sylvia)*, Anouk Aimee *(Maddalena)*, Yvonne Furneaux *(Emma)*, Magali Noel *(Fanny)*, Alain Cuny *(Steiner)*, Nadia Gray *(Nadia)*, Lex Barker *(Robert)*, Annibale Ninchi *(Marcello's Father)*, Walter Santesso *(Paparazzo)*, Jacques Sernas *(Matinee Idol)*, Valeria Ciangottini *(Paola)*, Alan Dijon *(Frankie Stout)*, Renee Longarini *(Signora Steiner)*, Polidor *(Clown)*, Giulio Questi *(Don Giulio)*, Cesarino Miceli Picardi *(Irate Man in Nightclub)*, Adriana Moneta *(Prostitute)*, Anna Maria Salerno *(Her Friend)*, Oscar Ghiglia, Gino Marturano *(Their Pimps)*, Leonardo Botta *(Doctor)*, Harriet White *(Sylvia's Secretary)*, Gio Staiano *(Effeminate Male)*, Carlo Di Maggio *(Producer)*, Adriano Celentano *(Rock-n-Roll Singer)*, Archie Savage *(Negro Dancer)*, Giacomo Gabriello *(Maddalena's Father)*, Giovanna and Massimo Busetti *(Lying Children Of The Miracle)*, Rina Franchetti *(Their Mother)*, Aurelio Nardi *(Their Uncle)*, Alfredo Rizzo *(Television Director)*, Marianna Leibl *(Yvonne's Companion)*, Iris Tree *(Poetess)*, *Lilly Granado (Lucy)*, Gloria Jones *(Gloria)*, Nico Otzak *(Sophisticated Prostitute)*, Vadim Wolkonsky *(Prince Mascalchi)*, Audrey McDonald *(Sonia)*, Rosemary Rennel Rodd *(English Medium)*, Ferdinando Brofferio *(Maddalena's Lover)*, Doris Pignatelli, Princess of Monteroduni *(Lady in White Coat)*, Ida Galli *(Debutante of the Year)*, Loretta Ramaciotti *(Woman in Seance)*, Giulio Girola *(Police Commissioner)*, Mino Doro *(Nadia's Lover)*, Antonio Jacono, Carlo Musto *(Transvestites)*, Tito Buzzo *(Muscle Man)*, Sandra Lee *(Spoleto Ballerina)*, Leontine Van Strein *(Matinee Idol's Girl Friend)*, Leo Coleman *(Negro Dancer)*, Laura Betti *(Laura)*, Riccardo Garrone *(Riccardo, The Villa Owner)*, Franca Pasut *(Girl Covered With Feathers)*, Prince Eugenio Ruspoli di Poggio Suasa *(Don Eugenio Mascalchi)*, Daniela Calvino *(Daniela)*, Enrico Glori *(Nadia's Admirer)*, Enzo Cerusico, Enzo Doria, Giulio Paradisi *(Photojournalists)*, Henry Thody, Donatella Della Nora, Maite Morand, Donato Castellaneta, John Francis Lane, Concetta Ragusa, Francois Dieudonne, Mario Mallarno, Nadia Balabine, Umberto Felici, Maurizio Guelfi *(Press Conference Journalists)*, Leonida Repaci, Anna Salvatore, Letizia Spadini, Margherita Russo, Winie Vagliani, Desmond O'Grady *(Steiner's Other Guests)*, Count Ivenda Dobrzensky *(Giovanni)*, Francesco Consalvo, Maria Teresa Vianello, Angela Giavalisco, Tiziano Cortini, Maria Mazzanti *(People at Airport)*, Tomas Torres, Gloria Hendy, Noel Sheldon, April Hennessy, Angela Wilson *(People at Via Veneto)*, Giovanni Querrel, I. Campanino, Teresa Tsao, Giulio Citti *(People at Nightclub)*, Lisa Schneider, Aldo Vasco, Francisco Lori, Romolo Giordani, Ada Passeri *(People in Miracle Sequence)*, Nina Hohenlohe, Maria Marigliano, Mario De Grenet, Franco Rossellini, Joan Antequera *(People at the Castle)*, Orietta Fiume, Katherine Denise, Mario Conocchia, Umberto Orsini, Domino, Lucia Vasilico.

There are those who found LA DOLCE VITA to be the perfect cure for insomnia. There are also those who felt it was one of the greatest Italian films ever made. It was long at three hours but unceasingly interesting. The title, which means "The Sweet Life," is satiric in itself because the theory that money brings one happiness is refuted over and over in the movie. Fellini claims that he based many of the incidents on real-life occurrences and we believe him because no one could have made up so many preposterous situations. Anyone who spent any time in Rome during the late 1950s and early 1960s will recognize many of the people being portrayed. The picture begins as Romans are shocked by seeing a large statue of Jesus being carried over the city by a helicopter. Following in a second chopper is Mastroianni, a gossip writer for the local scandal sheets. He aspires to serious writing but, like so many, never gets around to writing anything beyond what he writes for *lire*. While visiting a local nightspot, Mastroianni meets Aimee, a wealthy heiress suffering from a huge case of ennui in that everything bores her and she is constantly on the lookout for new thrills. Together, they pick up hooker Moneta and spend the night as a *menage a trois* in the prostitute's room. When Mastroianni gets home, he finds his regular mistress, Furneaux, has taken an overdose of sleeping pills. He rushes her to the hospital where he is assured that she'll recover, then races off to cover the arrival of Hollywood starlet Ekberg at the airport. He is soon infatuated with the buxom blonde and takes her for a tour around his Rome, including all the usual spots—Trevi, St. Peter's, the Caracalla Baths, etc. The tour is interrupted violently when Mastroianni is attacked by Ekberg's fiance Barker (who was her husband in real life). Now Mastroianni drives out of town to check on the story that two small children have had a vision of the Blessed Virgin. Hundreds of believers are there to be healed but it's soon learned that the kids were lying and just making sport. A rainstorm hits and the huge crowd flees. Mastroianni's father, Ninchi, arrives. He's a dear, gentle man and is shocked by his son's lifestyle and eventually decides to return to the provinces. Next, Mastroianni meets and falls for Ciangottini, an innocent waitress who is a breath of fresh air after his terrible bouts with his mistress, Furneaux. He is stunned to learn that one of his best friends, Cuny, has committed suicide and taken the lives of his two adorable children as well. There is no reason this intellectual should have done this and the news is shattering to Mastroianni. By this time, Mastroianni has given up all pretense of anything literary and decides to say the "hell with it" and live only for pleasure. He goes to an orgy at the seaside home of Gray, a divorcee, and in the morning, the crowd wanders on to the beach where a huge unidentifiable fish lies rotting in the hot sun. Across the canal, he sees Ciangottini wave at him and shout something, but he can't quite hear what she's saying. He finally gives up and walks off with his friends and the film ends. Confounding? Yes. Informative? Yes again. Can we ever hope to crawl inside Fellini's mind to see what he meant by this? Probably not. What we can do is settle in and watch a panorama of what Rome was like in those days and just accept it, without editorializing on anyone's part, and bask in the genius and originality that went into making the movie. In its own way, LA DOLCE VITA was just as much of a breakthrough as CITIZEN KANE in that Fellini pulled out all the stops to offer us a panoply of life in the big city. Much of the dialog is banal, when spoken by banal people, and much of the dialog is brilliant, when spoken by brilliant people. In other words, it's a depiction of the way it was. To dissect and analyze LA DOLCE VITA any further might be to do it a disservice. Some have called it satire, some say it's a slice of life, some say it's just an elaborate practical joke on Fellini's part. That's enough to realize that LA DOLCE VITA was many things to many people. It's a classic in that the breadth of vision, the humor, the darkness, the nobility, and the tawdriness all blend to become a total cinematic experience. Fellini, as is his usual custom, employed a great many amateurs along with the professional actors. Many of them never made another film and LA DOLCE VITA represented their moment in the sun. All of the actors, both pro and non-pro, were totally believable and the idea of using Mastroianni, a journalist, to be the lever on which the story rests, was excellent because it afforded us the opportunity to watch as well as participate in all the sequences through legitimate, if jaded, eyes. Never before has three hours gone by so rapidly. Forget any philosophy, don't look for any deep, underlying meanings, just let yourself become enmeshed in the sweet life and see if you don't agree that this was a monumental achievement, in any language.

p, Giuseppe Amato, Angelo Rizzoli; d, Federico Fellini; w, Fellini, Ennio Flaiano, Tullio Pinelli, Brunello Rondi (based on a story by Fellini, Flaiano, Pinelli); ph, Otello Martelli (Totalscope); m, Nino Rota; ed, Leo Catozzo; md, Franco Ferrara; art d, Piero Gherardi; cos, Gherardi; makeup, Otello Fava.

Drama **Cas.** **(PR:C MPAA:NR)**

LA FABULEUSE AVENTURE DE MARCO POLO
(SEE: MARCO THE MAGNIFICENT, 1966, Ital./Fr./Yugo./Egypt/Afghanistan)

LA FEMME AUX BOTTES ROUGES
(SEE: WOMAN WITH RED BOOTS, THE, 1974, Fr./Span.)

LA FEMME D'A COTE (SEE: WOMAN NEXT DOOR, THE, 1981, Fr.)

LA FEMME DU BOULANGERS (SEE: BAKER'S WIFE, THE, 1940, Fr.)

LA FEMME INFIDELE***
(1969, Fr./Ital.) 98m Les Films de Boetie-Cinegay/AA c (AKA: THE UNFAITHFUL WIFE)

Stephane Audran *(Helene Desvallees)*, Michel Bouquet *(Charles Desvallees)*, Maurice Ronet *(Victor Pegala)*, Serge Bento *(Bignon)*, Michel Duchaussoy *(Police Officer Duval)*, Guy Marly *(Police Officer Gobet)*, Stephane Di Napoli *(Michel Desvallees)*, Louise Chevalier *(Maid)*, Louise Rioton *(Mother-in-Law)*, Henri Marteau *(Paul)*, Francois Moro-Giafferi *(Frederic)*, Dominique Zardi *(Truck Driver)*, Michel Charrel *(Policeman)*, Henri Attal *(Man in Cafe)*, Jean-Marie Arnoux *(False Witness)*, Donatella Turri *(Brigitte)*.

Bouquet is a middle-aged insurance broker who lives in Versailles with his wife, Audran, and son, Di Napoli. He becomes suspicious that his wife is having an affair and hires a private eye to shadow her. It is soon discovered that she is spending her time with Ronet, a Parisian writer. Bouquet pays a visit to Ronet and after some civilized conversation, bludgeons him with a statuette, though not before commenting on his "ugly mug." He returns to his wife, and as the police close in, their romance reawakens. The finale has the wife and son watching the cops haul away Bouquet. A subtle murder drama which stresses character more than action.

p, Andre Genoves; d&w, Claude Chabrol; ph, Jean Rabier (Eastmancolor); m, Pierre Jansen; ed, Jacques Gaillard; md, Andre Girard, Dominique Zardi; art d, Guy Littaye; set d, Raoul Guiraud.

Crime/Drama **(PR:C MPAA:M)**

LA FERME DU PENDU* 1/2
(1946, Fr.) 90m Corona bw (AKA: HANGED MAN'S FARM)

Alfred Adam, Charles Vanel, Arlette Merry.

Full-blown melodrama, set in the French countryside, about the lustful, no-good son of a farming family and the ruin he brings down on his family. Director Dreville was an excellent craftsman who made a number of lurid dramas in this vein. Trash, but interesting trash.

d, Jean Dreville; w, Andre-Paul Antoine; ph, Andre Thomas.

Drama **(PR:C MPAA:NR)**

LA FETE A HENRIETTE (SEE: HOLIDAY FOR HENRIETTE, 1955, Fr.)

LA FEU FOLLET (SEE: FIRE WITHIN, THE, 1963, Fr.)

LA FILLE DE MATA HARI
(SEE: MATA HARI'S DAUGHTER, 1954, Fr./Ital.)

LA FILLE DE PUISATIER
(SEE: WELL-DIGGERS DAUGHTER, THE, 1946, Fr.)

LA FILLE DU DIABLE (SEE: DEVIL'S DAUGHTER, 1949, Fr.)

LA FILLE SANS VOILE (SEE: GIRL IN THE BIKINI, THE, 1958, Fr.)

LA FIN DU MONDE (SEE: THE END OF THE WORLD, 1930, Fr.)

LA FOLLE DES GRANDEURS
(SEE: DELUSIONS OF GRANDEUR, 1971, Fr.)

LA FORTUNA DI ESSERE DONNA
(SEE: LUCKY TO BE A WOMAN, 1955, Ital./Fr.)

LA FUGA**
(1966, Ital.) 92m Cine 3/International Classics (FOX) bw

Giovanni Ralli (*Piera Fabbri*), Anouk Aimee (*Luisa*), Paul Geurs (*Andrea Fabbri*), Enrico Maria Salerno (*Psychoanalyst*), Carol Walker (*Piera's Mother*), Guido Alberti (*Piera's Father*), Jone Salinas Musu (*Andrea's Mother*), Maurizio Arena, Anita Sanders, Ignazio Dolce.

Ralli, unsatisfied in her marriage to nuclear physicist Guers, gets involved in a lesbian relationship with the refined and intelligent Aimee. She convinces herself that she is happy, but after an argument Ralli drives her car into a truck and dies, a victim of loneliness too poignant to bear. Songs: "Topless" (sung by Peppino Di Capri), "La Tua Stagione" (sung by Milva).

p, Vittorio Glori Musy, Alberto Casati, Mario Mariani; d, Paolo Spinola; w, Sergio Amidei, Piero Bellanova (based on an idea by Spinola, Carla Conti); ph, Marcello Gatti, Armando Nannuzzi; m, Piero Piccioni; ed, Nino Baragli; prod d, Piero Gherardi; set d, Nedo Azzini; cos, Gherardi.

Drama   **(PR:O   MPAA:NR)**

LA GRANDE BOUFFE**
(1973, Fr.) 130m Mara Film-Capitolina/ABCKO c (AKA: THE BIG FEAST; THE GREAT FEED, THE GRANDE BOUFFE)

Marcello Mastroianni (*Airline Pilot*), Ugo Tognazzi (*The Chef*), Michel Piccoli (*TV Producer*), Philippe Noiret (*The Judge*), Andrea Ferreol (*The School-teacher*).

Four friends, overwhelmed by ennui, enter into a suicide pact, the weapon being total self-indulgence. They cloister themselves within a walled villa in the heart of Paris, and the vendors of viands trundle in bearing sides of beef and all the trimmings. Tognazzi, a chef, ecstatically begins his preparations, gourmet food for the gourmands, food without end. Three prostitutes arrive to share in the provender and to service the celebrants. Mastroianni, a vain, womanizing airline pilot whose passion is machinery, finds a Bugatti on blocks in an outbuilding and begins to work on the engine. Piccoli, an effete television producer with a thinly disguised yen for Mastroianni, plays classical piano and does barre stretches in the brief intervals between meals. Noiret, a judge, pontificates amusingly when he isn't eating. As a goose's feet are nailed to a board while it is stuffed with grain by means of a funnel to make it fat, the four have nailed themselves to their retreat, funneling delicious repasts into their digestive tracts, waiting for the terminal *mal de foie*, the revenge of the liver. Plump schoolteacher Ferreol arrives with some students on a tour. Instinctively grasping the situation, knowing the needs of the men, she stays on to nurture them, ministering to their sexual desires, helpmeet to their hedonism, duenna of death. Sated, the prostitutes depart: fun is fun, but enough is enough. One-by-one, the internal organs of the gross gourmands lash back at them. Mastroianni succumbs in his beloved Bugatti, having completed his repairs. The delicate Piccoli expires in an explosion of flatulence. Chef Tognazzi, architect of the outrage, dies on his marble pastry bench, too weak to bring food to his mouth, but helped to his finish by Ferreol. Noiret, lingering longest, lapses from life in the garden while being fed by Ferreol a pink blancmange shaped like an enormous pair of female breasts. An outrageous, funny, blackly humorous, well-acted work from writer-director Ferreri, the John Waters of Europe, the "master of bad taste."

p, Jean Pierre Rossau; d, Marco Ferreri; w, Ferreri, Rafael Azcona; ph, Mario Vulpiani, Pasquale Rachini (Eastmancolor); m, Philippe Sarde; ed, Claudine Merlin, Gina Pignier; art d, Michel de Bronin.

Satire   **(PR:C-O   MPAA:NR)**

LA GRANDE BOURGEOISE**
(1977, Ital.) 115m Lira-Filmarpa/Atlantic-Buckley Brothers c (AKA: THE MURRI AFFAIR)

Catherine Deneuve (*Linda Murri*), Giancarlo Giannini (*Tullio Murri*), Fernando Rey (*Augusto Murri*), Tina Aumont (*Rosa Bonetti*), Paolo Bonicelli (*Francesco Bonmartini*), Corrada Pani (*Pio Naldi*), Eltore Mani (*Carlo Secchi*), Marcel Bozzuffi (*Augusto Stanzani*).

A bland criminal drama which seems to attack the upper class purely as a reflex, falling into the usual "suffering bourgeoise" cliches. Deneuve is a member of the posh Murri family whose marriage to a vicious husband is met with the disapproval of her brother Giannini, a highly respected lawyer and Socialist leader. He decides, however, to murder Deneuve's husband, placing the family under heavy scrutiny and putting pressure on their father, Rey, a popular intellectual and doctor. Based on an actual murder case, the characters and the ensuing trial bring forth all the evils of the class system but never succeed in attracting one's interest as anything more than a socio-political exercise.

d, Mauro Bolognini; ph, Ennio Guarniier; m, Ennio Morricone.

Crime/Drama   **(PR:C   MPAA:R)**

LA GRANDE ILLUSION
(SEE: GRAND ILLUSION, 1937, Fr.)

LA GUERRE EST FINIE**
(1967, Fr./Swed.) 121m Sofracima-Europa/BRANDON bw (KRIGETAR SLUT; AKA: THE WAR IS OVER)

Yves Montand (*Diego*), Ingrid Thulin (*Marianne*), Genevieve Bujold (*Nadine Sallanches*), Jean Daste (*The Chief*), Jorge Semprun (*Narrator*), Dominique Rozan (*Jude*), Jean-Francois Remi (*Juan*), Marie Mergey (*Madame Lopez*), Jacques Wallet (*C.R.S. Policeman*), Michel Piccoli (*1st Customs Inspector*), Anouk Ferjac (*Madame Jude*), Roland Monod (*Antoine*), Pierre Decazes (*S.N.C.F. Employee*), Paul Crauchet (*Roberto*), Claire Dunhamel, Antoine Bourseiller (*Travelers*), Laurence

Badie (*Bernadette Pluvier*), Francoise Bertin (*Carmen*), Yvette Etievant (*Yvette*), Jean Bouise (*Ramon*), Annie Fargue (*Agnes*), Gerard Sety (*Bill*), Catherine de Seynes (*Jeanine*), Jacques Rispal (*Manolo*), Fylgia Zadig (*Woman at Meeting*), Pierre Leproux (*Maker of Forged Papers*), Roger Pelletier (*2nd Customs Inspector*), R.J. Chauffard (*Drunkard*), Jose-Maria Flotats (*Miguel*), Jean Bolo (*Agent*), Pierre Barbaud (*Client*), Gerard Lartigau (*Head of "Revolutionary Action"*), Jean Larrouquette (*Member of "Revolutionary Action"*), Martine Vatel (*Student*), Laure Paillette (*Old Lady*), Jacques Robnard (*Pierrot*), Marcel Cuvelier (*Inspector Chardin*), Bernard Fresson (*Sarlat*), Antoine Vitez (*Air France Employee*).

Some of Montand's best work has been as a political refugee or firebrand. This time, Montand is a long-time revolutionary who lives in Paris. He has been active against the Spanish government and is now returning from Madrid while carrying a false passport. The Guardia Civil stops him at the border and tries to discover who he really is but a call to his Paris phone number turns up Bujold, a student in the revolutionary movement who corroborates that he is who his papers say he is. Montand returns to Paris to learn that his pals have been captured in Madrid and that his local contact, Remi, went back to Spain at the same time Montand was returning to France. Montand wants to stop Remi, who is still on the road south, and asks Crauchet, the man in charge of travel for the underground, to help stop Remi from going to his death. Crauchet says he has more important things to concern him, such as the upcoming general strike. Montand gets together with Bujold, and they are immediately attracted to each other, so they make love. Soon after, Montand goes back to his usual mistress, Thulin, a divorcee who is raising a son on her own. Montand still wants to go to Madrid to aid the cause but the others in his cell forbid him from doing that as he is so recognizable to the authorities that he wouldn't last long on the street. Bouise is sent in Montand's place against Montand's wishes. Montand doesn't believe that the general strike will accomplish anything and he is censured by the others in his cell who feel that he is tired and unable to be objective. While resting in Paris, Montand spots police on Bujold's trail and then learns that Bujold and her student comrades are planning to terrorize tourists in Spain in order to publicize their political beliefs. Thulin is in complete accord with the students, which irks Montand. Now Montand learns that the man who went to Spain instead of him, Bouise, has been killed. Montand leaves for Madrid and things go awry almost instantly. Thulin is the only person who can save him and she boards a plane to Madrid in the hope that she can extricate her lover from the situation. There was more tension than action in this picture, which was typical of the way Resnais directs, as opposed to Costa-Gavras. Resnais is the man who gave us the perplexing and tedious LAST YEAR AT MARIENBAD, although screenwriter Semprun can do more active scripts, as he proved when he co-wrote Z. Filmed in and around Paris, LA GUERRE EST FINIE never did much at the box office and sank into the sunset quickly. (In French; English subtitles.)

p, Catherine Winter, Gisele Rebillon; d, Alain Resnais; w, Jorge Semprun; ph, Sacha Vierny; m, Giovanni Fusco; ed, Eric Pluet; set d, Jacques Saulnier; cos, Marie Martine; makeup, Alexandre and Eliane Marcus.

Drama   **(PR:C-O   MPAA:NR)**

LA HABANERA**
(1937, Ger.) 98m UFA bw

Zarah Leander (*Astree Sternhjelm*), Julia Serda (*Ana Sternhjelm*), Ferdinand Marian (*Don Pedro de Avila*), Karl Martell (*Dr. Sven Nagel*), Boris Alekin (*Dr. Luis Gomez*), Paul Bildt (*Dr. Pardway*), Edwin Jurgensen (*Shumann*), Michael Schulz-Dornburg (*Little Juan*), Rosita Alcaraz (*Spanish Dancer*), Lisa Helwig (*Nurse*), Geza von Foldessy (*Chauffeur*), Carl Kuhlmann.

One of Douglas Sirk's pre-American films (under his real name of Detlef Sierck), LA HABANERA tells the story of Leander who falls in love with Marian while on a Puerto Rico-bound cruise ship with her aunt Serda. With little hesitation they get married. Ten years later, living on an island, Leander is unhappy, consoled only by her son. When a mysterious disease threatens the island, Martell, a Swedish doctor, visits and falls in love with Leander. She leaves behind her greedy husband (who has been covering up the outbreak in an attempt to save his crops) and leaves for Sweden with Martell. Interesting only as a precursor to the brilliant melodramas Sirk would later produce in the U.S.

p, Bruno Duday; d, Detlef Sierck [Douglas Sirk]; w, Gerhard Menzel; ph, Franz Weihmayr; m, Lothar Bruhne; set d, Anton Weber, Ernst Albrecht; m/l, "Kinderlied," "Du Kannst es Nicht Wissen," Bruhne, Sierck.

Drama   **(PR:A   MPAA:NR)**

LA HIJA DEL ENGANO   (SEE: DAUGHTER OF DECEIT, 1977, Mex.)

LA JOVEN   (SEE: YOUNG ONE, THE, 1961, Mex.)

LA KERMESSE HEROIQUE   (SEE: CARNIVAL IN FLANDERS, 1936, Fr.)

LA LAMA NEL CORPO   (SEE: MURDER CLINIC, THE, 1967, Ital./Fr.)

LA LUNE DANS LE CANIVEAU
(SEE: THE MOON IN THE GUTTER, 1983, Fr./Ital.)

LA MALDICION DE LA MOMIA AZTECA
(SEE: CURSE OF THE AZTEC MUMMY, THE, 1965, Mex.)

LA MAMAM ET LA PUTAIN
(SEE: THE MOTHER AND THE WHORE, 1973, Fr.)

LA MANDARINE   (SEE: SWEET DECEPTION, 1972, Fr.)

LA MANDRAGOLA   (SEE: MANDRAGOLA, 1966, Fr./Ital.)

LA MARCA DEL MUERTO
(SEE: CREATURE OF THE WALKING DEAD, 1960, Mex.)

LA MARIE DU PORT*
(1951, Fr.) 100m Sacha Gordine/Bellon-Foulke bw (AKA: MARIE DU PORT)
Jean Gabin (Chatelard), Blanchette Brunoy (Odile), Nicole Courcel (Marie), Julien Carette (Viau), Claude Romain (Marcel), Jeanne Marken (Patronne).

The sense of impending doom so important to most of Carne's earlier works such as PORT OF SHADOWS and DAYBREAK takes on a much more subtle tone in this complex love story. When his sophisticated mistress' father dies, successful restaurateur Gabin travels to the small fishing village that was once Brunoy's home to attend the funeral. He begins to carry on what he considers to be an innocent affair with Courcel, the younger sister of mistress Brunoy. The girl, however, takes Gabin's attentions quite seriously. It is not until he discovers that Brunoy has been carrying on with the town's version of a Romeo that he finally realizes the value of Courcel's vitality. The slowly developing plot allows for ample exposure of the picturesque fishing village and a gradual examination of the characters. Both Gabin and Courcel go through intense changes, the girl learns those pains which accompany pleasure, while Gabin regains the youthful energy that he had lost in his petit bourgeois existence. The many twists of this convoluted love-cum-acquisition story reflect the life and times of its author, famed mystery writer Simenon, who confessed to a fantastic number of sexual conquests—averaging nearly one woman a day—during his mature years (one wonders how he can have been so prolific a writer with such a proliferation of amorous activities). The picture marks a change of character for Gabin, previously most often cast as a defeated fugitive. This time he is successful and wise, albeit with a hint of a checkered past; he was to repeat this characterization many times in his post-war films. (In French; English subtitles.)

p, Sacha Gordine; d, Marcel Carne; w, G. Ribemont-Dessaignes, Louis Chavance, Carne (based on the novel by Georges Simenon); ph, Henri Alekan; m, Joseph Kosma; ed, Leonide Azar.

Drama   (PR:C   MPAA:NR)

LA MARIEE ETAIT EN NOIR
(SEE: BRIDE WORE BLACK, THE, 1968, Fr./Ital.)

LA MARSEILLAISE*1/2** (1938, Fr.) 130m La Marseillaise Society/World bw
Pierre Renoir (Louis XVI), Lise Delamare (Marie Antoinette), Leon Larive (Picard), William Haguet (La Rochefoucald-Liancourt), Louis Jouvet (Roederer), Aime Clairond (M. de Saint-Laurent), Maurice Escande (Le Seigneur du Village), Andre Zibral (M. de Saint Merri), Andrex (Arnaud), Ardisson (Bomier), Paul Dullac (Javel), Fernand Flamant (Ardisson), Jean-Louis Allibert (Moissan), Nadia Siberskaia (Louison), Jeanna Hella (the interpellant), Edouard Delmont (Cabri, the farmer), Elisa Ruis (Mme. de Lamballe), G. Lefebure (Mme. Elizabeth), Pamela Stirling, Genia Vaury (servants), Jean Aquistapace (the mayor), Georges Spanelly (La Chesnaye), Pierre Nay (Dubouchage), Jaque Catelain (Capt. Langlade), Edmond Castle (Leroux), Jean Ayme (M. de Fougerolles), Irene Joachim (Mme. de Saint-Laurent), Alex Truchy (Cuculiere), Georges Peclet (Lt. Pignatel), Geo-Dorlys (A Marseillaise Leader), Jo Lastry (Capt. Massugue), Adolphe Autran (The Drummer), Gaston Modot, Carette (Two Volunteers), Severine Lerczinska (farm woman), Marthe Marty (Baumier's mother), Edmond Beauchamp (The Priest), Roger Pregor, Pierre Ferval, Fernand Bellon, Jean Boissemond, Blanche Destournelles, Lucy Kieffer.

The story is of the march on Paris by a battalion of 500 volunteers which arrives on time to capture the Tuilleries, leading to the publication of the Brunswick Manifesto and the overthrow of the monarchy of Louis XVI. Essentially the film is a grand march from Marseilles to Paris, contrasting the lives of the commoners with those of the aristocracy. With this march of course came the most patriotic of French songs, "La Marseillaise," and it is this song that the peasants energetically sing, allowing it to evolve from a little melody to an anthem. Renoir does what he does best by providing a naturalistic, nearly documentary portrayal of the characters. In one sense LA MARSEILLAISE is something of a western, with its march paralleling that of the wagon train. Released on the heels of the brilliant GRAND ILLUSION, this picture suffered from the prejudice that a director shouldn't make two masterpieces in a row. A vastly inferior 79-minute version was released in the U.S. in 1939. Interestingly, it was produced for a labor organization (Confederation Generale de Travail) on a rather unorthodox subscription basis in which people would buy tickets to see the film before it was even shot, thereby financing its production. Working as an assistant director was Jacques Becker, who directed the great CASQUE D'OR.

d, Jean Renoir; w, Renoir, Carl Koch, N. Martel Dreyfus, Mme. Jean-Paul Dreyfus; ph, Jean-Serge Bourgoin, Alain Douarinou, Jean-Marie Maillols, Jean-Paul Alphen, J. Louis; m, Lalande, Gretry, Jean Philippe Rameau, Johann Sebastian Bach, Wolfgang Amadeus Mozart, Rouget de l'Isle, Kosma, Sauveplane (orchestra under the direction of Roger Desormieres); ed, Marguerite Renoir, Marthe Huguet; set d, Leon Barsacq, Georges Wakhevitch, John Perier; cos, Granier Chanel.

Historical Drama   (PR:A   MPAA:NR)

LA MATERNELLE1/2**
(1933, Fr.) 100m Photosonor bw (AKA: CHILDREN OF MONTMARTRE)
Madeleine Renaud (Rose), Paulette Elambert (Marie Coeuret), Mady Berry (Mme. Paulin), Alice Tissot (Superintendent), Henri Debain (Dr. Libois), Sylvette Fillacier (Mme. Coeuret), Alex Bernard (Professor), Jany Delille (Singer), Gaston Severin (Inspector), Edmond van Daele (Pantin).

Renaud takes a job as a nurse in a children's day care center and befriends the lovable Elambert, who has been abandoned by her prostitute mother. The two grow fond of each other, but when Renaud announces her upcoming marriage, Elambert is deeply affected. The child proceeds to throw herself into the Seine in a suicide attempt, but is rescued. Directed by Benoit-Levy and Marie Epstein (the sister of director Jean), the films falls flat at the point of the child's suicide attempt, an action so grossly unrealistic as to negate much of the masterpiece status this picture had

attained. The real greatness of this film comes not from its script or directors, but from the setting and the bright-eyed children who people it. Comprised mainly of nonactors, the children just beg to be photographed. Benoit-Levy directed this picture in the midst of over 400 educational shorts from 1920 to 1940, finding his calling in his work for UNESCO in the mid 1940s.

d&w, Jean Benoit-Levy, Marie Epstein (based on the novel by Leon Frapie); ph, Georges Asselin; m, Edouard Flament; m/l, Alice Verlay.

Drama   (PR:A   MPAA:NR)

LA MORT EN CE JARDIN (SEE: DEATH IN THE GARDEN, 1977, Fr./Mex.)

LA MORTADELLA   (SEE: LADY LIBERTY, 1972, Ital.)

LA MORTE EN DIRECT   (SEE: DEATHWATCH, 1980, Fr./Ger.)

LA MORTE RISALE A IERI SERA
(SEE: DEATH TOOK PLACE LAST NIGHT, 1970, Ital./Ger.)

LA MORTE VIENE DALLA SPAZIO
(SEE: DAY THE SKY EXPLODED, THE, 1958, Fr./Ital.)

LA MUERTA EN EST JARDIN
(SEE: DEATH IN THE GARDEN, 1977, Mex.)

LA NAVE DE LOS MONSTRUOS zero (1959, Mex.) 82m Sotomayor bw
Eulalio Gonzalez Piporro, Ann Bertha Lepe, Lorena Velazquez, Consuelo Frank, Manuel Lopez, Jesus Rodriguez, Jose Pardave.

Piporro is a cowboy who is discovered by a strange group of aliens who, in the midst of their planet-hopping, have stopped on Earth to collect specimens. Included in this bizarre bunch are the Prince of Mars, Tor the Robot, a lady vampire, and a vivacious female captain, the latter two deciding to make Earth their home while the others continue their voyages. Bad, very bad . . . and with bad songs, too.

p, Jesus Sotomayor; d, Rogelio A. Gonzalez; w, Jose Maria Fernandez Unsain, Alfredo Varela, Jr.; ph, Raul Martinez Solares.

Science-fiction   (PR:C-O   MPAA:NR)

LA NOTTE*1/2**
(1961, Fr./Ital.) 122m Nepi-Silver-Sofitedip/DD bw (AKA: THE NIGHT)
Marcello Mastroianni (Giovanni Pontano), Jeanne Moreau (Lidia), Monica Vitti (Valentina Gherardini), Bernhard Wicki (Tommaso), Maria Pia Luzi (Patient), Rosy Mazzacurati (Resy), Guido A. Marsan (Fanti), Gitt Magrini (Signora Gherardina), Vincenzo Corbella (Gherardina), Giorgio Negro (Roberto), Roberta Speroni (Berenice), Ugo Fortunati (Cesarino), Vittorio Bertolini, Valentino Bompiani, Salvatore Quasimodo, Giansiro Ferrata, Roberto Danesi, Ottiero Ottieri.

Mastroianni and Moreau are husband and wife in this study of emptiness and sterility in modern life and relationships. It opens with their visit to a hospitalized friend dying of cancer. They are on their way to a party for the publication of Mastroianni's new novel, but the celebration is hampered by Moreau's informing him, en route, that he disgusts her and she no longer wants to live with him. She leaves the party and wanders the barren streets for the remainder of the night, while Mastroianni chases after young Vitti, the enticing daughter of an industrialist who has offered him a job. When Moreau and Mastroianni confront one another at home later, the news of their friend's death that night draws them together once again. The finale has them making love in a field as the camera shyly backs away. Much of Antonioni's greatness is evident in this picture—the seemingly hopeless relationship between a man and a woman, the overwhelming environment which is devoid of emotion, and the quietly observant camerawork. But at the same time Antonioni is painfully obvious with his use of symbolism. One of the film's major faults lies in its casting of Mastroianni who simply doesn't fit the role. A problematic film which serves more as a transition for Antonioni than anything else, and seems to make even less sense when screened without having seen his previous film, the masterful L'AV-VENTURA.

p, Emanuele Cassuto; d, Michelangelo Antonioni; w, Antonioni, Tonino Guerra, Ernio Flaiano (based on a story by Antonioni); ph, Gianni di Venanzio; m, Giorgio Gaslini; ed, Eraldo da Roma; set d, Piero Zuffi.

Drama   (PR:C-O   MPAA:NR)

LA NOTTE BRAVA1/2**
(1962, Fr./Ital.) 96m Ajace Cinematografica-Franco London/Miller-Medallion bw (LES GARCONS; AKA: ON ANY STREET; BAD GIRLS DON'T CRY)
Elsa Martinelli (Anna), Antonella Lualdi (Supplizia), Jean-Claude Brialy (Scintillone), Laurent Terzieff (Ruggeretto), Franco Interlenghi (Bella-Bella), Anna Maria Ferrero (Nicoletta), Mylene Demongeot (Laura), Rosanna Schiaffino (Rossana), Tomas Milian (Achille), Marcella Valeri (Rossana's Mother).

The English translation of this title would read "the kind night," a rather cynical description of the escapades of three Roman thugs as they spend an entire day and night causing havoc. Lualdi, Brialy, and Terzieff are the three buddies who start out their day by stealing guns, which they then try to sell but are temporarily distracted by three prostitutes. In fitting with the character of these three youths, they try to make off without paying for services rendered. But the prostitutes are one up on the thugs and wisely steal their money. It's back to the city for the boys where they continue their destructive games. Watching them take advantage of three homosexuals, then seeing their attempts to make it with some girls gets quite tiring after awhile, making one wish to see some form of redeeming qualities in these youths. But none are offered—a supposedly powerful statement about the wasted existence of modern youth. Pasolini was credited with the script, showing the beginnings of his obsession with moral decay, which would have its ultimate expression in SALO.

p, Antonio Cervi, Alessandro Jacovoni; d, Mauro Bolognini; w, Pier Paolo Pasolini, Jacques-Laurent Bost; ph, Armando Nannuzzi; m, Piero Piccioni; ed, Nino Baragli; art d, Carlo Egidi.

Drama   **(PR:O MPAA:NR)**

LA NUIT AMERICAINE   (SEE: DAY FOR NIGHT, 1973, Fr.)

LA NUIT DE VARENNES***   (1983, Fr./Ital.) 135m GAU-COL/Triumph c

Marcello Mastroianni (Casanova), Jean-Louis Barrault (Nicolas Edme Restif), Hanna Schygulla (Countess Sophie de la Borde), Harvey Keitel (Thomas Paine), Jean-Claude Brialy (Mons. Jacob), Daniel Gelin (De Wendel), Jean-Louis Trintignant (Mons. Sauce), Michel Piccoli (King Louis XVI), Eleonore Hirt (Queen Marie-Antoinette), Andrea Ferreol (Mme. Adelaide Gagnon), Michel Vitold (De Florange), Laura Betti (Virginia Capacelli), Enzo Jannacci (Italian Barker), Pierre Malet (Emile Delage), Hugues Quester (Jean-Louis Romeuf), Dora Doll (Nanette Precy), Caterina Boratto (Mme. Faustine), Didi Porego (Mme. Sauce), Evelyne Dress (Agnes Restif), Aline Messe (Marie Madeleine), Patrick Osmond (National Guard Commander), Jacques Peyrac (Outrider), Yves Collignon (Drouet), Agnes Nobecourt (Hubertine), Claude LeGors, Vernon Dobtcheff, Ugo Fangareggi, Roger Trapp, Annie Bell, Fausto di Bella, Jacques Zanetti, Antonella Cancellieri, Robert Nobaret, Bruno DuLouvat, Noelle Mesny, Jeanne Carre, Jeanne Tatu, Albert Michel, Enrico Bergier.

This good, often bizarre, historical drama takes a factual basis and runs wild with imaginative possibilities. King Louis (Piccoli) and his queen (Hirt) flee Paris to the safety of Varennes at the onslaught of the French Revolution. Close behind in a pursuing coach are Casanova (Mastroianni, in an excellent performance) and the American revolutionary Thomas Paine (Keitel). The latter pair bicker about life and politics as they travel; all the while, the revolution, a growing behemoth, looms in the future. Good direction, coupled with a lush photography which takes full advantage of the surrounding countryside, enhances the unusual premise. An enjoyable black comedy.

p, Renzo Rossellini; d, Ettore Scola; w, Scola, Sergio Amidei; ph, Armando Nannuzzi; m, Armando Travajoi; ed, Raimondo Crociani; art d, Dante Ferretti; cos, Gabriella Pescucci.

Historical Drama/Comedy   **Cas.**   **(PR:O MPAA:R)**

LA NUIT DES GENERAUX
                    (SEE: NIGHT OF THE GENERALS, THE, 1966, Fr./Brit.)

LA PARISIENNE***
(1958, Fr./Ital.) 85m Ariane-Cinetel-Filmsonor-Rizzoli/UA c (UNE PARISIENNE; PARISIENNE)

Brigitte Bardot (Brigitte Laurier), Charles Boyer (Prince Charles), Henri Vidal (Michel), Andre Luguet (Premier Laurier), Nadia Gray (Queen Greta), Madeleine Lebeau (Monique), Noel Roquevert (Herblay), Robert Pizani (Ambassador), Guy Trejean (Colonel), Claire Maurier (Caroline), Marcel Peres (General).

A lively humorous romp which puts Bardot in her finest comic role—the innocent yet enticing daughter of the French Premier. A marriage to Vidal, the Premier's private secretary, is arranged but when he takes to a flirtatious lifestyle BB decides to fight back. She makes eyes at Boyer, an aging Prince, and flies with him to a sunny Riviera vacation spot. Before long, after both Boyer and BB catch colds, the love-stricken newlyweds reunite and the prince goes on his way. One of the stronger arguments for Bardot's talent, with excellent support from Boyer and Boisrond's assured direction. (In French; English subtitles.)

p, Francis Cosne; d, Michel Boisrond; w, Annette Wademant, Jean Aurel, Jacques Emmanuel, Boisrond; ph, Marcel Grignon (Technicolor); m, Hubert Rostaing, Andre Hodeir, Henri Crolla; ed, Claudine Bouche; art d, Jean Andre.

Comedy   **(PR:C-O MPAA:NR)**

LA PART DE L'OMBRE   (SEE: BLIND DESIRE, 1948, Fr.)

LA PASSANTE***   (1983, Fr./Ger.) 106m Libra/Cinema 5 c

Romy Schneider (Elsa Weiner/Lina Baumstein), Michel Piccoli (Max Baumstein), Wendelin Werner (Max, As A Child), Helmut Griem (Michel Weiner), Gerard Klein (Maurice Bouillard), Dominique Labourier (Charlotte), Mathieu Carriere (Ruppert/Federico/Ambassador), Maria Schell.

A mysterious character study of Piccoli, a peace activist who inexplicably kills a Paraguayan ambassador when he learns that he is really a former Nazi. The concept of SS men altering their identities and rising in the South American political ranks is an interesting idea and is intelligently handled in LA PASSANTE, mainly due to a well-structured script which intercuts Piccoli's youth with the present. Schneider's final screen appearance as Piccoli's wife and the woman who cared for him as a young boy is a commendable way to finish a much-praised career. (In French; English subtitles.)

d, Jacques Ruffio; w, Ruffio, Jacques Kirsner; ph, Jean Jacques Cazoit; m, Georges Delerue.

Drama   **Cas.**   **(PR:C MPAA:NR)**

LA PEAU DOUCE   (SEE: SOFT SKIN, THE, 1964, Fr.)

LA PERMISSION   (SEE: STORY OF A THREE DAY PASS, THE, 1968, Fr.)

LA PETITE CAFE   (SEE: PLAYBOY OF PARIS, 1930)

LA PLANETE SAUVAGE   (SEE: FANTASTIC PLANET, 1973, Fr./Czech.)

LA POUPEE   (SEE: DOLL, THE, 1962, Fr.)

LA PRISE DE POUVOIR PAR LOUIS XIV
                             (SEE: RISE OF LOUIS XIV, THE, 1970, Fr.)

LA PRISONNIERE**
(1969, Fr./Ital.) 104m Corona-Vera-Fono Roma/AE c (LA PRIGIONIERA; AKA: THE FEMALE PRISONER) FEMALE PRISONER)

Laurent Terzieff (Stanislas Hassler), Bernard Fresson (Gilbert Moreau), Elisabeth Wiener (Jose), Dany Carrel (Maguy), Dario Riviere (Maurice), Michel Etcheverry, Claude Pieplu, Noelle Adam, Gilberte Geniat, Michel Piccoli, Charles Vanel, Andre Luguet, Annie Fargue, Germaine Delbat.

Wiener plays a woman whose secure and rather boring affair with an artist is sidetracked when she becomes attracted to suave art dealer Hassler. Her ardor cools when she discovers Terzieff's obsession with sadomasochistic photography—a hobby he indulges because of a problem he had with his mother, which can also partially account for his impotence. The two eventually do make some attempt at having a fling, but Fresson's boy friend finds out, and it turns into an ugly mess with the woman trying to commit suicide by leaving her car in front of a train. A far cry from some of Clouzot's earlier work such as WAGES OF FEAR, substituting an insight into the workings behind sexual obsession with a more shallow appeal to voyeurism. (In French; English subtitles.)

p, Robert Dorfman; d, Henri-Georges Clouzot; w, Clouzot, Monique Lange, Marcel Moussy; ph, Andres Winding (Eastmancolor); ed, Noelle Balenci; md, Gilbert Amy; art d, Jacques Saulnier; makeup, Michel Deruelle; English subtitles, Sonya Mays Friedman.

Drama   **(PR:O MPAA:M)**

LA PROMISE DE L'AUBE   (SEE: PROMISE AT DAWN, 1970, U.S./Fr.)

LA PROVINCIALE   (SEE: GIRL FROM LORRAINE, THE, 1982, Fr.)

LA QUESTION   (SEE: QUESTION, THE, 1977, Fr.)

LA RESIDENCIA   (SEE: HOUSE THAT SCREAMED, THE, 1970, Span.)

LA RONDE****   (1954, Fr.) 97m Commercial bw

Anton Walbrook (Raconteur), Simone Signoret (Leocadie the Prostitute), Serge Reggiani (Franz, the Soldier), Simone Simon (Marie, the Maid), Daniel Gelin (Alfred), Danielle Darrieux (Emma Breitkopf), Fernand Gravey (Charles, Emma's Husband), Odette Joyeux (The Grisette), Jean-Louis Barrault (Robert Kuhlenkampf), Isa Miranda (The Actress), Gerard Philipe (The Count), Robert Vattier (Prof. Schuller).

Released in Paris in 1950, LA RONDE, though quickly hailed as one of Max Ophuls' greatest achievements, was kept from U.S. shores for four years thanks to a judgment of "immoral" by the New York State censor board. A merry-go-round of romance is detailed in episodic fashion as characters drift from one sequence to the next, as they switch from one lover to another. Signoret, a young whore, meets Reggiani a soldier who leaves her for Simon. She then meets Gelin, who seduces the married Darrieux, whose husband is involved with Joyeux. She loves the poet Barrault, who in turn loves the actress Miranda, who gives her affections to Philipe. Love comes full circle when Philipe calls on Signoret, the hooker from the first episode. Each segment is held together by master of ceremonies Walbrook, who appears with the metaphorical carousel in each of his scenes. Originally Ophuls had planned to adapt a novel by Balzac with Greta Garbo in a lead role, but instead he turned his attentions to the heralded Arthur Schnitzler play. The Venice Film Fest awarded its "Best Screenplay" honors to LA RONDE, as did the Academy Awards. Britain's response was even more favorable, voting it the Best Film of 1951. Foolishly remade by Roger Vadim as CIRCLE OF LOVE, which is completely mangled by the director's maladroit hand.

p, Sasha Gordine; d, Max Ophuls; w, Ophuls, Jacques Natanson (based on the play "Der Reigen" by Arthur Schnitzler); ph, Christian Matras; m, Oscar Straus; ed, Leonide Azar; set d, D'Eaubonne.

Drama   **Cas.**   **(PR:O MPAA:NR)**

LA ROSE ESCORCHEE   (SEE: BLOOD ROSE, THE, 1970, Fr.)

LA ROUTE EST BELLE   (SEE: ROAD IS FINE, THE, 1930, Fr.)

LA RUE DES AMOURS FACILES
                             (SEE: RUN WITH THE DEVIL, 1963, Fr./Ital.)

LA SIGNORA SENZA CAMELIE
                             (SEE: LADY WITHOUT CAMELLIAS, THE, 1981, Ital.)

LA SIRENE DU MISSISSIPPI (SEE: MISSISSIPPI MERMAID, 1970, Fr./Ital.)

LA STRADA*****   (1956, Ital.) 115m Trans-Lux bw (AKA: THE ROAD)

Anthony Quinn (Zampano), Giulietta Masina (Gelsomina), Richard Basehart (Matto "The Fool"), Aldo Silvani (Columbiani), Marcella Rovere (La Vedova), Livia Venturini (La Suorina).

Fellini was at the top of his form and here is one case where nepotism paid off as he used his wife, Masina, in the lead and she was magnificent. Masina is a combination of Harry Langdon, Chaplin, and at least five other great silent comedians who could alternately make you laugh, then break your heart. The story of LA STRADA is so deceptively stark that it would have been turned down in screenplay form by most producers and probably was only made because two American stars were employed to assure a U.S. audience. It won countless awards including an Academy Award for Best Foreign Film, the New York Film Critics Award, Grand Prize at Venice, at Edinburgh, and perhaps 50 other accolades. Quinn is a traveling circus strongman who takes to Italy's villages on a motorcycle which tows his small house. His act consists of breaking chains by expanding his chest, then cadging donations from the assemblage. He realizes that he can't go on like this much longer and must have some extra added attraction to keep the *lire* coming in, so he "buys" a dim-witted girl, Masina, while visiting a seaside town. Her mother is poor and appreciates the chance to get rid of Masina and make a few coins while doing it (his prior purchase, Masina's sister, died before her warranty expired). The two of them begin traveling and Quinn treats Masina in not quite a loving fashion, as he might treat a pet schnauzer. He gives her performing lessons and she's soon able to beat a drum and play a trumpet, but little else. She is his chattel, his mistress, his assistant, and she is enjoying herself. Quinn sleeps with every woman he can find and is less than gentlemanly with Masina, but she keeps turning the other cheek. She wishes that he could pay a bit more attention to her but realizes that he is the way he is and there is no way she can change him. At one point, Quinn leaves her to sleep with a prostitute and she spends the night in tears, then sees a symbolic riderless horse go by her in the morning. The two perform at a wedding in the hinterlands and she is taken by the children to look at a deformed child in his bed. They play at fairs and functions and finally hook up with a tiny circus on the periphery of Rome where they meet Basehart, a clown and high-wire artist. Quinn and Basehart take an instant dislike to each other and Quinn attacks the clown with a knife, then gets thrown in jail for his crime. Basehart invites Masina to join him, but she is like a faithful puppy and refuses, as she feels she must stay outside the jail and wait for Quinn to be released. Quinn finally gets out and the loyal Masina is ready to serve him. They encounter Basehart on the road where he is busily changing a tire. Quinn goads Basehart into a fight and doesn't mean to, but kills the clown. Masina is thrown into a depression and begins to quietly cry like an animal whose master has died. Quinn takes it as long as he can but eventually strands her on a mountain, leaving her with the only remnant of their relationship: the trumpet. Many years later, Quinn is still traveling, and learns that Masina has died. It is only then that he realizes how much he cared for her. Grief descends on him; he gets drunk, goes to a quiet beach, and rinses himself in the water as an act of baptism, then begins to sob uncontrollably as all the love he never shared with her rolls down his cheeks in a torrent of deep emotion that may never stop. It's about love, loneliness, the need for someone with whom to share life and a mixture of smiles, tears, and angst. Fellini knows how to touch an audience down where very few filmmakers dare to go; to the soul. Quinn was marvelous in his role and his performance was a revelation to those who had only seen him as a lout or brute in various Hollywood films. He might have won the Oscar as Best Actor but he was already in the running as Best Supporting Actor for LUST FOR LIFE and won that. LA STRADA took almost three years to get the green light across the pond to the U.S., but the wait was worth it. Fellini hasn't made many movies when compared with the output of Hollywood-based directors. However, almost all of them have had something so unique and important that we can forgive his lack of quantity. There's a bit of symbolism in LA STRADA, though not nearly as much as Fellini has used in other films. This is probably the simplest film he's ever done, and it may also be his most beautiful. The picture of Masina, wearing a silly hat, playing that haunting theme on the trumpet, is one that you'll never forget.

p, Carlo Ponti, Dino De Laurentiis; d, Federico Fellini; w, Fellini, Tullio Pinelli, Ennio Flaiano (based on a story by Fellini and Pinelli); ph, Otello Martelli; m, Nino Rota; ed, Leo Cattozo, Lina Caterini; md, Franco Ferrara; art d, Mario Ravasco, E. Cervelli.

Drama **Cas.** **(PR:A-C MPAA:NR)**

LA STRADA PER FORT ALAMO
(SEE: ROAD TO FORT ALAMO, THE, 1966, Fr./Ital.)

LA SYMPHONIE PASTORALE
(SEE: SYMPHONIE PASTORALE, 1948, Fr.)

LA TENDA ROSSA (SEE: RED TENT, THE, 1971, Ital./USSR)

LA TERRA TREMA****
(1947, Ital.) 160m Universalia/Mario De Vecchi bw (AKA: EPISODA DEL MARE; THE EARTH WILL TREMBLE)

Luchino Visconti, Antonio Pietrangeli *(Narrators)*.

It would be very hard not to call LA TERRA TREMA one of the finest pieces of filmmaking to emerge from the Italian Neo-Realist movement; it possesses a lyrical quality that subtly combines photographic beauty with the cruel and harsh plight that is the fate of the film's subjects. Yet we remain a bit leary of naming this undoubtedly great film one of the masterpieces of all time, mainly as a result of its unnerving length and Visconti's tendency to lapse too heavily into preaching. Set in a small Sicilian fishing village with the entire cast consisting of members of the village—their weather-beaten faces lending a sense of realism to the account of the tragedy that is part of the village. The underlying theme involves the villagers' victimization by northern entrepreneurs who control the fishing market. One young man returns home from the war with the idea that the villagers do not have to be subject to such unfairness, but through their combined efforts can rearrange the system and eventually be relieved of their imposed poverty. His attempt at achieving this goal of independence is never successful, forcing him to rely once again upon the businessman he has been so vocal in fighting. He admits his defeat in order to insure that the family he supports will be able to survive without having to resort to begging. Though some of the situations appear a bit contrived, LA TERRA TREMA is still a powerful picture that exposes the incongruities inherent in a society where the privileged are allowed to take advantage of those whom they consider inferior. The photography is quite stunning, and although none of the actors were professionals, they were quite capable in transferring their underlying turmoil to the screen. After all, they were basically just playing themselves. Even though LA TERRA TREMA is considered to be quite a brilliant film, it met with near financial disaster, prompting a redubbing of the hard-to-understand Sicilian dialect into proper Italian and to cutting many of the scenes. The original version was not made available to the public again for another 17 years.

p, Salvo D'Anglo; d&w, Luchino Visconti (based on the novel *I Malavoglia* by Giovanni Verga); ph, G. R. Aldo; ed, Mario Serandrei; md, Willi Ferrero.

Drama **(PR:A MPAA:NR)**

LA TERRAZA (SEE: TERRACE, THE, 1964, Arg.)

LA TRAVIATA** (1968, Ital.) 110m B.L. Vision-I.C.I.T./Royal c

Anna Moffo *(Violetta Valery)*, Gino Bechi *(Giorgio Germont)*, Franco Bonisolli *(Alfredo Germont)*, Mafalda Micheluzzi *(Flora Bervoix)*, Afro Poli *(Dr. Grenvil)*, Glauco Scarlini *(Gastone)*, Arturo La Porta *(Baron Douphol)*, Athos Cesarini *(Giuseppe)*, Maurizio Piacenti *(Marquis d'Obigny)*, Gianna Lollini *(Annina)*, Chorus and Orchestra of the Rome Opera.

Absolutely nothing is gained by bringing this great Verdi opera to the screen except to sit back and listen to the wonderful music. The performances are flat and the staging is too theatrical. Verdi's name is the only thing that saves this one.

d&w, Mario Lanfranchi (based on the libretto by Francisco Maria Piave from the novel by Alexandre Dumas entitled *The Lady of the Camelias*); ph, Leonida Barboni (Eastmancolor); m, Giuseppe Verdi; ed, Gisa Levi Radicchi; prod d, Maurizio Monteverde; md, Giuseppe Patane; art d, Andrea Taccari; set d, Alberto Verso; ch, Gino Landi.

Opera **(PR:A MPAA:NR)**

LA TRAVIATA**** (1982) 105m Accent Films B.V.-R.A.I./UNIV c

Teresa Stratas *(Violetta Valery)*, Placido Domingo *(Alfredo Germont)*, Cornell MacNeil *(Giorgio Germont)*, Alan Monk *(Baron)*, Axelle Gall *(Flora Betvoix)*, Pina Cei *(Annina)*, Maurizio Barbacini *(Gastone)*, Robert Sommer *(Doctor Grenvil)*, Ricardo Oneto *(Marquis d'Obigny)*, Luciano Brizi *(Giuseppe)*, Tony Ammirati *(Messenger)*, Russell Christopher, Charles Antony, Geraldine Decker, Michael Best, Ferruccio Furlanetto, Ariel Bybee, Richard Vernon, Ekaterina Maksimova, Vladimir Vassiljev, Gabriella Borni.

The classic Verdi opera which has Violetta (played perfectly by Stratas) urged by Alfredo's father Germont to break off her affair with his son (played with equal fervor by Domingo). Eventually Alfredo tells Violetta what he really thinks of her in a damaging public outcry. The grand finale has Alfredo reunited with the dying Violetta. Director Zeffirelli has outdone himself this time, putting an opera on the screen better than anyone else in film. Immeasurably better than Saura's CARMEN (released later but which received an undeserved Academy Award nomination), LA TRAVIATA can boast not only the presence of Placido Domingo but some truly amazing camerawork. Cameraman Guarnieri and art director Quaranta have combined to deliver a flowing, sparkling set which is an elaborate feast for the viewer—a worthy accompaniment to the brilliant score. The camera dollies, zooms, cranes, and pans relentlessly showcase the gigantic and elaborately constructed set. The candlelit scenes often rival those of Kubrick's BARRY LYNDON, though Zeffirelli can back up his beauty with more than a hint of script. The exceptional final sequence (Violetta's death) is punctuated by a sweeping camera move which starts in closeup, pulls back and cranes up, then proceeds to practically dive onto a flower-laden table. After watching this film (whether or not you like opera) you'll begin to wonder what possessed the director to make ENDLESS LOVE. Or maybe there are two Franco Zeffirellis in the film world. (In Italian; English subtitles.)

p, Tarak Ben Ammar; d&w, Franco Zeffirelli (based on the libretto by Francesco Maria Piave from the novel by Alexandre Dumas entitled *The Lady of the Camelias*); ph, Ennio Guarnieri; m, Guiseppe Verdi; ed, Peter Taylor, Franca Sylvi; md, James Levine; prod d, Zeffirelli; art d, Gianni Quaranta; set d, Bruno Carlino; cos, Piero Tosi; ch, Alberto Testa.

Opera **(PR:A MPAA:G)**

LA TRUITE (SEE: TROUT, THE, 1982, Fr.)

LA VACCA E IL PRIGIONIERO
(SEE: COW AND I, THE, 1961, Fr./Itai./Ger.)

LA VACHE ET LE PRISONNIER
(SEE: COW AND I, THE, 1961, Fr./Ital./Ger.)

LA VALLEE DES PHARAOHS
(SEE: CLEOPATRA'S DAUGHTER, 1963, Fr./Ital.)

LA VENGANZA DEL SEXO (SEE: CURIOUS DR. HUMPP, 1967, Arg.)

LA VIA LATTEA (SEE: THE MILKY WAY 1969, Fr./Ital.)

LA VIACCIA**1/2
(1962, Fr./Ital.) 103m Titanus Galatea-S.G.C./EM c (AKA: THE LOVE MAKERS)

Jean-Paul Belmondo *(Amerigo Casamonti)*, Claudia Cardinale *(Bianca)*, Pietro Germi *(Stefano Casamonti)*, Paul Frankeur *(Ferdinando Casamonti)*, Romolo Valli *(Dante)*, Gabriella Pallotta *(Carmelinda)*, Gina Sanmarco *(Madam)*, Marcella Valeri *(Beppa)*, Emma Baron *(Giovanna)*, Franco Balducci *(Tognaccio)*, Claudio Biava *(Harlequin)*, Nando Angelini *(1st Young Man)*, Giuseppe Tosi *(Casamonti Relative)*, Duilio D'Amore *(Bernando)*, Paola Pitagora *(Anna)*, Gianna Giachetti *(Girl)*, Rosita Di Vera Cruz *(Margherita)*, Olimpia Cavalli *(Girl)*, Maurice Poli, Dante Posani, Rina Morelli, Renzo Palmer.

Late 19th-century period piece set in Florence and the nearby countryside centers on the escapades of Belmondo as the son of a struggling farm family. At the start he leaves the farm (entitled "La Viaccia") to go to Florence and live with his wealthy uncle in the hopes of getting on his good side and securing a piece of his will. But once in the city the youth's more passionate nature takes over, with him falling head-over-heels for prostitute Cardinale. She only views Belmondo as another paying customer, which doesn't stop the youth from pursuing her. At one point he is even sent back to the farm to keep him off the path of debauchery he has chosen.

But Belmondo is soon back in Florence and at the doorstep of Cardinale, getting himself deeper and deeper into an abyss which is his eventual undoing. This dark and dreary film was highlighted by superb performances from both Belmondo and Cardinale, though the bleakness of the story gives a very distorted view of their characters.

p, Alfredo Bini; d, Mauro Bolognini; w, Vasco Pratolini, Pasquale Festa Campanile, Massimo Franciosa (based on the novel *L'eredita* by Mario Pratesi); ph, Leonida Barboni (Eastmancolor); m, Claude Debussy (from "Rhapsodie"), Piero Piccioni; ed, Nino Baragli; md, Franco Ferrara; art d, Flavio Mogherini; set d, Piero Tosi; cos, Tosi.

Drama (PR:C-O MPAA:NR)

LA VICTOIRE EN CHANTANT
(SEE: BLACK AND WHITE IN COLOR, 1976, Fr.)

LA VIE CONTINUE★★ (1982, Fr.) 93m Triumph/COL c

Annie Girardot (*Jeanne*), Jean-Pierre Cassel (*Pierre*), Pierre Dux (*Max*), Michel Aumont (*Henri*), Giulia Salvatori (*Catherine*), Paulette Dubost (*Elizabeth*), Emmanuel Gayet (*Philippe*), Rivera Andres (*Jacquot*).

Life goes on for Girardot after she is widowed suddenly when her husband dies of a heart attack. When the initial shock of his loss wears off she must learn to cope with the new situation. An unflattering melodrama from France which sheds little light on widowhood.

p, Lise Fayolle, Giorgio Silvagni; d, Moshe Mizrahi; w, Mizrahi, Rachel Fabien; ph, Yves Lafaye; m, Georges Delerue; art d, Dominique Andre.

Drama **Cas.** (PR:A MPAA:PG)

LA VIE DE CHATEAU★★½
(1967, Fr.) 92m Ancinex-Cobela-Productions de la Gueville/Royal Films International bw (AKA: A MATTER OF RESISTANCE)

Catherine Deneuve (*Marie*), Philippe Noiret (*Jerome*), Pierre Brasseur (*Dimanche*), Mary Marquet (*Charlotte*), Henri Garcin (*Julien*), Carlos Thompson (*Klopstock*), Marc Dudicourt (*Schimmelbeck*), Alexis Micha (*The Boy*), Robert Moor (*Plantier The Gardener*), Donald O'Brien (*American Officer*), Paul Le Person (*Roger*), Pierre Rousseau (*German Orderly*), Marie Marc (*Dimanche's Housekeeper*), Annie Guegan (*Waitress In Bar*), Niksa Stefanini (*German General*), Christian Barbier (*French Colonel*), Jean-Pierre Moulin (*Lieutenant*), Valerie Camille (*English Girl*).

One of the more light-hearted treatments of the German Occupation in France during WW II, with Deneuve as the young beauty who turns everybody's head around and sets the whole plot going. Married to the lazy and oafish Noiret, who doesn't even seem to be aware that there is a war going on, a bit of spark is added to her life when Garcin comes knocking at her door. He's around to assist the French Resistance in setting up guidance for the American planes preparing to embark on the D-Day mission, but most of his time seems to be taken up pursuing Deneuve. The local German commander then notices the charms of the young woman and decides to make the Noiret's chateau his new headquarters. It is not long before Garcin shows up again, dead drunk and sad at having to part from Deneuve, creating quite a ruckus as they hide his identity from the Germans. None of the performers seemed to take the project very seriously and none of the performers was overserious in their portrayals (a departure for Deneuve, who at the time had been playing particularly intense dramatic roles) and the final product is all the better for it.

p, Nicole Stephane; d, Jean-Paul Rappeneau; w, Alain Cavalier, Claude Sautet, Rappeneau, Daniel Boulanger; ph, Pierre Lhomme; m, Michel Legrand; ed, Pierre Gillette; art d, Jacques Saulnier.

Comedy (PR:A MPAA:NR)

LA VIE DEVANT SOI (SEE: MADAME ROSA, 1977, Fr.)

LA VIOLENZA E L'MORE (SEE: MYTH, THE, 1965, Ital.)

LA VISITA★★ (1966, Ital./Fr.) 115m Zebra-Aera/Promenade bw

Sandra Milo (*Pina*), Francois Perier (*Adolfo*), Mario Adorf (*Cucaracha*), Angela Minervini (*Chiaretta*), Gastone Moschin (*Renato*), Didi Perego (*Nella*).

An intriguing but drawn-out tale of a woman in her late thirties looking for romance. Bored with her affair with a married truck driver, Milo gives a lonely hearts column a try. She is matched up with Perier, a seemingly reserved bookstore clerk who soon lets his vulgar, insulting, hard-drinking side show. After an evening of embarrassments he apologizes to Milo and she submits to his sexual advances. The following morning they go their separate ways, leaving open the possibility of further meetings.

p, Moris Ergas; d, Antonio Pietrangeli; w, Ettore Scola, Ruggero Maccari, Pietrangeli (based on the novel by Carlo Cassola); ph, Armando Nannuzzi; m, Armando Trovajoli; ed, Eraldo Da Roma; art d, Luigi Scaccianoce.

Drama (PR:O MPAA:NR)

LA VOGLIA MATTA (SEE: CRAZY DESIRE, 1964, Ital.)

LA VOIE LACTEE (SEE: THE MILKY WAY, 1969, Fr./Ital.)

LABBRA ROSSE (SEE: RED LIPS, 1964)

LABURNUM GROVE★★ (1936, Brit.) 73m Associated Talking Pictures/ABF bw

Edmund Gwenn (*Mr. Radfern*), Cedric Hardwicke (*Mr. Baxley*), Victoria Hopper (*Elsie Radfern*), Ethel Coleridge (*Mrs. Baxley*), Katie Johnson (*Mrs. Radfern*), Francis James (*Harold Russ*), James Harcourt (*Joe Fletten*), David Hawthorne (*Inspector Stack*), Frederick Burtwell (*Simpson*), Terence Conlin.

Gwenn is a well-respected man about town who really is a counterfeiter. In order to get rid of some pesky in-laws he sends them out shopping with his bogus bills and then leaves town before he gets hauled in. A harmless comedy which was one of director Reed's earliest ventures.

p, Basil Dean; d, Carol Reed; w, Gordon Wellesley, Anthony Kimmins (based on the play by J.B. Priestley); ph, John W. Boyle.

Comedy (PR:A MPAA:NR)

LABYRINTH (SEE: REFLECTION OF FEAR, A, 1973)

LACEMAKER, THE★★★½
(1977, Fr.) 108m Citel-Action F R 3-Filmproduktion Janus c (LA DENTELLIERE)

Isabelle Huppert (*Beatrice, "Pomme"*), Yves Beneyton (*Francois*), Florence Giorgetti (*Marylene*), Christian Baltauss (*Gerard*), Renata Schroeter (*Marianne*), Anne Marie Duringer (*Beatrice's Mother*), Michel De Re (*Painter*), Monique Chaumette (*Francois' Mother*), Jean Obe (*Francois' Father*), Odile Poisson (*Cashier*).

Huppert is a shy and passive girl nicknamed "Pomme" ("Apple") who travels to the Normandy coast with her best friend (Giorgetti) and meets Beneyton, a middle-class literature student. He is attracted to the sheepish, freckle-faced girl even though there is an obvious difference in class and education. They become lovers and get an apartment together in Paris. They are genuinely in love, but their differences begin to come to the surface. Giorgetti tries to convince Huppert to do more with her life than be a beautician. She is content, however, with simply loving Beneyton. When he brings her home to meet the family, he realizes that he should be with a woman who shares his interests in journalism. They soon drift apart and finally he asks her to leave. Huppert becomes ill and soon is admitted to a mental hospital. Her mother writes to Beneyton and asks him to pay her a visit. At the urging of his friends, he agrees. Their reunion is short-lived, however, and he returns to his friends, in tears and alone. A devastating look at the pain of love which was awarded a special prize at the Cannes Film Fest. The picture also marked the first starring role for the 22-year-old Huppert, who has gone on to become one of Europe's most breathtaking actresses, appearing in ENTRE NOUS and two recent Godard films, EVERY MAN FOR HIMSELF and PASSION. The unknown Huppert's performance was impressive enough to win critical acclaim from the British Film Academy, which honored her with their Award for the Most Promising Newcomer of the Year. (In French; English subtitles.)

d, Claude Goretta; w, Goretta, Pascal Laine (based on the novel by Laine); ph, Jean Boffety (Eastmancolor); m, Pierre Jansen; ed, Joelle Van Effenterre.

Romance/Drama (PR:O MPAA:R)

LACOMBE, LUCIEN★★★ (1974) 141m FOX c

Pierre Blaise (*Lucien*), Aurore Clement (*France*), Holger Lowenadler (*Albert Horn*), Therese Gieshe (*Bella Horn*), Stephane Bouy (*Jean Bernard*), Loumi Iacobesco (*Betty Beaulieu*), Rene Bouloc (*Faure*), Pierre Decazes (*Aubert*), Jean Rougerie (*Tonin*), Gilberte Rivet (*Mme. Lacombe*), Jacques Rispal (*Mons. Laborit*), Andre Cleveau, Irene de Trebert, Quintet from the Hot Club of France.

Director Louis Malle directs his intellectual pretensions at the Occupation this time around. Blaise is a young farm boy who tries to join the French Resistance but is rejected because of his youth. He instead joins the Gestapo, which gives him a kingly treatment and supplies him with liquor and anything else he requests. He then makes the mistake of falling in love with a Jewish girl, Clement, resulting in her father's deportation. With Clement and her mother in tow, Blaise sets out for Spain with the Resistance out to kill him. A turn for the better for Malle who normally has a tendency to shroud audience sympathy in fatty intellect. Much of Malle's motivation came from his own experiences growing up in France during the German Occupation. Even so, his fellow countrymen did not care very much for this cutting portrayal of the Resistance and were quite vocal in their opinions. This caused Malle to migrate to America where he made such films as ATLANTIC CITY and PRETTY BABY. There is a great score, too, by Django Reinhardt.

p&d, Louis Malle; w, Malle, Patrick Modiano; ph, Tonino Delli Colli (Eastmancolor); m, Django Reinhardt, Andre Claveau, Irene de Trebert; ed, Suzanne Baron; art d, Ghislain Uhry.

War Drama (PR:O MPAA:R)

LAD, THE★ (1935, Brit.) 72m Twickenham/UNIV bw

Gordon Harker (*Bill Shane*), Betty Stockfield (*Lady Fandon*), Jane Carr (*Pauline*), Gerald Barry (*Lord Fandon*), Geraldine Fitzgerald (*Joan*), Barbara Everest (*Mrs. Lorraine*), John Turnbull (*Inspector Martin*), David Hawthorne (*Maj. Grannitt*), Sebastian Shaw (*Jimmy*), Michael Shepley (*Arthur Maddeley*), Wilfred Caithness (*Tanner*), Ralph Truman (*O'Shea*).

A lame film which has Harker playing the part of an ex-con who is mistaken for a detective and is hired by a wealthy family to keep their affairs private. Tempted by his lavish surroundings, he is nevertheless persuaded to go straight by the family's housekeeper, an old flame of his. It's supposed to be a comedy.

p, Julius Hagen; d, Henry Edwards; w, Gerard Fairlie (based on the novel by Edgar Wallace); ph, Sydney Blythe.

Comedy (PR:A MPAA:NR)

LAD: A DOG★★½ (1962) 98m WB c

Peter Breck (*Stephan Tremayne*), Peggy McCay (*Elizabeth Tremayne*), Carroll O'Connor (*Hamilcar Q. Glure*), Angela Cartwright (*Angela*), Maurice Dallimore (*Lester*), Alice Pearce (*Hilda*), Jack Daly (*The Poacher*), Charles Fredericks (*Sheriff*), Tim Graham (*Constable*), Lillian Buyeff (*Miss Woodward*), Lad the Dog.

Somebody at Warners one day must have been watching LASSIE and decided to bring back the idea of canine stars with LAD: A DOG. Lad is an all-out wonder dog capturing the hearts and minds of movie-going kids. He first wins a dog show which is fixed in favor of a jealous neighbor's pup. Then he goes on to save 8-year-old Cartwright from a poisonous snake, only to be pistol-whipped by a presumptuous nurse. Poor old Lad, already suffering from a snake bite, crawls off into the woods and buries himself in the mud to draw out the venom. Lad's primitive medical technique is a success and he gets well in time to capture a poacher who sets fire to his owner's barn.

p, Max J. Rosenberg; d, Aram Avakian, Leslie H. Martinson; w, Lillie Hayward, Roberta O. Hodes (based on the novel by Albert Payson Terhune); ph, Bert Glennon (Technicolor); m, Heinz Roemheld; ed, Tom McAdoo; art d, Jack Poplin; set d, William H. Kuehl; makeup, Gordon Bau.

Drama (PR:AAA MPAA:NR)

LAD FROM OUR TOWN**
(1941, USSR) 65m Central Art Film Studio/Artkino bw

Nikolai Kruichkov (Lukonin), Nikolai Bogoliubov (Burmin), Anna Smirnova (Varya), Nikolai Mordvinov (Vasnyetsov), V. Stepanov (Sevostyanov), V. Melyedyev (Pyetka), A. Alekseyev (Volodya), P. Liubeshkin (Safonov).

A musically sparked Russian romance between a tank officer and his opera singing wife, which is set against civilian life, the Spanish Civil War, and WW II. Some vivid war battles featuring the rugged Kruichkov, a tank officer, who is engaging as well in his love scenes.

d, Alexander Stolper, Boris Ivanov (based on the play by Konstantin Simonov); ph, S. Uralov; m, Nikolai Kriukov; English titles, Charles Clement.

Romance/War (PR:A MPAA:NR)

LADDIE***
(1935) 70m RKO bw

John Beal (Laddie Stanton), Gloria Stuart (Pamela Pryor), Virginia Weidler (Little Sister), Charlotte Henry (Shelly Stanton), Donald Crisp (Mr. Pryor), Gloria Shea (Sally Stanton), Willard Robertson (Mr. Stanton), Dorothy Peterson (Mrs. Stanton), Jimmy Butler (Leon Stanton), Greta Meyer (Candace), Mary Forbes (Mrs. Pryor), Grady Sutton (Peter Dover).

George Stevens' reincarnation of the 1925 silent film about life on the farm in Indiana. Beal is cast in the title role as a youngster in love with the daughter of a neighboring country gentleman. Of course the old fellow doesn't think too much of the young clodhopper. Stevens' fine direction can be seen as a sign of things to come in SHANE (1953) and GIANT (1956). Producer Berman, displaying an obvious eye for talent, signed Stevens on to direct the Academy Award nominated ALICE ADAMS (1935).

p, Pandro S. Berman; d, George Stevens; w, Ray Harris, Dorothy Yost (based on the novel by Gene Stratton-Porter); ph, Harold Wenstrom; ed, James Morley.

Drama (PR:AAA MPAA:NR)

LADDIE**½
(1940) 69m RKO bw

Tim Holt (Laddie), Virginia Gilmore (Pamela), Joan Carroll (Sister), Spring Byington (Mrs. Stanton), Robert Barrat (Mr. Stanton), Esther Dale (Bridgette), Miles Mander (Mr. Pryor), Sammy McKim (Leon), Joan [Leslie] Brodel (Shelley), Martha O'Driscoll (Sally), Rand Brooks (Peter Dover), Mary Forbes (Mrs. Pryor), Peter Cushing (Robert Pryor).

The third version of LADDIE contains much of the homey charm of the previous two, but lacks the skillful directorial talent of George Stevens. In this familiar tale, Holt is the Indiana farm boy who falls in love with the daughter of his new neighbor, an English squire. Joan Carroll truly captivates as the kid sister whose mischief keeps the romance brewing. A small role for Cushing before he became a major star in English horror films.

p, Cliff Reid; d, Jack Hively; w, Bert Granet, Jerry Cady (based on the novel by Gene Stratton-Porter); ph, Harry Wild; m, Roy Webb; ed, George Hively; art d, Van Nest Polglase; spec eff, Vernon I. Walker.

Drama (PR:AAA MPAA:NR)

LADIES AND GENTLEMEN, THE FABULOUS STAINS**½
(1982) 87m PAR c

Diane Lane (Corinne Burns), Ray Winstone (Billy), Peter Donat (Harley Dennis), David Clennon (Dave Robell), John Lehne (Stu McGrath), Cynthia Sikes (Alicia Meeker), Laura Dern (Jessica McNeil), Marin Kanter (Tracy Burns), Paul Cook (Danny), Steve Jones (Steve), Paul Simonon (Johnny), John [Fee] Waybill (Lou Corpse), Christine Lahti (Aunt Linda), Janet Wright (Brenda), Vince Welnick (Jerry Jervey), Barry Ford (Lawnboy).

Lane heads an all-girl, no-talent punk band that gets to go on stage after a member of a heavy-metal band called the Metal Corpses becomes a real corpse. Touring with a punk band tagged The Looters, Lane's band reaches phenomenal heights before it ever cuts a single. Named the Fabulous Stains, the band's trademark is a skunk-ish dyed hair ("Just call us skunks") and the "We don't put out" motto. They become the target of the unscrupulous Clennon, who becomes their agent and turns them into a merchandiser's dream. An ending which shows the Stains receiving a gold record, being a *People* magazine cover story, and doing a rock video, leaves the audience wondering about the idea of "selling out." In terms of its portrayal of rock'n'roll on the road, THE FABULOUS STAINS is a pretty accurate picture, but as a piece it doesn't really play. Director Lou Adler is no stranger to the music scene, having produced the rock documentary MONTEREY POP (1968) as well as THE ROCKY HORROR PICTURE SHOW (1975), and directing Cheech and Chong's UP IN SMOKE (1978). Obviously he knows how to make a buck on the midnight circuit, but that's his limit. He has, however, compiled one heck of a cast. Diane Lane (who would later become Francis Coppola's pet actress—THE OUTSIDERS (1983), RUMBLE FISH (1983), and COTTON CLUB (1984)) bares some 15-year-

old flesh and dons some see-through clothes in a preview of her rock'n'roll role in STREETS OF FIRE, but she's a far cry from the gentle romantic in A LITTLE ROMANCE (a role which she will probably never recapture). Adding a genuine feel to the music are Paul Cook and Steve Jones (as members of The Looters) who should know a thing or two about selling out. They were two of the guys in the Sex Pistols, the ultimate punk band, which broke up after receiving too much press. Paul Simonon (bass player from The Clash) and Fee Waybill (lead vocalist of The Tubes) bring along some more authenticity. Songs include "The Professionals," "Waste of Time," "Road Map." (Steve Jones, Paul Cook).

p, Joe Roth; d, Lou Adler; w, Rob Morton; ph, Bruce Surtees; ed, Tom Benko; prod d, Leon Ericksen; art d, Graeme Murray; set d, Peter Young.

Musical/Drama/Comedy (PR:O MPAA:R)

LADIES COURAGEOUS**
(1944) 88m UNIV bw

Loretta Young (Roberta Harper), Geraldine Fitzgerald (Virgie Alford), Diana Barrymore (Nadine), Anne Gwynne (Gerry Vail), Evelyn Ankers (Wilhelmina), Phillip Terry (Tommy Harper), David Bruce (Frank Garrison), Lois Collier (Jill), June Vincent (Mary Francis), Samuel S. Hinds (Brig. Gen. Wade), Richard Fraser (Col. Brennan), Frank Jenks (Snapper), Janet Shaw (Bee Jay), Kane Richmond (Alex Anderson), Billy Wayne (Mechanic), Dorothy Moore (Emily Templeton), Gwen Crawford (Ann Templeton), Ruth Roman (WAF), Fay Helm (WAVE), Dennis Moore (Tower Man), Matt McHugh (Cab Driver), Steve Brodie (Tower Man), Blake Edwards (Pilot), Chester Carlyle (General), Grandon Rhodes (Briefing Officer), Doris Linden (Hilda), Don McGill (MP Sergeant), Marie Harmon (Genevieve).

Young is in charge of a couple of dozen WAFS (Women's Auxiliary Ferrying Squad) and wants to make sure that they get all the recognition they deserve. We see them serving the Army in top form, but also on the brink of disaster. Fitzgerald, as Young's hotshot sister, nearly wipes out the WAFS when she carelessly cracks up a plane. A piece of feminist propaganda during WW II that may have made women enlist but sure didn't entertain them. Future producer and director Blake Edwards appears in a bit role as a pilot in one of his earliest movie appearances.

p, Walter Wanger; d, John Rawlins; w, Norman Reilly Raine, Doris Gilbert (based on the novel Looking For Trouble by Virginia Spencer Cowles); ph, Hal Mohr; ed, Philip Cahn; art d, John Goodman.

War (PR:A MPAA:NR)

LADIES CRAVE EXCITEMENT**
(1935) 67m Mascot bw

Norman Foster (Don Phelan), Evalyn Knapp (Wilma Howell), Esther Ralston (Miss Winkler), Eric Linden (Bob Starke), Purnell Pratt (Amos Starke), Gilbert Emery (J. Fenton Howell), Irene Franklin (Vi), Syd Saylor (Flynn), Emma Dunn (Mary Phelan), Mary McLaren (Maid), Jason Robards (Nick), Matt McHugh (Johnson), Francis McDonald (Terry), George Hayes (Dan McCloskey), Stanley Blystone, Russell Hicks, Max Wagner, Lynton Brent, Edward Pell, Robert Frazer, Herbert Heywood, Christian Rub.

The "March of Time" newsreels are disguised as the "March of Events" in this tale of two rival news camerapersons—Foster and Knapp. A romance builds as they are continually involved in a series of newsworthy events. Audiences crave excitement, too, but they didn't get too much from this picture.

p, Nat Levine; d, Nick Grinde; w, Wellyn Totman (based on a story by John Rathmell); ph, Ernest Miller, William Nobles; ed, Joseph Lewis.

Drama/Romance (PR:A MPAA:NR)

LADIES' DAY**
(1943) 62m RKO bw

Lupe Velez (Pepita), Eddie Albert (Wacky), Patsy Kelly (Hazel), Max Baer (Hippo), Jerome Cowan (Updyke), Iris Adrian (Kitty), Joan Barclay (Joan), Cliff Clark (Dan), Carmen Morales (Marianna), George Cleveland (Doc), Jack Briggs (Marty), Russ Clark (Smokey), Nedrick Young (Tony), Eddie Dew (Spike), Tom Kennedy (Dugan, House Detective), Ralph Sanford, Frank Mills, Bud Geary, Kernan Cripps (Umpires), Richard Martin, Russell Wade, Wayne McCoy, Malcolm McTaggart, Mal Merrihugh, Charles Russell, Jack Shea, Jack Gargan, Cy Malis (Ballplayers), Rube Schaeffer (Runner), Jack Carrington (Announcer on Field), Sally Wadsworth (Cute Blonde), Mary Stuart, Ariel Heath, Mary Halsey, Ann Summers (Wives), Eddie Borden (Man on Field), Don Kerr (Pepita's Assistant), George O'Hanlon (Young Rube), Earle Hodgins (Old-Man Customer), Russell Hoyt (Assistant Director), Henry Hall (Dr. Adams), Wesley Barry (Reporter), Allen Wood (Locker Boy), Norman Mayes (Pullman Porter), Teddy Mangean (Upstairs Bellhop), Barrie Millman (Baby), Jack O'Connor (Cab Driver), Jack Stewart (Doorman), George Noisom (Airport Mess Boy), Freddie Carpenter (Bellhop), Ted O'Shea (Airport Attendant), John Sheehan (Producer), Vinton Haworth (Director).

Albert has trouble concentrating on his pitching form while thinking about that of his wife Velez. To insure that he doesn't mess up, the players' wives kidnap the saucy newlywed and try to keep her locked in a hotel room until the championship is over. This poses some problems, however, as Velez is tougher to keep still than a Mexican jumping bean.

p, Bert Gilroy; d, Leslie Goodwins; w, Charles E. Roberts, Dane Lussier (based on a play by Robert Considine, Edward Clark Lilley, Bertrand Robinson); ph, Jack Mackenzie; m, Roy Webb; ed, Harry Marker; art d, Albert S. D'Agostino, Feild Gray.

Comedy/Romance (PR:A MPAA:NR)

LADIES IN DISTRESS*½
(1938) 66m REP bw

Alison Skipworth (Josephine Bonney), Polly Moran (Lydia Bonney), Robert Livingston (Braddock), Virginia Grey (Sally), Max Terhune (Dave Evans), Berton Churchill (Morgan), Leonard Penn (Roman), Horace MacMahon (2nd Thug), Allen Vincent (Spade), Eddie Acuff (1st Thug), Anthony Hughes (Lieutenant), Jack Carr (Policeman), Walter Sande (Duncan), Billy Wayne (Brown).

Skipworth, the tough-old-lady mayor of Bonneyville, sets her sights on making her town a better place in which to live. She enlists the aid of an ex-pupil (she was previously a teacher), Livingston, who gets the job done.

p, Harry Grey; d, Gus Meins; w, Dorrell and Stuart McGowan (based on a story idea by Dore Schary); ph, Jack Marta; ed, Ernest Nims; md, Alberto Columbo.

Drama **(PR:A MPAA:NR)**

LADIES IN LOVE** (1930) 64m Hollywood/CHES bw

Alice Day *(Brenda Lascelle)*, Johnny Walker *(Harry King)*, Freeman Wood *(Ward Hampton)*, Marjorie Kane *(Marjorie)*, James Burtis *(Al Pine)*, Dorothy Gould *(Patsy Green)*, Elinor Flynn *(Mary Wood)*, Mary Carr *(Mrs. Wood)*, Mary Foy *(Mrs. Tibbs)*, Bernie Lamont *(Frank Jones)*.

Day is a radio singer who attracts the interest of country boy-songwriter Walker, who's determined to get his song air play. Jealousy and deception nearly come between the pair, but their love is strong enough to keep them together. Most of the action takes place in the radio studio and includes the tunes: "Oh How I Love You" (sung by Day) and "Big Boy" (sung by Kane).

d, Edgar Lewis; w, Charles Beahan; ph, M.A. Anderson; ed, James Morley.

Drama/Romance **(PR:A MPAA:NR)**

LADIES IN LOVE ** 1/2** (1936) 97m FOX bw

Janet Gaynor *(Martha Kerenye)*, Loretta Young *(Susie Schmidt)*, Constance Bennett *(Yoli Haydn)*, Simone Simon *(Marie Armand)*, Don Ameche *(Dr. Rudi Imre)*, Paul Lukas *(John Barta)*, Tyrone Power, Jr. *(Karl Lanyi)*, Alan Mowbray *(Paul Sandor)*, Wilfrid Lawson *(Ben Horvath)*, J. Edward Bromberg *(Brenner)*, Virginia Field *(Countess Helena)*, Frank Dawson *(Johann)*, Egon Brecher *(Concierge)*, Vesey O'Davoren *(Fritz)*, Jayne Regan *(Mrs. Dreker)*, John Bleifer *(Porter)*, Eleanor Wesselhoeft *(Charwoman)*, William Brisbane *(Chauffeur)*, Monty Woolley *(Man In Box Seat)*, Lynn Bari *(Clerk)*, Helen Dickson *(Woman)*, Paul Weigel *(Waiter)*, Tony Merlo *(Assistant Stage Manager)*, Paul McVey *(Actor)*, Maxine Elliott Hicks *(Girl in Audience)*, Edward Peil, Jr. *(Boy in Audience)*, Hector Sarno *(Turkish Waiter)*.

A tame multi-storied comedy based on a Hungarian play, LADIES IN LOVE had a most impressive cast but failed to catch fire at the box office because the jollity was very studied and almost forced. A brief look at the cast list will indicate the fact that just about every Fox contract player was impressed into this expensive ($750,000) flop. Three Hungarian working girls pool their savings to rent an expensive apartment in Budapest in order to impress the men they want to marry and attract a higher class of beau. Gaynor is a poverty-stricken peeress who hustles neckties to make a living and to support the feeding habits of the rabbits owned by Ameche, a doctor who uses the furry animals in his research. She supplements that by assisting Mowbray, an egotistical magician. Bennett wants Lukas to marry her but he is reluctant. Meanwhile, she is being chased by Lawson, a rich young man, and keeps him at bay, dangling her decision before him and never committing. Lukas eventually turns from her to marry innocent Simone, a young farm girl. Young is a naive singer-dancer who wants to nab Power, an engaging count she's met at a cocktail party. The ins and outs of the love affairs are the stuff of this film. Power decides to leave Young and marry Field, a woman of his own station. Young responds by planning a suicide attempt. By mistake, Gaynor drinks the poison potion and Ameche is called in to save her. In doing so, he convinces her that he loves her and wants to marry her. Bennett sees their joy and attempts to get Lukas but he is set to marry Simone the following day so she takes Lawson off the string by agreeing to marry him. Power is already gone and Young is depressed and Lawson gives her a reason to live by deeding her a hat shop so she'll have something to do with her life and give up the idea of suicide. The film ends as the women leave the apartment and go their separate ways. There were some high-priced and high-strung women in this cast and everyone expected fireworks on and off the screen but they never exploded. The actresses did their jobs, had little to say to each other, and the lack of chemistry resulted in a dud. This was a very calculated "woman's picture" on the part of Darryl F. Zanuck, although women found it as trivial as men did. Good dialog but with none of the bubbling insouciance that a picture of this sort needs. The stage-bound heritage of the story is constantly evident.

p, B. G. DeSylva; d, Edward H. Griffith; w, Melville Baker (based on a play by Ladislaus Bus-Fekete); ph, Hal Mohr; ed, Ralph Dietrich; md, Louis Silvers; art d, William Darling; set d, Thomas Little; cos, Gwen Wakeling.

Comedy **(PR:A MPAA:NR)**

LADIES IN RETIREMENT* 1/2** (1941) 91m COL bw

Ida Lupino *(Ellen Creed)*, Louis Hayward *(Albert Feather)*, Evelyn Keyes *(Lucy)*, Elsa Lanchester *(Emily Creed)*, Edith Barrett *(Louisa Creed)*, Isobel Elsom *(Leonora Fiske)*, Emma Dunn *(Sister Theresa)*, Queenie Leonard *(Sister Agatha)*, Clyde Cook *(Bates)*.

An eerie tale which casts Lupino as the housemaid-companion of Elsom, a wealthy British ex-actress. When Lupino decides to let her two deranged half sisters stay for a visit, they get on Elsom's nerves and are asked to leave. Lupino knows that if her sisters enter the real world they will be institutionalized, so she strangles Elsom. The murderous trio continue to live in the mansion, dodging any suspicion until a nosey relative (Hayward) pays a visit. It's not long before he figures out what has happened, but until they're caught the suspense builds to a dramatic chill. The original play was based on a true story that occurred in France, when Euphrasie Mercier murdered her companion, Elodie Menetret, in 1886 to get money for her two insane sisters. In this fine film version of the stage play, in which Flora Robson gave an outstanding performance as the housekeeper, Lupino struggled against her youth and movie star aura to give her role some intensity, and she succeeded admirably, using everything in her repertoire to build her characterization.

p, Lester Cowan, Gilbert Miller; d, Charles Vidor; w, Garrett Fort, Reginald Denham (based on a play by Denham and Edward Percy, from H. B. Irving's *French Crime and Criminals)*; ph, George Barnes; m, Ernst Toch; ed, Al Clark; md, M. W. Stoloff; art d, Lionel Banks.

Crime/Drama **(PR:C MPAA:NR)**

LADIES IN WASHINGTON (SEE: LADIES OF WASHINGTON, 1944)

LADIES LOVE BRUTES** (1930) 71m PAR bw

George Bancroft *(Joe Forziati)*, Mary Astor *(Mimi Howell)*, Fredric March *(Dwight Howell)*, Margaret Quimby *(Lucille Gates)*, Stanley Fields *(Mike Mendino)*, Ben Hendricks, Jr. *(Slattery)*, Lawford Davidson *(George Wyndam)*, Ferike Boros *(Mrs. Forziati)*, David Durand *(Joey Forziati)*, Freddie Burke Frederick *(Jackie Howell)*, Paul Fix *(Slip)*, Claude Allister *(Tailor)*, Crauford Kent, E. H. Calvert *(Committeemen)*, Henry Armetta *(Headwaiter)*.

Bancroft is a likable but crude building contractor worth millions who falls in love with society woman Astor. She, as the title suggests, does not love the brute back, and though he tries his best she refuses him. Meanwhile, March, Astor's estranged husband, just mingles around in the background trying to find something to do with his character. Some nice shots of an early New York City skyline.

d, Roland V. Lee; w, Waldemar Young, Herman J. Mankiewicz (based on the Zoe Akins play "Pardon My Glove"); ph, Henry Fischbeck; ed, Eda Warren.

Drama **(PR:A MPAA:NR)**

LADIES LOVE DANGER** (1935) 69m FOX bw

Mona Barrie *(Rita)*, Gilbert Roland *(Ricardo Souchet)*, Donald Cook *(Tom Lennox)*, Adrienne Ames *(Adele Michel)*, Hardie Albright *(Phil Morton)*, Herbert Mundin *(Giffins)*, Nick [Dick] Foran *(Sgt. Bender)*, John Wray *(Lt. Roberts)*, Marion Clayton, Ray Walker, Rita Rozelle, Snowflake, Leonard Carey, Henry Kolker, Russell Hicks.

The danger-loving lady is Barrie who, with the aid of playwright-private eye Roland, discovers who's behind the murder of a number of people in their theatrical crowd. It's average, but the suspense holds through until the end.

p, Edward T. Lowe; d, H. Bruce Humberstone; w, Samson Raphaelson, Robert Ellis, Helen Logan (based on the story by Ilya Zorn); ph, Daniel B. Clark.

Crime/Mystery **(PR:A MPAA:NR)**

LADIES' MAN ** 1/2** (1931) 76m PAR bw

William Powell *(Jamie Darricott)*, Kay Francis *(Norma Page)*, Carole Lombard *(Rachel Fendley)*, Gilbert Emery *(Horace Fendley)*, Olive Tell *(Mrs. Fendley)*, Martin Burton *(Anthony Fendley)*, John Holland *(Peyton Waldon)*, Frank Atkinson *(Valet)*, Maude Turner Gordon *(Therese Blanton)*, Hooper Atchley *(Headwaiter)*, Clarence Wilson *(Jeweler)*, Dick Cramer *(Private Detective)*, Edward Hearn *(Maitre D')*, Lee Phelps *(Desk Clerk)*, Frank O'Connor *(News Clerk)*, Bill O'Brien *(Elevator Starter)*, Lothar Mendes *(Lobby Extra)*.

Herman Mankiewicz always had a biting streak in his work (he co-authored CITIZEN KANE, among many credits) and that's evident from the start in LADIES' MAN, a picture that begins as a bubbling froth, then falls into a morbid, dreary tale that was, no doubt, a forerunner of AMERICAN GIGOLO. Powell is a professional squirer of rich women whose husbands are too busy coining money to take care of their emotional and physical needs. He takes the women around town and lives off the proceeds from the expensive trinkets and baubles they give him in return for his company. Tell is quite a bit older than Powell, but he lives well through her patronage. The large looming problem is that Tell's daughter, Lombard, also loves Powell, even though she knows her mother is trifling with him behind Emery's, her father's, back. Powell is not enough of a hard-heart to be able to stifle his own emotions and the one woman he loves is Francis. When Emery finds out that both his wife and daughter are seeing Powell, he is enraged. While his wife waits downstairs in a hotel ballroom, Emery throttles Powell and tosses him out the hotel window to his death. Not a million laughs, as you can see, LADIES' MAN clunked at the turnstiles as most people couldn't handle the downbeat ending. But the moral codes of the day demanded that the gigolo get his comeuppance (or, as in this case, his comedownance) and Powell had to be handed retribution, albeit a hard one at that. Powell married Lombard at about this time (1931 through 1933) and this was their second film together. It was also the fourth of a half-dozen duets with Francis. Director Mendes makes a cameo appearance in a lobby scene. The picture did absolutely nothing for any of the participants' careers.

d, Lothar Mendes; w, Herman J. Mankiewicz (based on a story by Rupert Hughes); ph, Victor Milner.

Drama **(PR:C MPAA:NR)**

LADIES' MAN** (1947) 91m PAR bw

Eddie Bracken *(Henry Haskell)*, Cass Daley *(Geraldine Ryan)*, Virginia Welles *(Jean Mitchell)*, Johnny Coy *(Johnny O'Connor)*, Virginia Field *(Gladys Hayden)*, Lewis Russell *(David Harmon)*, Georges Renevant *(Mr. Jones)*, Roberta Jonay *(Phone Operator)*, Spike Jones and His City Slickers.

After a hick from Oklahoma strikes oil he heads for New York where he gets suckered into playing Prince Charming on a radio program. He also gets himself mixed up with a gold digger who uses him to land an ad agency job. Tunes include: "I Gotta Girl I Love in North and South Dakota," "What Am I Gonna Do About You?" "I'm as Ready as I'll Ever Be," "Away Out West" (Jule Styne, Sammy Cahn), "Cocktails for Two" (Sam Coslow, Arthur Johnston), "Holiday for Strings" (David Rose), "Mama Yo Quiero" (Al Stillman, Jaraca, Vincente Paiva).

p, Daniel Dare; d, William D. Russell; w, Edmund Beloin, Jack Rose, Lewis Meltzer (based on the story "Manhattan at Midnight" by William Bowers, Robinson Holbert); ph, Stuart Thompson; m, Jule Styne, Sammy Cahn; ed, Everett Douglas; md, Irvin Talbot; art d, Hans Dreier, Walter Tyler; ch, Billy Daniels.

Musical **(PR:A MPAA:NR)**

LADIES MAN, THE**½   (1961) 106m PAR c

Jerry Lewis (*Herbert H. Heebert*), Helen Traubel (*Helen Welenmelon*), Pat Stanley (*Fay*), Kathleen Freeman (*Katie*), George Raft (*Himself*), Harry James (*Himself*), Marty Ingels (*Marty*), Buddy Lester (*Buddy*), Gloria Jean (*Gloria*), Hope Holiday (*Miss Anxious*), Jack La Lanne (*Himself*), Westbrook Van Voorhis (*Himself*), Sylvia Lewis (*Sylvia*), Eddie Quillan, Roscoe Ates, Jack Kruschen, Alex Gerry, Doodles Weaver, Dee Arlen, Francesca Bellini, Vicki Benet, Patricia Blair, Lillian Briggs, Bonnie Evans, Jacqueline Fontaine, Marianne Gaba, Gretchen Houser, Karyn Kupcinet, Paula Lane, Mary LaRoche, Shary Layne, Mary LeBow, Ann McCrea, Daria Massey, Fay Nuell, Madlyn Rhue, Caroline Richter, Sheila Rogers, Nancy Root, Lynn Ross, Joan Staley, Kay Tapscott, Patty Thomas, Gloria Tracey, Meri Welles, Beverly Wills.

Lewis leaves his home town after being jilted by the girl he loves, and heads for sunny California. He decides he will become a woman-hater, but this becomes tough when he gets a job in a boarding house full of vivacious ladies. Of course they are crazy about him, thinking that he's a lovable moron (they were half right). He's afraid, though, that he's not wanted and prepares to leave, but they persuade him to stay. Some odd cameos include Harry James doing a version of his tune, "Bang Tail," and George Raft as a tough guy who does the tango. There are also some elaborate multiroom, tri-level sets which reportedly cost $350,000 to construct. The film made more than enough at the box office to cover that expense. Among the players was Karyn Kupcinet, daughter of Irv Kupcinet, nationally syndicated columnist, in her only film role before her early death.

p&d, Jerry Lewis; w, Lewis, Bill Richmond; ph, W. Wallace Kelley (Technicolor); m, Walter Scharf; ed, Stanley Johnson; art d, Hal Pereira, Ross Bellah; set d, Sam Comer, James Payne; cos, Edith Head; ch, Bobby Van; m/l, Harry Warren, Jack Brooks, "Bang Tail," Harry James, played by James and his Band; makeup, Wally Westmore.

Comedy   (PR:A MPAA:NR)

LADIES MUST LIVE**   (1940) 58m WB bw (AKA: HOMETOWNERS)

Wayne Morris (*Lake*), Rosemary Lane (*Pat*), Roscoe Karns (*Pete*), Lee Patrick (*Mary*), George Reeves (*George*), Ferris Taylor (*Halliday*), Lottie Williams (*Mrs. Halliday*), DeWolf [William] Hopper (*Barton*), Cliff Saum (*Thunderbird*), Billy Dawson (*Tommy*), Mildred Gover (*Lettie*), Dana Dale, Mildred Coles (*Chorus Girls*).

Some good performances can't help a bad script which has Morris trying to keep his millionaire pal from marrying a gold digger. After lots of talk about big bucks, everyone is in the clear by the finale. From George M. Cohan's play "The Hometowners," first filmed in 1928.

d, Noel Smith; w, Robert E. Kent (based on the play "The Hometowners" by George M. Cohan); ph, Ted McCord; ed, Everett Dodd; songs; "I Could Make You Care," "It Shows You What Love Can Do," sung by Rosemary Lane.

Drama   (PR:A MPAA:NR)

LADIES MUST LOVE*   (1933) 71m UNIV bw

June Knight (*Jeannie*), Neil Hamilton (*Bill*), Sally O'Neil (*Dot*), Dorothy Burgess (*Peggy*), Mary Carlisle (*Sally Lou*), George E. Stone (*Joey*), Maude Eburne (*Mme. Fifi*), Oscar Apfel (*Nussbauer*), Edmund Breese (*Van Dyne*), Berton Churchill (*Gaskins*), Virginia Cherrill (*Society Girl*).

Knight stars in a mediocre comedy about a Broadway show girl who sticks up for a kind-hearted fellow when three of her girl friends want to make a sucker out of him. Knight's singing and dancing provide what little action there is in the film.

d, E. A. du Pont; w, John F. Larkin (based on a play by William Hurlbut); ph, Tony Gaudio; ed, Robert Carlisle; m/l, Harry Sauber, Lynn Cowan.

Comedy   (PR:A MPAA:NR)

LADIES MUST PLAY*   (1930) 70m COL bw

Dorothy Sebastian (*Norma*), Neil Hamilton (*Anthony Gregg*), Natalie Moorhead (*Connie*), John Holland (*Geoffrey*), Harry Stubbs (*Stormfield Button*), Shirley Palmer (*Marie*), Pauline Neff (*Mrs. Wheeler*).

A bleak cast stuck with an equally bleak script that fails to move in its 70 minutes. It's about a lady who is madly in love with her boss, though he doesn't know it. He, however, isn't much of a businessman and goes broke, but not without first concocting a scheme to make the money roll in. He involves the woman in a plot to make some cash by marrying her off to a wealthy bachelor. The ladies may be playing, but the customers are paying and they can't be too happy about laying down their cash for this one.

p&d, Raymond Cannon; w, Jo Swerling, Dorothy Howell, Lucile Gleason (based on a story by Paul Fox); ph, Joseph Walker; ed, Gene Milford.

Comedy/Drama   (PR:A MPAA:NR)

LADIES OF LEISURE**½   (1930) 98m COL bw

Barbara Stanwyck (*Kay Arnold*), Ralph Graves (*Jerry Strange*), Lowell Sherman (*Bill Standish*), Marie Prevost (*Dot Lamar*), Nance O'Neil (*Mrs. Strange*), George Fawcett (*Mr. Strange*), Johnnie Walker (*Charlie*), Juliette Compton (*Claire Collins*), Edith Ellison.

David Belasco, one of the grandfathers of the Broadway stage, presented this in New York under the title "Ladies of the Evening," but as that might have been construed as referring to professional prostitutes, they changed the title for the screen. Graves, in an absolutely granite performance, is a rich young man who would like to be an artist. Stanwyck is an attractive model who would like to snare a rich young man who would like to be an artist. Graves sees right through her gold-digging ways but likes her anyway and thinks he can make a silk purse out of her, so he offers her a job as his personal model. It isn't long before Graves falls hard

for Stanwyck and wants to marry her. Naturally, his parents, Fawcett and O'Neil, are shocked and totally against his marrying beneath his station. O'Neil goes so far as to have a confrontation with Stanwyck, pleading with her to stay away from the naive young man. Then Fawcett does the same. These are the two best scenes and could be an acting primer for soap-opera people even today. Stanwyck finally decides that it might be better if she leaves Graves so she takes off for Cuba with Graves' pal, Sherman, aboard a cruise ship. She becomes increasingly morose and eventually jumps overboard. After she is rescued, Graves, who knew about her background, comes to see her in the hospital and prevails upon her to forget whatever anyone else has said and to join him in marriage for the rest of their lives. What little comedy exists is provided by Prevost as an overweight gold-digger who is trying to lose poundage, plays with a reducing vibrator, and races up twenty flights of stairs in the funniest sequence. Capra kept everyone under tight rein and any tendency to emote was admirably stifled under his firm direction. The picture was remade seven years later as WOMEN OF GLAMOUR with Virginia Bruce in the Stanwyck role.

p, Harry Cohn; d, Frank Capra; w, Jo Swerling (based on the play "Ladies of the Evening" by Milton Herbert Gropper); ph, Joseph Walker; ed, Maurice Wright; art d, Harrison Wiley; cos, Edward Stevenson.

Drama/Comedy   (PR:A-C MPAA:NR)

LADIES OF THE BIG HOUSE**½   (1932) 76m PAR bw

Sylvia Sidney (*Kathleen Storm*), Gene Raymond (*Standish McNeil*), Wynne Gibson (*Susie Thompson*), Rockliffe Fellowes (*Martin Doremus*), Earle Foxe (*Kid Athens*), Frank Sheridan (*Warden Hecker*), Edna Bennett (*the Countess*), Fritzi Ridgeway (*Reno Maggie*), Louise Beavers (*Ivory*), Miriam Goldina (*The Mexican Woman*), Purnell Pratt (*John Hartman*), Esther Howard (*Clara Newman*), Ruth Lyons (*Gertie*), Hilda Vaughn (*Millie*), Jane Darwell (*Mrs. Turner*), Mary Foy (*Mrs. Lowry*), Noel Francis (*Thelma*), Theodore von Eltz (*Frazer*), Evelyn Preer (*Black Woman*).

A gripping prison drama which is fast-moving and economically cut, wasting not a single frame. Sidney devotes herself to freeing her imprisoned husband before he is to be executed for a crime he didn't commit. After a jailbreak attempt the whole mess is cleared up and the executioner doesn't get to do the deed. It's the gritty atmosphere of the prison and stark humanism that set this picture apart and gives it a ring of truth.

d, Marion Gering; w, Louis Weitzenkorn (based on the story by Ernest Booth); ph, David Abel.

Prison Drama   (PR:A MPAA:NR)

LADIES OF THE CHORUS**   (1948) 59m COL bw

Adele Jergens (*May Martin*), Marilyn Monroe (*Peggy Martin*), Rand Brooks (*Randy Carroll*), Nana Bryant (*Mrs. Carroll*), Eddie Carr (*Billy Mackay*), Steven Geray (*Salisbury*), Bill Edwards (*Alan Wakefield*), Marjorie Hoshelle (*Bubbles LaRue*), Frank Scannell (*Joe*), Dave Barry (*Hipple*), Alan Barry (*Hipple, Jr.*), Myron Healey (*Tom Lawson*), Gladys Blake (*Flower Shop Girl*), Almira Sessions (*Old Maid*), Claire Whitney (*Mrs. Windrift*), Robert Clarke, Emmett Vogan.

This chorus girl musical is worth watching for one reason only; in her second film appearance Monroe (in a sizable part) is cast as a leggy burlesque showgirl who shares the stage with her mom (Jergens) and another half dozen or so beauties. She falls in love with wealthy socialite Brooks, a romance met with disapproval by Jergens. It turns out that mother got herself into the same situation years before and is just watching out for little Marilyn. The picture ends with a double wedding—Monroe to Brooks and Jergens to longtime love Carr. Monroe delivered a pair of tunes, "Every Baby Needs a Da Da Daddy" and "Anyone Can Tell I Love You" (Allan Roberts, Lester Lee). Roberts and Lee also contributed "Crazy for You," "You're Never Too Old," and the title tune. This picture still wasn't enough to convince the studio executives that Marilyn was hot property. She was dropped by Columbia after this role and it was still a few years before she became a living legend.

p, Harry A. Romm; d, Phil Karlson; w, Harry Sauber, Joseph Carol (based on a story by Sauber); ph, Frank Redman; ed, Richard Fantl; md, Mischa Bakaleinikoff; art d, Robert Peterson; ch, Jack Boyle.

Musical/Romance   (PR:A MPAA:NR)

LADIES OF THE JURY**   (1932) 65m RKO bw

Edna May Oliver (*Mrs. Crane*), Ken Murray (*Wayne Dazy*), Roscoe Ates (*Andrew MacKaig*), Kitty Kelly (*Mayme Mixter*), Guinn Williams (*Steve Bromm*), Kate Price (*Mrs. McGuire*), Charles Dow Clark (*Jay J. Pressley*), Cora Witherspoon (*Lily Pratt*), Jill Esmond (*Mrs. Gordon*), Robert McWade (*Judge*), Helene Miller (*Evelyn Snow*), Suzanne Fleming (*Suzanne*), Tom Francis (*Jury Room Officer*), Leyland Hodgson (*Chauncey Gordon*), Alan Roscoe, Florence Lake, Lita Chevret, Morgan Galloway, George Andre Beranger, George Humbert.

An innocuous courtroom drama which has spunky society matron Oliver trying to convince her fellow jurors that Esmond isn't guilty of killing her husband. After an 11-1 vote against the girl, Oliver and the jury visit the scene of the crime, where it is discovered that the dead man's nephew and a housemaid are the guilty ones. Oliver is hilarious as she breaks precedent after precedent in her interrogations from the jury box.

p, William LeBaron; d, Lowell Sherman; w, Marion Dixon, Salisbury Field, John Frederick Ballard, Eddie Welch (based on a play by Ballard); ph, Jack MacKenzie; ed, Charles Kimball.

Drama/Comedy   (PR:A MPAA:NR)

LADIES OF THE MOB   (SEE: HOUSE OF WOMEN, 1962)

LADIES OF THE PARK***
(1964, Fr.) 84m Films Raoul Ploquin/Brandon bw (LES DAMES DU BOIS DE BOULOGNE)

Maria Casares *(Helene)*, Elina Labourdette *(Agnes)*, Lucienne Bogaert *(Mme. D)*, Paul Bernard *(Jean)*, Yvette Etievant *(Chambermaid)*, Jean Marchat *(Jacques)*, Bernard Lajarrige, Marcel Rouze, Emma Lyonnel, Lucy Lancy, Marguerite de Morlaye, Nicole Regnault, Katsou the Dog.

Originally made in 1945, while the last remnants of the German army were still occupying France, this was only Bresson's second feature film and his last using professional actors. It didn't make its way to the States until after this brilliant director had gained some international prominence. Adapted from a sequence in 18th-Century encyclopedist Diderot's brilliant novel but set in more modern times, Casares plays a jilted woman who sets out to destroy the man whose love she can no longer claim. To do so, she sets him up with a former prostitute (Labourdette) without revealing this woman's past. It is not until the actual day of the wedding between Labourdette and Bernard, after Casares has invited former patrons of the prostitute to the ritual, that Bernard discovers his wife-to-be's past. Bernard lays waste to Casares' knaving plans by accepting Labourdette despite the past that has been kept secret from him. Many of the themes which had meaning in the original book did not make the transfer to the modern setting, forcing the film to lose potential impact. The performances by both Casares and Labourdette were strikingly captivating, and were enough in themselves to carry the film. Other than this the main value of LADIES OF THE PARK is to see the development of the career of Bresson. (In French; English subtitles.)

p, Raoul Ploquin; d, Robert Bresson; w, Bresson, Jean Cocteau (based on the novel *Jacques le Fataliste et Son Maitre* by Denis Diderot); ph, Philippe Agostini, Maurice Pecqueux, Marcel Weiss; m, Jean-Jacques Grunenwald; ed, Jean Feyte; art d, Max Douy, James Allan, Robert Clavel.

Drama **(PR:C MPAA:NR)**

LADIES OF WASHINGTON** (1944) 61m FOX bw

Trudy Marshall *(Carol)*, Ronald Graham *(Dr. Mayberry)*, Anthony Quinn *(Michael)*, Sheila Ryan *(Jerry)*, Robert Bailey *(Stephen)*, Beverly Whitney *(Helen)*, Jackie Paley *(Adelaide)*, Carleton Young *(Investigator)*, John Philliber *(Mother Henry)*, Robin Raymond *(Vicky)*, Doris Merrick *(Amy)*, Barbara Booth *(Betty)*, Jo-Carroll Dennison *(Frieda)*, Lillian Porter *(Marjorie)*, Harry Shannon *(Lt. Lake)*, Ruby Dandridge *(Nellie)*, Charles D. Brown *(Inspector Saunders)*, Pierre Watkin *(Dr. Crane)*, Nella Walker *(Mrs. Crane)*, Inna Gest *(Dorothy)*, Rosalind Keith *(Nurse)*, Edna Mae Jones *(Susan)*, Bert McClay *(Ensign)*, J. Farrell MacDonald *(Watchman)*, Byron Foulger *(Clerk)*, Mary Field *(Nurse's Aide)*, Bess Flowers *(Bit Woman)*, Harry Depp *(Mr. Wethering)*, Lee Shumway *(Sgt. Martin)*.

Marshall invites college friend Ryan to stay with her in an apartment house for girls with government jobs. Ryan's high-faluting attitude soon alienates everyone in the co-op. She eventually gets involved in an affair with foreign spy Quinn, who is trying to pump her for information on the married steel executive she's been seeing. Before she can say "Capitol Hill" she is the accomplice to a murder committed by Quinn. Marshall, however, fares all right when she weds a doctor who sewed up a wounded Quinn. This picture contained two "firsts" for Quinn—his first starring role and his first screen kiss.

p, William Girard; d, Louis King; w, Wanda Tuchock; ph, Charles Clarke; m, Cyril Mockridge; ed, Nick DiMaggio; md, Emil Newman; art d, James Basevi, Leland Fuller; spec eff, Fred Sersen.

Crime **(PR:A MPAA:NR)**

LADIES SHOULD LISTEN** (1934) 62m PAR bw

Cary Grant *(Julian de Lussac)*, Frances Drake *(Anna Mirelle)*, Edward Everett Horton *(Paul Vernet)*, Rosita Moreno *(Marguerite Cintos)*, George Barbier *(Joseph Flamberg)*, Nydia Westman *(Susie Flamberg)*, Charles Ray *(Henri, the Porter)*, Charles Arnt *(Albert, the Manservant)*, Rafael Corio *(Ramon Cintos)*, Clara Lou [Ann] Sheridan *(Blanche, the Telephone Operator)*, Henrietta Burnside *(Operator)*, Joe North *(Butler)*.

Strained attempt at farce in the French style but much too heavy-handed. Grant is in Paris to work a deal. He's a French businessman who is trying to negotiate a concession option on some South American nitrate deposits. He's on vacation and has this apparently valuable contract in his possession when Moreno and Corio try to get it away from him with a badger-game type of flim-flam. Simultaneously, Westman, a spinster, puts her throbbing body before him. His phone is being listened to by Drake, the switchboard operator, who also is infatuated by him and seeks to protect him by exposing the machinations of Moreno and Corio. Drake is a nosy type who gets her thrills by listening in. Horton has been engaged to Westman for many years and is slightly jealous of the attention she showers on Grant. Grant loves the adulation and makes no moves to stop it. Complications happen, doors open and close, etc. Moreno tries to vamp Grant for profit, and Westman is just swooning. Drake attempts to keep Grant away from the two. In the end, Horton gets Westman back, Moreno and Corio are unmasked as scoundrels, and Grant will presumably wind up with Drake, his protector. They tried so hard to make this funny that they lost sight of any believability. Grant overplayed (as he did in many films) but this time he didn't have the material. Drake does her best work in many years and Horton, a rock of Gibraltar in so many films, does his usual excellent job. Horton could always be depended upon, from the time he first appeared in films in TOO MUCH BUSINESS in 1922 until his final film, COLD TURKEY, released after his death in 1971. This story began life as a play by Alfred Savoir, then was adapted by the prolific Guy Bolton (who worked so well with P.G. Wodehouse), but it never did make the big time. Some people must have thought it would make a funny movie. They were wrong.

p, Douglas MacLean; d, Frank Tuttle; w, Guy Bolton, Claude Binyon, Frank Butler (based on a story by Bolton and Alfred Savoir); ph, Harry Sharp; art d, Hans Dreier, Ernst Fegte.

Comedy **(PR:A MPAA:NR)**

LADIES THEY TALK ABOUT**
(1933) 68m WB bw (AKA: WOMEN IN PRISON)

Barbara Stanwyck *(Nan Taylor)*, Preston S. Foster *(David Slade)*, Lyle Talbot *(Don)*, Dorothy Burgess *(Susie)*, Lillian Roth *(Linda)*, Maude Eburne *(Aunt Maggie)*, Harold Huber *(Lefty)*, Ruth Donnelly *(Noonan)*, Robert Warwick *(The Warden)*, Helen Ware *(Miss Johnson)*, DeWitt Jennings *(Tracy)*, Robert McWade *(District Attorney)*, Cecil Cunningham *(Mrs. Arlington)*, Helen Mann *(Blondie)*, Grace Cunard *(Marie)*, Madame Sul-te-Wan *(Mustard)*, Harold Healy *(Dutch)*, Harry Gribbon *(Bank Guard)*, Snowball *(Parrot)*, William Keighley *(Man Getting a Shoeshine)*, Isabel Withers *(Convict)*, Harry C. Bradley *(Reformer)*, Davison Clark *(Chief at Jail)*, Ferris Taylor *(Reformer on Stage)*, Helen Dickson *(Matron with Cigar)*.

Pictures about women in prison have long been a staple in the theaters. This is just one more in the list that includes LADIES OF THE BIG HOUSE, PRISON WITHOUT BARS, GIRLS BEHIND BARS, WOMEN'S PRISON, GIRLS' PRISON, CAGED, I WANT TO LIVE, CHAINED HEAT, and on and on. Based on the true-life experiences of actress Dorothy Mackaye, who went to jail after her husband was killed in a battle with actor Paul Kelly, who was also sentenced to prison, LADIES THEY TALK ABOUT was presented in California as a play with Mackaye in the lead. Stanwyck is a tough-talking gun moll who is part of a gang of bank robbers. They are soon caught, and she's sent to the female division of San Quentin where life isn't nearly as bad as in some of the aforementioned pictures. The inmates fix their cells up like rooms in a resort, they seem to be able to roam around as they please, they play cards, and are apparently staying at a spa. The man who arranged to have her sentenced is an old boy friend, a combination evangelist and district attorney played by Foster. It should go without saying that Foster falls for Stanwyck, despite having to do his job by putting her away. Once inside, Stanwyck asserts herself and soon is the leader of the inmates, among whom are Roth and Eburne. Stanwyck leads a jailbreak but is double crossed and a pair of her fellow prisoners killed. She thinks that Foster blew the whistle. When she's eventually released, she goes after Foster, who is in the midst of running a revival meeting. She has a gun with her, shoots, hits him in the arm, and immediately regrets her deed as she realizes that she loves him. Roth sings "If I Could Be With You" to a photo of Joe Brown and Etta Moten does "St. Louis Blues" off-stage. Stanwyck must have liked being called a "lady" because she also made LADIES OF LEISURE, GAMBLING LADY, A LOST LADY, THE GREAT MAN'S LADY, LADY OF BURLESQUE, THE LADY GAMBLES, and TO PLEASE A LADY. Before settling on the final title, this was variously called "Betrayed," "Lady No. 6142," "Prisoner No. 6142" and "Women In Prison." The acting was pretty good and the film was pretty short, both plusses. The major problem was everything else.

p, Ray Griffith, d, Howard Bretherton, William Keighley; w, Sidney Sutherland, Brown Holmes, William McGrath (based on the play "Women in Prison" by Dorothy Mackaye, Carlton Miles); ph, John Seitz; ed, Basil Wrangel; md, Leo F. Forbstein; art d, Esdras Hartley; cos, Orry-Kelly.

Drama **(PR:A MPAA:NR)**

LADIES WHO DO** (1964, Brit.) 85m Fanfare-Bryanston/CD bw

Peggy Mount *(Mrs. Cragg)*, Robert Morley *(Col. Whitforth)*, Harry H. Corbett *(James Ryder)*, Miriam Karlin *(Mrs. Higgins)*, Avril Elgar *(Emily Parish)*, Dandy Nichols *(Mrs. Merryweather)*, Jon Pertwee *(Mr. Tait)*, Nigel Davenport *(Mr. Strang)*, Graham Stark *(Foreman)*, Ron Moody *(Inspector)*, Cardew Robinson *(Police Driver)*, John Laurie *(Dr. MacGregor)*, Arthur Howard *(Ryder's Chauffeur)*, Margaret Boyd *(Mrs. Parish)*, Joan Benham *(Miss Pensent)*, Brian Rawlinson *(Compressor Driver)*, Harry Fowler *(Driller)*, Ed Devereaux *(Mr. Gubbins)*, Marianne Stone *(Mrs. Gubbins)*, Carol White *(Sandra)*.

British cleaning lady Mount discovers scraps of paper in a wastepaper basket which contain stock market tips. With the help of Morley, Mount and her lady friends make a killing in the market. When they overhear a plot by financier Corbett to raze the street on which Mount lives, they organize a small but effective revolt and their houses are saved from the wrecking ball.

p, George H. Brown; d, C. M. Pennington Richards; w, Michael Pertwee (based on an idea by John Bignell); ph, Geoffrey Faithfull; m, Ron Goodwin; ed, Oswald Hafenrichter; md, Goodwin; art d, Harry White; makeup, Eddie Knight.

Comedy **(PR:A MPAA:NR)**

L'ADOLESCENT (SEE: ADOLESCENT, THE, 1978)

LADY AND GENT** (1932) 80m PAR bw

George Bancroft *(Slag Bailey)*, Wynne Gibson *(Puff Rogers)*, Charles Starrett *(Ted Streaver)*, James Gleason *(Pin Streaver)*, John Wayne *(Buzz Kinney)*, Morgan Wallace *(Cash Enright)*, James Crane *(McSweeley)*, William Halligan *(Doc Hayes)*, Billy Butts *(Tad, age 9)*, Joyce Compton *(Betty)*, Frank McGlynn, Sr. *(Principal)*, Charles Grapewin *(Grocer)*, Frederick Wallace *(Watchman)*, Lew Kelly *(Coroner)*, Sid Saylor *(Joe)*, Russell Powell *(2nd Bartender)*, Frank Darien *(Jim)*, Hal Price *(1st Bartender)*, A.S. Byron *(Judge)*, John Beck *(Workman)*, Tom Kennedy *(Small Arena Fighter)*, Frank Dawson *(Minister)*.

Bancroft is the "gent," a washed-up fighter named Slag, and Gibson, his nightclub-owner girl friend named Puff, is the "lady." When the pair end up taking care of an orphaned youngster, they give up their hopes and decide to raise the kid the right way. Eventually they send him to college where he becomes a football star, but is tempted to step into the ring like dad. Bancroft and the boy battle it out, but finally see eye-to-eye. Wayne makes an early screen appearance as a clean-cut kid turned punch-drunk fighter.

d, Stephen Roberts; w, Grover Jones, William Slavens McNutt; ph, Harry Fischbeck.

Drama   (PR:A MPAA:NR)

LADY AND THE BANDIT, THE**   (1951) 79m COL bw

Louis Hayward (Dick Turpin), Patricia Medina (Joyce Greene), Suzanne Dalbert(Cecile), Tom Tully (Tom King), John Williams (Archibald Puffin), Malu Gatica (Baroness Margaret), Alan Mowbray (Lord Willoughby), Lumsden Hare (Sir Robert Walpole), Barbara Brown (Lady Greene), Malcolm Keen (Sir Thomas DeVeil), Stapleton Kent (John Ratchett), Sheldon Jett (Ramsey Jostin), George Baxter (David Garrick), Ivan Triesault (King George), Norman Leavitt (B. Hedger), Frank Reicher (Count Eckhardt).

An 18th-Century costume drama set in England which has Hayward cast as Dick Turpin, a character in the English poet and essayist Alfred Noyes' best known single poem, "The Highwayman." He bravely rides 200 miles on horseback from London to York to clear his wife, in Noyes' version of the famous ride, who is about to be hanged as an accomplice to murder. He arrives on time, proving his wife's innocence but incriminating himself. At the end it is he whose neck is placed in the noose. The valor of Turpin never really makes it to the screen.

p, Harry Joe Brown; d, Ralph Murphy; w, Robert Libott, Frank Burt (based on a story by Jack DeWitt and Duncan Renaldo from a poem by Alfred Noyes); ph, Henry Freulich; m, George Duning; ed, Gene Havlick; md, Morris Stoloff; art d, George Brooks.

Adventure/Drama   (PR:A MPAA:NR)

LADY AND THE DOCTOR, THE
(SEE: LADY AND THE MONSTER, THE, 1944)

LADY AND THE MOB, THE***   (1939) 65m COL bw

Fay Bainter (Hattie Leonard), Ida Lupino (Lila Thorne), Lee Bowman (Fred Leonard), Henry Armetta (Zambrogio), Warren Hymer (Frankie O'Fallon), Harold Huber (Harry the Lug), Forbes Murray (District Attorney), Joseph Sawyer (Blinky Mack), Tom Dugan (Brains Logan), Joseph Caits (Bert the Beetle), Jim Toney (Big Time Tim), Tommy Mack (The Canary), Brandon Tynan (Mayor Jones), George Meeker (George Watson).

A unique and colorful gangster picture which has Bainter cast as a grand old dame who gets mixed up with the underworld. When she gets the brushoff from some chauvinistic mobsters, she hits on the idea of getting together her own gang. A pleasant mix of comedy and mobsters in this deviation from the gangster genre.

p, Fred Kohlmar; d, Ben Stoloff; w, Richard Maibaum, Gertrude Purcell (based on a story by George Bradshaw, Price Day); ph, John Stumar; ed, Otto Meyer.

Crime/Comedy   (PR:A MPAA:NR)

LADY AND THE MONSTER, THE**1/2
(1944) 86m REP bw (AKA: TIGER MAN; GB: THE LADY AND THE DOCTOR)

Erich von Stroheim (Prof. Franz Mueller), Vera Hruba Ralston (Janice Farell), Richard Arlen (Patrick Cory), Mary Nash (Mrs. Fame), Sidney Blackmer (Eugene Fulton), Helen Vinson (Chloe Donovan), Charles Cane (Grimes), William Henry (Roger Collins), Juanita Quigley (Mary Lou), Josephine Dillon (Mary Lou's Grandmother), Tom London, Jack Kirk (Husky Men), Sam Flint (G. Phipps), Edward Keane (Manning), Lane Chandler (White), Wallis Clark (Warden), Harry Hayden (Dr. Martin), Antonio Triano, Lola Montes (Dance Team), Maxine Doyle (Receptionist), Billy Benedict (Bellhop), Herbert Clifton (Bulter), Harry Depp (Bank Teller), Lee Phelps (Headwaiter), Janet Martin (Cafe Singer), Frank Graham (Narrator).

The stalwart Stroheim is cast as a scientist who keeps alive the brain of a dead criminal financier, which eventually takes over the mind of lab assistant Arlen. Stroheim does what he can to keep the malevolent brain under control, but it is able to force Arlen into killing the gangster's enemies. The plot is familiar and has had two sequels—DONOVAN'S BRAIN (1953) and VENGEANCE (1962), both based on the same novel. Republic president Herbert Yates continued to push the debatable talents of his future wife, then-skating star Ralston. Appearing in her first nonmusical role, Ralston suffers from her inability to handle the English language (she was a Czech), and the overpowering presence of Stroheim, who had the tendency to overshadow anyone he acted with. Director Sherman teamed with Stroheim and Arlen again with STORM OVER LISBON (1944), but it would be another six years before Stroheim would get a decent role in Billy Wilder's SUNSET BOULEVARD.

p&d, George Sherman; w, Dane Lussier, Frederick Kohner (based on the novel Donovan's Brain by Curt Siodmak); ph, John Alton; m, Walter Scharf; ed, Arthur Roberts; art d, Russell Kimball; set d, Otto Siegel; spec eff, Theodore Lydecker.

Horror   (PR:C MPAA:NR)

LADY AND THE OUTLAW, THE   (SEE: BILLY TWO HATS, 1974)

LADY AND THE TRAMP***1/2   (1955) 75m BV c

Voices of: Peggy Lee (Darling, Peg, Si, and Am), Barbara Luddy (Lady), Larry Roberts (Tramp), Bill Thompson (Jock, Bull, Dachsie), Bill Baucon (Trusty), Stan Freberg (Beaver), Verna Felton (Aunt Sarah), Alan Reed (Boris), George Givot (Tony), Dallas McKennon (Toughy, Professor), Lee Millar (Jim Dear), The Mello Men.

The classic tale of Lady, the prim and proper cocker spaniel who falls in love with the raggedy mutt Tramp. Lady runs away from her owner who has put a muzzle on the pup, and ends up being pursued by tough dogs in a bad part of town. Tramp rescues her and has his beaver friend cut through the muzzle. The two pups spend a night on the town, which includes the memorable spaghetti-eating scene when both Lady and Tramp are eating the same strand. Their lips (do dogs have lips?) are drawn closer and closer until at last—they kiss. They raid a chicken coop and are caught by a dog catcher who brings them to the pound. Lady is furious with Tramp, but by the finale they are happily raising their own litter of pups. Disney's first CinemaScope cartoon, LADY AND THE TRAMP had its moments but never really worked on the level of the great ones—DUMBO (1941), FANTASIA (1940), or BAMBI (1942). It simply lacked that certain charm, though it was a huge box office success. Its price tag was $4,000,000 and it took three years to complete, but it grossed over $25,000,000, making more money than any film from the 1950s except for THE TEN COMMANDMENTS (1956) and BEN-HUR (1959). Songs include: "He's A Tramp," "La La Lu," "Bella Notte," "Siamese Cat Song," "Peace on Earth" (Peggy Lee, Sonny Burke).

p, Walt Disney; d, Hamilton Luske, Clyde Geronimi, Wilfred Jackson; w, Erdman Penner, Joe Rinaldi, Ralph Wright, Donald DaGradi (based on the novel by Ward Greene); ph, (CinemaScope, Technicolor); m, Oliver Wallace; ed, Don Halliday; directing anim, Milt Kahl, Franklin Thomas, Oliver Johnston, Jr., John Lounsbery, Wolfgang Reitherman, Eric Larson, Hal King, Les Clark; anim, George Nicholas, Hal Ambro, Ken O'Brien, Jerry Hathcock, Erik Cleworth, Marvin Woodward, Ed Aardal, John Sibley, Harvey Toombs, Cliff Nordberg, Don Lusk, George Kreisl, Hugh Fraser, John Freeman, Jack Campbell, Bob Carson; backgrounds, Claude Coats, Dick Anthony, Ralph Hulett, Thelma Witmer, Eyvind Earle, Jimi Trout, Ray Huffine, Brice Mack; layout, Ken Anderson, Tom Codrick, Al Zinnen, A. Kendall O'Connor, Hugh Hennesy, Lance Nolley, Jacques Rupp, McLaren Stewart, Don Griffith, Thor Putnam, Collin Campbell, Victor Haboush, Bill Bosche; eff animation, George Rowley, Dan McManus.

Animated Feature   (PR:AAA MPAA:NR)

LADY AT MIDNIGHT**   (1948) 61m EL bw

Richard Denning (Peter Wiggins), Frances Rafferty (Ellen Wiggins), Lora Lee Michel (Tina Wiggins), Ralph Dunn (Al Garrity), Nana Bryant (Lydia Forsythe), Jack Searle (Freddy Forsythe), Harlan Warde (Ross Atherton), Claudia Drake (Carolyn Sugar), Ben Welden (Willie Gold).

Denning and Rafferty are a young couple who have to fight to keep their adopted 7-year-old daughter under their roof. When a mysterious murder begins to cloud things, some snooping proves that a greedy lawyer is trying to get his hands on the youngster's fortune.

p, John Sutherland; d, Sherman Scott; w, Richard Sale; ph, Jack Greenhalgh; m, Leo Erdody; ed, Martin Cohn; art d, Edward Jewell.

Drama   (PR:A MPAA:NR)

LADY BE CAREFUL*   (1936) 70m PAR bw

Lew Ayres (Dud "Dynamite"), Mary Carlisle (Billie), Larry "Buster" Crabbe (Jake), Benny Baker (Barney), Grant Withers (Loomis), Jack Chapin (Herb), Josephine McKim (Alice), Wilma Francis (Bernice).

Ayres is a seaman who is entered in a contest in Panama and inadvertently ends up winning a blue ribbon. He also wins the beauty contest gal Carlisle. Based on a Broadway stage play, it should have never made it to the silver screen.

p&d, J.T. Reed; w, Dorothy Parker, Alan Campbell, Harry Ruskin (based on the play "Sailor Beware" by Kenyon Nicholson, Charles Robinson); ph, Henry Sharpe; art d, Hans Dreier, Roland Anderson.

Comedy   (PR:A MPAA:NR)

LADY BE GAY   (SEE: LAUGH IT OFF, 1939)

LADY BE GOOD***   (1941) 110m MGM bw

Eleanor Powell (Marilyn Marsh), Ann Sothern (Dixie Donegan), Robert Young (Eddie Crane), Lionel Barrymore (Judge Murdock), John Carroll (Buddy Crawford), Red Skelton (Joe "Red" Willet), Virginia O'Brien (Lull), Tom Conway (Mr. Blanton), Dan Dailey, Jr. (Bill Pattison), Reginald Owen (Max Milton), Rose Hobart (Mrs. Carter Wardley), Phil Silvers (M.C.), Warren Berry, Nyas Berry, James Berry (Berry Brothers), Connie Russell (Singer), Doris Day (Debutante), Edward Gargan (Policeman).

All that remain from the 1924 stage smash are the wonderful tunes and the title in this second remake of the story (first done as a silent in 1928). The screenwriters took it upon themselves to rewrite the story, coming up with some meaningless drivel to fill up the dead space between songs. But it's the songs that please, especially the Academy Award winning "The Last Time I Saw Paris" (Jerome Kern, Oscar Hammerstein II, sung by Ann Sothern), which spawned controversy because it wasn't written for the movie. Other tunes include: "So Am I," "Oh Lady Be Good," "Fascinating Rhythm," "Hang on to Me" (George, Ira Gershwin), "You'll Never Know" (Roger Edens), "You're Words, My Music" (Edens, Arthur Freed), "Saudades" (Edens), "Alone" (Freed, Nacio Herb Brown). Oh, the story. Sothern and Young are songwriters in love who split up, can't live without each other, and get back together. Forget about the plot, just listen to the music.

p, Arthur Freed; d, Norman Z. McLeod; w, Jack McGowan, Kay Van Riper, John McClain, (uncredited) Ralph Spence, Arnold Auerbach, Herman Wouk, Robert McGunigle, Vincente Minnelli (based on a story by McGowan); ph, George Folsey, Oliver T. Marsh; ed, Frederick Y. Smith; md, George Stoll; art d, Cedric Gibbons, John S. Detlie; set d, Edwin B. Willis; cos, Adrian; ch, by Busby Berkeley.

Musical   (PR:A MPAA:NR)

LADY BEHAVE*1/2   (1937) 70m REP bw

Sally Eilers (Paula Kendall), Neil Hamilton (Stephens Cormack), Joseph Schildkraut (Michael Andrews), Grant Mitchell (Burton Williams), Patricia Farr (Clarice), Marcia Mae Jones (Patricia), George Ernest (Hank), Warren Hymer (Butch), Robert Greig

(Alfred), Charles Richman *(Howell)*, Spencer Charters *(Innkeeper)*, Mary Gordon *(Cook)*.

Farr, while under the influence, marries a millionaire even though she already has a husband. The millionaire doesn't know his new wife is spoken for, but Farr's sister, Eilers, gets her out of her jam by acting as her double. Lots of good old-line performers in this one give it a nostalgic interest.

p, Albert E. Levoy; d, Lloyd Corrigan; w, Joseph Krumgold, Olive Cooper (based on the story by Krumgold); ph, Harry Wild; ed, William Morgan; md, Alberto Colombo; art d, John Victor Mackay.

Comedy **(PR:A MPAA:NR)**

LADY BEWARE (SEE: THIRTEENTH GUEST, THE, 1932)

LADY BODYGUARD** (1942) 69m PAR bw

Eddie Albert *(Terry Moore)*, Anne Shirley *(A.C. Baker)*, Raymond Walburn *(Avery Jamieson)*, Ed Brophy *(Harry Gargan)*, Donald MacBride *(R.L. Barclay)*, Maude Eburne *(Mother Hodges)*, Clem Bevans *(Elmer Frawley)*, Roger Pryor *(George MacAlister)*, Gus Schilling *(Bughouse Sweeney)*, Olin Howlin *(Mr. Saunders)*, Charles Halton *(Edwards)*, Warren Ashe *(Fletcher)*, Jack Norton *(Henderson)*, Mary Treen *(Miss Tracy)*, Greta Granstedt *(Gertie)*, Oscar O'Shea *(Justice of the Peace)*, Emmett Vogan *(Stone)*, John H. Dilson *(Doctor)*, Harlan Briggs *(Gaston)*, George M. Carleton, Gordon DeMain *(Directors)*, Frances Morris *(Receptionist)*, Jack Stoney, Fred Graham, Kernan Cripps, Murray Alper *(Attendants)*, Charles R. Moore *(Porter)*, Sam Ash, Wilbur Mack, Jack Gardner *(Salesmen)*, Al Hill *(Mechanic)*, Matt McHugh *(Drunk)*, Peter Leeds *(Intern)*, Harry Tyler *(Weasel-faced Salesman)*, William Newell *(Chef)*, Stanley Blystone *(Police Officer)*, Gloria Williams, Ethel Clayton *(Women)*.

Shirley is an ad representative for an insurance agency, who bungles a publicity stunt and gives away a life insurance policy worth $1 million instead of $1,000. Test pilot Albert is the lucky recipient whose relatives won't let the girl worm out of the error. In keeping with film tradition, Albert and Shirley walk the aisle for the finale after their comic attempts at an elopement by plane.

p, Sol C. Siegel; d, William Clemens; w, Edmund Hartmann, Art Arthur (based on the story by Edward Haldeman, Vera Caspary); ph, Daniel Fapp; ed, William Shea; art d, Hans Dreier, Haldane Douglas.

Comedy/Romance **(PR:A MPAA:NR)**

LADY BY CHOICE*** (1934) 74m COL bw

Carole Lombard *("Alabam" Georgia Lee)*, May Robson *(Patsy Patterson)*, Roger Pryor *(John Mills)*, Walter Connolly *(Judge Daly)*, Arthur Hohl *(Charlie Kendall)*, Raymond Walburn *(Front O'Malley)*, James Burke *(Sgt. Brannigan)*, Mariska Aldrich *(Lucretia)*, William Faversham *(Malone)*, John Boyle *(Walsh)*, Henry Kolker *(David Opper)*, Lillian Harmer *(Miss Kennedy)*, Abe Dinovitch *(Louie)*, Fred "Snowflake" Toones *(Mose)*, Charles Coleman *(Butler)*, Hector V. Sarno *(Florist)*, Harry C. Bradley *(Court Clerk)*, Julius Tannen *(Brooke)*, Christian J. Frank *(Proprietor)*, Edith Conrad *(Miss Kingsley's Assistant)*, Elizabeth Jones *(Colored Woman)*, Irene Thompson *(Chorus Girl)*, Harold Berquist *(Bailiff)*, Adele Cutler Jerome *(Dancing Teacher/Double for Miss Lombard)*, Gino Corrado *(Head Waiter)*, Kit Guard, Jack Stone *(Brawling Waiters)*, Charles King, William Irving, Cy Slokum, Billy Mann *(Drunks)*, Lee Shumway, Allan Sears, Eddie Hearn *(Detectives)*, Charles Sullivan, Jimmie Dundee, Harry Tenbrook *(Sailors)*, Dennis O'Keefe *(Dancing Extra)*, Eddie Foster *(Radio Technician)*, Christine Signe *(Maid)*.

A charming comedy-drama that tugs the heart and smacks of Damon Runyon so it was not surprising that the screenwriter was tapped, many years later, to adapt Runyon's short stories for the Broadway smash, "Guys And Dolls." Robson is a drunken bag lady who is hauled before night-court judge Connolly for wrecking a bar. Pryor is the son of an old swain of Robson's and he talks Connolly into dropping the drunk and disorderly charges and allowing Robson to go to an old ladies' home. That same evening, Lombard, as a Sally Rand fan-dancer type, is arrested for a lewd and lascivious public performance. Mother's Day is coming up and Lombard's press agent, Walburn, suggests that they can get lots of good press if Lombard will agree to adopt a Mother. Lombard goes to the home and chooses Robson, who takes the new title to heart and encourages Lombard to quit fan dancing and strive for greater things. Robson begins serious lessons in acting, singing, and dancing. Robson also pushes Lombard and Pryor together and love happens. Pryor is a wealthy young man and we wonder if Lombard is after him because of love or money. Lombard also learns that Pryor will be cut off without a penny if he marries her so she tosses her serious career aside and returns to dancing with fans. Robson wants to see Pryor and her "daughter" marry so she arranges to have Lombard's show raided. Back in court, Robson and the judge conspire to bring the kids together and Lombard has to decide between a year in the slammer or marriage to Pryor. Can you guess which she chooses? Robson is a delight and Lombard gives early evidence of the light comedienne she was to become. Robson did a similar role in LADY FOR A DAY, a Runyon adaptation, and was nominated for an Oscar. You may catch a glimpse of dancing extra Dennis O'Keefe, the handsome, brash Irish leading man of the 1940s and 1950s. He had been an extra in many films between 1931 and 1938, using his real name, Edward "Bud" Flanagan. He began regularly using the moniker with the apostrophe only after signing on with MGM as a contract player in 1937. In this earlier film, he must have been testing his new handle.

p, Robert North; d, David Burton; w, Jo Swerling (based on a story by Dwight Taylor); ph, Ted Tetzlaff; ed, Viola Lawrence.

Comedy **(PR:A MPAA:NR)**

LADY CAROLINE LAMB*
(1972, Brit./Ital.) 122m GEC Pulsar-Vides-Tomorrow Enterprises/UA c

Sarah Miles *(Lady Caroline Lamb)*, Jon Finch *(William Lamb)*, Richard Chamber

Iain *(Lord Byron)*, John Mills *(Canning)*, Margaret Leighton *(Lady Melbourne)*, Pamela Brown *(Lady Bessborough)*, Silvia Monti *(Miss Milbanke)*, Ralph Richardson *(The King)*, Laurence Olivier *(Duke of Wellington)*, Peter Bull *(Government Minister)*, Charles Carson *(Mr. Potter)*, Sonia Dresdel *(Lady Pont)*, Nicholas Field *(St. John)*, Felicity Gibson *(Girl in Blue)*, Robert Harris *(Apothecary)*, Richard Hurndall *(Radical Member)*, Paddy Joyce *(Irish Housekeeper)*, Bernard Kay *(Benson)*, Janet Key *(Miss Fairfax)*, Mario Maranzana *(Coachman)*, Robert Mill *(Wellington's Aide de Camp)*, Norman Mitchell *(Restaurant Functionary)*, John Moffatt *(Murray)*, Trevor Peacock *(Agent)*, Maureen Pryor *(Mrs. Buller)*, Fanny Rowe *(Lady Holland)*, Stephen Sheppard *(Buckham)*, Roy Stewart *(Black Pug)*, Ralph Truman *(Admiral)*, Michael Wilding *(Lord Holland)*, Joyce Carey *(Marquise)*, Preston Lockwood *(1st Partner)*, John Rapley *(2nd Partner)*, Ivor Slater *(Chatsworth Domo)*.

The romantic Miles weds rising politician Finch, only to fall in love with Chamberlain. She makes no attempt at discretion, nearly ruining her husband's career. Chamberlain, however, tires of her, leading to a suicide attempt and another affair, this time with duke Olivier. An overly simplified script is the ruination of all the performances except Olivier's and Richardson's—two actors who have learned to overcome poor dialog. At the time, Miles was married to screenwriter Bolt, which may explain the poor result of this movie, as he wrote better things such as LAWRENCE OF ARABIA (1962), DOCTOR ZHIVAGO (1965), and A MAN FOR ALL SEASONS (1966).

p, Fernando Ghia; d&w, Robert Bolt; ph, Oswald Morris (Eastmancolor); m, Richard Rodney Bennett; ed, Norman Savage; md, Marcus Dods; art d, Carmen Dillon; set d, Vernon Dixon; cos, David Walker; ch, Eleanor Fazan; makeup, George Frost; hair styles, Bobbie Smith.

Historical Drama **Cas.** **(PR:A MPAA:PG)**

LADY CHASER*¹/₂ (1946) 58m PRC bw

Robert Lowery, Ann Savage, Inez Cooper, Frank Ferguson, William Haade, Ralph Dunn, Paul Bryar, Charlie Williams, Garry Owen, Marie Martino.

Played more for laughs than as a murder mystery, an innocent woman finds herself charged with murder when her uncle dies of poisoning from a pill she gave to him. Actually, she thought the pill was an aspirin, having accepted it from a mysterious woman. The rest of the film consists of a madcap chase of the woman responsible for dispensing the poisonous pill.

p, Sigmund Neufeld; d, Sam Newfield; w, Fred Myton (based on the story by G.T. Fleming-Roberts); ph, Jack Greenhalgh; ed, Holbrook N. Todd; art d, Frank Sylos.

Comedy/Mystery **(PR:A MPAA:NR)**

LADY CHATTERLEY'S LOVER**
(1959, Fr.) 102m Regie du Film-Orsay/Kingsley International bw (L'AMANT DE LADY CHATTERLEY)

Danielle Darrieux *(Constance Chatterley)*, Erno Crisa *(Oliver Mellors)*, Leo Genn *(Sir Clifford Chatterley)*, Berthe Tissen *(Mrs. Bolton)*, Janine Crispin *(Hilda)*, Jean Murat *(Winter)*, Gerard Sety *(Michaelis)*, Jacqueline Noelle *(Bertha)*.

A tame version of the D.H. Lawrence novel which was banned for 30 years in the U.S. This time the film version met the same fate. The story is by now a familiar one; Darrieux is the sexually insatiable Lady Chatterley, who, upon learning that her husband is impotent, takes the estate's gamekeeper as her lover. She gets pregnant and goes off with her lover at the finale. The book was known for its graphic sexual descriptions (relatively), but the film chooses instead to cut away from any sexual activity and in its place shots of burning embers in the fireplace. For some reason the New York censors felt that this was enough to warrant reediting before it was allowed to be released. The film, as they put it, "presented adultery as a desirable, acceptable, and proper pattern of behavior." The case went to the Supreme Court and was overturned. The fervor quickly died down, however, after the audiences realized that there wasn't anything to censor in the first place. Word of mouth spread and LADY CHATTERLEY'S LOVER was soon a box office lead balloon. (In French; English subtitles.)

p, Gilbert Cohn-Seat; d&w, Marc Allegret (based on the novel by D.H. Lawrence and the play by Gaston Bonheur, Philippe de Rothschild); m, Joseph Kosma.

Drama **(PR:A MPAA:NR)**

LADY CHATTERLEY'S LOVER zero
(1981, Fr./Brit.) 103m Producteurs Associes-Cannon/Prodis c

Sylvia Kristel *(Constance Chatterley)*, Shane Briant *(Clifford Chatterley)*, Nicholas Clay *(Oliver Mellors)*, Ann Mitchell *(Mrs. Bolton)*, Elizabeth Spriggs *(Lady Eva)*, Peter Bennett *(Butler)*, Pascale Rivault *(Hilda)*, Anthony Head, Frank Moorey, Bessie Love, John Tynan, Michael Huston, Fran Hunter, Ryan Michael, Mark Colleano.

A vapid adaptation of D.H. Lawrence's scorching novel which fizzles into nothingness on the screen. The director and star of the soft-porn classic EMMANUELLE, Jaeckin and Kristel, combine their debatable talents, with the latter playing the role of Lady Chatterley. Stuck with a husband who's paralyzed from the waist down, the sex-driven Kristel is encouraged to take on a lover. She vents her energies with gamekeeper Clay, and together they display their sexual prowess like peacocks their feathers. The kindest thing to say is that the production is attractive. Also released at 141m. (In English.)

p, Andre Djaoui, Christopher Pierce; d, Just Jaeckin; w, Christopher Wicking, Jaeckin, Marc Behm (based on the novel by D.H. Lawrence); ph, Robert Fraisse; m, Stanley Myers; ed, Eunice Mountjoy; prod d, Anton Furst; cos, Shirley Russell.

Drama **Cas.** **(PR:O MPAA:R)**

LADY CONFESSES, THE**　　　　　　(1945) 64m PRC bw

Mary Beth Hughes (Vicki McGuire), Hugh Beaumont (Larry Craig), Edmund MacDonald (Lucky Brandon), Claudia Drake (Lucille Compton), Emmett Vogan (Capt. Brown), Edward Howard (Harmon), Dewey Robinson (Steve), Carol Andrews (Marge), Ruth Brande (Gladys), Barbara Slater (Norma Craig), Jack George (Manager), Jerome Root (Bill), Edwina Patterson (Stand-in).

Standard stuff in which Beaumont's girl dons the Sherlock Holmes personality and does some sleuthing to save him from a murder charge. It's been seen a hundred times before, much better and much worse. This one's in between.

p, Alfred Stern; d, Sam Newfield; w, Helen Martin (based on a story by Irwin R. Franklin); ph, Jack Greenhalgh; m, Lee Zahler; ed, Holbrook Todd; art d, Paul Palmentola; m/l, Robert Unger, Al Seaman, Cindy Walker.

Mystery/Drama　　　　　　　　　　　(PR:A MPAA:NR)

LADY CONSENTS, THE**½　　　　　　(1936) 75m RKO bw

Ann Harding (Anne Talbot), Herbert Marshall (Dr. Michael Talbot), Margaret Lindsay (Jerry Mannerly), Walter Abel (Stanley Ashton), Edward Ellis (Jim Talbot), Hobart Cavanaugh (Yardley), Ilka Chase (Susan), Paul Porcasi (Joe), Willie Best (Sam), Mary Gordon (Apple Lady).

When Marshall's attentions shift from his wife (Harding) to a younger woman (Lindsay), Harding sits back and lets him play out his fantasy. Marshall takes Lindsay to the altar, but eventually gets back together with Harding after Marshall's dad has an accident. The most interesting thing about the picture, however, is the fact that in it beer was served in a tin can, which drew protests from American and Canadian glass blowers unions.

p, Edward Kaufman; d, Stephen Roberts; w, P.J. Wolfson, Anthony Veiller (based on the story "The Indestructible Mrs. Talbot" by Wolfson); ph, J. Roy Hunt; art d, Van Nest Polglase; cos, Bernard Newman.

Drama/Comedy　　　　　　　　　　　(PR:A MPAA:NR)

LADY CRAVED EXCITEMENT, THE*

　　　　　　　　　　(1950, Brit.) 69m Hammer/Exclusive bw

Hy Hazell (Pat), Michael Medwin (Johnny), Sidney James (Carlo), Thelma Grigg (Julia), Andrew Keir (Peterson), Danny Green (Boris), John Longden (Inspector James), Ian Wilson (Mugsy), Barbara Hamilton, Jasmine Dee, Gordon Mulholland.

Lacking what the title lady craves, this stiff programmer has Hazell as a cabaret singer who tires of her boring, humdrum routine and gets mixed up with the criminal world. She and her partner Medwin uncover a plot to smuggle priceless art works out of the country and manage to prevent any wrongdoing.

p, Anthony Hinds; d, Francis Searle; w, Edward J. Mason, John Gilling, Searle (based on the radio serial by Mason); ph, Walter Harvey.

Comedy　　　　　　　　　　　　　　(PR:A MPAA:NR)

LADY DANCES, THE　　　(SEE: MERRY WIDOW, THE, 1934)

LADY DOCTOR, THE**

(1963, Fr./Ital./Span.) 103m Gallus-Galliera-Les Films Fernand Rivers-S.G.G.C.-Jolly-Fenix/Governor bw (DITES 33; TOTO, VITTORIO E LA DOTTORESSA; MI MUJER ES DOCTOR)

Toto (Mike Spillone), Vittorio De Sica (Marquis De Vitti), Abbe Lane (Dr. Brigitte Baker), Darry Cowl (Patient), Pierre Mondy, Teddy Reno, German Cobos, Agostino Salvietti, Titina De Filippo, Fulvia Franco, Tecla Scarano.

Lane marries a lawyer who must stay in the good graces of his two aunts to receive an inheritance. When Lane begins to keep strange hours, Toto is hired to shadow the girl. He discovers that she has been meeting De Sica and things look grim for a time. She announces that she is pregnant, but in the end Lane is cleared of any adulterous deeds. Originally released in 1957 in Italy at 94m, and in Spain and Paris in 1958 at 90m.

p, Dario Sabatello; d, Camilio Mastrocinque, Ana Mariscal; w, Vittorio Metz, Marcello Marchesi, Roberto Gianviti, Sabatello; ph, Gabor Pogany, Adalberto Albertini, Alvaro Mancori, Manuel Berenguer; m, Carlo Innocenzi; ed, Roberto Cinquini, Juan Pison.

Comedy　　　　　　　　　　　　　　(PR:C MPAA:NR)

THE LADY DRACULA*

(1974) 80m Media Cinema c (AKA: THE LEGENDARY CURSE OF LEMORA; LEMORA, LADY DRACULA)

Lesley Gilb (Lemora), Cheryl "Rainbeaux" Smith (Lila), William Whitton (Alvin), Steve Johnson (Ticket Man), Monte Pyke (Bus Driver), Maxine Ballantyne (Old Lady), Parker West (Young Man), Richard Blackburn (Reverend).

Poor adolescent Smith is a hapless church singer who gets lured into the woods by Gilb. She soon discovers that Gilb is a vampire with a brood of children for followers, in addition to having a few lesbian tendencies. This bottom-of-the-barrel feature has a few interesting moments, which save it from near-bomb status. It was condemned by the Catholic Film Board. Smith went on to become an actress in Australian pornographic films.

p, Robert Fern; d, Richard Blackburn; w, Blackburn, Fern; m, Daniel Neufield; cos, Rosanna Norton.

Horror　　　　　　　　　　　　　　(PR:O MPAA:PG)

LADY ESCAPES, THE**　　　　　　(1937) 63m FOX bw

Gloria Stuart (Linda Ryan), Michael Whalen (Michael Hilton), George Sanders (Rene Blanchard), Cora Witherspoon (Fanny Worthington), Gerald Oliver-Smith (Reggie Farnsworth), June Brewster (Dolores), Howard Hickman (Judge), Joseph

Tozer (Drake), Don Alvarado (Antonio), Maurice Cass (Mons. Cheval), Franklin Pangborn (Pierre), Tom Ricketts (Uncle George).

Stuart and Whalen go their separate ways after endless arguing. Stuart takes off to France where she hooks a European playboy. Anxious to get his wife back, Whalen discovers that the playboy has another girl, and after persuading that pair to wed, Whalen gets Stuart back in his arms.

p, Leslie L. Landau; d, Eugene Forde; w, Don Ettlinger (based on the novel My Second Wife by Eugene Heltai); ph, Lucien Andriot; ed, Al de Gaetano; md, Samuel Kaylin.

Comedy　　　　　　　　　　　　　　(PR:A MPAA:NR)

LADY EVE, THE*****　　　　　　(1941) 97m PAR bw

Barbara Stanwyck (Jean Harrington), Henry Fonda (Charles Pike), Charles Coburn ("Colonel" Harry Harrington), Eugene Pallette (Mr. Pike), William Demarest (Muggsy-Ambrose Murgatroyd), Eric Blore (Sir Alfred McGlennan Keith), Melville Cooper (Gerald), Martha O'Driscoll (Martha), Janet Beecher (Mrs. Pike), Robert Greig (Burrows), Dora Clement (Gertrude), Luis Alberni (Pike's Chef), Frank Moran (Party Bartender), Wilda Bennett, Evelyn Beresford, Georgie Cooper, Gayne Whitman, Alfred Hall, Bertram Marburgh, George Melford, Arthur Stuart Hull, Kenneth Gibson (Party Guests), Joe North, Wilson Benge (Butlers at Party), Pauline Drake (Social Secretary), Harry Rosenthal (Piano Tuner), Abdullah Abbas (Man with Potted Palm), Julius Tannen, J.W. Johnston, Ray Flynn, Harry Bailey (Lawyers in Pike's Office), Wanda McKay, Ella Neal, Marcelle Christopher (Daughters on Boat), John Hartley (Young Man on Boat), Helen Dickson, Almeda Fowler, Betty Farrington, Eva Dennison (Mothers on Boat), Robert Warwick (Bank Manager), Torben Meyer (Purser), Jack Richardson (Father of Girl on Boat), Harry Depp (Man with Glasses on Boat), Ester Michelson (Wife on Boat), Robert Dudley (Husband on Boat), Norman Ainsley (Sir Alfred's Manservant), Jimmy Conlin, Alan Bridge, Victor Potel (Stewards), Reginald Sheffield (Prof. Jones), Arthur Hoyt (Lawyer at Telephone in Pike's Office), Frances Raymond (Old Lady on Boat).

Of all the masterpieces of mirth that Preston Sturges wrote and directed, many believe, and with good reason, that THE LADY EVE is his most brilliant and trenchant comedy, a battle of the sexes wonderfully acted by Stanwyck and Fonda. Son of a wealthy brewer, Pallette, whose slogan is "Pike's Pale, the Ale That Won for Yale," Fonda believes all women within a thousand miles of him are after his money. He occupies his time with scientific expeditions to exotic places, looking for strange snakes to trap and study. He is fond of summarizing his entire life with the line: "You know me, nothing but reptiles." Returning from an Amazon snake trip, Fonda is enroute to America and, as he boards ship, a fetching young lady, Stanwyck, sees him gangling up the gangway and promptly drops an apple on his head (ergo the film's title). He is attracted to her but wary. Stanwyck introduces Fonda to her crafty father, Coburn, and the two lipsmack their way into a plan to bilk the young man. Coburn, ever the gentleman, however, insists on style, reminding his daughter: "Let us be crooked, but never common." Luxury liners are common to this father-daughter act for they ply their trade as cardsharps on one oceangoing vessel after another. Stanwyck introduces herself and her father by simply tripping the naive Fonda as he strolls past their table, then, before he can recover, claiming that she has broken the heel of her shoe. She insists that he accompany her to her cabin and there he is sent into a groggy state by her perfume. She has soon inveigled Fonda into a friendly card game, while outwitting Fonda's dim-witted bodyguard, Demarest. It's all innocent fun, Stanwyck implies when Fonda sits down with her father: "He does card tricks." All the while, Fonda is falling deeper in love with Stanwyck, shyly telling her: "You have a definite nose." "Do you like the rest of me?" she responds. Stanwyck can't help herself; her victim is so innocent, so naive that she finds herself reluctantly falling in love with him. She makes a decision to be the sucker's ideal, telling her dumbfounded father that "I'm going to be exactly the way he thinks I am." When Coburn pushes her to maneuver Fonda into the big card game where the victim can be fleeced, Stanwyck puts him off. "Children don't respect their parents anymore," he grumbles. Yet Coburn is too crafty for the daughter he has honed into his own likeness, and manages to steer Fonda into the game. Stanwyck is clever, too, manipulating the game so that Fonda only loses a small amount to Coburn who is by then nearing apoplexy. Through a ruse, Coburn finagles a whopping payment from Fonda, pretending to be embarrassed at winning so much money from him, but he curtly adds, when Fonda is making out the check: "Just make it out to cash, $32,000 and no cents." Stanwyck is later livid with her father over the scam and he soothes her by tearing up Fonda's check, which he does not, substituting another check for the good one. Fonda then comes to Coburn and declares his love for his daughter, blurting that he intends to ask for her hand. Coburn responds by pretending to be shocked. All looks peachy for Stanwyck until Demarest, the bloodhound bodyguard, unearths Stanwyck's unsavory past. When this is made known to Fonda, he becomes incensed, confronting Stanwyck. She admits she did attempt to fleece him but fell in love with him instead. Fonda sneers: "Thought you were having a lot of fun with me, didn't you?" then tells her it's quits between them. Feeling "hurt and cheap," Stanwyck now vows to get even with Fonda for being dumped. She contacts Blore, a phony English aristocrat who has known Fonda and his family since Fonda was "a tall backward boy always toying with toads." He agrees to pass off Stanwyck as his niece and when Fonda meets her again he actually believes she's a titled British lady since she so closely resembles the old Stanwyck she has to be someone else, at least that's the logic Fonda employs. Stanwyck and Blore visit Pallette and family and Fonda is utterly captivated by the charming and beautiful Stanwyck in her new role; he promptly proposes. She accepts and they are married. But on the train en route to a honeymoon cottage, Stanwyck takes her sweet revenge in one of the most unforgettable scenes in any romantic comedy. Just as Fonda embraces her and is about to consummate the marriage, Stanwyck tells him that he should know about every man she's ever been with and begins to rattle off an endless string of ex-lovers and husbands, a recounting of disturbing, lurid affairs dwarfing the King Lists of Mentho. Fonda winces and cringes as he hears the lady's unsolicited confessions. (As Stanwyck describes the delicate details of each past romance the train conveniently enters a tunnel or the clack of the wheels and whine of the whistle from the engine drowns out her words to maintain the propriety of the day.) In a whirlwind move, Fonda leaves his new bride and demands an annulment. Coburn, hearing the news, urges Stanwyck to strike, to take Fonda for all his millions in a whopping settlement, but she refuses, admitting to her errant father that she still loves the sap, and all the revenge has gone out of her. Father and daughter then go back to the ocean liner and more victims, but, on a trip to the Amazon, Stanwyck spots Fonda once more and trips him, beginning the zany relationship all over again. Fonda is overjoyed at seeing her. "I'm married," she begins. "So am I," he answers. As they embrace she begins to make a real confession but he cuts her off. Fonda is wholly confused now, not sure whether Stanwyck is two women or one and he stops her admissions with: "I don't want to understand. I don't want to know. Whatever it is, keep it to yourself. All I know is I adore you. I'll never leave you again. We'll work it out somehow." And it looks like they will. THE LADY EVE stands as one of Sturges' best romantic comedies with just the right blend of satire and slapstick, most of the laughs coming from his clever and often inspired comedic lines. His direction is flawless and his cast, from stars to his stock players, Demarest, Warwick, Moran, etc., deliver beautifully. This may be one of the finest scripts ever written for films, one that surely should be studied by any apprentice filmmaker. It's taut but allows for all the flippancy and sparkle to heighten an already impossible situation. Sturges, who began as a contract scriptwriter for Paramount, promised Stanwyck that he would write a great comedy for her someday and this was it. Paramount was impressed by Sturges' earlier movie, THE GREAT MCGINTY which proved to be a box office bonanza, his first directorial chore. Paramount allowed him a big budget for THE LADY EVE but suggested Brian Aherne play the male lead. Paramount even toyed with casting Madeleine Carroll or Paulette Goddard in the lead role but Sturges insisted Stanwyck get the part, reminding studio moguls that he had promised the role to her and, if she didn't get it, Paramount could forget about THE LADY EVE. Sturges also insisted on Fonda and he was borrowed from Fox which made Stanwyck very happy. She later stated: "I think there was a great, compatible feeling between Sturges and myself. I loved the script . . . and I had an enormous plus by the name of Henry Fonda." Sturges affected extravagant apparel while directing the film, which came in under budget and only two days over shooting schedule. He wore a pastel-colored beret, knit muffler around his neck, and a loud polo shirt, explaining to one gossip columnist that this was necessary as he was always moving about his sets which were crowded with visitors—anyone could stroll into the sound stage and view his films, the more the merrier was Sturges' philosophy. Nothing seemed to bother him while directing and rewriting his script on the spot. Radios could be blaring, crew members shouting, scenes being set up, but Sturges would ignore the cacaphony and rewrite lines brilliantly. He made lightning decisions scene by scene while shooting and they always seemed to be right. As he later told gossip columnist Hedda Hopper: "I have no success formula. If I have attained any, it's an act of God. What I learned, I picked up on sets. I just kept my eyes opened and learned, as my Filipino chauffeur learned to drive an auto. For five years he rode on seats near the bus driver and watched the driver. Then he went out and started driving." The shooting scripts Sturges prepared made it easy for his cameramen to set up shots. In one instance for THE LADY EVE, Sturges had written: "Close shot—an annihilating pair of feet and ankles with some leg thrown in." The cast of THE LADY EVE soon got used to Sturges' unorthodox methods. He insisted that everyone acting in the film view each day's rushes, whether they were in the scenes or not. His longtime contract player, Demarest, one of the greatest character actors in films, later stated (in *Between Flops* by James Curtis): "We always had to look at them, every goddamned night. Then he'd start to put the picture together and you'd have to watch that too." Sturges received rave reviews for another of his films, CHRISTMAS IN JULY while THE LADY EVE was still in production and he happily read these accolades to any and all on the set. The raves for THE LADY EVE were even more widespread and the public loved the film, filling Paramount's coffers with so much profit that the studio realized that it had a "golden boy" in Sturges and he was given a free hand to go on making his superlative comedies which far surpass most comedies written and produced today. THE LADY EVE was remade as THE BIRDS AND THE BEES in 1956 with George Gobel, Mitzi Gaynor, and David Niven (as the cardsharp father) in the leads and directed by Norman Taurog. It was poorly produced and directed and bombed at the box office. Oddly, most of Sturges' funniest lines were rewritten and the script came out so lame that it never got off the floor.

p, Paul Jones; d&w, Preston Sturges (based on the story "The Faithful Heart" by Monckton Hoffe); ph, Victor Milner; ed, Stuart Gilmore; md, Sigmund Krumgold; art d, Hans Dreier, Ernst Fegte; cos, Edith Head; makeup, Wally Westmore.

Comedy/Romance **Cas.** **(PR:A MPAA:NR)**

LADY FIGHTS BACK** (1937) 61m UNIV bw

Irene Hervey *(Heather McHale)*, Kent Taylor *(Owen Merrill)*, William Lundigan *(Doug McKenzie)*, Willie Best *(McTavish)*, Frank Jenks *(Steve)*, Joe Sawyer *(Jannsen)*, Paul Hurst *(Maloney)*, Ernest Cossart *(Commissioner Allan)*, Chick Chandler *(Crowder)*, Si Jenks *(Villager)*, Gerald Oliver Smith *(Sir Daniel McAndrews)*.

A standard outdoor tale which has the ecology-minded Hervey working together with dam-builder Taylor in an attempt to save some local salmon. Of course, they save their fishy friends, as romance envelopes the pair. An eyeful of nature scenery is a pleasant change from the claustrophobic confines of the sound stage.

p, Edmund Grainger; d, Milton Carruth; w, Brown Holmes, Robert T. Shannon (based on the novel *Heather of the High Hand* by Arthur Stringer); ph, Milton Krasner; ed, Paul Landres; spec eff, John P. Fulton.

Drama/Romance **(PR:A MPAA:NR)**

LADY FOR A DAY* 1/2** (1933) 95m COL bw

Warren William *(Dave the Dude)*, May Robson *(Apple Annie)*, Guy Kibbee *(Judge Blake)*, Glenda Farrell *(Missouri Martin)*, Ned Sparks *(Happy)*, Jean Parker *(Louise)*, Walter Connolly *(Count Romero)*, Barry Norton *(Carlos)*, Robert Emmett O'Connor *(Inspector)*, Wallis Clark *(The Commissioner)*, Nat Pendleton *(Shakespeare)*, Hobart Bosworth *(The Governor)*, Barry Norton *(Carlos, Young Man)*, Blind Dad Mills *(Blind Man)*, "Shorty" *(Panhandler)*, Halliwell Hobbes.

A light-hearted, sentimental tale of "Apple Annie" (played by the charming 75-year-old Robson), an apple peddler who is known and loved by everyone in Times Square. The "queen" of the neighborhood, Robson is friend to the local bigwigs and her fellow panhandlers, the latter of whom she "extorts" in order to pay for the education of her secret daughter, Parker. Not having seen Parker since birth, Robson faithfully writes to her in Spain, pretending to be "Mrs. E. Worthington Manville," a wealthy *grande dame* who resides in a posh New York hotel. Robson writes her letters on hotel stationery and has conned the bellboy into forwarding her mail. Robson is thrown into a panic when Parker sends a letter announcing her imminent arrival. She is to be accompanied by her fiance of royal blood, Norton, and his father, Connolly, both of whom are anxious to meet her. Hot-shot gambler William hears of Robson's predicament and offers her a way out. (William's kindness comes from his superstition that Robson's apples provide him with luck in his high-stakes wagering). Involving everyone including the governor, William's plan calls for pulling the wool over the visitors' royal eyes. Robson is given a luxurious hotel suite, then fitted by dressmakers, pampered by servants, and treated like the lady Parker thinks she is. The situation nears the breaking point, but by the finale Parker and Norton are blissfully united. Having successfully married her daughter off, Robson seems content to return to her humble Times Square apple peddling. Nominated for four Academy Awards in the 1933 season, LADY FOR A DAY was an audience smash. Audiences laughed and cried, and director Capra had begun his long string of successes. Not only did Capra profit, but so did others involved. Robson, who was chosen when Capra was refused Marie Dressler, was given her finest and most memorable role after a prosperous stage and screen career which spanned decades. Riskin strengthened his collaboration with Capra (they would later co-pen IT HAPPENED ONE NIGHT, 1934, MR. DEEDS GOES TO TOWN, 1936, and MEET JOHN DOE, 1941) as well as getting his girl friend Farrell a supporting role. LADY FOR A DAY even boosted the popularity of writer Damon Runyon who sold the rights to his story "Madame La Gimp" to Capra for only $1,500. Given all the critical raves that LADY FOR A DAY garnered, Capra thought for sure that he had an Oscar winner in this film. Perhaps it would win all four awards it was nominated for. As Capra wrote in his biography *The Name Above The Title*: "No picture had ever won *four* major Oscars. It would set a *record*. Hot Damn! I wrote and threw away dozens of acceptance speeches; practiced shy humility before the mirror; rehearsed emotional breaks in my voice at just the right spots." All his preparation, however, went for nought. LADY FOR A DAY was shut out. CAVALCADE won for best picture and its director, Frank Lloyd, also won. The awards ceremony proved to be a major embarrassment for Capra. During the announcement of Best Director, Will Rogers tore open the envelope and, as Capra recounts, read: "Well, well, well, what do you know! I've watched this young man for a long time . . . Saw him come up from the bottom. It couldn't happen to a nicer guy. Come up and get it, Frank." Forgetting, as did Rogers, that there were two "Franks" nominated—Capra and Lloyd, Capra began making his way to the stage. Stuck halfway between his table and the stage, a confused Capra finally realised his mistake when he saw Lloyd approaching Rogers at the podium. "That walk back," Capra continues, "through applauding VIP's yelling 'Sit down! Down in front! Sit down!' as I obstructed their view was the longest, saddest, most shattering walk in my life. I wished I could have crawled under the rug like a miserable worm. When I slumped into my chair I felt like one. All my friends at the table were crying." The following year, however, Capra redeemed himself with IT HAPPENED ONE NIGHT. Capra did better than the "record" four major nominations—that picture took five. Capra and Riskin reworked LADY FOR A DAY in 1961 as POCKETFUL OF MIRACLES. Sequel: LADY BY CHOICE.

d, Frank Capra; w, Robert Riskin (based on the story "Madame La Gimp" by Damon Runyon); ph, Joseph Walker; ed, Gene Havlick; md, Constantin Bakaleinikoff; art d, Stephen Goosson; cos, Robert Kalloch.

Drama/Comedy **(PR:A MPAA:NR)**

LADY FOR A NIGHT** (1941) 87m REP bw

Joan Blondell *(Jenny Blake)*, John Wayne *(Jack Morgan)*, Ray Middleton *(Alan Alderson)*, Blanche Yurka *(Julia Alderson)*, Edith Barrett *(Katherine Alderson)*, Leonid Kinskey *(Boris)*, Philip Merivale *(Stephen Alderson)*, Hattie Noel *(Chloe)*, Dorothy Burgess *(Flo)*, Patricia Knox *(Mabel)*, Montagu Love *(Judge)*, Lew Payton *(Napoleon)*, Guy Usher *(Governor)*, Margaret Armstrong *(Governor's wife)*, Ivan Miller *(Mayor)*, Carmel Myers *(Mayor's Wife)*, Betty Hill *(Governor's Daughter)*, Marilyn Hare *(Mary Lou)*, Corinne Valdez *(Can-Can Dancer)*, Pierre Watkin *(Prosecutor)*, Jac George *(Orchestra Leader)*, Gertrude Astor *(Woman)*, Minerva Urecal *(Spinster)*, Dudley Dickerson, Paul White *(Black Specialty Dancers)*, Dolores Gray *(Dolores)*, Dewey Robinson *(Horse Dealer)*, The Hall Johnson Choir.

Blondell is a riverboat queen who runs her casino with the aid of political boss Wayne. When decadent society man Middleton drops a bundle while gambling, Blondell offers him a proposition—if he marries her, she'll wipe out his debts. It is her way of getting accepted by high society—her lifelong dream. Middleton's family doesn't take too kindly to her, in fact, they're downright nasty. A nasty old aunt tries to poison Blondell, but Middleton inadvertently drinks the brew and dies. Blondell is charged for the crime, but proven innocent. The tidy wrapup has her returning to life on the Mississippi with Wayne. There are several musical numbers, including Blondell singing "Up in a Balloon."

p, Albert J. Cohen; d, Leigh Jason; w, Isabel Dawn, Boyce DeGaw (based on a story by Garrett Fort); ph, Norbert Brodine; m, David Buttolph; ed, Murray Seldeen, Ernest Nims; md, Cy Feuer; art d, John Victor Mackey.

Drama   Cas.   (PR:A MPAA:NR)

LADY FRANKENSTEIN zero
(1971, Ital.) 99m Condor/New World c (LA FIGLIA DI FRANKENSTEIN; AKA: THE DAUGHTER OF FRANKENSTEIN; MADAME FRANKENSTEIN)

Joseph Cotten (*Baron*), Sarah Bay [Rosalba Neri] (*Tanya*), Mickey Hargity (*Captain*), Paul Muller (*Marsh*), Paul Whiteman, Herbert Fux.

Mel Welles, the flower shop owner in THE LITTLE SHOP OF HORRORS (1960), helmed this piece of trash with Cotten embarrassingly cast as Dr. Frankenstein. He is helped by daughter Bay, who desires to create a monster that can satisfy her sexual urges. Luckily, Cotton dies off early in the picture, but we're treated with the creation of yet another monster. One of the creatures is ugly and not so bad, and the other is rather dapper but a killer. He is anything but a romantic, killing Bay while having sex with her on an operating table. Cotton, a brilliant performer, must have been bound, gagged, and forced onto the set to do this abominable film.

p, Harry Cushing, Mel Welles [Ernst von Theumer]; d, Welles; w, Edward Di Lorenzo (based on a story by Dick Randall from a comic magazine story "For the Love of Frankenstein" by Bill Warren); ph, Richard Pallotin [Riccardo Pallotini]; m, Alessandro Alessandroni; ed, Cleo Converse; art d, Francis Mellon; spec eff, Cipa.

Horror   Cas.   (PR:O MPAA:R)

LADY FROM BOSTON, THE   (SEE: PARDON MY FRENCH, 1951)

LADY FROM CHEYENNE** 1/2   (1941) 87m UNIV bw

Loretta Young (*Annie*), Robert Preston (*Steve*), Edward Arnold (*Cork*), Frank Craven (*Hank Foreman*), Gladys George (*Elsie*), Jessie Ralph (*Mrs. McGuinness*), Stanley Fields (*Stover*), Willie Best (*George*), Samuel S. Hinds (*Gov. Howard*), Spencer Charters (*Mr. McGuinness*), Clare Verdera (*Mrs. Matthews*), Alan Bridge (*Mr. Matthews*), Joseph Sawyer (*Noisy*), Ralph Dunn, Harry Cording (*Cork's Henchmen*), Charles T. Aldrich (*Leo*), Dorothy Granger (*Myrtle*), Marion Martin (*Gertie*), Gladys Blake, Sally Payne, Iris Adrian, June Wilkins (*Chorus Girls*), Charles Williams (*Clerk*), Erville Alderson (*Fairchild*), Emmett Vogan (*Stanton*), Roger Imhof (*Uncle Bill*), William B. Davidson (*Dunbar*), James Kirkwood (*Politician*), Emory Parnell (*Crowley*), Dick Alexander, Griff Barnett (*Men*), Esther Howard (*Landlady*).

Young is a Quaker schoolteacher who battles gambler Arnold, and, in the process, establishes women's voting rights in Wyoming in 1869. She also secures for women the right to sit on a jury, enabling the ladies to convict racketeer Arnold. The characters are symbolically made-to-order—Young is the frail, liberated, educated, Quaker (the model woman) and Arnold is a vulgar, gambling, boozing mobster (the typical man)—pushing the picture barely over the top of being average.

p&d, Frank Lloyd; w, Kathryn Scola, Warren Duff (based on the story by Jonathan Finn, Theresa Oaks); ph, Milton Krasner; m, Charles Previn; md, Previn; art d, Jack Otterson; m/l, Previn, Sam Lerner.

Western   (PR:A MPAA:NR)

LADY FROM CHUNGKING**   (1943) 71m PRC bw

Anna May Wong (*Kwan Mei*), Harold Huber (*Gen. Kaimura*), Mae Clarke (*Lavara*), Rick Vallin (*Rodney Carr*), Paul Bryar (*Pat O'Rourke*), Ted Hecht (*Lt. Shimoto*), Louis [Ludwig] Donath (*Hans Gruber*), James Leong (*Chen*), Archie Got (*Mochow*), Walter Soo Hoo (*Lu-Chi*).

Wong is the leader of a group of Chinese guerrillas who have organized the farmers in preparation to fight the Japanese. Interesting historically, since the film was set against the Chinese-Japanese fighting prior to Pearl Harbor.

p, Alfred Stern, Arthur Alexander; d, William Nigh; w, Sam Robins (based on the story by Robins, Milton Raison); ph, Marcel Le Picard; ed, Charles Henkel, Jr.

War Drama   (PR:A MPAA:NR)

LADY FROM LISBON** 1/2
         (1942, Brit.) 75m BN-Shaftesbury/Anglo-American bw

Francis L. Sullivan (*Minghetti*), Jane Carr (*Tamara*), Martita Hunt (*Susan Wellington-Smythe*), Charles Victor (*Porter*), Antony Holles (*Anzoni*), George Street (*Hauptmann*), Gerhard Kempinsky (*Flugel*), Leo de Porkony (*Mario*), Wilfrid Hyde-White (*Ganier*).

A humorous espionage picture employing the dated "stolen Mona Lisa" plot which only shows up in early British films. Sullivan is a South American who makes a deal with the Nazis to do some spying in Lisbon in exchange for the priceless Leonardo DaVinci. All of a sudden (in keeping with this sort of "genre") numerous Mona Lisas begin popping up, all but one of them being fakes. Not until a British agent identifies the real one does Sullivan switch to the side of the Allies.

p, Elizabeth Hiscott; d, Leslie Hiscott; w, Michael Barringer; ph, Erwin Hillier.

Comedy/Espionage   (PR:A MPAA:NR)

LADY FROM LOUISIANA** 1/2   (1941) 82m REP bw

John Wayne (*John Reynolds*), Ona Munson (*Julie Mirbeau*), Ray Middleton (*Blackie Williams*), Henry Stephenson (*Gen. Mirbeau*), Helen Westley (*Mrs. Brunot*), Jack Pennick (*Cuffy*), Dorothy Dandridge (*Felice*), Shimen Ruskin (*Gaston*), Jacqueline Dalya (*Pearl*), Paul Scardon (*Judge Wilson*), Major James H. MacNamara (*Sen. Cassidy*), James C. Morton (*Littlefield*), Maurice Costello (*Edwards*).

Wayne, a young lawyer who is fighting against a local lottery racket, meets and falls in love with Munson, whose dad (Stephenson) runs the lottery. Munson tries to

convince him that the lottery isn't *that* bad, but when one of the recent winners is murdered, Wayne goes after the culprit full-force. Stephenson, however, is unaware that his assistant, Middleton, is skimming the profits instead of giving them to charity. Middleton's goon kills the boss and because Wayne is in charge of the anti-lottery squad he is blamed indirectly. With her dad murdered, Munson takes charge of the operation. The snooping Wayne comes up with the necessary proof to indict everyone involved with the racket, including Munson. When a ferocious storm deluges the courthouse with flood water, Middleton tries to escape, taking Munson with him. He hijacks a boat, leaving the doomed Munson waiting on a levee. Wayne also gets on the boat, and in an attempt to flee from his pursuer, Middleton drowns. As fate would have it, Wayne and Munson end up as Mr. and Mrs. Reynolds. Though it's highly implausible that this gal would ever run such a racket, the movie still is a nice piece of entertainment. Costello, a matinee idol in the old silent days, plays a small part in this film. He is also remembered today as being among the first important stage actors to turn to the screen, and the father of silent stars Helene and Dolores Costello.

p&d, Bernard Vorhaus; w, Vera Caspary, Michael Hogan, Guy Endore (based on a story by Edward James, Francis Faragoh); ph, Jack Marta; ed, Murray Seldeen, Edward Mann; md, Cy Feuer; art d, John Victor Mackay.

Drama   Cas.   (PR:A MPAA:NR)

LADY FROM NOWHERE zero   (1931) 65m CHES bw

Alice Day, John Holland, Phillips Smalley, Barbara Bedford, Mischa Auer, James Burtis.

A muddled and confused independent feature that tells the standard boy-girl tale of amateur detectives doing their best to bring justice down on the bad guys. A typical small part for bulging-eyed Auer before he hit his stride in MY MAN GODFREY (1936), which brought him an Oscar nomination.

p, George R. Batcheller; d, Richard Thorpe; w, Adrian Johnson, Barney Gerard; ph, M.A. Anderson; ed, Thorpe.

Crime   (PR:A MPAA:NR)

LADY FROM NOWHERE**   (1936) 60m COL bw

Mary Astor (*Polly*), Charles Quigley (*Earl*), Thurston Hall (*Mr. Barnes*), Victor Kilian (*Zeke*), Spencer Charters (*Gramp*), Norman Willis (*Ed Lustig*), Gene Morgan (*Mike*), Rita LaRoy (*Mabel*), Claudia Coleman (*Mrs. Banks*), Matty Fain (*Frankie*), John Tyrell (*Nick*).

Astor has the misfortune of being the only witness to a murder and both the mob and the cops are out to find her. She lies low, but the gangsters do a better job of sniffing her out than the police do. She runs into newspaperman Quigley and tells him that she's a lost heiress, but the mob still hunts her down. A nice Hollywood ending ties up all the loose ends.

d, Gordon Wiles; w, Fred Niblo, Jr., Arthur Strawn, Joseph Krumgold (based on the story by Ben G. Kohn); ph, Henry Freulich; ed, James Sweeney.

Drama/Crime   (PR:A MPAA:NR)

LADY FROM SHANGHAI, THE*** 1/2   (1948) 87m COL bw

Rita Hayworth (*Elsa Bannister*), Orson Welles (*Michael O'Hara*), Everett Sloane (*Arthur Bannister*), Glenn Anders (*George Grisby*), Ted de Corsia (*Sidney Broome*), Erskine Sanford (*Judge*), Gus Schilling (*Goldie*), Carl Frank (*District Attorney*), Louis Merrill (*Jake*), Evelyn Ellis (*Bessie*), Harry Shannon (*Cab Driver*), Wong Show Chong (*Li*), Sam Nelson (*Yacht Captain*), Tiny Jones (*Woman*), Edythe Elliott (*Old Lady*), Peter Cusanelli (*Bartender*), Joseph Granby (*Police Lieutenant*), Al Eben, Norman Thomson, Harry Strang, Steve Benton, Milton Kibbee, Edward Coke (*Policemen*), Gerald Pierce (*Waiter*), Maynard Holmes (*Truck Driver*), Jack Baxley (*Guard*), Dorothy Vaughan (*Old Woman*), Philip Morris (*Port Steward/Policemen/Peters*), Phil Van Zandt (*Toughie/Cop*), William Alland, Alvin Hammer, Mary Newton, Robert Gray, Byron Kane (*Reporters*), Ed Peil, Heenan Elliott (*Guards*), Charles Meakin (*Jury Foreman*), John Elliott (*Clerk*), Jessie Arnold (*Schoolteacher*), Doris Chan, Billy Louie (*Chinese Girls*), Joe Recht (*Garage Attendant*), Jean Wong (*Ticket Seller*), Mabel Smaney, George "Shorty" Chirello, Vernon Cansino (*People*), Grace Lem (*Chinese Woman*), Preston Lee (*Chinese Man*), Joseph Palma (*Cab Driver*), Artarne Wong (*Ticket Taker*), Richard Wilson (*District Attorney's Assistant*), Players of the Mandarin Theatre of San Francisco.

This *film noir* entry seems to improve with age, though its plot remains murky and its characters are never fully developed; all of them have too much of a past to be completely captured in a single film. Welles appears at the beginning, spouting a curious Irish brogue and an opening line that sums up most of what is to come: "When I start out to make a fool of myself, there's very little can stop me!" Strolling in Central Park, he sees a beautiful woman being molested and rushes to her rescue, beating off her attacker. She, Hayworth, flirts with him a bit and then disappears into the gloom. Welles, an unemployed sailor, is then hired as a crew member of a pleasure yacht owned by Sloane, a wealthy, crippled criminal lawyer, a ship headed for Mexican waters. Once on board, Welles quickly realizes that Hayworth, the very woman he aided, is Sloane's wife; she and Sloane act mysteriously toward him. He is introduced to Anders, Sloan's oddball law partner, and later is inveigled into a bizarre game wherein Welles will pretend to murder Anders. But Anders is killed for real and now Welles, after the ship has sailed to Acapulco where Welles has dallied with vixen Hayworth, stands accused of the murder. In short, Hayworth and Sloane have set him up. But Welles only learns of the insidious plan by bits and pieces, not fully realizing how he has been mainpulated until Hayworth explains some of it to him in the San Francisco aquarium, while giant, ugly fish swim behind her in huge tanks, her icy beauty still holding him captive. Welles is arrested and tried for Anders' murder and he is defended by legal genius Sloane who has never lost a case. But this time, Sloane does everything in his power to present an anemic, almost non-existent defense. Seeing Sloane throwing him to the wolves, Welles escapes before the jury brings in a verdict. He goes to a theater in Chinatown and hides there. Hayworth, accompanied by her Oriental friends, finds Welles and drugs him, removing him to the Hall of Mirrors at a neaarby amusement park. There, attorney Sloane finds Hayworth and Welles, believing she and Welles have been having an affair. Sloane and Hayworth hold guns on each other, but it's impossible for them—in the many-mirrored hall—to pinpoint their targets. They begin shooting at each other, Sloane shattering one mirror after another until he finds his target, and Hayworth also shooting him. With Sloane dead, Hayworth writhes on the floor. Welles comes out of his stupor and goes to the entrance, turning to hear Hayworth beg him to help her. He gives her a look of pity and goes out, leaving her to die with her husband, two schemers whose ugly deaths are entwined in their own strange machinations. Welles steps outside and, in a long shot showing a wide sky over distant San Francisco and Welles as a small figure retreating into the expansive scene, he is heard in voice-over to say: "I went to call the cops but I knew she'd be dead before they got there. I'd be free . . . Well, everybody is somebody's fool. The only way to stay out of trouble is to grow old, so I guess I'll concentrate on that. Maybe I'll live so long that I'll forget her. Maybe I'll die trying." THE LADY FROM SHANGHAI is as expermental as CITIZEN KANE in many ways—perhaps more so, as Welles used myriad jump cuts and optical devices that are surprisingly creative but tend to break up continuity, and the many subplots working at the same time. He shows his characters as reflected in windshields, water tumblers, and finally the dazzling mirror sequence. (Where Welles had employed the same techniques in CITIZEN KANE in subdued usage, he emphasizes those techniques here). In one shot, Welles stresses the one facial feature of his own that he disliked most, his nose, which is shown in extreme close-up, while Hayworth is shown as a speck in the distance on some rocks at Acapulco, an incredible depth-of-field shot. THE LADY FROM SHANGHAI was not Welles at his most spectacular, but it was vintage Welles, after all. The movie came into being because of Welles' own desperation for money. His then-marriage to Hayworth was in bad shape and he had used up his Hollywood welcome in producing several masterpieces that had failed to make money. Going East, Welles had joined Mike Todd in putting together a Broadway production of "Around the World in 80 Days," but Todd had run out of money, needing $50,000, and Welles turned to Columbia Studio mogul Harry Cohn. He phoned Cohn from backstage in the theater which he and Todd had rented. Getting Cohn on the line, Welles told him: "If you'll advance me the $50,000, I'll make a deal with you to write and direct a picture. I've got a suspense story that can be made inexpensively." Welles merely expected Cohn to agree but became frantic when the producer insisted upon knowing what the film was called. Desperately Welles looked about and spotted a wardrobe mistress reading a novel entitled The Lady from Shanghai (which he later bought), and rattled the title off to Cohn. Cohn told Welles that he would send the money. The $50,000 was not enough to save Todd's show—which closed after a short run—and Welles returned to Hollywood to make a film about which he knew nothing but the title. He did concoct enough of a story to boost Cohn's interest beyond a low-budget production. The mogul now wanted to star Hayworth, Welles' estranged wife, giving it the top production treatment. The film—originally scheduled as an Ida Lupino vehicle—was lavished with a huge budget and Hayworth reconciled with Welles, believing that the money Welles made from the film—he would get a percentage of the gross for his appearance as an actor—would help support their daughter Rebecca. Cohn's motives were, as usual, strictly mercenary. Hayworth's present contract with Columbia was running out and he wanted to reap whatever money her name would draw before she entered into films backed by her own production firm. The first thing Welles did was to order his wife and star to cut her long, luxuriant russet hair into a blonde bob. When Cohn heard about it, seeing the stills of Hayworth with shorn locks, he exploded, going into a titanic fit, cursing Welles left and right—but he stayed clear of the production, which jumped from its original two-month shooting to $2 million while Welles continued creating elaborate scenes and expensive on-location setups from Alcapulco to San Francisco, then inexplicably changed his mind and scrapped everything, starting once more from scratch. Welles, Hayworth, cast, and crew stayed on in the expensive resort town of Acapulco for twenty-eight days, lavishly spending Cohn's money. To make sure the fortunes of Welles' friend, Errol Flynn, improved, he rented the actor's yacht, which is the ship portrayed as Sloane's during THE LADY FROM SHANGHAI, and it is Flynn who is sailing the vessel during the trip. (Flynn can acutally be glimpsed in a brief scene in Acapulco outside a cantina.) Welles simply disregarded Cohn's warnings about going over budget. He constructed an involved chase through the amusement park which demanded an avenue of mirrors, then, after the enormous mirror set was completed, realized he could not use it as originally intended since it was impossible to light, given the configuration of the mirrors. He then changed it to the Hall of Mirrors funhouse scene. (The wizard who finally created the Hall of Mirrors sequence and solved Welles' dilemma was special effects expert Lawrence Butler who had brought forth Rex Ingram as the genie from the bottle, made toy horses and carpets fly, and constructed a host of wonderful photographic tricks for Alexander Korda's magnificent THE THIEF OF BAGDAD.) Nothing seemed to go right and when Welles finished production in February 1947 he realized he had a giant mess on his hands and admitted it to Harry Cohn. Virginia Van Upp, who had written many of Hayworth's films, was called in to patch the movie together; many scenes—including a lengthy montage and an airplane sequence—were cut, so the film stayed at ninety-one minutes. Then more minutes were cut to the release length of 87 minutes. Gossipmonger Louella Parsons, a longtime Hayworth booster, viciously attacked Welles, whom she called "awesome Orson, the self-styled genius," stating that he had purposely and maliciously set out to ruin his wife's career. She concluded that Welles, who had by then left for Europe to make films, was "washed up." Hayworth was also off to Europe to make her own films but she went alone. When she finished THE LADY FROM SHANGHAI, she was also finished with Welles, suing him for divorce. The decree was granted November 10, 1947, just after Hayworth declared on the witness stand: "Mr. Welles showed no interest in establishing a home. Mr.

Welles told me he never should have married in the first place, as it interfered with his freedom in his way of life."

p,d&w, Orson Welles (based on the novel The Lady From Shanghai, by [Raymond] Sherwood King); ph, Charles Lawton, Jr.; m, Heinz Roemheld; ed, Viola Lawrence; md, Morris Stoloff; art d, Stephen Goosson, Sturges Carne; set d, Wilbur Menefee, Herman Schoenbrun; cos, Jean Louis; spec eff, Lawrence Butler; m/l, "Please Don't Kiss Me," Allan Roberts, Doris Fisher (dubbed by Anita Ellis); makeup, Robert Schiffer, Clay Campbell.

Crime Drama   **Cas.**   **(PR:C MPAA:NR)**

LADY FROM TEXAS, THE ** 1/2   (1951) 78m UNIV c

Howard Duff (Dan Mason), Mona Freeman (Bonnie Lee), Josephine Hull (Miss Birdie), Gene Lockhart (Judge George Jeffers), Craig Stevens (Cyril Guthrie), Jay C. Flippen (Sheriff), Ed Begley (Dave Blodgett), Barbara Knudson (Mabel), Chris-Pin Martin (Jose), Lane Bradford, Kenneth Patterson, Morgan Farley (Lawyer Haddon).

Hull is a kind-hearted old lady who is the victim of Stevens' dishonest efforts to buy her ranch for much less than it's worth. Duff, with the aid of Freeman, stands up for Hull against the injustice. A courtroom battle, in which Stevens tries to prove Hull crazy, caps this unlikely Western. This was the last picture for Hull, who won an Oscar for Best Supporting Actress for her role in HARVEY.

p, Leonard Goldstein; d, Joseph Pevney; w, Gerald Drayson Adams, Connie Lee Bennett (based on a story by Harold Shumate); ph, Charles P. Boyle (Technicolor); ed, Virgil Vogel; md, Joseph Kish; art d, Bernard Herzbrun, Emrich Nicholson.

Western   **(PR:A MPAA:NR)**

LADY FROM THE SEA, THE **
                    (1929, Brit.) 62m FP-BIP/PAR bw (AKA: GOODWIN SANDS)

Moore Marriott (Old Roberts), Mona Goya (Claire le Grange), Raymond Milland (Tom Roberts), Bruce Gordon (Dick Roberts), Eugenie Amami (Rose), Anita Graham (Mrs. Roberts), Wilfred Shine (Doctor).

A satisfying romancer about a seaman who pulls an endearing Frenchwoman from the dangerous waters and takes a fancy to her. Of course he has a girl who really loves him waiting back on land and she's not too pleased with his catch. He learns his lesson, however, and before long the lovers are joyfully reunited. Originally filmed silent with sound added the following year.

d, Castleton Knight; w, Garnett Weston, Victor Kendall (based on a story by Joe Grossman); ph, James Rogers, Jack Cox, Theodor Sparkuhl.

Romance   **(PR:A MPAA:NR)**

LADY GAMBLES, THE ** 1/2   (1949) 98m UNIV bw

Barbara Stanwyck (Joan Boothe), Robert Preston (David Boothe), Stephen McNally (Corrigan), Edith Barrett (Ruth Phillips), John Hoyt (Dr. Rojac), Elliott Sullivan (Barky), John Harmon (Frenchy), Phil Van Zandt (Chuck), Leif Erickson (Tony), Curt Conway (Bank Clerk), Houseley Stevenson (Pawnbroker), Don Beddoe (Mr. Sutherland), Nana Bryant (Mrs. Sutherland), Anthony [Tony] Curtis (Bellboy), Peter Leeds (Hotel Clerk), Frank Moran (Murphy), Esther Howard (Cross Lady), John Indrisano (Bert), Polly Bailey (Woman at Slot Machine), Francis McDonald (Trainer), Rex Lease (Guide), Kenneth Cutler (Clerk), Al Bayne (Dice Shooter), George Spaulding (Dr. McCann), Billy Wayne (Stickman), Peter Brocco (1st Character), George Charleton (Macilwaine), Sherry Hall (1st Man), Eda Reiss Merin (Woman), Harold Goodwin (Westerner), Frank McFarland, Al Rhein, Beatrice Gray, Manuel Paris, Jim Toney, Eddie Le Baron, Bill Cartledge, William Hudson, Donna La Barr.

Nobody suffers as well as Stanwyck can. This is another of her nine films with the word "lady" or "ladies" in the title and is the story of addiction: not to drugs or alcohol, but to the gambling bug. Stanwyck is the happily married wife of Preston, a writer on assignment in Nevada where he is doing a story on the huge Boulder Dam. She accompanies him and has lots of time on her hands so she tries a little gambling at a casino and soon is hooked. She loses a fortune, hocks some of her goods, and lies about it to Preston. The marriage ends unhappily and she goes to work as a B-girl in the casino to support her habit. She's taken under McNally's wing. He's a tough casino operator who wants to use her to make a few bucks but she soon screws that up. Desperate and depressed, she climbs out on a window ledge to jump and is talked down by Preston, psychiatrist Hoyt, and Barrett, her sister. The picture stops short of truth by some specious mumbo-jumbo about her having a guilt complex as the reason for her gambling mania. It was similar to, but not nearly as effective as, THE LOST WEEKEND. Many films have been made about the subject (THE GAMBLER, CALIFORNIA SPLIT, etc.) though none has ever really captured the psychological need to lose everything that most gamblers have. McNally was excellent in his role although that may have been due to the fact that he had the sharpest dialog. Look hard for Tony Curtis (while he was still billed as "Anthony") as a hotel bellhop. This picture was shot many years before Las Vegas became as garish as it is now and the town appeared to be a very pleasant place to spend a holiday, if you could avoid the tables. In those days, the hotels offered such incredible deals (rooms for $10, breakfasts for a dollar, etc.) that Las Vegas was the best vacation bargain in the west. Parents might well be advised to allow their children to see THE LADY GAMBLES as it has a moral behind it that kids should learn about excesses.

p, Michael Kraike; d, Michael Gordon; w, Roy Huggins, Halsted Welles (based on a story by Lewis Meltzer, Oscar Saul); ph, Russell Metty; m, Frank Skinner; ed, Milton Carruth; art d, Alexander Golitzen; set d, Russell A. Gausman, Ruby Rolevitt; cos, Orry-Kelly; makeup, Bud Westmore, Bob Ewing.

Drama   **(PR:A MPAA:NR)**

LADY GANGSTER*
(1942) 62m WB bw

Faye Emerson (*Dot Burton*), Julie Bishop (*Myrtle Reed*), Frank Wilcox (*Kenneth Phillips*), Roland Drew (*Carey Wells*), Jackie C. Gleason (*Wilson*), Ruth Ford (*Lucy Fenton*), Virginia Brissac (*Mrs. Stoner*), Dorothy Vaughan (*Jenkins*), Dorothy Adams (*Deaf Annie*), Dewolf [William] Hopper (*John*), Vera Lewis (*Ma Silsby*), Herbert Rawlinson (*Lewis Sinton*), Peggy Diggins (*Mary*), Charles Wilson (*Detective*), Bill Phillips (*Stew*), Frank Mayo (*Walker*), Leah Baird (*Matron*), Sol Gorss, Fred Kelsey (*Cops*), Daisy Bufford (*Black Girl*), Joan Winfield (*Nurse*), Jack Mower (*Sergeant*), Ken Christy (*Bank Guard*).

An inconsistent movie with Emerson as a tough gang moll who is reformed by district attorney Wilcox. Florian Roberts was the pseudonym used by Robert Florey, ebullient director of many silents who chose the Roberts pseudonym for the first and only time in his career for LADY GANGSTER, and maybe with good reason.

d, Florian Roberts [Robert Florey]; w, Anthony Coldeway (based on the play "Gangstress, or Women in Prison" by Dorothy Mackaye, Carlton Miles); ph, Arthur Todd; ed, Harold McLernon; art d, Ted Smith.

Crime/Drama (PR:A MPAA:NR)

LADY GENERAL, THE**
(1965, Hong Kong) 106m Shaw Bros./Frank Lee International c (AKA: HUA MU-LAN)

Ivy Ling Po (*Hua Mu-lan*), Chin Han (*Li Kuang*), Chen Yen Yen (*Mrs. Hua*), Yang Chi-ching (*Hua Hu*), Chu Mu (*Hua Ming*), Wang Lan (*Jua Mu- hui*), Li Kun (*Chen Wei-han*), Chiang Kuang-chao (*Chang Teh-sheng*), Ching Miao (*Marshal Ho*), Feng I (*Wang Kuei*), Ho Ping (*Tribal King*), Chao Ming (*Wu Hsin-cheng*).

Ling Po is a young lady who wants nothing more than to be a soldier, but her father forbids it. She enlists, disguised as a boy. While in combat she secretly falls in love with her tentmate, Han. She is injured in battle and Han pays a visit, pleasantly surprised when he learns that she is a woman. He goes back to the army with the promise that he'll return to marry her. Implausible, but charming all the same.

p, Run Run Shaw; d, Yueh Feng; w, Ke Jui-feng.

War Drama (PR:A MPAA:NR)

LADY GODIVA*1/2
(1955) 89m UNIV c

Maureen O'Hara (*Lady Godiva*), George Nader (*Lord Leofric*), Eduard Franz (*King Edward*), Leslie Bradley (*Count Eustace*), Victor McLaglen (*Grimald*), Torin Thatcher (*Lord Godwin*), Rex Reason (*Harold*), Arthur Gould-Porter (*Thorold*), Robert Warwick (*Humbert*), Grant Withers (*Pendar*), Sim Iness (*Oswin*), Alec Harford (*Tom the Tailor*), Arthur Shields (*Innkeeper*), Anthony Eustrel (*Prior*), Kathryn Givney (*Abbess*), Thayer Roberts (*William*), Clint Eastwood (*1st Saxon*), Rhodes Reason (*Sweyn*), Olive Sturgess (*Girl*), Tom Cloud, Judith Brian (*Listeners*), Maya Van Horn (*Frenchwoman*), Jack Grinnage (*Blacksmith's Son*), Philo McCullough (*Captain*), Henry Brandon (*Bejac*).

In this period piece, set during the conflicts between the Normans and the Saxons, O'Hara is cast as the legendary woman who rode naked on horseback through the streets. Her fellow villagers prove their Saxon loyalty by not looking at her as she passes, except for one perverted soul who promptly has his eyes plucked out by an enraged McLagen. After a decent-sized role in FRANCIS IN THE NAVY (1955), Clint Eastwood is barely noticeable as an unnamed Saxon. Lucky Clint. There is little revelation here.

p, Robert Arthur; d, Arthur Lubin; w, Oscar Brodney, Harry Ruskin (based on a story by Brodney); ph, Carl Guthrie (Technicolor); ed, Paul Weatherwax; md, Joseph Gershenson; art d, Alexander Golitzen, Robert Boyle.

Drama (PR:A MPAA:NR)

LADY GODIVA RIDES AGAIN**
(1955, Brit.) 90m London/Carroll bw

Dennis Price (*Simon Abbott*), John McCallum (*Larry Burns*), Stanley Holloway (*Mr. Clark*), Pauline Stroud (*Marjorie Clark*), Gladys Henson (*Mrs. Clark*), Bernadette O'Farrell (*Janie*), George Cole (*Johnny*), Diana Dors (*Dolores August*), Eddie Byrne (*Eddie Mooney*), Kay Kendall (*Sylvie*), Renee Houston (*Beattie*), Dora Bryan (*Publicity Woman*), Sidney James (*Lew Beeson*), Dagmar [Dana] Wynter (*Myrtle Shaw*), Tommy Duggan (*Compere*), Eddie Leslie (*Comic*), Walford Hyden (*Conductor*), Edward Forsyth, Lisa Lee (*Singers*), Cyril Chamberlain (*Harry*), Lyn Evans (*Vic Kennedy*), Peter Martyn (*photographer*), Fred Berger (*Mr. Green*), Henry Longhurst (*Soap Director*), Felix Felton, Arthur Brander, Sidney Vivian (*Councilors*), Arthur Howard, Clive Baxter, Paul Connell (*Soap Publicity Men*), John Harvey (*Buller*), Rowena Gregory (*Waitress*), Tom Gill (*Receptionist*), Patricia Goddard (*Susan*), Richard Wattis (*Casting Director*), Michael Ripper (*Stage Manager*), Charlotte Mitchell (*Lucille*), Toke Townley (*Lucille's Husband*), Alastair Sim, Googie Withers, Trevor Howard, Myrette Morven, Leslie Mitchell, Russell Waters, Joan Collins, Violet Pretty [Anne Heywood], Jimmy Young, Greta Gray, Dorothy Hocking, Madeleine Mona, Dawn Chapple, Deirdre de Peyer, Rita Wheatley, June Charlier, Simone Silva, June Hart, Maureen O'Neill, Sylvia Wren, Kismet Shahani, Marlene Ann Dee, Suzanne Levesi, Ann Hanslip, Diana Russell, Gina Egan, Evelyn Buyers, Johnnie Johnson, Enid Smeedon, Phyllis Garnett, Noel Scott-Gorman, Peter O'Farrell, Syd Dean and His Band.

Stroud is a beauty who wins a national contest after a case of mistaken identity. Although she triumphs, she can't make up for her lack of talent which every casting agency all too clearly points out, frustrating her thespian ambitions. She finally resorts to taking a nude stage role. Funny in spots, tiresome in others.

p, Frank Launder, Sidney Gilliat; d, Launder; w, Launder, Val Valentine; ph, Wilkie Cooper; m, William Alwyn; ed, Thelma Connell; md, Muir Mathieson; art d, Joseph Bato; cos., Anna Duse.

Comedy (PR:A MPAA:NR)

LADY GREY zero
(1980) 100m Maverick c

Ginger Alden (*Lady Grey*), David Allen Coe (*Black Jack Donovan*), Paul Ott (*Don Sands*), Herman Bloodsworth (*Johnny Nyland*), Ed Grady (*Hubbard Jackson*), Paula Baldwin (*Pru*).

Elvis Presley's last girl friend, Alden, proves that she simply should stay as far out of the public eye as possible. Her performance as the country femme fatale who rises to the top but still isn't happy displays negative acting ability and ruins anything of value (a bold assumption) in the script. The picture features an abundance of good ole boys, some unwilling prostitutes, and the rape of an unconscious Alden (though not much different from Alden in a conscious state). Forget about this movie; do something more interesting instead, like watching water evaporate.

p, Earl Owensby; d, Worth Keeter; w, Tom McIntyre; ph, Darryl Cathcart (DeLuxe Color); m, Arthur Smith, Clay Smith; ed, Jim Laudenslager; art d, Sam Robbins.

Drama **Cas.** (PR:O MPAA:NR)

LADY HAMILTON
(SEE: THAT HAMILTON WOMAN, 1941)

LADY HAMILTON*1/2
(1969, Ger./Ital./Fr.) 98m Rapid-P.E.A.-S.N.C./Constantin c (AKA: THE MAKING OF A LADY)

Michele Mercier (*Lady Hamilton*), Richard Johnson (*Lord Nelson*), John Mills (*Lord Hamilton*), Harald Leipnitz (*Harry Featherstone*), Robert Hundar (*Capt. Hardy*), Mirco Ellis (*John Payne*), Boy Gobert (*George Romney*), Dieter Borsche (*Dr. Graham*), Nadja Tiller (*Queen of Naples*), Lorenzo Terzon (*Charles Greville*), Howard Ross (*Dick*).

Based on the novel by Alexandre Dumas pere, this picture has sex-kitten Mercier portraying the title character, a country bumpkin who melts men with her very presence. She weds Mills and becomes a "Lady" with a capital "L." She then has an affair with naval hero Horatio Nelson (Johnson). When Mills dies she marries and has a child by Johnson. She is rudely awakened, however, when she is not allowed to attend her famous husband's funeral, making her realize how little society thinks of her. It's Mercier's film from beginning to end, serving chiefly as a vehicle for her body—the romance is minimized (seemingly unintentionally) as is the script. Director Christian-Jaque has directed over 100 films; he's bound to turn out some losers every now and then.

p, Wolf C. Hartwig; d, Christian-Jaque; w, Werner P. Zibaso, Jameson Brewer, Christian-Jaque (based on the novel by Alexandre Dumas pere); ph, Pierre Petit (Panavision, Eastmancolor); m, Riz Ortolani.

Drama (PR:O MPAA:NR)

LADY HAS PLANS, THE**1/2
(1942) 77m PAR bw

Ray Milland (*Kenneth Harper*), Paulette Goddard (*Sidney Royce*), Roland Young (*Ronald Dean*), Albert Dekker (*Baron Von Kemp*), Margaret Hayes (*Rita Lenox*), Cecil Kellaway (*Peter Miles*), Addison Richards (*Paul Baker*), Edward Norris (*Frank Richards*), Charles Arnt (*Pooly*), Hans Schumm, Hans von Morhart (*Germans*), Genia Nikola (*German Maid*), Gerald Mohr (*Joe Scalsi*), Lionel Royce (*Guard*), Thomas W. Ross (*Abner Spencer*), Arthur Loft (*Mr. Weston*), Paul Phillips, Warren Ashe (*G-Men*), Lee Shumway (*Cop*), Terry Ray (*Taxi Driver*), Mel Ruick (*Announcer*), Keith Richards, George Dobbs, Hans Furberg (*Hotel Clerks*), Yola d'Avril (*Hotel Maid*), Richard Webb (*Hotel Information Clerk*), Nestor Paiva (*Portuguese Porter*), Sigfrid Tor (*German Guard*), Louis Mercier (*Bellhop*), Wolfgang A. Zilzer (*German Clerk, Baron's Office*), Hans Joby, William Yetter, Adolph Milar (*German Officials*), Francisco Maran (*Hotel Manager*), Jean Del Val (*Bartender*), Martin Garralaga (*Maitre D'*), Richard Webb (*Information Clerk at Hotel*), Bruce Wyndham (*German*), Ray Flynn (*Man*).

Milland is a radio broadcaster in Lisbon during WW II. Goddard, his assistant, is mistaken for a Nazi spy with a secret message tattooed on her back in invisible ink. The far-fetched but enjoyable plot is filled to the brim with spies and counterspies. This picture was one of four which Milland and Goddard appeared in together within a one year stretch, the others being STAR-SPANGLED RHYTHM, REAP THE WILD WIND, and THE CRYSTAL BALL.

p, Fred Kohlmar; d, Sidney Lanfield; w, Harry Tugend (based on a story by Leo Birinski); ph, Charles Lang; ed, William Shea.

Spy Drama/Comedy (PR:A MPAA:NR)

LADY ICE*1/2
(1973) 93m Tomorrow/NGP c

Donald Sutherland (*Andy Hammond*), Jennifer O'Neill (*Paula Booth*), Robert Duvall (*Ford Pierce*), Patrick Magee (*Paul Booth*), Eric [Hans Gudegast] Braeden (*Peter Brinker*), Jon Cypher (*Eddy Stell*), Buffy Dee (*Fat Man*), Perry Lopez (*Carlos*), Charles J. Swepeniser, Edward Biaganti (*Robbers*), Zvee Scooler, Sol Frieder (*Jewelers*), Berenice Clayre (*Head Matron*).

Sutherland, in a lackluster performance, is an insurance company detective battling a gang of jewel thieves for possession of $3 million worth of diamonds. Lots of fast-moving car chases and slow-moving pickup scenes between Sutherland and O'Neill are provided. It's Duvall, fresh off his Academy Award-nominated role in THE GODFATHER (1972), who makes the picture worthwhile. Unfortunately his role is far too small. Lucien Ballard's fine camerawork (his 101st time behind the camera) is the next best reason for watching.

p, Harrison Starr; d, Tom Gries; w, Alan Trustman, Harold Clemens (based on a story by Trustman); ph, Lucien Ballard (Panavision, Technicolor); m, Pierre Botkin, Jr.; ed, Robert Swink, William Sanda; prod d, Joel Schiller; set d, Nicholas Romanac; cos, Donfeld; makeup, Gary Liddiard.

Action/Crime **Cas.** (PR:CA MPAA:PG)

LADY IN A CAGE*   (1964) 94m American Entertainment/PAR bw

Olivia de Havilland (*Mrs. Hilyard*), Ann Sothern (*Sade*), Jeff Corey (*The Wino*), James Caan (*Randall*), Jennifer Billingsley (*Elaine*), Rafael Campos (*Essie*), William Swan (*Malcolm Hilyard*), Charles Seel (*Junkyard Proprietor*), Scatman Crothers (*Proprietor's Assistant*).

Luther Davis, who co-wrote "Kismet" for Broadway and whose credits for films are long and impressive, is a gentle man, not given to violence, so it came as a shock to those who knew him when he wrote and produced this realistic, shocking, and very intense drama. He claims that the material was based on truth and his desire was to bring the public out of its apathy toward violence and the easy way in which it is accepted. De Havilland had never done a role like this and later admitted that she had a share of the profits. The movie was banned in England due to the subject matter. De Havilland is a rich author who lives in New York in a multi-storied town house. There is a power failure and her elevator is stuck between floors. That shouldn't be a problem, as she has an alarm in the elevator (the "cage" of the title), which she rings. But it's July 4th and the streets are so noisy that no one hears the persistent ringing of the bell. De Havilland is using the elevator because she's recovering from a problem with her hip and is considerably less than mobile. A further complication is that her son, Swan, at the age of twenty-nine has left her since he can no longer put up with her doting ways. The bell is eventually heard by Corey, a drunk, who forces entry into the house, robs it of goods and booze, and pays no attention to the pleas of the trapped woman. He comes back later with Sothern, a buxom streetwalker, and a trio of teenage toughs, led by Caan in his first starring role after a bit in IRMA LA DOUCE. Caan is crazy and enjoys teasing de Havilland who attempts to convince them that she will give them anything if they free her. They respond by wrecking the house and she finally begins to harangue them. The destruction becomes a frenzy, then Corey is stabbed to death and Sothern is placed in the cellar. De Havilland finally manages to flee the elevator. Caan approaches her but she has two metal strips in her hand which she's pried from the side of the elevator. She plunges these into Caan's eyes, blinding him, and the other two, Billingsley and Campos, race out. She is in pain from having jumped from the elevator and she drags herself across the floor, out the door, and onto the street. Caan is blinded and attempts to block her, but he winds up on the street and is killed by a passing car as he stumbles in front of the motorist. De Havilland lies in the street screaming for help and is finally aided by some pedestrians. This probably was a play that never got produced because much of the action is interior. One can see the similarity between this and WAIT UNTIL DARK in that the heroine is unable to function and the villains take their pleasure with her until she exacts revenge. Director Grauman later went on to produce and direct many TV shows, including "Felony Squad." Its often sadistic moments are not for children.

p, Luther Davis; d, Walter Grauman; w, Davis; ph, Lee Garmes; m, Paul Glass; ed, Leon Barsha; md, Glass; prod d, Rudolph Sternad; art d, Hal Pereira; set d, Joseph Kish, Sam Comer; spec eff, Paul K. Lerpac; makeup, Wally Westmore, Gene Hibbs.

Drama   **Cas.**   **(PR:O   MPAA:NR)**

LADY IN A JAM****1/2**   (1942) 78m UNIV bw

Irene Dunne (*Jane Palmer*), Patric Knowles (*Dr. Enright*), Ralph Bellamy (*Stanley*), Eugene Pallette (*Mr. Billingsley*), Samuel S. Hinds (*Dr. Brewster*), Queenie Vassar (*Cactus Kate*), Jane Garland (*Strawberry*), Edward McWade (*Groundhog*), Robert Homans (*Faro Bill*), Charles Lane (*Government Man*), Hobart Cavanaugh (*Reporter*), Mira McKinney (*Lady of the Evening*), Sarah Padden (*Miner's Wife*), Clara Blandick (*Tourist*), Sam H. Underwood (*Desert Rat*), Kathleen Howard, Mona Barrie, Veda Ann Borg, Josephine Whittell, Kitty O'Neil, Claire Whitney, Isabel LaMal (*Women*), Russell Hicks (*Manager*), Irving Bacon (*Motel Proprietor*), Hardie Albright (*Chauffeur*), Fuzzy Knight, Eddie Fetherstone (*Cab Drivers*), Robert Emmett Keane (*Coupe Driver*), Charles Cane (*Cop*), Holmes Herbert, Garry Owen, Reed Hadley, Charles Coleman (*Men*), Phyllis Kennedy (*Drunk Tourist*), Rex Lease, Syd Saylor, Ruth Warren (*Drunks*), Eddie Dunn (*Bartender*), Thomas Kilshaw (*Auctioneer*), Chief Thundercloud (*Himself*), Eddy Chandler (*Waiter*), Lester Dorr (*Assistant Manager*), Al Bridge (*Furniture Mover*), Fred Stanley (*Tourist*), Dick Alexander (*Fighter*), Billy Benedict (*Barker*), Bess Flowers (*Nurse*), Casey MacGregor (*Case Keeper*), Jack Gardner (*Auctioneer's Clerk*).

The lady is Dunne; the jam is what she gets in after squandering the fortune left her by her grandfather. The guy who saves the day is psychiatrist Knowles, who takes her out West to visit her grandma. These jams have a way of working themselves out when a couple gets married, which is exactly what Dunne and Knowles do.

p&d, Gregory La Cava; w, Eugene Thackrey, Frank Cockrell, Otho Lovering; ph, Hal Mohr; m, Frank Skinner; ed, Russell Schoengarth; md, Charles Previn; art d, Jack Otterson.

Comedy   **(PR:A   MPAA:NR)**

LADY IN CEMENT**   (1968) 93m Arcola-Millfield/FOX c

Frank Sinatra (*Tony Rome*), Raquel Welch (*Kit Forrest*), Richard Conte (*Lt. Santini*), Martin Gabel (*Al Mungar*), Lainie Kazan (*Maria Baretto*), Pat Henry (*Rubin*), Steve Peck (*Paul Mungar*), Virginia Wood (*Audrey*), Richard Deacon (*Arnie Sherwin*), Frank Raiter (*Danny Yale*), Peter Hock (*Frenchy*), Alex Stevens (*Shev*), Christine Todd (*Sandra Lomax*), Mac Robbins (*Sidney, the Organizer*), Tommy Uhlar (*The Kid, Tighe Santini*), Ray Baumel (*Paco*), Pauly Dash (*McComb*), Andy Jarrell (*Pool Boy*), Dan Blocker (*Gronsky*), Joe E. Lewis (*Himself*).

A sequel to TONY ROME (1967), LADY IN CEMENT is not nearly so good as the original although both were written, in part, by the same author, Albert, who also wrote the novel from whence they came. Sinatra is again in Miami as a wise-cracking private eye. He's diving for buried treasure off the coast and comes across the corpse of a comely blonde who has been given cement shoes and dropped to the bottom of the sea. The autopsy reveals that she was murdered by stabbing and Blocker, a behemoth ex-con, hires Sinatra to learn whether the dead woman was his

former girl friend. Sinatra starts to gumshoe and asks Kazan, the missing woman's ex-roomie, if she's heard from her lately. Kazan says she saw Blocker's girl at a party given by Welch, an alcoholic heiress. Welch claims that she was too drunk to recall anything about her party. Gabel is a neighbor of Welch's and a one-time rackets boss. He tells Sinatra to lay off Welch. Later, Kazan is killed and a brace of Gabel's toughs try to knock off Blocker. Deacon is an artist and is able to reconstruct the face of the dead woman and identify her as Blocker's love. Now Sinatra discovers that Welch and the dead woman both had eyes for Gabel's son, Peck, and had argued over him. Sinatra is framed for the death of Kazan's boss, Raiter, a gay man. Conte is the local Miami cop who is both a pal and a nemesis of Sinatra and knows deep down that old blue eyes is innocent, but feels he must arrest Sinatra until the real killer is found. Sinatra gets away from Conte and moves in with Welch, whom he suspects is the killer. That suspicion begins to become a reality when Welch admits that she woke up after the boozy party with a knife in her hand and the dead girl lying next to her on the floor. It's too pat, and Sinatra thinks that she may also be the victim of a frame. He gets Blocker to admit that he and Peck were siphoning some money from Gabel's coffers. Now Sinatra comes to the conclusion that Peck must have murdered the lady in cement to get any money Blocker may have given her for safekeeping. He races to Welch's house because he feels hers may be the next body to be found. Once there, he saves Welch from the knife-wielding Peck. The case is closed when Sinatra hands the killer to Conte, then goes off to complete his underwater treasure hunt with Welch. Much too complex and with little of the humor of TONY ROME, it had the same producer, director, and cameraman as the former but none of the high spirits. There was some talk of this becoming a TV series starring Fox contract player Tony Scotti who was so laughable in VALLEY OF THE DOLLS. It didn't happen. The lack of success of LADY IN CEMENT effectively ended Tony Rome's career.

p, Aaron Rosenberg; d, Gordon Douglas; w, Marvin H. Albert, Jack Guss (based on the novel by Albert); ph, Joseph Biroc, Ricou Browning (Panavision, DeLuxe Color); m, Hugo Montenegro; ed, Robert Simpson; md, Montenegro; art d, Leroy Deane; set d, Walter M. Scott, Jerry Wunderlich; cos, Moss Mabry; spec eff, L. B. Abbott, Art Cruikshank; makeup, Layne Britton, Dan Striepke.

Crime Drama   **(PR:O   MPAA:R)**

LADY IN DANGER* **1/2**   (1934, Brit.) 68m GAU bw

Tom Walls (*Richard Dexter*), Yvonne Arnaud (*Queen of Ardenberg*), Leon M. Lion (*Dittling*), Anne Grey (*Lydia*), Hugh Wakefield (*King*), Marie Lohr (*Lady Brockley*), Alfred Drayton (*Quill*), Leonora Corbett (*Marcelle*), Cecil Parker (*Liker*), O.B. Clarence (*Nelson*), Harold Warrender (*Clive*), Hubert Harben (*Matterby*), Charles Lefeaux, Dorothy Galbraith, Jane Cornell, Mervyn Johns.

A vague comedy which refuses to commit itself to a romance between the leads. Walls is an English chap who lands his airplane in a revolution-torn country and ends up escorting a disguised queen (Arnaud) safely to England.

p, Michael Balcon; d, Tom Walls; w, Ben Travers (based on the play "O Mistress Mine" by Travers); ph, Phil Tannura.

Comedy   **(PR:A   MPAA:NR)**

LADY IN DISTRESS** **1/2**

(1942, Brit.) 62m Greenspan and Seligman Enterprises/GFD bw (GB: A WINDOW IN LONDON)

Michael Redgrave (*Peter*), Sally Gray (*Vivienne*), Paul Lukas (*Zoltini*), Hartley Power (*Max Preston*), Patricia Roc (*Pat*), Glen Alyn (*Andrea*), Gertrude Musgrove (*Telephonist*), George Carney (*Night Watchman*), Brian Coleman (*Constable*), Alf Goddard (*Tiny*), Wilfred Walter (*Foreman*), George Merritt (*Manager*), John Salew (*Reporter*), Pamela Randall, Kimberley and Page.

Illusions and murders that aren't really murders color this interesting tale. Redgrave sees what he thinks is a stabbing, but it turns out to be a rehearsal for a magician's show. After some more misconceptions, Gray, magician Lukas' wife-assistant, ends up killed by her unbearably jealous husband.

p, Josef Somlo, Richard Norton; d, Herbert Mason; w, Ian Dalrymple, Brigid Cooper (based on the screenplay by Herbert and Manet entitled "Metropolitan"); ph, Glen McWilliams; ed, Philip Charlot; art d, Ralph Brinton.

Drama   **(PR:A   MPAA:NR)**

LADY IN QUESTION, THE***

          (1940) 78m COL bw (AKA: IT HAPPENED IN PARIS)

Brian Aherne (*Andre Morestan*), Rita Hayworth (*Natalie Roguin*), Glenn Ford (*Pierre Morestan*), Irene Rich (*Michele Morestan*), George Coulouris (*Defense Attorney*), Lloyd Corrigan (*Prosecuting Attorney*), Evelyn Keyes (*Francoise Morestan*), Edward Norris (*Robert LaCoste*), Curt Bois (*Henri Lurette*), Frank Reicher (*President of the Court*), Sumner Getchell (*Fat Boy*), Nicholas Bela (*Nicholas Farkas*), William Stack (*Mariner*), Dorothy Burgess (*Antoinette*), Hamilton MacFadden, Allen Marlow (*Guards*), Julius Tannen (*2nd Judge*), Fern Emmett (*Nathalie Roguin*), James B. Carson (*Wine Salesman*), Frank Hilliard, Carlton Griffin, Ronald Alexander, Alexander Palasthy, Ted Lorch, Frank Pharr (*Jurors*), Fred Rapport (*Alternate Juror*), Louis Aldon (*Court Clerk*), Mary Bovard (*Miss Morlet*), Emma Tansey (*Flower Woman*), Ralph Peters (*Pedestrian*), George Davis (*Customer*), Leon Belasco (*Barber*), Eddie Laughton (*Bit Man*), Jack Raymond (*Expressman*), Vernon Dent (*Gendarme*), Jack Rice (*Newly Married Juror*), Harrison Greene (*Jury Foreman*), William Castle, Earl Gunn (*Angry Jurors*).

Bourgeois Parisian shop-owner Aherne is on a jury for a trial in which Hayworth is the defendant. He sees to it that she is convicted, but later finds her work in his store. Her spotted past is kept under cover until Aherne's son Ford falls in love with her. The secret is revealed and the couple elope, though everything ends on a bright and cheerful note. This marked the first time Ford and Hayworth appeared together. They would go on to become one of Hollywood's great screen couples, appearing in such films as the film-noir classic GILDA and THE LOVES OF CARMEN, both helmed by Charles Vidor. The picture's original title, IT HAPPENED IN PARIS, was dropped to prevent patrons from thinking it a war film—the French capital being occupied by the Nazis at that time. Aherne proved his versatility as an actor once again, taking on the rather bourgeois part—the second role as a father that he played that year, the other being in MY SON, MY SON. Besides Hayworth and Ford, another young actor appeared in THE LADY IN QUESTION who would go on to stardom, Evelyn Keyes. Based on the film HEART OF PARIS by Marc Allegret.

p, B. B. Kahane; d, Charles Vidor; w, Lewis Meltzer (based on the screenplay for HEART OF PARIS by H. G. Lustig, Marcel Archard); ph, Lucien Andriot; m, Lucien Moraweek; ed, Al Clark; md, M. W. Stoloff; art d, Lionel Banks; cos, Ray Howell, Robert Kalloch; makeup, William Knight.

Drama **(PR:A MPAA:NR)**

LADY IN RED, THE*** (1979) 93m New World c (AKA: GUNS, SIN AND BATHTUB GIN)

Pamela Sue Martin *(Polly Franklin)*, Robert Conrad *(John Dillinger)*, Louise Fletcher *(Anna Sage)*, Robert Hogan *(Jake Lingle)*, Laurie Heineman *(Rose Shimkus)*, Glenn Withrow *(Eddie)*, Rod Gist *(Pinetop)*, Peter Hobbs *(Pops Geissler)*, Christopher Lloyd *(Frognose)*, Dick Miller *(Patek)*, Nancy Anne Parsons *(Tiny Alice)*, Alan Vint *(Melvin Purvis)*.

A low-budget, New World (i.e. Roger Corman) quickie which turned out to be a good showcase for the budding talents of screenwriter Sayles and director Teague. THE LADY IN RED came at the end of the Corman gangster cycle which saw several uneven and violent biographies of real-life hoods Al Capone/Bugs Moran in THE ST. VALENTINE'S DAY MASSACRE (1967), Ma Barker in BLOODY MAMA (1970), John Dillinger in DILLINGER (1973), and, once again, "Scarface" Al in CAPONE (1975). Screenwriter Sayles twisted the formula a bit and decided to show the crime community of the 1920s and 1930s through the eyes of a young woman, Martin, who drifts into a life of crime. She is a small-town girl who, tired of boredom and abuse at home, decides to leave for Hollywood. She makes it as far as Chicago where she gets a low-paying job and falls subject to the same abuse she suffered back home. Martin rebels against her condition and causes enough trouble to land herself in prison. There the situation gets even worse when her sadistic guards become determined to quash her independent attitude. Nearly broken, Martin is released in the custody of the infamous Anna Sage (Fletcher), who employs the girl in her bordello. Though working as a prostitute, Martin is able to attain a certain (if seedy) status and gain a modicum of control over her own destiny. Unfortunately, Fletcher's bordello is closed down by the authorities, leaving Martin to scratch for a living once again. Soon afterward she meets a handsome, smart, and dashing man, Conrad, who claims he works at the Board of Trade. Conrad is, in fact, the notorious bank robber John Dillinger, though he keeps his identity a secret from Martin. The two begin a romance and become genuinely close to one another. Martin, for the first time in her life, is in love and she tells her friend Fletcher about Conrad. Fletcher realizes Conrad's true identity and, needing a bargaining chip to keep from being deported back to her native Rumania, she secretly informs the FBI and arranges to set the gangster up. One hot night in July Martin, Conrad, and Fletcher go to the air-conditioned Biograph theater to see a movie and cool off. When the film is over and the three leave, Conrad is gunned down by the FBI. Martin is traumatized by the shocking event and is horrified to learn that her lover was public enemy number 1. Though Fletcher was the real culprit, the press pegs Martin as the "lady in red" who set up John Dillinger. The notoriety drives Martin into a full-fledged life of crime and she commits several robberies before finally winding her way out to her original destination, Hollywood. Though the film plays hard and loose with the facts (especially since facts unearthed since Dillinger's "death" show that the killing was a hoax and another man was killed in Dillinger's place—facts that Hoover and the FBI tried to cover up) regarding Conrad's Dillinger and Martin's character (whose real name was Polly Hamilton), THE LADY IN RED succeeds on many levels. Sayles' script is an intelligent look at a woman's struggle in the society of the 1930s. Her decision to rebel against her small-farm-town life sets into motion a series of events that arise to quash her independence, driving her into the underworld to survive. Although the script is filled with fanciful assumptions and distortions of fact, it conveys the proper mood and feel for the character and the times. Teague's direction manages to capture the 1930s on a shoestring budget and the performances he gets from his cast are solid. Martin, who went all the way to break her "Nancy Drew" image from television, gives a likable, tough, and intelligent characterization. Conrad is surprisingly good as John Dillinger. He brings a strange melancholy to the character while still maintaining the charm and intelligence associated with the famous criminal. It is a quiet, reserved, very human interpretation of the legendary bank robber that does not succumb to traditional gangster movie sterotypes. While the film at times suffers from the obligatory Corman excesses of nudity and violence, THE LADY IN RED is more than just another exploitation film, it is an interesting addition to the gangster genre.

p, Julie Corman; d, Lewis Teague; w, John Sayles; ph, Daniel Lacambre; m, James Horner; ed, Larry Bock, Ron Medico, Teague; prod d, Joe McAnelly; art d, Philip Thomas; set d, Keith Hein; cos, Danny Morgan, Pat Tonema.

Crime **Cas.** **(PR:O MPAA:R)**

LADY IN SCARLET, THE* (1935) 65m CHES bw

Reginald Denny *(Oliver Keith)*, Patricia Farr *(Ella Carey)*, Claudia Dell *(Alice Sayre)*, James Bush *(Tom Pennyward)*, Dorothy Revier *(Julia Sayre)*, John St. Polis *(James Shelby)*, Jameson Thomas *(Dr. Boyer)*, Jack Adair, John T. Murray.

Sorely lacking in action is this mildly amusing murder mystery which has lawyer Denny donning his detective hat. Together with his spunky secretary, Denny follows the clues to outsmart the guilty party.

p, George R. Batcheller; d, Charles Lamont; w, Robert Ellis, Helen Logan (based on the story by Arthur Hoerl); ph, M. A. Anderson; ed, Roland Reed.

Crime/Romance **(PR:A MPAA:NR)**

LADY IN THE CAR WITH GLASSES AND A GUN, THE 1/2**
(1970, U.S./Fr.) 105m Lira-COL/COL c (LA DAME DANS L'AUTO AVEC DES LUNETTES ET UN FUSIL)

Samantha Eggar *(Dany Lang)*, Oliver Reed *(Michael Caldwell)*, John McEnery *(Philippe)*, Stephane Audran *(Anita Caldwell)*, Billie Dixon *(Secretary)*, Bernard Fresson *(Jean)*, Philippe Nicaud *(Highway Policeman)*, Marcel Bozzuffi *(Manuel)*, Jacques Fabbri *(Doctor)*, Yves Pignot *(Baptistin)*, Jacques Legras *(Policeman)*, Maria Meriko *(Mme. Pacaud)*, Andre Oumansky *(Bernard Thorr)*, Monique Melinand *(Barmaid)*, Martine Kelly *(Kiki)*, Claude Vernier *(Psychiatrist)*, Henri Czarniak *(Garage Proprietor)*, Edmond Ardisson *(Garage Night Man)*, Gilberte Geniat *(Village Storekeeper)*, Roger Lumont *(Hotel Clerk)*, Robert Deac *(Boy in Cassis)*, Lisa Jouvet, Fred Fisher *(Danish Tourists)*, Raoul Delfosse, Louise Rioton *(American Tourists)*, Jacqueline Porel *(2nd Secretary)*, Paule Noelle *(3rd Secretary)*.

Eggar plays a secretary at a Paris ad agency who one day impulsively heads for the Riviera. En route, however, she experiences a number of strange occurrences which point to her having been in places that she's never visited, and being recognized by people she's never met. As the bizarre coincidences become overly complicated, the plot gets more implausible, but there are still a number of good moments.

p, Raymond Danon, Anatole Litvak; d, Litvak; w, Richard Harris, Eleanor Perry (based on the novel by Sebastien Japrisot); ph, Claude Renoir (Panavision, Eastmancolor); m, Michel Legrand; ed, Peter Thornton; md, Legrand; art d, Willy Holt; cos, Christian Dior, Jean Zay; m/l, "On the Road," Legrand (sung by Petula Clark).

Drama **(PR:O MPAA:R)**

LADY IN THE DARK* 1/2** (1944) 100m PAR c

Ginger Rogers *(Liza Elliott)*, Ray Milland *(Charley Johnson)*, Jon Hall *(Randy Curtis)*, Warner Baxter *(Kendall Nesbitt)*, Barry Sullivan *(Dr. Brooks)*, Mischa Auer *(Russell Paxton)*, Mary Philips *(Maggie Grant)*, Phyllis Brooks *(Allison DuBois)*, Edward Fielding *(Dr. Carlton)*, Don Loper *(Adams)*, Mary Parker *(Miss Parker)*, Catherine Craig *(Miss Foster)*, Marietta Canty *(Martha)*, Virginia Farmer *(Miss Edwards)*, Fay Helm *(Miss Bowers)*, Gail Russell *(Barbara, Age 17)*, Kay Linaker *(Liza's Mother)*, Harvey Stephens *(Liza's Father)*, Rand Brooks *(Ben)*, Pepito Perez *(Clown)*, Charles Smith *(Barbara's Boyfriend)*, Audrey Young, Eleanor DeVan, Jeanne Straser, Lynda Grey, Christopher King, Maxine Ardell, Alice Kirby, Arlyne Varden, Angela Wilson, Dorothy O'Kelly, Betty Hall, Fran Shore, Louise LaPlanche *(Office Girls)*, Paul Pierce, George Mayon, James Notaro, Jacques Karre, Byron Poindexter, Kit Carson *(Specialty Dancers)*, Bunny Waters, Susan Paley, Dorothy Ford, Mary MacLaren *(Models)*, Paul McVey *(Librarian)*, Marten Lamont, Tristram Coffin, Dennis Moore, Jack Luden *(Men)*, Jack Mulhall *(Photographer)*, Murray Alper *(Taxicab Driver)*, Dorothy Granger *(Autograph Hunter)*, Emmett Vogan, Lester Dorr, Grandon Rhodes *(Reporters)*, Johnnie Johnson, John O'Connor, Buster Brodie *(Clowns)*, Herbert Corthell *(Senator)*, Herb Holcomb *(Aquatic Clown)*, Charles Bates *(David)*, Theodore Marc *(Daniel Boone Clown)*, Armand Tanny *(Strong-Man Clown)*, Stuart Barlow *(Accordion Clown)*, Leonora Johnson *(Bird's Nest Clown)*, Harry Bayfield *(Snow Clown)*, Larry Rio *(Farmer Clown)*, Buz Buckley *(Freckle-faced Boy)*, Priscilla Lyon *(Little Girl at Circus)*, Marjean Neville *(Liza, Ages 5 and 7)*, Phyllis Brooks *(Barbara, Age 7)*, Billy Dawson *(Boy at Circus)*, Billy Daniels *(Office Boy)*, Georgia Backus *(Miss Sullivan)*, George Calliga *(Captain of Waiters)*, Frances Robinson *(Girl with Randy)*, Hillary Brooke *(Miss Barr)*, Charles Coleman *(Butler)*, Miriam Franklin *(Dancer)*, Lester Sharpe *(Pianist)*, Bobby Beers *(Charley, as a Boy)*, Jan Buckingham *(Miss Shawn)*.

LADY IN THE DARK was a breakthrough play on the Broadway stage featuring Danny Kaye and Victor Mature supporting the luminous Gertrude Lawrence. Unfortunately, none of the above trio made it to the screen and the loss is evident. Also evident is the excising of several wonderful Weill/Gershwin tunes in favor of some others that neither advanced nor enhanced the bold plot. Rogers is the editor of a national magazine who realizes that she is about to have a nervous breakdown. The trio of men in her life are Milland, Baxter, and Hall; she seeks professional help in the office of psychiatrist Sullivan. Her sessions and various dream sequences make up the musical production numbers. Milland is the advertising manager for the magazine and sparks fly between him and Rogers. Baxter is recently divorced and wants Rogers but she can't handle him once he's become single and instead turns to Hall, a hunk, but eventually leaves him and winds up in Milland's arms at the fadeout, leaving Auer, the magazine photographer, to comment "This is the end, the absolute end" at the conclusion. LADY IN THE DARK cost a lot of money to make (almost 3 million) and it made a lot of money in the wartime atmosphere when audiences were clamoring for something light to relieve the news in the papers and on radio. The original score had the famous "Tschaikowsky" number by Kaye as well as the haunting "My Ship." Both tunes disappeared from the film except for a few bars of "My Ship" that made no sense. It's true that the limitations of the stage worked against the huge production numbers they were able to mount for the screen; however this is a case where better might have been smaller. Songs included: "Suddenly, It's Spring" (Johnny Burke, Jimmie Van Heusen), "Dream Lover" (Clifford Grey, Victor Schertzinger), "Artist's Waltz" (Robert Emmett Dolan), "This Is New," "Girl Of The Moment," "One Life To Live," "It Looks Like Liza," "The Saga Of Jenny" (Ira Gershwin, Kurt Weill). They attempted something different on several levels with LADY IN THE DARK. It was, at once, the story of a woman in a man's world, the story of a woman in a dangerous mental state, and the story of a woman who couldn't make a decision. In the early 1940s psychiatry was not nearly as prevalent as it later became and the play attempted to remove some of the mystery that surrounded Freud's discoveries. It was gaudy and glamorous and the photography in this, Rogers' first color film, was good enough to be nominated for an Oscar, as were the art direction and set decoration. Despite all of the flaws, anyone who sees the movie and has not seen the play will be pleased.

p, Richard Blumenthal; d, Mitchell Leisen; w, Frances Goodrich, Albert Hackett (based on the play by Moss Hart, Kurt Weill, Ira Gershwin); ph, Ray Rennahan, Farciot Edouart (Technicolor); m, Robert Emmett Dolan; ed, Alma Macrorie; md, Dolan; art d, Hans Dreier, Raoul Pene du Bois; set d, Ray Moyer; cos, du Bois, Edith Head, Leisen, Babs Wilomez; spec eff, Gordon Jennings, Paul Lerpae; ch, Billy Daniels, Don Loper; makeup, Wally Westmore.

Musical (PR:A MPAA:NR)

LADY IN THE DEATH HOUSE* (1944) 56m PRC bw

Jean Parker (Mary), Lionel Atwill (Finch), Douglas Fowley (Brad), Marcia Mae Jones (Suzy), Robert Middlemass (State's Attorney), Cy Kendall (Detective), John Maxwell (Snell), George Irving (Gregory), Forrest Taylor (Warden).

Parker is the lady wrongly accused of murder (is anybody ever rightly accused of murder anymore?) and saved from the "hot seat" by criminologist Atwill. This one is as short on ideas as it is on length.

p, Jack Schwarz; d, Steve Sekely; w, Harry O. Hoyt (based on a story by Fred C. Davis); ph, Gus Peterson; m, Jan Gray; ed, Robert O. Crandall; art d, Frank Sylos.

Drama Cas. (PR:A MPAA:NR)

LADY IN THE FOG (SEE: SCOTLAND YARD INVESTIGATOR, 1952, Brit.)

LADY IN THE IRON MASK**1/2 (1952) 78m FOX c

Louis Hayward (D'Artagnan), Patricia Medina (Princess Anne/Princess Louise), Alan Hale, Jr. (Porthos), Judd Holdren (Aramis), Steve Brodie (Athos), John Sutton (Duke De Valdac), Hal Gerard (Philip of Spain), Lester Matthews (Prime Minster).

The sexes are switched in this version of Dumas' The Man In The Iron Mask with Medina playing the twin sister roles—one being Anne, the ruling princess, the other her long-lost sister Louise. A kidnaping plot has Anne taken off to an island, fitted with a grotesque iron mask, and replaced by Louise. The Three Musketeers, led by the swashbuckling D'Artagnan (enthusiastically played by Hayward) rescue the princess but decide to take off for America and leave her sister minding the throne. In reality, the iron mask was actually made of fitted cloth, but reality isn't always very cinematic.

p, Walter Wanger, Eugene Frenke; d, Ralph Murphy; w, Jack Pollexfen, Aubrey Wisberg (based on "The Three Musketeers" characters in a novel by Alexandre Dumas); ph, Ernest Laszlo (Super-CineColor); m, Dimitri Tiomkin; ed, Merrill White; art d, Martin Obzina.

Adventure (PR:A MPAA:NR)

LADY IN THE LAKE**** (1947) 105m MGM bw

Robert Montgomery (Philip Marlowe), Lloyd Nolan (Lt. DeGarmot), Audrey Totter (Adrienne Fromsett), Tom Tully (Capt. Kane), Leon Ames (Derace Kingsby), Jayne Meadows (Mildred Havelend), Morris Ankrum (Eugene Grayson), Lila Leeds (Receptionist), Richard Simmons (Chris Lavery), Ellen Ross (Elevator Girl), William Roberts (Artist), Kathleen Lockhart (Mrs. Grayson), Ellay Mort (Chrystal Kingsby), Cy Kendall (Jaibi), Ralph Dunn (Sergeant), William McKeever Riley (Bunny), Wheaton Chambers (Property Clerk), Frank Orth (Greer), Robert Williams (Detective), Fred E. Sherman (Reporter), Jack Davis, John Gallaudet, Tom Murray, George Magrill, Budd Fine, John Webb Dillon (Policemen), Robert Spencer (Marlowe's Double), Billy Newell (Drunk), Eddie Acuff (Coroner), Nina Ross, Charles Bradstreet, George Travell, William O'Leary, Bert Moorhouse, Florence Stephens, Sandra Morgan, Fred Santley, Laura Treadwell, Kay Wiley, Frank Dae, David Cavendish, James Nolan, Sherry Hall, Ann Lawrence, and Roger Cole (Chirstmas Party Guests).

"YOU accept an invitation to a blonde's apartment! YOU get socked in the jaw by a murder suspect!" That's how the ads approached filmgoers in promoting this rugged, inventive film noir entry, the first to use the so-called "camera I" through 105 taut and chilling minutes. Under Montgomery's clever direction, the viewer is really in the film, so to speak, with all the action and characters addressing the camera which is really Montgomery, playing that incorruptible private eye, Philip Marlowe, Raymond Chandler's unforgettable character. The subjective camera performed almost all of Montgomery's chores with the actor's voice over its movements (one of the first uses of a hand-held camera with all the bouncing of a walking man, smoke before its lens as he puffed on a cigarette or received a puckering kiss from leading lady Totter). Marlowe, or Montgomery, is seen on occasions, but in mirrors or in the reflection of windows, but it's the camera that takes most of the beating. The film opens as the camera moves into Montgomery's office where he sits behind a desk; behind him is a window with his name on it (misspelled in the film as "Phillip Marlowe"). He begins to relate the "Lady in the Lake" caper and the subjective camera takes over, the story moving in flashback. Montgomery, tired of sleuthing for a living, has taken up writing; he has produced a number of detective stories and submitted them to Kingsby Publications. There, editor Totter reads Montgomery's most recent story and asks that he come to see her. When he arrives in the magazine office, he learns that she's not interested in his story but wants him to locate Ames' (Kingsby's) wife who has vanished. Montgomery learns that Totter plans to wed her boss, Ames, and that she really wants the detective to find the missing wife so Ames can divorce her and marry Totter. Montgomery's first call is to see well-to-do, musclebound gigolo Simmons. He is, at first, welcomed by the handsome young rake but asks one sensitive question too many and is suddenly punched silly. He wakes up in the Bay City jail where tough cop Nolan tells him he was picked up for drunk driving and gave the police a hard time, that he, Nolan, had to hit him again, knocking him out. Nolan hands him back his money, $18, and begins to read Totter's letter to him about his story, sarcastically reading the title, "If I Should Die Before I Live," and adds "so you're a story writer,

too, huh? The detective business must be on the skids. What are you trying to do—elevate yourself?" Nolan escorts Montgomery into his boss' office. Tully, the captain in charge, lectures Montgomery about drunk driving. Montgomery says he was framed, that he was knocked out, thrown into his car, booze poured over him, and his car driven wildly down the street and over a curb which is where he was picked up. Tully tells him to stop messing around in his district. Nolan threatens him with a beating and he is shown the door. Visiting Totter, he goes to a mirror in her office to reveal a closed black eye. Montgomery tells Totter that the $300 he was given to find Ames' wife was not enough for the beating he took. Then comes a report that the wife of the caretaker of Ames' retreat at Little Fawn Lake has been found murdered, her body found floating in the lake. Totter tells Montgomery that she believes the caretaker's wife was murdered by Ames' wife, and that she wants him to go up to the lake and prove her theory so Ames' wife can be prosecuted for murder. He goes to the lake and then returns to tell Totter that the caretaker's wife was really someone else. He hands Totter a pin engraved from Simmons to Ames' wife. He decides he'll pursue the matter and that he'll go and see Simmons again, allowing himself to be swayed by Totter's insistence. "You're so full of persuasion," he tells her, "what else would you say you're full of?" She tells him to go back to the lake and snoop around and stay away from Simmons. She also tells him not to fall in love with her. Montgomery immediately goes to see Simmons and finds Meadows, the landlady, marching around Lavery's house with a gun in her hand. Montgomery says he's from the finance company, that Simmons is behind on his car payments. She hands him the gun and says that Simmons left it on the stairs. Montgomery rushes Meadows out of the house, then looks upstairs and finds a handkerchief with Totter's initials on it, then, in the shower of an upstairs bathroom, Simmons, shot to pieces, bullet holes blasted through the glass shower door. Montgomery then attends a Christmas party given by Ames. He takes Totter into another office and gives her the gun that killed Simmons wrapped in her handkerchief. He as much as accuses Totter of killing Simmons but she, of course, denies it. Ames enters the office and learns that Totter has hired Montgomery to find his wife. He becomes angry, telling Totter he wants his errant wife left alone. Montgomery asks if Ames' wife owns a gun and Ames begins to believe his wife may have killed Simmons. Ames tells off Montgomery and informs Totter that he will never "say anything endearing to you again." Totter lashes out against Montgomery, telling him that he's lost her a million dollars, meaning the chance of marrying the rich Ames. She fires Montgomery and as he is about to leave, Ames hires him to find his wife so he can protect her against any possible murder charges. Montgomery then returns to Simmons' house and gives the murder gun to Tully, who shouts at him for withholding evidence. He demands to know whom he's working for and Montgomery doesn't hesitate in telling Tully that he's working for Ames. He explains to Tully that a woman has been found dead in Little Fawn Lake but Tully tells him he's only interested in the Simmons' death. When Tully goes into another room, Montgomery goads Nolan, telling him he knows that a "tough cop" visited the lake and the dead woman. Nolan slaps him. Montgomery then almost accuses Nolan of killing the woman and, before Nolan can sock him, he knocks the cop down. Tully walks back into the room and arrests Montgomery for assaulting an officer. Montgomery is released at the police station. He tells Tully that he suspects Nolan of killing the dead woman at the lake but Tully tells him he's wrong and sends Montgomery on his way. Totter visits Montgomery at his hotel to tell her she's fallen for him but he ignores her. As Montgomery drives down a road, Nolan, in another car, smashes into Montgomery's car, forcing it to crash. Nolan then runs over and dumps booze all over Montgomery, who is half conscious. A passing motorist with too much to drink later peeks into the smashed-up car and Montgomery changes identity cards with him. Police arrive and pick up the drunk and drive off; Montgomery staggers from hiding, falls down in the road, then crawls to a phone booth to call Totter, telling her to come and get him. He wakes up in Totter's bed, his head lacerated, as is revealed when Totter gives him a mirror. She bandages his head and tries to talk him out of being a detective. "Why eat," he says cynically, "you only get hungry again." Again she tells him she's in love with him and he with her. He mends in her apartment and the next day she buys him a Christmas present, a silk bathrobe, and he has breakfast with her. He has almost accepted her affection and wonders what "this new thing between us" will bring, also wondering how they will live. Later, they sit listening to "A Christmas Carol" on the radio, and Totter continues telling him the story of her life. Ames interrupts this idyllic setting, telling Montgomery that his wife has just called him and has asked for some money. Ames asks Montgomery to deliver $500 to his wife since two detectives are following him and he doesn't want to lead them to his wife. He offers Montgomery $5,000 to handle the affair and Montgomery jumps at the offer even though Totter tells him not to take it. Ames tells Montgomery to go to a place called the Peacock Room. Ames leaves and then Montgomery asks Totter to follow him in 10 minutes with the police. He expects Ames' wife to lead him to her hideout, and Totter is to follow a trail of rice he will leave for her. Montgomery meets Ames' wife, who turns out to be Meadows. He leaves his trail of rice to her apartment. There he tells her that he knows she has not only impersonated Simmons' landlady but the caretaker's wife and that Ames' real wife is the lady killed and dumped into the lake and that Meadows is also impersonating her to get money from Ames. She holds a gun on him but he takes it away from her and she becomes a frightened, nervous wreck, begging for her life. There's a knock at the door but instead of Totter and Tully it's Nolan, who knocks Montgomery down and grabs his gun. Nolan, it seems, has shown up to kill Meadows who jilted and used him in the past. Montgomery tells him to call the police but Nolan tells him he's going to shoot Meadows with Montgomery's gun and then Montgomery; he will later report finding both of them dead at each other's hands. Meadows pleads with him as he shoots her four times in the stomach. Half crazed, Nolan holds a gun on Montgomery, preparing to kill him, asking: "How does it feel dying in the middle of somebody else's dirty love affair?" He tells him he followed the rice trail and kicked it into the street so no one else would follow it. Tully and cops arrive on the fire escape and Nolan shoots at them. They return the fire, killing Nolan and saving Montgomery. At the finish,

Montgomery is again in his office, wrapping up the case for the viewer as Totter comes in and tells him she has their one-way train tickets to New York. LADY IN THE LAKE was an experiment Montgomery the actor had long dreamed of performing as Montgomery the director. Montgomery's decision to direct was not well received by his studio, MGM, but when John Ford fractured his leg three weeks before completing THEY WERE EXPENDABLE (1945) and Montgomery completed the film for him, he won plaudits from Ford and the studio. MGM agreed that Montgomery could direct LADY IN THE LAKE, which it had purchased from author Chandler for $35,000 (more money than Chandler had been paid for DOUBLE INDEMNITY (1944) and THE BLUE DAHLIA (1946) by Paramount). As early as 1938 Montgomery had been planning to make a film using the subjective camera. He originally wanted to direct John Galsworthy's *Escape*, but MGM moguls told him that the studio had just purchased the Chandler novel and he accepted the crime tale. When he informed studio executives how he would approach filming LADY IN THE LAKE, the bosses were first puzzled, then grew extremely nervous. One of the conditions allowing him to direct was that MGM could take advantage of his star power; he would have to appear in the film. But, while using the subjective camera, the tall, handsome actor appears in only four brief scenes, which made the studio bosses angry and feeling betrayed. They also disliked Montgomery's direct approach to the audience, challenging viewers to solve the mystery of the film right from his opening address: "You'll see it just as I saw it. You'll meet the people; you'll find the clues. And maybe you'll solve it quick and maybe you won't." MGM had set up another hurdle. Montgomery had to show executives the first reel for their approval before he would be allowed to continue. According to Stephen Pendo, writing in *Raymond Chandler on Screen*, one of the executives saw the first reel and said: "It's fine, just fine, but where's Bob Montgomery?" The star was behind the camera, or, more specific, under it, with harness strapped to the small camera and his chest or back while his fellow actors played to the lens. The film is extremely fluid as the camera floats from scene to scene, simulating Montgomery's movements. Moreover, much of the $1 million budget that went into making LADY IN THE LAKE was for elaborate sets, "breakaway sets," one writer dubbed them. In one instance, the camera approaches Montgomery's car and enters it, but the car was actually in two separate pieces and when the camera swung behind the wheel, it merely moved in back of the front part of the car, the rear being swung away to make room for it. The same involved technique had to be employed as the camera moved upstairs, into rooms. Montgomery told John Tuska (as related in *The Detective in Hollywood*): "The real challenge was the filming itself. We had to do a lot of rehearsing. Actors are trained *not* to look at the camera. I had to overcome all that training. I had a basket installed under the camera and sat there so that, at least, the actors could respond to me, even if they couldn't look directly at me . . . the most complicated scene . . . was where Marlowe crawls to the telephone booth. It took four people just to handle the action. We had to remove all the walls of the booth after Marlowe gets inside." Montgomery is undoubtedly the most polished, sophisticated, and urbane Philip Marlowe to grace the screen, and, according to Philip French, writing in *The World of Raymond Chandler*, "As for Robert Montgomery, one might think him the closest screen Marlowe in style and appearance to Chandler's professed ideal, Cary Grant." Yet Chandler not only disliked Montgomery in the film but hated the film itself, remarking sarcastically that it was "probably the worst picture ever made." The author's pessimism was certainly created by the unpleasant experience he endured in attempting to adapt his novel to the screen, the only time Chandler was ever paid to create a film script from one of his original works. The independent-minded writer was busy writing scripts at Paramount but they allowed him, in July 1945, to go to MGM to write the script for Montgomery's brainchild. He had little faith in the technique the actor-director was about to use, later commenting: "Every young writer or director has wanted to try it. 'Let's make the camera a character'; it's been said at every lunch table in Hollywood one time or another. I knew one fellow who wanted to make the camera the murderer which wouldn't work without an awful lot of fraud. The camera is too honest." Chandler's motive in taking on the script chore not only involved money. Frank MacShane, author of *The Life of Raymond Chandler* (the best book on this gifted, enigmatic writer), wrote that Chandler "had taken the job to protect his story and keep it from being ruined by a hack writer." The assignment didn't work out well for Chandler as he himself would later remember: "I worked at MGM once in that cold storage plant they call the Thalberg Building, fourth floor. Had a nice producer, George Haight, a fine fellow. About that time some potato-brain, probably [Eddie] Mannix, had decided that writers would do more work if they had no couches to lie on. So there was no couch in my office. Never a man to be stopped by trifles,I got a steamer rug out of the car, spread it on the floor and lay down on that. Haight, coming in for a courtesy call, rushed to the phone and yelled down to the story editor . . . that I was a horizontal writer and for Chrissake send up a couch. However, the cold storage atmosphere got to me too quick, and the coteries at the writers table in the commissary. I said I would work at home. They said Mannix had issued orders no writers to work at home. I said a man as big as Mannix ought to be allowed the privilege of changing his mind. So I worked at home, and only went over there three or four times to talk to Haight." When Chandler did arrive at the studio Haight was increasingly vexed at the copy he was turning in, all of it new and far departed from the original story. "Can't we have some of your books?" the producer would plead. "Isn't it one of your books we bought?" Chandler would reply: "I'm sick of it. It's so much easier to write new stuff." He went on, saying he was "stale" on LADY IN THE LAKE and that "it's just not my kind of story, or not any longer. When a writer breaks his heart to do a job and does it as well as he can, he just doesn't want to do it all over again and worse." A contract writer, Steve Fisher, was assigned to complete what Chandler had begun. Chandler first insisted that he receive credit, a demand that made Fisher balk. Then, when Chandler saw the completed script, he utterly refused to have his name associated with the screenplay. He was reportedly upset that the scenes at Little Fawn Lake had been eliminated and used only in reference by Montgomery. Chandler had written, according to Al Clark in *Raymond Chandler in Hollywood*, 220 pages during the 13 weeks of his contract and Haight brought in Fisher to boil it down to a 106 page shooting script. Fisher claimed that the film made $4 million during its first month of release but other reports vary widely with this figure. It did make money but not enough to please MGM boss Louis B. Mayer, whose opinion of Montgomery changed considerably. The actor received critical acclaim for his experiment but Mayer feared that his "family studio" might be turned into a haven for experimental and "arty" films. LADY IN THE LAKE, aside from a documentary for the U.S. Navy, would be Montgomery's last MGM film. It's obvious that Montgomery enjoyed this experiment, then bold by contemporary standards; he also implanted his little joke in the cast listings, crediting an "Ellay Mort" with the role of Chrystal Kingsby, a woman never seen since she has been drowned by the first reel, Montgomery spelling the nonexistent player phonetically with the French phrase, *elle est morte* ("she is dead"). Montgomery would go on to star and direct another offbeat but fascinating *film noir* entry, RIDE THE PINK HORSE, where he talked out of the side of his mouth and was a lot tougher than the Philip Marlowe he gently essayed here. Nolan is also superb as the vindictive, desperate, and thoroughly corrupt cop. Totter, appearing impressively in her first major role, was plucked out of the Hollywood backwaters by Montgomery to play the alluring love interest since she had a solid radio background and he felt this would lend well in her delivery to the subjective camera. Up to that time she had been the seductive voice in BEWITCHED (1945), a brassy friend of Lucille Ball's in ZIEGFELD FOLLIES (1946), and the sexy waitress John Garfield picks up in a train station after his lover, Lana Turner, leaves town in THE POSTMAN ALWAYS RINGS TWICE (1946). The attractive, statuesque Meadows does an outstanding job in playing three different parts, a landlady, a missing wife, and at the end, a neurotic killer of the ladies she's been impersonating, no simple task. LADY IN THE LAKE is no mere curiosity but a full-blown, well-told, and always arresting story, engulfing the viewer, as it were, into the action, the mystery, and the harrowing finale, Raymond Chandler and Louis B. Mayer notwithstanding.

p, George Haight; d, Robert Montgomery; w, Steve Fisher, (uncredited) Raymond Chandler (based on the novel by Chandler); ph, Paul C. Vogel; m, David Snell; ed, Gene Ruggiero; art d, Cedric Gibbons, Preston Ames; set d, Edwin B. Willis, Thomas Theuerkauf; cos, Irene; spec eff, A. Arnold Gillespie; makeup, Jack Dawn.

Crime Drama **(PR:A MPAA:NR)**

LADY IN THE MORGUE 1/2**

(1938) 70m UNIV bw (GB: CASE OF THE MISSING BLONDE; AKA: CORPSE IN THE MORGUE)

Preston Foster *(Detective Bill Crane)*, Patricia Ellis *(Mrs. Sam Taylor)*, Frank Jenks *(Doc Williams)*, Barbara Pepper *(Kay Renshaw)*, Thomas Jackson *(Strom)*, Rollo Lloyd *(Coroner)*, Gordon ["Wild Bill"] Elliott *(Chauncey Courtland)*, Roland Drew *(Sam Taylor)*, Joseph Downing *(Steve Collins)*, James Robbins *(Frankie French)*, Morgan Wallace *(Leyman)*, Al Hill *(Spitzy)*, Brian Burke *(Johnson)*, Donald Kerr *(Greening)*, Don Brodie *(Taxi Driver)*, Gordon Hart *(Col. Black)*.

Foster is a private eye who has to prove himself innocent when the body of a beautiful, but dead, woman disappears from the morgue. There's as much intrigue as there is confusion as he spends all his time trying to find out who made off with the body.

p, Irving Starr; d, Otis Garrett; w, Eric Taylor, Robertson White (based on the novel *Crime Club* by Jonathan Latimer); ph, Stanley Cortez; ed, Ted Kent.

Crime/Mystery **(PR:A MPAA:NR)**

LADY IS A SQUARE, THE** (1959, Brit.) 100m ABF-Pathe ABF bw

Anna Neagle *(Frances Baring)*, Frankie Vaughan *(Johnny Burns)*, Janette Scott *(Joanna Baring)*, Anthony Newley *(Freddy)*, Wilfrid Hyde-White *(Charles)*, Christopher Rhodes *(Greenslade)*, Kenneth Cope *(Derek)*, Josephine Fitzgerald *(Mrs. Eady)*, Harold Kasket *(Spolenski)*, John Le Mesurier *(Fergusson)*, Ted Lune *(Harry Shuttleworth)*, Mary Peach *(Mrs. Freddy)*, Marguerite Brennan, Bruno Barnabe, Walter Horsbrugh, Jeremy White, Robert Desmond, Gwynneth Tighe, Frederick Schiller, Derek Prentice, Myrette Morven, John Carson, Gerald Case, National Youth Orchestra.

Neagle is the aristocratic widow of a classical music impresario determined to continue on in his name. The problem is she's out of cash and in need of a conductor. When pop musician Vaughan poses as a piano tuner, he gains entrance into her house and soon falls in love with her daughter, Scott. Neagle looks down at Vaughan until he suddenly shoots to the top of the Hit Parade with a catchy pop number. He also makes enough money to secretly finance Neagle's concerts which gets her out of debt. She soon changes her tune about pop music and has a hand-clappin', foot-tappin', totally un-square time with the kids. The rockin' tunes include: "Love Is The Sweetest Thing," (Ray Noble). The square ones include Handel's "Largo."

p, Herbert Wilcox, Anna Neagle; d, Wilcox; w, Harold Purcell, Pamela Bower, Nicholas Phipps (based on a story by Purcell); ph, Gordon Dines; m, Wally Stott; ed, Basil Warren.

Comedy/Romance/Musical **(PR:A MPAA:NR)**

LADY IS FICKLE, THE** (1948, Ital.) 82m Minerva/Superfilm bw

Ferrucio Tagliavini *(Ferrucio Landini)*, Fioretto Dolfi *(Rosetta)*, Carlo Campanini *(Christopher)*, Carlo Micheluzzi *(Mr. Bonsi)*.

Tagliavini plays a schoolteacher striving to break into grand opera. He gets his chance when he loses his girl friend in a theater lobby but manages to land a job while searching for her. The film offers a fine display of Tagliavini's vocal talents, but as a whole the story falls into inappropriate slapstick, with the rest of the cast delivering mediocre performances. (In Italian; English subtitles.)

d, Mario Mattoli; ph, Alverto Fusi; subtitles, Armando Macaluso.

Musical **(PR:A MPAA:NR)**

LADY IS WILLING, THE½** (1934, Brit.) 66m COL bw

Leslie Howard *(Albert Latour)*, Cedric Hardwicke *(Gustav Dupont)*, Binnie Barnes *(Helene Dupont)*, Sir Nigel Playfair *(Prof. Menard)*, Nigel Bruce *(Welton)*, Claud Allister *(Brevin)*, W. Graham Browne *(Pignolet)*, Kendall Lee *(Valerie)*, Arthur Howard *(Dr. Germont)*, Virginia Field *(Maid)*, John Turnbull.

Howard plays a private detective hired by three businessmen to help them get even with Hardwicke, who has misused their investments in some property shares. Howard's plan of attack is to kidnap Hardwicke's wife, Barnes, whose signature is needed for property Hardwicke wants to sell. Howard manages the kidnap by falling in love with Barnes. A credible script and convincing performances are severely marred by direction which relies heavily upon stage techniques unsuitable for the screen.

p, Joseph Friedman; d, Gilbert Miller; w, Guy Bolton (based upon the play by Louis Verneuil); ph, Joseph Walker; art d, Oscar Werndorff.

Comedy **(PR:A MPAA:NR)**

LADY IS WILLING, THE*** (1942) 92m COL bw

Marlene Dietrich *(Elizabeth Madden)*, Fred MacMurray *(Dr. Corey McBain)*, Aline MacMahon *(Buddy)*, Stanley Ridges *(Kenneth Hanline)*, Arline Judge *(Frances)*, Roger Clark *(Victor)*, Marietta Canty *(Mary Lou)*, David James *(Baby Corey)*, Ruth Ford *(Myrtle)*, Sterling Holloway *(Arthur Miggle)*, Harvey Stephens *(Dr. Golding)*, Harry Shannon *(Detective Sergeant Barnes)*, Elisabeth Risdon *(Mrs. Cummings)*, Charles Lane *(K. K. Miller)*, Murray Alper *(Joe Quig)*, Kitty Kelly *(Nellie Quig)*, Chester Clute *(Income Tax Man)*, Robert Emmett Keane *(Hotel Manager)*, Eddie Acuff *(Murphy)*, Lorna Dunn *(Maid)*, Eugene Borden *(Wine Steward)*, Judith Linden *(Airline Stewardess)*, Neil Hamilton *(Charlie)*, Helen Ainsworth *(Interior Decorator)*, Lou Fulton *(Mop Man)*, Billy Newell *(Counter Man)*, Charles Halton *(Dr. Jones)*, Romaine Callender *(Man)*, Edward McWade *(Boston Doorman)*, Paul Oman *(Violinist)*, Ernie Adams *(Doorman)*, Frances Morris, Georgia Backus *(Nurses)*, Jimmy Conlin *(Bum)*, Myrtle Anderson *(Maid)*.

Bright, breezy romantic comedy with Dietrich playing an unaccustomed sympathetic role in which the audience didn't have to secretly like her. This time they could like her without hiding it. Dietrich is a renowned musical-stage star with no husband but a passion for motherhood. She finds an abandoned baby, James, and decides that she wants to raise it. But she has no idea what to do and never bothers to check whether it's a boy or a girl until she has to. James begins to cry and Dietrich is thrown into a tizzy and makes her manager, Ridges, and her secretary, MacMahon, nuts until they locate MacMurray, a divorced pediatrician, who straightens things out. He's puzzled by Dietrich and also intrigued by her. He explains that the child is male and was only bawling because its stomach was empty. Dietrich names the baby after MacMurray and plans to adopt it officially but that's thwarted when she learns that single parents aren't allowed to do that (remember, this was 1942 when that sort of thing was unheard of. Even today, it is frowned upon.) In order to get to keep the child, she makes MacMurray an offer. He prefers research to practice and she will marry him "in name only" and support his work. He accepts that and moves into a section of her huge apartment and she blithely continues her career in between raising her son. Do we have to tell you that the two fall in love? That causes a bit of woe when MacMurray's ex-wife, Judge, comes out of the woodwork. Dietrich resents Judge's interference in their lives and MacMurray's inability to deal with it, so she takes the baby and goes on tour. Then the baby gets sick and needs an operation. MacMurray flies in, does the surgery, and he and Dietrich make up and, it is presumed, will live happily ever after.

p&d, Mitchell Leisen; w, James Edward Grant, Albert McCleery (based on the story by Grant); ph, Ted Tetzlaff; m, W. Franke Harling; ed, Eda Warren; md, Morris W. Stoloff; art d, Rudolph Sternad, Lionel Banks; cos, Irene; ch, Douglas Dean; m/l, "Strange Thing (and I find You)," Jack King, Gordon Clifford.

Comedy **(PR:A MPAA:NR)**

LADY JANE GREY***

(1936, Brit.) 78m Gainsborough/GAU bw (GB: TUDOR ROSE; AKA: NINE DAYS A QUEEN)

Sir Cedric Hardwicke *(Earl of Warwick)*, John Mills *(Lord Guildford Dudley)*, Felix Aylmer *(Edward Seymour)*, Leslie Perrins *(Thomas Seymour)*, Frank Cellier *(Henry VIII)*, Desmond Tester *(Edward VI)*, Gwen Ffrangcon-Davies *(Mary Tudor)*, Martita Hunt *(Jane's Mother)*, Miles Malleson *(Jane's Father)*, Sybil Thorndike *(Ellen)*, Nova Pilbeam *(Lady Jane Grey)*, John Laurie, Roy Emerton, Albert Davies, Arthur Goullet, John Turnbull, Peter Croft.

A highly accurate and detailed costume drama concentrating on the brief reigns of Edward VI (Tester) and Lady Jane Grey (Pilbeam) after the death of Henry VIII (Cellier). The acute attention to costumes and sets, plus a smoothly scripted and directed effort, make this an intriguing look at English history. The majority of roles were performed marvelously by members of London's West End theater community, who were relatively unknown to the screen.

p, Michael Balcon; d, Robert Stevenson; w, Stevenson, Miles Malleson; ph, M. Greenbaum.

Drama/History **(PR:A MPAA:NR)**

LADY KILLER*½** (1933) 76m WB bw

James Cagney *(Dan Quigley)*, Mae Clarke *(Myra Gale)*, Leslie Fenton *(Duke)*, Margaret Lindsay *(Lois Underwood)*, Henry O'Neill *(Ramick)*, Willard Robertson *(Conroy)*, Douglas Cosgrove *(Jones)*, Raymond Hatton *(Pete)*, Russell Hopton *(Smiley)*, William Davidson *(Williams)*, Marjorie Gateson *(Mrs. Wilbur Marley)*, Robert Elliott *(Brannigan)*, John Marston *(Kendall)*, Douglas Dumbrille *(Spade Maddock)*, George Chandler *(Thompson)*, George Blackwood *(The Escort)*, Jack Don Wong *(Oriental)*, Frank Sheridan *(Los Angeles Police Chief)*, Edwin Maxwell *(Jeffries, Theater Manager)*, Phil Tead *(Usher Sargeant Seymour)*, Dewey Robinson *(Movie Fan)*, H. C. Bradley *(Man with Purse)*, Harry Holman *(J. B. Roland)*, Harry Beresford *(Dr. Crane)*, Olaf Hytten *(Butler)*, Harry Strang *(Ambulance Attendant)*, Al Hill *(Casino Cashier)*, Bud Flanagan [Dennis O'Keefe] *(Man in Casino)*, James Burke *(Hand-Out)*, Robert Homans *(Jailer)*, Clarence Wilson *(Lawyer)*, Sam McDaniel *(Porter)*, Spencer Charters *(Los Angeles Cop)*, Herman Bing *(Western Director)*, Harold Waldridge *(Letter-Handler)*, Luis Alberni *(Director)*, Ray Cooke *(Property Man)*, Sam Ash *(Hood)*.

This is one of those early madcap comedies that is acted and directed at whirlwind pace and is spritely with snappy dialog and Cagney's irrepressible personality. It's also a grand spoof of Hollywood and begins, ironically enough, in New York's Strand Theater, owned by Warner Bros. (Cagney's studio, of course), where Cagney is an usher. When he's fired, Cagney turns to crime, involving himself with Dumbrille, Hopton, Fenton and Hatton, along with blonde moll Clarke. They practice a "come-on" badger game where Clarke entices some married sucker into a compromising position and he pays off big rather than be exposed. Cagney finds the work repulsive and quits when a gang member is killed, taking the Super Chief to California and, once there, hiding out in Hollywood from the New York police. He takes a room in the Alexandria Hotel but believes he's been spotted by police; it turns out that a director, Davidson, has followed him, typecasting him for a prison movie he's making. Cagney takes the part and later graduates to bigger roles. One part calls for him to play an Indian chief in long headdress, riding a mechanical horse while a western scene is shown on rear-view projection, driven half crazy by a maniacal German director, Bing. Cagney's fan mail increases to the point where he becomes a star by popular demand. Meanwhile, he courts the genteel Lindsay, with whom he appears in an historical drama, a film lambasted by one particularly vicious critic. Cagney buttonholes the critic in the Cocoanut Grove restaurant and forces him to eat a copy of his review in the men's room, then shoves him into a toilet where, offscreen, he falls back to register the sound of loud flushing. Dumbrille and gang then show up and try to involve Cagney in another scheme, robbing the homes of movie stars, but Cagney resists them and later causes their roundup. It's all fast and furious fun with Cagney bantering his way through a film with exceptional direction and a smart script. The swaggering star is again united with Mae Clarke of PUBLIC ENEMY fame, but here he refrains from smashing a grapefruit into her face; he merely yanks her out of bed by her hair and hurls her down a corridor, the most violent act Cagney ever visited upon a female in any movie, yet it's played for laughs and gets them. Said Cagney later: "She [Mae Clarke] knew how to hold on to the wrists. I didn't pull her hair at all." This romp through movieland was one of five films the busy Cagney made for Warner Bros. in 1933, the others being PICTURE SNATCHER, HARD TO HANDLE, THE MAYOR OF HELL and FOOTLIGHT PARADE, the latter being one of his longtime favorites.

p, Henry Blanke; d, Roy Del Ruth; w, Ben Markson, Lillie Hayward (based on the story "The Finger Man" by Rosalind Keating Shaffer); ph, Tony Gaudio; ed, George Amy; md, Leo F. Forbstein; art d, Robert Haas; cos, Orry-Kelly; makeup, Perc Westmore.

Comedy/Satire **(PR:A MPAA:NR)**

LADY KILLERS, THE (SEE: LADYKILLERS, THE, 1956, Brit.)

LADY L* (1965, Fr./Ital.) 124m Champion-Concordia/MGM c

Sophia Loren *(Lady L)*, Paul Newman *(Armand)*, David Niven *(Lord Lendale)*, Cecil Parker *(Sir Percy)*, Claude Dauphin *(Inspector Mercier)*, Marcel Dalio *(Sapper)*, Philippe Noiret *(Ambroise Gerome)*, Michel Piccoli *(Lecoeur)*, Jean Wiener *(Krajewski)*, Daniel Emilfork *(Kobeleff)*, Eugene Deckers *(Koenigstein)*, Jacques Dufilho *(Beala)*, Tanya Lopert *(Agneau)*, Catherine Allegret *(Pantoufle)*, Hella Petri *(Madam)*, Peter Ustinov *(Prince Otto)*, Sacha Pitoeff *(Bomb-Throwing Revolutionary)*, Arthur Howard *(Butler)*, Roger Trapp, Jean Rupert, Joseph Dassin, Jacques Legras, Mario Feliciani, Dorothy Reynolds, Hazel Hughes, Jacques Ciron.

This is one of those cute little films made by a cute little cadre of actors with nothing much else to do. Loren, in preposterous and unbelievable makeup as an eighty-year-old woman, opens and closes the film while narrating her not-too-exciting life in between. Loren and Newman are married when a sexless Lord, Niven, spies the voluptuous Loren and asks her to wed. She does, creating a lackluster *menage a trois*, becoming a Lady but continuing to bed with Newman and having children by him. Newman is a part-time anarchist busy planning the overthrow of the capitalistic system and a full-time chauffeur for Niven who only wants Loren as a name-only wife. There are a few funny moments when Newman goes berserk and tries to bomb Prince Otto of Bavaria with backfiring results but for the most part this is a forced farce that does not come off at all. Ustinov directs without style, invention, pace, or continuity. The story seems to be made up as the production lolled along through a Victorian era not too carefully detailed. The depth of Ustinov's concentration on the film was limited, to say the least, since he wrote a play, "The Unknown Soldier and His Wife" while managing his rather off-handed helming of this film. Gina Lollobrigida and Tony Curtis were originally slated for the leading roles but were dropped. When Loren was approached to play the bed-hopping aristocrat she jumped at the chance but insisted that Ustinov direct, no doubt because he was a weak director and could be manipulated. Even before he took over more than $2 million had been spent on elaborate sets and background footage. Ustinov later admitted the film was an utter failure but he blamed the script: "The plot spanned decade after decade with ample opportunity for decoration but there was no real story there." Newman merely walks through his role, sporting a series of disguises as a French anarchist that make him all the more ridiculous-looking. Only Niven as the sad and cynical aristocrat is bearable, but even this sophisticated actor fumbles about with little to say or do. Loren's peasant posture and pedestrian street gestures suggest anything but the upper-crust lady she's supposed to be playing.

p, Carlo Ponti; d&w, Peter Ustinov (based on the novel by Romain Gary); ph, Henri Alekan (Panavision, Eastmancolor); m, Jean Francaix; ed, Roger Dwyre; art d, Jean d'Eaubonne, Auguste Capelier; set d, Maurice Barnathan; cos, Marcel Escoffier, Jacqueline Guyot; spec eff, Karl Baumgartner; makeup, William Tuttle, Michel Deruel, Giuseppe Annunziata.

Comedy **(PR:C MPAA:NR)**

LADY, LET'S DANCE** 1/2 (1944) 88m MON bw

Belita *(Herself)*, James Ellison *(Jerry)*, Frick *(Himself)*, Frack *(Himself)*, Walter Catlett *(Timber)*, Lucien Littlefield *(Snodgrass)*, Maurice St. Clair *(Manuelo)*, Eugene Mikeler *(Eugene)*, Henry Busse *(Himself)*, Harry Harvey *(Fraser)*, Jack Rice *(Given)*, Emmett Vogan *(Stack)*, Barbara Woodell *(Dolores)*, The Orchestras of Henry Busse, Eddie LeBaron, Mitch Ayres, Lou Bring.

This costly production is more a vehicle for portraying Belita's ice-skating and dancing abilities than it is for presenting a story. Belita is a quick replacement for the dance team of a California resort run by Ellison. Her career skyrockets into stardom, while Ellison loses his job and drifts around the country until he lands in the Army. Thin story line is glossed over by the entertaining dance and ice-skating numbers, all photographed excellently by Stengler. Songs include "Dream of Dreams," "Rio," "In The Days of Beau Brummel," "Lady, Let's Dance," "Happy Hearts," "Ten Million Men and a Girl" (Dave Oppenheim, Ted Grouya), "Silver Shadows and Golden Dreams" (Charles Newman, Lew Pollack), and the rhumba standard "Esperanza."

p, Scott R. Dunlap; d, Frank Woodruff; w, Peter Milne, Paul Gerard Smith (based on a story by Bradbury Foote and Dunlap); ph, Mack Stengler; ed, Richard Currier; md, Edward Kay; ch, Michael Panaieff, Dave Gould.

Musical **(PR:A MPAA:NR)**

LADY LIBERTY*

(1972, Ital./Fr.) 95m Champion-Concordia/UA c (LA MORTADELLA)

Sophia Loren *(Maddalena Ciarrapico)*, William Devane *(Jock Fenner)*, Luigi Proietti *(Michelle Brunj)*, Beeson Carroll *(Dominic)*, Bill Deprato *(Pasquale)*, Danny Devito *(Mancuso)*, David Doyle *(O'Henry)*, Charles Bartlett *(Wildflower)*, Tracy Hotchiner *(Wow Girl)*, Daniel Fortus *(Wow Boy)*, Irene Signoretti *(Hostess)*, Jack Aaron *(Steward)*, Mary Whelchel *(Kind Lady)*, Richard Libertini *(Tim)*, Adam Reed *(Witty Boy)*, Terry Thompson *(Bill)*, Alfred Hinckley *(Nolan)*, Dennis McMullen, Mark Dawson *(Cops)*, Randy Hines *(Teddy)*, Elsa Raven *(Policewoman)*, Sally DeMay *(Old Lady)*, Basil Hoffman *(Willett)*, Alex Fisher *(Lawrence)*, Tom Lacy *(City Editor)*, Darrell Zwerling *(Stan)*, Edward Herrmann *(Policeman)*, Packy McFarland *(Trix)*, Alan Feinstein, Garnett Smith, Robert Pickering, Donald Billett *(Aides)*, Dennis Helfend, Peter Landers, Frank Bara, Roger Ochs, Joel Wolfe *(Reporters)*, John Gerstad *(Martin)*, Chris Norris *(Lydia)*, Frank Hamilton *(TV Director)*, Dutch Miller *(Gallagher)*, Martin Abrams *(Young Man)*, Peter DeAnda *(Al)*, George Fisher, Charles Guardino, Alex Stevens *(Thugs)*, Fred J. Scollay *(Doctor)*, Bob Glaudini *(Georgie)*, Paul Ambrose *(Dora)*, Dick Sabol, William Ostroff *(Colleagues)*, Brian Chapin *(Copy Boy)*, Kathy Galvin *(Emily)*, Geordie Campbell *(Andrew)*, Susan Sarandon *(Sally)*, Michael Haley *(Cab Driver)*, Candy Darling *(Transvestite)*, K. Callan *(Subway Lady)*, Dick Ensslen, Thomas Murphy, Jack Dabdoub, Robert Cromwell *(Cops)*.

Another Italian comedy import with about as much plot as a bowl of spaghetti. Loren arrives in the U.S. to see her fiance, Proietti, carrying a large Mortadella sausage from her hometown of Bologna as a gift for him. When U.S. customs officials forbid Loren to bring the sausage into the country, she explodes and almost causes an international incident. Devane, a New York reporter, hears about Loren's fight for her rights and decides to exploit the story for his newspaper. Meanwhile, the curvacious, buxom Loren befriends meek-mannered customs official Carroll and together they eat the sausage. When Devane's story breaks, Loren is further enraged, though she is now free to enter the country sans sausage. She visits fiance Proietti, to find that he has been embarrassed by her actions, and she flees to Carroll but soon leaves him upon discovering that he's a mama's boy. Next she goes to Devane and spends the night with him. Proietti appears, full of conciliation, telling Loren that her stand on the sausage has caused business at his restaurant to boom and he now asks her to marry her. She sneers at his opportunism, then rejects Devane too upon learning he has a wife and children. She is last seen making her way into the canyons of Manhattan, looking for a decent man and, one can safely assume, an edible sausage. No bread, no mustard, just baloney.

p, Carlo Ponti; d, Mario Monicelli; w, Leonard Melfi, Suso Cecchi D'Amico, Don Carlos Dunaway, R. W. Spera, Mario Monicelli, Ring Lardner, Jr. (based on the story by Melfi); ph, Alfio Contini (Eastmancolor); m, Lucio Dalla; ed, Ruggero Mastroianni; prod d, Mario Garbuglia; art d, Rene D'Auriac, Richard Bianchi; set d, Paul Vogt; cos, Albert Wolsky; makeup, Giuseppe Annunziata, Fern Buchner.

Comedy **(PR:C MPAA:PG)**

LADY LIES, THE*** (1929) 75m PAR bw

Walter Huston *(Robert Rossiter)*, Claudette Colbert *(Joyce Roamer)*, Charles Ruggles *(Charlie Tyler)*, Patricia Deering *(Jo Rossiter)*, Tom Brown *(Bob Rossiter)*, Betty Gadde *(Hilda Pearson)*, Jean Dixon *(Ann Gardner)*, Duncan Penwarden *(Henry Tuttle)*, Virginia True Boardman *(Amelia Tuttle)*, Verna Deane *(Bernice Tuttle)*.

Huston plays a wealthy widower who falls for Colbert, a woman of the lower classes. This creates havoc in his household when his two children, Deering and Brown, fear she is only after his money and come up with several plans to stop the affair. The play has been excellently brought to the screen through the direction of Henley and further aided by superior performances from the entire cast, especially Colbert and Ruggles.

d, Hobart Henley; w, Garrett Fort, John Meehan (based on the play by Meehan); ph, William Steiner; ed, Helene Turner.

Comedy **(PR:A MPAA:NR)**

LADY LUCK** (1936) 62m CHES bw

Patricia Farr *(Mamie Murphy)*, William Bakewell *(Dave Holmes)*, Duncan Renaldo *(Tony Morelli)*, Iris Adrian *(Rita)*, Lulu McConnell *("Aunt" Mamie)*, Jameson Thomas *(Jack Conroy)*, Vivian Oakland *(Mrs. Hemingway)*, Claude Allister *(Briggs)*, Arthur Hoyt *(Mr. Hemingway)*, Lew Kelly, John Kelly, Joe Barton, Lupe Lupien.

Farr plays a manicurist who has mistakenly been chosen the winner of a large sweepstakes. She immediately becomes the target of fortune hunters Renaldo, a crooked night club owner, and Thomas, who wants to marry her to gain publicity and a stage contract. Eventually McConnell, the real winner, shows up letting Farr receive all the attention as long as she gets the money. Written and directed competently, though routinely, with performances on par.

p, George R. Batcheller; d, Charles Lamont; w, John Krafft (based on the story by Stuart and Dorrell McGowan); ph, M. A. Andersen; ed, Roland D. Reed.

Drama **(PR:A MPAA:NR)**

LADY LUCK** (1946) 97m RKO bw

Robert Young *(Larry Scott)*, Barbara Hale *(Mary Audrey)*, Frank Morgan *(William Audrey)*, James Gleason *(Sacramento Sam)*, Don Rice *(Eddie)*, Harry Davenport *(Judge Martin)*, Lloyd Corrigan *(Little Joe)*, Teddy Hart *(Little Guy)*, Joseph Vitale *(Happy Johnson)*, Douglas Morrow *(Dan Morgan)*, Robert Clarke *(Southern Officer)*, Larry Wheat *(Calm Card Player)*, Alf Haugan *(Sign Maker)*, Alvin Hammer *(Man in Book Store)*, Betty Gillette *(Stewardess)*, Russell Simpson *(Daniel Boone)*, Harry Depp *(Elderly Gent)*, Grace Hampton *(Woman in Book Shop)*, Pat Prest *(Girl)*, Eric Mayne, Major Sam Harris, Henry Herbert, J.W. Johnson, Carl Faulker, Forbes Murray, Billie Snyder, Sayre Deering, Clyde McAtee, Jack Ford, Jack Arkin, Sam Lufkin, Paul Lacy, Brick Sullivan, Sammy Shack *(Gamblers)*, Bert Moorhouse, Jack Stoney *(Billiard Players)*, Mary Field *(Tall, Thin Woman)*, Forrest Taylor *(Gen. Sherman)*, Dick Elliott *(Fat Man)*, Joe Whitehead, Jack Norton *(Bartenders)*, Al Rhein *(Croupier)*, Myrna Dell *(Mabel)*, Harry Harvey *(Desk Clerk)*, Eddie Dunn *(Police Lieutenant)*, Nancy Saunders *(Manicurist)*, Frank Dae *(Man in Hallway)*, Lorin Raker *(Process Server)*, Cosmo Sardo *(Barber)*.

Young is a newlywed whose wife, Hale, is descended from a long line of gamblers who all lost their shirts, giving her a strong aversion to any gambling on the part of her husband. When she catches him in a game of craps during their honeymoon she threatens to leave. Young's friends try to patch up the marriage by getting Hale hooked. The roles soon become reversed, with Young pursuing the honest working life while his wife opens a casino. Hale's grandpa, Morgan, tries to come to the rescue of his granddaughter by conceiving a plan that will knock her back to her senses. Effective performances are somewhat marred by a weak story line.

p, Warren Duff; d, Edwin L. Marin; w, Lynn Root, Frank Fenton (based on the story by Herbert Clyde Lewis); ph, Lucien Andriot; m, Leigh Harline; ed, Ralph Dawson; md, C. Bakaleinikoff; art d, Albert S. D'Agostino, Feild Gray; set d, Darrell Silvera, James Altwies; cos, Edward.

Comedy **(PR:A MPAA:NR)**

LADY MISLAID, A** (1958, Brit.) 60m Welwyn/ABF-Pathe bw

Phyllis Calvert *(Esther Williams)*, Alan White *(Sgt. Bullock)*, Thorley Walters *(Smith)*, Gillian Owen *(Jennifer Williams)*, Richard Leech *(George)*, Constance Fraser *(Mrs. Small)*, Sheila Shand Gibbs *(Betty)*.

Calvert and Owen are a pair of suspicious spinsters whose holiday at a rented cottage takes a comic turn when a police investigator shows up looking for the body of the former renter's wife. They turn up a skeleton but it is that of an ancient Englishman. Eventually Walters, the chap suspected of killing his spouse, proves his innocence and clears up all the confusion.

p, Robert Hall; d, David Macdonald; w, Frederick Gotfurt (based on the play by Kenneth Horne); ph, Norman Warwick.

Comedy **(PR:A MPAA:NR)**

LADY OBJECTS, THE* 1/2 (1938) 62m COL bw

Lanny Ross *(William Hayward)*, Gloria Stuart *(Ann Adams)*, Joan Marsh *(June Lane)*, Roy Benson *(George Martin)*, Pierre Watkin *(Mr. Harper)*, Robert Paige *(Ken Harper)*, Arthur Loft *(Charles Clarke)*, Stanley Andrews *(Baker)*, Jan Buckingham *(Mrs. Harper)*, Bess Flowers *(Miriam Harper)*, Ann Doran *(Miss Hollins)*, Vessy O'Davoren *(Langham)*.

Ross plays an ex-college football star who marries his college sweetheart, Stuart. Their relationship becomes shaky as her career as a criminal lawyer escalates, while he struggles as an unsuccessful architect. Once separated, Ross makes some extra money as a nightclub singer but is then wrongly accused of a murder. Stuart is called upon to bail him out in a tearful courtroom scene. The cast delivers strong performances, but is unable to lift this lame story. Songs include: "A Mist Over the Moon," "That Week in Paris," "Home in Your Arms," "When You're in the Room," "Sky High," "Naughty, Naughty," "Victory Song" (Hammerstein II, Oakland, Milton Drake).

p, William Perlberg; d, Erle C. Kenton; w, Gladys Lehman, Charles Kenyon; ph, Allen G. Siegler; m, Oscar Hammerstein II, Ben Oakland; ed, Al Clark.

Drama **(PR:A MPAA:NR)**

LADY OF BURLESQUE** 1/2

(1943) 91m Hunt Stromberg/UA bw (GB: STRIPTEASE LADY)

Barbara Stanwyck *(Dixie Daisy)*, Michael O'Shea *(Biff Brannigan)*, J. Edward Bromberg *(S.B. Foss)*, Iris Adrian *(Gee Gee Graham)*, Gloria Dickson *(Dolly*

Baxter), Victoria Faust *(Lolita La Verne)*, Charles Dingle *(Inspector Harrigan)*, Stephanie Bachelor *(Princess Nirvena)*, Marion Martin *(Alice Angel)*, Eddie Gordon *(Officer Pat Kelly)*, Pinky Lee *(Mandy)*, Frank Fenton *(Russell Rogers)*, Frank Conroy *(Stacchi)*, Lew Kelly *(The Hermit)*, Claire Carleton *(Sandra)*, Janis Carter *(Janine)*, Gerald Mohr *(Louie Grindero)*, Bert Hanlon *(Sammy)*, Sid Marion *(Joey)*, Lou Lubin *(Moey)*, Lee Trent *(Lee)*, Don Lynn *(Don)*, Beal Wong *(Wong)*, Freddie Walburn *(Messenger Boy)*, Isabel Withers *(Teletype Operator)*, George Chandler *(Jake, Stagehand)*, Kit Guard *(Hank, Stagehand)*, Eddie Borden *(Man in Audience)*, David Kashner *(Cossack)*, Florence Auer *(Policewoman)*, Joe Devlin, Louise La Planche, Elinor Troy, Virginia Gardner, Carol Carrolton, Dallas Worth, Mary Gail, Barbara Slater, Noel Neill, Marjorie Raymond, Jean Longworth, Joan Dale, Gerry Coonan, Valmere Barman, Joette Robinson.

Stripper Gypsy Rose Lee took some time out from doffing her clothes to write the mystery this film is based upon. In years to come, she would be the inspiration for the play and movie GYPSY and bear Otto Preminger's child out of wedlock. Stanwyck is a burlesque star at Bromberg's theater. O'Shea (who had been plucked from his stage performance in "The Eve of St. Mark" for this film) is the comic who chases after her in between "Take It Off!" cries and "Vas You Dere, Charlie?" routines. There are constant disagreements between the chorus girls and Stanwyck is always stepping in to arbitrate matters. Then Faust is strangled by a G-string. Cops arrive and there are motives and clues galore but they can't nail anyone. There's another strangulation and Stanwyck and O'Shea team up to find the murderer. In doing so, they fall in love. Stanwyck sings "Take It Off The E-String, Play It On the G-String" while doing a dynamic strip number. Fenton warbles "So This Is You" and a good time is had by all. A few laughs, some tension, and a very true-to-life depiction of what goes on backstage. This was Hunt Stromberg's first independent picture after nearly twenty years of hits at MGM. Lange took an Oscar nomination for his music. We hesitate telling you who the killer is because it would ruin the goings-on.

p, Hunt Stromberg; d, William A. Wellman; w, James Gunn (based on the novel *The G-String Murders* by Gypsy Rose Lee); ph, Robert DeGrasse; m, Arthur Lange; ed, James E. Newcomb; prod d, Joseph Platt; art d, Bernard Herzbrun; cos, Edith Head, Natalie Visart; ch, Danny Dare; m/l, Sammy Cahn, Harry Akst; makeup, Bob Stephanoff.

Mystery/Comedy Cas. (PR:C MPAA:NR)

LADY OF CHANCE, A** (1928) 79m MGM bw

Norma Shearer *(Dolly)*, Lowell Sherman *(Bradley)*, Gwen Lee *(Gwen)*, John Mack Brown *(Steve Crandall)*, Eugenie Besserer *(Mrs. Crandall)*, Buddy Messinger *(Hank)*

Shearer is a pretty blackmailer in league with gangster Sherman. She lures men up to her room, then Sherman bursts in pretending to be her husband. The terrified victim usually coughs up money to keep the matter quiet. After one episode of this kind, Sherman keeps the whole take, so Shearer robs him and goes into hiding. She meets and falls in love with Brown, the inventor of a revolutionary new concrete mix. When her former cohorts catch up to her, they scheme to bilk Brown out of his money, but rather than betray the man she loves, Shearer turns herself in to the law and is sent to a reformatory. Brown manages to swing her a parole and the lovers are happily reunited. This was Shearer's first talking (actually, part-talking) picture, although she herself did not talk in it; dialog sequences were sporadic and featured other players, and the film relied heavily on writer Spence's titles to carry the story. Shearer had been a star of silents for years, but she was filled with incertitude about her vocal capabilities. Fortunately, she had the help of young studio *wunderkind* Irving Thalberg, whom she had married a year previously. Following this film's completion, the Thalbergs took a long European vacation. On their return, Shearer went to experts at the University of Southern California to have her voice analyzed. Reassured, she underwent a talking screen test and was signed for the leading role in MGM's second all-talking picture, THE TRIAL OF MARY DUGAN (1929). Johnny Mack Brown, who in these late-1920s films played leads with such other ladies as Greta Garbo and Joan Crawford, had matriculated downward to B westerns by the early 1930s.

d, Hobart Henley, Robert Z. Leonard; w, A. P. Younger, John Lee Meehan, Ralph Spence, Edmund Scott (based on the story "Little Angel" by Leroy Scott); ph, Peverell Marley, William Daniels; ed, Margaret Booth; art d, Cedric Gibbons; cos, Adrian.

Comedy-Drama (PR:A MPAA:NR)

LADY OF DECEIT (SEE: BORN TO KILL, 1947)

LADY OF MONZA, THE*
(1970, Ital.) 98m Clesi-Finanziaria San Marco/Tower c (UNA STORIA LOMBARDA; AKA: THE NUN OF MONZA)

Anne Heywood *(Virginia de Leyva)*, Antonio Sabato *(Gian Paolo Osio)*, Hardy Kruger *(Father Arrigone)*, Carla Gravina *(Caterina Da Meda)*, Tino Carraro *(Monsignor Barca)*, Luigi Pistilli *(Count De Fuentes)*, Margarita Lozano *(Sister Benedetta)*, Anna Maria Alegiani *(Sister Octavia)*, Giovanna Galletti *(Sister Angela)*, Caterina Boratto *(Sister Francesca)*, Angelica Ippolito *(Sister Degnamerita)*, Maria Michi *(Sister Bianca)*, Renzo Giovampietro, Laura Belli, Rita Calderoni, Pier Paolo Capponi.

Heywood portrays a nun in 17th Century Italy who finds herself passionately responding as she is being raped by a nobleman, Sabato. Later, she is stricken with guilt over her behavior and has Sabato arrested. She soon finds herself pregnant and, after giving birth, Heywood arranges for his escape from prison. They once again begin their illicit relationship, which continues until a nun who witnessed their lovemaking is found dead. Heywood is sentenced to life imprisonment after being convicted of having sexual relations and of being an accomplice to murder. Pretty sleazy.

p, Silvio Clementelli; d, Eriprando Visconti; w, Visconti, Giampiero Bona (based on the novel by Mario Mazzucchelli); ph, Luigi Kuveiller (Eastmancolor); m, Ennio Morricone; ed, Sergio Montanari; art d, Flavio Mogherini; cos, Danilo Donati.

Historical Drama (PR:O MPAA:R)

LADY OF MYSTERY
(SEE: CLOSE CALL FOR BOSTON BLACKIE, A, 1946)

LADY OF SCANDAL, THE**
(1930) 76m MGM bw (GB: THE HIGH ROAD)

Ruth Chatterton *(Elsie)*, Basil Rathbone *(Edward)*, Ralph Forbes *(John)*, Nance O'Neil *(Lady Trench)*, Frederick Kerr *(Lord Trench)*, Herbert Bunston *(Lord Crayle)*, Cyril Chadwick *(Sir Reginald)*, Effie Ellsler *(Lady Minster)*, Robert Bolder *(Hilary)*, Moon Carroll *(Alice)*, MacKenzie Ward *(Ernest)*, Edgar Norton *(Morton)*.

Chatterton plays a stage actress who is brought to the aristocratic home of her fiance, Forbes. Here she meets his cousin Rathbone, a man of questionable moral attributes. The two have a brief affair before she leaves both men to return to the stage. Written with a bent toward sophisticated humor, the script is handled well by the entire cast. The theme song is entitled "Say It with a Smile."

d, Sidney Franklin; w, Hans Kraly, Claudine West, Edwin Justus Mayer (based on the play "The High Road" by Frederick Lonsdale); ph, Oliver T. Marsh, Arthur Miller; ed, Margaret Booth; art d, Cedric Gibbons; cos, Adrian.

Romance (PR:A MPAA:NR)

LADY OF SECRETS** (1936) 73m COL bw

Ruth Chatterton *(Celia Whittaker)*, Otto Kruger *(David)*, Lionel Atwill *(Mr. Whittaker)*, Marian Marsh *(Joan)*, Lloyd Nolan *(Michael)*, Robert Allen *(Richard)*, Elisabeth Risdon *(Mrs. Whittaker)*, Nana Bryant *(Aunt Harriet)*, Esther Dale *(Eccles)*.

Before her daughter marries a man she does not love, Chatterton reveals a dark family secret to her. Told in flashback, Chatterton's lover, Nolan, is killed in the war after being sent there by her domineering father, Atwill. When it is discovered that Chatterton is pregnant by Nolan, Atwill allows her to keep the baby girl as long as she tells everyone it is her sister. When Chatterton finally admits the truth to her daughter, Atwill claims she is crazy and has her committed. This uneven script is poorly handled by overdirection.

p, B. P. Schulberg; d, Marion Gering; w, Joseph Anthony, Zoe Akins (based on the story by Katherine Brush); ph, Ted Tetzlaff; ed, Viola Lawrence.

Drama (PR:A MPAA:NR)

LADY OF THE BOULEVARDS (SEE: NANA, 1934)

LADY OF THE PAVEMENTS** (1929) 93m Art Cinema Corp/UA bw

Lupe Velez *(Nanon del Rayon)*, William Boyd *(Count Karl von Arnim)*, Jetta Goudal *(Countess Diane des Granges)*, Albert Conti *(Baron Finot)*, George Fawcett *(Baron Haussmann)*, Henry Armetta *(Papa Pierre)*, William Bakewell *(A Pianist)*, Franklin Pangborn *(M'sieu Dubrey, Dance Master)*.

As an ordinary programmer and part talkie, this relatively light drama isn't bad. Velez, later to become famous as "the Mexican Spitfire" in the 1930s and 1940s, is paired off with Boyd, an actor discovered by Cecil B. DeMille, who later was to become the western's Hopalong Cassidy. The setting for this Ruritanian romance is Paris, 1868. As a Prussian count, Boyd is engaged to Goudal, a French countess. She enrages the man after engaging in an affair, so he vows to marry a "lady of the pavements." Goudal secretly arranges for Boyd to meet Velez, a cabaret singer whom she disguises as a sophisticate. The two marry, then a reception is held in their honor. There Goudal reveals Velez's true identity, and the frightened singer rushes out, returning to her old cabaret to resume singing. However, Boyd is in love and finds Velez for the happy conclusion. For any minor director, this would probably be considered a fairly good outing. The reviews were generally good, and Velez gives the part real zest. However, the director in this case was the great D. W. Griffith. Though the camera work shows some occasional flashes of his old touch, this represents both a personal and artistic failure. By now his career was well out of his control, ravaged by his genteel Southern ideals which were long out of date, as well as an unhappy problem with alcohol. Critics paid more attention to the film's fiery leading lady, complimenting her on the live performance she gave at the film's opening wherein she did impersonations of her costar Goudal, as well as Gloria Swanson and Dolores Del Rio. After suffering through the humiliation of the New York opening, Griffith, along with companions Jacob Kalich and Molly Picon, went off for a private party of their own. At the end of the evening's drinking, the beaten man, in a hazy depression perhaps increased by his alcoholic consumption, signed Picon's autograph book with the bitterness only fallen genius knows: "There is no more—D.W." There were some inventive techniques employed by the great Griffith, however. In one startling scene Griffith wanted to show the image of Boyd repeated 13 times, a multiple exposure filling an entire room, then merging into one image. Four special effects specialists were hired to achieve this image but they failed. Then Ned Mann created the scene by exposing the negative through the camera 36 times. Griffith also experimented with Velez as she sang a song, increasing the sound of her voice as she approached the camera and decreasing it as she retreated, almost employing the camera here as the subjective camera, as a character, or as one might really hear another person, but technicians failed to get the right sound in this early day talkie where synchronization was a crude and fumbling technique.

p, Joseph M. Schenck; d, D. W. Griffith; w, Sam Taylor, Gerrit Lloyd, George Scarborough (based on the story "La Paiva" by Karl Gustav Vollmoeller); ph, Karl Struss; ed, James Smith; set d, William Cameron Menzies; cos, Alice O'Neill; m/l, "Where is the Song of Songs for Me?" Irving Berlin; spec. eff, Ned Mann.

Drama (PR:A MPAA:NR)

LADY OF THE ROSE   (SEE: BRIDE OF THE REGIMENT, 1930)

LADY OF THE SHADOWS   (SEE: TERROR, THE, 1963)

LADY OF THE TROPICS*1/2   (1939) 92m MGM bw

Robert Taylor (*Bill Carey*), Hedy Lamarr (*Manon De Vargnes*), Joseph Schildkraut (*Pierre Delaroch*), Gloria Franklin (*Nina*), Ernest Cossart (*Father Antoine*), Mary Taylor (*Dolly Harrison*), Charles Trowbridge (*Alfred Z. Harrison*), Frederick Worlock (*Col. Demassey*), Paul Porcasi (*Lamartine*), Margaret Padula (*Madame Kya*), Cecil Cunningham (*Countess Bericki*), Natalie Moorhead (*Mrs. Hazlitt*), Gloria Franklin (*Singer*), Zeffie Tilbury.

Taylor took some time off from making LADY OF THE TROPICS to marry Barbara Stanwyck. He would have been wise to stay on his honeymoon for a year because they made him come back and finish this turkey. There's no question that Lamarr (whom Louis B. Mayer named after silent star Barbara La Marr: it was a lot more mellifluous than the name she had in Europe, Hedy Kiesler) had one of the most beautiful faces in pictures, but no one ever accused her of being a great actress. She proves that here as a half-caste in Indo-China for whom Taylor falls. Taylor is on holiday aboard a yacht when he meets Lamarr and he is soon crazy about her. He jumps ship, leaving his fiancee and her family sputtering, and stays in Saigon to marry Lamarr. The lovers enlist Schildkraut, a wealthy Eurasian, in helping them get her a passport so she can go to America. Schildkraut can do it, but he, also, pines for Lamarr and deliberately stalls the procedure. The lovers soon run out of money and Taylor can't find any work. Lamarr says she'll sleep with Schildkraut if he helps Taylor get a job and secures a passport for her. Schildkraut agrees and ships Taylor off to a rubber plantation in the thick Viet Nam jungle. Lamarr never does give herself to Schildkraut but does go out one night with him to the local opera. When Taylor returns to the city, he thinks that he's been cuckolded and wants to kill Schildkraut. Lamarr gets there first, and shoots Schildkraut and then herself. Taylor arrives and finds her dying, with the elusive passport in her hand. This was a surprisingly flat script from the typewriter of Ben Hecht. Occasionally, some flashes of his wit and originality show through, but one has the feeling that he did this one strictly for the money. Although technically Lamarr's third film, it was only the second one released. Work had been suspended on I TAKE THIS WOMAN which was then re-shot and released in 1940. That movie was, if you recall, waggishly dubbed "I Re-Take This Woman" because of the extensive extra shooting involved. One song: "Each Time You Say Goodbye, I Die A Little," sounds exactly like the first lines of Cole Porter's hit "Every Time You Say Goodbye."

p, Sam Zimbalist; d, Jack Conway; w, Ben Hecht; ph, George Folsey; m, Franz Waxman; ed, Elmo Vernon; art d, Cedric Gibbons, Paul Groesse; set d, Edwin B. Willis; cos, Adrian, Valles; m/l, Phil Ohlman, Foster Carlin.

Drama   (PR:C   MPAA:NR)

LADY OF VENGEANCE*   (1957, Brit) 75m Princess/UA bw

Dennis O'Keefe (*William T. Marshall*), Ann Sears (*Katie Whiteside*), Anton Diffring (*Karnak*), Patrick Barr (*Inspector Madden*), Vernon Greeves (*Larry Shaw*), Eileen Elton (*Melissa*), Frederick Schiller (*Schtegel*), Jacqueline Curtiss (*Penny*), George [G.H.] Mulcaster (*Bennett*), Gerald Case (*Hawley*), Jack McNaughton (*Coroner*), Colin Croft (*Bartender*), Andy Ho (*Houseman*), Humphrey Morton (*Corbey*).

O'Keefe is out to get vengeance on the man responsible for driving his ward to suicide. His plan of attack is slow mental torture. The plot is very confusing, making it hard to follow this picture. Slack direction does little to help the burdensome plot.

p, Burt Balaban, Bernard Donnenfield, William N. Boyle; d, Balaban; w, Irve Tunick; ph, Ian Struthers; m, Phil Cardew; ed, Eric Boyd-Perkins; art d, Harry White.

Drama   (PR:A   MPAA:NR)

LADY ON A TRAIN***1/2   (1945) 93m UNIV bw

Deanna Durbin (*Nikki Collins*), Ralph Bellamy (*Jonathan*), Edward Everett Horton (*Mr. Haskell*), George Coulouris (*Mr. Saunders*), Allen Jenkins (*Danny*), David Bruce (*Wayne Morgan*), Patricia Morison (*Joyce*), Dan Duryea (*Arnold*), Maria Palmer (*Margo*), Elizabeth Patterson (*Aunt Charlotte*), Samuel S. Hinds (*Mr. Wiggam*), William Frawley (*Sgt. Christie*), Jacqueline de Wit (*Miss Fletcher*), Thurston Hall (*Josiah Waring*), Clyde Fillmore (*Cousin*), Ben Carter (*Maxwell*), Mary Forbes, Sarah Edwards (*Cousins*), Nora Cecil (*Woman with Umbrella*), Hobart Cavanaugh (*Drunk*), Alfred "Lash" La Rue (*Waiter*), Poni Adams, Kathleen O'Malley (*Photographers*), Jean Trent, Barbara Bates (*Hatcheck Girls*), Karen Randle (*Cigarette Girl*), Tom Dugan (*Turnkey*), Addison Richards (*Captain*), Joseph Crehan (*Mr. Smith*), Chester Clute (*Conductor*), Ralph Peters (*Taxi Driver*), Charles Cane (*New York Policeman*), Andre Charlot (*Man with Carnation*), Eddie Bruce, George Lewis, Charles Sherlock, Bert Moorehouse (*Reporters*), Eddie Acuff (*New York Cab Driver*), Alice Fleming (*Mrs. Brown*), Ed Waller (*Mr. Brown*), Eddie Dunn (*Clerk*), Jack Norton (*Santa Claus*), Matt McHugh (*Drunk*), George Chandler (*Customer*), Charles Deschamps (*Hairdresser*), Bert Roach (*Fat Man*), Robert Dudley (*Honeywell*), George Lloyd, Al Ferguson (*Workmen*), Eddie Bartel (*Sound Track*), Mabel Forrest (*Wife*), Sam McDaniel, Ernest Anderson (*Doormen*), Dick Hirbe (*Newsboy*), Ethel Mae Halls (*Haughty Woman*).

A delightful thriller unusual in that it's also loaded with laughs, having been written by Beloin and O'Brien, who churned out the brilliant scripts for Jack Benny's radio shows. Durbin is charming and turns in a superb performance as a naive young lady en route to New York for a meeting with a family lawyer Horton. Just before the train pulls into Grand Central Station she sees from the window next to her seat a murder take place in a nearby office building, glimpsing the killer only from the back. She tells police but they think her imagination is working overtime. Desperately, Durbin turns to Bruce, a mystery writer, and both amateur detectives try to solve the crime. Recognizing the murdered man in a newsreel clip as a shipping tycoon, Durbin visits his family and is mistaken for the victim's mistress, a nightclub singer.

Durbin goes to the nightclub and finds the mistress murdered and barely manages to escape with her life. Later, in the same building where the murder occurred, Durbin flees from one of the family relatives, Duryea, believing him the killer, and ends up in the arms of Bellamy, another family relative who takes her into the very room where the killing took place. Duryea bursts into the room with a gun, followed by Bruce who takes the gun and gives it to Bellamy, who is the real killer, one who has murdered to inherit a fortune. Before the sinister Bellamy can do more damage, the police arrive and arrest him. This is a fast-paced movie with a bright and witty script and plenty of scary adventures which Durbin cleverly manages to survive. Cast member Alfred La Rue later turned to B westerns as Lash La Rue; he was first cast in a Durbin vehicle, CHRISTMAS HOLIDAY (1944), and later admitted that the young singing star, who was then queen of the Universal lot, aided his career greatly.

p, Felix Jackson; d, Charles David; w, Edmund Beloin, Robert O'Brien (based on a story by Leslie Charteris); ph, Woody Bredell; m, Miklos Rozsa; ed, Ted Kent; art d, John B. Goodman, Robert C. Clatworthy; set d, Russell A. Gausman; cos, Howard Greer; spec eff, John P. Fulton; m/l, "Gimme a Little Kiss, Will Ya, Huh?" Roy Turk, Jack Smith, Maceo Pinkhard, "Silent Night," "Night and Day," Cole Porter.

Comedy/Crime   (PR:A   MPAA:NR)

LADY ON THE TRACKS, THE**
        (1968, Czech.) 83m Barrandov/Royal c (DAMA NA KOLEJICH)

Jirina Bohdalova (*Marie Kucerova*), Radoslav Brzobohaty (*Vaclav Kucera*), Frantisek Peterka (*Bedrich*), Libuse Geprtova (*Katerina*), Stanislav Fiser (*Mr. Marek*).

While driving her trolley car through Prague, Bohdalova sees her husband kissing another woman. She abandons the train, takes all her money out of the bank, and becomes a new more fashionable and elegant woman. She tries to change her husband's desires and after the usual comic interludes the pair reunite. (In Czech; English subtitles.)

d, Ladislav Rychman; w, Vratislav Blazek; ph, Josef Hanus; art d, Olin Bosak; ch, Josef Konicek; m/l, Jiri Malasek, Jiri Bazant, Vlastimil Hala.

Musical Comedy   (PR:A   MPAA:G)

LADY OSCAR**   (1979, Fr./Jap.) 125m Kitty Music/Toho c

Catriona Maccoll (*Oscar*), Barry Stokes (*Andre*), Christina Bohm (*Marie Antoinette*), Jonas Bergstrom (*Fersen*).

A Japanese comic strip set in revolutionary France is the basis for this feature shot in English with little-known British players on French locations and backed with Japanese money. Macoll is the heroine, brought up as a boy by her martinet father. She adopts men's clothing and becomes a uniformed bodyguard to Marie Antoinette (Bohm). When the revolution breaks out she is reunited with her secret love, Stokes, the son of her family housekeeper, but the storming of the Bastille separates them again. Excellent production design makes this film a treat for the eye, though the Bastille-storming sequence, much-touted at the time, is something of a disappointment. Director Demy is best known for THE UMBRELLAS OF CHERBOURG (1964) and a handful of other nice-looking but rather empty features. LADY OSCAR was his first film in almost six years.

d, Jacques Demy; w, Patricia Louisiana Knop, Demy (based on the comic strip "Rose Of Versailles" by Ryoko Ikeda); ph, Jean Penzer (Eastmancolor); m, Michel Legrand; art d, Bernard Evein.

Historical Drama   (PR:C   MPAA:NR)

LADY PAYS OFF, THE**   (1951) 80m UNIV bw

Linda Darnell (*Evelyn Warren*), Stephen McNally (*Matt Braddock*), Gigi Perreau (*Diana Braddock*), Virginia Field (*Kay Stoddard*), Ann Codee (*Marie Luba*), Lynne Hunter (*Minnie*), Nestor Paiva (*Manuel*), James Griffith (*Ronald*), Billy Wayne (*Croupier*), Katherine Warren (*Dean Howell*), Paul McVey (*Speaker*), Tristram Coffin (*Carl*), Judd Holdren (*3rd Face*) Nolan Leary (*Doctor*), John Doucette (*Cab Driver*), Billy Newell (*Bartender*), Ric Roman (*Ricky*).

Darnell wins the award for America's "Teacher of the Year," but is found in an embarrassing situation when she loses $7,000 at a Reno casino. The nightclub owner, McNally, makes a deal with her to cover the debt and to keep her gambling spree from the press: she will be the private tutor of his daughter Perreau. Darnell plans to get vengeance on McNally by getting him to fall in love with her, then dumping him. However, Perreau sees Darnell and McNally as the perfect couple and lays plans to keep the two together. Unbelievable and obvious plot is further hampered by the miscasting of Darnell. Though smoothly directed, Sirk is quoted as saying, "I have no feeling for this picture at all," which is obvious in the final product.

p, Albert J. Cohen; d, Douglas Sirk; w, Frank Gill Jr., Cohen; ph, William H. Daniels; m, Frank Skinner; ed, Russell Schoengarth; md, Skinner; art d, Bernard Herzbrun, Robert Boyle; set d, Russell A. Gausman, Julia Heron; cos, Bill Thomas.

Drama/Comedy   (PR:A   MPAA:NR)

LADY POSSESSED*   (1952) 87m Portland/REP bw

James Mason (*Del Palma*), June Havoc (*Jean Wilson*), Stephen Dunne (*Tom Wilson*), Fay Compton (*Madame Brune*), Pamela Kellino (*Sybil*), Steven Geray (*Dr. Stepanek*), Diana Graves (*Medium*), Odette Myrtil (*Mrs. Burrows*), Eileen Erskine (*Violet*), John P. Monaghan (*Dave*), Enid Mosier (*Calypso Singer*), Judy Osborn (*Secretary*), Constance Cavendish, Alma Lawton, Anna Grevier, Tonyna Micky Dolly (*Nurses*), Hazel Franklyn (*Matron*).

This attempt at a psychological thriller has Havoc overhearing a conversation between pianist Mason and his wife in a hospital. He wants to disobey the doctor's regulations by taking her to their country home. When Havoc suffers a miscarriage, her husband rents a country home for her to rest at. The home turns out to be that of Mason, whose wife has recently passed away. Havoc recalls the conversation she overheard and, in her dazed state, imagines she is taking the place of Mason's dead wife. Neither the performances nor the narrow direction are able to help save this confusing script. Mason even sings in this one, which doesn't help the film one bit. Songs include: "My Heart Asks Why" (Hans May, Hermione Hannen), "It's You I Love" (Allie Wrubel), "More Wonderful Than These" (Spier, Kay Thompson).

p, James Mason; d, William Spier, Roy Kellino; w, Mason, Pamela Kellino (based on the novel *Del Palma* by Pamela Kellino); ph, Karl Struss; m, Nathan Scott; ed, Arthur Roberts; art d, Frank Arrigo.

Drama **(PR:A MPAA:NR)**

LADY REFUSES, THE* (1931) 70m RKO bw

Betty Compson, Gilbert Emery, John Darrow, Margaret Livingston, Ivan Lebedeff, Edgar Norton, Daphne Pollard, Reginald Sharland.

A wretched melodrama which has Compson down on her luck until she is befriended by the wealthy Emery. He hires her to woo his son, Darrow, away from the gold digger that he's involved with. She does so and in the process falls in love with Emery, a bit of news which comes as quite a surprise to sonny boy.

p, Bertram Millhauser; d, George Archainbaud; w, Wallace Smith (based on the story "Lady For Hire" by Robert Milton, Guy Bolton); ph, Leo Tover.

Drama **(PR:A MPAA:NR)**

LADY REPORTER (SEE: BULLDOG EDITION, 1936)

LADY SAYS NO, THE** (1951) 80m Stillman/UA bw

Joan Caulfield *(Dorinda)*, David Niven *(Bill)*, James Robertson Justice *(Uncle Matt)*, Lenore Lonergan *(Goldie)*, Frances Bavier *(Aunt Alice)*, Peggy Maley *(Midge)*, Henry Jones *(Potsy)*, Jeff York *(Goose)*, George Davis *(Bartender)*, Robert Williams *(General)*, Mary Laurence *(Mary)*.

Niven is a photographer assigned to do a layout on author Caulfield who has just written a book which takes an unpleasant perspective toward men. Well-paced direction and competent performances are unable to save the haphazardly written script.

p, Frank Ross, John Stillman, Jr.; d, Ross; w, Robert Russell; ph, James Wong Howe; m, Emil Newman; ed, George Amy; art d, Perry Ferguson.

Comedy **(PR:A MPAA:NR)**

LADY SCARFACE** (1941) 69m RKO bw

Dennis O'Keefe *(Lt. Mason)*, Judith Anderson *(Slade)*, Frances Neal *(Ann Rogers)*, Mildred Coles *(Mary Powell)*, Eric Blore *(Mr. Hartford)*, Marc Lawrence *(Lefty Landers)*, Damian O'Flynn *(Onslow)*, Andrew Tombes *(Seidel)*, Marion Martin *(Ruby)*, Rand Brooks *(Jimmy Powell)*, Arthur Shields *(Matt)*, Lee Bonnell *(George)*, Harry Burns *(Semenoff)*, Horace MacMahon *(Mullen)*, Eddy Conrad *(Hotel Waiter)*, Joey Ray *(Mr. Barlowe)*, Charles Halton *(Mr. Pinchbeck)*, Ruth Dietrich *(Pinchbeck's Secretary)*, Robert Middlemass *(Capt. Lovell, New York)*, Harry Humphrey *(Watchman)*, Bert Howard *(Mr. Tuckerman)*, Claire McDowell *(Mrs. Tuckerman)*.

This gangster film attempts to portray a female counterpart to the earlier SCARFACE. Anderson, the leader of a gang responsible for a number of robberies and murders, has a large scar which has left her permanently disfigured. Embittered, she has turned to a life of crime. O'Keefe, the police detective in charge of tracking down the gang leader, is unaware that she is a woman. Well-paced direction helps to gloss over the many weaknesses in the script. Performances are efficient, except for Anderson who is miscast as a toughened criminal.

p, Cliff Reid; d, Frank Woodruff; w, Arnaud D'Usseau, Richard Collins; ph, Nicholas Musuraca; ed, Harry Marker.

Crime **Cas.** **(PR:A MPAA:NR)**

LADY SINGS THE BLUES*1/2** (1972) 144m Motown-Weston-Furie/PAR c

Diana Ross *(Billie Holiday)*, Billy Dee Williams *(Louis McKay)*, Richard Pryor *(Piano Man)*, James Callahan *(Reg Hanley)*, Paul Hampton *(Harry)*, Sid Melton *(Jerry)*, Virginia Capers *(Mama Holiday)*, Yvonne Fair *(Yvonne)*, Scatman Crothers *(Big Ben)*, Robert L. Gordy *(Hawk)* Harry Caesar *(The Rapist)*, Milton Selzer *(The Doctor)*, Ned Glass *(The Agent)*, Paulene Myers *(Mrs. Edson)*, Isabel Sanford *(First Madame)*, Tracee Lyles *(Whore)*, Norman Bartold *(Detective)*, Clay Tanner, Jester Hairston, Bert Kramer, Paul Micale, Michelle Aller, Byron Kane, Barbara Minkus, Kay Lewis, Helen Lewis, George Wyner, Shirley Melline, Toby Russ, Larry Duran, Ernie Robinson, Don McGovern, Dick Poston, Charles Woolf, Denise Denise, Lynn Hamilton, Victor Morosco.

Inaccurate film biography that also suffers from being overly directed by Furie. The script, Ross, and the musical supervision took Oscar nominations, but the movie failed to win any of the coveted statuettes. It's the early 1930s and Ross is a teenager who is raped by Caesar, a drunk, in her empty house in Baltimore. She is understandably traumatized by the experience and her mother, Capers, sends her north to Harlem where she'll stay with a pal of hers, Sanford. Capers doesn't know at the time that Sanford is running a whorehouse. Ross becomes a maid and spends her idle time listening to records. Soon, however, she is performing other chores beyond dusting and is one of the more popular attractions at the brothel. She abandons that life for show business and tries to dance at a local club, but has two left feet. Pryor is the man who plays the piano in the bordello and encourages her to try singing. She changes her name and catches the eye of Williams, a local Sporting Life-type, and becomes his woman. While most black singers are doing raucous shout-singing, Ross decides to affect a more delicate manner of performing and is promptly nicknamed "Lady Day." Callahan and Hampton, two white musicians, invite her to join them on a road tour with their band. While working the Deep South, Ross is shocked to see a black man lynched. She also is treated terribly by the local Southerners and finds it increasingly hard to work as the spectre of injustice haunts her. Hampton offers her drugs to help give her balm and surcease and she is soon addicted. Williams tries to get her off the stuff to no avail. The band is booked on a New York radio show but the sponsors refuse to allow her to perform and now she turns to narcotics in a big way. Williams can handle her no longer and throws her out. When Capers dies, Ross increases the drugs, then realizes she's killing herself and walks into a sanitarium in an attempt to kick the habit. While still being treated, she's arrested and convicted on felonious drug usage, then sent to prison where she learns that her New York cabaret license has been taken away from her. That means she can never again work the jazz center of the world. She is released and, with Williams' help, starts a new life. She tours America and finally manages to convince the authorities that she is clean so she is allowed to do a concert at Carnegie Hall. In preparation for that, she travels to Los Angeles for another date, just before the big night. Williams leaves for New York and Ross is depressed at being alone. She visits Pryor and they get high together. Then some dope peddlers break into the apartment and beat Pryor to death. Williams comes back to Los Angeles to help her through this, they return to New York, the concert is a success, and she is happy. That lasts a brief time as she is again turned down for the cabaret license by the city. Shortly thereafter, she is jailed on drug charges again and the rest of the film is a quick look at her slide down the ladder of success until her death at age 44. If the true life story of Billie Holiday had not been so well documented, this might have been an interesting picture on its own merits, but the producers felt they had to alter reality in order to make the sale (otherwise it would have been a documentary in the eyes of co-producer Weston) and the result angered many. In the six years from 1939, Holiday was the lover of Lester Young, the famous sax man, then married Jimmy Monroe. She was discovered by John Hammond, the jazz critic, recorded for Benny Goodman, then sang for Count Basie and Artie Shaw and also recorded for Teddy Wilson. The name of Basie is briefly seen on a theatre and none of the others is ever mentioned. So much for historical accuracy. The number of liberties taken is enormous and caused great consternation among those who were aware of the truth. Nevertheless, this is a fairly good, if much too long, film and Ross proves that she can act. Everyone knew she could sing, although one wondered if she could take that Supremes voice and subjugate it in favor of the Holiday intonations. She could and did and managed to sound like the original without ever seeming to imitate her. Although Holiday was married three times and had countless other good friends, the only romantic interest in the film is played by Williams, another great mishandling of the facts. Look at LADY SINGS THE BLUES as a total fictional musical and you'll enjoy it far more. A raft of great songs include: "My Man" (Channing Pollock, Maurice Yvain), "Strange Fruit" (Lewis Allan), "God Bless the Child," "Don't Explain" (Billie Holiday, Arthur Herzog, Jr.), "T'Aint Nobody's Business If I Do" (Porter, Grainger, Graham Prince, Clarence Williams), "Lady Sings the Blues" (Holiday, H. Nichols), "All Of Me" (Seymour Simons, Gerald Marks), "The Man I Love," "Our Love Is Here To Stay" (George and Ira Gershwin), "I Cried For You" (Abe Lyman, Gus Arnheim, Arthur Freed), "Mean To Me" (Roy Turk, Fred Ahlert), "Them There Eyes" (Maceo Pinkard, William Tracy, Doris Tauber), "What a Little Moonlight Can Do" (Harry Woods), "Lover Man (Oh Where Can You Be?)" (Jimmy Davis, Jimmy Sherman, Roger "Ram" Ramirez), "You've Changed" (Bill Carey, Carl Fischer)," "Good Morning Heartache" (Irene Higginbotham, Ervin Drake, Dan Fisher), "Gimme a Pigfoot and a Bottle of Beer" ("Kid" Wesley, "Sox" Wilson). Executive Producer Berry Gordy, Jr., the man who established the incredible Motown Records dynasty, went on to produce and direct other films after this. Co-Producer Weston made several other movies. The man who co-wrote the book was married to Gloria Swanson in her waning years and later wrote a book about the perils of another white stuff. It was called "Sugar Blues" and railed against the dangers of that sweetness in your system.

p, Jay Weston, James S. White; d, Sidney J. Furie; w, Terence McCloy, Chris Clark, Suzanne De Passe (based on the book by Billie Holiday, William Dufty); ph, John A. Alonzo (Panavision, Eastmancolor); m, Michel Legrand; ed, Argyle Nelson; prod d, Carl Anderson; set d, Reg Allen; cos, Bob Mackie, Ray Aghayan, Norma Koch; makeup, Don Schoenfeld.

Musical Biography **Cas.** **(PR:O MPAA:R)**

LADY, STAY DEAD zero (1982, Aus.) 95m Ryntare c

Chard Hayward [Gordon], Louise Howitt, Deborah Coulls, Roger Ward.

Thinking he is through with his problems after murdering one woman, gardener Hayward quickly finds himself on the way to commit another—and possibly several more—before this dismal excuse for a movie unwinds. Lacks even the basics to entice fans of this type of stuff.

p,d&w, Terry Rourke; ph, Ray Henman; m, Bob Young; art d, Bob Hill.

Horror **(PR:O MPAA:NR)**

LADY SURRENDERS, A* (1930) 102m UNIV bw (GB: BLIND WIVES)

Conrad Nagel *(Winthrop Beauvel)*, Genevieve Tobin *(Mary)*, Basil Rathbone *(Carl Vaudry)*, Rose Hobart *(Isabel Beauvel)*, Carmel Myers *(Sonia)*, Vivian Oakland *(Mrs. Lynchfield)*, Franklin Pangborn *(Lawton)*, Edgar Norton *(Butler)*, Grace Cunard *(Maid)*, Virginia Hammond *(Woman)*.

On the assumption that his wife, Hobart, has gone to Europe to get a divorce, Nagel marries the woman he has been in love with, Tobin. Later, it is discovered Hobart decided not to go through with her original plan and refuses to give in to divorce until frustrated Tobin attempts suicide by stepping in front of a car. At this point, Hobart gives in and grants a divorce. Story moves much too slowly. This is further marred by actors using accents which are not suited to their parts.

p, Carl Laemmle, Jr.; d, John Stahl; w, Gladys Lehman, Arthur Richman, Albert Richman (based on the novel *Sincerity* by John Erskine); ph, Jackson Rose; ed, Maurice Pivar, William L. Cahn; set d, Walter Kessler.

Romance (PR:A MPAA:NR)

LADY SURRENDERS, A**

(1947, Brit.) 108m Gainsborough/UNIV bw (GB: LOVE STORY)

Margaret Lockwood *(Lissa Cambell)*, Stewart Granger *(Kit Firth)*, Patricia Roc *(Judy Martin)*, Tom Walls *(Tom Tanner)*, Reginald Purdell *(Albert)*, Moira Lister *(Carol)*, Dorothy Bramhall *(Susie)*, Vincent Holman *(Prospero)*, Joan Rees *(Ariel)*, Walter Hudd *(Ray)*, A. E. Matthews *(Col. Pitt Smith)*, Beatrice Varley *(Mrs. Rossiter)*, Harriet Cohen *(Pianist)*, Josephine Middleton *(Mrs. Pitt Smith)*, Brian Herbert *(Zed)*, Lawrence Hanray *(Angus Rossiter)*, Sydney Beer.

Lockwood plays a concert pianist dying from a weak heart who, wishing for one last fling, has an affair with ex-RAF pilot, Granger. Granger is also suffering from a disease which is causing him to go blind. Neither of the friends allows the other to know of the malady each is suffering, until Lockwood finds out through Granger's fiancee, Roc, that she has talked him into turning down a dangerous operation that has little chance of success. Roc tells Lockwood that she will leave the pilot if he has the operation. He has the surgery and it succeeds, so Roc goes through with her threat, leaving Lockwood and Granger free to fall in love. Competent performances are marred by uneven direction, but the film offers some nice scenic photography of the English coast.

p, Harold Huth; d, Leslie Arliss; w, Arliss, Doreen Montgomery, Rodney Ackland (based on the story by J. W. Drawbell); ph, Bernard Knowles; m, Hubert Bath; md, Louis Levy, Sydney Beer.

Romance/Drama (PR:A MPAA:NR)

LADY TAKES A CHANCE, A** 1/2

(1943) 86m Frank Ross-RKO/bw

Jean Arthur *(Mollie Truesdale)*, John Wayne *(Duke Hudkins)*, Charles Winninger *(Waco)*, Phil Silvers *(Smiley Lambert)*, Mary Fields *(Florrie Bendix)*, Don Costello *(Drunk)*, John Philliber *(Storekeeper)*, Grady Sutton *(Malcolm)*, Grant Withers *(Bob)*, Hans Conried *(Gregg)*, Peggy Carroll *(Jitterbug)*, Ariel Heath *(Flossie)*, Sugar Geise *(Linda Belle)*, Joan Blair *(Lilly)*, Tom Fadden *(Mullen)*, Eddy Waller *(Bus Station Attendant)*, Nina Quartero *(Carmencita)*, Alex Melesh *(Bartender)*, Cy Kendall *(Gambling House Boss)*, Paul Scott *(2nd Bartender)*, Charles D. Brown *(Dr. Humbolt)*, Butch and Buddy, The Three Peppers, Mysty Shot *(Sammy the Horse)*.

Arthur (wife of producer Ross) plays a working class girl from the big city on a bus tour of the West, when she runs into Wayne at a rodeo he's performing in. Then she misses her bus and is stranded with Wayne and his sidekick, Winninger. Wayne introduces her to the rougher aspects of the region, such as gambling and barroom brawls, and also steals her heart. She finally boards the bus for home but finds Wayne waiting at the station to take her back West. Strong performances and a witty script are marred by flat direction. Ardrey, screenwriter for the film, later became known for his best-selling books on behavorial evolution such as *African Genesis* and *The Territorial Imperative*.

p, Frank Ross; d, William A. Seiter; w, Robert Ardrey, (uncredited) Garson Kanin (based on the story by Jo Swerling); ph, Frank Redman; m, Roy Webb; ed, Theron Warth; md, C. Bakaleinikoff; art d, Albert S. D'Agostino, Alfred Herman; spec eff, Vernon L. Walker.

Comedy/Romance (PR:A MPAA:NR)

LADY TAKES A FLYER, THE**

(1958) 94m UNIV c

Lana Turner *(Maggie Colby)*, Jeff Chandler *(Mike Dandridge)*, Richard Denning *(Al Reynolds)*, Andra Martin *(Nikko Taylor)*, Chuck Connors *(Phil Donahue)*, Reta Shaw *(Nurse Kennedy)*, Alan Hale, Jr. *(Frank Henshaw)*, Jerry Paris *(Willie Ridgely)*, Dee J. Thompson *(Collie Minor)*, Nestor Paiva *(Childreth)*, James Doherty *(Tower Officer)*.

Inspired by the true story of a husband-and-wife airplane ferrying service ("the flying Fords"), Chandler and Turner star in this romanticized screen version. When she becomes pregnant, Turner is forced to remain grounded and tend house. Bored by the responsibilities of a family, Chandler begins seeking entertainment and companionship elsewhere. Neglected Turner, tired of waiting at home for her husband, takes a plane out on her own, only to find herself lost in a thick fog. Chandler saves her by relaying messages to her from the ground, saving her life and ultimately their marriage. Smooth direction and competent performances are hurt by an uneven and plodding script. Jack Arnold, the director, is better known for the science-fiction films he directed in the 1950s such as IT CAME FROM OUTER SPACE (produced by the same producer, Alland, who was the inquiring reporter in Orson Welles' CITIZEN KANE), THE CREATURE FROM THE BLACK LAGOON and THE INCREDIBLE SHRINKING MAN.

p, William Alland; d, Jack Arnold; w, Danny Arnold (based on the story by Edmund H. North); ph, Irving Glassberg (CinemaScope, Eastmancolor); m, Herman Stein; ed, Sherman Todd; md, Joseph Gershenson; art d, Alexander Golitzen, Richard H. Riedel; set d, Russell A. Gausman, Oliver Emert; cos, Bill Thomas; makeup, Bud Westmore.

Drama (PR:A MPAA:NR)

LADY TAKES A SAILOR, THE**

(1949) 99m WB bw

Jane Wyman *(Jennifer Smith)*, Dennis Morgan *(Bill Craig)*, Eve Arden *(Susan Wayne)*, Robert Douglas *(John Tyson)*, Allyn Joslyn *(Ralph Whitcomb)*, Tom Tully *(Henry Duckworth)*, Lina Romay *(Racquel Riviera)*, Fred Clark *(Victor Santell)*, William Frawley *(Oliver Harker)*, Charles Meredith *(Dr. McKewen)*, Craig Stevens *(Danvers)*, Stanley Prager *(Taxi Driver)*, Kenneth Britton *(Davis)*, Ruth Lewis *(Miss Clark)*, Ruth Lee *(Miss Brand)*, Sonia Bryden *(Arlette)*, Walter Shumway *(Dr. Coombs)*, Henrietta Taylor *(Dr. Anna Sparton)*, Emil Rameau *(Dr. Mittenwald)*, Leslie Kimmell *(Conrad Updike)*, John Halloran *(Homer Benton)*, Harry Cheshire *(Judge Vardon)*, Ray Erlenhorn *(Photographer)*, John McGuire *(Coast Guard Officer)*, Robert Malcolm *(Chief of Police)*, Frank Cady *(Mr. Crane)*, George Spaulding *(Adm. Morell)*, Jack Lee *(Capt. Cutter)*, Joe McTurk *(Waiter)*, Bridget Brown *(Hat Check Girl)*, Hallene Hill *(Flower Woman)*, Richard Ryan *(Apartment House Clerk)*, Wendy Lee *(Telephone Operator)*, Phyllis Godfrey *(Hilda)*, Jack Boyle *(Interne)*, Lute Crockett *(Doctor)*, Nina Prescott *(Tyson's Secretary)*, Olan Soule *(Secretary)*, John Morgan, Len Hendry, Russ Conway *(Constables)*, Josephine Whittell, Ken Patterson *(Reporters)*, Tom Stevenson *(Institute Guide)*, Ray Montgomery *(Lab Man)*.

Escapist entertainment has Wyman as the head of a research organization doing research at the bottom of the sea. Her work and career promise to boom until she runs into a secret investigator, Morgan, disguised as a sailor. After much resistance Wyman gives in to the advances of Morgan, letting her work go down the tubes. Well paced, smooth direction, and efficient performances are added to a script which delivers well but lacks enough seriousness to leave much of an impact.

p, Harry Kurnitz; d, Michael Curtiz; w, Everett Freeman (based on the story "The Octopus and Miss Smith" by Jerry Gruskin); ph, Ted McCord; m, Max Steiner; ed, David Weisbart; art d, Edward Carrere; cos, Milo Anderson; spec eff, Roy Davidson, H.F. Koenekamp; makeup, Perc Westmore.

Drama/Comedy (PR:A MPAA:NR)

LADY TO LOVE, A** 1/2

(1930) 92m MGM bw

Vilma Banky *(Lena Shultz)*, Edward G. Robinson *(Tony)*, Robert Ames *(Buck)*, Richard Carle *(Postman)* Lloyd Ingraham *(Father McKee)*, Anderson Lawler *(Doctor)*, Gum Chin *(Ah Gee)*, Henry Armetta *(Angelo)*, George Davis *(Georgie)*.

Robinson plays an aging grape grower in search of a wife. He spots Banky waitressing at a restaurant and asks for her hand in marriage by way of a letter and photograph of himself, as they have never met. But the photograph he encloses is actually that of his handsome young assistant, Ames, since Robinson fears Banky may turn him down if she knows he is old and a cripple as well. Anxious for a stable home, the waitress accepts the offer, only to be shocked when she discovers the true identity of her admirer. But she learns to love Robinson for his honest and pure heart and soon marries him. A romantic fling with Ames threatens their relationship at one point, but their love for one another is strengthened afterwards. Strong performances by the cast, especially Robinson, who evokes a lot of compassion. Victor Seastrom (Sjostrom) was a prominent Swedish director who did a few American films before he went back to Sweden. His American masterpiece was THE WIND (1928) with Lillian Gish.

d, Victor Seastrom; w, Sidney Howard (based on the play "They Knew What They Wanted" by Howard); ph, Merritt B. Gerstad; ed, Conrad A. Nervig, Leslie Wilder.

Drama (PR:A MPAA:NR)

LADY TUBBS**

(1935) 66m UNIV bw (GB: THE GAY LADY)

Alice Brady *(Henrietta "Mom" Tubbs)*, Douglass Montgomery *(Phil Ash-Orcutt)* Anita Louise *(Wynne Howard)*, Alan Mowbray *(Elyot Wembsleigh)*, Minor Watson *(Fishbaker)*, Russell Hicks *(Mr. Ash-Orcutt)*, Hedda Hopper *(Mrs. Ash-Orcutt)*, June Clayworth *(Jean LaGendre)*, Lumsden Hare *(Lord Abernathy)*, Harry Tyler *(Elmer)*, Walter Brennan *(Joseph)*, Rafael Storm *(Rinaldo)*, Mildred Harris, Mary Carewe, Phyllis Brooks, Mary Wallace, Virginia Hammond, Walter Lang, Pat O'Malley, Victor Potel, Perry Ivins, Sam McDaniel.

Social farce has Brady as a cook at a railroad construction site who becomes engaged to the wealthy Montgomery. With her new position in society, Brady exposes the shallowness of the upper class. Good performances help to gloss over the weaknesses in the story. Brady, who played comedy in films, spent much of her career performing tragedy on stage.

p, Lou Ostrow; d, Alan Crosland; w, Barry Trivers (based on the novel by Homer Croy); ph, Norbert Brodine; ed, Murray Seldeen.

Comedy (PR:A MPAA:NR)

LADY VANISHES, THE*****

(1938, Brit.) 97m GAU/Gainsborough/MGM bw

Margaret Lockwood *(Iris Henderson)*, Michael Redgrave *(Gilbert Redman)*, Paul Lukas *(Dr. Hartz)*, Dame May Whitty *(Miss Froy)*, Cecil Parker *(Eric Todhunter)*, Linden Travers *(Margaret Todhunter)*, Mary Clare *(Baroness)*, Naunton Wayne *(Caldicott)*, Basil Radford *(Charters)*, Emile Boreo *(Hotel Manager)*, Philip Leaver *(Signor Doppo)*, Zelma Vas Dias *(Signora Doppo)*, Catharine Lacey *(The Nun)*, Josephine Wilson *(Mme. Kummer)*, Googie Withers *(Blanche)*, Sally Stewart *(Julie)*, Charles Oliver *(Officer)*, Kathleen Tremaine.

Hitchcock suspends plausibility here for the sake of a fascinating story and characters everyone dreams of meeting on a train trip but without the hazards so expertly and chillingly presented in THE LADY VANISHES. The film opens in a resort town somewhere in the Balkans as a young English girl, Lockwood, nears the end of her vacation. The town is temporarily cut off from the outside world by an avalanche that has blocked the railroad. Passengers enter an inn looking for rooms which are in short supply. Lockwood is returning to London to wed an office worker, a prospect she does not particularly relish; she tells her friends, "I've been everywhere and done everything . . . what's left for me except marriage?" Other guests include an English politician, Parker, and his mistress, Travers, a pair of English gentlemen, Wayne and Radford, who are cricket fanatics and only concern themselves with getting back to England to see an important up-coming match, a musician, Redgrave, who is studying local mountain ballads, and a kindly grand-mother type, Whitty. When Whitty dines with Wayne and Radford she explains that she's a retired governess on holiday. When she hears a native singing outside, Whitty excuses herself and goes to her room where she listens to the singer, methodically counting out bars of music as he sings them. She's interrupted by a loud banging overhead and goes into the hall where she meets Lockwood, who has the room next door and is also annoyed at the banging. She complains to the manager, Boreo, who goes to Redgrave's room to find him with some native dancers performing clog dances so he can record the ritual. When Redgrave proves truculent, Lockwood pays Boreo to evict the musician. She later changes her mind when Redgrave confronts her. Meanwhile, Whitty continues listening to the local singer, strangely counting the beats of his song, then tosses him a coin from her window. The next day the train tracks are cleared of snow and the passengers board the transcontinental express. Lockwood sees Whitty struggling with her bags and leans over to help her; just then a flower pot drops from a balcony and strikes Lockwood on the head but it appears that the pot was meant for the old lady. Waving goodbye to her friends from the train, Lockwood is apparently in pain and has blurry vision for a moment. She and Whitty sit in the same compartment with other strangers, then go to the dining car for a cup of tea. When in the dining car, Whitty hands a tin of her own tea to the waiter and asks that he make her tea with her own brand. She introduces herself but the train goes over a bridge and the noise drowns out her words so she writes her name "Froy" on the window, outlining the letters on the condensation gathered there. Returning to the compartment, Lockwood goes to sleep. When she awakens and finds that Whitty is not there, she asks the other passengers in the compartment where the English lady has gone and they tell her that "there has been no English lady here." Lockwood is flabbergasted. Whitty's valise is gone. She begins to search the train but stewards, waiters, porters, and conductors have no record of Whitty's existence on the train. Lockwood finds Redgrave in the third class car watching native dancers perform and seeks his help. "If I thought you were going to be on this train, I'd have stayed another week in the hotel," he tells her. Lockwood explains that Whitty is missing and he helps search the train for her. Lukas, a wealthy doctor, offers his help but can recall no English lady. Clare, a baroness, also has not seen Whitty. Parker is approached but denies seeing her, too. "But you must have," Lockwood reminds him, "she almost fell into your compartment." He insists he hasn't seen her, then retreats nervously into his compartment where Travers is reading a magazine; their compartment, like their lives, is sealed off, the blinds pulled. Later Lukas suggests that Lockwood is suffering from a concussion after having been hit on the head with the pot and that she is hallucinating, that Whitty is most probably a figment of her imagination. The train makes a stop and Redgrave and Lockwood watch both sides of the train to see if Whitty gets off. She does not, but Lukas receives a patient on a stretcher which is put into his compartment. Meanwhile, Parker makes evasive remarks when Travers asks him when he will divorce his wife in England; he muses about his being made a judge. He then tells Travers that he would not admit to seeing Whitty because, if there were some trouble, they might have to testify as witnesses and their secret liaison would be revealed. Travers, angry at being treated like a scarlet woman, boldly steps into the corridor to tell Lockwood and Redgrave that she indeed did see Whitty pass her compartment with Lockwood. Lukas then introduces another woman, a foreigner, to Lockwood, one who is wearing the exact clothes Whitty wore when last seen by Lockwood. Lukas tells her she's still suffering from the head blow and that her subconscious substituted Whitty's face for the woman who is dressed like Whitty. Travers then sees the foreign woman and identifies her as the woman she saw with Lockwood. Travers hesitates, however, when making this statement and Lockwood later tells Redgrave that "she was lying, they're all lying." Redgrave, supportive but disbelieving, takes Lockwood to the dining car where he tells her about himself; he's obviously attracted to her and asks: "Do you like me?" "Not much," Lockwood replies perfunctorily. He plunges on, trying to make small talk. Then, just as the train begins to enter the tunnel, Lockwood notices the name "Froy" which Whitty had written on the window. Lockwood appears to get hysterical, loudly asking everyone to help her find the missing Whitty. When conductors try to subdue her, Lockwood runs to an emergency handle, pulls it, and stops the train. She passes out, later waking in her compartment with Lukas telling Redgrave that she is ill and he must look after her. Then Redgrave takes Lockwood into the corridor and tells her he believes her, that he's just seen the packet of tea Whitty gave the waiter. They begin to search the train, going to the baggage car where they find magician's equipment belonging to "The Great Doppo," one of the passengers in Lockwood's compartment (Leaver), along with a "disappearing cabinet" with a false back. While searching about, Lockwood finds Whitty's spectacles. Leaver arrives and demands the spectacles be given to him, that they are his. He and Redgrave struggle. Leaver pulls a knife and Lockwood bites his hand so he drops it and then Redgrave knocks Leaver out and puts him into one of the magician's chests, locking him in. They later go to Lukas' compartment and attempt to inspect the patient who is wrapped in bandages from head to foot. The nun, Lacey, attending the patient, does not respond when Redgrave asks her if she speaks English, French, or German. He leans over to separate the bandages of the patient when Lukas bursts into the compartment and demands to know what they are doing, saying that they are jeopardizing the life of his patient. He regains his composure, ushering them out of the compartment. He tells Redgrave and Lockwood that the nun is deaf and dumb. When Lukas returns to his compartment Lacey yells at him saying that "somebody must have tipped them off!" Redgrave later confronts Lukas in the dining car, asking him about the nun taking care of his patient and saying: "Don't you think it's rather peculiar that she's wearing high heel shoes." Lukas shrugs off the question. He gives them some wine which he has ostensibly drugged. Redgrave asks him if he knows for sure that his real patient is under all those bandages and Lukas promises that he will examine her. He takes the pair to a compartment adjoining his and tells them that, yes, his patient is Whitty, and that she will soon be taken off the train and he will operate on her, clearly meaning that he means to kill her. When Redgrave makes a move, he spots Lukas' gun which is aimed at them. Lukas admits that he is a part of "this conspiracy as you term it." He then tells them he has drugged their drinks and they will soon be unconscious, adding that he has been kind enough not to overdose them since a larger dosage would render them insane. Lockwood and Redgrave fall unconscious and Lukas leaves. But the couple have only been pretending and are soon breathing cool air from the open window. Redgrave then climbs outside the train and works his way to Lukas' compartment where he begins to remove the bandages from the patient. Lacey tells him "Go on, it is Miss Froy. You needn't worry. You haven't been drugged. He told me to put something in your drinks but I didn't do it." A woman conspirator enters the compartment and Redgrave substitutes her for Whitty whom he frees. Then, with Lacey resuming her vigil, Redgrave and Lockwood go back to the other compartment and pretend to be unconscious. The train halts at a station and the bandaged conspirator is taken off and put into an ambulance, Lukas going with her. He removes the bandages to find he has the wrong woman. He gets back on the train and informs the magician who has freed himself and the baroness that they must kill Whitty *and* Lockwood and Redgrave. Meanwhile, Redgrave discovers that the part of the train they are riding in has been detached and is being hauled along a branch line. He confronts Whitty, asking what and who she is and why she has gotten them all into so much trouble. She sputters that she's only a governess. They go to the dining car since "it's tea time and all the English will be there." In the dining car Redgrave explains the abduction and how the train is heading into danger, asking all for their help. The train stops in a wooded area. Lacey, the nun, staggers into the dining car. Then an officer gets on the train and politely asks them all to get off and get into the cars waiting outside. They refuse and Redgrave knocks out the officer. The officers outside with Lukas begin shooting at the train and Redgrave, using the officer's gun, fires back. Parker turns coward and tries to surrender under a white flag but is killed. Whitty takes Redgrave and Lockwood aside and tells them she must get away, she must deliver an urgent message to the foreign office at Whitehall in London. "Then you are a spy," Lockwood says. "I've always thought that was such a grim word," replies Whitty. She entrusts them with the message in case she does not get through, telling them they must remember "a tune that contains, in code, of course, a vital clause of a secret pact between two European countries. I want you to memorize it." She hums the tune to musician Redgrave. Then she slips off the train and disappears into the forest. Redgrave manages to get the engine moving and the train heads for the border with the military cars chasing it, Lukas and cronies firing at the moving train which reaches the border and chugs on to safety, leaving the foreign agents behind. When Redgrave and Lockwood reach London it's clear they will be together. Redgrave and Lockwood are later shown at the foreign office in London. They tell officials they are there to deliver an important message. Just then they hear the familiar tune being played on a piano and they walk into a room where Whitty sits at a piano, playing the vital song and its secret message. She smiles widely at her two young benefactors, reaching out for them, taking them gratefully into her arms. This clever, quick-paced spy classic was Hitchcock's most famous and celebrated British film and brought him to the attention of Hollywood. He would finish one more film in England, JAMAICA INN, before moving to the U.S. to make the rest of his films for American companies, his first being REBECCA in 1940 for Selznick International. THE LADY VANISHES was extremely popular in the U.S. and set the style for many a Hitchcock thriller to come. The cast performs marvelously, particularly Whitty, Redgrave, and Lockwood. The role of a disarming little old lady playing a spy was acted with unexpected shrewdness by Whitty but it was Hitchcock who really brought this veteran actress out of her comfortable cocoon. The venerable old lady was well into her first scene when Hitchcock ran screaming onto the set, shouting: "Stop! That's terrible! Aren't you ashamed of yourself?" This shock treatment caused Whitty to inject a great deal of vitality into the part. Such abrasive techniques were part of Hitchcock's methodology with actors. He later confided to producer Black: "Break them down right at the start. It's much the best way." Hitchcock and Redgrave did not get along in the production. Redgrave thought of himself as a theatrical actor, and was reluctant from the beginning to make the movie (one which made him an international star). He insisted upon having extensive rehearsals for his scenes which irritated Hitchcock. After one brief rehearsal for the first scene, Hitchcock announced to Redgrave that he was ready to shoot. The startled Redgrave blurted: "In the theater we'd have three weeks to rehearse this." Snorted Hitchcock: "I'm sorry. In this medium we have three minutes!" Throughout the production the actor and director matched temperaments, with Hitchcock getting the best of their little confrontations. Hitchcock, at one point, said to Redgrave: "You know, don't you, that Robert Donat wanted to play this role in the worst way?" Redgrave should have known better than to challenge Hitchcock; he had seen this single-minded genius in action before when playing a bit part in Hitchcock's SECRET AGENT (1936). Redgrave would later complain bitterly about Hitchcock not being "an actor's director" (whatever that might be, most likely a Robert Altman type who allows the actors to do whatever they feel with their parts). Yet, Redgrave, one of the finest actors in British films, was undoubtedly speaking while chewing on sour grapes and the memory of having been put in his place. The director's casting instincts were right on target here (as they usually were). He put two straight character actors, Wayne and Radford, into the roles of the cricket-obsessed Englishmen, men who had seldom played comedy, and they proved hilarious. The first 20 minutes of THE LADY VANISHES offer a slow pace but adroitly set up the accelerated speed of the story, just like a train getting up steam. Clearly, Hitchcock's imprint was everywhere in the film, particularly his ability to properly manipulate his actors to the story's needs. After finishing this classic spy thriller, Hitchcock was ready for Hollywood and its most boisterous vain stars, not one of whom would ever intimidate this master filmmaker. THE LADY VANISHES had a wide-ranging effect on young filmmakers of the time, not the least of whom was Orson Welles who reportedly saw this film 11 times. Writer James Thurber, another report had it, went Welles two times better. THE LADY VANISHES received the 1938 New York Critic's Award and Hitchcock was also selected as Best Director for the same film by that august group.

p, Edward Black; d, Alfred Hitchcock; w, Alma Reville, Sidney Gilliat, Frank Launder (based on the novel *The Wheel Spins* by Ethel Lina White); ph, Jack Cox; m, Louis Levy; ed, Alfred Roome, R. E. Dearing; set d, Alex Vetchinsky, Maurice Carter, Albert Jullion.

Spy Drama **Cas.** **(PR:A MPAA:NR)**

LADY VANISHES, THE*1/2   (1980, Brit.) 99m Hammer/RANK-Group I c

Elliot Gould (Robert Condon), Cybill Shepherd (Amanda Kelly), Angela Lansbury (Miss Froy), Herbert Lom (Dr. Hartz), Arthur Lowe (Charters), Ian Carmichael (Caldicott), Gerald Harper (Mr. Todhunter), Jean Anderson (Baroness Kisling), Jenny Runacre (Mrs. Todhunter), Vladek Sheybal (Trainmaster), Madlena Nedeva (Nun), Wolf Kahler (Helmut), Madge Ryan (Rose Flood-Porter), Rosalind Knight (Mrs. Barnes), Jonathan Hackett (Waiter), Barbara Markham (Mme. Kummer), Hillevi (Maid's Daughter), Garry McDermott (Manservant), Jacki Harding (Maid).

This remake of the 1930s Hitchcock thriller is a far cry from its predecessor, lacking in the styles and subtleties of humor the master was able to evoke. Lansbury plays the nanny who mysteriously disappears while on board a European passenger train. Gould and Shepherd are the couple who search for the missing lady, uncovering a German plot and falling in love in the process. Flat direction to a cast, most of whom are hard to take seriously, creates a mishmash of styles somewhere between comedy and suspense. The scenic photography is the film's best offering. Shepherd is terrible and Gould not much better.

p, Tom Sachs; d, Anthony Page; w, George Axelrod (based on the novel by Ethel Lina White); ph, Douglas Slocombe (Panavision); m, Richard Hartley; ed, Russell Lloyd; prod d, Wilfred Shingleton; art d, Bill Alexander, George von Kieseritzky; cos, Emma Porteus.

Drama   (PR:C MPAA:PG)

LADY WANTS MINK, THE*1/2   (1953) 92m REP c

Dennis O'Keefe (Jim Connors), Ruth Hussey (Nora Connors), Eve Arden (Gladys Jones), William Demarest (Harvey Jones), Gene Lockhart (Mr. Heggie), Hope Emerson (Mrs. Hoxie), Hillary Brooke (Mrs. Cantrell), Tommy Rettig (Ritchie Connors), Earl Robie (Sandy Connors), Mary Field (Janie), Isabel Randolph (Mrs. Frazier), Thomas Browne Henry (Mr. Swiss), Brad Johnson (Bud Dunn), Mara Corday (Model), Robert Shayne (Cecil), Jean Fenwick (Faye), Jean Vachon (Doris), Vici Raaf (Daisy), Mary Alan Hokanson (Marian), Angela Greene (Marge), Barbara Billingsley (Phyllis), Arthur Walsh (Motorcycle Postman), Howard J. Negley (Mr. Binyon), Max Wagner (Mr. Benson), Rodney Bell (Dave), Joseph Mell (Ralph), Sydney Mason (Newton), Frank Gerstle (Frank-Office Worker), Wayne Tredway (Mr. Murdock), Bobby Diamond (Melvin Potts), Dennis Ross (Augie), Gail Bonney (Landlady), Wade Crosby, Slim Duncan, Michael Barton (Movers).

This satire on mink crazy women has Hussey as a housewife whose husband, O'Keefe, can't afford to buy her a mink coat, so she actually tries to grow one of her own. In the process, her family is kicked out of their home by an irate landlady and forced to move out to the country. To top matters off, O'Keefe loses his job. When given the chance to move back to the city, however, the family refuses, preferring their new country life. Thin plot line is hampered by a script which doesn't manage to get the laughs across.

p&d, William A. Seiter; w, Dane Lussier, Richard Alan Simmons (based on a story by Leonard Neubauer, Lou Schor); ph, Reggie Lanning (Trucolor); m, Stanley Wilson; ed, Fred Allen; art d, Martin Obzina.

Comedy   (PR:A MPAA:NR)

LADY WHO DARED, THE*   (1931) 55m FN-WB bw

Billie Dove (Margaret Townsend), Sidney Blackmer (Charles Townsend), Conway Tearle (Jack Norton), Judith Vosselli (Julianne Boone-Fleming), Cosmo Kyrle Bellew (Seton Boone Fleming), Lloyd Ingraham (Farrell), Ivan Simpson (Butler), Mathilde Comont (Chambermaid).

Tearle is a South American diamond smuggler involved in a blackmail scheme centering around some pictures of a consulate's wife, Dove. In the final showdown, Tearle decides he can't go through with the plan. Lifeless performances are added to a script which relies heavily upon words instead of realistic portrayals.

d, William Beaudine; w, Forrest Halsey, Kathryn Scola (based on the story "Devil's Playground" by Kenneth J. Saunders); ph, Tony Gaudio; ed, LeRoy Stone.

Drama   (PR:A MPAA:NR)

LADY WINDERMERE'S FAN   (SEE; FAN, THE, 1949)

LADY WITH A LAMP, THE***
          (1951, Brit.) 110m Imperadio/BL bw (AKA: THE LADY WITH THE LAMP)

Anna Neagle (Florence Nightingale), Michael Wilding (Sidney Herbert), Gladys Young (Mrs. Bracebridge), Felix Aylmer (Lord Palmerston), Julian D'Albie (Mr. Bracebridge), Arthur Young (W. E. Gladstone), Edwin Styles (Mr. Nightingale), Helen Shingler (Parthenope Nightingale), Rosalie Crutchley (Mrs. Sidney Herbert), Maureen Pryor (Sister Wheeler), Mary MacKenzie (Nurse Johnson), Henry Edwards (Howard Russell), Andrew Osborn (Dr. Sutherland), Clement McCallin (Richard M. Milnes), Helena Pickard (Queen Victoria), Peter Graves (Prince Albert), Dame Sybil Thorndike (Miss Bosanquet), Monckton Hoffe (Lord Stratford), Cecil Trouncer (Sir Douglas Dawson), Barbara Couper (Mrs. Nightingale), Colin Gordon, Gordon Jackson, Charles Carson, Leslie Weston, Nigel Stock, Michael Brennan, Edie Martin, Peter Hobbes, Liam Gaffney, Ann Codrington, Betty Cooper, Edward Lexy, John Vere, Olive Bonham-Carter, Basil Dignam, Florence Nightingale Allebeury.

Romanticized version of Florence Nightingale's successful fight for sanitary medical treatment during the Crimean War. This version concentrates upon the political complexities the hard-headed nurse, played by Neagle, had to battle with. The cast gives fine impressions of the many historical personalities. The contrast of settings between stately British homes and the squalor of the hospital focuses the viewer's attentions on what the real battles were. Notable mention should be given to Lewthwaite's editing of the war sequences.

p&d, Herbert Wilcox; w, Warren Chetham Strode (based on the play by Reginald Berkeley); ph, Max Greene [Mutz Greenbaum]; m, Anthony Collins; ed, Bill Lewthwaite.

Biography   (PR:A MPAA:NR)

LADY WITH A PAST**   (1932) 70m RKO-Pathe bw (GB: REPUTATION)

Constance Bennett (Venice Muir), Ben Lyon (Guy Bryson), David Manners (Donnie Wainwright), Don Alvarado (The Argentine), Albert Conti (Rene), Merna Kennedy (Ann Duryea), Blanche Frederici (Nora), John Roche (Karl), Nella Walker (Aunt Emma), Astrid Allwyn (Lola), Helene Millard (Mrs. Bryson), Donald Dillaway (Jerry), Freeman Wood (Patterson), Cornelius Keefe (Spaulding), George Irving (Mr. Patridge), Arnold Lucy (Butler), Bruce Cabot (Dance Extra), Don Terry (Friend), Bill Elliott (Brown).

Farce has Bennett as a bashful, but beautiful, young girl, unhappy with her uneventful love life. Wishing to improve matters, she hires a private escort, Lyon, and skips off to Europe. She is so successful at projecting the image of a femme fatale that she is written up on the scandal page of a Parisian newspaper. The somewhat flimsy script is helped somewhat by the well-paced direction. Bennett looks wonderful in an array of extravagant gowns.

p, Charles Rogers, Harry Joe Brown; d, Edward H. Griffith; w, Horace Jackson (based on the story by Harriet Henry); ph, Hal Mohr; ed, Charles Craft.

Comedy/Romance   (PR:A MPAA:NR)

LADY WITH RED HAIR**   (1940) 78m WB bw

Miriam Hopkins (Mrs. Leslie Carter), Claude Rains (David Belasco), Richard Ainley (Lou Payne), John Litel (Charles Bryant), Laura Hope Crews (Mrs. Dudley), Helen Westley (Mrs. Frazier), Mona Barrie (Mrs. Brooks), Victor Jory (George Clifton), Fritz Leiber (Mr. Foster), Cecil Kellaway (Mr. Chapman), Florence Shirley (Daisy Dawn), Johnny Russell (Dudley Carter), Halliwell Hobbes (Judge), Selmer Jackson (Henry De Mille), William Davidson (Stock Company Manager), Doris Lloyd (Teacher), Thomas Jackson (Mr. Harper), Alexis Smith (Girl at Wedding), William Hopper (Theater Attendant), Creighton Hale (Eddie the Reporter), Maurice Cass (Scenic Artist), Russell Hicks (Host), Cyril Ring (Playwright), Huntley Gordon (Actor Playing John), Maris Wrixon (Miss Annie Ellis), Cornel Wilde (Mr. Williams), Helene Millard (Mrs. Ballard), Paul Stanton (Mr. Winter), John Hamilton (Mr. Graham), Frank Wilcox (Mr. Lynn), Virginia Brissac (Mrs. Humbert), John Ridgely (Actor Playing Paul).

Based on the true story inspired by the memoirs of little-known stage actress Leslie Carter is this touching story of a woman (Hopkins), divorced from her husband and separated from her son, who devotes her entire life to the stage. Her only goal is to regain her lost child by the wealth and fame she hopes to achieve. Through her constant efforts at approaching the famous producer Belasco (Rains) for a job, she eventually gets a part. Though her first show flops, the work and persistence of the producer enables her to star in several triumphant successes. After deciding that her son is lost to her forever she remarries. Though both the script and direction are a bit heavy-handed, the cast still manages to deliver some top-rate performances.

p, Jack L. Warner, Edmund Grainger; d, Kurt Bernhardt; w, Charles Kenyon, Milton Krims (based on the story "Portrait of a Lady with Red Hair" by N. Brewster Morse, Norbert Faulkner); ph, Arthur Edeson; m, Heinz Roemheld; ed, James Gibbon; md, Leo F. Forbstein; art d, Max Parker; cos, Milo Anderson.

Drama   (PR:A MPAA:NR)

LADY WITH THE DOG, THE**1/2
          (1962, USSR) 86m Lenfilm/Artkino bw (DAMA S SOBACHKOY)

Iya Savvina (Anna Sergeyovna), Aleksi Batalov (Dmitriy Gurov), Nina Alisova (Madame Gurov), Pyotr Krymov (von Didenitz), Dmitriy Zebrov (Frolov), Marya Safonova (Natasha), Yuriy Medvedev, T. Rozanov, Yuriy Svirin, Vladimir Erenberg, G. Barysheva, K. Gun, Z. Dorogova, M. Ivanov, G. Kurovskiy, S. Mazovetskaya, A. Orlov, P. Pervushin, L. Stepanov.

Batalov is a middle-aged Moscow banker during the early 1900s who meets the beautiful young Savvina on a vacation in Yalta. He becomes obsessed with this woman, while watching her walk her dog each day. Eventually they are involved in a serious affair, although both are married. When he returns to Moscow, the thought of Savvina still lingers. They engage in a number of rendezvous and realizing that they cannot go public with their love, they decide to continue on in secret brief encounters.

d&w, Iosif Kheyfits (based on a story by Anton Pavlovich Chekhov); ph, Andrey Moskvin, Dmitriy Meskhiyev; m, N. Simonyan; ed, Y. Bazhenova; art d, B. Manevich, I. Kaplan.

Drama   (PR:A MPAA:NR)

LADY WITH THE LAMP, THE
          (SEE: LADY WITH A LAMP, THE, 1951, Brit.)

LADY WITHOUT PASSPORT, A**   (1950) 72m MGM bw

Hedy Lamarr (Marianne Lorress), John Hodiak (Pete Karczag), James Craig (Frank Westlake), George Macready (Palinov), Steven Geray (Frenchman), Bruce Cowling (Archer Delby James), Nedrick Young (Harry Nordell), Steven Hill (Jack), Robert Osterloh (Lt. Lannahan), Trevor Bardette (Lt. Carfagno), Charles Wagenheim (Ramon Santez), Renzo Cesana (A. Sestina), Esther Zeitlin (Beryl Sandring), Carlo Tricoli (Mr. Sandring), Marta Mitrovitch (Elizabeth Alonescu), Don Garner (Dimitri Matthias), Richard Crane (Navy Flyer), Nita Bieber (Dancer), Martin Garralaga (Police Officer), Mario Siletti (Cafe Owner).

So-so picture with few thrills. Lamarr is a beautiful refugee and the U.S. government has a plan to stop illegal aliens from coming into the country. Heading up the effort is Hodiak, who pretends to be Hungarian and is apparently trying to make his way into the U.S. without a passport through Cuba. He gets involved with Lamarr and convinces her to work with him uncovering the racket. Macready is the villain behind the smuggling and Lamarr maneuvers her way into his inner sanctum. Once Macready realizes the Feds are on to him, he tries to escape with Lamarr and takes her north, in a light plane to Florida. The main problem is that he doesn't know how to fly and neither does she! They crash-land in the Everglades and he is shot and killed and she is rescued. This is an attempt at film noir but doesn't have enough noir to make it a film. The subject of illegal aliens was handled far better and much more excitingly by MGM when they did BORDER INCIDENT the year before. Hodiak was pleasant but never an exciting actor. Macready was his usual evil self but Lamarr needed better support in order to score and the result was an unintended B movie, produced by a man who had specialized in B movies but managed to overcome short budgets in the past and present such winners as LASSIE COME HOME.

p, Samuel Marx; d, Joseph H. Lewis; w, Howard Dimsdale, Cyril Hume (based on the story by Lawrence Taylor); ph, Paul C. Vogel; m, David Raksin; ed, Frederick Y. Smith; art d, Cedric Gibbons, Edward Carfagno.

Crime Drama **PR:A MPAA:NR)**

LADY WITHOUT CAMELLIAS, THE***

(1981, Ital.) 105m ENIC-Italtoons bw (LA SIGNORA SENZA CAMELIE; AKA: CAMILLE WITHOUT CAMILLIAS)

Lucia Bose *(Clara Manni)*, Andrea Cecchi *(Gianni Franchi)*, Gino Cervi *(Ercole "Ercolino")*, Ivan Desny *(Nardo Rusconi)*, Alain Cuny *(Lodi)*, Monica Clay *(Simonetta)*, Anna Carena *(Clara's Mother)*, Enrico Glori *(Director)*, Laura Tiberti, Oscar Andriani, Elio Steiner, Nino Del Fabbro.

An early feature from Antonioni released in the U.S. 28 years later, which again displays his interest in alienating a character from his or her surroundings. Here Bose is a working-class girl from Milan who is put into a low-budget film only to be catapulted to stardom by an image-making producer (Cecchi) who prefers to see her playing Joan of Arc. A marriage to Cecchi fails, as does their version of JOAN OF ARC, and a relationship with Desny, a diplomat with whom she's fallen in love. She soon finds that her stardom will come from the immoral, second-rate films representative of her working-class upbringing and not from "decent films" and fur coats. Antonioni, however, is again plagued by the same chronic miscasting that has tumbled some of his other films—David Hemmings in BLOW-UP and Steve Cochran in IL GRIDO—this time by trying to pass off the glamorous, sophisticated Bose as a peasant girl alienated from the upper class. (In Italian; English subtitles.)

p, Domenico Forges Davanzati; d, Michelangelo Antonioni; w, Antonioni, Suso Cecchi D'Amico, Francesco Maselli, P. M. Pasinetti (based on a story by Antonioni); ph, Enzo Serafin; m, Giovanni Fusco; set d, Gianni Polidori.

Drama **(PR:C-O MPAA:NR)**

LADYBUG, LADYBUG 1/2** (1963) 81m Francis/UA bw

Jane Connell *(Mrs. Maxton)*, William Daniels *(Mr. Calkins)*, James Frawley *(Truck Driver)*, Richard Hamilton *(JoAnn's Father)*, Kathryn Hays *(Mrs. Forbes)*, Jane Hoffman *(Mrs. Hayworth)*, Elena Karam *(Don and Trudy's Mother)*, Judith Lowry *(Luke's Grandmother)*, Nancy Marchand *(Mrs. Andrews)*, Estelle Parsons *(JoAnn's Mother)*, Doug Chapin *(Gary)*, Miles Chapin *(Joel)*, Bozo Dell *(Peter)*, Dianne Higgins *(Jill)*, Alan Howard *(Luke)*, Christopher Howard *(Steve)* David Komoroff *(Don)*, Donnie Melvin *(Brian)*, Susan Melvin *(Trudy)*, Linda Meyer *(JoAnn)*, Alice Playten *(Harriet)*, Marilyn Rogers *(Sarah)*, Jennifer Stone *(Pattie)*.

Based upon a true incident which occurred during the 1962 Cuban missile crisis, this terrifying account of life under the fear of nuclear war successfully illustrates the harm undue panic and thoughtlessness can provoke. Made on a shoestring budget, this is the story of a school where an air-raid warning accidently goes off. When the children are directed to go home, one 12-year old (Playten) invites several of her friends to stay in the air-raid shelter at her home. When another girl asks for admittance to the shelter, she is denied by Playten who insists there is not enough food to go around. The forsaken girl runs to find a hiding space and locks herself in an abandoned refrigerator where she suffocates. Though unevenly directed, the main emphasis of the film shines through very strongly. The children in this film are the highlights of the cast, giving a much more realistic portrayal than the adults involved. This was producer-director Perry's first film since his successful DAVID AND LISA.

p&d, Frank Perry; w, Eleanor Perry (based on an article by Lois Dickert); ph, Leonard Hirshfield; m, Robert Cohert; ed, Armond Lebowitz, Edith Hamlin; md, Cobert; art d, Albert Brenner; cos, Anna Hill Johnstone.

Drama **(PR:C MPAA:NR)**

LADYKILLERS, THE****

(1956, Brit.) 96m Ealing/CD c (AKA: THE LADY KILLERS)

Alec Guinness *(Professor Marcus)*, Cecil Parker *(The Mayor)*, Herbert Lom *(Louis)*, Peter Sellers *(Harry)*, Danny Green *(One-Round)*, Jack Warner *(Police Superintendent)*, Katie Johnson *(Mrs. Wilberforce)*, Philip Stainton *(Police Sergeant)*, Frankie Howard *(Barrow Boy)*, Fred Griffiths *(The Junkman)*, Kenneth Connor *(The Cab Driver)*, Edie Martin *(Lettice)*, Jack Melford *(Detective)*, Phoebe Hodgson *(4th Guest)*, Helen Burls *(Hypatia)*, Ewan Roberts *(Constable)*, Harold Goodwin *(Parcels Clerk)*, Leonard Sharp *(Pavement Artist)*, Stratford Johns *(Security Guard)*, Sam Kydd, Evelyn Kerry, Neil Wilson, Michael Corcoran, Robert Moore, John Rudling, Madge Brindley, Lucy Griffiths, Peter Williams, George Roderick.

British comedies are most successful when they are dark. The Anglo culture appears to be fascinated by the gangster mentality and many of their best comedies have been about the workings of the criminal mind. THE LADYKILLERS is a perfect example of the fun that Ealing had when delving into the world of the lawless. Guinness is a professor, a strange and quirky man who rents a room at the home of a dotty old woman, Johnson (who won a British Film Academy Award for this role). She is somewhat suspicious but lets him have the lodgings when he tells her that he is a musician and he will be practicing with his group in the house. Parker, Lom, Sellers, and Green are the others in the gang and they gather regularly at the house, but it's not to play Bach. They're in the midst of planning a daring robbery that will set them all up for life. They practice their music (using recordings to fool Johnson) and she is always bursting in on them with tea and various little goodies. The robbery takes place and they nab about 60,000 pounds which they place in a large trunk and check at the railway station. Rather than take a chance themselves, the crooks send Johnson to the station to get the loot in a cab. There's a bit of business with a street fight and Johnson is brought home with a police escort. The gang thinks they are going to have to silence the babbling old woman but none of them wants to do the dirty deed. They fear that she will inadvertently blurt something to the cops that will render them poundless and encaged for the rest of their natural lives. Even after drawing lots, none of them can bring himself to kill her. They try to get out of town and in a macabre (and funny) series of events, each member of the gang is killed until Guinness is the lone survivor and he's done in at a railway signal while trying to dispose of the last corpse. All of the deaths are in fun and never lower the levity of the piece (as in KIND HEARTS AND CORONETS, 1949). Johnson, it seems, has always been regaling the local constabulary with tall tales and when she goes to them with the money in hand to set the record straight, they don't believe her. Now thousands of pounds richer, Johnson shrugs and exits the police station, then gives a huge banknote to a passing hobo as the film ends. Johnson had many years in show business before finally achieving the award. She died two years later and this was a most fitting bow-off. Sellers is young and pudgy in this film and had not yet perfected the comic skills that became his trademark. Rose's script won an Oscar nomination and he went on to write many more comedies, most notably IT'S A MAD (4) WORLD with his wife, Tania. This was rare for another reason: it's one of the few 1950s comedies made in color. This was the last of the famed Ealing Studios comedy films; the studios were in the process of closing down by the time of the picture's British release in 1955. It was a fitting tribute to the great studios.

p, Seth Holt; d, Alexander Mackendrick; w, William Rose (based on his story); ph, Otto Heller (Technicolor); m, Tristram Cary; ed, Jack Harris; art d, Jim Morahan.

Crime Comedy **Cas.** **(PR:A-C MPAA:NR)**

LADY'S FROM KENTUCKY, THE** (1939) 67m PAR bw

George Raft *(Marty Black)*, Ellen Drew *(Penelope "Penny" Hollis)*, Hugh Herbert *(Mousey Johnson)*, ZaSu Pitts *(Dulcey Lee)*, Louise Beavers *(Aunt Tina)*, Lew Payton *(Sixty)*, Forrester Harvey *(Nonny Watkins)*, Harry Tyler *(Carter)*, Edward J. Pawley *(Spike Cronin)*, Gilbert Emery *(Pinckney Rodell)*, Jimmy Bristow *(Brewster)*, Mickey O'Boyle *(Roman Boy)*, Mike Arnold *(Cantankerous)*, Kentucky Lady *(Foal)*, Eugene Jackson *(Winfield)*, George Anderson *(Joe Lane)*, Stanley Andrews *(Doctor)*, Nell Craig, Carol Holloway *(Nurses in Corridor)*, Hooper Atchley *(Surgeon)*, Fern Emmett *(Attending Nurse)*, Roger Gray *(Waiter)*, Virginia Sale *(Cashier)*, Robert Perry *(Dealer)*, Oscar G. Hendrian, Paul Newlan, John Merton, Robert Stevenson *(Gamblers)*, Frank Moran, Jack Raymond *(Customers)*, Robert Milasch *(Big Longshoreman)*, Harry Tenbrook, George Turner *(Longshoremen)*, Gloria Williams *(Nurse)*, Frankie Van *(Taxi Driver)*, Archie Twitchell *(Radio Announcer)*, Hal K. Dawson, Tom Hanlon *(Announcers)*, William Cartledge *(Jones)*, Charles Trowbridge *(Charles Butler)*, George Melford, Carl Stockdale *(Veterinarians)*, Irving Bacon *(Information Clerk)*, Gus Glassmire *(Pole Judge)*, Charles Wilson, James Flavin *(Men)*, Helaine Moler, Paula De Cardo *(Girls)*.

Horse racing tale, centering on the conflicts between greedy bettors and the welfare of the horses, has Raft as a bookie gone broke with nothing left but partial ownership in a long-shot thoroughbred. The horse proves to be of weak stature but still a good runner. Against the advice of its other owner, Drew, the former bookie prepares the horse to compete in the Kentucky Derby. The horse wins, but is ruined physically by doing so. Competent performances are an asset to the uneven pace of the film.

p, Jeff Lazarus; d, Alexander Hall; w, Malcolm Stuart Boylan (based on the story by Rowland Brown); ph, Theodor Sparkuhl; ed, Harvey Johnson.

Drama **(PR:A MPAA:NR)**

LADY'S MORALS, A*** (1930) 86m COS/MGM bw (GB: JENNY LIND)

Grace Moore *(Jenny Lind)*, Reginald Denny *(Paul Brandt)*, Wallace Beery *(Barnum)*, Gus Shy *(Olaf)*, Gilbert Emery *(Broughm)*, Jobyna Howland *(Josephine)*, George F. Marion *(Innkeeper)*, Paul Porcasi *(Maretti)*, Giovanni Martino *(Zerga)*, Bodil Rosing *(Innkeeper's Wife)*, Joan Standing *(Louise)*, Mavis Villiers *(Selma)*, Judith Vosselli *(Rosatti)*.

Screen version of the life of the famous Swedish opera star Jenny Lind, otherwise known as the "Swedish Nightingale." Moore, of the Metropolitan Opera, portrays the singer in this film which seemed more like an excuse to display the vocal talents of Moore than anything else. There was, however, some room left for the development of a romance between Moore and Denny who pursues the diva from city to city, trying to gain her affection in any manner possible. He eventually does so, but only after the singer has temporarily lost her voice, and he has received a knock on the head which insures his eventual blindness. As expected, the highlight of the film is the singing virtuosity of Moore. Songs include: "Rataplan" from "The Daughter of the Regiment" (Donizetti), "Casta Diva" (from Bellini's "Norma"), "Is It Destiny," "The Student's Song," and "I Hear Your Voice" (Clifford Grey, Oscar Straus), "Oh Why" (Arthur Freed, Herbert Stothart, Henry M. Woods), "Swedish Pastoral" (Howard Johnson, Stothart), "Lovely Hour" (Carrie Jacobs Bond).

d, Sidney Franklin; w, Hans Kraly, Claudine West, John Meehan, Arthur Richman (based on the story by Dorothy Farnum); ph, George Barnes; ed, Margaret Booth; art d, Cedric Gibbons; cos, Adrian; ch, Sammy Lee.

Musical **(PR:A MPAA:NR)**

LADY'S PROFESSION, A*   (1933) 70m PAR bw

Alison Skipworth (Beulah Bonnell), Roland Young (Lord Reginald Withers), Sari Maritza (Cecily Withers), Kent Taylor (Dick Garfield), Roscoe Karns (Tony), Warren Hymer (Bolton), Georgie Barbier (James Garfield), Dewey Robinson (The Colonel), Billy Bletcher, DeWitt Jennings, Edgar Norton, Ethel Griffies, Claudia Braddock, James Burke.

Young plays a British nobleman who comes to America to try to regain his lost fortune. His plan of attack is the opening of a speakeasy during prohibition which serves only ginger ale, but the beverage is spiked by an unhappy racketeer. Cast and direction do well considering the material, which is filled with jokes that miss the mark.

d, Norman McLeod; w, Walter DeLeon, Malcolm Stuart Boylan (based on the story by Nina Wilcox Putnam); ph, Gilbert Warrenton.

Comedy   (PR:A MPAA:NR)

LAFAYETTE*½

(1963, Fr.) 110m Copernic-Cosmos/Maco c (LA FAYETTE; LAFAYETTE (UNA SPADA PER DUE BANDIERE))

Michel Le Royer (Lafayette), Howard St. John (George Washington), Jack Hawkins (Gen. Cornwallis), Wolfgang Preiss (Baron Kalb), Orson Welles (Ben Franklin), Vittorio De Sica (Bancroft), Edmund Purdom (Silas Deane), Pascale Audret (Adrienne Lafayette), Georges Riviere (Vergennes), Liselotte Pulver (Marie Antoinette), Jacques Castelot (Duc d'Ayen), Folco Lulli (Le Boursier), Albert Remy (Louis XVI), Renee Saint-Cyr (Duchesse d'Ayen), Rosanna Schiaffino (Comtesse de Simiane), Henri Amilien (Segur), Gilles Brissac (Monsieur), Roger Bontemps (La Bergerie), Jean-Roger Caussimon (Maurepas), Sylvie Coste (Aglae), Christian Melsen (Gen. Philip), Claude Naudes (Abbe de Cour), Roland Rodier (Mauroy), Rene Rozan (Lauzun), Henri Tisot, Lois Bolton, Jean Degrave, Jean-Jacques Delbo, Michel Galabru, Jean Lanier, Anthony Stuart.

This costume drama, set at the time of the American Revolution, follows a 20-year-old Lafayette (Le Royer) as he travels from his native France to the States-to-be. He aids in the colonial cause and eventually is hired by George Washington (St. John) to bring about the downfall of General Cornwallis (Hawkins). The picture, however, is weighed down by its need for spectacle, and displays little grace in its presentation. It can, at least, boast two of cinema's greatest directors as part of the cast—Welles, doing his best as Ben Franklin, and De Sica. (In French; English subtitles.)

p, Maurice Jacquin; d, Jean Dreville; w, Suzanne Arduini, Jacques Sigurd, Jean-Bernard Luc, Francois Ponthier, Dreville, Jacquin; ph, Claude Renoir, Roger Hubert (Supertechnirama 70, Technicolor); m, Steve Laurent, Pierre Duclos; ed, Rene Le Henaff; art d, Maurice Colasson; set d, Colasson; cos, Jacqueline Guyot, Francoise Tournafond, Leon Zay; spec eff, Bill Warrington; subtitles, John Hunter, Norbert Terry, Robert Braun.

Historical Biography   (PR:AA MPAA:NR)

LAFAYETTE ESCADRILLE**½

(1958) 93m WB-Fr bw (GB: HELL BENT FOR GLORY)

Tab Hunter (Thad Walker), Etchika Choureau (Renee Beaulieu), Bill Wellman, Jr. (Bill Wellman), Jody McCrea (Tom Hitchcock), Dennis Devine (Red Scanlon), Marcel Dalio (Drillmaster), David Janssen ("Duke" Sinclaire), Paul Fix (U.S. General), Veola Vonn (The Madam), Will Hutchins (Dave Putnam), Clint Eastwood (George Moseley), Bob Hover (Dave Judd), Tom Laughlin (Arthur Blumenthal), Brett Halsey (Frank Baylies), Henry Nakamura (Jimmy), Maurice Maraac (Sgt. Parris), Raymond Bailey (Mr. Walker), George Nardelli (Concierge), William A. Wellman, Jr. (Narrator).

This is a disappointing film from a premier director, one which promises epic at the beginning and delivers a soap opera in the middle and a dismal bath of banal tragedy for the finish. Hunter, whose acting efforts have always been, at best, mediocre, is one of many young American volunteers to a French air force group during WW I, known as the Lafayette Escadrille. Most of the beginning deals with the training of the recruits and their difficulties with crude training planes and the French language spoken by their impatient instructors. Hunter, when off duty, meets and falls in love with Choureau, a common streetwalker with some sensitivity; this "poule" quits the oldest profession and takes a job, reforming for Hunter's sake. He is a malcontented young man whose father, he relates while evoking little sympathy, beat him and therefore he resents any kind of authority (which might prompt one to ask why he joined the military in the first place). Strutting, arrogant French officer Dalio, irritated by Hunter's inability to understand his commands, strikes him. Hunter knocks the officer to the ground, a court martial offense. Before he can be jailed, Hunter's pals smuggle him out of camp and he spends a great deal of time hiding out in Paris in his sweetheart's apartment. The bulk of the film dwells on his hiding out in a murky loft. Tragedy comes to Hunter but he later redeems himself serving in the U.S. Air Corps when America comes into the war. There really isn't a lot here. The bloated Hunter segments are downright boring, but Clothier's aerial photography is stunning, what there is of it. One of the best scenes in the movie, near the beginning, shows the young recruits sleeping in makeshift quarters shortly after arrival at the training camp in France. Wellman, whose own son Bill Wellman, Jr. plays his father, then narrates in voice-over what will happen to these brave flying warriors in poignant, memorable lines, dripping with nostalgia and a personal loving memory. Wellman later denounced this film as a failure, stating that he had written the tale as a love story and Warner Bros. insisted on making it into a mini-epic, changing his title from C'EST LA GUERRE to LAFAYETTE ESCADRILLE. In his autobiography, A Short Time For Insanity, Wellman admitted the film collapsed "artistically, financially and spiritually. A bad picture is like a frightful birthmark on your face—it never leaves you, first run, second run, reruns, TV prime time, late time, lousy time; it's always there for people to stare at unbelievingly or turn away

from or, worse still, turn off, or should that be better still? It's your eternal badge of embarrassment."

p&d, William A. Wellman; w, A. S. Fleischman (based on the story "C'est La Guerre" by Wellman); ph, William Clothier; m, Leonard Rosenman; ed, Owen Marks; prod d, Donald A. Peters; art d, John Beckman; set d, Ralph Hurst; cos, Marjorie Best; makeup, Gordon Bau.

Aviation Drama/Romance   (PR:A MPAA:NR)

L'AFRICAN   (SEE: AFRICAN, THE, 1983, Fr.)

L'AGE D'OR****   (1979, Fr.) 60m Corinth bw (AKA: AGE OF GOLD)

Lya Lys (The Woman), Gaston Modot (The Man), Max Ernst (Bandit Chief), Pierre Prevert (Bandit), Caridad de Laberdesque, Lionel Salem, Madame Noizet, Jose Artigas, Jacques Brunius.

One of the most controversial films of all time, L'AGE D'OR— filmed in 1930—is a surrealistic Dadaistic inquiry into the traditions and standards of modern culture that have kept basic and truer passions from being freely expressed. Lys and Modot are the lovers who don't allow anything to keep them from expressing their feelings toward each other. They want to make love, but in order to do so they must overcome a number of seemingly insurmountable obstacles, representatives of the church, bourgeois social etiquette, and their own psychological hamperings. Their love never consummated, Lys is drawn by the music her father is conducting, taking her back to the basic bonds she cannot break. Told in surrealistic images that are incredibly funny, a cow lying on a bed and a frustrated man kicking an obnoxious poodle belonging to a socialite up into the air, to name just two of the many absurd images, the overall desire is to express the power of love at overcoming things placed in its path. During one of L'AGE D'OR's initial showings in Paris, a minor riot broke out in which paintings by artists such as Man Ray, Max Ernst, and Dali were destroyed. This eventually led to the picture being banned, but not before enough people saw it to create heated arguments printed up in both the left- and right-wing newspapers. Although Salvador Dali is credited with having collaborated on the script, this is really Bunuel's film, with only one of Dali's sequences actually being used. Many of the themes which were to appear throughout Bunuel's films first appeared here, in some instances as many as 30 years prior to the later works. L'AGE D'OR is most definitely a classic of sorts and a film that should be studied by any individual interested in the development of the cinema.

p, Le Vicomte de Noailles; d, Luis Bunuel; w, Bunuel, Salvador Dali; ph, Albert Duverger; m, Wagner, Mendelssohn, Beethoven, Debussy; ed, Bunuel.

Satire   (PR:C MPAA:NR)

LAILA   (SEE: MAKE WAY FOR LILA, 1962)

LAKE, THE*   (1970, Jap.) 94m Gendai Eiga/Shochiku c (ONNA NO MIZUUMI)

Mariko Okada (Miyuki Mizuki), Shinsuke Ashida (Yuzo), Shigeru Tsuyuguchi (Ginpei Momoi), Tamotsu Hayakawa (Kitano), Keiko Natsu (Machie), K. Ichikawa, Aiko Masuda, Hiroko Masuda, Sakae Umezu, Keisuke Nakai, Kazumi Higuchi, Mitsuyo Omata.

Okada is a housewife who falls in love with her interior decorator. Her affair takes her to trashy hotels where she allows her lover to take nude photographs of her. Later, the negatives are used against her by another man, Tsuyuguchi, who has seen the lovers entering the hotel. His blackmail attempt, coupled with the fact that the interior decorator has another mistress, brings about a beachside lovemaking encounter between Tsuyuguchi and Okada. When her husband learns the truth from the decorator, the married couple return home together.

p, Keinosuke Kubo; d, Yoshishige Yoshida; w, Yoshio Isihido, Yasuko Ono, Yoshida (based on the story "Mizuumi" by Yasunari Kawabata); ph, Tatsuo Suzuki; m, Sei Ikeno; ed, Sachiko Shimizu.

Drama   (PR:O MPAA:NR)

LAKE OF DRACULA**

(1973, Jap.) 82m Toho c (CHI O SUU ME; AKA: BLOODTHIRSTY EYES, DRACULA'S LUST FOR BLOOD)

Midori Fujita (Akiko), Choei Takahashi (Sacki), Sanae Emi (Natsuoke), Mori Kishida, Kaku Takashina.

An interesting tale of a young girl who is saved from a vampire attack by an elderly man and is affected by the incident for years. The people around her, however, have a tendency of dismissing her fright as a nightmare.

p, Fumio Tanaka; d, Michio Yamamoto.

Horror   (PR:O MPAA:NR)

LAKE PLACID SERENADE**   (1944) 85m REP bw

Vera Hruba Ralson (Vera Haschek), Robert Livingston (Jordan), Eugene Pallette (Carl Cermak), Barbara Jo Allen [Vera Vague] (Countess), Walter Catlett (Webb), William Frawley (Jiggers), Ruth Terry (Susan), Stephanie Bachelor (Irene), Lloyd Corrigan (Haschek), John Litel (Walter Benda), Ludwig Stossel (Mayor Of Lany), Andrew Tombes (Skating Club Head), Marietta Canty (Maid), Twinkle Watts, McGowan and Mack, Janina Frostova, Felix Sadovsky, Janet Martin, Ray Noble and Orchestra, Harry Owens and His Royal Hawaiians (Specialties), Roy Rogers (Guest Star), Mike Macy (Judge), Sewall Shurtz (Apprentice Boy), Janna De Loos (Friend at Lake), Demetrius Alexis (Tourist), Erno Kiraly, Hans Herbert (Judges), Ferdinand Munier (Kris Kringle), Nora Lane (Benda's Secretary), John Dehner (Radio Announcer), Frank Mayo, Pat Gleason, Dick Scott, Ernie Adams, Charles Williams, (Reporters), Ruth O. Warren (Cleaning Woman), Bert Moorehouse (Photographer), Eric Alden, Stewart Hall, Craig Lawrence (Candidates), Geoffrey Ingham (Good Looking Man), John Hamilton (Hopkins), Stanley Andrews (Exec-

utive), Virginia Carroll *(Receptionist)*, Eddie Kane *(Desk Clerk)*, Chester Clute *(Haines)*.

This Cinderella love story between European skater Ralston (actually a figure-skating star in Czechoslovakia before becoming an actress) and a competitor she meets in America is an excuse for this lavish spectacle of music, song, and dance. When representing her country at a Lake Placid carnival, Ralston is unable to return home due to the outbreak of war. While being taken care of by her wealthy uncle, she falls in love with his junior partner, Livingston. When she discovers that the young man is already engaged to be married, she runs off. But the romance proves true as Livingston follows in pursuit. Songs include: "Deep Purple" (Mitchel Parish, Peter De Rose), "My Isle of Golden Dreams" (Gus Kahn, Walter Blaufuss), "National Emblem March" (E.E. Bagley), "Winter Wonderland" (Dick Smith, Felix Bernard, sung by Roy Rogers), "Intermezzo" (Robert Henning, Heinz Provost), "Waiting for the Robert E. Lee" (L. Wolfe Gilbert, Lewis F. Muir), "When Citrus is in Bloom," "Drigo's Serenade" (Richard Drigo), "While Strolling in the Park" (Robert A. King).

p, Harry Grey; d, Steve Sekely; w, Dick Irving Hyland, Doris Gilbert (based on the story by Frederick Kohner); ph, John Alton; ed, Arthur Roberts; md, Walter Scharf; art d, Russell Kimball; set d, Earl Wooden; spec eff, Howard and Theodore Lydecker; ch, Jack Crosby.

Musical   **(PR:A MPAA:NR)**

LAMA NEL CORPO, LA   (SEE: MURDER CLINIC, THE, 1969, Ital.)

L'AMANT DE LADY CHATTERLEY
                                        (SEE: LADY CHATTERLEY'S LOVER, 1959, Fr.)

LAMBETH WALK, THE*¹/₂   (1940, Brit.) 67m CAPAD-Pinebrook/MGM bw

Lupino Lane *(Bill Snibson)*, Sally Gray *(Sally)*, Seymour Hicks *(Sir John)*, Norah Howard *(The Duchess)*, Enid Stamp-Taylor *(Jacqueline)*, Wallace Lupino *(Parchester)*, Wilfrid Hyde-White *(Lord Battersby)*, May Hallatt *(Lady Battersby)*, Mark Lester *(Sir Roger)*, Charles Heslop *(Oswald)*.

This screen adaptation of the long-running London play, "Me and My Girl," centers around a man from the poor side of town, Lane, who is granted an inheritance and title, but still marries his faithful Cockney girl friend, Gray. Cast is efficient, but their performances are marred by a humor which doesn't quite come across.

p, Anthony Havelock-Allan; d, Albert de Courville; w, Clifford Grey, Robert Edmunds, John Paddy Carstairs (based on the play "Me and My Girl" by Louis Rose, Douglas Furber, Noel Gay); ph, Francis Carver; ed, Dick Best.

Comedy   **(PR:A MPAA:NR)**

LAMENT OF THE PATH, THE   (SEE: PANTHER PANCHALI, 1958, India)

L'AMORE   (SEE: WAYS OF LOVE, 1950, Ital.)

L'AMORE DIFFICILE   (SEE: OF WAYWARD LOVE, 1964, Ital./Ger.)

L'AMOUR zero   (1973) 90m Altura c

Michael Sklar *(Michael)*, Donna Jordan *(Donna)*, Max Delys *(Max)*, Patti D'Arbanville *(Patti)*, Karl Lagerfeld *(Karl)*, Coral Labrie *(Coral)*, Peter Greenlaw *(Peter)*, Corey Tippin *(Corey)*, Jane Forth *(Jane)*.

Another Morrissey-and-Warhol combined effort that centers on individuals lost in a sea of decay and seediness. Sklar is the victim of the probing camera, as he gets to live out one of his crude fantasies. Strictly for those who consider Warhol an insightful artist.

p, Paul Morrissey; d&w, Andy Warhol, Morrissey; ph, Jed Johnson (Eastmancolor); m, Ben Weisman; ed, Lana Jokel, Jed Johnson; m/l, Weisman, Michael Sklar (sung by Cass Elliot).

Drama   **(PR:O MPAA:R)**

LAMP IN ASSASSIN MEWS, THE*¹/₂   (1962, Brit.) 65m Danziger/UA bw

Francis Matthews *(Jack)*, Lisa Daniely *(Mary Clarke)*, Ian Fleming *(Albert Potts)*, Amy Dalby *(Victoria Potts)*, Ann Sears *(Ruth)*, Anne Lawson *(Ella)*, Derek Tansey *(Jarvis)*, Ann Lancaster *(Mrs. Dowling)*, Colin Tapley *(Inspector)*.

An odd comedy about a stubborn couple who plan to defend a treasured possession from those who want to remove it. In their attempt to save the lamp in this typically British comedy, they try to kill a councillor and the contretemps goes on.

p, Brian Taylor; d, Godfrey Grayson; w, M. M. McCormack.

Comedy   **(PR:A MPAA:NR)**

LAMP STILL BURNS, THE***   (1943, Brit.) 90m TC/GFD bw

Rosamund John *(Hilary Clarke)*, Stewart Granger *(Larry Rains)*, Godfrey Tearle *(Sir Marshall Frayne)*, Sophie Stewart *(Christine Morris)*, John Laurie *(Mr. Hervey)*, Margaret Vyner *(Pamela Siddell)*, Cathleen Nesbitt *(Matron)*, Eric Micklewood *(Dr. Trevor)*, Joyce Grenfell *(Dr. Barratt)*, Joan Maude *(Sister Catley)*, Grace Arnold *(Sister Sprock)*, Jenny Laird *(Ginger Watkins)* Megs Jenkins *(Nurse)*, Wylie Watson *(Diabetic)*, Ernest Thesiger *(Chairman)*, Brefni O'Rorke *(Lorimer)*, John Howard, Mignon O'Doherty, Leslie Dwyer, Max Earle, Gordon Begg, Althe Parker, Paul Merton, Aubrey Mallalieu, Jane Gill-Davis, David Keir, Patric Curwen, Janette Scott.

Realistic portrayal of the less-than-adequate conditions in a British hospital during WW II. John plays a young architect who chucks her career in wartime to devote her life to nursing. Outstanding performances by the entire cast in this evenly directed and edited feature. The film is endowed with high production values which, for this time in British history, is unusual. Unfortunately, producer-actor Howard was shot down by the Germans while flying in a passenger plane soon after this picture was made, ending a brilliant career.

p, Leslie Howard; d, Maurice Elvey; w, Elizabeth Baron, Roland Pertwee, Major Neilson (based on the novel *One Pair of Feet* by Monica Dickens); ph, Jack Hildyard.

Drama   **(PR:A MPAA:NR)**

L'ANATRA ALL'ARANCIA   (SEE: DUCK IN ORANGE SAUCE, 1976, Ital.)

LANCASHIRE LUCK*¹/₂   (1937, Brit.) 74m British and Dominions/PAR bw

George Carney *(George Lovejoy)*, Wendy Hiller *(Betty Lovejoy)*, Muriel George *(Mrs. Lovejoy)*, Nigel Stock *(Joe Lovejoy)*, George Galleon *(Sir Gerald Maydew)*, Margaret Damer *(Lady Maydew)*, Bett Huth *(Lady Evelyn Brenton)*, Peter Popp.

The differences between the upper and lower classes are again stretched to comic lengths as the working class Carney wins a small fortune on the football pools and opens up a ritzy tea shop in a classy part of town. He enjoys his new lifestyle, as does his daughter Hiller, who becomes involved with a titled young man, much to the dismay of his Lady mother. By the finale, all the class creases are ironed out and love prevails.

p, Anthony Havelock-Allan; d, Henry Cass; w, A. R. Rawlinson (based on a story by Ronald Gow); ph, Francis Carver.

Comedy   **(PR:A MPAA:NR)**

LANCELOT AND GUINEVERE   (SEE: SWORD AND LANCELOT, 1963)

LANCELOT DU LAC   (SEE: LANCELOT OF THE LAKE, 1975, Fr.)

LANCELOT OF THE LAKE***
(1975, Fr.) 85m Mara Films-Laser Production-ORTF-Gerico Sound/CFDC-New Yorker Films c (LANCELOT DU LAC, LE GRAAL; AKA: THE GRAIL)

Luc Simon *(Lancelot)*, Laura Duke Condominas *(Queen Guinevere)*, Humbert Balsan *(Gawain)*, Vladimir Antolek-Oresek *(King Arthur)*, Patrick Bernhard *(Modred)*, Arthur De Montalembert *(Lionel)*.

The brilliant French director Robert Bresson applied his personal form of cinematic vision to the legend of Lancelot and the Knights of the Round Table to create a whole new rendition of the famous story. These knights are portrayed as anything but noble and conscientious individuals, rather as ruthless and greedy men whose main motivation is to obtain their desires. Disillusioned with their inabilities to discover the Holy Grail, the Knights on the quest return to England causing havoc along the way, which includes an excessive amount of fighting among themselves. Lancelot returns to the love of Guinevere, sparking new battles among the knights and Lancelot's own dismissal from Arthur's favor. This depiction of the famous legend takes on secondary importance in the wake of the moody visual style, low key performances, and an obtrusive soundtrack. All these combine to create an extremely disturbing effect, and a further example of Bresson's cinematic genius.

p, Jean-Pierre Rassam, Francois Rochas; d&w, Robert Bresson; ph, Pasqualino de Santis (Eastmancolor); m, Philippe Sarde; ed, Germaine Lamy; prod d, Pierre Charbonnier; cos, Gres.

Historical Drama   **(PR:C MPAA:NR)**

LANCER SPY***   (1937) 84m FOX bw

Dolores Del Rio *(Fraulein Dolores Daria)*, George Sanders *(Baron Kurt von Rohback/Lt. Michael Bruce)*, Peter Lorre *(Maj. Sigfried Gruning)*, Virginia Field *(Joan Bruce)*, Sig Rumann *(Lt. Col. Gottfried Hollen)*, Joseph Schildkraut *(Prince Ferdi zu Schwarzwald)*, Maurice Moscovich *(Gen. von Meinhardt)*, Lionel Atwill *(Col. Fenwick)*, Luther Adler *(Schratt)*, Fritz Feld *(Fritz Mueller)*, Lester Mathews *(Capt. Neville)*, Carlos J. de Valdez *(Von Klingen)*, Gregory Gaye *(Capt. Freymann)*, Joan Carol *(Elizabeth Bruce)*, Holmes Herbert *(Dr. Aldrich)*, Clyde Cook *(Orderly)*, John Burton *(Lieutenant)*, Herbert Evans, Victor Kolberg *(Sergeants)*, David Clyde, Neil Fitzgerald *(Orderlies)*, Fredrik Vogeding *(Danish Boat Captain)*, Kenneth Hunter *(Commandant)*, Claude King *(Captain)*, Olaf Hytten *(Barber)*, Ian MacLaren *(Plainclothesman)*, Dave Thursby *(Sentry)*, Boyd Irwin, Sr. *(Surgeon)*, Paul Weigel *(Hotel Manager Schreiber)*, Frank Reicher *(Admiral)*, Egon Brecher *(Bendiner)*, Elisabeth Frohlich *(Farmer's Wife)*, Lynn Bari *(Fenwick's Companion)*, Adia Kurnetzoff *(Major Domo)*, Michael S. Visaroff *(Referee)*, Leonard Mudie *(Statesman)*, Hans Joby *(Waiter)*, Bert Sprotte *(Conducter)*, Walter Bonn *(Officer on Train)*, Greta Meyer *(Woman on Train)*, Hans von Morhart *(Intelligence Officer)*, Frank Puglia, Feodor Chaliapin, Jr. *(Monks)*, Frederick Gehrmann, Arno Frey *(Soldiers)*, Bud Geary *(Captain's Aide)*, Maj. Sam Harris *(Officer at Party)*.

Although he was appearing in his ninth film (his fifth in the U.S.), this was the one that put Russian-born Sanders into another sphere and made him a star. He plays an Englishman who is recruited to go behind German lines due to his resemblance to a captured bigwig. (Don't forget, this was made in 1937, fully four years before the U.S. was in the war). His job is to masquerade as the German and come back with some important military secrets. Upon his arrival in Germany, Sanders has almost everyone duped by his looks and behavior. The one person who is not so sure is Lorre, head of the secret police, who assigns Del Rio to ferret out the truth. Del Rio is a nightclub singer who worms her way into Sanders' confidence. As the two get closer, need we say that they fall in love? Once that's in the hopper, her passion for the Englishman overwhelms her loyalty to Germany and she won't blow the whistle on him. A German spy in England sends some photos of Sanders, as his true British self, to Lorre and the secret is out. But Sanders, with Del Rio's help, has been accomplishing what he came to do; the robbery of the war plans of the High Command. Sanders is successful and escapes to Switzerland. However, Del Rio is captured and executed by the Germans for her complicity. The picture is related in a flashback as Sanders tells the story to Atwill, a captain of the British secret service. The sequence at the top, when Sanders is substituted for Sanders and effects a daring escape from the British jail, is as exciting a set of scenes as you'll ever see.

This was Ratoff's first directorial job after many years of producing, writing, and acting. He kept everyone on the edge of their seats with a snappy script by Phillip Dunne that even included a bit of comedy from Schildkraut as a German martinet. Schildkraut had a small role in this film but managed to squeeze in another job that year which won him an Oscar as Best Supporting Actor in THE LIFE OF EMILE ZOLA, when he played the tragic Capt. Dreyfus. But before the 1930s ended, both Sanders and Schildkraut would be heavies opposite Lorre who was MR. MOTO in at least eight low-budget crime stories.

p, Samuel G. Engel; d, Gregory Ratoff; w, Philip Dunne (based on a story by Martha McKenna); ph, Barney McGill; ed, Louis Loeffler; md, Arthur Lange; art d, Albert Hogsett.

Spy Drama (PR:A MPAA:NR)

LAND AND THE LAW (SEE: BLACK MARKET RUSTLERS, 1943)

LAND BEYOND THE LAW**½ (1937) 54m WB bw

Dick Foran (Chip Douglas), Linda Perry (Louise), Wayne Morris (Dave Massey), Irene Franklin (Cattle Kate), Joseph King (Governor Lew Wallace), Gordon Hart (Maj. Adair), Cy Kendall (Slade Henaberry), Frank Orth (Shorty), Glenn Strange (Bandy Malarkey), Harry Woods (Tascosa), Milton Kibbee (Sheriff Spence), Edmund Cobb (Mason), Henry Otho (Kirby), Tom Brower (Douglas, Sr.), Paul Panzer (Blake), Julian Rivero, Artie Ortego, Jim Corey, Bud Osborne, Wilfred Lucas, Gene Alsace, Frank McCarroll.

Fast-paced western has Foran as a young cowhand who unwisely becomes involved with a gang of cattle rustlers headed by Woods. After a change of heart, Foran helps save the rancher's cattle from his former gang. Performances are all adequate and well cast. Songs sung by Foran include: "Whistle While You're Waiting," "Song of the Circle Bar," and "The Prairie, My Home" (M. K. Jerome, Jack Acholl).

p, Bryan Foy; d, B. Reeves Eason; w, Luci Ward, Joseph K. Watson (based on a story, "The Last Bad Man" by Marion Jackson); ph, Ted McCord; ed, Thomas Richards.

Western/Musical (PR:A MPAA:NR)

LAND OF FIGHTING MEN** (1938) 55m MON bw

Jack Randall (Jack), Colorado Hillbillies (Themselves), Herman Brix [Bruce Bennett] (Fred), Louise Stanley (Connie), Dickie Jones (Jimmy), Bob Burns (Sheriff), Wheeler Oakman (Wallace), John Merton (Flint), Lane Chandler (Cliff), Rex Lease (Ed), Ernie Adams.

Run-of-the-mill western has Randall coming to the aid of his old buddy Brix to help him keep Oakman from snatching his land. Shortly after Randall arrives, Brix is killed and the evidence all points to Randall. Standard western performers deliver acceptably, with Randall managing to sing a couple of decent songs. Songs include: "Cowboy Band," "The West Was Meant for Me" (Connie Lee); and "King of the Trail" (Edward Cherkose, Charles Rosoff).

p, Maurice Conn; d, Alan James; w, Joseph O'Donnell (based on the story by Stanley Roberts); ph, Robert Cline; ed, Richard G. Wray.

Western (PR:A MPAA:NR)

LAND OF FURY** (1955 Brit.) 90m Group-Fanfare/UNIV c (GB: THE SEEKERS)

Jack Hawkins (Philip Wayne), Glynis Johns (Marion Southey), Noel Purcell (Paddy Clarke), Inia Te Wiata (Hongi Tepe), Kenneth Williams (Peter Wishart), Laya Raki (Moana), Patrick Warbrick (Awarua), Tony Erstich (Bangiruru), Edward Baker (Toroa), Maharaia Winiata (Hongi Tepe's Father), Thomas Heathcote (Sgt. Paul), Norman Mitchell (Grayson), James Copeland (Mackay), Francis de Wolff (Capt. Bryce), Henry Gilbert (Aspiti Tohunga), Ian Fleming, Patrick Rawiri, Mac Hata, J. Ward Holmes, Fred Johnson, F.B.J. Sharp, Kim Parker.

Typically British adventure saga starring Hawkins as a naval officer who steps ashore in New Zealand with an interpreter and is promptly captured by the natives for having walked upon sacred burial ground. The quick-thinking duo reason with the chief of the savages, and they soon have him begging them to stay and show them the ways of the white man. Eventually Hawkins returns to England, but is forced to leave due to some nasty legal difficulties. The sailor takes his lovely bride, Johns, back to New Zealand with him and sets up shop as a justice of the peace. Following the birth of his son, Hawkins falls victim to the seduction of the big chief's wily bride and soon finds himself in the middle of a war when one of the white settlers kills a native. Hawkins and his wife are killed in the battle, but the forgiving chieftain finds their baby alive and decides to raise it himself.

p, Earl St. John, George H. Brown; d, Ken Annakin; w, William Fairchild (based on the novel The Seekers by John Guthrie); ph, Geoffrey Unsworth (Eastmancolor); m, William Alwyn; ed, John Guthridge; md, Muir Mathieson; art d, Maurice Carter; cos, Julie Harris.

Drama (PR:A MPAA:NR)

LAND OF HUNTED MEN** (1943) 58m MON bw

Ray Corrigan, Dennis Moore, Max Terhune, Phyllis Adair, Charles King, John Merton, Ted Mapes, Frank McCarroll, Forrest Taylor, Steve Clark, Fred Toones, Carl Sepulveda.

A band of outlaws is terrorizing a town in the West. Leave it to Corrigan and his "Range Busters" to ride in and save the day in this entry of the 1940s series.

p, George W. Weeks; d, S. Roy Luby; w, Elizabeth Beecher (based on a story by William Nolte).

Western (PR:A MPAA:NR)

LAND OF MISSING MEN, THE** (1930) 55m Trem Carr/TIF bw

Bob Steele (Steve O'Neil), Al "Fuzzy" St. John (Buckshot), Edward Dunn (Sheriff Bower), Caryl Lincoln (Nita Madero), Al Jennings (John Evans, Ex-Sheriff), Fern Emmett (Martha Evans), Emilio Fernandez (Lopez), Noah Hendricks (Texas), C.R. Dufau (Senor Madero), S.S. Simon (Express Agent), Fred Burns.

Steele and sidekick St. John happen upon a saloon where a gunfight has just occurred. Inside they find a number of bodies and a wounded man who tells them of a plan to hold up the stagecoach carrying the dying man's daughter. The heroes reach the coach ahead of the robbers and stop it, kidnaping the girl (Lincoln). She escapes the care of Steele and goes to round up a posse. Steele and St. John enter the bandit camp and manage to subdue the bad guys and expose sheriff Dunn as their leader just as help arrives. Routine horse opera interesting mostly for the presence of Al Jennings in a minor role. A failure as a robber in the late 1880s, Jennings served seven years in prison for his part in a train robbery that netted all of $60 for Jennings and his three brothers. When he was released he travelled to California telling stories about his dangerous days as the Old West's most feared desperado. Not much better as an actor than as a robber, he managed to hang on in the film community, telling his increasingly ludicrous yarns to anyone who would listen. In 1951 Hollywood immortalized this legend-in-his-own-mind in AL JENNINGS OF OKLAHOMA, taking the myth even further from the reality. Jennings died in 1961 at the age of 98 raving about his fictitious accomplishments. This was one of eight films made by Steele in a series distributed by the short-lived Tiffany (the company went out of business after its next series, which featured Ken Maynard). Six of the eight were directed by McCarthy. The series had two firsts: Steele's premier all-talking picture, and the first film in which the diminutive cowboy sang (fortunately, he soon stopped that nonsense), a full four years before Gene Autry "introduced" the singing-cowboy concept.

p, Trem Carr; d, John P. McCarthy; w, McCarthy, Bob Quigley (based on a story by McCarthy); ph, Harry Neumann.

Western (PR:A MPAA:NR)

LAND OF NO RETURN, THE*½ (1981) 84m International Picture Show c (AKA: CHALLENGE TO SURVIVE; SNOWMAN)

Mel Torme (Zak O'Brien), William Shatner (Curt Benell), Donald Moffat (Air Traffic Controller), "Caesar" (The Eagle), "Romulus" (The Wolf).

Crooner Torme, known to millions as "The Velvet Fog" for his mellifluous song styling, plays a TV animal trainer whose private airplane crashes in the rugged mountains of Utah. Concealing his paucity of jawbone with a full beard, stocky singer Torme treks out of the snowy wilderness with the assistance of his trained eagle, which supplies the food by hunting. In cutaway sequences, a trained wolf that also escaped maiming in the crash similarly forages for survival. Shatner, as Torme's TV producer, does the back-home worrying during the long, slow, tedious, but colorful and scenic progress. First released in 1977, re-released in 1981.

p&d, Kent Bateman; w, Bateman, Frank Ray Perilli; ph, Joao Fernandes (DeLuxe Color); m, Ralph Geddes; ed, Dick Alweis.

Adventure (PR:A MPAA:PG)

LAND OF OZ (SEE: WONDERFUL LAND OF OZ, 1969)

LAND OF THE LAWLESS** (1947) 54m MON bw

Johnny Mack Brown, Raymond Hatton, Christine McIntyre, Tris Coffin, June Harrison, Marshall Reed, I. Stanford Jolley, Steve Clark, Edmund Cobb, Roy Butler, Cactus Mack, Gary Garrett, Carl Sepulveda, Victor Cox.

In the barren wastelands of no man's land, a group of outlaws create their own laws. An average action Western, with Brown and sidekick Hatton riding as always on the side of justice.

p, Barney Sarecky; d, Lambert Hillyer; w, J. Benton Cheney (based on a story by Cheney); ph, William A. Sickner; ed, Robert Crandall; md, Edward Kay.

Western (PR:A MPAA:NR)

LAND OF THE MINOTAUR*½ (1976, Gr.) 88m Crown International c (AKA: THE DEVIL'S MEN: THE DEVIL'S PEOPLE, MINOTAUR)

Donald Pleasence (Father Roche), Peter Cushing (Baron Corofax), Luan Peters (Laurie), Nikos Verlekis (Ian), Costas Skouras (Milo), Bob Behling (Tom), Vanna Revilli (Beth), Fernando Bislani (Police Sergeant), Anna Mantzourani.

The mythic Greek minotaur is revived in this unconvincing horrific nonsense. Cushing is the head of a modern day Greek cult that worships the man-bull, using female human sacrifices to honor their god. Local priest Pleasence comes in to stop the blasphemy. There's enough gratuitous violence and naked female flesh to satisfy horror genre fans. The music, surprisingly enough, is by esoteric rock composer Eno.

p, Frixos Constantine; d, Costa Carayiannis; w, Arthur Rowe; m, Brian Eno.

Horror Cas. (PR:O MPAA:PG)

LAND OF THE MISSING MEN (SEE: LAND OF MISSING MEN, 1930)

LAND OF THE OPEN RANGE** (1941) 60m RKO bw

Tim Holt (Dave), Ray Whitley (Smokey), Janet Waldo (Mary Cook), Lee "Lasses" White (Whopper), Hobart Cavanaugh (Pinky Gardner), Lee Bonnell (Stuart), Roy Barcroft (Gil Carse), John Elliot (Dad Cook), Frank Ellis (Dode), Tom London (Tonton), J. Merrill Holmes (Sam Walton).

This western has a new twist, with a dead crook bequeathing his land to any villain who has spent at least two years in jail. This attracts an assorted array of former jailbirds to the town where Holt is sheriff. It's his job to make sure the land is divided equally. Out-takes of the famous landrush sequence from the 1931 epic CIMARRON were used to upgrade this minor western. Songs include: 'Hi-o My Horse Is So Slow,'' "KI-O," and "Land of The Open Range" (Fred Rose, Ray Whitley).

p, Bert Gilroy; d, Edward Killy; w, Morton Grant (based on the story "Homesteads Of Hate" by Lee Bond); ph, Harry Wild; ed, Frederic Knudtson; md, Paul Sawtell.

Western **(PR:A MPAA:NR)**

LAND OF THE OUTLAWS** (1944) 56m MON bw

Johnny Mack Brown, Raymond Hatton, Stephen Keyes, Nan Holliday, Hugh Prosser, Charles King, John Merton, Steve Clark, Art Fowler, Tom Quinn, Ray Elder, Chick Hannon, Bob Cason, Kansas Moehring, Ben Corbett, George Morrell.

Some badmen are on the run and so they head out on the range, hoping to find a place that's safe from the law. Standard western fare with plenty of saddle play and gunslinging.

p, Charles J. Bigelow; d, Lambert Hillyer; w, Joe O'Donnell; ph, Harry Neumann; ed, John C. Fuller; md, Edward Kay.

Western **(PR:A MPAA:NR)**

LAND OF THE PHARAOHS** (1955) 103m Continental/WB c

Jack Hawkins *(Pharaoh)*, Joan Collins *(Princess Nellifer)*, Dewey Martin *(Senta)*, Alexis Minotis *(Hamar)*, James Robertson Justice *(Vashtar)*, Luisa Boni *(Kyra)*, Sydney Chaplin *(Treneh)*, James Hayter *(Vashtar's Servant)*, Kerima *(Queen Nailla)*, Piero Giagnoni *(Pharaoh's Son)*.

LAND OF THE PHARAOHS is a BIG movie, the spectacle of which has seldom been equalled. Hawks, a man who made so many smaller films, was at the helm of this epic that was destined to lose almost two-thirds of its six-million-dollar investment. To recreate it today would cost at least eight times that amount but would still be foolish. Hawks used more than 10,000 extras (the size of a middling Midwest town) and handled the DeMille-type hordes well enough. The problems arose in the shooting of the small moments, the times when actors had to speak to each other. Hawks usually had his actors talk at rat-tat-tat speed but he decelerated to an amoebic pace here. Hawkins is an Egyptian Pharaoh who returns to his palace after many feats of desert warriorship. In the past six years, he's been involved in five wars and has amassed the spoils of victory, which include a ton or so of gold. He tells his pal, Minotis, that he is finally contented, except for two matters; he wants his Queen, Kerima, to present him with a son, and he would like a suitable resting place once he's gone off to Egyptian heaven. He assigns his top architect, Justice, to the task of creating a fit and lasting monument where he can rest his head and surround himself with his treasures. Justice is a slave and tells Hawkins that he will only design the tomb if Hawkins agrees to allow his fellow slaves to be released upon the project's completion. Construction commences and thousands of slaves as well as native Egyptians are put to the task of building the pyramid. Kerima bears Hawkins a son, Giagnoni, and he and Justice's son, Martin, grow to manhood as best friends. While the pyramid is being built, Hawkins asks his neighboring countries to send a trinket of their esteem (gold, mostly) in his honor. Cyprus doesn't have much gold so they send him Joan Collins instead (age 22 and ravishing), who refuses to do Hawkins' bidding, namely, sleep with him. Hawkins is at once angered and intrigued by Collins so he makes her his second wife. But Collins, already playing a mean and vicious character in preparation for her later TV success on "Dynasty," has plans of her own. She conspires with Chaplin (son of Charlie), a palace guard, to kill Hawkins and Giagnoni so she can rule the civilized world. Both murder attempts are flubbed but Kerima dies in the process and Hawkins is only injured. Collins thinks fast and says that the whole cabal was planned by Chaplin. Hawkins gets in a battle with Chaplin, kills him, and is himself mortally wounded in the fight. Collins can help him but she prefers to watch him die (in a scene not unlike Bette Davis' response in THE LITTLE FOXES when her husband, Herbert Marshall, was suffering a heart attack and she made no move to get him his medicine). A few moments before his last breath, Hawkins finally understands that it was Collins all along who planned the assassination. At the suggestion of Minotis, Collins enters the pyramid to nab the gold as the funeral procession enters along with her. Minotis now informs her that the pyramid is about to be sealed, along with the funeral party and himself and they will all be entombed alive in there forever. Collins screams in agony while, outside, Justice and Martin lead their people to freedom as Collins goes through her histrionics. The original plan was to have Justice, who knew the secret of the pyramid, die with his king, but Minotis took his place and granted him freedom. Faulkner wrote the script with veteran Kurnitz and Coney Islander Bloom and it was more stentorian than dramatic. Much of the picture concerned the building of the pyramid, not an exceptionally exciting event to watch. Hawks would have been wise to cast a few big names as cameos to help, the way David Lean did with Anthony Quinn and Alec Guinness for LAWRENCE OF ARABIA, to bolster the unknown Peter O'Toole. Chaplin was allegedly Collins' boy friend at one time. She later married Anthony Newley, who portrayed Charlie Chaplin in a musical version of the great clown's life in 1983. LAND OF THE PHARAOHS grew out of Hawks' efforts to explore the new cinematic form of CinemaScope. Originally he had intended to film a story about the building of a U.S. airbase in China during WW II, which was completed in three weeks by using thousands of Chinese men and women to carry the necessary stones for the construction, but the political situation made cooperation with the Chinese impossible. It then occurred to him that the building of the pyramids was a story of that magnitude, and so he set to work on a script. Future Nobel Prize winner Faulkner always liked to promote the story that he suffered the tortures of the damned when he worked as a scriptwriter in Hollywood, and did it only because he was a poor scrivener trying to survive. Hawks tells a different story. Asked what part the writer played in scripting the scenario, Hawks said, "He contributed enormously . . . We are very old friends and understand each other perfectly and work well together." He went on to say that the pyramid story excited Faulkner's imagination and that any time he needed Faulkner's help he called for him.

p&d, Howard Hawks; w, William Faulkner, Harry Kurnitz, Harold Jack Bloom; ph, Lee Garmes, Russell Harlan (CinemaScope, Warner Color); m, Dimitri Tiomkin; ed, Rudi Fehr, V. Sagovsky; art d, Alexandre Trauner; cos, Mayo; spec eff, Don Steward; makeup, Emile Lavigne.

Historical Epic **(PR:A-C MPAA:NR)**

LAND OF THE SIX GUNS* 1/2 (1940) 54m MON bw

Jack Randall *(Rowan)*, Louise Stanley *(Carole)*, Frank LaRue *(Howard)*, Glenn Strange *(Manny)*, Bud Osborne *(Sheriff)*, George Chesebro *(Taylor)*, Steve Clark *(Stone)*, Kenne Duncan *(Max)*, Richard Cramer *(Joe)*, Jack Perrin *(Davis)*, Carl Mathews *(Drake)*.

Randall plays a deputy sheriff who tries to retire his gun and settle down on a ranch. But, as luck—and the plot line—would have it, his property turns out to be in the middle of a path used by rustlers to move illegal cattle from Mexico to the States. All this is accompanied by the usual "Hollywood Cowboy" song, sung here by Strange.

p, Harry S. Webb; d, Raymond K. Johnson; w, Tom Gibson; ph, Edward A. Kull, William Hyer; ed, Robert Golden.

Western **(PR:A MPAA:NR)**

LAND OF THE SILVER FOX** (1928) 55m WB bw

Rin-Tin-Tin *(Rinty the Dog)*, Leila Hyams *(Marie du Fronque)*, John Miljan *(James Crawford)*, Carroll Nye *(Carroll)*, Tom Santschi *(Butch Nelson)*, Princess Neola *(The Squaw)*.

After villainous Miljan brutally beats Rin-Tin-Tin, the dog is bought from him by Nye. Miljan sets Nye up with a sled-load of furs to be transported, then sends Santschi out to kill him and take the furs. Nye is left for dead but the heroic German Shepherd saves his master's life. When Nye is finally able to reach a settlement he is accused of stealing the furs and arrested, but Rin-Tin-Tin snarls at Santschi until he confesses. Rin-Tin-Tin lives up to his top billing, proving himself the most dynamic presence on the screen. Also released in a silent version.

d, Ray Enright; w, Howard Smith, Joseph Jackson (based on a story by Charles Condon); ph, Frank Kesson; ed, Owen Marks.

Adventure **(PR:AA MPAA:NR)**

LAND OF WANTED MEN** (1932) 60m MON bw

Bill Cody, Andy Shuford, Sheila Manners, Gibson Gowland, Jack Richardson, Frank Lackteen, James Marcus.

Average western has Cody as the newly appointed sheriff in cattle country, when sheep ranchers begin to intrude upon the cattle barons' property. It's Cody's job to maintain the peace, but his own legitimacy is brought into question. Satisfactory performances and direction.

p, Trem Carr; d&w, Harry Fraser; ph, Archie Stout.

Western **(PR:A MPAA:NR)**

LAND RAIDERS**
(1969) 101m COL c (AKA: DAY OF THE LANDGRABBERS)

Telly Savalas *(Vince Carden)*, George Maharis *(Paul Cardenas)*, Arlene Dahl *(Martha Carden)*, Janet Landgard *(Kate Mayfield)*, Jocelyn Lane *(Luisa Rojas)*, George Coulouris *(Cardenas)*, Guy Rolfe *(Maj. Tanner)*, Phil Brown *(Mayfield)*, Marcella St. Amant *(Luisa Montoya)*, Paul Picerni *(Carney)*, Robert Carricart *(Rojas)*, Gustavo Rojo *(Juantez)*, Fernando Rey *(Priest)*, Ben Tatar *(Loomis)*, John Clark *(Ace)*, Charles Stalnaker *(Willis)*, Susan Harvey *(Mrs. Willis)*.

Savalas plays an Apache-hating landowner, trying to rid the land of Indians, while at the same time claiming their land for himself. Government agents are sent in to maintain peace, but fail. When Savalas' brother Maharis arrives after many years' absence, an old feud is re-ignited concerning his old girl friend, now dead. Seeing the undue violence Savalas is causing gives Maharis a chance to get even. Adequate performances are marred by an over-abundance of action sequences.

p, Charles H. Schneer; d, Nathan H. Juran; w, Ken Pettus (based on a story by Pettus, Jesse Lasky, Jr., Pat Silver); ph, Wilkie Cooper (Technicolor); m, Bruno Nicolai; ed, Archie Ludski; md, Nicolai; art d, Jose Alguero.

Western **(PR:C MPAA:GP)**

LAND THAT TIME FORGOT, THE**
(1975, Brit.) 91m Rosenberg-Subotsky/AIP c

Doug McClure *(Bowen Tyler)*, John McEnery *(Capt. Von Schoenvorts)*, Susan Penhaligon *(Lisa Clayton)*, Keith Barron *(Bradley)*, Anthony Ainley *(Dietz)*, Godfrey James *(Borg)*, Bobby Farr *(Ahm)*, Declan Mulholland *(Olson)*, Colin Farrell *(Whiteley)*, Ben Howard *(Benson)*, Roy Holder *(Plesser)*, Andrew McCulloch *(Sinclair)*, Ron Pember *(Jones)*, Grahame Mallard *(Deusett)*, Andrew Lodge *(Reuther)*, Brian Hall *(Schwartz)*, Stanley McGeagh *(Hiller)*, Peter Sproule *(Hindle)*, Steve James *(1st Sto-Lu)*.

A thin plot about a couple of American survivors held captive on a German sub that goes off course is an excuse for a children's adventure film. The sub runs out of fuel and is forced to land on an uncharted island in the Antarctic. The island is filled with prehistoric animals and cave men. There is also a primitive oil refinery which the crew finally reaches by fighting off gigantic animals and unfriendly natives. The special effects are unrealistic as are the dialog and performances. However, despite everything, the picture still makes for great fun. Sequel: THE PEOPLE THAT TIME FORGOT.

p, John Dark; d, Kevin Conner; w, James Cawthorn, Michael Moorcock (based on the novel by Edgar Rice Burroughs); ph, Alan Hume (Technicolor); m, Douglas

Gamley; ed, John Ireland; art d, Bert Davey; set d, Maurice Carter; spec eff, Derek Meddings.

Fantasy/Adventure   Cas.   **(PR:A MPAA:PG)**

LAND UNKNOWN, THE**½   (1957) 78m UNIV bw

Jock Mahoney (*Cmdr. Harold Roberts*), Shawn Smith (*Margareth Hathaway*), William Reynolds (*Lt. Jack Carmen*), Henry Brandon (*Hunter*), Douglas R. Kennedy (*Capt. Burnham*), Phil Harvey (*Steve Miller*).

Superior special effects make this science fiction adventure a respectable endeavor. Mahoney heads an expedition to the Antarctic, but his helicopter is damaged when it collides with a giant flying bird. The group is forced to land in a place inhabited by creatures from the Mesozoic Era. Also stranded there is Brandon, a scientist from an expedition made 10 years earlier. He has gone insane during his stay, but has somehow managed to survive. The parts from his disabled helicopter allow the stranded crew to repair their helicopter and return to civilization. Well directed with believable performances, including that of Brandon who was an actual member of Adm. Richard Byrd's 1947 South Pole expedition.

p, William Alland; d, Virgil Vogel; w, William N. Robson, Laszlo Gorog (based on a story by Charles Palmer); ph, Ellis W. Carter (CinemaScope); m, Joseph Gershenson; ed, Fred MacDowell; art d, Alexander Golitzen, Richard H. Riedel; spec eff, Fred Knoth, Orien Ernest, Jack Kevan.

Fantasy/Adventure   **(PR:A MPAA:NR)**

LAND WE LOVE, THE   (SEE: HERO'S ISLAND, 1962)

LAND WITHOUT MUSIC   (SEE: FORBIDDEN MUSIC, 1936, Brit.)

LANDFALL**   (1953, Brit.) 86m ABF-Pathe/Stratford bw

Michael Denison (*Rick*), Patricia Plunkett (*Mona*), Edith Sharpe (*Rick's Mother*), Margaret Barton (*Rick's Sister*), Charles Victor (*Mona's Father*), Kathleen Harrison (*Mona's Mother*), Denis O'Dea (*Capt. Burnaby*), Margaretta Scott (*Mrs. Burnaby*), Sebastian Shaw (*Wing-Comdr. Dickens*), Maurice Denham (*Wing-Comdr. Hewitt*), A.E. Matthews (*Air Raid Warden*), David Tomlinson (*Binks*), Joan Dowling (*Miriam, the Barmaid*), Frederick Leister (*Admiral*), Nora Swinburne (*Admiral's Wife*), Stanley Rose (*Uncle Bill*), Walter Hudd (*Prof. Legge*), Ivan Samson (*Cmdr. Rutherford*), Hubert Gregg (*Lt. Cmdr. Dale*), Andrea Lea (*Willow*), Paul Carpenter (*P/O Morgan*), Laurence Harvey (*P/O Hooper*), Gerald Case (*Squadron Leader Peterson*), Bryan Coleman (*P/O Weaver*), Norman Watson (*P/O Jones*), James Carney (*Sgt. Plt. Hutchison*), Moultrie Kelsall (*Lt. James*), Dennis Vance (*Lt. Kitchen*), Cavan Watson (*Lt. Mitcheson*), Andrew Leigh (*Customer*), Teddy Foster and his Band.

Denison plays an RAF pilot who sinks what is supposed to be a British sub in the English Channel. He is dismissed from his position by a court of inquiry. Barmaid Plunkett helps gather the information which proves the sub was actually a disguised German vessel. The two start an affair, which Denison is hesitant to continue because of the differences in their social classes. Adequate performances are marred by a script burdened with some soap opera dramatics.

p, Victor Skutezky; d, Ken Annakin; w, Talbot Jennings, Gilbert Gunn (based on the novel by Nevil Shute); ph, Wilkie Cooper; ed, Peter Graham Scott.

Drama   **(PR:A MPAA:NR)**

LANDLORD, THE***   (1970) 112m Mirisch/Cartier UA c

Beau Bridges (*Elgar Enders*), Pearl Bailey (*Marge*), Diana Sands (*Fanny*), Louis Gossett (*Copee*), Lee Grant (*Mrs. Enders*), Douglas Grant (*Walter Gee*), Melvin Stewart (*Prof. Duboise*), Walter Brooke (*Mr. Enders*), Susan Anspach (*Susan*), Robert Klein (*Peter*), Will McKenzie (*William, Jr.*), Gretchen Walther (*Doris*), Stanley Green (*Heywood*), Marki Bey (*Lanie*), Oliver Clark, Florynce Kennedy, Joe Madden, Grover Dale, Trish Van Devere, Larry Cook, Hector Elizondo, John McCurry, Lionel G. Wilson, Marlene Clark, Gloria Henry, Willis Pinkett, Hannah Battle, Michael Ferguson, Bobby V. Garvin, Richard Usher, Chelle C. Mordecai, Christopher L. Calloway, Carl Lee, Van Kirksey, Louise Stubbs, Tony Major.

A comic, often satiric, look at racial tensions has sheltered rich kid Bridges buying a ghetto tenement with the intention of kicking the tenants out and remodeling it for his own use. His initial plans are changed when he begins to grow attached to the people who live in the building. They are an interesting assortment of "types" who spark emotions in Bridges he never knew he possessed. He falls in love with Bey, a black art student, and decides to marry her. These plans are temporarily postponed when he discovers he has gotten his neighbor Sands pregnant. The film offers some top-notch performances, and the direction by Ashby allows the individual personalities of the characters to shine through. There are a few uneven moments in the script, but they can be easily dismissed. Willis is able to capture the atmosphere of both the rich and poor New York lifestyles with impressive skill. Film was shot on location throughout New York City.

p, Norman Jewison; d, Hal Ashby; w, William Gunn (based on the novel by Kristin Hunter); ph, Gordon Willis (DeLuxe Color); m, Al Kooper; ed, William Abbott Sawyer, Edward Warschilka; prod d, Robert Boyle; set d, John Godfrey; cos, Domingo A. Rodriguez; makeup, Mike Maggi.

Drama/Comedy   **(PR:C MPAA:R)**

LANDRU**½

(1963, Fr./Ital) 114m Rome Paris-C.C. Champion/EMP c (AKA: BLUEBEARD)

Charles Denner (*Henri-Desire Landru*), Michele Morgan (*Celestine Buisson*), Danielle Darrieux (*Berthe Heon*), Hildegard Neff (*Madame X*), Juliette Mayniel (*Anna Collomb*), Stephane Audran (*Fernande Segret*), Catherine Rouvel (*Andree Babelay*), Denise Provence (*Madame Lacoste*), Francoise Lugagne (*Madame Landru*), Mary Marquet (*Mme. Guillin*), Robert Burnier (*Presiding Judge*), Huguette

Forge (*Mme. Vidal*), Jean-Louis Maury (*Commissioner Belin*), Gisele Sandre (*Georgette*), Mario David (*Prosecutor*), Claude Mansard (*Defense Attorney*), Sacha Briquet (*Assistant Prosecutor*), Serge Bento (*Maurice Landru*), Denise Lepvrier (*Catherine Landru*), Diana Lepvrier (*Landru's Daughter*), Raymond Queneau (*Clemenceau*), Jean-Pierre Melville (*Mandel*), Henri Attal, Dominique Zardi (*Gendarmes*), Claude Chabrol.

An inconsistent black comedy based on the exploits of French mass murderer Henri-Desire Landru, who romanced, swindled, and then dismembered at least 10 women during WW I. Denner coldly plays the balding, bearded villain who places ads in the lonelyhearts section of a newspaper to find his victims. He picks out profitable targets—women in their fifties with large fortunes. He then romances them in his villa, cons them into signing over their assets, kills them, dismembers their bodies, and burns them in his incinerator. Denner's reason, however, is not that of a psychotic, but of a responsible member of the bourgeoisie (a favorite target of Chabrol's). Denner insists that he only kills for the money, which he needs to support his family. The killings become ritualistic, each ending with smoke pouring from his chimney. His killing spree continues through the war until he is recognized by the sister of one of his victims. He is later brought to trial (where he refuses to comment on his guilt or innocence) and, on February 25, 1922, guillotined. Scripted by famed French author Sagan (at age 19 she wrote the critically acclaimed *Bonjour Tristesse*, which was filmed by Otto Preminger in 1959), LANDRU takes a casual approach to the murderer's legend, concerning itself more with the condemnation of bourgoise ideals than the psychology of crime. This was not the first attempt to bring Landru's escapades to the screen. In 1947 Charles Chaplin released MONSIEUR VERDOUX, a thinly disguised version which was eventually pulled from distribution. (Dubbed in English).

p, Carlo Ponti, Georges de Beauregard; d, Claude Chabrol; w, Francoise Sagan; ph, Jean Rabier (Eastmancolor); m, Pierre Jansen; ed, Jacques Gaillard; md, Andre Girard; art d, Jacques Saulnier; cos, Maurice Albray.

Crime   **(PR:O MPAA:NR)**

LANDRUSH*   (1946) 53m COL bw

Charles Starrett (*Steve Harmon/Durango Kid*), Smiley Burnette (*Smiley*), Doris Houck (*Mary Parker*), Emmett Lynn (*Jake Parker*), Bud Geary (*Hawkins*), Stephen Barclay (*Caleb Garvey*), Robert Kortman (*Sackett*), George Chesebro (*Bill*), Bud Osborne (*Sheriff Collins*), Ozie Waters and his Colorado Rangers.

Generic western format has Starrett (the Durango Kid) as a masked lawman who saves helpless squatters from greedy villains. It seems the government is giving away Indian property that has become a refuge for ne'er-do-wells. Performances are stiff and direction is uneven—at best. (See DURANGO KID series, Index.)

p, Colbert Clark; d, Vernon Keays; w, Michael Simmons; ph, George B. Meehan; ed, James Sweeney; art d, Charles Clague; m/l, Burnette, Ozie Waters.

Western   **(PR:A MPAA:NR)**

LANDSLIDE**   (1937, Brit.) 67m Crusade/PAR bw

Jimmy Hanley (*Jimmy Haddon*), Dinah Sheridan (*Dinah Shaw*), Jimmy Mageean (*Harry McGovern*), Ann Cavanagh (*Lena Petrie*), Elizabeth Inglis (*Vera Grant*), Bruno Barnabe (*Bob White*), David Arnold (*Sgt. Lewellyn*), Dora Mayfield, Ernie Tate, Robert Moore, Ben Williams, Edward Kennedy, Jean Scott.

When a company of actors is trapped inside their theater after a landslide, a night of terror ensues. The cashier is found dead and the cashbox is gone. Two more company members are almost done in until a stage hand is found guilty. He himself is accidentally killed when a support beam falls on the man, crushing him to death. The story has some real promise with its claustrophobic setting, but the tension is never built and the film's potential is never reached.

p, Victor M. Greene; d&w, Donovan Pedelty.

Crime   **(PR:A MPAA:NR)**

L'ANEE DERNIERE A MARIENBAD

     (SEE: LAST YEAR AT MARIENBAD, 1962, Fr./Ital.)

LANGTAN   (SEE: NIGHT GAMES, 1966)

LARAMIE*½   (1949) 55m COL bw

Charles Starrett (*Steve Holden/Durango Kid*), Smiley Burnette (*Smiley*), Fred Sears (*Col. Dennison*), Tommy Ivo (*Ronald Dennison, Jr.*), Elton Britt (*Sergeant*), George Lloyd (*Sgt. Duff*), Bob Wilke (*Cronin*), Myron Healey (*Lt. Reed*), Shooting Star (*Chief Eagle*), Jay Silverheels (*Running Wolf*), Marjorie Stapp, Ethan Laidlaw, Bob Cason.

An episode of the Durango Kid series features Starrett as a Federal Peace Commission officer called in to bring peace to two feuding Indian tribes. The fight is instigated by a gang of outlaws, setting off an uprising in order to sell guns to the Indians. Written and directed without conviction. Performances are adequate, with a few welcome moments of comic relief. (See DURANGO KID series, Index.)

p, Colbert Clark; d, Ray Nazarro; w, Barry Shipman; ph, Rex Wimpy; ed, Paul Borofsky; art d, Charles Clague.

Western   **(PR:A MPAA:NR)**

LARAMIE MOUNTAINS*½   (1952) 54m COL bw

Charles Starrett (*Steve Holden/The Durango Kid*), Smiley Burnette (*Smiley Burnette*), Fred Sears (*Maj. Markham*), Jack "Jock" Mahoney (*Swift Eagle*), Marshall Reed (*Lt. Pierce*), Rory Mallinson (*Paul Drake*), Zon Murray (*Carson*), John War Eagle (*Chief Lone Tree*), Bob Wilke (*Mandel*).

Another in the "Durango Kid" series, this one has Starrett trying to stop a war between Indians and the U.S. Cavalry from escalating into an Indian massacre. It turns out that a couple of outlaws disguised as Indian scouts are trying to instigate the war to lay claim to gold that has been discovered on the Indians' land. Stale directing and routine performances make this a below-par addition to the series. (See DURANGO KID Series, Index.)

p, Colbert Clark; d, Ray Nazarro; w, Barry Shipman; ph, Fayte M. Brown; ed, Paul Borofsky; md, Mischa Bakaleinikoff; art d, Charles Clague; set d, James Crowe.

Western   **(PR:A   MPAA:NR)**

LARAMIE TRAIL, THE**½   (1944) 55m REP bw

Robert Livingston, Smiley Burnette, Linda Brent, Emmett Lynn, John James, George J. Lewis, Leander de Cordova, Slim Whitaker, Bud Osborne, Bud Geary, Roy Barcroft, Kenne Duncan, Marshal Reed, Martin Garralaga.

A Virginian goes out West where he meets a young man facing a trumped up murder rap. He saves the victim from a false conviction and all ends happily. This is a predictable enough Western, but it moves at a fast clip.

p, Louis Gray; d, John English; w, J. Benton Chaney (based on the story "Mystery at Spanish Hacienda" by Jackson Gregory); ph, Ellis Thackery; m, Mort Glickman; ed, Harry Keller; art d, Fred Ritter.

Western   **(PR:A   MPAA:NR)**

LARCENY***   (1948) 89m UNIV bw

John Payne (Rick Maxon), Joan Caulfield (Deborah Owens Clark), Dan Duryea (Silky Randall), Shelley Winters (Tory), Dorothy Hart (Madeline), Richard Rober (Max), Dan O'Herlihy (Duke), Nicholas Joy (Walter Vanderline), Percy Helton (Charlie Jordan), Walter Greaza (Mr. Owens), Patricia Alphin (Waitress), Harry Antrim (Mr. McNulty), Russ Conway (Detective), Paul Brinegar (Mechanic), Don Wilson (Master of Ceremonies), Barbara Challis (Maid), Grandon Rhodes (Harry Carson), Ruth Lee (Patricia Carson), Gene Evans (Horace), Bill Walker (Butler), Sam Edwards (Y.A.A. President), Don Garner (College Boy), Pat Walker (Peggy), Jack Chefe (Bald-Headed Waiter), John Carpenter (Man Bidder), Jasper Weldon (Porter), Oliver Hartwell (Black Porter), Bob E. Perry (Bartender), Alex Davidoff (Waiter), Donald Dewar (Boy).

A gang of confidence tricksters led by Duryea descends on a small town in southern California intending to cheat Caulfield, the widow of a war hero, out of her savings by having her put up money for a memorial to him. Payne is the smooth-talking front man for the gang who finds himself unable to go through with the scheme when he falls in love with the mark. Further complications are added by Winters, Duryea's moll, who has a hankering for Payne. The unhappy ending has Payne turning himself and the whole gang in to the police. Well-crafted entertainment moves at a good clip and features fine performances by Duryea as the dangerous gang leader and, especially, Winters as the amorous moll. Winters, however, was not happy with the film as it was the first of more than 20 she made in the space of seven years while she was under contract to Universal. Forced by studio heads to appear in a number of programmers like LARCENY, Winters was so unhappy with the first rushes when she saw them that she cut off most of her hair. The next day the makeup and hair people were shocked, but they managed to do her hair into curls and since the film was shooting in sequence they wrote a line into the script about Winters getting her hair done. Universal took advantage of the situation by promoting the cut in fan magazines and in *Life* magazine. Winters liked the new style so much she kept it permanently.

p, Leonard Goldstein, Aaron Rosenberg; d, George Sherman; w, Herbert F. Margolis, Louis Markein, William Bowers (based on the novel *The Velvet Fleece* by Lois Ely, John Fleming); ph, Irving Glassberg; m, Leith Stevens; ed, Frank Gross; art d, Bernard Herzbrun, Richard Reidel.

Crime   **(PR:A-C   MPAA:NR)**

LARCENY IN HER HEART**   (1946) 68m PRC bw

Hugh Beaumont (Michael Shayne), Cheryl Walker (Phyllis), Ralph Dunn (Sgt. Rafferty), Paul Bryar (Tim Rourke), Charles Wilson (Chief Gentry), Douglas Fowley (Doc Patterson), Gordon Richards (Burton Stallings), Charles Quigley (Arch Dubler), Julia McMillan (Lucille), Marie Harmon (Helen Stallings), Lee Bennett (Whit Marlowe), Henry Hall (Dr. Porter), Milton Kibbee (Joe Morell).

Run-of-the-mill murder mystery features Beaumont as a private investigator on the case after a corpse turns up on his front porch. Good performances are marred by a plot that loses steam. There are some good comic moments, however, when Beaumont tries to dodge the police.

p, Sigmund Neufeld; d, Sam Newfield; w, Raymond L. Schrock (based on the story by Brett Halliday); ph, Jack Greenhalgh; ed, Holbrook N. Todd; md, Leo Erdody; art d, Edward C. Jewell.

Mystery   **(PR:A   MPAA:NR)**

LARCENY, INC.***   (1942) 95m WB bw

Edward G. Robinson (J. Chalmers "Pressure" Maxwell), Jane Wyman (Denny Costello), Broderick Crawford (Jug Martin), Jack Carson (Jeff Randolph), Anthony Quinn (Leo Dexter), Edward S. Brophy (Weepy Davis), Harry Davenport (Homer Bigelow), John Qualen (Sam Bachrach), Barbara Jo Allen [Vera Vague] (Mademoiselle Gloria), Grant Mitchell (Aspinwall), Jack C. [Jackie] Gleason (Hobart), Andrew Tombes (Oscar Engelhart), Joseph Downing (Smitty), George Meeker (Mr. Jackson), Fortunio Bonanova (Anton Copoulos), Joseph Crehan (Warden), Jean Ames (Florence), William Davidson (McCarthy), Chester Clute (Buchanan), Creighton Hale (Carmichael), Emory Parnell (Officer O'Casey), Joe Devlin (Umpire), John Kelly (Batter), Jimmy O'Gatty, Jack Kenney (Convicts), Eddy Chandler (1st Guard), Oscar "Dutch" Hendrian (Chuck), Bill Phillips (Muggsy), Hank Mann, Eddie Foster, Cliff Saum, Charles Sullivan (Ballplayers), James Flavin (2nd Guard), Charles Drake (Driver), Vera Lewis (Woman), Ray Montgomery (Young Man), Lucien Littlefield (1st Customer), Grace Stafford (Secretary), DeWolfe [William]

Hopper (2nd Customer), Pat O'Malley (Policeman), Arthur Q. Bryan (Stout Man), Roland Drew (Man), Philo Reh, Fred Walburn (Urchins), Don Barclay (Drunk), Kitty Kelly (Woman), Wallace Scott (Sandwich Man), Fred Kelsey (Bronson).

In a role which has roots in the gangster spoof BROTHER ORCHID (1940), Robinson again plays a criminal who decides to go straight. On the day before his release from Sing Sing prison, he discusses plans to open a dog track with Crawford. Quinn, a fellow inmate, hears their future plans and tries to pressure them into pulling a bank job for him. They listen to his idea—buying a luggage store next to a bank and tunneling their way into the vault—but politely decline. Things change, however, upon their release the following day, when Robinson and Crawford discover that their partner, Brophy, lost their investment. Robinson, in dire financial straits, buys the luggage shop Quinn spoke of, and takes charge of the digging operation. While Crawford and Brophy struggle with the shovels in the basement, Robinson is upstairs trying to deal with customers. To his surprise, the store is frequented by a steady flow of customers, most of whom just pay a visit in order to chat and wish Robinson luck. Their increasing visits soon push Robinson's patience to the breaking point since the noisy digging must be halted when visitors arrive. Robinson soon hires his niece, Wyman, to manage the store while he oversees Crawford and Brophy, neither of whom can do anything right. Much to Robinson's chagrin, Wyman proves to be an overly enthusiastic worker, needlessly overstocking the store with expensive luggage sold to her by the pushy Carson. Back in prison, Quinn learns that Robinson has gone ahead with the plan without his knowledge. Quinn escapes from prison and bursts into the shop armed with a gun. He takes over the tunneling operation and decides to dynamite his way in. The charge is far too powerful, however, and the entire luggage shop is blown up. The police rush to the scene and arrest Quinn, whom they think acted alone. Robinson, whose reputation as an upstanding community member is still intact, decides to open up another shop and renew his attempt to go straight. Robinson's final film under his Warner Bros. contract, LARCENY, INC. was the star's third association with director Lloyd Bacon on a spoof of the genre that made Robinson a star. Like its superior predecessors A SLIGHT CASE OF MURDER (1938) and BROTHER ORCHID (1940), LARCENY, INC. provided Robinson with a chance to tear down that gangster facade that forever cloaked his career. Disturbed by this typecasting, Robinson went on to play an attorney twice in his next three films (TALES OF MANHATTAN, 1942, and FLESH AND FANTASY, 1943, both directed by Julien Duvivier, who earned his reputation with the 1936 gangster classic PEPE LE MOKO) and a naval hero, in DESTROYER (1943).

p, Hal B. Wallis, Jack Saper, Jerry Wald; d, Lloyd Bacon; w, Everett Freeman, Edwin Gilbert (based on the play "The Night Before Christmas" by Laura and S. J. Perelman); ph, Tony Gaudio; m, Adolph Deutsch; ed, Ralph Dawson; md, Leo F. Forbstein; art d, John Hughes.

Crime/Comedy   **Cas.**   **(PR:A   MPAA:NR)**

LARCENY LANE   (SEE: BLONDE CRAZY, 1931)

LARCENY ON THE AIR**   (1937) 67m REP bw

Robert Livingston (Baxter), Grace Bradley (Jean Sterling), Willard Robertson (McDonald), Pierre Watkin (Kennedy), Granville Bates (Professor), William Newell (Andrews), Byron Foulger (Pete), Wilbur Mack (Thompson), Matty Fain (Burke), Smiley Burnette, Josephine Whittell, Charles Timblin, William Griffith, DeWolf [William] Hopper, Frank DuFrance, Florence Gill.

Livingston plays a righteous doctor determined to stop the corrupt selling of quack cures. Starting out by delivering talks over the radio, he continues his work through an investigation that gets him mixed up with the mob. In the process he falls in love with Bradley, daughter of the hood he's after. Fast, well-paced direction helps the slight script. Performances are adequate. The song, "Sittin' on the Moon," lifted from a 1936 film of the same name, was thrown in for good measure.

p, Nat Levine, Sol C. Siegal; d, Irving Pichel; w, Endre Bohem, Richard English (based on a story by English); ph, Jack Marta; m, Harry Grey; ed, Edward Mann.

Drama   **(PR:A   MPAA:NR)**

LARCENY STREET*½

(1941, Brit.) 62m Jack Buchanan/Film Alliance of the U.S. bw (GB: SMASH AND GRAB)

Jack Buchanan (John Forrest), Elsie Randolph (Alice Forrest), Arthur Margetson (Malveen), Anthony Holles (Palino), Edmund Willard (Cappellano), David Burns (Bellini), Lawrence Grossmith (Rankin), Zoe Wynn (Carole), Edward Lexy (Inspector McInery), Lawrence Hanray (Praskins), Sara Seegar (Miss Quincey), Nigel Fitzgerald.

Jewels are being stolen around London and it's up to detective Buchanan, with the help of wife Randolph, to find out who's behind the crime. The trail leads him to a barber shop that's used for fencing the hot gems. Buchanan nearly has a close shave (literally) but is saved in the nick of time. Though Buchanan gives a funny performance, using his comic gifts with finesse, the film is well below his talents. Direction shows no sense at all for suspense or comedy, instead relying on rudimentary filmmaking cliches that were old-fashioned well before silents started to talk.

d, Tim Whelan; w, Ralph Spence (based on a story by Whelan); ph, Henry Harris, Roy Clark.

Suspense/Comedy   **(PR:A   MPAA:NR)**

LARCENY WITH MUSIC**   (1943) 64m UNIV bw

Allan Jones (Ken Daniels), Kitty Carlisle (Pamela Mason), Leo Carrillo (Gus Borelli), William Frawley (Mike Simms), Gus Schilling (Austin J. Caldwell), Lee Patrick (Agatha Parkinson), Samuel S. Hinds (Brewster), Sig Arno (Zybisco), King Sisters (Themselves), John Hamilton (Important Banker), Murray Alper (Cab Driver),

George Lloyd (Peitro), Jack Gardner (Customer), Marte Faust (Bus Driver), Alvino Rey and his Orchestra.

This comeback for Carlisle stars her as the vocalist of a chamber music quintet that has seen better days. They lose their nightclub gig when a scheming orchestra manager persuades nightclub owner Carrillo to book his orchestra. Frawley, as the manager, concocts the story that orchestra vocalist Jones is heir to a fortune, and that Carrillo, by giving the band a spot, can get a chunk of the inheritance. But the scheme is exposed after Carlisle, in disguise as a chambermaid in the nightclub, figures it out. All ends well, despite—or because of—the complications. The film delivers some entertaining musical performances, especially by the King Sisters, but the thin script and weak direction don't add up to a stellar musical. Songs: "For the Want of You" (Jule Styne, Eddie Cherkoss, sung by the King Sisters), "They Died with Their Boots Laced," "Do You Hear Music?" "Please, Louise" (Don Raye, Gene DePaul), "Only in Dreams" (Sam Lerner, Charles Previn), "When You Wore a Tulip" (Jack Mahoney, Percy Wenrich, sung by the King Sisters).

p, Howard Benedict; d, Edward Lilley; w, Robert Harari; ph, Paul Ivano; ed, Paul Landres; md, Charles Previn; art d, John Goodman.

Musical/Romance   **(PR:A MPAA:NR)**

LARGE ROPE, THE*   (1953, Brit.) 72m Insignia/UA bw

Donald Houston (Tom Penney), Susan Shaw (Susan Hamble), Robert Brown (Mick Jordan), Vanda Godsell (Amy Jordan), Peter Byrne (Jeff Stribling), Richard Warner (Inspector Harmer), Christine Finn (May), Thomas Heathcote (James Gore), Carl Bernard (Alfred Hamble), Douglas Herald (Simon Penney), Leonard White, Margaret Anderson, Barbara Cavan, Natalie Kent, Michael Mulcaster, Edward Judd.

Tiresome depiction in which Houston tries to lead a peaceful and hardworking existence in his village, after being released from prison for a murder he didn't commit. But when another murder occurs in Houston's town, suspicion quicklypoints to the ex-con. Things work out for the best, however, as Houston manages to clear his name on both accounts, and solve the murders as well.

p, Victor Hanbury; d, Wolf Rilla; w, Ted Willis; ph, Geoffrey Faithfull.

Crime/Drama   **(PR:A MPAA:NR)**

LARGE ROPE, THE   (SEE: LONG ROPE, 1961)

L'ARMEE DES OMBRES*½
(1969, Fr./Ital.) 140m Corona-Fono c (AKA: THE ARMY OF SHADOWS)

Lino Ventura (Philippe Gerbier), Paul Meurisse (Luc Jardie), Simone Signoret (Mathilde), Jean-Pierre Cassel (Jean-François), Claude Mann (Le Masque), Christian Barbier (Le Bison), Serge Reggiani (The Barber), Alain Libolt (Dounat), Paul Crauchet (Felix), Alain Bottet (Camp Commandant).

A dark portrayal of the French Resistance movement has Ventura cast as a brave fighter who escapes from Gestapo Headquarters after killing a guard. He returns to Marseilles where he and his group apprehend an informer and strangle him. Ventura's group, with the aid of Signoret, attempts to rescue an arrested Resistance fighter in Lyons but Ventura is captured and Cassel is killed. Ventura makes a daring escape while on his way to the firing squad and returns to the fight. The group learns that Signoret has been arrested. Threatened with forced prostitution, Signoret gives the names of some of her countrymen to the Gestapo. While driving down the street, one of Ventura's group sees the released Signoret walking along and kills her in the name of the Resistance. Based on the novel by Joseph Kessel, L'ARMEE DES OMBRES was the pet project of Jean Pierre Melville for nearly 25 years and he referred to it as "the book about the Resistance." What he brought to the screen was a film which was as personal as Kessel's novel, creating a war film which had all the markings of Melville's usual gangster stylings. Himself a member of the Resistance for two years, Melville portrays those who fought against the Occupation in a romantic light which was subsequently de-mythicized in Marcel Ophuls' documentary THE SORROW AND THE PITY (1970).

d&w, Jean-Pierre Melville (based on the novel Army of Shadows by Joseph Kessel); ph, Pierre Lhomme (Eastmancolor); m, Eric de Marsan; ed, Françoise Bonnot.

War Drama   **(PR:C MPAA:NR)**

LAS CUATRO VERDADES
(SEE: THREE FABLES OF LOVE, 1963, Fr./Ital./Span.)

L'AS DES AS   (SEE: ACE OF ACES, 1982, Fr./Ger.)

LAS RATAS NO DUERMEN DE NOCHE*
(1974, Span./Fr.) 93m Mezquirez/Eurocine-Europrodis c

Paul Naschy, Richard Palmer, Carlos Otero, Oliver Mathot, Silvia Solar, Victor Israel, Evelyn Scott, Richard Kolin, Gilda Anderson.

Naschy is a gang boss who is bopped over the head and needs a new brain. Scientist Palmer has just the thinking cap for the ailing mobster—that of a decapitated rival gangster. Not surprisingly, the rival's brain begins to take over. Lots of sadism and medical images lace this routine crime thriller.

d&w, Juan Fortuny; ph, Raymond Heil.

Crime/Drama/Horror   **(PR:O MPAA:NR)**

LAS VEGAS 500 MILLIONS
(SEE: THEY CAME TO ROB LAS VEGAS, 1969)

LAS VEGAS FREE-FOR-ALL*½
(1968, Jap.) 157m Toho-Watanabe c (KUREIZI OGON SAKUSEN)

Hitoshi Ueki (Shinran Machida), Hajime Hana (Shigekane Itagaki), Kei Tani (Kaneo Nashimoto), Mie Hama (Tsukiko), Mari Sono (Yuriko), Peggy Neal (Mary), The Peanuts.

A Japanese gambler wins big after being given a poker chip from Las Vegas, and requests a transfer to his company's Los Angeles branch. A young doctor receives a property deed worth $1 million after a man is hit and killed by a taxi. A politician is sent to the States after a disagreement with his superiors on an assignment to inspect sanitation facilities. These three men meet on an L.A.-bound plane from Tokyo, and, upon landing, each receives some bad news. They decide to go to Las Vegas and make a fortune, but don't have much luck. Crooks learn that the doctor's property contains a gold mine and try to seize control, but the Japanese trio gets there first. They discover a cache of gold coins which has already been pledged to build a hospital. A pretty odd crime comedy.

d, Takashi Tsuboshima; w, Ryozo Kasahara, Yasuo Tanami; ph, Shoji Utsumi [Masaharu Utsumi] (Tohoscope, Eastmancolor); m, Yasushi Miyagawa, Tessho Hagiwara.

Crime/Comedy   **(PR:C MPAA:NR)**

LAS VEGAS HILLBILLYS*
(1966) 90m Woolner Brothers c (AKA: COUNTRY MUSIC, U.S.A.)

Ferlin Husky (Woody), Mamie Van Doren (Boots), Don Bowman (Jeepers), Billie Bird (Aunt Clementine), Jayne Mansfield, Louis Quinn, Richard Kiel, John Harmon, Sonny James, Del Reeves, Roy Drusky, Bill Anderson, Wilma Burgess, The Duke of Paducah, Connie Smith.

Country singer Husky stars as a farm boy from Tennessee who inherits a Las Vegas casino. He packs his bags and heads West, meeting Mansfield on the way. They arrive to find that the casino is a dilapidated old barn which is in desperate need of fixing. Barmaid Van Doren lends a hand in putting on a country music jamboree which nets enough cash to do the repair work. A strange cast and a strange idea. Includes the song, "Money Greases the Wheel," sung by Husky. (Sequel: HILLBILLYS IN A HAUNTED HOUSE.)

p, Larry E. Jackson; d, Arthur C. Pierce; w, Jackson.

Comedy/Musical   **(PR:A MPAA:NR)**

LAS VEGAS LADY*½   (1976) 87m Crown International c

Stella Stevens (Lucky), Stuart Whitman (Vic), George DiCenzo (Eversull), Lynne Moody (Carole), Linda Scruggs (Lisa), Joseph Della Sorte (A.C.), Jesse White (Big Jake), Hank Robinson, Karl Lukas, Emilia Dallenbach, Max Starkey, Andrew Stevens, Frank Bonner, Walter Smith, Jack Gordon, Stephanie Faulkner, Ava Readdy, Gene Slott, Tony Bill.

Predictable plot has Stevens and Whitman involved in a scheme to heist $500,000. By so doing they can satisfy—and pay for—their dreams. Problem is that Stevens does not necessarily want to stick it out with Whitman. The director and cast did all they could to move this unfulfilling script along. Included in the cast is Andrew Stevens, son of the lead, Stella Stevens.

p, Joseph Zappala, Gene Slott; d, Noel Nosseck; w, Walter Dallenbach; ph, Stephen Katz; m, Alan Silvestri; ed, Robert Gordon.

Drama   **Cas.**   **(PR:A MPAA:PG)**

LAS VEGAS NIGHTS*½   (1941) 90m PAR bw (GB: THE GAY CITY)

Phil Regan (Bill Stevens), Bert Wheeler (Stu Grant), Tommy Dorsey and His Orchestra, Constance Moore (Norma Jennings), Virginia Dale (Patsy Lynch), Lillian Cornell (Mildred Jennings), Betty Brewer (Katy), Hank Ladd (Hank Bevis), Eddie Kane (Maitre D'), Eleanor Stewart (Hat Check Girl), Catherine Craig, Marcelle Christopher, Ella Neal, Jean Phillips (Girls With Bill), Wanda McKay (Cigarette Girl), Francetta Malloy (Gloria Stafford), Henry Kolker (William Stevens, Sr.), Nick Moro (Guitar and Violin Player), Frank Yaconelli (Concertina Player), Earl Douglas (Guitar Player), Frank Sinatra, Red Donahue and His Mule Uno.

Frank Sinatra made his film debut in this picture, with a brief performance as a nightclub singer proving to be the only bright spot in a haphazard musical. Story evolves around three sisters, accompanied by Wheeler, who come to Las Vegas to lay claim to an inheritance. In the process they make a fortune gambling, quickly lose it, then panhandle enough money to open their own club, but this falls through. Eventually they get around to the business of the estate which requires outwitting a crooked lawyer. Except for a few musical numbers, this picture has little to offer. The plot is weak and often tedious, and the script fails to integrate musical numbers into the story line. Sinatra sings "I'll Never Smile Again" (Ruth Lowe). Other songs include: "Song of India" (Nikolai Andreevich Rimski-Korsakov, arranged by "Red" Bone), "On Miami Shore" (William LeBaron, Victor Jacobi), "I've Gotta Ride," "Mary, Mary, Quite Contrary" (Frank Loesser, Burton Lane), "Dolores" (Loesser, Louis Alter).

p, William LeBaron; d, Ralph Murphy; w, Ernest Pagano, Harry Clork, Eddie Welch (based on a story by Pagano); ph, William C. Mellor; ed, Arthur Schmidt; md, Victor Young; art d, Hans Dreier, Earl Hedrick.

Musical   **(PR:A MPAA:NR)**

LAS VEGAS SHAKEDOWN**½   (1955) 79m AA bw

Dennis O'Keefe (Joe Barnes), Coleen Gray (Julia Rae), Charles Winninger (Mr. Raff), Thomas Gomez (Sirago), Dorothy Patrick (Dorothy Reid), Mary Beth Hughes (Mabel), Elizabeth Patterson (Mrs. Raff), James Millican (Wheeler Reid), Robert Armstrong (Doc), Joseph Downing (Matty), Lewis Martin (Collins), Mara McAfee (Angela), Charles Fredericks (Sheriff Woods), Regina Gleason (Maxine Miller), Murray Alper (House Manager), James Alexander (Sam Costar), Frank Hanley (Martin), Allen Mathews (Rick).

O'Keefe plays the operator of a Las Vegas casino that serves as the backdrop for a potpourri of characters and situations. One incident involves hood Gomez' desperate attempts to buy the hotel including threats on O'Keefe's life. Performances are adequate and direction is well paced, making up for script weaknesses which may stem from an unrealistic perspective of Las Vegas life.

p, William F. Broidy; d, Sidney Salkow; w, Steve Fisher; ph, John Martin; m, Edward J. Kay; ed, Chandler House; cos, Tommy Thompson.

Drama **(PR:A MPAA:NR)**

LAS VEGAS STORY, THE* (1952) 87m RKO bw

Jane Russell *(Linda Rollins)*, Victor Mature *(Dave Andrews)*, Vincent Price *(Lloyd Rollins)*, Hoagy Carmichael *(Happy)*, Brad Dexter *(Thomas Hubler)*, Gordon Oliver *(Drucker)*, Jay C. Flippen *(Harris)*, Will Wright *(Fogarty)*, Bill Welsh *(Martin)*, Ray Montgomery *(Desk Clerk)*, Colleen Miller *(Mary)*, Robert Wilke *(Clayton)*, Syd Saylor *(Matty)*, George Hoagland, Roger Creed, Jimmy Long, Bert Stevens, Norman Stevens, Ben Harris, Ted Jordan, Philip Ahlm *(Men)*, Mary Bayless, Mary Darby, Barbara Freking, Jean Corbett, Hazel Shaw, Evelyn Lovequist *(Women)*, Clarence Muse *(Pullman Porter)*, Dorothy Abbott, Joan Mallory, Jane Easton *(Waitresses)*, Mavis Russell *(Blonde)*, Midge Ware *(Chief Money Changer)*, John Merrick *(Gus)*, Brooks Benedict *(Stickman Dealer)*, Paul Frees *(District Attorney)*, Carl Sklover, Ralph Alley, Mitchell Rhein, Forrest Lederer, Charles Cross *(Dealers)*, Connie Castle *(Guest)*, Milton Kibbee *(Coroner)*, Al Murphy, Harry Brooks, Dick Ryan *(Bartenders)*, Howard Darbeen *(Stickman)*, Wallis Clark *(Witwer)*, Oliver Hartwell *(Redcap)*, Roy Darmour, Pat Collins, Sam Finn, Joe Gilbert *(Stickmen)*, Carolyn Block, Betty Onge, Helen Blizard, Mona Knox *(Change Girls)*, Robert Milton *(Sheriff)*, Steve Flagg *(Deputy)*, Suzanne Ames, Annabelle Applegate, Joyce Niven, Shirley Tegge, Anne Dore, Chili Williams, Sylvia Lewis *(Guests)*, Barbara Thatcher, Beverly Thomas, Sue Casey.

A routine drama meant to be a thriller has Price and Russell as a married couple on a trip to Las Vegas, where she runs into her ex-flame Mature. Price proceeds to lose heavily at the dice tables, losing Russell at the same time. Meanwhile, he reveals himself to be an embezzler. Mature plays the righteous sheriff who gets Price out of a jam, even though Price is married to the woman he loves. At the release of this picture, Howard Hughes refused to give Paul Jarrico credit for his contribution to the script because of his alleged Communist sympathies. This led to a lengthy legal battle, as well as to hostilities between the Screenwriters Guild and Hughes. Performances in this picture are for the most part lifeless, mainly due to the ill-scripted dialog and poorly motivated situations.

p, Robert Sparks; d, Robert Stevenson; w, Earl Felton, Harry Essex (based on the story by Jay Dratler); ph, Harry J. Wild; m, Leigh Harline; ed, George Shrader; md, C. Bakaleinikoff; art d, Albert S. D'Agostino, Feild Gray; set d, Darrell Silvera, John Sturdevant; cos, Howard Greer; spec eff, Harold Wellman; m/l, "My Resistance Is Low," Carmichael, Harold Adamson (sung by Russell), "I Get Along Without You Very Well," (sung by Russell), "The Monkey Song," Carmichael (sung by Carmichael); makeup, Mel Burns.

Drama **Cas.** **(PR:A MPAA:NR)**

LASCA OF THE RIO GRANDE½** (1931) 60m UNIV bw

Leo Carrillo *(Jose Santa Cruz)*, Dorothy Burgess *(Lasca)*, Johnny Mack Brown *(Miles Kincaid)*, Slim Summerville *(Crabapple)*, Frank Campeau *(Jehosaphat)*.

Carrillo is a Texas Ranger who's fallen in love with dance hall girl Burgess. Unfortunately, she's wanted for murder and it's up to her lover to bring her in. But Burgess won't let him do it and sacrifices her life by throwing herself into a cattle stampede. An unusual theme for a program western.

d, Edward Laemmle; w, Randall Faye (based on the poem "Lasca" by Frank Duprez, and a story by Tom Reed); ph, Harry Neumann.

Western **(PR:A MPAA:NR)**

LASERBLAST*½ (1978) 85m Irwin Yablans c

Kim Milford *(Billy Duncan)*, Cheryl Smith *(Kathy Farley)*, Gianni Russo *(Tony Craig)*, Ron Masak *(Sheriff)*, Dennis Burkley *(Peter Ungar)*, Barry Cutler *(Jesse Jeep)*, Mike Bobenko *(Chuck Boran)*, Eddie Deezen *(Froggy)*, Keenan Wynn *(Col. Farley)*, Roddy McDowall *(Dr. Mellon)*.

Messy science fictioner has Milford as an abused teenager finding an alien laser in the desert. He uses the gun to seek revenge on all the people who have done him harm in the past, in the process taking on the guise of the alien who had previously owned the gun. Directed and scripted with a bias toward action rather than story development. Except for the makeup, the special effects fail to lend this picture any believability.

p, Charles Band; d, Michael Rae; w, Franne Schacht, Frank Ray Perilli; ph, Terry Bowen (Technicolor); m, Joel Goldsmith, Richard Band; ed, Jodie Copeland; cos, Jill Sheridan, Barbara Scott; spec eff & makeup, Harry Woolman, Paul Gentry, Dave Allen.

Fantasy **Cas.** **(PR:C MPAA:PG)**

LASH, THE** (1930) 76m FN-WB bw

Richard Barthelmess *(Francisco Delfino)*, James Rennie *(David Howard)*, Mary Astor *(Rosita Garcia)*, Marian Nixon *(Dolores Delfino)*, Fred Kohler *(Peter Harkness)*, Barbara Bedford *(Lupe)*, Robert Edeson *(Mariano Delfino)*, Mathilde Comont *(Concha)*, Arthur Stone *(Juan)*, Erville Alderson *(Judge Travers)*.

Set in California shortly after the American conquest of the Spanish, THE LASH stars Barthelmess as a Mexican rancher who becomes a sort of Latin Robin Hood in his efforts to avenge the injustices suffered by his people. He battles the evil American land commissioner and defends the virtue of the beautiful Astor. He eventually succeeds in delivering his precious cattle to the commissioner—in the form of a stampede which wrecks the corrupt bureaucrat's office. Barthelmess nevertheless collects what he is due. The film was meant to be a starring vehicle for the dashing Barthelmess, so other roles are diminished. Some suspension of belief may be required to accept Barthelmess in western garb. Directed with little belief in the project. THE LASH, it should be noted, is surprisingly anti-American for its time. This early western was also part of an experiment in widescreen projection by Warner Bros., called Vitascope by this particular studio. The other major studios also attempted their initial ventures into the larger format, in westerns, around this same time.

d, Frank Lloyd; w, Bradley King (based on the story "Adios" by Lanier and Virginia Stivers Bartlett); ph, Ernest Haller (Vitascope); ed, Harold Young.

Western **(PR:A MPAA:NR)**

LASH, THE½** (1934, Brit.) 63m REA/RKO bw

Lyn Harding *(Bronson Haughton)*, John Mills *(Arthur Haughton)*, Joan Maude *(Dora Bush)*, Leslie Perrins *(Alec Larkin)*, Mary Jerrold *(Margaret Haughton)*, Aubrey Mather *(Col. Bush)*, D.J. Williams *(Mr. Charles)*, Roy Emerton *(Steve)*, S. Victor Stanley *(Jake)*, Peggy Blythe.

Harding is a man who has worked his way to the top and is now a millionaire. Mills plays his self-centered son who continually lets him down with his devil-may-care attitude. When Mills jumps a ship bound for Australia to continue his affair with a married woman, Maude, it's the last straw for Harding. He beats his son to near death with a horsewhip. This film's passionate study of the violent relationship between a father and son leaves the audience to conclude on its own whether either party has learned anything from their mistakes.

p, Julius Hagen; d, Henry Edwards; w, Brock Williams, Vera Allinson, H. Fowler Mear (based on a play by Owen Davis, Sewell Collins, Cyril Campion); ph, Ernest Palmer.

Drama **(PR:C MPAA:NR)**

LASH OF THE PENITENTES (SEE: PENITENTE MURDER CASE, 1937)

LASKY JEDNE PLAVOLASKY
(SEE: LOVES OF A BLONDE, 1965, Czech.)

L'ASSASSIN HABITE AU 21
(SEE: MURDERER LIVES AT NUMBER 21, THE, 1947, Fr.)

LASSIE, COME HOME**** (1943) 90m MGM c

Roddy McDowall *(Joe Carraclough)*, Donald Crisp *(Sam Carraclough)*, Edmund Gwenn *(Rowlie)*, Dame May Whitty *(Dolly)*, Nigel Bruce *(Duke of Rudling)*, Elsa Lanchester *(Mrs. Carraclough)*, Elizabeth Taylor *(Priscilla)*, J. Patrick O'Malley *(Hynes)*, Ben Webster *(Dan'l Fadden)*, Alec Craig *(Snickers)*, John Rogers *(Buckles)*, Arthur Shields *(Jock)*, Alan Napier *(Andrew)*, Roy Parry *(Butcher)*, George Broughton *(Allen)*, Howard Davies *(Cobbler)*, John Power *(Miner)*, Nelson Leigh *(Teacher)*, May Beatty *(Fat Woman)*, Charles Irwin *(Tom)*, Pal *(Lassie)*, Larry Kert *(Stunt Boy for Roddy McDowall)*.

In case you didn't know it, Lassie was a male dog named Pal. He'd been bought for $10 by trainer Rudd Weatherwax who had worked for MGM training animals for PECK'S BAD BOY and THE CHAMP. The studio wanted a female and Weatherwax was chosen to select the proper female dog, but when shooting began the female shed heavily and was replaced by Pal, who was a stunt double until he proved his stuff. Since then, there have been many dogs to play Lassie, all of them male. Moderate box office had been predicted for this low-budget movie out of Dore Schary's "B" unit, but it's spawned many sequels as well as both a radio and a long-running TV show. Marx, the producer, had been walking the streets as a volunteer civil defense warden at night when he met Taylor's father, a recent British emigre, who prevailed on Marx to give his 11 year old a chance. Marx did and the rest is film history. Marx stayed with MGM for more then 40 years, on and off, until he retired to write the best-seller about his aunt, QUEEN OF THE RITZ. Contrary to popular belief, this was not Taylor's first film. She had been signed to a brief contract by Universal and appeared in THERE'S ONE BORN EVERY MINUTE but was dropped quickly, an indication of the talent-spotting ability of the studio executives at the Valley lot at that time. Taylor's screen test proved positive and she was put into this film, a boy and his dog story that no one thought would be such an enormous success. It's the dark days after WWI in Yorkshire, England. Lanchester and Crisp are an impoverished couple and need money so they sell their son's dog to Bruce, a Duke who can give it a good home as he has a huge estate and many dogs. McDowall, the boy, is terribly hurt but realizes it's probably best for his dog's welfare. Lassie escapes time and again from Bruce's kennels and comes home to McDowall. Then Bruce takes the dog north to Scotland for the hunting season where he is allowed to escape again by Bruce's sympathetic granddaughter, Taylor. Now Lassie begins a long journey back to McDowall's family. He encounters many adventures along the way including a visit with Whitty and Webster, an aged farm couple, as well as a stay with handyman Gwenn. He continues south through dreadful weather and several problems before finally arriving, exhausted, at McDowall's home. Just when it seems that this dog will never be happy, Bruce decides to hire Crisp to help with the kennels on his estate and the picture ends. Lassie was one of many dogs that achieved stardom in the movies although he (she) has lasted longer than any of the dogs before or since. Some of them include Asta (owned by Nick and Nora of THIN MAN fame), Rin-Tin-Tin, the biggest of all silent screen canines, and Benji, among many. McDowall had scored earlier in MY FRIEND FLICKA for Fox and was loaned out by the studio to make this film. Taylor, McDowall, Crisp, Lanchester, Bruce, Whitty, Gwenn, Shields, Napier, and several of the other actors were part of the London-to-Hollywood crowd who made so many wonderful films for American studios. Director Wilcox had been a studio publicist, then King Vidor's script clerk before becoming a screen test director and finally film director. Although he was one of the boss' sons-in-law (Nick Schenck), nepotism may have helped him get the job but it was his talent that sustained him and he went on to helm THE COURAGE OF LASSIE, HILLS OF HOME, and FORBIDDEN PLANET among his credits. One of his best pictures was THE

SECRET GARDEN. Sharp-eyed viewers will recognize the lean Napier as the man who later played "Alfred" on the "Batman" TV show in the 1960s. If Arthur Shields looks and sounds familiar, it may be due to the fact that he is Barry Fitzgerald's brother and the two of them had near-identical voices. (See LASSIE series, Index.)

p, Samuel Marx; d, Fred M. Wilcox; w, Hugo Butler (based on the novel by Eric Knight); ph, Leonard Smith (Technicolor); m, Daniele Amfitheatrof; ed, Ben Lewis; art d, Cedric Gibbons, Paul Groesse; set d, Edwin B. Willis, Mildred Griffiths; spec eff, Warren Newcombe; Lassie's trainer, Rudd Weatherwax.

Drama (PR:AAA MPAA:NR)

LASSIE FROM LANCASHIRE**¹/₂ (1938, Brit.) 81m BN/ABF bw

Marjorie Browne (Jenny), Hal Thompson (Tom), Marjorie Sandford (Margie), Mark Daly (Dad), Vera Lennox (Daisy), Elsie Wagstaffe (Aunt Hetty), Johnnie Schofield (Cyril), Billy Caryll, Hilda Mundy, Joe Mott, Leslie Phillips.

Browne, a struggling young actress, joins her father Daly when he moves into his sister's boarding house. The woman works the pair to death, but Browne manages to find love in the form of Thompson, a would-be songwriter. The two begin a romance, but this is nearly dashed when the star actress of the local pierrot company becomes jealous and conspires to destroy their love. In the end, Browne and Thompson overcome the star's attempts to bust the romance, and the two dream of big things after being offered a theater contract in London's West End. An amusing little romantic comedy.

p, John Corfield; d, John Paddy Carstairs; w, Doreen Montgomery, Ernest Dudley; ph, Bryan Langley.

Comedy (PR:AA MPAA:NR)

LASSIE'S GREAT ADVENTURE** (1963) 103m Wrather/FOX c

June Lockhart (Ruth Martin), Hugh Reilly (Paul Martin), Jon Provost (Timmy Martin), Robert Howard (Sgt. Sprague), Will J. White (Constable MacDonald), Richard Kiel (Chinook Pete), Walter Stocker (John Stanley), Walter Kelley (Control Tower Operator), Patrick Waltz (Pilot), Leo Needham (Ranger Henty), Richard Simmons, Patrick Westwood, Lassie the Dog.

Little Provost and faithful pup Lassie (the sixth generation) are carried off in a hot air balloon which is being used as a promotional display at a country fair. They drift into Canada and are befriended by a giant mute Indian (Kiel). Lockhart and Reilly are frantic, but a Mountie-organized helicopter search brings them back unscathed. Standard kid stuff which was originally presented as a four-part television program entitled "The Journey." (See LASSIE series, Index.)

p, Robert Golden; d, William Beaudine, Sr.; w, Monroe Manning, Charles O'Neal (based on a story by Sumner Arthur Long); ph, Ed Fitzgerald (Eastmancolor); ed, Monica Collingwood; art d, George Troast; set d, Frank Rafferty; cos, Walt Hoffman; spec eff, Harold Murphy; makeup, Don Schoenfeld.

Adventure (PR:AAA MPAA:NR)

L'ASSOCIE (SEE: ASSOCIATE, THE, 1982, Fr./Ger.)

LAST ACT OF MARTIN WESTON, THE*¹/₂ (1970, Can./Czech.) 98m Barrandov Studio/Jacot c

Jon Granik (Martin Weston), Milena Dvorska (Secretary), Nuala Fitzgerald (Weston's Ex-Wife), Albert Waxman.

An American businessman living in Europe for the past 18 years and divorced from his wife lays an elaborate suicide plan involving a bomb hidden in a coat hanger. Incoherent ending shows that it was all in his head. Awfully dull feature unlikely ever to be revived anywhere.

p,d&w, Michael Jacot; ph, Jiri Tarantik; m, Milan Kymlicka; ed, Anthony Bower; art d, Jiri Hlupy.

Drama (PR:C MPAA:NR)

LAST ADVENTURE, THE*¹/₂
(1968, Fr./Ital.) 102m S.N.C.-Compagnia Generale Finanziaria Cinematografica/UNIV c (LES AVENTURIERS; I TRE AVVENTURIERI)

Alain Delon (Manu), Lino Ventura (Roland), Joanna Shimkus (Letitia), Serge Reggiani (Pilot), Hans Meyer, Thérèse Quentin, Guy Delorme, Jean Darie, Jean Trognon, Odile Poisson, Irène Tunc, Paul Crauchet.

After losing his pilot's license because of an attempted flight through the Arc de Triomphe, flyer Delon and his racing mechanic friend Ventura set off for the Congo. They drag along failed sculptress Shimkus and start searching for a downed plane which is supposed to be full of great riches. They are tracked by a gang of mercenaries who kill Shimkus, whom both men have fallen in love with, and follow them to locate the treasure. The hunted pair plan instead to open a restaurant on a deserted island, but soon drift apart. Nothing too adventurous here.

p, Rene Pigneres, Gerard Beytout; d, Robert Enrico; w, Jose Giovanni, Enrico, Pierre Pelegri (based on the novel Les Aventuriers by Giovanni); ph, Jean Boffety (Techniscope, Eastmancolor); m, François de Roubaix; ed, Jacqueline Méppiel; art d, Jacques d'Ovidio; cos, Paco Rabanne; spec eff, Jean Falloux.

Crime/Adventure (PR:A MPAA:NR)

LAST ADVENTURERS, THE*
(1937, Brit) Conway/Sound City bw (AKA: DOWN TO THE SEA IN SHIPS)

Niall McGinnis (Jeremy Bowker), Roy Emerton (John Arkell), Linden Travers (Ann Arkell), Peter Gawthorne (Fergus Arkell), Katie Johnson (Susan Arkell), Johnnie Schofield (Stalky), Norah Howard (Mary Allen), Ballard Berkeley (Fred Delvin), Esma Cannon (Polly Shepherd), Tony Wylde (Glory Be), Kay Walsh (Margaret Arkell), Billy Shine, Howard Douglas, Bernard Ansell.

Singularly provocative shots of storms at sea make this romantic adventure film peculiarly British. Two shipwrecks help eat away the footage as McGinnis is rescued in the first one by a man (Emerton) skippering a ship carrying the love interest, his daughter, with whom McGinnis is smitten. In the second wreck, McGinnis again is saved by Emerton, along with Emerton's brother-in-law, with whom he has been feuding. Everything is patched up by the time the wind dies down.

p, H. Fraser Passmore; d, Roy Kellino; w, Denison Clift; ph, Kellino.

Adventure (PR:A MPAA:NR)

LAST AFFAIR, THE* (1976) 80m Chelex c

Jack Wallace, Ron Dean, Del Close, Betty Thomas, Marigray Jobes, Debbie Dan, William Norris, Jack Hafferkamp.

This unevenly written and directed mess revolves around the efforts of a married couple to have a baby. Not a very interesting subject for a film in the first place, so a bit of spice is thrown in by having the male half of the marriage unable to produce viable sperm cells. Adoption is out; this leaves the woman to find another means of conception, first via the singles bar route, and then with a male prostitute. Some interesting ideas—such as the husband being a real macho type who is sterile, and the bizarre men the lady encounters—are thrown into the goings-on but nothing is there to hold these situations together. Stuart Gordon, who later directed REANIMATOR (1985), winner at Cannes for best science-fiction film, had a part in staging the action scenes. Writer-director Charbakshi must be held responsible for the dialog, which is as sterile as the husband. The cast includes some excellent way-off-Broadway stage actors, most of them centered in Chicago, especially the extremely talented Wallace.

p,d&w, Henri Charbakshi; ph, Robin Rutledge; m, Sooren Alexander; ed, Charbakshi; ch, Stuart Gordon.

Drama (PR:O MPAA:R)

LAST AMERICAN HERO, THE* (1973) 95m Fox c (AKA: HARD DRIVER)

Jeff Bridges (Elroy Jackson, Jr.), Valerie Perrine (Marge), Geraldine Fitzgerald (Mrs. Jackson), Ned Beatty (Hackel), Gary Busey (Wayne Jackson), Art Lund (Elroy Jackson, Sr.), Ed Lauter (Burton Colt), William Smith II (Kyle Kingman), Gregory Walcott (Morley), Tom Ligon (Lamar), Ernie Orsatti (Davie Baer), Erica Hagen (Trina), James Murphy (Spud), Lane Smith (Rick Penny).

Sympathetic look at a moonshiner, Bridges, who puts his car racing talents to use as a means of raising money to get his father out of jail. Backed by a pushy promoter, Beatty, and a clinging floozie, Perrine, Bridges becomes a professional stock car racer to turn the trick. Excellent performances are captured by subtle direction. Script is well written, concentrating on human values without sinking into sentimentality.

p, William Roberts, John Cutts; d, Lamont Johnson; w, Roberts (based on articles by Tom Wolfe); ph, George Silano (Panavision, DeLuxe Color); m, Charles Fox; ed, Tom Rolf, Robbe Roberts; art d, Lawrence Paull; set d, James Berkey; m/l, "I Got a Name," Norman Gimbell (sung by Jim Croce).

Drama/Action (PR:C MPAA:PG)

LAST AMERICAN VIRGIN, THE* (1982) 90m Cannon c

Lawrence Monoson (Gary), Diana Franklin (Karen), Steve Antin (Rick), Joe Rubbo (David), Louisa Moritz (Carmela), Brian Peck (Victor), Kimmy Robertson (Rose), Tessa Richarde (Brenda), Winifred Freedman (Millie), Gerri Idol (Roxanne), Sandy Sprung (Mother), Paul Keith (Father), Phil Rubenstein (Gino), Roberto Rodriguez (Paco), Blanche Rubin (Librarian), Michael Chieffo (Soda Jerk), Leslie Simms (Mrs. Applebaum), Harry Bugin (Doctor), Julianna McCarthy (Counselor), Mel Wells (Druggist), Sylvia Lawler (Assistant), Nancy Brock (Ruby), Lyla Graham (Mrs. Roswell), Mordo Dana (Jeweler), Robert Doran (Earl), Noel Scott, Peter Ellenstein, Rob Reese.

What could have been a sensitive look at the problems of growing up is shattered when THE LAST AMERICAN VIRGIN becomes a formula picture aimed at the exploitation of the teenage market. The story centers around three high school friends as they discover sex and search for fulfillment. Director Davidson manages to elicit warm performances from inexperienced actors, but this is all in vain as the script turns into another formula treatment of a delicate subject. The soundtrack features Blondie, The Cars, The Police, The Waitresses, and Devo.

p, Menahem Golan, Yoram Globus; d&w, Boaz Davidson; ph, Adam Greenburg (MGM Color); ed, Bruria Davidson; art d, Jim Dultz.

Comedy/Drama Cas. (PR:O MPAA:R)

LAST ANGRY MAN, THE**¹/₂ (1959) 100m COL bw

Paul Muni (Dr. Sam Abelman), David Wayne (Woodrow Wilson Thrasher), Betsy Palmer (Anne Thrasher), Luther Adler (Dr. Max Vogel), Joby Baker (Myron Malkin), Joanna Moore (Alice Taggart), Nancy R. Pollock (Sarah Abelman), Billy Dee Williams (Josh Quincy), Claudia McNeil (Mrs. Quincy), Robert F. Simon (Lyman Gattling), Dan Tobin (Ben Loomer), Godfrey Cambridge (Nobody Home), Helen Champan (Miss Bannahan), Cicely Tyson (Girl Left on Porch), David Winters (Lee Roy).

Though the direction of this sensitive film sometimes lags, the powerful performance by Muni makes the movie exceptional. Muni is a rugged individualist, an idealistic physician who has worked out of his own clinic in a Brooklyn slum for 45 years with faithful wife Pollock at his side. Muni's nephew, Baker, a young journalist, writes an article about his dedicated uncle and this attracts the attention of TV producer Wayne who, with the urging of the ambitious nephew looking for a job on a TV production, decides he will do a show on Muni. But Muni wants no part of a network show and Wayne turns to Adler who went to school with Muni, asking him to persuade the old man to cooperate. Adler agrees, but on the condition that Wayne promises to buy Muni and his wife a nice home in a decent neighborhood. Adler then successfully argues Muni into appearing on the show in order to express his beliefs about the rampant hypocrisy in the medical profession. Williams, a black street tough in Muni's neighborhood, has meanwhile become Muni's latest cause; the doctor believes that Williams is suffering from a brain tumor and is forever tracking Williams down to administer aid. On the night of the show, Muni hears that Williams has been arrested for car theft and he leaves before the first telecast, suffering a lethal heart attack while in the police station on his errand of mercy. Muni is riveting as the elderly idealist whose life is devoted to medicine and strong support comes from the veteran Adler and Williams, making his film debut here. Williams later admitted his debt to Muni who taught him much, even how to fake an arm-wrestling scene since Muni stated, when the two really went at it for a few minutes: "I'm not as young as I used to be." This was Muni's first movie in 13 years and he only consented to appear in the film if it was understood that he would have his way. To that end, he lectured director Mann for hours on how to interpret a scene. At one point, according to one of Muni's biographers, the brilliant actor told Mann that a particular scene had to be "filtered, sifted, refined, and distilled." When Muni walked off Mann said to Adler: "What does he think we're making—matzoh balls?" Originally, Columbia had thought to cast Peter Ustinov in the physician's role but studio chief Harry Cohn felt he would not be strong enough and the temperamental and mercurial Muni was slated. Muni received his fifth Oscar nomination for his telling portrait.

p, Fred Kohlmar; d, Daniel Mann; w, Gerald Green, Richard Murphy (based on the novel by Green); ph, James Wong Howe; m, George Duning; ed, Charles Nelson; md, Morris W. Stoloff; art d, Carl Anderson; set d, William Kiernan; cos, Jean Louis; makeup, Clay Campbell.

Drama   **(PR:A   MPAA:NR)**

LAST BANDIT, THE**¹/₂   (1949) 78m REP c

William Elliott (*Frank Norris/Frank Plummer*), Adrian Booth (*Kate Foley*), Forrest Tucker (*Jim Plummer*), Andy Devine (*Casey Brown*), Jack Holt (*Mort Pemberton*), Minna Gombell (*Winnie McPhall*), Grant Withers (*Ed Bagley*), Virginia Brissac (*Kate's Mother*), Louis R. Faust (*Hank Morse*), Stanley Andrews (*Jeff Baldwin*), Martin Garralaga (*Patrick Moreno*), Joseph Crehan (*Engineer of Local No. 44*), Charles Middleton (*Circuit Rider*), Rex Lease, Emmett Lynn, Eugene Roth, George Chesebro, Hank Bell, Jack O'Shea, Tex Terry, Steve Clark.

This remake of the 1941 version of the picture of the same name has added action. This film revolves around two brothers, Elliott and Tucker, partners in an outlaw band. Elliott tries to go straight as a security officer on a train. Tucker, thinking his brother will make it easy for him to rob it, decides to hold up the train Elliott is protecting. The film is smoothly directed and written. Performances are adequate, although the love scenes are a bit shaky.

p&d, Joseph Kane; w, Thomas Williamson (based on the story by Luci Ward, Jack Natteford); ph, Jack Martin (Trucolor); m, Dale Butts; ed, Arthur Roberts; art d, Frank Arrigo.

Western   **(PR:A   MPAA:NR)**

LAST BARRICADE, THE**   (1938, Brit.) 58m FOX British bw

Frank Fox (*Michael Donovan*), Greta Gynt (*Maria*), Paul Sheridan (*Valdez*), Meinhart Maur (*Don Jose*), Dino Galvani (*Lopez*), Vernon Harris (*Capt. Lee*), Hay Petrie (*Capt. MacTavish*), Andrea Malandrinos (*General*), Alfred Atkins, Rosarito, Dominick Sterlini.

This film takes place during the Spanish Civil War, where Fox is a journalist who meets and falls in love with Gynt. He wants her to run off with him, but when Gynt learns that her father is involved in espionage, she plots to destroy a garrison with explosives before its soldiers can evacuate. Gynt then hurries to the garrison where Fox is holed up at a factory there in order to warn him. The two escape before the place is blown to bits, but Gynt winds up in prison. Her lover manages to spring her, however, and they return to England. A wild, far-fetched but lively plot.

p, John Findlay; d&w, Alex Bryce (based on a story by R. F. Gore-Brown, Lawrence Green); ph, Stanley Grant.

War/Romance   **(PR:C   MPAA:NR)**

LAST BLITZKRIEG, THE**¹/₂   (1958) 85m COL bw

Van Johnson (*Richardson/Kroner*), Kerwin Mathews (*Wilitz*), Dick York (*Sgt. Ludwig*), Larry Storch (*Ennis*), Lise Bourdin (*Monique*), Hans Bentz van den Berg (*Col. von Ruppel*), Leon Askin (*Sgt. Steiner*), Robert Boon (*Kirsch*), Ton Van Duinhoven (*Hoffner*), Gijsbert Tersteeg (*Col. Eindorf*), Charles Rosenblum (*Schwarz*), Steve Van Brandenberg (*Lt. Wheeler*), Montgomery Ford (*Capt. Levin*), Herb Grika (*Cpl. Wilson*), Chris Baay (*Capt. Bruger*), Ronnie Ianderweer (*Pierre*), Fred Oster (*Fielding*), Karl Kent (*Pvt. 1st Class Manning*), Jan Verkoren (*German Officer*), Howard Jaffe (*Cpl. Charlie Two*), T. Bolland (*Weapons Instructor*), Jack Kelling (*Auto Instructor*), John T. Greene (*American Truck Driver*), Hans Hagemeyer (*German Lieutenant*), Pieter Goemans (*German Orderly*).

Filmed entirely in Holland, this WW II adventure has a different twist. Johnson is a Nazi who had lived in the U.S. prior to the war. He and his English-speaking Germans infiltrate American troops in France. His mission is to sabotage the American war effort. By the end of the film he is discovered and changes sides. The film is evenly paced and directed, with a competent cast.

p, Sam Katzman; d, Arthur Dreifuss; w, Lou Morheim; ph, Ted Scaife; m, Hugo De Groot; ed, Lien d'Olliveyra; art d, Nico van Baarle.

War   **(PR:A   MPAA:NR)**

LAST BRIDGE, THE***¹/₂

(1957, Aust.) 90m Cosmopol Film Union bw (DIE LETZTE BRUECKE)

Maria Schell (*Helga Reinbeck*), Bernhard Wicki (*Boro*), Barbara Rutting (*Militza*), Carl Mohner (*Sgt. Martin Berger*), Horst Haechler (*Lt. Scherer*), Pable Mincie (*Momcillo*), Tilla Durieux (*Old Peasant Woman*), Radolcic Dragoslav (*English Officer*), Robert Meyn (*German Doctor*).

A beautiful, moving anti-war film, THE LAST BRIDGE garnishes much of its quiet dignity from Schell's moving performance. It is war-torn Europe and Schell plays a German doctor captured by the Yugoslavians. At first she is reluctant to help her wounded enemies, but gradually she softens her stance, learning that all people are entitled to equal treatment. The film develops its simple plot with slow detail, letting Schell's learning process gradually build. THE LAST BRIDGE proved to be a turning point in her career, as it won Schell the 1954 Best Actress award at the Cannes Film Festival.

d, Helmut Kautner; w, Kautner, Norbert Kunzie; ph, Fred Kollhanck; m, Carl de Groof.

Drama   **(PR:O   MPAA:NR)**

LAST CASTLE, THE   (SEE: ECHOES OF A SUMMER, 1976)

LAST CHALLENGE, THE**¹/₂   (1967) 96m MGM c

Glenn Ford (*Marshal Dan Blaine*), Angie Dickinson (*Lisa Denton*), Chad Everett (*Lot McGuire*), Gary Merrill (*Squint Calloway*), Jack Elam (*Ernest Scarnes*), Delphi Lawrence (*Marie Webster*), Royal Dano (*Pretty Horse*), Kevin Hagen (*Frank Garrison*), Florence Sundstrom (*Outdoors*), Marian Collier (*Sadie*), Robert Sorrells (*Harry Bell*), John Milford (*Turpin*), Frank McGrath (*Ballard Weeks*), Amanda Randolph (*Lisa's Maid*), Bill Walker (*Servant*), Letitia Paquette (*Girl with Lot*), Beverly Hills (*Saloon Hostess*), Jack Bighead, Henry O'Brien, George Little Buffalo, Eddie Little Sky.

This polished version of the standard western tale has Ford as the town sheriff with the "fastest gun in the West" reputation. Everett is a young gunslinger out to kill Ford and capture the title. Seeing himself in the young Everett, Ford tries to dissuade him, but Everett is intent on a gunfight. Dickinson is the saloon hostess who wants to keep Ford, her love, alive. The cast gives credible performances, and the direction keeps the action evenly paced. The first picture directed by Thorpe after 44 competent years behind the camera.

p&d, Richard Thorpe; w, John Sherry, Robert Emmett Ginna (based on the novel *Pistolero's Progress* by Sherry); ph, Ellsworth Fredericks (Panavision, Metrocolor); m, Richard Shores; ed, Richard Farrell; art d, George W. Davis; makeup, William Tuttle.

Western   **(PR:A   MPAA:NR)**

LAST CHANCE, THE**¹/₂   (1937, Brit.) 70m Welwyn Pathe bw

Frank Leighton (*Alan Burmister*), Judy Kelly (*Mary Perrin*), Lawrence Hanray (*Mr. Perrin*), Wyndham Goldie (*John Worrall*), Franklyn Bellamy (*Inspector Cutts*), Aubrey Mallalieu (*Judge Croyle*), Billy Milton (*Michael Worrall*), Jenny Laird (*Betty*), Charles Sewell (*Brough*), Alfred Wellesley (*Ivor Connell*), Charles Paton, Harry Hutchinson, Arthur Hambling, Edgar Driver.

Leighton plays a man wrongly convicted of murder, who escapes from prison to try and clear his name. Kelly is his fiancee. She marries Leighton's lawyer who, it turns out, committed the murder. Kelly eagerly hides Leighton while he attempts to clear his name. The writing is fairly even but doesn't match the arresting plot.

p, Warwick Ward; d, Thomas Bentley; w, Harry Hughes (based on the play by Frank Stayton); ph, Ernest Palmer.

Drama   **(PR:A   MPAA:NR)**

LAST CHANCE, THE***¹/₂   (1945, Switz.) 105m MGM bw

E.G. Morrison (*Maj. Telford*), John Hoy (*Lt. Halliday*), Ray Reagan (*Sgt. Braddock*), Luisa Rossi (*Tonina*), Odeardo Mosini (*Innkeeper*), Giuseppe Gaieati (*Carrier*), Romano Calo (*Priest*), Tino Erier (*Muzio*), Leopold Biberti (*Swiss Lieutenant*), Sigfrit Steiner (*Military Doctor*), Emil Gerber (*Frontier Guard*), Therese Glehse (*Frau Wittels*), Robert Schwarz (*Bernard*), Germaine Tournier (*Mme. Monnier*), M. Sakhnowsky (*Hillel Sokolowski*), Berthe Sakhnowsky (*Chanele*), Jean Martin (*Professor*), Rudolf Kampf (*Professor*), Jean Martin (*Dutchman*), Gertrudien Cate (*Dutchwoman*), Carlo Romatko (*Yugoslav Worker*).

This is a realistic portrayal of three WWII Allied officers' attempts to help a group of refugees escape from Italy, through the Alps, to freedom in Switzerland. The players are not actors, but actual victims of the war portraying their struggles to escape the Nazis. Likewise, the three officers are pilots, shot down over Switzerland, who tried acting before returning home. Despite the actors' amateur status, they deliver surprisingly good performances. An overriding message is the unity of all people. This comes alive in a scene in which the refugees sing a song together in different languages.

p, L. Wechsler; d, Leopold Lindtberg; w, Richard Schweitzer; ph, Emil Berna; m, Robert Blum; ed, Herman Haller.

War/Drama   **(PR:A   MPAA:NR)**

LAST CHASE, THE**   (1981) 101m Crown International c

Lee Majors (*Frank Hart*), Burgess Meredith (*Capt. Williams*), Chris Makepeace (*Ring*), Alexandra Stewart (*Eudora*), George Touliatos (*Hawkings*), Ben Gordon (*Morely*), Diane D'Aquila (*Santana*).

Majors plays a former race car driver in a futuristic society where cars and gasoline have been outlawed by an oppressive government. He reassembles his Porsche to take him to freedom in California. College dropout Makepeace accompanies Majors and the government sends former fighter pilot Meredith to stop the rebels.

Performances are adequate, but the script lacks balance between car racing and the human aspects of the picture.

p&d, Martyn Burke; w, C. R. O'Christopher, Taylor Sutherland, Burke; ph, Paul Van Der Linden (DeLuxe Color); ed, Steve Weslake; m, Gil Melle; art d, Roy Forge Smith; spec eff, M. Lennick, David Stringer, Paul Davidson, James Liles; aerial ph, Clay Lacey.

Fantasy/Science Fiction　　Cas.　　　(PR:A　MPAA:PG)

LAST COMMAND, THE, 1942　　(SEE: PRISONER OF JAPAN, 1942)

LAST COMMAND, THE* 1/2**　　　　　　(1955) 110m REP c

Sterling Hayden (*James Bowie*), Anna Maria Alberghetti (*Consuela*), Richard Carlson (*William Travis*), Arthur Hunnicutt (*Davy Crockett*), Ernest Borgnine (*Mike Radin*), J. Carrol Naish (*Santa Anna*), Ben Cooper (*Jeb Lacey*), John Russell (*Lt. Dickinson*), Virginia Grey (*Mrs. Dickinson*), Jim Davis (*Evans*), Eduard Franz (*Lorenzo de Quesada*), Otto Kruger (*Stephen Austin*), Russell Simpson (*The Parson*), Roy Roberts (*Dr. Sutherland*), Slim Pickens (*Abe*), Hugh Sanders (*Sam Houston*).

Hayden is American hero and big knife inventor Jim Bowie, a Mexican citizen living in Texas and friends with general Naish. When neighbors Borgnine and Carlson, American citizens, begin agitating for secession from Mexico, Hayden tries to recommend a course of moderation, even fighting a knife duel with Borgnine over the matter. When Naish's repressive reactions to the unrest finally bring tensions to the breaking point, Hayden sides with his Texan neighbors. They settle into the Alamo and wait for the siege, while Hayden finds time to court Alberghetti, the daughter of a friendly Mexican landowner. What happens to the defenders is known to every schoolchild; the 187 men inside hold off 7,000 Mexican regulars for 13 days before the walls are breached and everyone within is killed. Wounded earlier, Hayden puts up a final fight with his knife from his cot. John Wayne had wanted to do this project for a long time, but his negotiations fell through because either Republic head Herbert Yates shrank from the high projected cost of the project for his struggling studio, or Wayne rejected the film when Yates refused to fund it unless Wayne's costar was Vera Hruba Ralston, the no-talent Czechoslovakian refugee figure skater, resident star at Republic, and Yates' mistress. Wayne had already worked with her on THE FIGHTING KENTUCKIAN (1949) and walked rather than do it again. Wayne's version of the story, THE ALAMO, would not be released until 1960, but Yates, seemingly to spite his departing star, rushed this version into production. Although in sheer spectacle and production value it can't compare to the film Wayne was to make, THE LAST COMMAND offers compensatory pleasures like Hayden, Borgnine, and Carlson, a good script, and some exciting battle scenes.

p&d, Frank Lloyd; w, Warren Duff (based on the story by Sy Bartlett); ph, Jack Marta (Trucolor); m, Max Steiner; ed, Tony Martinelli; md, Steiner; art d, Frank Arrigo; cos, Adele Palmer; m/l, "Jim Bowie" by Steiner and Sidney Clare (sung by Gordon MacRae).

Historical Drama/Western　　Cas.　　　(PR:A　MPAA:NR)

LAST COUPON, THE 1/2**　　　　　(1932, Brit.) 84m BIP/Wardour bw

Leslie Fuller (*Bill Carter*), Mary Jerrold (*Polly Carter*), Molly Lamont (*Betty Carter*), Binnie Barnes (*Mrs. Meredith*), Gus McNaughton (*Lord Bedlington*), Jack Hobbs (*Dr. Sinclair*), Marian Dawson (*Mrs. Bates*), Harry Carr (*Jocker*), Jimmy Godden (*Geordie Bates*), Hal Gordon (*Rusty Walker*), Ellen Pollock, Clive Morton, Syd Crossley.

Well-conceived farce revolving around the excitement a miner, Fuller, has when he thinks he's won a hefty football pool. Sending his wife into anguish, he draws up plans for all of the money, but luckily never has a chance to blow the small fortune as he winds up not having won the pool after all. A good vehicle for Fuller, who was given better material than usual with which to work.

p, John Maxwell; d, Thomas Bentley; w, Frank Launder, Syd Courtenay (based on the play by Ernest E. Bryan); ph, Jack Cox, Bryan Langley.

Comedy　　　　　　　　　　　(PR:A　MPAA:NR)

LAST CROOKED MILE, THE 1/2**　　　(1946) 67m REP bw

Donald Barry (*Tom Dwyer*), Ann Savage (*Sheila Kennedy*), Adele Mara (*Bonnie*), Tom Powers (*Floyd Sorelson*), Sheldon Leonard (*Ed MacGuire*), Nestor Paiva (*Ferrara*), Harry Shannon (*Lt. Blake*), Ben Welden (*Haynes*), John Miljan (*Lt. Mayrin*), Charles D. Brown (*Detrich*), John Dehner (*Jarvis*), Anthony Caruso (*Charlie*).

This variation on the standard gangster theme has private detective Barry hired to recover $300,000. The thieves robbed a bank and died in a car accident. Barry eventually uncovers the real criminals. Script weaknesses are camouflaged by smooth direction and realistic performances. Savage sings one song: "The One I Love Belongs To Somebody Else."

p, Randolph E. Abel; d, Philip Ford; w, Jerry Sackheim (based on the radio play by Robert L. Richards); ph, Alfred Keller, Howard and Theodore Lydecker; m, Joseph Dubin.

Crime　　　　　　　　　　　　(PR:A　MPAA:NR)

LAST CURTAIN, THE* 1/2　　(1937, Brit.) 67m British and Dominions/PAR bw

Campbell Gullan (*Sir Alan Masterville*), Kenneth Duncan (*Joe Garsatti*), Greta Gynt (*Julie Rendle*), John Wickham (*Bob Fenton*), Sara Seager (*Molly*), Joss Ambler (*Ellis*), W.G. Fay (*Milligan*), Eric Hales (*Barrington*), Evan John, Arthur Sinclair.

Uneven crime drama in which Wickham plays an insurance detective on the trail of a gang of notorious jewel thieves who use the novel idea of putting the jewels inside of donuts, which Gullan then purchases. Wickham manages to join up with this bakery gang to further his investigation, almost getting himself mixed up in the

murder of Gullan. Gullan names his killer before he dies, however, and Wickham wraps up the crime scenario, crooks, jewels, and all.

p, Anthony Havelock-Brown; d, David Macdonald; w, A. R. Rawlinson (based on the story by Derek B. Mayne); ph, Francis Carter.

Crime/Comedy　　　　　　　　　(PR:A　MPAA:NR)

LAST DANCE, THE**　　　　　　(1930) 69m Audible Pictures bw

Vera Reynolds (*Sally Kelly*), Jason Robards (*Tom Malloy*), George Chandler (*Sam Wise*), Gertrude Short (*Sybil Kelly*), Harry Todd (*Pa Kelly*), Lillian Leighton (*Ma Kelly*), Miami Alvarez (*Babe La Marr*), Lynton Brent (*Jones*), James Hertz (*Edgar*), Henry Roquemore (*Lucien Abbott*), Fred Walton (*Weber*).

This comedy spoof features Reynolds as a taxi dancer for a Broadway club marrying a millionaire. The performances are adequate although the settings are inaccurate and characterizations mundane. The theme song, "Sally, I'm Lovin' You, Sally," is sung by Chandler.

d, Scott Pembroke, Jack Townley; ph, M. A. Andersen; ed, Scott Himm; m/l, Ray Canfield, Neil Moret.

Comedy/Romance　　　　　　　　(PR:A　MPAA:NR)

LAST DAY OF THE WAR, THE**
(1969, U.S./Ital./Span.) 96m Prodi Cinematografica-Atlantida-Valencia/Sagittarius c
(L'ULTIMO GIORNO DELLA GUERRA; EL ULTIMO DIA DE LA GUERRA)

George Maharis (*Sgt. Chips Slater*), Maria Perschy (*Elena Truppe*), John Clarke (*Hobbs*), James Philbrook (*Lt. Poole*), Gerard Herter (*Maj. Skorch*), Gustavo Rojo (*Hawk*), Jack Stuart [Giacomo Rossi Stuart] (*Kendall*), Gerard Tichy (*Bronc*), Sancho Gracia (*Martinez*), Tomas Blanco (*Martin Truppe*), Ruben Rojo (*O'Brien*), Ralph Browne (*Maj. Garrick*), Carl Rapp (*Burgomaster*), Jorge Rigaud, Claudia Gravy, Matilde Munoz Sampedro.

Maharis is a U.S. Army sergeant ordered to locate a German scientist who favors the Allied cause. The scientist is also being hunted by an SS member who wants him executed. The scientist's daughter is brought in from the U.S. to help in the search, but the SS man gets to him first. However, an angry mob of concentration camp escapees kills the SS member and the scientist is rescued.

p, Sam X. Abarbanel; d, Juan Antonio Bardem; w, Abarbanel, Bardem, Howard Berk (based on the story by Berk); ph, Romolo Garroni (Eastmancolor); m, Franco Pezzullo; ed, Margarita Ochoa; art d, Rafael Ablanque; set d, Santiago Ontanon.

War/Drama　　　　Cas.　　　　(PR:A　MPAA:NR)

LAST DAYS OF BOOT HILL**　　　　(1947) 55m COL bw

Charles Starrett (*Steve Waring/The Durango Kid*), Smiley Burnette (*Himself*), Virginia Hunter (*Paula Thorpe*), Paul Campbell (*Frank Rayburn*), Mary Newton (*Mrs. Forrest Brent*), Bill Free (*Reed Brokaw*), J. Courtland Lytton (*Dan McCoy*), Bob Wilke (*Bronc Peters*), Alan Bridge (*Forrest Brent*), the Cass County Boys.

Another film in the Durango Kid series features Starrett as a U.S. marshal trying to uncover gold stolen years before. The story is told almost completely in flashback, using footage from old films in the series to cut costs. The direction is evenly paced to a cast of standard performances. The story suffers too many gunfights and chases. (See DURANGO KID, series, Index.)

p, Colbert Clark; d, Ray Nazarro; w, Norman S. Hall; ph, George F. Kelley; ed, Paul Borofsky; art d, Charles Clague.

Western　　　　　　　　　　　(PR:A　MPAA:NR)

LAST DAYS OF DOLWYN, THE* 1/2**
(1949, Brit.) 95m LFP bw (AKA: DOLWYN; WOMAN OF DOLWYN)

Dame Edith Evans (*Merri*), Emlyn Williams (*Rob*), Richard Burton (*Gareth*), Anthony James (*Dafydd*), Barbara Couper (*Lady Dolwyn*), Alan Aynesworth (*Lord Lancashire*), Andrea Lea (*Margaret*), Hugh Griffith (*Minister*), Roddy Hughes (*Caradoc*), David Davies (*Septimus*), Edward Rees (*Gruffyd*), Tom Jones (*John Henry*), Sam Hinton (*Idris*), Prysor Williams (*Old Tal*), Kenneth Evans (*Jabbez*), Maurice Browning (*Huw*), Pat Glyn (*Dorcas*), Joan Griffiths (*Eira*), Betty Stanley (*Nurse Pugh*), Dudley Jones (*Hughes*), Aubrey Richards (*Ellis*), Madoline Thomas (*Mrs. Thomas*), Dorothy Langley (*Lizzie*), Doreen Richards (*Mrs. Septimus*), Bryan V. Thomas (*Alwyn*), Frank Dunlop (*Ephrain*), Daffyd Howard (*Will*), Eileen Dale (*Mrs. Ellis*), Betty Humphries (*Mrs. John Henry*), Rita Crailey (*Hen Ann*), Emrys Leyshon (*Watkins*), Constance Lewis (*Mrs. Richards*), Hywel Wood (*Hywel*).

Williams returns to his boyhood village in Wales in the hope of buying out the entire district to be used for a water-reservoir project. This is his own revenge against the village which had him exiled as a thief. Due to resistance from Evans, he fails at his land deal, so he tries to burn the village down. He is stopped by Burton and killed in a fight. Evans then floods the village herself to conceal his body, protecting her stepson Burton from the fruits of his crime. The story is well developed, with even and subtle direction. The cast is equally subtle, but effective in their portrayals of modest Welsh villagers. This was stage actor Burton's first feature film (which resulted in his first marriage; he met his first wife, Welsh actress Sybil Williams, on the set), and one of his first acting jobs since returning from WW II service in the Royal Air Force as a navigator.

p, Anatole de Grunwald; d&w, Emlyn Williams; ph, Otto Heller, Gus Drisse; m, John Greenwood; ed, Maurice Rootes; prod d, Wilfred Shingleton; cos, Michael Wright.

Drama　　　　　　　　　　　　(PR:A　MPAA:NR)

LAST DAYS OF MAN ON EARTH, THE* 1/2**
(1975, Brit.) 81m Goodtimes Enterprises-Gladiole/New World c (AKA: THE FINAL PROGRAMME)

Jon Finch (*Jerry Cornelius*), Jenny Runacre (*Miss Brunner*), Hugh Griffith (*Prof.*

Hira), Patrick Magee (*Dr. Baxter*), Sterling Hayden (*Maj. Wrongway Lindbergh*), Harry Andrews (*John*), Graham Crowden (*Dr. Smiles*), George Coulouris (*Dr. Powys*), Basil Henson (*Dr. Lucas*), Derrick O'Connor (*Frank*), Gilles Milinaire (*Dimitri*), Ronald Lacey (*Shades*), Julie Ege (*Miss Ege*), Sandy Ratcliff (*Jenny*), Sarah Douglas (*Catherine*), Dolores Del Mar (*Fortune Teller*).

The planet is on its last legs. Finch plays a rebellious scientist with potential answers to society's problems. But in his selfishness he creates a new messiah through a child by Runacre. The result is an apelike monster. The special effects crew created a believable surreal world, but the material is handled in a mishmash of styles, garbling any possible message. The cast is solid, though ill-used.

p, John Goldstone, Sandy Lieberson; d&w Robert Fuest (based on the novel *The Final Programme* by Michael Moorcock); ph, Norman Warwick (Technicolor); m, Paul Beaver, Bernard Krause, Gerry Mulligan; ed, Barrie Vince, Barbara Pokras; art d, Philip Harrison.

Fantasy/Science Fiction   **Cas.**   **(PR:O MPAA:R)**

LAST DAYS OF MUSSOLINI***
(1974, Ital.) 126m Aquila Cinematografica/PAR c (MUSSOLINI: ULTIMO ATTO; AKA: THE LAST FOUR DAYS)

Rod Steiger (*Benito Mussolini*), Lisa Gastoni (*Clara Petacci*), Henry Fonda (*Cardinal Schuster*), Franco Nero (*Col. Valerio*), Lino Capolicchio (*Pedro*).

Steiger plays the infamous Italian dictator in this realistic view of the few days prior to his execution. Four different groups are hunting him: the Nazis who want to get him out of Italy, the Allies who want to try him as a war criminal, the provincial Italian government, and the Italian freedom fighters. Steiger gives a wonderful portrayal of the inner confusion and conflict the dictator feels. Lizzani's direction shows the opposing factions in a well-balanced manner.

p, Enzo Peri; d, Carlo Lizzani; w, Lizzani, Fabio Pittorru; ph, Roberto Geradi (Eastmancolor); m, Ennio Morricone; art d, Amedeo Fago.

War/Drama   **(PR:A MPAA:NR)**

LAST DAYS OF PLANET EARTH
(SEE: PROPHECIES OF NOSTRADAMUS: CATASTROPHE 1999, 1974, Jap.)

LAST DAYS OF POMPEII, THE***
(1935) 96m RKO bw

Preston Foster (*Marcus*), Alan Hale (*Burbix*), Basil Rathbone (*Pontius Pilate*), John Wood (*Flavius as a Man*), Louis Calhern (*Prefect*), David Holt (*Flavius as a Boy*), Dorothy Wilson (*Clodia*), Wyrley Birch (*Leaster*), Gloria Shea (*Julia*), Frank Conroy (*Gaius*), William V. Mong (*Cleon*), Edward Van Sloan (*Calvus*), Henry Kolker (*Warder*), Zeffie Tilbury (*Wise Woman*), John Davidson, Ward Bond, Edwin Maxwell.

This film bears no resemblance to the novel by Sir Edward Bulwer-Lytton, except as it is set in the same historical time period and as it depicts the eruption of Mount Vesuvius at the climactic finale. Foster is solid, if not moving, as an honest, powerful blacksmith whose son and wife are crushed beneath the wheels of a nobleman's chariot. His perception turns black and his heart parsimonious. He decides that the only thing in life that matters is money and power and he goes after it in the gladiatorial arena, slaying his opponents mercilessly. Then he kills a valiant adversary and finds the man's son waiting for his father after the combat. In shame and remorse, he adopts the boy, Holt, who grows up to be Wood. Foster wants his son to be educated properly and a wise old woman, Tilbury, tells him to see "the greatest man in Judea." Foster assumes she means Rathbone, who is playing Pontius Pilate the Roman administrator (as no one ever played him before or after). Rathbone suggests Foster raid a neighboring tribe to steal horses and gold, a partnership that later makes both men rich. But during the raid, Holt is injured in a fall from a horse. Foster is frantic to save the boy's life and he is directed to a "great prophet," Jesus Christ. The boy is healed by Jesus and Foster later hears from Rathbone that he is haunted by having had to condemn "the King of the Jews," the very Healer who restored his son to him. He later sees Christ being driven to his crucifixion but when the followers of Jesus beg him to intervene, Foster refuses to risk his life. After many years, Foster is now one of Pompeii's wealthiest citizens, in charge of the gladiatorial arena, a position his son, Wood, finds repulsive. The idealistic Wood, who is in love with a Christian slave girl, Wilson, conspires to allow the Christians to escape slaughter in the arena, but he is apprehended and sentenced to die with the Christians. Foster attempts to free his son at the fatal hour but is held back. Just as the Christians are being led into the arena, Vesuvius erupts, cascading death and destruction down upon wicked Pompeii. Foster realizes that all his worldly riches cannot save his son and the girl he loves so he renounces his pagan world, helping the Christians to get to the docks and take flight on boats reserved for Roman aristocrats. Foster holds the gates to the docks closed while the city is destroyed about him, along with the Romans who finally spear him to death. As he dies he sees a vision of Christ, who blesses him. THE LAST DAYS OF POMPEII is somewhat static and the cast, excepting Rathbone, only slightly above average. Even the special effects from specialist O'Brien are not that effective, but some of the earthquake scenes are exciting. The matting and rear projection of some of the ongoing disaster are obvious. Rathbone is a marvel as Pilate, giving one of his finest performances, even though all his scenes were shot in a week. "The part was me and I was the part," he later commented . . . . "It was magnificently written with economy of words—truly a sublime characterization." One of Rathbone's unforgettable scenes takes place in the luxurious palace Foster has built for himself on a mountain overlooking the seaport of Pompeii. Wood tells Rathbone that he remembers meeting "a great man" as a child. Rathbone replies with incredible depth of feeling: "There was such a man. I crucified him." This film, the product of Cooper and Schoedsack, makers of the fantastic KING KONG two years earlier, does not quite come off, but it remains entertaining. The film lost $237,000 and did not begin to make money until its re-release in 1949, when it was double-billed with SHE.

p, Merian C. Cooper; d, Ernest B. Schoedsack; w, Ruth Rose, Boris Ingster (based on a story by James Ashmore Creelman, Melville Baker); ph, Eddie Linden, Jr., Ray Hunt; m, Roy Webb; ed, Archie Marschek; spec eff, Willis O'Brien, Vernon Walker, Harry Redmond.

Historical Epic   **Cas.**   **(PR:A MPAA:NR)**

LAST DAYS OF POMPEII, THE**½
(1960, Ital.) 103m Cineproduzioni-Procusa-Transocean/UA c (ULTIMI GIORNI DI POMPEII)

Steve Reeves (*Glaucus*), Cristine Kaufmann (*Ione*), Barbara Carroll (*Nydia*), Anne Marie Baumann (*Julia*), Mimmo Palmara (*Gallinus*), Fernando Rey (*High Priest*), Carlo Tamberlani (*Leader of the Christians*), Angel Aranda (*Antonius*), Mino Doro (*2nd Consul*), Guglielmo Marin (*Askinius*), Mario Berroatua, Mario Morales, Angel Ortiz (*Praetorian Guards*).

This gladiator spectacle from Italy has Reeves as the man of superhuman strength trying to rid Pompeii of its undesirable elements. Throughout he battles wild animals and armed warriors. Though the story is far-fetched, for spectacle it is magnificent entertainment. The film has been shot in Supertotalscope, which captures the fantastic events, especially the fireworks of the erupting volcano in graphic scale. Co-scripter Leone was soon to become the doyen of spaghetti westerns.

p, Paolo Moffa; d, Mario Bonnard; w, Ennio De Concini, Sergio Leone, Duccio Tessari, Sergio Corbucci; ph, Antonio Ballesteros (Supertotalscope, Eastmancolor); m, Angelo Francesco Lavagnino; ed, Eraldo Da Roma; cos, Vittorio Rossi.

Fantasy   **(PR:A MPAA:NR)**

LAST DAYS OF SODOM AND GOMORRAH, THE
(SEE: SODOM AND GOMORRAH, 1962, Fr./Ital.)

LAST DETAIL, THE****
(1973) 103m COL c

Jack Nicholson (*Buddusky SM1*), Otis Young (*Mulhall GM1*), Randy Quaid (*Meadows SN*), Clifton James (*Chief Master-At-Arms*), Michael Moriarty (*Marine Duty Officer*), Carol Kane (*Young Whore*), Luana Anders (*Donna*), Kathleen Miller (*Kathleen*), Nancy Allen (*Nancy*), Gerry Salsberg (*Henry*), Don McGovern (*Bartender*), Pat Hamilton (*Madame*), Michael Chapman (*Taxi Driver*), Jim Henshaw (*Sweek*), Derek McGrath, Gilda Radner, Jim Horn, John Castellano (*Nichiren Shoshu Members*).

If all the four-letter words had been removed from this movie, it might have been half the length. And yet, the foul language seems right for the movie. THE LAST DETAIL is a grim portrayal of a trip taken by three men, one of whom is to lose his freedom by journey's end. Two career sailors, Nicholson and Young, are randomly selected to escort Quaid from their West Virginia base to a prison in Massachusetts. Quaid had been caught stealing from the polio charity box and since that was the favorite charity of the admiral's wife, he is sentenced to eight years in jail, or five dollars per year—a sentence only eclipsed by Jean Valjean in LES MISERABLES. Nicholson and Young got a lot more than they bargained for when they were assigned this detail. At first, they think it's just another shore leave with liberty to be enjoyed and lots of carousing. The two hardened sailors are soon won over by Quaid's bumbling ways and the difficulty of his plight. This causes them to take a paternal attitude toward him as they travel from one dim location to another. It seems that only the characters in the film are alive as everywhere they travel appears to have been filtered by pale grays and yellows. Nicholson and Young try to show Quaid a good time before his long stay in the brig. They encounter Anders, who takes them to a Nicheren Shoshu meeting where religious zealots (including Gilda Radner before she became a TV star) chant "Nam-Myoho-Renge-Kyo" and dance happily in their scented environment. Now Anders takes Quaid to her room when she learns of his bleak future and tells him that she's going to do something that will be very important. The naive Quaid thinks she's about to seduce him but instead she begins to chant, which confuses him at first, then leads to a poignant scene later. Nicholson and Young can't make any time with Anders' pals so it's off to another adventure; this time to a brothel where they offer Quaid a good time with Kane, which they'll pay for. Quaid unsuccessfully tries to escape (while chanting the liturgy Anders taught him) but Nicholson and Young capture him after an agonizing chase across a frozen park, and deliver him to prison. We get the feeling that Nicholson and Young, if their naval careers did not depend on it, would have taken off with Quaid. They try hard not to be emotional as Quaid is escorted up a small staircase to the room where he will spend the rest of his youth. THE LAST DETAIL is a gritty look at the military life and the people who are attracted to it. It is dark in its message and gray to the eye. Locations are all washed out as though there were a thin membrane of filth spread across everyone except the three leads, who pop out colorfully like a trio of strawberries in a bowl of Cream of Wheat. This is Nicholson's best work since FIVE EASY PIECES, perhaps because his character seems to be an extension of that film's Bobby DuPea. Ashby's direction is superlative as is his use of music to help secure the mood. Ashby was able to get Nicholson's least-mannered performance in many a day, after bombs with THE KING OF MARVIN GARDENS, A SAFE PLACE, and DRIVE, HE SAID. Ponicsan also wrote the naval-based novel, *Cinderella Liberty*, which was made into a film this same year. THE LAST DETAIL won no Oscars but did get nominations for Quaid, Nicholson, and Robert Towne for his screenplay. Towne and Nicholson collaborated later for CHINATOWN.

p, Gerald Ayres; d, Hal Ashby; w, Robert Towne (based on the novel by Darryl Ponicsan); ph, Michael Chapman (Metrocolor); m, Johnny Mandel; ed, Robert C. Jones; prod d, Michael Haller; cos, Ted Parvin; makeup, Maureen Sweeney.

Drama   **Cas.**   **(PR:O MPAA:R)**

LAST EMBRACE**½
(1979) 103m UA c

Roy Scheider (*Harry Hannan*), Janet Margolin (*Ellie Fabian*), John Glover (*Richard Peabody*), Sam Levene (*Sam Urdell*), Charles Napier (*Dave Quittle*), Christopher

Walken (Eckart), Jacqueline Brookes (Dr. Coopersmith), David Margulies (Rabbi Drexel), Andrew Duncan (Bernie Meckler), Marcia Rodd (Adrian), Gary Goetzman (Tour Guide), Lou Gilbert (Rabbi Jacobs), Mandy Patinkin, Max Wright (Commuters), Sandy McLeod (Dorothy Hannan), Cynthia Scheider (Adrian's Friend), Sasha von Scherler (Shopper), George Hillman (Ukelele Player), Gary Gunter (Newscaster), Burt Santos, Joe Spinell, Jim McBride (Men in Cantina), Jonathan Demme (Man On Train).

This thriller owes much of its technique to Alfred Hitchcock, though it is more in homage to the master than a ripoff. Scheider is a government agent recovering from a nervous breakdown resulting from his wife's murder and his losing a job. He inadvertently becomes involved in a murder. Direction is uneven at times, but manages to maintain suspense. The performances are good and the photography creates the proper mysterious atmosphere. The score is by Miklos Rosza, who also scored Hitchcock's SPELLBOUND. Actor Mandy Patinkin has a small part five years before he hit it big on Broadway in "Sunday In The Park With George" and, in 1983, played the love interest to Barbra Streisand (star/producer/director/co-writer) in YENTL.

p, Michael Taylor, Dan Wigutow; d, Jonathan Demme; w, David Shaber (based on the novel The Thirteenth Man by Murray Teigh Bloom); ph, Tak Fujimoto (Technicolor); m, Miklos Rosza; ed, Barry Malkin; art d, James A. Taylor.

Mystery (PR:O MPAA:R)

LAST ESCAPE, THE** (1970, Brit.) 90m Oakmont/UA c

Stuart Whitman (Capt. Lee Mitchell), John Collin (Sgt. Harry McBee), Martin Jarvis (Lt. Donald Wilcox), Pinkas Braun (Von Heinken), Gunther Neutze (Maj. Hessel), Margit Saad (Karen Gerhardt), Patrick Jordan (Maj. Griggs), Johnny Briggs (Cpl. O'Connell), Harald Dietl (Maj. Petrov), Gert Vespermann (Blucher), Andy Pap (Curt), Andrew Lodge (Gregory), David Taylor (Morse), Richard Abbott (Billings), Paul Bentley (Jarvis), Christian Skrobek (Russian Signal Officer), Chuck Stanford (American Lieutenant), Frank Guarente (American Signal Officer), Michael Hinz (Junior SS Officer), Helmut Heisler.

This WWII action picture, filmed in Munich, stars Whitman as an American officer who joins British soldiers trying to rescue a German scientist from the Nazis. They infiltrate Germany, take the scientist and several refugees, but are chased by SS officers and Russian tanks. The script is laden with cliches, but the director handles the action sequences well. Performances are adequate.

p, Irving Temaner; d, Walter Grauman; w, Herman Hoffman (based on the story by John C. Champion, Barry Trivers); ph, Gernot Roll (DeLuxe Color); ed, Peter Elliot, Bud Molin; art d, Rolf Zehetbauer; spec eff, Karl Baumgartner.

War (PR:A MPAA:G)

LAST EXPRESS, THE** (1938) 63m UNIV bw

Kent Taylor (Duncan MacLain), Dorothea Kent (Amy Arden), Don Brodie (Spud Savage), Greta Granstedt (Gladys Hewitt), Paul Hurst (Springer), Samuel Lee (Trilby), Albert Shaw (Shane), Edward Raquello (Paul Zarinka), Robert Emmett Keane (Howard Hewitt), Charles Trowbridge (Meredith), Addison Richards (Frank Hoefle).

This standard detective piece is perplexing enough to keep the audience guessing. Taylor, with his pal Brodie, is hired to investigate the murder of a prosecuting attorney who had been appointed to rid New York of its hoods. The two private detectives uncover ties between the crime cartel and city hall, get in trouble with the mob, and are arrested. The script is taut and suspense rules throughout. Several interesting sequences are shot in the New York subway system.

p, Irving Starr; d, Otis Garrett; w, Edmund L. Hartmann (based on a story by Bayard Kendrick); ph, Stanley Cortez; ed, Maurice Wright.

Crime (PR:A MPAA:NR)

LAST FIGHT, THE*½ (1983) 86m Movie and Pictures International/Best Film and Video c

Willie Colon (Joaquin Vargas), Ruben Blades (Andy "Kid" Clave), Fred Williamson (Jesse Crowder), Joe Spinell (Boss), Darlanne Fluegel (Sally), Nereida Mercado (Nancy), Anthony Sirico (Frankie), Det. Pantane (Vinny Argiro), Jose "Chegui" Torres (Ex-Champ), Nick Corello (Pedro), Sal Corolio (Papa), Izzy Sanabria (Slim), Don King, Salvador Sanchez, Bert Sugarman.

Slow-moving drama features Blades as a singer who turns to the ring when his gambling debts accumulate. Night club owner Colon allows Blades the services of his girl friend. Blades makes it to the title bout, but loses to Salvador Sanchez. Sanchez was the featherweight champion, who was killed in an auto accident shortly after this film was shot. The direction creates a film-noirish atmosphere, but in so doing stifles the performances.

p, Jerry Masucci; d&w, Fred Williamson (based on a story by Masucci); ph, James Lemmo; m, Jay Chattaway; ed, Daniel Loewenthal; m/l, Cary King, Ruben Blades.

Drama Cas. (PR:O MPAA:R)

LAST FLIGHT, THE*** (1931) 80m FN bw

Richard Barthelmess (Cary Lockwood), Johnny Mack Brown (Bill Talbot), Helen Chandler (Nikki), David Manners (Shep Lambert), Elliott Nugent (Francis), Walter Byron (Frink), Luis Alberni (Spectator at Bullfight).

This sensitive look at the "lost generation" following World War I features Barthelmess as a flying ace unable to return to his family after his combat experience. He stays in Paris with comrades who feel the same way. They run into Chandler, a female counterpart to their style of fun, and the group lives it up for a while. Eventually the group heads to Spain, where all but Barthelmess and Chandler meet early deaths. The film showcases well-paced direction of the script, which relies on a delicate balance between comedy and drama. Characterizations are adequate.

d, Wilhelm [William] Dieterle; w, John Monk Saunders (based on the novel Single Lady by Saunders); ph, Sid Hickox; ed, Al Hall; art d, Jack Okey; cos, Earl Luick.

Drama (PR:A MPAA:NR)

LAST FLIGHT OF NOAH'S ARK, THE** (1980) 97m Disney/BV c

Elliott Gould (Noah Dugan), Genevieve Bujold (Bernadette Lafleur), Ricky Schroder (Bobby), Tammy Lauren (Julie), Vincent Gardenia (Stoney), John Fujioka (Cleveland), Yuki Shimoda (Hiro), Dana Elcar (Benchley), Ruth Manning (Charlotte Braithwaite), Arthur Adams (Leipzig Manager), Pete Renaday (Irate Pilot), Bob Whiting (Chaplain), John P. Ryan (Coslough), Austin Willis (Slabotsky).

Another Disney family film which stresses, to the point of ridiculousness, the importance of treating animals kindly. In this film, Gould is a crabby airline pilot talked into flying animals to an island desperately in need of some living beasts. Unbeknownst to Gould, Schroder and Lauren stow aboard to watch over the animals, but all they do is cry, demanding attention and their way. The plane crashes off a small island inhabited by two Japanese soldiers who do not realize WWII is over. The plane is converted into a sailboat, and the animals float off to their destiny. The script is written without any adherence to realistic conditions, nevertheless it is directed with a strong belief in the project, Gould and Bujold giving the needed strong performances.

p, Ron Miller; d, Charles Jarrott; w, Steven W. Carabatsos, Sandy Glass, George Arthur Bloom (based on the story by Earnest K. Gann); ph, Charles F. Wheeler (Technicolor); m, Maurice Jarre; ed, Gordon D. Brenner; art d, John B. Mansbridge; spec eff, Art Cruickshank, Eustace Lycett, Danny Lee.

Children/Fantasy Cas. (PR:AA MPAA:G)

LAST FOUR DAYS, THE (SEE: LAST DAYS OF MUSSOLINI, 1974, Ital.)

LAST FRONTIER, THE**

(1955) 97m COL c (AKA: SAVAGE WILDERNESS)

Victor Mature (Jed), Guy Madison (Capt. Riordan), Robert Preston (Col. Frank Marston), James Whitmore (Gus), Anne Bancroft (Corinna Marston), Russell Collins (Capt. Clark), Peter Whitney (Sgt. Maj. Decker), Pat Hogan (Mungo), Manuel Donde (Red Cloud), Guy Williams (Lt. Benton), Mickey Kuhn (Luke), William Calles (Spotted Elk), Jack Pennick (Corporal), Robert St. Angelo (Sentry), William Traylor (Soldier).

Routine western showcases Mature as part of a trio of trappers who lose a year's worth of skins to marauding Indians. The three arrive at a cavalry outpost and take jobs as scouts. But all is not well at the fort. Those living at the fort fear Indian attack and hate the new commander, Preston. Mature chases after Preston's woman, Bancroft. Performers make the best of weak scripting and direction in this sometimes absurd story about the taming of a "noble savage." Oddly, and adding to its negative aspects, much of the film was shot at night.

p, William Fadiman; d, Anthony Mann; w, Philip Yordan, Russell S. Hughes (based on the novel The Gilded Rooster, by Richard Emery Roberts); ph, William Mellor (CinemaScope, Technicolor); m, Leigh Harline; ed, Al Clark; md, Morris Stoloff; art d, Robert Peterson; m/l, "The Last Frontier," Lester Lee, Ned Washington (sung by Rusty Draper).

Western (PR:A MPAA:NR)

LAST FRONTIER UPRISING*½ (1947) 67m REP c

Monte Hale (Himself), Adrian Booth (Mary Lou Gardner), James Taggart (Vance Daley), Roy Barcroft (Boyd), Tom London (Skillet), Philip Van Zandt (Lyons), Edmund Cobb (Sheriff Hanlon), John Ince (Sam Chisholm), Frank O'Connor (Rancher), Bob Blair (Texan), Doyle O'Dell (Rancher), Foy Willing and the Riders of the Purple Sage.

Hale plays a government agent sent to Texas to buy horses. He fights horse thieves while falling in love with Booth. The cast gives the stock western performance to this overbaked loaf of entertainment whose yeast failed to make it rise.

p, Louis Gray; d, Lesley Selander; w, Harvey Gates (based on the story by Jerome Odlum); ph, Bud Thackery (Trucolor); m, Mort Glickman; ed, Charles Craft; art d, Fred A. Ritter.

Western (PR:A MPAA:NR)

LAST GAME, THE***

(1964, USSR) 88m Mosfilm/Artkino bw (TRETIY TAYM)

Yu. Volkov, V. Kashpur, Mazarov Kuravlyov, Yuriy Nazarov, V. Nevinny, Gleb Strizhenov, Gennadiy Yukhtin, A. Eybozhenko, A. Metyolkin, Ye. Paptsov (Soviet Team), V. Skulme, V. Tomingas, V. Lange, V. Chyornyy, M. Ogonkov, O. Savelyev, L. Novikov, B. Kvin, L. Ilyukhin, A. Zinovyev (German Team), I. Stravinskiy, E. Knausmyuller, T. Gurko, E. Barens, V. Markova, V. Sharykina, L. Dranovskaya, N. Abramov, I. Borisov, L. Biryulin, L. Galanov, Yu. Dmitriyev, Kolya Kozlov, Vova Kolotygin, Nikolay Novlyanskiy, Sasha Petrov, V. Pitsek, I. Pushkaryov, A. Danilova, G. Svetlani, Z. Chekulayeva.

Based on a WWII incident, the film depicts a soccer match between the Germans and the Russian soldiers. The game takes place in occupied Kiev and the Nazis give an ultimatum to the Soviets: lose or die. As the crowd gathers the Soviets become increasingly nationalistic and defeat the Germans. With their propaganda attempt erased, the Nazis lead the Soviet team to a firing squad. A powerful kick in the face to the Nazi forces, even if it is Soviet propaganda.

d, Y. Karelov; w, A. Borshchagovskiy (based on the novel by Borshchagovskiy); ph, Sergey Zaytsev; m, Andrey Petrov; ed, K. Aleyeva; art d, B. Tsaryov.

War/Drama (PR:C MPAA:NR)

LAST GANGSTER, THE*   (1937) 81m MGM bw

Edward G. Robinson (*Joe Krozac*), James Stewart (*Paul North*), Rose Stradner (*Talva Krozac*), Lionel Stander (*Curly*), Douglas Scott (*Paul North, Jr.*), John Carradine (*Casper*), Sidney Blackmer (*San Francisco Editor*), Edward Brophy (*Fats Garvey*), Alan Baxter ("*Acey*" *Kile*), Edward Marr (*Frankie Kile*), Grant Mitchell (*Warden*), Frank Conroy (*Sid Gorman*), Moroni Olson (*Shea*), Ivan Miller (*Wilson*), Willard Robertson (*Broderick*), Louise Beavers (*Gloria*), Donald Barry (*Billy Ernst*), Ben Welden (*Bottles Bailey*), Horace McMahon (*Limpy*), Edward Pawley (*Brockett*), John Kelly (*Red*), David Leo Tillotson, Jim Kaehner, Billy Smith, Reggie Streeter, Dick Holland (*Boys*), Pierre Watkin (*Editor*), William Benedict (*Office Boy*), Douglas McPhail (*Reporter*), Cy Kendall (*Editor*), Frederick Vogeding (*Ambassador*), Victor Adams, George Magrill, Jerry Jerome (*Hoods*), Walter Miller (*Mike Kile*), Wade Boteler (*Turnkey*), Larry Sims (*Jo Krozac*), Lee Phelps (*Train Guard*), Frederick Burton (*Boston Editor*), Phillip Terry (*1st Reporter*), Ernest Wood (*Reporter*), Charles Coleman (*Krozac's Butler*), Jack Pennick (*Convict in Dinner Hall Fight*), Allen Mathews, Eddie Foster, All Hill, Huey White, Sammy Finn, Charlie Sullivan, Brooks Benedict, Jack Raynold (*Convicts*), Martin Turner (*Train Cook*), Eddie Parker, Lee Powell (*Federal Men*), Priscilla Lawson, Shirley Chambers (*Girls in Dive*), Arthur Howard, Broderick O'Farrell, Mitchell Ingraham, Billy Arnold, Cyril Ring (*Fathers*), Charles Coleman (*Krozac's Butler*).

Only the extravagant acting of Robinson brings this rather routine crime yarn above the average. He is a big-shot crime czar who returns from Europe after marrying youthful Stradner. But much of Robinson's empire has been eroded by rival gang activities. He launches a gang war and is about to regain the upper hand when one of his opponents fingers him to the police. Robinson is sent to jail and his wife promises to stick by him. She and her newly delivered baby take a lot of abuse from authorities and San Francisco newspapers, so much so that Stewart, a sympathetic reporter, writes a number of articles showing her in a good light and is fired for his efforts. Stradner, meanwhile, visits Robinson in prison and he reveals a barbaric nature that destroys her love for him. Stewart befriends Stradner and later marries her after persuading her to divorce her gangster husband. Stewart and Stradner move to Massachusetts where Stewart adopts Robinson's child and becomes a successful editor. After ten years, Robinson is released from prison; he has only one thing on his mind, finding his ex-wife and son. One of his goons, Stander, convinces Robinson to take over the old gang but when he arrives at a meeting, his old partners in crime beat him up and then torture him in order to find out where he has buried the money he hid before going into prison. When Robinson won't talk, Stander and gang kidnap his ten-year-old son and threaten to injure him unless Robinson talks. He does, and when the gang runs for the money, he and the boy escape. The boy, Scott, refuses to acknowledge Robinson as his father, which incenses the gangster. He is so embittered by now that he vows to kill Stewart and Stradner for allowing his son to forget him. But when Robinson arrives with Scott at Stewart's home, he realizes that the editor and his ex-wife are warm, considerate people who have given the boy a fine home. He leaves his son, realizing that Scott will have a better life without him and his tainted name. Baxter, one of the gangsters Robinson tried to kill years earlier, tracks him down and shoots him; Robinson dies holding his son's merit badges in his hand. This was Robinson's first film at MGM since 1929, and, years later, Robinson marveled at taking the part of the aging gangster, especially after he had informed his home studio, Warner Bros., that he would no longer play snarling hoodlums and had demanded and got script approval for his films. It was supposed to be a swan song for the gangster, one that went on wailing for years to come; Robinson would be playing the crime czar for decades to come in such films as KEY LARGO and HELL ON FRISCO BAY. This was one of Stewart's first substantial leading roles at MGM, where he was being groomed for stardom. He made a favorable impression playing the do-good editor but looked a bit ludicrous in a mustache. Stradner, an accomplished Viennese actress, failed to excite American audiences and her film career in Hollywood quickly faded.

p, J. J. Cohn; d, Edward Ludwig; w, John Lee Mahin (based on a story by William A. Wellman, Robert Carson); ph, William Daniels; ed, Ben Lewis; art d, Cedric Gibbons, Daniel Cathcart; set d, Edwin Willis; montages, Slavko Vorkapich.

Crime Drama   **(PR:A MPAA:NR)**

LAST GANGSTER, THE, 1944 (SEE: ROGER TOUHY, GANGSTER, 1944)

LAST GENTLEMAN, THE **1/2   (1934) 78m 20th Century/UA bw

George Arliss (*Cabot Barr*), Edna May Oliver (*Augusta*), Janet Beecher (*Helen*), Charlotte Henry (*Marjorie*), Frank Albertson (*Allan*), Rafaela Ottiano (*Retta*), Ralph Morgan (*Loring*), Edward Ellis (*Claude*), Donald Meek (*Judd*), Joseph Cawthorn (*Dr. Wilson*), Harry C. Bradley (*Prof. Schumacker*).

Arliss plays an eccentric millionaire nearing death who won't let go of his strong hold over the rest of his family. Even dead, he continues to haunt his family, having himself filmed for the reading of his will. Arliss is effective in his part, but the rest of the cast suffers from overplaying their roles, especially in the comedy sequences. The plot is uneven, but does have some interesting moments.

d, Sidney Lanfield; w, Leonard Praskins (based on the play by Katherine Clugston); ph, Barney McGill; ed, Maurice Wright.

Comedy   **(PR:A MPAA:NR)**

LAST GLORY OF TROY   (SEE: AVENGER, THE, 1962, Ital.)

LAST GRAVE, THE   (SEE: NAVAJO RUN, 1964)

LAST GREAT TREASURE, THE   (SEE: MOTHER LODE, 1982)

LAST GRENADE, THE**   (1970, Brit.) 94m Cinerama c

Stanley Baker (*Maj. Harry Grigsby*), Alex Cord (*Kip Thompson*), Honor Blackman (*Katherine Whiteley*), Richard Attenborough (*Gen. Charles Whiteley*), Ray Brooks (*Lt. David Coulson*), Rafer Johnson (*Joe Jackson*), Andrew Keir (*Gordon MacKenzie*), Julian Glover (*Andy Royal*), John Thaw (*Terry Mitchell*), Philip Latham (*Adams*), Neil Wilson (*Wilson*), Gerald Sim (*Dr. Griffiths*), A.J. Brown (*Governor*), Pamela Stanley (*Governor's Wife*), Kenji Takaki (*Te Ching*), Paul Dawkins (*Commissioner Doyle*).

Baker and Cord are mercenary comrades fighting in the Congo. Cord jumps sides and turns his guns on Baker's troops, wiping out most of them. The action continues in Hong Kong, where Baker has followed Cord in order to get revenge. In Hong Kong Baker falls in love with Blackman, the wife of pompous general Attenborough, but she is killed in a car blown up by Cord. Baker finally gets his revenge when he throws a grenade which kills Cord, even as Baker lays dying himself. The script is flat, filled with predictable sequences and unrealistic dialog, and there is little the performers can do to overcome these weaknesses.

p, Josef Shaftel; d, Gordon Flemyng; w, Kenneth Ware, James Mitchell, John Sherlock (based on the novel *The Ordeal of Major Grigsby* by Sherlock); ph, Alan Hume (Panavision, Eastmancolor); m, John Dankworth; ed, Ernest Hosler, Ann Chegwidden; art d, Anthony Pratt; set d, Terence Morgan, II; cos, Beatrice Dawson; spec eff, Pat Moore; makeup, Wally Schneiderman.

War   **(PR:C MPAA:M)**

LAST GUNFIGHTER, THE*

(1961, Can.) 56m Dalry/Brenner bw (AKA: HIRED GUN; THE DEVIL'S SPAWN)

Don Borisenko, Tass Tory, Jay Shannon, Michael Zenon, Ken James, Gordon Clark, James Beggs [Hagan Beggs], Art Jenoff, Buddy Ferens, Jim Peddie, Ed Holmes, Bill William, James Barron, Mike Conway, Spud Abbot, Al Waxman, Bert Hilckman, Garrick Hagon.

An anti-western in which a gunfighter passing through town is hired to protect some farmers from a bullying rancher. The gunfighter gets involved with a farmer's wife and a fight ensues, leaving the rancher and the gunman dead, the latter a victim of the farmer.

p,d&w, Lindsay Shonteff; ph, Herbert S. Alpert; m, Fred Tudor; ed, Shonteff; set d, Edgar Keenan; cos, Malabar; m/l, Leslie Pouliot.

Western   **(PR:A MPAA:NR)**

LAST GUNFIGHTER, THE   (SEE: DEATH OF A GUNFIGHTER, 1969)

LAST HARD MEN, THE* 1/2   (1976) 103m FOX c

Charlton Heston (*Sam Burgade*), James Coburn (*Zach Provo*), Barbara Hershey (*Susan Burgade*), Jorge Rivero (*Cesar Menendez*), Michael Parks (*Sheriff Noel Nye*), Larry Wilcox (*Mike Shelby*), Morgan Paull (*Portugee Shiraz*), Thalmus Rasulala (*George Weed*), Bob Donner (*Lee Roy Tucker*), John Quade (*Will Gant*), Christopher Mitchum (*Hal Brickman*).

This western adventure in the style of Sam Peckinpah has Coburn escaping from jail and seeking revenge on ex-lawman Heston, the man who put him in jail and killed his wife. To draw Heston out of retirement, Coburn kidnaps his daughter, threatening to rape her. The story is a rough and realistic portrait of the final days of the Wild West as it is now subdued by civilization. Heston is an archaic type of hero, but his ways are the only ones which can battle those of Coburn. The cast gives believable and realistic performances, with script and direction contributing a sleek smoothness, though the underlying messages have too much emphasis placed upon them.

p, Russell Thacher, Walter Seltzer; d, Andrew V. McLaglen; w, Guerdon Trueblood (based on the novel *Gun Down* by Brian Garfield); ph, Duke Callaghan (Panavision, DeLuxe Color); m, Jerry Goldsmith; ed, Fred Chulack; art d, Edward Carfagno; set d, Bob Signorelli; stunts, Joe Canutt.

Western   **(PR:O MPAA:R)**

LAST HERO   (SEE: LONELY ARE THE BRAVE, 1962)

LAST HILL, THE**   (1945, USSR) 86m Tbilisi/Artkino bw

Nikolai Kruichkov (*Comdr. Boris Likachev*), Marina Pastukhova (*Maria Perventseva*), Boris Andreyev (*Maj. Zhukovsky*), Anton Khorava (*Vice-Admiral*), Nikolai Dorokhin (*Sgt. Sizov*), Feodor Ischenko, Nikolai Gorlov, Evgeni Preov, Yegor Tkachuk, Zurab Lezhava (*Sailors*).

A below-par Russian entry dealing with the heroic 250-day stand at Sevastopol during the Nazi siege. The film suffers from a lack of realistic portrayals and uneven technical work. (In Russian; English subtitles.)

d, Alexander Zarkhi, Josef Heifitz; w, Zarkhi, Boris Voyetekho, Heifitz (based on the novel *The Last Days of Sevastopol* by Voyetekhov); ph, Arcady Kalzaty; m, A. Balanchivadze; English subtitles, Charles Clement.

War   **(PR:A MPAA:NR)**

LAST HOLIDAY**

(1950, Brit.) 89m Associated British Picture Corp.-Watergate/Stratford bw

Alec Guinness (*George Bird*), Beatrice Campbell (*Sheila Rockingham*), Kay Walsh (*Mrs. Poole*), Bernard Lee (*Inspector Wilton*), Wilfrid Hyde-White (*Chalfont*), Muriel George (*Lady Oswington*), Helen Cherry (*Miss Mellows*), Jean Colin (*Daisy Clarence*), Brian Worth (*Derek Rockingham*), Sidney James (*Joe Clarence*), Coco [Gregoire] Aslan (*Gambini*), Ernest Thesiger (*Sir Trevor Lampington*), David McCallum, Sr. (*Blind Fiddler*), Esma Cannon, Campbell Cotts, Moultrie Kelsall, Madame E. Kirkwood-Hackett, Eric Maturin, Hal Osmond, Brian Oulton, Heather Wilde, Ronald Simpson, Meirer Tzelniker, Leslie Weston, Lockwood West, Harry Hutchinson, Norman Astridge, Arthur Howard.

This snappy, light-hearted British film features Guinness as a man who has contracted an incurable disease and only has a short time left to live. He withdraws his life savings and moves to a fancy hotel for one last fling. Ironically, he is offered several new prospects, after having struggled his entire life, earning a meager salary as a salesman. Cleverly written, the film is moved along by a direction which smoothly combines the various caricatures. Guinness delivers a well-polished performance.

p, Stephen Mitchell, A.D. Peters, J.B. Priestley; d, Henry Cass; w, Priestley; ph, Ray Elton; m, Francis Chagrin; ed, Monica Kimick; md, Louis Levy; art d, Duncan Sutherland.

Comedy   **(PR:A   MPAA:NR)**

LAST HORSEMAN, THE**   (1944) 54m COL bw

Russell Hayden (*Lucky Rawlins*), Dub Taylor (*Cannonball*), Bob Wills (*Bob*), Ann Savage (*Judy Ware*), John Maxwell (*Cash Watson*), Frank La Rue (*Rance Williams*), Nick Thompson (*Karp*), J. P. "Blackie" Whiteford (*Slade*), Ted Mapes (*Cudlow*), Forrest Taylor (*Bert Saunders*), Curley Dresden.

Hayden plays a ranch foreman who has $12,000 stolen from him. To get the money back, Hayden and his pals disguise themselves as women and nab the crooks. Adequate performances, with an evenly paced development of action. When their leader isn't busy acting, Bob Wills and His Texas Playboys provide the music.

p, Leon Barsha; d, William Berke; w, Ed Earl Repp; ph, George Meehan; ed, Jerome Thoms; art d, Lionel Banks.

Western   **(PR:A   MPAA:NR)**

LAST HOUR, THE**1/2   (1930, Brit.) 77m But bw

Stewart Rome (*Prince Nicola*), Richard Cooper (*Byron*), Kathleen Vaughan (*Mary Tregellis*), Alexander Field (*Smarty Walker*), Wilfred Shine (*Tregellis*), James Raglan (*Charles Lister*), George Bealby (*Blumfeldt*), Frank Arlton (*George*), Billy Shine (*Ben*).

Brisk-moving early British comedy with Rome as a prince who has just stolen the top-secret plan for a death ray. He wanders into a party at a local inn, secret service men on his tail. It appears as if Rome is a dead duck, but the half-witted police still manage to make a mess of things. Performances are overacted, a leftover from the days of silent screen acting, but the direction is well paced.

p, Archibald Nettleford; d, Walter Forde; w, H. Fowler Mear (based on the play by Charles Bennett); ph, Geoffrey Faithfull.

Comedy   **(PR:A   MPAA:NR)**

LAST HOUSE ON DEAD END STREET zero

(1977) 90m Cinematic-Production Concepts/L.B.S. c (AKA: THE FUN HOUSE)

Steven Morrison, Janet Sorley, Dennis Crawford, Lawrence Bornman, Paul Phillips, Elaine Norcross, Alex Kregar, Franklin Statz, Barbara Amusen, Geraldine Sanders.

Grotesque film about a brief investigation into the makings of snuff films. This picture attempted to be a cult classic, but fell far short, as classics are chosen by audiences, not moviemakers.

p, Norman F. Kaiser; d, Victor Janos; w, Brian Lawrence.

Horror   **Cas.**   **(PR:O   MPAA:R)**

LAST HOUSE ON THE LEFT**1/2   (1972) 91m Hallmark/AIP c

David Hess (*Krug*), Lucy Grantham (*Phyllis*), Sandra Cassel (*Mari Collingwood*), Marc Sheffler (*Junior*), Jeramie Rain (*Sadie*), Fred Lincoln (*Weasel*), Gaylord St. James (*Dr. Collingwood*), Cynthia Carr (*Mrs. Collingwood*), Ada Washington (*Lady Truck Driver*).

An extremely controversial cult favorite (the original "Just keep repeating: It's only a movie . . . only a movie" movie), especially with the gore fanatics, LAST HOUSE ON THE LEFT is a much more complex (albeit crudely made) film than its bloody reputation allows for. Loosely based on Ingmar Bergman's THE VIRGIN SPRING, LAST HOUSE ON THE LEFT details the atrocities committed by a group of escaped convicts (including the teenage drug addict brother of the leader of the group, and a woman who seems to float her favors among the other members, though she's supposed to be the leader's girl) that kidnap, rape, and murder two teenage girls who are on their way to a concert. After hiding the bodies, the convicts make their way through the dense New Jersey woods and take refuge in the home of a suburban couple while posing as a family whose car has broken down. Little do the killers know that the house they have picked happens to be owned by the parents of one of the girls. Eventually the parents find out that these strangers have murdered their daughter, and the once-nice, gentle suburban couple enact a savage revenge on the killers that makes them just as vile as those they seek to punish. As stated earlier, the film was crudely made on a miniscule budget, but what the film lacks in technical competence, it makes up for in characterization and insight into violent behavior. The killers initially toy with (torture) the girls, as if playing a game, but when the game gets out of hand and the girls wind up dead, the killers look at their corpses with saddened confusion, as if they had broken something; these people are not unthinking monsters, but deeply disturbed, nearly childlike (but admittedly very deadly) individuals who represent the dark underbelly of American society. (Craven has said the film came out of his feelings of rage and frustration over the Viet Nam war, but the relevancy of this can be debated.) The moment is brief, but without it, the film would be just another sickening exploitation piece. Director Craven (who would go on to polish his themes in the high-budgeted and slicker THE HILLS HAVE EYES) never for a moment allows the viewer to *sympathize* with the killers, but he does provide a window of *understanding* into how senseless acts of violence occur. Then he poses a moral question to the viewer: Who is worse, the sick, depraved convicts who have made murder a way of life, or the girls' affluent, God-fearing parents, who allow themselves to throw away their value system to enact a bloody, torturous revenge? Craven poses the question and leaves it hanging for the viewer to decide. A deeply disturbing film that should only be viewed by those prepared for it.

p, Sean S. Cunningham; d,w&ed, Wes Craven; ph, Victor Hurwitz (Movielab color); m, Steve Chapin, David Hess.

Crime   **Cas.**   **(PR:O   MPAA:R)**

LAST HOUSE ON THE LEFT, PART II

(SEE: TWITCH OF THE DEATH NERVE, 1972, Ital.)

LAST HUNT, THE***1/2   (1956) 108m MGM c

Robert Taylor (*Charles Gilson*), Stewart Granger (*Sandy McKenzie*), Lloyd Nolan (*Woodfoot*), Debra Paget (*Indian Girl*), Russ Tamblyn (*Jimmy*), Constance Ford (*Peg*), Joe DeSantis (*Ed Black*), Ainslie Pryor (*1st Buffalo Hunter*), Terry Wilson (*Buffalo Hunter*), Ralph Moody (*Indian Agent*), Fred Graham (*Bartender*), Ed Lonehill (*Spotted Hand*), Dan White (*Deputy*), William "Bill" Phillips (*Man*), Jerry Martin (*Barber*), Roy Barcroft (*Barfly*), Rosemary Johnston (*Woman*).

Chilling look at Taylor as a sadistic buffalo hunter who kills purely for the enjoyment of killing. He also hunts down defenseless Indians he accuses of stealing his horses. He teams up for a short bit with Granger, a soft-spoken former buffalo hunter, but the two personalities clash. Taylor's sadistic nature forces him to seek revenge on Granger; he waits in ambush, but dies from exposure. The frozen face that serves as the picture's last shot is a fitting visual metaphor for the type of man Taylor portrays (not unlike Jack Nicholson's fate in Stanley Kubrick's THE SHINING). The film was shot entirely in Custer National Park, offering some stunning scenery. The shots of the buffalo being mowed down come from actual footage of buffalo being shot in order to keep them controlled. The script's in-depth look into the motivating forces behind the characters is complemented by striking performances. Well-paced direction helps to keep the movie from lapsing into even a moment of dullness.

p, Dore Schary; d&w, Richard Brooks (based on the novel by Milton Lott); ph, Russell Harlan (CinemaScope, Eastmancolor); m, Daniele Amfitheatrof; ed, Ben Lewis; md, Amfitheatrof; art d, Cedric Gibbons, Merril Pye.

Western   **(PR:C   MPAA:NR)**

LAST HURRAH, THE***1/2   (1958) 121m COL bw

Spencer Tracy (*Frank Skeffington*), Jeffrey Hunter (*Adam Caulfield*), Dianne Foster (*Maeve Caulfield*), Pat O'Brien (*John Gorman*), Basil Rathbone (*Norman Cass, Sr.*), Donald Crisp (*The Cardinal*), James Gleason (*Cuke Gillen*), Edward Brophy (*Ditto Boland*), John Carradine (*Amos Force*), Willis Bouchey (*Roger Sugrue*), Basil Ruysdael (*Bishop Gardner*), Ricardo Cortez (*Sam Weinberg*), Wallace Ford (*Charles J. Hennessey*), Frank McHugh (*Festus Garvey*), Anna Lee (*Gert Minihan*), Jane Darwell (*Delia Boylan*), Frank Albertson (*Jack Mangan*), Charles FitzSimons (*Kevin McCluskey*), Carleton Young (*Mr. Winslow*), Bob Sweeney (*Johnny Degnan*), Edmund Lowe (*Johnny Byrne*), William Leslie (*Dan Herlihy*), Ken Curtis (*Monsignor Killian*), O. Z. Whitehead (*Norman Cass, Jr.*), Arthur Walsh (*Frank Skeffington, Jr.*), Helen Westcott (*Mrs. McCluskey*), Ruth Warren (*Ellen Davin*), Mimi Doyle (*Mamie Burns*), Dan Borzage (*Pete*), James Flavin (*Police Captain*), William Forrest (*Doctor*), Frank Sully (*Fire Chief*), Charlie Sullivan (*Chauffeur*), Ruth Clifford (*Nurse*), Jack Pennick (*Policeman*), Richard Deacon (*Plymouth Club Director*), Harry Tenbrook (*Footsie*), Eve March, Bill Henry, James Waters, Rand Brooks, Harry Lauter (*Young Politicians*), Harry Tyler (*Retainer*), Robert Levin (*Jules Kowalsky*), Julius Tannen (*Mr. Kowalsky*), Hal K. Dawson (*Managing Editor*), Clete Roberts (*News Commentator*), Edmund Cobb, Charles Trowbridge (*Men*), Tommy Earwood (*Gregory McCluskey*), Tommy Jackson.

Tracy breezes through this colorful study of a political boss, the perennial mayor of an Eastern city, presumably Boston, which is predominately Irish-American. He rises each morning to put a rose beneath the portrait of his deceased wife. He has a son, Walsh, who does nothing but play jazz and run after girls, an empty-headed good-for-nothing. Through Tracy is surrounded by cronies and political associates, he is essentially friendless, except for a young and idealistic nephew, Hunter, who works as a reporter for an opposition newspaper run by Carradine, leader of the patrician class which has always been at odds with Tracy and his minions. Hunter, however, sees greatness in his down-to-earth uncle, one who does his utmost to represent the people, not a privileged few. These patricians include Rathbone, the city's most powerful banker from whom Tracy seeks a loan to back the city's new housing project. Rathbone refuses and Tracy retaliates by making Rathbone's non compes mentis son, Whitehead, acting fire commissioner. Rather than see his childlike son disgrace the family, Rathbone grants the loan but takes his revenge by financially backing the opposition. Hunter records Tracy's last political campaign, his "last hurrah" for the city's mayoralty, a campaign packed with old-time street marches, slogans, banners, the kind of thing that went out with Boss Richard Daley of Chicago and Mayor Curley of Boston. Tracy loses but heroically, suffering a heart attack and dying in bed after his political pals make their final goodbyes—O'Brien, Gleason, Brophy, McHugh. For Tracy, this comical, light-hearted movie, well-directed by the venerable Ford, was like old home week. He was reunited with his Irish drinking cronies, McHugh, Gleason, Brophy, O'Brien and showed nothing but respect for helmsman Ford. He thought at the time that this might be the right film in which to make his bow-out from the movies, saying: "I've joked about retiring but this could be the picture. I'm superstitious—you know that's part of being Irish—and I'm back with John Ford again for the first time since I started out with him 28 years ago. (Tracy had made his first film, UP THE RIVER, in 1930, with Ford directing.) I feel this is the proper place for me to end. Even the title is prophetic." But Tracy would have a few more hurrahs, six of them. This would be the last film made by Brophy, a veteran character actor, who died shortly thereafter. Rathbone is particularly good as the vindictive banker and even though his background was theatrical, an area of experience usually derided by Ford, he was treated with special consideration by the director who had great respect for his talent. Ford's approach here is rather somber, despite the comedic aspects of the script, placing emphasis on death; his scenes are deeply shadowed and there is a pervasive gloom to almost every scene, heralding, as it were, Tracy's demise as a politician and human. There are nevertheless some sterling moments as Tracy defies the forces of power and wealth and momentarily triumphs. O'Brien, who was on the outs with several moguls for arcane reasons, had a hard time being cast for this film and he later stated that Ford had to go to bat for him: "John Ford, pal since AIR MAIL, asked for me in THE LAST HURRAH."

p&d, John Ford; w, Frank Nugent (based on the novel by Edwin O'Conner); ph, Charles Lawton, Jr.; ed, Jack Murray; art d, Robert Peterson; set d, William Kiernan.

Drama   Cas.   **(PR:A MPAA:NR)**

LAST JOURNEY, THE**   (1936, Brit.) 55m Twickenham/Atlantic bw

Godfrey Tearle (The Specialist), Hugh Williams (The Man), Judy Gunn (The Girl), Mickey Brantford (The Boy), Julien Mitchell (The Driver), Olga Lindo (The Wife), Michael Hogan (The Fireman), Frank Pettingell (The Drunk), Eliot Makeham (The Light-Fingered Gentleman), Eve Gray (The Light-Fingered Lady), Sydney Fairbrother (The Crank), Sam Wilkinson (The Stutterer), Viola Compton (The Chatterer), John Lloyd (The Steward), Nelson Keys (The Frenchman).

Mitchell plays an aging railroad engineer who goes crazy when he discovers he is being forced to retire. Prompted by a fit of jealousy at seeing his wife flirting with his fireman (Hogan), he decides that his last ride as engineer will culminate in crashing the train into a concrete wall. Tearle plays the psychiatrist who talks him out of it. An unbelievable story with additional subplots, including one that has a crooked biagamist who schemes to marry a rich girl.

p, Julius Hagen; d, Bernard Vorhaus; w, John Soutar, H. Fowler Mear (based on the story by J. Jefferson Farjeon); ph, William Luff, Percy Strong.

Drama   **(PR:A MPAA:NR)**

LAST LOAD, THE**   (1948, Brit.) 57m Elstree Independent/GFD bw

Douglas Barr (David Eden), Ivor Bowyer (Monty), Angela Glynne (Susan Potter), Angela Foulds (Betty Potter), David Hannaford (Bobby), Ian Colin (Mr. Eden), John Longden (Mr. Potter), Frank Atkinson (Jenkins).

Barr and Glynne play two tots, both children of men in the trucking business, instrumental in uncovering a scheme by a gang of crooks to steal a shipment before it reaches its launching point. Well paced effort highlighted by the energy provided by the children.

p&d, John Baxter; w, Geoffrey Orme, Mary Cathcart Borer; ph, Jo Jago.

Children's Adventure   **(PR:AAA MPAA:NR)**

LAST MAN**   (1932) 65m COL bw-c

Charles Bickford (Bannister), Constance Cummings (Marian), Alec B. Francis (Mr. Wingate), Alan Roscoe (Marsden), Robert Ellis (English Charlie), Jimmy Wang (Won-Le-Ton), Johnny Eberts (Egyptian Spy), Bill Williams (Gibbs), Al Smith (Halborn), Hal Price (Captain of the Ballentyne), Kit Guard (1st Mate of the Ballentyne), Jack Carlisle (1st Mate of the Glencoe), Ed Le Saint (Captain of the Glencoe), George Magrill (2nd Mate of the Ballentyne), Jack Richardson (Doctor), Bill Sundholm (Swede Sailor), Bob St. Angelo (Joe).

A derelict ship is found floating off the coast of Port Said, with no one left alive but a crazed man and a woman. Bickford is the detective called in to uncover the plot to destroy the ship and collect the insurance money, knowledge of which has provoked a mutiny. Color is introduced as a new medium for film, but unfortunately this at-that-time experimental technique is emphasized more than a believable story-line. For the most part, the script is slow moving, with little suspense.

d, Howard Higgin, Francis Faragoh; w, Keene Thompson (based on the story by Thompson); ph, Benjamin Kline; ed, Gene Havlick.

Mystery   **(PR:A MPAA:NR)**

LAST MAN, THE** ½
     (1968, Fr.) 82m Dovidis-Annouchka bw (LE DERNIER HOMME)

Sofia Torkeli, Corinne Brill, Jean-Claude Bouillon.

Bouillon, his wife (Torkeli), and their friend (Brill) are below the ground on a cave expedition when a nuclear holocaust strikes, killing everyone on Earth except them. Upon the discovery that they are the last people alive, Bouillon begins to mistreat his pregnant wife and woo Brill. Torkeli runs away and when she returns she finds her husband and friend dying of radiation poisoning. Not a well-acted film, although it did win the Golden Asteroid at the 1969 Trieste festival of Science Fiction.

d&w, Charles Bitsch; ph, Pierre Lhomme; ed, Armand Prenny.

Science-Fiction/Drama   **(PR:C MPAA:NR)**

LAST MAN ON EARTH, THE**
(1964, U.S./Ital.) 86m AP-Produzioni La Regina/AIP bw (L'ULTIMO UOMO DELLA TERRA)

Vincent Price (Robert Morgan), Franca Bettoia (Ruth), Emma Danieli (Virginia), Giacomo Rossi-Stuart (Ben Cortman), Umberto Rau, Christi Courtland, Tony Corevi, Hector [Ettore] Ribotta.

Price plays a scientist who is the last survivor on Earth after a plague has turned the rest of the population into vampires. He manages to escape contagion, due to a jungle virus he had once, which makes him immune to the epidemic. Price spends his time clearing the streets of dead bodies and driving stakes into the hearts of sleeping vampires. He falls for Bettoia who belongs to a group of vampires claiming to have found a temporary antidote to the virus. He frees her from vampire-ism by giving her a transfusion of his blood. She, in turn, informs him that her fellow group members intend to kill him for destroying other vampires. Although Price is idealistic in the belief that there is hope for the future, the semi-vampires kill the last man on Earth anyway. Remade as THE OMEGA MAN.

p, Robert L. Lippert; d, Ubaldo Ragona, Sidney Salkow; w, William P. Leicester, Logan Swanson (based on the novel I Am Legend, by Richard Matheson); ph, Franco Delli Colli; m, Paul Sawtell, Bert Shefter; ed, Gene Ruggiero; art d, Giorgio Giovannini; makeup, Piero Mecacci.

Horror/Suspense   **(PR:O MPAA:NR)**

LAST MAN TO HANG, THE* ½   (1956, Brit.) 75m ACT Films/COL bw

Tom Conway (Sir Roderick Strood), Elizabeth Sellars (Daphne Strood), Eunice Gayson (Elizabeth), Freda Jackson (Mrs. Tucker), Hugh Latimer (Mark), Ronald Simpson (Dr. Cartwright), Victor Maddern (Bonaker), Anthony Newley (Gaskin), Margaretta Scott (Mrs. Cranshaw), Leslie Weston (Mayfield), Bill Shine (Underhay), Anna Turner (Lucy Prynne), Jack Lambert (Maj. Forth), Harold Goodwin (Cheed), Joan Newell (Mrs. Iseley), Thomas Heathcote (Bracket), Tony Quinn (Nywood), Hal Osmond (Coates), Joan Hickson (Lucy's Mother), Gillian Lynne (Gaskin's Girl), Shelagh Fraser (Bracket's Wife), Olive Sloane (Mayfield's Wife), Michael McKeag (Mayfield's Son), Harold Siddons (Cheed's Doctor), Maya Koumani (Cheed's Nurse), Walter Hudd (The Judge), Raymond Huntley (Attorney General), David Home (Antony Harcombe, Queen's Counsel), Dan Cunningham (Clerk of The Court), Russell Napier (Detective Sgt. Bolton), Martin Boddey (Detective Sgt. Horne), John Schlesinger (Dr. Goldfinger), Conrad Phillips (Dr. Mason), Sheila Manahan (Senior Sister), Rosamund Waring (Nurse Tomkins).

Tedious courtroom drama has Conway on trial for the murder of his neurotic wife, Sellars, through a sedative overdose. The jury must decide on whether her death was premeditated or accidental. Conway is found not guilty, and later it emerges that his housekeeper, Jackson, has had him framed by identifying the wrong body as his wife. Sellars is indeed alive, having been given the wrong card in the hospital.

p, John W. Gossage; d, Terence Fisher; w, Gerald Bullett, Ivor Montagu, Max Trell, Maurice Elvey (based on the novel The Jury by Bullett); ph, Desmond Dickinson; m, John Wooldridge; ed, Peter Taylor; md, Wooldridge; art d, Alan Harris.

Drama   **(PR:C MPAA:NR)**

LAST MARRIED COUPLE IN AMERICA, THE**   (1980) 103m UNIV c

George Segal (Jeff Thomson), Natalie Wood (Mari Thomson), Richard Benjamin (Marv Cooper), Arlene Golonka (Sally Cooper), Alan Arbus (Al), Marilyn Sokol (Alice Squib), Oliver Clark (Max Dryden), Priscilla Barnes (Helena Dryden), Dom DeLuise (Walter Holmes), Valerie Harper (Barbara), Bob Dishy (Howard), Mark Lonow (Tom), Sondra Currie (Lainy), Robert Wahler (Rick), Catherine Hickland (Rebecca), Charlene Ryan (Oriana), Murphy Dunne, David Rode, David Comfort, Ricky Segall, Stewart Moss, Colby Chester, Delia Salvi, Bebe Drake-Hooks, Edgy Lee, Mieko Kobayshi, Yvonne Wilder, Billy Holms, George Pentecost, David Bennett, Shari Summers, Jenny O'Hara, William Bogert, Robert Perault, Brad Maule, Jan Jorden, Vernon Weddle, G. Lewis Cates, Jenny Neumann, Lynne Marie Stewart, Oz Tortora.

Another 1950s-like suburban couple film with swearing to boot, as if to show us that this movie was indeed made in the 1980s. Segal and Wood star as a couple confused by the numerous divorces among their friends. They believe they're completely happy and immune to breakup, until Harper comes on the scene as the other woman. Predictable ending has Segal and Wood reunited. Songs include: "We Could Have It All" (sung by Maureen McGovern), "Do You Think I'm Sexy" (sung by Rod Stewart), "Got To Be Real" (sung by Cheryl Lynn).

p, Edward S. Feldman, John Herman Shaner; d, Gilbert Cates; w, Shaner; ph, Ralph Woolsey (Technicolor); m, Charles Fox; ed, Peter E. Berger; art d, Peter Smith; cos, Edith Head; ch, Scott Salmon.

Comedy   Cas.   **(PR:O MPAA:R)**

LAST MERCENARY, THE**
(1969, Ital./Span./Ger.) 100m Orbita-Roxy-Protor/Excelsior c (L'ULTIMO MERCENARIO; EL MERCENARIO; EL ULTIMO MERCENARIO; DIE GROSSE TREIBJAGD)

Ray Danton (Mark Anderson), Pascale Petit (Isabel), Georges Rigaud (Manuel de Lagos), Carl Mohner, Gunther Stoll, Salvo Basile, Vicente Roca, Irma de Santis, Tomas Torres, Piergiuseppe Sciume.

Mercenary Danton is hired by a wealthy industrialist to stop a gang of Brazilian saboteurs from gaining control of his ore mines. By arming the miners, Danton successfully repels the saboteurs.

p, George Ferrer; d, Dieter Muller; w, Ricardo Ferrer Bosch, Julio Salvador, Manfred R. Kohler (based on the story by Bosch); ph, Juan Gelpi (Techniscope, Technicolor); m, Bruno Nicolai; ed, Edith Schuman; art d, Luciano De Nardi

Action/Drama   **(PR:C MPAA:M)**

LAST METRO, THE*** ½
(1981, Fr.) 133m Les Films Du Carrosse-Sedif-T.F.1-Societe Francaise de Production/UA c (LE DERNIER METRO)

Catherine Deneuve (Marion Steiner), Gerard Depardieu (Bernard Granger), Jean Poiret (Jean-Loup Cottins), Heinz Bennent (Lucas Steiner), Andrea Ferreol (Arlette Guillaume), Paulette Dubost (Germaine Fabre), Sabine Haudepin (Nadine Marsac), Jean-Louis Richard (Daxiat), Maurice Risch (Raymond, the Stage Manager), Marcel Berbert (Merlin), Richard Bohringer (Gestapo Agent), Jean-Pierre Klein (Christian Leglise), Master Franck Pasquier (Jacquot [Eric]), Renata (German Nightclub Singer), Jean-Jose Richer (Rene Bernardini), Martine Simonet (Martine the Thief), Laszlo Szabo (Lt. Bergen), Henia Ziv (Yvonne, the Chambermaid), Jessica Zucman (Rosette Goldstern), Alain Tasma (Marc), Rene Dupre (Valentin), Pierre Belot (Desk Clerk), Christian Baltauss (Bernard's Replacement), Alexandra Aumond (1st Nurse), Marie-Dominique Henry (2nd Nurse), Jacob Weizbluth (Rosen), Les Petits Chanteurs De L'Abbaye (Boys' Choir), Rose Thierry (Jacquot's Mother [Concierge]).

A precise and somewhat restrained picture set during the German occupation of France and taking place almost entirely in a theater building. Deneuve, in an arresting performance, is the wife of a top stage director, Bennent, who is forced to go underground in order to avoid the anti-Semitism of the Nazis. Instead of fleeing Paris, however, Bennent hides in the cellar of the theater, secretly listening to and watching the rehearsals of his new play which co-stars Deneuve and Depardieu. As time passes, the lives of the theater personnel become more open and strained, especially in the case of Deneuve and Depardieu who fight their attraction to each other. Politics and romance are placed on parallel tracks as Deneuve tries to remain as loyal to her husband as she is to her countrymen. Truffaut addresses this conflict in an ending which delivers two possible outcomes—on stage (in a performance of Bennent's play) Deneuve is united with Depardieu while off stage she remains at her husband's side. While often scolded for not addressing political issues in his pictures, Truffaut finally found a suitable vehicle in THE LAST METRO—one which deals with the Occupation in human, romantic terms. What Truffaut has done even more than film a realistic portrayal of the Occupation is to capture Paris of the 1940s as it has been mythicized in the films of that period. Not surprisingly Truffaut's image of Occupied France is more formed by the films he saw than by history itself—a true sign of a person obsessed by movies. Songs include: "Bei Mir Bist Du Schon" (Sholom Secunda, Chan-Chaplin, Jacob Jacobs, Jacques Larue), "Priere A Zumba" (A. Lara, Larue), "Mon Amant De Saint-Jean" (E. Carrara, L. Agel), "Sombreros Et Mantilles (J. Vaissade-Chanty) and "Cantique: Pitie Mon Dieu (A. Kunk). (In French; English subtitles.)

d, Francois Truffaut; w, Truffaut, Suzanne Schiffman, Jean-Claude Grumberg (based on a story by Truffaut, Schiffman); ph, Nestor Almendros; m, Georges Delerue; ed, Martine Barraque; art d, Jean-Pierre Kohut-Svelko; cos, Lisele Roos.

Drama   **Cas.**   **(PR:C-O MPAA:R)**

LAST MILE, THE*½   (1932) 75m KBS/World Wide bw

Preston S. Foster (Killer Mears), Howard Phillips (Richard Walters), George E. Stone (Berg), Noel Madison (D'Amoro), Alan Roscoe (Kirby), Paul Fix (Eddie Werner), Al Hill (Fred Mayer), Daniel L. Haynes (Sonny Jackson), Frank Sheridan (Warden Frank Lewis), Alec B. Francis (Father O'Connors), Edward Van Sloan (Rabbi), Louise Carter (Mrs. Walters), Ralph Theodore (Pat Callahan the Principal Keeper), Albert J. Smith (Drake), Kenneth MacDonald (Harris), Walter Walker (Governor Blaine), Francis McDonald (Holdup Man), William Scott (Peddie), Jack Kennedy (O'Flaherty).

Convicted, though innocent, of the murder of his partner, Phillips is sentenced to die in the electric chair and is sent to death row to await the day. Within hours of his arrival one of the other men on the row, Stone, is taken for that last walk while Phillips remembers how he was arguing with his partner when some robbers came in and killed him. As life in the death house settles into its horrible routine of waiting, Phillips gets to know the other prisoners and the sadistic guards. One of the prisoners, Foster, is a hardened criminal who's been bound for this fate all his life and seems resigned to it, but the taunting of Smith—the cruelest of the turnkeys—finally pushes him over the edge. When Smith makes the mistake of leaning against Foster's cell, the convict strangles him and takes his keys. The other prisoners are let out of their cells, except for Fix, whose long wait for death has broken his mind and who refuses to come out. Armed with Smith's gun, Foster manages to capture several more guards and lock them into the cells; then he phones the warden, demanding a fast car and four hours' start. Guards besiege the prisoners and when it becomes obvious that the rebellion is doomed, Foster steps into the open and is gunned down. The obligatory happy ending comes when Phillips is proved innocent and released, in contrast to the play, where his character is guilty of the murder of his girl friend and goes to the chair rather quickly. The only film ever directed by Sam Bischoff, best known as a producer (THE CHARGE OF THE LIGHT BRIGADE, YOU'LL NEVER GET RICH, etc.) THE LAST MILE is a gritty, strong work with excellent performances and a message driven home in a prolog in which a real prison warden speaks out against capital punishment. One of the best of a spate of prison films inspired by prison uprisings at Auburn and Dannemora in New York State in 1929. In 1930 "The Last Mile" appeared on stage in New York with Spencer Tracy as "Killer" Mears. When the show went to Los Angeles, Clark Gable took the part and within a year both men had moved to gangster roles in the movies and then to stardom. The play was adapted from a memoir entitled The Law Takes Its Toll, written by Robert Blake while he was awaiting execution in Texas.

p, E. W. Hammons; d, Sam Bischoff; w, Seton I. Miller (based on the play by John Wexley); ph, Arthur Edeson; ed, Martin G. Cohn, Rose Loewinger; md, Val Burton; set d, Ralph DeLacy.

Crime Drama   **(PR:A MPAA:NR)**

LAST MILE, THE*   (1959) 81m UA bw

Mickey Rooney ("Killer" John Mears), Alan Bunce (The Warden), Frank Conroy (O'Flaherty, the Guard), Leon Janney (Callahan, the Guard), Frank Overton (Father O'Connors), Clifford David (Convict Richard Walters), Harry Millard (Convict Fred Mayor), John McCurry (Convict Vince Jackson), Ford Rainey (Convict Red Kirby), John Seven (Convict Tom D'Amoro), Michael Constantine (Convict Ed Werner), John Vari (Convict Jimmy Martin), Donald Barry (Drake, the Guard), Clifton James (Harris, the Guard), Milton Selzer (Peddie, the Guard), George Marcy (Convict Pete Rodrigues).

The remake of the 1932 prison movie classic is inferior to it in most respects but does feature a host of excellent supporting portrayals and one of Rooney's better adult performances in the role that made stars of Spencer Tracy and Clark Gable on the stage and that Preston Foster essayed on the screen. Death row inmates wait for their time to come, slowly going crazy (Constantine is already there), endlessly tormented by sadistic guard Barry until the day he makes the fatal mistake of leaning against Rooney's cell. The hardened killer, with nothing to lose, strangles Barry and

uses his keys and gun to free the other inmates and capture more of the guards. Priest Overton, who had been rebuffed by Rooney when he tried to talk to the convict earlier, is also taken hostage and is the only one not terrified by their predicament. One by one the convicts fall victim to the guns that surround the cellblock, and when Rooney sees that his demands are never going to be met, he ends his wait for death by stepping into a hail of bullets. A powerful film, grim and tense. Former B-western star Barry's sadistic guard and Overton's compassionate, fearless priest stand out in a fine cast composed mostly of people from the stage, and although Rooney tends to chew the scenery on occasion, it doesn't seem too out of place given the extraordinary circumstances in which he finds himself.

p, Max J. Rosenberg, Milton Subotsky; d, Howard W. Koch; w, Subotsky, Seton I. Miller (based on the play by John Wexley); ph, Joseph Brun; m, Van Alexander; ed, Robert Brockman, Patricia Jaffe; prod d, Paul Barnes; set d, Jack Wright, Jr.; cos, Frank Thompson; spec eff, Milton Olson, Vincent Brady; makeup, Robert Jiras.

Crime   **(PR:C MPAA:NR)**

LAST MOMENT, THE*   (1954, Brit.) 51m Douglas Fairbanks Jr./BL bw

Douglas Fairbanks Jr. (George Griffin), Cyril Cusack, Greta Gynt, Paul Carpenter, MacDonald Parke, Mary Merrall, Barbara Mullen, Fulton Mackay, Valerie Carton.

With his stay in London, Fairbanks produced a number of short segment films whose main target seemed to be British TV. More so than not, these things were pretty bad, dull, and not worth serious consideration. Two such short films were combined to be released theatrically, following the same sloppy pattern of the rest in the series. The first of these stars Fairbanks as a disillusioned inventor of a new miracle drug who is saved from the ultimate act of a depressive individual when he gets a chance to use the drug to save a young boy. The other story centers around the fear that envelops an Irish family when its patriarch becomes obsessed with a scheme presented by a devious double-talker. Luckily the local priest intervenes and makes the man understand a more logical path for all involved.

p, Tom D. Connochie, Roy Goddard; d, Lance Comfort; w, Selwyn Jepson, Paul Vincent Carroll; ph, Jimmy Wilson, Brendan J. Stafford.

Drama   **(PR:A MPAA:NR)**

LAST MOMENT, THE zero   (1966) 83m A-Y/Headliner bw

Melora Conway, Nick Dimitri, Byrd Holland, Terry Olson, Stasa Damascus, Victoria Moreno, Tanya Lemani.

A melodrama about a dying leukemia patient whose uninformed husband thinks she is having an affair with her doctor. She decides her husband doesn't love or trust her, and so she does have an affair with a Hollywood nightclub singer. He soon learns of her supposed tryst with the doctor and leaves. Distraught, the woman jumps to her death from a cliff, leaving behind her diary which tells the two men the real reasons for her visits to the doctor.

p,d&w, Al Yasin; m/l, George Michaelides.

Drama   **(PR:C MPAA:NR)**

LAST MOVIE, THE*   (1971) 108m UNIV/CIC c (AKA: CHINCHERO)

Julie Adams (Mrs. Anderson), Dennis Hopper (Kansas), Daniel Ades (Thomas Mercado), Rod Cameron (Pat), John Alderman (Jonathan), Michael Anderson, Jr. (Mayor's Son), Rich Aguilar (Gaffer), Donna Baccala (Miss Anderson), Tom Baker (Member of Billy's Gang), Toni Basil (Rose), Poupee Bocar (Singer), Anna Lynn Brown (Dance Hall Girl), Bernard Casselman (Doctor), James Contreras (Boom-man), Eddie Donno (Stunt Man), Severn Darden (Mayor), Lou Donelan (Prop Man), Roy Engel (Anderson), Warren Finnerty (Banker), Peter Fonda (Sheriff), Fritz Ford (Citizen), Sam Fuller (Director), Stella Garcia (Maria), Michael Greene (Hired Gun), Samya Greene (Baby), William Gray (In Billy's Gang), Don Gordon (Neville), Al Hopson (Sheriff), Bud Hassink (In Gang), George Hill (Key Grip), Henry Jaglom (Minister's Son), Gray Johnson (Stunt Man), Kris Kristofferson (Minstrel Wrangler), Clint Kimbrough (Minister), John Phillip Law (Little Brother), Ted Markland (Big Brother), Victor Maymudes (In Gang), Cynthia McAdams (Dance Hall Girl), Tomas Milian (Priest), Sylvia Miles (Script Girl), Jim Mitchum (Art), Al Monroe (Citizen), Jorge Montoro (Jorge), Owen Orr (Hired Gun), Michelle Phillips (Banker's Daughter), Robert Rothwell (Citizen), Richard Rust (Pisco), John Stevens (Cameraman), Toni Stern (Dance Hall Girl), Dennis Stock (Still Man), Dean Stockwell (Billy), Russ Tamblyn (In Gang), Alan Warnick (Assistant Director), John Buck Wilken (Minstrel Wrangler).

Hopper, Nicholson, and Fonda came off the success of EASY RIDER to make their own movies. Nicholson did DRIVE, HE SAID, Fonda directed THE HIRED HAND, and Hopper did this. Put them all together and you still won't have half the fun of EASY RIDER so it was a case of divide and conquer when they set out on their own. Universal gave Hopper $1 million and he came back with more than 40 hours of film. His first cut was more than six hours and his final cut, after more than a year of editing, was incomprehensible to the studio, the public, and just about everyone else who saw it except for the people at the Venice Film Festival who, amazingly, gave it an award. Take a look at the cast list and you'll see that Hopper called in many of his pals to do cameos but all that talent couldn't help. It's supposedly based on some experiences Hopper had while filming THE SONS OF KATIE ELDER in Mexico. He'd hoped to shoot this in Mexico but was refused so he took the entire company to Peru. It begins at the end, flashes back to the beginning, and winds up somewhere in the middle as Hopper plays a movie stunt man who stays behind on a film location after the company has moved off. The filming (directed by Fuller as a director) has Stockwell, as Billy The Kid, getting killed doing a stunt. Hopper now takes up with a local whore, Garcia, then goes off to find gold with Gordon. The local priest, Milian, is angered by all the violence and blames movies for the introduction of death and destruction to his naive villagers. Gordon commits suicide, inexplicably, and Hopper feels guilty. (He spends most of the film feeling guilty.) Hopper is then adopted by the local Peruvian Indians who have taken the left-behind movie equipment and made it part of their religion. In the end, the Indians plan to crucify Hopper, as they have cast him as Billy The Kid in *their* production. This film has more meaningless scenes than a Warhol movie. There are blank frames, inserts that read "Scene Missing," and endless pretentiousness. Kovacs can usually make anything look good but he comes a cropper in this case, so what we have is an immense pile of cinematic manure, wrapped in a silk ribbon. It looks as though Hopper called all his pals, said "Hey, I have a million bucks. Wanna go down to Peru with me and make a movie?" And, surprisingly enough, many of them did, including three directors, Fuller, Jaglom, and Fonda, all of whom should have known better. In Jaglom's case, however, perhaps not, for he is the man who lensed some of the most yawnable films in history, including 1985's ALWAYS and the somewhat-better CAN SHE BAKE A CHERRY PIE? The only reason to see THE LAST MOVIE is to marvel at the fact that a studio was dumb enough to finance it and that so many people were involved with such garbage. Hopper, to this day, thinks that it's a masterpiece, but there are very few who agree with him.

p, Paul Lewis; d, Dennis Hopper; w, Stewart Stern (based on a story by Hopper and Stern); ph, Laszlo Kovacs (Technicolor); m, Kris Kristofferson, John Buck Wilkin, Chabuca Granda, Severn Darden, the Villagers of Chinchero, Peru; ed, Hopper, David Berlatsky, Antranig Mahakian; art d, Leon Erickson; set d, Peter Cornberg; cos, Gerald Alpert; spec eff, Milton Rice; m/l, "Maria Suenos," Chabuca Granda (sung by Poupee Bocar); makeup, Ted Coodley; stunts, Charles Bail.

Drama (PR:O MPAA:R)

LAST MUSKETEER, THE** (1952) 67m REP bw

Rex Allen *(Himself)*, Mary Ellen Kay *(Sue)*, Slim Pickens *(Slim)*, James Anderson *(Russ Tasker)*, Boyd "Red" Morgan *(Barney)*, Monte Montague *(Matt Becker)*, Michael Hall *(Johnny Becker)*, Alan Bridge *(Lem Shaver)*, Stan Jones *(Sheriff Blake)*, Republic Rhythm Riders, Koko the Horse.

Western yarn has Allen trying to keep an ambitious Anderson from taking over all the land in the district from the cattle ranchers. Anderson tries to dry up the valley so that land will become cheap. He can then buy it all, build a dam, and become wealthy on electric power. Allen spoils the scheme when he discovers another watering hole. Songs include: "I Still Love the West" (Foy Willing), "Aura Lee," "Down In the Valley."

p, Edward J. White; d, William Witney; w, Arthur E. Orloff; ph, John MacBurnie; m, Nathan Scott; ed, Harold Minter; art d, Frank Arrigo; m/l, Foy Willing.

Western (PR:A MPAA:NR)

LAST OF MRS. CHEYNEY, THE½** (1929) 94m MGM bw

Norma Shearer *(Mrs. Cheyney)*, Basil Rathbone *(Lord Arthur Dilling)*, George Barraud *(Charles)*, Herbert Bunston *(Lord Elton)*, Hedda Hopper *(Lady Maria)*, Moon Carroll *(Joan)*, Madeline Seymour *(Mrs. Wynton)*, Cyril Chadwick *(Willie Wynton)*, Maude Turner Gordon *(Mrs. Webley)*, Finch Smiles *(William)*, George K. Arthur *(George)*.

This was the first and, arguably, the best of three versions of Lonsdale's play, which had starred Ina Claire and Roland Young on Broadway. It was done with Joan Crawford, William Powell, and Robert Montgomery in 1937, then again as THE LAW AND THE LADY with Greer Garson, Fernando Lamas, and Michael Wilding. Rathbone made his sound debut in the film and audiences were thrilled by that mellifluous voice, despite hit-and-miss recording on the part of the studio's sound department which was just learning the newfangled technique. Shearer poses as a rich widow while visiting Monte Carlo but she is little more than an adventuress with larceny on her mind. She and Barraud conspire to steal an expensive necklace of pearls from Gordon but she thinks better of it after meeting Rathbone, Gordon's nephew and a lord in his own right. Shearer travels with a retinue of crooks who pose as her servants and she is immediately accepted by the society types. Later, she is invited to Gordon's country mansion in England where she intends to purloin the pearls. She's caught by Rathbone but wins him over with her charm. Now Rathbone says he'll keep mum about her doings if she agrees to have an affair with him. Shearer may be a crook but she's not a hussy so she calls for everyone at the home to be her judge and jury and confesses what she's done and what Rathbone had suggested. The guests find her guilty and are about to call in the police when Bunston steps forward and admits that he once wrote Shearer a letter that would prove embarrassing to all if the contents are revealed. The gathered aristocrats buy her off with a large sum of money in a check. Shearer proves her mettle by destroying the check and the letter, and the others are so thrilled by her selflessness that they welcome her into their social set. Rathbone is totally taken by this and the picture ends as the two of them plan a life together. Certainly it's unbelievable and, yes, it's filled with constructional faults, but the whole thing is so airy and delicate as played by a marvelous cast that we can forgive all of the above. The dialog is sometimes too clever, almost Oscar Wilde-like, though the bon mots come so thick and fast and you laugh so hard that you have no time to realize it's all a lot of silliness. Shearer and producer Thalberg were married at the time this was made. Until their marriage in 1927, she had not been a star but once she wed the studio chief, she had her choice of plums and got a beauty with this role.

p, Irving Thalberg; d, Sidney Franklin; w, Hans Kraly, Claudine West (based on the play by Frederick Lonsdale); ph, William Daniels; ed, Conrad V. Nervig; art d, Cedric Gibbons; cos, Adrian.

Comedy (PR:A MPAA:NR)

LAST OF MRS. CHEYNEY, THE** (1937) 98m MGM bw

Joan Crawford *(Fay Cheyney)*, Robert Montgomery *(Lord Arthur Dilling)*, William Powell *(Charles)*, Frank Morgan *(Lord Elton)*, Nigel Bruce *(Sir William)*, Jessie Ralph *(Duchess)*, Benita Hume *(Kitty)*, Melville Cooper *(William)*, Ralph Forbes *(John)*, Colleen Clare *(Joan)*, Leonard Carey *(Ames)*, Sara Haden *(Anna)*, Lumsden Hare *(Inspector Witherspoon)*, Wallis Clark *(George)*, Aileen Pringle *(Marie)*, Bob Cory *(Deck Steward)*, Vesey O'Davoren *(Steward)*, Wilson Benge *(Butler)*, Thomas Braidon *(Head Steward)*, Barnett Parker *(Purser)*.

This film, marred by the tragedy of director Boleslawski's death, was a moderate success at the box office although a cut below the original, which starred Norma Shearer. Crawford is a schemer who roams the parties of the London elite posing as a landed woman (with no land to speak of). What she really is is a jewel thief and she has her dark eyes on the gem-draped necks and wrists of the British society types. Oozing charm, she worms her way into the good graces of everyone and plans a huge heist at a weekend party. With her accomplished aide, Powell, at her side portraying a butler (he'd done it to great plaudits three pictures before as MY MAN GODFREY), they descend upon the mansion in the country where she takes everyone in with her grace and style. At the estate, Crawford attracts Montgomery, a lord, by showing a lot more class than either Hume or Pringle, two debutantes. Montgomery eventually reveals himself to be a scoundrel and Powell and Crawford are uncovered as thieves. She gets them out of it, though, when she threatens to reveal the contents of some letters sent to her by Morgan, another lord, in which he painted his society compatriots in less than glowing colors. If Crawford and Powell are taken in by the police, she'll be forced to offer the letters as evidence in court and they will be reprinted by, shudder, the press. The bluebloods back off and Crawford and Powell are free to leave. The comedy is handled well, including Crawford, who hadn't done many laugh movies until this time. Powell and Morgan shine in their roles, but Montgomery, in an unsympathetic part, doesn't have much of an opportunity to engage the audience. The camera work was by George Folsey. His son, George Folsey, Jr., followed in his footsteps and will, unfortunately, always be remembered as the man behind the camera when tragedy hit the set of THE TWILIGHT ZONE and actor Vic Morrow died, with two underage children who shouldn't have been working that late in the first place. Hume later married Ronald Colman and was his wife until his death, then she married George Sanders. After director Boleslawski's untimely death the chore was taken over by George Fitzmaurice.

p, Lawrence Weingarten; d, Richard Boleslawski, George Fitzmaurice; w, Leon Gordon, Samson Raphaelson, Monckton Hoffe (based on the play by Frederick Lonsdale); ph, George Folsey; m, Dr. William Axt; ed, Frank Sullivan; art d, Cedric Gibbons; cos, Adrian.

Drama (PR:A MPAA:NR)

LAST OF SHEILA, THE* (1973) 120m WB c

Richard Benjamin *(Tom)*, Dyan Cannon *(Christine)*, James Coburn *(Clinton)*, Joan Hackett *(Lee)*, James Mason *(Philip)*, Ian McShane *(Anthony)*, Raquel Welch *(Alice)*, Yvonne Romain *(Sheila)*, Pierro Rosso *(Vittorio)*, Serge Citon *(Guido)*, Robert Rossi *(Captain)*, Elaine Geisinger, Elliot Geisinger *(American Couple)*, Jack Pugeat *(Silver Salesman)*, Martial *(Locksmith)*, Maurice Crosnier *(Concierge)*.

THE LAST OF SHEILA is about as difficult to figure out as a calculus problem but not nearly as much fun. Screenwriters Perkins and Sondheim try to outsmart the audience and succeed only in outsmarting themselves with a plot that no amount of talented actors could save from literary self-indulgence. It's more of a board game than a screenplay, but the stereotypical characters are so bolluxed up in the convoluted plot that they seem like lost wanderers in a desert of failed bon mots. Coburn is a wealthy Hollywood producer whose wife was killed by a hit-and-run driver at a party a year ago. He's invited six people, all suspects, to his yacht in the South of France in the hopes of uncovering the culprit. He winds up getting killed after the most unlikely sequence of events you've ever squirmed in your seat watching. He hands out cards to everyone with secrets written on them having to do with each of the sextet. None of the suspects have a card that pertains to them; Coburn hopes that one will step forward and claim the "I Am the Hit-And-Run Driver" card and solve the case. Now we go into a series of endless flashbacks and backbiting. A confession also occurs that comes too early to be taken seriously. There follows a progression of more twists and turns than one finds on California's Route One, none of them interesting or provocative. Both authors are puzzle freaks and they have set up a puzzle that has too many tangents leading off into nowheresville. Benjamin, a failed screenwriter, is married to rich neurotic Hackett. Welch, a movie star, is married to her manager, McShane; Mason is an aging film director; and Cannon is a parody of a high-powered agent. Someone tries to kill Cannon, then Coburn is found dead. Hackett admits she drove the car and that she's also killed Coburn, but when Hackett is also found dead, having done herself in (or so it seems), no one believes her earlier admission. Mason thinks about it and posits that Benjamin really killed Coburn (he knew that his wife had killed Coburn's wife) and preyed on the woman's deranged mind to kill herself. Benjamin would like to kill Mason but Welch arrives, stopping that. Now that Benjamin is rich (his late wife left him everything), the survivors decide to make a movie together called, you guessed it, THE LAST OF SHEILA. The cast is much better than the material, but it's a shame that so many talents had to be wasted on this pretentious tripe. Ross' direction does little for the film and meandered so much that even he didn't seem to understand what was going on. It just goes to show that if you have a name in New York or Hollywood, you can sell anything. But you can't fool the public all of the time and this picture sank like a stone. Bette Midler sings "Friends," the song that has become her trademark, and that's one of the few things to recommend about this film.

p&d, Herbert Ross; w, Anthony Perkins, Stephen Sondheim; ph, Gerry Turpin (Technicolor); m, Billy Goldenberg; ed, Edward Warschilka; prod d, Ken Adam; art d, Tony Roman; set d, John Jarvis; m/l, "Friends," Goldenberg.

Mystery/Comedy Cas. (PR:C MPAA:PG)

LAST OF SUMMER (SEE: EARLY AUTUMN, 1962, Jap.)

LAST OF THE BADMEN** (1957) 79m AA c

George Montgomery *(Dan Barton)*, James Best *(Ted Hamilton)*, Douglas Kennedy

(Hawkins), Keith Larsen (Roberts), Robert Foulk (Taylor), Willis Bouchey (Marshal Parker), John Doucette (Johnson), Meg Randall (Lila), Tom Greenway (Dallas), Addison Richards (Dillon), Michael Ansara (Kramer), John Damler (Elkins), Harlan Warde (Green).

Montgomery plays a Chicago detective investigating a bunch of stage coach robberies. He goes undercover to expose a gang that breaks prisoners out of jail, then kills them when the reward on their heads has risen. Montgomery succeeds in exposing the outlaws, before they do him in.

p, Vincent M. Fennelly; d, Paul Landres; w, Daniel B. Ullman, David Chantler (based on the story by Ullman); ph, Ellsworth Fredricks (CinemaScope, De Luxe Color); m, Paul Sawtell; ed, William Austin; art d, David Milton; m/l, Gwen Davis.

Western   (PR:A MPAA:NR)

LAST OF THE BUCCANEERS**1/2   (1950) 78m COL c

Paul Henreid (Jean Lafitte), Jack Oakie (Sgt. Dominick), Karin Booth (Belle Summers), Mary Anderson (Swallow), Edgar Barrier (George Mareval), John Dehner (Sgt. Beluche), Harry Cording (Cragg Brown), Eugene Borden (Capt. Perez), Pierre Watkin (Gov. Claiborne), Sumner Getchell (Paul DeLorie), Paul Marion (Jose Cabrillo), Rusty Wescoatt (Col. Parnell), Jean Del Val (Sauvinct).

Henreid plays the legendary pirate of the Gulf of Mexico, Lafitte. This tale occurs after the British have been driven from New Orleans, with the help of the pirate. Henreid is unable to retain his boats from the American government, so he captures one and sets up shop on a small island off the coast. The government lets them go through with their plundering as long as they lay off American ships. Unfortunately, one of Henreid's pirate captains raids an American ship, forcing Henreid and his eloquent bride-to-be, Booth, to escape to safety. Action is well paced, with the cast giving adequate performances.

p, Sam Katzman; d, Lew Landers; w, Robert E. Kent; ph, Vincent Farrar (Technicolor); ed, Henry Batista; md, Mischa Bakaleinikoff; art d, Paul Palmentola.

Adventure/Drama   (PR:A MPAA:NR)

LAST OF THE CAVALRY, THE   (SEE: ARMY GIRL, 1938)

LAST OF THE CLINTONS, THE*   (1935) 59m Ajax bw

Harry Carey (Trigger Carson), Betty Mack (Edith Elkins), Del Gordon (Marty Todd), Victor Potel (Jed Clinton), Earl Dwire (Luke Todd), Tom London (Elkins), Ruth Findlay, Slim Whitaker, Ernie Adams, William McCall, Lafe McKee.

Prospector Potel lends a hand to cattle detective Carey, as Carey tries to round up the usual gang of rustlers. Battles rage, guns fire, and horses stampede, but in the end Carey takes the gang to the cleaners.

p, William Berke; d, Harry Fraser; w, Weston Edwards (based on the story by Monroe Talbot); ph, Robert Cline; ed, Arthur A. Brookes.

Western   (PR:A MPAA:NR)

LAST OF THE COMANCHES**
                 (1952) 85m COL c (AKA: THE SABRE AND THE ARROW)

Broderick Crawford (Sgt. Matt Trainor), Barbara Hale (Julia Lanning), Johnny Stewart (Little Knife), Lloyd Bridges (Jim Starbuck), Mickey Shaughnessy (Rusty Potter), George Mathews (Romany O'Rattigan), Hugh Sanders (Denver Kinnaird), Ric Roman (Martinez), Chubby Johnson (Henry Ruppert), Martin Milner (Billy Creel), Milton Parsons (Prophet Satterlee), Jack Woody (Cpl. Floyd), John War Eagle (Black Cloud), Carleton Young (Maj. Lanning), William Andrews (Lt. Floyd), Bud Osborne (Wagon Driver), George Chesebro (Pete), Jay Silverheels, Rod Redwing (Indians).

Crawford embarks on a 100-mile mission with a small group of surviving soldiers. Water provisions run short and thirst sets in, a fate also suffered by a band of Indians. The soldiers hole up in an abandoned mission, while the Comanches prepare to attack. Luckily (and predictably), another cavalry group shows up in the nick of time.

p, Buddy Adler; d, Andre de Toth; w, Kenneth Gamet; ph, Charles Lawton, Jr., Ray Cory (Technicolor); m, George Duning; ed, Al Clark; md, Morris Stoloff; art d, Ross Bellah; set d, Frank Tuttle.

Western   (PR:A MPAA:NR)

LAST OF THE COWBOYS, THE
                 (SEE: GREAT SMOKEY ROADBLOCK, THE, 1978)

LAST OF THE DESPERADOES**1/2   (1956) 70m ARC bw

James Craig (Pat Garrett), Jim Davis (John W. Poe), Barton MacLane (Mosby), Margia Dean (Sarita), Donna Martel (Paulita), Myrna Dell (Clara), Bob Steele (Bowdre), Stanley Clements (Bert).

Craig takes on the role of sheriff Pat Garrett who, after killing Billy the Kid, is targeted by the Kid's gang. After a number of innocent townsfolk are killed, Craig tries to rally the support of the locals but finds them unwilling. He resorts to an alias and moves to a different town, but still the killings continue. He gets back his badge and knocks the gang down one by one. A fine cast makes this one still eminently watchable.

p, Sigmund Neufeld; d, Sam Newfield; w, Orville Hampton (based on the story by Hampton); ph, Eddie Linden; m, Paul Dunlap; ed, Holbrook Todd.

Western   (PR:A MPAA:NR)

LAST OF THE DUANES*1/2   (1930) 62m FOX bw

George O'Brien (Buck Duane), Lucile Brown (Ruth Garrett), Myrna Loy (Lola), Walter McGrail (Bland), James Bradbury, Jr. (Euchre), Nat Pendleton (Bossamer), Blanche Frederici (Mrs. Duane), Frank Campeau (Luke Stevens), James Mason

(Morgan), Lloyd Ingraham (Mr. Garrett), Willard Robertson (Captain of the Rangers).

O'Brien is an honest cowboy who kills a man in self-defense and then has to flee to escape the law. While on the run, he proves his worth by helping out a rancher, saving a woman from a gang of outlaws, and defeating the gang that wronged him. One of a number of Tom Mix silents based on the Zane Grey novels that were remade with the advent of sound.

p, Edward Butcher, Harold B. Lipsitz; d, Alfred Werker; w, Ernest Pascal (based on a story by Zane Grey); ph, Daniel B. Clark; ed, Ralph Dietrich; art d, William Darling; cos, Sophie Wachner; m/l, "Cowboy Dan," "The Outlaw Song," Cliff Friend.

Western   (PR:A MPAA:NR)

LAST OF THE DUANES**   (1941) 57m FOX bw

George Montgomery (Buck Duane), Lynne Roberts (Nancy Bowdrey), Eve Arden (Kate), Francis Ford (Luke Stevens), George E. Stone (Euchre), William Farnum (Maj. McNeil), Joseph Sawyer (Bull Lossomer), Truman Bradley (Capt. Laramie), Russell Simpson (Tom Duane), Don Costello (Jim Bland), Harry Woods (Red Morgan), Andrew Tombes (Sheriff), Tom London (Deputy), Tim Ryan (Bartender), Ann Carter (Cannon's Daughter), Harry Hayden (Banker), Walter McGrail, Russ Clark (Ranger Guards), Lew Kelly (Old Timer), Jack Stoney, Tom Moray, Syd Saylor (Men), Ethan Laidlaw, Lane Chandler, LeRoy Mason (Henchmen), Arthur Aylesworth (Old Man), Paul Sutton (Tired Man), J. Anthony Hughes (Cannon), Paul Burns (Horseshoe Player), Erville Alderson (Zeke).

A remake of the thrice-filmed Zane Grey novel from 1914, which was filmed this time as a sequel to RIDERS OF THE PURPLE SAGE. Montgomery stars as an honest cowboy on the run to clear his name of a killing done in self-defense. He battles an outlaw gang who are terrorizing dance hall entertainer Arden, and then sides up with the Texas Rangers to bring the gang to justice.

p, Sol M. Wurtzel; d, James Tinling; w, Irving Cummings, Jr., William Conselman, Jr. (based on story by Zane Grey); ph, Charles Clarke; ed, Nick De Maggio; md, Cyril J. Mockridge; art d, Richard Day, Chester Gore.

Western   (PR:A MPAA:NR)

LAST OF THE FAST GUNS, THE**   (1958) 82m UNIV c

Jock Mahoney (Brad Ellison), Gilbert Roland (Miles Lang), Linda Cristal (Maria O'Reilly), Eduard Franz (Padre Jose), Lorne Greene (Michael O'Reilly), Carl Benton Reid (John Forbes), Edward C. Platt (Samuel Grypton), Eduardo Noriega (Cordoba), Jorge Trevino (Manuel), Rafael Alcayde (Alcalde), Lee Morgan (Johnny Ringo), Milton Bernstein (James Younger), Stillman Segar (Ben Thompson), Jose Chavez Trowe (Garcia), Francisco Reyguera (Pablo), Richard Cutting (Sheriff), Ralph Neff (Bartender).

This film's title states that with Billy the Kid and Jesse James dead, Mahoney is the "last of the fast guns." The plot has Mahoney hired by millionaire Reid to find his long lost brother, Franz, who disappeared into Mexico many years ago. If Franz isn't found, his share of the business goes to Reid's conniving partner, Roland. Roland is determined to get control of the business, but can't do so if Franz is found. Mahoney finds Franz and persuades him to return home, but only after the brother is nearly kidnaped and killed in the process.

p, Howard Christie; d, George Sherman; w, David P. Harmon; ph, Alex Phillips (CinemaScope, Eastmancolor); m. Joseph Gershenson; ed, Patrick McCormack; art d, Alexander Golitzen, Roberto Silva.

Western   (PR:A MPAA:NR)

LAST OF THE KNUCKLEMEN, THE***   (1981, Aus.) 93m Hexagon c

Gerard Kennedy (Tarzan), Michael Preston (Pansy), Peter Hehir (Tom), Michael Duffield (Methuselah), Dennis Miller (Horse), Stephen Bisley (Mad Dog), Michael Caton (Monk), Stewart Faichney (Tassie), Steve Rackman (Carl), Saviour Sammut (Cook), Sean Myers (Engineer), Gerry Duggan (Old Arthur), Denise Drysdale, Helen Watts (Whores).

A tale from Down Under which has Kennedy in charge of a group of disgruntled workers, one of whom is named Pansy (Preston), a perpetual braggart. His loud-mouthing finally gets on Kennedy's nerves and he challenges him to a fight, handing him his just deserts. An effectively gritty atmosphere set in a mining town with an ample collection of hookers, gambling tables, and hard-edged workers.

p,d&w, Tim Burstall (based on the play by John Powers); ph, Dan Burstall (Atlab Color); m, Bruce Smeaton; ed, Edward McQueen-Mason; art d, Leslie Binns.

Drama   (PR:A MPAA:NR)

LAST OF THE LONE WOLF**   (1930) 70m COL bw

Bert Lytell (Michael Lanyard), Patsy Ruth Miller (Stephanie), Lucien Prival (Varril), Otto Matieson (Prime Minister), Alfred Hickman (King), Maryland Morne (Queen), Haley Sullivan (Camilla, Queen's Maid), Pietro Sosso (M.C.), Henry Daniell (Count von Rimpau), James Liddy (Hoffman).

This Lone Wolf entry, the first talkie of the series, tells the tale of jealousies between the King and his flirtatious wife, the Queen. The King learns that his wife has given away a ring, a gift from the King, to her military attache lover. The King then plans a grand ball, ordering the Queen to wear the ring. She has her lady-in-waiting set off to retrieve her gift, meeting, along the way, a thief, who unknown to her, was hired by the King to steal the ring from the attache's safe. They venture through a series of events together, with the thief remaining faithful to the Queen and returning the ring to her instead of the King. (See LONE WOLF series, Index.)

d, Richard Boleslawsky; w, John T. Neville, James Whitaker (based on the book by Louis Joseph Vance); ph, Ben Kline; ed, Dave Berg.

Adventure   (PR:A MPAA:NR)

LAST OF THE MOHICANS, THE**** (1936) 91m Small/UA bw

Randolph Scott *(Hawkeye, Colonial Scout)*, Binnie Barnes *(Alice Munro)*, Heather Angel *(Cora Munro)*, Hugh Buckler *(Col. Munro, British Father of Girls)*, Henry Wilcoxon *(Maj. Duncan Heyward, British)*, Bruce Cabot *(Magua, Treacherous Spy)*, Robert Barrat *(Chingachgook, Mohican Chief)*, Phillip Reed *(Uncas, His Son)*, Willard Robertson *(Capt. Winthrop, Colonial)*, Frank McGlynn, Sr. *(David Gamut)*, Will Stanton *(Jenkins, Heyward's Orderly)*, William V. Mong, Olaf Hytten, Lumsden Hare, Reginald Barlow, Lionel Belmore.

Packed with excitement and adventure, this entry is undoubtedly the finest film version of any Cooper tale with Scott and Wilcoxon giving superlative performances and Cabot, as a vicious, lascivious Indian, rendering one of the most hateful roles in film history. Following the outlines of the Cooper novel, the script is literate and sprightly. Scott, as the indefatigable Hawkeye, has a great love for the wilderness, its creatures and fauna, including the Indians who reside there. But he's no idealistic fool; he shrewdly determines what Indians cannot be trusted and knows the wily ways of the treacherous Hurons who have sided with the French in the French-Indian wars. The setting is upper New York State, 1756, a year in which French Gen. Montcalm besieged old Fort William Henry on Lake George. Fighting alongside the French against the British are the merciless Hurons, one of whom is Cabot, a spy working inside British lines. Scott is ordered to escort a British officer, Wilcoxon, and Barnes and Angel, the daughters of Buckler, commander of Fort William Henry, to the fort through hostile lines. Accompanying Scott are Barrat (Chingachgook) and Reed (Uncas), his son, the last survivors of the Mohican tribe which has been wiped out in a mass slaughter by the Hurons. The small party treks through the wilderness, into dense forests and over mountain trails. Barnes falls in love with the tight-lipped Scott much to the consternation of Wilcoxon who loves her. Angel also falls in love with the kind and affectionate Reed. Cabot leads the Hurons in a wild chase after the party. In one sequence Scott and the others steal Huron canoes but are followed down river by a strong war party, a spectacular chase that ends with Cabot, who lusts after Angel, trapping the terrified girl on a cliff. Rather than surrender to him, she hurls herself into space and doom. Reed, catching up with the vile Huron, struggles with Cabot who knocks him off the cliff. He falls on the rocks next to Angel and the hands of the Indian and the white girl reach out and clasp in death. Barrat arrives and kills Cabot, later performing a ceremony for his dead son and the girl he loved, stating sorrowfully that he is now "last of Mohicans." The small party struggles onward and finally reaches the safety of the fort, but only because Scott holds back a pack of pursuing Hurons and is captured. He is tortured and then put to the stake to be burned alive. Meanwhile, French and Indian forces overwhelm Fort William Henry, Montcalm's troops having to drive off their own looting allies. A special contingent under Wilcoxon's command makes its way to the Huron village and rescues Scott at the last minute, just as he is about to be put to the torch. Producer Small spared no expense in making this a superbly crafted frontier epic. Seitz directs with elan and Planck's lensing, shot on location in California's high Sierras, is magnificent. The battle scenes are well staged and the acting is above average on all levels. Scott reached stardom with this major production, having boosted his career in 1933 with WILD HORSE MESA, the first of nine western films from Paramount that were based on Zane Grey tales. The frontier yarns spun so floridly by James Fenimore Cooper had been converted many times to film. The great director D. W. Griffith made LEATHERSTOCKING for Biograph in 1909, a short film shot on location at Cuddebackville, New York, with the legendary Billy Bitzer behind the cameras. Two one-reelers, both filmed in 1911, were entitled THE LAST OF THE MOHICANS. Bela Lugosi, believe it or not, played Uncas in another German version, released in the U.S. in 1921 as THE DEERSLAYER. The following year Maurice Tourneur and Clarence Brown directed a smashing feature-length silent version of THE LAST OF THE MOHICANS with Wallace Beery playing the heavy, Magua. Seitz directed a 10-chapter serial version called LEATHERSTOCKING in 1924 for Pathe which featured Edna Murphy, Harold Miller, and Frank Lackteen, the director therefore having a great deal of experience that qualified him for the best of the films based on the Cooper tale, the version starring Scott. Little Mascot Films, a poverty row production firm, filmed the first talkie version of THE LAST OF THE MOHICANS in 1932 as a 12-chapter serial with Harry Carey and Edwina Booth. In 1947, Columbia produced another version entitled LAST OF THE REDMEN, starring Jon Hall, Evelyn Ankers, and Buster Crabbe as Uncas.

p, Edward Small, Harry M. Goetz; d, George B. Seitz; w, Philip Dunne, John Balderston, Paul Perez, Daniel Moore (based on the novel by James Fenimore Cooper); ph, Robert Planck; ed, Jack Dennis; md, Roy Webb; art d, John Ducasse Schulze.

Historical Epic/Adventure Cas. (PR:A MPAA:NR)

LAST OF THE PAGANS** (1936) 72m MGM bw

Mala *(Taro)*, Lotus Long *(Lilleo)*, Telo A. Tematua *(Native Chief)*, Ae A Faaturia *(Boy Hunter)*, Rangapo A Taipoo *(Taro's Mother)*.

MGM reunites its two stars from ESKIMO, Mala and Long, and sends them to the South Sea islands to act alongside the natives. Based on Herman Melville's novel *Typee*, this picture covers the romantic adventures of the two and their battles with nature. In between their romancing, they overcome numerous island obstacles including an underwater battle with a shark, a cave-in at tropical mines, a hurricane, plus lots of hula dancing. In the end, love conquers all.

p, Philip Goldstone; d, Richard Thorpe; w, John Villiers Farrow (based on a story by Farrow, suggested by the book *Typee* by Herman Melville); ph, Clyde De Vinna; m, Nat W. Finston; ed, Martin G. Cohn.

Romance/Adventure (PR:A MPAA:NR)

LAST OF THE PONY RIDERS** (1953) 58m COL bw

Gene Autry *(Himself)*, Smiley Burnette *(Himself)*, Kathleen Case *(Katie McEwen)*, Dick Jones *(Johnny Blair)*, John Downey *(Tom McEwen)*, Howard Wright *(Clyde Vesey)*, Arthur Space *(Jess Hogan)*, Gregg Barton *(Dutch Murdoch)*, Buzz Henry *(Yank)*, Harry Mackin *(Cliff Patrick)*, Harry Hines *(Bindlestiff)*, Champion the Horse.

In his final appearance in the singing cowboy series, Autry stars as an ex-Pony Express rider who is trying to protect his mail franchise in the transition from Pony Express to stage coach and telegraph. He plans to set up a new stage line, but Wright as the local banker is scheming a stage coach line for himself. Part of Wright's foils include fake Indian attacks on relay stations, plus a conspiracy with the town blacksmith. Case is Autry's romantic interest and Burnette is reunited as his best friend. Predictable ending has good triumphing over evil. Songs include "Song on the Prairie" (sung by Autry) and "Sugar Babe" (duet by Autry and Burnette).

p, Armand Schaefer; d, George Archainbaud; w, Ruth Woodman; ph, William Bradford; ed, James Sweeney; art d, Ross Bellah.

Western Cas. (PR:A MPAA:NR)

LAST OF THE RED HOT LOVERS*1/2 (1972) 98m PAR c

Alan Arkin *(Barney Cashman)*, Sally Kellerman *(Elaine Navazio)*, Paula Prentiss *(Bobbi Michele)*, Renee Taylor *(Jeanette Fisher)*, Bella Bruck *(Cashier)*, Sandy Balson *(Charlotte)*, Frank Loverde *(Mel Fisher)*, Burt Conroy *(Bert)*, Charles Woolf *(Jesse)*, Ben Freedman *(Mickey)*, Buddy Lewis, Mousey Garner *(Waiters)*, Bernie Styles *(Man with Boxes)*, John Batiste *(Truckman's Helper)*, Lois Aurino *(Girl in Car)*, Sully Boyar, J. J. Barry, Paul Larson *(Men in Coffee Shop)*, Ruth Jaroslow *(Lady in Coffee Shop)*, Oliver Steindecker *(Cabbie)*, Leonard Parker *(Parking Lot Attendant)*, Liesha Gullisson *(Girl on Corner)*.

Based on the humorous Neil Simon play of the same name, this film is not nearly so funny. The story centers on Arkin, a successful sea food restaurant owner who, depressed about being middle-aged, dreams of having just one passionate love affair in his life. He acquires the key to his mother's unoccupied apartment and then attempts to carry on an affair with three different women, Kellerman, Prentiss, and Taylor. Each tryst ends unsuccessfully, and in the end Arkin telephones his wife and asks her to meet him at his mother's apartment. Arkin does his comedic best as a man surviving a mid-life crisis. Prentiss sounds as if she's strangling on a pretzel so garbled is her delivery.

p, Howard W. Koch; d, Gene Saks; w, Neil Simon (based on the play by Simon); ph, Victor J. Kemper; m, Neal Hefti; ed, Maury Winetrobe; art d, Ben Edwards; set d, Jack Stevens; cos, Albert Wolsky; m/l, "Alfie," "What the World Needs Now," Burt Bacharach, Hal David; makeup, John Inzerella.

Comedy Cas. (PR:A MPAA:PG)

LAST OF THE REDMEN1/2** (1947) 78m COL c

Jon Hall *(Major Heyward)*, Michael O'Shea *(Hawk-Eye)*, Evelyn Ankers *(Alice Munro)*, Julie Bishop *(Cora Munro)*, Buster Crabbe *(Magua)*, Rick Vallin *(Uncas)*, Buzz Henry *(Davy)*, Guy Hedlund *(Gen. Munro)*, Frederic Worlock *(Gen. Webb)*, Emmett Vogan *(Bob Wheelwright)*, Chief Many Treaties.

This adaptation of *The Last of the Mohicans* has Hall leading three children, Ankers, Bishop, and Henry, through dangerous Indian territory at the request of their British general father. Along the way they encounter a number of adventurous obstacles and the life-threatening presence of the Uncas, the last tribe of the Mohican Indians. A dressing up of a classic tale may thrill the kids, but adults might give it a dressing down for some plot manhandling that Natty Bumppo would not have liked.

p, Sam Katzman; d, George Sherman; w, Herbert Dalmas, George H. Plympton (based on the book *The Last of the Mohicans*, by James Fenimore Cooper); ph, Ray Fernstrom, Ira H. Morgan (Vitacolor); ed, James Sweeney; md, Mischa Bakaleinikoff; art d, Paul Palmentola.

Adventure (PR:AA MPAA:NR)

LAST OF THE REDSKINS (SEE: LAST OF THE REDMEN, 1947)

LAST OF THE RENEGADES**

(1966, Fr./Ital./Ger./Yugo.) 93m Rialto-S.N.C.-Jadran-Atlantis/COL c (LE TRESOR DES MONTAGNES BLEUES; GIORNI DI FUOCO; WINNETOU II TEIL; VINETU II)

Lex Barker *(Old Shatterhand)*, Pierre Brice *(Winnetou)*, Anthony Steel *(Forrester)*, Karin Dor *(Ribanna)*, Klaus Kinski *(Luke)*, Mario Girotti *(Lt. Merril)*, Renato Baldini *(Col. J.F. Merril)*, Eddi Arent *(Lord Castlepool)*, Marie Noelle, Ilija Ivezic, Velimir Hitil, Mirko Boman, Rikard Brezeska.

A Europeanized western which has Kinski and Steel greedily trying to get to the oil that they know is sitting beneath an Indian reservation. Brice is an Indian chief who is determined to keep peace between the white man and the Indian, but things prove difficult when Steel tries to wrongly blame the Indians for a wagon attack. The finale has Brice and his braves riding to the rescue as they follow through on his earlier vow of assuring peace. Europeans flex their muscles again on the universal western motif and make the going exciting. Shot entirely in beautiful locations in Yugoslavia.

p, Horst Wendlandt, Wolfgang Kuhnlenz; d, Harold Reinl; w, Harald G. Petersson (based on the story by Karl Friedrich May); ph, Ernst W. Kalinke (CinemaScope, Eastmancolor); m, Martin Bottcher; ed, Hermann Haller; art d, Vladimir Tadej; cos, Irms Pauli.

Western (PR:A MPAA:NR)

LAST OF THE SECRET AGENTS?, THE* (1966) 92m PAR c

Marty Allen *(Marty Johnson)*, Steve Rossi *(Steve Donovan)*, John Williams *(J. Frederick Duval)*, Nancy Sinatra *(Micheline)*, Lou Jacobi *(Papa Leo)*, Carmen *(Baby May Zoftig)*, Theo Marcuse *(Zoltan Schubach)*, Connie Sawyer *(Florence)*, Ben Lessy *(Harry)*, Remo Pisani *(Them 1)*, Larry Duran *(Them 2)*, Wilhelm Von

Homburg, Loren Ewing *(GGI men)*, Aida Fries *(Belly Dancer)*, Harvey Korman *(German Colonel)*, Sig Ruman *(Prof. Werner Von Koenig)*, Thordis I. Brandt *(Fred Johnson)*, Edy Williams, Phyllis Davis *(Beautiful Girls)*, Don Keefer *(Over-Vain Spy)*, Emanuel Thomas *(Frogman)*, Philip Sascombe *(Englishman)*, Paul Daniel *(Milkman)*, Ed Sullivan *(Himself)*, Mark G. Baker *(Wardrobe Man)*, Eddie Carroll, Eddie Donno *(Slate Boys)*, Hoke Howell *(Man in Adolph Hitler Uniform)*, Allen Durlin Jung *(Kurawa from Japan)*, Louise Colombet, Paul C.R. Deville *(French Peasants)*, Henry Dar-Boggia *(Conductor)*, Chester A. Hayes *(Organ Grinder)*, Kathy Martin *(Duval's Companion)*, Tommy H. Lee *(Montgomery)*, Almira Sessions, Madge Blake *(Middle-Aged Ladies)*, Joe Devlin *(Waiter)*, Susan Jean *(Girl Spy)*, John Sterling *(2nd Story Man)*, Matty Jordan *(Italian Man)*, William Yip *(Chinese Man)*, Charles La Torre *(Frenchman)*, Victoria Carroll *(Female Approaching Umbrella)*, Makee K. Blaisdell *(King)*, Kay Hughes *(Book Ends)*, Alain Mehrez *(French Boy)*, Mike H. deAnda *(Robust Frenchman)*, Mark Harris, Scott Elliott *(Distinguished Englishmen)*, Robert Goodwin *(Ngumba Nurumbru)*, George Dega *(Boris Tulchinsky)*, Ray Dannis *(Man on TV)*.

Allen and Rossi star as two American tourists in France who get talked into working for GGI (Good Guys, Inc.) against THEM, an organization of art thieves. In the path of their adventures, they learn that THEM plans on stealing the Venus di Milo at the London World's Fair. They thwart the bad guys' efforts with the help of a secret weapon, The Umbrella. The thieves are apprehended and Allen and Rossi are heroes. Songs include the title song (Lee Hazelwood), "You Are" (Neal Hefti), "Don Jose Ole!" (Pete King, Mel Tolkin, Norman Abbott). All songs sung by Steve Rossi, with the exception of the title song, barely sung by Nancy Sinatra.

p&d, Norman Abbott; w, Mel Tolkin (based on the story by Abbott, Tolkin); ph, Harold Stine (Technicolor); m, Pete King; ed, Otho Lovering; prod d, William C. Davidson; art d, Hal Pereira, Roland Anderson; set d, Robert R. Benton, James Payne; cos, Edith Head; ch, Andre Tayir; spec eff, Paul K. Lerpae; makeup, Wally Westmore.

Comedy **(PR:A MPAA:NR)**

LAST OF THE VIKINGS, THE* **1/2**
(1962, Fr./Ital.) 102m Tiberius-Galatea-Cyclope-Criterion/Medallion c (LE DERNIER DES VIKINGS; L'ULTIMO DEI VICHINGHI)
Cameron Mitchell *(Harald)*, Edmund Purdom *(Sven)*, Isabelle Corey *(Hilde)*, Helene Remy *(Elga)*, Aldo Bufi Landi *(Londborg)*, Andrea Aureli *(Haakon)*, Giorgio Ardisson *(Guntar)*, Carla Calo *(Herta)*, Nando Tamberlani *(Gultred)*, Corrado Annicelli *(Godrun)*, Broderick Crawford, Andrea Checchi, Piero Lulli, Mario Feliciani, Benito Stefanelli.

Viking prince Mitchell returns home to Viken and discovers that King Sven of Norway (Purdom) has killed his father. He also learns that Purdom is planning to force marriage upon his sister in order to form an alliance with the Danes. Mitchell rounds up some faithful Vikings and breaks into Purdom's heavily guarded fortress, killing the king, saving his sister, Corey, and restoring order to Viken.

p, Roberto Capitani, Luigi Mondello; d, Giacomo Gentilomo; w, Arpad De Riso, Guido Zurli, Mondello; ph, Enzo Serafin (Dyaliscope, Eastmancolor); m, Roberto Nicolosi; ed, Gino Talamo; art d, Saverio D'Eugenio; cos, Tigano, Lo Faro.

Adventure/Drama **(PR:A MPAA:NR)**

LAST OF THE WARRENS, THE* (1936) 60m Supreme bw
Bob Steele *(Ted Warren)*, Margaret Marquis *(Mary Burns)*, Charles King *(Kent)*, Lafe McKee *(Sheriff)*, Charles K. French *(Bruce Warren)*, Horace Murphy *(Grizzly)*, Blackie Whiteford *(Slip)*, Steve Clark *(Spike)*.

The legendary Kentucky feud between the Warrens and the Selbys is transposed to a western genre with Steele and his father as the last of the Warrens. The opposing Selby clan is represented by King, who is determined to finish off the Warrens. Battles blaze and Steele's father, French, is nearly killed. A western setting fails to help this mediocre story.

p, A.W. Hackel; d&w, Robert N. Bradbury; ph, Bert Longnecker; ed, S. Roy Luby.

Western **Cas.** **(PR:A MPAA:NR)**

LAST OF THE WILD HORSES** (1948) 84m Screen Guild bw
James Ellison *(Duke Barnum)*, Mary Beth Hughes *(Terry Williams)*, Jane Frazee *(Jane Cooper)*, Douglas Dumbrille *(Charlie Cooper)*, James Millican *(Sheriff Harrison)*, Reed Hadley *(Riley)*, Olin Howlin *(Remedy Williams)*, Grady Sutton *(Curly)*, William Haade *(Rocky Rockford)*, Rory Mallinson *(Hank)*, Stanley Andrews *(Ferguson)*.

Beautifully photographed in southern Oregon, this average western is the usual tale of a powerful rancher who bullies his neighboring ranchers into doing things his way. Hadley is the villainous foreman of a big ranch who tries to frame Ellison for murder. Ellison is brought to trial, but, after escaping, proves his innocence. Traditional except for the opening scene, which foreshadows the climactic battle.

p, Robert L. Lippert, Carl K. Hittelman; d, Lippert; w, Jack Harvey; ph, Benjamin Kline (Sepiatone); ed, Paul Landres; md, Albert Glasser.

Western **(PR:A MPAA:NR)**

LAST OUTLAW, THE** (1936) 62m RKO bw
Harry Carey *(Dean Payton)*, Hoot Gibson *(Chuck Wilson)*, Henry B. Walthall *(Calvin Yates)*, Margaret Callahan *(Sally Mason)*, Frank M. Thomas, Sr. *(Dr. Mason)*, Russell Hopton *(Billings)*, Tom Tyler *(Al Goss)*, Harry Jans *(Joe)*, Ray Mayer *(Jess)*, Frank Jenks *(Tom)*, Maxine Jennings *(Billings' Secretary)*, Fred Scott *(Larry Dixon)*, Joe Sawyer.

From a story by John Ford (which he filmed as a two-reeler in 1919), THE LAST OUTLAW is a long-forgotten western more concerned with characterization and setting than with action. Carey emerges from a 25-year prison term to discover that

his quiet old town of Broken Knee has burgeoned into the modern Center City, with bustling inhabitants who are entirely engrossed in expansion. He also finds that his infant daughter has blossomed beautifully. He and his fellow old-timers grow less and less patient with their younger, more boisterous successors. When a gang robs a local bank and takes his daughter hostage, Carey shows them that he may be old, but he's not going without a fight. Especially interesting for its time.

p, Robert Sisk; d, Christy Cabanne; w, John Twist, Jack Townley, E. Murray Campbell (based on a story by John Ford, Campbell); ph, Jack MacKenzie; ed, George Hively; m/l, "My Heart's on the Trail," Nathaniel Shilkret, Frank Luther.

Western **(PR:A MPAA:NR)**

LAST OUTPOST, THE** **1/2** (1935) 72m PAR bw
Cary Grant *(Michael Andrews)*, Claude Rains *(John Stevenson)*, Gertrude Michael *(Rosemary Haydon)*, Kathleen Burke *(Ilya)*, Colin Tapley *(Lt. Prescott)*, Akim Tamiroff *(Mirov)*, Billy Bevan *(Cpl. Foster)*, Georges Renavent *(Turkish Major)*, Margaret Swope *(Nurse Rowland)*, Jameson Thomas *(Cullen)*, Nick Shaid *(Haidor)*, Harry Semels *(Amrak)*, Meyer Ouhayoun *(Armenian Patriarch)*, Frazier Acosta *(Armenian Officer)*, Malay Clu *(Armenian Guard)*, Elspeth Dudgeon *(Head Nurse)*, Beulah McDonald *(Nurse)*, Robert Adair *(Sergeant in General's Office)*, William Brown *(Sgt. Bates)*, Claude King *(General)*, Olaf Hytten *(Doctor)*, Frank Elliott, Ward Lane *(Colonels)*, Frank Dawson *(Surgeon)*, Ramsey Hill *(Captain)*, Mark Strong, Carey Harrison *(Officers)*.

An interesting picture which adds steam to the argument that there should only be one director in charge of a film. THE LAST OUTPOST is plagued with a pair of directors, Barton and Gasnier, resulting in a film that is sometimes good and sometimes bad. It begins with Grant being saved by Rains from a tribe of Kurds in the desert. Together the British officers cooperate in transporting an Armenian tribe, allies of the Brits, to safer territory. Their trek takes them over majestic mountain ranges and through dangerous passages. At this point, however, the picture nose-dives into a familiar Hollywood melodrama, as if no one could decide how to end the first half. While recovering in a Cairo hospital, an injured Grant falls in love with his nurse, Michael. It turns out that Michael is Rains' wife, though they haven't seen each other since their wedding three years ago. Grant and Rains are sent out together with their troops to attack an enemy fort, resulting in Rains' death. The doors are then left wide open for the romance to begin.

p, E. Lloyd Sheldon; d, Charles Barton, Louis Gasnier; w, Philip MacDonald, Frank Partos, Charles Brackett (based on the novel *The Drum* by F. Britten Austin); ph, Theodor Sparkuhl; ed, Jack Dennis; art d, Hans Dreier, Earl Hedrick.

Adventure **(PR:A MPAA:NR)**

LAST OUTPOST, THE** (1951) 88m PAR c
Ronald Reagan *(Vance Britten)*, Rhonda Fleming *(Julie McCloud)*, Bruce Bennett *(Jeb Britten)*, Bill Williams *(Sgt. Tucker)*, Peter Hanson *(Lt. Crosby)*, Noah Beery, Jr. *(Sgt. Calhoun)*, Hugh Beaumont *(Lt. Fenton)*, John Ridgely *(Sam McCloud)*, Lloyd Corrigan *(Mr. Delacourt)*, Charles Evans *(Chief Grey Cloud)*, James Burke *(Gregory)*, Richard Crane *(Lt. McReady)*, Ewing Mitchell *(Maj. Riordan)*, John War Eagle *(Geronimo)*, Tarbaby the Horse.

Reagan and Bennett are brothers who choose opposite sides during the Civil War, Reagan going to the defense of the Confederacy and Bennett to the Union side. Both become cavalry officers and come into conflict when Bennett is sent out to Arizona to defend gold shipments that Reagan is raiding. Some of the Northerners try to persuade the Apaches to attack the Confederates, but Reagan confers with the chief and tells him not to get involved in the white man's fight, realizing that once the Indians take to the warpath they will wipe out every white man and woman in the territory, including his ex-fiancee, Fleming, and her husband, Ridgely. A white man recklessly murders an Apache chief and the Indians attack the Union fort Bennett is defending and in which Fleming and Ridgely are seeking protection. Things look grim for the besieged outpost until Reagan and his men charge to the rescue and, fighting side by side with the Yankees, put the Apaches to rout. The red menace vanquished, Reagan and his men ride back to Dixie. Producers Pine and Thomas were the resident B movie unit at Paramount, known as "The Dollar Bills" for their penny-pinching ways, but they occasionally veered into minor "A" pictures like THE LAST OUTPOST, their biggest budgeted and biggest grossing picture to that time. Reagan had his own horse, Tarbaby, shipped to the Arizona location at Paramount's expense to ride in the film. The fine thoroughbred was looked at dubiously by the wranglers acting as extras who doubted the horse's ability to stand the desert heat and constant action. By the end of the first day of shooting, so many of the other horses were out of commission they had trouble getting enough together for some of the shots, while Tarbaby was still going strong. An enjoyable action western with some excellent color photography and solid performances by Reagan, Bennett, and the supporting cast, particularly Beery as Reagan's aide.

p, William H. Pine, William C. Thomas; d, Lewis R. Foster; w, Geoffrey Homes, George Worthing Yates, Winston Miller; ph, Loyal Griggs (Technicolor); m, Lucien Calliet; ed, Howard Smith; art d, Lewis H. Creber.

Western **(PR:A MPAA:NR)**

LAST PAGE, THE (SEE: MAN BAIT, 1952, Brit.)

LAST PARADE, THE** (1931) 82m COL bw
Jack Holt *(Cookie Leonard)*, Tom Moore *(Mike O'Dowd)*, Constance Cummings *(Molly Pearson)*, Gaylord Pendleton *(Larry Pearson)*, Robert Ellis *(Marino)*, Earle D. Bunn *(Lefty)*, Vivi *(Vivi)*, Jess De Vorska *(Rosenberg)*, Ed Le Saint *(Chief of Police)*, Edmund Breese *(City Editor)*, Clarence Muse *(Alabam')*, Gino Corrado *(Joe)*, Robert Graham *(Danny Murphy)*.

Holt and Moore are WWI buddies who return to the U.S.; Moore gets work as a police sergeant, but Holt is left jobless. Holt starts running booze for a small-time bootlegger, but becomes enterprising and goes into business for himself, creating an enemy in his former employer. When Holt's brother is killed, Holt retaliates by killing the bootlegger. He is caught, however, by Moore. The two of them, plus nurse Cummings who served with them in the war, walk arm in arm to the electric chair. Not everyone loves a parade, especially if it's their last one.

p, Jack Cohn; d, Erle C. Kenton; w, Dorothy Howell (based on a story by Casey Robinson); ph, Teddy Talzlaff; ed, Gene Havtick.

Crime **(PR:A MPAA:NR)**

LAST PERFORMANCE, THE*** (1929) 69m UNIV bw

Conrad Veidt *(Erik the Great)*, Mary Philbin *(Julie)*, Leslie Fenton *(Buffo)*, Fred MacKay *(Mark Royce)*, Gustav Partos *(Theater Manager)*, William H. Turner *(Booking Agent)*, Anders Randolph *(Judge)*, Sam De Grasse *(District Attorney)*, George Irving *(Defense Attorney)*.

Veidt, the hulking zombie from THE CABINET OF DR. CALIGARI, is an older magician who has fallen in love with his young assistant, Philbin. She does not return the feelings though and instead has romantic feelings for Fenton, a thief who has become Veidt's pupil. MacKay is another of the magician's assistants who becomes jealous of the young couple's romance and exposes it all to the magician. Fenton kills MacKay and subsequently commits suicide at his murder trial. The plot is standard crime of passion material but strong direction and some imaginative and stylish camera work give the film excellent boosting. For the film's Hungarian distribution, an unknown actor named Bela Lugosi dubbed Veidt's lines.

d, Paul Fejos; w, James Ashmore Creelman, Walter Anthony, Tom Reed (based on a story by Creelman); ph, Hal Mohr; ed, Edward Cahn, Robert Carlisle, Robert Jahns.

Crime **(PR:C MPAA:NR)**

LAST PICTURE SHOW, THE***** (1971) 118m BBS/COL bw

Timothy Bottoms *(Sonny Crawford)*, Jeff Bridges *(Duane Jackson)*, Cybill Shepherd *(Jacy Farrow)*, Ben Johnson *(Sam the Lion)*, Cloris Leachman *(Ruth Popper)*, Ellen Burstyn *(Lois Farrow)*, Eileen Brennan *(Genevieve)*, Clu Gulager *(Abilene)*, Sharon Taggart *(Charlene Duggs)*, Randy Quaid *(Lester Marlow)*, Joe Heathcock *(Sheriff)*, Bill Thurman *(Coach Popper)*, Barc Doyle *(Joe Bob Blanton)*, Jessie Lee Fulton *(Miss Mosey)*, Gary Brockette *(Bobby Sheen)*, Helena Humann *(Jimmie Sue)*, Loyd Catlett *(Leroy)*, Robert Glenn *(Gene Farrow)*, John Hillerman *(Teacher)*, Janice O'Malley *(Mrs. Clarg)*, Floyd Mahaney *(Oklahoma Patrolman)*, Kimberly Hyde *(Annie-Annie Martin)*, Noble Willingham *(Chester)*, Marjory Jay *(Winnie Snips)*, Joye Hash *(Mrs. Jackson)*, Pamela Keller *(Jackie Lee French)*, Gordon Hurst *(Monroe)*, Mike Hosford *(Johnny)*, Faye Jordan *(Nurse)*, Charlie Seybert *(Andy Fanner)*, Grover Lewis *(Mr. Crawford)*, Rebecca Ulrick *(Marlene)*, Merrill Shepherd *(Agnes)*, Buddy Wood *(Bud)*, Kenny Wood *(Ken)*, Leon Brown *(Cowboy in Cafe)*, Bobby McGriff *(Truck Driver)*, Jack Mueller *(Oil Pumper)*, Robert Arnold *(Brother Blanton)*, Frank Marshall *(Tommy Logan)*, Otis Elmore *(Mechanic)*, Charles Salmon *(Roughneck Driver)*, George Gaulden *(Cowboy in the Cafe)*, Will Morris Hannis *(Gas Station Man)*, Leon Miller Band.

Bogdanovich is a very talented director. He has made many films, with the exception of THEY ALL LAUGHED and DAISY MILLER, which have brought loads of entertainment value to the public. None of his films stand up to THE LAST PICTURE SHOW when it comes to dramatic flair and authenticity. He seems comfortable doing period pieces and also scored well with PAPER MOON, but in this, his third picture (his first was TARGETS, the second was a documentary on John Ford), he captures the era so accurately that the viewer can feel the hopelessness of living in a dying Texas town that is destined to atrophy as the slow wave of modernism destroys what once was and will never be again. Bridges and Bottoms are the stars of the local high school football team—not much of an achievement as the team has a dismal record. Bridges is aggressive and Bottoms is sensitive and the two complement each other as best friends (just as the black-and-white film complemented the story telling). The story unfolds seamlessly, detailing relationships in a small town. Sam Bottoms is a retarded young boy (he got the part after he showed up to watch brother Tim's first day of shooting) who is the butt of cruel jokes by the no-gooders who hang around the cafe-pool hall-theater owned by Johnson, a one-time cowboy who seems to be every boy's idol and surrogate father. Tim Bottoms takes up the cudgel as Sam Bottom's protector and is soon befriended, then bedded down by Leachman, the sexy wife of the school's basketball coach, Thurman. The affair continues for most of the picture, heating up and cooling down a few times. To keep it up, Tim Bottoms ceases dating his regular girl friend, Taggart. Bridges continues dating his girl, Shepherd, but is not happy about her self-centered behavior. She attends a nude bathing party in order to meet rich Brockette. This is at the behest of her mother, Burstyn, who knows that Bridges is poor and she wants her daughter to marry wealthily. Brockette rejects Shepherd because he doesn't want to be bothered with a virgin. Bridges and Tim Bottoms take a short and wild trip south of the border to Mexico and when they return they are saddened to learn that Johnson has died. The pool hall has been left to Bottoms, the cafe to long-time waitress Brennan, and the movie house has been willed to Fulton, an old woman who has been the concession manager since before anyone can recall. Shepherd seduces Bridges in order to lose her virginal status, then runs back to Brockette, who scorns her again and marries someone else. Bridges takes a job in the oil fields as Shepherd takes up with Gulager, foreman at her father's place of business and Burstyn's occasional lover. Not content with that, she lures Bottoms away from Leachman. Bridges returns to town, hears of Bottoms and Shepherd, and retaliates by hitting Bottoms in the face with a bottle. Bottoms convalesces as Bridges goes off to join the Army. Shepherd and Bottoms are about to get married when intercepted by her parents, Burstyn and Glenn. Glenn takes Shepherd home and Burstyn stays with Bottoms a while and confesses that she and the late Johnson had also been lovers. Later, Bridges comes back to the dying town for a brief stay before being shipped off to Korea. Time has healed Bottom's wounds, both physically and mentally, and the two get together for one last night at the picture show. It's about to be shuttered due to the onslaught of television. They spend the night talking about the good old times, then Bridges asks Bottoms to take care of his car until he comes home from Korea. Bottoms walks back to the pool hall and Sam Bottoms, the retarded boy, races across the street to see him but is struck and killed by a motorist. Bottoms is enraged, frustrated, doesn't know what to do, so he climbs into Bridges' car and begins to drive but he has nowhere to go to get away. He finally stops at Leachman's house and she yells at him for what she thinks is his cruel treatment of her. She soon calms down and blushes as he takes her hand and we know that their sexual relationship is not yet over. THE LAST PICTURE SHOW was a refreshing look *backward* in movies. While others were outfoxing themselves with multiscreen techniques, Bogdanovich made a movie that could have been shot years before and the result was critically and financially rewarding. The director is an admirer of Ford and Hawks and this is a homage to their styles, rather than the kind of ripoffs Colin Higgins and Brian De Palma have done with Hitchcock. The only element that separates this from an early film is the use of frontal nudity and the frank treatment accorded the adult themes that never would have been allowed by the censors. Bogdanovich was hailed as another Orson Welles (one more of Bogdanovich's mentors and friends) by everyone, although his career did not have the same tragedies as Welles' when everyone applauded him in public and refused to take his phone calls in private. Many emotions are stirred in THE LAST PICTURE SHOW, emotions that have been forgotten in the wake of spacemen and the near-porno sex and patriotic blood-letting seen today. It's a little story, episodic, but it lives and breathes with more power than any Darth Vader or Rambo or Rocky. This is a movie about humans, not ray guns or robots, and will continue to touch audiences whenever and wherever it is seen. There was a time when Bogdanovich considered Jimmy Stewart, among others, to appear in the film, then he wisely opted for "no-names" and many of them are *huge* names today. Johnson and Leachman each won Oscars and the picture was nominated as Best Picture, Best Script, Best Direction, Best Cinematography as well as Bridges for Best Supporting Actor and Burstyn as Best Supporting Actress. That was the year for THE FRENCH CONNECTION, KLUTE, and FIDDLER ON THE ROOF and the competition was too stiff. Bogdanovich was married to designer Platt when the film began but that was soon over in the wake of an alleged affair with Shepherd. He went on to have a well-chronicled romance with the late Dorothy Stratten (STAR 80) and, after making an excellent film called MASK, he went personally bankrupt in late 1985. Burstyn had formerly acted under the name of Ellen McRae then changed her name when she married Neil Burstyn (nee Burstein; aka: Neil Nephew) who also worked for the producing company that made this movie as a story consultant on "The Monkees" TV show. Look for "Magnum's" John Hillerman in a small role as a teacher. THE LAST PICTURE SHOW could have been a tawdry, sleazy soap opera but the 31-year-old former film critic kept a tight rein on matters and presented it as a slice of a life that has all but disappeared.

p, Stephen J. Friedman; d, Peter Bogdanovich; w, Bogdanovich, Larry McMurtry (based on the novel by McMurtry); ph, Robert Surtees; m, (various recordings) Hank Williams, Bob Wills and the Texas Playboys, Eddie Arnold, Eddie Fisher, Phil Harris, Pee Wee King, Hank Snow, Tony Bennett, Lefty Frizzell, Frankie Laine, Johnny Ray, Johnny Strindley, Kay Starr, Hank Thompson, Webb Pierce, Joe Stafford; ed, Donn Cambern; prod d, Polly Platt; art d, Walter Scott Herndon.

Drama **(PR:C-O MPAA:R)**

LAST PORNO FLICK, THE zero
(1974) 88m Bryanston c (AKA: THE MAD, MAD MOVIEMAKERS)

Frank Calcagnini, Michael Pataki, Mike Kellin, Jo Anne Meredith, Robyn Hilton, Tom Signorelli, Marianna Hill, Carmen Zapata, Anthony Carbone.

An unnecessary spoof of the X-rated DEEP THROAT which is already a parody of itself. The humor is far from funny and tries too hard to be "hip," an automatic deathblow to a spoof. As in FRIDAY THE 13th: THE FINAL CHAPTER, the title lies.

p, Steve Bono; d, Ray Marsh; w, Larry Ditillio.

Comedy **Cas.** **(PR:O MPAA:PG)**

LAST POSSE, THE 1/2** (1953) 73m COL bw

Broderick Crawford *(Sheriff Frazier)*, John Derek *(Jed Clayton)*, Charles Bickford *(Sampson Drune)*, Wanda Hendrix *(Deborah Morley)*, Warner Anderson *(Robert Emerson)*, Henry Hull *(Stokely)*, Will Wright *(Todd Mitchell)*, Tom Powers *(Frank White)*, Raymond Greenleaf *(Albert Hagen)*, James Kirkwood *(Judge Parker)*, Eddy Waller *(Dr. Pryor)*, Skip Homeier *(Art Romer)*, James Bell *(Will Romer)*, Guy Wilkerson *(George Romer)*, Mira McKinney *(Mrs. Mitchell)*, Helen Wallace *(Mrs. White)*, Harry Hayden *(Davis)*, Monte Blue *(Kane)*.

A confusing but compelling western complicated by flashbacks and flash forwards. Essentially it is about a posse of model citizens chasing down the three outlaws who stole a fortune from a cattle baron. After catching the trio, the "respectable" folk decide to hang onto the cash, refusing to divulge their secret to sheriff Crawford, who was mortally wounded on the trail and is expected to die at any moment.

p, Harry Joe Brown; d, Alfred Werker; w, Seymour and Connie Lee Bennett, Kenneth Gamet (based on a story by the Bennetts); ph, Burnett Guffey; ed, Gene Havelick; art d, George Brooks.

Western **(PR:A MPAA:NR)**

LAST POST, THE* 1/2 (1929, Brit.) 89m BRIT/GAU bw

John Longden *(David/Martin)*, Frank Vosper *(Paul)*, Alf Goddard *(Tiny)*, Cynthia Murtagh Haynes *(Christine)*, J. Fisher White *(Mr. Blair)*, A.B. Imeson *(Rollo)*, Johnny Butt *(Goodson)*, Rolf Leslie *(Stefan)*, Aggie Brantford *(Girl)*.

In a dual role Longden plays a soldier who shoulders blame after his revolutionary brother kills a fellow soldier during a workers strike. Things look bad for him but finally the brother turns himself in and faces a firing squad for his crime. Originally this film had been a silent feature but sound was added in 1930 to take advantage of the new technology. It did not help any for the film is melodramatic pulp without any honest emotions. Still, THE LAST POST remains something of a historical oddity as it's one of the few films of the time to be written and directed by women.

p&d, Dinah Shurey; w, Shurey, Lydia Hayward; ph, D.P. Cooper.

Drama   **(PR:C MPAA:NR)**

LAST REBEL, THE**

(1961, Mex.) 83m Hispano Continental/STER c (EL ULTIMO REBELDE)

Carlos Thompson (*Joaquin Murrieta*), Ariadne Welter (*Clara*), Rodolfo Acosta ("*Three Fingers*" *Jack*), Charles Fawcett (*Capt. Harry Love*), Lee Morgan (*Lang*), Eduardo Noriega, John Kelly, Rebeca Iturbide, Carlos Muzquiz, Eduardo Gonzalez Pliego, Federico Curiel, Leopoldo Ortin, Manuel Arvide, Tony Carbajal, Antonio Raxell, Claudio Brook, Bertha Lehar.

After his wife is slain by a group of miners, Thompson gathers together a gang of outlaws and goes on a killing spree, slaying literally hundreds of miners. Fawcett and his Texas Rangers, however, finally put an end to the gringo-hating gunslinger.

p&d, Miguel Contreras Torres; w, Torres, Manuel R. Ojeda (based on a story by Ojeda); ph, Jose Ortiz Ramos (Eastmancolor); m, Federico Ruiz; ed, Jose Bustos; art d, Ramon Rodriguez Granada.

Western/Drama   **(PR:C MPAA:NR)**

LAST REBEL, THE*   (1971) 90m Glendinning, U.S. Capital/COL c

Joe Namath (*Burnside Hollis*), Jack Elam (*Matt Graves*), Woody Strode (*Duncan*), Ty Hardin (*Sheriff*), Victoria George (*Pearl*), Renato Romano (*Virgil*), Marina Coffa (*Camelia*), Annamaria Chio (*Mme. Dupres*), Mike Forrest (*Cowboy Pool Hustler*), Bruce Eweka (*Black Boy*), Jessica Dublin (*Ruby*), Herb Andress (*Lieutenant*), Larry Laurence (*Bedroom Man*), Sebastian Segriff (*Union Officer*), Al Hassan (*Barman*), Art Johnson (*Tall Soldier*), Paul Sheriff (*Old Soldier*), Troy Patterson (*1st Rancher*), Rick Wells (*2nd Rancher*), Dominic Barto (*Stagecoach Agent*), Jim Garbo, Tomas Rudy (*Sheriff's Men*).

New York Jets' quarterback Joe Namath should have stayed in the huddle instead of going to Spain and Italy to make this terrible western. The setting is Missouri at the end of the Civil War; the story features the rebellious Namath and his equally rebellious partner, Elam, raising a ruckus in a small town after they rescue Strode from a lynching. A poorly scripted picture, THE LAST REBEL would be lame even if John Wayne had taken Namath's part.

p, Larry G. Spangler; d, Denys McCoy; w, Warren Kiefer; ph, Carlo Carlini (Technicolor); m, Jon Lord, Tony Ashton; ed, Fritz Mueller; art d, Guido Josia; cos, Gaia Romanini; m/l, "I'm Dying for You," "Oh, Matilda," Ashton, "You, Me and a Friend of Mine," Ashton, Lord.

Western   **(PR:C MPAA:PG)**

LAST REMAKE OF BEAU GESTE, THE* ¹/₂   (1977) 84m UNIV c

Ann-Margret (*Lady Flavia Geste*), Marty Feldman (*Digby Geste*), Michael York (*Beau Geste*), Peter Ustinov (*Sgt. Markov*), James Earl Jones (*Sheikh Abdul*), Trevor Howard (*Sir Hector Geste*), Henry Gibson (*Gen. Pecheur*), Terry-Thomas (*Prison Governor*), Roy Kinnear (*Cpl. Boldini*), Spike Milligan (*Crumble*), Avery Schreiber (*Used Camel Salesman*), Hugh Griffith (*Judge*), Irene Handl (*Miss Wormwood*), Sinead Cusack (*Isabel Geste*), Michael McConkey (*Young Digby*), Bekki Bridge (*Young Isabel*), Martin Snaric (*Valentino*), Ed McMahon (*Arab Horseman*), Henry Polic II (*Capt. Merdmanger*), Ted Cassidy (*Blindman*), Burt Kwouk (*Father Shapiro*), Val Pringle (*Dostoyevsky*), Gwen Nelson (*Lady in Courtroom*), Roland MacLeod (*Dr. Crippen*), Stephen Lewis (*Henshaw*), Philip Bollard (*Young Beau, age 6*), Nicholas Bridge (*Young Beau, age 12*).

Directing his first feature, Marty Feldman follows the route of associates Mel Brooks and Gene Wilder in spoofing earlier genres. Here Foreign Legion sagas are roasted, especially the William Wellman classic BEAU GESTE (1966), which starred Gary Cooper. Feldman plays the title character (the twin brother of Michael York) who carries on in the desert with utter lunacy, and gets in trouble after supposedly stealing a priceless gem. The irreverently handled plot doesn't seem to matter to Feldman, at least not as much as his often infantile gags. Only diehard fans of this sort of classless humor will get laughs from this effort. Feldman emerges as a second-rate Brooks, who many already consider second-rate.

p, William S. Gilmore; d, Marty Feldman; w, Feldman, Chris Allen (based on a story by Feldman and Sam Bobrick); ph, Gerry Fisher (Panavision, Technicolor); m, John Morris; prod d, Brian Eatwell; ed, Jim Clark, Arthur Schmidt; art d, Les Dilley; set d, Roger Christian; cos, May Routh, Ron Beck; spec eff, Albert Whitlock; stunts, Buddy Van Horn; makeup, Del Armstrong.

Comedy   **(PR:C MPAA:PG)**

LAST RHINO, THE**

(1961, Brit.) 56m World Safari/Children's Film Foundation c

David Ellis (*David*), Susan Millar-Smith (*Susan*), Tom Samuels (*Warden*), Tony Blane (*Commissioner*), John Taylor (*Pilot*), Shabani Hamisi (*Shabani*), Mlonga Muli (*Baaba*).

A tribe of native Africans are after a rhinoceros. The beast is wounded but its life is saved by some plucky children of a Kenyan game warden. This adventure is strictly for the kids.

p, Henry Geddes, Johnnie Coquillon; d&w, Geddes; ph, (Eastmancolor).

Children's adventure   **(PR:AAA MPAA:NR)**

LAST RIDE, THE zero   (1932) 64m Richmount/UNIV bw

Charles Morton (*The Reporter*), Dorothy Revier, Virginia Brown Faire (*The Girls*), Frank Mayo (*Picardi*), Tom Santschi (*Big Boy*), Francis Ford, Bobby Dunn.

A rookie news reporter is assigned to cover a feud between a bootlegger and a hijacker in which the police don't wish to interfere. The reporter is actually the kid brother of the hijacker, who eventually is killed by the bootlegger. The reporter sides with the dead man's gang and gets revenge on the murderer. Standard gangster dealings, but short on gunplay.

d, Duke Worne; w, Arthur Hoerl; ph, M.A. Anderson.

Crime   **(PR:A MPAA:NR)**

LAST RIDE, THE*   (1944) 56m WB bw

Richard Travis (*Pat Harrigan*), Charles Lang (*Mike Harrigan*), Eleanor Parker (*Kitty Kelly*), Jack LaRue (*Joe Genna*), Cy Kendall (*Capt. Butler*), Wade Boteler (*Delaney*), Mary Gordon (*Mrs. Kelly*), Harry Lewis (*Harry Bronson*), Michael Ames (*Fritz Hummel*), Virginia Patton (*Hazel Dale*), Ross Ford (*Joe Taylor*), Jack Mower (*Shannon*), Frank Mayo (*Walters*), Stuart Holmes (*Maltby*), Leah Baird (*Mrs. Bronson*).

A slow-moving gangster story about a clean detective, and his gangster brother, Lang, both of whom love the same girl. Involved with a black market car-tire racket, Lang is shot and dies in his brother's arms after the latter exposes the ring.

d, D. Ross Lederman; w, Raymond L. Schrock; ph, James Van Trees; ed, Harold McLernon; art d, Leo E. Kuter.

Crime   **(PR:A MPAA:NR)**

LAST RITES zero

(1980) 88m New Empire/Cannon c (AKA: DRACULA'S LAST RITES)

Patricia Lee Hammond, Gerald Fielding, Victor Jorge, Michael Lally, Mimi Weddell.

A horrible film about a bald vampire mortician in cahoots with the local sheriff and doctor, who bring him bodies so he can suck out their blood. The script, however, makes it seem that someone sucked out the screenwriter's brains—it simply hits new lows in stupidity. They do have some fun with names, calling the vampire Lucard (that's Dracul backwards), and giving his victims the names of the Fonda clan. Why? No one knows. Incredibly inept on technical terms, giving the audience a chance to play "spot the camera equipment," or camera cases, or light stands, or microphones. . . .

p, Kelly Van Horn; d, Domonic Paris; w, Ben Donnelly, Paris; ph, Paris (Deluxe Color); m, Paul Jost, George Small; ed, Elizabeth Lombardo.

Horror   **(PR:O MPAA:R)**

LAST ROMAN, THE   (SEE: FIGHT FOR ROME-PART 1, 1969, Ger./Rum.)

LAST ROSE OF SUMMER, THE* ¹/₂   (1937, Brit.) 60m MGM bw

John Garrick (*Thomas More*), Kathleen Gibson (*His Sweetheart*), Malcolm Graham (*Lord Byron*), Marian Spencer, Cecil Ramage, R. Meadows White.

Graham portrays the famed poet Lord George Gordon Byron in this film biography. His life is presented in a musical, with poorly strung together sequences that make for a confusing, wholly unrealistic story.

p&d, James Fitzpatrick; w, W.K. Williamson.

Musical/Biography   **(PR:A MPAA:NR)**

LAST ROUND-UP, THE* ¹/₂   (1934) 61m PAR bw

Randolph Scott (*Jim Cleve*), Barbara Fritchie (*Joan Randall*), Monte Blue (*Jack Kells*), Fred Kohler (*Sam Gulden*), Fuzzy Knight (*Bunko McGee*), Richard Carle (*Judge Savin*), Barton MacLane (*Charley Benson*), Charles B. Middleton (*Sheriff*), Frank Rice (*Shrimp*), Dick Rush (*Rush*), Buck Connors (*Old Man Tracy*), Ben Corbett, James Mason, Bud Osborne, Bob Miles, Jim Corey, Sam Allen, Jack M. Holmes.

A standard B western which pays more attention to Blue than to the top-billed Scott. Blue is an outlaw who gives up his life to help starry-eyed lovers Scott and Fritchie defeat the cattle-rustling Kohler. Based on a Zane Grey novel, THE LAST ROUND-UP is a remake of a 1919 silent and a 1930 version called THE BORDER LEGION, and incorporates stock footage from both films.

p, Harold Hurley; d, Henry Hathaway; w, Jack Cunningham (based on the novel "THE BORDER LEGION" by Zane Grey); ph, Archie Stout; art d, Earl Hedrick.

Western   **(PR:A MPAA:NR)**

LAST ROUND-UP, THE*** ¹/₂   (1947) 77m COL bw

Gene Autry (*Himself*), Jean Heather (*Carol*), Ralph Morgan (*Mason*), Carol Thurston (*Lydia Henry*), Mark Daniels (*Matt Mason*), Bobby Blake (*Mike*), Russ Vincent (*Jeff Henry*), George "Shug" Fisher (*Marvin*), Trevor Bardette (*Indian Chief*), Lee Bennett (*Goss*), John Halloran (*Taylor*), Sandy Sanders (*Jim*), Roy Gordon (*Smith*), Silverheels Smith [Jay Silverheels] (*Sam Luther*), Frances Rey (*Cora Luther*), Bob Cason (*Carter*), Dale Van Sickle, Don Kay Reynolds, Nolan Leary, Ted Adams, Jack Baxley, Steve Clark, Chuck Hamilton, Bud Osborne, Frankie Marvin, Kernan Cripps, Jose Alvarado, J. W. Cody, Iron Eyes Cody, Blackie Whiteford, Robert Walker, Virginia Carroll, Arline Archuletta, Louis Crosby, Brian O'Hara, Rodd Redwing, Alex Montoya, The Texas Rangers, Ed Piel, Sr., George Carleton, Billy Wilkinson, Champion, Jr. the Horse.

Autry is placed in charge of rounding up a tribe of Indians who are sitting on a barren plot of land. The construction of an aqueduct is planned so the tribe must be relocated, a move the Indians understandably are not too excited about. The first film produced by Gene Autry Productions, THE LAST ROUND-UP is reportedly Autry's personal favorite. A well-written, fast-paced entry with a number of likable tunes: "You Can't See the Sun When You're Crying," "160 Acres in the Valley," "An Apple for the Teacher," "Comin' Round the Mountain," and "The Last Round-up." Includes a fair amount of stock footage from the 1940 film ARIZONA.

p, Armand Schaefer; d, John English; w, Jack Townley, Earle Snell; ph, William Bradford; ed, Aaron Stell; md, Mischa Bakaleinikoff; art d, Harold MacArthur.

Western   **(PR:AA   MPAA:NR)**

LAST RUN, THE   (1971) 99m MGM c

George C. Scott (Harry Garmes), Tony Musante (Paul Ricard), Trish Van Devere (Claudie Scherrer), Colleen Dewhurst (Monique), Aldo Sanbrell (Miguel), Antonio Tarruella (Motorcycle Policeman), Robert Coleby (Hitchhiker), Robert J. Zurica (1st Man), Rocky Taylor (2nd Man).

A confusing and muddled film directed by Fleischer but begun by John Huston. The film stars Scott, a former driver for the Chicago mob, who is talked into making one last run. His job is to drive escaped convict Musante and his girl friend, Van Devere, from Spain to France. Scott pays for this one last job with his own death. Most interesting is the appearance of Dewhurst, the former Mrs. Scott, and Van Devere, the future Mrs. Scott, in the same film. Photography by Nykvist is an asset.

p, Carter De Haven; d, Richard Fleischer; w, Alan Sharp; ph, Sven Nykvist (Panavision, Metrocolor); m, Jerry Goldsmith; ed, Russell Lloyd; art d, Roy Walker, Jose Maria Tapiador; makeup, Del Acevedo, Mariano Garcia.

Crime/Action   **(PR:A   MPAA:GP)**

LAST SAFARI, THE   (1967, Brit.) 110m PAR c

Kaz Garas (Casey), Stewart Granger (Miles Gilchrist), Gabriella Licudi (Grant), Johnny Sekka (Jama), Liam Redmond (Alec Beaumont), Eugene Deckers (Refugee Leader), David Munyua (Chongu), John De Villiers (Rich), Wilfred Moore (Game Warden), Jean Parnell (Mrs. Beaumont), Bill Grant (Commissioner), John Sutton (Harry), Kipkoske (Gavai), Labina (Village Chief), Masai Tribe Wakamba Tribal Dancers.

Tourist Garas plans a leisurely vacation on safari in Africa, but changes those plans when he meets Granger, a troubled safari guide. Garas learns that Granger blames himself, in part, for the death of a close friend. Refusing to work for Garas, Granger sets out to kill the elephant that took his friend's life, more to overcome his guilt than out of revenge. Garas follows and together they locate the animal, but Granger cannot find the courage to fire. The elephant charges and Garas refrains from shooting, realizing that it must be Granger who does the deed. Granger finally finds the necessary bravery and, with his finger on the trigger, decides not to kill the elephant—the rediscovery of his courage being enough for him.

p&d, Henry Hathaway; w, John Gay (based on the novel Gilligan's Last Elephant by Gerald Hanley); ph, Ted Moore (Technicolor); m, John Dankworth; ed, John Bloom; prod d, Geoffrey Helman; art d, Maurice Fowler; cos, Brian Owen-Smith; makeup, Neville Smallwood.

Action   **(PR:A   MPAA:NR)**

LAST SHOT YOU HEAR, THE*   (1969, Brit.) 86m Lippert/FOX bw

Hugh Marlowe (Dr. Charles Nordeck), Zena Walker (Eileen), Patricia Haines (Anne Nordeck), William Dysart (Peter Marriott), Thorley Walters (Gen. Jowett), Joan Young (Mrs. Jowett), Lionel Murton (Rubens), Helen Horton (Dodie Rubens), John Nettleton (Det. Insp. Nash), John Wentworth (Chambers), Alistair Williamson (CID Officer), Daphne Barker (Reporter), Lynley Laurence (Girl), Julian Holloway (Young Man), James Mellor, Ian Hamilton (Reporters), Shaun Curry (Diver), Stephen Moore (Peter's Colleague), Job Stewart (Policeman), Janet Kelly (Receptionist).

A technical mess, this tired picture starts out with an interesting premise but doesn't know what to do with it. Marlowe is a well-respected marriage counselor, lecturer, and writer, who is shocked to learn that his wife is having an affair. In light of his standing, he refuses to grant her a divorce, angering not only his wife but her lover, who decides to murder Marlowe. A plot twist has Marlowe being shot with blanks and recording the murder attempt on tape, causing the lover's plan to backfire.

p, Jack Parsons; d, Gordon Hessler; w, Tim Shields (based on the play "The Sound of Murder" by William Fairchild); ph, David Holmes; m, Bert Shefter; ed, Robert Winter; prod d, Pat Green; art d, Ken Ryan; m/l, "Only Yesterday," Jack Ackerman, Stella Stevens, Bert Shefter (sung by Stevens, Bill Henderson); makeup, Ricky Rickerby.

Crime   **(PR:C   MPAA:R)**

LAST STAGE, THE   (SEE; LAST STOP, THE, 1949, Pol.)

LAST STAGECOACH WEST, THE   (1957) 67m Ventura/REP bw

Jim Davis (Bill Cameron), Mary Castle (Louise McCord), Victor Jory (Rand McCord), Lee Van Cleef, Grant Withers, Roy Barcroft, John Alderson, Glenn Strange, Franics McDonald, Willis Bouchey, Lewis Martin, Tristram Coffin.

A late western from fading Republic Studios, THE LAST STAGECOACH WEST is not all that different from any of their productions in the 1940s. Jory and daughter Castle operate a mail stagecoach that is competing with the new railroad mail service. Davis is a railway detective who must stop numerous saboteurs of the new system. It turns out that Jory is behind the nefarious doings, leaving heartbroken Castle to be consoled in Davis' arms. The plot is not much but like so many westerns, this is packed with action from beginning to end. This makes up for the story's rather lean moments with some particularly nasty performances from henchmen Van Cleef and Barcroft.

p, Rudy Ralston; d, Joe Kane; w, Barry Shipman; ph, Jack Marta (Naturama); ed, Joseph Harrison; md, Gerald Roberts; art d, Ralph Oberg.

Western   **(PR:A   MPAA:NR)**

LAST STAND, THE   (1938) 57m UNIV bw

Bob Baker (Tip), Constance Moore (Nancy), Fuzzy Knight (Pepper), Earl Hodgins (Thorn), Marjorie Reynolds (Nancy), Forrest Taylor (Turner), Glenn Strange (Joe), Jack Kirk (Ed), Jimmy Phillips (Tom), Sam Flint (Calhoun), Frank Ellis, Jack Montgomery.

Baker impersonates a cattle rustler to find out who killed his father. He deceptively becomes part of a bandit gang and soon finds the fellow he is looking for. An appropriate trio of tunes includes "Let Me Ride Once More," "Adios, Old Kid From Laredo," "Lost Dogie" (Atze Taconis, Homer Gayne, sung by Bob Baker).

p, Trem Carr; d, Joseph H. Lewis; w, Norton S. Parker, Harry O. Hoyt; ph, Harry Neumann; ed, Charles Craft.

Western   **(PR:A   MPAA:NR)**

LAST STOP, THE**

(1949, Pol.) 110m Films Polski/Times bw (OSTATNI ETAP; AKA: THE LAST STAGE)

Huguette Faget (Michele), W. Bartowna (Helene), T. Gorecka (Eugenie), A. Gorecka (Anna), M. Winogradowa (Nadia), B. Drapinska (Marthe), B. Fijewska (Agnes), A. Slaska (Superintendent), B. Rachwalska (Elsa), H. Drohocka (Lala).

This grim film is a portrait of life among the women inmates of Auschwitz. Shot on location, THE LAST STOP recreates the horror of Nazi concentration camps with startling accuracy, telling the story about the survival and eventual rescue of one woman from this hell. THE LAST STOP is not an easy film to watch but certainly an important work about what previously had been considered beyond human capabilities or thought. Made only a few years after the end of the war, its creators were two Auschwitz survivors themselves.

p&d, Wanda Jakubowska; w, Jakubowska, Gerda Schneider; ph, Borys Monastyrski; m, R. Palester; art d, J. Rybowski; set d, R. Mann, C. Piakowski.

Drama   **(PR:O   MPAA:NR)**

LAST SUMMER*   (1969) 97m Alsid-Francis/AA c

Barbara Hershey (Sandy), Richard Thomas (Peter), Bruce Davison (Dan), Cathy Burns (Rhoda), Ernesto Gonzalez (Anibal), Peter Turgeon (Mr. Caudell), Lou Gary, Andrew Krance, Wayne Mayer (Town Hoods), Ralph Waite (Peter's Father), Conrad Bain (Dan's Father), Eileen Letchworth (Dan's Mother), Maeve McGuire (Younger Woman), Ed Stevlingson (Sidney), Glen Walker (Boy at Dance), Lydia Wilen (Waitress).

An interesting and daring "youth film" from the 1960s, which throws together a group of kids in their early teens. Without parental supervision the youngsters are practically abandoned on New York's Fire Island. The teens get drunk, play the revealing teen game of "truth or dare," smoke pot, and experiment with sex. A rivalry builds between the promiscuous Hershey and the shy Burns with the former taking off her bikini top and daring the latter to do the same. Hershey then helps the boys hold Burns down while one of them rapes her. A brutal film, as well as an insightful one, LAST SUMMER was given an X-rating when it was first released, but after some cuts were made, it was amended to an R-rating by the MPAA. Hershey, who changed her name to Seagull and then back again (coincidentally, perhaps, Hershey kills a seagull in this picture), has appeared in a number of minor, well-acted roles, the most notable being the 1980 film THE STUNT MAN.

p, Alfred W. Crown, Sidney Beckerman; d, Frank Perry; w, Eleanor Perry (based on a novel by Evan Hunter); ph, Gerald Hirschfeld (Eastmancolor); m, John Simon; prod d, Phil Goldfarb; ed, Sidney Katz, Marion Kraft; art d, Peter Dohanos; cos, Theoni V. Aldredge.

Drama   **Cas.**   **(PR:O   MPAA:R)**

LAST SUNSET, THE*   (1961) 112m Byrnaprod/UNIV c

Rock Hudson (Dana Stribling), Kirk Douglas (Brendan O'Malley), Dorothy Malone (Belle Breckenridge), Joseph Cotten (John Breckenridge), Carol Lynley (Missy Breckenridge), Neville Brand (Frank Hobbs), Regis Toomey (Milton Wing), Rad Fulton (Julesburg Kid), Adam Williams (Calverton), Jack Elam (Ed Hobbs), John Shay (Bowman), Margarito De Luna (Jose), Jose Torvay (Rosario), Chichuahua (Chihuahua), Jose Frowe, Manuel Vergara, (Men at Cock Fight).

A perverse western from Robert Aldrich rooted more in Greek tragedy than in genre expectations. Douglas is a fugitive wanted by lawman Hudson for the murder of Hudson's brother-in-law. Douglas, on the run, stops to see Malone, a flame from 16 years ago, who is now married to Cotten and the mother of 16-year-old Lynley. Douglas takes the job of driving Cotten's herd to Texas, but is quickly found by Hudson. However, instead of taking the fugitive back to Texas, Hudson decides to help with the herd, considering he is going that direction anyway. Along the way Hudson falls in love with Malone, Cotten is killed in a barroom brawl, and Douglas becomes attracted to the young Lynley. Hudson and Douglas also gain each other's respect. When they reach Texas, Douglas tells the lawman that he is heading across the border with Lynley, who he has begun to romance. Malone informs her ex-flame that Lynley is his daughter, sending Douglas into a suicidal rage. He draws on Hudson with an empty gun and Hudson, unaware that the gun isn't loaded, fires and kills Douglas. Part western, part soap opera, and part romance, but when added up, the whole is an underrated, superbly cast picture which draws the dark side of Aldrich into the public eye.

p, Eugene Frenke, Edward Lewis; d, Robert Aldrich; w, Dalton Trumbo (based on the novel Sundown at Crazy Horse by Howard Rigsby); ph, Ernest Laszlo (Eastmancolor); m, Ernest Gold; ed, Edward Mann; prod d, Joseph Behm; md, Joseph Gershenson; art d, Alexander Golitzen, Alfred Sweeney; set d, Oliver Emert; cos, Norma Koch; m/l, "Pretty Little Girl in the Yellow Dress," Dimitri Tiomkin, Ned Washington; makeup, Bud Westmore.

Western   **(PR:C-O   MPAA:NR)**

LAST TEN DAYS, THE***
(1956, Ger.) 113m Cosmopolfilm/COL bw (DER LETZE AKT; AKA: LAST TEN DAYS OF ADOLF HITLER)

Albin Skoda *(Adolf Hitler)*, Oskar Werner *(Capt. Wuest)*, Lotte Tobisch *(Eva Braun)*, Willy Krause *(Joseph Goebbels)*, Erich Stuckmann *(Heinrich Himmler)*, Edmund Erlandsen *(Albert Speer)*, Kurt Eilers *(Martin Bormann)*, Leopold Hainisch *(Field Marshall Keitel)*, Otto Schmoele *(Gen. Alfred Jodl)*, Herbert Herbe *(Gen. Krebs)*, Hannes Schiel *(SS Gunsche)*, Erik Frey *(Gen. Burgdorf)*, Otto Woegerer *(Field Marshal Greim)*, Julius Jonak *(SS Fegelein)*, Helene Areon.

As one of the final films of his long career, the great G.W. Pabst undertook a film depiction of the possible goings-on in the bunker as Adolf Hitler, his wife Eva, and some of the higher-ups await their eventual end. While these maniacs are trying to cope with the turn of events, there is still a war going on in which they are supposed to be making important decisions. In walks Werner, a soldier just following orders who wants Hitler to approve orders to send reinforcements to the front. Werner acts as a contrast to other people who are inhabiting this bunker, apparently a means of showing that not all Germans were maniacal Nazis, but normal people just trying to live. Pabst's political stance had always been a bit mysterious; at one point he denounced the Nazis then fled to France. Yet a couple of years later he was back in Germany making films for the Nazi party. THE LAST TEN DAYS seems to be another of his efforts in which he exonerates himself of any possible connection with Nazi ideals. That aside, he was still a capable filmmaker at this point, effectively depicting a period that many people want to forget. (In German; English subtitles.)

p, Carl Szokoil; d, G.W. Pabst; w, Erich Maria Remarque (based on the novel *Ten Days to Die* by M.A. Mussanno); ph, Gunther Anders; English titles, Herman Weinberg.

Drama **(PR:A MPAA:NR)**

LAST TIME I SAW ARCHIE, THE1/2**
(1961) 103m Mark VII Ltd.-Manzanita-Talbot/UA bw

Robert Mitchum *(Archie Hall)*, Jack Webb *(Bill Bowers)*, Martha Hyer *(Peggy Kramer)*, France Nuyen *(Cindy Hamilton)*, Joe Flynn *(Pvt. Russell Drexel)*, James Lydon *(Pvt. Billy Simpson)*, Del Moore *(Pvt. Frank Ostrow)*, Louis Nye *(Pvt. Sam Beacham)*, Richard Arlen *(Col. Martin)*, Don Knotts *(Capt. Little)*, Robert Strauss *(M. Sgt. Stanley Erlenheim)*, Harvey Lembeck *(Sgt. Malcolm Greenbriar)*, Claudia Barrett *(Lola)*, Theona Bryant *(Daphne)*, Elaine Davis *(Carole)*, Marilyn Burtis *(Patsy Ruth)*, James Mitchum *(Corporal)*, Gene McCarthy *(Bartender)*, John Nolan *(Lt. Oglemeyer)*, Martin Dean *(2nd Lieutenant)*, Bill Kilmer, Phil Gordon, Dick Cathcart, *(Soldiers)*, Howard McNear *(Gen. Williams)*, Robert Clarke *(Officer)*, Nancy Kulp *(Miss Willoughby)*, Art Ballinger.

Jack Webb directed his only comedy here from the actual WWII experiences of pilot William Bowers, who also served as screenwriter. The film stars Mitchum as the title character and Webb as Bowers. Together they con everyone on their Army base into believing that they are part of a special operation. As a result, they get much free time away from the base and are usually found in the company of Nuyen and Hyer. Eventually they get out of the service and go to Hollywood, where Mitchum becomes a big-time studio executive and Webb becomes a scriptwriter.

p&d, Jack Webb; w, William Bowers; ph, Joseph MacDonald; m, Frank Comstock; ed, Robert Leeds; md, Comstock; art d, Feild Gray; set d, John Sturtevant; cos, Jesse Munden, Sabine Manela; spec eff, A. Paul Pollard; makeup, Stanley Campbell.

Comedy **(PR:A MPAA:NR)**

LAST TIME I SAW PARIS, THE* 1/2** (1954) 116m MGM c

Elizabeth Taylor *(Helen Ellswirth)*, Van Johnson *(Charles Wills)*, Walter Pidgeon *(James Ellswirth)*, Donna Reed *(Marie Ellswirth)*, Eva Gabor *(Lorraine Quarl)*, Kurt Kasznar *(Maurice)*, George Dolenz *(Claude Matine)*, Roger Moore *(Paul)*, Sandy Descher *(Vicki)*, Celia Lovsky *(Mama)*, Peter Leeds *(Barney)*, John Doucette *(Campbell)*, Odette *(Singer)*, Luis Urbina, Gilda Fontana *(Flamenco Dance Team)*, Christian Pasques *(Boy)*, Ed Hinton, Richard Emory, Steve Wayne *(American Officers)*, Loulette Sablon *(Nurse)*, Jean Heremans *(Leon)*, Josette Deegan, Mary Ann Hawkins *(Two Girls Fighting)*, Matt Moore, Paul Power, Harry Cody *(English Men)*, Ann Codee *(Another Nurse)*, Gene Coogan *(Gendarme)*.

F. Scott Fitzgerald's tragic love story was brought to the screen with surprising vitality under Brooks' expert hand, one where he drew forth fine performances from Taylor, Johnson, and others, surrounding his cast in a sumptuous MGM production that captured the flavor of expatriate life in the City of Light. Where Fitzgerald set his poignant tale in the 1920s, this film begins just after WW II; Johnson is a GI with literary ambitions who goes to Paris and meets wealthy Taylor. They fall in love and he settles down there, attempting to write his first novel. All goes well for a while until failure to sell his writing causes Johnson to turn to the bottle. His excessive drinking soon causes the couple to fall out and Taylor to be accidentally locked out of their Parisian quarters during a rainstorm (when Johnson passes out from drink). She catches pneumonia and later dies. Their child is raised by Taylor's sister, Reed, who has always disapproved of Johnson; he returns to the U.S. and becomes a successful novelist. Once back in Paris (which is how the film opens, the Johnson-Taylor love story shown in flashback), Johnson begs for custody of his little girl. Reed relents at the last moment and the child is reunited with her reformed father. Taylor was never more lovely and turns in a superior performance as the star-crossed lady in love with Johnson. She later told an interviewer: "Rather curiously . . . THE LAST TIME I SAW PARIS first convinced me I wanted to be an actress, instead of yawning my way through parts. That girl was off-beat with mercurial flashes of instability—more than just glib dialog." Johnson, who also turns in a good effort, although he's a bit glib in spots, was first teamed with Taylor in 1950 in THE BIG HANGOVER and got top billing. With THE LAST TIME I SAW PARIS, Taylor received the top slot as she had become one of the big box office draws for MGM. Producer Lester Cowan had originally purchased the rights from Fitzgerald to this story for $3,000, intending to film it as a Mary Pickford vehicle in the 1920s for Goldwyn. Cowan sold the story to Paramount for a Gregory Peck-William Wyler production that fell through. But MGM purchased the rights from Paramount specifically for Taylor, assigning the clever Epstein twins to write a sparkling script that kept the flavor if not the brilliance of Fitzgerald's story intact. MGM shot two weeks on location in Paris and on the Riviera, mostly at Cannes, producing the balance of the film on the Culver City lot.

p, Jack Cummings; d, Richard Brooks; w, Brooks, Julius J., Philip G. Epstein (based on the story "Babylon Revisited" by F. Scott Fitzgerald); ph, Joseph Ruttenberg (Technicolor); m, Conrad Salinger; ed, John Dunning; art d, Cedric Gibbons, Randall Duell; set d, Edwin B. Willis, Jack D. Moore; cos, Helen Rose; spec eff, A. Arnold Gillespie; m/l, "The Last Time I Saw Paris" Jerome Kern, Oscar Hammerstein II.

Romance **(PR:A MPAA:NR)**

LAST TOMAHAWK, THE**
(1965, Ger./Ital./Span.) 89m International Germania Film-Cineproduzioni Associate-P.C. Balcazar bw (DER LETZE MOHIKANER)

Anthony Steffens [Antonio De Teffe], Karin Dor, Dan Martin, Joachim Fuchsberger, Carl Lange, Marie France.

Another of Reinl's films influenced by Karl May; this time an adaptation of James Fenimore Cooper's *The Last of the Mohicans.* De Teffe stars as the Indian Strongheart (Leatherstocking in the novel), who, with the aid of Martin, gets Lange and his daughters to safety. Includes some fine action sequences which help along an oddly paced plot.

p, Franz Thierry; d, Harald Reinl; w, Joachim Bartsch; ph, Ernst Kalinke, Francisco Marin.

Western **(PR:A MPAA:NR)**

LAST TOMB OF LIGEIA (SEE: TOMB OF LIGEIA, THE, 1965, Brit.)

LAST TRAIL, THE* 1/2 (1934) 59m FOX bw

George O'Brien, Claire Trevor, El Brendel, Lucille LaVerne, Matt McHugh, Edward J. LeSaint, J. Carrol Naish, Ruth Warren, George Reed, Luis Alberni.

O'Brien undermines the scheme of an outlaw gang that plans to swindle his land away. They hire him to pose as an heir to the property without realizing he really is the owner. He performs his task well, but not to the specifications of the crooks, who are soon brought to justice.

d, James Tinling; w, Stuart Anthony (based on a story by Zane Grey); ph, Arthur Miller; m, Arthur Lange; ed, Barney Wolf; cos, Royer.

Western **(PR:A MPAA:NR)**

LAST TRAIN FROM BOMBAY* 1/2 (1952) 73m COL bw

Jon Hall *(Martin Viking)*, Christine Larson *(Mary Anne Palmer)*, Lisa Ferraday *(Charlane)*, Douglas R. Kennedy *(Kevin O'Hara)*, Michael Fox *(Captain Tamil)*, Donna Martell *(Nawob's Daughter)*, Matthew Boulton *(Col. Palmer)*, James Fairfax *(Bartender)*, Gregory Gay *(B. Vornin)*, Kenneth Terrell, Frederic Berest *(Ceylonese)*, Barry Brooks *(Porters)*.

A fast-moving adventure tale that comes close to being swallowed up by its own bulky plot. Hall is an American diplomat who travels to India only to find the country on the brink of civil war. He then discovers that an old pal, Kennedy, is behind the plan to spark the fighting. Kennedy is soon murdered but informs Hall that a train full of explosives is going to blow up a train carrying an Indian prince. Knowing of the plot, Hall becomes the assassins' target and also a suspect in Kennedy's murder. He puts his life on the line to save the prince, and by doing so clears his own name and prevents the war.

p, Sam Katzman; d, Fred F. Sears; w, Robert Yale Libott; ph, Henry Freulich; ed, Richard Fant; md, Mischa Bakaleinikoff; art d, Paul Palmentola; set d, Sidney Clifford.

Adventure **(PR:A MPAA:NR)**

LAST TRAIN FROM GUN HILL* 1/2** (1959) 94m Bryna/PAR c

Kirk Douglas *(Matt Morgan)*, Anthony Quinn *(Craig Belden)*, Carolyn Jones *(Linda)*, Earl Holliman *(Rick Belden)*, Ziva Rodann *(Catherine Morgan)*, Brad Dexter *(Beero)*, Brian Hutton *(Lee)*, Bing Russell *(Skag)*, Val Avery *(Bartender)*, Walter Sande *(Sheriff Bartlett)*, Lars Henderson *(Petey Morgan)*, Henry Wills *(Jake)*, John R. Anderson *(Salesman at Bar)*, William Newell *(Hotel Clerk)*, Len Hendry *(Man in Lobby)*, Dabbs Greer *(Andy)*, Mara Lynn *(Minnie)*, Raymond A. McWalters *(Wounded Gunman)*, Sid Tomack *(Roomer)*, Charles Stevens *(Keno)*, Julius Tanner *(Cleaning Man)*, Glenn Strange *(Saloon Bouncer)*, Jack Lomas *(Charlie)*, Tony Russo *(Pinto)*, Ricky William Kelman *(Boy)*, Walter (Tony) Merrill *(Conductor)*, Eric Alden, Carl H. Saxe, Frank Hagney *(Craig's Men)*, Hank Mann *(Storekeeper)*, Frank Carter *(Cowboy on Train)*, Mike Mahoney *(Drummer on Train)*, Bob Scott *(Conductor)*, Ty Hardin *(Cowboy)*.

An atmospheric, psychological western from much the same team responsible for GUNFIGHT AT THE O.K. CORRAL: director Sturges, actors Douglas and Holliman and cinematographer Lang, as well as editor, art directors and composer. Douglas is determined to bring to justice the man who killed and raped his wife, but is shocked to learn the culprit is Holliman, the son of Quinn, Douglas' best friend and a powerful cattle baron. His plan is to get the boy onto the last train out of Gun Hill before Quinn's henchmen can stop him. A final shootout at the train station ends with Douglas the only one left standing. Extremely well done on all fronts.

p, Hal B. Wallis; d, John Sturges; w, James Poe (based on the story "Showdown" by Les Crutchfield); ph, Charles B. Lang, Jr. (VistaVision, Technicolor); m, Dimitri Tiomkin; ed, Warren Low; md, Tiomkin; art d, Walter Tyler, Hal Pereira.

Western Cas. (PR:C MPAA:NR)

LAST TRAIN FROM MADRID, THE*** (1937) 85m PAR bw

Dorothy Lamour *(Carmelita Castillo)*, Lew Ayres *(Bill Dexter)*, Gilbert Roland *(Eduardo de Soto)*, Karen Morley *(Helene Rafitte)*, Lionel Atwill *(Col. Vigo)*, Helen Mack *(Lola)*, Robert Cummings *(Juan Ramos)*, Olympe Bradna *(Maria Ferrer)*, Anthony Quinn *(Capt. Ricardo Alvarez)*, Lee Bowman *(Michael Balk)*, Evelyn Brent *(Women's Battalion Officer)*, Jack Perrin *(Guard)*, Frank Leyva *(Chauffeur)*, Roland Rego *(Officer)*, George Lloyd *(Intelligence Officer)*, Ralf Harolde *(Lola's Friend)*, Hooper Atchley *(Martin)*, Louise Carter *(Rosa Delgado)*, Harry Semels *(Guard)*, Francis McDonald *(Mora)*, Francis Ford *(Pedro Elias)*, Charles Middleton *(Warden)*, Sam Appel *(2nd Warden)*, Stanley Price *(Clerk)*, Otto Hoffman *(Fernando)*, Henry Brandon *(Announcer)*, Maurice Cass *(Waiter)*, Harry Worth *(Gomez)*, [Paul] Tiny Newland *(Turnkey)*, Rollo Lloyd *(Hernandez)*, Charles Stevens *(Escaped Prisoner)*, Bess Flowers *(Saleswoman)*, Harry Woods *(Government Man)*, Alan Ladd *(Bit Soldier)*, Cecil B. DeMille *(Man Coming from Bungalow)*, Stanley Fields *(Avila)*.

This was the first Hollywood production dealing with the controversial Spanish Civil War, then much in the headlines and debated hotly across the nation as the bloody testing ground between Democracy and Fascism. Yet the film makes little political comment, dealing instead with a group of refugees fleeing war-ravaged Madrid (then in the hands of the Loyalists). The impressive cast and solid story line, fragmented into the lives of the passengers on the train, makes this one enjoyable and often exciting, even though it's really little more than GRAND HOTEL on wheels. The passengers include army deserter Cummings, wealthy baroness Morley, prostitute Mack, Ayres, a cynical newsman, and Bradna, an orphan who is attached to him. The main story concerns Lamour, who is Roland's ex-girl friend but who is now friendly with Quinn, the officer charged by commander Atwill to see that the train gets safely away to Valencia. Roland is an ex-army man, now a political fugitive who falls out with old friend Quinn over Lamour's affections. In the end, he is allowed to stay on the train, reuniting with Lamour, thanks to Quinn. When Atwill learns that Roland is one of the passengers, he orders Quinn to take Roland off and shoot him. But Quinn, for Lamour's sake, holds Atwill at gunpoint until the train is safely away, and is later captured and shot for his insubordination. Temperamental Roland insisted during this production that all other male actors shave their mustaches so that he would be the only actor wearing one and thereby be distinctive. Future superstar Alan Ladd can be fleetingly seen as a trooper, as can famed director Cecil B. DeMille, who has a walk-through part, a good luck gesture toward his new son-in-law Quinn who had married DeMille's adopted daughter Katherine. During this production all the makeup and hairdresser personnel went on strike and the actors had to fend for themselves, a hardship on actresses such as Lamour, who later admitted in her autobiography, *My Side of the Road*: ". . . after doing it all myself I had new respect for those artists who never appear on camera and whose work comes off with cold cream at the end of the day."

p, George M. Arthur; d, James Hogan; w, Louis Stevens, Robert Wyler (based on a story by Paul Harvey Fox, Elsie Fox); ph, Harry Fischbeck; ed, Everett Douglass; md, Boris Morros.

War Drama (PR:A MPAA:NR)

LAST TYCOON, THE** 1/2** (1976) 122m PAR c

Robert De Niro *(Monroe Stahr)*, Tony Curtis *(Rodriguez)*, Robert Mitchum *(Pat Brady)*, Jeanne Moreau *(Didi)*, Jack Nicholson *(Brimmer)*, Donald Pleasence *(Boxley)*, Ingrid Boulting *(Kathleen Moore)*, Ray Milland *(Fleishacker)*, Dana Andrews *(Red Ridingwood)*, Theresa Russell *(Cecilia Brady)*, Peter Strauss *(Wylie)*, Tige Andrews *(Popolos)*, Morgan Farley *(Marcus)*, John Carradine *(Guide)*, Jeff Corey *(Doctor)*, Diane Shalet *(Stahr's Secretary)*, Seymour Cassell *(Seal Trainer)*, Angelica Huston *(Edna)*, Bonnie Bartlett, Sharon Masters *(Brady's Secretaries)*, Eric Christmas *(Norman)*, Leslie Curtis *(Mrs. Rodriguez)*, Lloyd Kino *(Butler)*, Brendan Burns *(Assistant Editor)*, Carrie Miller *(Lady in Restaurant)*, Peggy Feury *(Hairdresser)*, Betsey Jones-Moreland *(Lady Writer)*, Patricia Singer *(Girl on Beach)*.

The unfinished novel by F. Scott Fitzgerald converts awkwardly to the screen but is saved from oblivion by that always fascinating actor De Niro, who essays the role of the movie mogul (which was based on MGM's Irving Thalberg). The film opens with De Niro very much in power at his studio, backed by his mentor and friend Mitchum, and guiding the careers of such people as matinee idol Curtis, who is going through an identity crisis. (Curtis burlesques his role and is unbelievably bad as a cross between John Gilbert and Ramon Novarro.) De Niro spots an attractive young girl, Boulting, who strolls onto the set and floats around on a huge prop in the studio tank one night. He attempts to make love to her, she reminding him of his dead wife, while dealing with the power struggles within the studio. Boulting, a much-touted new discovery, proved to be without acting talent, a totally vacuous personality. Mitchum again sleepwalks his way through his studio-boss role, taking women into his office washroom to fornicate and being discovered by his embarrassed daughter Russell, who is hell-bent to capture the elusive De Niro. Nicholson appears briefly as a truculent union leader and plays a vicious game of ping-pong with De Niro, then vanishes. There's simply not enough to this story since there was never an end to it, and the middle is soggy, with Pinter's movie musings that mean nothing to the average viewer. At one point Mitchum and De Niro are screening a new film in a posh screening room and Mitchum passes a remark about the film they are watching, a comment which is more than apt for THE LAST TYCOON: "It just lays there and goes to sleep."

p, Sam Spiegel; d, Elia Kazan; w, Harold Pinter (based on the novel by F. Scott Fitzgerald); ph, Victor Kemper (Panavision, Technicolor); m, Maurice Jarre; ed, Richard Marks; prod d, Gene Callahan; art d, Jack Collis; set d, Bill Smith, Jerry Wunderlich; cos, Anna Hill Johnstone.

Drama Cas. (PR:C MPAA:PG)

LAST UNICORN, THE** 1/2** (1982) 84m ITC c

Voices: Alan Arkin *(Schmendrick the Magician)*, Jeff Bridges *(Prince Lir)*, Mia Farrow *(The Last Unicorn/Lady Amalthea)*, Tammy Grimes *(Molly Grue)*, Robert Klein *(The Butterfly)*, Angela Lansbury *(Mommy Fortuna)*, Christopher Lee *(King Haggard)*, Keenan Wynn *(Capt. Cully)*, Paul Frees *(The Talking Cat)*, Rene Auberjonois *(The Speaking Skull)*.

Written by Peter S. Beagle and based on his best-selling novel, this animated children's film focuses on a unicorn and her mission to free the rest of her breed from the tyranny of an evil king. During her travels, she meets up with a cast of colorful characters, and at one point is temporarily transfomed into a young damsel.

p&d, Arthur Rankin, Jr., Jules Bass; w, Peter S. Beagle (based on a novel by Beagle); ph, Hiroyasu Omoto; m, Jimmy Webb; ed, Tomoko Kida; prod d, Rankin; animators, Yoshiko Sasaki, Masahiro Yoshida, Kayoko Sakano, Fukuo Suzuki, Ioru Hara, Guy Kubo.

Animated Feature Cas. (PR:AAA MPAA:G)

LAST VALLEY, THE** (1971, Brit.) 125m ABC/Cinerama c

Michael Caine *(The Captain)*, Omar Sharif *(Vogel)*, Florinda Bolkan *(Erica)*, Nigel Davenport *(Gruber)*, Per Oscarsson *(Father Sebastian)*, Arthur O'Connell *(Hoffman)*, Madeline Hinde *(Inge Hoffman)*, Yorgo Voyagis *(Pirelli)*, Miguel Alejandro *(Julio)*, Christian Roberts *(Andreas)*, Ian Hogg *(Graf)*, Michael Gothard *(Hansen)*, Brian Blessed *(Korski)*, George Innes *(Vornez)*, Irene Prador *(Frau Hoffman)*, Vladek Sheybal *(Mathias)*, John Hallam *(Geddes)*, Andrew McCulloch *(Shutz)*, Jack Shepherd *(Eskesen)*, Leon Lissek *(Czeraki)*, Chris Chittell *(Svenson)*, Kurt Christian *(Tsarus)*, Mark Edwards *(Sernen)*, Claudia Butenuth *(Helga)*, Michaela *(Peasant Girl)*, Larry Taylor *(Garnak)*, Paul Challen *(Zollner)*, Tony Vogel *(Tub)*, Patrick Westwood *(Rethman)*, Frazer Hines *(Corg)*, Edward Underdown *(Gnarled Peasant)*, Holly Du Marreck *(Little Girl)*, Ralph Arliss *(Claus)*, Seyton Pooley *(Nansen)*, Dave Crowley *(Pastori)*, Mike Douglas *(Stoffel)*, Richard Graydon *(Yuri)*, Joe Powell *(Kaas)*, Lisa Jager *(Rape Girl)*, Terry Richards *(Norseman)*.

Sharif, a former teacher seeking refuge from the ravages of the Thirty Years War, settles down in a peaceful village in a lush Alpine valley. Caine, an army captain, and his men are urged by Sharif to set up camp when the village is threatened by a band of murderous mercenaries. Written, produced, directed, and heavily financed by James Clavell, this extravagant costume drama ended up with a reported $7 million loss. Clavell went on to write the blockbuster novels *Shogun* and *Noble House*.

p,d&w, James Clavell (based on a novel by J.B. Pick); ph, John Wilcox (Todd-AO, Eastmancolor); m, John Barry; ed, John Bloom; md, Barry; art d, Peter Mullins; cos, Yvonne Blake; spec eff, Pat Moore; makeup, Wally Schneiderman, Alberto De Rossi; stunt arr, John Sullivan.

Action Adventure Cas. (PR:A MPAA:GP)

LAST VICTIM, THE (SEE: FORCED ENTRY, 1975)

LAST VOYAGE, THE*** (1960) 91m MGM c

Robert Stack *(Cliff Henderson)*, Dorothy Malone *(Laurie Henderson)*, George Sanders *(Capt. Robert Adams)*, Edmond O'Brien *(2nd Engineer Walsh)*, Woody Strode *(Hank Lawson)*, Jack Kruschen *(Chief Engineer Pringle)*, Joel Marston *(3rd Officer England)*, George Furness *(Osborne)*, Marshall Kent *(Quartermaster)*, Richard Norris *(3rd Engineer Cole)*, Andrew Hughes *(Radio Operator)*, Robert Martin *(2nd Mate Mace)*, Bill Wilson *(Youth)*, Tammy Marihugh *(Jill Henderson)*.

Stack and Malone (brother and sister Hadley from WRITTEN ON THE WIND) are a married couple whose ocean voyage turns sour upon the opening credit's explosions. Fire and quickly rising waters begin to take their toll, placing everyone on board in grave danger. Malone, who becomes trapped in the ship's lowest level, eventually is rescued by Strode and the others. This early disaster film is made watchable by a number of fine performances and the excellent camerawork of Hal Mohr, who described this picture (and his collaboration with the Stones) as the most difficult he'd ever made. The Stones purchased the French liner *Ile de France*, which was headed for the scrapyard, and used it for the realistic sinking scenes.

p, Andrew L. Stone, Virginia Stone; d&w, Andrew L. Stone; ph, Hal Mohr (Metrocolor); m, Rudy Schrager; ed, Virginia L. Stone.

Disaster (PR:A MPAA:NR)

LAST WAGON, THE*** (1956) 99m FOX c

Richard Widmark *(Todd)*, Felicia Farr *(Jenny)*, Susan Kohner *(Jolie)*, Tommy Rettig *(Billy)*, Stephanie Griffin *(Valinda)*, Ray Stricklyn *(Clint)*, Nick Adams *(Ridge)*, Carl Benton Reid *(Gen. Howard)*, Douglas Kennedy *(Col. Normand)*, George Mathews *(Bull Harper)*, James Drury *(Lt. Kelly)*, Ken Clark *(Sergeant)*, Timothy Carey *(Cole Harper)*, George Ross *(Sarge)*, Juney Ellis *(Mrs. Clinton)*, Abel Fernandez *(Apache Medicine Man)*.

Widmark, a tough trapper who has killed the men responsible for murdering his wife and children, is captured by a local sheriff and chained to a wagon train. A band of Apaches attacks and kills everyone except Widmark, who is left for dead, and the teen occupants of one wagon. Widmark takes on the task of leading the group to safety. A hard-driving, fast-paced physical western.

p, William B. Hawks; d, Delmer Daves; w, James Edward Grant, Daves, Gwen Bagni Gielgud (based on a story by Gielgud); ph, Wilfrid Cline (CinemaScope, DeLuxe Color); m, Lionel Newman; ed, Hugh S. Fowler; art d, Lyle R. Wheeler, Lewis H. Creber; cos, Mary Wills.

Western (PR:C MPAA:NR)

LAST WALTZ, THE   (1936, Brit.) 74m Warwick/AP&D bw

Jarmilla Novotna (*Countess Vera Lizavetta*), Harry Welchman (*Count Dmitri*), Gerald Barry (*Prince Paul*), Josephine Huntley Wright (*Babushka*), Tonie Edgar Bruce (*Countess*), Betty Huntley Wright, Bruce Winston, Jack Hellier, Paul Sheridan, Pamela Randall, Elizabeth Arkell, MacArthur Gordon, E. Fitzclarence, Madge Snell, Bella Milo.

In the ever mythical European country of Ruritania, Barry plays a prince who must marry in order to satisfy his ministers. A countess and three of her four daughters are brought for the playboy monarch's choosing. However, some complications set in when Novotna, Barry's would-be bride, is more attentive to her escort, Welchman. The jealous prince has Welchman imprisoned but all is righted when the missing fourth daughter arrives and gives Barry's heart a whirl. Shot on location in Paris, this production of a Viennese operetta is not nearly so gay as it should be, resulting in a tired and rather boring production.

p, Gina Carlton; d, Leo Mittler, Gerald Barry; w, Reginald Arkell (based on the opera "Der Letzewalzer" by Oscar Strauss, Max Wallner, Georg Weber).

Operetta   **(PR:A MPAA:NR)**

LAST WAR, THE*

(1962, Jap.) 110m TOHO bw (SEKAI DAISENSO; AKA: THE FINAL WAR)

Frankie Sakai, Nobuko Otowa, Akira Takarada, Yuriko Hoshi, Yumi Shirakawa.

A nuclear holocaust picture from Japan in which impending WW III destruction draws close after a 38th Parallel disagreement and an air collision between two superpower jets. The angry governments respond by pressing the button, resulting in total nuclear devastation. The concentration is on those dying, slowly and painfully. It is interesting to note that sentiments that made the television film THE DAY AFTER possible also existed across the globe 20 years earlier. Special effects by the masterful Tsuburaya are far above average. An 80-minute version also has been shown.

p, Tomoyuki Tanaka; d, Shue Matsubayashi; w, Toshio Yasumi, Takeshi Kimura; ph, Rokuro Nishigaki; spec eff, Eiji Tsuburaya.

Science Fiction/Drama   Cas.   (PR:C MPAA:NR)

LAST WARNING, THE*1/2   (1929) 87m UNIV bw

Laura La Plante (*Doris*), Montagu Love (*McHugh*), Roy D'Arcy (*Carlton*), Margaret Livingston (*Evalinda*), John Boles (*Qualie*), Burr McIntosh (*Josiah*), Mack Swain (*Robert*), Bert Roach (*Mike*), Carrie Daumery (*Barbara*), Slim Summerville (*Tommy*), Torben Meyer (*Gene*), D'Arcy Corrigan (*Woodford*), Bud Phelps (*Sammy*), Charles K. French (*Doctor*), Francisco Maran (*Jeffries*), Ella McKenzie (*Ann*), Fred Kelsey, Tom O'Brien (*Inspectors*), Harry Northrup (*Coroner*).

When a theater company's leading man is killed during a performance suspicions run high but the mystery remains. Five years later, a producer reopens the theater and presents the same play with the same cast. An eerie chain of events follows, culminating in the disappearance of the new leading man. The mystery is unlocked when it is discovered that a masked stage manager a la PHANTOM OF THE OPERA (1925), to get the company's stockholders to pull out of the production, has set up the entire scheme. Another similarity to PHANTOM OF THE OPERA exists with the film's use of the old theater built for the Phantom's Paris Opera sequences. The picture, which is a part-talkie, also features some unusual photography by Hal Mohr, who had already shot some 25 features and would continue working until the end of the 1960s. It was remade in 1939 as HOUSE OF FEAR.

d, Paul Leni; w, Alfred A. Cohn, Tom Reed, Robert F. Hill (based on the story "House of Fear" by Wadsworth Camp and on the play by Thomas F. Fallon); ph, Hal Mohr; m, Joseph Cherniavsky; ed, Robert Carlisle.

Mystery   **(PR:A MPAA:NR)**

LAST WARNING, THE*1/2   (1938) 62m UNIV bw

Preston Foster (*Det. Bill Crane*), Frank Jenks (*Doc Williams*), Joyce Compton (*Dawn Day*), Kay Linaker (*Carla Rodriguez*), E.E. Clive (*Maj. Barclay*), Frances Robinson (*Linda Essex*), Raymond Parker (*John Essex*), Robert Paige (*Tony Henderson*), Albert Dekker (*Higgs*), Roland Drew (*Paul Gomez*), Clem Wilenchick (*Slocumbe*), Orville Caldwell (*Wilson*), Richard Lane.

Private detectives Foster and Jenks are called to the estate of wealthy playboy Parker and his sister, Robinson, after Parker has received some threatening letters. While Foster searches for clues to who wrote the notes, Robinson is kidnaped, giving the sleuths another mystery to solve. (See Crime Club series, Index.)

p, Irving Starr; d, Al Rogell; w, Edmund L. Hartmann (based on the novel *The Dead Don't Care* by Jonathan Latimer); ph, George Meehan; ed, Maurice Wright; md, Charles Previn; art d, Jack Otterson.

Mystery/Comedy   **(PR:A MPAA:NR)**

LAST WARRIOR, THE   (SEE: FLAP, 1970)

LAST WAVE, THE**

(1978, Aus.) 106m Ayer-South Australian-Australian Film Commission/World Northal c

Richard Chamberlain (*David Burton*), Olivia Hamnett (*Anne Burton*), Gulpilil (*Chris Lee*), Frederick Parslow (*Rev. Burton*), Vivean Gray (*Dr. Whitburn*), Nanjiwarra Amagula (*Charlie*), Walter Amagula (*Gerry Lee*), Roy Bara (*Larry*), Cedric Lalara (*Lindsey*), Morris Lalara (*Jacko*), Peter Carroll (*Michael Zeadler*), Athol Compton (*Billy Corman*), Hedley Cullen (*Judge*), Michael Duffield (*Andrew Potter*), Wallas Eaton (*Morgue Doctor*), Jo England (*Babysitter*), John Frawley (*Policeman*), Jennifer de Greenlaw (*Zeadler's Secretary*), Richard Henderson (*Prosecutor*), Merv Lilley (*Publican*), John Meagher (*Morgue Clerk*), Guido Rametta (*Guido*), Malcolm

Robertson (*Don Fishburn*), Greg Rowe (*Carl*), Katrina Sedgwick (*Sophie Burton*), Ingrid Weir (*Grace Burton*).

A powerful, yet subtle, picture from Australian director Weir, who has proven to have quite a flair for themes dealing with mystical events. Like his earlier work, PICNIC AT HANGING ROCK, this picture takes full advantage of unexplainable events and their connection with the aborigine world and the ancient Australian landscape. The picture opens as a raging thunderstorm from a clear blue sky drenches a small desert settlement, switching quickly to Sydney, which is also in the midst of a torrential downpour. A voice over the radio unconvincingly attempts to explain the phenomenon as a reaction to cold winds from the Antarctic. An earlier shot of an aborigine painting on a cave wall lets the viewer know there is something at work here that goes beyond the realm of scientific explanation, setting the mood for the rest of the film. The contrast between the Western viewpoint, which attributes everything to facts, and the aboriginal perspective of a cosmos that is beyond the grasp of conscious thought, creates a tension that is carried throughout the film. Chamberlain plays a Sydney lawyer who becomes involved in the trial of those suspected of murdering an aborigine, despite his lack of experience with both aborigines and criminal law. One of the defendants, Gulpilil, begins to appear in his dreams, even though the two men have never met. Through his later conversations with Gulpilil and an ancient aborigine, Chamberlain begins to understand the dreams' significance. Weir does a fine job of weaving real events with dream sequences and developing the aborigine perspective. This is one of the few films that does not portray aborigines as a defeated people at the mercy of white settlers and, instead, treats them with great respect. Chamberlain is convincing as a wealthy lawyer and family man who becomes possessed by a vision beyond his grasp. Although the plot falters in a few instances, it maintains a high level of suspense overall.

p, Hal McElroy, James McElroy; d, Peter Weir; w, Weir, Tony Morphett, Peter Popescu; ph, Russell Boyd (Artlab Color); m, Charles Wain; ed, Max Lemon; art d, Neil Angwin; set d, Bill Malcolm; cos, Annie Bleakley; spec eff, Angwin, Monty Fieguth.

Drama   Cas.   (PR:A MPAA:PG)

LAST WILL OF DR. MABUSE, THE

(SEE: TESTAMENT OF DR. MABUSE, THE, 1933, Ger.)

LAST WOMAN OF SHANG, THE**

(1964, Hong Kong) 107m Shaw Brothers/Frank Lee c (TA CHI)

Lin Dai (*Ta Chi*), Pat Ting Hung (*Chi Yen*), Shin Yung-kyoon (*King Chou*), Ching Miao (*Duke of Sipa*), Chiang Kuang-chao (*Yiu Hun*), Yang Chihching (*Pei Kan*), Li Ye-chuan (*Fei Chung*), Nam Koong-woon (*Chi Fa*), Tien Feng (*Su Fu*), Chen Yung-hua (*Queen Chiang*), Fung Yee, Li Yuen-chung, Lam Way-li.

Lin sets out to avenge the death of her father, who crumbled under the pressures of 12th-century B.C. emperor Shin. She gets him under her amorous spell and asks him to build her a tower. The project soaks the emperor's bankroll, placing undue hardship on the workers. Eventually a rebel army unites to overthrow the emperor. Lin, trapped by the army in the burning tower, dies in the process.

p, Run Run Shaw; d, Yueh Feng; w, Wang Yueh-ting; ph, Ho Lan-shan (Shawscope, Eastmancolor); m, Wang Fu-ling; ed, Chiang Hsing-lung; art d, Chen Chi-jui, Chen Chin-shen.

Adventure/Drama   **(PR:A MPAA:NR)**

LAST WOMAN ON EARTH, THE*1/2   (1960) 71m Filmgroup c

Anthony Carbone (*Harold*), Betsy Jones-Moreland (*Evelyn*), Edward Wain [Robert Towne] (*Martin*).

When a sudden reduction of the earth's oxygen kills off the entire population, only three survivors are left—gangster Carbone, his wife, Jones-Moreland, and lawyer Wain. While harbored in a boat near Puerto Rico, the trio debate whether or not they should begin rebuilding their future, while Wain and Carbone battle for the affections of the only female left. This Corman quickie was written by rookie Wain, who also adopted the name Robert Towne and took on one of the acting roles. Wain, who went on to write CHINATOWN, is far better in front of the typewriter than the camera.

p&d, Roger Corman; w, Edward Wain [Robert Towne]; ph, Jack Marquette (VitaScope, Eastmancolor); m, Ronald S. Stein; ed, Anthony Carras.

Science Fiction   **(PR:A MPAA:NR)**

LAST WORD, THE*1/2

(1979) 105m Variety/International c (AKA: DANNY TRAVIS)

Richard Harris (*Danny Travis*), Karen Black (*Paula Herbert*), Martin Landau (*Capt. Garrity*), Dennis Christopher (*Ben Travis*), Biff McGuire (*Gov. Davis*), Christopher Guest (*Roger*), Penelope Milford (*Denise Travis*), Bonnie Bartlett, Jorge Cervera, Nathan Cook, Linda Dangcil, Alex Henteloff, Pat McNamara, Michael Pataki, Natasha Ryan, Charles Siebert, James Staley, Richard Venture.

Harris portrays a likable Irish inventor whose bad business sense keeps him and his children in dire financial straits. He gets entangled in a fight with city hall after the rundown building he lives in is slated for demolition. He also discovers an unlawful redevelopment project that will stuff the pockets of the governor, McGuire. Facing eviction, Harris abducts a sheriff and holds him prisoner in the apartment until the crooked McGuire can be exposed. The film pokes fun at the media and the power they hold over public opinion. Black plays an opportunist TV anchorwoman who smells a good story and a possible Pulitzer Prize. The film was co-scripted by Carson (Black's husband), who also penned PARIS, TEXAS.

p, Richard C. Abramson, Michael C. Varhol; d, Roy Boulting; w, Varhol, Greg Smith, L.M. Kit Carson (based on a story by Horatius Haeberle); ph, Jules Brenner;

m, Carol Lees; ed, George Grenville; prod d, Jack Collins; set d, Dennis Peeples; spec eff, Henry Millar.

Comedy/Drama   **Cas.**   **(PR:A MPAA:PG)**

LAST YEAR AT MARIENBAD**
(1962, Fr./Ital.) 94m Terra-Societe Nouvelle des Films Cormoran-Precitel-Como-Tamara-Silver Films Cineriz/Astor bw (L'ANEE DERNIERE A MARIENBAD; L'ANNO SCORSO A MARIENBAD)

Delphine Seyrig (A/Woman), Giorgio Albertazzi (X/Stranger), Sacha Pitoeff (M/Escort/Husband), Francoise Bertin, Luce Garcia-Ville, Helena Kornel, Francois Spira, Karin Toeche-Mittler, Pierre Barbaud, Wilhelm von Deek, Jean Lanier, Gerard Lorin, Davide Montemuri, Gilles Queant, Gabriel Werner.

Undoubtedly one of the most important and influential films to emerge from the early 1960s, LAST YEAR AT MARIENBAD created a hotbed of discussion that has far outlived its original distribution. Working in close collaboration with Alain Robbe-Grillet, one of France's leading novelists and a spokesman for the "new novel" movement (Marguerite Duras, the scripter for HIROSHIMA MON AMOUR, was of a similar background), Resnais set out to scrutinize the barest elements of a film and in this manner redefine the rules that had such strong control over the narrative of cinema. Jean-Luc Godard's BREATHLESS, produced a year earlier, had approached the nature of film in a similar manner, yet without totally dissolving the narrative form as is done with LAST YEAR AT MARIENBAD. As in HIROSHIMA MON AMOUR, Resnais' concern is with the relationship between time, memory, and the imagination, and how these work in film structure, yet LAST YEAR AT MARIENBAD broke completely with the normal forms of cinematic narrative to create one of the hardest and most frustrating films to watch. Even those people who take pleasure in fitting narrative puzzles together were at a loss with what to do with this film. Nonetheless, MARIENBAD is still an immensely fascinating exercise, which upon viewing will change the way in which a person watches a film. What there is of a story takes place in one of those cold chateaus that were such popular meeting places for the upper-class elitists of an earlier generation. Albertazzi, denoted simply as X, comes across A (Seyrig), a woman he is positive he met the previous year at a different spa and had arranged to meet at the present time and place. Yet Seyrig is emphatic in denying that any such meeting ever took place, that she and Albertazzi ever had an affair, and suggests that they are, in fact, complete strangers. Albertazzi's attempts to convince Seyrig that such an event actually took place, will take place in the future, or should take place, is the minimal plot that takes up the duration of the film. Included in this love affair is the presence of Pitoeff, a man accompanying Seyrig at the chateau, and in all likelihood her husband, though this fact is one that is never fully revealed. Likewise, the viewer cannot be fully aware of whether Albertazzi and Seyrig met beneath the structures of the chateau before, or if the events Albertazzi is describing are simply images that are taking place inside his head. Adding to the ambiguous image is the voice of Albertazzi narrating as the camera wanders about the baroque corridors of the chateau, further enhancing the viewpoint that this entire film is simply a depiction of events as they occur inside Albertazzi's mind. Thus, the film's structure is one that most closely resembles the way the mind works, its recalling of past events in totally random fashion, the introduction of possible ways an event could have occurred, and at guessing (or dreaming) what will take place in the future. This can explain the seemingly unrelated juxtapositions of shots and fragments of speech that create the structure of LAST YEAR AT MARIENBAD. The viewer is left with a puzzle whose pieces need to be fitted together in order to attain a conclusion. Characters, plot, and emotional responses have all become secondary to what is on the screen at any precise moment, and to the manner Resnais has chosen to string these together. The elements of the cinema have been exposed at their barest minimum, the story a simple love triangle similar to those that had existed in theatrical film throughout its short history. Even the macho battle between Albertazzi and Pitoeff is one that takes on the form of a classic situation. Yet, though all the elements have been brought to extreme simplicity, performances are little more than statuesque poses. Dialog is delivered without inflection; every single shot is highly detailed, having the stamp of Resnais' keen sense of style. This makes LAST YEAR AT MARIENBAD a much more visual than narrative film, though many viewers insist that it is aimed solely at a highbrow literary audience. In fact, the opposite is true; the classical form of narrative storytelling that had so dominated film since its inception was precisely what Resnais and Robbe-Grillet wished to break away from. It was time the cinema became an art form which separated itself completely from the same rules which governed the novel. How successful they were with this little experiment is perhaps best revealed in the prominent styles of television commercials and music videos. Not exactly the most flattering responses to the intellectual genius of Resnais, but proof of the primacy of visuals over the spoken word in film syntax. (In French; English subtitles.)

p, Pierre Courau, Raymond Froment; d, Alain Resnais; w, Alain Robbe-Grillet; ph, Sacha Vierny (Dyaliscope); m, Francis Seyrig; ed, Henri Colpi, Jasmine Chasney; md, Andre Girard; art d, Jacques Saulnier; set d, Georges Glon, Andre Piltant, Jean-Jacques Fabre; cos, Bernard Evein, Chanel; makeup, Alexandre Marcus.

Drama   **Cas.**   **(PR:C MPAA:NR)**

L'ATALANTE***
(1947, Fr.) 89m J.L. Nounez/Argui bw (AKA: LE CHALAND QUI PASSE)

Michel Simon (Pere Jules), Jean Daste (Jean), Dita Parlo (Juliette), Gilles Margaritis (Peddler), Louis Lefevre (Cabin Boy), Fanny Clar (Juliette's Mother), Raphael Diligent (Juliette's Father), Maurice Gilles (Office Manager), Rene Bleck (Best Man), Charles Goldblatt (Thief), Jacques Prevert, Pierre Prevert (Extras at Station).

Vigo's poetic love story about the barge L'Atalante's captain (Daste), who marries an ordinary country girl (Parlo) and takes her with him as he sails. Bored with life on the barge, Parlo becomes anxious to see Paris. After arguing with Daste, she is befriended by his eccentric seamate Simon. Giving in to his wife's request, Daste

takes the girl to a cabaret in Paris where they meet a flirtatious peddler. The following day an angry and jealous Daste leaves the ship without his wife, who is later visited by the peddler. Upon Daste's return, the peddler is promptly thrown off L'Atalante. Parlo sneaks off to Paris, and when Daste notices she's gone he orders the barge to depart. She returns only to find that L'Atalante has set sail. Her purse having been stolen and with no way to catch up with the barge, Parlo takes a job in town. Meanwhile, Daste is too preoccupied with his lost love to man the barge properly and Simon takes over. Each of the lovers is shown restlessly suffering during their separation. Simon, tired of seeing Daste distraught, locates Parlo and returns her to L'Atalante for the splendid reunion. Vigo made only four films before his untimely death at age 29. This picture was his final one and also his masterpiece. It takes a simple love story and treats it in both a realistic and surrealistic manner by combining and contrasting styles. In one scene, Daste, stricken with loneliness, dives into the surrounding waters and sees an image of a smiling Parlo swimming in her wedding gown. An early scene has Simon (a French character actor who had previously worked for Jean Renoir) in perhaps the best role of his career. In it he shows Parlo his odd assortment of collectibles, including a pair of severed hands in a jar, kept as mementos of a dead friend. Upon its initial screening in 1934, L'ATALANTE received the same negative reaction as Vigo's ZERO FOR CONDUCT. The distributors (Gaumont, at the time) inserted a popular song, "Le Chaland Qui Passe" ("The Passing Barge") by Cesare Andrea Bixio and re-edited nearly all the scenes. The film was a box-office disaster, and three weeks later Vigo was dead. It wasn't until 1940 that Paris was to see a partially restored version. A complete version was finally constructed for the Biarritz Festival (a short-lived alternative to Cannes) thanks to Cinematheque Francais and Henri Langlois. After the negative response to ZERO FOR CONDUCT, Vigo reassured himself by stating (and this can easily be applied to all his films), "I knew I hadn't made a real film, like the others." L'ATALANTE isn't a film like the others, it's a masterpiece.

p, Jacques Louis Nounez; d, Jean Vigo; w, Vigo, Albert Riera (based on a scenario by Jean Guinee [R. de Guichen]); ph, Boris Kaufman; ed, Louis Chavance; m/l, Maurice Jaubert, Charles Goldblatt.

Romance   **Cas.**   **(PR:C MPAA:NR)**

LATE AT NIGHT*   (1946, Brit.) 69m Bruton Films/Premier bw

Daphne Day (Jill Esdaile), Barry Morse (Dave Jackson), Noel Dryden (Tony Cunningham), Paul Demel (The Spider), Don Avory, Monica Mallory, Paul Sheridan.

Poorly acted, directed, and scripted project taking the investigations of reporter Morse into an illegal booze production operation as the means to bore an audience for a little over an hour. In an incredibly unconvincing manner he hooks up with other members of the gang who seem overhappy to see the head of the operation receive his just rewards.

p, Herbert Wynne; d, Michael Corlton; w, Henry C. James; ph, Jan Sikorski.

Crime   **(PR:A MPAA:NR)**

LATE AUTUMN*   (1973, Jap.) 127m New Yorker c (AKIBIYORI)

Setsuko Hara (The Mother), Yoko Tsukasa (The Daughter), Chishu Ryu (The Uncle), Mariko Okada (The Daughter's Friend), Keiji Sada (The Young Man).

One of the final efforts from one of the great masters of Japanese cinema, Ozu, LATE AUTUMN was originally made in 1960 but not brought to the American shores until 10 years after the director's death. Tsukasa plays the daughter of Hara, a woman recently widowed who suddenly finds old friends of her husband taking an extreme interest in getting the daughter married. But Hara really does not seem all that interested in walking to the altar quite yet, something that shocks men bogged down in a tradition that does not have much place for a woman unless she is married. Eventually Hara does agree to marry, out of a desire to please the insistent elders, but her ideas of marriage are still something that seem quite obscure to the traditionalists. Ozu made 54 films in his long career, most marked by his subtle style which consisted of no camera movement and the placement of the camera only a few feet above the floor. He became quite a master in this technique that allowed him to place more concentration on plot and character development. The latter portion of his career saw Ozu extremely concerned about the effects of Westernization upon traditional Japan; in LATE AUTUMN this is shown in Hara's views that bring consternation to the elders. Yet she is so versed in traditional culture she is unable to make a total break from old values.

d, Yasujiro Ozu; w, Kogo Noda, Ozu; ph, Ushun Atsuta (Agfacolor); m, Takanobu Saito; art d, Tatsuo Hamada.

Drama   **(PR:A MPAA:NR)**

LATE EDWINA BLACK, THE   (SEE: OBSESSED, 1951, Brit.)

LATE EXTRA*1/2   (1935, Brit.) 69m FOX bw

Virginia Cherrill (Janet), James Mason (Jim Martin), Alastair Sim (Mac), Ian Colin (Carson), Clifford McLaglen (Weinhardt), Cyril Cusack (Jules), David Horne (Editor), Antoinette Cellier (Sylvia), Donald Wolfit (Inspector Greville), Hannen Swaffer (Himself), Ralph Truman, Andrea Malandrinos, Billy Shine, Desmond Tester, Michael Wilding.

Mason is a rookie reporter from the Daily Gazette who is trying to track down bank robber McLaglen. The newspaper offers a reward for his capture, prompting a woman to give some information, but she is killed before Mason gets to her. He finally catches up to McLaglen in Soho and turns him over to the police. Though he had made a number of appearances in films known as "quota quickies," this was the first real movie role for Mason, embarking upon a career that would last nearly half a century. Look for Elizabeth Taylor's second husband, Wilding, in a bit role before he became a polished leading man.

p, Ernest Garside; d, Albert Parker; w, Fenn Sherie, Ingram d'Abbes (based on a story by Anthony Richardson); ph, Alex Bryce.

Crime (PR:A MPAA:NR)

LATE GEORGE APLEY, THE**** (1947) 93m FOX bw

Ronald Colman *(George Apley)*, Peggy Cummins *(Eleanor Apley)*, Vanessa Brown *(Agnes)*, Richard Haydn *(Horatio Willing)*, Charles Russell *(Howard Boulder)*, Richard Ney *(John Apley)*, Percy Waram *(Roger Newcombe)*, Mildred Natwick *(Amelia Newcombe)*, Edna Best *(Catherine Apley)*, Nydia Westman *(Jane Willing)*, Francis Pierlot *(Wilson)*, Kathleen Howard *(Margaret)*, Paul Harvey *(Julian Dole)*, Helen Freeman *(Lydia)*, Theresa Lyon *(Chestnut Vendor)*, William Moran *(Henry Apley)*, Clifford Brooke *(Charles)*, David Bond *(Manager Of Modiste Shop)*, Diana Douglas *(Sarah)*, Ottola Nesmith *(Madame At Modiste Shop)*, Wyndham Standing, Stuart Hall *(Gentlemen)*, Mae Marsh *(Maid)*, Cordelia Campbell *(Child Skater)*, Richard Shaw *(Man)*, J. Pat Moriarity *(Policeman)*.

Content to live his happy home life, Colman was very choosy about his next project (after a couple of whopping flops) and by the time the script for this film hit his desk, he was ready. Until that time, he'd been busy with other endeavors and made it clear to the moviemakers that he would only accept the very best material and was not about to make more than one film per year. His desire for quality was more than fulfilled by THE LATE GEORGE APLEY, which had first been a best-selling Pulitzer Prize-winning novel, then was adapted into a play. Colman is Apley, a man who believes his beloved Boston to be the hub of the universe. He further thinks that any place not within 10 miles of Beacon Hill to be as savage as Borneo. Colman demands that his son, Ney, attend Harvard and that his daughter, Cummins, only marry a man who has grown up within earshot of the Charles Street Church. But as fate would have it, Ney falls for Brown, a girl from Worcester, and Cummins begins dating a man who is a "Yaley" (perish the thought!). What's a Brahmin to do? The situation is not hopeless, though, as Cummins' boy friend, Russell, does show some signs of culture by regularly quoting Emerson, Colman's favorite author. Ney is forbidden to marry his love and by film's end, we discern that he will wind up like his father, watching birds and upholding all the moral standards that their ancestors handed down. There are some similarities to LIFE WITH FATHER in that both leading men are concerned with the status quo. The treatment is different, though, as Colman's Apley is rather sympathetic underneath it all, while William Powell's Day was probably the same on the inside as he was on the outside. Colman also shows some concessions to change, much in contrast to the ultimate New Yorker, Clarence Day. As an Englishman, Colman had no problem slipping into the highbrow quasi-English accent of the Back Bay. On the stage, Leo G. Carroll played it even more clipped for greater humor. Cummins (an English import in her first U.S. film) is excellent and Ney, who later married Greer Garson and eventually gave up acting to become an investment counselor, does his best work. Natwick and Best score in the supporting cast and Haydn is superb as a prissy Boston type. It is said that Marquand pictured no one else but Colman to play his creation. His desire came to pass with excellent results although the film did not catch the eye of the Motion Picture Academy and no Oscar awards were given or nominated. Mankiewicz, who had been known primarily as a writer and producer before directing DRAGONWYCK, handles the directional chores with aplomb and keeps the comedy coming with regularity. Bostonians, who are notorious for not liking being spoofed, flocked to the theaters to see THE LATE GEORGE APLEY and laughed their heads off.

p, Fred Kohlmar; d, Joseph L. Mankiewicz; w, Philip Dunne (based on the novel by John P. Marquand and the play by Marquand and George S. Kaufman); ph, Joseph La Shelle; m, Cyril J. Mockridge; ed, James B. Clark; md, Alfred Newman; art d, James Basevi, J. Russell Spencer; set d, Edwin B. Willis, Paul Fox; cos, Rene Hubert; spec eff, Fred Sersen.

Comedy (PR:A MPAA:NR)

LATE LIZ, THE zero (1971) 119m Dick Ross/Gateway c

Anne Baxter *(Liz Addams Hatch)*, Steve Forrest *(Jim Hatch)*, James Gregory *(Sam Burns)*, Coleen Gray *(Sue Webb)*, Joan Hotchkis *(Sally Pearson)*, Jack Albertson *(Rev. Gordon Rogers)*, Eloise Hardt *(Laura Valon)*, Steve Dunne *(Si Addams)*, Reid Smith *(Alan Trowbridge)*, Bill [William] Katt *(Peter Addams)*, Ivor Francis *(Dr. Murray)*, Gail Bonney *(Maid)*, Jackson Bostwick *(Randall Trowbridge)*, Don Lamond *(Steve Blake)*, Buck Young *(Logan Pearson)*, Lee Delano *(Joe Vito)*, Virginia Capers *(Martha)*, Alvy Moore *(Bill Morris)*, Nancy Hadley *(Edie Morris)*, John Baer *(Arthur Bryson)*, Mark Tapscott *(Tony Webb)*.

A cliche-ridden film which casts Baxter as a high-society alcoholic who finds the strength to put down the bottle after seeking guidance from minister Albertson. She had found fulfillment in a life of empty bottles, bad marriages, and suicide attempts. May only be of interest to die-hard do-gooders. Actor Katt, boozer Baxter's second son, is in real life the son of players Bill Williams and Barbara Hale. He went on to appear in CARRIE (1976) and FIRST LOVE (1977).

p&d, Dick Ross; w, Bill Rega (based on an autobiography by Gert Behanna, pen name Elizabeth Burns); ph, Harry Stradling, Jr. (Metrocolor); m, Ralph Carmichael; ed, Mike Pozen; md, Carmichael; art d, Bill Malley; set d, James W. Payne; cos, Patricia Morris; makeup, Tom Ellingwood.

Religious Drama Cas. (PR:A MPAA:GP

LATE SHOW, THE* 1/2** (1977) 94m Lion's Gate/WB c

Art Carney *(Ira Wells)*, Lily Tomlin *(Margo Sperling)*, Bill Macy *(Charlie Hatter)*, Eugene Roche *(Ron Birdwell)*, Joanna Cassidy *(Laura Birdwell)*, John Considine *(Lamar)*, Ruth Nelson *(Mrs. Schmidt)*, John Davey *(Sgt. Dayton)*, Howard Duff *(Harry Regan)*.

A fine, overlooked film which paired Carney and Tomlin as a detective duo. It never caught on with audiences and by the time the word of mouth began, it was out of the theaters. Carney is an aging private eye who depressingly watches parts of his body begin to fail. One night, while relaxing at home, his former sidekick, Duff, shows up for a visit. The stay is short, however, as Duff has been the recipient of a large bullet wound. Carney goes out to avenge the death of his pal. Duff, it seems, had been on the trail of a missing cat, having been hired by Tomlin to find the far-ranging feline. The pussy had been catnaped by a former associate of Tomlin's. She's a personal manager, fence, dealer in stolen goods, and she'd held out on a payment to this guy, so he nabbed her pet. Macy is a pal of Duff's who prevails on Carney to take the case. Tomlin arranges a meeting with the catnaper for herself and Macy and Carney, but the guy is shot to death. Now they find some valuable stamps on his body, stamps that had been stolen from a wealthy collector whose wife was murdered during the theft. The trio figure that the dead man and his partner did that deed and that Duff was killed for trying to get his share of the proceeds. They break into the dead man's flat and find the cat, as well as Cassidy, the sexy wife of a fence, Roche. She admits that she and the stamp collector had been having an affair and that she'd come to the apartment to get Tomlin's late associate's associate, who had been blackmailing her. Now they find that guy dead in the refrigerator. Cassidy escapes and Tomlin and Carney pursue her in a chase through the city. Tomlin likes the experience and fancies herself and Carney as the new Mr. and Mrs. North or Nick and Nora Charles. When Carney understands that she is attracted to him, Carney exits. Later, Carney visits Roche and tells him that Cassidy was being blackmailed for having an affair. Roche now hires Macy to find a weapon before Carney does because he thinks that it may have been the gun that killed the stamp collector's wife in the robbery. Cassidy contacts Carney and they go to visit the collector, but he's dead as well. Tomlin finds the missing gun in her cat's carrying case, calls Carney, can't get him, so she calls Macy, who shows up post haste with Roche's henchman, Considine. They want the gun. Carney and Cassidy arrive and Carney sees there's danger here so he pretends he's having an ulcer attack, then uses the ruse to disarm Considine. With gun in hand, and in the best Holmesian tradition, Carney does the denouement and says that Cassidy arranged for her boy friend's wife's death, then faked the stamp robbery to establish a *raison morte*. Her boy friend balked and wanted to tell the police, so she killed him as well and attempted to put the frame on husband Roche. Roche, who killed Duff, was hip to that and wanted the murder weapon so he could hold it over Cassidy's head forever. Guns blast and Carney shoots Roche, Considine, and Macy. At Macy's funeral, Carney decides he's been alone too long and when he's invited to depart his furnished room, he rents the apartment next to Tomlin's. This should have been the first of many pictures with the duo, as they worked wonderfully together. Tomlin's quirky character could have been laughable and caricaturish but she went for the subtleties, under Benton's direction, and was charming. This was her second film, after NASHVILLE, and her first lead. Carney was superb in his return to the screen after having won the Oscar as Best Actor for HARRY AND TONTO. His portrayal of a man whose body is beginning to betray him and whose spirit won't throw in the towel is nothing short of elegant. A lovely film on many levels, it was Benton's second, and he showed immense sensitivity and the ability to spin a good yarn. We have to thank our stars above that the producer, Robert Altman, did not choose to also direct. All technical credits are excellent, particularly the sound, which in many of Altman's films is deliberately fuzzy and overlapped, in what he perceives to be a reflection of reality, when all it is is annoying.

p, Robert Altman; d&w, Robert Benton; ph, Chuck Rosher (Panavision, MGM Color); m, Ken Wannberg; ed, Lou Lombardo, Peter Appleton; set d, Bob Gould; m/l, "What Was," Wannberg, Stephen Lehner (sung by Bev Kelly); stunts, Paul Baxley; makeup, Monty Westmore.

Crime Cas. (PR:A-C MPAA:PG)

LATIN LOVE 1/2** (1930, Brit.) 85m GAU bw (GB: GREEK STREET)

Sari Maritza *(Anna)*, William Freshman *(Rikki)*, Martin Lewis *(Mansfield Yates)*, Berte Coote *(Sir George Ascot)*, Renee Clama *(Lucia)*, Bruce Winston *(Max)*, Peter Haddon, Rex Maurice, Stanelli *(Businessmen)*, Max Rivers' Trocadero Girls.

Freshman owns a small cafe where Maritza sings. Nightclub owner Lewis notices the talented woman and gives her both stardom and a fancy flat. Freshman becomes jealous despite her new-found fame and the attentions paid to her by Lewis. But as in all good musicals, Freshman and Maritza are reunited for a happy ending in this light, enjoyable formula piece. The Soho atmosphere gives the film some added appeal.

p, L'Estrange Fawcett; d, Sinclair Hill; w, Ralph Gilbert Bettinson, Leslie Howard Gordon (based on a story by Robert Stevenson); ph, Percy Strong.

Musical (PR:A MPAA:NR)

LATIN LOVERS*** (1953) 104m MGM c

Lana Turner *(Nora Taylor)*, Ricardo Montalban *(Roberto Santos)*, John Lund *(Paul Chevron)*, Louis Calhern *(Grandfather Santos)*, Jean Hagen *(Anne Kellwood)*, Eduard Franz *(Dr. Lionel Y. Newman)*, Beulah Bondi *(Woman Analyst)*, Joaquin Garay *(Zeca)*, Archer MacDonald *(Howard G. Hubbell)*, Dorothy Neumann *(Mrs. Newman)*, Robert Burton *(Mr. Cumberly)*, Rita Moreno *(Christina)*, Beatrice Gray *(Receptionist)*, Lois Kimbrell *(Secretary)*, Matt Moore *(Man)*, Gloria Noble, Lynn Sousa, Suzanne Alexander *(Brazilian Girls)*, Tristram Coffin *(Paul's Business Associate)*, Melba Meredith *(Mrs. Costa)*, Paul Maxey *(Mr. Costa)*.

Watching LATIN LOVERS is like sitting atop an enormous bowl of lush tropical fruits. An escapist movie from the first fade-in, it has everything you might want in a picture if you were trying to forget the travails of the day. Turner is a wealthy heiress ($37 million dollars worth) who can't decide whether men love her for herself or for her lucre. She has some funny scenes with her analyst, Franz, and his wife, Neumann, who makes some cogent comments on psychiatry. The quandary is bogus because her boy friend Lund, is richer than she is ($48 million, to be exact). Lund flies off to Brazil and she follows him, thinking that the new location might spice up their waning love life. Lund, it seems, is more interested in being a businessman than a swain. Once in Brazil, Turner meets Montalban, who is also wealthy but nowhere in the class of Lund or Turner. (Montalban replaced Fernando Lamas at the last minute because Turner and Lamas were making divorce noises at the time and the studio chiefs didn't want to jeopardize the film.) He sweeps Turner off her feet and pledges his Latin love to her. Lund reacts mildly and Turner responds to that ennui by handing all of her money over to Montalban because the cash has brought her nothing but self-doubt. Lund winds up with Hagen, Turner's secretary, and no loose end is left untied. There are any number of snappy song-and-dance numbers, one of which sees Montalban and Turner high-stepping with a great deal of finesse. And this is not easy for Montalban, who had a bout with polio (before the vaccine was discovered) and has managed to keep that slight disability under wraps. Turner is gorgeous and looks even better whenever Helen Rose does her costumes, which she did for this film. The Lennart dialog is as flowery as the background flora but not out of place for the situation and the settings. Lots of sidebar humor in the script, all well handled by the participants. The studio wanted to capitalize on Turner's popularity in THE BAD AND THE BEAUTIFUL so they even used that as the key line in the advertising for LATIN LOVERS. She was billed as "The Bad And Beautiful" girl, just in case anyone missed that. LeRoy did a competent directorial job and all supporting roles were well cast. The original choice for the Lund role was Michael Wilding, but he balked at being cast as a "second male lead" and stepped out just prior to shooting. The music is good and tinged with a Latin flavor, thanks to Stoll's musical direction and his treatment of the Brodszky-Robin tunes which included: "Night and You," "Carlotta, You Gotta Be Mine," "A Little More Of Your Amor," "Come To My Arms," "I Had To Kiss You." Even with those songs, LATIN LOVERS doesn't really qualify as one of MGM's super musicals. Instead, this is a romantic comedy with music and might have been just as successful without the songs. Look for Rita Moreno in a small role, before she catapulted to success in Broadway's "West Side Story." Montalban went on to become a star of TV, screen, and Chrysler commercials. Lamas divorced Turner to marry Arlene Dahl and fathered their son, Lorenzo, who has since become a TV star. After divorcing Dahl, he married another MGM star, Esther Williams, in 1967 and they swam happily together in their Beverly Hills home until his death in the mid-1980s. For the record, neither Lamas nor Montalban was Brazilian. Lamas was born in Buenos Aires, Argentina, and Montalban is from Mexico City. Set decorator Mapes later became a producer in association with his longtime pal, one-time B-musical star Ross Hunter.

p, Joe Pasternak; d, Mervyn LeRoy; w, Isobel Lennart; ph, Joseph Ruttenberg (Technicolor); m, Nicholas Brodszky; ed, John McSweeney, Jr.; md, George Stoll; art d, Cedric Gibbons, Gabriel Scognamillo; set d, Edwin B. Willis, Jacques Mapes; cos, Helen Rose, Herschel McCoy; spec eff, A. Arnold Gillespie, Warren Newcombe; ch, Frank Veloz; m/l, Brodszky, Leo Robin.

Musical/Comedy   **(PR:A MPAA:NR)**

LATIN QUARTER   (SEE: FRENZY, 1946, Brit.)

LATITUDE ZERO**
(1969, U.S./Jap.) 99m Toho-Don Sharp/NGP c (IDO ZERO DAISAKUSEN)

Joseph Cotten (*Capt. Craig McKenzie*), Cesar Romero (*Malic*), Richard Jaeckel (*Perry Lawton*), Patricia Medina (*Lucretia*), Linda Haynes (*Dr. Anne Barton*), Akira Takarada (*Dr. Ken Tashiro*), Masumi Okada (*Dr. Jules Masson*), Hikaru Kuroki (*Kroiga*), Mari Nakayama (*"Tsuroko" Okada*), Tetsu Nakamura (*Pirate*), Akihiko Hirata, Kin Omae.

A volcanic eruption causes an underwater exploration sub filled with Japanese scientists to lose instrument control. Sea captain Cotten rescues the crew and takes them to an underwater city devoted to humankind. Another Japanese scientist, the inventor of an anti-radiation serum, is the subject of a kidnaping plot by the wicked Romero, who plans to transplant the scientist's brain. In Cotten's attempt to rescue the kidnap victim, he is pitted against an entourage of giant rats, man-bats, and a flying lion which has the brain of Romero's one-time mistress. Of course, mankind is saved, thanks to Cotten's derring-do. A Jules Verne-styled picture from GODZILLA director Honda with some less-than-spectacular special effects from the normally convincing Tsuburaya.

p, Tomoyuki Tanaka; d, Inoshiro Honda; w, Ted Sherdeman, Shinichi Sekizawa (based on the "Latitude Zero" stories by Sherdeman); ph, Taiichi Kankura (Eastmancolor); m, Akira Ifukube; ed, Ume Takeda; set d, Takeo Kita; cos, Kiichi Ichida, Linda Glazman; spec eff, Eiji Tsuburaya.

Science Fiction   **(PR:AAA MPAA:G)**

L'ATLANTIDE, 1932, Ger.
(SEE: MISTRESS OF ATLANTIS, THE, 1932, Ger.)

L'ATLANTIDE, 1967, Fr./Ital.
(SEE: JOURNEY BENEATH THE DESERT, 1967, Fr./Ital.)

L'ATTENTAT   (SEE: FRENCH CONSPIRACY, THE, 1973, Fr.)

LAUGH AND GET RICH**
(1931) 72m RKO bw

Hugh Herbert (*Joe Austin*), Edna May Oliver (*Sarah Austin*), Dorothy Lee (*Alice Austin*), Robert Emmett Keane (*Phelps*), John Harron (*Hepburn*), Charles Sellon (*Biddle*), George Davis (*Vincentini*), Maude Fealy (*Miss Teasdale*), Russell Gleason (*Larry*), Louise MacIntosh, Lita Chevret, Joyce Davis.

Set in a boarding house, this domestic comedy casts Herbert as Oliver's well-meaning but lazy husband whose get-rich-quick schemes put pressure on their relationship. He steals Oliver's money to invest in oil, but instead makes a killing by backing an invention of his daughter's boy friend. Much of this limp comedy seemed old hat even in 1931. LaCava would go on to make much better, much faster-paced comedies.

p, Douglas MacLean; d, Gregory LaCava; w, LaCava, Ralph Spence (based on a story by MacLean); ph, Jack MacKenzie; ed, Jack Kitchen.

Comedy   **(PR:A MPAA:NR)**

LAUGH IT OFF*
(1939) 64m UNIV bw (GB: LADY BE GAY)

Johnny Downs (*Stephen Hannis*), Constance Moore (*Ruth Spencer*), Marjorie Rambeau (*Sylvia Swan*), Cecil Cunningham (*Tess Gibson*), Hedda Hopper (*Elizabeth Rockingham*), Janet Beecher (*Mary Carter*), Edgar Kennedy (*Judge McGuinnis*), Tom Dugan (*Rod Bates*), William Demarest (*Barney Cole*), Chester Clute (*Eliot Rigby*), Horace McMahon (*Phil Ferranti*), Paula Stone (*Linda Lane*), Lillian West (*Sarah*), Louise Bates (*Ellen*), Tony Cabooch (*Italian Man*), Jack Norton (*Drunk*), Alan Edwards (*Carter*), Tom Chatterton (*Politician*), Betty Roadman (*Woman at Apartment*), Danny Webb (*Indian Wahoo*), Ruth Rickaby (*Mrs. McGinnis*), John Dilson (*Swan*), Gertrude W. Hoffman (*Carrie*), Pat West (*Ice Cream Truck Driver*), Claire Whitney (*Miss Martin*), Jack Kenney (*Moving Man*), Brooks Benedict (*Croupier*), Dick Rush (*Plainclothesman*), Francis Sayles (*Clerk*), Charles McMurphy (*Cop*), Frank O'Connor (*Doorman*), Jack Gardner (*Reporter*).

Four unemployed showgirls find work when The Home for Retired Ladies goes bankrupt. They take over an ailing nightclub and revitalize their own careers by putting on a glamour-filled show. A collection of gangsters is tossed in for good measure (what would a nightclub be without them?). Songs include: "My Dream and I," "Doin' the 1940," "Laugh It Off," "Who's Gonna Keep Your Wigwam Warm?" (Sam Lerner, Ben Oakland).

p&d, Albert S. Rogell; w, Harry Clork, Lee Loeb (based on the story "Listen Kids" by Loeb, Mort Braus); ph, Stanley Cortez; ed, Milton Carruth; md, Charles Previn.

Musical   **(PR:A MPAA:NR)**

LAUGH IT OFF** 1/2
(1940, Brit.) 78m BN/Anglo bw

Tommy Trinder (*Tommy Towers*), Jean Colin (*Sally*), Anthony Hulme (*Lt. Somers*), Marjorie Browne (*Peggy*), Edward Lexy (*Sgt. Maj. Slaughter*), Ida Barr (*Mrs. McNab*), Charles Victor (*Colonel*), Peter Gawthorne (*General*), Wally Patch (*Sergeant*), Warren Jenkins (*Pat*), John Laurie (*Jock*), Geraldo and His Orchestra, Darville & Shires, The Three Maxwells, Joan Davis Dancers, Julias Ladies Choir, Sydney Burchell, Georgian Singers, The Scottish Sextette.

After WWII begins, British entertainer Trinder is drafted into service. He immediately falls on the bad side of his commanding officer Lexy, but after saving the camp show with his show-biz expertise, Trinder is granted a commission. This is a fairly entertaining effort, designed as a showcase for many talents in a glorious show of support for England's military forces. Though Trinder is billed as the star, the film is at its best when he is off-screen and the other talents strut their stuff.

p, John Corfield; d, John Baxter; w, Bridget Boland, Austin Melford (based on a story by Boland); ph, James Wilson.

Musical   **(PR:A MPAA:NR)**

LAUGH PAGLIACCI**
(1948, Ital.) 89m Itala/Continental bw

Alida Valli (*Julia*), Beniamino Gigli (*Morelli/Canio*), Paolo Hoerbiger (*Real-Life Canio*), Carlo Romano (*Leoncavallo*), Dagny Servaes (*Valmondi*), Adriana Perris (*Nedda*), Pacci (*Tonio*), Mario Boviello (*Silvio*), Adelio Zagonara (*Beppe*).

An operatic film which stars the young Valli (THE PARADINE CASE) as the daughter of Hoerbiger, a traveling clown who was convicted of murdering his wife and her lover. After serving a 20-year sentence, he sets out to find his daughter, locating her in the home of a wealthy woman. In order to make certain she will not turn him away, Hoerbiger has musician Romano compose an opera which tells his story. The girl sympathizes with the clown's fate, thereby securing the relationship between father and daughter. (In Italian: English subtitles.)

d, Giuseppe Fatigati; w, Cesare Viola; m, Ruggiero Leoncavallo, Gaetano Donizetti.

Opera   **(PR:A MPAA:NR)**

LAUGH YOUR BLUES AWAY*
(1943) 65m COL bw (AKA: LET'S HAVE FUN)

Jinx Falkenburg (*Pam Crawford/Olga*), Bert Gordon (*Boris Rascalnikoff*), Douglass Drake [Johnny Mitchell] (*Jimmy Westerly*), Isobel Elsom (*Mrs. Westerly*), Roger Clark (*Blake Henley*), George Lessey (*Mr. Westerly*), Vivian Oakland (*Mrs. Conklin*), Dick Elliott (*Mr. Conklin*), Phyllis Kennedy (*Priscilla Conklin*), Robert Greig (*Wilfred*), Frank Sully (*Buck*), Clyde Fillmore (*Senator Hargrave*), Barbara Brown (*Mrs. Hargrave*), Edna Holland (*Mrs. Watson*), Edward Earle (*Mr. Larkin*), Wyndham Standing (*Mr. Jamison*), Florence Wix (*Mrs. Jamison*), Walter Baldwin (*Clerk*), Eddie Kane (*Headwaiter*), John T. Murray (*Judge Watson*), Bess Flowers (*Mrs. Larkin*), Shirley Patterson (*Mrs. Knox*), Ken Christy (*Mr. Burke*), Louise Squires (*Blonde*), Hallene Hill (*Woman*), Eddie Laughton (*Man*), John Tyrell (*Decorator*), Joel Friedkin, James Morton, Earle Hodgins (*Actors*), Arthur A. Wenzel, Richard Robert Rinehart, Eugene Walsh, Jack Lewis (*Musicians*), Nora Lou [Martin] and the Pals of the Golden West.

A silly comedy which has Elsom trying to match her son Drake with Kennedy, the daughter of a wealthy Texas cattle tycoon. The conniving Elsom hires a couple of unemployed actors, Gordon and Falkenburg, to pose as members of Russian royalty in order to impress the Texans. Madcap romantic misfires occur with nobody marrying the person he was supposed to marry, but by the finale, everyone emerges unscathed. The picture was originally titled LET'S HAVE FUN, but that title was deferred to another Bert Gordon starrer released in 1943. Gordon, known as "the Mad Russian," was a popular radio comedian of the time. Some audiences felt that his role name was most appropriate: that the film was a crime and that they were undergoing considerable punishment. Songs include: "Dark Eyes," "Prairie Parade," "Down in the Heat of Smetna," "Gin Rhumba," "He's My Guy" (Larry Marks, Dick Charles).

p, Jack Fier; d, Charles Barton; w, Harry Sauber, Ned Dandy; ph, Philip Tannura; ed, Richard Fantl; art d, Lionel Banks, Paul Murphy.

Comedy   (PR:A MPAA:NR)

LAUGHING ANNE zero   (1954, Brit./U.S.) 90m Imperadio/REP c

Wendell Corey (Capt. Davidson), Margaret Lockwood (Laughing Anne), Forrest Tucker (Jem Farrell), Ronald Shiner (Nobby Clark), Robert Harris (Joseph Conrad), Jacques Brunius (Frenchie), Daphne Anderson (Blonde Singer), Helen Shingler (Susan Davidson), Danny Green (Nicholas), Harold Lang (Jacques), Edgar Norfolk (Conrad's Companion), Sean Lynch (David), Gerard Lohan (Davy), Andy Ho (Chinese Merchant), Maurice Bush (Battling Brunius), Dave Crowley (1st Boxer), Jack Cooper (2nd Boxer), Rudolph Offenbach (M.C.), Christopher Rhodes (1st Escort), John Serret (2nd Escort), Michael Oldham (3rd Escort), Bernard Robel (Pianist), Joe Powell (Pierre), Julian Sherier (Bartender), Nandi (Charlie).

A lifeless adaptation of Conrad's Between The Tides, set against the backdrop of the South Seas. Lockwood is a Parisian chanteuse who sets sail with her former boxer husband, Tucker. En route, she stows away on Corey's schooner, but when he proposes marriage, she goes running back to Tucker. Years later, the three come together again with Tucker planning to raid Corey's ship for a load of its silver. The twist ending has both Lockwood and Tucker getting killed, and Corey taking care of the couple's young son. Songs include: "I've Fallen in Deep Water" (Ted Grouya, Geoffrey Parsons), "All the World Is Mine on Sunday" (Pierre Roche, Parsons), both sung by Lockwood.

p, Herbert J. Yates, Herbert Wilcox; d, Wilcox; w, Pamela Wilcox Bower (based on the novel Between the Tides by Joseph Conrad); ph, Max Greene (Technicolor); m, Anthony Collins; ed, Basil Warren; ch, Philip and Betty Buchel.

Adventure   (PR:A MPAA:NR)

LAUGHING AT DANGER*¹/₂   (1940) 63m MON bw

Frankie Darro (Frankie Kelly), Joy Hodges (Mary Baker), George Houston (Dan Haggerty), Mantan Moreland (Jefferson), Kay Sutton (Mrs. Inez Morton), Guy Usher (Alvin Craig), Lillian Elliott (Mrs. Kelly), Veda Ann Borg (Celeste), Betty Compson (Mrs. Van Horn), Rolfe Sedan (Pierre), Maxine Leslie (Florence), Ralph Peters (Dugan), Gene O'Donnell (Chuck Benson).

A murder yarn set in a beauty parlor has the owners hiding microphones throughout the shop to record the incriminating chatter of the socialite customers. They proceed to use the recordings to blackmail the women. When a couple of murders and a suicide are mixed up with the blackmailing racket, it's up to Darro, the beauty shop page boy, and his bumbling assistant Moreland to get to the bottom of things—and save the day.

p, Lindsley Parsons; d, Howard Bretherton; w, John Krafft, Joseph West (based on a story by West); ph, Fred Jackman, Jr.; ed, Jack Ogilvie.

Mystery/Comedy   (PR:A MPAA:NR)

LAUGHING AT LIFE*¹/₂   (1933) 72m Mascot/Nat Levine bw

Victor McLaglen, Conchita Montenegro, William "Stage" Boyd, Lois Wilson, Henry B. Walthall, Regis Toomey, Ruth Hall, Dewey Robinson, Guinn Williams, Ivan Lebedeff, Mathilde Comont, Noah Beery, Tully Marshall, J. Farrell MacDonald, Henry Armetta, Edmund Breese, Frankie Darro, Buster Phelps, Pat O'Malley, William Desmond, Lloyd Whitlock, Philo McCullough, George Humbert.

A mercenary, who cares little for the feelings of his loved ones, leaves his wife and child to go off and fight. Years later, after establishing himself as a revolutionary leader in South America, he meets an engineer. This man (by the sheer coincidence that B movies seem to thrive on) just happens to be his son. Dumb and forgettable nonsense.

d, Ford Beebe; w, Prescott Chaplin, Thomas Dugan (based on a story by Beebe); ph, Ernie Miller, Tom Galligan; ed, Ray Snyder.

Drama/Adventure   (PR:A MPAA:NR)

LAUGHING AT TROUBLE**   (1937) 66m FOX bw

Jane Darwell (Glory Bradford), Sara Haden (Jennie Nevins), Lois Wilson (Alice Mathews), Margaret Hamilton (Lizzie Beadle), Delma Byron (Mary Bradford), Allan ["Rocky"] Lane (John Campbell), Pert Kelton (Ella McShane), John Carradine (Alec Brady), James Burke (Bill Norton), Russell Hicks (Cyrus Hall), Edward Acuff (Jamie Bradford), Frank Reicher (Dr. Larson), William Benedict (Wilbur), Edward McWade (Harvey).

A fairly engaging innocent-man-accused-of-murder film set against the background of a small-town newspaper. Publisher Darwell helps her niece's fiance, Lane, escape from jail and clear his name. She harbors the "criminal" in her home and then discovers the identity of the real killer, tricking him into a confession.

p, Max Golden; d, Frank R. Strayer; w, Robert Ellis, Helen Logan (based on a story by Adelyn Bushnell); ph, Barney McGill; ed, Nick DeMaggio; md, Samuel Kaylin.

Mystery   (PR:A MPAA:NR)

LAUGHING BOY*   (1934) 75m MGM bw

Ramon Novarro (Laughing Boy), Lupe Velez (Slim Girl), William B. Davidson (Hartshorne), Chief Thunderbird (Father), Catalina Rambula (Mother), Tall Man's Boy (Wounded Face), F.A. Armenta (Yellow Singer), Deer Spring (Squaw's Son), Pellicana (Red Man), Harlan Knight, Julius Bogua, Preston Scott.

An unintentionally funny film, and perhaps director Van Dyke's weakest picture. The film stars Novarro and Velez as an Indian couple whose Mexican accents and inability to act like Indians make them wildly inappropriate for their roles. The story, which was cut in a few spots by 1934 censors, concerns Velez as the Indian maiden who wishes to live as the white folks do. She marries Novarro, but has an affair with a white man. Novarro discovers Velez in the arms of the white man and shoots an

arrow at him. He hits Velez by accident and she dies in front of the two men she loves. Based on the Pulitzer Prize-winning novel of 1929.

p, Hunt Stromberg; d, W.S. Van Dyke; w, John Colton, John Lee Mahin (based on the novel by Oliver La Farge); ph, Lester White; m, Herbert Stothart; ed, Blanche Sewell; m/l, Gus Kahn, Stothart.

Drama   (PR:A MPAA:NR)

LAUGHING IN THE SUNSHINE*¹/₂
                    (1953, Brit./Swed.) 81m Martin Films-Swint Films/UA c

Jane Hylton (Princess), Bengt Logardt (Gustav), Peter Dyneley, Gene Anderson, Marjorie Fielding, Adolf Jahr, Stanley Maxted.

It is the old story of prince meeting princess, and falling in love without realizing they have royal blood. Hylton is the princess on vacation in Sweden when she runs into Logardt, establishing the usual apprehensions about falling in love with a commoner. The color photography by Nykvist (known primarily for his work with Ingmar Bergman) is the highlight of this film.

p, John Martin; d, Dan Birt; w, Tim Carew (based on the play by Sven Cederstrand); ph, Sven Nykvist.

Drama   (PR:A MPAA:NR)

LAUGHING IRISH EYES**   (1936) 70m REP bw

Phil Regan (Danno O'Keefe), Walter C. Kelly (Pat Kelly), Evalyn Knapp (Peggy Kelly), Ray Walker (Eddie Bell), Mary Gordon (Mrs. O'Keefe), Warren Hymer (Tiger O'Keefe), Betty Compson (Molly), J.M. Kerrigan (Tim), Herman Bing (Weisbecher), Raymond Hatton (Gallagher), Clarence Muse (Deacon), Russell Hicks (Silk), Maurice Black (Tony), John Indrisano, John Sheehan, Robert E. Homans.

Regan plays an Irish blacksmith with aspirations of being a singer. When American fight promoter Kelly goes to Ireland to find a topnotch boxer, he mistakenly picks Regan who is quickly shuffled off to the States and given a chance in the ring. He soon ends up with the middleweight title, as well as Kelly's daughter Knapp. Nothing new here, but the performances are authentic and the fight scenes leave you pulling for Regan. Songs include: "All My Life," "Bless You Darling Mother," "Laughing Irish Eyes" (Sidney Mitchell, Sammy Stept, sung by Regan), and "Londonderry Air."

p, Colbert Clark; d, Joseph Santley; w, Olive Cooper, Ben Ryan, Stanley Rauh (based on a story by Sidney Sutherland, Wallace Sullivan); ph, Milton Krasner, Reggie Lanning; ed, Joseph H. Lewis, Murray Seldeen.

Drama/Musical   (PR:A MPAA:NR)

LAUGHING LADY, THE**   (1930) 77m PAR bw

Ruth Chatterton (Marjorie Lee), Clive Brook (Daniel Farr), Dan Healy (Al Brown), Nat Pendleton (James Dugan), Raymond Walburn (Hector Lee), Dorothy Hall (Flo), Hedda Harrigan (Cynthia), Lillian B. Tonge (Parker), Marguerite St. John (Mrs. Playgate), Herbert Druce (Hamilton Playgate), Alice Hegeman (Mrs. Collop), Joe King (City Editor), Helen Hawley (Rose), Betty Bartley (Barbara).

Well-acted film that stars Chatterton as a high-society woman who's often in the headlines and more gets written when she nearly drowns at a beach party. She is rescued by a handsome lifeguard, who later seduces her, causing her husband to file for divorce. Brook plays her mate's attorney who ends up falling for the charms of Chatterton. It's all very high class deportment on a barnyard theme. A remake of the 1924 silent Gloria Swanson vehicle, A SOCIETY SCANDAL.

d, Victor Schertzinger; w, Bartlett Cormack, Arthur Richman (based on a story by Alfred Sutro); ph, George J. Folsey.

Drama   (PR:A MPAA:NR)

LAUGHING LADY, THE**   (1950, Brit.) 100m BN/Four Continents c

Anne Ziegler (Denise Tremayne), Webster Booth (Andre), Francis L. Sullivan (Sir William Tremayne), Peter Graves (Prince of Wales), Chili Bouchier (Louise), Felix Aylmer (Sir Felix Mountroyal), Ralph Truman (Lord Mandeville), Charles Goldner (Robespierre), Jack Melford (Lord Barrymore), Paul Dupuis (Pierre), John Ruddock (Gilliatt), George de Warfaz (Tinville), Mary Martlew (Lady Langley), Frederick Burtwell (Jenkins), Hay Petrie (Tom), Anthony Nicholls (Mr. Pitt), D. Whittingham (Highwayman), Hay Petrie (Tom the Coachman), John Serret (Dumas, President of the Tribunal), Clare Lindsay (Duchess of Loraine), Capt. Younghusband (Garrat), Harry Fine (O'Hara), Griffiths Moss (Major Domo No. 1), Geoffrey Wilmer (Gaoler), Laurence Archer (St. Juste), James Hayter (Ostler, Turk's Head), John Clifford (1st Flunkey, Great Dene), Hugh Owens (Major Domo, Royal Pavilion), Harry Terry (Watchman, Knightsbridge), Robert Conner (Executioner), George Dudley (1st Judge), Maurice Bannister (2nd Judge), Yulius Dobringer (Priest), Willi Werder (Brigoyne the French Coachman), E. Francois (Potman), Andre Belhomme (2nd Flunkey, Great Dene), Beatrice Campbell.

Set during the French Revolution, this British musical casts Goldner as the murderous Robespierre. Before guillotining a duchess, he makes a deal with her son, Booth. If he can travel to England and locate a pearl necklace given as a gift to Marie Antoinette, his mother will not get her head lopped off. He falls in love with Ziegler, who now has the necklace, a gift from her future husband, the Prince of Wales. Booth decides not to return the pearls to Goldner, but eventually Ziegler brings them to France herself. Released in England in 1946.

p, Louis H. Jackson; d, Paul L. Stein; w, Jack Whittingham (based on a play by Ingram d'Abbes); ph, Geoffrey Unsworth (Technicolor); m, Hans May; ed, Alan Osbiston; md, May, art d, R. Holmes Paul; ch, Eileen Baker; portrait painted by James Proudfoot.

Musical/Drama   (PR:A MPAA:NR)

LAUGHING POLICEMAN, THE** ½

(1973) 111m FOX c (GB: AN INVESTIGATION OF MURDER)

Walter Matthau *(Jake Martin)*, Bruce Dern *(Leo Larsen)*, Lou Gossett *(Larrimore)*, Albert Paulsen *(Camerero)*, Anthony Zerbe *(Lt. Steiner)*, Val Avery *(Pappas)*, Cathy Lee Crosby *(Kay Butler)*, Mario Gallo *(Bobby Mow)*, Joanna Cassidy *(Monica)*, Shirley Ballard *(Grace Martin)*, William Hansen *(Schwermer)*, Jonas Wolfe *(Collins)*, Paul Koslo *(Havgood)*, Lou Guss *(Gus Niles)*, Lee McCain *(Prostitute)*, David Moody *(Pimp)*, Ivan Bookman *(Rodney)*, Cliff James *(Maloney)*, Gregg Sierra *(Vickery)*, Warren Finnerty *(Ripple)*, Matt Clark *(Coroner)*, Joe Bernard *(Avakian's Brother)*, Melvina Smedley *(Maydola)*, Leigh French *(Porno Cashier)*, Jim Clawin *(Fowler)*, Tony Costello *(Dave Evans)*, John Francis *(Russo)*, John Vick *(Terry)*, Wayne Grace *(Brennan)*, Cheryl Christiansen *(Nurse)*, Jimmy Christy *(Avakian)*, Dave Belrose *(Ralph Martin)*, Dawn Frame *(Debbie Martin)*, Ellen Nance, Lavelle Robey *(Receptionists)*, Hobart Nelson *(Jail Guard)*, Gus Bruneman *(Squad Captain)*, The San Francisco Strutters.

Although an extremely violent movie, one not for youngsters, the pace and literate script, coupled to Matthau's top performance, make this crime yarn appealing. A bloody prolog soaks the screen with gore as a busload of people are slaughtered on a San Francisco street. Enter police detective Matthau who has been recently teamed with new partner Dern, both opposites and clashing from the beginning. Matthau is the laughing cop who finds less and less to guffaw about as the investigation takes him and Dern through homosexual cesspools in search of a cop killer. Paulsen, a wealthy gay with a taste for violence, is finally tracked down as the culprit but not before a number of chases and shootouts ensue. Matthau's offbeat humor is a saving factor in an otherwise repulsive setting. Dern gives his usual "I dont't give a damn" performance. Dern, with his rodent-like expressions, arrogant attitude, and monotone nasal delivery is an actor who is fascinating for his lack of ability, and how he has managed to glean one sizable part after another with a minimum of talent is a perplexity of casting. Obnoxious, unappealing, and definitely on the weird side, Dern has managed to give the impression that he represents an element of enviable nonconformity in present day filmmaking when, in truth, he is only obnoxious, unappealing, and weird.

p&d, Stuart Rosenberg; w, Thomas Rickman (based on the novel by Per Wahloo, Maj Sjowall); ph, David Walsh (DeLuxe Color); m, Charles Fox; ed, Robert Wyamn; set d, Doug Von Koss.

Crime Drama **Cas.** **(PR:O MPAA:PG)**

LAUGHING SINNERS** (1931) 71m MGM bw

Joan Crawford *(Ivy Stevens)*, Neil Hamilton *(Howard Palmer)*, Clark Gable *(Carl Loomis)*, Marjorie Rambeau *(Ruby)*, Guy Kibbee *(Cass Wheeler)*, Cliff Edwards *(Mike)*, Roscoe Karns *(Fred Geer)*, Gertrude Short *(Edna)*, George Cooper *(Joe)*, George F. Marion *(Humpty)*, Bert Woodruff *(Tink)*, Henry Armetta *(Tony The Chef)*, Lee Phelps *(Salesman)*.

LAUGHING SINNERS had already finished shooting when the studio bosses saw the response to Gable as Crawford's man in DANCE, FOOLS, DANCE, so they cut all the already-shot footage with Johnny Mack Brown and re shot the scenes with Gable, who was billed under Neil Hamilton. Crawford is a nightclub thrush who gets tossed aside by a shifty traveling salesman, Hamilton, whom she thinks the sun rises and falls upon. When he dumps her, she thinks there's nothing left to live for so she takes a dive off a bridge into the local river. Gable, a Salvation Army worker, saves her and begins to redo her life. Under his tutelage, she forswears the nightery existence and begins to work next to him in his evangelistic occupation. Soon enough, she's also in uniform, pounding the tambourine on street corners. All is well until she again meets Hamilton at a local hotel and her passion for him outstrips her good sense. It isn't long before she's in Hamilton's power. Gable breaks in on the two of them, knocks Hamilton for a loop, then says he's willing to take Crawford back into his life if she's willing to try it again. Crawford understands that a life with Hamilton would only wind her up in the river she'd been rescued from in reel one, so she tosses him aside and goes off with Gable. The picture was originally released as COMPLETE SURRENDER before Thalberg saw sparks in the Crawford-Gable combination and ordered the new scenes. The two were having an off-screen romance at the time and that could readily be recognized on the screen. Crawford was a blonde for LAUGHING SINNERS and, as a woman of easy morals, was in training for the part that would make her an international star in RAIN, the following year. "What Can I Do? I Love That Man" is sung well by Crawford, who was a musical performer before giving her vocal cords a rest as a dramatic actress. The play upon which this was based was not a hit, so one wonders why they chose to make it as a film.

d, Harry Beaumont; w, Bess Meredyth, Martin Flavin, Edith Fitzgerald (based on the play "Torch Song" by Kenyon Nicholson); ph, Charles Rosher; ed, George Hively; m/l, Martin Broones, Arthur Freed.

Drama **(PR:C MPAA:NR)**

LAUGHTER**** (1930) 85m PAR bw

Fredric March *(Paul Lockridge)*, Nancy Carroll *(Peggy Gibson)*, Frank Morgan *(C. Mortimer Gibson)*, Glenn Anders *(Ralph Le Saint)*, Diane Ellis *(Marjorie Gibson)*, Leonard Carey *(Benham)*, Ollie Burgoyne *(Pearl)*.

Director and co-story writer D'Arrast had a brief career that included a stint with Chaplin. If he did nothing else but work on LAUGHTER, his place in movie history should be secure. This is a dandy, far ahead of its time in content, photography, and style. Carroll is a dancer in The Follies surrounded by amorous stage-door Johnnies. She gives them all up in favor of Morgan, a multimillionaire who denies her nothing. Composer March, a one-time suitor, is stunned and travels to Paris to forget. Morgan spends too much time watching ticker tapes instead of Carroll, so she seeks new ways to relieve her loneliness and has her limousine take her to Greenwich Village where she visits Anders, also a former beau. Anders is a sculptor who has had little success and when she arrives, he's just destroyed a statue and has finished penning a suicide note. He is very depressed but Carroll's appearance helps him out of his torpor. Then Ellis, Morgan's daughter by a former marriage, comes home from Europe. Carroll meets her at the ocean liner's dock and the two women, who are close in age, become fast friends. March comes home from Paris and seeks to reawaken his relationship with Carroll. In the beginning, she tries to stay away from him, but he is so charming that she is soon seeing him on the side, while Morgan sits with his stock quotations. March sees that Carroll no longer has the old *joie de vivre* and encourages her to put some laughter back into her now-barren life. Meanwhile, Anders and Ellis also meet and they are soon attracted to each other. March and Carroll are riding in the country when a sudden rainstorm causes them to seek shelter in a small, empty house, as they run out of gas. They have to remove their clothes and dry off. While doing that, they are seen by local people and the village police arrest them for breaking and entering. They are taken to the small town's hoosegow and Carroll has to embarrassedly ask Morgan for the needed money to get them out of jail. Evidently Morgan's name is important enough to quash the problem and they are soon back in the city. There's a huge ball at the Morgan mansion and Carroll sees Ellis get a phone call, then surreptitiously slip away. Carroll quietly tails Ellis to Anders' flat and now learns that the two lovebirds mean to wed. Carroll suspects that Anders is marrying her stepdaughter because he can't have her, so she takes a bold step and makes Anders state publicly that Ellis is his one true love. Anders cannot answer and Ellis is enraged at Carroll's behavior so she slaps her and exits. Anders picks up a gun and threatens to kill Carroll but doesn't. When she leaves his building, she hears a shot. Anders has killed himself, something he's planned from the first reel. The cops are called in and Carroll is grilled but they believe, quite rightly, that Anders took his own life. By the time Carroll returns home, the press is already there, having heard via the radio of Anders' death and her involvement with it. Morgan wants an explanation and she tells him that she is leaving him. Morgan is thunderstruck and offers her anything she wants to stay, but she says she needs the one commodity that money can't buy, love. She leaves that night with March on an ocean liner and the last scene shows them sharing champagne on a wide Parisian street with her laughing once more. This could have been as soapy as a tubful of Tide, but it was swiftly and funnily paced with a patina of sophistication that didn't arrive in other movies until Lubitsch came on the horizon. March is elegant, Carroll is sweet, the script crackles with pointed wit, and everything works. A neglected film from a neglected director, LAUGHTER has lost none of the luster that it had almost six decades ago. It could be shown today and never have the feeling that it was made when Herbert Hoover was president.

d, Harry D'Abbadie D'Arrast; w, Donald Ogden Stewart (based on a story by D'Abbadie D'Arrast, Douglas Doty); ph, George Folsey; ed, Helene Turner; m/l, "Little Did I Know," Irving Kahal, Pierre Norman, Sammy Fain.

Comedy/Drama **(PR:A-C MPAA:NR)**

LAUGHTER IN HELL* (1933) 68m UNIV bw

Pat O'Brien *(Barney Slaney)*, Tom Conlon *(Barney Slaney as a Boy)*, Merna Kennedy *(Marybelle Evans)*, Berton Churchill *(Mike Slaney)*, Gloria Stuart *(Lorraine)*, Tom Brown *(Barton)*, Lew Kelly *(Mileaway)*, Arthur Vinton *(Grover Perkins)*, Mickey Bennett *(Grover Perkins as a Boy)*, Clarence Muse *(Jackson)*, Douglas Dumbrille *(Ed Perkins)*, Dick Winslow *(Ed Perkins as a Boy)*, Noel Madison *(Brownfield)*, Tom Ricketts *(Judge)*, William H. Turner *(I.N. Tree)*.

A tolerable chain-gang drama with a great title. O'Brien stars as a tough Irishman who murders his wife and her lover, a deed which sends him to prison. He runs into more trouble in the lockup, when he discovers that the lover's brother, Dumbrille, is the hard-edged warden. An escape follows, but O'Brien fares no better after hiding out in a house contaminated with a contagious fever. Eventually, thanks to the help of Stuart, a happy fate does lie in store for O'Brien.

d, Edward L. Cahn; w, Tom Reed, Russell Hopton (based on a story by Jim Tully); ph, John Stumar.

Drama **(PR:A MPAA:NR)**

LAUGHTER IN PARADISE** ½

(1951, Brit.) 94m Transocean/ABF-Pathe bw

Alastair Sim *(Deniston Russell)*, Fay Compton *(Agnes Russell)*, Beatrice Campbell *(Lucille Grayson)*, Veronica Hurst *(Joan Webb)*, Guy Middleton *(Simon Russell)*, George Cole *(Herbert Russell)*, A.E. Matthews *(Sir Charles Robson)*, Joyce Grenfell *(Elizabeth Robson)*, Anthony Steel *(Roger Godfrey)*, John Laurie *(Gordon Webb)*, Eleanor Summerfield *(Sheila Wilcott)*, Ronald Adam *(Mr. Wagstaffe)*, Leslie Dwyer *(Police Sergeant)*, Ernest Thesiger *(Endicott)*, Hugh Griffith *(Henry Russell)*, Michael Pertwee *(Stuart)*, Audrey Hepburn *(Cigarette Girl)*, Mackenzie Ward *(Benson)*, Charlotte Mitchell *(Ethel)*, Colin Gordon, Mary Germaine, Noel Howlett, Martin Boddey.

Keen pacing and a fresh, witty script are two of the factors which helped this amusing British comedy become that country's top moneymaker in 1951. A practical joker leaves $140,000 to each of four relatives with the condition that they must follow specific instructions. Compton, his sister, has the tables turned on her; instead of bossing maids around, she must become one for 28 days. Likewise, cousin Sim, who writes trashy crime novels, must spend that many days in prison to receive his share. Cole, a meek bank clerk, has to perform a daring robbery of his bank. The last to be included is Middleton, who must put aside his playboy habits and marry the first girl he meets. Audrey Hepburn appears in a minor role as a cigarette girl.

p&d, Mario Zampi; w, Michael Pertwee, Jack Davies; ph, William McLeod; m, Stanley Black; ed, Giulio Zampi; art d, Ivan King.

Comedy **(PR:AA MPAA:NR)**

LAUGHTER IN THE AIR (SEE: MYRT AND MARGE, 1934)

LAURA***** (1944) 88m FOX bw

Gene Tierney *(Laura Hunt)*, Dana Andrews *(Mark McPherson)*, Clifton Webb *(Waldo Lydecker)*, Vincent Price *(Shelby Carpenter)*, Judith Anderson *(Ann Treadwell)*, Dorothy Adams *(Bessie Clary)*, James Flavin *(McAvity)*, Clyde Fillmore *(Bullitt)*, Ralph Dunn *(Fred Callahan)*, Grant Mitchell *(Corey)*, Kathleen Howard *(Louise)*, Harold Schlickenmayer, Harry Strang, Lane Chandler *(Detectives)*, Frank La Rue *(Hairdresser)*, Alexander Sacha, Dorothy Christy, Aileen Pringle, Terry Adams, Jean Fenwick, Yolanda Lacca, Forbes Murray, Cyril Ring, Nester Eristoff, Kay Linaker, Cara Williams, Gloria Marlin, Beatrice Gray, Kay Connors, Frances Gladwin, William Forrest *(People)*, Buster Miles *(Office Boy)*, Jane Nigh *(Secretary)*, John Dexter *(Jacoby)*.

Undoubtedly one of the most stylish and taut murder mysteries ever put on film, LAURA presents stunning performances from Tierney, Andrews, Price, and Anderson. And, in one of the most delectable roles of his career, Webb, as a monied, pampered, self-loving cynical columnist, along with Preminger's deft direction and La Shelle's marvelous lensing (which won an Oscar), makes this film a must for any lover of *film noir*. Its face destroyed by a blast from a shotgun, a body is discovered in Tierney's apartment by her maid. Police detective Andrews begins his investigation into Tierney's death by interviewing a group of prominent but distasteful citizens, not the least of whom is the acerbic-minded Webb, a deft and powerful columnist whom Andrews finds writing in his bathtub. Webb relates how Tierney first approached him in the Algonquin Hotel dining room, asking him to endorse a pen her ad agency was promoting. In a flashback we see Tierney being refused by the arrogant Webb, who is nevertheless attracted by her ravishing beauty. He later appears at her agency and apologizes, then makes her his protege, promoting her career and taking bows for her success. Webb goes on to relate how, using his waspish intellectuality, he was able to dominate Tierney, as well as drive off any potential suiter, all except witty playboy Price, whom Webb detests. Andrews next visits Tierney's rich spinster aunt, Anderson, who admits that even though Price was engaged to Tierney he was seeing her. The detective, who visits Tierney's apartment several times and becomes enamored of the dead woman, fascinated by her portrait, later learns that Price, her fiance, was also seeing a model named Diane Redfern. Later confronted with this fact, callous cad Price admits to philandering about with many females while stringing the lovely Tierney along. Andrews, once more back at Tierney's apartment, is shocked to see the murder victim walk through the door, returning from a country vacation. He explains that she was supposed to be murdered and it is later revealed that the real victim was the model Redfern. Later Andrews compels Price to come clean; the playboy confesses that he had taken Redfern to Tierney's apartment but when someone rang the doorbell, he hid in a closet and the model opened the door. He then heard a shot and found Redfern dead, then he was afraid to reveal what happened to police lest he be thought the killer. He admits that he fled and kept silent about the murder, hoping Tierney would later return and the real killer would be identified. Tierney at first is testy with the probing Andrews but she later comes to love him. Her reincarnation shocks everyone; when Webb comes into her apartment and sees her alive he faints dead away. In a surprise move, Andrews arrests Tierney for the Redfern killing, but he later tells her that he really does not intend to charge her, that he wants to draw out the actual murderer. He takes her home and later returns to find Webb there. Both men begin to argue, Webb obviously incensed at the attention Tierney shows to Andrews. Webb leaves in a huff. Later, Andrews finds the shotgun used to kill Redfern, hidden by Webb in the base of a grandfather clock. Andrews explains to Tierney that Webb meant to kill her but mistook Redfern in the dark and believed he had murdered Tierney, killing her in a jealous rage over her engagement to ne'er-do-well Price. Andrews then leaves Tierney alone, using her as bait, believing that Webb will attempt to kill the woman he loves once again, this time because she's in love with Andrews. He's right. Webb does act, but first he prepares a clever alibi. Instead of giving his weekly broadcast live, he runs a tape from an earlier program so that Andrews will believe he's at the station. Then he goes to Tierney's apartment, retrieves the shotgun, loads it, and casually walks into her bedroom as she is preparing to retire. Andrews by this time is on to Webb and arrives at the last minute, Tierney running into his arms just as Webb wheels about and fires, blowing away the clock. Andrews and other detectives shoot the berserk columnist as he marches forward, firing the other barrel. Webb falls dead, uttering Tierney's name. LAURA is an unusual *film noir* entry in that it is, at the beginning, actually narrated by the killer, Webb, who has begun to write Tierney's life story at the start of the film. Moreover, Webb half admires Andrews, the detective, when meeting him, having written about Andrews' former exploits with criminals and himself being a devout criminologist on the amateur side. He, like many an egotistical real-life killer, offers to help Andrews in his investigation. He tells Andrews arrogantly while dressing: "How singularly innocent I look this morning. Have you ever seen such candid eyes?" When he tells Andrews he had, for Tierney's sake, become "the kindest, gentlest, the most sympathetic man in the world," he adds: "I should be sincerely sorry to see my neighbors' children devoured by wolves." Webb takes exception to Andrews' tone and demeanor, sneering when telling Tierney later: "A *dame* in Washington Heights once got a fox fur out of him!" Everywhere Andrews goes there is the image of the lovely, radiant Tierney and he is greeted by the great theme song "Laura" written by Raksin especially for the film. It's played on records, by string quartets in restaurants. The Webb character is also present in one form or another in every scene, representing the superior airs of New York's *haute societe*, right from the beginning when he tells Tierney that he writes "with a goose quill dipped in venom." His is the world of wit, wisdom, the bon mot, the cleverly turned phrase and his overall character is highly reminiscent of the acerbic-tongued New York critic Alexander Woollcott, who presided at the famous Algonquin "Round Table." (The scene where Webb is seated at the most advantageous table at the Algonquin dining room is not without an endorsement of the Woollcott character.) Making this murder mystery all the more fascinating is that it does not occur in dingy, dark rooms or damp back alleys, but in the svelte world of the upper crust, within the privileged ranks of Manhattanites where such ugly works of the lower classes rarely occur. And it is the allure of this world, along with Tierney's beauteous mystique staring down from her portrait, that obsesses Andrews. In one scene he visits her apartment, stares at the portrait, then takes off his coat, sits in front of it nervously smoking a cigarette. Then he goes into her bedroom, inspects her closets, smells her perfume, then out to the living room to pour himself a stiff drink, a taut scene which graphically shows how much he desires this dead girl, an almost perverted obsession bordering on necrophilia. Webb himself points this out to Andrews when saying: "Ever strike you—that you're acting strangely? . . . You'll end up in a psychiatric ward. I don't think they've ever had a patient who fell in love with a corpse." The pervasive presence of Tierney is only superceded by that of her sophisticated, self-loving Svengali, Webb, who loves only one thing more in life, Tierney, and will do anything to keep her, his creation, to himself. He finds her dating another writer and destroys the man in print. When she becomes engaged to Price he prepares a dossier on his background, telling her how Price bounced checks and took money from every woman he ever deceived. When he learns that Price is seeing Anderson on the side, he takes Tierney to her aunt's apartment and shows her the two dining together. Price at that time is smooth as silk, telling Tierney that he was only dining with Anderson to inform her of the impending marriage between himself and Tierney. Snorts Webb: "In a moment of supreme disaster, he's trite." Webb, of course, is never at a loss for a brilliant retort, even when trapped, reveling in his own narcissism. "In my case," he says, "self-absorption is justified." His supreme self confidence is his own undoing. Webb tips his hand in another scene to Andrews by announcing in front of Andrews, Anderson, and Price that, since Tierney is now dead, he intends to reclaim certain priceless items he "only lent" to Tierney, mentioning a vase, fire screen, and the grandfather clock, the latter being the place where he has hidden the murder weapon. He is so insistent on taking back these items that the cool, shrewd Andrews, the man of the people who triumphs in the end over the superior, intellectual elitist, cannot help but investigate the clock and he finds the shotgun used to kill the hapless Miss Redfern, a woman never seen on the screen, even as a corpse. Andrews further compounds the puzzle for the viewer when telling Tierney upon her return from the country where she has been incommunicado that he "suspects nobody and everybody," including her. (This was a line to be oft-repeated in detective films for decades to come, used to comedic heights by Peter Sellers as the inept Inspector Clouseau in the PINK PANTHER series.) There is much debate to this day regarding the true genius behind this classic film, either director Preminger, who produced the film and selected the Caspary novel from the start for Fox, or Rouben Mamoulian who was first assigned the directorial role for the film and was later removed by Fox mogul Darryl Zanuck. Preminger had been brought from Austria in 1935 to Hollywood by super mogul Joseph Schenck; he had been a theater director but Schenck thought he would be perfect as a film director and he went to work at Fox where Zanuck, who immediately disliked his German ways, assigned him to several low-budget films, finally giving him KIDNAPPED (1938) to helm. But Zanuck, viewing the rushes for KIDNAPPED, took issue with a ridiculous point in the script, asking Preminger why he didn't follow a scene where the script indicated that Freddie Bartholomew was to speak to his dog. Preminger denied that such a scene was ever written and Zanuck fired him on the spot, replacing him with a mediocre director, Alfred L. Werker. When Zanuck went into the service during WW II, the studio was guided by William Goetz, who allowed Preminger to act in and direct a substantial film, MARGIN FOR ERROR, giving him a seven-year contract at Fox. This irked Zanuck no end when he returned from the service. Meanwhile, Preminger read the Caspary novel and went to B production chief Bryan Foy, telling him he wanted to produce and direct the film. Goetz and Zanuck were then in a mortal struggle for control of the studio and Zanuck announced that he would not step foot onto studio property until Goetz resigned. Zanuck ran the studio from his luxurious beachhouse in Santa Monica, summoning producers and directors to him there, one of these being Preminger. In his autobiography Preminger remembered how "a butler escorted me through the house to the garden where Zanuck was sitting in swimming trunks beside his pool. His back was to me. He glanced around briefly and then gave me the back of his head again. He picked up a piece of paper and said: "I see you are working on a few things. I don't think much of them, except for one, LAURA. I've read it and it isn't bad. You can produce it but as long as I am at Fox you will never direct." He was dismissed like a servant and went back to Foy. LAURA was designated as a B film for Fox, even though Zanuck had hired Tierney, a popular magazine model before entering the world of Hollywood. Zanuck had originally wanted Jennifer Jones to play the lead in LAURA but she turned it down. Hedy Lamarr was then approached but she too declined the role. Oddly, when Lamarr divorced Texas oil man Howard Lee in 1960, Tierney married him shortly thereafter. Preminger worked on the script with Dratler but found that the dialog had no zip so he hired Betty Reinhardt and the poet Samuel Hoffenstein to punch up the dialog. "Hoffenstein practically created the character of Waldo Lydecker for Clifton Webb," Preminger later stated. "He was in the habit of overwriting but after the scenes were edited his dialog was brilliant." (Hoffenstein, it might be noted, was a contemporary and friend of the previously mentioned Woollcott, and a sometimes member of the Algonquin Round Table, drawing most assuredly upon his intimate knowledge of Woollcott's expansive, egotistical, and brilliant character for the Webb part.) The story line was completely changed and novelist Caspary objected to not only the new plot and added characters, but the fact that Zanuck had made it a B production. Foy didn't like it either and told Zanuck so in a meeting, but the unpredictable mogul said he did like the approach Preminger's writers had taken and stated: "The fact that it doesn't have a routine scene in a police station is exactly what I like about it. I'll take over the supervision of the picture." This meant that the film would now be an A picture with a considerable budget. Nothing shoddy, slipshod, or half-measured was ever released by Fox with Zanuck overlooking it as a special project of his own. However, Zanuck still refused to let Preminger direct the film. He asked Walter Lang and then Lewis Milestone to helm the picture, but both directors, knowing that their friend Preminger wanted to direct the film, turned down the assignment. Zanuck finally got Rouben Mamoulian to accept the chore. Preminger desperately wanted the sophisticated Webb to play the all-important role of Waldo Lydecker but when he mentioned this to the casting director, he was told: "You can't have Clifton Webb play this part. Darryl would blow a gasket." "Why?" asked Preminger. "Because he flies," answered the casting director, according to Leonard Mosley writing in *Zanuck*. Replied Preminger: "I'm just a poor foreigner and I don't understand the American language, so tell me what you are talking about. Clifton Webb, he flies. What do you mean?" He was then told that Webb was a homosexual and that Zanuck would never give him a substantial role, but Preminger refused to believe it and insisted upon Webb. Zanuck balked, saying that Webb wouldn't be right for the role. Preminger asked Zanuck to attend a stage production of Noel Coward's "Blithe Spirit" at the Biltmore Theater in Los Angeles and watch Webb in the lead role, but Zanuck refused. Preminger then filmed Webb's best scene and showed this to Zanuck, who finally yielded. Bit by agonizing bit the film became Preminger's with Zanuck reluctantly turning more and more over to the purposeful director. Preminger had rushes sent to Zanuck when the mogul was in New York on a business trip; Zanuck grew angry over Andrews' reserved performance, calling him an "agreeable school boy," and saying that he wasn't tough enough to play the detective. He added: "I was afraid of this all along and this is why I wanted John Hodiak but stupidly listened to Preminger." Zanuck didn't like Mamoulian's style, shots, setup, nothing he did on LAURA and finally, at the studio commissary, turned to Preminger and said: "What do you think? Shall I take Mamoulian off the picture?" Preminger tensed and said "yes," and later quoted Zanuck as saying: "Monday you can start directing LAURA from scratch." According to another report, Zanuck merely stated: "You're on." Mamoulian always insisted that the film as seen today was chiefly his product and that of his veteran cameraman, Lucian Ballard. Oddly, however, Zanuck clung to one dictate on the film; he wanted Webb's closeups kept to a minimum. All along, Zanuck had wanted the heavyset, offbeat character actor Laird Cregar to enact the Webb role and he hoped Webb would be awful but he was wonderful, which Zanuck later had to admit. Preminger threw out Mamoulian's sets, costumes, all of his footage, according to the director. Ballard ignored Preminger, smoking cigars and reading the paper while he was supposed to be setting up shots. Engaged to actress Merle Oberon, Ballard, according to Preminger, wanted to be fired so he could do a film at MGM with his intended. Preminger did fire him but Zanuck insisted that Ballard fulfill his Fox contract and demoted him to the test stage, the lowest job a cinematographer could perform, Preminger brought in La Shelle, whose superb high contrast lensing won him an Academy Award and established him as a foremost cameraman in Hollywood. When scrapping the Mamoulian sets, Preminger even got rid of the portrait of Tierney which Mamoulian's wife had painted, feeling it was unrealistic. He had a blow-up photo of the actress smeared with paint to give it the image of an oil painting but one which was easily identified as Tierney, mounting it in an expensive frame so Andrews could stare at it and fall in love with this beautiful ghost. Except for Webb, the cast was hostile to Preminger. Mamoulian, before departing, had told the actors that Preminger hated their acting. Anderson confronted the director with this, saying: "I hear that you don't like the way I'm playing my part." He agreed and she snapped: "All right, then show me how to do it better." With that Preminger stepped forward and, in front of the entire cast, acted out one of Anderson's scenes step by step. Zanuck viewed the film upon completion and insisted that the ending be remade, the last 15 minutes to be reshot from Tierney's point of view, almost as if everything shown earlier had been a dream. This, of course, destroyed Preminger's carefully constructed scenes. Zanuck told Preminger either he reshoot the ending or he would get another director. Preminger agreed to shoot a new ending which baffled the entire cast and crew, all believing that a classic film was already in the can. Zanuck screened the film with Preminger and his close friend Walter Winchell, then the most powerful newspaper columnist in America. Winchell and an unnamed woman sat in the deep leather chairs behind Zanuck in the screening room, laughing at Webb's lines which caused the amazed Zanuck to turn around and look at them in wonder. At the finish, Winchell yelled: "Bigtime! Bigtime! Bigtime, Darryl! But the end—I don't get it. You're going to change it?" It was then that Zanuck finally gave in completely to Preminger. Said the mogul: "After all these arguments—you want your old ending back?" Preminger nodded and got the film his way. Zanuck then stated: "If this is a big success, it will be all to Preminger's credit." And it was, except for the exquisite theme song. Preminger originally wanted to employ Duke Ellington's "Sophisticated Lady," but composer David Raksin fought hard to provide his own theme song. Preminger said that he would have to compose it immediately, giving him this order on a Friday, saying it must be completed by Monday. By Monday Raksin had produced "Laura," and Johnny Mercer later added the words. It became a classic American ballad, as popular as this unforgettable *film noir* production.

p&d, Otto Preminger; w, Jay Dratler, Samuel Hoffenstein, Betty Reinhardt, Ring Lardner, Jr., Jerome Cady (based on the novel by Vera Caspary); ph, Joseph La Shelle; m, David Raksin; ed, Louis Loeffler; prod d, Thomas Little, Paul S. Fox; md, Emil Newman; art d, Lyle Wheeler, Leland Fuller; set d, Thomas Little, Paul S. Fox; cos, Bonnie Cashin; spec eff, Fred Sersen.

Crime Drama **Cas.** **(PR:A MPAA:NR)**

LAUTLOSE WAFFEN (SEE: DEFECTOR, THE, 1966, Ger./Fr.)

LAVENDER HILL MOB, THE**** (1951, Brit.) 82m Ealing/UNIV bw

Alec Guinness *(Henry Holland)*, Stanley Holloway *(Pendlebury)*, Sidney James *(Lackery)*, Alfie Bass *(Shorty)*, Marjorie Fielding *(Mrs. Chalk)*, John Gregson *(Farrow)*, Edie Martin *(Miss Evesham)*, Clive Morton *(Station Sergeant)*, Ronald Adam *(Turner)*, Sydney Tafler *(Clayton)*, Jacques Brunius *(Official)*, Meredith Edwards *(P.C. Edwards)*, Gibb McLaughlin *(Godwin)*, Patrick Barr *(Inspector)*, Marie Burke *(Senora Gallardo)*, Audrey Hepburn *(Chiquita)*, John Salew *(Parkin)*, Arthur Hambling *(Wallis)*, Frederick Piper *(Cafe Proprietor)*, Peter Bull *(Joe the Gab)*, Patric Doonan *(Craggs)*, Alanna Boyce *(Schoolgirl with Paperweight)*, William [James] Fox *(Gregory)*, Michael Trubshawe *(Ambassador)*, Ann Heffernan, Eugene Deckers, Paul Demel, Andrea Malandrinos, Cyril Chamberlain, Tony Quinn, Moutrie Kelsall, Christopher Hewett, David Davies, Joe Clarke, Charles Lamb, Archie Duncan, Fred Griffiths, Frank Forsyth, Arthur Mullard, Jacques Cey, Marie Ney, John Warwick, Robert Shaw.

THE LAVENDER HILL MOB is a hilarious tongue-in-cheek crime comedy, one of the many to come out of Ealing Studios during their most prolific years. Guinness stars as a mild-mannered transporter of gold bullion, a quiet messenger whose job it is to bring the yellow stuff from the smelter to the bank. His eyes have been watering for 20 years as thousands of pounds of gold have passed before him. Eventually, and with seemingly no premeditation, he decides he will steal one million pounds of it. But how? Guinness enlists Holloway, an old pal who is a paperweight manufacturer and a bit of a sculptor. They team up with James and Bass, two cockney professional crooks, and the scheme is launched. They hijack the bank's armored car in a very funny comedic series of events, get the gold bars, and bring them to Holloway's place of business. Once there, they melt the gold and form it in the likeness of small, souvenir Eiffel Towers. While the police rant and rave and say that it will be impossible to smuggle that much gold out of England, the booty is passed before the eyes of customs officials and sent off to Paris. Guinness and Holloway follow the gold and learn too late that six of the Eiffel Towers have been purchased by a group of English schoolgirls on a day's trip to the City of Light. Now the search begins in earnest, as the two men bribe, cajole, and plead with the girls for their towers and retrieve them all, save one. Boyce has the final Eiffel Tower and she won't give it up. She eventually shows it to a local bobby who's working at a convention hall where the police are giving an exhibition of their crime and detection abilities. Guinness and Holloway snatch it from Boyce and a chase ensues inside the jam-packed hall. Once outside, the two men steal a police car and begin issuing confusing instructions via the police radio to throw their pursuers off the track. There's a huge pileup of fender-benders as the strains of "Old MacDonald Had a Farm" are heard on all the police radios. Holloway and Guinness run through the streets and wind up in the London Underground (subway) and it seems that they've gotten away with it. However, since the film begins with Guinness telling this story in a swank Rio restaurant, it returns there for the conclusion and we see that Guinness is not only having a drink with the other chap, he is also handcuffed to him. In that opening sequence, Guinness hands a cute young woman some money and tells her to buy a little gift. She says, "Oh, but how sweet of you." You'll have to look fast to recognize Audrey Hepburn as the young girl. Guinness is winning as the last man on earth you'd suspect of being a criminal. Clarke's screenplay won an Oscar and rightly so. Guinness was nominated but lost to Gary Cooper (for HIGH NOON). Although made and released in 1951, it was not up for the awards until 1952. Crichton's direction was first-rate and he again proved his mettle when he helmed THE TITFIELD THUNDERBOLT and THE BATTLE OF THE SEXES. Many of England's best comic actors were seen in small roles, including Sidney Tafler, Peter Bull, and John Gregson. In a tiny role, you may notice James Fox (brother of Edward), still being billed as William. The one flaw is that if Guinness had truly gone to Brazil, the British police would have never been able to extradite him as there is no agreement between the two countries and that is where the main perpetrator of England's "Great Train Robbery" wound up happily drinking coffee and raising a second family.

p, Michael Balcon; d, Charles Crichton; w, T.E.B. Clarke; ph, Douglas Slocombe; m, Georges Auric; ed, Seth Holt; md, Ernest Irving; art d, William Kellner.

Crime/Comedy **Cas.** **(PR:A MPAA:NR)**

L'AVEU (SEE: CONFESSION, THE, 1970, Fr.)

LAVIRINT SMRTI (SEE: FLAMING FRONTIER, 1968, Ger./Yugo.)

L'AVVENTURA***** (1960, Ital.) 145m CDD/Janus bw

Monica Vitti *(Claudia)*, Gabriele Ferzetti *(Sandro)*, Lea Massari *(Anna)*, Dominique Blanchar *(Giulia)*, James Addams *(Corrado)*, Renzo Ricci *(Anna's Father)*, Esmeralda Ruspoli *(Patrizia)*, Lelio Luttazi *(Raimondo)*, Dorothy De Poliolo *(Gloria Perkins)*, Giovanni Petrucci *(Young Prince)*, Enrico Bologna, Franco Cimino, Giovanni Danesi, Rita Mole, Renato Pincicoli, Angela Tommasi di Lampedusa, Vincenzo Tranchina.

A group of wealthy Italians embarks on a yachting excursion to an island of rock which jabs out of the waters near Sicily. After they arrive they notice that Massari is missing. Everyone joins the search. They look along the wave-battered cliffs which dress the shoreline and scout out the endless crevices which may have swallowed her up. Her best friend, Vitti, pairs with Massari's lover, Ferzetti, in the search. Eventually they give up the search, thinking she may have left the island. They return to the mainland, making various inquiries as to her whereabouts, occasionally meeting someone who thinks they might know her. Ferzetti gets more involved with Vitti and soon they are lovers, with the latter becoming Massari's substitute for Ferzetti (earlier in the film, Massari had even given Vitti a dress of hers to wear). The two lovers arrive at a luxurious hotel where they meet their former hostess from the yacht. Vitti remains in her room to sleep, while Ferzetti makes the rounds without her. Vitti awakens to find Ferzetti gone and wanders away. The end has Ferzetti searching for Vitti and finding her near a bench, staring out into the distance. Together, but separate, they stare into the emptiness before them. Voted in the prestigious *Sight and Sound* poll as one of the 10 greatest films of all time, L'AVVENTURA is not only Antonioni's masterpiece, but one of cinema's most important films, especially in terms of narrative form. The pressing question the plot raises, "What happened to Anna (Massari)?" is simply ignored. The plot becomes irrelevant—the adventure the title alludes to does not exist. Instead, the greatest adventure the picture offers is the changing lives of Vitti and Ferzetti, or perhaps what *will* happen to them after the film ends. Photographed almost entirely outdoors, the shooting took months to complete and sent the then-production company, Imeria, into debt. Cino Del Duca came to Antonioni's aid and filming continued, though many of the summer shots actually took place in the winter. Some four months later, the Cannes Film Festival premier greeted the picture with an unparalleled assault of hisses and boos. A couple of months later L'AVVENTURA was setting box office records in Paris, and by the time it hit America it had received a "condemned" rating from the National League of Decency, apparently for its lack of morality. The film's producer, in fact, had clearly told Antonioni, "Now listen Michelangelo, have it prohibited to children under 16." As with all of Antonioni's films, the photography and composition are unsurpassed. A breathtaking film which should not be missed by anyone with an interest in film aesthetics.

p, Cino Del Duca; d, Michelangelo Antonioni; w, Antonioni, Elio Bartolini, Tonino Guerra (based on the story by Antonioni); ph, Aldo Scavarda; m, Giovanni Fusco; ed, Eraldo da Roma; set d, Piero Polletto.

Drama (PR:A MPAA:NR)

L'AVVENTURIERO (SEE: ROVER, THE, 1967, Ital.)

LAW, THE, 1940 (SEE: LAW AND ORDER, 1940)

LAW, THE, 1958 (SEE: WHERE THE HOT WIND BLOWS, 1958)

LAW AND DISORDER**½ (1940, Brit.) 74m British Consolidated/RKO bw

Barry K. Barnes (Larry Preston), Diana Churchill (Janet Preston), Alastair Sim (Samuel Blight), Edward Chapman (Inspector Bray), Austin Trevor (Heinrichs), Ruby Miller, Leo Genn, Geoffrey Sumner, Glen Alyn, Torin Thatcher, Carl Jaffe, Cyril Smith.

When hotshot young lawyer Barnes defends some saboteurs with successful results, he amazes those close to him and angers the police. Later Barnes is drafted into the service and learns the same group now is using radio transmitters to guide enemy missiles to their intended targets. Barnes has just enough time to save the day and all ends happily. The plot is not much but the script is packed with wisecracks and one-liners that give this picture some needed pizazz. Enjoyable on its own level.

p, K.C. Alexander; d, David MacDonald; w, Roger MacDonald.

Crime/Comedy (PR:A MPAA:NR)

LAW AND DISORDER*** (1958, Brit.) 76m Hotspur-BL/CD bw

Michael Redgrave (Percy Brand), Robert Morley (Sir Edward Crichton), Elizabeth Sellars (Gina Lasalle), Ronald Squire (Col. Masters), George Couloris (Bennie), Joan Hickson (Aunt Florence), Lionel Jeffries (Maj. Proudfoot), Jeremy Burnham (Colin Brand), Harold Goodwin (Blacky), Meredith Edwards (Sgt. Bolton), Brenda Bruce (Mary Cooper), David Hutcheson (Freddie Cooper), John Le Mesurier (Sir Humphrey Pomfret), Mary Kerridge (Lady Crichton), Allan Cuthbertson (Police Inspector), Sam Kydd (Shorty), John Warwick (Police Superintendent), Reginald Beckwith (Vickery), Michael Trubshawe, Moultrie Kelsall, Irene Handl, John Hewer, Nora Nicholson, Anthony Sagar, John Paul, Alfred Burke, Michael Brennan, Arthur Howard.

A slick comedy characteristic of British movies of the era, LAW AND DISORDER is a beer keg of laughs squeezed into a brief 76 minutes. Redgrave is a crook who has made scads of pounds with various cons and schemes. His success is somewhat tempered by the fact that he is regularly sent away by a stern and pompous judge, Morley. That doesn't bother Redgrave too much, but what does concern him is that his son, Burnham, does not find out what daddy does for a living. So Redgrave fills young Burnham with malarkey about being a missionary to cover his stays in the clink. Burnham grows up believing that Redgrave is a religious do-gooder instead of a crooked do-badder. The scenes between Redgrave and Burnham indicate that Redgrave is not a bad chap, just a dishonest one. Burnham grows up to be a barrister and becomes Morley's aide in court. Meanwhile, Redgrave has retired to a seaside fishing village to live off his years of swag, but old habits are hard to break and he soon becomes involved with a gang of brandy smugglers who work out of the tiny town. He gets in touch with his old gang but things come to a mess and the gang is caught. Redgrave and his cohorts concoct a fantastic scheme whereby they intend to frame Morley and get him disbarred. In the end, that doesn't work out and Redgrave is again sent to jail. His one consolation is that Burnham never does find out what he does to earn his livelihood. A tight screenplay, with nary a wasted word, and sharp acting by some of England's best characters. This is a good example of the 1950s "Brit-Coms" and there is so much joy in watching Morley acting with Redgrave that it seems a shame a series of films weren't made with these two characters pitted against each other.

p, Paul Soskin, George Pitcher; d, Charles Crichton; w, T.E.B. Clarke, Patrick Campbell, Vivienne Knight (based on the novel Smuggler's Circuit by Denys Roberts); ph, Ted Scaife; m, Humphrey Searle; ed, Oswald Hafenrichter; md, Muir Mathieson; art d, Allan Harris.

Comedy (PR:A MPAA:NR)

LAW AND DISORDER***

(1974) 103m Memorial-Leroy Street-Ugo-Fadsin/COL c

Carroll O'Connor (Willie), Ernest Borgnine (Cy), Ann Wedgeworth (Sally), Anita Dangler (Irene), Leslie Ackerman (Karen), Karen Black (Gloria), Jack Kehoe (Elliott), David Spielberg (Bobby), Joe Ragno (Peter), Pat Corley (Ken), J. Frank Lucas (Flasher), Ed Grover (Capt. Malloy), Pepper Wormser (Yablonsky), Lionel Pina (Chico), Gary Springer (F.U. Kid), Jay Fletcher (Jogger), Bill Richert (Desk Sergeant), Jack Stamberger (Morris), Ed Madsen (Frank), Adam Lessuck (Eddie), Sydney Sherrif (Ralph), Alan Arbus (Dr. Richter), Theodorina Bello (Chico's Mother), Peter Lago (Chico's Father), Rita Gam (Woman in Cab), Michael Medwin (Man in Cab).

An offbeat comedy from Czech director Passer starring O'Connor and Borgnine as part of a vigilante citizens' group. Incensed with their community's rising crime rate,

taxi driver O'Connor and former marine-hairdresser Borgnine set out to restore law and order by forming an auxiliary police group, but instead, cause more problems than they prevent. Though intelligently directed by Passer (CUTTER'S WAY), the approach to the subject matter is alternately serious and comic, resulting in a lack of a consistent point of view which is ultimately confusing and unsatisfying to the viewer.

p, William Richert; d, Ivan Passer; w, Passer, Richert, Kenneth Harris Fishman; ph, Arthur J. Ornitz (Panavision); m, Andy Badale; ed, Anthony Protenza; art d, Gene Rudolf; set d, Paul Vogt; cos, Ann Roth.

Comedy/Drama (PR:O MPAA:R)

LAW AND JAKE WADE, THE*** (1958) 86m MGM c

Robert Taylor (Jake Wade), Richard Widmark (Clint Hollister), Patricia Owens (Peggy Carter), Robert Middleton (Ortero), Henry Silva (Rennie), DeForest Kelley (Wexler), Burt Douglas (Lieutenant), Eddie Firestone (Burke).

An admirably scripted western from Sturges which casts Taylor as a former bank robber turned marshal. Years before donning the badge, he was a member of Widmark's gang, but after robbing a local savings and loan he took the money and ran. When news reaches Taylor that Widmark is the guest of honor at a necktie party, the marshal arranges to have his life spared. Widmark, still holding a grudge, is less than amiable to Taylor. He and his henchmen kidnap Taylor and his girl, forcing them into the Sierras, where the stolen money was buried. Taylor manages to pull a few quick moves which end in the death of Widmark's entire gang, saving the last shot for Widmark himself. A movie with interesting morals—Taylor is given the power to save the life of his nemesis, only to take it away in the finale. A gripping picture from the opening credits to the final shootout.

p, William Hawks; d, John Sturges; w, William Bowers (based on the novel by Marvin H. Albert); ph, Robert Surtees (CinemaScope, Metrocolor); ed, Ferris Webster; art d, William A. Horning, Daniel B. Cathcart; set d, Henry Grace, Otto Siegel; cos, Walter Plunkett; spec eff, Lee LeBlanc; makeup, William Tuttle.

Western (PR:A MPAA:NR)

LAW AND LAWLESS** (1932) 59m Majestic bw

Jack Hoxie, Hilda Moore, Wally Wales, Yakima Canutt, Julian Rivero, Jack Mower, J. Frank Glendon, Edith Fellows, Helen Gibson, Robert Burns, Alma Rayford, Joe De La Cruz, Fred Burns, Elvero Sonchez, William Quinn, Al Taylor, Dixie Starr.

Bad men in the old West are stealing cattle and no one can stop them. Things change pretty quickly in the territory though when a lone rider comes in the area and saves the day. Typical filler western.

p, Larry Darmour; d, Armand Schaefer; w, Oliver Drake (based on a story by Drake).

Western (PR:A MPAA:NR)

LAW AND LEAD** (1937) 60m REP bw

Rex Bell (Jimmy Sawyer), Wally Wales (Steve), Harley Wood (Hope Hawley), Earl Dwire (Hawley), Soledad Jiminez (Senora Gonzales), Donald Reed (Pancho Gonzales), Roger Williams (Jeff), Lane Chandler (Ned Hyland), Karl Hackett, Lloyd Ingraham, Edward Cassidy, Lew Meehan.

This routine western stars Bell as the hero intent on capturing a masked bandit who is pretending to be a reformed outlaw pal of Bell's. He also manages to fall in love with Wood, who just happens to be the daughter of the masquerading outlaw. When Bell unmasks the mysterious cowpoke he clears his friend's name. The director offered a welcome change of pace with guitar music in between the barroom action, virtually heralding the coming onslaught of singing cowboys who sent Rex and other nonsingers out to pasture.

p, Arthur and Max Alexander; d, Bob Hill; w, Basil Dickey (based on the story by Rock Hawley [Bob Hill]); ph, Charles Henkel.

Western (PR:A MPAA:NR)

LAW AND ORDER***½ (1932) 70m UNIV bw (AKA: GUNS A' BLAZING)

Walter Huston (Frame Johnson), Harry Carey (Ed Brant), Raymond Hatton (Deadwood), Russell Simpson (Judge Williams), Russell Hopton (Luther Johnson), Ralph Ince (Poe Northrup), Harry Woods (Walt Northrup), Richard Alexander (Kurt Northrup), Alphonz Ethier (Fin Elder), Andy Devine (Johnny Kinsman), Dewey Robinson (Ed Deal), Walter Brennan (Lanky Smith), Lois Wilson (Girl), Nelson McDowell, D'Arcy Corrigan, George Dixon, Arthur G. Wanzer, Neal Hart.

Co-scripted by a young John Huston and starring his father, Walter, this serious, well-conceived western tells the tale of how law and order must be achieved, even with endless violence. Huston is a Wyatt Earp sort who teams with Carey in a fight to clean up the legendary corpse-producing town of Tombstone. He knocks the cowardly judicial system of the town to its knees, while allowing justice to stand tall. His reign begins by ordering the hanging of a farmer who accidentally killed someone. He continues his attacks until Tombstone is a safe place to live, not a difficult statement to make after killing a good portion of the population. With his job finished, Huston rides on. Remade in 1940 and 1953, getting progressively worse each time.

d, Edward L. Cahn; w, John Huston, Tom Reed (based on the story "Saint Johnson" by W.R. Burnett); ph, Jackson Rose; ed, Milton Carruth.

Western (PR:A MPAA:NR)

LAW AND ORDER, 1936 (SEE: FUGITIVE SHERIFF, THE, 1936)

LAW AND ORDER, 1936 (SEE: FAST BULLETS, 1936)

LAW AND ORDER** (1940) 57m UNIV bw (AKA: THE LAW)

Johnny Mack Brown (Bill Ralston), Fuzzy Knight (Deadwood), Nell O'Day (Sally

Dixon), James Craig (*Brant*), Harry Cording (*Poe Daggett*), Earle Hodgins (*Elder*), Robert Fiske (*Deal*), James Dodd (*Jimmy*), William Worthington (*Judge Williams*), Ethan Laidlaw (*Kurt Daggett*), Ted Adams (*Walt*), Harry Humphrey (*Dixon*), George Plues (*Stage Driver*), Kermit Maynard, Jack Shannon, Scoop Martin, Cliff Parkinson, Bob Kortman (*Henchmen*), Frank McCarroll, Frank Ellis, Jim Corey, Lew Meehan, Charles King, The Notables Quartet.

Brown is a retired marshal who dons his badge one more time in order to rid his town of the ruthless gang who killed O'Day's father. Besides being the girl Brown courts, O'Day also does some shooting when she feels it necessary. A loose remake of the like-titled Edward L. Cahn picture of 1932 and WILD WEST DAYS (1940 serial), in both of which Brown also starred.

p, Joseph Sanford; d, Ray Taylor; w, Sherman Lowe, Victor McLeod (based on the novel *Saint Johnson* by W.R. Burnett); ph, Jerome Ash; md, H.J. Salter; m/l, "Those Happy Old Days," (sung by Fuzzy Knight), "Oklahoma's Oke with Me" (sung by Jimmy Dodd, Nell O'Day), Milton Rosen, Everett Carter, James Dodd.

Western **(PR:A MPAA:NR)**

LAW AND ORDER* ½ (1942) 57m PRC bw

Buster Crabbe (*Billy the Kid*), Al St. John (*Fuzzy Q. Jones*), Tex O'Brien (*Jeff*), Sarah Padden (*Aunt Mary*), Wanda McKay (*Linda*), Charles King (*Crawford*), Hal Price (*Simms*), John Merton (*Turtle*), Kenne Duncan (*Dungan*), Ted Adams (*Sheriff*), Budd Buster, Kermit Maynard.

Crabbe does double duty in this standard oater, first as outlaw Billy the Kid and then as the cavalry lieutenant he bears a resemblance to. After a plan to con a blind woman out of her life savings, the guilty party gets his just deserts.

p, Sigmund Neufeld; d, Sherman Scott [Sam Newfield]; w, Sam Robins; ph, Jack Greenhalgh; ed, Holbrook N. Todd.

Western **(PR:A MPAA:NR)**

LAW AND ORDER* ½ (1953) 80m UNIV c

Ronald Reagan (*Frame Johnson*), Dorothy Malone (*Jeannie Bristow*), Alex Nicol (*Lute Johnson*), Preston Foster (*Kurt Durling*), Ruth Hampton (*Maria*), Russell Johnson (*Jimmy Johnson*), Barry Kelley (*Fin Elder*), Chubby Johnson (*Denver Cahoon*), Dennis Weaver (*Frank Durling*), Jack Kelly (*Jed*), Valerie Jackson (*Clarissa*), Don Garner (*Johnny Benton*), Tom Browne Henry (*Dixon*), Richard Garrick (*Judge Williams*), Tristram Coffin (*Parker*), Gregg Barton (*Wingett*), William O'Neal (*Ben Wiley*), Wally Cassell (*Durango Kid*), Bill Tannen (*Stranger*), Jack Daly (*Allie Marshall*), James Stone (*Martin*), Harry Harvey (*Land Agent*), Martin Garralaga (*Mexican Man*), Mike Ragan (*Horseman*), Ken MacDonald (*Rancher*), Britt Wood (*Drunk*), William Gould, Jack Ingram, Ethan Laidlaw, Jimmy Gray, Edwin Parker (*Men*), Dick Cutting (*Card Player*), Watson Downs (*Doctor*), Thor Holmes (*Stable Boy*), Kermit Maynard (*Onlooker*), John Carpenter, Buddy Roosevelt, Victor Romito.

The third remake of 1932's stark and sobering LAW AND ORDER, here starring Ronald Reagan, is a budget-minded and tired tale of a marshal who puts on his holster again after planning to retire. He puts off his plan to leave Tombstone with his saloon-keeper fiancee when the citizens ask him to rid their town of Foster's despicable gang. Reagan is a success, doing in the outlaws and then retiring with wife Malone. Little remains of the bleakness involved in the cleaning up of the old Wild West that made the 1932 version so memorable.

p, John W. Rogers; d, Nathan Juran; w, John and Owen Bagni, D.D. Beauchamp (based on the story "Saint Johnson" by W.R. Burnett); ph, Clifford Stine (Technicolor); m, Joseph Gershenson; ed, Ted J. Kent; art d, Alexander Golitzen, Robert Clatworthy.

Western **(PR:A MPAA:NR)**

LAW AND THE LADY, THE* ½ (1951) 104m MGM bw

Greer Garson (*Jane Hoskins*), Michael Wilding (*Nigel Duxbury/Lord Minden*), Fernando Lamas (*Juan Dinas*), Marjorie Main (*Mrs. Wortin*), Hayden Rorke (*Tracy Collins*), Margalo Gillmore (*Cora Caighn*), Ralph Dumke (*James H. Caighn*), Phyllis Stanley (*Lady Minden*), Rhys Williams (*Inspector McGraw*), Natalie Schafer (*Pamela Femberson*), Soledad Jiminez (*Princess Margarita*), Lalo Rios (*Fanchito*), Stanley Logan (*Sir Roland Epping*), Holmes Herbert (*English Colonel*), John Eldredge (*Assistant Manager*), Andre Charlot (*Maitre d'Hotel*), Victor Sen Yung (*Chinese Manager*), Anna Q. Nilsson (*Mrs. Scholmm*), Bess Flowers (*Mrs. Bruno Thayar*), Stuart Holmes (*Mr. Bruno Thayar*), Betty Farrington (*Mrs. Belpayasa*), Nikki Juston (*Miss Belpayasa*), Richard Hale (*Sheriff*), Spencer Chan (*Servant*), Matt Moore (*Sen. Scholmm*).

A spotty, overlong tale set in London at the turn-of-the-century. After being accused of stealing her boss' jewelry, maid Garson hooks up with Wilding and together they go on a rampage of conning folks out of their valuables. Their escapades take them to San Francisco where they decide to make their partnership legal through marriage.

p&d, Edwin H. Knopf; w, Leonard Spigelgass, Karl Tunberg (based on the play "The Last of Mrs. Cheney" by Frederick Lonsdale); ph, George J. Folsey, m, Carmen Dragon; ed, James E. Newcom, William Gulick; art d, Cedric Gibbons, Daniel Cathcart; m/l, "Sari," Emmerich Kalman.

Crime **(PR:A MPAA:NR)**

LAW AND TOMBSTONE, THE (SEE: HOUR OF THE GUN, 1967)

LAW BEYOND THE RANGE** (1935) 60m COL bw

Tim McCoy (*Colonel*), Billie Seward, Robert Allen, Guy Usher, Harry Todd, Walter Brennan, Si Jenks, J.B. Kenton, Ben Hendricks, Jr., Jules Cowles, Tom London, Jack Rockwell, Alan Sears.

Outlaws are controlling a territory and are seemingly unstoppable. Enter McCoy to fight back and regain the area for law-abiding citizens. Typical western action.

d, Ford Beebe; w, Lambert Hillyer; ph, Benjamin Kline; ed, Ray Snyder.

Western **(PR:A MPAA:NR)**

LAW COMES TO TEXAS, THE** ½ (1939) 61m COL bw

Bill Elliott (*John Haynes*), Veda Ann Borg (*Dora Lewis*), Bud Osbourne (*Judge Dean*), Charles Whittaker (*Barney*), Leon Beaumon (*Jeff*), Paul Everton (*Governor*), Charles King (*Kaintucky*), Slim Whitaker, Edmund Cobb, Lee Shumway, Frank Ellis, Jack Ingram, Frank LaRue, David Sharpe, Forrest Taylor, Budd Buster, Lane Chandler, Dan White, Ben Corbett.

Elliott is a tough cowboy who tosses aside his law books to become a Texas state trooper. At the request of the governor, he poses as an outlaw to lure a gang of bandits into a trap. Then, enlisting the help of his sidekick, King, he leads a trooper raid against the outlaws. Hand-to-hand battles in the climax lend spirit to this rugged drama of the cleaning up of some lawless elements plaguing Texas.

p, Larry Darmour; d, Joseph Levering; w, Nate Gatzert; ph, James S. Brown; ed, Dwight Caldwell.

Western **(PR:A MPAA:NR)**

LAW COMMANDS, THE* (1938) 58m Crescent bw

Tom Keene (*Dr. Kenton*), Lorraine Hayes (*Mary*), Budd Buster (*Kentuck*), Mathew Betz (*Frago*), Robert Fiske (*Abbott*), John Merton (*Clark*), Carl Stockdale (*Johnson*), David Sharpe (*Danny*), Marie Stoddard (*Min*), Horace B. Carpenter, Fred Burns.

Keene courts Hayes, the daughter of an Iowa settler, in this standard cowboy film which delivers the usual good guy vs. bad guy routine. Unique only for its Iowa setting, an unlikely place for a western but which, before its tall corn era, was prime acreage for land-grabbers to hustle in.

p, E.B. Derr; d, William Nigh; w, Bennett Cohen; ph, Arthur Martinelli; ed, Donald Barrett.

Western **(PR:A MPAA:NR)**

LAW DEMANDS, THE (SEE: RECKLESS RIDER, 1931)

LAW FOR TOMBSTONE* ½ (1937) 59m UNIV bw

Buck Jones (*Alamo Bowie*), Muriel Evans (*Nellie Gray*), Harvey Clark (*Doc Holliday*), Carl Stockdale (*Judge Hart*), Earle Hodgins (*Jack Dunn/Twin Gun Jack*), Alexander Cross (*Bull Clanton*), Chuck Morrison, Mary Carney, Charles LeMoyne, Ben Corbett, Harold Hodge, Arthur Van Slyke, Ezra Paluette, Francis Walker, Bob Kortman, Slim Whitaker, Tom Forman, Bill Patton, Frank McCarroll, D.V. Tannlinger, Carlos Bernardo, Silver the Horse.

A very minor Jones outing, this film has him bring justice to the infamous Arizona trouble spot. He is hired by a stagecoach line to put the lid on an increasing number of gold shipment robberies. The six-gunner learns fast that Tombstone is being run by a mysterious outlaw, Twin Gun Jack (Hodgins), who is rendered helpless by Jones with the help of Clark (Doc Holliday).

p, Buck Jones; d, Jones, B. Reeves Eason; w, Frances Guihan (based on a story by Charles M. Martin); ph, Allen Thompson, John Hickson.

Western **(PR:A MPAA:NR)**

LAW IN HER HANDS, THE* (1936) 53m FN-WB bw

Margaret Lindsay (*Mary Wentworth*), Glenda Farrell (*Dorothy Davis*), Warren Hull (*Robert Mitchell*), Lyle Talbot (*Frank Gordon*), Eddie Acuff (*Eddie O'Malley*), Dick Purcell (*Marty*), Al Shean (*Franz*), Joseph Crehan (*Thomas Mallon*), Matty Fain (*Augie Simelli*), Addison Richards (*William McGuire*), Milt Kibbee (*Herman Sturm*), Eddie Shubert (*Harry Morton*), Mabel Colcord (*Fishcake Fanny*), Billy Wayne (*Mug*).

A crippled tale of a female lawyer, Lindsay, who sets out to prove herself as an attorney and soon becomes a successful underworld defender. She falls in love with the district attorney, Hull, and her career goals are cast aside when she opts to become her adversary's wife.

p, Bryan Foy; d, William Clemens; w, George Bricker, Luci Ward (based on the story "Lawyer Woman" by Bricker); ph, Sid Hickox; ed, Clarence Kolster.

Romance/Comedy **(PR:A MPAA:NR)**

LAW IS THE LAW, THE** ½ (1959, Fr.) 103m Les Film Ariane-FS-France Cinema/CD bw

Fernandel (*Ferdinand Pastorelli*), Toto (*Giuseppe la Paglia*), Noel Roquevert (*Malandain*), Mario Besozzi (*Marozzi*), Rene Genin (*Donadieu*), Nathalie Nerval (*Helene Pastorelli*), Leda Gloria (*Antonietta la Paglia*), Jean Brochard (*Bonnefond*), Henri Cremieux (*Bourride*), Albert Dinan (*Peloffi*), Anna Maria Lucciani (*Marisa*), Luciano Marin (*Mario*), Henri Arius (*Mayor of Assola*).

Top French comic Fernandel was teamed with his popular Italian counterpart, Toto, for this enjoyable little comedy that complements the duo's respective talents. The pair live in a house that sits squarely on the Italian-French border where some rooms are in Italy, some in France. Toto is an Italian smuggler, married to French customs man Fernandel's ex-wife. The two engage in an on-going battle and somewhat strange partnership in their unique smuggling operation. The ending is a nicely orchestrated bit of funny business. The two comedy stars work well together, with neither overshadowing the other. The comedy is basic, but fun and quite enjoyable. (In French; English subtitles)

p, A. Mnouchkine, G. Danciger; d, Christian-Jaque; w, Jacques Emmanuel, Jean-Charles Tacchella, Age, Jean Manse, Scarpelli; ph, Gianni Di Venanzo; m, Nino Rota; ed, Jacques Desagneaux.

Comedy **(PR:A MPAA:NR)**

LAW MEN*   (1944) 58m MON bw

Johnny Mack Brown (Nevada), Raymond Hatton (Sandy), Jan Wiley (Phyllis), Kirby Grant (Clyde Miller), Robert Frazer (Bradford), Edmund Cobb (Slade), Art Fowler (Gus), Harry F. Price (Haynes), Marshall Reed (Killifer), Isabel Withers (Auntie Mac), Ben Corbett (Simmons), Ted Mapes (Curley), Steve Clark (Wilson), Bud Osborne (Hardy), Jack Rockwell, George Morrell, Ray Jones.

A formula Brown western in which he teams up with Hatton to investigate a string of bank and stage robberies. Hatton disguises himself as a shoemaker, while Brown manages to join the gang of thieves. In the end, justice prevails.

p, Charles J. Bigelow; d, Lambert Hillyer; w, Glenn Tryon; ph, Harry Neumann; ed, John C. Fuller; md, Edward Kay.

Western   (PR:A MPAA:NR)

LAW OF THE BADLANDS**   (1950) 59m RKO bw

Tim Holt (Dave), Joan Dixon (Velvet), Robert Livingston (Dirkin), Leonard Penn (Cash), Harry Woods (Conroy), Larry Johns (Simms), Robert Bray (Benson), Kenneth MacDonald (Capt. McVey), John Cliff (Madigan), Richard Martin (Chito Rafferty), Sam Lufkin, Danny Sands, Art Felix, Booger McCarthy.

Holt and sidekick Martin are Texas Rangers who go undercover, at the request of the U.S. government, to find the source of phony bills making their way east. The two join the counterfeiters and are about to bring them to justice, when Martin's ex-girl friend, Dixon, pops into town and accidentally blows their cover. It takes their fellow Rangers to get them out of the fix.

p, Herman Schlom; d, Lesley Selander; w, Ed Earl Repp; ph, George E. Diskant; m, C. Bakaleinikoff; ed, Desmond Marquette, art d, Albert S. D'Agostino, Feild Gray.

Western   (PR:A MPAA:NR)

LAW OF THE BARBARY COAST* 1/2   (1949) 65m COL bw

Gloria Henry (Julie Adams), Stephen Dunne (Phil Morton), Adele Jergens (Lita), Robert Shayne (Michael Lodge), Stefan Schnabel (Alexis Boralof), Edwin Max (Arnold), Ross Ford (Wayne Adams), J. Farrell MacDonald (Sgt. O'Leary).

Crusading district attorney Shayne sets his sights on ridding San Francisco's Bowery of a crime ring that is killing off state witnesses and organizing megabuck gambling operations. Schnabel is the big-shot mobster who tries to thwart Shayne's efforts.

p, Wallace MacDonald; d, Lew Landers; w, Robert Libott, Frank Burt; ph, Henry Freulich; ed, Henry Batista; md, Mischa Bakaleinikoff; art d, Harold MacArthur.

Crime   (PR:A MPAA:NR)

LAW OF THE GOLDEN WEST** 1/2   (1949) 60m REP bw

Monte Hale (William F. Cody), Paul Hurst (Otis Ellis), Gail Davis (Ann Calvert), Roy Barcroft (Clete Larrabee), John Holland (Quentin Morell), Scott Elliott (Wayne Calvert), Lane Bradford (Belden), Harold Goodwin (Gibson), John Hamilton (Isaac).

Hale, as a young Buffalo Bill Cody, is intent on finding out who murdered his father. With only a hotel room key as a clue, he sets out to find the persons responsible for the killing, which took place during a train robbery. The key eventually leads him to unscrupulous lawyer Holland and chief villain Barcroft. Hale had dispensed with "singing cowboy" roles at this point. This film was cleverly constructed to make use of Republic's excess footage from its bigger budgeted productions.

p, Melville Tucker; d, Philip Ford; w, Norman S. Hall; ph, Ernest Miller; m, Stanley Wilson; ed, Richard L. Van Enger; art d, Frank Hotaling.

Western   (PR:A MPAA:NR)

LAW OF THE JUNGLE* 1/2   (1942) 61m MON bw

Arline Judge, John King, Mantan Moreland, Martin Wilkins, Arthur J. O'Connell, C. Montague Shaw, Guy Kingsford, Victor Kendal, Feodor Chaliapin, Lawrence Criner.

The American film industry gave WW II plenty of support, turning out war-based stories as fast as possible. This one is definitely *not* one of its more inspired efforts. A group of Nazis are operating out of a secret jungle headquarters. It's up to a lady fugitive and a brave scientist to find out the Germans' location and put a stop to their nefarious doings.

p, Lindsley Parsons; d, Jean Yarbrough; w, George Bricker; ph, Max Stengler; ed, Jack Ogilvie.

Adventure   **Cas.**   (PR:A MPAA:NR)

LAW OF THE LASH**   (1947) 53m PRC bw

Al "Lash" LaRue (Cheyenne), Al "Fuzzy" St. John (Fuzzy), Lee Roberts (Lefty), Mary Scott (Jane Hilton), Jack O'Shea (Decker), Charles King (Sheriff), Carl Mathews (Blackie), Matty Roubert (Pee Wee), John Elliott (Dad Hilton), Charles Whitaker (Bart), Ted French (Smitty), Richard Cramer (Bartender), Brad Slavin (Sam).

A standard horse opry with LaRue going undercover to aid prospector St. John in his battles against a gang of outlaws led by O'Shea and Roberts. Full of action, with LaRue using his fists, guns, and, above all, his whip.

p, Jerry Thomas; d, Ray Taylor; w, William L. Nolte; ph, Robert Cline; ed, Hugh Winn.

Western   **Cas.**   (PR:A MPAA:NR)

LAW OF THE LAWLESS** 1/2   (1964) 87m PAR c

Dale Robertson (Judge Clem Rogers), Yvonne De Carlo (Ellie Irish), William Bendix (Sheriff Ed Tanner), Bruce Cabot (Joe Rile), Barton MacLane (Big Tom Stone), John Agar (Pete Stone), Richard Arlen (Bartender), Jody McCrea (George Stapleton), Kent Taylor (Rand McDonald), Bill Williams (Silas Miller), Rod Lauren

(Deputy Tim Ludlow), George Chandler (Hotel Clerk), Lon Chaney, Jr., (Tiny), Donald "Red" Barry (Tuffy), Roy Jenson, Jerry Summers, Reg Parton (Johnson Brothers), Alex Sharp (Drifter), Wally Wales (Rider/Stunts), Lorraine Bendix, Joe Forte, Leigh Chapman, Dick Ryan, Romo Vincent.

The first of 11 westerns produced by Lyles, which casts a number of veteran stars from the 1930s through 1950s. Robertson is a gunfighter-turned-judge who butts heads with MacLane after sentencing the latter's son to die. MacLane tries to rally the locals into shooting Robertson, but his efforts end up backfiring. A bit lacking in action, but still enjoyable, if only to see some familiar old faces back in action.

p, A.C. Lyles; d, William F. Claxton; w, Steve Fisher; ph, Lester Shorr (Techniscope, Technicolor); ed, Otho Lovering; art d, Hal Pereira, Al Roelofs; set d, Sam Comer, Darrell Silvera; spec eff, Paul K. Lerpae; makeup, Wally Westmore.

Western   (PR:A MPAA:NR)

LAW OF THE NORTH*   (1932) 56m MON bw

Bill Cody, Andy Shuford, Nadine Dore, Al "Fuzzy" St. John, William L. Thorne, Heinie Conklin, Gil Pratt, Jack Carlyle, Lew Short.

An implausible western in which Cody is brought to trial for murder, even though no one can find the body. No one, that is, except for Dore, who has taken the "dead" man into her house and revived him without telling anyone. Cody soon uncovers Dore's scheme and finds the proof he needs.

p, Trem Carr; d&w, Harry Fraser; ph, Archie Stout, Will Cline.

Western   (PR:AA MPAA:NR)

LAW OF THE NORTHWEST* 1/2   (1943) 57m COL bw

Charles Starrett (Steve King), Shirley Patterson (Michel Darcy), Arthur Hunnicutt (Arkansas), Stanley Brown (Neal Clayton), Douglas Leavitt (George Bradley), Donald Curtis (Frank Mason), Douglass Drake (Paul Darcy), Davison Clark (Tom Clayton), Reginald Barlow (Jean Darcy).

This Starrett vehicle sets him in the north woods of Canada in 1943 as a Mountie pitted against a devious group of Nazis trying to block transport of valuable war minerals for Allied forces. Starrett does all he can to rush construction of a road being used to route the supplies.

p, Jack Fier; d, William Berke; w, Luci Ward; ph, Benjamin Kline; ed, Jerome Thoms; art d, Lionel Banks.

Western   (PR:A MPAA:NR)

LAW OF THE PAMPAS**   (1939) 72m PAR bw

William Boyd (Hopalong Cassidy), Russell Hayden (Lucky Jenkins), Steffi Duna (Chiquita), Sidney Toler (Don Fernando Rameriez), Sidney Blackmer (Ralph Merritt), Pedro de Cordoba (Jose Valdez), William Duncan (Buck Peters), Anna Demetrio (Dolores Rameriez), Eddie Dean (Curly), Glenn Strange (Slim), Jo Jo La Savio (Ernesto "Tito" Valdez), Tony Roux (A Gaucho), Martin Garralaga (Bolo Carrier), The King's Men.

This film, No. 24 in the "Hopalong Cassidy" series, sees Boyd and Hayden heading down to South America to deliver a herd of cattle when they run into the villainous Blackmer. This is the first Hopalong film made since the departure of Gabby Hayes who played the beloved sidekick here played by Toler who replaced Hayes briefly. (See HOPALONG CASSIDY series, Index.)

p, Harry Sherman; d, Nate Watt; w, Harrison Jacobs (based on characters created by Clarence E. Mulford); ph, Russell Harlan; m, Victor Young; ed, Carroll Lewis; art d, Lewis J. Rachmil.

Western   (PR:A MPAA:NR)

LAW OF THE PANHANDLE* 1/2   (1950) 55m MON bw

Johnny Mack Brown (Johnny Mack), Jane Adams (Margie Kendal), Riley Hill (Tom Stocker), Marshall Reed (Rance), Myron Healey (Henry Faulkner), Ted Adams (Fred Kendal), Lee Roberts (Judd), Carol Henry (Ace Parker), Milburn Morante (Ezra Miller), Kermit Maynard (Luke Winslow), Bob Duncan (Evans), Boyd Stockman, George DeNormand, Tex Palmer, Ray Jones.

U.S. Marshal Brown assists a sheriff, Hill, in rounding up a gang of outlaws that is intimidating a group of ranchers. The outlaws are led by Healey, who is out to claim the ranchers' land and sell it to the railroad at a profit.

p, Jerry Thomas; d, Lewis Collins; w, Joseph Poland; ph, Harry Neumann; ed, William Austin; md, Edward Kay.

Western   (PR:A MPAA:NR)

LAW OF THE PLAINS***   (1938) 56m COL bw

Charles Starrett (Chuck Saunders), Iris Meredith (Marion), Bob Nolan (Bob), Robert Warwick (Willard McGowan), Dick Curtis (Jim Fletcher), Edward Le Saint (William Norton), Edmund Cobb (Slagle), Art Mix (Grant), Jack Rockwell (Marshal), George Chesebro (Bartender), Jack Long, John Tyrell, Sons of the Pioneers.

A fine Starrett entry which has a plot as old as the genre from which it springs, but containing the added tonic of the Sons of the Pioneers warbling their way through gunsmoke and fisticuffs. Starrett helps out a farming community that is terrorized by a gang of outlaws, under the secret control of banker Warwick. Denouement winds it all up with the banker exposed as a counterfeit good guy.

p, Harry Decker; d, Sam Nelson; w, Maurice Geraghty; ph, Benjamin Kline; ed, Gene Havlick; md, Morris Stoloff; m/l, Bob Nolan.

Western   (PR:A MPAA:NR)

LAW OF THE RANGE*   (1941) 59m UNIV bw

Johnny Mack Brown (Steve), Fuzzy Knight (Chaparral), Nell O'Day (Mary), Roy Harris (The Kid), Pat O'Malley (Steve's Father), Elaine Morey (Virginia), Ethan

Laidlaw (Hobart), Al Bridge (Squint Jamison), Hal Taliaferro (Tim O'Brien), Lucille Walker and the Texas Rangers, Jack Rockwell, Charles King, Terry Frost, Jim Corey, Bud Osborne, Slim Whitaker, Bob Kortman.

A slow-paced Brown picture which finds him settling an old feud with O'Day's family. When he discovers that Bridge killed her father, the feud is laid to rest and spirited O'Day and the hero come together for the clinch. A remake of THE IVORY HANDLED GUN (1935), starring Buck Jones.

p, Will Cowan; d, Ray Taylor; w, John Green; ph, Charles Van Enger; m, Robert Crawford, Gomer Cool, Milton Rosen, Everett Carter.

Western   **(PR:A   MPAA:NR)**

LAW OF THE RANGER*   (1937) 58m COL bw

Bob Allen (Bob), Elaine Shepard (Evelyn), John Merton (Nash), Hal Taliaferro (Wally), Lafe McKee (Polk), Tom London (Pete), Charles "Slim" Whitaker (Steve), Ernest Adams (Zeke), Lane Chandler (Williams), Bud Osborne, Jimmy Aubrey.

The "law of the ranger" is above the fat cats and their wallets in this Allen vehicle, where Merton tries to snatch a town's water rights, for which he receives a blast in McKee's newspaper. Thereupon Merton shoots McKee as a signal that he's had enough of media nosiness. Allen rides into town with a couple of ranger friends and shows Merton that nobody stands taller than the ranger. And that's the law, stranger.

p, Larry Darmour; d, Spencer Gordon Bennett; w, Nate Gatzert (based on a story by Jesse Duffy, Joseph Levering); ph, James S. Brown, Jr.; ed, Dwight Caldwell.

Western   **(PR:A   MPAA:NR)**

LAW OF THE RIO   (SEE: RIDERS OF THE RIO, 1931)

LAW OF THE RIO GRANDE*   (1931) 50m Webb-Douglas/SYN bw

Bob Custer, Betty Mack, Edmund Cobb, Nelson McDowell, Harry Todd.

A familiar oater which has Custer shooting it out with a group of cattle thieves. The outlaws think they can get away with breaking Rio Grande law, but the sheriff and his deputies prove them wrong.

p, F.E. Douglas; d, Bennett Cohen, Forrest Sheldon; w, Betty Burbridge, Cohen; ph, Archie Stout; ed, Fred Bain.

Western   **(PR:A   MPAA:NR)**

LAW OF THE SADDLE*   (1944) 59m PRC bw

Bob Livingston (Rocky Cameron), Al "Fuzzy" St. John (Fuzzy Jones), Betty Miles (Gayle), Lane Chandler (Steve Kinney), John Elliott (Dan Kirby), Reed Howes (Dave), Curley Dresden (Joe), Al Ferguson (Bart), Frank Ellis (Vic), Frank Hagney, Jimmy Aubrey.

Livingston comes to the aid of a group of townsfolk living in terror of a mysterious gang of outlaws. It turns out that the newly elected sheriff is behind the looting and this town is just one of many which he and his gang have been hounding. With the aid of St. John and Miles, whose father was killed by the gang, Livingston brings the sheriff and his boys to justice.

p, Sigmund Neufeld; d, Melville De Lay; w, Fred Myton; ph, Robert Cline; ed, Holbrook N. Todd.

Western   **Cas.**   **(PR:A   MPAA:NR)**

LAW OF THE SEA zero   (1932) 64m MON bw

Ralph Ince, Sally Blane, William Farnum, Rex Bell, Priscilla Dean, Eve Southern, Sid Saylor, Jack Clifford, Frank Larue, Wally Albright.

A vicious sea captain rescues a group of castaways and makes a play for one of their wives. When her sea captain husband objects, he is blinded and sent adrift. After 20 years, however, he runs into the man who took his wife, remembers the sound of his treacherous laughter, and kills him in revenge. Poorly scripted make-believe from the land of Snooze.

d, Otto Brower; ph, Archie Stout.

Drama   **(PR:A   MPAA:NR)**

LAW OF THE TEXAN*   (1938) 54m COL bw

Buck Jones (Buck), Dorothy Fay (Helen), Kenneth Harlan (Spencer), Don Douglas (Hackett), Matty Kemp (Bryant), Joe Whitehead (Flaherty), Forrest Taylor (Capt. Moore), Jose Tortosa (Sanchez), Melissa Sierra (Rosa), Tommy Mack (Juan), Bob Kortman (Quinn), Dave O'Brien, Silver the Horse.

Full of action, but lacking anything else, this Buck Jones film has him going undercover to gain the confidence of a gang of thieves. With Harlan as their leader, they plan to steal all of the town's silver bullion. Jones, however, brings Texas law down on their backs with a thwang that rattles the teeth of youngsters who love this stuff.

p, Monroe Shaff; d, Elmer Clifton; w, Shaff, Arthur Hoerl; ph, Eddie Linden; ed, Charles Hunt.

Western   **(PR:A   MPAA:NR)**

LAW OF THE TIMBER*1/2   (1941) 63m PRC bw

Marjorie Reynolds, Monte Blue, J. Farrell MacDonald, Hal Brazeal, George Humbert, Sven Hugo, Earl Eby, Milt Moroni, Betty Roadman, Eddie Phillips.

After the death of her logger father, Reynolds takes over the company and works to fulfill an order from the U.S. government. After a number of sabotage attempts, she discovers that her foreman is responsible. Routine programmer from Poverty Row.

p&d, Bernard B. Ray; w, Jack Natteford (based on the story "The Speck On The Wall" by James Oliver Curwood); ed, Carl Himm; md, Clarence E. Wheeler.

Drama   **(PR:A   MPAA:NR)**

LAW OF THE TONG zero   (1931) 61m SYN bw

Phyllis Barrington (Joan), Jason Robards, Sr. (Charlie Wong), John Harron (Doug), Dorothy Farley (Mme. Duval), Mary Carr (Mother McGregor), Frank Lackteen (Yuen Lee), William Mahlen (Capt. McGregor), Richard Alexander (Davy Jones).

Gangsters populating San Francisco's Chinatown dance halls are brought to the screen in this substandard crime tale mixed with doses of Oriental philosophy. Of interest still are the scenes of San Francisco's Chinatown, a cheap dancehall of the time, and a Depression-era Salvation Army shelter.

p, Willis Kent; d, Lew Collins; w, Oliver Drake; ph, William Nobles.

Crime   **(PR:A   MPAA:NR)**

LAW OF THE TROPICS*1/2   (1941) 76m WB bw

Constance Bennett (Joan Madison), Jeffrey Lynn (Jim Conway), Regis Toomey (Tom Marshall), Mona Maris (Rita Marshall), Hobart Bosworth (Boss Frank Davis), Frank Puglia (Tito), Thomas Jackson (Lt. Maquire), Paul Harvey (Alfred King, Sr.), Craig Stevens (Alfred King, Jr.), Roland Drew (Hotel Clerk), Charles Judels (Captain of River Boat), Cliff Clark (Bartender), Rolfe Sedan (Julio the Tailor), Luis Alberni (Native), Martin Garralaga (Pedro the Bookkeeper), Creighton Hale (Wilson the Clerk), Demetrius Emanuel (Waiter), Paco Moreno (Vendor), Anna Demetrio (Maria the Vendor), Don Orlando (Messenger), John Eberts, Juan Duval (Natives), Mayta Palmera (Dancer), Dale Van Sickel (Double for Craig Stevens).

An innocuous tearjerker, this film tells the story of a rubber planter in South America, Lynn, who is jilted by his fiancee back in the U.S. He has trouble gaining the respect of the natives, but is soon befriended by Bennett, a nightclub singer who looks after him. Lynn's employers disapprove when he marries the woman, saving her from a detective in the U.S. who is investigating her past. To protect her, Lynn pretends that she is his stateside fiancee. It is all for naught because the private eye finds out her real identity and drags her back to stand trial in the U.S. Lynn goes along to clear her name. This is a remake of OIL FOR THE LAMPS OF CHINA (1935).

p, Ben Stoloff; d, Ray Enright; w, Charles Grayson (based on the novel Oil for the Lamps of China by Alice Tisdale Hobart); ph, Sid Hickox; m, Howard Jackson; ed, Frederick Richards.

Drama   **(PR:A   MPAA:NR)**

LAW OF THE UNDERWORLD*1/2   (1938) 58m RKO bw

Chester Morris (Gene Fillmore), Anne Shirley (Annabelle), Eduardo Ciannelli (Rockey), Walter Abel (Rogers), Richard Bond (Tommy), Lee Patrick (Dorothy), Paul Guilfoyle (Batsy), Frank M. Thomas (Capt. Gargan), Eddie Acuff (Bill), Jack Arnold (Eddie), Jack Carson (Johnny), Paul Stanton (Barton), George Shelley (Frank), Anthony Warde (Larry).

Two innocent lovers, Shirley and Bond, get caught up in the gang activities of Morris, a "respectable" citizen who keeps his underworld dealings a secret. The trouble occurs when the lovers are framed for a jewelry store robbery where a clerk is killed. They are arrested and it is up to Morris to let them be executed or admit to his underworld connections. He puts his own life on the line in the finale. A remake of THE PAY OFF (1930).

p, Robert Sisk; d, Lew Landers; w, Bert Granet, Edmund L. Hartmann (based on the stage play "Crime" by John B. Hymer and Samuel Shipman); ph, Nicholas Musuraca; ed, Ted Cheesman.

Crime   **(PR:A   MPAA:NR)**

LAW OF THE VALLEY**   (1944) 52m MON bw

Johnny Mack Brown, Raymond Hatton, Lynne Carver, Edmund Cobb, Charles King, Kirk Barron, Tom Quinn, Marshall Reed, Hal Price, George DeNormand, Steve Clark, George Morrell, Charles McMurphy.

Typical adventure-packed Western with plenty of two-fisted action, as Brown and long-time sidekick Hatton lead the way to gain a small town's freedom. Another competent outing for veteran western director Bretherton.

p, Charles J. Bigelow; d, Howard Bretherton; w, Joseph O'Donnell; ph, Marcel LePicard; m, Edward Kay; ed, Pierre Janet; md, Kay.

Western   **(PR:A   MPAA:NR)**

LAW OF THE WEST zero   (1949) 54m MON bw

Johnny Mack Brown (Johnny Mack), Tax Terhune (Alibi), Bill Kennedy (Nixon), Gerry Pattison (Tennessee), Jack Ingram (Burke), Eddie Parker (Mike), Riley Hill (Charley), Steve Clark (Lane), James Harrison (Sheriff), Bob Woodward (Spence), Marshall Reed (Drago), Kenne Duncan (Stevens), Bud Osborne (Brook), Frank Ellis.

A well-trodden path is walked by Brown in this tale of a real estate agent who doctors landowners' deeds in his favor. To discover his plan, Brown serves as his bodyguard and learns that Kennedy is the culprit. When Kennedy gets word of Brown's involvement, he tells his henchmen to kill Brown and the agent he is supposed to be guarding, but only the latter is killed. Ventriloquist Terhune uses his vocal trickery to get himself and Brown out of a trap set by Kennedy's thugs, restoring order to the community.

p, Barney Sarecky; d, Ray Taylor; w, J. Benton Cheney; ph, Harry Neumann; m, Edward Kay; ed, Johnny Fuller.

Western   **(PR:A   MPAA:NR)**

LAW RIDES, THE**   (1936) 57m Supreme/William Steiner bw

Bob Steele, Harley Wood, Charles King, Buck Connors, Margaret Mann, Jack Rockwell, Norman Neilsen, Barney Furey, Ted Mapes.

After a cache of gold coins turns up, robbery and murder abound. Leave it to ever-present good guy Steele to ride in and save the day in this typical Western actioneer.

p, A.W. Hackel; d, Robert N. Bradbury; w, Al Martin (based on a story by Forbes Parkhill).

Western   **Cas.**   **(PR:A MPAA:NR)**

LAW RIDES AGAIN, THE*½   (1943) 56m MON bw

Ken Maynard (Ken), Hoot Gibson (Hoot), Betty Miles (Betty), Jack LaRue (Dillon), Emmett Lynn (Eagle Eye), Kenneth Harlan (Hampton), Chief Thunder Cloud (Indian), Bryant Washburn (Commissioner Lee), John Bridges (Jess), Fred Hoose (Hank), Charles Murray, Jr. (Marshal), Hank Bell (Sheriff), Chief Many Treaties (Barking Fox), John Merton.

The fast-paced second entry in the Trail Blazers series has Gibson and Maynard enlisting the aid of LaRue to bring down a deceitful Indian agent, Harlan. The blazing good guys do their best with the meager budget and bottom rung cinematography. (See TRAIL BLAZERS series, Index).

p, Robert Tansey; d, Alan James; w, Frances Kavanaugh; ph, Marcel Le Picard; ed, Fred Bain; md, Frank Sanucci.

Western   **(PR:A MPAA:NR)**

LAW RIDES WEST, THE   (SEE: SANTA FE TRAIL, THE, 1930)

LAW VS. BILLY THE KID, THE**   (1954) 72m COL c

Scott Brady (Billy the Kid), Betta St. John (Nita Maxwell), James Griffith (Pat Garrett), Alan Hale, Jr. (Bob Ollinger), Paul Cavanagh (John H. Tunstall), William "Bill" Phillips (Charlie Bowdre), Benny Rubin (Arnold Dodge), Steve Darrell (Tom Watkins), George Berkeley (Tom O'Folliard), William Tannen (Dave Rudabaugh), Richard Cutting (Pete Maxwell), John Cliff (Carl Trumble), Otis Garth (Gov. Wallace), Martin Garralaga (Miguel Bolanos), Frank Sully (Jack Poe), William Fawcett (Parsons), Robert Griffin (L.G. Murphy).

Another account of the title character's infamous career which has director Castle sacrificing factual accuracies for the more commercial aspects—shootouts and fist fights. While working on Cavanagh's ranch, Brady hangs around with Griffith and falls in love with rancher's daughter, St. John. Eventually Griffith becomes a lawman, chasing Brady after a string of murders. Griffith catches Brady, when the latter arranges to meet St. John.

p, Sam Katzman; d, William Castle; w, John T. Williams; ph, Henry Freulich (Technicolor); ed, Aaron Stell.

Western   **(PR:A MPAA:NR)**

LAW WEST OF TOMBSTONE, THE**½   (1938) 72m RKO bw

Harry Carey (Bill Parker), Tim Holt (The Tonto Kid), Evelyn Brent (Clara Martinez), Jean Rouverol (Nitta Moseby), Clarence Kolb (Sam Kent), Allan Lane (Danny), Esther Muir (Mme. Mustache), Bradley Page (Doc Howard), Paul Guilfoyle (Bud McQuinn), Robert Moya (Chuy), Ward Bond (Mulligan), George Irving (Mort Dixon), Monte Montague (Clayt McQuinn), Bob Kortman, Kermit Maynard.

An above average western is the first cowboy appearance of 20-year-old Holt. He plays a "Billy the Kid" type who falls in love with the daughter of the local barroom judge, modeled after Judge Roy Bean, dispensing justice from a saloon.

p, Cliff Reid; d, Glenn Tryon; w, John Twist, Clarence Upson Young (based on a story by Young); ph, J. Roy Hunt; md, Roy Webb; art d, Van Nest Polglase.

Western/Comedy   **Cas.**   **(PR:A MPAA:NR)**

LAWFUL LARCENY**   (1930) 66m RKO bw

Bebe Daniels (Marion Dorsey), Kenneth Thomson (Andrew Dorsey), Lowell Sherman (Guy Tarlow), Olive Tell (Vivian Hepburn), Purnell B. Pratt (Judge Perry), Lou Payne (Davis), Bert Roach (French), Maude Turner Gordon (Mrs. Davis), Helene Millard (Mrs. French), Charles Coleman (Butler).

An entertaining picture which features Thomson as a buffoon who loses his fortune to the gambling and loving ways of the crafty Tell. After a three-month absence, Thomson's wife, Daniels, returns and must concoct a plot to retrieve her husband's wealth. She is hired as Tell's secretary, and before long proves that Tell is a lyin', cheatin', stealin', no-good hussy. Daniels does a fine job of portraying the hurt wife who fights to protect her husband's integrity.

p, William Le Baron; d, Lowell Sherman; w, Jane Murfin (based on the play "Lawful Larceny" by Samuel Shipman); ph, Roy Hunt; ed, Marie Halvey.

Drama   **(PR:A MPAA:NR)**

LAWLESS, THE***   (1950) 83m PAR bw (GB: THE DIVIDING LINE)

Macdonald Carey (Larry Wilder), Gail Russell (Sunny Garcia), John Sands (Joe Ferguson), Lee Patrick (Jan Dawson), John Hoyt (Ed Ferguson), Lalo Rios (Paul Rodriguez), Maurice Jara (Lopo Chavez), Walter Reed (Jim Wilson), Guy Anderson (Jonas Creel), Argentina Brunetti (Mrs. Rodriguez), William Edmunds (Mr. Jensen), Gloria Winters (Mildred Jensen), John Davis (Harry Pawling), Martha Hyer (Caroline Tyler), Frank Fenton (Mr. Prentis), Paul Harvey (Chief Of Police Blake), Felipe Turich (Mr. Rodriguez), Ian MacDonald (Sgt. Al Peters), Noel Reyburn (Fred Jackson), Tab Hunter (Frank O'Brien), Russ Conway (Eldredge), James Bush (Anderson), Julia Faye (Mrs. Jensen), Howard Negley (Pete Cassell), Gordon Nelson (Cadwallader), Frank Ferguson (Carl Green), Ray Hyke (Motorcycle Officer), Pedro de Cordoba (Mr. Garcia), Robert B. Williams (Boswell), John Murphy (Mayor).

Daniel Mainwaring wrote the book and the script, but he may not have liked the way the film came out so he used a pseudonym on the screenplay. He shouldn't have turned away from this as THE LAWLESS is a fast-paced, expertly edited tale of

racial intolerance and violence that is just as timely today as it was then. The picture revolves around a group of "Fruit Tramps," those impoverished souls who follow the crops and eke out a living picking various fruits and vegetables. They are given small salaries and large disdain by the wealthy Californians who own the land. There's a fight at a dance between the white kids and the Mexicans (almost the same scene was done between the Puerto Ricans and the white kids in WEST SIDE STORY) and Rios runs off after the battle. The melee is used by the friends and families of the white bullies to instigate a lynch mob and to raze the office of Carey, a newspaper man who is sympathetic to the plight of the farm workers. Rios is eventually captured and the Mexicans revolt. Carey is excellent as the newsman who, at first, straddles the issue, then comes out as a champion of the underdog. The action never stops and the result is a well-made B movie that doesn't betray its age. Look for Martha Hyer and Tab Hunter in small roles.

p, William H. Pine, William C. Thomas; d, Joseph Losey; w, Geoffrey Homes [Daniel Mainwaring] (based on the novel The Voice of Stephen Wilder by Mainwaring); ph, Roy Hunt; m, Mahlon Merrick; ed, Howard Smith; md, David Chudnow; art d, Lewis H. Creber; set d, Al Kegerris.

Drama   **(PR:A-C MPAA:NR)**

LAWLESS BORDER**   (1935) 58m Spectrum bw (AKA: LAWLESS BORDER) (GB: BORDER PATROL)

Bill Cody, Molly O'Day, Martin Garralaga, Ted Adams, Joe De La Cruze, John Elliott, Merrill McCormack, Roger Williams, Curly Baldwin, Budd Buster, William McCall.

There's a murder out in the West that raises the wrath of one man, Cody. The cowpoke boards his horse and sets out to find the killer. An average Western.

p, Ray Kirkwood; d, John P. McCarthy; w, Zara Tazil; ph, Robert Cline.

Western   **(PR:A MPAA:NR)**

LAWLESS BREED, THE**   (1946) 58m UNIV bw (AKA: LAWLESS CLAN)

Kirby Grant, Fuzzy Knight, Jane Adams, Harry Brown, Dick Curtis, Charles King, Karl Hackett, Hank Worden, Claudia Drake, Ernie Adams, Harry Wilson, Artie Ortego.

Grant and Knight are a G-man and his sidekick investigating a strange death in the West. It seems that a local banker has died, but the team discovers this was just a scam to collect insurance money. Adams is the love interest for Grant in this typical western outing.

p&d, Wallace W. Fox; w, Bob Williams; md, Milton Rosen.

Western/Crime Drama   **(PR:AA MPAA:NR)**

LAWLESS BREED, THE***   (1952) 83m UNIV c

Rock Hudson (John Wesley Hardin), Julia Adams (Rosie), John McIntire (J.C. Hardin/John Clements), Mary Castle (Jane Brown), Hugh O'Brian (Ike Hanley), Forrest Lewis (Zeke Jenkins), Lee Van Cleef (Dirk Hanley), Tom Fadden (Chick Noonan), William Pullen (Joe Hardin), Dennis Weaver (Jim Clements), Glenn Strange (Ben Hanley), Richard Garland (Joe Clements), Race Gentry (Young John Hardin), Carl Pitti (Sheriff Conlon), Ned Davenport (Blunt), Robert Anderson (Wild Bill Hickok), Stephen Chase (Judge), Richard Wessel (Marv, the Bartender), Emory Parnell (Bartender), Tom Jackson (McNelly), George Wallace (Bully Brady), Edward Earle (Henry Johnson), Michael Ansara (Gus), Paul "Tiny" Newland (Race Track Judge), Gertrude Graner (Aunt Em), Francis Ford (Old Timer), I. Stanford Jolley (Another Bartender), Buddy Roosevelt (Deputy Sheriff), Ethan Laidlaw (Clerk), Stanley Blystone (Card Player), Charles B. V. Miller (Bit), Wheaton Chambers (Doc), Bobbie Hoy, Bob Anderson.

An above-average oater, THE LAWLESS BREED loosely chronicles the life of real-life Texas outlaw and gunman John Wesley Hardin, a man who claimed in his own autobiography to have killed no fewer than 40 men, nineteen more than Billy the Kid is said to have slain. Hudson energetically plays Hardin, whose criminal career is shown in flashback—how he was compelled to adopt a life of crime, a rather hackneyed excuse—and his exploits with Union soldiers, Indians, and, most of all, other gunslingers. Interspersed into this episodic tale is his sporadic love affair with Adams and the son they produce, one whom Hudson stops from repeating his own tragic life at the risk of his neck. The portrait is fatalistic and somewhat glum in spots but Walsh directs with great vitality, providing plenty of action. Hudson, in his first starring role, does an above-average job, as does the lovely Adams. Universal put enough behind this production to raise it from the hum-drum values of a B-western.

p, William Alland; d, Raoul Walsh; w, Bernard Gordon (based on a story by Alland); ph, Irving Glassberg (Technicolor); m, Joseph Gershenson; ed, Frank Gross; art d, Bernard Herzbrun, Richard Riedel; set d, Russell A. Gausman, Oliver Emert.

Western   **(PR:A MPAA:NR)**

LAWLESS CLAN   (SEE: LAWLESS BREED, THE, 1946)

LAWLESS CODE**   (1949) 58m MON bw

Jimmy Wakely, Dub "Cannonball" Taylor, Bud Osborne, Riley Hill, Tristram Coffin, Terry Frost, Myron Healey, Kenne Duncan, Ellen Hall, Bob Curtis, Steve Clark, Frank MacCarroll, Beatrice Maude, Carl Deacon Moore, Michael Royal.

A group of nefarious outlaws murder a man, then try to pin the blame on his innocent nephew. Things don't look too well for him, but it all comes out right in the end.

p, Louis Gray; d, Oliver Drake; w, Basil Dickey (based on a story by Dickey); ph, Harry Neumann; md, Edward Kay.

Western   **(PR:A MPAA:NR)**

LAWLESS COWBOYS*   (1952) 58m MON bw

Whip Wilson (Whip), Jim Bannon (Himself), Fuzzy Knight (Smithers), Lee Roberts (Hanson), Pamela Duncan (Nora Clayton), Lane Bradford (Ace Malloy), I. Stanford Jolley (Sheriff), Bruce Edwards (Bob Rank), Richard Emory (Jeff), Marshall Reed (Paul Maxwell), Ace Malloy, Stanley Price.

Wilson comes to the rescue when the Wild West's most popular sport—rodeo—is endangered by an outlaw crime ring during stagecoach days. The Central City Rodeo Committee calls on Wilson when it is suspected that a gang of crooks is paying riders to throw their events. He enlists the aid of Bannon, a local rider, and Knight, a crusading newspaperman in exposing the criminals.

p, Vincent M. Fennelly; d, Lewis Collins; w, Maurice Tombragel; ph, Ernest Miller; ed, Samuel Fields.

Western   **(PR:A   MPAA:NR)**

LAWLESS EIGHTIES, THE½**   (1957) 70m Ventura/REP bw

Buster Crabbe, John Smith, Marilyn Saris, Ted de Corsia, Anthony Caruso, John Doucette, Frank Ferguson, Sheila Bromley, Walter Reed, Buzz Henry, Will J. White, Bob Swan.

Crabbe is a circuit rider who comes upon some masked men abusing a group of Indians. He runs off to inform the authorities, but is shot and wounded. Left to die, Crabbe is found by a gunfighter who helps the man out. Okay action western with a somewhat different plot than others.

p, Rudy Ralston; d, Joe Kane; w, Kenneth Gamet (based on the story "Brother Van" by Alson Jesse Smith); ph, Jack Marta (Naturama); ed, Joseph Harrison; md, Gerald Roberts; art d, Ralph Oberg.

Western   **(PR:C   MPAA:NR)**

LAWLESS EMPIRE*   (1946) 58m COL bw

Charles Starrett (Steve Random), Tex Harding (Rev. Tex Harding), Dub Taylor (Cannonball), Mildred Law (Vicky), Johnny Walsh (Marty Foster), Jim Calvert (Blaze Howard), Ethan Laidlaw (Duke Flinders), Forrest Taylor (Doc Weston), Jack Rockwell (Jed Stevens), George Chesebro (Lenny), Boyd Stockman (Skids), Lloyd Ingraham (Mr. Murphy), Jessie Arnold (Mrs. Murphy), Tom Chatterton (Sam Enders), Bob Wills and His Texas Playboys, Ray Jones.

A typical western plot has Starrett bringing the law down on a gang of rustlers who are making life tough for the ranchers and settlers. Harding is a hard-edged, no-nonsense preacher who builds a church to rid the people of the lawless elements. (See DURANGO KID series, Index).

p, Colbert Clark; d, Vernon Keays; w, Bennett Cohen (based on a story by Elizabeth Beecher); ph, George Meehan; ed, Paul Borofsky; art d, Charles Clague.

Western   **(PR:A   MPAA:NR)**

LAWLESS FRONTIER, THE**   (1935) 59m Lone Star/MON bw

John Wayne (John Tobin), Sheila Terry (Ruby), George "Gabby" Hayes (Dusty), Earl Dwire (Zanti), Yakima Canutt (Joe), Jack Rockwell (Sheriff), Gordon D. [Demain] Woods (Miller), Lloyd Whitlock, Eddie Parker, Artie Ortego, Buffalo Bill, Jr., Herman Hack.

Wayne tries to clear himself of a crime a sheriff has pinned on him. The sheriff is in cahoots with rustlers led by Whitlock. Wayne goes gunning for the gang to clear his name and avenge the murders of his parents which were committed by Whitlock.

p, Paul Malvern, d&w, Robert N. Bradbury; ph, Archie Stout; ed, Carl Pierson.

Western   **Cas.**   **(PR:A   MPAA:NR)**

LAWLESS LAND*½   (1937) 60m REP bw

Johnny Mack Brown (Jeff), Louise Stanley (Letty), Ted Adams (Clay), Julian Rivero (Ortego), Horace Murphy (Lafe), Frank Ball (Bill), Edward Cassidy (Sheriff), Ana Camargo (Lolita), Roger Williams, Frances Kellogg, Chiquita Hernandez Orchestra.

A second-rate plot and limited action make this somewhat less than a routine B western, despite the charisma of the reliable Brown. The latter is a Texas Ranger who rides into town to solve a string of killings. The villain, clearly recognizable by his hairline mustache, proves to be Adams. Murphy is fine in comic relief, and Stanley as the lovely Letty, is on loan from Warner Bros.

p, A.W. Hackel; d, Albert Ray; w, Andrew Bennison; ph, Jack Greenhalgh; ed, S. Roy Luby.

Western   **Cas.**   **(PR:A   MPAA:NR)**

LAWLESS NINETIES, THE**   (1936) 58m REP bw

John Wayne (John Tipton), Ann Rutherford (Janet Carter), Harry Woods (Charles K. Plummer), George "Gabby" Hayes (Maj. Carter), Al Bridge (Steele), Lane Chandler (Bridger), "Snowflake" [Fred Toones] (Mose), Etta McDaniel (Mandy Lou), Tom Brower (Marshall), Cliff Lyons (Davis), Jack Rockwell (Smith), Al Taylor (Red), Charles King (Hartley), George Chesebro (Green), Tom London (Ward), Sam Flint (Pierce), Earl Seaman (T. Roosevelt), Tracy Lane (Belden), Philo McCullough (Outlaw Leader), Chuck Baldra (Tex), Lloyd Ingraham (Palmer), Monte Blue (Outlaw), Jimmie Harrison (Telegraph Operator), Lew Meehan, Horace B. Carpenter, Sherry Tansey, Curley Dresden, Tex Palmer, Jack Kirk, Edward Hearn, Steve Clark.

With a plot closely resembling Republic's later big-budget western of 1940, THE DARK COMMAND, this effort deals with government man Wayne's efforts to attain an honest election despite the efforts of Woods, who secretly heads a band of raiders. At issue is the possible statehood of the Wyoming territories. Hayes, beardless, is outstanding as a crusading newspaper editor whose courage costs him his life. Assuming the editorial reins following father Hayes' demise is Rutherford. Wayne masses the good citizens, who barricade the town and turn the rebels out.

The referendum is fairly balloted; the territories achieve statehood. The first of a series of three westerns starring Wayne to be directed by Kane.

p, Paul Malvern; d, Joseph Kane; w, Joseph Poland (based on a story by Joseph Poland, Scott Pembroke); ph, William Nobles.

Western   **(PR:A   MPAA:NR)**

LAWLESS PLAINSMEN*½   (1942) 59m COL bw

Charles Starrett (Steve Rideen), Russell Hayden ("Lucky" Bannon), Luana Walters (Baltimore Bonnie), Cliff Edwards (Harmony Stubbs), Raphael Bennett (Seth McBride), Gwen Kenyon (Madge Mason), Frank LaRue (Bill Mason), Stanley Brown (Tascosa), Nick Thompson (Ochella), Eddie Laughton (Slim), Carl Mathews (Outlaw).

Ranch foreman Starrett and the boss' son, kid sidekick Hayden, get caught in the middle of a battle in the saloon run by beautiful but brassy Walters, little realizing that the fight was engineered by Bennett, her ex-husband. The fight is no more than a diversion which permits bad man Bennett to loot the safe. Ruined by the plot, Walters accepts an offer of transit from the territory in a passing wagon train. The wounded Hayden, needing medical attention, also is a passenger, safeguarded by the steel-jawed Starrett. Bennett, his devilishness yet undisclosed, joins the procession with a wagonload of weapons for the rampaging redskins. Bennett kills the wagonmaster and a friendly Indian, but is himself killed by Starrett in a shootout. Starrett tries to make peace with the dead Indian's father, a chief, but is taken captive. Rescued through the efforts of the newly healthy Hayden, Starrett returns to the wagon train, defending it from a score or more of attacks. At the showdown, the Seventh Cavalry arrives to save the day. Director Berke, who had produced many of the films starring the adult-youngster duo, began his one-take technique with this film, cheapening the series substantially.

p, Jack Fier; d, William Berke; w, Luci Ward; ph, Benjamin Kline; ed, William Lyon; art d, Lionel Banks.

Western   **(PR:A   MPAA:NR)**

LAWLESS RANGE**   (1935) 54m Trem Carr-MON/REP bw

John Wayne (John Middleton), Sheila Mannors (Anne), Earle Dwire (Emmett), Frank McGlynn, Jr. (Carter [Martin]), Jack Curtis (Marshal), Yakima Canutt (Burns), Wally Howe (Mason), Glenn Strange, Jack Kirk, Charles Baldra, Charley Sargent, Fred Burns, Slim Whitaker, Julia Griffin.

Wayne plays a government agent again who is sent to investigate a series of raids and cattle rustling on the Pequeno Valley settlers. A banker, McGlynn, is the mastermind. Wayne discovers that he wants to make the valley a ghost town to get his hands on a secret gold mine. This film was shot for Monogram though it was released as a Republic picture. Wayne warbles a tune or two, and not too badly, in an attempt to keep pace with his peers in the genre.

p, Paul Malvern; d, Robert N. Bradbury; w, Lindsley Parsons; ph, Archie Stout; ed, Carl Pierson.

Western   **Cas.**   **(PR:A   MPAA:NR)**

LAWLESS RIDER, THE**   (1954) 62m Royal West/UA bw

Johnny Carpenter (Rod Tatum), Frankie Darro (Jim Bascom), Douglass Dumbrille (Marshal Brady), Frank "Red" Carpenter (Big Red), Noel Neill (Nancy James), Kenne Duncan (Freno Frost), Weldon Bascom (Sheriff Brown), Rose Bascom (Texas Rose Bascom), Bud Osborne (Tulso), Lou Roberson (Black Jack), Bill Coontz (Red Rooks), Bill Chaney (Bill), Roy Canada (Andy), Tap Canutt (Young Marshal), Hank Caldwell and his Saddle Kings.

A band of criminals raids the ranchers, murdering and rustling cattle. Carpenter, who produced and wrote this film, is the marshal who, with the help of trick rope champion Bascom, puts a stop to the raids. An average story which is pumped up by the well-directed action sequences by Yakima Canutt. This was the last film Canutt directed; he put most of his remaining efforts into stunt work, building it into the profession it is today. Canutt would also continue to work as a second-unit director.

p, John Carpenter, Alex Gordon; d, Yakima Canutt; w, Carpenter; ph, William C. Thompson; m, Rudy DeSaxe; ed, John Fuller; m/l, "Thinking of You," Marguerite McFarlane.

Western   **(PR:A   MPAA:NR)**

LAWLESS RIDERS*   (1936) 58m COL bw

Ken Maynard (Ken Manley), Geneva Mitchell (Edith Adams), Harry Woods (Bart), Frank Yaconelli (Pedro), Wally Wales [Hal Taliaferro] (Carl), Slim Whitaker (Prod), Frank Ellis (Twister), Jack Rockwell (Sheriff), Bob McKenzie, Hank Bell, Bud Jamison, Horace B. Carpenter, Jack King, Bud McClure, Pascale Perry, Oscar Gahan, Tarzan the Horse.

Nothing worthwhile in this Maynard oater as he tries to prove his innocence on a murder charge. Mitchell is the banker's daughter who is in love with the cowboy, and Yaconelli and Wales provided what might be called the comic relief. Loads of battling, and Maynard essays one song in an attempt to keep up with the competition, demonstrating conclusively that he battles better than he belts out a tune.

p, Larry Darmour; d, Spencer Gordon Bennet; w, Nate Gatzert; ph, Herbert Kirkpatrick; ed, Dwight Caldwell.

Western   **(PR:A   MPAA:NR)**

LAWLESS STREET, A***   (1955) 78m Scott-Brown/COL c

Randolph Scott (Calem Ware), Angela Lansbury (Tally Dickinson), Warner Anderson (Hamer Thorne), Jean Parker (Cora Dean), Wallace Ford (Dr. Amos Wynn), John Emery (Cody Clark), James Bell (Asaph Dean), Ruth Donnelly (Molly

Higgins), Michael Pate *(Harley Baskam)*, Don Megowan *(Dooley Brion)*, Jeanette Nolan *(Mrs. Dingo Brion)*, Peter Ortiz *(Hiram Hayes)*, Don Carlos *(Juan Tobrez)*, Frank Hagney *(Dingo Brion)*, Charles Williams *(Willis)*, Frank Ferguson *(Abe Deland)*, Harry Tyler *(Tony Cabillo)*, Harry Antrim *(Mayor Kent)*, Jay Lawrence, Reed Howes, Guy Teague, Hal K. Dawson, Pat Collins, Frank Scannell, Stanley Blystone, Barry Brooks, Edwin Chandler.

Scott is a lawman who moves from town to town in the Colorado Territory ridding each of its outlaws. His dedication to his job causes his wife, Lansbury, to leave him. She will not come back to him until he has hung up his guns for good. He is determined to clean up the town of Medicine Bend—run by Anderson and Emery—who don't want to see the territory become a state. They hire gunman Pate to take care of Scott, but Scott's gun is faster. With his mission completed, Scott *does* put his guns down and get back together with his wife. A well-written western with Scott's character more complex than the usual western hero.

p, Harry Joe Brown; d, Joseph H. Lewis; w, Kenneth Gamet (based on the novel *Marshal of Medicine Bend* by Brad Ward); ph, Ray Rennahan (Technicolor); m, Paul Sawtell; ed, Gene Havlick; md, Sawtell; art d, George Brooks; ch, Jerry Antes.

Western **(PR:A MPAA:NR)**

LAWLESS VALLEY** ½ (1938) 59m RKO bw

George O'Brien *(Larry Rhodes)*, Walter Miller *(Bob North)*, Kay Sutton *(Norma Rogers)*, Fred Kohler, Sr. *(Tom Marsh)*, Fred Kohler, Jr. *(Jeff Marsh)*, George McQuarrie *(Tim Wade)*, Lew Kelly *(Fresno)*, Earle Hodgins *(Sheriff Heck Hampton)*, Chill Wills *(Speedy McGow)*, Dot Farley *(Anna)*, Dick Hunter *(Henchman)*, Robert Stanton [Kirby Grant], George Chesebro, Carl Stockdale, Ben Corbett, Robert McKenzie.

Railroaded to prison by corrupt sheriff Hodgins, the vassal of Kohler, Sr., who rules Shadow Valley, O'Brien serves his sentence and returns, hoping to clear himself of stigma and to discover his slain father's killers. In a Romeo-Juliet romance, Sutton is the winsome ward of the villainous Kohler, Sr., who wishes her to wed his equally evil son, Kohler, Jr. Hoping to help the hectored heroine escape, O'Brien is captured by the devilish duo and their henchmen, his life being made surety to their demands for her compliance. The honorable O'Brien forces a confession from the chagrined sheriff and all ends well. A well-handled B western.

p, Bert Gilroy; d, David Howard; w, Oliver Drake (based on the story "No Law in Shadow Valley" by W.C. Tuttle); ph, Harry Wild; ed, Frederich Knudtson; md, Roy Webb.

Western **(PR:A MPAA:NR)**

LAWLESS WOMAN, THE* ½ (1931) 63m CHES bw

Vera Reynolds, Carroll Nye, Thomas Jackson, Wheeler Oakman, James Burtis, Gwen Lee, Phillips Smalley, June Page, Kitty Adams.

Burtis is a cub reporter in the big city, determined to impress his bosses. That he does, outsmarting veteran writers, lawmen, and a car full of gangsters as he solves a pair of murders. He also finds love, in the form of Page, as he saves a good girl gone wrong from the clutches of the badmen. It is, as Burtis exclaims, "all in a day's work" for a beginning reporter. The story is packed with cliches like that, as well as unbelievable situations and circumstances.

d, Richard Thorpe; w, Barney Gerard (based on a story by Arthur Hoerl, Barney Gerard, Thorpe); ph, M.S. Anderson; ed, Tom Persons.

Crime **(PR:A MPAA:NR)**

LAWMAN*** (1971) 98m Scimitar/UA c

Burt Lancaster *(Marshal Jered Maddox)*, Robert Ryan *(Marshal Cotton Ryan)*, Lee J. Cobb *(Vincent Bronson)*, Sheree North *(Laura Shelby)*, Joseph Wiseman *(Lucas)*, Robert Duvall *(Vernon Adams)*, Albert Salmi *(Harvey Stenbaugh)*, J.D. Cannon *(Hurd Price)*, John McGiver *(Mayor Sam Bolden)*, Richard Jordan *(Crowe Wheelwright)*, John Beck *(Jason Bronson)*, Ralph Waite *(Jack Dekker)*, William Watson *(Choctaw Lee)*, Charles Tyner *(Minister)*, John Hillerman *(Totts)*, Robert Emhardt *(Hersham)*, Richard Bull *(Dusaine)*, Hugh McDermott *(Moss)*, Lou Frizell *(Cobden)*, Walter Brooke *(Luther Harris)*, Bill Brimley *(Marc Corman)*.

Though directed by an Englishman, Winner, in his first try at the western genre, there's more spaghetti than steak-and-kidney pie in this ferocious film. Exploring the age-old political question, "Does the end justify the means?" letter-of-the-lawman Lancaster pursues rancher Cobb and his six hired hands home after the carefree cowboys have accidentally killed an old man in a drunken, playful spree. Following regulations, Lancaster enlists the aid of Ryan, the local marshal; the latter deliberately diverts him from his quest, as do the rest of the citizens. Doggedly doing his duty, Lancaster confronts Cobb, who tries to cut a deal, reasoning that the killing was an accident, as everyone is aware. Cobb's rambunctious ranchhands, realizing the futility of trying to sway the fanatical Lancaster from what he regards as his mission, goad him to a gunfight, in which foreman Salmi is killed. Tracking the fleeing felons, Lancaster wounds Cannon, then takes the wounded man to the nearby home of Duvall. The latter has flown his own coop, leaving behind his wife North, who once was intimate with the malevolent marshal. Following a night of reminiscence, Lancaster relents, electing to lay down his guns to halt yet more mayhem. Too late: the ranchers and their neighbors stage a showdown. Cobb's son Beck draws on Lancaster, who is forced to the fray in a gory close, one which leaves but a single survivor of the seven unwitting miscreants. Lancaster rides away, chastened or no, no one knows. A humorless Greek-tragedy western with little going for it save its inexorable momentum toward the obvious end.

p&d, Michael Winner; w, Gerald Wilson; ph, Bob Paynter (Technicolor); m, Jerry Fielding; ed, Freddie Wilson; prod d, Stan Jolley; art d, Herbert Westbrook; set d, Ray Moyer; cos, Ron Beck; spec eff, Leon Ortega; makeup, Richard Mills.

Western **(PR:C MPAA:GP)**

LAWMAN IS BORN, A*** (1937) 58m A.W. Hackel/REP bw

Johnny Mack Brown *(Tom Mitchell)*, Iris Meredith *(Beth Graham)*, Warner Richmond *(Kane Briscoe)*, Mary MacLaren *(Martha Lance)*, Dick Curtis *(Lefty Doogan)*, Earle Hodgins *(Sheriff Lance)*, Charles King *(Bert Moscrip)*, Frank LaRue *(Graham)*, Al St. John *(Root)*, Steve Clark *(Sam Brownlee)*, Jack C. Smith *(Ike Manton)*, Sherry Tansey, Wally West, Budd Buster, Lew Meehan, Tex Palmer.

A well-done series western with Brown stopping a gang of landgrabbing cattle rustlers and throwing them behind bars. The story is simple but totally realistic, except for the more-than-six-shot six-shooters, but otherwise for a low-budget western the eye on detail is unusual. The acting is better than expected, especially by Meredith, Brown's love interest.

p, A.W. Hackel; d, Sam Newfield; w, George H. Plympton (based on a story by Harry F. Olmstead); ph, Bert Longenecker; ed, Roy Claire.

Western **(PR:A MPAA:NR)**

LAWRENCE OF ARABIA***** (1962, Brit.) 220m Horizon/COL c

Peter O'Toole *(T.E. Lawrence)*, Alec Guinness *(Prince Feisal)*, Anthony Quinn *(Auda Abu Tayi)*, Jack Hawkins *(Gen. Allenby)*, Jose Ferrer *(Turkish Bey)*, Anthony Quayle *(Col. Harry Brighton)*, Claude Rains *(Mr. Dryden)*, Arthur Kennedy *(Jackson Bentley)*, Donald Wolfit *(Gen. Murray)*, Omar Sharif *(Sherif Ali Ibn El Kharish)*, I.S. Johar *(Gasim)*, Gamil Ratib *(Majid)*, Michel Ray *(Ferraj)*, Zia Mohyeddin *(Tafas)*, John Dimech *(Daud)*, Howard Marion Crawford *(Medical Officer)*, Jack Gwillim *(Club Secretary)*, Hugh Miller *(RAMC Colonel)*, Kenneth Fortescue *(Allenby's Aide)*, Stuart Saunders *(Regimental Sergeant-Major)*, Fernando Sancho *(Turkish Sergeant)*, Henry Oscar *(Reciter)*, Norman Rossington *(Cpl. Jenkins)*, John Ruddock *(Elder Harith)*, M. Cher Kaoui, Mohammed Habachi.

When asked where he wanted his seats for the road show premiere of LAWRENCE OF ARABIA, one wag said, "I'll have two on the shady side, please." And he was right. The intensity of the screen was such that audiences could almost get tanned by the scenes in the desert. Were it not for a last-minute change of heart for Lean, he might have gone ahead with a proposed biography of Ghandi and forgotten about T.E. Lawrence. That would have been a loss as this is acknowledged as one of the greatest adventure-biographies ever filmed. Lean chose O'Toole, then an obscure Irishman who had just scored in the London stage version of "Hamlet." He wasn't sure of his decision as O'Toole is tall and Lawrence was small. O'Toole is dashing and Lawrence was shy and yet the lanky actor turned out to be perfection in the role and successfully captured the enigmatic quality of the man upon whom the film was based. We must applaud Lean for his bold step in selecting O'Toole, as well as bless him for saving us the spectre of 220 minutes with Charlton Heston. Lean exhibited the same type of fascination for the desert as Lawrence had and took more than a year filming and studying the terrain of Saudi Arabia before commencing work on the film. Lean is a man who takes great pains in what he does and spends sometimes four and five years on a project. That attention to detail is evident in every frame of this huge epic that did not get away (something we've seen often in lesser hands, such as Cimino's HEAVEN'S GATE). LAWRENCE OF ARABIA begins with the death of Lawrence. He had already taken the name of Ross, to avoid any publicity, and was riding a Vincent Black Shadow motorcycle along a country road in May, 1935, when he crashed mysteriously. Some thought it was suicide, others think he may have been ridden off the road, but the consensus is that his death was accidental. The film does not pose any questions, merely reports the facts as Lean and screenwriter Bolt (with uncredited assistance from Michael Wilson) saw them. Suddenly we're in British headquarters in Cairo during the WWI. O'Toole is a 29-year-old General Staff desk man and not very interested in his work, as it provided none of the adventure for which he joined the service. He requests, and is granted, a transfer to Arabia and, once there, helps promote an Arab rebellion against the Turks who rule the area. In order to do this, he must unite the warring Arab factions, which he does. Then, with men supplied to him by Quinn, he and Sharif cross the burning sands of the Nefud Desert to capture the port of Aqaba from a superior, but disorganized Turkish garrison. Along the way, O'Toole must take the life of a man he's saved because that man had done something that would have split the tribes. Realizing that one man's death will save the lives of many others, he shoots him. The result is a baffling and perturbing feeling for O'Toole, almost a sadistic glee in the taking of another person's life. Now it's back to Cairo again where Hawkins, one of his superiors, convinces O'Toole that he must return to the desert to continue his work as he seems to be the only Briton whom the Arabs believe. Equipped with arms and men and money, O'Toole begins a period of guerrilla warfare. He is deified by his Arab men, and his exploits are made even larger as Kennedy, an American journalist, goes with him and dutifully reports the forays to a waiting world. (The Kennedy character is loosely based on the real-life travels of Lowell Thomas, a journalist, then a CBS radio commentator for almost five decades. Thomas wrote a book entitled *With Lawrence In Arabia.*) O'Toole is captured by the Turks, tortured and sodomized by the vicious Ferrer, then released. (The film only hints at the possibility that Lawrence actually enjoyed this brutal treatment and may have had underlying homosexual and masochistic tendencies.) O'Toole returns to Cairo and is given a new assignment by Hawkins. Damascus is to be attacked and the Arabs need "Arens" to lead them. (They could never pronounce "Lawrence," hence the name "Arens" was accorded him.) O'Toole and his charges slaughter a column of Turks, then he leads his men to Damascus where an Arab council is set up. But the Arabs of that era are not unlike many of them today and the attempt at unification is a disaster, with all of the factions bickering and threatening each other at a time when their joy should have been supreme. The council is dissolved, Hawkins and the big cheese, Guinness (as Feisal), attempt to hammer out an accord, and O'Toole returns to England in the sadness that he has failed. (After the years depicted in the film, Lawrence took the name of Ross, reenlisted in the service and his true identity was eventually unmasked.) This is a film of grandeur and epic measurements. The sweeping desert vistas and the stark story combine to totally immerse the viewer. We never get close to the persona of

Lawrence in the film and perhaps that is as it should be, for no one was able to get close to him in real life. If there is any flaw in this gem of a movie, that dispassionate manner of O'Toole's is it. Lean chose to avoid Lawrence's personal life and concentrate on the heroic story, the immense successes and the bitter disappointments. Shot partly on location in Saudi Arabia, temperatures often went so high that thermometer readings could not be taken. The actual city of Aqaba had become so modern that it was impossible to shoot, so a duplicate was built along the sea at Seville in Spain, where Damascus, Cairo, and Jerusalem were also constructed. The slaughter of the Turks was filmed in Morocco. LAWRENCE OF ARABIA won Oscars as Best Film, for Best Direction, Best Music, Best Photography, Best Art Direction, Best Sound and Best Editing. The screenplay, O'Toole, and Sharif were also nominated, but lost out that year to TO KILL A MOCKINGBIRD, Gregory Peck, and Ed Begley for SWEET BIRD OF YOUTH. The number of awards is not surprising as the Academy is often impressed by historical pieces that work. Many thought O'Toole was a flash in the cinematic pan. This was proven incorrect when he returned, in his next film, to take plaudits in BECKET. The supporting cast in LAWRENCE OF ARABIA is one of the best ever assembled. The only question mark is the sometimes caricaturish work done by Quinn, wearing a huge putty nose. Any adventure film, no matter what the cost, would be hard-pressed to rival LAWRENCE OF ARABIA in scope or content. It cost $15 million in 1962, a sum that might be triple that today. The battle scenes are among the most horrifying ever shot and show the brutality, rather than the glory, of war. One of the second unit cinematographers was Nicholas Roeg, who later went on to direct many puzzling films. He should have stayed closer to Lean, who is anything but puzzling. Lean's career includes examples of the best of any genre, in that BRIEF ENCOUNTER is the perfect bittersweet romance, GREAT EXPECTATIONS is one of the finest period pieces, and THE BRIDGE ON THE RIVER KWAI, perhaps the best of the Japanese theater war movies. Screenwriter Wilson also worked, uncredited, on that one, as he was one of the "Hollywood Ten" who refused to talk to the House Un-American Activities Committee and paid the price by being blackballed for many years.

p, Sam Spiegel, David Lean; d, Lean; w, Robert Bolt, Michael Wilson (based on *The Seven Pillars of Wisdom* by T.E. Lawrence); ph, F.A. Young (Super Panavision 70, Technicolor); m, Maurice Jarre; ed, Anne V. Coates; prod d, John Box; md, M.W. Stoloff; art d, John Stoll; set d, Dario Simoni; cos, Phyllis Dalton; makeup, Charles Parker; hairstyles, A.G. Scott.

Adventure **Cas.** **(PR:C MPAA:NR)**

LAWTON STORY, THE** (1949) 101m Hallmark c

Ginger Prince *(Ginger)*, Forrest Taylor *(Uncle Mark)*, Millard Coody *(Himself/Jesus)*, Ferris Taylor *(Uncle Jonathan)*, Maude Eburne *(Henrietta)*, Gwyn Shipman *(Jane)*, Darlene Bridges *(Herself/Virgin Mary)*, Willa Pearl Curtis *(Willa Pearl)*, Ray Largay *(Dr. Martin)*, A.S. Fischer *(Himself/Simon)*, Hazel Lee Becker *(Herself/Mary Magdalene)*, Knox Manning *(Narrator)*, Lee "Lasses" White.

A cheap independent film that circles around the Easter pageant in Lawton, Oklahoma. The actors are mostly residents of the town who act as themselves and as characters in the story of Christ. The last 50 minutes of the film is of the pageant itself, and was shot in color. Hallmark also did an exploitation film titled MOM AND DAD.

p, Kroger Babb; d, William Beaudine, Harold Daniels; w, Scott Darling, De Vallon Scott (based on stories by Milton Raison, Mildred A. Horn, Rev. A. Mark Wallock); ph, Henry Sharp (Cinecolor); ed, Dick Currier; md, Edward J. Kay; art d, Dave Milton; m/l, Lee "Lasses" White, Steven Edwards, Andy Page, Vachel Lindsey.

Drama **(PR:A MPAA:NR)**

LAWYER, THE** (1969) 117m Furie Productions/PAR c

Barry Newman *(Tony Petrocelli)*, Harold Gould *(Eric P. Scott)*, Diana Muldaur *(Ruth Petrocelli)*, Robert Colbert *(Jack Harrison)*, Kathleen Crowley *(Alice Fiske)*, Warren Kemmerling *(Sergeant Moran)*, Booth Colman *(Judge Crawford)*, Ken Swofford *(Charlie O'Keefe)*, E.J. Andre *(F.J. Williamson)*, William Sylvester *(Paul Harrison)*, Jeff Thompson *(Andy Greer)*, Tom Harvey *(Bob Chambers)*, Ivor Barry *(Wyler)*, Melendy Britt *(Ann Greer)*, John Himes *(Myron McCauley)*, Ralph Thomas *(Mike Peterson)*, Mary Wilcox *(Wilma Harrison)*, Gene O'Donnell *(Judge Swackhammer)*, Walter Mathews *(Mr. Andre)*, Ray Ballard *(Mr. Canon)*, James McEachin *(Striker)*, Robert L. Poyner *(J.C. Hornby)*.

Newman plays a midwestern lawyer defending a doctor, Colbert, accused of murdering his wife. Colbert asserts that he was knocked unconscious and when he awoke he found his wife dead in their bedroom. During the trial, it's revealed that the doctor was having an affair with a divorcee, and the case gets much prejudiced press coverage. Colbert is found guilty; Newman calls for an appeal and in the retrial Colbert is found innocent because of the testimony of a witness who says that Colbert's wife might have been murdered by the wife of the man with whom she was having an affair. The trial is loosely based on the Sam Sheppard murder case. The film would be the basis for a TV series.

p, Brad Dexter; d, Sidney J. Furie; w, Furie, Harold Buchman; ph, Ralph Woolsey (Technicolor); m, Malcolm Dodds; ed, Argyle Nelson, Jr.; art d, Pato Guzman; set d, Audrey Blasdel.

Drama **(PR:O MPAA:R)**

LAWYER MAN** (1933) 68m WB bw

William Powell *(Anton Adam)*, Joan Blondell *(Olga Michaels)*, Helen Vinson *(Barbara Bentley)*, Alan Dinehart *(Granville Bentley)*, Allen Jenkins *(Issy Levine)*, David Landau *(John Gilmurry)*, Claire Dodd *(Virginia St. Johns)*, Sheila Terry *(Flo)*, Kenneth Thomson *(Dr. Frank Gresham)*, Jack LaRue *(Spike)*, Rockliffe Fellowes *(Kovak)*, Roscoe Karns *(Merritt)*, Dorothy Christy *(Chorus Girl)*, Ann Brody *(Mrs. Levine)*, Curley Wright *(Giuseppi)*, Edward McWade *(Moyle)*, Tom Kennedy *(Jake, the Iceman)*, Sterling Holloway *(Olga's Dining Friend)*, Vaughn Taylor *(Reporter)*, Wade Boteler *(Court Officer)*, Hooper Atchley *(Anton's Aide)*, Irving Bacon *(Court Guard)*, Frederick Burton *(Judge)*, Henry Hall *(Juryman)*, Wilfred Lucas *(Jury Foreman)*, Dewey Robinson *(Client)*.

Powell is a small-time lawyer who moves up the forensic ranks to assistant prosecutor. On the way to the top he's charged with blackmailing Dodd, but he's found innocent. Blondell plays his secretary, and Landau is the political boss who sets him up with the blackmail charge. Few courtroom scenes; the action focuses on Powell's ascension to suavity in cultured society. He and Blondell are excellent, even though mismatched.

p, Hal Wallis; d, William Dieterle; w, Rian James, James Seymour (based on a novel by Max Trell); ph, Robert Kurrle; ed, Thomas Pratt.

Drama **(PR:A MPAA:NR)**

LAWYER'S SECRET, THE* 1/2 (1931) 70m PAR bw

Clive Brook *(Drake Norris)*, Charles "Buddy" Rogers *(Laurie Roberts)*, Richard Arlen *(Joe Hart)*, Fay Wray *(Kay Roberts)*, Jean Arthur *(Beatrice Stevens)*, Francis McDonald *("The Weasel")*, *Harold Goodwin ("Madame X")*, *Syd Saylor ("Red")*; *Lawrence LaMarr, Robert Perry, Wilbur Mack.*

Brook is a lawyer who defends his soon-to-be brother-in-law, Rogers, on a murder charge. A sailor, Arlen, has been charged with the murder because he had gambled away his gun, which was used as the murder weapon. He has been sentenced to death. Rogers comes forward with a confession in the final minutes. Wray is Brook's fiancee and Arthur plays Arlen's girl friend. One of the first of many films to explore the sanctity of the lawyer/client confidence (remarkably resembling the popular priest/penitent theme), this features an excellent portrayal by Arlen. Rogers, Mary Pickford's husband, does well as the ne'er- do-well accessory to murder.

d, Louis Gasnier, Max Marcin; w, Lloyd Corrigan, Marcin (based on a story by James Hilary Finn); ph, Arthur Todd.

Drama **(PR:A MPAA:NR)**

LAXDALE HALL (SEE: SCOTCH ON THE ROCKS, 1954, Brit.)

LAY THAT RIFLE DOWN* 1/2 (1955) 71m REP bw

Judy Canova *(Judy)*, Robert Lowery *(Nick Stokes)*, Jil Jarmyn *(Betty)*, Jacqueline de Wit *(Aunt Sarah)*, Richard Deacon *(Glover Speckleton)*, Robert Burton *(Professor)*, James Bell *(Mr. Fetcher)*, Leon Tyler *(Horace Speckleton)*, Tweeny Canova *(Tweeny)*, Pierre Watkin *(Mr. Coswell)*, Marjorie Bennett *(Mrs. Speckleton)*, William Fawcett *(Wurpie)*, Paul E. Burns *(Mr. Gribble)*, Edmund Cobb *(Sheriff Cushing)*, Donald MacDonald *(Johnny)*, Mimi Gibson *(Terry)*, Rudy Lee *(Billy)*.

Another rustic Cinderella story, the last of Canova's second and final series at Republic, has the country comedienne a domestic drudge at the small hotel of her outrageous aunt, De Wit. Eager to enhance her meager existence, the downtrodden damsel enrolls in a correspondence charm course. Swindling associates of the school descend upon her, intending to use her as a dupe in their duplicitous plot to do De Wit and bank president Deacon out of their fortunes. Confidence man Lowery, witnessing Canova's good works in aiding orphans on her family farm, undergoes a conversion. Down-to-earth goodness gains great things as oil is discovered under the farm and Canova, as always, turns princess-like. While continuing her successful TV career, Canova dropped out of films for five years until her appearance in MGM's ADVENTURES OF HUCKLEBERRY FINN (1960). Songs include: "I'm Glad I Was Born on My Birthday," "Sleepy Serenade," "The Continental Correspondence Charm School" (Donald Kahn, Jack Elliott).

p, Sidney Picker; d, Charles Lamont; w, Barry Shipman; ph, John L. Russell, Jr.; m, R. Dale Butts; ed, Arthur E. Roberts; md, Butts; art d, Carroll Clark; spec eff, Howard and Theodore Lydecker.

Comedy **(PR:A MPAA:NR)**

LAZARILLO*

(1963, Span.) 100m Hesperia/Union bw (EL LAZARILLO DE TORMES)

Marco Paoletti *(Lazarillo)*, Juan Jose Menendez *(The Squire)*, Carlos Casaravilla *(Blind Man)*, Memmo Carotenuto *(The Actor)*, Margarita Lozano *(Lazarillo's Mother)*, Antonio Molino *(The Bailiff)*, Emilio Santiago *(Priest)*, Ana Prehan, Mary Paz Pondal, Enrique Avila, Pilar Sanclemente, Carlo Pisacane.

Orphaned youngster Paoletti, abandoned by his mother, wanders from a blind beggar to a priest to an actor. He earns a living with the latter by masquerading as a priest and selling papal indulgences. He has discovered that a full belly is more important than a serene conscience. Released in its native Spain in 1959. (In Spanish; English subtitles.)

p, Carlos Couret; d&w, Cesar Ardavin (based on the anonymous novel *Lazarillo de Tormes)*; ph, Manuel Berenguer; m, Emilio Lehurberg; ed, Magdalena Pulido, Salvador Ruiz de Luna; art d, Eduardo Torre de la Fuente; cos, Humberto Cornejo; English subtitles, Travers Clement.

Drama **(PR:A MPAA:NR)**

LAZY BONES (SEE: HALLELUJAH, I'M A BUM, 1933)

LAZY RIVER* 1/2 (1934) 75m MGM bw

Jean Parker *(Sarah)*, Robert Young *(Bill Drexel)*, Ted Healy *(Gabby)*, C. Henry Gordon *(Sam Kee)*, Nat Pendleton *(Tiny)*, Ruth Channing *(Ruby)*, Maude Eburne *(Miss Minnie)*, Raymond Hatton *(Captain Orkney)*, Irene Franklin *(Suzanne)*, Joseph Cawthorn *(Ambrose)*, Erville Alderson *(Sheriff)*, George Lewis *(Armand)*, Purnell B. Pratt *(Lawyer)*, Walter Long *(Buck)*, Donald Douglas *(Officer)*, John Larkin *(Black Man)*.

Bayou belle Parker is a charmer as she helps three ex-convicts, Healy, Pendleton, and ne'er-do-well scion of wealth Young to follow the path of righteousness. They take the path in their own peculiar style, robbing a rascal's riverboat safe to assist an old woman who would otherwise have lost her store. The improbable villain, the half-Chinese Gordon, overacts prodigiously as we see how he filled his safe, smuggling contraband Chinese emigrants into the country, dumping their weighted bodies overboard when approached by authorities. When he tries to do the same to Young, the latter is rescued by the heroic efforts of his friends, the former miscreants. All works out well as one-time black sheep Young bares his past to Parker and they unite.

p, Lucien Hubbard; d, George B. Seitz; w, Hubbard (based on the play "Ruby" by Lea David Freeman); ph, Gregg Toland; m, Dr. William Axt; ed, William LeVanway.

Drama (PR:A MPAA:NR)

LAZYBONES**1/2 (1935, Brit.) REA/RKO bw

Claire Luce (*Kitty McCarthy*), Ian Hunter (*Sir Reginald Ford*), Sara Allgood (*Bridget*), Bernard Nedell (*Mike McCarthy*), Michael Shepley (*Hildebrand Pope*), Bobbie Comber (*Kemp*), Denys Blakelock (*Hugh Ford*), Marjorie Gaskell (*Marjory Ford*), Pamela Carme (*Lottie Pope*), Harold Warrender (*Lord Melton*), Miles Malleson (*Pessimist*), Fred Withers, Frank Morgan, Fewlass Llewellyn, Paul Blake.

Hunter is a ne'er-do-well baronet who's lost his patrimony. After meeting American heiress Luce, Hunter thinks a marriage will help him recoup his lost fortune, but after the nuptials, it proves she's been swindled and is just as penniless. Her nefarious cousin Nedell steals some official government papers and tries to blackmail Luce into leaving her husband. She won't do it and with the aid of Hunter—dubbed "Lazybones" by his family—Nedell is stopped and forced to return to America. There are some good moments in this enjoyable romantic comedy. An early directorial effort for the maker of THE RED SHOES and PEEPING TOM.

p, Julius Hagen; d, Michael Powell; w, Gerard Fairlie (based on the play by Ernest Denny); ph, Ernest Palmer.

Comedy (PR:A MPAA:NR)

LE AMICHE***
(1962, Ital.) 104m Titanus-Trionfalcine/Premiere Films bw (AKA: THE GIRL FRIENDS)

Eleonora Rossi-Drago (*Clelia*), Gabriele Ferzetti (*Lorenzo*), Franco Fabrizi (*Cesare Pedoni*), Valentina Cortese (*Nene*), Yvonne Furneaux (*Momina de Stefani*), Madeleine Fischer (*Rosetta Savoni*), Anna Maria Pancani (*Mariella*), Maria Gambarelli (*Clelia's Employer*), Ettore Manni (*Carlo*), Luciano Volpato.

Originally made in 1955, LE AMICHE was not shown in the U.S. until L'AVVENTURA had established Antonioni as an important figure in the international cinema. Without relying too heavily upon plot or story development, Antonioni dwells deep beneath exteriors of his characters to explore their mental make-up. Opening with Rossi-Drago returning from Rome to her home town of Turin, she becomes involved with a group of the local young fashionables. She attempts to have an affair with a young architect, Manni, but ends it when she becomes convinced that marriage to him will only result in a life of poverty. Her friends include Ferzetti, an artist who is married to Cortese, and who is also having an affair with Fischer. Fischer commits suicide when Ferzetti announces that his art means more to him than his women, and eventually Rossi-Drago returns to Rome after she is fired from her job. LE AMICHE was an example in the development of Antonioni's style that would reach its fulfillment in L'AVVENTURA and LA NOTTE. A concern with man's psychological relationship to a continually isolated environment was the prime factor in establishing this approach.

p, Giovanni Addessi; d, Michelangelo Antonioni; w, Suso Cecchi D'Amico, Alba De Cespedes, Antonioni (based on the story "Tre donne sole" by Cesare Pavese); ph, Gianni Di Venanzo; m, Giovanni Fusco; ed, Eraldo Da Roma; art d, Gianni Polidori, cos, Sorelle Fontana [Roma].

Drama (PR:C MPAA:NR)

LE AVVENTURE E GLI AMORI DI MIGUEL CERVANTES
(SEE: YOUNG REBEL, THE, 1969, Fr./Ital./Span.)

LE BEAU MARIAGE****
(1982, Fr.) 97m Les Films du Losanger-Les Films du Carosse/UA c (AKA: A GOOD MARRIAGE; THE WELL-MADE MARRIAGE)

Beatrice Romand (*Sabine*), Andre Dussollier (*Edmond*), Feodor Atkine (*Simon*), Huguette Faget (*Antique Dealer*), Arielle Dombasle (*Clarisse*), Thamila Mezbah (*Mother*), Sophie Renoir (*Lise*), Herve Duhamel (*Frederic*), Pascal Greggory (*Nicolas*), Virginie Thevenet (*The Bride*), Denise Bailly (*The Countess*), Vincent Gauthier (*Claude*), Ann Mercier (*Secretary*), Catherine Rethi (*Client*), Patrick Lambert (*Traveler*).

The second of Eric Rohmer's "Comedies and Proverbs" series (the first being THE AVIATOR'S WIFE), LE BEAU MARIAGE is a brilliant and hopelessly charming tale of a university student with a flat in Paris who decides one day, quite arbitrarily, to get married . . . all she is lacking is a husband, a minor detail in her plan. She leaves her painter boy friend, quits her antique-store job, and begins her pursuit of lawyer Dussolier. He, however, is a few years older than she and absorbed by his work. Innocently infatuated with Dussolier (after all, she has decided that he will be her husband), she invites him to a birthday party at her mother's house. Hours into the party it appears he will not show up but he does, though Romand's hopes are soon shattered. He is obviously uncomfortable, exhausted, and uninterested in a relationship. He tries to be as kind and understanding as possible to Romand, but she pesters him on the phone and at his office until he is brutally blunt with her. Instead of taking the rejection too hard, she simply carries on without him. A thoroughly enjoyable picture which is carried by Romand's spunky performance (she previously appeared in Rohmer's CLAIRE'S KNEE, 12 years earlier), allowing

you to leave the theater with a smile on your face. You'll also be humming the fine synthesized score by Gure. (In French; English subtitles.)

p, Margaret Menogoz; d&w, Eric Rohmer; ph, Bernard Lutic, Romain Winding, Nicolas Brunet; m, Ronan Gure, Simon Des Innocents; ed, Cecile Decugis, Lisa Heredia.

Drama/Comedy (PR:C-O MPAA:PG)

LE BEAU SERGE***1/2
(1959, Fr.) 97m United Motion Picture (AKA: HANDSOME SERGE)

Gerard Blain (*Serge*), Jean-Claude Brialy (*Francois*), Bernadette Lafont (*Marie*), Edmond Beauchamp (*Glomaud*), Michelle Meritz, (*Yvonne*), Jeanne Perez, Claude Cerval, Andre Dino.

Generally considered the film that put the French New Wave in the history books (though Rivette's PARIS BELONGS TO US was the first to go into production), LE BEAU SERGE received overwhelming critical support for its use of non-professional actors, raw black-and-white photography (masterfully executed by Decae), and its personal vision. A tale of two old friends, LE BEAU SERGE, stars Brialy as a city dweller who returns to the provincial French village of his childhood and is reunited with Blain, a successful architect-turned-drunkard. After the birth of a malformed son, Blain's life and marriage tailspin as he collapses under a tremendous guilt. He not only denies the aid of the local priest, but refuses to accept the advice of Brialy, a theology student. Brialy persists, suggesting that Blain leave his wife—an action which only worsens his depressed state and causes him to take up with Lafont, his wife's half-sister. It takes the birth of a healthy baby to relieve the guilt that Blain carries with him. Unfortunately the film is cluttered with a high degree of Catholicism, which Chabrol had the good sense to diminish in his later films. Though highly acclaimed, LE BEAU SERGE's popularity was quickly overshadowed by the success of Truffaut's 400 BLOWS, Godard's BREATHLESS, and Resnais' HIROSHIMA MON AMOUR, all of which were released the same year (1959 in France). A companion piece to LE BEAU SERGE which also starred Brialy and Blain, LES COUSINS, appeared the following year to an equally enthusiastic reception. (In French; English subtitles.)

d&w, Claude Chabrol; ph, Henri Decae; m, Emile Delpierre; ed, Jacques Gaillard; English subtitles, Ben Smith.

Drama (PR:C-O MPAA:NR)

LE BLE EN HERBE (SEE: GAME OF LOVE, THE 1954, Fr.)

LE BONHEUR**1/2 (1966, Fr.) 87m Parc/Clover c (AKA: HAPPINESS)

Jean-Claude Drouot (*Francois*), Claire Drouot (*Therese*), Sandrine Drouot (*Gisou*), Oliver Drouot (*Pierrot*), Marie-France Boyer (*Emilie*).

Offbeat in its idyllic nature LE BONHEUR centers on a man's desire to have both a wife and a mistress, even though his marriage seems satisfactory. Drouot, a French carpenter, takes a vacation with his wife and two children (played by Drouot's real-life wife and children) and, while enjoying the airy countryside, encounters Boyer, a postal clerk. The two are impelled to begin a passionate affair. Rather than ruining his marriage, Drouot finds that his infidelity actually brings him closer to his wife. She, however, responds to his liberal outlook by killing herself. His grief is quickly forgotten and, instead of breaking off with his mistress, moves in with her. What makes this seem so unrealistic is the flowery Mozart score and the impressionistic Renoir atmosphere which replaces the expected sorrow and death. Varda, one of the few consistently interesting woman directors, has here acknowledged her debt to Jean Renoir's 1960 film PICNIC ON THE GRASS, but she unfortunately lacks the grace to make it succeed. An interesting idea that is, unfortunately, not all that interesting to watch. Selections from Mozart include: "The Piano Quintet in E-Flat Major," "Music For Two Pianos," "The Fugue in C-Minor for Piano, Four Hands," "Adagio and Fugue in C-Minor for String Orchestra," and a movement from an unfinished symphony. (In French; English subtitles.)

p, Mag Bodard; d&w, Agnes Varda; ph, Jean Rabier, Claude Beausoleil (Eastmancolor); m, Wolfgang Amadeus Mozart; ed, Janine Verneau; art d, Hubert Monloup.

Drama (PR:C MPAA:NR)

LE BOUCHER**1/2
(1971, Fr./Ital.) 93m Films La Boetie Euro International Film/Cinerama c (AKA: THE BUTCHER)

Stephane Audran (*Helene*), Jean Yanne (*Popaul*), Antonio Passalia (*Angelo*), Mario Beccaria (*Leon Hamel*), Pasquale Ferone (*Pere Cahrpy*), Roger Rudel (*Police Inspector Grumbach*), William Guerault (*Charles*).

A calculated and slowly-paced thriller set in the French countryside, where schoolteacher Audran begins a new assignment. She is soon romanced by the village butcher, Yanne, though she seems more concerned with her schoolchildren than with finding a lover. In the meantime, the village is stricken with random murders. Audran finds herself directly involved when a young girl's body is found near the schoolyard. With another murder, Audran finds herself frighteningly close to the incident. During a school outing, she and the children take a lunch break and eat their sandwiches outdoors. One girl, who is sitting next to a cliff, suddenly finds blood dripping onto her bread. Above her is discovered yet another butchered body. Audran's suspicions are raised when she finds a cigarette lighter of Yanne's next to the body, but the clever, deranged killer is one step ahead of her and buys another identical lighter. By the finale Audran's concern has turned into deadly fear as she barricades herself inside her house while Yanne pleads for her to let him in. He manages to get in and, armed with a butcher knife threatens Audran, but instead plunges the weapon into himself. Audran, whose love and compassion for him has grown during the incident, drives him during the night to a hospital, where he dies after their first kiss. An occasionally compelling psychological thriller which often gets bogged down in tedium, failing to reach the level of suspense that could have been achieved. The action takes place in a small town near the caves of Lascaux, with their prehistoric Cro-Magnon drawings perhaps redolent of the beast that may lurk within the seemingly gentle purveyor of meats. Like the psychopathic killer of little girls in Fritz Lang's M, Yanne's character is evoked in a manner which is calculated to stir a measure of audience sympathy: he is unable to help himself; he has his good qualities. The likely murderer of little girls, like Alfred Hitchcock's ladykiller in FRENZY, is depicted in an almost heroic light. Audran, the real-life wife of director Chabrol and star of three of his films, gives a compelling performance flawed only slightly by an excessive *panache*: she is simply too sophisticated to come across as a country schoolteacher. (In French; English subtitles.)

p, Andre Geneves; d&w, Claude Chabrol; ph, Jean Rabier (Eastmancolor); m, Pierre Jansen; ed, Jacques Gaillard; cos, Joseph Poulard.

Crime Drama   **(PR:O   MPAA:GP)**

LE CAPORAL EPINGLE   (SEE: ELUSIVE CORPORAL, THE, 1963, Fr.)

LE CAVE SE REBIFFE
                        (SEE: COUNTERFEITERS OF PARIS, THE, 1962, Fr./Ital.)

LE CERVEAU   (SEE: BRAIN, THE, 1969, Fr./U.S.)

LE CHARME DISCRET DE LA BOURGEOISIE
            (SEE: DISCREET CHARM OF THE BOURGEOISIE, THE, 1972, Fr.)

LE CHAT   (SEE: CAT, THE, 1975, Fr.)

LE CHAT DANS LE SAC   (SEE: CAT IN THE SACK, THE, 1967, Can.)

LE CHEVAL D'ORGEUIL   (SEE: HORSE OF PRIDE, 1980, Fr.)

LE CIEL EST A VOUS***
(1957, Fr.) 105m Les Films Raoul Ploquin/UFA bw (AKA: THE SKY IS YOURS)

Madeleine Renaud *(Therese Gauthier)*, Charles Vanel *(Pierre Gauthier)*, Jean Debucourt *(Larcher)*, Leonce Corne *(Dr. Maulette)*, Albert Remy *(Marcel)*, Robert Le Fort *(Robert)*, Anne Marie Labaye *(Jacqueline)*, Raoul Marco *(M. Noblet)*, Raymonde Vernay *(Mme. Brissard)*, Michel Francois *(Claude)*, Anne Vandenne *(Lucienne Ivry)*, Renee Thorel *(Neighbor)*.

Arguably Gremillon's finest directorial achievement, this picture tells the true tale (based on the 1938 Flight of Mme. Dupeyron) of a garage owner (Vanel) and his wife (Renaud) who both become fascinated with flying. They sacrifice everything for this passion and are rewarded when Renaud sets the woman's distance flying record. Gremillon was one of the few French directors who refused to flee during the Nazi occupation of France, choosing instead to make pictures which could take on a second meaning. It was said that this flying allegory represents the goals and ideals of those fighting for the Resistance—the Nazis never second guessed him, however.

d, Jean Gremillon; w, Charles Spaak (based on the story by Albert Valentin); ph, Louis Page; m, Roland-Manuel; ed, Louisette Hautecoeur; art d, Max Douy.

Drama   **(PR:A   MPAA:NR)**

LE CLOCHARD   (SEE: MAGNIFICENT TRAMP, THE, 1962, Fr./Ital.)

LE COMTE DE MONTE CRISTO
            (SEE: STORY OF THE COUNT OF MONTE CRISTO, THE, 1962, Fr./Ital.)

LE CORBEAU   (SEE: RAVEN, THE, 1948, Fr.)

LE CORNIAUD   (SEE: SUCKER, THE, 1966, Fr./Ital.)

LE CRIME DE MONSIEUR LANGE
                        (SEE: CRIME OF MONSIEUR LANGE, THE, 1936, Fr.)

LE DANGER VIENT DE L'ESCAPE
                        (SEE: DAY THE SKY EXPLODED, THE, 1958, Fr./Ital.)

LE DENIER MILLIARDAIRE ** 1/2   (1934, Fr.) 90m Pathe-Natan bw

Max Dearly *(Banco)*, Marthe Mellot *(Queen)*, Renee Saint-Cyr *(Princess)*, Sinoel *(Prime Minister)*, Paul Olivier *(Chamberlain)*, Charles Redgie *(Crown Prince)*, Raymond Cordy *(Valet)*, Jose Noguero *(Band Leader)*, Marcel Carpentier *(Detective)*, Aimos, Jean Ayme, Christiane Ribes.

A fictitious country, Casinaria, depends on gambling foreigners to support its economy, and finds itself on the verge of bankruptcy. Queen Mellot lures financier Dearly to her country intending to marry him to her daughter (St. Cyr), although the girl loves Noguero, leader of the national band (whose entire repertoire consists of the national anthem played in a variety of tempos). Dearly is appointed dictator and suffers a blow to the head, resulting in some very strange behavior. St. Cyr elopes with Noguero and Dearly ends up engaged to the queen before revealing that he is not the millionaire he pretended to be. A major letdown after his earlier successes, this Clair offering provoked rioting in France, then in the midst of a wave of conservatism (provoked by the rise of Hitler next door). Although a major failure in its native country, the film became a major success in the USSR and Japan. Worth seeing for a number of funny scenes revolving around the collapse of the nation's currency. Clair had originally contracted with Tobis (Les Films Sonores) to make the film, but the German-owned French company rejected his script for obvious reasons; the finished film was banned in the Italy of Mussolini and the Germany of Hitler. Some of the funniest scenes in the film had to do with achingly evocative economic conditions in those recently depression-torn countries. A farmer pays a waiter for his dinner with a hen, and receives as change two chicks and an egg; he leaves the latter as a tip. In another scene which presaged the later craze for aerobic exercise, mad dictator Dearly decrees that all citizens must run for hours around the public square. After this film Clair left France and made the wonderful THE GHOST

GOES WEST in England and several excellent features in the U.S. (AND THEN THERE WERE NONE and I MARRIED A WITCH among them) before returning to his homeland after the war. (In French; English subtitles.)

d&w, Rene Clair; ph, Rudolph Mate, Louis Nee; m, Maurice Jaubert; ed, Jean Pouzet; art d, Lucien Aguettand, Lucien Carre.

Comedy   **(PR:A   MPAA:NR)**

LE DESERT DES TARTARES
                        (SEE: DESERT OF THE TARTARS, THE, 1976, Fr./Ital./Iran)

LE DESERT ROUGE   (SEE: RED DESERT, 1964, Fr./Ital.)

LE DIABLE AU CORPS   (SEE: DEVIL IN THE FLESH, THE, 1949, Fr.)

LE DIABLE PAR LA QUEUE
                        (SEE: DEVIL BY THE TAIL, THE, 1969, Fr./Ital.)

LE DIABLE PROBABLEMENT   (SEE: DEVIL PROBABLY, THE, 1977, Fr.)

LE DIABOLIQUE DOCTEUR MABUSE
            (SEE: THOUSAND EYES OF DR. MABUSE, THE, 1960, Fr./Ital./Ger.)

LE DISTRAIT   (SEE: DAYDREAMER, THE, 1975, Fr.)

LE FANTOME DE LA LIBERTE
                        (SEE: PHANTOM OF LIBERTY, THE, 1974, Fr.)

LE FARCEUR   (SEE: JOKER, THE, 1961, Fr.)

LE FATE   (SEE: QUEENS, THE, 1968, Ital./Fr.)

LE GAI SAVOIR****
(1968, Fr.) 95m O.R.T.F.-Anouchka-Bavaria Atelier c (AKA: THE JOY OF LEARNING; MERRY WISDOM; HAPPY KNOWLEDGE)

Juliet Berto *(Patricia Lumumba)*, Jean-Pierre Leaud *(Emile Rousseau)*.

A fascinating film from the master of cinematic discourse, Jean-Luc Godard, in which he makes a profound attempt to dissolve narrative structure to its most base elements—sound and image. Commissioned by the French government as a television adaptation of Jean Jacques Rousseau's "Emile," LE GAI SAVOIR instead turned out to be a study of language—or more precisely film language. It is completely absent of plot and leaves Berto and Leaud (two of the most prominent acting figures in the French New Wave) sitting in the black void of a sound stage, lit only by a single light. Not surprisingly the French government was furious with Godard for his failure to deliver an "acceptable" movie and refused to televise it, allowing him to buy back the rights. What results is a wealth of philosophy relating to Godard's radical thoughts on filmmaking, delivered in the form of a conversation between Leaud and Berto. Intercut with their thoughts are some compelling word association tests which further exemplify Godard's love of language. It's no CASABLANCA, but for those with adventurous tastes and an interest in questioning the status quo, LE GAI SAVOIR's language deserves the same consideration as the literature of such contemporaries as Jean-Paul Sartre.

d&w, Jean-Luc Godard (based on "Emile" by Jean Jacques Rousseau); ph, Georges Leclerc (Eastmancolor); ed, Germaine Cohen; m/l, "Cuban Revolutionary Hymn."

Experimental   **(PR:A   MPAA:NR)**

LE GENDARME ET LES EXTRATERRESTRES zero
                                                      (1978, Fr.) 91m SNC bw

Louis de Funes, Michel Galabru, Maurice Risch, Jean-Pierre Rambal, Maria Mauban, Guy Grosso, Michel Modo, Jacques Francois.

A farcical science-fiction film about a flying saucer which lands on St. Tropez. The aliens look just like us humans but make the sound of an empty can if you bump into them. They drink oil, too. It's about 90 minutes too long. One of a string of comedies featuring De Funes, a Jerry Lewis clone. Here, he's the policeman who investigates the strange pheonomenon.

d, Jean Girault; w, Jacques Vilfrid; ph, Marcel Grignon, Didier Tarot.

Science-Fiction/Comedy   **(PR:C   MPAA:NR)**

LE GENTLEMAN DE COCODY
                                        (SEE: MAN FROM COCODY, 1966, Fr./Ital.)

LE GORILLE A MORDU L'ARCHEVEQUE
                                        (SEE: DEADLY DECOYS, THE, 1962, Fr.)

LE GRAND CHEF   (SEE: BIG CHIEF, THE, 1960, Fr.)

LE GRAND JEU   (SEE: BIG GAME, THE, 1954, Fr./Ital.)

LE JEUNE FOLLE   (SEE: DESPERATE DECISION, 1954, Fr.)

LE JOUER D'ECHECS   (SEE: DEVIL IS AN EMPRESS, THE, 1939, Fr.)

LE JOUEUR   (SEE: GAMBLER, THE, 1958, Fr.)

LE JOUR ET L'HEURE   (SEE: DAY AND THE HOUR, THE, 1963, Fr./Ital.)

LE JOUR SE LEVE   (SEE: DAYBREAK, 1940, Fr.)

LE JOURNAL D'UNE CURE DE CAMPAGNE
                        (SEE: DIARY OF A COUNTRY PRIEST, 1954, Fr.)

LE JUGE ET L'ASSASSIN
                        (SEE: JUDGE AND THE ASSASSIN, THE, 1979, Fr.)

LE LONG DES TROITTORS (SEE: DIARY OF A BAD GIRL, 1958, Fr.)

LE MAGNIFIQUE (SEE: MAGNIFICENT ONE, THE, 1974, Fr.)

LE MANS*** (1971) 108m Solar/NG c

Steve McQueen (*Michael Delaney*), Siegfried Rauch (*Erich Stahler*), Elga Andersen (*Lisa Belgetti*), Ronald Leigh-Hunt (*David Townsend*), Fred Haltiner (*Johann Ritter*), Luc Merenda (*Claude Aurac*), Christopher Waite (*Larry Wilson*), Louise Edlind (*Anna Ritter*), Angelo Infanti (*Lugo Abratte*), Jean-Claude Bercq (*Paul Jacques Dion*), Michele Scalera (*Vito Scalise*), Gino Cassani (*Loretto Fuselli*), Alfred Bell (*Tommy Hopkins*), Carlo Cecchi (*Paolo Scandenza*), Richard Rudiger (*Bruno Frohm*), Hal Hamilton (*Chris Barnett*), Jonathan Williams (*Jonathan Burton*), Peter Parten (*Peter Wiese*), Conrad Pringle (*Tony Elkins*), Erich Glavitza (*Josef Hauser*), Peter Huber (*Max Kummel*).

McQueen is a top Grand Prix driver out to beat his rival, Rauch, in the 24-hour French race. Between laps McQueen falls in love with widow Andersen, whose husband was killed in a race accident in which McQueen was also involved. The film was shot in documentary style and more attention was put into shooting the race than the story. McQueen, an experienced racer, did his own driving in the racing sequences. Director John Sturges began this film but was replaced by Katzin when Sturges had creative differences with McQueen. Originally this project was started by Warner Brothers to get in the theaters before John Frankenheimer's GRAND PRIX. It didn't, and was temporarily shelved.

p, Jack N. Reddish; d, Lee H. Katzin; w, Harry Kleiner; ph, Robert B. Hauser, Rene Guissart, Jr.; (Panavision, DeLuxe Color); m, Michel Legrand; ed, Donald W. Ernst, John Woodcock, Ghislaine Des Jonqueres; md, Legrand; prod d, Phil Abramson; art d, Nikita Knatz; cos, Ray Summers; spec eff, Sass Bedig; makeup, Emile Lavigne.

Drama (PR:A MPAA:G)

LE MARIAGE DE FIGARO (SEE MARRIAGE OF FIGARO, THE, 1963, Fr.)

LE MEPRIS (SEE: CONTEMPT, 1963, Ital./Fr.)

LE MERAVIGLIOSE AVVENTURE DI MARCO POLO
(SEE: MARCO THE MAGNIFICENT, 1966, Ital./Fr./Yugo./Egypt/Afghanistan)

LE MERCENARIRE (SEE: SWORDSMAN OF SIENA, THE, 1962, Fr./Ital.)

LE MILLION (SEE: THE MILLION, 1931, Fr.)

LE MIROIR A DEUX FACES
(SEE: MIRROR HAS TWO FACES, THE, 1959, Fr.)

LE MONDAT (SEE: MANDABI, 1970, Fr.)

LE MONDE TREMBLERA**
(1939, Fr.) 108m CICC bw (AKA: LA REVOLTE DES VIVANTS)

Madeleine Sologne, Mady Berry, Armand Bernard, Erich von Stroheim, Claude Dauphin, Roger Duchesne, Christiane Delyne, Sonia Bessis, Nina Sainclair, Julien Carette.

When a scientist invents a machine which can predict a person's death, panicked citizens begin to riot, bringing about the death of the inventor, as the machine has predicted. Henri-Georges Clouzot, in his pre-directorial days (WAGES OF FEAR, LES DIABOLIQUES) co-wrote the script, which featured the inimitable Erich von Stroheim. As usual, Stroheim had to resort to acting in mediocre-to-bad films when his own projects went unrealized. This picture was surrounded by the aborted LA COURONNE DE FER (1938) and LA DAME BLANCHE (1939), the latter of which was to have been co-scripted by Jean Renoir.

p, Leopold Schlosberg; d, Richard Pottier; w, Jean Villard, Henri-Georges Clouzot (based on the novel *La Machine A Predire La Mort* by C.R. Dumas and R.F. Didelot); ph, Robert Le Febvre; art d, Leon Barsacq.

Science-Fiction/Drama (PR:A MPAA:NR)

LE NOTTI BIANCHE (SEE: WHITE NIGHTS, 1957, Fr./Ital.)

LE PASSAGER DE LA PLUIE (SEE: RIDER ON THE RAIN, 1970, Fr./Ital.)

LE PASSE MURAILLE (SEE: MR. PEEK-A-BOO, 1951, Fr.)

LE PAYS BLEU (SEE: BLUE COUNTRY, THE, 1977, Fr.)

LE PERE TRANQUILLE (SEE: MR. ORCHID, 1948, Fr.)

LE PETIT SOLDAT**1/2
(1965, Fr.) 88m Georges de Beauregard-SNC/West End bw (GB: THE LITTLE SOLDIER)

Michel Subor (*Bruno Forestier*), Anna Karina (*Veronica Dreyer*), Henri-Jacques Huet (*Jacques*), Paul Beauvais (*Paul*), Laszlo Szabo (*Laszlo*), Georges de Beauregard (*Activist Leader*), Jean-Luc Godard (*Bystander At Railway Station*), Gilbert Edard.

In Godard's followup to his landmark BREATHLESS (1959), Subor, a French army deserter with ties to a right-wing terrorist group, is assigned to kill a journalist who sympathizes with the Algerians. He becomes the target of a gang of Leftist thugs who want information about his political allies—information he refuses to give them. After successfully avoiding them, he meets Karina who, unknown to him, works for the Left. He is soon captured and, in a superbly discomforting scene (the most famous in the film), tortured in the gang's bathroom. He is handcuffed to the shower fixtures, burned with matches, and nearly suffocated by a wet cloth which is hooded over his head— brutalities which leave little or no physical scarring. He manages to escape by jumping out of a window, though he is unsure which floor he is on.

Luckily, he lands safely just one floor below where Karina, whom he's since fallen in love with, is waiting. She rescues him and they escape to her apartment with plans of taking off for South America. However, after he goes off to assassinate the journalist she is kidnaped by members of the Right. Only after Subor commits the murder (which he carried out only to earn his and Karina's freedom) does he learn that Karina has been killed. Intended for release in France in 1960 it was banned because of the censor's sensitivity to the Algerian content. They succeeded in keeping LE PETIT SOLDAT off the screens until 1963 (during which time Godard completed four more films), though it took another two years for it to cross the Atlantic. While historical comprehension of the French-Algerian situation is helpful, it is unnecessary for an understanding of the film, especially since Godard admits that he himself held a confused viewpoint on the subject at the time. LE PETIT SOLDAT is far more confusing than BREATHLESS, jumping in and out of scenes without letting the audience get a grasp on the narrative. The film also contains some early signs of Godard's fascination with cinema, including the now-legendary quote, "The cinema is truth 24 frames a second." It also marked the first feature film appearance for Anna Karina, whom Godard married the following year. They met in a manner which seems suited for one of his own pictures. He placed an ad in a trade paper which read: "Wanted: very pretty young woman, 18–20 years old to become my star and my friend." She became both—his wife and one of the most popular French actresses of the 1960s.

p, Georges de Beauregard; d&w, Jean-Luc Godard; ph, Raoul Coutard; m, Maurice Leroux; ed, Agnes Guillemot, Nadine Marquand, Lila Herman.

Crime Drama (PR:C MPAA:NR)

LE PETIT THEATRE DE JEAN RENOIR****
(1974, Fr.) 100m Son et Lumiere-ORTF/Phoenix

"The Last New Year's Eve": Nino Fornicola (*The Bum*), Minny Monti (*The Female Bum*), Roger Trapp (*Max Vialle*), Roland Martin, Frederic Santaya, Pierre Gulda; "The Electric Floor Waxer": Marguerite Cassan (*Isabelle*), Pierre Olaf (*The Husband*), Jacques Dynam (*The Second Husband*), Jean-Louis Tristan (*Agent*), Claude Guillaume, Denis de Gunsburg (*Young Couple*); "When Love Dies": Jeanne Moreau (*The Singer*); "The King Of Yvetot": Fernand Sardou (*Duvallier*), Francoise Arnoul (*Isabelle*), Jean Carmet (*Feraud*), Andrex (*Blanc*), Dominique Labourier (*The Maid*), Roger Fregois (*Jolly*), Edmond Ardisson (*Cesar, the Tramp*).

An exceptional coda to the long and magnificent career of Jean Renoir which sums up his world in a personal manner. Divided into four parts, each introduced by the charming 75-year-old director himself, the picture moves from the artificially theatrical to the naturally realistic. The first episode, "The Last New Year's Eve," has Fornicola, a ragged and seemingly lonely bum, standing outside the window of an upper-class restaurant. One of the rich people inside pays to have the bum watch them eat from the outside. Of course, the diners lose their appetites, and as a consolation they have the food given to the bum. One of the rich women also gives her coat to the man. He is then seen returning to his riverside shelter, where he is greeted by his equally ragged wife. Together, in the night, they peacefully die. Shot entirely on a stage, Renoir, narrating, enjoyed its staginess by paying homage to Hans Christian Andersen. The second episode, "The Electric Floor Waxer," is an odd little piece for those familiar with Renoir (and for anyone, for that matter). Based on an earlier project entitled "It's Revolution," this tale is a satirical opera complete with singing choruses of office workers rising up from the lower depths of the Metro station. They sing repetitive refrains about their offices and their jobs. One woman (Cassan) goes through life obsessed with giving the floor a good waxing, causing heartache among her successive husbands. Dynam, her second mate, finally saves Cassan from waxing by throwing the vibrating, whirling machine out the window. As it crashes to the ground below, Cassan leaps from the window to join her plug-in lover. The third episode is hardly an episode at all; in one long dolly in-dolly out Jeanne Moreau sings that tune called "When Love Dies" (Oscar Cremieux). It is included to, as Renoir puts it, "take us for a little while outside our century of sleazy progress." The fourth episode, "The King Of Yvetot," is the most purely realistic, shot entirely on location. At the introduction Renoir shows us his little theater (a miniature model of a stage) and briefly explains the sport of *petanque*, the values and the rules of this game. He takes a tiny metal ball and rolls it along the little stage, and with one quick edit, we are transported into the world of cinema as a large *petanque* ball rolls along the ground. An old man is seen playing. He is revealed to have a young wife, who in turn has an even younger lover. The conflicts of this triangle are resolved peacefully and with respect to set morals in a final game of *petanque*, which Renoir "firmly believes to be an instrument of peace." The film's finale is also the end of the end of Renoir's little theater as the members of the cast come out for a closing bow. The actors thank us for watching and we cannot help but feel thanks for Renoir's humble presentation. One can think of no more appropriate way for one of film's greatest directors (and probably the greatest in Europe) to wrap up his genuinely profound career. Originally made for French television in 1969. (In French; English subtitles).

p, Pierre Long; d&w, Jean Renoir; ph, Georges Leclerc (Eastmancolor); m, Joseph Kosma, Jean Wiener; ed, Genevieve Winding; prod d, Gilbert Margerie; English subtitles, Herman Weinberg.

Drama (PR:C MPAA:NR)

LE PLAISIR***1/2
(1954, Fr.) 95m Stera-C.C.F.C./Meyer-Kingsley bw (AKA: HOUSE OF PLEASURE)

"The Mask": Claude Dauphin (*The Doctor*), Jean Galland (*Ambroise, "The Mask"*), Gaby Morlay (*Denise, His Wife*), Gaby Bruyere (*Frimousse, The Mask's Partner*); "The Model": Daniel Gelin (*Jean*), Simone Simon (*Josephine*), Jean Servais (*The Friend*), Michel Vadet (*Journalist*), Rene Pascal, Marcel Reuze; "The House of Madame Tellier": Madeleine Renaud (*Mme. Tellier*), Jean Gabin (*Joseph Rivet*), Danielle Darrieux (*Rosa*), Pierre Brasseur (*Julien Ledentu, the Salesman*),

Ginette Leclerc *(Flora)*, Paulette Dubost *(Fernande)*, Mira Parely *(Raphaele)*, Mathilde Casadesus *(Louise)*, Helena Manson *(Marie)*, Joelle Jany *(Constance)*, Louis Seigner *(Mr. Tourneveau)*, Rene Blanchard *(Mayor)*, Michel Vadet *(Sailor)*, Joe Dest *(The German)*, Claire Olivier *(Mme. Tourneveau)*, Georges Vitray *(The Captain)*, Arthur Devere *(Employee)*, Charles Vissiere *(Old Man from Normandy)*, Zelie Yzelle *(His Wife)*, Antoine Balpetre, Marcel Peres, Louis Seigner, Robert Lombard, Henri Cremieux, Jean Mayer, Palau and Georges Baconnet *(Clients of the Maison Tellier)*; Voice of Guy de Maupassant: Peter Ustinov *(English Version)*, Jean Servais *(French Version)*, Anton Walbrook *(German Version)*.

Following the success of LA RONDE, Max Ophuls decided to adapt three stories by Guy de Maupassant for this picture, which was released in France in 1952. The first of the stories, "The Mask," concerns an aging roue who, with his wife's compliance, wears a mask to a dance hall in order to hide his wrinkles. The second story, "The House Of Madame Tellier," has Renaud closing her brothel so she and her girls can go to their niece's first communion. The final episode, "The Model," has Simon, a model in love with a painter, throw herself from a window to express her love. The painter marries the girl and devotes his life to her care since, by her action, she becomes crippled for life. Ophuls' goal was to show the pain of pleasure in people's lives—pleasure and old age in "The Mask;" pleasure and purity in "Madame Tellier," and pleasure and marriage in "The Model." His original intention was to film the story "Paul's Wife" instead of "The Model," but at his producer's insistence Ophuls omitted this sequence dealing with pleasure and death. As with LA RONDE, this film's episodes are joined by a narrator, Peter Ustinov (English), Anton Walbrook (German), and Jean Servais (French). The dollying and craning camera technique which has nearly become synonymous with Ophuls' name is awesomely evident in the "Madam Tellier" episode, which allows the camera to survey, in all its fluidity, the activities of the brothel.

p&d, Max Ophuls; w, Ophuls, Jacques Natanson (based on three stories by Guy de Maupassant, "The Mask" ["Le Masque" 1889], "The House of Madame Tellier" ["La Maison Tellier" 1881], "The Model" ["Le Modele"] 1883); ph, Christian Matras, Philippe Agostini; m, Joe Hajos, Maurice Yvain (based on themes of Offenbach); ed, Leonide Azar; art d, Jean d'Eaubonne; cos, Georges Annenkov.

Drama   **Cas.**   **(PR:C-O   MPAA:NR)**

LE PUITS AUX TROIS VERITES
(SEE: THREE FACES OF SIN, 1963, Fr./Ital.)

LE QUATTRO VERITA
(SEE: THREE FABLES OF LOVE, 1963, Fr./Ital./Span.)

LE ROI DE COEUR   (SEE: KING OF HEARTS, 1967, Fr./Ital.)

LE ROMAN D'UN TRICHEUR (SEE: STORY OF A CHEAT, THE, 1938, Fr.)

LE ROUBLE A DEUX FACES
(SEE: DAY THE HOTLINE GOT HOT, THE, 1968, Fr./Span.)

LE ROUGE AUX LEVRES
(SEE: DAUGHTERS OF DARKNESS, 1971, Bel./Gr./Ger./Ital.)

LE ROUGE ET LA NOIR (SEE: THE RED AND THE BLACK, 1954, Fr./Ital.)

LE ROUTE DE CORINTH
(SEE: WHO'S GOT THE BLACK BOX?, 1970, Fr./Gr./Ital.)

LE SANG D'UN POETE   (SEE: BLOOD OF A POET, 1930, Fr.)

LE SERPENT   (SEE: SERPENT, THE, 1973, Fr./W. Ger.)

LE SILENCE EST D'OR   (SEE: MAN ABOUT TOWN, 1947, Fr.)

LE SOUFFLE AU COEUR
(SEE: MURMUR OF THE HEART, 1971, Fr./Ital./Ger.)

LE TEMPS DES ASSASSINS
(SEE: DEADLIER THAN THE MALE, 1957, Fr.)

LE TESTAMENT DU DR. MABUSE
(SEE: TESTAMENT OF DR. MABUSE, THE, 1933, Ger.)

LE VENT D'EST   (SEE: WIND FROM THE EAST, 1970, Fr./Ital./Ger.)

LE VICOMTE REGLE SES COMPTES
(SEE: VISCOUNT, THE, 1967, Fr./Span./Ital./Ger)

LE VIOL***
(1968, Fr./Swed.) 90m Parc Film-Argos Films-Sandrews/Freena Films-G. G. Prod.
c (OVERGREPPET; LE VIOL OU UN AMOUR FOU; AKA: THE RAPE)

Bibi Andersson *(Marianne Pescourt)*, Bruno Cremer *(Walter)*, Frederic de Pasquale *(Henri Pescourt)*, Katerina Larsson *(Jacqueline, the Maid)*.

After her husband and maid leave her posh apartment, Andersson is unexpectedly confronted by mysterious visitor Cremer. He comes to her door with gun in hand and chloroforms the woman. Upon waking, Andersson finds herself tied to a couch. Cremer tells her to keep quiet and nothing will happen. The two talk; Cremer hints that her husband (de Pasquale) may be in some sort of danger. The strange situation is periodically interrupted by phone calls wherein Cremer informs the caller that everything is fine. Andersson is finally let loose to cook a meal for herself and her captor. She attempts to call the police but stops after Cremer shoots, narrowly missing her. Attracted by his intelligence, Andersson permits Cremer to take her to the bedroom for a liaison. Her husband calls to say he's on his way home; Cremer leaves, stating that his job is through. Andersson prepares her home for a scheduled party that evening as de Pasquale returns. At the party is Cremer, who had been on the guest list. After finally going to bed, Andersson is restless as de Pasquale sleeps.

The doorbell rings; once more Andersson finds Cremer at the door. Another of the European riddle films, in which audiences must make up their own minds about what's going on. Dream, reality, waking fantasy, game? Do you know which? Do you *care* which?

p, Goran Lindgren, Mag Bodard; d&w, Jacques Doniol-Valcroze; ph, Rune Ericson (Eastmancolor); m, Michel Portal; ed, Sophie Bhaud; art d, Jan Boleslaw; cos, Eva-Lisa Nelstedt.

Drama   **(PR:O   MPAA:NR)**

LE VOILE BLEU   (SEE: BLUE VEIL, THE, 1947, Fr.)

LE VOLEUR   (SEE: THIEF OF PARIS, THE, 1967, Fr./Ital.)

LE VOYAGE EN AMERIQUE   (SEE: VOYAGE TO AMERICA, 1952, Fr.)

LE VOYOU   (SEE: CROOK, THE, 1971, Fr.)

LEAD LAW   (SEE: CROOKED TRAIL, 1936)

LEADBELLY****1/2   (1976) 126m PAR c

Roger E. Mosley *(Huddie Ledbetter)*, Paul Benjamin *(Wes Ledbetter)*, Madge Sinclair *(Miss Eula)*, Alan Manson *(Prison Chief Guard)*, Albert P. Hall *(Dicklicker)*, Art Evans *(Blind Lemon Jefferson)*, James E. Brodhead *(John Lomax)*, John Henry Faulk *(Governor Neff)*, Vivian Bonnell *(Old Lady)*, Dana Manno *(Margaret Judd)*, Timothy Pickard *(Gray Man)*, Lynn Hamilton *(Sally Ledbetter)*, Loretta Greene *(Lethe)*, Valerie Odell *(Amy)*, Rozaa Jean *(Sugar Tit)*.

Good film/biography about the life and times and songs and misfortunes of Huddie Ledbetter, the famed blues singer. Ledbetter, a man neither educated nor lucky, spent much of his adult life in prisons or on chain gangs or just trying to stay alive. In LEADBELLY, we see the type of attitude he encountered as a black living in pre-enlightened times. Often a slave to his own temper tantrums, Ledbetter spent many years on a Texas chain gang for killing a man in a fight and a term in a different prison for stabbing another. A man of enormous strength, he had little outlet for his fury other than violence and then, more constructively, with his music. Several classic folk songs are interspersed and rendered beautifully by HiTide Harris (accompanied by Brownie McGhee, David Cohen, Dick Rosmini and Sonny Terry). Most of the film takes place in flashbacks, loooking deep into Ledbetter's past and trying to fathom the reason for his behavior. Mosley is excellent as the misunderstood bluesman, creating a role that is as multi-dimensional as one could wish. We see the anger, the generosity, and the musical abilities of a man who might have become a household word were it not for the fact that the cards were stacked against him from the first deal. Although the film purports to examine the life of a great artist, we don't see enough of that and are only witness to his dour personal problems. Still, this is a very informative film with fine performances offered by almost everyone in the cast, most notably Benjamin as Ledbetter's sharecropper father; Sinclair as a Louisiana madame; and Manson, whose complex role as a southern prison guard captain should have merited an Oscar nomination at least. It's too bad that hardly anyone took note of this picture as the subject material failed to merit much press or word of mouth. It's beautifully photographed by Surtees (who could turn a garbage dump into a wonderland of images) and everyone involved with it should be proud. The executive producer was British TV star David Frost and it seemed to be aimed at the European market, where Leadbelly has remained popular. The information for the film was prepared by the Lomaxes, well-known musicologists, and John Lomax is seen in the film as played by Brodhead. There have been many films made by tax shelter groups that have been awful, although that didn't matter to those who invested their money. In this case, they've made a good biography (that was too light on the showbusiness side and too heavy on the dreary) whether they wanted to or not. Faulk, you may recall, was the one-time TV star whose life was ruined by allegations on the part of misled Red-baiters. He sued successfully and won, in a landmark decision, and that story was later seen on TV in a film.

p, Marc Merson; d, Gordon Parks; w, Ernest Kinoy; ph, Bruce Surtees (Eastmancolor); m, Fred Karlin; ed, Harry Howard; prod d, Robert Boyle; set d, John Kuri; stunts, Harold Jones.

Musical/Biography   **(PR:C-O   MPAA:PG)**

LEADVILLE GUNSLINGER* 1/2   (1952) 54m REP bw

Allan "Rocky" Lane *(Allan "Rocky" Lane)*, Black Jack *(His Stallion)*, Eddy Waller *(Nugget Clark)*, Grant Withers *(Jonathan Graves)*, Elaine Riley *(Carol Davis)*, Roy Barcroft *(Chet/Pete Yonker)*, Richard Crane *(Jim Blanchard)*, I. Stanford Jolley *(Cliff Saunders)*, Kenneth MacDonald *(Sheriff Nichols)*, Mickey Simpson *(Monk)*, Ed Hinton *(Deputy Ned Smith)*, Art Dillard *(Sentry)*, Wesley Hudman *(Driver)*.

Lane is a U.S. marshal who comes into the town of Leadville to pick up a prisoner and stays to help out his friend, Waller. Waller is having trouble with a gang of outlaws who are trying to get him to leave his ranch. Lane masquerades as one of the bandits and finds out that banker Withers is the leader; he wants the land because of the oil sitting below.

p&d, Harry Keller; w, M. Coates Webster; ph, Bud Thackery; m, Stanley Wilson; ed, Robert M. Leeds; art d, Fred A. Ritter.

Western   **(PR:A   MPAA:NR)**

LEAGUE OF FRIGHTENED MEN*   (1937) 71m COL bw

Walter Connolly *(Nero Wolfe)*, Lionel Stander *(Archie Goodwin)*, Eduardo Ciannelli *(Paul Chapin)*, Irene Hervey *(Evelyn Hibbard)*, Victor Kilian *(Pitney Scott)*, Nana Bryant *(Agnes Burton)*, Allen Brook *(Mark Chapin)*, Walter Kingsford *(Ferdinand Bowen)*, Leonard Mudie *(Prof. Hibbard)*, Kenneth Hunter *(Dr. Burton)*, Charles Irwin *(Augustus Farrell)*, Rafaela Ottiano *(Dora Chapin)*, Edward McNamara

(Inspector Cramer), Jameson Thomas *(Michael Ayers)*, Ian Wolfe *(Nicholas Cabot)*, Jonathan Hale *(Alexander Drummond)*, Herbert Ashley *(Fritz)*, James Flavin *(Joe)*.

A boring mystery with Connolly playing Wolfe and solving the case from his study. Action is limited and the villain is obvious from the beginning of the film. Stander is Connolly's assistant who does all the running around and tries unsuccessfully to be the comic relief. Stander played the same character in MEET NERO WOLFE, the first film in the series, but the fat, cerebral, orchid-loving Wolfe was played by Edward Arnold. (See NERO WOLFE Series, Index.)

d, Alfred E. Green; w, Eugene Solow, Guy Endore (based on a story by Rex Stout); ph, Henry Freulich; ed, Gene Milford.

Murder Mystery **(PR:A MPAA:NR)**

LEAGUE OF GENTLEMEN, THE*1/2** (1961, Brit.) 116 Allied Film Makers/Kingsley bw

Jack Hawkins *(Hyde)*, Nigel Patrick *(Peter Graham Race)*, Roger Livesey *(Mycroft)*, Richard Attenborough *(Edward Lexy)*, Bryan Forbes *(Martin Porthill)*, Kieron Moore *(Stevens)*, Robert Coote *(Bunny Warren)*, Terence Alexander *(Rupert Rutland-Smith)*, Melissa Stribling *(Peggy)*, Norman Bird *(Frank Weaver)*, Nanette Newman *(Elizabeth)*, David Lodge *(C.S.M.)*, Patrick Wymark *(Wylie)*, Lydia Sherwood *(Hilda)*, Doris Hare *(Molly Weaver)*, Gerald Harper *(Capt. Saunders)*, Brian Murray *(Grogan)*.

Near perfection to the last detail is accorded to THE LEAGUE OF GENTLEMEN. Unfortunately, for the perpetrators of the cinematic crime, the same "near perfection" is what does them in. Hawkins is angry at having been mandatorily retired by the British Army; so angry, in fact, that he decides to put his service experience to devious use with a huge bank robbery. He contacts a group of his old buddies and enlists them in his plan. Each of the men will receive a share in the proceeds of the million pound heist. Every painstaking phase of the operation is shown (we've all seen films like this: RIFIFI, TOPKAPI, THIEF, etc.) in an interesting, yet never tedious, fashion. Further, the psyches of all the miscreants are also shown in a fascinating manner, with heavy emphasis on humor and a tangible feeling that we, the audience, like these guys and want them to succeed. When the moment arrives, the men jump into action with military precision and use all of their expertise to make it a success. Gas masks, smoke bombs, radio jamming—the lot—are utilized and they get away with it, for a while, anyhow. However, we've all learned that "crime doesn't pay" (at least not in the 1960s when there was still some sort of censorship applied to screen stories) and the cabal is uncovered when Coote, a drunken pal of Hawkins's, arrives unexpectedly. Through his stupidity, the authorities are led to the den of thieves where they are nabbed before they can divvy the cash. THE LEAGUE OF GENTLEMEN starts a bit slow as the plot is unraveled but then begins to move like lightning and is more than satisfying on all levels. It might have been played straight for thrills and intrigue, but the screenplay (by Forbes, who also played the role of Porthill) and the direction were light-hearted and all of the characterizations had some comedic quirk that made them stand out from the others. For an example of how this kind of caper film should *not* be done, see THE BRINK'S JOB.

p, Michael Relph; d, Basil Dearden; w, Bryan Forbes (based on the novel *The League of Gentlemen* by John Boland); ph, Arthur Ibbetson; m, Philip Green; ed, John D. Guthridge; prod d, Peter Proud; md, Green; art d, Proud; set d, Arthur Taksen; cos, Joan Ellacott; makeup, Harry Frampton.

Crime/Comedy **(PR:A-C MPAA:NR)**

LEAP INTO THE VOID*** (1982, Ital.) 120m Summit c

Michel Piccoli *(Judge Ponticelli)*, Anouk Aimee *(Marta Ponticelli)*, Michele Placido *(Giovanni)*, Gisella Burinato *(Anna)*, Antonio Piovanelli *(Quasimodo)*, Anna Orso *(Marilena)*, Giampaolo Saccarola *(Insane Brother)*, Adriana Pecorelli *(Sonia)*, Paola Ciampi *(Ponticelli's Mother)*, Piergiorgio Bellocchio *(Giorgio)*, Mario Prosperi, Enrico Bergier *(Ponticelli's Brothers)*, Elisabeth Labi *(Ponticelli's Fiancee)*, Mario Ravasio *(Brother of Suicide)*, Gaetano Campisi, Marino Cenna *(Actors)*, Lamberto Consani, Marina Sassi *(Friends of Giovanni)*, Giancarlo Sammartano, Oreste Rotundo *(Passersby)*, Remo Remotti *(Thief)*, Rossano Weber *(Fire-Eater)*, Alessandro Antonucci, Daria Fago, Matteo Fago, Giovanni Frezza, Maria Pia Frezza *(Ponticelli Children)*.

Piccoli is a magistrate whose sister Aimee is mentally ill. He uses his friend Placido in an attempt to drive Aimee to suicide, but the plot goes awry. Despite the seemingly unfunny ideas in the plot this is a good comedy that shows genuine compassion for the characters.

d, Marco Bellocchio; w, Bellocchio, Piero Natoli, Vincenzo Cerami (based on a story by Bellocchio); ph, Beppe Lanci (Eastmancolor); m, Nicola Piovani; ed, Roberto Perpignani; prod d, Amedeo Fago, Andrea Crisanti; cos, Lia Morandini .

Comedy **(PR:O MPAA:NR)**

LEAP OF FAITH*** (1931, Brit.) 77m Imperator bw

Edward Chapman *(Lee)*, Lilian Harvey *(Betty)*, Jack Raine *(Billy)*, Victor Vos *(Luther)*, Sheryl Gunn *(Gale)*, Anthony Lauren *(Reilly)*, Ames Hardy *(Gabriel)*.

A charming comedy about a group of priests and nuns who are attempting to raise money for an orphanage that has fallen upon hard times. It was bold for its day as there was an undertone of attraction between Chapman, a priest in charge of the running of the orphanage, and Harvey, the sister who ruled the children. The relationships between the religious people were so off-hand that they referred to each other by their first names, thus Sister Elizabeth was known as "Betty" and this caused a scandal in the small town just outside Birmingham. The orphanage is leased by the church and the real estate man who owns the property wants to take it over and build a workers apartment block but he can't take it over if the orphanage continues to make the small, but difficult, rent payments. In a forerunner of films to come from MGM, they decide to put on a show, charge admission, and use that money to pay their lease. Using all the children in the orphanage as the stars, they stage a show and are prepared to make it happen when their lead trumpet player, Raine, splits a lip playing soccer. Since he is the best musician and leads the small band, there is no way they can make this happen until an itinerant musician happens into the orphanage. This is Hardy and all he carries is a small suitcase and a trumpet case. He's willing to take any kind of work in order to pay for his room and board and they immediately get him to lead the band. What is never answered is if he is the angel Gabriel who has come to save them. The show is a great success, townsfolk from all around the area come in to see it and enough money is raised to keep the orphanage afloat. Ames Hardy was actually a trumpeter with several British bands of the era and this was his only acting role. In a small role as the Blighty version of Shirley Temple, eight-year-old Gunn was outstanding. She later married a peer of the realm and is currently a duchess in an area near Northumberland. The title refers to the need to accept the fact that Hardy was, in truth, Gabriel.

p, David Murray-Smith; d&w, Ed Greenwood; ph, T.B. Lynch; m, Bradley Haynes; ed, Michael Aarons; set d, Lillian Hayton; art d, Jill Mitwell.

Comedy **(PR:A MPAA:NR)**

LEAP YEAR*1/2 (1932, Brit.) 91m British and Dominions/GAU bw

Tom Walls *(Sir Peter Traillon)*, Anne Grey *(Paula Zahren)*, Edmond Breon *(Jack Debrant)*, Ellis Jeffreys *(Mrs. Debrant)*, Jeanne Stuart *(Angela Mallard)*, Charles Carson *(Sir Archibald Mallard)*, Lawrence Hanray *(Hope)*, Joan Brierley *(Girl)*, Franklyn Bellamy *(Silas)*.

A sprightly tale of an aristocratic Foreign Office agent (Walls, working solo after having been successfully paired with Ralph Lynn for years) who finds romance for one magic weekend with a mysterious lady who fails to give him her name. After years of searching for his lost love, he gives up his quest and opts to further his career by marrying his boss' daughter. Virtually on the eve of his wedding, he is sent to the south of France, where he fortuitously finds the mysterious mademoiselle and bags her as his bride.

p, Herbert Wilcox; d, Tom Walls; w, A.R. Rawlinson; ph, F.A. Young.

Comedy **(PR:A MPAA:NR)**

LEARN, BABY, LEARN (SEE: LEARNING TREE, THE, 1969)

LEARNING TREE, THE1/2** (1969) 107m Winger Enterprises/WB c (AKA: LEARN, BABY, LEARN)

Kyle Johnson *(Newt Winger)*, Alex Clarke *(Marcus Savage)*, Estelle Evans *(Sarah Winger)*, Dana Elcar *(Sheriff Kirky)*, Mira Waters *(Arcella Jefferson)*, Joel Fluellen *(Uncle Rob)*, Malcolm Atterbury *(Silas Newhall)*, Richard Ward *(Booker Savage)*, Russell Thorson *(Judge Cavanaugh)*, Peggy Rea *(Miss McClintock)*, Carole Lamond *(Big Mabel)*, Kevin Hagen *(Doc Cravens)*, James "Jimmy" Rushing *(Chappie Logan)*, Dub Taylor *(Spikey)*, Felix Nelson *(Jack Winger)*, George Mitchell *(Jake Kiner)*, Saundra Sharp *(Prissy)*, Stephen Perry *(Jappy)*, Don Dubbins *(Harley Davis)*, Jon Lormer *(McCormack)*, Morgan Sterne *(Mr. Hall)*, Thomas Anderson *(Pastor Broadnap)*, Philip Roye *(Pete Winger)*, Hope Summers *(Mrs. Kiner)*, Carter Vinnegar *(Seansy)*, Bobby Goss *(Skunk)*, Alfred Jones *(Cap'n Tuck)*, Zooey Hall *(Chauncey Cavanaugh)*.

A moving, though sometimes melodramatic, story of a black teenager growing up in a Kansas town in the 1920s. Adapted from Renaissance man Parks' own novel, the film tells the story of Newt (Johnson) who, through the people he encounters, learns of the happiness and pains of life, and the hardships and discrimination thrown on his race. One of the best things about this film is that Parks shows varying racial attitudes from the white and black people of the town. This gives the film a complexity not found in other films dealing with racial prejudice. The latter portion of the film revolves around the murder of a white man by another white—and blamed on a black— that Johnson witnesses. He is afraid to come forward because of what the white community might do, but finally does. The white man responsible for the murder commits suicide and the black is eventually killed by the town's bigoted sheriff. Johnson leaves town, sickened by the violence and prejudice.

p,d&w, Gordon Parks (based on his novel); ph, Burnett Guffey (Panavision, Technicolor); m, Parks; ed, George R. Rohrs; md, Tom McIntosh; art d, Edward Engoron; set d, Joanne MacDougall; sp eff, Albert Whitlock; m/l, "The Learning Tree," Gordon Parks, sung by O.C. Smith, "My Baby's Gone," sung by James "Jimmy" Rushing.

Drama **(PR:O MPAA:M)**

LEASE OF LIFE*** (1954, Brit.) 93m EAL-Michael Balcon/GFD c

Robert Donat *(William Thorne)*, Kay Walsh *(Vera Thorne)*, Adrienne Corri *(Susan Thorne)*, Denholm Elliott *(Martin Blake)*, Walter Fitzgerald *(The Dean)*, Cyril Raymond *(Headmaster)*, Reginald Beckwith *(Foley)*, Robert Sandford *(Boy with Book)*, Frank Atkinson *(Verger)*, Alan Webb *(Dr. Pembury)*, Richard Wattis *(Solicitor)*, Frederick Piper *(Jeweler)*, Vida Hope *(Mrs. Sproatley)*, Beckett Bould *(Sproatley)*, Richard Leech *(Carter)*, Jean Anderson *(Mrs. Calthorpe)*, Mark Daly *(Spooner)*, Russell Waters *(Russell)*, John Salew *(Doctor)*, Edie Martin *(Mrs. Calthorpe's Friend)*, Mark Dignam, Charles Saynor, Sheila Raynor.

Donat is a village parson who discovers he has only a year to live. He accepts the news calmly, but faces the problem of raising money for his daughter's schooling. She is a talented musician; Donat wants to see her go to school in London. A dying member of Donat's parish wills all his money to Donat to spite his wife. The parson's wife, Walsh, takes some of that money to pay for their daughter's tuition without Donat's knowledge. Donat, who played Mr. Chips in GOODBYE, MR. CHIPS (1939), boosts the weak story with his engaging performance.

p, Jack Rix; d, Charles Frend; w, Eric Ambler (based on a story by Frank Baker, Patrick Jenkins); ph, Douglas Slocombe (Eastmancolor); m, Alan Rawsthorne; ed, Peter Tanner; art d, Jim Morahan.

Drama **(PR:A MPAA:NR)**

LEATHER AND NYLON**
(1969, Fr./Ital.) 95m Copernic-Fida/Ben Barry c (LE SOLEIL DES VOYOUS; IL PIU GRANDE COLPO DEL SECOLO; AKA: ACTION MAN) GRANDE COLPO DEL SECOLO; AKA: ACTION MAN)

Jean Gabin (*Denis Farrand*), Robert Stack (*Jim Beckley*), Margaret Lee (*Betty*), Suzanne Flon (*Marie-Jeanne Farrand*), Jean Topart (*Monsieur Henri*), Lucien Bogaert (*Old Woman*), Walter Giller (*Maurice Labrousse*), Georges Aminel (*Commissioner Leduc*), Albert Michel, Carol Vell, Mino Doro.

Gabin is a retired crook-turned-legitimate businessman in this caper film. Bored with his peaceful life, he lets himself get talked into a bank robbery by American adventurer Stack. The heist is successful, but a gang of drug dealers who have been giving Gabin a hard time kidnap his wife and demand the loot as ransom. Stack and Gabin manage to rescue her, though at the cost of Stack's life. Gabin is his usual able self, and Stack his usual wooden self. This was the type of action feature that caused the youthful French cinema critics of the 1950s to categorize talented director Delannoy (THE ETERNAL RETURN) as "emotionally frigid."

p, Raymond Danon; d, Jean Delannoy; w, Alphonse Boudard, Delannoy (based on the novel *The Action Man* by J.M. Flynn); ph, Walter Wottitz (Franscope, Eastmancolor); m, Francis Lai; ed, Henri Taverna.

Crime   **(PR:A-C   MPAA:NR)**

LEATHER BOYS, THE***   (1965, Brit.) 108m Raymond Stross/AA bw
Rita Tushingham (*Dot*), Colin Campbell (*Reggie*), Dudley Sutton (*Pete*), Gladys Henson (*Gran*), Avice Landon (*Reggie's Mother*), Lockwood West (*Reggie's Father*), Betty Marsden (*Dot's Mother*), Martin Mathews (*Uncle Arthur*), Johnny Briggs (*Boy Friend*), James Chase (*Les*), Geoffrey Dunn (*Mr. Lunnis*), Dandy Nichols (*Mrs. Stanley*), Valerie Varnam (*Brenda*), Jill Mai Meredith (*June*), Elizabeth Begley (*Receptionist*), Brian Phelan (*Man-in-Jeans*), Oliver MacGreevey (*Merchant Seaman*), Sylvia Kay (*Schoolteacher*), Sandra Caron, Tracey Rogers (*Schoolgirls*), Carmel McSharry (*Bus Conductor*), Joyce Hemson (*Publican's Wife*).

An English drama of a teenage girl who marries a motorcycle buff. Tushingham marries Campbell to escape from her parents; the relationship never gets off the ground. She doesn't do any housework, and only cooks cans of beans. Campbell moves out and goes to live with his friend Sutton, whom Campbell begins to suspect is a homosexual. He moves back when he hears that his wife is pregnant, and discovers that she's sleeping with another man. He and the sociable Sutton decide to run off to sea, but Sutton enjoys himself too much with a gay group of sailors; Campbell is left bereft of bride and of friend.

p, Raymond Stross; d, Sidney J. Furie; w, Gillian Freeman (based on the novel by Eliot George [Freeman]); ph, Gerald Gibbs (CinemaScope); m, Bill McGuffie; ed, Reginald Beck; art d, Arthur Lawson.

Drama   **Cas.**   **(PR:O   MPAA:NR)**

LEATHER BURNERS, THE**   (1943) 66m UA bw
William Boyd (*Hopalong Cassidy*), Andy Clyde (*California Carlson*), Jay Kirby (*Johnny Travers*), Victor Jory (*Dan Slack*), George Givot (*Sam Bucktoe*), Shelley Spencer (*Sharon Longstreet*), Bobby Larson (*Bobby Longstreet*), George Reeves (*Harrison Brooke*), Hal Taliaferro (*Lafe*), Forbes Murray (*Bart*), Robert Mitchum (*Randall*).

Boyd sets out to learn whether Jory is a cattle rustler and goes to work on his ranch. He is framed for murder when he's discovered by Jory's men. Young Larson is the one who proves Boyd is innocent and enables him to finish his task. Boyd discovers that Jory is working with mine owner Givot and they turned the mine into a giant cattle pen. Robert Mitchum has a small part in this, his third bit part in the Hopalong series. (See HOPALONG CASSIDY series, Index.)

p, Harry Sherman; d, Joseph E. Henabery; w, Jo Pagano (based on a story by Bliss Lomax); ph, Russell Harlan; m, Samuel Kaylin; ed, Carroll Lewis; md, Irvin Talbot; art d, Ralph Berger.

Western   **(PR:A   MPAA:NR)**

LEATHER GLOVES**   (1948) 75m COL (GB: LOSER TAKE ALL) bw
Cameron Mitchell (*Dave Collins*), Virginia Grey (*Janet Gilbert*), Jane Nigh (*Cathy*), Sam Levene (*Bernie*), Henry O'Neill (*Dudley*), Blake Edwards (*Vince Reedy*), Bob Castro (*Huerta Fernandez*), Sally Corner (*Mrs. Hubbard*), Stanley Andrews (*Mr. Hubbard*), Eddie Acuff (*Duke*), Ralph Volkie (*Referee*), Walter Soderling (*Trimble*).

Mitchell wanders into a small town and gets himself put on an upcoming fight card. He falls in love with Grey and promises the promoter he signed with that he'll throw the fight. He discovers that Grey has her eye on the man he's going to fight and so, to drive him out of the dirty fight game, Mitchell gives him a beating and goes back on the bum, leaving several lives changed by his brief appearance among them.

p&d, Richard Quine, William Asher; w, Brown Holmes (based on a story "No Place to Go" by Richard English); ph, Henry Freulich, ed, Viola Lawrence.

Drama   **(PR:A   MPAA:NR)**

LEATHER-PUSHERS, THE*¹/₂   (1940) 64m UNIV bw
Richard Arlen (*Dick*), Andy Devine (*Andy Grogan*), Astrid Allwyn (*Pat*), Douglas Fowley (*Slick*), Charles D. Brown (*Stevens*), Shemp Howard (*Sailor*), Horace MacMahon (*Slugger*), Charles Lane (*Mitchell*), Wade Boteler (*Commissioner*), George Lloyd (*Joe*), Eddie Gribbon (*Pete*), Frank Mitchell (*Grogan's Manager*), Reid Kilpatrick (*Commentator*), Ben Alexander (*Announcer*).

Arlen is wrestler Devine's trainer and when a brawl breaks out in the local gym promoter Fowley figures that Arlen has a mean left hook. He sets the trainer up as a boxer and tries to get him some press. Sportswriter Allwyn (her readers think she's a man) gives Arlen a hard time so Fowley raffles his boxer off and makes sure that

Allwyn wins. Arlen then proves to himself and to Allwyn that he is a boxer by winning the championship.

p, Ben Pivar; d, John Rawlins; w, Larry Rhine, Ben Chapman, Maxwell Shane; ph, Stanley Cortez; ed, Arthur Hilton; md, H.J. Salter; art d, Jack Otterson.

Action/Comedy   **(PR:A   MPAA:NR)**

LEATHER SAINT, THE**   (1956) 86m PAR bw
Paul Douglas (*Gus MacAuliffe*), John Derek (*Father Gil Allen*), Jody Lawrence (*Pearl Gorman*), Cesar Romero (*Tony Lorenzo*), Richard Shannon (*Tom Kelly*), Ernest Truex (*Father Ritchie*), Ricky Vera (*Pepito*), Thomas B. Henry (*Bishop Hardtke*), Lou Nova (*Tiger*), Robert Cornthwaite (*Dr. Lomas*), Edith Evanson (*Stella*), Baynes Barron (*Henchman*), Mary Benoit (*Nurse*), Bill Baldwin (*Flight Announcer*), Courtland Shepard, Ralph Montgomery, Estelle Etterre, Jan Bradley, Babette Baine, Richard Bender, Cheryl Callaway, Edward G. Pagett, Raymond Winston, Donald Wittenberg, Bill Meader, Lawrence A. Williams.

Derek is a minister on Sundays and a boxer on Saturdays, when he goes into the ring to help raise funds to help some children in his parish who have been struck down with polio. Douglas is his fight manager who has no idea of Derek's true guidance, and Lawrence is a torch singer that the leather minister reforms from alcohol addiction. A moving story about a clergyman whose creed takes him beyond the church, into the world of the suffering.

p, Norman Retchin; d, Alvin Ganzer; w, Retchin, Ganzer; ph, Haskell B. Boggs (VistaVision); m, Irvin Talbot; ed, Floyd Knudtson; art d, Hal Pereira, Henry Bumstead.

Drama   **(PR:A   MPAA:NR)**

LEATHERNECK, THE*¹/₂   (1929) 76m Pathe bw
William Boyd (*Joseph Hanlon*), Alan Hale (*Otto Schmidt*), Robert Armstrong (*William Calhoun*), Fred Kohler (*Heckla*), Diane Ellis (*Tanya*), James Aldine (*Tanya's Brother*), Paul Weigel (*Petrovitch*), Jules Cowles (*Cook*), Wade Boteler (*Gunnery Sergeant*), Philo McCullough (*Judge Advocate*), Joe Girard (*Colonel*), Mitchell Lewis (*Capt. Brand*), Joseph Girard, Richard Neill, Lloyd Whitlock, Lee Shumway, Jack Richardson (*Officers of the Court Martial*).

Boyd is a Marine charged with desertion and the murder of a Marine buddy. The film cuts back and forth from the trial to events during WW I that led to the charges. Ellis is the Russian woman Boyd married in Europe who arrives to save her husband at the last moment. Film has only 10 percent dialog to help it lamely along.

p, Ralph Block, d, Howard Higgin; w, Elliott Clawson; ph, John Mescall; ed, Doane Harrison.

Drama   **(PR:A   MPAA:NR)**

LEATHERNECKING*¹/₂   (1930) 72m RKO bw-c (GB: PRESENT ARMS)
Irene Dunne (*Delphine*), Ken Murray (*Frank*), Louise Fazenda (*Hortense*), Ned Sparks (*Ned Sparks*), Lilyan Tashman (*Edna*), Eddie Foy, Jr. (*Chick*), Benny Rubin (*Stein*), Rita Le Roy (*Fortuneteller*), Fred Santley (*Douglas*), Baron William Von Brinken (*Richter*), Carl Gerrard (*Colonel*), Werther & Wolfgang Weidler (*Richter's Sons*).

A silly musical with Foy as a Marine private pursuing socialite Dunne. He goes to great lengths to win her heart, stealing his captain's uniform and masquerading as an officer. That backfires and he then fakes a shipwreck which ends up in a real shipwreck of Dunne's yacht. And even through all of that Foy gets his girl. Adapted from the 1928 Broadway Musical "Present Arms" (musical numbers directed by Busby Berkeley), the film version is a pale imitation of the original. This was Dunne's screen debut. Songs included, "You Took Advantage of Me," "A Kiss for Cinderella" (Rodgers and Hart), "All My Life," "Careless Kisses," "Evening Star," "Brightly Nice And So Peculiar" (Benny Davis, Harry Akst), "Shake It Off and Smile" (Sidney Clare, Oscar Levant).

d, Eddie Cline; w, Alfred Jackson, Jane Murfin (based on the play "Present Arms" by Herbert Fields, Richard Rodgers, Lorenz Hart); ph, J. Roy Hunt; m, Oscar Levant; md, Victor Baravalle; art d, Max Ree; ch, Pearl Eaton.

Musical   **(PR:A   MPAA:NR)**

LEATHERNECKS HAVE LANDED, THE*¹/₂   (1936) 67m REP bw
Lew Ayres (*Woody Davis*), Isabel Jewell (*Brooklyn*), Jimmy Ellison (*Mac MacDonald*), James Burke (*Corrigan*), J. Carrol Naish (*Brenov*), Clay Clement (*Capt. Halstead*), Maynard Holmes (*Tubby Waters*), Ward Bond (*Tex*), Paul Porcasi (*Rico*), Christian Rub (*Schooner Captain*), Joseph Sawyer (*Sgt. Regan*), Henry Mowbray (*British Army Major*), John Webb Dillion (*Marine Captain*), Claude King (*British Agent*), Louis Vincenot, Lal Chand Mehra, Frank Tang, Ray Corrigan, Beal Wong, Robert Strange, Victor Wong, Montagu Shaw.

Ayres is a Marine stationed in China where he and a buddy brawl in a barroom and the buddy is accidentally killed. Ayres is cashiered out of the service and takes up with gunrunner Burke, and with Jewell, who also is stranded in the Far East. Conclusion has Ayres shooting it out with arch villain Naish and getting out of the chop suey melange all in one piece. Some stock shots of cruisers at sea and Marines in Shanghai are handled adroitly and help keep this one interesting.

p, Ken Goldsmith; d, Howard Bretherton; w, Seton I. Miller (based on a story by Wellyn Totman, James Gruen); ph, Ernest Miller, Jack Marta; ed, Robert Jahns.

Thriller   **(PR:A   MPAA:NR)**

LEAVE HER TO HEAVEN***   (1946) 110m FOX c
Gene Tierney (*Ellen Berent*), Cornel Wilde (*Richard Harland*), Jeanne Crain (*Ruth Berent*), Vincent Price (*Russell Quinton*), Mary Phillips (*Mrs. Berent*), Ray Collins (*Glen Robie*), Gene Lockhart (*Dr. Saunders*), Reed Hadley (*Dr. Mason*), Darryl Hickman (*Danny Harland*), Chill Wills (*Leick Thorne*), Paul Everton (*Judge*), Olive

Blakeney (*Mrs. Robie*), Addison Richards (*Bedford*), Harry Depp (*Catterson*), Grant Mitchell (*Carlson, the Bank Vice President*), Milton Parsons (*Medcraft, the Mortician*), Earl Schenck (*Norton*), Hugh Maguire (*Lin Robie*), Betty Hannon (*Tess Robie*), Kay Riley (*Nurse*), Mae Marsh (*Fisherwoman*), Audrey Betz (*Cook at Robie's Ranch*), Guy Beach (*Sheriff*), Jim Farley (*Conductor*), Charles Tannen (*Man*).

Beautiful Tierney betrays her lovely countenance here by playing one of the most evil creatures ever to slink across the screen. She meets and falls desperately in love with Wilde, an author who resembles her father. Tierney is pathologically possessive of Wilde, jealous of any and all who might share his affections. The two settle down in a rustic spot called "Back of the Moon," but Tierney intends to have Wilde all to herself. She dismisses the local handyman and then drowns his crippled half-brother Hickman. Tierney becomes pregnant but cannot bear having a child in her life—which might divert some of Wilde's love from her—so she goes to the head of a staircase and purposely throws herself down, causing a miscarriage. Her foster sister, Crain, comes into her life and Tierney begrudges even the smallest cordiality Wilde shows her. Tierney unburdens herself with Wilde by telling him how she drowned Hickman and killed their child so they could always be together. Wilde, who's been thick-headed about his insane wife to this time—if not criminally negligent— shudders at her hideous confession and makes plans to rid himself of this cuckoo. Believing she will soon lose Wilde to Crain, Tierney poisons herself in such a way as to put blame on her husband and foster sister. Both are tried, viciously prosecuted by Price, a former lover of the dead Tierney. His overreaching methods and sugar-coated portrait of Tierney—her story is told in flashback—is obvious to the jury, which frees Wilde and Crain of murder charges. However, Wilde is found guilty of being an accessory to Tierney's murders through not having revealed them following her confession to him. Crain is waiting for Wilde when he steps from prison. Tierney is fascinating as the ravishing killer but Wilde and Crain are too tame by comparison. Price is his usual flamboyant self. Stahl's direction is well done and the lensing by Shamroy in rich color is lush and eye-pleasing, the focus soft enough in the on-location shots in Arizona, Georgia, and Maine to qualify as *film noir*. (The misunderstanding exists that if a film is shot in color instead of stark black-and-white it cannot exist as genuine *film noir*. This, of course, is nonsense; *film noir* is dictated by the script and character development, not the technical process, although much in this special film category has been shot in the traditional black-and-white.)

p, William A. Bacher; d, John M. Stahl; w, Jo Swerling (based on the novel by Ben Ames Williams); ph, Leon Shamroy (Technicolor); m, Alfred Newman; ed, James B. Clark; art d, Lyle Wheeler, Maurice Ransford; set d, Thomas Little, Ernest Lansing; cos, Kay Nelson; spec eff, Fred Sersen; makeup, Ben Nye.

Romance/Crime Drama   **(PR:O   MPAA:NR)**

LEAVE IT TO BLANCHE*   (1934, Brit.) 51m WB-FN bw

Henry Kendall (*Peter Manners*), Olive Blakeney (*Blanche Wetherby*), Miki Hood (*Doris Manners*), Griffith Jones (*Philip Amesbury*), Rex Harrison (*Ronnie*), Hamilton Keene (*Brewster*), Julian Royce (*Patteridge*), Elizabeth Jenns (*Blossom*), Harold Warrender (*Guardee*), Phyllis Stanley (*Singer*), Molly Clifford, Denise Sylvester, Margaret Gunn, Kenneth Kove, Hermione Hannen.

Inane domestic farce with Hood, on the advice from Blakeney, trying to add some spice to her marriage by making her husband jealous. Hood manages to convince Kendall that she has a lover—which she really doesn't—piquing the man into committing murder. Of course no one really gets killed, and everything ends on a happy note.

p, Irving Asher; d, Harold Young; w, Brock Williams (based on the story by Roland Brown).

Comedy   **(PR:A   MPAA:NR)**

LEAVE IT TO BLONDIE**   (1945) 74m COL bw

Penny Singleton (*Blondie*), Arthur Lake (*Dagwood*), Larry Simms (*Alexander*), Marjorie Weaver (*Rita Rogers*), Jonathan Hale (*J.C. Dithers*), Chick Chandler (*Eddie Baxter*), Danny Mummert (*Alvin*), Marjorie Ann Mutchie (*Cookie*), Eula Morgan (*Mrs. Meredith*), Arthur Space (*Mr. Fuddle*), Eddie Acuff (*Mailman*), Fred Graff (*Henry*), Jack Rice (*Ollie*), Maude Eburne (*Magda*), Anne Loos (*Mary*), Marilyn Johnson (*Secretary*), Daisy (*Herself*).

The Bumsteads (Singleton and Lake) enter a song-writing contest hoping to win the prize money to cover checks that have been written for charity, neither knowing the other had done so. Hale, Lake's boss, is trying to make a real estate deal and wants his employee to soften up the female dealer. Misunderstandings and screwball situations arise and end in the usual fashion. Columbia re-started the BLONDIE series after a two-year hiatus. (See BLONDIE series, Index.)

p, Burt Kelly; d, Abby Berlin; w, Connie Lee (based on characters in a comic strip created by Chic Young); ph, Franz F. Planer; ed, Al Clark; art d, Perry Smith.

Comedy   **(PR:A   MPAA:NR)**

LEAVE IT TO HENRY**   (1949) 57m MON bw

Raymond Walburn (*Henry Latham*), Walter Catlett (*Mayor Colton*), Gary Gray (*David Latham*), Mary Stuart (*Barbara Latham*), Barbara Brown (*Mrs. Latham*), Houseley Stevenson (*Mr. McCluskey*), Ida Moore (*Aunt Martha*), Olin Howlin (*Milo Williams*), Pat Phelan (*Jim McCluskey*), George McDonald (*Georgie Colton*), Maynard Holmes (*Truck Driver*), Burk Symon (*Judge*), William Vedder (*Jeweler*), Harry Harvey (*Attorney*).

Walburn is on trial for burning up the toll bridge and through flashbacks we are told the story that led to his arrest. The town is planning its centennial celebration and the ladies club wants to re-enact a moment from the town's history. Walburn is hired to build a replica of a steamboat that caught on fire. He carries things too far when he puts the model on a barge, sets it on fire, and floats it down the river. It runs into the bridge and puts Walburn before the judge.

p, Peter Scully; d, Jean Yarbrough; w, D.D. Beauchamp (based on a story "Cruise of the Prairie Queen" by Beauchamp); ph, William Sickner; ed, Scully; md, Edward J. Kay.

Comedy   **(PR:A   MPAA:NR)**

LEAVE IT TO ME½   (1933, Brit.) 76m British International/Wardour bw

Gene Gerrard (*Sebastian Help*), Olive Borden (*Peavey*), Molly Lamont (*Eve Halliday*), George Gee (*Coots*), Gus McNaughton (*Baxter*), Clive Currie (*Lord Emsworth*), Tonie Edgar Bruce (*Lady Constance*), Peter Godfrey (*Siegfried Velour*), Syd Crossley (*Beach*), Melville Cooper (*Hon. Freddie*), Wylie Watson (*Client*).

To protect his aunt's jewels from thieves Gerrard, a professional "helper," takes on the guise of a poet. His plan is almost undone by Borden, a lady thief who is also disguised as a woman of words. Based on an enormously popular British play, this is a highly spirited comedy that never quite manages to achieve everything it sets out to do but is entertaining enough for what it is.

p, John Maxwell; d, Monty Banks; w, Gene Gerrard, Frank Miller, Cecil Lewis (based on the play "Leave it to Psmith" by P. G. Wodehouse and Ian Hay).

Comedy   **(PR:A   MPAA:NR)**

LEAVE IT TO ME**   (1937, Brit.) 71m BL bw

Sandy Powell (*Sandy*), Iris March (*Joan*), Franklin Dyall (*Sing*), Garry Marsh (*Sergeant*), Davy Burnaby (*Sir William*), Jack Hobbs (*Guest*), Claude Horton (*Butler*), Dora Hibbert, Nicholas Bird, George Pencheff, Jack Pye.

When March is bullied by her stepfather, ambitious but bumbling young policeman Powell comes to the rescue. Inadvertently he gets mixed up with a gang of Chinese thieves who drug him. After being dismissed from the force for this blunder, Powell recovers a stolen gem from the gang and is reinstated to the force. This is accomplished only after numerous gimmicky costume changes by Powell in a drawn-out comedy.

p, Tom Arnold; d, Herbert Smith; w, Fenn Sherie, Ingram d'Abbes; ph, George Stretton.

Comedy   **(PR:A   MPAA:NR)**

LEAVE IT TO SMITH*½   (1934) 69m GAU bw (GB: JUST SMITH)

Tom Walls (*Smith*), Carol Goodner (*Mary Linkley*), Anne Grey (*Lady Moynton*), Allan Aynesworth (*Lord Trench*), Eva Moore (*Lady Trench*), Reginald Gardiner (*Lord Redwood*), Veronica Rose (*Lady Susan Redwood*), Hartley Power (*John Mortimer*), Basil Radford (*Sir John Moynton*), Peter Gawthorne (*Rolls*), Leslie Perrins (*Duke of Bristol*), Margaret Moffat.

Walls is a thief who helps Goodner out of a jam. Things seem to go all right until Walls finds himself in more trouble because of his good deed. A lot of veddy British diction makes this one hard to understand.

p, Michael Balcon; d, Tom Walls; w, John O.C. Orton (based on the play "Never Come Back" by Frederick Lonsdale).

Comedy   **(PR:A   MPAA:NR)**

LEAVE IT TO THE IRISH*½   (1944) 61m MON bw

James Dunn (*Terry Moran*), Wanda McKay (*Nora O'Brien*), Jack La Rue (*Maletti*), Arthur Loft (*Timothy O'Brien*), Vince Barnett (*Harry*), Barbara Woodell (*Mrs. Hamilton*), Joseph DeVillard (*Gus*), Olaf Hytten (*Butler*), Ted Stanhope (*Joe*), Eddie Allen (*Slim*), Dick Scott (*Biff*).

Dunn and McKay are private investigators who team up to solve the murder of a fur dealer. After a couple of comical incidents, Dunn finds himself the murder suspect. A low-budget comedy that deals out the laughs like hoarded dollars.

p, Lindsley Parsons; d, William Beaudine; w, Tim Ryan, Eddie Davis; ph, Ira Morgan; ed, Dick Currier; art d, David Milton.

Comedy   **(PR:A   MPAA:NR)**

LEAVE IT TO THE MARINES*   (1951) 65m Lippert bw

Sid Melton (*Gerald Meek*), Mara Lynn (*Myrna McAllister*), Gregg Martell (*Sgt. McTaggert*), Ida Moore (*Grandma Meek*), Sam Flint (*Col. Flenge*), Doug Evans (*Gen. Garvin*), Margia Dean (*Cpl. Tootie*), Richard Monohan (*Partridge*), William Haade (*Sgt. Delaney*), Jack George (*Dr. Suture*), Paul Bryar (*Pappadopoli*), Ezelle Poule (*Mrs. McAllister*), Will Orleans (*Pvt. White*), Richard Farmer (*Colonel's Clerk*), Jimmy Cross (*Court Clerk*).

A witless comedy with Melton signing up for military service when he confuses the office for the marriage license bureau. His bride-to-be, Lynn, signs up, too, and they end in a Marine boot camp. Melton causes problems for his outfit and his sergeant, Martell, and gets the medal of bravery for saving the company mascot. The slapstick humor has been done too many times and far better.

p, Sigmund Neufeld; d, Samuel Newfield; w, Orville Hampton; ph, Jack Greenhalgh; ed, Carl Pierson.

Comedy   **(PR:A   MPAA:NR)**

LEAVENWORTH CASE, THE*   (1936) 66m REP bw

Donald Cook (*Dr. Harwell*), Jean Rouverol (*Elenore*), Norman Foster (*Bob*), Erin O'Brien-Moore (*Gloria*), Maude Eburne (*Phoebe*), Warren Hymer (*O'Malley*), Frank Sheridan (*Silas Leavenworth*), Gavin Gordon (*Henry Clavering*), Clay Clement (*Inspector Holmes*), Ian Wolfe (*Hudson*), Peggy Stratford (*Miss Owens*), Archie Robbins (*Duke*), Lucille Ware, Belle Mitchell, Marie Rice, Carl Stockdale, Dagmar Oakland, Bess Stafford.

Another murder mystery with all the suspects gathered at the house of the victim, a wealthy man. The murderer is apparent the moment of the deed because of careless direction, and so there is little reason to watch the rest of the film. Too bad, because the novel the picture is made from, written in the 1880s, was the granddaddy of many mystery stories to follow.

d, Lewis D. Collins; w, Albert DeMond, Sidney Sutherland (based on a novel by Anna Katharine Green); ph, Ernest Miller, Jack Marta; ed, Dan Milner.

Murder Mystery (PR:A MPAA:NR)

LEBENSBORN (SEE: ORDERED TO LOVE, 1963, Ger.)

LEBENSZEICHEN (SEE: SIGNS OF LIFE, 1981, Ger.)

L'ECLIPSE (SEE: ECLIPSE, 1962, Fr./Ital.)

L'ECLISSE (SEE: ECLIPSE, 1962, Fr./Ital.)

L'ECOLE BUISSONIERE (SEE: PASSION FOR LIFE, 1948, Fr.)

LEDA (SEE: WEB OF PASSION, 1961, Fr.)

LEECH WOMAN, THE** (1960) 77m UNIV bw

Coleen Gray *(June Talbot)*, Grant Williams *(Neil Foster)*, Phillip Terry *(Dr. Paul Talbot)*, Gloria Talbott *(Sally)*, John Van Dreelen *(Bertram Garvay)*, Estelle Hemsley *(Old Malla)*, Kim Hamilton *(Young Malla)*, Arthur Batanides *(Jerry)*, Murray Alper, Chester Jones.

Gray is the wife of scientist Terry who is experimenting with prolonging youth. They travel to Africa where Gray discovers that her husband has been using her as a guinea pig for his laboratory work. She kills him when she learns through a tribal ritual that she can preserve her youth with the pineal gland of males, and then she goes on a killing rampage to keep that youthful look. Williams arrives on the scene to put a stop to her rejuvenating process. Striking makeup by Bud Westmore.

p, Joseph Gershenson; d, Edward Dein; w, David Duncan (based on a story by Ben Pivar, Francis Rosenwald); ph, Ellis Carter; m, Irving Gertz; ed, Milton Carruth; art d, Alexander Golitzen, Robert Clatworthy; cos, Bill Thomas; makeup, Bud Westmore.

Horror (PR:C MPAA:NR)

LEFT HAND OF GOD, THE* 1/2** (1955) 87m FOX c

Humphrey Bogart *(Jim Carmody)*, Gene Tierney *(Ann Scott)*, Lee J. Cobb *(Mieh Yang)*, Agnes Moorehead *(Beryl Sigman)*, E.G. Marshall *(Dr. Sigman)*, Jean Porter *(Mary Yin)*, Carl Benton Reid *(Rev. Cornelius)*, Victor Sen Yung *(John Wong)*, Philip Ahn *(Jan Teng)*, Benson Fong *(Chun Tien)*, Richard Cutting *(Father O'Shea)*, Leon Lontoc *(Pao-Ching)*, Don Forbes *(Father Keller)*, Noel Toy *(Woman in Sarong)*, Peter Chong *(Feng-Merchant)*, Marie Tsien *(Woman in Kimona)*, Stephen Wong *(The Boy)*, Sophie Chin *(Celeste)*, George Chan *(Li Kwan)*, Walter Soo Hoo *(Hospital Orderly)*, Henry S. Quan *(Orderly)*, Doris Chung *(Nurse)*, Moy Ming *(Old Man)*, George Lee *(Mi Lu)*, Beal Wong *(Father)*, Stella Lynn *(Pao Chu)*, Robert Burton *(Rev. Marvin)*, Soo Yong *(Midwife)*, May Lee.

It is 1947 and Bogart is a soldier of fortune, a one-time American fighter pilot who has crashed in China and has thrown his lot in with warlord Cobb, living in the mountains with the bandits and taking as a mistress a Eurasian girl, Porter. Yet Bogart is uncomfortable in his role of adviser and captain of Cobb's ragtag army. When one of Cobb's men kills a priest, Bogart decides to escape his friendly captor, knowing that Cobb has given orders to shoot all deserters. He takes on the priest's identification and robes, making his way to a village where missionaries Marshall and Moorehead take him in. He is attracted to stunning mission nurse Tierney but can do nothing about it and is even forced to enact some religious ceremonies in order to preserve his disguise. Bogart falls in love with Tierney and she feels uncomfortable in his presence, having a strong physical attraction to him which makes them both feel ashamed. Bogart can stand it no longer and writes the bishop that he is an impostor, even though he has brought great comfort to the impoverished village and its bedraggled parisioners. Cobb arrives and insists that Bogart rejoin him as companion and adviser but Bogart demands he be set free. Unless Bogart returns to the ranks, Cobb threatens, he will destroy the village and all in it. Bogart then appeals to Cobb's considerable sporting blood, offering to roll the dice. If he wins, he goes free and the village remains unmolested. If he loses he will return with Cobb and serve five years as military counsel. Cobb loses and graciously pays his debt. The bishop's emmissary arrives and chastises Bogart for his sacrilege but Marshall and Moorehead, who were originally hostile to Bogart, come to his defense and point out the good he has done for the village. Bogart is ordered to report to higher authorities on the coast. When he leaves it is understood that Tierney will follow him and the two of them will share a life together as man and wife. The story is improbable but Bogart's fine job of acting and Tierney's luscious presence heighten the tame script which is directed with great energy by Dmytryk and beautifully lensed by Planer. Tierney had not appeared in films for several years and had recently been released from a sanitarium after suffering a bout with mental illness. Zanuck, who had made her a star at Fox, asked Bogart and Dmytryk if they would consider her as their leading lady and both agreed. Bogart's performance, as usual, was flawless but he nevertheless enjoyed his libations. At 4 p.m., when the major portion of shooting was completed for the day, Bogart would ask Dmytryk if he had any more important scenes for him to shoot. If the answer was no, Bogart would go to a small refrigerator in his dressing room and pull forth a bottle of scotch, pouring himself a stiff one. He was, however, in considerable pain, having recently suffered a slipped disc and having to perform lengthy scenes while riding horseback. By then, Dmytryk remembered, Bogart was endlessly chain smoking and, before doing a scene, would step aside and "slip into a paroxysm of coughing" which was self-induced to avoid coughing during his scenes. "Nearly every one on the set begged him to cut down on his smoking, but Bogey would just shrug his shoulders and light another cigarette." The cigarettes, of course, would kill him; he would be dead of cancer of the esophagus by 1957. For Bogart enthusiasts this film remains a high camp production and it is obvious that the expansive Cobb played his part for laughs but it is nevertheless entertaining. Fox made much of the Bogart-Tierney relationship of priest and lover in their ads which overstated the case. At the film's premiere an interviewer trapped Bogart coming out of the theater and asked: "How does it feel to be a priest?" Bogart snapped back: "How would *I* know?" and walked off. End of interview.

p, Buddy Adler; d, Edward Dmytryk; w, Alfred Hayes (based on the novel by William E. Barrett); ph, Franz Planer (CinemaScope, Deluxe Color); m, Victor Young; ed, Dorothy Spencer; art d, Lyle Wheeler, Maurice Ransford; set d, Walter M. Scott, Frank Wade, cos, Travilla; spec eff, Ray Kellogg.

Adventure/Romance Cas. (PR:A MPAA:NR)

LEFT-HANDED GUN, THE* 1/2** (1958) 102m WB bw

Paul Newman *(Billy Bonney)*, Lita Milan *(Celsa)*, John Dehner *(Pat Garrett)*, Hurd Hatfield *(Moultrie)*, James Congdon *(Charlie Boudre)*, James Best *(Tom Folliard)*, Colin Keith-Johnston *(Tunstall)*, John Dierkes *(McSween)*, Bob Anderson *(Hill)*, Wally Brown *(Moon)*, Ainslie Pryor *(Joe Grant)*, Martin Garralaga *(Saval)*, Denver Pyle *(Ollinger)*, Paul Smith *(Bell)*, Nestor Paiva *(Maxwell)*, Jo Summers *(Mrs. Garrett)*, Robert Foulk *(Brady)*, Anne Barton *(Mrs. Hill)*.

A good but distrubing psychological western (is there really such a thing?), well directed by Penn and acted to strange fascination by Newman. This is the story, once more, of Billy the Kid, a legend around whom all sorts of lies and glories have been spun. Penn, however, and to his credit, de-myths the Kid and Newman probably plays him more honestly than any other before or since. He was a slow-witted illiterate with a streak of sadistic bloodlust in him, fiercely loyal to his few friends and deadly to all those who became his enemy. And it is a matter of record that Billy was a backstabbing, backshooting murderer who never stood up in a fair fight and bested any opponent with gun, knife, or fist. He was a sneak, aptly described in another version of his life simply in the title DIRTY LITTLE BILLY (1972). Newman is nothing but a western guttersnipe until Keith-Johnston, playing the kindly rancher John Tunstall, whom Billy had known in real life, treats him with understanding. Newman reacts as would any loveless human, becoming fanatically devoted to the rancher. When the unarmed Keith-Johnston is shot to death by a deputy and three others in a range war, Newman goes crazy. He and his equally empty-headed saddlemates Best and Congdon track down the killers and murder them one by one. This leads to Newman's arrest and subsequent jailing. He escapes and crosses the border where he has a brief, awkward affair with Milan, a blacksmith's wife, which leads to another killing. When he returns, Newman is gunned down by Dehner, playing Pat Garrett, lawman and harsh real-life father figure to Billy the Kid. Dehner vows revenge on his one-time pal Newman after Newman kills one of the guests, the last of the foursome sought by Newman for Keith-Johnston's death, at Dehner's wedding party. Flitting in and out of Newman's life is a neurotic pulp writer, Hatfield, who creates the myth of Billy the Kid and then condemns Newman for not living up to his lies, finally screaming at him: "You're not *him*!" Weird and definitely not wonderful is Hatfield. This debunking film by Penn, his first chore at directing, stems from Gore Vidal's wacky and self-serving teleplay "The Death of Billy the Kid," which was directed by Penn for TV in 1955. Penn toned down Vidal's blatant portrait of the Kid as a rampant homosexual which served the author's interests more than that of true history and accurate biography. Newman, as he had in SOMEBODY UP THERE LIKES ME, took a role here which was originally coveted by James Dean, who died prematurely in a car accident, but he does a masterful job in portraying the ruthless little killer whose reputation only existed beyond his grave.

p, Fred Coe; d, Arthur Penn; w, Leslie Stevens (based on the teleplay "The Death of Billy the Kid" by Gore Vidal); ph, J. Peverell Marley; m, Alexander Courage; ed, Folmar Blangsted; art d, Art Loel; set d, William Kuehl; cos, Marjorie Best; m/l, William Goyen, Courage.

Western Cas. (PR:C MPAA:NR)

LEFT-HANDED LAW* 1/2 (1937) 63m UNIV bw

Buck Jones *(Alamo Bowie)*, Noel Francis *(Betty Golden)*, Matty Fain *(One-Shot Brady)*, George Regas *(Sam Logan)*, Robert Frazer *(Tom Willis)*, Lee Phelps *(Sheriff Grant)*, Frank LaRue, Lee Shumway, Nena Quartaro, Charles LeMoyne, Budd Buster, Frank Lackteen, Jim Toney, Bill Wolfe, Silver Tip Baker, Jack Evans, Jim Corey, Silver the Horse.

Jones rids a town in New Mexico of Fain and his gang of outlaws. The cowboy hero also finds time to take charge of the ranch of Francis' father and make a few jokes. The small kids and the kid in us all will find enjoyment in this dust-covered western filled with he-man action and all the western cliches that could be gathered at the time.

p, Buck Jones; d, Lesley Selander; w, Frances Guihan (based on a story by Charles M. Martin); ph, Allen Thompson, William Sickner.

Western (PR:A MPAA:NR)

LEFT-HANDED WOMAN, THE***
(1980, Ger.) 119m Road Movies Filmproduktion/New Yorker c

Edith Clever *(The Woman)*, Markus Muhleisen *(Stefan)*, Bruno Ganz *(Bruno)*, Michel Lonsdale *(Waiter)*, Angela Winkler *(Franziska)*, Bernhard Wicki *(Publisher)*, Nicholas Novikoff *(Driver)*, Bernhard Minetti *(Father)*, Rudiger Vogler *(Actor)*, Jany Holt *(Woman at the Meeting)*, Gerard Depardieu *(Man with T-shirt)*, Phillippe Calzergues *(Stefan's Friend)*, Ines de Lonchamps *(Woman with Child)*, Hanns Zischler, Simone Benmuse, Erika Krallk, Walter Greinhart, Sam Cuzelin, Mr. and Mrs. Borg, Rene, Mechild Kalisky.

An extremely alienating glimpse of a married woman who, on a whim, decides that she doesn't want to remain living with her husband and separates from him. Though there is little drama or narrative and the acting is so subtle the players almost appear to be ghostwalking, THE LEFT-HANDED WOMAN is very powerful in showing this woman's emotional state. Her life is empty and boring, as is revealed in the stunning photography of Robby Muller, who captures sparse spaces that resemble the woman's inner blandness. To many people this may seem boring, but one cannot deny the power of such an approach to reveal modern personal traumas in an alienating universe. (In German; English subtitles.)

p, Renee Gundelach; d&w, Peter Handke; ph, Robby Muller; ed, Peter Pryzgodda; cos, Domenica Kaesdorf.

Drama   (PR:C-O MPAA:NR)

LEFT, RIGHT AND CENTRE**½   (1959) 95m BL bw
Patricia Bredin (Stella Stoker), Eric Barker (Bert Glimmer), Jack Hedley (Bill Hemingway), Leslie Dwyer (Alf Stoker), Russell Waters (Mr. Bray), Hattie Jacques (Woman in Car), Ian Carmichael (Robert Wilcot), Richard Wattis (Harding-Pratt), Moyra Fraser (Annabel), William Kendall (Pottle), George Benson (Egerton), Anthony Sharp (Peterson), Moultrie Kelsall (Grimsby-Armfield), Alastair Sim (Lord Wilcot), Gordon Harker (Hardy), Frederick Leister (Dr. Rushall), John Salew (Mayor), Bill Shine (Basingstoke), Jeremy Hawke (TV Interviewer), Irene Handl (Mrs. Maggs), Eamonn Andrews, Gilbert Harding, Josephine Douglas, Carole Carr (TV Panel), Philip Morant (Bulson), Fred Griffiths (Fish Porter), Olwen Brookes (Mrs. Samson), Peter Elliott (Satterwaite), Erik Chitty (Returning Officer), Frank Atkinson (Robert's Porter), Redmond Phillips (Mr. Smithson), John Sharp (Mr. Reeves), Olaf Pooley (TV Newscaster), Douglas Ives, Sidney Gilliat.

Carmichael is a British TV game show host and becomes the local candidate for the Conservative Party. Bredin is the candidate for the Socialists and the two fall madly in love. Their agents go to great lengths to wreck the relationship and save the election. A funny film if the viewer has some knowledge of Britain's political system.

p, Frank Launder, Sidney Gilliat; d, Gilliat; w, Gilliat (based on a story by Gilliat, Val Valentine); ph, Gerald Gibbs; m, Humphrey Searle; ed, Geoffrey Foot.

Comedy   (PR:A MPAA:NR)

LEFTOVER LADIES*   (1931) 65m TIF bw (GB: BROKEN LINKS)
Claudia Dell (Patricia), Marjorie Rambeau (The Duchess), Walter Byron (Ronny), Alan Mowbray (Jerry), Dorothy Revier (Amy), Rita LaRoy (Vera), Roscoe Karns ("Scoop"), Selmer Jackson (Churchill), Buster Phelps (Buddy), Franklyn Farnum (Benson).

This low-budget yawn concerns two couples who go through divorce only to realize that they still need each other. Dell and Byron are one of the couples, and Mowbray and Revier the other. Unskilled handling from the production end to the writing makes it one to avoid.

d, Eric C. Kenton; w, Robert R. Presnell (based on a story by Ursula Parrott); ph, John Stumar; ed, Martin Cohn.

Drama   (PR:A MPAA:NR)

LEGACY**½   (1976) 90m Kino International c
Joan Hotchkis (Woman), George McDaniel (Husband), Sean Allan (Lover), Dixie Lee (Mother).

Hotchkis, who also wrote the screenplay and the play this one is based on, is a poor little rich girl who grows bored with her life. She engages in mind games, self denigration, and slowly dips down into madness. Her performance is a genuine tour-de-force, but unfortunately the direction never matches it and the ending is anticlimactic.

d, Karen Arthur; w, Joan Hotchkis (based on her play); ph, John Bailey, m, Roger Kellaway; ed, Carol Littleton.

Drama   (PR:O MPAA:R)

LEGACY, THE*½
          (1979, Brit.) 100m UNIV c (AKA: THE LEGACY OF MAGGIE WALSH)
Katharine Ross (Maggie Walsh), Sam Elliott (Pete Danner), John Standing (Jason Mountolive), Ian Hogg (Harry), Margaret Tyzack (Nurse Adams), Charles Gray (Karl), Lee Montague (Jacques), Hildegard Neil (Barbara), Marianne Broome (Maria), William Abney (Butler), Patsy Smart (Cook), Mathias Kilroy (Stable Lad), Reg Harding (Gardener), Roger Daltrey (Clive).

An American couple, Ross and Elliott, arrive in England and end up staying at a country mansion when their car is forced off the road. The other guests at the house, Gray, Neil, Daltrey, Montague, and Broome, begin dying in strange ways. The new couple discover that the victims had sold their souls to the devil and bedridden millionaire Standing is the man who is collecting the debts. Ross is destined to take the old man's place, but Elliott makes sure this doesn't come to pass. Uninspired visit with Satan, who turns out to be a pretty tame fellow.

p, David Foster; d, Richard Marquand; w, Jimmy Sangster, Patric Tilley, Paul Wheeler (based on a story by Sangster); ph, Dick Bush, Alan Hume (Technicolor); m, Michael J. Lewis; ed, Anne V. Coates; prod d, Disley Jones; cos, Shura Cohen; spec eff, Ian Wingrove.

Fantasy   (PR:O MPAA:R)

LEGACY OF A SPY   (SEE: A DOUBLE MAN, 1968)

LEGACY OF BLOOD*
          (1973) 90m Universal Entertainment c (AKA: BLOOD LEGACY)
Rudolfo Acosta (Sheriff Dan Garcia), Merry Anders (Laura Dean), Norman Bartold (Tom Drake), John Carradine (Christopher Dean), Faith Domergue (Victoria Dean), Jeff Morrow (Gregory Dean), Ivy Bethune (Elga), Richard Davalos (Johnny Dean), Buck Kartalian (Igor), John Smith (Carl Isenburg), John Russell (Frank Mantee), Brooke Mills (Leslie Dean), Mr. Chin (Chin).

Carradine is a millionaire who leaves his vast riches to his children. Of course there's just one catch: the offspring must spend a week in the old man's house to collect. This leads to a myriad of nasty doings, and none of them new or original.

p&d, Carl Monson; w, Eric Norden; ph, B. Rombouts, Jack Beckett; prod d, Mike McCloskey.

Horror   Cas.   (PR:O MPAA:R)

LEGACY OF BLOOD zero
          (1978) 82m Take One Film Group/Ken Lane Films c (AKA: BLOOD LEGACY)
Elaine Boies, Chris Broderick, Marilee Troncone, Jeannie Cusick, Pete Barcia, Louise Gallandra, Stanley Schwartz, Dale Hansen, Joe Downing, Julia Curry, Martin Reymert.

An extremely low budget horror film that drags along to a bloody climax. Three sisters and their husbands arrive at an inn for the reading of their father's will and are murdered one by one. Production qualities are nil and the acting could have been handled better by children.

p,d,w,ph&ed, Andy Milligan; set d, Joe Cook; makeup, Walter Ballesten.

Horror   (PR:O MPAA:NR)

LEGACY OF MAGGIE WALSH   (SEE: LEGACY, THE, 1979)

LEGACY OF THE 500,000, THE**½
          (1964, Jap.) 98m Toho bw (GOJUMAN-NIN NO ISAN)
Toshiro Mifune (Matsuo), Tatsuya Mihashi, Tatsuya Nakadai, Tsutomu Yamazaki.

Kurosawa favorite Mifune directs and stars in this fairly routine adventure as a man who finds himself abducted by the rich president of a maritime trading company because he knows the whereabouts of 10,000 gold coins left in the Philippines by the Japanese army during WW II. Mifune is brought to a boat captained by the businessman's brother and the small group (which includes a driver and bodyguard) enter the Philippines disguised as U.S. Army troops and Chinese merchants. Eventually the treasure hunters make their way through the rugged, mountainous region of North Luzon and run in with a group of native headhunters, but they never do find the gold. Mifune is okay in his dual role as actor/director, but he doesn't have that spark that only Kurosawa was able to bring out of him in their collaborations.

d, Toshiro Mifune; w, Ryuzo Kikushima; ph, Takao Saito (Tokoscope).

Adventure   (PR:A MPAA:NR)

LEGAL LARCENY   (SEE: SILVER CITY RAIDERS, 1943)

LEGEND IN LEOTARDS
          (SEE: RETURN OF CAPTAIN INVINCIBLE, THE, 1983, Aus./U.S.)

LEGEND OF A BANDIT, THE**
          (1945, Mex.) 82m Clasa bw (LA LEYENDA DE BANDIDO)
Raul de Anda (Benito Canaies), Susana Guizar (Isabel), Miguel Angel Ferriz (Priest), Tito Junco (Capt. Rogenio), Miguel Arenas (Isabel's Father), Agustin Isunza ("The Tall One"), El Chicote ("The Short One").

Anda is a peasant-turned-bandit when the town constable wants to marry his girlfriend, and accuses Anda of murder. The military chases after Anda and his companions, but he eludes them and tries to stop the forced marriage. (In Spanish.)

d, Fernando Mendez; m, Trio Calaveras.

Western   (PR:A MPAA:NR)

LEGEND OF BLOOD MOUNTAIN, THE*   (1965) 76m Craddock c
George Ellis (Bestoink Dooley), Zenas Sears, Glenda Brunson, Erin Fleming, Sheila Stringer.

Cheap, obscure horror film has small-town reporter Ellis meeting beautiful girls and an ugly monster while working on a story. Fleming, who has a minor role here, later became Groucho Marx's secretary/companion in the great comedian's final years.

p, Don Hadley; d, Massey Cramer; w, Cramer, Hadley, Bob Corley.

Horror   (PR:O MPAA:NR)

LEGEND OF BOGGY CREEK, THE**   (1973) 90m Howco International c
Vern Stearman (Narrator), Willie E. Smith, John P. Hixon, John W. Oates, Jeff Crabtree, Buddy Crabtree, Herb Jones, Inhabitants of Fouke, Arkansas.

Docudrama about a Bigfoot-like creature that allegedly terrorizes the small town of Fouke, Arkansas near the Texas border. Usually seen as a dark, shambling shape running across someone's headlight beams on stark country roads, the creature makes several attacks on people, tossing their garbage cans around, rocking trailer homes, and occasionally sticking its arm in someone's window, scaring the kids. The film is crudely made, but quite effective, and its G rating attracted lots of little kids not usually able to see a horror movie in a theater and gave them a couple of good scares. A sequel, RETURN TO BOGGY CREEK, was released in 1977.

p&d, Charles B. Pierce; w, Earl E. Smith; ph, Pierce (Technicolor); m, Jamie Mendoza-Nava; ed, Thomas F. Boutress.

Drama/Horror/Adventure   (PR:A-C MPAA:G)

LEGEND OF COUGAR CANYON**
          (1974) 89m James Flocker Productions/Gold Key c
Rex Allen (Storyteller), Holger Kasper (Walter), Steven Benally, Jr. (Steve), Johnny Guerro (Indian Guide), Members of the Navajo Nation.

Two 12-year-olds go wandering and end up in a mysterious old cave where they are trapped by a vicious cougar. This adventure story is a terror and suspense piece aimed directly at younger audiences.

p&d, James T. Flocker; ph, David E. Jackson (Eastmancolor); m, William Loose.

Children's Adventure   (PR:A MPAA:G)

LEGEND OF FRENCHIE KING, THE*

(1971, Fr./Ital./Span./Brit.) 96m Franco-Vides-Coper Hemdale Films c (LES PETROLEUSES; AKA: THE PETROLEUM GIRLS; THE OIL GIRLS) AKA: THE PETROLEUM GIRLS; THE OIL GIRLS)

Brigitte Bardot (Frenchie), Claudia Cardinale (Maria), Michael J. Pollard (Marshal), Emma Cohen (Sister), Micheline Presle (Aunt Amelie), Patty Shepard (Petite Pluie), Teresa Cimpera (Caroline), Oscar Davis (Mathieu), Georges Beller (Marc), Patrick Prejan (Luc), Rocardo Salvino (Jean), Valery Inkijnoff (Spitting Bull), Denise Provence (Mlle. Letellier), Leroy Hayns (Marquis), Jacques Jouanneau (Mons. Letellier), Raoul Delfosse (Le Cornac), France Dougnac (Elisabeth), Henri Czarniak.

Set in New Mexico (shot in Spain) in 1880, this bad western exploits the sex-kitten attributes of Bardot and her four eye-appealing sisters. They keep their father's legend alive by robbing trains while disguised as men. After stealing the deed to the Little P Ranch, the five gals move in and discover they are sitting on a fortune in oil. BB's rival, Cardinale, also learns the property's worth and tries to buy the land. After a fair amount of feuding, with marshal/dogcatcher Pollard in the middle, BB and CC become the best of friends. The bumbling, camera-mugging Pollard closes the pic by stating "The West ain't no place fer a man!" This pic, combining the worst parts of SHALAKO and VIVA MARIA, was begun by Guy Casaril. After disagreements with the producer, Casaril split and was replaced by Christian-Jaque. This caused a great deal of confusion among the industry folks, who believed that two BB/CC pictures were being filmed—FRENCHIE KING by Christian-Jaque and LES PETROLEUSES by Casaril. Christian-Jaque (who insisted that Pollard had won an Oscar for BONNIE AND CLYDE) simply didn't know what to do with Pollard, allowing him far too much freedom in a role which should have been handled by someone twice his age. Even for devotees of the luscious BB and CC this one is nonlegendary.

p, Raymond Erger, Francis Cosne; d, Guy Casaril, Christian-Jaque; w, Casaril, Daniel Boulanger, Marie-Ange Anies, Jean Nemours, Clement Bywood; ph, Henri Persin (Eastmancolor); m, Francis Lai; ed, Nicole Guadauchon.

Western/Comedy (PR:C MPAA:R)

LEGEND OF HELL HOUSE, THE**

(1973, Brit.) 94m James H. Nicholson's Academy Pictures/FOX c

Pamela Franklin (Florence Tanner), Roddy McDowall (Ben Fischer), Clive Revill (Dr. Chris Barrett), Gayle Hunnicutt (Ann Barrett), Roland Culver (Rudolph Deutsch), Peter Bowles (Hanley), Michael Gough.

Four people are hired to stay in a haunted house for a week to determine whether or not ghosts are inhabiting the house. Franklin is a medium who believes she is able to communicate with the spirit world. McDowall is a physical medium who had stayed in the house before, and Revill is a skeptical physicist who brings along his wife, Hunnicutt. The man who is paying for their stay is millionaire Culver. There are a few scary moments in the film, but very few. The ending and explanation of the haunting spirits is anti-climactic.

p, Albert Fennell, Norman T. Herman; d, John Hough; w, Richard Matheson (adapted from his novel Hell House); ph, Alan Hume (DeLuxe Color); m, Brian Hodgson, Delia Derbyshire; ed, Geoffrey Foot; prod d, Ron Fry; set d, Robert Jones.

Horror Cas. (PR:C MPAA:PG)

LEGEND OF HILLBILLY JOHN, THE

(SEE: WHO FEARS THE DEVIL, 1972)

LEGEND OF LOBO, THE**1/2

(1962) 67m Disney/BV c

Rex Allen (Narrator and Singer).

A Disney animal film told in visuals and narration. Lobo is a wolf and the film follows him from birth to when he becomes the leader of a new pack. When his mate is captured by a hunter, Lobo outsmarts the man and gets his mate back. The wolf then leads his pack to an unpopulated area. Field producer and cameraman Jack Couffer would later coproduce another Disney film on wolves, the superb NEVER CRY WOLF.

d, James Algar; w, Dwight Hauser, Algar (based on a story by Ernest Thompson-Seton); ph, Jack Couffer, Lloyd Beebe (Technicolor); m, Oliver Wallace; ed, Norman R. Palmer; m/l, "The Legend of Lobo," Richard M. Sherman, Robert B. Sherman.

Adventure (PR:AA MPAA:NR)

LEGEND OF LYLAH CLARE, THE**1/2

(1968) 127m Associates & Aldrich/MGM c

Kim Novak (Lylah Clare/Elsa Brinkmann), Peter Finch (Lewis Zarkan), Ernest Borgnine (Barney Sheean), Milton Selzer (Bart Langner), Rossella Falk (Rossella), Gabriele Tinti (Paolo), Valentina Cortese (Countess Bozo Bedoni), Jean Carroll (Becky Langner), Michael Murphy (Mark Peter Sheean), Lee Meriwether (Young Girl), James Lanphier (1st Legman), Robert Ellenstein (Mike), Nick Dennis (Nick), Dave Willock (Cameraman), Coral Browne (Molly Luther), Peter Bravos (Butler), Ellen Corby (Script Girl), Michael Fox (Announcer), Hal Maguire (2nd Legman), Tom Patty (Bedoni's Escort), Vernon Scott (Himself), Queenie Smith (Hairdresser), Sidney Skolsky (Himself), Barbara Ann Warkmeister, Mel Warkmeister (Aerialists), George Kennedy (Matt Burke in ANNA CHRISTIE, 1930).

Originally a teleplay presented on NBC's "DuPont Show of the Week," this is a pretty good drama with some stand-out acting and will attract those who enjoy the 1980s brand of TV soap opera. Novak plays two roles: one is a young Chicago actress (which she was in real life), and the other is a legendary dead movie queen. She's hired by Selzer to play the late actress in an upcoming film biography, if Finch, husband of the dead star, can be convinced that she's the woman who can handle it. Finch (whose name is Zarkan, which sounds more like a space villain than a

director) reluctantly meets with Novak and is struck by the similarity between this sweet, young thing and his late wife (and why not?). Finch hasn't worked since his wife died on their wedding night, but he is soon eager to direct Novak in the film and appeals to Borgnine, the studio chief, for financing. Borgnine agrees and Finch begins to mold Novak into the same personality as his late wife. She balks at first but realizes this is a chance she may never have again, so she allows herself to be manipulated until she is almost becoming the dead woman. Soon enough, Novak and Finch are lovers, a fact that does not go unnoticed by Falk, the housekeeper, who pays unusual attention to their trysts. Falk is a drug addict and a lesbian and was the dead actress' dialog coach until her death. Novak, by this time, thinks she really is Finch's former wife and insults powerful movie gossip columnist Browne in much the same way Clare did. Novak now realizes that Finch doesn't love her, but he does cherish the memory of his late wife. Her manner of retaliation is to have an affair with the handsome gardener, Tinti. When Finch learns of this, he changes the end of the film and writes in a scene that puts Novak in jeopardy—a dangerous trapeze stunt which she will probably not survive. Both women suffer from vertigo (Novak couldn't seem to get away from that rare ailment), a fact of which Finch is well aware. Novak falls to her death and the last moments of Clare's life are revealed. We see that Finch killed her when he learned that she and Falk were having a lesbian liaison. He pushed her down a flight of stairs and she went into film history. Finch leaves the studio and returns home, filled with a mixture of grief and guilt for having killed the only two women he's ever loved. He reaches home, where Falk is waiting for him with a loaded gun. Before she fires the fatal shot, the picture ends. THE LEGEND OF LYLAH CLARE combines Aldrich's eerie direction with a script that takes pot-shots at the movie business. The elements work from time to time, but clash more often. This was Novak's return to the screen after a two-year absence, and she does a fine job in two roles that are alike and yet different, as Novak must use a German accent when portraying Clare. The supporting cast is uniformly good, especially Italian actress Falk, who is frighteningly evil. The gowns by Renie are excellent and all technical credits are good. Hollywood spent a lot of time trying to figure out who the characters were based upon, but that was fruitless as there are so many people who resemble Novak, Finch, Selzer, and Borgnine that the choices were many.

p&d, Robert Aldrich; w, Hugo Butler, Jean Rouverol (based on the teleplay "The Legend of Lylah Clare" by Robert Thom, Edward DeBlasio); ph, Joseph Biroc (Metrocolor); m, Frank De Vol; ed, Michael Luciano; art d, George W. Davis, William Glasgow; set d, Henry Grace, Keogh Gleason; cos, Renie; spec eff, Al Burke; m/l, "Lylah," De Vol, Sibylle Siegfried (sung by Siegfried); makeup, William Tuttle, Robert Schiffer; hairstyles, Sydney Guilaroff, Agnes Flanagan; stunts, John Indrisano.

Drama (PR:A-C MPAA:R)

LEGEND OF NIGGER CHARLEY, THE**

(1972) 98m PAR c

Fred Williamson (Nigger Charley), D'Urville Martin (Toby), Don Pedro Colley (Joshua), Gertrude Jeanette (Theo), Marcia McBroom (Julia), Alan Gifford (Hill Carter), John Ryan (Houston), Will Hussung (Dr. Saunders), Mill Moor (Walker), Thomas Anderson (Shadow), Jerry Gatlin (Sheriff Rhinehart), Tricia O'Neil (Sarah Lyons), Doug Rowe (Dewey Lyons), Keith Prentice (Nils Fowler), Tom Pemberton (Willie), Joe Santos (Reverend), Fred Lerner (Ollokot).

Williamson, Martin, and Colley are slaves who escape from Ryan's plantation and head west. They are pursued by bounty hunter Prentice, joined by Anderson and Pemberton, and become friends with Rowe and his half-breed wife, O'Neil. The group cleans out a bar, kills a band of outlaws led by Santos, and keeps heading west. A fair black exploitation film with a surprisingly large budget and good production values. (Sequel: SOUL OF NIGGER CHARLEY.)

p, Larry G. Spangler; d, Martin Goldman; w, Spangler, Goldman (based on a story by James Warner Bellah); ph, Peter Eco; m, John Bennings; ed, Howard Kuperman; art d, Merrill Sindler; cos, Joseph Garibaldi Aulisi; spec eff, Joe Day; makeup, Enrico Cortese; stunts, Jerry Gatlin.

Western (PR:C MPAA:PG)

LEGEND OF ROBIN HOOD, THE

(SEE: CHALLENGE FOR ROBIN HOOD, 1968, Brit.)

LEGEND OF SPIDER FOREST, THE*

(1976, Brit.) 88m New Line c (AKA: VENOM)

Neda Americ, Simon Brent.

A young artist decides to take a holiday in Bavaria. Before he can enjoy the rustic countryside, he encounters the "Spider Goddess" and her henchmen scientists who use spider venom to kill their victims. Cheap and bad.

d, Peter Sykes.

Horror (PR:C MPAA:PG)

LEGEND OF THE BAYOU

(SEE: EATEN ALIVE!, 1976)

LEGEND OF THE LONE RANGER, THE zero

(1981) 98m UNIV/Associated Film Distribution c

Klinton Spilsbury (The Lone Ranger), Michael Horse (Tonto), Christopher Lloyd (Cavendish), Matt Clark (Sheriff Wiatt), Juanin Clay (Amy Striker), Jason Robards (President Grant), John Bennett Perry (Dan Reid), David Hayward (Collins), John Hart (Lucas Striker), Richard Farnsworth (Wild Bill Hickok), Lincoln Tate (General Custer), Ted Flicker (Buffalo Bill Cody), Marc Gilpin (Young John Reid), Patrick Mantoya (Young Tonto), David Bennett (Gen'l. Rodriguez), Rick Traeger (German), James Bowman (Gambler), Kit Wong (Chinese), Daniel Nunez (Agent), R. L. Tolbert (Stagecoach Driver), Clay Boss (Shotgun), Ted White (Reid), Chere Bryson (Mrs. Reid), James Lee Crite (Waiter), Min Burke (Stephenson), Jeff Ramsey (Alcott), Bennie Dobbins (Lopez), Henry Wills (Little), Greg Walker (Rankin), Mike

Adams (*Palmer*), Ben Bates (*Post*), Bill Hart (*Carner*), Larry Randles (*Stacy*), Robert Hoy (*Perimutter*), Ted Gehring (*Stillwell*), Buck Taylor (*Gattlin*), Tom R. Diaz (*Eastman*), Chuck Hayward (*Wald*), Tom Laughlin (*Neeley*), Terry Leonard (*Valentine*), Steve Meador (*Russell*), Joe Finnegan (*Westlake*), Roy Bonner (*Richardson*), John M. Smith (*Whitloff*).

This film is one of the worst films of the '80s. It could almost be considered camp. Spilsbury's lines were all dubbed over by another actor because of his nonexistent acting abilities and unmanly voice. The tale of how the Lone Ranger came to be has been left alone, which is the only interesting part of the film (the first 15 minutes), but then dullness reigns for 50 minutes because the Ranger doesn't put on his mask. Then the action is quite violent and bloody for a film aimed at the younger set. The Ranger's archenemy, Lloyd, kidnaps the President, Robards, and not only do Tonto and the Lone Ranger come to his rescue, but so does General Custer, Wild Bill Hickok, and Buffalo Bill. Rhetorical question: If the Lone Ranger is such a hero, isn't it conceivable that he could rescue the Prez with just the aid of his faithful companion? This was the first film for director Fraker since MONTE WALSH.

p, Walter Coblenz; d, William A. Fraker; w, Ivan Goff, Ben Roberts, Michael Kane, William Roberts, Jerry Berloshan (based on stories and characters created by George W. Trendle); ph, Laszlo Kovacs (Panavision, Technicolor); m, John Barry; ed, Thomas Stanford; prod d, Albert Brenner; art d, David M. Haber; set d, Phillip Abramson; cos, Noel Taylor.

Western **Cas.** **(PR:C MPAA:PG)**

LEGEND OF THE LOST*

(1957, U.S./Panama/Ital.) 108m Batjac-Haggiag-Dear/UA c

John Wayne (*Joe January*), Sophia Loren (*Dita*), Rossano Brazzi (*Paul Bonnard*), Kurt Kasznar (*Prefect Dukas*), Sonia Moser, Angela Portaluri (*Girls*), Ibrahim El Hadish (*Galli Galli*).

Despite the fact that he was one of the most facile screenwriters in film history, and probably the highest paid, Ben Hecht did pen some clinkers. This is one of them. Wayne is a down-and-out adventurer who finds himself in a Timbuktu jail for lack of funds and brawling. He is hired by idealist and dreamer Brazzi to guide him to remote and near-mythical ruins in the middle of the Sahara Desert where a great treasure reportedly awaits discovery, one Brazzi's own vanished father sought years earlier. Wayne doesn't for a minute believe Brazzi but goes along for wages and to breathe free air. Joining them against Wayne's will is street girl Loren, who is out for adventure and a wedding ring from Brazzi, who seems indifferent to her and the voluptuous body jiggling beneath her paper-thin dress. As Wayne predicts, rivalry over the girl develops between him and Brazzi, particularly when Wayne makes his dislike of slovenly Loren known, a disguise for his own attraction to the earthy wench. She knocks Wayne cold with a skillet when he and Brazzi get into a fist fight just to prove she's interested in Wayne. The bedraggled trio finally arrives in the deserted ruins of ancient Timgad, and there Brazzi finds the skeletons of his father and his guide, both obviously having killed each other over the affections of a woman who accompanied their expedition years earlier. This revelation sends Brazzi off the deep end and he inexplicably changes into a lethal killer intent on destroying Loren and Wayne. He dies at Loren's hands before he can kill Wayne. Before Wayne and Loren die of thirst, a passing caravan picks them up and takes them back to Timbuktu. LEGEND OF THE LOST is an exercise in senseless brutality and insanity and presents a *menage a trois* that could only be likened to the Three Stooges. Wayne took the entire production as a joke, his words aptly describing the script: "We're out in the middle of nowhere looking for nothing in the wrong season." He looks with a grimace at his pack mule and adds: "Damn it, you have a pal on this trip, a fellow jackass—that's me!" He then loudly heehaws. He later states, in a line that sums up this mess churned out mindlessly by the normally gifted Hathaway: "Two men and a dame put a strain on any civilization." The strain is also on the viewer, who must plod over sand dunes with this mismatched trio, through a dull story and a dismal ending. Even Loren's well-worn dress, torn in all the places that will reveal as much thigh and mammary allowable, does not enhance this misadventure. Wayne was quoted as admiring Loren for bravely trekking through the desert: "She's been bitten by scorpions, marooned in sandstorms, but nothing can stop that gal. She makes all us men look like ninnies. I came here to find hidden treasure and I've found a gold mine. When she gets to Hollywood, she'll slay them!" Said the towering Amazon Loren about Wayne: "At last I'm playing with an actor who is my own size." Not exactly; Loren never did measure up to Big Duke Wayne at her best filmic moments.

p&d, Henry Hathaway; w, Robert Presnell, Jr., Ben Hecht; ph, Jack Cardiff (Technirama, Technicolor); m, A. F. Lavagnino; ed, Bert Bates; md, Lavagnino; art d, Alfred Ybarra.

Adventure **(PR:C MPAA:NR)**

LEGEND OF THE SEA WOLF (SEE: WOLF LARSEN, 1974)

LEGEND OF THE SEVEN GOLDEN VAMPIRES, THE
(SEE: DRACULA AND THE SEVEN GOLDEN VAMPIRES, 1974, Brit./Hong Kong)

LEGEND OF THE TREE OF LIFE
(SEE: IGOROTA, THE LEGEND OF THE TREE OF LIFE, 1970)

LEGEND OF THE WOLF WOMAN, THE zero
(1977, Span.) 84m Dimension c (LA LUPA MANNURA)

Annik Borel, Frederick Stafford, Dagmar Lassander, Howard Ross.

A scummy little nothing of a movie which perversely mixes sex and horror as a hairy naked woman kills a townsperson. Two hundred years later, a woman possessed by her spirit starts doing the same thing.

p, Diego Alchimede; d&w, Rino Di Silvestro.

Horror **Cas.** **(PR:O MPAA:R)**

LEGEND OF TOM DOOLEY, THE* (1959) 79m COL bw

Michael Landon (*Tom Dooley*), Jo Morrow (*Laura*), Jack Hogan (*Charlie Grayson*), Richard Rust (*Country Boy*), Dee Pollock (*Abel*), Ken Lynch (*Father*), Howard Wright (*Sheriff*), Ralph Moody (*Doc Henry*), John Cliff (*Lieutenant*), Cheerio Meredith (*Meg*), Gary Hunley (*The Kid*), Anthony Jochim (*Preacher*), Jeff Morris (*Confederate Soldier*), Jason Johnson (*Frank*), Joe Yrigoyen (*Bix*), Sandy Sanders (*Rand*), Juney Ellis (*1st Old Maid*), Maudie Prickett (*2nd Old Maid*).

The film is based on a traditional folk song made popular in the late 1950s by the Kingston Trio (the group sings the song over the titles). A very somber western, with Landon in the title role as a Confederate soldier who robs a Union stagecoach along with Pollock and Rust and kills two soldiers, not knowing the war is over. Knowing that they will be tried for murder, they head south, but first Landon gets his northern girl friend, Morrow. They elope and then she's accidentally killed. This leads the authorities to Landon, and he's tried and hanged. An engaging and downbeat film, with good performances from Landon and Rust.

p, Stan Shpetner; d, Ted Post; w, Shpetner; ph, Gibert Warrenton; m, Ronald Stein; ed, Robert S. Eisen; art d, Don Arment.

Western **(PR:A MPAA:NR)**

LEGEND OF WITCH HOLLOW (SEE: WITCHMAKER, THE, 1969)

LEGENDARY CURSE OF LEMORA (SEE: LADY DRACULA, 1973)

LEGION OF LOST FLYERS*1/2 (1939) 63m UNIV bw

Richard Arlen ("*Loop*" *Gillan*), Andy Devine ("*Beef*" *Brumley*), Anne Nagel (*Paula Perry*), William Lundigan (*Ralph Perry*), Guinn "Big Boy" Williams (*Jake*), Ona Munson (*Martha*), Jerry Marlowe (*Freddy*), Leon Ames (*Smythe*), Theodore Von Eltz (*Bill Desert*), Leon Belasco (*Frenchy*), David Willock (*Blinkey*), Jack Carson (*Barrigan*), Edith Mills (*Bertha*), Pat Flaherty (*Sam*), Eddy Waller (*Petey*).

Arlen is a pilot in the Alaskan wilderness and Devine is his mechanic. Arlen has been accused of causing a plane crash in which his passengers die. He sets out to find the real culprit and, of course, also finds time to romance Nagel. Devine and Mills, an Eskimo woman, provide comic relief. Strictly kiddie fare.

p, Ben Pivar; d, Christy Cabanne; w, Maurice Tombragel (based on a story by Pivar); ph, Jerome Ash; ed, Maurice Wright.

Adventure **(PR:A MPAA:NR)**

LEGION OF MISSING MEN* (1937) 63m MON bw

Ralph Forbes (*Bob Carter*), Ben Alexander (*Don Carter*), George Regas (*Garcia*), Hala Linda (*Nina*), James Aubrey (*Bilgey*), Paul Hurst (*Muggsy*), Frank Leigh (*Col. Laurente*), Roy D'Arcy (*Sheik*).

Monogram's standard "good guys-versus-bad guys" plot is transplanted from the western movies to this poorly made epic involving the Foreign Legion. Blood-thirsty Arabs are on the warpath but just can't defeat the hard-fighting Legionnaires. Badly directed and making poor use of stock footage, the story gets at best only a little help from the better-deserving cast.

p, I.E. Chadwick; d, Hamilton MacFadden; w, Sherman L. Lowe, Harry O. Hoyt (story by Norman S. Hall); ph, Marcel Le Picard; m/l, "Your Are My Romance," Richard Gump, Flo Brown, sung by Hala Linda.

Adventure **Cas.** **(PR:A MPAA:NR)**

LEGION OF TERROR* (1936) 62m COL bw

Bruce Cabot (*Frank Marshall*), Marguerite Churchill (*Nancy Foster*), Crawford Weaver (*Slim Hewitt*), Ward Bond (*Don Foster*), Charles Wilson (*McCollom*), John Hamilton (*Cummings*), Arthur Loft (*Gardner*), Nicholas Copeland (*Lefty*), John Tyrell (*Francy*), Ed Le Saint (*Breardon*).

Cabot and Weaver are postal inspectors sent to put an end to the title organization. The gang controls most of the town and specializes in murder, blackmail, and sending bombs to Congressmen. Cabot gets involved with Churchill, whose brother, Bond, was killed by the Legion. In the end, Cabot saves his girl and partner from execution with the help of the state police.

d, C.C. Coleman; w, Bert Granet; ph, George Meehan; ed, Al Clark.

Crime Drama **(PR:A MPAA:NR)**

LEGION OF THE DOOMED* (1958) 75m AA bw

Bill Williams (*Lt. Smith*), Dawn Richard (*Dalbert Marcheck*), Anthony Caruso (*Sgt. Calvelli*), Kurt Krueger (*Capt. Marcheck*), Tom Hubbard (*Brodie*), John Damler (*Darjon*), Rush Williams (*Canuck*), George Baxter (*Col. Lesperance*), Saul Gorss (*Tordeau*), Joseph Abdullah (*Karaba*), Hal Gerard (*Garabi*).

Inept and cliched nonsense involving the psuedo-dangerous lives of a group of Foreign Legionnaires. The plucky troops have to fight off hostile natives, of course, and they do it with standard heroics.

p, William F. Broidy; d, Thor Brooks; w, Tom Hubbard, Fred Eggers; ph, John J. Martin; ed, Herbert R. Hoffman; art d, George Troast.

Adventure **(PR:A MPAA:NR)**

LEGION OF THE LAWLESS* (1940) 59m RKO bw

George O'Brien (*Jeff Toland*), Virginia Vale (*Ellen*), Herbert Heywood (*Doc Denton*), Norman Willis (*Leo Harper*), Hugh Sothern (*Henry Ives*), William Benedict (*Edwin*), Eddy Waller (*Lafe Barton*), Delmar Watson, Bud Osborne, Monte Montague, Slim Whitaker, Mary Field, Richard Cramer, John Dilson, Martin Garralaga, Ed Piel, Lloyd Ingraham, Henry Wills, Wilfred Lucas.

O'Brien is a lawyer in the western town of Ivestown. The mayor of the town has set up a vigilante group to help keep law and order, but soon the group oversteps their authority. O'Brien rallies the citizens of the town and puts an end to the vigilantes in a climactic gun fight.

p, Bert Gilroy; d, David Howard; w, Doris Schroeder (based on a story by Berne Giler); ph, Harry Wild; ed, Frederic Knudtson.

Western **Cas.** **(PR:A MPAA:NR)**

LEGIONS OF THE NILE**

(1960, Ital.) 87m Fox c (LE LEGIONI DI CLEOPATRA)

Linda Cristal (Cleopatra), Ettore Manni (Curridius), Georges Marchal (Mark Antony), Maria Mahor (Marianne), Alfredo Mayo (Ottaviano), Daniela Rocca, Mino Doro, Andrea Aureli, Rafael Calvo, Conrado San Martin, Stefano Terra, Stefano Oppedisano, Mary Carillo, Jany Clair, Salvatore Furnari, Juan Majan, Rafael Duran, Tomas Blanco.

An Italian spectacular from the neo-mythological Cottafavi which retells the tale of Antony and Cleopatra. The only reason Fox is involved is because it was planning its own CLEOPATRA and acquired this one to keep it off the market.

p, Virgile De Blasi, Italo Zingarelli; d, Vittorio Cottafavi; w, Cottafavi, Giorgio Cristallani, Arnoldo Marrousu, Ennio de Concini; ph, Mario Pacheco (CinemaScope, DeLuxe Color); m, Renzo Rossellini; cos, Vittorio Rossi; ch, Pieter Van Der Sloot.

Biographical Drama **(PR:A MPAA:NR)**

L'ELISIR D'AMORE (SEE: THIS WINE OF LOVE, 1948, Ital.)

LEMON DROP KID, THE*** (1934) 71m PAR bw

Lee Tracy (Wally Brooks), Helen Mack (Alice Deering), William Frawley (The Professor), Minna Gombell (Maizie), Baby LeRoy (The Baby), Robert McWade (Mr. Griggsby), Henry B. Walthall (Jonas Deering), Clarence H. Wilson (Martin Potter), Charles Wilson (Warden), Kitty Kelley (Cora), Edward J. Le Saint, Robert E. Homans, Grace Goodall, William B. Davidson, Del Henderson, Edward Gargan, James Burke, Jules Cowles, C. L. Sherwood, Bee McCune, Jean McCune, Sam McDaniel, Tammany Young, Al Hill, Tempe Pigott, Charles McEvoy, Edwin Baker, Walter McGrail, Lee Shumway, Stanley Blystone, Eddie Peabody, Marshall Ruth.

Tracy is a fast-talking racetrack bum who swindles $100 from an old, ailing man. He takes it on the lam and ends up in a small town where he marries Mack. She talks him out of going back to the big city and they settle down and have a child. Things are going perfectly until Tracy's wife discovers that she has a potentially terminal ailment. Tracy robs a bank to pay for a specialist, but he's caught and his wife dies. In prison, Tracy finds out that his son has been adopted by friends he knew at the racetrack. They're holding on to him until father serves his sentence. It also turns out that the old man Tracy swindled never pressed charges—because lemon drops he had given the old man helped his arthritis and he's written a large check in Tracy's name. A melodramatic, but moving film. It's one of those movies that after it's over you ask, "Why don't they make them like that anymore?" Bob Hope did a remake in 1951 which didn't follow this storyline.

p, William Le Baron; d, Marshall Neilan; w, Howard J. Green, J. P. McEvoy (based on the story by Damon Runyon); ph, Henry Sharp; art d, Hans J. Dreier, John B. Goodman.

Drama **(PR:A MPAA:NR)**

LEMON DROP KID, THE*** (1951) 91m PAR bw

Bob Hope (Lemon Drop Kid), Marilyn Maxwell (Brainey Baxter), Lloyd Nolan (Charlie), Jane Darwell (Nellie Thursday), Andrea King (Stella), Fred Clark (Moose Moran), Jay C. Flippen (Straight Flush), William Frawley (Gloomy Willie), Harry Bellaver (Sam the Surgeon), Sid Melton (Little Louie), Ben Welden (Singin' Solly), Ida Moore (Bird Lady), Francis Pierlot (Henry Regan), Charles Cooley (Goomba), Society Kid Hogan (Society Kid), Harry Shannon (Policeman John), Bernard Szold (Honest Harry), Tor Johnson (Super Swedish Angel), Tom Dugan (No Thumbs Charlie).

Hope is a racetrack bookie who gets in trouble with a big-time gangster. Hope tips Nolan on a sure thing and the gangster puts down a large sum of money and loses. He wants his money back, or Hope's head. The rest of the film focuses on the bookie's attempts to get the dough. Hope works well as a fast-talking bookie and the comic situations he's thrown in are hilarious. Hope also played the radio version of the Lemon Drop Kid. Songs include "Silver Bells," "It Doesn't Cost a Dime to Dream," "They Obviously Want Me to Sing" (Ray Evans, Jay Livingston).

p, Robert L. Welch; d, Sidney Lanfield; w, Edmund Hartmann, Frank Tashlin, Robert O'Brien (based on a story by Edmund Beloin and Damon Runyon); ph, Daniel L. Fapp; m, Jay Livingston and Ray Evans; ed, Archie Marshek; art d, Hal Pereira, Franz Bachelin.

Musical/Comedy **(PR:A MPAA:NR)**

LEMON GROVE KIDS MEET THE MONSTERS, THE**1/2

(1966) 89m Steckler c

Cash Flagg [Ray Dennis Steckler], Carolyn Brandt.

What do you do when there's nothing good on TV? Why not get some friends together and make a movie? That's exactly what happened with this strange and sort of enjoyable homage (of sorts) to the Bowery Boys. Flagg (the stage name for director Steckler) sent his friends and neighbors running around in this oddball story involving a race entered by his modern-day Dead End Kids. Along the way to the finish line, they encounter various creatures like a gorilla, a mummy, a vampiress, men from space, and a late-era beatnik who is also in the spy business. This originally was two short features Flagg combined for a theatrical release. In its original run actors were hired to run around in the audience while decked out in monster suits. Flagg went on to make the semi-cult favorite THE INCREDIBLY

STRANGE CREATURES WHO STOPPED LIVING AND BECAME MIXED UP ZOMBIES.

p&d, Ray Dennis Steckler; w, Ron Haydock, Jim Harmon.

Horror/Comedy **(PR:C MPAA:G)**

LEMONADE JOE***

(1966, Czech.) 90m Barrandov-Ceskoslovensky/AA bw (LIMONADOVY JOE; AKA: KONSKA OPERA)

Karel Fiala (Lemonade Joe), Milos Kopecky (Horace Badman), Kveta Fialova (Tornado Lou), Olga Schoberova (Winifred Goodman), Rudolf Deyl (Doug Badman), Bohus Zahorsky (Goodman), Josef Hlinomaz (Grimpo), Karel Effa (Panjo Kid), Waldemar Matuska (Banjo Kid), Eman Fiala (Pianist), Vladimir Mensik, Jiri Lir (Barmen), Jiri Steimar (Kolalok), Jaroslav Stercl (Postmaster), Oldrich Lukes (Sheriff), Alois Dvorsky (Deaf Old Man), Milos Nedbal (Long-Haired Player), Jaroslav Mares, Antonin Sura (Gunmen), Rudolf Cortez, Stanislav Litera (Shooters), Viktor Ocasek (Undertaker), Ruda Princ (Barber), Milos Vavruska, Jan Pohan (Bandits), Stella Zazvorkova (Mother), Vlastimil Bedrna (Photographer), Lubomir Bryg (Cashier), Stanislaw Navratil, Ladislav Gzela (Musicians), Antonin Jedlicka, Jaroslav Klenot (Fighters), Jiri Jelinek, Jiri Schulz (Poker Players), Jiri Lansky (Cowboy), Vaclav Stekl, Bretislav Dolejsi, Karel Engel, Vladimir Erlebach, Jiri Hanzl, Vaclav Havelka, Gustav Jankovsky, Jan Kasik, Jaroslav Maran, R. Rademacher, Sobeslav Sejk, Zdenek Srstka, J. Stastny, Jaroslav Tetiva, Jaroslav Tomsa, K. Vitek, Ludvik Wolf, Lubomir Zacek, Yvetta Simonova, Jarmila Vesela, Karel Gott.

A western spoof which has Fiala in the title role, an Arizona cowboy who gets strength by drinking Kolaloka lemonade. This is the Czech BLAZING SADDLES, with Lemonade Joe visiting an all-soda saloon, passing out on whiskey, and getting his all-white outfit stained with jam by the bad guys. The culprits are promptly shot, but later brought back to life with the help of a lemonade elixir. Justice wins out in the end as Lemonade Joe rides off into the proverbial sunset. A lot of fun can be had if you can stand the lousy dubbing job.

p, Jaroslav Jilovec; d, Oldrich Lipsky; w, Jiri Bredecka, Lipsky (based on the novel and play by Bredecka); ph, Vladimir Novotny (CinemaScope); m, Jan Rychlik, Vlastimil Hala; ed, Miroslav Hajek, Jitka Sulcova; art d, Karel Skvor, Jan Knakal; cos, Bredecka, Fernand Vacha; spec eff, Vladimir Novotny, Ludvik Maly; ch, Josef Konicek.

Western/Satire **(PR:A MPAA:NR)**

LEMORA THE LADY DRACULA (SEE: LADY DRACULA, 1973)

LENA RIVERS*1/2 (1932) 60m TIF bw

Charlotte Henry (Lena Rivers), Beryl Mercer (Grandmother), James Kirkwood (Graham), Morgan Galloway (Durrie Graham), Joyce Compton (Caroline), Betty Blythe (Mrs. Nichols), John St. Polis (Nicholas), Russell Simpson (Grandfather), Clarence Muse.

A sappy, melodramatic drollery about a girl (Henry) who moves in with her rich aunt after her fisherman grandfather dies. Next door lives the girl's real father, and she falls in love with his ward.

d, Phil Rosen; w, Stuart Anthony, Warren B. Duff (based on a novel by Mary J. Holmes); ph, Ira Morgan; ed, Martin G. Cohn, Maurice Wright.

Drama **(PR:A MPAA:NR)**

LEND ME YOUR EAR (SEE: THE LIVING GHOST, 1942)

LEND ME YOUR HUSBAND*1/2 (1935, Brit.) 61m EM/RKO bw

John Stuart (Jeff Green), Nora Swinburne (Virgie Green), Nancy Burne (Ba-ba), Evan Thomas (Tony), Annie Esmond (Mother).

Stuart is a married man who has grown bored with his wife. He decides that he's mad for Burne, his wife's best friend, and the two run off together. But soon he learns that Burne is as daft as they come, and the beleaguered man returns to his wife once more. This one-joke comedy grows stale quickly and drags on until the inevitable conclusion.

p, George King, Randall Faye; d, Frederick Hayward; w, Faye (based on a story by Michael Trevellyan).

Comedy **(PR:A MPAA:NR)**

LEND ME YOUR WIFE** (1935, Brit.) 61m Grafton/MGM bw

Henry Kendall (Tony Radford), Kathleen Kelly (Grace Harwood), Cyril Smith (Charles Harwood), Jimmy Godden (Uncle Jerry), Marie Ault (Aunt Jane), Hal Gordon (Nick Larkin), Gillian Maude (Ruth).

In order to claim an inheritance from his rich uncle, perennial bachelor Kendall must marry before he reaches age 40. Though in no hurry to wed, Kendall does want the cash, so he talks Kelly, his best pal's wife, into posing as his betrothed. Some funny moments ensue, though the comedy is entirely predictable.

p, Fred Browett; d, W. P. Kellino; w, Fred Duprez, Edmund Dalby, Kellino (based on the play by Duprez and Dalby).

Comedy **(PR:A MPAA:NR)**

L'ENFANCE NUE (SEE: ME, 1970, Fr.)

L'ENIGMATIQUE MONSIEUR PARKES** (1930) 70m PAR bw

Adolphe Menjou (Courtenay Parkes), Claudette Colbert (Lucy de Stavrin), Emile Chautard (H. Sylvester Corbett), Adrienne D'Ambricourt (Mrs. Corbett), Sandra Ravel (Edith Corbett), Armand Kaliz (Malatroff), Frank O'Neill (Jimmy Weyman), Andre Cheron (Commissaire de Police), Jacques Jou-Jerville.

French language version of SLIGHTLY SCARLET, with a vastly superior cast led by Menjou and Colbert in their native language debuts. They play a pair of jewel thieves who meet in front of a safe at the estate where they are guests. They fall in love, but are threatened by a master criminal. Menjou manages to subdue the fiend in a fist fight, and he and Colbert are exonerated of their crimes at the fadeout.

d, Louis Gasnier; w, Henri Bataille (based on a story by Percy Heath); ph, Allen Siegler; ed, Bataille.

Crime (PR:A MPAA:NR)

LENNY*** (1974) 111m UA bw

Dustin Hoffman *(Lenny Bruce)*, Valerie Perrine *(Honey Bruce)*, Jan Miner *(Sally Marr)*, Stanley Beck *(Artie Silver)*, Gary Morton *(Sherman Hart)*, Rashel Novikoff *(Aunt Mema)*, Guy Rennie *(Jack Goldstein)*, Frankie Man *(Baltimore Strip Club MC)*, Mark Harris *(San Francisco Defense Attorney)*, Lee Sandman *(San Francisco Judge)*, Susan Malnick *(Kitty Bruce at Age 11)*, Martin Begley *(San Francisco Judge)*, Phil Philbin *(New York Cop)*, Ted Sorrell, Clarence Thomas *(New York Attorneys)*, Mike Murphy *(New York District Attorney)*, Buddy Boylan *(Marty)*, Mickey Gatlin *(San Francisco Cop)*, George DeWitt *(Comic)*, Judy LaScala *(Chorus Girl)*, Glen Wilder, Frank Orsati *(Hunters)*, Michelle Young *(Nurse's Aide)*, Allison Goldstein *(Kitty at Age 1)*, Bridghid Glass *(Kitty at Age 2)*, Jack Nagle *(Rev. Mooney)*.

Harsh, funny, grim, and as truthful a film biography as you will ever see, LENNY took Academy nominations for Hoffman, Perrine, Surtees, Fosse, Best Screenplay, and Best Picture but didn't win any as THE GODFATHER, PART II won most of the statuettes. Produced by one-time gag writer Worth, LENNY proved that it isn't easy to be ahead of your time. By today's liberal standards, much of what comedian Lenny Bruce said on stage would be allowed without any police interference. There are those who say he would be just another comic today, but they don't realize his quest was to always stay ahead of his time and, if Bruce were alive, he'd be off in some other far-out comedy sphere. Bruce was an immensely intelligent commentator on the current scene, who was crushed on the cogs of society's mechanism. This was Fosse's third picture (after CABARET and SWEET CHARITY), and he showed some of the problems he had with this movie when making his own biography, ALL THAT JAZZ. At times, LENNY looks like an autobiography as Hoffman *becomes* the famed comedian and pours his guts out on stage, using many of the same routines Bruce did in real life. The movie has three separate sections and looks like a play (where it actually began)—a conscious decision on Fosse's part, due either to his stage background or the fact that he wanted it to have the intimacy of the stage rather than the scope of the screen. The first part shows Hoffman's courtship of Perrine, a stripper with a surprising amount of class and smarts (at least, that's the way she's portrayed by Perrine). Hoffman refers to her as his "shicksa goddess"—a reference to her flaxen hair and distinct lack of Hebraic blood. All the while, Hoffman is enjoying greater popularity as a performer in a more standard fashion, before he decided to experiment and opt for more controversial material. Hoffman and Perrine have an auto accident that nearly costs her life and we see the comedian shown as, perhaps, a too-loving husband, with an obsession about his wife. He had a penchant for obsessions that was to stand him in bad stead for the rest of his life as he never seemed to know when to let go of something. He becomes hooked on drugs, another obsession, then he becomes obsessed with the various police departments who seek to stop his shows wherever he performs. Rather than pay a fine or do a few days' time, Hoffman decides that he *can* fight City Hall, and that takes up about a third of the film. In the end, it is his obsession with death that is seen, and we never know if he has a predisposition for his own destruction or not. The film is done in a series of interviews and flashbacks conducted by an off-camera party, a la CITIZEN KANE. Perrine, who had not been thought of as a good actress before this, is solid as Hoffman's former wife. Miner essays the role of Sally Marr, mother of the comedian. Marr, in real life, was not like the actress who played her. She is a manager of comedians, an actress in her own right, and a funny woman who adored her son and was his best audience. Beck, playing Hoffman's agent, is a long-time pal of Hoffman's, but that nepotism had little to do with his getting the role as he does a fine job. The disjointed interviews become part of a patchwork quilt and bring to light the ongoing struggle that an "original" must face in order to become a success. It's interesting to watch the private life of the comic against the public one. In real life, Bruce seldom used foul language and even remonstrated those who did if there was a woman present. What he wanted was the *right* to use four-letter words in his act. When the police begin to harass him, Hoffman's greatest performances are given in court, to less-than-wonderful reviews from the judges and juries who hear them. The film was shot in black and white. One wonders if it is Fosse's or the comedian's obsession with death that takes hold at the end, because the director's work in ALL THAT JAZZ, as well as his STAR 80, is heavily concerned with morbidity. Bruce made gifts to a lot of people, of money, items and, most of all, himself. His daughter, Kitty, married Freddie Prinz, Lenny's greatest fan. Prinz later died tragically as the result of a gun accident (some claimed suicide) at the height of his television popularity. Many comedians, such as George Carlin, Richard Pryor, and Eddie Murphy owe a debt of gratitude to Bruce for his pioneering ways in getting all censorship lifted from the nightclub stage. Without him, one wonders if the other comedians would have made it so quickly. Bruce died as the result of a drug overdose. Hoffman won an Oscar for KRAMER VS. KRAMER, but this is one of his greatest roles. Background music includes some older Miles Davis recordings.

p, Marvin Worth; d, Bob Fosse; w, Julian Barry (based on his play); ph, Bruce Surtees; ed, Alan Heim; prod d, Joel Schiller; set d, Nicholas Romanac; cos, Albert Wolsky.

Biography Cas. (PR:C-O MPAA:R)

LEO AND LOREE** (1980) 97m UA c

Donny Most, Linda Purl, David Huffman, Jerry Paris, Shannon Farnon, Allan Rich, Susan Lawrence.

Would-be actor Most moves to Hollywood in an attempt to break into the movies. There he meets Purl, the daughter of an Oscar-winning actor, who is also trying to get into pictures. Their romance and fledgling film careers are at the center of this somewhat awkward, though occasionally charming little film. As a feature film it's passable, but the material and cast are better suited to a television-movie format. Most, director Paris, and executive producer Ron Howard (on the verge of a strong directing career himself) were all veterans of the popular TV sitcom "Happy Days."

p, Jim Begg; d, Jerry Paris; w, James Ritz; ph, Costa Petals (CFI Color); m, Lance Rubin; ed, Ed Cotter; art d, Linda Pearl.

Romance (PR:A MPAA:PG)

LEO THE LAST* 1/2 (1970, Brit.) 104m UA c

Marcello Mastroianni *(Leo)*, Billie Whitelaw *(Margaret)*, Calvin Lockhart *(Roscoe)*, Glenna Forster Jones *(Salambo)*, Graham Crowden *(Max)*, Gwen Ffrangcon Davies *(Hilda)*, David DeKeyser *(David)*, Vladek Sheybal *(Laszlo)*, Keefe West *(Jasper)*, Kenneth J. Warren *(Kowalski)*, Patsy Smart *(Mrs. Kowalski)*, Ram John Holder *(Black Preacher)*, Thomas Bucson *(Mr. Madi)*, Tina Solomon *(Mrs. Madi)*, Brinsley Forde *(Bip)*, Robert Redman, Malcolm Redman, Robert Kennedy *(Madi Children)*, Phyllis McMahon *(Blonde Whore)*, Princess Patience *(Black Whore)*, Bernard Boston, Roy Stewart *(Bodyguards)*, Lucita Lijertwood *(Wailing Lady)*, Ishaq Bux *(Supermarket Manager)*, Doris Clark *(Singing Lady)*, Lou Gossett, Alba, Marcia Redman, Billy Russell.

Mastroianni is an exiled European monarch who returns to London after many years away. The area where his mansion is located has become a black ghetto, but Mastroianni is oblivious to his surroundings, absorbed in bird watching. In time, Mastroianni notices the plight of his neighbors through his telescope, but he moves into action only after Jones is forced into prostitution. He takes her in as his ward and tries to involve himself in the problems of the ghetto. The monarch's royal guard revolts, taking over his house and arming themselves. Mastroianni and the neighborhood folk band together, defeat the guards with fireworks, and burn down the mansion. A pretentious, heavy-handed satire of the class structure and European royalty. Director Boorman seems to be trying to say many things in this film, none of which is clearly stated.

p, Irwin Winkler, Robert Chartoff; d, John Boorman; w, William Stair, Boorman (based on the play *The Prince* by George Tabori); ph, Peter Suschitzky (DeLuxe Color); m, Fred Myrow; ed, Tom Priestly; prod d, Tony Woollard; set d, Peter Young; cos, Joan Woollard; spec eff, John Richardson; m/l, Myrow (sung by Ram John Holder, The Swingle Singers); makeup, Alex Garfath.

Drama (PR:O MPAA:R)

LEONOR* (1977, Fr./Span./Ital.) 100m New Line c

Liv Ullmann *(Leonor)*, Michel Piccoli *(Richard)*, Ornella Mutti *(Catherine)*, Antonio Ferrandis *(Thomas)*, Jose Maria Caffarel *(Doctor)*, Angel Del Pozo *(Chaplain)*.

Even good talent can have off moments, as Ullmann so drearily proves in this tedious mess. She plays a medieval wife who returns to haunt husband Piccoli ten years after he sealed her in a tomb. The direction is plodding and further hampered by a thoroughly idiotic script. Ullmann was obviously capable of better things, to say the least.

d, Juan Bunuel; w, Bunuel, Philippe Nuridzany, Pierre Maintigneux, Jean-Claude Carriere, Clement Biddle Wood (based on a story by Ludwig Tieck); ph, Luciano Tovoli (Eastmancolor); m, Ennio Morricone; ed, Pablo Del Amo.

Drama Cas. (PR:O MPAA:R)

LEOPARD, THE 1/2**
(1963, Ital.) 165m Titanus/FOX c (IL GATTOPARDO; LE GUEPARD)

Burt Lancaster *(Prince Don Fabrizio Salina)*, Alain Delon *(Tancredi)*, Claudia Cardinale *(Angelica Sedara/Bertiana)*, Rina Morelli *(Maria Stella)*, Paolo Stoppa *(Don Calogero Sedara)*, Romolo Valli *(Father Pirrone)*, Lucilla Morlacchi *(Concetta)*, Serge Reggiani *(Don Ciccio Tumeo)*, Ida Galli *(Carolina)*, Ottavia Piccolo *(Caterina)*, Pierre Clementi *(Francesco Paolo)*, Carlo Valenzano *(Paolo)*, Anna Maria Bottini *(Governess Mademoiselle Dombreuil)*, Mario Girotti *(Count Cavriaghi)*, Leslie French *(Cavalier Chevally)*, Olimpia Cavalli *(Mariannina)*, Marino Mase *(Tutor)*, Sandra Chistolini *(Youngest Daughter)*, Brook Fuller *(Little Prince)*, Giuliano Gemma *(Garibaldino General)*, Giovanni Melisendi *(Don Onofrio Rotolo)*, Howard Nelson-Rubien *(Don Diego)*, Lola Braccini *(Donna Margherita)*, Ivo Garrani *(Col. Pallavicino)*, Vittorio Duse, Carlo Lolli, Franco Gula, Giovanni Materassi, Carmelo Artale, Anna Maria Surdo, Alina Zalewska, Winni Riva, Giuseppe Spagnitti, Rosolino Bua, Dante Posani, Stelvio Rosi, Tina Lattanzi, Marcella Rovena, Rina De Liguoro, Valerio Ruggeri, Carlo Palmucci.

There were many walkouts at the huge Hollywood premiere of this picture and the sound of the footsteps was almost totally muffled by the snores and yawns of those who stayed to the end. Nevertheless, it took the Golden Palm as Best Film at Cannes. Based on di Lampedusa's best-seller, THE LEOPARD is a rambling movie of epic proportions. Originally released at close to three and one half hours in length, it was trimmed, somewhat, for the English-speaking market but that didn't help it at the wickets. Lancaster is a prince desperately attempting to maintain a life style he has grown up with. It is the 1860s and Italy is a region made up of many city-states (most people don't recall that Italy did not become a country until united by Garibaldi) and about to form into a nation. That would put an end to the life of elegance that Lancaster lives. A new business class is arising that threatens the modus operandi of the aristocrats. Lancaster gets his nephew, Delon, to marry Cardinale, daughter of wealthy Stoppa. He wants to keep the bullheaded business types from overrunning the grace and culture of his life and thinks that the wedding between the two will help him stave off the rebels. Cardinale ascends into a caste of society where she is unfit to govern, which symbolizes the changing society of Italy and Europe at that time. Lancaster's daughter, Morlacchi, loves Delon, but he discourages the romance and pushes her into a wedding with Stoppa, whose infusion of money will help Lancaster marry off his other two daughters. A new government is formed, and Lancaster declines an offer to be part of it as he feels he is a man caught between two worlds, the new and the ancient. Cardinale is debuted at a fancy ball (one of the most gorgeous scenes ever shot) and Lancaster walks outside to ruminate about what is to come. This is a leisurely account of a period that has little meaning to anyone except the Sicilians who know the era from reading about it in their history books. It had little appeal in the U.S., just as a film about the French and Indian wars might mean nothing in Palermo. Lancaster gives an excellent performance as the proud prince who refuses to allow his world to fall apart. Much of the film revolves around him and what he is feeling, and he can let us sense that with an eyebrow raise, rather than a lengthy diatribe. Lots of detail went into making this as authentic as possible. It's sumptuous and sensitive, but it is also boring in many scenes, and one wishes that they'd just get on with it. Filmed on location in Sicily, no expense was spared in order to make the film, which is dubbed in English, and the money is all up there on screen. The scene at the ball is exquisite but, in it's own way, just as tiresome as the wedding scene in THE DEER HUNTER. Visconti seemed determined to create a highly aesthetic-looking film, no matter what lengths he had to go. On one particularly grueling hot day, he insisted a number of retakes be done on a particular shot in which a horse, on the frame's edge, kept flicking its tail. This infuriated the director, who felt this uncalled for swishing was destroying the entire *mise-en-scene* of the shot!

p, Goffredo Lombardo; d, Luchino Visconti; w, Visconti, Suso Cecchi D'Amico, Pasquale Festa Campanile, Enrico Medioli, Massimo Franciosa (based on the novel *Il Gattopardo* by Giuseppe Tomasi di Lampedusa); ph, Giuseppe Rotunno (CinemaScope, DeLuxe Color); m, Nino Rota ("Unpublished Waltz" by Giuseppe Verdi); ed, Mario Serandrei; md, Franco Ferrara; art d, Mario Garbuglia; set d, Giorgio Pes, Laudomia Hercolani; cos, Piero Tosi, Reanda, Sartoria Safas; makeup, Alberto De Rossi.

Period Drama (PR:A-C MPAA:PG)

LEOPARD IN THE SNOW 1/2**
(1979, Brit./Can.) 90m Harlequin-Seastone-Leopard in the Snow/New World c

Keir Dullea, Susan Penhaligon, Kenneth More, Billie Whitelaw, Gordon Thomson, Jeremy Kemp, Yvonne Manners.

After being caught in a snow storm Penhaligon is rescued by Dullea, who sports a leopard as a pet. Naturally, the woman falls for her rescuer and eventually discovers the silent recluse is a former race-car driver. For what it is, this film is really not bad, though emotions are perfunctory at best. Dullea had certainly come a long way from 2001: A SPACE ODYSSEY. If the story seems like a formula romance, it should come as no surprise, as this is the first film production from the popular Harlequin Romance publishing company.

p, John Quested, Chris Harrop; d, Gerry O'Hara; w, Anne Mather, Jill Hyem (based on a novel by Mather); ph, Alfie Hicks (Technicolor); m, Kenneth Jones.

Romance Cas. (PR:A MPAA:PG)

LEOPARD MAN, THE* 1/2** (1943) 63m RKO bw

Dennis O'Keefe *(Jerry Manning)*, Margo *(Clo-Clo)*, Jean Brooks *(Kiki Walker)*, Isabel Jewell *(Maria)*, James Bell *(Dr. Galbraith)*, Margaret Landry *(Teresa Delgado)*, Abner Biberman *(Charlie How-Come)*, Richard Martin *(Raoul Belmonte)*, Tula Parma *(Consuelo Contreras)*, Ben Bard *(Chief Robles)*, Ariel Heath *(Eloire)*, Fely Franquelli *(Rosita)*, Robert Anderson *(Dwight)*, Jacqueline De Wit *(Helene)*, Bobby Spindola *(Pedro)*, William Halligan *(Brunton)*, Kate Lawson *(Senora Delgado)*, Russell Wade *(Man in Car)*, Jacques Lory *(Philippe)*, Ottola Nesmith *(Senora Contreras)*, Margaret Sylva *(Marta)*, Charles Lung *(Manuel)*, John Dilson *(Coroner)*, Mary Maclaren *(Nun)*, Tom Orosco *(Window Cleaner)*, Eliso Gamboa *(Senor Delgado)*, Joe Dominguez *(Cop)*, Betty Roadman *(Clo-Clo's Mother)*, Rosa Rita Varella *(Clo-Clo's Sister)*, John Piffle *(Flower Vendor)*, Rene Pedrini *(Frightened Waiter)*, Brandon Hurst *(Gatekeeper)*, Rose Higgins *(Indian Weaver)*, George Sherwood *(Police Lieutenant)*, John Tettemer *(Minister)*.

Another atmospheric thriller from producer Val Lewton and director Jacques Tourneur (CAT PEOPLE, I WALKED WITH A ZOMBIE). O'Keefe, a public relations man from a New Mexico nightclub, rents a leopard as a publicity stunt. The animal escapes and kills a little girl. In the film's most frightening scene, the girl's mother locks her out of the house for returning late from an errand, and all the viewer sees when the girl is attacked by the leopard is blood coming from under the door. Two subsequent murders are blamed on the leopard, but O'Keefe and Margo unmask the real—human—killer. This film, along with Lewton and Tourneur's other collaborations, proves once again that money is not the most essential element in good filmmaking. Robert de Grasse's photography plays an important role in creating the mood for this film.

p, Val Lewton; d, Jacques Tourneur; w, Ardel Wray, Edward Dein (based on the novel *Black Alibi* by Cornell Woolrich); ph, Robert de Grasse; m, Roy Webb; ed, Mark Robson; md, Constantin Bakaleinikoff; art d, Albert D'Agostino, Walter E. Keller; set d, Darrell Silvera, Al Fields.

Thriller Cas. (PR:O MPAA:NR)

LEPKE 1/2** (1975, U.S./Israel) 109m AmeriEuro/WB c

Tony Curtis *(Louis "Lepke" Buchalter)*, Anjanette Comer *(Bernice Meyer)*, Michael Callan *(Robert Kane)*, Warren Berlinger *(Gurrah Shapiro)*, Gianni Russo *(Albert Anastasia)*, Vic Tayback *(Lucky Luciano)*, Mary Wilcox *(Marion)*, Milton Berle *(Mr. Meyer)*, Jack Ackerman *(Little Augie)*, Louis Guss *(Max Rubin)*, Vaughn Meader *(Walter Winchell)*, Lillian Adams *(Mama Meyer)*, Albert Cole *(Gross)*, Zitto Kazan *(Abe "Kid Twist" Reles)*, Johnny Silver *(Schwartz)*, J. S. Johnson *(Mendy Weiss)*, Simmy Bow *(Tannenbaum)*, John Durren *(Dutch Schultz)*, Barry Miller *(Young Lepke)*, John Ian Jacobs *(Big Hesh)*, Matt Greene *(Skinny)*, Richard C. Adams *(Thomas Dewey)*, Sam Solomon *(Butcher)*, Jeannine Brown *(Prostitute)*, Raymond Cavaleri *(Gino)*, Norman Pauker *(Rabbi)*, Ida Mae McKenzie *(Mrs. Shea)*, Jack Tesler *(Feldman)*, Joseph Kim *(Lin Phoo)*, Casey Morgan *(Young Gurrah)*, Wesley Lau, Jim Hayes *(Detectives)*, Guy Christopher *(Reporter)*, Marco Goldstein *(Cantor)*, Crane Jackson *(Judge)*, To Castronova *(Policeman)*, Robin Chesler *(Sarah)*, Josef Behrens *(Violinist)*.

In an effort to capitalize on the tremendous success of Francis Ford Coppola's GODFATHER films, wily producer/director Golam (with help from partner Yoram Globus, who served as executive producer) set out to make the definitive screen biography of notorious Jewish gangster Louis "Lepke" Buchalter, the only top mobster ever to be executed by the U.S. government. The film follows the gangster from the time he was a youngster committing petty crimes in the streets of Manhattan's Lower East Side. Eventually caught, the boy is sent to prison where, during his adolescence, he learns more about crime. Upon his release, Curtis and his friend Berlinger join a gang of strikebreakers. Curtis swiftly rises through the ranks and finds himself in full control of the vicious gang. He soon becomes a force to be reckoned with in the underworld, and gains the respect of men like "Lucky" Luciano (Tayback—a dubious piece of casting) and Albert Anastasia (Russo). When psychopathic gangster "Dutch" Schultz (Durren) ignores the mob's protests and vows to kill District Attorney Thomas E. Dewey (Adams), Curtis has the "Dutchman" killed with full approval from the other top mobsters. Eventually Curtis moves the operation to Brooklyn and invents "Murder Inc.," an insidious, independent organization which mob rulers can hire to do their killing on approval of the outfit council. The new scheme is a bloody success. With murder turning a profit, Tayback and Curtis enter the drug trade and the men earn additional millions. Ironically, the man whose life he helped to save, Adams, goes after the powerful Curtis and actually manages to indict him on a minor charge. Curtis loses his cool and orders the execution of a witness, but his commands drift back to the district attorney's office and he is arrested. Determined to avoid jail, Curtis jumps bail and goes underground. Leaderless, Curtis' criminal empire begins to crumble. Tayback and the other mob chieftains find the government harassing their operations in an effort to extricate Curtis from the bowels of the underworld. The other gangsters soon get fed up with the government's meddling and tell Curtis to give himself up or face their lethal wrath. Employing crusading columnist Walter Winchell (Meader) as a go-between, Curtis strikes a deal with J. Edgar Hoover and the FBI, giving himself up. The Feds renege on the agreement however, and Curtis soon finds himself being taken to the electric chair. Despite several attempts to stay the execution, Curtis is electrocuted. Though certainly one of the more historically accurate real-life gangster screen biographies, LEPKE suffers from a cold, just-the-facts presentation that fails to infuse the material with life. Curtis was a good choice to play Lepke, but the script never gives the actor a chance to display any range, intelligence, or insight into the complex man. In the film, Lepke is a one-dimensional gangster who rose through the ranks to a place of unparalleled power and influence—just like any other low-budget movie gangster, factual or ficitonal. In life, Lepke was a fascinating, intelligent, vicious man whose influence on organized crime is still being felt today. LEPKE offers no new understanding of the gangster or his times, and ultimately fails as a gangster picture because it has nothing new to say.

p&d, Menahem Golam; w, Wesley Lau, Tamar Hoffs (based on a story by Lau); ph, Andrew Davis (Panavision, Deluxe Color); m, Ken Wannberg; ed, Dov Hoenig, Aaron Stell; prod d, Jack Degovia; set d, Vincent Cresciman; cos, Jodie Tillen; spec eff, Cliff Wenger; stunts, George P. Wilbur.

Crime/Biography Cas. (PR:O MPAA:R)

LES ABYSSES* 1/2 (1964, Fr.) 90m Lenox/Kanawha bw

Francine Berge *(Michele)*, Colette Berge *(Marie-Louise)*, Pascale de Boysson *(Elisabeth)*, Colette Regis *(Mme. Lapeyre)*, Paul Bonifas *(Mons. Lapeyre)*, Jean-Louis Le Goff *(Philippe)*, Lise Daubigny, Marcel Roche, Robert Benois *(Buyers)*.

The Berge sisters play a pair of orphaned sisters (more than a little fond of each other) reduced to near-slave laboring for a destitute wine-grower. When it appears that wine-grower Bonifas is going to sell his farm and vineyard, the sisters set about destroying the place, fearing the loss of their slim livelihood. When the sale is made, the girls go berserk, brutally murdering Bonfias' wife and daughter. This odd tale is based on a notorious French murder case of the 1930s.

p&d, Nico Papatakis; w, Jean Vauthier; ph, Jean-Michel Boussaguet; m, Pierre Barbaud; ed, Denise de Casablanca, Pascale Laverriere, Edwige Bernard; md, Konstantin Simonovic; makeup, Marie-Louise Gillet.

Drama (PR:O MPAA:NR)

LES AMANTS (SEE: LOVERS, THE, 1959, Fr.)

LES AMANTS DE VERONE (SEE: LOVERS OF VERONA, 1951, Fr.)

LES ANGES DU PECHE (SEE: ANGELS OF THE STREET, 1950, Fr.)

LES AVENTURES EXTRAORDINAIRES DE CERVANTES
(SEE: YOUNG REBEL, THE, 1969, Fr./Ital./Span.)

LES BAS FONDS (SEE: LOWER DEPTHS, THE, 1937, Fr.)

LES BELLES-DE-NUIT 1/2**
(1952, Fr.) Franco London-Rizzoli/Lopert-UA bw (AKA: BEAUTIES OF THE NIGHT)

Gerard Philipe *(Claude)*, Martine Carol *(Edmee)*, Gina Lollobrigida *(Leila)*, Magali Vendeuil *(Suzanne)*, Marilyn Buferd *(Bonny, Madame Bonacieux)*, Raymond Cordy *(Gaston, the Father)*, Paola Stoppa *(Opera Director)*, Raymond Bussieres *(Roger, the Mechanic)*, Bernard Lajarrige *(Leon, the Policeman)*, Jean Paredes *(Paul, the Pharmacist)*, Palau *(The Old Gentleman)*, Albert Michel *(Postman)*.

This whimsical film stars Philipe as a young composer whose environment is too noisy and whose head is too filled with dreams to allow him to accomplish much of anything in real life. He loses the teaching job which supplied the meager wages with which he paid for his human needs. The beautiful girl who lives next to him—Vendeuil—appears ready and willing to start up an affair, yet Philipe never pays her the slightest attention. Instead, he lives in a dream world that has him a great composer in the 19th Century being surrounded by beauties, a musketeer in the service of King Louis XIII, and a number of other equally incredible situations. At one point Philipe even confuses his identity between dreams, then starts distorting reality and making his friends question his sanity. With such a bizarre premise it would seem that the film could easily lose control of its development. Yet, with a master such as Clair at the helm, things remain within bounds, briefly making slips into a realm that allows for some delightful insights. Composer Van Parys introduces a different theme for each of Philipe's fantasies, which include a noisy nightmare of cacophony in which he conducts an orchestra of vacuum cleaners, pots and pans, and other household items. His historical fantasies are invariably evoked by real happenings and real people; harem girl Lollobrigida, for example, is in reality the cashier in his local cafe. One thread ties the succession of fantasies together: in each, an old man bitterly bewails the present and longs for "the good old days," heralding another jump to an even earlier period. At the conclusion, Philipe races from prehistory to the present in a Jeep in this remarkable return to pure social comedy by a master of the art. (In French; English subtitles.)

d&w, Rene Clair; ph, Armand Thiraud, Robert Juillard; m, Georges Van Parys; ed, Louisette Hautecoeur; prod d, Leon Barsacq.

Comedy   **(PR:C   MPAA:NR)**

LES BICHES***½**
(1968, Fr.) 104m Films la Boetie-Alexandra/Jack H. Harris c (AKA: HETEROSEX-UALS, THE)

Stephane Audran (*Frederique*), Jaqueline Sassard (*Why*), Jean-Louis Trintignant (*Paul Thomas*), Nane Germon (*Violetta*), Serge Bento (*Bookseller*), Dominique Zardi (*Riais*), Henri Attal (*Robeque*), Claude Chabrol (*Filmmaker*), Henri Frances.

A strange and intense film from the Nouvelle Vague's master of suspense. An architect shows romantic interest in an elegant, elderly lesbian. A young girl, who loves both of the older people, is confused by the relationship and finally cracks. Her descent into madness takes frightening twists as she murders the lesbian and begins wearing the woman's clothing. Chabrol's direction is up to his usual excellence, and he handles this unusual material sympathetically.

p, Andre Genoves; d, Claude Chabrol; w, Paul Gegauff, Chabrol; ph, Jean Rabier (Eastmancolor); m, Pierre Jansen; ed, Jacques Gaillard; md, Jacques Baudry; cos, Maurice Albray.

Drama   **(PR:O   MPAA:R)**

LES CAMARADES   (SEE: ORGANIZER, THE, 1964, Fr./Ital./Yugo.)

LES CAPRICES DE MARIE   (SEE: GIVE HER THE MOON, 1970, Fr./Ital.)

LES CARABINIERS**½**
(1968, Fr./Ital.) 80m Rome-Paris-Laetitia/New Yorker bw (GB: THE SOLDIERS)

Marino Mase (*Ulysses*), Albert Juross (*Michel-Ange*), Genevieve Galea (*Venus*), Catherine Ribero (*Cleopatre*), Gerard Poirot (*1st Carabinier*), Jean Brassat (*2nd Carabinier*), Alvaro Gheri (*3rd Carabinier*), Barbet Schroeder (*Car Salesman*), Odile Geoffroy (*Young Communist Girl*), Roger Coggio, Pascale Audret (*Couple In Car*), Catherine Durante (*Heroine of the Film-Within-The-Film*), Jean Gruault ("*Bebe's*" *Father*), Jean-Louis Comolli (*Soldier With The Fish*), Wladimir Faters (*Revolutionary*), Jean Monsigny (*Soldier*), Gilbert Servien (*Soldier*).

Released in Paris in 1963, Godard's fifth film is an ultra-impersonal exercise in the subject of war. Juross and Mase are a pair of soldiers called upon to fight for the King. They leave their wives behind when they hear of the promises of great riches in return for their fighting. They send their wives letters and inform them of their activities—saluting the Statue of Liberty, endlessly executing a woman, buying a Masarati, and going to the cinema. They return home and show their wives their great conquests—a massive collection of postcards including the Grand Canyon, The Eiffel Tower, The Empire State Building, and the pyramids. The war ends, but they are not on the winning side. They decide to search for the King so they can collect their booty, but are gunned down. A tremendous box-office bomb, which caused Godard to personally address every critic who panned the film. For the first hour it is a difficult viewing experience. Godard went to great length to develop unsympathetic characters, creating a distance between the screen and the audience. He purposely shot the film on a grainy film stock and made it even grainier in the processing. The effect was like the days of newsreels, even incorporating actual stock footage into the final film. After the first hour, however, the audience is treated to an Eisensteinian montage consisting of 12 minutes of conquests—the postcard sequence. In LES CARABINIERS Godard has succeeded in portraying war as an ugly and ignoble atrocity in a manner unlike that which he calls "the beautiful Zanuck-ian style." A film which serves better as a liberating step in cinematic convention, than as a dramatic work.

p, Georges de Beauregard, Carlo Ponti; d, Jean-Luc Godard; w, Godard, Jean Gruault, Roberto Rossellini (based on the play "I Carabinieri" by Benjamino Joppolo); ph, Raoul Coutard; m, Philippe Arthuys; ed, Agnes Guillemot, Lila Lakshmanan; art d, Jean-Jacques Fabre.

War Drama   **(PR:O   MPAA:NR)**

LES CHOSES DE LA VIE   (SEE: THINGS OF LIFE, THE, 1970, Fr./Ital.)

LES CLANDESTINS   (SEE: CLANDESTINE, 1948, Fr.)

LES COUSINS   (SEE: COUSINS, THE, 1959, Fr.)

LES CREATURES*****
(1969, Fr./Swed.) 91m Parc-Madeleine-Sandrews/New Yorker c/bw (VAREL-SERNA)

Catherine Deneuve (*Mylene*), Michel Piccoli (*Edgar*), Eva Dahlbeck (*Michele Quellec*), Jacques Charrier (*Rene de Montyon*), Nino Castelnuovo (*Jean Modet*), Ursula Kubler (*Vamp*), Britta Pettersson (*Lucie de Montyon*), Louis Falavigna (*Pierre Roland*), Marie-France Mignal (*Vivian Quellec*), Bernard Lajarrige (*Doctor*), Pierre Danny (*Max Picot*), Alain Roy (*Pere Quellec*), Lucien Bodard (*Recluse*), Jeanne Allard, Roger Dax.

Piccoli stars as a novelist who, after being scarred in an auto accident, takes his pregnant wife Deneuve to the French seaside to recover from their trauma. He spends his time finishing a novel, using the townspeople as the story's characters. Varda, the leading woman New Wave director, combines reality and fantasy in a provocative manner, while drawing comparison with Alain Resnais.

p, Mag Bodard; d&w, Agnes Varda; ph, Willy Kurant (Franscope); m, Pierre Barbaud; ed, Janine Verneau; set d, Claude Pignot.

Drama   **(PR:A   MPAA:NR)**

LES DAMES DE BOIS DE BOULOGNE
                                     (SEE: LADIES OF THE PARK, 1964, Fr.)

LES DEMOISELLES DE ROCHEFORT
                                     (SEE: YOUNG GIRLS OF ROCHEFORT, 1967, Fr.)

LES DEMONS DE MINUIT   (SEE: MIDNIGHT FOLLY, 1962, Fr.)

LES DERNIERES VACANCES*****   (1947, Fr.) 95m Pathe bw

Berthe Bovy, Renee Devillers, Pierre Dux, Jean d'Yd, Odile Versois, Michel Francois.

Two families vacation together at a summer house in the south of France. While the adults carry on their long-standing affairs and talk about plans to sell the house, their children begin their own amorous escapades. A very well done film by documentarist Leenhardt, who would make only one other feature, fourteen years later.

d, Roger Leenhardt; w, R. Breuil, Leenhardt; ph, Philippe Agostini; m, Guy Bernard; ed, Myriam; art d, Leon Barsacq.

Drama   **(PR:A-C   MPAA:NR)**

LES DIABOLIQUES   (SEE: DIABOLIQUE, 1955, Fr.)

LES DOIGTS CROISES   (SEE: CATCH ME A SPY, 1971, Brit./Fr.)

LES ENFANTS DU PARADIS (SEE: CHILDREN OF PARADISE, 1945, Fr.)

LES ENFANTS TERRIBLES*****
                                     (1952, Fr.) 107m Melville bw (AKA: THE STRANGE ONES)

Nicole Stephane (*Elisabeth*), Edouard Dermit (*Paul*), Jacques Bernard (*Gerard*), Renee Cosima (*Dargelos, Agathe*), Roger Gaillard (*Gerard's Uncle*), Melvyn Martin (*Michael*), Maurice Revel (*Doctor*), Adeline Aucoc (*Mariette*), Maria Cyliakus (*The Mother*), Jean-Marie Robain (*Headmaster*), Emile Mathis (*Vice-Principal*), Jean Cocteau (*Narrator*).

Dermit is a young Parisian severely injured when he is hit by a snowball thrown by Cosima, the school bully whom he idolizes. He is cared for by his sister, Stephane, with whom he shares a bedroom, even though they are both in their teens. The near-incestuous pair are brought closer by the death of their ailing mother and are constantly joined by Dermit's friend, Bernard, who is infatuated with Stephane. The trio becomes a quartet when Dermit meets a friend of his sister's, Cosima (who now plays the role of a girl). Stephane secretly dates a wealthy American, and when he dies, she inherits his large townhouse. The foursome pile in and everyone's emotions are carried to an unbearable level. Dermit and Cosima (as Stephane's friend) fall in love, causing Stephane to admit her attraction to her brother. Bernard confesses his love for Stephane, and she arranges to sabotage Cosima's desire for her brother, which eventually leads to a marriage between Cosima and Bernard. The finale has Dermit dying after receiving a poisonous plant from the bully Cosima, and a distraught Stephane committing suicide. Based on Jean Cocteau's celebrated play, the film was directed by Jean-Pierre Melville, who was given such a prestigious chance after Cocteau saw an early 16mm film of his. LES ENFANTS TERRIBLES was shot in Melville's apartment, which he rented with the intention of using it as a location, though his wife was somewhat less enthusiastic. The film unmistakeably bears Cocteau's stamp, and he even directed one scene (the beach) when Melville fell ill.

p&d, Jean-Pierre Melville; w, Melville, Jean Cocteau (from Cocteau's novel, *The Holy Terrors*); ph, Henri Decae; m, Johann Sebastian Bach, Antonio Vivaldi; ed, Monique Bonnot.

Drama   **(PR:A-C   MPAA:NR)**

LES ESPIONS   (SEE: SPIES, THE, 1957, Fr.)

LES FELINS   (SEE: JOY HOUSE, 1964, Fr.)

LES GARCONS   (SEE: LA NOTTE BRAVA, 1962, Fr./Ital.)

LES GAULOISES BLEUES*
                                     (1969, Fr.) 93m Treize-Ariane-Artistes Associes/Lopert c

Annie Girardot (*The Mother*), Jean-Pierre Kalfon (*Ivan, age 30*), Nella Bielski (*Jeanne*), Bruno Cremer (*The Father*), Henri Garcin, Jean Lescot (*Hunters*), Georges Demestre (*Ivan, age 6*), Francois Perier (*Judge*), Anne Wiazemsky (*Nurse*), Marcel Pagliero (*Gypsy Merchant*), Tsilla Chelton (*Delegate*), Jose Varella (*Lawyer*), Tanya Lopert (*Death*), Karina Gondy (*Welfare Agent*), Elizabeth Braconnier (*Bailiff-Nurse*), Francis Girod, Claude Degliame, Sofie Maltzeff, Dominique Vielleville, Tania Becker, Maxmilien Decroux, Isabelle Felder, Andre Ancel, Jacques Baudry.

Kalfon ventures into a tobacco shop for a pack of Gauloises Bleues cigarettes and falls in love with shopgirl Bielski. The couple marry, but soon their relationship is on the rocks. He gets into trouble with the law, bringing them closer to divorce, when Bielski learns she is pregnant. While sitting in the waiting room, Kalfon looks back over his crime-spotted childhood. After an overdose of flashbacks, Kalfon is brought back into the real world with the news that his child was stillborn. Co-produced by Claude Lelouch.

p, Alexandre Mnouchkine, Claude Lelouch, Georges Dancigers; d&w, Michel Cournot; ph, Alain Levent (Eastmancolor); m, Monteverdi, Penderecki; ed, Agnes Guillemot; art d, Guy Littaye, E. Fress; makeup, Aida Carange.

Drama **(PR:A MPAA:G)**

LES GIRLS*** (1957) 114m MGM c

Gene Kelly *(Barry Nichols)*, Mitzi Gaynor *(Joy Henderson)*, Kay Kendall *(Lady Wren)*, Taina Elg *(Angele Ducros)*, Jacques Bergerac *(Pierre Ducros)*, Leslie Phillips *(Sir Gerald Wren)*, Henry Daniell *(Judge)*, Patrick MacNee *(Sir Percy)*, Stephen Vercoe *(Mr. Outward)*, Philip Tonge *(Associate Judge)*, Owen McGiveney *(Court Usher)*, Francis Ravel *(French Stage Manager)*, Adrienne d'Ambricourt *(Wardrobe Woman)*, Maurice Marsac *(French House Manager)*, Cyril Delevanti *(Fanatic)*, George Navarro *(Waiter)*, Nestor Paiva *(Spanish Peasant Man)*, Maya Van Horn *(Stout French Woman)*, Louisa Triana *(Flamenco Dancer)*, Genevieve Pasques *(Shopkeeper)*, Lilyan Chauvin *(Dancer)*, Dick Alexander *(Stagehand)*.

Some of MGM's greatest successes were their musicals of the 1930s and 1940s. They took the tradition into the 1950s and scored with this relatively minor effort that had some of the company's finest creative talents behind it. Kelly, Elg, Gaynor, and Kendall are a popular act in Europe who have been playing to ovations for years. Some time later, long after the group has dissolved, Kendall, now the wife of an English peer, Phillips, decides to write her autobiography and cites, with brutal candor, her memories of what went on behind the scenes in the now-defunct act. Elg, now married to French industrialist Bergerac, is outraged by the revelations and institutes a libel suit against Kendall. The case comes to Daniell's court and the picture becomes a musical RASHOMON as each of the stars tells stories the way they remember them. No one is lying, it's merely that they recall matters very differently. The testimony concerns personal and interpersonal relationships. Kendall had written that Elg attempted to seduce Kelly while she, Kendall, was engaged to him. When Kelly declined the offer, Elg attempted suicide. Elg doesn't see it that way and her story comes out precisely the opposite. Kelly says he never had a crush on either of them but preferred Gaynor—to whom he is now married—all along. Kelly testifies that neither Kendall nor Elg attempted suicide but had both been unfortunate enough to be in a room with a faulty gas heater and improper ventilation. The picture ends with everyone having had a say and a host of musical numbers sung and danced. The script was too long-winded and short-witted to be a breezy paean to the MGMusicals. This was Kelly's last acting job at the studio and he never quite mustered the energy needed to sock it over. It was sort of, but not quite, a later version of IDIOT'S DELIGHT, which was also about an American song and dance man, Clark Gable, with a bevy of cuties, who gets trapped at a mountain resort as war breaks out in Europe. Kelly stayed away from the choreographing chores until Cole became ill and Kelly had to take over the dancing reins. This was Porter's last Hollywood score and not one of his best. Porter thought that Patrick's script was excellent and not really in need of tunes to further the action so he was not challenged and it was only when Porter had to dig deeply that his best songs emerged. Kendall, in her first U.S. picture, was a blazing success with critics and the public but her life was cut short by leukemia before she was 33. Elg, who wasn't made up well, proved her mettle singing, dancing and acting, yet her career never took off. Gaynor, who was professionally wholesome in most of her roles, was exactly that here. Although chosen to be the Royal Command Film in November, 1957, in London, LES GIRLS never did make much money and signalled the end of the "original musical" era for Hollywood until many years later when rock and roll films took over. With Kelly, Cole Porter and Jack Cole bowing out, LES GIRLS was a picture of endings. Once the sixties arrived, with psychodramas, anti-heros, and political films, the studios didn't want to make big musicals unless they were adapted from proven Broadway hits. And even then, as with Gaynor's SOUTH PACIFIC, that was no assurance of success. Although Porter's score was pale, and not up to his usual lofty standards, it would have been a feather in any other composer's cap. The tunes include: "Les Girls," "Flower Song," "You're Just Too, Too," "Ca C'est L'Amour," "Ladies In Waiting," "La Habanera," and a delicious satire of Brando's THE WILD ONE entitled "Why Am I So Gone (About That Gal)?" Cukor didn't do many musicals and his biggest one, MY FAIR LADY, was not nearly his best film. Although shot entirely in Hollywood, except for stock shots, Cukor and his color consultant, George Hoyningen-Huene, made it look authentically European. A later attempt at a TV series starring Larry Blyden was an abysmal flop.

p, Sol C. Siegel; d, George Cukor; w, John Patrick (based on a story by Vera Caspary); ph, Robert Surtees (CinemaScope, Metrocolor); m, Cole Porter; ed, Ferris Webster; md, Adolph Deutsch; art d, William A. Horning, Gene Allen; set d, Edwin B. Willis; cos, Orry-Kelly; ch, Jack Cole; m/l, Porter.

Musical/Comedy **(PR:A MPAA:NR)**

LES GRANDES MANOEUVRES
(SEE: GRAND MANUEVERS, 1956, Fr./Ital.)

LES HOMMES EN BLANC (SEE: DOCTORS, THE, 1956, Fr.)

LES INNOCENTS AUX MAINS SALES
(SEE: DIRTY HANDS, 1976, Fr./Ital./Ger.)

LES JEUX INTERDIT (SEE: FORBIDDEN GAMES, 1953, Fr.)

LES JEUX SONT FAITS**
(1947, Fr.) 91m Les Films Gibe/Lopert bw (AKA: THE CHIPS ARE DOWN)

Micheline Presle *(Eve Charlier)*, Michel Pagliero *(Pierre)*, Marguerite Moreno *(Bookkeeper)*, Fernand Fabre *(Andre Charlier)*, Jacques Irwin *(Dictator)*, Charles Dullin *(The Noble)*, Colette Ripert *(Lucette)*, Mouloudji *(Lucien)*.

Pagliero is a Communist killed during an uprising and Presle the wife of a fascist official who poisoned her; both died at the same time. They meet in the afterlife and fall in love and are granted permission to return to life to see if they could be lovers in the real world. The rules are that physical consummation must take place within 24 hours. Instead they argue over politics until they are both returned to death. Fascinating though depressing feature written by Sartre, his first dalliance with the movies. Predictably, the film was panned by the critics when it made its debut at Cannes.

d, Jean Delannoy; w, Jean Paul Sartre, Jacques Laurent Bost, Delannoy; ph, Christian Matras; m, Georges Auric.

Drama **(PR:A-C MPAA:NR)**

LES LACHES VIVENT D'ESPOIR (SEE: MY BABY IS BLACK!, 1965, Fr.)

LES LETTRES DE MON MOULIN
(SEE: LETTERS FROM MY WINDMILL, 1955, Fr.)

LES LIAISONS DANGEREUSES**
(1961, Fr./Ital.) 106m Marceau-Cocinor-Laetitia/Astor bw (RELAZIONI PERICOLOSE; AKA: DANGEROUS LOVE AFFAIRS)

Gerard Philipe *(Valmont de Merteuil)*, Jeanne Moreau *(Juliette de Merteuil)*, Jeanne Valerie *(Cecile Volanges)*, Annette Vadim *(Marianne Tourvel)*, Simone Renant *(Mme. Volanges)*, Jean-Louis Trintignant *(Danceny)*, Nicolas Vogel *(Court)*, Boris Vian *(Prevan)*, Frederic O'Brady, Gillian Hills.

This Vadim film casts Philipe and Moreau as a married couple who thrive on extramarital affairs. When Philipe finds himself emotionally involved with Annette Vadim (nee Stroyberg, Vadim's wife after Brigitte Bardot), the relationship with Moreau falls apart. Eventually Philipe is killed and Moreau disfigured in a fire which she set to burn her husband's incriminating letters. Vadim, who made a name for himself by showing Bardot's flesh, tries the same thing here with Annette.

d, Roger Vadim; w, Vadim, Roger Vailland, Claude Brule (from the novel by Pierre Ambroise Francois Choderlos de Laclos); ph, Marcel Grignon; m, Thelonius Monk, Jack Murray (played by Barney Wilem's Orchestra and Art Blakey's Jazz Messengers); ed, Victoria Mercanton.

Drama **(PR:O MPAA:NR)**

LES LIENS DE SANG (SEE: BLOOD RELATIVES, 1978, Fr./Can.)

LES LOUVES (SEE: DEMONIAQUE, 1958, Fr.)

LES MAINS SALES **
(1954, Fr.) 103m MacDonald bw (AKA: DIRTY HANDS)

Pierre Brasseur *(Hoederer)*, Daniel Gelin *(Hugo Barine)*, Claude Nollier *(Olga)*, Monique Artur *(Jessica)*, Jacques Castelot *(The Prince)*, Marcel Andre *(Karski)*, Georges Chamarat *(Barine)*, Roland Bailly, Eddy Rasimi *(Bodyguards)*.

Gelin, an idealistic young Communist fighting the Nazis in some unnamed occupied country, is convinced by a rival faction within the party that his boss (Brasseur) is going to sell out the cause by advocating an alliance with the reactionaries in the country and that he must be killed. Assigned to the task, he takes his flighty wife (Artur) with him to do the job, but when he arrives in Brasseur's presence he is unable to pull the trigger, instead engaging his victim in a number of the interminable philosophical discussions obligatory in a play by Sartre. It is not until he finds Brasseur kissing his wife that he is able to muster up the gumption to shoot the man. Dying, Brasseur forgives his act as one of jealousy, and when Gelin returns to the Communist faction that put him up to it, the party line has changed; he finds them now advocating the course of alliance with the reactionary forces and Brasseur regarded as a martyred hero. Gelin is executed. Static filming of a popular and controversial play which originally starred Charles Boyer in the Brasseur part.

p&d, Fernand Rivers; w, Rivers, Jacques Bost, Jean-Paul Sartre (based on the play by Sartre); ph, Jean Bachelet.

Drama **(PR:A-C MPAA:NR)**

LES MAITRES DU TEMPS ** 1/2** (1982, Fr./Switz./Ger.) 78m c

Some fine animation with renowned artist Moebius as chief graphic designer is a good reason for seeing this science fiction picture. Bogged down in a metaphysical rescue mission, it is still more interesting than Ralph Bakshi's work in this territory.

p, Roland Gritti, Jacques Dercourt; d, Rene Laloux; w, Laloux, Moebius (Jean Giraud), Jean-Patrick Manchette; spec eff, Sandor Reisenbuchler.

Animated Science-Fiction **(PR:A MPAA:NR)**

LES MAUDITS (SEE: DAMNED, THE, 1948, Fr.)

LES MISERABLES***** (1935) 108m FOX/UA bw

Fredric March *(Jean Valjean)*, Charles Laughton *(Javert)*, Cedric Hardwicke *(Bishop Bienvenu)*, Rochelle Hudson *(Big Cosette)*, Marilyn Knowlden *(Little Cosette)*, Frances Drake *(Eponine)*, John Beal *(Marius)*, Jessie Ralph *(Mme. Magloire)*, Florence Eldridge *(Fantine)*, Ferdinand Gottschalk *(Thenardier)*, Jane Kerr *(Mme. Thenardier)*, Eily Malyon *(Mother Superior)*, Vernon Downing *(Brissac)*, Lyons Wickland *(Lamarque)*, John Carradine *(Enjolras)*, Charles Haefeli *(Brevet)*, Leonid Kinskey *(Genflon)*, John Bleifer *(Chenildieu)*, Harry Semels *(Cochepaille)*, Mary

Forbes *(Mme. Baptiseme)*, Florence Roberts *(Toussaint)*, Lorin Raker *(Valain)*, Perry Ivins *(M. Devereux)*, Thomas Mills *(L'Estrange)*, Lowell Drew *(Duval)*, Davison Clark *(Marcin)*, Ian McClaren *(Head Gardener)*.

March is overwhelming as the sensitive, persecuted Jean Valjean who steals a loaf of bread to survive, is captured, and given 10 years at hard labor in prison. When finally escaping the prison galley, March is a hardbitten, stone-hearted, and utterly unsympathetic creature whose compassion for his fellow man has been hammered out of him by the cruelty of confinement. He is taken in by Hardwicke, a Bishop who refuses to prosecute him for stealing two silver candlesticks, and, through Hardwicke's kindness and understanding, March regains his sensitivity, totally reforming. He works night and day to build a new life for himself using another name, taking a young child as his own. He becomes a well-to-do businessman and, moving to another town, becomes so widely liked that he is elected mayor. His grown daughter, Drake, and he live in a resplendent house and every waking day of March's life is devoted to benefiting his fellow man. His chief of police, Laughton, is less than convivial, however. He is a police bloodhound, one of those cold, unimpassioned officials who knows no humanity, only the letter of the law. To the single-minded Laughton the law is to be upheld and enforced at all costs, with no mercy shown to anyone causing the slightest infraction. Laughton and March clash repeatedly over the interpretation of the law and the policeman becomes incensed when March intercedes on behalf of social pariah, Eldridge (March's real-life wife). One day March sees a villager trapped beneath a heavy wagon and, with what seems to be superhuman strength, he puts his back to the wagon and lifts it so the man can be saved. Laughton watches this feat and is reminded of a galley prisoner he once encountered. He begins to investigate March's past and identifies March as Jean Valjean, the wanted criminal. He is then confused when another prisoner is found, a mindless inmate who amazingly resembles March, and who admits he is Jean Valjean. He is put on trial but the honest-to-the-bone March (who plays both parts) admits he is the real Jean Valjean. Before he can be jailed he again escapes with Drake to Paris where he assumes yet another identity. His daughter falls in love with Beal, a young radical who works for prison reform. Laughton arrives in Paris and is assigned to watch the revolutionaries. He gets onto March's trail once more as March becomes more and more involved with Beal and his revolutionary friends. Half of Paris revolts against inhuman conditions and Drake suddenly runs to her father with the news that her love Beal has been injured in the fighting. March goes to the barricades and finds the young man, carrying him to safety, but Laughton is right behind him. March escapes into the Paris sewers, carrying Beal through the treacherous chest-high waters until depositing him with his daughter. When he realizes that his daughter and Beal will be safe to lead a happy life together, March goes to surrender to Laughton. But the dogged policeman, who has witnessed March's selfless sacrifice, finds compassion stirring in his heart, an emotion he cannot understand and one that so confuses and vexes him that he is willing to break the law, the very fibre of his being, and allow the noble March his freedom. But this he cannot do either. Laughton solves his traumatic dilemma by hurling himself into the Seine and drowning himself. March is free to rejoin his daughter and Beal, living out his life among those who love him. This full-scale production was meticulous in every detail and faithful to the Hugo novel, except for allowing March to live in the end where he dies in the original tale. Boleslawski, a largely forgotten director today, was truly masterful in his handling of LES MISERABLES, adhering faithfully to Hugo's scenes and working diligently from Lipscomb's compact 108-minute script, which is literate and moving. Among Boleslawski's fine films are RASPUTIN AND THE EMPRESS (1932), starring Lionel, John, and Ethel Barrymore and THE PAINTED VEIL (1934). March gives one of his greatest performances as the hunted victim Jean Valjean, far superior to that essayed in a French version in 1936 and the crude 1918 silent version, also made by Fox and starring William Farnum. The film was remade in 1952 with Michael Rennie as Jean Valjean and Robert Newton as Javert, the policeman, but it was only a pale imitation of the 1935 classic. A number of other actors would essay the great Hugo created character, including Richard Jordan in a British remake of the film in 1979, but no one has ever approached March's depthful characterization.

p, Darryl F. Zanuck; d, Richard Boleslawski; w, W.P. Lipscomb (based on the novel by Victor Hugo); ph, Gregg Toland; ed, Barbara McLean; md, Alfred Newman.

Historical Drama (PR:A MPAA:NR)

LES MISERABLES*** (1936, Fr.) 305m Pathe-Nathan bw

Harry Baur *(Jean Valjean, Mons. Madeleine, Mons. Fauchelevent)*, Charles Vanel *(Javert)*, Henry Krauss *(Bishop Myriel)*, Charles Dullin *(Thenardier)*, Marguerite Moreno *(Mme. Thenardier)*, Odette Florelle *(Fantine)*, Gaby Triquet *(Cosette, as a Child)*, Jean Servais *(Marius)*, Josseline Gael *(Cosette, as an Adult)*, Orane Demazis *(Eponine, as an Adult)*, Robert Vidalin *(Enjolras)*, Emile Genevois *(Gavroche)*, Cailloux *(Maboeuf)*, Max Dearly *(Gillenormand)*.

One of many versions of the classic novel by Victor Hugo about a thief who tries to make good but is hounded by a determined detective. At 305 minutes it is arguably the most faithful to the novel, but it still doesn't equal the 1935 U.S. version. When it was released in Paris in 1933 it was oddly shown in three parts—TEMPETE SOUS UN CRANE (120m), LES THENARDIERS (90m), LIBERTE, LIBERTE CHERIE (95m)—and in three different theaters. It was later cut to a single 165 minute version, and later edited again into two parts—JEAN VALJEAN (109m) and COSETTE (100m).

d, Raymond Bernard; w, Bernard, Andre Lang (based on the novel by Victor Hugo); ph, Jules Kruger; m, Arthur Honneger.

Drama (PR:A MPAA:NR)

LES MISERABLES*** (1952) 105m FOX bw

Michael Rennie *(Jean Valjean)*, Debra Paget *(Cosette)*, Robert Newton *(Javert)*, Edmund Gwenn *(Bishop)*, Sylvia Sidney *(Fantine)*, Cameron Mitchell *(Marius)*, Elsa Lanchester *(Madame Magloire)*, James Robertson Justice *(Robert)*, Joseph Wiseman *(Genflou)*, Rhys Williams *(Brevet)*, Florence Bates *(Mme. Bonnet)*, Merry Anders *(Cicely)*, John Rogers *(Bonnet)*, Charles Keane *(Corporal)*, John Dierkes *(Bosun)*, John Costello *(Cochepaille)*, Norma Varden *(Mme. Courbet)*, William Cottrell *(Dupuy)*, Queenie Leonard *(Valjean's Maid)*, Bobby Hyatt *(Gavroche)*, Sanders Clark *(Lieutenant)*, Patsy Weil *(Cosette, age 7)*, Jean Vachon *(Nun)*, Sean McClory *(Bamatabois)*, June Hillman *(Mother Superior)*, James Craven *(Vero)*, Lester Matthews *(Mentou, Sr.)*, Jimmie Moss *(Mentou's Grandson)*, Ian Wolfe *(Presiding Judge)*, Alfred Linder *(Genet)*, John O'Malley *(Worker)*, Leslie Denison *(Mounted Policeman)*, Alex Frazer *(Silversmith)*, Jack Raine *(Captain)*, John Sherman *(Town Corporal)*, Dayton Lummis *(Defense)*, Victor Wood *(Prosecutor)*, Robert Adler *(Valjean's Coachman)*, Victor Romito *(Man)*, Charlotte Austin *(Student)*, Olaf Hytten, Frank Baker *(Judges)*, Michael Granger, Jerry Miley, Jack Baston *(Policemen)*, Mary Forbes, Moyna McGill *(Nuns)*, Tudor Owen, Leonard Carey, William Dalzell *(Citizens)*, Charles Fitzsimons *(Noel, Student)*, Roger Anderson *(Revolutionary)*.

This was the fifth version of Victor Hugo's novel (Fox Film Co. in 1918, Universal in 1927, United Artists in 1935, and a French production in 1936). The story of justice and the law is told in three episodes: Rennie's arrest for stealing bread and his imprisonment; his becoming a mayor and adoption of Paget; and Newton's hounding of Rennie because of his missed parole. The film ends when Newton lets Rennie go and commits suicide for going against his own principles. A well crafted production, but it doesn't hold up as well as the 1935 U.A. version.

p, Fred Kohlmar; d, Lewis Milestone; w, Richard Murphy (based on the novel by Victor Hugo); ph, Joseph La Shelle; m, Alex North; ed, Hugh Fowler; md, Lionel Newman; art d, Lyle Wheeler, J. Russell Spencer; set d, Thomas Little, Walter M. Scott.

Drama (PR:A MPAA:NR)

LES MISERABLES** (1982, Fr.) 187m GEF-CCFC/TF-1 Film Prods. SFP/Del Duca Films/CCFC c

Lino Ventura *(Jean Valjean)*, Michel Bouquet *(Inspector Javert)*, Jean Carmet *(Thenardier)*, Francoise Seigner *(La Thenardier)*, Evelyne Bouix *(Fantine)*, Christine Jean *(Cosette)*, Franck David *(Marius)*, Candice Patou *(Eponine)*, Louis Seigner *(Monseigneur Myriel)*, Fernand Ledoux *(Guillenormand)*, Emmanuel Curtil *(Gavroche)*, Paul Preboist *(Fauchelevent)*, Herve Furic *(Enjolras)*.

This is the sixth French version of Hugo's classic novel and the weakest. The two best French versions are the 1927 silent version directed by Henri Fescourt (over seven hours long) and Raymond Bernard's 1936 version (six hours and fifteen minutes). This was a French film and T.V. co-production (six 52-minute episodes for television) at a cost of $10,000,000. The film is heavy-handed and because so much of the book has been squeezed in, many scenes aren't given enough time to develop. This makes the film seem forced and many sequences melodramatic.

p, Dominique Harispuru; d, Robert Hossein; w, Hossein and Alain Decaux (adapted from Victor Hugo's novel); ph, Edmond Richard (Eastmancolor); ed, Martine Baraque-Curie; art d, Francois de Lamothe.

Drama (PR:A MPAA:NR)

LES NOCES DU SABLE (SEE: DAUGHTER OF THE SANDS, 1952, Fr.)

LES NUITS DE L'EVPOUVANTE (SEE: MURDER CLINIC, THE, 1967, Ital./Fr.)

LES OGRESSES (SEE: QUEENS, THE, 1968, Ital./Fr.)

LES PARENTS TERRIBLES**** (1950, Fr.) 105m Ariane bw (AKA: THE STORM WITHIN)

Jean Marais *(Michel)*, Yvonne de Bray *(Yvonne-Sophie)*, Gabrielle Dorziat *(Aunt Leo)*, Marcel Andre *(Georges)*, Josette Day *(Madeleine)*, Jean Cocteau *(Narrator)*.

Cocteau's brilliant domestic drama which many consider to be his greatest achievement, including Cocteau himself. Based on his stage play (performed ten years earlier with much the same cast) it casts de Bray as the dangerously possessive mother who is wed to Andre, a weak and defeated man. De Bray opposes the marriage of her young son Marais to the beautiful Day. It turns out that Day is the mistress of Andre, who happens to be the subject of Marais' aunt's (Dorziat) desires. When the tangled affairs come into the open, de Bray commits suicide, unable to accept the loss of her magnetic hold over her family. Set in only two locations—de Bray's family's apartment and Day's apartment—the film is, as Cocteau said, a record "of the acting of an incomparable cast." Georges Auric's score is a prime example of sound in perfect unity with the picture. A far-inferior remake, INTIMATE RELATIONS, was released in Britain in 1953. Various lengths exist, with both a 98m and 86m cut being shown in the U.S.

d&w, Jean Cocteau (based on his play); ph, Michel Kelber; m, Georges Auric; ed, Jacqueline Sadoul; art d, Christian Berard, Guy de Gastyne.

Drama (PR:A MPAA:NR)

LES PEMPS DES AMANTS (SEE: PLACE FOR LOVERS, A, 1969, Ital./Fr.)

LES PERLES DES COURONNE (SEE: PEARLS OF THE CROWN, 1938, Fr.)

LES PETROLEUSES (SEE: LEGEND OF FRENCHIE KING, THE, 1971, Fr./Ital./Span./Brit.)

LES PORTES DE LA NUIT (SEE: GATES OF THE NIGHT, 1950, Fr.)

LES QUATRES CENTS COUPS (SEE: FOUR HUNDRED BLOWS, THE, 1959, Fr.)

LES QUATRES VERITES

(SEE: THREE FABLES OF LOVE, 1963, Fr./Ital./Span.)

LES SOMNAMBULES
(SEE: MON ONCLE D'AMERIQUE, 1980, Fr.)

LES TITANS
(SEE: MY SON, THE HERO, 1963, Ital./Fr.)

LES TRICHEURS
(SEE: CHEATERS, THE, 1961, Fr.)

LES TRIPES AU SOLEIL
(SEE: CHECKERBOARD, 1969, Fr.)

LES VACANCES DE MONSIEUR HULOT
(SEE: MR. HULOT'S HOLIDAY, 1954, Fr.)

LES VALSEUSES
(SEE: GOING PLACES, 1974, Fr.)

LES VISITEURS DU SOIR
(SEE: DEVIL'S ENVOYS, THE, 1947, Fr.)

LES YEUX SANS VISAGE
(SEE: HORROR CHAMBER OF DR. FAUSTUS, THE, 1962, Fr./Ital.)

LESBIAN TWINS
(SEE: VIRGIN WITCH, THE, 1973, Brit.)

LESNAYA PESNYA
(SEE: SONG OF THE FOREST, 1963, USSR)

L'ESPION
(SEE: DEFECTOR, THE, 1966, Ger./Fr.)

LESSON IN LOVE, A***
(1960, Swed.) 95m SvenskFilmindustri/Janus Films, Inc. bw (EN LEKTION I KARLEK)

Eva Dahlbeck (Marianne Erneman), Gunnar Bjornstrand (Dr. David Erneman), Yvonne Lombard (Suzanne), Harriet Andersson (Nix), Ake Gronberg (Carl Adam), Olof Winnerstrand (Prof. Henrik Erneman), Renee Bjorling (Svea Erneman), Birgitte Reimar (Lise), John Elfstrom (Sam), Dagmar Ebbeson (Nurse), Helge Hagerman (Travelling Salesman), Sigge Furst (Priest), Gosta Pruzelius (Train Guard) Carl Strom (Uncle Axel), Arne Lindblad (Hotel Manager), Torsten Lilliecrona (Porter), Yvonne Brosset (Ballerina).

Bergman's reputation is as a cinema artiste of dark, complex films, but this early comedy (released in Sweden in 1954) shows the master's often overlooked comic side. Bjornstrand is a gynecologist who becomes involved with Lombard, a 21-year-old patient. The story is told in flashback as the doctor shares a train compartment with strangers on his way to Copenhagen. With a fine mix of compassion and humor, Bjornstrand's story of a love that blooms before its inevitable fading unfolds. Bergman's camera lovingly records the story with a fine sense of control, the humor often bitter-sweet and never maudlin. Bergman wrote and shot the film in a relatively short period of time, with the idea of creating a light, frivolous story. He later stated A LESSON IN LOVE was made only for the passing moment, though it's filled with genuine love and caring. (In Swedish; English subtitles.)

p,d&w, Ingmar Bergman; ph, Martin Bodin; m, Dag Wiren; ed, Oscar Rosander; set d, P.A. Lundgren.

Comedy   **(PR:C   MPAA:NR)**

LEST WE FORGET**
(1934, Brit.) 60m Sound City/MGM bw

Stewart Rome (Captain Rayner), George Carney (Sgt. Jock), Esmond Knight (Pat Doyle, Jr.), Ann Yates (Sylvia Rayner), Roddy Hughes (Taffy), Tony Quinn (Pat Doyle), Wilson Coleman (Butler).

Four soldiers—an Englishman, a Scotsman, a Welshman, and an Irishman—are trapped in a fox hole during a heavy battle. The quartet vow to meet after the war should they survive. Of course they do survive and a reunion is planned. However, Rome, the Englishman, has come on hard times in post-war life and is experiencing financial troubles. Rather than let his friends know of his troubles, Rome feigns great wealth when the quartet is reunited. This film followed the 1932 REUNION, which employed the same producer, writer, and star (Rome).

p, Norman Loudon; d, John Baxter; w, Herbert Ayres.

Drama   **(PR:C   MPAA:NR)**

LET 'EM HAVE IT*** (1935) 96m Reliance/Astor/UA bw (GB: FALSE FACES)

Richard Arlen (Mal Stevens), Virginia Bruce (Eleanor Spencer), Alice Brady (Aunt Ethel), Bruce Cabot (Joe Keefer), Harvey Stephens (Van Rensseler), Eric Linden (Buddy Spencer), Joyce Compton (Barbara), Gordon Jones (Tex), J. Farrell Macdonald (Mr. Keefer), Bodil Rosing (Mrs. Keefer), Paul Stanton (Department Chief), Robert Emmett O'Connor (Police Captain), Hale Hamilton (Ex-Senator Reilly), Dorothy Appleby (Lola), Barbara Pepper (Milly), Matthew Betz (Thompson), Harry Woods (Big Bill), Clyde Dillson (Pete), Matty Fain ("Brooklyn"), Paul Fix (Sam), Donald Kirke (Curley), Eugene Strong ("Dude"), Christian Rub (Henkel), Eleanor Wesselhoeft (Mrs. Henkel), Wesley Barry (Walton), Ian Maclaren (Reconstructionist), George Pauncefort (Dr. Hoffman), Joseph King (Instructor), Clarence Wilson (Reynolds), Katherine Clare Ward (Ma Harrison), Landers Stevens (Parole Chairman), Sidney Bracy (Butler).

The depression was still in full swing when the crime movie became a main staple of the film industry. The Hayes office in Hollywood made it a rule that the moviemakers could not idolize big-time criminals by making movies about them. There were many ways to get around this and this film is one example. Based loosely on the career of John Dillinger, federal agent Arlen is after Cabot who killed Cabot's brother, also an agent of the FBI. This is the routine story with plenty of car chases and gun battles with Cabot finally being brought to justice. The best sequence of the film is when Cabot goes to a plastic surgeon and finds after the operation that the doctor has branded the criminal's initials on his face. This impossible tale, loosely based on G-MEN, was suggested and overseen by J. Edgar Hoover, one of the greatest spinners of tall tales in the federal government at that time.

p, Edward Small; d, Sam Wood; w, Joseph Moncure March, Elmer Harris; ph, J. Peverell Marley, Robert Planck; ed, Grant Whytock.

Crime   **(PR:A   MPAA:NR)**

LET FREEDOM RING***
(1939) 85m MGM bw

Nelson Eddy (Steve Logan), Virginia Bruce (Maggie Adams), Victor McLaglen (Chris Mulligan), Lionel Barrymore (Thomas Logan), Edward Arnold (Jim Wade), Guy Kibbee (Judge David Bronson), Charles Butterworth ("The Mackerel"), H.B. Warner (Rutledge), Raymond Walburn (Editor Underwood), Dick Rich ("Thumper" Jackson), Trevor Bardette (Cagan), George F. Hayes ("Pop" Wilkie), Louis Jean Heydt (Ned Wilkie), Sarah Padden ("Ma" Logan), Eddie Dunn ("Curley," Bartender), C. E. Anderson (Sheriff Hicks), Maude Allen (Hilda), Adia Kuznetzoff (Pole), Luis Alberni (Tony), Emory Parnell (Swede), Tenen Holtz (Hunky), Mitchell Lewis (Joe), Victor Potel (2nd Swede), Constantine Romanoff (Russian), Lionel Royce (German), Billy Bevan (Cockney), Syd Saylor, Ted Thompson (Surveyors), Hank Bell (Stage Driver), Harry Wilson (Workman), Philo McCullough, Harry Fleischmann, Ralph [Francis X., Jr.] Bushman (Cagan Henchmen), Bruce Mitchell, Cyril Ring, Heinie Conklin, Jimmy Aubrey (Ranchers), Art Mix, Harry Tenbrook, James Mason (Barflies).

Eddy is a Harvard lawyer who returns to his small western hometown to find the railroad trying to take over the town. Arnold heads the railroad and has bought out the town judge, making it easier to do whatever he likes. Eddy stands up to Arnold and the railroad thugs burn his house down. The lawyer then pretends to be on Arnold's side as he masquerades as "The Hornet." Under this guise, Eddy kidnaps the town's publisher and printing press, and has leaflets made to continue the fight against Arnold. The railroad henchmen take chase and Eddy is wounded in a shoot-out. Arnold still doesn't know the identity of the mysterious crusader and this enables Eddy to convince McLaglen, Arnold's top henchman, to join forces with the town. Arnold is then quickly herded out of town for good. The film is a sappy celebration of the American spirit that works in spite of itself. The main reason for that is Ben Hecht's script. Film was printed in a sepia tone. Songs include "Dusty Road" (Leon and Otis Rene), "Love Serenade" (Riccardo Drigo, Bob Wright, Chet Forrest), "Home Sweet Home" (Sir Henry R. Bishop, John Howard Payne), "When Irish Eyes Are Smiling" (Ernest R. Ball, Chauncey Olcott, George Graff, Jr.), "America" (Henry Carey, Rev. Samuel Francis Smith), "Pat Sez He" (Foster Carling, Phil Ohman), "Where Else But Here" (Sigmund Romberg, Edward Heyman), "Funiculi Funicula" (Luigi Denza), "Ten Thousand Cattle Straying" (Owen Wister), "I've Been Working On the Railroad" (traditional).

p, Harry Rapf; d, Jack Conway; w, Ben Hecht; ph, Sidney Wagner; ed, Fredrick Y. Smith; md, Arthur Lange; art d, Cedric Gibbons, Daniel B. Cathcart; set d, Edwin B. Willis; cos, Dolly Tree, Vales.

Musical   **(PR:A   MPAA:NR)**

LET GEORGE DO IT**
(1940, Brit.) 73m EAL-ATP/Film Alliance bw

George Formby (George), Phyllis Calvert (Mary), Garry Marsh (Mendez), Romney Brent (Slim), Bernard Lee (Nelson), Coral Browne (Ivy), Diana Beaumont (Greta), Torin Thatcher (U-boat Commander), Hal Gordon (Arbuckle), Donald Calthrop (Strickland), Ronald Shiner (Musician), Albert Lieven (Radio Operator), Bill Shine (Steward), Helena Pickard, Percy Walsh.

Formby is a ukelele player in Norway who's mistaken for a Nazi spy. German agents think that the musician is one of their own and Formby gets entangled in a number of comic situations with them. In the end, Formby reveals band leader Marsh as the real spy. This was the first of the famed Ealing Studios comedies to deal directly with WW II. Many more were to follow. Songs include: "Oh, Don't the Wind Blow Cold," "Mr. Wu Is a Window Cleaner Now," "Grandad's Flannelette Nightshirt," and "Count Your Blessings and Smile."

p, Michael Balcon; d, Marcel Varnel; w, John Dighton, Austin Melford, Angus Macphail, Basil Dearden; ph, Ronald Neame; ed, Ray Pitt; md, Ernest Irving; art d, Wilfred Shingleton.

Comedy   **(PR:A   MPAA:NR)**

LET JOY REIGN SUPREME***
(1977, Fr.) 120m Fildebroc-UPF-La Gueville/Specialty Films c (QUE LA FETE COMMENCE)

Philippe Noiret (Philippe D'Orleans), Jean Rochefort (Abbe), Jean-Pierre Marielle (Marquis Pontcallec), Christine Pascal (Emilie), Marina Vlady (Madame Parabere de Bourbon), Gerard Desarthe (Duc De Bourbon), Alfred Adam (Villeroi), Gilles Guillot (Caussimon).

Noiret stars as Philippe D'Orleans, an aesthetically minded regent to the young Louis XV. Though Noiret holds power in early 18th-century France, he has no real standing in the royal scheme of things, though he tries his best to keep his countrymen cultured and content, thus delaying a peasant uprising. Gradually, however, rage grows in the servile class. Noiret tries to avoid violence by teaming with Marielle, a power-hungry priest with no concern for God or man. The regent then is shaken by the death of his daughter, with whom he has been accused of incest. He becomes embittered when he is forced to execute a group of revolutionaries, but the finale makes it quite apparent that the joy that will reign supreme will be that of the peasants. Noiret turns in a superb performance (a feat he would equal in Tavernier's 1981 COUP DE TORCHON) as the humanistic regent, allowing the audience to become wholly absorbed in his characterization. A special treat is the soundtrack music which was written by Philippe D'Orleans himself, providing demonstrable evidence of his interest in the arts.

p, Michelle de Broca; d, Bertrand Tavernier; w, Tavernier, Jean Aurenche; ph, Pierre William Glenn (Eastmancolor); m, Philippe D'Orleans; ed, Armand Psenny.

Historical Drama (PR:C MPAA:NR)

LET ME EXPLAIN, DEAR**¹/₂**
(1932) 75m British International Pictures/Wardour bw

Gene Gerrard (*George Hunter*), Viola Lyel (*Angela Hunter*), Claude Hulbert (*Cyril Merryweather*), Jane Carr (*Mamie*), Amy Veness (*Aunt Fanny*), Henry Longhurst (*Dr. Coote*), Hal Gordon (*Parrott*), C. Denier Warren (*Jeweller*), Reginald Bach (*Taxi-driver*).

Gerrard is a married man who's having an affair with Hulbert. She has broken the clasp of her expensive necklace and Gerrard takes it with him to have fixed. His wife finds it and thinks it's a present for her. She tells him how sorry she is for accusing him of cheating and Gerrard can't get himself to tell her the truth. So, to buy a new necklace for Hulbert, he fakes an injury to collect on the insurance money. But things don't work as planned.

p, John Maxwell; d&w, Gene Gerrard, Frank Miller (adapted from the play "A Little Bit of Fluff" by Walter Ellis).

Comedy (PR:A MPAA:NR)

LET NO MAN WRITE MY EPITAPH** (1960) 105m COL bw

Burl Ives (*Judge Bruce Mallory Sullivan*), Shelley Winters (*Nellie Romano*), James Darren (*Nick Romano*), Jean Seberg (*Barbara Holloway*), Ricardo Montalban (*Louie Ramponi*), Ella Fitzgerald (*Flora*), Rudolph Acosta (*Max*), Philip Ober (*Grant Holloway*), Jeanne Cooper (*Fran*), Bernie Hamilton (*Goodbye George*), Walter Burke (*Wart*), Francis DeSales (*Magistrate*), Michael Davis (*Nick, as a Child*), Dan Easton (*Eddie*), Nesdon Booth (*Mike*), Roy Jenson (*Whitey*), Joel Fricano (*Barney*), Joe Gallison (*Lee*).

Adapted from Willard Motley's novel about life on Chicago's South Side, the film falls flat because of poor performances from the cast. Winters plays a junkie mother trying to raise her kid right. Darren is her son who becomes a concert pianist. Montalban is a drug dealer who is killed by Ives, who commits the crime because he believed the dealer had harmed Darren. Winters' overacting is a real problem in this film since she's on the screen the majority of the time. With better actors this would have been a very powerful film because director Leacock captures the gritty atmosphere of skid row and the people that inhabit it. The acting will remind the viewer that the people on the screen are Hollywood actors who have no idea of the characters they are playing.

p, Boris D. Kaplin; d, Phillip Leacock; w, Robert Presnell, Jr. (adapted from a novel by Willard Motley); ph, Burnett Guffey; m, George Dunning; ed, Chester W. Schaeffer.

Drama (PR:A MPAA:NR)

LET THE BALLOON GO* (1977, Aus.) 92m Film Australia/Inter Planetary c

Robert Bettles (*John Sumner*), Jan Kingsbury (*Mrs. Sumner*), Ben Gabriel (*Mr. Sumner*), Sally Whiteman (*Mamie*), Matthew Wilson (*Cecil*), Terry McQuillan (*Harry*), Bruce Spence (*Acting Fire Chief Gifford*), John Ewart (*Police Constable Baird*), Kenneth Goodlet (*Maj. Fairleigh*), Ray Barrett (*Dr. McLeod*), Nigel Lovell (*The Parson*), Babette Stephens (*Mrs. Braithwaite*), Brian Anderson, Charles Metcalfe, Phillip Ross, Scott Griffiths, Goff Vockler, Bob Lee.

With children's films there is an occasional tendency to underestimate the audience, resulting in sloppy and inept productions. Such is the case with LET THE BALLOON GO, a potentially sensitive film for younger audiences that completely shortchanges their intelligence. Bettles, delivering a good performance in spite of the production, is a disabled youngster living in WW I-era Australia. Despite many setbacks, the boy achieves his goal by film's end, as he gains an independence from those around him. The director really doesn't know what to do with the story, focusing on the crueler elements of Bettles' struggle, rather than on the uplifting aspects. The film's possibilities are further hampered by what is clearly a lack of concern for the audience by the producers, confirmed by the poor set design and almost amateurish costuming. This was the first children's film produced by the Australian government, which normally works on well-made documentaries for adults. It's a shame they didn't give the children enough credit as filmgoers, for they are often the toughest audiences to please.

p, Richard Mason; d, Oliver Howes; w, Mason, Howes, Ivan Southall, Cliff Green (based on the novel by Southall); ph, Dean Semler; m, George Dreyfus; art d, David Copping; stunts, Grant Page.

Children's Drama Cas. (PR:A MPAA:G)

LET THE PEOPLE LAUGH (SEE: SING AS YOU SWING, 1937, Brit.)

LET THE PEOPLE SING** (1942, Brit.) 105m BN/Anglo-American bw

Alastair Sim (*The Professor*), Fred Emney (*Sir George Denberry-Baxter*), Edward Rigby (*Timmy Tiverton*), Oliver Wakefield (*Sir Reginald Foxfield*), Patricia Roc (*Hope Ollerton*), Annie Esmond (*Lady Foxfield*), Marian Spencer (*Lady Shepshod*), Olive Sloane (*Daisy Barley*), Maire O'Neill (*Mrs. Mitterley*), Gus McNaughton (*Ketley*), Charles Hawtrey (*Orton*), Peter Gawthorne (*Maj. Shiptonthorpe*), Aubrey Mallalieu (*Cmdr. Spofforth*), G. H. Mulcaster (*Inspector*), Wally Patch (*Sam*), Horace Kenney (*Walter*), Morris Harvey (*Jim Flagg*), Ida Barr (*Katie*), Spencer Trevor (*Col. Hazelhead*), David Keir, Charles Doe, Eliot Makeham, Alexander Field, Leopold Glasspoole, Ian Fleming, Robert Aitken, Mignon O'Doherty, Michael Martin-Harvey, Richard George, Diana Beaumont, Stanley Paskin, George Merritt.

A British comedy about an out-of-work comedian and a drunk trying to stop the town council from shutting down the public hall. Sim is a Czech refugee professor.

p&d, John Baxter; w, Baxter, Barbara K. Emary, Geoffrey Orme (based on the novel by J. B. Priestley); ph, James Wilson; m, Kennedy Russell; m/l, Desmond O'Connor, Noel Gray, Frank Eyton.

Comedy (PR:A MPAA:NR)

LET THEM LIVE** (1937) 72m UNIV bw

John Howard (*Dr. Paul Martin*), Nan Grey (*Judith Marshall*), Edward Ellis (*Pete Lindsey*), Judith Barrett (*Rita Johnson*), Robert Wilcox (*Dr. Donald Clipton*), Bennie Bartlett (*Mike*), Henry Kolker (*Judge Lederer*), Robert Warwick (*The Mayor*), William B. Davidson (*The Editor*), Ralph Remley (*Danny*).

Howard is a young doctor trying to break down a crooked political machine. A dying judge gives him a signed confession concerning the political sharks' wrongdoings. Howard also stops an epidemic and falls in love with Grey.

p, Edmund Grainger; d, Harold Young, Donald Gallagher; w, Bruce Manning, Lionel Houser (based on the story "The Stones Cry Out" by Richard Wormser); ph, James Van Trees; ed, John Rawlins; md, Lou Forte.

Drama (PR:A MPAA:NR)

LET US BE GAY** (1930) 82m MGM bw

Norma Shearer (*Kitty Brown*), Rod La Rocque (*Bob Brown*), Marie Dressler (*Mrs. Boucicault*), Gilbert Emery (*Townley*), Hedda Hopper (*Madge Livingston*), Raymond Hackett (*Bruce*), Sally Eilers (*Diane*), Tyrrell Davis (*Wallace*), Wilfred Noy (*Whitman*), William O'Brien (*Struthers*), Sybil Grove (*Perkins*).

When she finds that husband La Rocque has been cheating on her, Shearer divorces him and travels to Paris. There she is transformed from a plain housewife into a glamorous sophisticate. Dressler, a wealthy old woman, wants Shearer to help end the affair between Dressler's granddaughter, Hedda Hopper, and La Rocque. Shearer returns to the States and throws a party with La Rocque and Hopper among the guests. La Rocque doesn't recognize his ex-wife at first, but when he does, the old flame is rekindled and they are reunited.

d, Robert Z. Leonard; w, Frances Marion, Lucille Newmark (based on the play by Rachel Crothers); ph, Norbert Brodine; ed, Basil Wrangell; art d, Cedric Gibbons; cos, Adrian.

Romantic Comedy (PR:A MPAA:NR)

LET US LIVE*** (1939) 66m COL bw

Maureen O'Sullivan (*Mary Roberts*), Henry Fonda ("*Brick*" *Tennant*), Ralph Bellamy (*Lt. Everett*), Alan Baxter (*Joe Lindon*), Stanley Ridges (*District Attorney*), Henry Kolker (*Chief of Police*), Peter Lynn (*Joe Taylor*), George Douglas (*Ed Walsh*), Philip Trent (*Frank Burke*), Martin Spellman (*Jimmy Burke*), Charles Trowbridge (*Judge*), Dick Elliott (*Rotarian Juror*), Alec Craig (*Bookkeeper Juror*), Byron Foulger (*Defense Attorney*), Harry Holman (*Businessman Juror*), Emmett Vogan (*Bank Cashier*), Arthur Loft (*Warden*), Joe De Stefani (*Dentist Juror*), Harry Bradley (*Driver*), Betty Farrington (*Mother Juror*), Al Herman (*Garage Attendant Juror*), Jessie Perry (*Head of P.T.A. Juror*), Billy Lee (*Public Accountant Juror*), Harry Bailey (*Drug Clerk Juror*), Phil Dunham (*Nervous Man Juror*), John Qualen (*Dan*), William Mong (*Joe Taylor, Sr.*), Ian Maclaren (*Priest*), Clarence Wilson (*Lunchroom Proprietor*), Ray Walker (*Fred Robinson*), Beatrice Curtis (*Waitress*), Eddie Laughton (*Cab Driver*), Ann Doran (*Secretary Juror*), Dick Curtis (*Cell Mate*), Jim Blaine, Monte Vandergrift, Ted Oliver (*Detectives*), Herbert Heywood (*Theater Watchman*), William Royle (*Prison Guard*), Edmund Cobb (*Blair*), Tom London (*Police Sergeant*), George Chesebro (*Jail Guard*), Lee Shumway (*Warden's Attendant*), Bess Wade (*Woman*), Philip Morris, Eric Alden, Lee Phelps (*Cops*).

One needn't be a psychic to know how LET US LIVE will end, after just a few minutes of the innocent-man-being-sentenced-to-death-but-beating-the-rap-at-the-last-minute-story. Fonda and Baxter are two innocent men arrested for robbery and murder. They are tried, convicted, and sent to jail to await their execution. O'Sullivan is Fonda's fiancee and believes him to be innocent so she persuades Bellamy, a police lieutenant, to help her clear Fonda and Baxter. Fonda spends most of the movie pacing his cell bewilderedly. Bellamy and O'Sullivan manage to find the real villains and make their evidence known just one hour before Fonda and Baxter are to meet their fates. It is a short, tight film that the studio offered either as a top or bottom feature for a double bill. At the same time, there was a case pending in the Massachusetts courts which was quite similar to the film and the Commonwealth insisted that the studio not trespass too deeply into the reality of the situation. In the actual case, the accused cab drivers were also innocent. Fonda made two other films with nearly the same theme, YOU ONLY LIVE ONCE and Alfred Hitchcock's THE WRONG MAN. Both were superior to this in critical and box office success.

p, William Perlberg; d, John Brahm; w, Anthony Veiller, Allen Rivkin (based on a story by Joseph F. Dineen); ph, Lucien Ballard; m, Karol Rathaus; ed, Al Clark; md, Morris W. Stoloff; art d, Lionel Banks.

Crime (PR:A MPAA:NR)

L'ETOILE DU NORD* (1983, Fr.) 124m Sara-Antenne 2-Gala/UA c

Simone Signoret (*Madame Baron*), Philippe Noiret (*Edouard*), Fanny Cottencon (*Sylvie*), Julie Jezequel (*Antoinette*), Jean Rougerie (*Monsiur Baron*), Jean-Pierre Klein (*Moise*), Jean-Yves Chatelais (*Valesco*), Michel Koniencny (*Domb*), Jean Dautremay (*Engineer*), Patricia Malvoisin (*Arlette*), Gamil Ratib (*Nemrod*), Liliana Gerace (*Jasmina*), Pierre Forget (*Albert*), Julien Bukowsky, Abdallah Chahed, Serge Coursan, Michele Couty, Malek Eddine, Kateb, Slim Mahfoudh, Mohsen Zaaza, Dominique Zardi, Dany Jacquet.

A sickly and insubstantial portrayal by Noiret of a classic psychopath. After meeting a young adventuress (Cottencon) in Egypt, Noiret introduces her to a rich Egyptian, who makes her his mistress. The jealous Noiret gets on the same Brussels-bound train as the Egyptian. The next evening he shows up at a boarding house owned by Signoret, Cottencon's mother. Noiret is a mess and his clothes are bloodstained. He learns that the Egyptian was killed on the train; however, he claims that he remembers nothing. Based on a novel by George Simenon, L'ETOILE DU NORD (the name of the train) is a failure on all fronts, except in the characterization of the killer, but that is so sparse that it is quickly overshadowed by the moronic use of flashbacks. Apparently employed to add intrigue, they only multiply the boredom. Cottencon is inexplicably absent for the picture's second half, while an aging Signoret is unfortunately present. 79-year-old Jean Aurenche, once one of France's "Quality of Tradition" screenwriters, displays none of the talent with which he made his reputation.

p, Alain Sarde; d, Pierre Granier-Deferre; w, Jean Aurenche, Michel Grisolia, Granier-Deferre (based on the novel *La Locataire* by George Simenon); ph, Pierre-William Glenn (Fujicolor); m, Philippe Sarde; ed, Jean Ravel; art d, Dominique Andre; cos, Catherine Letterier.

Crime/Drama **(PR:O MPAA:PG)**

L'ETRANGER (SEE: STRANGER, THE, 1967, Algeria/Fr./Ital.)

LET'S BE FAMOUS** ½

(1939, Brit.) 83m Ealing-Associated Talking Picture/ABE bw

Jimmy O'Dea *(Jimmy Houlihan)*, Betty Driver *(Betty Pinbright)*, Sonnie Hale *(Finch)*, Patrick Barr *(Johnnie Blake)*, Basil Radford *(Watson)*, Milton Rosmer *(Albert Pinbright)*, Lena Brown *(Polly Pinbright)*, Garry Marsh *(BBC Official)*, Alf Goddard *(Battling Bulger)*, Henry Hallett *(Grenville)*, Hay Plumb *(Announcer)*, Franklin Bellamy.

O'Dea leaves his small town in Ireland to get what he thinks is his big singing break on BBC radio. It turns out he's a contestant in a spelling bee, and O'Dea throws a fit on the air. This gets him some publicity and talent agent Hale picks him up. Hale thinks the free press will make O'Dea a singing star; all it does is get Hale fired from his job. The two get drunk, take over a sports broadcast, provide some tipsy hilarity, and are hired as comics.

p, Michael Balcon; d, Walter Forde; w, Roger MacDougal, Allan Mackinnon; ph, Ronald Neame, Gordon Dines; ed, Ray Pitt; art d, O. F. Werndorff.

Comedy **(PR:A MPAA:NR)**

LET'S BE HAPPY** (1957, Brit.) 107m ABE-Pathe/AA c

Vera Ellen *(Jeannie MacLean)*, Tony Martin *(Stanley Smith)*, Robert Flemyng *(Lord James MacNairn)*, Zena Marshall *(Helene)*, Helen Horton *(Sadie Whitelaw)*, Beckett Bould *(Reverend MacDonald)*, Alfred Burke *(French Ticket Clerk)*, Vernon Greeves *(Air Line Steward)*, Richard Molinas *(Bearded Man)*, Eugene Deckers *(Diner Attendant)*, Russell Waters *(Hotel Clerk)*, Paul Young *(Page Boy)*, Peter Sinclair *(MacTavish)*, Magda Miller *(Mrs. MacTavish)*, Brian Oulton *(Hotel Valet)*, Guy Middleton *(Mr. Fielding)*, Katherine Kath *(Mrs. Fielding)*, Charles Carson *(Mr. Ferguson)*, Jock McKay *(Elderly Dancer)*, Michael Anthony *(Monsieur Flor)*, Jean Cadell *(Mrs. Cathie)*, Gordon Jackson *(Dougal MacLean)*, Carl Duering *(Customs Inspector)*, Molly Weir *(Flower Girl)*, Jameson Clark, Ewan Roberts.

Ellen uses her inheritance to visit Scotland, the land of her ancestors. En route she meets salesman Martin, who tries to win her heart. Ellen quickly spends all her money, unbeknownst to once-prosperous Lord Fleming, who is under the impression that she is loaded. When he discovers that she is as poor as he is, he ceases courting her. Returning to the States, Ellen finds Martin waiting for her. This film is a musical reworking of the Aimee Stuart play that also provided the inspiration for JEANNIE (1941) and LET'S BE HAPPY (1952).

p, Marcel Hellman; d, Henry Levin; w, Diana Morgan, Dorothy Cooper (based on the play "Jeannie" by Aimee Stuart); ph, Erwin Hillier (CinemaScope, Technicolor); m, Nicholas Brodszky; ed, E. B. Jarvis; md, Louis Levy; art d, Terence Verity; cos, Anna Duse; ch, Pauline Grant, Alfred Rodrigues; m/l, Paul Francis Webster.

Musical/Comedy **(PR:A MPAA:NR)**

LET'S BE RITZY** (1934) 71m UNIV bw

Lew Ayres *(Jimmie)*, Patricia Ellis *(Ruth)*, Isabel Jewell *(Betty)*, Frank McHugh *(Bill Damroy)*, Berton Churchill *(Pembrook)*, Robert McWade *(Splevin)*, Hedda Hopper *(Mrs. Burton)*, Betty Lawford *(Mrs. Pembrook)*, Clay Clement *(Mr. Hildreth)*, Addison Richards *(Spaulding)*, Adrian Morris *(Henry)*, Lois January *(Stenographer)*.

Ayres and Ellis are newlyweds with no money between them. Poverty strains their marriage and almost gets them kicked out of their apartment. Ayres gets himself and his wife into a number of difficult situations trying to make a buck.

d, Edward Ludwig; w, Harry Sauber, Earle Snell (based on a play by William Anthony McGuire); ph, Charles Stumar; ed, Nathan Carruth.

Comedy **(PR:A MPAA:NR)**

LET'S DANCE** ½ (1950) 112m PAR c

Betty Hutton *(Kitty McNeil)*, Fred Astaire *(Donald Elwood)*, Roland Young *(Mr. Edmund Pohlwhistle)*, Ruth Warrick *(Carola Everett)*, Lucile Watson *(Serena Everett)*, Gregory Moffett *(Richard Everett)*, Barton MacLane *(Larry Channock)*, Shepperd Strudwick *(Timothy Bryant)*, Melville Cooper *(Mr. Charles Wagstaffe)*, Harold Huber *(Marcel)*, George Zucco *(Judge)*, Peggy Badley *(Bubbles Malone)*, Virginia Toland *(Elsie)*, Sayre Dearing *(Process Server)*, Ida Moore *(Mrs. McGuire)*, Nana Bryant *(Mrs. Bryant)*, Boyd Davis *(Butler)*, Bobby Barber *(Bartender)*, Herbert Vigran *(Chili Parlor Owner)*, Rolfe Sedan *(Jewelry Clerk)*, Ralph Peters *(Cab Driver)*, Paul A. Pierce *(Square Dance Caller)*, Eric Alden *(Captain)*, Milton Delugg *(Himself)*, Harry Woods *(Police Lieutenant)*, Chester Conklin *(Watchman)*, Major Sam Harris, Bess Flowers, Marion Gray *(Guests)*, Peggy O'Neill *(Woman)*.

After the enormous success of ANNIE GET YOUR GUN, Paramount decided to pair their top musical star, Hutton, with Astaire, but it didn't work. Filled with cliches, a generally lackluster and witless screenplay, and a failure to ignite, LET'S DANCE has Astaire billed under Hutton. Although he attempted to save the hackneyed story with his feet and grace, it was unsalvageable, and the result is a flat piece of business. Astaire and Hutton are performing overseas for the troops when she reveals that she's just been married to a flier in the service. Dissolve to years later in a Boston brownstone where we discover that her husband died in action, and that she now has a 5-year-old son, Moffett. The house belongs to her late hubby's mother, Watson, a stuffed blouse. Hutton is stifled by the Boston Brahmin life and decides to leave her mean mother-in-law and take up the showbiz cudgels once more. Watson has other plans for Moffett and would never allow that, so Hutton and son leave surreptitiously. Hutton finds Astaire, who is earning a few bucks in a nightspot by evening, but trying to make it as a businessman by day. Astaire helps Hutton get a job at the boite and everyone in the club immediately takes to Hutton and Moffett. But Watson can't stand the thought of her grandson growing up in such a tawdry atmosphere and sends her lawyers out to get the boy back. A custody suit is begun, but when Astaire and Hutton fall in love and decide to make their lives one, Watson has no recourse. There's little entertainment value in LET'S DANCE until the two stars begin to dance, and then the magic of the Astaire feet takes over. There are two numbers that are usually featured in Astairetrospectives (a new word that has no value in the English language for anything other than what it seems); one where he dances on a piano, and the other when he and Hutton have a fleeting moment in which they actually seem to like each other during a cowboy number with the same energy, laughs, and rough-and-tumble moves that Astaire and Garland used in the hobo dance "A Couple of Swells" from EASTER PARADE (1948). It's innovatively choreographed by Pan (a man with whom Astaire worked often and well) and played with great fun by Hutton and Astaire. Other than that, there's not much electricity. LET'S DANCE is far too long and Loesser's score is not nearly as good as much of his other work. Tunes include: "Tunnel of Love," "The Hyacinth," "Piano Dance," "Jack and the Beanstalk," "Can't Stop Talking," "Oh, Them Dudes," and the one song that stepped out to become sort of a standard, "Why Fight the Feeling?" Cooper and Young provide what little humor there is in the movie with their portrayals of two attorneys whom Watson has hired to do the dirty deed of nabbing Moffett away from his mother. Some judicious editing of the long, dull dialog sequences would have helped matters, but the fault lies in the fact that Hutton and Astaire, like smoked salmon on an English muffin, just don't seem to blend.

p, Robert Fellows; d, Norman Z. McLeod; w, Allan Scott, Dane Lussier (based on the story "Little Boy Blue" by Maurice Zolotow); ph, George Barnes (Technicolor); ed, Ellsworth Hoagland; md, Robert Emmett Dolan; art d, Hans Dreier, Roland Anderson; ch, Hermes Pan; m/l, Frank Loesser.

Musical/Comedy **(PR:A MPAA:NR)**

LET'S DO IT (SEE: JUDY'S LITTLE NO-NO, 1969)

LET'S DO IT AGAIN** (1953) 95m COL c

Jane Wyman *(Constance Stuart)*, Ray Milland *(Gary Stuart)*, Aldo Ray *(Frank McGraw)*, Leon Ames *(Chet Stuart)*, Valerie Bettis *(Lilly Adair)*, Tom Helmore *(Courtney Craig)*, Karin Booth *(Deborah Randolph)*, Mary Treen *(Nelly)*, Kathryn Givney *(Mrs. Randolph)*, Herbert Heyes *(Mr. Randolph)*, Maurice Stein *(Willie)*, Frank Remley *(Pete)*, Don Rice *(Hal)*, Don Gibson *(Gas Station Attendant)*, Richard Wessel, Bob Hopkins *(Movers)*, Anthony De Mario *(Wine Steward)*, Herb Vigran *(Charlie the Theater Manager)*, Walter Clinton *(Attendant)*, Frank Connor *(Man)*, Major Sam Harris, Leoda Richards *(Bits)*, Howard Negley *(Charlie the Cop)*, Douglas Evans *(Black Cat Club Manager)*, Joey Ray *(Chauffeur)*.

Wyman is married to womanizing composer Milland and sets out to give him some of his own medicine. She has a harmless affair, but her ploy backfires and the couple get a divorce. Once separated, they try every way to make each other jealous. Wyman is chased by Alaskan millionaire Ray, and Milland uses Booth to try to win back his wife. The film lacks any surprises; it is obvious Wyman and Milland will get back together. LET'S DO IT AGAIN was a musical remake of Columbia's THE AWFUL TRUTH (1937). The songs include "Call of the Wild," "Give Me a Man Who Makes Music," "There Are Things I Remember," "Anyone" (Lester Lee, Ned Washington), "Takin' a Slow Burn" (Lee, Washington—sung by Jane Wyman), "Anyone But You" (Lee, Washington—sung by Dick Haymes).

p, Oscar Saul; d, Alexander Hall; w, Mary Loos, Richard Sale (based on the play "The Awful Truth" by Arthur Richman); ph, Charles Lawton, Jr. (Technicolor); m, George Duning; ed, Charles Nelson; md, Morris Stoloff; art d, Walter Holscher; set d, William Kiernan; cos, Jean Louis; ch, Lee Scott, Valerie Bettis.

Musical/Comedy **(PR:A MPAA:NR)**

LET'S DO IT AGAIN*** (1975) 112m First Artists/WB c

Sidney Poitier *(Clyde Williams)*, Bill Cosby *(Billy Foster)*, Calvin Lockhart *(Biggie Smalls)*, John Amos *(Kansas City Mack)*, Denise Nicholas *(Beth Foster)*, Lee Chamberlin *(Dee Dee Williams)*, Mel Stewart *(Ellison)*, Julius Harris *(Bubbletop Woodson)*, Paul E. Harris *(Jody Tipps)*, Val Avery *(Lt. Bottomley)*, Jimmie Walker *(Bootney Farnsworth)*, Ossie Davis *(Elder Johnson)*, Talya Ferro, Doug Johnson, Richard Young, Cedric Scott *(Biggie's Gang)*, Morgan Roberts *(Fish 'n' Chips Freddie)*, Billy Eckstine *(Zack)*, George Foreman *(Factory Worker)*.

The sequel to UPTOWN SATURDAY NIGHT with Poitier and Cosby again in the starring roles. And again they're trying to raise money for their club, "The Sons And Daughters Of Shaka Lodge." They find a potential bonanza in bony boxer Walker. Poitier hypnotizes him and Walker becomes a boxing dynamo. A solid comedy with Poitier directing.

p, Melville Tucker; d, Sidney Poitier; w, Richard Wesley (based on a story by Timothy March); ph, Donald M. Morgan (Technicolor); m, Curtis Mayfield; ed,

Pembroke J. Herring; prod d, Alfred Sweeney; set d, Ruby R. Levitt; stunts, Henry Kingi.

Comedy   **Cas.**   **(PR:A MPAA:PG)**

LET'S FACE IT** ½   (1943) 76m PAR bw

Bob Hope (*Jerry Walker*), Betty Hutton (*Winnie Potter*), ZaSu Pitts (*Cornelia Pidgeon*), Phyllis Povah (*Nancy Collister*), Dave Willock (*Barney Hilliard*), Eve Arden (*Maggie Watson*), Cully Richards (*Frankie Burns*), Marjorie Weaver (*Jean Blanchard*), Dona Drake (*Muriel*), Raymond Walburn (*Julian Watson*), Andrew Tombes (*Judge Henry Clay Pidgeon*), Arthur Loft (*George Collister*), Joe Sawyer (*Sgt. Wiggins*), Grace Hayle (*Mrs. Wigglesworth*), Evelyn Dockson (*Mrs. Taylor*), Andria Moreland, Brook Evans (*Milk Maids*), Kay Linaker (*Canteen Hostess*), Nicco & Tanya (*Dance Team*), Fredric Nay (*Walsh*), George Meader (*Justice of the Peace*), Joyce Compton (*Wiggins' Girl*), Florence Shirley (*Woman in Sun Shell Cafe*), Barbara Pepper (*Daisy*), Robin Raymond (*Mimi*), Phyllis Ruth (*Lulu*), Lionel Royce (*Submarine Commander*), Emory Parnell (*Colonel*), Don Kerr (*Specialty Dancer*), Edward Dew (*Sergeant*), Eddie Dunn (*Cop*), Elinor Troy (*Elinor*), Eleanor Prentiss (*Joan, A Woman in Court*), Cyril Ring (*Headwaiter*), William B. Davidson (*Man in Boat*), Yvonne De Carlo, Noel Neill, Julie Gibson, Jayne Hazard (*Girls*), Hal Rand, Allen Ray, Jerry James (*Men*), Lena Belle (*Lena*), Helena Brinton (*Helena*), Tommye Adams (*Tommye*), Barbara Brooks (*Barbara*), Ellen Johnson (*Ellen*), Debbra Keith (*Betty*).

A screwball comedy adapted from a stage show by Cole Porter and Herbert and Dorothy Fields (which, in turn, was based on the play "Cradle Snatchers"). Danny Kaye starred on Broadway and Hope takes over his role in this film version. Three wives get tired of their husbands' cheating and hire soldiers to be their escorts. The wives and their military dates end up at the same place their husbands have come with the soldiers' girl friends. This sends up sparks and things snowball from there. The best sequence finds Hope atop a Nazi submarine, sending it aground by flashing a mirror down the periscope. The songs include "Let's Not Talk About Love" (Cole Porter—sung by Betty Hutton), "Let's Face It" (Porter—sung by Dave Willock, Cully Richards), "Who Did? I Did" (Jule Styne, Sammy Cahn—sung by Bob Hope, Hutton).

p, Fred Kohlmar; d, Sidney Lanfield; w, Harry Tugend (based on a musical play by Dorothy and Herbert Fields, Cole Porter from the play "Cradle Snatchers" by Norma Mitchell, Russell G. Medcraft); ph, Lionel Lindon; ed, Paul Weatherwax; md, Robert Emmett Dolan; art d, Hans Dreier, Earl Hedrick; set d, Raymond Moyer.

Musical/Comedy   **(PR:A MPAA:NR)**

LET'S FALL IN LOVE**   (1934) 64m COL bw

Edmund Lowe (*Ken*), Ann Sothern (*Jean*), Miriam Jordan (*Gerry*), Gregory Ratoff (*Max*), Tala Birell (*Forsell*), Arthur Jarrett (*Composer*), Marjorie Gateson (*Agatha*), Betty Furness (*Linda*), Ruth Warren, Greta Meyer, Kane Richmond, John Qualen, Selmer Jackson, Niles Welch, Consuelo Baker, Sven Borg.

Ratoff is a film producer who must find a new leading lady when his Swedish star walks off the set. The director, Lowe, finds Sothern, a sideshow performer, and convinces his producer to use her. Ratoff promotes her as his new Swedish discovery. Sothern and Lowe fall in love during the shooting of the film and Lowe's fiancee goes to the newspaper and spills the beans on Sothern. Songs include "Let's Fall In Love," "Breakfast Ball," "This Is Only The Beginning," "Love Is Love Anywhere" (Harold Arlen, Ted Koehler).

d, David Burton; w, Herbert Fields; ph, Benjamin Kline; ed, Gene Milford; md, Constantin Bakaleinikoff.

Musical   **(PR:A MPAA:NR)**

LET'S GET MARRIED**   (1937) 68m COL bw

Ida Lupino (*Paula Quinn*), Walter Connolly (*Joe Quinn*), Ralph Bellamy (*Kirk Duncan*), Reginald Denny (*George Willoughby*), Raymond Walburn (*Harrington*), Robert Allen (*Charles*), Nana Bryant (*Mrs. Willoughby*), Edward McWade (*Tom*), Emmett Vogan (*Dick*), Will Morgan (*Harry*), Granville Bates (*Hank Keith*), Charles Irwin (*Mike*), Arthur Hoyt (*Minister*), George Ernest (*Billy Norris*), James Flavin (*Dolan*), Vesey O'Davoren (*Butler*), Ted Oliver (*Cop*), Clyde Davis (*Waiter*), Ed Cook (*Boy*), Sherry Hall (*Reporter*).

Lupino's politician father tries to boost the political career of his daughter's socialite suitor. The socialite wins election to Congress but loses Lupino to weatherman Bellamy. Connolly's and Lupino's performances rise above the average material.

p, Everett Riskin; d, Alfred E. Green; w, Ethel Hill (based on a story by A.H.Z. Carr); ph, Henry Freulich; ed, Al Clark.

Comedy   **(PR:A MPAA:NR)**

LET'S GET MARRIED**   (1960, Brit.) 91m Viceroy/Eros bw

Anthony Newley (*Dickie Bird*), Anne Aubrey (*Anne Linton*), Bernie Winters (*Bernie*), Hermione Baddeley (*Mrs. O'Grady*), James Booth (*Photographer*), Lionel Jeffries (*Marsh*), Diane Clare (*Glad*), John Le Mesurier (*Dean*), Victor Maddern (*Works Manager*), Joyce Carey (*Miss Finch*), Sydney Tafler (*Pendle*), Betty Marsden (*Miss Kaplan*), Cardew Robinson (*Salesman*), Meier Tzelniker (*Schutzberger*), Nicholas Parsons (*RAF Officer*), Paul Whitson-Jones (*Uncle Herbert*).

Newley, a medical student who lacks confidence, takes a job as a laundry delivery boy, hoping to become more comfortable with people. He meets and marries Aubrey, a pregnant model whose boy friend has left her. Newley gains the confidence he needs when he is forced to deliver the baby. Newley sings "Do You Mind" and "Let's Get Married." Aubrey sings "Confessions."

p, John R. Sloan; d, Peter Graham Scott; w, Ken Taylor (based on the novel

Confessions of a Kept Woman); ph, Ted Moore; m, Edwin Astley; ed, Ernest Walker.

Drama   **(PR:A MPAA:NR)**

LET'S GET TOUGH**   (1942) 62m BAN/MON bw

Leo Gorcey (*Ethelbert "Muggs" McGinnis*), Huntz Hall (*Glimpy*), Bobby Jordan (*Danny Collins*), "Sunshine Sammy" Morrison (*Scruno*), Bobby Stone (*Skinny*), David Gorcey (*Peewee*), Tom Brown (*Phil Connors*), Florence Rice (*Nora Stevens*), Robert Armstrong (*Officer "Pops" Stevens*), Gabriel Dell (*Fritz Hienbach*), Philip Ahn (*Joe Matsui*), Sam Bernard (*Hienbach Sr.*), Jerry Bergen (*Music Teacher*), Pat Costello (*Navy Recruiter*).

The Bowery Boys fight for their country by giving the once-over to an antique shop owned by a Japanese man. They are shocked to find the man stabbed in his store. It's not long before they get their hands on a secret Japanese message which exposes a Black Dragon Society plot to overthrow the government. Shot during WW II, LET'S GET TOUGH (titled LITTLE MACARTHURS during production) illustrates the country's "anti-Jap" sentiments but is careful to avoid confusion between them and the Chinese. Today the film still doesn't show up on television stations in places like San Francisco and Los Angeles, in deference to those cities' Japanese communities. (See BOWERY BOYS series, Index.)

p, Sam Katzman, Jack Dietz; d, Wallace Fox; w, Harvey Gates (based on the story "I Am An American" by Gates); ph, Art Reed; ed, Robert Golden; md, Johnny Lange, Lew Porter; art d, David Milton.

Comedy   **(PR:A MPAA:NR)**

LET'S GO COLLEGIATE* ½   (1941) 62m MON bw

Frankie Darro (*Frankie*), Marcia Mae Jones (*Bess Martin*), Jackie Moran (*Tad*), Keye Luke (*Buck Wing*), Mantan Moreland (*Jeff*), Gale Storm (*Midge*), Frank Sully (*Herk Bevans*), Barton Yarborough (*Coach*), Frank Faylen (*Speed*), Paul Maxey (*Bill*), Billy Griffith (*Professor*), Marvin Jones (*Homer*), Marguerite Whitten, Tristram Coffin, Gene O'Donnell.

Darro and Moran are members of their college's crew and they've promised their girl friends that the team will win it all. Things go wrong when their best oarsman is drafted. The two college kids get truck driver Sully to take his place and nobody is the wiser. Songs include "Look What You've Done to Me," "Sweet 16" (Harry Tobias, Edward Kay—sung by Gale Storm), "Let's Do A Little Dreaming" (Tobias, Kay—sung by Marcia Mae Jones).

p, Lindsley Parsons; d, Jean Yarbrough; w, Edmond Kelso; ph, Mack Stengler; ed, Jack Ogilvie; md, Edward Kay; art d, Charles Clague.

Musical/Comedy   **(PR:A MPAA:NR)**

LET'S GO NATIVE* ½   (1930) 75m PAR bw

Jack Oakie (*Voltaire McGinnis*), Jeanette MacDonald (*Joan Wood*), James Hall (*Wally Wendell*), William Austin (*Basil Pistol*), Kay Francis (*Constance Cooke*), Charles Sellon (*Grandpa Wendell*), David Newell (*Chief Officer Williams*), Eugene Pallette (*Deputy Sheriff Careful Cuthbert*), Richard "Skeets" Gallagher (*King of the Island*), Rafael Storm (*An Argentinian*), Charlie Hall (*Charlie, a Mover*), Earl Askam, Harry Bernard (*Movers*), Pat Harmon (*Policeman*), Virginia Bruce (*Grandpa Wendell's Secretary*), E. H. Calvert (*Diner Eating Duck*), Grady Sutton (*Diner*), John Elliott (*Captain*), Oscar Smith (*Cook*), The King's Men (*Singers*).

LET'S GO NATIVE is another variation of THE ADMIRABLE CRICHTON (which preceded it), TIGHT LITTLE ISLAND (which followed it) and "Gilligan's Island" (which should put a stop to this kind of picture forever). The only difference is that LET'S GO NATIVE has some songs, and the other movies of the same theme were far funnier. Director McCarey couldn't make the trite script work at all, and the picture didn't have much success, despite starring Oakie and MacDonald, two of the more popular actors of the day. Sellon is a millionaire who wants his son, Hall, to marry MacDonald, a girl of his choosing. Hall rebels and hops a boat going to Argentina. He stokes alongside Oakie, a Brooklyn cab driver who had an accident and can't pay off, so he's departing the U.S. Hall's fiancee, MacDonald, is on board as well, trying to raise money for a show she hopes to present in Buenos Aires. The boat is wrecked and everyone winds up on a lush, tropical island. Gallagher, a dancer, was shipwrecked there sometime before and has taught the natives how to sing and dance. Once on the island, everyone has to wear the theatrical clothing that washed up on shore. MacDonald buys the island from the natives by offering them the costumes for her show (does that sound like the Indians selling Manhattan for $24 in trinkets?). Sellon, who arrives with a rescue party as MacDonald and Hall are falling in love, buys the island from MacDonald (it's filled with oil and gems). But just as the deal is completed, the island sinks as a result of an earthquake. Oakie and Francis have also fallen in love by this time and the picture ends. The idea of Hall and MacDonald, who at first want nothing to do with each other, being thrown together by fate and falling in love, is not new. Matter of fact, very little of the picture is anything but old hat. The best line is spoken by Gallagher, who remarks "This was one of the Virgin Islands, before I got here." Tunes include: "I've Got a Yen for You," "Let's Go Native," "My Mad Moment," "It Seems To Be Spring," "Joe Jazz," and a background music piece by Victor Schertzinger, "Gotta Be Good." Two other songs were written for the film but were either never shot or cut from the release print. They were "Pampa Rose" and "Don't I Do." Co-writer Marion had been a famous silent film title writer before this foray into sound films, which did not enhance his career.

p&d, Leo McCarey; w, George Marion, Jr., Percy Heath; ph, Victor Milner; ch, David Bennett; m/l, Richard A. Whiting, Marion, Jr.

Musical/Comedy   **(PR:A MPAA:NR)**

LET'S GO NAVY***   (1951) 68m MON bw

Leo Gorcey (*Terrence Aloysius "Slip" Mahoney/Dalton B. Dalton*), Huntz Hall

(Horace Debussy "Sach" Jones/Hobenocker), Billy Benedict (Whitey/Schwartz), David Gorcey (Chuck/Merriweather), Buddy Gorman (Butch/Stevenson), Bernard Gorcey (Louie Dumbrowski), Allen Jenkins (Mervin Longnecker), Charlita (Princess Papoola), Paul Harvey (Cmdr. Tannen), Tom Neal (Joe), Richard Benedict (Red), Emory Parnell (Sgt. Mulloy), Douglas Evans (Lt. Smith), Frank Jenks (Shell Game Operator), Tom Kennedy (Donovan, Cop), Dorothy Ford (Kitten), Harry Lauter (Dalton B. Dalton), Dave Willock (Horatio Hobenocker), Peter Mamakos (Nuramo), Ray Walker (Lt. Bradley), Jonathan Hale (Captain), Paul Bryar (Policeman), Richard Monahan (Merriweather), William Lechner (Stevenson), George Offerman, Jr. (Harry Schwartz), Mike Lally (Detective Snyder), Russ Conway (Lt. Moss), Harry Strang (Petty Officer Grompkin), William Vincent (Sailor), Lee Graham (Storekeeper), Pat Gleason (Disbursing Officer), George Eldridge (3rd Officer), William Hudson (1st Aide), Bob Peoples (2nd Aide), John Close (Officer), Emil Sitka (Postman), Ray Dawe (Fat Sailor), Murray Alper (Sailor With Nuramo Tattoo), Jimmy Cross (1st Sailor), Bill Chandler (2nd Sailor), Don Gordon (3rd Sailor), Neyle Morrow (4th Sailor), Joey Ray (5th Sailor).

One of the best from the "Bowery Boys" series with Gorcey and cohorts enlisting in the Navy to catch two thieves. The boys are holding $1600 in charity funds for the Bowery and have it stolen by two men in sailor uniforms. Gorcey and crew join the Navy under assumed names (so they can leave the service when they get the money) and are at sea for a year with no luck in finding the two men. They leave the Navy when Hall wins $2,000 gambling, but this money is stolen by the same two crooks. The boys' captain retrieves the money and through a bureaucratic mistake the boys are reenlisted. This was the 23rd film in the "Bowery Boys" series and the last to be produced by Jan Grippo. (See BOWERY BOYS series, Index.)

p, Jan Grippo; d, William Beaudine; w, Max Adams, Bert Lawrence; ph, Marcel Le Picard; ed, William Austin; md, Edward Kay; art d, Dave Milton; set d, Otto Siegel.

Comedy   **(PR:A MPAA:NR)**

LET'S GO PLACES**   (1930) 70m FOX bw

Joseph Wagstaff (Paul Adams), Lola Lane (Marjorie Lorraine), Sharon Lynn (Virginia Gordon), Frank Richardson (J. Speed Quinn), Walter Catlett (Rex Wardell), Dixie Lee (Dixie), Charles Judels (Du Bonnet), Ilka Chase (Mrs. Du Bonnet), Larry Steers (Ben King), Betty Grable (Chorus Girl), Eddie Kane (Frenchman).

Wagstaff is a young singer who goes to Hollywood to get into films. When he arrives he's mistaken for a famous opera tenor and is given the royal treatment. Wagstaff stays at his look-alike's mansion and gets his start in the movies. Wagstaff loses his girl friend when the tenor's wife claims the impostor (without seeing him) as hers. The tenor arrives and it's discovered that he is Wagstaff's uncle. Originally, the Fox Studios had made a great deal about creating a film musical which would expose some of the things which actually happen in off-screen Hollywood. However, LET'S GO PLACES never lived up to this premise, and hardly differs from other backstage musicals except in locale.

d, Frank Strayer; w, William K. Wells (based on a story by Andrew Bennison); ph, Conrad Wells; ed, Al DeGaetano; ch, Danny Dare.

Musical/Comedy   **(PR:A MPAA:NR)**

LET'S GO STEADY**   (1945) 60m COL bw

Pat Parrish (Linda), Jackie Moran (Roy Spencer), June Preisser (Mable Stack), Jimmy Lloyd (Henry McCoy), Arnold Stang (Chet Carson), Skinnay Ennis (Larry Tyler), Mel Torme ("Streak" Edwards), William Moss (Andy), Byron Foulger (Waldemar Oates), Gladys Blake (Miss Schlepheimer), Eddie Bruce (Fred Williams), William Frambes (Bertram Quill), Skinnay Ennis' Band.

A group of kids from a small town is swindled out of $50 by a phony New York publisher. Looking to be stars, the kids begin to promote themselves by getting a bandleader and a radio station to help with their show. Songs include "Tantza Babele," "Sioux Falls S.D.," "Baby Boogie" (Mel Torme).

p, Ted Richmond; d, Del Lord; w, Erna Lazarus (based on a story by William B. Sackheim); ph, Benjamin Kline; ed, Richard Fantl; art d, Charles Clague; m/l, Mel Torme.

Musical/Comedy   **(PR:A MPAA:NR)**

LET'S GO, YOUNG GUY!*

               (1967, Jap.) 92m Toho c (LET'S GO WAKADAISHO)

Yuzo Kayama (Yuichi Tanuma), Yuriko Hoshi, Bibari Maeda, Akira Takarada, Chen Man Ling, Hoei Tanaka, To Man Rei, Choko Iida.

Poor Japanese comedy features college-boy Kayama getting into a string of not-so-hilarious misadventures at home and in Hong Kong on a soccer trip, where he meets a Chinese lovely. Hard-nosed Japanese prejudice against such "miscegenation" comes to the fore. Proof positive that the Japanese cinema is just as loaded with bad exploitation films as anyone else's.

p, Sanezumi Fujimoto; d, Katsumi Iwauchi; w, Yasuo Tanami; ph, Yuzuru Aizawa (Eastmancolor); m, Kenjiro Hirose.

Comedy   **(PR:A MPAA:NR)**

LET'S HAVE A MURDER   (SEE: STICK 'EM UP, 1950, Brit.)

LET'S HAVE FUN   (SEE: LAUGH YOUR BLUES AWAY, 1943)

LET'S KILL UNCLE***   (1966) 92m UNIV c

Nigel Green (Maj. Harrison), Mary Badham (Chrissie), Pat Cardi (Barnaby Harrison), Robert Pickering (Travis), Linda Lawson (Justine), Reff Sanchez (Ketchman), Nestor Paiva (Steward).

One of producer-director Castle's chilling productions. Cardi is a 12-year-old boy whose father died and left him a great deal of money. His uncle, Green, summons

him to a tropical island where he plans to kill the boy and collect the inheritance. Badham is the young girl who helps Cardi combat his uncle. Green, who wrote a book on how to kill, uses sharks, poison mushrooms, tarantulas, fire, and hypnotism to try to put the kid six feet under. The children begin to pursue the uncle and the affair becomes a constantly shifting game of cat and mouse. Green finally tires, calls it a draw, and leaves the island. A well-paced thriller with good performances from the two young stars (Badham played the young girl in TO KILL A MOCKINGBIRD).

p&d William Castle; w, Mark Rodgers (based on the novel by Rohan O'Grady); ph, Harold Lipstein (Technicolor); m, Herman Stein; ed, Edwin H. Bryant; art d, Alexander Golitzen, William D. DeCinces; set d, John McCarthy, Julia Heron.

Thriller   **(PR:C MPAA:NR)**

LET'S LIVE A LITTLE**   (1948) 85m United California/EL bw

Hedy Lamarr (Dr. J. O. Loring), Robert Cummings (Duke Crawford), Anna Sten (Michele Bennett), Robert Shayne (Dr. Richard Field), Mary Treen (Miss Adams), Harry Antrim (James Montgomery), Hal K. Dawson (M.C.), Billy Bevan (Morton), Curt Bois (Chemist), John Newland (Newcomb), Jimmy Dodd (Lewis), Frank Sully (Artist), Oliver Blake (Photographer), John Dehner (Dempster), Frank Wilcox (Salesman), Eve Whitney (Miss O'Reilly), Eddie Parks (Cruickshank), Norma Varden (Nurse Brady), Leo Mostovoy (Pierre), Lillian Randolph (Sarah), Virginia Farmer (Mrs. Harris), Paul Maxey (Mr. Stevens), Lucien Littlefield (Mr. Tinker), Regina Wallace (Mrs. Lansworth), Byron Foulger (Mr. Hopkins).

LET'S LIVE A LITTLE is like an Indianapolis racer that leads the pack for several laps then runs out of gas a mile or so from the checkered flag. Cummings is an advertising man who is vainly attempting to extricate himself from a lingering love affair with Sten. Unfortunately, Sten's bank account is huge and she also holds the strings on a large account for his company that she won't renew unless he agrees to keep their flame fanned. Cummings is driven to fits of neurosis and is removed from Sten's account, then is assigned to promote a new tome by Lamarr, a gorgeous psychiatrist. He meets her and is soon in her spell, confessing his problems to her. He says he is being driven to hallucinations by the whole matter and Lamarr suggests, as only a movie analyst might, that he shower Sten with attention. It may help matters. Cummings takes Sten to a nightspot and Lamarr is off to the side to watch the tactics. When Lamarr and Sten meet, Sten, no dummy she, suspects that Cummings may have more on his mind than a patient-doctor relationship with Lamarr. Sten starts an argument and Cummings crumbles, something he did for many years so well on television. Lamarr thinks that Cummings could use some rest so she takes him off to the country where they, of course, fall head over couch for each other. That is threatened when Cummings hears Lamarr tell a colleague that she is using Cummings as a case study and becomes one more off the handle. Cummings returns to Gotham and Sten who insists that they become affianced before she'll sign the renewal agreement with his company. When Lamarr hears that Cummings and Sten are to marry, she forgets her Hippocratic oath, becomes as nervous as Cummings was in the first reel, and eventually wins him back. LET'S LIVE A LITTLE begins quickly and tight, then starts to unravel somewhere in the middle. Cummings, who also co-produced, was adequate and Lamarr was, as usual, beautiful, but she was never a great comedian and that's a gift that an actor has or hasn't. She hasn't. Laszlo's photography was a definite plus and made the picture look better than it was.

p, Eugene Frenke, Robert Cummings; d, Richard Wallace; w, Howard Irving Young, Edmund Hartmann, Albert J. Cohen (based on a story by Cohen, Jack Harvey); ph, Ernest Laszlo; m, Werner Heymann; ed, Arthur Hilton; md, Irving Friedman; art d, Edward L. Ilou; set d, Armor Marlowe, Robert P. Fox; cos, Elois Jenssen; spec eff, George J. Teague; makeup, Ern Westmore, Joe Stinton.

Comedy   **(PR:A MPAA:NR)**

LET'S LIVE AGAIN**   (1948) 68m FOX bw

John Emery, James Millican, Taylor Holmes, Diana Douglas, Hillary Brooke, Charles D. Brown, Jeff Corey, Percy Helton, John Parrish, Earle Hodgins, Dewey Robinson, Ralph D. Sanford, Rags the Dog.

An enjoyably stupid picture about an atomic scientist who imagines that his missing adventurer-brother has been reincarnated as a dog. Of course, everyone thinks he's nuts and they put him in the loony bin. It all gets straightened out by the end, though.

p, Frank Seltzer; d, Herbert I. Leeds; w, Rodney Carlisle, Robert Smiley (based on a story by Herman Wohl, John Vlahos); ph, Mack Stengler; m, Ralph Stanley; ed, Bert Jordan; md, David Chudnow; art d, Jerome Pycha, Jr.

Comedy   **(PR:A MPAA:NR)**

LET'S LIVE TONIGHT*½   (1935) 75m COL bw

Lillian Harvey (Kay Routledge), Tullio Carminati (Nick Kerry), Janet Beecher (Mrs. Routledge), Hugh Williams (Brian Kerry), Tala Birell (Countess Margot De Legere), Luis Alberni (Mario), Claudia Coleman (Lily Montrose), Arthur Treacher (Ozzy Featherstone), Gilbert Emery (Maharajah).

Two rich brothers, Carminati and Williams, chase after the same woman, Harvey. The chasing goes on in ritzy Monte Carlo and it's Carminati, the older brother, who finally wins out.

p, Robert North; d, Victor Schertzinger; w, Gene Markey (based on a story by Bradley King); ph, Joseph Walker; ed, Gene Milford; m/l, "Love Passes By," Schertzinger (sung by Tullio Carminati).

Romantic Comedy   **(PR:A MPAA:NR)**

LET'S LOVE AND LAUGH   (SEE: BRIDEGROOM FOR TWO, 1932, Brit.)

LET'S MAKE A MILLION*½   (1937) 61m PAR bw

Charlotte Wynters (Caroline), Edward Everett Horton (Harrison Gentry), Porter

Hall *(Spencer)*, J.M. Kerrigan *(Sam Smith)*, Margaret Seddon *(Aunt Martha)*, Margaret McWade *(Aunt Lucy)*, Purnell Pratt *(Gilbert)*, Irving Bacon *(Jerry)*, Ivan Miller *(Peter Winton)*.

A dull comedy about a WW I veteran (Horton) who gets his bonus money from the government and the problems it causes him. He gets married, his aunts try to tell him how he should spend the money, and he finally invests in oil. Con artists show up in his town and swindle everybody who buys their fake petroleum futures. Horton sets up his drill and at the end of the film hits a gusher.

p, Harold Hurley; d, Ray McCarey; w, Robert Yost, Manuel Seff (based on a story by Lawrence Pohle, Thomas Ahearne); ph, Karl Struss.

Comedy **(PR:A MPAA:NR)**

LET'S MAKE A NIGHT OF IT* 1/2 (1937, Brit.) 92m ABF/UNIV bw

Charles "Buddy" Rogers *(Jack Kent)*, June Clyde *(Peggy Boydell)*, Claire Luce *(Viola Vanders)*, Fred Emney *(Henry Boydell)*, Iris Hoey *(Laura Boydell)*, Jack Melford *(Count Castelli)*, Claud Allister *(Monty)*, Steve Geray *(Luigi)*, Antony Holles *(Headwaiter)*, Lawrence Anderson *(Harold)*, Zelma O'Neal *(Kitty)*, Bertha Belmore *(Policewoman)*, Syd Walker *(Policeman)*, Oliver Wakefield *(Wedding Guest)*, Dan Donovan *(Street Singer)*, Afrique *(Impersonations)*, Brian Michie *(Compere)*, Irene Prador, Molly Picon, Four Franks, Peggy and Ready, Four Aces, Josephine Bradley, Percy Athos Follies, Jack Jackson and His Band, Jack Harris and His Band, Sydney Lipton and His Band, Joe Loss and His Band, Eddie Carroll and His Band, Harry Acres and His Band, Rudy Starita's Marimba Band.

A British musical comedy about a husband and wife who own competing nightclubs. The comedy seems to be missing, the music isn't worth humming, and you'll probably fall asleep after the first 10 minutes.

p, Walter C. Mycroft; d, Graham Cutts; w, F. McGrew Willis, Hugh Brooke (based on the radio play "The Silver Spoon" by Henrik N. Ege); ph, Otto Kanturek, Claude Friese-Greene; md, Harry Acres; m/l, Michael Carr, Jimmy Kennedy, Ray Noble, Allan Murray.

Musical/Comedy **(PR:A MPAA:NR)**

LET'S MAKE IT LEGAL 1/2** (1951) 77m Robert Bassler/FOX bw

Claudette Colbert *(Miriam)*, Macdonald Carey *(Hugh)*, Zachary Scott *(Victor)*, Barbara Bates *(Barbara Denham)*, Robert Wagner *(Jerry Denham)*, Marilyn Monroe *(Joyce)*, Frank Cady *(Ferguson)*, Jim Hayward *(Gardener)*, Carol Savage *(Miss Jessup)*, Paul Gerrits *(Milkman)*, Betty Jane Brown *(Secretary)*, Vici Raaf *(Hugh's Secretary)*, Joan Fisher *(Baby Annabella)*, Kathleen Freeman, Rennie McEvoy, Wilson Wood, James Magill, Roger Moore, Beverly Thompson *(Reporters)*, Abe Dinvitch, Frank Sully *(Laborers)*, Jack Mather, Michael Ross *(Policemen)*, Harry Denny *(Hotel Manager)*, Harry Harvey, Sr. *(Mailman)*, Ralph Sanford *(Police Lieutenant)*.

Colbert divorces her husband, Carey, after being married for twenty years. She leaves him because he's a chronic gambler. Their daughter, Bates, tries to get them back together. Colbert's old flame, Scott, comes back into town and he's become a millionaire. He begins seeing her again and when Carey finds out he goes out of his way to try to split them apart. Scott informs her that he and Carey had rolled dice to see who would get her. Scott lost and left town. She finds out from her ex-husband that he rolled with loaded dice to ensure that he didn't lose her. The two make up and everything ends on an upbeat note. Marilyn Monroe has a co-starring role as a man-hunter.

p, Robert Bassler; d, Richard Sale; w, F. Hugh Herbert, I. A. L. Diamond (based on a story by Mortimer Braus); ph, Lucien Ballard; m, Cyril J. Mockridge; ed, Robert Fritch; md, Lionel Newman; art d, Lyle Wheeler, Albert Hogsett.

Comedy **(PR:A MPAA:NR)**

LET'S MAKE LOVE 1/2** (1960) 118m FOX c

Marilyn Monroe *(Amanda)*, Yves Montand *(Jean-Marc Clement)*, Tony Randall *(Howard Coffman)*, Frankie Vaughan *(Tony Danton)*, Wilfrid Hyde-White *(John Wales)*, David Burns *(Oliver Burton)*, Michael David *(Dave Kerry)*, Mara Lynn *(Lily Nyles)*, Dennis King, Jr. *(Abe Miller)*, Joe Besser *(Lamont)*, Madge Kennedy *(Miss Manners)*, Ray Foster *(Jimmy)*, Mike Mason *(Yale)*, John Craven *(Comstock)*, Harry Cheshire *(Minister)*, Larry Thor *(Wilson)*, Richard Fowler *(Van Cliburn)*, John Gatti *(Elvis Presley)*, Marian Manners *(Maria Callas)*, Oscar Beregi *(Chauffeur)*, Geraldine Wall *(Miss Hansen)*, Milton Berle, Bing Crosby, Gene Kelly *(Guest Stars)*.

Monroe's 28th picture was supposed to be a satire of Howard Hughes entitled "The Billionaire," but Fox's lawyers must have advised nix, and it became a sort of later version of ON THE AVENUE, made in 1937 by the same studio. Montand is a billionaire industrialist who is told by his attorney, Hyde-White, and his public relations man, Randall, that an off-Broadway satire of him is being planned and is now in rehearsals. Montand and Randall go to the theater and see Monroe doing "My Heart Belongs To Daddy" (in one of her very best song renditions ever). The show has no one to play Montand, and the director thinks he is an actor who has come to audition for the role. As Montand looks a great deal like the lead, he is hired instantly by producer Burns. He accepts the job to get closer to Monroe, who says that she doesn't care a whit for rich men. Montand needlessly fears Monroe and Vaughan, the star of the revue, are an item. It turns out that Montand's firm owns the building, and some of his aides intend to close it down. Randall gets drunk and tells off Montand for the deed, but Montand, who didn't even know he owned the place, stops the foreclosure. Now, using Hyde-White as his agent, Montand puts money into the show. Montand knows that he has no show-business talent, so what does a billionaire do when he wants to learn to sing, dance, and be funny? He hires Crosby, Kelly, and Berle to teach him the tricks of the trade. Several more plot twists until Montand and Monroe wind up in an elevator and realize they are in love. This was Vaughan's first U.S. film after a highly successful music-hall career in England. LET'S MAKE LOVE was glossy, glitzy, glamorous, and had as much wit as one finds in the average Frankenstein film—in other words, hardly any. Surprising when you look at the authors, both veterans of comedy. The only redeeming qualities of the picture are Monroe's luminescence and Randall's delicious underplaying. Director Cukor would work together again with Monroe in 1962 in the film SOMETHING'S GOT TO GIVE during which she suddenly died. Tunes include: "Let's Make Love," "Specialization," "Incurably Romantic," "Sing Me a Song That Sells," "You with the Crazy Eyes" (Jimmy Van Heusen, Sammy Cahn); "Give Me the Simple Life" (Rube Bloom, Harry Ruby); and Cole Porter's classic mentioned earlier.

p, Jerry Wald; d, George Cukor; w, Norman Krasna, Hal Kanter; ph, Daniel L. Fapp (CinemaScope, DeLuxe Color); m, Lionel Newman; ed, David Bretherton; md, Newman; art d, Lyle R. Wheeler, Gene Allen; cos, Dorothy Jeakinsch; ch, Jack Cole.

Musical Comedy **(PR:AA MPAA:NR)**

LET'S MAKE MUSIC** (1940) 82m Howard Benedict/RKO bw

Bob Crosby *(Himself)*, Jean Rogers *(Abby Adams)*, Elisabeth Risdon *(Malvina Adams)*, Joseph Buloff *(Joe Bellah)*, Joyce Compton *(Betty)*, Bennie Bartlett *(Tommy)*, Louis Jean Heydt *(Mr. Stevens)*, Bill Goodwin *(Announcer)*, Frank Orth *(Mr. Botts)*, Grant Withers *(Headwaiter)*, Walter Tetley *(Eddie)*, Benny Rubin *(Music Publisher)*, Jacqueline Nash *(Singer)*, Donna Jean Dolfer *(Pianist)*, Bob Crosby's Orchestra with The Bobcats.

Bandleader Bob Crosby's feature film debut. The screenplay by famed author Nathanael West is little more than a mildly comical vehicle for a few tunes. Crosby's radio-show scriptwriters provided the puerile passages issuing from Bing's brother's own mouth. The story deals with a maiden-lady music teacher whose corny composition is adopted by a hip musical group as a novelty number. The song's a smash, and the teacher is invited to join the ensemble and make with the boogie. Songs include the sudden smash, "Fight On For Newton High" (Roy Webb, Dave Dreyer, Herman Ruby), "The Big Noise From Winnetka" (Bob Crosby, Ray Haggart, Gil Rodin, Ray Bauduc), "Central Park" (Johnnie Mercer, Matt Malneck), "You Forgot About Me" (Richard Robertson, Sammy Mysels, Jimmy Hanley).

p, Howard Benedict; d, Leslie Goodwins; w, Nathanael West (special dialog by Helen Phillips, Bernard Dougall); ph, Jack Mackenzie; ed, Desmond Marquette; md, Roy Webb; art d, Van Nest Polglase.

Musical **(PR:A MPAA:NR)**

LET'S MAKE UP**
(1955, Brit.) 94m Everest/UA bw/c (GB: LILACS IN THE SPRING)

Anna Neagle *(Carole Beaumont/Lillian Grey/Queen Victoria/Nell Gwyn)*, Errol Flynn *(John Beaumont)*, David Farrar *(Charles King/King Charles)*, Kathleen Harrison *(Kate)*, Peter Graves *(Albert Gutman/Prince Albert)*, Helen Haye *(Lady Drayton)*, Scott Sanders *(Old George)*, Alma Taylor *(1st Woman)*, Hetty King *(2nd Woman)*, Alan Gifford *(Hollywood Director)*, Jennifer Mitchell *(Young Carole)*, Gillian Harrison *(Very Young Carole)*, George Margo *(Reporter)*, Sean Connery.

Producer Wilcox offered to help bail out the near-bankrupt, aging actor Flynn in return for the latter's services in this vehicle for the producer's wife, Neagle, based on a successful stage play in which she had starred. Neagle plays a WW II stage star who is uncertain about which of two suitors, Farrar or Graves, to accept as husband. Injured during an air raid, she dreams (with a sudden switch from black-and-white to color) while unconscious that she is famed historical courtesan Nell Gwyn, hotly pursued by rakehell King Charles, played by Farrar. Recovering from her injury, she seeks rest in the country house of the German-born grandmother of suitor Graves. Blacking out again, she dreams herself to be a young Queen Victoria, introducing the waltz to her domain, with Graves as her consort, Prince Albert. In a third flight of imagination, Neagle reprises her own mother's history—an entertainer like herself who, in an earlier war, married song-and-dance man Flynn. Husband Flynn plays Svengali to her Trilby, helping her achieve stardom, then steps aside into obscurity. Flynn travels to America, attaining fame in films, and ultimately the two stars are reunited. Awakening again, and fully recovered, Neagle decides about her two suitors. The aging Flynn, ravaged by drink, handled his singing-dancing part surprisingly well; he had, after all, done a great deal of well-choreographed swordplay. Neagle was her usual charming self. Look for Sean Connery in an early bit part. Songs include the music-hall classics "Lily of Laguna," "Blighty," "We'll Gather Lilacs," and "Tipperary," as well as "Lassie From Lancashire" (John Neal) and "Dance Little Lady" (Noel Coward).

p&d, Herbert Wilcox; w, Harold Purcell (based on the play "The Glorious Days" by Robert Nesbitt); ph, Max Greene (Trucolor); m, Harry Parr Davies; ed, Reginald Beck; ch, Philip and Betty Buchel.

Fantasy **(PR:A MPAA:NR)**

LET'S ROCK* 1/2 (1958) 78m COL bw (GB: KEEP IT COOL)

Julius La Rosa *(Tommy Adane)*, Phyllis Newman *(Kathy Abbott)*, Conrad Janis *(Charlie)*, Joy Harman *(Pickup Girl)*, Fred Kareman *(Monk)*, Pete Paull *(Gordo)*, Charles Shelander *(Clinch)*, Wink Martindale *(Himself)*, Harold Gary *(Shep Harris)*, Jerry Hackady *(Floor Manager)*, Ron McLewdon *(Engineer)*, Ned Wertimer *(Studio Manager)*, Tony Brande *(Bartender)*, Danny and the Juniors, Paul Anka, The Royal Teens, Della Reese, Roy Hamilton, The Tyrones.

A routine 1950s rock 'n' roll movie with La Rosa as a ballad singer who won't change over to rock. Janis is his manager and Newman his sweetheart and together the two convince the ballad singer that the only way to sell records is to rock and roll. Only stand-outs are Danny and the Juniors doing "At The Hop" and the Royal Teens with "Short Shorts." Other songs include, "Crazy, Crazy Party," "Two Perfect Strangers," "Casual," "There Are Times," "Here Comes Love," "The Secret Paths Of Love," and "Lonelyville."

p&d, Harry Foster; w, Hal Hackady; ph, Jack Etra; ed, S. Charles Rawson; art d, Paul Barnes.

Musical Drama (PR:A MPAA:NR)

LET'S SCARE JESSICA TO DEATH** (1971) 89m Jessica-PAR c

Zohra Lampert *(Jessica)*, Barton Heyman *(Duncan)*, Kevin O'Connor *(Woody)*, Gretchen Corbett *(Girl)*, Alan Manson *(Dorker)*, Mariclare Costello *(Emily)*.

Lampert is released from a mental hospital and moves to a farmhouse in Connecticut with her husband Heyman and family friend O'Connor. A strange woman, Corbett, is found at their house and Lampert discovers that she's a vampire. There are also living dead parading around town, and no one believes Lampert's stories. She begins to think she's having another breakdown. It seems her husband and friends may have something planned for Lampert, but they're the ones who are getting killed. A fair horror film, thanks to director Hancock (director of BANG THE DRUM SLOWLY). This was his debut film and he was able to work over the poor script and pull off an adequate shocker. Lampert does her usual mindlessly groping performance.

p, Charles B. Moss, Jr.; d, John Hancock; w, Norman Jonas, Ralph Rose; ph, Bob Baldwin; m, Orville Stoeber (electronic music, Walter Sear); ed, Murray Soloman, Joe Ryan; set d, Norman Kenneson; cos, Mariette Pinchart; makeup, Irvin Carlton.

Horror Cas. (PR:C MPAA:GP)

LET'S SING AGAIN** (1936) 70m Principal Productions/RKO bw

Bobby Breen *(Billy Gordon)*, Henry Armetta *(Joe Pasquale)*, George Houston *(Leon Albe)*, Vivienne Osborne *(Rosa Donelli)*, Grant Withers *(Diablo)*, Inez Courtney *(Marge)*, Lucien Littlefield *(Perkins)*, Richard Carle *(Carter)*, Clay Clement *(Jackson)*, Ann Doran *(Alice Albe)*.

Eight-year-old boy soprano Breen runs away from an orphanage and joins a traveling show. He's "adopted" by washed-up opera singer Armetta, who helps develop the young boy's singing voice. When he becomes ill, Armetta takes Breen to New York and during an opera performance Breen is reunited with his real father. This was Breen's screen debut and the first of a series of Breen musicals produced by Sol Lesser's Principal Productions. Breen got his start in show business on the Eddie Cantor radio show. Songs include "Let's Sing Again" (Jimmy McHugh, Gus Kahn), "Lullaby" (Hugo Riesenfeld, Selma Hautzik), "Farmer In The Dell" (Samuel Pokrass, Charles O. Locke, Richard E. Tyler), "La Donna e Mobile" from Giuseppe Verdi's opera "Rigoletto."

p, Sol Lesser; d, Kurt Neumann; w, Don Swift, Dan Jarrett; ph, Harry Neumann; ed, Robert Crandall; md, Hugo Reisenfeld.

Musical (PR:A MPAA:NR)

LET'S TALK ABOUT WOMEN***
(1964, Fr./Ital.) 108m Fair-CON/EM bw (SE PERMETTETE; PARLIAMO DI DONNE)

1st Episode: Vittorio Gassman *(Stranger)*, Maria Fiore *(Fearful Wife)*; 2nd Episode: Gassman *(Practical Joker)*, Donatella Mauro *(His Wife)*, Mario Lucidi *(Son)*; 3rd Episode: Gassman *(Client)*, Giovanna Ralli *(Prostitute)*, Umberto D'Orsi *(Old Friend)*; 4th Episode: Gassman *(Lover)*, Antonella Lualdi *(Fiancee)*; 5th Episode: Gassman *(Impatient Lover)*, Sylva Koscina *(Reluctant Girl)*, Edda Ferronao *(Willing Maid)*; 6th Episode: Gassman *(Waiter)*, Heidi Stroh *(Pick-Up)*; 7th Episode: Gassman *(Timid Brother)*, Rosanna Gherardi *(Dishonored Sister)*, Olga Romanelli *(Distraught Mother)*, Walter Chiari *(Philanderer)*, Ivy Olsen *(Pick-Up)*; 8th Episode: Gassman *(Rag Man)*, Eleonora Rossi-Drago *(Indolent Lady)*; 9th Episode: Gassman *(Prisoner)*, Jeanne Valerie *(His Wife)*, Marco Tulli *(Other Man)*, Attilio Dottesio *(Prison Official)*.

A captivating Italian comedy made up of nine episodes about Gassman's encounters with various women, including prostitutes and married ladies. One of the better skits has Gassman visiting a hooker and recognizing a picture of her husband as an old chum. She brings him back to her house for a reunion, during which the husband refuses to let Gassman pay for the wife/hooker's services. In another episode, Gassman is a rag dealer who pays a visit to a wealthy and promiscuous woman for her rag collection. She tries instead to give him her body, but he declines, stating that he prefers material goods.

p, Mario Cecchi Gori; d, Ettore Scola; w, Scola, Ruggero Maccari; ph, Sandro D'Eva; m, Armando Trovaioli; ed, Marcello Malvestiti; art d, Arrigo Breschi; m/l, "Ogni Volta" by C. A. Rossi (sung by Paul Anka).

Comedy (PR:C MPAA:NR)

LET'S TALK IT OVER*½ (1934) 68m UNIV bw

Chester Morris *(Mike McGann)*, Mae Clarke *(Pat Rockland)*, Frank Craven *(Mr. Rockland)*, John Warburton *(Alex Winters)*, Irene Ware *(Sandra)*, Andy Devine *(Gravel)*, Russ Brown *(Bill)*, Anderson Lawler *(Peter)*, Goodee Montgomery *(Helen Wray)*, Douglas Fowley *(Sailor Jones)*, Herbert Corthell *(Butler)*, Jane Darwell *(Mrs. O'Keefe)*, Willard Robertson *(Dr. Preston)*, Frank Reicher *(Richards)*, Henry Armetta *(Tony)*, Otis Harlan *(Purser)*, Tom Dugan *(Tough Man)*.

A princess-and-the-plebian romantic comedy with the clever Clarke, a moneyed miss, attempting to catch the attention of an insouciant playboy. Failing to meet him through more conventional channels, she fakes a mishap with a watery one, hoping that he will play lifeguard and fish her out of the briny deep. Instead, brash roughneck sailor Morris reacts and pulls off the "rescue." Amidst her snooty friends, she amuses herself by patronizing the gabby gob, betting her peers that she can pull a Pygmalion and make him socially acceptable. Clarke lands Morris a job with her uncle's (Craven) brokerage house and proceeds to turn him into a silk purse. Morris discovers the terms of the bet and reacts with rage (you can dress him up, but you can't take him anywhere), crashing her car and injuring himself. Reacting to the reality of his pain, she discovers she loves the macho miscreant. Predictable but pleasant.

p, B.F. Zeldman; d, Kurt Neumann; w, John Meehan, Jr. (based on the story "Loves of a Sailor" by Dore Schary, Lewis Foster); ph, Charles Stumar.

Drama (PR:A MPAA:NR)

LET'S TRY AGAIN** (1934) 64m RKO bw (GB: MARRIAGE SYMPHONY)

Diana Wynyard *(Alice Overton)*, Clive Brook *(Dr. Jack Overton)*, Irene Hervey *(Marge)*, Helen Vinson *(Nan Duval)*, Theodore Newton *(Paul)*, Arthur Hoyt *(Phillips)*, Henry Kolker.

Brook is a physician who is married to Wynyard and both are contemplating affairs and divorce. Wynyard starts an affair with Newton and when Brook finds out, he's surprised that he doesn't really care. The couple begin divorce proceedings, but find that even after being married for ten years, there is still a spark in their relationship. That's about the only spark in this tedious, moralistic film.

p, Myles Connolly; d, Worthington Miner; w, Miner, Allen Scott (based on the play "Sour Grapes" by Vincent Lawrence); ph, J. Roy Hunt; m, Max Steiner; ed, Ralph Dietrich.

Drama (PR:A MPAA:NR)

LETTER, THE* (1929) 62m PAR bw

Jeanne Eagels *(Leslie Crosbie)*, O. P. Heggie *(Joyce)*, Reginald Owen *(Robert Crosbie)*, Herbert Marshall *(Geoffry Hammond)*, Irene Brown *(Mrs. Joyce)*, Lady Tsen Mei *(Li-Ti)*, Tamaki Yoshiwara *(Ong Chi Sing)*, Kenneth Thomson.

Western Electric disc sound synchronization was used for this, the first feature film made at Paramount's Long Island studio, and audiences found it to be very well done. Maugham's play about a married woman in the far-eastern colonies who kills her faithless lover is filled with shades of gray; its non-judgmental author was essentially concerned with presenting the subtleties of the human condition to his audience. From its shock opening—Eagels firing shots into her lover's already lifeless body—to its equally dramatic finale, the film bears the mark of a masterful playwright. The willowy, charismatic Eagels made three silent films; this was her first talkie. She died of a heroin overdose shortly after the film's release. The picture marked the American screen debuts of actors Marshall and Owen; Marshall later played the husband opposite Bette Davis in the 1940 remake.

p, Monta Bell; d, Jean De Limur; w, Garrett Fort, Bell, De Limur (based on the play by Somerset Maugham); ph, George Folsey; ed, De Limur, Bell.

Drama (PR:A MPAA:NR)

LETTER, THE**** (1940) 95m WB bw

Bette Davis *(Leslie Crosbie)*, Herbert Marshall *(Robert Crosbie)*, James Stephenson *(Howard Joyce)*, Gale Sondergaard *(Mrs. Hammond)*, Bruce Lester *(John Withers)*, Elizabeth Earl *(Adele Ainsworth)*, Cecil Kellaway *(Prescott)*, Victor Sen Yung *(Ong Chi Seng)*, Doris Lloyd *(Mrs. Cooper)*, Willie Fung *(Chung Hi)*, Tetsu Komai *(Head Boy)*, Leonard Mudie *(Fred)*, John Ridgely *(Driver)*, Charles Irwin, Holmes Herbert *(Bob's Friends)*, Douglas Walton *(Well-Wisher)*, David Newell *(Geoffrey Hammond)*, Frieda Inescort, Roland Got, Otto Hahn, Pete Kotehernaro, Ottola Nesmith, Lillian Kemple-Cooper.

Newell visits Davis' Malayan rubber plantation while her husband Marshall is away on business and Davis shoots him to death. She later states that old family friend Newell tried to attack her and she merely defended herself. Marshall, the ever-faithful husband, believes her without question and asks Stephenson, an accomplished lawyer, to defend her. Stephenson then receives word that Newell's Eurasian widow, Sondergaard, has a letter written by Davis to her deceased husband, asking him to come to her on the night he was killed. When confronted with this news, Davis coldly admits murdering Newell and that he was her lover. Taking pity on her, Stephenson agrees to buy the letter for $10,000 from Sondergaard, her blackmail price. Meanwhile, he makes little of the missive to Marshall who tells him to buy it back. Sondergaard insists that she will not turn the letter over unless Davis claims it personally. Davis is freed of a murder charge in court and returns home to Marshall. When he discovers that all his savings have been spent for the letter, he demands Davis tell him what it contains. She admits everything but the always forgiving Marshall tells her he loves her still, but he is a shambles. As Davis walks into the garden, Sondergaard appears with a henchman and stabs Davis to death. Police stop them when they attempt to flee. Maugham's story could have been easily turned into sappy melodrama but under Wyler's magnificent handling of the story and Davis' taut and calculated performance, high art was attained. THE LETTER is as good today as it was when first filmed. Marshall, who had played the lover in an earlier version of the film, is excellent as the long-suffering husband, but Stephenson really steals all his scenes as the honest lawyer putting his career in jeopardy for a friend. Oddly, the unpredictable Jack Warner asked Wyler to test Stephenson for the role and when the director stated that he was superior to anything he expected, Warner balked at casting him as the lawyer. "I didn't realize this was such an important part," Warner told Wyler, "I mean this fellow is just in stock here. Maybe you should use a better name." Wyler insisted upon keeping Stephenson, oddly having to fight for an actor Warner had originally suggested. Davis and her famous temperament sometimes vexed Wyler but the ever patient director persuaded her to play the scenes his way. At the point where Davis is to tell her husband Marshall of her posthumous devotion to her dead lover, the very man she killed, uttering the line: "I still love the man I killed," Davis felt that she could not say such a line face to face to Marshall, her understanding husband. Wyler insisted she not turn away, but say it to his face to be most effective. Then Davis walked off the set, but returned to follow Wyler's instructions. "I did it his way," she later commented. "It played validly, heaven knows, but to this day I think my way was the right way." Davis wanted to play the lead in THE LETTER in the worst way; not only was her role meaty and challenging but it represented an image of another actress who had always fascinated her, the tragic and electric Jeanne Eagels, who had died of an overdose of heroin in 1929, premature and hallucinatory. Eagels had mesmerized Broadway audiences for three years, from 1922 to 1925, playing Sadie Thompson in another Maugham work, "Rain." She went on to a stellar but short-lived career in films, including a starring role in Paramount's early sound version of THE LETTER. By the time this dope-crazed actress finished the film she was ready for a lunatic asylum. She was shown a working print of THE LETTER and went crazy, clawing the screen and yelling that the studio reshoot the film with another leading man. They did, and this bizarre actress was even more macabre in her role, the very one Davis attempted to duplicate, for Eagels was her secret idol. She watched Eagels' silent films in utter amazement and found her strangely captivating. She even emulated some of her gestures and quirky style. Much of it worked its way into Davis' version (or Wyler's, really) of THE LETTER which earned the actress another Oscar nomination. Warner Bros. produced a remake in 1947 entitled THE UNFAITHFUL with Ann Sheridan.

p, Hall B. Wallis, Robert Lord; d, William Wyler; w, Howard Koch (based on the story by W. Somerset Maugham); ph, Tony Gaudio; m, Max Steiner; ed, George Amy; md, Leo F. Forbstein; art d, Carl Jules Weyl; cos, Orry-Kelly.

Drama **Cas.** **(PR:A MPAA:NR)**

LETTER FOR EVIE, A** (1945) 88m MGM bw

Marsha Hunt *(Evie O'Connor)*, John Carroll *(Edgar "Wolf" Larsen)*, Hume Cronyn *(John Phineas McPherson)*, Spring Byington *(Mrs. McPherson)*, Pamela Britton *(Barney Lee)*, Norman Lloyd *(Dewitt Pyncheon)*, Percival Vivian *(Mr. McPherson)*, Donald Curtis *(Captain Budlow)*, Esther Howard *(Mrs. Edgewaters)*, Robin Raymond *(Eloise Edgewaters)*, Therese Lyon *(Mrs. Jackson)*, Lynn Whitney *(Miss Jenkins)*, Cameron Mitchell *(Wounded Soldier)*.

Edmund Rostand's play "Cyrano de Bergerac" in olive drab. On the home front, Hunt writes a letter to an unknown WW II soldier and places it in the pocket of an army shirt later issued to Carroll, a hedonistic hero in uniform. Carroll, preferring his birds in the hand rather than in the bush, ignores the letter. Instead his friend, scholarly soldier Cronyn, starts a correspondence with Hunt in Carroll's name, sending her a snapshot of his well-built buddy. Transferred to New York, Hunt's city, Cronyn strikes up a friendship with his patriotic pen pal, Hunt, who is now smitten with the missives she believes to have been written by Carroll. When the latter discovers Cronyn's secret, the lecherous lover-boy attempts to move in on Hunt. Naturally, all ends well. This was a remake of the 1922 silent film DON'T WRITE LETTERS.

p, William H. Wright; d, Jules Dassin; w, De Vallon Scott, Alan Friedman (based on the story "Don't Write Letters" by Blanche Brace); ph, Karl Freund; m, George Bassman; ed, Chester W. Schaeffer; art d, Cedric Gibbons, Hubert Hubson.

Comedy/Drama **(PR:A MPAA:NR)**

LETTER FROM A NOVICE (SEE: RITA, 1963, Fr./Ital.)

LETTER FROM AN UNKNOWN WOMAN*½** (1948) 86m Rampart/UNIV bw

Joan Fontaine *(Lisa Berndle)*, Louis Jourdan *(Stefan Brand)*, Mady Christians *(Frau Berndle)*, Marcel Journet *(Johann Stauffer)*, John Good *(Lt. Leopold von Kaltnegger)*, Leo B. Pessin *(Stefan Jr.)*, Art Smith *(John)*, Carol Yorke *(Marie)*, Howard Freeman *(Herr Kastner)*, Erskine Sanford *(Porter)*, Otto Waldis *(Concierge)*, Sonja Bryden *(Frau Spitzer)*, Audrey Young *(Pretty)*, William Trenk *(Fritzel)*, Fred Nurney *(Officer on Street)*, Torben Meyer *(Carriage Driver)*, Hermine Sterler *(Mother Superior)*, C. Ramsey Hill *(Col. Steindorf)*, Will Lee, William Hall *(Movers)*, Lotte Stein *(Woman Musician)*, Ilka Gruning *(Woman Ticket Taker)*, Paul E. Burns *(2nd Concierge)*, Roland Varno *(Second)*, Leo Mostovoy, Shimen Ruskin *(Older Men)*, Celia Lovsky *(Flower Vendor)*, Lester Sharpe *(Critic)*, Michael Mark *(Cafe Customer)*, Lois Austin *(Elderly Woman)*, Lisa Golm *(Woman Musician)*, Rex Lease *(Station Attendant)*, Edmund Cobb *(2nd Carriage Driver)*, Betty Blythe *(Frau Kohner)*, Diane Lee Stewart, Vera Stokes, Doretta Johnson, Lorraine Gale *(Girl Friends)*, Cy Stevens, Doug Carter, Jack Gargan *(Men)*, Arthur Lovejoy *(Footman)*, Guy L. Shaw *(Cafe Patron)*, June Wood *(Cashier)*, Jean Ransome *(Maid)*, Judith Woodbury *(Model)*, Manuel Paris *(Baron's Second)*, John McCallum *(Store Helper)*, Robert W. Brown *(First Officer)*.

Fontaine falls in love with her neighbor Jourdan, a concert pianist. She follows his career and then they finally meet on the eve of his departure on a concert tour. Jourdan promises to return for her, but that doesn't happen; she marries another man when she discovers that she's pregnant with Jourdan's child. She meets the pianist some time later, but he doesn't remember her. The story is told in flashbacks as Jourdan reads a letter from Fontaine just before she dies of typhus. The first production from the production company formed by Fontaine and William Dozier. Superb direction by Max Ophuls.

p, John Houseman; d, Max Ophuls; w, Howard Koch (based on the novel *Brief Einer Unbekannten* by Stefan Zweig); ph, Franz Planer; m, Daniele Amfitheatrof; ed, Ted J. Kent; art d, Alexander Golitzen; set d, Russell A. Gausman, Ruby R. Levitt; cos, Travis Banton; makeup, Bud Westmore.

Drama **(PR:A MPAA:NR)**

LETTER FROM KOREA (SEE: YANK IN KOREA, A, 1951)

LETTER OF INTRODUCTION½** (1938) 100m UNIV bw

Adolphe Menjou *(John Mannering)*, Andrea Leeds *(Kay Martin)*, Edgar Bergen *(Himself)*, George Murphy *(Barry Paige)*, Rita Johnson *(Honey)*, Ann Sheridan *(Lydia Hoyt)*, Eve Arden *(Cora)*, Charlie McCarthy *(Himself)*, Ernest Cossart *(Andrews)*, Jonathan Hale *(Woodstock)*, Frank Jenks *(Joe)*, Walter Perry *(Backstage Doorman)*, Frances Robinson *(Hatcheck Girl)*, Constance Moore *(Autograph Seeker)*, Eleanor Hansen *(Stagestruck Girl)*, Raymond Parker *(Call Boy)*, May Boley *(Mrs. Meggs)*, Armand Kaliz *(Jules, the Barber)*, Russell Hopton *(Process Server)*, Stanley Hughes *(Kibitzer)*, William B. Davidson *(Mr. Raleigh)*, Kathleen Howard *(Aunt Jonnie)*, Esther Ralston *(Mrs. Sinclair)*, Irving Bacon, Ray Walker *(Reporters)*, Leonard Mudie *(Critic)*, Doris Lloyd *(Charlotte)*, Morgan Wallace *(Editor)*, Richard Tucker *(Gossip)*, George Humbert *(Musician on Stage)*, Frank Reicher, Theodore Von Eltz, Chester Clute *(Doctors)*, Natalie Moorhead *(Mrs. Raleigh)*, Crauford Kent *(Mr. Sinclair)*, Gordon "Bill" Elliott *(Backgammon Man)*, Sam Hayes *(Announcer)*, Wade Boteler *(Policeman)*, Donald "Red" Barry, Philip Trent *(Men at Party)*, Dick Winslow *(Elevator Boy)*, Rolfe Sedan *(Fitter)*, Alphonse Martell *(Maitre D'Hotel)*, Sharon Lewis *(Bridge Player)*, Edith Craig, Kitty McHugh *(Girl Singers)*, Claire Whitney *(Nurse)*, Sandy Sanford *(Fireman)*, John Archer, Allen Fox *(Photographers)*, Charlie Sherlock, Don Brodie *(Reporters)*, Kane Richmond *(Man)*, Inez Courtney, Dorothy Granger *(Women at Party)*, Mortimer Snerd *(Himself)*.

Menjou is a Hollywood actor who finds his daughter (Leeds) from one of his early marriages showing up at his doorstep. The matinee idol hasn't seen his daughter since she was a baby. Leeds wants to be an actress and wants daddy's help. Her boy friend Murphy becomes very jealous because Menjou, out of vanity, doesn't want to admit that Leeds is his daughter. To save their relationship Murphy is told; the only other one who knows of Leeds' true identity is Menjou's butler. The film ends sadly when Menjou drunkenly steps in front of a car and is killed.

p&d, John M. Stahl; w, Sheridan Gibney, Leonard Spigelgass (based on a story by Bernice Boone); ph, Karl Freund; ed, Ted Kent.

Comedy/Drama **Cas.** **(PR:A MPAA:NR)**

LETTER THAT WAS NEVER SENT, THE**

(1962, USSR) 98m Mosfilm/Artkino c (NEOTPRAVLENNOYE PISMO; AKA: THE UNSENT LETTER; THE LETTER THAT WAS NOT SENT)

Innokentiy Smoktunovskiy *(Konstantin Sabinin)*, Tatyana Samoylova *(Tanya)*, Vasiliy Livanov *(Andrey)*, Yevgeniy Urbanskiy *(Sergey)*, G. Kozhakina *(Vera)*.

A group of Soviet geologists searches for diamonds in Siberia, spending months on their project. One by one they die, leaving only the group leader, who is rescued by helicopter from the icy ocean waters. Made by the team that created THE CRANES ARE FLYING (1959, USSR).

d, Mikhail Kalatozov; w, Grigoriy Koltunov, Valeriy Osipov, Viktor Rozov (based on a story by Osipov); ph, Sergey Urusevskiy; m, Nikolay Kryukov; ed, N. Anikina; md, A. Roytman; art d, David Vinitskiy.

Adventure/Drama **(PR:A MPAA:NR)**

LETTER TO THREE WIVES, A**** (1948) 103m FOX bw

Jeanne Crain *(Deborah Bishop)*, Linda Darnell *(Lora May Hollingsway)*, Ann Sothern *(Rita Phipps)*, Kirk Douglas *(George Phipps)*, Paul Douglas *(Porter Hollingsway)*, Barbara Lawrence *(Babe)*, Jeffrey Lynn *(Brad Bishop)*, Connie Gilchrist *(Mrs. Finney)*, Florence Bates *(Mrs. Manleigh)*, Hobart Cavanaugh *(Mr. Manleigh)*, Patti Brady *(Kathleen)*, Ruth Vivian *(Miss Hawkins)*, Thelma Ritter *(Sadie)*, Stuart Holmes *(Old Man)*, George Offerman, Jr. *(Nick)*, Ralph Brooks *(Character)*, James Adamson *(Butler)*, Joe Bautista *(Thomasino)*, John Davidson *(Waiter)*, Carl Switzer, John Venn *(Messengers)*, Celeste Holm *(Voice of Addie Ross)*, Sammy Finn *(Waiter)*.

Ingeniously constructed, this film is one of the finest movies ever made about marriage, the doubts, fears and recriminations of female spouses who, in this case three lovely wives, believe they are soon to lose their husbands to another woman. Crain, Darnell, and Sothern are about to leave on a boat trip along the Hudson River, escorting a group of youngsters, when a messenger delivers letters to each of them, all from the same woman, Addie Ross, never shown on screen and heard only through the voice of Holm. Holm has written the same message to all three wives; that she has run off with *one* of their husbands but she does not mention which one, devilishly leaving them to figure out who has lost out, providing the subtlest kind of emotional torture. All three women live in comfortable homes in the Hudson Valley and have ostensibly happy marriages but the letters cause them to frantically review their marriages. Crain, while the boat makes its way up the Hudson, thinks back to her meeting with Lynn, a Navy officer, when she was a WAVE, how they married, and her constant fear that she would never fit into his upperclass social set. She is shown at her first country club dance with Lynn, wearing a dress all wrong for the occasion and drinking so much that she makes a fool of herself. Moreover, she hears Addie Ross' name mentioned and how Lynn has never forgotten this woman. Driving her to anxiety is the nagging memory of Lynn telling her that he would not be home that night and would be staying overnight out-of-town on business. Sothern also reviews her marriage with Kirk Douglas. He is an underpaid, idealistic school teacher who has a decidedly skeptical view of commerce, particularly critical of the radio shows Sothern writes to supplement their income. Her soap opera, however, becomes so successful that she takes over his role as breadwinner, which Douglas obviously resents. During a dinner party for the sponsors of the show, Douglas goes on a vitriolic rampage, insulting the sponsors and condemning rampant radio commercialism, saying that his wife, an intelligent woman, has been turned by this insidious medium into a "fearful, sniveling writer of drooling pap." Douglas goes on to deliver a scathing indictment of radio which applies to TV equally, a speech that is often deleted by TV stations to this day so that advertisers might not be offended. Says Kirk with his best snide delivery: "The purpose of radio writing, as far as I can see, is to prove to the masses that a deodorant can bring happiness, a mouthwash guarantee success, and a laxative attract romance. 'Don't think,' says the radio, and we'll pay you for it! 'Can't spell 'cat'? Too bad—buy a yacht and a million dollars to the gentleman for being in our audience tonight! 'Worry,' says the radio! Will your friends not tell you? Will you lose your teeth? Will your body function after you're thirty-five? Use our product or you'll lose your husband, your job, and die! Use our product and we'll make you rich, we'll make you famous!" Sothern recalls with increasing discomfort that her husband left the house Saturday morning—the day he usually reserved for fishing—wearing his best blue serge suit. She is convinced that he, a one-time friend of Addie Ross, is the one who has gone off with "the other woman." Darnell, a beauteous spouse who is utterly materialistic, thinks back on how she trapped self-made, wealthy Paul Douglas. She is a poor girl who literally lives on the wrong side of the tracks. When Douglas first courts her, he comes to her mother's little house which rattles and shakes with the passing of each train rumbling down the nearby tracks. (One of the funniest scenes in this or any other movie shows Darnell's mother, Gilchrist, and friend Ritter drinking beer and pretending all is normal while Douglas watches the house being shaken to pieces as he waits for Darnell to ready herself for a date.) Darnell has been a sly fox and played hard to get, insisting that Douglas marry her before she bestows any favors. He does and would have anyway, being a gentle, kind man. Both have a running fight for a marriage and both repeatedly tell the other how they have no love for each other. Darnell has no doubt that it's her husband, Paul Douglas, who has run off with old friend Addie Ross. When the boat docks, all three women rush home. Kirk and Paul Douglas are at home but Lynn is not and when the group attends a club dinner that night all assume that Lynn is the one who has gone off with home-breaker Ross. But Crain soon learns that her husband is really away on business and still loves her. Paul Douglas is the one who ran off with Ross, he confesses, which confuses Darnell. But he has returned because he does love Darnell and he tells her so. The acting of the six leading players here is outstanding, with Darnell giving the finest performance of her career as the supposedly hard-hearted lady with only wealth on her mind. Paul Douglas is also exceptional as the lovable tough businessman and, for the first time in his career, Kirk Douglas, usually a louse, is appealing as the principled school teacher. The dialog is sharp, pungent, and witty, which earned Mankiewicz an Oscar for his script and his direction was equally taut and moving, which earned him another Oscar as Best Director. Mankiewicz developed the story from a John Klempner short story first appearing in *Cosmopolitan*, entitled "One of Our Hearts." Klempner later expanded the piece to an overlong, repetitious novel, retitled *A Letter to Five Wives*, and Mankiewicz's screenplay was originally called A LETTER TO FOUR WIVES but Fox boss Zanuck thought the screenplay overreached the idea. He called the director-writer into his office and told him: "You've got one wife too many." He ordered Mankiewicz to eliminate one story which he did and the film became A LETTER TO THREE WIVES, working beautifully. Originally, Zanuck wanted Ernst Lubitsch to direct the film, fighting producer Siegel on his selection of Mankiewicz. "I can't get along with him," Zanuck told Siegel. "If he gets a hit with this, he'll be unlivable!" The selection of Holm as the omniscient narrator of the film, the vixen Addie Ross, was a stroke of genius by Mankiewicz as she has the perfect voice for such an off-camera role, sweet and sour, kind and bitchy. The writer called Holm and asked: "How would you like to be a character who is never seen in a movie?" Replied Holm caustically: "Oh, that's wonderful. My wooden leg won't have to show." Mankiewicz and Darnell began a tempestuous affair during the production of this film, one that did not end for several years. The film was a landmark achievement for Mankiewicz who became so famous because of this film on the Fox lot that Zanuck became deeply resentful. He personally blamed Mankiewicz years later for almost destroying Fox with his hugely expensive production of CLEOPATRA.

p, Sol C. Siegel; d, Joseph L. Mankiewicz; w, Mankiewicz, Vera Caspary (based on the novel by John Klempner); ph, Arthur Miller; m, Alfred Newman; ed, J. Watson Webb; md, Newman; art d, Lyle Wheeler, J. Russell Spencer; set d, Thomas Little, Walter M. Scott; cos, Kay Nelson; spec eff, Fred Sersen; makeup, Ben Nye.

Drama **(PR:A MPAA:NR)**

LETTERS FROM MY WINDMILL* 1/2**
(1955, Fr.) 116m Mediterranean/Tohan Pictures bw (LES LETTRES DE MON MOULIN)

"The Three Low Masses": Henri Vilbert *(Dom Balaguere/Garrigou)*, Daxely *(The Devil)*, Yvonne Gamy *(The Old Woman)*, Keller *(The Marquis)*, Viviane Mery *(The Marchioness)*, Clara Michel *(The Countess)*, Rene Sarvil *(The Chef)*; "The Elixir of Father Gaucher": Rellys *(Father Gaucher)*, Robert Vattier *(The Abbot)*, Christian Lude *(Father Sylvestre)*, Fernand Sardou *(M. Charnigue)*, Guy Alland *(Brother Ulysse)*, Joseph Riozet *(Father Hyacinthe)*, Jean Toscane *(Father Virgile)*; "The Secret of Master Cornille": Roger Crouzet *(Alphonse Daudet)*, Pierrette Bruno *(Vivette)*, Delmont *(Master Cornille)*, Arius *(M. Decanis)*, Luce Dassas *(Sylvie)*, Breols *(The Mayor)*.

Noted French director Pagnol adapted three stories by 19th century Gallic writer Alphonse Daudet for this fine episodic film. Crouzet plays the writer, who comes to an abandoned windmill in Provence in order to write his stories. This is the link which holds the film together, a device Pagnol uses with some imagination, as the writer himself is even incorporated into one episode. The first story involves the adventures of a gourmand clergyman who has a mass stolen from him by the Devil. The second, and best of the three, is the story of some monks who manufacture liqueur so they can raise the funds to do the Lord's work. The final tale is of an impoverished miller who nearly kills himself in trying to prove the existence of a fictional client. Though Pagnol's film has a touch too much dialog, the film delivers its simple stories with a genuine freshness. The camerawork shows a love for the French countryside setting and the people who live there. His mixture of humor and pathos is well handled without ever becoming maudlin or cruel. Highly enjoyable. Famed director Preston Sturges wrote the subtitles. (In French; English subtitles.)

p,d&w, Marcel Pagnol (based on the stories of Alphonse Daudet); ph, Willy Factorouitch; m, Henri Tomasi; ed, Jacqueline Gaudin; art d, Robert Giordani.

Drama/Comedy **(PR:A MPAA:NR)**

LETTING IN THE SUNSHINE**
(1933, Brit.) 73m British International/Wardour bw

Albert Burdon *(Nobby Green)*, Renee Gadd *(Jane)*, Molly Lamont *(Lady Anne)*, Henry Mollison *(Duvine)*, Tonie Edgar Bruce *(Lady Warminster)*, Herbert Langley *(Foreman)*, Eric Le Fre *(Bill)*, Ethel Warwick *(Housekeeper)*, Syd Crossley *(Jenkyns)*, Henry Longhurst.

A sweet young girl, Gadd, is maid for a house that is sublet to a band of robbers. She and window cleaner Burdon overhear a conversation wherein the crooks plan to rob an heiress of a valuable necklace during a ball. The plan calls for the lights to go out and the real necklace to be substituted with a fake. The working-class couple decides not to call the cops but rather to go to the ball themselves and stop the crooks. Some good laughs along the way, but mostly this film resorts to pratfalls and mugging for the humor. The actors aren't bad, though, giving nice if uninspired comic performances.

p, John Maxwell; d, Lupino Lane; w, Con West, Herbert Sargent, Frank Miller (based on a story by Anthony Asquith); ph, J. J. Cox, Bryan Langley.

Comedy **(PR:A MPAA:NR)**

LETTY LYNTON 1/2** (1932) 84m MGM bw

Joan Crawford *(Letty Lynton)*, Robert Montgomery *(Hale Darrow)*, Nils Asther *(Emile Renaud)*, Lewis Stone *(Mr. Haney)*, May Robson *(Mrs. Lynton)*, Louise Closser Hale *(Miranda)*, Emma Dunn *(Mrs. Darrow)*, Walter Walker *(Mr. Darrow)*, William Pawley *(Hennessey)*.

LETTY LYNTON is a better-than-average example of the work of a woman who gave the phrase "Mommy Dearest" new meaning. Crawford is a wealthy socialite on vacation in South America, where she is pursued by charming Asther. She doesn't love him a bit, but he's amusing for a time, and they dally together. After a while, she becomes bored with him, and the sultry climate, and the lush foliage, so she decides to return to New York. This doesn't sit well with Asther who has, by this time, fallen hard for her. In order to keep her from leaving, he says he will reveal the nature of some steamy letters she's written to him while she was in an indiscreet mood, thus ruining her image up north. She's unruffled by his threats and gets on an ocean liner pointed north with her maid-companion, Hale. On board the ship she meets Montgomery and before the cruise is over, they are engaged. Talk about a hussy! Meanwhile, Asther is not taking this lying down, so he flies to New York and is waiting for her at the dock. Crawford goes home to her cold-hearted mother, Robson, whom she has never liked. Asther shows up at the Crawford manse and repeats his threat to bare the letters. This is overheard by Robson and the dirt is now out of the bag. Later, Crawford goes to Asther's apartment (it must have been much easier to find a flat in New York in those days) with a vial of poison that she dumps into his drink after he ignores all her pleas to cease and desist. He drinks the stuff and dies right away. She is immediately horrified and goes to the Long Island estate of Montgomery's parents, Dunn and Walker. But the cops trail her there after tracing her whereabouts. She's all smiles and laughter at the party until the law steps in and takes her to the police station where it looks as though the whole thing is an open-and-shut case. Then Montgomery, her *deus ex* machoman, arrives with Robson and they have concocted an alibi which the district attorney quickly believes and Crawford is allowed to leave and, presumably, spend the rest of her life with Montgomery. This also serves to bring her closer to Robson. Good drama with a couple of solid comedic licks tossed in by Hale. Some unbelievable plot turns mar the effect, such as the district attorney's fast dismissal of a murder charge after the false alibi. Several minutes could have been cut, most of all in the Crawford-Asther scenes. A bit of overplaying also serves to lose credibility. Adrian's gowns for Crawford were exceptional.

d, Clarence Brown; w, John Meehan, Wanda Tuchock (based on the novel by Marie Belloc Lowndes); ph, Oliver T. Marsh; ed, Conrad A. Nervig; cos, Adrian.

Drama **(PR:A-C MPAA:NR)**

LETYAT ZHURAVIT (SEE: CRANES ARE FLYING, THE, 1960, USSR)

L'EVANGILE SELON SAINT MATTHIEU
(SEE: GOSPEL ACCORDING TO SAINT MATTHEW, THE, 1966, Fr./Ital)

LEVIATHAN*** (1961, Fr.) 92m Valois bw

Louis Jourdan *(Paul)*, Marie Laforet *(Angele)*, Lilli Palmer *(Wife)*, Georges Wilson *(Husband)*, Madeleine Robinson *(Mrs. Londe)*.

Jourdan plays a married tutor in a small French town. He meets Laforet, a young girl who lives in the village, and becomes wildly infatuated with her. This grows into obsession and he begins following her everywhere. But it is revealed that she is the mistress of the man whose son Jourdan has been tutoring. When he confronts her, she denies this, and Jourdan makes a pass. When she resists his advances he tries to kill her, disfiguring her face permanently. From there he's on the run, killing an older man along the way. Moody and slightly eerie, relying heavily on suggestions and symbolism. Characterizations, though well acted by the cast (particularly Robinson in her supporting role), are not as well written as perhaps could be. For a first directorial effort, Keigel shows an able hand for narration and style, though, which redeems the film's lesser qualities.

d, Leonard Keigel; w, Keigel, Rene Gerard, Julien Green (based on the novel by Green); ph, Nicolas Hayer; ed, Armand Paenny

Drama **(PR:O MPAA:NR)**

L'HOMME AU CHAPEAU ROND
(SEE: ETERNAL HUSBAND, THE, 1946, Fr.)

L'HOMME DE RIO (SEE: THAT MAN FROM RIO, 1964, Fr./Ital.)

L'HOMME DU MINNESOTA
(SEE: MINNESOTA CLAY, 1966, Ital./Fr./Span.)

L'HOMME EN COLERE (SEE: ANGRY MAN, THE, 1979, Fr./Can.)

L'HOMME QUI AIMAT LES FEMMES
(SEE: MAN WHO LOVED WOMEN, THE, 1977, Fr.)

LIANG SHAN-PO YU CHU YING-TAI (SEE: LOVE ETERNE, THE, 1964)

LIANNA*** (1983) 110m Winwood/UA c

Linda Griffiths *(Lianna)*, Jane Hallaren (Ruth), Jon DeVries *(Dick)*, Jo Henderson *(Sandy)*, Jessica Wight MacDonald *(Theda)*, Jesse Solomon *(Spencer)*, John Sayles *(Jerry)*, Stephen Mendillo *(Bob)*, Betsy Julia Robinson *(Cindy)*, Nancy Mette *(Kim)*, Maggie Renzi *(Sheila)*, Madelyn Coleman *(Mrs. Hennessy)*, Robyn Reeves *(Job Applicant)*, Christopher Elliott *(Lighting Assistant)*, Marta Renzi, D. David Porter *(Dancers)*, Rochelle Oliver *(Betty)*, Nancy-Elizabeth Kammer *(Liz)*, Jean Passanante *(Rose)*, Maggie Task *(Evelyn)*, Marisa Smith, Amanda Carlin *(Dick's Students)*, Madeline Lee *(Supermarket Customer)*, Deborah Taylor *(Receptionist)*.

Griffiths is the unsure wife of DeVries, an egotistical and domineering college professor. He ridicules her decision to return to school, but she continues to pursue her degree in spite of him. Hallaren is one of her teachers, a supporting and caring person who helps Griffiths with her internal struggles. Gradually the two women grow closer until their friendship blossoms into a love affair, with Griffiths leaving her husband for Hallaren. This is a wise and caring film and never preachy about its lesbian theme. Sayles was noted for writing such films as THE HOWLING and ALLIGATOR so he could finance his own independent features. The comic campiness of his B horror writing is not evident here. The directorial style and the wonderful dialog are completely natural, allowing the characters to tell the story; not a single moment within the film seems the least bit false or contrived. The two female lead roles are sensitively portrayed, as is DeVries' performance. His sexual confusions and anger towards Griffiths and Hallaren are nicely handled. Sayles also has a bit part as a friend supportive of the new relationship. There are some technical problems within the film, reflective of its low budget. However this doesn't hamper an otherwise fine and sensitively told story. That such a subject could be so delicately and intelligently handled by a male writer-director certainly sounds a note of high progress within the so-called battle between the sexes.

p, Jeffrey Nelson, Maggie Renzi; d&w, John Sayles; ph, Austin de Besche (DuArt Color); m, Mason Daring; ed, Sayles; art d, Jeanne McDonnell; cos, Louise Martinez; ch, Marta Renzi.

Drama **Cas.** **(PR:O MPAA:R)**

LIARS, THE**

(1964, Fr.) 90m Mediterranee/Shawn-Ellis bw (LES MENTEURS; AKA: TWISTED LIVES)

Dawn Addams *(Norma O'Brien)*, Jean Servais *(Paul Dutraz)*, Claude Brasseur *(Dominique)*, Francis Blanche *(Blanchin)*, Roland Lesaffre *(Clement)*, Wim Patten *(Herve)*, Anne-Marie Bellini *(Maud)*, Anne-Marie Coffinet *(Valentine)*, Gaston Modot *(Carloti)*.

Servais places a newspaper ad in the hope of finding himself a wife. Addams, a 40-ish looking Australian actress, responds, but she warns him that she has a 20-year-old son, Brasseur. Servais begins to get suspicious when he finds that Addams is wearing make-up to appear older, and discovers that Brasseur is really her lover. He then uncovers a plot to kill him for his money and confronts the pair. Brasseur flees and dies in a car crash and Servais plans a return trip to Africa. Before it's too late, however, Addams attempts to kill herself, which tells Servais how much she really loves him. They depart together.

p, Georges Cheyko; d, Edmond T. Greville; w, Frederic Dard, Max Montagu (based on the novel *Cette Mort Dont tu Parlais* by Dard); ph, Armand Thirard; m, Andre Hossein; ed, Jean Ravel; set d, Rino Mondellini.

Drama **(PR:A MPAA:NR)**

LIAR'S DICE1/2** (1980) Makdissy-Eubanks 95m c

Robert Ede *(Joe)*, Terry Eubanks-Makdissy *(Anne)*, Issam B. Makdissy *(Samir)*, Frank Triest *(Jack)*, D. G. Buckles *(Pete)*, Norma Small *(Dottie)*, Phran Gauci *(Janice)*, Rafik Assad *(Jamil)*, Shirley James *(Sharon)*, Phil De Carla *(Tony)*, Jerry La Rue *(Mel)*, Judd Strelo *(Boy)*, Jeannette Mignola *(New Waitress)*, John Lovell *(Boy's Father)*.

A fairly interesting independent feature, LIAR'S DICE was put together on a shoestring budget of just $40,000. Eubanks-Makdissy, the director's wife—who also did the film's script and art pieces—is a lonely artist who must work as a cocktail waitress to support herself. She becomes involved with two men—a married foreigner (Makdissy, the film's director), and an older man (Ede)—to help take away her pain. While the film never quite explores this theme as fully as needed for dramatic impact, there is a certain honesty to this such as is so often found in small, independent features. Ede's performance is the standout, a genuine portrait of an old man's plight. Despite the low budget, LIAR'S DICE makes its point well with a sincerity lacking in bigger-budgeted Hollywood productions of similar themes.

p, Butros Makdissy, Ed Eubanks; d, Issam B. Makdissy; w, Terry Eubanks-Makdissy; ph, Douglas Murray; m, Coleman Burke, Gary Yamani; ed, Issam B. Makdissy.

Drama **(PR:O MPAA:NR)**

LIAR'S MOON* (1982) 106m Crown International c

Matt Dillon, Cindy Fisher, Christopher Connelly, Hoyt Axton, Yvonne DeCarlo, Maggie Blye, Susan Tyrrell, Broderick Crawford.

An annoying teen love story with tough/sensitive poor-boy Dillon eloping with Fisher, a rich banker's daughter. The script relies solely on this cliched class difference, turning out a cardboard cut-out of teeny-boppers. The film's lack of direction is obvious in its twin-ending release. One version has Fisher dying from a messed-up abortion, the other has her remaining alive. It's not enough that we have to plop down five bucks, but now we have to tell them how to cut their movies.

p, Don P. Behrns; d&w, David Fisher (based on a story by Janice Thompson, Billy Hanna); ph, John Hora (Metrocolor); ed, Christopher Greenbury.

Drama/Romance **Cas.** **(PR:O MPAA:PG)**

LIBEL1/2** (1959, Brit.) 100m MGM bw

Dirk Bogarde *(Sir Mark Loddon/Frank Welney/Number Fifteen)*, Olivia de Havilland *(Lady Maggie Loddon)*, Paul Massie *(Jeffrey Buckenham)*, Robert Morley *(Sir Wilfred)*, Wilfrid Hyde-White *(Hubert Foxley)*, Anthony Dawson *(Gerald Loddon)*, Richard Wattis *(Judge)*, Richard Dimbleby *(Himself)*, Martin Miller *(Dr. Schrott)*, Millicent Martin *(Maisie)*, Bill Shine *(Guide)*, Ivan Samson *(Adm. Loddon)*, Sebastian Saville *(Michael Loddon)*, Gordon Stern *(Maddox)*, Josephine Middleton *(Mrs. Squires)*, Kenneth Griffith *(Fitch)*, Joyce Carey *(Miss Sykes)*, Robert Shaw *(1st Photographer)*, Geoffrey Bayldon *(2nd Photographer)*, Arthur Howard *(Car Salesman)*, Barbara Archer *(Barmaid)*, Anthony Doonan *(Man at Bar)*, Vanda Hudson *(Girl in Street)*.

LIBEL is a confusing film that does little to enhance the careers of any of the people involved. Bogarde stars as a man who may or may not have been the person he claims to be. When Bogarde is seen on television (he's a wealthy Londoner and a peer) by Massie, a former inmate at the same POW camp, Massie wonders if Bogarde is the man he seems to be—or is he an actor who was at the camp at the same time and looked like the peer? Massie, a Canadian airline pilot, accuses Bogarde of being an impostor and the British press has its teeth in one of its patented smarmy stories. Bogarde's wife, de Havilland, urges him to hire well-known barrister Morley to bring libel charges. What makes the case difficult is that Bogarde has suffered in the war (or has he?) and stutters, as well as having periods of amnesia. The court trial commences and the action flows back and forth between Morley and the other attorney, Hyde-White, and Bogarde's guilt or innocence seems to change with each witness. Then a surprise witness is ushered in. It's Bogarde (as the actor), now a hulk of a man who lives in a mental institution where he is known as Number 15. Seeing him stuns the peer into recalling what happened when the two men escaped from the camp. The actor had attempted to kill the Sir, who responded by defending himself and beating the attacker into submission. The actor had hoped to replace the peer in his life style and fool everyone. (This was a real happening in France several centuries before and was eventually made into a movie as THE RETURN OF MARTIN GUERRE). It's improbable and even the courtroom scenes fail to catch fire. Bogarde was excellent in the two roles and played them so differently that he could make you believe he was two people.

p, Anatole de Grunwald; d, Anthony Asquith; w, De Grunwald, Karl Tunberg (based on a play by Edward Wooll); ph, Robert Krasker; m, Benjamin Frankel; ed, Frank Clarke; art d, Paul Sheriff; cos, Christian Dior; spec eff, Tom Howard.

Drama **(PR:A MPAA:NR)**

LIBELED LADY**** (1936) 98m MGM bw

William Powell *(Bill Chandler)*, Myrna Loy *(Connie Allenbury)*, Jean Harlow *(Gladys Benton)*, Spencer Tracy *(Warren Haggerty)*, Walter Connolly *(James B. Allenbury)*, Charley Grapewin *(Hollis Bane)*, Cora Witherspoon *(Mrs. Burns-Norvell)*, E. E. Clive *(Evans the Fishing Instructor)*, Bunny Lauri Beatty *(Babs Burns-Norvell)*, Otto Yamaoka *(Ching)*, Charles Trowbridge *(Graham)*, Spencer Charters *(Magistrate McCall)*, George Chandler *(Bellhop)*, Greta Meyer *(Connie's Maid)*, William Benedict *(Joe)*, Hal K. Dawson *(Harvey Allen)*, Fred Graham *(Press Man)*, William Stack *(Editor)*, Selmer Jackson *(Adams, Editor of Washington Chronicle)*, William Newell *(Divorce Detective)*, Duke York *(Taxi Driver)*, Pat West *(Detective)*, Ed Stanley *(Clerk)*, Wally Maher, Pinky Parker, Harry Lash, Pat Somerset *(Photographers)*, Tom Mahoney *(Alex)*, Richard Tucker *(Barker)*, Libby Taylor *(Tiny, Gladys' Maid)*, Eric Lonsdale, Olaf Hytten *(Reporters)*, Charles Irwin *(Steward)*, Eddie Shubert *(Mac the Circulation Editor)*, George Davis *(Waiter)*, Thomas Pogue *(Minister)*, Myra Marsh *(Secretary)*, Hattie McDaniel *(Maid in Hall)*, Howard Hickman *(Cable Editor)*, James T. Mack *(Pop)*, Jack Mulhall, Dennis O'Keefe, Charles King *(Barkers)*, Nick Thompson *(Hot Dog Stand Man)*, Inez Palange *(Fortune Teller)*, Harry C. Bradley *(Justice of Peace)*, Bodil Ann Rosing *(Wife of Justice of Peace)*, Barnett Parker *(Butler)*, Robin Adair *(Palmer the English Reporter)*, Charles Croker King *(Charles Archibald the Lawyer)*, Sherry Hall *(Denver Courier Editor)*, Alphonse Martel *(Table Captain)*, Eric Wilton *(Steward on Dock)*, Jay Eaton, Ralph Brooks *(Dance Extras)*.

Take four first-rate farceurs, add a crackling script, give them an ace director, and what do you have? A smash, that's what. You almost need a scorecard to keep track of the twists in the story so don't try to make any sense of it when you see it, just enjoy the merry meanderings of a cast that seemed to be having a bang-up time making this movie. Tracy is the managing editor of a newspaper and he erroneously prints a story saying that wealthy Loy is busy nabbing another woman's husband, a British peer. The story is totally false and Loy sues the paper for $5 million. Tracy is about to marry Harlow, a woman he's left at the altar several times. He does it again and the festivities have to be postponed as Tracy is going to get to the bottom of the story and attempt to remove the lawsuit which could cost him his job. Tracy hires Powell, a former co-worker who doesn't like him but needs a job. The task is to marry Harlow (in name only), thus clearing the way for Tracy to woo Loy. If that works, Harlow can sue Loy for alienation of affections, then agree to drop that suit if Loy drops hers. Powell is a lawyer with a devious and devilish mind. He boards the ocean liner bringing Loy and her father, Connolly, back to the States. Connolly is a fishing buff and Powell reads up on that sport to impress the old man, but Loy will have little to do with Powell as she thinks he is just one more fortune hunter. Connolly invites Powell to fish with him up at his mountain retreat and Powell luckily catches a legendary trout that Connolly's been trying to net for years. Now Powell and Loy begin to fall in love (as they did in so many films) and he tries to talk her out of her libel suit. Tracy learns that Powell is in love with Loy and urges Harlow to file her alienations suit until Powell convinces her to drop it, lest it ruin his relationship with Loy. Loy now discovers that Powell is married to Harlow and tests his love for her by asking that they get married. Without batting an eyelash, Powell accepts and they are married by a justice of the peace. Tracy and Harlow hear of this and come to Powell's hotel where Loy says she's dropped the suit. Tracy is delighted, but Harlow is annoyed at Powell for charming her and then marrying Loy, thus making him a bigamist. Powell retorts that Harlow's first marriage (to an unseen person) wasn't legally dissolved with the mail-order divorce she'd gotten from Mexico, therefore his marriage to her wasn't legal. Now Harlow hits Powell with a bombshell and says that she did get a legal split in Reno before they had their sham wedding. Thinking fast, Powell whacks Tracy, thus eliciting the sympathy from Harlow that he needs to get out of this pickle. Harlow agrees to divorce Powell and marry her long-time love, Tracy. Loy has known about all of this for a while and is happy that she and Powell can now tie the knot in a more permanent fashion. The punch that Powell threw was a fake, for Harlow's benefit, and it worked. The laughs come rolling off the screen in just about every sequence and this ranks as one of the best "screwball" comedies of the 1930s. Powell and Harlow were conducting an off-screen romance at the time he was having his on-screen romances with Loy. They were engaged to be married when she died.

p, Lawrence Weingarten; d, Jack Conway; w, Maurine Watkins, Howard Emmett Rogers, George Oppenheimer (based on a story by Wallace Sullivan); ph, Norbert Brodine; m, Dr. William Axt; ed, Frederick Y. Smith; art d, Cedric Gibbons, William A. Hornung; set d, Edwin B. Willis; cos, Dolly Tree.

Comedy (PR:A MPAA:NR)

LIBERATION OF L.B. JONES, THE** (1970) 102m Liberation/COL c

Lee J. Cobb (*Oman Hedgepath*), Anthony Zerbe (*Willie Joe Worth*), Roscoe Lee Browne (*L. B. Jones*), Lola Falana (*Emma Jones*), Lee Majors (*Steve Mundine*), Barbara Hershey (*Nella Mundine*), Yaphet Kotto (*Sonny Boy Mosby*), Arch Johnson (*Stanley Bumpas*), Chill Wills (*Mr. Ike*), Zara Cully (*Mama Lavorn*), Fayard Nicholas (*Benny*), Joseph Attles (*Henry*), Lauren Jones (*Erleen*), Dub Taylor (*Mayor*), Brenda Sykes (*Jelly*), Larry D. Mann (*Grocer*), Ray Teal (*Police Chief*), Eve McVeagh (*Miss Griggs, Secretary*), Sonora McKeller (*Miss Ponsella*), Robert Van Meter (*Blind Man*), Jack Grinnage (*Driver*), John S. Jackson (*Suspect*).

Majors and Hershey are a young married couple who head South to live with his uncle, Cobb, who is a leading lawyer. Majors has come to join his uncle's law practice. Arriving on the same train is Kotto, who is returning to the same town to avenge a brutal beating once inflicted on him by Johnson. Browne is a local funeral director, a wealthy man who wants to divorce his wife (Falana in her American film debut) for having an affair with Zerbe, a local white policeman. Though he does not want the case, Cobb is persuaded by his nephew to handle the suit. Fearful of the scandal such a legal battle would cause, Zerbe implores Falana not to contest the divorce. But she needs money to raise Zerbe's child. Angry, he severely beats her. Then, with the help of Johnson, he arrests Browne on false pretenses. The undertaker escapes; the two policemen pursue him and, tired of running, Browne confronts the men. They shoot and castrate him but despite the policemens' confession no legal action is taken. Kotto, still after Johnson, avenges the murder when he pushes crooked cop Johnson into a harvester. He thinks he is retaliating for his long-ago beating as he unknowingly avenges his compatriot's murder. Though this is a film stocked with very strong performances, ultimately it is an empty affair. The questions of racism and Southern prejudice had been well handled by other films long before this. Had it been made ten years earlier it would have been a landmark, but in 1970 it was no longer fresh material. The script is pockmarked with cliches and stereotypes, though the technical aspects were fine. This last film of director Wyler was nothing special. For what it's worth, this film generated some anonymous complaints from the Ku Klux Klan.

p, Ronald Lubin; d, William Wyler; w, Stirling Sillphant, Jesse Hill Ford (based on the novel *The Liberation of Lord Byron Jones* by Ford); ph, Robert Surtees (Eastmancolor); m, Elmer Bernstein; ed, Robert Swink, Carl Kress; prod d, Kenneth A. Reid; set d, Frank Tuttle; cos, Seth Banks, Gene Ashman, Vi Alford; makeup, Ben Lane.

Drama Cas. (PR:O MPAA:R)

LIBIDO**1/2 (1973, Aus.) 118m Producers & Directors Guild of Australia/MGM c

"The Husband": Elkey Neidhart (*Penelope*), Byron Williams (*Jonathan*), Mark Albiston (*Harold*); "The Child": Bruce Barry (*David*), Jill Forster (*The Mother*), Judy Morris (*Sybil*), John Williams (*Martin*), Louise Homfray (*Housekeeper*), George Fairfax (*Father*); "The Priest": Arthur Dignam (*Father Burn*), Robyn Nevin (*Sister Caroline*), Vivean Gray (*Elderly Nun*); "The Family Man": Jack Thompson (*Ken*), Max Gillies (*Gerry*), Debbie Nankervis (*First Girl*), Sue Brady (*Second Girl*).

Four different directors and four different writers were assigned by the Producers and Directors Guild of Australia to film short episodes on the topic "libido". The result is a mixed bag; one wonders what grades their efforts might have rated had their snippets been made as a classroom project. "The Husband", directed by Murray and written by McGregor, deals with a man who enhances his sexual relations with his wife by fantasizing her engaging in extramarital sexual activities. One of his fantasies has her secretly trysting with Albiston, his best friend; another has her gang-raped by five men (in a dance-like choreographed dream set to music). When Williams rises from the bed of his fantasies and leaves for work, Neidhart telephones Albiston, inviting him to join her and leaving the audience wondering whether the yet-more-exotic fantasies of her husband might have some substance. "The Child", written by Porter and directed by Burstall, deals with a woman,

Forster, whose husband drowns in the Titanic tragedy. She begins an affair with the wordly Barry, who is deeply resented by her young son Williams. Vacationing with Barry, Forster leaves Williams in the care of governess Morris, whom he comes to adore. When the lovers return, Williams fears that Morris will be found expendable. Upset, he wanders afield and chances on his idealized governess making love to his mother's lover. Shattered, he makes his way to a nearby river and attempts to escape his hateful confines in a rowboat. Barry, realizing the boy's state of mind, races after him and tries to leap into the boat. Williams strokes the oars strongly and Barry, a non-swimmer, falls into the water and drowns. "The Priest", written by Keneally and directed by Schepisi, is a dialog between a love-smitten priest, Dignam, and his inamorata, nun Nevin, punctuated by flashbacks accenting their history. He is impatient to leave his vocation in order to marry; she insists that they follow the conventional bureaucratic route, which takes time. Quarreling, the two part. "The Family Man", written by Williamson and directed by Baker, deals with a pair of good old Aussie rowdies who celebrate the confinement of Thompson's wife—it's their third child—by picking up two party girls and playing with them in Thompson's beach house. Offended by the men's uncaring attitude, the girls leave. When Thompson returns to the beach house some time later with his wife and three children he finds that the girls have draped it with a sign accusing him of having assaulted them during his wife's stay in the hospital. All in all, an academically interesting tour de force from down under.

p, John B. Murray, Christopher Muir; d, Murray, Tim Burstall, Fred A. Schepisi, David Baker; w, Craig McGregor, Hal Porter, Thomas Keneally, David Williamson; ph, Robin Copping, Bruce McNaughton.

Episodic Drama (PR:O MPAA:NR)

LICENSED TO KILL
(SEE: SECOND BEST AGENT IN THE WHOLE WIDE WORLD, THE, 1965, Brit.)

L'IDIOT (SEE: IDIOT, THE, 1948, Fr.)

LIDO MYSTERY, THE
(SEE: ENEMY AGENTS MEET ELLERY QUEEN, 1942)

LIE DETECTOR, THE (SEE: TRUTH ABOUT MURDER, THE, 1946)

LIEBESSPIELE (SEE: SKI FEVER, 1969)

LIES MY FATHER TOLD ME** (1960, Brit.) 60m Emmet Dalton bw

Harry Brogan (*Grandfather*), Betsy Blair (*Mother*), Edward Golden (*Father*), Rita O'Dea (*Grandmother*), Terry Raven (*David*), Gearold O'Lochlain, John Cowley (*Old Gentlemen*).

A young boy who lives in Dublin adores his grandfather, a simple rag-and-bone seller. This relationship displeases his parents, who try to separate the pair. This is the first version of Ted Allan's story of Jewish life in Montreal, transplanted to Dublin for this British low-budget feature. It was later remade with the original setting with much better results in 1975.

p, Don Chaffey, Charles Leeds; d, Chaffey; w, Ted Allan (based on his story).

Drama (PR:A MPAA:NR)

LIES MY FATHER TOLD ME***1/2
(1975, Can.) 103m Pentimento-Pentacle VIII/COL c

Yossi Yadin (*Zaida*), Len Birman (*Harry Herman*), Marilyn Lightstone (*Annie Herman*), Jeffrey Lynas (*David*), Ted Allan (*Mr. Baumgarten*), Barbara Chilcott (*Mrs. Tannebaum*), Mignon Elkins (*Mrs. Bondy*), Henry Gamer (*Uncle Benny*), Carole Lazare (*Edna*), Cleo Paskal (*Cleo*).

Set in 1920s Montreal, this nostalgic tale centers on the binding relationship between a wide-eyed seven-year-old boy and his aging, Orthodox Jewish grandfather. The latter, played by Israeli actor Yadin, has a broken-down wagon (drawn by an equally ailing horse) that the man rides about the town in. The boy accompanies him on these trips, finding in the old man an adult with whom he can relate. His parents are too selfish to give their son the needed attention and the rest of the residents of the area are equally self-absorbed, unwilling or unable to give the boy any form of human understanding. Czech director Kadar was treading on extremely touchy ground in this story, having to be very careful not to fall into over-indulgent sentimentalism. Kadar managed to keep a firm hand over the material and created a genuinely absorbing look into a touching moment of childhood.

p, Anthony Bedrich, Harry Gulkin; d, Jan Kadar; w, Ted Allan; ph, Paul Van Der Linden; m, Sol Kaplan; ed, Edward Beyer, Richard Marks; prod d, Francois Barbeau.

Drama (PR:A MPAA:PG)

LIEUTENANT DARING, RN*** (1935, Brit.) 85m But bw

Hugh Williams (*Lt. Bob Daring*), Geraldine Fitzgerald (*Joan Fayre*), Frederick Lloyd (*Capt. Mayne*), Jerry Verno (*AB Swallow*), John Rorke (*Marine Fish*), Ernest Butcher (*AB Singer*), Martin Walker (*Neville Mayne*), Ralph Truman (*Mung*), Richard Norris (*Briggs*), Edwin Ellis (*Sergeant*), George Carr, Robb Wilton, Geoffrey Clark, Ellen Tai, Grace Tai, Arthur Brander, Charles Cantley, Douglas Bell, A. E. J. Walker, Douglas Phillips, Pat Hagan, Victor Hagan, Hugh Selwyn, K. Wing, Chee Foo, Su Yee Troupe, Neil McKay, Horace Sheldon and his Orchestra.

When some important documents are stolen, naval hero Williams is framed by his commander's son. Things don't look good for him until love interest Fitzgerald is kidnaped by Chinese pirates. Williams rescues her from the nefarious villains and manages to prove his innocence at the same time in this rousing, up-and-at-'em adventure. This story was taken from a silent film character's adventures and projects many of the same filmmaking values. There's a hearty sense of daring coupled with a genuine naive goodness that makes this an enjoyable feature. Naturally, it's full of improbabilities, but that's half the fun.

p, Lawrence Huntington; d, Reginald Denham; w, Gerald Elliott (based on a story by Frank H. Shaw); ph, George Dudgeon Stretton.

Adventure   **(PR:A MPAA:NR)**

LT. ROBIN CRUSOE, U.S.N.*   (1966) 115m Disney/BV c

Dick Van Dyke (*Lt. Robin Crusoe*), Nancy Kwan (*Wednesday*), Akim Tamiroff (*Tanamashu*), Arthur Malet (*Umbrella Man*), Tyler McVey (*Captain*), Pete L. Renoudet (*Pilot*), Peter Duryea (*Co-pilot*), John Dennis (*Crew Chief*), Nancy Hsueh, Yvonne Ribuca, Victoria Young, Bebe Louie, Lucia Valero (*Native Girls*), "Floyd" (*The Chimpanzee*).

Van Dyke is a navy pilot who is forced to abandon his plane when it catches fire. He washes up on an abandoned island, where he meets Floyd, an astro-chimp whose space capsule has crashed onto this isle as well. Together they build themselves a small civilization containing everything from living quarters to a South Seas golf course. One day he spots footprints and follows them to find Kwan, a beautiful island girl (Daniel Defoe's hero should have been so lucky) who has been exiled by her father for not marrying the man of his choice. Van Dyke dubs her "Wednesday" and organizes her and her disgruntled sisters into an all-woman army. They fight off an attack by her father, native chief Tamiroff, but when Kwan and Van Dyke do a victory dance, the white man accidentally discovers his dancing is an exact replica of a native marriage-proposal dance. Just in the nick of time a Navy helicopter comes to rescue him, taking Floyd along as well. Van Dyke, who was a great clown in his popular television series as well as MARY POPPINS, is completely wasted in this witless and insipid outing. He's reduced to pratfalls and mugging without much opportunity to show his real talents. The Robinson Crusoe update is wholly contrived and not really creative. The story is credited to a "Retlaw Yensid" which is backwards for Walter Disney. His name is not the only backwards thing here, considering the usual standards he set for his films. Despite the overall weaknesses of the film, it grossed a fairly impressive eight million dollars. The kids will love it.

p, Bill Walsh, Ron Miller; d, Byron Paul; w, Walsh, Donald DaGradi (based on a story by Retlaw Yensid [Walt Disney]); ph, William Snyder (Technicolor); m, Bob Brunner; ed, Cotton Warburton; art d, Carroll Clark, Carl Anderson; set d, Emile Kuri, Frank R. McKelvy; cos, Bill Thomas; spec eff, Eustace Lycett, Peter Ellenshaw, Robert A. Mattey; makeup Pat McNalley.

Children's Comedy   **(PR:AAA MPAA:NR)**

LIEUTENANT WORE SKIRTS, THE***   (1956) 98m FOX c

Tom Ewell (*Gregory Whitcomb*), Sheree North (*Katy Whitcomb*), Rita Moreno (*Sandra Gaxton*), Rick Jason (*Capt. Barney Sloan*), Les Tremayne (*Henry Gaxton*), Alice Reinhart (*Capt. Briggs*), Gregory Walcott (*Lt. Sweeney*), Jean Willes (*Joan Sweeney*), Sylvia Lewis (*Takitoff*), Edward Platt (*Maj. Dunning*), Jacqueline Fontaine (*Buxom Date*), Arthur Q. Bryan (*Mr. Curtis*), Paul Glass (*Sam*), Keith Vincent (*Delivery Boy*), Kathy Marlowe (*Gloria*), Joe Locke (*Roger Wilkins*), Bette Arlen (*WAF Officer*), Franklin James (*Sentry*), Maury Hill (*Officer at Gate*), Janice Carroll (*WAF Sergeant*), Dorothy Gordon (*WAF*), Ralph Sanford (*Gateman*), Pat Marshall (*Chorus Girl*), Helene Marshall (*Mildred Walkins*), Sam Bagley (*Comedian*), Marjorie Stapp (*Mother in Laundromat*), Michael Ross (*M.P.*), Marianne Candace Kelly, Leslie Parrish (*Girls*), Pat McMahon (*WAF*), Suzanne Ridgeway (*Hula Dancer*).

Fun little farce features Ewell as an aging war hero, now a television writer married to the somewhat younger North, an ex-WAC herself. Despite his better efforts, the Air Force calls him up though he is rejected eventually for medical reasons. But North is accepted and Ewell becomes a sort of male serviceman's wife, stuck on the base while his wife is out on patrols. He schemes to get her out of the military, failing everytime until nature solves the problem when North gets pregnant. Ewell is wonderful in his follow-up to THE SEVEN YEAR ITCH, handling the role of the frustrated husband with a wonderful sense of frenzy. Tashlin's script and direction are at their usual best, keeping the dialog witty with rare forays into lesser quality slapstick. Fun for all.

p, Buddy Adler; d, Frank Tashlin; w, Tashlin, Albert Beich (based on a story by Beich); ph, Leo Tover (CinemaScope, DeLuxe Color); m, Cyril J. Mockridge; ed, James B. Clark; md, Lionel Newman; art d, Lyle R. Wheeler, Leland Fuller; m/l, "Rock Around the Island," Ken Darby.

Comedy   **(PR:A MPAA:NR)**

LIFE AFTER DARK   (SEE: GIRLS IN THE NIGHT, 1953)

LIFE AND DEATH OF COLONEL BLIMP, THE
           (SEE: COLONEL BLIMP, 1945, Brit.)

LIFE AND LOVES OF BEETHOVEN, THE***1/2
(1937, Fr.) 135m General Productions/WORLD bw (UN GRAND AMOUR DE BEETHOVEN)

Harry Baur (*Ludwig van Beethoven*), Annie Ducaux (*Therese von Brunswick*), Jany Holt (*Giulietta Guicciardi*), Jean Debucourt (*Count Gallenberg*), Paul Pauley (*Schuppanzigh*), Lucien Rozenberg (*Count Guicciardi*), Yolande Laffon (*Countess Guicciardi*), Jane Marken (*Esther*), Lucas Gridoux (*Smeskall*), Roger Blin (*de Ries*), Jean-Louis Barrault (*Karl*), Marcel Dalio (*Steiner*).

Abel Gance's film biography of one of the world's greatest composers, which focuses on what Gance saw to be his only true loves—music and Holt. As in his classic NAPOLEON, Gance views Beethoven as being one of the great men of history, the very essence of music. Baur is superb in the lead role and adds believability to the genius' character. The most stirring scene is one of silence, when the composer's anomalous deafness is made manifest as the visuals recount the ringing of a blacksmith's anvil, the singing of birds, the chattering of villagers, a street

musician's music, all unheard. Unfortunately, however, this picture was never given the attention that NAPOLEON received and sits disintegrating, waiting restoration.

p&d, Abel Gance; w, Gance, Steve Passeur; ph, Robert LeFebvre, Marc Fossard; m, Ludwig van Beethoven (arranged by Louis Masson); ed Marguerite Beauge; md, Louis Masson.

Biography   **(PR:A MPAA:NR)**

LIFE AND LOVES OF MOZART, THE***
(1959, Ger.) 87m Cosmopol/Bakros International c (REICH MIR DIE HAND MEIN LEBEN; AKA: GIVE ME YOUR HAND MY LOVE; MOZART)

Oskar Werner (*Wolfgang Amadeus Mozart*), Johanna Matz (*Annie Gottleib*), Gertrud Kuekelmann (*Constanze Mozart*), Nadja Tiller (*Aloysia Weber*), Erich Kunz (*Impresario Schikaneder*), Angelika Hauff (*Susi Girl*), Annie Rosar (*Mother Weber*), the voices of: Hilda Gueden (*Pamina*), Anton Dermota, Gottlob Frick, Erika Koeth, Else Liebesburg, members of the State Opera in Vienna and the Vienna Philharmonic Orchestra under the direction of Hans Sinarowsky.

The convention among novelists and screenplay writers appears to be that artists can only create masterworks when they have an erection; thoughts of a beautiful damsel must enter their minds before artistic fulfillment occurs. This is another filmic biography in that trite living-muse mold. Mozart was as inveterate a letter writer as he was a composer; his diatribes and his penchant for scatological jokes are too well known to excuse such cliches as this, which is not even up to the level of the later AMADEUS (the latter had the great composer as an *idiot savant*, nonfunctional in any but musical terms). Like many such composer biographies, this one is partly saved by its music. It has the added advantage of a charismatic performance by Werner, and good work by the others in the cast. The English title aside, the film depicts only Mozart's later years, a time of poverty, strife, and disgrace. His problems were political, more the fault of his librettist, Emmanuel Schikaneder (Kunz) than himself. The two were devoted Freemasons at a time when the espousal of such a philosophy was outlaw heresy in Austria and much of the rest of Europe. The picture takes place during the premiere of "Die Zauberflote" ("The Magic Flute"), which was widely viewed as a paean of praise to Freemasonry. Werner's supposed Mozart-muse is Matz, who plays Pamina in the opera (with vocal assistance from Gueden). With the inspiration of Matz—at the expense of the long-suffering Frau Mozart, Kuekelmann—Werner completes some wonderfully melodic works before his demise, leaving a lyrical legacy for the lovelorn Matz, who dolefully trails his funeral wagon in a howling nonmusical wind at the film's conclusion. (In German, English subtitles.)

d&w, Karl Hartl; ph, Oskar Snirch (Eastmancolor); m, Wolfgang Amadeus Mozart.

Drama   **(PR:C MPAA:NR)**

LIFE AND TIMES OF CHESTER-ANGUS RAMSGOOD, THE**
           (1971, Can.) 80m West-Ridge Films c

Robert Matson, Mary-Beth McGuffin, Michael Sorgeoff, Judi Sommer, Ed Astley, Craig Peterson, Margaret Hunter, Cecil Glass, Victor A. Young, Janet Pollock, Carol Briggs, Ellen Seaborn, Ruth Nichol, Kevan Moore, John Young, Becky Sharp, Norman Puchalski, Bill Brenie, George Tobin.

Any charm that results from this low-budget independent feature is mainly a result of director-writer Curnick's ability to take advantage of a naive young man's first attempts at romance. Matson is the young college student with the hots for McGuffin, something he is unable to do much about, except make baby eyes, even though some of his buddies do everything within their powers to try to get the couple together. Thin plot line allows for an abundance of well-placed laughs, but little in terms of depth. The low budget shows in the production techniques. The 16mm picture was partly funded by the Canadian Film Development Corporation.

p, Don Wilson; d,w&ph, David Curnick; m, Frewer and Buckley; ed, Curnick.

Drama/Comedy   **(PR;C MPAA:NR)**

LIFE AND TIMES OF GRIZZLY ADAMS, THE*1/2
           (1974) 93m Sunn International/Sunn Classic c

Dan Haggerty (*James Capen Adams*), Don Shanks (*Indian Brave*), Marjorie Harper (*Adult Peg*), Lisa Jones (*Young Peg*), "Ben" (*The Bear*).

After being falsely accused of murder in the 1880's, Haggerty must leave his young daughter in order to save his life. He heads off to the wilderness to hide out and there begins his life as a "mountain man," communing with nature and inevitably becoming just as much a part of the area as the hopelessly cute animals he befriends. After many years of this peaceful existence Haggerty is confronted by a young woman who, to no one's surprise, turns out to be his now-grown-up daughter. She tells him he can return home now—that his name has been cleared—but everyone who has seen a Sunn Classic picture of this ilk surely knows what the man's answer is. The story is banal and completely lacking in any real honesty. The filmmaking matches this as well with long silent passages that feature an unnecessary narration by Haggerty telling exactly what's taking place. Sunn Classic knew exactly what they were doing with this film. It contains the same cute "man and nature" components as their other films like THE ADVENTURES OF THE WILDERNESS FAMILY and CHALLENGE TO BE FREE. It's filmmaking at its most basic commodity level, which worked well, based on this film's success. Despite the complete lack of quality, GRIZZLY ADAMS was well received by the public—and inspired a television series, to boot.

p, Charles E. Sellier, Jr.; d, Richard Friedenberg; w, Lawrence Dobkin; ph, George Stapleford (DeLuxe Color); m, Thom Pace; ed, Stapleford; set d, Richard Heavirland.

Family Adventure   Cas.   **(PR:AAA MPAA:G)**

LIFE AND TIMES OF JUDGE ROY BEAN, THE*
(1972) 120m First Artists/NG c

Paul Newman *(Judge Roy Bean)*, Jacqueline Bisset *(Rose Bean)*, Ava Gardner *(Lily Langtry)*, Tab Hunter *(Sam Dodd)*, John Huston *(Grizzly Adams)*, Stacy Keach *(Bad Bob)*, Roddy McDowall *(Frank Gass)*, Anthony Perkins *(Rev. LaSalle)*, Victoria Principal *(Marie Elena)*, Ned Beatty *(Tector Crites)*, Anthony Zerbe *(Hustler)*, Jim Burk *(Bart Jackson)*, Matt Clark *(Nick the Grub)*, Steve Kanaly *(Whorehouse Lucky Jim)*, Bill McKinney *(Fermel Parlee)*, Francesca Jarvis *(Mrs. Jackson)*, Karen Carr *(Mrs. Grubb)*, Dolores Clark *(Mrs. Whorehouse Jim)*, Lee Meza *(Mrs. Parlee)*, Neil Summers *(Snake River Rufus Krile)*, Jack Colvin *(Pimp)*, Howard Morton *(Photographer)*, Billy Pearson *(Miner/Station Master)*, Stan Barrett *(Killer)*, Don Starr *(Opera House Manager)*, Alfred G. Bosnos *(Opera House Clerk)*, John Hudkins *(Man at Stage Door)*, David Sharpe *(Doctor)*, Barbara J. Longo *(Fat Lady)*, Frank Soto *(Mexican Leader)*, Roy Jenson, Gary Combs, Fred Brookfield, Ben Dobbins, Dick Farnsworth, LeRoy Johnson, Fred Krone, Terry Leonard, Dean Smith *(Outlaws)*, Margo Epper, Jeannie Epper, Stephanie Epper *(Whores)*.

A rambling revisionist western whose episodic nature spawned only marginal success, and which didn't come close to BUTCH CASSIDY AND THE SUNDANCE KID on any level. Newman is a self-proclaimed judge in the tiny, West Texas town of Vinegaroon. He's a sot with megalomanic tendencies with whom no one wishes to associate when he rides into the small burg and draws a moustache on his own wanted poster. Matter of fact, they tie him to the back of a horse that drags him out to the middle of the Badlands where he is saved by a young Mexican girl, Principal. He returns to the saloon and kills everyone there, then sets himself up as the only real man in town and renames the place "Langtry" in honor of the legendary Lily. The town prospers as Newman robs anyone who comes through and hangs anyone with money. Newman's world begins to disintegrate when Principal dies and his fellow townsfolk start to turn on him. There's one death after another and a series of cameo appearances with actors waltzing into town, getting killed or waltzing out, developing little sense of who they are or why they are in this movie. Newman departs, then returns to murder the people who took the town away from him. A few of the characters talk directly to the camera, as though this were a documentary, and offer their remembrances of Newman, moments that are totally out of whack with the rest of the movie. The picture ends as Gardner, playing Langtry, arrives to see the town named after her. This $4 million production is not an homage; it is a travesty of the Old West. It depicts the last days of the horse era, then, after Newman leaves for several years, it's the start of the automobile period. Newman dies in a hail of gunfire (and none too soon), shouting "For Texas and for Miss Lily." It's surrealistic, sometimes funny, violent, and, most of all, confused. Huston plays Grizzly Adams and Keach almost steals the show with a weird role as a man who drinks hot coffee from the pot and eats raw onion when he orders an entire horse roasted as his dinner. The song "Marmalade, Molasses and Honey" was nominated for an Oscar but lost out to "The Morning After" from THE POSEIDON ADVENTURE. In another surprise, Newman warbles "The Yellow Rose of Texas" to Gardner.

p, John Foreman; d, John Huston; w, John Milius; ph, Richard Moore (Panavision, Technicolor); m, Maurice Jarre; ed, Hugh S. Fowler; md, Jarre; art d, Tambi Larsen; set d, Robert Benton; cos, Edith Head; spec eff, Butler-Glouner; m/l, "Marmalade, Molasses and Honey," Jarre, Marilyn and Alan Bergman (sung by Andy Williams); stunts, James Arnett; makeup, William Tuttle, Monty Westmore.

Western Comedy Cas. (PR:C MPAA:PG)

LIFE AT STAKE, A (SEE: KEY MAN, 1957, Brit.)

LIFE AT THE TOP*½** (1965, Brit.) 116m Romulus/COL bw

Laurence Harvey *(Joe Lampton)*, Jean Simmons *(Susan Lampton)*, Honor Blackman *(Norah Hauxley)*, Michael Craig *(Mark)*, Donald Wolfit *(Abe Brown)*, Robert Morley *(Tiffield)*, Margaret Johnston *(Sybil)*, Ambrosine Phillpotts *(Mrs. Brown)*, Allan Cuthbertson *(George Aisgill)*, Paul A. Martin *(Harry)*, Frances Cosslett *(Barbara)*, Ian Shand *(Hethersett)*, George A. Cooper *(Graffham)*, Nigel Davenport *(Mottram)*, Andrew Laurence *(McLelland)*, Geoffrey Bayldon *(Industrial Psychologist)*, Denis Quilley *(Ben)*, David Oxley *(Tim)*, David McKail *(Oscar)*, Paul Whitsun-Jones *(Keatley)*, Charles Lamb *(Wincastle)*, Michael Newport *(Newspaper Boy)*, Richard Leech *(Doctor)*, Ingrid Anthofer *(Stripper)*, Harry Fowler *(Magic Beans Man)*.

A sequel to ROOM AT THE TOP, this was written and directed by two Canadians who later teamed again for THE APPRENTICESHIP OF DUDDY KRAVITZ. This film later spawned a British TV series called "Man At The Top" and then a movie, MAN AT THE TOP, in 1973. It's 10 years after ROOM AT THE TOP and Harvey has ascended the ranks of business and shed his working-class mannerisms to hold an important position in his father-in-law's (Wolfit) mill business. Harvey is an ambitious man but riddled with self-doubt and he wonders if he would have achieved such a lofty position if he'd not married into it. He rises to power in the company, as well as in local politics where he runs as a Conservative and wins a membership on the town council. His marriage to Simmons is rapidly becoming "in name only" and his relationship with Wolfit is such that when Wolfit asks his advice on a matter, it is completely disregarded. Harvey's life takes a further tumble when he votes on a slum clearing matter with his conscience, instead of with his company loyalty. Then he finds Simmons in bed with his best friend, Craig, and the two occurrences combine to send him off in the arms of Blackman, a London TV newshen. That wobbles quickly as he loses interest both in Blackman and the pleasures of London. Further, he is not able to secure any employment because he's never been schooled in anything. Simmons follows him to London and prevails upon him to return to the small town where he is a big fish. He agrees and they go back. It's there that he learns that Wolfit actually likes him and that the old fellow is planning to leave him the whole business upon his retirement. He is still unsure of himself and his abilities to run a large company but will give it the old school try (even though he never went to the old school). Harvey is excellent and offers some very subtle shadings to the role, even more than he did in his earlier portrayal in ROOM AT THE TOP, for which he took an Oscar nomination. Simmons is good in an unsympathetic role and Wolfit repeats the fine job he did in the original. Morley is seen briefly and effectively as a London businessman and Johnston registers her presence as Craig's unhappy wife. LIFE AT THE TOP suffers from some slipshod lighting and some other mistakes in the technical area, but that's quibbling stuff as the impression made is memorable. In years to come, American TV would take up these same subjects in various soap operas and do them with a great deal more glitz but in a far more shallow fashion. LIFE AT THE TOP shows that being at the apex of a mountain is not all that it's cracked up to be. Why they replaced Heather Sears with Jean Simmons as the wife is not apparent because Sears did well in the first film. Not much humor to speak of, although Davenport does do one scene with Harvey that stands out as he leads the confused young man through a tour of some London strip clubs. Harvey's brief career ended when he died of cancer at 45. He'd been married to actress Margaret Leighton and to the widow of Columbia chief Harry Cohn. Born Larushka Skikne in Lithuania, he went to South Africa to escape the Nazi holocaust of Jews and eventually joined the navy there at the age of 14. That ruse was discovered shortly and he was returned home at 15. When he turned 18, he joined the army and fought bravely until the end of the war. That odd background belied his British upper-class accent and he made many films playing roles that had little to do with his real history, a tribute to his acting ability.

p, James Woolf, William Kirby; d, Ted Kotcheff; w, Mordecai Richler (based on the novel *Life at the Top* by John Braine); ph, Oswald Morris; m, Richard Addinsell; ed, Derek York; md, Marcus Dods; art d, Edward Marshall; set d, David Ffolkes; cos, Beatrice Dawson; makeup, George Frost.

Drama (PR:C MPAA:NR)

LIFE BEGINS*** (1932) 71m FN/WB-FN bw (GB: DREAM OF LIFE)

Loretta Young *(Grace Sutton)*, Eric Linden *(Jed Sutton)*, Aline MacMahon *(Miss Bowers)*, Glenda Farrell *(Florette)*, Dorothy Peterson *(Psychopathic Patient)*, Vivienne Osborne *(Mrs. MacGilvary)*, Frank McHugh *(Banks)*, Gilbert Roland *(Tony)*, Hale Hamilton *(Doctor Cramm)*, Herbert Mundin *(Mr. MacGilvary)*, Clara Blandick *(Mrs. West)*, Gloria Shea *(Mrs. Banks)*, Elizabeth Patterson *(Mrs. Tubby)*, Preston Foster *(Dr. Brett)*, Walter Walker *(Dr. Tubby)*, Helena Phillips *(Prison Matron)*, Reginald Mason *(Dr. Lee)*, Ruthelma Stevens *(Rose)*, Dorothy Tree *(Rita)*, Mary Phillips *(Miss Pinty)*, Terrance Ray *(Student)*.

A nice slice of life film dealing with the different characters found in a hospital's maternity ward. The central story revolves around Young, a convicted murderess who is about to give birth. Other mothers-to-be include Peterson as a non-pregnant psychopath who is always sneaking into the ward, convinced she is about to give birth and Farrell, a hardened nightclub singer who wants nothing to do with her children once her twins are born. (But when she sees them she cannot help but sing "Frankie and Johnny," the closest she can come to a lullaby.) The ensemble cast works well together and the directors handle the various threads of the plot with sympathy and understanding, rarely letting the different stories get confused with each other. Young's death scene in childbirth is especially well handled. Originally, this was a student play created at Columbia University, later moving to Broadway, though closing after only a week. The studio was impressed enough to buy the rights, however, for the paltry sum of $6000. This was remade in 1939 as A CHILD IS BORN.

p, Ray Griffith; d, James Flood, Elliott Nugent; w, Earl Baldwin (based on the play by Mary M. Axelson); ph, James Van Trees; ed, George Marks.

Drama (PR:C MPAA:NR)

LIFE BEGINS ANEW½**
(1938, Ger.) 106m UFA bw (ZU NEUEN UFERN; AKA: TO NEW SHORES)

Zarah Leander *(Gloria Vane)*, Willy Birgel *(Sir Albert Finsbury)*, Hilde von Stolz *(Fanny)*, Carola Hohn *(Mary)*, Viktor Staal *(Henry)*, Erich Ziegel *(Dr. Hoyer)*, Edwin Jurgensen *(Governor)*, Jakob Tiedtke *(Wells Senior)*, Robert Dorsay *(Bobby Wells)*, Iwa Wanja *(Violet)*, Ernst Legal *(Stout)*, Siegfried Schurenberg *(Gilbert)*, Lina Lossen *(Head Warden)*, Lissi Arna *(Nelly)*, Herbert Hubner *(Music Hall Proprietor)*, Curd [Curt] Jurgens.

Leander pleads guilty to a crime which her spineless lover committed and ends up in the Paramatta Penitentiary in Australia. When her lover realizes that she's been transported he moves to Australia and makes an unsuccessful attempt to contact her. Instead, he marries the daughter of the governor, while Leander marries respectable settler Staal and thereby gets out of prison. She is saddened to learn that her former paramour has found someone else so she runs off and tries to start anew as a nightclub singer. Ultimately, she returns voluntarily to the prison, but her selfless husband again retrieves her. One of Detlef Sierck's final German films before coming to America and changing his name to Douglas Sirk. Interesting as a precursor of the brilliant melodramas which were to come later.

p, Bruno Duday; d, [Hans] Detlef Sierck [Douglas Sirk]; w, Sierck, Kurt Heuser (based on the novel *Zu Neuen Ufern* by Louis H. Lorenz); ph, Franz Weihmayr; ed, Milo Harbich; set d, Fritz Maurischat; cos, Arno Richter; m/l, Ralph Benatzky.

Drama (PR:A MPAA:NR)

LIFE BEGINS AT COLLEGE (SEE: LIFE BEGINS IN COLLEGE, 1937)

LIFE BEGINS AT 8:30**
(1942) 84m FOX bw (GB: THE LIGHT OF HEART)

Monty Woolley *(Madden Thomas)*, Ida Lupino *(Kathi Thomas)*, Cornel Wilde *(Robert)*, Sara Allgood *(Mrs. Lothian)*, Melville Cooper *(Barty)*, J. Edward Bromberg *(Gordon)*, William Demarest *(Officer)*, Hal K. Dawson *(Producer)*, Milton Parsons *(Announcer)*, William Halligan *(Sgt. McNamara)*, Inez Palange *(Mrs.*

Spano), Charles La Torre *(Mr. Spano)*, James Flavin *(Policeman)*, Colin Campbell *(Dresser)*, Fay Helm *(Ruthie)*, George Holmes *(Jerry)*, Wheaton Chambers *(Floor-walker)*, Bud Geary *(Cab Driver)*, Netta Packer *(Maid)*, Alec Craig *(Santa Claus)*, Cyril Ring *(Box Office Man)*, Lee Phelps *(Bartender)*.

Despite Johnson's well-crafted adaptation of the play, this remains a talk piece that shows its stage heritage throughout. Woolley is a famed theater actor who has recently gone downhill as a result of his dependence upon grain spirits. His crippled daughter, Lupino, is concerned about his well-being, but he rewards her, and everyone around him, with darts of his caustic wit. As his drinking gets heavier, he finds it increasingly difficult to find employment and his barbs become sharper. Lupino continues to stay by daddy's side until Wilde, a composer, arrives to fetch her heart away. He helps Lupino in her desire to reacquaint the theatrical community with Woolley's talents. The bearded one is wary at first of Wilde's motives and fears that he will lose Lupino to the dark and dashing man. After some odd jobs (including one as a department store Santa Claus), Woolley accepts an offer to appear as "King Lear," and he is triumphant. He then takes up with a rich old flame, Allgood, and allows Wilde and Lupino to have their moment together. Wilde and Lupino do well in the roles conceived by Johnson, who changed the locale from London to New York in his screenplay. Simply wonderful in one of his patented acerbic roles, Woolley, who was very much the same off-stage as he was on, could always be counted on for a fine performance.

p, Nunnally Johnson; d, Irving Pichel; w, Johnson (based on the play "The Light of the Heart" by Emlyn Williams); ph, Edward Cronjager; m, Alfred Newman; ed, Fred Allen; art d, Richard Day, Boris Leven; set d, Thomas Little, Al Orenbach.

Comedy/Drama **(PR:A MPAA:NR)**

LIFE BEGINS AT 40*** (1935) 73m FOX bw

Will Rogers *(Kenesaw H. Clark)*, Rochelle Hudson *(Adele Anderson)*, Richard Cromwell *(Lee Austin)*, George Barbier *(Colonel Joseph Abercrombie)*, Jane Darwell *(Ida Harris)*, Slim Summerville *(T. Watterson Meriwether)*, Sterling Holloway *(Chris)*, Thomas Beck *(Joe Abercrombie)*, Roger Imhof *("Pappy" Smithers)*, Charles Sellon *(Tom Cotton)*, John Bradford *(Wally Stevens)*, Ruth Gillette *(Mrs. Cotton)*, Clair Du Brey *(Mrs. T. Watterson Meriwether)*, Jed Prouty *(Charles Beagle)*, John Ince *(Storekeeper)*, T. Roy Barnes *(Simonds, Salesman)*, James Donlan *(Farmer)*, Robert Kerr *(Bank Teller)*, Katherine Clare Ward *(House-wife)*, Crete Sipple *(Townswoman)*, Guy Usher *(Sheriff)*, Watson Children *(Meriwether Children)*, Creighton Hale *(Drug Clerk)*, Robert Dalton *(Steven's Henchman)*, Barbara Barondess *(Abercrombie's Maid)*, Edward McWade *(Doctor)*, John Wallace *(Peg-Leg Man)*, Billy Bletcher *(Hog Caller)*, Frank Darien, William Burress, Harry Dunkinson *(Abercrombie's Friends)*, Edward Le Saint, Jac Hoffman, Rhody Hathaway, Ernest Shields, Robert McKenzie, Rodney Hildebrand, Jack Waters, J. B. Kenton, Larry Fisher, E. W. Borman, John Webb Dillon, Jack Henderson, James Marcus, Allan Sears, Carl Miller, Bill Baxter *(Townsmen)*, Herbert Hayward, W. J. Kolberg *(Rural Characters)*, Gloria Roy *(Bit Girl)*, Gordon Carveth, William Sundholm, Floyd Criswell *(Stunts)*, Len Trainer *(Stand-in for Rogers)*, Emily Baldwin *(Stand-In for Hudson)*.

Delightful little film finds Rogers as a small-town newspaperman who befriends Cromwell, a youth framed on bank robbery charges. Barbier is the bank manager who forecloses on Rogers in retaliation, but Rogers and Cromwell start their own small one-page sheet. When Barbier runs for mayor, Rogers sets up former silent comedy star Summerville, the town bum, as the opposing candidate. An investigation proves Cromwell to be innocent and the banker's son the guilty party. The film ends happily with Cromwell cleared (as well as winning the heart of schoolteacher Hudson), Rogers back in business, and Summerville off to the woodpile. A nice folksy picture, full of the wry humor and jokes for which Rogers was famous. The ensemble is a good bunch, handling the comic turns with great ease. The film holds up well today and, as with most of Rogers work, seems surprisingly contemporary.

p, Sol M. Wurtzel; d, George Marshall; w, Lamar Trotti, Robert Quillen, Dudley Nichols, William M. Conselman (based on the book by Walter B. Pitkin); ph, Harry Jackson; ed, Alexander Troffey; md, Samuel Kaylin; art d, Duncan Cramer, Albert Hogsett; cos, Lillian; ch, Jack Donohue.

Comedy **(PR:AAA MPAA:NR)**

LIFE BEGINS AT 17 1/2** (1958) 74m Clover/COL bw

Mark Damon *(Russ Lippincott)*, Dorothy Johnson *(Elaine Peck)*, Edward [Edd] Byrnes *(Jim)*, Ann Doran *(Virginia Peck)*, Hugh Sanders *(Harry Peck)*, Luana Anders *(Carol Peck)*, Cathy O'Neill *(Pooky Peck)*, George Eldredge *(Mr. Lippincott)*, Tommy Ivo *(Earl Williamson)*, Bob Dennis *(Allen Sperry)*, Robert Moechel *(George Tewksbury)*, Maurice Manson *(Mr. Tilling)*.

Tepid teenage Cinderella tale features Anders as the not-so-beautiful younger sister of Johnson. Damon wants to date the older girl so he uses the young sibling in order to get to Johnson. But Anders discovers she's being badly used and in order to get revenge she announces that Damon is the father of her nonexistent child-to-be. Aimed at the typical teenaged audience of the late 1950s, this is well acted and directed for what it is. It was advertised as "a family drama of adolescent love." The mostly teenaged cast handles the script fairly well. Byrnes, who was a national star with his television show "77 Sunset Strip" is featured as Johnson's boy friend.

p, Sam Katzman; d, Arthur Dreifuss; w, Richard Baer; ph, Fred Jackman; ed, Saul A. Goodkind; art d, Paul Palmentola.

Teenage Drama/Romance **(PR:C MPAA:NR)**

LIFE BEGINS FOR ANDY HARDY* 1/2** (1941) 100m MGM bw

Mickey Rooney *(Andy Hardy)*, Lewis Stone *(Judge Hardy)*, Judy Garland *(Betsy Booth)*, Fay Holden *(Mrs. Hardy)*, Ann Rutherford *(Polly Benedict)*, Sara Haden *(Aunt Milly)*, Patricia Dane *(Jennitt Hicks)*, Ray McDonald *(Jimmy Frobisher)*, George Breakston *(Beezy)*, Pierre Watkin *(Dr. Waggoner)*, Frances Morris *(Operator)*, Tommy Kelly *(Chuck)*, Robert Winkler *(Private)*, William Forrest *(Commandant)*, Paul Newlan, Duke York *(Truckmen)*, Byron Shores *(Jackson)*, Hollis Jewell *(Ted)*, Sidney Miller, Roger Daniel *(Boys)*, Arthur Loft, James Flavin *(Policemen)*, Charlotte Wynters *(Elizabeth Norton)*, Bob Pittard *(Delivery Boy)*, Lester Matthews *(Mr. Maddox)*, Don Brodie *(Clerk)*, John Harmon *(Taxi Driver)*, Gladden James *(Man)*, Frank Ferguson *(Stationer)*, Leonard Sues *(Kelly)*, George Carleton *(Florist)*, George Ovey *(Janitor)*, Robert E. Homans *(Watchman)*, William J. Holmes *(Dr. Griffin)*, Manart Kipen *(Rabbi Strauss)*, Ralph Byrd *(Father Gallagher)*, Ann Morriss *(Miss Dean)*, Mira McKinney *(Miss Gomez)*, Nora Lane *(Miss Howard)*, John Eldredge *(Paul McWilliams)*, Joseph Crehan *(Peter Dugan)*, Mary Jo Ellis *(Drugstore Cashier)*, Yolande Mollot *(Drugstore Waitress)*, Estelle Etterre, Bess Flowers *(Secretaries)*, Kent Rogers *(Tough Boy)*, Purnell Pratt *(Dr. Storfen)*.

A serious departure in MGM's highly successful ANDY HARDY series finds Rooney as the prodigal. The recent high school graduate has a heart-to-heart discussion with his father, Stone, about his future. Not wanting to follow immediately in his father's footsteps, Rooney's ambition is to go off to New York and "find himself." Though they don't agree with him, the Hardys let their son go off to New York City. There he joins his long-suffering friend Garland (in her third and last film in the HARDY series, though she continued to work on-screen with Rooney in other films). After much difficulty, Rooney finds a job as an office boy for the paltry sum of $10 a week. He meets McDonald, a struggling dancer, and sneaks the penniless, homeless young man into his hotel room so he can have someplace to stay. But Rooney is startled one evening when he comes home to find his new friend dead of a heart attack. He gets a loan on his jalopy so McDonald can have a decent funeral rather than a pauper's grave. Rooney has befriended Dane, an older divorcee—the receptionist in his employer's office—who invites the young man up to her apartment for an evening. The offer is tempting, but Rooney's homespun value system—along with the arrival of his father in the big city—help him make a proper choice (one which any redblooded boy would regret all his life). Looking over the events that have happened since his arrival in New York, Rooney decides that his home town and college are his real future and he returns to Carvel with Stone. Though the critics attacked the film as too far a departure from the ANDY HARDY series' normal vein, this is a fine addition. Rooney and Garland both show great maturity with their characters. Garland is a fine counterbalance for Rooney, constantly watching over him like a loving mother and calling his father when things look dark. Though she truly wants to be in love with him, she can circumvent her feelings to help the skittish young man when he really needs her. The National Legion of Decency surprised everyone in the film world by rating this film A-2, an objectional film for children. They felt that Rooney's heart-to-heart talks with Stone were too "daring" for children, to say nothing of his scenes with Dane. (See ANDY HARDY series, Index).

d, George B. Seitz; w, Agnes Christine Johnston (based on characters created by Aurania Rouverol); ph, Lester White; ed, Elmo Veron; md, Georgie Stoll; art d, Cedric Gibbons; cos, Kalloch.

Family Drama **(PR:A MPAA:NR)**

LIFE BEGINS IN COLLEGE 1/2**
(1937) 90m FOX bw (GB: THE JOY PARADE)

Ritz Brothers *(Themselves)*, Joan Davis *(Inez)*, Tony Martin *(Band Leader)*, Gloria Stuart *(Janet O'Hara)*, Fred Stone *(Coach O'Hara)*, Nat Pendleton *(George Black)*, Dick Baldwin *(Bob Hayner)*, Joan Marsh *(Cuddles)*, Dixie Dunbar *(Polly)*, Edward Thorgersen *(Radio Announcer)*, Jed Prouty *(Oliver Stearns, Sr.)*, Maurice Cass *(Dean Moss)*, Marjorie Weaver *(Miss Murphy)*, J. C. Nugent *(T. Edwin Cabot)*, Robert Lowery *(Sling)*, Elisha Cook, Jr. *(Ollie Stearns)*, Lon Chaney, Jr. *(Gilks)*, Fred Kohler, Jr. *(Bret)*, Brewster Twins *(Emmy and Mary Lou)*, Charles Wilson *(Coach Burke)*, Frank Sully *(Acting Captain)*, Robert Murphy *(Rooter)*, Norman Willis *(Referee)*, Dick Klein, Ron Cooley *(Cheerleaders)*, Jim Pierce, Jeff Cravath *(Coaches)*, Hal K. Dawson *(Graduate Manager)*, Edward Arnold, Jr., Thomas Kellard, Grant Peters *(Huskies)*, Sarah Edwards *(Teacher)*, Spec O'Donnell *(Ugly Student)*.

One of the many football comedies of the 1930s, this features the zany Ritz Brothers as three college students in their seventh year of school, working their long way through the halls of higher learning (and low comedy) as tailors. They long for a chance to play on the football team. When the coach (Stone) is fired, Pendleton—who is a rich Indian student—gives the school a heavy sum of money to keep Stone. Stuart is the coach's daughter, who gets mad at boy friend Baldwin when she thinks he's trying to expose Pendleton as a former professional footballer. Of course, it turns out that Baldwin is innocent; when he is injured in the big game, the Ritzes at last have their chance to play ball, cultimating in a zany finish. Not a great football comedy like the Marx Brothers' HORSEFEATHERS, but this is fun in its own way. There are some good song-and-dance numbers including "Sweet Varsity Sue" (Al Lewis, Charles Tobias, Murray Mencher), and "The Rhumba Goes Collegiate," "Big Chief Swing It," "Our Team Is On the Warpath," "Fair Lombardy," "Why Talk About Love" (Sidney Mitchell, Lew Pollack). The Ritzes also have a minor classic comedy routine with their "Spirit of '76" number. The direction keeps a steady pace and the humor rarely lags. Thorgersen, who was the regular sports announcer for Movietone newsreels has a cameo as the football radio announcer. This was released in the fall of 1937 to capitalize on the football season.

p, Harold Wilson; d, William A. Seiter; w, Karl Tunberg, Don Ettlinger, Sidney Kuller, Ray Golden, Samuel Pokrass (based on stories by Darrell Ware); ph, Robert Planck; ed, Louis Loeffler; md, Louis Silvers; art d, Hans Peters; ch, Nick Castle, Geneva Sawyer.

Comedy **(PR:AA MPAA:NR)**

LIFE BEGINS TOMORROW**
(1952, Fr.) 86m International Pictures bw (LA VIE COMMENCE DEMAIN)

Jean-Pierre Aumont *(The Man of Today)*, Andre Labarthe *(The Man of Tomorrow)*,

Jean-Paul Sartre (Existentialist), Daniel Lagache (Psychiatrist), Le Corbusier (Architect), Pablo Picasso (Artist), Andre Gide (Author), Jean Rostand (Biologist), Dominique.

Aumont is the innocent abroad in the high country of the intelligentsia; Labarthe, a journalist, is his guide in this think piece co-starring some of the major shakers and movers of its time. As the artists and scientists pedantically plead not guilty to the prospect of the world's destruction, Aumont is advised to prepare himself for future shock. Newsreel clips and classroom cuts are interspersed through the tale, suggesting what technology has in store for humanity in the age of nuclear destruction. Perhaps the most compelling asseveration is that the minds of the maniacs who control the world's institutions might be surgically altered for the better. The film was made with the cooperation of UNESCO; it features a fine score by Milhaud.

p, Arthur Mayer, Edward Kingsley; d&w, Nicole Vedres; ph, Fred Langenfeld; m, Darius Milhaud; ed, Marinette Cadix.

Philosophical Drama   **(PR:C   MPAA:NR)**

LIFE BEGINS WITH LOVE**   (1937) 72m COL bw

Jean Parker (Carole), Douglass Montgomery (Drake IV), Edith Fellows (Dodie), Leona Maricle (Millicent), Lumsden Hare (Col. Drake), Aubrey Mather (Roberts), James Burke (McGraw), Minerva Urecal (Mrs. Murphy), Scotty Beckett (Manchild), Joel Davis (Stevie), Joyce Kay (Maggie), Si Wills (Photographer).

Montgomery is an heir to millions who pledges his fortune to charity while in the midst of a drunken bout. Parker is a nursery school teacher. Montgomery hides out, disguised as a janitor for the school, in order to avoid redeeming his drunken pledge and also to avoid Maricle. She's a beauty who's also after his money. Fellows, Davis, and Beckett are Parker's charges, often stealing the show with their inherent movie-kid cuteness. Parker must go down in history as the best-dressed nursery school teacher of all time. It's no wonder her school is broke if her clothes budget is as high as it appears to be. Technical credits are standard for this highly forgettable number.

d, Raymond B. McCarey; w, Thomas Mitchell, Brown Holmes (based on a story by Dorothy Bennett); ph, Lucien Ballard; ed, Viola Lawrence.

Romance   **(PR:A   MPAA:NR)**

LIFE DANCES ON, CHRISTINE   (SEE: UN CARNET DE BAL, 1938, Fr.)

LIFE FOR RUTH   (SEE: WALK IN THE SHADOW, 1966, Brit.)

LIFE GOES ON**
(1932, Brit.) 78m British and Dominions/PAR bw (AKA: SORRY YOU'VE BEEN TROUBLED)

Hugh Wakefield (Ridgeway Emsworth), Elsie Randolph (Phoebe Selsey), Betty Stockfield (Lady Sheridan), Wallace Geoffreys (Robert Kent), Warwick Ward (Ronald St. John), Jeanne Stuart (Clare Armore), Dennis Hoey (Anthony Carlisle), Antony Holles (John Collis), Robert Horton (Sir George Sheridan).

After attracting the amorous attention of hotel switchboard operator Randolph, Wakefield learns he's checked into a trouble-filled place. A stockbroker in the room next to his has died and a woman is being framed for his killing. It seems the hotel manager and another individual want to keep the death quiet before rearranging the clues in order to manipulate money markets. Typical low-budget British programmer.

p, Herbert Wilcox; d, Jack Raymond; w, [uncredited] (based on a play by Walter Hackett).

Crime   **(PR:A-C   MPAA:NR)**

LIFE IN DANGER*   (1964, Brit.) 63m Parroch/AA bw

Derren Nesbitt (The Man), Julie Hopkins (Hazel Ashley), Howard Marion Crawford (Maj. Peters), Victor Brooks (Tom Baldwin), Jack Allen (Jack Ashley), Christopher Witty (Johnny Ashley), Carmel McSharry (Mrs. Ashley), Mary Manson (Jill Shadwell), Bruce Seton (Landlord), Peter Swanwick (Dr. Nichols), Bryan Coleman (Chief Constable Ryman), Humphrey Lestocq (Inspector Bennet), Richard Pearson (Sgt. Norris), Celia Hewitt (Woman at Bus Stop), Brian Rawlinson (Male Nurse).

Drifter Nesbitt befriends teen Hopkins and the two spend some time in a nearby barn. She tries to get him to take her away from her parents, but he refuses. In the light of a search for an escaped child murderer, a police hunt is begun for the missing Hopkins. They search the barn, but the pair is too well hidden to be found. Later, a mob led by Crawford sniffs out the barn again and finds Nesbitt, believing he's the killer. Wounded, he's saved from the angry mob when news arrives that the real murderer has been captured. Released in England in 1959.

p, Jack Parkins; d, Terry Bishop; w, Malcolm Hulke, Eric Paice; ph, Peter Hennessy; m, William Davies; ed, John Trumper; md, Davies; art d, Peter Proud.

Drama   **(PR:A   MPAA:NR)**

LIFE IN EMERGENCY WARD 10***   (1959, Brit.) 86m Eros bw

Michael Craig (Dr. Stephen Russell), Wilfrid Hyde-White (Professor Bourne-Evans), Dorothy Alison (Sister Janet Fraser), Glyn Owen (Dr. Paddy O'Meara), Rosemary Miller (Nurse Pat Roberts), Charles Tingwell (Dr. Alan Dawson), Frederick Bartman (Dr. Simon Forrester), Joan Sims (Mrs. Pryor), Rupert Davies (Dr. Tim Hunter), Sheila Sweet (Anne Hunter), David Lodge (Mr. Phillips), Dorothy Gordon (Mrs. Phillips), Christopher Witty (David Phillips), Tony Quinn (Joe Cooney), Douglas Ives (Potter), George Tovey (Mr. Pryor), Pauline Stroud (Nurse Vincent), Christina Gregg (Nurse April Andrews), Jean Aubrey, Maurice Kaufmann, Geoffrey Adams, John Baker, Enid Lindsey, Peter Greenspan, Henry Momberg, Howard Knight, Mark Mylam.

Hospital drama features Craig as a new surgeon plugging an experimental heart-lung machine he has brought to England from America. The other surgeons are wary about the new device, especially after it fails on an older patient. But when a young boy with a hole in his heart needs emergency surgery the device is put to good use and Craig proves himself. In between are vignettes involving other patients, including a woman expecting quadruplets as well as the usual doctor-nurse romances. A lot of this is just standard hospital-film follies but it's told in an intriguing and fresh manner. The acting has sincerity, and the comedy and drama of the situations are nicely balanced. The Royal College of Surgeons served as technical consultants for the film, which was based on a popular British TV series.

p, Ted Lloyd; d, Robert Day; w, Tessa Diamond, Hazel Adair (based on the TV series); ph, Geoffrey Faithfull; m, Phillip Green; ed, Lito Carruthers.

Drama   **(PR:C   MPAA:NR)**

LIFE IN HER HANDS***1/2   (1951, Brit.) 58m Crown Film Unit/UA bw

Kathleen Byron (Ann Peters), Bernadette O'Farrell (Mary Gordon), Jacqueline Charles (Michele Rennie), Jenny Laird (Matron), Robert Long (Jack Wilson), Grace Gaven (Sister McTavish), Jean Anderson (Night Sister), Joan Maude (Sister Tutor), Elwyn Brook-Jones (Surgeon), Irish Ballard (Nurse Soper), Susan Richmond (Mrs. Wilson), Grace Arnold (Children's Sister), Audrey Teasdale.

When her husband is killed Byron blames herself for his death. In order to get over her grief she becomes a nurse. Though she passes through the training period, Byron snaps after a patient dies, and begins to rebel against authority. Only after helping doctors during a caesarian birth is her humanity restored as Byron realizes that new life balances out death. Though a bit simplistic, this is well enough acted to work as good drama. The documentary shooting style adds to the film's quality, as well.

p, Frederick Wilson; d, Philip Leacock; w, Monica Dickens, Anthony Stevens; ph, Fred Gamage.

Drama   **(PR:C   MPAA:NR)**

LIFE IN THE BALANCE, A**1/2   (1955) 74m Panoramic/FOX bw

Ricardo Montalban (Antonio Gomez), Anne Bancroft (Maria Ibinia), Lee Marvin (The Murderer), Jose Perez (Paco Gomez), Rodolfo Acosta (Lt. Fernando), Carlos Muzquiz (Capt. Saldana), Jorge Trevino (Sergeant), Jose Torvay (Andres Martinez), Eva Calvo (Carla Arlotta), Fanny Schiller (Carmen Martinez), Tamara Garina (Dona Lucrecia), Pascual G. Pena (Porter), Antonio Carbajal (Pedro).

A nice little thriller featuring Marvin as a psychotic killer, who murders people he believes are sinners. He kills a woman in the building where Montalban and his son Perez live in Mexico City. Circumstantial evidence points towards Montalban, who is arrested for the crime. But Perez has witnessed the murderer and goes after Marvin to prove his father's innocence. The climactic ending has the boy smashing police call boxes, leaving a trail for the cops before Marvin finds him out and captures him. The technical values are good with the script and direction taking the story along nicely. The acting is nothing spectacular, with the strong exception of Perez, who outshines the adults easily. Bancroft has a supporting role as Montalban's lover. Filmed in cooperation with the police department of Mexico City, with a nice use of the locale.

p, Leonard Goldstein; d, Harry Horner; w, Robert Presnell, Jr., Leo Townsend (based on a story by Georges Simenon); ph, J. Gomez Urquiza; m, Raul Lavista; ed, George Gittens, George Crone; md, Lavista; art d, Bunther Gerzo.

Thriller   **(PR:O   MPAA:NR)**

LIFE IN THE RAW**1/2   (1933) 62m FOX bw

George O'Brien, Claire Trevor, Warner Richmond, Francis Ford, Greta Nissen, Gaylord Pendleton, Alan Edwards, Nigel De Brulier.

Above-average western has Trevor (in her film debut) framing the man she loves so that the real culprit, her brother, can get away. Excellent photography and nice pacing.

d, Louis King; w, Stuart Anthony (based on a story by Zane Grey); ph, Robert Planck; m, Arthur Lange; set d, Duncan Cramer; ch, Sammy Lee.

Western   **(PR:A   MPAA:NR)**

LIFE IS A CIRCUS**1/2   (1962, Brit.) 84m Vale/Schoenfeld bw

Bud Flanagan (Bud), Teddy Knox (Sebastian), Jimmy Nervo (Cecil), Jimmy Gold (Goldie), Charlie Naughton (Charlie), Eddie Gray (Eddie), Chesney Allen (Ches), Shirley Eaton (Shirley Winter), Michael Holliday (Carl Rickenbeck), Lionel Jeffries (Genie), Joseph Tomelty (Joe Winter), Eric Pohlmann (Rickenbeck), Fred Johnson (Mr. Deaken), Harold Kasket (Hassan), Maureen Moore (Rose of Baghdad), Edwin Richfield (Driver), Peter Glaze (1st Hand), Sam Kydd (Removal Man), Geoffrey Denton (Policeman).

The Crazy Gang (Flanagan, Nervo, Knox, Naughton, Gold and Gray) is a popular British comedy troupe featured here in their first film appearance. The story—a remake of ALF's BUTTON AFLOAT—has them serving as sweepers for a financially strapped circus. Pohlmann is the owner of a rival carnival who wants to put them out of business. But when a magical lamp containing a genie is purchased, the Crazies manage to save the day. The thin plot is merely a showcase for the various talents of the troupe which include a comedy trapeze act, some juggling, magic, and a number of corny jokes. Though the stage business of the troupe doesn't translate well to the big screen, this isn't too bad a comedy. Songs include "Life is a Circus" (Bernie Loren, Horace Linsley), "For You, For You" (Dave Goddard, Gene McCarthy, Larry Vannata), "Underneath the Arches" (Bud Flanagan).

p, E. M. Smedley-Aston; d, Val Guest; w, Guest, John Warren, Len Heath; ph, Arthur Graham (CinemaScope); m, Philip Green; ed, Bill Lenny; art d, Tony Masters; ch, Denys Palmer.

Comedy (PR:A MPAA:NR)

LIFE LOVE DEATH*

(1969, Fr./Ital.) 115m Treize-Ariane-Artistes Associes-P.E.A./Lopert c-bw (LA VIE, L'AMOUR, LA MORT)

Souad Amidou *(Francois Toledo)*, Caroline Cellier *(Caroline)*, Janine Magnan *(Jeanne)*, Marcel Bozzufi *(Inspector Marchand)*, Pierre Zimmer *(Police Officer)*, Lisette Bersy *(Helene)*, Albert Naud *(Defense Lawyer)*, Jean-Pierre Sloan *("Partie Civile")*, Nathalie Durrand *(Sophie)*, Sylvia Saurel, Denyse Roland, Rita Maiden *(Prostitutes)*, Claudia Morin *(Girl at Dance)*, Catherine Samie *(Julie)*, Pierre Collet *(Chief Executioner)*, Albert Rajau, Jacques Henry, Jean-Marc Allegre *(Executioner's Assistants)*, Colette Taconnat *("Assistante Sociale")*, Jean Collomb *(Motel Owner)*, Robert Hossein *(Man in Film)*, Annie Girardot *(Woman in Film)*, El Cordobes *(Bullfighter)*, Jacques Portet, Yves Gabrielli, Jean-Pierre Hazi *(Police)*.

Amidou is arrested for murder and condemned to death. In prison he reflects on his prostitute-strewn past and the murders that followed—a whore who insulted him because of his impotence, and another he met after a bullfight. The next morning he is taken out to the prison courtyard and beheaded. And rightly so.

p, Alexandre Mnouchkine, Georges Dancigers; d, Claude Lelouch; w, Peter Uytterhoeven, Lelouch; ph, Jean Collomb; m, Francis Lai; ed, Claude Barrois; md, Christian Gaubert.

Drama (PR:O MPAA:R)

LIFE OF A COUNTRY DOCTOR**

(1961, Jap.) 104m Toho/Toho International bw (FUNDOSHI ISHA; AKA: LIFE OF THE COUNTRY DOCTOR, THE COUNTRY DOCTOR)

Hisaya Morishige *(Keisai Koyama)*, Setsuko Hara *(Iku, His Wife)*, Yosuke Natsuki *(Hangoro)*, Chiemi Eri *(Osaki)*, So Yamamura *(Dr. Meikai Ikeda)*.

A doctor in Japan during the late 1800s takes on an assistant much younger than himself, raising questions about his traditional methods and modernized techniques. It takes an epidemic of typhus to make him come around. Directed by one-time actor Inagaki.

p, Tomoyuki Tanaka; d, Hiroshi Inagaki; w, Ryuzo Kikushima; ph, Kazuo Yamada (Tohoscope); m, Ikuma Dan; English adapter, Victor Suzuki.

Historical Drama (PR:A MPAA:NR)

LIFE OF BRIAN

(SEE: MONTY PYTHON'S LIFE OF BRIAN, 1979, Brit.)

LIFE OF EMILE ZOLA, THE*****

(1937) 123m WB bw

Paul Muni *(Emile Zola)*, Gale Sondergaard *(Lucie Dreyfus)*, Joseph Schildkraut *(Capt. Alfred Dreyfus)*, Gloria Holden *(Alexandrine Zola)*, Donald Crisp *(Maitre Labori)*, Erin O'Brien-Moore *(Nana)*, John Litel *(Charpentier)*, Henry O'Neill *(Col. Picquart)*, Morris Carnovsky *(Anatole France)*, Louis Calhern *(Maj. Dort)*, Ralph Morgan *(Commander of Paris)*, Robert Barrat *(Maj. Walsin-Esterhazy)*, Vladimir Sokoloff *(Paul Cezanne)*, Harry Davenport *(Chief of Staff)*, Robert Warwick *(Maj. Henry)*, Charles Richman *(Monsieur Delagorgue)*, Dickie Moore *(Pierre Dreyfus)*, Rolla Gourvitch *(Jeanne Dreyfus)*, Filbert Emery *(Minister of War)*, Walter Kingsford *(Col. Sandherr)*, Paul Everton *(Assistant Chief of Staff)*, Montagu Love *(Cavaignac)*, Frank Sheridan *(Van Cassell)*, Lumsden Hare *(Mr. Richards)*, Marcia Mae Jones *(Helen Richards)*, Florence Roberts *(Madame Zola)*, Grant Mitchell *(Georges Clemenceau)*, Moroni Olsen *(Capt. Guignet)*, Egon Brecher *(Brucker)*, Frank Reicher *(M. Perrenx)*, Walter O. Stahl *(Senator Scheurer-Kestner)*, Frank Darien *(Albert)*, Countess Iphigeni Castiglioni *(Madame Charpentier)*, Arthur Aylesworth *(Chief Censor)*, Frank Mayo *(Mathieu Dreyfus)*, Alexander Leftwich *(Maj. D'Aboville)*, Paul Irving *(La Rue)*, Pierre Watkin *(Prefect of Police)*, Holmes Herbert *(Commander of Paris)*, Robert Cummings, Sr. *(Gen. Gillian)*, Harry Worth *(Lieutenant)*, William von Brincken *(Schwartzkoppen)*.

In his early career, Muni was the unofficial actor who was designated to play Great Men. He won an Oscar as Louis Pasteur, and also played Benito Juarez, French explorer Pierre Radisson, Chopin's teacher (Joseph Elsner), a gangster based on the life of Al Capone, as well as Napoleon, Schubert, and Don Juan (plus four more) in 1929's SEVEN FACES. So it wasn't a surprise when he was cast as Zola for this flawless film that took the Oscar as Best Picture of 1937. It won awards for Best Script as well as a Best Supporting Actor statuette for Joseph Schildkraut. Nominations went to Muni, Dieterle, Steiner, and for Best Story. Despite being literate, pointed, and informative, it was a huge box office success, which says a lot for the intelligence of the moviegoers of the late thirties. THE LIFE OF EMILE ZOLA depicted a famous historical episode where one man took a stand against injustice and bigotry and won. The producers never thought such a film would be a huge winner but the intelligence of the script and Muni's towering portrayal (as well as those of all the other actors) caused word-of-mouth to begin and it was as financially rewarding as it was prestigious. The script was originally shown to Ernst Lubitsch at Paramount who liked it but felt he had no actor in his stable worthy of the role so he suggested it be brought to Blanke, a pal and competitor at Warner Bros., as Blanke had Muni and Lubitsch felt Muni was the only actor in Hollywood who could handle such an assignment. Lubitsch was right, as he was on so many other occasions, and proved that there are a few people in the movie business who have conscience and generosity. Muni is Zola, a beleaguered author who has problems with the censors as well as his fellow Frenchman. Much of the populace and the government thought his work too scandalous and sought to keep it off the shelves. When his book, *Nana*, is published (based on his own experiences with O'Brien-Moore, a Gallic prostitute), he is soundly thrashed by everyone for his frank treatment of social injustice, but the book becomes very popular and that consoles the anguished writer. As the years pass, he is acknowledged as France's greatest author as well as the champion of those who cannot speak for themselves during the country's bloodless "after revolution" when words are exchanged rather than swords and bullets. One night, Muni is visited by Sondergaard, wife of Schildkraut, an army captain who has been accused of treason. Muni agrees to help, begins to study the case, and publishes his famous article "J'Accuse" which plainly states the truth about Schildkraut's railroading and accuses Barrat as the man who betrayed his country. The French did not know who the actual culprit was at the time so they elected the Jewish Schildkraut as a scapegoat. He was tried, convicted, discharged, and sent to Devil's Island for a life term. Muni gets the support of France (Carnovsky) and his attorney (Crisp), and the article is published. The army feels it has been libeled; Zola is put on trial and is convicted in a room full of prejudiced army officers. He escapes to England, rather than face jail, but won't stop writing about the Dreyfus affair. The French public starts to believe its laureate and much pressure is brought to bear until the government decides to look more deeply into the matter. The facts are learned and Barrat is brought up for a court martial but the military people are so embarrassed by their mistake that they refuse to convict Barrat and he is acquitted in the reverse of a kangaroo court. Schildkraut is vindicated and allowed to leave Devil's Island and Muni can now return to France. Unfortunately, Muni dies before he can meet the man upon whom he has spent so much time and effort. In real life, Dreyfus outlived everyone else concerned with the situation; he died in 1935 at the age of 75. Muni had played Dreyfus in a Maurice Schwartz Yiddish Art Theatre play in 1924 when he was 29. He later did this again on radio for Lux Soap on CBS in 1939. The entire supporting cast is perfection and each character crucial to the story is given a well-balanced tale to tell. The period sequences are all authentic and nothing was spared to recreate the settings. Dieterle did a magnificent job of interpreting the screenplay, which was especially effective during the courtroom scenes. The religious theme, so crucial to the case, was handled effectively and was not hammered home heavily. Matter of fact, the word "Jew" was never mentioned, although that had a great deal to do with the wall of hatred that had been built around Dreyfus until the truth was uncovered. Dieterle handled Muni in two more biographical winners, JUAREZ and THE STORY OF LOUIS PASTEUR. As was his custom, Muni steeped himself in the character he was to play. For this, he read all of Zola's works, pored over every account of the trial, and attempted many different makeup variations before settling on the one he finally used. A beautiful biography, perfectly acted and brilliantly filmed. The 1958 remake, I ACCUSE, was anything but.

p, Hal B. Wallis, Henry Blanke; d, William Dieterle, Irving Rapper; w, Norman Reilly Raine, Heinz Herald, Geza Herczeg (based on the story by Heinz Herald and Geza Herczeg); ph, Tony Gaudio; m, Max Steiner; ed, Warren Lowe; md, Leo F. Forbstein; art d, Anton Grot; set d, Albert C. Wilson; cos, Milo Anderson, Ali Hubert; makeup, Perc Westmore.

Biography Cas. (PR:AA MPAA:NR)

LIFE OF HER OWN, A**

(1950) 108m MGM bw

Lana Turner *(Lily Brannel James)*, Ray Milland *(Steve Harleigh)*, Tom Ewell *(Tom Caraway)*, Louis Calhern *(Jim Leversoe)*, Ann Dvorak *(Mary Ashlon)*, Barry Sullivan *(Lee Gorrance)*, Margaret Phillips *(Nora Harleigh)*, Jean Hagen *(Maggie Collins)*, Phyllis Kirk *(Jerry)*, Sara Haden *(Smitty)*, Hermes Pan *(Lily's Dance Partner)*, Carol Brannan, Beth Douglas, Roberta Johnson, Alice Wallace, Bunny Waters, Pat Davies, Dorothy Abbott, Bridget Carr, Charlene Hardey, Marlene Hoyt *(Models)*, Tom Seidel *(Bob Collins)*, Hilda Plowright *(Desk Clerk)*, Elizabeth Flournoy *(Caraway Receptionist)*, Dorothy Tree *(Caraway Secretary)*, Robert Emmett Keane, Richard Anderson *(Hosiery Men)*, Wilson Wood *(Cab Driver)*, Harry Barris *(Piano Player)*, Beverly Garland *(Girl at Party)*, Whit Bissell *(Rental Agent)*, Kathleen Freeman *(Peg)*, Gertrude Graner *(Woman Photographer)*, Major Sam Harris *(Man Model)*, Frankie Darro *(Bellboy)*, Queenie Leonard *(Hotel Matron)*, Paul Kramer *(Airport Gateman)*, Kenny Garcia, Arthur Loew, Jr., Peter Thompson, Walter McGrail, Joan Valeries, Kerry O'Day, Carol Brewster, Beverly Thompson, Lee Lynn, Meredith Leeds *(People at Party)*, Geraldine Wall *(Hosiery Woman)*, Percy Helton *(Hamburger Proprietor)*, Sarah Padden *(Overseer)*, Kenne Duncan *(Man Asking Invitation)*, Maura Murphy *(Vogue Receptionist)*.

Although uncredited, much of the story owes its derivation to Rebecca West's novel *The Abiding Vision*. Several top screenwriters attempted to adapt it, including Donald Ogden Stewart, Samson Raphaelson, and others. Eventually, Isobel Lennart's version was used and she received sole credit. It also marked Turner's return to movies after having married millionaire Bob Topping and going on an extended honeymoon around the world. It was not a particularly intriguing story and the studio chiefs thought they could breathe some box-office life into it by casting some heavyweights. They were mistaken. Turner is a model who goes to New York in search of fame and fortune. She signs with an agency and is soon befriended by an over-the-hill model, Dvorak, who is seen only briefly (and effectively) in the film as she despondently jumps out a window before reel two ends. Turner vows that she won't go the same way as her pal and takes to modeling with a vengeance. She soon rises to the top of her field, becomes the 1950s version of Christie Brinkley, and is seen everywhere. She meets Milland, a Montanan, who sets her up in a chic penthouse with the money he's made in his copper business. Now Turner learns that Milland is married to a crippled woman, Phillips, and that the chances of divorce are slim to none. She sets out to enjoy the high life in New York and plays with Manhattan's elite until that begins to pale and she decides to confront Phillips and tell her of her love for Milland. Upon meeting the disabled woman, Turner sees that her feelings about Milland don't compare with the need that Phillips has. So she quickly changes her mind and calls a stop to the affair, determined not to wind up the way Dvorak did, as a sidewalk pizza. MGM did its best to stack the odds in favor of the film by hiring Cukor, a director well known for his ability to handle "women's pictures" but nothing helped. Both James Mason and Wendell Corey turned down the Milland role. Mason felt he was too British and Corey thought he "wasn't right."

There was no ending and the picture sort of fizzled out. The original ending called for Turner to be working as a 45-year-old maid in a New York hotel. They filmed an ending that had Turner follow Dvorak in suicide, but audiences winced at it in previews and retakes were called for, with the new ending being the one that concludes the picture. Turner and Cukor enjoyed the experience of working together and regretted that the material wasn't better. Some interesting sidelight casting includes choreographer Hermes Pan dancing with Turner, veteran comedienne Kathleen Freeman (before she was a veteran), tough guy Frankie Darro as a bellhop, and character actors Whit Bissell, Beverly Garland, and Richard Anderson in small bits.

p, Voldemar Vetluguin; d, George Cukor; w, Isobel Lennart; ph, George Folsey; m, Bronislau Kaper; ed, George White; md, Johnny Green; art d, Cedric Gibbons, Arthur Lonergan; set d, Edwin B. Willis, Henry W. Grace; cos, Helen Rose; makeup, William Tuttle; hairstyles, Sydney Guilaroff.

Drama   **(PR:A-C MPAA:NR)**

LIFE OF JIMMY DOLAN, THE**1/2
(1933) 85m WB bw (GB: THE KID'S LAST FIGHT)

Douglas Fairbanks, Jr. *(Jimmy Dolan)*, Loretta Young *(Peggy)*, Aline MacMahon *(The Aunt)*, Guy Kibbee *(Phlaxer)*, Lyle Talbot *(Doc Woods)*, Fifi D'Orsay *(Budgie)*, Shirley Grey *(Goldie)*, George Meeker *(Magee)*, Harold Huber *(Reggie Newman)*, Farina *(Sam)*, Dawn O'Day [Anne Shirley] *(Mary Lou)*, David Durand *(George)*, Mickey Rooney *(Freckles)*, Arthur Hohl *(Malvin)*, Arthur Dekuh *(Louie Primaro)*, John Wayne *(Smith)*.

Better than average fight film features the younger Fairbanks as a boxer who becomes a champ, then accidentally kills a newspaperman. His manager double-crosses him and tries to flee, only to have his car flip over and his body burn beyond recognition. Seeing his chance for escape, Fairbanks takes the manager's identity going underground and ending up at a home for crippled children. They need money to pay off the mortgage so Fairbanks re-enters the ring to raise the cash. Don't miss two future big names in bit parts, Rooney as one of the crippled kids and Wayne as a fighter. This was remade as THEY MADE ME A CRIMINAL in 1939 with John Garfield.

d, Archie Mayo; w, David Boehm, Erwin Gelsey (based on the play "The Sucker" by Bertram Milhauser and Beulah Marie Dix); ph, Arthur Edeson; ed, Bert Levy.

Sports/Drama   **(PR:A MPAA:NR)**

LIFE OF OHARU***1/2
(1964, Jap.) 146m Shin Toho/Toho International bw (SAIKAKU ICHIDAI ONNA; AKA: DIARY OF OHARU)

Kinuyo Tanaka *(Oharu)*, Tsukie Matsura *(Tomo, Oharu's Mother)*, Ichiro Sugai *(Shonzaemon, Oharu's Father)*, Toshiro Mifune *(Katsunosuke)*, Toshiaki Konoe *(Lord Tokitaka Matsudaira)*, Hisako Yamane *(Lady Matsudaira)*, Jukichi Uno *(Yakichi Senya)*, Eitaro Shindo *(Kohei Sasaya)*, Akira Oizumi *(Fumikichi, Sasaya's Friend)*, Masao Shimizu *(Kikuno Koji)*, Daisuke Kato *(Tasaburo Hishiya)*, Toranosuke Ogawa *(Yataemon Isobei)*, Eijiro Yanagi *(Daimo Enaka)*, Yuriko Hamada *(Yoshioka)*, Hiroshi Oizumi *(Manager Bunkichi)*, Haruo Ichikawa *(Iwabashi)*, Kikue Mori *(Myokai, the Old Nun)*, Chieko Hagashiyama, Sadako Sawamura.

LIFE OF OHARU is a later film in the long and brilliant career of masterful director Mizoguchi. The plot details the life of Tanaka, a 50-year-old prostitute in the 17th Century. She prays before Buddha and relives her past. In flashback we see that she was once the young daughter of a samurai employed by the imperial palace of Kyoto. She falls in love with a lower-class man and, as punishment, her lover is decapitated and her family banished from the city. She attempts suicide but fails and soon after becomes the mistress of a prince. The prince, however, sends her away after she bears him a son. Her father then sells Tanaka and she is put to work as a prostitute. A wealthy client buys her, but he is discovered to be a criminal and soon she is forced to sell herself again. She meets and marries a merchant and lives with him until he dies, once again forcing her into prostitution, this time at the age of 50. After she finishes her prayers, she is confronted by her son, now a prince, and asked to live in his home. Demoralized by her experiences, she soon leaves his home and spends the rest of her life as a beggar. In LIFE OF OHARU, Mizoguchi concentrates on the formal style which he had developed so successfully in his earlier works, extremely long takes of meticulously composed shots with a minimal amount of cutting, a style that lends itself to an almost literary interpretation of the material. In LIFE OF OHARU we see the master honing his art.

d, Kenji Mizoguchi; w, Yoshikata Yoda, Mizoguchi (based on the novel *Koshuku ichidai onna* by Saikaku Ibara); ph, Yoshimi Kono, Yoshimi Hirano; m, Ichiro Saito; ed, Toshio Goto; art d, Hiroshi Mizutani.

Drama   **Cas.**   **(PR:C MPAA:NR)**

LIFE OF RILEY, THE***
(1949) 87m UNIV bw

William Bendix *(Chester A. Riley)*, Rosemary DeCamp *(Peg Riley)*, James Gleason *(Gillis)*, Bill Goodwin *(Sidney Monohan)*, Beulah Bondi *(Miss Bogle)*, Meg Randall *(Babs Riley)*, Richard Long *(Jeff Taylor)*, Lanny Rees *(Junior Riley)*, Mark Daniels *(Burt Stevenson)*, Ted De Corsia *(Norman)*, John Brown *("Digger" O'Dell)*, Victoria Horne *(Lucy Monohan)*, William E. Green *(Carl Stevenson)*, Mary Philips, Jerry Elliot, Virginia Bradley *(Girls)*.

Bendix repeats his role from the popular radio series in this easy-to-take comedy. As a riveter in an airplane factory, he longs for a better job, and soon after his daughter (Randall) begins dating the boss' son (Daniels) he finds himself elevated to an executive job. Only later does he find out that the promotion was arranged by his daughter, who now must marry Daniels to make good her end of the deal. Bendix is outraged and breaks up the wedding in mid-ceremony seeing that his daughter is reunited with the man she really loves, Long. Adapted from a radio show that began

in 1944. The show was later turned into two television series, the first running twenty-six weeks in 1949 and 1950 starring Jackie Gleason, the second running five years from 1953 through 1958 with Bendix repeating his role from radio and screen.

p,d&w, Irving Brecher (based on the radio program); ph, William Daniels; m, Frank Skinner; ed, Milton Carruth; art d, Bernard Herzbrun, John De Cuir.

Comedy   **(PR:A MPAA:NR)**

LIFE OF THE COUNTRY DOCTOR
(SEE: LIFE OF A COUNTRY DOCTOR, 1963, Jap.)

LIFE OF THE PARTY, THE**1/2
(1930) 78m WB c

Winnie Lightner *(Flo)*, Irene Delroy *(Dot)*, Jack Whiting *(A. J. Smith)*, Charles Butterworth *(Col. Joy)*, Charles Judels *(Mons. LeMaire)*, John Davidson *(Fake Mr. Smith)*, Arthur Edmund Carewe *(Fake Count)*, Arthur Hoyt *(Secretary)*, William Irving.

The always funny Lightner, along with her pal Delroy, play a pair of shop clerks. They're out for some better times and go searching for rich gentlemen to keep them in the opulence they feel suits them. They chase two men named Smith (Whiting and Davidson), one poor and one rich. The trail takes them to Havana for a rousing comical finish. This is an amusing film in the GOLD DIGGERS tradition with some fine comic performances by Lightner and Judels. But the film suffered from some severe cutting. Originally it was filmed as a musical but the genre was beginning to lose popularity at the time of release. Consequently the studio pared out many songs and production numbers, leaving only "Can It Be Possible?" (Sidney Mitchell, Archie Gottler, Joseph Mayer), "One Robin Doesn't Make a Spring," and "Somehow" (Frederick Loewe, Earle Crooker). This was also one of the first all-Technicolor films.

d, Roy Del Ruth; w, Arthur Caesar (based on a story by Melville Crossman [Darryl F. Zanuck]); ph, Dev Jennings (2-color Technicolor); ed, William Holmes.

Comedy   **(PR:A MPAA:NR)**

LIFE OF THE PARTY*
(1934, Brit.) 53m WB-FN bw

Jerry Verno *(Arthur Bleeby)*, Betty Astell *(Blanche Hopkins)*, Eric Fawcett *(Harry Hopkins)*, Vera Boggetti *(Caroline Bleeby)*, Kenneth Kove *(Andrew Larkin)*, Hermione Hannen *(Dora Reeves)*, Phyllis Morris *(Clarice)*.

A man is constantly trying to get his wife away from people for whom she loves to throw parties. Some wives try to keep the fun-loving woman away from their husbands as well. The title is thoroughly misleading in this weak, unappealing comedy.

p, Irving Asher; d, Ralph Dawson; w, Brock Williams (based on the play "Twin Beds" by Margaret Mayo and Salisbury Field).

Comedy   **(PR:A MPAA:NR)**

LIFE OF THE PARTY, THE**
(1937) 86m RKO bw

Joe Penner *(Penner)*, Gene Raymond *(Barry Saunders)*, Parkyakarkus *(Parky)*, Harriet Hilliard *(Mitzi)*, Victor Moore *(Oliver)*, Helen Broderick *(Pauline)*, Billy Gilbert *(Dr. Molnac)*, Ann Miller *(Betty)*, Richard Lane *(Hotel Manager)*, Franklin Pangborn *(Beggs)*, Margaret Dumont *(Mrs. Penner)*, Ann Shoemaker *(Countess Martos)*, Jane Rhodes *(Susan)*, George Irving *(Mr. Van Tuyl)*, Winifred Harris *(Mrs. Van Tuyl)*, Charles Judels *(Maitre d'Hotel)*.

Penner is a wealthy but irresponsible man chosen by Shoemaker to be the husband for Hilliard, her crooning daughter. But the aspiring singer wants nothing to do with him, instead setting her sights on Raymond, with whom she winds up at the end. Moore is a detective assigned to keep Raymond out of woman trouble but obviously he can't fulfill his assignment. The star-studded cast can't do much with the simplistic script, RKO's last-ditch attempt to turn radio performers Penner and Parkyakarkus into movie stars. The two are good but limited in what they can do on the screen. Support is only average, despite some heavyweight second bananas like Gilbert, Pangborn, and the long-suffering Dumont as Penner's mother. The big production number features dancer Miller with Hilliard on the vocal. Ultimately this is little more than a hodge-podge of music and dance, interspersed with comedy. Songs included: "So You Won't Sing," "Let's Have Another Cigarette," "The Life of the Party," "Chirp a Little Ditty," "Yankee Doodle Band" (Herb Magidson, Allie Wrubel), "Roses in December" (George Jessel, Ben Oakland, Magidson).

p, Edward Kaufman; d, William A. Seiter; w, Bert Kalmar, Harry Ruby, Viola Brothers Shore (based on a story by Joseph Santley); ph, J. Roy Hunt; ed, Jack Hively; md, Roy Webb; ch, Sammy Lee; art d, Van Nest Polglase; set d, Darrell Silvera; cos, Edward Stevenson; spec eff, Vernon L. Walker.

Musical Comedy   **(PR:A MPAA:NR)**

LIFE OF VERGIE WINTERS, THE**1/2
(1934) 75m RKO bw

Ann Harding *(Vergie Winters)*, John Boles *(John Shadwell)*, Helen Vinson *(Laura Shadwell)*, Betty Furness *(Joan at Age 19)*, Frank Albertson *(Ranny Truesdale)*, Lon [Creighton] Chaney, Jr. *(Hugo McQueen)*, Sara Haden *(Winnie Belle)*, Molly O'Day *(Sadie)*, Ben Alexander *(Barry Preston)*, Donald Crisp *(Mike Davey)*, Maidel Turner *(Ella Heenan)*, Cecil Cunningham *(Pearl Turner)*, Josephine Whittell *(Madame Claire)*, Wesley Barry *(Herbert Somerby)*, Edward Van Sloan *(Jim Winters)*, Wallis Clark *(Mr. Preston)*, Edwin Stanley *(Mr. Truesdale)*, Bonita Granville *(Joan as a Girl)*, Walter Brennan *(Roscoe, a Gossiper)*, Jed Prouty *(Reverend)*, Mary McLaren *(Nurse)*, Betty Mack *(Della the Maid)*.

THE LIFE OF VERGIE WINTERS was not a happy life but it seemed to be just right for audiences who liked this sort of STELLA DALLAS and BACK STREET story. Unrequited love is always a good subject and when you add a child born out of wedlock, well, you're sure to have the hankies wringing wet. Harding is an attractive young woman in love with a man on the rise, Boles. The only drawback is that Boles is married to a hissable type, Vinson, whom he has wed out of convenience, rather than love. She's the "right woman" for a young guy on the go, but his heart belongs to Harding and they conceive a daughter without benefit of clergy. It's all kept on the hush-hush and Boles continues promising he'll divorce Vinson and make an honest woman out of Harding. Harding won't hear of that, though, because any sort of scandal might make mincemeat out of his promising career in politics. So the child grows up from Granville into Furness while Harding sighs a great deal in a dress shop. Eventually, Boles can take the double life no longer and tells Vinson that he wants out to marry Harding, whom he's been seeing regularly. Vinson follows Boles to Harding's residence and shoots the man. Harding, in a move so martyr-like that she might be eligible for unwed-mother sainthood, takes the rap, rather than besmirch her late lover's name. She is sent to prison, where we meet her in the first reel (the whole film is a flashback) as she watches Boles' funeral procession out the barred windows. Vinson, on her deathbed, finally absolves Harding of the crime and Furness arrives to take her mom home from the slammer. Well directed by Santell, this could have slipped into a quagmire of sentimental slush had it not been for the sharp screenplay and the sharper editing. Steiner's score also helped mightily. Anyone familiar with the mores of the 1930s knew from the start that Harding had to pay, in some way, for her pleasure, so there's no suspense, just wondering how they'll get to giving her what-for because of her affair with, sigh, a married man. Note Bonita Granville (who later married millionaire Jack Wrather), Betty Furness (who became a consumer advocate on TV), Walter Brennan (before winning any of his three Oscars), and Ben Alexander (who went on to be Jack Webb's sidekick on "Dragnet").

p, Pandro S. Berman; d, Alfred Santell; w, Jane Murfin (based on the novel *A Good Woman* by Louis Bromfield); ph, Lucien Andriot; m, Max Steiner; ed, George Hively.

Drama (PR:C MPAA:NR)

LIFE RETURNS*¹/₂ (1939) 62m UNIV/Scienart bw

Dr. Robert E. Cornish, Onslow Stevens, Lois Wilson, George Breakston, Valerie Hobson, Stanley Fields, Frank Reicher, Richard Carle, Dean Benton, Lois January, Richard Quine, Maidel Turner, George McQuarrie, Otis Harlan.

On May 22, 1934, Cornish filmed a famous experiment where he brought a dead dog back to life. This footage is incorporated in a film featuring Breakston as a cute movie kid whose dog gets the gas from nasty dogcatcher Fields. Dull and overlong at just over an hour's running time, the story is padded with some nonsense about gangsters being behind the operation. The performers could stand to undergo Cornish's procedure; they're all lifeless and need to be resuscitated.

p, Lou Ostrow; d, Eugen Frenke; w, Arthur T. Horman, John F. Goodrich (story by Frenke, James Hogan); ph, Robert Planck; ed, Harry Marker.

Drama (PR:C MPAA:NR)

LIFE STUDY** (1973) 99m Nebbco c

Bartholomew Miro, Jr. *(Angelo Corelli)*, Erika Peterson *(Myrna Clement)*, Tom Lee Jones *(Gus)*, Ziska *(The Model)*, Gregory D'Alessio *(Adrian Clement)*, Rosetta Garuffi *(Grandma)*, Anthony Forest *(John Clement)*, Yvonne Sherwell *(Peggy Clement)*, Emmett Priest *(Jim Rowe)*, Ed Mona *(Vinnie)*, John Toland *(Ken Lambert)*, Fritzi Kopell *(Helen Hopkinson)*, Priscilla Bardonille *(Veda)*, Lynette Dupret *(Angelo's Mother)*, John Feeney *(Joe Levine)*, Candy Latson *(Frank Walker)*, Bob Roberts *(Angelo's Father)*, Efigenio Miha *(Pedro)*, Max Andersson *(Father Gunnarson)*.

Peterson is a pregnant 17 year old, determined not to fall into the social traps set up by her rich parents. She flees to New York City's Greenwich Village. There she meets Miro, a struggling filmmaker who is wrestling with his own psyche over the problem of his childhood. He finally returns to his Virginia home, accompanied by Peterson, to confront his parents and come to terms with his past. The pop psychology of the film doesn't quite work, going for simplistic and easy outs rather than taking on the issues. Nebbia's direction is spotty: he handles the outdoor sequences with flair but the more intimate moments are awkward. This independent feature is his directorial debut.

p&d, Michael Nebbia; w, Arthur Birnkrant (based on a story by Nebbia); ph, Nebbia (DeLuxe Color); m, Emanuel Vardi; ed, Ray Sandiford, Sidney Katz.

Drama (PR:O MPAA:NR)

LIFE UPSIDE DOWN**
(1965, Fr.) 92m A. J. Films/Landau-AA bw (LA VIE A L'ENVERS; AKA: INSIDE OUT)

Charles Denner *(Jacques Valin)*, Anna Gaylor *(Viviane)*, Guy Saint-Jean *(Fernand)*, Nicole Gueden *(Nicole)*, Jean Yanne *(Kerbel)*, Yvonne Clech *(Mme. Kerbel)*, Robert Bousquet *(Paul)*, Francoise Moncey *(Ina)*, Jean Dewever *(Major)*, Gilbert Meunier *(Park Keeper)*, Andre Thorent *(Doctor)*, Bernard Sury *(Inspector)*, Jenny Orleans *(Concierge)*, Nane Germon *(Mother)*.

A strange and darkly funny drama starring Denner as a real-estate agent who delves deeper and deeper into meditation until it destroys his mind. Denner lives with his girl friend Gaylor, a fashion model. She begins to get concerned about her boy friend when he is discovered spending an inordinate amount of time staring into space. To calm her Denner agrees to marry her but on the day of the wedding he is nowhere to be found. Soon after, he loses his job, but Denner is thrilled to have that much more time to meditate. Eventually he is committed to an asylum where he can meditate in peace.

p, Michel Peynet; d&w, Alain Jessua; ph, Jacques Robin; m, Jacques Loussier; ed, Nicole Marko; art d, Olivier Girard.

Drama (PR:C MPAA:NR)

LIFE WITH BLONDIE**¹/₂ (1946) 69m COL bw

Penny Singleton *(Blondie)*, Arthur Lake *(Dagwood)*, Larry Simms *(Alexander)*,

Marjorie Kent *(Cookie)*, Jonathan Hale *(Dithers)*, Ernest Truex *(Glassby)*, Marc Lawrence *(Pete)*, Veda Ann Borg *(Hazel)*, Jack Rice *(Ollie)*, Bobby Larson *(Tommy)*, Doug Fowley *(Blackie)*, George Tyne *(Cassidy)*, Edward Gargan *(Dog-catcher)*, Francis Pierlot *(Rutledge)*, Ray Walker *(Anthony)*, Eddie Acuff *(Postman)*, Robert Ryan *(2nd Policeman)*, Steve Benton *(Driver)*, Daisy the Dog.

A better-than-average entry in the Columbia series based on the famous comic strip. This time the family dog, Daisy, becomes the moneymaker of the household. She wins a contest to be a Navy model and then is the hottest canine photographic pinup around. Lake gets jealous of the dog when his position as head of the house is threatened by the pooch. Some gangsters kidnap Daisy but she is rescued and all is resolved within the family. A standard programmer for 1940s movie houses features some nice comic acting by Lake and Singleton, with good support from Truex and from Fowley as a gangster. (See BLONDIE series, Index.)

p, Burt Kelly; d, Abby Berlin; w, Connie Lee (based on the comic strip created by Chic Young); ph, L. W. O'Connell; ed, Jerome Thoms; md, Mischa Bakaleinikoff.

Comedy (PR:AAA MPAA:NR)

LIFE WITH FATHER**** (1947) 118m WB c

William Powell *(Clarence Day)*, Irene Dunne *(Vinnie Day)*, Elizabeth Taylor *(Mary)*, Edmund Gwenn *(Rev. Dr. Lloyd)*, ZaSu Pitts *(Cora)*, Jimmy Lydon *(Clarence)*, Emma Dunn *(Margaret)*, Moroni Olsen *(Dr. Humphries)*, Elisabeth Risdon *(Mrs. Whitehead)*, Derek Scott *(Harlan)*, Johnny Calkins *(Whitney)*, Martin Milner *(John)*, Heather Wilde *(Annie)*, Monte Blue *(Policeman)*, Nancy Evans *(Delia)*, Mary Field *(Nora)*, Queenie Leonard *(Maggie)*, Clara Blandick *(Mrs. Wiggins)*, Frank Elliott *(Dr. Somers)*, Clara Reid *(Scrub Woman)*, Philo McCullough *(Milkman)*, Loie Bridge *(Corsetierre)*, George Meader *(Salesman)*, Douglas Kennedy *(Mr. Morley)*, Phil Van Zandt *(Clerk)*, Russell Arms *(Stock Quotation Operator)*, Faith Kruger *(Hilda)*, Jean De Val *(Francois)*, Michael and Ralph Mineo *(Twins)*, Creighton Hale *(Father of Twins)*, Jean Andren *(Mother of Twins)*, Elaine Lange *(Ellen)*, Jack Martin *(Chef)*, Arlene Dahl *(Girl in Delmonico's)*, Gertrude Valerie, David Cavendish, Henry Sylvester, Hallene Hill, Laura Treadwell *(Churchgoers)*, John Beck *(Perkins the Clerk)*, James Metcalf *(Customer)*, Joe Bernard *(Cashier)*, Lucille Shamberger *(Nursemaid)*.

From the moment the decision was made to film LIFE WITH FATHER, it was destined to succeed. As a play, LIFE WITH FATHER ran 3,224 performances on Broadway, a total that was only eclipsed by "Fiddler On The Roof." If there is such a thing as being time-tested, that would have to apply to this story. Based on that play and the book by Clarence Day, Jr., it's a true series of memories with Powell as the Father whom everyone recalls. Powell is a stern but loving authoritarian who rules his Victorian household with an iron hand and a bamboo cane. Dunne, his wife, loves the man, as do all of his red-headed children, but she does occasionally become rankled by his chauvinistic ways, which can be epitomized by a conversation he has with Lydon (Clarence, Jr.) when he states that "women have no capacity for thought. They simply get all stirred up." He then tells Lydon that he now knows everything that need be known about women and urges him to run along. Powell's character embodies the spirit of the male Victorian of the late 1880s and the film revolves around him and the urban, urbane life the family leads. There's not much of a plot, just a lot of alternately quiet and raucous moments of love and laughter. Dunne becomes ill and that so throws Powell that he promises he will get baptized (something he never did) if and when she recovers. When she does come back from death's door, he reluctantly, in the last line of the play (cut from the film) says to a pal who asks where he is going one Sunday morning: "I'm going to be baptized, dammit!" LIFE WITH FATHER was a hit despite having no plot to speak of. It was enough to laugh and listen to the mustached philosopher, who was charismatic enough to charm spots off a leopard. Director Curtiz made films that were so varied that he must be recognized as a prodigious talent. Anyone who could do this film, as well as CASABLANCA, YANKEE DOODLE DANDY, ANGELS WITH DIRTY FACES, THE ADVENTURES OF ROBIN HOOD, and KING CREOLE is a force to reckon with. Powell was the perfect choice to play Father, and all the other roles were equally well-cast. Stewart's adaptation remained faithful to the play but added the dimension of cinema to the intimate stage setting, making it seem effortless. The movie goes far beyond the Day family. It also delves deeply into the life style of the wealthy of that bygone day. It was originally sent out as a "road show" film and no one balked at paying the slightly higher ticket price to see it in first run. Taylor, Milner, Lydon, and Gwenn all contributed to the overall charm of the movie, but it truly belongs to Powell who was nominated for an Oscar for his performance along with Marley, Skall, and Steiner. There was an attempt at a sequel, LIFE WITH MOTHER, that couldn't hold a candle to this. It also inspired a brief TV series in 1955. Look for a very young and beautiful Arlene Dahl in a scene at Delmonico's Restaurant. Older TV fans will also recognize singer Russell Arms as the stock quotation operator. Milner, of course, went on to star in a few TV series and Taylor went on to be Taylor, 'nuf said.

p, Robert Bucker; d, Michael Curtiz, Herschel Daugherty; w, Donald Ogden Stewart (based on the play by Howard Lindsay, Russel Crouse and the book by Clarence Day, Jr.); ph, Peverell Marley, William V. Skall (Technicolor); m, Max Steiner; ed, George Amy; md, Leo F. Forbstein; art d, Robert Hass; set d, George James Hopkins; cos, Milo Anderson; spec eff, Ray Foster, William McCann; makeup, Perc Westmore; tech adv, Mrs. Clarence Day.

Comedy Cas. (PR:AAA MPAA:NR)

LIFE WITH HENRY** (1941) 80m PAR bw

Jackie Cooper *(Henry Aldrich)*, Leila Ernst *(Kathleen Anderson)*, Eddie Bracken *(Dizzy Stevens)*, Fred Niblo *(Mr. Aldrich)*, Hedda Hopper *(Mrs. Aldrich)*, Kay Stewart *(Mary Aldrich)*, Moroni Olsen *(Sylvanus Q. Sattherwaite)*, Rod Cameron *(Bill Van Dusen)*, Pierre Watkin *(Mr. Anderson)*, Lucien Littlefield *(Mr. Stevens)*, Frank M. Thomas *(Joe Nye)*, Etta McDaniel *(Cleo Johnson)*, Hanley Stafford

(Theater Manager), Edith Evanson *(Anne, the Swedish Maid)*, Rand Brooks *(Daniel Gordon)*, Doris Lloyd *(Mrs. Anderson)*, Frances Carson *(Mrs. Stevens)*, Josephine Whittel *(Aunt Harriett)*, Charlotte Treadway *(Mrs. Joe Nye)*, Thurston Hall *(Mr. Woodring)*, Winifred Harris *(Mrs. Woodring)*, Theodore Von Eltz *(Mr. Rappaport)*, Mary Currier *(Mrs. Rappaport)*, Wanda McKay *(Girl on Stage)*.

The second of Columbia's HENRY ALDRICH films, based on a popular radio series and an answer to MGM's ANDY HARDY movies. This time Cooper plays the gawky hero, though Jimmy Lydon would return to play the title role for the remainder of the series. This time the hapless lad is trying to raise $100 so he can go to Alaska. But his earnest and well-meaning spirit can't stop the bungling the character is famous for. Here he gets caught up in trouble, ending up accidentally closing a factory. The script stretches the believability factor beyond reason and the laughs are not as plentiful as the producers hoped. Still, like all of the ALDRICH films, time has given it a certain corny charm, reflective of a more innocent time. Gossip queen Hopper plays Cooper's mother. (See HENRY ALDRICH series, Index.)

p&d, Jay Theodore Reed; w, Clifford Goldsmith, Don Hartman; ph, Leo Tover; ed, William Shea.

Comedy **(PR:AAA MPAA:NR)**

LIFE WITH THE LYONS (SEE: FAMILY AFFAIR, 1954, Brit.)

LIFEBOAT***** (1944) 96m FOX bw

Tallulah Bankhead *(Connie Porter)*, William Bendix *(Gus)*, Walter Slezak *(The German)*, Mary Anderson *(Alice)*, John Hodiak *(Kovak)*, Henry Hull *(Rittenhouse)*, Heather Angel *(Mrs. Higgins)*, Hume Cronyn *(Stanley Garrett)*, Canada Lee *(Joe)*, William Yetter, Jr. *(German Sailor)*, Alfred Hitchcock *(Man in "Before and After" Ad)*.

One of Hitchcock's most intensive thrillers has a handful of survivors climb into a lifeboat after their ship is torpedoed by a German U-boat which is also sunk during the battle. The captain of the submarine, Slezak, swims to the boat and is taken aboard by the kind-hearted survivors. Since he is the only man capable of handling the craft in rough weather and navigating it to a safe harbor, he is elected helmsman. The survivors are an odd lot—Bankhead, a brilliant fashion writer, Hull, a tycoon industrialist, Hodiak, a socially conscious seaman, Bendix, a wounded stoker, Cronyn, a meek radio operator, Anderson, a bewildered nurse, Angel, a mother unbalanced by the dead child she holds (which is quickly buried at sea), and Lee, a black steward. Slowly, and with insidious cleverness, Slezak steers a course, not for land, but to a rendezvous with a German mother ship, planning and executing the deaths of several on board before he is discovered and beaten to death by an aroused group of allies who toss his carcass overboard. When another German sailor, whose ship has been sunk in a naval battle toward the end of the film, tries to enter the boat, he is attacked and left to drown in the sea by a hardened and wiser group. Bankhead is superb as the spoiled, wealthy dilettante writer whose expensive furs and jewelry are worth more to her than the lives of her fellow survivors. At one point, however, she uses her diamond bracelet to catch a fish and it vanishes beneath the waves. Bendix is terrific as the dumb but compassionate stoker and Hodiak puts up electric charges as the sailor with Czech ancestry, "one of them bozos," as Hull puts it, who lashes out against the Nazis and the injustices they visit upon the world. Hull is excellent as the cigar-smoking protocapitalist who becomes a democrat on the voyage but reverts to type when it becomes obvious that he will be rescued. Though Hitchcock employed his favorite device of rear-projection or process shots of rough, gray seas (stock footage taken off the Florida coastline), the director put his small cast into a lifeboat inside a studio tank and mercilessly sloshed the actors with water for many weeks during production. He had huge wind fans, water-spraying machines, and giant water-activators whirring, whirling, and gyrating all the time, creating studio hazards for the crew and cast. Cronyn, who was dragged beneath the water of the studio tank and almost drowned while being trapped underneath one of the underwater activators, was saved from death by an alert lifeguard whom Hitchcock had posted near the tank for just such emergencies. Cronyn later stated: "We were covered with crude oil and when we finished a scene there might be an hour waiting for a new camera setup. We would climb down, go to our dressing rooms and change to dry clothes, then go back to the raft and start over again." It was tricky work for the inventive Hitchcock, especially the setup shots. As Hitchcock told Jay Robert Nash in *The Innovators*: "LIFEBOAT—well, you couldn't have very well gone to sea to do that. You could never get the mobility of the shots . . . There would have been no way to get level with the people. As it was, in order to get at the people in the boat, I had to have three lifeboats—one full-length, a half of one, and a half of one split down the middle—and we brought up whichever one was useful for the shot. It wasn't just shot in one boat." Steinbeck, who wrote the original story and was first assigned to script the film, thought himself too restricted with a single set and considered Hitchcock's "obsession" with a single set too limiting. When he stalled on the script, Hitchcock brought in MacKinlay Kantor who also failed to realize sharp scenes and smart dialog and he was replaced by veteran Swerling, although, as was his custom, Hitchcock brought the talented Ben Hecht in at the last moment to tighten up the scenes and sharpen the dialog (he is uncredited). The director overcame all technical obstacles for his masterpiece but was momentarily faced with a dilemma having to do with his customary cameo appearance. How would he get himself into a movie where everyone was confined in a lifeboat on the high seas? Hitchcock had recently taken off a great deal of weight and used two photos of himself, profiles, before, bloated, and after, slimmer, in an ad appearing in an old newspaper which Bendix reads while the cast drifts along. The ad promoted a mythical diet product, "Reduco," which caused the director another minor headache. After the film was released, he received a great deal of mail from obese viewers demanding to know where they might buy "Reduco." As usual, Hitchcock had little to do with any of the cast, except for the beautiful, unpredictable Bankhead. Youthful Mary Anderson, attempting to learn more about filmmaking, especially an appraisal of her own image by master filmmaker Hitchcock, approached the director and asked what he thought was her best profile. "What do you think is my best side," she asked. "My dear," he replied, not looking at her, "you're sitting on it." From the opening to the closing, this was Bankhead's film. Hitchcock had more or less rescued the actress who had made six unsuccessful films in the past and whose theatrical career was sagging. He offered her $75,000 for her leading part and she leaped at the opportunity. He opens his shots by panning across debris-strewn, oil-streaked waters following the sinking of the ship, traveling to a lifeboat where, her hair coiffured, her makeup perfect, her body draped in mink and adorned with diamonds, is the incomparable Bankhead. She appears ready to attend a first-night Broadway opening rather than endure a life-and-death survival test in wild seas. But as the film progressed Bankhead proved her mettle on and off screen. Said Hitchcock later: "She stood up to being doused with 5,400 gallons of water and got a round of applause from the stageheands." She also came down with pneumonia twice and was wobbly-legged through the last third of the film. Her portrayal was magnificent and won for her the coveted New York Screen Critics award for Best Actress. She would write in her memoirs: "At last I had licked the screen, a screen which had six times betrayed me. Did I get an Academy Oscar? No! The people who vote in that free-for-all know on which side their *crepes Suzette* are buttered. I wasn't under contract to any of the major studios, hence was thought an outlaw." She added cryptically: "News of my salty antics in LIFEBOAT seeped through the blockade." Her reference had, no doubt, to do with the fact that during the production, Bankhead discarded the use of underwear, which disturbed a visiting editor from a powerful woman's magazine when she saw the star climbing into the lifeboat with a bottom exposed to one and all on the set. Studio boss Zanuck was told and became alarmed, sending one of his producers to ask Hitchcock to remedy the delicate situation. Said the representative to Hitchcock: "The women on the set are complaining about Miss Bankhead—she's got nothing on! And they want me to speak to her." Snorted Hitchcock: "Well, you know she's a firebrand and she'll tear you to pieces . . . and she probably hates your guts anyway." "What am I to do?" begged the producer. "Will you tell her?" Hitchcock shook his head: "Not me. First of all, I'm on loan from Selznick and I don't even work for 20th Century Fox. You better go and see Zanuck up front or ask Lou Shriver, his assistant." The producer was back shortly, glumly reporting to Hitchcock that he, the producer, had been given orders to tell Bankhead to clean up her act. "I wouldn't if I were you," warned Hitchcock. "I don't think it's your department." The producer looked at him, puzzled. "Then whose department is it?" "Either hairdressing or makeup," answered Hitchcock. Hitchcock did spend time with the tempestuous actress off-camera. Bankhead took him to several art galleries and, at her urging, he purchased the first of his collection of modern paintings, one by Milton Avery. When LIFEBOAT was released it ran into some severe criticism from a few critics who felt that Hitchcock had sold out democratic ideals by making Slezak a superman, staying healthy and strong during the ordeal when the rest of those in the lifeboat became weak and demoralized. They obviously chose to ignore the fact that Slezak was shown to horde a private cache of water and food with which he nourished himself secretly. Hitchcock defended himself by saying that the profile of Slezak was to act as a warning about the devious ways of the Nazis. The public responded well, however, to this film, and Hitchcock received another Oscar nomination as Best Director. Bankhead, however, developed a deep-seated hatred for Slezak during the production. Although he was a self-avowed anti-Nazi, the German actor was nevertheless abused by Bankhead. When passing him on the set she would kick him viciously in the legs and shout: "You goddamned Nazi!" The bewildered Slezak could only painfully protest that he was merely playing a role. But then it was Bankhead who was forever playing a role. Upon her return East she held a press press conference in the Louis XIV Room of the St. Regis Hotel in New York. She began to answer routine questions about LIFEBOAT when she spotted a female reporter from *PM*, a liberal newspaper not of her liking. "Of all the filthy, rotten Communist rags that is," she roared. "It's the most vicious, dangerous, hating paper that's ever been published. . . It's a dirty Communist sheet! I loathe it! I loathe it! I wouldn't even touch it with my hands. It's cruel, unfair, and rotten . . . I have the maid bring the paper to me with *tongs*, but I do love 'Barnaby' [a cartoon strip appearing in *PM*]." Another reporter tried to calm Bankhead down but she shouted: "Don't shush me. This isn't your cocktail party! If you don't like what I'm saying, get the hell out!" Bankhead later appeared to be conciliatory to the *PM* reporter, telling her: "You know you look just like a dear friend of mine." The reporter got up and started to leave, walking to the door. Bankhead shouted after her: "She committed suicide!"

p, Kenneth Macgowan; d, Alfred Hitchcock; w, Jo Swerling (based on the story by John Steinbeck); ph, Glen MacWilliams; m, Hugo W. Friedhofer; ed, Dorothy Spencer; md, Emil Newman; art d, James Basevi, Maurice Ransford; spec eff, Fred Sersen.

Drama **Cas.** **(PR:A MPAA:NR)**

LIFEGUARD*** (1976) 96m PAR c

Sam Elliott *(Rick Carlson)*, Anne Archer *(Cathy)*, Stephen Young *(Larry)*, Parker Stevenson *(Chris)*, Kathleen Quinlan *(Wendy)*, Steve Burns *(Machine Gun)*, Sharon Weber *(Tina)*, Mark Hall, Scott Lichtig.

This quickie is a real surprise: a sensitive, thought-provoking story involving a man forced to look at himself. Elliott is the title character, an old-timer in the profession at age 30. Though he enjoys the life, outside pressures from his parents and peers force Elliott to realize that the beach life can't go on forever. His performance is intelligent, with some good support by Archer as Elliott's high school sweetheart and Quinlan as a young girl with a crush on him. Unfortunately, this was sold to the public as merely another beach movie and consequently had little box office success.

p, Ron Silverman; d, Daniel Petrie; w, Ron Koslow; ph, Ralph Woolsey (CFI Color); m, Dale Menten; ed, Argyle Nelson, Jr.; m/l, Menten, Paul Williams.

Drama **(PR:C MPAA:PG)**

LIFESPAN**   (1975, U.S./Brit./Neth.) 85m Whitepal c

Hiram Keller (Doctor), Tina Aumont (Girl), Klaus Kinski (Industrialist).

Keller is a doctor investigating the apparent suicide of another doctor. He learns that the dead man was working on a drug to stop the aging process, gets involved with the dead man's mistress (Aumont), and is almost driven insane by an evil industrialist who wants the drug for himself. Some interesting premises totally wasted in a boring movie.

d, Alexander Whitelaw; w, Whitelaw, Judith Roscow, Alva Ruben; ph, Eddy Van Der Eden (Eastmancolor); m, Terry Riley.

Science Fiction   **(PR:C MPAA:NR)**

LIFT, THE* 1/2   (1965, Brit./Can.) 85m Libra Films bw

Helen Ryan (Margot Maxwell), Alastair Williamson (Mr. Maxwell), Holly Doone (Jane Maxwell), Job Stewart (Joe), Shirley Rogers (Fanny).

A young man convinces a London millionaire to use his airplane for business purposes. After meeting the man's two daughters, he seduces them. He tries to return to an old girl friend but ends up alone. The script never quite makes it, often rambling and with poorly drawn characters. But the direction, like many independent first directorial efforts, is imaginative, giving a new look at London locales. The cast gives it their best despite script weaknesses. Though laughable in many parts (especially a poorly done nude scene) this has a freshness to it that makes it worth a look.

p, Julius Rascheff; d&w, Burt Krancer; ph, Rascheff; m, Andre Hajdu.

Drama   **(PR:O MPAA:NR)**

LIFT, THE**   (1983, Neth.) 99m Sigma/WB c (DER LIFT)

Huub Stapel, Willeke Van Ammelrooy, Josine Van Dalsum, Piet Romer, Gerard Thoolen, Hans Veerman, Manfred De Graaf, Onno Molenkamp, Siem Vroom, Carola Gijbers Van Wijk, Pieter Lutz, Huib Broos, Dick Scheffer, Serge-Henri Valcke, Ab Abspoel, Peer Mascini, Cor Witschge, Michiel Kerbosch, Liz Snoijink, Wiske Sterringa, Arnica Elsendoorn, Ad Noyons, Hans Dagelet, Kees Prins, Aat Ceelen.

Surprisingly effective horror-science-fiction film about an organic computer-controlled elevator that goes insane and kills its passengers. Stapel plays its arch enemy, a maintenance engineer, who, with the help of tabloid reporter Van Ammelrooy, defeats the crazed lift. Not really scary, but interesting nevertheless.

p, Matthijs Van Heijningen; d&w, Dick Maas; ph, Marc Felperlaan (Eastmancolor); ed, Hans Van Dongen; art d, Harry Ammerlaan; spec eff, Leo Cahn, Rene Stouthamer.

Science Fiction   **(PR:C MPAA:NR)**

LIGEA   (SEE: TOMB OF LIGEA, 1965)

LIGHT   (SEE: LUMIMERE, 1976, Fr.)

LIGHT ACROSSS THE STREET, THE** 1/2

(1957, Fr.) 98m Entreprise Generale-Fernand Rives/United Motion Picture Organization bw (LA LUMIERE D'EN FACE) (AKA: FEMALE AND THE FLESH, THE)

Brigitte Bardot (Olivia Marceau), Raymond Pellegrin (Georges Marceau), Roger Pigaut (Pietri), Claude Romain (Barbette), Guy Pierraud (Antoine), Lucien Herbert (Gaspard), Berval (Albert), Jacques Gauthier (Doctor), Jean Debucourt (La Professeur), Hennery (Ernest), Lucien Hubert (Gaspard), Daniel Ceccaldi (L'Amoreux), Christine Gouze-Renal.

After a serious truck accident, Pellegrin is ordered to avoid any excitement. He goes through with his plan to marry Bardot, though, and they start a roadside truckstop. While Pellegrin is forbidden to sleep with Bardot, his jealousy runs wild when he sees how the other truckers look at her. She begins to see the gas station owner across the road and when Pellegrin finds out about it he tries to kill her. She escapes and runs across the road. Pellegrin follows with a gun but is run over by a truck. A standard melodrama, but significant as the film that firmly established Bardot as the sex object of the era after her innocent appearances in DOCTOR AT SEA and others. Bardot had contracted to work in two more films with producer Gauthier (who played the role of the doctor here), but his untimely death led to the obligation being taken over by Ray Ventura—uncle of one of Bardot's lovers-to-be, crooner Sacha Distel—who later went into partnership with Raoul Levy, who produced the blockbuster Bardot vehicle, AND GOD CREATED WOMAN. (In French; English subtitles.)

p, Jacques Gauthier; d, Georges Lacombe; w, Louis Chavance, Rene Masson, Rene Lefebvre (based on a story by Jean-Claude Aurel); ph, Louis Page; m, Norbert Glanzberg; ed, Raymond Leboursier; art d, Alexandre Trauner.

Drama   **(PR:O MPAA:NR)**

LIGHT AT THE EDGE OF THE WORLD, THE* 1/2

(1971, U.S./Span./Lichtenstein) 120m NG c

Kirk Douglas (Will Denton), Yul Brynner (Jonathan Kongre), Samantha Eggar (Arabella), Jean Claude Drouot (Virgilio), Fernando Rey (Capt. Moriz), Renato Salvatori (Montefiore), Massimo Ranieri (Felipe), Aldo Sambrell (Tarcante), Tito Garcia (Emilio), Victor Israel (Das Mortes), Tony Skios (Santos), Luis Barbo (Calsa Larga), Tony Cyrus (Valgolyo), Raul Castro (Malapinha), Oscar Davis (Amador), Alejandro de Enciso (Morabbito), Martin Uvince (Balduino), John Clark (Matt), Maria Borge (Emily Jane), Juan Cazalilla (Capt. Lafayette).

In 1865 Argentine sets up a lighthouse staffed by three very different personalities: Rey, a fanatical seaman; Ranieri, a loyal assistant; and Douglas, an American drifter. When an unusual schooner comes near the lighthouse, Rey and Ranieri go out to investigate. They are brutally murdered by the ship's crew: a marauding band of

pirates led by Brynner, out to take over the lighthouse to attract ships for their own wicked purposes. Douglas is captured but escapes. Soon the pirates are in business, taking over a ship carrying Eggar, an English noblewoman, and Salvatori, the ship's engineer. She is raped and murdered and Douglas avenges her by blowing up the pirate ship with cannon. He meets Brynner in a one-on-one battle. The pirate falls to his death after the lighthouse catches fire from a pirate gun shot. Overlong, dull, and sadistic, this is a film too fanciful for adults and too gory for kids. The direction is weak, taking little interest in anything but the brutality. Brynner is the only standout here, mostly for his hambone performance.

p, Kirk Douglas; d, Kevin Billington; w, Tom Rowe, Rachel Billington, Bertha Dominguez (based on the novel by Jules Verne); ph, Henri Decae (Panavision, Eastmancolor); m, Piero Piccioni; ed, Bert Bates; art d, Enrique Alarcon; cos, Deirdre Clancy, Manuel Mampaso; spec eff, Antonio Molina, Richard M. Parker.

Adventure   **Cas.**   **(PR:O MPAA:GP)**

LIGHT BLUE   (SEE: BACHELOR OF HEARTS, 1958)

LIGHT FANTASTIC, THE   (SEE: LOVE IS BETTER THAN EVER, 1952)

LIGHT FANTASTIC**   (1964) 85m Seneca/EM bw

Dolores McDougal (Beverly), Barry Bartle (Stephen), Jean Shepherd (Frank), Lesley Woods (Mrs. Sharpe), Alan Bergmann (Bill), Cathy Sullivan, Drummond Erskine, Jane Ross, Flicka McKenna, Corrinne Orr, Nicolas Coster, Robert Mandan, Sara Berk.

Fairly routine romantic drama concerning McDougal, a homely and lonely secretary in New York City, who wins three free dance lessons. Her instructor, Bartle, tells her she has a unique talent for dancing and convinces her to sign a long-term lesson agreement. McDougal falls for Bartle and they begin an affair. Much to Bartle's surprise, he begins to fall in love with McDougal. McDougal learns it was all a sham when she dances with instructor Shepherd, who gives her the same sales pitch. McDougal refuses to see Bartle anymore, despite his protestations that he does indeed love her. Her loneliness, however, drives her back to him.

p, Robert Gaffney; d, Robert McCarty; w, Joseph Hochstein, McCarty (based on a story by Hochstein); ph, J. Burgi Contner; m, Joseph Liebman; ed, James Gaffney; md, Judd Woldin; set d, Albert Brenner; m/l, "My Secret World" by Doris Menkes, Liebman (sung by Eydie Gorme).

Romance   **(PR:A MPAA:NR)**

LIGHT FINGERS**   (1929) 60m COL bw

Ian Keith (Light Fingers), Dorothy Revier (Dorothy Madison), Carroll Nye (Donald Madison), Ralph Theodore (Kerrigan), Tom Ricketts (Edward Madison), Charles Gerrard (London Tower), Pietro Sosso (Butler).

Keith, a criminal ne'er-do-well, meets Revier, a sweet young thing who inspires him to reform his ways, and they live happily ever after. This simple story was one of the many early talkies that was completely self-conscious about the new era, and the actors talk up a storm. And well they might, with the magical microphones lying about, and their careers on the line.

d, Joseph Henabery; w, Jack Natteford (based on a story by Alfred Henry Lewis); ph, Ted Tetzlaff.

Crime/Romance   **(PR:A MPAA:NR)**

LIGHT FINGERS* 1/2   (1957, Brit.) 86m Parkside/Archway bw

Roland Culver (Humphrey Levenham), Eunice Gayson (Rose Levenham), Guy Rolfe (Dennis Payne), Ronald Howard (Michael Lacey), Hy Hazell (Cynthia Lacey), Avril Angers (Miss Manley), Lonnie Donegan (Himself), Reginald Beckwith (Gates), Nora Nicholson (Lady Shepley-Cooke), Guy Middleton (Colonel), Kynaston Reeves (Sir Charles Shepley-Cooke), Michael Balfour (The Major), Charles Lamb, Olga Dickie.

Gayson is a woman who can't resist auctions, but Culver, her skinflint husband, is convinced that the things she brings home are a result of kleptomania. He hires Rolfe to keep an eye on Gayson, then sends her to psychiatrist Howard. Gayson catches on to the plot and exposes her would-be watchdog as a thief, which causes Culver to mend his miserly ways. Though there's an occasional spot of humor to be found, the film drags on interminably.

p, Roger Proudlock; d, Terry Bishop; w, Alfred Shaughnessy; ph, Jimmy Harvey; m, Lonnie Donegan.

Comedy   **(PR:A MPAA:NR)**

LIGHT IN THE FOREST, THE***   (1958) 93m BV c

James MacArthur (Johnny Butler/True Son), Carol Lynley (Shenandoe Hastings), Fess Parker (Del Hardy), Wendell Corey (Wilse Owens), Joanne Dru (Milly Elder), Jessica Tandy (Myra Butler), Joseph Calleia (Chief Cuyloga), John McIntire (John Elder), Rafael Campos (Half Arrow), Frank Ferguson (Harry Butler), Norman Fredric (Niskitoon), Marian Seldes (Kate Owens), Stephen Bekassy (Col. Henry Bouquet), Sam Buffington (George Owens).

MacArthur, a white raised by Indians, is forced to return to white society following the signing of a peace treaty. Parker is an Army scout assigned to oversee the young man's readjustment. Difficulties arise when MacArthur meets his uncle, Corey, a brutal man who takes part in murderous attacks on Indian villages. Lynley is Corey's indentured servant who initially despises MacArthur because her parents were killed by marauding Indians. As MacArthur adapts to the white society, the two begin to fall in love. When Corey kills an Indian friend of MacArthur, he becomes enraged and returns to his tribe, only to find that they want to use him as a decoy to ambush innocent whites. He refuses and returns to confront Corey, whom he beats senseless. He and Lynley then head off for the forest to build a peaceful life together, while Parker settles down with Dru, the local minister's daughter. The "young-man-at-odds-with-his-surroundings" theme was a typical one for Disney films of the 1950s, and this is a worthy treatment. Good characters and a reasonably intelligent examination of the issues are its strong points. There's some chemistry between Lynley and MacArthur, and their love scenes are sensitively handled. The socially aware Disney films of the 1950s were far superior to his rather bland live-action output during the following decade (with the notable exception of MARY POPPINS). This film marked Lynley's debut and was the start of a long relationship between the studio and MacArthur. It was, however, the end of Parker's work for Disney, as he had grown weary of playing what he felt was the same character over and over again and left the studio. Iron Eyes Cody, who had filled Indian roles in several films, served as a technical director on THE LIGHT IN THE FOREST.

p, Walt Disney; d, Herschel Daugherty; w, Lawrence Edward Watkin (based on the novel by Conrad Richter); ph, Ellsworth Fredericks (Technicolor); m, Paul J. Smith; ed, Stanley Johnson; md, Franklyn Marks; art d, Carroll Clark; set d, Emile Kuri, Fred MacLean; cos, Chuck Keehne, Gertrude Casey; makeup, Pat McNalley; m/l, title song, Smith, Gil George, "I Asked My Love A Favor," Smith, Lawrence E. Watkin.

Drama **(PR:AAA MPAA:NR)**

LIGHT IN THE PIAZZA*½** (1962) 102m MGM c

Olivia de Havilland *(Margaret Johnson)*, Rossano Brazzi *(Signor Naccarelli)*, Yvette Mimieux *(Clara Johnson)*, George Hamilton *(Farizio Naccarelli)*, Barry Sullivan *(Noel Johnson)*, Isabel Dean *(Miss Hawtree)*, Moultrie Kelsall *(The Minister)*, Nancy Nevinson *(Signora Naccarelli)*, Rosella Spinelli *(Guiseppi Naccarelli)*, William Greene *(The Consular Agent)*, Robert Rietty *(The Priest)*, Steve Plytas *(Concierge)*, Luciano Barontino *(Marchese)*, Bonas Eugevio *(Policeman)*, Peppino Demartino *(Train Conductor)*.

It's a shame that LIGHT IN THE PIAZZA was not more of a box-office success. It had much going for it: the stars were well known, the literate script by a literate writer, and sensational locations beautifully photographed. Then why did it fail to deliver patrons? Probably, the fault lies in the story, which was alternately depressing and more depressing. Mimieux is 26, but was mentally retarded to the age of 10 when she sustained an accident. Her mother, de Havilland, takes her on a mini "grand tour" of Europe in the hopes of brightening her child's life. Sullivan, de Havilland's husband, thinks that Mimieux would be better in one of those places where the inmates get three hots and a cot and some minor therapy. The two women visit Rome, then Florence, and those two cities look like postcards come alive. In Florence, Mimieux is noticed by Hamilton, a dashing young Florentine (and when was Hamilton ever not dashing?) who immediately falls for the gentle, sweet Mimieux and asks her to marry him. This puts de Havilland squarely on the horns of a dilemma until she reckons, why not? It just might work. Especially since Hamilton is hardly an Einstein himself. Neither family is hurting for money and de Havilland thinks that the kids can be co-supported by them and probably have normal children. Sullivan is against it and would prefer Mimieux go away somewhere. This may be due to his desire to reawaken the relationship he once had with his wife, before their daughter's problem arose. Brazzi, a much-married type, is Hamilton's father, and takes somewhat more than an in-law stance to de Havilland, who is a comely woman. Eventually, de Havilland tells Brazzi of her daughter's mental condition, but it makes no never mind and the two kids are happily married. Mother de Havilland leaves the church feeling she did the right thing. Her performance was a small gem and she stayed off the screen for three years between this and her next film, a loss for the public's eyes. The film was touching but may have kept audiences away because of the theme of mental retardation. Mimieux played her part with a childlike quality rather than an over-the-top depiction of someone who is unable to communicate and interact with others. MGM might have made this happen with a different title and a different marketing strategy as there is much to recommend the finished product, including a first-time-ever look at the priceless treasures of the Uffizi Museum.

p, Arthur Freed; d, Guy Green; w, Julius J. Epstein (based on the novel by Elizabeth Spencer); ph, Otto Heller (CinemaScope, Metrocolor); m, Mario Nascimbene; ed, Frank Clarke; md, Dock Mathieson; art d, Frank White; cos, Christian Dior; spec eff, Tom Howard; makeup, Tom Smith.

Drama **(PR:A MPAA:NR)**

LIGHT OF HEART, THE (SEE: LIFE BEGINS AT 8:30, 1942)

LIGHT OF WESTERN STARS, THE*** (1930) 70m PAR bw

Richard Arlen *(Dick Bailey)*, Mary Brian *(Ruth Hammond)*, Fred Kohler *(Stack)*, Harry Green *("Pie Pan" Pultz)*, Regis Toomey *(Bob Drexell)*, William LeMaire *(Grif Meeker)*, George Chandler *(Slig Whalen)*, Syd Saylor *("Square-Toe" Boots)*, Guy Oliver *(Sheriff Jarvis)*, Gus Saville *(Pop Skelly)*.

Brian is a young woman from the east who comes to claim her late brother's ranch. Arlen, a drunken cowpoke, meets and falls madly in love with her. It turns out his best friend was her murdered brother, and he does a quick sober-up job to impress her. Kohler is the leader of some bad guys who want to take over the ranch but are stopped by Arlen. This could have been a standard western programmer, but maintains a freshness not normally found in horse operas. There's a good deal of humor and slapstick, though none of it is overdone or detracts from the plot. Some good performances and brisk direction (with two men in the director's chair!). This was the third version of the Grey novel; silent versions were made in 1918 and 1925. A fourth version was made with the same producer in 1940. This was Paramount's first talking adaptation of a Grey novel.

p, Harry Sherman; d, Otto Brower, Edwin H. Knopf; w, Grover Jones, William Slavens McNutt (based on the novel by Zane Grey); ph, Charles Lang; ed, Jane Loring.

Western **Cas.** **(PR:A MPAA:NR)**

LIGHT OF WESTERN STARS, THE** (1940) 67m PAR bw

Victor Jory *(Gene Stewart)*, Jo Ann Sayers *(Madeline "Majesty" Hammond)*, Russell Hayden *(Alfred Hammond)*, Morris Ankrum *(Nat Hayworth)*, Noah Beery, Jr. *(Poco)*, J. Farrell MacDonald *(Bill Stillwell)*, Ruth Rogers *(Flo Kingsley)*, Tom Tyler *(Sheriff Tom Hawes)*, Rad Robinson *(Monty)*, Eddie Dean *(Nels)*, Esther Estrella *(Bonita)*, Alan Ladd *(Danny)*, Georgia Hawkins *(Helen)*, Earl Askam *(Sneed)*, Lucio Villegas *(Marco)*.

Fourth and weakest version of the Grey novel. Sayers is a proper easterner who goes out West only to meet the often inebriated Jory. Naturally she's repelled by his uncouth ways, but before you know it we've got true love on our hands. The pace is far too slow and the story was pretty dated at this point. It was produced by Sherman, who held that title on the 1930 version.

p, Harry Sherman; d, Lesley Selander; w, Norman Houston (based on the novel by Zane Grey); ph, Russell Harlan; m, Victor Young; ed, Sherman A. Rose; art d, Lewis J. Rachmil.

Western **Cas.** **(PR:A MPAA:NR)**

LIGHT THAT FAILED, THE**** (1939) 97m PAR bw

Ronald Colman *(Dick Heldar)*, Walter Huston *(Terpenhow)*, Muriel Angelus *(Maisie)*, Ida Lupino *(Bessie Broke)*, Dudley Digges *(The Nilghai)*, Ernest Cossart *(Beeton)*, Ferike Boros *(Mme. Binat)*, Pedro de Cordoba *(Mons. Binat)*, Colin Tapley *(Gardner)*, Fay Helm *(Red-Haired Girl)*, Ronald Sinclair *(Dick as a Boy)*, Sarita Wooten *(Maisie as a Girl)*, Halliwell Hobbes, Colin Kenny *(Doctors)*, Charles Irwin *(Soldier Model)*, Francis McDonald *(George)*, George Regas *(Cassavetti)*, Wilfred Roberts *(Barton)*, Clyde Cook, James Aubrey *(Soldiers)*, Maj. Sam Harris *(Wells)*, Connie Leon *(Flower Woman)*, Harry Cording *(Soldier)*, Cyril Ring *(War Correspondent)*, Barbara Denny *(Waitress)*, Pat O'Malley *(Bullock)*, Clara M. Blore *(Mother)*, George Chandler, George H. Melford *(Voices)*, Leslie Francis *(Man with Bandaged Eyes)*, Barry Downing *(Little Boy)*, Harold Entwistle *(Old Man with Dark Glasses)*, Joe Collings *(Thackery)*, Carl Voss *(Chops the Officer)*, Hayden Stevenson *(War Correspondent)*, Gerald Rogers *(Sick Man)*.

This tragic Kipling tale, from his first novel, displays Wellman's consummate directorial skills in following the story faithfully, unlike earlier versions with sugar-coated endings. Colman is a gifted artist who receives a sabre cut during a battle. He returns to England where he becomes a famous painter, his masterpiece being that of a lowly London prostitute, Lupino, who poses for the painting. She is driven half mad with desire for him, a part so intensely played by Lupino that it brought her to stardom. Realizing that her station in life will prevent her from ever having Colman, Lupino viciously destroys the painting of her but Colman does not realize that the work is ruined. The old wound has caused him to slowly go blind. In one shattering scene Colman proudly displays the portrait to his devoted friend, Huston, without realizing that Lupino has slashed it to pieces. His sight almost gone, Colman bids goodbye to his childhood sweetheart and returns to the Sudan with friend Huston. At the first sound of battle, Colman begs Huston to put him into the fight, and is sent blindly charging on his white stallion to his death. This moving, haunting film reinforces Kipling's love of honor, male friendship, and nobility of spirit. Wellman handles the story and gaslight era with great care, developing his characters with incisive scenes. But it was a chore for the director. Wellman and Colman argued throughout the film, the director refusing Colman's perfectionist demands for endless takes, as well as ignoring the actor's insistence that Vivien Leigh play the slatternly Bessie. Lupino got that emotion-charged part by barging into Wellman's office to tell him that no other woman in the world could play Bessie as well as she and Lupino enacted the part right then and there. She got the role and audiences around the world were stunned by her marvelous portrayal. Of Colman, the director would later comment: "Ronald Colman and Wellman, an odd combination to say the least. He didn't like me; I didn't like him—the only two things we agreed fully on. The most beautiful voice [Colman's] in the whole motion picture business."

p&d, William A. Wellman; w, Robert Carson (based on the novel by Rudyard Kipling); ph, Theodor Sparkuhl; m, Victor Young; ed, Thomas Scott; art d, Hans Dreier, Robert Odell; set d, A. E. Freudeman; stunts, Yakima Canutt.

Drama **(PR:A MPAA:NR)**

LIGHT TOUCH, THE** (1951) 110m MGM bw

Stewart Granger *(Sam Conride)*, Pier Angeli *(Anna Vasarri)*, George Sanders *(Felix Guignol)*, Kurt Kasznar *(Mr. Aramescu)*, Joseph Calleia *(Lt. Massiro)*, Larry Keating *(Mr. R. F. Hawkley)*, Rhys Williams *(Mr. MacWade)*, Norman Lloyd *(Anton)*, Mike Mazurki *(Charles)*, Hans Conried *(Leopold)*, Renzo Cesana *(Father Dolzi)*, Robert Jefferson *(Bellboy)*, Aram Katcher *(Butler)*, Andre Charisse *(Guest)*, Gladys Holland, Louise Colombet *(French Women)*, George Dee *(French Man)*, Paul de Corday *(French Telephone Clerk)*, Robert Conte *(Waiter)*, Louis Velarde *(Arab Boy Juggler)*, Albert Ben Astar *(Hamadi Mahmoud)*.

Angeli is a naive young artist. She becomes involved with Sanders, whom she thinks is an art dealer. In reality he is a member of a gang of art thieves, led by master crook Granger. Before she realizes what's going on Angeli is caught up in the international art smuggling underground. Though the locales are nicely photographed, this is a pretty dull picture. No suspense is maintained and there is an overabundance of stereotypes and cliches. Brooks, who had only recently begun directing his screenplays at this point, shows little of the talent that he would display in IN COLD BLOOD.

p, Pandro S. Berman; d&w, Richard Brooks (based on a story by Jed Harris and Tom Reed); ph, Robert Surtees; m, Miklos Rozsa; ed, George Boemler; md, Rozsa; art d, Cedric Gibbons, Gabriel Scognamillo.

Crime **(PR:C MPAA:NR)**

LIGHT TOUCH, THE*
(1955, Brit.) 85m EAL/UNIV c (GB: TOUCH AND GO)

Jack Hawkins (Jim Fletcher), Margaret Johnston (Helen Fletcher), June Thorburn (Peggy Fletcher), Roland Culver (Reg Fairbright), John Fraser (Richard Kenyon), James Hayter (M. B. Kimball), Alison Leggatt (Alice Fairbright), Margaret Halstan (Mrs. Pritchett), Henry Longhurst (Mr. Pritchett), Basil Dignam (Stevens), Bessie Love (Mrs. Baxter), Gabrielle Brune (Waitress), Warwick Ashton (Policeman), Dorothy White, Elizabeth Winch [Liz Fraser], Alfred Burke, Eric Phillips, Michael Corcoran, Margaret Courtney, John Carroll, Jacques Cey, Peter Hunt, Arthur Howard, Heathcliff the Cat.

Comedy follows the adventures of Hawkins and family when they plan a move from England to Australia. Every problem imaginable pops up right on schedule, from trouble with the family cat to daughter Thorburn's refusal to leave her new boy friend Fraser. The humor is slight and most of the players miscast.

p, Seth Holt; d, Michael Truman; w, William Rose (based on a story by William and Tania Rose); ph, Douglas Slocombe (Technicolor); m, John Addison; ed, Peter Tanner; art d, Edward Carrick; m/l, Ray Noble.

Comedy   (PR:A   MPAA:NR)

LIGHT UP THE SKY**
(1960, Brit.) 90m Criterion/Bryanston-BL bw

Ian Carmichael (Lt. Ogleby), Tommy Steele (Eric McCaffey), Benny Hill (Syd McCaffey), Sydney Tafler (Ted Green), Victor Maddern (Lance Bombardier Tomlinson), Harry Locke (Roland Kenyon), Johnny Briggs (Leslie Smith), Cyril Smith ("Spinner" Rice), Dick Emery (Harry the Driver), Cardew Robinson (Compere), Susan Burnet (Jean), Sheila Hancock (Theater Act), Fred Griffiths (Mr. Jennings).

In 1941 a British army searchlight unit is staffed with a group of zanies, including a girl-chaser, a cook, a nice, if stupid, officer, and other assorted characters. Interspersed with their various cut-ups are moments of war-time tragedy. Episodic and ultimately plotless, meandering about with no real handle on what it wants to say. Comedian Hill exhibits the form that would later make him a popular television star in both the U.K. and U.S. Gilbert, who directed the fine SINK THE BISMARK! does a half-hearted job and the film is occasionally amusing.

p&d, Lewis Gilbert; w, Vernon Harris (based on the play "Touch it Light" by Robert Storey); ph, John Wilcox; m, Douglas Gamley; ed, Peter Tanner; m/l, Lionel Bart, Michael Pratt.

Comedy/Drama   (PR:A   MPAA:NR)

LIGHT YEARS AWAY**
(1982, Fr./Switz.) 107m LPA-Phenix-Slotint-SSR/New Yorker c (LES ANNEES LUMIERES)

Trevor Howard (Yoshka), Mick Ford (Jonas), Bernice Stegers (Betty), Henri Virlogeux (Lawyer), Odile Schmitt (Dancer), Louis Samier (Trucker), Joe Pilkington (Thomas), John Murphy (Man in Bar), Mannix Flynn (Drunk Boy), Don Foley (Cafe Owner), Jerry O'Brien (Bar Owner), Vincent Smith (Cop), Gabrielle Keenan (Girl at Village Dance).

Something of a sequel to Tanner's JONAH WHO WILL BE 25 IN THE YEAR 2000 (1976) starring Ford, who hooks up with bizarre old man Howard, who is trying to build a one-man flying machine in his garage. There are some nice moments, but the film is very slow, too simple, and burdened with too much "meaningful" dialog to be as charming as Tanner's earlier success.

p, Pierre Heros; d&w, Alain Tanner (based on the novel La Voie Sauvage by Daniel Odier); ph, Jean-Francois Robin (Eastmancolor); m, Arie Dzierlatka; ed, Brigitte Sousselier; art d, John Lucas; makeup, M. Autret.

Science Fiction   (PR:C   MPAA:NR)

LIGHTHOUSE**
(1947) 62m PRC bw

Don Castle, June Lang, John Litel, Marian Martin, Charles Wagenheim, Richard Bailey.

A romantic triangle set on an island, with two men, both lighthouse keepers, in love with the same girl. Piqued at the one she really loves, the girl marries the other, causing quite a bit of tension until the rejected lover leaves.

p, Franklin Gilbert; d, Frank Wisbar; w, Robert Churchill (based on the story by Don Martin); ph, Walter Strenge; m, Ernest Gold; ed, Robert Jahns, art d, Glenn T. Thompson.

Drama   (PR:A   MPAA:NR)

LIGHTHOUSE KEEPER'S DAUGHTER, THE
(SEE: GIRL IN THE BIKINI, THE, 1958, Fr.)

LIGHTNIN'***
(1930) 94m FOX bw

Will Rogers ("Lightin'" Bill Jones), Louise Dresser (Mrs. Mary Jones), Joel McCrea (John Marvin), Helen Cohan (Milly Jones), Sharon Lynn (Mrs. Lower), J. M. Kerrigan (Judge Lem Townsend), Jason Robards [Sr.] (Thomas, a Lawyer), Ruth Warren (Margaret Davis), Joyce Compton (Diana), Rex Bell (Ronald), Luke Cosgrave (Zeb), Thomas Jefferson (Walter Lannon), Goodee Montgomery (Mrs. Brooks), Philip Tead (Monte Winslow), Walter Percival (Everett Hammond), Charlotte Walker (Mrs. Thatcher), Frank Campeau (Sheriff Brooks), Blanche Le Clair (Mrs. Leonard), Bruce Warren (Mr. Leonard), Antica Nast (Mrs. Lord), Moon Carroll (Mrs. Blue), Bess Flowers (Mrs. Weeks), Gwendolyn Faye (Mrs. Starr), Eva Dennison (Mrs. George), Betty Alden (Mrs. Graham), Lucille Young (Mrs. Young), Betty Sinclair (Mrs. Bigg), Roxanne Curtis (Flapper Divorcee).

Rogers is the proprietor of a hotel near Reno, Nevada, and the majority of his guests are women en route to and from the town where they obtain quickie divorces. This was a successful play in 1918, offering a role Rogers really wanted. He's perfect as the wise sage, spinning humorous stories and providing advice with the right mix of innocence and maturity. There's no real story, just wonderful performances by Rogers and his supporting players.

p, John Golden; d, Henry King; w, S.N. Behrman, Sonya Levien (based on the play by Winchell Smith and Frank Bacon); ph, Chester Lyons; ed, Louis Loeffler; art d, Harry Oliver; cos, Sophie Wachner; m/l, "Reno Blues," Joseph McCarthy, James F. Hanley (sung by Goodee Montgomery).

Comedy   (PR:A   MPAA:NR)

LIGHTNIN' CRANDALL**
(1937) 60m REP bw

Bob Steele (Bob Crandall), Lois January (Sheila Shannon), Charlie King (Carson Blaine), Frank LaRue (Wes Shannon), Ernie Adams (Texas), Earl Dwire (Parson Durkin), Dave O'Brien (Tommy Shannon), Lew Meehan (Bull Prescott), Horace Murphy (Travis), Lloyd Ingraham (Judge), Dick Cramer, Jack C. Smith, Sherry Tansey, Tex Palmer, Ed Carey, Art Felix.

Steele is a gunman who opts for a quieter life. He heads off for Arizona, only to find himself in the middle of a feud among cattle ranchers. LaRue is the good rancher who must fight off bad guys Dwire and King. Of course he gets help from Steele and the gunman ends up with January, the rancher's daughter.

p, A.W. Hackel; d, Sam Newfield; w, Charles Francis Royal (based on a story by E.B. Mann); ph, Bert Longenecker; ed, S. Roy Luby.

Western   (PR:A   MPAA:NR)

LIGHTNIN' IN THE FOREST**
(1948) 58m REP bw

Lynne Roberts (Jerry Vail), Donald Barry (Stan Martin), Warren Douglas (Dave Lamont), Adrian Booth (Dell Parker), Lucien Littlefield (Joad), Claire DuBrey (Martha), Roy Barcroft (Lt. Bain), Paul Harvey (Judge Waterman), Al Eben (Bud), Jerry Jerome (Stinger), George Chandler (Elevator Operator), Eddie Dunn (Police Officer), Dale Van Sickel (Valtin), Bud Wolfe (Prichard), Hank Worden (Bartender).

Douglas plays a vacationing psychiatrist who meets thrill-seeker Roberts, leading to involvement in a variety of wild situations. Competent cast and rapid pace make up for some ragged scripting.

p, Sidney Picker; d, George Blair; w, John K. Butler (based on a story by J. Benton Cheney); ph, John MacBurnie; m, Mort Glickman; ed, Irving M. Schoenberg; md, Glickman, art d, Frank Arrigo; spec eff, Howard and Theodore Lydecker.

Crime   (PR:C   MPAA:NR)

LIGHTNING BILL CARSON*
(1936) 75m Puritan/Excelsior bw

Tim McCoy, Lois January, Rex Lease, Harry Worth, Karl Hackett, John Merton, Lafe McKee, Frank Ellis, Slim Whitaker, Edmund Cobb, Jack Rockwell, Jimmy Aubrey, Artie Ortego, Oscar Gahan.

Minor western features McCoy as a good guy fighting off rustlers, hombres, and gunslingers. Poorly written and directed, with some standard action sequences.

p, Sigmund Neufeld, Leslie Simmonds; d, Sam Newfield, w, Joseph O'Donnell (based on a story by George Arthur Durlam); ph, Jack Greenhalgh; ed, Jack English.

Western   (PR:A   MPAA:NR)

LIGHTNING BOLT*
(1967, Ital./Sp.) 96m Seven Film-B.G.A.-Balcazar/Woolner c (OPERAZIONE GOLDMAN; OPERACION GOLDMAN)

Anthony Eisley (Harry Sennet), Wandisa Leigh (Kary), Folco Lulli (Rethe), Diana Lorys (Capt. Patricia Flanagan), Ursula Parker (Luisa Rivelli), Paco Sanz, Jose Maria Caffarel, Orste Palella, Renato Montalbano, Luciana Petri, Tito Garcia.

Cheap action drama starring Eisley (who made quite a few of these unintentional howlers) as an American secret agent sent out to investigate the sabotage of a number of Cape Kennedy moon rockets. The trail leads to the undersea submarine base of the evil Lulli who plans to conquer the world with a laser cannon. The heroic Eisley puts an end to Lulli's insidious plot when he triggers an explosion that destroys the villain's compound.

p, Cleto Fontini, Giuseppe De Blasio; d, Anthony Dawson [Antonio Margheriti]; w, Alfonso Balcazar, Jose Antonio de la Loma (based on a story by Balcazar); ph, Riccardo Pallottini (Techniscope, Technicolor); m, Riz Ortolani; ed, Otello Colangeli; art d, Juan Alberto Soler, Antonio Visone.

Action   (PR:A   MPAA:NR)

LIGHTNING CONDUCTOR**1/2
(1938, Brit.) 79m Pinebrook/GFD bw

Gordon Harker (Albert Rughouse), John Lodge (Anderson), Sally Gray (Mary), Ernest Thesiger (Professor), George Moon (George), Steven Geray (Morley), Charles Eaton (Royle), Charles Hambling (Bus Inspector), Roy Findlay (Dakers).

Harker is a Cockney bus conductor who amuses himself and his passengers by performing magic tricks. Spies steal defense plans and plant them on the unknowing man. A series of comic misadventures follows as the spies try to regain the plans. A suspenseful comedy with some good characterizations.

p, Anthony Havelock-Allan; d, Maurice Elvey; w, J. Jefferson Farjeon, Ivor McLaren, Laurence Green (based on a story by Evadne Price); ph, Francis Carver.

Comedy/Suspense   (PR:A   MPAA:NR)

LIGHTNING FLYER**
(1931) 65m COL bw

James Hall, Dorothy Sebastian, Walter Merrill, Robert E. Homans, Albert J. Smith, Ethan Allen, Eddie Boland, George Meadows.

When a railroad owner kicks his carefree son, Hall, out of the house, the young man uses a pseudonym to get a job at his father's railroad yard, hoping to make good. The chance for redemption comes when an escaped convict cuts a freight loose.

Hall thrashes the villain and sidetracks the runaway freight. Some good action in an otherwise standard drama.

d, William Nigh; w, Barry Barringer (based on his story); ph, Ted Tetzlaff; ed, James Sweeney.

Drama (PR:A MPAA:NR)

LIGHTNING GUNS**¹/₂ (1950) 55m COL bw (AKA: TAKING SIDES)

Charles Starrett (Steve Brandon/The Durango Kid), Smiley Burnette (Himself), Gloria Henry (Susan Atkins), William Norton Bailey (Luke Atkins), Edgar Dearing (Capt. Dan Saunders), Raymond Bond (Jud Norton), Jock O'Mahoney (Rob Saunders), Chuck Roberson (Hank Burch), Frank Griffin (Jim Otis), Joel Friedkin (Crawley), George Chesebro (Blake), Ken Houchins (Musician), Merrill Mc-Cormack.

A good entry in Columbia's DURANGO KID series finds Starrett helping old buddy Dearing, a rancher. Seems he's having problems with Bailey, another rancher, over the building of a dam. Dearing is being blamed for a lot of problems since he doesn't want the dam built, but Starrett proves his old pal is innocent. Plenty of action and good comic relief by Burnette, who sings "The Bathtub King" and "Our Whole Family's Smart." Another song is "Rambling Blood in My Veins." This was O'Mahoney's first screen role after long being Starrett's stunt man. (See DURANGO KID series, Index.)

p, Colbert Clark; d, Fred F. Sears; w, Victor Arthur (based on a story by Bill Milligan); ph, Fayte Browne; m, Mischa Bakaleinikoff; ed, Paul Borofsky; art d, Charles Clague.

Western (PR:A MPAA:NR)

LIGHTNING RAIDERS** (1945) 61m PRC bw

Buster Crabbe (Billy Carson), Al "Fuzzy" St. John (Fuzzy), Mady Lawrence (Jane), Henry Hall (Wright), Steve Darrell (Hayden), I. Stanford Jolley (Kane), Karl Hackett (Murray), Roy Brent (Phillips), Marin Sais (Mrs. Murray), Al Ferguson (Lorrin).

A stagecoach is robbed of its mail delivery. St. John has been expecting some important mail and gets suspicious when it doesn't arrive. He calls in his buddy Crabbe and the two ride off to save the day. One of the last Crabbe/St. John westerns and not one of their better efforts. St. John, a former silent comic and distant relation of Fatty Arbuckle, had the unique distinction of being the only western serial player to have the same role in more than one series. His "Fuzzy" shows up in the LONE RIDER series with George Houston, as well as Crabbe's BILLY THE KID series.

p, Sigmund Neufeld; d, Sam Newfield; w, Elmer Clifton; ph, Jack Greenhalgh; ed, Holbrook N. Todd; md, Lee Zahler.

Western (PR:A MPAA:NR)

LIGHTNING RANGE** (1934) 53m Superior bw

Buddy Roosevelt, Patsy Bellamy, Betty Butler, Denver Dixon, Jack Evans, Si Jenks, Boris Bullock, Ken Broeker, Clyde McClary, Bart Carre, Olin Francis, Jack Bronston, Jack Evans, Lafe McKee, Genee Boutell, Anne Howard, Merrill Mc-Cormack.

When a woman is threatened by a gang of outlaws, it's up to Roosevelt to save the day. He gets back her money, defeats the bad guys, and wins the girl's heart in the process. Typical western outing.

p&d, Victor Adamson [Denver Dixon]; w, L. V. Jefferson.

Western (PR:A MPAA:NR)

LIGHTNING STRIKES TWICE* (1935) 64m RKO bw

Ben Lyon (Stephen Brewster), "Skeets" Gallagher (Wally Richards), Thelma Todd (Judy Nelson), Johnathan Hale (Capt. Nelson), Laura Hope Crews (Aunt Jane), Walter Catlett (Gus), Pert Kelton (Fay), Chick Chandler (Marty Hicks), Margaret Armstrong (Delia), John Davidson (Phillips), Fred Kelsey (Dugan), Edgar Deering (Lt. Foster), Roger Grey (Casey), Walter Long (Policeman).

Some real possibilities with a great cast are wasted in this unfunny comedy. It's a murder mystery with every cliche in the book, from a suspicious butler to jewel theft. This was referred to by the studio as a "commitment special" as many of its stars owed it a picture. There is some genuine talent here but it's all for naught as the script never lets the performers show what they can do.

p, Lee Marcus; d, Ben Holmes; w, Joseph A. Fields, John Gray (based on a story by Holmes and Marion Dix); ph, Edward Cronjager; ed, Arthur Roberts.

Comedy/Mystery (PR:A MPAA:NR)

LIGHTNING STRIKES TWICE** (1951) 91m WB bw

Richard Todd (Richard Trevelyan), Ruth Roman (Shelley Carnes), Mercedes McCambridge (Liza McStringer), Zachary Scott (Harvey Turner), Frank Conroy (J.D. Nolan), Kathryn Givney (Myra Nolan), Rhys Williams (Father Paul), Darryl Hickman (String), Nacho Galindo (Pedro).

Todd is cleared of murdering his wife by a hung jury. However his friends and neighbors still think he's guilty. He meets Roman, an actress taking a vacation. She believes in his innocence and tries to help him. Along the way they fall in love and marry. They discover that McCambridge was the real killer, as she nearly succeeds in doing away with Todd's new wife. But Roman escapes and McCambridge is killed in an auto accident. Though the mystery is a little thin and sometimes muddled, there are some nice moments here. The cast is not bad despite the script troubles. Vidor's direction is okay, though his fans will surely be disappointed knowing full well that he had done much better with his earlier work.

p, Henry Blanke; d, King Vidor; w, Lenore Coffee (based on the novel A Man Without Friends by Margaret Echard); ph, Sid Hickox; m, Max Steiner; ed, Thomas Reilly; art d, Douglas Bacon.

Mystery (PR:C MPAA:NR)

LIGHTNING STRIKES WEST** (1940) 56m Colony bw

Ken Maynard (Morgan), Claire Rochelle (Mae), Robert Terry (Grant), Michael Wallon (Taggart), Charles King (Laikon), Reed Howes (Frank), Dick Dickinson (Mack), George Chesebro (Sheriff), John Elliott (Doctor), William Gould (Marshal), Chick Hannon, Tex Palmer, Carl Mathews, Tarzan the Horse.

A routine effort for Maynard finds him chasing a bad guy escapee that he had once sent to prison. Quickly made on a low budget, it isn't the worst film Maynard ever did though it certainly doesn't stand out in his career. Stock situations and characters, each neatly fitted into its appropriate slot.

p, Max and Arthur Alexander; d, Harry Fraser; w, Martha Chapin (based on a story by Monroe Talbot); ph, Elmer Dyer; m, Lew Porter; ed, Charles Henkel.

Western (PR:A MPAA:NR)

LIGHTNING SWORDS OF DEATH
(SEE: SHOGUN ASSASSIN, 1974, Jap.)

LIGHTS AND SHADOWS (SEE: WOMAN RACKET, THE, 1930)

LIGHTS OF NEW YORK** (1928) 57m WB bw

Helene Costello (Kitty Lewis), Cullen Landis (Eddie Morgan), Gladys Brockwell (Molly Thompson), Mary Carr (Mrs. Morgan), Wheeler Oakman (Hawk Miller), Eugene Pallette (Gene), Robert Elliott (Detective Crosby), Tom Dugan (Sam), Tom McGuire (Collins), Guy D'Ennery (Tommy), Walker Percival (Mr. Jackson), Jere Delaney (Mr. Dickson).

There's nothing special to this routine crime yarn; in fact it's so crudely made that one wonders at the professional talent behind the film, or the lack of it. The film does have one historic distinction; it was the first all-talking motion picture and it was a great sensation, costing only $75,000 to make and returning to Warner Bros. a whopping $2 million. Landis and Pallette move to Manhattan and open a barbershop which they later discover is being used as a front for a large bootlegging operation. Nightclub owner and racket boss Oakman is later killed and Landis is framed for the murder, a gun belonging to Costello, who works in Oakman's club as a singer, being found on Landis. But before the innocent is sent to the electric chair, Brockwell, Oakman's mistress, confesses to the killing. The sound on this film, although carrying 100 percent dialog, is simply dreadful, worse than the quality of phonograph records at the turn of the century. Oakman does, however, deliver an underworld line that would become a cliche in scores of future gangster movies. Oakman orders one of his henchmen to get rid of a rival gangster, stating: "Take him for a ride!" Foy, son of the famed comedian Eddie Foy, directs the film sloppily, as if he had something better to do and was rushing the job. He would later go on to become head of B productions at Warners and other studios, grinding out films that were little better than this historic but inept film.

d, Bryan Foy; w, Hugh Herbert, Murray Roth (based on a story by Charles R. Gaskill); ph, Edwin Du Par; ed, Jack Killifer.

Crime Drama (PR:A MPAA:NR)

LIGHTS OF OLD SANTA FE**¹/₂ (1944) 78m REP bw

Roy Rogers (Roy), George "Gabby" Hayes (Gabby), Dale Evans (Marjorie Brooks), Lloyd Corrigan (Marty Maizely), Richard Powers (Frank Madden), Claire Du Brey (Rosie McGerk), Arthur Loft (Bill Wetherbee), Roy Barcroft (Ken Ferguson), Lucien Littlefield (The Judge), Sam Flint (The Sheriff), Bob Nolan and the Sons of the Pioneers (Themselves), Trigger the Horse.

Rogers and his faithful horse Trigger are the star attractions for Powers' rodeo show. But bad guy Powers won't let them do any of their fancier footwork and they leave him for Hayes, who owns a struggling rodeo and is tempted by Powers' offer to buy him out. But Rogers saves the day and manages to woo Evans from the crooked man as well. A typical Rogers horse-and-songfest, with the right amount of action as well. This was the first directorial assignment for McDonald in the Rogers series, after working with the singing cowpoke on two of the WEAVER FAMILY series, JEEPERS CREEPERS (1939), and ARKANSAS JUDGE (1941).

p, Harry Grey; d, Frank McDonald; w, Gordon Kahn, Bob Williams; ph, Reggie Lanning; m, Morton Scott; ed, Ralph Dixon; md, Scott; art d, Frank Hotaling; ch, Larry Ceballos.

Western **Cas.** (PR:A MPAA:NR)

LIGHTS OF VARIETY (SEE: VARIETY LIGHTS, 1965, Ital.)

LIGHTS OUT (SEE: BRIGHT VICTORY, 1951)

LIKE A CROW ON A JUNE BUG***
(1972) 84m Futurama c (AKA: SIXTEEN)

Mercedes McCambridge, Parley Baer, Ford Rainey, Beverly Powers, John Lozier, Simone Griffeth, Maidie Norman.

A young girl, played by Griffeth, reaches her 16th birthday while living in a deep South backwoods area. This is a sympathetic coming-of-age story with a nicely utilized setting.

p, Harvey Bernard; d, Larry Dobkin; w, Curtis Brown Taylor.

Drama (PR:C MPAA:R)

LIKE A TURTLE ON ITS BACK**¹/₂ (1981, Fr.) 110m New Line Cinema c

Bernadette LaFont (Camille), Jean-Francois Stevenin (Paul), Virginia Thevenet (Nathalie), Veronique Silver (Mme. Beuve), Claude Miller (Pierre), Marion Game

(Sylvie), Valerie Quenessen *(Nietzsche Student)*, Veronique Dancigers *(Arrogant Girl)*, Jean Daste *(Bad-Tempered Invalid)*, Francois LaFarge *(Jean-Louis No. 1)*, Etienne Chicot *(Jean-Louis No. 2)*, Michel Blanc *(Reveler Who Reads Manuscript)*, Sandy Whitelaw *(Prokosh)*, Souare Bhime *(Black Man)*, Jo Perque *(Usherette)*, Florence L. Afuma *(Ava)*.

The day-to-day life and anxieties of a frustrated writer are portrayed as the film's protagonist continually bangs on his typewriter in his search for self. Though the film is uneven there is an honesty to it that is often absorbing. (In French; English subtitles.)

p, Luc Beraud, Hubert Niogret; d, Beraud; w, Beraud, Claude Miller; ph, Bruno Nuytten; ed, Joele Van Effenterre.

Drama (PR:O MPAA:NR)

LIKE FATHER LIKE SON** (1961) Tom Laughlin 90m bw

Tom Laughlin *(Christopher Wotan)*, Taffy Paul *(Ginny Miller)*, William Wellman, Jr. *(John)*, Jim Stacey *(Art)*, Chris Robinson *(Bobby)*, Dennis O'Flaherty *(Marty)*, Bob Colona *(Harry)*, Chuck Siebert *(Lee)*, Roxanne Heard *(Joan Meyers)*, Charles Heard *(Mr. Wotan)*, Dorothy Downey *(Mrs. Wotan)*, Linda March *(Tury Martin)* , Ed Cook *(Coach Webster)*, John Burns *(Coach Ferguson)*, Jack Starrett *(Coach Jennings)*.

Laughlin, who serves not only as star but also producer, director, and writer, is a sensitive yet volatile high school athlete. He has problems on all fronts: his father is an alcoholic, his coach a sadistic bully, and he has dissatisfying relationships with women. The film is flat, save for Laughlin. It's his film so he gave himself the juiciest role and the most flattering photography. The other characters are one-dimensional stereotypes and the dialog is often laughable. Laughlin is allowed three emotions: sullenness, happiness, and depression. His direction is all right and there's an occasional flash of real talent in the camera work. This was the first of a projected three-part series that never materialized.

p,d&w, Tom Laughlin; ph, James Crabe; m, Shelly Manne; ed, Don Henderson.

Drama (PR:C MPAA:NR)

LIKE FATHER, LIKE SON, 1965 (SEE: YOUNG SINNER, THE, 1965)

LIKELY LADS, THE* (1976, Brit.) 90m EMI bw

Rodney Bewes, James Bolam, Brigit Forsyth, Mary Tamm, Sheila Fearn, Zena Walker.

A British television series of the late 1960s is revived with Bewes and Bolam returning to their old roles. The Northern English duo take to the road on holiday, their female companions in tow. This material worked better on television and it didn't work at all on this side of the ocean.

p, Aida Young; d, Michael Tuchner; w, Dick Clement, Ian La Frenais; ph, Tony Imi; m, Mike Hugg.

Comedy (PR:A MPAA:NR)

LIKELY STORY, A** (1947) 89m RKO bw

Barbara Hale *(Vickie North)*, Bill Williams *(Bill Baker)*, Lanny Rees *(Jamie)*, Sam Levene *(Louie)*, Dan Tobin *(Phil Bright)*, Nestor Paiva *(Tiny)*, Max Willenz *(Mr. Slepoff)*, Henry Kulky *(Tremendo)*, Robin Raymond *(Ticket Girl)*, Mary Young *(Little Old Lady)*, Nancy Saunders *(Blonde on Train)*, Bill Shannon *(Major)*, Charles Pawley, Drew Miller, Carl Hanson, Larry Randall *(Reporters)*, Sam Flint, Emmett Vogan *(Doctors)*, Isabel Withers, Mary Treen, Dorothy Curtis *(Nurses)*, Paul Newlan *(Truck Driver)*, Joe Green *(Senator)*, Jack Rice *(Secretary to Senator)*, Cy Schindell *(Criminal)*, Jack Arkin, Mike Lally, Hal Craig *(Photographers)*, Clarence Muse *(Porter)*, Dick Rush *(Detective)*, Tom Noonan, Sam Lufkin, Jack Gargan *(Taxi Drivers)*, George Magrill *(Express Man)*, Chester Clute *(Dr. Brown)*, Pat McKee *(Smoky)*, Hal K. Dawson *(Dr. Fraser)*, Jason Robards, Sr. *(Cop)*, Eddie Parks *(Drunk)*, Bill Wallace *(Limousine Driver)*, Lee Phelps *(Cop at Intersection)*, Jessie Arnold *(Landlady)*, Semion J. Grenvold, Katherine Lytle, Ethelreda Leopold *(Artists)*, Al Murphy, Charles Sullivan, Joseph Palma, Philip Friedman, Cy Malis *(Poker Players)*, Patsy O'Bryne *(Flower Woman)*, Kid Chissell *(Gym Attendant)*, William Gould *(Doorman)*, Phil Warren *(Intern)*, Dick Elliott *(Conductor)*, Alan Wood *(Elevator Operator)*, William Self, Phil Warren *(Interns)*.

Williams is a former soldier who convinces himself he has a fatal heart condition. He meets artist Hale, a young girl from the Midwest who's trying to make it in the Big Apple. He convinces some gangsters to insure him, collecting a fee which he gives Hale. Of course, he's not going to die and finds himself not only getting better, but falling for Hale as well. In the end the gangsters try to get back their money but are fooled by the tricky Williams. At times this is droll, but it often falls flat. Hale and Williams do have a good chemistry, but direction and script push too hard for big laughs where subtlety would have been more appropriate. This was the first film produced by Berger, who had been the director-manager of the St. Louis Municipal Opera.

p, Richard H. Berger; d, H.C. Potter; w, Bess Taffell (based on a story by Alexander Kenedi); ph, Roy Hunt; m, Leigh Harline; ed, Harry Marker; md, C. Bakaleinikoff; art d, Alberto S. D'Agostino, Feild Gray; set d, Darrell Silvera; spec eff, Russell A. Cully.

Comedy (PR:A MPAA:NR)

LI'L ABNER** (1940) 78m Vogue/RKO bw (GB: TROUBLE CHASER)

Granville Owen *(Li'l Abner)*, Martha O'Driscoll *(Daisy Mae)*, Mona Ray *(Mammy Yokum)*, Johnnie Morris *(Pappy Yokum)*, Buster Keaton *(Lonesome Polecat)*, Billie Seward *(Cousin Delightful)*, Kay Sutton *(Wendy Wilecat)* Maude Eburne *(Granny Scraggs)*, Edgar Kennedy *(Cornelius Cornpone)*, Charles A. Post *(Earthquake McGoon)*, Bud Jamison *(Hairless Joe)*, Dick Elliott *(Marryin' Sam)*, Johnny Arthur,

Walter Catlett, Lucien Littlefield, Frank Wilder, Chester Conklin, Mickey Daniels, Doodles Weaver.

An unfunny rendition of Al Capp's delightful comic strip finds Owen running about the town of Dogpatch to elude that most dreaded of institutions, marriage. O'Driscoll is the hillbilly lady who wants him just as much as he doesn't want her. The potential for comedy was enormous considering the source material but LI'L ABNER never does the comic strip justice. Everyone runs around with a variety of southern dialects which make much of the film incomprehensible. The direction shows no sense at all of what to do with the material and the comic talents of such names as Keaton, Kennedy, and Conklin are wasted. A musical version of LI'L ABNER, based on the Broadway show, followed in 1959.

p, Herman Schlom; d, Albert S. Rogell; w, Charles Kerr and Tyler Johnson (based on the comic strip by Al Capp); m/l, title song, Ben Oakland, Milton Drake, Milton Berle.

Comedy Cas. (PR:AAA MPAA:NR)

LI'L ABNER*** (1959) 113m PAR c

Peter Palmer *(Li'l Abner)*, Leslie Parrish *(Daisy Mae)*, Stubby Kaye *(Marryin' Sam)*, Julie Newmar *(Stupefyin' Jones)*, Howard St. John *(General Bullmoose)*, Stella Stevens *(Appassionata Von Climax)*, Billie Hayes *(Mammy Yokum)*, Joe E. Marks *(Pappy Yokum)*, Bern Hoffman *(Earthquake McGoon)*, Al Nesor *(Evil Eye Fleagle)*, Robert Strauss *(Romeo Scragg)*, William Lanteau *(Available Jones)*, Ted Thurston *(Sen. Jack S. Phogbound)*, Carmen Alvarez *(Moonbeam McSwine)*, Alan Carney *(Mayor Dawgmeat)*, Stanley Simmonds *(Rasmussen T. Finsdale)*, Joe Ploski, DiKi Lerner.

Broadly played musical comedy based on the Broadway show that itself was based on the comic strip by Al Capp. In this faithful adaptation of the stage version, the town of Dogpatch has been deemed "the most useless town in all of America," thus making it the perfect site for testing the A-bomb. The citizenry fights back. They look for something to give the town importance, finally settling on Hayes and her formula for "Yokumberry Tonic," an elixir for both health and romance. Naturally the government gets interested and all ends happily. The cast, nearly all from the original show, are wonderful in their cartoonish roles, providing the right amount of energy and yokel innocence. The costuming and choreography are as lively as the music. The dance sequences are particularly well edited, which goes to show there's more to movie dance numbers than just some fancy footwork. Though it's aged a little bit, this is still good fun. Songs: "Jubilation T. Cornpone," "Don't Take That Rag Off'n the Bush," "A Typical Day," "If I Had My Druthers," "Room Enuff for Us," "Namely You," "The Country's in the Very Best of Hands," "Unnecessary Town," "I'm Past My Prime," "I Wish It Could Be Otherwise," "Put 'Em Back the Way They Wuz," "Matrimonial Stomp" (Gene De Paul, Johnny Mercer).

p, Norman Panama; d, Melvin Frank; w, Panama, Frank (based on their musical and characters from the comic strip created by Al Capp); ph, Daniel L. Fapp (VistaVision, Technicolor); m, Nelson Riddle; ed, Arthur P. Schmidt; md, Joseph Lilley, Riddle; art d, Hal Pereira, J. MacMillan Johnson; spec eff, John P. Fulton; ch, Michael Kidd, Dee Dee Wood.

Musical Comedy (PR:AA MPAA:NR)

LILA, 1962 (SEE: MAKE WAY FOR LILA, 1962)

LILA, 1968 (SEE: MANTIS IN LACE, 1968)

LILA—LOVE UNDER THE MIDNIGHT SUN
(SEE: MAKE WAY FOR LILA, 1962, Swed.)

LILAC DOMINO, THE* (1940, Brit.) 65m Grafton-Capitol-Cecil/UA bw

Michael Bartlett *(Count Anatole)*, June Knight *(Shari de Gonda)*, S. Z. Sakall *(Sandor)*, Athene Seyler *(Mme. Alary)*, Richard Dolman *(Stephen)*, Cameron Hall *(Arnim)*, Fred Emney *(Baron de Gonda)*, Paul Blake *(Andor)*, Jane Carr *(Leonie)*, Morris Harvey *(Janosch)*, Robert Nainby *(Dr. Biro)*, Joan Hickson *(Maid)*, Julie Suedo, Joan Newall, Isobel Scaife.

Bartlett stars as a philandering, gambling count who is attracted to a masked woman at a masquerade ball. The mystery woman is Knight, a daughter of a baron, who sets out to reform the count. Based on a minor operetta, the film was badly dated even at the time of its release. Uninspired direction and weak casting make it one to be avoided.

p, Max Schach, Isadore Goldschmidt, Lee Garmes; d, Frederick Zelnik; w, Basil Mason, Neil Gow, R. Hutter, Derek Neam (based on the play by Rudolf Bernauer, E. Gatti, B. Jenbach); ph, Roy Clarke, Bryan Langley; ed, Lynn Harrison; ch, Derra de Morods; m/l Charles Cuvillier, Hans Mey, Clifford Grey.

Operetta (PR:A MPAA:NR)

LILACS IN THE SPRING (SEE: LET'S MAKE UP, 1955, Brit.)

LILI***½ (1953) 81m MGM c

Leslie Caron *(Lili Daurier)*, Mel Ferrer *(Paul Berthalet)*, Jean Pierre Aumont *(Marc)*, Zsa Zsa Gabor *(Rosalie)*, Kurt Kasznar *(Jacquot)*, Amanda Blake *(Peach Lips)*, Alex Gerry *(Proprietor)*, Ralph Dumke *(Mons. Corvier)*, Wilton Graff *(Mons. Tonit)*, George Baxter *(Mons. Enrique)*, Eda Reiss Merin *(Fruit Peddler)*, George Davis *(Workman)*, Mitchell Lewis *(Concessionaire)*, Fred Walton *(Whistler)*, Richard Grayson *(Flirting Vendor)*, Dorothy Jarnac *(Specialty Dancer)*.

An absolute charmer. Caron is a 16 year old who runs off to become a waitress with a carnival. She falls in love with Aumont, a magician who is more amused by the young innocent than anything else. Fired for paying too much attention to the dashing gentleman, Caron is comforted by a group of puppets, operated by Ferrer. This is probably the film's nicest moment, as Caron and the dancing figures sing the now-famed song "Hi-Lili, Hi-Lo." Caron despises Ferrer, whom she thinks is a cruel man. He is a bitter former dancer, crippled by a war injury. Driven mad with jealousy by Caron's infatuation with the magician, he slaps her. She discovers that Gabor (in what was probably the only decent performance in an otherwise undistinguished career) is Aumont's wife as well as assistant. Caron packs her things but as she walks away she begins to realize that Ferrer truly loves her and is only able to express this through his puppets. She turns around and returns to his waiting arms. Caron is wonderful as the girl. The character's growth is natural and beautiful to watch. Caron was rightly nominated for an Oscar, as were Walters for his direction and Deutsch for her adaptation of Gallico's short story. LILI did pick up an Oscar for Kaper's music. It was the basis for a hit Broadway musical in 1961 called "Carnival," with Anna Maria Alberghetti in the Caron role. At the time, creating Broadway shows from movies was unheard of, though this became a regular pattern in the mid-1970s.

p, Edwin H. Knopf; d, Charles Walters; w, Helen Deutsch (based on the story by Paul Gallico); ph, Robert Planck (Technicolor); m, Bronislau Kaper; ed, Ferris Webster; art d, Cedric Gibbons, Paul Groesse; set d, Edwin B. Willis, Arthur Krams; cos, Mary Anne Nyberg; spec eff, Warren Newcombe; ch, Walters, Dorothy Jarnac; m/l, "Hi-Lili, Hi-Lo," Kaper, Deutsch; makeup, William Tuttle.

Drama **Cas.** **(PR:AA MPAA:NR)**

LILI MARLEEN** (1981, Ger.) 120m Roxy-CIP-Rialto/UA c

Hanna Schygulla *(Wilkie Bunterberg)*, Giancarlo Giannini *(Robert Mendelsson)*, Mel Ferrer *(David Mendelsson)*, Karl Heinz von Hassel *(Henkel)*, Christine Kaufmann *(Miriam)*, Hark Bohm *(Tascher)*, Karin Baal *(Anna Lederer)*, Udo Kier *(Drewitz)*, Erik Schumann *(Von Strehlow)*, Gottfried John *(Aaron)*, Elisabeth Volkmann *(Marika)*, Barbara Valentin *(Eva)*, Helen Vita *(Grete)*, Adrian Hoven *(Ginsberg)*, Willy Harlander *(Prosel)*, Roger Fritz *(Kauffmann)*, Franz Buchwieser *(Thorne)*, Rainer Will *(Bernt)*, Lilo Pempeit *(Tamara)*, Raul Gimenez *(Blonsky)*, Alexander Allerson *(Goedecke)*, Rudolf Lenz *(Dr. Glaubrecht)*, Traute Hoss *(Polin)*, Brigitte Mira *(Neighbor)*, Herb Andress *(Reintgen)*, Michael McLernon *(Swiss Officer)*, Jurgen Drager *(Journalist)*, Toni Netzle *(Mrs. Prosel)*, Rainer Werner Fassbinder *(Guenter Weissenborn Rainer)*.

Fassbinder was surely one of the world's most prolific filmmakers, producing an enormous body of work before his early death, which ironically occurred as he was editing film. With such a large output there were bound to be a few pictures that fell short of the director's normally high quality, LILI MARLEEN being an example. "The story of a song!" claimed the advertising copy which is more or less truth in advertising. "Lili Marleen" was a song made famous in Germany by Lale Andersen and later Marlene Dietrich. It was very popular with the German forces during WW II. However, Fassbinder's film has little to do with the true story of the song. The film opens in 1938 with the lovely and accomplished Schygulla, a cabaret singer in Zurich. She discovers boy friend Giannini, a Swiss Jew, is not only a musical composer but also a member of the underground resistance movement. During a trip to Germany, her song becomes a hit, and no less than the Fuhrer himself wants to meet her. She becomes a big star, while Giannini's father blocks her return to Switzerland. Giannini sneaks into Berlin and meets once more with his now-famous lover. She becomes blacklisted and is forced to leave the country while Giannini is arrested. After the war, they meet once more, but he is now married and well on his way to success. Though Fassbinder's camera work is excellent, including some filmic allusions to the famous German studio UFA, his themes are never really developed. The political and social messages so often found in his work give way to more melodramatic story telling. Schygulla, who is usually a shining performer, is spotty here. Her singing makes one wonder how the song got to be such a hit. (In English.)

p, Luggi Waldleitner, Enzo Peri; d, Rainer Werner Fassbinder; w, Manfred Purzer, Joshua Sinclair, Fassbinder (based on the song by Lale Andersen); ph, Xavier Schwarzenberger; m, Peer Raben; ed, Franz Walsch, Juliane Lorenz; prod d, Rolf Zehetbauer; art d, Herbert Stravel; cos, Barbara Baum; spec eff, Joachim Schulz; ch, Dr. Dieter Gackstetter; m/l, title song, Hans Leip, Norbert Schultze.

Drama **(PR:O MPAA:R)**

LILI MARLENE (SEE: LILLI MARLENE, 1951, Brit.)

LILIES OF THE FIELD*** (1930) 58m FN-WB bw

Corinne Griffith *(Mildred Harker)*, Ralph Forbes *(Ted Willing)*, John Loder *(Walter Harker)*, Eve Southern *(Pink)*, Jean Bary *(Gertie)*, Tyler Brooke *(Bert Miller)*, Freeman Wood *(Lewis Conroy)*, Ann Schaeffer *(1st Maid)*, Clarissa Selwynne *(2nd Maid)*, Patsy Page *(Baby)*, Andre Beranger *(Barber)*, Douglas Gerrard *(Head-waiter)*, Rita La Roy *(Florette)*, Betty Boyd *(Joyce)*, May Boley *(Maizie)*, Virginia Bruce *(Doris)*, Charles Mailes *(Judge)*, Ray Largay *(Harker's Lawyer)*, Joe Bernard *(Mildred's Lawyer)*, Tenen Holtz *(Paymaster)*, Wilfred Noy *(Butler)*, Alice Moe *(3rd Maid)*.

Griffith stars as a woman who loses custody of her child during a bitter divorce. She takes to the world of jazz nightclubs, eventually becoming a gold digger. But her descent in social status continues with her arrest for vagrancy. Some nice nightclub song and dance numbers including "I'd Like To Be a Gypsy" are the few brief moments of happiness in Griffith's otherwise doomed story. Though well done and convincingly realistic, the audiences of 1930 found the film too depressing and the box office receipts were an embarrassment. Korda's direction is excellent, however, taking the story nicely toward its inevitable conclusion. Remake of a 1924 film of the same name, also starring Griffith.

p, Walter Morosco; d, Alexander Korda; w, John F. Goodrich (based on the novel by William Hurlbut); ph, Lee Garmes; ch, Roy Mack; m/l, "I'd Like To Be a Gypsy," Ned Washington, Herb Magidson, Michael H. Cleary.

Drama **(PR:O MPAA:NR)**

LILIES OF THE FIELD** (1934, Brit.) 75m British and Dominions/UA bw

Winifred Shotter *(Betty Beverley)*, Ellis Jeffreys *(Mrs. Carmichael)*, Anthony Bushell *(Guy Mallory)*, Claude Hulbert *(Bryan Rigby)*, Judy Gunn *(Kitty Beverley)*, Jack Raine *(George Belwood)*, Bobbie Comber *(Withers)*, Hubert Harben *(Rev. John Beverley)*, Maud Gill *(Mrs. Beverley)*, Tonie Edgar Bruce *(Lady Rocker)*, Gladys Jennings *(Hon. Monica Flane)*, Elsie French, John Mott *(The Aspidistras)*.

Shotter and Gunn are sisters competing for the heart of Bushell. Shotter poses as a proper Victorian maiden and ends up with the man of her dreams. Nicely acted and excellent production credits make this a charming romantic comedy.

p, Herbert Wilcox; d, Norman Walker; w, Dion Titheradge (based on the play by John Hastings Turner); ph, Cyril Bristow.

Romance/Comedy **(PR:A MPAA:NR)**

LILIES OF THE FIELD* 1/2** (1963) 94m Rainbow/UA bw

Sidney Poitier *(Homer Smith)*, Lilia Skala *(Mother Maria)*, Lisa Mann *(Sister Gertrude)*, Isa Crino *(Sister Agnes)*, Francesca Jarvis *(Sister Albertine)*, Pamela Branch *(Sister Elizabeth)*, Stanley Adams *(Juan)*, Dan Frazer *(Father Murphy)*, Ralph Nelson *(Mr. Ashton)*.

LILIES OF THE FIELD is a "feel-good" movie that blazed new trails in the motion picture world. Not that it had any particular special effects or innovations in movies. It had no spectacular action or dance sequences and surely no violence. But it was a trendsetter in that it marked the first time that the Academy of Motion Picture Arts and Sciences ever awarded an Oscar to a black actor, Poitier. It was also nominated as Best Picture, Best Screenplay, Best Cinematography, and Best Supporting Actress. Poitier is an ex-GI roaming around the Southwest, taking odd jobs and seeing what there is to see when he stops at a small farm to refill his car radiator. The farm is run by five German nuns who immediately set upon him to help them with their manual labors. They are new to these shores and don't speak much English but the Mother Superior, Skala, convinces Poitier to stay a while and help work the farm that was willed to them. He fixes their leaky roof and they send up prayers in honor of the man whom "God has sent." Now Skala asks if he will stay on to help with some other chores. Poitier is a little tired of his aimless wanderings and not much convincing is necessary, even though they prevail on him to do a major project—the building of a chapel. Poitier agrees, as long as they will supply the needed materials. He teams up with Nelson (doing double chores as director and actor), a contractor, and they start to build the chapel. Meanwhile, he donates his small salary back to the nuns to buy food and spends his spare time teaching the nuns how to speak English, in one of many touching scenes. When the materials run out, so does Poitier and the nuns think he's abandoned them, but he does return a few weeks later to complete the job he started for the nuns who he has come to love. Now, however, he is finally assisted by the local townspeople who refused to help him the first time around. On the night before the sanctification of the chapel, Poitier leaves with as little fanfare as he came with. It was a small, low budget picture that went straight for the heart and succeeded critically as well as financially. Director Nelson also helmed another Oscar-winning performance when he did Cliff Robertson's CHARLY, and his work on FATHER GOOSE helped screenwriters Frank Tarloff and Peter Stone win Oscars.

p&d, Ralph Nelson; w, James Poe (based on the novel by William E. Barrett); ph, Ernest Haller; m, Jerry Goldsmith; ed, John McCafferty.

Drama **Cas.** **(PR:A MPAA:NR)**

LILIOM** (1930) 89m FOX bw

Charles Farrell *(Liliom)*, Rose Hobart *(Julie)*, Estelle Taylor *(Mme. Muskrat)*, Lee Tracy *(Buzzard)*, Walter Abel *(Carpenter)*, Mildred Van Dorn *(Marie)*, Guinn "Big Boy" Williams *(Hollinger)*, Lillian Elliott *(Aunt Hulda)*, Bert Roach *(Wolf)*, H.B. Warner *(Chief Magistrate)*, Dawn [Anne Shirley] O'Day *(Louise)*, Nat Pendleton, James Marcus.

Farrell runs the merry-go-round at a Budapest amusement park and falls in love with Hobart. She becomes pregnant and he resorts to robbery to supplement his meager income, but when his plans go awry he commits suicide to avoid capture by the police. A celestial train transports him to heaven where he is told he can return to Earth after 10 years. Upon returning, he realizes that he is better off as a memory and returns to the heavenly train. A clever premise, but Farrell is hopelessly miscast in the title role and Borzage, who had been so successful in silent films, was yet to achieve competence with talking pictures. A silent version of the story was released in 1921 under the title A TRIP TO PARADISE.

d, Frank Borzage; w, S.N. Behrman, Sonya Levien (based on the play by Ferenc Molnar); ph, Chester Lyons; m, Richard Fall; ed, Margaret V. Clancey; art d, Harry Oliver; cos, Sophie Wachner; m/l, "Dream of Romance," "Thief Song," Fall, Marcella Gardner.

Drama/Fantasy **(PR:C MPAA:NR)**

LILIOM*** (1935, Fr.) 85m SAF-FOX Europa/FOX bw

Charles Boyer *(Liliom)*, Madeleine Ozeray *(Julie)*, Florelle *(Mme. Muskat)*, Alcover *(Alfred)*, Roland Toutain *(Sailor)*, Robert Arnoux *(Strong Arm)*, Alexandre Rignault *(Hollinger)*, Henri Richaud *(Commissary)*, Richard Darencet *(Purgatory Cop)*, Raoul Marco *(Detective)*, Antonin Artaud *(Knife Grinder)*, Leon Arnel *(Clerk)*, Rene Stern *(Cashier)*, Maximilienne, Mimi Funes, Viviane Romance, Mila Parely, Rosa Valetti, Lily Latte.

A better version of the 1930 film by the fine producer-director team of Pommer and Lang. Boyer is a man taken to heaven by a pair of angels. He is tried by a judge and confronted by various characters from his past to see if he is deserving of his wings. Fantastic elements are well-handled by the normally ice-cold realist Lang. The heaven photography is beautiful with other-worldly sets that don't seem the least bit pretentious. This was Lang's first picture after fleeing Nazi Germany. The original release ran two hours, though it was cut by some 35 minutes for its American release.

p, Erich Pommer; d, Fritz Lang; w, Lang, Robert Liebman, Bernard Zimmer (based on the play by Ferenc Molnar); ph, Rudolph Mate, Louis Nee; m, Jean Lenoir, Franz Waxman; art d, Paul Cohn, Rene Renoux.

Drama/Fantasy (PR:A MPAA:NR)

LILITH✶✶ (1964) 110m COL bw

Warren Beatty (Vincent Bruce), Jean Seberg (Lilith Arthur), Peter Fonda (Stephen Evshevsky), Kim Hunter (Bea Brice), Anne Meacham (Mrs. Yvonne Meaghan), James Patterson (Dr. Lavrier), Jessica Walter (Laura), Gene Hackman (Norman), Robert Reilly (Bob Clayfield), Rene Auberjonois (Howie), Lucy Smith (Vincent's Grandmother), Maurice Brenner (Mr. Gordon), Jeanne Barr (Miss Glassman), Richard Higgs (Mr. Palakis), Elizabeth Bader (Girl at Bar), Alice Spivak (Lonely Girl), Walter Arnold (Lonely Girl's Father), Kathleen Phelan (Lonely Girl's Mother), Cecilia Ray (Lilith's Mother in Dream), Gunnar Peters (Her Chauffeur in Dream), L. Jerome Offutt (Tournament Judge), W. Jerome Offutt (Tournament Announcer), Robert Jolivette (Older Watermelon Boy), Jason Jolivette (Younger Watermelon Boy), Jeno Mate (Assistant to Dr. Lavrier), Ben Carruthers (Benito), Dina Paisner (Psychodrama Moderator), Pawnee Sills (Receptionist), Luther Foulk, Kenneth Fuchs, Steve Dawson, Michael Paras (Doctors), Morton Taylor (Ambulance Doctor), Joavan Curran, Rick Branda, Wade Taylor, Tony Lombard, David Barry, Frank Nanoia (Ambulance Attendants), Joanne Bayes, Barbara Lowe, Patsy Klein, Gwen Van Dam, Eadie Renaud (Nurses), Rosalie Posner, Thom Brann, Louis Jenkins, Tracee Towers, Virginia Schneider, Robert Miller, Bruce Powers, Don Donnellan, Ken Naarden, Ron Cunningham (Occupational Therapists), Katherine Gregg, Edith Fellows, Page Jones, Olympia Dukakis, Mildred Smith, Cynthia McAdams, Wendell Phillips, Jr., Tony Grey, Elizabeth Lawrence, Harvey Jason, Gordon Phillips, Robert Dahdah, B.J. DeSimone, Marie-Antoinette, Cornelius Frizell, Janet Banzet, Tina Rome, Thelma Ray, Katha Cale, Harry Northrup, G.K. Osborne, Charles Tyner, Sonya Zomina, Anna Van Der Heida, Jocella Jackson, Amelie Barleon, Bess Carlton, Sylvia Gassel, David Craig, Bud Truland, Ruth Baker, Ceil Ray, Jeanne DeFlorio, Joe Rankin, Paul Varro, Stuart Goodman, Billie Erlich, and Peter Bosche (Patients).

LILITH is another example of attempting to hew too closely to a novel and failing. LILITH may have been a book that should have not been brought to the screen. Not even Rossen (who died shortly after finishing the movie, a man who had given us some memorable works, such as THE HUSTLER and ALL THE KING'S MEN, could solve the inherent problems. Beatty is a Korean War veteran who returns to his Maryland home and takes a job at the occupational therapy department of a local mental hospital where he will help reorient the wealthy patients to reality. While employed, he meets Seberg, an intriguing young woman who lives in her own little world and seldom comes out to visit with society. Beatty falls for Seberg and they begin having a taboo affair. Now he learns that she is two-timing him with a woman, Meacham, and that her nyphomaniacal tendencies dominate her existence. Fonda, another patient, appears to be the only person whom Seberg will not sleep with and he commits suicide due to that rejection. Fonda's death destroys what little sanity remains in Seberg and she now begins to trespass in the realm of total madness. The incident also ruins the mental health of Beatty and he seeks out the help of the doctors with whom he'd been colleagued earlier. Beatty is most lethargic in LILITH, his first film after having been so critically acclaimed in ALL FALL DOWN. He waits too long to deliver his lines and, when they are finally spoken they have all the power and punch of a nerf ball. Rossen and Beatty were at odds while making the movie with Beatty having all sorts of suggestions as to how to improve it and Rossen not heeding much from the man who would eventually prove to be a good filmmaker as a producer and later a director. Seberg is believable as the demented titler, as are Fonda and Walter, a woman who can play nutso with the best of them (she more than proved that in PLAY MISTY FOR ME) but this time she's mentally sound as Beatty's old flame who wouldn't wait for him to come home from Korea, so she married Hackman instead. The interesting novel upon which it is based examines the inner workings of mad minds but when put on the screen it becomes a murky, boring, and seldom entertaining attempt at an American "art film." Seberg had come a long way since her 1956 debut as Joan Of Arc and she was to improve greatly as the years passed until her tragic and mysterious death at 41.

p,d&w, Robert Rossen (based on the novel by J.R. Salamanca); ph, Eugen Shuftan, Tibor Sands; m, Kenyon Hopkins; ed, Aram Avakian; md, Hopkins; prod d, Richard Sylbert; set d, Gene Callahan; cos, Ruth Morley; makeup, Irving Buchman, Bill Herman, Robert Jiras; puppets, The Zoo, Gene Carlough.

Drama **Cas.** (PR:C MPAA:NR)

LILLI MARLENE✶¹/₂ (1951, Brit.) 75m Monarch/RKO bw

Lisa Daniely (Lilli Marlene), Hugh McDermott (Steve Moray), Richard Murdoch (Capt. Wimpole), Stanley Baker (Evans), John Blythe (Holt), Russell Hunter (Scottie), Arthur Lawrence (Lieber), Irene Prador (Nurse Schmidt), Aud Johansen (Nurse Melk), Estelle Brody (Estelle), Carl Jaffe (Propaganda Chief), Philo Hauser (Fratzell), Walter Gotell (Herr Direktor), Richard Marnery (S.S. Colonel), Rufus Cruickshank (Sgt. Bull), Olaf Olsen (Nazi Officer), Leslie Dwyer (Berry), Judith Warden (Auntie), Cecil Brock (O'Riley), Ben Williams (Brownie), Marcel Poncin (Lestoque), Michael Ward (Winterton), Laurence O'Madden (Col. Wharton), Stuart Lindsell (Maj. Phillips), Barbara Cummings (Shirley), Kenneth Cleveland, Conrad Phillips (Security Officers).

Daniely is a singer who, during WW II, popularizes a song with the same name as her character. While entertaining British troops in north Africa, a Nazi officer hears her and offers her a good salary to inspire the German front lines. She refuses and McDermott, an American broadcaster who has fallen in love with her, takes her to Cairo. She is kidnaped by Nazis and forced to sing for Hitler's troops. When the war ends, she returns to London, is cleared of collaboration with the enemy, and reunites with McDermott. This is a poorly made picture, with overwritten dialog and amateurish direction. The story is wholly unbelievable, though Daniely is appealing.

The song "Lili Marlene" (sometimes, as in this title, spelled "Lilli") was popular during WW II, and inspired not only this film, but the German LILI MARLEEN in 1981 as well.

p, William J. Gell; d, Arthur Crabtree; w, Leslie Wood; ph, Jack Asher; m, Stanley Black; ed, Lister Laurence; art d, R. Holmes Paul.

Drama (PR:C MPAA:NR)

LILLIAN RUSSELL✶✶¹/₂ (1940) 127m FOX bw

Alice Faye (Lillian Russell), Don Ameche (Edward Solomon), Henry Fonda (Alexander Moore), Edward Arnold (Diamond Jim Brady), Warren William (Jesse Lewisohn), Leo Carrillo (Tony Pastor), Helen Westley (Grandma Leonard), Dorothy Peterson (Cynthia Leonard), Ernest Truex (Charles Leonard), Lynn Bari (Edna McCauley), Nigel Bruce (William Gilbert), Claud Allister (Arthur Sullivan), Joe Weber, Lew Fields (Themselves), Una O'Connor (Marie), Eddie Foy, Jr. (Eddie Foy, Sr.), Joseph Cawthorn (Leopold Damrosch), William B. Davidson (President Cleveland), Hal K. Dawson (Chauffeur), Robert Emmett Keane (Jeweler), Frank Darien (Coachman), Irving Bacon, William Haade, Paul Burns (Soldiers), Milburn Stone, Charles Tannen (Reporters), Leyland Hodgson (Hotel Clerk), Philip Winter (Tenor), Thaddeus Jones (Mose), Alex Pollard (Waiter), Tom London (Frank), Stella Shirpsor (Baby), Robert Shaw (Man), A.S. "Pop" Byron (Policeman), Floyd Shackelford (Valet), Diane Fisher (Dorothy), Charles Halton (Dr. Dobbins), Ferike Boros (Mrs. Rose), Frank Thomas (Official), Cecil Cunningham (Mrs. Hobbs), Elyse Knox, Joan Valerie, Alice Armand (Lillian Russell's Sisters), Paul McVey (Stage Manager), Dennis Kaye (New Born Baby), Harry Hayden (Mr. Sloane, Newspaper Editor), Frank Sully, Richard Carle, Ottola Nesmith, Robert Homans.

The real Lillian Russell was far more interesting than the one Fox presented to a waiting world. She'd been married four times and had a fantastic life before settling down with her final husband, a newspaper publisher. In this padded version (more than two hours in length, a good deal more footage than Fox usually ascribed to their musicals), Faye is seen as one of several Iowa sisters (Knox, Valerie, and Armand are the others) who move to New York at the conclusion of the Civil War. With her grandfather, Truex, standing firmly behind her desire to sing, she is given a chance to study under Cawthorn (the famed Leopold Damrosch) who quickly sees that she has a fine voice, though not nearly powerful enough for opera. Lillian's mother, Peterson, has political ambitions and runs for the mayor's job but only gets a tiny number of votes. Faye is practicing in her back yard when she's overheard by Carrillo (Tony Pastor, a well-known turn of the century impresario) who hires her to sing in his theater. He changes her name to Lillian Russell (it had been Helen Leonard) and she is soon the toast of New York. Early on, she and her grandmother, Westley, had been rescued when their horse carriage was frightened by a band of suffragettes. Despite her success, she can't get the picture of the man who saved them, Fonda, out of her mind. Time passes and she has shows written for her, products named after her, and a host of boy friends waiting in line for her favors, including William (as Jesse Lewisohn, the rich man after whom New York's Lewisohn Stadium is named) and Arnold as Diamond Jim Brady (this was his second time in that role. He'd also played Brady in a Universal film of the same name five years before.). She has one other beau, a quiet and serious musician, Ameche. Faye makes her name worldwide when she sings for Davidson (as President Grover Cleveland) via the long distance telephone (which Ameche had invented in another movie). She and Ameche marry and go off to London where Gilbert and Sullivan (Bruce and Allister) are hard at work and arguing as they write a show for her. Now Fonda re-enters her life and commissions several articles on her for his newspaper. Faye gives birth to a child and Ameche is writing a show for her when he dies suddenly. Unbearably depressed, Faye refuses any further interviews and Fonda is gone from her life, for a while, anyhow. Before leaving Europe, Faye makes one appearance and sings a song cleffed by her late husband. Returning to the U.S., she continues to perform, becomes a living legend and appears with some other famed personalities, Weber and Fields. (playing themselves). She stars in a new show and Fonda comes backstage where he and Faye meet again and later marry. If this were filmed in color, it would have been far more effective and no one seems to know why it wasn't. Wonderful costumes and sensational sets. The furniture from the film stayed with the studio until auctioned in 1971 by Sotheby-Parke-Bernet. Tunes from a fleet of songwriters include: "The Band Played On," "After the Ball," "My Blushin' Rose," "Come Down, Ma' Evenin' Star," "Blue Love Bird," "Waltz Is King," "Adored One," "Comin' Thro' the Rye," "Back in the Old Days of Old Broadway," and "He Goes To Church on Sunday." The screenwriter knew his way around musical biographies, having also written THE GREAT ZIEGFELD. The shallow role displeased Fonda, who had just played one of the great roles in movie history in THE GRAPES OF WRATH. Thereafter, any time the name of the movie came up, Fonda would grunt in disgust. However, Zanuck was aiming at a blockbuster at the box office and wanted all the strength he could get in the billings, and, after all, Fonda had had to sign a Fox contract to get THE GRAPES OF WRATH role, and now he was paying the price.

p, Darryl F. Zanuck; d, Irving Cummings; w, William Anthony McGuire; ph, Leon Shamroy; ed, Walter Thompson; md, Alfred Newman; art d, Richard Day, Joseph C. Wright; set d, Thomas Little; cos, Travis Banton; ch, Seymour Felix; m/l, Gus Kahn, Bronislau Kaper, Mack Gordon, Alfred Newman, Charles Henderson, John E. Palmer, Charles B. Ward, John Stromberg, Robert B. Smith.

Musical/Biography (PR:A MPAA:NR)

LILLY TURNER✶ (1933) 75m WB-FN bw

Ruth Chatterton (Lilly Turner), George Brent (Bob Chandler), Frank McHugh (Dave Dixon), Ruth Donnelly (Edna), Guy Kibbee (Doc McGill), Gordon Westcott (Rex Durkee), Marjorie Gateson (Mrs. McGill), Arthur Vinton (Sam), Robert Barrat (Fritz), Grant Mitchell (Dr. Hawley), Margaret Seddon (Mrs. Turner), Hobart Cavanaugh (Earle), Mayo Methot (Mrs. Durkee), Katherine Claire Ward (Mrs. Flint), Lucille Ward (Mother), Mae Busch (Hazel).

Chatterton is the only saving grace in this mess of a film. She marries a man she later discovers to be a bigamist. She has a baby by him but marries a drunk so her child will know a father. She falls in love with another man, but when her husband breaks his back defending her from a killer, she stays with him after all. The film has no logic, veering off on too many turns to be believable. Hardly one of Wellman's finer efforts.

d, William A. Wellman; w, Gene Markey, Kathryn Scola (based on a play by Philip Dunning and George Abbott); ph, Sid Hickox; ed, James Morley.

Drama **(PR:C MPAA:NR)**

LILY CHRISTINE* (1932, Brit.) PAR British bw

Corinne Griffith *(Lily Christine Summerset)*, Colin Clive *(Rupert Harvey)*, Margaret Bannerman *(Mrs. Abbey)*, Miles Mander *(Ambatriadi)*, Jack Trevor *(Ivor Summerset)*, Anne Grey *(Muriel Harvey)*, Barbara Everest *(Hempel)*, Peter Graves.

Griffith made her final film appearance in this movie, marrying Morosco shortly after the film's release (she divorced him in 1934). The wife of Trevor, she becomes stranded and has to spend the night with friend Clive. It's an innocent evening, but Trevor, who wants to dissolve the marriage anyway, immediately sues for divorce. Her reputation ruined, she commits suicide by jumping in front of a speeding truck. A dismal failure and an unfortunate career finish for an actress who had been called "the most beautiful woman on the silent screen."

p, Walter Morosco; d, Paul Stein; w, Tobert Gore-Brown, Michael Arlen (based on the novel by Arlen).

Drama **(PR:C MPAA:NR)**

LILY OF KILARNEY (SEE: BRIDE OF THE LAKE, 1934, Brit.)

LILY OF LAGUNA*½ (1938, Brit.) 84m BUT bw

Nora Swinburne *(Gloria Grey)*, Richard Ainley *(Roger Fielding)*, Talbot O'Farrell *(Mike)*, G.H. Mulcaster *(Gerald Marshall)*, Jenny Laird *(Jane Marshall)*, Edgar Driver *(Tommy Thompson)*, Desmond Roberts *(Arnold Egerton)*, Violet Graham *(Margaret Marshall)*, Dudley Rolph, Richard Newton, Claire Arnold, Scott Harold, John Payne's Negro Choir.

Swinburne renounces her theatrical career to marry a scientist. After having a child, the lure of the stage proves to be too strong and Swinburne returns. Her husband divorces her. Twenty years go by and the daughter has grown up. She falls for a radio producer for whom Swinburne has fallen for as well. Realizing this is the man her daughter loves, Swinburne gives him up but the story's not over yet. She is shot by an ex-suitor who feels she used him. Then she reunites with the scientist who still loves her. A boring tale.

p, Sidney Morgan; d, Oswald Mitchell; w, Mitchell, Ian Walker (based on a story by Joan Wentworth Wood); ph, Geoffrey Faithfull.

Drama **(PR:C MPAA:NR)**

LIMBO (SEE: REBEL ROUSERS, 1970)

LIMBO***

(1972) 111m UNIV c (AKA: WOMEN IN LIMBO, CHAINED TO YESTERDAY)

Kate Jackson *(Sandy Lawton)*, Katherine Justice *(Sharon Dornbeck)*, Stuart Margolin *(Phil Garrett)*, Hazel Medina *(Jane York)*, Kathleen Nolan *(Mary Kay Buell)*, Russell Wiggins *(Alan Weber)*, Joan Murphy *(Margaret Holroyd)*, Michael Bersell *(Joe Buell)*, Kim Nicholas *(Kathy Buell)*, *Ken Kornbluh (Pete Buell)*, *Laura Kornbluh (Julie Buell)*, Richard Callinan *(Col. Lloyd)*, Charles Martin *(Col. Gunderson)*, Frank Logan *(Gen. Gibbs)*, Andrew Jarrell *(Ed Baldwin)*, Mike Phillips *(Lt. Phillips)*.

A small Vietnam era film that deals with the problems facing a group of women married to men who are missing in action. This is a slice of life film with each woman representing a different category: Nolan is the mother of four, whose husband has been missing for years; Justice is a socialite who refuses to believe, despite strong evidence, that her husband has been killed; and Jackson gives a fine performance as a young woman, married only two weeks before her husband went off to war. He is missing in action and she has met another man. This is one of the few films about Vietnam's effect on the home front and certainly one of the only films made while the war was in progress. It also is a stand-out for the number of women involved in production. Silver wrote the story and collaborated on the screenplay. In addition, the film was edited and scored by women.

p, Linda Gottlieb; d, Mark Robson; w, Joan Silver, James Bridges (based on a story by Silver); ph, Charles Wheeler (Technicolor); m, Anita Kerr; ed, Dorothy Spencer; art d, James Sullivan; set d, Don Ivy; cos, Marjorie Wahl, Mickey Sherrard; makeup, Guy Del Russo.

Drama **(PR:O MPAA:PG)**

LIMBO LINE, THE** (1969, Brit.) 98m LIP c

Craig Stevens *(Manston)*, Kate O'Mara *(Irina)*, Eugene Deckers *(Cadillet)*, Moira Redmond *(Ludmilla)*, Vladek Sheybal *(Oleg)*, Yolande Turner *(Pauline)*, Rosemary Rogers *(Joan Halst)*, Jean Marsh *(Dilys)*, Hugo De Vernier *(Hulst)*, Alan Barry *(Williams)*, James Thornhill *(Pieter)*, Norman Bird *(Chivers)*, Frederick Jaeger *(Alex)*, Eric Mason *(Castle)*, Denys Peek *(Jan)*, Robert Urquhart *(Hardwick)*, Ferdy Mayne *(Sutcliffe)*, Joan Benham *(Lady Faraday)*, John Horsley *(Richards)*.

The Limbo Line is an operation in which Russians kidnap defectors and take them back to Moscow for brainwashing. Stevens is an intelligence agent who wants to stop this. Next on the list is O'Mara, a beautiful Russian ballerina with whom he falls in love. She is kidnaped and he follows the Line to a Communist headquarters in Germany. There he is faced with a choice: to kill the man behind the operation and lose the girl, or save her and let the Line continue. But his duty as an agent must override his emotions and he sacrifices his love in the name of justice. It's an interesting idea, though the screenplay is occasionally laughable with some unbelievably corny dialog. Stevens is fine as the agent and there's enough action to please any fan of this genre.

p, Frank Bevis; d, Samuel Gallu; w, Donald James (based on the novel by Victor Canning); ph, John Wilcox (Eastmancolor); m, Johnnie Spence; ed, Peter Weatherley; art d, Scott Macgregor.

Spy Drama **(PR:O MPAA:NR)**

LIMEHOUSE BLUES* (1934) 63m PAR bw (AKA: EAST END CHANT)

George Raft *(Harry Young)*, Jean Parker *(Toni)*, Anna May Wong *(Tu Tuan)*, Kent Taylor *(Eric Benton)*, Montagu Love *(Pug Talbot)*, Billy Bevan *(Herb)*, John Rogers *(Smokey)*, Robert Lorraine *(Inspector Sheridan)*, E. Alyn Warren *(Ching Lee)*, Wyndham Standing *(Assistant Commissioner Kenyon)*, Louis Vincenot *(Rhama)*, Eily Malyon *(Woman Who Finds Pug)*, Forrester Harvey *(McDonald)*, Robert "Bob" A'Dair *(Policeman in Pug's House)*, Elsie Prescott *(Woman Employment Agent)*, James May *(Taxi Driver)*, Colin Kenny *(Davis)*, Eric Blore *(Man Slummer)*, Colin Tapley *(Man Fighting with Wife)*, Rita Carlyle *(Wife)*, Desmond Roberts *(Constable)*, Tempe Pigott *(Maggie)*, Otto Yamaoka *(Chinese Waiter on Boat)*, Dora Mayfield *(Flower Woman)*, Clara Lou [Ann] Sheridan *(Girl with Couples)*, Keith Kenneth.

Casting George Raft as a Chinese man makes as much sense as casting Eddie Murphy as a Swede. But Hollywood liked to do things like that and often used Occidentals in Oriental roles. Sometimes it worked, as in THE GOOD EARTH, and sometimes it didn't, as in this. Raft is an Asian gangster, but this time he can't flip a coin as he has 2-inch fingernails. He's a New York half-breed who leaves for London's Limehouse section and quickly becomes the No. 1 smuggler. There, he falls for Parker, a Caucasian tart, who is grateful to him, not passionate. This throws a year-of-the-monkey wrench into his plans as he attempts to cross the racial roadblock. His regular mistress, Wong, hears about this and is more than annoyed. When Raft learns that Parker loves Taylor, owner of a pet store, he too, is annoyed. Wong wreaks revenge by telling Scotland Yardsman Lorraine about Raft's illegal business, then she commits suicide. Raft plans to murder Taylor but is picked up by the cops before his men can perform the deed. Raft braves a hail of bullets to get to Taylor and save him, but he dies in the attempt, and none too soon, as the performances have, by now, annoyed everyone who saw the film. Wong scores best, perhaps because she is the only one of the leads cast correctly. Otherwise, every other actor goes too far in their work. America never bought Raft as a Chinese and Hollywood persisted in it's policy for too many years. There are rare exceptions to the failure of that policy, most notably Paul Muni as Wang Lung in THE GOOD EARTH, but Muni was so gifted he could have probably played an alligator with believability. This is another of the more than 20 films Ann Sheridan appeared in as a starlet under her real name before her career picked up in 1936.

d, Alexander Hall; w, Arthur Phillips, Cyril Hume, Grover Jones (based on the story by Phillips); ph, Harry Fischbeck; m, Sam Coslow.

Crime **(PR:A-C MPAA:NR)**

LIMELIGHT, 1937 (SEE: BACKSTAGE, 1937, Brit.)

LIMELIGHT****** (1952) 145m Chaplin/UA bw

Charles Chaplin *(Calvero)*, Claire Bloom *(Terry, a Ballet Dancer)*, Sydney Chaplin *(Neville, a Composer)*, Andre Eglevsky *(Harlequin)*, Melissa Hayden *(Columbine)*, Charles Chaplin, Jr., Wheeler Dryden *(Clowns)*, Nigel Bruce *(Postant, an Impresario)*, Norman Lloyd *(Stage Manager)*, Buster Keaton *(Piano Accompanist)*, Marjorie Bennett *(Mrs. Alsop, Landlady)*, Geraldine Chaplin, Michael Chaplin, Josephine Chaplin *(Street Urchins)*, Snub Pollard *(Street Musician)*.

Chaplin, as usual, is the whole show here and, as usual, he is superb in this swansong statement about his own career and the old-style entertainment he best represented. He is a one-time great of the British music halls at the turn of the century (which is exactly where Chaplin himself began), who finds a young dancer, Bloom, depressed over setbacks, attempting suicide in their cheap boarding house. He takes Bloom in, nurses her back to health, and supports her efforts to become a success. As her star rises, his fades, but he bows out with magnificent aplomb in the place he most loves, the theater. Chaplin plays comic and dramatic scenes with great skill. He is simply wonderful when exercising his astounding pantomime routines, particularly his act where he tames a flea and, in another act, where he imagines himself a great lion tamer. Chaplin is a delight when he sits with Bloom and teaches her his "laughter therapy." He ends his career and his life with an hilarious routine with the great comic Keaton, collapsing of exhaustion, falling into the orchestra pit and getting wedged in a large drum, commenting: "Ladies and gentlemen, I would like to say something, but I am stuck." He dies happy in that he believes that Bloom is in love not with him but with a young composer, played by Chaplin's real-life son, Sydney. Other children, from his marriage with Oona O'Neill (daughter of the great American playwright), appear as street urchins. The overlong film is extraordinary in that Chaplin produced, directed, wrote the script, and composed the haunting, lyrical score (winning an Oscar for the latter; the film's main love theme, "Eternally," becoming a popular ballad). LIMELIGHT is a direct comment on Chaplin's own fabulous career, one which saw the triumph and decline of physical comedy, slapstick as it were, which stemmed from the worlds of the circus and music halls and reached is greatest popularity during the silent film era when Chaplin reigned supreme as the greatest filmic artist. Yet he had fallen out of favor with a public that believed him to be a wild-eyed leftist radical, if not an outright Communist, and LIMELIGHT suffered by virtue of this public posture, yielding little profit at the box office. LIMELIGHT pays homage to the past, one where a simple, nuance-free entertainment gave joy and laughter to millions. Bloom, at age 19, became an overnight star with her appearance in LIMELIGHT (she had debuted in the film THE BLIND GODDESS at age 16). She later recalled in her memoirs, *Limelight and After*: "Chaplin was the most exacting director, not because he expected you to produce wonders on your own but because he expected you to follow unquestioningly his every instruction. I was surprised at how old-fashioned much of what he prescribed seemed—rather theatrical effects that I didn't associate with the modern cinema."

p,d&w, Charles Chaplin; ph, Karl Struss; m, Chaplin; ed, Joe Inge; art d, Eugene Laurie; ch, Chaplin, Andre Eglevsky, Melissa Hayden.

Drama/Comedy   Cas.   (PR:A MPAA:G)

LIMIT, THE**

(1972) 90m New Era Communications/Cannon c (AKA: SPEED LIMIT: 65)

Yaphet Kotto (Mark Johnson), Quinn Redeker (Jeff McMillan), Virgil Frye (Kenny), Corinne Cole (Judy), Ted Cassidy (Big Donnie), Pamela Jones (Margret), Gary Littlejohn (Pete), Irene Forrest (Delores), Nancy Ashe (Waitress), John Bellah (Pickup Truck Driver), Frank Belt (Man in Restaurant), Ed Cambridge (Police Captain), Vic Canupe (Bartender), Bobby Clark, Richard Kennedy (Men in Bar Fight), Douglas Forward (BMW Driver), Richard Hale (Man in Park), Stuart Herschman (Messenger on Beach) Joyce Hutton (Girl in Park), Peaches Jones (Woman in Station Wagon), Natascha Kotto (Carol Southern), Fred Krone, Jack Perkins (Drunks), Frank Roh (John Woods/Mr. America), Buddy Pantsary (Gas Station Attendant), John Roh (Boy with Kite), Diane Regis, Nina Tresoff (Virgin Girl Friends).

An atypical biker picture directed by star Kotto. Kotto plays a Los Angeles police officer who befriends a white officer and a tough black biker leader. With those usual sources of conflict taken care of, director Kotto introduces a vengeful biker who is second in command in the gang. He beats up his girl friend and takes the biker leader's woman for a motorcycle ride which nearly kills her and her unborn child. A chase through the city streets ensues and Kotto finally catches the thug but not before getting his throat slit. In an unexpected ending, Kotto is taken to the hospital while his friends and wife await his recovery. While the production appears raw and Kotto's direction relatively weak, THE LIMIT must receive some credit for bending the usual conventions of the genre.

p&d, Yaphet Kotto; w, Sean Cameron (based on a story by Kotto); ph, Fenton Hamilton (Metrocolor); ed, Norman Schwartz; cos, Nancy Brown, Mr. Guy, Gazebo.

Crime   (PR:C MPAA:PG)

L'IMMORTELLE***

(1969, Fr./Ital./Turkey) 100m Les Films Tamara-Dino De Laurentiis-Cocinor-Colo-Hamle/Grove bw (L'IMMORTALE)

Francoise Brion (L, the Woman), Jacques Doniol-Valcroze (N, the Man), Guido Celano (M, the Stranger), Catherine Carayon (Catherine), Sezer Sezin (Turkish Woman), Ulvi Uraz (Antique Dealer), Belkis Mutlu (Servant), Catherine Blisson.

This is the first film from French novelist Alain Robbe-Grillet. Released in Paris in 1963, the film concerns a character known as N who becomes obsessed with a woman known as L. She is followed by a Turkish man, M, and his two dogs. N follows L around the city's crowded streets and persuades her to take a vacation with him. While they are driving away, one of M's dogs runs into the street. To avoid hitting the dog, they swerve off the road and L is killed. Some time later, the man takes the same trip and the other dog runs into the street. He swerves to avoid the dog and dies. An interesting film which, not surprisingly, is quite similar to the work of director Alain Resnais. After seeing Resnais' HIROSHIMA, MON AMOUR, Robbe-Grillet and the director discussed a collaboration. The idea for L'IM-MORTELLE was one idea, but the pair instead chose LAST YEAR AT MARIENBAD.

d&w, Alain Robbe-Grillet (based on a story by Robbe-Grillet); ph, Maurice Barry; m, Georges Delerue, Tashin Kavalcioglu; ed, Bob Wade; art d, Konnell Melissos.

Drama   (PR:C MPAA:NR)

LIMONADOVY JOE   (SEE: LEMONADE JOE, 1966, Czech.)

LIMPING MAN, THE* 1/2

(1931, Brit.) 79m BIP/Powers bw (GB: CREEPING SHADOWS)

Franklin Dyall (Disher), Arthur Hardy (Sir Edwin Paget), Margot Grahame (Gloria Paget), Lester Matthews (Brian Nash), Jeanne Stuart (Olga Hoyt), Gerald Rawlinson (Paul Tegle), David Hawthorne (Peter Hoyt), Charles Farrell (Chicago Joe), Henrietta Watson (Lady Paget), Matthew Boulton (Insp. Potter), Percy Parsons (Limping Man), Hal Gordon, Ernest Stilwell, Samuel Pringle.

A trio of vengeful ex-cons try to spook Matthews when he moves into an estate he inherited. They cut his phone wires, empty his gas tanks, and cause the bells to chime inexplicably to repay him for turning informer, an act that sent them to prison years earlier. One of the three men limps around the grounds, further raising Matthews' suspicions. With the help of detective Dyall, Matthews' life is saved and the criminals are punished.

p,d&w, John Orton (based on the play "The Limping Man" by Will Scott).

Crime   (PR:A MPAA:NR)

LIMPING MAN, THE* 1/2   (1936, Brit.) 72m Pathe bw

Francis L. Sullivan (Theodore Disher), Hugh Wakefield (Col. Paget), Iris Hoey (Mrs. Paget), Patricia Hilliard (Gloria Paget), Robert Cochran (Philip Nash), Leslie Perrins (Paul Hoyt), Judy Kelly (Olga Hoyt), Frank Atkinson (Inspector Cable), Arthur Brander (Sandall), Syd Crossley (Sparrow), George Pugh (Chicago Joe), Harry Hutchinson ("Limpy"), John Turnbull (Inspector Potts).

Another version of the 1931 film where a limping man and thieves try to do in the inheritor of an estate, all in the name of mistaken identity and greed. Lots of spooky effects, screaming, and other inanities before the evil one is killed and the whole business is solved by a criminologist fortuitously placed in the center of the action.

p,d&w, Walter Summers (based on the play "The Limping Man" by Will Scott); ph, Bryan Langley, Cyril Bristow.

Crime   (PR:A MPAA:NR)

LIMPING MAN, THE**   (1953, Brit.) 76m Lippert bw

Lloyd Bridges (Franklyn Prior), Moira Lister (Pauline French), Alan Wheatley (Inspector Braddock), Leslie Phillips (Cameron), Helene Cordet (Helene Castle), Andre Van Gyseghem (Stage Doorman), Tom Gill (Stage Manager), Bruce Beeby (Kendall-Brown), Rachel Roberts (Barmaid), Lionel Blair (Dancer), Verne Morgan (Stone), Marjory Hume (Landlady), Robert Harbin (Magician), Charles Bottrill (Xylophonist), Irissa Cooper, Raymond Rollett.

Bridges plays a former American soldier returning once more to London. He wants to find his wartime love, Lister, but instead gets involved in solving a sniper murder. Ignoring the advice of police, he trails the limping man who killed someone with whom Bridges had been speaking. Along the way he discovers that Lister is involved with gangsters. But wouldn't you know it! He wakes up on the plane to London for this was only a dream! This impossibly hokey ending detracts from what is otherwise an average thriller with a little bit of suspense. Bridges is good and a nice leisurely mood is set, building to a mounting suspense. But the dream ending soils the entire film.

p, Donald Ginsberg; d, Charles De Lautour, Cy Endfield; w, Ian Stuart, Reginald Long (based on a story by Anthony Verney); ph, Jonah Jones; m, Eric Robinson; ed, Stan Willis; art d, Cedric Dawe; m/l, Hugh Baker and Arthur Wilkinson, Cyril Ornadel and David Croft.

Crime   (PR:A MPAA:NR)

LINCOLN CONSPIRACY, THE*   (1977) 90m Sunn Classic c

Bradford Dillman (John Wilkes Booth), John Dehner (Col. Lafayette C. Baker), John Anderson (Abraham Lincoln), Robert Middleton (Edwin M. Stanton), James Greene (Capt. James William Boyd), Whit Bissell (Sen. John Conness), Dick Callinan (Sen. Benjamin Wade), E.J. Andre (Rep. Thaddeus Stevens), Gregory J. Oliver (Rep. George Julian), J. Don Ferguson (Lt. Luther Baker), Billy Johnson (Sen. Zachariah Chandler), William Travis (Sen. George Boutwell), Maurice Hunt (Rep. A.J. Rogers), Patrick Wright (Maj. Thomas Eckert), Frank Schuller (Lt. Everton Conger), John Cooler (Maj. Henry Rathbone), Fred Buch (Capt. D.H. Gleason), Ned Hartnett (Christopher C. Auger), Jerry Fleck (Edward Spangler), Joe A. Dorsey (Lt. Edward P. Doherty), William Gribble (Capt. Willie Jett), Wallace K. Wilkinson (Dr. Samuel Mudd), Fred Grandy (David Herold), Mimi Honce (Mary Surratt), Bill Dial (George Atzerodt), Ken Kercheval (John Surratt), Sonny Shroyer (Lewis Paine), Ben Jones (Samuel Arnold), Christopher Allport (Michael O'Laughlin), Charlie Briggs (Andrew Potter), Mark Harris (Luther Potter), Paul Brown (Thomas Caldwell), Ed Lupinski (Edwin Henson), Frances Fordham (Mary Todd Lincoln), Liz Dent (Clara Harris), Bruce Atkins (John Parker), Howard Brunner (Louis J. Weichmann), Len Wayland (Ward H. Lamon), Larry Quackenbush (Harry Ford), Ralph Flanders (Richard Garrett), Dan Fitzgerald (Sanford Conover), Ben Mayo (Richard Montgomery), Ted Henning (Robert Campbell), John Mackay (James Merritt), Doug Kaye (Lincoln's Secretary), Albert Smith (Ferryman), Brad Crandall (Narrator).

A dubious historical "re-enactment" which proposes that Lincoln (portrayed by Anderson) was the victim of a conspiracy organized by Secretary of War Edward Stanton (portrayed by Middleton). Supposedly the secretary and his supporters were displeased with Lincoln's willingness to rebuild the South so they secretly met and plotted to abduct the president. The "official" plan is to have confederate spy Boyd (played by Greene) kidnap Lincoln from the historic Ford's Theater. Booth, (portrayed by Dillman), however, learns of the plan and takes advantage of the opportunity to assassinate the president. A massive search takes place and a suspect is gunned down—Boyd, not Booth. The natural coverup follows and the rest is history, sort of. The only thing THE LINCOLN CONSPIRACY actually reveals is America's fascination with conspiracies in general. Coming on the heels of Watergate and capitalizing on the Lincoln-Kennedy connections (a trendy topic of discussion in the mid-1970s), THE LINCOLN CONSPIRACY leads us to believe that John Wilkes Booth is living in exile (perhaps on the mountain where Noah's Arc supposedly is located) with a senile old Hitler, a Russian double of Lee Harvey Oswald and an aging John F. Kennedy who is still running the country from his invalid's bed.

p, Charles E. Sellier, Jr., Rayland D. Jensen; d, James L. Conway; w, Jonathan Cobbler (based on the book by David Balsiger, Sellier, Jr.); ph, Henning Schellerup; m, Bob Summers; ed, Martin Dreffke; md, Don Perry; art d, William Cornford; set d, Charles Bennett; cos, Cheryl Beasley; makeup, Melanie Leavitt.

Historical Drama   Cas.   (PR:A MPAA:G)

LINDA**   (1960, Brit.) 61m Independent Artists/Brynston bw

Carol White (Linda), Alan Rothwell (Phil), Cavan Malone (Chief), Edward Cast (Vicar), Vivienne Lacey (Rosie), Lois Dane (Clara), Keith Faulkner (Joe).

White is cast as the teen-age star of the title who helps young Rothwell defeat his battle with adolescent loneliness and despair. It all builds to a rather disappointing gang fight during a church social, but love carries the two leads through the melee safely.

p, Arthur Alcott; d, Don Sharp; w, Bill MacIlwraith.

Drama   (PR:A MPAA:NR)

LINDA BE GOOD**   (1947) 67m PRC bw

Elyse Knox (Linda Prentiss), John Hubbard (Roger Prentiss), Marie Wilson (Margie LaVitte), Gordon Richards (Sam Thompson), Jack Norton (Jim Benson), Ralph Sanford (Nunnally LaVitte), Joyce Compton (Mrs. LaVitte), Frank Scannell (Eddie Morgan), Sir Lancelot (Himself), Lenny Bremen (Sgt. Hrublchka), Gerald Oliver

Smith (Butler), Claire Carlton (Myrtle), Alan Nixon (Officer Jones), Byron Foulger (Book Shop Owner), Edward Gargan (Frankie), Muni Seroff (Maitre d'Hotel), Myra McKinney (Mrs. Thompson), Professor Lamberti.

Novelist Knox checks out the action at a local nightclub to get background material for her next book. Her husband is out of town on business and knows nothing about this. As it turns out, his boss (Richards) is dating a stripper (Wilson) and shows up at the club. Knox blackmails him into promoting her hubby so she won't spill the beans about where and with whom he spends time and money. This is a mildly amusing comedy with some good musical numbers by Lancelot. The script is a little underwritten but the straight-forward direction and some tight editing help smooth things out.

p, Matty Kemp; d, Frank McDonald; w, Leslie Vale, George Halasz (based on a story by Richard Irving Hyland and Howard Harris); ph, George Robinson; ed, Norman A. Cerf; art d, Lew Creber; m/l, "Old Woman with the Rolling Pin," "Young Girls of Today," Sir Lancelot (sung by Sir Lancelot), "Linda Be Good," Jack Mason, Charles Herbert, "My Mother Says I Mustn't," Mason, Sy Miller (sung by Marie Wilson).

Comedy   **(PR:A   MPAA:NR)**

LINE   (SEE: PASSIONATE DEMONS, THE, 1961, Norway)

LINE, THE*   (1982) 95m Enterprise c

Russ Thacker, Lewis J. Stadlen, Brad Sullivan, Kathleen Tolan, Jacqueline Brookes, David Doyle, Andrew Duncan, Russell Horton, James Catusi, Stephan Weyte, Cliff Collings, Gil Rodgers, Raymond Baker, David Ramsey, Sab Shimono, James Kelly, Mary Doyle, Sue Lain, Don Blakely, Robert Capece, Michael Heit, Tim Riley, Michael McGowan, Erik Estrada.

THE LINE is a poor attempt at filmmaking which is really one-third of a 1972 picture called PARADES. For some reason director Siegel decided to resurrect his previous film and gives us this one about a Vietnam deserter and his days in a California military stockade during a sit-down strike with his fellow prisoners. The inclusion of Erik Estrada at the bottom of the credits during the prime of his career (his fame came with the television series C.H.I.P.S.) is a dead giveaway to this film's age.

p&d, Robert J. Siegel; w, Reginald Shelborne, Patricia Maxwell; ph, Sol Negrin; m, Rod McBrien; ed, Dennis Golub, Shelborne; art d, Robert Wrightman.

Prison Drama   **Cas.**   **(PR:C   MPAA:NR)**

LINE ENGAGED*   (1935, Brit.) 68m BL bw

Bramwell Fletcher (David Morland), Jane Baxter (Eva Rutland), Arthur Wontner (Insp. Morland), Mary Clare (Mrs. Gardner), Leslie Perrins (Gordon Rutland), George Merritt (Sgt. Thomas), Kathleen Harrison (Maid), John Turnbull (Supt. Harrison), Coral Browne (Doreen), Ronald Shiner (Ryan), Francis James.

Fletcher is accused of murdering the husband of Baxter, the woman he is in love with. Fletcher's father, Wontner, is quick to pin the murder on him, but it is soon revealed that the guilty one is Baxter's mother. Because he is an author with a "perfect murder" plot in his latest book, Fletcher is the natural choice for a criminal but film experience tells us that this just isn't so.

p, Herbert Smith; d, Bernard Mainwaring; w, Jack De Leon, Jack Celestin (based on the play by De Leon, Celestin); ph, George Dudgeon Stretton.

Crime   **(PR:A   MPAA:NR)**

LINE OF DUTY   (SEE: INCIDENT IN AN ALLEY, 1962)

LINEUP, THE*   (1934) 75m COL bw (GB: IDENTITY PARADE)

William Gargan (Bob), Marian Nixon (Peggy), Paul Hurst (Doyle), John Milian (Fields), Harold Huber (Mile-a-Way), Greta Meyer (Mrs. Peterson), Joseph Crehan (McGrath), Noel Francis (Mable), Francis McDonald (Trigger), Charlie Browne (Chuck).

One of the many short gangster pictures put out in the 1930s to serve as the lower half of a double bill, this tale has nothing new to say. Nixon is a checkroom girl who accidentally gets caught up with some gangsters who frequent the club where she works. She is accused of stealing furs from the cloakroom and the only one who believes her innocence is detective Gargan. He absolves her, gets a promotion, and wins her heart as well. Hurst plays his goofy sidekick. The direction keeps things moving sensibly along.

d, Howard Higgin; w, George Waggner; ph, Benjamin Kline; ed, Jack Rawlins.

Crime   **(PR:A   MPAA:NR)**

LINEUP, THE*   (1958) 85m COL bw

Eli Wallach (Dancer), Robert Keith (Julian), Warner Anderson (Lt. Guthrie), Richard Jaeckel (Sandy McLain), Mary La Roche (Dorothy Bradshaw), William Leslie (Larry Warner), Emile Meyer (Inspector Al Quine), Marshall Reed (Inspector Fred Asher), Raymond Bailey (Philip Dressler), Vaughan Taylor (The Man), Cheryl Callaway (Cindy), Bert Holland (Porter), George Eldredge (Dr. Turkel), Robert Bailey (Staples), Charles Stewart, Jack Carol (Lab Men), Dee Pollock, Chuck Courtney (Boys), Junius Mathews (Jeffers), Frank Tang (Housekeeper), Clayton Post (Communications Sergeant), Francis de Sales (Chester McPhee), Kay English (Supervisor), Al Merin (Porter Foreman), Billy Snyder (Salisbury), Bill Marsh (Manager), John Maxwell (Norm Thompson), Kathleen O'Malley (Stewardess), Jack Moyles (Attendant).

A brutal but absorbing crime tale, THE LINEUP stars character actor Wallach as a killer-for-hire, working for the mob. Three packets of heroin are smuggled into San Francisco and it's Wallach's job to recover them from the unsuspecting travelers they have been planted on. He is accompanied by Keith, a strange criminal associate obsessed with writing down the last words of Wallach's victims. A seaman who realizes what he has been given is killed by Wallach and so too is the servant

of a couple who have been given the second packet. The third shipment is contained inside a Japanese doll owned by a little girl. Wallach befriends her mother and discovers that the child has opened the doll and used the heroin to powder her dolly's face. Rather than kill the mother and child, Wallach goes to see the underworld boss, Taylor, a vicious, cold-hearted cripple who meets Wallach in his wheelchair on the balcony overlooking a skating rink. Taylor refuses to accept Wallach's explanation about the missing heroin, believing the killer has grabbed off the dope for his own purposes. Taylor says with a sneer to Wallach: "You're dead." Wallach goes berserk and hurls Taylor off the balcony, killing him. He flees with Keith and Jaeckel, a nervous get-away driver. Police detectives Anderson and Meyer, who have been tracking Wallach, now catch up with him after a wild chase where Keith and Jaeckel are killed. Rather than surrender, the stoic Wallach shoots it out with the cops and is himself killed. This is vintage Siegel, a director who specialized in film noir productions but always on the ultra-violent side, as depicted in such films as THE BIG STEAL (1949), RIOT IN CELL BLOCK 11 (1954), CRIME IN THE STREETS (1956), and BABY FACE NELSON (1957). THE LINEUP is no exception as it probes the evil character of a contract killer who murders without mercy until it comes to the child and mother and he is faced with a dilemma which causes his downfall. Wallach is riveting in this film as the automaton killer with a spark of decency that bursts forth and engulfs him in flaming passion.

p, Jaime De Valle; d, Don Siegel; w, Stirling Silliphant (based on characters created by Lawrence L. Klee in the TV series "The Lineup"); ph, Hal Mohr; m, Mischa Bakaleinikoff; ed, Al Clark; art d, Ross Bellah; set d, Louis Daige; tech ad, Inspector John Kane, San Francisco Police Department.

Crime Drama   **(PR:O   MPAA:NR)**

LINKS OF JUSTICE*   (1958) 68m PAR bw

Jack Watling (Edgar Mills), Sarah Lawson (Clare Mills), Robert Raikes (Averill), Denis Shaw (Heath), Kay Callard (Stella), Michael Kelly (Robert Lane), Jacques Cey (Dr. Zelderman), Jan Holden (Elsie), Geoffrey Hibbert (Edward Manning), Honor Sheperd, Hal Osmond, Totti Truman Taylor, Diana Chesney, Vernon Smythe, Andrea Malandrinos, Frank Henderson, Graydon Gould, John Drake, Peter Bathurst, Brian Weske, Adrian Cairns, Robert Dorning, Harold Lang.

Watling and his mistress, Callard, plan to kill Lawson, his wife, for her money. The plan goes awry and Watling is murdered. Lawson is suspected but is able to prove she acted in self-defense when a burglar who witnessed the crime comes forth.

p, Edward J. Danziger, Harry Lee Danziger; d, Max Varnel; w, Brian Clemens, Eldon Howard; ph, Jimmy Wilson.

Crime   **(PR:A   MPAA:NR)**

L'INTRIGO   (SEE: DARK PURPOSE, 1964)

LIOLA   (SEE: VERY HANDY MAN, A, 1966)

LION, THE**   (1962, Brit.) 96m FOX c

William Holden (Robert Hayward), Trevor Howard (John Bullitt), Capucine (Christine), Pamela Franklin (Tina), Makara Kwaiha Ramadhani (Bogo), Zakee (Ol' Kalu), Paul Oduor (Oriunga), Samuel Obiero Romboh (Kihoro), Christopher Agunda (Elder of Masai), Zamba the Lion.

THE LION was not exceptionally fascinating but it had advantages over some of the jungle pictures made afterwards. First, there was a real story to go with the lush flora and fauna. Second, it had some fine acting by all concerned. Holden is an American lawyer summoned to the Dark Continent by his ex-wife, Capucine, who fears that their young daughter, Franklin, has become overly fond of the jungle and too attached to Zamba, a lion she has raised from birth. That's no surprise as Capucine's current husband, Howard, is a game warden attached to oversee a preserve. Howard is skeptical about Holden's appearance and doesn't mask his jealousy well. When an old tribal chieftain is left to die at the mercy of the elements (the custom of that tribe), Holden can't bear it and saves the man's life, who is grateful. The chieftain returns to the tribe and tells his son, Oduor, that he won't relinquish the title. Oduor had wanted to take over the helm and claim Franklin as his woman. (Since the girl is only eleven or so, that doesn't sit well.) The old man says that his son will never be a man until he has killed a lion so Oduor chooses Franklin's pet as his prey. Franklin won't hear of that and orders Zamba to kill the prince. Now Howard has to kill the lion. Franklin, who never really knew her father, Holden, is brought closer to him when she sees Howard destroy Zamba. Howard has, by now, noted the growing attraction between Holden and Capucine and gives his assent for them all to return to the U.S. By the early 1960s, Holden had fallen in love with Africa and Capucine and the two factors that determined his decision to make this movie were that she co-star and that the film be done on location in Africa. Franklin underplays her role with none of the cloying cutsiness that could have been present, a fitting followup to her first film, THE INNOCENTS. Howard is in a seething rage most of the time, as he should be when he sees his wife and stepdaughter being pulled from him. Zamba the lion acquits himself well and might have signed a multi-picture deal with MGM, except that they already had their own Leo. (Okay, it's a joke, but we can't keep all of the reviews scholarly and serious, can we?) The picture was filmed in Uganda, Kenya, and Tanganyika.

p, Samuel G. Engle; d, Jack Cardiff; w, Irene and Louis Kamp (based on the novel by Joseph Kessel); ph, Ted Scaife (CinemaScope, DeLuxe Color); m, Malcolm Arnold; ed, Russell Lloyd; md, Arnold; art d, Alan Withy, John Hoesli; makeup, George Frost; tech adv, Maj. W.H.M. Taberer; animal supr, Ralph Helfer.

Drama   **(PR:A   MPAA:NR)**

LION AND THE HORSE, THE* 1/2   (1952) 83m WB c

Steve Cochran (Ben Kirby), Ray Teal (Dave Tracy), Bob Steele (Mat Jennings), Harry Antrim (Cas Bagley), George O'Hanlon ("Shorty" Cameron), Sherry

Jackson (Jenny), Ed Hinton (Al Richie), William Fawcett ("Pappy" Cole), House Peters Jr. ("Rocky" Steuber), Lee Roberts (Riggs), Lane Chandler (The Sheriff), Charles Stevens (Deputy Britt), Jack Williams (Steve Collier), Tom Tyler (Bud Sabin), Billy Dix (Clint Adams), Steve Peck (Jiggs Dalton), Wildfire the Horse.

This simple-minded story had one good thing going for it: it was the first released film with Warner Brothers' new process WarnerColor. The backgrounds are wonderful and scenery is used well. Too bad it had this story stuck onto it. Cochran is a cowboy who tracks down a wild horse with the rather unoriginal name of Wildfire. The horse is sold to bad guy Teal's rodeo and is maltreated. Wildfire escapes with a circus lion. When the king of the beasts starts attacking humans, Wildfire puts a stop to it and is reunited with Cochran. Cochran is OK in his sympathetic role, which cast him against his usual hardboiled type. Lots of action pads out the thin story line and direction is mediocre at best. Though this was the first released WarnerColor, CARSON CITY, another western released after this, was the first film shot with the new process.

p, Bryan Foy; d, Louis King; w, Crane Wilber; ph, Edwin Du Par (WarnerColor); m, Max Steiner; ed, William Ziegler; art d, Stanley Fleischer.

Western   **(PR:A   MPAA:NR)**

LION AND THE LAMB*   (1931) 74m COL bw

Walter Byron (Dave), Carmel Myers (Inez), Raymond Hatton (Muggsy), Montagu Love (Tottie), Miriam Seegar (Madge), Charles Gerrard (Bert), Will Stanton (Ruebin), Charles Wildish (First Lascar), Harry Semels (Second Lascar), Robert Milasch (Lem), Yorke Sherwood (Wister), Sidney Bracey (Stanton).

After returning to London from an around the world trip, Byron finds he has been named an earl. In addition, he accidentally gets involved with the criminal underground. He gets out before they kidnap a wealthy young woman and tries to stop them. This poorly written film is so bad it's unintentionally funny. Implausibilities, played as straight as can be, pile up, resulting in great—if unintended—camp.

d, George B. Seitz; w, Matt Taylor (based on the story by E. Phillips Oppenheim); ph, Henry Sharpe; ed, Gene Milford.

Crime   **(PR:A   MPAA:NR)**

LION AND THE MOUSE, THE*   (1928) 65m WB bw

May McAvoy (Shirley Rossmore), Lionel Barrymore (John "Ready Money" Ryder), Alec Francis (Judge Rossmore), William Collier, Jr. (Jefferson Ryder), Emmett Corrigan (Dr. Hays), Jack Ackroyd (Smith, Jeff's Valet).

With the introduction of sound, the studios scrambled to put together any film that would talk. Often these films were slipshod efforts that were poorly recorded and part silent as well. THE LION AND THE MOUSE is a classic example. The story is simplistic and the dialog stiff and formal. The actors, with the strong exception of Barrymore, cannot grasp the concept of talking and acting at the same time. The film starts off with speech for about the first third, then mysteriously reverts to title cards. It ends with sound, though as with the first section, it's poorly recorded. The actors drift in and out of comprehensibility as they move around the microphones. The synchronization is also a mess. It was billed as "the first talking motion picture," though this hardly was truth in advertising. Barrymore, for what it's worth, seems to be ignoring the stiff dialog and interpreting it to fit his character. He gives the only real performance to be found. The story has him as a powerful financier, with McAvoy as the young pretty who tries to do him in.

d, Lloyd Bacon; w, Robert Lord (title cards by Jimmie Starr; based on the play by Charles Klein); ph, Norbert Brodine; ed, Harold J. McCord.

Drama   **(PR:A   MPAA:NR)**

LION HAS WINGS, THE**   (1940, Brit.) 76m London/UA bw

Merle Oberon (Mrs. Richardson), Ralph Richardson (Wing Cmdr. Richardson), June Duprez (June), Robert Douglas (Briefing Officer), Anthony Bushell (Pilot), Derrick de Marney (Bill), Brian Worth (Bobby), Austin Trevor (Schulemburg), Ivan Brandt (Officer), G.H. Mulcaster (Controller), Herbert Lomas (Holveg), Milton Rosmer (Head of Observer Corps), Robert Rendel (Chief of Air Staff), Archibald Batty (Air Officer), Ronald Adam, John Longden, Ian Fleming, Miles Malleson, Bernard Miles, Charles Carson, John Penrose, Frank Tickle, John Robinson, Carl Jaffe, Gerald Case, Torin Thatcher, Ronald Shiner, Lowell Thomas (Narrator).

Though today this film seems ridiculous, for its time it was an important piece. This was a propaganda film released during WW II, combining actual documentary footage with a slight story to explain British involvement in the war. The story is little more than an excuse to show the British home front and the creation of airplanes. In addition to newsreel and documentary footage, scenes from FIRE OVER ENGLAND and THE GAP also were incorporated. In 1940, this was an important morale booster but it, like many other propaganda pieces, shows no insight for the post-war population. Korda, who produced, also directed some sequences, though he is not credited as a director.

p, Alexander Korda; d, Michael Powell, Brian Desmond Hurst, Adrian Brunel; w, Brunel, E.V.H. Emmett (based on a story by Ian Dalrymple); ph, Harry Stradling, Osmond Borradaile; m, Richard Addinsell; ed, Henry Cornelius, Charles Frend; prod d, Vincent Korda; md, Muir Mathieson.

War Drama   **Cas.**   **(PR:A   MPAA:NR)**

LION HUNTERS, THE* 1/2

(1951) 75m MON bw (GB: BOMBA AND THE LION HUNTERS)

Johnny Sheffield (Bomba), Morris Ankrum (Forbes), Ann Todd (Jean), Douglas Kennedy (Martin), Smoki Whitfield (Jonas), Robert Davis (Lohu), Woodrow Strode (Walu).

Sheffield, who had played "Boy" in the TARZAN films, got his chance at a Tarzan-like role, playing the young white boy who grows up in the jungle. The

BOMBA series was not one of Monogram studios' best efforts, though the kids did (and still do) enjoy them. Here, he stops some evil lion hunters with a pre-Rachel Carson plot. He tells them that the lions were meant to run free but do you think those hunters listen? He saves the king of beasts and Todd for good measure. Plenty of bad acting and an overabundance of cheap stock shots do not help much unless this is watched for camp's sake.

p, Walter Mirisch; d&w, Ford Beebe (based on the "Bomba" books created by Roy Rockwood); ph, William Sickner; m, Marlin Skiles; ed, Otho Lovering; md, Skiles; art d, Dave Milton.

Adventure   **(PR:AA   MPAA:NR)**

LION IN THE STREETS, A   (SEE: LION IS IN THE STREETS, A, 1953)

LION IN WINTER, THE****   (1968, Brit.) 134m Haworth/AE c

Peter O'Toole (King Henry II), Katharine Hepburn (Queen Eleanor of Aquitaine), Jane Merrow (Princess Alais), John Castle (Prince Geoffrey), Timothy Dalton (King Philip of France), Anthony Hopkins (Prince Richard the Lion-Hearted), Nigel Stock (William Marshall), Nigel Terry (Prince John), Kenneth Griffith (Strolling Player), O. Z. Whitehead (Bishop of Durham), Kenneth Ives (Eleanor's Guard), Henry Wolff, Karol Hagar, Mark Griffith.

O'Toole, the all-powerful Henry II, summons his politically ambitious family to a reunion in 1183, including his wife, Hepburn, whom he has kept in a remote castle to keep her from meddling with his empire. His three sons—all coveting his wide kingdom—Castle, Terry, and Hopkins are also present, along with O'Toole's mistress Merrow and her brother Dalton, playing King Philip of France. The members of this tempestuous family jockey for position and brutally squabble among each other, rekindling every injury suffered and adding new, Homeric insults to their already bruised reputations. Merrow expects that O'Toole will discard his estranged wife Hepburn and get rid of his three grown sons so that they can marry and her child with him will become the next king. Yet Hepburn weaves her old magic and manages to preserve the family and the kingdom for her politically obsessed sons—notably Hopkins, the eldest—playing the future English king, Richard the Lion-Hearted. Hepburn is simply wonderful as the scheming and shrewd Eleanor of Aquitaine and her verbal duels with the equally impressive O'Toole (here playing a man of fifty behind a beard and heavy makeup) are spellbinding. Hepburn won her third Oscar for this superlative performance, becoming the first actress in history to do so (her previous Oscars were for MORNING GLORY, 1933 and GUESS WHO'S COMING TO DINNER, 1967). O'Toole holds his own with the magnificent Hepburn in one of the wittiest, most literate and inventive scripts ever written for the screen. Although some critics at the time of release lambasted A LION IN WINTER as nothing more than a filmed stage play, this is really a specious argument (which could also be wrongly applied to such stellar movies as LONG DAY'S JOURNEY INTO NIGHT). The claim that costume dramas are never successful was mightily disproved by this film, which enjoyed a booming box-office business and the wide respect of the public. Hepburn enjoyed filming this sprightly historical drama, telling a newsman at the time that her character, Eleanor, "must have been tough as nails to have lived to be 82 years old and full of beans. Both she and Henry II were big-time operators who played for whole countries. I like big-time operators." She manipulated O'Toole with abandon during the production, telling him on the set to "stop towering over me. Come and sit down and try to look respectable." Despite O'Toole's reputation as a fierce and temperamental actor, he complied meekly with Hepburn's commands. The actor later moaned that Hepburn had turned him into "a shadow of my former gay-dog self . . . . She is terrifying. It is sheer masochism working with her. She has been sent by some dark fate to nag and torment me." This was the second time O'Toole played Henry II, portraying him as an ineffectual monarch in BECKET. Shot on location in Ireland, Wales, and France.

p, Martin Poll; d, Anthony Harvey; w, James Goldman (based on his play); ph, Douglas Slocombe (Panavision, Eastmancolor); m, John Barry; ed, John Bloom; md, Barry; art d, Peter Murton, Gilbert Margerie; set d, Peter James; cos, Margaret Furse; makeup, Bill Lodge.

Historical Drama   **Cas.**   **(PR:A   MPAA:PG)**

LION IS IN THE STREETS, A*** 1/2   (1953) 88m WB c

James Cagney (Hank Martin), Barbara Hale (Verity Wade), Anne Francis (Flamingo), Warner Anderson (Jules Bolduc), John McIntire (Jeb Brown), Jeanne Cagney (Jennie Brown), Lon Chaney, Jr. (Spurge), Frank McHugh (Rector), Larry Keating (Robert J. Castleberry), Onslow Stevens (Guy Polli), James Millican (Mr. Beach), Mickey Simpson (Tim Peck), Sara Haden (Lulu May), Ellen Corby (Singing Woman), Roland Winters (Prosecutor), Burt Mustin (Swith), Irene Tedrow (Sophy), James Griffith (Mayor's Clerk), Fay Roope (Gov. Snowden), Henry Kulky (Polli's Butler), Sarah Selby (Townswoman), James Griffith (Castleberry's Secretary), William "Bill" Phillips (Deputy Lewis), Sam McDaniel (Moses, Bolduc's Butler).

In another virtuoso performance, Cagney is a crafty backwaters peddler in a Deep South state. He begins campaigning for political office, making the downtrodden sharecroppers his crusade. With his wife Hale at his side, Cagney rises with the help of the masses—winning a significant victory when he proves that the weights used to scale cotton are crooked, exposing the corrupt practices of Keating, the state's most powerful businessman—and this is at the risk of his life. He is catapulted into a vicious, mud-slinging race for the governorship and is himself corrupted along the way, betraying his own people. Just when the high office is within Cagney's grasp, he shot to death by Jeanne Cagney, the wife of one of his betrayed followers. Though the story is a hackneyed one—the rise of an itinerant to a position of power—Cagney is so dynamic that he rivets the viewer's attention. Hale is appealing as the patient wife and Francis gives a bizarre performance as a wild swampwater girl known as Flamingo. Walsh directs with his usual vitality, but there's no mistaking the similarity of this film to ALL THE KING'S MEN, which had captured the Huey Long personality three years earlier, duplicated on a more primitive level by Cagney. But in ALL THE KING'S MEN, Broderick Crawford won an Oscar and the type of southern tyrant he portrayed retained its image in the public's minds. The entire Cagney clan got into this act, with Jimmy in the lead, his sister Jeanne in a supporting role and his brothers William as producer and Edward as story editor.

p, William Cagney; d, Raoul Walsh; w, Luther Davis (based on the novel by Adria Locke Langley); ph, Harry Stradling (Technicolor); m, Franz Waxman; ed, George Amy; prod d, Wiard Ihnen; set d, Fred M. MacLean; cos, Kay Nelson; spec eff, Roscoe Cline; makeup, Otis Malcolm.

Drama **(PR:A MPAA:NR)**

LION OF ST. MARK**(1967, Ital.) 87m Liber c (IL LEONE DI SAN MARCO)

Gordon Scott (Manrico Masiero), Gianna Maria Canale (Rosanna), Rick Battaglia (Dandolo), Alberto Farnese (Titta), Giulio Marchetti (Gualtiero), Franca Bettoja (Isabella Fieschi).

This Italian swashbuckler stars Scott as the son of the Doge of Venice whose rule is threatened by plundering pirates. Scott mobilizes a mercenary force to combat the invaders and dons a mask, calling himself "The Lion of St. Mark" to protect his identity. After a few run-ins with the pirates, Scott falls in love with female pirate Canale, and he frees her when she is captured by the mercenaries. Canale is grateful, but she refuses to renounce the pirates until she learns that the "Lion" is actually Scott. The pirates are defeated, Scott's uncle adopts Canale (so that she may achieve the social standing necessary to associate with Scott), and the couple are wed.

p, Ottavio Poggi; d, Luigi Capuano, Richard McNamara; w, Arpad De Riso, Capuano (based on a story by Poggi); ph, Alvaro Mancori (Totalscope, Eastmancolor); m, Carlo Rustichelli; ed, Antonietta Zita; art d, Ernesto Kromberg; cos, Giancarlo Bartolini Salimbeni.

Adventure **(PR:A MPAA:NR)**

LION OF SPARTA (SEE: 300 SPARTANS, THE, 1962)

LION OF THE DESERT*1/2

(1981, Libya/Brit.) 162m Falcon International/United Film Distribution c (AKA. OMAR MUKHTAR)

Anthony Quinn (Omar Mukhtar), Oliver Reed (Gen. Rodolfo Graziani), Rod Steiger (Benito Mussolini), John Gielgud (Sharif El Gariani), Irene Papas (Mabrouka), Raf Vallone (Diodiece), Gastone Moschin (Maj. Tomelli), Stefano Patrizi (Lt. Sandrini), Sky Dumont (Prince Amadeo), Robert Brown (Al-Fadeel), Eleonora Stathopoulou (Ali's Mother), Andrew Keir (Salem), Adolfo Lastretti (Col. Sarsani), Pietro Gerlini (Barillo), George Sweeney (Capt. Biagi), Mario Feliciani (Lobitto), Claudio Gora (President of Court), Massimiliano Baratta (Capture Captain), Franco Fantasia (Gen. Graziani's Aide), Rodolfo Bigotti (Ismail), Ihab Werfali (Ali), Gianfranco Barra (Sentry), Mark Colleano (Infantry Corporal), Scott Fensome (Machine Gun Sergeant), Aisha Hussein (Aisha), Mukhtar Aswad (Collaborator), Pietro Tordi (Field Marshal), Takis Emmanuel (Bu-Matari), Ewen Solon, Loris Bazoki, Alec Mango, Filippo Degara, Luciano Catenacci, Victor Baring, Pietro Brambilla, Lino Capolicchio.

INCHON, the film produced by the Rev. Sun Myung Moon, may have set a trend among the madmen of the world. Libya's dictator Col. Muammar Qadhafi, after putting up the money for the controversial and unbelievably awful MOHAMMAD: MESSENGER OF GOD, decided to do his own WW II film. Like Moon's Korea, Qadhafi had a disaster or two in Libya's past that apparently was aching to become a bad movie. Quinn, looking strangely like Iran's Ayatollah Khomeini, is the famed Arab hero who fights off Italian Fascists led by Reed. Though the acting is awful (Gielgud once more trying to destroy his reputation for a buck) this is not quite so bad as INCHON, though that is not saying much. The battle scenes do have some intelligent staging and the narrative runs straight forward. But the film is pockmarked with cliche after cliche and is far longer than necessary. Jarre's music is merely a rehash of his fine LAWRENCE OF ARABIA score. Qadhafi put up $35 million for this film that grossed approximately 1/35th of its cost.

p&d, Moustapha Akkad; w, H.A.L. Craig; ph, Jack Hildyard (Panavision, Eastmancolor); m, Maurice Jarre; ed, John Shirley; prod d, Mario Garbuglia, Syd Cain; art d, Giorgio Desideri, Maurice Cain, Bob Bell; cos, Orietta Nasallirocca, Piero Cicoletti, Hassan Ben Dardaf; spec eff, Kit West.

War/Adventure **Cas.** **(PR:O MPAA:PG)**

LIONHEART** (1968, Brit.) 57m Children's Film Foundation c

James Forlong (Andrew Fowler), Louise Rush (Belinda), Ian Jessup (Robert), Robert Dean (Father), Pauline Yates (Mother), Robert Davis (Corporal), Joe Brown (Pvt. Worms), Ben Aris (Capt. Harris), Wilfred Brambell (Dignett), Jimmy Edwards (Butcher), Irene Handl (Lil), Leslie Dwyer (Carpenter).

A standard children's film which merely serves youngsters with the usual cute entertainment. This time a boy befriends a lion which has wandered away from the circus and saves it from an untimely demise. One gets the feeling that LIONHEART would have worked just as well as a cartoon.

p&d, Michael Forlong; w, Forlong, Alexander Fullerton (based on a novel by Fullerton).

Children's Film **(PR:AA MPAA:NR)**

LION'S DEN, THE** (1936) 59m Puritan bw

Tim McCoy (Tim Barton), Joan Woodbury (Ann Merwin), Arthur Millett (Merwin), Dick Curtis (Slim), John Merton (Single-Shot Smith), Don Barclay (Paddy), J. Frank Glendon (Nate Welsh), Art Felix, Jack Rockwell, Karl Hackett, Jack Evans.

Simplistic McCoy Western has him disguised as a bad guy to capture a bunch of outlaws terrorizing Millett's ranch. Barclay is McCoy's sidekick, providing comic

relief. Woodbury is the romantic interest. There is only one shootout, which is highly unusual for B Westerns. Other than that, this is standard stuff.

p, Sig Neufeld, Leslie Simmonds; d, Sam Newfield; w, John T. Neville (based on a story by L.V. Jefferson); ph, Jack Greenhalgh; ed, Neville.

Western **(PR:A MPAA:NR)**

LIONS LOVE*** (1969) 115m Raab c

Viva, Gerome Ragni, James Rado, Shirley Clarke, Carlos Clarens, Eddie Constantine, Agnes Varda, Max Laemmle, Hal Landers, Steve Kemis, Peter Bogdanovich, Billie Dixon, Richard Bright.

An interesting improvisational film with a sort of Godardian style and wit to it. The story follows Clarke, an independent filmmaker who wants to do a movie with Rado, Ragni (the creators of "Hair"), and Warhol's star Viva. When her studio backs out on her, Clarke attempts suicide. The film is an unusual hodge-podge, including television footage of Robert Kennedy's assassination, the shooting of Andy Warhol, and scenes from Michael McClure's "The Beard" featuring Dixon and Bright. Varda, the film's director (who went on to make the wonderful feminist film ONE SINGS, THE OTHER DOESN'T) also makes an appearance as do Constantine and Bogdanovich, before he became a noted director himself. Varda's use of camera style and natural light is fresh and original. Despite its improvisational style, the film looks professional and well planned. Viva is one of the few actresses who can actually live up to her name.

p,d&w, Agnes Varda; ph, Stefan Larner (Technicolor); m, Joseph Byrd; ed, Robert Dalva; art d, Jack Wright III.

Comedy **(PR:O MPAA:NR)**

LIPSTICK**

(1965, Fr./Ital.) 89m Europa Cinematografica-Explorer-CFPC/Medallion bw (IL ROSSETTO; JEUX PRECOCES)

Laura Vivaldi (Sylvana), Pierre Brice (Gino), Georgia Moll (Lorella), Bella Darvi (Nora), Pietro Germi (Insp. Fioresi), Lia Angeleri, Ivano Staccioli, Nino Marchetti, Renato Mambor.

Italian mystery starring Vivaldi as a 13-year-old schoolgirl who becomes involved in a murder case because she is infatuated with Brice, her handsome neighbor. A prostitute is found murdered in the building where Vivaldi and Brice live, and the police begin nosing around. Because Brice knows that Vivaldi saw him leave the dead woman's apartment, he encourages her interest to establish an alibi. Eventually Vivaldi becomes disenchanted with Brice and tells the police what she knows. The police, however, think she is just being vengeful, and do not believe her. A sympathetic inspector, Germi, advises Vivaldi's mother to send the girl to a private convent for protection, and then decides to investigate. He soon finds that Vivaldi was telling the truth and arrests Brice just as he is about to marry an heiress, leaving Vivaldi exonerated and able to resume her life.

p, Murray J. King (U.S. only); d, Damiano Damiani; w, Damiani, Cesare Zavattini; ph, Pier Ludovico Pavoni; m, Giovanni Fusco; ed, Fernando Cerchio; art d, Sergio Baldacchini.

Mystery **(PR:C-O MPAA:NR)**

LIPSTICK zero (1976) 89m PAR c

Margaux Hemingway (Chris McCormick), Chris Sarandon (Gordon Stuart), Perry King (Steve Edison), Anne Bancroft (Carla Bondi), Robin Gammell (Nathan Cartwright), Mariel Hemingway (Kathy McCormick), Francesco (Photographer), Bill Burns (Judge), Meg Wylie (Sister Margaret), Inga Swenson (Sister Monica), John Bennett Perry (Martin McCormick).

Mean little film that pretends to say something about rape, but panders to the cheap exploitation values of bad thriller films. Margaux Hemingway, a fashion model, makes her film debut playing—what else?—a fashion model. Sarandon is a music teacher who goes crazy and rapes her. He tries to get her little sister as well but Margaux Hemingway blows him away with a handy shotgun. She is tried for murder but is acquitted, thanks to Bancroft's legal skills. The elder Hemingway, granddaughter of the famous writer, is absolutely awful. Sarandon, who was excellent as the transsexual in DOG DAY AFTERNOON, is equally el stinko as her co-star. The real saving grace of the film is Margaux Hemingway's teenage sister, Mariel. This was her film debut as well and she shows real accomplishment at a surprisingly young age.

p, Freddie Fields; d, Lamont Johnson; w, David Rayfiel; ph, Bill Butler, William A. Fraker (Technicolor); m, Michel Poinareff, Jimmie Haskell; ed, Marion Rothman; prod d, Robert Luthardt; set d, Donfeld.

Drama **Cas.** **(PR:O MPAA:R)**

LIQUID SKY***1/2 (1982) 118m Z Films c

Anne Carlisle (Margaret/Jimmy), Paula E. Sheppard (Adrian), Susan Doukas (Sylvia), Otto von Wernherr (Johann), Bob Brady (Owen), Elaine C. Grove (Katherine), Stanley Knap (Paul), Jack Adalist (Vincent), Lloyd Ziff (Lester), Harry Lum (Deliveryman), Roy MacArthur (Jack), Sara Carlisle (Nellie), Nina V. Kerova (Designer), Alan Preston (Photographer), Christine Hatfull (Hairstylist), Calvin Haugen (Makeup Artist), Deborah Jacobs, Inansi, Tom Cote, Michael Drechsler, Jose Preval, David Ilku, Neke Carson, Jenifer Chang, Vincent Pandoliano, Benjamin Liu, Angelo, Lucille, Jerre Edmunds, Marcel Fieve, Mariann Marlow, Perry Iannaconi, Rodger Martencen.

Outrageous fun, this film is New Wave chic, satire, self-parody, science fiction, and certainly one of the more accessible independent features ever made. The story has something to do with aliens who are after the heroin-like substance produced by the human brain at the point of orgasm. Carlisle, who co-wrote the screenplay, plays a lesbian punk model and a homosexual punk model to boot. It's a difficult job but somebody's got to do it and she does. As the woman, Carlisle discovers a special sexual power: at orgasm she can make her lover disappear into thin air, courtesy of some wonderful solarized special effects. A subplot involves von Wernherr as a government scientist trying to find out about the UFO on Carlisle's roof. He holes up across the street in the apartment of a horny and hysterically funny socialite. His low-key performance, coupled with Doukas' frustration, is great stuff. This off-beat film was directed by Tsukerman, a classically trained Soviet-born filmmaker. His observations of modern America, as well as the beautiful New York City photography, are right on the money. LIQUID SKY deservedly became a cult classic shortly after its release.

p&d, Slava Tsukerman; w, Tsukerman, Anne Carlisle, Nina V. Kerova; ph, Yuri Neyman (TVC Color); m, Tsukerman, Brenda I. Hutchinson, Clive Smith; ed, Sharyn Leslie Ross; prod d, Marina Levikova; cos, Levikova; spec eff, Neyman; m/l, Tsukerman; makeup, Rashkovsky-Kaleva, Fieve.

Science Fiction/Satire **Cas.** **(PR:O MPAA:R)**

LIQUIDATOR, THE** 1/2 (1966, Brit.) 104m MGM c

Rod Taylor *(Boysie Oakes)*, Trevor Howard *(Col. Mostyn)*, Jill St. John *(Iris MacIntosh)*, Wilfrid Hyde-White *(Chief)*, David Tomlinson *(Quadrant)*, Eric Sykes *(Griffen)*, Akim Tamiroff *(Sheriek)*, Gabriella Licudi *(Corale)*, John Le Mesurier *(Chekov)*, Derek Nimmo *(Fly)*, Jeremy Lloyd *(Young Man)*, Jennifer Jayne *(Janice Benedict)*, Betty McDowall *(Frances Anne)*, Colin Gordon *(Vicar)*, Louise Dunn *(Jessie)*, Henry Cogan *(Yakov)*, Daniel Emilfork *(Gregory)*, Richard Wattis *(Flying Instructor)*, David Langton *(Station Commander)*, Tony Wright *(Flying Control)*, Suzy Kendall *(Judith)*, Jo Rowbottom *(Betty)*, Scot Finch *(Operations Officer)*, Ronald Leigh-Hunt *(Mac)*.

Based on the novel by espionage writer Gardner, this Bondish-style feature finds Taylor as a playboy who's afraid to fly and gets sick at the sight of blood. He is not the spy type but he did save Howard's life during WW II and that is good enough for Howard. He sets up his old comrade with expensive penthouses, cars, and women, eventually springing on Taylor that his mission is to be an assassin for hire. Taylor wants nothing to do with this and hires someone to do the dirty work for him. But he ends up doing it all himself, complete with a political assassination, pretty counterspies, and a climactic finish where Taylor pilots a jet plane after knocking out its hijacker. The plot has more holes than Swiss cheese but the pace is swift. In parts, this is funny, but it often seems to be amusing its players more than the audience. However, slick production values and Taylor's off-beat performance give this some tongue-in-cheek charm.

p, Jon Pennington; d, Jack Cardiff; w, Peter Yeldham (based on the novel by John Gardner); ph, Ted Scaife (Panavision, Metrocolor); m, Lalo Schifrin; ed, Ernest Walter; md, Schifrin; art d, John Blezard; cos, Elizabeth Haffenden, Joan Bridge; m/l, Peter Callender, Schifrin.

Spy Drama **(PR:C MPAA:NR)**

LISA** 1/2 (1962, Brit.) 112m FOX c (GB: THE INSPECTOR)

Stephen Boyd *(Peter Jongman)*, Dolores Hart *(Lisa Held)*, Leo McKern *(Brandt)*, Hugh Griffith *(Van der Pink)*, Donald Pleasence *(Sgt. Wolters)*, Harry Andrews *(Ayoob)*, Robert Stephens *(Dickens)*, Marius Goring *(Thorens)*, Finlay Currie *(De Kooi)*, Harold Goldblatt *(Dr. Mitropoulous)*, Neil McCallum *(Browne)*, Geoffrey Keen *(Commissioner Bartels)*, Jean Anderson *(Mrs. Jongman)*, Jack Gwillim *(Insp. Cobb)*, Arthur Gross *(Railway Conductor)*, Tibby Brittain *(M.P. Sergeant)*, Ann Dickins *(Rachael)*, Vi Stephens *(Barge Woman)*, Derek Francis *(Detective Inspector)*, John Welsh *(Agriculture Officer)*, Victor Brooks *(Sgt. Greninger)*, Geoffrey Fredrick *(Soldier)*, Clifford Elkin *(Signaler)*, Michael David *(Capt. Berger)*, Jane Jordan Rogers *(Anaka Jongman)*.

Hart is an Auschwitz survivor who desperately wants to emigrate to Palestine. She meets Goring, whom she thinks will help her. He is actually a dealer in white slaves and plans to ship her to South America where some of his ex-Nazi friends have set up a market. Boyd is a Dutch police officer, wracked with guilt over his girl friend's death in Auschwitz. He accidentally kills Goring and decides to atone for his past by helping Hart in her quest. He gets them passage on a ship, where a medical examination proves Hart unable to produce children as a result of Nazi experiments on her. Word reaches them that Boyd is wanted for questioning in Goring's death. Since Hart's immigration is illegal, he strikes a deal: allow her into Palestine and he will turn himself in. At times this is a fascinating film, with fine performances by the two leads. However, there is a tendency to play some things in a somber, heavy-handed manner that makes them seem more psychologically revealing than they truly are. Some nice location work in Holland, London, Tangiers, and Israel.

p, Mark Robson; d, Philip Dunne; w, Nelson Gidding (based on the novel by Jan de Hartog); ph, Arthur Ibbetson (CinemaScope, DeLuxe Color); m, Malcolm Arnold; ed, Ernest Walter; md, Arnold; art d, Elliot Scott; set d, John Jarvis; makeup, John O'Gorman, Wally Schneiderman.

Drama **(PR:O MPAA:NR)**

LISA AND THE DEVIL (SEE: HOUSE OF EXORCISM, THE, 1976, Ital.)

LISA, TOSCA OF ATHENS* 1/2

(1961, Gr.) 84m Delta/Hellenic bw (AKA: LISA, THE GREEK TOSCA)

Xenie Kalogeropoulos *(Lisa)*, Kostas Kakavas *(Nicky)*, Kostas Hadjichristos *(Bulfos)*, D. Papagianopoulos *(Johnny)*.

Kalogeropoulos plays a woman trapped in a loveless marriage who meets and falls in love with Papagianopoulos. After many lengthy and emotional arguments with her parents, she is eventually able to persuade them that she and he are meant for each other.

d, Sokrates Kapsaskis; w, Giannis Maris; m/l, Nana Moushouri.

Drama **(PR:A MPAA:NR)**

LISBON** (1956) 90m REP c

Ray Milland *(Capt. Robert John Evans)*, Maureen O'Hara *(Sylvia Merrill)*, Claude Rains *(Artistides Mavros)*, Yvonne Furneaux *(Maria Maddalena Masanet)*, Francis Lederer *(Serafim)*, Percy Marmont *(Lloyd Merrill)*, Jay Novello *(Joao Casimiro Fonseca)*, Edward Chapman *(Edgar Selwyn)*, Harold Jamieson *(Philip Norworth)*, Humberto Madeira *(Tio Rabio)*.

O'Hara is the wife of a rich man held behind the Iron Curtain. She can get his money only when he returns, dead. She talks to Rains, a killer for hire, who agrees to carry out her plan to kill him. He hires Milland, an unassuming boat captain, to ferry him and O'Hara under the pretense of rescuing the man from the Communists. But in a moment of amour, she tells Milland the real story and he is appalled. He ruins their plans and takes off with Furneaux, one of Rains' many girl friends. Some interesting moments, though Milland's direction is lacking the necessary punch the film needs. His performance helps, though. Rains is good as the mercenary, though there is a particularly cruel and unnecessary scene where he smashes a bird with a tennis racket. The film has a nice look to it, with good location photography.

p&d, Ray Milland; w, John Tucker Battle (based on a story by Martin Rackin); ph, Jack Marta (Naturama, Trucolor); m, Nelson Riddle; ed, Richard L. Van Enger; art d, Frank Arrigo.

Thriller **(PR:O MPAA:NR)**

LISBON STORY, THE** 1/2 (1946, Brit.) 100m BN/Anglo-American bw

Patricia Burke *(Gabrielle Girard)*, David Farrar *(David Warren)*, Walter Rilla *(Karl von Schriner)*, Richard Tauber *(Andre Joubert)*, Lawrence O'Madden *(Michael O'Rourke)*, Austin Trevor *(Maj. Lutzen)*, Paul Bonifas *(Stephan Corelle)*, Harry Welchman *(George Duncan)*, Esme Percy *(Mariot)*, Noele Gordon *(Panache)*, John Ruddock *(Pierre Sargon)*, Joan Seton *(Lisette)*, Allan Jeayes *(Dr. Cartier)*, Martin Walker *(Journalist)*, Stephane Grappelly, Lorely Dyer, Halamar & Konarski, Ralph Truman, Michelle de Lys, Jan van Loewen, Uriel Porter, Hannah Watt, F. Wendhausen, Morgan Davies, Leo de Pokorny.

This better-than-average musical surely has one of the oddest plots the genre ever saw. Burke is a singer in a cabaret. She meets Farrar, a British agent, and agrees to go with him to Nazi Germany to rescue a kidnaped French atomic scientist. The production looks good and the two leads handle the unusual material with ease. Occasionally the film falls short of its intentions but the pace is so smooth that such rifts are overlooked. Based on a show that originally played the famous Hippodrome Theater, its most famous song "Pedro the Fisherman" (Harry Parr-Davis) was a big hit in postwar England.

p, Louis H. Jackson; d, Paul L. Stein; w, Jack Whittingham (based on the play by Harold Purcell, Harry Parr-Davies); ph, Ernest Palmer, Gerald D. Moss; m, Harry Parr-Davis.

Musical/Thriller **(PR:A MPAA:NR)**

LISETTE* 1/2

(1961) 83m Medallion bw (AKA: FALL GIRL; A CROWD FOR LISETTE)

Greta Chi *(Lisette)*, John Agar *(Joe McElroy)*, Walter Klavun *(Amos Culpepper)*, John Cestare *(Buck Culpepper)*, Jim Pritchett *(Howard Shaner)*, Susan Ellis *(Ruth McElroy)*.

Sleazy melodrama filmed in Florida and starring Agar as a newspaper editor who sponsors an orphaned refugee from Indochina as a good-will gesture to aid his father-in-law, Klavun, in his race for a Senate seat. Much to everyone's surprise, the orphan, Chi, turns out to be a stunning Eurasian woman. Agar soon finds himself in bed with her but, nonetheless, she publicly denounces the publicity scheme. To get revenge, Klavun attempts to discredit Chi. Agar, ashamed of his feelings toward the girl, goes along with the ambitious politician's plan hoping she will leave town. Chi leaves with Klavun's son, Cestare, but when she struggles against his advances, he throws her out of his speeding car and runs her down. Cestare turns himself in, and Agar resigns his post and goes back to his wife.

p,d&w, John Hugh; ph, Charles O'Roark; m, Les Baxter; m/l, "Goodbye Lisette," Baxter (sung by John Agar).

Drama **(PR:C MPAA:NR)**

LIST OF ADRIAN MESSENGER, THE*** 1/2 (1963) 98m UNIV bw

George C. Scott *(Anthony Gethryn)*, Dana Wynter *(Lady Jocelyn Brutenholm)*, Clive Brook *(Marquis of Gleneyre)*, Gladys Cooper *(Mrs. Karoudjian)*, Herbert Marshall *(Sir Wilfred Lucas)*, Jacques Roux *(Raoul le Borg)*, John Merivale *(Adrian Messenger)*, Marcel Dalio *(Anton Karoudjian)*, Bernard Archard *(Inspector Pike)*, Walter Anthony Huston *(Derek)*, Roland DeLong *(Carstairs)*, Anita Sharp-Bolster *(Mrs. Slattery)*, Alan Caillou *(Inspector Seymour)*, John Huston *(Lord Ashton)*, Noel Purcell *(Countryman)*, Richard Peel *(Sgt. Flood)*, Bernard Fox *(Lynch)*, Nelson Welch *(White)*, Tim Durant *(Hunt Secretary)*, Barbara Morrison *(Nurse)*, Jennifer Raine *(Student Nurse)*, Constance Cavendish *(Maid)*, Eric Heath *(Orderly)*, Anna Van Der Heide *(Stewardess)*, Delphi Lawrence *(Airport Stewardess)*, Tony Curtis *(Italian)*, Kirk Douglas *(George Brougham)*, Burt Lancaster *(Woman)*, Robert Mitchum *(Jim Slattery)*, Frank Sinatra *(Gypsy Stableman)*, Mona Lilian *(Proprietress)*, Stacey Morgan *(Whip Man)*, Joe Lynch *(Cyclist)*.

This convoluted but absorbing mystery begins when Scott, a retired British colonel, is given a list of 11 names by his friend Merivale, and asked to check on the whereabouts of those on the list. A short time later Merivale's plane blows up and this causes Scott to look into the fates of those on the list. He soon discovers that all have met a similar fate and begins to investigate, learning that the killer is a master of disguises, adopting a new identity for every victim. Scott also learns that all the victims were POWs in Burma during WW II and that they all knew the traitor in their midst who informed on them, telling the Japanese guards when they would be attempting their escape. The killer also plans to murder the only person who stands to inherit a vast estate, the murderer being another family member after the estate. At the last minute, before the boy is killed, Scott turns the tables on the killer, who flees and dies in the trap he himself has set for the boy. Huston directs this film with calculating care, setting up a number of red herrings who are all played by superstars in disguise. These cameo appearances are made by Mitchum, Sinatra, Lancaster, Douglas, Curtis, and even Huston himself. It was all eerily effective and provided many a scary moment. Location shooting was conducted in Ireland.

p, Edward Lewis; d, John Huston; w, Anthony Veiller (based on the novel by Philip MacDonald); ph, Joe MacDonald; m, Jerry Goldsmith; ed, Terry Morse, Hugh Fowler; art d, Akexander Golitzen, Stephen Grimes, George Webb; set d, Oliver Emert; makeup, Bud Westmore.

Crime Drama **Cas.** **(PR:A MPAA:NR)**

LISTEN, DARLING*** (1938) 72m MGM bw

Judy Garland *(Pinkie Wingate)*, Freddie Bartholomew *(Buzz Mitchell)*, Mary Astor *(Dottie Wingate)*, Walter Pidgeon *(Richard Thurlow)*, Alan Hale *(J.J. Slattery)*, Scotty Beckett *(Billie Wingate)*, Barnett Parker *(Abercrombie)*, Gene Lockhart *(Mr. Drubbs)*, Charles Grapewin *(Uncle Joe)*.

Astor plays a widow who wants to insure the futures of her two children by marrying Lockhart. Garland is the daughter who, along with her teenage friend Bartholomew, knows he is all wrong for her and manages to get her fixed up with Pidgeon by the film's end. This was Garland's first real acting role and she was marvelous, delivering an innocent, yet polished performance. She sings "Zing! Went the Strings of My Heart!" (James Hanley), which became one of her signature tunes throughout her career. This was her only teaming with Bartholomew and they worked well together, although his career was soon over. Garland's career, on the other hand, was to skyrocket within the next two years with the making of THE WIZARD OF OZ. Astor, by the way, would be Garland's mother once again in MEET ME IN ST. LOUIS. Other tunes in this film included: "Ten Pins in the Sky" (Joseph McCarthy, Milton Ager), and "On the Bumpy Road to Love" (Al Lewis, Al Hoffmann, Murray Mencher).

p, Jack Cummings; d, Edwin L. Marin; w, Elaine Ryan, Anne Morrison Chapin (based on a story by Katherine Brush), ph, Charles Lawton, Jr.; ed, Blanche Sewell; md, George Stoll; art d, Cedric Gibbons.

Musical/Comedy **(PR:AAA MPAA:NR)**

LISTEN, LET'S MAKE LOVE* ½

(1969, Fr./Ital.) 91m P.E.A.-Les Productions Artistes Associes/Lopert c (ET SI ON FAISAIT L'AMOUR?; SCUSI, FACCIAMO L'AMORE?)

Pierre Clementi *(Lallo)*, Beba Loncar *(Aunt Lidia)*, Carlo Caprioli *(Uncle Carlo)*, Edwige Feuillere *(Giuditta Passani)*, Juliette Mayniel *(Gilberta)*, Tanya Lopert *(Flavia Menobo)*, Claudine Auger *(Ida Bernasconi)*, Valentina Cortese *(Lallo's Mother)*, Massimo Girotti *(Tassi)*, Martine Malle *(Sveva)*, Roberto Gatto *(Ida's Husband)*, Mario Meniconi *(Mr. Breuner)*, Anna Maria Covacci *(Mrs. Breuner)*, Franca Valeri *(Diraghi)*, Fabian Fabre *(Puccio Picco)*, Antonietta Fiorita *(Cloakroom Attendant)*, Ivan Scratuglia *(Lallo's Friend)*, Ornella Polito Santoliquido *(Amparo Botti)*, Americo Tot *(Baron von Tummler)*.

Distasteful drama starring Clementi as a young Neapolitan who arrives in Milan for the funeral of his father, who was a gigolo. Clementi decides to follow in his father's footsteps and seek the company of rich women also. After passing through the lives of many older women, he finds himself the object of a bid between a rich steel heiress and an aging, wealthy homosexual, Tot. The homosexual wins the bidding, but Clementi chooses an affair with the heiress. This soon wears off and Clementi finds himself falling in love with a young lady, Malle, but his hopes are dashed when he discovers that she is his half-sister. Remembering the advice that one of his father's friends had once given him ("it's better for a young man to attach himself to a rich homosexual") Clementi opts for the affections of Tot.

p, Alberto Grimaldi; d, Vittorio Caprioli; w, Caprioli, Franca Valeri, Enrico Medioli; ph, Pasquale De Santis (Techniscope, Technicolor); m, Ennio Morricone; ed, Ruggero Mastroianni; md, Bruno Nicolai; art d, Ferninando Scarfiotti; set d, Nedo Azzini; cos, Scarfiotti; makeup, Franco Freda.

Drama **(PR:O MPAA:R)**

LISZTOMANIA* ½ (1975, Brit.) 104m Goodtime Enterprises/WB c

Roger Daltrey *(Franz Liszt)*, Sara Kestelman *(Princess Carolyn)*, Paul Nicholas *(Richard Wagner)*, Fiona Lewis *(Countess Marie)*, Veronica Quilligan *(Cosima Wagner)*, Nell Campbell *(Olga)*, Andrew Reilly *(Hans von Bulow)*, Ringo Starr *(Pope)*, John Justin *(Count d'Agoult)*, Anulka Dziubinska *(Lola Montez)*, Imogen Claire *(George Sand)*, Peter Brayham *(Bodyguard)*, David English *(Captain)*.

Hot on the heels of his success with The Who's rock opera TOMMY, Russell turned his attentions to classical composer, Liszt. Daltrey, who co-wrote and starred in TOMMY, plays the famed composer as the first rock idol, along with Nicholas (also from TOMMY) as his fellow composer, Wagner. Both handle their roles well in this bizarre, sexually obsessed biographical fantasy. Russell's style works in some parts but often ends up in self-indulgence disguised as surrealism. The result is a shockfest. Wakeman's re-working of Liszt and Wagner music as rock numbers is an interesting, if not entirely successful touch. Russell fans undoubtedly will love it, but the longhairs may wonder what he was trying to prove. Songs include: "Love's Dream," "Orpheus Song," "Peace At Last" (sung by Daltrey), "Excelsior Song" (sung by Nicholas), and "Hell" (sung by Linda Lewis).

p, Roy Baird, David Puttnam; d&w, Ken Russell; ph, Peter Suschitzky (Technicolor); m, Rick Wakeman, Jonathan Benson, Franz Liszt, Richard Wagner; ed, Stuart Baird; md, Wakeman; art d, Philip Harrison; cos, Shirley Russell.

Biography **Cas.** **(PR:O MPAA:R)**

LITTLE ACCIDENT** (1930) 82m UNIV bw

Douglas Fairbanks, Jr. *(Norman Overbeck)*, Anita Page *(Isabel)*, Sally Blane *(Madge)*, ZaSu Pitts *(Monica)*, Joan Marsh *(Doris)*, Roscoe Karns *(Gilbert)*, Slim Summerville *(Hicks)*, Henry Armetta *(Rudolpho Amendelara)*, Myrtle Stedman *(Mrs. Overbeck)*, Albert Gran *(Mr. Overbeck)*, Nora Cecil *(Dr. Zernecke)*, Bertha Mann *(Miss Hemingway)*, Gertrude Short *(Miss Clark)*, Dot Farley *(Mrs. Van Dine)*.

Fairbanks is about to marry for the second time, but problems arise when his ex-wife informs him that he is the father of her new-born child. He puts off his wedding plans temporarily but eventually ends up with his first wife, Page. This fairly simplistic and overlong comedy went through a few changes before the cameras started rolling. Based on a play of the same title (which in turn had its basis in a novel by Dell), the censorship offices found the material a little risque and some dialog and scene cutting proved necessary. The result was far tamer than its original intent. A remake in 1939 had the same title and a third version made in 1944 was called CASANOVA BROWN.

p, Carl Laemmle; d, William James Craft; w, Gladys Lehman, Anthony Brown, Gene Towne (based on the play "The Little Accident" by Floyd Dell, Thomas Mitchell and the novel *An Unmarried Father* by Dell); ph, Roy Overbaugh; ed, Harry Lieb.

Comedy **(PR:A MPAA:NR)**

LITTLE ACCIDENT** (1939) 65m UNIV bw

Hugh Herbert *(Herbert Pearson)*, Sandra Lee Henville *(Baby Sandy)*, Florence Rice *(Alice Pearson)*, Richard Carlson *(Perry Allerton)*, Ernest Truex *(Tabby Morgan)*, Joy Hodges *(Joan Huston)*, Fritz Feld *(Malisse)*, Kathleen Howard *(Mrs. Allerton)*, Howard Hickman *(Mr. Allerton)*, Edgar Kennedy *(Paper Hanger)*, Etienne Girardot *(Prof. Artemus Glenwater)*, Charles D. Brown *(Jeff Collins)*, Anne Gwynne *(Blonde Girl)*, Peggy Moran *(Tall Girl)*, Frances Robinson *(3rd Model)*, Olaf Hytten *(Meggs)*, Robert Greig *(Butler)*, Emory Parnell *(Policeman)*, Charles Irwin *(Announcer)*, Arthur Q. Bryan *(Customer)*, Virginia Sale *(Nurse)*, Ruth Gillette *(Woman)*, Frederic Santley *(1st Man)*, Milton Kibbee *(2nd Man)*, Ralph Sanford *(Conductor)*, Mary Field *(Miss Wilson)*, William Newell *(Photographer)*, Hattie Noel *(Melissa)*, Margaret Brayton *(Receptionist)*, Eddie Coke *(Salesman)*, Harrison Greene *(Sobol)*, Frank Mitchell *(Customer)*, Minerva Urecal *(Woman)*, Betty Mack *(1st Woman)*, Clara Blore *(3rd Woman)*, Harry Depp *(Meek)*, Hugh McArthur *(Hauser)*, Joey Ray *(2nd Cameraman)*, Frank Parker *(1st Cameraman)*, Frank Marlowe *(Taxi Driver)*, Dave Willock *(Attendant)*, Fay McKenzie *(Woman)*, Al Thompson *(Laundry Worker)*, Ray Turner *(Colored Man)*, Bert Young *(Laundry Worker)*, Marjorie "Babe" Kane *(Woman Ironer)*, Ronnie Rondell *(Cameraman)*, Frank O'Connor *(Newspaperman)*, Bobbe Trefts *(Nurse)*, Eva McKenzie *(Woman)*.

Herbert is a newspaper advice columnist who needs a little advice of his own when little bundle of joy, Henville, is dumped on his desk. From there on it's a series of cute antics involving the baby and every adult in the film. This was Henville's third film and the first one where she plays a member of her gender. She's a born scene stealer, greatly helped by lots of "cute kid" shots plastered all over the screen. The grownups get either aggravated (like Kennedy in another one of his masterful "slow burns") or find the antics of the precocious brat adorable. This remake of the 1930 film was tailor-made for Henville. The story was done once more as CASANOVA BROWN in 1944.

p&d, Charles Lamont; w, Paul Yawitz, Eve Greene (based on the play "The Little Accident" by Floyd Dell, Thomas Mitchell and the novel *An Unmarried Father* by Dell); ph, Milton Krasner; ed, Frank Gross; md, Charles Previn; art d, Jack Otterson.

Comedy **(PR:A MPAA:NR)**

LITTLE ADVENTURESS, THE* ½ (1938) 60m COL bw

Edith Fellows *(Pinky Horton)*, Richard Fiske *(Dick Horton)*, Jacqueline [Julie Bishop] Wells *(Helen Gould)*, Cliff Edwards *(Handy)*, Virginia Howell *(Aunt Hattie)*, Harry C. Bradley *(Henry Lowell)*, Charles Waldron *(Herkimer Gould)*, Kenneth Harlan *(Tom Eagan)*.

Typical "girl and her horse" story has Fellows taking her beloved steed out West after her carnival-performing parents are killed in an accident. There she hooks up with her cousin, Fiske, a racing enthusiast, and the two train the horse to run for a big race. If you can't guess how the picture turns out from there, then you're not up on your movie cliches. This formula film is poorly written and directed, with more implausibilities than most of this genre.

d, D. Ross Lederman; w, Michael L. Simmons (based on a story by Simmons, Paul Jarrico); ph, Henry Freulich; ed, Al Clark.

Drama **(PR:AA MPAA:NR)**

LITTLE ANGEL**

(1961, Mex.) 90m Peliculas Rodriguez/K. Gordon Murray-Trans-International c (LA SONRISA DE LA VIRGEN)

Maria Gracia *(Marita)*, Jorge Martinez de Hoyos *(Farmhand)*, Prudencia Griffel, Emma Rodriguez, Miguel Manzano, Manuel Santoyo, Hugh Downs *(Narrator)*.

This rural drama from Mexico stars Gracia as a young farm girl who, through constant prayer and deep religious conviction, is able to save the farm from disaster when a pregnant cow cannot give milk.

p, Jose Luis Celis, K. Gordon Murray; d, Roberto Rodriguez, Ken Smith; w, Rodriguez, Celis, Rafael Garcia Travesi (based on a story by Rodriguez, Celis, Ricardo Garibay); ph, Gabriel Figueroa (Eastmancolor); m, Raul Lavista; ed, Fernando Martinez; art d, Salvador Lozano Mena.

Drama **(PR:A MPAA:NR)**

LITTLE ARK, THE*** (1972) 100m NG c

Theodore Bikel *(Captain)*, Genevieve Ambas *(Adinda)*, Philip Frame *(Jan)*, Max

Croiset *(Father Grijpma)*, Johan De Slaa *(Cook, U.K. 516)*, Lo Van Hensbergen *(Mr. Tandema)*, Truss Dekker *(Mother Grijpma)*, Edda Barends *(Miss Winter)*, Lex Schoorel *(Sparks)*, Heleen Van Meurs *(Nurse)*, Guus Verstraete *(Pieters)*, Heleen Pimentel *(Mrs. Ool)*, Riek Schagen *(Vrouu Brodfelder)*, Martin Brozius *(Farmer)*, Maurits Koek *(Farmer's Son)*, John Soer *(Man with Dog)*, Tim Beekman *(Launch Officer)*, Jos Knipscheer *(Doctor)*, Jeroen Krabbe *(1st Man)*, Jos Bergman *(Young Man)*, Renier Heidemann *(1st Photographer)*, Manfred De Graff *(2nd Photographer)*, Wik Jongsma *(2nd Man)*, Monica Achterberg *(Little Girl)*, Bussy, Noisette, Ko, Prince.

A pair of adopted children, one Caucasian and the other Malaysian, get separated from their parents during the famous Holland flooding of 1953. They get picked up by Bikel, the captain of a houseboat, who takes care of them and their pets. In the end the children are re-united with their father, but sadly the mother has drowned. This latter fact, along with some of the flooding sequences, may make this a little too intense for very young children, but other than that it's a fine family film. Bikel is wonderful as the pseudo-gruff boatman, and the racial mixing of the children is honest. There is a wonderful animated sequence, narrated by Bikel, that tells the old Dutch legend of a maiden who gives up her soul to save her true love. Production values are first rate, especially the scenic photography of Holland, and the film's song "Come Follow Me" (Fred Karlin, Tylwyth Kymry) was nominated for an Oscar.

p, Robert B. Radnitz; d, James B. Clark; w, Joanna Crawford (based on the novel by Jan De Hartog); ph, Austin Dempster, Denys Coop (Panavision, Technicolor); m, Fred Karlin; ed, Fred A. Chulack; art d, Massino Gotz; set d, Jan Andre; cos, Nen Rosterdinck; makeup, Ton Van Den Heurel; animation, Fred Calvert Productions; animal trainer, Frank Weatherwax.

Children's Adventure **(PR:AAA MPAA:G)**

LITTLE AUSTRALIANS zero (1940, Aus.) 62m O'Brien/UNIV bw

Charles McCallum *(Capt. Woolcot)*, Patricia McDonald *(Ester)*, Sandra Jaques *(Meg)*, Robert Gray *(Pip)*, Mary McGowan *(Judy)*, Ron Rousel *(Bunty)*, Janet Gleeson *(Nell)*, Nancy Gleeson *(Baby)*, Don Tall *(The General)*.

Had this been a film for adults it might have been an interesting psycho-drama. But as it's aimed at children it instead comes across as mean and thoroughly unsuitable for its intended audience. McCallum is a father who doesn't understand the crazy behavior of his kids. There's no attempt at humor at all in his character; he comes off more like a tyrant than a father. This was based on a charming children's story, but you'd never guess by the results. Collins was originally a Hollywood director who left the U.S. for Australia.

d, Arthur Greville Collins; w, Pat Ryan (based on a story by Ethel Turner); ph, George D. Malcolm.

Drama **(PR:C MPAA:NR)**

LITTLE BALLERINA, THE** (1951, Brit.) 61m GAU-BI/UNIV bw

Yvonne Marsh *(Joan)*, Marian Chapman *(Sally)*, Doreen Richards *(Lydia)*, Kay Henderson *(Pamela)*, Anita Holland *(Carol)*, Beatrice Varley *(Mrs. Field)*, Herbert C. Walton *(Grandpa)*, George Carney *(Bill)*, Anthony Newley *(Johnny)*, Martita Hunt *(Miss Crichton)*, Leslie Dwyer *(Barney)*, Eliot Makeham *(Mr. Maggs)*, Margot Fonteyn *(Herself)*, Michael Somes, Sydney Tafler.

The perfect film for young ballet aspirants. Marsh is a schoolgirl trying to get into the famed Sadler's Wells Ballet Company. Coming from a modest background, she is in need of a scholarship and tries to win the attention of Fonteyn, who plays herself. There's some nice sequences with the girls going through their steps and a chance to see Fonteyn perform a number from "Les Sylphides." It's nicely directed and acted, and though it's no RED SHOES, children undoubtedly will adore it.

p, Geoffrey Barkas; d, Lewis Gilbert; w, Michael Barringer, Mary Cathcart Borer, Gilbert (based on a story by Barringer); ph, Frank North.

Ballet **(PR:AAA MPAA:NR)**

LITTLE BIG HORN***

(1951) 86m Lippert bw (GB: THE FIGHTING SEVENTH)

Lloyd Bridges *(Capt. Phillip Donlin)*, John Ireland *(Lt. John Haywood)*, Marie Windsor *(Celia Donlin)*, Reed Hadley *(Sgt. Maj. Peter Grierson)*, Jim Davis *(Cpl. Doan Moylan)*, Wally Cassell *(Pvt. Danny Zecca)*, Hugh O'Brian *(Pvt. Al DeWalt)*, King Donovan *(Pvt. James Corbo)*, Richard Emory *(Pvt. Mitch Shovels)*, John Pickard *(Sgt. "Vet" McCloud)*, Robert Sherwood *(Pvt. David Mason)*, Sheb Wooley *(Quince)*, Larry Stewart *(Bugler Stevie Williams)*, Rod Redwing *(Cpl. Arika)*, Richard Paxton *(Pvt. Ralph Hall)*, Gordon Wynne *(Pvt. Arndst Hofstetter)*, Ted Avery *(Pvt. Tim Harvey)*, Barbara Woodell *(Mrs. Owens)*, Anne Warren *(Little Girl)*.

Based on a true story, this film tells of a small band of cavalry men trying to get to Gen. Custer and warn him of a probable Sioux ambush. As they move through the hostile territory, the men are killed off one by one from the arrows of an unseen enemy until only Bridges and Ireland are left. Bridges is convinced that Ireland has stolen his wife, which adds to the tension. The building of mood and character in this film is terrific, with suspense tightly wired throughout. The two leads are good in their nerve-racking roles. This was Lippert's most expensive film to date and the directoral debut of Warren, who had previously served as a western novelist and later a screenwriter. He guides the film with a steady hand and the results are remarkable for a first effort. Eventually he would go on to produce some of the 1960's most successful television programs, including "Gunsmoke" and "Rawhide."

p, Carl K. Hittleman; d&w, Charles Marquis Warren (based on a story by Harold Shumate); ph, Ernest W. Miller; m, Paul Dunlap; ed, Carl Pierson; art d, F. Paul Sylos; m/l, "On the Little Big Horn," Stanley Adams, Maurice Sigler, Larry Stock.

Western **(PR:C MPAA:NR)**

LITTLE BIG MAN 1/2** (1970) 147m NG c

Dustin Hoffman *(Jack Crabb)*, Faye Dunaway *(Mrs. Pendrake)*, Martin Balsam *(Allardyce T. Merriweather)*, Richard Mulligan *(Gen. George A. Custer)*, Chief Dan George *(Old Lodge Skins)*, Jeff Corey *(Wild Bill Hickok)*, Amy Eccles *(Sunshine)*, Kelly Jean Peters *(Olga)*, Carole Androsky *(Caroline)*, Robert Little Star *(Little Horse)*, Cal Bellini *(Younger Bear)*, Ruben Moreno *(Shadow that Comes at Night)*, Steve Shemayne *(Burns Red in the Sun)*, William Hickey *(Historian)*, James Anderson *(Sergeant)*, Jesse Vint *(Lieutenant)*, Alan Oppenheimer *(Major)*, Thayer David *(Rev. Silas Pendrake)*, Philip Kenneally *(Mr. Kane)*, Jack Bannon *(Captain)*, Ray Dimas *(Young Jack Crabb)*, Alan Howard *(Adolescent Jack Crabb)*, Jack Mullaney *(Card Player)*, Steve Miranda *(Younger Bear as a Child)*, Lou Cutell *(Deacon)*, M. Emmet Walsh *(Shotgun Guard)*, Emily Cho *(Digging Bear)*, Cecelia Kootenay *(Little Elk)*, Linda Dyer *(Corn Woman)*, Dessie Bad Bear *(Buffalo Wallow Woman)*, Len George *(Crow Scout)*, Norman Nathan *(Pawnee)*, Helen Verbit *(Madame)*, Bert Conway *(Bartender)*, Earl Rosell *(Giant Troop)*, Ken Mayer *(Sergeant)*, Bud Cokes *(Man at Bar)*, Rory O'Brien *(Assassin)*, Tracy Hotchner *(Flirtatious Girl)*, Don Brodie *(Stage Passenger)*, Herb Nelson.

Nothing could be stranger than this story, recounted by a decrepit, 121-year-old man, Hoffman (in makeup that would have scared off Karloff) who claims to be the only survivor of the Custer Massacre at the Little Big Horn. The incredible story is seen in flashback as Hoffman describes how he and his older sister, Androsky, became lost on the plains and were taken in by Cheyenne Indians. Androsky escapes but 10-year-old Howard (Hoffman as a boy) remains with the Indians and six years later saves one of the tribe's braves, Bellini, causing him to be dubbed Little Big Man and making Bellini indebted to him. Later white men trap part of the tribe and are about to kill Hoffman when he declares he is white and denounces his Indian heritage. Hoffman is taken in by preacher David and his lusty wife Dunaway, who is busy trying to seduce him and everybody else in town. Hoffman leaves to become a drummer with Balsam, a fake medicine man who is so inept that he constantly loses limbs to those he has conned (until he is later stumbling about armless and legless). Hoffman becomes a gunfighter known as "The Soda Pop Kid," but abandons this dangerous career when he witnesses Wild Bill Hickok (Corey) in a bloody shootout. After other adventures as a scout for Custer and a brief wedding to a huge Swedish woman, Hoffman settles down with Eccles, an Indian maiden, and has a child, both killed by Custer in his massacre of the Indians on the Washita River. Hoffman and his adopted grandfather George are the only survivors. Hoffman then becomes a drunk who is rescued by Corey, meets Dunaway again after she has turned whore, and leads Custer to the Little Big Horn where the general, Mulligan, attacks the Indians and is wiped out, Hoffman being spared by his old friend Bellini. The tale told, Hoffman bemoans the Indians' fate as an old, useless man. It's all a hairy dog story with a few amusing moments, but mostly it's mindless historical revisionism the way a hippy might view less-than-great events of the Old West.

p, Stuart Millar; d, Arthur Penn; w, Calder Willingham (based on the novel by Thomas Berger); ph, Harry Stradling, Jr. (Panavision, Technicolor); m, John Hammond; ed, Dede Allen; prod d, Dean Tavoularis; art d, Angelo Graham; set d, George R. Nelson; cos, Dorothy Jeakins; spec eff, Logan Frazee; stunts, Hal Needham; makeup, Dick Smith, Terry Miles.

Western **Cas.** **(PR:C-O MPAA:GP)**

LITTLE BIG SHOT** (1935) 80m WB bw

Sybil Jason *(Gloria Gibbs)*, Glenda Farrell *(Jean)*, Robert Armstrong *(Steve Craig)*, Edward Everett Horton *(Mortimer Thompson)*, Jack LaRue *(Jack Dore)*, Arthur Vinton *(Kell Norton)*, J. Carrol Naish *(Bert)*, Edgar Kennedy *(Onderdonk)*, Addison Richards *(Gibbs)*, Emma Dunn *(Matron)*, Tammany Young *(Rajah Louis)*, Joseph [Sawyer] Sauers, Ward Bond, Murray Alper, Marc Lawrence, Guy Usher, Mary Foy.

This tailor-made film was especially for Warner Bros.' new discovery—5-year-old Jason, who was to be the studio's answer to Shirley Temple. Jason wasn't bad; she could sing, dance, and charm her way into anyone's heart. But her only average looks and sometimes unintelligible South African accent were hardly enough to sink the Good Ship Lollipop. Here she plays a gangster's daughter who is taken in charge by a couple of street people shortly before her father is killed. She goes through the typical "cute kid in the underworld" adventures which, in spite of the cliche plot, are well scripted. Armstrong warbles "My Kid's a Crooner;" among Jason's obligatory numbers were "I'm a Little Big Shot Now" and "Rolling in the Money" (Mort Dixon, Allie Wrubel). The kids should enjoy it. Director Curtiz and screenwriter Epstein later collaborated again for CASABLANCA.

p, Sam Bischoff; d, Michael Curtiz; w, Jerry Wald, Julius J. Epstein, Robert Andrews (based on a story by Harrison Jacobs); ph, Tony Gaudio; m, Leo F. Forbstein; ed, Jack Killifer; md, Forbstein; art d, Hugh Retticher.

Musical/Crime/Children's **(PR:AAA MPAA:NR)**

LITTLE BIG SHOT* 1/2 (1952, Brit.) 90m Byron/ABF bw

Ronald Shiner *(Henry Hawkwood)*, Marie Lohr *(Mrs. Maddox)*, Derek Farr *(Sgt. Wilson)*, Manning Whiley *(Mike Connor)*, Danny Green *(Big Mo)*, Yvette Wyatt *(Ann)*, Digby Wolfe *(Peter Carton)*, Marjorie Stewart *(Mrs. Crane)*, Victor Baring *(Little Mo)*, Cyril Conway, Gabrielle Daye, Daphne Barker, Lawrence Douglas, Steve Knight, Arthur Dibbs, Tony Bradley.

Shiner plays a bungling gang member whose father was the group's head crook until his death. The surviving members keep Shiner involved in their operation only out of respect. When they finally send him out on his own caper—the ransacking of a mansion full of jewels—he turns it into a fiasco which results in the rounding up of the entire gang except, of course, Shiner.

p, Henry Halstead; d, Jack Raymond; w, John Paddy Carstairs (based on a play by Janet Allan); ph, James Wilson, Gerald Moss.

Comedy/Crime **(PR:A MPAA:NR)**

LITTLE BIT OF BLUFF, A*½ (1935, Brit.) 61m GS Enterprises/MGM bw

Reginald Gardiner *(Hugh Rigby)*, Marjorie Shotter *(Joyce Simcox)*, H. F. Maltby *(Adm. Simcox)*, Margaret Watson *(Mrs. Simcox)*, Clifford Heatherley, Clifford McLaglen, Molly Fisher, Peggy Novak.

Gardiner gets a chance to do some sleuthing when his fiancee's father, stodgy old admiral Maltby, has his family heirlooms lifted. He disguises himself as a detective and manages to track down the crooks. In keeping with tradition, Maltby's faith in the young fellow is then restored, making him worthy of marriage into the family. Maltby does a fine job as the admiral, but one sometimes gets the feeling that he saved all the *really* funny lines for himself.

p, A. George Smith; d, Maclean Rogers; w, H. F. Maltby, Kathleen Butler.

Comedy **(PR:A MPAA:NR)**

LITTLE BIT OF HEAVEN, A** (1940) 87m UNIV bw

Gloria Jean *(Midge)*, Robert Stack *(Bob)*, Hugh Herbert *(Pop)*, C. Aubrey Smith *(Grandpa)*, Stuart Erwin *(Cotton)*, Nan Grey *(Janet)*, Eugene Pallette *(Herrington)*, Billy Gilbert *(Tony)*, Butch & Buddy *(Tony's Kids)*, Nana Bryant *(Mom)*, Tommy Bond *(Jerry)*, Frank Jenks *(Uncle Dan)*, Noah Beery, Sr. *(Uncle Sherm)*, Maurice Costello *(Uncle Louie)*, Charles Ray *(Uncle Wes)*, Monte Blue *(Uncle Pat)*, Fred Kelsey *(Uncle Pete)*, Tom Dugan *(Uncle Ed)*, William Desmond *(Uncle Francis)*, Edgar Deering *(Uncle Jack)*, Kenneth Harlan *(Uncle Burt)*, Pat O'Malley *(Uncle Mike)*, David Oliver *(Uncle Freddie)*, Charles Previn *(Radio Conductor)*, Kitty O'Neil *(Mrs. Mitchell)*, Helen Brown *(Secretary)*, Sig Arno *(Francois)*, Rafaela Ottiano *(Mme. Lupinsky)*, Chester Clute *(Mr. Dixon)*, Renie Riano *(Mrs. Dixon)*.

Jean is a 12-year-old girl from a New York City East Side family. She takes to singing, eventually making it big on the radio. The family members go wild with their newfound wealth and ignore all their old friends. Angered, Jean pretends to lose her voice and the family quickly mends its ways. Despite the simplistic script and lackluster direction, Jean really comes off well in this, her second feature. She not only sings up a storm, but also proves she can act as well. Songs include: "What Did We Learn at School?" (Vivian Ellis, sung by Jean), "After Every Rain Storm" (Sam Lerner, Frank Skinner, sung by Jean), "A Little Bit of Heaven" (J. Keirn Brennan, Ernest Ball, sung by Jean), "Dawn of Love" (Ralph Freed, Charles Previn).

p, Joe Pasternak; d, Andrew Marton; w, Daniel Taradash, Gertrude Purcell, Harold Goldman (based on a story by Grover Jones); ph, John Seitz; ed, Laslo Benedek; md, Charles Previn; art d, Jack Otterson.

Musical **(PR:AAA MPAA:NR)**

LITTLE BOY BLUE*

(1963, Mex.) 86m K. Gordon Murray/Trans-International c

A bizarre fantasy produced by K. Gordon Murray who is notorious for his other bizarre fantasies, such as LITTLE RED RIDING HOOD AND THE MONSTERS, THE CURSE OF THE DOLL PEOPLE, and THE TURKISH CUCUMBER. This one has the title youngster taking off on an adventure to find his pet monkey, but getting mixed up with a gang of outlaws in the Mexican jungle instead. All goes well for the boy and his monkey by the finale.

p, K. Gordon Murray.

Fantasy **(PR:A MPAA:NR)**

LITTLE BOY LOST*** (1953) 95m PAR bw

Bing Crosby *(Bill Wainwright)*, Claude Dauphin *(Pierre Fernier)*, Christian Fourcade *(Jean)*, Gabrielle Dorziat *(Mother Superior)*, Nicole Maurey *(Lisa Garret)*, Collette Dereal *(Nelly)*, Georgette Anys *(Madame Quilleboeuf)*, Henri Letondal *(Tracing Service Clerk)*, Michael Moore *(Attache)*, Peter Baldwin *(Lt. Walker)*, Gladys de Segonzac *(Helene)*, Yola d'Avril *(Madame Le Blanc)*, Bruce Payne *(Ronnie)*, Jean Del Val *(Dr. Birous)*, Adele St. Maur *(Nurse)*, Ninon Straty *(Suzanne Pitou)*, Jacques Gallo *(Paul)*, Karin Vengay *(Stewardess)*, Tina Blagoi *(Sister Therese)*, Arthur Dulac *(Waiter)*, Paul Magranville, Roger Etienne Everaert, Allan Douglas, Michel Champommier, Pierre Plauzales, Rene de Loffre, Jean Champommier, Claude Guy, Christian Pasques, Ferard Seidl.

As a war correspondent in occupied France, Crosby married and fathered a son. The war is now over and his wife is dead, executed by the Nazis for being active in the resistance movement. He has lost track of his son and is determined to find the boy. At a Parisian orphanage he is introduced to Fourcade, an eight-year-old boy with some resemblance to Crosby's late wife. In order to ascertain whether the boy is really his son, he takes the lad to their old apartment, but the child doesn't seem to remember it. However, a few days later the boy seems to know everything quite well. Crosby is almost convinced until Fourcade mentions a shop that was built after the war. He discovers that the boy has been coached by Dorziat, the nun in charge of the orphanage. She explains herself by telling Crosby that she would do anything to see one of the war orphans have a chance at a good life. Crosby has grown attached to the child, but the memory of his wife continues to haunt him. Dauphin, an old friend, confronts him. He too has lost a wife to the war and tells Crosby that the dead should be laid to rest, and that Fourcade needs a father, not an orphanage. With this in mind Crosby returns to adopt the child. Crosby and Fourcade are quite a team. Both give sensitive and moving performances. Fourcade is all the more amazing in his first role. The eight-year-old pulls off a difficult characterization like a seasoned veteran. Seaton's direction tends to run a little on the sentimental side, but holds interest throughout. The on-location Paris backgrounds are nicely used. Crosby also sings a few songs, "The Magic Window," "Cela M'Est Egal," "A Propos de Rien" (Johnny Burke, James Van Heusen) and a French version of "Oh Susanna" (Stephen Foster), that really aren't necessary for the film's development, though they probably helped the box office. This was the second version of the story by Laski. An earlier telling was made for television a year or so before this.

p, William Perlberg; d&w, George Seaton (based on a story by Marghanita Laski); ph, George Barnes; m, Victor Young; ed, Alma Macrorie; art d, Hal Pereira, Henry Bumstead; set d, Sam Comer and Ross Dowd; cos, Edith Head; m/l, Johnny Burke and James Van Heusen.

Drama **(PR:A MPAA:NR)**

LITTLE CAESAR****** (1931) 80m FN/WB bw

Edward G. Robinson *(Cesare Enrico Bandello/Rico—Little Caesar)*, Douglas Fairbanks, Jr. *(Joe Massara)*, Glenda Farrell *(Olga Strassoff)*, William Collier, Jr. *(Tony Passa)*, Ralph Ince *(Diamond Pete Montana)*, George E. Stone *(Otero)*, Thomas Jackson *(Lt. Tom Flaherty)*, Stanley Fields *(Sam Vettori)*, Armand Kaliz *(DeVoss)*, Sidney Blackmer *(The Big Boy)*, Landers Stevens *(Commissioner McClure)*, Maurice Black *(Little Arnie Lorch)*, Noel Madison *(Peppi)*, Nick Bela *(Ritz Colonna)*, Lucille La Verne *(Ma Magdalena)*, Ben Hendricks, Jr. *(Kid Bean)*, George Daly *(Machine Gunner)*, Ernie Adams *(Cashier)*, Larry Steers *(Cafe Guest)*, Louis Natheaux *(Hood)*, Kernan Cripps *(Detective)*.

This is the landmark film that launched the gangster movie cycle, a powerful movie that chronicled for the first time in talkies the sleazy and slick underworld, epitomized by a snarling and ambitious creature who had no redeeming virtues, Robinson. He was rotten through and through, and even watching him decades later the viewer can only wonder at his incredibly perceptive performance. Robinson is a dedicated killer and thief right from the opening scenes of LITTLE CAESAR. He stops in a gas station and enters the building. There is a flash of gunfire and Robinson emerges with the money from the till, presumably having killed the owner. His driver, Fairbanks, nervously wheels the coupe into the darkness. Later, Robinson and Fairbanks are in a diner, ordering "spaghetti and coffee for two," so that no doubt will be left as to their national origin. In the diner Robinson reads of underworld bigshots in the big city and tells Fairbanks that he, too, will some day be a rackets czar, that he intends to make something of himself, that he's not "just another mug." When he arrives in the big city, presumably Chicago, Robinson goes to the Palermo Club where Fields is the resident boss and one of the underworld kingpins. Robinson tells him he can be of great service to Fields and that he's good with a gun. Fields tells him that the gun "stuff doesn't go," but accepts him as a new gunsel and takes him into a room to meet his mob, saying "I want you all to meet a new guy what's gonna be with us." The camera pans the room to show a motley, mean looking crew, including Stone, Madison, Collier, and Hendricks. Robinson swaggers and struts in front of the mob and quickly earns their respect with Stone becoming Robinson's lickspittle sidekick. As Robinson grows in stature following one caper after another where he proves his fearlessness and becomes the No. 2 man under Fields, Fairbanks pursues another career. He has met and fallen in love with Farrell, a dancer in a club run by Black, and becomes her dancing partner. Jackson, head of the detective squad, begins applying the pressure to the Fields mob. Robinson stands up to him, telling him that "no mug like you will ever put the cuffs on Little Rico." Later, when Fields loses his nerve, Robinson sneers contemptuously at him and says: "Sam, you're getting soft. You're getting so you can dish it out but you can't take it." Robinson takes over the mob after the hoodlums back him in a robbery both Fields and the city's crime czar, Ince, oppose. Ince has already told Black, Fields, and other bosses to go easy on the violence, that Stevens, the crime commissioner, is cracking down and everyone is to keep a low profile. Yet Robinson and his gang make a raid on Black's nightclub, robbing the till and the customers. When commissioner Stevens appears in the lobby and reaches for his gun to battle the gangsters, Robinson kills him. Fairbanks, who has acted as a lookout, has been pressured into his role by Robinson, who has told him nobody ever quits him or his gang, and that becoming a ballroom dancer is tantamount to turning "sissy." Following the robbery, Robinson becomes gang chief and later meets "Mr. Big," the cultured and all-powerful Blackmer, a high society tycoon who pulls all the underworld strings. Robinson marvels at his huge mansion and exquisite furnishings and apes his boss by setting himself up in similar surroundings. He is given a testimonial dinner at the Palermo Club where he is awarded a gold watch as a gift from "the boys," but he sours on the gift when he finds it's been stolen. The next day he buys several newspapers which feature his picture at the banquet and, while strolling down the street, is fired on by a machinegunner in a speeding truck. But Robinson survives with only a flesh wound, which makes him believe that he is invincable. Stone comes to Robinson and tells him that Collier is guilt-ridden over the Stevens killing and is going to his local priest to confess. Robinson tries to convince the young hoodlum that to tell the priest is betraying the mob. Collier won't listen and, when Robinson finds Collier climbing the steps of the church on his way to the confessional, he shoots and kills him. (These were the same steps that would later serve as James Cagney's death spot in THE ROARING TWENTIES.) Robinson is now near the top of the heap and he plans to get rid of even Blackmer, asking Fairbanks to come back to the mob and be his right hand man. Fairbanks, a weakling, refuses, but only when the iron-willed Farrell stands up to Robinson. Robinson, a truly asexual person in love with only money and power, tells Fairbanks that "dames" will be his downfall and that "being somebody" and "having your own way or nothing" is the only real reason for living. Farrell calls cop Jackson, telling him that her boy friend Fairbanks knows who killed Stevens. Robinson hears that Fairbanks is about to inform on him and he and Stone confront the failed gangster. Yet Robinson cannot bring himself to shoot his pal Fairbanks and he flees with Stone just as Jackson and cops arrive. Stone is shot to death but Robinson escapes. His gang and fortune quickly evaporate. Robinson pays an old harridan, La Verne, almost his entire fortune to hide him out in a secret back room of her rundown store. She gives him back only a pittance of the money he has stowed away with her for safekeeping and then kicks him out. Robinson hits the skids, living on the streets and, when he can afford it, in flophouses. He reads in the newspapers how he has disappeared because he is a coward and won't face Jackson and the police, stories deliberately planted to draw him out of hiding. It works; Robinson calls Jackson and threatens him, his call being traced to the warehouse district. Jackson and cops track Robinson down as he walks a deserted street. He sees the police car coming and ducks behind a billboard. Jackson orders him to come out but Robinson, pulling a pistol, yells back: "Come in and get me!" Jackson aims a machinegun at the billboard and rakes it, the bullets ploughing into Robinson. He collapses and Jackson steps behind the billboard to see the once powerful gangster moan out: "Mother of Mercy, is this the end of Rico?" He dies on the spot, thus fulfilling the prophetic words first shown at the beginning of the film (quoted from St. Matthew): "For all them that take the sword shall perish by the sword." There were actually two endings to LITTLE CAESAR. In another version, Robinson's words were "Mother of *God*, is this the end of Rico?" but this was softened to "Mother of *Mercy*" for Bible belt states where the former statement was thought to be too strong. LITTLE CAESAR was the first talking movie to portray the American gangster outside of prison walls, coming after such early day talkies as THE LAST MILE, THE BIG HOUSE, and NUMBERED MEN. And it was as ruthless as the real-life gangster upon which author Burnett, from Chicago, based his tale. The prototype for this story is undoubtedly Al Capone, Chicago's crime czar, who rose as does Robinson, through the ranks, from goon bodyguard to overall crime czar. The part of Ince was based upon Big Jim Colisimo whom Capone murdered for Johnny Torrio in 1920 on his way up the bloody ladder of crime. The underworld banquet held in Robinson's honor, however, is based upon a notorious fete given on the North Side of Chicago in the early 1920s, honoring other gangsters, Dion "Deanie" O'Bannion and Samuel J. "Nails" Morton, one attended by aldermen and high society potentates, reported widely in the press which further scandalized "that toddlin' town." The Blackmer role of Mr. Big was surely based upon the utterly corrupt Big Bill Thompson, mayor of Chicago and Capone's hip pocket politician. The film was all the idea of director LeRoy, who read the Burnett novel in galley proofs and then went to Warner Bros. production chief Darryl Zanuck, later boss of Fox, and asked to film it. Zanuck read the book and quickly agreed, saying: "Every other underworld picture has had a thug with a little bit of good in him. He reforms before the fadeout. This guy is no good at all. It'll go over big!" Moreover, Zanuck let the shrewd, expert LeRoy make the film his own way and he proved to be a master of *film noir*, producing a fast-paced film that kept up with its lightning-fast star. The 37-year-old Robinson was not new to films; he had been acting in movies since 1923 but went largely unnoticed. Robinson was not originally intended to play the lead role. According to the actor, producer Wallis called him into his office and offered him the supporting role of Otero, later played by Stone, and he refused, coming back later to demand the starring role. Wallis, who took full credit for the development of the story, recalled it another way, saying in his memoirs, *Starmaker*: "He walked into my office one day wearing a homburg, heavy black overcoat, and white evening scarf, a cigar clenched between his teeth. He *was* Rico." Wallis assigned Robinson the part but the sensitive actor found it difficult to adjust to the killer beast he was playing, so much so that director LeRoy could not prevent Robinson from wildly blinking every time he fired a gun. LeRoy solved the problem by affixing little transparent bands of tape to Robinson's upper eyelids so that when he did blast away his eyes remained wide open, which gave him an even more menacing, heartless appearance. LeRoy, the ultimate craftsman who approached filmmaking as if he were the average viewer, had a cavalier attitude on the set which irritated Robinson, so much so that he complained to Wallis (according to Wallis) and the producer paid a visit to the set, asking LeRoy to stop the clowning, which he did. After Robinson was cast, Farrell was scheduled to play the dancer, but Robinson's sidekick was still unslated. LeRoy heard of a dark featured young actor appearing in the Los Angeles production of "The Last Mile," and signed him, Clark Gable, to a screen test for the role. Zanuck saw the test and exploded, shouting at LeRoy: "What the hell have you done, Mervyn? I'll tell you what you've done. You've just thrown away $500 on a test! Didn't you see the size of that guy's ears?" Gable was out and Fairbanks was later cast as the reluctant sidekick, but Robinson felt that he was a little too sophisticated, too polished to be convincing as an apprentice hoodlum. The author Burnett also didn't like the actor when watching him act on the set, telling Wallis that they were portraying the Fairbanks role as a homosexual. Said Wallis later: "No such thing was on our minds." This notion by Burnett later gave birth to a spate of speculation by latter day critics in search of something more to say about LITTLE CAESAR, so they promoted the idea of the homosexual liaison between Robinson and Fairbanks, an idea that is silly at best. Burnett was a young writer in Chicago, age 28, when, according to Wallis, he was listening to a radio one night, a broadcast from a local night club where his friend was playing in a jazz band and actually heard guns go off, gangsters killing his friend while spraying the audience with bullets to kill rival hoodlums. "He heard the shooting and the death cries over the air," stated Wallis. "As a result he wrote *Little Caesar*, a bitter, savage portrait of hoodlums in the big city." Burnett had no experience as a writer, although he did send his finished manuscript to the great editor at Scribner's, Maxwell Perkins. Though Perkins wanted to publish the book, the publishing board, or so the story goes, refused to print a novel about gangsters. Burnett threw the book in a trunk and forgot about it, going to work in a hotel owned by his uncle. He hauled the book out a year later and sent it to Dial Press and it was immediately accepted and published, becoming an overnight sensation and establishing Burnett as a master of crime tales. (He would later author such crime masterpieces as THE ASPHALT JUNGLE.) Burnett was asked by Wallis to write the film script but he refused. Robert Lord did a rough draft but Wallis thought it too sophisticated and assigned Faragoh to tone it down into gangster lingo and the script was greatly improved. Zanuck also had a hand in bringing the story to the gutter level where it would be believable adding more underworld argot. The film, made for a then hefty $700,000, was a box office smash and so indelibly did Robinson implant his gangster image that he was woefully consigned to playing the role over and over again. The film was not the first movie to deal with the criminal underworld. The great silent film director D. W. Griffith portrayed the underworld of New York in a one-reeler, THE MUSKETEERS OF PIG ALLEY (1912), in which Griffith actually employed some hoodlums in the Lower East Side where he shot the film on location. Then, in 1927, came the silent film UNDERWORLD, directed by Josef von Sternberg and written by Ben Hecht, a portrait of Capone and his rise to gangland bigshot. But it took LITTLE CAESAR to quickly establish the popular gangster genre which was quickly followed by a host of other films such as PUBLIC ENEMY, SMART MONEY, THE FINGER POINTS, and SCARFACE. Oddly, LITTLE CAESAR depicted a minimum of violence, although the intent was there always in Robinson's menacing presence. The actor was not the risk Wallis, Zanuck, and even LeRoy later presented him to be, when claiming that he had only portrayed meek mannered sorts prior to LITTLE CAESAR. They either forgot or ignored the fact the Robinson appeared as a gangland boss in a Warner Bros. programmer, THE WIDOW FROM CHICAGO, with Alice White in 1930. No matter, he remains, thanks to his unforgettable role as Rico Bandello, the definite movie gangster who wouldn't give up till he died, going out with a whine through his lips, begging for mercy from a Heaven he had profaned.

p, Hal Wallis (for Darryl Zanuck); d, Mervyn LeRoy; w, Robert N. Lee, Zanuck, Francis Edward Faragoh (uncredited), Robert Lord (based on the novel by W. R. Burnett); ph, Tony Gaudio; m, Erno Rapee; ed, Ray Curtiss; md, Leo Forbstein; art d, Anton Grot; cos, Earl Luick.

Crime Drama **Cas.** **(PR:C MPAA:NR)**

LITTLE CIGARS** 1/2 (1973) 92m AIP c

Angel Tompkins *(Cleo)*, Billy Curtis *(Slick)*, Jerry Maren *(Cadillac)*, Frank Delfino *(Monty)*, Emory Souza *(Hugo)*, Felix Silla *(Frankie)*, Joe De Santis *(Travers)*, Todd Susman *(Buzz)*, Jon Cedar *(Faust)*, Phil Kenneally *(Ganz)*.

THE TERROR OF TINY TOWN was the first all-midget Western. Thirty-five years after that epic's release someone got the bright idea of doing an all-midget gangster picture. Here the film's heavies are a five-midget group of racketeers. Tompkins is a normal sized gun moll on the run from her boy friend. She gets involved with the quintet, who stage a medicine show as a ruse so they can rob cars. She becomes the star attraction of their show, performing with two of the gang while the other three go about their crooked task. Highly off-beat and a lot better than one might suspect. Jokes about the diminutive sizes abound, but the film is not at all insulting, unlike the awful UNDER THE RAINBOW a few years later. Despite their size, these midgets can sure take a punch as well as any movie tough guy.

p, Albert Band; d, Chris Christenberry; w, Louis Garfinkle, Frank Ray Perilli; ph, John M. Stephens (DeLuxe Color); m, Harry Betts; ed, Eve Newman; art d, Alfeo Bocchicchio.

Crime/Comedy **(PR:A MPAA:PG)**

LITTLE COLONEL, THE*** 1/2 (1935) 80m FOX bw-c

Shirley Temple *(Lloyd Sherman, the Little Colonel)*, Lionel Barrymore *(Col. Lloyd)*, Evelyn Venable *(Elizabeth Lloyd Sherman)*, John Lodge *(Jack Sherman)*, Sidney Blackmer *(Swazey)*, Alden Chase *(Hull)*, William Burress *(Dr. Scott)*, David O'Brien *(Frank Randolph)*, Hattie McDaniel *(Mom Beck)*, Geneva Williams *(Maria)*, Avonne Jackson *(May Lily)*, Nyanza Potts *(Henry Clay)*, Frank Darien *(Nebler)*, Bill "Bojangles" Robinson *(Walker)*, Lillian West *(Neighbor Woman)*, Robert Warwick *(Commanding Officer)*, Harry Strang *(Sergeant)*.

Barrymore is a Southern colonel, bitter over losing both the Civil War and daughter Venable. It's not just that she's getting married—she's eloped with a Yankee! But when the couple get financially strapped, Barrymore grudgingly takes in Venable and her northern husband Lodge. They also have a daughter, the little charmer herself. Of course the little girl succeeds, through pluck and determination, in reconciling her grandfather and her parents, and the film ends happily. Temple is an absolute natural, coming across as an honest and sincere child rather than just a movie brat. The film is black-and-white with a "Pink Party" technicolor sequence for the happy finale. The film's highlight is the famous "Stair Dance" between old-time vaudeville hoofer Robinson and his diminutive partner. They are a charming pair and play off each other nicely. Unfortunately, as in most Hollywood films of the era, blacks are reduced to playing comic buffoons or good-natured "darkies." Temple's innocence cuts through the racism somewhat, but even today, the film may be offensive in some spots.

p, B. G. De Sylva; d, David Butler; w, William Conselman (based on a story by Annie Fellows Johnston); ph, Arthur Miller (Technicolor sequence by William Skall); m, Thomas Moore; ed, Irene Morra; md, Arthur Lange; m/l, "Love's Young Dream," Moore.

Drama **(PR:AAA MPAA:NR)**

LITTLE CONVICT, THE** (1980, Aus.) 90m Roadshow c

Rolf Harris *(Grandpa)*.

Tolerable children's film has Harris narrating, acting, and singing along with the animated-cartoon adventures of an English lad of thirteen convicted of aiding a highwayman by holding his horse and sentenced to be deported to Australia. There he falls in with the tough but fair convicts and wins favor from the governor by helping to save his wife's life. The animated characters are super-imposed on live action backgrounds shot in an amusement park called Old Sydney Town. Okay for kids, though adults will find it hard to take.

p&d, Yoram Gross; w, John Palmer; animation, Paul McAdam; art d, Athol Henry.

Children **(PR:AA MPAA:G)**

LITTLE DAMOZEL, THE** (1933, Brit.) 73m British & Dominions/W&F bw

Anna Neagle *(Julie Alardy)*, James Rennie *(Recky Poole)*, Benita Hume *(Sybil Craven)*, Athole Stewart *(Capt. Partington)*, Alfred Drayton *(Walter Angel)*, Clifford Heatherley *(Papa Bertholdy)*, Peter Northcote *(Abraham)*, Franklyn Bellamy *(Franz)*, Aubrey Fitzgerald *(Fritz)*.

Rennie is a gambler who accepts a wager to marry Neagle, an independent showgirl. They wed and eventually fall in love but she decides to dissolve their bond and return to show business. The dejected Rennie plans to kill himself, making it appear accidental so Neagle will receive some cash. Before he can go through with the act, however, she returns to him and they begin an idyllic existence together.

p&d, Herbert Wilcox; w, Donovan Pedelty (based on the play by Monckton Hoffe); ph, F. A. Young.

Musical/Romance   **(PR:A MPAA:NR)**

LITTLE DARLINGS**   (1980) 92m PAR c

Tatum O'Neal (Ferris), Kristy McNichol (Angel), Armand Assante (Gary), Matt Dillon (Randy), Maggie Blye (Ms. Bright), Nicolas Coster (Whitney), Krista Errickson (Cinder), Alexa Kenin (Dana), Abby Bluestone (Chubby), Cynthia Nixon (Sunshine), Simone Schachter (Carrots), Jenn Thompson (Penelope), Troas Hayes (Diane), Mary Betten (Miss Nichols), Marianne Gordon (Mrs. Whitney), Paige Connor, Edith Ivey, J. Don Ferguson, Laura Whyte, Suzanne Hlavacek, Scott MacLellan, Martha Wolbrinck, Bill Gribble, Cathy Larson.

O'Neal is a lonely rich girl. McNichol is a kid from the wrong side of the tracks. They meet at summer camp, take an instant dislike to each other, and end up betting which one of them will lose her virginity first. The two leads are honestly played, and there is a nice feel for the real scariness that sex has for adolescents. However, the screenplay gets bogged down in some silly sub-plots and stereotypes. Assante, though a better actor than this film deserves, gives a nice performance and has a good chemistry with O'Neal. When it's briefly good, this film is really tender.

p, Stephen J. Friedman; d, Ronald F. Maxwell; w, Kimi Peck, Dalene Young; ph, Fred Batka (Panavision, Metrocolor); m, Charles Fox; ed, Pembroke J. Herring; prod d, William Hiney; set d, Charles Forian; cos, Joseph Aulisi; m/l, Fox, Carole Bayer Sager.

Teenage Romance   **Cas.**   **(PR:O MPAA:R)**

LITTLE DOLLY DAYDREAM*½   (1938, Brit.) 82m Argyle-British/But bw

Binkie Stuart (Dolly), Talbot O'Farrell (Old Moe), Jane Welsh (Claire), Warren Jenkins (Jack Kelly), Eric Fawcett (Richard), Cathleen Nesbitt (Miss Parker), Sydney Fairbrother (Mrs. Harris), G. H. Mulcaster (Warton), Arthur E. Owen (Spider), Billy Watts, Gerald Vane, Henry Adnes, Syd Crossley, Douglas Stewart, Guy Jones and His Band.

An innocuous homespun tale of a young girl, Stuart, who is taken from the loving care of her mother and placed under the wicked control of her aunt. She manages to sneak away and is befriended by an organ-grinder, O'Farrell, helping him round up a gang of crooks. The cheery finale has mother and daughter returning to each other's arms with the expected dose of sentimentality.

p, John Argyle; d&w, Oswald Mitchell (based on a story by Ian Walker); ph, Geoffrey Faithfull.

Musical   **(PR:AA MPAA:NR)**

LITTLE DRAGONS, THE*½   (1980) 90m Eastwind/Aurora c

Charles Lane (J. J.), Ann Sothern (Angel), Chris Petersen (Zack), Pat Petersen (Woody), Sally Boyden (Carol), Rick Lenz (Dick Forbinger), Sharon Weber (Ruth Forbinger), Joe Spinell (Yancey), John Chandler (Carl), Clifford A. Pellow (Sheriff), Stephen Young (Lunsford), Pat Johnson (Karate Instructor), Master Bong Soon Han (The Master), Donnie Williams (Motorcycle Gang Leader), Tony Bill (Niles), Brad Gorman (Deputy).

Boyden is on vacation in the country with her parents. She's kidnapped by two local yokels, Spinell and Chandler, who live with mama Sothern in an abandoned car. The police are too dumb to solve the crime so the young karate experts, the Petersen brothers, end up saving the day. This one is strictly for the under-ten set. The story, acting, and production values are as simplistic as can be.

p, Hannah Hempstead, Curtis Hanson; d, Hanson; w, Harvey Applebaum, Louis G. Attlee, Rudolph Borchert, Alan Ormsby; ph, Stephen Katz; m, Ken Lauber; art d, Spencer Quinn.

Martial Arts   **Cas.**   **(PR:A-C MPAA:PG)**

LITTLE EGYPT**½   (1951) 82m UNIV c (GB: CHICAGO MASQUERADE)

Mark Stevens (Wayne Cravat), Rhonda Fleming (Izora), Nancy Guild (Sylvia Graydon), Charles Drake (Oliver Doane), Tom D'Andrea (Max), Minor Watson (Cyrus Graydon), Steven Geray (Pasha), Verna Felton (Mrs. Doane), Kathryn Givney (Cynthia Graydon), John Litel (Shuster), Dan Riss (Prosecutor), Jack George (Meheddi), Ed Clark (Judge), John Gallaudet (O'Reilly), Freeman Lusk (Spinelli), Fritz Feld (Professor), Leon Belasco (Moulai).

An entertaining but rather shallow programmer, LITTLE EGYPT uses as a backdrop the famous cooch dancer who quivered her belly for the boys at the 1893 Chicago Exposition, bringing down a wrathful storm from reform groups who found her dances obscene. Stevens is a con man who is joined by an opportunistic red-headed, statuesque Fleming, a girl from the New Jersey slums. They are both after Watson's millions and go through an elaborate scheme to bilk the tobacco tycoon. The windup is that Fleming, adorned with scanty costume, performs the hip-shaking, belly-bouncing, thigh-thumping dance made infamous by Izora and gets arrested for her efforts on charges of indecent exposure. It's all really tame stuff with a story less than inspirational. Fleming is nevertheless sensually appealing.

p, Jack Gross; d, Frederick de Cordova; w, Oscar Brodney, Doris Gilbert (based on the story by Brodney); ph, Russell Metty; ed, Joseph Curtiss; md, Joseph Gershenson; art d, Bernard Herzbrun, Robert Clatworthy; ch, Harold Belfer.

Historical Drama   **(PR:A MPAA:NR)**

LITTLE FAUSS AND BIG HALSY**   (1970) 98m PAR c

Robert Redford (Big Halsy), Michael J. Pollard (Little Fauss), Lauren Hutton (Rita

Nebraska), Noah Beery, Jr. (Seally Fauss), Lucille Benson (Mom Fauss), Ray Ballard (Photographer), Linda Gaye Scott (Mometh), Erin O'Reilly (Sylvene McFall), Ben Archibek (Rick Nifty), Shara St. John (Marcy).

Pollard is a drunken, slow-witted kid barred from motorcycle racing for his constant inebriation. He meets Redford after a race one day and the two men strike up a bargain. Redford will ride using Pollard's name, with Pollard as mechanic. Redford is a big mouth and constantly abuses the ever-admiring Pollard. The two characters go through a series of misadventures, and both fall in love with rich girl Hutton. Of course she goes for Redford and is amused by Pollard's attentions. Pollard ends up breaking his leg and goes home to his parents, Benson and Beery, who never approved of Redford to start with. The film ends with the two facing off in a race. Redford has a breakdown and leaves the track as Pollard takes the lead. This is a real mixed bag. Originally it was to be directed by the screenwriter, but the studio decided to give it to Furie. He wanted no part of it, though he had some admiration for the screenplay. Nevertheless, he gave it his best shot, with little help from his two leads. They were constantly fighting with each other, if they spoke at all. Motorcycle action is nicely coordinated, despite the helter-skelter feel of the plot. Some good background music by Johnny Cash, Carl Perkins, and Bob Dylan helps give the film some authentic atmosphere.

p, Albert S. Ruddy; d, Sidney J. Furie; w, Charles Eastman; ph, Ralph Woolsey (Panavision, Movielab); ed, Argyle Nelson, Jr.; art d, Lawrence G. Paull; set d, Audrey Blasdel; m/l, "Rollin' Free," Johnny Cash (sung by Cash), "Ballad of Little Fauss and Big Halsy," Carl Perkins (sung by Cash), "Wanted Man," Bob Dylan (sung by Cash), "True Love is Greater Than Friendship," Perkins (sung by Perkins), "706 Union Avenue," Perkins (sung by The Tennessee Three).

Drama   **(PR:O MPAA:R)**

LITTLE FOXES, THE*****   (1941) 115m RKO bw

Bette Davis (Regina Hubbard Giddens), Herbert Marshall (Horace Giddens), Teresa Wright (Alexandra Giddens), Richard Carlson (David Hewitt), Patricia Collinge (Birdie Hubbard), Dan Duryea (Leo Hubbard), Charles Dingle (Ben Hubbard), Carl Benton Reid (Oscar Hubbard), Jessica Grayson (Addie), John Marriott (Cal), Russell Hicks (William Marshall), Lucien Littlefield (Sam Naders), Virginia Brissac (Lucy Hewitt), Terry Nibert (Julia), Alan Bridge (Dawson the Hotel Manager), Charles R. Moore (Simon), Kenny Washington (Servant), Lew Kelly (Train Companion), Henry Roquemore (Depositor), Hooper Atchley (Guest), Henry Thomas (Bit).

THE LITTLE FOXES is one of the best play adaptations ever put on film. It was nominated for eight Oscars but won none and more's the pity. Kudos went for Best Director, Best Actress, Best Supporting Actress (Wright and Collinge), Best Screenplay, Best Scoring, Best Editing, and Best Art/Set Design (Goosson and Bristol). Louisiana-born Hellman has continued the story she began with ANOTHER PART OF THE FOREST (although that one was written as a pre-quel several years later) of the Hubbards, as shifty a family as ever drank bourbon and branch water. Davis is asked by her brothers, Dingle and Reid, if she will lend them money to erect a cotton mill that will utilize the cheap labor available at the turn-of-the-century. They need $75,000, a not unsubstantial sum, and she recognizes the fact that she can benefit greatly by the move. She invites Hicks, the Yankee financier who has suggested the enterprise, to her home for a dinner so she can have a closer look at him. Next, Davis has her daughter, Wright, travel north to Maryland to return with her husband, Marshall, who has been recuperating from a heart attack at a Baltimore sanitarium. Marshall comes home with Wright and Davis begins to nag him about financing for the new venture but he remains firmly against it for several reasons. He thinks the idea is morally wrong as it will exploit the labor and do nothing more than establish a southern sweatshop, and he is not sure of Davis' brothers and whether they are trustworthy. Reid and Dingle realize they'll never be able to extract the money from Marshall so they get Reid's son, the weak-willed Duryea, who works in the family banking business, to rob a handful of negotiable bonds from Marshall's private vault in order to be able to put up their share of the money. Davis, as avaricious a woman as ever seen on stage or screen, instantly suspects what's happened and attempts to blackmail her own brothers into giving her a percentage of their business in return for her keeping quiet about the theft. That's throttled when Marshall steps forward and says that the bonds weren't stolen at all. Rather, Marshall says he gave them to Duryea as an interest-free loan. Davis is annoyed that Marshall is siding with Duryea and continues to verbally badger and rankle Marshall until his heart gives out and he has an attack. He collapses and pleads for his medicine but Davis sits there, like a cake of ice. Marshall musters all of his strength to climb the stairs to his bedroom where the heart stimulant is. When he collapses, she finally calls for help from Marriott, her black butler. Later, Marshall is dying and Davis and Wright stand by his bed. Davis again asks Marshall to admit the truth but Marshall uses his last strength to warn his daughter about marrying her cousin, Duryea. Instead, he gasps, marry Carlson, a bright newspaper editor whom she dearly loves. Marshall dies and Davis is relieved. She begins to blackmail Reid and Dingle and now wants the lioness' share of their business (66 2/3 percent) in return for her keeping mum about the felony Duryea has committed. Wright hears Davis' demands and confronts her, saying that she can't stay a moment longer in the same house as the woman who killed her father. Wright races outside to Carlson, who has been waiting in the rain for her, and Davis is left alone. She is rich, powerful, and on top of the world, but she has no one with whom to share her success. Along the way, there are many memorable revelations. Collinge, Reid's wife, has a terrific scene where the booze takes over and she admits she hates both her husband and her son and that she knows full well that Reid married her to gain control of her family's successful plantation. She talks about her headaches that Reid always refers to when she doesn't show up for family functions. The truth is that she's a quiet drunk and he uses those headaches as an excuse to cover her problem. Every scene in the picture worked like a play and that may be due, in part, to the fact that several of the actors were repeating their stage success; Collinge, Reid, Dingle, Marriott, and Duryea. Carlson's role was not seen in the stage presentation. Hellman gets sole screenplay credit but there is the odd qualifying line of "additional scenes and dialog by Arthur Kober, Dorothy Parker and Alan Campbell" so the determination is unclear. Kober had been Hellman's husband at one time and Parker and Campbell were also married. There have been many cinematic articles written about Wyler and Toland in regard to this. Toland had been known for his deep-focus work on CITIZEN KANE and used it to great advantage again in THE LITTLE FOXES. One of the most chilling scenes is when the camera stays on Davis in the foreground as Marshall suffers his heart attack in the background. Davis never blinks, never acknowledges her husband's plight, just sits there like a haughty statue as Marshall goes through his pain out-of-focus as Wyler wanted the audience to concentrate on Davis' face and see just what a cold-hearted woman she was. This is a cynical, mean film and the leads are all blackguards (except for Wright, Marshall, Collinge, and Carlson) so it's hard to garner any emotion for them other than disgust. But as a technical achievement and as a film that stirs emotions, it's hard to top THE LITTLE FOXES. The title is drawn from The Song Of Solomon, 2:15, which states: "Take us the foxes, the little foxes, that spoil the vines . . . for our vines have tender grapes." There was another movie done in 1945 which was titled OUR VINES HAVE TENDER GRAPES that had nothing whatsoever to do with this one. Davis didn't feel that she gave a good performance and she and Wyler argued from dawn to dusk about the interpretation. Davis was wrong and the result was one of her finest films. In later years, Elizabeth Taylor attempted it in a road show that toured America with great financial success and poor critical notices. Her interpretation of it was more Woolf than Fox, as she raved and ranted and showed none of the subtlety Davis had on screen or Tallulah Bankhead demonstrated in the Broadway play. For Duryea and Wright, THE LITTLE FOXES was their screen debut.

d, William Wyler; w, Lillian Hellman, Arthur Kober, Dorothy Parker, Alan Campbell (based on a play by Hellman); ph, Gregg Toland; m, Meredith Willson; ed, Daniel Mandell; md, Willson; art d, Stephen Goosson; set d, Howard Bristol; cos, Orry-Kelly.

Drama **Cas.** **(PR:A-C MPAA:NR)**

LITTLE FRIEND*** (1934, Brit.) 80m GAU bw

Matheson Lang *(John Hughes)*, Lydia Sherwood *(Helen Hughes)*, Nova Pilbeam *(Felicity Hughes)*, Arthur Margetson *(Hilliard)*, Jean Cadell *(Miss Drew)*, Jimmy Hanley *(Leonard Parry)*, Gibb McLaughlin *(Thomson)*, Diana Cotton *(Maud)*, Cecil Parker *(Mason)*, Clare Greet *(Mrs. Parry)*, Jack Raine *(Jeffries)*, Finlay Currie *(Grove)*, Robert Nainby *(Uncle Ned)*, Atholl Fleming *(Shepherd)*, Basil Goth *(Doctor)*, Charles Childerstone *(Solicitor)*, Gerald Kent *(Butler)*, Allan Aynesworth *(Col. Amberley)*, Lewis Casson *(Judge)*, Marcell Rogez, Robert Kay, Joan Davis.

A tailor-made film for Pilbeam, who was the studio's newest child star, finds her caught between Lang and Sherwood. Seems her parents are going through a messy divorce and she's the pawn between them. When her father has her go on the witness stand against her mother, Pilbeam is emotionally wrought. She goes home and attempts suicide. This crisis is just the thing that brings her parents back together. The ending is hard to swallow, but otherwise this isn't too bad a film. Pilbeam's a natural at age 14, giving a sensitive performance as an adolescent caught in affairs beyond her comprehension. The adult cast, largely British film regulars of the day, give just the support the girl needs. Lang is nicely restrained, trying hard not to let his feelings toward his wife affect his relationship with his daughter. Ultimately this fails, but Lang makes it believable. The director handles the material nicely. This was a brave topic for its time and it's never melodramatic. Script was co-written by Isherwood, whose later stories of Berlin in the days shortly before Hitler were turned into the evocative CABARET.

p, Robert Stevenson; d, Berthold Viertel; w, Viertel, Christopher Isherwood, Margaret Kennedy (based on a novel by Ernst Lothar); ph, Gunther Krampf; md, Louis Levy.

Drama **(PR:C MPAA:NR)**

LITTLE FUGITIVE, THE* 1/2** (1953) 75m Joseph Burstyn bw

Richie Andrusco *(Joey)*, Ricky Brewster *(Lennie)*, Winifred Cushing *(The Mother)*, Jay Williams *(Pony Ride Man)*, Will Lee *(Photographer)*, Charlie Moss *(Harry)*, Tommy De Canio *(Charlie)*.

An honest, independently produced slice of Americana which was barely noticed when placed against the mega-structure of Hollywood. The almost neo-realistic approach deals with Andrusco, a seven-year-old Brooklyn boy, and the 10-year-old brother who gets stuck babysitting for him. In order to weasel out of his responsibility, big brother cons Andrusco into thinking he has killed another youngster with his cap gun. Being a stout devotee of Gene Autry, Andrusco believes his brother's trick and runs away. He takes refuge at Coney Island, forgetting his guilt long enough to enjoy the rides, games, and animals. He remains absorbed in this fantasy outlet until a suspicious pony ride operator takes notice and calls Andrusco's worried mother. Andrusco, as natural as can be, turns in one of the most unprecocious child performances in film, a far cry from the usual studio "brats." Produced on a shoestring by three former journalists and still photographers, THE LITTLE FUGITIVE stood beside the films of Mizoguchi, Fellini, Huston, and Carne to receive a Silver Lion from the Venice Film Fest. Except for a single Oscar nomination, it unfortunately was soon forgotten in its home country and today is hardly remembered. Once seen, however, it will probably never be forgotten.

p, Morris Engel, Ray Ashley; d&w, Ashley, Engel, Ruth Orkin; ph, Engel; m, Eddy Manson; ed, Orkin, Lester Troos.

Drama **(PR:A MPAA:NR)**

LITTLE GEL (SEE: KING OF HEARTS, 1936, Brit.)

LITTLE GIANT, THE*** (1933) 70m FN-WB bw

Edward G. Robinson *(James Francis "Bugs" Ahearn)*, Helen Vinson *(Polly Cass)*, Mary Astor *(Ruth Wayburn)*, Kenneth Thomson *(John Stanley)*, Russell Hopton *(Al Daniels)*, Shirley Grey *(Edith Merriam)*, Donald Dillaway *(Gordon Cass)*, Louise Mackintosh *(Mrs. Cass)*, Berton Churchill *(Donald Hadley Cass)*, Helen Mann *(Frankie)*, Selmer Jackson *(Voice of Radio Announcer)*, Dewey Robinson *(Butch Zanqutoski)*, John Kelly *(Ed "Tim")*, Sidney Bracey *(Butler)*, Bob Perry, Adrian Morris *(Joe Milano's Hoods)*, Rolfe Sedan *(Waiter)*, Charles Coleman *(Charteris)*, Bill Elliott *(Guest)*, Leonard Carey *(Ingelby)*, Nora Cecil *(Maid)*, Lester Dorr, Lorin Raker *(Investment Clerks)*, Guy Usher *(Detective)*, John Marston *(District Attorney)*, Harry Tenbrook *(Pulido)*, Joan Barclay, Loretta Layson, Maxine Cantway, Jayne Shadduck, Loretta Andrews, Ann Hovey, Lynn Browning, Renee Whitney, Margaret LaMarr, Alice Jans, Barbara Rogers, Bonny Bannon, Toby Wing, Pat Wing *(Society Girls)*, James H. Doyle.

Quick gangster spoof starring Robinson in a role satirizing the parts he'd been playing for real. This was Robinson's first comedic effort and he proved he could handle it well. Robinson is a Chicago beer magnate about to go bust because Roosevelt has been elected and Prohibition has been repealed. Rather than find new illegal ways to make a buck, he decides to pull up stakes and move to Santa Barbara and a new life dedicated to the proposition that all polo ponies are created equal. Having left ChiTown with lots of money and very little class, he attempts to crack the Montecito moguls but they see right through him. Vinson, a wealthy young woman, takes him to meet her family, whom Robinson thinks is the upper crust. They turn out to be connivers and wind up defrauding Robinson out of his sudsy fortune. They sell him stocks and he inadvertently takes the rap for the scheme. Before he can be convicted, he talks the district attorney, Marston, into letting him try to regain the money. Now he contacts his gang in Chicago and institutes "The Chicago Plan" and his cohorts strong-arm the con men into getting the money back. Along the way, he meets and falls for Astor, a poor girl in whose heavily mortgaged house he's been living. After the money is retrieved, Robinson gets his engagement ring back from Vinson and it is presumed he will present it to Astor. Robinson is wonderful as the bumbling gangster out of his element and when he tries to blend in with the rich, horsey set, you'll laugh until tears flow. At times, the comedy gets heavy-handed but there's enough good fun to satisfy everyone. Good technical work by all concerned and a machine-gun script from Lord and Mizner set this apart from many of the other gangster spoofs of the time, such as RACKETY RAX and WHAT! NO BEER?

p, Ray Griffith; d, Roy Del Ruth; w, Wilson Mizner, Robert Lord (based on the story by Lord); ph, Sid Hickox; ed, George Marks; md, Leo F. Forbstein; art d, Robert Haas.

Crime/Comedy **(PR:A MPAA:NR)**

LITTLE GIANT** (1946) 91m UNIV bw (GB: ON THE CARPET)

Bud Abbott *(John Morrison/Tom Chandler)*, Lou Costello *(Benny Miller)*, Brenda Joyce *(Ruby)*, Jacqueline De Wit *(Hazel)*, George Cleveland *(Uncle Clarence)*, Elena Verdugo *(Martha Hill)*, Mary Gordon *(Mom Miller)*, Pierre Watkin *(President Van Loon)*, Donald MacBride *(Pullman Conductor)*, Victor Kilian *(Gus)*, Margaret Dumont *(Mrs. Hendrickson)*, George Chandler *(O'Brien, Salesman)*, Beatrice Gray *(Miss King, Secretary)*, Ed Gargan *(Policeman)*, Ralph Peters *(Jim)*, Bert Roach *(Bartender)*, George Holmes *(Hercules)*, Eddy Waller *(Driver)*, Ralph Dunn *(Man in Lower Berth)*, Dorothy Christy *(Wife)*, Chester Conklin *(Tailor)*, William "Red" Donahue *(Farmer Perkins)*, Florence Lake, Mary Field, Anne O'Neal, Lane Chandler, Joe Kirk, Ethelreda Leopold, Donald Kerr, Milly Bronson, Pat Costello, Sebastian Cristillo, Eunahad the Mule.

An interesting Abbott and Costello entry which doesn't team them as the usual comedy duo. Chubby Lou ventures to the city to make enough money to marry his country girl. He is hired by Abbott to work as a vacuum cleaner salesman, but becomes the laughingstock of the firm, publicly humiliated by the company president (also played by Abbott). He becomes the butt of his co-workers' nasty joke which convinces him that he can read minds. This revelation gives him a new lease on life, and the following day he sells a record number of vacuums. He is invited to meet president Abbott and given a hero's welcome. After he exposes an embezzlement scheme, a mix-up occurs and he is sent back to the country humiliated and penniless. Everything comes to a happy end as he gets a hefty bonus check from the company, a new position, and his country sweetheart. Clearly a vehicle for Costello, who proves that he can carry a film all by himself.

p, Joe Gershenson; d, William A. Seiter; w, Walter DeLeon (based on a story by Paul Jarrico and Richard Collins); ph, Charles Van Enger; m, Edgar Fairchild; ed, Fred R. Feitshans, Jr.; md, Fairchild; art d, John B. Goodman, Martin Obzina.

Comedy **(PR:A MPAA:NR)**

LITTLE GIRL WHO LIVES DOWN THE LANE, THE* 1/2**
(1977, Can.) 91m RANK/AIP c

Jodie Foster *(Rynn Jacobs)*, Martin Sheen *(Frank Hallet)*, Alexis Smith *(Mrs. Hallet)*, Mort Shuman *(Officer Miglioriti)*, Scott Jacoby *(Mario Podesta)*, Dorothy Davis *(Town Hall Clerk)*, Clesson Goodhue *(Bank Manager)*, Hubert Noel, Jacques Famery *(Bank Clerks)*, Mary Morter, Judie Wildman *(Tellers)*.

While not the horror film it was billed to be, this Foster vehicle is a disturbing, wonderfully acted, expertly scripted, and suspenseful study of a murderous 13-year-old girl (Foster). Living alone in her father's home, Foster makes up stories that her father is away, when in fact he is dead. She handles the bills, the upkeep, and her own survival, admirably putting into practice what her father taught her. When a snooping neighbor makes a nuisance of herself, foster knocks her down the stairs. Matter-of-factly, Foster lets the cellar door close and gets back to her work. Soon Sheen is making a pest of himself, wanting both answers and Foster's barely pubescent body. Meanwhile, Foster becomes genuinely attracted to Jacoby, a youngster her own age. Their friendship builds to a bedroom scene, which while showing an unclothed Foster, still has a touching innocence to it. Sheen, knowing that something is odd about Foster's situation, presses her for answers about her father. His insistence threatens to ruin the private, self-sustaining, child-as-adult world which she has created with Jacoby. The finale has Foster lacing Sheen's tea with arsenic. Catching on to her game, Sheen tries the age-old game of switcheroo, and drinks her cup of tea. Foster is one step ahead of him, however, and Sheen dies, ending up under the floorboards. In trying to protect her world, Foster seems almost justified in her killings, leading the audience to second-guess their own morals. A minor but brilliant expose of a murderess.

p, Zev Braun; d, Nicolas Gessner; w, Laird Koenig (based on his novel); ph, Rene Verzier (Panavision); m, Christian Gaubert; ed, Yves Langlois; md, Mort Shuman; art d, Robert Prevost; set d, Ronald Fauteux; cos, Denis Sperdouklis, Valentino.

Crime   **Cas.**   **(PR:O MPAA:PG)**

LITTLE HUMPBACKED HORSE, THE**1/2

(1962, USSR) 82m Central Documentary Film/Artkino c (SKAZKA O KONKE-GORBUNKE)

Maya Plisetskaya (Queen Maiden), Vladimir Vasilyev (Ivan), Alla Shcherbinina (The Little Humpbacked Horse), Aleksandr Radunskiy (The King), Aleksandr Pavlinov (Old Man), I. Peregudov (Danila), A. Simachyov (Gavrila), L. Shvachkin (King's Groom), Natalya Taborko (Water Spirit), Vasya Vorokhobko (Fish), Georgiy Farmanyants, Gennadiy Ledyakh, Bolshoi Theater Ballet.

A filmed version of the ballet performance at the Bolshoi Theater. The plot concerns a simple-minded stable boy, Vasilyev, and his pet, Shcherbinina, as they venture to the court of the king, Radunskiy. Radunskiy orders the boy to fetch his love from under the sea, Plisetskaya, and bring her to him. The lovely maiden is repulsed by the ugly king, and she insists that he bathe in boiling water before she will marry him. The king orders Vasilyev to test the bath, and he emerges incredibly handsome. The king then dives into the waters, but he is killed, leaving the maiden and the stable boy to marry.

p,d&w, Aleksandr Radunskiy (based on the ballet, "Konyok-Gorbunok," by Rodion Konstantinovich Shchedrin, Vasiliy Ivanovich Vaynonen, Pavel Grigoryevich Malyarevskiy); ph, Mikhail Silenko, Yevgeniy Yatsun (Magicolor); m, Shchedrin; md, A. Zhyuraytis; art d, B. Volkov; anim, V. Krestyaninov, K. Aleksandrova, I. Znamenskiy, B. Chani

Ballet   **(PR:A MPAA:NR)**

LITTLE HUT, THE**

(1957) 78m MGM c

Ava Gardner (Lady Susan Ashlow), Stewart Granger (Sir Philip Ashlow), David Niven (Henry Brittingham-Brett), Walter Chiari (Mario), Finlay Currie (The Rev. Brittingham-Brett), Jean Cadell (Mrs. Brittingham-Brett), Jack Lambert (Captain MacWade), Henry Oscar (Mr. Trollope), Viola Lyel (Miss Edwards), Jaron Yaltan (Indian Gentleman).

A bedroom farce set on an island, starring Granger and Niven as shipwrecked males and Gardner as the voluptuous female. Granger is a busy government worker who has little time for his wife, Gardner. Gardner turns to Granger's best friend, Niven, for romance, causing the sexual tension to approach unbearable heights.

p, F. Hugh Herbert, Mark Robson; d, Robson; w, Herbert (based on the play by Andre Roussin and English stage adaptation by Nancy Mitford); ph, Freddie Young (Eastmancolor); m, Robert Farnon; ed, Ernest Walter; art d, Elliot Scott; cos, Christian Dior; m/l, "The Little Hut," Eric Maschwitz, Marcel Stellman, Peggy Cochrane.

Comedy/Romance   **(PR:A MPAA:NR)**

LITTLE IODINE**

(1946) 57m UA bw

Jo Ann Marlowe (Little Iodine), Marc Cramer (Marc Andrews), Eve Whitney (Janis Payne), Irene Ryan (Mrs. Tremble), Hobart Cavanaugh (Mr. Tremble), Lanny Rees (Horace), Leon Belasco (Simkins), Emory Parnell (Mr. Bigdome), Sarah Selby (Mrs. Bigdome), Jean Patriquin (Grandma Jones).

A standard comedy programmer with standard youngster Marlowe as the title character, based on a King Features cartoon strip. The little tyke makes life tough for her folks, Cavanaugh and Ryan, by raising her dad's suspicions of a language records salesman who visits Ryan. Family life returns to normal, however, by the picture's finale, with Cavanaugh learning of his daughter's trickery.

p, Buddy Rogers, Ralph Cohn; d, Reginald LeBorg; w, Richard Landau; ph, Robert Pittack; m, Alexander Steinert; ed, Lynn Harrison; art d, George Van Marter.

Comedy   **(PR:A MPAA:NR)**

LITTLE JOE, THE WRANGLER*1/2

(1942) 61m UNIV bw

Johnny Mack Brown (Neal Wallace), Tex Ritter (Bob Brewster), Fuzzy Knight (Little Joe Smith), Jennifer Holt (Janet Hammond), Florine McKinney (Mary Brewster), James Craven (Lloyd Chapin), Hal Taliaferro (Wally Wales), Glenn Strange (Jeff Corey), The Jimmy Wakely Trio (Jimmy Wakely, Cyrus Bond, Eddie Snyder), Ethan Laidlaw (Bit), Evelyn Cooke (Helen), Slim Whitaker (Charlie), Carl Sepulveda (Norton), Michael Vallon (Clem), Robert F. Hill (Hammond), Dave Allen, Bill Patton (Miners).

A fast-paced punchfest which has Brown and Ritter teaming to clear Brown's name from a robbery and murder frame-up. Ritter has a hunch that Brown is innocent and keeps his sheriff's badge by proving it.

p, Oliver Drake; d, Lewis D. Collins; w, Sherman Lowe, Elizabeth Beecher (based on a story by Lowe); ph, William Sickner; ed, Russell Schoengarth; md, H. J. Salter; art d, Jack Otterson; m/l, "I'll Saddle My Pony," Jimmy Wakely, sung by the

Wakely Trio, "Get Along, Little Dogie," sung by the Wakely Trio, "Little Joe, the Wrangler," sung by Tex Ritter with the Wakely Trio, later by Fuzzy Knight.

Western   **(PR:A MPAA:NR)**

LITTLE JOHNNY JONES**

(1930) 73m FN-WB bw

Eddie Buzzell (Johnny Jones), Alice Day (Mary Baker), Edna Murphy (Vivien Dale), Robert Edeson (Ed Baker), Wheeler Oakman (George Wyman), Donald Reed (Lopez), Raymond Turner.

Second time around for this story of Cohan's. The first was in 1923 and director LeRoy acted in that one. It's a dated piece, as are many films of this era, but for those who lean toward artistic pentimenti, it's worth a watch. Cohan, the Horatio Alger of Broadway, wrote and starred in the original Broadway play (there's a bit of it seen in YANKEE DOODLE DANDY) about a jockey, Buzzell, who comes to New York to seek fame and fillies. He falls for Day, a city girl, and after the requisite misunderstandings, they are united after he goes to England and wins the Derby. Buzzell, who was a Broadway mega-star in the early part of this century, is chipper in his first screen appearance but his emoting is quite broad and doesn't sit well under the scrutiny of the close-up camera. Two of Cohan's songs are featured, "Yankee Doodle Dandy" and "Give My Regards To Broadway," while several more from other writers include: "Go Find Somebody To Love" (Herb Magidson, Michael Cleary) "She Was Kicked In The Head By A Butterfly," "My Paradise" (Magidson, James Cavanaugh) "Painting The Clouds With Sunshine" (Al Dubin, Joe Burke), "Straight, Place And Show" (Herman Ruby, M. K. Jerome). The screenplay was co-written by Buzzell, and that accounts for whatever humor is found in the thin tale. LeRoy was already directing his ninth movie and just turning 30 when this was made. Many years later, there was an attempt to make this again into a stage musical with no success. Buzzell later abandoned his career as an actor and took up directing with such films as GO WEST, BEST FOOT FORWARD, A WOMAN OF DISTINCTION, and many more.

d, Mervyn LeRoy; w, Adelaide Heilbron, Edward Buzzell (based on the play by George M. Cohan); ph, Faxon Dean; ed, Frank Ware.

Musical/Comedy   **Cas.**   **(PR:A MPAA:NR)**

LITTLE JUNGLE BOY*1/2

(1969, Aus.) 78m Mass-Brown c (AKA: MOMMAN, LITTLE JUNGLE BOY)

Rahman Rahman, Michael Pate, Noel Ferrier, Willie Fennell, Mike Dorsey, Niki Huen, Leslie Berryman, Nicki Turner.

Routine tale of a jungle boy brought into civilization out of the Malayan jungle by a husband-wife doctor team. The boy is kidnaped by an evil reporter, but he escapes into the streets of Singapore and makes his way back to the kind doctors who took him out of the jungle. The boy is asked by the sultan to help guide men to the northern part of his province so that they can administer penicillin to natives suffering from dysentery. The native medicine man trusts the boy because he sees his power over animals, and he allows the men to inoculate the tribe. The tribe saved, the boy returns to the jungle.

p,d&w, Mende Brown; ph, Brendon Brown (Eastmancolor); md, Tommy Tycho.

Adventure   **(PR:A MPAA:NR)**

LITTLE KIDNAPPERS, THE***1/2

(1954, Brit.) 93m UA bw (GB: THE KIDNAPPERS)

Duncan Macrae (Granddaddy), Jean Anderson (Grandma), Adrienne Corri (Kirsty), Theodore Bikel (Willem Bloem), Jon Whiteley (Harry), Vincent Winter (Davy), Francis de Wolff (Jan Hooft, Sr.), James Sutherland (Arron McNab), John Rae (Andrew McCleod), Jack Stewart (Dominie), Jameson Clark (Tom Cameron), Eric Woodburn (Sam Howie), Christopher Beeny (Jan Hooft, Jr.), Howard Connell (Archibald Jenkins).

Wonderful family film set in Nova Scotia at the turn of the century. Macrae, the stern, bigoted grandfather of two orphaned children, Winter and Whiteley, tries to inculcate in them his own prejudices against the Boers. When the boys ask for a dog, Macrae forbids it. But their desire to express love is so overwhelming that they adopt a baby. This is a warm, human film that conveys its message to the viewer nicely without being heavy handed. At the film's heart are the delightfully natural performances of Winter and Whiteley. These are children we can believe in. The direction by Leacock is sensitive and caring. Recommended for family viewing.

p, Sergei Nolbandov, Leslie Parkyn; d, Philip Leacock; w, Neil Paterson; ph, Eric Cross; m, Bruce Montgomery; ed, John Trumper.

Family Drama   **(PR:AAA MPAA:NR)**

LITTLE LAURA AND BIG JOHN**

(1973) 82m Crown International c

Fabian Forte (John), Karen Black (Laura), Ivy Thayer (Laura's Mother), Kenny Miller, Paul Gleason, Cliff Frates, Evie Karafotias, Phil Philbin, Margaret Fuller.

Forte and Black take to the road as outlaws in 1900s Florida. A surprisingly good cast lifts this exploitation item above the ranks. Allegedly based on a true story. The leading man was known only by his first name, Fabian, in such beach-blanket musicals as RIDE THE WILD SURF (1964).

p, Lou Wiethe; d&w, Luke Moberly, Bob Woodburn (based on a story by Philip Weidling); m, Bill Walker.

Crime   **Cas.**   **(PR:O MPAA:R)**

LITTLE LORD FAUNTLEROY***

(1936) 98m UA bw

C. Aubrey Smith (Earl of Dorincourt), Freddie Bartholomew (Ceddie), Dolores Costello Barrymore ("Dearest," Mrs. Errol), Henry Stephenson (Havisham), Guy Kibbee (Mr. Hobbs), Mickey Rooney (Dick), Eric Alden (Ben), Jackie Searl (The Claimant), Reginald Barlow (Newick), Ivan Simpson (Rev. Mordaunt), E. E. Clive (Sir Harry Lorridaile), Constance Collier (Lady Lorridaile), Una O'Connor (Mary),

May Beatty *(Mrs. Mellon)*, Joan Standing *(Dawson)*, Jessie Ralph *(Apple Woman)*, Lionel Belmore *(Higgins)*, Gilbert Emery *(Purvis)*, Joseph Tyzack *(Thomas)*, Alex Pollard *(Footman)*, Daisy Belmore *(Mrs. Baines)*, Walter Kingsford *(Mr. Snade)*, Eric Alden, Helen Flint, Tempe Pigott, Lawrence Grant, Walter Kingsford, Eily Malyon, Fred Walton, Robert Emmett O'Connor, Elsa Buchanan, "Prince."

This was the third of four versions of the durable Burnett story. Originally done in 1914, then again in 1922, it was later a TV movie with Ricky Schroder and Alec Guinness. Bartholomew is a nice young Brooklyn boy whose mother, Barrymore, is the widow of an Englishman. Her late husband's father, Smith, hates Americans for no other reason than they are Americans. When it's discovered that the boy is the heir to a fortune and a title, he has to go to England and claim his inheritance as well as win over his grumpy grandfather's heart. Once that's done, Bartholomew and his pals bypass an attempt by a false claimant and all winds up well. The expression "Little Lord Fauntleroy" has become anathema to many and we tend to think of the little lord as a prissy type, but that's not the case at all, as Bartholomew demonstrates his manliness against a bunch of Brooklyn toughs. Mickey Rooney does a small bit as a shoeshine boy and, as always, stands out. Kibbee, as a Brooklyn grocer, is also excellent in a role that could have been a parody in the hands of a lesser actor. Terrific technical work in a highly professional manner plus a script that goes right for the heart.

p, David O. Selznick; d, John Cromwell; w, Hugh Walpole (based on the book by Frances Hodgson Burnett); ph, Charles Rosher; m, Max Steiner; ed, Harold Kern; art d, Sturges Carne.

Drama **Cas.** **(PR:AAA MPAA:NR)**

LITTLE MALCOLM*** (1974, Brit.) 112m Apple Films/Multicetera c

John Hurt *(Malcolm Scrawdyke)*, John McEnery *(Wick Blagdon)*, Raymond Platt *(Irwin Ingham)*, Rosalind Ayres *(Ann Gedge)*, David Warner *(Dennis Charles Nipple)*.

Produced by ex-Beatle George Harrison, this keenly written look at the "angry young men" of Britain is based on a popular London stage play. It stars Hurt as a youngster who joins up with a rebellious pair to plot an uprising, while reveling in the socio-political attitudes of the time. Producer Harrison would go on to bring the comic talents of the Monty Python troupe to the screen. Photographed by John Alcott, who also worked on A CLOCKWORK ORANGE and BARRY LYNDON.

p, Gavric Losey, George Harrison; d, Stuart Cooper; w, Derek Woodward (based on the play "Little Malcolm and His Struggle Against the Eunuchs" by David Halliwell); ph, John Alcott (Panavision); m, Stanley Myers; ed, Ray Lovejoy.

Drama/Comedy **(PR:C MPAA:NR)**

LITTLE MAN, WHAT NOW?* 1/2** (1934) 95m UNIV bw

Margaret Sullavan *(Lammchen Pinneberg)*, Douglass Montogmery *(Hans Pinneberg)*, Alan Hale *(Jachman)*, Catherine Doucet *(Mia Pinneberg)*, Fred Kohler *(Communist)*, Mae Marsh *(His Wife)*, DeWitt Jennings *(Emil Kleinholz)*, Alan Mowbray *(Franz Schluter, the Actor)*, Muriel Kirkland *(Marie Kleinholz)*, Hedda Hopper *(Nurse)*, Sarah Padden *(Widow Scharrenhofer)*, Earle Foxe *(Frenchman)*, George Meeker *(Shultz)*, Bodil Rosing *(Frau Kleinholz)*, Donald Haines *(Kleinholz, Jr.)*, Monroe Owsley *(Kessler)*, G. P. Huntley, Jr. *(Heilbut)*, Paul Fix *(Lauderback)*, Frank Reicher *(Lehman)*, Christian Rub *(Puttbreese)*, Etienne Girardot *(Spannfuss)*, Max Asher *(Chauffeur)*, Carlos de Valdez *(Dr. Sesam)*, Thomas Ricketts *(Mr. Sesam)*.

After the news of their secret marriage leaks out, newlyweds Sullavan and Montgomery leave their small town for pre-Hitler Berlin. They live with Doucet, the groom's stepmother, in what turns out to be a well-disguised, high-class bordello. Montgomery quits his meager department store job and they pack their bags. Enroute to nowhere in particular, they stay in a loft owned by an old wagon driver, where Sullavan gives birth to a son (the "little man" of the title). Soon thereafter, Montgomery is offered a job in Holland, leaving Germany just as the Weimar Republic is about to fall. One of the finest films of the 1930s to deal with Germany's political and social crisis, and a wonderful romance from Borzage.

p, Carl Laemmle; d, Franz Borzage; w, William Anthony McGuire (based on the novel by Hans Fallada [Rudolf Ditzen]; ph, Norbert Brodine; ed, Milton Carruth.

Romance **(PR:A MPAA:NR)**

LITTLE MARTYR, THE***

(1947, Ital.) 91m Superfilm bw (I BAMBINI CI GUARDANO; IL PICCOLO MARTIRE; AKA: THE CHILDREN ARE WATCHING US)

Emilio Cigoli *(Andrew)*, Luciano De Ambrosis *(Prico)*, Isa Pola *(Nina)*, Adriano Rimoldi *(Roberto)*, Giovanna Cigoli *(Agnese)*, Ione Frigerio *(Nonna)*, Maria Gardena *(Mrs. Uberti)*, Dina Pechellini *(Aunt Berelli)*, Nicoletta Parodi *(Giuliana)*, Tecia Scarano *(Mrs. Berelli)*, Ernesto Calindrini *(Claudio)*, Olinto Cristina *(Painter)*, Mario Gallina *(Doctor)*, Zaira La Fratta *(Paolina)*, Armando Migliari *(Commendatore)*, Guido Morisi *(Gigi Sharlani)*.

Originally released in Italy in 1943, THE LITTLE MARTYR tells the moving story of a dejected 5-year-old boy, De Ambrosis, who must cope with his mother's affair. The sensitive and insightful child tries to put a stop to his mother's flings, hoping to protect his father. He is sent away to a private school, after which his father commits suicide. The boy, aware that his mother is responsible, turns his back on her. An emotional picture which was one of the forerunners of Italy's neo-realist movement, scripted by that period's finest writer, Cesare Zavattini (BICYCLE THIEF, UMBERTO D). (In Italian; English subtitles.)

p, Franco Magli; d, Vittorio De Sica; w, Cesare G. Viola, Marguerite Maglione, Cesare Zavattini, Adolfo Franci, Ghererdo Ghereradi, De Sica (based on the novel by Viola); ph, Mario Benotti.

Drama **(PR:A MPAA:NR)**

LITTLE MELODY FROM VIENNA**

(1948, Aust.) 100m Excelsior/Fritz Erban bw (KLEINE MELODIE AUS WIEN)

Paul Hoerbiger *(Professor)*, Maria Andergast *(Widow)*, Annie Rosar, Fritz Imhoff, Fritz Lehmann, Theodor Danegger, Herta Dolezel.

A pleasant little tale about a war widow who after losing her home, boards with a local professor. Their relationship is tense initially, but the professor soon grows to love her.

d, E. W. Emo; w, Emo, Franz Tassie (based on a story by Fritz Koselka and Lillian Belmont); ph, Fritz Woditzke; m/l, "Little Melody from Vienna," "Violet Blue," "Three Brownies," Robert Stolz, Aldo Pinelli.

Romance **(PR:A MPAA:NR)**

LITTLE MEN** (1935) 72m Mascot bw

Ralph Morgan *(Prof. Bhaer)*, Erin O'Brien-Moore *(Jo)*, Junior Durkin *(Franz)*, Cora Sue Collins *(Daisy)*, Phyllis Fraser *(Mary Anne)*, Frankie Darro *(Dan)*, David Durand *(Nat)*, Dickie Moore *(Demi)*, Tad Alexander *(Jack)*, Buster Phelps *(Dick)*, Ronnie Crosby *(Rob)*, Tommy Bupp *(Tommy)*, Bobby Cox *(Stuffy)*, Dickie Jones *(Dolly)*, Richard Quine *(Ned)*, Donald Buck *(Billy)*, Eddie Dale Heiden *(Teddy)*, George Ernest *(Emil)*, Gustav von Seyffertitz, Jacqueline Taylor, Margaret Mann, Hattie McDaniel.

When one considers the phenomenal success of LITTLE WOMEN, it isn't surprising that a sequel would come along, nor is it surprising that it wouldn't measure up to its predecessor. Morgan has married and is now operating a Boys Town sort of school for any boy who cares to enter. Hollywood tossed in all their best boys, including Darro and Moore, but didn't come up with much. Overly sappy.

p, Ken Goldsmith; d, Phil Rosen; w, Gertrude Orr (based on the novel by Louisa May Alcott); ph, Ernie Miller, William Nobles; m, Dr. Hugo Riesenfeld; ed, Joseph Kane.

Drama **(PR:A MPAA:NR)**

LITTLE MEN* (1940) 84m RKO bw

Kay Francis *(Jo)*, Jack Oakie *(Willie)*, George Bancroft *(Maj. Burdie)*, Jimmy Lydon *(Dan)*, Ann Gillis *(Nan)*, Charles [Carl] Esmond *(Professor)*, Richard Nichols *(Teddy)*, Casey Johnson *(Robby)*, Francesca Santoro *(Bess)*, Johnny Burke *(Silas)*, Lillian Randolph *(Asia)*, Sammy McKim *(Tommy)*, Edward Rice *(Demi)*, Anne Howard *(Daisy)*, Jimmy Zaner *(Jack)*, Bobbie Cooper *(Adolphus)*, Schuyler Standish *(Nat)*, Paul Matthews *(Stuffy)*, Tony Neil *(Ned)*, Fred Estes *(Emmett)*, Douglas Rucker *(Billy)*, Donald Rackerby *(Frank)*, William Demarest *(Constable)*, Sterling Holloway *(Reporter)*, Isabel Jewell *(Stella N.)*, Elsie the Cow *(Buttercup)*, Bud Jamison *(Cop)*, Sarah Edwards *(Landlady)*, Duke York *(Poker Player)*, Howard Hickman *(Doctor)*, Stanley Blystone *(Bartender)*.

The least inspired of the Louisa May Alcott adaptations, this version of LITTLE MEN falls short of the 1935 picture, and isn't even in the same league as the 1933 gem, LITTLE WOMEN. It's the same story of a group of youngsters who are taught about life in a small, caring school. The prize-winning Elsie the Cow has a sizable role, which should tell you a little something about this one's quality.

p, Gene Towne, Graham Baker; d, Norman Z. McLeod; w, Mark Kelly, Arthur Caesar (based on the novel by Louisa May Alcott); ph, Nicholas Musuraca; m, Roy Webb; ed, George Hively; art d, Van Nest Polglase, Al Herman.

Drama **Cas.** **(PR:AA MPAA:NR)**

LITTLE MINISTER, THE*** (1934) 104m RKO bw

Katharine Hepburn *(Babbie)*, John Beal *(Gavin)*, Alan Hale *(Rob Dow)*, Donald Crisp *(Dr. McQueen)*, Lumsden Hare *(Thammas)*, Andy Clyde *(Wearyworld)*, Beryl Mercer *(Margaret)*, Billy Watson *(Micah Dow)*, Dorothy Stickney *(Jean)*, Mary Gordon *(Nanny)*, Frank Conroy *(Lord Rintoul)*, Eily Malyon *(Evalina)*, Reginald Denny *(Capt. Halliwell)*, Leonard Carey *(Munn)*, Herbert Bunston *(Carfrae)*, Harry Beresford *(John Spens)*, Barlowe Borland *(Snecky)*, May Beatty *(Maid)*.

THE LITTLE MINISTER was one of Sir James Barrie's most enduring works. He published the novel in 1891. It was adapted into a play in 1897 in England, then brought to the USA in 1907 starring Maude Adams. She revived it in 1915, then Ruth Chatterton played it on Broadway again in the middle 1920s. Adams did two radio versions in 1934 and two silent screen pictures were released by two different companies in 1921. Paramount's starred Betty Compson and George Hackathorne; Vitagraph's starred Alice Calhoun and Jimmy Morrison. In this, Hepburn is a peeress who enjoys dressing up as a gypsy and running around the area with the impoverished weavers in 1840 Scotland. They are little more than slaves to the city folks who own the manufacturing facilities and finally decide to rebel. Conroy is Hepburn's guardian and orders the soldiers in to stem the tide of rebellion but Hepburn works undercover against Conroy and warns the weavers of the attacks so they are always able to escape. She encounters Beal, the new cleric of the local church, and the two of them fall in love. He doesn't know that she is anything but a gypsy girl and the conservative congregation is totally against the romance; they make no bones about their feelings. The love affair between the two is not hidden and the dour parishioners are making plans to fire Beal when it is learned that Hepburn is not a gypsy at all, rather she is the ward of Conroy. Once that's discovered, all is well with the stiff Scots and Beal is allowed to stay on. The play was far more whimsical than the film and the comedy was rampant. In this, the writers have elected to go for drama and that may have been an error. Barrie loved to write for women and many of his works eluded synopsizing and only worked in the execution (PETER PAN, etc). This is sort of Hollywood's version of the Scots and served to make us believe that most of those folks were unsmiling, rigid people. Anyone who has ever ventured to Scotland knows that's not true. They are probably (along with the Irish) the most hospitable, fun-loving and, unfortunately, hard-drinking lot you'll ever meet. Their New Year's holiday, Hogmany, makes

Mardi Gras in New Orleans and Carnival in Rio and Fasching in Munich look like church socials. You'll have to listen hard to hear the dialog through the Scots burr but it's worth your concentration.

p, Pandro S. Berman; d, Richard Wallace; w, Jane Murfin, Sarah Y. Mason, Victor Heerman, Mortimer Offner, Jack Wagner (based on the novel and play by Sir James M. Barrie); ph, Henry Gerrard; m, Max Steiner; ed, William Hamilton; art d, Van Nest Polglase, Carroll Clark; set d, Hobe Erwin; cos, Walter Plunkett; spec eff, Vernon Walker; makeup, Mel Burns; tech adv, Robert Watson.

Drama   **Cas.**   **(PR:A   MPAA:NR)**

LITTLE MISS BIG* ½   (1946) 60m UNIV bw (GB: BAXTER'S MILLIONS)

Beverly Simmons (*Nancy Bryan*), Fay Holden (*Mary Jane Baxter*), Frank McHugh (*Charlie Bryan*), Fred Brady (*Eddie Martin*), Dorothy Morris (*Kathy Bryan*), Milburn Stone (*Father Lennergan*), Samuel S. Hinds (*Wilfred Elliott*), John Eldredge (*Sanford Baxter*), Houseley Stevenson (*Duncan*), Jeff York (*Clancy*), Peggy Webber (*Ellen*), Jim Nolan (*Detective Lieutenant*), Arthur Loft (*Mayor*), Warren Ashe (*Attorney Hartley*), Minerva Urecal (*Woman*), Frank Ferguson (*Dr. Raymond*), Barbara Woodell (*Secretary*), Beatrice Gray (*Woman Cousin*), William Ruhl (*Man Cousin*), Rod Bell (*Nephew*), Dick Wessel (*Private Detective*), Dorothy Christy (*Mrs. Baxter*), Teddy Infuhr, Vincent Graeff, Donald Davis (*Boys*).

A weak comedy that stars Holden as a temperamental millionairess who is committed to an insane asylum by her nephew because she wants to leave all her money to her dog and not to him. She escapes from the looney bin and seeks refuge with a poor barber's family, where her ill temper is smoothed by Simmons, the barber's young daughter. After proving her sanity, Holden makes sure that the barber's family never again has financial problems.

p, Marshall Grant; d, Erle C. Kenton; w, Erna Lazarus (from story by Harry H. Poppe, Chester Beecroft, Mary Marlind); ph, Paul Ivano; m, H. J. Salter; ed, Russell Schoengarth; art d, Jack Otterson, Abraham Grossman; m/l, "Peter, Peter, Pumpkin Eater," "A Tisket, A Tasket," special lyrics by Jack Brooks.

Comedy   **(PR:A   MPAA:NR)**

LITTLE MISS BROADWAY** ½   (1938) 70m FOX bw

Shirley Temple (*Betsy Brown*), George Murphy (*Roger Wendling*), Jimmy Durante (*Jimmy Clayton*), Phyllis Brooks (*Barbara Shea*), Edna Mae Oliver (*Sarah Wendling*), George Barbier (*Fiske*), Edward Ellis (*Pop Shea*), Jane Darwell (*Miss Hutchins*), El Brendel (*Ole*), Donald Meek (*Willoughby Wendling*), Patricia Wilder (*Flossie*), Claude Gillingwater, Sr. (*Judge*), George and Olive Brasno (*Themselves*), Charles Williams (*Mike Brody*), Charles Coleman (*Simmons*), Russell Hicks (*Perry*), Brian Sisters (*Themselves*), Brewster Twins (*Guests*), Claire DuBrey (*Miss Blodgett*), Robert Gleckler (*Detective*), C. Montague Shaw (*Miles*), Frank Dae (*Pool*), Clarence Hummel Wilson (*Scully*), Eddie Collins, Syd Saylor, Jerry Colonna, Heinie Conklin (*Members of the Band*), Ben Welden (*Taxi Driver*).

A delightful Shirley Temple vehicle in which she again does what she does best—portray a singing, dancing, pouting orphan girl. This time she is living with a group of washed-up vaudevillians in a hotel run by the heartless Oliver. Being entertainers, the hotel's inhabitants make a fair amount of noise, especially Murphy and Durante, whose swing band keeps Oliver up nights. She threatens to close the place down if they don't all pay their back rent. None of them has any cash, but when little Shirley hits on the idea of a fund-raising vaudeville show their future is secured. Shirley lays on the charm for Oliver, who, of course, realizes how mean she's been and has a change of heart. Songs include: "Be Optimistic," "How Can I Thank You," "I'll Build a Broadway for You," "Little Miss Broadway," "If All the World Were Paper," "Thank You for the Use of the Hall," "We Should Be Together," "Swing Me an Old-Fashioned Song" (Walter Bullock, Harold Spina), "When You Were Sweet Sixteen" (James Thornton), "Happy Birthday to You" (Patty Smith Hill, Mildred J. Hill) and "Auld Lang Syne" (traditional).

p, Darryl F. Zanuck; d, Irving Cummings; w, Harry Tugend, Jack Yellen; ph, Arthur Miller; m, Walter Bullock, Harold Spina; ed, Walter Thompson; md, Louis Silvers; ch, Nick Castle, Geneva Sawyer.

Musical   **(PR:A   MPAA:NR)**

LITTLE MISS BROADWAY* ½   (1947) 70m COL bw

Jean Porter, John Shelton, Ruth Donnelly, Doris Colleen, Edward P. Gargan, Vince Barnett, Douglas Wood, Milton Kibbee, Charles Jordan, Ben Welden, Kirk Alyn, Jack Norman, Stan Ross, Jack George, Jerry Wald and His Orchestra.

Porter plays an orphaned girl who mistakenly believes that her newly discovered relatives are wealthy socialites. Loath to set her straight, the "relatives" move into a temporarily abandoned mansion in order to entertain the girl and her fiance. Unfortunately, they offer very little entertainment for the audience. Songs include: "That's Good Enough For Me," "A Man is a Brother to a Mule" (Alan Roberts, Doris Fisher), "Judy and Dick" (Betty Wright, Victor McLeod, Fred Karger), "Cheer for the Team" (Walter G. Samuels, Charles Newman, McElbert Moore).

p, Sam Katzman; d, Arthur Dreifuss; w, Dreifuss, Victor McLeod, Betty Wright; ph, Ira H. Morgan; ed, Richard Fantl; md, Mischa Bakaleinikoff; art d, Paul Palmentola.

Musical Comedy   **(PR:A   MPAA:NR)**

LITTLE MISS DEVIL* ½   (1951, Egypt) 95m Oriental Film bw

Farid El Atrache (*Asfour*), Samia Gamal (*Kahramana/Semsema*), Lola Sedky (*Aleya*), Ismail Yassine (*Asfour's Comedian Friend*), Abed Salam Nabilsy (*Mimi Bey*), Estephen Rosty (*Aleya's Father*), Zaky Abraham (*Man of Destiny*), the Christa Ballet.

An average story about a singer, Atrache, who falls for a singer, Sedky, who will have nothing to do with him. She only has eyes for a millionaire. Leggy dancer Gamal appears before Atrache as a genie from a lamp and with her wildly suggestive

dancing gyrations, quickly causes him to forget Sedky. Gamal, a beautiful belly dancer, had recently wed oil-rich Texas playboy Sheppard King. The film's distributors took full advantage of the attendant publicity, featuring full-sized cutouts of the jewel-naveled houri. (In Arabic; English subtitles.)

p, Farid El Atrache; d, Mohammed Ragaky; w, Barakat (based on a story by Abou Saud Abiari); ph, Julio De Luca, Amberto Lanzano, Ahmed Adley; m, Atrache, Ahmed Ramy, Mahmoun Shanawy, Joseph Badrous; ch, Izek Dickson.

Musical   **(PR:A   MPAA:NR)**

LITTLE MISS MARKER*** ½   (1934) 78m PAR bw (GB: GIRL IN PAWN)

Adolphe Menjou (*Sorrowful Jones*), Dorothy Dell (*Bangles Carson*), Charles Bickford (*Big Steve*), Shirley Temple (*Miss Marker*), Lynn Overman (*Regret*), Frank McGlynn, Sr. (*Doc Chesley*), Jack Sheehan (*Sun Rise*), Garry Owen (*Grinder*), Willie Best (*Dizzy Memphis*), Puggy White (*Eddie White*), Tammany Young (*Buggs*), Sam Hardy (*Bennie the Gouge*), Edward Earle (*Marky's Father*), John Kelly (*Sore Toe*), Warren Hymer (*Canvas-Back*), Frank Conroy (*Dr. Ingalls*), James Burke (*Detective Reardon*), Mildred Gover (*Sarah*), Lucille Ward (*Mrs. Walsh*), Crauford Kent (*Doctor*), Nora Cecil (*Head of Home Finding Society*), Ernie Adams, Don Brodie (*Bettors*), Stanley Price (*Bookie*).

This was the first of several versions of Damon Runyon's charming and durable story. It was remade in 1949 as SORROWFUL JONES, then in 1963 as 40 POUNDS OF TROUBLE, and finally in 1980 as LITTLE MISS MARKER again. None of them compared with the original because none of them had the amazing Shirley Temple (who was on loan-out from Fox at the time; this was the picture that sent her soaring to the top of the popularity charts). Temple is an adorable tyke who is left with long-faced bookie Menjou as a marker for a $20 bet. When Temple's father dies by his own hand, Menjou is left with a child. He has no idea of what to do with Temple and reads her the racing tout sheet as a bedtime story. As the story continues, Menjou and Temple get closer. She is fascinated by King Arthur and Menjou's pals are all dubbed names by her. He also gets religion while bringing up Temple and, in a deed that astounds his friends, he lays out money to buy her clothes and even spends money for a new suit. This is a great shock to his pals as he had been known as a most parsimonious fellow indeed. In order to make a proper home for Temple, Menjou eventually marries his long-time amour, Dell, who sings in a nightclub. Now, if that sounds familiar, think of the relationship of Nathan Detroit and his ever-loving Adelaide and you'll see that Runyon was not afraid to steal from himself. Dell was only 19 years old when she made the picture and her career was tragically cut short by a fatal car accident as the film was released. Four tunes liven up matters: "Laugh You Son-Of-A-Gun," "Low-Down Lullaby," "I'm a Black Sheep Who's Blue," and "Sidewalks of New York." Menjou held his own against the histrionics of Temple (a not-so-easy task) and once commented that she was a "six-year-old Ethel Barrymore" (although she was only five at the time). Lots of funny complications including a running battle with Menjou's enemy, Bickford, and a hysterical sequence with all the Broadway characters in medieval costumes at a nightclub. The scene finishes when they bring in a doped horse in full trappings. Special plaudits for the casting of all the minor parts. It's the standard Broadway yarn that Runyon told well and often; hard-hearted wise guys melt when they have to put aside their tough talk and show their true emotions. No one did it as well, before or since, as he did. For the record, the picture opened at New York's Paramount and, for under a buck, you could see this film as well as a stage show that featured Dave Apollon, Danzi Goodell, Diffin and Draper, Bob Rips, Nora Williams, Jean, Ruth and Gail, the Eight Debutantes, and Apollon's Hawaiian Band, household names all.

p, B. P. Schulberg; d, Alexander Hall; w, William R. Lipman, Sam Hellman, Gladys Lehman (based on the story by Damon Runyon); ph, Alfred Gilks; m, Ralph Rainger; ed, William Shea; m/l, Leo Robin, Ralph Rainger.

Comedy   **Cas.**   **(PR:AAA   MPAA:NR)**

LITTLE MISS MARKER* ½   (1980) 103m UNIV c

Walter Matthau (*Sorrowful Jones*), Julie Andrews (*Amanda*), Tony Curtis (*Blackie*), Bob Newhart (*Regret*), Lee Grant (*The Judge*), Sara Stimson (*The Kid*), Brian Dennehy (*Herbie*), Kenneth McMillan (*Brannigan*), Andrew Rubin (*Carter*), Joshua Shelley (*Benny*), Randy Herman (*Clerk*), Nedra Volz (*Mrs. Clancy*), Jacquelyn Hyde (*Lola*), Tom Pedi (*Vittorio*), Jessica Rains (*Clerk*), Henry Slate (*Teller*), Alvin Hammer (*Morris*), Don Bexley (*Sam*), Jack DeLeon (*Manager*), John P. Finnegan (*Clerk*), Ralph Manza, Jack Mullaney, Mark Anger, Lennie Bremen, Maurice Marks, Colin Gilbert, Wynn Irwin, Joseph Knowland, Stanley Lawrence, Louis Basile, Ed Ness, H. B. Newton, Stanley E. Ritchie, William Ackridge, Alan Thomason, Charles A. Venegas, Sharri Zak, Robert E. Ball, Simmy Bow, Jorge B. Cruz.

A stale, often-filmed remake of the 1934 Shirley Temple vehicle which in this version features Sara Stimson in Curly Top's role. The little tyke is left in the care of a stodgy bookie, Matthau, as a down payment for one of her father's bets. Matthau gets involved in some life-threatening situations with the sleazy Curtis, who is trying to open a casino in Andrews' mansion. Initially Matthau is annoyed by Stimson's presence, but he softens and grows fond of her before long. This is the directorial debut of screenwriter Bernstein. Other versions of the same story are the 1949 SORROWFUL JONES and 1963 40 POUNDS OF TROUBLE, which starred Tony Curtis.

p, Jennings Lang; d&w, Walter Bernstein (based on a story by Damon Runyon); ph, Philip Lathrop (Technicolor); m, Henry Mancini; ed, Eve Newman; prod d, Edward C. Carfagno; set d, Hal Gausman; cos, Ruth Morley.

Comedy   **Cas.**   **(PR:C   MPAA:PG)**

LITTLE MISS MOLLY**   (1940) 64m Alliance (GB: MY IRISH MOLLY)

Maureen O'Hara (*Eileen O'Shea*), Binkie Stuart (*Molly Martin*), Tom Burke (*Danny Gallagher*), Philip Reed (*Bob*), Maire O'Neill (*Mrs. O'Shea*), C. Denier Warren

(Chuck), Maureen Moore *(Hannah Delaney)*, Franklyn Kelsey *(Liam Delaney)*, Leo McCabe *(Corney)*, Paddy the Dog.

Stuart is a five-year-old orphan, mistreated by her aunt. However, she knows the secret of her father's will and who the money is to go to. Stuart keeps this information from her big sister O'Hara. She's in love with Reed, an American writer. The entire film is an inept Irish version of Cinderella, with Stuart trying desperately to sing and dance her way into your heart. But the kid is no Shirley Temple and her scenes look and sound awful. O'Hara and Reed are the real drawing cards here, overcoming the weak dialog and so-so direction to give some interest to the story.

p, John Argyle; d, Alex Bryce; w, Ian Walker, Bryce (based on a story by Argyle); ph, Ernest Palmer; ed, F. H. Bickerton.

Drama/Musical **(PR:A MPAA:NR)**

LITTLE MISS NOBODY** (1933, Brit.) 52m WB-FN/WB bw
Winna Winifried *(Karen Bergen)*, Sebastian Shaw *(Pat Carey)*, Betty Huntley Wright *(Tilly)*, Alice O'Day *(Mrs. Merridew)*, A. Bromley Davenport *(Mr. Romary)*, Drusilla Wills *(Birdie May)*, Ben Field *(Sam Brightwell)*, Ernest Sefton *(Mr. Morrison)*, Abraham Sofaer *(Mr. Beal)*.

A young Norwegian girl wants to become a movie star and will go to any length to achieve her goal. After meeting a gentleman who believes in her, a wild publicity stunt is concocted to gain her a studio contract. Standard hokum.

p, Irving Asher; d, John Daumery.

Comedy **(PR:A MPAA:NR)**

LITTLE MISS NOBODY*¹/₂ (1936) 65m FOX bw
Jane Withers *(Judy Devlin)*, Jane Darwell *(Martha Bradley)*, Ralph Morgan *(Gerald Dexter)*, Sara Haden *(Teresa Lewis)*, Harry Carey *(John Russell)*, Betty Jean Hainey *(Mary Dorsey)*, Thomas Jackson *(Dutch Miller)*, Jackie Morrow *(Junior Smythe)*, Jed Prouty *(Hector Smythe)*, Claudia Coleman *(Sybil Smythe)*, Donald Haines *(Harold Slade)*, Clarence H. Wilson *(Herman Slade)*, Lillian Harmer *(Jessica Taggert)*.

Child star Withers gets a shaky starring vehicle in this film. She plays a spirited and moralistic little girl who is a virtual prisoner in an orphanage. When she hears that an attorney is looking for his long lost daughter, Withers discovers that she is that child. In an effort to get another child adopted, Withers changes her papers with the girl, but she is discovered and reunited with her father.

p, Sol M. Wurtzel; d, John Blystone; w, Lou Breslow, Paul Burger, Edward Eliscu (based on a story by Frederick Hazlitt Brennan); ph, Bert Glennon; ed, Al DeGaetano; md, Samuel Kaylin; m/l, Jack Stern, Henry H. Tobias, Harry Tobias, Sidney Claire.

Comedy **(PR:AA MPAA:NR)**

LITTLE MISS ROUGHNECK* (1938) 64m COL bw
Edith Fellows *(Foxine LaRue)*, Leo Carrillo *(Pascual)*, Scott Colton *(Partridge)*, Jacqueline [Julie Bishop] Wells *(Mary)*, Margaret Irving *(Gert)*, Inez Palange *(Mercedes)*, George McKay *(Edwards)*, Thurston Hall *(Crowley)*, Frank C. Wilson *(DeWilde)*, John Gallaudet *(Larkin)*, Walter Stahl *(Von Hemmer)*, Ivan Miller *(Yerkes)*, Al Bridge *(Sheriff)*, Wade Boteler *(Carr)*, Guy Usher *(Dorn)*.

A backstage Hollywood comedy that stars Fellows as a would-be child star, pushed to the brink of failure by her pathetic stage mother, Irving. Colton is the talent scout, who becomes Fellows' agent to be close to her non-theatrical sister, Wells. Because of her mother's obnoxious behavior, Fellows is booted out of every major studio. Fellows devises a kidnap hoax for publicity, and when her story makes the front page she signs a deal for a seven-year contract . . . and a happy ending.

d, Aubrey Scotto; w, Fred Niblo, Jr., Grace Neville, Michael L. Simmons; ph, Benjamin Kline; ed, James Sweeney.

Comedy **(PR:AA MPAA:NR)**

LITTLE MISS SOMEBODY* (1937, Brit.) 78m Mondover/But bw
Binkie Stuart *(Binkie Sladen)*, John Longden *(Jim Trevor)*, Kathleen Kelly *(Mary Grey)*, Jane Carr *(Mrs. Borden)*, George Carney *(Angus Duncan)*, D. A. Clarke-Smith *(Mr. Borden)*, Margaret Emden *(Mrs. Peacher)*, Vivienne Chatterton *(Amelia Sparkes)*, C. Denier Warren *(Jonas)*, Hal Walters *(Albert Sims)*, J. Fisher White *(Tom Shirley)*, Ernest Sefton, Cynthia Stock, Roddy Hughes, Oliver Gordon.

Overly sentimentalized tear-jerker about an orphan girl forced to reside with the evil Carney so he can attempt to capitalize on the girl's future inheritance. Stuart, the girl, puts up enough of a battle to go back to the farm couple with whom she was so happy. A saccharine treatment.

p, Walter Tennyson, Alfred D'Eyncourt; d, Tennyson; w, H. Fowler Mear, Mary Dunn (based on the story by Tennyson); ph, Geoffrey Faithfull.

Drama **(PR:A MPAA:NR)**

LITTLE MISS THOROUGHBRED*¹/₂ (1938) 65m WB bw
John Litel *("Nails" Morgan)*, Ann Sheridan *(Madge Perry)*, Frank McHugh *(Todd Harrington)*, Janet Chapman *(Mary Ann)*, Eric Stanley *(Col. Whitcomb)*, Robert E. Homans *(Officer O'Reilly)*, Charles Wilson *(Dutch Fultz)*, John Ridgely *(Slug)*, Jean Benedict *(Sister Margaret)*, Maureen Rodin-Ryan *(Sister Patricia)*, Lottie Williams *(Mother Superior)*, James Nolan *(Interne)*, Cy Kendall *(District Attorney)*, Paul Everton *(Judge Stanhope)*, Dorothy Vaughn *(Mrs. O'Reilly)*.

The orphaned Chapman decides that her father is still alive and well and just needs to be discovered. And this is what the little tot sets out to do, much to the dismay of the nuns who have acted as her guardians. Her father never pops up, but she manages to get a substitute by stealing the heart of gambler Litel. A real tear-jerker

designed to tug at the audience's heartstrings, which it does but in a sickeningly sweet manner.

p, Bryan Foy; d, John Farrow; w, Albert DeMond, George Bricker (based on the story "Little Lady Luck" by DeMond); ph, L. William O'Connell; ed, Everett Dodd.

Drama **(PR:AA MPAA:NR)**

LITTLE MISTER JIM*¹/₂ (1946) 92m MGM bw
Jackie "Butch" Jenkins *(Little Jim Tukker)*, James Craig *(Capt. Big Jim Tukker)*, Frances Gifford *(Jean Tukker)*, Luana Patten *(Missey Choosey)*, Spring Byington *(Mrs. Starwell)*, Chingwah Lee *(Sui Jen)*, Laura La Plante *(Mrs. Glenson)*, Henry O'Neill *(Chaplain)*, Morris Ankrum *(Col. Starwell)*, Celia Travers *(Miss Martin)*, Ruth Brady *(Miss Hall)*, Sharon McManus *(Elsie)*, Buz Buckley *(Ronnie)*, Carol Nugent *(Clara)*, Jean Van *(Mary)*.

A tear-jerker about a poor little boy, Jenkins, who lives on an army base with his mother, Gifford, and officer father, Craig. The mother dies and the father, who cannot handle his loss, begins drinking and neglects Jenkins. Chinese servant Lee adds some Oriental philosophy making a sugary ending possible.

p, Orville O. Dull; d, Fred Zinnemann; w, George Bruce (based on the novel, *Army Brat*, by Tommy Wadelton); ph, Lester White; m, George Bassman; ed, Frank Hull; art d, Cedric Gibbons, Hubert Hobson.

Drama **(PR:A MPAA:NR)**

LITTLE MOTHER*¹/₂
(1973, U.S./Yugo./Ger.) 90m Peter Carstein Films-Jadran/Audubon c (AKA: BLOOD QUEEN)
Christiane Kruger *(Marina Pinares)*, Siegfried Rauch *(Col. Pinares)*, Ivan Desny *(Col. Umberia)*, Mark Damon *(Riano)*, Anton Diffring *(The Cardinal)*, Elga Sorbas *(Annette)*, Radley Metzger *(American Surgeon)*.

Using the Eva Peron legend as its basis, filmmaker Metzger managed to turn a pretty good story about political intrigue and a relentless urge for power into little more than suggestive pulp. Kruger plays the cancer-stricken woman who met her husband while she was a prostitute and aided his political career through her connections. Now that she is dying, she attempts to achieve canonization from the Catholic Church. But first she must get rid of people who know about her lowly beginnings as a prostitute. Flashbacks explain how Kruger helped enable her husband to become the uncontested ruler of the country. She used the bedroom to secure power, but the people still view her as a "saint." Kruger gives a performance that is the film's only redeeming feature, but the rest of the cast is incredibly flat, and overly concerned with what seems to be the main object of the picture: to tease sexually rather than an intriguing expose of political corruption. (In English.)

p&d, Radley Metzger; w, Brian Phelan; ph, Hans Jura (Eastmancolor); m, George Craig; ed, Amadeo Salfa.

Drama **(PR:O MPAA:R)**

LITTLE MURDERS*¹/₂** (1971) 110m FOX c
Elliott Gould *(Alfred Chamberlain)*, Marcia Rodd *(Patsy Newquist)*, Vincent Gardenia *(Mr. Newquist)*, Elizabeth Wilson *(Mrs. Newquist)*, Jon Korkes *(Kenny)*, John Randolph *(Mr. Chamberlain)*, Doris Roberts *(Mrs. Chamberlain)*, Donald Sutherland *(Minister)*, Lou Jacobi *(Judge)*, Alan Arkin *(Detective)*.

It flopped as a play in 1967 (with Gould, Barbara Cook, David Steinberg, Heywood Hale Broun, and Ruth White), then went to London where it was chosen as the first American play by the Royal Shakespeare Company and received the award as Best Foreign Play. Two years later, Arkin directed it successfully at New York's Circle In The Square with a cast that included Linda Lavin, Fred Williard, Vincent Gardenia, Jon Korkes and Elizabeth Wilson. At the time of the first production, it was looked upon as being surrealistic. Unfortunately, life has imitated art and, today, it is painfully accurate in many ways. In other words, the world has caught up with Feiffer's vision. This was Arkin's first, and perhaps his best, attempt at directing as he brought this black comedy to the screen and added some marvelous touches that were not evident in the stage version. It's early in the morning in a New York apartment. Rodd (in her first film) hears the unmistakable sounds of a man being mugged outside her bedroom. She can't get through to the police so she attempts to save the man and is mugged herself as the man, Gould, walks away unconcerned. She fights the hoods, then races after Gould as he walks into his photography studio. He calmly explains that he lives by the moral code of Apathy. He had once been a successful commercial photographer but now prefers to spend his time making films of excrement (a definite satire of Andy Warhol's choice of subjects). Despite his weirdness, Rodd thinks that Gould might make a good husband. Rodd is an incurable Pollyanna and thinks that the world will get better and that she would like to spend the rest of her days with Gould. She takes him home to meet the family and Gardenia thinks he's just another one of Rodd's gay friends. Wilson, in a role not unlike the dotty mother in YOU CAN'T TAKE IT WITH YOU, doesn't much care about what Gould does or his sexual proclivities, as long as he's a nice person and can become part of the family. Korkes is a closet gay and pays no attention to Gould. Rodd and Gould take a Catskills vacation together and her happy attitude overcomes Gould's ennui. He agrees to marry her, as long as it's a civil, rather than a religious, ceremony. The judge turns out to be hippie Sutherland and the wedding is a mad melange of his philosophy. Rodd convinces Gould to see his parents from whom he has been estranged. Randolph and Roberts welcome him and Gould is now happy in the thought that he has found, in Rodd, someone who loves him and will only do what's best for him. The happiness is shattered when Rodd is killed by a sniper in the apartment. Gould tries to get Arkin, the police detective, to help, but it's no use; there's just too much violence happening in the city to work on investigating one little murder. There are more than 300 unmotivated killings in the city and Arkin is a shivering mass of trembles due to them. Gardenia freaks out and begins screaming, Gould visits a local park and begins to take photographs of humans, rather than offal. He comes back to the apartment with a bouquet and a rifle and asks Gardenia and Korkes to join him at the window where they begin sniping at pedestrians. After all three have successfully killed an innocent victim, they sit down to a celebratory dinner and Wilson says she's so happy that her family is happy again. For a while, she was actually worried. LITTLE MURDERS was not a success the first time around as it was too bold for the sensibilities of the early 1970s. Today, it's right on the nose and a chilling example of Feiffer's prophecies. Gould, who also coproduced, was superb, and all of the other actors must take equal credit for the excellence of the movie. TV versions will edit some of the saltier language but there is enough left to realize that this, in its own way, is a classic film that must not be missed. Gould and Steinberg (who costarred in the play) have remained friends into the 1980s and Steinberg recently directed Gould in a cable version of "Casey At The Bat" in 1985. This picture, like Haut Brion or Chateau Lafite Rothschild, gets better as it ages. It was made in New York City with location shots at Kiamesha Lake, a resort area in the "Borscht Belt."

p, Jack Brodsky, Elliott Gould; d, Alan Arkin; w, Jules Feiffer (based on his play); ph, Gordon Willis (DeLuxe Color); m, Fred Kaz; ed, Howard Kuperman; prod d, Gene Rudolph; set d, Philip Smith; cos, Albert Wolsky; makeup, John Alese.

Satire **(PR:O MPAA:R)**

LITTLE NELLIE KELLY 1/2** (1940) 96m MGM bw

Judy Garland *(Nellie Kelly/Little Nellie Kelly)*, George Murphy *(Jerry Kelly)*, Charles Winninger *(Michael Noonan)*, Douglas McPhail *(Dennis Fogarty)*, Arthur Shields *(Timothy Fogarty)*, Rita Page *(Mary Fogarty)*, Forrester Harvey *(Moriarity)*, James Burke *(Sgt. McGowan)*, George Watts *(Keevan)*, John Raitt *(Intern)*, Pat O'Malley *(Mounted Cop)*.

Though it was only a year after THE WIZARD OF OZ, little Judy Garland had grown up some and was now playing an Irish wife to Murphy. After making the trip to New York, she dies in childbirth. The film skips ahead 20 years, where we see Garland playing Murphy's daughter. She falls in love with McPhail against the wishes of her father and grandfather (Winninger), but they eventually see things her way. The darling Garland does her best with the weak script, contributing her vocal talents to the following tunes: "Nellie Kelly I Love You" (George M. Cohan), "Nellie Is A Darling," "It's A Great Day For The Irish" (Roger Edens), "A Pretty Girl Milking Her Cow" (adapted by Edens), "Danny Boy," and a swing version of "Singing In The Rain" (Arthur Freed, Nacio Herb Brown). Reportedly, studio chief Louis B. Mayer was quite upset at the very thought of young Miss Garland playing the dual role of a girl and her mother, leaving the man to cry to anyone within earshot "We can't let that baby have a baby!"

p, Arthur Freed; d, Norman Taurog; w, Jack McGowan (based on the musical comedy by George M. Cohan); ph, Ray June; m, Roger Edens; ed, Frederick Y. Smith; md, Georgie Stoll; art d, Cecric Gibbons; set d, Edwin B. Willis; cos, Dolly Tree, Gile Steele; makeup, Jack Dawn.

Musical **(PR:A MPAA:NR)**

LITTLE NIGHT MUSIC, A** (1977, Aust./U.S./Ger.) 124m New World c

Elizabeth Taylor *(Desiree Armfeldt)*, Diana Rigg *(Charlotte Mittelheim)*, Len Cariou *(Frederick Egerman)*, Lesley-Anne Down *(Anne Egerman)*, Hermione Gingold *(Mme. Armfeldt)*, Laurence Guittard *(Carl-Magnus Mittelheim)*, Christopher Guard *(Erich Egerman)*, Chloe Franks *(Fredericka Armfeldt)*, Heinz Maracek *(Kurt)*, Lesley Dunlop *(Petra)*, Jonathan Tunick *(Conductor)*, Hubert Tscheppe *(Franz)*, Rudolf Schrympf *(Band Conductor)*, Franz Schussler *(Mayor)*, Johanna Schussler *(Mayoress)*, Jean Sincere *(Box Office Lady)*, Dagmar Koller *(1st Lady)*, Ruth Brinkman *(2nd Lady)*, Anna Veigl *(Concierge)*, Stefan Paryla *(Uniformed Sergeant)*, Eva Dvorska *(1st Whore)*, Lisa De Cohen *(2nd Whore)*, Kurt Martynow *(Major Domo)*, Gerty Barek *(Cook)*, James De Graot *(Footman)*.

An uninspired screen version of Steven Sondheim's stage play, which in turn was based on Ingmar Bergman's SMILES OF A SUMMER NIGHT. It has nothing in common with Bergman's picture except the basic premise: that of a group of people meeting for dinner at a country estate. Those on the guest list include Taylor, a lively actress who wants to settle down; Cariou a newly married lawyer who had a past fling with Taylor; Down, his 18-year-old virgin bride; and Rigg, the wife of Taylor's current lover, Guittard. Prince, the stage director of Sondheim's play, cannot handle the screen version, and fails to build any of the pace that the play had on Broadway. Songs include: "Send In The Clowns," "Every Day A Little Death," "The Glamorous Life," "Love Takes Time," "Now," "You Must Meet My Wife," "Soon," "Later," and "A Weekend In the Country" (Stephen Sondheim).

p, Elliott Kastner; d, Harold Prince; w, Hugh Wheeler (based on the musical play by Stephen Sondheim, Wheeler and suggested by the film SMILES OF A SUMMER NIGHT by Ingmar Bergman), ph, Arthur Ibbetson (Eastmancolor); ed, John Jympson; prod d, Laci von Ronay; md, Paul Gemignani; art d, Herta Pischinger, Thomas Riccabona; cos, Florence Klotz; ch, Patricia Birch.

Musical **Cas.** **(PR:C MPAA:PG)**

LITTLE NUNS, THE 1/2**
(1965, Ital.) 100m Hesperia/EM bw (LE MONACHINE)

Catherine Spaak *(Sister Celeste)*, Sylva Koscina *(Elena)*, Amedeo Nazzari *(Livio Bertana)*, Didi Perego *(Mother Rachele)*, Umberto D'Orsi *(Spugna)*, Sandro Bruni *(Damiano, the Orphan)*, Annie Gorassini *(Bertana's Secretary)*, Alberto Bonucci *(Mr. Batistucchi)*, Lando Buzzanca.

A charming Italian comedy which begins in a tiny village which has a problem with commercial jets flying overhead. It seems the jets' sound waves are destroying the town convent's ancient fresco of St. Domitilla. The Mother Superior, Perego, and a naive nun, Spaak, set out for Rome to speak with the airline owner. Stowing away on the trip is a curious orphan, Bruni. Intent upon their mission, the nuns accomplish much more than they had planned, saving the airline owner's job and securing a wife for him in the process. (Dubbed in English.)

p, Ferruccio Brusarosco; d, Luciano Salce; w, Franco Castellano, Giuseppe Moccia; ph, Erico Menczer; m, Ennio Morricone; ed, Roberto Cinquini; md, Morricone; prod d, Gianni Minervini; set d, Aurelio Crugnola; cos, Giuliano Papi.

Comedy **(PR:A MPAA:NR)**

LITTLE OF WHAT YOU FANCY, A* 1/2 (1968, Brit.) 75m Border c

Mark Eden, Helen Shapiro, Barry Cryer, Sheila Bernette, Sidney Bromley, Mary King, Terry Day, John Rutland.

A tour down memory lane is delivered through an abundance of music, aimed at evoking a sense of the history that surrounds the British music hall. There's almost no plot in this slight showcase of some little-known musical talents.

p, O. Negus-Fancey; d, Robert Webb; w, Ray Mackender.

Musical **(PR:A MPAA:NR)**

LITTLE OLD NEW YORK 1/2** (1940) 99m FOX bw

Alice Faye *(Pat O'Day)*, Fred MacMurray *(Charles Browne)*, Richard Greene *(Robert Fulton)*, Brenda Joyce *(Harriet Livingstone)*, Andy Devine *(Commodore)*, Henry Stephenson *(Chancellor Livingstone)*, Fritz Feld *(Tavern Keeper)*, Ward Bond *(Regan)*, Clarence Hummel Wilson *(Stout)*, Robert Middlemass *(Nicholas Roosevelt)*, Roger Imhof *(John Jacob Astor)*, Theodor von Eltz *(Washington Irving)*, Virginia Brissac *(Mrs. Brevoort)*, Ben Carter *(Noah)*, O. G. Hendrian *(Blackie)*, Victor Kilian *(DeWitt)*, Jody Gilbert *(Hilda)*, Arthur Aylesworth *(Sea Captain)*, Stanley Andrews *(Patrol Captain)*, Harry Tyler *(Helmsman)*, Paul Sutton *(Wolf)*, Tyler Brooke *(Singer)*, Herbert Ashley *(Ticket Taker), Herbert Heywood (Horace)*, Maj. James H. McNamara *(Banker)*, Marion Briscoe *(Banker's Wife)*, Chick Collins *(Captain)*, Harry Strang *(Fireman)*, Pat Hartigan *(Regan's Henchman)*, Herbert Evans *(Footman)*, Keith Hitchcock *(Butler)*, Jessie Arnold *(Woman)*, Iva Stewart *(Mrs. Irving)*.

LITTLE OLD NEW YORK is not much more than a romantic comedy history lesson that would have benefited greatly if the film had been a musical. Greene is Robert Fulton and he arrives in New York in 1807 after having made several experiments of his theories in France. He moves into a tavern run by Alice Faye, then calls upon Stephenson, the Chancellor, to help him secure financing for his steamboat. Fay's boyfriend, MacMurray, is a sailor and jealous of the attention Faye showers on Greene, but that's temporarily set aside when Greene falls for Stephenson's niece, Joyce. With that out of the way, MacMurray helps Greene in building the boat but a group of sailors think that the new form of transportation will put them out of work so they burn the ship. Bond is the leader of the gang and is thrilled when the ship is left a smoldering ruin. Stephenson stops donating money so Faye rallies some of her friends and they raise the cash. She does this by buying booze from supplier Wilson on credit, then selling the stuff to her competitors for less than what she's promised to pay back. She thinks Greene is in love with her and MacMurray is again miffed and refuses to work on the construction. Faye prevails on him and he agrees but he and Greene look daggers at each other. An embargo against foreign goods is signed and Bond works for the harbor patrol in keeping the British materials from the city, but Greene and MacMurray sail out to sea under fog and darkness cover to secure the steam engine from a waiting British ship. The engine is placed in Fulton's boat and everyone in New York is there to see "Fulton's Folly," but the steamship works, much to their surprise. Faye finally understands that Greene loves Joyce so she abandons her infatuation and will marry MacMurray. This had been a silent movie with Marion Davies in 1923 and the clunkiness of the dialog leads one to believe that it might have been better left silent.

p, Darryl F. Zanuck; d, Henry King; w, Harry Tugend (based on the story by John Balderson); ph, Leon Shamroy; m, Alfred Newman; ed, Barbara MacLean; art d, Richard Day, Rudolph Sternad, James Havens; set d, Thomas Little; cos, Royer; spec eff, Fred Sersen; m/l, "Who Is the Beau of the Belle of New York?" Mack Gordon.

Comedy **(PR:A MPAA:NR)**

LITTLE ONES, THE** (1965, Brit.) 66m Goldhawk/COL bw

Carl Gonzales *(Jackie)*, Kim Smith *(Ted)*, Dudley Foster *(Insp. Carter)*, Derek Newark *(Detective Sgt. Wilson)*, Jean Marlow *(Ted's Mum)*, Peter Thomas *(Ted's Dad)*, Derek Francis *(Paddy)*, Cyril Shaps *(Child Welfare Officer)*, John Chandos *(Lord Brantley)*, Diane Aubrey *(Peggy)*, George Betton, Tom Crossman, Norman Mitchell, Michael McKenzie, Anne Padwick, Bob Payne, Anthony Wager, Gillian Hayes, Harry Goodier, Valerie Jayne, Ken Jones.

Two London lads—Smith, a white child who is abused at home, and Gonzales, a neglected child whose prostitute mother ignores him— attempt to flee their unhappy surroundings. The two decide to stow away on a ship bound for Jamaica where Gonzales' father supposedly lives. To get some cash, they steal a suitcase from a Rolls Royce belonging to a shipping tycoon, but are soon apprehended, given a lecture and sent home. However, they are told that there are always ships leaving for Jamaica which gives them some hope of escape. Background music is played by The Turnkeys.

p, Freddie Robertson; d&w, Jim O'Connolly; ph, David Holmes; m, Robertson; ed, Henry Richardson; md, Malcolm Lockyer; art d, Derek Barrington; set d, Arthur Fell; cos, Ernie Farrer; makeup, Harry Webber.

Children's Drama **(PR:AA MPAA:NR)**

LITTLE ORPHAN ANNIE** (1932) 60m RKO bw

Mitzi Green *(Annie)*, Buster Phelps *(Mickey)*, May Robson *(Mrs. Stewart)*, Kate Lawson *(Mrs. Burgin)*, Matt Moore *(Dr. Griffith)*, Edgar Kennedy *(Daddy Warbucks)*, Sidney Bracey *(Butler)*.

"Leapin' lizards!," this harmless picture, based on the famous comic strip of the same name, is the story of a winsome little girl, Green, who is deserted by her poor father. She hangs around with fellow orphan Phelps and the pair end up in an orphanage which, of course, is full of adventure. Phelps soon is adopted by a wealthy old woman, Robson, and Green happily ends up with Kennedy.

d, John Robertson; w, Wanda Tuchock, Tom McNamara (based on the comic strip of Harold Gray, Al Lowenthal); ph, Jack McKenzie.

Children's Drama   **(PR:AAA MPAA:NR)**

LITTLE ORPHAN ANNIE*   (1938) 57m Colonial/PAR bw

Ann Gillis (*Annie*), Robert Kent (*Johnny Adams*), June Travis (*Mary Ellen*), J. Farrell MacDonald (*Pop Corrigan*), J.M. Kerrigan (*Tom Jennings*), Sarah Padden (*Mrs. Moriarity*), James Burke (*Mike Moriarity*), Ian MacLaren (*Soo Long*), Margaret Armstrong (*Mrs. Jennings*), Dorothy Vaughn (*Mrs. Milligan*), Ben Welden (*Spot McGee*).

A mindless screen adaptation of the popular cartoon character with Gillis weakly portraying Annie. She meets Kent, a one-time boxing champ who now lives in a tenement building. She persuades his neighbors to help defray his training expenses, and thereby sharing the profits when he wins the big fight. A group of gangsters do not like the idea, however, and lock Kent in the gym before the fight. He gets out in the nick of time and wins with a knockout.

p, John Speaks; d, Ben Holmes; w, Budd Schulberg, Samuel Ornitz (based on a story by Ornitz, Endre Bohem from the comic strip by Harold Gray, Al Lowenthal); ph, Frank Redman; ed, Robert Bischoff; md, Lou Forbes; art d, Feild Gray.

Children's Drama   **(PR:A MPAA:NR)**

LITTLE ORVIE*¹/₂   (1940) 65m RKO bw

John Sheffield (*Orvie Stone*), Ernest Truex (*Frank Stone*), Dorothy Tree (*Clara Stone*), Ann Todd (*Patsy Balliser*), Emma Dunn (*Mrs. Welty*), Daisy Mothershed (*Corbina*), Fay Helm (*Mrs. Balliser*), Virginia Brissac (*Mrs. Green*), Paul Burns (*Grocer*), Del Henderson (*Mr. Brown*), Fern Emmett (*Mrs. Jackson*), Edgar Dearing (*Policeman*), Ray Turner (*Jefferson*).

Small town Indiana kid Sheffield is told he cannot have a dog, but when he finds a stray and keeps it for a day, he cannot seem to get rid of it. Sheffield bends the will of his mother and father, Tree and Truex, until things work out his way.

p, William Sistrom; d, Ray McCarey; w, Lynn Root, Frank Fenton, Robert Chapin (based on the novel *Little Orvie* by Booth Tarkington); ph, Roy Hunt; ed, Theron Warth.

Children's Drama   **(PR:AA MPAA:NR)**

LITTLE PRINCE, THE**   (1974, Brit.) 88m PAR c

Richard Kiley (*The Pilot*), Steven Warner (*The Little Prince*), Bob Fosse (*The Snake*), Gene Wilder (*The Fox*), Joss Ackland (*The King*), Clive Revill (*The Businessman*), Victor Spinetti (*The Historian*), Graham Crowden (*The General*), Donna McKechnie (*The Rose*).

A disappointing adaptation of the internationally known fable by Antoine de Saint-Exupery, brought to the screen by a group that reads like a who's who of musicals. Unfortunately, this supergroup misses the mark, turning out a visually exciting piece of fluff which fails on almost all other levels. Warner is the title character, a philosophical space inhabitant who shares his experiences with pilot Kiley while he is grounded in the desert. Besides Fosse, whose superbly self-choreographed "snake in the grass" sequence is a film highlight, the supporting players lack the necessary spark. It could have been great, but instead it's forgettable. Songs include: "It's A Hat," "I Need Air," "I'm On Your Side," "Be Happy," "You're A Child," "I Never Met A Rose," "Why Is The Desert (Lovely To See)?," "Closer and Closer And Closer," "Little Prince (From Who Knows Where)" (Frederick Loewe, Alan Jay Lerner).

p&d Stanley Donen; w, Alan Jay Lerner (based on the children's novel by Antoine de Saint-Exupery); ph, Christopher Challis (Technicolor); m, Frederick Loewe; ed, Peter Boita, John Guthridge; prod d, John Barry; art d, Norman Reynolds; cos, Shirley Russell, Tim Goodchild; ch, Ronn Forella, Bob Fosse.

Musical   **Cas.**   **(PR:AAA MPAA:G)**

LITTLE PRINCESS, THE*¹/₂**   (1939) 91m FOX c

Shirley Temple (*Sara Crewe*), Richard Greene (*Geoffrey Hamilton*), Anita Louise (*Rose*), Ian Hunter (*Capt. Crewe*), Cesar Romero (*Ram Dass*), Arthur Treacher (*Bertie Minchin*), Mary Nash (*Amanda Minchin*), Sybil Jason (*Becky*), Miles Mander (*Lord Wickham*), Marcia Mae Jones (*Lavinia*), Beryl Mercer (*Queen Victoria*), Deidre Gale (*Jessie*), Ira Stevens (*Ermengarde*), E.E. Clive (*Mr. Barrows*), Keith Kenneth (*Bobbie*), Will Stanton and Harry Allen (*Grooms*), Holmes Herbert, Evan Thomas, Guy Bellis (*Doctors*), Kenneth Hunter (*General*), Lionel Braham (*Colonel*), Eily Malyon (*Cook*), Clyde Cook (*Attendant*), Olaf Hytten (*Man*), Rita Page (*Girl*).

This top-flight Shirley Temple charmer has the lovable moppet off to boarding school after the reported death of her father, killed in the Boer War. She is severely mistreated by the wicked Nash, but gets away long enough to search the military hospitals for her dad (Hunter). She finds him, but discovers that he has amnesia. The sight of his long-lost daugher, however, brings him around. This is the sort of film that made Temple a legend.

p, Darryl F. Zanuck; d, Walter Lang; w, Ethel Hill, Walter Ferris (based on the novel *The Fantasy* by Frances Hodgson Burnett); ph, Arthur Miller, William Skall (Technicolor); m, Walter Bullock, Samuel Pokrass; ed, Louis Loeffler; md, Louis Silvers; art d, Bernard Herzbrun, Hans Peters; m/l, Walter Bullock, Samuel Pokrass.

Drama/Musical   **Cas.**   **(PR:AAA MPAA:NR)**

LITTLE RED MONKEY   (SEE: CASE OF THE RED MONKEY, 1954, Brit.)

LITTLE RED RIDING HOOD*¹/₂**   (1963, Mex.) 85m Peliculas Rodriguez/Murray Productions c (LA CAPERUCITA ROJA)

Maria Gracia, Manuel Valdes, Rafael Munoz, Beatriz Aguirre, Guillermo Alvarez Bianchi, Prudencia Griffel, Irma Torres, Santanon.

Mexican film version of the famous fairy tale filmed and released in Mexico in 1960, but not distributed in the U.S. until 1963. It spawned two sequels: LITTLE RED RIDING HOOD AND THE MONSTERS and LITTLE RED RIDING HOOD AND HER FRIENDS. (In English.)

p, K. Gordon Murray; d, Roberto Rodriguez; w, Fernando Morales Ortiz, Ricardo Garibay, Rafael Garcia Travesi (based on the story "Le petit Chaperon rouge" from *Recueil de Pieces Curieuses et Nouvelles*, by Charles Perrault); ph, Alex Phillips (Eastmancolor); m Sergio Guerrero; ed, Jose Bustos; set d, Edward Fitzgerald.

Fantasy   **(PR:A MPAA:NR)**

LITTLE RED RIDING HOOD AND HER FRIENDS**   (1964, Mex.) 90m Peliculas Rodriguez/K. Gordon Murray Productions c (CAPERUCITA Y SUS TRES AMIGOS; AKA: LITTLE RED RIDING HOOD AND HER THREE FRIENDS)

Manuel Valdes (*The Wolf*), Maria Gracia (*Little Red Riding Hood*), Santanon (*The Fox*), Consuelo Guerrero de Luna, Alfredo Vergara, Luis Manuel Pelayo, Beatriz Aguirre, Prudencia Griffel, Eduardo Alcaraz, Guillermo Alvarez Bianchi, Armando Lujan, Enrique Edwards, Edmundo Espino, Leticia Roo, Roberto Meyer, Elvira Lodi.

The second in the Mexican LITTLE RED RIDING HOOD series, this film sees Gracia and her friends—the wolf, the fox, and the dog—going on various adventures, including a run-in with gypsies and an encounter with a fairy princess in her enchanted kingdom. (In English.)

p, K. Gordon Murray; d, Roberto Rodriguez; w, Rodriguez, Rafael A. Perez (based on a story by Rodriguez); ph, Jose Ortiz Ramos (Eastmancolor); m, Sergio Guerrero; ed, Jose Bustos; set d, Gunther Gerszo.

Fantasy   **(PR:A MPAA:NR)**

LITTLE RED RIDING HOOD AND THE MONSTERS**   (1965, Mex.) 82m Peliculas Rodriguez/K. Gordon Murray Productions c (CAPERUCITA Y PULGARCITO CONTRA LOS MONSTRUOS)

Maria Gracia (*Little Red Riding Hood*), Jose Elias Moreno, Manuel Valdes, Cesareo Quesada, Ofelia Guilmain, Quintin Bulnes, Santanon, Magda Donato, Armando Gutierrez.

The third and strangest of the LITTLE RED RIDING HOOD series sees Gracia, Tom Thumb, and various animal friends doing battle with a bad witch, a vampire, and other monsters in a haunted forest. (In English.)

p, K. Gordon Murray; d, Roberto Rodriguez, Manuel San Fernando; w, Fernando Morales Ortiz, Adolfo Torres Portillo, Rodriguez, Sergio Magana; ph, Rosalio Solano (Eastmancolor); m, Raul Lavista; ed, Jose Bustos; set d, Roberto Silva; m/l, Ortiz.

Fantasy   **(PR:C MPAA:NR)**

LITTLE RED SCHOOLHOUSE*¹/₂**   (1936) 66m CHES bw

Frank "Junior" Coghlan, Jr. (*Frank Burke*), Dickie Moore (*Dickie Burke*), Ann Doran (*Mary Burke*), Lloyd Hughes (*Roger Owen*), Richard Carle (*The Professor*), Ralf Harolde (*Pete Scardoni*), Frank Sheridan (*Warden Gail*), Matthew Betz (*Bill*), Kenneth Howell (*Schuyler Tree*), Sidney Miller (*Sidney Levy*), Gloria Browne (*Shirley*), Don Brodie (*Ed*), Lou Davis (*Mac*), Corky the Dog.

Coghlan is a teenaged student who attends the title organization of lower learning, being taught more about practical jokes than multiplication. He leaves for the big city, where he soon gets mixed up with a gang of delinquents and winds up in reform school. It takes the efforts of a lovebird pair of schoolteachers to set him straight. Moore shines above the rest of the cast in this uneventful, poorly written picture.

p, George R. Batcheller; d, Charles Lamont; w, Paul Perez; ph, M. A. Anderson; ed, Rowland Reed.

Drama   **(PR:AA MPAA:NR)**

LITTLE ROMANCE, A**   (1979, U.S./Fr.) 108m Pan Arts-Trinacra/Orion c

Laurence Olivier (*Julius*), Diane Lane (*Lauren*), Thelonious Bernard (*Daniel*), Arthur Hill (*Richard King*), Sally Kellerman (*Kay King*), Broderick Crawford (*Brod*), David Dukes (*George de Marco*), Andrew Duncan (*Bob Duryea*), Claudette Sutherland (*Janet Duryea*), Graham Fletcher-Cook (*Londet*), Ashby Semple (*Natalie*), Claude Brosset (*Michel Michon*), Jacques Maury (*Insp. Leclerc*), Anna Massey (*Mrs. Siegel*), Peter Maloney (*Martin*), Dominique Lavanant (*Mme. Corier*), Mike Marshall (*1st Assistant Director*), Michel Bardinet (*French Ambassador*), Alain David Gabison (*French Representative*), Isabelle Duby (*Monique*), Jeffrey Carey (*Makeup Man*), John Pepper (*2nd Assistant Director*), Denise Glaser (*Woman Critic*), Jeanne Herviale (*Woman In Metro*), Carlo Lastricati (*Tour Guide*), Judy Mullen (*Secretary*), Philippe Briguad (*Theater Manager*), Lucienne Legrand (*Cashier*).

Defining the word "charming," this teenage romantic comedy tells the innocent tale of a pair of 13-year-olds who fall in love in France. Lane (in her first and best role) is living in Paris with her capitalist stepfather (Hill) and her floozy mother (Kellerman). While visiting the set of a movie production directed by Kellerman's budding love interest (Dukes), Lane meets Bernard. Bernard is a lower-class youngster with a system for playing the horses and a fascination with both Robert Redford (he steals lobby cards from BUTCH CASSIDY AND THE SUNDANCE KID, another George Roy Hill picture) and Humphrey Bogart. With Lane's character being named Lauren, Bernard has endless chances to play Bogie to her

Bacall. The two grow attached to each other when they discover they both have extremely high IQ's and interests in philosophy, facets of themselves which they are usually too embarrassed to admit. They soon meet Olivier, giving a gloriously hammed-up performance as a friendly old scoundrel. He tells them tall tales of his widowed ex-wife, his love for Elizabeth Barrett Browning, and a legend that if two lovers kiss under Venice's Bridge of Sighs in a gondola at sunset when the bells toll, their love will last forever. Lane falls in love with the legend and with Bernard. At a combination birthday party for Lane, and "rap party" for the film crew, Dukes, the obnoxious director, crudely insults Bernard and Lane, and ends up with the youngster punching him. Bernard promptly gets himself kicked out of the party by a furious Kellerman, who forbids her daughter to ever speak to him again. The young lovers decide to run away to Venice when Lane hears the news that her father accepted a transfer to the States. Bernard tries his luck at the Longchamps racetrack, ending up with enough cash to take a train to Venice. In order to cross the Italian border they bring Olivier along as their guardian, under the ruse that Lane's sick mother is staying there. Lane's plans get mixed up when she forgets to warn her friend (Semple, in a lovable role) not to call her house, inadvertently leading her parents to believe she was kidnaped. The police soon discover that she is traveling with Olivier, who is identified as a well-known pickpocket. Olivier soon realizes that the police are on a manhunt for the trio, and he is angry that he is now wanted for kidnaping. Lane and Bernard nearly give up their goal when Olivier tells them that the legend was his invention created "to bring a little romance" into his life. Bernard and Lane try even harder to get to a gondola by sunset, hiding out in a moviehouse (again a Hill picture, THE STING), while Olivier turns himself in. Every character is developed to the fullest, especially Arthur Hill as the jealous husband who respects Bernard's convictions and his stepdaughter's nonconformity. Crawford, playing himself, serves as one of the picture's highlights. His brightest scene occurs directly after Bernard punches Dukes, when the youngster compares his own right hook to Crawford's in SIN TOWN, in which he smacks Ward Bond. Crawford, his memory failing him, insists that it was Richard Widmark he connected with. Bernard is correct, however, when he informs Crawford that he never made a picture with Widmark. The unfaltering performances are complemented by Delerue's Oscar-winning score. Orion Picture's first release.

p, Robert L. Crawford, Yves Rousset-Rouard, d, George Roy Hill; w, Allan Burns (based on the novel $E = MC^2$, *Mon Amour* by Patrick Cauvin); ph, Pierre William Glenn (Panavision, Technicolor); m, Georges Delerue; ed, William Reynolds; prod d, Henry Bumstead; art d, Francois De Lamothe; cos, Rosine Delamare.

Romance/Comedy   **Cas.**   **(PR:A   MPAA:PG)**

LITTLE SAVAGE, THE**   (1959) 73m FOX c

Pedro Armendariz (*Capt. Tiburon*), Rodolfo Hoyos (*Taursus*), Terry Rangno (*Frank as a Boy*), Christiane Martel (*Nanoa*), Robert Palmer (*Frank as a Man*).

Set on a Caribbean island in the 1700s, this adventure tale will turn on more kids than adults. Young Rangno helps Armendariz get back on his feet after the pirate is left for dead by his ungrateful captain (Hoyos). Armendariz, who had come to the island to bury a couple of treasure chests, becomes friends with the youngster who grows to manhood during the course of the film (Palmer plays the boy as an adult). When Hoyos returns 10 years later, the two pirates die in a shootout, leaving Palmer with the treasure and a native girl friend.

p, Jack Leewood; d, Byron Haskin; w, Eric Norden (based on the novel by Frederick Marryat); ph, George Stahl, Jr. (CinemaScope, DeLuxe Color); m, Paul Lavista; ed, Albert E. Valenzuela; art d, John Mansbridge, Ramon Rodriguez.

Adventure   **(PR:A   MPAA:NR)**

LITTLE SEX, A*   (1982) 94m MTM Enterprises/UNIV c

Tim Matheson (*Michael Donovan*), Kate Capshaw (*Katherine*), Edward Herrmann (*Tommy*), John Glover (*Walter*), Joan Copeland (*Mrs. Harrison*), Susanna Dalton (*Nancy Barwood*), Wendie Malick (*Philomena*), Wallace Shawn (*Oliver*), Betsy Aidem (*Passerby*), Sharon Bamber (*Theresa Donovan*), Tanya Berezin (*Joyce*), Michael Bias (*Wedding Photographer*), Kim von Brandenstein (*Bubble Girl*), Barbara Bratt (*Office Girl*), Christy Brown (*Mindy*), Robert Burr (*Joe Donovan*), Melinda Culea (*Betty*), Leigh Curran (*Marie Donovan*), Lisa Dunsheath (*Lucy*), Frankie Faison (*Electrician*), Sara Felcher (*Old Lady*), Sharon Foote (*Salesgirl*), Donna R. Fowler, Jennine Marie Gourine, Sam Gray, James Greene, Delphi Harrington, Frances Helm, Carolyn Houlihan, Elva Josephson, Wayne Kell, Ann Lange, Sagan Lewis, Renee Lippin, Merry Lommis, Jim Lovelett, J. Frank Lucas, Ron Maccone, P.J. Mann, Winston May, Patricia Mertens, Joshua Michaels, Sharron Miller, Linda G. Miller, Carolyn Perry, Nick Petron, Don Philips, Isabel Price, Kathleen Purrman, Eric Ratcliff, Mary Ritter, Janine Robbins, Lauren Sautner, Sara Schedeen, Carol Lee Shahid, Bill Smitrovich, Kimberly Stern, Alex Stevens, Melanie Strauss, John Tillinger, Victoria Vanderkloot, Chris Westwood, David Wilkins.

The first feature from television's MTM Enterprises is so full of cliches it's pathetic, amounting to nothing more than a made-for-TV movie with the title ingredient thrown in. Matheson's life is unfulfilled as a director of TV commercials, though he's a big hit with the girls. He decides he's had enough and marries his live-in love of 10 months. He soon gets bored, has an affair, gets caught, his girlfriend gets mad, leaves him, etc. One can't help thinking his girlfriend (Capshaw, who would later star in INDIANA JONES AND THE TEMPLE OF DOOM, in her full screen debut) gets everything she deserves, considering her lousy husband was cheating on her for the 10 months that they lived together. What did she expect after the wedding, Andy Hardy?

p, Robert DeLaurentis, Bruce Paltrow; d, Paltrow; w, DeLaurentis; ph, Ralf D. Bode (Panavision, Technicolor); m, Georges Delerue; ed, Bill Butler; prod d, Stephen Hendrickson; cos, Patrizia von Brandenstein.

Comedy   **Cas.**   **(PR:O   MPAA:R)**

LITTLE SHEPHERD OF KINGDOM COME** 1/2

(1961) 108m Associated/FOX c

Jimmie Rodgers (*Chad*), Luana Patten (*Melissa Turner*), Chill Wills (*Major Buford*), Linda Hutchins (*Margaret Dean*), Robert Dix (*Caleb Turner*), George Kennedy (*Nathan Dillon*), Kenny Miller (*Reuben*), Neil Hamilton (*General Dean*), Shirley O'Hara (*Mrs. Turner*), Lois January (*Mrs. Dean*), John Holland, Edward Faulkner, Russ Bender, Morris Ankrum, Nelson Leigh, Lane Chandler, Diana Darrin, Dan Simmons, Glen Marshall, Helen Scott, Ollie O'Toole, I. Stanford Jolley, Don Giovanni, Jerry Summers, Glen Walters.

Rodgers plays an orphaned Kentucky teenager who flees the home of his brutal guardian and eventually winds up in the town of Kingdom Come and at the home of kindly schoolteacher Dix and his family. He soon falls in love with Dix's daughter Patten, but their romance is interrupted by the Civil War in which Rodgers volunteers to fight (he joins the Union side). After the war, much more mature and wiser, Rodgers returns to build a future with Patten. Pleasant without being too maudlin.

p, Maury Dexter; d, Andrew V. McLaglen; w, Barre Lyndon (based on the novel by John Fox, Jr.); ph, Floyd Crosby (CinemaScope, Deluxe Color); m, Henry Vars; ed, Jodie Copelan, Carl Pierson; md, Vars; art d, John Mansbridge; set d, Joseph Kish; m/l, "When Love Is Young," "The Little Shepherd of Kingdom Come," by Dunham, Vars (sung by Jimmie Rodgers).

Drama   **(PR:A   MPAA:NR)**

LITTLE SHOP OF HORRORS***   (1961) 70m Filmgroup bw

Jonathan Haze (*Seymour Krelboin*), Jackie Joseph (*Audrey*), Mel Welles (*Gravis Mushnik*), Jack Nicholson (*Wilbur Force*), Dick Miller (*Fouch*), Myrtle Vail (*Winifred Krelboin*), Leola Wendorff (*Mrs. Shiva*).

Roger Corman's super-low budget cult favorite which also happens to be one of the funniest black comedies ever made. The plot details the sorry existence of dim-witted schlep Haze who works in Welles' Skid Row flower shop. To impress his girl, Joseph, Haze invents a carnivorous little flower which he names Audrey Jr. (after his girlfriend). Soon Haze's flower is all the rage among the chlorophyll critics and botanists alike. The only problem is, the little flower needs human blood to grow. After discovering this gruesome detail, *and* the fact that the plant can talk (everytime it's hungry it yells "Feed Me!") Haze becomes slowly possessed by the flora and commits several murders in order to stop his plant's tummy from growling. Along with these feedings come rapid growth by the plant and soon it overgrows the whole flower shop bellowing "Feeeed Meee!" in a monstrously loud and obnoxious voice. In the end, Haze decides enough is enough and jumps into his plant wielding a knife, killing himself and his creation. While not very funny reading, LITTLE SHOP OF HORRORS is a hilarious (and yes, quite silly) film filled to the brim with enough little vignettes and character quirks to sustain laughter throughout its brief 70 minute running time. Shot in two days on a dare by Roger Corman who was challenged by a studio employee to come up with a script and shoot a movie in the brief time left before the storefront set was torn down (it was left standing from another production), LITTLE SHOP OF HORRORS is surprisingly well shot and performed. Corman contacted screenwriter Chuck Griffith from his other camp hit A BUCKET OF BLOOD and together they hacked out the killer plant story in less than a week. Aided by on-the-set inspiration, Corman and his cast and crew (including a very young Jack Nicholson in a side-splitting cameo as a masochistic dental patient begging for more pain) threw together a small masterpiece of taut, economical filmmaking in the space of two days and one night that has passed the test of time and has even been revived as a very successful off-broadway musical in the 1980s (a film version of the musical has been announced).

p&d, Roger Corman; w, Charles B. Griffith; ph, Archie Dalzell; m, Fred Katz; ed, Marshall Neilan Jr.; art d, Daniel Haller.

Comedy/Horror   **Cas.**   **(PR:C-O   MPAA:NR)**

LITTLE SISTER   (SEE: MARLOWE, 1969)

LITTLE SOLDIER, THE   (SEE: LE PETIT SOLDAT, 1965, Fr.)

LITTLE STRANGER*   (1934, Brit.) 51m MGM bw

Nigel Playfair (*Sam Collins*), Eva Moore (*Jessie Collins*), Norah Baring (*Millie Dent*), Hamilton Keene (*Tom Hale*).

After unmarried and pregnant Baring moves into a boarding house owned by Moore, she finds friendship with her landlady's husband Playfair. Baring later dies giving birth, leaving her child an orphan. This film wrings every last bit of emotional sap from the tear-jerking story as Playfair tells his wife the child is a foundling. The couple, to no one's surprise, adopt the child and raise it as their own. A dumb, maudlin soap opera, which holds no surprises for anyone.

p, d&w, George King; ph, Gunther Krampf.

Drama   **(PR:A   MPAA:NR)**

LITTLE THEATER OF JEAN RENOIR, THE
(SEE: LE PETIT THEATRE DE JEAN RENOIR, 1974, Fr./Ital./Ger.)

LITTLE TOKYO, U.S.A.*   (1942) 64m FOX bw

Preston Foster (*Michael Steele*), Brenda Joyce (*Maris Hanover*), Harold Huber (*Takimura*), Don Douglas (*Hendricks*), June Duprez (*Teru*), George E. Stone (*Kingoro*), Abner Biberman (*Satsuma*), Charles Tannen (*Marsten*), Frank Orth (*Jerry*), Edward Soohoo (*Suma*), Beal Wong (*Shadow*), Daisy Lee (*Mrs. Satsuma*), Leonard Strong (*Fujiama*), J. Farrell MacDonald (*Captain Wade*), Richard Loo (*Oshima*), Sen Yung (*Okono*), Melie Chang (*Mrs. Okono*).

This story takes place just before the attack on Pearl Harbor. Los Angeles policeman Foster, along with his reporter girlfriend, Joyce, puts the heat on Japanese spies in

Los Angeles' "Little Tokyo." Huber is the American-born Japanese spy ring leader who frames Preston for murder, but the cop clears himself and exposes the ring.

p, Bryan Foy; d, Otto Brower; w, George Bricker; ph, Joseph MacDonald; ed, Harry Reynolds; md, Emil Newman; art d, Richard Day, Maurice Ransford.

Spy Drama (PR:A MPAA:NR)

LITTLE TOUGH GUY** (1938) 83m UNIV bw

Billy Halop (*Johnny Boylan*), Huntz Hall (*Carl "Pig" Adams*), Gabriel Dell (*String*), Bernard Punsley (*Ape*), David Gorcey (*Sniper*), Hally Chester (*Dopey*), Helen Parrish (*Kay Boylan*), Robert Wilcox (*Paul Wilson*), Jackie Searl (*Cyril Gerrard*), Marjorie Main (*Mrs. Boylan*), Peggy Stewart (*Rita Belle Warren*), Edward Cehman (*Carl*), Edward Pawley (*Jim Boylan*), Olin Howland (*Baxter*), Robert E. Homans (*Truant Officer*), Eleanor Hanson (*Cashier*), Charles Trowbridge, Selmer Jackson (*Judges*), Buster Phelps, George Billings (*Kids*), Ben Taggart, William Ruhl (*Detectives*), Hooper Atchley (*Mr. Randall*), Clara Macklin Blore (*Mrs. Daniels*), Jason Robards, Sr. (*Supervisor*), John Fitzgerald (*Eddie*), Richard Selzer (*Bud*), Frank Bischell (*Band Leader*), Johnny Green (*Usher*), James Zahner (*Bertis*), Stanley Hughes (*Clerk*), Raymond Parker (*Secretary*), Pat C. Flick (*Peddler*), Helen MacKellar (*Mrs. Wanamaker*), Alan Edwards (*Mr. Gerrard*), Jack Carr (*Domino Cop*), Edwin Stanley (*D.A.*), Harry Hayden (*Superintendent*), Janet McLeavy (*Dot LaFleur*), Victor Adams (*Secretary*), Edward Arnold, Jr. (*Fat*), Paul Dubov (*Chuck*), Paul Weigel (*Proprietor*), J. Pat O'Malley (*Police Sergeant*), Bert Young (*Truck Driver*), George Sherwood (*Detective*), Georgia O'Dell (*Woman*), John Estes (*Office Boy*), Gwen Seager (*Salesgirl*), Mike Pat Donovan, Jack Daley, Monty Montague (*Policemen*).

Not using the tag "Dead End Kids," this pre-"Bowery Boys" outing casts part of the usual lineup in a direct lift from 1937's DEAD END and 1938's CRIME SCHOOL. Billy Halop, the lead "little tough guy," takes to the streets when his father gets framed for inciting a riot and murder. When Halop fails to clear his father's name, he takes the side of the criminals, joining up with a local gang of young crooks. During a robbery in which they get surrounded by cops, fellow delinquent Hall makes a run for it and is gunned down. Halop is talked out and winds up in a reform school where, unlike this picture's predecessors, the young criminal is actually reformed. (See BOWERY BOYS series, Index).

p, Ken Goldsmith; d, Harold Young; w, Gilson Brown, Brenda Weisberg (based on a story by Weisberg); ph, Elwood Bredell; ed, Philip Cahn; md, Charles Previn; art d, Jack Otterson.

Crime **Cas.** (PR:A MPAA:NR)

LITTLE TOUGH GUYS IN SOCIETY*1/2 (1938) 76m UNIV bw

Mischa Auer (*Dr. Trenkle*), Mary Boland (*Mrs. Berry*), Edward Everett Horton (*Oliver*), Helen Parrish (*Penny*), Jackie Searl (*Randolph*), Peggy Stewart (*Jane*), Harold Huber (*Uncle Buck*), David Oliver (*Footman*), Frankie Thomas (*Danny*), Harris Berger (*Sailor*), Hally Chester (*Murphy*), Charles Duncan (*Monk*), David Gorcey (*Yap*), William Benedict (*Trouble*).

This film sees the six little j.d.'s escaping from a crime they committed in their slum neighborhood, getting themselves invited to a country mansion by their rich crime loving pal, Searl. The gang practically wrecks the place as they try to adjust to their ritzy surroundings. The boys, even though they have found temporary refuge, soon find that they must go back to the city to stand trial for the crimes they have committed. (See BOWERY BOYS series, Index).

p, Max H. Golden; d, Erle C. Kenton; w, Edward Eliscu, Mortimer Offner; ph, George Robinson; ed, Bernard W. Burton; md, Charles Previn; art d, Jack Otterson.

Comedy (PR:A MPAA:NR)

LITTLE WILDCAT, THE** (1928) 62m WB bw

Audrey Ferris (*Audrey*), James Murray (*Conrad Burton*), Robert Edeson (*Joel Ketchum*), George Fawcett (*Judge Holt*), Hallam Cooley (*Victor Sargeant*), Doris Dawson (*Sue*).

Primitive talkie has Murray a flying ace and barnstormer who lands in a small southern town. Ferris and Dawson each vow to wed the flier but Dawson gets the jump by going to Murray's apartment to spend the weekend, hoping to compromise her reputation so much that he will be forced to marry her. Decent comedy with some good writing. Also released in a silent version.

d, Ray Enright; w, E. T. Lowe, Jr. (based on a story by Gene Wright); ph, Ben Reynolds; ed, George Marks.

Comedy (PR:A MPAA:NR)

LITTLE WOMEN***** (1933) 117m RKO bw

Katharine Hepburn (*Jo*), Joan Bennett (*Amy*), Paul Lukas (*Prof. Fritz Bhaer*), Edna May Oliver (*Aunt March*), Jean Parker (*Beth*), Frances Dee (*Meg*), Henry Stephenson (*Mr. Laurence*), Douglass Montgomery (*Laurie*), John Davis Lodge (*Brooke*), Spring Byington (*Marmee*), Samuel S. Hinds (*Mr. March*), Mabel Colcord (*Hannah*), Marion Ballou (*Mrs. Kirke*), Nydia Westman (*Mamie*), Harry Beresford (*Dr. Bangs*), Marina Schubert (*Flo King*), Dorothy Gray, June Filmer (*Girls at Boarding House*), Olin Howland (*Mr. Davis*).

An unabashedly sentimental adaptation of Alcott's novel that remains, to this day, an example of Hollywood's best filmmaking. David O. Selznick was running the studio but left before the picture went into production so those chores were chaired by executive producer Merian C. Cooper and Macgowan, with Cukor at the helm. It had been made as a silent, then remade with June Allyson and Elizabeth Taylor in 1949, but the former and the latter pale by comparison to this. The book, if you recall, was episodic and that is never easy to put on screen, but the Oscar-winning script by Mason and Heerman managed to do it well. The picture was also Oscar-nominated as was the direction, but that was the year when CAVALCADE

took those two nods. It's the Civil War era and the setting is at Concord, Massachusetts, where four sisters, Hepburn, Bennett, Dee, and Parker, are being raised by their mother, Byington, while Hinds, their father, is off fighting for the cause of the Blue. It's not easy raising these independent girls but Byington is doing a fine job of it. Hepburn wants to write, go it alone, but she is very close to her sisters and can't bring herself to leave, especially at this time when they must stick together. Dee, however, accepts the marriage proposal of Lodge and Hepburn fears that the family will disintegrate. She's been seeing Montgomery and he would like to marry her but she decides, instead, to go to New York City. It's there that she meets Lukas, a professor, who helps her through her anger and begins to teach her about writing and expression. While Hepburn is in New York, Montgomery finds that he loves Bennett and they marry. Meanwhile, Parker is dying and Hepburn leaves New York to be with her sister during the last days. Parker dies around the time the Civil War is concluding. Hinds returns home and the family is reunited, with the addition of Lukas who comes north to be with Hepburn. The story is simple enough, almost soap opera (without the sex), so what is the great charm of the film? First, there is the brilliance of the cast. Hepburn was magnificent and kept in tow by Cukor's direction. They became great friends and he also handled many other films for her. The script called for great production and RKO didn't stint at all. The party scene at Montgomery's is as great an evocation of what America was like in those days as GONE WITH THE WIND was. The sets, the costumes, the lighting, and Cukor's ability to handle actors all contribute to the overall effectiveness of the narrative. LITTLE WOMEN was a hit at the box office despite the fact that most of the smashes of the era were far more hard-edged, mainly dealing in crime and sex. So it was a courageous move on the part of the studio to put such a nostalgic venture into the works. There's no question that Selznick took a long, hard look at the elements that made LITTLE WOMEN successful before he decided to independently film GONE WITH THE WIND. In essence, that was the southern version of LITTLE WOMEN in that both stories were allegedly taking place at the same time. There are laughs, tears, and just about everything in between in this movie. Children in school were asked to see it by their teachers as it presented a slice of American history in such a palatable fashion that no one could dislike learning. The only thing missing was color and that can be handled these days when they can add color to a film electronically. Someone would be wise to do just that. It was released at the depths of the Depression and served to buoy the spirits of hapless Americans at a time when the country needed to be taken back to a day when life was simpler. It did that and will do that again and again no matter when it is seen. An American classic.

p, Kenneth Macgowan; d, George Cukor; w, Sarah Y. Mason, Victor Heerman (based on the novel by Louisa May Alcott); ph, Henry Gerrard; m, Max Steiner; ed, Jack Kitchin; art d, Van Nest Polglase; set d, Hobe Erwin; cos, Walter Plunkett; spec eff, Harry Redmond; makeup, Mel Burns.

Drama **Cas.** (PR:AAA MPAA:NR)

LITTLE WOMEN**1/2 (1949) 121m MGM c

June Allyson (*Jo March*), Peter Lawford (*Laurie Laurence*), Margaret O'Brien (*Beth March*), Elizabeth Taylor (*Amy March*), Janet Leigh (*Meg March*), Rossano Brazzi (*Professor Bhaer*), Mary Astor (*Marmee March*), Lucile Watson (*Aunt March*), Sir C. Aubrey Smith (*Mr. Laurence*), Elizabeth Patterson (*Hannah*), Leon Ames (*Mr. March*), Harry Davenport (*Dr. Barnes*), Richard Stapley (*John Brooke*), Connie Gilchrist (*Mrs. Kirke*), Ellen Corby (*Sophie*), Will Wright (*Mr. Grace*), Olin Howlin (*Schoolteacher*), Harlan Briggs, Frank Darian (*Cronies*), Arthur Walsh (*Young Man*), Eloise Hardt (*Sally Gardiner*), Isabel Randolph (*Mrs. Gardiner*).

This version is a well-handled retelling of the classic Louisa May Alcott tale. The novel was turned into a silent film in 1919 and the 1933 version featured Katharine Hepburn. This time director LeRoy had a star-studded group playing the four sisters who are left to fend for themselves during the Civil War. While none of the actresses was nominated for an award, the technical crew nabbed a pair of nominations for cinematography and art direction.

p&d, Mervyn LeRoy; w, Andrew Solt, Sarah Y. Mason, Victor Heerman (based on the novel *Little Women* by Louisa May Alcott); ph, Robert Planck, Charles Schoenbaum (Technicolor); m, Adolph Deutsch; ed, Ralph E. Winters; art d, Cedric Gibbons, Paul Groesse; set d, Edwin B. Willis, Jack D. Moore; cos, Walter Plunkett; spec eff, Warren Newcombe; makeup, Jack Dawn.

Drama (PR:AA MPAA:NR)

LITTLE WORLD OF DON CAMILLO, THE***

(1953, Fr./Ital.) 96m Rizzoli-Amato/IFE-London Film bw (LE PETIT MONDE DE DON CAMILLO)

Fernandel (*Don Camillo*), Gino Cervi (*Peppone*), Sylvie (*Christina*), Vera Talqui (*Gina*), Franco Interlenghi (*Mariolino*), Charles Vissieres (*Bishop*), Cuciano Manara (*Filotti*), Armando Migliari (*Brusco*).

This delightful farce stars Fernandel as a small town priest at odds with the local mayor, a close friend who has joined the Communist ranks. Their confrontations assume a number of creatively staged formats, including a scene in which Fernandel obnoxiously rings the church bells to drown the Communists' noisy celebration of a decisive political victory. But when it comes to the welfare of the village, the two work together. Fernandel is excellent, smoothly changing moods throughout the film. Orson Welles is the narrator in the English version of this film.

d, Julien Duvivier; w, Duvivier, Rene Barjavel (based on the novel by Giovanni Guareschi); m, Alessandro Cicognini.

Comedy (PR:A MPAA:NR)

LITTLEST HOBO, THE**1/2 (1958) 77m AA bw

Buddy Hart (*Tommy*), Wendy Stuart (*Molly*), Carlyle Mitchell (*Gov. Malloy*), Howard Hoffman (*Captain in Mission*), Robert Kline (*Mike*), Pat Bradley (*Joe*), Bill Coontz (*Attendant*), Dorothy Johnson (*Sister Ophelia*), William Marks (*Dr. Hunt*),

Pauline Moore (*Nurse*), Larry Thor (*Police Captain*), Norman Bartold (*Police Sergeant*), London the Dog, Fleecie the Lamb.

The title dog rides into town on a freight train and rescues a small lamb from an untimely end in a slaughterhouse. The pair wander on to the lawn of the governor's mansion inspiring the governor's paralyzed daughter to walk.

p, Hugh M. Hooker; d, Charles R. Rondeau; w, Dorrell McGowan; ph, Perry Fennerman, Walter Strenge; m, Ronald Stein; ed, Howard Epstein, Arthur H. Nadel.

Children's Drama   **(PR:AAA   MPAA:NR)**

LITTLEST HORSE THIEVES, THE***
         (1977) 104m BV c (GB: ESCAPE FROM THE DARK)

Alastair Sim (*Lord Harrogate*), Peter Barkworth (*Richard Sandman*), Maurice Colbourne (*Luke Armstrong*), Susan Tebbs (*Violet Armstrong*), Geraldine McEwan (*Miss Coutt*), Joe Gladwin (*Bert*), Andrew Harrison (*Dave Sadler*), Benjie Bolgar (*Tommy Sadler*), Chloe Franks (*Alice Sandman*), Prunella Scales (*Mrs. Sandman*), Leslie Sands (*Foreman Sam Carter*), Jeremy Bulloch (*Ginger*), Derek Newark, Duncan Lamont, Ian Hogg, Richard Warner, Don Henderson, Tommy Wright, John Hartley, Ken Kitson, Peter Geddis, Roy Evans, Gordon Kaye, James Marcus, Donald Bisset, Gordon Christie, Walter Hall, Grimethorpe Colliery Band.

A well-done Disney period piece set in turn-of-the century England about three youngsters who attempt to rescue a herd of pit ponies from their hazardous and cruel duties in the Yorkshire coal mines. Aided by the mine manager's spirited daughter Franks, the two boys, Harrison and Bolgar, join forces with the old groom to hoist the ponies from the depths of the mine. When the animals are at last discovered in the abandoned chapel where the children hid them, they are again prepared for the slaughter. It's then up to the boys' stepfather to plead their case—to such an extent that the miners vote to strike if the animals are killed. When financial conditions force the workers to continue, an explosion takes place, trapping some miners. Through the valiant efforts of one special pony, the blind Flash, the miners are saved. And, in turn, their value is recognized, the children are honored and a local peer, Sim, throws a party to signal the happy-ever-after ending.

p, Ron Miller; d, Charles Jarrott; w, Rosemary Anne Sisson (based on a story by Sisson, Burt Kennedy); ph, Paul Beeson (Technicolor); m, Ron Goodwin; ed, Richard Marden; md, Goodwin; art d, Robert Laing; set d, Hugh Scaife; cos, John Furniss; m/l, "Flash's Theme," Goodwin; makeup, Roy Ashton, Harry Frampton; pony trainer, James Prine.

Drama   **(PR:AAA   MPAA:G)**

LITTLEST OUTLAW, THE***
         (1955) 73m BV c

Pedro Armendariz (*Gen. Torres*), Joseph Calleia (*Padre*), Rodolfo Acosta (*Chato*), Andres Velasquez (*Pablito*), Matador Pepe Ortiz, (*Himself*), Laila Maley (*Celita*), Gilberto Gonzales (*Tiger*), Jose Torvay (*Vulture*), Ferrusquilla (*Senor Garcia*), Enriqueta Zazueta (*Senora Garcia*), Senor Lee (*Gypsy*), Carlos Ortigoza (*Doctor*), Margarito Luna (*Silvestre*), Ricardo Gonzales (*Marcos*), Maria Eugenia (*Bride*), Pedrito Vargas (*Groom*).

A charming Disney feature which approaches "neo-realism" by casting Spanish non-actors (with the exception of Calleia) and shooting entirely on location. The story is simple but effective. A young boy, Velasquez, grows fond of a horse his nasty stepfather is training to jump by torturing it. The horse is owned by a general who orders it destroyed after it bucks his daughter, who asked the horse to jump. Velasquez steals the animal and runs away, seeking refuge with padre Calleia. In the meantime, the horse and Velasquez are separated. While at a bullfight with the padre, the boy spots the horse in the ring, about to be gored by a charging bull. Velasquez jumps in, hops on the horse, and rides to safety. He turns himself in to the general, whose temper has cooled. The general spares the horse's life and Velasquez and the general's daughter ride together. Filmed in both Spanish and English it included one scene which does not fit the Disney mold—bullfighter Pepe Ortiz, in an actual piece of footage—is gored by a wild bull. Otherwise, this is a top-notch example of what Disney could do on a limited budget.

p, Larry Lansburgh; d, Roberto Gavaldon; w, Bill Walsh (based on a story by Lansburgh); ph, Alex Phillips, J. Carlos Carbajal (Technicolor); m, William Lava; ed, Carlos Savage; prod d, Luis Sanchez Tello; set d, Rafael Suarez.

Children's Drama   **(PR:AAA   MPAA:NR)**

LITTLEST REBEL, THE***1/2
         (1935) 73m FOX bw

Shirley Temple (*Virginia Houston Cary*), John Boles (*Confederate Capt. Herbert Cary*), Jack Holt (*Union Col. Morrison*), Karen Morley (*Mrs. Cary*), Bill Robinson (*Uncle Billy*), Guinn "Big Boy" Williams (*Sgt. Dudley*), Willie Best (*James Henry*), Frank McGlynn, Sr. (*President Lincoln*), Bessie Lyle (*Mammy*), Hannah Washington (*Sally Ann*), James Flavin (*Guard*).

A wonderful Shirley Temple picture set in the South during the Civil War, with Temple trying to keep the plantation afloat with the help of the tap-dancing Robinson. When her mother takes ill, Temple's father, Boles, tries to sneak through enemy lines to see her. Union troops catch him and arrest him as a spy. Holt, a Union colonel, helps Boles escape, but he is caught again and sentenced to die. Temple takes her appeal all the way to the top, and drops in on President Lincoln. In one of Temple's most captivating scenes, she appeals to "Honest Abe" while sharing an apple with him. They chat for a bit, exchange patriotic speeches and finally Lincoln guarantees Boles' safety. Includes the song: "Believe Me If All Those Endearing Young Charms" (Thomas Moore, Matthew Locke) and a great duet with "Bojangles" Robinson, "Polly Wolly Doodle."

p, Darryl F. Zanuck, B. G. DeSylva; d, David Butler; w, Edwin Burke, Harry Tugend (based on the play by Edward Peple); ph, John Seitz; ed, Irene Morra; md, Cyril Mockridge; art d, William Darling; set d, Thomas K. Little; cos, Gwen Wakeling.

Musical/Drama   **(PR:AAA   MPAA:NR)**

LIVE A LITTLE, LOVE A LITTLE*1/2
         (1968) 89m MGM c

Elvis Presley (*Greg*), Michele Carey (*Bernice*), Don Porter (*Mike Lansdown*), Rudy Vallee (*Penlow*), Dick Sargent (*Harry*), Sterling Holloway (*Milkman*), Celeste Yarnall (*Ellen*), Eddie Hodges (*Delivery Boy*), Joan Shawlee (*Woman in Apartment*), Mary Grover (*Miss Selfridge*), Emily Banks (*Receptionist*), Michael Keller (*Art Director*), Merri Ashley (*1st Secretary*), Phyllis Davis (*2nd Secretary*), Ursula Menzel (*Perfume Model*), Susan Shute, Edie Baskin, Gabrielle, Ginny Kaneen, Thordis Brandt (*Models*), Susan Henning (*Mermaid*), Morgan Windbeil, Benjie Bancroft (*Motorcycle Cops*).

Presley put his public image on the line slightly by playing a *Playboy* magazine-type photographer who occasionally says "dammit." The character also has a second job, in the same building and at the same time, working for a strict, conservative publisher. He manages to juggle his schedules and coffee breaks, but not for long. His life becomes more complicated when he falls in love with model Carey, who leaves him and later returns. Songs include: "Almost In Love" (Randy Starr, Luiz Bonfa), "A Little Less Conversation" (Billy Strange, Scott Davis), "Edge of Reality" (Bill Giant, Bernie Baum, Florence Kaye), and "Wonderful World," all sung by Presley in his 28th film.

p, Douglas Laurence; d, Norman Taurog; w, Michael A. Hoey, Dan Greenburg (based on the novel *Kiss My Firm But Pliant Lips* by Greenburg); ph, Fred Koenekamp (Panavision, Metrocolor); m, Billy Strange; ed, John McSweeney; art d, George Davis, Preston Ames; set d, Henry Grace, Don Greenwood Jr.; ch, Jack Regas, Jack Baker; makeup, William Tuttle.

Musical   **(PR:A   MPAA:NR)**

LIVE A LITTLE, STEAL A LOT
         (SEE: MURPH THE SURF, 1974)

LIVE AGAIN*
         (1936, Brit.) 74m Morgan Films/National Provincial bw

Noah Beery, Sr. (*Morton Meredith*), Bessie Love (*Kathleen Vernon*), John Garrick (*John Wayne*), Stan Paskin (*Joshua Bloggs*), Cecil Gray (*Vivian Turnbull*), Pamela Randall (*Grace Felton*), Lynwood Roberts (*Maj. Cannon*), Frank Stanmore (*Magistrate*), Vi Kaley (*Jane Bloggs*), Gertrude Bibby.

Outdated and boring musical focuses on aging opera star Beery, who hopes that Garrick will follow in his footsteps. The latter agrees, but is temporarily sidetracked from operatic stardom when he falls in love with a young woman. Decent cast was absolutely wasted in this stale story.

p, G. B. Morgan; d, Arthur Maude; w, John Quin; ph, Horace Wheddon.

Drama/Musical   **(PR:A   MPAA:NR)**

LIVE AND LET DIE**1/2
         (1973, Brit.) 121m Eon/UA c

Roger Moore (*James Bond*), Yaphet Kotto (*Kananga/Mr. Big*), Jane Seymour (*Solitaire*), Clifton James (*Sheriff Pepper*), Julius W. Harris (*Tee Hee*), Geoffrey Holder (*Baron Samedi*), David Hedison (*Felix Leiter*), Gloria Hendry (*Rosie*), Bernard Lee ("M"), Lois Maxwell (*Miss Moneypenny*), Tommy Lane (*Adam*), Earl Jolly Brown (*Whisper*), Roy Stewart (*Quarrel*), Lon Satton (*Strutter*), Arnold Williams (*Cab Driver*), Ruth Kempf (*Mrs. Bell*), Joie Chitwood (*Charlie*), Madeline Smith (*Beautiful Girl*), Michael Ebbin (*Dambala*), Kubi Chaza (*Salesgirl*), B. J. Arnau (*Singer*).

This James Bond entry marked the first appearance of Roger Moore, the fourth 007 after David Niven, the inimitable Sean Connery and George Lazenby (who?). As clean-cut as Moore was, making die-hard Connery fans cringe, he was actually closer to creator Fleming's conception of the superspy. The plot line of this film, however, was increasingly less Fleming-like. This time Kotto was cast as Bond's archrival. In a double role, he plays Kananga, Caribbean diplomat, and Mr. Big, a New York drug dealer. His plan for world domination calls for supplying everyone in America with free heroin, thereby turning the entire population into junkies dependent on him for survival. Needless to say, Bond stops him, resorting to the usual high-speed chases and gadgetry. Providing the obligatory sexpot role is Seymour, a tarot reader whose powers will vanish if she loses her virginity. As fate, and Bond, would have it, Seymour's skills are soon rendered ineffective. The real stars of this picture (to take nothing away from Moore's debonair performance) are the stunt coordinators and stuntmen. Two of the most memorable escapes in the Bond series appear in this picture. The most dangerous and destructive is a breathtaking motorboat race in which Kotto's henchmen (an all-black cast of hoods, which offers an intelligent contrast to the period's wave of black exploitation films) tail Bond through lowland marshes at speeds of 70 mph. Countless crashes occur both on and off the screen. A scene in which a boat flies through a wedding cake required several takes, as did others where boats skid onto a front lawn and slide into a pool. In Moore's getaway, his motorboat jumps over a swampside road, smashes into a bungling sheriff's car and safely lands on the other side. Moore did several of his own stunts, some of which resulted in minor injuries, including a jammed, fractured tooth and bruises. Another scene required Bond, stuck on an island surrounded by hungry crocodiles, to jump over their backs while the startled man eaters snap at his legs. To execute this stunt, a crocodile farmer (ironically named Kananga) was hired to devise a way to safely pull it off. The farmer, who also was to perform the stunt, tied weights to the crocodiles' feet, immobilizing all but their jaws and tails (which isn't much of a consolation). After a few attempts, which landed the farmer in the water (he was bitten only once, on the shoe), the stunt was successfully completed. Paul McCartney and Wings supplied the theme song, which became a Top 10 hit for some time. Former Beatles' producer George Martin scored the music.

p, Albert R. Broccoli, Harry Saltzman; d, Guy Hamilton; w, Tom Mankiewicz (based on the novel by Ian Fleming); ph, Ted Moore (DeLuxe Color); m, George Martin; ed, Bert Bates, Raymond Poulton, John Shirley; prod d, Syd Cain; art d, Cain, Stephen Hendrickson; cos, Julie Harris; spec eff, Derek Meddings; ch, Geoffrey Holder; m/l, "Live and Let Die," Paul and Linda McCartney; stunts, Eddie Smith,

Ross Kananga, Joie Chitwood, Jerry Comeaux, Bill Bennett, Bob Simmons, Roger Moore.

Spy Drama/Adventure   **Cas.**   **(PR:C MPAA:PG)**

LIVE FAST, DIE YOUNG*¹/₂   (1958) 82m B.R.K./UNIV bw

Mary Murphy (*Kim Winters*), Norma Eberhardt (*Jill Winters*), Sheridan Comerate (*Jerry*), Michael Connors (*Rick*), Peggy Maley (*Sue*), Jay Jostyn (*Knox*), Troy Donahue (*Artie*), Carol Varga (*Violet*), Joan Marshall (*Judy Tobin*), Gordon Jones (*Pop*), Dawn Richard (*Mona*), Jamie O'Hara (*Mary*), Dorothy Provine.

The consequences of bringing big sister on a diamond heist are brought to the screen in this tame entry, which doesn't come close to living up to its title. A black sheep sister splits from her older, more sensible sibling and joins up with a gang of thieves. She is able to enjoy the good life for a while, zipping up and down San Francisco's hilly streets, until her big sister shows up during a diamond heist and gets everyone tossed in the slammer.

p, Harry Rybnick, Richard Kay; d, Paul Henreid; w, Allen Rivkin, Ib Melchior (based on a story by Melchior, Edwin B. Watson); ph, Philip Lathrop; m, Joseph Gershenson; ed, Edward Curtiss; md, Gershenson; art d, Alexander Golitzen, Robert E. Smith; cos, Bill Thomas.

Crime   **(PR:A MPAA:NR)**

LIVE FOR LIFE**

(1967, Fr./Ital.) 130m Films Ariane-Vides Films-Artistes Associes/UA-Lopert c (VIVRE POUR VIVRE; VIVERE PER VIVERE)

Yves Montand (*Robert Colomb*), Candice Bergen (*Candice*), Annie Girardot (*Catherine Colomb*), Irene Tunc (*Mireille*), Anouck Ferjac (*Jacqueline*), Uta Taeger (*Maid*), Jean Collomb (*Waiter*), Jacques Portet (*Photographer*), Michel Parbot (*Michel*), Maurice Seveno (*Himself*), Louis Lyonnet.

A weak follow-up to Lelouch's A MAN AND A WOMAN, the flashy, pseudo-intellectual tale that achieved great commercial success, as well as critical acclaim at Cannes. LIVE FOR LIFE focuses on Montand, a television newsman, and his on-the-rocks marriage to Girardot. He takes on the young Bergen as a lover in Kenya, but upon returning to his Paris home, feels compelled to take Girardot on a second honeymoon. Bergen follows him to Paris and rekindles their affair. Montand confesses the affair to his wife, who then leaves him. He moves in with Bergen, but finds the relationship unfulfilling, so he leaves for Viet Nam to work on a news documentary. He returns to Paris to find Bergen has left for the States and Girardot has found her independence. Girardot eventually takes him back, but their relationship has clearly changed. Lelouch's (as well as countless other directors') interest in Viet Nam was high, and that same year he contributed to the collective work LOIN DU VIET NAM.

p, Alexandre Mnouchkine, Georges Danciger; d, Claude Lelouch; w, Pierre Uytterhoeven, Lelouch; ph, Lelouch, Patrice Pouget (DeLuxe Color); m, Francis Lai; ed, Lelouch; cos, Yves Saint-Laurent; spec eff, Jean Beylieu; m/l, "Des Ronds dans l'Eau," Raymond Le Senechal, Pierre Barouh (sung by Nicole Croisille, Girardot); makeup, Michel Deruelle.

Drama   **(PR:A MPAA:NR)**

LIVE IT UP   (SEE: SING AND SWING, 1964, Brit.)

LIVE, LOVE AND LEARN**   (1937) 78m MGM bw

Robert Montgomery (*Bob Graham*), Rosalind Russell (*Julie Stoddard*), Robert Benchley (*Oscar*), Helen Vinson (*Lily Chalmers*), Mickey Rooney (*Jerry Crump*), Monty Woolley (*Mr. Bawltitude*), E. E. Clive (*Mr. Palmiston*), Charles Judels (*Pedro Filipe*), Maude Eburne (*Mrs. Crump*), Harlan Briggs (*Justice of the Peace*), Al Shean (*Fraum*), George Cooper (*Bus Driver*), Billy Gilbert (*Newsboy*), Dorothy Appleby (*Lou*), Ena Gregory (*Bessie*), Kate Price (*Wilma*), Heinie Conklin (*Elmer*), Billy Dooley (*Fritz*), John Kelly, Joe Caits, Philip Tully, John Quillan, Frank Marlowe (*Sailors*), James Flavin, Jack Perrin, Frank Sully, Jerry Miley, Russ Clark (*Marines*), June Clayworth (*Annabelle Post*), Ann Rutherford (*Class President*), Minerva Urecal, Virginia Sale, Maxine Elliott Hicks (*Sisters*), Rollo Lloyd (*Agent*), Soledad Jimenez (*Spanish Woman*), Don Barclay, Harry Lash, Milton Kibbee, Ralph McCullough (*Reporters*), Chester Clute (*Jess, a Reporter*), Edith Kingdon, Mariska Aldrich (*Dowagers*), Ramsey Hill, Edward Earle, Carl Leviness (*Salesmen*), Arthur Stuart Hull (*Marsden*), Adrienne d'Ambricourt (*The Duchess*), John Davidson (*Wingate*), Robert Emmett Keane (*Apartment House Manager*), William Austin (*Butler*), Winifred Harris (*Mrs. Colfax-Baxter*), Billy Engle (*Dittenfuss*), Zeffie Tilbury (*Mrs. Venable*), Wilbur Mack (*Yacht Salesman*), Tenen Holtz (*Socialist*), Charles Irwin (*Magazine Salesman*), Eddie Gribbon (*Masseur*), Robert Spindola (*Italian Boy*), Margaret Lynar (*Movie Star*), Leila McIntyre (*Miss Cross*).

A harmless screwball comedy that casts Russell as a wealthy socialite who falls in love with Bohemian artist Montgomery, forcing him to adapt to his free-and-easy life style. She is happy living in their meager art studio-apartment, until Montgomery gets a taste of success and drives her away. Montgomery comes to his senses when he realizes that success has robbed him of his creative drive. The two reunite and continue to live their poor but happy existence.

p, Harry Rapf; d, George Fitzmaurice; w, Charles Brackett, Cyril Hume, Richard Maibaum (based on the story by Marion Parsonnet, suggested by a story by Helen Grace Carlisle); ph, Ray June; ed, Conrad A. Nervig.

Comedy   **(PR:A MPAA:NR)**

LIVE NOW—PAY LATER**   (1962, Brit.) 104m Woodland/RF bw

Ian Hendry (*Albert Argyle*), June Ritchie (*Treasure*), John Gregson (*Callendar*), Liz Fraser (*Joyce Corby*), Geoffrey Keen (*Reggie Corby*), Jeanette Sterke (*Grace*), Peter Butterworth (*Fred*), Nyree Dawn Porter (*Marjorie Mason*), Ronald Howard (*Cedric Mason*), Harold Berens (*Solly Cowell*), Thelma Ruby (*Hetty*), Monty Landis

(*Arnold*), Kevin Brennan (*Jackson*), Malcolm Knight (*Ratty*), Bridget Armstrong (*Gloria*), Judith Furse (*Mrs. Ackroyd*), Joan Heal (*Mrs. Pocock*), Michael Brennan (*Bailiff*), William Kendall (*Maj. Simpkins*), Georgina Cookson (*Lucy*), Justine Lord (*Coral Wentworth*), Geoffrey Hibbert (*Price*), Andrew Cruickshank (*Vicar*), John Wood (*Curate*).

A tolerable comedy starring Hendry as a philandering door-to-door salesman whose trips to the boudoir with female customers almost always result in a big sale. In the meantime, he is scheming his boss out of profits, trying his hand at blackmail and attempting a reconciliation with girlfriend Ritchie. Includes a pleasant little ditty, "Live Now—Pay Later," by Ruth Batchelor and Clive Westlake.

p, Jack Hanbury; d, Jay Lewis; w, Jack Trevor Story (based on the novel *All on the Never-Never* by Jack Lindsey); ph, Jack Hildyard; m, Ron Grainer; ed, Roger Cherrill.

Comedy   **(PR:A MPAA:NR)**

LIVE TO LOVE   (SEE: DEVIL'S HAND, THE, 1961)

LIVE TODAY FOR TOMORROW   (SEE: ACT OF MURDER, AN, 1948)

LIVE WIRE, THE**   (1937, Brit.) 69m Tudor-Olympic/BL bw

Bernard Nedell (*James Cody*), Jean Gillie (*Sally Barton*), Hugh Wakefield (*Grantham*), Arthur Wontner (*Montell*), Kathleen Kelly (*Phoebe*), Irene Ware (*Jane*), David Burns (*Snakey*), Felix Aylmer (*Wilton*), H. F. Maltby (*Hodgson*), C. M. Hallard (*Sir George Dawson*).

Typical British comedy casts Nedell as an American con man hiding out in England. In pursuit of a pretty young girl, he enters an office building and stumbles upon a company president on the verge of committing suicide. Learning that the executive is involved in an embezzling scheme, Nedell talks the man into taking a six-month leave and letting him take over the company. With a little book juggling, Nedell rescues the firm from bankruptcy.

p, Herbert Wynne; d, Herbert Brenon; w, Stafford Dickens, John E. Lewis, Leslie H. Gordon (based on the play "Plunder in the Air" by Dickens); ph, George Stretton.

Comedy   **(PR:A MPAA:NR)**

LIVE WIRES**¹/₂   (1946) 64m MON bw

Leo Gorcey (*Terrence "Slip" Mahoney*), Huntz Hall (*Sach*), Bobby Jordan (*Bobby*), Billy Benedict (*Whitey*), William Frambes (*Homer*), Claudia Drake (*Jeanette*), Pamela Blake (*Mary Mahoney*), Patti Brill (*Mabel*), Mike Mazurki (*Patsy Clark*), John Eldredge (*Herbert L. Sayers*), Pat Gleason (*John Stevens*), William Ruhl (*Construction Foreman*), Rodney Bell (*George*), Bill Christy (*Boy Friend*), Nancy Brinkman (*Girl Friend*), Robert Emmett Keane (*Barton*), Earle Hodgins (*Barker*), Bernard Gorcey (*Jack Kane*), Frank Marlowe (*Red*), Gladys Blake (*Ann Clark*), Eddie Borden (*Shill*), Charlie Sullivan, Henry Russell (*Ditch Diggers*), John Indrisano, Steve Taylor (*Bouncers*), Beverly Hawthorne (*1st Pretty Girl*), Jack Chefe (*Head Waiter*), Malcolm McClean (*Emcee and Announcer*), George Eldredge (*Cop*).

LIVE WIRES was the first in the series of Bowery Boys films which continued until 1957. It's practically Leo Gorcey's film, however, with the rest of the gang in subordinate roles. Gorcey is a tough guy who still answers to his even tougher sister, played by Pamela Blake. He loses his job at a construction firm, where Blake also works, when he punches out the foreman. He soon finds himself employed, along with Hall, at the district attorney's office. They get themselves into trouble when they try to bring in gangster Mazurki on their own. Their amateur investigation leads them to an even rougher gangster, John Eldredge, who runs the construction company that fired Gorcey. Setting a pattern that the series (and most every film of the era) would not break, Gorcey and the boys bring Eldredge to justice before he can get away. Bernard Gorcey, who would in subsequent pictures be known as drugstore owner Louie, is here playing the role of a small time bookie. (See BOWERY BOYS series, Index.)

p, Lindsley Parsons, Jan Grippo; d, Phil Karlson; w, Tim Ryan, Josef Mischel (based on a story by Jeb [Dore] Schary); ph, William Sickner; ed, Fred Maguire; md, Edward J. Kay; art d, Dave Milton; set d, Charles Thompson.

Comedy   **(PR:A MPAA:NR)**

LIVE YOUR OWN WAY**

(1970, Jap.) 98m Gekidan Haiyuza Shinsei Eigasha/Shochiku bw (WAKAMONO TACHI)

Kunie Tanaka (*Taro*), Isao Hashimoto (*Jiro*), Kei Yamamoto (*Saburo*), Orie Sato (*Orie*), Shoji Matsuyama (*Suekichi*), Yasushi Nagata, Mie Minami, Michiko Otsuka.

Japanese drama about four boys and their sister, who are left to fend for themselves after their parents' death. The film details the problems faced by the orphans as they struggle to establish their own lives and at the same time care for one another.

d, Tokihisa Morikawa; w, Hisashi Yamanouchi (based on the Japanese television series "Wakamono Tachi"); ph, Yoshio Miyajima; m, Masaru Sato; art d, Totetsu Hirakawa.

Drama   **(PR:A MPAA:NR)**

LIVELY SET, THE**   (1964) 95m UNIV c

James Darren (*Casey Owens*), Pamela Tiffin (*Eadie Manning*), Doug McClure (*Chuck Manning*), Joanie Sommers (*Doreen Grey*), Marilyn Maxwell (*Marge Owens*), Charles Drake (*Paul Manning*), Peter Mann (*Stanford Rogers*), Russ Conway (*Moody*), Carole Wells (*Mona*), Frances Robinson (*Celeste*), Greg Morris (*Policeman*), Ross Elliott (*Ernie Owens*), Martin Blaine (*Prof. Collins*), Capt. Max Schumacher, Dick Whittinghill, Mickey Thompson, James Nelson, Ron Miller, Duane Carter, Billy Krause (*Themselves*).

A lively teen-oriented picture with Darren as an ex-GI who devotes more time to hot rods than to either girls or college. He finally takes notice of the opposite sex when Tiffin shows up on the scene. They get engaged and head for San Francisco, where Darren starts running in racing circles. After cracking up a prototype car he builds for racing hero Mann, he scrounges up enough cash to build his own. His snazzy hot rod takes him across the finish line first, and with the prize money he weds Tiffin and returns to college. This mindless entertainment includes a decent selection of early 1960s music: "If You Love Him" and "Casey Wake Up" (Bobby Darin, sung by Joanie Sommers), "Look At Me" (Darin, Randy Newman, sung by Wink Martindale) and "Boss Barracuda" (Darin, Terry Melcher, sung by the Surfaris), and "The Lively Set" (Darin, sung by Darren).

p, William Alland; d, Jack Arnold; w, Mel Goldberg, William Wood (based on a story by Goldberg, Alland); ph, Carl Guthrie (Eastmancolor); m, Bobby Darin; ed, Archie Marshek; md, Joseph Gershenson; art d, Walter Simonds, Alexander Golitzen; set d, John McCarthy, Joe Kish; cos, Rosemary Odell; spec eff, Sass Bedig, makeup, Bud Westmore, Keester Sweeney.

Action **(PR:A MPAA:NR)**

LIVER EATERS, THE (SEE: SPIDER BABY, 1968)

LIVES OF A BENGAL LANCER**** (1935) 109m PAR bw

Gary Cooper *(Lt. McGregor)*, Franchot Tone *(Lt. Fortesque)*, Richard Cromwell *(Lt. Stone)*, Sir Guy Standing *(Col. Stone)*, C. Aubrey Smith *(Maj. Hamilton)*, Monte Blue *(Hamzulia Khan)*, Kathleen Burke *(Tania Volkanskaya)*, Colin Tapley *(Lt. Barrett)*, Douglas Dumbrille *(Mohammed Khan)*, Akim Tamiroff *(Emir)*, Jameson Thomas *(Hendrickson)*, Noble Johnson *(Ram Singh)*, Lumsden Hare *(Maj. Gen. Woodley)*, J. Carrol Naish *(Grand Vizier)*, Rollo Lloyd *(The Ghazi, a Prisoner)*, Charles Stevens *(McGregor's Servant)*, Boswhan Singh *(Nuim Shah)*, Abdul Hassan *(Ali Hamdi)*, Mischa Auer *(Afridi)*, Clive Morgan *(Lt. Norton)*, Eddie Das *(Servant)*, Leonid Kinskey *(Snake Charmer)*, Hussain Hasri *(Muezzin)*, James Warwick *(Lt. Gilhooley)*, George Regas *(Kushal Khan)*, Maj. Sam Harris, Carli Taylor *(British Officers)*, James Bell, Jamiel Hasson, Ram Singh, Gen. Ikonnikoff, F. A. Armenta *(Indian Officers)*, Claude King *(Experienced Clerk)*, Reginald Sheffield *(Novice)*, Ray Cooper *(Assistant to Grand Vizier)*, Myra Kinch *(Solo Dancer)*, Lya Lys *(Girl on Train)*.

In this rousing adventure film that features no love story, Hathaway's direction of LIVES OF A BENGAL LANCER provides a galloping pace with excitement all the way in a lavish production. Cooper is a seasoned frontier fighter who takes two new officers under his wing when they arrive at a remote British outpost in Northwest India. The new lieutenants are Tone and Cromwell, the former a brash and cocky character seeking adventure and as little discipline as possible, the latter being the son of the commander, Standing. When Standing greets his new officers on parade he coldly shakes Cromwell's hand, giving no indication that he acknowledges him as his son, refusing to show the slightest sign of favoritism. This prompts Cooper to label him "ramrod," a word he injudiciously carves onto a table while watching the review of new officers. Cromwell becomes embittered as his father treats him as a stranger, despite the encouragement to "speak to the boy" from Standing's second-in-command, the venerable and understanding Smith. Cooper takes a ribbing from wise guy Tone about shepherding Stone through his troubled times, calling him "Mother McGregor." But Cooper witnesses retribution when Tone takes to playing a snakecharmer's horn and actually produces a deadly python which weaves in front of the terrified Tone who must go on playing and playing until Cooper takes pity on him and kills the lethal snake. Cooper is ordered to find a British spy, Tapley, who has not appeared after disguising himself as an Indian and trying to penetrate the operations of the evil-minded Dumbrille, a local chieftan planning bloody revolt. Cooper, joined by Tone and Cromwell, finds Tapley and learns that Dumbrille is collecting the mountain tribes for a massive attack against the British garrison, as well as planning to steal two million rounds of ammunition which has just been shipped to Tamiroff, a friendly chief. Standing and his officers journey to Tamiroff's stronghold, paying a friendly visit but really scouting the location of the ammunition. During a "pig-sticking" hunt organized by Tamiroff for the amusement of the British officers, Standing is injured while protecting his son. Cromwell is later kidnaped by Burke and her agents and taken to Dumbrille's mountain fortress. Standing refuses to send his lancers in to save his son, stating that that is exactly what Dumbrille wants after baiting the trap. Cooper thinks him heartless and he and Tone go after the young man, disguising themselves as native peddlers. They are quickly discovered, however, and taken to a torture chamber where sticks are jammed under their fingernails and then set afire. The pain is excruciating but Cooper and Tone will not inform Dumbrille when and where the ammunition will be delivered. Cromwell, however, his morale crushed and having no belief in a service epitomized by his cold-hearted father, cracks and tells Dumbrille what he wants to know. Days later the three officers see the ammunition enter Dumbrille's fortress and they are informed that Standing and his 300 lancers have arrived outside the gates and will be systematically destroyed. Cooper and Tone break free and take over a machinegun as Standing and his lancers attack. They mow down Dumbrille's vicious mountain troops while Cromwell also breaks free and attacks Dumbrille, killing him in a hand-to-hand combat. Cooper then sprints to the arsenal with a burning torch and ignites it, blowing it and himself up, along with half the enemy. Standing enters the vanquished fortress and later bestows posthumous honors upon the deceased Cooper, along with Tone and the young man he now gratefully acknowledges as his son. The Victoria Cross is pinned on the saddle of Cooper's horse. The action in LIVES OF A BENGAL LANCER is non-stop and it remains one of the great adventure films, nominated for six Oscars (for Best Picture, Best Director, Best Screenplay, Best Editing, and for recording and second-unit direction, assistant directors Clem Beauchamp and Paul Wing winning in the latter category.) So superbly mounted were the sets created by Dreier and Anderson that the fussy Cecil B. DeMille had them only slightly revamped before using them in his lavish epic, THE CRUSADES. Paramount bought the book by Maj. Francis Yeats-Brown in 1930 and spent five years shooting background footage in Northwest India. Everything about the production was authentic, down to the last button on a lancer's tunic. The lancers had had a celebrated history in the British army, having served in the Sikh and Afghan wars and having aided the British in quashing the awful Sepoy Rebellion of 1857. Hathaway should be given special credit for a great deal of footage he himself shot in India and later wove without discernible gaps into the film, a pet project of the director's. Hathaway had always wanted Cooper for the role he played in LIVES OF A BENGAL LANCER and told Paramount that he was determined to create Cooper into one of America's great film heroes. This was Hathaway's first significant film as a director, one that became immensely popular with the public and returned enormous box office receipts to Paramount for many years through myriad re-releases.

p, Louis D. Lighton; d, Henry Hathaway; w, Waldemar Young, John L. Balderston, Achmed Abdullah, Grover Jones, William Slavens McNutt, (based on the novel by Maj. Francis Yeats-Brown); ph, Charles Lang, Ernest Schoedsack; m, Milan Roder; ed, Ellsworth Hoagland; art d, Hans Dreier, Roland Anderson; cos, Travis Banton; ch, LeRoy Prinz.

Adventure **Cas.** **(PR:A MPAA:NR)**

LIVING (SEE: IKIRU, 1960, Jap.)

LIVING BETWEEN TWO WORLDS** (1963) 75m Empire bw

Maye Henderson *(Mom)*, Anita Poree *(Bucky)*, Mimi Dillard *(Helen)*, Horace Jackson *(Harvey)*, Irvin Mosley *(Papa)*, Kyle Johnson *(Larry)*, Derrick Lewis *(Norman)*, Geraldine West *(Mrs. Peters)*, DeForest Covan *(Orderly)*, *Lawrence LaMarr (Janitor)*, Napoleon Whiting *(Rev. Williamson)*, John Shaner, David Morrow.

An insightful picture about a young black man, Jackson, who is brought up by a deeply religious mother who wants him to enter the ministry. Having second thoughts about this type of life, he decides to pursue a career as a jazz musician instead. Meanwhile, Jackson's fiancee, Dillard, tries to free him from his mother's hold. After Dillard is brutally raped by two white men, Jackson turns a deaf ear to his musical ambitions and heads straight for the pulpit.

p, Horace Jackson; d, Bobby Johnson; w, Jackson; ph, Willie Zsigmond [Vilmos Zsigmond]; m, Gordon Zahler; ed, Gene Evans; set d, Carl Randell.

Drama **(PR:A MPAA:NR)**

LIVING COFFIN, THE* 1/2

(1965, Mex.) 72m Alameda/Murray-Trans-International c (EL GRITO DE LA MUERTE)

Gaston Santos, Maria Duval, Pedro d'Aguillon, Hortensia Santovena, Guillermo Alvarez Bianchi, Antonio Raxell, Eugenia Galindo, Carlos Ancira, Quintin Bulnes, Carolina Barret.

More Mexican horror! This one's loosely based on Edgar Allan Poe's "The Premature Burial" and details a woman's obsession with being buried alive. She even has an alarm bell rigged into her coffin for just such emergencies. Filmed and released south-of-the-border in 1958, but it didn't make it to the U.S. until 1965.

p, Cesar Santos Galindo, K. Gordon Murray; d, Fernando Mendez; w, Ramon Obon; ph, Victor Herrera; m, Gustavo Cesar Carrion; ed, Charles Kimball; art d, Gunther Gerszo.

Horror **(PR:C MPAA:NR)**

LIVING CORPSE, THE** (1940, Fr.) 82m Alliance/Juno bw (NUITS DE FEU)

Victor Francen *(Fedor Andreiev)*, Gaby Morlay *(Lisa Andreiev)*, Simone Signoret *(Bodinine)*, Georges Rigaud *(Serge Rostoff)*, Madeleine Robinson *(Macha)*, Mia Slavenska *(Ballerina)*.

Released in Paris in 1937, THE LIVING CORPSE is yet another disappointment from one of France's greatest directors of silent films. In this Tolstoy tale, a public prosecutor decides to commit suicide so that his unfaithful wife can be with her lover. The man is saved from his demise and decides to enter the army, but is presumed by everyone to be dead. His wife, now engaged to her lover, is hauled to jail for her husband's murder but is released when he turns up later. She pleads with him to come back to her, but he ignores her and walks off. She vows to await his return. Notable mainly for the early appearance of Signoret, who received an Oscar for ROOM AT THE TOP. (In French; English subtitles.)

d, Marcel L'Herbier; w, L'Herbier, T. H. Robert (based on the play by Leo Tolstoy); ph, Armand Thirard; m, Jean Wiener; ch, Serge Lifar.

Drama **(PR:A MPAA:NR)**

LIVING DANGEROUSLY** (1936, Brit.) 69m BIP/Wardour bw

Otto Kruger *(Dr. Stanley Norton)*, Leonora Corbett *(Helen Pryor)*, Francis Lister *(Dr. Henry Pryor)*, Aileen Marson *(Vera Kennedy)*, Lawrence Andersen *(Lloyd)*, Eric Stanley *(Sir George Parker)*, Charles Mortimer *(Insp. Webster)*, Hubert Harben *(President of Council)*, Iris Hoey *(Lady Annesley)*, James Carew *(Lingard)*, Jimmy Godden *(Member of Council)*, Hartley Power *(District Attorney)*.

A mediocre suspense drama about a doctor, Kruger, who is dealing morphine. Lister, his former partner, catches Kruger with his ex-wife and decides to blackmail him. Kruger then is forced to kill Lister in order to protect his reputation.

p, Walter C. Mycroft; d, Herbert Brenon; w, Geoffrey Kerr, Marjorie Deans, Dudley Leslie (based on the play by Reginald Simpson, Frank Gregory); ph, Bryan Langley; ed, Flora Newton.

Crime **(PR:A MPAA:NR)**

LIVING DEAD, THE*
(1936, Brit.) 63m BIP/FD bw (GB: THE SCOTLAND YARD MYSTERY)

Gerald du Maurier (Inspector Stanton), George Curzon (Dr. Masters), Grete Natzler (Irene), Belle Chrystal (Mary Stanton), Leslie Perrins (Dr. John Freeman), Wally Patch (George), Henry Victor (Floyd), Herbert Cameron (Paxton), Frederick Peisley (Bailey), Paul Graetz (Paston).

Curzon devises a scheme to kill people, collect the insurance money, and then bring them back to life. It's far from believable, as are the inept techniques of Scotland Yard inspector du Maurier. It takes the inspector's future son-in-law, who happens to be employed by the insurance firm as a doctor, to bring Curzon to justice. It doesn't say too much for the Yard.

p, Walter C. Mycroft; d, Thomas Bentley; w, Frank Miller (based on a play by Wallace Geoffrey); ph, James Wilson; ed, Walter Stokvis.

Crime/Mystery   (PR:A MPAA:NR)

LIVING DEAD AT MANCHESTER MORGUE
(SEE: DON'T OPEN THE WINDOW, 1974, Ital./Span.)

LIVING FREE**1/2
(1972, Brit.) 90m Open Road-Highroad/COL c

Nigel Davenport (George Adamson), Susan Hampshire (Joy Adamson), Geoffrey Keen (John Kendall), Edward Judd (Game Warden Weaver), Peter Lukoye (Nuru), Shane De Louvres (Madedde), Robert Beaumont (Billy Collins), Nobby Noble (Bank Manager), Aludin Quershi (Bank Clerk), Charles Hayes (Herbert Baker), Jean Hayes (Mrs. Herbert Baker), Elsa The Lioness, Jespah, Gopa, Little Elsa (Her Cubs), James Kamau.

Davenport and Hampshire star in this sequel to BORN FREE, replacing Virginia McKenna and Bill Travers as lion-lovers Joy and George Adamson. This time the couple is determined to keep Elsa's three lion cubs "living free" after the death of their mother. Again the filmmakers have their finger on the "heart-warming emotions" button and press it at will. But after just a short while, it becomes predictable and ineffective. As in BORN FREE, the nature photography is awe-inspiring. Both films were shot on location in Kenya.

p, Paul Radin; d, Jack Couffer; w, Millard Kaufman (based on the books by Joy Adamson); ph, Wolfgang Suschitzky, Couffer; m, Sol Kaplan; ed, Don Deacon; prod d, John Stoll; md, Kaplan; m/l, "Living Free," Kaplan, Freddie Douglas (sung by Julie Budd); makeup, Jill Carpenter; wildlife sup, Hubert Wells.

Drama   (PR:A MPAA:G)

LIVING GHOST, THE*
(1942) 61m MON bw (GB LEND ME YOUR EAR)

James Dunn, Joan Woodbury, Paul McVey, Vera Gordon, Norman Willis, J. Farrell MacDonald, Minerva Urecal, George Eldredge, Jan Wiley, Edna Johnson, Danny Beck, Gus Glassmire, Lawrence Grant, Howard Banks, J. Arthur Young, Frances Richards, Harry Depp.

In this meager horror film effort, a mad scientist thinks up a recipe for zombies and proceeds to put the cast—as well as the audience—to sleep. Dunn hams it up, and everyone else tries to look scared.

p, A. W. Hackel; d, William Beaudine; w, Joseph Hoffman (based on the story by Howard Dimsdale); ph, Mack Stengler; ed, Jack Ogilvie; md, Frank Sanucci.

Horror   (PR:A MPAA:NR)

LIVING HEAD, THE*1/2
(1969, Mex.) 75 m Cinematografica A.B.S.A./Trans-International bw (LA CABEZA VIVIENTE)

Mauricio Garces, Ana Luisa Peluffo, German Robles, Guillermo Cramer, Abel Salazar, Antonio Raxell.

Archeologists unearth the tomb of an Aztec chief and discover the severed heads of the entombed, the Grand Priest and the chief's mummified bride who was buried alive. The mummy disintegrates, but the severed heads survive. When one of the archeologists brings the relics home, he soon discovers his daughter has become possessed by the heads, which have come to life and command her to begin making human sacrifices. Eventually the evil heads are defeated, and their hypnotic spell is broken. Pretty silly, but done well enough for the indiscriminating horror fan.

p, Abel Salazar; d, Chano Urueta; w, Frederick Curiel, Adolfo Lopez Portillo; ph, Jorge Stahl, Jr., Jose Ortiz Ramos; m, Gustavo Cesar Carrion; ed, Alfredo Rosas Priego; art d, Roberto Silva.

Horror   Cas.   (PR:O MPAA:NR)

LIVING IDOL, THE*1/2
(1957) 101m MGM c

Steve Forrest (Terry Matthews), Liliane Montevecchi (Juanita), James Robertson Justice (Dr. Alfred Stones), Sara Garcia (Elena), Eduardo Noriega (Manuel).

A perfect example of a film that one must watch with a completely void mind, for any attempt to find logic in the characters' actions will be utterly worthless. Justice is an archaeologist who believes that Montevecchi's soul is that of an Aztec sacrifice made to jaguar gods in a previous century. He lets loose a jaguar to see if he's on the mark, but before it rips her to shreds, Forrest comes to her aid.

p, Albert Lewin, Gregorio Walerstein; d&w, Lewin; ph, Jack Hildyard (Cinema-Scope, Eastmancolor); m, Manuel Esperon, Rudolfo Halffter; ed, Rafael Ceballos; art d, Edward Fitzgerald; cos, Armando Valdez Peza, Ramon Valdiosera; ch, Jose Silva, David Campbell; m/l, "Tepo," Ismael Diaz.

Adventure   (PR:C-O MPAA:NR)

LIVING IN A BIG WAY**
(1947) 102m MGM bw

Gene Kelly (Leo Gogarty), Marie McDonald (Margaud Morgan), Charles Winninger (D. Rutherford Morgan), Phyllis Thaxter (Peggy Randall), Spring Byington (Mrs. Morgan), Jean Adair (Abigail Morgan), Clinton Sundberg (Everett Hanover

Smythe), John Warburton (Stuart), William Phillips (Schultz), John Alexander (Attorney Ambridge), Phyllis Kennedy (Annie Pearl), Bernadine Hayes (Dolly).

It wasn't a musical, it wasn't a comedy, it wasn't much of anything except an example of Kelly's ability to take a sow's ear and make half a silk purse out of it. He was saddled by a costar who was known as "The Body" and for good reason; she didn't have much of anything else. La Cava had a story but not much more than that when the studio decided to make the movie, so Ravetch was writing as the film was being lensed. There were also many improvised moments in the picture which proves again that old adage; "If it ain't on the page, it ain't on the stage." Kelly is an Army lieutenant who marries McDonald after a whirlwind courtship. He is sent overseas within hours of the wedding. Dissolve through the three years of service and Kelly returns to find that McDonald wants a divorce. She believes they married too quickly and that wartime romances are never successful. Kelly doesn't want to give her a divorce and he is aided in that by her parents, Byington and Winninger, who like Kelly and think he makes a fine son-in-law. They let him stay at a house they own where returning servicemen are allowed to take refuge until they get on their feet. Now we learn that Winninger made all his money by a bit of war profiteering and his doting attitude toward McDonald has caused her to become a spoiled brat. Winninger would like Kelly to straighten out her pampered head, as does Adair, McDonald's crusty grandmother, who is solidly behind Kelly's plan to build apartments for war veterans. The love between Kelly and McDonald goes up and down for a few reels and they eventually agree on a divorce, though neither will admit that they love each other. The hearing judge decides not to grant the split and they are both secretly happy about that and will attempt to make it go. Thaxter does well as a war widow who likes Kelly because he reminds her of her late husband. It was after they began this that Kelly (with the help of Donen) added some musical numbers to push this picture. The songs included "It Had To Be You," "Fido And Me," and a few traditionals like "Yankee Doodle," "Ring Around The Rosy," "Loo By Loo," and "In And Out The Window." The theme of poor boy marrying rich girl has been seen many times and it might have worked better if Kelly had been teamed with just about anyone else in the MGM stable. McDonald's life went the way of her career and she died in 1965 at the young age of 42. This was La Cava's last picture after a stellar career that included such excellent work as STAGE DOOR and MY MAN GODFREY. Kelly and Donen did some wonderful choreography with children, a forerunner of what was to come to pass in four years with AN AMERICAN IN PARIS.

p, Pandro S. Berman; d, Gregory La Cava; w, La Cava, Irving Ravetch (based on a story by La Cava); ph, Harold Rosson; m, Lennie Hayton; ed, Ferris Webster; art d, Cedric Gibbons, William Ferrari; ch, Gene Kelly, Stanley Donen; m/l, Louis Alter, Edward Heyman, Gus Kahn, Isham Jones.

Comedy   (PR:A MPAA:NR)

LIVING IT UP***1/2
(1954) 94m PAR c

Dean Martin (Steve), Jerry Lewis (Homer), Janet Leigh (Wally Cook), Edward Arnold (The Mayor), Fred Clark (Oliver Stone), Sheree North (Jitterbug Dancer), Sammy White (Waiter), Sid Tomack (Master of Ceremonies), Sig Rumann (Dr. Egelhofer), Richard Loo (Dr. Lee), Raymond Greenleaf (Conductor), Walter Baldwin (Isaiah), Marla English, Kathryn [Grant/Crosby] Grandstaff (Manicurists), Emmett Lynn (Station Attendant), Dabbs Greer (Head Ranger), Clancy Cooper (Slugger), John Alderson (Catcher), Booth Colman (Fernandez), Stanley Blystone (Engineer), Fritz Feld (Barber), Torben Meyer (Chef), Grady Sutton (Gift Shop Proprietor), Frankie Darro (Bellboy Captain).

Perhaps the best of the Martin and Lewis series, this outlandish tale concerns Lewis, a midwestern station master who is exposed to radioactive material and told by his doctor, Martin, that he only has a few months to live. Though the diagnosis turns out to be wrong, Martin convinces Lewis to accept an all-expense paid trip, offered as a "last hurrah" by newspaper reporter Leigh, anyway. A remake of the 1937 film NOTHING SACRED, which starred Carole Lombard. Songs include "How Do You Speak to an Angel," "That's What I Like," "Every Street's a Boulevard in Old New York," "Money Burns a Hole in My Pocket," "You're Gonna Dance with Me Baby," and "Champagne and Wedding Cake" (Styne, Hilliard).

p, Paul Jones; d, Norman Taurog; w, Jack Rose, Melville Shavelson (based on the musical comedy "Hazel Flagg" by Ben Hecht, Jule Styne, Bob Hilliard, from the story by James Street); ph, Daniel Fapp (Technicolor); ed, Archie Marshek; art d, Albert Nozaki, Hal Pereira; ch, Nick Castle.

Comedy Musical   (PR:A MPAA:NR)

LIVING LEGEND zero
(1980) 92m Maverick Pictures International c

Earl Owensby (Eli Canfield), William T. Hicks (Jim Cannon), Ginger Alden (Jeannie Loring), Jerry Rushing (Chad), Greg Carswell (Teddy), Toby Wallace (Dean), Kristina Reynolds (Susan).

A pitiful waste of celluloid about a super famous country rock star who wears glittery clothes, takes pills, lives a high-pressure life, is pursued by crazed fans, and has a conniving manager. If it sounds like the Elvis Presley story . . . well, it can't be. The disclaimer says so. We're supposed to believe that casting Alden, Elvis' female companion at the time of his death, is purely coincidental. Owensby lip-synchs some good songs, though, actually sung by Roy Orbison.

p, Earl Owensby; d, Worth Keeter; w, Tom McIntyre; ph, Darrell Cathcart (CFI Color); ed, Richard Aldridge.

Drama   (PR:O MPAA:PG)

LIVING ON LOVE**
(1937) 60m RKO bw

James Dunn (Gary), Whitney Bourne (Mary), Joan Woodbury (Edith), Solly Ward (Eli), Tom Kennedy (Pete), Franklin Pangborn (Oglethorpe), Kenneth Terrell, James Fawcett (Ghonoff Brothers), Chester Clute (Jessup), Evelyn Carrington (Mme. Valley), Etta McDaniel (Lizbeth).

An improbable but amusing comedy starring Dunn and Bourne as roommates who've never met. They share an apartment, but he works nights and sleeps during the day, and she works days and uses the abode at night. As strangers, they meet and eventually fall in love. A remake of the 1933 film, RAFTER ROMANCE.

p, Maury Cohen; d, Lew Landers; w, Franklin Coen (based on the novel by John Wells); ph, Nicholas Musuraca; ed, Harry Marker; art d, Van Nest Polglase.

Comedy **(PR:A MPAA:NR)**

LIVING ON VELVET 1/2** (1935) 80m FN-WB bw

Kay Francis *(Amy Prentiss)*, George Brent *(Terry Parker)*, Warren William *(Walter Pritcham)*, Helen Lowell *(Aunt Martha)*, Henry O'Neill *(Thornton)*, Samuel S. Hinds *(Henry L. Parker)*, Russell Hicks *(Major)*, Maude Turner Gordon *(Mrs. Parker)*, Martha Merrill *(Cynthia Parker)*, Edgar Kennedy *(Counterman)*, Sam Hayes *(Announcer)*, Lee Shumway, Emmet Vogan *(Officers)*, Selmer Jackson *(Captain)*, Walter Miller *(Leader)*, Stanley King *(Soldier)*, Niles Welch *(Major's Aide)*, May Beatty, Mrs. Wilfred North *(Dowagers)*, Grace Hayle *(Woman)*, Harry Bradley, Jay Eaton, Lloyd Whitlock *(Men)*, Olaf Hytten *(Travis)*, Harry Holman *(Bartender)*, Wade Boteler *(Desk Sergeant)*, Eric Wilton *(Lawton)*, Harold Nelson *(Sexton)*, Frank Dodd *(Minister)*, William Norton Bailey *(Drew)*, David Newell *(Smalley)*, John Cooper *(Messenger Boy)*, Jack Richardson *(Taxi Driver)*, Eddy Chandler *(Policeman)*, Paul Fix *(Intern)*, Frank Fanning *(Doorman)*, Bud Geary *(Aunt Martha's Chauffeur)*, Austa *(Max, the Dachshund Dog)*, Eddie Phillips *(Eddie at Party)*, William Wayne *(Butler)*, Bill Elliot *(Commuter)*.

Brent is an amateur pilot whose plane goes down. His parents and sister are killed in the accident, and his guilt causes him to adopt a reckless lifestyle. He marries Francis, and the two live in squalor until Brent comes into an $8,000 inheritance. He uses the money to buy a plane to haul passengers short distances, and puts the couple back into debt. Francis leaves him, but returns after he is injured in a car accident.

p, Edward Chodorov; d, Frank Borzage; w, Jerry Wald, Julius Epstein; ph, Sid Hickox; ed, William Holmes; md, Leo F. Forbstein; art d, Robert M. Haas; cos, Orry-Kelly; m/l, "Living on Velvet," Al Dubin, Harry Warren.

Drama **(PR:A MPAA:NR)**

LIVING VENUS zero (1961) 74m Mid-Continent/Creative Services bw

William Kerwin *(Jack Norwall)*, Danica D'Hondt *(Peggy Brandon)*, Harvey Korman *(Ken Carter)*, Jeanette Leahy, Lawrence J. Aberwood, Robert Bell, Linne Ahlstrand, Billy Falbo, Bob Scobey and His Band.

H. G. Lewis helmed this drama about an assistant publisher of a girlie magazine, Kerwin, who decides to start his own publication. With the help of photographer Korman, Kerwin transforms model D'Hondt into the living image of Venus. Both men are soon fighting for their creation's affections. Things start going downhill, however, and the magazine collapses, the model commits suicide, and Kerwin is left a broken man. Filmed in Chicago, the late Mayor Daley apparently swore off movie production in his fair city after this picture was made.

p&d, Herschell Gordon Lewis.

Drama **(PR:O MPAA:NR)**

LIZA zero (1976, Fr./Ital.) 100m Lira-Pegaso/CRDC-Pathe-Sirus-Oceanic c

Catherine Deneuve *(Liza)*, Marcello Mastroianni *(Giorgio)*, Corinne Marchand *(Wife)*, Michel Piccoli *(Friend)*, Pascal Laperrousaz *(Son)*.

An outlandish look at modern society that has Mastroianni living on a Mediterannean island with his dog in a round cement house. Deneuve comes to the island, the pair meet, and she soon becomes Mastroianni's lover. Jealous of the dog, Deneuve kills it and becomes its replacement, wearing its collar and fetching sticks. It turns out that Mastroianni has a suicidal wife, and when he goes to visit her, Deneuve follows and brings him back to their island retreat. Before long French Legionnaires are scouting the island for deserters, and the lovers are painting a Nazi airplane pink. A lot of "artistic" nonsense and a waste of time and money.

d, Marco Ferreri; w, Ferreri, Jean-Claude Carriere (based on the book by Ennio Flaiano); ph, Mario Vulpiano (Eastmancolor); m, Philippe Sarde; art d, Theo Meurisse.

Drama **(PR:O MPAA:NR)**

LIZZIE 1/2** (1957) 81m Bryna/MGM bw

Eleanor Parker *(Elizabeth Richmond)*, Richard Boone *(Dr. Neal Wright)*, Joan Blondell *(Aunt Morgan)*, Hugo Haas *(Walter Brenner)*, Ric Roman *(Johnny Valenzo)*, Dorothy Arnold *(Elizabeth's Mother)*, John Reach *(Robin)*, Marion Ross *(Ruth Seaton)*, Johnny Mathis *(Nightclub Singer)*, Jan Englund *(Helen Jameson)*, Carol Wells *(Elizabeth, 13-years-old)*, Karen Green *(Elizabeth, 9-years-old)*, Gene Walker *(Guard)*, Pat Golden *(Man in Bar)*, Dick Paxton *(Waiter)*, Michael Mark *(Bartender)*.

Released the same year as THE THREE FACES OF EVE, this picture treads much the same water, but not nearly as well. Based on Jackson's novel, *The Bird's Nest*, it stars Parker as a troubled woman with three personalities: Elizabeth, the dreary museum employee who feels mentally unbalanced; Beth, the pleasant, likable girl; and the title character Lizzie, a wild woman who goes out nights, gets insanely drunk and winds up in strangers' beds. Director Haas stars as a kindly neighbor who, with Blondell, an alcoholic aunt, brings her to psychiatrist Boone. Through treatment and shock therapy, he is able to rid Parker of the boisterous Lizzie. Haas' finest film, which isn't saying all that much.

p, Jerry Bresler; d, Hugo Haas; w, Mel Dinelli (based on the novel *The Bird's Nest* by Shirley Jackson); ph, Paul Ivano; m, Leith Stevens; ed, Leon Barsha; md, Stevens; art d, Rudi Feld; cos, Norman Martien, Sabine Manela; m/l, "It's Not for Me to Say" (Albert Stillman, Robert Allen; sung by Johnny Mathis), "Warm and Tender" (Hal David, Burt Bacharach; sung by Mathis).

Drama **(PR:C MPAA:NR)**

LJUBAVNI SLUJAC ILI TRAGEDIJA SLUZBENICE P.T.T.
(SEE: LOVE AFFAIR; OR THE CASE OF THE MISSING SWITCHBOARD OPERATOR, 1968, Yugo.)

LLANO KID, THE* 1/2 (1940) 68m PAR bw

Tito Guizar *(The Llano Kid)*, Alan Mowbray *(John Travers)*, Gale Sondergaard *(Lora Travers)*, Jane Clayton *(Lupita)*, Emma Dunn *(Donna Teresa)*, Minor Watson *(Sheriff McLane)*, Harry Worth *(Dissipated Mexican)*, Anna Demetrio *(Fat Maria)*, Chris-Pin Martin *(Sixto)*, Carlos De Valdez *(Don Pedro)*, Glenn Strange *(Henderson)*, Tony Roux *(Jose)*, Eddie Dean.

Mexican singing star Guizar appears in this attempt to cash in on the success of the Cisco Kid movies. Guizar robs a stagecoach and manages to kiss Sondergaard, who is the only person to see him with his mask off. Later when Guizar is arrested, Sondergaard refuses to identify him. The two team up to bilk a Mexican woman of her fortune by having Guizar pose as her son. Guizar's conscience gets to him, and he decides not to steal the money but become a good son to the old woman instead. Guizar rejects Sondergaard and eventually marries Clayton, the old woman's adopted daughter.

p, Harry Sherman; d, Edward Venturini; w, Wanda Tuchock (based on the story "The Double-Dyed Deceiver" by O. Henry); ph, Russell Harlan; ed, Sherman A. Rose; art d, Lewis J. Rachmil.

Western **(PR:A MPAA:NR)**

LLOYDS OF LONDON* 1/2** (1936) 115m FOX bw

Freddie Bartholomew *(Young Jonathan Blake)*, Madeleine Carroll *(Lady Elizabeth Stacy)*, Sir Guy Standing *(John Julius Angerstein)*, Tyrone Power *(Jonathan Blake)*, George Sanders *(Lord Everett Stacy)*, C. Aubrey Smith *(Old "Q")*, Virginia Field *(Polly)*, Montagu Love *(Hawkins)*, Una O'Connor *(Widow Blake)*, J. M. Kerrigan *(Brook Watson)*, Gavin Muir *(Sir Gavin Gore)*, Douglas Scott *(Young Horatio Nelson)*, Forrester Harvey *(Percival Potts)*, E. E. Clive *(Magistrate)*, Miles Mander *(Jukes)*, John Burton *(Lord Horatio Nelson)*, Lester Matthews *(Capt. Hardy)*, Lumsden Hare *(Capt. Suckling)*, Vernon Steel *(Sir Thomas Lawrence)*, Barlowe Borland *(Joshua Lamb)*, Robert Greig *(Lord Drayton)*, Murray Kinnell *(Reverend Nelson)*, May Beatty *(Lady Markham)*, Hugh Huntley *(Prince of Wales)*, Will Stanton *(Smitt)*, Holmes Herbert *(Spokesman)*, Charles Crokerking *(Willoughby)*, Thomas Pogue *(Benjamin Franklin)*, Yorke Sherwood *(Dr. Sam Johnson)*, William Wagner *(Boswell)*, Ann Howard *(Catherine)*, Winter Hall *(Dr. Beatty)*, Fay Chaldecott *(Sunghnah)*, Yvonne Severn *(Ann)*, Arthur Hohl *(1st Captain)*, Reginald Barlow *(2nd Captain)*, Charles Coleman, Charles McNaughton, Leonard Mudie *(Waiters at Lloyds')*, Rita Carlyle *(Pawn Seller)*, Ivan F. Simpson *(Old Man)*, D'Arcy Corrigan *(Chimney Sweep)*, Cecil Watson *(Woman)*, Leonard Walker *(Fiddler)*, Georges Renavent *(French Lieutenant)*, Olaf Hytten *(Telescope Man)*, Thomas A. Braiden *(Chaplain)*, Jean DeBriac *(Fisherman)*, Constance Purdy *(Singer)*, Captain John Blood *(Doorman)*, Ralph Cooper, Elsa Buchanan.

Although this Fox epic, lavishly produced but thin on historical accuracy, starred Power—then fourth billed—the top star was listed as the precocious Bartholomew, the studio's *wunderkind*, who plays Power as a boy. Bartholomew and his pal Scott, playing a young Horatio, later Lord Nelson, one of England's greatest naval heroes, overhear pirates in 1770 planning to scuttle a ship and steal its cargo. Both boys run off to inform the great insurance brokers, Lloyds of London, but Scott gets sidetracked and only Bartholomew finds his way to the brokerage house. He cannot enter until a kindly Benjamin Franklin (Pogue) escorts him inside. He finds the senior official, Standing, and reports his terrible findings. Standing takes quick action and then rewards Bartholomew with an apprenticeship with the firm. He grows up to be Power, a man who stands high in the company, especially after inventing a message relay system to bring news to England from the continent and because of his lifelong friendship with Nelson, played as a grownup by Burton. Sanders, the haughty nephew of the First Lord of the Admiralty, hates Power for his influential position. When Napoleon Bonaparte comes to power in France, Power goes to the continent to aid some of his friends who are trapped in the Reign of Terror, rescuing a beautiful English girl, Carroll. He smuggles her back to England but she vanishes. Power learns that Carroll is the wife of his nemesis, Sanders, and he tries to put her out of his mind by swamping himself with work. Power has a bit of sweet revenge when Sanders requests a loan from Lloyds to cover his enormous gambling debts. The strutting Sanders is turned down, becoming a mortal enemy of Power's as well as Lloyds'. The insurance brokerage firm itself falls upon hard times when it refuses to insure ships after England begins to lose its war with Bonaparte. Carroll gives her fortune to help shore up the company at Power's request and Sanders almost goes crazy when he hears of this. Moreover, he believes that Power has lied when bringing news through his relay service that his friend Nelson has won a great naval victory over the French at Trafalgar. He begins to spread the word that Power and Lloyds are complete frauds—which almost ruins the company—but, at the last minute, confirmation of Nelson's victory and tragic death arrives and the day is saved. Sanders finds Carroll in Power's arms and explodes, challenging Power to a duel. Power is wounded but Sanders dies of a fatal wound. Carroll now nurses the man she really loves back to health and happiness. The production is rich and historically correct in costume and props but the events have been twisted about a bit, a habit of Fox boss Zanuck who took great liberties with the facts in most of the historical epics he made in the 1930s, including THE HOUSE OF ROTHSCHILD, CLIVE OF INDIA, and others, causing critics of his studio to dub the studio "16th Century-Fox." This was the first of eleven films director King would make with Power, who was nothing more than a lowly contract player until Zanuck decided to risk a big-budget film on him. LLOYDS OF LONDON made Power an overnight sensation, and he became one of Fox's greatest stars. Actually King was the man who urged Zanuck to give Power the break; Power had been a studio stock player and was literally pulled from the ranks, replacing Don Ameche, whom Zanuck originally cast in the lead part. Carroll was also a replacement. Loretta Young had originally signed to play the femme lead against Ameche, but when King began building Power's part—at the expense of her own role, she believed—Young exploded in fury at the upstart youngster's part being padded and left the production. The studio spent $850,000 on the film, its biggest budget to date, and soon had a hit.

p, Kenneth MacGowan; d, Henry King; w, Ernest Pascal, Walter Ferris (based on the story by Curtis Kenyon); ph, Bert Glennon; ed, Barbara McLean; md, Louis Silvers; art d, William S. Darling; set d, Thomas Little; cos, Royer.

Historical Epic Cas. (PR:A MPAA:NR)

LO STRANIERO (SEE: STRANGER, THE, 1967, Algeria/Fr./Ital.)

LOADED DICE (SEE: CROSS MY HEART, 1937, Brit.)

LOADED PISTOLS**¹/₂ (1948) 79m Autry/COL bw

Gene Autry (Himself), Barbara Britton (Mary Evans), Chill Wills (Sheriff Cramer), Jack Holt (Dave Randall), Russell Arms (Larry Evans), Robert Shayne (Don Mason), Vince Barnett (Sam Gardner), Leon Weaver (Jake Harper), Fred Kohler, Jr. (Bill Otis), Clem Bevans (Jim Hedge), Sandy Sanders (Rancher), Budd Buster, John R. McKee, Stanley Blystone, Hank Bell, Felice Raymond, Dick Alexander, Frank O'Connor, Reed Howes, William Sundholm, Snub Pollard, Heinie Conklin, Champion, Jr. (The Horse).

A fast-action Autry western, with the singing cowboy harboring a youngster accused of murder, while hunting down the actual culprits. Sheriff Wills and the real killer, Shayne, make Autry's job a little tougher, but in the end, Autry fools Shayne into a confession. When not tracking lawbreakers, Autry finds time to sing: "Loaded Pistols," "When the Bloom Is on the Sage," "A Boy From Texas and a Girl From Tennessee," "Pretty Mary," and "Blue Tail Fly."

p, Armand Schaefer; d, John English; w, Dwight Cummins, Dorothy Yost; ph, William Bradford; ed, Aaron Stell; md, Mischa Bakaleinikoff; art d, Harold MacArthur.

Western Cas. (PR:A MPAA:NR)

LOAN SHARK** (1952) 79m Lippert bw

George Raft (Joe Gargen), Dorothy Hart (Ann Nelson), Paul Stewart (Donelli), Helen Westcott (Martha Haines), John Hoyt (Phillips), Henry Slate (Paul Nelson), William Phipps (Ed Haines), Russell Johnson (Thompson), Benny Baker (Tubby), Larry Dobkin (Walter Karr), Charles Meredith (Rennick), Harlan Warde (Lt. White), Spring Mitchell (Nancy), Margia Dean (Ivy), Ross Elliott (Norm), Robert Bice (Steve Casmer), Robert Williams (Scully), Michael Ragan (Maxie), Virginia Caroll (Netta), William "Bill" Phillips (Baski), George Eldredge (George), William Tannen (Rourke), Jack Daley (Borrower).

A good crime film that has Raft heavily entangled in the loan shark racket. Raft finds work with the Acme Tire Company in order to uncover a loan shark operation that is not only emptying the pockets of factory workers, but is also responsible for his brother-in-law's murder. Raft worms his way into the gang, headed by the vicious Dobkin. After a shoot-out in a theater, Dobkin is left dead and the racket is smashed. Film contains some fine camerawork and *film noir* lighting.

p, Bernard Luber; d, Seymour Friedman; w, Martin Rackin, Eugene Ling (based on an unpublished story by Rackin); ph, Joseph Biroc; ed, Al Joseph; art d, Feild Gray.

Crime (PR:A MPAA:NR)

LOCAL BAD MAN*¹/₂ (1932) 59m Allied bw

Hoot Gibson, Sally Blane, Edward Piel, Sr., Hooper Atchley, Milt Brown, Edward Hearn, Skeeter Bill Robbins, Jack Clifford.

Gibson is a railroad agent who is the targeted fall guy in an attempted railroad insurance swindle. Two brothers, who are bankers, wish to steal one of their own money shipments, frame Gibson for the theft, and then keep that money as well as the insurance money reimbursed to them by the railroad. Gibson narrowly stops their first robbery attempt, but when the two brothers try it again, Gibson is prepared and captures the scheming pair.

p, M. H. Hoffman; d, Otto Brower; w, Philip White (based on the story "All for Love" by Peter B. Kyne); ph, Harry Neumann, Tom Galligan; ed, Mildred Johnston.

Western (PR:A MPAA:NR)

LOCAL BOY MAKES GOOD** (1931) 67m FN-WB bw

Joe E. Brown (John Miller), Dorothy Lee (Julia Winters), Ruth Hall (Marjorie Blake), Edward Woods (Spike Hoyt), Edward J. Nugent (Wally Pierce), John Harrington (Coach Jackson), Wade Boteler, William Burress, Robert Bennett.

A silly but tolerable comedy starring Joe E. Brown as a sheepish florist who writes a note to Lee, the girl of his dreams. He has no intentions of dropping the note in the mail, but one of his prankster pals does. As a result, Brown must pretend to be the collegiate track athlete he claimed to be in his letter. He makes the team in a rather unorthodox manner—he throws the javelin and nearly impales the coach, who chases him around the track in record time. A typical college comedy which serves only to showcase Brown.

p, Robert Lord; d, Mervyn LeRoy; w, Lord (based on the play "The Poor Nut" by J. C. and Elliott Nugent); ph, Sol Polito; ed, Jack Killifer; md, Leo F. Forbstein.

Comedy (PR:A MPAA:NR)

LOCAL COLOR zero (1978) 116m Rappaport bw

Jane Campbell (Andrea), Bob Herron (Fred), Dolores Kenan (Lil), Michael Burg (Alvin), Tom Bair (Andrew), Barry de Jasu (Brian), Randy Danson (Viv), Temmie Brodkey (Debbie).

Incomprehensible 16mm soap opera disguised as an art film. Eight characters interact in different ways, dreams and reality converge, and a gun is passed around. Produced, written, edited, and directed by Rappaport, so he is the one to blame for foisting this on the world.

p,d&w, Mark Rappaport; ph, Fred Murphy; ed, Rappaport.

Drama (PR:O MPAA:NR)

LOCAL HERO**** (1983, Brit.) 111m Enigma-Goldcrest/WB c

Burt Lancaster (Happer), Peter Riegert (Mac), Fulton Mackay (Ben), Denis Lawson (Urquhart), Norman Chancer (Moritz), Peter Capaldi (Oldsen), Rikki Fulton (Geddes), Alex Norton (Watt), Jenny Seagrove (Marina), Jennifer Black (Stella), Christopher Rozycki (Victor), Christopher Asante (Rev. MacPherson), John Jackson (Cal), Dan Ammerman (Donaldson), Tam Dean Burn (Roddy), Luke Coulter (Baby), Karen Douglas (Mrs. Wyatt), Kenny Ireland (Skipper), Harlan Jordan (Fountain), Charles Kearney (Peter), David Mowat (Gideon), John Poland (Anderson), Anne Scott Jones (Linda), Ian Stewart (Bulloch), Tanya Ticktin (Russian), Jonathan Watson (Jonathan), David Anderson (Fraser), Mark Winchester, Alan Clark, Alal Darby, Roddy Murray, Dale Winchester, Brian Rowan (Ace Tones), Caroline Guthrie (Pauline), Ray Jeffries (Andrew), Willie Joss (Sandy), James Kennedy (Edward), Buddy Quaid (Crabbe), Edith Ruddick (Old Lady), John Gordon Sinclair (Ricky), Sandra Voe (Mrs. Fraser), Jimmy Yuill (Iain), Betty Macey, Michele McCarel, Anne Thompson (Switchboard Operators).

Charming, whimsical, and near perfect, LOCAL HERO proves again that you don't need a lot of money to make a good film. Scottish writer-director Forsyth, coming off his hit GREGORY'S GIRL, has outdone himself with an original idea carried out with intelligence. It's funny and touching and, except that the scenes with Lancaster in the U.S. seem to have been directed and written by someone else, it's a terrific example of superior film making. Lancaster is the head of a huge oil company in Texas. He is so ashamed of his success that he has Chancer, a psychiatrist, come in regularly and abuse him with verbal insults. Chancer winds up outside Lancaster's skyscraper window and writing obscenities. Lancaster is obviously nuts and he speaks his version of astronomy, which seems to be the credo by which he lives his life. Meanwhile, Riegert, a young executive of the oil company, has been dispatched to Scotland to buy an entire town so the company can drill for North Sea oil reserves. Riegert, a Hungarian-descent young man, has taken the name of MacIntyre for business reasons and so he was chosen for the task although the closest he ever came to anything Scottish was with soda and a twist. Once in the little town, Riegert meets Lawson, a Scots sharper who represents everyone in the town as a lawyer, while tending the only inn. The obvious plot turn would be to show the Americans as nasty and rapacious but it turns out that the Scots would be only too happy to depart the area, if the price is right. Capaldi is the local Scot who works for the oil company and he's romantically involved with Seagrove, a diver who also works for the company. Asante, whose screen name is MacPherson, is the vicar and Riegert is surprised to see he is a black. Matter of fact, nothing is what it seems to Riegert and he finds himself falling in love with the simple life of Scotland after the hustle of Houston. A deal is about to be struck but there's a problem and Lancaster must show up to straighten matters out. Meanwhile, we see that Soviet trawler captain Rozycki makes regular stops at the village where he deals with Lawson who makes sundry investments for him in real estate and securities. The denouement is so unexpected that we feel it would do you a disservice to know it ahead of time. Just be prepared for an ending that will knock you for a loop. Scotland is a gorgeous country and the shots of it, vis-a-vis Houston, make one long to be there. Every actor, down to the smallest role, is well chosen. LOCAL HERO is a very funny movie and Lancaster was never better in a parody of the role he's played straight so many times before; the blustery military-industrial type who raves and rants. Lancaster has always had a good sense of humor and showed it in THE CRIMSON PIRATE as well as in many other films, but the audience may have a tendency to remember him mainly for his dramatic work. Forsyth is to be congratulated for a delightful and unique job. He will be heard from in the years to come.

p, David Puttnam; d&w, Bill Forsyth; ph, Chris Menges; m, Mark Knopfler; ed, Michael Bradsell; prod d, Roger Murray-Leach; art d, Richard James, Adrienne Atkinson, Frank Walsh, Ian Watson; spec eff, Wally Veevers.

Comedy Cas. (PR:A-C MPAA:PG)

LOCK UP YOUR DAUGHTERS zero (1969, Brit.) 102m Domino/COL c

Christopher Plummer (Lord Foppington), Susannah York (Hilaret), Glynis Johns (Mrs. Squeezum), Ian Bannen (Ramble), Tom Bell (Shaftoe), Elaine Taylor (Cloris), Jim Dale (Lusty), Kathleen Harrison (Lady Clumsey), Roy Kinnear (Sir Tunbelly Clumsey), Georgia Brown (Nell), Vanessa Howard (Hoyden Clumsey), Roy Dotrice (Gossip), Fenella Fielding (Lady Eager), Paul Dawkins (Lord Eager), Peter Bayliss (Mr. Justice Squeezum), Richard Wordsworth (Coupler), Peter Bull (Bull), Wallas Eaton (Staff), Trevor Ray (Quill), Blake Butler (Faithful), Arthur Mullard (Night Watchman), Edward Atienza (Mr. Justice Worthy), Patricia Routledge (Nurse), Roy Pember (Bottle), Fred Emney (Earl of Ware), John Morley (Nobleman), Tony Sympson (Clerk of the Court), Michael Darbyshire (La Verole), Clive Morton (Bowsell), Roger Hammond (Johnsonian Figure), Martin Crosbie, Cecil Sheehan, Tom Irwin, Danny O'Connor, Vernon Hayden (Constables).

A confusing, complicated 18th Century romp through the love affairs of three bawdy girls who get involved with three wanton sailors. What director Coe thinks is sexy and erotic only turns out to be repulsive and vulgar. The characters are entirely unlikeable, and the script is undeniably uninspired. The film even includes a pie-in-the-face scene, which has long ago worn out its welcome. Lock up the producers!

p, David Deutsch; d, Peter Coe; w, Keith Waterhouse, Willis Hall (based on the Mermaid Theater presentation by Lionel Bart, Laurie Johnson, and Bernard Miles, derived from Henry Fielding's play "Rape Upon Rape" and from John Vanbrugh's play "The Relapse"); ph, Peter Suschitzky (Technicolor); m, Ron Grainer; ed, Frank Clarke; prod d, Tony Woollard; set d, Ian Whittaker, Peter Young; cos, Alan Barrett; makeup, W. T. Partleton.

Comedy **(PR:C-O MPAA:M)**

LOCK YOUR DOORS (SEE: APE MAN, THE, 1943)

LOCKED DOOR, THE*½ (1929) 74m UA bw

Rod La Rocque *(Frank Devereaux)*, Barbara Stanwyck *(Ann Carter)*, William "Stage" Boyd *(Lawrence Reagan)*, Betty Bronson *(Helen Reagan)*, Harry Stubbs *(The Waiter)*, Harry Mestayer *(District Attorney)*, Mack Swain *(Hotel Proprietor)*, ZaSu Pitts *(Telephone Girl)*, George Bunny *(The Valet)*, Purnell Pratt *(Police Officer)*, Fred Warren *(Photographer)*, Charles Sullivan *(Guest)*, Edgar Dearing *(Cop)*, Mary Ashcraft, Violet Bird, Eleanor Fredericks, Martha Stewart, Virginia McFadden, Lita Chevret, Leona Leigh, Greta von Rue, Dorothy Gowan, Kay English *(Girls on Rum Boat)*, Edward Dillon, Clarence Burton, Robert Schable, Earle Browne, Pauline Curley, Fletcher Norton, Gilbert Clayton.

Barbara Stanwyck's first Hollywood-made film, shot partly in director Fitzmaurice's home, begins with Stanwyck being taken to an illegal, floating cabaret by wealthy La Rocque. He locks her in a private room and, when police raid the club, her photograph is taken with La Rocque. Some time later, Stanwyck marries her new boss, Boyd, while La Rocque gets involved with Stanwyck's sister-in-law, Bronson. La Rocque and Boyd quarrel over Stanwyck, and Boyd shoots and kills La Rocque. Stanwyck is later found locked in her room and admits to the crime to spare her husband. Boyd's confession, however, saves her. Like other early talkies, the film is stagy, and therefore stilted and flat. Not surprisingly, this is one of Stanwyck's least favorite pictures. The flim is a remake of THE SIGN ON THE DOOR (1922) with Norma Talmadge.

p&d, George Fitzmaurice; w, C. Gardner Sullivan, George Scarborough, Earle Brown (based on the play "The Sign on the Door" by Channing Pollock); ph, Ray June; ed, Hal Kern; art d&set d, William Cameron Menzies.

Drama **(PR:A MPAA:NR)**

LOCKER 69*½ (1962, Brit.) 56m Merton Park/AA bw

Eddie Byrne *(Simon York)*, Paul Daneman *(Frank Griffiths)*, Penelope Horner *(Julie Denver)*, Walter Brown *(Craig)*, Edward Underdown *(Bennett Sanders)*, Clarissa Stolz *(Eva Terila)*, John Carson *(Miguel Terila)*, John Glyn-Jones *(Inspector Roon)*.

One of those mystery thrillers that relies on far-fetched plot devices to keep the story moving; in this case missing dead bodies, mysterious papers in a safety deposit box, and a private detective who can't get the police interested in the murder of his boss. Eventually the poor man takes up the investigation on his own. Moderate entertainment value in uncovering how the film sustains suspense.

p, Jack Greenwood; d, Norman Harrison; w, Richard Harris (based on the story by Edgar Wallace).

Mystery **(PR:A MPAA:NR)**

LOCKET, THE** (1946) 86m RKO bw

Laraine Day *(Nancy Blair)*, Brian Aherne *(Dr. Blair)*, Robert Mitchum *(Norman Clyde)*, Gene Raymond *(John Willis)*, Sharyn Moffett *(Nancy, Age 10)*, Ricardo Cortez *(Mr. Bonner)*, Henry Stephenson *(Lord Wyndham)*, Katherine Emery *(Mrs. Willis)*, Reginald Denny *(Mr. Wendall)*, Fay Helm *(Mrs. Bonner)*, Helene Thimig *(Mrs. Monks)*, Nella Walker *(Mrs. Wendall)*, Queenie Leonard *(Woman Singer)*, Lillian Fontaine *(Lady Wyndham)*, Myrna Dell *(Thelma)*, Johnny Clark *(Donald)*, Vivian Oakland *(Mrs. Donovan)*, Nancy Saunders *(Miss Wyatt)*, George Humbert *(Luigi)*, Trina Varella *(Luigi's wife)*, Nick Thompson *(Waiter)*, Connie Leon *(Bonner Maid)*, Dave Thursby *(Dexter)*, Tom Chatterton *(Art Critic)*, Sam Flint *(District Attorney)*, Tom Coleman *(Stenotypist)*, J. W. Johnston, Allen Schute, Eddie Borden *(Men)*, Virginia Keiley *(Ambulance Driver)*, Wyndham Standing *(Butler)*, Fred Worlock, Henry Mowbray *(Doctors)*, Cecil Weston *(Nurse)*, Colin Kenny *(Chauffeur)*, Leonard Mudie *(Air Raid Warden)*, Pat Malone *(London Bobby)*, Jacqueline Frost *(Girl)*, Polly Bailey *(Cook)*, Ellen Corby, Jean Ransom *(Kitchen Girls)*, Keith Hitchcock *(Orville)*, Gloria Donovan *(Karen)*, Carol Donell, Martha Hyer, Kay Christopher *(Bridesmaids)*, Ben Erway *(2nd Willis Butler)*, Mari Aldon *(Mary)*, Charles Flynn, Joe Ray, Bob Templeton *(Photographers)*, Broderick O'Farrell *(Minister)*, Dorothy Curtis (Maid).

They should have named this picture "Flashback" because that's what it is; one flashback after another with the tale told in the style of Akira Kurosawa from several points of view. The technique gets in the way of the story. Not that there is that much of a story, and it winds up being a confused picture about a confused woman. Two years later, a better film was made on the subject of a mental breakdown. It was THE SNAKE PIT. Here, Day is about to marry rich Raymond when Aherne, a psychiatrist, shows up and warns Raymond to break it off. He'd once been married to Day for five years and knows that she is seriously disturbed. He tells Raymond that Mitchum, another Day fiance, found a stolen bracelet in Day's purse and Day explained that she'd once been accused of stealing a locket as a child and was innocent but that left her with a kleptomaniac complex. Mitchum had her promise she'd never do that again but then she was arrested in a robbery-murder case and was exonerated when the dead man's valet confessed. Mitchum came to Aherne for help, as Aherne was her doctor. She denied having anything to do with the killing, so the valet got the hot seat and Mitchum did himself in. Aherne married Day, then found a cache of gems she'd heisted from pals. Raymond doesn't believe these accusations and is convinced by Day that Aherne suffers from delusions. On the way to the altar, Emery, Raymond's mother, gives Day a locket and Day recalls that it was the same one she'd been charged with stealing as a child. That triggers an emotional outburst and Day has a mental collapse, winding up in a mental hospital. Much too convoluted and a lot of psychological mishmash. Look for Hyer in a tiny role and note Joan Fontaine's and Olivia de Havilland's mother, Lilian Fontaine, as Lady Wyndham. A good cast in a diffuse film.

p, Bert Granet; d, John Brahm; w, Sheridan Gibney; ph, Nicholas Musuraca; m, Roy Webb; ed, J. R. Whittredge; md, Constantin Bakaleinikoff; art d, Albert S. D'Agostino, Alfred Herman; set d, Darrell Silvera, Harley Miller; cos, Michael Woulfe, spec eff, Russell A. Cully.

Drama **(PR:C MPAA:NR)**

LODGER, THE (SEE: PHANTOM FIEND, THE, 1935, Brit.)

LODGER, THE**** (1944) 84m FOX bw

Merle Oberon *(Kitty)*, George Sanders *(John Garrick)*, Laird Cregar *(The Lodger)*, Sir Cedric Hardwicke *(Robert Burton)*, Sara Allgood *(Ellen)*, Aubrey Mather *(Supt. Sutherland)*, Queenie Leonard *(Daisy)*, David Clyde *(Sgt. Bates)*, Helena Pickard *(Anne Rowley)*, Lumsden Hare *(Dr. Sheridan)*, Frederick Worlock *(Sir Gerard)*, Olaf Hytten *(Harris)*, Colin Campbell *(Harold)*, Anita Bolster *(Wiggy)*, Billy Bevan *(Publican)*, Forrester Harvey *(Cobbler)*, Skelton Knaggs *(Costermonger)*, Charles Hall *(Comedian)*, Edmund Breon *(Manager)*, Harry Allen *(Conductor)*, Raymond Severn *(Boy)*, Heather Wilde *(Girl)*, Colin Kenny, Bob Stephenson, Les Sketchley, Clive Morgan *(Plainclothesmen)*, Crauford Kent, Frank Elliott *(Aides)*, Stuart Holmes *(King Edward)*, Walter Tetley *(Call Boy)*, Boyd Irwin *(Policeman)*, Herbert Clifton *(Conductor)*, Jimmy Aubrey *(Cab Driver)*, Will Stanton *(Newsboy)*, Gerald Hamer *(Milkman)*, Montague Shaw *(Stage Manager)*, Cyril Delevanti *(Stage Hand)*, Connie Leon *(Woman)*, Kenneth Hunter *(Mounted Inspector)*, Donald Stuart *(Concertina Player)*, John Rogers *(Down and Outer)*, Wilson Benge, Charles Knight *(Vigilantes)*, Alec Harford *(Conductor)*, Yorke Sherwood, Colin Hunter *(Policemen)*, Dave Thursby *(Sergeant)*, John Rice *(Mounted Police)*, Herbert Evans *(Constable)*, Douglas Gerrard *(Porter)*, Ruth Clifford *(Hairdresser)*, Harold De Becker *(Charlie)*, Doris Lloyd *(Jennie)*.

Cregar is absolutely chilling in this Jack the Ripper tale, perhaps the best ever produced about Bloody Jack. The screen is soaked with fog and dampness of Victorian London, its cobblestones sweating, its gaslights flickering, as blood-chilling screams pierce the night air and a dark figure goes running, running. Oberon is a beautiful singer whose parents, Allgood and Hardwicke, rent a room to the mysterious Cregar who tells them he won't be joining them for breakfast, lunch, or dinner, because he works at night. During the night, Cregar slips out into the fog carrying his little black bag and during the dawn hours can be heard pacing back and forth in his rooms which are always kept locked, a place where he performs what he calls his "experiments." Cregar eyes Oberon and fences with her friend Sanders, a Scotland Yard inspector developing new criminology techniques, but, in the end, he cannot resist ridding the world of Oberon's terrible beauty as he has done with hapless others. But before he can murder Oberon, the police and Sanders interrupt the attack and chase Cregar wildly through a theater. Trapped like a salivating and maniacal bear, Cregar hurls himself through a huge window and into the Thames to drown rather than surrender, an ending not in keeping with the superlative novel written by Marie Belloc-Lowndes. In this film, unlike the original story, no doubt is left that Cregar is Jack the Ripper. The huge actor is superb in this grand *film noir* production; he and Sanders would almost repeat their parts in a similar movie, HANGOVER SQUARE. Only 28 at the time, Cregar longed for the image of the matinee idol and, shortly after the release of THE LODGER, went on a crash water diet and literally starved himself to death. This was a remake of the Alfred Hitchcock silent film starring Ivor Novello and it's probably better with Brahm directing with a tight rein. The script is brilliant and Ballard's photography a marvel of fluid action, mightily aided by Friedhofer's strange and unnerving score.

p, Robert Bassler; d, John Brahm; w, Barre Lyndon (based on the novel by Marie Belloc Lowndes); ph, Lucien Ballard; m, Hugo W. Friedhofer; ed, J. Watson Webb; md, Emil Newman; art d, James Basevi, John Ewing; set d, Thomas Little, Walter M. Scott; spec eff, Fred Sersen; ch, Kenny Williams.

Crime Drama **Cas.** **(PR:C-O MPAA:NR)**

L'OEIL DU MALIN (SEE: THIRD LOVER, THE, 1963, Fr./Ital.)

LOGAN'S RUN½** (1976) 118m MGM/UA c

Michael York *(Logan)*, Jenny Agutter *(Jessica)*, Richard Jordan *(Francis)*, Roscoe Lee Browne *(Box)*, Farrah Fawcett-Majors *(Holly)*, Peter Ustinov *(Old Man)*, Michael Anderson, Jr. *(Doc)*, Gary Morgan *(Billy)*, Denny Arnold *(Runner #1)*, Glen Wilder *(Runner #2)*, Lara Lindsay *(Woman Runner)*, Bob Neil *(1st Sanctuary Man)*, Randolph Roberts *(2nd Sanctuary Man)*, Camilla Carr *(Sanctuary Woman)*, Greg Michaels *(Ambush Man)*, Roger Borden *(Daniel)*, Michelle Stacy *(Mary Two)*, Ann Ford *(Woman on Lastday)*, Laura Hippe *(New You Shop Customer)*.

A hit-and-miss futuristic film about a world where nobody is allowed to live past 30 years. The story takes place in a manmade self-contained city, where there is no crime, hunger, or strife. The catch is that at the age of 30, everyone must go through a ritual called "renewal," in which the participants float toward the top of an arena where they will be obliterated by disintegration rays. Supposedly, if a participant makes it to the top, he will live another 30 years, but the ritual is fixed and nobody ever lives. Some discover the ruse and become "runners," those who try to escape the city rather than face elimination. York's job is to hunt down runners and kill them; but, after meeting Agutter, a potential runner, he takes up their cause. Agutter and York escape, with York's friend, Jordan, in hot pursuit. Once the couple is clear of the city, they see the outside world for the first time. Traveling through the ruins of Washington, D.C., they meet Ustinov, the first person they have ever met over

30. They bring him back to their futuristic city to show him the rest of the populace; and eventually they destroy the computer that runs the city. Fawcett-Majors makes her film debut as an assistant to a devious cosmetic surgeon.

p, Saul David; d, Michael Anderson; w, David Zelag Goodman (based on the novel by William F. Nolan, George Clayton Johnson); ph, Ernest Laszlo (Todd-AO, Metrocolor); m, Jerry Goldsmith; ed, Bob Wyman; prod d, Dale Hennesy; set d, Robert De Vestel; cos, Bill Thomas; spec eff, L. B. Abbott, Frank Van Der Veer; stunts, Glen Wilder, Bill Couch.

Science Fiction   **Cas.**   **(PR:A MPAA:PG)**

LOLA, 1933   (SEE: YOUNG BLOOD, 1933)

LOLA***
(1961, Fr./Ital.) 90m Rome Paris-Euro International/Films Around the World bw
(DONNA DI VITA)

Anouk Aimee *(Lola)*, Marc Michel *(Roland)*, Elina Labourdette *(Mme. Desnoyers)*, Alan Scott *(Frankie)*, Annie Duperoux *(Cecile)*, Jacques Harden *(Michel)*, Margo Lion *(Jeanne, Michel's Mother)*, Catherine Lutz *(Claire, the Waitress)*, Corinne Marchand *(Daisy)*, Yvette Anziani *(Mme. Frederique)*, Gerard Delaroche *(Yvon, Lola's Son)*, Jacques Goasguen *(Librarian)*, Ginette Valton *(Beauty Shop Proprietor)*, Jacques Lebreton *(Bookshop Owner)*, Carlo Nell *(Dancing Teacher)*, Dorothee Blank *(Dolly)*, Isabelle Lunghini *(Nelly)*, Annik Noel *(Ellen)*, Anne Zamire *(Maggie)*, Babette Barbin *(Minnie)*.

Free-flowing debut feature from French director Jacques Demy, who, with his wife, director Agnes Varda, flourished during the New Wave. Because of the abundance of sweeping camera movement (superbly engineered by Raoul Coutard) it has often been called a musical without music. (Demy would later go to Hollywood and make a real musical with Gene Kelly.) Aimee plays the title role, a cabaret singer who awaits the return of Harden, her husband who has been away for seven years. In the meantime she has a few affairs, her strongest affections going to childhood friend Michel. He has dreams of settling down with Aimee, but those are shattered when Harden returns on the scene and sweeps Aimee away in his glaring white Cadillac. Filled with cinematic allusions (a fondness of French New Wave directors) to Robert Bresson, Gary Cooper, Max Ophuls (especially his camera work), and Josef von Sternberg. Demy received a helping hand from Jean-Luc Godard who offered his talents as a production consultant. (In French; English subtitles.)

p, Carlo Ponti, Georges de Beauregard; d&w, Jacques Demy; ph, Raoul Coutard (Franscope); m, Michel Legrand, Johann Sebastian Bach ("The Well-Tempered Clavier"), Wolfgang Amadeus Mozart ("Concerto For Flute in D-Major"), Carl Maria von Weber ("Invitation to the Waltz"); ed, Anne-Marie Cotret, Monique Teisseire; art d, Bernard Evein; m/l, "C'est moi, c'est Lola," Agnes Varda, "Moi j'etais pour elle," Marguerite Monnot (sung by Anouk Aimee); English subtitles, Rose Sokol.

Drama   **(PR:C MPAA:NR)**

LOLA*   (1971, Brit./Ital.) 98m World-Eurofilm/AIP c (GB: TWINKY)

Charles Bronson *(Scott Wardman)*, Susan George *(Lola "Twinky" Londonderry)*, Michael Craig *(Daddy)*, Honor Blackman *(Mummy)*, Orson Bean *(Hal)*, Paul Ford *(Scott's Father)*, Kay Medford *(Scott's Mother)*, Jack Hawkins *(Judge Millington-Draper)*, Trevor Howard *(Grandfather)*, Lionel Jeffries *(Mr. Creighton)*, Robert Morley *(Judge Roxburgh)*, Elspeth March *(Secretary)*, Eric Chitty *(Client)*, Cathy Jose *(Felicity)*, Leslie Schofield *(1st Policeman)*, Derek Steen *(2nd Policeman)*, Gordon Waller *(Marty)*, Jimmy Tarbuck *(1st TV Comic)*, Norman Vaughan *(2nd TV Comic)*, Reg Lever *(Old Gentleman)*, Tony Arpino *(New York Judge)*, Eric Barker *(Marriage Clerk)*, John Rae *(Hotel Receptionist)*, John Wright *(Hotel Waiter)*, Polly Williams *(Lola's Sister)*, Anthony Kemp *(Lola's Brother)*, Peggy Aitchison *(Mrs. Finchley)*.

Fairly laughable Bronson vehicle which sees him as a rapidly aging American writer living in London who falls into a romantic involvement with 16-year-old George. Driven out of the country by her parents after they marry, the couple flee to New York City for a better life, but they find the same set of prejudices and raised eyebrows from *his* parents. Eventually the age difference rips the relationship apart. Seeing almost no way to make money from this Bronson film, AIP changed the title of the film to a more suitable exploitation moniker, CHILD BRIDE, but then opted for LOLA perhaps because of the association that title could conjure up with Stanley Kubrick's LOLITA. Luckily the plan didn't work and LOLA faded from memory.

p, Clive Sharp; d, Richard Donner; w, Norman Thaddeus Vane; ph, Walter Lassaly (Technicolor); m, John Scott; ed, Norman Wanstall, md, Scott; art d, Michael Wield; m/l "Twinky," "The Lonely Years," "Go Where the Sun Goes," Jim Dale (sung by Dale).

Drama   **(PR:C-O MPAA:PG)**

LOLA*1/2**   (1982, Ger.) 113m Rialto-Trio/UA c

Barbara Sukowa *(Lola)*, Armin Mueller-Stahl *(Von Bohm)*, Mario Adorf *(Schuckert)*, Matthias Fuchs *(Esslin)*, Helga Feddersen *(Hettich)*, Karin Baal *(Lola's Mother)*, Ivan Desny *(Wittich)*, Karl-Heinz von Hassel *(Timmerding)*, Sonia Neudorfer *(Mrs. Fink)*, Elisabeth Volkmann *(Gigi)*, Hark Bohm *(Mayor Voelker)*, Rosel Zech *(Mrs. Schuckert)*, Isolde Barth *(Mrs. Voelker)*, Christine Kaufmann *(Susi)*, Karsten Peters *(Editor)*, Nino Korda *(TV Man)*, Raul Gimenez, Udo Kier *(Waiters)*, Kary Baer, Rainer Will *(Demonstrators)*, Andrea Keuer *(Librarian)*, Aurike Vigo *(Little Marie)*, Herbert Steinmetz *(Pfortner)*, Gunther Kaufmann *(G.I.)*, Helmut Petigk *(Drunk)*, Juliane Lorenz *(Saleslady)*, Marita Pleyer *(Rahel)*, Maxim Oswarl *(Grandpa Berger)*, Y Sa Lo, Andrea Heuer.

The third installment of Fassbinder's war trilogy, which he called "The Entire History of the German Federal Republic" (VERONIKA VOSS and THE MARRIAGE OF MARIA BRAUN being the other two parts). Set in the post WW II 1950s, it stars

Sukowa as a steamy cabaret singer who drifts between halves of a double life. She spends half her time dancing at the Villa Frink, a decadent club/brothel. The rest of the time she is carrying on a relationship with Mueller-Stahl, the honest, newly hired building inspector. He has every intention of fighting corruption, especially that of property developer Adorf, until he sees Sukowa one day performing at the Villa Frink. Unaware of this side of her, Mueller-Stahl goes mad, running away from her and the club. Sexual desire prevails over his integrity and he returns to her. In the finale, he marries Sukowa, who receives the Villa Frink as a wedding present from Adorf. In the end they've all gotten what they want—Mueller-Stahl gets Sukowa; Sukowa gets to continue life at the club; and Adorf can continue in his corrupt ways now that he has given the newlyweds the club. Shot before VERONIKA VOSS (the second part), LOLA was announced as the third installment with more to follow, though none ever did. Essentially an update of THE BLUE ANGEL, the film suffers from a less-than-memorable (though skilled) performance by Sukowa, who has nowhere near the presence of Marlene Dietrich or Fassbinder regular Hanna Schygulla. Frightened with the thought of making this film, Sukowa in one scene, received reassurance from Fassbinder, who sat under a table and caressed her legs as she delivered her lines. She had no problem, however, with another, more difficult scene in which she was to perform a striptease, jump over a table, and land on Adorf's shoulders. She did it perfectly with no rehearsals and on the first take. (German; English Subtitles.)

p, Horst Wendlandt; d, Rainer Werner Fassbinder; w, Peter Marthesheimer, Pea Froehlich, Fassbinder; ph, Xaver Schwarzenberger; m, Peer Raben; ed, Juliane Lorenz; art d, Rolf Zehetbauer; cos, Barbara Baum.

Drama   **(PR:O MPAA:R)**

LOLA MONTES***
(1955, Fr./Ger.) 110m Gamma-Florida-Union/Brandon c (AKA: THE SINS OF LOLA MONTES; GB: THE FALL OF LOLA MONTES)

Martine Carol *(Lola Montes)*, Peter Ustinov *(Circus Master)*, Anton Walbrook *(Ludwig I, King of Bavaria)*, Ivan Desny *(Lt. James)*, Will Quadflieg *(Franz Liszt)*, Oskar Werner *(Student)*, Lise Delamare *(Mrs. Craigie)*, Henri Guisol *(Maurice)*, Paulette Dubost *(Josephine)*, Helena Manson *(James' Sister)*, Willy Eichberger *(Doctor)*, Jacques Fayet *(Steward)*, Daniel Mendaille *(Captain)*, Jean Gallard *(Baron's Secretary)*, Claude Pinoteau *(Orchestra Leader)*, Beatrice Arnac *(Circus Rider)*, Werner Finck *(Painter)*, Germaine Delbat *(Stewardess)*, Walter Kiaulehn *(Theater Attendant)*, Willy Rosner *(1st Minister)*, Friedrich Domin *(Circus Director)*, Gustav Waldou *(Rhino Trainer)*, Helene Iawkoff, Betty Philipsen.

One of the masterpieces of French cinema, and certainly director Max Ophuls' greatest film. Through flashback, the picture takes a fascinating look at the life and loves of the passionate Lola Montes (Carol). With an introduction by a New Orleans circus master (Ustinov), the aging Carol does her pantomime act and answers personal questions from the audience in exchange for a quarter. The ringmaster relates her story to the audience—both circus and film. He tells of her encounters with men in France, Italy, Russia, Poland, of her early affair with Franz Liszt, and finally of her romance with the King of Bavaria. In the final scene, Carol (who has throughout the film been performing various circus acts) stands at the top of a high platform preparing for a dangerous jump. Appearing as if she will faint, she requests that no net be used. She successfully does her act, receiving a proposal from Ustinov and one dollar apiece from the men in the audience who line up just to kiss her hand. Born Max Oppenheimer in 1902, Ophuls began as an assistant to director Anatole Litvak. He left Germany as Hitler rose to power, and eventually, in 1941, came to the U.S. It wasn't until 1949, however, that Ophuls would make his four finest, and final, films—LA RONDE (1950), LE PLAISIR (1951), THE EARRINGS OF MADAME DE . . . (1953), and LOLA MONTES. The idea for LOLA MONTES came after Ophuls heard about Judy Garland's nervous breakdown and Zsa Zsa Gabor's illustrious romances on the radio. What interested the director was not the main character herself (Lola, Judy, or Zsa Zsa), but the reaction of the people around her. Photographed in Eastmancolor and CinemaScope, the film is breathtaking visually, even though Ophuls tried to lessen the effect of the wide screen by placing pillars and curtains on both the left and right sides of the frame. It also displayed the brilliant camera choreography that has become an Ophuls trademark, and has rarely been equalled since. However, none of this interested the audience and it opened as a flop in France. The producers, who intended it to be a great commercial spectacle, took the matter into their own hands. While Ophuls lay on his deathbed (he died in 1957), they began snipping away. The 140-minute film soon became a meager 90-minute chronological version. Needless to say, this version faired no better and a 110-minute version was finally agreed upon. It wasn't until 1969 that the film made it to the U.S. in its restored form. Film critics who had heard the praises garnished upon LOLA MONTES by the French New Wave critics finally saw the film for themselves. Its chief proponent was Andrew Sarris, whose unfaltering assessment instantly elevated the picture to cult status. A wonderful film, which despite much criticism against Carol's wooden performance, is the epitome of craftsmanship and technique. Pure elegance.

d, Max Ophuls; w, Ophuls, Jacques Natanson, Franz Geiger, Annette Wademant (based on the unpublished novel *La Vie Extraordinaire de Lola Montes* by Cecil Saint-Laurent); ph, Christian Matras (CinemaScope, Eastmancolor); m, Georges Auric; ed, Madeleine Gug; art d, Jean d'Eaubonne, Willy Schatz; cos, Georges Annenkov, Marcel Escoffier.

Drama   **(PR:C MPAA:NR)**

LOLA'S MISTAKE   (SEE: THIS REBEL BREED, 1960)

LOLITA*1/2**   (1962) 152m Seven Arts-A.A.-Anya-Transworld/MGM bw

James Mason *(Humbert Humbert)*, Sue Lyon *(Lolita Haze)*, Shelley Winters *(Charlotte Haze)*, Peter Sellers *(Clare Quilty)*, Marianne Stone *(Vivian Darkbloom)*, Diana Decker *(Jean Farlow)*, Jerry Stovin *(John Farlow)*, Gary Cockrell *(Dick)*,

Suzanne Gibbs (*Mona Farlow*), Roberta Shore (*Lorna*), Eric Lane (*Roy*), Shirley Douglas (*Mrs. Starch*), Roland Brand (*Bill*), Colin Maitland (*Charlie*), Cec Linder (*Physician*), Irvin Allen (*Hospital Attendant*), Lois Maxwell (*Nurse Mary Lore*), William Greene (*Swine*), C. Denier Warren (*Potts*), Isobel Lucas (*Haze Maid*), Maxine Holden (*Hotel Receptionist*), Marion Mathie (*Miss Lebone*), Craig Sams (*Rex*), John Harrison (*Tom*), James Dyrenforth (*Beale Senior*), Terence Kilburn.

When the novel was released, it was a smash hit and an outrage to many bluenoses because it dared to tell a love story between a fortyish man and a 12-year-old girl. In the film, they've advanced the age of the nymphet to about 15 and removed much of the controversy. It's far too long and having Nabokov do his own screen adaptation may have been a mistake because he attempted to cram all of the content from the book into the screenplay, whereas another adaptor might not have been as faithful and that could have resulted in a tighter film. Nevertheless, it was a fun movie with enough black humor to make all the black humor-lovers laugh and enough room for Mason, Sellers, Winters, and Lyon to show their wares. Sellers is an alcoholic and totally jaded television writer who has made a fortune purveying his works. Mason walks into a messy mansion and, after taunting him, shoots Sellers, then settles down, in flashback, to recall how it is he came to do this deed. Mason is a middle-aged British professor who is on his way to take a position at an Ohio college but stops for a while in New Hampshire before wending his way west. He is to make a few speeches in the area and when his host's home has been damaged in a fire, he is sent to stay at the house of Winters, a buxom, wealthy, pseudo-intellectual widow, which is precisely the kind of woman Mason detests. But she has a nubile daughter, Lyon, and so he stays at the house and allows himself to be wooed by the effervescent and fluttery Winters. Mason would like to leave but, upon seeing Lyon, he changes his mind. Winters is very sexual and makes no bones about wanting Mason. He, in turn, is fascinated and then aroused by Lyon. He attempts to analyze this and thinks it may be because he once loved a young girl when he was a boy and never recovered from it. In Lyon, he has found that same girl and has regressed in age to the time when the youthful affair was aborted. In order to be near the seductive Lyon, Mason marries Winters and begins writing his feelings in a personal diary. Winters is so cloying and jealous that Mason entertains thoughts of snuffing her out but that problem is resolved when Winters finds the diary, reads how he hates her and loves Lyon, then madly rushes into the street and is smashed by a passing car. Lyon had been away in summer camp and Mason is now her official guardian. He takes her from the camp and they drive to Ohio where he enrolls her in a private school. For a brief while they are happy together, then Lyon discovers boys and begins to make Mason insanely jealous. He is like a love slave to her and allows her to have her way. She is appearing in a play written by Sellers and lies to Mason in order to spend some time with the rakehell. Mason and Lyon argue and eventually set out on a long drive, but Mason gets the feeling they are being followed which, of course, they are—by Sellers. The latter gets the chance to wear several disguises in much the same way he did in a later Kubrick film, DR. STRANGELOVE. Sellers is a total degenerate and just waiting for the moment to pounce. Then Mason and Lyon get sick, are hospitalized, and she uses the opportunity to slip out of the hospital and run off with Sellers. Many years later, Mason hears from Lyon. She's now married to Cockrell, an unskilled laborer, and pregnant. She needs money and calls on Mason for help. Mason now learns that it was Sellers who took her away but she left him because he wanted her to do "weird things." Mason pleads with her to come back but she refuses. Mason gives her all his money, then sets out to find Sellers and wreak revenge. Once at Sellers' home, he forces the man into a mad ping-pong match before he kills him. To satisfy the moral code of the 1960s, an epilog was added to the effect that Mason died in stir of a heart attack. As you have read, it's not all that shocking and the most erotic part of the film is a pedicure. Kubrick exhibited great subtle taste (he had to or they would have given this a hard time in the theaters) and that was the failing. If made today by another director, all the tawdry bedroom details would have been included and that would have swung the pendulum too far in the other direction. The script was nominated for an Oscar but that was the extent of the accolades. Too bad. At two and a half hours, you'll squirm a bit in your seat. By today's standards, the film is tame enough to watch with your maiden aunt or teenage granddaughter. Winters and Mason are magnificent, Sellers is less than his usual self and Lyon looks the part, but that's about it.

p, James B. Harris; d, Stanley Kubrick; w, Vladimir Nabokov (based on his novel); ph, Oswald Morris; m, Nelson Riddle; ed, Anthony Harvey; art d, Bill Andrews; set d, Andrew Low, Peter James; cos, Gene Coffin; m/l, Lolita theme, Bob Harris; makeup, George Partleton.

Comedy/Drama   Cas.   **(PR:C-O MPAA:NR)**

LOLLIPOP**
(1966, Braz.) 89m Producoes Cinematograficas Herbert Richers/Times bw (AKA: ASFALTO SELVAGEM; FORBIDDEN LOVE AFFAIR)

Vera Vianna (*Lollipop*), Jece Valadao (*Silvio*), Maria Helena Dias (*Leticia*), Fregolente (*Nono*), Odilon Azevedo (*Dr. Arnaldo*), Jorge Doria (*Dr. Bergamini*), Nestor Montemar (*Zozimo*), Milton Carneiro (*Dr. Vaconcelos*), Alberico Bruno (*Father Fidelis*), Licia Magna (*Madame Zeze*), Tina Goncalves (*Aunt Ceci*), Thelma Reston (*Gina*), Rodolfo Arena (*Captain*).

Vianna plays an unholy vixen named Lollipop who has loved her orphaned cousin Valadao since childhood and would rather destroy him than watch him marry another. When Valadao announces his engagement to Dias, Vianna sets out to seduce her cousin and succeeds. Soon after, Vianna declares that she is pregnant. This severs Valadao's engagement to Dias, but Vianna's father forbids their marriage to her cousin and arranges for an abortion. When Vianna attempts to run off with Valadao, her father is forced to reveal that Valadao is actually her illegitimate son. Horrified by his act of incest, Valadao kills himself. Vianna's guilt-ridden father also takes his life leaving Vianna totally alone.

p, Herbert Richers; d&w, J. B. Tanko (based on a novel by Nelson Rodrigues); ph, Toni Rabatoni; m, Joao Negrao; ed, Rafael Justo; set d, Alexandre Horvath.

Drama   **(PR:O MPAA:NR)**

LOLLIPOP, 1976   (SEE: FOREVER YOUNG, FOREVER FREE, 1976)

LOLLIPOP COVER, THE**1/2   (1965) 82m International/Continental bw/c

Don Gordon (*Nick Bartaloni*), Carol Seflinger (*Felicity*), George Sawaya, Annette Valentine, Bek Nelson, David White, John Marley, Bert Remsen, Midge Ware, Cliff Carnell, Carolyn Hughes, Lee Philips.

An admirable independent feature about a former boxer, Gordon, and an abandoned 9-year-old girl, Seflinger, who hitchhike together to California. There, Gordon hopes to find a drug addict who was given Gordon's life savings by his late sister. His search is futile, but along the way he learns through his contact with Seflinger to be less cynical. The title stems from the youngster's habit of looking at everything through colored cellophane candy wrappers, a blatant but intriguing symbol.

p&d, Everett Chambers; w, Chambers, Don Gordon (based on an idea by Nancy Valentine); ph, Michael Murphy; m, Ruby Raksin; ed, James D. Mitchell; m/l, "If You Love Me," Raksin, "When I See a Rainbow," Raksin, Mitchell (sung by Sally Kellerman).

Drama   **(PR:A MPAA:NR)**

LOLLY MADONNA WAR, THE   (SEE: LOLLY MADONNA XXX, 1973)

LOLLY-MADONNA XXX**
       (1973) 105m MGM c (AKA: THE LOLLY-MADONNA WAR)

Rod Steiger (*Laban Feather*), Robert Ryan (*Pap Gutshall*), Jeff Bridges (*Zack Feather*), Scott Wilson (*Thrush Feather*), Katherine Squire (*Mrs. Chickie Feather*), Tresa Hughes (*Mrs. Elspeth Gutshall*), Timothy Scott (*Skylar Feather*), Kiel Martin (*Ludie Gutshall*), Ed Lauter (*Hawk Feather*), Joan Goodfellow (*Sister Gutshall*), Season Hubley (*Roonie Gill*), Randy Quaid (*Finch Feather*), Gary Busey (*Seb Gutshall*), Paul Koslo (*Villum Gutshall*).

A pointless film with an excellent cast, LOLLY-MADONNA XXX tells the story of a family feud in the South, sparked by a land dispute and fueled by bitterness and mistaken ideas. The families are headed by Steiger on one side and Ryan on the other, with a mistaken identity in a rape case leading to the climactic slaughter of both families.

p, Rodney Carr-Smith; d, Richard C. Sarafian; w, Carr-Smith, Sue Grafton (based on the novel *The Lolly Madonna War* by Grafton); ph, Philip Lathrop (Panavision, Metrocolor); m, Fred Myrow; ed, Tom Rolf; art d, Herman Blumenthal; set d, Jim Payne; m/l, "Peaceful Country," Kim Carnes, David Ellingson (sung by Carnes).

Drama   **(PR:A MPAA:PG)**

LONDON BELONGS TO ME   (SEE: DULCIMER STREET, 1948, Brit.)

LONDON BLACKOUT MURDERS**   (1942) 58m REP bw

John Abbott (*Jack Rawlings*), Mary McLeod (*Mary Tillet*), Lloyd Corrigan (*Inspector Harris*), Lester Matthews (*Madison*), Anita Bolster (*Mrs. Pringle*), Louis Borell (*Peter Dongen*), Billy Bevan (*Air Raid Warden*), Lumsden Hare (*Supt. Neil*), Frederick Worlock (*Caldwell*), Carl Harbord (*George*), Keith Hitchcock (*Constable*), Tom Stevenson (*Doctor*).

A low-budget thriller set during the WW II bombing raids on London. The story involves a psychotic surgeon, Abbott, who, during blackouts, murders those he believes to be enemies of England via a deadly hypodermic needle. It's never proven that these people are actually enemies, but he kills them just the same. In the end, he is arrested and tried for the killing of his wife several years earlier, a crime which had just been uncovered. The trial occurs in a basement courthouse while London is under attack.

p&d, George Sherman; w, Curt Siodmak; ph, Jack Marta; ed, Charles Craft; md, Morton Scott; art d, Russell Kimball.

Crime   **(PR:A MPAA:NR)**

LONDON BY NIGHT*1/2   (1937) 70m MGM bw

George Murphy (*Michael Denis*), Rita Johnson (*Patricia Herrick*), Virginia Field (*Bessie*), Leo G. Carroll (*Correy*), George Zucco (*Inspector Jefferson*), Montagu Love (*Sir Arthur Herrick*), Eddie Quillan (*Bill*), Leonard Mudie (*Squires*), J. M. Kerrigan (*Times*), Neil Fitzgerald (*Inspector Sleet*), Harry Stubbs (*Postman*), Ivan Simpson (*Burroughs*), Corky (*Jones*).

Set in London, this thriller concerns a would-be blackmailer who fakes two murders to build up his reputation as someone not to fool with. He instigates a blackmail and kidnaping scheme, but soon gets involved with some real murders as he tries to escape with the blackmail money. An average, well-crafted script.

p, Sam Zimbalist; d, William Thiele; w, George Oppenheimer (based on the play, "The Umbrella Man," by Will Scott); ph, Leonard M. Smith; m, Dr. William Axt; ed, George Boemler; art d, Cedric Gibbons; m/l, Bob Wright, Chet Forrest.

Crime   **(PR:A MPAA:NR)**

LONDON CALLING   (SEE: HELLO LONDON, 1958, Brit.)

LONDON MELODY*   (1930, Brit.) 58m British Screen/Audible Filmcraft bw

Lorraine La Fosse (*Molly Smith*), Haddon Mason (*Sam Austin*), Betty Naismith (*Betty Smith*), Ballard Berkeley (*Jan Moor*), David Openshaw (*Singer*), Helen Debroy Summers, Bobby Kerrigan.

Thin plot serves as the basis for some equally undeveloped songs. La Fosse plays the young beauty who grabs her man by pretending to be a French musical revue star. He eventually discovers the truth, but doesn't take the news too hard at all. p,d&w, Geoffrey Malins, Donald Stuart.

Musical   **(PR:A MPAA:NR)**

LONDON MELODY, 1938   (SEE: GIRL IN THE STREET, 1938, Brit.)

LONDON TOWN   (SEE: MY HEART GOES CRAZY, 1953, Brit.)

LONE AVENGER, THE**   (1933) 58m KBS/World Wide-FOX bw

Ken Maynard, Muriel Gordon, Jack Rockwell, Charles King, Al Bridge, James Marcus, Niles Welch, William Norton Bailey, Ed Brady, Clarence Geldert, "Tarzan", Lew Meehan, Horace B. Carpenter, Jack Ward, Roy Bucko, Buck Bucko, Bud McClure.

Average oater has Maynard a mysterious stranger out to clear his father's name. He gets the villain narrowed down to one of two choices, and bluffs knowing which one it is until the guilty man cracks and gives himself away.

p, Paul Kelly, Sam Bischoff, William Saal; d, Alan James; w, James, Forrest Sheldon, Betty Burbridge (based on a story by Sheldon, Burbridge).

Western   **Cas.**   **(PR:A MPAA:NR)**

LONE CLIMBER, THE**1/2   (1950, Brit./Aust.) 59m GB Instructional/GFD bw

Gerty Jobstmann (Fraulein Huber), Fritz Langer (Karl Behrens), Eleanore Kulicek (Lisel Bauer), Herbert Nitsch (Hans Schneider), Fritz von Friedl (Rudi), Herbert Navratil, Elfriede Kaspar, Ernestine Frauenberger.

Well-made children's film centering around an excursion to the Alps and the excitement that ensues as the result of one child's insistence upon climbing a mountain without the permission of his guardian. Instead of telling their teacher about their comrade's disobedience, several children undertake the job of getting him back into camp without the teacher's knowledge, leading to one child's injury which requires a detailed rescue mission. Effectively portrays the problems of breaking set rules. (In German: English commentary).

p, Mary Field; d, William C. Hammond; w, Patricia Latham; ph, Walter Riml.

Adventure   **(PR:AAA MPAA:NR)**

LONE COWBOY*1/2   (1934) 68m PAR bw

Jackie Cooper (Scooter O'Neal), Lila Lee (Eleanor Jones), John Wray (Bill O'Neal), Addison Richards ('Dobe Jones), Gavin Gordon (Jim Weston), Barton MacLane (J. J. Baxter), J. M. Kerrigan (Mr. Curran), Del Henderson (Mr. Burton), William LeMaire (Buck), Herbert Corthell (Cowboy Cook), Charles B. Middleton (Marshal), George Pearce, Irving Bacon, Lillian Harmer, William Robyns, Leonard Kilbrick, Rose Levine, Buster Guelich, Col. Starrett Ford, Henry C. Bradley, Charles Kean, Harold Goodwin, Jerome Storm, James Adamson, Joe Barton.

A somewhat contrived western that tried to live up to Cooper's successful THE CHAMP. This plot has Cooper living with his father, Richards, the Lone Cowboy, after his wife, Lee, has run off with their foreman. The two go looking for Lee, with Richards getting injured in a rodeo when he spots his wife in the grandstands. After a short hospital stay, the foreman, played by Gordon, pulls a gun on Richards. A wild gun fight leaves Cooper shot and Gordon dead. The wife forgives her husband for killing her lover and the family is reunited.

d, Paul Sloane; w, Sloane, Bobby Vernon, Agnes Brand Leahy (based on the book by Will James); ph, Theodor Sparkuhl.

Western   **(PR:A MPAA:NR)**

LONE GUN, THE*1/2   (1954) 74m World Films/UA c

George Montgomery (Cruz), Dorothy Malone (Charlotte Downing), Frank Faylen (Fairweather), Neville Brand (Tray Moran), Skip Homeier (Cass Downing), Douglas Kennedy (Gad Moran), Robert Wilke (Hort Morgan), Fay Roope (Mayor Booth), Douglas Fowley (Charlie).

A lackluster formula western that contains the usual cowboy story cliches. It's the tale of Montgomery, a poor but honest marshal who is determined to bring justice to a town full of outlaws. In the process, he wins the hand of a rancher's daughter, Malone.

p, Edward Small; d, Ray Nazarro; w, Don Martin, Richard Schayer (based on the story by L. L. Foreman); ph, Lester White (Color Corp. of America); ed, Bernard Small.

Western   **(PR:A MPAA:NR)**

LONE HAND, THE**1/2   (1953) 79m UNIV c

Joel McCrea (Zachary Hallock), Barbara Hale (Sarah Jane Skaggs), Alex Nicol (Jonah Varden), Charles Drake (George Hadley), Jimmy Hunt (Joshua Hallock), Jim Arness (Gus Varden), Roy Roberts (Mr. Skaggs), Frank Ferguson (Mr. Dunn), Wesley Morgan (Daniel Skaggs), Cherokee (Cherokee).

McCrea and his son Hunt head out west to begin a quiet life of farming. McCrea is asked to join forces with a vigilante group intent on bringing justice to the community, but refuses, much to the dismay of his idolizing son. Before long, McCrea is actually fighting along with the outlaws in order to support his son and his new wife, Hale. All turns out fine in the end, however, when McCrea reveals that he has been acting undercover in an effort to expose the bandits.

p, Howard Christie; d, George Sherman; w, Joseph Hoffman (based on the story by Irving Ravetch); ph, Maury Gertsman (Technicolor); ed, Paul Weatherwax; art d, Alexander Golitzen, Erie Orsom.

Western   **(PR:A MPAA:NR)**

LONE HAND TEXAN, THE**   (1947) 54m COL bw (AKA: THE CHEAT)

Charles Starrett (Steve Driscoll), Smiley Burnette (Smiley), Mary Newton (Mrs. Adams), Fred Sears (Sam Jason), Mustard & Gravy (Themselves), Maude Prickett (Hattie Hatfield), George Chesebro (Scanlon), Robert Stevens (Boemer Kildea), Bob Cason (First Outlaw), Jim Diehl (Strawboss), George Russell (Second Outlaw), Jasper Weldon (Coachman), Ernest Stokes.

Another vehicle with Starrett as the Durango Kid. This time Starrett is in oil country, trying to help a buddy fight off the local bad guys who are scheming to steal his land. After being shot at and almost framed for a hold-up, Starrett discovers that the gang is working for a respectable old woman, Newton, who wants the property for herself. (See DURANGO KID series. Index.)

p, Colbert Clark; d, Ray Nazarro; w, Ed Earl Repp (based on the story by Repp); ph, George F. Kelley; ed, Paul Borofsky.

Western   **(PR:A MPAA:NR)**

LONE PRAIRIE, THE*1/2   (1942) 58m COL bw (GB: INSIDE INFORMATION)

Russell Hayden, Dub Taylor, Bob Wills and his Texas Playboys, Lucille Lambert, John Merton, John Maxwell, Jack Kirk, Edmund Cobb, Ernie Adams, Kermit Maynard.

The lonesome prairie is left wide open for a gang of hoods to continue with their ruthless exploitation of the hardworking settlers, because there's no form of solidified lawkeepers to stand in their way. That is, until Hayden comes along and makes the prairie safe once again.

p, Leon Barsha; d, William Berke; w, Fred Myton (based on the story by Ed Earl Repp, J. Benton Cheney).

Western   **(PR:A MPAA:NR)**

LONE RANGER, THE**1/2   (1955) 86m Jack Wrather/WB c

Clayton Moore (The Lone Ranger), Jay Silverheels (Tonto), Lyle Bettger (Reece Kilgore), Bonita Granville (Welcome Kilgore), Perry Lopez (Ramirez), Robert Wilke (Cassidy), John Pickard (Sheriff Kimberley), Beverly Washburn (Lila), Michael Ansara (Angry Horse), Frank De Kova (Red Hawk), Charles Meredith (The Governor), Mickey Simpson (Powder), Zon Murray (Goss), Lane Chandler (Whitebeard).

After over a decade of playing the masked hero on TV and radio, Moore made the leap to the big screen with his trusty Indian companion, Silverheels, by his side. Aimed particularly at children, Moore was more energetic than ever. The story has Moore investigating a recent series of Indian uprisings. What looks like treaty-breaking by the Indians, however, is really a scheme by a greedy rancher (Bettger), who wants to mine silver on Indian land. But the mountain Bettger wants to mine is sacred to the Indians. Moore and Silverheels uncover the plot and restore peace between the Indians and the whites. Of course, the end has Moore and Silverheels riding off into the sunset with the cry of the Lone Ranger, "Hi-ho Silver!" (See LONE RANGER series, Index.)

p, Willis Goldbeck; d, Stuart Heisler; w, Herb Meadow (based on, "The Lone Ranger" legend); ph, Edwin DuPar (Warner Color); m, David Buttolph; ed, Clarence Kolster; md, Buttolph; art d, Stanley Fleischer.

Western   **(PR:AA MPAA:NR)**

LONE RANGER AND THE LOST CITY OF GOLD, THE**   (1958) 80m UA c

Clayton Moore (The Lone Ranger), Jay Silverheels (Tonto), Douglas Kennedy (Ross Brady), Charles Watts (Oscar Matthison), Noreen Nash (Frances Henderson), Lisa Montell (Paviva), Ralph Moody (Padre Vincente Esteban), Norman Frederic (Dr. James Rolfe), John Miljan (Tomache), Maurice Jara (Redbird), Bill Henry (Travers), Lane Bradford (Wilson), Belle Mitchell (Caulama), Silver the Horse.

This film marked the 25th anniversary of the Lone Ranger and Tonto saga. When three Indians are killed by hooded bandits, Moore and Silverheels enter the picture to solve the mysterious deaths. They discover that each Indian was wearing a medallion at the time of his death. Further investigation reveals that the medallions are part of a puzzle that, solved, form a map leading to a lost city of gold. Moore's quest is to find the two Indians wearing the remaining medallions before Kennedy's gang does. In a hot gun battle, Moore and Silverheels foil the outlaws' plan, discover the ancient riches, and return the lost city of gold to the Indians. (See LONE RANGER series, Index.)

p, Sherman A. Harris, Jack Wrather; d, Lesley Selander; w, Robert Schaefer, Eric Freiwald (based on the Lone Ranger legend); ph, Kenneth Peach (Eastmancolor); m, Les Baxter; ed, Robert S. Golden, art d, James D. Vance; set d, Charles Thompson; m/l, "Hi Ho Silver," Baxter, Lenny Adelson.

Western   **(PR:AA MPAA:NR)**

LONE RIDER, THE*1/2   (1930) 57m Beverly/COL bw

Buck Jones (Jim Lanning), Vera Reynolds (Mary), Harry Woods (Farrell), George Pearce (Judge), Silver the Horse.

Jones is a cowboy who becomes the leader of a vigilante group, hiding his darkened past from the other members. When outlaw Woods digs up Jones' skeletons, the vigilantes turn on him and start their chase. Jones saves his reputation by bringing Woods in to stand trial, thereby clearing his own name. This was Buck Jones' first all-talkie western, after a long successful career in silent movies for Fox.

p, Sol Lesser; d, Louis King; w, Forrest Sheldon (based on the story by Frank H. Clark); ph, Ted D. McCord; ed, James Sweeney.

Western   **(PR:A MPAA:NR)**

LONE RIDER AMBUSHED, THE*½   (1941) 67m PRC bw

George Houston (*Tom Cameron/Keno Harris*), Al St. John (*Fuzzy*), Maxine Leslie (*Linda*), Frank Hagney (*Blackie Dawson*), Jack Ingram (*Charlie Davis*), Hal Price (*Sheriff*), Ted Adams (*Deputy*), George Chesebro (*Pete*), Ralph Peters (*Bartender*), Charles King (*Foreman*), Steve Clark, Carl Mathews.

Houston stars as the Lone Rider who assumes the identity of a former outlaw in an effort to learn where the latter has stowed the loot from his last big heist. Hagney is the former partner whom Houston tries to milk for information, but he soon grows suspicious. Eventually, Houston captures Hagney and his band and brings them all to justice. (See LONE RIDER series, Index.)

p, Sigmund Neufeld; d, Sam Newfield; w, Oliver Drake; ph, Jack Greenhalgh; ed, Holbrook N. Todd; m/l, Johnny Lange, Lew Porter ("Without You," "If It Hadn't Been For You").

Western   **(PR:A MPAA:NR)**

LONE RIDER AND THE BANDIT, THE*½   (1942) 54m PRC bw

George Houston (*Tom*), Al St. John (*Fuzzy*), Dennis Moore, Vicki Lester, Glenn Strange, Jack Ingram, Milt Kibbee, Carl Sepulveda, Slim Andrews, Eddie Dean, Slim Whitaker, Hal Price, Kenne Duncan, Curley Dresden.

As the "Lone Rider" Houston uses the disguise of a musician to obtain information about local miners who are being terrorized. The greedy brains behind the scheme has devised a means to make the miners sell cheap in the hope of lining his own pocket, a plan that works well until Houston puts a stop to the proceedings. St. John is around to supply a chuckle or two while doing his duty in aiding Houston. (See LONE RIDER series, Index.)

p, Sigmund Neufeld; d, Sam Newfield; w, Steve Braxton; ph, Jack Greenhalgh; ed, Holbrook N. Todd.

Western   **(PR:A MPAA:NR)**

LONE RIDER CROSSES THE RIO, THE*½   (1941) 58m PRC bw

George Houston (*Tom*), Roquell Verria (*Rosalie*), Al St. John (*Fuzzy*), Charles King (*Jarvis*), Alden Chase (*Hatfield*), Julian Rivero (*Pedro*), Thornton Edwards (*Torres*), Howard Masters (*Francisco*), Frank Ellis (*Fred*), Phillip Turich (*Lt. Mendoza*), Jay [Buffalo Bill, Jr.] Wilsey (*Bart*), Frank Hagney, Curley Dresden, Sherry Tansey, Steve Clark.

A so-so entry in the Lone Rider series, which takes place in Mexico, and has Houston and side-kick St. John, seeking refuge from a gang of outlaws. The two get mixed up with a Mexican official's son and the cabaret singer he loves, a relationship the boy's father disapproves of. Houston and St. John fake a kidnaping of the son so he may be with his love. But when a real group of kidnapers steals the boy, Houston and St. John are naturally accused of the crime. Eventually they rescue the son, capture the crooks, unmask the leader, and set the boy's father straight. (See LONE RIDER series, Index.)

p, Sigmund Neufeld; d, Sam Newfield; w, William Lively; ph, Jack Greenhalgh; m, Johnny Lange, Lew Porter; ed, Holbrook N. Todd.

Western   **(PR:A MPAA:NR)**

LONE RIDER FIGHTS BACK, THE*½   (1941) 64m PRC bw

George Houston (*Tom*), Al St. John (*Fuzzy*), Dorothy Short, Frank Hagney, Dennis Moore, Charles King, Frank Ellis, Hal Price, Jack O'Shea, Merrill McCormack.

Relying more upon his wits than his fists and six-gun, Houston infiltrates the band of outlaws responsible for the death of one of his buddies. It doesn't take long before the others are fighting among themselves and letting out the information that will put them behind bars. (See LONE RIDER series, Index.)

p, Sigmund Neufeld; d, Sam Newfield; w, Joe O'Donnell (based on the story by Fred McConnell); ph, Jack Greenhalgh; ed, Holbrook N. Todd.

Western   **(PR:A MPAA:NR)**

LONE RIDER IN CHEYENNE, THE*½   (1942) 59m PRC bw

George Houston (*Tom*), Al St. John (*Fuzzy*), Dennis Moore, Ella Neal, Roy Barcroft, Kenne Duncan, Lynton Brent, Milt Kibbee, Jack Holmes, Karl Hackett, Jack Ingram, George Chesebro.

In one of his final appearances in the shortlived "Lone Rider" series, Houston is out to clear the name of a man wrongly accused of murdering a prison guard. A bit more plot than usual was added to the series which seemed to concentrate on nothing other than two-fisted action. (See LONE RIDER series, Index.)

p, Sigmund Neufeld; d, Sam Newfield; w, Oliver Drake, Elizabeth Beecher; m, Johnny Lange, Lew Porter.

Western   **(PR:A MPAA:NR)**

LONE RIDER IN GHOST TOWN, THE*½   (1941) 64m PRC bw

George Houston (*Tom/Lone Rider*), Al St. John (*Fuzzy*), Alaine Brandes (*Helen*), Budd Buster (*Mooseclide*), Frank Hagney (*O'Shead*), Alden Chase (*Sinclair*), Reed Howes (*Gordon*), Charles King (*Roberts*), George Chesebro (*Jed*), Edward Piel, Sr. (*Clark*), Archie Hall (*Roper*), Jay [Buffalo Bill, Jr.] Wilsey, Karl Hackett, Don Forrest, Frank Ellis, Curley Dresden, Steve Clark, Byron Vance, Jack Ingram, Augie Gomez, Lane Bradford.

This addition to the Lone Rider series has Houston and St. John checking out a supposedly haunted ghost town, which is really the hideout for an outlaw gang. They live in the deserted town and scare off strangers in order to protect their hidden ore mine. Houston and St. John aren't easily frightened and get to the bottom of the mystery in typical fashion. (See LONE RIDER series, Index.)

p, Sigmund Neufeld; d, Sam Newfield; w, Joe O'Donnell; ph, Jack Greenhalgh; ed, Holbrook N. Todd; m/l Johnny Lange, Lew Porter.

Western   **(PR:A MPAA:NR)**

LONE STAR**½   (1952) 94m MGM bw

Clark Gable (*Devereaux Burke*), Ava Gardner (*Martha Ronda*), Broderick Crawford (*Thomas Craden*), Lionel Barrymore (*Andrew Jackson*), Beulah Bondi (*Minniver Bryan*), Ed Begley (*Sen. Anthony Demmett*), William Farnum (*Sen. Tom Crockett*), Lowell Gilmore (*Capt. Elliott*), Moroni Olsen (*Sam Houston*), Russell Simpson (*Sen. Maynard Cole*), William Conrad (*Mizzette*), James Burke (*Luther Kilgore*), Ralph Reed (*Bud Yoakum*), Ric Roman (*Curau*), Victor Sutherland (*President Anson Jones*), Jonathan Cott (*Ben McCulloch*), Charles Cane (*Mayhew*), Nacho Galindo (*Vincente*), Trevor Bardette (*Sid Yoakum*), Harry Woods (*Dellman*), Dudley Sadler (*Ashbel Smith*), George Hamilton (*Noah*), Roy Gordon, Stanley Andrews, William E. Green (*Men*), Earle Hodgins (*Windy Barton*), Warren MacGregor (*Rancher*), Rex Lease, Davison Clark (*Senators*), Chief Yowlachie (*Indian Chief*), Emmett Lynn (*Josh*), Tony Roux (*Chico*), Lucius Cook, Rex Bell.

Like the state of Texas, everything about this film is big—big stars, big budget, big horizons. Gable is a cattle baron selected by Andrew Jackson (Barrymore) to seek out Sam Houston (Olsen) and persuade him not to make a separate peace with Mexico. The Mexican-Texas war is over and the Alamo and San Jacinto are memories, but forces in Texas are now serious about making the state a separate country. It's Gable's job to persuade Olsen and others to bring Texas into the Union. En route to see Olsen, Gable runs into rough and tumble Crawford, a state senator who is pushing for a treaty with Mexico and is backed not only by many influential persons but by the British ambassador. Gable bucks Crawford and also has eyes for his girl, Gardner, a fiery newspaper editor. When Gable does get to Olsen, he is pondering the fate of Texas in Comanche Territory. Gable persuades him to stay with the Union and Olsen gives Gable a letter to deliver to the Texas senate which will endorse this move. Crawford, who has already tried to ambush Gable, knowing his mission, masses an army to prevent the senate from meeting and Gable gathers a loyal band to fight this horde. The groups clash but Olsen appears at the last minute and brings peace, winning over even Crawford to the cause of annexation which all know will mean another war with Mexico. At the finish they all march forward to meet the Mexican menace. The story is cliche-ridden but there's plenty of action. Sherman's direction lacks fire but Gable and Crawford make up for the faulty helmsmanship and potholed script. Gable was drinking heavily during this production and one report had it that he was suffering from early stages of Parkinson's disease. Though he had gotten along well with Gardner in THE HUCKSTERS, Gable now steered clear of the sensuous star; some said he was resentful of her youthful energy but most likely he was merely tired.

p, Z. Wayne Griffin; d, Vincent Sherman; w, Howard Estabrook, Borden Chase (based on the story by Chase); ph, Harold Rosson; m, David Buttolph; ed, Ferris Webster; art d, Cedric Gibbons, Hans Peters.

Western   **(PR:A MPAA:NR)**

LONE STAR LAW MEN*   (1942) 58m MON bw

Tom Keene (*Tom*), Frank Yaconelli (*Lopez*), Sugar Dawn (*Sugar*), Betty Miles (*Betty*), Gene Alsace (*Brady*), Glenn Strange (*Scott*), Charles King (*Dude*), Fred Hoose (*James*), Stanley Price (*Mason*), James Sheridan (*Red*), Reed Howes (*Ace*), Franklyn Farnum, Jack Ingram.

Keene stars as a deputy marshal in a border town overflowing with bandits. The lead outlaw is King, who has his men kill a U.S. marshal. Keene goes undercover and joins the gang in a successful attempt to thwart their crooked efforts.

p&d, Robert Tansey; w, Robert [Tansey] Emmett, Frances Kavanaugh; ph, Robert Cline; ed, Fred Bain.

Western   **(PR:A MPAA:NR)**

LONE STAR LAWMAN   (SEE: TEXAS LAWMEN, 1951)

LONE STAR PIONEERS**   (1939) 54m COL bw

Bill Elliott (*Pat*), Dorothy Gulliver (*Virginia*), Charles Whitaker (*Buck*), Charles King (*Pete*), Lee Shumway (*Bill*), Budd Buster (*Crittenden*), Jack Ingram (*Coe*), Harry Harvey (*Eph*), Buzz Barton (*Chuck*), Frank LaRue (*Joe*), David Sharpe, Frank Ellis, Kit Guard, Merrill McCormack, Jack Rockwell, Tex Palmer.

U.S. marshal Elliott is sent to Texas to track down guerrillas who have been looting supply shipments. He dons a black hat and joins a gang led by Whitaker and King. He discovers that the outlaws are hiding out on a ranch, and are holding the rancher, his son and daughter prisoner while receiving information on the next shipment of goods. Elliott manages to foil the gang's plans and bring them to justice.

p, Larry Darmour; d, Joseph Levering; w, Nate Gatzert; ph, James S. Brown, Jr.; ed, Dwight Caldwell.

Western   **(PR:A MPAA:NR)**

LONE STAR RAIDERS*   (1940) 57m REP bw

Robert Livingston (*Stony Brooke*), Bob Steele (*Tucson Smith*), Rufe Davis (*Lullaby Joslin*), June Johnson (*Linda*), George Douglas (*Martin*), Sarah Padden (*Granny*), John Elliott (*Cameron*), John Merton (*Dixon*), Rex Lease (*Fisher*), Bud Osborne (*Blake*), Jack Kirk (*Bixby*), Tom London (*Jones*), Hal Price (*Sheriff*).

Livingston, Steele, and Davis continue their fight for law and order in the West when they come to the aid of an old woman, Padden, who inherits a horse ranch. The ranch is in financial disaster because of a drought that is killing off the horses. Padden is trying to sell her horses to the U.S. Army, but her competitors go to dirty means to get the contract away from her. The Three Mesquiteers make sure that the contract isn't stolen away, after she wins an influential horse race. (See THREE MESQUITEERS series, Index.)

p, Louis Gray; d, George Sherman; w, Joseph Moncure March, Barry Shipman (based on the original by Charles Francis Royal, based on characters created by William Colt MacDonald); ph, William Nobles; m, Cy Feuer; ed, Tony Martinelli.

Western (PR:A MPAA:NR)

LONE STAR RANGER, THE*¹/₂ (1930) 64m FOX bw

George O'Brien (Buck Duane), Sue Carol (Mary Aldridge), Walter McGrail (Phil Lawson), Warren Hymer (The Bowery Kid), Russell Simpson (Col. Aldridge), Roy Stewart (Capt. McNally), Lee Shumway (Red Kane), Colin Chase (Tom Laramie), Richard Alexander (Jim Fletcher), Joel Franz (Hank Jones), Joe Rickson (Spike), Oliver Eckhardt (Lem Parker), Caroline Rankin (Mrs. Parker), Elizabeth Patterson (Sarah Martin), Billy Butts (Bud Jones), Delmar Watson (Baby Jones), William Steele (1st Deputy), Bob Fleming (2nd Deputy), Ralph Le Fevre (Stage Driver).

In O'Brien's first all-talking western, he plays an outlaw-turned-rancher in order to receive a pardon and win Carol's heart. He is sent on a mission to round up some cattle rustlers, and in the process discovers that the head of the gang is Carol's father. Plenty of shoot 'em up action abounds.

p&d, A. F. Erickson; w, Seton I. Miller, John Hunter Booth (based on the novel by Zane Grey); ph, Daniel Clark; ed, Jack Murray.

Western (PR:A MPAA:NR)

LONE STAR RANGER*¹/₂ (1942) 58m FOX bw

John Kimbrough (Buck Duane), Sheila Ryan (Barbara Longstreth), Jonathan Hale (Judge Longstreth), William Farnum (Maj. McNeil), Truman Bradley (Phil Lawson), George E. Stone (Euchre), Russell Simpson (Tom Duane), Dorothy Burgess (Trixie), Tom Fadden (Sam), Fred Kohler, Jr. (Red), Eddy C. Waller (Mitchell), Harry Hayden (Sheriff), George Melford (Hardin), Tom London.

In this remake of the 1930 film of the same name, former football player Kimbrough stars as a Texas Ranger on the trail of a gang of crooks led by Hale and Farnum, who are gathering up Texas land for themselves by scaring off potential buyers. Kimbrough befriends Ryan, the niece of Hale, who doesn't know about her uncle's illegal doings. Through Ryan, he traps Hale and brings the outlaw gang to justice.

p, Sol M. Wurtzel; d, James Tinling; w, William Conselman, Jr., Irving Cummings, Jr., George Kane (based on the novel by Zane Grey); ph, Lucien Andriot; ed, Nick De Maggio; md, Emil Newman; art d, Richard Day, Chester Gore.

Western (PR:A MPAA:NR)

LONE STAR TRAIL, THE**¹/₂ (1943) 57m UNIV bw

Johnny Mack Brown (Blaze Barker), Tex Ritter (Fargo Steele), Fuzzy Knight (Angus MacAngus), Jennifer Holt (Joan Winters), George Eldredge (Doug Ransom), Michael Vallon (Jonathan Bentley), Harry Strang (Sheriff Waddell), Earle Hodgins (Maj. Cyrus Jenkins), Jack Ingram (Dan Jason), Bob Mitchum (Ben Slocum), Ethan Laidlaw (Steve Bannister), William Desmond (Bartender), Henry Rocquemore (Bank Teller), Denver Dixon, Carl Mathews (Townsmen), Eddie Parker (Lynch), Billy Engle (Stage Passenger), Bob Reeves (Barfly), Tom Steele (Mitchum's Double), Fred Graham, Jimmy Wakely Trio.

Brown, having served two years in prison for a train robbery he didn't commit, is paroled from prison and attempts to clear his name. Since he is not allowed to wear a gun, he enlists the aid of U.S. marshal Ritter to find the real culprits. Along with sidekick Knight, Ritter is able to exonerate Brown.

p, Oliver Drake; d, Ray Taylor; w, Drake (based on the story by Victor Halperin); ph, William Sickner; ed, Ray Snyder; md, H. J. Salter; art d, John Goodman; m/l, Drake, Milton Rosen, Jimmy Wakely.

Western (PR:A MPAA:NR)

LONE STAR VIGILANTES, THE** (1942) 58m COL bw

Bill Elliott (Wild Bill Hickok), Tex Ritter (Tex Martin), Frank Mitchell (Cannonball), Virginia Carpenter (Shary Monroe), Luana Walters (Marcia Banning), Budd Buster (Col. Monroe), Forrest Taylor (Dr. Banning), Gavin Gordon (Maj. Clark), Lowell Drew (Peabody), Edmund Cobb (Charlie Cobb), Ethan Laidlaw (Benson), Rick Anderson (Lige Miller), George Chesebro, Paul Mulvey, Steve Clark, Al Haskell.

Set in post-Civil War Texas, this story has Elliott, Ritter, and Mitchell coming home to find that their community is controlled by outlaws. When they discover that the gang is headed by a phony lawman, they expose the plot and the bad guys. Plenty of gun-fighting action.

p, Leon Barsha; d, Wallace W. Fox; w, Luci Ward; ph, Benjamin Kline; ed, Mel Thorsen.

Western (PR:A MPAA:NR)

LONE TEXAN**¹/₂ (1959) 71m RF/FOX bw

Willard Parker (Clint Banister), Grant Williams (Greg Harvey), Audrey Dalton (Susan Harvey), Douglas Kennedy (Phillip Harvey), June Blair (Florrie Stuart), Dabbs Greer (Doc Jansen), Barbara Heller (Amy Todd), Rayford Barnes (Finch), Tyler McVey (Henry Biggs), Lee Farr (Riff), Jimmy Murphy (Ric), Dick Monahan (Jesse), Robert Dix (Carpetbagger), Gregg Barton (Ben Hollis), I. Stanford Jolley (Trades), Sid Melton (Gus Pringle), Shirle Haven (Nancy), Hank Patterson (Jack Stone), Frank Marlowe (Charlie), Boyd Stockman, Jerry Summers, Bill Coontz (Indians), Tom London (Old Dan), Elena Davinci, Doe Swain (Women Passengers).

Parker stars as a post-Civil War soldier returning to his home town, only to find that the townsfolk have labeled him a "turncoat" for fighting on the side of the Union. His brother, Williams, has taken over as sheriff and is leading a reign of outlaw terror over the inhabitants. Parker is determined to bring back law and order to his town. During the final confrontation, Williams goes for his gun in an attempt to kill a deputy who is about to shoot Parker in the back. But Parker, thinking his younger brother is drawing on him, fatally shoots Williams.

p, Jack Leewood; d, Paul Landres; w, James Landis, Jack Thomas (based on the novel by Landis); ph, Walter Strenge (RegalScope); m, Paul Dunlap; ed, Robert Fritch.

Western (PR:A MPAA:NR)

LONE TEXAS RANGER*¹/₂ (1945) 56m REP bw

Bill Elliott (Red Ryder), Bobby Blake (Little Beaver), Alice Fleming, Roy Barcroft, Helen Talbot, Jack McClendon, Rex Lease, Tom Chatterton, Jack Kirk, Nelson McDowell, Larry Olson, Dale Van Sickel, Frank O'Connor, Bob Wilke, Bud Geary, Budd Buster, Hal Price, Horace B. Carpenter, Nolan Leary, Tom Steele, LeRoy Mason (Voice only), Earl Dobbins, Bill Stevens.

As Red Ryder, Elliott discovers that a man has been using his position as sheriff to cover up for a number of illegal activities, including murder. Eventually Elliott is forced to kill the crook, a deed that doesn't set well with those who admired the sheriff, especially his son. (See RED RYDER series, Index.)

p, Louis Gray; d, Spencer Gordon Bennett; w, Bob Williams; ph, Bud Thackery; ed, Charles Craft; md, Richard Cherwin; art d, Russell Kimball.

Western (PR:A MPAA:NR)

LONE TRAIL, THE*¹/₂ (1932) 61m SYN bw

Rex Lease (Tom Lanning), Edmund Cobb (Fred), Billy O'Brien (Bud), Virginia Brown Faire (Ruth Farnum), Jack Mower (Butch Kohler), Robert Walker (Joe), Harry Todd (Jed), Muro (King, the Dog), Joe Bonomo, Josephine Hill, Al Ferguson, Jack Perrin.

Lease shows some Western heroics after his sister Faire is abducted by an outlaw known only as "The Tiger." With the help of his crafty canine, Muro, Lease rescues Faire and captures "The Tiger" and his cohorts. A feature-length version of the 1931 serial THE SIGN OF THE WOLF.

p, Harry S. Webb; d, Forrest Sheldon, Webb; w, Betty Burbridge, Bennett Cohen.

Western (PR:A MPAA:NR)

LONE TROUBADOR, THE (SEE: TWO-GUN TROUBADOR, 1939)

LONE WOLF AND HIS LADY, THE** (1949) 60m COL bw

Ron Randell (Michael Lanyard), June Vincent (Grace Duffy), Alan Mowbray (Jamison), William Frawley (Inspector Crane), Collette Lyons (Marta Frisbie), Douglas Dumbrille (John J. Murdock), James Todd (Tanner), Steven Geray (Van Groot), Robert H. Barrat (Steve Taylor), Arthur Space (Fisher), Philip Van Zandt (Joe Brewster), Jack Overman (Bill Slovak), Lee Phelps (Sgt. Henderson), Robert B. Williams (Lt. Martin), Fred Sears (Tex Talbot), William Newell (Ava Rockling), George Tyne (Paul Braud), Lane Chandler (4th Cop), Harry Hayden (Shemus O'Brien), Will Lee (Walter).

The last of the long-running LONE WOLF series (see Index), this entry has Randell as a former jewel thief turned reporter, who gets into trouble when he is assigned to cover the exhibition of a famous diamond. When the jewel disappears, Randell is accused of stealing it. It is all Randell can do to keep out of the police's reach in order to track down the real culprits. (See LONE WOLF series, Index.)

p, Rudolph C. Flothow; d, John Hoffman; w, Malcolm Stuart Boylan (based on the story by Edward Dein from the work by Louis Joseph Vance); ph, Philip Tannura; ed, James Sweeney; md, Mischa Bakaleinikoff; art d, Sturges Carne.

Mystery (PR:A MPAA:NR)

LONE WOLF IN LONDON*¹/₂ (1947) 64m COL bw

Gerald Mohr (Michael Lanyard), Nancy Saunders (Ann Kelmscott), Eric Blore (Jamison), Evelyn Ankers (Iris Chatham), Richard Fraser (David Woolerton), Queenie Leonard (Lily), Alan Napier (Monty Beresford), Denis Green (Garvey), Frederic Worlock (Inspector Broome), Tom Stevenson (Henry Robards), Vernon Steele (Sir John Kelmscott), Paul Fung (Bruce Tang), Guy Kingsford (Mitchum).

Mohr is the former jewel thief working on the side of the law. He is accused of stealing gems from Scotland Yard's safe. The film's plot keeps tripping over itself with story twists and sub-plots. In the end, Mohr apprehends the real thief and the jewels are put back into the safe. Mohr is one of the weaker actors to play the Lone Wolf character. (See LONE WOLF series, Index.)

p, Ted Richmond; d, Leslie Goodwins; w, Arthur E. Orloff (based on the story by Barbara Weisberg, Orloff); ph, Henry Freulich; ed, Henry Batista; art d, Robert Peterson; md, Mischa Bakaleinikoff.

Mystery (PR:A MPAA:NR)

LONE WOLF IN MEXICO, THE*¹/₂ (1947) 69m COL bw

Gerald Mohr (Michael Lanyard), Sheila Ryan (Sharon Montgomery), Jacqueline de Wit (Liliane Dumont), Eric Blore (Jamison), Nestor Paiva (Carlos Rodriguez), John Gallaudet (Henderson), Bernard Nedell (Leon Dumont), Winifred Harris (Mrs. Van Weir), Peter Brocco (Emil), Alan Edwards (Charles Montgomery), Fred Godoy (Capt. Mendez), Theodore Gottlieb (Watchman).

One-time sophisticated burglar Mohr uses the skills he learned in his illegal trade to aid the police in tracking down a gang of diamond smugglers. He finds himself in the midst of a number of murders which are ineffective in keeping him from achieving his goal. (See LONE WOLF series, Index.)

p, Sanford Cummings; d, D. Ross Lederman; w, Maurice Tombragel, Martin Goldsmith (based on the story by Louis Joseph Vance); ph, Allen Siegler; ed, William Lyon; md, Mischa Bakaleinikoff; art d, Charles Clague.

Mystery (PR:A MPAA:NR)

LONE WOLF IN PARIS, THE** (1938) 67m COL bw

Francis Lederer (*Michael Lanyard*), Frances Drake (*Princess Thania*), Olaf Hytten (*Jenkins*), Walter Kingsford (*Grand Duke Gregor*), Leona Maricle (*Baroness Cambrell*), Albert Van Dekker (*Marquis de Meyervon*), Maurice Cass (*Monsieur Fromont*), Bess Flowers (*Davna*), Ruth Robinson (*Queen Regent*), Pio Peretti (*King*), Eddie Fetherston (*Mace*), Dick Curtis (*Guard*), Al Herman (*Otto*).

Lederer plays the reformed jewel thief who is hired to steal back a cache of gems. The crown jewels have been pawned to a grand duke and he doesn't want to give them up. Lederer is sent to do what he does best, steal. (See LONE WOLF series, Index.)

d, Albert S. Rogell; w, Arthur T. Horman (based on a story by Louis Joseph Vance); ph, Lucien Ballard; ed, Otto Meyer.

Mystery (PR:A MPAA:NR)

LONE WOLF KEEPS A DATE, THE*1/2 (1940) 65m COL bw

Warren William (*Michael Lanyard*), Frances Robinson (*Patricia Lawrence*), Bruce Bennett (*Scotty*), Eric Blore (*Jamison*), Thurston Hall (*Inspector Crane*), Jed Prouty (*Capt. Moon*), Fred Kelsey (*Dickens*), Don Beddoe (*Big Joe Brady*), Lester Matthews (*Mr. Lee*), Edward Gargan (*Chimp*), Eddie Laughton (*Measles*), Mary Servoss (*Mrs. Colby*), Francis McDonald (*Santos*).

The Lone Wolf, William, is in Havana and helps Robinson retrieve $10 thousand that was stolen from her. The money is for her boy friend's release from prison for a crime he didn't commit. William locates the gang of crooks and plays both sides of the law in order to return the money to Robinson. (See LONE WOLF series, Index.)

p, Ralph Cohn; d, Sidney Salkow; w, Salkow, Earl Fenton (based on the character by Louis Joseph Vance); ph, Barney McGill; ed, Richard Fantl; md, Morris Stoloff.

Mystery (PR:A MPAA:NR)

LONE WOLF McQUADE** (1983) 107m 1818 Prod.-Topkick/Orion c

Chuck Norris (*J. J. McQuade*), David Carradine (*Rawley Wilkes*), Barbara Carrera (*Lola Richardson*), Leon Isaac Kennedy (*Jackson*), Robert Beltran (*Kayo*), L. Q. Jones (*Dakota*), Dana Kimmell (*Sally*), R. G. Armstrong (*T. Tyler*), Jorge Cervera, Jr. (*Jefe*), Sharon Farrell (*Molly*), Daniel Frishman (*Falcon*), William Sanderson (*Snow*), John Anderson (*Burnside*), Robert Arenas, Tommy Ballard, Jeff Bannister, Anthony E. Caglia, Eli Cummins, Oscar Hildago, Robert Jordan, Joe Kaufenberg, Susan Kaufenberg, Velma Nieto.

Norris is a legendary Texas Ranger who is after Carradine and cohorts. Carradine is a gun runner stealing U.S. Army shipments and selling them to Central American terrorist groups. As the title states, Norris is again a one-man army, but surprisingly he gets help from Beltran (EATING RAOUL), a rookie patrolman, and Kennedy, an F.B.I. agent. These two stay in the background whenever Norris can showcase his awesome martial arts skills or pull off the implausible (plowing his truck from its ten foot deep grave). Carrera is Norris' and Carradine's love interest and it gets confusing as to whose side she is on from scene to scene. After his ex-partner, Jones, his dog, and his daughter are kidnaped, Norris goes down to Mexico with an Eastwood glint for revenge. He reluctantly lets Beltran and Kennedy join him and they take on Carradine's compound. Norris does most of the work, shooting, kicking, dodging bullets, with a climactic karate battle with Carradine. One of the better Norris action films, but the film loses a lot towards the end when the action bends reality a little too much. Director Carver seems to try to imitate Sergio Leone's style, but that crumbles shortly after the opening scene.

p, Yoram Ben-Ami, Steve Carver; d, Carver; w, B. J. Nelson (based on a story by H. Kaye Dyal, Nelson); ph, Roger Shearman (Deluxe Color); m, Francesco De Masi; ed, Anthony Redman; prod. d, Norm Baron; set d, Robert Zilliox.

Action/Adventure **Cas.** (PR:C-O MPAA:PG)

LONE WOLF MEETS A LADY, THE** (1940) 71m COL bw

Warren William (*Michael Lanyard*), Jean Muir (*Joan Bradley*), Eric Blore (*Jamison*), Victor Jory (*Clay Beaudine*), Roger Pryor (*Pete Rennick*), Warren Hull (*Bob Pennion*), Thurston Hall (*Inspector Crane*), Fred A. Kelsey (*Dickens*), Robert Emmett Keane (*Peter Van Wyck*), Georgia Caine (*Mrs. Pennion*), William Forrest (*Arthur Trent*), Marla Shelton (*Rose Waverly*), Bruce Bennett (*McManus*), Luis Alberni (*Pappakontus*).

William comes to the aid of Muir who is charged with robbery and murder. The Wolf breaks the mystery of the real murderer and gets Muir off the hook. To do this, William has to deal with and double cross everyone from a gangster to detective Hall. (See, LONE WOLF series, Index.)

p, Ralph Cohn; d, Sidney Salkow; w, John Larkin (based on the story by Larkin, Wolfe Kaufman, from the character by Louis Joseph Vance); ph, Henry Freulich; ed, Al Clark.

Mystery (PR:A MPAA:NR)

LONE WOLF RETURNS, THE**1/2 (1936) 68m COL bw

Melvyn Douglas (*Michael Lanyard*), Gail Patrick (*Marcia Stewart*), Tala Birell (*Liane*), Henry Mollison (*Mollison*), Thurston Hall (*Inspector Crane*), Raymond Walburn (*Jenkins*), Douglas Dumbrille (*Morphew*), Nana Bryant (*Aunt Julie*), Robert Middlemass (*McGowan*), Robert Emmet O'Connor (*Benson*), Wyrley Birch (*Mr. Cole*), Eddy Chandler, John Thomas, William Howard Gould (*Detectives*), Arthur Rankin, Harry Depp (*Men*), George McKay (*Maestro*), Frank Reicher (*Coleman*), Harry Holman (*Friar*), Archie Robbins (*Terry*), Lois Lindsey (*Baby*), Fred Malatesta (*French Official*), Olaf Hytten (*Bancroft Butler*), Monte Vandergrift, Lew Kelly (*Custom Officials*), Maude Truax (*Fat Woman*), Thomas Pogue (*Old Man*), Pat West (*Mugg*), Jack Clifford, Roger Gray, Hal Price, Jack Gray, Kernan Cripps, Lee Shumway (*Cops*), Gennaro Curci (*Flute Player*), John Piccori (*Assistant

to Official*), Henry Roquemore, Ned Norton (*Suburbanites*), Arthur Loft (*Oscar*), Lloyd Whitlock (*Drunk*), Mort Greene (*Crooner*), Eddie Fetherston (*Reporter*), Harry Harvey (*Photographer*), Vesey O'Davoren (*Stewart Butler*), Dorothy Bay (*Marjorie*), Pat Somerset (*Gladiator*), Arthur Stuart Hull (*Jackson*), George Webb (*Tarzan*), David Horsley (*Robin Hood*), Ivan Christy, Tony Merlo, Arthur Raymond Hill (*Waiters*), Harry Hollingsworth (*Doorman*), Helen Leyser (*Young Girl*), Earl Pingree (*New York Traffic Cop*).

One of the better films in the Lone Wolf series, with Douglas doing a fine job as the title character. Again, he is after a jewel thief and this one has an army of gangsters protecting him. Dumbrille is Douglas' opponent in this above-average B production. (See LONE WOLF series, Index.)

d, Roy William Neill; w, Joseph Krumgold, Bruce Manning, Lionel Houser, Robert O'Connell (based on the story by Louis Joseph Vance); ph, Henry Freulich; ed, Viola Lawrence; md, Howard Jackson.

Mystery (PR:A MPAA:NR)

LONE WOLF SPY HUNT, THE*** (1939) 67m COL bw (GB: THE LONE WOLF'S DAUGHTER)

Warren William (*Michael Lanyard*), Ida Lupino (*Val Carson*), Rita Hayworth (*Karen*), Virginia Weidler (*Patricia Lanyard*), Ralph Morgan (*Spiro Gregory*), Tom Dugan (*Sgt. Devan*), Don Beddoe (*Inspector Thomas*), Leonard Carey (*Jameson*), Ben Welden (*Jenks*), Brandon Tynan (*Sen. Carson*), Helen Lynd (*Marie Templeton*), Irving Bacon (*Sergeant*), Marek Windheim (*Waiter*), Jack Norton (*Charlie Fenton, the Drunk*), Dick Elliott (*Little Cop*), Alec Craig (*Marriage Bureau Clerk*), Dick Curtis, Lou Davis, John Tyrrell (*Heavies*), Marc Lawrence (*Heavy-Leader*), Stanley Brown, Beatrice Curtis, Lola Jensen, James Craig (*Guests*), Tony Hughes, Bud Jamison (*Bartenders*), Eddie Laughton (*Footman*), Forbes Murray (*Angus Palmer*), James Blaine (*Cop*), Frank Baker (*Evans*), Russ Clark (*Evans*), Landers Stevens (*Thatcher*), Lee Phelps (*Police Broadcaster*), Vernon Dent (*Fat Man at Party*), Adrian Booth (*Girl Whom Lanyard Meets in Club*), Eddie Fetherston (*Man*), Jim Millican (*Cab Driver*), Jack Hill, George DeNormand, Ed Brandenberg, Dick Jensen, Ed Randolph (*Doubles*), Eddie Hearn (*Police Sergeant*), Eddie Cobb (*Police Clerk*), I. Stanford Jolley (*Doorman*).

The best of the LONE WOLF series with William making his debut as the jewel thief. The Wolf is abducted by a band of crooks who force him to steal secret anti-aircraft plans. William only takes half the plans and this enables him to track down the crooks and the documents. Lupino is William's girl friend and Weidler is the ex-thief's daughter. This was the only Michael Lanyard adventure to include the Lone Wolf's daughter and had been filmed twice before, in 1919 and 1929 under its original title, THE LONE WOLF'S DAUGHTER. This film was also the first time Rita Hayworth had her own specially designed wardrobe and stand-in (Ellen Duffy). One of the best things about this film is the natural blending of action and comedy. (See LONE WOLF series, Index.)

p, Joseph Sistrom; d, Peter Godfrey; w, Jonathan Latimer (based on the novel, *The Lone Wolf's Daughter* by Louis Joseph Vance); ph, Allen G. Siegler; ed, Otto Meyer; md, Morris W. Stoloff; art d, Lionel Banks; cos, Kalloch.

Mystery/Adventure (PR:A MPAA:NR)

LONE WOLF STRIKES, THE** (1940) 57m COL bw

Warren William (*Michael Lanyard*), Joan Perry (*Delia Jordan*), Eric Blore (*Jamison*), Alan Baxter (*Jim Ryder*), Astrid Allwyn (*Binnie Weldon*), Montagu Love (*Emil Gorlick*), Robert W. Wilcox (*Ralph Bolton*), Don Beddoe (*Conroy*), Fred A. Kelsey (*Dickens*), Addison Richards (*Stanley Young*), Roy Gordon (*Phillip Jordan*), Harland Tucker (*Alberts*), Peter Lynn (*Dorgan*), Murray Alper (*Pete/Bartender*), Eddie Cobb (*Third Cop*).

William comes to the aid of heiress Perry who has had her pearl necklace stolen. William tracks down Baxter and Allwyn, the thieves, and switches the real pearls with fakes. He returns Perry's necklace and turns the crooks over to the police. (See LONE WOLF series, Index.)

p, Fred Kohlmar; d, Sidney Salkow; w, Harry Segall, Albert Duffy (based on a story by Dalton Trumbo based on the characters by Louis Joseph Vance); ph, Henry Freulich; ed, Al Clark.

Mystery (PR:A MPAA:NR)

LONE WOLF TAKES A CHANCE, THE** (1941) 76m COL bw

Warren William (*Michael Lanyard*), June Storey (*Gloria Foster*), Henry Wilcoxon (*Frank Jordan*), Eric Blore (*Jamison*), Thurston Hall (*Inspector Crane*), Don Beddoe (*Sheriff Haggerty*), Evalyn Knapp (*Evelyn Jordan*), Fred Kelsey (*Dickens*), William Forrest (*Vic Hilton*), Walter Kingsford (*Dr. Hooper Tupman*), Lloyd Bridges (*Johnny Baker*), Ben Taggart (*Conductor*), Richard Fiske (*Brakeman*), Regis Toomey (*Wallace*), Irving Bacon (*Projectionist*), Tom London (*1st Cop*).

William bets Police Inspector Hall that he can stay out of trouble for 24 hours. But as usual, William finds himself caught in the middle of many implausible situations. First, there's a murder, then a robbery of treasury engraving plates from a newly invented car, plus car chases, kidnapings and wild train rides. The pace is break-neck, but the story can't keep up. (See LONE WOLF series, Index.)

p, Ralph Cohn; d, Sidney Salkow; w, Salkow, Earl Felton (based on a story by Salkow and Felton based on the characters by Louis Joseph Vance); ph, John Stumar; ed, Viola Lawrence.

Mystery (PR:A MPAA:NR)

LONE WOLF'S DAUGHTER, THE*1/2 (1929) 72m COL bw

Bert Lytell (*Michael Lanyard*), Gertrude Olmstead (*Helen Fairchild*), Charles Gerrard (*Count Polinac*), Lilyan Tashman (*Velma*), Donald Keith (*Bobby

Crenshaw), Florence Allen *(Adrienne)*, Robert Elliott *(Ethier)*, Ruth Cherrington *(Mrs. Crenshaw)*.

Lytell as the Lone Wolf travels to America to see his adopted daughter and in the process stops a jewel robbery. He also captures two men wanted by Scotland Yard, falls for a good-looking woman and still finds time for his daughter. The movie is silent, except for the opening dialog between Lytell and a police inspector. (See LONE WOLF series, Index.)

d, Albert S. Rogell; w, Sig Herzig, Harry Revier (based on the characters by Louis Joseph Vance); ph, James Van Trees; ed, William Hamilton; art d, Harrison Wiley.

Mystery/Suspense (PR:A MPAA:NR)

LONE WOLF'S DAUGHTER, THE, 1939
(SEE: LONE WOLF SPY HUNT, THE, 1939)

LONELINESS OF THE LONG DISTANCE RUNNER, THE****
(1962, Brit.) 104m Woodfall-Bryanston-Seven Arts/CD bw (AKA; REBEL WITH A CAUSE)

Tom Courtenay *(Colin Smith)*, [Sir] Michael Redgrave *(The Governor)*, Avis Bunnage *(Mrs. Smith)*, Peter Madden *(Mr. Smith)*, James Bolam *(Mike)*, Julia Foster *(Gladys)*, Topsy Jane *(Audrey)*, Dervis Ward *(Detective)*, Raymond Dyer *(Gordon)*, Alec McCowen *(Brown)*, Joe Robinson *(Roach)*, Philip Martin *(Stacey)*, Arthur Mullard *(Chief Officer)*, Ray Austin *(Craig)*, Anthony Sayger *(Fenton)*, John Thaw *(Bosworth)*, Peter Kriss *(Scott)*, James Cairncross *(Jones)*, Peter Duguid *(Doctor)*, John Bull *(Ronalds)*, William Ash *(Gunthorpe)*, Dallas Cavell *(Lord Jaspers)*, Anita Oliver *(Alice Smith)*, Brian Hammond *(Johnny Smith)*, Christopher Parker *(Bill Smith)*, John Brooking *(Green)*, Frank Finlay *(Booking Office Clerk)*, Robert Percival *(Tory Politician)*, Christopher Williams *(Public School Boy)*.

Courtenay had been starring in the British stage production of "Billy Liar" when director Richardson found him and made this his film debut. It was auspicious enough for Courtenay to win the British Academy's most promising newcomer award. The movie was not a success when first released, but has stood up well under the test of time and now is regarded as one of the best "angry young men" movies of the 1960s. Courtenay is a rebellious teen-ager from Nottingham in England. His mother, Bunnage, is a slattern and a slut. They are poor and she tells Courtenay that he has to contribute to the household. But there is no way an ill-educated youth can get a job so he robs a bakery, stashes the money in a drainpipe, and is caught when a rainstorm forces the cash out of the makeshift hiding place. The result is that he goes to Borstal (reformatory) where Redgrave is the authoritarian chief. Redgrave thinks that the boys can be reformed if they use their high spirits in athletic endeavors and so he emphasizes that in his running of the institution. Courtenay has no use for anyone involved with Borstal and has but one friend, Bolam. He treats the officials with disdain and is marking time until he can be back on the streets again. He is a natural runner and explains that he had a lot of practice running away from the police. Redgrave puts him into training for a meet against a nearby public school. He lets Courtenay know that if he wins the race, there will be all sorts of perks for the boy. Courtenay begins practicing and we see a series of flashbacks as the lad recalls why it is he came to be in this predicament. He thinks about his beloved father who died of cancer; his mother who blew what little insurance money they received on a minor-league gigolo and a new television set; his sweetheart, Jane; his best pal, Bolam. (The training sequence is similar to the one in ROCKY but without Bill Conti's music. Case in point: Next time ROCKY appears on TV, turn the sound down as he does his road work and see how ineffective it is without those trumpets and that tune.) The day of the big race dawns and Redgrave is delighted that Courtenay is representing the school as he feels sure the boy will triumph. After all, what youth wouldn't give his all in order to secure extra privileges? The race begins and Courtenay steps out to an early lead and easily outclasses the competition. But just as he nears the finish line, he stops short and watches as the others pass him. Redgrave is thunderstruck by Courtenay's move because this is the biggest thing in his life. Courtenay looks up at the man, doesn't say anything, doesn't break a smile, just stares, and we know that it is his ultimate gesture of rebelliousness. Sure, he knows that he'll be punished for this but it's his way of saying nobody owns me, I do what I want, and you're not going to make me just another number in your prison." Two years before, writer Sillitoe had already explored the estrangement of the British working-class man against society with his excellent SATURDAY NIGHT AND SUNDAY MORNING and some of the same ground was trod upon in this, although not with the same intensity. One year after the release of this film, Courtenay repeated his stage success with the film of BILLY LIAR and has since become one of England's brightest lights on stage and screen.

p&d, Tony Richardson; w, Alan Sillitoe (based on a story by Sillitoe); ph, Walter Lassally; m, John Addison; ed, Anthony Gibbs; prod d, Ralph Brinton; art d, Ted Marshall; set d, Josie Macavin; cos, Sophie Harris; makeup, Jimmy Evans.

Drama (PR:C-O MPAA:NR)

LONELY ARE THE BRAVE**** (1962) 107m UNIV bw

Kirk Douglas *(Jack Burns)*, Gena Rowlands *(Jerri Bondi)*, Walter Matthau *(Sheriff Johnson)*, Michael Kane *(Paul Bondi)*, Carroll O'Connor *(Hinton)*, William Schallert *(Harry)*, Karl Swenson *(Rev. Hoskins)*, George Kennedy *(Guitierrez)*, Dan Sheridan *(Deputy Glynn)*, Bill Raisch *("One Arm")*, William Mims *(1st Deputy in Bar)*, Martin Garralaga *(Old Man)*, Lalo Rios *(Prisoner)*.

In one of his finest portrayals, one where he will not compromise one moment of his freedom, Douglas plays a genuine cowboy, one of the last of the real cowboys, engulfed in a modern world ever crushing the Old West. Douglas is resting beneath clear and spacious western skies at the opening, the broad peace split by the sound of a jet plane passing overhead which brings a wry smile to his face. He rides his horse into Albuquerque to visit friends Kane and Rowlands and Rowlands tells him that her husband has been jailed for helping illegal Mexicans into the U.S. Douglas starts a brawl in a saloon and gets put into jail; this he has done on purpose so he can get close to his friend Kane, but his pal does not want his help in breaking out. He will serve his brief time, telling Douglas he intends to play out his hand with the law, and refuses to become a fugitive. Douglas is deeply hurt but his nature remains unchanged. He breaks out himself and heads for the hills, compassionate sheriff Matthau organizing a pursuit. During the pursuit Douglas second-guesses Matthau and his men at every turn, which earns Matthau's respect. He secretly admires Douglas and his individualistic ways but he knows the cowboy represents a wild way of life that is no more and that "either you go by the rules or you lose." Matthau pursues Douglas with his posse, using a Jeep, short wave communications, and a helicopter borrowed from the Army, but Douglas dodges and shifts his trail through the mountains, crossing over high ridges to freedom. Descending into the valley on the other side during a rainstorm, he attempts to cross a heavily trafficked super highway and is run over and killed by a huge truck driven by O'Connor. Douglas is superb as the cowboy who will not yield to the modern world and Miller's direction is excellent, this being the finest film in his otherwise up-and-down career. Matthau is also convincing as the understanding sheriff who tries his best to capture a man he does not want to see in irons. Douglas found great satisfaction in a role that reflected his own perspective, later stating: "It happens to be a point of view I love. This is what attracted me to the story—the difficulty of being an individual today." Lathrop's sharp black and white photography and Goldsmith's evocative score add measurably to this outstanding film. Trumbo's script is both sensitive and apt in describing the last anachronistic hours of a man out of his own time. A sense of doom is captured by Miller in his unobtrusive cross-cutting which shows truck driver O'Connor relentlessly driving toward the fatal rendezvous with the man on horseback. Shot on location near Albuquerque, New Mexico.

p, Edward Lewis; d, David Miller; w, Dalton Trumbo (based on the novel *Brave Cowboy* by Edward Abbey); ph, Philip Lathrop (Panavision); m, Jerry Goldsmith; ed, Leon Barsha, Edward Mann; art d, Alexander Golitzen, Robert E. Smith; set d, George Milo; makeup, Bud Westmore.

Western Cas. (PR:C MPAA:NR)

LONELY HEART BANDITS (SEE: LONELY HEARTS BANDITS, 1950)

LONELY HEARTS1/2** (1983, Aus.) 95m Samuel Goldwyn c

Wendy Hughes *(Patricia Curnow)*, Norman Kaye *(Peter Thompson)*, Jon Finlayson *(George, Theater Director)*, Julia Blake *(Pamela, Peter's Sister)*, Jonathan Hardy *(Bruce, Pamela's Husband)*, Irene Inescort *(Patricia's Mother)*, Vic Gordon *(Patricia's Father)*, Ted Grove-Rogers *(Peter's Father)*, Ronald Falk *(Wig Salesman)*, Chris Haywood *(Detective)*, Diana Greentree *(Sally Gordon)*, Margaret Steven *(Psychiatrist)*, Kris McQuade *(Rosemarie)*, Laurie Dobson *(Priest)*, Myrtle Roberts, Irene Hewitt *("Bye Bye Blackbird" Sisters)*, Jean Campbell, Ernest Wilson *(Old Couple in Park)*, Tony Llewellyn-Jones *(Martin)*, Dawn Klingberg *(Flower Seller)*, Lola Russell *(Mrs. Eddy)*, Jack Hill *(Bingo Caller)*, Christine Calcutt *(Dorothy)*, Ernie Bourne *(Man in Toilet)*, Barry Chambers *(Pianist)*, Sue Chapman *(Girl in Bank)*, Isobel Harley *(Bank Customer)*.

An off-beat comedy from down under that uses the affair between Hughes and Kaye to show off a number of eccentricities. He is an extremely outgoing piano tuner rapidly approaching middle age, while she has spent her time hiding out in an office unaware of many of life's experiences. This odd couple manage to hit it off quite well, supplying a number of light-hearted moments.

p, John B. Murray; d, Paul Cox; w, Cox, John Clarke; ph, Yuri Sokol; m, Norman Kaye; ed, Tim Lewis; art d, Neil Angwin.

Comedy Cas. (PR:O MPAA:R)

LONELY HEARTS BANDITS**
(1950) 60m REP bw (AKA: LONELY HEART BANDITS)

Dorothy Patrick *(Louise Curtis)*, John Eldredge *(Tony Morell, alias Wade Antrim)*, Barbara Fuller *(Laurel Vernon)*, Robert Rockwell *(Lt. Carroll)*, Ann Doran *(Nancy Crane)*, Richard Travis *(Aaron Hart)*, Dorothy Granger *(Belle)*, Eric Sinclair *(Bobby Crane)*, Kathleen Freeman *(Bertha)*, Frank Kreig *(Cal)*, Harry Cheshire *(Sheriff Polk)*, William Schallert *(Dave Clark)*, Howard J. Negley *(Elmer Jayson)*, John Crawford *(Stevedore)*, Eddie Dunn *(Sheriff York)*, Sammy McKim *(Jimmy Ward)*, Leonard Penn *(Detective Stanley)*.

This tightly packaged movie has Eldredge as a gangster who figures there's money to be made in the lonely hearts business. He marries Patrick and together they begin their escapade of conning lovelorn victims out of their money and then murdering them. After unsuccessfully courting a wealthy widow, Travis becomes suspicious of the pair when she mysteriously disappears. The manhunt is on and the film concludes with the police nabbing the husband-and-wife team. This film was inspired by The Lonely Heart Murders that took place in the late 1940s.

p, Stephen Auer; d, George Blair; w, Gene Lewis; ph, Ellis W. Carter; m, Stanley Wilson; ed, Harry Keller.

Crime/Drama (PR:A MPAA:NR)

LONELY HEARTS KILLER (SEE: HONEYMOON KILLERS, THE, 1969)

LONELY HEARTS KILLERS (SEE: HONEYMOON KILLERS, THE 1969)

LONELY LADY, THE, 1955 (SEE: STRANGERS, THE, 1955, Ital.)

LONELY LADY, THE zero (1983) 92m UNIV c

Pia Zadora *(Jerilee)*, Lloyd Bochner *(Walter)*, Bibi Besch *(Veronica)*, Joseph Cali *(Vincent)*, Anthony Holland *(Guy)*, Jared Martin *(George)*, Ray Liotta *(Joe)*, Carla Romanelli *(Carla)*, Olivier Pierre *(George)*, Kendal Kaldwell *(Joanne)*, Lou Hirsch *(Bernie)*, Kerry Shale *(Walt, Jr.)*, Sandra Dickinson *(Nancy)*, Shane Rimmer *(Adolph)*, Nancy Wood *(Janie)*, Ed Bishop *(Dr. Baker)*, Giovanni Rizzo *(Gino)*, Mickey Knox *(Tom)*, Kenneth Nelson *(Bud)*, Jay Benedict *(Dr. Sloan)*, Robyn Mandell *(Kim)*, Cecily Browne Laird *(Mrs. Stone)*, Billy J. Mitchell *(Gross)*, Glory

Annen *(Marion)*, Harrison Muller, Jr. *(Martin)*, Mary D'Antin *(Margaret)*, Carolynn DeFonseca *(Joanna)*, Cyrus Elias *(Nick)*, Kieran Canter *(Gary)*, David Mills.

This is the second film Zadora made with the encouragement of her multimillionaire husband, but unfortunately, it does nothing to convince one of her acting ability. The shallow script starts out with an introduction of Zadora in pigtails as an aspiring high school writer. She weds a much older Hollywood writer, Bochner, but his impotency and jealousy soon corrode the marriage. After leaving him, Zadora begins a whirlwind of heterosexual and lesbian orgies. She gets what she wants, however, success, but if there is some deep and hidden meaning to this story, it is certainly lost on the audience. Garbage unwrapped.

p, Robert R. Weston; d, Peter Sasdy; w, John Kershaw, Shawn Randall (based on the adaptation by Ellen Shepard, based on the novel by Harold Robbins); ph, Brian West (Technicolor); m, Charles Calello; ed, Keith Palmer; prod. d, Enzo Bulgarelli, art d, Adriana Bellone, Luciano Spadoni; cos, Giorgio Armani; m/l, Calello, Roger Voudouris (Title song sung by Larry Graham).

Drama Cas. (PR:O MPAA:R)

LONELY LANE*** (1963, Jap.) 124m Toho bw (HOROKI)

Hideko Takamine *(Fumiko Hayashi)*, Kinuyo Tanaka, Daisuke Kato, Akira Takarada, Mitsuko Kusabue, Noboru Nakaya, Toko Tsukasa.

A dramatized biography of Fumiko Hayashi, the noted Japanese writer. The story begins with her birth to impoverished parents. After a premature end to her education, Hayashi (Takamine) takes a variety of odd jobs to support herself. She also becomes involved with various men, some good and some bad. Eventually she writes the story of her life, which becomes a highly successful novel. She continues her career as a writer until her eventual death in 1951. Director Naruse had previously adapted a number of Hayashi's popular novels to the screen, and after her death he conceived of this filmization of her autobiography as a final tribute. Like most of Naruse's work, relentlessly downbeat.

p, Sanezumi Fujimoto, Mikio Naruse, Tadahiro Teramoto; d, Naruse; w, Toshiro Ide, Sumie Tanaka (based on *Horoki* by Fumiko Hayashi); ph, Jun Yasumoto (Tohoscope); m, Yuji Koseki.

Drama (PR:O MPAA:NR)

LONELY MAN, THE 1/2** (1957) 87m PAR bw

Jack Palance *(Jacob Wade)*, Anthony Perkins *(Riley Wade)*, Neville Brand *(King Fisher)*, Robert Middleton *(Ben Ryerson)*, Elaine Aiken *(Ada Marshall)*, Elisha Cook, Jr. *(Willie)*, Claude Akins *(Blackburn)*, Lee Van Cleef *(Faro)*, Harry Shannon *(Dr. Fisher)*, James Bell *(Judge Hart)*, Adam Williams *(Lon)*, Denver Pyle *(Sheriff)*, John Doucette *(Sundown Whipple)*, Paul Newlan *(Fence Green)*, Philip Van Zandt *(Burnsey)*, Moody Blanchard, Milton Frome, Tudor Owen, Russell Simpson, Taggert Casey, Daniel White, Richard Ryan, Billy Dix, Wesley Hudman, Zon Murray, Dirk London, Alan Page, Kenneth Hooker, Bill Meader.

Seventeen years after deserting his family, Palance decides to put his gunbelt on the shelf and make amends with his son, Perkins. But Perkins blames his father for his mother's death and the gunfighter has a hard time winning him back. Palance's enemies don't want to forget the past either, including Brand as a gambler looking to kill Palance for taking his woman. Van Cleef is Brand's henchman and Middleton is a gunfighter who vacillates his allegiance between Brand and Palance. Action is put on the back burner to concentrate on Palance's and Perkins' relationship, and Palance's struggle to escape his past and start anew. Based on the 1941 film SHEPHERD OF THE HILLS.

p, Pat Duggan; d, Henry Levin; w, Harry Essex, Robert Smith; ph, Lionel Lindon (VistaVision); m, Van Cleave; ed, William B. Murphy; art d, Hal Pereira, Roland Anderson; spec eff, John P. Fulton; m/l, Jack Brooks, Cleave (sung by Tennessee Ernie Ford).

Western (PR:A MPAA:NR)

LONELY MAN, THE, 1969 (SEE: GUN RIDERS, 1969)

LONELY ROAD, THE (SEE: SCOTLAND YARD COMMANDS, 1937, Brit.)

LONELY STAGE (SEE: I COULD GO ON SINGING, 1963)

LONELY TRAIL, THE** (1936) 58m REP bw

John Wayne *(John)*, Ann Rutherford *(Virginia)*, Cy Kendall *(Holden)*, Bob Kortman *(Hays)*, Snowflake [Fred Toones] *(Snowflake)*, Etta McDaniel *(Mammy)*, Sam Flint *(Governor)*, Denny [Dennis Moore] Meadows *(Terry)*, Jim Toney *(Jed)*, Yakima Canutt *(Horell)*, Lloyd Ingraham *(Tucker)*, Bob Burns *(Rancher)*, James Marcus *(Mayor)*, Rodney Hildebrand *(Capt. of Cavalry)*, Eugene Jackson *(Dancer)*, Floyd Shackelford *(Armstrong)*, Jack Kirk, Jack Ingram, Bud Pope, Tex Phelps, Tracy Layne, Clyde Kenney *(Troopers)*, Leon Lord *(Blaine)*, Horace B. Carpenter, Oscar Gahan, Francis Walker, Clifton Young.

Wayne returns to his home in Texas after serving with the Union army, and finds the state overrun by corrupt carpetbaggers. The Governor, Flint, hires Wayne to clean up the state, and the Duke always takes care of business. He has problems getting help from the ranchers and townspeople because he was a Union soldier, but in the end they come to his rescue and help kick out the carpetbaggers.

p, Nat Levine; d, Joseph Kane; w, Bernard McConville, Jack Natteford (based on the original by McConville); ph, William Nobles; ed, Lester Orlebeck.

Western Cas. (PR:A MPAA:NR)

LONELY WIVES* 1/2 (1931) 87m Pathe/RKO-Pathe bw

Edward Everett Horton *(Mr. Smith/Mr. Zero)*, Esther Ralston *(Mrs. Smith)*, Laura La Plante *(Diane)*, Patsy Ruth Miller *(Minter)*, Spencer Charters *(Andrews)*, Maude Eburne *(Mrs. Mantel)*, Georgette Rhoades *(Muzette)*, Maurice Black.

Horton has a dual role in this film as a married attorney and a vaudeville impersonator. It seems that Horton's mother-in-law has come to stay while his wife is away, but Horton has other plans for the evening. He wants to play with La Plante, so he hires the impersonator to fool his mother-in-law. Unfortunately for him, his wife, Ralston, decides to return home that very night, which causes a number of comical complications.

d, Russell Mack; w, Walter DeLeon (based on the stage play by A. H. Woods); ph, Edward Snyder; ed, Joseph Kane.

Comedy Cas. (PR:A MPAA:NR)

LONELY WOMAN, THE (SEE: STRANGERS, THE, 1955, Ital.)

LONELYHEARTS* 1/2** (1958) 108m UA bw

Montgomery Clift *(Adam White)*, Robert Ryan *(William Shrike)*, Myrna Loy *(Florence Shrike)*, Dolores Hart *(Justy Sargent)*, Maureen Stapleton *(Fay Doyle)*, Frank Maxwell *(Pat Doyle)*, Jackie Coogan *(Ned Gates)*, Mike Kellin *(Frank Goldsmith)*, Frank Overton *(Mr. Sargent)*, Don Washbrook *(Don Sargent)*, John Washbrook *(Johnny Sargent)*, Onslow Stevens *(Mr. Lassiter)*, Mary Alan Hokanson *(Edna)*, John Gallaudet *(Bartender)*, Lee Zimmer *(Jerry)*, J. B. Welch *(Charlie)*, Charles Wagenheim *(Bartender)*, Frank Richards *(Taxi Driver)*, Dorothy Neumann *(Mrs. Cannon)*.

Nathanael West is probably one of the most disregarded major novelists in this century and his dark, brooding, brilliant works do not translate well to the screen. Here his powerful novel about the lovelorn is brilliantly enacted, tautly directed, and comes from a script that is as faithful as producer Schary's compassion for the public would allow. Clift, in one of his best roles, is a reporter who is made the lovelorn columnist of his paper by cynical publisher Ryan, who is also superb in his role. Clift comes to be known as "Miss Lonelyhearts" and, at first, does not take his job seriously. Then he begins to feel compassion for the poor, lonely, love-starved creatures pouring out their hearts to him. Some of his correspondents, like Stapleton, are only neurotic sociopaths feeding their own egos by inveigling Clift not only into correspondence but confrontations that almost prove lethal. Meanwhile, Loy, Ryan's wife, who has lost all respect for her husband, makes a friend of Clift which the jaded Ryan both encourages and condemns. Ryan is the terrible goad who keeps prodding Clift to open his soul to strangers reading his column, a task that turns Clift into an emotionally torn man and confuses his relationship with girl friend Hart. It's the perverse Ryan who insists that Clift go that one step further in consoling the unbalanced Stapleton, wife of a cripple, and having a sordid sexual affair with her (one that resulted in the hero's death in the novel at the hands of a crippled husband). Clift survives all the trauma and then goes off with Hart, leaving Ryan and his rag in the lurch. Hart is the only person Clift has room enough to love in the end, telling her at one time: "I love you because you love me and because you're warm and soft." He has tried desperately to become an emotional sponge for humanity's sake, at least before the disillusionment sets in, saying early on: "If someone is in trouble, how can you not take them seriously?" To Ryan, the ever cynical publisher, it's all a perverse little game; he comments in one scene: "I enjoy seeing youth betray their promises." But much of his seething hatred for humanity is reserved for wife Loy who, long ago, had had a brief affair, a tryst that Ryan will never let her forget, keeping alive the idea that she is nothing more than a tramp and encouraging her to wallow in her alcoholism. Clift is fascinating in this jumbled film as he plays a man of emotional indecision who must arbitrate the emotional destinies of nameless others. Donehue does a commendable job with a meaningful but multi-directional script. Producer Schary got the backing for this film from United Artists only on the proviso that he bring in the entire production for less than $1 million. He prevailed upon Clift to accept only half of his usual fee, $100,000, to appear in the film, Schary's first after leaving MGM. All of the cast members worked for half salary and were all personal friends. Donehue directed the film by blocking it out like a play, which pleased Clift and the others. The effect, however, was to give a confining look to the overall film. Clift by then was drinking heavily and could only work until about 2 p.m. when he would show signs of fatigue and the entire production had to shut down. LONELY HEARTS took 45 days to complete and when it was released it did only spotty business at the box office. Loy, then yet an attractive female in middle-age, reportedly fell in love with Clift during the shooting. Despite Loy being 15 years older than Clift, one report had it that she wanted to marry the troubled young man. The West novel had been filmed once before, as ADVICE TO THE LOVELORN in 1933, starring Lee Tracy, who played the story strictly for laughs.

p, Dore Schary; d, Vincent J. Donehue; w, Schary (based on the novella *Miss Lonelyhearts* by Nathanael West and the play by Howard Teichmann); ph, John Alton; m, Conrad Salinger; ed, Aaron Steele, John Faure; md, Adolph Deutsch; art d, Serge Krizman; set d, Darrell Silvera; cos, Chuck Arrico, Angela Alexander; makeup, Abe Haberman, Frank Laure.

Drama (PR:C MPAA:NR)

LONER, THE (SEE: RUCKUS, 1981)

LONERS, THE* 1/2 (1972) 79m Four Leaf/Fanfare c

Dean Stockwell *(Stein)*, Pat Stich *(Julio)*, Todd Susman *(Allan)*, Scott Brady *(Policeman Hearn)*, Gloria Grahame *(Annabelle)*, Alex Dreier *(Police Chief Peters)*, Tim Rooney *(Howie)*, Ward Wood *(Sheriff)*, Hortense Petra *(Mrs. Anderson)*, Richard O'Brien *(Driver)*, Hal Jon Norman *(Stein's Father)*, Duane Grey *(Man in Diner)*, Jean Dorl *(Woman in Diner)*, Stuart Nisbet *(Bridegroom)*, Larry O'Leno *(Policeman)*.

Stockwell plays a half-Navajo who is on the run from police for accidentally running a car off the road with his motorcycle. Along the way he picks up Stich, a rebellious teenager fleeing from her shrewish mother, and Susman, a retarded teen devoted to Stockwell. The spree across country involves a robbery where Susman accidentally kills the owner. The three hide out in a church where Susman performs a mock wedding ceremony for Stockwell and Stich. Things get worse when Susman goes into town for food and, when provoked by a jealous husband, guns down a half dozen people. Thinking they can fly his father's plane to South America, Stockwell takes his pals back to the reservation, only to find out his father no longer owns the plane and is disappointed that his son has rejected the Indian way of life. The melodrama ends when the three renegades decide to leave the reservation and are gunned down by surrounding police.

p, Jerry Katzman; d, Sutton Roley; w, John Lawrance, Barry Sandler (based on a story by Lawrance); ph, Irving Lippman (Metrocolor); m, Fred Karger; ed, John Woelz.

Crime/Drama   **Cas.**   **(PR:O   MPAA:R)**

LONESOME**   (1928) 60m UNIV bw

Barbara Kent (Mary), Glenn Tryon (Jim), Fay Holderness (Overdressed Woman), Gustav Partos (Romantic Gentleman), Eddie Phillips (The Sport).

Kent and Tryon are two lonely people living in the same New York City boarding house. They have no idea of each other until they meet at Coney Island and fall in love. They spend the day together until they are separated by the outbreak of a fire. Both return to the boarding house to discover they're neighbors. This was Universal's first sound film with only three dialog scenes (all on the beach).

p, Carl Laemmle, Jr.; d, Paul Fejos; w, Edward T. Lowe, Jr., Tom Reed (based on a story by Mann Page); ph, Gilbert Warrenton; ed, Frank Atkinson.

Drama   **(PR:A   MPAA:NR)**

LONESOME COWBOYS zero   (1968) 110m Factory Films c

Viva, Tom Hompertz, Eric Emerson, Taylor Mead, Louis Walden, Joe D'Alessandro, Julian Burroughs, Francis Francine.

One of a string of Factory films of the 1960s, with homosexual sex and perverse humor. Slim story-line has a gang of gay cowboys riding into a desert town, where a frustrated Viva and Mead welcome them with open arms. Francine is the transvestite sheriff and Hompertz is the boy everyone wants to bed down. There's sex with horses, gay and straight sex, plus a Viva strip show, too. Morrisey is the uncredited director behind Warhol. Today, the film seems so out-of-date, that it's funnier than ever intended, and shows that Warhol and his bunch were just looking to shock, not break ground. By today's standards, however, LONESOME COWBOYS seems pretty tame.

p,d&w, Andy Warhol; ph, Paul Morrisey (Eastmancolor).

Western   **(PR:O   MPAA:NR)**

LONESOME TRAIL, THE*¹⁄₂   (1930) 69m G.A. Durlam/Syndicate bw

Charles Delaney (Judd Rascomb), Ben Corbett (Sweetheart), Jimmy Aubrey (Tenderfoot), Monte Montague (Gila Red), Virginia Brown Faire (Martha), William McCall (Rankin), George Berliner (Crabb), George Hackathorne (Oswald), William von Brincken (Man in White Sombrero), George Rigas (The Ring-Tailored Roarer), Lafe McKee (Sheriff), Yakima Canutt (Two Gun), Bob Reeves (Alkali), Art Mix (Slim).

A low-budget independent western with Delaney singing "Oh, Susannah" and other tunes. This singing cowboy western foreshadowed the surge of tune-carrying cowpokes to come. Mix and Canutt are the bad guys and this was Delaney's only starring role.

d, Bruce Mitchell; w, G. A. Durlam; ph, Paul H. Allen; ed, Durlam.

Western   **(PR:A   MPAA:NR)**

LONESOME TRAIL, THE**   (1955) 73m Lippert bw

Wayne Morris, John Agar, Margia Dean, Edgar Buchanan, Adele Jergens, Earle Lyon, Ian MacDonald, Douglas Fowley, Richard Bartlett, Betty Blythe.

Routine cowboy story is taken out of the ordinary format by having the good guys use bows and arrows to fight their battles; in this case against landgrabbers trying to run them off their ranch. Needless to say, guns prove no match for the traditional weapons of the American Indians.

p, Earle Lyon; d, Richard Bartlett; w, Bartlett, Ian MacDonald (based on the novel Silent Beckoning by Gordon D. Shirreffs); m, Leon Klatzken.

Western   **(PR:A   MPAA:NR)**

LONG ABSENCE, THE***

(1962, Fr./Ital.) 85m Societe Cinematographique Lyre-Procinex-Galatea/Commercial bw (UNE AUSSI LONGUE ABSENCE; L'INVERNO TI FARA TORNARE)

Alida Valli (Therese Langlois), Georges Wilson (Tramp), Jacques Harden (Truck Driver), Diana Lepvrier (Martine), Catherine Fontenay (Alice), Amedee (Marcel), Charles Blavette (Fernand), Paul Faivre (Pensioner), Charles Bouillaud (Favier), Pierre Parel (Manager), Nane Germon (Simone), Pierre Mirat (Druggist), Jean Luisi, Corrado Guarducci (Workmen), Georges Bielec, Michel Risbourg (Young Men), Clement Harari (Man at Juke Box).

A moving, poignant film starring Valli as a lonely Parisian cafe owner who spots a humming tramp, Wilson, walking past her cafe. Valli becomes convinced that the man is her husband whom she lost in the war sixteen years ago. She follows Wilson to his little shack by the Seine and learns that he has had amnesia since the war. She invites Wilson back to her cafe where she tries to reawaken his memory. When she sees the deep scar on the back of his head, Valli knows deep-down that he will never remember, but she is determined to spend the rest of her life trying to evoke his memories. Winner of the Pix Louis Dellux and shared the Grand Prize at Cannes with Luis Bunuel's VIRIDIANA.

d, Henri Colpi; w, Marguerite Duras, Gerard Jarlot (based on the story by Duras); ph, Marcel Weiss; m, Georges Delerue (based on themes by Gioacchino Antonio Rossini, Gaetano Donizetti); ed, Jasmine Chasney, Jacqueline Meppiel; art d, Maurice Colasson.

Drama   **(PR:A   MPAA:NR)**

LONG AGO, TOMORROW***

(1971, Brit.) 110m EMI/Cinema 5 c (AKA: THE RAGING MOON)

Malcolm McDowell (Bruce Pritchard), Nanette Newman (Jill Mathews), Georgia Brown (Sarah Charles), Bernard Lee (Uncle Bob), Gerald Sim (Rev. Corbett), Michael Flanders (Clarence Marlow), Margery Mason (Matron), Barry Jackson (Bill Charles), Christopher Chittell (Terry), Geoffrey Whitehead (Harold), Jack Woolgar (Bruce's Father), Norman Bird (Dr. Mathews), Constance Chapman (Mrs. Mathews), Michael Lees (Geoffrey), Geoffrey Bayldon (Mr. Latbury), Patsy Smart (Bruce's Mother), Theresa Watson (Gladys), Sylvia Coleridge (Celia), Brook Williams (Hugh Collins), Richard Moore (Arnold Foster), George Hilsdon (George), Nellie Hanham (Margaret), Aimee Delamain (Alice), Anne Dyson (Gladys' Mother) Norman Tyrrell (Gladys' Father), Petra Markham (Mary), Winifride Shelley (Mrs. Hetherington), John Savident (Fete Guest), Michael Nightingale (Mr. Thomas), Jackie Agrique (Edna), Paul Darrow (Doctor), Lee Carter (Wedding Singer), Sarah Forbes, Emma Forbes (Bridesmaids).

This moving story is about McDowell, a 24-year-old, arrogant, self-centered youth who contracts an incurable crippling disease that paralyzes him from the waist down. He is confined to a wheelchair and is transferred to a home for paraplegics, where he becomes bitter and withdrawn, as well as rebellious against the rules and regulations of the home. He spends his time alone, writing short stories and poetry, until he meets Newman, a surprisingly cheerful girl who has polio. But before he can make his feelings known, she leaves the institution for her home, where her parents try to talk her into marrying her long-time fiance, Lees. She decides to break off the engagement and return to the home, and from that moment on, McDowell and Newman are inseparable. Against the wishes of her parents and everyone else, they decide to marry. But before the plans become a reality, Newman dies and McDowell is left to contemplate life's ironies alone. Songs include: Title song (Burt Bacharach, Hal David, sung by B. J. Thomas), "A Time For Winning" (Tony Macaulay, Roger Cook, Tony Greenaway, sung by Blue Mink), "Many Loving Things" (Stanley Myers, Roger Cook, sung by Cook).

p, Bruce Cohn Curtis; d&w, Bryan Forbes (based on the novel The Raging Moon by Peter Marshall); ph, Tony Imi (Technicolor); m, Stanley Myers; ed, Timothy Gee; art d, Robert Jones; cos, Laurel Staffell.

Drama   **Cas.**   **(PR:C   MPAA:GP)**

LONG AND THE SHORT AND THE TALL, THE***

(1961, Brit.) 105m Warner-Pathe bw (AKA: JUNGLE FIGHTERS)

Richard Todd (Sgt. Mitchem), Laurence Harvey (Pvt. Bamforth), Richard Harris (Cor. Johnstone), Ronald Fraser (Lance-Cor. MacLeish), John Meillon (Pvt. Smith), David McCallum (Pvt. Whitaker), John Rees (Pvt. Evans), Kenji Takaki (Tojo).

A war drama set in the jungles of Burma has a British patrol, led by Todd, capturing a Japanese scout, Takaki. Todd wants to bring the prisoner alive to headquarters to be interrogated, but his men want to kill the scout. Harvey is ordered to watch Takaki, and while the tension builds among the men, he and the prisoner become friends. A rock slide blocks the patrol's only path back to their base and while they contemplate their fate, they discover that the Japanese soldier has looted them. Again, the men want him shot and McCallum finally does it. Unfortunately for them, nearby Japanese troops hear the shot and advance on the patrol. Harris and McCallum are the only ones to survive the fighting, and when the Japs find Takaki's canteen on McCallum, trouble again ensues. With a weird twist of fate Harris and McCallum are now the prisoners that the patrol (this time Japanese) want to shoot.

p, Michael Balcon; d, Leslie Norman; w, Wolf Mankowitz, Willis Hall (based on a play by Hall); ph, Edwin Hillier; m, Stanley Black; ed, Gordon Stone; md, Stanley Black; art d, Terence Verity, Jim Morahan; cos, Ernie Farrer; spec eff, George Blackwell; makeup, L.V. Clark.

War Drama   **(PR:A   MPAA:NR)**

LONG ARM, THE   (SEE: THIRD KEY, THE, 1957, Brit.)

LONG CORRIDOR   (SEE: SHOCK CORRIDOR, 1963)

LONG DARK HALL, THE**   (1951, Brit.) 80m Five Oceans/Cusick/EL bw

Rex Harrison (Arthur Groome), Lilli Palmer (Mary Groome), Denis O'Dea (Sir Charles Morton), Raymond Huntley (Chief Inspector Sullivan), Patricia Wayne (Rose Mallory), Anthony Dawson (The Man), Anthony Bushell (Clive Bedford), Meriel Forbes (Marjorie Danns), Brenda de Banzie (Mrs. Rogers), William Squires (Sgt. Cochran), Michael Medwin (Leslie Scott), Colin Gordon (Pound), Eric Pohlmann (Polaris), Tania Heald (Sheila Groome), Henrietta Barry (Rosemary Groome), Dora Stevening (Mary's Mother), Ronald Simpson (Mary's Father), Ballard Berkeley (Supt. Maxey), Henry Longhurst (Judge), Douglas Jeffries, Fletcher Lightfoot, Anthony Shaw, Lily Molnar, Frank Tickle, Tom Macauley, Richard Littledale, Jenny Laird, Tony Quinn, Jill Bennett.

A minor league courtroom drama from a script by Nunnally Johnson while he was at Universal. It was later sold to A&P heir Huntington Hartford who eventually had it produced in England. Harrison is a married man with a couple of children. He has a wonderful relationship with his wife, Palmer, but can't help a bit of dalliance on the side. When his mistress is murdered, all the circumstantial evidence points to him. We know from the start that he's innocent as they have chosen to make this an "open mystery" (like the old "Columbo" TV series) rather than a "closed mystery" (like most of the Agatha Christie novels). Harrison is put on trial and most of the film takes place in the courtroom as the web of evidence is carefully wrapped around the suspect. He is defended by the producer and co-director, Bushell, who should have stayed behind the camera. Dawson, the real killer, thinking that Harrison is about to be hanged, sends a letter to the police confessing that he did it. But the mail is not delivered on time because of a Parliamentary decision and the letter gets to the police before the hangman gets to Harrison. A few sparkling moments between the at the time real-life husband and wife team of Palmer and Harrison is all that distinguishes this from a thousand other courtroom dramas. Excellent work by Huntley who played comedy (MAKE MINE MINK) as well as he played drama (THE LAST HOLIDAY).

p, Peter Cusick; d, Anthony Bushell, Reginald Beck; w, Nunnally Johnson, William E.C. Fairchild (based on the novel *A Case to Answer* by Edgar Lustgarden); ph, Wilkie Cooper; m, Benjamin Frankel; ed, Tom Simpson; art d, George Patterson; set d, Ronald Kinnoch.

Drama **Cas.** **(PR:A-C MPAA:NR)**

LONG, DARK NIGHT, THE (SEE: PACK, THE, 1977)

LONG DAY'S DYING, THE* (1968, Brit.) 93m Junction/PAR c

David Hemmings *(John)*, Tom Bell *(Tom)*, Tony Beckley *(Cliff)*, Alan Dobie *(Helmut)*.

A heavy-handed war melodrama with three British paratroopers caught behind German lines. Hemmings, Bell, and Beckley are the men who wait in a burned-out building for their sergeant's arrival. Hemmings is a pacifist, Bell is the oldest and most experienced, and Beckley is a war-loving sadist. They capture a German officer, Dobie, who tricks them into letting him live, and set out to find their sergeant, only to discover his throat slit. They spend the night in a farmhouse before heading back to their own lines and get into a skirmish with a German patrol. Beckley is killed, and so are the Germans. The remaining two men and their prisoner make it to the British lines, only to be cut down by their own men.

p, Peter Collinson, Harry Fine; d, Collinson; w, Charles Wood (based on a novel by Alan White); ph, Brian Probyn (Techniscope, Technicolor); ed, John Trumper; art d, Disley Jones; spec eff, Pat Moore; makeup, Bob Lawrence.

War Drama **(PR:C-O MPAA:R)**

LONG DAY'S JOURNEY INTO NIGHT***** (1962) 174m Landau/Embassy bw

Katharine Hepburn *(Mary Tyrone)*, Ralph Richardson *(James Tyrone, Sr.)*, Jason Robards, Jr. *(James Tyrone, Jr.)*, Dean Stockwell *(Edmund Tyrone)*, Jeanne Barr *(Cathleen)*.

This greatest of Eugene O'Neill plays is brought to the screen with an overpowering wealth of talent: Hepburn, Richardson, and Robards giving magnificent once-in-a-lifetime performances as members of the doomed Tyrone family. It is one long, long day and night in the year 1912 at the Tyrone summer home in New London, Connecticut. The elder Tyrone, Richardson, was once a fine Shakespearean actor but has been making good money in recent years by playing the same role over and over again in a commercial play. He is also entering old age and is fearful of dying broke, further nurturing lifelong habits of being a skinflint. His wife, Hepburn, has just returned from a sanitarium. She is all lady, an Irish Catholic with strong and deep moral principles, but she is also strangely withdrawn. The oldest son, Robards, has attempted to follow his father in the acting profession but has failed miserably and he takes solace in drink, having become an alcoholic cynic who would rather destroy all around him than show the deep affections he feels. The younger brother, Stockwell, is recovering from tuberculosis and has spent time in a sanitarium himself, a second-rate institution which his tightwad father has sent him to in order to save money. Stockwell is a budding writer and he not only struggles with his craft but his deep and contradictory feelings toward his family. Richardson dwells on the past as he recalls his theatrical triumphs of yesterday, eloquently impressing his amused sons with his stature in the theater. Hepburn, meanwhile, spends lengthy periods of time in her room which begins to unnerve Richardson. As the day wears on, Richardson insists that only a few lights be turned on to save money; he is a man who cannot help his own quirks. None of the family, except the youthful Stockwell, can help the way they are, although they struggle against their secret vices for the sake of a family that exists in name only. At first Robards is congenial and loving toward his younger brother, but when Hepburn appears in a daze he and his father sink into murky depths of emotion and Robards begins to lambast Richardson, blaming him for Hepburn's condition. She is a dope addict, he finally blurts to the unsuspecting Stockwell, and he, Stockwell, is also to blame for her horrid state. When Stockwell was born, Richardson hired a quack who attended Hepburn in a hotel to save money, Robards relates with delicious perversity, and it was this doctor who injected Hepburn with addictive morphine to deal with her pain. Moreover, Hepburn is burdened with guilt since her father died of tuberculosis and she feels that she's passed this illness onto her son Stockwell. Richardson, too, blames Stockwell for his wife's condition and shows it by consigning his boy to a state-run health resort where his care will be less than professional. Robards, pretending comraderie, takes Stockwell carousing through the town, introducing him to his whore friends and treating his sleazy ways as good clean masculine fun, but he gets drunk and his truthful feelings come out; he drunkenly attacks Stockwell, telling him to "Watch out for me, kid." Hepburn is now in a different world, entering the family room late at night, her own devils possessing her mind and controlling her words, although through the haze she still makes a feeble attempt to perceive of this group of strangers as a family still rooted together. Hepburn is a marvel as she makes one fantastic transition after another, from girlish coquette remembering her apple blossom youth, to maddened dope fiend, from loving mother to a mindless creature groping for identity. All of this she somehow accomplishes in one of the most masterful performances on film. Richardson isn't close behind and Robards is a wonder as he embodies the truly tortured older brother. Stockwell is the only one in the cast who is thin on believability but this may be an unjust appraisal in that he is merely overwhelmed by the magnetic actors with whom he must interact. Hepburn took on the role of the dope-addicted mother for a pittance and tried to get Spencer Tracy to play the father, but he adamantly refused. Tracy was exhausted after working in JUDGMENT AT NUREMBERG and told producer Landau: "Look, Kate's the lunatic—she's the one who goes off and appears at Stratford in Shakespeare—'Much Ado' and all that stuff. I don't believe in that nonsense. I'm a movie actor." He then asked for $500,000 to appear in the movie which, of course, on Landau's limited budget, was impossible. Richardson was brought in just after Hepburn agreed to play the role, one which earned her an Oscar nomination where she lost out to Anne Bancroft for THE MIRACLE WORKER. It is her finest portrait. The film, shot on location in New York City, followed the superb O'Neill play almost word for word. O'Neill, at age 50 began writing the play in 1939 and finished the following year, calling it a work "of old sorrow, written in tears and blood." It is completely autobiographical. His father, James O'Neill, was once an accomplished Shakespearean actor who had become successful and rich playing "The Count of Monte Cristo," enacting the part season after season. His wife, O'Neill's mother, was addicted to morphine from the time of O'Neill's birth, and his brother Jamie was a would-be actor who died prematurely of acute alcoholism. According to O'Neill's will, the play was not to be produced until 25 years after his death, which occurred in 1951. But his widow, Carlotta, decided otherwise and the play was performed in 1956, becoming an overnight classic. The play starred Fredric March, Florence Eldridge, Robards, and Bradford Dillman.

p, Ely Landau, Jack J. Dreyfus, Jr.; d, Sidney Lumet; w, Eugene O'Neill (based on his play); ph, Boris Kaufman; m, Andre Previn; ed, Ralph Rosenblum; prod d, Richard Sylbert; art d, Sylbert; cos, Motley.

Drama **Cas.** **(PR:C MPAA:NR)**

LONG DISTANCE (SEE: HOT MONEY GIRL, 1962, Brit./Ger.)

LONG DUEL, THE** (1967, Brit.) 115m RANK-LIP/PAR c

Yul Brynner *(Sultan)*, Trevor Howard *(Freddy Young)*, Harry Andrews *(Superintendent Stafford)*, Andrew Keir *(Gungaram)*, Charlotte Rampling *(Jane Stafford)*, Virginia North *(Champa)*, Laurence Naismith *(McDougal)*, Maurice Denham *(Governor)*, Imogen Hassall *(Tara)*, Paul Hardwick *(Jamadar)*, Antonio Padilla Ruiz *(Munnu)*, David Sumner *(Gyan Singh)*, Rafiq Anwar *(Pahelwan)*, George Pastell *(Ram Chand)*, Shivendra Sinha *(Abdul)*, Zohra Segal *(Devi)*, Norman Florence *(Nathu)*, Kurt Christian *(Babu)*, Dino Shafeek *(Akbar)*, Terry Yorke *(Moti)*, Tommy Reeves *(Sentry)*, Jimmy Lodge *(Guard)*, Patrick Newell *(Colonel)*, Jeremy Lloyd *(Crabbe)*, Terence Alexander *(Major)*, Marianne Stone *(Major's Wife)*, Edward Fox *(Hardwicke)*, Bakshi Prem *(High Priest)*, Toni Kanal *(Kamala)*, Ramon Serrano *(Bhim)*, Ben Tatar *(Sandhu)*, Aldo Sambrel *(Prem)*, Monish Bose, Naseem Khan, Shymala Devi, Shirley Sen Guptha, Jamila Massey *(Dancing Girls)*.

An overblown adventure picture set in the 1920s stars Howard as a British police officer in India who opposes his country's treatment of the local Bhantas. The Bhantas' leader, Brynner, is regarded as a dangerous man by the British, and when he resolves to free his people, the English send Howard out to capture the rebel. Howard is stymied by his lack of conviction for the assignment and his respect for Brynner, so he sets out to bring him back alive. After a few run-ins with the rebel, Howard meets Brynner face-to-face and pleads with him to give himself up. Brynner refuses, and Howard returns to his base camp with the news. Frustrated, the British plan to attack Brynner's stronghold, and in the ensuing battle Brynner is mortally wounded. Admitting a respect for his pursuer, Brynner asks Howard to raise his young son as his own.

p&d, Ken Annakin; w, Ernest Bornemann, Peter Yeldham, Geoffrey Orme (based on a story by Ranveer Singh); ph, Jack Hildyard (Panavision/Technicolor); m, Patrick John Scott; ed, Bert Bates; md, Scott; art d, Alex Vetchinsky; set d, Arthur Taksen; cos, John Furness; spec eff, Dick Parker; m/l, "When the World Is Ready," Scott, Don Black (sung by Vince Hill).

Adventure **(PR:A MPAA:NR)**

LONG GOOD FRIDAY, THE*½** (1982, Brit.) 105m Calendar-Black Lion/EM c

Bob Hoskins *(Harold)*, Helen Mirren *(Victoria)*, Eddie Constantine *(Charlie)*, Dave King *(Parky)*, Bryan Marshall *(Harris)*, George Coulouris *(Gus)*, Derek Thompson *(Jeff)*, Bruce Alexander *(Mac)*, Paul Barber *(Errol)*, Pierce Brosnan *(1st Irishman)*, Charles Cork *(Eric)*, Bill Cornelius *(Pete)*, Stephen Davis *(Tony)*, Alan Devlin *(Priest)*, Christopher Driscoll *(Phil)*, Brian Hall *(Alan)*, P. H. Moriarty *(Razors)*, Paul Freeman *(Colin)*, Patti Love *(Carol)*.

An English gangster thriller, the film stars Hoskins as a mob boss who finds his world crumples violently. During the Easter weekend, Hoskins tries to work a massive land deal connected with the 1988 London Olympics with his American counterparts. Business is interrupted when his buildings are bombed and men are murdered. Hoskins goes after his rival gang bosses only to learn they have had no part in the "hits". The gangster soon finds out that the IRA is behind the violence because one of Hoskins' men robbed protection money from the IRA. Hoskins gets revenge on the IRA, but the terrorists have the last word. The film is a taut, violent thriller with an intense performance by Hoskins. Eddie Constantine makes a welcome appearance as the key U.S. negotiator in the criminal deal.

p, Barry Hanson; d, John Mackenzie; w, Barrie Keefe; ph, Phil Meheux; m, Francis Monkman; ed, Mike Taylor; art d, Vic Symonds.

Crime Drama **Cas.** **(PR:O MPAA:R)**

LONG GOODBYE, THE* (1973) 112m UA c

Elliott Gould *(Philip Marlowe)*, Nina van Pallandt *(Eileen Wade)*, Sterling Hayden *(Roger Wade)*, Mark Rydell *(Marty Augustine)*, Henry Gibson *(Dr. Verringer)*, David Arkin *(Harry)*, Jim Bouton *(Terry Lennox)*, Warren Berlinger *(Morgan)*, Jo Ann

Brody *(Jo Ann Eggenweiler)*, Jack Knight *(Hood)*, Pepe Callahan *(Pepe)*, Vince Palmieri, Arnold Strong *(Hoods)*, Rutanya Alda, Tammy Shaw *(Marlowe's Neighbors)*, Jack Riley *(Piano Player)*, Ken Sansom *(Colony Guard)*, Danny Goldman *(Bartender)*, Sybil Scotford *(Real Estate Lady)*, Steve Coit *(Detective Farmer)*, Tracy Harris *(Detective)*, Jerry Jones *(Detective Green)*, Rodney Moss *(Supermarket Clerk)*, Pancho Cordoba *(Doctor)*, Enrique Lucero *(Jefe)*, John Davies *(Detective Davies)*, Herb Kerns *(Herbie)*.

Of all the Philip Marlowes to stride across the screen—Humphrey Bogart, Dick Powell, Robert Montgomery—Gould is the most unlikely and the most unbelievable. Having this marshmallow actor playing a hard-boiled detective is like having Leo Gorcey play the Ringo Kid in STAGECOACH. Gould is lying about his pad waiting for a case to show up but his friend Bouton appears instead and asks him to drive him to Tijuana, which he does. Later the L.A. police arrest Gould and charge him with helping Bouton escape; Bouton has apparently killed his wife but Gould refuses to believe it. He is later released when police receive word from Mexico that Bouton has committed suicide. Van Pallandt then shows up and hires Gould to find her missing husband, Hayden, an unpredictable author of some note. Gould finds Hayden in a sanitorium run by greedy little Gibson; the author is drying out but Gould persuades Hayden to return home. Here Van Pallandt and Hayden fall to arguing and the author exhibits a violent temper, one so pronounced that Gould thinks he might have had something to do with the death of Bouton's wife. In the middle of the night, with Gould still mourning the loss of his temperamental cat, gangster Rydell shows up with his goons and demands that Gould return the money that Bouton, who had worked for Rydell as a money runner, had taken before fleeing to Mexico. Gould doesn't know a thing about it and is abused for his ignorance. He is warned that he must return the money or face destruction. Later, the unperturbed Gould gets contradictory stories about Bouton from both Van Pallandt and Hayden. He goes to Mexico and verifies Bouton's death with local officials but is puzzled by it all. Then he attends a party given by Hayden and Van Pallandt where Hayden is utterly humiliated by Gibson who slaps the author and demands his medical fee, which is paid. That night, a drunken Hayden walks into the ocean and drowns himself. Van Pallandt tries to put the killing of Bouton's wife on her dead husband, saying he was a violent man and something must have gone wrong with Hayden's affair with the dead woman. Gould asks police to reopen the Bouton case but they refuse. Then the money Rydell has been demanding unexpectedly shows up and is returned to the gangster. Gould sees Van Pallandt meet with Rydell and when he tries to follow her, he is struck by a car and hospitalized. He gets out of his sick bed and journeys to Mexico where he tracks down a very much alive Bouton. It has all been a setup, Gould learns and explodes, shooting Bouton to death. As he leaves the Mexican hideout, a luxurious spot, he passes Van Pallandt who is going to meet her lover and it is obvious that both have murdered their spouses to be with each other. Perversely, Gould does a weird little dance as he passes Van Pallandt and is captured in freeze-frame for a less than rewarding finish. This is another one of those disjointed, unintelligible Altman films which has no real plotline, character development, or a single memorable line. The whole unprofessional mess is an insult to the memory of that fine writer, Raymond Chandler. Gould is simply no-talented here and wholly miscast. Van Pallandt's presence came about because of the notoriety she gleaned as a former mistress of swindler Clifford Irving who tried to scam the world into believing he had authored an official biography of Howard Hughes. She is a nonentity as an actress, wholly without talent. Rydell isn't much better as he does an imitation of Roman Polanski's gangster from CHINATOWN. Gibson is interesting in his offbeat role and Hayden is the only real actor in the bunch. This is a definite waste of time, larded with gratuitous violence and a moronic point of view.

p, Jerry Bick; d, Robert Altman; w, Leigh Brackett (based on the novel by Raymond Chandler); ph, Vilmos Zsigmond (PanaVision, Technicolor); m, John Williams; ed, Lou Lombardo; cos, Kent James, Marjorie Wahl; m/l, title song, John Williams, Johnny Mercer; makeup, Bill Miller.

Crime Drama **(PR:O MPAA:R)**

LONG GRAY LINE, THE*½** (1955) 138m COL c

Tyrone Power *(Marty Maher)*, Maureen O'Hara *(Mary O'Donnell)*, Robert Francis *(James Sundstrom, Jr.)*, Donald Crisp *(Old Martin)*, Ward Bond *(Capt. Herman J. Koehler)*, Betsy Palmer *(Kitty Carter)*, Phil Carey *(Charles Dotson)*, William Leslie *(Red Sundstrom)*, Harry Carey, Jr. *(Dwight Eisenhower)*, Patrick Wayne *(Cherub Overton)*, Sean McClory *(Dinny Maher)*, Peter Graves *(Cpl. Rudolph Heinz)*, Milburn Stone *(Capt. John Pershing)*, Erin O'Brien Moore *(Mrs. Koehler)*, Walter D. Ehlers *(Mike Shannon)*, Willis Bouchey *(Maj. Thomas)*, Don Barclay *(McDonald)*, Martin Milner *(Jim O'Carberry)*, Chuck Courtney *(Whitney Larson)*, Maj. Philip Kieffer *(Superintendent)*, Norman Van Brocklin *(Gus Dorain)*, Diane DeLaire *(Nurse)*, Donald Murphy *(Army Captain)*, Lisa Davis *(Eleanor)*, Dona Cole *(Peggy)*, Robert Roark *(Cadet Pirelli)*, Robert Ellis *(Cadet Short)*, Ken Curtis *(Specialty Bit)*, Jack Pennick *(Recruiting Sergeant)*, Mimi Doyle *(Nun)*, James Sears *(Knute Rockne)*, Fritz Apking, Mary Benoit, Raoul Freeman, Jack Mower, Jack Ellis, Leon McLaughlin *(Bits)*, Tom Hennesy *(Peter Dotson)*, John Herbin *(Cadet Ramsey)*, Mickey Roth *(Cadet Curly Stern)*, Elbert Steele *(The President)*, Jean Moorhead *(Girl)*, Mickey Simpson *(New York Policeman)*, Pat O'Malley, Harry Denny *(Priests)*, Pat Harding, Dorothy Seese *(Ad-Lib Girls)*.

This is an affectionate look at West Point, its cadets, and, in particular, one colorful individual, Martin Maher, (pronounced Marr), played wonderfully by Power, an Irish immigrant who found a home in the Army. The story begins as Power, an old man, is about to be retired from the service. He protests personally to a former West Point cadet, President Dwight D. Eisenhower, Steele, who was nurtured at the Point by Power when Eisenhower was a lowly cadet. Power recounts the story of his life and we see the film unfold in flashback, beginning with Power's migration from Ireland in 1903. He gets a job as a waiter at the Point. He is a poor waiter and broken dishes abound, charges for which soon exceed his wages. To compensate for the charges, Power enlists in the Army and is assigned duties at the Point but he is constantly getting into trouble because of his volatile temperament. Then the athletic director, Bond, takes notice of him and, after the two have a boxing match—Bond beats the pants off Power—the truculent Irishman is made assistant athletic director. When Bond notices that Power has an eye for O'Hara, an Irish maid at the Point, he encourages a courtship which results in marriage. With O'Hara to temper his raucous ways, Power settles down. The couple are given a small cottage on the campus grounds and Power has soon saved enough money to bring his elderly father, Crisp, to America from Ireland. The couple have a child but the baby dies soon after birth and O'Hara is informed that she can never have another. Power and O'Hara then transfer their affections to the young cadets, adopting them as though they were their own, their favorite being Francis. He disappoints them and himself when, on the eve of graduation, he violates Academy rules and, enacting the honor system, confesses his guilt and resigns without receiving his commission. He nevertheless joins the Army at the outbreak of WW II and proves himself worthwhile by distinguishing himself in combat. O'Hara dies and Power goes on and on, becoming an institution at the Point, a person remembered as a father figure by scores of cadets. When he receives orders to retire, Power pleads his case with Steele. The President realizes that Power has become a great part of the Academy's traditions and allows him to stay on at the Point until the end of his days. This rousing film ends with Power taking the review of "The Long Gray Line," the uniformed companies of cadets marching before him to honor a lifetime of service to the Army and the Corps. Ford directs with loving care and lets just the right amount of sentiment through to capture the spirit and image of West Point. Shot on location, the story moves briskly under Ford's sure hand and Power gives one of his most memorable performances, while O'Hara renders a vivid part as his wife. The director reluctantly accepted the CinemaScope process here but made the most of it, showing the wide vistas of the Academy and its splendid formations of cadets. The film cost $2 million to produce but turned out to be a box office bonanza, yielding more than $5 million in its initial release.

p, Robert Arthur; d, John Ford; w, Edward Hope (based on the novel *Bringing Up the Brass* by Marty Maher and Nardi Reeder Campion); ph, Charles Lawton, Jr. (CinemaScope, Technicolor); m, Morris Stoloff; ed, William Lyon; art d, Robert Peterson; set d, Frank Tuttle; cos, Jean Louis.

Drama **(PR:A MPAA:NR)**

LONG HAUL, THE** (1957, Brit.) 100m Marksman/COL bw

Victor Mature *(Harry Miller)*, Gene Anderson *(Connie Miller)*, Patrick Allen *(Joe Easy)*, Diana Dors *(Lynn)*, Liam Redmond *(Casey)*, Peter Reynolds *(Frank)*, Michael Wade *(Butch Miller)*, Dervis Ward *(Mutt)*, Murray Kash *(Jeff)*, Jameson Clark *(MacNaughton)*, John Harvey *(Supt. Macrea)*, Roland Brand *(Army Sergeant)*, Stanley Rose *(Foreman)*, Raymond Barry *(Depot Manager)*, John Welsh *(The Doctor)*, Susan Campbell *(Mabel)*, Meier Tzelniker *(Nat Fine)*, Freddie Watts, Harcourt Curacao, Van Boolen, Martin Shaban *(Drivers)*, Norman Rossington *(Young Liverpool Driver)*, Madge Brindley *(Fat Woman)*, Ewen Solon, Wensley Pithey.

Mature is an ex-GI who is married to Anderson, an English woman from Liverpool. She convinces him to stay in England and her uncle gets him a job driving a truck. When he stops the robbery of a fellow driver, not knowing that it's staged and the driver is getting a cut of the loot, he loses his job. He gets involved with Allen, a racketeer, and starts an affair with Allen's girlfriend, Dors. The police go after Mature when an ex-friend is killed in a faked accident. Mature hits the road with the gangster, Dors, and a truckload of stolen furs. When Allen is killed as the trio comes in sight of the freighter taking them to freedom, Mature turns back to try to straighten things out.

p, Maxwell Setton; d&w, Ken Hughes (based on the novel by Mervyn Mills); ph, Basil Emmott; m, Trevor Duncan; ed, Raymond Poulton; md, Richard Taylor; art d, John Hoesli.

Drama **(PR:A MPAA:NR)**

LONG, HOT SUMMER, THE**** (1958) 115m FOX c

Paul Newman *(Ben Quick)*, Joanne Woodward *(Clara Varner)*, Anthony Franciosa *(Jody Varner)*, Orson Welles *(Will Varner)*, Lee Remick *(Eula Varner)*, Angela Lansbury *(Minnie Littlejohn)*, Richard Anderson *(Alan Stewart)*, Sarah Marshall *(Agnes Stewart)*, Mabel Albertson *(Mrs. Stewart)*, J. Pat O'Malley *(Ratliff)*, William Walker *(Lucius)*, George Dunn *(Peabody)*, Jess Kirkpatrick *(Armistead)*, Val Avery *(Wilk)*, I. Stanford Jolley *(Houstin)*, Nicholas King *(John Fisher)*, Lee Erickson *(Tom Shortly)*, Ralph Reed *(J. V. Bookright)*, Terry Rangno *(Pete Armistead)*, Steve Widders *(Buddy Peabody)*, Jim Brandt *(Linus Olds)*, Helen Wallace *(Mrs. Houstin)*, Brian Corcoran *(Harry Peabody)*, Byron Foulger *(Harris)*, Victor Rodman *(Justice of the Peace)*, Eugene Jackson *(Waiter)*.

Martin Ritt, a one-time New York actor, fell in love with the Deep South while directing this picture and continued to explore the hinterlands in several more films afterward. He teamed again with Newman and screenwriters Ravetch and Frank many times with great success on such films as HUD and HOMBRE and later directed other Southern-based films such as CONRACK, SOUNDER, and NORMA RAE. Other than INTRUDER IN THE DUST, William Faulkner's novels have had a hard time on screen. This is an exception as they decided to use parts of Faulkner's work, rather than faithfully adapting an entire novel. Their decision was correct and THE LONG, HOT SUMMER is an excellent film that served to shoot Newman, Woodward, Remick, and Franciosa to stardom. Newman had come over on a loan-out from Warners and the result was that fireworks exploded when he and Woodward met. She'd already won an Oscar for THE THREE FACES OF EVE and they fell in love while making this one, eventually being married at the end of January 1958. Newman plays a Mississippi man given to hot-tempered behavior. His late father had settled disputes by burning down his opponent's barns and

Newman appears to be following in his father's arsonist footsteps. He arrives in a town dominated by porky Welles, the large land owner who cows everyone with his behavior. Franciosa is his child-like son, a man with absolutely no backbone. Welles's daughter is Woodward, already deemed an old maid by the town but still feisty enough to sass her daddy. Newman becomes a sharecropper on the Welles property and Welles is impressed by the young man's independence. Remick is Franciosa's wife and dedicated to him, albeit a little disappointed in his weakling attitude. Woodward is seeing Anderson, who is ruled by his mother, Albertson, and is just as under her thumb as Franciosa is under Welles's. Welles thinks that Newman might just make a fine son-in-law who could take over the vast holdings and do something with it. He attempts to get his daughter and Newman together but she rebels. It's not that she doesn't find Newman attractive, she just resents being told what to do. She also thinks that Newman is beneath her station and finds him a bit vulgar. Welles tells Franciosa that he intends to put Newman and Woodward together as he prefers Newman to his own son. Franciosa responds by trapping Welles in a burning barn, thinking that Newman will be accused of it because of his prior record, albeit heresay. But before the flames can claim Welles, Franciosa rescues the man. Woodward eventually realizes that she loves Newman and decides to marry him. At the same time, Lansbury, Welles's long-time mistress, prevails on him to marry her and the film ends. Welles, who looked awful, was only 42 at the time, just nine years older than Newman, 14 years older than Woodward, 12 years older than Franciosa. Lansbury, who has always been cast older than she was, was the same age as Newman at the time. The script was superior to most of these cornpone films and much of the dialog was worthy of Tennessee Williams at his best. Lots of tension, some humor and excellent characterizations are what set this one apart. The difference between this and Otto Preminger's abysmal HURRY SUNDOWN is as wide as the Mississippi is long. Several years later a TV show was attempted, based on THE LONG, HOT SUMMER. All it was was long.

p, Jerry Wald; d, Martin Ritt; w, Irving Ravetch, Harriet Frank Jr. (based on "Barn Burning," "The Spotted Horse," the novel *The Hamlet* by William Faulkner); ph, Joseph La Shelle (CinemaScope, DeLuxe Color); m, Alex North; ed, Louis R. Loeffler; md, Lionel Newman; art d, Lyle R. Wheeler, Maurice Ransford; set d, Walter M. Scott; cos, Adele Palmer; spec eff, L.B. Abbott; m/l, "The Long Hot Summer," Sammy Cahn, North (sung by Jimmie Rodgers); makeup, Ben Nye.

Drama **Cas.** **(PR:A-C MPAA:NR)**

LONG IS THE ROAD***

(1948, Ger.) 77m International Film Organization/Lopert bw

Israel Becker (*David Jelin*), Bettina Moissi (*Dora Berkowitz*), Berta Litwina (*Hanna Jelin*), Jakob Fischer (*Jakob Jelin*), Otto Wernicke (*Senior Doctor*), Paul Dahlke (*2nd Doctor*), Alexander Hardini (*Farmer*), David Hart (*Mr. Liebermann*), Mischa Nathan (*Partisan*), H. L. Fischer (*Chodetzki*).

Becker is separated from his Jewish parents when the Germans invade Poland. The young man joins the Polish partisans while his parents are taken to the concentration camps. His father is killed after being determined "unfit", and his mother is moved from one labor camp to another. After the war, the son and mother reunite and must find a new homeland. This was the first film made in what would become West Germany after WW II. Author Becker plays the lead well, and the professional cast does nicely. Several Yiddish folk tunes are included. (In Yiddish, German, Polish; English subtitles.)

p, Abraham Weinstein; d, Herbert B. Fredersdorf, Marek Goldstein; w, Karl Georg Kulb and Israel Becker (based on a story by Becker); ph, Franz Koch; m, Lothar Bruhne; art d, C. L. Krimse.

Drama **(PR:A MPAA:NR)**

LONG JOHN SILVER1/2**

(1954, Aus.) 108m Distributors Corporation of America c (AKA: LONG JOHN SILVER RETURNS TO TREASURE ISLAND)

Robert Newton (*Long John Silver*), Kit Taylor (*Jim Hawkins*), Connie Gilchrist (*Purity Pinker*), Eric Reiman (*Trip Fenner*), Syd Chambers (*Ned Shill*), Grant Taylor (*Patch*), John Brunskill (*Old Stingley*), Harry Hambleton (*Big Eric*), Henry Gilbert (*Billie Bowlegs*), Elwyn Daniel (*Dodd Perch*), Al Thomas (*Harry Grip*), Harvey Adams (*Governor Strong*), Muriel Steinbeck (*Lady Strong*), Lloyd Berrell (*Mendoza*), Tony Arpino (*Kling*), Billy Kay (*Ironhand*), Frank Ransom (*Sentry*), Don McNiven (*Sgt. Cover*), Charles McCallum (*Elderly Naval Officer*), Rodney (Rod) Taylor (*Israel Hand*), Hans Stern (*Father Monaster*), Thora Smith (*Elizabeth Strong*), George Simpson Little (*Capt. McDougal*), John Pooley (*Young Naval Officer*).

Newton plays the character he portrayed in Walt Disney's TREASURE ISLAND in this Australian swashbuckler. The pace is quick and the action plentiful as the pirate saves the governor's daughter, loots the king's treasure, and battles his arch-rival on Treasure Island. Newton is perfect for the role and adds a light sense of humor that makes the ruthless pirate appealing. One of two Australian films featuring stage actor Rod Taylor before he went to Hollywood and made it big.

p, Joseph Kaufman; d, Byron Haskin; w, Martin Rackin; ph, Carl Guthrie (CinemaScope, Eastmancolor); m, David Buttolph; ed, Mike Del Campo.

Adventure **Cas.** **(PR:A MPAA:NR)**

LONG JOHN SILVER RETURNS TO TREASURE ISLAND

(SEE: LONG JOHN SILVER, 1954)

LONG KNIFE, THE** (1958, Brit.) 57m Merton Park/Anglo-Amalgamated bw

Joan Rice (*Jill Holden*), Sheldon Lawrence (*Ross Waters*), Dorothy Brewster (*Angela/The Boy*), Ellen Pollock (*Mrs. Cheam*), Victor Brooks (*Superintendent Leigh*), Alan Keith (*Dr. Ian Probus*), Arthur Gomez (*Sgt. Bowles*).

Well-paced crime drama centers around the strange happenings at a nursing home where Rice works as a nurse. Her innocent snoopings uncover a gang that takes advantage of helpless patients; a discovery that makes her the prime suspect when one of the elderly patients is murdered. A mounting level of suspense is maintained throughout the movie.

p, Jack Greenwood; d, Montgomery Tully; w, Ian Stuart Black (based on the novel *The Long Night* by Seldon Truss).

Crime **(PR:C MPAA:NR)**

LONG, LONG TRAIL, THE*1/2** (1929) 58m UNIV bw

Hoot Gibson (*The Ramblin' Kid*), Sally Eilers (*June*), Walter Brennan ("*Skinny*" *Rawlins*), James Mason (*Mike Wilson*), Kathryn McGuire (*Ophelia*), Archie Ricks (*Jyp*), Howard Truesdale (*Uncle Josh*).

Gibson is the Ramblin' Kid who is entered in the annual rodeo. He's doped by bad guy Mason, but Gibson, being the hero, still can ride and stop Mason from stealing the sweepstakes money. This western was the first talking film for Gibson. An early film for veteran character actor Brennan, and no, that isn't the English actor Mason. The exciting concluding scenes of this film were done in an early large-screen process, Magnascope, a precursor of the later anamorphic-lens processes such as CinemaScope.

p, Hoot Gibson; d, Arthur Rosson; w, Howard Green (based on the novel *The Ramblin' Kid* by Earl Wayland Bowman); ph, Harry Neumann; ed, Gilmore Walker.

Western **(PR:A MPAA:NR)**

LONG, LONG TRAIL, THE, 1942 (SEE: TEXAS TO BATAAN, 1942)

LONG, LONG TRAILER, THE** (1954) 96m MGM c

Lucille Ball (*Tracy Collini*), Desi Arnaz (*Nicholas Collini*), Marjorie Main (*Mrs. Hittaway*), Keenan Wynn (*Policeman*), Gladys Hurlbut (*Mrs. Bolton*), Moroni Olsen (*Mr. Tewitt*), Bert Freed (*Foreman*), Madge Blake (*Aunt Anastacia*), Walter Baldwin (*Uncle Edgar*), Oliver Blake (*Mr. Judlow*), Perry Sheehan (*Bridesmaid*), Charles Herbert (*Little Boy*), Herb Vigran (*Trailer Salesman*), Karl Lukas (*Inspector*), Emmett Vogan (*Mr. Bolton*), Edgar Dearing (*Manager*), Geraldine Carr, Sarah Spencer (*Girl Friends*), Ruth Warren (*Mrs. Dudley*), Dallas Boyd (*Minister*), Howard McNear (*Mr. Hittaway*), Jack Kruschen (*Mechanic*), Edna Skinner (*Mrs. Barrett*), Alan Lee (*Mr. Elliott*), Robert Anderson (*Carl Barrett*), Phil Rich (*Mr. Dudley*), John Call (*Shorty*), Wilson Wood (*Garage Owner*), Dorothy Neumann (*Aunt Ellen*), Howard Wright (*Uncle Bill*), Connie Van (*Grace*), Dennis Ross (*Jody*), Christopher Olsen (*Tom*), Ruth Lee (*Mrs. Tewitt*), Dick Alexander (*Father*), Frank Gerstle (*Attendant*), Peter Leeds (*Garage Manager*), Judy Sackett (*Bettie*), Juney Ellis (*Waitress*), Janet Sackett (*Kay*), Norman Leavitt (*Driver*).

A light comedy with a number of slapstick gags, the film works thanks to the stars' chemistry and Ball's timing. Ball and Arnaz buy a trailer that cost them five times what they were planning to spend, and the travels in their house-on-wheels are the nucleus of the laughs. Credit must be given to director Minnelli and script writers Goodrich and Hackett for keeping the humor flowing smoothly and not letting things become heavy-handed. Ball and Arnaz made this film when their T.V. show *I Love Lucy* was a national hit.

p, Pandro S. Berman; d, Vincente Minnelli; w, Albert Hackett, Frances Goodrich (based on a novel by Clinton Twiss); ph, Robert Surtees (Ansco Color); m, Adolph Deutsch; ed, Ferris Webster; art d, Cedric Gibbons, Edward Carfagno; set d, Edwin B. Willis, Keogh Gleason; spec eff, A. Arnold Gillespie, Warren Newcombe; m/l, "Breezin' Along With the Breeze," Haven Gillespie, Seymour Simmons, Richard A. Whiting.

Comedy **(PR:A MPAA:NR)**

LONG LOST FATHER1/2** (1934) 64m RKO bw

John Barrymore (*Carl Bellaire*), Helen Chandler (*Lindsey Lane*), Donald Cook (*Dr. Bill Strong*), Alan Mowbray (*Sir Anthony Gelding*), Claude King (*Inspector*), Reginald Sharland (*Lord Vivyan*), Ferdinand Gottschalk (*Lawyer*), Phyllis Barry (*Phylis Mersey-Royds*), Tempe Pigott (*Flower*), Herbert Bunston (*Bishop*), E. E. Clive, Natalie Moorhead, Doris Lloyd, Charles Irwin, John Rogers.

Barrymore is the manager of a London night club who had abandoned his family years ago. His daughter, Chandler, shows up at the club as a performer, but wants nothing to do with her father. She becomes involved with a criminal type and her father gets her off a robbery charge and introduces her to respectable Cook.

d, Ernest B. Schoedsack; w, Dwight Taylor (based on a novel by G. B. Stern); ph, Nick Musuraca; ed, Paul Weatherwax.

Drama **(PR:A MPAA:NR)**

LONG MEMORY, THE** (1953, Brit.) 96m Europa British/GFD bw

John Mills (*Davidson*), John McCallum (*Detective Inspector Lowther*), Elizabeth Sellars (*Fay Lowther*), Eva Bergh (*Elsa*), Geoffrey Keen (*Craig*), Michael Martin-Harvey (*Jackson*), John Chandos (*Boyd*), John Slater (*Pewsey*), Thora Hird (*Mrs. Pewsey*), Vida Hope (*Alice Gedge*), Harold Lang (*Boyd's Chauffeur*), Mary MacKenzie (*Gladys*), John Glyn-Jones (*Gedge*), John Horsley (*Bletchley*), Fred Johnson (*Driver*), Laurence Naismith (*Asprey*), Peter Jones (*Fisher*), Christopher Beeny (*Mickie*), Henry Edwards (*Judge*), Julian Somers (*Delaney*), Dennis Shaw (*Shaw*), Russell Waters (*Scotson*).

Mills is sentenced to life imprisonment after being framed for murder, and 12 years later he is released on parole, obsessed with finding the people who sent him to prison and getting revenge. He learns that the man he was accused of murdering heads a dockside business and that one of the perjurers is married to a Scotland Yard detective. Mills meets Bergh, a refugee cafe girl, and falls in love with her. But even she doesn't sidetrack his thirst for revenge.

p, Hugh Stewart; d, Robert Hamer; w, Hamer, Frank Harvey (based on a novel by Howard Clewes); ph, Harry Waxman; m, William Alwyn; ed, Gordon Hales.

Thriller (PR:A MPAA:NR)

LONG NIGHT, THE*** (1947) 101m RKO bw

Henry Fonda (Joe Adams), Barbara Bel Geddes (Jo Ann),Vincent Price (Maximilian), Ann Dvorak (Charlene), Howard Freeman (Sheriff), Moroni Olsen (Chief of Police), Elisha Cook, Jr. (Frank), Queenie Smith (Janitor's Wife), David Clarke (Bill), Charles McGraw (Policeman), Patty King (Peggy), Robert Davis (Freddie), Will Wright (Janitor), Ray Teal (Hudson), Pat Flaherty (Sergeant), Dick Reeves (Cop), Jack Overman (Man), Mary Gordon (Old Lady), Murray Alper (Bartender), Byron Foulger (Man with Bike).

In this sometimes less than effective remake of Marcel Carne's DAYBREAK (1939), Fonda is a WW II veteran trying to readjust to civilian life. Fonda opens the film by shooting to death a glib second-rate magician and con man, Price, and then taking refuge in his rooms, barricading himself from police and thinking back on how he got into this mess. He had taken a job as a sandblaster in a grimy mill town on the Ohio-Pennsylvania border, and we see in flashback how he meets and falls in love with daydreamer Bel Geddes who wants desperately to escape her drab life. Price and his sexy assistant Dvorak come to town with their magic show and Price immediately tries to seduce Bel Geddes while Fonda is attracted to the earthy Dvorak who tells him that Price is a heel and a wolf who cannot be trusted with Bel Geddes. When he confronts Price, Fonda is told by Price that he, Price, is really Bel Geddes' father—naturally, a lie—and that Fonda is a no-account and must stay away from her. Price later visits Fonda to apparently kill him for reasons less than clear. While threatening Fonda, Price boasts about sexually conquering Bel Geddes, which causes Fonda to explode. Both men struggle for a gun and Price is killed, which brings us back to the barricaded room and the grim present. As the police charge, Fonda fires back, battling all night long until he is killed. The story is intriguing but Litvak's direction is a bit heavy-handed and Price is so hammy that no amount of Fonda's considerable talent is able to overcome the mad magician's histrionics. The production values are above average with excellent lensing by Polito. Fonda chose this part when returning from the service following WW II, wanting to change his image from rich playboy and romatic lead in light comedies, but the story was too leaden and, despite his fine performance, the film failed at the box office.

p, Robert, Raymond Hakim, Anatole Litvak; d, Litvak; w, John Wexley (based on the screenplay to LE JOUR SE LEVE by Jacques Viot); ph, Sol Polito; m, Dmitri Tiomkin; ed, Robert Swank; md, Tiomkin; prod d, Eugene Lourie; set d, Darrell Silvera; spec eff, Russell A. Culley.

Drama (PR:A MPAA:NR)

LONG NIGHT, THE**½ (1976) 85m Woodie King Associates/Howard Mahler c

W. Geoffrey King (Fred "Steely" Brown), Dick Anthony Williams (Paul Brown), Peggy Kirkpatrick (Mae Brown).

A naturally acted film about a black teenage boy, King, who wanders the streets one evening after his Vietnam veteran father runs out on his easygoing mother. The film uses flashbacks to provide background on the boy's family life while, throughout the night he tries to scrape together enough money to repay a $27 debt to his mother. Directed by one of New York's top black theater producers, THE LONG NIGHT's fatal flaw is its inability to achieve an arresting degree of visual or cinematic understanding. Fine performances all the way around, especially from the young King, make the film a commendable effort.

p, Woodie King, Jr., St. Claire Bourne; d, King; w, King, Julian Mayfield (based on the novel by Mayfield); ph, James Malloy; m, William Daniels, Michael Felder; ed, Joe Staton, Ed McAllister.

Drama (PR:A MPAA:PG)

LONG RIDE FROM HELL, A*½ (1970, Ital.) 104m BRC/Cinerama c (VIVO PER LA TUA MORTE)

Steve Reeves (Mike Sturges), Wayde Preston (Mayner), Dick Palmer [Mimmo Palmara] (Freeman), Silvana Venturelli (Ruth), Lee Burton (Guido Lollabrigida) (Sheriff), Ted Carter (Shorty), Rosalba Neri (Prostitute), Franco Fantasia (Roy), Mario Maranzana (Bobcat), Enzo Fiermonte, Silvana Bacci, Spartaco Conversi, Ivan Scratuglia, Franco Balducci, Emma Baron, Bruno Corazzari, Sergio De Vecchi.

This was the last film the former Hercules Reeves would star in before retiring to raise horses on his ranch. He co-wrote this western in which he and his brother, Fantasia, are wrongly imprisoned for rustling. His brother is killed and Reeves escapes from prison and seeks out the real criminals.

d, Alex Burks [Camillo Bazzoni]; w, Roberto Natale, Steve Reeves (based on the novel Judas Gun by Gordon Shirreffs); ph, Enzo Barboni; m, Carlo Savina; ed, Roberta Perpignani; set d, Gastone Carsetti; cos, Franco Antonelli; m/l, "Go West Young Man," Savina; makeup, Marcello Ceccarelli; stunts, Remo De Angelis.

Western (PR:O MPAA:R)

LONG RIDE HOME, THE (SEE: TIME FOR KILLING, A, 1967)

LONG RIDERS, THE***** (1980) 99m UA c

David Carradine (Cole Younger), Keith Carradine (Jim Younger), Robert Carradine (Bob Younger), James Keach (Jesse James), Stacy Keach (Frank James), Dennis Quaid (Ed Miller), Randy Quaid (Clell Miller), Kevin Brophy (John Younger), Harry Carey, Jr. (George Arthur), Christopher Guest (Charlie Ford), Nicholas Guest (Bob Ford), Shelby Leverington (Annie Ralston), Felice Orlandi (Mr. Reddick), Pamela Reed (Belle Starr), James Remar (Sam Starr), Fran Ryan (Mrs. Samuel), Savannah Smith (Zee), Amy Stryker (Beth), James Whitmore, Jr. (Mr. Rixley), John Bottoms

(Mortician), West Buchanan (McCorkindale), Edward Bunker, Martina Deignan, Allan Graf, Chris Mulkey, Thomas R. Myers, Marlise Pieratt, Glenn Robards, Tim Rossovich, Lin Shaye, Gary Watkins, Peter Jason, Steve Chambers, Duke Stroud, William Traylor, J. Don Ferguson, Hugh McGraw, Prentiss E. Rowe, Stuart Mossman, Michael Lackey, Mitch Greenhill, Bill Bryson, Jimmy Medearis, Edgar McLeod, Luis Contreras, Kalen Keach, R. B. Thrift.

A superb, nitty-gritty retelling of the middle border outlaw story of the James-Younger gang, the most notorious American bandits of the 19th century. In a unique bit of casting, the principal players are made up of real life brothers, playing brothers of the gun. We see from the beginning the outlaw band in full action, robbing a bank. Later Dennis Quaid is kicked out of the gang for needlessly killing a man in the holdup. James Keach, playing Jesse James, tosses him his share of the loot and tells him to run for it or be gunned down, a sentiment echoed by Dennis' own brother, Randy. The gang splits up, the James boys going back to their wives and farms. David Carradine, playing the role of Cole Younger—who was really co-leader of the gang with Jesse—goes off to Texas to see his whore girl friend, Reed, playing Belle Starr. After trysting with her, he must battle her Indian paramour, Remar, in a saloon knife fight, where he kills Remar. Then it's back to Missouri and a meeting with the boys, who decide to rob the money bloated bank in Northfield, Minnesota.The ride north is full of hazard since the gang is out of its element and the raid ends in disaster as the gang is shot to pieces. The James-Younger brothers survive to hide out in the Minnesota woods, all the Carradine brothers severely wounded and Randy Quaid dying, while the Keach brothers are unscathed. James Keach decides that he and his brother Stacy must escape while they can and tells David Carradine that he and his brothers will be left behind. Carradine pulls his pistol and aims it at the bandit chieftain, then uncocks it and fires the stoic James Keach a grim grin, telling him that "the Youngers don't need the Jameses." The Carradine brothers are left behind to be made prisoners and the Keach brothers escape the closing net of the oncoming posses. Later, the Guest brothers make a deal with the Pinkerton detectives trailing the outlaws and shoot James Keach to death. Stacy Keach, last of the notorious band at large, turns himself in but tells authorities that he will surrender his gun under one condition, that he be allowed to bury his brother. This is granted and we see in the last scene Stacy Keach accompanying his brother's coffin on a train back to the old homestead. THE LONG RIDERS is one of the last great westerns made in America, directed tautly by Hill and working with an excellent script rich with great research. The lensing by Waite is magnificent, with not a wasted frame in the entire film, and the period is correctly and movingly captured. Cooder's outstanding score incorporates folk music of the era as succinctly and effectively as did Charles Strouse in his down-home compositions for BONNIE AND CLYDE. The whole feeling of this film is one of antiquity—as if the viewer is actually there in the 1870s when America was raw, unconventional, and full of the unpredictable—a marvelous atmosphere created by Hill and projected by a superb cast. James Keach may not be the romantic embodiment of Jesse James as he was played by Tyrone Power in JESSE JAMES (1939), but he more realistically enacts the taciturn, cold-blooded thief Jesse really was and Stacy Keach is perfect as the puzzled, Puritanical but loyal brother, Frank. David Carradine is excellent as the confident, bold Cole Younger and he and Randy Quaid provide the only backwoods humor seen and heard in this tough film. Keith and Robert Carrradine are very good as the other Younger brothers and the Guest brothers epitomize the treacherous Ford siblings. Though THE LONG RIDERS does not spare the violence, this is must for any adult western fan.

p, Tim Zinneman; d, Walter Hill; w, Bill Bryden, Steven Phillip Smith, Stacy Keach; ph, Ric Waite (Technicolor); m, Ry Cooder; ed, David Holden; prod d, Jack T. Collis; art d, Peter Romero; set d, Richard Goddard; cos, Bobbie Mannix; ch, Katina Sawidis.

Western Cas. (PR:O MPAA:R)

LONG ROPE, THE** (1961) 61m AP/Fox bw

Hugh Marlowe (Jonas Stone), Alan Hale (Sheriff John Millard), Robert J. Wilke (Ben Matthews), Lisa Montell (Alicia Alvarez), Chris Robinson (Reb Gilroy), Jeffrey Morris (Will Matthews), David Renard (Louis Ortega), Madeleine Holmes (Señora Dona Vega), John Alonzo (Manuel Alvarez), Jack Powers (Luke Simms), Kathryn Harte (Mrs. Creech), Jack Carlin, Scott Randall (Henchmen), Linda Cordova (Mexican Waitress), Stephen Welles (Jim Matthews), Alex Cordellis.

Marlowe is a federal judge who comes to the town of Tularosa to try Alonzo for the murder of Wilke's brother. Wilke is the local cattle baron and has very tight control over the town. Marlowe discovers that Alonzo's mother-in-law, Holmes, is the guilty party. She wanted Alonzo out of the way so her daughter, Montell, can marry Wilke, and get back the land the cattle baron had taken from her family. After the trial, Wilke challenges the judge to a gun battle and the sheriff intervenes and is killed by Wilke. Marlowe, with the help of Robinson, arrests the cattle baron. This western was shot in a one-week period.

p, Margia Dean; d, William Witney; w, Robert Hamner; ph, Kay Norton (CinemaScope); m, Paul Sawtell, Bert Shefter, Frankie Ortega; ed, Peter Johnson; art d, John Mansbridge; cos, Paula Giokaris; makeup, Ernie Park.

Western (PR:A MPAA:NR)

LONG SHADOW, THE** (1961, Brit.) 64m Argo/RFD bw

John Crawford (Kelly), Susan Hampshire (Gunilla), Willoughby Goddard (Schober), Humphrey Lestocq (Bannister), Rory O'Brine (Ruchi Korbanyi), Anne Castaldini (Magda), Margaret Robertson (Mother), William Nagy (Garity), Lilly Kann (Old Lady).

A British espionage picture with a little something for all nationalities. An American newsman in Austria saves a Hungarian child and a Swedish nurse from untimely demise. It turns out that the bad guys are actually Russian-backed Nazis. Unfortunately, this multinational plot fails to generate any real excitement outside of the norm.

p, Jack O. Lamont, John Pellatt; d, Peter Maxwell; w, Paddy Manning O'Brine.

Spy Drama **(PR:A MPAA:NR)**

LONG SHIPS, THE zero (1964, Brit./Yugo.) 124m Warwick-Avala/COL (DUGI BRODOVI)

Richard Widmark *(Rolfe)*, Sidney Poitier *(El Mansuh)*, Rosanna Schiaffino *(Aminah)*, Russ Tamblyn *(Orm)*, Oscar Homolka *(Krok)*, Lionel Jeffries *(Aziz)*, Edward Judd *(Sven)*, Beba Loncar *(Gerda)*, Clifford Evans *(King Harald)*, Colin Blakely *(Rhykka)*, Gordon Jackson *(Vahlin)*, David Lodge *(Olla)*, Paul Stassino *(Raschid)*, Jeanne Moody *(Ylva)*, Henry Oscar *(Auctioneer)*.

A disastrous Viking epic starring Poitier and Widmark as a Moorish chieftain and a Viking adventurer who butt heads over a golden bell. The press books stated "Sidney Poitier in his first non-Negro role!" That's a neat trick. A $6 million bomb that makes producer Allen's 1970s disaster films look like picnics in the park. Poitier said it most elegantly: "To say it was disastrous is a compliment."

p, Irving Allen; d, Jack Cardiff; w, Berkely Mather, Beverley Cross (based on the novel by Frans T. Bengtsson); ph, Christopher Challis (Technirama 70, Technicolor); m, Dušan Radic; ed, Geoffrey Foot; md, Borislav Pascan; art d, Zoran Zorčić, William Constable, Vlastimir Gavrik, John Hoesli; cos, Anthony Mendleson, David Ffolkes; spec eff, Syd Pearson, Bill Warrington.

Adventure **(PR:C MPAA:NR)**

LONG SHOT, THE** (1939) 69m FA/GN bw

Gordon Jones *(Jeff Clayton)*, Marsha Hunt *(Martha Sharon)*, C. Henry Gordon *(Lew Ralston)*, George Meeker *(Dell Baker)*, Harry Davenport *(Henry Sharon)*, George E. Stone *(Danny Welch)*, Tom Kennedy *(Mike Claurens)*, Emerson Treacy *(Henry Knox)*, Gay Seabrook *(Helen Knox)*, Jason Robards *(Doctor)*, Claire Rochelle *(Nurse)*, James Robinson *(Tucky)*, Dorothy Fay, Frank Darien, Earle Hodgins, Lee Phelps, Ben Burt, Denmore Chief, Joe Hernandez, James Keefe.

Gordon is out to ruin rival stable owner Davenport, thinking that then Davenport's niece, Hunt, will marry him. Davenport sees it coming, fakes his death, and wills his only horse to Hunt and his partner, Jones. The horse is a constant loser until the pair discover that the horse can't run in the rail position. With this solved the horse wins the Santa Anita handicap, Davenport comes back, Gordon and his henchman, Meeker, are foiled, and Hunt and Jones fall in love.

p, Franklyn Warner; d, Charles Lamont; w, Ewart Adamson (based on a story by Harry Beresford, George Callaghan); ph, Arthur Martinelli; ed, Bernard Loftus.

Drama **(PR:A MPAA:NR)**

LONG SHOT*** (1981, Brit.) 85m Mithras bw/c

Charles Gormley *(Charlie)*, Neville Smith *(Neville)*, Ann Zelda *(Anne)*, David Stone *(A Distributor)*, Suzanne Danielle *(Sue)*, Ron Taylor *(American Director)*, Wim Wenders *(Another Director)*, Stephen Frears *(Biscuit Man)*, Jim Haines *(Professor of Sexual Politics)*, Maurice Bulbulian *(French-Canadian Director)*, William Forsyth *(Bille)*, Richard DeMarco *(Gallery Owner)*, Alan Bennett *(Neville's Doctor)*, Sarah Boston *(TV Producer)*, Mel Claman *(Cartoonist)*, Susannah York *(An Actress)*, Dennis Selinger *(An Agent)*, Sandy Lieberson *(A Film Executive)*, John Boorman *(The Director)*, Mary Maddox, Jill Beck, Jacqui Byford.

An interesting independent film that deals with business and other hurdles one must go through to make a film. Most of the people acting in the film are non-actors: Gormley, who plays a producer, is a film producer, and directors Wenders and Boorman play men of their profession. Most of the film was shot during the 1977 Edinburgh Festival using part improvisation and part scripted scenes. Gormley plays a Scottish producer trying to get his so-called commercial film "Gulf and Western" off the ground. A somewhat bleak film that should be seen by anyone who ever thought they'd like to make a movie.

p&d, Maurice Hatton; w, Hatton, Eoin McCann, the cast; ph, Michael Davis, Michael Dodds, Ivan Strasburg, Hatton, Teo Davis; m, Terry Dougherty, Antonio Vivaldi; ed, Howard Sharp.

Drama **(PR:C MPAA:PG)**

LONG VOYAGE HOME, THE***** (1940) 105m Argosy/UA bw

John Wayne *(Ole Olsen)*, Thomas Mitchell *(Aloysius Driscoll)*, Ian Hunter *(Smitty)*, Barry Fitzgerald *(Cocky)*, Wilfrid Lawson *(Captain)*, Mildred Natwick *(Freda)*, John Qualen *(Axel Swanson)*, Ward Bond *(Yank)*, Joseph Sawyer *(Davis)*, Arthur Shields *(Donkeyman)*, J. M. Kerrigan *(Limehouse Crimp)*, Rafaela Ottiano *(Tropical Woman)*, David Hughes *(Scotty)*, Billy Bevan *(Joe, Limehouse Barman)*, Cyril McLaglen *(First Mate)*, Robert E. Perry *(Paddy)*, Jack Pennick *(Johnny Bergman)*, Constantin Frenke *(Narvey)*, Constantin Romanoff *(Big Frank)*, Dan Borzage *(Tim)*, Harry Tenbrook *(Max)*, Douglas Walton *(Second Lieutenant)*, Carmen Morales, Carmen d'Antonio *(Girls in Canoe)*, Harry Woods *(First Mate of "Amindra")*, Arthur Miles *(Captain of "Amindra")*, Edgar "Blue" Washington *(Cook)*, Lionel Pape *(Mr. Clifton)*, Jane Crowley *(Kate)*, Maureen Roden-Ryan *(Mag)*, Tina Menard, Judith Linden, Elena Martinez, Lita Cortez, Soledad Gonzales *(Bumboat Girls)*, James Flavin, Lee Shumway *(Dock Policemen)*, Wyndham Standing *(British Naval Officer)*, Lowell Drew *(Bald Man)*, Sammy Stein *(Seaman)*.

Based on 4 of O'Neill's finest one-act plays, THE LONG VOYAGE HOME is a grim, powerful saga of merchant seamen, the hardscrabble lives they lead and the hopes they nurture for a better future. Ford presents a magnificent portrayal of humanity at sea and its struggle to not only survive but remain civilized during the early stages of WW II. The crew of the tramp freighter *S.S. Glencairn* is enjoying a last night of liberty on a Caribbean island, attending a party with native women that ends in a brawl before the men stagger back to the freighter. Only Hunter has remained on board, refusing to join the raucous festivities. At Baltimore, the ship takes on a load of dynamite to be delivered to England, a cargo that makes the crew jumpy; each sailor knows that German U-boats lurk in the waters all around England, then at war with Germany, and that a single torpedo will blow the *Glencairn* to bits. Among the crew members is Wayne, playing a good-hearted young Swede whose only ambition is to make enough money to return home to settle down with his family on a small farm. To that end he is protected by his fellow seamen—chiefly Mitchell, Bond, Fitzgerald amd Qualen—who are all seasoned men of the sea having the same ambition, but who know they will only briefly return to the land. During the Atlantic crossing a raging storm engulfs the *Glencairn* and Bond is mortally injured in an accident. He dies painfully below deck as his friends stand by to comfort him. Ever watchful for submarines and feeding their own paranoid fears, crew members see a light flicker on and off from a porthole below decks and conclude that someone on board is sending signals, perhaps to a U-boat. Investigating, the crewmen find Hunter in their quarters acting furtive. Fitzgerald accuses him of being a spy, telling the others how he has observed Hunter writing secretly and storing his missives in a locked tin box. Mitchell and the others break into the box while Hunter protests and they find a letter which Hunter has written, reading it aloud and discovering—to their acute embarrassment, as Hunter agonizes—that it is a letter written to Hunter's wife, who has left him because of his excessive drinking. Mitchell breaks off the reading and the men sheepishly leave Hunter to his misery. Later, Hunter goes on deck to stand watch. Wayne asks from his post: "All's well, Smitty?" Replies Hunter: "All's well, Ole." The ship is later attacked by a German warplane which strafes the ship and kills Hunter. The ship arrives safely in England and crew members vow to put Wayne on a ship to Sweden; nothing will waylay the youth "this time." Qualen, a fellow Swede—who has paternalistically looked after Wayne through this voyage and others—sews Wayne's back pay into the lining of his coat and pins his ticket home to the lining. The crew then goes on its usual pub crawl with Wayne tagging along, allowed to take one "ginger beer." The seamen sink heavily into drink and do not notice prostitute Natwick taking Wayne aside and insisting he have a drink with her. Out of politeness he sips another ginger beer which she has dosed with a knockout drug. She waits, distracted but pretending to listen to Wayne's simple stories about home, until the drug takes effect. Kerrigan—a stooge for the cutthroat owners of a hated ship, the *Amindra*—engineers the drugged Wayne on board the vessel which must shanghai sailors to fill its necessary crew requirements. When Mitchell and the others learn that Wayne has been shanghaied, they storm the *Amindra* where a savage fight ensues. Wayne is rescued from the sinister ship but Mitchell is struck over the head and kept on board in Wayne's place without the knowledge of the others. Wayne is sent safely back home the next day but a newspaper, unseen by the crew, reports that the *Amindra* has been sunk by U-boats and all hands on board lost, including Mitchell. THE LONG VOYAGE HOME is one of Ford's great masterpieces, a startlingly well photographed movie which was based upon four of O'Neill's plays (in fact, Mitchell and Bond are essentially playing the same part in two different roles). The contrasting lighting, the wonderful atmospherics at sea and on the land, the configuration of shots were basically accomplished by cinematographer Toland. As Wayne later told one of his biographers, Maurice Zolotow: "Usually it would be Mr. Ford who helped the cinematographer get his compositions for maximum effect—bring out what was good in any set-up—help him light it—but it in this case it was Gregg Toland who helped Mr. Ford. LONG VOYAGE is about as beautifully photographed a movie as there ever has been." Wayne had to play a young Swedish sailor and Ford insisted he employ an accent which Wayne resisted, believing he would appear comic. But he had foreign actress, Osa Massen, help him with the accent and when he first employed the accent Ford congratulated him for getting it right. (Wayne neglected to tell him that his coach was Danish.) Wayne's performance is reserved and very effective as he appears to be what he is supposed to be, a simple man, but not a simpleton. Mitchell does a wonderful job as the old salt, and Hunter is moving as the tortured seaman who has ruined his life on land. There is a pervasive air about THE LONG VOYAGE HOME where the sun is always behind the clouds and omnipotent death lurks mostly on land. Although the seamen yearn for their long-lost homes, they know except for Wayne, that they will never leave the sea, will sail on the water until they are buried beneath the waves. THE LONG VOYAGE HOME was playwright O'Neill's favorite film; Ford gave him a print of the movie and he ran it over and over again until he wore it out.

p, Walter Wanger; d, John Ford; w, Dudley Nichols (based upon 4 one-act plays by Eugene O'Neill, "The Moon of the Caribbees," "In the Zone," "Bound East for Cardiff," "The Long Voyage Home" performed under the unifying title "S.S. Glencairn"); ph, Gregg Toland; m, Richard Hageman; ed, Sherman Todd; md, Edward Paul; art d, James Basevi; set d, Julia Heron; spec eff, Ray Binger, R. T. Layton.

Drama **Cas.** **(PR:A MPAA:NR)**

LONG WAIT, THE** 1/2 (1954) 94m Parklane/UA bw

Anthony Quinn *(Johnny McBride)*, Charles Coburn *(Gardiner)*, Gene Evans *(Servo)*, Peggie Castle *(Venus)*, Mary Ellen Kay *(Wendy)*, Shawn Smith *(Carol)*, Dolores Donlon *(Troy)*, Barry Kelley *(Tucker)*, James Millican *(Lindsey)*, Bruno Ve Sota *(Packman)*, Jay Adler *(Bellboy)*, John Damler *(Logan)*, Frank Marlowe *(Pop Henderson)*.

Quinn returns to his hometown after losing his memory and his fingerprints in a fiery car crash. There he finds he's the suspect for a bank robbery and the murder of the district attorney. The police can't arrest him because of his amnesia and lack of fingerprints. Quinn tries to track down a secretary of the bank who disappeared when he had left and gets involved with four women. He also encounters Evans, the local gangster, who puts a contract out on Quinn. Quinn learns that the bank owner, Coburn, was behind the bank holdup and is working with Evans. With the help of Kay, Quinn sees that Coburn is arrested and his own name cleared. The film was adapted from the novel by Mickey Spillane, and Quinn makes one of the better Spillane heroes.

p, Lesser Samuels; d, Victor Saville; w, Alan Green, Samuels (based on a novel by Mickey Spillane); ph, Franz Planer; m, Mario Castlenuovo-Tedesco; ed, Ronald Sinclair; md, Irving Gertz; art d, Boris Leven; m/l, "Once" by Harold Spina, Bob Russell.

Crime Drama **(PR:A MPAA:NR)**

LONG WEEKEND 1/2** (1978, Aus.) 100m Dugong c

John Hargreaves *(Peter)*, Briony Behets *(Marcia)*, Mike McEwen *(Truck Driver)*, Michael Aitkins *(Bartender)*, Roy Day *(Old Man)*, Sue Kiss von Soly *(City Girl)*.

Married couple Hargreaves and Behets take a vacation in the woods to try to work out their marital problems, but don't find the relaxation they were looking for. Nicely directed with a great sense of the oppressiveness of the outdoors. Nature is the villain in this well-filmed second feature picture by Australian director Eggleston.

p, Richard Brennan; d, Colin Eggleston; w, Everett De Roche; ph, Vincent Monton (Panavision, Eastmancolor); m, Michael Carlos; ed, Brian Kavanagh; art d, Larry Eastwood; set d, Tony Hunt; cos, Kevin Reagan.

Drama **(PR:C-O MPAA:NR)**

LONGEST DAY, THE**** (1962) 180m FOX bw

John Wayne *(Col. Benjamin Vandervoort)*, Robert Mitchum *(Brig. Gen. Norman Cota)*, Henry Fonda *(Brig. Gen. Theodore Roosevelt)*, Robert Ryan *(Brig. Gen. James Gavin)*, Rod Steiger *(Destroyer Commander)*, Robert Wagner *(U.S. Ranger)*, Richard Beymer *(Schultz)*, Mel Ferrer *(Maj. Gen. Robert Haines)*, Jeffrey Hunter *(Sgt. Fuller)*, Paul Anka *(U.S. Ranger)*, Sal Mineo *(Pvt. Martini)*, Roddy McDowall *(Pvt. Morris)*, Stuart Whitman *(Lt. Sheen)*, Eddie Albert *(Col. Newton)*, Edmond O'Brien *(Gen. Raymond O. Barton)*, Fabian *(Ranger)*, Red Buttons *(Pvt. Steele)*, Tom Tryon *(Lt. Wilson)*, Alexander Knox *(Maj. Gen. Walter Bedell Smith)*, Tommy Sands *(U.S. Ranger)*, Ray Danton *(Capt. Frank)*, Henry Grace *(Gen. Dwight D. Eisenhower)*, Mark Damon *(Pvt. Harris)*, Dewey Martin *(Pvt. Wilder)*, Steven Forrest *(Capt. Harding)*, John Crawford *(Col. Caffey)*, Ron Randell *(Joe Williams)*, Nicholas Stuart *(Gen. Omar Bradley)*, John Mellon *(Rear Adm. Alan G. Kirk)*, Fred Durr *(Major of the Rangers)*, Richard Burton *(RAF Pilot)*, Kenneth More *(Capt. Maud)*, Peter Lawford *(Lord Lovat)*, Richard Todd *(Maj. Howard)*, Leo Genn *(Gen. Parker)*, John Gregson *(Padre)*, Sean Connery *(Pvt. Flanagan)*, Jack Hedley *(Briefing Man)*, Michael Medwin *(Pvt. Watney)*, Norman Rossington *(Pvt. Clough)*, John Robinson *(Adm. Sir Bertram Ramsay)*, Patrick Barr *(Group Capt. Stagg)*, Donald Houston *(RAF Pilot)*, Trevor Reid *(Gen. Montgomery)*, Leslie Phillips *(RAF Officer)*, Richard Wattis *(British Soldier)*, Christopher Lee *(Bit)*, Irina Demick *(Janine)*, Bouvril *(Mayor)*, Jean-Louis Barrault *(Father Roulland)*, Christian Marquand *(Comdr. Philippe Kieffer)*, Arletty *(Mme. Barrault)*, Madeline Renaud *(Mother Superior)*, Georges Riviere *(Sgt. Montlaur)*, Georges Wilson *(Renaud)*, Jean Servais *(Adm. Jaujard)*, Fernand Ledoux *(Louis)*, Curt Jergens *(Gen. Blumentritt)*, Werner Hinz *(Marshal Rommel)*, Paul Hartmann *(Runstedt)*, Peter Van Eyck *(Lt. Col. Ocker)*, Gert Frobe *(Sgt. Kaffeeklatsch)*, Hans Christian Blech *(Maj. Pluskat)*, Wolfgang Priess *(Gen. Pemsel)*, Heinz Reincke *(Col. Priller)*, Richard Munch *(Gen. Marcks)*, Ernst Schroder *(Gen. Salmuth)*, Kurt Meisel *(During)*, Wolfgang Lukschy *(Gen. Alfred Jodl)*, Eugene Deckers *(Nazi Soldier)*, Peter Helm *(Young GI)*, Maurice Poli *(Jean)*, Hans C. Blech *(Maj. Pluskat)*, Simon Lack *(Air Chief Marshal Sir Trafford Leigh-Mallory)*, Louis Mounier *(Air Chief Marshal Sir Arthur William Tedder)*, Sian Phillips *(Wren)*, Howard Marion Crasford *(Doctor)*, Heinz Spitzner *(Lt. Col. Hellmuth Meyer)*, Robert Freytag *(Meyer's Aide)*, Til Kiwe *(Capt. Hellmuth Lang)*, Wolfgang Buttner *(Maj. Gen. Dr. Hans Spiedel)*, Ruth Hausmeister *(Frau Rommel)*, Michael Hinz *(Manfred Rommel)*, Paul Roth *(Col. Schiller)*, Harmut Rock *(Sgt. Bergsdorf)*, Karl John *(Luftwaffe General)*, Dietmar Schoenherr *(Luftwaffe Major)*, Riner Penkert *(Lt. Fritz Theen)*, Kurt Pecher *(German Commander)*, Serge Tolstoy *(German Officer)*, George Segal *(1st Commando Up Cliff)*, Maurice Poli *(Jean)*, Alice Tissot *(Housekeeper)*, Jo D'Avra *(Naval Captain)*, Daniel Gelin, Francoise Rosay, Patrick Barr.

This massive movie about a single day of WW II, perhaps the most important day of that terrible conflict, was long the pet project of Fox boss Zanuck and he used three directors, a staggering all-star cast, and a fortune to make it. Based on Ryan's popular compilation of interviews with D-Day (June 6, 1944) survivors, the invasion of Europe was presented in three segments by Zanuck, who directed, according to reports, all American and British interior scenes. The first segment surveys the Americans and British preparing for the invasion, then waiting anxiously for the weather to break so the greatest armada ever gathered could cross the treacherous English Channel to the French beachheads. The high command meets in long sessions and finally General Eisenhower, Grace, makes the decision to send the armada across the Channel. On the Continent the Free French underground busies itself by supplying last-minute secret information to the approaching allies and sabotaging bridges and railroads. The Germans, alerted to accelerated resistance activities, begin to suspect that the invasion is at hand and put coastal defense units on standby alert. The second segment begins with a wave of gliders carrying infantry inland, troops who take key positions while paratroopers land behind enemy lines and begin independent battles. Then the vast armada comes into view but the thousands of ships are seen at dawn by only a few German sentinels along Hitler's supposedly impregnagble sea wall. Of particular fascination is the scene in which Blech, playing the first German officer to actually spot the armada, calls headquarters and says: "Those thousands of ships you say the Allies don't have—well, they have them!" The third segment depicts the massive assault on the beachheads, the British at Sword, Gold and Juno Beaches, the Americans at Omaha and Utah Beaches, the French at Quistreham. The film focuses on the officers and infantrymen alike, concentrating on heroic commanders such as Fonda (as Brig. Gen. Theodore Roosevelt, Jr.), Wayne (as Lt. Col. Benjamin Vandervoort of the 82nd Paratroop Division), and Mitchum as Brig. Gen. Norman Cota who finally moves his hard-pressed men off bloody Omaha Beach where they were being slaughtered by German crossfire. Beymer is one of the infantrymen, a paratrooper lost on the previous night when dropping behind enemy lines, so is Buttons, an 82nd Airbone trooper who drops with dozens of others into heavily occupied St. Mere Eglise where crack German troops wipe out the Americans helplessly floating downward into the fire of their machine guns. Buttons' parachute gets caught on a church steeple and he watches the nightmare massacre while helplessly dangling from the roof, pretending to be dead. It is one of the most chilling scenes ever recorded in any war film. But it is the following day, D-Day, that sees all the action as the Allies storm the beaches and try to punch a hole through Hitler's defense lines. Scenes cross-cut to the Germans reacting to the invasion, front line commanders calling Hitler repeatedly only to be told that he has gone to bed, has taken a sleeping pill, and cannot be disturbed. When he is reached, Hitler refuses to commit his lethal panzer divisons (all of which is based on fact). Wayne, who was to play the role Mitchum later took over, replaced William Holden as the paratrooper commander when Holden dropped out of the production (one of the few of the hundreds who did not answer Zanuck's call to arms which brought forth almost all of Hollywood's talent). There are so many stars in this film that it's hard to keep up with their scenes. Steiger appears as a captain of one of the armada ships, drinking coffee and telling those on the bridge to never forget what they are witnessing, that they are seeing "the greatest armada ever assembled" on the face of the earth. Then there's Burton, a severely wounded British pilot who has crash landed and who has crawled to a small French farmhouse only to shoot it out with a resident Nazi officer; he is later found dying by Beymer. Hunter is marvelous as the courageous GI who sets land torpedoes that finally blow up the stubborn barricade holding the men back on Omaha Beach at the loss of his own life; his is one of the few parts that is part-fictional. According to Maj. George J. Mitchell, who was present on Omaha Beach at the time, Hunter plays "an imaginary character. What happened was this: General Cota discovered a bulldozer loaded with explosives and got a GI—unknown—to ram it into the tank barricade." The British were also well represented with Todd as a commando leader who, with his paratroopers, drops behind German lines and then takes a key bridge and holds it until Lawford, playing the colorful Lord Lovat, arrives the next day with relief forces. Lawford's flamboyant role was later criticized as unbelievable but Zanuck retorted: "The real Lord Lovat, believe it or not, performed and behaved on D-Day exactly as shown in the film, with bagpipes and everything else, including the light-colored khaki sweater. He actually had a batman following him with a brandy bottle, but this was just too much for me to accept. Incidentally, Lord Lovat was with us throughout all the Peter Lawford sequences, and Lawford copied him. Lovat is . . . a legendary character, and his bravado is geniune. On June 8, 1944 [two days after D-Day], he was shot in the belly and half of his stomach had to be removed. He was out of action for seven months, but returned to his commandoes in time to cross the Rhine. Lovat had had seven commando raids prior to D-Day, and was a symbol to the British." The film is undoubtedly the greatest overall production to profile WW II, and the most expensive black and white film up to that time, costing well over $10 million. It was the last great Hollywood epic produced by the last Hollywood mogul, Zanuck, who oversaw every frame edited by his right-hand production chief, Williams, who directed almost all the magnificent battle scenes. And these are outstanding, startling and shocking in their realistic depiction, achieved by marvelous technical talent. Zanuck ordered Williams to employ every trick in the book to make the CinemaScope process encompass his unforgettable epic and he did. Williams used traveling matte shots, process plates for the glider seqence, aerial shots for the strafing of the beaches (by Priller and another pilot, the only two German planes mustered to meet the invasion), helicopter shots and special effects of every kind. One of the most arresting sequences is shot from what seems to be a helicopter, a traveling camera shot whisking over vast terrain and encompassing the French coastal town of Quistreham, inexplicably coming to a standstill high overhead—too high for a crane shot—lingering to show the French assault on the casino the Germans had fortified and then moving on to sweep through other streets and over buildings, as if seen from the eye of a 500-foot giant. The sudden appearance of a group of nuns during this battle was recorded by Zanuck just as it occurred. The French commander Kieffer, who directed the attack, was on hand to advise Zanuck that the nuns actually did appear, walking through the shellfire to aid wounded French troops. Zanuck used up eight cameramen on the main shooting of the film, so much the perfectionist that he demanded that all scenes be shot in exactly the same kind of conditions and weather as were present when the real events happened. To further authenticate events, Zanuck insisted that the Germans and French speak their native languages during scenes covering their activities, subtitling their lines and dubbing nothing. The Germans are equally impressive, especially Jurgens, playing Gen. Blumentritt, Reincke, playing German flying ace Priller, and Hinz, enacting the part of Field Marshal Rommel. Few films have been so skillfully constructed and never on a scale as this, one where the sweep, dimension, and authenticity of that terrible day are captured masterfully on film. Few could have controlled such a monumental production and, to his credit, Zanuck accomplished the impossible. It was Zanuck who decided to cram the screen with one famous actor after another. He later said: "I wanted the audience to have a kick. Every time a door opened, it would be a well-known personality." Mitchum, who is superb as Gen. Cota, later gave an interview in which he stated that G.I.s, borrowed from Army camps in Germany for the film, had second thoughts about appearing in the invasion scenes. He was quoted as having said: "It was raining, the wind was blowing, and the sea was rough, and these troops were afraid to board. I had to hop aboard first myself with some other actors and stuntmen before they gave in." Mitchum quickly heard from the front office at Fox and retracted his statements. Fonda is one of the stars who gives a great performance even in his limited cameo appearance. He plays the 57-year-old General Teddy Roosevelt, Jr., son of the President of the U.S., a man who walked with a cane because of an old leg injury. Roosevelt had to insist that he lead his men ashore on Utah Beach as the commander of that sector, *his* commander, O'Brien, wanting to protect him against the possibilty of his being killed by denying his request. Fonda, as did Roosevelt, made the plea that his father was denied a command during WW I, and he must be allowed to uphold the family name by landing at Normandy. He does, hobbling across the sand, gathering his men around him and, with steady gaze and resolute voice, saying: "We're starting the war from right here." The most memorable star, of course, was Wayne, the rugged never-say-die commander of the indefatigable paratroopers. Zanuck started his all-star list with Wayne but the Duke turned him down flat for an old insult he still remembered. Zanuck persisted and Wayne told him he would do the cameo for $250,000 and would not budge from the price. Zanuck paid it for Wayne's four days before the cameras, some of the best scenes in this memorable film. Wayne was later to say: "Poor old Zanuck. I shouldn't have been that rotten, I guess. The other cameos, they were getting maybe twenty-five thousand, the most." But Zanuck considered Wayne an asset at almost any price and he had other problems, enormous dilemmas to solve. As he remarked to Lord Louis Mountbatten: "I believe I have a tougher job than Ike had on D-Day—at least he had the equipment. I have to find it, rebuild it, and transport it to Normandy." He did, producing a classic war film.

p, Darryl F. Zanuck; d, Andrew Marton, Ken Annakin, Bernhard Wicki, Gerd Oswald; w, Cornelius Ryan, Romain Gary, James Jones, David Pursel, Jack Seddon (based on the novel by Ryan); ph, Jean Bourgoin, Henri Persin, Walter Wottitz, Guy Tabary; m, Maurice Jarre; ed, Samuel Beetley; md, Mitch Miller; art d, Ted Haworth, Leon Barsacq, Vincent Korda; set d, Gabriel Bechir; spec eff, Karl Helmer, Karl Baumgartner, Augie Lohman, Robert McDonald, Alex Weldon; m/l, Paul Anka.

War Epic **Cas.** **(PR:C MPAA:G)**

LONGEST NIGHT, THE* 1/2 (1936) 50m MGM bw

Robert Young (*Charley Phelps*), Florence Rice (*Joan Sutten*), Ted Healy (*Sergeant*), Julie Haydon (*Eve Sutten*), Catharine Doucet (*Mrs. Wilson*), Janet Beecher (*Mrs. Briggs*), Leslie Fenton (*Carl Briggs*), Sidney Toler (*Capt. Holt*), Paul Stanton (*Grover*), Etienne Girardot (*Mr. Kinney*), Tommy Bupp, Samuel S. Hinds, Minor Watson, Kitty McHugh, Olin Howlin, Gertrude Sutton, John Hyams.

A dull film with Young as the department store head who falls in love with clerk Rice and has problems with gangsters. One gangster comes into the store and buys merchandise that the gang will later steal. This was the shortest feature MGM ever made.

p, Lucien Hubbard, Samuel Marx; d, Errol Taggert; w, Robert Andrews (based on the story "The Whispering Window" by Cortland Fitzsimmons); ph, Lester White; ed, Robert J. Kern.

Drama **(PR:A MPAA:NR)**

LONGEST SPUR (SEE: HOT SPUR, 1968)

LONGEST YARD, THE* 1/2 (1974) 121m PAR c

Burt Reynolds (*Paul Crewe*), Eddie Albert (*Warden Hazen*), Ed Lauter (*Capt. Knauer*), Michael Conrad (*Nate Scarboro*), Jim Hampton (*Caretaker*), Harry Caesar (*Granville*), John Steadman (*Pop*), Charles Tyner (*Unger*), Mike Henry (*Rassmeusen*), Bernadette Peters (*Warden's Secretary*), Pervis Arkins (*Mawabe*), Tony Cacciotti (*Rotka*), Anitra Ford (*Melissa*), Michael Ford (*Announcer*), Joe Kapp (*Walking Boss*), Richard Kiel (*Samson*), Pepper Martin (*Shop Steward*), Mort Marshall (*Assistant Warden*), Ray Nitschke (*Bogdanski*), Sonny Sixkiller (*Indian*), Dino Washington (*Mason*), Ernie Wheelwright (*Spooner*), Joseph Dorsey (*Bartender*), Dr. Gus Carlucci (*Team Doctor*), Jack Rockwell (*Trainer*), Sonny Shroyer (*Tannen*), Roy Ogden (*Schmidt*), Don Ferguson (*Referee*), Chuck Hayward, Alfie Wise (*Troopers*), Robert Tessier (*Shokner*), Tony Reese (*Levitt*), Steve Wilder (*J. J.*), George Jones (*Big George*), Wilbur Gillan (*Big Wilbur*), Wilson Warren (*Buttercup*), Joe Jackson (*Little Joe*), Howard Silverstein (*Howie*), Donald Hixon (*Donny*), Jim Nicholson (*Ice Man*).

Reynolds is an ex-football star playing stud for socialite Ford. When he takes off in her car, she calls the police and reports her car missing. The police take after Reynolds in a well choreographed car chase by second unit director Hal Needham. Reynolds is arrested and sent to Albert's prison. The warden forces the ex-football player to organize an inmate football team to play the guards' team headed by Lauter. Albert blackmails Reynolds to throw the climactic game which adds to the drama and suspense of the game. The final 47 minutes of the film are of the football game itself, and the laughs come as fast as the action. One of Reynolds' best performances thanks mainly to Aldrich's strong direction and THE LONGEST YARD ranks up there with Aldrich's THE DIRTY DOZEN (1967) and KISS ME DEADLY (1955).

p, Albert S. Ruddy; d, Robert Aldrich; w, Tracy Keenan Wynn (based on a story by Ruddy); ph, Joseph Biroc (Technicolor); m, Frank DeVol; ed, Michael Luciano, Frank Capacchione, Allan Jacobs, George Hively; prod d, James S. Vance.

Action/Comedy **Cas.** **(PR:O MPAA:R)**

LONGHORN, THE* (1951) 70m MON bw

Wild Bill Elliott (*Jim Kirk*), Phyllis Coates (*Gail*), Myron Healey (*Andy*), Lane Bradford (*Purdy*), Stan Jolley (*Robinson*), Marshall Reed (*Latimer*), Marshall Bradford (*Doctor*), William Fawcett (*Bartender*), Zon Murray (*Tyler*), Lee Roberts (*Clark*), John Hart (*Moresby*), Steve Clark (*Rancher*), Carol Henry (*Henchman*), Herman Hack, Carl Matthews.

Elliott plans to breed Herefords with Texas Longhorns. He heads for Oregon with Healey and the cowboys to buy new stock and drive them to Wyoming. But Healey is working with a band of rustlers who want to capitalize on Elliott's idea first. Midway through the drive to Wyoming, the cattle are stolen and Elliott and his cohorts go after Healey and the rustlers.

p, Vincent M. Fennelly; d, Lewis Collins; w, Dan Ullman; ph, Ernest Miller; ed, Richard Heermance; md, Raoul Kraushaar; art d, David Milton.

Western **(PR:A MPAA:NR)**

LONGING FOR LOVE* (1966, Jap.) 105m Nikkatsu bw (AKA: AI NO KAWAKI)

Ruriko Asaoka (*Etsuko*), Nobuo Nakamura (*Father-in-Law*), Tetsuo Ishitachi (*Gardener*), Akira Yamanouchi (*2nd Son*), Chitose Kurenai (*Servant Girl*), Tuko Kusunoki, Yoko Ozono.

Japanese melodrama based on a novel written by controversial and frequently brilliant author Yukio Mishima. Asaoka plays a young widow living on her husband's family estate. Nakamura, her widowed father-in-law, is remarried and supporting his wife and his second son. Nakamura is enamored with Asaoka and frequently forces himself on her. Lonely, isolated, and trapped, Asaoka looks for escape through a relationship with one of the estate's gardeners, Ishitachi. Her obsession is obvious to everyone in the household but Ishitachi himself, and when Asaoka discovers that he has gotten a servant girl pregnant, she forces the woman to get rid of her child. Driven somewhat mad by the futility of her existence, Asaoka orders Ishitachi into the greenhouse where she informs him of the death of his baby. Nakamura suddenly appears with a gun to shoot his rival, but when Ishitachi expresses joy over the news, Asaoka shoots him. Nakamura and Asaoka bury the body and she then flees the estate.

p, Kanou Otsuka; d, Koreyoshi Kurahara; w, Shigeya Fujita, Kurahara (based on the novel *Ai no kawaki* by Yukio Mishima); ph, Yoshio Mimiya; m, Toshiro Mayuzumi.

Drama **(PR:O MPAA:NR)**

LONNIE* (1963) 76m Dolphin/Futuramic bw

Scott Marlowe (*Lonnie*), Frank Silvera (*Paco*), Turina Hayes (*Ria*), Wilton Graff (*Mitchell*), Michael Constantine (*Gage*), Joan Anderson (*Lois*), Arthur Storch.

Marlowe plays the title loser who rents his car to Spanish revolutionary Silvera. Silvera and his accomplice, Graff, use the vehicle as a getaway car in a diamond robbery, the proceeds of which will go to fund the revolution. Upon investigating the whereabouts of his car, Marlowe learns that Anderson, his childhood sweetheart, is prostituting herself and giving Silvera the money to further his cause. Marlowe is captured by Silvera and forced to help the crooks escape by boat. He soon falls in love with the boat owner's daughter, Haynes, and together they defeat the slimy thief and his cohorts. Shot on location in Georgia. Johnny Chase sings the title song.

p, Herbert Skable; d, William Hale; w, William Copeland; ph, Haskell Wexler; m, Bob Cooper; ed, Melvin Sloan.

Drama **(PR:C MPAA:NR)**

LOOK BACK IN ANGER* (1959) 115m ABF-PATHE/WB bw

Richard Burton (*Jimmy Porter*), Claire Bloom (*Helena Charles*), Mary Ure (*Alison Porter*), Edith Evans (*Mrs. Tanner*), Gary Raymond (*Cliff Lewis*), Glen Byam Shaw (*Cpl. Redfern*), Phyllis Nielson-Terry (*Mrs. Redfern*), Donald Pleasence (*Hurst*), Jane Eccles (*Miss Drury*), S. P. Kapoor (*Kapoor*), George Devine (*Doctor*), Walter Hudd (*Actor*), Anne Dickins (*Girl A.S.M.*), Bernice Swanson (*Sally*), Chris Barber and His Jazz Band, Stanley Van Beers, Jordan Lawrence, John Dearth, Michael Balfour, Nigel Davenport, Alfred Lynch, Toke Townley, Maureen Swanson.

In the late 1950s and early 1960s, there were several "angry young men" films written and produced. Whether any of these authors had any talent is a matter of taste, but we can assure you they *were* angry. Very angry. Osborne was a forerunner of the genre and wrote a play that had enormous success in London and New York. This lensing was faithful to the original but it lost a bit in the translation from the intimacy of the stage to the screen. Canadian Harry Saltzman, who made his fortune in England, produced the picture before he decided to make films that had more commercial possibilities (i.e. the JAMES BOND series which he did with Albert Broccoli) and he is to be congratulated for taking a chance with an iffy property. Burton, in a no-holds-barred performance, is a university-educated malcontent who currently earns his keep by running a candy stall in a large market area run by Pleasence, in yet another of his fine roles. Burton seems to love his wife, Ure, but can't help verbally mistreating her. (She repeats the part she played on the stage. This was one of her very few film appearances. She had been married to playwright Osborne, then married playwright-actor Robert Shaw. She died at 42 after mixing whiskey with barbiturates.) Ure takes about as much as anyone can stand, then leaves him when her best friend, Bloom, persuades her that she must to save her sanity. Burton is now alone, with nobody to insult, and he takes up with Bloom, a woman he has despised for most of the first few reels. Ure has been pregnant all along but didn't tell Burton. When she loses the baby, she returns to Burton and Bloom thinks that's the time for her to leave, and she's right. Evans is a sweet old lady who helps Burton set up his business and Kapoor has a few good scenes as an Indian trader but most of the picture belongs to Burton's bravura performance. The major problem of the picture is that Osborne seems to have concocted the slight plot for one reason only; to vent his spleen against the church, society, the rich, the government, and whatever captured his fancy at the time. The dialog at times is endless and much too flip in the wrong situations. It's as though the author attempted to be a modern-day Oscar Wilde, but with a social conscience, and his "message" is heard loud, clear, and far too often. Although Burton has the range to be kind, funny, earthy, noble, and passionate, he is given little opportunity to get beyond letting that memorable voice of his bellow and roar. Still, for all the obvious drawbacks, LOOK BACK IN ANGER should be seen by anyone who is interested in learning about the England of that era. Burton had been making films for 10 years and had starred as Alexander in ALEXANDER THE GREAT as well as having been Edwin Booth in PRINCE OF PLAYERS. This seamy role, however, was the one that brought him to the attention of many who thought that he could only act when dressed in Biblical clothes, as in THE ROBE, or in doublet and hose.

He was only 34 at the time this was made and the ravages of high living were already beginning to show on his rugged Welsh face.

p, Harry Saltzman; d, Tony Richardson; w, Nigel Kneale, John Osborne (based on the play by Osborne); ph, Oswald Morris; m, Chris Barber; ed, Richard Best; md, John Addison; art d, Peter Glazier; cos, Jocelyn Richards; m/l, Tom Eastwood.

Drama/Play Adaptation   **Cas.**   **(PR:C-O MPAA:NR)**

LOOK BEFORE YOU LAUGH   (SEE: MAKE MINE A MILLION, 1965)

LOOK BEFORE YOU LOVE**   (1948, Brit.) 96m Burnham/GFD bw

Margaret Lockwood (*Ann Markham*), Griffith Jones (*Charles Kent*), Norman Wooland (*Ashley Morehouse*), Phyllis Stanley (*Bettina Colby*), Maurice Denham (*Fosser*), Frederick Piper (*Miller*), Bruce Seton (*Johns*), Michael Medwin (*Emile Garat*), Violet Farebrother (*Dowager*), Peggy Evans (*Typist*), June Elvin, Joan Rees, Nigel Lawlor, Alan Adair, Giselle Morlais, Stanley Quentin, Daphne Arthur, Dorothy Bramhall, Edwin Palmer, Peter Fontaine.

Lockwood works in the British Embassy in Rio and marries Jones, a man with a dubious past. After their wedding she discovers he is wanted for fraud and other crimes, but he promises that he will mend his wicked ways. They return to England by ship and meet millionaire Wooland, who pays the unscrupulous Jones $40,000 to disappear so he can marry Lockwood. Ridiculous story played straight; as a farce it might have had some chance.

p, John Corfield, Harold Huth; d, Huth; w, Reginald Long (based on a story by Ketti Frings); ph, Harry Waxman, Harold Haysom; m, Bretton Byrd; ed, John D. Guthridge.

Drama   **(PR:A MPAA:NR)**

LOOK DOWN AND DIE, MEN OF STEEL   (SEE: STEEL, 1980)

LOOK FOR THE SILVER LINING*¹/₂   (1949) 106m WB c

June Haver (*Marilyn Miller*), Ray Bolger (*Jack Donahue*), Gordon MacRae (*Frank Carter*), Charlie Ruggles (*Pop Miller*), Rosemary DeCamp (*Mom Miller*), Lee Wilde (*Claire Miller*), Lyn Wilde (*Ruth Miller*), Dick Simmons (*Henry Doran*), S. Z. Sakall (*Shendorf*), Walter Catlett (*Himself*), George Zorich, Oleg Tupine (*Ballet Specialty*), Lillian Yarbo (*Violet*), Paul E. Burns (*Mr. Beeman*), Douglas Kennedy (*Doctor*), Ted Mapes (*Driver*), Monte Blue (*St. Clair*), Will Rogers, Jr. (*Will Rogers*), Esther Howard (*Mrs. Moffitt*), Jack Gargan (*Stage Manager*).

An insipid musical biography of Marilyn Miller, with Bolger being the only noteworthy actor in the film and his tap dance rendition of Jerome Kern's "Who" the only highlight. Bolger is Haver's mentor on her climb from vaudeville to Broadway and her tale is told in flashbacks. Songs include: "Look For The Silver Lining," "Whip-Poor-Will," "A Kiss In The Dark" (Buddy De Sylva, Victor Herbert), "Pirouette" (Herman Finck), "Just A Memory" (De Sylva, Lew Brown, Ray Henderson), "Time On My Hands" (Mack Gordon, Harold Adamson, Vincent Youmans), "Wild Rose" (Clifford Grey, Kern), "Shine On Harvest Moon" (Nora Bayes, Jack Norworth), "Back, Back, Back To Baltimore" (Harry Williams, Egbert Van Alstyne), "Jingle Bells" (J. S. Pierpont), "Can't You Hear Me Callin', Caroline?" (William H. Gardner, Caro Roma), "Carolina In The Morning" (Gus Kahn, Walter Donaldson), "Yama Yama Man" (George Collin Davis, Karl Hoschna), "Dengozo" (Ernesto Nazareth), "Oh Gee! Oh Joy!" (P. G. Wodehouse, George and Ira Gershwin).

p, William Jacobs; d, David Butler; w, Phoebe and Henry Ephron, Marian Spitzer (based on a story "Life of Marilyn Miller" by Bert Kalmar, Harry Ruby); ph, Peverell Marley (Technicolor); m, Ray Heindorf; ed, Irene Morra; md, Ray Heindorf; art d, John Hughes; ch, LeRoy Prinz.

Musical   **(PR:A MPAA:NR)**

LOOK IN ANY WINDOW**   (1961) 87m AA bw

Paul Anka (*Craig Fowler*), Ruth Roman (*Jackie Fowler*), Alex Nicol (*Jay Fowler*), Gigi Perreau (*Eileen Lowell*), Carole Mathews (*Betty Lowell*), George Dolenz (*Carlo*), Jack Cassidy (*Gareth Lowell*), Robert Sampson (*Lindstrom*), Dan Grayam (*Webber*), Jacqueline Kruger, Norman Winston.

Another problem teen-ager movie with Anka as a peeping Tom because he has problem parents. His father, Nichol, is an alcoholic and his mother, Roman, fools around with any man that looks her way. Anka spies on his suburban neighbors, and comes close to being caught when he is peeping on the couple next door, Cassidy and Mathews. Anka's mother runs off to Las Vegas with Cassidy and the teen-ager tries to seduce Perreau, daughter of Cassidy and Mathews. She falls through a glass coffee table trying to escape Anka's advances, and the peeper runs. He is caught by a plainclothed police officer prowling around a pool party. This causes Anka's parents to examine their own lifestyle.

p, William Alland, Laurence E. Mascott; d, Alland; w, Mascott; ph, W. Wallace Kelly; m, Richard Shores; ed, Harold Gordon; art d, Hilyard Brown; m/l "Look In Any Window," Paul Anka, sung by Anka; makeup, Maurice Seiderman.

Drama   **(PR:A MPAA:NR)**

LOOK OUT FOR LOVE   (SEE: GIRLS IN THE STREET, 1938, Brit.)

LOOK OUT SISTER***   (1948) 64m Savini/Astor bw

Louis Jordan (*Himself*), Suzette Harbin (*Betty Scott*), Monte Hawley (*Mack Gordon*), Glenn Allen (*Billy*), Tommy Southern (*Cactus*), Jack Clisby (*Pistol Pete*), Maceo Sheffield (*Officer Lee/The Sheriff*), Peggy Thomas (*Dancer*), Louise Franklin (*Bathing Beauty*), Anice Clark, Dorothy Seamans (*Girl Exhibition Divers*), Bob Scott and Louis Jordan's Tymphany 6: Aaron Izenhall (*Trumpet*), Paul Quinchette (*Tenor Saxophone*), William Doggett (*Piano*), William Hadnott (*Bass*), Chris Colombus (*Drums*), James Jackson (*Guitar*).

A musical satire on the western with an all-black cast starring Jordan who dreams he is on a dude ranch. "Two Gun" Jordan wins Harbin's heart and saves the ranch from foreclosure by Hawley. The film is full of 1940s black culture and slang and great music performed by Jordan and his Tymphany Six. The humor is broad, but it's an enjoyable and historic film. Songs include "Caldonia," "Don't Burn the Candle at Both Ends," and nine others.

p, Berle Adams; d, Bud Pollard; w, John E. Gordon; ph, Carl Berger; ed, Pollard; m/l, Louis Jordan, Leroy Hickman, Dallas Bartley, Don Wilson, Wilhelmina Grey, Sid Robbins, Benny Carter, Irving Gordon, Lee Penny, Dick Miles, Walter Bishop, Fleecie Moore, Ben Lorre, Jeff Dane.

Musical Comedy   **(PR:A MPAA:NR)**

LOOK UP AND LAUGH*¹/₂
     (1935, Brit.) 64m Associated Talking Picture/ABF bw

Gracie Fields (*Grace Pearson*), Alfred Drayton (*Belfer*), Douglas Wakefield (*Joe Chirk*), Billy Nelson (*Alf Chirk*), Harry Tate (*Tumpenny*), Huntley Wright (*Old Ketley*), D. J. Williams (*Malpas*), Morris Harvey (*Rosenbloom*), Norman Walker (*Brierley*), Tommy Fields (*Sidney Pearson*), Robb Wilton (*The Mayor*), Arthur Hambling (*Horning*), Kenneth Kove (*Piano Assistant*), Jack Melford (*Journalist*), Vivien Leigh (*Marjorie Belfer*), Maud Gill (*Miss Canvey*), Helen Ferrers (*Lady Buster*), Kenneth More.

Fields stars in this comedy about a group of market stallholders who circumvent a chainstore when they discover a Royal Charter. The song "Love is Everywhere" is included. It was only the third film appearance for beautiful Leigh, who was then 22 years old.

p&d, Basil Dean; w, Gordon Wellesley (based on a story by J. B. Priestley); ph, Robert G. Martin; m, Harry Parr-Davies.

Comedy   **(PR:A MPAA:NR)**

LOOK WHO'S LAUGHING**¹/₂   (1941) 79m RKO bw

Edgar Bergen (*Himself*), Charlie McCarthy (*Himself*), Jim Jordan (*Fibber McGee*), Marian Jordan (*Molly McGee*), Lucille Ball (*Julie Patterson*), Lee Bonnell (*Jerry*), Dorothy Lovett (*Marge*), Harold Peary (*The Great Gildersleeve*), Isabel Randolph (*Mrs. Uppington*), Walter Baldwin (*Bill*), Neil Hamilton (*Hilary Horton*), Charles Halton (*Cudahy*), Harlow Wilcox (*Mr. Collins*), Spencer Charters (*Hotel Manager*), Jed Prouty (*Mayor Duncan*), George Cleveland (*Mayor Kelsey*), Bill Thompson (*Veteran*), Sterling Holloway (*Rusty, the Soda Jerk*), Florence Wright (*Evelyn*), Harlan Briggs, Arthur Q. Bryan (*Mayor Duncan's Aides*), Charles Lane (*Club Secretary*), Edna Holland (*Mrs. Hargrave*), Dell Henderson (*Mr. Wentworth*), Jack George (*Orchestra Leader*), Matty Kemp (*Harry*), Louise Currie (*Jane*), Louis Payne (*Butler*), Joe Hickey (*Dancing Partner*), Donald Kerr (*Father*), Sally Cairns (*Girl*), Eleanor Counts, Yvonne Chenal (*Bits*), Dorothy Lloyd (*Maisie/Matilda*).

Radio stars Edgar Bergen and Fibber McGee and Molly are top-billed in this B comedy. Bergen has his airplane factory built in Wistful Vista (McGee and Molly's radio hometown). Ball is Bergen's secretary who almost marries Bonnell, Bergen's business manager, but ends up in Bergen's arms. Halton is Bergen's rival and Hamilton is Bergen's millionaire friend who buys McGee's property to build an airport. Peary is McGee's pal and unwitting aid to Halton's schemes to ruin Bergen.

p&d, Allan Dwan; w, James V. Kern, Don Quinn, Leonard L. Levinson, Zeno Klinker, Dorothy Kingsley; ph, Frank Redman; m, Roy Webb; ed, Sherman Todd; md, Constantine Bakaleinikoff; art d, Van Nest Polglase; spec eff, Vernon L. Walker.

Comedy   **(PR:A MPAA:NR)**

LOOKER*¹/₂   (1981) 94m Ladd/WB c

Albert Finney (*Dr. Larry Roberts*), James Coburn (*John Reston*), Susan Dey (*Cindy*), Leigh Taylor-Young (*Jennifer Long*), Dorian Harewood (*Lt. Masters*), Tim Rossovich (*Moustache Man*), Darryl Hickman (*Dr. Jim Belfield*), Kathryn Witt (*Tina*), Terri Welles (*Lisa*), Michael Gainsborough (*Sen. Harrison*), Ashley Cox (*Candy*), Donna Benz (*Ellen*), Catherine Parks (*Jan*), Terry Kiser (*Commercial Director*), Georgann Johnson (*Cindy's Mother*), Richard Venture (*Cindy's Father*), Anthony Charnota (*Master's Assistant*), Terrence McNally (*Scanning Room Technician*), David Adams (*Guard*), John Sanderford, Scott Mulhern (*Policemen*), Jeana Tomasino (*Suzy*), Barry Jenner (*Commercial Producer*), Arthur Taxier, Richard Milholland, Darrel Maury, Paul Jasmin, Eloise Hardt, Melissa Prophet, Lila Christianson, Lorna Christianson, Gary Combs, Kelly Black, Jerry Douglas, Randi Brooks, Jesse Logan, Joe Medalis, Estelle Omens, Steve Strong, Tawny Moyer, Dick Christie, Katherine DeHetre, Allsion Balson, Adam Starr.

A muddled and silly film from writer/director Crichton about hypnotic TV commercials (written and produced for the film by Robert Chandler), murdered models, and stun guns. Finney is a plastic surgeon who becomes a murder suspect when two models he performed operations on are murdered. Finney ignores the police and takes it upon himself, with help from model Dey, to find the culprit. They discover that a Coburn-headed conglomerate is the murderer. The corporation makes three-dimensional images of the models to be used in subliminal ads. Coburn's henchmen chase Finney with stun guns that make the user invisible and send the victim into a trance. The film would have been more interesting if they just stuck with stun guns but Crichton goes overboard with the confusing storyline. Former Playboy Playmates are the models.

p, Howard Jeffrey; d&w, Michael Crichton; ph, Paul Lohmann (Panavision, Technicolor); m, Barry DeVorzon; ed, Carl Kress; prod d, Dean Edward Mitzner; art d, Jack Taylor, Jr.; cos, Betsy Cox; spec eff, Joe Day; stunts, Fred Waugh; makeup, Ken Chase; computer animation, Information International, Inc.

Science Fiction/Thriller   **Cas.**   **(PR:O MPAA:PG)**

LOOKIN' GOOD (SEE: CORKY, 1972)

LOOKIN' FOR SOMEONE (SEE: SINGING ON THE TRAIL, 1946)

LOOKIN' TO GET OUT** (1982) 104m Lorimar-Northstar International/PAR c

Jon Voight *(Alex Kovac)*, Ann-Margret *(Patti Warner)*, Burt Young *(Jerry Feldman)*, Bert Remsen *(Smitty)*, Jude Farese *(Harry)*, Allen Keller *(Joey)*, Richard Bradford *(Bernie Gold)*, Stacey Pickren *(Rusty-Redhaired Hooker)*, Samantha Harper *(Lillian-Jerry's Ex-Wife)*, Fox Harris *(Harvey-Elevator Operator)*, Marcheline Bertrand *(Girl in Jeep)*, Roger Rook, Howard Gray, Bill Borsella, Henry Robinson *(Poker Players)*, Sigmund Frohlich *(Dealer)*, Steven E. Pelzer *(Paul)*, Ruth Manning *(Shannon)*, Don Lake *(Alfred)*, Barbara Joyce Furman *(Desk Assistant)*, Wiley Harker *(Dr. Green)*, Barry Gootkind *(Floorman)*, Howard Witt *(Sid)*, Peter Lind Hayes, Mary Healy *(Tourists)*, Siegfried and Roy *(Magicians)*, Kris Kremo *(Juggler)*, Angelina Jolie Voight *(Tosh)*, Larry Alan Weisshart *(Bellhop)*, Patrick O'Neill *(Bartender)*, Frank Bella *(Maitre D')*, Robert S. Aumen, Dick Padgette, Tony Hawkins, Lee Nickerson, Tony Hawkson, Michael DeLuna, Michael D. Misuraca, Joseph Miller, Gloria Manos, Pam Parmelli, Roberta Greenberg, Martha Sheehan, John Ortstadt, Myrtle Elizabeth Lolatte, Effie Karath, Cis Rundle, Peter Kulas, Bob Buckingham, Jim DeCloss, Ken Cohen, Don Caldwell, Ron Skurow, Steve Vincent, Danny Tucker, Dacid Welch, Terry Fisher.

A 17 million dollar flop about a couple of New York losers, Voight and Young, who go to Las Vegas to make some big bucks. They left New York after Voight lost $10,000 that belonged to thugs Keller and Ferese in a poker game. In Vegas, the two hook up with ex-call girl Ann-Margret, set up headquarters in the MGM Grand Hotel, and break the bank in the casino. Much dialog seems improvised which hits and misses and makes the scripted plot developments seem forced. Director Ashby's cut of the film was chopped by Paramount, Voight, Schaffel, and Schwartz, and came up weaker for it. The film has problems, but it's no turkey.

p, Robert Schaffel; d, Hal Ashby; w, Al Schwartz, Jon Voight; ph, Haskell Wexler; m, Johnny Mandel; ed, Robert C. Jones; prod d, Robert Boyle; art d, James Schoppee.

Comedy **Cas.** **(PR:O MPAA:R)**

LOOKING FOR DANGER** (1957) 62m AA bw

Huntz Hall *(Sach)*, Stanley Clements *(Duke)*, Eddie LeRoy *(Blinky)*, David Condon *(Chuck)*, Jimmy Murphy *(Myron)*, Richard Avonde *(Ahmed)*, Otto Reichow *(Wolff)*, Michael Granger *(Sidi-Omar)*, Peter Mamakos *(Hassan)*, Lili Kardell *(Shareen)*, Joan Bradshaw *(Zarida)*, George Khoury *(Mustapha)*, Henry Rowland *(Wetzel)*, Percy Helton *(Mike Clancy)*, Harry Strang *(Sgt. Watson)*, Paul Bryar *(Maj. Harper)*, Jane Burgess *(Sari)*, John Harmon *(Bradfield)*, Michael Vallon *(Waiter)*, Dick Elliott *(Mike Clancy)*.

A late entry in the BOWERY BOYS series has Hall explaining (in flashback) how he and the boys were spies during WW II. In the war, Hall and Clements were sent on a mission to locate "The Hawk," an important member of the North African underground. Disguising themselves as Nazis, the boys make their way into the compound of sultan Granger, an Axis supporter who spots them as Americans right off. Granger gives the boys a message which they then give to one of the dancing girls, Kardell, who reveals herself as "The Hawk." Together the trio try to notify their commanders, but they are imprisoned by the sultan, and it takes the rest of the gang disguised as Nazis to break them out and capture Granger. Some moments of old Bowery Boys chemistry break through, but the material is pretty mundane. (See BOWERY BOYS series, Index.)

p, Ben Schwalb; d, Austen Jewell; w, Elwood Ullman (based on the story by Ullman, Edward Bernds); ph, Harry Neumann; ed, Neil Brunnenkant; md, Marlin Skiles; art d, David Milton, cos, Bert Henrikson; makeup, Emile LaVigne.

Comedy **(PR:A MPAA:NR)**

LOOKING FOR LOVE** (1964) 84m Euterpe-Franmet/MGM c

Connie Francis *(Libby Caruso)*, Jim Hutton *(Paul Davis)*, Susan Oliver *(Jan McNair)*, Joby Baker *(Cuz Rickover)*, Barbara Nichols *(Gaye Swinger)*, Jay C. Flippen *(Mr. Ralph Front)*, Jesse White *(Tiger Shay)*, Charles Lane *(Director)*, Joan Marshall *(Miss Devine)*, Johnny Carson, George Hamilton, Yvette Mimieux, Paula Prentiss, Danny Thomas *(Themselves)*, Mimi Dillard.

Francis is a switchboard operator with an eye on becoming a movie star and catching Hutton, in this teen romance film. Once the singing star has Hutton though, she realizes he's not for her, and grocery assistant Baker is. Hutton isn't left in the cold because he pairs up with Francis' roommate, Oliver. Cameo appearances by TV host Carson, and actors Hamilton, Mimieux, Prentiss, and Thomas. Songs include: "Let's Have a Party," "When the Clock Strikes Midnight," "Looking For Love" (Hank Hunter, Stan Vincent), "Whoever You Are, I Love You" (Peter Udell, Gary Geld), "This is My Happiest Moment" (Ted Murray, Benny Davis), "Be My Love" (Sammy Cahn, Nicholas Brodszky), (all songs sung by Connie Francis) "I Can't Believe That You're in Love With Me" (Jimmy McHugh, Clarence Gaskill, sung by Connie Francis, Danny Thomas).

p, Joe Pasternak; d, Don Weis; w, Ruth Brooks Flippen; ph, Milton Krasner (Panavision, Metrocolor); m, Georgie Stoll; ed, Adrienne Fazan; art d, George W. Davis, Urie McCleary; set d, Henry Grace, Charles S. Thompson; cos, Don Loper, Lambert Marks, Florence Hackett, William T. Zacha; spec eff, Glen Galvin; makeup, William Tuttle.

Romance Comedy/Musical **(PR:A MPAA:NR)**

LOOKING FOR MR. GOODBAR*½** (1977) 135m PAR c

Diane Keaton *(Theresa Dunn)*, Tuesday Weld *(Katherine Dunn)*, William Atherton *(James Morrissey)*, Richard Kiley *(Mr. Dunn)*, Richard Gere *(Tony Lopanto)*, Alan Feinstein *(Professor Engle)*, Tom Berenger *(Gary Cooper White)*, Priscilla Pointer *(Mrs. Dunn)*, Laurie Prange *(Brigid Dunn)*, Joel Fabiani *(Barney)*, Julius Harris *(Black Cat)*, Richard Bright *(George)*, Levar Burton *(Cap Jackson)*, Marilyn Coleman *(Mrs. Jackson)*, Elizabeth Cheshire *(Little Theresa)*.

In the hands of a less sure director, this could have been a tawdry mess, but Brooks exercises some good judgement in dealing with the material and the result is a somewhat satisfying adaptation of the Rossner novel. Keaton is a repressed teacher of deaf and dumb children who lives under the thumb of her macho father, Kiley, and her let's-make-everything-nice mother, Pointer. She would love to be free of them so she sets out to find "Mr. Right" but in all the wrong places. She haunts the singles bars and goes on a sexual voyage, sleeping with Atherton, a befuddled, sweet guy who loves her; Gere, a stud with sadistic tendencies that thrill her and finally, Berenger, the insane bisexual who eventually takes her life. Keaton is shown existing in two worlds; the safety of school, home and hearth; and the madcap life of the swingers who stay up late, drowning their loneliness in stingers and sex. This is the other side of Hoffman's and Farrow's JOHN AND MARY and we kept looking hard at the bar scenes to see if Dustin and Mia were in the background. There are many erotic scenes but they are handled well. Imagine Brian DePalma with the same script and you'll realize how disgusting it could have been. Feinstein is excellent as Keaton's first lover and Weld is sensational as Keaton's sister, a slightly dippy person who has found her happiness in following whatever trend is au courant. LOOKING FOR MR. GOODBAR made lots of money and showed that Keaton, who had just scored in ANNIE HALL, could get out from under Woody Allen's wing and be a star on her own. An added plus was the score by Artie Kane which evoked the solitude of living in a city with millions of people but still not having anyone with whom to really talk.

p, Freddie Fields; d&w, Richard Brooks (based on the novel by Judith Rosner); ph, William A. Fraker (Panavision, Metrocolor); m, Artie Kane; ed, George Grenville; art d, Edward Carfagno; set d, Ruby Levitt; cos, Jodie Lynn Tillen; m/l, "Don't Ask to Stay Until Tomorrow," Artie Kane, Carol Connors (sung by Marlena Shaw); makeup, Charles Schram.

Drama **Cas.** **(PR:C-O MPAA:R)**

LOOKING FOR TROUBLE, 1931 (SEE: TIP-OFF, THE, 1931)

LOOKING FOR TROUBLE*½ (1934) 77m FOX/UA bw

Spencer Tracy *(Joe Graham)*, Constance Cummings *(Ethel Greenwood)*, Jack Oakie *(Casey)*, Morgan Conway *(Dan Sutter)*, Arline Judge *(Mazie)*, Judith Wood *(Pearl La Tour)*, Paul Harvey *(James Regan)*, Joseph [Sawyer] Sauers *(Max Stanley)*, Franklyn Ardell *(Martin)*, Paul Porcasi *(Cabaret Manager)*.

Tracy and Oakie are repairmen for the telephone company in this sluggish action drama. Tracy is married to Cummings and he thinks that her boss, Conway, is a crook. Tracy drags Oakie with him to prove his point, and they're caught snooping by Conway's henchmen. They leave the pair to die in a burning building, but Tracy sets off the fire alarm and saves their lives. When Conway is killed, Cummings is the main suspect, and Tracy and Oakie go off to find the real murderer. During the Long Beach earthquake they find Wood, an old girl friend of Conway's who admits to killing the crook.

p, Darryl F. Zanuck; d, William Wellman; w, Leonard Praskins, Elmer Harris (based on a story by J. R. Bren); ph, James Van Trees; ed, Peter Fritch; md, Alfred Newman; art d, Richard Day, Joseph Wright.

Drama **(PR:A MPAA:NR)**

LOOKING FORWARD** (1933) 76m MGM bw

Lionel Barrymore *(Michael Benton)*, Lewis Stone *(Gabriel Service, Sr.)*, Benita Hume *(Isobel Service)*, Elizabeth Allan *(Caroline Service)*, Phillips Holmes *(Michael Service)*, Colin Clive *(Geoffrey Fielding)*, Alec B. Francis *(Birkenshaw)*, Doris Lloyd *(Mrs. Benton)*, Halliwell Hobbes *(Mr. Felton)*, Douglas Walton *(Willie)*, Viva Tattersall *(Elsie Benton)*, Lawrence Grant *(Philip Bendicott)*, George K. Arthur *(Mr. Tressitt)*, Charles Irwin *(Mr. Burton)*, Billy Bevan *(Mr. Barker)*.

The title of this film was taken from President Franklin Delano Roosevelt's book, but the story is adapted from an English play entitled, "Service." It is a Depression parable with Barrymore laid off from his position at a London shop because of tight times. He had worked there for 40 years and had come from a family of men who spent their lives working at the shop. Stone is the man who must let Barrymore go, only to sell his shop to a lower-priced competitor. Most of the film focuses on Stone and his family, with Barrymore essentially in a supporting role.

p&d, Clarence Brown; w, Bess Meredyth, H.M. Harwood (based on the play "Service" by C. L. Anthony [Dodie Smith]); ph, Oliver T. Marsh; ed, Hugh Wynn.

Drama **(PR:A MPAA:NR)**

LOOKING GLASS WAR, THE** (1970, Brit.) 106m Frankovich/COL c

Christopher Jones *(Leiser)*, Pia Degermark *(The Girl)*, Ralph Richardson *(Leclerc)*, Anthony Hopkins *(John Avery)*, Paul Rogers *(Haldane)*, Susan George *(Susan)*, Ray McAnally *(Starr)*, Robert Urquhart *(Johnson)*, Maxine Audley *(Babs Leclerc)*, Anna Massey *(Sarah)*, Frederick Jaeger *(Captain Lansen)*, Paul Maxwell *(C.I.A. Man)*, Timothy West *(Taylor)*, Vivien Pickles *(Carol)*, Peter Swanwick *(Peerson)*, Cyril Shaps *(East German Detective)*, Michael Robbins *(Truck Driver)*, Guy Deghy *(Fritsche)*, David Scheuer *(Russian Officer)*, John Franklin *(Pine)*, Linda Hedger *(Taylor's Child)*, Nicholas Stewart *(German Boy)*, Ernst Walder *(Radio Engineer)*, Partrick Wright *(Vopo)*, Sylva Langova *(East German Woman)*, Alan McClelland *(Doctor)*, Angela Down *(Chelsea Girl)*, Robert Wilde *(English Policeman)*, Russell Lewis *(Avery's Child)*.

A predictable espionage film adapted from John Le Carre's novel features screenwriter Pierson's debut as a director. The film is somewhat of a disappointment from the man who wrote CAT BALLOU and COOL HAND LUKE. Jones is a Polish refugee recruited by the head of British Intelligence, Richardson, to go into East Germany to verify the existence of missile sites. A German pilot had taken pictures, but he was murdered and the negatives lost. He is trained and then dropped across the East German border. He kills a guard and forgets to turn off his radio, which sends troops close on his heels. He takes a ride with a truck driver who threatens to turn him in if he doesn't have sex with him. Jones kills him and takes the truck. He picks up Degermark and her small son, and when he tries to send another radio message, the Germans track the signal and kill Jones and the woman. Degermark starred in the Swedish film, ELVIRA MADIGAN and Jones' first major role was in WILD IN THE STREETS.

p, John Box; d&w, Frank R. Pierson (based on the novel by John Le Carre); ph, Austin Dempster (Panavision, Technicolor); m, Wally Stott; ed, Willy Kemplen; art d, Terence Marsh; set d, Henry Federer, cos, Dinah Greet; m/l, "Fly Away, Love," Stott; makeup, Ernest Gasser.

Spy Drama   **Cas.**   **(PR:C MPAA:M)**

LOOKING ON THE BRIGHT SIDE**

(1932, Brit.) 81m Associated Talking Pictures/RKO bw

Gracie Fields (Gracie), Richard Dolman (Laurie), Julian Rose (Oscar Schultz), Wyn Richmond (Miss Joy), Tony de Lungo (Delmonico), Betty Shale (Hetty Hunt), Viola Compton (Sergeant), Bettina Montahners.

Fields plays a manicurist who falls in love wtih song-writing hairdresser Dolman, who is, unfortunately, in love with a glamorous singer. Generally considered to be Fields first major film hit.

p, Basil Dean; d, Dean, Graham Cutts; w, Dean, Archie Pitt, Brock Williams; ph, Robert Martin.

Musical   **(PR:A MPAA:NR)**

LOOKING UP**

(1977) 94m First American/Levitt-Pickman c

Marilyn Chris (Rose Lander), Dick Shawn (Manny Lander), Doris Belack (Libby Levine), Harry Goz (Sy Levine), Jacqueline Brookes (Becky), Naomi Riseman (Grandma), Will Hussing (Grandpa), Neva Small (Myra), George Reinholt (Stan), Gillian Goll (Ann Reeny), Ellen Sherman (Francine Levine), Susan McKinley (Barbara Lander), Anthony Mannino (Larry), Paul Lieber (Michael Lander), Paul Christopoulos (David Lander), Lee Wilson (Judy), Estelle Harris (Irma), Izzy Singer (Gene), Barry Burns (Harvey), Michael Vale (Sweedler), Andrew Smith (Burger Crown Man), Jack Weissbluth (Lou), Barbara Andress (Natalie), Ruth Franklin (Bernice), Miguel Pinero, Dadi Pinero, Lefty (Muggers), Jacqueline Tuteur (Checkout Girl), June Berry (Phyllis), Sally DeMay (Gussie), Edith Weissbluth (Mrs. G.), Jill Weissbluth (Genevieve), Sarah Phillips (Mrs. Combs), Ted Butler (Walter), Frederica Minte (Antique Customer), Joshua Freund (Jaymen), Ginger James (Cory), Gizella Mittleman (Lady in Window).

A soap opera-like, low-budget film about three generations of a modern middle-class New York Jewish family. Most of the cast are soap opera actors. Chris, the main character, tries to get a fast food franchise to help her husband's seltzer business. In addition, she must contend with a daughter popping pills and the care of her daughter's two neglected children. One of her sisters has a husband who is indicted in a real estate scam which destroys the marriage prospects for their daughter. To top it off, Chris discovers that her own husband fathered her sister's daughter. Of course what makes soap operas watchable is the engaging characters, and this is where the film fails hands down.

p, Linda Yellen, Karen Rosenburg; d, Yellen; w, Jonathan Platnick; ph, Arpad Makay, Lloyd Friedas (Movielab Color); m, Brad Fiedel; ed, John Carter; art d, John Annus; m/l, "Rose's Theme," Fiedel (sung by Robin Green).

Drama   **(PR:C MPAA:PG)**

LOOKS AND SMILES***

(1982, Brit.) 104m Black Lion-Kestrel-MK2/Artificial Eye bw

Phil Askham, Pam Darrell, Graham Green, Tracey Goodlad, Stuart Golland, Patti Nichols, Tony Pitts, Arthur Davies, Cilla Mason, Carolyn Nicholson, Les Hickin, Roy Haywood, Ted Beyer, Jackie Shinn, Ernest Johns, Rita May, Christine Francis, Marie Mason, Curtis May, Paul Tuke.

Powerful, gritty little drama shot in a documentary style about two high-school dropouts who are faced with the choice of going into the military or going on public aid. One of the boys enlists and finds himself in Belfast where he begins terrorizing Catholics; the other stays home and becomes increasingly destitute as he tries to find work. The cast are all amateurs, the visual style stunningly realistic. The result is a forceful examination of human waste.

p, Irving Teitelbaum; d, Kenneth Loach; w, Barry Hines; ph, Chris Menges; m, Marc Wilkinson, Richard & The Taxmen; ed, Steve Singleton; art d, Martin Johnson.

Drama   **(PR:C MPAA:NR)**

LOONIES ON BROADWAY

(SEE: ZOMBIES ON BROADWAY, 1945)

LOOPHOLE*1/2

(1954) 79m AA bw

Barry Sullivan (Mike Donovan), Charles McGraw (Gus Slavin), Dorothy Malone (Ruthie Donovan), Don Haggerty (Neil Sanford), Mary Beth Hughes (Vera), Don Beddoe (Herman Tate), Dayton Lummis (Mr. Starling), Joanne Jordan (Georgia), John Eldredge (Mr. Temple), Richard Reeves (Pete Mazurki).

Gentle Beddoe works at a bank as a teller. He walks into another bank and masquerades as one of the bank examiners. In doing so, he steals about $50,000 from Sullivan's station. Sullivan waits until the following Monday to report the loss and his bank manager, police officer Haggerty and even the federal agents believe he's innocent. But McGraw, the private eye who works for the bonding company that insures the bank, thinks Sullivan is lying. He trails Sullivan and makes sure that

Sullivan can not be bonded so the man is out of a job. Sullivan tries to find other employment but each time he gets it, McGraw arrives and says that Sullivan is a suspected criminal. Sullivan secures work as a cab driver and one day, he and his wife, Malone, are going to their bank when Sullivan recognizes Beddoe as the man who filched the lucre. Sullivan muscles Beddoe back to his apartment while pretending to want a piece of the action. Then Hughes, Beddoe's sweetie, arrives and is about to kill Sullivan. McGraw has been on Sullivan's heels the whole time and he arrives to break things up but he refuses to believe that Sullivan was tailing the crooks, not part of them. Sullivan gets away and follows Beddoe and Hughes to a Malibu beach house, now knowing that it's an ambush. Sullivan calls Haggerty who sends the police out, then Sullivan goes inside the house and Hughes insists that he hand over the money Beddoe gave him earlier. Beddoe has a gun and Hughes, a femme fatale if there ever was one, insists that Beddoe shoot Sullivan. He is not that kind of guy and won't do it so Hughes grabs the gun and plugs Beddoe and Sullivan but only wings our hero. He's able to wrest the gun away and hold her down until the Blue Knights arrive. In the end, Sullivan gets his old job back but we are left with a strange conclusion when we see McGraw standing off to the side and watching Sullivan. A fairly ordinary picture with not enough style to make it unusual, LOOPHOLE wouldn't even make a good TV movie these days.

p, Lindsley Parsons; d, Harold Schuster; w, Warren Douglas (based on a story by George Bricker, Dwight V. Babcock); ph, William Sickner; m, Paul Dunlap; ed, Ace Herman; art d, David Milton; set d, Ben Bone; makeup, Ted Larsen.

Crime Drama   **(PR:A MPAA:NR)**

LOOPHOLE*

(1981, Brit.) 105m Brent Walker c

Albert Finney (Mike Daniels), Martin Sheen (Stephen Booker), Susannah York (Dinah Booker), Colin Blakely (Gardner), Jonathan Pryce (Taylor), Alfred Lynch (Harry), Christopher Guard (Cliff), Robert Morley (Godfrey), Terence Hardiman (David), Bridget Brice (Emily), Ian Howarth (Matthew), Harriet Collins (Sarah), Gwyneth Powell (Doreen), Tony Doyle (Nolan), Jerry Harte (Maxwell), James Grout (Fairbrother).

Finney and Sheen, despite their talents, can't make this a worthwhile film. Finney has pulled together a group of thieves to pull off a heist on a large London bank. Sheen, an architect, joins the criminals to get himself out of debt. No surprises or anything original in this insubstantial script.

p, David Korda, Julian Holloway; d, John Quested; w, Jonathan Hales (based on the novel by Robert Pollock); ph, Michael Reed; m, Lalo Schifrin; ed, Ralph Sheldon; prod d, Syd Cain.

Crime Drama   **Cas.**   **(PR:C MPAA:NR)**

LOOSE ANKLES**1/2

(1930) 66m FN-WB bw

Loretta Young (Ann Harper Berry), Douglas Fairbanks, Jr. (Gil Hayden), Louise Fazenda (Aunt Sarah Harper), Ethel Wales (Aunt Katherine Harper), Otis Harlan (Maj. Rupert Harper), Daphne Pollard (Agnes), Inez Courtney (Betty), Norman Douglas Selby (Terry), Eddie Nugent (Andy), Raymond Keane (Linton).

Young will inherit a large sum of money from her grandmother if she follows the terms stated in the will. She must marry a man with a clean background and a good name, who can win the approval of her aunts. Young must also stay out of trouble herself, and for no good reason she doesn't follow any of the rules. She advertises for a man and her only taker is Fairbanks. They fall in love and Young does want to marry, but her aunts balk because Fairbanks is a gigolo. They change their tune when Fairbanks' friends threaten to reveal the time they escorted the aunts to a raided cafe.

d, Ted Wilde; w, Gene Towne (based on the play by Sam Janney); ph, Arthur Todd; ch, Roy Mack; m/l, "Loose Ankles," "Whoopin' It Up," Meskill, Wendling.

Comedy   **(PR:A MPAA:NR)**

LOOSE ENDS*1/2

(1930, Brit.) 84m BIP bw

Edna Best (Nina Grant), Owen Nares (Malcolm Ferres), Miles Mander (Raymond Carteret), Adrianne Allen (Brenda Fallon), Donald Calthrop (Winton Penner), Edna Davies (Deborah Price), Sybil Arundale (Sally Britt), J. Fisher White (Stranger), Gerard Lyley (Cyril Gayling).

An unimaginative drawing-room drama about a girl reporter who finds herself blackmailed after learning that Nares served a 15-year sentence for murdering his sister's betrayer.

d, Norman Walker; w, Dion Titherage, Walker (based on the play by Titherage); ph, Claude Friese-Greene; ed, S. Simmons, Emile DeAuelle.

Crime   **(PR:A MPAA:NR)**

LOOSE ENDS*1/2

(1975) 103m American Eagle-Fat Chance/Bauer International bw

Chris Mulkey (Billy Regis), John Jenkins (Eddie Hassit), Linda Jenkins (Jenny Hassit), Bobby Jenkins (Jason Hassit), Irv Fink (Mr. Farrell), Karlos Ozols (Drunk), Gerald Drake (Grocery Clerk), Judith Poplinski (Waitress), Christian Mulkey, Sr. (Shop Foreman), Pamela LaVarre (Girl in Jaguar), Faye Gallos (Nightclub Dancer), Darlette Engelmeier, Ruby Tuesday (Pickups), S. R. Griffis, Bill Tilton (Pool Players), Bret Larson, Bucky Jandrich (Bar Toughs).

A low budget, independent film about two beer-drinking, pool playing mechanics who grow tired of their lives. Jenkins is married, with one child and another on the way; his buddy Mulkey is divorced, and would like the two of them to break out and start over. Jenkins is unhappy with his home life, and when his wife yells at him for buying a Great Dane for his son, he packs up and leaves with Mulkey. Half way to another city, Jenkins changes his mind and goes back to his family. Why he changes his mind is left murky, like the despair the hero allows himself to settle into.

p, Victoria Wozniak; d, David Burton Morris; w, Morris, Wozniak; ph, Gregory M. Cummins; m, John Paul Hammond; ed, G. M. Cummins; art d, Ann Morris.

Drama (PR:C MPAA:NR)

LOOSE IN LONDON**½ (1953) 62 m AA/MON bw

Leo Gorcey (Slip), Huntz Hall (Sach), David Gorcey (Chuck), Bernard Gorcey (Louie), John Dodsworth (Sir Edgar Whipsnade), Norma Varden (Aunt Agatha), William Cottrell (Reggie), Angela Greene (Lady Marcia), Rex Evans (Herbert), Walter Kingsford (Earl of Walsingham), James Logan (Hoskins, Butler), Alex Frazer (Higby, Solicitor), Joan Shawlee (Tall Girl), James Fairfax (Steward), Wilbur Mack (Sir Talbot), Bennie Bartlett (Butch), Charles Keane (Bly), Clyde Cook (Taxi Driver), Teddy Mangean (Skinny Man), Gertrude Astor (Lady Hightower), Matthew Boulton (Ames), Charles Wagenheim (Pierre).

Lawyers discover Hall is related to a terminally ill British earl. Hall, Gorcey, and the boys go to London and discover that relatives are poisoning the earl, Dodsworth. When Hall tells Dodsworth, he is made sole heir of his estate, but a messenger shows up with a letter stating there is not any relation between the two. One of the funnier Bowery Boys films thanks to director Bernds, who cowrote the screenplay with Ullman. (See BOWERY BOYS series, Index.)

p, Ben Schwalb; d, Edward Bernds; w, Elwood Ullman, Bernds; ph, Harry Neumann; ed, John C. Fuller; md, Marlin Skiles; art d, David Milton; spec eff, Ray Mercer; makeup, Eddie Polo.

Comedy (PR:A MPAA:NR)

LOOSE PLEASURES

(SEE: TIGHT SKIRTS, LOOSE PLEASURES, 1966, Fr.)

LOOSE SHOES** (1980) 74m Brooksfilm/Atlantic c (AKA: COMING ATTRACTIONS)

Lewis Arquette (Warden), Danny Dayton (Bartender), Buddy Hackett (Himself), Ed Lauter (Sheriff), Jaye P. Morgan (Stop-it Nurse), Bill Murray (Lefty), Avery Schreiber (Theatre Manager), Susan Tyrrell (Boobies), Murphy Dunne (Tough G.I.), Howard Hesseman (Ernie Piles), Ira Miller (Blind Stranger), Misty Rowe (Louise), Steve Landesberg (Duddy Allen), Pamela Hottman, Gary Owens, Roger Peltz, Harry Shearer, Gary Goodrow (Narrator).

Hit-or-miss spoof of movie trailers featuring "Saturday Night Live" alumni Murray and Shearer in small roles. Patterned after other successful comedy anthologies such as KENTUCKY FRIED MOVIE and TUNNELVISION, LOOSE SHOES has a few moments of genuine hilarity. Highlights include: "The Last Mile" with Murray; "Skateboarders From Hell" a parody of biker films; "Welcome To Bacon County"; a parody of Woody Allen entitled "Sneakers"; and the funniest segment "Dark Town After Dark," a sepia-colored tribute to the black musicals of the 1930s. Technically crude at times, LOOSE SHOES has enough originality to merit a look.

p, Joel Chernoff; d, Ira Miller; w, Varley Smith, Ian Paiser, Royce D. Applegate, Miller; ph, John P. Beckett (CFI color); m, Murphy Dunne; ed, Alan Balsam; art d, Mike McCloskey; ch, Ceil Gruessing; animation, Phil Savenick, Suzan Green.

Comedy (PR:C MPAA:R)

LOOT*** (1971, Brit.) 101m Performing Arts/Cinevision c

Richard Attenborough (Inspector Truscott), Lee Remick (Fay), Hywel Bennett (Dennis), Roy Holder (Hal McLeavy), Milo O'Shea (Mr. McLeavy), Dick Emery (Mr. Bateman), Joe Lynch (Father O'Shaughnessy), John Cater (Meadows), Aubrey Woods (Undertaker), Enid Lowe (W.V.A. Leader), Andonia Katsaros (Police-woman), Harold Innocent (Bank Manager), Kevin Brennan (Vicar), Jean Marlow (Mrs. McLeavy), Robert Raglan (Doctor), Hal Galili, Douglas Ridley, Adrian Correger, Edwin Finn (Pallbearers).

An enjoyable comedy in which Bennett and Holder pull off a bank heist and hide the money in Holder's mother's coffin. Bennett is an undertaker at a funeral parlor next to the bank and the two blow a hole in the wall and grab the money. When they try to hide the money in the coffin, they discover that both the money and Holder's mother will not fit. So, they put the money in the coffin and mom in the bathroom. They keep moving the body until it ends up in the hotel owned by Holder's father, O'Shea. Police inspector Attenborough shows up and so does money-hungry Remick, who is sleeping with Bennett and trying to marry O'Shea. Attenborough thinks she is the woman who killed seven of her previous husbands. In the end Holder and Remick admit to their crimes, Remick's being that she killed O'Shea's wife.

p, Arthur Lewis; d, Silvio Narizzano; w, Ray Galton, Alan Simpson (based on the play by Joe Orton); ph, Austin Dempster (Eastmancolor); ed, Martin Charles; art d, Anthony Pratt; set d, Terence Morgan II; cos, Brian Cox; m/l, Keith Mansfield, Richard Willing-Denton (songs sung by Steve Ellis).

Comedy (PR:C MPAA:PG)

LOOTERS, THE** (1955) 87m UNIV bw

Rory Calhoun (Jesse Hill), Julie Adams (Sheryl Gregory), Ray Danton (Pete Corder), Thomas Gomez (George Parkinson), Frank Faylen (Stan Leppich), Rod Williams (Co-Pilot), Russ Conway (Maj. Knowles), John Stephenson (Stevenson), Emory Parnell (Joe, Sr.), James Parnell (Joe, Jr.).

Calhoun and his army buddy Danton climb Pike's Peak to rescue the survivors of a plane crash. Adams, a nude model; Faylen, a Navy petty officer; Gomez, a brokerage clerk; and the injured co-pilot, Williams are the only survivors. Two hundred and fifty thousand dollars also survives the crash and Danton teams with Gomez and forces his buddy to lead them back down the mountain. Danton plans to kill everyone when they are out of the wilderness. Calhoun leads them to an Army artillery target field and battles it out with Danton. The money is returned to the owners and Adams decides to live with Calhoun.

p, Howard Christie; d, Abner Biberman; w, Richard Alan Simmons (based on a story by Paul Schneider); ph, Lloyd Ahern; m, Joseph Gershenson; ed, Russell Schoengarth; art d, Alexander Golitzen, Alfred Sweeney.

Action/Adventure (PR:A MPAA:NR)

L'OR ET L'AMOUR (SEE: GREAT DAY IN THE MORNING, 1956)

LORD BABS** (1932, Brit.) 65m Gainsborough/Ideal bw

Bobby Howes (Lord Basil "Babs" Drayford), Jean Colin (Nurse Foster), Pat Paterson (Helen Parker), Alfred Drayton (Ambrose Parker), Arthur Chesney (Mr. Turpin), Clare Greet (Mrs. Parker), Hugh Dempster (Dr. Neville), Joseph Cunningham (Chief Steward), Walter Forde.

Howes stars in this musical comedy as a ship's steward who inherits an earldom and the accompanying fortune. He is less than enthusiastic about the prospect and is persuaded by his friend Dempster to pretend he has reverted back to his youth. By doing so he also is able to dump his fiancee Paterson.

p, Michael Balcon; d, Walter Forde; w, Clifford Grey, Angus Macphail, Sidney Gilliat (based on the play by Keble Howard); ph, Leslie Rowson.

Musical/Comedy (PR:A MPAA:NR)

LORD BYRON OF BROADWAY** (1930) 66m MGM bw/c

Charles Kaley (Roy), Ethelind Terry (Ardis), Marion Shilling (Nancy), Cliff Edwards (Joe), Gwen Lee (Bessie), Benny Rubin (Phil), Drew Demarest (Edwards), John Byron (Mr. Millaire), Rita Flynn (Red Head), Hazel Craven (Blondie), Gino Corrado (Riccardi), Paulette Paquet (Marie).

Kaley is a composer who bounces through relationships just to get another hit song. This process goes on until he meets Shilling whom Kaley eventually marries. Kaley and Terry, Broadway stars, make their film debut and exit with this box-office flop. In the musical sequence "Blue Daughter Of Heaven" overhead shots were used, a year before Busby Berkeley would. Also, two musical scenes were shot in Technicolor. Songs include, "A Bundle Of Love Letters," "Should I," "The Woman In The Shoe," "Only Love Is Real," "When I Met You," "You're The Bride And I'm The Groom" (Arthur Freed, Nacio Herb Brown), "Love Ain't Nothing But The Blues" (Joe Goodwin, Louis Alter), "Blue Daughter Of Heaven" (Dimitri Tiomkin, Raymond B. Eagan).

d, William Nigh, Harry Beaumont; w, Crane Wilbur, Willard Mack (based on the novel by Nell Martin); ph, Henry Sharp (Technicolor); ed, Anne Bauchens; ch, Sammy Lee.

Musical (PR:A MPAA:NR)

LORD CAMBER'S LADIES** (1932, Brit.) 80m BIP bw

Gerald du Maurier (Dr. Napier), Gertrude Lawrence (Shirley Neville), Benita Hume (Janet King), Nigel Bruce (Lord Camber), Clare Greet (Peach), A. Bromley Davenport (Sir Bedford Slufter), Betty Norton (Hetty), Harold Meade (Ainley), Hugh E. Wright (Old Man), Hal Gordon (Stage Manager), Molly Lamont (Actress).

Hume runs a florist's store and falls in love with Bruce, a regular customer. He is trapped into marriage with an actress, Lawrence. Heartbroken, Hume becomes a nurse. One day Bruce's wife shows up, accuses Hume of having an affair wtih her husband, and dies. Bruce and Hume are charged with the woman's death, but they are found innocent and the two are able to begin their romance.

p, Alfred Hitchcock; d, Benn W. Levy; w, Levy, Gilbert Wakefield, Edwin Greenwood (based on "The Case of Lady Camber" by Horace Annesley Vachell); ph, James Wilson.

Drama (PR:A MPAA:NR)

LORD EDGEWARE DIES** (1934, Brit.) 81m REA/RKO bw

Austin Trevor (Hercule Poirot), Jane Carr (Lady Edgeware), Richard Cooper (Capt. Hastings), John Turnbull (Inspector Japp), Michael Shepley (Capt. Ronald Marsh), Leslie Perrins (Bryan Martin), C. V. France (Lord Edgeware), Esme Percy (Duke of Merton).

Fair adaptation of an Agatha Christie murder mystery has Trevor in the role of one of her favorite detectives, Poirot. When an aging and wealthy aristocrat is the victim of foul play, all evidence points to Carr, the young wife who obviously wanted his money for herself. With what seems like the greatest of ease, Trevor proves this not to be the case at all.

p, Julius Hagen; d, Henry Edwards; w, H. Fowler Mear (based on the novel by Agatha Christie); ph, Sydney Blythe.

Mystery (PR:A MPAA:NR)

LORD JEFF**½ (1938) 78m MGM bw (GB: THE BOY FROM BARNADO'S)

Freddie Bartholomew (Geoffrey Braemer), Mickey Rooney (Terry O'Mulvaney), Charles Coburn (Capt. Briggs), Herbert Mundin ("Crusty" Jelks), Terry Kilburn (Albert Baker), Gale Sondergaard (Doris Clandon), Peter Lawford (Benny Potter), Walter Tetley (Tommy Thrums), Peter Ellis (Ned Saunders), George Zucco (Jim Hampstead), Matthew Boulton (Inspector Scott), John Burton (John Cartwright), Emma Dunn (Mrs. Briggs), Monty Woolley (Jeweler), Gilbert Emery (Magistrate), Charles Irwin (Mr. Burke), Walter Kingsford (Superintendent).

Bartholomew is sent to the Russell-Cotes merchant marine training school after being arrested as an accessory to a jewel robbery. The boy rebels at first, but with the help of his classmates, Bartholomew gets an apprenticeship with the Queen Mary and captures the jewel thieves.

p, Frank Davis; d, Sam Wood; w, James K. McGuinness (based on a story by Bradford Ropes, Val Burton, Endre Bohem); ph, John Seitz; m, Edward Ward; ed, Frank E. Hill; art d, Cedric Gibbons.

Drama (PR:AA MPAA:NR)

LORD JIM**** (1965, Brit.) 154m COL c

Peter O'Toole *(Lord Jim)*, James Mason *(Gentleman Brown)*, Curt Jurgens *(Cornelius)*, Eli Wallach *(The General)*, Jack Hawkins *(Marlow)*, Paul Lukas *(Stein)*, Akim Tamiroff *(Schomberg)*, Daliah Lavi *(The Girl)*, Ichizo Itami *(Waris)*, Tatsuo Saito *(Chief Du-Ramin)*, Eric Young *(Malay)*, Andrew Keir *(Brierly)*, Jack MacGowran *(Robinson)*, Walter Gotell *(Captain of the S.S. 'Patna')*, Noel Chester *(Capt. Chester)*, Serge Reggiani *(French Lieutenant)*, Rafik Anwar *(Moslem Leader)*, Marne Maitland *(Elder)*, Newton Blick *(Doctor)*, Christian Marquand *(French Officer)*.

A stunning exotic filming of Conrad's classic sees O'Toole superbly convey the character of the title role. He serves an apprenticeship at sea under the protective eye of Hawkins and later graduates to first officer of a tramp liner, the *Patna*, loaded with religious passengers in an awful passage where the ship is mercilessly lashed by a hurricane. In a moment of desperation, the idealistic O'Toole abandons the ship and leaves its passengers to their fate. The ship survives, however, with many passengers drowned and O'Toole loses his license and sinks into waterfront obscurity, his spiritual mortification complete. To redeem himself, O'Toole agrees to take a shipment of dynamite from Lukas and deliver it to a tribe of natives in uncharted territory. The tribe is in bondage to feudal warlord Wallach who oppresses them at will. Surviving ambushes and treachery from his own crew members, O'Toole manages to get the explosives to the settlement and hide the barrels, exploding one to make Wallach and his henchmen believe that the entire shipment has been destroyed. Wallach captures O'Toole and tortures him inside his fortress but native girl Lavi helps him escape. He joins the natives and organizes an attack on the fortress, a seesaw battle that finally sees O'Toole and the natives triumph and Wallach killed. Jurgens, however, escapes to join river pirate Mason and they muster their forces to return to the fortress to obtain Wallach's fabulous cache of jewels, stolen from the natives, of course. O'Toole greets the thieves with a cannon shot that decimates them but the son of the native chief is killed in the encounter and, to make up for his death to the native chief, O'Toole nobly sacrifices his own life at the finish. Beautifully photographed by Young and tightly directed by Brooks, LORD JIM is both moving and suspenseful, without losing any of the literate and psychological nature of the original story. Shot on location in Cambodia and Hong Kong.

p,d&w, Richard Brooks (based on the novel by Joseph Conrad); ph, Freddie Young (Super Panavision, Technicolor); m, Bronsilau Kaper; ed, Alan Osbiston; prod d, Geoffrey Drake; md, Muir Matheson; art d, Bill Hutchinson, Ernest Archer; cos, Phyllus Dalton; spec eff, Cliff Richardson; makeup, Charles Parker.

Historical Drama/Adventure Cas. (PR:A MPAA:NR)

LORD LOVE A DUCK*** (1966) 105m Charleston Enterprises/UA bw

Roddy McDowall *(Alan "Mollymauk" Musgrave)*, Tuesday Weld *(Barbara Ann Greene)*, Lola Albright *(Marie Green)*, Martin West *(Bob Barnard)*, Ruth Gordon *(Stella Barnard)*, Harvey Korman *(Weldon Emmett)*, Sarah Marshall *(Miss Schwartz)*, Lynn Carey *(Sally Grace)*, Max Showalter *(Howard Greene)*, Donald Murphy *(Phil Neuhauser)*, Joseph Mell *(Dr. Lippman)*, Dan Frazer *(Used Car Salesman)*, Martine Bartlett *(Inez)*, Jo Collins *(Kitten)*, Hal Baylor *(Jack)*, Laurie Mitchell *(Jack's Wife)*, David Draper *(Billy Gibbons)*, Donald Foster *(Mr. Beverly)*, Judith Loomis *(Mrs. Butch Neuhauser)*, Martin Gabel *(Harry Belmont)*.

A wacky satire/black comedy with high-school senior McDowall helping schoolmate Weld get whatever she desires. McDowall's I.Q. is so high that he knows what everyone wants before they speak. He gets Weld into the sorority of her choice and insures that she will get good grades by getting her a secretarial job with the high school principal, Korman. She meets West, a rich college senior, at a sex seminar at a drive-in church. Weld is tested for a beach party movie with West's help, but problems arise when West's mother, Gordon, doesn't approve of Weld. McDowall fixes that by introducing Gordon to booze. Weld's mother, Albright, kills herself when she thinks she has ruined her daughter's relationship and life. Weld and West marry and he becomes a marriage counselor. When he objects to his wife's movie career, McDowall decides to get rid of him. His attempts fail until he runs him over at the high school graduation with a bulldozer (killing everyone on the speaker's platform as well). The film is told in flashback with McDowall in the prison psychiatric wing telling his story to a tape recorder. Directed by the man who wrote THE SEVEN YEAR ITCH and WILL SUCCESS SPOIL ROCK HUNTER?

p&d, George Axelrod; w, Axelrod, Larry H. Johnson (based on a novel by Al Hine); ph, Daniel L. Fapp; m, Neal Hefti; ed, William A. Lyon; art d, Malcolm Brown; set d, Raphael Bretton; cos, Paula Giokaris; spec eff, Herman Townsley; m/l, Ernie Sheldon, Hefti; makeup, Lou Hippe; title song sung by The Wild Ones.

Comedy (PR:A MPAA:NR)

LORD MOUNTDRAGO (SEE: THREE CASES OF MURDER, 1955)

LORD OF THE FLIES** (1963, Brit.) 90m Allen-Hogdon-Two Arts/CD bw

James Aubrey *(Ralph)*, Tom Chapin *(Jack)*, Hugh Edwards *(Piggy)*, Roger Elwin *(Roger)*, Tom Gaman *(Simon)*, The Surtees Twins *(Sam and Eric)*, Roger Allen, David Brunjes, Peter Davy, Kent Fletcher, Nicholas Hammond, Christopher Harris, Alan Heaps, Jonathan Heaps, Burnes Hollyman, Andrew Horne, Richard Horne, Timothy Horne, Erik Jordan, Peter Ksiezopolski, Anthony McCall-Hudson, Malcolm Rodker, David St. Clair, Rene Sanfiorenzo, Jr., Jeremy Scuse, John Stableford, Nicholas Valkenburg, Patrick Valkenburg, Edward Valencia, John Walsh, David Walsh, Jeremy Willis.

Disappointing rendition of the Golding novel with overacting and poor direction on Brook's part. It's some time in the near future and a plane carrying some wealthy British school boys is flown out of London as a war is about to erupt. Their plane is going to the safety of the South Pacific and crashes on a remote island (actually, it was Puerto Rico and Vieques in the Caribbean). None of the adults makes it to shore and 40 of the boys are left to fend for themselves. Aubrey is made the leader and the lads begin to set up a sub-society so they can survive until rescued. Aubrey takes myopic Edwards' spectacles and uses them to start a fire with the sun's rays that might be seen from the sky. Chapin, the toughest of the lot, names himself as the great white hunter and leads the boys on a boar hunt. They catch and kill a pig, slice off its head and put that on a pointed stick which they point to the "beast" on the top of the mountain. That creature is actually the dead body of the airplane pilot who parachuted from the plane and died in the process. The boys are a microcosm of society and eventually two different groups emerge, one led by Aubrey, the other by Chapin. The factions split and Chapin leads the boys who dress up as Indians and paint their faces like savages. These once-mannered boys are becoming increasingly feral, worse than any mad pygmies one might find. Their dancing is frenzied as they chant and initiate rituals. Then Gaman, one of the quiet lads in the other group, arrives to tell them that the "beast" has been discovered to be their late pilot but they kill Gaman in a blood-letting. Next, they murder Edwards, a defenseless fat boy, and they refuse to believe that the "beast" is not a beast. They now plan to kill Aubrey and use him as a sacrifice to appease their new god. There's a chase across the small island and they are stopped short of another murder when a rescue group appears. They suddenly realize what they've done and cease chasing Aubrey, then they begin crying, like the little boys they were before all this happened. It was a provocative idea but so overwrought that, in the end, it was hardly more than a pre-teen version of MOST DANGEROUS GAME or THE ISLAND OF DR. MOREAU. In his haste to get to the savagery, Brook neglected to honestly motivate their actions and the result left audiences wondering how it could have come to pass that this meek melange of youngsters could have become evil so quickly. Pre-teeners, the very group they were portraying, found little to warrant word-of-mouth and the picture sank in a morass of its own pseudo-philosophy.

p, Lewis Allen; d&w, Peter Brook (based on the novel by William Golding); ph, Tom Hollyman; m, Raymond Leppard; ed, Brook, Gerald Feil, Jean-Claude Lubtchansky.

Drama Cas. (PR:A-C MPAA:NR)

LORD OF THE JUNGLE* (1955) 69m AA bw

Johnny Sheffield *(Bomba)*, Wayne Morris *(Jeff Woods)*, Nancy Hale *(Mona Andrews)*, Paul Picerni *(Paul Gavin)*, William Phipps *(Kenny Balou)*, Smoki Whitfield *(Eli)*, Leonard Mudie *(Com. Andy Barnes)*, James Adamson *(Elisha)*, Harry Lauter *(Pilot)*, Joel Fluellen *(Molu)*, Juanita Moore *(Molu's Wife)*.

No it's not about Tarzan, it's the last of the BOMBA THE JUNGLE BOY movies starring Sheffield who finally decided to retire the role at the age of 24. In this final outing Sheffield is ordered to slaughter some wild elephants that have been trampling the local natives. However the Jungle Boy can't bring himself to destroy the entire herd, instead doing away with only the leader who started all the problems. (See BOMBA series, Index.)

p,d&w Ford Beebe (based on characters created by Roy Rockwood in the "Bomba" books); ph, Harry Neumann; ed, Neil Brunnenkant; md, Marlin Skiles; art d, David Milton.

Adventure (PR:A MPAA:NR)

LORD OF THE MANOR** ½** (1933, Brit.) 71m British and Dominions/PAR bw

Betty Stockfeld *(Barbara Fleeter)*, Fred Kerr *(Sir Henry Bovey)*, Harry [Henry] Wilcoxon *(Jim Bridge)*, Kate Cutler *(Lady Bovey)*, Frank Bertram *(George Tover)*, Joan Marion *(Kitty Carvell)*, April Dawn *(Lily Tover)*, Deering Wells *(Robert Bovey)*, David Horne *(Gen. Sir George Fleeter)*, Frederick Ross.

A decent romantic comedy in which the proposed marriage of two aristocrats, an engagement not made in heaven but in the local club, goes awry when the prospective mates fall for members of the lower class. Along with all the laughs are some insightful jabs at social prejudice.

p, Herbert Wilcox; d, Henry Edwards; w, Dorothy Rowan (based on the play by John Hastings Turner); ph, Henry Harris.

Comedy (PR:A MPAA:NR)

LORD OF THE RINGS, THE** ½** (1978) 131m Fantasy Films/UA c

Animator Ralph Bakshi's adaptation of J. R. R. Tolkien's *Lord Of The Rings* trilogy is an entertaining film which keeps faithful to the novels, and that is where the one problem lies. The film tries to squeeze in too much information, and in the process some segments seem shallower than others. The film also ends abruptly, leaving us to believe that a second installment will be coming, but it doesn't look likely. Tolkien fans will enjoy this adaptation and newcomers to the stories will want to pick up the books where the film leaves off. Bakshi's rotoscope technique (animating live action) works well.

p, Saul Zaentz; d, Ralph Bakshi; w, Chris Conkling, Peter S. Beagle (based on the stories by J. R. R. Tolkien); m, Leonard Roseman.

Fantasy Cas. (PR:A MPAA:PG)

LORD RICHARD IN THE PANTRY* ½** (1930, Brit.) 85m Twickenham/WB bw

Richard Cooper *(Lord Richard Sandridge)*, Dorothy Seacombe *(Sylvia Garland)*, Marjorie Hume *(Lady Violet Elliott)*, Leo Sheffield *(Carter)*, Fred Volpe *(Sir Charles Bundleman)*, Barbara Gott *(Cook)*, Alexander Field *(Sam)*, Viola Lyel *(Evelyn Lovejoy)*, Gladys Hamer *(Gladys)*, Charles Stone, Harry Terry, Helena Pickard.

Cooper gets into financial trouble and rents his house to Seacombe, a widow. When he finds that the police have a warrant for his arrest on a framed charge of theft he plays the butler in his own home.

p, Julius Hagen, Henry Edwards; d, Walter Forde; w, H. Fowler Mear (based on a play by Sidney Blow, Douglas Hoare).

Comedy **(PR:A MPAA:NR)**

LORD SHANGO** (1975) 91m Bryanston c

Lawrence Cook *(Jabo)*, Marlene Clark *(Jenny)*, Wally Taylor *(Memphis)*, Bill Overton *(Femi)*, Avis McCarthur *(Billie)*, John Russell *(Rev. Slater)*, Stanley Greene *(Deacon Tibbles)*, B. A. Ward *(Deacon Davis)*, Maurice Woods *(Cult Leader)*, Dwayne Oliver *(Assistant Leader)*, Sandi Franklin *(Bebe)*, Ella Mitchell *(Lead Singer)*, Ethel Ayler *(Lady in Bar)*.

An interesting but flawed horror film dealing with the clash between black Christians and primal African superstitions. A cult priest is drowned when he tries to disrupt a traditional baptism. The young girl, McCarthur, and her mother, Clark, are caught between their Christian beliefs and the Yoruban cultism, and the dead priest who comes back to life. A nonexploitative black horror film that suffered at the box office because of poor marketing.

p, Steve Bono, Ronald Hobbs; d, Raymond Marsh; w, Paul Carter Harrison; ph, Edward Brown (Technicolor); m, Howard Roberts; ed, George Norris; art d, Hank Aldrich.

Horror **(PR:O MPAA:R)**

LORDS OF DISCIPLINE, THE** ½ (1983) 102m PAR c

David Keith *(Will)*, Robert Prosky *(Bear)*, G. D. Spradlin *(Gen. Durrell)*, Barbara Babcock *(Abigail)*, Michael Biehn *(Alexander)*, Rick Rossovich *(Pig)*, John Lavachielli *(Mark)*, Mitchell Lichtenstein *(Trado)*, Mark Breland *(Pearce)*, Malcolm Danare *(Poteete)*, Judge Reinhold *(Macabbee)*, Greg Webb *(Braselton)*, "Wild" Bill Paxton *(Gilbreath)*, Dean Miller *(Gooch)*, Ed Bishop *(Commerce)*, Stuart Milligan *(McIntyre)*, Katharine Levy *(Teresa)*, Jason Connery *(MacKinnon)*, Rolf Saxon *(Rowland)*, Michael Horton *(Bobby)*, Ian Tyler *(Cadet Colonel)*, Tony Sibbald *(TAC Major)*, Norman Chancer *(TAC Captain)*, Ronald Fernee, Michael Fitzpatrick, Richard Oldfield *(TAC Officers)*, Sarah Brackett *(Mrs. Durrell)*, Mary Ellen Ray *(Mrs. Bear)*, Helena Stevens *(Librarian)*, Valerie Colgan *(General's Secretary)*, Matt Frewer, Williams Hope, Peter Hutchinson, Peter Merrill, Sheridan Earl Russell, Simon Shepherd, Aaron Swartz, Graham Cull, Mark Eadie, Tom Fry, Lee Galpin, Dean Lawrence, Martin Phillips, Joe Searby, Christopher Warrick, Nicola King, Sallyanne Law, Elizabeth Morton, Kim Thomson, Sophie Ward, Natasha Fraser.

Military training became the rage after AN OFFICER AND A GENTLEMAN and this film and TAPS were hustled into production. The year is about 1964 and a Southern military academy is "welcoming" the first black cadet, Breland. Most of the other cadets seem to be graduates of the Hitler youth movement, with the exception of Keith. The others begin a routine that rivals Auschwitz. Keith is given the job of looking after Breland to shield him from any difficulties. But there is a group called The Ten who almost kill the new recruit and want nothing more than to castrate Breland. Keith is a senior and takes his job seriously so he enlists pals Rossovich, Lichtenstein, and Lavachielli to try and find out who are The Ten. Their investigation leads them higher and higher in the administration of the school and what we are shown is a miniature Watergate scandal (the parallels are all too obvious). Breland keeps turning the other cheek until one particular scene where he explains why he is taking all this guff from the others in a moment reminiscent of Jackie Robinson's plight when he cracked lily-white major league baseball. While cloaked in the guise of social relevance, THE LORDS OF DISCIPLINE seemed more like an exploitation of it than a condemnation. All acting roles are well-drawn, especially Spradlin, who seems to be making a career out of playing crusty types who run schools (ONE ON ONE, etc). It was shot in London but you'd never know it as this film is as American as Mom's Apple Pie and the Ku Klux Klan. Distasteful, but fascinating, sort of like watching a boa eat a live mouse.

p, Herb Jaffe, Gabriel Katzka; d, Franc Roddam; w, Thomas Pope, Lloyd Fonvielle (based on the novel by Pat Conroy); ph, Brian Tufano (Eastmancolor); m, Howard Blake; ed, Michael Ellis; prod d, John Graysmark; art d, Alan Cassie; set d, Peter Howitt, George DeTitto; cos, John Mollo.

Drama **Cas.** **(PR:O MPAA:R)**

LORDS OF FLATBUSH, THE*** (1974) 86m COL c

Perry King *(Chico)*, Sylvester Stallone *(Stanley Rosiello)*, Henry Winkler *(Butchey Weinstein)*, Paul Mace *(Wimpy Murgalo)*, Susie [Susan] Blakely *(Jane Bradshaw)*, Maria Smith *(Frannie Malincanico)*, Renee Paris *(Annie Yuckamanelli)*, Paul Jabara *(Crazy Cohen)*, Bruce Reed *(Mike)*, Frank Steifel *(Arnie)*, Martin Davidson *(Birnbaum)*, Joe Stern *(Eddie)*, Ruth Klinger *(Mrs. Tyrell)*, Joan Newman *(Miss Molina)*, Dolph Sweet *(Rosiello)*, Lou Byrne *(Mrs. Bradshaw)*, Bill Van Sleet *(Bradshaw)*, Margaret Bauer *(Nancy)*, Lillian Davidson, Ann Lefkowitz, Florence Schissler, Mildred Deutsch *(Mah Jong Players)*, Ralph Rogers Trio *(Wedding Band)*, Ray Sharkey, Geraldine Smith, Darryl Peck, Bernardo Hiller, Karen Kaye, Phyllis Gibbs, Helen Calahan, Dana Foley, Barbara Foley, Thomas Clarke, Bonnie Sylvano, Linda Troiano, Mark Flanagan *(Students)*, Armand Assante, Antonia Rey, Rose Rothman, George Goomishian, Arlene Gelb, Jamie Gelb, Stacy Gelb, Peter Mints, Tom Bauer, David Stein *(Wedding Guests)*.

Anyone who grew up in the Brooklyn of the 1950s will recognize the essential honesty of this picture but it might as well be taking place in Korea for everyone else. It's a rambling movie with a good mix of drama and comedy and served to introduce several actors who went on to much greater fame in other movies. The Lords of Flatbush are a tough street gang, but not one of those groups that pillage and vandalize. Rather, they are a social club, one of thousands in Brooklyn at the time. (The small area of Coney Island had, at least, a dozen alone including The Mariners, The Acwans [A Club Without A Name acronym], the Emanons [Nonames backwards], et al.) Stallone and King are best pals in Brooklyn's Flatbush area (and is there a more ugly name for a neighborhood?). Stallone gets his girl friend, Smith, pregnant then takes her to a local jewelry shop to buy a ring. King's girl friend is Blakely (while she was still "Susie" and not Susan) and she eventually dumps him. In between are several small, but compelling, incidents that serve to truly indicate life in Brooklyn. It's a character piece that wanders and roams from place to place with no single impetus although one gets the feeling that the people behind the film had that in mind. Co-director Verona must like the area because he used it for BRIGHTON BEACH. The actors who distinguished themselves later include: Blakely; Henry Winkler ("Happy Days"); Armand Assante (I, THE JURY); Ray Sharkey (THE IDOLMAKER); Dolph Sweet ("Gimme A Break"); Paul Jabara (who became a songwriter and won an Oscar) and, of course, Stallone, who was making his leading-man debut after an unbilled bit in Woody Allen's BANANAS and a few roles in films that will never reach a Saturday matinee for kids. Co-director Verona eventually became one of the prime movers of music video as well as a best-selling artist. Joe Brooks did the music with some help from Paul Nicholas and Jabara. Brooks will be best remembered (or forgotten) for scripting, producing, directing and writing the song for YOU LIGHT UP MY LIFE.

p, Stephen F. Verona; d, Verona, Martin Davidson; w, Verona, Davidson, Gayle Glecker, Sylvester Stallone; ph, Joseph Mangine, Edward Lachman (Technicolor); m, Joe Brooks, Paul Jabara, Paul Nicholas; ed, Stan Siegel, Muffie Meyer; art d, Glenda Miller.

Drama **(PR:C MPAA:PG)**

LORNA DOONE** (1935, Brit.) 90m Associated Talking Pictures/ABF bw

Victoria Hopper *(Lorna Doone)*, John Loder *(Jan Ridd)*, Margaret Lockwood *(Annie Ridd)*, Roy Emerton *(Carver Doone)*, Mary Clare *(Mistress Ridd)*, Edward Rigby *(Reuben Huckaback)*, Roger Livesey *(Tom Faggus)*, George Curzon *(King James II)*, D. A. Clarke-Smith *(Counsellor Doone)*, Lawrence Hanray *(Parson Bowden)*, Amy Veness *(Betty Muxworthy)*, Eliot Makeham *(John Fry)*, Wyndham Goldie *(Judge Jeffries)*, Frank Cellier *(Jeremy Stickles)*, Herbert Lomas *(Sir Ensor Doone)*, Peggy Blythe, Peter Penrose, Thea Holme, Toska von Bissing, Arthur Hambling, Alexis France, June Holden.

Loder is an English country farmer in the 1600s who seeks revenge on the Doones, a family of criminals who terrorize farmers and settlements. When Loder was a boy, he saw the clan kill his father. He falls in love with Lorna Doone (Hopper), and takes her to live with him on the farm. A St. James court messenger arrives and takes Hopper. She was kidnaped as a baby by the outlaws and raised as one of their own. She goes to the castle to be raised as a proper lady. Loder kills a number of Doones, becomes a knight, marries Hopper and brings her back to his farm.

p&d, Basil Dean; w, Dorothy Farnum, Miles Malleson, Gordon Wellesley (based on the novel by R. D. Blackmore); ph, Bob Martin.

Drama **(PR:A MPAA:NR)**

LORNA DOONE** (1951) 88m COL c

Barbara Hale *(Lorna Doone)*, Richard Greene *(John Ridd)*, Carl Benton Reid *(Sir Ensor Doone)*, William Bishop *(Carver Doone)*, Ron Randell *(Tom Faggus)*, Sean McClory *(Charleworth Doone)*, Onslow Stevens *(Counsellor Doone)*, Lester Matthews *(King Charles II)*, John Dehner *(Baron de Wichehalse)*, Gloria Petroff *(Lorna Doone as a Child)*, Orley Lindgren *(John Ridd as a Child)*, Dick Curtis *(Garth)*, Anne Howard *(Annie Ridd)*, Katherine Warren *(Sarah Ridd)*, Malcolm Keen *(Lord Lorne)*, Queenie Leonard *(Gweeny)*, Trevor Bardette *(Jan Fry)*, Myron Healey *(Todd Darcy)*, Harry Lauter *(Calvin Oates, Jr.)*, Norman Rainey *(Parson Bowden)*, Tudor Owen *(Farmer Snowe)*, Trevor Ward *(Farmer Dyke)*, Betty Fairfax *(Mrs. Lacy)*, Allen Pinson *(Jonas)*, Ted Jordan *(Gurney)*, Glenn Thompson *(Billy)*, Bruce Lester *(Walt Snowe)*, Leonard Mudie *(Cal Oates, Sr.)*, Ray Teal *(Farmer Ridd)*, Fred Graham *(Outrider)*, Paul Collins *(Charleworth as a Child)*, Jerry Mickelsen *(Carver Doone as a Child)*, Sherry Jackson *(Annie Ridd as a Child)*, James Logan *(Farmer)*, Pat Aherne *(Judge Jeffries)*, Wheaton Chambers *(Priest)*, Eric Wilton, Gerald Hamer *(Doctors)*, House Peters, Jr., Bill Hale *(Patrol Leaders)*.

Greene is the English farmer who leads villagers in overthrowing the ruthless Doone family. Hale is the woman with whom he falls in love. She was kidnaped from a royal family and raised by the Doones. After Greene defeats the outlaw family, he marries Hale. A good amount of action in this castle drama.

p, Edward Small; d, Phil Karlson; w, Jesse L. Lasky, Jr., Richard Schayer (based on the novel by Richard D. Blackmore); ph, Charles Van Enger (Technicolor); m, George Duning; ed, Al Clark; md, Morris Stoloff; art d, Harold MacArthur.

Drama **(PR:A MPAA:NR)**

LOS AMANTES DE VERONA
(SEE: ROMEO AND JULIET, 1968, Ital./Span.)

LOS AMIGOS (SEE: DEAF SMITH AND JOHNNY EARS, 1973, Ital.)

LOS ASTRONAUTAS**
(1960, Mex.) 85m Producciones Zacarias bw (AKA: TURISTAS INTERPLANETARIOS; DOS VIAJEROS DEL ESPACIO)

Marco Antonio Campos *(Viruta)*, Gaspar Henaine *(Capulina)*, Gina Romand, Norma Mora, Erna Martha Bauman, Antonio Raxel, Armando Saenz, Tito Novaro, Jorge Casanova, Rica Osorio.

Science fiction comedy starring the Mexican equivalent of Abbott and Costello, Campos and Henaine. The film opens with the planet Venus, which is ruled by women. Trouble arises when the men on the planet demand a bigger share of power because they no longer are allowed to have fun. Two Venusian women, Romand and Mora, are sent to Earth to find men to bring back to Venus as examples of the "old fashioned" male. The aliens choose Campos and Henaine and it is only a matter of time before the two comics have the whole planet in stitches.

p, Mario A. Zacarias; d, Miguel Zacarias; w, Miguel Zacarias, Roberto Gomez Bolanos; ph, Manuel Gomez Urquiza.

Comedy/Science Fiction (PR:A MPAA:NR)

LOS AUTOMATAS DE LA MUERTE*

(1960, Mex.) 80m Estudios America/Producciones Corsa bw

Wolf Ruvinskis (Neutron), Julio Aleman (Caronte), Armando Silvestre, Roberto Ramirez, Rodolfo Landa, Grek Martin, Ernesto Finance, David Lama, Los Tres Ases, Trio Los Diamantes.

The third and final chapter in the Neutron the Black Masked Wrestler trilogy sees our hero pitted against the evil robot army of mad doctor Aleman while the crazed mastermind frantically tries to blackmail the world into surrendering under the threat of his neutron bomb. This film, as are the other two films in the series, NEUTRON EL ENMASCARADO NEGRO and NEUTRON CONTRA EL DR. CARONTE, is bogged down by obnoxious musical interludes.

p, Emilio Gomez Muriel; d, Federico Curiel; w, Alfredo Ruanova; ph, Fernando Alvarez Garces Colin.

Science Fiction (PR:A MPAA:NR)

LOS INVISIBLES* (1961, Mex.) 90m Filmadora Chapultepec bw

Marco Antonio Campos (Viruta), Gaspar Henaine (Capulina), Edouardo Fajardo (Jewel Thief), Martha Elena Cervantes (Susana), Rosa Maria Gallardo (Patricia), Daniel Chino Herrera, Jose Jasso, Chucho Salinas, Lucila de Cordova.

Once again the Mexican Abbott and Costello, Campos and Henaine, romp about in this adventure which sees the duo after a jewel thief. They are aided by a special spray paint, invented by Herrera, that makes people and objects invisible. Though the film was made one full year after the comedy team's LOS ASTRONAUTAS, it was released in the U.S. before it.

p, Pedro Galindo; d, Jaime Salvador; w, Roberto Gomez Bolanos; ph, Jose Ortiz Ramos.

Comedy/Science Fiction (PR:A MPAA:NR)

LOS OLVIDADOS***
(1950, Mex.) 88m Estudios Cinematograficos Del Tepeyac/Mayer-Kingsley bw
(AKA: THE YOUNG AND THE DAMNED)

Estela Inda (The Mother), Alfonso Mejia (Pedro), Roberto Cobo (Jaibo), Jesus Navarro (The Lost Boy), Miguel Inclan (The Blind Man), Alma Fuentes (The Young Girl), Francisco Jambrino (The Principal), Hector Portillo, Salvador Quiros, Victor Manuel Mendoza.

Set in the slums of Mexico City, this ruthless account of "Reckless Youth," whose dismal and directionless existence has become a vicious web from which they cannot escape, marked Bunuel's re-emergence as a prominent filmmaker after a long absence. The two films he made with Salvador Dali, UN CHIEN ANDALOU (1928) and L'AGE D'OR (1930), were both shocking exercises filled with insightful and surrealistic images. Likewise with the semi-documentary LAS HURDES (1932), a devastating account of the depths into which individuals fall when they succumb to the wretchedness of poverty. It is in this vein that LOS OLVIDADOS followed, with a gap of 18 years in which Bunuel made a couple of films of virtually no consequence for the same producer for whom he made this film. Because he was working in a more commercial format than in the earlier productions, the images he depicted had to be much more subdued. However, working in Mexico did allow Bunuel enough freedom to take complete control of the project. Mejia and Cobo are the two youths whose relationship makes up the main thrust of LOS OLVIDADOS. Cobo is the older of the two, his personality having been formed to the point where it cannot change; a selfish and vicious nature that has allowed him to take advantage of those less fortunate than himself will continue with him into manhood, if he makes it that far. At the film's opening, Cobo has just been released from jail, immediately coming back to take control of the gang of boys who hang out in the streets and instigating inane and criminal deeds, something they do not do so much for the needed cash as for the pleasure in seeing those less fortunate than themselves suffer. These include taking a legless man off his cart and leaving him lying helpless on the street, and throwing stones at a blind man who strums his guitar in the plaza to make a few bucks. One of the boys most eager to follow Cobo is the childlike Mejia, whose innocent eyes reveal a spark of goodness lacking in the other boys. Yet he becomes so involved in these sorry deeds that when he does try and set himself in a different direction, he meets with a fatalistic ending at the hands of the boy he had loved. At one point Mejia gets a job to help his mother support her three children. The diligence with which he attends to his job is destroyed when Cobo comes to visit him and steals a knife. Mejia is accused of the crime and sent to a detention center that strives to instill those values the boys need to function in an adult world. They are given a chance to be out in the open air and to learn a bit about wildlife while developing relations between themselves and their adult supervisors that are based upon trust. When one supervisor thinks Mejia has shown dependable qualities, he asks him to run an errand which will require that the boy leave the camp and return later. Once out, Mejia runs into Cobo, who is all set to take advantage of his "friend." He forces the boy to hand over the money the supervisor had given him, and then won't allow Mejia to return to the camp. Mejia remains insistent and makes demands of Cobo, but to no avail. Cobo stresses his will one last time over the boy and Mejia winds up dead. The influence of the Italian neo-realists upon Bunuel is obvious. Shades of BICYCLE THIEF (1949) and OPEN CITY (1946) can be felt in LOS OLVIDADOS, especially themes of the poor and common folk forced into situations they cannot handle regardless of how hard they try. Likewise, Bunuel used mainly nonprofessional actors, was limited in terms of a production budget and shooting schedule, and shot everything in the streets instead of in the studio (an oddity during this period). Yet he differs—and this is what makes LOS OLVIDADOS such a masterpiece—in that he remains objective as the camera records the material.

In this way the viewer is allowed to make a judgment for himself, to investigate what the screen is holding before him without the influence of the filmmaker. Reportedly Bunuel's producer asked him to come up with an idea for a children's film; the director responded with LOS OLVIDADOS. Winner of the 1951 Best Director Award at Cannes Film Festival. (In Spanish; English subtitles.)

p, Oscar Dancigers; d, Luis Bunuel; w, Bunuel, Luis Alcoriza; ph, Gabriel Figueroa; m, Rodolfo Halffter (from the themes of Gustavo Pittaluga); ed, Carlos Savage; set d, Edward Fitzgerald.

Drama Cas. (PR:O MPAA:NR)

LOS PLATILLOS VOLADORES zero

(1955, Mex.) 95m Mier y Brooks bw (AKA: LOS PLATOS VOLADORES)

Adalberto Martinez Resortes (Marciano), Evangelina Elizondo (Saturnina), Andres Soler (Prof. Saldana), Famie Kaufman Vitola, Jose Bronco Venegas, Bertha Lehar, Amalia Aguilar.

Totally vapid Mexican musical comedy starring Resortes and Elizondo as an inventor and his fiancee who have perfected a car with an airplane engine. In the hopes of winning a large prize so they will have enough money to get married, Resortes enters the car in a race. A freak accident lands the couple in a small village where the people look at them as Martians. Soler, a professor, and his colleagues perform a series of tests on the couple and they play along with him while helping the poor villagers. Eventually Resortes and Elizondo confess to Soler that they are not Martians. Soler tells them he knew it all along but could not say anything for fear of bursting the villagers' bubble. As the couple prepare to leave the village for their honeymoon, real Martians arrive and take them away.

p, Felipe Mier, Oscar J. Brooks; d, Julian Soler; w, Carlos Leon, Carlos Orellana, Pedro de Urdimales; ph, Agustin Martinez Solares.

Musical/Science Fiction (PR:A MPAA:NR)

LOSER TAKE ALL (SEE: LEATHER GLOVES, 1948)

LOSER TAKES ALL* (1956, Brit.) 86m BL c

Rossano Brazzi (Bertrand), Glynis Johns (Cary), Robert Morley (Dreuther), Tony Britton (Philip), Felix Aylmer (The Other), Albert Lieven (Hotel Manager), A. E. Matthews (Elderly Man), Joyce Carey (Bird's Nest), Geoffrey Keen (Reception Clerk), Peter Illing (Stranger), Walter Hudd (Arnold), Charles Lloyd Pack (Sir Walter Blixon), Guido Lorraine (Room Waiter), Joan Benham (Miss Bullen), Gloria Ashley (Organino Girl), Carl Bernard (Steward), Mona Washburn (Nurse), Hal Osmond (Liftman), Andre Maranne (Bar Waiter), Andre Mikhelson (Head Waiter), John Moffatt (Barman), Orest Orloff (Casino Barman), Bryan Coleman (Elegant Man at Casino), Murray Kash (Proprietor of Taxi Bar), Shirley Ann Field (Attractive Girl in Salle Privee), Alexis de Galien (Casino Attendant), Marianne Deeming (Hotel Maid), Armand Guinle (Official at Mairir).

Johns and Brazzi are a young British couple planning to get married. Johns' boss, Morley, insists that they be married in Monte Carlo and spend their honeymoon on his yacht. Morley never shows up, the couple's money soon runs out and Johns starts gambling. While Johns is at the tables, Brazzi starts an affair with Britton.

p, John Stafford; d, Ken Annakin; w, Graham Greene (adapted from Greene's novel); ph, Georges Perinal (CinemaScope, Eastmancolor); m, Alessandro Cicognini; ed, Jean Barker.

Comedy (PR:A MPAA:NR)

LOSERS, THE zero (1968) 75m Cleveland Syndicate c

Sandy Roberts (Dena Miller), Jeff Baker (Michael Baron), Miles Mutchler (Samuel Hart), Helen Murray (Florence Hart).

A cheap sexploitation film independently shot in Cleveland for $30,000 features Roberts as a hooker who gets involved with spies when her john is murdered. Baker, a gay ex-cop, helps Roberts to find the killer and $200,000. Sex scenes are tame and the production quality compares with home movies.

p&d, Edward Montoro, James Somich.

Crime Drama (PR:O MPAA:NR)

LOSERS, THE zero (1970) 95m Fanfare c

William Smith (Link Thomas), Bernie Hamilton (Capt. Jackson), Adam Roarke (Duke), Houston Savage (Dirty Denny), Eugene Cornelius (Speed), Paul Koslo (Limpy), John Garwood (Sgt. Winston), Ana Korita (Kim Sue), Lillian Margarejo (Suriya), Paraluman (Mama-san), Paul Nuckles (Kowalski), Ronnie Ross (Lt. Hayworth), Armando Lucero (Screw), Jack Starrett (Chet Davis), Fran Dinh Hy (Charlie), Alan Caillou (Albanian), Paquito Salcedo (Tac Houn), Von Deming (Shillick), Herman Robles (Inspector), Monica Phillips (Negro Baby), Daniel Kemp (Maj. Thomas), Vic Diaz (Diem-Nuc).

The CIA hires five Hells Angels to go into Cambodia and rescue a presidential advisor. It sounds ridiculous and it is. The bikers have armored motorcycles and roar into a Chinese or maybe North Vietnamese (it is never clear) camp, saving the aide, director Starrett, and getting killed in the process. A dimwitted action film that makes the Vietnam war seem like a western. Though the politics of the film seem to swing more to the left, THE LOSERS falls into the same trash heap as John Wayne's THE GREEN BERETS and Chuck Norris' MIA and MIA II.

p, Joe Solomon; d, Jack Starrett; w, Alan Caillou; ph, Nonong Rasca (Eastmancolor); m, Stu Phillips; ed, James Moore, Richard Brockway; sp eff, Roger George, Joe Zoomar; makeup, Ricardo Villamin.

War Drama Cas. (PR:O MPAA:R)

LOSIN' IT* (1983) 104m EM c

Tom Cruise (Woody), Jackie Earle Haley (Dave), John Stockwell (Spider), Shelley Long (Kathy), John P. Navin, Jr. (Wendell), Henry Darrow (El Jefe), James Victor (Lawyer), Hector Elias (Chuey), Daniel Faraldo, Enrique Castillo (Cab Drivers), Mario Marcelino (Pablo), Rick Rossovitch (Marine), Kale Browne (Larry), John Valby (M.C.), Cornelio Hernandez, Hector Morales, Santos Morales, Laura James, Rita Rogers, Victoria Wells, Irma Garcia, Sosimo Hernandez, Jesse Aragon, Margarita Garcia, Joe Spinell, Susan Saldivar, Bell Hernandez, Rick Powell, Dean R. Miller, Jack M. Nietzsche, Jr., Timothy Brown, Amando Ogaz, Steve Gonzales.

Another creatively barren teen-age sex film with the high school seniors going to Tijuana to do it Mexican style. The jokes and situations are the same, interchangeable with the countless number of other hormone crazed teen-age films. Long is along for the ride to get a quick divorce and is able to pass on most of the low-brow scenes. Cruise, before his star-making role in RISKY BUSINESS, Haley of BREAKING AWAY fame, Stockwell and Navin are the hot schoolboys searching for a whorehouse. The Mexican characters and women, with the exception of Long, are stereotypes.

p, Bryan Gindoff, Hannah Hempstead; d, Curtis Hanson; w, B. W. L. Norton (based on a story by Norton); ph, Gil Taylor (DeLuxe Color); m, Ken Wannberg; ed, Richard Halsey; prod d, Robb Wilson King; art d, Vance Lorenzini; m/l, title song, J. Alan, T. Shenale (performed by the Jeff Alan Band).

Comedy **Cas.** **(PR:O MPAA:R)**

LOSING GAME, THE (SEE: PAY-OFF, THE, 1930)

LOSS OF FEELING1/2
(1935, USSR) 85m Mezrapbom bw (GIBEL SENSATY)

S. Vecheslov, V. Gardin, M. Volgina, A. Chekulaeva, V. Orlov, N. Ablov, N. Rybikov, P. Poltoratski.

This Russian film is an adaptation of a classic Czech novel from which the term "robot" sprang. The plot centers on an inventor who creates robots to do the work of humans. His machines are stong and intelligent, but they have no souls. Soon a class struggle ensues between the displaced human workers and the factory bosses who want to convert their operations entirely to robots. Not as interesting or as skillful as Fritz Lang's METROPOLIS, but not bad either. Quite a deviation from Capek's original play, which had no humans in it at all. Director Andreievsky is noted for having made the first color-stereoscopic film in the U.S.S.R.

d, Aleksander Andreievsky, w, G. Grebner (based on the novel R.U.R.-Rossum's Universal Robots by Czech author Karel Capek); ph, M. Magidson.

Science Fiction **(PR:A MPAA:NR)**

LOSS OF INNOCENCE*
(1961, Brit.) 99m P.K.L./COL c (GB: THE GREENGAGE SUMMER)

Kenneth More (Eliot), Danielle Darrieux (Madame Zizi), Susannah York (Joss Grey), Claude Nollier (Madame Corbet), Jane Asher (Hester Grey), Elizabeth Dear (Vicky Grey), Richard Williams (Willmouse Grey), David Saire (Paul), Raymond Gerome (Inspector Renard), Maurice Denham (Uncle William Bullock), Andre Maranne (Monsieur Dufour), Harold Kasket (Monsieur Prideaux), Jacques Brunius (Monsieur Foubert), Joy Shelton (Mrs. Grey), Balbina (Mauricette), Will Stamp (Monsieur Armand), Jean Ozenne (Champagne Director), Jacques Dhery (Bargee), Bessie Love, Fred Johnson (American Tourists).

York plays a British 16-year-old left stranded at a French hotel during her vacation with her three younger siblings when their mother becomes ill and is hospitalized. The proprietor, Darrieux, reluctantly takes the children in, and her handsome lover More volunteers to entertain them. More takes the children on a tour of the countryside and, during their excursion, York finds herself increasingly attracted to their guide, much to the dismay of Darrieux who begins to distrust the youngster. One evening York goes into a jealous rage when she sees More and Darrieux heading for bed, and she gets drunk with scullery boy Saire. The next day, York decides to get revenge on More by sending his picture to the police, having recognized him as a wanted jewel thief. That evening, Saire encouraged by York's drunkenness the night before, enters the girl's room and tries to rape her. Alerted by her screams, More rushes into the room and accidentally pushes Saire out the window and to his death. York confesses her betrayal to More, and he makes good his escape. Still concerned about the children, More wires their uncle asking him to come to the hotel and retrieve the youngsters and the wire tips the police to More's whereabouts and he is captured.

p, Victor Saville, Edward Small; d, Lewis Gilbert; w, Howard Koch (based on the novel The Greengage Summer by Rumer Godden); ph, F.A. Young (Eastmancolor); m, Richard Addinsell; ed, Peter Hunt; md, Muir Mathieson; cos, Julie Harris; makeup, George Partleton.

Romance/Drama **(PR:C MPAA:NR)**

LOST (SEE: TEARS FOR SIMON, 1957, Brit.)

LOST AND FOUND1/2 (1979) 106m COL c

George Segal (Adam), Glenda Jackson (Tricia), Maureen Stapleton (Jemmy), Hollis McLaren (Eden), John Cunningham (Lenny), Paul Sorvino (Reilly), Kenneth Pogue (Julian), Janie Sell (Zelda), Diana Barrington (Ellie), Leslie Carlson (Jean-Paul), John Candy (Carpentier), James Morris (Gendarme), Bruno Engler (Ski Patrol), David Bolt (French Doctor), Richard Adams (Attendant), Mary Pirie, Nicole D'Amour, Denise Baillargeon (French Nurses), Roger Periard (French Lawyer), Lois Maxwell (English Woman), Douglas Campbell (British Professor), John Anthony Robinow (Conductor), Robert Goodier (Mayor), Sandy Webster (Bryce), Barbara Hamilton (Mrs. Bryce), Patricia Collins (Helen), Rob Garrison (Ed), Cecil Linder

(Sanders), James Hurde (Hurley), Martin Short (Engel), John Baylis (Schuster), Dennis Strong (Porter).

Many of the same people came back from their success in A TOUCH OF CLASS to make this film but it didn't come close to the original in wit, style, or box office receipts. Executive producer Arnold Kopleson (formerly Johnny Carson's attorney and a renowned deal-maker in the film business) put together a team that looked good on paper but just didn't seem to work on celluloid. Segal is a widowed English professor who meets Jackson, a divorced Englishwoman, at a French ski resort, when they break each other's legs in an accident. They fall in love, decide to marry, and move back to the U.S. The first few reels are funny, with Segal and Jackson having excellent material with which to work as they explore each other's personalities and agree to wed. Once in the States, Segal is eager to obtain tenure at the college and he is competing with Cunningham. The picture goes downhill as the tension of "will they or won't they marry?" has already been relieved. The remainder of the movie is a series of slapstick scenes, including the obligatory drunken one where staid Jackson gets swacked at a conservative university party and it just sort of fizzles out. Segal has played the Jewish boy being dominated by the mother so many times (NO WAY TO TREAT A LADY, WHERE'S POPPA, etc) that it's about time he retires that trophy. What's funny is very good and what's bad isn't all that terrible. Look for SCTV types John Candy and Martin Short in small roles, before they became famous.

p&d, Melvin Frank; w, Frank, Jack Rose; ph, Douglas Slocombe (Panavision, Technicolor); m, John Cameron; ed, Bill Butler; prod d, Trevor Williams; art d, Ted Tester; set d, Gerry Holmes; cos, Julie Harris.

Comedy **Cas.** **(PR:A-C MPAA:PG)**

LOST ANGEL* (1944) 91m MGM bw

Margaret O'Brien (Alpha), James Craig (Mike Regan), Marsha Hunt (Katie Mallory), Philip Merivale (Prof. Peter Vincent), Keenan Wynn (Packy), Alan Napier (Dr. Woodring), Henry O'Neill (Prof. Pringle), Sara Haden (Rhoda Kitterick), Donald Meek (Prof. Catty), Elizabeth Risdon (Mrs. Pringle), Kathleen Lockhart (Mrs. Catty), Walter Fenner (Prof. Endicott), Howard Freeman (Prof. Richards), Bobby Blake (Jerry), Bobby Driscoll (Boy On Train), Jack Lambert (Lefty Moran), Naomi Childers (Matron), Kay Medford, Gloria Grafton (Operators), Edward McWade (Old Man), Russell Gleason, William Bishop, Lee Phelps, Edward Hearn (Reporters), Mike Mazurki (Fighter), Allen Wood (Tough Kid), Ava Gardner (Hat Check Girl), Al Hill (Mug), Joe Yule (Tenant).

O'Brien is picked by a group of scientists to be made into a child prodigy. Police reporter Craig steps in and shows little Margaret the joys of being a normal child. The script was tailored to build O'Brien's stardom, by order of the boss, Louis B. Mayer, and that it did.

p, Robert Sisk; d, Roy Rowland; w, Isobel Lennart (based on an idea by Angna Enters); ph, Robert Surtees; m, Daniele Amfitheatrof; ed, Frank E. Hall; art d, Cedric Gibbons, Lynden Sparhawk; set d, Edwin B. Willis, Helen Conway.

Drama **(PR:A MPAA:NR)**

LOST BATTALION*1/2 (1961, U.S./Phil.) 83m Alta Vista/AIP bw

Leopoldo Salcedo (Ramon, Guerrilla Leader), Diane Jergens (Kathy, the Girl), Johnny Monteiro (Bruno, Bandit Leader), Joe Dennis (Landis), Jennings Sturgeon (Hughes), Joe Sison (Pepe), Bruce Baxter (Jimmy), Renato Robles (2nd Guerrilla), Rosi Acosta (Pepe's Wife), Arsenio Alonso (3rd Guerrilla).

A low-budget WW II picture shot in the Philippines, the film stars Salcedo as the leader of a group of guerrillas battling the Japanese invaders. One of the guerrillas' goals is to aid American refugees stranded by the war. A refugee, Jergens, falls in love with Salcedo, but she is soon kidnapped by bandits. Salcedo rescues the girl but is wounded in the process. The guerrillas are aided by friendly pygmies, but the bandit leader, Hughes, follows and fights Salcedo to the death. Salcedo kills the bandit, but is bitten by a deadly cobra and stays behind to die when an American submarine arrives to save the group.

p&d, Eddie Romero; w, Romero, Cesar Amigo; ph, Felipe Sacdalan; ed, Joven Calub; art d, Vincente Bonus; spec eff, Santos Hilario; makeup, Remy Amazan.

War **(PR:A MPAA:NR)**

LOST BOUNDARIES* (1949) 99m De Rochemont/FC bw

Beatrice Pearson (Marcia Carter), Mel Ferrer (Dr. Scott Carter), Richard Hylton (Howard Carter), Susan Douglas (Shelley Carter), Canada Lee (Lt. Thompson), Rev. Robert Dunn (Rev. John Taylor), Grace Coppin (Mrs. Mitchell), Carleton Carpenter (Andy), Seth Arnold (Clint Adams), Wendell Holmes (Mr. Mitchell), Parker Fennelly (Alvin Tupper), Ralph Riggs (Loren Tucker), William Greaves (Arthur Cooper), Rai Saunders (Jesse Pridham), Leigh Whipper (Janitor), Morton Stevens (Dr. Walter Brackett), Maurice Ellis (Dr. Cashman), Alexander Campbell (Mr. Bigelow), Edwin Cooper (Baggage Man), Royal Beal (Detective Staples), Peggy Kimber (Joan), Emory Richardson (Dr. Howard), Patricia Quinn O'Hara (Mrs. Taylor), Margaret Barker (Nurse Richmond), John Glendinning (Lt. Lacey), John Gerstad (George Turner), Peter Hobbs, Horace Mitchell, William G. Wendell, Lee Nugent, Nancy Heye.

The true story of a light-skinned black doctor and his family who have passed for white in a New England town. The film concentrates on the problems the doctor, Ferrer (in his screen debut) has maintaining the lie, and the radical adjustment the children are forced to make when their real race is known. The film neatly stays away from melodrama and makes a strong statement against prejudice. Producer de Rochemont displays his documentary colors in this film, reflecting his strong experience in the field: he was the originator of the "March of Time" series of news/documentary shorts and brought many of his cohorts in that venture with him when he formed his own production company.

p, Louis de Rochemont; d, Alfred L. Werker; w, Virginia Shaler, Eugene Ling, Charles A. Palmer, Furland de Kay (based on an article by W. L. White); ph, William J. Miller; m, Louis Applebaum; ed, David Kummins; md, Jack Shaindlin; art d, Herbert Andrews; m/l, Albert Johnston, Jr., Carleton Carpenter, Herbert Taylor.

Drama   **(PR:A   MPAA:NR)**

LOST CANYON*   (1943) 61m UA bw

William Boyd (*Hopalong Cassidy*), Jay Kirby (*Breezy Travers*), Andy Clyde (*California*), Lola Lane (*Laura*), Douglas Fowley (*Jeff Burton*), Herbert Rawlinson (*Clark*), Guy Usher (*Rogers*), Karl Hackett (*Haskell*), Hugh Prosser, Keith Richards, Herman Hack, Merrill McCormack, George Morrell.

Kirby is charged with robbing a bank and he flees into the hills to escape jail. Boyd arrives to prove the kid's innocence and capture the real crooks. This was the second of the Hopalong Cassidy series that United Artists distributed. The Sportsman Quartet is tossed in by producer Sherman to sing, "Jingle, Jangle, Jingle." (See HOPALONG CASSIDY series, Index.)

p, Harry Sherman; d, Lesley Selander; w, Harry O. Hoyt (based on a story by Clarence E. Mulford); ph, Russell Harlan; ed, Sherman A. Rose; art d, Ralph Berger.

Western   **(PR:A   MPAA:NR)**

LOST CHORD, THE* 1/2   (1937, Brit.) 70m Twickenham/Treo bw

Elizabeth Allan (*Joan Elton*), John Stuart (*David Graham*), Mary Glynne (*Countess Madeleine*), Leslie Perrins (*Count Carol Zara*), Anne Grey (*Pauline*), Jack Hawkins (*Dr. Jim Selby*), Bernard Ansell (*Benito Levina*), Eliot Makeham (*Bertie Pollard*), Garry Marsh (*Joseph Mendel*), Betty Astell (*Madge*), Frederick Ranalow (*Beppo*), Barbara Everest (*Mother Superior*), Billy Mayerl, Tudor Davis.

Stuart is a composer who falls in love with a concert singer, Glynne, but she gets involved with a count. Stuart kills the count in a duel and loses the use of his right arm. Then Glynne dies and Stuart drops out of music. Twenty years later, he falls in love with her daughter Allan and writes an operetta for her. The film was originally released in 1934, and a silent U.S. version was done in 1925 by Arrow Productions.

p, Julius Hagen; d, Maurice Elvey; w, H. Fowler Mear (based on a song by Sir Arthur Sullivan); ph, Sidney Blyth.

Drama   **(PR:A   MPAA:NR)**

LOST COMMAND, THE* 1/2   (1966) 129m Red Lion/COL c

Anthony Quinn (*Lt. Col. Pierre Raspeguy*), Alain Delon (*Capt. Philippe Esclavier*), George Segal (*Lt. Ben Mahidi*), Michele Morgan (*Countess de Clairefons*), Maurice Ronet (*Capt. Boisfeuras*), Claudia Cardinale (*Aicha*), Gregoire Aslan (*Ben Saad*), Jean Servais (*Gen. Melies*), Maurice Sarfati (*Merle*), Jean-Claude Bercq (*Orsini*), Jacques Marin (*Mayor*), Jean Paul Moulinot (*DeGuyot*), Sly Lamont (*Verte*), Andres Monreal (*Ahmed*), Gordon Heath (*Dia*), Simino (*Sapinsky*), Rene Havard (*Fernand*), Armand Mestral (*Administration Officer*), Burt Kwouk (*Viet Officer*), Al Mulock (*Mugnier*), Marie Burke (*Mother Raspeguy*), Aldo Sanbrell (*Ibrahim*), Jorge Rigaud (*Priest*), Roberto Robles (*Manuel*), Emilio Carrer (*Father Mihidi*), Carmen Tarrazo (*Mother Mihidi*), Howard Hagan (*Pilot*), Mario De Barros (*Geoffrin*), Walter Kelly (*Major V.P.*), Robert Sutton (*Yusseff*), Simon Benzakein (*Arab Customer*), Hector Quiroga (*Bakhti*), Felix De Pomes (*Aged Speaker*).

Action film that could have used some judicious editing. The French are bested in Indochina and a unit of paratroopers, led by Quinn, is returning to France in 1954 after the disastrous defeat at Dienbienphu. The ship stops at Algiers where Segal, playing an Arab officer in the French service, disembarks to visit his family. When Quinn arrives in France, he takes up with Morgan, a rich countess who was widowed when her general husband was killed in Asia. Quinn is well below her station but the attraction is such that she gets him posted to Algeria where she hopes he can raise his rank from lieutenant colonel to general. If he comes back as a general, she will marry him. Quinn takes over a raggedy unit and convinces his two wartime comrades, Delon and Ronet, to help him get the rag-tags into shape. Quinn is shocked to discover that Segal has joined the Arab terrorists who are conducting a campaign to get the French out of Algeria. Quinn, Delon, and Ronet train the men and they set out to quash the Arabs. Meanwhile, Delon is having an affair with Cardinale and doesn't know that she is Segal's sister! She is now on the inside of Quinn's plans and tells Segal everything. Delon learns of her duplicity and whacks her around until she reveals Segal's hideout. He makes Quinn promise that Segal will be taken alive, then gives him the location. There's a huge shoot-out and Ronet deliberately shoots Segal. Delon is disgusted and quits the regiment just as they are being decorated for bravery. Cardinale has been sent to jail for collaboration, Morgan watches proudly as Quinn gets his general's rank, and Delon notes some youngsters scrawling the word "Independence" on the barracks walls, a portent of what was to come. THE LOST COMMAND was filmed in Spain. All technical credits are excellent and special plaudits for Waxman's music. Quinn, in the unsympathetic role of a quasi-mercenary who is fighting for personal glory (and the hand of Morgan), is dynamic. At the time the picture was being made, the U.S. was fighting in Vietnam. The Joint Chiefs of Staff should have watched this film to see the folly of their ways.

p&d, Mark Robson; w, Nelson Gidding (based on the novel *The Centurions* by Jean Larteguy); ph, Robert Surtees (Panavision, Pathe Color); m, Franz Waxman; ed, Dorothy Spencer; art d, John Stroll; set d, Vernon Dixon; cos, Tanine Autre; spec eff, Manuel Baquero, Kit West; makeup, Harold Fletcher, Francisco Puyol; special military advisors, Rene Lepage, Antonio Sanz Ridriejo.

Action/Adventure   **(PR:A-C   MPAA:NR)**

LOST CONTINENT* 1/2   (1951) 83m Lippert bw

Cesar Romero (*Maj. Joe Nolan*), Hillary Brooke (*Maria Stevens*), Chick Chandler (*Lt. Danny Wilson*), John Hoyt (*Michael Rostov*), Acquanetta (*Native Girl*), Sid

Melton (*Sgt. Willie Tatlow*), Whit Bissell (*Stanley Briggs*), Hugh Beaumont (*Robert Phillips*), Murray Alper (*M.P.*), William Green (*Simmons*).

An American rocket ship crashes on a Pacific island where the dinosaurs still roam. Romero leads a rescue team to recover the rocket and a secret device on board. Acquanetta is the island girl who helps the stranded explorers back to the real world. When the rescue team arrives, the film takes on a green tint, due to a green filter projectionists used. Scenes from the film ROCKETSHIP X-M were cut into this film, and it was directed by the man who did TERROR OF TINY TOWN.

p, Sigmund Neufeld; d, Samuel Newfield; w, Richard H. Landau (based on a story by Carroll Young); ph, Jack Greenhalgh; m, Paul Dunlap; ed, Phil Cahn; spec eff, Augie Lohman.

Science Fiction   **(PR:A   MPAA:NR)**

LOST CONTINENT, THE* *   (1968, Brit.) 89m Seven Arts-Hammer/FOX c

Eric Porter (*Capt. Lansen*), Hildegard Knef [Hildegarde Neff] (*Eva*), Suzanna Leigh (*Unity*), Tony Beckley (*Harry Tyler*), Nigel Stock (*Dr. Webster*), Neil McCallum (*1st Officer Hemmings*), Benito Carruthers (*Ricaldi*), Jimmy Hanley (*Pat*), James Cossins (*Chief*), Dana Gillespie (*Sarah*), Victor Maddern (*Mate*), Reg Lye (*Helmsman*), Norman Eshley (*Jonathan*), Michael Ripper (*Sea Lawyer*), Donald Sumpter (*Sparks*), Alf Joint (*Jason*), Charles Houston (*Braemar*), Shivendra Sinha (*Hurri Curri*), Darryl Read (*El Diablo*), Eddie Powell (*Inquisitor*), Frank Hayden (*Sergeant*), Mark Heath, Horace James (*Customs Men*).

A ship captained by Porter carries a cargo of illegal explosives and a group of shady characters. During a storm the crew abandons ship and ends up on an island with killer seaweed, giant crabs and jellyfish, prehistoric sharks, and a lost race of Spanish conquistadors. An action film that makes for enjoyable viewing.

p&d, Michael Carreras; w, Michael Nash (based on the novel *Uncharted Seas* by Dennis Wheatley); ph, Paul Benson (DeLuxe Color); m, Gerard Schurmann; ed, Chris Barnes; art d, Arthur Lawson; cos, Carl Toms; spec eff, Cliff Richardson, Robert A. Mattey; m/l, Roy Philips (sung by The Peddlers); makeup, George Parleton.

Science Fiction/Adventure   **(PR:A   MPAA:G)**

LOST FACE, THE* *

(1965, Czech.) 85m Svabik-Prochazka bw (ZTRACENA TVAR)

Vlastimil Brodsky, Fred Demare, Jana Brezkova, Frantisek Filipovsky, Marie Vasova, Martin Rurek, Nina Popelikova, Jiri Vala, Zdenka Prochazkova.

Brodsky stars as a successful transplant doctor whose best efforts are frustrated by lack of interest and money from official clinics. This forces him to become involved with a gangster who pays him big money to remove the face of a priest the gangster has murdered and transplant it to himself. After a few face changes, Brodsky realizes that it is better to be unrecognized in a pure environment than to be a genius in a corrupt one, and he reverts back to his original facial features. The film is a bit too preachy, but funny and interesting nonetheless.

d, Pavel Hobl; w, Hobl, Josef Nesvadba; ph, Jiri Vojta.

Science Fiction/Comedy   **(PR:C   MPAA:NR)**

LOST HAPPINESS* 1/2   (1948, Ital.) 78m ICI/Saturnia bw

Leonardo Cortese (*Giorgio Viglieri*), Dina Sossoli (*Anna*), Manuel Roero (*Franco*), Giuseppe Poreli (*Sabastriaro*), Arnaoldo Toeri (*Nicola*), Adriana De Roberto (*Maria*).

A routine love-triangle stars Cortese as a famous violinist whose wife, Sossoli, has a brief fling with his accompanist Roero, who uses the tryst to blackmail the woman into continuing the affair. His ambition overrides his sense when he fakes evidence that he has been murdered by Cortese. Eventually Roero is caught and killed by the violinist. (In Italian; English subtitles.)

d, F. M. Ratti.

Crime   **(PR:A   MPAA:NR)**

LOST HONEYMOON* 1/2   (1947) 71m Bryan Foy/EL bw

Franchot Tone (*Johnny Gray*), Ann Richards (*Amy Atkins*), Tom Conway (*Dr. Davis*), Frances Rafferty (*Lois Evans*), Clarence Kolb (*Mr. Evans*), Una O'Connor (*Mrs. Tubbs*), Winston Severn (*Johnny, Jr.*), Adele Davenport (*Joyce*), Sandra Roger (*Mrs. Jenkins*), John Wald (*Major*).

Tone recovers from amnesia and isn't sure if he has married Richards in this entertaining farce featuring Tone's comic timing. Some of the better moments are when Tone engages in a wrestling match with the plastic wrapping of his new shirt, tries to regain amnesia by bouncing his head off a street lamp, and runs down the highway in his pajamas to get advice from a friend.

p, Lee Marcus, Bryan Foy; d, Leigh Jason; w, Joseph Fields; ph, L. W. O'Connell; m, Werner Heyman; ed, Norman Colbert; md, Irving Friedman; art d, Edward C. Jewell.

Comedy   **(PR:A   MPAA:NR)**

LOST HONOR OF KATHARINA BLUM, THE* 1/2

(1975, Ger.) 104m PAR-Orion-WDR-Bioskop Film/Cinema International c (DIE VERLORENE EHRE DER KATHARINA BLUM)

Angela Winkler (*Katharina Blum*), Mario Adorf (*Beizmenne*), Dieter Laser (*Werner Toetgess*), Heinz Bennent (*Dr. Blorna*), Hannelore Hoger (*Trude Blorna*), Harald Kuhlmann (*Moeding*), Karl Heinz Vosgerau (*Alois Straubleder*), Juergen Prochnow (*Ludwig Goetten*), Rolf Becker (*Hach*), Regine Lutz (*Else Woltersheim*), Werner Eichhorn (*Konrad Beiters*).

This film adaptation of the Heinrich Boll novel does a fairly capable job of transferring the themes and narrative structure Boll emphasized. Winkler plays the waitress and trustworthy ideal citizen who suddenly finds herself the victim of an unorthodox police investigation and media destruction of her private life after a brief affair with a man wanted by the police for political reasons. Before this, she had been a woman respected by her employers for her efficiency and by her friends because of her level head. Winkler's calm and uneventful life is made a shambles by one particularly ruthless reporter who will stop at nothing, including a grueling interview with Winkler's sickly mother, to read something into the simple facts. Labeled a communist conspirator in the headlines, Winkler erupts from the cool demeanor she had been maintaining throughout this trying ordeal and shoots the nauseating reporter. The plotting of these occurrences takes the format of a series of tidbits of information gathered about Winkler. In this manner various viewpoints about Winkler's character are revealed in an effort to take a more objective stance. At times this comes off as being much too cold and distanced to gain much audience empathy, but is quite effective in transferring the type of oppressive atmosphere the story requires. Winkler's performance is equally cool, exposing a woman who seems almost incapable of revealing her emotions. A result of attempting to exist in a society which breeds alienation, a world in which Winkler is finally able to release all the anger she has been harboring when she shoots the reporter.

p, Willim Benninger, Eberhard Junkersdorf; d, Volker Schloendorff, Margarethe von Trotta; w, Schloendorff, von Trotta (based on the novel by Heinrich Boll); ph, Jost Vacano (Eastmancolor); m, Hans-Werner Henze; ed, Peter Przygodda.

Drama **Cas.** **(PR:C MPAA:R)**

LOST HORIZON***** (1937) 133m COL bw

Ronald Colman *(Robert Conway)*, Jane Wyatt *(Sondra)*, Edward Everett Horton *(Alexander P. Lovett)*, John Howard *(George Conway)*, Thomas Mitchell *(Henry Barnard)*, Margo *(Maria)*, Isabel Jewell *(Gloria Stone)*, H. B. Warner *(Chang)*, Sam Jaffe *(High Lama)*, Hugh Buckler *(Lord Gainsford)*, John Miltern *(Carstairs)*, Lawrence Grant *(1st Man)*, John Burton *(Wynant)*, John T. Murray *(Meeker)*, Max Rabinowitz *(Seiveking)*, Willie Fung *(Bandit Leader)*, Wryley Birch *(Missionary)*, John Tettener *(Montaigne)*, Boyd Irwin *(Assistant Foreign Secretary)*, Leonard Mudie *(Senior Foreign Secretary)*, David Clyde *(Steward)*, Neil Fitzgerald *(Radio Operator)*, Val Durand *(Talu)*, Ruth Robinson *(Missionary)*, Margaret McWade *(Missionary)*, Noble Johnson *(Leader of Porters)*, Dennis D'Auburn *(Aviator)*, Milton Owen *(Fenner)*, Victor Wong *(Bandit Leader)*, Carl Stockdale *(Missionary)*, Darby Clarke *(Radio Operator)*, George Chan *(Chinese Priest)*, Eric Wilton *(Englishman)*, Chief Big Tree *(Porter)*, Richard Loo *(Shanghai Airport Official)*, Beatrice Curtis, Mary Lou Dix, Beatrice Blinn, Arthur Rankin *(Passengers)*, The Hall Johnson Choir.

In the wonderful world of Frank Capra, this film ranks with his other masterpieces, MR. SMITH GOES TO WASHINGTON, MR. DEEDS GOES TO TOWN, IT'S A WONDERFUL LIFE, IT HAPPENED ONE NIGHT, except that it is unlike anything this evocative director did before or after. It's the tale, of course, that sets this film apart from Capra's usual middle-class genre, one of strange adventure and near fantasy that caught the imagination of the viewing public. Faithful to the immensely popular Hilton novel, the film opens with Colman, the gallant, suave British diplomat, author, and Far Eastern historian, saving refugees during a Chinese revolution. The group takes off in a small passenger plane, a motley collection. With Colman is his younger impressionable brother, Howard, a swindler wanted by the law, Mitchell, a prostitute with tuberculosis, Jewell, and a fussy fossil scientist, Horton. Colman notices, however, that the plane is not headed for a safe city but is ever climbing into the high mountains, as it soars above the towering snow-coated Himalayas, to Tibet, known as "The Roof of the World." The passengers cannot enter the pilot's compartment, discovering he is a strange Oriental, not the European they thought to be at the controls. The plane crashes and the passengers struggle out of the damaged plane, sinking into deep snow. As time passes the survivors almost give up hope of being rescued; then an odd-looking group appears, led by an ancient Chinese, Warner, who appears to have been looking for the Europeans. He provides them with warm clothing and they join the caravan and are taken over the mountains to a remote, small pass. They cross over a narrow bridge between towering mountains and the blizzard suddenly vanishes, the snow disappears, and they stand inside a beautiful, sun-filled world known as the Valley of the Blue Moon, looking down upon magnificent landscapes that make up the lamasery of Shangri-La. Taken to a magnificent structure and given luxurious rooms, the Europeans soon discover the marvelous tranquility of this hidden unknown land where nothing is known of greed, war, hatred, and crime. Colman, while trying to learn more of this mysterious place, is told by Warner, assistant to the High Lama, that Shangri-La was discovered and founded by Father Perrault, a missionary who established the lamasery in 1713 as a place for contemplation, free from earthly pressures and worries. Wyatt, a beautiful young girl, is seen by Colman and he quickly falls in love with her before being summoned by the High Lama, Jaffe. Colman listens to Jaffe relate the history of Shangri-La and is shocked to realize that the High Lama and the founding father, Perrault, are the same person, that this wise old man is older than any living man on earth, more than 250 years old. He realizes he is dying, Jaffe tells Colman, and he has selected Colman to replace him as High Lama. That is why his plane was hijacked and flown into the high mountains. Jaffe predicts devastating wars in the outside world and that his Shangri-La will serve as a safe haven for those wishing to preserve ideals and civilization. Says Jaffe: "Against that time is why I avoided death and am here and why you were brought here. For when that day comes, the world must begin to look for a new life and it is our hope that they may find it here. For here we shall be with their books and their music and a way of life based on one simple rule—be kind. When that day comes, it is our hope that the brotherly love of Shangri-La will spread throughout the world." Colman is perfectly content to shed his worldly burdens and assume the role Jaffe has designated for him, planning to marry the beautiful Wyatt. But to Howard, the beauteous valley where no one ages is nothing more than a lovely prison from which he insists they escape. He too has fallen in love, with Margo, an exotic Oriental beauty. Though she looks 20, Warner tells Colman that she is Russian and she is really 60 years old; Shangari-La and its eternal peace has kept her young, Warner explains, but Howard won't believe him. Colman is finally convinced when Margo tells him that Warner and Jaffe are lying, that she is not an old woman and the old men are insane. Margo bribes some porters and she and Howard and Colman climb through the pass into the outer world, working through the snow. The porters fall to their deaths in a ravine and Howard and Colman are horrified when Margo's face begins to wither into old age before their eyes. She dies a shriveled old hag that night. (Margo's deeply wrinkled face at death is one of the most shocking scenes in film history.) Howard's mind snaps at the sight of Margo's decomposing body and he commits suicide by throwing himself over a cliff. Colman, now lost in the snows, wanders for days until he stumbles into a native village, his memory erased. He is taken back to England to recuperate and there he suddenly remembers Shangri-La and all its wonders, particularly the woman he loves, Wyatt. He leave immediately for Tibet, determined to somehow find his way back to the wonderful Valley of the Blue Moon. One of his admirers, Lord Gainsford, Buckler, returns to his club to tell fellow members that he failed in his attempt to find the missing Colman, that the adventurer somehow slipped past him and vanished in the high mountains. Buckler lifts his glass in a toast: "Here is my hope that Robert Conway will find his Shangri La. Here is my hope that we all find our Shangri-La." Unlike the novel where the hero is not seen again, leaving the doubt as to whether or not he was able to find his way back to Shangri-La, Capra relents to hope and shows Colman struggling through the snow and miraculously finding the pass that will lead him back into the fabled valley and a reunion with Wyatt and almost eternal happiness. It is fairly certain that novelist Hilton based the character Colman so expertly played upon real-life adventurer and mountaineer George Leigh-Mallory who vanished in 1924 while attempting to conquer Mount Everest and was lost in a blizzard near the summit. LOST HORIZON epitomized everyone's concept of Utopia, Shangri-La being a place where pure air, bright sun, and untroubled time allowed a person to live for centuries in blissful peace. So entrenched did this film become in the imagination of the public that Shangri-La became a household word. When U.S. planes struck back at Japan for the first time, in the famous Doolittle raid of 1942, President Franklin D. Roosevelt explained jocularly that American planes had taken off from "Shangri-La." Where Hilton had written the novel is six weeks (published in 1933) Capra took two years to transfer the tale to celluloid. The magnificent set constructed by Goosson (for which he won an Oscar) displaying the wonders of Shangri-La, was the largest ever built in Hollywood. For two months 150 workmen labored to build the 1,000-foot-long, 500-foot wide lamasery, with its deep flights of marbled stairs and huge patio, broad terraces, rich gardens, and lily coated pools. The main building was a sort of art deco design borrowed heavily from Frank Lloyd Wright's conceptions. Everything about the film was expensive and little Columbia Studios staggered under the burden of a $2,500,000 budget for LOST HORIZON. Its boss, Harry Cohn, moaned every day he reviewed the mounting cost, which amounted to half of the studio's entire yearly budget. True to his adventurous spirit, Capra cast two relatively unknowns in the leading female parts, Wyatt, a recent college graduate with only a few minor films to her credit, and Mexican dancer Margo who had appeared in a few films, notably Ben Hecht's CRIME WITHOUT PASSION. Colman was in Capra's mind from the beginning as the lead even though Cohn did not like the actor, considered him too polished, too refined. Here the mogul was being his usual truculent self for he knew that Colman was box office dynamite. The actor had been selected at age 44 in 1935 as the most handsome man on the screen by 51 female stars, receiving 22 votes with Clark Gable placing second with only eight votes and Fredric March third with seven votes. When it came to casting the High Lama, however, Capra was in a hair-pulling quandary. He finally opted for A. E. Anson, a 90-year-old stage actor who had seldom been seen on the screen. Anson was ancient and on his last legs, found in retirement in the San Gabriel Valley. Capra had him brought in for a screen test, shot without makeup and decided he was perfect. He called Anson's home and got his housekeeper on the phone, telling her to inform the old actor that he had the role. The housekeeper wept for joy but called back within an hour. She had told the actor the good news, she reported to Capra, and he had smiled broadly, then died! Next Capra cast Henry B. Walthal in the part of the 250-year-old Lama. Walthal, who had played the Little Colonel in D. W. Griffith's masterpiece, THE BIRTH OF A NATION, was also in failing health and died before Capra could get him on film. The director even toyed with casting Charles Laughton in the role until he tested veteran character actor Jaffe who won the part immediately and so effectively played the delicate role—he is on the screen for only a few minutes—that he is forever remembered as the ancient missionary. When Colman stepped onto the LOST HORIZON set it was with some apprehension. He heard about the brutish Cohn and wanted no part of him, having his lawyers insert a special clause into his contract which specified that he would not have to deal with the mogul, only with Capra. Colman and Capra got along famously, the director, having a high regard for the actor, later stating: "There was too much written and said about Colman as a star-personality. He was far more than that—a true actor, one of singular gifts." Actually, Cohn had thought he might convince Capra to use Brian Aherne in the lead role of LOST HORIZON, to save money, of course, but Capra prevailed. Oddly, Aherne lost two significant parts to Colman, one in LOST HORIZON, the second in A TALE OF TWO CITIES, but he was always gracious about it, later remarking: "You see, I have never taken acting very seriously." Howard, playing the role of the weak-willed younger brother, was borrowed by Capra from Paramount where he was a contract player. It was one of the two best roles he would ever play, the other being the snob fiance in THE PHILADELPHIA STORY, directed by George Cukor, who, like Capra, requested his services. At the time, Howard disliked the role of the younger brother, and also loathed playing Hepburn's arrogant fiance in THE PHILADELPHIA STORY, but he would later look back in gratitude at the two directors singling him out: "If it hadn't been for Frank Capra and George Cukor, I would be remembered only as the man who made love to THE INVISIBLE WOMAN." Howard's remark made reference to a

1941 potboiler where he played opposite the disappearing Virginia Bruce. To provide an authentic-looking set for the the snow-bound mountain scenes, Capra used a huge cold storage warehouse where frozen swordfish were stacked to the ceiling like logs. Here about 20 percent of the film was shot in freezing temperatures so that actual snow could be created. It was in this warehouse that the plane crash, the climbing sequences, the avalanche that destroys the porters, were all shot. For distant shots Capra employed some stock footage from an adventure documentary directed by Andrew Marton in 1930 (the same footage was later used by economy-minded Columbia for its 1952 production of STORM OVER TIBET). Capra, ever the stickler for authenticity, found a rare horn collection owned by a California collector and obtained ancient Tibetan musical instruments, some as long as eight feet, one battered instrument coming from the temple of Lhasa in the Tibetan mountains. He simulated yaks by covering yearling steers with long hair and did the same with Shetland ponies to simulate the tiny Tibetan horses. All of the painstaking care Capra took with LOST HORIZON shows; the film is directed with swift pace, inventive shots, and evident vitality. This was Capra's high water mark, so it would be for Colman, a stirring achievement that was not obvious to the premiere audience first seeing the film. During the opening scenes viewers began to snicker, then laugh, which caused Capra to break out in out a cold sweat. He left his seat next to the worried Cohn and went to the lobby for a drink of water. The man taking a drink in front of him said: "Did you ever see such a goddamned Fu-Manchu thing?" Capra lost control, raced out into a rain storm and did not return to the theater until the film was over. He later told Cohn that they should dump the first two reels into the studio incinerator. When the film was released in its cut version, 118 minutes, it was universally applauded and Columbia walked away with a box office blockbuster which returned many millions to its depleted coffers, the film remaining in rerelease state for decades. Everything about LOST HORIZON reflects quality work, from Riskin's bright and literate script to Tiomkin's stirring music. Walker's soft focus photography enhances every scene and the special effects are outstanding. The film was nominated for a Best Picture Oscar but lost out to THE LIFE OF EMILE ZOLA.

p&d, Frank Capra; w, Robert Riskin (based on the novel by James Hilton); ph, Joseph Walker; m, Dimitri Tiomkin; ed, Gene Havlick, Gene Milford; md, Max Steiner; art d, Stephen Goosson; set d, Babs Johnstone; cos, Ernest Dryden; spec eff, E. Roy Davidson, Ganahl Carson.

Adventure   **Cas.**   **(PR:A MPAA:NR)**

LOST HORIZON zero   (1973) 150m Ross Hunter/COL c

Peter Finch (Richard Conway), Liv Ullmann (Catherine), Sally Kellerman (Sally Hughes), George Kennedy (Sam Cornelius), Michael York (George Conway), Olivia Hussey (Maria), Bobby Van (Harry Lovett), James Shigeta (Brother To-Lenn), Charles Boyer (High Lama), John Gielgud (Chang), Larry Duran (Oriental Pilot), Kent Smith, John Van Dreelan, Miiko Taka, Tybee Brascia, Neil Jon, Hedley Mattingly, Virginia Ann Lee, Paul De Lucca.

Adapted from Hilton's novel and Frank Capra's classic film translation of 1937, this film was one of the bigger bombs at the box office in the 1970s. The picture opens with foreigners being evacuated by plane from a revolution in Southeast Asia and crashing into the Himalayas. There they find Shangri-La. The production cost more than $7 million and returned only half of that to Columbia. During shooting the film was criticized by the Japanese-American Citizens League for casting Gielgud as an Oriental. Songs include "Lost Horizon" (sung by Shawn Phillips), "Share the Joy," "The World is a Circle," "The Dance of the Fathers," "Living Together, Growing Together," "I Might Frighten Her Away," "The Things I Will Not Miss," "If I Could Go Back," "Where Knowledge Ends (Faith Begins)," "Question Me An Answer," "I Come to You," and "Reflections" (Burt Bacharach, Hal David). Kellerman, Kennedy, Van, and Shigeta did their own singing, while Finch, Ullmann, and Hussey were dubbed by, respectively, Jerry Whitman, Diana Lee, and Andra Willis. Before word got out of the ineptitude of this film, it was chosen for a Command Performance before Queen Elizabeth—the first U.S. film in 17 years to get such an honor. The choreography by Pan received widespread criticism. Originally there had been a "fertility dance" featuring muscular bikini-clad men dancing in a "ring-around-the-rosy" fashion. Supposedly the preview audience laughed so hysterically that it was cut from the final print.

p, Ross Hunter; d, Charles Jarrott; w, Larry Kramer (based on the novel by James Hilton); ph, Robert Surtees (Panavision, Metrocolor); ed, Maury Winetrobe; md, Burt Bacharach; art d, Preston Ames; set d, Jerry Wunderlich; cos, Jean Louis; spec eff, Butler-Glounder; ch, Hermes Pan.

Musical   **(PR:A MPAA:G)**

LOST ILLUSION, THE   (SEE: FALLEN IDOL, THE, 1949, Brit.)

LOST IN A HAREM**   (1944) 89m MGM bw

Bud Abbott (Peter Johnson), Lou Costello (Harvey Garvey), Marilyn Maxwell (Hazel Moon), John Conte (Prince Ramo), Douglas Dumbrille (Nimativ), Lottie Harrison (Teema), J. Lockard Martin (Bobo), Murray Leonard (The Derelict), Adia Kuznetzoff (Chief Ghamu), Milton Parsons (Crystal Gazer), Ralph Sanford (Mr. Ormulu), Bud Wolfe, Carey Loftin (Chase Guards), Harry Cording (Police Chief), Eddie Abdo (Native), Sammy Stein (Native Jailor), Duke York (Jailor), Katharine Booth (Beautiful Girl), Frank Penny (Bearded Vendor), Frank Scannell (Fruit Vendor), Nick Thompson (Native), Tor Johnson (Majordomo), Jody Gilbert (Native Laundry Woman), Paul "Tiny" Newland (Guard), Eddie Dunn (Sentry), Sondra Rogers (Zaida, Maid), Dick Alexander (Executioner), Tom Herbert (Drunk), Heinie Conklin, Ernest Brenck (Natives in Cafe), Toni LaRue, Frances Ramsden, Margaret Savage, Jan Bryant, Margaret Kelly, Elinor Troy, Symona Boniface (Slave Girls), The Pinas (Acrobatic Act), Jimmy Dorsey and his Orchestra.

Abbott and Costello star in this harem musical comedy, where an American troupe is stranded in a desert land ruled by evil sheik Dumbrille, who has ousted the rightful

heir, his nephew, from the throne. Conte, as the nephew, knows his uncle has a weakness for blondes, so he hires Maxwell to seduce Dumbrille and the troupe's magical act, Abbott and Costello, to steal the sheik's magical rings. Costello returned after a year of illness to team up again with Abbott, both playing the usual slapstick comedy in this film to the hilt. Musical numbers were supplied by Jimmy Dorsey and His Orchestra. An elaborate ballet scene set to "Scheherazade" music more than makes up for leftover props and costumes from the movie KISMET.

p, George Haight; d, Charles Riesner; w, John Grant, Harry Crane, Harry Ruskin; ph, Lester White; m, Johnny Green, Nicolai Andreyevich Rimsky-Korsakov; ed, George Hively; md, David Snell; art d, Cedric Gibbons, Daniel B. Cathcart; m/l, Don Raye, Gene de Paul, Sammy Fain, Ralph Freed, Toots Camarata ("What Does It Take," "It is Written").

Comedy   **(PR:A MPAA:NR)**

LOST IN ALASKA**

(1952) 76m UNIV bw (AKA: ABBOTT AND COSTELLO LOST IN ALASKA)

Bud Abbott (Tom Watson), Lou Costello (George Bell), Mitzi Green (Rosette), Tom Ewell (Nugget Joe McDermott), Bruce Cabot (Jake Stillman), Emory Parnell (Sherman), Jack Ingram (Henchman), Rex Lease (Old-Timer), Joseph Kirk (Henchman), Minerva Urecal (Mrs. McGillicuddy), Howard Negley (Higgins), Maudie Pricket (Woman in Window), Billy Wayne (Croupier), Paul Newlan (Captain Chisholm), Michael Ross (Willie), Julia Montoya (Eskimo Woman), Iron Eyes Cody (Nanook), Fred Aldrich (Bearded Prospector), Donald Kerr (Multolah), George Barton (Bit), Bobby Barber (Bit Chief).

Considered to be one of the weaker of the comedy team's efforts, this film has Abbott and Costello up in Alaska where they save gold prospector Ewell from committing suicide over the unrequited love of Green. Unfortunately, Ewell's greedy friends, headed by saloon owner Cabot, want to get their hands on his $2,000,000 fortune, and the rest of the plot consists of Abbott, Costello, and Ewell in a climactic dog sled chase, dodging bullets left and right.

p, Howard Christie; d, Jean Yarbrough; w, Martin Ragaway, Leonard Stern (based on a story by Elwood Ullman); ph, George Robinson; m, Joseph Gershenson; ed, Leonard Weiner; md, Gershenson; art d, Bernard Herzbrun, Robert Boyle; set d, Russell A. Gausman, Ray Jeffers; ch, Harold Belfer.

Comedy   **(PR:AAA MPAA:NR)**

LOST IN THE LEGION*½   (1934, Brit.) 66m BIP/Wardour bw

Leslie Fuller (Bill), Renee Houston (Mary McFee), Betty Fields (Sally Hogg), Hal Gordon (Alf), H. F. Maltby (Kaid), Alf Goddard (Sgt. Mulligan), James Knight (Ryan), Mike Johnson (Fritz), A. Bromley (Colonel), Syd Courtenay, Ernest Fuller, Santos Casani, Lola Harvey.

Plot has Fuller and Gordon as ship's cooks who accidentally get themselves inducted into the Foreign Legion. Their madcap adventures include saving two fair maidens from becoming slaves in an Arab's harem.

p, Walter C. Mycroft; d, Fred Newmeyer; w, Syd Courtenay, John Paddy Carstairs (based on the story by Courtenay, Lola Harvey); ph, Jack Parker.

Comedy   **(PR:A MPAA:NR)**

LOST IN THE STARS**   (1974) 114m American Film Theatre c

Brock Peters (Stephen Kumalo), Melba Moore (Irina), Raymond St. Jacques (John Kumalo), Clifton Davis (Absalom), Paul Rogers (James Jarvis), Paulene Myers (Grace), Paula Kelly (Rose), H.B. Barnam III (Alex), Ji-Tu Cumbuka (Johannes), Alan Weeks (Matthew), John Williams (Judge), Ivor Barry (Carmichael), Harvey Jason (Arthur Jarvis), John Holland (Van Jarsdale), John Hawker (Paulus), Myrna White (Linda), Michael-James Wixted (Edward Jarvis), William Glover (Eland).

A poor adaptation of the Anderson/Weill musical play that was based on Alan Paton's moving South African novel, Cry, the Beloved Country. Peters stars as a black Zulu minister who loses his faith when he travels to Johannesburg in search of his fugitive son. Davis is the son who, in a bungled robbery attempt, murders the son of a white bigot (Rogers). What could have been a powerfully moving film with a statement about segregation and racism falls far short in its attempt. Songs include: title song, "Cry the Beloved Country," "Little Gray House," "Trouble Man," "Bird of Paradise," "Big Mole," "Train Go Now to Johannesburg."

p, Ely A. Landau; d, Daniel Mann; w, Alfred Hayes (based on the play by Maxwell Anderson, Kurt Weill, suggested by the novel Cry, The Beloved Country by Alan Paton); ph, Robert Hauser (Technicolor); m, Kurt Weill; ed, Walt Hannemann; md, Alex North; art d, Jack Martin Smith; ch, Paula Kelly; m/l, Kurt Weil, Maxwell Anderson.

Musical/Drama   **(PR:A MPAA:G)**

LOST IN THE STRATOSPHERE*   (1935) 65m MON bw

William Cagney (Lt. Cooper), Edward Nugent (Wood), June Collyer (Evelyn), Lona Andre (Sophie), Edmund Breese (Col. Brooks), Frank McGlynn, Sr. (Col. Worthington), Pauline Garon (Hilda Garon), Matt McHugh (O'Toole), Rudd Clark, Jack Mack, June Gittleson, Hattie McDaniel.

This film is about two junior officers who are best friends and like to play practical jokes on each other until a girl breaks them apart. Unfortunately, the involvement of stratosphere balloons only comes into play during the last 20 minutes of the movie, where the two friends are put in charge and come back heroes. But as life would have it, only one can have the girl.

p, W. T. Lackey; d, Melville Brown; w, Albert DeMond (based on a story by Tristram Tupper); ph, Ira Morgan; ed, Carl Pierson.

Comedy   **(PR:A MPAA:NR)**

LOST JUNGLE, THE*½ (1934) 70m Mascot bw

Clyde Beatty *(Clyde Beatty)*, Cecilia Parker *(Ruth Robinson)*, Syd Saylor *(Larry Henderson)*, Warner Richmond *(Sharkey)*, Wheeler Oakman *(Kirby)*, Edward J. Le Saint *(Capt. Robinson)*, Maston Williams *(Thompson)*, J. Crauford Kent *(Explorer)*, Lloyd Whitlock *(Howard)*, Lloyd Ingraham *(Bannister)*, Lew Meehan *(Flynn)*, Max Wagner *(Slade)*, Wes Warner *(Jackman)*, Jack Carlyle *(The Cook)*, Jim Corey *(Steve)*, Wally Wales *(Sandy)*, Ernie S. Adams *(Pete)*, Charles Whittaker *(Slim)*, Harry Holman *(Maitland)*, Mickey Rooney *(Mickey)*, The Hagenbeck-Wallace Circus Wild Animals.

Once the world's most famous wild animal trainer, Beatty stars as himself in this film. After the circus season is over, he takes a trip with his jealous assistant, Richmond, and press agent, Saylor, in search of new animals. A storm wrecks their ship on an uncharted island where Beatty discovers members of another crew who were stranded months before in search of a lost treasure. Among them is the captain, Le Saint, and his beautiful daughter, Parker. Le Saint's crew is ready to mutiny and when Oakman, the leader of the dissenters, discovers the location of the treasure with Richmond, they decide to keep the treasure for themselves. Beatty protects everyone from constant encounters with tigers, lions, bears, crocodiles, and gorillas. In the end, Richmond and Oakman pay for their treachery with their lives. The treasure is discovered by Le Saint and Beatty, and everyone is saved.

p, Nat Levine; d, Armand Schaefer, Dave Howard; w, Barney Sarecky, David Howard, Schaefer, Wyndham Gittens (based on the story by Colbert Clark, John Rathmell, Sherman Lowe, Al Martin); ph, Alvin Wyckoff, William Nobles; m, Hal Chasnoff; ed, Earl Turner.

Action/Adventure **(PR:A MPAA:NR)**

LOST LADY, THE (SEE: SAFE IN HELL, 1931)

LOST LADY, A** (1934) 61m FN/WB bw (GB: COURAGEOUS)

Barbara Stanwyck *(Marian Ormsby)*, Frank Morgan *(Daniel Forrester)*, Ricardo Cortez *(Ellinger)*, Lyle Talbot *(Neil)*, Phillip Reed *(Ned Montgomery)*, Hobart Cavanaugh *(Robert)*, Rafaela Ottiano *(Rosa)*, Henry Kolker *(John Ormsby)*, Walter Walker *(Judge Hardy)*, Mary Forbes *(Mrs. Hardy)*, Samuel S. Hinds *(Jim Sloane)*, Jameson Thomas *(Lord Verrington)*, Edward Keane *(Man)*, Colin Kenny *(Butler)*, Eddie Shubert, Harry Seymour *(Reporters)*, Tom Parsons *(Doctor)*, Willie Fung *(Chinese Cook)*, Edward McWade *(Simpson)*, Lorena Layson *(Young Matron)*, John Elliott *(Man)*, Edward Le Saint *(Mr. Cannon)*, Howard Hickman *(Dr. Barlow)*, Addison Richards *(State Attorney)*, Lee Beggs *(Old Gardener)*, Joseph Crehan, Sam Godfrey *(Doctors)*, Ethelreda Leopold *(Blonde Dancer)*, Eulalie Jensen *(Mrs. Sloane)*, John Hale, Virginia Hammond, Mary Russell.

This was the second time around for the Pulitzer Prize-winning novel and author Willa Cather was so disgusted by what was done that she forbade the sale of her literary work to films ever again. Irene Rich starred in the silent 1925 version and that was just fine, but this was hardly more than a fashion show for Stanwyck, who wore more dresses in the picture than Milton Berle did in a season of TV shows. Stanwyck is about to be married when her fiance is killed by the irate husband of a woman with whom he'd once dallied. This event so traumatizes Stanwyck that she believes herself to be incapable of another love. She hies herself to a mountain retreat, wallowing in self-pity. One afternoon, while hiking through rough terrain, she falls and is hurt. Then along comes genial Morgan, a lawyer in his dotage (he was actually only 44 at the time but they made him look considerably older). He helps her back to mental and physical health and she is drawn to him, more out of affection than passion, and eventually marries him. Soon after, she meets Cortez, a dashing type, and sparks fly immediately. She is unhappy again and resents having married Morgan but it all works out when she tells Morgan how she feels about Cortez and the old codger drops dead of a heart attack. It's all so pat and predictable (until Morgan keels over) that we're never caught up in the drama. This was one of the many "lady" pictures that Stanwyck made and, when you come to think of it, she seldom played a lady in any of them. Cather based the character of Marian Ormsby on the wife of Silas Gerber, governor of Nebraska in 1875, who lived in a big house in Red Cloud, Cather's home as a girl.

d, Alfred E. Green; w, Gene Markey, Kathryn Scola (based on the novel by Willa Cather); ph, Sid Hickox; ed, Owen Marks; art d, Jack Okey; cos, Orry-Kelly.

Drama **(PR:A MPAA:NR)**

LOST LAGOON*½ (1958) 79m UA bw

Jeffrey Lynn *(Charlie Walker)*, Peter Donat *(David Burnham)*, Leila Barry *(Elizabeth Moore)*, Jane Hartley *(Bernadine Walker)*, Roger Clark *(Millard Cauley)*, Don Gibson *(Mr. Beakins)*, Celeste Robinson *(Colima)*, Stanley Seymour, Isabelle Jones *(Natives)*, Herbert Smith and his Coral Islanders.

Unhappy husband Lynn is a castaway on a Caribbean island after a storm sinks the fishing boat he was on. He starts a new life with Barry and they set up a holiday resort. His wife's insurance investigator finds him and takes him back to his wife, while Barry marries a former boy friend.

p&d, John Rawlins; w, Milton Subotsky, Rawlins, Jeffrey Lynn; ph, Harry W. Smith; m, Hubert Smith, Terry Brannon; ed, David Rawlins; art d, Fay W. Van Hessen; m/l, Smith, Darwin Venneri.

Drama **(PR:A MPAA:NR)**

LOST, LONELY AND VICIOUS*½ (1958) 73m Bon Aire/Howco-States Rights bw

Ken Clayton *(Johnnie)*, Barbara Wilson *(Preach)*, Lilyan Chauvin *(Tanya)*, Richard Gilden *(Walt)*, Carole Nugent *(Pinkie)*, Sandra Giles *(Darlene)*, Allen Fife *(Buddy)*, Frank Stallworth *(Father)*, Johnny Erben *(Young Actor)*, Clint Quigley *(Reporter)*, T. Earl Johnson *(Psychiatrist)*.

Loosely based on the life of James Dean, with Clayton playing a Hollywood actor who has a fixation with death, fast cars, and women. Between movies he bounces from one woman to another until he meets Wilson, a drugstore clerk. She gets him to drop his preoccupation with killing himself in his sports car.

p, Charles M. Casinelli; d, Frank Myers; w, Norman Graham; ph, Ted and Vincent Saizis; m, Fredrick David; ed, Herb Hoffman.

Drama **(PR:A MPAA:NR)**

LOST MAN, THE½** (1969) 113m UNIV c

Sidney Poitier *(Jason Higgs)*, Joanna Shimkus *(Cathy Ellis)*, Al Freeman, Jr. *(Dennis Laurence)*, Michael Tolan *(Hamilton)*, Leon Bibb *(Eddie Moxy)*, Richard Dysart *(Barnes)*, David Steinberg *(Photographer)*, Beverly Todd *(Sally)*, Paul Winfield *(Orville)*, Bernie Hamilton *(Reggie Page)*, Richard Anthony Williams *(Ronald)*, Dolph Sweet *(Police Captain)*, Arnold Williams *(Terry)*, Maxine Stuart *(Miss Harrison)*, George Tyne *(Plainclothesman)*, Paulene Myers *(Grandma)*, Lee Weaver *(Willie)*, Morris Erby *(Miller)*, Doug Johnson *(Teddy)*, Lincoln Kilpatrick *(Minister)*, John Daheim *(Officer Parsons)*, Sonny Garrison *(Miller's Assistant)*, Virginia Capers *(Theresa)*, Vonetta McGee *(Diane)*, Frank Marth *(Warren)*.

Poitier plays the leader of a militant black group that robs a factory to provide money for families of jailed demonstators. In the escape Poitier kills a man and one of his men is killed. Poitier hides out in a movie theater while the others go to a whorehouse. They're killed in a police shoot-out when the madam makes a phone call. Unable to get the money to the civil rights organization because of police patrols, Poitier enlists the help of white social worker Shimkus, and they're cornered by police when they try to reach a waiting ship. Both are shot down when Shimkus shoots Poitier's gun into the ground. Previously filmed as ODD MAN OUT—with an Irish orientation—with James Mason in 1947.

p, Edward Muhl, Melville Tucker; d&w, Robert Alan Aurthur (based on the novel *Odd Man Out* by F. L. Green); ph, Jerry Finnerman (Panavsion, Technicolor); m, Quincy Jones; ed, Edward Mann; art d, Alexander Golitzen, George C. Webb; set d, John McCarthy, John Austin; cos, Edith Head; m/l, Jones, Ernie Shelby, Willie Cooper.

Drama **(PR:C MPAA:M)**

LOST MEN (SEE: HOMICIDE SQUAD, THE, 1931)

LOST MISSILE, THE** (1958, U.S./Can.) 70m William Berke/UA bw

Robert Loggia *(David Loring)*, Ellen Parker *(Joan Woods)*, Larry Kerr *(Gen. Barr)*, Philip Pine *(Joe Freed)*, Marilee Earle *(Ella Freed)*, Fred Engleberg *(TV Personality)*, Kitty Kelly *(Ella's Mother)*, Selmer Jackson *(Secretary of State)*, Joe Hyams *(Young)*, Bill Bradley *(Bradley)*.

An alien missile circles the earth at such a rate that the heat caused by its velocity destroys Ottawa, and New York City is next on the list. Scientist Loggia saves the day by building a minute hydrogen warhead inside a nuclear missile which blows away the lost missile of the title in the final moments. This was the last film directed by Berke (he died shortly after production), who specialized in series westerns.

p, Lee Gordon; d, Lester William Berke; w, John McPartland, Jerome Bixby (based on a story by Berke); ph, Kenneth Peach; m, Gerald Fried; ed, Ed Sutherland.

Science Fiction **(PR:A MPAA:NR)**

LOST MOMENT, THE½** (1947) 89m UNIV bw

Robert Cummings *(Lewis Venable)*, Susan Hayward *(Tina Borderau)*, Agnes Moorehead *(Juliana Boderau)*, Joan Loring *(Amelia)*, Eduardo Ciannelli *(Father Rinaldo)*, John Archer *(Charles)*, Frank Puglia *(Pietro)*, Minerva Urecal *(Maria)*, William Edmunds *(Vittorio)*, Martin Garralaga *(Waiter)*, Eugene Borden *(Proprietor)*, Micholas Khadarik *(Singer)*, Julian Rivero *(Storyteller)*, Lillian Molieri, Donna De Mario *(Pretty Girls)*, Robert Verdaine *(Young Man)*, Wallace Stark *(Sketch Artist)*, Saverio Lo Medico *(Waiter)*, Chris Drake.

Confined drama based on Henry James's novel *The Aspern Papers* that was adapted by a radio scribe and directed by a radio actor so there is lots of dialog and not that much visual excitement. Cummings is an American publisher who is told of the existence of a cache of love letters written by a missing poet in Venice by his pal, Archer. This intrigues Cummings so he goes to Venice under another name, and meets the object of the love letters, Moorehead (as a 105-year-old woman in a triumph of makeup) and her niece, Hayward. Cummings finds Hayward attractive (who wouldn't?). However, she shows him little more than disdain. The old house is creaky and frightening and Cummings stays on, learns that Moorehead is blind, and does his best to placate Hayward. Loring, a maid, agrees to aid Cummings in his quest. Then the weirdness begins. Cummings hears piano playing one night, decides to investigate, and finds Hayward at the keyboard in sort of a trance. She thinks that Cummings is the missing poet and that she is her own aunt. Cummings calls on the local cleric, Ciannelli, who explains that Hayward's mind is askew because of the love letters and the still-missing poet. Cummings attempts to bring her out of her fog with wining and dining, then, once he's learned the location of the letters, steals them. Hayward goes into another fuzzy state, looks for the letters and can't find them, so she attempts to kill Moorehead because she suspects the old woman took them. Cummings arrives, admits he took the letters, and then Moorehead says the poet isn't missing at all; he's dead, and she killed him when she believed he was going to drop her. (There's a spot in the garden where nothing grows. That must be the grave.) Hayward hits the carpeted floor in a dead faint and Cummings takes her outside as the blind Moorehead tries to find the letters which Cummings had dropped on the floor. In doing so, she knocks over a candle that sets the place on fire. Cummings does the brave thing by going into the inferno to save the old lady, but it's not soon enough and she dies. The death of Moorehead causes Hayward to come out of her mental fog forever. The picture ends with Cummings and Hayward watching the old house burn. Hayward and Gabel didn't agree and the battles on the set were heard across the city. Some good suspense moments and excellent acting by all concerned, but a disappointment at the turnstiles. Hayward was 29 at the time and never more ravishing.

p, Walter Wanger; d, Martin Gabel; w, Leonardo Bercovici (based on the novel *The Aspern Papers* by Henry James); ph, Hal Mohr; m, Daniele Amfitheatrof; ed, Milton Carruth; art d, Alexander Golitzen.

Drama **Cas.** **(PR:A MPAA:NR)**

LOST ON THE WESTERN FRONT 1/2**
(1940, Brit.) 62m Franco-London/Standard bw (GB: A ROMANCE IN FLANDERS)

Paul Cavanagh *(John Morley)*, Marcelle Chantal *(Yvonne Berry)*, Garry Marsh *(Rodd Berry)*, Olga Lindo *(Madame Vlandermaere)*, Alistair Sim *(Col. Wexton)*, Evelyn Roberts *(Capt. Stanford)*, P. Kynaston Reeves *(Maj. Burke)*, Arthur Hambling *(Col. Kennedy)*, C. Denier Warren *(Bill Johnson)*, Frank Atkinson *(Joe Stuggins)*, Bobbie Comber *(Chauffeur)*, Andrea Malandrinos *(Mayor)*, Denise Sydney *(Muriel)*, Kathleen Weston *(Bessie)*, Muriel Pavlow.

Chantal marries again after hearing that her first husband has been killed during the war. She later recognizes her "dead" husband in a crowd and learns that he is suffering from amnesia, caused by a wound suffered when her new mate sent him to his "death."

p, F. Deutschmeister; d, Maurice Elvey; w, Harold Simpson (based on the novel *Widow's Island* by Mario Fort, Ralph Vanio); ph, William Luff.

Drama **(PR:A MPAA:NR)**

LOST ONE, THE* 1/2**
(1951, Ger.) 97m National Filmgesellschaft (DER VERLONE)

Peter Lorre *(Dr. Karl Rothe)*, Karl John *(Hoesch)*, Helmut Rudolf *(Colonel Winkler)*, Renate Mannhardt *(Inge Hermann)*, Johanna Hofer *(Frau Hermann)*, Eva-Ingeborg Scholz *(Ursula Weber)*, Lotte Rausch *(Helene)*, Gisela Trowe *(Prostitute)*, Kurt Meister *(Prefect)*, Hansi Wendler *(Secretary)*, Alexander Hunzinger *(Drunk)*, Josef Dahmen *(Canteen Bartender)*.

Inspired by what he experienced when he returned to his native Germany in 1949, famed Hollywood character actor Lorre directed the only film of his long career, THE LOST ONE. Lorre is a doctor working in a postwar refugee camp in Germany. He has assumed a new identity and calls himself "Neumeister" ("new man"). He is confronted by John who has just begun working at the camp as Lorre's new medical assistant, whom Lorre recognizes immediately as an old nemesis from the war days. John seeks a truce between himself and Lorre because he needs the doctor to secure false identity papers for him so that he may escape the Allies. Lorre invites John to the camp's canteen for a drink and dismisses the bartender so that they may speak privately. John, getting drunk, reminds Lorre how he had helped him during the war, and, although Lorre never asked for his assistance, agrees that there is a debt to be repaid. A flashback then takes us to 1943 where we see Lorre working for the Nazis as an immunologist. John is his lab assistant, and he enters accompanied by Gestapo officer Rudolf who informs the doctor that they have obtained information that leads them to believe that Lorre's fiancee Mannhardt has sold the results of his secret experiments to the British. Rudolf suggests that Lorre "end" the relationship, and that night, after confronting Mannhardt, Lorre fondles her pearl necklace and puts his hands around her throat. Back in the present, Lorre confesses to John that he remembers nothing of the murder, but he felt that he should be punished. The punishment never came however, because John and Rudolf covered up the crime. Flashback to 1943 and we see that a young woman, Hofer, has taken Mannhardt's room in the boarding house where Lorre lives. Lorre begins to have romantic feelings for the girl, but these emotions soon turn murderous. His homicidal instincts overtaking him, Lorre leaves the apartment rather than give in to his impulses. He picks up a prostitute in a bar and she leads him to her home. When she gets a good look at him, she suddenly becomes terrified and begins to scream that he is a murderer. He flees the apartment building and takes a late train home where he meets Rausch, a lonely, sexually frustrated woman who tries to seduce him. When an air-raid warning sounds, all the passengers leave the train and head for shelter except Lorre and Rausch. When the passengers return, they find the strangled corpse of Rausch. Stricken with guilt, Lorre decides to end his life, but first he will kill John who started the whole vicious cycle. While searching for John, Lorre stumbles across an anti-Nazi conspiracy planned by none other than Rudolf. When his headquarters are raided by Nazis, Rudolf and Lorre escape through the bombed out streets of Hamburg and witness the conspirators killed or captured by the soldiers. Rudolf then disappears, requesting that Lorre complete his job on John. Lorre survives the war, assumes his new identity, but has never been able to locate John. Returning to the present, John's reappearance illustrates for Lorre that there is no hiding from one's past. John, quite drunk at this point, dares Lorre to kill him. Lorre calmly pulls a gun and shoots John, completing his lengthy quest for vengeance. Lorre then leaves the refugee camp, walks on the railroad tracks, and when he hears the train coming, stops with his back to it and puts his hand over his face before the train runs him over. Unrelentingly grim, THE LOST ONE is a dark examination of life in Germany during, and shortly after, WW II. Lorre evokes the visual style of Fritz Lang who directed him in his finest film, M. Though critics at the time claimed that Lorre was just retreading Lang's M for his own use, THE LOST ONE is a quite different film and, in fact, could be considered an extension of his character in M. Lorre, as the compulsive killer, confronts himself and must deal with the guilt that stifles his existence in a way that the child-killer in M never did. THE LOST ONE was badly received in Germany upon its release which came quite late in the post-war cycle of filmmaking. The grim, bleak conscience-raising German films had fallen out of favor with a public that was now only interested in escapist entertainment, thus dooming Lorre's film at the box office. Seldom seen in America, THE LOST ONE could only be viewed in an unsubtitled print donated by Lorre himself to U.C.L.A. Recently, Fred Pressburger, son of producer Arnold Pressburger, has revived the film, rerecorded the soundtrack, added sub-titles, and rereleased it in art houses in the U.S.

p, Arnold Pressburger; d, Peter Lorre; w, Lorre, Benno Vigny, Axel Eggebrecht; ph, Vaclav Vich; ed, C. O. Bartning; art d, Franz Schroedter, Karl Weber.

Drama **(PR:C MPAA:NR)**

LOST PATROL, THE,* 1/2** (1934) 74m RKO bw

Victor McLaglen *(The Sergeant)*, Boris Karloff *(Sanders)*, Wallace Ford *(Morelli)*, Reginald Denny *(George Brown)*, J. M. Kerrigan *(Quincannon)*, Billy Bevan *(Herbert Hale)*, Alan Hale *(Cook)*, Brandon Hurst *(Bell)*, Douglas Walton *(Pearson)*, Sammy Stein *(Abelson)*, Howard Wilson *(Aviator)*, Neville Clark *(Lt. Hawkins)*, Paul Hanson *(Jock Mackay)*, Francis Ford.

There's not a woman in the cast of this strange but fascinating Ford film which gives a feeling of impending doom from frame to frame but is nevertheless an absorbing adventure drama. The story deals with a British cavalry patrol in the Mesopotamian desert during WW I. Ford shows the shadows of the mounted men before showing the men themselves while the credits come up. A single shot rings out and the leader, an officer, falls dead from his horse, his face buried in the sand. With him goes the purpose of the mission and even the direction in which the patrol is traveling. McLaglen, the sergeant who takes over, finds nothing in the officer's map case to indicate where they are and tells his men that the officer kept everything in his head. McLaglen leads the group to an oasis, but the men find themselves under occasional deadly sniper fire from unseen Arabs who have surrounded them and lie in wait, out of sight in the stretching dunes. In fact, the soldiers—except for McLaglen—never see the Arabs and this insidious enemy takes on an almost mythical image. One by one the soldiers are picked off until only McLaglen, Ford, and Karloff are left. Then a British plane flies overhead, answering their frantic signals. The pilot lands, gets out of his plane, and tucks a walking stick under his arm, strolling leisurely toward the oasis, McLaglen and Ford yelling at him to take cover. He is shot down and killed, which sends religious zealot Karloff round the bend. Karloff suddenly appears as a mendicant, adorned in rags and carrying a makeshift cross, running wildly into the desert, screaming out to the unseen Arabs to accept the way of the cross. He is shot to death. Ford—who races after the lunatic—is also shot, leaving McLaglen alone to bury his comrades. He places their sabers, gleaming in the intense sunlight, at the heads of their graves and then digs his own grave as, gun in hand, he waits for the Arabs. (This scene was duplicated for the finale of a Robert Taylor WW II film, BATAAN and the plotline would be employed in BAD LANDS (1939) and SAHARA (1943).) The Arabs now attack in force but McLaglen mows them down with the Lewis gun from the plane. A British relief column later appears and the numb McLaglen greets his rescuers as if they are a mirage. When an officer asks where McLaglen's men are, the sergeant can only point to the row of graves and the upturned sabers. THE LOST PATROL, shot on location in the desert around Yuma, Arizona, is a much superior remake of a 1929 British film with Agnew McMaster in Karloff's role and, ironically, Victor's brother, Cyril McLaglen, as the sergeant. The schedule for this film was grueling, with the relentless Ford shooting the entire film in 110-degree heat within ten days. Karloff is outstanding—if not completely overwhelmed by his own insane character—as the religious nut, and McLaglen does yeoman service as the resolute sergeant. Ford, as usual, keeps the pace hectic and paints his picture of destiny with master strokes.

p, Cliff Reid; d, John Ford; w, Dudley Nichols, Garrett Fort (based on the novel *Patrol* by Philip MacDonald): ph, Harold Wenstrom; m, Max Steiner; ed, Paul Weatherwax; art d, Van Nest Polglase, Sidney Ullman.

War/Adventure **Cas.** **(PR:C MPAA:NR)**

LOST PEOPLE, THE 1/2** (1950, Brit.) 89m Gainsborough/GFD bw

Dennis Price *(Capt. Ridley)*, Mai Zetterling *(Lili)*, Richard Attenborough *(Jan)*, Siobhan McKenna *(Marie)*, Maxwell Reed *(Peter)*, William Hartnell *(Sgt. Barnes)*, Gerard Heinz *(Professor)*, Zena Marshall *(Anna)*, Olaf Pooley *(Milosh)*, Harcourt Williams *(Priest)*, Philo Hauser *(Draja)*, Jill Balcon *(Rebecca)*, Grey Blake *(Capt. Saunders)*, Marcel Poncin *(Duval)*, Tutte Lemkow, Paul Hardtmuth, Nelly Arno, Pamela Sterling, Peter Bull, George Benson.

Price is a British captain and Hartnell a sergeant under him, and the two take command of a group of displaced persons after WW II. The group is being kept at a large German theater as they wait to be transported to different countries. Price's biggest problem is trying to keep the peace between people of different nationalities until a dying man is believed to have the plague. When the theater is quarantined, the people drop their differences and band together. They jump at each other's throats again as soon as the plague theory is discounted. When an innocent young woman is murdered, Price declares over her body that there can only be peace in the world when people put aside their differences and learn to live as brothers.

p, Gordon Wellesley; d, Bernard Knowles, Muriel Box; w, Bridget Boland, Box (based on the play "Cockpit" by Boland); ph, Jack Asher; m, John Greenwood; ed, Gordon Hales.

War Drama **(PR:A MPAA:NR)**

LOST RANCH* (1937) 57m Victory bw

Tom Tyler *(Wade)*, Jeanne Martel *(Rita)*, Marjorie Beebe *(Minnie)*, Howard Bryant *(Happy)*, Ted Lorch *(Merkle)*, Slim Whitaker *(Sheriff)*, Forrest Taylor *(Garson)*, Lafe McKee *(Carroll)*, Roger Williams *(Terry)*.

Tyler is again working for the Cattlemen's Protective Association and going after a band of kidnapers led by Taylor. They've taken McKee hostage, and Martel, McKee's daughter, takes up with Tyler to save her father. A terrible western that has Tyler attempting to sing.

p&d, Sam Katzman; w, Basil Dickey; ph, Bill Hyer; ed, Holbrook N. Todd.

Western **(PR:A MPAA:NR)**

LOST RIVER   (SEE: TRAIL OF THE RUSTLERS, 1950)

LOST SEX**¹/₂   (1968, Jap.) 97m Kindai Eiga Kyokai/Chevron bw (HONNO)

Hideo Kanze *(The Master)*, Nobuko Otowa *(The Housemaid)*, Eijiro Tono *(Neighbor/Writer)*, Yoshinobu Ogawa *(Neighbor/Son)*, Kaori Shima *(Neighbor/Son's Wife)*.

Japanese drama directed by Shindo, one of the first Japanese filmmakers to deal directly with the horrible aftermath of the nuclear bomb. Kanze stars as a respected drama teacher who has gone to his mountain villa for a vacation. He lives alone, seeing only his housekeeper, a war widow from the local village. One day, Kanze spots two young lovers embracing and tells Otowa of his sexual frustration. He explains that he has been impotent ever since he was caught in the bomb blast at Hiroshima while stationed there during the war. Though a nurse aided him in regaining his virility so that he could marry, he soon became impotent again and was divorced. Sympathetic to his plight, Otowa suggests that he observe a custom practiced in the village every spring. The custom entails that men of the village sneak into the bedrooms of available women and have sex with them. Otowa invites Kanze into her bedroom to witness. When three men attempt to enter her home, Kanze becomes aroused and prevents them from entering. The next evening he disguises himself, enters her room, and is finally able to make love. This is repeated night after night until Kanze suddenly becomes convinced that Otowa is having other affairs. He confronts her with his suspicions and then leaves the village. In autumn Kanze returns to the village and learns that Otowa has died due to a tubal pregnancy. He also discovers that she had hired men in the village to simulate the spring ritual in order to arouse Kanze. Learning that her reputation in the village was beyond reproach, the guilt-ridden and remorseful Kanze stands alone watching the snows cover the mountains.

d&w, Kaneto Shindo; ph, Kiyomi Kuroda; m, Hikaru Hayashi.

Drama   **(PR:O MPAA:NR)**

LOST SOULS*¹/₂   (1961, Ital.) 84m Oscar/Ellis bw (VITE PERDUTE)

Virna Lisi *(Anna)*, Sandra Milo *(Giulia)*, Jacques Sernas *(The Baron)*, Gabriele Tinti *(Carlo)*, Marco Guglielmi *(Toni)*, John Kitzmiller *(Luca)*, Roberto Mauri, Anna Alberti, Arturo Dominici, Gustavo De Nardo, Gennaro Sebastiani.

Italian crime film about five convicts led by Sernas who have escaped from the island of Elba and enter an iron mine payroll office in order to rob it. There they are met with stiff resistance from Tinti, the mine owner's son, who refuses to hand over the payroll checks. When Tinti's sister Lisi and two of her friends happen to wander into the office, the criminals try to hold them hostage. One of the girls tries to run for help, but she is captured by one of the convicts who subsequently tries to rape her. In the struggle the convict is shot in the arm by the girl, and he kills her. Tinti finally gives the criminals the checks, but Sernas orders Guglielmi to take Lisi with him to the bank to endorse them. Seeing her opportunity, Lisi scribbles a note on the back of a check for the police. When the con and his hostage return, they find the bloody corpse of Sernas, who was killed by one of the other cons. In the ensuing gunfight, all the criminals kill each other off, leaving Tinti, Lisi, and her friend to await the arrival of the police.

p, Federico Teti; d&w, Adelchi Bianchi, Roberto Mauri; ph, Aldo Tonti.

Crime   **(PR:O MPAA:NR)**

LOST SQUADRON, THE***   (1932) 72m RKO bw

Richard Dix *(Capt. Gibson)*, Mary Astor *(Follette Marsh)*, Erich von Stroheim *(Von Furst)*, Dorothy Jordon *(The Pest)*, Joel McCrea *(Red)*, Robert Armstrong *(Woody)*, Hugh Herbert *(Fritz)*, Ralph Ince *(Detective)*, Dick Garce, Art Gobel, Leo Nomis, Frank Clark *(Fliers)*.

This bizarre but absorbing film depicts WW I fighter pilots working in Hollywood as daredevil stunt pilots, under the orders of maniacal German director Von Stroheim. Dix, McCrea, and Armstrong are the pilots he punishes by making them perform impossible death-kissing feats. Making matters worse is Von Stroheim's discovery that Dix and his wife, Astor, are in love. The pathological director decides he will murder Dix and coats corrosive acid on the control wires of Dix's biplane, causing it to crash. It is not Dix who is killed but his pal Armstrong. Dix and friends take just revenge on the killer Von Stroheim. McCrea shoots him and then he is taken up in a stunt plane by Dix who dives with Von Stroheim's body to earth in a fiery crash. Actually, Von Stroheim was performing an adroit parody of himself in THE LOST SQUADRON. He is shown strutting about on sets, calling his actors idiots, and, when Astor displeases him, twisting her wrists so forcefully that they almost appear to break off. His attire is strictly Saville Row and he wears white gloves everywhere. He rages about while stroking a horrid scar on his forehead, grabbing the many megaphones available to him at every turn, all monogrammed with his name ("Mr. Von Furst"), so he can bellow at his cowed actors. He laces every direction with sarcastic insults and, in one scene where he is displeased with the performances, he explodes, discarding his coat and throwing it to the ground, screaming like a maniac, his Teutonic words running together so that he sounds like a rabid dog, which, of course, is a parody of himself when he was directing some of his classics (THE MERRY WIDOW, THE WEDDING MARCH, FOOLISH WIVES, BLIND HUSBANDS) during the silent era. The aerial stunts in THE LOST SQUADRON are stupendous, with dogfights simulating WW I combat that look as real as anything achieved by Howard Hughes in HELL'S ANGELS or William Wellman in the silent classic WINGS. In his first production for RKO, Selznick pulled out all the stops and produced a high quality, expensive-looking film. When releasing the film, RKO hyped it mightily to the public, trying to encompass in its PR copy the many facets of the complex story. Wrote their office flaks: "Wingmen of the Hollywood skies courting death as they courted women—dangerously, glamorously! A wave of the hand . . . and off they streaked! Plunging, zooming, climbing, crashing . . . that a madman below might create on film the supreme thrill to shock the world!" This

was not the first and certainly not the last film to caricature the eccentric Von Stroheim. In the silent era he was profiled as a manic foreign director, "Eric von Greed" in MY NEIGHBOR'S WIFE, 1925, as "Von Strogoff" in HIGH HAT, 1927, and in the talkie era as "Kolofski" in the Leslie Howard-Humphrey Bogart comedy, STAND-IN (1937), and in Red Skelton's spoof of Hollywood, MERTON OF THE MOVIES (1947) as "Von Strutt." But it was in THE LOST SQUADRON that the priceless scenes of Von Stroheim satirizing Von Stroheim appear (or maybe he was just playing himself for the fun of it), a film director who will do anything to achieve realism, even if it costs the lives of a horde of extras. Paul Sloane was originally scheduled to direct this film but he grew ill during the production and was replaced by the competent Archainbaud. Many believed, however, that Von Stroheim really directed the film, especially when realizing that it was typically overlong in the Von Stroheim tradition and much had to be cut from it, bringing it down to 80 minutes for its initial release. It was later cut to 72 minutes. There are some marvelous early talkie scenes of Hollywood, a crowd-packed premiere witnessed by the hobo fliers who arrive in Los Angeles looking for jobs after being on the bum for a decade, and the outdoor aerial stunts with Von Stroheim directing his cameramen below, shouting: "Listen you—be sure and keep them in the cameras. We might catch a nice crackup!" In another scene Von Stroheim directs the leading man in one of his films by telling him how to fly his plane and to be sure that stunt pilot Armstrong "doesn't knock your head off" when he swoops close with his plane. Adds Von Stroheim: "There's one consolation—you'll never miss it!"

d, George Archainbaud; w, Wallace Smith, Herman J. Mankiewicz, Robert Presnell (based on a story by Dick Grace); ph, Leo Trover, Edward Cronjager (air ph, Rob Robison, Elmer Dyer); ed, William Hamilton; cos, Max Ree.

Adventure/Drama   **Cas.**   **(PR:C MPAA:NR)**

LOST STAGE VALLEY   (SEE: STAGE TO TUCSON, 1950)

LOST TRAIL, THE*¹/₂   (1945) 53m MON bw

Johnny Mack Brown *(Nevada)*, Raymond Hatton *(Sandy)*, Jennifer Holt *(Jane Burns)*, Riley Hill *(Ned Turner)*, Kenneth MacDonald *(John Corbett)*, Lynton Brent *(Hall)*, John Ince *(Bailey)*, John Bridges *(Dr. Brown)*, Eddie Parker *(Bill)*, Frank McCarroll *(Joe)*, Dick Dickinson *(Ed)*, Milburn Morante *(Zeke)*, Frank LaRue *(Jones)*, Steve Clark *(Mason)*, George Morrell, Carl Mathews, Victor Cox, Cal Shrum and his Rhythm Rangers.

MacDonald is the operator of a stagecoach line competing with Holt's company. His men start robbing Holt's stagecoaches and killing her men in order to force her out of the business. U.S. marshal Brown, with the help of fellow-marshal Hatton, puts a stop to it after a few chases and gun battles.

p, Charles J. Bigelow; d, Lambert Hillyer; w, Jess Bowers [Adele Buffington]; ph, Marcel LePicard; ed, Danny Milner.

Western   **(PR:A MPAA:NR)**

LOST TREASURE OF THE AMAZON   (SEE: JIVARO, 1954)

LOST TRIBE, THE**   (1949) 72m COL bw

Johnny Weissmuller *(Jungle Jim)*, Myrna Dell *(Norina)*, Elena Verdugo *(Li Wanna)*, Joseph Vitale *(Calhoun)*, Ralph Dunn *(Capt. Rawling)*, Paul Marion *(Chot)*, Nelson Leigh *(Zoron)*, George J. Lewis *(Whip Wilson)*, Gil Perkins *(Dojek)*, George DeNormand *(Cullen)*, Wally West *(Eckle)*, Rube Schaffer *(Lerch)*.

Based on the cartoon strip "Jungle Jim" with Weissmuller playing the cartoon adventurer. The former Tarzan comes to the rescue of a lost African city (the natives are white) that is under siege by a band of crooks who want to steal its treasures. He also takes on a lion in hand-to-hand combat, wrestles a couple of sharks, and performs other impossible feats. Verdugo and Dunn are the crooks and Dell is the woman who catches Jungle Jim's attention, when he's not doing battle with countless numbers of humans and animals. Kids will enjoy this pre-RAIDERS OF THE LOST ARK adventure. (See JUNGLE JIM series, Index.)

p, Sam Katzman; d, William Berke; w, Arthur Hoerl, Don Martin (based on a story by Hoerl inspired by the King Features comic strip "Jungle Jim"); ph, Ira H. Morgan; ed, Aaron Stell; md, Mischa Bakaleinikoff; art d, Paul Palmentola.

Action/Adventure   **(PR:A MPAA:NR)**

LOST VOLCANO, THE**   (1950) 67m MON bw

Johnny Sheffield *(Bomba)*, Donald Woods *(Paul Gordon)*, Marjorie Lord *(Ruth Gordon)*, John Ridgely *(Barton)*, Elena Verdugo *(Nona)*, Tommy Ivo *(David)*, Don Harvey *(Higgins)*, Grandon Rhodes *(Charles Landley)*, Robert Lewis *(Daniel)*.

Jungle adventure has Sheffield, muscle-clad king of the jungle, saving young Ivo from two hunting guides who have kidnaped Ivo to force him to lead them to a lost city. It is located in the center of an active volcano, and Sheffield manages to get to Ivo just before it erupts. Picture used a lot of stock animal footage in a realistic manner. Script and direction are well-paced, with Sheffield fitting the part of Bomba well. (See BOMBA series, Index.)

p, Walter Mirisch; d&w, Ford Beebe (based on characters created by Roy Rockwood); ph, Marcel LePicard; m, Ozzie Caswell; ed, Richard Heermance; md, Caswell; art d, Dave Milton.

Adventure   **(PR:AA MPAA:NR)**

LOST WEEKEND, THE*****   (1945) 101m PAR bw

Ray Milland *(Don Birnam)*, Jane Wyman *(Helen St. James)*, Phillip Terry *(Nick Birnam)*, Howard Da Silva *(Nat the Bartender)*, Doris Dowling *(Gloria)*, Frank Faylen *(Bim)*, Mary Young *(Mrs. Deveridge)*, Anita Bolster *(Mrs. Foley)*, Lilian Fontaine *(Mrs. St. James)*, Lewis L. Russell *(Charles St. James)*, Frank Orth *(Opera Attendant)*, Gisela Werbiseck *(Mrs. Wertheim)*, Eddie Laughton *(Mr. Brophy)*, Harry Barris *(Piano Player)*, Jayne Hazard *(M. M.)*, Craig Reynold *(M. M.'s Escort)*,

Walter Baldwin *(Albany)*, Fred "Snowflake" Toones, Clarence Muse *(Washroom Attendants)*, Gene Ashley, Jerry James, William Meader *(Male Nurses)*, Emmett Vogan *(Doctor)*, Milton Wallace *(Pawnbroker)*, Pat Moriarty, William O'Leary *(Irishmen)*, Lester Sharpe, Bertram Warburgh *(Jewish Men)*, Theodora Lynch, John Garris *(Opera Singers)*, Byron Foulger *(Shopkeeper)*, Helen Dickson *(Mrs. Frink)*, David Clyde *(Dave)*.

THE LOST WEEKEND, the most celebrated of the "problem films" of the 1940s, was a movie that barely missed being shelved let alone being released. The script by Wilder and Brackett is merciless and unrelenting but literate and even poetic in spots. Wilder's direction is excruciatingly effective in its set shots and unusual framing. And Milland's virtuoso performance as the hopeless alcoholic is startling, shocking, and utterly riveting. There was nothing like this film until its chancy appearance and there have been few like it since, certainly no film that approaches its power and persuasiveness. Milland is a struggling writer who is losing the battle at the typewriter which causes him to water down his writer's block with booze. The film opens with the camera zooming through the window of a New York apartment building and into an apartment Milland shares with his responsible brother Terry, who is about to go on a weekend vacation. He is concerned about leaving Milland alone but his brother assures him all will be fine, that he will be settling down to do some serious writing. But right from that moment we know his sneaking, manipulative drunk nature because he is hiding a bottle of liquor at the time he is reassuring his brother all will be well. Milland makes a feeble attempt to write but he knows from the offset that it's a useless effort for his real ambition is to consume the contents of those quart bottles he has secreted about the apartment in every conceivable hiding place. After Milland uses up the booze in the apartment he takes the money his brother has left for the cleaning lady and slips down to his favorite watering hole where bartender Da Silva, a congenial sort, hates to see him coming, knowing he is not a social drinker but a stone boozer. Da Silva begins to pour and Milland sinks deeper into his alcoholic world. He is at first charming and wonderfully imaginative, spewing forth the literature that has not gone onto a manuscript page, squandering it verbally at the bar. "That's not Third Avenue out there, Nat," Milland waxes sloppily but eloquently. "It's the Nile." And he goes into a description of an ancient world visiting the modern in his now distorted perception of reality. He is fascinating and the liquor allows his intelligence and creativity to beguile Da Silva and others but it's a fading charm and he fades with it as he counts the rings left on the bar by the shot glasses of booze he has consumed. He runs out of money and Da Silva cuts him off, not because of the money but because he pities him and wants to help him; Da Silva encourages Milland to go home and take care of himself. From there it's all downhill fast. While his girl friend, Wyman, a magazine editor, calls and later searches for him, Milland sinks to a level of utter debasement. To buy more booze he takes money from a prostitute, then goes to a cocktail lounge where he sits next to a couple, rifling through the woman's purse when she goes to the washroom, taking money, again for booze. He is caught but the woman, attracted to him, pitying him, begs he not be prosecuted. Milland then undergoes a night of horror. Drunk, alone in his apartment, he hallucinates the image of a bat flying wildly about the room, diving at him, so that he sinks back in fear in a chair to next see a small mouse appear in a crack in the wall, and the bat diving down at the mouse, tearing at it so that the blood runs wickedly down the wall in a gory stream, sending Milland into paroxysms of screaming terror. In a more sober moment he thinks back on the one person he loves and is ashamed to face, Wyman, and we see in flashback their first meeting at a concert and how they meet at the coat room, their claim checks mixed and how embarrassed he is when she discovers a small bottle of booze in his coat. In desperation, Milland later pawns Wyman's prized possession, her fur coat, to buy liquor. Then he attempts to trade his typewriter, the instrument of his future, the tool of his hope, but bartender Da Silva refuses to take it in exchange for booze. "You're the writer, Mr. Birnam, not me," protests Da Silva. Frantic, Milland staggers down Third Avenue, attempting to pawn the typewriter but he finds to his horror that all the pawnshops are closed, it being Yom Kippur. Weak from lack of food, dehydrated, exhausted, he falls into the gutter and is picked up by the police and taken to the alcoholic ward of New York's Bellevue Hospital. There he awakens to a new and more devastating nightmare inside the drunk ward. A sadistic male nurse, bitingly played by Faylen, preps Milland for a night of sheer fright by telling him that all the drunks about him hallucinate, see animals of all sorts, scream, and some have to be strapped down. He ends his brutal catalog of fears by smilingly telling Milland that he was talking to the "doctor the other day and he told me that delerium tremens is a disease of the night . . . Well . . . good night." Faylen, although only on the screen for a few moments, makes a terrific impact as the insidious and utterly repulsive male nurse. He had been chosen over Lee Tracy and Jack Oakie but even director Wilder, who knew he was right for the role of the vindictive nurse, didn't like him. His is only one of many roles played in the film by fine character actors, Da Silva being the most potent as the sympathetic and conscientious bartender. The lights go out and soon the ward is wild with men turning into raving beasts, screaming, yelling out their hallucinations, squirming and fighting the straps that hold them, quaking and shivering and jerking about as if in the throes of epileptic fits. Finally, Milland can no longer stand it and, through a ruse, escapes Bellevue and returns home. He is a disheveled, fatigued, and emotionally exhausted wreck when Wyman and Terry find him. Milland realizes that he has hit bottom and begs forgiveness from his brother and girl friend, vowing he will not drink again and this self promise seems valid at the close of this depressing but enlightening film as Milland sits down to his typewriter and begins to write the only tale he really knows best, his own descent into self-destruction through drinking. He determinedly types out a title page to his novel: "The Bottle by Don Birnam." THE LOST WEEKEND is beautifully written by Wilder and Brackett, pulling no punches and Wilder's direction is just as candid, brilliantly conceived from shot to shot. He slowly builds his scenes, presenting low-key lighting and deep-focus photography. Wilder emphasizes objects that reinforce the menace of booze, shooting scenes through whiskey shot glasses and bottles. And shots of Milland—he appears in almost every scene as a blistering point of view—oftimes encompass in wide and long views a hidden bottle, dangling from a string out of a window, hidden in a lampshade, waiting to be consumed and to consume its imbiber. There is much that is surrealistic in Wilder's approach, reminescent of Goya's paintings or the work of filmmaker Bunuel, particularly LOS OLIVADADOS. (Roman Polanski would lean heavily upon the cat-and-mouse scene from THE LOST WEEKEND when making his film REPULSION in 1965, depicting a cracking wall.) Of course, Milland is superb as the romantic alcoholic, a masterstroke of casting. Up to the time of the LOST WEEKEND, Milland had been a matinee idol who made his mark in light comedy and romances. And his casting, like that of Wyman, also a veteran of light comedies, was revolutionary and startling. Milland was given the Jackson novel to read by Buddy DeSylva, Paramount mogul, with a note reading: "Read it. Study it. You're going to play it." Milland was apprehensive and, when reading the stark story, believed that the film might earn some critical praise as a social document but not much else. He also felt that he was not equipped to handle such a serious role, but his wife encouraged him to try it. He was encouraged also by the fact that Wilder and Brackett, the geniuses behind the film, had never had a flop. (Brackett would later state: "THE LOST WEEKEND was the easiest script we wrote, thanks to the superb novel." Wilder credited the film with establishing his name in Hollywood: "It was after this picture that people started noticing me.") Milland, to achieve that gaunt, haggard look of the alcoholic, went on a crash diet and took off many pounds. Not a tippler at that time, he even tried over-drinking, and got sick. He believed he had to sink himself into the quagmire of the drunk and, when the company went to New York to shoot location footage, Milland checked himself into Bellevue with the help of resident doctors. It was a horror he would later repeat on camera. He was given an iron bed and was locked into the drunk ward. "The place was a multitude of smells," he recalled in his autobiography, *Wide-Eyed in Babylon*, "but the dominant one was that of a cesspool. And there were the sounds of moaning, and quiet crying. One man talked incessantly, just gibberish, and two of the inmates were under restraint, strapped to their beds." He was told by the male nurses that most of the inmates had been professional men in the advertising field and one had been the mayor of a large city. He was given a drink of paraldehyde mixture, which the inmates were given nightly to quiet their stomachs, which caused the actor to retch. That night Milland was awakened by screams and the noise from guards struggling with a new arrival, a hysterical man who set off the whole ward. "The screaming didn't stop and the other inmates began growling in the foulest language imaginable . . . Suddenly the room was bedlam. I knew I was looking into the deepest pit." Barefooted, and only wearing a robe, Milland ran from the ward while the door was open and slipped past the desk and outside, to run through the gates on to Thirty-fourth Street where he tried to hail a cab. Completely unnerved, the actor turned around and found a policeman looking at him suspiciously. He told the officer that he was Ray Milland the movie star and that he was staying at the Waldorf and was doing some research on a movie. The cop scowled, apparently not a movie-goer, and then grabbed Milland when he saw the Bellevue stamp on his bathrobe. When Milland struggled, the cop stamped on his bare toes which caused him to painfully submit. The actor was hustled back to Bellevue where it took him a half hour to explain to newly arrived male nurses unfamiliar with his research arrangements who he was and that he wanted out of Bellevue, *immediately*. He was released but when Wilder learned of his exploits, he delightfully employed the very same ward for his Bellevue scenes. Authorities at the hospital later regretted allowing the film company to use the premises for THE LOST WEEKEND. When they saw the film they vowed never again to cooperate with Hollywood. Director George Seaton later wanted to use interiors of Bellevue when he was shooting THE MIRACLE ON 34TH STREET, those showing Edmund Gwen, claimant to the exclusive title of Santa Claus, being examined, but he ran into a brick wall with authorities. Said Seaton: "Wilder's a tough man to follow . . . The hospital manager practically threw me out beause he was still mad at himself for having given Wilder permission to shoot at the hospital. What made him particularly angry was that the picture showed a male nurse brutalizing an alcoholic." Milland not only experienced difficulty in researching his role but gleaned undeserved publicity when supposedly shooting his streetwalking scenes in New York City where he was supposedly incognito. During his trek down Third Avenue to pawn the typewriter, Milland, his clothes a mess, his face black with beard stubble, hollow-eyed, and looking as if on death's door, stopped to look into a window. Wilder's camera followed him, hidden in trucks and cars and shops along the way. "At that moment," Milland later related, "two well-dressed women approached with the obvious intention of looking in the window. They saw me and stopped dead. Slowly a look of shock came over their faces. Then they dropped their heads and hurried away, stopping after a dozen steps to look back." Both were friends of his wife who quickly reported back to Hollywood that Ray Milland was on a Homeric bender in New York. Gossip columnists soon placed items in the West Coast papers to that effect and Milland got a call from his wife telling him that he had better correct the story and pronto. Milland called Paramount's front office and yelled that he was being framed for appearing in a scene and having people believe he had turned into the worst kind of drunk. The publicity department worked overtime correcting his image. The on-camera drinking (ice tea) continued when the company moved back to Hollywood to finish the film. The legendary saloon, P. J. Clarke's, on New York City's Third Avenue, was reconstructed down to the last detail on Paramount's Stage Five and it is here where Milland and Da Silva have their confrontations. Every day during the shooting of the bar scenes, sharply at five a.m., a man would walk through the sound stage door and step onto the set, going to the bar. Da Silva would take a bottle of real Bourbon from beneath the bar and pour him a shot. The man would belt it down and give Milland and the other actors a painful little grin, put fifty cents on the bar, and depart. When the man entered, all shooting stopped. The actors remained silent and director Wilder only stared mutely at the man, tolerating this little eccentricity of a native New Yorker taking solace in having a drink on the set that recreated one of the city's great watering holes. The man was Robert Benchley, humorist, writer, critic, imbiber. Milland's outstanding performance would win for him an Oscar as Best Actor and THE LOST WEEKEND would also take Oscars for Best Picture, Best Director, and Best Screenplay. Milland's triumph, however, was not without social side effects; he was the butt of drunk jokes for years. When going out with his wife he was accosted by idiotic drinkers who wanted to buy him drinks and watch him fall flat on his face in an alcoholic stupor. Worse, Milland was painfully pestered by legions of drunks who wrote to him for years, begging for help. Oddly, Paramount executives took one look at the finished film and told Wilder they were seriously considering not releasing THE LOST WEEK-END. They had received an avalanche of protest, ironically from temperance advocates, who felt the film would encourage drinking. Powerful lobbyists for the liquor industry offered as much as $5 million for the negative of the film so it could be destroyed. But, at Wilder's urgings, Paramount released the film on a limited engagement in New York City and the critics fell all over themselves praising the magnificent job. The public responded by packing the theater and the same thing happened in some West Coast theaters. Paramount released the film across the country and it proved to be one of the biggest hits of 1945. When Milland accepted his Oscar for his startling role, he completely forgot the speech he had prepared. He could only smile and bow and exit, Oscar in hand. Emcee Bob Hope stepped forward gingerly and quipped: "I'm surprised they just handed it to him. I thought they'd hide it in the chandelier!" Milland was later being driven to a Paramount party when he asked the limousine driver to take a short detour to Hillcrest off Sunset. He got out of the car at this point, looking down upon the dazzling lights of the city spreading out before him. Fifteen years earlier his agent had taken him to this spot and told the then novice actor that "it all belongs to Ramon Novarro. He is the reigning romantic star at the moment, so tonight it belongs to him." Milland remembered that time and then said in a soft voice: "Mr. Novarro. Tonight they belong to me!"

p, Charles Brackett; d, Billy Wilder; w, Brackett, Wilder (based on the novel by Charles R. Jackson); ph, John F. Seitz; m, Miklos Rozsa, Guiseppe Verdi; ed, Doane Harrison; md, Victor Young; art d, Hans Dreier; spec eff, Gordon Jennings; Earl Hedrick; set d, Bertram Granger, Armando Agnini; cos, Edith Head; m/l, "Libiamo" from La Traviata by Verdi (sung by John Garris, Theodora Lynch); makeup, Wally Westmore.

Drama   **Cas.**   (PR:C-O   MPAA:NR)

LOST WOMEN   (SEE: MESA OF LOST WOMEN, 1952)

LOST WORLD, THE* 1/2   (1960) 97m FOX c

Michael Rennie (Lord Roxton), Jill St. John (Jennifer Holmes), David Hedison (Ed Malone), Claude Rains (Professor Challenger), Fernando Lamas (Gomez), Richard Haydn (Professor Summerlee), Ray Stricklyn (David), Jay Novello (Costa), Vitina Marcus (Native Girl), Ian Wolfe (Burton White), John Graham (Stuart Holmes), Colin Campbell (Professor Waldron).

Irwin Allen is truly an amazing filmmaker. Anyone who can take an exciting Arthur Conan Doyle story, cast some excellent performers, and then make a dull movie must be reckoned with as a man of amazing talents. Doyle was, of course, best known for Sherlock Holmes and Dr. Watson, but he also had a penchant for the occult as well as a lively fantasy imagination. The novel was written in 1912, filmed as a silent in 1925 with Wallace Beery and some innovative techniques, then remade by Allen into a film where special effects were the stars. Rains is a British zoology professor who claims he found the "lost world" in South America on a prior trip. This time he leads another group to the Amazon area where he intends to prove that dinosaurs and their compatriots still live. His cadre includes St. John, the daughter of a William Randolph Hearst-type who is putting up the money for the expedition; Rennie, a playboy-adventurer; Haydn, a serious scientist who doesn't believe Rains; Stricklyn, St. John's brother; and Hedison, a photographer/reporter. Once south of the border, they are joined by guitar-playing 'copter pilot Lamas and Novello, a guide. Into the dense jungle they go and are quickly set upon by prehistoric beasts, Indians who want to eat them, huge arachnids, and the sort of stuff that Bert Gordon specialized in with such films as THE FOOD OF THE GODS and EMPIRE OF THE ANTS. The beasts destroy their gear and the explorers are stranded on a plateau, cut off from the world. Eventually, they make their way back to civilization through several more gauntlets and Rains has a little relic with him; a small dinosaur egg that he plans to take back to England. Most of the "beasts" seemed to be blow-ups of various reptiles and insects and only pre-teeners would believe it for a minute. The screenplay is typical of Allen's work; plodding, expositional, and tiresome. If it should come on TV, turn down the sound and listen to something by Mozart as you watch the visuals. You'll enjoy that far more than the speeches. St. John looks gorgeous and Hedison is handsome. Allen must have liked his work, for he starred the actor in the TV series "Voyage to the Bottom of the Sea" several years later.

p&d, Irwin Allen; w, Allen, Charles Bennett (based on the novel by Sir Arthur Conan Doyle); ph, Winton Hoch (CinemaScope, DeLuxe Color); m, Bert Shefter, Paul Sawtell; ed, Hugh S. Fowler; art d, Duncan Cramer, Walter M. Simonds; set d, Walter M. Scott, Joseph Kish, John Sturtevant; cos, Paul Zastupnevich; spec eff, L. B. Abbott, Emil Kosa, James B. Gordon; makeup, Ben Nye.

Science Fiction   (PR:A   MPAA:NR)

LOST WORLD OF SINBAD, THE**
        (1965, Jap.) 94m Toho/AIP c (DAITOZOKU; AKA: SAMURAI PIRATE)

Toshiro Mifune, Makoto Satoh, Jun Funado, Ichiro Arishima, Miye Hama, Kumi Mizuno, Eiko Wakabayashi, Mitsuko Kusabue, Tadao Nakumura, Jun Tazaki, Takaashi Shimura.

A Japanese exploitation-adventure film became a tale of the mythic hero Sinbad in this English-dubbed version. This is a result of America's familiarity with Sinbad. Mifune plays the hero in this story about an evil premier trying to take over the kingdom. Mifune foils his attempts when he gets a group of pirates together to rid

the land of evil, which includes an old witch who can turn people into stone. Performances are overly stiff, with the script lacking in proper pacing of the action sequences. Direction is adequate, and the special effects are passable, in this film which came from the makers of GODZILLA.

p, Yuko Tanaka; d, Senkichi Tangiguchi; w, Takeshi Kimura; ph, Shinichi Sekizawa (Colorscope, Pathecolor); m, Masaru Satoh; spec eff, Eiji Tsuburaya.

Fantasy   (PR:A   MPAA:NR)

LOST ZEPPELIN**   (1930) 73m TIF bw

Conway Tearle (Cmdr. Hall), Virginia Valli (Mrs. Hall), Ricardo Cortez (Tom Armstrong), Duke Martin (Lt. Wallace), Kathryn McGuire (Nancy), Winter Hall (Mr. Wilson).

Adventure tale has a group of explorers battling the elements in the Antarctic. For the time this picture was made, the miniatures and special effects look very impressive. Obviously a lot of money and effort went into making the action sequences look realistic, with the cast giving very good performances to back up the production techniques.

d, Edward Sloman; w, Frances Hyland, Charles Kenyon (based on a story by Hyland, Jack Natteford); ph, Jackson Rose; ed, Martin G. Cohn, Donn Hayes.

Adventure   (PR:A   MPAA:NR)

LOTNA***   (1966, Pol.) 88m Kadr/Pol-Ton bw/c

Adam Pawlikowski (Lt. Wadnicki), Jerzy Moes (Ens. Grabowski), Jerzy Pichelski (Capt. Chodakiewicz), Mieczyslaw Loza (Sgt. Maj. Laton), Bozena Kurowska (Ewa), Roman Polanski, B. Dardzinski, H. Dzieszynski, Wieslaw Golas, Tadeusz Kosudarski, Henryk Hunko, Artur Mlodnicki, Irena Malkiewicz, Karol Rommel, T. Somogi, W. Wozniak, M.Wisniewski.

Fine war film directed by famed Polish director Wajda which follows the path of a beautiful white mare named Lotna through Poland's struggle against the Nazis in 1939. The film begins as a Polish cavalry captain acquires the horse from a dying landowner. Soon after that the captain is killed and the horse falls into the hands of a young ensign whose company is temporarily stationed in a small village. There the ensign falls in love with a young schoolteacher and they are married. But as the company celebrates the couple's marriage, Polish infantry pass through the village in retreat. The next morning the horse runs off and the ensign is killed while trying to catch her. Next, a lieutenant retrieves the horse and rides her into a desperate charge against the Nazis. He too is killed, and a sergeant-major finds the horse standing over the officer's body. The soldier takes the horse, but rides her so hard that she breaks a leg, forcing the man to shoot her. He buries the beautiful horse under a pine tree. Future director Polanski plays a small role.

p, Stanislaw Adler; d, Andrzej Wajda; w, Wojciech Zukrowski, Wajda; ph, Jerzy Lipman (Agfacolor, Sepiatone); m, Tadeusz Baird; ed, Janina Niedzwiecka, Lena Deptula; md, W. Rowicki; art d, Roman Wolyniec; cos, Lidia Grys, Jan Banucha; makeup, Stefan Szezpanski, Roman Baszkiewicz.

War   (PR:C   MPAA:NR)

LOTTERY BRIDE, THE zero   (1930) 80m UA bw/c

Jeanette MacDonald (Jenny Swanson), John Garrick (Chris Svenson), Joe E. Brown (Hoke Curtis), ZaSu Pitts (Hilda), Robert Chisholm (Olaf Svenson), Joseph Macaulay (Alberto), Harry Gribbon (Battleaxe Boris), Carroll Nye (Nels Swanson), Max Davidson (Marriage Broker), Frank Brownlee (Guard), Paul Hurst (Lottery Agent), Robert E. Homans (Miner).

An awful hodge-podge that nearly ended the brief musical era before it really started. MacDonald is a sweet Norwegian girl who is the lottery bride of the brother of the man she loves. The story has more twists than California's Route One with many attempts at comedy (by Joe E. Brown as a bandleader in a nightclub known as "The Jazzy Viking") that all fall flat under Stein's heavy-handed Teutonic direction. Garrick, a handsome British actor recruited from the stage, does what he can with the convoluted material as does Chisholm, playing Garrick's brother. In an attempt to pack a lot of story and songs into this frozen story, they've made it denser than a glacier, and just about as fast-moving. It's somewhere between an opera and an operation as far as the enjoyment quotient is concerned. Pitts was cute and this film was her watershed in that she was given almost 10 more jobs that year but for everyone else, it was a failure and an embarrassment. The lyrics were from hunger, cliche-ridden and exemplifying everything bad about the operetta. Friml's music was as singable as a chorus of burps and the whole thing is better left in the dim memories of those responsible for it. Songs by Rudolph Friml and J. Keirn Brennan include: "You're An Angel," "My Northern Lights," "Come Drink to the Girl that You Love" (sung by chorus), "Yubla" (sung by MacDonald), "My Northern Light" (sung by Garrick, MacDonald), "Round She Whirls" (sung by male chorus), "Shoulder to Shoulder" (sung by Garrick, Chisholm with male chorus), "High and Low" (sung by chorus), "Napoli" (sung by Macauley), "Two Strong Men" (sung by Gribbon, Brown), "You're an Angel" (sung by Chisholm), "High and Low" reprise (sung by chorus), "I'll Follow the Trail" (sung by Chisholm), and a host of orchestral music that makes Gregorian chants sound like the lightest Bach fugue in comparison.

p, Arthur Hammerstein; d, Paul Stein; w, Horace Jackson, Howard Emmett Rogers (based on the story "Bride 66" by Herbert Stothart); ph, Ray June, Karl Freund (Two Color Technicolor); m, Rudolph Friml; ed, Robert J. Kern; md, Hugo Riesenfeld; prod d, William Cameron Menzies, Park French; art d, Menzies, French; cos, Alice O'Neill.

Musical   **Cas.**   (PR:A   MPAA:NR)

LOTTERY LOVER* 1/2   (1935) 82m FOX bw

Lew Ayres (Cadet Frank Harrington), "Pat" Paterson (Patty), Peggy Fears (Gaby

Aimee), Sterling Holloway (Cadet Harold Stump), Walter King (Prince Midanoff), Alan Dinehart (Tank), Reginald Denny (Capt. Payne), Eddie Nugent (Gibbs), Nick [Dick] Foran (Cadet Allen Taylor), Rafaela Ottiano (Gaby's Maid).

Overused story line has a bunch of American naval cadets arriving in Paris with the sole intent of living it up. Fears is the beautiful chorus girl the cadets draw lots for, and the winner is the shy Ayres. Songs include: "There's A Bit Of Paree In You," "Ting-A-Ling-A-Ling," "Close Your Eyes And See," "All For The Love Of A Girl" (Don Hartman, Jay Corney). Performances are all shallow, with the direction failing to do an even job of combining songs with action.

p, Al Rockett; d, William Thiele; w, Franz Schulz, Sam Hellman, Billy Wilder (based on a story by Siegried M. Herzig, Maurice Hanline); ph, Bert Grennon.

Comedy (PR:A MPAA:NR)

LOTUS LADY* (1930) 68m Audible/Greiver bw

Fern Andra (Tamarah), Ralph Emerson (Larry Kelland), Betty Francisco (Claire Winton), Lucien Prival (Castro), Frank Leigh (Brent), Edward Cecil (George Kelland), Junior Pironne (Laddie), Jimmy Leong (Li), Joyzelle (The Dancer).

Emerson heads off to Indochina to clean up some shady deals made by his brother. While there, he's sold some worthless land and meets Andra and her oppressive boss Prival. Within five years he manages to marry the native girl and establish himself in business. Enter Francisco, Emerson's old girl friend, who tries to mess up everything. She's stopped, to no one's surprise, and miracle of miracles: there's oil discovered on Emerson's land! Minor programmer with an absolutely ridiculous plot development.

p, Lon Young; d, Phil Rosen; w, Harry Sinclair Drago; ph, M. A. Anderson; ed, Carl Himm.

Drama (PR:A MPAA:NR)

LOUDEST WHISPER, THE (SEE: CHILDREN'S HOUR, THE, 1961)

LOUDSPEAKER, THE** (1934) 70m MON bw

Ray Walker (Joe Miller), Jacqueline Wells [Julie Bishop] (Janet Melrose), Noel Francis (Dolly), Charles Grapewin (Pop Calloway), Lorin Baker (Green), Wilbur Mack (Walker), Spencer Charters (Burroughs), Sherwood Bailey (Ignatz), Billy Irvin (Caleb Hawkins), Ruth Romaine (Amy), Lawrence Wheat (Thomas), Mary Carr (Grandma).

Entertaining spoof has Walker as a railroad worker whose big ambition in life is to become a radio star. He goes around trying out his gags and routines on everyone he comes in contact with, which leads to him getting dumped by his girl, Wells, due to his thoughtless conceit. The story suffers from a lack of any dramatic intent.

d, Joseph Santley; w, Albert De Mond, Ralph Spence (based on the story by Spence); ph, Gilbert Warrenton; ed, Jack Ogilvie; m/l, "Who But You," "Doo Ah Doo Ah Know What I'm Doing" (Lew Brown, Harry Akst).

Comedy (PR:A MPAA:NR)

LOUIE, THERE'S A CROWD DOWNSTAIRS (SEE: START THE REVOLUTION WITHOUT ME, 1970)

LOUISA** (1950) 90m UNIV bw

Ronald Reagan (Hal Norton), Charles Coburn (Mr. Burnside), Ruth Hussey (Meg Norton), Edmund Gwenn (Mr. Hammond), Spring Byington (Louisa Norton), Piper Laurie (Cathy Norton), Scotty Beckett (Jimmy Blake), Connie Gilchrist (Gladys), Willard Waterman (Dick Stewart), Jimmy Hunt (Chris Norton), Marjorie Crosland (Lil Stewart), Ann Pearce (Miss Randall), Dave Willock (Joe Collins), Frank Ferguson (Park Attendant), Billy Newell (Usher), Eddie Parker (Motorcycle Cop), George Eldredge (Policeman), Bill Clauson (Charleston Dancer), Dell Henderson, Scotty Groves, Bob Bowman (Men), Charles Courtney (Delivery Boy), Howard Keiser (Kid in Levis), Robert Miles (Hot Rod), Donna and Diana Norris (Twins), Sherry Jackson (Girl), John Collum (Boy), Richard Michelson (Teenager), Martin Milner (Bob Stewart), Terry Frost (Stacy Walker), Rev. Neal Dodd (Minister).

Charming and heartwarming love story shows that it is never too late to fall in love. Reagan plays a successful suburban family man, whose household goes topsy-turvy when his mother, Byington, comes to live with him. She becomes the love interest of the local grocer, Edmund Gwenn, and Reagan's tycoon boss, Coburn, who fight over the elderly lady like two teenagers in love for the first time. Written without dabbling into unwarranted sentimentality, assisted by well-suited performances.

p, Robert Arthur; d, Alexander Hall; w, Stanley Roberts; ph, Maury Gertsman; m, Frank Skinner; ed, Milton Carruth; art d, Bernard Herzbrun, Robert Boyle.

Comedy (PR:A MPAA:NR)

LOUISE*½ (1940, Fr.) 72m European Film Distributors/Mayer and Burstyn bw

Grace Moore (Louise), Georges Thill (Julien), Andre Pernet (Father), Suzanne Despres (Mother), Ginette Leclerc (Lucienne), Le Vigan (Gaston), Jacqueline Gautier (Alphonsine), Beauchamp (Philosophe).

Dull, slow-moving attempt at transferring opera to the screen has Moore as a seamstress saved from a life of shame by her father, Pernet. Good singing and performances are not good enough to hold audience interest for very long. Released in 1939, the promoters claimed, at the film's London premiere, that this was the first time grand opera had been transposed to the screen. A disappointing effort by the great director of silent epics, Gance. (In French; English subtitles.)

d, Abel Gance; w, Steve Passeur (based on the opera by Gustave Charpentier); ph, Kurt Coutant.

Opera (PR:A MPAA:NR)

LOUISIANA** (1947) 82m MON bw

Jimmie Davis (Jimmie Davis), Margaret Lindsay (Alvern Adams), John Gallaudet (Charlie Mitchell), Freddie Stewart (Freddie Stewart), Dottye Brown (Laura), Mollie Miller (Mollie Miller), Ralph Freeto (Jimmie Davis as a Boy), Russell Hicks (Fred Astor), Lee "Lasses" White (Old Timer), John Harmon (Steve), Tristram Coffin (Tomlins), Eddy Waller (Mr. Davis), Mary Field (Mrs. Davis), Joseph Crehan (Neilson), Charles Lane (McCormack), Raymond Largay (Dr. Dodd), Ford Pearson (Ford Pearson), Charles Mitchell, Jimmy Thomason, Lloyd Ellis, Logan Conger, Gib Thompson, Slim Harbert (The Sunshine Serenaders).

Based on the true story of Davis' (playing himself) rise from a sharecropper's son to become the governor of Louisiana. The plot concentrates on Davis' desire for a good education, his career as a professor in a women's college, and his time spent as a toughened police commissioner. Davis' eccentric way of getting voter interest was through his singing. In this picture he performs several numbers: "You Are My Sunshine," "Nobody's Darling But Mine," "It Makes No Difference," "There's A New Moon Over My Shoulder," "Let's Be Sweethearts Again," and "You Won't Be Satisfied That Way." Miller performs "Basin Street" and "Old Man Mose." The performances are adequate, though Davis is a bit self-conscious; the direction is documentary in style, with an authentic Louisiana setting.

p, Lindsley Parsons; d, Phil Karlson; w, Jack De Witt, Vick Knight, Scott Darling (based on the story by Steve Healy); ph, William Sickner; ed, Ace Herman; m/l, Jimmie Davis, Charlie Mitchell, Floyd Tillman, Ekko Whelan, Lee Blastic, Vaughan Morton, Lloyd Ellis.

Biography (PR:A MPAA:NR)

LOUISIANA GAL (SEE: OLD LOUISIANA, 1938)

LOUISIANA HAYRIDE* (1944) 67m COL bw

Judy Canova (Judy Crocker), Ross Hunter (Gordon Pearson), Richard Lane (J. Huntington McMasters), Lloyd Bridges (Montague Price), Matt Willis (Jeb Crocker), George McKay (Canada Brown), Minerva Urecal (Maw Crocker), Hobart Cavanaugh (Malcolm Cartwright), Eddie Kane (Warburton), Nelson Leigh (Wiffle), Arthur Loft (Director), Robert E. Homans (Officer Conlon), Russell Hicks (Forbes), Harry Wilson, Dirk Thane (Listeners on Train), Eddie Bruce, Si Jenks, Syd Saylor, Pat West (Men), Ben Taggart (Conductor), Ernie Adams (Pawnbroker), Charles Sullivan, Jack Gardner, Brian O'Hara (Cab Drivers), Jack Rice (Hotel Clerk), Walter Baldwin (Lem), Earl Dewey (Governor), George Magrill, George Ford (Troopers), Bud Jamison (Doorman), Lane and Eddie Chandler (Plainclothesmen), Constance Purdy (Mrs. Vandergrift), Frank Hagney (Bartender), Christine McIntyre (Female Star), Jessie Arnold (Aunt Hepzibah), Eddie Bartell (Salesman), Reba King, Betty Jane Graham (Girls), Teddy Mangean (Messenger), Joe Palma (Cameraman), Danny Desmond (Bellboy), Charles Sherlock, Charles Marsh (Photographers), Buddy [George Tyne] Yarus (Joe, Assistant Director), Gene Stutenroth (Studio Guard), Art Miles (Brakeman), Louis Mason (Farmer), Edwin Stanley (Producer), Fred Graff (Testing Director).

Canova plays a star-struck hillbilly chasing after a film career, despite the adversity that comes her way in the form of con men Lane and McKay. The story suffers from the film's low budget and misplaced gags, but the singing is well done. Songs include, "You Gotta Go Where The Train Goes," "Rainbow Road" (Kim Gannon, Walter Kent), "I'm a Woman of the World" (Jerry Seelen, Saul Chaplin).

p&d, Charles Barton; w, Paul Yawitz (based on a story by Yawitz, Manny Seff); ph, L. W. O'Connell; ed, Otto Meyer; md, M. R. Bakaleinikoff; art d, Lionel Banks, Walter Holschier; m/l, Kim Gannon and Walter Kent, Jerry Seelen and Saul Chaplin, Junie McCree and Albert Von Tilzer.

Comedy (PR:A MPAA:NR)

LOUISIANA HUSSY* (1960) 66m Bon Aire/Howco bw

Nan Peterson (Nina Duprez), Robert Richards (Pierre Guillot), Peter Coe (Jacques Guillot), Betty Lynn (Lily), Howard Wright (Cob), Harry Lauter (Clay Lanier), Rosalee Calvert (Minette Lanier), Tyler McVay (Doc Opie), Smoki Whitfield (Burt), Helen Forrest (Callie).

Melodramatic tale of an evil Cajun beauty who ruins the lives of everyone she meets. She breaks up families, causes trouble, and even provokes the suicide of a young bride.

p, Charles M. Casinelli; d, Lee Sholem; w, Charles Lang.

Drama (PR:C MPAA:NR)

LOUISIANA PURCHASE*½ (1941) 95m PAR c

Bob Hope (Jim Taylor), Vera Zorina (Marina Von Minden), Victor Moore (Sen. O. P. Loganberry), Irene Bordoni (Madame Bordelaise), Dona Drake (Beatrice), Raymond Walburn (Col. Davis, Sr.), Maxie Rosenbloom (The Shadow), Frank Albertson (Davis, Jr.), Phyllis Ruth (Emmy-Lou), Donald MacBride (Police Captain Whitfield), Andrew Tombes (Dean Manning), Robert Warwick (Speaker of the House), Charles LaTorre (Gaston), Charles Lasky (Danseur), Emory Parnell (Lawyer), Iris Meredith (Lawyer's Secretary), Frances Gifford, Catherine Craig (Saleslaties), Jack Norton (Jester), Sam McDaniel (Sam), Kay Aldridge (Louisiana Belle), Katherine Booth, Alaine Brandes, Barbara Britton, Brooke Evans, Blanche Grady, Lynda Grey, Margaret Hayes, Louise La Planche, Barbara Slater, Eleanor Stewart, Jean Wallace.

This successful screen adaptation of the popular Broadway musical included many performers from the original cast. Moore is a righteous U.S. Senator investigating political corruption; Hope plays the innocent who has inadvertently been set up. The musical numbers are performed well and the costumes are lavish. Hope and Moore effectively change from comedy to seriousness when the script calls for it. The songs include, "Louisiana Purchase" (Irving Berlin—sung by Dona Drake), "You're Lonely and I'm Lonely" (sung by Vera Zorina, Victor Moore), "It's a

Lovely Day Tomorrow" (Berlin), "Prologue: Take a Letter To Paramount Pictures," "Before the Picture Starts," "Dance With Me (At the Mardi Gras)."

p, B. G. "Buddy" DeSylva, Harold Wilson; d, Irving Cummings; w, Jerome Chodorov, Joseph Fields (based on the stage musical by Morrie Ryskind, DeSylva); ph, Harry Hallenberger, Ray Rennahan (Technicolor); ed, LeRoy Stone; art d, Hans Dreier, Robert Usher.

Musical Comedy **(PR:A MPAA:NR)**

LOUISIANA STORY* 1/2** (1948) 77m Flaherty/Lopert bw

Joseph Boudreaux *(Boy)*, Lionel Le Blanc *(Father)*, Mrs. E. Bienvenu *(Mother)*, Frank Hardy *(Driller)*, C. T. Guedry *(Boilerman)*.

By 1948 Robert Flaherty was a respected name in the film world for his documentaries, particularly NANOOK OF THE NORTH and MAN OF ARAN. Flaherty had experienced corporate sponsorship before; NANOOK OF THE NORTH was funded by Revillon Freres, the furriers. Discovering this fact, and in consideration of his quality reputation, Standard Oil of New Jersey struck up an unusual arrangement that remained unprecedented. He was given an initial budget of $175,000 (which later totaled up to $258,000) and told to make a film about oil exploration. He was given total creative freedom, as well as distribution rights. Perhaps the most unusual move was Standard Oil's request not to be identified as a sponsor. Corporate sponsorship was heavily influential on documentarists of the era, making this final point a surprising move. Flaherty took his crew to the Bayou country of Louisiana and created a simple story from that which he observed. The local Cajun population at the time was faced with the threat of oncoming oil derricks and modern technology. Flaherty's scenario showed the struggle of one family, as seen through the eyes of a small boy, as it maintains its backroads life while adjusting to the modern era. Flaherty's camera lovingly records the bayou life, with lush photography that he hoped would hold audiences "spellbound by the mystery of the wilderness." Boudreaux, Flaherty's child protaganist, goes through his everyday life, trapping racoons and fighting off a swamp alligator. But gradually the technology of oil creeps onto this seeming utopia. Oil workers are friendly though, trying to peacefully co-exist with the Cajuns. In a climactic moment (which actually took place some sixty miles from the main shooting location) an oil rig blows, threatening the land. But the workers are able to cap the drill, thus keeping the natural environment safe while continuing to progress with their work. Flaherty's docu-drama is a wholly natural story. The simple framework was beautifully fleshed out by his cast of non-actors. The results are clear, and above all, honest. Unlike so many corporate-sponsored films, LOUISIANA STORY is not propaganda but a genuine story with realistic situations. The score nicely backs the film, with Eugene Ormandy and the Philadelphia Orchestra providing the music. Flaherty's cameraman was Richard Leacock, who would become a noted filmmaker in his own right.

p&d, Robert J. Flaherty; w, Robert J. and Frances Flaherty; ph, Richard Leacock; m, Virgil Thomson; ed, Helen Von Dongren.

Docu-Drama **Cas.** **(PR:AAA MPAA:NR)**

LOUISIANA TERRITORY* 1/2 (1953) 65m RKO c

Val Winter *(Robert Livingston)*, Leo Zinser *(Charles Talleyrand)*, Julian Meister *(George Benton)*, Phyliss Massicot *(Phyliss Caldwell)*, Marlene Behrens *(Jane Benton)*.

Winter plays the ghost of Robert Livingston, who helped negotiate the Louisiana Purchase. The spirit has returned to modern day New Orleans to marvel at what has become of the land, and more importantly, to provide a flimsy plot for what is essentially a travelog in 3-D.

p, Jay Bonafield, Douglas Travers; d, Harry W. Smith; w, Jerome Brondfield; ph, Smith (3-D, Pathe Color); m, George Bassman; ed, Milton Shifman.

Travel/Drama **(PR:A MPAA:NR)**

LOULOU*** (1980, Fr.) 110m Gaumont Action Films/New Yorker c

Isabelle Huppert *(Nelly)*, Gerard Depardieu *(Loulou)*, Guy Marchand *(Andre)*, Humbert Balsan *(Michel)*, Bernard Tronczyk *(Remy)*, Christian Boucher *(Pierrot)*, Frederique Cerbonnet *(Dominique)*, Jacqueline Dufranne *(Loulou's Mother)*, Willy Safar *(Jean-Louis)*, Agnes Rosier *(Cathy)*, Patricia Coulet *(Marite)*, Jean-Claude Meilland *(Man with Knife)*, Patrick Playez *(Thomas)*, Gerald Garnier *(Lulu)*, Catherine de Guirchitch *(Marie-Jo)*, Jean Van Herzeele *(Rene)*, Patrick Polvey *(Philippe)*, Xavier St. Macary *(Bernard)*.

By placing emphasis on his characters and the elements which bring them together rather than the normal forms of plot development, director Pialat managed to create an immensely enjoyable film that doesn't end when the final credits are flashed over the screen. Huppert is the cute and sexy (in an earthy sort of way) Parisian who throws over her secure life with the rather stuffy Marchand in order to be with the street-wise Depardieu. The latter has no steady income, resorts to robbery when in need of cash, and can be a bit of a brute, yet radiates a certain innocence which begs for attention. Obviously he has those qualities which Huppert needs in order to feel fulfilled; things she never received from Marchand, a man too concerned with maintaining his place in bourgeoise society. Marchand goes to extremes in order to regain Huppert, even offering her a job in his office under the stipulation that he wants her just because she is a good worker. The image of Marchand remains somewhat repugnant throughout the film, yet one cannot help but feel quite a bit of sympathy for his plight, even hoping that he and Huppert may have a chance to get back together. This almost happens briefly when Huppert decides to sleep with him again in what appears to be a whim on her part. Afterwards she goes right back to her loving Depardieu to continue a life whose future has no direct line to success, but will always remain shakily held together by bonds that go much deeper than those of the exterior. The bare-bones philosophy, somewhat resembling that of Jean-Luc Godard's BREATHLESS, is the triumph of irresponsible, egotistical charm over substance and security, expressing the theory of the inborn masochism of women: if one is nice to a girl, some utter rotter will run off with her. The success of such a project relies almost entirely upon the ability of the director to bring those qualities from his actors which will capture the audience's empathy. Pialat has done just this, his three leading actors all excellent choices. (In French; English subtitles.)

d, Maurice Pialat; w, Pialat, Arlette Langmann (based on a story by Langmann); ph, Pierre William Glenn, Jacques Loiseleux (Eastmancolor); ed, Yann Dedet, Sophie Coussein; set d, Max Berto.

Drama **(PR:O MPAA:NR)**

L'OURS (SEE: BEAR, THE, 1963, Fr.)

LOVABLE AND SWEET (SEE: RUNAROUND, THE, 1931)

LOVABLE CHEAT, THE** (1949) 76m Skyline/FC bw

Charles Ruggles *(Claude Mercadet)*, Peggy Ann Garner *(Julie Mercadet)*, Richard Ney *(Jacques Minard)*, Alan Mowbray *(Justin)*, Iris Adrian *(Madame Mercadet)*, Ludwig Donath *(Violette)*, Fritz Feld *(Monsieur Louis)*, John Wengraf *(Pierquin)*, Otto Waldis *(Bailiff)*, Edna Holland *(Madame Pierquin)*, Minerva Urecal *(Virginie)*, Helen Servis *(Madame Goulard)*, Jody Gilbert *(Madame Violette)*, Buster Keaton *(Goulard)*, Curt Bois *(Count de la Brive)*, Albin Roeheling *(Butcher)*, Fred Fox *(Baker)*, Jack Del Rio *(Wine Seller)*, Jerry Austin *(Grocer)*, Andre Pola *(Policeman)*, Terri Daniels, Gerry Ganzer *(Tailor's Assistants)*, George Ramsey *(Henri)*, Charles Vincent *(Pierre)*, Bud Hooker *(Coachman)*, Judith Trafford *(Therese)*.

Fairly boring adaptation of Balzac's play about a Parisian flimflam man who coerces money from his friends while trying to arrange a suitable marriage for his daughter. The story suffers from an overabundance of talk without supporting action. The costuming is an asset, with the performers fitting their roles well.

p, Richard Oswald, Edward Lewis; d, Oswald; w, Oswald, Lewis (based on the play "Mercadet Le Falseur" by Honore De Balzac); ph, Paul Ivano; m, Karl Hajos; ed, Douglas Bagier; art d, Boris Leven.

Drama **(PR:A MPAA:NR)**

LOVE*** (1972, Hung.) 92m Mafilm Studio/Ajay bw (SZERELEM)

Lili Darvas *(Old Lady)*, Mari Torocsik *(Luca)*, Ivan Darvas *(Janos)*, Erzsi Orsolya, Laszlo Mensaros, Tibor Bitskei.

This extremely touching film has a young woman (Torocsik) giving up her own material needs in order to watch over her dying mother-in-law. The old woman—L. Darvas—is unable to get out of bed, has a hard time distinguishing events out of the past from those of the present, and hardly recognizes the sacrifices that Torocsik has been making for her. The son, Torocsik's husband, has been put in prison for a ten-year sentence as a political undesirable, but Torocsik writes letters, presumably from him, to his mother telling her that he is in America working on a movie and is being treated as if he were a king. Darvas is kept happy with the illusion that her son is doing well, though one can never be sure whether she is just putting on an act herself in order to keep Torocsik content. LOVE is an extreme rarity in the cinema in that it manages to be a moving portrayal of people in a seemingly intolerable situation, yet never becomes overly sentimental or begs for audience sympathy. Toward the end, L. Darvas—appearing here in her last film before her actual death— begins to fantasize about her past, recounting adventures of her youth in Imperial Vienna reciprocally to Torocsik. Ultimately, the latter's husband, I. Darvas, returns from prison, unexpectedly released after only one year of suffering, on the very eve of his mother's death. The experience has aged her spouse, but Torocsik can deal with age. Director Makk's 13th film, but his first to be released in the U.S., won a Special Jury Prize at the Cannes festival. L. Darvas returned to her native land—which she had departed for the U.S. with Hitler's invasion—to make this picture. She had lived in the U.S. since WW II, acting on stage (her husband, playwright Ferenc Molnar, wrote a play for her annually during his productive years) and in such films as CIMARRON (1960) and MEET ME IN LAS VEGAS (1956). LOVE, her last appearance in film, is a suitable memorial for this remarkable bilingual actress. (In Hungarian; English subtitles.)

d, Karoly Makk; w, Tibor Dery (based on two novellas by Dery); ph, Janos Toth; m, Andras Mihaly; ed, Gyorgy Sivo; art d, Jozsef Romvary.

Drama **(PR:C MPAA:NR)**

LOVE 1/2** (1982, Can.) 105m Levinson-Velvet c

Episode 1—"Love From The Marketplace": Maureen Fitzgerald *(Mum)*, Gordon Thomson *(Tony)*; Episode 2—"The Black Cat in the Black Mouse Socks": Joni Mitchell *(Paula)*, Winston Rekert *(John)*; Episode 3—"Por Vida/For Life": Nicholas Campbell *(Danny)*, Toni Kalem *(The Girl)*; Episode 4—"Love On Your Birthday": Marilyn Lightstone *(Marilyn)*, Moses Znaimer *(Marvin)*, Linda Rennhofer *(Shirley)*; Episode 5—"Julia": Lawrence Dane *(Mr. Wiseman)*, Janet-Laine Green *(Julia)*, Elizabeth Shepherd *(Mrs. Wiseman)*; Episode 6— "Parting": Charles Jolliffe *(Old Man)*, Rita Tuckett *(Wife)*.

Four female directors look at love in this film composed of six segments. LOVE FROM THE MARKETPLACE centers on the importance of food in a love affair. BLACK CAT, written by and starring singer Mitchell, is a mood piece coordinated with its musical accompaniment. JULIA is the story of a renewed affair that had backfired earlier. LOVE ON YOUR BIRTHDAY has a wife giving her husband her best friend on his birthday, and getting jealous in the process. POR VIDA centers on a WW II G.I. returning home to his old girl friend. PARTING, directed by Liv Ullmann, is the touching story of an old man's affection for his paralyzed wife. Of the six segments, PARTING and MARKETPLACE are the most successful and powerful; the others need more time to develop their stories.

p, Renee Perlmutter; d, Mai Zetterling (Episodes 1,2,5), Liv Ullmann (Episode 6), Nancy Dowd (Episode 3), Annette Cohen (Episode 4); w, Zetterling (Episode 1), Joni Mitchell (Episode 2), Dowd (Episode 3), Gael Greene (Episode 4), Edna

O'Brien (Episode 5), Ullmann (Episode 6); ph, Reginald Morris, Norman Leigh; m, Tim McCauley; ed, Donald Ginsberg, Wayne Griffin, Stephan Fanfara; prod d, Claude Bonniere; m/l, Mitchell.

Drama   (PR:C MPAA:NR)

LOVE A LA CARTE** 1/2
(1965, Ital.) 98m Zebra/Promenade bw (ADUA E LE COMPAGNE; AKA: ADUA AND HER FRIENDS, ADUA AND HER COMPANIONS)

Simone Signoret (Adua), Marcello Mastroianni (Piero), Gina Rovere (Milly), Sandra Milo (Lolita), Emmanuelle Riva (Marilina), Claudio Gora (Ercoli), Ivo Garrani (Lawyer), Gianrico Tedeschi (Stefano), Domenico Modugno.

Four prostitutes (Signoret, Rovere, Milo, Riva) are forced to go into the restaurant business when the brothels of Rome are closed down by official order. The women strike a deal with landlord Gora to buy a run-down restaurant with their savings. He agrees to use his name to buy their food license on the condition that they also run a small brothel upstairs. The restaurant is a success due to the best efforts of the ladies, but soon trouble develops in their personal lives that threatens the business. Signoret falls in love with a car salesman, Mastroianni, who is actually using her to further his career. Rovere falls in love with a young man and makes plans to marry and quit the business to settle down. Riva takes her daughter out of a foster home to live with her. But only Milo maintains a lifestyle uncomplicated by responsibilities. Soon their lives collapse due to Gora's insistence that they return to prostitution. Signoret learns of Mastroianni's unfaithfulness; Rovere is trapped into admitting her profession to her boy friend; Riva is forced to return her child to the foster home; and the food license is revoked. The women decide to get their revenge by trashing the building, but it is only a momentary victory, as all the women are faced with the reality of having to walk the streets again.

p, Moris Ergas; d, Antonio Pietrangeli; w, Ruggero Maccari, Ettore Scola, Pietrangeli, Tullio Pinelli; ph, Armando Nannuzzi; m, Piero Piccioni; ed, Eraldo Da Roma; art d, Luigi Scaccianoce.

Drama   (PR:O MPAA:NR)

LOVE AFFAIR**   (1932) 68m COL bw
Dorothy Mackaill (Carol Owen), Humphrey Bogart (Jim Leonard), Jack Kennedy (Gilligan), Barbara Leonard (Felice), Astrid Allwyn (Linda Lee), Bradley Page (Georgie), Halliwell Hobbes (Kibbee), Hale Hamilton (Mr. Hardy), Harold Minjir (Antone).

Bogart plays an aviator and airplane mechanic who falls in love with Mackaill while giving her flying lessons. The problem with the two getting hitched is that she is wealthy, while he is broke. Bogart has also invented a new motor, which Mackaill is willing to finance, until she finds her fortune no longer exists. The difficulties multiply until Mackaill tries suicide, but Bogart is Johnny-on-the-spot and the clouds part to reveal the film's romantic silver lining.

d, Thornton Freeland; w, Jo Swerling, Dorothy Howell (based on the story by Ursulla Parrott); ph, Teddy Tetzlaff; ed, Jack Dennis.

Drama   (PR:A MPAA:NR)

LOVE AFFAIR****   (1939) 87m RKO bw
Irene Dunne (Terry McKay), Charles Boyer (Michel Marnet), Maria Ouspenskaya (Grandmother Janou), Lee Bowman (Kenneth Bradley), Astrid Allwyn (Lois Clarke), Maurice Moscovich (Maurice Cobert), Scotty Beckett (Boy on Ship), Bess Flowers, Harold Miller (Couple on Deck), Joan Leslie (Autograph Seeker), Dell Henderson (Cafe Manager), Carol Hughes (Nightclub Patron), Ferike Boros (Boarding House Keeper), Frank McGlynn, Sr. (Orphanage Superintendent [Picklepuss]), Oscar O'Shea (Priest), Tom Dugan (Drunk with Christmas Tree), Lloyd Ingraham, Leyland Hodgson (Doctors), Phyllis Kennedy (Maid), Gerald Mohr (Extra).

A superb romantic comedy-drama that deftly mixes humor with pathos, passion, and ennui, and takes us on an emotional voyage that never fails to please. Boyer is engaged to Allwyn and Dunne is engaged to Bowman when the two meet onboard ship and the attraction is instant. In the cases of their amours, they like the people they are to marry but there is no deep-seated love. Bowman and Allwyn are both wealthy and would make excellent spouses yet is that enough? Evidently not. Boyer and Dunne flirt, then realize that this is not merely a shipboard fling, there is much more to their feelings about each other. They resolve to meet in six months, at the top of the Empire State Building. If they both still feel the way they do now, they'll jettison their respective spouses-to-be and reactivate their fires. The months pass and Dunne has a bit of luck working as a nightclub singer while Boyer is content to bide his time as a painter. Neither has married and both count the days until they meet again. On the way to the building, Dunne is hurt in an automobile accident and it would appear that she's going to be permanently crippled. She doesn't want Boyer to feel sorry for her so she doesn't get in touch with him. Boyer waits at the rendezvous for hours then leaves, thinking she must have married Bowman. When they finally are reunited by chance, he understands her motives in staying away and he feels deep in his heart that he can help her walk again. There are many wonderful moments in the picture, both comedic and touching. As Boyer's mother, Ouspenskaya, is dying, Dunne underplays her farewell to the old woman and Boyer can't help but fall in love with her. The first half of the picture is the breezy, witty and chic half. The second part, however, opts for a more serious tone but we never have the feeling that they are divided even though the emphasis does shift. Legend has it that the writers were writing new pages every day and the actors never had a finished script. If that's true, more power to director McCarey who kept it all together and didn't betray the fact with jumpy direction. In the Philadelphia nightclub scene, Dunne gets to warble "Sing My Heart" and when she briefly works at an orphanage, we hear "Wishing" as done by the tykes. Look for veteran TV actor Gerald Mohr in a tiny extra bit and Joan Leslie, in her fourth film, at the age of 14.

Nominated for Oscars for Best Picture, Best Screenplay, Best Actress, Best Supporting Actress, and Best Song but this was the year of GONE WITH THE WIND, STAGECOACH, and THE WIZARD OF OZ (among others) so there was no chance. This was remade as AN AFFAIR TO REMEMBER.

p&d, Leo McCarey; w, Delmer Daves, Donald Ogden Stewart (story by McCarey, Daves, Mildred Cram); ph, Rudolph Mate; m, Roy Webb; ed, Edward Dmtryk, George Hively; spec eff, Vernon L. Walker; m/l, "Wishing," B. G. DeSylva (sung by chorus), "Sing My Heart," Harold Arlen, Ted Koehler (sung by Irene Dunne).

Comedy/Drama   (PR:A MPAA:NR)

LOVE AFFAIR OF THE DICTATOR, THE
                                     (SEE: DICTATOR, THE, 1935, Brit.)

LOVE AFFAIR; OR THE CASE OF THE MISSING SWITCHBOARD OPERATOR***
(1968, Yugo.) 70m Avala/Brandon bw (LJUBAVNI SLUCAJ ILI TRAGEDIJA SLUZBENICE P.T.T.; AKA: AN AFFAIR OF THE HEART)

Eva Ras (Isabela), Slobodan Aligrudic (Ahmed), Ruzica Sokic (Ruza, Isabela's friend), Miodrag Andric (Mica, the Postman), Aleksandar Kostic (Sexologist), Zivojin Aleksic (Criminologist), Dragan Obradovic.

An early film from frequently brilliant Yugoslavian filmmaker Dusan Makavejev (WR - MYSTERIES OF THE ORGANISM (1971)), whose films defy any sane person's attempt at synopsis. LOVE AFFAIR seemingly deals with the deterioration of a relationship between a rat catcher (Aligrudic) and a switchboard operator (Ras). Infidelity and jealousy lead to Ras' accidental murder. Makavejev's films combine documentary footage with disjointed and somewhat obtuse narrative scenes that mix together into a crazy-quilt of meanings. The early films juxtapose subject matter pertaining to politics, sex, traditional values, and repression (and a great deal of humor), producing a confusing array of ideas and problems that are not at all *solved* for the viewer, but *presented* before him in a unique manner. Definitely not for average moviegoers, but greatly rewarding for those willing to be challenged by the cinema.

d&w, Dusan Makavejev; ph, Aleksandar Petkovic; m, Hanns Eisler; ed, Katarina Stojanovic; art d, Vladislav Lazic.

Comedy   (PR:O MPAA:NR)

LOVE AMONG THE MILLIONAIRES* 1/2   (1930) 74m PAR bw
Clara Bow (Pepper Green), Stanley Smith (Jerry Hamilton), Skeets Gallagher (Boots McGee), Stuart Erwin (Clicker Watson), Mitzi Green (Penelope Green), Charles Sellon (Pop Green), Theodore Von Eltz (Jordan), Claude King (Mr. Hamilton), Barbara Bennett (Virginia Hamilton).

Another rendition of the ageless story of rich boy wanting to marry poor girl, but being hampered by a domineering father who doesn't want the marriage to come off. In this one Bow is a waitress in an eatery near a railroad yard. When the owner of the railroad's son wanders into the restaurant, he falls hopelessly in love with Bow. She gives a charming performance, but the role is not a good vehicle for her talents. Some vaudeville-type gags manage to get some laughs. Songs include: title song, "Believe It or Not, I've Found My Man," "That's Worth While Waiting For," "Rarin' to Go," "Don't Be a Meanie."

d, Frank Tuttle; w, Grover Jones, William Conselman, Herman J. Mankiewicz (based on the story by Keene Thompson); ph, Allen Siegler; m/l, L. Wolfe Gilbert, Abel Baer.

Drama   (PR:A MPAA:NR)

LOVE AND ANARCHY** 1/2
(1974, Ital.) 108m Peppercorn-Wormser c (FILM D'AMORE E D'ANARCHIA)
Giancarlo Giannini (Tunin), Mariangela Melato (Salome), Lina Polito (Tripolina), Eros Pagni (Spatoletti), Pina Cei (Madame Aida), Elena Fiore (Donna Carmela).

Director-writer Lina Wertmuller attempted to portray the elements which force a man to become an anarchist, primarily to show how a naive romanticism as a motivating source does not usually face up well to the realities of a situation. Giannini, a humble farmer who hooks up with an antifascist revolutionary group in 1930s Italy, is assigned the task of assassinating Mussolini. He comes to the city, where he stays in a whorehouse run by Melato, a woman who turned to prostitution and political idealism when her boy friend was killed by fascist hands. Though Giannini passionately wants to see Mussolini dead and is dead set in carrying out his plan, ultimately, he must fail. Being too good a person, oversensitive to the people he encounters, and falling in love with one of the prostitutes, he is distracted from ever successfully achieving his goal. That fact makes him more and more distraught, until he is eventually forced to vent his disturbed emotional state in a violent act that precipitates his own end. Though LOVE AND ANARCHY is a very insightful look into how political situations affect humble citizens, it is filled with too many of Wertmuller's excesses to be totally effective as a film. However, she does a splendid job in detailing the atmosphere of 1930s Italy; both characters and settings are faithful renditions of this turbulent period.

p, Herbert R. Steinmann, Billy Baxter; d&w, Lina Wertmuller; ph, Giuseppe Rotunno (Technicolor); m, Nino Rota; ed, Franco Fraticelli; set d& cos, Enrico Job.

Drama   Cas.   (PR:O MPAA:R)

LOVE AND BULLETS* 1/2
                 (1979, Brit.) 95m Lew Grade/Associated Film Distribution c
Charles Bronson (Charlie Congers), Rod Steiger (Joe Bomposa), Jill Ireland (Jackie Pruit), Strother Martin (Louis Monk), Bradford Dillman (Brickman), Henry Silva (Vittorio Farroni), Paul Koslo (Huntz), Sam Chew (Cook), Michael V. Gazzo (Lobo), Val Avery (Caruso), Bill Gray (Mike Durant), Andy Romano (FBI Agent Marty), Robin Clarke (FBI Agent George), Cliff Pellow (Police Captain), Lorraine Chase

(Vittorio's Girl Friend), Joseph Roman *(Coroner)*, Albert Salmi *(Andy Minton)*, John Belluci *(Alibisi)*, Rick Colliti *(Carlo)*.

Scenic Switzerland serves as the backdrop for much of this dull, routine thriller. Bronson is the cop hired by the F.B.I. to rescue Ireland, girl friend of powerful mobster Steiger, with the belief that she may have some incriminating evidence against her old flame. It turns out she doesn't really know anything, but is killed by the mobster anyhow, but not before Bronson has fallen in love with her. This sets Bronson out on his own type of predictable revenge. Steiger and Ireland manage to give believable performances, but Bronson is unable to evoke a sense of hardness. The direction suffers from lack of effective pacing, and too much concentration on the pretty scenery.

p, Pancho Kohner; d, Stuart Rosenberg; w, Wendell Mayes, John Melson; ph, Fred Koenekamp (Technivision, Technicolor); m, Lalo Schifrin; ed, Michael Anderson, Tom Priestley, Lesley Walker; prod d, John De Cuir; art d, Colin Grimes; cos, Dorothy Jeakins.

Crime **Cas.** **(PR:C MPAA:PG)**

LOVE AND DEATH*½** (1975) 85m UA c

Woody Allen *(Boris)*, Diane Keaton *(Sonja)*, Georges Adet *(Old Nehamkin)*, Frank Adu *(Drill Sergeant)*, Edmond Ardisson *(Priest)*, Feodor Atkine *(Mikhail)*, Albert Augier *(Waiter)*, Yves Barsacq *(Rimsky)*, Lloyd Battista *(Don Francisco)*, Jack Berard *(Gen. Lecoq)*, Eva Bertrand *(Woman in Hygiene Class)*, George Birt *(Doctor)*, Yves Brainville *(Andre)*, Gerard Buhr *(Servant)*, Brian Coburn *(Dimitri)*, Henry Coutet *(Minskov)*, Patricia Crown *(Cheerleader)*, Henry Czarniak *(Ivan)*, Despo Diamantidou *(Mother)*, Sandor Eles *(Soldier No. 2)*, Luce Fabiole *(Grandmother)*, Florian *(Uncle Nikolai)*, Jacqueline Fogt *(Ludmilla)*, Sol L. Frieder *(Voskovec)*, Olga Georges-Picot *(Countess)*, Harold Gould *(Anton)*, Harry Hankin *(Uncle Sasha)*, Jessica Harper *(Natasha)*, Tony Jay *(Vladimir Maximovitch)*, Tutte Lemkow *(Pierre)*, Jack Lenoir *(Krapotkin)*, Leib Lensky *(Father Andre)*, Ann Lonn Berg *(Olga)*, Roger Lumont *(Baker)*, Alfred Lutter III *(Young Boris)*, Ed Marcus *(Raskov)*, Jacques Maury *(Second)*, Narcissa McKinley *(Cheerleader)*, Aubrey Morris *(Soldier No. 4)*, Denise Peron *(Spanish Countess)*, Beth Porter *(Anna)*, Alan Rossett *(Guard)*, Shmen Ruskin *(Borslov)*, Persival Russel *(Berdykov)*, Chris Sanders *(Joseph)*, Zvee Scooler *(Father)*, C. A. R. Smith *(Father Nikolai)*, Fred Smith *(Soldier)*, Bernard Taylor *(Soldier No. 3)*, Clement-Thierry *(Jacques)*, Alan Tilvern *(Sergeant)*, James Tolkan *(Napoleon)*, Helen Vallier *(Madame Wolfe)*, Howard Vernon *(Gen. Leveque)*, Glenn Williams *(Soldier No. 1)*, Jacob Witkin *(Suskin)*, The Dimtrievitch Gypsy Orchestra.

Woody Allen seldom makes movies that last more than 90 minutes, which should be a lesson to others who think that they have to justify their work by making it endless. This time, Allen takes on Russia and satirizes just about every author and director who ever stepped off the Steppes. Like many Allen movies, the plot defies description, but here goes; Allen is impressed into the Russian Army in the early 1800s and he and his distant cousin, Keaton, plan to put an end to all this carnage by assassinating Napoleon, whom they believe is the source of woes that trouble Europe. Along the way, they encounter numerous adventures in their DR. ZHIVAGO-like hegira across the frozen wastes. Allen one-liners come thick and quick and hardly a moment goes by without some bon mot from his lips. He'd obviously seen FIDDLER ON THE ROOF and been so bored he decided to take the same sort of material and make it funny. And he did. It was filmed in Hungary and France so the chances are you may not recognize anyone in the cast, other than Keaton and Allen. This works for the film, not against it, as we believe these people are who Allen says they are. The only actor we can find in the cast who did anything later was Jack Lenoir who starred as the rapscallion chauffeur to Wayne Rogers in the much-underrated ONCE IN PARIS.

p, Charles H. Joffe; d&w, Woody Allen; ph, Ghislain Cloquet (Panavision, DeLuxe Color); m, Sergei Prokofiev; ed, Ron Kalish, Ralph Rosenblum; art d, Willy Holt; set d, Claude Reytinas; cos, Gladys DeSegonzac.

Comedy **Cas.** **(PR:A-C MPAA:PG)**

LOVE AND HISSES** (1937) 83m FOX bw

Walter Winchell *(Himself)*, Ben Bernie *(Himself)*, Simone Simon *(Yvette Guerin)*, Bert Lahr *(Sugar Boles)*, Joan Davis *(Joan)*, Dick Baldwin *(Steve Nelson)*, Ruth Terry *(Specialty)*, Douglas Fowley *(Webster)*, Chick Chandler *(Sidney Hoffman)*, Charles Williams *(Irving Skolsky)*, Georges Renavent *(Count Pierre Raoul Guerin)*, Brewster Twins *(Specialty)*, Chilton and Thomas *(Specialty)*, Peters Sisters *(Specialty)*, Charles Judels *(Oscar)*, Robert Battier *(Gangster)*, Hal K. Dawson *(Music Store Clerk)*, June Storey, Phillippa Hilbere, Lynne Berkeley, June Wilkins *(Girls)*, Lon Chaney, Jr. *(Attendant)*, Edward McWade *(Ticket Seller)*, Hooper Atchley *(Joe Moss)*, Charles Tannen *(Desk Clerk)*, Fred Kelsey *(Officer)*, George Humbert *(Chef)*, Ben Welden *(Bugsy)*, Pop Byron *(Policeman)*, John Hiestand *(Announcer)*, Donald Haines *(Newsboy)*, Rush Hughes, Gary Breckner *(Announcers)*, Harry Stubbs *(Producer)*.

Routine musical has Winchell and Bernie playing themselves, columnist and bandleader respectively. They feud over singer Simon, a sensation just over from France. Without Winchell's knowledge, Bernie manages to get free publicity for this new singing act in Winchell's column. Musical pieces help to give this stale script (which suffers from overused jokes) some life. Though not professionals, Winchell and Bernie manage enough acting to be convincing, with the rest of the performances up to par. Songs include "Sweet Someone," "Broadway Gone Hawaiian," "I Want To Be In Winchell's Column," "Be A Good Sport," "Lost In Your Eyes" (Mack Gordon, Harry Revel), "Power House" (Raymond Scott), "The Wolf Song" (Norman Zeno), "Darling, Je Vous Aime Beaucoup" (Anna Sosenko), "Bell Song" (from the opera "Lakeme"—sung by Simone Simon), "Little Love, Little Kiss" (sung by Simon).

p, Darryl F. Zanuck; d, Sidney Lanfield; w, Curtis Kenyon, Art Arthur (based on a story by Arthur); ph, Robert Planck; ed, Robert Simpson, William Forsyth; md, Louis Silvers; art d, Bernard Herzbrun, Mark-Lee Kirk, Thomas Little; ch, Nick Castle, Geneva Sawyer; m/l, Mack Gordon, Harry Revel, Lew Pollack, Sydney D. Mitchell, Raymond Scott, Norman Zeno, Will Irwin.

Musical **(PR:A MPAA:NR)**

LOVE AND KISSES** (1965) 87m UNIV c

Rick Nelson *(Buzzy Pringle)*, Jack Kelly *(Jeff Pringle)*, Kristin Harmon Nelson *(Rosemary Cotts)*, Jerry Van Dyke *(Freddy)*, Pert Kelton *(Nanny)*, Madelyn Himes *(Carol Pringle)*, Sheilah Wells *(Elizabeth Pringle)*, Howard McNear *(Mr. Frisby)*, Ivan Bonar *(Assemblyman Potter)*, Barry Livingston *(Bobby)*, Alvy Moore *(Officer Jones)*, Angelo Brovelli *(Stage Manager)*, Betty Rowland, Nancy Lewis, Anita Mann *(Dancers)*.

Family household is upturned when, freshly graduated from high school, Rick and Kristin Nelson decide to marry and move in with the groom's parents. Problems arise because Rick's big sister, Wells, feels her upcoming marriage is being impinged upon, while the new bride does not act up to the expectations of one recently wed. Rick manages to sing a few numbers. Written and directed with an aim at the teen market, filled with the properly placed jokes, the film was based on a play by Anita Rowe Black.

p,d&w, Ozzie Nelson (based on the play by Anita Rowe Black); ph, Robert Moreno (Technicolor); m, William Loose, Jimmie Haskell; ed, Newell P. Kimlin; md, Joseph Gershenson; art d, Alexander Golitzen, Frank Arrigo; set d, John McCarthy, Julia Heron; cos, Seth Banks, Dolores Sheppard; m/l, "Love and Kisses," "Say You Love Me," Sonny Curtis, "Come Out Dancin'," Clint Ballard, Jr., Angela Reila (songs sung by Rick Nelson); makeup, Monte Westmore.

Comedy **(PR:A MPAA:NR)**

LOVE AND LARCENY***

(1963, Fr./Ital.) 94m Maxima-Ceilncom-S.G.C./Major bw (IL MATTATORE: L'HOMME AUX CENT VISAGES)

Vittorio Gassman *(Gerardo)*, Anna Maria Ferraro *(Annalise)*, Dorian Gray *(Elena)*, Peppino De Filippo *(Chinotto)*, Mario Carotenuto *(Lallo Cortina)*, Alberto Bonucci *(Gloria Patri)*, Fosco Giachetti *(The General)*, Luigi Pavese *(Rebuschini)*, Linda Sini *(Laura)*, Aldo Bufi Landi *("Commissioner")*, Fernando Bruni, Enrico Glori, Mario Scaccia, Mario Frera, Piera Arico, Salvatore Cafiero, Fanfulla, Armando Bandini, Dina DeSantis, Walter Santesso, Ignazio Leone, Giovanni Baghino, Armando Annuale, Mimmo Poli, Enzo Petito, Pierugo Gragnani, Andrea Petricca, Enzo Cerusico, Vincenzo Talarico.

Pleasant comedy from Italy has Gassman as a third-rate actor who is sent to jail for impersonating a businessman, and who comes out a first rate con artist. Teaming with jailmate De Filippo, he manages a number of successful escapades, including Gassman's impersonation of Greta Garbo searching for a spot on a beach. Eventually, his girl friend, Ferraro, tricks him into marriage, and he's forced to settle down to a quiet home life. This doesn't last for long, as De Filippo comes to his rescue. The direction is well-paced, with the continual comic scenes never losing their effectiveness. The performers manage to deliver their roles in an efficient manner.

p, Mario Cecchi Gori; d, Dino Risi; w, Sandro Continenza, Sergio Pugliese, Ettore Scola (based on the story by Agee Scarpelli); ph, Massimo Dallamano (Totalscope); m, Pippo Barzizza; ed, Eraldo Da Roma; art d, Sergio Giovaninni.

Comedy **(PR:A MPAA:NR)**

LOVE AND LEARN*½ (1947) 84m WB bw

Jack Carson *(Jingles)*, Robert Hutton *(Bob Grant)*, Martha Vickers *(Barbara Wyngate)*, Janis Paige *(Jackie)*, Otto Kruger *(Andrew Wyngate)*, Barbara Brown *(Victoria Wyngate)*, Tom D'Andrea *(Wells)*, Florence Bates *(Mrs. Davis)*, Craig Stevens *(Willard)*, Don McGuire *(Delaney)*, John Alvin *(William)*, Herbert Anderson *(Pete)*, Jane Harker *(Receptionist)*, Lou Nova *(Marty)*, Angela Greene *(Phyllis McGillicuddy)*.

Tried and true plot line is delivered here in a less than satisfactory manner. Carson and Hutton are impoverished musicians looking for a break, when the wealthy but sheltered Vickers comes to their rescue. Vickers is disguised as a poor working girl, in order to get a just feel for life. When her impersonation is uncovered, the boys throw a fit. Cast manages to deliver effectively, despite a script that is laden with predictability and jokes that never get off the ground. Songs include "Would You Believe Me" (Charles Tobias, M. K. Jerome, Ray Heindorf, sung by Carson, reprised by Trudy Erwin), "If You Are Coming Back To Me," "Happy Me" (Jerome, Jack Scholl, sung by Carson).

p, William Jacobs; d, Frederick de Cordova; w, Eugene Conrad, Francis Swann, I. A. L. Diamond (based on the story "Gentlemen Are Born" by Harry Sauber); ph, Wesley Anderson; m, Max Steiner; ed, Frank McGee; md, Leo F. Forbstein; art d, Stanley Fleischer.

Musical **(PR:A MPAA:NR)**

LOVE AND MARRIAGE½**

(1966, Ital.) 106m Panda/EM bw (L'IDEA FISSA)

"The First Night": Lando Buzzanca *(Concetto)*, Maria Grazia Buccella *(Enea)*, Umberto D'Orsi *(Roro)*, Luciana Angelillo *(Lady on Yacht)*, Gianni Del Balzo *(Baron)*, Amedeo Girard *(Hotel Clerk)*, "One Moment Is Enough": Ingeborg Schoener *(Marina)*, Renato Tagliani *(Giancarlo)*, Sandro Moretti *(Barman)*, Steve Forsyth *(Young Man In Cinema)*, Enzo Carra *(Andrea)*, Marino Mase *(Fisherman)*, Armando Tarallo *(Don Eugenio)*, Flora Volpe *(Amelia)*; "The Last Card": Eleonora Rossi-Drago *(Elsa)*, Aldo Giuffre *(Antonio)*, April Hennessy *(Gladys)*, June Weaver *(Ann)*, Ethel Levin *(Linda)*, Gioia Durrell *(Manicurist)*, Carlo Loffredo *(1st Man)*,

Bruno Scipioni *(2nd Man)*; "Saturday, July 18": Sylva Koscina *(Diana)*, Philippe Leroy *(Mario)*; Alrise Estense, Roberto Fabbri, Nino Falanga.

Four short segments which all concentrate upon the theme of infidelity, coming up with some clever and ingenious situations that make light of the possessiveness of the Italian male "macho." The first, and probably best, follows a young Sicilian couple on their honeymoon in Naples, where they are invited aboard a millionaire's yacht. The rich gentleman offers the groom one million lire to sleep with the bride. The drunken groom accepts but the next morning, when the expensive hotel he has checked into will not accept his check, he is faced with either relating his experience or going to jail. "Moment" has Tagliani as an extremely jealous husband, who keeps a continual eye on his wife wherever she goes, even to the rest room. He boasts of her faithfulness, but his clever wife manages to sneak numerous affairs right under her husband's nose. When Tagliani finds out about his wife's promiscuity he attempts to drown her. Leaving her for dead, he returns to find her making love to a fisherman. In "The Last Card" Giuffre plays an unemployed soccer player whose wife, Drago, arranges for him to become a male prostitute to help alleviate their trying financial situation. But Giuffre has such a hard time at this new profession, that he runs back to his wife, declaring the desire to find a job. The last segment, "Saturday, July 18," has Koscina vacationing on the island of Capri for a month, joined for the last two weeks by her husband Leroy. The first day Leroy arrives on the island, he brags about his wife's faithfulness, only to find out later how wrong he has been.

p, Ermanno Donati, Luigi Carpentieri; d, Gianni Puccini ("The First Night"; "Saturday, July 18"), Mino Guerrini ("One Moment Is Enough"; "The Last Card"); w, Bruno Baratti, Oreste Biancoli, Eliana De Sabata, Jaja Fiastri, Guerrini, Puccini, Ennio De Concini; ph, Luciano Trasatti, Alfio Contini, Riccardo Pallottini; m, Marcello Giombini; ed, Mario Forges Davanzati, Bruna Malaguti; art d, Aurelio Crugnola; cos, Luciana Marinucci.

Comedy **(PR:C MPAA:NR)**

LOVE AND MONEY*** (1982) 90m Lorimar/PAR c

Ray Sharkey *(Byron Levin)*, Ornella Muti *(Catherine Stockheinz)*, Klaus Kinski *(Frederick Stockheinz)*, Armand Assante *(Lorenzo Prado)*, King Vidor *(Walter Klein)*, Susan Heldfond *(Vicky)*, William Prince *(Ambassador Paultz)*, Tony Sirico *(Raoul)*, Jacqueline Brooks *(Mrs. Paultz)*, Daniel Faraldo *(Hector)*, Rodolfo Hoyos *(Gen. Sanzer)*, Terry Jastrow *(Clem Dixon)*, Tom McFadden *(Blair)*, Cynthia Allison *(Newscaster)*, Sonny Gibson *(Bodyguard)*, Tony Plana *(National Guard General)*, Nick Powers *(Youth Counselor)*, Stephen Keep *(Hankland)*, Kathy Spring *(Melanie Dixon)*, Susan Welsh *(Sandy)*, Breck Costin *(Hotel Doorman)*, Laura Grayson *(Adela)*, Gene Rutherford *(Hotel Waiter)*.

Another piece of obsessive work by the maker of FINGERS, this picture lacks the sadistic qualities of the earlier film, making it a much more accessible movie. Still, its showings have been extremely limited. Sharkey plays an investment counselor bored with his routine life and with his relationship with his girl friend, librarian Heldfond. Business magnate Kinski asks for his assistance in convincing the new leader of a small, silver-rich Latin American country to allow Kinski's company to set up shop there. This is after Sharkey has been involved in an intense affair with Kinski's wife, Muti. Kinski is trying to extend his power, and Sharkey gets more excitement than he bargained for, as he is drawn into violence and intrigue while all the time chasing after Muti. Sharkey lacks the passion required for his role, and he is totally outshone by the performances of Kinski and Muti. The Los Angeles backlots are unconvincing as a substitute for the Latin American country. Originally Warren Beatty had signed the New York critic Pauline Kael, to assist Toback in the production, but Toback and Kael failed to see eye-to-eye. This would have been the famous reviewer's first escapade into the actual production of a film. LOVE AND MONEY was the Hollywood debut for Italian star Muti and also featured a performance by legendary director King Vidor, who was then 87 years of age.

p,d,&w, James Toback; ph, Fred Schuler (Metrocolor); m, Aaron Copland; ed, Dennis Hill; md, Copland art d, Lee Fischer.

Drama **(PR:O MPAA:R)**

LOVE AND PAIN AND THE WHOLE DAMN THING*** (1973) 110m COL c

Maggie Smith *(Lila Fisher)*, Timothy Bottoms *(Walter Elbertson)*, Don Jaime de Mora y Aragon *(The Duke)*, Emiliano Redondo *(Spanish Gentleman)*, Charles Baxter *(Dr. Elbertson)*, Margaret Modlin *(Mrs. Elbertson)*, May Heatherly *(Melanie Elbertson)*, Lloyd Brimhall *(Carl)*, Elmer Modlin *(Dr. Edelheidt)*, Andres Monreal *(Tourist Guide)*.

A scenic Spanish background serves well this sensitive love story about two misfits, both finding a sense of belonging for the first time. Bottoms plays the dropout son of a successful father. He is on a bicycle tour of Spain when he runs into Smith, an aging spinster, timid to the point of neurosis. After a set of bumbling attempts by Bottoms to make love to Smith, she eventually gives in. Both Smith and Bottoms give convincing performances in difficult roles; they manage to display their inner emotions without falling into cliched histrionics. The whole story almost falls apart, though, when the script injects the terminal illness theme (Smith is dying). Material is subtly handled by the director, with photography that captures the scenery without allowing it to become overpowering. Shot in 1971 and originally titled THE WIDOWER, the film was released two years later with its present title.

p&d, Alan J. Pakula; w, Alvin Sargent; ph, Geoffrey Unsworth; m, Michael Small; ed, Russell Lloyd; md, Small; art d, Enrique Alarcon; cos, Germinal Rangel, Mitzou; makeup, Mariano Garcia Rey.

Drama **(PR:C MPAA:R)**

LOVE AND THE FRENCHWOMAN***

(1961, Fr.) 143m Films Metzger et Woog-Paris-Elysee-Unidex/Auerbach-Kingsley bw (LA FRANCAISE ET L'AMOUR)

"Childhood": Pierre-Jean Vaillard *(Mon. Bazouche)*, Jacqueline Porel *(Mme. Bazouche)*, Darry Cowl *(Dr. Dufieux)*, Noel Roquevert *(Col. Chappe)*, Martine Lambert *(Gisele)*, Bibi Morat *(Jaja)*, Jacques Duby *(Young Man)*, Paulette Dubost *(Mme. Tronche)*, Micheline Dax *(Lulu)*, Pierre Paulet *(Driver)*; "Adolescence": Sophie Desmarets *(Mother)*, Pierre Mondy *(Father)*, Annie Sinigalia *(Bichette)*, Roger Pierre *(Prince Charming)*, Francois Nocher *(Jacques)*, Pierre-Louis, Simone Paris; "Virginity": Valerie Lagrange *(Ginette)*, Pierre Michael *(Francois)*, Paul Bonifas *(Father)*, Nicole Chollet *(Mother)*; "Marriage": Marie-Jose Nat *(Line)*, Claude Rich *(Charles)*, Yves Robert *(Man With The Moustache)*, Liliane Patrick *(Lady With Cigarette)*, Jacques Fabbri *(Ticket Collector)*; "Adultery": Dany Robin *(Nicole)*, Paul Meurisse *(Jean-Claude)*, Jean-Paul Belmondo *(Gil)*, Alice Kessler, Ellen Kessler *(Twins)*, Claude Pieplu; "Divorce": Annie Girardot *(Danielle)*, Francois Perier *(Michel)*, Denise Grey *(Mother)*, Jean Poiret, Michel Serrault *(Lawyers)*, Francis Blanche *(Marceroux)*, Alfred Adam *(Friend)*, Georges Chamarat *(Judge)*; "A Woman Alone": Martine Carol *(Elaine)*, Sylvia Montfort *(Gilberte)*, Robert Lamoureux *(Desire)*, Simone Renant *(Lawyer)*, Suzanne Nivette *(Mme. Mangebois)*, Paul Ville *(Tribunal President)*.

A charming French anthology film that traces the nature of love in typical French women from childhood to old age. The first episode "Childhood", details a 9-year-old's confusion when her parents tell her that babies come from cabbages. The parents have a hysterical little girl on their hands when the child sees a cabbage fall from a vegetable truck. "Adolescence" shows a girl's first kiss and the exciting world of diaries, stolen kisses, and daydreams of charming princes. "Virginity" takes on the sticky problem of a young couple having trouble waiting until marriage to consummate their love. Due to financial problems, the pair must continually postpone their marriage, and they are about to give in to temptation, when reason clears their heads and they definitely decide to wait. "Marriage" details a newlywed couple's first turbulent experiences with petty arguments and frustrating personal habits, as they drive to their honeymoon spot. In "Adultery" a bored wife takes a young lover, and when her husband finds out, he invites the young man to lunch and tries to scare him off with tales of his wife's lavish spending habits. Having succeeded, the husband returns to his repentant wife, but he is interrupted by a phone call from *his* mistress. "Divorce" sees a couple trying to part on friendly terms and remain friends, but the obnoxious demands of their lawyers prevent them from having a civilized divorce. "A Woman Alone" concerns a professional bigamist who attempts to bilk a lonely woman; but he falls in love with her roommate and reveals his plot. The women have him prosecuted, but upon his release he meets up with the lonely lady lawyer who had defended him in his trial.

p, Jacques Remy, Robert Woog; ph, Robert Lefebvre; art d, Lucien Aguettand; animation, Jabely; English commentary, Jacques Bruinius; "Childhood": d, Henri Decoin; w, Felicien Marceau; m, Joseph Kosma; ed, Claude Durand; "Adolescence": d, Jean Delannoy; w, Louise de Vilmorin, Jacques Robert; m, Paul Misraki; ed, Henri Taverna; "Virginity": d, Michel Boisrond; w, Annette Wademant; m, Jean Constantin; ed, Taverna; "Marriage": d&w, Rene Clair; m, Jacques Metehen; ed, Louisette Hautecoeur; "Adultery": d, Henri Verneuil; w, France Roche, Michel Audiard; m, Norbert Glanzberg; ed, Borys Lewin; "Divorce": d, Christian-Jacque; w, Charles Spaak; m, Henri Crolla; ed, Jacques Desagneau; art d, Robert Gys, Lucien Aguettand; "A Woman Alone": d&w, Jean-Paul Le Chanois (based on a story by Marcel Ayme); m, Georges Delerue; ed, Emma Le Chanois.

Comedy **(PR:C-O MPAA:NR)**

LOVE AND THE MIDNIGHT AUTO SUPPLY*

(1978) 93m Producers Capitol c

Michael Parks *(Duke)*, Linda Cristal *(Annie)*, Scott Jacoby *(Justin)*, Bill Adler *(Ramon)*, Colleen Camp *(Billie Jean)*, Monica Gayle *(Kathy)*, Sedena Spivey *(Violet)*, George McCalister *(Peter Santore)*, John Ireland *(Tony Santore)*, Rory Calhoun *(Len Thompson)*, Rod Cameron *(Sheriff Dawson)*, Bert Freed *(Mayor John Randolph)*.

This messy project has Parks as the head of a car-theft ring. He is approached by Jacoby and McCalister to donate half of the crooks take to the righteous cause of displaced farmworkers. Parks agrees to do so because McCalister's dad is about to become the town's next mayor. Credible performances aid this otherwise uneven mishmash of styles.

p,d,&w, James Polakof; ph, Lawrence Raimond (Movielab Color): m, Ed Bofas; ed, Irving Rosenblum; art d, Perry Ferguson II: stunts, Richard Butler.

Comedy **(PR:C-O MPAA:PG)**

LOVE AT FIRST BITE 1/2** (1979) 96m Melvin Simon/AIP c

George Hamilton *(Count Dracula)*, Susan Saint James *(Cindy Sondheim)*, Richard Benjamin *(Dr. Jeff Rosenberg)*, Dick Shawn *(Lt. Ferguson)*, Arte Johnson *(Renfield)*, Sherman Hemsley *(Rev. Mike)*, Isabel Sanford *(Judge)*, Barry Gordon *(Flashlight Vendor)*, Ronnie Schell *(Gay in Elevator)*, Bob Basso *(TV Repairman)*, Bryan O'Byrne *(Priest)*, Michael Pataki *(Mobster)*, Beverly Sanders *(Lady in Elevator)*, Basil Hoffman *(Desk Clerk)*, Stanley Brock *(Cab Driver)*, Danny Dayton *(Billy)*, Robert Ellenstein *(W.V. Man)*, David Ketchum *(Customs Inspector)*.

Spoof of the famous vampire legend finds Hamilton as the count searching among the New York City night life for the girl of his dreams. The film is permeated with obvious satire, but the jokes really work. In a funny scene set in a disco, Hamilton and Benjamin (boy friend to Saint James, the woman coveted by the count) try to hypnotize each other, while Saint James third-wheels around and storms out. Overall though, the script is uneven; the jokes are not paced to sustain the plot. Also there's a romance somewhere beneath it all, but this is never properly developed.

Hamilton gives a convincing performance, though occasionally he has problems with the accent he affects.

p, Joel Freeman; d, Stan Dragoti; w, Robert Kaufman (based on a story by Kaufman, Mark Gindes); ph, Edward Rosson (CFI Color); m, Charles Bernstein; ed, Mort Fallick, Allan Jacobs; prod d, Serge Krizman; ch, Alex Romero; m/l, "I Love The Night Life" (sung by Evelyn "Champagne" King).

Comedy   Cas.   **(PR:C MPAA:PG)**

LOVE AT FIRST SIGHT**   (1930) 65m CHES bw

Norman Foster (*Richard Norton*), Suzanne Keener (*June Vernon*), Doris Rankin (*Mrs. Vernon*), Lester Cole (*Paul Russell*), Abe Reynolds (*Abe Feinstein*), Hooper L. Atchley (*Frank Belmont*), Burt Matthews (*Master of Ceremonies*), Dorothee Adam ("*Jig-a-Boo*" *Singer*), Jim Harkins, Paul Specht, and His Orchestra, Tracy and Elwood, Chester Hale Girls.

After getting Reynolds to back their first Broadway show, Foster and Cole begin searching for a singer. Foster spies Keener and thinks she's just right for the part, mostly because he's highly infatuated with the lass. She's faced with choosing between the show and a nightclub that her mother would rather have her sing at. Of course, after the usual trials and errors, things turn out happily for the couple and a new show is begun. Songs include: "Sunshine," "Jig-a-Boo Jig," "What Is Living Without You?" "Love at First Sight" (Lester Lee, Charles Levison).

d, Edgar Lewis; w, Lester Lee, Charles Levison; ph, Dal Clawson; ed, Russell Shields; m/l, Lee, Levison.

Musical   **(PR:A MPAA:NR)**

LOVE AT FIRST SIGHT*1/2   (1977, Can.) 85m Quadrant Films/Movietime c

Mary Ann McDonald (*Shirley*), Dan Aykroyd (*Roy*), Jane Mallett (*Grandma*), George Murray (*Frank*), Barry Morse (*William*), Mignon Elkins (*Edna*), Les Carlson (*Stu*), Grace Louis.

Dreadful attempt at comedy has Aykroyd as a blind man and the object of McDonald's love. They want to get married, but Murray, as McDonald's father doesn't want a blind son-in-law. But the two persist. Storyline is never fully developed, it depends too much upon jokes which are either predictable or just are not funny. Even though, the cast manages to take their parts seriously and to deliver some worthwhile performances. The title song, "Love at First Sight," is sung by Dionne Warwick.

p, Peter O'Brian; d&w, Rex Bromfield; ph, Henri Fiks; m, Roy Payne; ed, Alan Collins; art d, Tony Hall.

Comedy   **(PR:A MPAA:NR)**

LOVE AT NIGHT**

(1961, Fr.) 97m SLPF/Lutetia/Sonodis/Selb/William Mishkin bw (IMPASSE DES VERTUS; AKA: SEX AT NIGHT)

Isabelle Pia (*Monique*), Christian Marquand (*Eugene*), Simone Paris (*Denise*), Raymond Bussieres (*Gilbert*), Daniel Cauchy (*Fanfan*), Jean-Louis Le Goff, Jacqueline Carrel, Monique Clarence, Genvieve Morel, Jacques Clancy, Georges Chamarat, Gaston Rey, Emile Prudhomme, Claudy Chapeland.

Paris plays a beautiful widow who falls in love with Marquand, a young hustler many years her junior, and decides to support him with her inheritance. When the money runs out, Marquand gets ready to leave for greener pastures, but his departure is delayed when Paris's lovely 19-year-old daughter Pia returns home from a sanitarium. Marquand becomes obsessed with seducing Pia but she rejects him. Pia decides to keep the incident to herself. Marquand joins a gang of smugglers to raise money. Soon after Marquand decides to force himself on Pia. Paris catches them and accuses Pia of trying to steal her lover. Pia leaves the house to live with an aunt, but Marquand wants to marry her. When the smugglers realize that the police are closing in on their operations, they frame Marquand to take the fall. Marquand suspects as much and goes to the police, but when Pia is kidnaped by the gang, he returns to save her and is killed in the attempt.

p, Geroges Senamaud; d&w, Pierre Mere (based on a story by Jean Perine); ph, Joseph Brun; m, Jean Marion; ed, Jacques Mavae; m/l, Rene Denoncin; makeup, Odette Berroyer.

Drama   **(PR:C-O MPAA:NR)**

LOVE AT SEA*1/2   (1936, Brit.) 70m British and Dominions/PAR bw

Rosalyn Boulter (*Betty Foster*), Carl Harbord (*Dick Holmes*), Aubrey Mallalieu (*John Brighton*), Frank Birch (*Mr. Godwin*), Dorothy Dewhurst (*Mrs. Hackworth Pratt*), Maud Gill (*Emily Foster*), Beatrix Fielden-Kaye (*Katherine Foster*), Billy Bray (*Slippery Joe*), George Merritt (*Inspector*), Raymond Ellis, Eve Riley, George Dewhurst, Vi Kaley, Hector McGregor.

Early British farce that puts madcap humor and a far-fetched plot aboard a luxury liner. Totally by chance a reporter and a girl meet and fall in love on the ship. Neither of them had originally planned to go on the cruise, but are substitutes for other people who had planned to meet at sea.

p, Anthony Havelock-Allan; d, Adrian Brunel; w, Beaufoy Milton (based on the story by Jane Browne); ph, Francis Carver.

Comedy   **(PR:A MPAA:NR)**

LOVE AT SECOND SIGHT   (SEE: GIRL THIEF, THE, 1938, Brit.)

LOVE AT TWENTY***

(1963, Fr./Ital./Jap./Pol./Ger.) 110m Ulysse-Unitec-Cinescolo-Toho-Towa-Kamera-Film Polski-Beta/EM bw (L'AMOUR A VINGST ANS, AMORE A VENT'ANNI, HATACHI NO KOI, MILOSC DWUDZIESTOLATKOW, LIEBE MIT ZWANZIG)

France: Jean-Pierre Leaud (*Antoine Doinel*), Marie-France Pisier (*Colette*), Francois Darbon (*Colette's Father*), Rosy Varte (*Colette's Mother*), Patrick Auffay (*Rene*), Jean-Francois Adam (*Albert Tazzi*); Italy: Eleonora Rossi-Drago (*Valentina*), Cristina Gajoni (*Christina*), Geronimo Meynier (*Leonardo*); Japan: Koji Furuhata (*Hiroshi*), Nami Tamura (*Fukimo*); West Germany: Christian Doermer (*Tonio*), Barbara Frey (*Ursula*), Vera Tschechowa, Werner Finck; Poland: Barbara Lass (*Basia*), Zbigniew Cybulski (*Sbyssek*), Wladyslaw Kowalski (*Wladek*).

An international compilation film which is best known for its Truffaut episode "Antoine and Colette," the second installment of his "Antoine Doinel" series begun in THE 400 BLOWS. Conceived by French producer Roustang, the film is built on the theme of being 20-years-old, or as he would put it, "the inscrutable youth of the atomic age and technological civilization." Five young film-makers contributed: Francois Truffaut (France), Renzo Rossellini (Italy), Shintaro Ishihara (Japan), Marcel Ophuls (West Germany), and Andrzej Wajda (Poland). Truffaut's episode had Leaud moving across the street from the girl he loves, and discovering that her parents like him more than she does. Rossellini's has a young man involved in relationships with a young woman and an older woman. Ishihara's piece has a love-maddened working-class lad killing his girl friend and the wealthy girl, he cannot attain because of class differences. Ophuls' segment is far more optimistic. A photographer on a stopover in Munich gets a girl pregnant. After arriving home, he learns what he has done and returns to the girl, marries her, and soon falls in love with her. Wajda's episode is different from the rest (which is not surprising considering he was the eldest, at age 35). It is told from the point of view of an older generation. A middle-aged man saves a young girl who slipped into a polar bear pit in a zoo. He is invited back to the home of a pair of teen-age witnesses who are throwing a party. He tells the partygoers of his past as a resistance fighter. They get him drunk, tease him, and sing him a song about a "sleepy old bear," and kick him out.

p, Pierre Roustang; m, Georges Delerue (linking episodes); ed, Claudine Bouche; France: d, Francois Truffaut; w, Yvon Samuel, Truffaut; ph, Raoul Coutard; Italy: d&w, Renzo Rossellini; ph, Mario Montuori; Japan: d&w, Shintaro Ishihara; ph, Shigeo Hayashida; m, Toru Takemitsu; West Germany: d&w Marcel Ophuls; ph, Wolf Wirth; Poland: d, Andrzej Wajda; w, Jerzy Stefan Stawinski; ph, Jerzy Lipman; m, Jerzy Matuszkiewicz.

Drama   **(PR:C MPAA:NR)**

LOVE BAN, THE

(SEE: IT'S A 2'6" ABOVE THE GROUND WORLD, 1972, Brit.)

LOVE BEFORE BREAKFAST**1/2   (1936) 65m UNIV bw

Carole Lombard (*Kay Colby*), Preston Foster (*Scott Miller*), Cesar Romero (*Bill Wadsworth*), Janet Beecher (*Mrs. Colby*), Betty Lawford (*Contessa Janie Campanella*), Richard Carle (*Brinkerhoff*), Forrester Harvey (*First Mate*), Ed Barton (*Jerry/Cabby*), Sam Tong (*Steward*), Bob Thom (*Chauffeur*), Alphonse Martell, William Arnold (*Waiters*), Dennis O'Keefe, Robert Kent, Ralph Malone, Howard "Red" Christie, Ralph Brooks, David Tyrell, David Worth (*College Boys*), Earl Eby (*Entertainer*), Albert Richman (*Proprietor*), Pat Flaherty (*Bouncer*), Nick De Ruiz (*Chef*), Harry Tracy (*Groom*), Bert Roach (*Fat Man*), Joyce Compton (*Mary Lee Jackson*), Pushface Lombard (*Junior*), Charles Tannen, Bert Moorhouse, Jay Easton, Theodore von Eltz (*Clerks*), Edward Earle (*Quartermaster*), E. E. Clive (*Captain*), Jimmy Aye (*Petty Officer*), Lester Dorr (*Attendant*), John King (*Johnny*), Nan Grey (*Telephone Girl*), Mia Ichioka (*Yuki*), John Rogers (*Dickson*), Douglas Blackley (*College Boy*), Don Briggs (*Stuart Farnum*), Andre Beranger (*Charles*), Diana Gibson (*Clerk*).

The big mystery about this film was what the title had to do with anything. Yes, it was about love, but there wasn't a bit of it before breakfast. Romero works for Foster, a wealthy man who dabbles in black gold; oil, that is. Both of them are understandably in love with Lombard. Foster has a way to get rid of his competition so he offers Romero the chance to run the company's operations in a place as far away as he can send him, Japan. Romero snaps at the opportunity, much to Lombard's dismay. At the same time, Foster arranges for comely Lawford to sail on the same ship. She's a countess with charm oozing from every delicate pore. Foster reckons that Romero will never be able to resist the combination of title, money, and beauty. Given a choice between the two, Lombard would have selected Romero but now that he's out of the way, Foster moves in. She tolerates him, with virtually no show of affection, until Romero sends her an overseas telegram saying that he's going to marry Lawford. That settles it and she decides to give Foster her hand. Then, just before the wedding is to take place, she thinks that she's made the wrong move so she pleads with Romero to come back. Further, once she figures out that Foster arranged the whole thing between Romero and Lawford, she feels that he has gone beyond mere matchmaking and into the realm of manipulation, so she breaks off their engagement. Later, on Foster's yacht, she understands that he did it all because he loves her. There's a contrived fall off the ship and the two are finally united by the ship's captain, a totally bogus piece of business but needed to put a cute capper on the film. LOVE BEFORE BREAKFAST is a noisy picture with harangues by the handful, some of them funny, some of them flat. Everyone in the picture is good but the script let them down. Even so, it's a fair example of what passed for "screwball" comedy of the 1930s, albeit in lesser hands than those of Howard Hawks.

p, Edmund Grainger; d, Walter Lang; w, Herbert Fields, Gertrude Princell (based on the novel *Spinster Dinner* by Faith Baldwin); ph, Ted Tetzlaff; ed, Maurice Wright; md, Franz Waxman; art d, Albert D'Agostino; cos, Travis Banton, Brymer.

Comedy   **(PR:A MPAA:NR)**

LOVE BEGINS AT TWENTY**

(1936) 60m FN-WB bw (GB: ALL ONE NIGHT)

Warren Hull (*Jerry Wayne*), Patricia Ellis (*Lois Gillingwater*), Hugh Herbert (*Horatio*

Gillingwater), Hobart Cavanaugh (Jake Buckley), Dorothy Vaughan (Evalina Gillingwater), Clarence Wilson (Jonathan Ramp), Robert Gleckler (Mugsy O'Banion), Mary Treen (Alice Gillingwater), Anne Nagel (Miss Perkins), Arthur Aylesworth (Justice Felton), Saul Gorss (Jim), Henry Otho (Lumpy), Max Wagner (Lester), Tom Brower (Bert Hanson), Milt Kibbee (Wilbur), Tom Wilson (Fred).

Herbert plays a henpecked husband who finds the courage to stand up to his wife through the gin bottle. Herbert manages to play his part without falling into slapstick, with the rest of the cast holding their own. Direction is smooth.

p, Bryan Foy; d, Frank McDonald; w, Tom Reed, Dalton Trumbo (based on the play "Broken Dishes" by Martin Flavin); ph, George Barnes; ed, Terry Morse.

Comedy (PR:A MPAA:NR)

LOVE BIRDS*½ (1934) 61m UNIV bw

Slim Summerville (Henry Whipple), ZaSu Pitts (Araminta Tootle), Mickey Rooney (Gladwyn Tootle), Frederick Burton (Barbwire), Emmett Vogan (Forbes), Dorothy Christy (Kitten), Maude Eburne (Mme. Bertha), Hugh Enfield (Bus Driver), Arthur Stone (Janitor), Ethel Mandell (Teacher), Gertrude Short (Burlesque Girl), Clarence H. Wilson (Blewitt), John T. Murray (Dentist).

Slim plot line which never has a chance to take off, has Summerville and Pitts owners of the same property. Rumors of gold on the property send the community into gold fever. It all proves to be a hoax in the end, and Pitts and Summerville get their money back. Except for a couple of humorous situations, the story offers little to sustain itself.

p, Carl Laemmle, Jr.; d, William A. Seiter; w, Doris Anderson (based on a story by Clarence Marks, Dale Van Every); ph, Norbert Brodine; ed, Clarence Wilson.

Comedy (PR:A MPAA:NR)

LOVE BOUND* (1932) 67m PEER bw

Natalie Moorhead, Jack Mulhall, Edmund Breese, Montagu Love, Clara Kimball Young, Roy D'Arcy.

Listless piece of work concerning a woman who leaves her husband because she thinks he has been fooling around with the actress whose career he manages. She takes a ship to Europe, which also has the actress aboard. There is an attempt to find out the truth, but it never materializes. Lifeless performances, and below par photography serve as a barrier in developing any type of story.

d, Robert Hill; w, J. Gilbert, George Plympton.

Drama (PR:A MPAA:NR)

LOVE BUG, THE*** (1968) 108m Disney/BV c

Dean Jones (Jim Douglas), Michele Lee (Carole), David Tomlinson (Thorndyke), Buddy Hackett (Tennessee Steinmetz), Joe Flynn (Havershaw), Benson Fong (Mr. Wu), Joe E. Ross (Detective), Barry Kelley (Police Sergeant), Iris Adrian (Carhop), Andy Granatelli (Himself), Dale Van Sickel, Regina Parton, Bob Drake, Hal Brock, Rex Ramsey, Lynn Grate, Richard Warlock, Everett Creach, Bill Couch, Robert Hoy, Jack Mahoney, Richard Brill, Rudy Doucette, Jim McCullough, Glenn Wilder, Robert James, Bob Harris, Richard Geary, Jack Perkins, Ronnie Rondell, Reg Parton, Tom Bamford, Marion J. Playan, Bill Hickman, Hal Grist, Larry Schmitz, Dana Derfus, Gerald Jann, Ted Duncan, Gene Roscoe, Charles Willis, Roy Butterfield, J. J. Wilson, Bud Ekins, Gene Curtis, John Timanus, Fred Krone, Jesse Wayne, Fred Stromsoe, Kim Brewer, (The Drivers), Ned Glass, Gil Lamb, Nicole Jaffe, Russ Caldwell, Pete Renoudet, Alan Fordney, Gary Owens, Robert Foulk, Wally Boag, Max Balchowsky, Brian Fong, Stan Duke, Chick Hearn, Pedro Gonzalez-Gonzalez, Herbie the Car.

First in the "Herbie" series, this is one of the most successful Disney films ever. They all star a cute little Volkswagen named Herbie, which has a mind of its own. In this episode, unsuccessful driver Jones rescues Herbie from Tomlinson, a slick race-car driver who mistreats the little car. The car takes to Jones and begins winning races for him without Jones ever knowing of Herbie's special attributes. Tomlinson becomes jealous of the car's success, and continually tries to buy it back. Entire cast gives standout performances, but Herbie manages to steal the acting awards. Direction is smooth and well paced.

p, Bill Walsh; d, Robert Stevenson; w, Don DaGradi, Walsh (based on a story by Gordon Buford); ph, Edward Colman (Technicolor); m, George Bruns; ed, Cotton Warburton; art d, Carroll Clark, John B. Mansbridge; set d, Emile Kuri, Hal Gausman; cos, Bill Thomas; spec eff, Eustace Lycett, Alan Maley, Peter Ellenshaw, Robert A. Mattey, Howard Jensen, Danny Lee; makeup, Otis Malcolm.

Comedy Cas. (PR:AAA MPAA:G)

LOVE BUTCHER, THE*½ (1982) 83m Desert/Mirror Releasing c

Erik Stern (Caleb/Lester), Kay Near (Florence), Jeremiah Beecher (Russell), Edward Roehm (Capt. Stark), Robin Sherwood (Sheila).

This low-budget slasher film is about a crippled gardener who seems to be constantly mistreated by his female employers. He gets his revenge when his alter-ego rapes them and kills them with a gardening tool. Script is filled with heavy handed dialog, mainly for the comic effect. Stern does a decent job handling the two roles, but the rest of the cast is devoid of any life. The film is well photographed.

p, Gary Williams, Micky Belski; d, Mikel Angel, Don Jones; w, Jones, James Evergreen; ph, Jones, Austin McKinney (Techniscope, Technicolor) m, Richard Hieronymous; ed, Robert Freeman; art d, Val West, Ron Foreman; makeup, Gail Peterson.

Horror Cas. (PR:O MPAA:R)

LOVE CAGE, THE (SEE: JOY HOUSE, 1964, Fr.)

LOVE CAPTIVE, THE**½ (1934) 63m UNIV bw

Nils Asther (Dr. Alexis Collender), Gloria Stuart (Alice Trask), Paul Kelly (Dr. Norman Ware), Alan Dinehart (Roger Loft), Renee Gadd (Valerie Loft), Virginia Kami (Mary Williams), Russ Brown (Larry Chapman), Addison Richards (Dr. Collins), John Wray (Jules Glass), Jane Meridith (Mrs. Forndyce), Ellalee Ruby (Annie Nolan), Franklyn Ardell (Pete Noland), Robert Greig, Sam Godfrey Demetrius Alexis.

Asther plays a gifted psychiatrist with a dark side. He has a thing for beautiful women who are already spoken for, which leads him to hypnotize them so they fall in love with him. Direction and performances are smooth.

d, Max Marcin; w, Karen de Wolf (based on a story "The Humbug" by Marcin); ph, Gilbert Warrenton; ed, Ted Kent.

Drama/Crime (PR:A MPAA:NR)

LOVE CHILD**½ (1982) 97m Ladd/WB c

Amy Madigan (Terry Jean Moore), Beau Bridges (Jack Hansen), Mackenzie Phillips (J. J.), Albert Salmi (Capt. Ellis), Joanna Merlin (Superintendent Sturgis), Margaret Whitton (Jacki Steinberg), Lewis Smith (Jesse Chaney), Dennis Lipscomb (Arthur Brady), Anna Maria Horsford (Mara), Michael Shane (Judge Hare), Randy Dreyfuss (Striker), Rhea Pearlman (June Burns), Juanita Mahone (Cecily), Richard Whiting (Judge Weston), Luis Avalos (Tony), Mary McCusker (Jeanette), Patrick Sullivan, Richard Liberty (Police), Jody Wilson (Sgt. Benson), William Leonard (Judge Powell), Madeline Kiggins (Guard), Mathew Pearce (Boy in Car), Dara Murphy (Nancy), Candy Trabuco (Vanessa), Sarah Zinsser (Sarah), Cheryl King (Van Inmate), Pat Mann (Parker), Jack Stevens (Jack's Son), John Archie (Guard), Ellen Beck (Rabbit), Susan Batson (Brenda), Patricia Williams (Lida), Carole Russo (Evelyn), Jill-Rene Weissman (Stefanie), Terry Jean Moore (Amy), Zelda Patterson (Other Girl), Richard Hunsinger, Al Kiggins, Raymond Peters (Correctional Officers), Carol Chaput (Guard), Annette Foosaner (Woman in Yard), Ronne Mickey (Faith), Tame Connolly (Norma), Norma Davids (Bonnie).

True story has Madigan as a prisoner, convicted of a crime her cousin committed. She befriends guard Bridges, which eventually leads to a love affair and she becomes pregnant. Instead of giving up the baby, she fights to raise the child while in prison. MacKenzie is a fellow prisoner who helps guide Madigan through her ordeal. Madigan gives a solid performance in a complicated role. Supporting cast is adequate.

p, Paul Maslansky; d, Larry Peerce; w, Anne Gerard, Katherine Specktor (based on a story by Gerard); ph, James Pergola (Capital Telecine Color); m, Charles Fox; ed, Bob Wyman; art d, Don Ivey; m/l, Carly Simon, Fox.

Drama Cas. (PR:O MPAA:R)

LOVE CHILDREN (SEE: PSYCHOUT, 1968)

LOVE COMES ALONG*½ (1930) 77m RKO bw

Bebe Daniels (Peggy), Lloyd Hughes (Johnny Stark), Montagu Love (Sangredo), Ned Sparks (Happy), Alma Tell (Carlotta), Lionel Belmore (Brown), Evelyn Selbie (Bianca), Sam Appel (Gomez).

Daniels plays an actress stranded on a Caribbean island, where she has a stormy affair with a carefree sailor and a run-in with the local power. Daniels' voice, either in voice or in song, is a spark to performances which suffer from miscasting. Direction and screenplay are choppy.

d, Rupert Julian; w, Wallace Smith (based on the play "Conchita" by Edward Knoblock); ph, J. Roy Hunt; m, Sidney Claire; ed, Archie Marshek; m/l, Oscar Levant, Claire, "Until Love Comes Along," "Night Winds" (both sung by Daniels).

Drama (PR:A MPAA:NR)

LOVE CONTRACT, THE** (1932, Brit.) 90m British and Dominions/GAU bw

Winifred Shotter (Antoinette), Owen Nares (Neville Cardington), Sunday Wilshin (Mrs. Savage), Miles Malleson (Peters), Gibb McLaughlin (Hodge), Spencer Trevor (Mr. Savage), Frank Harvey (Bank Manager), Cosmo Kryle Bellew (Sir George), The Mangan Tillerettes.

Crude plot has a rich girl losing all her savings in the stockmarket. She is forced to sell her house. The interested buyer is her stock broker, who soon turns his interest toward the fallen girl. Well-paced script is marred by uneven direction. Performances are adequate, with top-notch production values.

p, Herbert Wilcox; d, Herbert Selpin (based on the play "Chauffeur Antoinette" by De Latraz, C. Desty, R. Blum); m, Ralph Benatsky; ph, F. A. Young.

Drama (PR:A MPAA:NR)

LOVE CRAZY**** (1941) 97m MGM bw

William Powell (Steven Ireland), Myrna Loy (Susan Ireland), Gail Patrick (Isobel Grayson), Jack Carson (Ward Willoughby), Florence Bates (Mrs. Cooper), Sidney Blackmer (George Hennie), Vladimir Sokoloff (Dr. Klugle), Kathleen Lockhart (Mrs. Bristol), Sig Rumann (Dr. Wuthering), Donald MacBride ("Pinky" Grayson), Sara Haden (Cecilia Landis), Fern Emmett (Martha), Elisha Cook Jr. (Elevator Boy), Joseph Crehan (Judge), Jimmy Ames (Taxi Driver), George Meeker (DeWest), Aldrich Bowker (Doorman), George Guhl, Harry Fleischmann (Drivers), Barbara Bedford (Secretary), Clarence Muse (Robert), Jay Eaton, Larry Steers, James H. McNamara, Richard Kipling, Broderick O'Farrell (Guests), Ian Wolfe, Edward Van Sloan, George Irving, Douglas Wood, Byron Shores, Roy Gordon, Emmett Vogan, Selmer Jackson (Doctors), William Tannen (Attendant), Jesse Graves (Butler), Jack Mulhall (Court Clerk), Joan Barclay (Telephone Operator), Ralph Bushman, Lee Phelps, George Magrill, Bill Lally, Ken Christy (Guards), Harry Strang (Sergeant), Wade Boteler (Captain of Detectives), Ed Peil Sr., Dick Allan, Eddie Hart, Philo McCullough, Kai Robinson, George Lollier, James Millican, Paul Palmer, Charles McMurphy, Pat Gleason, James Pierce, Rudy Steinbock (Detectives).

A mile-a-minute breakneck farce that looks as good today as it did back then. Powell and Loy made a dozen films together, six as Nick and Nora Charles. This time, they're a happily married couple about to celebrate their fourth anniversary when their domestic tranquility is shattered as Loy's mother, Bates, arrives to spend some time. In short order, Bates sprains an ankle and will stay a lot longer than anyone anticipated. Powell has to tend the old battleaxe while Loy goes out on an errand to meet her aunt. Powell is bored by the meddling matriarch and decides to have a few sips with Patrick, an old flame who lives in the same apartment building but now is married to MacBride. Bates has listened to the conversation with Patrick and misconstrued it so when Loy comes home, Bates fills her ears with gossip. Loy thinks that she can make Powell jealous by doing the same thing so she goes to Patrick's apartment (or so she thinks) but winds up in the flat of Carson instead. Carson is an archery champion who is nuttier than a pound of pecans. He wants to show her how good he is with the bow and arrow and when she wants out, Carson follows her in the apartment building's halls, stripped to the waist. Then the two of them run into Powell who is less than thrilled by his lovely wife being pursued by a madman. An argument ensues when Powell, who is a bit tipsy, tells her that it was just an innocent evening with Patrick. Loy won't hear of it and walks out on him. Later, Loy decides she wants a divorce and Powell, at first, agrees, then realizes that he loves her and would like to renege. His lawyer, Blackmer, says that the law states a woman can't divorce an insane person so he advises Powell to play wacky until she comes to her senses. In attempting that, Powell pretends to be Abe Lincoln and frees his black servants, but Loy sees through his charade and has him committed to a mental institution to teach him a lesson. Inside the hospital, one wonders who is nuts, the patients or the doctors, Rumann and Sokoloff. Now he has to convince everyone that he is sane and that's something that all of the mental patients believe so it isn't easy. He escapes from the place and learns that the police are after him so he shaves off the trademark mustache, dresses in drag, and pretends to be his own sister. Bates believes it and when Loy and Powell (still in full woman's regalia) go to sleep in the next room, Bates tells them to "sleep well." Loy and Powell are reconciled and all ends for the best. There are several superb set pieces, including a scene in a disabled elevator with Patrick in which Powell gets his head stuck between the doors; the dumping of Bates into a swimming pool (the audience just up and clapped at that) and the highlight sequence with Powell, using a silly falsetto, and masquerading as his spinster sister. There was more slapstick than verbal wit in this picture than one usually saw in a Powell-Loy teaming, although enough raillery to satisfy most of their sophisticated-language fans. Conway's direction was deft and the scenes go by so quickly that you'll be laughing so hard at one, you won't notice that you're half-way through the next

p, Pandro S. Berman; d, Jack Conway; w, William Ludwig, Charles Lederer, David Hertz (based on a story by Hertz, Ludwig); ph, Ray June; m, David Snell; ed, Ben Lewis; art d, Cedric Gibbons.

Comedy　　　　　　　　　　　　　　　　**(PR:A　MPAA:NR)**

LOVE CYCLES**
(1969, Gr.) 87m Transit/Europix bw (DAMA SPATHI; AKA: QUEEN OF CLUBS)

Elena Nathanael (Elena), Spiros Focas (Alexander), Theo Roubanis (Vassilis), Despo Diamantidou (Marianthe), Dimos Starenios (Teacher), Aris Malliagross (Doctor).

Nathanael plays the unhappy wife of sailor Roubanis who becomes irresistibly infatuated with innkeeper Focas while on a vacation with her husband. Guilty, she confesses her obsession to her husband and in return he beats her and returns home. In retaliation, she sleeps with Focas and returns to Athens with her new lover on her heels. She agrees to get rid of Focas and resume her life with Roubanis and go on a trip with him. She has sex with Focas for one last time and goes to the docks to meet her husband. Roubanis, who has had enough of her games, goes off alone, leaving her on the dock.

p, Theiphanis A. Damaskinos, Viktor G. Michaelides; d, Georges Skalenakis; w, Yannis Djiotis; ph, Andrea Anastassatos; m, Yannis Markopoulos.

Drama　　　　　　　　　　　　　　　　**(PR:C　MPAA:NR)**

LOVE DOCTOR, THE*½　　　　　　　(1929) 60m PAR bw

Richard Dix (Dr. Gerald Sumner), June Collyer (Virginia Moore), Morgan Farley (Bud Woodbridge), Miriam Seegar (Grace Tyler), Winifred Harris (Mrs. Woodbridge), Lawford Davidson (Preston De Witt), Gale Henry (Lucy).

Slow-moving spoof about a recent medical graduate, Dix, who gives advice on matters concerning love, and falls victim to his own advice when a new nurse, Collyer, shows up. Not much suspense but good performances carry it through.

d, Melville Brown; w, Guy Bolton, Herman J. Mankiewicz, J. Walter Ruben (based on the play "The Boomerang: Comedy in Three Acts" by Winchell Smith, Victor Mapes); ph, Edward Cronjager; ed, Otto Ludwig.

Comedy　　　　　　　　　　　　　　　　**(PR:A　MPAA:NR)**

LOVE ETERNAL　　　　　　(SEE; ETERNAL RETURN, THE, 1943, Fr.)

LOVE ETERNE, THE**½
(1964, Hong Kong) 126m Shaw Bros./Frank Lee c LIANG SHAN-PO YU CHU YING-T'AI)

Betty Loh Tih (Chu Ying-tai), Ivy Ling Po (Liang Shan-po), Jen Chieh (Ying Hsin), Chen Yen Yen (Lady Chu), Li Kun (Ssu Chiu), Kao Pao-shu (Headmaster's Wife), Ching Miao (Chu Kung-yuan), Yang Chi-ching (Headmaster), Au-yang Sha-fei (Lady Liang), Chiang Kuang-chao.

Fairy-tale like romance from Hong Kong set in fourth-century China sees Tih as a young woman who persuades her parents to allow her to study at the university disguised as a boy. There she falls in love with fellow student Po, but she cannot reveal her identity for fear of losing her chance at higher education. Years later, Po

learns of the deceit and travels to Tih's home to see her. Once there, he learns that she is about to marry another and he commits suicide. Learning of his death, Tih discards her wedding gown for mourning clothes and visits Po's grave. A vicious storm erupts and Po's grave opens pulling Tih in. When the storm passes the grave again opens permitting Po and Tih to emerge transformed into butterflies.

p, Run Run Shaw; d&w, Li Han-hsiang; ph, Ho Lan-shan (Shawscope, Eastmancolor); m, Chou Lan-ping; art d, Chen Chi-jui.

Romance　　　　　　　　　　　　　　　　**(PR:A　MPAA:NR)**

LOVE FACTORY**
(1969, Ital.) 94m Alma/Borde bw/c (BIANCO, ROSSO, GIALLO, ROSA; AKA: WHITE, RED, YELLOW, AND PINK)

"White—The Unkindest Cut": Anita Ekberg (Alberchiaria), Carlo Giuffre (Vitaliano), Sandro Dori (The Mute), E. Caruso; "Red—Veni, Vidi, Vici": Carlo Giuffre (Apollodorus), Maria Grazia Buccella (Poppaea), Giancarlo Cobelli (Nero), Marcella Ruffini (Sulpicia); "Yellow—Suicides Anonymous": Carlo Giuffre (Brighenti), Agnes Spaak (Enrichetta), Claudia Giannotti (Mrs. Brighenti), Leopoldo Trieste; "Pink—The First": Carlo Giuffre (Johnny), Yoko Tani (Yoko), Pietro Carloni, Giusi Raspani Dandolo.

An episodic Italian sex comedy told in four parts. "The Unkindest Cut," has veterinarian Giuffre become the lover of Ekberg who makes her living castrating pigs. When the cowardly vet leaves her standing alone at the altar, Ekberg vows to perform professional duties on him. "Veni, Vidi, Vici", the second episode, is set in Imperial Rome and sees Nero go mad and burn Rome because his wife enjoys taking milk baths with her many lovers. The third; "Suicides Anonymous," features a rich Milan businessman losing his fortune when he is abandoned by his teen-age mistress. The last, and most bizarre episode, "The First," sees a Japanese stripper seduce a young playboy and he becomes pregnant. Due to his promiscuous reputation, the stripper denies the baby is hers.

p, Francesco Mazzei; d, Massimo Mida; w, Bruno Baratti; ph, Marcello Gatti, Gianni Narzisi (Technicolor); m, Piero Umiliani.

Comedy　　　　　　　　　　　　　　　　**(PR:C-O　MPAA:NR)**

LOVE FEAST, THE*½
(1966, Ger.) 88m Achtmann/Globe bw (IMMER WEN ES NACHT WIRD)

Jan Hendricks (Bobby Elkins), Hannelore Elsner (Elke Gerdes), Karin Kernke (Karin Klausen), Walter Wilz (Dr. Harold Goetz), Elisabeth Volkman (Kitty), Almut Berg (Lollo), Adeline Wagner (Mudy), Edith Mill (Gloria Elkins), Gerhard Kittler (Professor Elkins).

Overwrought melodrama starring Hendriks as the bored, perverted young son of Doctor Wilz, who, suddenly decides to dump his 17-year-old plaything, Elsner, with whom he has indulged in all manner of sexual activity. Broke and on her own, Elsner seeks advice from Wilz's lab assistant Kernke, and the women decide to take revenge on Hendriks. Kernke accepts Hendriks' invitation to attend one of his parties, but is frustrated when he ignores her for a young starlet, Volkman. That evening Elsner is arrested for prostitution and and taken to a hospital where it is discovered that she is seriously ill. Kernke and Hendriks' paths cross again, and she soon begins to pity his lonely lifestyle, and seeks to help him. Kernke attempts to force Hendriks into visiting Elsner in the hospital, but he refuses and drives off in his car only to be killed in an accident.

d, Hans Dieter Bove; w, Christoph Baal, Klaus Peter Schulze; ph, Erich Kuchler; m, Wolfram Roehrig; set d, Fritz Graf.

Drama　　　　　　　　　　　　　　　　**(PR:O　MPAA:NR)**

LOVE FINDS A WAY　　　　　　(SEE: ALIAS FRENCH GERTIE, 1930)

LOVE FINDS ANDY HARDY***　　　　　(1938) 90m MGM bw

Lewis Stone (Judge James Hardy), Mickey Rooney (Andrew Hardy), Judy Garland (Betsy Booth), Cecilia Parker (Marian Hardy), Fay Holden (Mrs. Hardy), Ann Rutherford (Polly Benedict), Betty Ross Clarke (Aunt Milly), Lana Turner (Cynthia Potter), Marie Blake (Augusta), Don Castle (Dennis Hunt), Gene Reynolds (Jimmy MacMahon), Mary Howard (Mrs. Tompkins), George Breakston (Beezy), Raymond Hatton (Peter Dugan), Frank Darien (Bill Collector), Rand Brooks (Judge), Erville Alderson (Court Attendant)

Another in the "Andy Hardy" series, this picture proved to be one of the highest grossing films for MGM in 1938 and marked Garland's first appearance in the series. These films are another example of movie mogul Louis B. Mayer's obsession with a naive set of values extolling the virtues of the nuclear family in small town America. The public obviously wanted to see these virtues personified as they flocked to the theaters and prompted 16 "Andy Hardy" films. The insertion of Garland proved to be a big plus, if not for her vocal abilities than for her pleasant girl-next-door image. This episode has Rooney in trouble with his girl friend, Rutherford, when he agrees to escort his buddy's girl, Turner, a real "dish" around for a fee to pay off the car he just bought. This is Turner's first screen appearance for MGM. Suddenly Garland pops up when she pays her aunt and uncle a visit. Rooney quickly dismisses her as nothing but a kid. That is until he hears her sing at a local dance. She quickly becomes another girl problem for Rooney but she sets him straight by pointing out the proper girl, Rutherford. The entire cast gives excellent performances and are helped by a fine director. The script suffers from a wholesomeness that is difficult to swallow. It was written by William Ludwig, a young lawyer from New York, who had moved west for his health, and got a job in MGM's Junior Writing Department. In 1942 the "Andy Hardy" Series won an award certificate at the Oscar ceremonies for the series' "Achievement in representing an American Way of Life." (See ANDY HARDY series, Index.)

p, Carey Wilson; d, George B. Seitz; w, William Ludwig (based on stories by Vivian B. Bretherton and characters by Aurania Rouverol); ph, Lester White; m, David

Snell; ed, Ben Lewis; art d, Cedric Gibbons, Stan Rogers; set d, Edwin B. Willis; cos, Jeanne; m/l, "Meet the Beat of My Heart," "It Never Rains but it Pours" Mack Gordon, Harry Revel, "In Between" Roger Edens, (all sung by Judy Garland).

Comedy/Drama (PR:AA MPAA:NR)

LOVE FROM A STRANGER**** (1937, Brit.) 86m Trafalgar/UA bw

Ann Harding *(Carol Howard)*, Basil Rathbone *(Gerald Lovell)*, Binnie Hale *(Kate Meadows)*, Bruce Seton *(Ronald Bruce)*, Jean Cadell *(Aunt Lou)*, Bryan Powley *(Dr. Gribble)*, Joan Hickson *(Emmy)*, Donald Calthrop *(Hobson)*, Eugene Leahy *(Mr. Tuttle)*.

This top notch thriller is the essence of the macabre and provides some brilliant acting between the fencing Harding and Rathbone. Both actress and actor parry and thrust in a game of deadly wits that far surpasses such theatrical exercises as SLEUTH. For this is no game Harding and Rathbone play. It's murder, plain and simple, Harding trying to prevent her own, Rathbone trying to take her life without her suspecting he's about to kill her. But she knows. Harding is a sweet and unsuspecting lady of beauty and no little refinement who wins a lottery while on a European vacation. A short time later she encounters suave and charming Rathbone who walks her to the altar. Rathbone uses some of Harding's money to buy a luxurious home in the country and all seems blissful until Rathbone quite casually asks Harding to sign a document, claiming it is a mortgage transfer, but this little act, Harding discovers, has deeply sinister undertones. The document, if signed, would turn over her entire fortune to Rathbone. Up to this point, the viewer has no inkling that he is even dishonest. But he is worse than that, as Harding learns when Seton, another stranger, warns her that Rathbone is a regular bluebeard, that he has killed many women for their money. From that point on, Harding desperately maneuvers to save her own life as her husband tries a variety of subtle ways to kill her. In the end, he tries poisoning her coffee but Harding is aware of the ploy and turns the tables on him, or appears to, and, in one of the most blood-curdling cat-and-mouse games ever filmed, the two verbally fence with each other. Harding finally convinces Rathbone that he is the one who has swallowed the poisoned cup of coffee. His weak heart gives out and he dies, without a drop of poison in his veins. Rathbone is both charming and frightening in his sophisticated role of subtle mass murderer and this film remains one of his finest. Harding is also excellent as the victim desperate to preserve her life. This was the American actress' first British film. All the vagaries and nuances of the original Agatha Christie story remain in tact and Lee's direction and Marion's script shines.

p, Max Schach; d, Rowland V. Lee; w, Frances Marion (based on the short story by Agatha Christie and the play by Frank Vosper); ph, Philip Tannura; ed, Howard O'Neill; cos, Samuel Lange.

Crime Drama (PR:C MPAA:NR)

LOVE FROM A STRANGER ½**
(1947) 81m EL bw (GB: A STRANGER WALKED IN)

John Hodiak *(Manuel Cortez)*, Sylvia Sidney *(Cecily Harrington)*, Ann Richards *(Mavia)*, John Howard *(Nigel Lawrence)*, Isobel Elsom *(Auntie Loo-Loo)*, Frederic Worlock *(Inspector Hobday)*, Ernest Cossart *(Billings)*, Philip Tonge *(Dr. Gribble)*, Anita Sharp-Bolster *(Ethel the Maid)*, Billy Bevan *(Cab Driver)*, John Goldsworthy *(Clerk)*, David Cavendish, Keith Hitchcock *(Policemen)*, Phyllis Barry *(Waitress)*, Gerald Rogers *(Postman)*, Colin Campbell *(Bank Teller)*, Bob Corey *(Cab Driver)*, Eugene Eberle *(Bellboy)*, Charles Coleman *(Hotel Doorman)*, Nolan Leary *(Man in Bar)*, Donald Kerry, Abe Dinovitch *(Men)*.

An unconvincing variation on the story of infamous mass murderer "Bluebeard" nee Henri-Desire Landru) starring Hodiak in an all-too obvious portrayal of the killer. Having killed a number of his previous wives, the secretive Latin American chooses as his next victim the young and innocent Sydney after she wins a hefty London lottery. She falls for his charms, but soon realizes his true nature. She turns to her friend, Richards, and her daffy aunt, Elsom, for help, eventually receiving it from her former suitor Howard. Hodiak realizes his game is up and flees during a nighttime thunderstorm. He is pursued through the rain by police and climactically run over by a stampeding team of horses. LOVE FROM A STRANGER was simply further proof that Sidney's once-monumental popularity had slid to an irretrievable low, though she did all she could with the material and turned in the film's finest performance. Splitting her energy between stage and film, she was relegated to appearing in low-budget, small-studio quickies like this one. LOVE FROM A STRANGER did so poorly at the box office (mostly due to it's spotty screenplay) that it was quickly sold to television where it could be seen with unfortunate regularity. LOVE FROM A STRANGER was filmed previously in England in 1937, and also was seen on the legitimate circuit, starring its adaptor, Frank Vosper, in the role of the maniacal killer. It's successful first run in England led to a dreadful opening in New York. Vosper headed back for England via ship, but mysteriously vanished. Some time later he reappeared—when his body washed up on the coast of France.

p, James J. Geller; d, Richard Whorf; w, Philip MacDonald (based on the short story, "Philomel Cottage" by Agatha Christie and the play by Frank Vosper); ph, Tony Gaudio; m, Irving Friedman; ed, Fred Allen; art d, Perry Smith.

Crime Drama Cas. (PR:A MPAA:NR)

LOVE GOD?, THE* ½ (1969) 101m UNIV c

Don Knotts *(Abner Audubon Peacock)*, Anne Francis *(Lisa LaMonica)*, Edmund O'Brien *(Osborn Tremain)*, James Gregory *(Darrell Evans Hughes)*, Maureen Arthur *(Eleanor Tremain)*, Margaret Ann Peterson *(Rose Ellen Wilkerson)*, B. S. Pully *(J. Charles Twilight)*, Jesslyn Fax *(Miss Love)*, Jacques Aubuchon *(Carter Fenton)*, Marjorie Bennett *(Miss Pickering)*, Jim Boles *(Amos Peacock)*, Ruth McDevitt *(Miss Keezy)*, Roy Stuart *(Joe Merkel)*, Herbert Voland *(Attorney General Fred Snow)*, James Westerfield *(Rev. Wikerson)*, John Hubbard *(Craig Frazier)*, Bob Hastings *(Shrader)*, Larry McCormick *(Rich)*, Robert Lieb *(Rayfield)*, Willis Bouchey *(Judge Claypool)*, Herbie Faye *(Lester Timkin)* Johnny Seven *(Petey)*, Joseph Perry *(Big Joe)*, Jim Begg *(Hotchkiss)*, Carla Borelli *(Erica Lane)*, Nancy Bonniwell *(Toma)*, Shelly Davis *(Ingrid)*, A'Leshia Lee *(Sherry)*, Terri Harper *(Delilah)*.

Tasteless attempt at satirizing American morals, finds Knotts as the editor of a bird watcher's magazine, becoming a national sex hero. This happens when O'Brien buys out the magazine and turns it into a girlie book. Problems arise when Knotts must admit he is still a virgin, though he really doesn't know what one is, who longs for the simple life. Poor production values and incredible plot make it impossible for the cast to portray anything that could be taken seriously.

p, Edward J. Montagne; d&w, Nat Hiken; ph, William Margulies (Technicolor); m, Vic Mizzy; ed, Sam E. Waxman; art d, Alexander Golitzen, George Patrick; set d, John McCarthy, Marvin March; cos, Helen Colvig; ch, Wilda Taylor; m/l, "Mr. Peacock" Walter Slivinski (performed by The Blossoms, Orange Colored Sky), "Summer in the Meadow" Lyn Murray, Hiken; makeup, Bud Westmore.

Comedy (PR:A MPAA:M)

LOVE HABIT, THE ½** (1931, Brit.) 72m British International bw

Seymour Hicks *(Justin Abelard)*, Margot Grahame *(Julie Dubois)*, Edmund Breon *(Alphonse Dubois)*, Ursula Jeans *(Rose Pom Pom)*, Clifford Heatherley *(Santorelli)*, Walter Armitage *(Max Quattro)*, Elsa Lanchester *(Mathilde)*.

Another effort from the early British cinema to transfer a play to the screen. This one, however, reveals some acceptance of the need to approach the cinema as an art form, differing from the stage in many respects. The subtler and slicker editing help add a better sense of pacing than is normally found in the British film of this period. Story centers around a man who becomes hopelessly infatuated with a married woman. To be near her he gets a job as her husband's valet, and through blackmail moves up to private secretary. Throughout the man makes advances toward the woman, who continuously rebuffs him on the grounds that she cannot be unfaithful knowing her own husband to be true. Unfortunately the witty script is still hampered by the British adherance to the stage, with the performances overacted in a sense ill-suited to the screen.

p, John Maxwell; d, Harry Lachman; w, Seymour Hicks, Val Valentine (based on a play by Louis Verneuil); ph, John J. Cox; ed, E. B. Jarvis.

Comedy (PR:A MPAA:NR)

LOVE HAPPY ½** (1949) 91m UA bw

Harpo Marx *(Himself)*, Chico Marx *(Faustino The Great)*, Ilona Massey *(Madame Egilichi)*, Vera-Ellen *(Maggie Phillips)*, Marion Hutton *(Bunny Dolan)*, Raymond Burr *(Alphonse Zoto)*, Bruce Gordon *(Hannibal Zoto)*, Groucho Marx *(Detective Sam Grunion, Narrator)*, Melville Cooper *(Throckmorton)*, Leon Belasco *(Mr. Lyons)*, Paul Valentine *(Mike Johnson)*, Eric Blore *(Mackinaw, Grunion's Assistant)*, Marilyn Monroe *(Grunion's Client)*.

This is the last film the Marx Brothers made as a team, and though it suffers from a script that does little to develop the story, the film shines with Marx Bros. humor. Story revolves around the search by detective Groucho for some diamonds that have been stashed in a sardine can. Also in search of the diamonds, is the ruthless Massey and her gang. When the sardine can turns up at a grocer, Harpo steals it, thinking it food for the group of downtrodden performers he is helping to sustain. Massey tracks the can to the group and decides to sponsor the troupe in hopes of getting her hands on the sardine can. Story suffers from uneven pacing, and comic situations which are overly contrived. As always, the Marx Brothers deliver outstanding performances. Film includes a brief walk-on by Marilyn Monroe.

p, Lester Cowan; d, David Miller; w, Frank Tashlin, Mac Benoff (based on the story by Harpo Marx); ph, William C. Mellor; ed, Basil Wrangell, Al Joseph; md, Paul Smith; art d, Gabriel Scognamillo; spec eff, Howard A. Anderson; ch, Billy Daniel; m/l, "Willow Weep For Me," "Mama Wants To Know," "Love Happy," Ann Ronell.

Comedy Cas. (PR:A MPAA:NR)

LOVE HAS MANY FACES** (1965) 104m COL c

Lana Turner *(Kit Jordan)*, Cliff Robertson *(Pete Jordan)*, Hugh O'Brian *(Hank Walker)*, Ruth Roman *(Margot Eliot)*, Stefanie Powers *(Carol Lambert)*, Virginia Grey *(Irene Talbot)*, Ron Husmann *(Chuck Austin)*, Enrique Lucero *(Lt. Riccardo Andrade)*, Carlos Montalban *(Don Julian)*, Jaime Bravo *(Manuel Perez)*, Fannie Schiller *(Maria)*, Rene Dupreyon *(Ramos)*.

Lana Turner is beautiful and Edith Head has swathed her in equally gorgeous clothing but that's all you can say about this dime novel story of love among the rich and bored in Acapulco. Turner is currently wed to Robertson, a former beachboy-gigolo who married her for her money and is now thinking he may have made a mistake. The body of another beachboy washes ashore and it's another young man with whom millionairess Turner had once flung a fling. Robertson thinks that the dead boy committed suicide because Turner left him. Now Powers arrives in town. She's the dead beachboy's fiancee and wants to get to the bottom of the case. Robertson starts to show some interest in Powers and Turner contents herself with yet another man in her seemingly endless string of amours, Bravo, a bullfighter. Meanwhile, O'Brian, also a beachboy-gigolo, is dancing attendance on Roman, another wealthy American, but his real goal is Turner and he is just waiting until Robertson and Turner founder on the shoals of matrimony so he can move in on her. Robertson continues falling for Powers as Acapulco police officer Lucero investigates the suicide. At a bull training ring run by Montalban, Turner hears Powers demand that Robertson leave Turner. Turner responds by jumping her horse over the barrier and being gored by a bull in the ring. Robertson leaps to the rescue, ole's the bull's next charges, then rushes Turner away for medical help. This selfless act brings Turner and Robertson back together and Powers, realizing that there's no room for a third party in this relationship, exits for Michigan, from whence she came. It's the kind of plot they could keep going for two years on "All My Children." Thank heaven it only lasted 104 minutes. Robertson is as wooden as a cigar store Indian but is animated compared to O'Brian, an actor whose expressions resemble the faces on Mount Rushmore. Nancy Wilson's rendition of the title song is better than the tune deserves. The movie was filmed on location in Mexico City and Acapulco.

p, Jerry Bresler; d, Alexander Singer; w, Marguerite Roberts; ph, Joseph Ruttenberg (Eastmancolor); m, David Raksin; ed, Alma Macrorie; art d, Alfred Sweeney; set d, Noldi Schreck; cos, Edith Head; m/l, "Love Has Many Faces," Mack David, Raksin (sung by Nancy Wilson); makeup, Ben Lane, Del Armstrong, Del Acevedo.

Drama　　　　　　　　　　　　　　　**(PR:C　MPAA:NR)**

LOVE, HONOR AND BEHAVE**½　　　　(1938) 70m WB bw

Wayne Morris (Ted Painter), John Litel (Jim Blake), Dick Foran (Pete Martin), Mona Barrie (Lisa Blake), Donald Briggs (Yale Tennis Coach), Gregory Gaye (Count Humbert), Audrey Leonard (Barbara, as a Child), Priscilla Lane (Barbara Blake), Thomas Mitchell (Dan Painter), Barbara O'Neil (Sally Painter), Minor Watson (Dr. MacConaghey), Margaret Irving (Nan Bowleigh), Dickie Moore (Ted, as a Child), Crauford Kent (Announcer).

Morris plays a Yale tennis star who wanted to be a good loser. He falls in love with Lane, the two run off, marry, and settle down. When Morris is away on business, Lane begins to start up an affair with an old flame. Morris finds out, tosses out his gentlemanly code and gives the boyfriend a thorough beating. He then proceeds to spank his unfaithful wife. Script and direction manage to maintain a touchy balance between light comedy and tragic overtones.

p, Hal B. Wallis; d, Stanley Logan; w, Clements Ripley, Michel Jacoby, Robert Buckner, Lawrence Kimble (based on the story "Everybody Was Very Nice" by Stephen Vincent Benet); ph, George Barnes; ed, Owen Marks; m/l, "Bei Mir Bist du Schoen," Sammy Cahn, Saul Chaplin, Sholom Secunda.

Drama　　　　　　　　　　　　　　　**(PR:A　MPAA:NR)**

LOVE, HONOR AND GOODBYE*½　　　(1945) 87m REP bw

Virginia Bruce (Roberta Baxter), Edward Ashley (William Baxter), Victor McLaglen (Terry), Nils Asther (Tony Linnard), Helen Broderick (Mary Riley), Veda Ann Borg (Marge), Jacqueline Moore (Sally), Robert Greig (Charles, the Butler), Victoria Horne (Miss Whipple), Ralph Dunn (Detective), Therese Lyon (Miss Hopkin).

A dull domestic comedy, has actress Bruce walking out on her lawyer husband, when she suspects him of infidelity. The husband takes in a tattoo artist and his child ward. Bruce manages to sneak her way back in, disguised as the child's nurse, in the hopes of catching her husband being unfaithful.

p, Harry Grey; d, Albert S. Rogell; w, Arthur Phillips, Lee Loeb, Dick Irving Hyland (based on a story by Art Arthur, Rogell); ph, Jack Alton; m, Roy Webb; ed, Richard L. Van Enger; md, Walter Scharf; art d, Russell Kimball, Hilyard Brown; m/l, "These Foolish Things," "Close Those Eyes," Scharf, Ned Washington, Jack Strachey, Holt Marvell, Harry Link (both sung by Bruce).

Comedy　　　　　　　　　　　　　　　**(PR:A　MPAA:NR)**

LOVE, HONOR, AND OH BABY!*½　　　(1933) 60m UNIV bw

Slim Summerville (Mark Reed), ZaSu Pitts (Connie Clark), George Barbier (Jasper B. Ogden), Lucille Gleason (Flo Bowen), Verree Teasdale (Elsie Carpenter), Donald Meek (Luther Bowen), Purnell Pratt (Marshall Durant), Adrianne Dore (Louise), Dorothy Grainger (Mrs. Brown), Neely Edwards (Mr. Brown), Henry Kolker (The Judge).

Shyster lawyer Summerville manages to help his fiancee win a $100,000 lawsuit, instigated to frame her boss. Story loses its comic impact by falling into slapstick.

d, Eddie Buzzell; w, Norman Krasna, Buzzell (based on the play "Oh, Promise Me" by Howard Lindsay, Bertrand Robinson); ph, George Robinson.

Comedy　　　　　　　　　　　　　　　**(PR:A　MPAA:NR)**

LOVE, HONOR AND OH, BABY*½　　　(1940) 59m UNIV bw

Donald Woods (Brian McGrath), Kathryn Adams (Susan), Wallace Ford (Joe Redmond), Marc Lawrence (Tony), Warren Hymer (Bull), Mona Barrie (Deedee Dore), Hobart Cavanaugh (Darnell), Irving Bacon (Cab Driver), Frank Puglia (Headwaiter), Tom Jackson (District Attorney), Eddy Waller (Panhandler), Jack Arnold (Man with Susan), Matt McHugh (Taxi Driver), Robert Frazer (Investigator), David Oliver (Taxi Driver), Gay Seabrook (Radio Voice), Bob McKenzie (Farmer), Fay McKenzie (Waitress), Ralph Brooks (Dr. Smith), Frank O'Connor (Investigator), Leonard Sues, Gerald Pierce (Newsboys), Eddy Chandler (Motor Cop).

Far-fetched plot has Woods deciding there is no use living after splitting from his girl and that he should do something worthwhile by taking care of his sister. The best way for him to do this is to have her collect on his life insurance policy. So he hires a gunman to knock him off. His plan goes haywire when another girl steps into his life and gives him a reason to live, only the killer, whose identity remains unknown to Woods, is still set on accomplishing his task. Basic idea is of some interest, but quickly loses steam.

d, Charles Lamont; w, Clarence Upson Young (based on the story "No Exit" by Elizabeth Troy); ph, Stanley Cortez; ed, Ted Kent.

Comedy　　　　　　　　　　　　　　　**(PR:A　MPAA:NR)**

LOVE HUNGER*

　　　　　　(1965, Arg.) 72m Cambist Films bw/c (LA FLOR DEL IRUPE)

Libertad Leblanc, Hector Pellegrini, Mario Hmaya, Mario Casado, Luis Alarcon, Hector Carrion, Jill Robin, George Fosati, Nancy Arnold, Steve Hollister, Amelia Folcini, Rick Angeline, Alberto Barcel, Carl Garcia.

Grim crime drama about a group of bank robbers who invade the shack of an old trapper while on the lam from a recent heist. Their stay is lengthy, and the men begin to complain about the lack of female contact. The trapper tells them the legend of "The Naked Flower" in which the only daughter of an aristocratic family is assaulted by the crazed groundskeeper. On her honeymoon, years later, the groundskeeper returns to kill the groom and rape the bride. The hysterical girl escapes into the swamp, but returns on moonlit nights in search of her husband. Soon after the trapper's tale, one of the robbers encounters a beautiful woman near the swamp and the couple make love. Meanwhile the gang's solidarity disintegrates when one man kills another over the loot, and in the struggle the trapper sees his opportunity and kills the surviving man. When the remaining thief returns with the beautiful girl, he decides to renounce his past and start a new life.

p, Emilio Spitz; d, Albert Dubois; w, Dubois, Albert Diego; ph, Juan Levaggi (Eastmancolor); m&md, Ted Simon, makeup, Edith Bell.

Crime　　　　　　　　　　　　　　　**(PR:O　MPAA:NR)**

LOVE IN A BUNGALOW*　　　　　　(1937) 67m UNIV bw

Nan Grey (Mary Callahan), Kent Taylor (Jeff Langan), Louise Beavers (Millie), Jack Smart (Wilbur Babcock), Minerva Urecal (Mrs. Kester), Hobart Cavanaugh (Mr. Kester), Richard Carle (Mr. Bisbee), Marjorie Main (Miss Emma Bisbee), Margaret McWade (Miss Lydia Bisbee), Robert Spencer (Tracy), Arthur Hoyt (Man), Florence Lake (The Ga-Ga Prospect), Armand "Curley" Wright (Janitor), Del Henderson (Manager), Otto Fries (Policeman), William Benedict (Telegraph Boy), Sherry Hall, Edward Earle, Art Yeoman, James T. Mack, John Iven, and Burr Carruth (Clerks in Bisbee's Office), Bobby Watson (Barker), Henry Roquemore (James), Stanley Blystone (Policeman), Betty Mack (Girl), Jerry Tucker (Junior), Joan Howard, Joan Breslau (Darlings).

Grey and Taylor put their wits together to win a radio contest for married couples only. The problem is they are not married, so the two, not really caring that much for each other, must pretend to be happily wed. Performances are not up to the professional standards of the actors; it is the same story for the direction and script.

p, E. M. Asher; d, Raymond B. McCarey; w, Austin Parker, Karen DeWolf, James Mulhauser (based on a story by Eleanore Griffin, William Rankin); ph, Milton Krasner, ed, Bernard Burton, Irving Burnbaum; md, Charles Previn; art d, John Harkrider.

Comedy　　　　　　　　　　　　　　　**(PR:A　MPAA:NR)**

LOVE IN A FOUR LETTER WORLD*

　　　　　　(1970, Can.) 93m Multivision-Multipix/AA c

Michael Kane (Harry Haven), Andre Lawrence (Walt), Kayle Chernin (Sam), Helen Whyte (Vera Haven), Candy Greene (Susan Haven), Pierre Letourneau (Pierre), Monique Mercure (Louise).

The Canadian Film Development Corporation wound up giving lots of money to finance the filming of a script which turned out to be little more than a sex-ploitation film. The story does have something to do with the problems of disillusioned people trying to live in an undisciplined society. But this is lost through all the sex scenes. Project is further marred by very low production values, and the absence of any professional acting, or any acting at all, for that matter.

p, Arthur Voronka; d, John Sone; w, Voronka, Sone; ph, Rene Verzier (Eastmancolor); ed, Glen Ludlow; art d, Jerome Couelle; cos, Marcel Carpenter; m/l, Dean Morgan, Paul Baillargeon, Ronnie Abramson.

Drama　　　　　　　　　　　　　　　**(PR:O　MPAA:R)**

LOVE IN A GOLDFISH BOWL**½　　　(1961) 88m PAR c

Tommy Sands (Gordon Slide), Fabian (Giuseppe "Seppi" La Barba), Jan Sterling (Sandra Slide), Toby Michaels (Blythe Holloway), Edward Andrews (Sen. Clyde Holloway), John McGiver (Dr. Frowley), Majel Barrett (Alice), Shirley O'Hara (Clara Dumont), Robert Patten (Lt. J. G. Marchon), Phillip Baird (Gregory), Denny Miller (Oscar Flegler), Susan Silo (Jenny), Elizabeth MacRae (Jackie), Joe Hyams, Mike and Marlin McKeever, Dee J. Thompson, Tom Quinn, Tiger.

1960s teen picture has something more to offer than the usual product of this genre, though some of the promotional elements are there, such as the appearance of Fabian and a pop soundtrack. Story revolves around two college freshmen, Sands and Michaels, drawn to each other platonically because they both feel neglected by their parents. Vacation time comes and the two decide to spend their vacation together at Sands' mother's home. When Michaels is sailing and her boat capsizes, she is saved by the amorous Coast Guardsman Fabian. Fabian takes to Michaels, and starts to hang around the house, accompanied by several of his buddies. During one wild party Sands' mother shows up, and immediately jumps to the wrong conclusion about Sands and Michaels. When they go back to school, Sands and Michaels have a revelation on their true feelings for one another, sparking a case of puppy love. The script suffers from a lack of credibility, but this is glossed over by realistic performances.

p, Martin Jurow, Richard Shepherd; d&w Jack Sher; (based on a story by Irene Kamp, Sher); ph, Loyal Griggs (Panavision, Technicolor); m, Jimmie Haskell; ed, Terry O. Morse; md, Haskell; art d, Hal Pereira, Roland Anderson; set d, Sam Comer, Ray Moyer; cos, Edith Head; spec eff, John P. Fulton; m/l, "Love in a Goldfish Bowl," Hal David, Burt Bacharach (sung by Tommy Sands), "You're Only Young Once," Russell Faith, Robert Marcucci, Peter De Angelis (sung by Fabian); makeup, Wally Westmore.

Drama　　　　　　　　　　　　　　　**(PR:A　MPAA:NR)**

LOVE IN A HOT CLIMATE**

(1958, Fr./Span.) 100m Cite Films-Cocinor/Hoffberg c (SANG ET LUMIERES; AKA: BEAUTY AND THE BULLFIGHTER)

Daniel Gelin (Ricardo), Zsa Zsa Gabor (Marilena), Henri Vilbert (Naguera), Arnoldo Foa (Riera), Christine Carrere (Pili), Jacques Dufilho (Chispa), Eugenio Domingo (Federico).

Gelin plays a bullfighter who attempts to retire from the ring after a good friend of his is killed by a bull. The peaceful existence out on a ranch raising bulls is never fully realized for Gelin as he is forced back to fight one more time as a result of a pesty mistress (Gabor) who desires her man to remain an athletic hero. The reentry into the ring is fatal for Gelin as a bull gores him to death, sending the crowd into an uproarious stampede. Bull-fighting sequences are staged quite well, but their overall effect is lost in the mundane plotting of the sentimentalized dramatics.

d, Georges Rauquie; w, Maurice Gerry, Michel Audiard (based on the novel by Joseph Peyre); ph, Maurice Barry (Eastmancolor); ed, Christian Gaudin; set d, Jean Mandaroux.

Drama (PR:A MPAA:NR)

LOVE IN A TAXI***

(1980) 90m Davey c

Diane Sommerfield (Carine), James H. Jacobs (Sam), Earl Monroe (Gary), Malik Murray (Davey), Lisa Jane Persky (Marian), Lyle Kessler (Jimmy), Karen Grannum (Norman), Phil Rubinstein (Mel), Al Fann (Monk), Dorothy Leon (Dowager), Bill Moor, Hannibal Penney Jr., Tony Capra (Hoods).

Warm-hearted story about the romance between a New York Jewish cabbie, Jacobs, and a black bank clerk, Sommerfield. The two are brought together when Sommerfield's adventurous son pops up in Jacobs' cab. Director Sickinger handles tensions in a subtle manner. Film was made on an extremely low budget, and shot entirely on location in New York City. Sommerfield and Jacobs allow a lot of personality to shine through their performances. Production values are polished for such a low-budget film.

p&d, Robert Sickinger; w, Michael Kortchmar; ph, Joseph Mangine; m, Susan Minsky; ed, Bill Freda; art d, Steven Vickers.

Drama (PR:A MPAA:NR)

LOVE IN BLOOM*1/2

(1935) 76m PAR bw

George Burns (George), Gracie Allen (Gracie), Joe Morrison (Larry Deane), Dixie Lee (Violet Downey), J. C. Nugent (Col. "Dad" Downey), Lee Kohlmar (Pop Heinrich), Richard Carle (Sheriff), Mary Foy (Mrs. Cassidy), Wade Boteler (The Cop), Marian Mansfield (Edith Bowen), Julia Graham, Sam Godfrey, Jack Mulhall, Frances Raymond, Bernadene Hayes, Harry Bradley, Douglas Wood, William Gorsman, Douglas Blackley, Benny Baker.

Dull reworking of classic romance theme has Lee and Morrison as a young couple hopelessly in love, unable to get hitched because Lee doesn't feel herself worthy of her lover. Slack direction and predictable script are saved somewhat by solid performances and a good score.

p, Benjamin Glazer; d, Elliott Nugent; w, J. P. McEvoy, Keene Thompson, John P. Medbury (based on a story by Frank R. Adams); ph, Leo Tover; ed, William Shea; m/l, "Lookie, Lookie, Lookie, Here Comes Cookie," "My Heart is an Open Book," "Got Me Doin' Things," Mack Gordon, Harry Revel.

Drama (PR:A MPAA:NR)

LOVE IN COLD BLOOD

(SEE: ICE HOUSE, THE, 1969)

LOVE IN EXILE**

(1936, Brit.) 63m CAP/GAU bw

Clive Brook (King Regis VI), Helen Vinson (Countess Xandra St. Aurion), Mary Carlisle (Emily Stewart), Ronald Squire (Paul), Cecil Ramage (John Weston), Will Fyffe (Doc Tate), Tamara Desni (Tanya), Edmund Breon (Baron Zarroy), Henry Oscar (Dictator), Barbara Everest (Anna).

Charming romance about Brook, as the king of an imaginary kingdom, who abdicates his throne for the love of a foreign-born woman, Vinson. However, the real reason for his abdication is that greedy businessmen want to put their own man in power. Brook spends his exile on the Riviera, while Vinson stays in Holland, refusing to be with the king because she believes she is the cause of his abdication. A coincidence is it that within weeks of this picture's U.S. release, Edward, Prince of Wales, abdicated the throne to pursue his romance. Adequate script is marred by lifeless performances.

p, Max Schach; d, Alfred L. Werker; w, Herman Mankiewicz, Roger Burford, Ernest Betts (based on the novel His Majesty's Pajamas by Gene Markey); ph, Otto Kanturek, Alfred Black.

Drama (PR:A MPAA:NR)

LOVE IN 4 DIMENSIONS**1/2

(1965 Fr./Ital.), 105m Adelphia Compagnia/ Eldorado bw (L'AMOUR EN 4 DIMENSIONS, AMORE IN 4 DIMENSIONI)

"Love and Language": Carlo Giuffre (Gerlando, the Sicillian), Franca Rame (Susy), Carlo Bagno (Trapattoni, the Taxi Driver), "Love and Life": Sylva Koscina (Irma, the Wife), Gastone Moschin (The Husband), France Polesello (Rosa, the Maid), Isa Crescenzi; "Love and Art": Philippe Leroy (Franco Lampredi, the Husband), Elena Martini (Livia Lampredi, his Wife), Fabrizio Capucci (Benito Mingozzi, the Typist), Alberto Bonucci (Pallotta, the Producer); "Love and Death": Michele Mercier (Luisa), Alberto Lionello (Matteo).

Well-done Italian comedy anthology told in four parts. The first, "Love and Language," stars Giuffre as a Sicilian who arrives in Milan and finds himself unable to communicate because of the dialect he speaks. A taxi driver, Bagno, takes pity upon the stranger and takes him home to meet his daughter Rame, who teaches him proper Italian. Soon the couple marry and Giuffre becomes a cab driver who enjoys hanging around the train station and ridiculing ignorant Sicilians upon their arrival. "Love and Life," the second story, stars Koscina as an insanely jealous wife, who has taken on a lover to provoke her husband to set her free. Knowing his weakness for women, Koscina hires a gorgeous model, Polesello, to work as the family maid in the hopes of catching her husband being unfaithful. Her plan works, but backfires when she phones Polesello to thank her and it is her lover who answers the phone. The third part, "Love and Art," tells the tale of an overworked screenwriter, Leroy, who hires a beautiful secretary to help with the typing. His wife, Martini, becomes insanely jealous and forces him to replace the woman with a male secretary, Capucci, who is also an aspiring screenwriter. Soon the young man is doing all the work and Leroy reaping all the acclaim. In fact he becomes so successful, that he does not even mind his wife's affair with Capucci. The last episode, "Love and Death," stars Lionello as a middle-aged businessman who encounters a young widow, Mercier, at the cemetery while visiting his wife's grave. Lionello drives the distraught woman home, and sympathetic to each other's grief, they soon become lovers. Mercier reveals that the stonecarver of her husband's tomb has demanded a large amount of money to finish the monument, and Lionello gladly writes her a check. Given a new burst of youthfulness by the affair, Linello returns to work a new man. However, when he returns to Mercier's home, he finds that she has moved and left no forwarding address. Crushed, he returns to the cemetery and sees Mercier collapsing in the arms of another rich old man.

"Love and Language": d&w, Massimo Mida; ph, Dario Di Palma; "Love and Life": d, Jacques Romain; w, Bruno Baratti; ph, Tonino Delli Colli; "Love and Art": d&w, Gianni Puccini; ph, Carlo Di Palma; "Love and Death"; d&w Mino Guerrini; ph, Colli; m, Franco Mannino; ed, Franco Fraticelli.

Comedy/Drama (PR:C MPAA:NR)

LOVE IN LAS VEGAS

(SEE: VIVA LAS VEGAS, 1964)

LOVE IN MOROCCO*

(1933, Fr.) 74m GAU bw (GB: BAROUD)

Felipe Montes (Si Allal, Caid of Ilouet), Rosita Garcia (Zinah, his Daughter), Pierre Batcheff (Si Hamed, his Son and Spahi Sergeant), Rex Ingram (Andre Duval, Spahi Sergeant), Arabella Fields (Mabrouka, a Slave), Andrews Engelmann (Si Amarok, Bandit Chief), Dennis Hoey (Capt. Labry), Laura Salerni (Arlette).

Typical western theme is transposed to the Moroccan desert in this story about two warring tribes. The bad guys are closing in on the good guys trapped in a fortress, when a messenger sneaks out to deliver information to the Marines. (In English.)

p, Ingram, Mansfield Markham; d, Ingram, Alice Terry; w, Ingram, Peter Spencer (based on a story by Ingram, Benno Vignay); ph, L. H. Burel, P. Portier, A. Allegier, Marcel Lucien, T. Tomatis; ed, Lothar Wolff; md, Louis Levy; art d, Henri Menessier, Jean Lafitte.

Drama (PR:A MPAA:NR)

LOVE IN PAWN**1/2

(1953, Brit.) 82m Tempean/Eros Films bw

Bernard Braden (Roger Fox), Barbara Kelly (Jean Fox), Walter Crisham (Hilary Stitfall), Tom Gill (Fred Pollock), Alan Robinson (Arnold Bibcock), Reg Dixon (Albert Trusslove), Avice Landone (Amelia Trusslove), Jean Carson (Amber Trusslove), Dorothy Gordon (Marlene), Laurence Naismith (Uncle Amos), John Laurie (Mr. McCutcheon), Benita Lydell, Hal Osmond.

Farce about an impoverished artist, Braden, and his wife, Kelly, who are offered a sizable fortune by Kelly's wealthy uncle to go legit. The uncle sends an attorney to visit the couple and judge their worth. To enable herself to get the money to properly entertain the attorney, Kelly pawns her husband, but loses the ticket and decides to leave him at the pawnshop. Well paced direction and good performances help a script that suffers from implausibility.

p, Robert Baker, Monty Berman; d, Charles Saunders; w, Guy Morgan, Frank Muir, Denis Norden (based on a story by Humphrey Knight); ph, Berman; m, Temple Abady; ed, Gordon Pilkington.

Comedy (PR:A MPAA:NR)

LOVE IN THE AFTERNOON***

(1957) 130m AA bw

Gary Cooper (Frank Flannagan), Audrey Hepburn (Ariane Chavasse), Maurice Chevalier (Claude Chavasse), Van Doude (Michel), John McGiver (Mons. X), Lise Bourdin (Mme. X), Bonifas (Commissioner of Police), Audrey Wilder (Brunette), Gyula Kokas, Michel Kokas:, George Cocos, Victor Gazzoli (Four Gypsies), Olga Valery (Lady with Dog), Leila Croft, Valerie Croft (Swedish Twins), Charles Bouillard (Valet at the Ritz), Minerva Pious (Maid at the Ritz), Filo (Flannagan's Chauffeur), Andre Priez (1st Porter at the Ritz), Gaidon (2nd Porter at the Ritz), Gregory Gromoff (Doorman at the Ritz), Janine Dard, Claude Ariel (Existentialists), Francois Moustache (Butcher), Gloria France (Client at Butcher's) Jean Sylvain (Baker), Annie Roudier (1st Client at Baker's), Jeanne Charblay (2nd Client at Baker's), Odette Charblay (3rd Client at Baker's), Gilbert Constant, Monique Saintey (Lovers on Left Bank), Jacques Preboist, Anne Laurent (Lovers Near The Seine), Jacques Ary, Simone Vanlancker (Lovers on Right Bank), Richard Flagy (Husband), Jeanne Papir (Wife), Marcelle Broc (1st Rich Woman), Marcelle Praince (2nd Rich Woman) Guy Delorme (Gigolo), Olivia Chevalier (Little Girl in the Gardens), Solon Smith (Little Boy in the Gardens), Eve Marley, Jean Rieubon (Tandemists) Christian Lude, Charles Lemontier, Emile Mylos (Generals), Alexander Trauner (Artist), Betty Schneider, Georges Perrault, Vera Boccadoro, Marc Aurian (Couples Under Water Wagon), Bernard Musson (Undertaker), Michele Selignac (Widow), Diga Valery Gypsies.

Filmed in Paris at the Studios de Boulogne, the Opera, the Chateau de Vitry, and in various suburban settings, there's no question that LOVE IN THE AFTERNOON had great locations going for it. It also had the winsome charm of Hepburn, the elfin puckishness of Chevalier, a literate script by Wilder and Diamond, and an airy feeling that wafted the audience along. What it didn't have going for it was a leading man, Gary Cooper could be many things but as the lead in a romantic comedy, he fell short. Not that he'd never done it before. Cooper had made several pictures in which he handled comedy lines with aplomb but he was pushing 56 at the time and looking too long in the tooth to be playing opposite the gamine Hepburn. Chevalier is a Parisian private eye who uses a long lens to espy that Cooper, a rich American, is cavorting with Bourdin, who is married to McGiver. Chevalier imparts that information to the outraged husband as Hepburn, Chevalier's daughter, is listening outside the door. She is fascinated by Cooper's activities so she rushes to his hotel to alert him that an irate man is about to shoot him. Cooper is amused by Hepburn, who is masquerading as a woman with a past. Thus begins a series of tete-a-tetes in the afternoon as Hepburn regales him with imaginary tales of her many lovers. Then she slips away and he doesn't know where or how to find her. As the film continues, Cooper is falling for Hepburn and desperately wants to know more about her. He's in a steam room one day and meets Chevalier, who hears Cooper's tale of love and offers his services, never knowing that the woman in question is his daughter. After a bit of investigating and putting two and two together, Chevalier realizes that the girl is Hepburn and he prevails on Cooper to forget her and leave Paris as soon as possible before any further emotional damage is done. Cooper goes to the railway station in preparation for a holiday in the South of France when Hepburn arrives to bid him adieu. It's then that they both understand that May and December *can* work and he takes her with him as the picture ends. Cooper just didn't work as a roué, and the picture is stolen by Chevalier's bravura turn. From what we have learned, Chevalier's good humor was just as evident off screen and he kept both cast and crew happy and content throughout the shooting while Cooper withdrew. He was on foreign territory, in his first film away from the States, and his discomfort was discernible. Wilder saw that and deliberately shot Cooper in shadows, keeping him elusive most of the time and choosing odd angles to accomplish this. For old radio fans, look at the lady in the Ritz hotel and see if you can tell who she is from her voice. It's Minerva Pious, the lady who played "Mrs. Nussbaum" on Fred Allen's radio feature "Allen's Alley." The brunette with Cooper at the opera was Wilder's wife, the former Audrey Young. LOVE IN THE AFTERNOON had many faults and yet, as the song goes: "with all it's faults, we love it still," There are a few tunes to spice up the romance: "Fascination" (F. D. Marchetti, Maurice de Feraudy), "L'Ame des Poetes" (Charles Trenet), "C'est Si Bon" (Henri Betti, Andre Hornez), "Love in the Afternoon," "Ariane," and "Hot Paprika" (Marty Malneck).

p&d, Billy Wilder; w, Wilder, I. A. L. Diamond (based on the novel *Ariane* by Claude Anet); ph, William Mellor; m,, Franz Waxman ed, Leonid Azar; art d, Alexander Trauner; cos, Hubert de Givenchy.

Comedy/Drama   **Cas.**   **(PR:A MPAA:NR)**

LOVE IN THE DESERT*¹/₂   (1929) 68m RKO bw

Olive Borden (*Zarah*), Hugh Trevor (*Bob Winslow*), Noah Beery (*Abdullah*), Frank Leigh (*Harim*), Charles Brinley (*Hassan*), Pearl Varvell (*Fatima*), William H. Tooker (*Mr. Winslow*), Ida Darling (*Mrs. Winslow*), Gordon Magee (*Sears*), Alan Roscoe (*Houdish*), Fatty Carr (*Briggs*).

Trevor plays the spoiled son of wealthy parents, sent to the desert as punishment for the troubles he has with some chorus girls. Trevor is kidnapped by a warring Arab tribe, but is saved by the beautiful princess, Borden. He decides to marry the girl, sending his mother into hysterics when Trevor sends her a telegraph indicating his intentions. After the silent film was made, dialog was inserted in the beginning and end to explain the story and give the film a gimmick. Script suffers from undeveloped pacing of individual scenes.

d, George Melford; w, Harvey Thew, Paul Percy, Randolph Bartlett (based on a story by Thew, Louis Sarecky); ph, Paul Perry; ed, Mildred Richter; cos, Walter Plunkett.

Comedy   **(PR:A MPAA:NR)**

LOVE IN THE ROUGH*¹/₂   (1930) 75m MGM bw

Robert Montgomery (*Kelly*), Dorothy Jordan (*Marilyn*), Benny Rubin (*Benny*), J. C. Nugent (*Waters*), Dorothy McNulty [Penny Singleton] (*Virgie*), Tyrell Davis (*Tewksbury*), Harry Burns (*Gardener*), Allan Lane (*Johnson*), Catherine Moylan (*Martha*), Edwards Davis (*Williams*), Roscoe Ates (*Proprietor*), Clarence H. Wilson (*Brown*).

The rather sketchy story of a golf-pro, Montgomery, romancing Jordan, serves as a backdrop for some nice musical numbers and some good comic routines by Rubin. Songs by Dorothy Fields and Jimmy McHugh include: "I'm Doing That Thing," "I'm Learning a Lot From You," "Like Kelly Can," and "Go Home and Tell Your Mother" (sung by Montgomery and Jordan). Remake of MGM's silent SPRING FEVER (1927).

d, Charles F. Reisner; w, Sarah Y. Mason, Joe Farnham, Robert E. Hopkins (based on the play "Spring Fever" by Vincent Lawrence) ph, Henry Sharp; ed, Basil Wrangell; cos, David Cox; ch, Sammy Lee.

Musical   **(PR:A MPAA:NR)**

LOVE IN WAITING*   (1948, Brit.) 60m Production Facilities/GFD bw

David Tomlinson (*Clitheroe*), Andrew Crawford (*Dick Lambert*), Peggy Evans (*Goldy*), Elspet Gray (*Brenda*), Patsy Drake (*Mary*), John Witty (*Harry*), Linda Grey (*Miss Bell*), George Merritt (*Pepperfield*), Johnnie Schofield (*Inspector Bates*), Eliot Makeham, Diana Chesney, James Lomas, Duncan Lewis, Grace Arnold, Richard Gilbert, Charles Paton, Sam Kydd, Patricia Dainton, Patience Rentoul.

Uninteresting farce revolving around the romances that develop when two young women, Evans and Gray, take on jobs as waitresses at a restaurant. Sparks of jealousy fly when Evans impedes upon an established worker's territory, forcing her to plot to have Evans convicted of stealing money from the cash register. Her plan fails; as does this film.

p, Henry Passmore; d, Douglas Pierce; w, Arthur Reid, Martin Lane (based on the story by Monica Dickens); ph, Roy Fogwell.

Comedy   **(PR:A MPAA:NR)**

LOVE-INS, THE**   (1967) 85m Four Leaf/COL c

Richard Todd (*Dr. Jonathan Barnett*), James MacArthur (*Larry Osborne*), Susan Oliver (*Patricia Cross*), Mark Goddard (*Elliot*), Carol Booth (*Harriet*), Marc Cavell (*Mario*), Janee Michelle (*Lamelle*), Ronnie Eckstine (*Bobby*), Michael Evans (*Reverend Spencer*), Hortense Petra (*Mrs. Sacaccio*), James Lloyd (*Mr. Henning*), Mario Roccuzzo (*Hippie on LSD*), Joe Pyne, (*Himself*) The Chocolate Watch Band, The U.F.O.'s, The New Age, Donnie Brooks.

Spinoff on the San Francisco hippie scene loses much of its impact in retrospect, mainly because it's hard to take the memories of these situations and characters from the late 1960s seriously. Story revolves around a professor, Todd, who resigns his position when two of his students, MacArthur and Oliver, publishers of an underground newspaper, are expelled. Todd becomes something of a cult hero, who promotes the use of LSD. Evicted from his apartment Todd moves in with MacArthur and Oliver, taking advantage of his messianic role to seduce Oliver. MacArthur is disillusioned by what Todd is offering, and uses his newspaper to criticize him. Script offers some strong satire on the mass hippie movement, but is somewhat hampered by roles which have been miscast.

p, Sam Katzman; d Arthur Dreifuss; w, Hal Collins, Dreifuss; ph, John F. Warren (PatheColor); m, Fred Karger; ed, Ben Lewis; md, Karger; art d, George W. Davis, Charles K. Hagedon; set d, Henry Grace, James Berkey; ch, Hal Belfer; makeup, William Tuttle.

Drama   **(PR:C MPAA:NR)**

LOVE IS A BALL**   (1963) 113m UA c (GB: ALL THIS AND MONEY TOO)

Glenn Ford (*John Davis*), Hope Lange (*Millie Mehaffey*), Charles Boyer (*Mons. Etienne Pimm*), Ricardo Montalban (*Gaspard*), Telly Savalas (*Dr. Gump*), Ruth McDevitt (*Mathilda*), Ulla Jacobsson (*Janine*), Georgette Anys (*Mme. Gallou*), Roberto Bettoni (*Milkman*), Mony Dalmes (*Mme. Fernier*), Laurence Hardy (*Priory*), Jean Lemaitre (*Carlo*), Andre Luguet (*Zoltan*), Olga Valery (*Mme. Girardin*), Jean Paredes (*Freddie*), Redmond Phillips (*Stacy*), Aram Stephan (*Gallou*), Erika Soucy (*Gretl*), John Wood (*Soames*), Jeane Pierre Zola (*Mueller*).

Boyer plays a matchmaker on the French Riviera, trying to wed heiress Lange to Montalban groomed for the part. Ford is hired by Boyer as Lange's chauffeur and to help Montalban. In the process however, Lange and Ford fall in love, with everyone else winding up with their true romances. Filmed on location in the Riviera. Though naive script lacks believability, expert performances make this picture entertaining.

p, Martin H. Poll; d, David Swift; w, Swift, Tom Waldman, Frank Waldman (from the novel "The Grand Duke and Mr. Pimm" by Lindsay Hardy); ph, Edmond Sechan (Panavision, Technicolor); m, Michel Legrand; ed, Tom McAdoo, Cathy Kelber, art d, Jean d'Eaubonne; set d, Fernand Bernardi; cos, Frank Thompson, Marie-Therese; makeup, Jean-Paul Ulysse.

Comedy   **(PR:A MPAA:NR)**

LOVE IS A CAROUSEL*   (1970) 77m Temarro/Roma c

Icarus (*Musicians*), Eleanor Gary (*Herself*), Tee Jay Johnston (*Himself, an Artist*), Maria Robles (*Doria*), Kay K. Kelly (*Stepmother*), Anita Moran (*Go-Go Dancer*), John Savage (*Boy Friend*), Ellen Marion (*Jackie the Lesbian*), Julio Susana (*Himself, an Artist*), Bob Moore (*Messenger*), Claudia Renito (*Laura*), Capt. Jack Ott (*Skipper of "Shark VII"*), Bill Hewett (*Crew*), Muriel Marshall (*Waitress*).

Nothing other than what could be expected is offered in this tired story about a young woman who is forced to leave home after being sexually abused, quickly finding herself enmeshed in a counterculture, which includes lesbianism and drugs. Unlike other films which indulge in the same subject, this girl finds her move away from home and the new experiences she encounters to be quite rewarding.

p, Roy P. Cheverton, Marvin C. Spero; d, Cheverton; ph, Cheverton, (Eastmancolor); m, Eleanor Gary; ed, Cesar A. Cruz; art d, Tee Jay Johnston; m/l, "Love Is a Carousel," "End Part II," "Thought," "Some Will Come," "Yesterday's Memories," "If I Could," "Ninth Epitaph," "New York Street," "Fred Song," Icarus, "Lucerito," "Buenos Dias," "Esta Noche," "Sonando," "Contigo," "Dos Mundos," Julio Susana.

Drama   **(PR:O MPAA:R)**

LOVE IS A DAY'S WORK   (SEE: FROM A ROMAN BALCONY, 1961)

LOVE IS A FUNNY THING**

(1970, Fr./Ital.) 110m Ariane-Treize-Les Productions Artistes Associes-Produzioni Associate Delphos-Majestic/UA c (AKA: AGAIN A LOVE STORY: UN TIPO CHI MI PLACE, HISTOIRE D'AIMER)

Jean-Paul Belmondo (*Henri*), Annie Girardot (*Francoise*), Maria-Pia Conte (*Henri's Wife*), Marcel Bozzufi (*Francoise's Husband*), Farrah Fawcett (*Patricia*), Peter Bergman (*Director*), Kaz Garas (*Paul*), Bill Quinn (*Passenger*), Arturo Dominici (*Customs Officer*), Timothy Blake ("*The Dominos*"), Jerry Cipperley (*Waiter in Cafe*), Forester Hood (*Indian*), Sweet Emma (*Herself*), Simone Renant, Susan Albert.

Fair romantic film told with a light touch starring Belmondo as a composer and Girardot as a French film actress whose paths cross while working on a film shot in the United States. Though they are both married, the couple fall into an affair as they tour the sights of America (Monument Valley and Las Vegas are given special attention). Guilty, Girardot phones her husband and tells him of the affair. Belmondo and Girardot decide to end their fling and go their separate ways.

However, Belmondo re-establishes contact with Girardot and arranges to meet her in Nice. She shows up for the romantic rendezvous, but he never arrives.

p, Alexandre Mnouchkine, Georges Dancigers; d, Claude Lelouch; w, Lelouch, Pierre Uytterhoeven; ph, Lelouch (DeLuxe Color); m, Francis Lai; ed, Claude Barrois; cos, Marie Osborne.

Romance (PR:C MPAA:GP)

LOVE IS A HEADACHE**   (1938) 68m MGM/bw

Franchot Tone (*Peter Lawrence*), Mickey Rooney (*Mike*), Ralph Morgan (*Reggie Odell*), Jessie Ralph (*Sheriff*), Barnett Parker (*Hotchkiss*), Gladys George (*Carlotta Lee*), Ted Healy (*Jimmy Slattery*), Frank Jenks (*Joe Cannon*), Virginia Weidler ("*Jake*"), Fay Holden (*Mary*), Julius Tannen (*Mr. Hiller*), Henry Kolker.

George plays an actress unable to get any good roles. As a publicity stunt she adopts two orphans, Rooney and Weidler, who respond by making a shambles of her life and her attempts to romance Tone. Good direction aids the absurdly written script. Performances are of a varied quality.

p, Frederick Stephani; d, Richard Thorpe; w, Marion Parsonnet, Harry Ruskin, William R. Lipman, Lou Heifetz, Herbert Klein; ph, John Seitz; m, Edward Ward; ed, Conrad A. Nervig; art d, Cedric Gibbons.

Comedy (PR:A MPAA:NR)

LOVE IS A MANY-SPLENDORED THING**   (1955) 102m FOX c

William Holden (*Mark Elliot*), Jennifer Jones (*Han Suyin*), Torin Thatcher (*Mr. Palmer-Jones*), Isobel Elsom (*Adeline Palmer-Jones*), Murray Matheson (*Dr. Tam*), Virginia Gregg (*Ann Richards*), Richard Loo (*Robert Hung*), Soo Young (*Nora Hung*), Philip Ahn (*3rd Uncle*), Jorja Curtright (*Suzanne*), Donna Martell (*Suchen*), Candace Lee (*Oh-No*), Kam Tong (*Dr. Sen*), James Hong (*5th Brother*), Herbert Heyes (*Father Low*), Angela Loo (*Mei Loo*), Marie Tsien (*Rosie Wu*), Barbara Jean Wong, Hazel Shon, Jean Wong (*Nurses*), Kei Chung (*Interne*), Henry S. Quan (*Officer*), Ashley Cowan (*British Sailor*), Marc Krah (*Wine Steward*), Joseph Kim (*Gen. Song*), Salvador Basquez (*Hotel Manager*), Edward Colmans (*Dining Room Captain*), Leonard Strong (*Fortune Teller*), Aen Ling Chow, Stella Lynn, Irene Liu (*Wives*), Beulah Kwoh (*Aunt*), Howard Soo Hoo (*2nd Brother*), Walter Soo Hoo (*3rd Brother*), Keye Luke (*Elder Brother*), Lee Tung Foo (*Old Loo*), John W. T. Chang (*Gate Keeper*), Weaver Levy (*Soldier*), Eleanor Moore (*English Secretary*).

A literate screenplay by Patrick is what elevates this from sheer bathos to just plain bathos. Based on the best-selling novel by Han Suyin, the title is from Frances Thompson's religious work, *The Kingdom Of God* and a very apt one indeed. What helped to sell the movie was the incredibly successful song based on the title by Fain and Webster. One must marvel at Webster's facility in taking such an odd phrase and making it work in a pop tune. Jones is a Eurasian physician in Hong Kong who falls for Holden, a married war correspondent from the United States. Their love grows, despite several problems. She finds an undercurrent of prejudice at the medical facility where she is employed. The bluenoses of British Hong Kong are nettled by this miscegenation and there is no way for the lovers to unite forever as his wife refuses to grant him freedom. Their affair continues until he is sent to Korea to cover the "police action" there and, like so many others sent there, he is killed. Jones goes back to the high and windy hill where the two shared so many happy hours and the film concludes. Jones wears some lovely Chinese dresses, Hong Kong looks like a place we'd like to spend some time, and Holden does a fine job. Despite all that, this is basically a sappy story that does not hold up and it is so obviously designed to elicit tissue-pulling that it often appears to be a parody of a love story. The best thing about the movie is that it gave Hollywood's excellent Asian actor's community a chance for some work. One of the reasons why Patrick was chosen for this adaptation is that he wrote the play, "The Teahouse Of The August Moon" and the producers thought Eurasians and Okinawans were the same.

p, Buddy Adler; d, Henry King; w, John Patrick (based on the novel *A Many Splendored Thing* by Han Suyin); ph, Leon Shamroy (Cinemascope, De Luxe Color); m, Alfred Newman; ed, William Reynolds; art d, Lyle R. Wheeler, George W. Davis; cos, Charles Le Maire; m/l, "Love is a Many-Splendored Thing," Sammy Fain, Paul Francis Webster.

Romance Cas. (PR:A MPAA:NR)

LOVE IS A RACKET***
          (1932) 72m WB-FN bw (GB: SUCH THINGS HAPPEN)

Douglas Fairbanks Jr. (*Jimmy Russell*), Ann Dvorak (*Sally*), Frances Dee (*Mary*) Lee Tracy (*Stanley Fiske*), Lyle Talbot (*Eddie Shaw*), Warren Hymer (*Burney Olds*), Andre Luguet (*Max Boncour*), William Burress (*Ollie*), Terrence Ray (*Seeley*), Marjorie Peterson (*Hat Check Girl*), Edward Kane (*Captain of Waiters*), Cecil Cunningham (*Hattie*), John Marston (*Curley John*), Matt McHugh (*Tipster*), George Ernest (*Little Boy*), Lillian Worth (*Girl*), Gino Corrado (*Waiter*), Snowflake (*Elevator Operator*), George Raft (*Sneaky*).

Fairbanks plays a newspaper gossip columnist in love with Broadway actress Dee, but she belongs to a gangster who covers the bad checks Dee likes to write. When Dee's aunt kills the gangster Dee runs off with a producer who promises her a part, leaving Fairbanks out in the cold. Good caricatures and witty dialog give this picture a fitting atmosphere. Well paced direction aids the script.

d, William A. Wellman; w, Courtney Terrett (based on the novel by Rian James); ph, Sid Hickox; ed, Bill Holmes; art d, Jack Okey

Drama/Comedy (PR:A MPAA:NR)

LOVE IS A SPLENDID ILLUSION*1/2   (1970, Brit.) 86m Piccadilly/RSE c

Simon Brent (*Christian Dubarry*), Andree Flamand (*Michele Howard*), Lisa Collings (*Amanda Dubarry*), Peter Hughes (*Maurice Howard*), Mark Kingston (*Bernard*

Collins), Fiona Curzon (*Liz*), Maxine Casson (*Debbie*), Anna Matisse (*Sophie*), Carl Ferber (*Jason*), Nancy Nevinson (*Mother*).

Modernistic weeper set in Italy in which a man is forced to accept the newly acquired knowledge that his love has had an affair with one of his friends. Best if kept a secret for all involved.

p, Bachoo Sen; d, Tom Clegg; w, David Baker, Sen.

Drama (PR:O MPAA:NR)

LOVE IS A WEAPON (SEE: HELL'S ISLAND, 1955)

LOVE IS A WOMAN*1/2
(1967, Brit.) 88m Pathe/Hemisphere c (AKA:DEATH IS A WOMAN; SEX IS A WOMAN)

Patsy Ann Noble (*Francesca*), Mark Burns (*Dennis*), Shaun Curry (*Joe*), William Dexter (*Malo*), Wanda Ventham (*Priscilla*), Terence De Marney (*Jacomini*), Caron Gardner (*Mary*), Mark Singleton (*Costello*), Michael Brennan (*Bonelli*), Blake Butler (*Lift Operator*), Dulcie Bowman (*Old Lady*), Anita Harris (*Herself*).

Convoluted British mystery starring Burns as an undercover narcotics agent who travels to the Mediterranean to stop smuggler Dexter and his partner. Soon after Burns' arrival, the partner is beaten by Curry and then shot and killed by his mistress, Noble. After Burns goes to great lengths to get into the confidence of Dexter, he is shocked to discover Dexter stabbed to death and that he is being considered the prime suspect by local detective Singleton. Enter Ventham, another undercover agent who was sent by the home office to help Burns solve the murder case and clear his name. Eventually it is revealed that Noble is the true mastermind behind the crimes and she even kills her lover and partner Curry so she may reap a fortune in heroin by herself. Unfortunately for her, Burns and Ventham arrive in time to stop her recovery of the drugs.

p, Harry Field; d, Frederic Goode; w, Wally Bosco; ph, William Jordan, Stephen Halliday; (Technicolor) ed, Fredrick Ives; md, John Shakespeare; art d, Peter Moll; m/l, "Who's Foolish," Joan Shakespeare (sung by Anita Harris), "Francesca," Shakespeare (sung by Dennis Lotis).

Mystery (PR:C MPAA:NR)

LOVE IS BETTER THAN EVER**1/2
          (1952) 81m MGM bw (GB: THE LIGHT FANTASTIC)

Larry Parks (*Jud Parker*), Elizabeth Taylor (*Anastacia Macaboy*), Josephine Hutchinson (*Mrs. Macaboy*), Tom Tully (*Mr. Macaboy*), Ann Doran (*Mrs. Levoy*), Elinor Donahue (*Pattie Marie Levoy*), Kathleen Freeman (*Mrs. Kahrney*), Doreen McCann (*Albertina Kahrney*), Alex Gerry (*Hamlet*), Dick Wessel (*Smittie*), Gene Kelly (*Guest Star*), Richard Karlan (*Siddo*), Dive Willock (*Davey*), Frank Hyers (*Bernie*), Bertil Unger (*Randie Dean*), Nancy Saunders (*Pauline*), Margaret Lloyd (*Mrs. Culpepper*), George Matkovich (*Cahoogit*), Lucille Curtis (*Mother*), Mae Clarke (*Mrs. Ireland*), William "Bill" Phillips (*Mr. Khourney*), Ann Tyrell (*Mrs. Whitney*), Gail Bonney (*Mrs. Oelschlager*), Tom Hanlon (*Announcer*), Jack George, Dan Foster.

Light-hearted romantic-comedy has Taylor as a small town dancing instructor in the Big Apple for a convention, when she meets and falls for the bigtime talent agent Parks. Parks shows Taylor the sights, than quickly dismisses her. But Taylor is persistent, using all the feminine charm she can muster to land the wolf. Good script is marred by an uneven direction, and leads which are not always up to the energy of the project. The release of this picture had to be withheld because of Parks' blacklisting by the McCarthy committee.

p, William H. Wright; d, Stanley Donen; w, Ruth Brooks Flippen; ph, Harold Rosson; m, Lennie Hayton; ed, George Boemler md, Hayton; art d, Cedric Gibbons, Gabriel Scognamillo;

Romance/Comedy (PR:A MPAA:NR)

LOVE IS LIKE THAT, 1930 (SEE; JAZZ CINDERELLA, 1930)

LOVE IS LIKE THAT*   (1933) 67m CHES bw

Bradley Page (*Dean Scarsdale*), Judith Vosselli (*Emily Scarsdale*), Dorothy Revier (*Pat Ormsby*), Albert Conti (*R. J. Ormsby*), Rochelle Hudson (*Gwendolyn*), Herta Lind (*Paula*), May Beatty (*Gloria*), John Warburton (*Steve*), Lorin Raker (*Tom*), Mary Foy, Betty Mack, Sam Adams.

Domestic comedy has Page as a drunken husband, Vosselli his irate wife, and Hudson the daughter in search of romance. Despite attempts by the cast to move this cumbersome piece along, it never takes off.

d, Richard Thorpe; w, Stuart Anthony (based on a story by Beulah Poynter); ph, M.A. Anderson.

Comedy (PR:A MPAA:NR)

LOVE IS MY PROFESSION**1/2
(1959, Fr.) 111m Iena-UCIL-Incom/Kingsley International bw (EN CAS DE MALHEUR; GB: IN CASE OF ADVERSITY)

Jean Gabin (*Gobillot*), Brigitte Bardot (*Yvette*), Edwige Feuillere (*Viviane*), Franco Interlenghi (*Mazetti*), Julien Bertheau (*The Inspector*), Nicole Berger (*Jeanine*), Mathilde Casadesus (*Anna*), Madeleine Barbulee (*Bordenave*), Jacques Clancy (*Duret*), Annick Allieres (*Naomi*).

The man considered to be one of France's all-time greatest actors (Gabin) nearly had to be brought to court to share the bill with the hottest and trendiest thing in film at the time, the voluptuous Bardot. At first filled with disgust at playing opposite a woman who used body movements as an excuse for acting (though he was probably more afraid that people would be coming to see Bardot instead of him), he found the girl a pleasure to work with. Gabin plays a high-class lawyer who defends street urchin Bardot in a robbery case. He gets her off the charge only to discover that she has no money with which to pay him, so she offers the one thing that has helped her survive on the street, her body. This starts an affair between Bardot and Gabin which has the lawyer setting her up in an apartment while he attempts to maintain an outward appearance of the righteous husband. Eventually, one of Bardot's boy friends becomes so jealous of Gabin he kills Bardot. For 1959, Bardot was shown in poses that were considered quite risque, but by today's standards would hardly create a stir. This feature kept many viewers from realizing the underlying psychological and social subthemes lurking in the script, namely a man who has been forced to live in a very strict and confining environment finally getting a chance to breathe a little. Bardot wasn't called on to add much depth to her character, nevertheless she is perfect in expressing the type of sexual directness and lower-class morals the part required. (In French; English subtitles.)

p, Raoul J. Levy; d, Claude Autant-Lara; w, Jean Aurenche, Pierre Bost (based on the novel *In Case of Emergency* by Georges Simenon); ph, Jacques Natteau; m, Rene Cloerec; ed, Madaleine Gug; art d, Max Douy.

Drama **(PR:O MPAA:NR)**

LOVE IS NEWS*** (1937) 78m FOX bw

Tyrone Power *(Steve Leyton)*, Loretta Young *(Tony Gateson)*, Don Ameche *(Martin Canavan)*, Slim Summerville *(Judge Hart)*, Dudley Digges *(Cyrus Jeffrey)*, Walter Catlett *(Eddie Johnson)*, George Sanders *(Count de Guyon)*, Jane Darwell *(Mrs. Flaherty)*, Stepin Fetchit *(Penrod)*, Pauline Moore *(Lois Westcott)*, Elisha Cook Jr. *(Egbert Eggleston)*, Frank Conroy *(A. G. Findlay)*, Edwin Maxwell *(Kenyon)*, Charles Williams *(Joe Brady)*, Julius Tannen *(Logan)*, George Humbert *(Mike Allegretti)*, Frederick Burton *(J. D. Jones)*, Charles Coleman *(Bevins)*, Paul McVey *(Alvord)*, Carol Tevis *(Tessie)*, Ed Deering *(Motorcycle Officer)*, George Offerman Jr. *(Copy Boy)*, Art Dupuis *(Tony's Chauffeur)*, Charles Tannen, Sidney Fields, Arthur Rankin, Jack Byron, Sterling Campbell, Dick French, Paul Frawley, Ray Johnson, Al Jenson *(Reporters)*, Richard Powell *(Insurance Salesman)*, Jack Mulhall *(Yacht Salesman)*, Sam Ash *(Tailor)*, Charles King, Harry Hayden, Harry Depp, Sherry Hall, Emmett Vogan, Larry Steers, Gladden James, Babe Green, Paddy O'Flynn *(Salesmen)*, Eddie Anderson, Dot Farley, Etta McDaniel *(Bits)*, Lynn Bari *(Secretary)*, Dorothy Christy *(Girl)*, John Dilson *(Clerk)*, Charles E. Griffin *(Desk Man)*, Harry Watson, Leonard Kibrick *(Newsboys)*, Mugsy Meyers *(Gambler)*, Jack Baxley *(Deputy)*, Joe Smith Marba *(Carpenter)*, Pop Byron, Wade Boteler, Fred Kelsey, Bruce Mitchell, Eddy Chandler *(Cops)*, Maidel Turner *(Dowager)*, Herbert Ashley *(Gateman)*, Alan Davis *(Pilot)*, Lillian West *(Maid in Tony's Bathroom)*, Antonio Filauri *(Head Waiter)*, Davison Clark *(Foreman of Print Shop)*, Edward Cooper *(Butler)*.

An often hilarious screwball comedy about the gentlemen of the press, LOVE IS NEWS was remade two more times as SWEET ROSIE O'GRADY and THAT WONDERFUL URGE but neither captured the essence of this delightful, well-made tale. Young is a Doris Duke, poor-little-rich-girl-type. She is forever tailed by the 1930s version of the paparazzi and spends most of her time avoiding The Fourth Estate. Power, who is in danger of being fired by his boss, Ameche, tricks Young into an interview. She is so angered that she decides to show this newshound just how little fun public notice can be. She tells every paper in town, with the exception of Power's, that she is leaving her fiance, Sanders, in favor of Power and settling a million dollar wedding gift on him. Wedding banns will be posted shortly. Ameche is rankled that Power didn't give him the scoop and fires the confused newsman. Now Power is the center of the news and surrounded by reporters and photographers and men who try to sell him things. Despite his protests, nobody believes Power. By this time, Young and Power have actually fallen in love although neither will admit it so what transpires is a love-hate relationship which everyone knows will wind up with them in a clinch when "The End" flashes on the screen. They wind up in jail where they occupy adjacent cells and shout through the bars. She wants a puff from his last cigarette and he agrees to it but she takes the butt and bites his fingers. Later, he dumps her in a mud puddle as revenge. Now they learn that Sanders, a gigolo-type who seeks rich women, is about to marry Young's cousin, Moore. In order to forestall that, Young announces to the press that she will once again marry Sanders. Upon hearing that, the mercenary Sanders drops Moore. Power doesn't know why she is doing that and angrily tells Young off. Before she can explain her reasons, he's out the door. Next day, Power is offered the job of managing editor at the paper that fired him and he can't understand why until he learns that Young's uncle, Digges, now owns a large share in it. The lovers are finally united and the picture predictably winds up happily. Power is splendid as the tough newspaperman who tames the heiress but anyone who saw IT HAPPENED ONE NIGHT will recognize the derivation of the story, right down to the various adventures in the hinterlands. This was the era for those breezy comedies and Fox thought they could do what Frank Capra was doing at Columbia. It worked well, but not brilliantly. The picture starts slowly, revs up in the second reel, and takes off like a rocket for the remainder. It was a terrific book for a musical so that's what it became in the first remake, SWEET ROSIE O'GRADY, then they went back to a straight comedy for the next one.

p, Earl Carroll, Harold Wilson; d, Tay Garnett; w, Harry Tugend, Jack Yellen (based on a story by William R. Lipman, Frederick Stephani); ph, Ernest Palmer; ed, Irene Morra; md, David Buttolph; art d, Rudolph Sternad; set d, Thomas Little; cos, Royer; m/l, "Love is News," Sidney Mitchell, Lew Pollack.

Comedy **(PR:A MPAA:NR)**

LOVE IS ON THE AIR**
(1937) 61m WB FN bw (GB; THE RADIO MURDER MYSTERY)

Ronald Reagan *(Andy McLeod)*, June Travis *(Jo Hopkins)*, Eddie Acuff *(Dunk Glover)*, Ben Welden *(Nicey Carter)*, Robert Barrat *(J.D. Harrington)*, Addison Richards *(E. E. Nichols)*, Raymond Hatton *(Weston)*, Tommy Bupp *(Mouse)*, Dickie Jones *(Bill)*, Spec O'Donnell *(Pinky)*, William Hopper *(Eddie Gould)*, Willard Parker *(Lee Quimby)*, Herbert Rawlinson *(Mr. Copelin)*, Mary Hart *(Mrs. Copelin)*, Jack Mower *(Lang)*, Harry Hayden *(Mr. Butler)*, Don Deering *(Announcer)*, Sonny Bupp *(Billie)*, Marianne Edwards *(Barbara)*, Fern Berry *(Girl)*, John Pirrone *(Curly)*, Henry Hanna *(Tiger)*, George Billings *(Pee-Wee)*, Jerry Tucker *(Youngster)*, Margaret Davis *(Fudge Girl)*, Julia Perkins *(Another Girl)*, John Harron *(Clerk)*, John H. Elliott *(Mr. McKenzie)*, Edwin Stanley *(Mr. Brown)*, Ann Howard *(Brunette Girl)*, Lee Shumway, Cliff Saum *(Cops)*.

Reagan plays a newscaster who digs into the town's criminal activities. He broadcasts his findings which puts pressure on the station's sponsors. Reagan is demoted to handling a childrens' hour but this doesn't stop the crusading journalist. This picture marked Reagan's film debut which he saluted by giving a somewhat erratic performance. The rest of the cast is adequate.

d, Nick Grinde; w, Morton Grant (from the story "Hi Nellie" by Roy Chanslor); ph, James Van Trees, ed, Bryan Foy.

Drama **(PR:A MPAA:NR)**

LOVE ISLAND* 1/2 (1952) 64m Astor c

Paul Valentine *(Lt. Richard Taber)*, Eva Gabor *(Sarna)*, Malcolm Lee Beggs *(Jaraka)*, Kathryn Chang *(Klepon)*, Dean Norton, Frank McNellis, Bruno Wick, Richard Shankland, Howard Blain, Vicki Marsden.

Color photography which makes the characters look purple make this shoddy story even worse. Plot centers around an airplane pilot who is forced to land on the island of Bali. He falls for the chief's daughter, Gabor, who is being pursued by a number of other men, including the local corrupt politician. Gabor is being forced to marry the politician to help save her father's hide. Acting is stereotyped, writing is cliched, and the direction is uneven. Stock footage of Java and Hawaii are interspersed, without really meshing with the rest of the footage.

p, Hall Shelton; d, Budd Pollard; w, Daniel Kusell, John E. Gordon; ph, George Hinners (Cinecolor).

Drama **(PR:A MPAA:NR)**

LOVE ITALIAN STYLE (SEE: LOVE, THE ITALIAN WAY, 1964, Ital.)

LOVE KISS, THE* 1/2 (1930) 71m Celebrity bw (GB: KISS ME)

Olive Shea *(Annabelle Lee)*, Forrest Stanley *(Roger Jackson)*, Joan Bourdelle *(Helen Foster)*, Alice Hegeman *(Miss Prim)*, Donald Meek *(William)*, Terry Carroll *(Ruth)*, Rita Crane *(Joan)*, Bertha Donn *(Mary)*, Sally Mack *(Sally)*.

Shea and Bourdelle are students at an all-girls school and rivals for the attentions of their teacher, Stanley. The two make a bet to see who will be the first to be kissed by him and Bourdelle wins, forcing Shea to work in the kitchen as the loser. The ending sees her as the winner, however, as Shea turns out to be the object of her teacher's affections all the time. A romance too ridiculous to take with any degree of seriousness.

p, P. A. Powers; d, Robert R. Snody; w, Harry G. Smith (based on a story by Snody); ph, Dal Clawson, Walter Strenge.

Romance/Drama **(PR:A MPAA:NR)**

LOVE LAUGHS AT ANDY HARDY* 1/2 (1946) 93m MGM bw

Mickey Rooney *(Andrew Hardy)*, Lewis Stone *(Judge Hardy)*, Sara Haden *(Aunt Milly)*, Bonita Granville *(Kay Wilson)*, Lina Romay *(Isobel Gonzales)*, Fay Holden *(Mrs. Hardy)*, Dorothy Ford *(Coffy Smith)*, Addison Richards *(Mr. Benedict)*, Hal Hackett *(Duke Johnson)*, Richard Simmons *(Dane Kittridge)*, Clinton Sundberg *(Haberdashery Proprietor)*, Geraldine Wall *(Miss Geeves)*, Charles Peck *(Tommy Gilchrest)*, John Walsh *(Freshman)*, Lucien Littlefield *(Telegraph Clerk)*, Holmes Herbert.

MGM attempted to cash in again with another chapter in the life of everyone's favorite family, but the appeal in the nine-year saga was beginning to wane. This one has Rooney back from the war and ready to finish his freshman year at college. He develops a walloping crush on Granville, who breaks his heart by marrying someone else. Dejected, Rooney decides to go off to South America when Romay, a south of the border cutie, steals his heart. Performances are standard though Rooney is getting too old to be totally convincing as Andy Hardy. The thin plot is padded with unnecessary humor. (See ANDY HARDY Series, Index.)

p, Robert Sisk; d, Willis Goldbeck; w, Harry Ruskin, William Ludwig (based on a story by Howard Dimsdale); ph, Robert Planck; ed, Irvine Warburton; art d, Cedric Gibbons; m/l, Earl K. Brent.

Comedy **Cas.** **(PR:A MPAA:NR)**

LOVE LETTERS 1/2** (1945) 101m PAR bw

Jennifer Jones *(Singleton)*, Joseph Cotten *(Alan Quinton)*, Ann Richards *(Dilly Carson)*, Anita Louise *(Helen Wentworth)*, Cecil Kellaway *(Mack)*, Gladys Cooper *(Beatrice Remington)*, Byron Barr *(Derek Quinton)*, Robert Sully *(Roger Morland)*, Reginald Denny *(Defense Attorney)*, Ernest Cossart *(Bishop)*, James Millican *(Jim Connings)*, Lumsden Hare *(Mr. Quinton)*, Winifred Harris *(Mrs. Quinton)*, Ethel May Halls *(Bishop's Wife)*, Matthew Boulton *(Judge)*, David Clyde *(Postman)*, Ian Wolfe *(Vicar)*, Alec Craig *(Dodd)*, Arthur Hohl *(Jupp)*, Conrad Binyon *(Boy in Library)*, Nina Borget *(Barmaid in Italian Inn)*, Louise Currie *(Clara Foley)*, Mary Field, Connie Leon *(Nurses)*, George Humbert *(Proprietor of Italian Inn)*, Clifford Brooke *(Cart Driver)*, Constance Purdy *(Old Hag)*, Ottola Nesmith, Helena Grant *(Attendants)*, Catherine Craig *(Jeanette Campbell)*, Harry Allen *(Farmer)*, Anthony Marsh *(Young Man at Party)*.

Sensitive story about two British soldiers in Italy, Cotten and Sully. Sully has Cotten write letters to his girl back home for him. The girl, Jones, falls in love with Sully but he is nothing like the man of the letters. Jones marries Sully, but is quickly disillusioned by the rough way in which she is treated. One night after a drunk Sully beats Jones and Jones' stepmother stabs Sully to death. The girl goes into shock which makes her an amnesiac, while her stepmother suffers a stroke and becomes speechless. Jones is accused of murder and sentenced to one year in jail. Hearing of his former friend's mysterious murder, Cotten visits Jones and immediately falls in love with her. Excellent performances and a guiding directorial hand aid this overly sentimental script.

p, Hal B. Wallis; d, William Dieterle; w, Ayn Rand (based on *Pity My Simplicity* by Chris Massie); ph, Lee Garmes; m, Victor Young; ed, Anne Bauchens; art d, Hans Dreier, Roland Anderson; set d, Ray Moyer; spec eff, Gordon Jennings; m/l, "Love Letters," Young.

Drama (PR:A MPAA:NR)

LOVE LETTERS*** (1983) 98m New World c (AKA: MY LOVE LETTERS)

Jamie Lee Curtis (*Anna*), James Keach (*Oliver*), Amy Madigan (*Wendy*), Bud Cort (*Danny*), Matt Clark (*Winter*), Bonnie Bartlett (*Mrs. Winter*), Phil Coccioletti (*Ralph*), Shelby Leverington (*Edith*), Rance Howard (*Chesley*), Betsy Toll (*Marcia*), Sally Kirkland (*Sally*).

Sensitive and moving portrayal of a young woman's (Curtis) introduction into a world of romance via an affair with an older man. At the same time she comes across some of her mother's old love letters to a man with whom she had been having an affair, a discovery that changes her attitude toward her mother and women in general. Curtis gives a performance which proves she is possessed of talent that should not be limited to exploitation pictures.

p, Roger Corman; d&w, Amy Jones; ph, Alec Hirschfeld; m, Ralph Jones; ed, Wendy Greene; art d, Jeannine Oppewall.

Drama **Cas.** (PR:C MPAA:R)

LOVE LETTERS OF A STAR*** 1/2 (1936) 66m UNIV bw

Henry Hunter (*John Aldrich*), Polly Rowles (*Lydia Todd*), C. Henry Gordon (*Lt. Valcour*), Walter Coy (*Charley Warren*), Hobart Cavanaugh (*Chester Blodgett*), Mary Alice Rice (*Jenny Aldrich*), Ralph Forbes (*Meredith Landers*), Alma Kruger (*Veronica Todd*), Samuel S. Hinds (*Artemus Todd*), Rollo Lloyd (*Sigurd Repellen*), Virginia Brissac (*Mrs. Blodgett*), Howard C. Hickman (*Dr. Webster*), Sam McDaniel (*Garage Attendant*), Olin Howland, John Hamilton, Reynolds Denniston, Warren Hymer, Halliwell Hobbes, Pierre Watkin.

A wealthy girl commits suicide when a potential blackmailer threatens to expose letters she has written to a popular stage star. This brings an investigation which concludes that the girl had been murdered. Tale is very suspenseful, with the mystery deepening as the story moves along. The plot never gets out of hand because of well balanced direction. Performances are adequate.

p, E. M. Asher; d, Lewis R. Foster, Milton Carruth; w, Foster, Carruth, James Mulhauser (based on a story by Rufus King); ph, Milton Krasner ed, Frank Gross.

Mystery (PR:A MPAA:NR)

LOVE LIES** (1931, Brit.) 65m BIP/Wardour bw

Stanley Lupino (*Jerry Walker*), Dorothy Boyd (*Joyce*), Jack Hobbs (*Rolly Rider*), Dennis Hoey (*Cyrus Watt*), Binnie Barnes (*Junetta*), Sebastian Smith (*Nicholas Wich*), Wallace Lupino (*Lord Lletgoe*), Arte Ash (*Butler*), Charles Courtneidge (*Inspector*).

British farce about a boy who decides to marry against the wishes of his uncle. The uncle visits the boy who then attempts to pan his bride off as his best friend's girl. Despite good performances and some witty dialog, the plot is too predictable.

p, Stanley Lupino; d, Lupino Lane; w, Lupino, Arthur Rigby, Frank Miller (based on a play by Lupino); ph, Walter Harvey, Horace Wheddon.

Comedy (PR:A MPAA:NR)

LOVE, LIFE AND LAUGHTER** (1934, Brit.) 83m ATP/ABF bw

Gracie Fields (*Nellie Gwyn*), John Loder (*Prince Charles*), Norah Howard (*Princess Grapfel*), Allan Aynesworth (*King*), Esme Percy (*Goebschen*), Veronica Brady (*Mrs. Gwyn*), Horace Kenney (*Mr. Gwyn*), Robb Wilton (*Magistrate*), Fred Duprez (*Greenbaum*), A. Bromley Davenport (*Menkenburg*), Ivor Barnard (*Troubetski*), Eric Maturin (*Director*), Elizabeth Jenns (*Actress*), Esme Church.

Loder is the prince of that mythical kingdom known as Ruritania. His responsibilities are more than he wants when he falls head-over-heels for showgirl Fields. Forsaking his royal heritage, Loder follows her across the continent, returning to his position only when his father's death makes Fields realize she cannot continue her affair when his country needs him. Premise is a bit far-fetched, but makes for a solid piece of entertainment.

p, Basil Dean; d, Maurice Elvey; w, Robert Edmunds (based on a story by Maurice Braddell).

Drama/Comedy (PR:A MPAA:NR)

LOVE, LIVE AND LAUGH* (1929) 81m FOX bw

George Jessel (*Luigi*), Lila Lee (*Margharita*), David Rollins (*Pasquale Gallupi*); Henry Kolker (*Enrico*), Kenneth MacKenna (*Dr. Price*), John Reinhart (*Mario*), Dick Winslow Johnson (*Mike*), Henry Armetta (*Tony*), Jerry Mandy (*Barber*), Marcia Manon (*Sylvia*).

Plodding story has Jessel as an Italian accordion player who gets a job in a music store owned by the father of the girl Jessel desires. The best scene in the entire film takes place in a nursery, where the kids show up the adults in acting abilities.

d, William K. Howard; w, Dana Burnet, Edwin Burke, George Jessel (based on the play "The Hurdy-Gurdy Man" by Leroy Clemens, John B. Hymer); ph, Lucien Andriot; ed, Al De Gaetano. m/l, L. Wolfe Gilbert, Abel Baer.

Comedy (PR:A MPAA:NR)

LOVE LOTTERY, THE** 1/2 (1954, Brit.) 89m EAL/GFD c

David Niven (*Rex Allerton*), Peggy Cummins (*Sally*), Anne Vernon (*Jane*), Herbert Lom (*Amico*), Charles Victor (*Jennings*), Gordon Jackson (*Ralph*), Felix Aylmer (*Winant*), Hugh McDermott (*Rodney Wheeler*), Stanley Maxted (*Stanton*), June Clyde (*Viola*), John Chandos (*Gulliver Kee*), Sebastian Cabot (*Suarez*), Eugene Deckers (*Vernet*), Hattie Jacques (*Chambermaid*), Humphrey Bogart (*Bit*), John Glyn-Jones (*Prince Borris*), Nellie Arno (*Russian Woman*), Gabrielle Blunt (*Doreen*), Mark Baker (*Maxie*), Marcel Poncin (*Priest*), Andrea Malandrinos (*Fodor*), Nicholas Stuart (*American Radio Announcer*), Michael Ward, Helena Pickard, Alexis Chesnakov, Boscoe Holder, Michael Craig.

Clever British satire on the Hollywood star system has Niven as a top-ranking studio star, who, in a publicity stunt, is being raffled off for a week. When Niven makes the satirical statement that a week is not enough, make it life, the press takes him seriously. In an attempt to get out of the mess, he runs to London but finds hordes of fans waiting there. He finally winds up at Lake Como, but still cannot find peace. All the while he has the continual nightmare of having to deal with a bobbysoxer fan. Performances are adequate with some beautiful color photography of Lake Como.

p, Monja Danischewsky; d, Charles Crichton; w, Harry Kurnitz (based on the story by Charles Neilson-Terry, Zelma Bramley-Moore); ph, Douglas Slocombe (Technicolor); m, Benjamin Frankel; ed, Seth Holt.

Comedy (PR:A MPAA:NR)

LOVE MACHINE, THE,* 1/2 (1971) 108m COL c

John Phillip Law (*Robin Stone*), Dyan Cannon (*Judith Austin*), Robert Ryan (*Gregory Austin*), Jackie Cooper (*Danton Miller*), David Hemmings (*Jerry Nelson*), Jodi Wexler (*Amanda*), William Roerick (*Cliff Dorne*), Maureen Arthur (*Ethel Evans*), Shecky Greene (*Christie Lane*), Clinton Greyn (*Alfie Knight*), Sharon Farrell (*Maggie Stewart*), Alexandra Hay (*Tina St. Claire*), Eve Bruce (*Amazon Woman*), Greg Mullavey (*Bob Summers*), Edith Atwater (*Mary*), Gene Baylos (*Eddie Flynn*), Ben Lessy (*Kenny Ditto*), Elizabeth St. Clair (*Susie*), Claudia Jennings (*Darlene*), Mary Collinson (*Debbie*), Madeleine Collinson (*Sandy*), Ann Ford (*Model*), Gayle Hunnicutt (*Astrological Girl at Party*), Jerry Dunphy, Michael Jackson, Ted Meyers (*Newscasters*).

Screen adaptation of the popular Jacqueline Susann novel about the goings on at a television network, which relegates all executive decisions as to what goes on to the bedroom. The main story is how far Cannon, wife to a top executive, can use her influence to push newsman Law to the top. The cast delivers erratic performances. The supporting cast outperforms the leads. Director Haley puts forth a sincere effort in presenting the sterile script, filled with soap opera dramatics.

p, M. J. Frankovich; d, Jack Haley Jr.; w, Samuel Taylor (based on *The Love Machine* by Jacqueline Susann); ph, Charles B. Lang (Eastmancolor); m, Artie Butler; ed, David Blewitt; set d, George Hopkins; cos, Moss Mabry; m/l "He's Moving On," Brian Wells, Ruth Batchelor (sung by Dionne Warwicke), "Amanda's Theme," Artie Butler, Mark Lindsay (sung by Warwicke); makeup, Hank Edds; titles, Maury Nemoy.

Drama (PR:O MPAA:R)

LOVE MADNESS (SEE: REEFER MADNESS, 1936)

LOVE MAKERS, THE (SEE: LA VIACCIA, 1962, FR./ITAL.)

LOVE MATCH, THE** 1/2 (1955, Brit.) 85m Group 3/BL bw

Arthur Askey (*Bill Brown*), Thora Hird (*Sal Brown*), Glenn Melvyn (*Wally Binns*), Robb Wilton (*Mr. Muddlecombe*), James Kenney (*Percy Brown*), Shirley Eaton (*Rose Brown*), Edward Chapman (*Mr. Longworth*), Danny Ross (*Alf Hall*), Anthea Askey (*Vera*), William Franklyn (*Arthur Ford*), Maurice Kaufmann (*Harry Longworth*), Patricia Hayes, Derek Kirby, Russel Waters, Peter Swanwick, Vi Stevens, Jill Adams, Dorothy Blythe, Ben Williams, Reginald Hearne, George Hirste, Iris Vandeleur, Sydney Bromley, June Martin, Bob Vossler, Leonard Williams, Richard Ford, Peter Godsell, Isabel George.

Highly enjoyable farce in which Askey and Melvyn play two overzealous football fans whose roughing up of the referee sets off a string of mishaps which almost costs them their railroad jobs. Their misadventures set the pace for a continual bombardment of well placed gags. An early screen appearance for Shirley Eaton as Askey's daughter, her most memorable appearance being the gold painted woman in GOLDFINGER.

p, John Baxter, Maclean Rogers; d, David Paltenghi; w, Geoffrey Orme, Glenn Melvyn (based on the play by Melvyn); ph, Arthur Grant.

Comedy (PR:A MPAA:NR)

LOVE MATES* (1967, Swed.) 90m Sandrews/Altura Films International c (ANGLAR, FINNS DOM?)

Jarl Kulle (*Jan Froman*), Christina Schollin (*Margareta Gunther*), Edvin Adolphson (*Admiral Gunther*), Isa Quensel (*Louise Gunther*), Sigge Furst (*Bert Hagson*), Gunnar Sjoberg (*Karl Evert Raeder*), George Fant (*Rolf*), Margit Carlqvist, Ake Claesson, Toivo Pawlo.

Dull romantic comedy starring Kulle as an independently wealthy young man (he comes from old money) who resolves to become rich on his own by taking a lowly bank job and working his way up the ladder. To speed his climb, he romances bank employee Schollin, who happens to be the daughter of the very influential Adolphson. Soon Kulle really falls in love with Schollin, and he becomes rich on his own by using the market tips he overhears in the bank.

p, Sven Lindberg; d&w, Lars-Magnus Lindgren (based on *Anglar, finns dom, Pappa?* by John Einar Aberg); ph, Rune Erickson (Eastmancolor); m, Torbjorn Lundquist, Evert Taube; ed, Lennart Wallen; art d, Jan Boleslaw; cos, Linda.

Romance/Comedy (PR:A MPAA:NR)

LOVE MATES, THE (SEE: MADLY, 1970, Fr.)

LOVE ME DEADLY* (1972) 88m Cinema National c

Mary Wilcox, Lyle Waggoner, Christopher Stone.

Pretty bad psychological horror flic starring Wilcox as a distraught young woman who has a thing for corpses and a homosexual mortician. Yes that's Lyle Waggoner of "The Carol Burnett Show" and "Wonder Woman" TV fame.

p, Buck Edwards, d&w, Jacques Lacerte.

Horror (PR:O MPAA:R)

LOVE ME FOREVER½** (1935) 91m COL bw (GB: ON WINGS OF SONG)

Grace Moore (*Margaret Howard*), Leo Carrillo (*Steve Corelli*), Michael Bartlett (*Himself*), Robert Allen (*Philip Cameron*), Spring Byington (*Fields*), Thurston Hall (*Maurizzio*), Douglas Dumbrille (*Miller*), Luis Alberni (*Luigi*), Gavin Gordon, Harry Barris, Arthur Kaye.

Successful attempt at combining opera and crime (film ranks as a predecessor to Francis Ford Coppola's COTTON CLUB), has Carrillo as a hood with a weakness for opera. He hears Moore sing and immediately falls for her. He spends all his time and money promoting her career, even to the point of building a club for her. Moore, however has her affections pointed toward someone else. Carrillo gets into a jam with a rival gang when he cannot pay his debts. Direction remains fairly even, blending the gangster story with the opera. Script gets a bit sappy at points. Production values are high, with realistic replicas of the Metropolitan Opera and a fancy nightclub. Musical numbers are all sung brilliantly by Moore and include: "Love Me Forever," "Whoa" (Gus Kahn, Victor Schertzinger), selections from the operas "La Boheme" (Puccini), and "Rigoletto" (Verdi), and "Il Bacio" (Luigi Arditi), and "Funiculi-Funicula" (Luigi Denza).

d, Victor Schertzinger; w, Jo Swerling, Sidney Buchman (based on a story by Schertzinger); ph, Joseph Walker; m, Louis Silvers; ed, Gene Milford, Viola Lawrence; md, Silvers, Gaetano Muola.

Musical/Crime (PR:A MPAA:NR)

LOVE ME OR LEAVE ME*** (1955) 122m MGM c

Doris Day (*Ruth Etting*), James Cagney (*Martin "The Gimp" Snyder*), Cameron Mitchell (*Johnny Alderman*), Robert Keith (*Bernard V. Loomis*), Tom Tully (*Frobisher*), Harry Bellaver (*Georgie*), Richard Gaines (*Paul Hunter*), Peter Leeds (*Fred Taylor*), Claude Stroud (*Eddie Fulton*), Audrey Young (*Jingle Girl*), John Harding (*Greg Trent*), Dorothy Abbott (*Dancer*), Phil Schumacher, Otto Reichow, Henry Kulky (*Bouncers*), Jay Adler (*Orry*), Mauritz Hugo (*Irate Customer*), Veda Ann Borg (*Hostess*), Claire Carleton (*Claire*), Benny Burt (*Stage Manager*), Robert B. Carson (*Mr. Brelston, Radio Station Manager*), James Drury (*Assistant Director*), Richard Simmons (*Dance Director*), Michael Kostrick (*Assistant Director*), Roy Engel (*1st Reporter*), John Damler (*2nd Reporter*), Genevieve Aumont (*Woman*), Roy Engel (*Propman*), Dale Van Sickel, Johnny Day (*Stage-Hands*), Larri Thomas, Patti Nestor, Winona Smith, Shirley Wilson (*Chorus Girls*), Robert Malcolm (*Doorman*), Robert Stephenson (*Waiter*), Paul McGuire (*Drapery Man*), Barry Regan (*Guard*), Jimmy Cross, Henry Randolph (*Photographers*), Chet Brandenberg (*Chauffeur*).

In a radical departure from the standard musicals of the day, LOVE ME OR LEAVE ME provides a hard-edged love story with Jazz Age tunes surrounding it, chronicling the life and times of Prohibition-era torch singer Ruth Etting. This was a once-in-a-lifetime role for songbird Day and she is simply great in a role unlike any other she ever played, sensuous and sexy in her performances, innocent and naive offstage. Cagney, the ruthless gangster obsessed with her to the point of murder, is equally magnificent, and even Mitchell, normally a lightweight talent, excels as Day's true love. Cagney, a Chicago gangster who owns a large laundry and services many saloons and nightclubs first sees Day in a rent-a-dancer hall where she resists the advances of one of the customers and is fired. Cagney goes to bat for her, getting her a job in a nightclub as a member of the chorus line but her real ambition is to become a singer. He pushes nightclub owner Tully into giving her a small singing bit, introducing a headliner. Meanwhile, pianist in the band Mitchell, who has an eye for the lady, helps her develop as a singer. At Day's conniving suggestion, Cagney arranges for the lead singer to be absent one night and Day goes on to make a hit with an audience packed with Cagney stooges. Soon, without his help, Day is a genuine success as she belts out one popular Jazz Age tune after another. Cagney next promotes Day into a popular radio singer and then gets her a spot in the Ziegfeld Follies in New York. But he does not fit in along the Great White Way, arguing with dance directors and making a fool of himself. Day does nothing to acknowledge his existence inside her new-found fame and Cagney responds by tearing up her contract with Ziegfeld. He then takes her on a national road tour and finally to Hollywood where she again meets up with Mitchell and the pianist resumes his subtle courting of her. Day, about to appear in movies, takes to drink over having to live with Cagney, a man she does not love. He, to establish his own identity, takes over a broken down nightclub, sinking all his money into refurbishing it. His worst nightmare occurs when he catches Mitchell kissing Day and he shoots the pianist and is arrested. Mitchell survives to wind up in Day's arms, and Cagney is released from prison to see his club opened with Day headlining for him as a gesture of gratitude for all he's done for her, an act he accepts, finally, with some grace, for the finale. The chemistry between Cagney and Day is electric and the overall production lavishly and accurately reproduces the 1920s era. The music is outstanding and Day never sang better. Vidor's direction is lively and inventive. There were several numbers that called for Day to display a lot of body and leg and it was expected that

the very prim actress would balk at such scenes, but producer Pasternak convinced her that showing the flesh was in keeping with the part so she agreed to the skimpy costumes, particularly where she and a chorus line do a sort of hippy coochie dance, flashing leg, thigh, and bosom. Cagney is simply magnetic as Martin "The Gimp" Snyder, Day's hoodlum mentor, although someone faltered in the research; Cagney's decided limp and roll is on the right leg when Snyder's left leg was the one afflicted. He sizzles the screen in another bravura performance with many a wiseguy line that remains memorable. In one scene, trying to impress Day, he tells her how he told off a film producer and that "his last three pictures were stinkeroos!" Snyder, however, was actually married to Etting, not just a man keeping her, as the film implies, and Etting did not meet Myrl Alderman (called Johnny in the film) until 1935, toward the end of her spectacular career. He was not, as the film indicates, her accompanist and instructor in the early 1920s. MGM went all out for this production; this was the first time for both Cagney and Day in making a film for that studio. Originally, George Cukor was slated to direct and Ava Gardner was scheduled to play the 1920s thrush but Gardner turned down the role, rightly believing that the studio would dub her singing voice as it had done in SHOWBOAT, 1951. The studio paid $50,000 just for the rights to the many songs used in the film and substantial but unstated sums to Etting, Alderman, and Snyder for the right to film their lives, even the most sordid aspects. After Etting (born November 23, 1896) saw the film she told reporters: "Oh, what a ___ mess that was. . . I never at any time was a dancehall girl. It was just a means of working in 'Ten Cents a Dance'. They took a lot of liberties with my life but I guess they usually do with that kind of thing." She was encouraged by friends to sue the studio but declined, recalling how Walter Winchell had once cautioned her that by suing one would only alert the gossip hounds to create even more scandal. The film was a great success, returning $4,153,000 the first time around to MGM's bank account. Two new songs were specifically composed for the film: "I'll Never Stop Loving You" (Nicholas Brodszky, Sammy Cahn) and "Never Look Back" (Chilton Price). Other songs include: "Shaking the Blues Away" (Irving Berlin, production number created by Alex Romero), "Mean to Me" (Roy Turk, Fred Ahlert), "Love Me or Leave Me" (Walter Donaldson, Gus Kahn), "Sam, the Old Accordian Man" (Donaldson), "At Sundown" (Donaldson), "Everybody Loves My Baby" (Jack Palmer, Spencer Williams), "Five Foot Two" (Sam M. Lewis, Joe Young, Ray Henderson), "I'm Sitting on Top of the World" (Lewis, Young, Henderson), "Stay on the Right Side, Sister" (Ted Koehler, Rube Bloom), "It All Depends on You" (Buddy DeSylva, Nacio Herb Brown, Ray Henderson), "Ten Cents A Dance" (Richard Rodgers, Lorenz Hart), "My Blue Heaven" (Donaldson, Richard Whiting), "You Made Me Love You" (Joseph McCarthy, James V. Monaco).

p, Joe Pasternak; d, Charles Vidor; w, Daniel Fuchs, Isobel Lennart (based on the story by Fuchs); ph, Arthur E. Arling (Eastmancolor, Cinemascope); m, Percy Faith (for Doris Day); ed, Ralph E. Winters; md, Georgie Stoll; art d, Cedric Gibbons, Urie McCleary; set d, Edwin B. Willis; cos, Helen Rose; spec eff, Warren Newcombe; ch, Alex Romero.

Musical/Drama (PR:A MPAA:NR)

LOVE ME TENDER* ½ (1956) 94m FOX bw

Richard Egan (*Vance*), Debra Paget (*Cathy*), Elvis Presley (*Clint*), Robert Middleton (*Siringo*), William Campbell (*Brett Reno*), Neville Brand (*Mike Gavin*), Mildred Dunnock (*The Mother*), Bruce Bennett (*Maj. Kincaid*), James Drury (*Ray Reno*), Russ Conway (*Ed Galt*), Ken Clark (*Kelso*), Barry Coe (*Davis*), Paul Burns (*Jethro*), L. Q. Jones (*Fleming*), Jerry Sheldon (*Conductor*).

This marked Elvis Presley's first screen appearance and turned what would have been a routine western into one of the best box-office successes for 20th Century-Fox. The story takes place near the end of the Civil War, with Presley the youngest of four brothers, and the only one to stay home from the war. Believing his brother to have died, Presley marries his girl, Paget. But the three brothers, return home, not before robbing a federal payroll and hiding the money. Finding his girl married to his brother, Egan decides to take off and return the stolen money. Stirred on by a confederate who does not want the money returned, Presley goes after his brother. The original title of this Elvis debut was to have been THE RENO BROTHERS, but was wisely changed to LOVE ME TENDER to take advantage of the song of the same name, even though this title is quite misleading. The performances, including Presley's, are lifeless, the script is overly dramatic, and the direction routine. As to be expected the high points are the Elvis songs, but they are not added to the plot in an even manner. Presley sings. "Love Me Tender" (W.W. Fosdick, George R. Poulton), "Poor Boy," "We're Gonna Move," and "Let Me" (Presley, Vera Matson).

p, David Weisbart; d, Robert D. Webb; w, Robert Buckner (based on a story by Maurice Geraghty); ph, Leo Tover (CinemaScope); m, Lionel Newman; ed, Hugh S. Fowler; art d, Lyle R. Wheeler, Maurice Ransford; cos, Mary Wills; spec eff, Ray Kellogg.

Western Cas. (PR:A MPAA:NR)

LOVE ME TONIGHT*** (1932) 104m PAR bw (AIMEZ-MOI CE SOIR!)

Maurice Chevalier (*Maurice Courtelin*), Jeanette MacDonald (*Princess Jeanette*), Charlie Ruggles (*Vicomte Gilbert de Vareze*), Charles Butterworth (*Count de Savignac*), Myrna Loy (*Countess Valentine*), Sir C. Aubrey Smith (*The Duke*), Elizabeth Patterson, Ethel Griffies, Blanche Frederici (*Aunts*), Joseph Cawthorn (*Dr. Armand de Fontinac*), Major Sam Harris (*Bridge Player*), Robert Greig (*Major-Domo Flamond*), Ethel Wales (*Madame Dutoit, Dressmaker*), Marion "Peanuts" Byron (*Bakery Girl*), Bert Roach (*Emile*), Tyler Brooke (*Composer*), Clarence Wilson (*Shirtmaker*), William H. Turner (*Bootmaker*), Tony Merlo (*Hatmaker*), Rolfe Sedan (*Taxi Driver*), Gordon Westcott (*Collector*), George "Gabby" Hayes (*Grocer*), Mary Doran (*Madame Dupont*), George Davis (*Pierre Dupont*), Edgar Norton (*Valet*), Cecil Cunningham (*Laundress*), Herbert Mundin (*Groom*), Rita Owin (*Chambermaid*), George Humbert (*Chef*), Tom Ricketts (*Bit*).

LOVE ME TONIGHT is one of the best musical films ever made. It is also the first "integrated" musical with the score being so seamlessly sewn into the story that it's hard to believe script and score were a collaboration among five people. The innovation is indicated immediately as Chevalier, a Parisian tailor, awakens at dawn to the sounds of the city stirring. The workers' tools are orchestrated like a piece for the Philharmonic as we hear the swish of a broom, the clang of a shovel, the whir of a grinding wheel, the scrape of a pick. Each sound is in rhythm, oh so subtly, then a young woman drops a needle on an old phonograph and an orchestra joins the sounds of Paris in one of the most charming and noteworthy openings ever lensed. Chevalier is seen in his window, sings "The Song of Paree," and we are off on a delightful experience. We soon learn that he is a tailor. Roach arrives at Chevalier's shop to pick up his wedding clothes, then they are both attracted by something outside. There's a marathon going past with many runners. Suddenly, Ruggles enters. He is in his shorts and holds a scrawled fruit peddler's sign that is obviously not an official runner's number. Ruggles is a local rakehell count who had been dallying with a woman the night before but her husband returned unexpectedly so he made haste and joined the runners. (This same scene was almost duplicated by Terry-Thomas in MAKE MINE MINK.) Now he asks Chevalier for the loan of some clothing and cash which Chevalier grants him instantly. Ruggles exits and Roach and Chevalier begin some rhyming dialog that winds up as the song "Isn't It Romantic?" Roach leaves, humming the tune. It's overheard by a cab driver who takes up the melody with a whistle. The driver's fare, a composer, writes it down. Later, he puts words to it while riding on a train where it is taken up by a group of Army men. Later, the men march across a field singing the song and a gypsy plays it on his violin until it is eventually heard by MacDonald in her chateau, completing the chain from Chevalier to MacDonald and establishing a link between them, even though they won't meet for awhile. MacDonald is badgered by Butterworth, an adoring swain, but she wants nothing to do with him and faints in her room. Meanwhile, her maiden aunt attendants, Griffies, Frederici, and Patterson, are attempting to mix up a cure for MacDonald's fainting spells. At the same time, Loy is downstairs asking her uncle, Smith, for an advance on her allowance. Ruggles arrives and we learn that he is titled but impoverished and lives off the largesse of Smith. He tries to borrow money from Loy to no avail. Back in Paris, a trio of Chevalier's pals, Merlo, Wilson, and Turner, are complaining that Ruggles owes them all money and they had only extended him credit on Chevalier's recommendation. Now Westcott walks in. He's a bill collector and informs them that Ruggles *never* pays his debts. The men want Ruggles' neck, but Chevalier says he will take care of recovering their bills. Davis, the husband of neighbor Doran, is to chauffeur his boss' limo to Biarritz and will take Chevalier to the suburban chateau. The car breaks down on a thin road and along comes MacDonald singing "Lover." Chevalier is off to the side watching repairs being attempted as MacDonald tries to slip through but her horse rears, overturns her carrriage, and tosses her into the muddy ditch. Chevalier extricates her, dubs her "Mimi," and sings the song of the same name that became his trademark. The small carriage is soon righted and she returns to the chateau where she has another fainting spell. Her doctor, Cawthorn, tells her that she needs a man. Unfortunately, there are only two eligible men of her station in all of France. One is in his 80s and the other isn't 13 yet. MacDonald has been a widow for a few years, having married a 70-year-old when she was 16. Chevalier comes to the house, pounds the massive door but no one answers so he enters, meets Loy, then Smith, who mistakes him as a pal of Ruggles. The two men get into conversation and Smith is rather taken by Chevalier, who is dressed in a most elegant suit. Ruggles enters, turns white at the sight of Chevalier, and hastily tells Smith that Chevalier is a great pal. Smith leaves and Ruggles pleads with Chevalier not to blow the whistle. He'll raise the money somehow and promises that Chevalier won't leave empty-handed. Ruggles tells Loy and the assemblage that Chevalier is a baron. Several very funny incidents follow, namely a hysterical early-morning workout with Smith, a challenge for Chevalier to ride a horse (the same scene was repeated in AUNTIE MAME and MAME), and the continuing investigation of Chevalier's supposed lineage by Smith. When Smith announces that he's read through every volume of French genealogy and could find no one with Chevalier's assumed name, Ruggles assures Smith that Chevalier is a Hapsburg, incognito. Chevalier is finally unmasked but by that time he has charmed everyone so completely that it doesn't matter much although Chevalier decides it would be better if he left. MacDonald races after his train on her horse, stops the train, and gets Chevalier off. They embrace in a gigantic puff of steam from the engine and the picture ends as the three aged attendants finish a huge tapestry upon which they have been working all film that reveals a prince on a white horse and his lady love in a tower. What you have just read only skims the surface of the story. The screenplay is incessantly witty with many quotable lines, none of which has aged in the years since the picture was released. The songs include the aforementioned plus: "How Are You?," "Poor Apache" (sung by Chevalier), "Love Me Tonight" (sung by Chevalier and MacDonald), "A Woman Needs Something Like That" (sung by Cawthorn and MacDonald), and "The Son of a Gun is Nothing But a Tailor" (sung by Smith, Greig, Cunningham, Byron, Norton, Owin, and Humbert). All the songs were composed by Richard Rodgers and Lorenz Hart. LOVE ME TONIGHT shimmered with sophistication from the moment it came on screen. It was the kind of movie that Lubitsch was known for and he helmed Chevalier and MacDonald two years later in MERRY WIDOW, an excellent musical comedy but nowhere near as flawless as LOVE ME TONIGHT. There was yet another tune written and shot but cut from the print before release. It was "The Man For Me" and no one has ever heard of it since. Loy played a sort-of nymphomaniac in the film and most of her lines were as risque as something by Mae West but she did them with such open-faced naiveté that even the bluest of noses couldn't turn up at her performance. LOVE ME TONIGHT is the reverse of CINDERELLA in that the poor boy winds up with the princess. It's a total "entertainment" and, although not as successful as they'd hoped when first released, it aged well (like Chevalier) and remains, to this day, a bubbling broth of wit, music, and love.

p&d, Rouben Mamoulian; w, Samuel Hoffenstein, Waldemar Young, George Marion Jr. (based on the play "Tailor in the Chateau" by Leopold Marchand, Paul

Armont); ph, Victor Milner; ed, Billy Shea; md, Nathaniel Finston; art d, Hans Dreier; set d, A. E. Freudeman; cos, Edith Head, Travis Banton; m/l, Richard Rodgers, Lorenz Hart.

Musical/Comedy   **(PR:A   MPAA:NR)**

LOVE MERCHANT, THE*
(1966) 80m General Studios/Cannon bw (AKA: LOVE MERCHANTS; ANOTHER WOMAN, ANOTHER DAY)

Loraine Claire (*Peggy Johns*), Judson Todd (*Kendall Harvey III*), Jim Chisholm (*Click*), George Wolfe (*Roger Johns*), Joanna Mills (*Bobbi*), Patti Paget (*Polly Fields*), Penni Peyton (*Dixie*), Cleo Nova (*Valery*), Francine Ashley (*Sandy*), Michael Lawrence (*Vince*), Annette Godette (*Hillary*), Shep Wild (*Zug*), Steve Barton (*Nat*), Phil Mason (*Gig*), Robin Marks (*Go-go Girl*), Carl Olsen (*Head Waiter*).

Melodrama features Claire as the newlywed wife of a floundering advertising executive, Wolfe, who decides to help bail out her husband by sleeping with bored millionaire playboy Todd. Much to her surprise, Claire is forced by Todd to participate in an orgy he has thrown for the occassion. Wolfe gets wind of the incident and angrily leaves his wife, but Claire's low opinion of Todd changes when the playboy tells her he has fallen in love with her. This illusion is soon shattered when Claire finds Todd in bed with a hooker, and she goes off in search of Wolfe to beg forgiveness.

d&w, Joe Sarno; ph, Bruce Sparks; m, Richard Cove; ed, George Binkey; md, Cove.

Drama   **(PR:O   MPAA:NR)**

LOVE MERCHANTS   (SEE: LOVE MERCHANT, THE 1966)

LOVE NEST, THE**   (1933, Brit.) 69m BIP/Wardour bw

Gene Gerrard (*George*), Camilla Horn (*Fifi*), Nancy Burne (*Angela*), Gus McNaughton (*Fox*), Garry Marsh (*Hugo*), Amy Veness (*Ma*), Charles Paton (*Pa*), Marion Dawson (*Mrs. Drinkwater*), Judy Kelly (*Girl*).

One rainy evening Horn, a married woman, locks herself out of her home. Having no where else to go, she turns to her neighbor Gerrard. He puts her up for the night though he's to be married the next day. Of course, this leads to a host of misunderstandings, and complications, all of which are worked out in time for a happy ending. The comedy isn't much, but Gerrard's lively performance helps things out somewhat.

p, Walter C. Mycroft; d, Thomas Bentley; w, H. F. Maltby, Frank Miller, Gene Gerrard.

Comedy   **(PR:A   MPAA:NR)**

LOVE NEST**   (1951) 84m FOX bw

June Haver (*Connie Scott*), William Lundigan (*Jim Scott*), Frank Fay (*Charley Patterson*), Marilyn Monroe (*Roberta Stevens*), Jack Paar (*Ed Forbes*), Leatrice Joy (*Eadie Gaynor*), Henry Kulky (*George Thompson*), Marie Blake (*Mrs. Quigg*), Patricia Miller (*Florence*), Maude Wallace (*Mrs. Arnold*), Joe Ploski (*Mr. Hansen*), Martha Wentworth (*Mrs. Thompson*), Faire Binney (*Mrs. Frazier*), Caryl Lincoln (*Mrs. McNab*), Robert H. [Clifton] Young (*Meter Reader*), Michael Ross (*Mr. McNab*), Bob Jellison (*Mr. Fain*), John Costello (*Mailman*), Leo Clary (*Detective Donovan*), Charles Calvert (*Mr. Knowland*), Jack Daly (*Mr. Clark*), Ray Montgomery (*Mr. Gray*), Florence Auer (*Mrs. Braddock*), Edna Holland (*Mrs. Engstrand*), Liz Slifer (*Mrs. Healy*), Alvin Hammer (*Glazier*), Tony DeMario (*Wine Steward*).

Light-hearted story about a couple who invest their life savings in a tenant building shortly after WW II. Lundigan plays the husband whose life ambition is to become a writer, but between fixing the building for the assortment of characters, which includes Monroe and Paar, and scraping up money to meet the mortgage, this dream doesn't seem very probable. One of his tenants, Fay, turns out to be an elderly Casanova, who has been living off wealthy widows. When he lands in jail, this becomes a hot news item. From the clink, Fay dictates his memoirs to Lundigan, who is able to publish a successful book and pay off his mortgage.

p, Jules Buck; d, Joseph Newman; w, I. A. L. Diamond (based on the novel by Scott Corbett); ph, Lloyd Ahern; m, Cyril Mockridge; ed, J. Watson Webb, Jr.; md, Lionel Newman; art d, Lyle Wheeler, George L. Patrick.

Comedy   **(PR:A   MPAA:NR)**

LOVE NOW . . . PAY LATER zero
(1966) 50m William Mishkin bw (AKA: NUDES ON CREDIT; SIN NOW . . .PAY LATER)

Lisa Palmer, Herman Rose.

Sleazy look at a couple of dopey guys who mistakenly get involved in espionage when they find an abandoned brief case. The exploits they become involved in as a result of their find lead to their eventual arrest.

d, Don Rolos.

Crime/Drama   **(PR:O   MPAA:NR)**

LOVE NOW . . . PAY LATER**
(1966, Ital.) 82m William Mishkin bw (AKA: SIN NOW PAY LATER; L'INFERNO ADDOSSO)

Annabella Incontrera (*Micki*), Sandro Luporini (*Marco*), Sandra Pizzorni (*Andre [Andrea]*), Jeanine (*Gigi [Guiguitte]*), Marie Harlow, Barbara Hill, Jack Nasome, Carmen Luster, Pat Plumet, Jackie Kamen.

Crime drama starring Luporini as a starving engineering student who concocts a plan to raise some money with the help of his friend Pizzorno, who is the son of a wealthy businessman. Pizzorno agrees to fake his own kidnaping and hide out at Luporini's apartment until his father pays the ransom. All goes smoothly until Luporini's girl friend, Incontrera, and her bookworm friend, Jeanine, arrive. Incontrera falls for Pizzorno, and in a fit of jealous rage, Luporini kills his friend. At a party, Luporini confesses the crime to his girl friend and she agrees to help him with a cover-up. Eventually a clever family lawyer of Pizzorno's father tracks down the killers.

p, Gianni Vernuccio, N. Negri; d&w Vernuccio; ph, Romolo Garroni.

Crime　　　　　　　　　　　　　　　　　　　　　　**(PR:C　MPAA:NR)**

LOVE OF THREE QUEENS (SEE: LOVES OF THREE QUEENS, 1953, Ital.)

LOVE ON A BET**　　　　　　　　　　　　　　　(1936) 75m RKO bw

Gene Raymond (Michael), Wendy Barrie (Paula), Helen Broderick (Aunt Charlotte), William Collier, Sr. (Uncle Carlton), Walter Johnson (Stephan), Addison [Jack] Randall (Jackson Wallace), Eddie Gribbon (Donovan), Morgan Wallace (Morton), William B. Davidson (A. W. Hutchinson), William Gould (Estimator), Minerva Urecal (Secretary), Billy Gilbert (Cop), Irving Bacon (Farmer), Marc Lawrence (Barker), Eddie Kane (Coutourier), Spencer Charters.

Unpretentious comedy has Raymond in a bet with his rich uncle that he can start out in New York with nothing but his underwear and wind up in Los Angeles, ten days later, wearing a new suit of clothes, $100 in his pocket, and engaged to a pretty girl. He then goes about proving it. Barrie and Broderick are the motorists who give him a lift. Story is not enough to hold up throughout, but the witty dialog comes to its aid.

p, Lee Marcus; d, Leigh Jason; w, P. J. Wolfson, Phil G. Epstein (based on the story by Kenneth Earl); ph, Robert de Grasse; ed, Desmond Marquette.

Comedy　　　　　　　　　　　　　　　　　　　　　**(PR:A　MPAA:NR)**

LOVE ON A BUDGET**　　　　　　　　　　　(1938) 60m Max Golden/FOX bw

Jed Prouty (John Jones), Shirley Deane (Bonnie Thompson), Spring Byington (Mrs. John Jones), Russell Gleason (Herbert Thompson), Kenneth Howell (Jack Jones), George Ernest (Roger Jones), June Carlson (Lucy Jones), Florence Roberts (Granny Jones), Billy Mahan (Bobby Jones), Alan Dinehart (Uncle Charlie), Dixie Dunbar (Betty), Marvin Stephens (Tommy McGuire), Paul Harvey (Emory Fisher), Joyce Compton (Millie Brown).

This is the eighth entry in the saga of the Jones family. In this one, Deane and Gleason are newlyweds involved in a get-rich scheme by their uncle, Dinehart. He almost wrecks their marriage, until the investment pays off. By this time in the series the characters have devloped stronger emotional traits which shine through in the performances. (See JONES FAMILY series, Index.)

p, Sol M. Wurtzel; d, Herbert I. Leeds; w, Robert Ellis, Helen Logan (based on the characters created by Katherine Kavanaugh); ph, Edward Snyder; m, Samuel Kaylin; ed, Harry Reynolds; md, Kaylin; art d, Bernard Herzbrun, Chester Gore.

Comedy　　　　　　　　　　　　　　　　　　　　　**(PR:A　MPAA:NR)**

LOVE ON A PILLOW**

(1963, Fr./Ital.) 102m Francos-Incei/Royal c (LE REPOS DU GUERRIER, IL RIPOSO DEL GUERRIERO; AKA: WARRIOR'S REST)

Brigitte Bardot (Genevieve Le Theil), Robert Hossein (Renaud Sarti), James Robertson Justice (Katov), Macha Meril (Raphaele), Yves Barsacq (Hotel Manager), Jacqueline Porel (Genevieve's Mother), Jean-Marc Bory (Pierre), Christian Melsen (Police Inspector), Michel Serrault (Varange), Ursula Kubler (Nurse), Robert Dalban (Police Sergeant), Jean Tuscano (Jazz Musician), Jean-Marc Tennberg (Coco).

In Bardot and director Vadim's second-to-last collaboration (it would be ten years until their last film together, IF DON JUAN WERE A WOMAN), Bardot plays a 25-year-old rich Parisian who goes to Dijon to collect an inheritance. There she unwittingly foils the suicide attempt of Hossein, a penniless alcoholic, who is somewhat manic and tells Bardot that he owes her his soul and that he is hers. Fascinated by this crazed man, Bardot allows herself to be seduced by him and soon they are living together. Their life is less than blissful however, as all that interests Hossein is drinking, reading mystery novels, and sex. He constantly abuses Bardot, but she stays with him because she is hopelessly in love with him. Despite his strong attempts at totally alienating her, Bardot stays with him until at a party, he seduces a prostitute in front of her. She leaves him, but they are reunited when he declares his love and proposes marriage. A less than successful film that Bardot admitted she made as a favor to Vadim, to whom she felt she owed a debt after he helped her make a comeback following her own suicide attempt in 1960. (In French; English subtitles.)

p, Francis Cosne; d, Roger Vadim; w, Vadim, Claude Choublier (based on the story Le repos du guerrier by Christiane Rochefort); ph, Armand Thirard (Franscope, Eastmancolor); m, Michel Magne; ed, Victoria Mercanton; art d, Jean Andre; cos, Tanine Autre; makeup, Pierre Berroyer, Odette Berroyer; English subtitles by Herman G. Weinberg.

Romance/Drama　　　　　　　　　　　　　　　　**(PR:O　MPAA:NR)**

LOVE ON SKIS*½　　　　　　　　　　　　　　　(1933, Brit.) 65m Sokal/BL bw

Bull and Buster, Joan Austin, Ralph Rogan, Jack Lester.

A conventional romance story about two tramps from Canada who are really professional skiers and skaters. Winter sports enthusiasts will thrill at the daredevil expertise of these two comedians. This picture was filmed around St. Moritz, and shows some of the finest skating, skiing, and ski-jumping experts in action.

d, L. Vadja.

Romance　　　　　　　　　　　　　　　　　　　　**(PR:A　MPAA:NR)**

LOVE ON THE DOLE***　　　　　　　　　　(1945, Brit.) 99m BN/Four Continents bw

Deborah Kerr (Sally Hardcastle), Clifford Evans (Larry Meath), Joyce Howard (Helen Hawkins), Frank Cellier (Sam Grundy), Mary Merrall (Mrs. Hardcastle), George Carney (Mr. Hardcastle), Geoffrey Hibbert (Harry Hardcastle), Maire O'Neill (Mrs. Dorbell), A. Bromley Davenport (Pawnbroker), Peter Gawthorne (Police Inspector), Martin Walker (Ned Narkey), Iris Vandeleur (Mrs. Nattle), Marie Ault (Mrs. Jilke), Marjorie Rhodes (Mrs. Bull), Kenneth Griffith (Tom Hare), B. John Slater (Jackson), Muriel George (Landlady), Charles Williams (Bill Simmons), Collin Chandler (Jack Lindsay), Denis Wyndham (Jim), Jordan Lawrence, James Harcourt, Philip Godfrey, Terry Conlin, Charles Groves.

Filmed in the North Country of England, this is the story of a penniless family struggling through the depression years. Kerr is a mill girl in love with Evans, who loses his job and refuses to marry her on "dole money." He is killed in a demonstration against pay, conditions, and unemployment, and so Kerr marries an old bookie she doesn't love in order to get jobs for her father and brother. This picture is realistic in its portrayal of poverty-stricken families, and although a depressing subject, the writers manage to place some well-timed humor into the script, with sepia-tinted photography capturing the North Country atmosphere and its poverty. Released in England in 1941.

p&d, John Baxter; w, Walter Greenwood, Barbara K. Emary, Rollo Gamble (based on the play by Ronald Gow, from the novel by Greenwood); ph, James Wilson; m, Richard Addinsell; ed, Michael Chorlton; art d, Holmes Paul.

Drama　　　　　　　　　　　　　　　　　　　　　**(PR:A　MPAA:NR)**

LOVE ON THE RIVIERA**

(1964, Fr./Ital.) 88m Cei-Incom-Maxima-Monteluce-Gallus/Ultra c (FEMMES D'UN ETE; RACCONTI D'ESTATE; AKA: SUMMER TALES)

Alberto Sordi (Aristarco Bertolini), Michele Morgan (Micheline), Marcello Mastroianni (Police Inspector), Sylva Koscina (Renata), Gabriele Ferzetti (Ferrari), Dorian Gray (Dorina), Franca Marzi (Clara), Lorella De Luca (Lina), Franco Fabrizi (Sandro), Enio Girolami (Walter), Jorge Mistral (Beach Attendant), Dany Carrel (Jacqueline), Marta Marcelli (Ada), Anita Allan (Bather).

Another Italian romantic-comedy anthology, this containing five vignettes. The first details the doomed romance of a police officer and his female prisoner, who become lovers after being left behind by the train that was transporting her to prison. Though he loves her, the officer cannot, and will not, betray his duty and he finishes his mission. Part two is a brief segment which sees the efforts of a gigolo to bilk a young opera diva frustrated by the girl's mother who insists they wed. The third segment concerns a beautiful, bikini-clad vamp who tries to extort money from wealthy men, but who falls in love with a penniless lifeguard instead. Part four details the efforts of a failing businessman to convince a rich investor to seduce his wife in exchange for a check bailing out his business. The wife refuses the rich man's advances, but the investor writes the check anyway. The last part has a young man involved with both a mother and her daughter. When he begins to pay more attention to the mother, the daughter soon becomes jealous. When he borrows money from the older woman, the daughter uses this as an excuse to kick the bum out. Though her mother becomes depressed, the daughter repays the money and tells her mother that the gigolo has returned it.

p, Mario Cecchi Gori; d, Gianni Franciolini; w, Alberto Moravia, Alberto Sordi, Sergio Amidei, Ennio Flajano, Edoardo Anton, Rodolfo Sonego, Rene Barjavel, Gianni Franciolini (based on a story by Moravia); ph, Enzo Serafin (Totalscope, Eastmancolor); m, Piero Piccioni; ed, Adriana Novelli; art d, Giorgio Giovannini; cos, Ugo Pericoli; spec eff, Goffredo Rocchetti.

Comedy/Drama　　　　　　　　　　　　　　　　**(PR:C　MPAA:NR)**

LOVE ON THE RUN ***　　　　　　　　　　　(1936) 80m MGM bw

Joan Crawford (Sally Parker), Clark Gable (Michael Anthony), Franchot Tone (Barnabas Pells), Reginald Owen (Baron Spandermann), Mona Maris (Baroness), Ivan Lebedeff (Prince Igor), Charles Judels (Lieutenant of Police), William Demarest (Editor), Dewey Robinson (Italian Father), Bobby [Bobs] Watson (Italian Boy), Betty Jane Graham (Italian Girl), Charles Trowbridge (Express Company Manager), George Davis (Sergeant of Police), Donald Meek (Caretaker), Harry Allen (Chauffeur), James B. Carson (French Waiter), Billy Gilbert (Cafe Manager), Reynolds Denniston (Inspector McCaskill), Egon Brecher (Dr. Gorsay), Richard Lancaster (English News Photographer), Donald Kerr, Charles Irwin (Movie Cameraman), Otto H. Fries (Mechanic), Elsa Buchanan, Viola Moore, Iris Moore (English Department Store Girls), Nanette Lafayette (French Maid), Lilyan Irene (Bit), Norman Ainsley (Newspaper Reporter), Jimmy Aubrey (Airplane Mechanic), Bob Cory (Assistant to Inspector McCaskill), Gunnis Davis (Hotel Elevator Man), Douglas Gordon (Cockney Comic Chauffeur), Frank Du Frane (Assistant to Editor), H. L. Fisher-Smith (Reporter), John Power (English Major-Domo), Montague Shaw (Motel Manager), Yorke Sherwood (London Bobby), Tom Herbert (Comic Taxi Driver), Adi Kuznetzoff (Rudolph, Baron's Servant), Phillips Smalley, Richard Powell, Margaret Marquis, Eleanor Stewart, Leonard Kinsky, Jack Dewees (Bits), Alice Ardell (French Maid), Joe Mack (Hack Driver), Duke York (Paul, Baron's Chauffeur), Agostino Borgat (French Comptroller), Fred Cavens, Fred W. Malatesta (French Waiters), Gennaro Curci (French Train Announcer), Alphonse Martel (French Spy), Frank Mayo (Traveling Man), Frank Puglia (Waiter), Genaro Spagnoli (French Taxi Driver), Jacques Vanair (French Telegraph Operator), Viola Moore (Cockney Telephone Girl), Robert du Couedic (French Clerk), Bobby Watson (Assistant Manager), George Andre Berenger (Comedy Reactionary).

Lightweight comedy on the order of IT HAPPENED ONE NIGHT and LOVE IS NEWS in that it concerns a rich American heiress and her various shenanigans. Tone (Crawford's real husband at the time) and Gable are journalists stationed in Europe. Gable and Tone are rivals and Gable is always beating Tone who is forever rankled by that. One of their assignments is to cover an international aviator, Owen, who turns out to be a mean-spirited spy. Another job is to cover the upcoming wedding of devil-may-care madcap Crawford, who is about to marry Lebedeff, an obvious fortune hunter. (The same situation occurred between Loretta Young and George Sanders, with Tyrone Power as the newsman, in LOVE IS NEWS.) Crawford hates newsmen but she doesn't know that's what Gable does for a living when she asks him to help her get out of her marriage to Lebedeff. Gable and Crawford steal Owen's plane and go across Europe by air, car, and draycart while Gable is still pursuing the Owen story and seeking to unmask him as an international agent. Tone is along for the ride and soon enough the trio is marked for assassination by the spies. A long chase ensues and they finally wind up at Fontainebleau in France where the dotty caretaker, Meek, thinks that the long-dead king and queen have come back. Gable cables the story to his paper and the next day Crawford realizes who he is, then angrily takes off for Nice with Tone. On the train, Owen nabs Crawford and Tone is tossed off. Gable gets to a farmhouse where Owen is planning to take off in his plane with the stolen plans for the British fortifications. Tone arrives at the farmhouse and finds Gable tied to a chair. Gable persuades Tone to change places with him and Tone agrees, albeit reluctantly. When the spies return, Gable captures and binds them, then takes off in the plane with Crawford, leaving Tone, the odd man out, still tied to the chair. The creators of the film borrowed a little from here and a bit from there and concocted a pleasant comedy with some excellent set pieces, especially the one at the castle with Meek, as Gable and Crawford don some aging costumes and perform a clunky minuet that winds up as a hula.

p, Joseph L. Mankiewicz; d, W. S. Van Dyke II; w, John Lee Mahin, Manuel Seff, Gladys Hurlbut (based on the story "Beauty and the Beast" by Alan Green, Julian Brodie); ph, Oliver T. Marsh; m, Franz Waxman; ed, Frank Sullivan; art d, Cedric Gibbons; cos, Adrian.

Comedy   (PR:A   MPAA:NR)

LOVE ON THE RUN*1/2**
                    (1980, Fr.) 94m Les Films Du Carosse c (L'AMOUR EN FUITE)
Jean-Pierre Leaud (Antoine Doinel), Marie-France Pisier (Colette), Claude Jade (Christine), Dani (Liliane), Dorothee (Sabine), Rosy Varte (Colette's Mother), Marie Henriau (Divorce Judge), Daniel Mesguich (Xavier the Librarian) Julien Bertheau (Mons. Lucien), Jean-Pierre Ducos (Christine's Lawyer), Pierre Dios (Maitre Renard), Alain Ollivier (Judge Aix), Monique Dury (Mme. Ida), Emmanuel Clot (Antoine's Friend), Christian Lentretien (Train Wolf), Roland Thenot (Angry Telephonist), Julien Dubois (Alphonse Doinel), Alexandre Janssen, Chantal Zaugg (Restaurant Car Children).

The fifth and final entry in Francois Truffaut's "Antoine Doinel" series which began in 1959 with THE 400 BLOWS. By now the young, unruly star of THE 400 BLOWS, Leaud, has grown into a man of 34—able to reminisce about his past loves and put them into his new book. The picture opens with Leaud and his newest love, Dorothee (in a wonderfully charming debut performance), awakening to a sunny morning—the morning that he is to get a divorce from his wife, Jade ("Christine" from 1971's "Doinel" adventure BED AND BOARD). Before the day is out Leaud meets up with his first love Pisier, who we've met years before as "Colette" in the episode Truffaut contributed to LOVE AT TWENTY (1963). There is actually very little in LOVE ON THE RUN that resembles a story. The chief purpose (and the force that drives Leaud) is to take a look back at the women he has loved. Leaud, like so many of Truffaut's characters, is obsessed by the desire to love. Here Leaud tells how he found a ripped-up, discarded picture of Dorothee in a phone booth and set out to find her. In the process, clips are repeatedly shown from THE 400 BLOWS, LOVE AT TWENTY, STOLEN KISSES, and BED AND BOARD, amounting to little more than an overview of the life of Doinel (as well as the lives of both Leaud and Truffaut). By the finale, Leaud has explained to Dorothee how he came to fall in love with her. They embrace (intercut with the rotor scene from THE 400 BLOWS) and decide to "pretend" that they will live happily ever after—the greatest commitment one can expect from the half-baked Doinel character. For those who haven't seen any of the previous "Doinel" pictures, LOVE ON THE RUN will probably be a difficult picture to sit through. But for those who have grown as these characters have grown, this film is a true charmer. As one can expect from Truffaut, LOVE ON THE RUN includes a superb score from Delerue and a perfectly hummable title song from Alain Souchon.

d, Francois Truffaut; w, Truffaut, Marie-France Pisier, Jean Aurel, Suzanne Schiffman; ph, Nestor Almendros; m, Georges Delerue; ed, Martine Barraque; art d, Jean-Pierre Kohut-Svelko; m/l, "L'Amour En Fuite" by Alain Souchon, Laurent Voulzy (sung by Souchon).

Drama/Comedy   **Cas.**   (PR:A-C   MPAA:PG)

LOVE ON THE SPOT**
                    (1932, Brit.) 64m Associated Talking Pictures/RKO bw
Rosemary Ames (Joan Prior), Richard Dolman (Bill Maitland), Aubrey Mather (Mr. Prior), Helen Ferrers (Lady Witchell), W. Cronin Wilson (Inspector MacAndrews), Patrick Ludlow (Mr. Terrington), J. Hubert Leslie (Manager), Margery Binner (Maid), Johnny Singer (Pageboy), Patrick Susands (Cartwright), Elizabeth Arkell.

Musical love story has Mather and Ames as a father-daughter con team. There is a schism between the two, though, when Ames learns that her father has tried to sell some illegal shares to Dolman, her current love interest. But when Dolman turns out to be just as crooked as Mather and Ames (he's after the jewels of hotel guests), the three realize it's time to change their lifestyles for more honest means of support.

p, Basil Dean; d, Graham Cutts; w, John Paddy Carstairs, Reginald Purdell (based on the novel Three of a Kind by Sapper).

Musical   (PR:A   MPAA:NR)

LOVE ON TOAST*1/2   (1937) 65m PAR bw
John Payne (Bill Adams), Stella Adler (Linda Craven), Luis Alberni (Joe Piso), Benny Baker (Egbert), Katherine "Sugar" Kane (Polly Marr), Grant Richards (Clark Sanford), Isabel Jewell (Belle Huntley), Edward Robins (Boswell), William Davidson (Jonathan), Franklin Pangborn (Finley), Daisy Buffert (Hyacinth).

Routine slapstick comedy story revolves around an advertiser's attempt to launch a successful campaign for a soup company. Her angle is to find a Mr. Manhattan who must then choose a Miss Brooklyn as his bride. Payne plays the contestant winner who chooses Kane as his mate. Story ends on a pie-throwing note. Songs include: "I'd Like to Play a Love Scene" (Sam Coslow) and "I Want a New Romance" (Coslow, Burton Lane).

p, Emanual Cohen; d, E. A. Dupont; w, Richard Connell, Jane Storm, Doris Malloy; ph, Charles Schoenbaum; ed, Ray Curtiss; art d, Wiard Ihnen.

Comedy   (PR:A   MPAA:NR)

LOVE ON WHEELS*1/2   (1932, Brit.) 80m Gainsborough/GAU bw
Jack Hulbert (Fred Hopkins), Edmund Gwenn (Philpotts), Leonora Corbett (Jane Russell), Gordon Harker (Briggs), Tony de Lungo (Bronelli), Percy Parsons (Crook), Roland Culver (Salesman), Lawrence Hanray (Commissionaire), Miles Malleson (Porter), Martita Hunt (Demonstrator).

This British musical has Hulbert as a shop assistant who tells Corbett that he is the manager in an effort to impress her. He gets fired, however, and she leaves him. But when he catches some thieves trying to rip off the shop, he is rehired as the store manager. Corbett comes back and he puts her in charge of the store's music department.

p, Michael Balcon; d, Victor Saville; w, Saville, Angus Macphail, Robert Stevenson, Douglas Furber (from the story by Franz Schulz, Ernest Angel); ph, Mutz Greenbaum.

Musical   (PR:A   MPAA:NR)

LOVE PARADE, THE*1/2** (1929) 107m PAR bw (FR: PARADE D'AMOUR)
Maurice Chevalier (Count Alfred Renard), Jeanette MacDonald (Queen Louise), Lupino Lane (Jacques), Lillian Roth (Lulu), Edgar Norton (Major-Domo), Lionel Belmore (Prime Minister), Albert Roccardi (Foreign Minister), Carl Stockdale (Admiral), Eugene Pallette (Minister of War), E. H. Calvert (Sylvanian Ambassador), Russell Powell (Afghan Ambassador), Margaret Fealy (First Lady in Waiting), Virginia Bruce, Josephine Hall, Rosaline Charles, Helen Friend (Ladies in Waiting), Yola D'Avril (Paulette), Andre Cheron (Paulette's Husband), Winter Hall (Priest), Ben Turpin (Cross-Eyed Lackey), Anton Vaverka, Albert De Winton, William Von Hardenburg (Cabinet Ministers), Jean Harlow (Extra in Theater Audience, and on Left Side of Box), Jiggs The Dog.

Students of film lore will find much to recommend in THE LOVE PARADE. It was Lubitsch's first sound film, MacDonald's debut, Chevalier's second picture, and the first of four that they made together. The others were: ONE HOUR WITH YOU, LOVE ME TONIGHT, and THE MERRY WIDOW. This was a rare commodity at the time, in that most musicals of the era were backstage types with wise-cracking chorus girls and songs that stopped, rather than advanced the flow of the action. MacDonald had been discovered on Broadway after appearing in "Yes, Yes, Yvette" (an obvious play on "No No, Nanette"), "Boom Boom," and "Angela". LOVE PARADE broke so much new ground that it was nominated for Oscars in six categories: Best Picture, Best Director, Best Actor, Best Cinematography, Best Decoration, and Best Sound Recording. But the awards were dominated by ALL QUIET ON THE WESTERN FRONT, DISRAELI, and THE BIG HOUSE. Once again, the story is a featherweight item that takes place in a mythical land that seems to exist only in the minds of Hungarian playwrights and their ilk. MacDonald is the Queen of Sylvania and is desperately lonely for male companionship. Chevalier is her emissary to France and has been raking hell so patently that he has been recalled to Sylvania. MacDonald reads of Chevalier's caddishness with a bevy of cuties and wonders if he could make her happy. She has him to her chambers and blatantly asks why he is so renowned as a lover and would he kindly demonstrate, by royal decree, what it is he does that endears him to so many distaffs. He does that eagerly and MacDonald is terribly impressed so she marries him. The country is in need of money and MacDonald is in the middle of attempting to borrow a bundle so Chevalier keeps his place in the background although he knows he could do a better job than she could. This subservient position is anathema to such a chauvinist and he begins to balk at her requests when they become regal demands. The opera is about to open and he is ordered to squire her but refuses so she attends alone. Later, Chevalier shows up and she is thrilled, but he's only come to tell her that he is about to seek a divorce. This job of prince consort does not appeal to him and he feels like the royal gigolo, rather than her husband. He plans to leave the next day for Paris and the attorney who will dissolve this mistaken marriage. Late that night, she returns from the opera and goes to his apartment where she agrees to make him king. They embrace and the picture ends. It's as thin as a fast food burger in story but the execution is so insouciant and bubbly that we don't care about the frail plot. Chevalier has the distinction of performing the first musical soliloquy in a talking picture with "Nobody's Using It Now." Good supporting work from Lillian Roth, Lupino Lane, and Eugene Pallette. Look for Jean Harlow as an extra in two places, in the orchestra and in a theater box, and Ben Turpin does his cross-eyed bit. Although this was a sound picture, large stretches were shot silently, then inserted with sound sequences in an attempt to make it coherent, which it wasn't. Lubitsch was from Germany, where they like their women slightly on the plump side, so he darn near force-fed the svelte MacDonald with heavy foods and milkshakes in order to Rubens her up. Songwriter Schertzinger also directed films from 1917, THE CLODHOPPER to 1941, THE FLEET'S IN (for which he also wrote the tunes.). All the music was written by Victor Schertzinger and Clifford Grey except for "Valse Tatjana" ballet by O. Potoker. Songs include: "Champagne" (sung by Lane),

"Paris, Stay the Same" (sung by Chevalier, Lane, and Jiggs), "Dream Lover" (sung by MacDonald, Fealey, Bruce, Friend, Hall, and Charles), "Anything to Please the Queen" (sung by MacDonald and Chevalier), "Sylvania's Queen" (sung by the chorus), "Let's Be Common" (sung by Lane and Roth), "March of the Grenadiers" (sung by MacDonald and male chorus), "The Queen is Always Right" (sung by Roth, Lane, and chorus).

p, Ernst Lubitsch; d, Lubitsch, Perry Ivins; w, Ernst Vajda, Guy Bolton (based on the play "The Prince Consort" by Leon Xanrof, Jules Chancel); ph, Victor Milner; ed, Merrill White; art d, Hans Dreier; set d, Dreier.

Musical Comedy (PR:A-C MPAA:NR)

LOVE PAST THIRTY* ½ (1934) 64m Monarch bw

Aileen Pringle (Caroline Burt), Theodore von Eltz (Charles Browne), Phyllis Barry (Beth Ramsden), John Marston (Walter Ramsden), Robert Fraser (Don Meredith), Gertrude Messinger (Zelda Burt), Gaylord Pendleton (Sam Adair), Virginia Sales (Nettie), Ben Hall (Junior Bert), Pat O'Malley (Lon Burt), Dot Farley (Dressmaker), Mary Carr (Grandma Nelson).

This picture has von Eltz as the city boy come home to marry his fiancee of 16 years, Pringle. But upon seeing her dowdy appearance, he is sidetracked by Messinger and becomes engaged to her as well. Come to find out, he becomes engaged to every girl he kisses. Pringle dumps him and takes the small fortune she made from her shop and moves into a beauty factory. She returns home to capture her niece's ex-boyfriend, which prompts von Eltz to return to her side and marry her.

p, Vin Moore; w, Earle Snell (based on the novel by Priscilla Wayne); ph, Irving Akers; ed, Fred Bain.

Comedy (PR:A MPAA:NR)

LOVE PLAY (SEE: PLAYTIME, 1963, Fr.)

LOVE PROBLEMS* (1970, Ital.) 101m Salaria-Cormons/RAF Industries c (L'ETA DEL MALESSERE)

Haydee Politoff (Enrica), Jean Sorel (Giorgio), Eleonora Rossi-Drago (Countess), Gabriele Ferzetti (Guido), Salvo Randone, Yorgo Voyagis, Giovanna Galletti, Edy Nogara, Gianni De Luigi, Claudio Gora.

Depressing drama concerning Politoff, a 17-year-old computer student, who seeks to get out of her unhappy home by becoming the mistress of Sorel, a selfish law student. Bored with him, she has affairs with a fellow student and another lawyer, Ferzetti. She becomes pregnant by Sorel, who arranges an abortion through a rich and eccentric countess, Rossi-Drago. Soon after, Politoff becomes Rossi-Drago's secretary, and witnessing the troubles with men encountered by the older woman, she resolves to spend the rest of her life alone.

p, Giancarlo Segarelli; d, Giuliano Biagetti; w, Dacia Maraini, Luciano Lucignani, Biagetti (based on the story, "L'eta Del Malessere" by Maraini); ph, Antonio Borghesi (Eastmancolor); m, Stefano Rossi; ed, Marcella Bevilacqua; art d, Franco Bottari; spec eff, Pino Ferranti.

Drama (PR:C MPAA:R)

LOVE RACE, THE* (1931, Brit.) 83m BIP/Pathe bw

Stanley Lupino (Reggie Powley), Jack Hobbs (Bobbie Mostyn), Dorothy Boyd (Ida Mostyn), Dorothy Bartlam (Rita Payne), Frank Perfitt (Mr. Powley), Wallace Lupino (Ferdinand Fish), Artie Ash (Eustace), Florence Vie (Mrs. Mostyn), Doris Rogers (Nernice Dawn).

Lupino is a race car-driving son of an automobile magnate. His fiancee jumps to conclusions and nearly dumps Lupino when he arrives at a party bearing the wrong suitcase, full of lingerie. Only after Lupino wins a big race against his rival does he win back the woman's heart.

p, Stanley Lupino; d, Lupino Lane, Pat Morton; w, Edwin Greenwood (based on a play by Lupino).

Comedy (PR:A MPAA:NR)

LOVE RACE (SEE: GIRL O' MY DREAMS, 1935)

LOVE RACKET, THE* ½ (1929) 74m FN bw

Dorothy Mackaill (Betty Brown), Sidney Blackmer (Fred Masters), Edmund Burns (George Wayne), Myrtle Stedman (Marion Masters), Edward Davis (Judge Davis), Webster Campbell (Prosecuting Attorney), Clarence Burton (Defense Attorney), Alice Day (Grace Pierce), Edith Yorke (Mrs. Pierce), Martha Mattox (Mrs. Slade), Tom Mahoney (Detective McGuire), Jack Curtis (John Gerrity).

After telling Mackaill that she is not legally married to him, the woman's husband walks out on her. Years go by, and Mackaill ends up on a jury for a murder trial involving similar circumstances. As it turns out, the murder victim proves to be the very man who walked out on Mackaill in the first place. Unfortunately, lack of strong direction and too many impossible coincidences result in a most unbelievable drama.

d, William A. Seiter; w, John F. Goodrich, Adele Commandini (based on the play "Woman on the Jury" by Bernard K. Burns); ph, Sid Hickox; ed, John Rawlins.

Drama (PR:A MPAA:NR)

LOVE REDEEMED (SEE: DRAGNET PATROL, 1932)

LOVE ROBOTS, THE* (1965, Jap.) 63m Olympic International bw

Hidekatsu Shibata, Hideo Sakei, Tamami Wakahara.

Beautiful young girls are snatched off the streets, brainwashed into mindless "robots" who will love or kill on command, and sold to the highest bidder. Enter tough detective Shibata, his sister a victim, who, despite being thrown off the police

force, manages to bust up the crime ring. Routine Japanese crime programmer, heavily re-edited for release in the U.S.

p&d, Koji Wakamatsu; ph, (CinemaScope).

Crime (PR:C MPAA:NR)

LOVE ROOT, THE (SEE: MANDRAGOLA, 1966, Fr./Ital.)

LOVE SLAVES OF THE AMAZONS* (1957) 81m UNIV c

Don Taylor (Dr. Peter Masters), Gianna Segale (Gina), Eduardo Ciannelli (Crespi), Harvey Chalk (Adhemar Silva), John Herbert (Hotel Clerk), Wilson Vianna (Fernando), Eugenio Carlos (Fernando's Brother), Anna Marie Nabuco (Queen), Tom Payne (Mario), Gilda Nery (Ugly Girl), Louis Serrano (Pilot).

Ridiculous attempt at an adventure film, has archaeologist Taylor, together with Ciannelli, stumbling into the land of The Amazons, ferocious, green-skinned women of cat-like nature. Taylor is captured by them, but manages to escape with a white woman played by Segale who's been held captive a while. Script and direction are horribly uneven, making for some unintentionally funny scenes. Performances are lifeless, but a plus can be given to the photography for capturing the beauty of the Brazilian jungle.

p,d,&w, Curt Siodmak; ph, Mario Page (Eastmancolor); m, Radames Gnattali; ed, Terry Morse; md, Joseph Gershenson; art d, Pierino Massenzi; ch, David Condi, Fernanda Condi; m/l, Gnattali.

Fantasy (PR:A MPAA:NR)

LOVE, SOLDIERS AND WOMEN (SEE: DAUGHTERS OF DESTINY, 1953, Fr./Ital.)

LOVE SPECIALIST, THE* (1959, Ital.) 104m GESI/Medallion c (LA RAGAZZA DEL PALIO)

Diana Dors (Diana Wilson), Vittorio Gassman (Prince Bruno), Franca Valeri (Bruno's Aunt), Bruce Cabot (Mike), Teresa Pellati (Laura), Tina Lattanzi (The Princess), Enrico Viarisio (Bruno's Uncle), Nando Bruno (Ferrari), Ronaldino (Tino).

Idiotic film starring Dors as a Texan who wins a quiz show jackpot after demonstrating her grasp of Italian history. She uses her winnings to fund a trip to Italy where she meets up with Gassman (who appeared in far too many of these dim Italian fluffs), an Italian prince who thinks she's rich. She believes he's loaded also, but, like herself, he is broke too. The romance, as well as the film, reach their climax at the Palio horse race where, after learning that Gassman has bribed the rival jockey into throwing the race so that his horse may win, Dors fast-talks the rival horse's owner into letting her ride the pony just to show the haughty prince up. Of course she goes on to win the race and the respect and admiration of Gassman. This really vapid English-dubbed film was a sad waste of Cabot in a small, unimportant role.

p, Maleno Malenotti; d, Luigi Zampa; w, Michael Pertwee, Ennio de Concini, Liani Ferri, Zampa (based on the novel by Raffaello Giannelli); ph, Giuseppe Rotunno (Technirama, Technicolor); ed, Eraldo Da Roma.

Romance (PR:A MPAA:NR)

LOVE STARVED (SEE: YOUNG BRIDE, 1932)

LOVE STORM, THE* ½ (1931, Brit.) 61m BIP/Wardour bw (GB: CAPE FORLORN)

Fay Compton (Eileen Kell), Frank Harvey (William Kell), Ian Hunter (Gordon Kingsley), Edmund Willard (Henry Cass), Donald Calthorp (Parsons).

Melodrama concerning a dance hall girl, Compton, who meets and marries the captain of a lighthouse. She quickly learns to hate the life and becomes embroiled in a torrid affair with her husband's assistant. One day a handsome crook is washed ashore after a storm and the lighthouse floozie falls into his arms. The assistant and the crook get into a violent fight over the woman, but it is Compton who kills her husband's employee. The cops arrive and cart off the crook, but somehow they never arrest Compton for the murder. She finally leaves her husband and waits in sleazy dance halls for her convict/lover's release. Unbelievable and overblown, this film is only worth watching for the fine cinematography by Claude Friese-Greene.

p&d, E. A. Dupont; w, Dupont, Victor Kendall (based on the stage play "Cape Forlorn" by Frank Harvey); ph, Claude Friese-Greene, Walter Blakely, Hal Young, John J. Cox; ed, A. C. Hammond.

Drama (PR:A MPAA:NR)

LOVE STORY (SEE: LADY SURRENDERS, A, 1947, Brit.)

LOVE STORY**

(1949, Fr.) 90m L'Industrie Cinematographique/Cine Classics-French Ideal Films bw (DOUCE)

Odette Joyeux (Douce), Roger Pigaut (Fabien Marani), Marguerite Moreno (Countess de Bonafe), Madeleine Robinson (Irene), Jean Debucourt (Douce's Father).

At a French manor, adolescent Joyeux falls in love with the manager of the estate (Pigaut). The girl is hampered in the romance because of her jealous governess (Robinson) who dreams of a higher station. Joyeux is supported, though, by her father (Debucourt) and the drama comes to a satisfying conclusion. Joyeux gives a rich, honest portrayal of a young girl in love and makes the seemingly tired plot line fresh and energetic. She's given good support by the cast under tightly controlled direction and design which accurately captures Paris in the 1880s. Released in France in 1943, four years before the director's hugely successful DEVIL IN THE FLESH, LOVE STORY appeared nearly simultaneously with the later film in the U.S. It suffered by comparison, and was also hampered by poor subtitling. (In French; English subtitles.)

p&d, Claude Autant-Lara; w, Autant-Lara, Jean Aurenche, Pierre Bost (based on the novel by Michel Davet); ph, Philippe Agostini; m, Rene Cloerec; ed, Madeleine Gug; prod d, Jacques Krauss.

Drama **(PR:C MPAA:NR)**

LOVE STORY*** (1970) 99m PAR c

Ali MacGraw *(Jenny Cavilleri)*, Ryan O'Neal *(Oliver Barrett IV)*, Ray Milland *(Oliver Barrett III)*, Katherine Balfour *(Mrs. Oliver Barrett III)*, John Marley *(Phil Cavilleri)*, Russell Nype *(Dean Thompson)*, Sydney Walker *(Dr. Shapely)*, Robert Modica *(Dr. Addison)*, Walker Daniels *(Ray)*, Tom [Tommy] Lee Jones *(Hank)*, John Merensky *(Steve)*, Andrew Duncan *(Rev. Blauvelt)*, Bob O'Connell *(Tommy the Doorman)*, Sudie Bond, Milo Boulton, Julie Garfield, Charlotte Ford.

"Love Means Never Having To Say You're Sorry" was the catch phrase that helped make this a huge grosser. LOVE STORY was a unique picture because it was actually better than Segal's bestseller from whence it sprang. To show how poorly some actors and directors are when it comes to knowing what's best for them, John Voight, Beau Bridges, and three Michaels—York, Douglas, and Sarrazin—all nixed the script. Directors Anthony Harvey and Larry Peerce (who may hold the record for consecutive bombs) also rejected the script before Hiller took it on. In other hands, it might have been sentimental slush but Hiller's work is excellent and the movie was nominated by the Academy for Best Picture, Best Director, Best Actor, Best Actress, Best Supporting Actor, Best Music, and Best Screenplay From Another Medium. Only the music took the Oscar as PATTON, AIRPORT, and M*A*S*H dominated the proceedings. O'Neal is at Harvard (where much of this was made) in his final pre-law year, when he meets and falls for MacGraw, a Radcliffe student studying music. She's a poor girl from a lower class family and he is one of the Boston Brahmins. O'Neal's father, Milland, won't hear of his son and heir marrying the daughter of an Italian baker and says he'll cut him off without a farthing. Love triumphs over money and O'Neal and MacGraw wed. With no money coming in, O'Neal has to apply for a scholarship to study law but the dean, Nype, thinks it ludicrous that a millionaire's son is asking for financial aid and decrees that O'Neal must pay his own tuition if he wants to have the prestigious Harvard degree. MacGraw has already bypassed a scholarship to study music in France in favor of the wedding. O'Neal takes a series of jobs to support them and they move into an apartment in a poor section of the Hub City that they can barely afford on MacGraw's salary as a vocal coach for a school choir. Still, they are ecstatically happy with each other. He graduates high in the class and gets a job with an important New York law firm. They move into a nice apartment and decide it's time to have a baby. Though they try hard, it's not working and so they go to see a doctor about what to do regarding her barren condition (or is it his fault?). Their physician, Walker, now tells O'Neal that MacGraw is dying. O'Neal is reeling with shock but must put on a happy face for his wife, whom he assumes knows nothing about her impending demise. Then he learns that she also knows and she declines his offer to take her to France, a place she's always wanted to see. She would prefer, instead, to spend her last days with him at home. Time passes. She's taken to the hospital and O'Neal has to borrow money from his father to pay for the expenses, but he won't tell Milland why. She dies in O'Neal's arms and Milland comes to the hospital to apologize for his earlier behavior, saying that he's sorry. O'Neal retorts with the famous line mentioned above, then walks past the old, bald man, and out into Central Park to think about what might have been. It's touching, well-made, and expertly intentioned to wring hankies. Segal's dialog is often sappy and not nearly as good as the actors who must deliver it. The same subject was examined in TERMS OF ENDEARMENT many years later. That picture nailed several awards but was inferior to this one on most levels. It had, however, Jack Nicholson to add humor to the grim proceedings and that may have been the reason for its success. A picture that touched everyone who saw it, LOVE STORY can take its place with DARK VICTORY and LOVE AFFAIR in the ranks of the excellent romantic films for which Hollywood is so famous.

p, Howard G. Minsky; d, Arthur Hiller; w, Erich Segal (based on his novel); ph, Dick Kratina (Movielab Color); m, Francis Lai; ed, Robert C. Jones; art d, Robert Gundlach; set d, Phil Smith; cos, Alice Manougian Martin, Pearl Somner; makeup, Martin Bell.

Drama **Cas.** **(PR:A-C MPAA:GP)**

LOVE—TAHITI STYLE (SEE: NUDE ODYSSEY 1962, Fr./Ital.)

LOVE TAKES FLIGHT* (1937) 70m Condor/GN bw

Bruce Cabot *(Neil Bradshaw)*, Beatrice Roberts *(Joan Lawson)*, John Sheehan *(Spud Johnson)*, Astrid Allwyn *(Diane Audre)*, Elliot Fisher *(Tommy)*, Gordon [William] Elliott *(Bill Parker)*, Edwin Maxwell *(Dave Miller)*, Harry Tyler *(Stone)*, William Moore *(Rice)*, Grady Sutton *(Donald)*, Arthur Hoyt *(Grey)*, William Thorn *(Parker, Sr.)*, Brooks Benedict *(Eddie)*, Henry Roquemore *(Bartender)*, Carol Tevis.

Actor Nagel's first and last try at directing had the full cooperation of American Airlines, and a grateful Nagel made the film virtually a commercial sales vehicle for that company. Cabot is a pilot who deserts his craft for a career in films. His jilted lady friend, airline stewardess Roberts, retaliates by trying to make a solo flight in a commandeered aircraft. Cabot catches on to her scheme and stows away to save the day, parachuting to earth just in time to ensure that she receives due credit for the feat. Not a nice maiden flight as director for Nagel.

p, George A. Hirliman; d, Conrad Nagel; w, Lionel Mervin Houser (based on a story by Ann Morrison Chapin); ph, Mack Stengler; ed, Tony Martinelli; md, Abe Myer; art d, F. Paul Sylos.

Drama **(PR:A MPAA:NR)**

LOVE TEST, THE** (1935, Brit.) 63m FOX bw

Judy Gunn *(Mary)*, Louis Hayward *(John)*, David Hutcheson *(Thompson)*, Morris Harvey *(President)*, Googie Withers *(Minnie)*, Aubrey Dexter *(Vice-President)*, Eve Turner *(Kathleen)*, Bernard Miles *(Allan)*, Gilbert Davis, Shayle Gardner, James Craig, Jack Knight.

A comedy of the sexes has a group of laboratory chemists upset when they learn Gunn may soon be put in charge of their group. Hayward attempts to seduce her in order to keep her in her place but ends up falling in love with her instead. In a dire attempt to stop Gunn, Hutcheson steals an important formula with the idea of blaming it on Gunn, but his plot is discovered and all ends happily. A minor British programmer and an early directorial effort for Powell.

p, John Findlay; d, Michael Powell; w, Selwyn Jepson (based on a story by Jack Celestin).

Comedy **(PR:A MPAA:NR)**

LOVE THAT BRUTE 1/2** (1950) 85m FOX bw

Paul Douglas *(Big Ed Hanley)*, Jean Peters *(Ruth Manning)*, Cesar Romero *(Pretty Willie)*, Keenan Wynn *(Bugs)*, Joan Davis *(Mamie)*, Arthur Treacher *(Quentin)*, Peter Price *(Harry)*, Jay C. Flippen *(Biff)*, Barry Kelley *(Burly Detective)*, Leon Belasco *(Ducray)*, Edwin Max *(Puggy)*, Sid Tomack *(Louie)*, Phil Tully *(Detective Lieutenant)*, Clara Blandick *(Landlady)*, Jimmie Hawkins *(Freddie Van Zandt)*, Judith Ann Vroom *(Gwendolyn)*, Grayce Hampton *(Dowager)*, Leif Erickson *(Commandant)*, Marion Marshall *(Dawn O'Day)*, Dick Wessel, John Doucette, Arthur O'Connell, Eugene Gericke *(Reporters)*, Lester Allen *(Agent)*, Billy Chaney, Dan Riss, Charles Lane, Frank "Billy" Mitchell, Tiny Timbrell, Sid Marion, Charles Evans, Stan Johnson, Mauritz Hugo.

Cute 1920s gangster spoof about a racketeer, Douglas, who turns out to be a soft-hearted slob (the kind of role he played so well and so often) over Peters, the recreational director of a city park. Douglas is nuts about her and wants to get her into his house so he decides to masquerade as a widower and hire her as his children's governess. Since he doesn't have any children, he sends underling Wynn out to hire a couple of kids who will fill the bill. There's a very funny interview with prospective child Price, a street tough, and the kid begins to talk like Bogart, Cagney, and Robinson all in one. Peters eventually realizes she's been duped and thinks Douglas may be another Capone, so she exits. Meanwhile, Douglas and Romero have been battling over control of the city and they agree to cease and desist after it appears that Douglas has eliminated Romero's left- and righthand men. The truth is that the two hoods are locked in Douglas' cellar. In the end, Romero tries to rub out Douglas but another body is switched for Douglas' and Romero is caught and convicted for a crime that never happened, thus leaving Douglas to go straight in order to please Peters, the woman he loves. The story owes a lot to Damon Runyon although he is not credited anywhere. Many of the gangster characters are the lovable Broadway sort which is, of course, just fanciful, as they are anything but lovable. Most of the picture is familiar stuff but there's enough of a twist on the tried-and-true material to give it some originality. Peters also gets to sing the old Rodgers and Hart standard, "You Took Advantage Of Me."

p, Fred Kohlmar; d, Alexander Hall; w, Karl Tunberg, Darrell Ware, John Lee Mahin; ph, Lloyd Ahern; m, Cyril Mockridge; ed, Nick DeMaggio; md, Lionel Newman; art d, Lyle Wheeler, Richard Irvine; m/l, Richard Rodgers, Lorenz Hart.

Crime/Comedy **(PR:A MPAA:NR)**

LOVE, THE ITALIAN WAY**

(1964, Ital.) 90m Serena/Trans-Lux c (FEMMINE DI LUSSO; AKA: LOVE ITALIAN STYLE)

Elke Sommer *(Greta)*, Walter Chiari *(Walter)*, Sylva Koscina *(Luciana)*, Ugo Tognazzi *(Hugo)*, Gabriele Ferzetti *(Count Luca di Sauvin/Albert Bressan)*, Belinda Lee *(Elena/Adriana Bressan)*, Gino Cervi *(Lemeni)*, Massimo Serato *(Sicilian Nobleman)*, Caprice Chantal *(Adrienne)*, Gisella Sofio *(Marilla)*, Ivan Desny *(Albert)*, Mario Scaccia *(Butler)*, Malo St. George *(Indian Girl)*, Gino Bartali.

A complicated romantic comedy detailing the sexual escapades of a shipful of rich zanies out for a cruise on a millionaire's yacht. The guests include a French businessman, his opera-star wife, his mistress, his wife's lover, a Count that the businessman has hired to seduce his wife so that he can obtain a divorce, the millionaire's girl friend, and his son, a gorgeous model hired by the millionaire to spark his son's interest in women, and, of course, a photographer who documents the activities. Eventually the confusion clears and everyone finds someone to fall in love with.

p, Dario Sabatello; d, George White [Giorgio Bianchi]; w, Roberto Gianviti, Vittorio Metz, Oreste Biancoli; ph, Tino Santoni (Technicolor); art d, Franco Fontana; cos, Elio Costanzi, Guiulia Mafai; m/l, "Femmine de Lusso," Domenico Modugno (sung by Modugno), "Te Voglio Stasera," "Per un Attimo," Carlo Rustichelli (sung by Peppino Di Capri), "Casta Diva" (sung by Gina Cigna).

Romance/Comedy **(PR:C MPAA:NR)**

LOVE THY NEIGHBOR** (1940) 82m PAR bw

Jack Benny *(Jack Benny)*, Fred Allen *(Fred Allen)*, Mary Martin *(Mary Allen)*, Verree Teasdale *(Barbara Allen)*, Eddie Anderson *(Rochester)*, Virginia Dale *(Virginia Astor)*, Theresa Harris *(Josephine)*, Richard Denning *(Joe)*, Jack Carson *(Policeman)*, Mary Kelley *(Chambermaid)*, Chester Clute *(Judge)*, Judd McMichael, Ted McMichael, Joe McMichael, Helen Carroll *(The Merry Macs)*, Russell Hicks *(Mr. Harrington)*, Barnett Parker *(George)*, The Merriel Abbott Dancers.

The four-year radio feud between Allen and Benny is brought to the screen here, but not in as successful a fashion as in their radio programs. The picture was highly promoted before its release, but this didn't help it at the box office. Allen's niece, Martin, attempts to be a go-between in the continual feud. She and Benny eventually fall in love and marry. Apart from the weak story line, there are plenty of moments for some good humor—mainly on the part of Anderson as Rochester—and some snappy vocal tunes. Direction manages to keep pace with the actors. Songs include: "Do You Know Why," "Isn't That Just Like Love," "Dearest Darest

I'' (Johnny Burke, Jimmy Van Heusen) and "My Heart Belongs To Daddy" (Cole Porter—sung by Mary Martin).

p&d, Mark Sandrich; w, William Morrow, Edmund Beloin, Ernest Pagano, Z. Myers; ph, Ted Tetzaff; ed, LeRoy Stone.

Comedy   **(PR:A MPAA:NR)**

LOVE TIME*   (1934) 72m FOX bw

Pat Paterson (*Valerie*), Nils Asther (*Franz Schubert*), Herbert Mundin (*Caesar*), Harry Green (*Adam*), Henry B. Walthall (*Duke Johann von Hatzfeld*), Lucien Littlefield (*Willie Obenbiegler*), Henry Kolker (*Emperor Francis 1st*), James Burke (*Benjamin*), Josephine Whittell (*Mrs. Obenbiegler*), Albert Conti, Herman Bing, Roger Imhof, Earle Foxe, Georgia Caine, Paul England, Mary Blackford.

Romanticized version of the love life of composer Franz Schubert. Paterson plays the daughter of a Duke exiled by the Emperor because of her mother's marriage. She tries to make plans for an elopement with the composer, Asther, but he flees because he does not want to ruin Paterson's life. But the girl never gives up in her pursuit of the composer. The story is thin, with an attempt to pad it with unneeded dramatics and misplaced comic relief. The direction is uneven, with Paterson poorly cast. The rest of the performances are good, but wasted.

d, James Tinling; w, William Conselman, Henry Johnson, Lynn Starling, Sally Sandlin (based on a story by Richard Carroll); ph, Arthur Miller; ed, Alex Troffey; m/l, Samuel Kaylin, Sidney Clare.

Drama   **(PR:A MPAA:NR)**

LOVE TRADER*   (1930) 66m TIF bw (GB: ISLAND OF DESIRE)

Leatrice Joy (*Martha Adams*), Roland Drew (*Tonia*), Henry B. Walthall (*Capt. Adams*), Barbara Bedford (*Luane*), Noah Beery, Jr. (*Capt. Morton*), Chester Conklin (*Nelson*), Clarence Burton (*John*), William Welsh (*Benson*), Tom Mahoney, Jack Curtis.

Dull, romantic yarn has a wife accompanying her New England sea captain husband on a journey to the South Seas. She is a woman of puritanical upbringing, subordinate to the wishes of her husband. When docked on an island, the captain goes ashore, making his wife stay on board the ship. Her singing and guitar playing attract a local islander, and the two fall in love. The wife is torn between her duty to her husband and the freedom the islander offers her. Thin story suffers from characters that are never fully developed.

p, Joseph Henabery, Harold Shumate; d, Henabery; w, Shumate; ph, Ernest Miller, Pliny Goodfriend.

Drama   **(PR:A MPAA:NR)**

LOVE TRAP, THE**   (1929) 63m UNIV bw

Laura La Plante (*Laura Todd*), Neil Hamilton (*Peter Cadwallader*), Robert Ellis (*Guy Emory*), Jocelyn Lee (*Bunny*), Norman Trevor (*Judge Cadwallader*), Clarissa Selwynne (*Mrs. Cadwallader*), Rita Le Roy (*Mary Cadwallader*).

Light-hearted entertainment has La Plante as a chorus girl out of her job, and soon after, out of her apartment. She is saved by a cabbie who offers his taxi as shelter. The two eventually marry, to the disdain of his stuffy, but wealthy uncle. This early talkie features both captions and dialog.

d, William Wyler; w, John B. Clymer, Clarence J. Marks, Clarence Thompson, Albert De Mond (based on a story by Edward J. Montagne); ph, Gilbert Warrenton; ed, Maurice Pivar.

Comedy   **(PRL:A MPAA:NR)**

LOVE UNDER FIRE*1/2   (1937) 70m FOX bw

Loretta Young (*Myra Cooper*), Don Ameche (*Tracy Egan*), Borrah Minevich and His Gang (*Themselves*), Frances Drake (*Pamela Beaumont*), Walter Catlett (*Tip Conway*), John Carradine (*Capt. Delmar*), Sig Rumann (*Gen. Montero*), Harold Huber (*Lt. Chavez*), Katherine de Mille (*Rosa*), E. E. Clive (*Capt. Bowden*), Don Alvarado (*Lt. Cabana*), Georges Renavent (*Capt. Contreas*), Clyde Cook (*Bert*), George Regas (*Lt. de Vega*), Claude King (*Cunningham*), Francis McDonald (*Officer*), David Clyde (*McWhirter*), Egon Brecher (*Civilian*), Juan Torena (*Captain*), Holmes Herbert (*Darnley*), George Humbert (*Porter*), Alphonse Martell (*French Official*), Martin Garralaga (*Luis*).

Confusing plot has Young as the alleged robber of a valuable necklace, which belongs to her boss. Ameche, a Scotland yard investigator, tracks Young down in Spain at the outbreak of the civil war. He falls in love with her, and the two attempt a get away to a British ship. It is never made clear whether Young actually *stole* the diamonds. The script is confusing, with a mishmash of unresolved items. The uneven direction offers no aid, placing musical numbers in at inappropriate times.

p, Nunnally Johnson; d, George Marshall; w, Gene Fowler, Allen Rivkin, Ernest Pascal (based on the play "The Fugitives" by Walter Hackett); ph, Ernest Palmer, ed, Barbara McLean; md, Arthur Lange; art d, Rudolph Sternad; m/l, "Language of Love," Samuel Pokrass.

Drama   **(PR:A MPAA:NR)**

LOVE UNDER THE CRUCIFIX**

(1965, Jap.) 102m Shochiku/Shochiku Films of America c (O-GIN SAMA)

Ineko Arima (*Gin Sama*), Ganjiro Nakamura (*Rikyu Senno*), Mieko Takamine (*Riki*), Tatsuya Nakadai (*Ukon Takayama*), Osamu Takizawa (*Hideyoshi Toyotomi*), Yumeji Tsukioka (*Yodo Gimi*), Koji Nanbara (*Mitsunari Ishida*), Keiko Kishi, Manami Fuji.

Set in 16th Century Japan, this film traces the ordeal of a young woman (Arima) who has fallen in love with Nakadai, a Christian and a married man. Though Arima does marry, she never ceases to love him. Years pass before the pair have an affair, but the circumstances which surround their meeting are less than perfect. Christi-

anity has been outlawed, so Nakadai has been forced into hiding, while Arima finds herself trapped inside a loveless marriage with a husband who attempts to use his wife to gain influence with the local political chieftain. A tragic end comes to Arima when word is leaked out about their affair with the Christian; she takes her life. LOVE UNDER THE CRUCIFIX was directed by Tanaka, at one time an actress and a rarity in the Japanese cinema in that she was perhaps the only woman director in that male-dominated society. She uses the story to explore the societal restrictions which keep individuals from expressing their true desires, concentrating on the problems which arise when a woman attempts to assert herself in a society where men make all the rules. (In Japanese; English subtitles.)

p, Sennosuke Tsukimori, Shigeru Wakatsuki; d, Kinuyo Tanaka; w, Masashige Narusawa (based on the novel *O-gin Sama* by Toko Kon); ph, Yoshio Miyajima (Shochiku Grandscope, Eastmancolor); m, Hikaru Hayashi; art d, Jun-ichi Osumi.

Drama   **(PR:A MPAA:NR)**

LOVE UP THE POLE*1/2   (1936, Brit.) 82m British Comedies/BUT bw

Ernie Lotinga (*Jimmy Josser*), Vivienne Chatterton (*Mrs. Berwick*), Wallace Lupino (*Maj. Toulonge*), Jack Frost (*Spud Walker*), Davina Craig (*Annie Noakes*), Lorna Hubbard (*Joan*), Harold Wilkinson (*Ramolini*), Fred Schwartz (*Mosenstein*), Phyllis Dixey (*Patient*), John Kevan (*Jack*), Max Avieson, Teddy Brogden, Bobbie Slater, Clarence Blakiston, Fred Gretton, Henry Wolston, Langley Howard, Frank Tilton, Doyle Crossley, John Dudley.

When two waiters (Lotinga and Frost) are mistaken for a pair of jewel thieves, the *garcons* must take it on the lam. They find out who the real culprits are, and from then on it's one long chase on land and water until they catch the crooks. The comedy had potential but the treatment here is a complete waste. The film drags on and on much longer than need be and the direction is thoroughly incompetent.

p, Norman Hope-Bell; d, Clifford Gulliver; w, Con West, Herbert Sargent, Ernest Lotinga (based on the play by West, Sargent); ph, Jack Parker.

Comedy   **(PR:A MPAA:NR)**

LOVE WAGER, THE**   (1933, Brit.) 64m Anglo-European/PAR bw

Pat Paterson (*Peggy*), Frank Stanmore (*Shorty*), Wallace Douglas (*Peter Neville*), Morton Selten (*Gen. Neville*), Moira Dale (*Auntie Prue*), H. Saxon-Snell (*Huxter*), Hugh E. Wright (*Noakes*), Philip Godfrey (*Ed Grimes*), Harry Terry.

Selten is a general who bets his novelist-son Douglas that the boy can't earn 1500 pounds in one year. Douglas wants the money in order to marry sweetheart Paterson, and he finally seizes the opportunity to make the cash when some jewels of Selten's are stolen. Enter Dale, a local advice columnist and friend of Douglas. She convinces his father to put up a reward in the exact amount of the bet and then helps Douglas to catch the thieves. Lots of plot twists in this silly, low-budget British production.

p, E. A. Fell; d, A. Cyran; w, Moira Dale

Comedy   **(PR:A MPAA:NR)**

LOVE WALTZ, THE**   (1930, Ger.) 70m UFA bw (LIEBESWALZER)

Julia Serda (*Duchess of Lauenburg*), Lilian Harvey (*Princess Eva*), Karl Ludwig Diehl (*Court Marshal*), Lotte Spira (*Archduchess Melany*), Georg Alexander (*Archduke Peter Ferdinand*), Hans Junkermann (*Fould*), Willy Fritsch (*Bobby*), Victor Schwannecke (*Dr. Lemke*), Karl Ettlinger (*Dr. Popper*), John Batten, Gertrude de Lolsky, Lilian Mower.

Light-hearted love story about a princess engaged to a duke who runs out on the engagement, allowing a young man to take his place. While impersonating the duke, the young man falls in love with the princess and they eventually marry, but not before complications arise. The script moves well, though lapsing in predictability. Harvey and Batten deliver their lines in their native English, but the rest of the dialog is dubbed, not always successfully.

p, Erich Pommer; d, Wilhelm Thiele, C. Winston; w, Hans Meueller, Robert Liebmann; ph, Werner Brandes; m, Werner R. Heymann.

Comedy   **(PR:A MPAA:NR)**

LOVE WITH THE PROPER STRANGER***

(1963) 102m Boardwalk-Rona/PAR bw

Natalie Wood (*Angie Rossini*), Steve McQueen (*Rocky Papasano*), Edie Adams (*Barbie, Barbara of Seville*), Herschel Bernardi (*Dominick Rossini*), Tom Bosley (*Anthony Colombo*), Harvey Lembeck (*Julio Rossini*), Penny Santon (*Mama Rossini*), Virginia Vincent (*Anna*), Nick Alexander (*Guido Rossini*), Augusta Ciolli (*Mrs. Papasano*), Ann Hegira (*Beetie*), Mario Badolati (*Elio Papasano*), Elena Karam (*Woman Doctor*), Nina Varela (*Mrs. Colombo*), Marilyn Chris (*Gina*), Wolfe Barzell (*The Priest*), Keith Worthey (*Negro Boy*), Henry Howard (*Lou*), Frank Marth (*Carlos*), Richard Bowler (*Flower Vendor*), Lennie Bremen (*Truck Driver*), Nobu McCarthy (*Yuki*), Jean Shulman (*Charlene*), Lou Herbert (*Harold*), M. Enserro (*Moish*), Barney Martin (*Sidney*), Louis Guss (*Flooey*), Tony Mordente (*Fat*), Val Avery (*Stein*), Richard Mulligan (*Louie*), Paul Price (*Klepp*), Arlene Golonka (*Marge*), Richard Dysart (*Accountant*), Loraine Abate (*Maria*), Vincent Deadrick (*Call Boy*), Victor Tayback (*Cye*).

This is sort of the female version of MARTY in that Wood, who got her third Oscar nomination for the role, is a quiet Italian girl tossed into a situation she finds difficult to handle. The major flaw in it is that Wood is portrayed as such a sweet and traditional type that it's not easy to believe she would have done what she's done; i.e. get pregnant in a one-night stand with McQueen. They'd been up at a summer hotel where he was working as a jazz musician and when she comes to his union hall one day Wood tells him what's happened and says she needs his help to find a doctor who will help them out of this pickle. He asks Adams, his regular girl friend, for advice and she is angered by his affair and tosses him out. At the same time,

Wood's family, mama Santon and brothers Bernardi and Lembeck, have no idea she's expecting and are pushing her to marry Bosley, a pudgy, self-effacing owner of a small restaurant. McQueen attempts to raise the money for the abortionist, then takes Wood to meet his parents, who fall under her charm. McQueen hates the thought of Wood having to go through the surgery but she realizes he is not a great prospect for marriage. Further, Bosley now knows that she is pregnant and has told people that it is his child, so he is more than willing to marry her. McQueen and Wood attempt to reconcile and the film ends as they embrace. The theme of unmarried pregnancy had been seen often before (e.g. BLUE DENIM) but was not usually handled as deftly as in this picture. Lots of earthy Italian humor from Bosley, Lembeck, and Bernardi (all Jewish, by the way) in the earthy Italian screenplay by Shulman (who is as Italian as gefilte fish). Matter of fact, none of the leads were Italian and the casting was slightly off for that reason. Adams almost steals the picture as McQueen's stripper girl friend. She always had a way with comedy and showed it early when playing the foil for her late genius husband, Ernie Kovacs. In small roles, look for Richard Mulligan, Arlene Golonka, Vic Tayback, and Richard Dysart, all of whom later achieved success on TV. Harvey Lembeck was just starting his phenomenally successful improvisation class that graduated many stars. Oscar nominations went to the screenplay and the cinematography in addition to Wood.

p, Alan J. Pakula; d, Robert Mulligan; w, Arnold Schulman; ph, Milton Krasner; m, Elmer Bernstein; ed, Aaron Stell; art d, Hal Pereira, Roland Anderson; set d, Sam Comer, Grace Gregory; cos, Edith Head; m/l, title song, Schulman, Bernstein (sung by Jack Jones); makeup, Wally Westmore, Ed Butterworth.

Comedy/Drama **(PR:C MPAA:NR)**

LOVED ONE, THE*** (1965) 116m MGM bw

Robert Morse *(Dennis Barlow)*, Jonathan Winters *(Wilbur Glenworthy/Harry Glenworthy)*, Anjanette Comer *(Aimee Thanatogenos)*, Rod Steiger *(Mr. Joyboy)*, Dana Andrews *(Gen. Brinkman)*, Milton Berle *(Mr. Kenton)*, James Coburn *(Immigration Officer)*, John Gielgud *(Sir Francis Hinsley)*, Tab Hunter *(Guide)*, Margaret Leighton *(Mrs. Kenton)*, Liberace *(Mr. Starker)*, Roddy McDowall *(D. J., Jr.)*, Robert Morley *(Sir Ambrose Abercrombie)*, Lionel Stander *(Guru Brahmin)*, Ayllene Gibbons *(Joyboy's Mother)*, Bernie Kopell *(Assistant to Guru Brahmin)*, Asa Maynor *(Secretary to D. J. Jr.)*, Alan Napier *(English Club Official)*, Martin Ransohoff *(Lorenzo Medici)*, Roxanne Arlen, Pamela Curran, Claire Kelly *(Whispering Glades Hostesses)*, John Bleifer *(Mr. Bogaloff)*, Bella Bruck *(Mrs. Bogaloff)*, Ed Reimers *(Whispering Glades Minister)*, Paul H. Williams *(Gunther Fry)*, "Miss Beverly Hills" *(Orgy Dancer)*, Chick Hearn *("Resurrection Now" TV Announcer)*, Brad Moore, Dort Clark, Robert Easton, Don Haggerty, Warren Kemmerling, Reta Shaw, Barik Trone.

This spoof on morticians, funerals and, in general, the dearly departed, captures much of the macabre hilarity in the Waugh novel but failed to impress critics at the time of release. It often sinks into broad burlesque under Southern's heavy-handed script but the dark laughs are still there. Morse, a naive, rather gawky character from England, visits his uncle, Gielgud, an aging, fussy art director living in a dilapidated Hollywood mansion. When his studio fires him, Gielgud hangs himself and Morley arrives as head of the British community of Hollywood talent and instructs Morse to arrange to have Gielgud buried at Whispering Glades Memorial Park (another name for the real life Forest Lawn), the most resplendant funeral grounds in America, run by Winters. Morse, while contacting morticians, obtains a job at a pet cemetery run by Winters'twin brother, also played by Winters, and the various schemes, scams, and unconcern by morticians for both humans and pets are revealed in all their callous glories. A host of bizarre characters then parade through Morse's life, including Comer, a sultry naive beauty he covets and who is lusted after by Winters (the one running the high-class mortuary) and Steiger, a crackpot cosmetologist who works with her. Comer is repelled by Steiger's obese and gluttonous mother and is almost won over by Morse who reads poetry (stolen from Steiger) to her. Then Comer's ideals are smashed by Winters, head of Whispering Glades, when he tries to seduce her and she commits suicide by injecting herself with embalming fluid. A further plot develops when Morse discovers that Winters, in collusion with Andrews, an Air Force general, plans to get rid of all the bodies on his property by sending them into space so he can transform his cemetery into a luxurious spa for retirees, making even more millions. He is foiled by Morse who replaces the body of a dead astronaut, the first to be shot into space, with Comer's comely corpse. Having exposed Winters and sent him to ruin, Morse returns to England to try and forget his morbid, morose, and strange experience in America. Morse is unappealing but the supporting players, especially Winters, and bits performed by Stander, Coburn, and Hunter are very funny.

p, John Calley, Haskell Wexler; d, Tony Richardson; w, Terry Southern, Christopher Isherwood (based on the novel by Evelyn Waugh); ph, Haskell Wexler; m, John Addison; ed, Antony Gibbs; prod d, Rouben Ter-Arutunian; art d, Sydney Z. Litwack; set d, James Payne; cos, Nat Tolmach, Ter-Arutunian, James Kelly, Marie T. Harris; spec eff, Geza Gaspar; makeup, Emile La Vigne, Bunny Armstrong.

Comedy **(PR:C MPAA:NR)**

LOVELESS, THE½** (1982) 83m Pioneer/Mainline c

William Dafoe, Robert Gordon, Marin Kanter, J. Don Ferguson, Tina L'Hotsky, Lawrence Matarese, Danny Rosen, Phillip Kimbrough, Ken Call, Elisabeth Gans, Margaret Jo Lee, John King, Bob Hannah, Jane Berman.

This independent film, made by a pair of recent film school graduates, pays homage to THE WILD ONE with a mise-en-scene heavily influenced by the paintings of Edward Hopper. The simple plot has a group of bikers stopping in a small town on their way to a big race in Daytona. There's not much more to THE LOVELESS than that, as the story just ambles along, packed with rockabilly tunes and not much dialog. As independent features go, it's not bad for a first effort, boasting of an often fascinating mise-en-scene. Overall though, this really isn't much more than an exercise by young filmmakers eager to show what they can do.

p, Grafton Nunes, A. Kitman Ho; d&w, Kathryn Bigelow, Monty Montgomery; ph, Doyle Smith; m, Robert Gordon; ed, Nancy Kantner; prod d, Lilly Kivert.

Drama **Cas.** **(PR:O MPAA:R)**

LOVELY TO LOOK AT (SEE: THIN ICE, 1937)

LOVELY TO LOOK AT*** (1952) 101m MGM c

Kathryn Grayson *(Stephanie)*, Red Skelton *(Al Marsh)*, Howard Keel *(Tony Naylor)*, Marge Champion *(Clarisse)*, Gower Champion *(Jerry Ralby)*, Ann Miller *(Bubbles Cassidy)*, Zsa Zsa Gabor *(Zsa Zsa)*, Kurt Kasznar *(Max Fogelsby)*, Marcel Dalio *(Pierre)*, Diane Cassidy *(Diane)*.

Okay remake of RKO's ROBERTA with lots of splash, color, and some excellent interpretations of a sensational score. Skelton, Champion, and Keel want to put a show on Broadway but can't raise the necessary. Miller is a chorine who is sweet on Keel and she offers them everything she has but they decline, knowing how risky that business is. Skelton's aunt has just passed away and left him a portion of her dress salon in Paris so the trio depart for the City Of Light in the hopes of selling Skelton's share and raising enough for their show. Once in Paris, they meet Grayson and Champion (Marge), two sisters who had been adopted by the old lady and who now own the other half of the store. The guys are shocked to learn that the salon is on its last needles and pins. To make the place successful enough to sell, Keel comes up with an idea: how about making this into a musical fashion show and get famed designer Adrian to create some new gowns? The shop's creditors, realizing that unless they do something they will be out of a lot of money, put some francs into the enterprise and hope for a miracle. Keel is falling for Grayson, much to the annoyance of Miller, who has by now come in from New York. Champion is falling for Champion (what did you expect? They were married at that time) and Skelton also has the warms for Grayson. Gabor is a model in rehearsal for the show and introduces them to her beau, Kasznar, a producer who will put up the money for their show on the proviso that they leave Paris at once. Skelton, Champion, and Miller refuse to walk out on Grayson and Champion but Keel goes to New York, only to realize that he can't do it alone. Kasznar and Keel return to Paris and the musical fashion show is a smash. Keel and Grayson are in love, the Champions are in love, and Miller and Skelton begin to see something in each other at the fade. The score included: "Opening Night," "Smoke Gets In Your Eyes," "Lovely To Look At," "The Touch of Your Hand," "Yesterdays," "I Won't Dance," "You're Devastating," "The Most Exciting Night," and "I'll Be Hard to Handle." The humor is slight, the fashions are gaudy, and the story is a trifle but all this is more than compensated for by Kern's music and Pan's choreography.

p, Jack Cummings; d, Mervyn LeRoy; w, George Wells, Harry Ruby, Andrew Solt (based on the Jerome Kern-Dorothy Fields-Otto Harbach musical comedy "Roberta" from the novel by Alice Duer Miller); ph, George J. Fosley (Technicolor); ed, John McSweeney, Jr.; md, Carmen Dragon, Saul Chaplin; art d, Cedric Gibbons, Gabriel Scognamillo; set d, Edwin B. Willis, Jack D. Moore; cos, Adrian; spec eff, A. Arnold Gillespie; ch, Hermes Pan; m/l, Jerome Kern, Dorothy Fields, Otto A. Harbach, Jimmy McHugh, Oscar Hammerstein II; makeup, Sydney Guilaroff.

Musical Comedy **(PR:A MPAA:NR)**

LOVELY WAY TO DIE, A**

(1968) 103m UNIV c (GB: A LOVELY WAY TO GO)

Kirk Douglas *(Jim Schuyler)*, Sylva Koscina *(Rena Westabrook)*, Eli Wallach *(Tennessee Fredericks)*, Kenneth Haigh *(Jonathan Fleming)*, Martyn Green *(Finchley)*, Sharon Farrell *(Carol)*, Ruth White *(Biddy, Cook)*, Philip Bosco *(Fuller)*, Ralph Waite *(Sean Magruder)*, Meg Myles *(Mrs. Magruder)*, William Roerick *(Loren Westabrook)*, Dana Elcar *(Layton)*, Dolph Sweet *(Haver)*, Dee Victor *(Mrs. Gordon)*, Lincoln Kilpatrick *(Daley)*, Doris Roberts *(Feeney)*, Carey Nairnes *(Harris)*, John Rogers *(Cooper)*, Gordon Peters *(Eric)*, Alex Stevens *(Lumson)*, Richard Woods, Conrad Bain *(James Lawrence)*, Robert Gerringer *(Connor)*, John Ryan *(Harry Samson)*, Sydney Walker, Jay Barney *(The Real Finchley)*, Marty Glickman *(Racetrack Announcer)*, Gino Piserchio *(Michel)*, Leslie Charleson *(Julie)*, Ali MacGraw *(Melody)*.

This picture starts with Douglas, a tough detective, turning in his badge, rather than face charges of police brutality. He is hired to guard a woman (Koscina) who is charged with the murder of her husband. Douglas quickly figures out that the woman is being set up and goes about proving her innocence, while falling in love with the lovely Koscina. The plot is improbable and predictable in several sequences. A well-suited cast and sure-handed direction help gloss over some of the script's weakness.

p, Richard Lewis; d, David Lowell Rich; w, A. J. Russell, ph, Morris "Moe" Hartzband; (Techniscope, Technicolor); m, Kenyon Hopkins; ed, Sidney Katz, Gene Palmer; art d, Alexander Golitzen, Willard Levitas, set d, John McCarthy, John Ward; cos, Mary Merrill; m/l, "A Lovely Way To Die," Hopkins, Judy Spencer (sung by Jackie Wilson), "A Lovely Way to Live," Hopkins, Spencer (sung by Marge Dodson); makeup, Bud Westmore.

Crime **(PR:C MPAA:NR)**

LOVELY WAY TO GO, A (SEE: A LOVELY WAY TO DIE, 1968)

LOVEMAKER, THE (SEE: MAIN STREET, 1956, Span.)

LOVEMAKERS, THE (SEE: LA VIACCIA, 1962)

LOVER BOY (SEE: LOVERS, HAPPY LOVERS!, 1954)

LOVER COME BACK* 1/2   (1931) 73m COL bw

Constance Cummings (*Connie*), Jack Mulhall (*Tom Evans*), Betty Bronson (*Vivian*), Jameson Thomas (*Yates*), Frederic Santley (*Schultzy*), Jack Mack (*Henry*), Katherine Givney (*Mrs. March*), Loretta Sayers (*Loretta*), Susan Fleming (*Susan*).

The goings on in an office serve as the backdrop for this burdensome picture. Cummings plays a stenographer who falls for the office manager. When he marries someone else, Cummings decides to accept a marriage proposal from the big boss, who never stops pestering her. The direction lacks any sort of pacing, and the lack of a skillful hand at the helm is obvious in the performances. Cummings, in particular, promises more than she delivers. Mulhall sings "Cigarette."

d, Erle C. Kenton; w, Robert Shannon, Dorothy Howell (based on the story by Helen Topping Miller); ph, Joseph Walker; ed, Gene Havlick.

Comedy   **(PR:A MPAA:NR)**

LOVER COME BACK** 1/2

(1946) 90m UNIV bw (AKA: WHEN LOVERS MEET)

George Brent (*Bill Williams*), Lucille Ball (*Kay Williams*), Vera Zorina (*Madeline Laslo*), Charles Winninger (*Pa Williams*), Carl Esmond (*Paul*), Raymond Walburn (*J. P. Winthrop*), Elisabeth Risdon (*Ma Williams*), Louise Beavers (*Martha*), Wallace Ford (*Tubbs*), Franklin Pangborn (*Hotel Clerk*), William Wright (*Jimmy Hennessey*), George Chandler (*Waiter*), Joan Shawlee [Fulton] (*Janie*), Pat Alphin, Audrey Young, Dorothy Christy (*Receptionists*), Ellen Corby (*Rita*), Lloyd Ingraham (*Partner*), Mary Moore, Joan Graham, Shirley O'Hara, Gwen Donovan (*Showgirls*), Eddy Waller (*Mr. Russel*), George Davis (*Maitre D'*), Dorothy Ford (*Brunette*), Edward Martendel (*Slocum*), Anne O'Neal (*Mrs. Tubbs*), Frank Scannell, Harold Goodwin, Perc Launders (*Reporters*), Lane Chandler, Jack Shutta, Jerome Root (*Bellhops*), Geraldine Jarman (*Blonde*), Louis Wood (*Room Steward*), Lottie Harrison (*Mother*), Katherine York (*Redhead*), Bill Hudson (*Young Man*).

Comic reworking of tried and true material has Brent as an overseas war correspondent coming home to his waiting wife, Ball. When she finds out that he's been fooling around while away, she goes into a jealous huff and tries some of the same medicine on Brent. When this doesn't work Ball heads to Las Vegas for a quick divorce, but Brent is close on her tail. Brent and Ball play well off each other, helping to make the film better than the material offered.

p, Michael Fessier, Ernest Pagano; d, William A. Seiter; w, Fessier, Pagano; ph, Joseph Valentine; m, Hans J. Salter; ed, Ray Snyder; art d, Jack Otterson, Martin Obzina; set d, Russell A. Gausman, Ted Offenbecker; cos, Travis Banton.

Comedy   **(PR:A MPAA:NR)**

LOVER COME BACK*** 1/2

(1961) 107m Seven Picture-Nob Hill-Arwin/UNIV c

Rock Hudson (*Jerry Webster*), Doris Day (*Carol Templeton*), Tony Randall (*Peter Ramsey*), Edie Adams (*Rebel Davis*), Jack Oakie (*J. Paxton Miller*), Jack Kruschen (*Dr. Linus Tyler*), Ann B. Davis (*Millie*), Joe Flynn (*Hadley*), Howard St. John (*Brackett*), Karen Norris (*Kelly*), Jack Albertson (*Fred*), Charles Watts (*Charlie*), Donna Douglas (*Deborah*), Ward Ramsey (*Hodges*), John Litel (*Board Member*), Chet Stratton (*Leonard*), Mina Vaughn, Barbara Frederick (*Party Girls*), Nelson Leigh (*Northcross*), Richard Deacon (*Dr. Melnick*), Hilda Plowright, Kathleen Mulqueen (*Cleaning Women*), Joan Patrick (*Ramsey Receptionist*), Al Hodge (*Bass Player*), William Benedict (*Musician*), Ted Bessell (*Elevator Operator*) Barbara Dorothy Clarke (*Dancer*).

Perhaps the best Hudson-Day film, LOVER COME BACK features the popular screwball couple as advertising agents pitted against each other in the high-tension world of Madison Avenue. Working for rival agencies, Hudson and Day are mortal enemies, who are aware of each others existence, but have never met. Fed up with Hudson's questionable tactics (he entices big accounts from clients using martinis and beautiful women), Day reports him to the Advertising Council. To combat this, Hudson sends beautiful chorus girl Adams to speak on his behalf, and she seduces the tribunal into dropping the charges. As a reward for a job well done, Hudson makes Adams his "VIP" girl and films a series of commercials for a nonexistent product. The nervous and confused president of the firm, Randall, mistakenly televises the spots, forcing the company to invent a product named "VIP". Nutty scientist Kruschen is hired to perform the task, and Day, determined to get a piece of the action for her firm, decides to do anything to steal the account. She mistakes Hudson for the inventor and allows Hudson to wine and dine her. When she learns the truth, she again reports him to the Advertising Council, accusing him of selling a nonexistent product. Luckily Kruschen comes up with a new mint-flavored candy to be sold as "VIP," and Hudson brings it to the hearing as evidence, letting everyone, including Day, sample a piece. Unfortunately, the candy has the same effect as drinking several triple martinis, and the next morning Day awakes in bed with Hudson and a marriage license. Outraged, she has the marriage annulled and she transfers to the California branch of the company. Nine months later they are remarried in the maternity ward. Very funny, with a great cast of supporting players, especially Randall.

p, Stanley Shapiro, Martin Melcher; d, Delbert Mann; w, Shapiro, Paul Henning; ph, Arthur E. Arling (Eastmancolor); m, Frank DeVol; ed, Marjorie Fowler; art d, Alexander Golitzen, Robert Clatworthy; set d, Oliver Emert; cos, Irene; m/l, "Lover Come Back," Alan Spilton, DeVol, "Should I Surrender," Adam Ross, William Landan (songs sung by Doris Day); makeup, Bud Westmore.

Comedy   **(PR:A MPAA:NR)**

LOVER FOR THE SUMMER, A

(SEE: MISTRESS FOR THE SUMMER, A, 1964, Fr./Ital.)

LOVER, WIFE   (SEE: WIFE MISTRESS, 1977, Ital.)

LOVERS, THE**

(1959, Fr.) 90m Nouvelle Editions des Films/Zenith bw (LES AMANTS)

Jeanne Moreau (*Jeanne Tournier*), Alain Cuny (*Henri Tournier*), Jean-Marc Bory (*Bernard Dubois-Lambert*), Judith Magre (*Maggy Thiebaut-Leroy*), Jose-Luis de Villalonga (*Raoul Flores*), Gaston Modot (*Coudray*), Patricia Garcin (*Catherine, Jeanne's Daughter*), Claude Mansard (*Marcelot*), Georgette Lobbe (*Marthe*).

Notorious for its extended seminude love-making scene when first released in 1959, Louis Malle's THE LOVERS seems tame today when compared with average "R" rated films of the 1980's. The film tells the simple tale of Moreau, a bored mother and wife, who meets, falls in love with, and sleeps with young archeologist Bory—all, in the course of one evening. The next morning she abandons her family and runs off with her new lover to an uncertain future. Overrated due to the censorship it incurred overseas and in the U.S. (A suburban Cleveland theatre manager was prosecuted for showing an obscene film. The case went to the Supreme Court and was eventually thrown out.) The film is a good, but not great examination of a female mid-life crisis. (In French; English subtitles).

d, Louis Malle; w, Malle, Louise de Vilmorin (based on the novel *Point de Lendemain* by Dominique Vivant); ph, Henri Decae (Dyaliscope); m, Johannes Brahams ("Sextet No. 1 in B Flat, Op. 18"); ed, Leonide Azar; prod d, Bernard Evein, Jacques Saulnier; English titles, Herman Weinberg.

Drama   **(PR:O MPAA:NR)**

LOVERS, THE* 1/2   (1972, Brit.) 89m Gildor/BL c

Richard Beckinsale, Paula Wilcox, Joan Scott, Susan Littler, John Comer, Stella Moray, Nikolas Simmonds.

A humorous look at the frustrations of a young man seeking sex with a girl friend who thinks it is best to wait until marriage. Some of the situations which one would expect to accompany such a theme are quite funny, but as a whole this meager idea is carried on far too long.

d, Herbert Wise; w, Jack Rosenthal; ph, Bob Huke (Eastmancolor); m, Carl Davis.

Comedy   **(PR:C MPAA:NR)**

LOVERS AND LIARS* 1/2

(1981, Ital.) 94m Levitt-Pickman c (AKA: A TRIP WITH ANITA, TRAVELS WITH ANITA)

Goldie Hawn (*Anita*), Giancarlo Giannini (*Guido*), Claudine Auger (*Elisa*), Aurore Clement (*Cora*), Laura Betti (*Laura*), Andrea Ferreol (*Noemi*).

Not released in America until Hawn made a big hit with PRIVATE BENJAMIN, and for good reason. The ridiculous premise of the story, which an excellent cast can do little to save, revolves around American tourist Hawn, who is being picked up while hitchhiking by the macho Giannini. Giannini is on his way to his father's funeral, something he does not tell Hawn, for no apparent reason. Instead he keeps her locked in the hotel room, while he is out for hours at a time visiting his father's village. The cast manages to go through their performances with some conviction. Morricone offers his usual exceptional score. (In English.)

p, Alberto Grimaldi; d, Mario Monicelli, Lee Kressel (English version); w, Paul Zimmerman, Monicelli; ph, Tonino Belli Colli (MovieLab Color); m, Ennio Morricone; ed, Ruggero Mastroianni.

Comedy   **Cas.**   **(PR:O MPAA:R)**

LOVERS AND LOLLIPOPS** 1/2   (1956) 80m Trans-Lux bw

Lori March (*Ann*), Gerald S. O'Loughlin (*Larry*), Cathy Dunn (*Peggy*), William Ward (*Peter*).

After becoming a widow, a woman tries to rekindle her love life in a romance with a businessman. The affair, however, has one unforseen setback when the widow's daughter grows jealous for her mother's attention. This is an amateur budget film, but not bad on that level. The film was made by the husband and wife team of Engel and Orkin and shows some truly interesting shots of New York City in the middle 1950s.

p&d, Morris Engel, Ruth Orkin; w, Engel, Orkin, Mary-Madeleine Lanphier; ph, Engel; ed, Orkin; md, Eddy Manson.

Drama/Comedy   **(PR:A MPAA:NR)**

LOVERS AND LUGGERS*** (1938, Aus.) 99m Cinesound/British Empire bw

Lloyd Hughes (*Daubeney Carshott*), Shirley Ann Richards (*Lorna*), James Raglan (*Craig*), Elaine Hamill (*Stella Raff*), Sydney Wheeler (*Capt. Quid*), Alec Kellaway (*McTavish*), Ronald Whelan (*Mendoza*), Campbell Copelin (*Archie*), Leslie Victor (*Dormer*), Marcelle Mamey (*Lotus*), Charles Chan (*Kishimuni*).

Suspenseful drama from down-under concerns a celebrated concert pianist leaving the stage to go pearl diving, just to please a whimsical woman. The direction manages to build up the pace to the dramatic conclusion. Except for the lead played by Hughes, the performances are exceptional.

d, Ken G. Hall; w, Frank Harvey (based on the novel by Gurney Slade); ph, Frank Hurley, George Heath; art d, Eric Thompson.

Drama   **(PR:A MPAA:NR)**

LOVERS AND OTHER STRANGERS*** 1/2 (1970) 104m ABC/Cinerama c

Gig Young (*Hal Henderson*), Bea Arthur (*Bea Vecchio*), Bonnie Bedelia (*Susan Henderson*), Anne Jackson (*Cathy*), Harry Guardino (*Johnny*), Michael Brandon (*Mike Vecchio*), Richard Castellano (*Frank Vecchio*), Robert Dishy (*Jerry*), Marian Hailey (*Brenda*), Joseph Hindy (*Richie*), Anthony Holland (*Donaldson*), Diane Keaton (*Joan*), Cloris Leachman (*Bernice*), Mort Marshall (*Father Gregory*), Anne Meara (*Wilma*), Bob Baliban (*Hotel Clerk*), Amy Stiller (*Flower Girl*), Charlotte Jones (*Johnny's Mother*).

A well-done, many-faceted comedy containing several romantic vignettes that take place before and during the wedding of a young couple, Brandon and Bedelia, who have decided to marry after living together for a year and a half. Though both the couples' families are thrilled by the news, the tension and excitement leading up to, and during the wedding, bring out many family squabbles heretofore repressed. Castellano is wonderful (it was his first major role and led to his being cast as a major character in THE GODFATHER) as the groom's father whose happiness is disturbed by the news that his other son, Hindy, is considering divorcing his wife, Keaton (this was also Keaton's first major role). On the other side of the family, Young, the rich, strict Irish-Catholic father-of-the-bride, finds himself trapped by his long-time mistress, Jackson, who suddenly decides to force him into choosing between her and his wife. Meanwhile, the bride's sister's (Meara) marriage is collapsing because her husband, Guardino, has become more interested in television than sex. The evening before the wedding, Brandon and Bedelia arrange a blind date between her cousin Hailey, and one of the ushers, Dishy. Dishy, hoping to score with Hailey, finds his efforts at seduction frustrated by the girl's non-stop chatter. The next day, all the emotional turmoil seems to work itself out and the wedding proceeds smoothly. LOVERS AND OTHER STRANGERS is a charming, hilarious film that skillfully balances the many divergent storylines into a fascinating, entertaining whole. Well cast (a fine example of ensemble acting), and well paced, it is a comedy that holds up to several viewings. For some mysterious reason the film was given an undue "R" rating by the MPAA, but there is no nudity or foul language to be found, and the sexual aspects of the story are handled tastefully. Songs were sung by Country Coalition, Larry Meredith.

p, David Susskind; d, Cy Howard; w, Renee Taylor, Joseph Bologna, David Zelag Goodman (based on the play by Bologna, Taylor); ph, Andrew Laszlo (Metrocolor); m, Fred Karlin; ed, David Bretherton, Sidney Katz; prod d, Ben Edwards; set d, John Allen Hicks; cos, Albert Wolsky; m/l, "For All We Know," Karlin, Robb Wilson, Robb Royer.

Comedy   **(PR:C MPAA:R)**

LOVERS COURAGEOUS**   (1932) 77m MGM bw

Robert Montgomery (Willie Smith), Madge Evans (Mary), Roland Young (Jeffrey), Frederick Kerr (Admiral), Reginald Owen (Jimmy), Beryl Mercer (Mrs. Smith), Evelyn Hall (Lady Blayne), Halliwell Hobbes (Mr. Smith), Jackie Searle (Willie as a Child), Norman Phillips, Jr. (Walter as a Child), Alan Mowbray (Lamone).

Formula material in this male Cinderella story has Montgomery as a playwright who's had nothing but hard luck his entire life: from his childhood, where he is continually beaten for cutting the school he hates, to his 2-pound-a-week job on a South African plantation. Evans walks into the picture while Montgomery is in South Africa, and the two immediately take to each other. She drops her intended, Owen, to marry Montgomery, who finally gets a chance to produce some plays because Owen comes from a wealthy, aristocratic family. Cast plods its way through the script, which adds some witty dialog to try and make up for the formulistic approach.

d, Robert Z. Leonard; w, Frederick Lonsdale; ph, William Daniels; ed, Margaret Booth.

Drama   **(PR:A MPAA:NR)**

LOVERS, HAPPY LOVERS!**
(1955, Brit.) 85m Transcontinental/FOX bw (GB: KNAVE OF HEARTS; AKA: LOVER BOY)

Gerard Philipe (Andre Ripois), Natasha Parry (Patricia), Valerie Hobson (Catherine), Joan Greenwood (Norah), Margaret Johnson (Anne), Germaine Montero (Marcelle), Diana Decker (Diana), Percy Marmont (Catherine's Father), Bill Shine, Mai Bacon, Margot Field, Julie Anslow, Harry Towb, Gerald Campion, Martin Benson, Eric Pohlmann, Eileen Way, Arthur Howard, Beryl Cooke, Judith Nelmes, David Coote, Richard Hart.

Philipe stars as an amorous Frenchman who goes off to London to charm a number of women, finally marrying Hobson. Soon after, boredom sets in and Philipe pursues Parry. When she spurns his advances, he desperately fakes a suicide attempt to gain her sympathy, but the trick goes awry and he plunges off a balcony to his death. An ironic but sympathetic look at some naive women and a genuine knave, a man who is a failed cynic pursuing women almost as an addiction. To achieve authenticity in background shots, director Clement resorted to shooting the streets of London with a hidden camera.

p, Paul Graetz; d, Rene Clement; w, Hugh Mills, Raymond Queneau, Clement (based on a novel by Louis Hemon); ph, Oswald Morris; m, Roman Vlad.

Drama   **(PR:C MPAA:NR)**

LOVERS IN LIMBO   (SEE: NAME OF THE GAME IS KILL, THE, 1968)

LOVERS LIKE US   (SEE: SAVAGE, THE, 1975, Fr.)

LOVERS MUST LEARN   (SEE: ROME ADVENTURE, 1962)

LOVER'S NET**
(1957, Fr.) 123m Enterprise Generale-Hoche-Fides/Times Film Corp. bw (LES AMANTS DU TAGE; AKA: PORT OF SHAME: GB: LOVERS OF LISBON)

Francoise Arnoul (Kathleen Dinver), Daniel Gelin (Pierre Roubier), Trevor Howard (Inspector Lewis), Amalia Rodrigues (Amalia), Dalio (Porfirio), Jacques Moulieres (Manuel [Moustique]), Ginette LeClerc (Maria), Betty Stockfield (Maisie).

The much-filmed love drama of a widower who meets a woman whose husband has recently died is spiced up a bit by adding murder to the plot. The result is a moody depiction of individuals driven by desperation. Gelin plays a man who killed his wife when, upon returning home from war, he discovered she was unfaithful. Now unable to trust women, he travels to Lisbon where he meets and falls in love with Arnoul, whose husband has recently died. What he is unaware of is that Arnoul

caused the death of her aristocratic British spouse, and is under intense investigation by Howard, who uses the unstable condition of Gelin to trap her. But before this ensues the shaky affair between Gelin and Arnoul is exposed as a volatile relationship that is doomed from the start. The lead characters are composed of emotional complexities that make falling in love seem like a grueling enterprise. A realistic treatment uncommon in film romances. (In French.)

p, Jacques Gauthier; d, Henri Verneuil; w, Marcel Rivet, Joseph Companeez (based on the novel by Joseph Kessel).

Romance/Drama   **(PR:C MPAA:NR)**

LOVERS OF LISBON   (SEE: LOVER'S NET, 1957, Fr.)

LOVERS OF MONTPARNASSE, THE
(SEE: MODIGLIANI OF MONTPARNASSE, 1961, Fr./Ital.)

LOVERS OF TERUEL, THE**
(1962, Fr.) 90m Monarch/CD c (LES AMANTS DE TERUEL)

Ludmilla Tcherina (Isa), Rene-Louis Lafforgue (Barker), Milko Sparemblek (Manuel), Milenko Banovitch (Diego), Stevan Grebel (Grebelito), Jean-Pierre Bras (Father), Antoine Marin (Pablo), Roberto (Dwarf).

Nicely done film featuring Tcherina as the star dancer in a troupe of gypsies whose own life begins to parallel the tragic 17th-century Spanish legend she interprets. The dance tells the story of Isabella, whose lover, Diego, goes off for three years to prove himself worthy of her. After waiting many years, Isabella reluctantly agrees to marry an unsavory duke, thinking Diego is dead. However, Diego soon returns, and when he learns of Isabella's marriage he kills himself. Grief stricken, Isabella commits suicide. (In French; English subtitles.)

d, Raymond Rouleau; w, Rouleau, Rene-Louis Lafforgue; ph, Claude Renoir (Totalscope, Eastmancolor); m, Mikis Theodorakis, Henri Sauguet; ed, Marinette Cadix; md, Kasimir Sipush; set d&cos, Jacques Dupont; ch, Milko Sparemblek; English subtitles, Herman G. Weinberg, Norbert Terry.

Dance   **(PR:A MPAA:NR)**

LOVERS OF TOLEDO, THE*1/2
(1954, Fr./Span./Ital.) 82m Lux-Athenea/Gaston Hakim bw (LES AMANTS DE TOLEDO)

Alida Valli (Inez), Pedro Armendariz (Don Blas), Gerard Landry (Fernando), Francoise Arnoul (Sancha).

Highly contrived romance drama with Armendariz playing a tough, crooked police chief who is willing to set prisoner Landry free on condition that Landry give up his beloved Valli so he can marry her. Other than the fancy set decorations which accurately capture the flavor of 19th-Century Spain, there is little here of interest.

p, Raymond Eger; d, Henri Decoin; w, Claude Vermorel (based on the novel The Ghost and the Cheat by Stendhal); ph, Michel Kelber; m, Jean-Jacques Grunenwald.

Drama   **(PR:A MPAA:NR)**

LOVERS OF VERONA, THE**
(1951, Fr.) 110m Souvaine Selective Pictures bw (LES AMANTS DE VERONE)

Serge Reggiani (Angelo), Pierre Brasseur (Raffaele), Anouk Aimee (Georgia Maglia), Marcel Dalio (Amedeo Maglia), Louis Salou (Ettore Maglia), Martine Carol (Bettina Verdi), Marianne Oswald (Laetitia), Charles Deschamps (Sandrini), Armontel (Blanchini).

An intriguing romance that is a modern version of "Romeo and Juliet," as the title suggests. Story takes place while a film crew is attempting a literal translation of the play, with Aimee and Reggiani as stand-ins for the film's leads who fall in love on the set. Instead of two feuding families, troubles erupt because Reggiani comes from a family of the working class while Aimee's parents were powerful Fascists and aristocrats who no longer enjoy the power they had during the war. Family stress leads the affair to a tragic end; Reggiani is killed by one of Aimee's relatives in the studio where the filming is taking place, and Aimee takes her own life, falling across the prostrate body of her lover. Aimee was only 17 when she starred in THE LOVERS OF VERONA, and was already on her way to enticing audiences with the mystifying grace with which she filled the screen. (In French; English subtitles.)

p, Raymond Borderie; d, Andre Cayatte; w, Jacques Prevert (based on the story by Cayatte); ph, Henri Alekan; m, Joseph Kosma; English titles, Herman G. Weinberg.

Drama   **(PR:A MPAA:NR)**

LOVERS ON A TIGHTROPE**
(1962, Fr.) 83m Panda/Interworld bw (LA CORDE RAIDE)

Annie Girardot (Cora), Francois Perier (Daniel), Gerard Buhr (Henri), Georges Descrieres (Simon), Genevieve Brunet (Isabelle), Hubert Deschamps (Lawyer), Henri Cremieux (Doctor), Henri Virlogeux, Piella Sorano, Michel Seldow, Pierre Moncorbier.

Routine romantic melodrama starring Girardot as the bored wife of wealthy Parisian businessman Perier, who unwittingly becomes involved in an affair with sleazy garage mechanic Buhr, who just wants to bilk the woman out of her fortune. Her husband suspects his brother and business partner, Descrieres, as being his wife's lover, but the truth is revealed when Descrieres is killed because Buhr sabotaged Perier's car (the evil mechanic assumed Perier was going to drive it). Girardot confesses her misdeeds, Buhr is arrested, and the husband and wife try to go on with their normal lives.

p, Robert Ciriez Daubigny; d, Jean-Charles Dudrumet; w, Roland Laudenbach,

Dudrumet; ph, Pierre Gueguen; m, Maurice Jarre; ed, Janine Verneau; art d, Olivier Girard.

Drama **(PR:A MPAA:NR)**

LOVERS' ROCK** (1966, Taiwan) Shaw Brothers bw

Cheng Pei-pei *(Lin Chiu-tse)*, Chiao Chuang *(Chin Yu)*, Hsang Tsung-hsin *(So Ta-kuei)*, Wen Ling *(Tseng Ah-feng)*.

Heavy-handed melodrama takes place in a small Chinese fishing village with two young fishermen rivals for the hand of a woman. Though the woman is in love with only one of the men, she keeps from marrying him out of obligation to the other. The expected tragic ending is avoided when the unwanted suitor falls in love with someone else. But tragedy lifts its head anyway in fatal irony when the two men, now again friends, sail out to sea and vanish. According to tradition, two new rock figures appear on the beach, representing women who have lost their men at sea.

p, Run Run Shaw; d&w, Pan Lei; ph, Hung Ching-yun; m, Loh Ming Tao.

Drama **(PR:A MPAA:NR)**

LOVE'S A LUXURY (SEE: CARETAKER'S DAUGHTER, THE, 1952, Brit.)

LOVES AND TIMES OF SCARAMOUCHE, THE* 1/2
(1976, Ital.) 91m, AE c (AKA: SCARAMOUCHE)

Michael Sarrazin *(Scaramouche)*, Ursula Andress *(Josephine)*, Aldo Maccione *(Napoleon)*, Giancarlo Prete, Michael Forest, Nico Il Grande, Romano Puppo, Massimo Vanni, Alex Togni, Damir Mejovsek, Lucia De Oliveira.

Sarrazin is the noted French lover who spends his time in and out of bed with various females as he is followed by an ever persistent Napoleon (Maccione). The latter is pretty funny but the rest of the film does not match his comic turns. The story is told at a frenzied pitch, trying to hide its empty plot under the guise of speed. It does not work well, resulting in a pale imitation of TOM JONES.

p, Federico Aicardi; d, Enzo G. Castellari; w, Tito Carpi, Castellari; ph, Giovanni Bergamini (Telecolor); m, Dammico Bixio; ed, Gian-franco Amicucci; art d, Enzo Bulgarelli.

Farce **Cas.** **(PR:C MPAA:PG)**

LOVES OF A BLONDE* 1/2**
(1966, Czech.) 88m Barrandov-Ceskoslovensky/Prominent-CBK bw (LASKY JEDNE PLAVOVLASKY; AKA: A BLONDE IN LOVE)

Hana Brejchova *(Andula)*, Vladimir Pucholt *(Milda)*, Vladimir Mensik *(Vacovsky)*, Ivan Kheil *(Manas)*, Jiri Hruby *(Burda)*, Milada Jezkova *(Milda's Mother)*, Josef Sebanek *(Milda's Father)*, Marie Salacova *(Marie)*, Jana Novakova *(Jana)*, Jana Crkalova *(Jaruska)*, Zdenka Lorencova *(Zdena)*, Tana Zelinkova *(Girl with Guitar)*, Jan Vostrcil *(Colonel)*, Josef Kolb *(Pokorny)*, Antonin Blazejovsky *(Tonda)*, M. Zednickova *(Educator)*.

Charming and frequently touching romantic comedy directed by Milos Forman and starring Brejchova as a young woman who works in a shoe factory and dreams of love. Dissatisfied with the men in her town, she is forced to cope with Blazejovsky, an ardent admirer, but less than what she perceives to be her ideal man. When their plant manager arranges for a dance to be held in honor of some soldiers who are to be stationed in the town, Brejchova looks forward to meeting a handsome military man. To her disappointment, the soldiers all turn out to be middle-aged reservists and so she sets her romantic sights on the piano player, Pucholt. After some uneasy introductions, Brejchova spends the night with Pucholt. Now in love, she travels to his parents' home in Prague where the shocked couple is outraged by their son's actions. When he arrives home, his mother drags him off screaming and yelling about the state of his morality. When Pucholt insists he barely knows the girl and never gave her any sort of encouragement or commitment, she dejectedly returns to the factory, but tells her girl friends of the wonderful weekend she spent with Pucholt and his parents in Prague.

d, Milos Forman; w, Jaroslav Papousek, Ivan Passer, Forman, Vaclav Sasek; ph, Miroslav Ondricek; m, Evzen Illin; ed, Miroslav Hajek; art d, Karel Cerny.

Comedy **Cas.** **(PR:A MPAA:NR)**

LOVES OF A DICTATOR (SEE: DICTATOR, THE, 1935, Brit.)

LOVES OF ARIANE, THE (SEE: ARIANE, 1931, Ger.)

LOVES OF CARMEN, THE 1/2** (1948) 99m Beckworth/COL c

Rita Hayworth *(Carmen Garcia)*, Glenn Ford *(Don Jose)*, Ron Randell *(Andres)*, Victor Jory *(Garcia)*, Luther Adler *(Dancaire)*, Arnold Moss *(Colonel)*, Joseph Buloff *(Remendado)*, Margaret Wycherly *(Old Crone)*, Bernard Nedell *(Pablo)*, John Baragrey *(Lucas)*, Philip Van Zandt *(Sergeant)*, Anthony Dante *(Groom)*, Veronika Pataky *(Bride)*, Rosa Turich *(Bride's Mother)*, Leona Roberts *(Ancient Old Gypsy)*, Vernon Cansino, Peter Virgo *(Soldiers)*, Fernando Ramos, Roy Fitzell, Jose Cansino *(Specialty Dancers-Gypsies)*, Joaquin Elizonda, Paul Bradley, Lala DeTolly, Marie Scheue, Barbara Hayden *(People on Stagecoach)*, Wally Cassell *(Dragoon)*, Nenette Vallon *(Woman with Broom)*, Kate Drain Lawson *(Woman Relative)*, Inez Palange, Eula Morgan *(Women in Crowns)*, Peter Cusanelli *(Man in Crown)*, Joseph Malouf *(Orderly)*, George Bell, Rosita Delva, Lucille Charles, Thomas Malinari, Delores Corral, Andrew Roud, Al Caruso, Roque Ybarra, Dimas Sotello, Julio Rojas *(Bits)*, Frances Rey, Roselyn Strangis *(Girls)*, Claire DuBrey *(Woman in Window)*, Tessie Murray, Angella Gomez, Lulu Mae Bohrman, Virginia Vann *(Women)*, David Ortega, Cosmo Sardo, Alfred Paix, Jerry De Castro, Paul Fierro, John J. Verros *(Men)*, Celeste Savoi *(Ad Lib Bit)*, Alma Beltran, Florence Auer *(Trinket Sellers)*, Lupe Gonzalez, Nina Campana *(Chestnut Sellers)*, Robert Sidney *(Specialty Dancer)*, Francis Pierlot *(Beggar)*, Juan Duval *(Toreador)*, Trevor Bardette *(Footman)*, Paul Marion *(Sergeant of Dragoons)*.

Prosper Merimee's heroine, Carmen, is one of the most durable ladies to have ever been created. Bizet first adapted the story as an opera that was introduced in 1875, then came a series of films that has never stopped. It was done by the Edison company in 1904. Marguerite Snow, Marion Leonard, and Pearl Sindelar all made their own versions in 1913, then Cecil B. DeMille starred Geraldine Farrar in his depiction in 1915 while William Fox used Theda Bara that same year. Charles Chaplin spoofed it in 1916, then a rest was given to the cigarette girl until Ernst Lubitsch directed Pola Negri in 1921. In 1927, Dolores Del Rio was tapped and, in 1928, the French did a version with Raquel Meller. 1931 marked her first talking picture as Marguerite Namara essayed the role in England. In 1933, the Germans made a funny version with Lotte Reiniger, then the Mexicans did it their way in 1940 with Imperio Argentina in the lead. Viviane Romance starred in the 1947 Italian-made picture and this one followed. But there were others to come. CARMEN JONES, an all-black picture, was released in 1954 and even more followed. The last one, to date, was a Spanish version in the 1980s and you may be sure we've missed a few. Carmen is Hayworth. She's a conscienceless and amoral wench married to gypsy Jory. She's had a series of lovers, many run-ins with the law, and a host of robberies to her discredit. A fortune teller predicts that Hayworth will die at the hands of her great love. This comes true as Ford, playing Don Jose as though he were a Kansas cowboy, stabs Hayworth after first dispatching Jory in a knife fight. Ford had been legitimate until he battled with Moss in a sword clash. When Moss was killed, Ford became a criminal and his downfall is assured when he encounters Hayworth. The central California town of Lone Pine was location headquarters for the movie and much of it was also shot in the area of Mt. Whitney. Lone Pine was doubled for many European locations and was a favorite of filmmakers in the 1930s. Although Vidor gets producer credit, it was actually produced by Hayworth's company, Beckworth. The assistant director was Earl Bellamy who became a successful TV director in later years with "The Waltons" and many other shows. This film, unfortunately, shed no new light on Carmen but did make scads of money and showed everyone that Hayworth was not just another pretty set of legs. One forgettable song: "The Love of a Gypsy" (M. W. Stoloff, Fred Karger).

p&d, Charles Vidor: w, Helen Deutsch (based on the story "Carmen" by Prosper Merimee); ph, William Snyder (Technicolor); m, Mario Castelnuovo-Tedesco; ed, Charles Nelson; md, M. W. Stoloff; art d, Stephen Goosson, Cary Odell; set d, Wilbur Menefee, William Kiernan; cos, Jean Louis; ch, Robert Sidney, Eduardo Cansino; m/l, Stoloff, Fred Karger; makeup, Clay Campbell.

Drama **(PR:C MPAA:NR)**

LOVES OF EDGAR ALLAN POE, THE** (1942) 67m FOX bw

Linda Darnell *(Virginia Clemm)*, John Shepperd [Shepperd Strudwick] *(Edgar Allan Poe)*, Virginia Gilmore *(Elmira Royster)*, Jane Darwell *(Mrs. Clemm)*, Mary Howard *(Frances Allan)*, Frank Conroy *(John Allan)*, Henry Morgan *(Ebenezer Burling)*, Walter Kingsford *(T. W. White)*, Morris Ankrum *(Mr. Graham)*, Skippy Wanders *(Poe, Age 3)*, Freddie Mercer *(Poe, Age 12)*, Erville Alderson *(Schoolmaster)*, Peggy McIntyre *(Elmira, Age 10)*, William Bakewell, Jr. *(Hugh Pleasant)*, Frank Melton *(Turner Dixon)*, Morton Lowry *(Charles Dickens)*, *Gilbert Emery (Thomas Jefferson)*, Ed Stanley *(Dr. Moran)*, Francis Ford *(Tavern Keeper)*, Harry Denny *(Kennedy)*, Hardie Albright *(Shelton)*, Jan Clayton *(Poe's Young Mother)*, Mae Marsh *(Mrs. Phillips)*, Alec Craig *(Printer)*, Leon Tyler *(Boy)*, Arthur Shields *(Somes, the Proctor)*.

Loosely based on the actual life of the famed poet-author, the film follows him from childhood as an adopted son of a Virginia tabacco dealer to his early death from alcoholism. The story attempts to blame a lot of Poe's later problems on his mistreatment by his foster father. Shepperd plays the matured Poe who is jilted by his childhood sweetheart, Gilmore, for a more affluent man. He eventually marries his first cousin, Darnell, before drinking himself to death. The entire cast gives competent performances, though the story focuses little on romantic relations, as the title would promise. The script suffers from weaknesses in motivation.

p, Bryan Foy; d, Harry Lachman; w, Samuel Hoffenstein, Tom Reed, Arthur Caesar; ph, Lucien Andriot; ed, Fred Allen; md, Emil Newman; art d, Richard Day, Nathan Juran.

Drama **(PR:A MPAA:NR)**

LOVES OF HERCULES, THE*
(1960), Ital./Fr.) 94m c (AKA: HERCULES AND THE HYDRA)

Jane Mansfield, Mickey Hargitay.

Another film in the "so bad it's good" category. Mansfield plays a dual role of an innocent queen who meets Hercules and the evil Amazon who wants Hargitay for her own. It's full of preposterous scenes and situations including Hargitay saving the hapless, spread-eagled Mansfield from her bindings via a neatly tossed axe. Other gems include talking trees, a cyclops, and an action scene where Hargitay saves the day by decapitating a three-headed dragon. This last sequence was later used in THE WILD WILD WORLD OF JAYNE MANSFIELD. Complete with poor dubbing, this is unintended hilarity at its best.

d, Carlo Ludnico Bragalia; w, Continenza, Doria.

Mythology **(PR:A MPAA:NR)**

LOVES OF ISADORA, THE (SEE: ISADORA, 1968, Brit.)

LOVES OF JOANNA GODDEN, THE* 1/2 (1947, Brit.) 89m EAL/GFD bw

Googie Withers *(Joanna Godden)*, Jean Kent *(Ellen Godden)*, John McCallum *(Arthur Alce)*, Derek Bond *(Martin Trevor)*, Henry Mollison *(Harry Trevor)*, Chips Rafferty *(Collard)*, Sonia Holm *(Louise)*, Josephine Stuart *(Grace Wickens)*, Alec Faversham *(Peter Relf)*, Edward Rigby *(Stuppen)*, Frederick Piper *(Isaac Turk)*, Fred Bateman *(Young Turk)*, Barbara Leake *(Miss Luckhurst)*, Ronald Simpson *(Rev. Brett)*, Douglas Jefferies *(Huggett)*, Gilbert Davis *(Godfrey)*, Grace Arnold *(Martha)*,

Ethel Coleridge (*Lighthouse Keeper's Wife*), William Mervyn (*Huxtable*), Betty Shale (*Mrs. Vennal*), Ernie Flisher (*Fuller*), Charles Whiteley (*Hook*), Dave Turk (*Wilson*), Albert Thompson (*Elphic*).

Nicely photographed story about a young woman, Withers, who inherits her father's sheep farm, the hope of her father being that she will marry her next-door-neighbor McCallum. But Withers outrages the countryside by remaining single and running the farm on her own. She becomes quite successful, packing her sister, Kent, off to a finishing school. Withers has a brief affair with one of her workers, Rafferty, before becoming engaged to a local aristocrat. Kent comes back from school and marries McCallum, but ditches him for a wealthy older man. When Withers' betrothed drowns, she finally latches onto McCallum. The photography is the only high point of the picture, and is also responsible for much of the film's dragginess. The filmmakers put forth too much effort in displaying the scenery, taking away from the development of the story. Withers is fairly dull in the lead, but looks nice. Kent as the sister is unconvincing.

p, Michael Balcon; d, Charles Frend; w, H. E. Bates, Angus MacPhail (based on the novel *Joanna Godden* by Sheila Kaye-Smith); ph, Douglas Slocombe; m, Ralph Vaughn Williams; ed, Michael Truman; md, Ernest Irving; art d, Duncan Sutherland; cos, Mark Luker; spec eff, Cliff Richardson, Lionel Banes.

Drama							(PR:A MPAA:NR)

LOVES OF MADAME DUBARRY, THE**
(1938, Brit.) 90m British International/J.H. Hoffberg bw (GB: I GIVE MY HEART; GIVE ME YOUR HEART)

Gitta Alpar (*Jeanne*), Patrick Waddington (*Rene*), Owen Nares (*Louis XV*), Arthur Margetson (*Count Dubarry*), Margaret Bannerman (*Marechale*), Hugh Miller (*Choiseul*), Gibb McLaughlin (*De Brissac*), Iris Ashley (*Margot*), Hay Petrie (*Cascal*), Helen Haye, Ellen Pollock.

Hefty Hungarian soprano Alpar is a milliner courted by aristocrats. She first has an affair with Waddington, a young writer for Margetson. She then marries Margetson in order to become Nares' mistress. Not only does Alpar get to chase a number of men, she also sings a couple of tunes. A rather stiff British production that is well done but not compelling. Alpar's first English-language film did not make her a star.

p, Walter C. Mycroft; d, Marcel Varnel; w, Frank Launder, Robert Burford, Kurt Siodmak, Paul Perez (based on the operetta "The Dubarry" by Paul Knepler, J. M. Welleminsky); ph, Claude Friese-Greene.

Drama							(PR:A MPAA:NR)

LOVES OF ROBERT BURNS, THE**
(1930, Brit.) 100m British and Dominions/W and F bw

Joseph Hislop (*Robert Burns*), Dorothy Seacombe (*Jean Armour*), Eve Gray (*Mary Campbell*), Nancy Price (*Posie Nancy*), Jean Cadell (*Mrs. Burns*), C. V. France (*Lord Farquhar*), Neil Kenyon (*Tam the Tinkler*), George Baker (*Soldier*), H. Saxon-Snell (*Gavin Hamilton*), Craighall Sherry (*James Armour*), Wilfred Shine (*Sailor*).

Poorly produced life of the famed writer that is short on fact and long on fancy. Hislop, a noted operatic tenor, is about the best thing the film has going. He gives a fairly good performance and handles the songs well. However the script is a joke. Though the title implies that several affairs will be dealt with, in reality there are only two. Gray and Seacombe are the two respective lovers, both historically inaccurate. The film shows Seacombe being seduced and being made into "an honest woman" by Burns when in reality they married and had several children. This story gives them no family at all. The Scottish settings are used nicely but the actors keep forgetting what country they are in and their accents change from scene to scene. Better to buy an anthology of Burns' work than to deal with the mess here.

p&d, Herbert Wilcox; w, Wilcox, P. Maclean Rogers (based on a story by Reginald Berkeley, Wilcox); ph, Dave Kesson.

Drama							(PR:A MPAA:NR)

LOVES OF SALAMMBO, THE*
(1962, Fr./Ital.) 72m FOX c (SALAMMBO; SALAMBO)

Jeanne Valerie (*Salammbo*), Jacques Sernas (*Mathos*), Edmund Purdom (*Narr Havas*), Riccardo Garrone (*Hamilcar*), Arnoldo Foa (*Spendius*), Charles Fawcett, Kamala Devi, Brunella Bovo.

A confusing mess based on a minor story by Gustave Flaubert finds Valerie, the daughter of Carthage's leader Garrone, in love with hired mercenary Sernas. He is the leader of a band of men causing strife within the city because Garrone refuses to pay them for their heroics. She promises her lover jewels as repayment but problems arise when local politico Purdom fills the jewel chests with rocks, taking the real gems for himself. The mercenaries attack once more, but Purdom's plot is revealed and he is executed. Valerie and Sernas are reunited once more. This simple story is lost in a myriad of poor production values. The script is dopey with an amateurish job on the photography and incoherent editing. The actors are stiff and unnatural as they so often are in cheap historical epics. The American version was also hampered by a poor dubbing job.

p, Fides-Stella; d, Sergio Grieco; w, Andre Tabet, John Blamy, Barbara Sohmers (based on a story by Gustave Flaubert); ph, Piero Portalupi (CinemaScope, DeLuxe Color); m, Alexandre Derevitsky; ed, Enzo Alfonzi.

Historical Drama						(PR:A MPAA:NR)

LOVES OF THREE QUEENS, THE**1/2
(1954, Ital./Fr.) 90m CDD-P.C.E. c (ETERNA FEMMINA; L'AMANTE DI PARIDE; AKA: ETERNAL WOMAN; FACE THAT LAUNCHED A THOUSAND SHIPS, THE; LOVE OF THREE QUEENS)

Hedy Lamarr (*Hedy Windsor/Helen of Troy/Empress Josephine/Genieve de Bra-*

bant), Gerard Oury (*Napoleon Bonaparte*), Massimo Serato (*Paris*), Robert Beatty (*Menelaus*), Cathy O'Donnell (*Oenone*), Guido Celano (*Jupiter*), Enrico Glori (*Priamus*), Seren Michelotti (*Cassandra*), Alba Arnova (*Venus*), Terence Morgan, Caesar Danova.

Lamarr must decide which costume to wear to a prestigious ball so she asks for advice from three male friends. One suggests she come as Helen of Troy, another says she is like Empress Josephine, Napoleon's mistress, and the third says Genieve de Brabant. But Lamarr doesn't feel that any of them fully suit her personality. Essentially the idea is best signified in the Italian title ETERNAL WOMAN, which tells us that the film is about the immortal essence of women. Not exceptionally well-made, the picture can boast an interesting combination of directors—France's Marc Allegret and our own Edgar Ulmer, who after beginning as an assistant to Max Reinhardt and F. W. Murnau, found that he didn't quite fit into the Hollywood mold. The picture was produced by the production company which Lamarr formed, but found little, if any, success. Originally the picture ran over three hours, but was mercifully cut. A fine score by Nino Rota helps.

p, Victor Pahlen; d, Marc Allegret, Edgar Ulmer; w, Allegret, Nino Novarese, Salka Viertel (based on a story by Mackenzie, Vadim Plenianikoy, Allegret, Hugh Gray); ph, Desmond Dickinson, Fernando Risi (Technicolor); m, Nino Rota; ed, Manuel Del Campo; art d, Virgilio Marchi, Mario Chiari.

Drama							(PR:A MPAA:NR)

LOVE'S OLD SWEET SONG**
(1933, Brit.) 79m Argyle/But bw (AKA: THE MISSING WITNESS)

John Stuart (*Paul Kingslake*), Joan Wyndham (*Mary Dean*), William Freshman (*Jimmy Croft*), Julie Suedo (*Iris Sinclair*), Ronald Ward (*Eric Kingslake*), Moore Marriott (*Old Tom*), Marie Wright (*Sarah*), Ivor Maxwell (*Podger Kingslake*), Barbara Everest (*Nurse*), Malcolm Tod (*Announcer*), Charles Courtney, Picot Schooling, Dora Levis, Sidney Arnold.

Wyndham is a singer whose manager (Stuart) loves her. She marries Ward, Stuart's no-good half brother, and becomes pregnant by him. When Ward's mistress is murdered, Stuart confesses to the crime to protect his brother and he goes to prison. Ward leaves Wyndham with her baby and is later killed in a gunfight. Wyndham realizes the truth and waits for Stuart's release. Depressing melodrama competently done.

p, John Argyle; d, Manning H. Hayes; w, Lydia Hayward; ph, Desmond Dickinson.

Drama							(PR:A MPAA:NR)

LOVESICK**
(1983) 95m Ladd/WB c

Dudley Moore (*Saul Benjamin*), Elizabeth McGovern (*Chloe Allen*), Alec Guinness (*Sigmund Freud*), Christine Baranski (*Nymphomaniac*), Gene Saks (*Frantic Patient*), Renee Taylor (*Mrs. Mondragon*), Kent Broadhurst (*Gay*), Lester Rawlins (*Silent Patient*), Wallace Shawn (*Otto Jaffe*), Suzanne Barrie (*His Wife*), Anne Kerry (*Katie*), Lotte Palfi Andor, Paul Andor, Anna Berger, Sol Frieder, Merwin Goldsmith, Fred Kareman, Mohindra Nath Kawlra, E. Katherine Kerr, Arthur Klein, Fred Melamed, Benjamin Rayson, Jonathan Reynolds, Stewart Steinberg (*Analysts*), Ron Silver (*Ted Caruso*), Ann Gillespie (*Actress*), John Tillinger (*Director*), Jeff Natter (*Stage Manager*), Peggy LeRoy Johnson (*Actress*), Larry Rivers (*Applezweig*), Richard B. Shull (*Dr. Fessner*), David Strathairn (*Zuckerman*), Yanni Sfinias (*Vendor*), Jack Sevier, Raynor Scheine (*In Shelter*), Mark Blum (*Intern*), Isabelle Monk (*Nurse*), Anne DeSalvo (*Interviewer*), Ray Ramirez (*Menendez*), Ellen Whyte (*Waitress*), Armalie Collier (*Maid*), John Huston (*Dr. Larry Geller*), Kaylan Pickford (*Anna*), Alan King (*Dr. Lionel Gross*), Selma Diamond (*Dr. Singer*), Stefan Schnabel (*Dr. Bergsen*), Otto Bettman (*Dr. Waxman*).

This second feature from writer-director Brickman reveals the influence of his friend Woody Allen. Just as Allen's character in PLAY IT AGAIN SAM carried on a dialogue with an apparition of Humphrey Bogart, so too does Moore, the star of Brickman's film, talk with a spectral Sigmund Freud. Moore plays a psychiatrist who falls in love with patient McGovern. The roles are all neatly done, but Brickman's script is nearly directionless. The film has its cute moments, but in the end, it is a sad waste of fine talent.

p, Charles Okun; d&w, Marshall Brickman; ph, Gerry Fisher (Technicolor); m, Philippe Sarde; ed, Nina Feinberg; prod d, Philip Rosenberg; set d, Gary Brink; cos, Kristi Zea.

Comedy			Cas.			(PR:C MPAA:PG)

LOVIN' MOLLY** (1974) 98m COL c (AKA: THE WILD AND THE SWEET)

Anthony Perkins (*Gid*), Beau Bridges (*Johnny*), Blythe Danner (*Molly*), Edward Binns (*Mr. Fry*), Susan Sarandon (*Sarah*), Conrad Fowkes (*Eddie*), Claude Traverse (*Mr. Taylor*), John Henry Faulk (*Mr. Grinsom*).

Forty years of a *menage a trois*, Texas-style. Danner is the liberated lady who manages to hold the long-term attention of two close buddies, played by Perkins and Bridges. The film opens in 1925, introducing the two farm boys and the woman they both love. Through the use of a voice-over we are propelled to 1945: Danner has married Fowkes but he soon leaves her a widow; Perkins has gotten married and fathered two kids; Bridges remains single. She still holds the two men at bay as the affairs continue. The film climaxes in 1964 with Perkins finally succumbing to a heart attack, and Danner and Bridges ending up together. Danner is the real standout here, giving an excellent performance. The sense of wildness she captures, and the slow aging she affects, are completely natural. She is given something few American film actresses ever get their hands on, a role she can really sink her teeth into. However, the story covers too large a time frame, and Lumet's direction has no feeling for the story or the place. He didn't seem to realize that Texas is a world of its own. This could easily have been New Jersey for all the uniqueness to be found in the direction. McMurtry, who wrote the original novel the film was based on, spoke out against the film's direction, claiming it had not been a true reflection of his work.

p, Stephen Friedman; d, Sidney Lumet; w, Friedman (based on the novel *Leaving Cheyenne* by Larry McMurtry); ph, Edward Brown (Movielab Color); m, Fred Hellerman; ed, Joanne Burke; prod d, Gene Coffin; set d, Robert Drunheller, Paul Hefferan.

Drama **(PR:O MPAA:R)**

LOVIN' THE LADIES** (1930) 65m RKO bw

Richard Dix *(Peter)*, Lois Wilson *(Joan Bently)*, Allen Kearns *(Jimmy Farnsworth)*, Rita La Roy *(Louise Endicott)*, Renee Macready *(Betty Duncan)*, Virginia Sale *(Marie)*, Selmer Jackson *(George Van Horne)*, Anthony Bushell *(Brooks)*, Henry Armetta *(Sagatelli)*.

Kearns, in order to win a bet with his pal Jackson, tries to get a young couple together and then engaged in just a month's time. Socialite Macready and Dix, an electrician, are his subjects. He has Dix dress as a society gentleman in order to impress Wilson, but the experiment goes awry when the electrician falls for Kearns' fiancee Wilson instead. In desperation Kearns reveals Dix's identity. In the meantime, Macready has fallen for a common butler. Some entertaining moments in this comic mix-up, but overall it's a fairly routine and predictable comedy.

p, William Le Baron; d, Melville Brown; w, J. Walter Ruben (based on the play "I Love You" by Le Baron); ph, Edward Cronjager; art d, Max Ree.

Comedy **(PR:A MPAA:NR)**

LOVING** (1970) 89m COL c

George Segal *(Brooks Wilson)*, Eva Marie Saint *(Selma Wilson)*, Sterling Hayden *(Lepridon)*, Keenan Wynn *(Edward)*, Nancie Phillips *(Nelly)*, Janis Young *(Grace)*, David Doyle *(Will)*, Paul Sparer *(Marve)*, Andrew Duncan *(Willy)*, Sherry Lansing *(Susan)*, Roland Winters *(Plommie)*, Edgar Stehli *(Mr. Kramm)*, Calvin Holt *(Danny)*, Mina Kolb *(Diane)*, Diana Douglas *(Mrs. Shavelson)*, David Ford *(Al)*, James Manis *(Charles)*, Mart Hulswit *(Ted)*, John Fink *(Brad)*, William Duffy *(Jay)*, Irving Selbst *(Benny)*, Martin Friedberg *(Roger)*, Lorraine Cullen *(Lizzie)*, Cheryl Bucher *(Hannah)*, Ed Crowley *(Mr. Shavelson)*, Roy Scheider *(Skip)*, Sab Shimono *(Byron)*, Eileen O'Neill *(Cindy)*, Diane Daives *(Barbie)*.

Sometimes funny, sometimes dramatic, LOVING is most times dull. Based on a novel by J. M. Ryan, it's the story of freelance artist Segal and his wife, Saint, as they try to keep their rocky marriage together in suburban Connecticut. Segal is having an in-town affair with Young and his work situation is teetering. The combination serves to place him on the precipice of a breakdown. He has a chance at a large commission and is supposed to meet with mogul Hayden at a private dining club that caters to admen. Segal drinks too much and gets vicious with the club's prexy. Hayden finds that behavior amusing, and says he'll think about giving Segal the business. At a party tossed by his mistress's aunt and uncle, Segal finds out that Hayden liked him enough to award him the art business. He tells neither Saint (who feels it's time they had a new house) nor Young (who feels it's time they had a more permanent relationship) and when Phillips, the nympho wife of neighbor Doyle, begins to come on to him, Segal falls for it. The two of them go to a child's playroom that has closed-circuit TV (for parents to keep tabs on the kids) and Segal and Phillips are observed by the entire party crowd as they make love. Saint watches and the crowd howls until Segal realizes what's happening as he spies the camera. He runs outside, not wearing his pants, where Doyle whacks him around. Then Saint begins to pound him with her purse until she can't hit him any longer. When her arms get tired, Segal tells her he's won Hayden's account and we are left with the feeling that she might just stay with him. Scheider does a small role and Lansing, who later became a film executive and ran FOX studios for years before beginning her own independent company, plays a sexpot. Her business ability was far greater than her acting prowess and acting's loss became producing's gain when she doffed the sock and buskin in favor of the executive suite.

p, Don Devlin; d, Irvin Kershner; w, Devlin (based on the novel *Brooks Wilson, Ltd.* by J. M. Ryan); ph, Gordon Willis (Eastmancolor); m, Bernardo Segall; ed, Robert Lawrence; prod d, Walter Scott Herndon; set d, John Godfrey; cos, Albert Wolsky; m/l, title song Segall, Willam B. Dorsey (sung by Chris Morgan); makeup, Joe Cranzano.

Comedy/Drama **(PR:C MPAA:R)**

LOVING COUPLES** (1966, Swed.) 113m Prominent bw (ALSKANDE PAR)

Harriet Andersson *(Agda)*, Gunnel Lindblom *(Adele Holstrom)*, Gio Petre *(Angela)*, Anita Bjork *(Aunt Petra)*, Gunnar Bjornstrand *(Dr. Jacob Lewin)*, Inga Landgre *(Mrs. Lewin)*, Jan Malmsjo *(Stellan von Pahlen)*, Frank Sundstrom *(Dir. Ola Landborg)*, Eva Dahlbeck *(Mrs. Landborg)*, Heinz Hopf *(Bernhard Landborg)*, Hans Straat *(Thomas)*, Bengt Brunskog *(Tord Holstrom)*, Toivo Pawlo *(Mr. Macson)*, Margit Carlqvist *(Dora Macson)*, Jan-Erik Lindqvist *(Peter)*, Barbro Hiort af Ornas *(Lilian)*, Marta Dorff *(Alexandra)*, Lissi Alandh *(Bell)*, Ake Gronberg *(Elderly Lecher in Street)*, Isa Quensel *(Fredrika)*, Hans Sundberg *(Organist)*, Sten Lonnert *(Kisse)*, Axel Fritz *(Per)*, Henrik Schildt *(Sam)*, Berit Gustafsson *(Henrika)*, Lars Grundtman, Lennart Grundtman *(Twin Brothers Nick and Nock)*, Dan Landgre *(Cecil)*, Lo Dagerman *(Angela, Age 10)*, Rebecca Pawlo *(Adele, Age 10)*, Katarina Edfeldt *(Agda, Age 13)*, Anja Boman *(Stanny)*, Nancy Dalunde *(Adele's Mother)*, Meta Velander *(The Woman)*, Claes Thelander *(Priest)*, Kai Norstrom *(Daniel)*, Eva Alw *(Housekeeper)*, Ulf Johansson, Borje Mellvig *(Lawyers)*, Kai Reiners *(Good Man)*, Sonja Hjort *(Patient)*, Birger Asander *(Band Leader)*, Stig de la Berg *(Sore Loser)*, Bo Hederstrom, Arne Lindblad, Holger Rosenqvist, Axeline Le Mon *(Guests)*.

An early film in the directorial career of Scandinavian actress and feminist filmmaker Zetterling, set in 1915, that traces the lives of three women in a hospital about to give birth and examines how they became pregnant and how they feel about it. Lindblom is a bitter woman who resents the middle class and has married a servant of a wealthy family. Though she really doesn't love her husband she conceives a child out of spite and receives the news coldly when informed by doctors that the baby is stillborn. Andersson is a wild and irresponsible woman who was introduced to sex at a very early age by an old man who seduced her with sweets. Since then she has become a model and occasional thief who sleeps around. Through a series of events she winds up seducing the son of the rich family that employs Lindblom's husband and she becomes pregnant by him. He agrees to support the child if she will consent to marry a homosexual friend and pretend the child is his. She agrees and has the baby while flirting with the doctor who delivers it. Petre is a quiet and unassuming woman, who had a brief lesbian encounter while in school, but then fell in love with an archeologist and became pregnant by him. When he refuses to take responsibility for the act, she becomes outraged and joins a feminist movement to break the taboo of having illegitimate children. Eventually she has her baby and is the only one of the three women who looks forward to being a mother. Zetterling's films were considered quite controversial at the time of their release, but upon historical reflection, it is apparent that her earlier works delighted in their taboo-breaking stance, and tended to ignore some of the weaknesses in characterization and execution.

p, Rune Waldekranz, Goran Lindgren; d, Mai Zetterling; w, Zetterling, David Hughes (based on *Froknarna von Pahlen* by Agnes von Krusenstjerna); ph, Sven Nykvist; m, Rodger Wallis; ed, Paul Davies; art d, Jan Boleslaw; cos, Birgitta Hahn; ch, Holger Rosenqvist; makeup, Gullan Westfelt.

Drama **(PR:O MPAA:NR)**

LOVING COUPLES** (1980) 97m FOX c

Shirley MacLaine *(Evelyn)*, James Coburn *(Walter)*, Susan Sarandon *(Stephanie)*, Stephen Collins *(Gregg)*, Sally Kellerman *(Mrs. Liggett)*, Nan Martin *(Walter's Nurse)*, Shelly Batt *(Dulcy)*, Bernard Behrens *(Elegant Doctor)*, Anne Bloom *(Nurse)*, Fred Carney *(Hotel Clerk)*, Helena Carroll *(Prudence)*, Marilyn Chris *(Sally)*, Pat Corley *(Delmonico Clerk)*, Michael Curry *(Ken)*, John Davis *(Cop Partner)*, John deLancie *(Allan)*, Edith Fields *(Evelyn's Nurse)*, Estelle Omens *(Mrs. Herzog)*, Peter Hobbs *(Frank)*, Paula Jones *(Salesgirl)*, Art Kassul *(Drunk Doctor)*, Hap Lawrence *(Nudist)*, Bob Levine, John Medici, David Murphy, June Sanders, Tony Travis, Sam Weisman.

This dopey little sex farce tries to be the BOB AND CAROL AND TED AND ALICE of the 1980s but falls far short of that goal. MacLaine and Coburn are a pair of workaholic doctors who barely know each other after years of marriage. Collins is a younger man, living with TV weathergirl Sarandon. After a meeting that could only take place in the movies (and unfortunately does) MacLaine and Collins have an affair. Coburn in turn takes up with Sarandon and from there it's a wild sex romp through motels and hot tubs. Sarandon is a delight, giving one of her sweet, zany characterizations while MacLaine and Coburn fight it out to see which one of these two veterans has more ham than Porky Pig. Everything is resolved nice and neat, just as you knew it would be. Fortunately the otherwise average formula direction moves the film along briskly. But the script plays into every trendy California icon of 1980, including disco music and "heart-rending" ballads. Bring a checklist so you do not miss anything.

p, Renee Valente; d, Jack Smight; w, Martin Donovan; ph, Philip Lathrop (Metrocolor); m, Fred Karlin; ed, Grey Fox, Frank Urioste; art d, Jan Scott.

Comedy **Cas.** **(PR:O MPAA:PG)**

LOVING MEMORY*½ (1970, Brit.) 57m Scott Free-BFI-Memorial Enterprises/BFI c

David Pugh *(Young Man)*, Roy Evans *(Man)*, Rosamund Greenwood *(Woman)*.

In this strange British tale an older woman becomes obsessed with her late brother's memory. After finding the cold corpse of a bike rider she begins to treat the cadaver as her own brother. As strange as it sounds.

p, Steve Bayley; d&w, Anthony Scott.

Drama **(PR:O MPAA:NR)**

LOVING YOU*** (1957) 101m PAR c

Elvis Presley *(Deke Rivers)*, Lizabeth Scott *(Glenda Markle)*, Wendell Corey *(Walker "Tex" Warner)*, Dolores Hart *(Susan Jessup)*, James Gleason *(Carl Meade)*, Paul Smith *(Skeeter)*, Ken Becker *(Wayne)*, Jana Lund *(Daisy)*, Ralph Dumke *(Tallman)*, The Jordanaires *(Themselves)*, Yvonne Lime *(Sally)*, Skip Young *(Teddy)*, Vernon Rich *(Harry Taylor)*, David Cameron *(Castle)*, Grace Hayle *(Mrs. Gunderson)*, Dick Ryan *(Mack)*, Steve Pendleton *(O'Shea)*, Sydney Chatton *(Grew)*, Jack Latham *(TV Announcer)*, William Forrest *(Mr. Jessup)*, Irene Tedrow *(Mrs. Jessup)*, Hal K. Dawson *(Lieutenant)*, Joe Forte *(Editor)*, Almira Sessions, Madge Blake *(Women)*, Beach Dickerson *(Glenn)*, Gail Lund *(Candy)*, Harry Cheshire *(Mayor)*, Gladys Presley *(Extra in Audience)*.

Presley's second film was a fictionalized version of how he made it to the top. "The Pelvis" more or less plays himself, a young hillbilly truckdriver who overnight becomes a rock'n'roll star. After delivering a load of beer to a political rally, Presley is talked into doing a number by a press agent (Scott) and the band's leader (Corey). Naturally he's a big hit and they talk him into joining them. He does and soon he is the sensation of Texas. He falls for Hart, a singer in the band, but gradually develops an interest in Scott. She begins throwing outrageous publicity stunts that bring great attention to her singer. As his fame grows, Presley is booked by Gleason to do a one man show at an important theater outside Dallas. Scott pulls off another of her promotional bonanzas by buying Presley a convertible and telling the press it is a gift from an admiring, though anonymous, oil man's widow. But in order to pay for the car, the band has to lose a member, namely Hart. Consoling his former love, Presley drives her out to her family home. There he discovers the wonderful simplicity of farm life but the idyll is interrupted when Scott fetches her singer and brings him back for the concert. But he discovers that she and Corey are divorced from each other and once more he drives off, this time in his old car. He crashes the old clunker but Scott finds him once more and brings him back for the show. Finally he ends up with Hart and a TV contract, and Scott gets back with Corey. This ranks as one of Presley's better films. He gives a fine performance, singing his heart out in some wonderful concert footage as well as emoting with some substance rarely found in his later, highly cartoonish features. Reportedly Presley surprised producer Wallis by explaining that what made great movie actors like Brando the talents they were was that they never smiled on screen. Kanter directs with vigor. Col. Tom Parker, Presley's money-mad manager, served as technical advisor. Look for Presley's mom as an extra. In addition to not smiling, Presley sings some great rock 'n'roll songs including "Loving You" (Jerry Lieber, Mike Stoller) and the classic "Teddy Bear" (Kal Mann, Bernie Lowe). Presley had an affinity for teddy bears, receiving them by the hundreds from fans in the early days. Presley also sings: "Lonesome Cowboy" (Sid Tepper, Roy C. Bennett), "Got A Lot of Livin' To Do" (A. Schroeder, Ben Weisman), "Party" (Jessie Mae Robinson), "Mean Woman Blues" (Claude DeMetrius), and "Hot Dog" (Lieber, Stoller).

p, Hal B. Wallis; d, Hal Kanter; w, Kanter, Herbert Baker (based on the story "A Call From Mitch Miller" by Mary Agnes Thompson); ph, Charles Lang Jr. (Vistavision, Technicolor); m, Walter Scharf; ed, Howard Smith; md, Scharf; art d, Hal Pereira, Albert Nozaki; cos, Edith Head; spec eff, John P. Fulton; ch, Charles O'Curran; makeup, Wally Westmore.

Drama/Musical   **Cas.**   **(PR:A MPAA:NR)**

LOWER DEPTHS, THE***
(1937, Fr.) 92m Albatros/Mayer-Burstyn (LES BAS-FONDS)

Jean Gabin (Pepel), Louis Jouvet (The Baron), Suzy Prim (Vassilissa), Jany Holt (Nastia), Vladimir Sokoloff (Kostyley), Junie Astor (Natacha), Robert Le Vigan (The Actor), Camille Bert (The Count), Rene Genin (Luka), Paul Temps (Satine), Robert Ozanne (Jabot), Saint-Iles (Kletsch), Maurice Bazuel (Allochka), Gabreillo (The Inspector), Larive (Felix), Nathalie Alexeeff (Anna).

An interesting adaptation of the famed Gorki play from its original Russian setting to the streets of Paris. Jouvet is fine as the French nobleman who loses his fortunes and must live in the Parisian slums. Gabin and Astor are the two lovers and Sokoloff a cruel landlord. Reportedly, Gorki saw the script shortly before his death and gave the film his approval. It was voted "Best Film of the Year" by French critics and director Renoir was consequently made a knight in the French government's Legion of Honor. A remake by Japanese director Akira Kurosawa was done in 1957, released in the U.S. in 1962. (In French; English subtitles).

p, Arthur Mayer, Joseph Burstyn; d, Jean Renoir; w, Renoir, Charles Spaak, E. Zamiatine, J. Companeez (based on the play by Maxim Gorki); ph, F. Bourgas; m, Jean Wiener; English subtitles, Julian Leigh.

Drama   **(PR:C MPAA:NR)**

LOWER DEPTHS, THE***
(1962, Jap.) 125m Toho/Brandon bw (DONZOKO)

Toshiro Mifune (Sutekichi, the Thief), Isuzu Yamada (Osugi, the Landlady), Ganjiro Nakamura (Rokubei, her Husband), Kyoko Kagawa (Okayo, her Sister), Bokuzen Hidari (Kahei, the Priest), Minoru Chiaki (The Ex-Samurai), Kamatari Fujiwara (The Actor), Eijiro Tono (Tomekichi, the Tinker), Eiko Miyoshi (Asa, his Wife), Akemi Negishi (Osen, the Prostitute), Koji Mitsui (Yoshisaburo, the Gambler), Nijiko Kiyokawa (Otaki), Haruo Tanaka (Tatsu), Kichijiro Ueda (Police Agent), Yu Fujiki.

Once again Kurosawa looked to Russian drama for his source material (he had ventured in this area before with CRIME AND PUNISHMENT and THE IDIOT, which were only marginally successful). Based on a play by Gorki and set in 19th-century Japan, THE LOWER DEPTHS is an ensemble film filled with fine performances (Mifune, as usual, has the edge). The action takes place in a small hostel which houses an odd assortment of eccentric characters who talk incessantly. The landlady, Yamada, hates her boarders and treats them shabbily, all except for Mifune, a thief, for whom she feels a great deal of passion. Mifune, however, is in love with Yamada's sister and when the landlady learns of this, she kills her husband in a jealous rage. Mifune is arrested and charged with the murder. Yamada goes mad with loneliness and the other boarders happily drink sake and laugh at the proceedings. Kurosawa was attracted to the material because of the inherent black comedy value which he felt illustrated the absurd nature of life.

p, Sojiro Motoki, Akira Kurosawa; d, Kurosawa; w, Hideo Oguni, Kursosawa, Shinobu Hashimoto; (based on the play "Na dne" by Maxim Gorki); ph, Ichio Yamazaki; m, Masaru Sato; art d, Yoshiro Muraki.

Drama/Comedy   **(PR:C MPAA:NR)**

LOYAL HEART**   (1946, Brit.) 80m BN-Strand/Anglo American bw

Percy Marmont (John Armstrong), Harry Welchman (Sir Ian), Patricia Marmont (Joan Stewart), Philip Kay (Tommy), Eleanor Hallam (Mary Armstrong), Beckett Bould (Burton), Valentine Dunn (Alice Burton), Cameron Hall (Edwards), Alexander Field (Blinkers), James Knight (Police Sergeant), Sydney Bromley, Mac Harry Picton, Gerald Pring, Joseph Ralph, Harry Herbert, John England, Arthur E. Owen, Charles Doe, Carl Lacey, Dorothy Dark, Fleet the Dog.

One farmer tries to buy the loyal sheepdog of his rival, but the canine is not for sale. The two fight, and the dog's owner is charged by his enemy with sheep stealing. Fortunately a local squire and one of the men's sons smooth things out for a happy ending. The story has some enjoyable moments, rising above a seemingly dull plot line. One critic of the film observed that Fleet the Dog was "far and away the best actor in the film."

p, Louis H. Jackson; d, Oswald Mitchell; w, George A. Cooper (based on the novel *Beth the Sheepdog* by Ernest Lewis); ph, Arthur Grant, Gerald Gibbs.

Drama   **(PR:AAA MPAA:NR)**

LOYALTIES** 1/2
(1934, Brit.) 70m Associated Talking Picture/Harold Auten bw

Basil Rathbone (Ferdinand de Levis), Heather Thatcher (Margaret Orme), Miles Mander (Capt. Ronald Dancy, D.S.O.), Joan Wyndham (Mabel, His Wife), Philip Strange (Maj. Colford), Alan Napier (Gen. Canynge), Algernon West (Charles Winsor), Cecily Byrne (Lady Adela, His Wife), Athole Stewart (Lord St. Erth), Patric Curwen (Sir Frederic Blair), Marcus Barron (The Lord Chief Justice), Ben Field (Gilman), Griffith Humphreys (Inspector Jones), Patrick Waddington (Augustus Borring), Lawrence Hanray (Jacob Twisden), Arnold Lucy (Googie), Robert Mawdesley (Edward Graviter), Mike Johnson (Jenkins), Anthony Holles (Ricardos), Stafford Hilliard (Treisure), Robert Coote (Robert), Aubrey Dexter (Kentman), Maxine Sandra (Ricardo's Daughter).

Rathbone plays a rich young Jewish man who runs into anti-Semitism at a weekend house party. When his wallet is stolen, Rathbone deduces that the culprit is Mander. Rather than risk scandal, some of the guests offer him membership in an exclusive club to forget about it. But when others balk at this because of his religion, Rathbone decides to press charges. He takes it to court and when Mander is proven guilty, the captain commits suicide. Based on a popular British play, this film is a definite mix. Rathbone, who created the role on stage, is good in the lead. Direction is awkward, though, and sometimes the plot seems to move in jerks rather than an even flow. The British accents are also a little hard on American ears, with the actors occasionally slurring their dialog as well. Galsworthy died shortly before filming began but was said to have been pleased with the adaptation of his play. British audiences enjoyed the film and applauded after screenings.

p&d, Basil Dean; w, W. P. Lipscomb (based on the play by John Galsworthy); ph, Robert Martin; art d, Edward Carrick.

Drama   **(PR:A MPAA:NR)**

LOYALTY OF LOVE**   (1937, Ital.) 90m Nuovo Mundo bw

Marta Abba (Teresa Confalonieri), Elsa de Giorgi (Princess Jablonowscka), Tina Lottanzi (Empress Carolina), Nerio Bernardi (Count Federico Confalonieri), Luigi Carini (Count Vitaliano Confalonieri, His Father), Luigi Cimara (Prince Metternich), Filippo Scelzo (Baron Salvotti), Riccardo Tassani (Franz the First), Romolo Costa (Governor of Milan), Achille Maieroni (Field Marshal Bubna), Erminio d'Olivo (Cav. De Castilla), Giovanni Barreila (Bolchesi).

Abba is excellent as the long-suffering wife of Bernardi. He is cheating on her with a variety of women, and remaining one step ahead of the law in his political activities. Eventually he is caught and sentenced to death, but through Abba's efforts the sentence is commuted to life imprisonment. Abba is the high point of the film, overshadowing the other performers with the intensity of her characterization. Unfortunately she is ultimately undermined by the uninspired direction and choppy editing of the film. The sound recording and photography also left much to be desired. At the time of this film's U.S. release, Abba was starring in the Broadway play "Tovarich." (In Italian; English subtitles.)

d, Guido Brignone; w, Tomaso Smith (based on a story by Rino Alessi); ph, Anchise Brizzi; m, S. A. M. Bixio.

Drama   **(PR:A MPAA:NR)**

LSD, I HATE YOU
(SEE: MOVIE STAR, AMERICAN STYLE OR, LSD, I HATE YOU, 1966)

LUCI DEL VARIETA   (SEE: VARIETY LIGHTS, 1965)

LUCIANO**   (1963, Ital.) 80m Vorona bw

Luciano Morelli (Luciano), Valentina Piacente (Wife), Anna Bragaglia (Mother), Franco Cluffi (Father), Paola Carlini (Rich Man).

Baldi, a noted Italian documentary filmmaker, made his feature-film debut with this piece, which was an expansion of a short documentary he had created earlier. Morelli, who was the subject of the original short, plays more or less himself. He is a young man, home after serving time in prison. His mother has died and his father pretends to be ill while having an affair with a woman. Confused and angered, Morelli leaves home and is taken under the wing of a rich man, who has attained his position by marriage. Baldi's camera style is clearly influenced by his documentaries. He has a nice style, using the mobile camera well. His use of non-actors, reminiscent of the earlier Italian neo-realism filmmaking is nicely handled as well. But the film suffers from its length. Though only 80 minutes, too many social and human issues are touched on without really focusing on any of them. The result is a thinly spread film that tries for dramatic and social impact but falls far short of this ideal.

p, Mario Lanfranchi; d, Luigi Baldi; w, Baldi, M. Jemma; ph, Ennio Guarnieri; m, Luciano Chailly.

Drama   **(PR:C MPAA:NR)**

LUCIFER PROJECT, THE   (SEE: BARRACUDA, 1978)

LUCK OF A SAILOR, THE**
(1934, Brit.) 66m British International Pictures/Wardour bw

Greta Nissen (Queen Helena), David Manners (Capt. Colin), Clifford Mollison (Shorty), Camilla Horn (Louise), Hugh Wakefield (King Karl), Lawrence Grossmith (Silvius), Reginald Purdell (Jenkins), H. F. Maltby (Admiral), Jimmy Godden (Betz), Jean Cadell (Princess Rosanna), Cecil Ramage (Owner), Gus McNaughton (Official), Arnold Lucy, J. H. Roberts.

Wakefield is an exiled Ruritanian monarch who marries Nissen, a poverty stricken commoner. After the nuptials, Wakefield is called back to the throne and takes his bride home on a British battleship. There Nissen meets commander Manners and the two fall in love. Fortunately for her, this is the movies where complications like marriage are easily smoothed out by unlikely endings. This one has Wakefield's people asking her to give up the king so he can marry an heiress, a task Nissen joyfully accepts. The rest of the film is as unbelievable as the ending in this routine, low-budget romance.

p, Walter C. Mycroft; d, Robert Milton; w, Clifford Grey, Wolfgang Wilhelm (based on the play "Contraband" by Horton Giddy).

Romance **(PR:A MPAA:NR)**

LUCK OF GINGER COFFEY, THE***
(1964, U.S./Can.) 100m Roth-Kershner-Crawley/CD c

Robert Shaw *(Ginger Coffey)*, Mary Ure *(Vera)*, Liam Redmond *(MacGregor)*, Tom Harvey *(Joe McGlade)*, Libby McClintock *(Paulie)*, Leo Leyden *(Brott)*, Powys Thomas *(Fox)*, Tom Kneebone *(Kenny)*, Leslie Yeo *(Stan Melton)*, Vern Chapman *(Hawkins)*, Paul Guevremont *(Marcel)*, Barry Stewart *(Clarence)*, Arch McDonnell *(O'Donnell)*, Oliva Legare *(Judge)*, Jacques Godin *(Policeman)*, Maurice Beaupre *(Mons. Beaulieu)*, Sydney Brown *(Old Billy)*, Juliette Huot *(Mme. Beaulieu)*, Paul Hebert *(Court Clerk)*, Barney McManus *(Newspaper Foreman)*, Clarence Goodhue *(Hickey)*.

A well-intentioned and noncommercial Canadian-based film starring real-life husband and wife Shaw and Ure, playing, oddly enough, a husband and wife. Shaw is pushing forty and can't hold a job in Dublin so he and his family emigrate to Montreal in the hope of a new life. His teenager daughter, McClintock, doesn't like the move but that's the way it is with kids and Shaw and Ure hope she'll adjust. Shaw has little success in Canada and his family asks to return to Ireland. They've kept a nest egg of money for the trip home but Shaw has spent it and now they must stay. Ure leaves Shaw, taking McClintock, but soon the child returns to live with her father. Shaw has apparently settled down and is working at two jobs; as a proofreader at a newspaper under hard-hearted Redmond, and next to Thomas, a bitter comrade, and as a laundry delivery man by day. Shaw thinks he may get a better job as a reporter so he jettisons his delivery job, despite getting a good offer from the folks who run the laundry. Suddenly, for no apparent reason, he is fired from the newspaper and it's too late to get back into the laundry so he is left low and wet (as opposed to high and dry). He talks Ure into coming home to help him control McClintock, who is now out of hand. Shaw looks for work, can't find anything, and winds up drenched with what the Irish call "the curse" of whiskey. He's soon arrested and tossed in the clink. Kindly judge Legare lets him out with a rap on the knuckles and he is heartened to see that Ure is standing outside the court waiting for him, open-armed. A nice picture and an interesting look at immigrants who have no language problem. It's about little people in a big predicament and succeeds on its own terms, but we are left with the thought that if we'd seen another two hours of this, Shaw would have wound up beating his wife and daughter, then stealing a car, and drunkenly driving off a bridge.

p, Leon Roth; d, Irvin Kershner; w, Brian Moore (based on his novel); ph, Manny Wynn; m, Bernardo Segall; ed, Anthony Gibbs; md, Segall; prod d, Harry Horner; art d, Albert Brenner; set d, Claude Bonniere.

Drama **(PR:A-C MPAA:NR)**

LUCK OF ROARING CAMP, THE*½ (1937) 61m MON bw

Owen Davis, Jr. *(Davy)*, Joan Woodbury *(Elsie)*, Charles Brokaw *(Oakhurst)*, Ferris Taylor *(Judge Brandt)*, Bob Kortman *(Yuba Bill)*, Charles King, Jr. *(Sandy)*, Byron Foulger *(Kentuck)*, Robert McKenzie *(Tuttle)*, John Wallace.

This was one of the many inconsequential programmers put out by Monogram studios. Davis is an orphan in the middle of the California gold rush. He teams up with gambler Brokaw and singer Woodbury for some rather uninspired adventures. The situations and dialog are laughably bad and the direction moves the film at a snail's pace.

p, Scott R. Dunlap; d, I. V. Willat; w, Harvey Gates (based on the story by Bret Harte); ph, Paul Ivano.

Western **(PR:A MPAA:NR)**

LUCK OF THE GAME (SEE: GRIDIRON FLASH, 1935)

LUCK OF THE IRISH, THE*** (1937, Ireland) 80m PAR/Guaranteed bw

Richard Hayward *(Sam Mulhern)*, Kay Walsh *(Eileen O'Donnel)*, Niall MacGinnis *(Derek O'Neill)*, J. R. Mageean *(Sir Brian O'Neill)*, R. H. MacCandless *(Gavin Grogan)*, Charles Fagan *(Sgt. Doyle)*, Harold Griffin *(Simon Reid)*, Charlotte Tedlie *(Hortense O'Neill)*, Nan Cullen *(Widow Whistler)*, John M. Henderson *(Sir Richard O'Donnel)*, Meta Grainger *(Lady O'Donnel)*.

This amiable comedy features Hayward as an Irishman who finds his wealth rapidly disappearing. In order to save himself, he hocks his stately manor and bets it all on his horse during the Grand National Steeplechase. There are some good Irish tunes as well as a comedy bar scene. The ensemble is made up of the members of the Belfast Repertory Company, who know how to play off each other. Pedelty made his directorial debut with this film after working his way up from being Paramount's London film scout.

p, Richard Hayward, Donovan Pedelty; d&w, Pedelty (based on the novel by Victor Haddick); ph, Jack Willson.

Comedy **(PR:A MPAA:NR)**

LUCK OF THE IRISH*** (1948) 99m FOX bw

Tyrone Power *(Stephen Fitzgerald)*, Anne Baxter *(Nora)*, Cecil Kellaway *(Horace)*, Lee J. Cobb *(D. C. Augur)*, James Todd *(Bill Clark)*, Jayne Meadows *(Frances Augur)*, J. M. Kerrigan *(Taedy)*, Phil Brown *(Higginbotham)*, Charles Irwin *(Cornelius)*, Louise Lorimer *(Augur's Secretary)*, Tim Ryan *(Patrolman Clancy)*, Harry Antrim *(Sen. Ransom)*, Margaret Wells *(Mrs. Augur)*, John Goldsworthy *(Butler)*, Douglas Gerrard *(Receptionist)*, Tito Vuolo *(Greek Vendor)*, William Swingley *(Terrance)*, Tom Stevenson *(Gentleman's Gentleman)*, Dorothy Neumann *(Employment Agency Manager)*, Ruth Clifford *(Secretary)*, Hollis Jewell *(Cab Driver)*, Eddie Parks *(Pickpocket)*, John Roy *(Subway Guard)*, Norman Leavitt *(Milkman)*, Albert Morin *(Captain of the Waiters)*, Ann Frederick *(Hatcheck Girl)*, J. Farrell MacDonald *(Captain)*, George Melford *(Doorman)*, Frank Mitchell *(Irish Dancer)*, Jimmy O'Brien *(Singer)*, Marion Marshall *(Secretary)*, Claribel Bessel *(The Bride)*, John Davidson, Wilson Wood, Don Brodie, Gene Garrick, Robert Adler, Robert Karnes *(Reporters)*.

Power is a hardboiled, ambitious newsman in this delightful fantasy which sees his world turned upside down by a precocious leprechaun, Kellaway, in one of the character actor's most impressive and hilarious roles. (Kellaway had earlier enacted a similar role in the comedy-fantasy I MARRIED A WITCH, essaying a long-dead warlock.) Power, on a trip to Ireland, stumbles across Kellaway when his car breaks down on a lonely road. Kellaway sends him to a nearby inn where he meets Baxter, the owner. She relates Irish lore and how there are many plots of gold buried thereabouts by leprechauns. Late that night Power spots Kellaway and follows him to a small glen, wrestling him to the ground and compelling him to reveal his pot of gold. But Power refuses to take the gold away with him and therefore obligates Kellaway who vows to repay the favor. When Power takes Baxter to the glen to show her the spot where he captured a leprechaun she thinks he's gone a bit daft. Once back in New York, Power is corrupted by Cobb, a right-wing publisher who hires him as a speech writer, wowing him with a heavy salary and a luxury apartment, plus introducing him to his attractive daughter, Meadows. Power is a bit amazed at the valet provided for him; he is an exact twin to Kellaway, the leprechaun. Kellaway criticizes the speeches Power writes for Cobb which propose ideas Power does not believe in. Then the leprechaun arranges for Power to "accidentally" meet Baxter once more on the subway, learning that she has come to the U.S. to collect an inheritance. He falls deeper in love with her but Baxter leaves him and returns to Ireland when she sees him with Meadows. Under Kellaway's subtle guidance, Power grows discontented with Cobb and, just as the big shot is to make a coast-to-coast broadcast, Power grabs the microphone and denounces his boss, upholds his ideals, and quits, returning to Ireland and Baxter. The debonair Power is surprisingly good in this comedic role and Kellaway is absolutely fascinating as the gnome-like, mischievous leprechaun, a part originally designed for Barry Fitzgerald.

p, Fred Kohlmar; d, Henry Koster; w, Philip Dunne (based on the novel by Guy Jones, Constance Jones); ph, Joseph La Shelle; m, Cyril J. Mockridge; ed, J. Watson Webb, Jr.; md, Lionel Newman; art d, Lyle Wheeler, J. Russell Spencer; set d, Thomas Little, Paul S. Fox; cos, Charles LeMaire, Bonnie Cashin; spec eff, Fred Sersen.

Comedy/Fantasy **(PR:A MPAA:NR)**

LUCK OF THE NAVY (SEE: NORTH SEA PATROL, 1939, Brit.)

LUCK OF THE TURF½** (1936, Brit.) 64m RKO bw

Jack Melford *(Sid Smith)*, Moira Lynd *(Letty Jackson)*, Wally Patch *(Bill Harris)*, Moore Marriott *(Mr. Jackson)*, Sybil Grove *(Mrs. Jackson)*, Tom Helmore *(Lord Broadwater)*, Peggy Novak *(Maisie)*.

Melford is a man with the ability to pick winning horses for his pals, though never placing a bet for himself. When he finally places his own bet in order to raise the funds to marry, he loses almost everything. However all is saved when he finds some money and puts it on a 50-to-1 shot which naturally turns up a big winner. Despite the simplicity of the plot, this has some charming moments with all-around good humor.

p&d, Randall Faye; w, John Hunter; ph, Geoffrey Faithfull.

Comedy **(PR:A MPAA:NR)**

LUCKIEST GIRL IN THE WORLD, THE** (1936) 70m UNIV bw

Jane Wyatt *(Pat Duncan)*, Louis Hayward *(Anthony McClellan)*, Nat Pendleton *(Dugan)*, Eugene Pallette *(Campbell Duncan)*, Catherine Doucet *(Mrs. Rosalie Duncan)*, Phillip Reed *(Percy Mayhew)*, Viola Callahan *(Mrs. Olson)*.

Wyatt is a poor little rich girl who bets her wealthy pop (Pallette) that she can live in big bad New York City on the paltry sum of $150 week. She wants to prove to him that she can handle poverty as her fiance, Reed, is not exactly rich. She arrives in the big town and proves herself right. However her plans for marriage change slightly when she meets another poverty-stricken young man, Hayward. He's a resident at the house she lodges in, projecting the right amount of boyish charm to win her heart. This was made with a definite female audience in mind, having been adapted from a story in *The Ladies Home Journal*. The script is not terribly complicated, though you may want to bring out a dustcloth for some of the gags. Buzzell's direction gives the film a certain kind of charm, moving it along at the right pace. Wyatt does a cute little job as the ingenue, ultimately carrying the film.

p, Charles R. Rogers; d, Eddie Buzzell; w, Herbert Fields, Henry Myers (based on a story by Anne Jordan); ph, Merritt Gerstad; ed, Dorothy Spencer.

Comedy **(PR:A MPAA:NR)**

LUCKY (SEE: BOY, A GIRL, AND A DOG, A, 1946)

LUCKY BOOTS (SEE: GUN PLAY, 1936)

LUCKY BOY** (1929) 97m TS bw

George Jessel *(Georgie Jessel)*, Rosa Rosanova *(Momma Jessel)*, William K. Strauss *(Poppa Jessel)*, Margaret Quimby *(Eleanor)*, Gwen Lee *(Mrs. Ellis) Richard Tucker (Mr. Ellis)*, Gayne Whitman *(Mr. Trent)*, Mary Doran *(Becky)*.

Jessel is featured in a role and story heavily inspired by Jolson and his 1927 feature THE JAZZ SINGER. Jessel plays a son of Jewish parents. Strauss is a jeweler, letting his son Jessel clerk the store. But the boy's heart really lies on the Broadway stage and he tries his hand at singing. Eventually he works his way to San Franscisco and an amateur competition. His parents hear him on the radio and are delighted with son's success. But Rosanova falls ill and Jessel hurries home. He finally becomes a star in a Broadway show called "Lucky Boy". Aside from the obvious parallels to THE JAZZ SINGER, this film is noted for a few other attributes of its own. The "Momma" motif became a famous one for Jessel, who often used to "telephone" his mother in his comedy routines. Here the theme is probably the strongest of the picture. Like THE JAZZ SINGER, this is part silent, part sound. This is one of the first films recorded in the R.C.A. Photophone process, which for its time was quite advanced over other recording processes. This was a routine early talkie that was enlivened by the music. Jessel sings: "Lucky Boy," "My Mother's Eyes" (L. Wolfe Gilbert, Abel Baer), "Old Man Sunshine," "My Real Sweetheart," "In My Bouquet of Memories" (Sam M. Lewis, Joe Young, Harry Akst), "My Blackbirds are Bluebirds Now" (Irving Caesar, Cliff Friend), and "California Here I Come" (Al Jolson, B.G. De Sylva, Joseph Meyer).

p, Norman Taurog, Charles C. Wilson, Rudolph Flothow; w, George Jessel (based on a story by Viola Brothers Shore); ph, Harry Jackson, Frank Zukor; m, Dr. Hugo Riesenfeld; ed, Desmond O'Brien, Russell Shields; md, Sacha Bunchuk; art d, Hervey Libbert; set d, George Sawley.

Musical/Drama   **(PR:A   MPAA:NR)**

LUCKY BRIDE, THE**½   (1948, USSR) 62m Mosfilm/Artkino c

Makolm Shtgaukh (*Ivan Mordashov*), Elena Shevetsova (*His Daughter*), Anna Lyslanskaya (*Maid*), Nikolai Gritsenko (*Lt. Fadeyev*), Sergei Stoltarov (*Faddei*), Alexandra Panova (*Rich Aunt*).

Shortly after the conclusion of the Napoleonic war Shtgaukh must marry off his daughter, Shevetsova, so she can inherit the fortune of her aunt, Panova. There is one stipulation however in that the intended must have the initials A.F. It seem Panova was once engaged to a man with those initials. The engagement broke off and she was left with linens, silverware, and other personal items all monogrammed with those letters. The film has a wonderful sense of slapstick and silliness that unfortunately is marred by a poor job of subtitling. Nevertheless, the wonderful comic performances manage to overcome the language barrier. Costuming and set designs are lushly photographed, though some of the outdoor scenes are obviously studio sets. (In Russian; English subtitles).

d&w, Igor Savchenko; ph, Eugene Andrikanis; m/l, Sergei Potonky, Dmitri Fliangoltz

Musical/Comedy   **(PR:AA   MPAA:NR)**

LUCKY CISCO KID**½   (1940) 67m FOX bw

Cesar Romero (*Cisco Kid*), Mary Beth Hughes (*Lola*), Dana Andrews (*Sgt. Dunn*), Evelyn Venable (*Mrs. Lawrence*), Chris-Pin Martin (*Gorditos*), Willard Robertson (*Judge McQuade*), Joseph Sawyer (*Stevens*), John Sheffield (*Tommy Lawrence*), William Royle (*Sheriff*), Francis Ford (*Court Clerk*), Otto Hoffman (*Storekeeper*), Dick Rich (*Stage Coach Driver*), Harry Strang (*Corporal*), Gloria Roy (*Dance Hall Girl*), Frank Lackteen (*Bandit*), Spencer Charters (*Hotel Guest*), Bob Hoffman, Boyd Morgan (*Soldiers*), Adrian Morris, Jimmie Dundee, William Pagan (*Stagecoach Passengers*).

In this fourth "Cisco Kid" movie, Romero replaces Warner Baxter in the role as the Kid, with Martin as his trusty sidekick. The pair investigate an impostor and his gang who are rustling cattle under the Kid's name. Hughes is the dance hall girl-cum-love interest, and Venable is the widow he finally falls for. Though the story is all formula and action, Romero is appropriately suave and debonair in the role. The film is directed at a fast pace, making this an exciting and above average picture. Dana Andrews' screen debut.

p, Sol M. Wurtzel; d, H. Bruce Humberstone; w, Robert Ellis, Helen Logan (based on a story by Julian Johnson, based on the character created by O. Henry); ph, Lucien Andriot; ed, Fred Allen; md, Cyril J. Mockridge.

Western   **(PR:A   MPAA:NR)**

LUCKY DAYS*½   (1935, Brit.) 67m British and Dominions/PAR bw

Chili Bouchier (*Patsy Cartwright*), Whitmore Humphries (*Paul Cartwright*), Leslie Perrins (*Jack Hurst*), Ann Codrington (*Eve Tandring*), Derek Gorst (*Prosser*), Ronald Simpson (*Smedley*), Eric Cowley (*Eric*), Alexander Archdale (*Alec*), Sally Gray (*Alice*), Elsie Irving, Eric Hales, Deering Wells.

Bouchier is a superstitious woman who relies on every word of an Eastern astrologer, Wells. This causes her some big trouble that almost means divorce when Bouchier uses the stars to provide her husband with business tips. These tips, however, prove to be surprisingly successful.

p, Anthony Havelock-Allan; d, Reginald Denham; w, Margaret MacDonnell (story by MacDonnell, Gordon MacDonnell); ph, Francis Carver.

Comedy   **(PR:A   MPAA:NR)**

LUCKY DAYS, 1943   (SEE: SING A JINGLE, 1943)

LUCKY DEVILS***   (1933) 64m RKO bw

Bill Boyd (*Skipper*), William Gargan (*Bob*), Bruce Cabot (*Happy*), William Bakewell (*Slugger*), Creighton [Lon, Jr.] Chaney (*Frankie*), Bob Rose (*Rusty*), Dorothy Wilson (*Fran*), Sylvia Picker (*Toots*), Julie Haydon (*Doris*), Gladden James (*Neville*), Edwin Stanley (*Spence*), Roscoe Ates (*Gabby*), Phyllis Fraser (*Midge*), Betty Furness (*Ginger*), Alan Roscoe (*Director*), Charles Gillette (*Cameraman*), Ward Bond.

A behind-the-scenes look at Hollywood stuntmen, this was based on a story co-written by Rose, a real-life stuntman. The wafer-thin story finds Boyd as a star stuntman who will do just about anything until he gets married to Wilson. She gets pregnant and he suddenly gets cold feet. They start going broke until he finally

overcomes his fears with one super-stunt for the climax. This is really nothing more than a chance to see some great stunts staged for the film, including men going through plate glass windows, automobile crashes, a fight on a burning roof, and other hair-raising excitements. Roscoe has a delightfully satirical role as a possessed director. It's a must for action freaks.

p, David O. Selznick; d, Ralph Ince; w, Ben Markson, Agnes Christine Johnson (based on a story by Casey Robinson, Bob Rose); ph, J. Roy Hunt; ed, Jack Kitchin.

Action   **(PR:A   MPAA:NR)**

LUCKY DEVILS**   (1941) 66m UNIV bw

Richard Arlen (*Dick*), Andy Devine (*Andy*), Dorothy Lovett (*Norma*), Janet Shaw (*Gwendy*), Gladys Blake (*Secretary*), Vinton Haworth (*Bradford*), Gus Schilling (*Grimshaw*), Tim Ryan (*Momser*), Ralf Harolde (*Ritter*), Edwin Stanley (*Official*), Walter Soderling (*Cordall*), Mildred Shaw (*Agnes*), Dora Clement (*Duchess*), Frank Mitchell (*Foreigner*), Hugh Huntley (*Duke*), William Forrest (*Chandler*), Eddie Bruce (*Myers*), Robert Winkler (*Mopey*), Dick Terry (*Berko*), Kathryn Sheldon (*Malinda*), Arthur O'Connell (*Pilot*), Dick Wessel (*Simmons*), James Morton (*Exposition Guard*), Lew Kelly (*Process Server*), Frank Brownlee (*Farmer*), Charles Smith (*Copy Boy*), Jack Smith (*Dam Guard*), J. Paul Jones (*Cassidy*), David Oliver (*Carter*), Victor Zimmerman (*Guard*), Roger Haliday (*Policeman*), Guy Kingsford (*Lab Man*), Ed Peil, Sr. (*Jail Guard*), Maria Montez (*Bathing Beauty Being Interviewed*).

Arlen and Devine are paired up once more in this lesser effort from their fictional newreel reporter series. Arlen is the breakneck reporter ever in search of a scoop, and Devine his comic relief sidekick. This time they're in love with Lovett and Shaw respectively, and get caught up with foreign saboteurs. Though the production values are fine for what this is, the story is hopelessly trite with an overdose of cliches. This was meant to be nothing more than a quick "B" program filler for the forties audiences.

p, Ben Pivar; d, Lew Landers; w, Alex Gottlieb (based on the story by Sam Robins); ph, Charles Van Enger; m, H. J. Salter; ed, Ed Curtiss; md, Charles Previn.

Comedy/Drama   **(PR:C   MPAA:NR)**

LUCKY DOG**½   (1933) 60m UNIV bw

Chic Sale, Tom O'Brien, Harry Holman, Clarence Geldert, Buster The Dog.

A simple comedy follows the adventures of Buster the dog. The loyal canine stays with his master despite some bad times which, of course, are balanced out by the good.

d, Zion Myers; w, Myers, Roland Asher; ph, Jerry Ash; ed, Myers.

Comedy   **(PR:AAA   MPAA:NR)**

LUCKY GIRL*½   (1932, Brit.) 75m BIP/Wardour bw

Gene Gerrard (*Stephan Gregorovitch*), Molly Lamont (*Lady Moira Cavendish-Gascoyne*), Gus McNaughton (*Hudson E. Greener*), Spencer Trevor (*Duke Hugo*), Tonie Edgar Bruce (*Duchess Amelia*), Hal Gordon (*Police Constable*), Ian Fleming (*Lord Henry*), Frank Stanmore (*Mullins*).

While traveling incognito, Ruritanian king Gerrard and his chancellor, McNaughton, attend a duke's party. There two are mistaken for jewel thieves, but the duke's daughter Lamont, for whom Gerrard has fallen, clears up the mess for a happy ending.

p, John Maxwell; d&w, Gene Gerrard, Frank Miller (based on the play "Mr. Abdulla" by Reginald Berkeley, Douglas Furber, R.P. Weston, Bert Lee); ph, John J. Cox, Bryan Langley.

Musical   **(PR:A   MPAA:NR)**

LUCKY IN LOVE*½   (1929) 76m Pathe bw

Morton Downey (*Michael O'More*), Betty Lawford (*Lady Mary Cardigan*), Colin Keith-Johnston (*Capt. Brian Fitzroy*), Halliwell Hobbes (*Earl of Balkerry*), J. M. Kerrigan (*Connors*), Edward McNamara (*Tim O'More*), Edward O'Connor (*Rafferty*), Richard Taber (*Paddy*), Mary Murray (*Kate*), Mackenzie Ward (*Cyril*), Louis Sorin (*Abe Feinberg*), Sonia Karlov (*Lulu Bellew*), Tyrrell Davis (*Potts*), Elizabeth Murray (*Landlady*).

Downey is the singing American stableboy for wealthy Irishman Hobbes. Lawford is Hobbes' granddaughter and love interest for Downey. He eventually goes back to America where his singing is noticed by Sorin, a department store owner. He immediately puts the tenor behind the music counter. Meanwhile, Keith-Johnston twitches his mustache and prepares to foreclose on Lawford's estate. Songs include: "Love is a Dreamer," "For the Likes O' You and Me," "When They Sing 'The Wearing of the Green' in Syncopated Blues" (Bud Green, Sam M. Stept).

d, Kenneth Webb; w, Gene Markey; ph, Philip Tannura, Harry Stradling; ed, Edward Pfitzenmeier; md, Sacha Bunchuk; set d, Clark Robinson.

Musical   **(PR:A   MPAA:NR)**

LUCKY JADE**   (1937, Brit.) 69m Welwyn Studios/PAR bw

Betty Ann Davies (*Betsy Bunn*), John Warwick (*John Marsden*), Claire Arnold (*Mrs. Sparsley*), Syd Crossley (*Rickets*), Derek Gorst (*Bob Grant*), Gordon Court (*Ricky Rickhart*), Richard Littledale (*Dingbat Eisan*), Tony Wylde (*Whitebait*), Boyer and Ravel, Leonard Shepherd.

In order to further her theatrical career, housemaid Davies takes advantage of her employer's absence by posing as an actress and throwing a giant party. Unfortunately, two thieves crash the party and steal the owner's valuable jade. In order to recover the pieces and save face, Davies grabs two of the partygoers to assist in recovering the jade. The pacing is lightning fast, giving a genuine frenetic atmosphere to this delightful British comedy.

p, Fred Browett; d&w, Walter Summers (based on the story by Jane Brown); ph, Horace Wheddon.

Crime/Comedy (PR:A MPAA:NR)

LUCKY JIM**¹/₂ (1957, Brit.) 95m Charter/Kingsley International bw

Ian Carmichael (*Jim Dixon*), Terry-Thomas (*Bertrand Welch*), Hugh Griffith (*Prof. Welch*), Sharon Acker (*Christine Callaghan*), Jean Anderson (*Mrs. Welch*), Maureen Connell (*Margaret Peel*), Clive Morton (*Sir Hector Gore-Urquhart*), Reginald Beckwith (*University Porter*), Kenneth Griffith (*Cyril Johns*), Jeremy Hawk (*Bill Atkinson*), John Welch (*The Principal*), Charles Lamb (*Contractor*), Jeremy Longhurst (*Waiter*), Henry Longhurst (*Prof. Hutchinson*), John Cairney (*Roberts*), Penny Morrell (*Miss Wilson*), Ronald Cardew (*Registrar*), Harry Fowler (*Taxi Driver*), Ian Wilson (*Glee Singer*).

Carmichael is a junior lecturer in history at an English university. On a certain weekend he finds himself involved in a series of slapstick misadventures, first at a party given by a colleague, then at some important school ceremonies. The film is a slap-dash comic spree with some excellent support by a fine group of comic actors including the always wonderful Terry-Thomas. The direction keeps things running at a merry pace, rarely getting away from itself in the frenzy. This was the third comic success from the producing/directing Boulting brothers after PRIVATE'S PROGRESS and BROTHERS IN LAW, both of which also featured Carmichael. But fans of the novel this is based upon will probably be disappointed. All the subtlety in Amis' book is dropped for broader comedy, which ultimately sacrifices the heart of the book. On its own, though, the film is still quite funny.

p, Roy Boulting; d, John Boulting; w, Jeffrey Dell, Patrick Campbell (based on the novel by Kingsley Amis); ph, Max Greene; m, John Addison; ed, Max Benedict; md, Addison.

Comedy **Cas.** (PR:C MPAA:NR)

LUCKY JORDAN*** (1942) 84m PAR bw

Alan Ladd (*Lucky Jordan*), Helen Walker (*Jill Evans*), Sheldon Leonard (*Slip Moran*), Mabel Paige (*Annie*), Marie McDonald (*Pearl*), Lloyd Corrigan (*Ernest Higgins*), Russell Hoyt (*Eddie*), Dave Willock (*Angelo Palacio*), Miles Mander (*Kilpatrick*), John Wengraf (*Kesselman*), Charles Cane (*Sergeant*), George F. Meader (*Little Man*), Virginia Brissac (*Woman with Little Man*), Al M. Hill, Fred Kohler, Jr. (*Killers*), Jack Roberts (*Johnny*), Clem Bevans (*Gas Station Attendant*), Olaf Hytten (*Charles, the Servant*), William Halligan (*Miller, the Gateman*), Kitty Kelly (*Mrs. Maggotti*), George Humbert (*Joe Maggotti*), Dorothy Dandridge (*Maid at Hollyhock School*), Paul Phillips, Joseph Downing (*Stick-Up Men*), Danny Duncan (*Clerk in Cigar Store*), Carol Hughes (*Girl in Back Room*), Ralph Dunn, Lyle Latell (*Army Guards*), Kenneth Christy (*Sergeant*), Edward Earle, Jack Baxley (*Men*), Edwin Miller (*Officer*), John Harmon (*Mug with Big Ears*), Edythe Elliott (*Secretary*), Jimmy O'Gatty (*Mug*), John Hamilton, Roy Gordon (*Colonels*), Albert Ferris, Crane Whitley (*Gardeners*), Otto Reichow (*Nazi Hood*), Ralph Dumke (*Sergeant*), Kirk Alyn (*Pearl's Boy Friend*), Frederick Giermann (*Bulky Gardener*), Arthur Loft (*Hearndon*), Frank Benson (*Cab Driver*), Ronnie Rondell (*Florist*), Terry Ray (*Sentry*), Elliott Sullivan, Bud McTaggart, Keith Richards (*Soldiers*), Sara Berner (*Helen*), William Forrest (*Commanding Officer*), Paul Stanton (*Draft Official*), Virginia Farmer (*Lady*), Ethel Clayton (*Woman*), Georgia Backus (*Saleslady in Toy Shop*), Harold Minjir (*Clerk in Flower Shop*), Marcella Phillips, Alice Kriby, Yvonne De Carlo (*Girls*), Harry V. Cheshire (*Garden Gatekeeper*), Ralph Peters (*Brig Sergeant*), Anthony L. Caruso (*Gunman*).

Released just a few short months after Ladd's electric debut in THIS GUN FOR HIRE and his follow-up THE GLASS KEY, this entry marks Ladd's first top billing—a fact which thrilled his growing throng of fans. Ladd, in nearly the same persona as his previous two pictures, plays an unpatriotic louse of a gangster who runs his territory with an iron fist. His biggest enemy is not from the underworld, however, but from the draft board. Ladd's pal, Corrigan, tries to get him classified as "4-F"—"socially undesirable," but that attempt fails. Ladd then tries to get himself adopted by a dependent old woman, Paige, but the draft board still serves him his papers. Ladd is shipped off to boot camp where he acts as the perfect antithesis to the model soldier. Not only does he have an aversion to rising early, but he has a habit of sleeping in silk pajamas. Before long Ladd goes AWOL, taking with him canteen girl Walker who tries in vain to convince him to surrender to the MPs. During the escape, Ladd steals a car belonging to an Army engineer. Walker in a fit of stubbornness throws a briefcase out the car window thinking it belongs to Ladd. When Ladd returns home, he finds that Leonard has seized control of his gang and his moll, McDonald. Leonard, who is selling government secrets to the Nazis, tells Ladd that the briefcase contains valuable documents. A fight ensues between Ladd and Leonard, ending with Ladd and Walker taking off to locate the briefcase. In the process Ladd loses Walker, who manages to escape by flirting with her captor. Ladd does find the briefcase, however, and hides out with Paige. She mothers him no end and even brags to her lady friends about her new "son." When a gang of fifth columnists beats up Paige to get the briefcase, Ladd gets infuriated and plans vengeance. He sets out after the spies not because of their political connections (this isn't something that Ladd's character can relate to) but because he "don't want this country run by guys who beat up old ladies." Assuming his personal patriotic stance, Ladd comes out swinging and rounds up the subversive thugs, gaining the respect of both the U.S. government and his new sweetheart, Walker. Although LUCKY JORDAN heads downhill after the two-thirds point (falling into cliched patriotism which isn't surprising considering that director Tuttle was one of the star witnesses for the House Un-American Activities Committee, informing on a number of his co workers), it is still a surprisingly fresh picture with a dose of comedy. Ladd even gets an opportunity to smile a bit, as well as show off his original blond hair color. Fans, who would soon make Ladd one of *Photoplay*'s most popular stars, just couldn't get enough of him. Paramount was well aware it had a hot property and cranked out as many Ladd vehicles as possible, just in case Ladd (like Lucky

Jordan) got sent off to fight in the Pacific and never came back. The picture also introduced Walker, a fresh young actress with a pleasing mien, in her screen debut.

p, Fred Kohlmar; d, Frank Tuttle; w, Darrell Ware, Karl Tunberg (based on the story by Charles Leonard); ph, John Seitz; ed, Archie Marshek; md, Adolph Deutsch; art d, Hans Dreier, Ernst Fegte.

Crime Drama (PR:A MPAA:NR)

LUCKY LADIES*¹/₂ (1932, Brit.) 74m WB-FN bw

Sydney Fairbrother (*Angle Tuckett*), Emily Fitzroy (*Cleo Honeycutt*), Tracy Holmes (*Ted*), Janice Adair (*Pearl*), Syd Crossley (*Hector Ramsbottom*), Charles Farrell (*Bookmaker*).

Two sisters who run an oyster bar win some big money in the Irish Sweepstakes. One of the pair ends up losing it all, though, when a phony count manages to trick her out of the winnings. He leaves her some seemingly bogus tickets, but these coupons turn out to be just as valuable as the original winnings. The humor is never developed in the situations as it should be, resulting in a minor, forgettable comedy.

p, Irving Asher; d, John Rawlings; w, W. Scott Darling, Randall Faye.

Comedy (PR:A MPAA:NR)

LUCKY LADY*¹/₂ (1975) 117m FOX c

Gene Hackman (*Kibby*), Liza Minnelli (*Claire*), Burt Reynolds (*Walker*), Geoffrey Lewis (*Capt. Aaron Mosley*), John Hillerman (*Christy McTeague*), Robby Benson (*Billy Webber*), Michael Hordern (*Capt. Rockwell*), Anthony Holland (*Mr. Tully*), John McLiam (*Rass Huggins*), Val Avery (*Dolph*), Louis Guss (*Bernie*), William H. Bassett (*Charley*), Emilio Fernandez (*"Ybarra"*), Duncan McLeod (*Auctioneer*), Milt [Lewis] Kogan (*Supercargo*), Suzanne Zenor (*Brunette*), Marjorie Battles (*Redhead*).

A very expensive stinker that cost more than $12 million to make after paying $400,000 for a dreadful script. It's an attempt at recreating the screwball comedies of the 1930s but the screenwriters have neither the wit nor the constructive ability to compete with the worst of that era. Filmed in Mexico, LUCKY LADY is the story of an unlikely *menage a trois* between two rumrunners, Hackman and Reynolds, and nightclub thrush Minnelli. Both fall for her as they haul booze up and down the coast, alternately escaping from the Coast Guard and another gang, led by Hillerman, who wants the action all to himself. At one point, Hackman and Reynolds masquerade as Coast Guardsmen to climb aboard the competition's boat and slaughter them (the best action sequence but hardly comedic). The first time around, both Hackman and Reynolds were killed but preview audiences nixed that so a new ending was added in which both men lived, but by that time it was too late. The picture suffered from forced slapstick, out-of-place violence, and a mixture of acting styles that clashed under Donen's unsure direction. Screenwriters Huyck and Katz have yet to recapture the success they had with AMERICAN GRAFFITI which may have been due to the fact that they wrote that one with George Lucas. They have failed to infuse this story with any sexuality as Hackman (who replaced George Segal in the film when Segal took ill) is more like Minnelli's father and Reynolds seems more like a high school playmate. Benson plays a cabin boy with his customary dullness although, when compared to the others, he was positively radiant. The best part of the movie was the brief action sequence utilizing several small boats. Two songs by Ebb and Kander that are better left as forgotten as this movie should be. Minnelli can be wonderful, Burt Reynolds is usually charming, and Gene Hackman has seldom given a less-than-wonderful performance, but together they are as explosive as wet matches.

p, Michael Grushkoff; d, Stanley Donen; w, Willard Huyck, Gloria Katz; ph, Geoffrey Unsworth (DeLuxe Color); m, Ralph Burns; ed, Peter Boita, George Hively, Tom Rolf; prod d, John Barry; art d, Norman Reynolds; m/l, Fred Ebb, John Kander.

Comedy/Drama (PR:C-O MPAA:PG)

LUCKY LARRIGAN*¹/₂ (1933) 56m MON bw

Rex Bell, Helen Foster, George Chesebro, John Elliott, Stanley Blystone, Julian Rivero, G. D. Wood [Gordon DeMain], Wilfred Lucas.

Bell plays a famous eastern polo hero who refuses to go west with his girl, Foster, whose father is a ranching partner with his dad. In the end, however, he winds up following her to the West where he undoubtedly will be too effete for the 10-gallon hatters. A silly notion and a failed effort to get away from routine western fare.

p, Trem Carr; d, J. P. McCarthy; w, Wellyn Totman; ph, Archie Stout.

Western/Comedy (PR:A MPAA:NR)

LUCKY LEGS*¹/₂ (1942) 64m COL bw

Jinx Falkenburg (*Gloria Carroll*), Leslie Brooks (*Jewel Perkins*), Kay Harris (*Calamity Jane*), Elizabeth Patterson (*Annabelle Dinwiddie*), Russell Hayden (*James Abercrombie*), William Wright (*Pinkie Connors*), Don Beddoe (*Ned McLane*), Adele Rowland (*Hettie Dinwiddie*), Edward Marr (*Mike Manley*), George McKay (*Red Fenton*), James C. Morton (*Pat*), Eddie Kane (*J. N. Peters*), Shirley Patterson (*Chambermaid*), Dick Talmadge (*Sam*), Charles Sullivan (*Lou*), Harry Tenbrook (*Dan*), Ralph Sanford (*Bartender*), Rita and Rubins (*Dance Team*), Brick Sullivan (*Policeman*), Adele Mara (*Secretary*), Billy Curtis (*Newsboy*), Romaine Callender (*Crump*), John Tyrell (*Dance Director*), Jack Gardner, Al Hill (*Reporters*), Ethan Laidlaw (*Duke*), Tyler Brooke (*Jenkins*), Gohr Van Vleck (*Doorman*), Jack Rice (*Jewelry Salesman*), John Holland (*Fur Salesman*), Franklin Parker (*Real Estate Salesman*), Frank Swales (*Inventor*), Jack Carr (*Food Vendor*), Cyril Ring (*Yacht Salesman*), Ernest Hilliard (*Salesman*), Blake McEdwards (*Red Arrow Messenger*), Frank Skully.

A young woman gets more than she counted on when she finds herself the recipient of a $1 million inheritance, the trouble coming in the form of a hood who is only too happy to latch onto this girl with newly acquired wealth. A few good chuckles. Another chorus girl romp for one-time model Falkenburg, who seemed to make a career of this role.

p, Wallace McDonald; w, Stanley Rubin, Jack Hartfield; ph, Philip Tannura; ed, Arthur Seid; md, M. W. Stoloff; m/l, "Lucky Legs," Sammy Cahn, Saul Chaplin.

Comedy **(PR:A MPAA:NR)**

LUCKY LOSER** (1934, Brit.) 68m British and Dominions/PAR bw
Richard Dolman (*Tom O'Grady*), Aileen Marson (*Kathleen Willoughby*), Anna Lee (*Ursula Hamilton*), Annie Esmond (*Mrs. Hamilton*), Roland Culver (*Pat Hayden*), Noel Shannon (*Peters*), Joan White (*Alice*), Gordon McLeod (*Auctioneer*), Alice Lane, Mary Gaskell.

After winning a fortune in a sweepstakes, the horrified Dolman finds he's left the winning ticket in an antique desk he recently sold. From there it's one long chase in his desperate efforts to find the desk and thus, his winning ticket.

p, Herbert Wilcox; d, Reginald Denham; w, Anne Smith, Basil Mason (based on the play "The Big Sweep" by Matthew Brennan).

Comedy **(PR:A MPAA:NR)**

LUCKY LOSERS** (1950) 69m MON bw
Leo Gorcey (*Slip Mahoney*), Huntz Hall (*Sach*), Hillary Brooke (*Countess*), Gabriel Dell (*Gabe Moreno*), Lyle Talbot (*Bruce McDermott*), Bernard Gorcey (*Louie Dumbrowsky*), William Benedict (*Whitey*), Joseph Turkel (*Johnny Angelo*), Harry Tyler (*Buffer McGee*), Buddy Gorman (*Butch*), David Gorcey (*Chuck*), Harry Cheshire (*Chick*), Douglas Evans (*Tom Whitney*), Wendy Waldron (*Carol Thurston*), Glen Vernon (*Andrew Stone III*), Dick Elliott (*1st Conventioner*), Chester Clute (*2nd Conventioner*), Selmer Jackson (*David Thurston*), Frank Jenks (*Bartender*).

This average entry in the Bowery Boys series finds Gorcey and Hall working in a Wall Street brokerage firm owned by Jackson. But when Jackson is found dead and it's reported a suicide, Dell, a newscaster in television, suspects foul play. When Gorcey finds some dice on his late boss' desk, he, too, figures that Jackson must have been in trouble with gamblers at the High Hat Club. Meanwhile, Dell reports his lead on the air and is severely beaten by some mobsters. But this doesn't stop him, and he delivers another report from his hospital bed, linking high society man Cheshire with gangsters and Jackson's death. Gorcey then sets up a trap for Cheshire by having the boys learn the gambling trade from Tyler, who once had connections with both Jackson and the notorious Club. The case is solved and all ends well for the East End Kids. Audiences might find a problem with LUCKY LOSERS, as it starts off on a humorous note and then turns deadly serious. (See BOWERY BOYS series, Index.)

p, Jan Grippo; d, William Beaudine; w, Charles R. Marion, Bert Lawrence; ph, Marcel Le Picard; ed, Otho Lovering, William Austin; md, Edward J. Kay; art d, David Milton; set d, Raymond Boltz, Jr.

Comedy **(PR:C MPAA:NR)**

LUCKY LUCIANO (SEE: RE: LUCKY LUCIANO, 1974, U.S./Fr./Ital.)

LUCKY LUKE** (1971, Fr./Bel.) 76m Dargaud Films/Artistes Associes bw
Voice of Rich Little.

Animated feature based on the exploits of the chain-smoking cowboy, Lucky Luke (whom Little impersonates with the voice of Gary Cooper) that appeared in Goscinny's popular European comic strip. The action takes place in a small western town known as Daisy Town, where villains of every shape and size arrive, but the biggest threats are the Daltons (whom Little impersonates with Bogart and Cagney). Fairly entertaining.

p, Rene Goscinny, Morris; d, Goscinny; w, Goscinny, Morris, Pierre Tchernia; ph, Francois Leonard.

Western/Animated **(PR:A MPAA:NR)**

LUCKY MASCOT, THE* ½ (1951, Brit.) 84m Diadem-Alliance/AA bw (AKA: THE BRASS MONKEY)
Carole Landis (*Kay Sheldon*), Carroll Levis (*Himself*), Herbert Lom (*Peter Hobart*), Avril Angers (*Herself*), Ernest Thesiger (*Ryder-Harris*), Henry Edwards (*Inspector Miller*), Edward Underdown (*Max Taylor*), Terry-Thomas, Carroll Levis' Discoveries, Albert and Les Ward, Leslie "Hutch" Hutchinson, Carole Lester [*Lesley*].

Levis is a radio personality who meets a connoisseur of Buddhist art. He's after "the brass monkey," a rare artifact, and will stop at nothing to get it. With the help of the "Discoveries" radio talent, Levis stops the man from carrying out his plans. An early appearance for noted British comic actor Terry-Thomas.

p, Nat A. Bronsten, David Coplan; d, Thornton Freeland; w, Alec Coppel, Freeland, C. Denis Freeman (based on the story by Coppel); ph, Bert Mason.

Comedy/Thriller **(PR:A MPAA:NR)**

LUCKY ME** (1954) 99m WB c
Doris Day (*Candy Williams*), Robert Cummings (*Dick Carson*), Phil Silvers (*Hap Snyder*), Eddie Foy, Jr. (*Duke McGee*), Nancy Walker (*Flo Neely*), Martha Hyer (*Lorraine Thayer*), Bill Goodwin (*Otis Thayer*), Marcel Dalio (*Anton*), Hayden Rorke (*Tommy Arthur*), James Burke (*Mahoney*), Herb Vigran (*Theater Manager*), George Sherwood (*Smith*), Percy Helton (*Brown*), James Hayward (*Jones*), Jack Shea (*Cop*), William Bakewell (*Motorist*), Cliff Ferre (*Orchestra Leader*), Charles Cane (*Sergeant*), Jean DeBriac (*Captain*), Ann Tyrrell (*Fortune Teller*), Ray Teal, Tom Powers (*Cronies*), Angie Dickinson, Lucy Marlow, Dolores Dorn, Emmaline Henry (*Party Guests*), Gladys Hurlbut (*Dowager*), Jac George (*Waiter Captain*).

This routine, lackluster musical has Day, Walker, Silvers, and Foy, Jr. as theatrical entertainers stranded in Miami, forced to work in a hotel kitchen. Then Day meets Cummings, a successful song writer who has set his hopes of his own musical production on a wealthy oilman, Goodwin. Unfortunately, this requires being nice to Goodwin's spoiled daughter, Hyer. He offers Day the lead role in his musical, which enrages Hyer, and when he arranges a party for Goodwin in order to show off his numbers, Hyer tries every trick in the book to thwart his efforts. In the end, Day and her gang succeed in convincing Goodwin to invest in Cummings' show. Songs include: "Lucky Me," "Superstition Song," "I Speak to the Stars," "Take a Memo to the Moon," "Love You Dearly," "Bluebells of Broadway," "Parisian Pretties," "Wanna Sing Like an Angel," "High Hopes," "Men."

p, Henry Blanke; d, Jack Donohue; w, James O'Hanlon, Robert O'Brien, Irving Elinson (based on a story by O'Hanlon); ph, Wilfrid M. Cline (CinemaScope, Warner Color); ed, Owen Marks; md, Ray Heindorf; art, d, John Beckman; set d, William Wallace; m/l, Sammy Fain, Paul Francis Webster.

Musical **(PR:A MPAA:NR)**

LUCKY NICK CAIN* ½ (1951) 87m Kaydor-Romulus/FOX bw (GB: I'LL GET YOU FOR THIS)
George Raft (*Nick Cain*), Coleen Gray (*Kay Wonderly*), Enzo Staiola (*Toni*), Charles Goldner (*Massine*), Walter Rilla (*Mueller*), Martin Benson (*Sperazza*), Peter Illing (*Ceralde*), Hugh French (*Travers*), Peter Bull (*Hans*), Elwyn Brook-Jones (*The Fence*), Constance Smith (*Nina*), Greta Gynt (*Claudette Ambling*), Margot Grahame (*Mrs. Langley*), Donald Stewart (*Kennedy*).

James Hadley Chase's novel, "I'll Get You For This" (aka: "High Stakes") was the basis for this crime adventure that had the plusses of Italian scenery and the minuses of some shabby acting in the secondary roles. Raft is an American gambler vacationing in Italy and the management of a gambling resort invites him to stay and be a front man for them as his name means something in the international gaming community (this actually happened to Raft when he went to live in England and fronted a gaming club) but it's a ruse. Raft is slipped a Mickey and when he wakes up he's been framed for the murder of a U.S. Treasury agent who was on the trail of an interesting conspiracy; the casino bosses have been manufacturing counterfeit dollars using Nazi plates that the Germans had hoped to use in WW II to undermine U.S. currency. Gray is an American who has lost her money at the tables and she and Raft get involved in the various plot turns, racing through the Riviera scenery with Goldner, an Italian police-type, and Staiola, a little boy they pick up. (You might recall him in THE BICYCLE THIEF.) He succeeds in nabbing the culprits and clearing his name, then returns to the tables and his vacation, with Gray in hand. A few good lines in the picture including one very "inside" scene where Raft takes Gray's hand at a nightclub. A tango begins in the background and she innocently inquires, "Do you tango?" Raft lets a hint of a glint come into his eye, then answers, "I used to." A lovely remembrance of the days when Raft tripped the light fantastic. British actor Goldner will be best recalled as the first mate on Alec Guinness's ship in THE CAPTAIN'S PARADISE.

p, Joseph Kaufman; d, Joseph M. Newman; w, George Callahan, William Rose (based on the novel *I'll Get You For This* by James Hadley Chase); ph, Otto Heller; m, Walter Goehr; ed, Russell Lloyd; art d, Ralph Brinton.

Crime/Drama **(PR:A MPAA:NR)**

LUCKY NIGHT* (1939) 90m MGM bw
Robert Taylor (*Bill Overton*), Myrna Loy (*Cora Jordan*), Joseph Allen, Jr. (*Joe Hilton*), Henry O'Neill (*Calvin Jordan*), Douglas Fowley (*George*), Charles Lane (*Carpenter*), Bernadene Hayes (*Blondie*), Gladys Blake (*Blackie*), Bernard Nedell (*Dusty Cormack*), Lillian Rich (*Secretary*), Carl Stockdale (*Clerk*), Jessie Arnold (*Forelady*), Charles Dorety, George Cooper, Jack Daley (*Passersby*), Edward Gargan (*Cop in Park*), Hal Price (*Waiter*), Donald Kerr (*Seller in Arcade*), Frank Faylen (*Announcer*), Oscar O'Shea (*Lt. Murphy*), Garry Owen (*Bandit*), Howard Mitchell (*Cop*), Irving Bacon (*Bus Conductor*), Bobby Watson (*Orchestra Leader*), Raymond Kelly (*Bellboy*), Henry Roquemore (*Mr. Applewaite*), Fern Emmett (*Mrs. Applewaite*), Marjorie Main (*Mrs. Briggs*), Barbara Norton (*Mrs. Briggs' Servant*), Josephine Whittell (*Lady in Paint Store*), Frank Coghlan, Jr. (*Boy in Paint Store*), Harold Schlickenmayer (*Cab Driver*), Baldy Cook (*Waiter in George's*), Al Thompson (*Bum*), C. L. Sherwood (*Tramp*).

Insipid attempt at yet another IT HAPPENED ONE NIGHT comedy that falls like a bad souffle. Long dialog passages with nothing witty being said, half-hearted direction, strained attempts at slapstick, and perhaps the dullest film either Loy or Taylor ever made. Loy is the madcap heiress (aren't they always?) to O'Neill's steel fortune. O'Neill wants her to marry a hand-picked twerp but she rebels and walks out into the world without a penny. On a park bench, she meets Taylor, who is unemployed. Sparks fly. They borrow a half dollar from a cop to eat on, risk it on a gambling venture, win a lot of money, then lose it all. In the process they fall in love, take an apartment, and Taylor gets a job selling plants for $35 a week. The young marrieds battle a lot, break up, and she goes home to Daddy. Taylor eventually finds her and they reconcile. A bore from start to finish, LUCKY NIGHT is a listless yarn that turned out to be a yawn.

p, Louis D. Lighton; d, Norman Taurog; w, Vincent Lawrence, Grover Jones (based on a story by Oliver Claxton); ph, Ray June; ed, Elmo Vernon.

Comedy **(PR:A MPAA:NR)**

LUCKY NUMBER, THE* (1933, Brit.) 72m Gainsborough/ID bw
Clifford Mollison (*Percy Gibbs*), Gordon Harker (*Hackney Man*), Joan Wyndham (*Winnie*), Joe Hayman (*MacDonald*), Frank Pettingell (*Brown*), Esme Percy (*Chairman*), Alfred Wellesley (*Pickpocket*), D. Hay Petrie (*Photographer*), Betty Hartley, The Arsenal Football Club.

After his girl leaves him for another guy, professional soccer player Mollison heads off to France for some rest and relaxation. At a side show, he meets Wyndham and the two become friends. Later Mollison realizes he's lost his wallet and is allowed to pay for drinks with a lottery ticket. Of course, the ticket proves to be a big winner so Mollison, along with Wyndham, begins searching for the precious scrap of paper. Eventually it's found, but the lottery's promoter has absconded with the funds. No matter, for Mollison and Wyndham have fallen in love and decide to get married. All's well that ends well, and Mollison returns to pro-soccer.

p, Michael Balcon; d, Anthony Asquith; w, Franz Schulz; ph, Gunther Krampf; m, Mischa Spoliansky; ed, Dan Birt; art d, Alex Vetchinsky.

Comedy										**(PR:A MPAA:NR)**

## LUCKY PARTNERS*½									(1940) 102m RKO bw

Ronald Colman (David Grant), Ginger Rogers (Jean Newton), Jack Carson (Freddie Harper), Spring Byington (Aunt), Cecilia Loftus (Mrs. Sylvester), Harry Davenport (Judge), Billy Gilbert (Charles), Hugh O'Connell (Niagara Clerk), Brandon Tynan (Mr. Sylvester), Leon Belasco (Nick No. 1), Edward Conrad (Nick No. 2), Olin Howland (Tourist), Benny Rubin, Tom Dugan (Spielers), Walter Kingsford (Wendell), Otto Hoffman (Clerk), Lucile Gleason (Ethel's Mother), Helen Lynd (Ethel), Dorothy Adams (Maid in Apartment), Fern Emmett (Hotel Maid), Grady Sutton (Reporter), Nora Cecil (Clubwoman), Lloyd Ingraham (Chamber of Commerce Member), Edgar Dearing (Desk Sergeant), Al Hill (Motor Cop), Murray Alper (Orchestra Leader), Jane Patten (Bride), Bruce Hale (Bridegroom), Frank Mills (Bus Driver), Alex Melesh (Art Salesman), Billy Benedict (Bellboy), Robert Dudley (Bailiff), Harlan Briggs (Mayor), Gayne Whitman (Announcer's Voice).

There is nothing duller than a dull comedy because when the jokes fail to hit the funny bone, the dialog can seem very tired indeed. Colman proved he could play the devil out of comedies (CHAMPAGNE FOR CAESAR is the best example) but not if he didn't have the material in the script or the right direction. Milestone may have been terrific for ALL QUIET ON THE WESTERN FRONT and OF MICE AND MEN, but asking him to direct a comedy is like asking Mickey Rooney to slam-dunk. Colman is an artist in New York's Greenwich Village. He meets Rogers, wishes her good luck, and the next thing she knows a stranger has given her a gorgeous gown. Rogers attributes her good fortune to Colman and she asks him to split a sweepstakes ticket purchase with her. He agrees and says that if they win, will she accompany him on a strictly platonic honeymoon to Niagara Falls? She agrees and do we have to tell you that they win? Carson is Rogers's fiance and not too thrilled about his love going off with another man to the very place he would have chosen for their honeymoon, so he follows them there. Rogers is, of course, falling for Colman, much to Carson's dismay. Some bogus bedroom farce tactics occur and the trio is hauled up before judge Davenport who orders them to stop all this nonsense. They should have stopped it before it started. The original was far lighter and funnier when written in France by Guitry who also starred and directed in 1935. The best thing about this dud was Carson's miffed suitor. Few actors could ever miff as well as Carson.

p, Harry E. Eddington, George Haight; d, Lewis Milestone; w, Allan Scott, John Van Druten (based on the story "Bonne Chance" by Sacha Guitry); ph, Robert DeGrasse; m, Dimitri Tiomkin; ed, Henry Berman; art d, Van Nest Polglase, Carroll Clark; set d, Darrell Silvera; cos, Irene; spec eff, Vernon L. Walker; makeup, Mel Burns.

Comedy						**Cas.**		**(PR:A MPAA:NR)**

## LUCKY RALSTON							(SEE: LAW AND ORDER, 1940)

## LUCKY STAR**									(1929) 85m FOX bw

Janet Gaynor (Mary Tucker), Charles Farrell (Timothy Osborn), Guinn "Big Boy" Williams (Martin Wrenn), Paul Fix (Joe), Hedwiga Reicher (Mrs. Tucker), Gloria Grey (Milly), Hector V. Sarno (Pop Fry).

This home-spun story features Gaynor as a lonely woman living on a rundown farm with her widowed mother. Reicher wants her children to have a better life than she and is convinced that Gaynor should marry Williams, a soldier home from WW I. He has returned to his former job, a power lineman, and Reicher thinks he's the best thing for her daughter. But Gaynor's heart belongs to Farrell, who also was a lineman before the war. But his crippling war wounds have forced him into menial tasks and Reicher doesn't consider him worthy of her daughter. Just before the marriage is to take place Williams, Farrell miraculously regains his strength, soundly beats his rival and marries his own true love. This simplistic story was certainly below the talents of its stars, but the studio felt that the company would take it and make it something special. The real novelty of this picture is that it talked! For the first time the public got to hear Gaynor and Farrell's voices. This alone was gimmick enough to make most of the viewing public ignore the vacuousness of the plot. There was a myriad of sound effects as well, including trains, trees, and Farrell's crippled legs dragging on the floor.

p, William Fox; d, Frank Borzage; w, Sonya Levien, John Hunter Booth (based on the story "Three Episodes in the Life of Timothy Osborn" by Tristram Tupper); ph, Chester Lyons, William Cooper Smith; ed, Katherine Hilliker, H. H. Caldwell; art d, Harry Oliver.

Drama										**(PR:A MPAA:NR)**

## LUCKY STAR, THE***				(1980, Can.) 110m Tele Metropole Internationale c

Rod Steiger (Col. Gluck), Louise Fletcher (Loes Bakker), Lou Jacobi (Elia Goldberg), Brett Marx (David Goldberg), Helen Hughes (Rose Goldberg), Yvon Dufour (Burgomaster), Jean Gascon (Priest), Isabelle Mejias (Marijke), Kalman Steinberg (Salomon), Guy L'Ecuyer (Antique Dealer), Johnny Krykamp (Kees), Peter Farber, Lex Goudsmith (Gendarmes), Rijk DeGooyer, Hans Cornelis (Ge-

stapo Men), Irene Kessler (Mrs. Stein), Tom Rack (Odd-job Man), Syd Libman (Rabbi), Fred DeGrote (Telephone Operator), Henry Gamer (Commissionaire).

Marx is a young Jewish boy whose parents (Jacobi and Hughes) are arrested and taken away by the Nazis. The boy is a dreamer and lover of Hollywood B westerns. He runs off and hides out as a farmhand on Fletcher's farm. Steiger is a German officer who comes around and is promptly taken prisoner by Marx, much in the same fashion as his western heroes take the bad guys. This is an absolute sweetheart of a movie with nice performances by the ensemble. The film's director lets the story unfold naturally and lets the comedy within its drama reveal itself in a subtle and not-so-subtle fashion. Filmed in Canada and Holland, it may be a bit upsetting to young viewers.

p, Claude Leger; d, Max Fischer; w, Fischer, Jack Rosenthal (based on an original idea by Roland Topor); ph, Frank Tidy; m, Art Philipps; ed, Yves Langlois.

Drama										**(PR:A MPAA:PG)**

## LUCKY STIFF, THE**							(1949) 99m Amusement Enterprises/UA bw

Dorothy Lamour (Anna Marie St. Claire), Brian Donlevy (John J. Malone), Claire Trevor (Marguerite Seaton), Irene Hervey (Mrs. Childers), Marjorie Rambeau (Hattie Hatfield), Robert Armstrong (Von Flanagan), Billy Vine (Joe Di Angelo), Warner Anderson (Eddie Britt), Virginia Patton (Millie Dale), Richard Gaines (District Attorney Logan), Joe Sawyer (Tony), Larry Blake (Louie Perez), Bob Hopkins (MacDougal), Sidney Miller (Bernstein), Charles Meredith (Mr. Childers), Jimmy Ames (Rico Di Angelo).

Donlevy is a detective out to discover the truth behind a protection scheme. Lamour is a singer who was electrocuted for murder but now her ghost has come back to haunt some gangsters. Ultimately, Donlevy discovers this to be a ruse: Lamour lives and is the brains behind the protection outfit. This weird, offbeat idea (based on the Rice novel) is not handled nearly as cleverly as it could be. The confusing screenplay goes off on a series of wild and diversified tangents before settling down with the main story line. This was the first picture for the Amusement Enterprises Company run by Jack Benny.

p, Jack Benny; d&w, Lewis R. Foster (based on the novel by Craig Rice); ph, Ernest Laszlo; ed, Howard Smith; md, David Chudnow; art d, Lewis H. Creber; m/l, "Loneliness," Victor Young, Ned Washington.

Comedy/Drama								**(PR:A MPAA:NR)**

## LUCKY SWEEP, A*							(1932, Brit.) 58m National Talkies/PDC bw

John Longden (Bill Higgins), Diana Beaumont (Polly), A.G. Poulton (Joshua), Marie Wright (Martha), Sybil Jane (Miss Grey), Elsie Prince (Secretary), Elsie Moore.

Longden is a fanatical anti-gambler who is sent a sweepstakes ticket in the mail as a joke by his fiancee. Unfortunately, the joke goes bad when Longden is accused of stealing the ticket. This was to be the saving grace of Bramble, a popular director-actor during the silent era, but it ended up doing his career more harm than good.

p, Harry Rowson; d, A. V. Bramble.

Comedy										**(PR:A MPAA:NR)**

## LUCKY TERROR*									(1936) 61m FD bw

Hoot Gibson (Lucky), Lona Andre (Ann), Charles Hill (Doc), Frank Yaconelli (Tony), Bob McKenzie (Sheriff), George Chesebro (Thorton), Jack Rockwell (Batt), Art Mix (Scooter), Fargo Bussey (Skeeter), Wally [Hal Taliaferro] Wales (Spike), Charles King (Lawyer), Nelson McDowell (Coroner), Horace Murphy, Hank Bell.

Some outlaws want to gain possession of a gold mine. Of course they've got to tangle with Gibson first in this simple-minded formula Western. Hill has some moments as a shyster operator of a medicine show, but the script is weak, never really giving the players a chance to do much of anything beyond standing around and waiting for the action to begin in the last two reels. The courtroom scene is completely out of place for the B western genre, coming off more weird than the apparently comedic intentions.

p, Walter Futter; d, Alan James; w, James, Roger Allman (based on a story by Allman); ph, Art Reed.

Western						**Cas.**		**(PR:A MPAA:NR)**

## LUCKY TEXAN, THE**½							(1934) 56m Lone Star/MON bw

John Wayne (Jerry Mason), Barbara Sheldon (Betty), George "Gabby" Hayes (Jake Benson), Yakima Canutt (Cole), Gordon DeMaine [Gordon D. Woods] (Sheriff), Edward Parker (Sheriff's Son), Earl Dwire (Banker), Lloyd Whitlock, Artie Ortego, Tex Palmer, Tex Phelps, George Morrell.

Wayne plays a tough Easterner gone West to meet Hayes, the mining partner of his father. Whitlock and Canutt are a pair of bad guys out to get their mine after Wayne and Hayes discover gold. They frame Hayes on trumped-up charges of murder, but Wayne ultimately proves that the sheriff's son is the real guilty party. The film ends with an exciting, and often funny chase between Wayne on a horse, the bad guys on a railroad handcar and Hayes in a broken down jalopy. This was Hayes' first role as a comic sidekick, a part he was born to play. He went on to making a career out of his "Gabby" characterization. The film is okay for a B western, developing at a nice pace. The photography is somewhat marred by rapid panning that blurs the image at points but otherwise production values are fine. A good chance to see Wayne before he became the legend that he was.

p, Paul Malvern; d&w, Robert N. Bradbury; ph, Archie J. Stout, ed, Carl Pierson.

Western						**Cas.**		**(PR:A MPAA:NR)**

LUCKY TO BE A WOMAN*

(1955, Ital.) 91m Le Louvre-Documento/International Film Distributors bw (LA FORTUNA DI ESSERE DONNA)

Sophia Loren (Antoinette), Charles Boyer (Count Gregorio), Marcello Mastroianni (Corrado), Nino Besozzi (Film Producer), Titina de Filippo (Antoinette's Mother), Giustino Duran (Antoinette's Father), Elisa Gegani, Mauro Sacripante, Memmo Carotenuto.

Sexpot Loren poses for some sexy shots taken by news photographers, and one shot showing the statuesque, voluptuous Loren hiking her skirt to adjust her stockings, is seen by impresario Boyer who decides to guide her future. The man who took the photo, Mastroianni, is secretly in love with Loren and schemes to win her heart and body. Loren is given the star treatment while Boyer makes plans to wed his new creation. Sultry Sophia, however, has second thoughts, and, after some clandestine meetings with shutterbug Mastroianni, decides she is better off not being a rich lady but the peasant wife of an impoverished photographer and she runs into Mastroianni's arms at the end. The whole miserable film is unbelievable but it could have been based on Loren's actual rise to stardom through a barrage of pinup photos where she bared her body to promote a fledgling film career and was subsequently spotted by producer Carlo Ponti who made her a star in Italian movies, then financed her Hollywood career. This was just another grinder for Loren, her 17th movie in three years, and as forgettable as most of her films.

p, Raymond Alexandre; d, Alessandro Blasetti; w, Susso Cecchi d'Amico, Ennio Flaiano, Alessandro Continenza, Blasetti; ph, Otello Martelli; m, Alessandro Cicognini; ed, Mario Serandrei; art d, Franco Lolli.

Drama/Comedy **(PR:C-O MPAA:NR)**

LUCKY TO ME*1/2

(1939, Brit.) 69m ABF bw

Stanley Lupino (Potty), Phyllis Brooks (Pamela), Barbara Blair (Minnie), Gene Sheldon (Hap Hazard), Antoinette Cellier (Kay), David Hutcheson (Peter Malden), Bruce Seton (Lord Tyneside).

When office clerk Lupino secretly marries secretary Brooks, the expected complications follow. Lupino must go off to the country to advise a rich client on money matters and ends up solving the man's romantic troubles as well. Only after this can Lupino and his bride take their honeymoon. This is farce at its most basic and lukewarm level. It marked a rather unfitting end to Lupino's fine screen comedy career.

p, Walter C. Mycroft; d, Thomas Bentley; w, Clifford Grey (based on the story by Stanley Lupino and Arthur Rigby); ph, Derek Williams.

Comedy **(PR:AA MPAA:NR)**

LUCRECE BORGIA**1/2

(1953, Ital./Fr.) 95m Ariane-FS-Francinex-Rizzoli/Cinedis c (AKA: LUCRETIA BORGIA; SINS OF THE BORGIAS)

Martine Carol (Lucrece Borgia), Pedro Armendariz (Cesar Borgia), Massimo Serrato (Duke of Aragon), Valentine Tessier (Julie Farmesa), Louis Seigner (Mage, Soothsayer), Arnoldo Foa (Micheletto), Christian Marquand (Paolo), Tania Fedor (Vanna), Georges Lannes (Ambassador), Maurice Ronet (Perott), Pieral (Midget).

An interesting, if a little overblown, version of the infamous Italian family of the Renaissance. Armendariz is the sadistic, cruel brother of Carol. He controls her every move in his drive for power. She's got her own troubles after a terrible sexual experience with her first husband. She is now in love with Serato, and ultimately tries poisoning her brother to save his life. A nice feel for the times is created within the film's mise-en-scene through historically accurate costuming and set design. The wide-screen is also well employed, particularly in the highly brutal battle scenes, as well as some orgies. The latter displayed an abundant amount of naked female flesh, which the American audiences of 1953 were certainly unaccustomed to. Though in parts it starts to drag, the direction manages to hold an interest.

p, Alexandre Mnouchkine, Francis Cosne, George Danciger; d, Christian-Jacque; w, Jaque, Jacques Sigurd, Cecil Saint-Laurent; ph, Christian Matras (Technicolor); m, Maurice Thiriet; ed, Jacques Carrere, Lucien Lacharmoise; cos, Marcel Escoffier.

Historical Drama **(PR:O MPAA:NR)**

LUCRETIA BORGIA

(SEE: LUCRECE BORGIA, 1953, Fr./Ital.)

LUCREZIA BORGIA**1/2

(1937, Fr.) 80m Compagnie du Cinema/European Films bw

Edwige Feuillere (Lucrezia Borgia), Gabriel Gabrio (Cesar Borgia), Aime Clariond (Machiavelli), Roger Karl (Alexander VI), Escande (Duke of Gandia), Josette Day (Sancia), Dumesnil (Sforza), Artault (Savonaroia), Max Michel (Alfonso of Aragon).

Famed French director of historical epics Gance (NAPOLEON) misfired with this somewhat muddled telling of the story of Cesar Borgia (Gabrino) who, in the 15th century, controlled the Papacy and used his sister Lucrezia (Feuillere) for his own, personal aggrandizement. Eventually the church pulled itself free of his grasp, and the people of Italy struggled to unify the country. Filled with the usual court intrigue, murders, rebellion and drama filmed in grand scale and period detail, LUCREZIA BORGIA falls a bit flat and suffers from an overblown, dated production that may have fared better in the silent days. Not one of the master's better efforts, though it does have its moments of brilliance. (In French; English subtitles.)

d, Abel Gance; w, Leopold Marchand, Henry Vendresse; m, M. Lattes.

Historical Drama **(PR:A MPAA:NR)**

LUCY GALLANT**

(1955) 104m PAR c (AKA: OIL TOWN)

Jane Wyman (Lucy Gallant), Charlton Heston (Casey Cole), Claire Trevor (Lady MacBeth), Thelma Ritter (Molly Basserman), William Demarest (Charles Madden), Wallace Ford (Gus Basserman), Tom Helmore (Jim Wardman), Gloria Talbott

(Laura Wilson), James Westerfield (Frank Wilson), Mary Field (Irma Wilson), Governor Allan Shivers of Texas (Himself), Edith Head (Herself), Joel Fluellen (Summertime), Louise Arthur (Sal), Jay Adler (Station Master), Frank Marlowe (Nolan), Roscoe Ates (Anderson), Howard Negley, Jack Pepper, Bill Hunter, Barbara Stewart, Edmund Cobb, Gene Roth, Max Wagner, Frank Hagney, Jack Shea, Robert Williams, Joey Ray, Ben Burt, Charles Regan, Beatrice Maude, Fern Barry, Emily Getchell, Mary Boyd, Elizabeth Cloud-Miller.

Wyman has her heart broken when her cad of a fiance leaves her high and dry at the altar. Trying to forget her sorrow, she runs off to a Texas oil town and opens a dress shop, where she catches the attention of leading designers as well as wealthy rancher Heston. He falls for Wyman who prefers to give herself totally to her career. A disheartened Heston joins the Army to forget Wyman and there becomes a hero. When he returns to civilian life, Wyman realizes that love is more important than a career and gives it all up to marry her man. The soap opera plot and yards of fashionable gowns were designed specifically with a female audience in mind, and the real designer, Head, makes a cameo appearance. While this is an entertaining film, one can see the motivations clearly in the forefront. Heston is fine, though this is certainly not as well realized a character for him as he has portrayed in biblical epics.

p, William H. Pine, William C. Thomas; d, Robert Parrish; w, John Lee Mahin, Winston Miller (based on the novel The Life of Lucy Gallant by Margaret Cousins); ph, Lionel Lindon (VistaVision/Technicolor); m, Van Cleave; ed, Howard Smith; md, Cleave; art d, Hal Pereira, Henry Bumstead; cos, Edith Head; m/l, "How Can I Tell Her," Jay Livingston, Ray Evans.

Drama **(PR:C MPAA:NR)**

LUDWIG**

(1973, Ital./Ger./Fr.) 186m Mega-Cinitel-Dieter Geissler Filmproduktion/MGM c

Helmut Berger (Ludwig), Romy Schneider (Empress Elizabeth), Trevor Howard (Richard Wagner), Silvana Mangano (Cosima Von Bulow), Gert Frobe (Father Hoffman), Helmut Griem (Capt. Durcheim), Isabella Telezynska (Queen Mother), Umberto Orsini (Count Von Holstein), John Moulder Brown (Prince Otto), Sona Petrova (Sophie), Folker Bohnet (Joseph Kainz), Heinz Moog (Prof. Gudden), Adriana Asti (Lila Von Buliowski), Marc Porel (Richard Hornig), Nora Ricci (Countess Ida Ferenczy), Mark Burns (Hans Von Bulow), Maurizio Bonuglia (Mayor), Alexander Allerson, Bert Bloch, Manfred Furst, Kurt Grosskurt, Anna Maria Hanschke, Gerhard Herter, Jan Linhart, Carla Mancini, Gernot Mohner, Clara Moustawcesky, Alain Naya, Allesandro Perrella, Karl Heinz Peters, Wolfram Schaerf, Henning Schluter, Helmut Stern, Eva Tavazzi, Louise Vincent, Gunnar Warner, Karl Heinz Windhorst, Rayka Yurit.

A handsome and stylish film, this biography of the Bavarian "mad king" is ultimately hollow and historically inaccurate. Berger plays the title role in a distanced manner that never expresses him to the audience. A good deal of time is spent showing his patronage of the famed composer Wagner, played by Howard, in what is probably the film's best performance. His love life is also explored in his platonic affair with Austrian princess Schneider, as well as the monarch's seduction of young men. Gradually Berger becomes quite insane, and ends up dead from mysterious causes. The production is marvelously directed, with Ludwig's actual castles for sets. Color and costume are nicely done and the mise-en-scene is a pleasure to the eye. Wagner's music as background works well. Visconti's directing is good and his sense of grandeur is firmly in place. But the script is overlong and boring, trying to do too much in too short a time (over three hours!) MGM had hoped this would be a hit on the art circuit, but that dream was never realized.

p, Ugo Santalucia; d, Luchino Visconti; w, Visconti, Enrico Medioli, Suso Cecchi D'Amico, William Weaver; ph, Armando Nannuzzi (Panavision, Technicolor); m, Robert Schumann, Richard Wagner, Jacques Offenbach; ed, Ruggero Mastroianni; md, Franco Mannino; art d, Mario Chiari, Mario Scisci; set d, Enzo Eusepi; cos, Piero Tosi.

Biography **(PR:O MPAA:R)**

LUGGAGE OF THE GODS**1/2

(1983) 74m GEN c

Mark Stolzenberg (Yuk), Gabriel Barre (Tull), Gwen Ellison (Hubba), Martin Haber (Zoot), Rochelle Robins (Kono), Lou Leccese (Flon), Dog Thomas (Gum), John Tarrant (Whittaker), Conrad Bergschneider (Lionel).

A group of cavemen and cavewomen live a peaceful, serene life until a strange occurrence changes their lives forever. It's no mythic black obelisk that intrudes onto the scene, but rather a mysterious set of luggage that drops from a passing jet liner. Though the title is probably more clever than most of the gags, this does have some rather good moments within the silliness.

p, Jeff Folmsbee; d&w, David Kendall; ph, Steven Ross; m, Cengiz Yaltkaya; ed, Jack Haigis; art d, Joshua Harrison; cos, Dawn Johnson; spec eff., Glenn Van Fleet; makeup, Arnold Gargiulo.

Comedy **(PR:C MPAA:NR)**

LULLABY, THE

(SEE: SIN OF MADELON CLAUDET, 1931)

LULLABY**

(1961, USSR) 90m Moldova/Artkino bw (KOLYBELNAYA; AKA: THE LULLABY)

Nikolay Timofeyev (Losev, The Pilot), Viktoria Lepko (Aurika), Lida Pigurenko (Aurika, as a Little Girl), Lyubov Chernoval (Aurika, the Archivist's Daughter), Viktor Chetverikov (Pavel), Yuriy Solovyov (Sgt. Mikheyev, the Orphanage Director), K. Kramarchuk (George Nistryanu), Shura Kuznetsov (Niku), Mark Troyanovskiy (The Archivist), V. Zamanskiy (Andrey Petryanu), L. Kruglyy (Levka), Katya Savinova (Olga, the Girl in the Truck), V. Ratomskiy (Demushkin), K. Polovikova (Anfisa), Yevgeniy Teterin (Mikhail Yakovlevich), Ada Voytsik (Yekaterina Borisovna), Tatyana Guretskaya (Zinaida Vasilyevna), S. Svetlichnaya

(Nata), I. Radchenko, Ye. Shutov, Ye. Izmaylova, I. Sedykh, L. Popovchenko, N. Krasnoshchyokov, I. Kolin, N. Zaytsev, K. Kozlenkova, V. Markin, B. Sokolov, V. Shchyolokov, Vera Kuznetsova.

Russian drama about an airline pilot, Timofeyev, who finds the passport of a woman he believes to be his long-lost daughter, who he thought had been killed in WW II. After recalling his long and painful search for the infant, he immediately sets out to find her in adulthood. The woman has become a nurse and now lives in Siberia. One day on her way home, when she insists that her fiance stop their car to aid a mother with a sick child, she and her boyfriend quarrel. So she hails a cab, coincidentally the same taxi her father has been traveling in through town in search of her, and father and daughter are happily reunited.

d, Mikhail Kalik; w, Avenir Zak, Isai Kuznetsov; ph, Vadim Derbenyov; m, D. Fedov; ed, Kalik; md, V. Dudarova; art d, S. Bulgakov, A. Roman; m/l, M. Sobol, A. Konunov.

Drama **(PR:A MPAA:NR)**

LULLABY OF BROADWAY, THE**¹/₂ (1951) 91m WB c

Doris Day (Melinda Howard), Gene Nelson (Tom Farnham), S. Z. Sakall (Adolph Hubbell), Billy De Wolfe ("Lefty" Mack), Gladys George (Jessica Howard), Florence Bates (Mrs. Hubbell), Anne Triola (Gloria Davis), Hanley Stafford (George Ferndel), Page Cavanaugh Trio (Themselves), The DeMattiazzis (Specialty), Sheldon Jett (Gus), Murray Alper (Joe the Bartender), Edith Leslie (Nurse), Hans Herbert (Headwaiter), Herschel Dougherty (Sidney), Elizabeth Flournoy (Secretary), Donald Kerr (Driver), Arlyn Roberts (Blonde Showgirl), Philo McCullough (Waiter), Jimmy Aubrey (Stewart), Bess Flowers (Passenger on Ship), Charles Williams (Reporter).

A flimsy musical that suffers from too many songs (albeit some wonderful ones) and not enough concentration on a story. Day is a musical comedy actress newly arrived from London to New York where she doesn't know that her mother, George, is no longer a major star but is now a drunken performer in a tacky Greenwich Village cabaret. Sakall is a rich man who lives in a huge house with his wife, Bates (in one of her patented battleaxe characterizations), and his valet, De Wolfe. He keeps George's charade alive when he tells Day that he is only renting his mansion from George. Bates thinks that Sakall is having an affair with Day and Sakall means to clear that up but the situation worsens when George is too swacked to appear at a party where she is to meet her daughter again. Nelson is a musical comedy star and he meets Day at that party. Love happens and Nelson prevails on Stafford, his producer, to use her in a show. Bates and Sakall are near divorce, then Day and Nelson have a spat. Eventually, they can't keep the news of George's descent into booziness from Day and when she learns about it she is depressed enough to buy a return ticket to England. George gets sober long enough to meet Day and they reconcile. Day and Nelson do the same and they team up for their first (of what will be many, they hope) smash show. Sounds like a good story but so little time is taken for motivation that the scenes shoot past the eye as little more than stage waits for the musical numbers. Tunes include: "Lullaby of Broadway," "You're Getting To Be a Habit With Me," "Just One of Those Things," "Somebody Loves Me," "I Love the Way You Say Goodnight," "Fine and Dandy," "Please Don't Talk About Me When I'm Gone," "A Shanty In Old Shanty Town," "We'd Like to Go On a Trip," "Zing! Went the Strings Of My Heart," "You're Dependable," and any movie with such great songs can't be all bad. If the voice of the producer in the film sounds familiar to older readers, that's because it belongs to the man who played Baby Snooks's long-suffering father for so many years on radio, Hanley Stafford.

p, William Jacobs; d, David Butler; w, Earl Baldwin (based on his story "My Irish Molly O"); ph, Wilfred M. Cline (Technicolor); ed, Irene Morra; md, Ray Heindorf; art d, Douglas Bacon; set d, Lyle B. Reifsnider; cos, Milo Anderson; ch, Al White, Eddie Prinz; m/l, Cole Porter, Harry Warren, Al Dubin, George Gershwin, Ballard MacDonald, B. G. De Sylva, Sam Stept, Sidney Clare, James F. Hanley, Joe Young, Jack Little, John Siras, Eddie Pola, George Wyle.

Musical Comedy **(PR:A MPAA:NR)**

L'ULTIMO UOMO DELLA TERRA
(SEE: LAST MAN ON EARTH, THE, 1964, U.S./Ital.)

LULU** (1962, Aus.) 100m Gloria bw

Nadja Tiller (Lulu), O. E. Hasse (Schon), Hildegard Knef (Baroness), Mario Adorf (Trainer), Rudolf Forster (Father), Leon Askin (Son), Georges Regnier (Jack the Ripper).

This remake of the famous Pabst film, PANDORA'S BOX (DIE BUECHSE DER PANDORA, 1929) features Tiller in the lead role. At age 14, she tries to steal the watch off a doctor, but is instead caught and becomes his kept woman. He transforms her into a worldly woman and marries her off to a wealthy man. Her new husband enjoys watching her dance au natural, but dies of a heart attack after catching her in liaison with a young artist. The young man becomes her next husband, but he also passes on, committing suicide. Finally, she marries the doctor, but kills him in a fight over a pistol. Sent to prison, the dead man's son, along with his lesbian admirer friend, free her and they run off to Paris. Eventually, she ends up in London, transformed into a prostitute who is finally murdered herself. Unfortunately, Tiller does not have the sex appeal needed to carry this film, though Hasse and Knef do give the movie some redeeming value.

p, Otto Durer; d&w, Rolf Thiele (based on the plays of Frank Wedekind); ph, Michel Kelber; m, Carl DeGroof.

Drama **(PR:O MPAA:NR)**

LULU*¹/₂ (1978) 94m Chase c

Paul Shenar (Ludwig Schon), Elisa Leonelli (Lulu), John Roberdeau (Alwa Schon), Norma Leistiko (Countess Geschwitz), Stephen Ashbrook (Walter), Warren Pierce (Dr. Goll), Michael Anderson (Prince Escerny), Thomas Roberdeau (Jack the Ripper).

Another version of the Pabst film, which had its basis in the dramatic plays of Frank Wedekind and the Alban Berg opera. This American version of the story is certainly different from the others in that it is told silently, with title cards rather than the spoken word. It's the story of a nymphomaniac's rise in society through a succession of successful marriages, and then her ultimate fall when she murders one husband and then is killed by Jack the Ripper. Told mainly in tight close-ups, the film is explicitly violent and never quite gets the intended silent film "feel," as there is one speaking character that seems to kill this attempt.

p&d, Ronald Chase; w, Frank Wedekind (based on the plays of Wedekind); ph, Chase; m, Alban Berg; ed, Chase, Jay Miracle, Todd Boekelheide, Bonnie Koehler; art d, Vance Martin, Donald Eastman.

Drama **(PR:O MPAA:NR)**

LULU BELLE*¹/₂ (1948) 86m COL bw

Dorothy Lamour (Lulu Belle), George Montgomery (George Davis), Albert Dekker (Mark Brady), Otto Kruger (Harry Randolph), Glenda Farrell (Molly Benson), Greg McClure (Butch Cooper), Charlotte Wynters (Mrs. Randolph), Addison Richards (Commissioner Dixon), William Haade (Duke Weaver), Ben Erway (Doctor), Clancy Cooper (Bartender), John Indrisano, Bud Wiser (Brady's Bodyguards), George Lewis (Capt. Ralph), Harry Hays Morgan (Maitre'D), Jack Norman (Wells), Martha Holliday (Pearl).

Lamour is a saloon singer, circa 1900. She marries attorney Montgomery and then heads off on a succession of lovers ranging from boxer McClure to his manager Dekker, and finally Kruger, a railroad magnate who takes her to New York. There she becomes a Broadway star until her wild ways finally catch up with her and she is shot. Based on a Broadway play by MacArthur and Sheldon, the original character had been a prostitute instead of a chanteuse. But that never would have been accepted for a star like Lamour by the audiences (to say nothing of studio heads), and the profession was changed for the film. Songs included: Title song (Edgar DeLange, Henry Russell), "Sweetie Pie" (John Lehman, Russell), "I'd Be Lost Without You" (Russell), "Ace in the Hole" (George Mitchell, James Dempsey), "Sweetheart of the Blues" (Lester Lee, Allan Roberts).

p, Benedict Bogeaus; d, Leslie Fenton; w, Everett Freeman, Karl Kamb (based on the play by Charles MacArthur, Edward Sheldon); ph, Ernest Laszlo; m, Henry Russell; ed, James Smith; art d, Duncan Cramer.

Drama/Musical **(PR:A MPAA:NR)**

LUM AND ABNER ABROAD* (1956) 72m Howco bw

Chester Lauck (Lum), Morris Goff (Abner), Jill Alis (Marianne), Lila Audres (Collette), Branko Spoylar (Papa Possavetz), Gene Gary (Nicky), Vern Mesita (Duchess), Valdo Stephens (Mischa), Steven Voyt (Frankenshpinin), Nada Nuchich (Lisa), Chris Peters (Croupier), Jim Kiley (Tommy Ellis), Joseph Batistich (Dignitary).

This originally was three short television shows based on the famous radio comedy team. However, they were linked together by a narration and released as a sort of three-part film. The first story finds Lauck and Goff helping out Alis, a ballerina unlucky in love. She's crazy about a journalist who's missing and the two kindly gents, with the help of the U.S. Embassy, get the lovers back together. Next it's off to Paris where they accidentally get involved with some smugglers. Finally they end up in Monte Carlo, breaking the bank, but settling for $14.80 so that the good citizens won't have to pay any taxes. For their efforts, they are admirably decorated. The film painfully shows its television background with a simplistic script and poor connections. The low-budget production includes the sound fading before the picture. Lauck and Goff still have a nice folksiness about them that sneaks through, despite the poor quality of the film.

p&d, James Kern; w, Carl Herzinger (based on stories by Kern, Herzinger); ph, Octhvian Miletich; ed, Maurice Wright, Blanche Jens.

Comedy **(PR:AA MPAA:NR)**

LUMBERJACK** (1944) 65m UA bw

William Boyd (Hopalong Cassidy), Andy Clyde (California Carlson), Jimmy Rogers (Jimmy Rogers), Herbert Rawlinson (Buck), Ellen Hall (Julie), Ethel Wales (Abbey), Douglas Dumbrille (Keeper), Francis McDonald (Fenwick), John Whitney (Jordan), Hal Taliaferro (Taggart), Henry Wills (Slade), Charles Morton (Big Joe), Frances Morris (Mrs. Williams), Jack Rockwell (Sheriff), Bob Burns (Justice), Hank Worden, Earle Hodgins, Pierce Lyden.

Number 52 in the HOPALONG CASSIDY series finds Boyd helping widow Hall. Her husband has been murdered under mysterious circumstances and now two land agents want her to sign away her property. She does so, despite the warnings of Boyd. Because of some lazy lumberjacks, it looks like she won't be able to deliver the virgin timber on time to the smarmy gents, but thanks to Boyd's derring-do (as well as some local homesteaders), she is able to keep her end of the bargain. Boyd solves the murder to boot. A standard programmer with some nice riding tricks by Boyd, as well as Clyde's usual comic support. Filmed in the High Sierras, this picture has a nice look to it that was different than most of the other films in this series. (See HOPALONG CASSIDY series, Index.)

p, Harry A. Sherman; d, Lesley Selander; w, Norman Houston, Barry Shipman (based on characters created by Clarence E. Mulford); ph, Russell Harlan.

Western **(PR:A MPAA:NR)**

LUMIERE**¹/₂ (1976, Fr.) 95m Orphee Arts-FR-3-GAU/New World c

Jeanne Moreau (Sarah Dedieu), Francine Racette (Juliene), Lucia Bose (Laura), Caroline Cartier (Caroline), Marie Henriau (Flora), Monique Tarbes (Claire), Keith

Carradine (David Foster), Bruno Ganz (Heinrich Grun), Francois Simon (Gregoire), Francis Huster (Thomas), Niels Arestrup (Nano), Georges Wod (Liansko), Patrice Alexsandre (Petard), Rene Feret (Julien), Anders Holmquist (Anders), Jacques Spiesser (Saint-Loup).

Moreau's first self-directed effort tells the story of four actresses and the special friendship they share. The tale opens up with three of the actresses gathered at the estate of the eldest and most successful, Moreau. Each carries her own set of troubles with career and romance. Moreau is ending a long affair with Huster, a writer/director, in order to move on to novelist Ganz. Still, she clings to old friend Simon, a research scientist. Bose is a former actress who gave up a career to become wife and mother. Cartier is just struggling to begin her career while attempting to resolve conflicts with her lover Arestrup. Racette is in a similar situation, trying to choose between theatrical success or husband and child. Racette winds up having a one-night stand with Carradine, playing a brief role here as the American rock star. (His career in "art films" constantly fluctuates between sensational and mediocre; here the latter applies.) Bose reveals to Moreau that she is expecting her fifth child in an attempt to hold on to her husband, whom she believes is having an affair. Story concludes with Moreau finally admitting to Ganz about her new love interest and at the same time, losing her friend Simon, who is dying of leukemia, to suicide. (In French; English subtitles.)

p, Claire Duval; d&w, Jeanne Moreau; ph, Ricardo Aronovich (Eastmancolor); m, Astor Piazzola; ed, Albert Jurgenson; cos, Christian Gasc; makeup, Ronaldo Abrev.

Drama   **(PR:O   MPAA:R)**

LUMIERE D'ETE*   (1943, Fr.) 112m Discina bw

Paul Bernard, Pierre Brasseur, Madeleine Renaud, Madeleine Robinson, Georges Marchal, Aimos Blavette, Marcel Levesque, Jane Marken.

Its main objective being an almost grotesque cutting up of the upper classes, LUMIERE D'ETE follows an innocent (Robinson) as she makes sojourn to a mountain resort to be with her fiance. This trip proves anything but the romantic outing she expected, as she discovers herself enveloped in decay by individuals who seem merely a shadow of real humans. Robinson's fiance also has become one of these leeches, as he nonchalantly drops her once he tires of her. A meeting with Marchal, a worker on a nearby dam, saves Robinson from this gang, especially from the greedy hands of Bernard, with the two eventually making an escape to a better future. Though some of the symbolism might appear heavy-handed, the characterizations, notably that of Bernard as an idle millionaire, and the contrast between the rich and working classes, make a powerful impression. (In French; English subtitles.)

p, Andre Paulve; d, Jean Gremillion; w, Jacques Prevert, Pierre Laroche; ph, Louis Page; m, Roland Manuel; art d, Max Douy, Leon Barsacq.

Drama   **(PR:C   MPAA:NR)**

LUMMOX*   (1930) 88m UA bw

Winifred Westover (Bertha Oberg), Dorothy Janis (Chita), Lydia Yeamans Titus (Annie Wennerberg), Ida Darling (Mrs. Farley), Ben Lyon (Rollo Farley), Myrta Bonillas (Veronica Neidringhouse), Cosmo Kyrle Bellew (John Bixby), Anita Bellew (Mrs. John Bixby), Robert Ullman (Paul Bixby, age 5), Clara Langsner (Mrs. Wallenstein, Sr.), William Collier, Jr. (Wally Wallenstein), Edna Murphy (May Wallenstein), Torben Meyer (Silly Willie), Fan Bourke (Mrs. McMurtry), Myrtle Stedman (Mrs. Ossetrich), Danny O'Shea (Barney), William Bakewell (Paul Charvet), Sidney Franklin (Mr. Meyerbogen).

Westover is an impoverished servant girl, working at a variety of menial tasks in order to support her illegitimate son. Crisis arises when she gives the boy up for a rich couple to adopt. The story is somewhat dull, though Westover's performance as a woman smarter than her employers credits her with a nice characterization. Her first lover, the father of her son, is a poet of greeting card talent, which the film would have us believe is great writing. There is sometimes overdramatization to the point of being comical.

d, Herbert Brenon; w, Elizabeth Brenon (based on the novel by Fannie Hurst); ph, Karl Struss; ed, Marie Halvey.

Drama   **(PR:A   MPAA:NR)**

L'UN ET L'AUTRE   (SEE: OTHER ONE, THE, 1967, Fr.)

LUNA*1/2   (1979, Ital.) 139m Fiction Film/FOX c (LA LUNA)

Jill Clayburgh (Caterina Silveri), Matthew Barry (Joe, Her Son), Veronica Lazar (Marina), Renato Salvatori (Communist), Fred Gwynne (Douglas Winter, Her Husband), Tomas Milian (Giuseppe), Alida Valli (Giuseppe's Mother), Elisabetta Campeti (Arianna), Franco Citti (Man In Bar), Roberto Benigni (Upholsterer), Carlo Verdone (Director of Caracalla), Peter Eyre (Edward), Stephane Barat (Mustafa), Pippo Campanini (Innkeeper), Rodolfo Lodi (Maestro Giancarlo Calo), Shara Di Nepi (Concetta, Caterina's Maid), Iole Silvani (Wardrobe Mistress), Francesco Mei, Ronaldo Bonacchi (Barmen), Mimmo Poli, Massimiliano Filoni (Piano Movers), Alessandro Vlad (Caracalla Conductor).

Bernardo Bertolucci's excessive look into the life of a troubled teenager created quite a stir upon its original release because of controversial subject matter, which included an incestuous relationship between mother and son. There really seems to be no reason to include such a scene beyond box office possibilities and Bertolucci's own desire to see just how far he could go. Clayburgh is the mother-opera singer, married to Gwynne who believes that the boy is his. Barry is the son without a father figure, spoiled beyond any reasonable means by his mother, and desperately in need of a strong father to keep him in line, a role Gwynne cannot provide. He finally gets his much needed guidance by the end of the film; the real father is hiding out in Italy teaching children. But before this happens, Barry has to watch Gwynne, whom he believes to be his father, commit suicide. Clayburgh and son move to Italy after this, where she tries to revive her fading singing career, while Barry becomes

a heroin addict after getting involved with the wrong people. This almost drives Clayburgh to the point of a nervous breakdown, as the relationship between mother and son deepens to the point where they almost make love. Luckily for audiences, they don't go all the way, though there are rumors that Bertolucci had originally planned to show them in the sexual act, but was kept from doing so for fear of moral censorship.

p, Giovanni Bertolucci; d, Bernardo Bertolucci; w, Giuseppe Bertolucci, Clare Peploe, B. Bertolucci, George Malko (based on the story by Franco Arcalli, Giuseppe and Bernardo Bertolucci); ph, Vittorio Storaro (Eastmancolor); m, Giuseppe Verdi; ed, Gabriella Cristiani; art d, Maria Paola Maino, Gianni Silvestri; cos, Lina Taviani.

Drama   **(PR:O   MPAA:R)**

LUNCH HOUR*   (1962, Brit.) 64m Eyeline/Bry bw

Shirley Anne Field (Girl), Robert Stephens (Man), Kay Walsh (Manageress), Hazel Hughes (Aunty), Michael Robbins (Harris), Nigel Davenport (Manager), Neil Culleton (Ronnie), Sandra Leo (Susan), Vi Stephens (Waitress).

A junior executive sets up a romantic interlude with a designer. Unfortunately for the two, everything that can go wrong, does, and therein lies the comedy.

p, John Mortimer, Harold Orton, Alfred Shaughnessy; d, James Hill; w, Mortimer (based on a play by Mortimer).

Comedy   **(PR:C   MPAA:NR)**

LUNCH ON THE GRASS   (SEE: PICNIC ON THE GRASS, 1959, Fr.)

LUNCH WAGON*   (1981) 88m Seymour Borde & Associates/Bordeaux c (AKA: LUNCH WAGON GIRLS; COME 'N GET IT)

Pamela Bryant (Marcy), Rosanne Katon (Shannon), Candy Moore (Diedra), Rick Podell (Al Schmeckler), Rose Marie (Mrs. Schmeckler), Chuck McCann (The Turtle), Jimmie Van Patten (Biff), Nels Van Patten (Scotty), Michael Tucci (Arnie), Louisa Moritz (Sunshine), Vic Dunlop (Ralph), Maurice Sneed (Ben), Michael Mislove (Danny Death), Biff Manard (Wino), Anthony Charnota (Herman), George Memmoli (Andy), Gary Levy (Larry), Peggy Mannix (Bertha), Steve Tannen (Harry), John Thompson, Dale Bozzio, Peter Marc, Bobby Sandler, Odis McKinney, Debrah Kelly, Terry Bozzio, Warren Cucurullo.

Three out-of-work young ladies, Bryant, Katon, and Moore, inherit a lunch wagon and set up business along construction sights in the San Fernando Valley. They call their business "Love Bites" and are they ever popular! They get involved with a rival lunch wagon, which is really a front for a gang of jewel thieves. Memmoli, as the gas station attendant, has a few witty jabs. Dialog is wittier than most films of this nature and the leading trio have a certain freshness about them.

p, Marke Borde; d, Ernest Pintoff; w, Leon Phillips, Marshall Harvey, Terrie Frankle; ph, Fred Lemler (DeLuxe Color); m, Richard Band; ed, Edward Salier.

Comedy   **Cas.**   **(PR:O   MPAA:R)**

LUNCH WAGON GIRLS   (SEE: LUNCH WAGON, 1981)

L'UNE CHANTE L'AUTRE PAS
                          (SEE: ONE SINGS, THE OTHER DOESN'T, 1977, Fr.)

LUNG-MEN K'O-CHAN   (SEE: DRAGON INN, 1968, China)

L'UOMO DALLE DUE OMBRE   (SEE: COLD SWEAT, 1974, Ital./Fr.)

LUPE zero   (1967) 60m Film-Makers Cooperative c

Mario Montez (Lupe Velez), White Pussy (A Cat), Medea Reid, Bill Vehr, Charles Frehse, Charles Ludlam, Charles Levine, Dorrie, Maxwell Reid, Salvador Cruz, Norman Holden.

An experimental satire on the life and career of Hollywood actress Lupe Velez, who is played by transvestite Montez. Musical numbers included.

p&d, Jose Rodriguez-Soltero.

Satire/Musical   **(PR:O   MPAA:NR)**

LURE, THE*   (1933, Brit.) 65m Maude/PAR bw

Anne Grey (Julia Waring), Cyril Raymond (Paul Dane), Alec Fraser (John Baxter), Billy Hartnell (Billy), Philip Clarke (Peter Waring), P.G. Clark (Merritt), Doris Long (Dorothy), Jean Ormond.

Raymond and Fraser are two guests at a house party. Both are in love with another guest, Grey, a widow each wishes to charm. Fraser has taken a valuable stone from his rival's brother, so the two have more than a woman to argue over. That night Fraser is murdered but Raymond comes up with a brilliant plan, involving a fake suicide, which unmasks the true killer.

p&d, Arthur Maude; w (based on the play by J. Sabben-Clare); ph, Eric Cross.

Thriller   **(PR:A   MPAA:NR)**

LURE OF THE ISLANDS*   (1942) 61m MON bw

Margie Hart, Robert Lowery, Guinn "Big Boy" Williams, Ivan Lebedeff, Warren Hymer, Gale Storm, John Bleifer, Satini Puailoa, John Casey, Jerome Sheldon, Kam Tong, Angelo Cruz.

Another Jean Yarbrough quickie is set on an island where Federal agents go undercover in order to do a bit of snooping. Nothing happens that isn't telegraphed a mile ahead of time.

p, Lindsley Parsons; d, Jean Yarbrough; w, Edmond Kelso, George Bricker, Scott Littleton; ph, Mack Stengler; ed, Jack Ogilvie; md, Eddie Kaye.

Crime   **(PR:A   MPAA:NR)**

LURE OF THE JUNGLE, THE**½

(1970, Den.) 88m Laterna/G.G. bw (PAW; AKA: BOY OF TWO WORLDS)

Jimmy Sterman (*Paw*), Edvin Adolphson (*Anders Nilsson*), Ninja Tholstrup (*Aunt Frieda*), Asbjorn Andersen (*Yvonne*), Sacha Wamberg (*Squire*), Freddy Pedersen (*Marius*), Karl Stegger, Preben Neergaard, Karen Lykkehus, Helge Kjaerulff-Schmidt, Grethe Hoholdt, Poul Smyrner, Mogens Hermansen, Finn Lassen, Svend Bille, Arthur Jensen, Ebba Amfeldt, Otto Hallstrom, Rigmor Hvidtfeldt, Ego Bronnum-Jacobsen.

A touching children's story centering on the prejudice Sterman faces as a result of having moved to Denmark from the West Indies when his Indian mother and white father die. The boy befriends a poacher and is given shelter from the hurt he receives at the hands of the townspeople. But this man is captured for his illegal activities, resulting in Sterman being sent to reform school, a fate from which he is saved only after he escapes and finds refuge in the home of a squire. Originally made in 1959, this film did not find its way to America until 1970.

d, Astrid Henning-Jensen; w, Astrid Henning-Jensen, Bjarne Henning-Jensen (based on the story *Paw, the Young Indian* by Torry Gredsted); ph, Henning Bendtsen, Niels Carstens, Arthur Christiansen; m, Herman D. Koppel; ed, Anker.

Drama　　　　　　　　　　　　　　　　　　　　　　　　**(PR:AAA　MPAA:G)**

LURE OF THE SWAMP**

(1957) 74m FOX bw

Marshall Thompson (*Simon Lewt*), Willard Parker (*James Lister*), Joan Vohs (*Cora Payne*), Jack Elam (*Bliss*), Joan Lora (*Evie Dee*), James Maloney (*August Dee*), Leo Gordon (*Steggins*), Skip Homeier.

After killing his partner in crime, Parker hires Florida swamp guide, Thompson, to take him into the marshes where $20,000 in stolen bank money has been hid. But Parker himself is killed by two others, Vohs, the first gangster's widow, and Elam, an insurance investigator. They want the money as well, and will let nothing stand in their way. In the end, Thompson is wounded and Elam and Vohs are killed. She has the money in hand, but sinks into the quicksand, taking the treasure with her. What could have been a fine suspense thriller, instead was a long, fairly tedious film, thanks to the uninspired direction of Cornfield. Build-ups are dragged out and the payoffs aren't as suspenseful as they could have been. Vohs is okay in her role, as is Lora, who plays Thompson's free-spirited girl friend.

p, Sam Hersh; d, Hubert Cornfield; w, William George (based on a novel by Gil Brewer); ph, Walter Strenge (Regalscope); m, Paul Dunlap; ed, Robert Fritch.

Thriller　　　　　　　　　　　　　　　　　　　　　　　**(PR:C　MPAA:NR)**

LURE OF THE WASTELAND**

(1939) 52m MON c

Grant Withers (*Smitty*), Karl Hackett (*Parker*), Marion Arnold (*Heroine*), LeRoy Mason (*Butch*), Henry Roquemore (*Judge Carleton*), Tom London (*Ranch Foreman*), Snub Pollard (*Cookie*), Sherry Tansey.

Going undercover to recover a stolen $25,000, marshal Withers poses as a convict to join Mason's gang. They go on some cattle raids, ending up at the ranch where former gang member Pollard is now a cook. He's hidden the money in the safe and Mason's come to reclaim it. But Withers reveals himself and after a knockdown, dragout fight, he brings in his man and recovers the loot. This was one of the few western programmers of the 1930s that actually was filmed in color. Unfortunately the color is not well balanced and often comes out muddied. The story is otherwise formula material, with Mason not too convincing as a bad guy. Arnold is supposed to be a romantic image, but mostly stands around looking pretty. The gang does stop their looting every once in awhile for a song, including the old favorite "Home on the Range."

p, Al Lane; d, Harry Fraser; w, Munro Talbot (based on a story by Talbot); ph, Francis Corby (Telco Color); ed, Charles V. Henkel, Jr.

Western　　　　　　　　　　　　　　　　　　　　　　　　**(PR:A　MPAA:NR)**

LURE OF THE WILDERNESS**

(1952) 92m FOX c

Jean Peters (*Laurie Harper*), Jeffrey Hunter (*Ben Tyler*), Constance Smith (*Noreen*), Walter Brennan (*Jim Harper*), Tom Tully (*Zack Tyler*), Harry Shannon (*Pat McGowan*), Will Wright (*Sheriff Brink*), Jack Elam (*Dave Longden*), Harry Carter (*Ned Tyler*), Pat Hogan (*Harry Longden*), Al Thompson (*Shep Rigby*), Robert Adler (*Will Stone*), Sherman Sanders (*Square Dance Caller*), Robert Karnes (*Jack Doran*), George Spaulding (*Sloan*), Walter Taylor (*Sheriff Jepson*), Ted Jordan (*Young Man*).

At the turn of the century Brennan is falsely accused of murder. He takes his daughter, Peters, and together they hide out in the depths of a swamp for eight years. One day Hunter loses his dog and goes searching in the area, finding the outcasts. They hold him captive but after he promises to help them get a fair trial they let him go. He sells the pelts Brennan has accumulated in order to raise money for an attorney. The real killers find out the plan and go after Brennan. One of them is killed, forcing the other to confess. Brennan returns to society and Peters marries Hunter. A remake of the 1941 film SWAMP WATER, this was not quite as moody as the original. The color photography does not help create the ambiance the black-and-white lensing had, though it does make the film seem more realistic. Essentially a straightforward story, with some suspenseful moments. Production values and acting are standard efforts.

p, Robert L. Jacks; d, Jean Negulesco; w, Louis Lantz (based on a story by Vereen Bell); ph, Edward Cronjager (Technicolor); m, Franz Waxman; ed, Barbara McLean; art d, Lyle Wheeler, set d, Thomas Little, Fred J. Rode.

Drama/Suspense　　　　　　　　　　　　　　　　　　　　**(PR:C　MPAA:NR)**

LURED***

(1947) 102m Oakmont-UA bw (GB: PERSONAL COLUMN)

George Sanders (*Robert Fleming*), Lucille Ball (*Sandra Carpenter*), Charles Coburn (*Inspector Temple*), Boris Karloff (*Artist*), Alan Mowbray (*Maxwell*), Cedric Hardwicke (*Julian Wilde*), George Zucco (*Officer Barrett*), Joseph Calleia (*Dr. Moryani*), Tanis Chandler (*Lucy Barnard*), Alan Napier (*Inspector Gordon*), Robert Coote (*Officer Barret*), Jimmie Aubrey (*Nelson*), Dorothy Vaughan (*Mrs. Miller*), Sam Harris (*Old Man at Concert Asking For Whiskey*).

An engaging thriller which casts Ball in a surprisingly good dramatic performance. An American taxi-dancer working in London, Ball loses her friend Chandler to a mysterious killer who advertises in the newspaper for attractive, lonely young ladies. A fan of French poet Baudelaire, the killer taunts Scotland Yard with clues written in verse about his next victim. Ball agrees to help the investigators catch this madman by acting as a decoy. One suspect, Karloff—in a red herring role as a dress designer—proves to be crazed, but not the murdering type. Another suspect is Calleia who is involved in trafficking white slaves between England and South America. In the meantime Ball has fallen for Sanders, a womanizing nightclub owner who wants to marry her. His friend and business partner Hardwicke is a quiet, repressed man who, of course, turns out to be the man Scotland Yard is looking for. Hardwicke nearly beats the law by attempting to pin the crimes on Sanders and kill Ball in the process. By the finale, however, London streets are once again made safe. Somewhat lengthy at 102 minutes, LURED succeeds because of a pair of fine performances by Ball (whose singing voice is dubbed by Annette Warren) and police inspector Coburn, both better known to the public as comedy stars. As familiar as the plot may seem, LURED proves to be a reliable crime melodrama in the classic Hollywood vein—complete with a top-notch cast of players and Sirk's sure-handed direction in the days before he became synonymous with the term "melodrama." Based on Robert Siodmak's 1939 French film PIEGES (SNARES) which starred Maurice Chavalier and Eric von Stroheim (in Karloff's role). Sirk insists that he never saw that film and that it must have been screenwriter Rosten's idea to adapt it.

p, James Nasser; d, Douglas Sirk; w, Leo Rosten (based on a story by Jacques Companeez, Ernest Neuville, Simon Gantillon); ph, William Daniels; m, Michel Michelet; ed, John M. Foley, James E. Newcom; md, David Chudnow; art d, Nicolai Remisoff; makeup, Don Cash.

Crime　　　　　　　　　　　　　　　　　　　　　　　　**(PR:A　MPAA:NR)**

LUST FOR A VAMPIRE**

(1971, Brit.) 95m Hammer-EMI/Levitt-Pickman c (AKA: TO LOVE A VAMPIRE)

Ralph Bates (*Giles Barton*), Barbara Jefford (*Countess Herritzen*), Suzanna Leigh (*Janet Playfair*), Michael Johnson (*Richard Lestrange*), Yutte Stensgaard (*Mircalla/Carmilla*), Mike Raven (*Count Karnstein*), Helen Christie (*Miss Simpson*), David Healy (*Pelley*), Michael Brennan (*Landlord*), Pippa Steel (*Susan*), Jack Melford (*Bishop*), Erik Chitty (*Prof. Hertz*), Luan Peters (*Trudie*), Christopher Cunningham (*Coachman*), Judy Matheson (*Amanda*), Caryl Little (*Isabel*), Christopher Neame (*Hans*), Harvey Hall (*Heinrich*), Erica Beale, Jackie Leapman, Melita Clarke, Patricia Warner, Christine Smith, Vivienne Chandler, Sue Longhurst, Melinda Churcher (*Schoolgirls*).

Silly, campy vampire fun features Stensgaard as a beautiful vampire enrolled in an exclusive finishing school located in Karnstein Castle, the former site of various black magic rituals. Bates, the school's headmaster, falls in love with his alluring pupil, and is ultimately her victim, but not before confronting her with charges about her true identity. A school professor, Johnson, also falls in love with Stensgaard, and this time, she returns the emotion. However, evil triumphs—almost—as she returns to her vampire ways and is dramatically struck down at film's end by a fiery beam. The role of this entrancing female vampire has been taken by Annette Vadim in Roger Vadim's BLOOD AND ROSES and by Ingrid Pitt in Roy Ward Baker's THE VAMPIRE LOVERS. This film version never takes itself too seriously, and the actors seem to be enjoying themselves. The direction is crisp and appropriately cocky, though an overabundance of zooms onto neck bites gets somewhat tiresome after a while. Originally the MPAA rated this "X" but after some cuts it was lowered to "R."

p, Michael Style, Harry Fine; d, Jimmy Sangster; w, Tudor Gates (based on characters created by J. Sheridan Le Fanu in his novel *Carmilla*); ph, David Muir (Technicolor); m, Harry Robinson; ed, Spencer Reeve; md, Philip Martell; art d, Don Mingaye; ch, Babbie McManus; m/l, "Strange Love," Robinson, Frank Godwin; makeup, George Blackler.

Horror　　　　　　　　**Cas.**　　　　　　　　**(PR:O　MPAA:R)**

LUST FOR EVIL

(SEE: PURPLE NOON, 1961, Fr./Ital.)

LUST FOR GOLD**

(1949) 90m COL bw

Ida Lupino (*Julia Thomas*), Glenn Ford (*Jacob Walz*), Gig Young (*Pete Thomas*), William Prince (*Barry Storm*), Edgar Buchanan (*Wiser*), Will Geer (*Deputy Ray Covin*), Paul Ford (*Sheriff Lynn Early*), Jay Silverheels (*Walter*), Eddy Waller (*Coroner*), Will Wright (*Parsons*), Virginia Mullen (*Matron*), Antonio Moreno (*Ramon Peralta*), Arthur Hunnicutt (*Ludi*), Myrna Dell (*Lucille*), Tom Tyler (*Luke*), Elspeth Dudgeon (*Mrs. Bannister*), Paul E. Burns (*Bill Bates*), Hayden Rorke (*Floyd Buckley*), Fred Sears (*Hotel Clerk*), Kermit Maynard (*Man in Lobby*), William J. Tannen (*Eager Fellow*), Edmund Cobb, Richard Alexander, George Chesebro (*Men*), Arthur Space (*Old Man*), Percy Helton (*Barber*).

Prince plays a young man trying to locate the fabled Lost Dutchman Gold Mine by searching through some public records. The body of the story about the mine's original discovery is then told in flashback. Ford plays the Dutchman, a money-mad miner who first runs across the mine during the days of the Old West. He has an affair with Lupino, an equally greedy woman, who wants to control the mine for herself and her husband (Young). Ford kills her and her husband when he catches on to her motives. Their deaths are revenged by nature when Ford is killed in an earthquake. The film flashes forward to Prince and his own search for the mine. On the verge of finding the gold, he gets into a fight with corrupt deputy Geer. The two engage in a to-the-death finish for the rights to the mine. Shot in black and white, the film was released in sepia tone, and also includes some stock footage. The narrative unfolds in a straightforward style, and the cast does the standard job. Originally the film was to be directed by George Marshall, but he was replaced by Simon shortly before shooting began. The new director simplified the plot of the original novel, and named Prince's character after the novel's author, Barry Storm. Storm was furious over the interpretations of his book's events in the film and sued for misrepresentation, among other counts.

p&d, S. Sylvan Simon; w, Ted Sherdeman, Richard English (based on the novel *Thunder God's Gold* by Barry Storm); ph, Archie Stout; m, George Duning; ed, Gene Havlick; md, Morris Stoloff; art d, Carl Anderson; cos, Jean Louis; makeup, Clay Campbell.

Western   **(PR:O   MPAA:NR)**

LUST FOR LIFE***   (1956) 122m MGM c

Kirk Douglas *(Vincent Van Gogh)*, Anthony Quinn *(Paul Gauguin)*, James Donald *(Theo Van Gogh)*, Pamela Brown *(Christine)*, Everett Sloane *(Dr. Gachet)*, Niall MacGinnis *(Roulin)*, Noel Purcell *(Anton Mauve)*, Henry Daniell *(Theodorus Van Gogh)*, Madge Kennedy *(Anna Cornelia Van Gogh)*, Jill Bennett *(Willemien)*, Lionel Jeffries *(Dr. Peyron)*, Laurence Naismith *(Dr. Bosman)*, Eric Pohlmann *(Colbert)*, Jeanette Sterke *(Kay)*, Toni Gerry *(Johanna)*, Wilton Graff *(Rev. Stricker)*, Isobel Elsom *(Mrs. Stricker)*, David Horne *(Rev. Peeters)*, Noel Howlett *(Commissioner Van Den Berghe)*, Ronald Adam *(Commissioner De Smet)*, John Ruddock *(Ducrucq)*, Julie Robinson *(Rachel)*, David Leonard *(Camille Pissarro)*, William Phipps *(Emile Bernard)*, David Bond *(Seurat)*, Frank Perls *(Pere Tanguy)*, Jay Adler *(Waiter)*, Laurence Badie *(Adeline Ravoux)*, Rex Evans *(Durand-Ruel)*, Marion Ross *(Sister Clothilde)*, Mitzi Blake *(Elizabeth)*, Anthony Sydes *(Cor)*, Antony Eustrel *(Tersteeg)*, Ernestine Barrier *(Jet)*, Jerry Bergen *(Henri de Toulouse Lautrec)*, Belle Mitchell *(Mme. Tanguy)*, Alec Mango *(Dr. Rey)*, Fred Johnson *(Cordan)*, Norman MacGowan *(Pier)*, Mickey Maga *(Jan)*.

There are many amazing things about this superlative film, not the least of which is the obvious fact that its stars, Douglas and Quinn, bore startling likenesses to the biographical parts they enacted. They were almost dead ringers for Van Gogh (Douglas) and Gauguin (Quinn). LUST FOR LIFE is also amazing in that it got made in the first place. The film was optioned by MGM in 1947 but it took almost nine years before the studio got around to filming Stone's immensely popular novel. Douglas, a loner full of religious zeal, leaves his native Holland in 1878, going to Le Borinage province in Belgium to inspire the coal miners there with the word of God. Instead of converting the rough miners to the church, Douglas, full of pity for their impoverished situation, gives away all his earthly belongings, as well as the church's. This generosity to the miners brings down a censure from church authorities. He denounces the church officials as hypocrites and, found by his brother, Donald, to be living in squalor, returns home to regain his health. There he recuperates by developing his natural talent and interest in art. His ever-restless nature upsets the Van Gogh household and, after he proposes to a cousin who violently rejects him (he holds his hand over a candle, letting the flames burn him, telling her that he will keep it there until she accepts him), his sister asks him to leave the house. In the Hague, Douglas sets up in a small house and takes Brown, a prostitute, as his housekeeper and lover. Purcell, playing the part of successful painter Anton Mauve, a relative of Van Gogh's, helps Douglas but Douglas resists Purcell's direction in painting and his fierce independence soon loses him Purcell's economic support and friendship. Douglas leaves for Paris to live with brother Donald and there meets the high critics and successful artists of the painting world, including Quinn, playing the equally eccentric Paul Gauguin, whom Douglas befriends, believing Quinn to be the one true artist who understands what he is attempting to achieve in art. Douglas is sent to the south of France to paint by his supportive brother and Donald later convinces Quinn to join him. But it's a conflicting friendship at best. Douglas is feverish in his pursuit of art, explosive and impulsive, blurting out his theories, his fiery passion. Quinn, quietly pipe-smoking, is contemplative, reserved, and a moderate by comparison. The two soon clash in belief and lifestyle and Quinn departs, unable to put up with Douglas' eccentricities and constant demand for attention. Douglas, left alone, falls deeply into moody fits and dark depression. In the dark night of his anguish, he grabs a razor and, in a seizure of self-accusation, cuts off his ear, as would a flagellant of old. He commits himself to a mental institution at St. Remy. Partly recovered, he still has fits and leans heavily on his brother for support. Donald sends him to Sloane, a physician who tries to cure Douglas' fits but it's no good. Douglas goes to live in Auvers where in July, 1890, he paints his last brilliant canvas, a gleaming wheatfield slashed by a purple road and singularly coated with hovering crows, the birds being harbingers of death in Douglas' mind. Upon completing the canvas, Douglas shoots himself and dies in his brother's arms. LUST FOR LIFE is often morose and even morbid, but it is, at the same time, inspirational, as Douglas masterfully portrays one of the world's great geniuses groping for an elusive talent, never satisfied with what he is able to capture on canvas, always questing for perfection and losing, losing, until the agony of loss, including all those whom he has loved in life, consumes his mind and lifts the pistol to his head. Unlike most other great talents, Van Gogh, as he is expertly portrayed here, could not or would not compromise on perfection, which is what drove him mad and to an early death. Douglas exudes a fire that never burned as brightly nor as high in any of his other films and it remains his most accomplished work. Quinn, though seen briefly, is excellent as the moody Gauguin, a man who vainly attempted to befriend a fellow genius, as futile as an earthquake befriending a volcano. MGM had been interested in filming the Stone novel since the book's first appearance in 1934 but not until producer Arthur Freed demanded it be filmed in 1946 did plans for the production develop. Freed's commitments to the studio, however, prevented him from putting the film together until 1955. By then producer Houseman took over the project and immediately launched a second unit to Europe to scout and film the exact locations of Van Gogh's life. Director Minnelli fought against using CinemaScope for this film. He would later relate in his autobiography

I Remember It Well: "If ever a picture shouldn't have been filmed in CinemaScope, it was LUST FOR LIFE, since the dimensions of the wider screen bear little relation to the conventional shape of paintings." Studio executive Arthur Loew, however, insisted that CinemaScope be employed and his was the last word. But Minnelli did win one technical battle. He realized that the Eastmancolor used by MGM did not offer the soft, subdued tones he felt necessary for reproducing Van Gogh's world and paintings. The color process had been developed by Fox for its production of THE ROBE in 1953 and it was picture postcard hard, or, as Minnelli described it, "straight from the candy box, a brilliant mixture of blues, reds, and yellows that resembled neither life nor art." Minelli, to his everlasting credit, fought hard for a different process, almost as if he knew this would be the most important film of his career, which it was. He opted for Ansco film but the company had stopped making that line of color negatives by that time, conceding that CinemaScope and Eastmancolor were inseparable, a point of view shared by unartistic film producers, who insisted that the public wanted attacking color and vowed to make color films as loud and garish as possible. Minnelli and Houseman hounded MGM's front office and finally convinced executives to use the Ansco process. The studio bought up all the remaining stock, about 300,000 feet of Ansco film, exhausting the firm's inventory and then had Ansco open a special laboratory to process what the company shot. The second unit, under Minnelli's direction, went to Europe to begin filming scenes right out ot Van Gogh's life. The director had remembered how, in THE GREAT WALTZ (1938) a brilliant montage of flowers had been used and he drew diagrams for the second unit, instructing it to capture the fruit trees in blossom at Arles, to match the view first seen by Van Gogh when he traveled to that town and opened the shutters of his room to the brilliant spread of budding flowers. Filming Van Gogh's paintings was another severe task. Houseman agreed that no movie camera could capture the brilliance and subtlety of Van Gogh's paintings (or any other painting for that matter). The light required for motion picture cameras radiated intense heat and this could ruin any painting. Houseman and Minnelli then devised a technical approach that would work when their technicians went into the homes of private collectors and museums around the world to put 200 of Van Gogh's masterpieces on film. As Houseman explained in his lengthy autobiography, *Front & Center:* ". . . we would send experts. . .armed with special portrait-cameras, with which they would make time-exposures without excessive light; these would then be converted into enlarged transparencies, which, in turn, would be backlit and rephotographed by movie cameras with insert equipment and special lenses. . . Except for a tendency to show the colors of the paintings a trifle brighter than they really were, the results were perfect—owing in part to the special film we used." Douglas himself immersed himself in the role, living it on and off camera as is his habit. Douglas had had a long time relationship with Minnelli and Houseman, all three of them working on the brilliant THE BAD AND THE BEAUTIFUL, 1952, and it was during this production that they seriously discussed doing LUST FOR LIFE, agreeing that only Douglas could play the role of Van Gogh. His wife, Anne, writing in *The Saturday Evening Post,* later reported how "Kirk always brings home his roles with him. . . He came home in that red beard of Van Gogh's, wearing those big boots, stomping around the house—it was frightening." Douglas also took intense instructions from a French artist. Minnelli instructed Douglas to add crows to a reproduction of Van Gogh's brilliant painting of the wheatfield in the final scene, as real crows were released nearby and swooped down on him, attracted by hidden food, all of this going onto film. Said Douglas later: "In practice sessions I painted more than 900 crows. I am not one of the art world's immortals, but at least I can now catch a crow in flight." Douglas was later nominated for a well-deserved Oscar for his greatest role but he lost out to Yul Brynner for THE KING AND I. Quinn, as the truculent, contemplative Gauguin, did win an Oscar as Best Supporting Actor, although he is on screen for a brief time, albeit he is magnificent. There is one delicious moment, among many, that Quinn provides when, disgusted with Douglas' sloppy ways, he hurriedly cleans up Douglas' palette, grumbling: "If there's one thing I despise, that's emotion in painting." Quinn appeared with Douglas in three films, this being the second, the others being SEVEN CITIES OF GOLD and MAN FROM DEL RIO. The film fairly drips with authenticity and Minnelli and Houseman, in their exhaustive research beyond Stone's novel, even dug up two elderly citizens in Arles who had known Van Gogh 60 years earlier, one being "The Baby Roulin," who was painted by the genius. Location shots were made at The Hague, in Provence, France, and a great deal around Le Borinage, Nuenen, and at Arles.

p, John Houseman; d, Vincente Minnelli; w, Norman Corwin (based on the novel by Irving Stone); ph, F. A. Young, Russell Harlan (CinemaScope, Metrocolor, Ansco Color); m, Miklos Rozsa; ed, Adrienne Fazan; md, Rozsa; art d, Cedric Gibbons, Hans Peters, Preston Ames; cos, Walter Plunkett.

Drama   **Cas.**   **(PR:C   MPAA:NR)**

LUST OF EVIL   (SEE: PURPLE NOON, 1961)

LUSTY BRAWLERS   (SEE: THIS MAN CAN'T DIE, 1970)

LUSTY MEN, THE***   (1952) 113m RKO bw

Susan Hayward *(Louise Merritt)*, Robert Mitchum *(Jeff McCloud)*, Arthur Kennedy *(Wes Merritt)*, Arthur Hunnicutt *(Booker Davis)*, Frank Faylen *(Al Dawson)*, Walter Coy *(Buster Burgess)*, Carol Nugent *(Rusty Davis)*, Maria Hart *(Rosemary Maddox)*, Lorna Thayer *(Grace Burgess)*, Burt Mustin *(Jeremiah)*, Karen King *(Ginny Logan)*, Jimmy Dodd *(Red Logan)*, Eleanor Todd *(Babs)*, Riley Hill *(Hoag the Ranch Hand)*, Bob Bray *(Fritz)*, Sheb Wooley *(Slim)*, Marshall Reed *(Jim-Bob)*, Paul E. Burns *(Waite)*, Sally Yarnell, Jean Stratton, Nancy Moore, Louise Saraydar, Mary Jane Carey, Alice Kirby *(Girls)*, Chuck Roberson *(Tall Cowboy)*, Lane Bradford *(Jim-Bob Tyler)*, Chili Williams, Hazel [Sonny] Boyne, Barbara Blaine *(Women)*, Sam Flint *(Doctor)*, Emmett Lynn *(Travis White)*, Glenn Strange *(Rig Ferris the Foreman)*, Denver Pyle *(Niko)*, Dan White, Lane Chandler *(Announcers)*, Ralph Volkie *(Slicker)*, George Sherwood *(Vet)*, Dennis Moore *(Cashier)*

Director Ray was a master of the offbeat film and this is no exception, a contemporary western that is probably the best of its kind ever produced with bravura performances from Mitchum, Hayward, and Kennedy. Mitchum is a washed up rodeo king, a world's champion who has seen his heyday, reveled in it, and slipped it into his back pocket. After being thrown and gored by a Brahma bull, Mitchum resigns himself to fence-sitting; he limps across an empty rodeo arena, suffering from myriad injuries, and heads for his Oklahoma homestead to retrieve a cache, hidden when he was a boy under the floorboards of a ramshackle home he once escaped from. The building is now owned by a talkative old man who allows him to take his boyhood treasure, two nickels and a rodeo program. Mitchum now has this to add to the meager money he has been able to save after 20 years of bouncing through the rodeo circuit. A married couple, Kennedy and Hayward, appear, looking to buy the property, and Kennedy recognizes Mitchum and gives him a job on his small ranch. Kennedy explains that he has entered a few events at an upcoming rodeo and asks that Mitchum help train him, Mitchum does, on the proviso that they split Kennedy's winnings. Hayward is wary of the bronc-riding champion but tolerates the arrangement since the winnings will help buy a new ranch and end money difficulties. Mitchum has weary eyes for the lusty Hayward; she leads him on so that he will continue to aid her husband. Kennedy begins to win one important event after another and he is soon a rising star in the rodeo circuit. Along with a fat wallet, Kennedy's heart also gets fat and he swaggers and struts about, lavishing money on booze, women, and especially those hangers-on who shower him with praise. Hayward begs Mitchum for help but he only suggests she get rid of her swell-headed husband and go off with him. She rejects him and her loyalty convinces Mitchum to guide his pupil in a new direction. Kennedy, however, does not take kindly to personal advice and he turns on the man who has boosted him to rodeo stardom, calling Mitchum a coward and a has-been. Mitchum bristles under the tongue-lashing and goes head to head against Kennedy in a rodeo, performing one hazardous event after another, winning the events hands down and proving he's still the best. In the final event, however, Mitchum catches his foot in a stirrup and is trapped beneath the hoofs of a bronc which stomps him near to death. Dying, the great rodeo star is carried out of the arena. He dies in the arms of Hayward and Kennedy, telling them not to mourn his going, that he's lived the life he wanted, that he "made a thousand bartenders rich." Mitchum's death shocks Kennedy into reality and he takes his winnings and goes off with wife Hayward to buy the ranch and settle down. THE LUSTY MEN is full of action and dangerous stunts, photographed beautifully by master cinematographer Garmes. Ray's direction is superb as he contrasts Hayward's intense desire for domestic security and Mitchum's world of the vagabond, a nomadic, dirty world hidden behind the dangerous arena. Everything about the film is basically "American" in social posture and earthy philosophies. Based on a *Life* magazine story by Stanush and scripted by cowboy Dortort, the screenplay presents classical situations and is full of poetry and destiny. Mitchum is excellent in this film, one where he really gets into his part and does not do his usual sleepwalking bit. Kennedy, an actor who never gave a bad performance, is moving and intense, and Hayward is just right as the forceful western ranch lady with ambitions she won't let die. This was Hayward's fourth film for RKO and she was called upon to perform another hair-pulling brawl, this time with Todd, over the affections of her errant husband. Garmes, who was noted as having filmed the burning of Atlanta in GONE WITH THE WIND, shooting the largest set ever filmed up to that time, did a turnabout and filmed Hayward in what was probably the smallest set up to that time, a shower in her house trailer which was reportedly 28 by 32 inches, while Hayward is lathering down, of course. Ray took his cameras on location, filming rodeos in Tuscon, Arizona; Spokane, Washington; Pendleton, Oregon; and Livermore, California, using a host of real rodeo stars such as Gerald Roberts, Jerry Ambler, and Les Sanborn. This film was originally entitled COWPOKE, then retitled THIS MAN IS MINE, and was shelved for a year before being released as THE LUSTY MEN. Other films have explored the genre such as RODEO, ARENA, and JUNIOR BONNER, but none compare to this landmark cowboy production.

p, Jerry Wald, Norman Krasna; d, Nicholas Ray; w, Horace McCoy, David Dortort (based on a story by Claude Stanush); ph, Lee Garmes; m, Roy Webb; ed, Ralph Dawson; md, C. Bakaleinikoff; art d, Albert S. D'Agostino, Alfred Herman; set d, Darrell Silvera, Jack Mills; cos, Michael Woulfe.

Western **Cas.** **(PR:C MPAA:NR)**

LUTHER** ½ (1974) 112m American Film Theatre c

Stacy Keach *(Martin Luther)*, Patrick Magee *(Hans)*, Hugh Griffith *(Tetzel)*, Robert Stephens *(Von Eck)*, Alan Badel *(Cajetan)*, Judi Dench *(Katherine)*, Leonard Rossiter *(Weinand)*, Maurice Denham *(Staupitz)*, Julian Glover *(The Knight)*, Peter Cellier *(Prior)*, Thomas Heathcote *(Lucas)*, Malcolm Stoddard *(King Charles)*.

An extremely well-acted addition of the American Film Theatre project. Keach plays the great 16th Century religious leader, giving the performance of his career. He takes the character from a young, somewhat muddled seminarian to the leader of the Reformation in a completely believable, mannered characterization. Unfortunately Osborne's play does not adapt well to film, which drags on longer than it should and reveals its theatrical background through an awkward narration that links the acts together. This is a classic example of how some of the best written plays are inherently noncinematic. The uniformily excellent cast, however, makes this worthwhile viewing.

p, Ely A. Landau; d, Guy Green; w, Edward Anhalt (based on the play by John Osborne); ph, Freddie Young; m, John Addison; ed, Malcolm Cook; prod d, Peter Mullins; cos, Elizabeth Haffenden, Joan Bridge.

Drama **(PR:C MPAA:G)**

LUTRING (SEE: WAKE UP AND DIE, 1967)

LUV* (1967) 93m COL c

Jack Lemmon *(Harry Berlin)*, Peter Falk *(Milt Manville)*, Elaine May *(Ellen Manville)*, Nina Wayne *(Linda)*, Eddie Mayehoff *(Attorney Goodhart)*, Paul Hartman *(Doyle)*, Severn Darden *(Vandergrist)*, Alan DeWitt *(Dalrymple)*.

On stage, it worked like an Audemars Piquet wristwatch because we were in Schisgal's surrealistic world, a bridge on which three people met, lived, loved, argued, and nearly died. Director Donner, working from Baker's screenplay, has attempted to expand it, to add characters for the sake of padding, and the result is a seldom funny (when Schisgal's original lines are used) and often dreary picture. Loser Lemmon is about to leap from the Manhattan Bridge when he is stopped from drowning himself and his sorrows by former schoolmate Falk, an ambitious and wealthy man who trades on Wall Street daily and deals in junk nightly. Lemmon is thrilled that he has been halted in his suicide attempt and can't thank Falk enough. Falk has a way that Lemmon can repay him, though. It seems that Falk has been trifling with Wayne, a pneumatic gym teacher, and he would like to shed himself of his neurotic wife, May. Lemmon and May meet, waltz around a bit, and eventually fall in love and marry, once the divorce is done. Then trouble erupts in Paradise for Falk and Wayne. He's given May everything to get the divorce and now he and Wayne are living in poverty. Furthermore, her once sleek figure is getting plumper. Lemmon and May aren't any better and Lemmon is twice as indifferent as Falk ever was to her. Falk and May realize they still love each other and decide that Lemmon and Wayne might make a nice couple, so they introduce them to each other but that doesn't work as neither Lemmon nor Wayne have any interest in each other. Lemmon had left a suicide note in the first reel and Falk and May now plan to murder the man and use the old note to justify his death to the police. Falk takes Lemmon to the bridge and is about to throw him off when he slips and falls off himself. Lemmon and May leap into the water to save Falk, and Wayne, who just happens to be jogging by, jumps in with the other three. It all happens so quickly that we're not sure who threw who into the water and, frankly, the picture is such a disappointment that we didn't care to see it again to find out. It's tedious and plodding and tries much too hard to be funny. Mulligan's music is a plus; everything else isn't. Hard to believe that this came from such a funny play.

p, Martin Manulis; d, Clive Donner; w, Elliott Baker (based on the play by Murray Schisgal); ph, Ernest Laszlo (Panavision, Eastmancolor); m, Gerry Mulligan; ed, Harold F. Kress; prod d, Albert Brenner; set d, Frank Tuttle; cos, Donfeld; spec eff, Geza Gaspar; m/l, "Love Casts Its Shadow Over My Heart," Irving Joseph, Schisgal; makeup, Ben Lane.

Comedy **Cas.** **(PR:A C MPAA:NR)**

LUXURY GIRLS** (1953, Ital.) 96m UA c

Susan Stephen *(Lorna Whitmore)*, Anna Maria Ferrero *(Valerie De Beranger)*, Jacques Sernas *(Jean-Jacques)*, Steve Barclay *(George Whitmore)*, Marina Vlady *(Eljay)*, Brunella Bovo *(Jeannie Gordon)*, Rosanna Podesta *(Pereira)*, Elisa Cegani *(Mme. Charpentier)*, Claudio Gora *(Prof. Charpentier)*, Estelle Brody *(Mrs. Whitmore)*, Lawrence Ward *(Greg Wilson)*, Paula Mori *(Beejay)*, Robert Risso *(Steve)*, Eva Vanicek *(Statistician)*, Vera Palumbo *(Knitter)*, Anna Casini *(Albino)*, Colette Laurent *(Boopie)*, Bianca Manenti *(Maid)*, Charles Rutherford *(Jean-Jacques' Friend)*, Mary Alcaide *(Ballet Mistress)*, Liana Del Balzo *(Princess de Vick-Beranger)*, Fronco Lodi *(Riding Instructor)*, Leopold Savona *(Boy Friend of Val)*.

A character film that shows the various lives of a group of girls studying at a Swiss finishing school. Though no men are allowed at the school, the girls concentrate on the town bachelors rather than their schoolwork. This framework sets up the different personalities explored by the film. Stephen plays an American who is eventually removed by her mother after it is discovered what her daughter's education really consists of. Of course there are scenes of girls pillow fighting, pulling hair, and a threatened suicide for dramatic overtones. Though the direction and photography are both excellent, using the Swiss scenery nicely, the film lacks authenticity and originality. Instead the script relies on formula situations and standard personalities. (In Italian: English subtitles.)

p, Carlo Civallero; d, Piero Mussetta; w, Ennio Flaiano; ph, Piero Portalupi; m, Nino Rota; ed, Gabriel Varriale.

Comedy/Drama **(PR:C MPAA:NR)**

LUXURY LINER zero (1933) 68m PAR bw

George Brent *(Dr. Thomas Bernhard)*, Zita Johann *(Miss Morgan)*, Vivienne Osborne *(Sybil Bernhard)*, Alice White *(Milli Stern)*, Verree Teasdale *(Luise Marheim)*, C. Aubrey Smith *(Edward Thorndyke)*, Frank Morgan *(Alex Stevanson)*, Henry Wadsworth *(Fritz)*, Wallis Clark *(Dr. Veith)*, Billy Bevan *(Schultz)*, Theodore Von Eltz *(Exl)*.

Love and life aboard a luxury liner from first class to crew members. The plot is as empty as they come and totally unbelievable. The actors are going through the motions, waving bon voyage to stock shots of their friends ashore. From there on out it's all downhill. Forty-five years later Aaron Spelling created a television series with a similar story line, "The Love Boat."

p, B. P. Schulberg; d, Lothar Mendes; w, Gene Markey, Kathryn Scola (based on the novel by Gina Kaus); ph, Victor Milner.

Drama **(PR:A MPAA:NR)**

LUXURY LINER** (1948) 97m MGM c

George Brent *(Capt. Jeremy Bradford)*, Jane Powell *(Polly Bradford)*, Lauritz Melchior *(Olaf Eriksen)*, Frances Gifford *(Laura Dene)*, Marina Koshetz *(Zita Romanka)*, Xavier Cugat *(Himself)*, Thomas E. Breen *(Denis Mulvy)*, Richard Derr *(Charles Worton)*, John Ridgely *(Chief Officer Carver)*, Chuck Lowry, Harold Hopper, Clark Yocum, June Hutton *(The Pied Pipers)*, Connie Gilchrist *(Bertha)*, Lee Tung Foo *(Fu Dong)*, Georgette Windsor *(Perdita)*, Romo Vincent *(Pierre)*,

Michael Dugan *(Officer)*, Kay Norton *(Ship's Hostess)*, Shirley Johns *(Count Karper)*, Betty Blythe *(Miss Fenmoor)*, Juanita Quigley *(Jean)*, Roger Moore, Wes Hopper *(Waiters)*, May McAvoy *(Woman)*.

A pre-"Love Boat" musical features Powell trying to marry off her widowed father, Brent, the captain of a luxury liner. Gifford plays a widowed passenger taking a cruise, wholly unprepared for the matchmaking efforts that she is about to be the victim of. Powell had been forbidden to go with her father on the cruise, but stowed away much to her father's chagrin. Brent also played the ship's captain in the 1933 film LUXURY LINER, though his position and the title are about all the two films have in common. Though this film is slight at best, the direction never takes the subject for anything more than it is and the film ends up being a good time. In between the slight plot are an abundance of those musical numbers that MGM is famous for. Cugat plays himself, doing a number he wrote called "Cugat's Nougat;" Koshetz sings a comedy version of Cole Porter's "I've Got You Under My Skin." Other songs include "Spring Came Back to Vienna" (Janice Toree, Fred Spielman, Fritz Rotter—sung by Jane Powell), "The Peanut Vendor" (L. Wolfe Gilbert, Marion Sunshine, Moises Simons—sung by Powell), "Yes We Have No Bananas" (Frank Silver, Irving Cohn—sung by The Pied Pipers), "Come Back to Sorrento" (Ernesto De Curtis, Claude Aveling— sung by Lauritz Melchior), "Gavotte" (from Massenet's "Manon"—sung by Powell), and "Con Maracas" (Cugat, Candido Dimanlig— performed by Cugat).

p, Joe Pasternak; d, Richard Whorf; w, Gladys Lehman, Richard Connell, Karl Lamb; ph, Robert Planck (Technicolor); ed, Robert J. Kern; md, George Stoll; art d, Cedric Gibbons, Paul Groesse; set d, Edwin B. Willis, Arthur Krams; cos, Jean Louis; ch, Nick Castle.

Musical Comedy (PR:A MPAA:NR)

LYCANTHROPUS

(SEE: WEREWOLF IN A GIRL'S DORMITORY, 1961, Ital.)

LYDIA** 1/2 (1941) 104m UA bw

Merle Oberon *(Lydia MacMillan)*, Edna May Oliver *(Granny)*, Alan Marshall *(Richard Mason)*, Joseph Cotten *(Michael Fitzpatrick)*, Hans Yaray *(Frank Andre)*, George Reeves *(Bob Willard)*, John Halliday *(Fitzpatrick the Butler)*, Sara Allgood *(Johnny's Mother)*, Billy Ray *(Johnny)*, Frank Conlon *(Old Ned)*.

A romantic drama that owes much to the French UN CARNET DE BAL which was directed by the same man who did this one. Oberon is the granddaughter of wealthy Oliver, a matriarch of an old New England family. Oberon dearly loves Marshall and spends one idyllic weekend with him at her family's estate on a small island off the coast of Maine. Afterwards, he tells her that he has to go off briefly to take care of another romantic liaison but he will be back to claim her for life. He doesn't return and she spends the rest of her life, a period of 40 years, thinking about him (in much the same way the lady did in GREAT EXPECTATIONS). She's had a chance to choose from one of three other suitors; Reeves, a drunken boor of a football player; Yaray, who is a blind musician; or Cotten, a doctor who is the son of Oberon's family's butler. Cotten stays by her side too long and is eventually tossed aside by Oberon who lives in the hope that Marshall, like General Douglas MacArthur, will return. In the ensuing years, Oberon becomes a benefactress of various charitable organizations, most notably homes for the blind. The decades go by and they all get old. Oberon and Cotten meet and he arranges for a party of all her old beaus. Reeves arrives, fat and boozy; Yaray is there, now white-haired and so thin he's almost transparent, and, of course, Cotten. Then a surprise guest walks in. It's Marshall, white-maned and bearded, but still handsome. He is introduced to Oberon and doesn't know who she is, almost crushing Oberon in the process. Oberon walks out on the terrace and Cotten, ever faithful like a pooch, tells her that he would know her anywhere, even after all these years. Oberon finally gives up the ghost, realizes that she's been living in a fool's dream, and takes Cotten's hand, now knowing that his love has lasted for a lifetime and she can accept it. It's nice to think that these two people have found each other at last but the overall feeling is "what a waste their lives have been." Perhaps that's the point Hecht and Hoffenstein wanted to make in their adaptation of the story—take life while you can.

p, Alexander Korda; d, Julien Duvivier; w, Ben Hecht, Samuel Hoffenstein (based on a story by Duvivier, Laslo Bush-Fekete); ph, Lee Garmes; m, Miklos Rozsa; ed, William Hornbeck; prod d, Vincent Korda; art d, Jack Okie; set d, Julie Heron; cos, Marcel Vertes, Walter Plunkett; spec eff, Lawrence Butler.

Romance Cas. (PR:A MPAA:NR)

LYDIA** (1964, Can.) 83m Libra c

Gordon Pinset *(Thomas)*, Anna Hagen *(Lydia)*, Benentino Costa *(Miki)*, Malena Anousaki *(Marella)*.

After learning he has a mysterious terminal illness, Pinsent goes off to the Greek Isles to think things through. At first he is put off by the local myths and legends but soon he comes to an understanding of the value that the population puts into these stories. Through Costa, a youngster well versed in local mythology, he meets another American, Hagen, and the two fall in love. But he knows that death is imminent and he leaves the island. Though at times simplistic and overly sentimental, the film has a pleasing naivete to it. The camera does give the scenery an almost ethereal look, but the direction is too slow, with the film also in need of tighter editing.

p, Julius Rascheff; d, Cedric d'Ailly; w, Rascheff, Binton Krancer; ph, Rascheff (Technicolor); m, A. Hajdu; ed, Krancer.

Drama (PR:O MPAA:NR)

LYDIA ATE THE APPLE (SEE: PARTINGS, 1962)

LYDIA BAILEY** 1/2 (1952) 89m FOX c

Dale Robertson *(Albion Hamlin)*, Anne Francis *(Lydia Bailey)*, Charles Korvin *(d'Autremont)*, William Marshall *(King Dick)*, Luis Van Rooten *(Gen. LeClerc)*, Adeline de Walt Reynolds *(Madame d'Autremont)*, Angos Perez *(Paul)*, Bob Evans *(Soldier)*, Gladys Holland *(Pauline Bonaparte)*, Will Wright *(Consul)*, Roy E. Glenn *(Mirabeau)*, Ken Renard *(Toussaint)*, Juanita Moore *(Marie)*, Carmen de Lavallade *(Specialty Dancer)*, Martin Wilkins *(Voodoo Priest)*, Albert Morin *(Lieutenant)*, William Washington *(Deckhand)*, Clancy Cooper *(Codman)*, Muriel Bledsoe *(Ametiste)*, Mildred Boyd *(Marmeline)*, Marjorie Elliott *(Roside)*, Sizette Harbin *(Floreal)*, Roz Hayes *(Aspodelle)*, Dolores Mallory *(Claireine)*, Lena Torrence *(Attenaire)*, Frances Williams *(Cloryphene)*, Ken Terrell *(Barbe)*, Louis Mercier *(Millet)*, William Walker *(Gen. LaPlume)*, Fred Cavens *(Fencing Instructor)*.

During Napoleon's attempted takeover of Haiti, American attorney Robertson must get the signature of island aristocrat Francis in order to settle an estate. She is the fiancee of Korvin, a wealthy plantation owner, and finds her alliances fall with the French rather than the Haitian rebels. Robertson hires Marshall, a rebel leader, to get him through the jungle to find Francis. After they arrive, the situation becomes very dangerous as French troops approach. Robertson and Marshall save Francis as well as her maid, Korvin, and Korvin's son. Francis eventually switches her alliances both politically and romantically as she ends up falling for Robertson. Lushly photographed in Technicolor, the film is a limited, though entertaining, adaptation of the epic novel by Kenneth Roberts. Robertson is appropriately dashing in the lead, though Francis seems too young for her role. The final sequences are especially well put together and very exciting.

p, Jules Schermer; d, Jean Negulesco; w, Michael Blankfort, Philip Dunne (based on the novel by Kenneth Roberts); ph, Harry Jackson (Technicolor); m, Hugo Friedhofer; ed, Dorothy Spencer; md, Lionel Newman; art d, Lyle Wheeler, J. Russell Spencer.

Adventure (PR:A MPAA:NR)

LYONS IN PARIS, THE** 1/2 (1955, Brit.) 81m Hammer/Exclusive bw

Bebe Daniels *(Bebe Lyon)*, Ben Lyon *(Himself)*, Barbara Lyon *(Herself)*, Richard Lyon *(Himself)*, Reginald Beckwith *(Capt. le Grand)*, Martine Alexis *(Fifi le Fleur)*, Pierre Dudan *(Charles)*, Dino Galvani *(Gerrard)*, Horace Percival *(Mr. Wimple)*, Molly Weir *(Aggie)*, Doris Rogers *(Florrie Wainwright)*, Gwen Lewis *(Mrs. Wimple)*, Hugh Morton *(Col. Price)*.

A simple but breezy British comedy based on a popular radio series of the time. The Lyons family is off to gay Paris for a holiday. When the father (Ben Lyon) tries to get some tickets from the mysterious Alexis, his children (Barbara and Richard) assume he's having an affair. After arriving in Paris, both father and son have some complications with the woman. Ben ends up in a duel over honor, but all works out nicely in the end. Told in a light-hearted manner that makes the seemingly skimpy material work.

p, Robert Dunbar; d&w, Val Guest (based on the radio series "Life with the Lyons" by Bebe Daniels, Bob Block, Bill Harding); ph, Jimmy Harvey.

Comedy (PR:A MPAA:NR)

LYONS MAIL, THE** (1931, Brit.) 76m Twickenham/Woolf and Freedman bw

Sir John Martin Harvey *(Lesurques/Dubosc)*, Norah Baring *(Julie)*, Ben Webster *(Jerome Lesurques)*, Moore Marriott *(Choppard)*, George Thirlwell *(Jean Didier)*, Michael Hogan *(Courriole)*, Sheila Wray *(Mme. Courriole)*, Eric Howard *(Fouinnard)*, Charles Paton, Earle Grey, John Garside, Gabrielle Casartelli.

A story of mixed-up identities as Harvey plays the dual role of virtuous silversmith and notorious highwayman. Set in France, the silversmith is arrested for a murder committed by the highwayman. He's condemned to die but fortunately the truth comes out in the end. This is the second film version of this adventure tale.

p, Julius Hagen; d, Arthur Maude; w, H. Fowler Mear (based on a play by Charles Reade).

Adventure (PR:A MPAA:NR)

LYSISTRATA (SEE: DAUGHTERS OF DESTINY, 1954, Fr.)

M

M***** (1933, Ger.) 117m Nero Film/Star Film GMBH/PAR bw
Peter Lorre *(Franz Becker)*, Otto Wernicke *(Inspector Karl Lohmann)*, Gustav Grundgens *(Schraenker)*, Theo Lingen *(Bauernfaenger)*, Theodore Loos *(Police Commissioner Groeber)*, Georg John *(Blind Peddler)*, Ellen Widmann *(Mme. Becker)*, Inge Landgut *(Elsie)*, Ernst Stahl-Nachbaur *(Police Chief)*, Paul Kemp *(Pickpocket)*, Franz Stein *(Minister)*, Rudolf Blumner *(Defense Attorney)*, Karl Platen *(Watchman)*, Gerhard Bienert *(Police Secretary)*, Rosa Valetti *(Servant)*, Hertha von Walter *(Prostitute)*, Fritz Odemar *(The Cheater)*, Fritz Gnass *(Burglar)*, Heinrich Gretler, Lotte Lobinger, Isenta, Leonard Steckel, Karchow, Edgar Pauly, Kepich, Gunther Neumann, Krehan, Almas, Kurth, Balthaus, Leeser, Behal, Rosa Lichenstein, Carell, Lohde, Doblin, Loretto, Eckhof, Mascheck, Else Ehser, Matthis, Elzer, Mederow, Faber, Margarete Melzer, Ilse Furstenberg, Trude Moss, Gelingk, Hadrian, M. Netto, Goldstein, Nied, Anna Goltz, Klaus Pohl, Heinrich Gotho, Polland, Hadank, Rebane, Hartberg, Rehkopf, Hempel, Reihsig, Hocker, Rhaden, Hoermann, Ritter, Sablotski, Sascha, Agnes Schulz-Lichterfeld, Stroux, Swinborne, Trutz, Otto Waldis, Walth, Wanka, Wannemann, Wulf, Bruno Ziener, Josef Damen, Maja Norden.

This is unquestionably Lang's most chilling and provocative film, if not his greatest production. It is the story of a child molester and murderer, an uncompromising and stark film which brought Lorre, as the killer, to international prominence; he would never again equal this tour de force. Although he later denied it, Lang most certainly based his character (he wrote the script with his wife, Thea von Harbou) upon the worst mass killer in Germany at the time, Peter Kurten, child molester and murderer. Berlin is in the grip of terror as an unknown child molester continues to kill little girls while the police search frantically and produce no clues to the identity of the murderer. Frenzied citizens turn against each other and inform on their neighbors, making havoc for the police. Raids conducted by the police produce an army of criminals, from forgers to prostitutes, but none can be charged with the killings. Moreover, the underworld is incensed with the intense heat put upon them, and its leading members resolve to find the murderer themselves, ordering the criminal community to find the killer and bring him to an underworld tribunal where he will be tried and, if found guilty, executed. In the streets the children play a mindless game with sinister words, skipping down the pavements chanting: "Just you wait a little while/The evil man in black will come/With his little chopper/He will chop you up." (Lang was undoubtedly inspired to insert this chilling chant when recalling the children of London who made famous a little ditty they chanted long after the bloody reign of Jack the Ripper: "Jack the Ripper's dead/And lying on his bed/He cut his throat/With Sunlight Soap/Jack the Ripper's dead.") A mother prepares supper for her little girl who is playing in the street. The girl bounces a ball off a billboard to which is tacked a reward poster for the child killer and a shadow crosses her face. She looks up and follows the man who buys her a balloon, whistling bars from Grieg's "Peer Gynt" ("Hall of the Mountain King"). The mother calls frantically for her child and then a ball is shown rolling out of some shrubbery and the balloon sails upward to be caught on a telegraph wire. Newspapers blare the latest killing while the killer, Lorre, writes a desperate letter to a newspaper, scrawling the words on his missive: "I haven't finished yet." (Again, Lang employs a Jack the Ripper technique; bloody Jack delighted in writing London newspapers about his upcoming murders.) Chief of detectives Wernicke concludes after this latest killing, that the murderer is mentally unbalanced and has his force sift through underworld suspects for the criminally insane. Other detectives are ordered to interview former mental patients and a plainclothesman following leads goes to the dingy apartment of Lorre but he finds him gone. Lorre is lurking on a streetcorner, watching a little girl, her image reflected in a store window. He begins to follow her whistling the haunting bars from "Peer Gynt," but he suddenly halts when the child's mother appears. Police searching Lorre's room find an Ariston cigarette wrapper, the same found at the sites of previous murders. Lorre is now following another child, buying a balloon for her and whistling the same tune which is this time recognized by the blind balloon salesman who calls another beggar and tells him that Lorre is the killer. The beggar chalks an M in the palm of his hand and, when passing Lorre, presses this tell-tale sign on his back. The little girl tries to wipe it off and Lorre turns to see he has been marked with the sign of Cain, the M reflected in a store window. He flees in panic, taking refuge in a deserted office building as word spreads through the criminal ranks that Lorre has been identified and where he is hiding. Disguised as policemen, gangsters rush into the building and drag Lorre from a storeroom where he has been cowering. He is taken to the cavernous basement of a warehouse where the criminals have set up a court. The jury has no sympathy for Lorre as he pleads his case. Staring at him with agonized looks are the mothers of his victims. Lorre, his soft, round, porcine features distorted horribly, screams, whimpers, and whines as only Lorre could do, a trapped animal fighting for his life, shrieking: "I can't help myself! I haven't any control over this evil thing that's inside me. . . It's there all the time, driving me out to wander through the streets. . . . It's me, pursuing myself!. . .I want to escape. . .to escape from myself! . . But, it's impossible . . . I have to obey!" The court-appointed lawyer echoes Lorre's chant, not too convincingly telling the judges and jury that Lorre is a sick man "and a sick man should be handed over, not to the executioner, but to the doctor." Lorre is nevertheless convicted and sentenced to death, but before he can be executed the police burst into the underworld hideout and take away the screaming Lorre. One of the victim's mothers states sorrowfully: "We, too, should keep closer watch on our children." In the original 117-minute version (later cut to 99 minutes), Lang showed Lorre sentenced in a legitimate court and three women, all mothers of victims, weeping, one saying: "We should learn to look after our children more." As with all his masterpieces, Lang tells his grim tale in murky shadow, the low-key lighting being a hallmark of German cinema, his characters here, especially Lorre,

being creatures of the night and, during the daytime hours, being shown as shadow figures. No child is shown being murdered but Lang achieves an equally chilling effect through brilliant opticals—distorted camera angles, weird, unnatural images and setups, even crude symbols at times—in one scene Lang shows a frustrated Lorre missing his intended victim and then he cuts to a neon sign with a jiggling phallic arrow that jumps up and down inside a whirling circle. He makes the most of the frenzy among the citizens, police and criminals alike, cross-cutting into these wholly different worlds to produce the same effect, fear. He takes full advantage of the wide-ranging scope of his story by using the city of Berlin, its broad streets and narrow alleyways, its ancient ruins and run-down slums where corruption seems to thrive on centuries of immorality, sweating on the walls of decrepit buildings, coating its furrowed streets, coursing through the veins of Lorre and others of his ilk. M is truly a film of the sinister soul but, enlightened for its day, insists that judgment be made by all, as Lang tells the story of the killer from the killer's point of view, as well as the outside world searching for him. This would remain Lang's favorite film, although he always insisted that he made up Lorre's character from whole cloth, not from the ghastly career of Peter Kurten, known as the "Monster of Dusseldorf." This is contrary to all evidence. Lang later claimed that he had announced his plan to make his film before Kurten was apprehended but Kurten was turned in by his wife (at the murderer's request) two months before Lang made his announcement and it is known that he spent time personally investigating the Kurten case with his wife, plus spending time in mental institutions checking on the lives of other child molesters and killers. Perhaps the great director did not wish to be thought of as imitating life, that his films were pure creations, but his entire career belies this stance. His first big American film, FURY, was based upon an actual lynching in San Jose, California, and YOU ONLY LIVE ONCE is certainly based on the exploits of the southwestern American bandits Bonnie Parker and Clyde Barrow. Further, Lang's color film, THE RETURN OF FRANK JAMES with Henry Fonda, chronicles with historical exactitude the exploits of the brother of America's most famous bandit, Jesse James. Quite simply, Fritz Lang took his best films right out of the headlines of the world's newspapers. Lang later admitted this fact in a 1947 article, stating: "If I were the only producer to be making murder films or if my interest in murder were abnormal or unique there would be no point in pursuing the question publicly, but the fact is that millions of people, peaceable, law-abiding American citizens are fascinated by murder. Why else. . .would the newspapers devote capitals three inches high and millions of words to print the gory details?. . .It seems that there is a latent fascination in murder, that the word arouses a tangle of submerged and suppressed emotion. Shall I ask, why are we interested in murder? First of all, a murder story, whether it is a work of fiction or an actual murder case reported in the newspapers. . .is a puzzle against which to match the sharpness of the mind." Lang knew well what it was to be suspected of murder. His first wife committed suicide when she found him embracing Thea von Harbou and he was initially thought to be guilty of killing her. Always a stickler for reality, even though he conveyed it in expressionistic terms, Lang interviewed police and even criminals at large when going into production for M. He actually employed real criminals for his film as underworld characters (not unusual for directors seeking authenticity; D. W. Griffith had done the same thing decades earlier when making his silent film, the first of the gangster genre, THE MUSKETEERS OF PIG ALLEY). But this ploy backfired; the criminals working in M were so active off-camera that 24 of them were arrested for various offenses before the film was completed. This was Lang's first sound film and he made the most of it, using sound to further emphasize the terror on the screen, the sound of Lorre's knife snapping open—not to stab a small boy standing nearby as the viewer might suspect but to peel an orange— the rattling of an attic door by a guard who shouts out: "Is anybody there?" before departing, and then Lorre's heavy breathing in the dark to let the viewer know he is there, lurking. The originally released American version was in German with English subtitles, but this was reportedly replaced by a dubbed version made in England. This version, however, is no longer available and one doubts whether it ever existed other than in some unsubstantiated reports, since Lorre supposedly traveled to England to record his voice in 1932 for the English language version, recorded by Eric Hakim. But Lorre, according to most reports, did not arrive in England until 1934 when requested to appear in films by Alfred Hitchcock. Lorre was a complete unknown when Lang saw him in a play then running in Berlin. The Hungarian-born actor (christened Laszlo Lowenstein), continued to act in the play at night, "Squaring the Circle" while shooting scenes during the day for M. He was so effective in the role of the heinous killer that he would be typecast for life, and would go on playing repulsive, frightening little psychopaths for the rest of his days. Two scenes will always stay in the viewer's mind, images of Lorre, after seeing M. The first when he looks at himself in a mirror inside his room, his bulbous, fear-haunted eyes staring back at the face of a murderer, his own face, and he suddenly accents his guilt and despicable compulsion by putting two fingers to his mouth and drawing the flesh downward so that he reshapes his appearance as a grotesque gargoyle, the image he really has of himself. The other is the abject fear showing on Lorre's face when he discovers the chalky M on his back, knowing that he is exposed and the nightmare he has long lived with will now explode and mean his own death. M was originally entitled MORDER UNTER UNS (MURDERERS AMONG US) and, because of this title, Lang was almost stopped from making his classic crime film. He approached an official at the Zeppelin hangars outside of Berlin where he had shot some previous films and asked for permission to shoot M on the premises. To his surprise his routine request was met with a firm no. "Why not?" asked Lang. "You know," the official replied cryptically. "What do you mean, 'you know.' Don't be stupid, I have a lot of things to do." Said the official: "No, no, and, by the way I think you shouldn't make this picture. You know why. You will hurt the feelings of many who will become very important. It will be very bad for you." Lang grew indignant, then asked: "Tell me, why should a story about a child murderer hurt anybody's feelings?" "What? What is this story about?" asked the official, surprised. "A child murderer!" yelled Lang and grabbed the lapels of the official. He felt something and turned over the lapel to find a swastika button. The official was a member of the Nazi Party who thought that the title, MURDERERS AMONG US, meant a film about the Nazis! The censors later gave Lang a hard time before allowing the release of the film which quickly met with universal praise and shocked the world with its frank exposure of a human beast. (No one made mention, however, that the beggars profiled in M are very much like those found in "The Three Penny Opera," a popular play during the corrupt Weimar Republic that did not escape Lang's ever alert eye.) Lang rightly feared the Nazis. Minister of Propaganda Josef Goebbels met with him and told him that he and Hitler had, years earlier, seen Lang's silent classic, METROPOLIS, in a small-town German theater and both were impressed. Goebbels insisted that Lang stay in Germany and make films for the Nazis. But Lang feared that Goebbels would discover that his mother was Jewish and he soon fled Germany, leaving considerable funds, all his memoirs, and a primitive art collection behind. Lorre, who was also Jewish and who was Hitler's favorite actor (Der Fuhrer not knowing of his Semitic background) also fled to England as soon as he could. The Nazis later sullied M. Nazi film producer Fritz Hippler made a phony documentary, "THE ETERNAL JEW," in 1940 and Lorre's confession at the end of M was taken from Lang's masterpiece and shown out of context as an absurd confession of a Jew who was incapable of controlling his perversions, and that he represented all Jews, who were unfit to live in a moral civilization. Nebenzal, who produced the original M, remade an English-speaking version for Columbia in 1950. Lang declined to direct it when asked and Lorre was too old to play a role he would rather forget anyway, thanks to the typecasting it earned him. David Wayne took on the difficult assignment under Joseph Losey's direction but it came nowhere near the original. Lang's distinctive images would influence many a filmmaker to come. The bouncing ball, the elaborate creation of a trap, and police evidence mounted through montage would appear in Carol Reed's THE THIRD MAN. Remade in 1951.

p, Seymour Nebenzal; d, Fritz Lang; w, Lang, Thea von Harbou, Paul Falkenberg, Adolf Jansen, Karl Vash (based on an article by Egon Jacobson); ph, Fritz Arno Wagner, Gustav Rathje; m, Edvard Grieg (abstract from "Peer Gynt"); ed, Paul Falkenberg; prod d, Emil Hasler, Karl Vollbrecht; art d, Hasler, Vollbrecht.

Crime Drama/Horror   Cas.   (PR:O   MPAA:NR)

M*   (1951) 88m COL bw

David Wayne (*Martin Harrow*), Howard Da Silva (*Carney*), Luther Adler (*Langley*), Martin Gabel (*Marshall*), Steve Brodie (*Lt. Becker*), Raymond Burr (*Pottsy*), Glenn Anders (*Riggert*), Karen Morley (*Mrs. Coster*), Norman Lloyd (*Sutro*), John Miljan (*Blind Vendor*), Walter Burke (*MacMahan*), Roy Engel (*Regan*), Benny Burt (*Jansen*), Lennie Bremen (*Lemke*), Jim Backus (*The Mayor*), Janine Perreau (*Intended Victim*), Robin Fletcher (*Elsie Coster*), Bernard Szold (*Nightwatchman*), Jorja Curtwright (*Mrs. Stewart*).

The film is a surprisingly good remake of Fritz Lang's German masterpiece of 1931, also produced by Seymour Nebenzal. Director is Joseph Losey, who set the action in contemporary Los Angeles. The film is an almost exact duplicate of the original, but with more emphasis on the sexual perversions that obsess child-killer Wayne who has a special fascination with the shoelaces of his victims. Losey's direction, combined with the L.A. locations, lend a *film noir* flavor to the work.

p, Seymour Nebenzal; d, Joseph Losey; w, Norman Reilly Raine, Leo Katcher, Waldo Salt (based on the script by Thea von Harbou, Fritz Lang, Paul Falkenberg, Adolf Jansen, Karl Vash, from an article by Egon Jacobson); ph, Ernest Laszlo; m, Michel Michelet; ed, Edward Mann; md, Bert Shefter; art d, Martin Obzina; set d, Ray Robinson; makeup, Ted Larsen.

Crime   (PR:C   MPAA:NR)

M*A*S*H**   (1970) 116m Aspen/FOX c

Donald Sutherland (*Hawkeye Pierce*), Elliott Gould (*Trapper John McIntyre*), Tom Skerritt (*Duke Forrest*), Sally Kellerman (*Maj. Hot Lips Houlihan*), Robert Duvall (*Maj. Frank Burns*), Jo Ann Pflug (*Hot Dish*), Rene Auberjonois (*Dago Red*), Roger Bowen (*Col. Henry Blake*), Gary Burghoff (*Radar O'Reilly*), David Arkin (*Sgt. Major Vollmer*), Fred Williamson (*Spearchucker*), Michael Murphy (*Me Lay*), Kim Atwood (*Ho-Jon*), Tim Brown (*Cpl. Judson*), Indus Arthur (*Lt. Leslie*), John Schuck (*Painless Pole*), Ken Prymus (*Pfc. Seidman*), Dwayne Damon (*Capt. Scorch*), Carl Gottlieb (*Ugly John*), Tamara Horrocks (*Capt. Knocko*), G. Wood (*Gen. Hammond*), Bobby Troup (*Sgt. Gorman*), Bud Cort (*Pvt. Boone*), Danny Goldman (*Capt. Murrhardt*), Corey Fisher (*Capt. Bandini*), J. B. Douglas (*Col. Douglas*), Yoko Young (*Japanese Servant*), Ben Davidson, Fran Tarkenton, Howard Williams, Jack Concannon, John Myers, Tom Woodeschick, Tommy Brown, Buck Buchanan, Nolan Smith (*Football Players*), Monica Peterson (*Pretty WAC*), Cathleen Cordell (*Nurse Corps Captain*), Sumi Haru (*Japanese Nurse*), Susan Ikeda, Masami Saito (*Japanese Caddies*), John Mamo (*Japanese Golf Pro*), Samantha Scott (*Nurse/Pin-up Model*), Tom Falk (*Corporal*), Harvey Levine (*2nd Lieutenant*), Diane Turley (*Correspondent*), Weaver Levy, Dale Ishimoto (*Korean Doctors*), Jerry Jones (*Motor Pool Sergeant*), Stephen Altman (*Hawkeye's 5-Year-Old Son*), Hiroko Watanabe (*Korean Prostitute*), H. Lloyd Nelson, Ted Knight, Marvin Miller (*Offstage Dialog*).

M*A*S*H was made before Robert Altman began to think of himself as ROBERT ALTMAN and the result is a superb comedy-drama of war that took chances and made lots of money. The story of the Mobile Army Surgical Hospital had been told before, in a Bogart movie, BATTLE CIRCUS, about the very same Korean War. But that film was made in 1953, shortly after the conflict in Korea had been resolved, and thus it was too soon to poke fun, as the scars of battle were still fresh. Lenny

Bruce once remarked that satire is "tragedy, plus time," and enough time had elapsed by 1970 to make us laugh at what we saw. Working from Richard Hooker's book, scenarist Lardner has amassed as wild and wacky a corps of characters as has ever been run across a screen. Sutherland and Skerritt are two happy army surgeons who steal a jeep in order to get them to their new assignment, which is very near the war zone. Most of the activity takes place in the camp, which is a microcosm of a much larger locale, with every possible madness that can happen. The camp's loudspeaker is a character on its own as the voice intones the various films that will be shown as well as the silliest announcements ever heard. Religious services are called in between a Japanese version of an American song, "My Blue Heaven," and, at one point, the sounds of Duvall and Kellerman making love. Neither Skerritt nor Sutherland can stomach priggish Duvall, a by-the-book officer who spends his off-hours reading the Bible. Skerritt and Sutherland are joined by Gould, another surgeon whose fuse is so short that he physically throttles Duvall after the man has erroneously shifted the blame for a soldier's death on a male nurse. Kellerman, a chief of nurses, arrives and she and Duvall form a front against the young surgeons, so the place is soon divided into two camps. Duvall and Kellerman find a lot to like in each other and are soon lovers, a fact that is shared by everyone, as Burghoff, a pal of the unholy trio, places a live microphone in Duvall's quarters and the unmistakable sounds of lovemaking are broadcast over the ubiquitous loudspeaker. Before dawn, Kellerman is nicknamed "Hot Lips" and Duvall, a blithering idiot for having been exposed, is taken away in a straitjacket. Schuck is the resident dentist, a man dedicated to filling cavities other than in people's teeth. He is suddenly and inexplicably impotent, and, without that ability, he figures his life is over and it's time to kill himself. The surgeons toss him a final dinner at which he is given a "suicide pill" that is, in reality, a tranquilizer. Sutherland has been dallying with Pflug, a married nurse, and he prevails on her to toss her morals totally to the wind and sleep with Schuck in a successful encounter that causes his impotence to go away. The men have been wondering if Kellerman is or isn't a real blonde and there's only one way to find out, so they fix the tent shower to make it collapse while she is inside bathing. The truth is witnessed by a gathering of interested parties. Gould is an expert at thoracic surgery and he is called to Japan to perform some delicate work on a congressman's son. He takes Sutherland along to aid in the surgery and later, the two men enjoy a somewhat long and away-from-the-story sojourn at a golf course. Kellerman has been bitching about what's going on in the camp and Wood, the general, arrives to personally investigate her allegations. When Sutherland mouths off about the ability of the camp to play football, Wood bets that his team can beat them. Five thousand dollars are wagered and the final sequence is a hilarious football game where the surgeons use hypos filled with sedatives and a pro football player, Williamson, to defeat the other team, which has some real players on it that include Fran Tarkenton, Ben Davidson, and Buck Buchanan. The film ends as Skerritt and Sutherland say goodbye and return to the U.S., their service complete. M*A*S*H successfully melds comedy and carnage, giggles and gore and takes pot shots at just about every sacred cow in the herd. Lardner won an Oscar for his screenplay and nominations were given for Best Picture, Best Direction, and to Kellerman as Best Supporting Actress. The film spawned one of the most successful TV series in the history of the cathode tube, although only one of the actors felt it would make it, Burghoff, who eventually left the show and probably still regrets it. Altman must have liked Cort's work because he used him in his next film, BREWSTER McCLOUD. In a small role, look for Carl Gottlieb, who later went on to write and direct. His biggest screenplay was JAWS. M*A*S*H had many flaws, some of them glaring, but the overall impact was important in the film industry and made Sutherland and Gould full-fledged stars, where they remained until they appeared in so many ill-conceived films that both fell from the audience's favor in the late 1970s. Both actors are usually better than the material they select. Altman has gone on to make some of the most confounding and pretentious films ever.

p, Ingo Preminger; d, Robert Altman; w, Ring Lardner, Jr. (based on the novel by Richard Hooker [Dr. H. Richard Hornberger, William Heinz]); ph, Harold E. Stine (Panavision, DeLuxe Color); m, Johnny Mandel; ed, Danford B. Greene; md, Herbert Spencer; art d, Jack Martin Smith, Arthur Lonergan; set d, Walter M. Scott, Stuart A. Reiss; spec eff, L. B. Abbott, Art Cruickshank; m/l, "Suicide Is Painless," Mike Altman, Mandel; makeup, Dan Striepeke, Lester Berns.

Comedy/War   Cas.   (PR:C-O   MPAA:R)

MA AND PA KETTLE½   (1949) 76m UNIV bw

Marjorie Main (*Ma Kettle*), Percy Kilbride (*Pa Kettle*), Richard Long (*Tom Kettle*), Meg Randall (*Kim Parker*), Patricia Alphin (*Secretary*), Esther Dale (*Mrs. Birdie Hicks*), Barry Kelley (*Mr. Tomkins*), Harry Antrim (*Mayor Swiggins*), Isabel O'Madigan (*Mrs. Hicks's Mother*), Ida Moore (*Emily*), Emory Parnell (*Billy Reed*), Boyd Davis (*Mr. Simpson*), O.Z. Whitehead (*Mr. Billings*), Ray Bennett (*Sam Rogers*), Alvin Hammer (*Alvin*), Lester Allen (*Geoduck*), Chief Yowlachie (*Crowbar*), Rex Lease (*Sheriff*), Dale Belding (*Danny Kettle*), Teddy Infuhr (*George Kettle*), George McDonald (*Henry Kettle*), Robin Winans (*Billy Kettle*), Gene Persson (*Ted Kettle*), Paul Dunn (*Donny Kettle*), Margaret Brown (*Ruthie Kettle*), Beverly Wook (*Eve Kettle*), Diane Florentine (*Sara Kettle*), Gloria Moore (*Rosie Kettle*), Melinda Plowman (*Susie Kettle*), Harry Tyler (*Ticket Agent*), Dewey Robinson (*Giant Man*), Sam McDaniel (*Waiter*), Ted Stanhope (*Steward*), Harry Cheshire (*Fletcher*), Eddy C. Waller (*Mr. Green*), John Wald (*Dick Palmer*), Donna Leary (*Salty Kettle*), Elena Schreiner (*Nancy Kettle*), George Arglen (*Willie Kettle*).

Kilbride and Main star in this spin-off of THE EGG AND I a 1947 film in which they were supporting characters and which spawned a lengthy series of comedies that lasted well into the 1950s. Kilbride and Main, the down-and-out parents of fifteen kids, are on the verge of being evicted from their ramshackle home. Things begin to look up when Kilbride wins the grand prize in a tobacco slogan contest, and the family is awarded a brand-new fully automated house. Local grouch Dale is jealous of the family's new fortune and accuses Kilbride of plagiarizing the slogan. Luckily, dedicated magazine writer Randall proves otherwise and marries Kilbride and Main's oldest son Long to boot. (See MA AND PA KETTLE series, Index.)

p, Leonard Goldstein; d, Charles Lamont; w, Herbert Margolis, Louis Morheim, Al Lewis (based on characters from the novel *The Egg And I* by Betty MacDonald); ph, Maury Gertsman; m, Milton Schwarzwald; ed, Russell Schoengarth; art d, Bernard Herzbrun, Emrich Nicholson.

Comedy **(PR:A MPAA:NR)**

MA AND PA KETTLE AT HOME** (1954) 80m UNIV bw

Marjorie Main *(Ma Kettle)*, Percy Kilbride *(Pa Kettle)*, Alan Mowbray *(Alphonsus Mannering)*, Ross Elliott *(Pete Crosby)*, Alice Kelley *(Sally Maddocks)*, Brett Halsey *(Elwin Kettle)*, Mary Wickes *(Miss Wetter)*, Irving Bacon *(Mr. Maddocks)*, Emory Parnell *(Bill Reed)*, Virginia Brissac *(Mrs. Maddocks)*, Stan Ross *(Crowbar)*, Oliver Blake *(Geoduck)*, Guy Wilkerson *(Jones)*, Edmund Cobb *(Jefferson)*, Edgar Dearing *(Perkins)*, Betty McDonough, Helen Gibson *(Ranch Wives)*, Judy Nugent *(Betty Kettle)*, Carol Nugent *(Nancy Kettle)*, Richard Eyer *(Billie Kettle)*, Donald MacDonald *(Benjamin Kettle)*, Coral Hammond *(Eve Kettle)*, Patrick Miller *(Teddy Kettle)*, Nancy Zane *(Sara Kettle)*, Gary Pagett *(George Kettle)*, Donna Cregan Moots *(Ruthie Kettle)*, Whitey Haupt *(Henry Kettle)*, Pat Morrow *(Susie Kettle)*, Tony Epper *(Danny Kettle)*, James Flavin, Robert Nelson *(Motorcycle Cops)*, Rick Vallin, Hank Worden, Ken Terrell *(Indians)*..

One of Kilbride's and Main's 15 offspring, Halsey, is a finalist in an essay competition that could win him a scholarship to an agricultural college. The judges, Mowbray and Elliott, decide to spend the weekend at the homes of the two finalists in order to determine who will be the winner. Upon hearing the news, Kilbride flies into a panic and attempts to spruce up his tumble-down farm so that the judges will look more favorably on Halsey. The improvements, of course, are merely cosmetic, and when a vicious rain kicks up during the judges' stay and washes off Kilbride's work, it appears that the scholarship is washed away as well. Fortunately the judges are more impressed with the quality of Halsey's solid family life than with the farm, and they grant him the scholarship. Filled with the usual collection of rustic characters, this MA AND PA KETTLE outing is another entertaining affair. (See MA AND PA KETTLE series, Index.)

p, Richard Wilson; d, Charles Lamont; w, Kay Lenard; ph, Carl Guthrie; ed, Leonard Weiner; md, Joseph Gershenson; art d, Bernard Herzbrun, Robert Boyle.

Comedy **(PR:A MPAA:NR)**

MA AND PA KETTLE AT THE FAIR** (1952) 78m UNIV bw

Marjorie Main *(Ma Kettle)*, Percy Kilbride *(Pa Kettle)*, Lori Nelson *(Rosie Kettle)*, James Best *(Marvin Johnson)*, Esther Dale *(Birdie Hicks)*, Russell Simpson *(Clem Johnson)*, Emory Parnell *(Billy Reed)*, Oliver Blake *(Geoduck)*, Hallene Hill *(Mrs. Hicks' Mother)*, Rex Lease *(Sheriff)*, James Griffith *(Medicine Man)*, Edmund Cobb, Roy Regnier *(Men)*, Teddy Infuhr *(Benjamin Kettle)*, George Arglen *(Willie Kettle)*, Ronald R. Rondell *(Danny Kettle)*, Margaret Brown *(Ruth Kettle)*, Jackie Jackson *(Henry Kettle)*, Billy Clark *(George Kettle)*, Donna Leary *(Sally Kettle)*, Elana Schreiner *(Nancy Kettle)*, Eugene Persson *(Teddy Kettle)*, Jenny Linder *(Sara Kettle)*, Sherry Jackson *(Susie Kettle)*, Gary Lee Jackson *(Billy Kettle)*, Beverly Mook *(Eve Kettle)*, Zachary Charles *(Crowbar)*, Frank Ferguson *(Sam, the Jailer)*, Syd Saylor *(Postman)*, Harry Harvey *(Chairman)*, Harry Cheshire *(Preacher)*, Wheaton Chambers *(Injured Man)*, Harry Cording *(Ed)*, William Gould, Frank McFarland *(Judges)*, Claire Meade *(Sarah)*, James Guilfoyle *(Birdie's Trainer)*, Mel Pogue *(Delivery Boy)*, Doug Carter *(Ticket Seller)*, Bob Donnelly *(Clown)*.

Another rustic comedy starring Kilbride and Main, the film features the proud-but-poor parents trying their best to win enough money at the county fair to send one of their daughters, Nelson, to college. Main tries her hand in the baking competition, while Kilbride rustles up enough dough to buy an old trotter and some silks in order to enter the fair's horse race. Of course the dedicated parents triumph over adversity, and daughter Nelson hooks up with dashing young man Best for the fadeout. (See MA AND PA KETTLE series, Index.)

p, Leonard Goldstein; d, Charles Barton; w, Richard Morris, John Grant (based on a story by Martin Ragaway, Leonard Stern, Jack Henley); ph, Maury Gertsman; ed, Ted J. Kent; md, Joseph Gershenson; art d, Bernard Herzbrun, Eric Orbom.

Comedy **(PR:A MPAA:NR)**

MA AND PA KETTLE AT WAIKIKI** (1955) 79m UNIV bw

Marjorie Main *(Ma Kettle)*, Percy Kilbride *(Pa Kettle)*, Lori Nelson *(Rosie Kettle)*, Byron Palmer *(Bob Baxter)*, Loring Smith *(Rodney Kettle)*, Lowell Gilmore *(Robert Coates)*, Mabel Albertson *(Mrs. Andrews)*, Fay Roope *(Fulton Andrews)*, Oliver Blake *(Geoduck)*, Teddy Hart *(Crowbar)*, Esther Dale *(Birdie Hicks)*, Russell Johnson *(Eddie Nelson)*, Ben Welden *(Shorty Bates)*, Dick Reeves *(Lefty Conway)*, Myron Healey *(Marty)*, Ric Roman *(Chuck Collins)*, Hilo Hattie *(Mama Lotus)*, Charles Lung *(Papa Lotus)*, Byron Kane *(Prof. Gilfallen)*, Sandra Spence *(Pa's Secretary)*, Harold Goodwin *(Dr. Barnes)*, Norman Field *(Dr. Fabian)*, Elana Schreiner *(Nancy Kettle)*, Beverly Mook *(Eve Kettle)*, Jenny Linder *(Sara Kettle)*, Ronnie Rondell *(Dannie Kettle)*, Tim Hawkins *(Teddy Kettle)*, Margaret Brown *(Ruthie Kettle)*, Billy Clark *(George Kettle)*, George Arglen *(Willie Kettle)*, Jon Gardner *(Benjamin Kettle)*, Jackie Jackson *(Henry Kettle)*, Donna Leary *(Sally Kettle)*, Bonnie Kay Eddy *(Susie Kettle)*, Luukiuluana *(Masseuse)*, Cindy Garner, Claudette Thornton *(Secretaries)*, Ida Moore *(Miss Pennyfeather)*.

The last MA AND PA KETTLE film for Kilbride, who retired upon its release, features Ma and Pa answering a cry for help from their cousin in Hawaii, Smith, who has been hit with health and finance problems. Kilbride, Main, and oldest daughter Nelson venture to the islands to run Smith's pineapple farm while he recovers from his illness. In a matter of moments, Kilbride manages to cause a massive explosion in the pineapple factory, *and* get himself kidnaped. Yet, all works out for the best by the fadeout. MA AND PA KETTLE AT WAIKIKI actually was filmed a few years before its release, but distribution was not until 1955. This was the last MA AND PA KETTLE film for producer Leonard Goldstein who died soon after its release. (See MA AND PA KETTLE series, Index.)

p, Leonard Goldstein; d, Lee Sholem; w, Jack Henley, Harry Clork, Elwood Ullman (based on a story by Connie Lee Bennett); ph, Cliff Stine; ed, Virgil Vogel; md, Joseph Gershenson; art d, Bernard Herzbrun, Eric Orbom.

Comedy **(PR:A MPAA:NR)**

MA AND PA KETTLE BACK ON THE FARM** (1951) 80m UNIV bw

Marjorie Main *(Ma Kettle)*, Percy Kilbride *(Pa Kettle)*, Richard Long *(Tom Kettle)*, Meg Randall *(Kim Kettle)*, Ray Collins *(Jonathan Parker)*, Barbara Brown *(Elizabeth Parker)*, Emory Parnell *(Billy Reed)*, Peter Leeds *(Manson)*, Teddy Hart *(Crowbar)*, Oliver Blake *(Geoduck)*.

This third film in the MA AND PA KETTLE series picks up where the last one left off with the farm family abandoning the modern home won by Kilbride in the previous film to move back to its plot of land in the country in search of uranium. Unfortunately, the only radioactive items in the country are Kilbride's army-surplus overalls which cause all manner of strange things to happen including car horns to honk and light bulbs to flash. A subplot involves Main's frustrations with son Long's mother-in-law (Brown) who wants her grandchild raised "hygienically." (See MA AND PA KETTLE series, Index.)

p, Leonard Goldstein; d, Edward Sedgwick; w, Jack Henley; ph, Charles Van Enger; ed, Russell Schoengarth; md, Joseph Gershenson; art d, Bernard Herzbrun, Emrich Nicholson.

Comedy **(PR:A MPAA:NR)**

MA AND PA KETTLE GO TO PARIS

(SEE: MA AND PA KETTLE ON VACATION, 1953)

MA AND PA KETTLE GO TO TOWN**

(1950) 79m UNIV bw (GB: GOING TO TOWN)

Marjorie Main *(Ma Kettle)*, Percy Kilbride *(Pa Kettle)*, Richard Long *(Tom Kettle)*, Meg Randall *(Kim Kettle)*, Ray Collins *(Jonathan Parker)*, Barbara Brown *(Elizabeth Parker)*, Esther Dale *(Birdie Hicks)*, Ellen Corby *(Emily)*, Teddy Hart *(Crowbar)*, Oliver Blake *(Geoduck)*, Emory Parnell *(Billy Reed)*, Peter Leeds *(Manson)*, Dale Belding *(Danny Kettle)*, Teddy Infuhr *(Benjamin Kettle)*, Rex Lease *(Sheriff)*, Diane Florentine *(Sara Kettle)*, Paul Dunn *(George Kettle)*, Eugene Persson *(Willie Kettle)*, Margaret Brown: *(Ruthie Kettle)*, Donna Leary *(Sally Kettle)*, Lynn Wood Coleman *(Billy Kettle)*, Mary Ann Jackson *(Rosie Kettle)*, Jackie Jackson *(Henry Kettle)*, Sherry Jackson *(Susie Kettle)*, Beverly Mook *(Eve Kettle)*, Elana Schreiner *(Nancy Kettle)*, Joyce Holden *(Miss Trent)*, Edmund Cobb *(Engineer)*, Jack Ingram *(State Trooper)*, Henry Hausner *(Burley)*, Verna Kornman *(Mrs. Quinlan)*, Alice Richey *(Mrs. Tullet)*, Steve Wayne *(Mr. Chadwick)*, Ann Pearce *(Miss Clyde)*, Lucille Barkley *(Miss Cooper)*, Edward Clark *(Dr. Bagley)*, Dee Carroll *(Miss Stafford)*, Elliott Lewis *(Boxer)*, Gregg Martell *(Louie)*, Charles McGraw *("Shotgun" Mike Munger)*, Kathryn Givney *(Mrs. Masterson)*, Jim Backus *(Little Joe)*, Paul McVey *(Harold Masterson)*, Bert Freed *(Dutch)*, Hal March *(Eskow)*.

The film features more down-home nonsense from Kilbride and Main as they venture to the Big Apple after Pa wins a jingle-writing contest. There they run into gangsters on the lam and agree to deliver some stolen loot to one of the mobster's buddies. Unfortunately, Kilbride loses the dough and the gangster who is supposed to take delivery thinks the old farmer is trying to muscle his way into the mob. As usual, all works out in the end. (See MA AND PA KETTLE series, Index.)

p, Leonard Goldstein; d, Charles Lamont; w, Martin Ragaway, Leonard Stern; ph, Charles Van Enger; ed, Russell Schoengarth; md, Milton Schwarzwald; art d, Bernard Herzbrun, Van Enger.

Comedy **(PR:A MPAA:NR)**

MA AND PA KETTLE ON VACATION**

(1953) 79m UNIV bw (GB: MA AND PA KETTLE GO TO PARIS)

Marjorie Main *(Ma Kettle)*, Percy Kilbride *(Pa Kettle)*, Ray Collins *(Jonathan Parker)*, Bodil Miller *(Inez Kraft)*, Sig Ruman *(Cyrus Kraft)*, Barbara Brown *(Elizabeth Parker)*, Ivan Triesault *(Henri Dupre)*, Oliver Blake *(Geoduck)*, Teddy Hart *(Crowbar)*, Peter Brocco *(Adolph Wade)*, Jay Novello *(Andre)*, Jean De Briac *(Chef Chantilly)*, Larry Dobkin *(Farrell)*, Harold Goodwin *(Harriman)*, Jack Kruschen *(Jacques Amien)*, Rosario Imperio, Andre D'Arcy *(Apache Team)*, Ken Terrell *(Taxicab Driver)*, Alice Kelley *(Stewardess)*, Rita Moreno *(Soubrette)*, John Eldredge *(Masterson)*, Zachary Yaconelli *(Maitre D')*, Sherry Jackson *(Susie Kettle)*, Gary Lee Jackson *(Billy Kettle)*, Billy Clark *(George Kettle)*, Jackie Jackson *(Henry Kettle)*, Elana Schreiner *(Nancy Kettle)*, Ronnie Rondell *(Dannie Kettle)*, Margaret Brown *(Ruthie Kettle)*, Jon Gardner *(Benjamin Kettle)*, Jenny Linder *(Sara Kettle)*, Beverly Mook *(Eve Kettle)*, Donna Leary *(Sally Kettle)*, Robert Scott *(Teddy Kettle)*, George Arglen *(Willie Kettle)*, Gloria Pall *(French Girl)*, Major Sam Harris *(Plane Passenger)*, Carli Elinor *(Orchestra Leader)*, Eddie Le Baron *(Wine Steward)*, Dave Willock *(Franklin)*.

This film features Kilbride and Main as the country couple on vacation in Paris accompanied by their daughter-in-law's wealthy parents Collins and Brown. Between attempts to buy racy postcards and ogle cancan girls, Kilbride finds himself unwittingly involved in espionage when a spy gives him a letter to be delivered to Brocco. To complicate matters, Brocco is knocked off by rival spies Ruman and Miller and soon the chase through the streets of Paris is on. (See MA AND PA KETTLE series, Index.)

p, Leonard Goldstein; d, Charles Lamont; w, Jack Henley; ph, George Robinson; ed, Leonard Weiner; art d, Bernard Herzbrun, Robert Boyle.

Comedy **(PR:A MPAA:NR)**

MA BARKER'S KILLER BROOD** (1960) 82m Filmservice bw

Lurene Tuttle *(Ma Barker)*, Tris Coffin *(Arthur Dunlop)*, Paul Dubov *(Alvin Karpis)*, Nelson Leigh *(George Barker)*, Myrna Dell *(Lou)*, Vic Lundin *(Machine Gun Kelly)*, Donald Spruance *(Herman Barker)*, Don Grady *(Herman as a Boy)*, Ronald Foster *(Doc Barker)*, Gary Ammann *(Doc as a Boy)*, Roy Baker *(Lloyd Barker)*, Donald Towers *(Lloyd as a Boy)*, Eric Morris *(Fred Barker)*, Michael Smith *(Fred as a Boy)*, Byron Foulger *(Dr. Guelffe)*, Eric Sinclair *(John Dillinger)*, Robert Kendall *(Baby Face Nelson)*, Irene Windust *(Mrs. Khortney)*, John McNamara *(Mr. Khortney)*, Dan Riss *(Baxter)*, David Carlile *(Avery)*, Charles Tannen *(1st Sheriff)*, Daniel White *(2nd Sheriff)*, Riley Hill *(Deputy)*, Bernard Pludow *(Charlie)*, Owen Bush *(Carney)*, Paul Power *(Minister)*, George Dockstader, Wally Rose, Bill Couch *(Guards)*.

Tuttle gives a lively performance in this otherwise dry film based on the true adventures of America's most notorious mother. The story begins with Tuttle's early career in dust-bowl Oklahoma, leading her sons astray as well as providing advice to such infamous names as Dillinger, Baby Face Nelson, and Machine Gun Kelly. The law finally catches up with her at her plush Florida hideout as the film climaxes with an action-packed shoot-out. Some good action sequences help keep this from being boring. The low-budget film was derived from a teleseries, with various episodes edited together.

p, William J. Faris; d, Bill Karn; w, F. Paul Hall; ph, Clark Ramsey; m, Gene Kauer; md, William Hinshaw; art d, Paul E. Mullen; set d, Harry Reif; m/l, "Little Joe Carew," Arna Lou Barnes (sung by Ginny Barry and Roye Baker).

Crime (PR:O MPAA:NR)

MA, HE'S MAKING EYES AT ME*½ (1940) 60m UNIV bw

Tom Brown *(Tommy Shaw)*, Constance Moore *(Connie Curtiss)*, Richard Carle *(C.J. Woodbury)*, Anne Nagel *(Miss Lansdale)*, Jerome Cowan *(Ted Carter)*, Elizabeth Risdon *(Minerva)*, Fritz Feld *(Forsythe)*, Larry Williams *(Joe Porter)*, Vivian Fay *(Vivian)*, Peggy Chamberlain *(Peggy)*, Frank Mitchell *(Frank)*, Marie Greene *(Marie)*, Wade Boteler *(Cop)*, Eddie Acuff, Henry Roquemore *(Counter Men)*, Grace Hayle *(Mrs. Smythe)*, Dora Clement *(Woman)*, Mary Field *(Girl Customer)*, Fay McKenzie, Kitty McHugh *(Brooklyn Girls)*, Stanley Blystone *(Doorman)*, Mary Currier *(Secretary)*, Michael Mark *(Small Thief)*.

Brown stars as a not-so-clever press agent who hooks up with unemployed chorus girl Moore and declares her "Miss Manhattan" in order to promote a line of inexpensive clothes. Brown then creates a "Mr. Manhattan" to escort Moore in public and even goes so far as to arrange a fake marriage for the two. At the last minute Brown realizes that he's in love with Moore and he fires "Mr. Manhattan" and goes to the altar himself. Songs include: "Ma, He's Making Eyes At Me" (Sidney Clare, Con Conrad—sung by Moore); "Unfair To Love" (Sam Lerner, Frank Skinner—sung by Moore); and "A Lemon In The Garden Of Love" (M.E. Rourke, Richard Carle).

p, Joseph Sanford; d, Harold Schuster; w, Charles Grayson, Edmund L. Hartmann (based on a story by Ed Sullivan); ph, Elwood Bredell; ed, Ed Curtiss; md, Charles Previn; art d, Jack Otterson.

Musical Comedy (PR:A MPAA:NR)

MA NUIT CHEZ MAUD (SEE: MY NIGHT AT MAUD'S, 1970, Fr.)

MA POMME (SEE: JUST ME, 1950, Fr.)

MAARAKAT ALGER (SEE; BATTLE OF ALGIERS, THE, 1967, Algeria/Ital.)

MACABRE** (1958) 73m AA bw

William Prince *(Dr. Rodney Barrett)*, Jim Backus *(Jim Tyloe)*, Christine White *(Nancy Wetherby)*, Jacqueline Scott *(Polly Baron)*, Susan Morrow *(Sylvia Stevenson)*, Philip Tonge *(Jode Wetherby)*, Jonathan Kidd *(Ed Quigley)*, Dorothy Morris *(Alice Barrett)*, Howard Hoffman *(Hummel)*, Ellen Corby *(Miss Kushins)*, Linda Guderman *(Marge)*, Voltaire Perkins *(Preacher)*.

Producer-director William Castle insured filmgoers for $1,000 each against "death by fright" before they viewed this movie, based on a novel written by thirteen individuals. The story involves a small-town doctor, Prince, who leads the search for his daughter whom some maniac has buried alive in a graveyard. In the end the whole thing turns out to be a hoax perpetrated by Prince in order to scare his dead wife's father into a heart attack. Prince then can collect the family inheritance.

p&d, William Castle; w, Robb White (bassed on the novel by Theo Durrant [Terry Adler, Anthony Boucher, Eunice Mays Boyd, Florence Ostern Faulkner, Allen Hymson, Cary Lucas, Dana Lyon, Lenore Glen Offord, Virginia Rath, Richard Shattuck, Darwin L. Teilhet, William Worley]); ph, Carl E. Guthrie; m, Les Baxter; ed, John F. Schreyer; art d, Jack T.Collis, Robert Kinoshita; spec eff, Jack Rabin, Louis Dewitt, Irving Block.

Horror (PR:C MPAA:NR)

MACAO*** (1952) 80m RKO bw

Robert Mitchum *(Nick Cochran)*, Jane Russell *(Julie Benson)*, William Bendix *(Lawrence Trumble)*, Thomas Gomez *(Lt. Sebastian)*, Gloria Grahame *(Margie)*, Brad Dexter *(Halloran)*, Edward Ashley *(Martin Stewart)*, Philip Ahn *(Itzumi)*, Vladimir Sokoloff *(Kwan Sum Tang)*, Don Zelaya *(Gimpy)*, Emory Parnell *(Ship Captain)*, Nacho Galindo *(Bus Driver)*, Philip Van Zandt *(Customs Official)*, George Chan *(Chinese Photographer)*, Seldon Jett *(Dutch Tourist)*, Genevieve Bell *(Woman Passenger)*, Tommy Lee *(Coolie Knifed in Water)*, Alex Montoya *(Coolie Bartender)*, James B. Leong *(Knifer)*, Alfredo Santos, *(Hoodlum)*, Marc Krah *(Desk Clerk)*, May Taksugi *(Barber)*, Lee Tung Foo *(Chinese Merchant)*, Maria Sen Young, Iris Wong *(Croupiers)*, Manuel Paris *(Bartender)*, Art Dupuis *(Portuguese Pilot)*, William Yip *(Rickshaw Driver)*, Michael Visaroff *(Russian Doorman)*, W. T. Chang *(Old Fisherman)*, Weaver Levy *(Chang)*, Trevor Bardette *(Bus Driver)*, Rico Alaniz *(Alvaris)*, Walter Ng *(Fisherman)*, Abdullah Abbas *(Arabian)*, Everett Glass *(Garcia)*, Phil Harron *(Sikh)*.

This was not one of von Sternberg's favorite films but the dynamic and utterly visual director made of MACAO, with its hodge-podge script and melodramatic meanderings, an exciting *film noir* entry, steaming up the screen with sultry, sexy Russell and a somnambulistic Mitchum who manage to clinch often, despite their sneering disregard for each other. Mitchum is on the run, having been convicted of a crime he did not commit. He meets nightclub singer Russell, who dislikes men in general, while both are on a steamer bound for Macao. Also on board is wise-cracking detective Bendix, who uses both Russell and Mitchum to identify jewel smugglers operating on the Portuguese islands off the coast of China; he's really after Dexter, a kingpin of crime in Macao. Mitchum steps in to help the buxom Russell who has difficulty resisting the pushy advances of a drunk; she repays Mitchum for getting rid of the pest by stealing his wallet while kissing him. Moreover, when the trio get to Macao, corrupt local police detective Gomez looks over the contents of Mitchum's wallet and concludes that he's another plainclothes detective sent to investigate Dexter's operations. He tells Dexter, who has already had three previous detectives killed, and, for her stealing efforts, Russell is rewarded with a job singing in Dexter's club. Dexter begins to make advances against the raven-haired Russell which infuriates his girl friend, Grahame, who works as a croupier in the club. Dexter next offers Mitchum a sizable sum to leave Macao but he stalls. When the real detective, Bendix, learns of the attempted bribe, he enlists Mitchum's help in setting up a trap for the smugglers and luring Dexter beyond the three-mile limit where he can be arrested. But the plan backfires and Mitchum is beaten up and Bendix knifed. The mortally wounded cop tells Mitchum to bring in Dexter and, if he does, his trouble in the States will be cleared up. Mitchum sneaks onto Dexter's yacht and, just after Dexter and Russell board it en route to Hong Kong and a quick tryst, Mitchum steers a course beyond the limit, where, after a fierce battle, Interpol police pick up the crime boss and his remaining henchmen. Mitchum and Russell leave for the U.S., ostensibly to begin a tempestuous life together. Russell got the usual sex-star buildup for this film, her role heralded with reams of publicity about a revealing gold and silver mesh lame dress which was affixed to her Amazonian body, RKO's publicity department pointed out, not with needle and thread but with steel pliers! She sings throatily if not handsomely "One for My Baby" (Johnny Mercer, Harold Arlen), "You Kill Me," and "Ocean Breeze" (Jule Styne, Leo Robin). She and Mitchum compete in shedding their clothes, a battle of cheesecake against beefcake. Russell wins flaps down, causing Mitchum to ogle her in one scene where she wears a very low-cut gown, revealing much of her famous topside, causing Jane to give out with her usual sneer and the line: "Enjoying the view?" Mitchum's retort is a classic of sorts: "It ain't the Taj Mahal or the Hanging Gardens of Babylon, but it'll do." Von Sternberg directed this melodramatic *film noir* entry with less than an enthusiastic approach, wrapping it up in two months on the RKO back lot. The stylistic director later stated in his autobiography, *Fun In a Chinese Laundry*: "After JET PILOT, I made one more film in accordance with the RKO contract I had foolishly accepted. This was made under the supervision of six different men in charge. It was called MACAO, and instead of fingers in that pie, half a dozen clowns immersed various parts of their anatomy in it." Nicholas Ray was brought in to shoot some of the final scenes, especially the fist fight between Mitchum and Dexter at the end, but most of the film remains von Sternberg's. His distinctive style is in evidence in such scenes where Bendix is seen being knifed through elaborate fishnetting, a cleverly planned chase across water and through bobbing floats, the shadowy world of Macao and its denizens. He later denounced the film when Ray was given some credit. Von Sternberg was also unhappy with Russell and Grahame who argued with him about his setups, failing to understand his motivations, which, in Russell's case, is not hard to believe. Russell delivers her lines like a huge wind-up doll and she is as alluring as she is sullen. The best acting in the film is done by the shifty, greasy-looking Gomez and ancient Sokoloff who plays a blind coolie spouting platitudes while running Russell and Mitchum about Macao's back streets.

p, Alex Gottlieb; d, Josef von Sternberg, (uncredited) Nicholas Ray; w, Bernard C. Schoenfeld, Stanley Rubin (based on a story by Bob Williams); ph, Harry J. Wild; m, Anthony Collins; ed, Samuel E. Beetley, Robert Golden; md, C. Bakaleinikoff; art d, Albert S. D'Agostino, Ralph Berger; cos, Michael Woulfe; m/l, "One for My Baby," Johnny Mercer, Harold Arlen, "Ocean Breeze," "Talk to Me Tomorrow," Jule Styne, Leo Robin; makeup, Mel Berns.

Crime Drama Cas. (PR:C MPAA:NR)

MACARIO** (1961, Mex.) 91m Clasa Films Mundiales/Azteca bw

Ignacio Lopez Torres *(Macario)*, Pina Pellicer *(Macario's Wife)*, Enrique Lucero *(Death)*, Jose Galvez *(The Devil)*, Jose Luis Jimenez *(God)*, Mario Alberto Rodriguez *(Don Ramiro)*, Sonia Infante, Eduardo Fajardo, Consuelo Frank, Jose Dupeyron, Celia Tejada, Enrique Garcia Alvarez.

An old Mexican peasant fable is brought to the screen with slick professionalism and adherence to the period the fable depicts. Tired of his extreme poverty, Torres goes on a hunger strike until the day when he can have an entire turkey to himself. To appease her husband, Pellicer steals a turkey and gives it to her husband even though her children went to bed hungry. While Torres is about to consume the turkey in the woods he is persuaded by Death to share some of it in return for magical powers which will allow him to heal the sick, on condition that Death agrees to the person being cured. His new power makes Torres a celebrity until he is accused of being an instrument of the devil. The last chance for him to vindicate himself is to come to the aid of the Viceroy's son. But Death decides that this boy should not be cured, so Torres is forced to flee, later dying.

p, Armando Orive Alba; d, Roberto Gavaldon; w, Emilio Carballido, Gavaldon (based on the story "The Third Guest" by Bruno Traven); ph, Gabriel Figueroa; m,

Raul Lavista; ed, Gloria Schoemann; art d, Manuel Fontanals; spec eff, Juan Munoz Ravelo.

Drama/Fantasy (PR:AA MPAA:NR)

MAC ARTHUR* 1/2** (1977) 128m UNIV c

Gregory Peck *(Gen. Douglas MacArthur)*, Ed Flanders *(President Truman)*, Dan O'Herlihy *(President Roosevelt)*, Ivan Bonar *(Gen. Sutherland)*, Ward Costello *(Gen. George Marshall)*, Nicholas Coster *(Col. Huff)*, Marj Dusay *(Mrs. MacArthur)*, Art Fleming *(The Secretary)*, Russell D. Johnson *(Adm. King)*, Sandy Kenyon *(Gen. Wainwright)*, Robert Mandan *(Rep. Martin)*, Allan Miller *(Col. Diller)*, Dick O'Neill *(Col. Whitney)*, Addison Powell *(Adm. Chester Nimitz)*, Tom Rosqui *(Gen. Sampson)*, G. D. Spradlin *(Gen. Eichelberger)*, Kenneth Tobey *(Adm. "Bull" Halsey)*, Gary Walberg *(Gen. Walker)*, Lane Allan *(Gen. Marquat)*, Barry Coe *(TV Reporter)*, Everett Cooper *(Gen. Krueger)*, Charles Cyphers *(Gen. Harding)*, Manuel De Pina *(Prettyman)*, Jesse Dizon *(Castro)*, Warde Donovan *(Gen. Shepherd)*, John Fujioka *(Emperor Hirohito)*, Jerry Holland *(Aide)*, Philip Kenneally *(Adm. Doyle)*, John McKee *(Adm. Leahy)*, Walter O. Miles *(Gen. Kenney)*, Gerald S. Peters *(Gen. Blamey)*, Eugene Peterson *(Gen. Collins)*, Beulah Quo *(Al Cheu)*, Alex Rodine *(Gen. Derevyanko)*, Yuki Shimoda *(Prime Minister Shidehara)*, Fred Stuthman *(Gen. Bradley)*, Harvey Vernon *(Adm. Sherman)*, William Wellman, Jr. *(Lt. Bulkeley)*.

General of the Army Douglas MacArthur was not a modest man but he was brilliant in military matters, perhaps the greatest strategic genius of WW II (given the considerable conjecture that Eisenhower's thinking was done for him by Gen. George Marshall). MacArthur was also charismatic, dashing, eloquent, and, thankfully for America, symbolic of an undying spirit, a will that would not quit and not only promised victory but insisted upon it as a Heavenly mandate given to him personally from on high. This dynamic and exceptionally historic man saw no better personification then in the wonderful enactment of his life by Peck. The film opens with Peck addressing a class at his alma mater, West Point, and his resonant words: "Duty . . . honor . . . country." It is Peck's final address at age 82, and, as he looks over the bright faces of the cadets in the main mess hall, he thinks back to his own graduation from the Point 59 years earlier and then forward through the decades to encompass one of the most spectacular careers of any American military officer. The scene fades and it is 1942 with Peck on beleaguered Corregidor, last American bastion in the Philippines, with hordes of Japanese forces attempting to bomb and bombard it into submission. Peck receives a direct order from President Franklin D. Roosevelt to evacuate "The Rock." an order at which he bristles. He complains to aides that, instead of sending him the promised reinforcements, the ships and planes that have never arrived, to save his American and Filipino forces from annihilation, Washington has ordered him to leave his men. His aides counsel him to obey, telling him "it's a direct order from the President of the United States." Peck reluctantly complies, departing with some staff members, his wife, and small boy, bidding farewell to Kenyon, playing Gen. Wainwright, promising him he will return with an army. But, after a hazardous journey through the islands and an exhausting flight to Australia, Peck finds no relief army waiting, only scattered, untrained troops. He announces that "I came through and I will return" to the Philippines. Later, with anger and regret, he learns that Kenyon has surrendered the Philippines, condemning him for submitting. Peck quickly builds an army of Americans and Australians and goes on the attack, taking back the islands from the Japanese through a brilliant island-hopping stretegy, bypassing Japanese strongholds and cutting off their supply lines, leaving these outposts to "wither on the vine." Peck is shown, to the consternation of aides, at the very front lines where he comes under fire but continues his observation of enemy lines without taking shelter. His strategy working, Peck begins to expand his sphere of military influence, coming into conflict with the Navy to the point where a showdown occurs in Hawaii with President Roosevelt, O'Herlihy, considering two plans to retake the Pacific from the Japanese, one, the Navy's, as espoused by Powell, as Nimitz, the other being MacArthur's. At first O'Herlihy seems to favor Powell's plan of bypassing the Philippines and striking at Formosa and from there to hit the Japanese home islands. But Peck steps forth and makes an impassioned plea to return to the Philippines, saying that if America does not return to aid its staunchest ally, now sorely oppressed by occupying Japanese troops, it will be thought of as an act of betrayal, that the word of America is no good and that the world will believe what the Japanese keep broadcasting, that America will not spill the blood of whites for another race. To further emphasize his point, Peck withdraws a personal letter from O'Herlihy he had received many months earlier which promised America would liberate the Philippines. O'Herlihy decides in Peck's favor and soon Peck is on board a battleship, amid a great invasion fleet, as Americans go ashore at Leyte. To Peck, he is fullfilling his promise of "I shall return," a phrase he refused to change to "*We* shall return." (This, of course, is based on fact. When Filipino leader Carlos Romulo was asked about the phrase, he agreed with MacArthur, stating: "America has let us down and won't be trusted. But the people still have confidence in MacArthur. If *he* says *he* is coming back, he will be believed . . . . They knew his word was his bond.") Peck comes ashore while the beaches are still under fire, wading through the water while commenting to those around him that the world is about to realize that "I can't walk on water." Peck duplicates MacArthur's stirring rallying cry to the Filipino guerrillas, broadcasting from the beach at Leyte: "People of the Philippines: I have returned. By the grace of Almighty God, our forces stand again on Philippine soil—soil consecrated in the blood of our two peoples . . . . Rally to me. Let the indomitable spirit of Bataan and Corregidor lead on. As the lines of battle roll forward to bring you within the zone of operations, rise and strike. Strike at every favorable opportunity! For your homes and hearths, strike! In the name of your sacred dead, strike! Let no heart be faint. Let every arm be steeled. The guidance of Divine God points the way. Follow in His name to the Holy Grail of righteous victory." Peck is later shown entering a prisoner-of-war camp and being greeted as a savior by the starved survivors. He finds some of his old comrades from Bataan and Corregidor and embraces them emotionally, these being some of the most moving scenes in the film. Soon Peck is accepting the Japanese surrender on board the battleship *Missouri*, warning that if the world does not find a way to solve its disputes, it faces Armageddon. Peck then becomes the military governor of a ruined Japan but through his enlightened policies he quickly rebuilds the nation, its economy, and national spirit. Then the Korean war breaks out and Peck conducts a brilliant retreat, saving countless American troops from capture. He retaliates against the communist forces with a surprise flanking movement, landing forces at Inchon and bagging whole North Korean armies. He chases the enemy to the Chinese border at the Yalu River but is ordered by President Truman, played by Flanders, to stop at the Yalu. Peck is told that, to prevent the enemy from crossing back into Korea, he can bomb the southern half of the Yalu bridges. "In all my days as a soldier," Peck rages, "I have never learned how to blow up half a bridge!" Not only does Peck order the complete bridges bombed but states publicly that China is the culprit behind the South Korean invasion and should be attacked before it unleashes its millions of troops into Korea. When the Chinese do attack, Peck rails against Washington and urges Nationalist Chinese troops be sent into China to attack the heart of communism. He defies Flanders and the President removes Peck from his command. He returns home a great hero, makes a farewell speech, the famous "old soldier" address, to Congress and retires. This brings the story full circle back to Peck's final speech at West Point where he says goodbye to the Corps. MACARTHUR is an enormous undertaking, a subject much too big to encompass in a single film and so the slices of MacArthur's life appear sometimes disjointed. But Peck is memorable and believable in one of his best parts, capturing the general's eccentricities, vanities, and heroism. The film lacks the panache of PATTON but presents a more introspective look at one of this century's most celebrated warriors. Critics were reluctant to hail this film as above average but Peck's forceful approach and Sargent's honest effort to encompass an unwieldy story compelled many to later acknowledge the film as a superior production. Both O'Herlihy and Flanders as presidents Roosevelt and Truman overact to the point of becoming caricatures.

p, Frank McCarthy; d, Joseph Sargent; w, Hal Barwood, Matthew Robbins; ph, Mario Tosi (Panavision, Technicolor); m, Jerry Goldsmith; ed, George Jay Nicholson; prod d, John J. Lloyd; set d, Hal Gausman; spec eff, Albert Whitlock; stunts, Joe Canutt; makeup, Jim McCoy, Frank McCoy.

Biography/War Cas. (PR:A MPAA:PG)

MACBETH** (1948) 106m Mercury/REP bw

Orson Welles *(Macbeth)*, Jeanette Nolan *(Lady Macbeth)*, Dan O'Herlihy *(Macduff)*, Roddy McDowall *(Malcolm)*, Edgar Barrier *(Banquo)*, Alan Napier *(A Holy Father)*, Erskine Sanford *(Duncan)*, John Dierkes *(Ross)*, Keene Curtis *(Lennox)*, Peggy Webber *(Lady Macduff)*, Lionel Braham *(Siward)*, Archie Heugly *(Young Siward)*, Christopher Welles *(Macduff Child)*, Morgan Farley *(Doctor)*, Lurene Tuttle *(Gentlewoman)*, Brainerd Duffield *(1st Murderer)*, William Alland *(2nd Murderer)*, George Chirello *(Seyton)*, Gus Schilling *(A Porter)*, Duffield, Tuttle, Webber *(The Three)*, Jerry Farber *(Fleance)*, Charles Lederer *(Witch)*.

Welles' MACBETH, as opposed to Roman Polanski's version, chose to emphasize the dark, dour moods of the Scottish countryside and Welles thought he had a winner here but he didn't. Shot in 23 days during the summer of 1947, it's a melange of styles with cardboard sets and scenery that only barely manages to escape the furious chewing of the actors. Welles took considerable license with the original text and gave himself a screenplay credit, which should have William Shakespeare turning, nay *spinning*, in his grave. Whereas the oblique camera angles worked well in CITIZEN KANE because Welles was creating his own universe, here they serve to do little more that distract. There was an attempt at an ersatz Scottish accent on most of the actors' parts and it lay like silly putty on the ear. Would that there might be more to recommend this retelling of the famous story of a thane who falls prey to his own vanity under the prodding of women and decides to murder in order to secure his kingdom. It is, however, such a personalized film (just as Olivier personalized his HAMLET to far greater plaudits) that we lose sight of the original tragedy by the Bard and we are nothing more than bored. McDowall, still a young lad, is okay and so is Napier. The second murderer may be of more than passing interest, as he is portrayed by the man who walked all through CITIZEN KANE trying to uncover the secret of "Rosebud,"William Alland, who later went into the production business and was responsible for such films as THE CREATURE FROM THE BLACK LAGOON (1954). In a small role, you'll also note Keene Curtis, who later shaved his head to play Daddy Warbucks in the stage version of "Annie." Despite having some fine support, Welles totally dominates the film, both on screen and off, and more's the pity. Nolan does her "Out Out, damned spot," but it sounds more like she's inviting the dog to do his business on the lawn. Welles playing Shakespeare is like asking Brando to play Neil Simon; no one wins. Originally released at 106 minutes, the film was later edited down to 89 minutes.

p, Orson Welles; d, Welles, William Alland (dialog director); w, Welles (based on the play by William Shakespeare); ph, John L. Russell, William Bradford; m, Jacques Ibert; ed, Louis Lindsay; md, Efrem Kurtz; art d, Fred Ritter; set d, John McCarthy, Jr., James Redd; cos, Welles, Fred Ritter, Adele Palmer; spec eff, Howard and Theodore Lydecker; makeup, Bob Mark.

Drama Cas. (PR:A MPAA:NR)

MACBETH 1/2** (1963) 107m Grand Prize Films/Prominent c

Maurice Evans *(Macbeth)*, Judith Anderson *(Lady Macbeth)*, Michael Hordern *(Banquo)*, Ian Bannen *(Macduff)*, Felix Aylmer *(Doctor)*, Malcolm Keen *(Duncan)*, Megs Jenkins *(Gentlewoman)*, Jeremy Brett *(Malcolm)*, Barry Warren *(Donalbain)*, William Hutt *(Ross)*, Charles Carson *(Caithness)*, Trader Faulkner *(Seyton)*, George Rose *(Porter)*, Valerie Taylor *(1st Witch)*, Anita Sharp Bolster *(2nd Witch)*, April Olrich *(3rd Witch)*, Brewster Mason *(Angus)*, Simon Lack *(Menteith)*, Scot Finch *(Fleance)*, Robert Brown *(Bloody Sergeant)*, Michael Ripper *(1st Murderer)*, Douglas Wilmer *(2nd Murderer)*.

Originally released in 1960 as an 80-minute "Hallmark Hall of Fame" broadcast on NBC television, this film is a faithful adaptation of Shakespeare's classic play. Evans is masterful as Macbeth, whose wife, Anderson, urges him to murder his way to the throne. The movie was filmed on location in Scotland.

p, Phil C. Samuel; d, George Schaefer; w, Schaefer, Anthony Squire (based on the play by William Shakespeare); ph, F. A. Young (Technicolor); m, Richard Addinsell; ed, Ralph Kemplen; art d, Edward Carrick; md, Muir Mathieson; cos, Beatrice Dawson; makeup, Bob Lawrence.

Drama   **(PR:A   MPAA:NR)**

MACBETH*1/2   (1971, Brit.) 140m Playboy/COL c

Jon Finch (Macbeth), Francesca Annis (Lady Macbeth), Martin Shaw (Banquo), Nicholas Selby (Duncan), John Stride (Ross), Stephan Chase (Malcolm), Paul Shelley (Donalbain), Terence Bayler (Macduff), Andrew Laurence (Lennox), Frank Wylie (Mentieth), Bernard Archard (Angus), Bruce Purchase (Caithness), Keith Chegwin (Fleance), Noel Davis (Seyton), Noelle Rimmington (Young Witch), Maisie Farquhar (Blind Witch), Vic Abbott (Cawdor), Elsie Taylor (1st Witch), Bill Drysdale (1st King's Groom), Roy Jones (2nd King's Groom), Patricia Mason (Gentlewoman), Ian Hogg (1st Minor Thane), Geoffrey Reed (2nd Minor Thane), Nigel Ashton (3rd Minor Thane), Mark Dignam (Macduff's Son), Diane Fletcher (Lady Macduff), Richard Pearson (Doctor), Sydney Bromley (Porter), William Hobbs (Young Seyward), Alf Joint (Old Seyward), Michael Balfour, Andrew McCulloch (Murderers), Howard Lang, David Ellison (Old Soldiers), Terence Mountain (Soldier), Paul Hennen (Boy Apprentice), Beth Owen, Maxine Skelton, Janie Kells, Olga Anthony, Roy Desmond, Pam Foster, John Gordon, Barbara Grimes, Aud Johansen, Dickie Martyn, Christina Paul, Don Vernon, Anna Willoughby (Dancers).

Roman Polanski's graphically violent version of the classical Shakespeare play casts Finch and Annis as the murderously obsessed couple in debt to witchcraft and prophesies. Polanski's first film after the murder of his wife Sharon Tate, MACBETH may or may not be related to the brutality of the much-publicized slayings. In any case, this version, if not the best Shakespearean adaptation, is certainly the most faithful to the original time reference. The vulgarity and gore that is seen on the screen is not exploitative or irresponsible, but a faithful translation of the play without being dictated by conventional theatrical techniques. While Annis' nude sleepwalking scene has been criticized as a result of Playboy Enterprise's involvement (in fact the script was written before Playboy agreed to produce the film), it is true to the times. The project was originally offered to Allied Artists, then to Universal, but both deals fell through. Hugh Hefner, who was anxious to get into film, felt this would be the perfect vehicle for the growing Playboy Enterprises. It turned out to be his first major failure instead. Polanski had originally intended to cast Tuesday Weld in the part of Lady Macbeth, but she declined after learning about the nude scene. Photographed in Wales during incessant downpours and enveloping fog, the picture was completed way behind schedule and lost about $3.5 million dollars. The orginal cut received an "X" rating.

p, Andrew Braunsberg, Roman Polanski; d, Polanski; w, Polanski, Kenneth Tynan (based on the play by William Shakespeare); ph, Gilbert Taylor (Todd AO 35, Technicolor); m, The Third Ear Band; ed, Alastair McIntyre; prod d, Wilfred Shingleton; art d, Fred Carter; set d, Bryan Graves; cos, Anthony Mendleson; spec eff, Ted Samuels; ch, Sally Gilpin.

Drama   **(PR:O   MPAA:R)**

MACDONALD OF THE CANADIAN MOUNTIES
                                          (SEE: PONY SOLDIER, 1951)

MACHETE*   (1958) 75m UA bw

Mari Blanchard (Jean), Albert Dekker (Don Luis Montoya), Juano Hernandez (Bernardo), Carlos Rivas (Carlos), Lee Van Cleef (Miguel), Ruth Cains (Rita).

This boring film stars Blanchard as the evil wife of sugar cane plantation owner Dekker. She sets her romantic sights on foreman Rivas, whom Dekker raised from birth. Since both men respect each other, the solution is for Blanchard to die in the convenient field fire at the climax of the movie, shot on location in Puerto Rico.

p&d, Kurt Neumann; w, Carroll Young, Neumann; ph, Karl Struss; m, Paul Sawtell, Bert Shefter; ed, Jodie Copelan.

Drama   **(PR:A   MPAA:NR)**

MACHINE GUN KELLY*1/2   (1958) 84m El Monte Productions/AIP bw

Charles Bronson (Machine Gun Kelly), Susan Cabot (Flo), Morey Amsterdam (Fandango), Jack Lambert (Howard), Wally Campo (Maize), Bob Griffin (Vito), Barboura Morris (Lynn), Richard Devon (Apple), Ted Thorpe (Teddy), Mitzi McCall (Harriet), Frank de Kova (Harry), Shirley Falls (Martha), Connie Gilchrist (Ma), Mike Fox (Clinton), Larry Thor (Drummond), George Archambeault (Frank), Jay Sayer (Philip Ashton).

This was typical of the gangster films made in the 1950s which capitalized on infamous 1930s gangsters, using the formulas found in such potboilers as THE RISE AND FALL OF LEGS DIAMOND, BABY FACE NELSON, and PORTRAIT OF A MOBSTER (about Dutch Shultz). Bronson is aptly cast as the phlegmatic Kelly, a bootlegger put out of business at the end of Prohibition, one who turns to bank robbing. His thrill-seeking moll, Cabot, insists Bronson pull a big caper so they can retire to a life of ease. To that end, Bronson plans the kidnaping of an industrialist's daughter but things go sour when Bronson gets jealous of henchman Amsterdam who makes a play for Cabot. He kicks Amsterdam out of the mob and he, Amsterdam, informs the police of Bronson's whereabouts. The feared gangster is captured and sent to prison for life. Of course, this being a Roger Corman film, none of the film is based upon the real facts which would have proved to be much more interesting. Kelly was known among friends as "Popgun Kelly," his outside reputation promoted by his scheming, avaricious wife Kathryn, the real brains and

guts behind the Kelly kidnaping gang. This was Bronson's first film as a star at age 37; it would typecast him as a brooding, cold-blooded killer, a character he would exploit to the hilt in DEATH WISH and its idiotic sequels.

p&d, Roger Corman; w, R. Wright Campbell; ph, Floyd Crosby; m, Gerald Fried; ed, Ronald Sinclair; art d, Daniel Haller; set d, Harry Reif; cos, Margo Corso; makeup, Dave Newell.

Crime Drama   **(PR:C-O   MPAA:NR)**

MACHINE GUN MAMA zero   (1944) 61m PRC bw

Armida (Nita Cordova), El Brendel (Ollie Swenson), Wallace Ford (John O'Reilly), Jack La Rue (Jose), Luis Alberni (Ignacio), Ariel Heath (The Blonde), Julian Rivero (Alberto Cordova), Eumenio Blance (First Detective), Anthony Warde (Carlos).

Dull, technically inept programmer about two hayseeds, Ford and Brendel, who sell an elephant to a traveling carnival and suddenly become trapped in a series of harrowing adventures involving the big beast.

p, Jack Schwarz; d, Harold Young, w, Sam Neuman; ph, Gus Peterson; m, Mort Glickman, David Chudnow; ed, Robert O. Crandall; md, Glickman, Chudnow; art d, Frank Sylos; m/l, Sam Neuman, Michael Breen.

Drama   **(PR:A   MPAA:NR)**

MACHINE GUN McCAIN**
                    (1970, Ital.) 94m Euroatlantica/COL c (GLI INTOCCABILI)

John Cassavetes (Hank McCain), Britt Ekland (Irene Tucker), Peter Falk (Charlie Adamo), Gabriele Ferzetti (Don Francesco DeMarco), Salvo Randone (Don Salvatore), Pierluigi Apra (Jack McCain), Gena Rowlands (Rosemary Scott), Florinda Bolkan (Joni Adamo), Margherita Guzzinati (Margaret DeMarco), Stephen Zacharias (Abe Stilberman), Luigi Pistilli (Duke Mazzanga), Jim Morrison (Joby Cuda), Claudio Biava (Barclay), Tony Kendall (Pete Zacari), Ermanno Consolazione (Gennarino Esposito), Annabella Andreoli (Assunta Esposito), Val Avery (Chuck Regan), Dennis Sallas (Fred Tecosky), Jack Ackerman (Britten), Billy Lee (Pepe).

This little gangster film features Cassavetes as a hardened criminal released from prison after twelve years thanks to the political influence of Falk, a Mafia chieftain. Cassavetes' son Apra gets his old man to help him in the robbery of a small Las Vegas casino on behalf of Falk's West Coast crime empire. When Falk learns that the casino is owned by some East Coast mobsters he calls off the robbery. Cassavetes mets Ekland and the two are hastily married. Apra is killed by some of Falk's goons and the newlyweds take to bombing various Las Vegas casinos. After disguising himself as a fireman, Cassavetes pulls off a two-million-dollar robbery from a hotel safe and the East Coast mobsters want him dead. Falk is killed and Cassavetes's ex-love-crime partner Rowlands (who was Cassavetes' real-life wife) helps her old amour and his new wife escape. Rather than tell all to the Mob, Rowlands commits suicide. The film climaxes with Ekland shot en route to a rendezvous with her man and Cassavetes dying in a hail of machine-gun fire. This cheap little Italian feature was made originally in 1968. Its two-lovers-on-the-run theme and death-by-machine-gun sequence give it more than a striking resemblance to BONNIE AND CLYDE, which undoubtedly was no accident. This was the sort of junk film in which Cassavetes continually appeared in order to finance his own artistic endeavors, such as FACES (1968).

p, Marco Vicario, Bino Cicogna; d, Giuliano Montaldo; w, Montaldo, Mino Roli (based on a story by Roli from the novel Candyleg by Ovid Demaris, English adaptation by Israel Horovitz); ph, Erico Menczer (Techniscope, Technicolor); m, Ennio Morricone; ed, Franco Fraticelli; art d, Flavio Mogherini; set d, Roberto Veloccia; cos, Enrico Sabbatini; m/l, "The Ballad of Hank McCain," Morricone, Audrey Nohra (sung by Jackie Lynton); makeup, Michele Trimarchi.

Crime   **(PR:O   MPAA:GP)**

MACHISMO—40 GRAVES FOR 40 GUNS*1/2
                    (1970) 95m PI/Boxoffice International c (AKA: 40 GRAVES FOR 40 GUNS)

Robert Padilla (Hidalgo), Dirk Peno (Lopez), Frederico Gomez (Vicente), Louis Ojena (Fernandez), Leslie York (Ruby), Rita Rogers (Lil), Stanley Adams (Granger), Sue Bernard (Julie), Bruce Gordon (Burt), Nancy Caroline (Louise), Royal Dano (Zach), Chuey Franco (Garcia), Jose Jasd (Rodriquez), Liberty Angelo (Dugan), Mike Robelo (Capt. Ramirez), Patti Heider (Phyllis), Noble "Kid" Chissell (Doc Peters), Lilyan Chauvin (Kate), Sean Kenney (Wichita), Joseph Tornatore (Jake), Gary Kent (Jim Harris), James Lemp (Ed Harris), Gary Graver (Tim Harris), Randy Starr (Roper), Hank Adams, Vincent Barbi, Buckalew, Bartlett Carson, Thomas Duran, Frisco Estes, Silas Everett, Bob Feiner, Michael Ford, Robert Gerald, Leonard Goodman, Lou Joffred, Walter Kray, Jeff Latham, Ray Lester, Steve McKinney, Biff Maynard, Harry Novak, Richard Paradise, David Schneider, Duke Wilmoth, William Wilson, Terry Woolman (The Harris Gang).

The Harris Gang is a notorious group of outlaws led by brothers Kent, Lemp, and Graver. They have attacked the Mexican town of Tecate, murdering and raping its citizens and stealing a pure gold cross from a church. Robelo, the head of the Federales, knows that only some equally ruthless outlaws would be capable of bringing in the gang. He springs Padilla from prison with the promise of a pardon if he can lead a group of men to bring back the Harrises and the cross. The newly formed posse heads north to the town of Gila Bend, where the outlaws have holed up. Gomez, a younger member of the band, is sent into town to scout out the area, only to be insulted and abused by the racists who live there. After bedding down with a few local women, one Mexican (Ojena) discovers the gold cross in a barmaid's bedroom. He steals the cross and it is placed in the town square to lure the Harris gang into an ambush. A bloody battle ensues and a number of the white outlaws are severely wounded. The Mexicans remain in the town, protecting a wounded member of their band as well as the remaining townsfolk. Meanwhile, the Harris gang recoups in a nearby valley. Rogers, the late Kent's girl friend, tells the gang she knows who the attackers are. After providing the information she rejects the sexual overtures of Kenney, the new leader. Angered, he rapes her and the remaining members all have their way with her. The next morning the final battle begins with almost all being killed. Adams, a local racist, decides that the heroic Mexicans aren't worth time or effort enough for a decent funeral and dumps their bodies in a ditch. Though extremely violent, the film is directed with much energy. The technique is not what it could be but what the film lacks in artistic form it makes up in vigor. Padilla carries the film as the Mexican *bandido* in this unusual mixture of THE WILD BUNCH and THE MAGNIFICENT SEVEN. Chuey Franco sings the songs.

p, Ronald V. Garcia; d, Paul Hunt; w, Garcia, Hunt; ph, Richmond Aguilar (Eastmancolor); additional ph, Garcia; m, Jack Preisner; ed, Hunt, Garcia, Mike Bennett; md, Preisner; art d, Rahn Vickery, Ben Adams; set d, Hank Adams, Ben Adams; cos, Sherri Tilley; spec eff, Harry Woolman; makeup, Dennis Marsh, Gordon Freed; stunts ch, Randy Starr, Joseph Tornatore.

Western **(PR:O MPAA:R)**

MACHISTE AGAINST THE CZAR
(SEE: ATLAS AGAINST THE CZAR, 1964, Ital.)

MACISTE NELLA TERRA DEI CICLOPI
(SEE: ATLAS AGAINST THE CZAR, 1964, Ital.)

MACHO CALLAHAN* (1970) 99m Felicidad/AE c

David Janssen *(Diego "Macho" Callahan)*, Jean Seberg *(Alexandra Mountford)*, Lee J. Cobb *(Duffy)*, James Booth *("King Harry" Wheeler)*, Pedro Armendariz, Jr. *(Juan Fernandez)*, David Carradine *(Col. David Mountford)*, Bo Hopkins *(Yancy)*, Richard Anderson *(Senior Officer)*, Diane Ladd *(Girl)*, Matt Clark *(Jailer)*, Richard Evans *(Mulvey)*, Robert Morgan *(McIntyre)*, Anne Revere *(Crystal)*, James Gammon *(Cowboy)*, Ron Soble *(2nd Cowboy)*, Diana Iverson *(2nd Girl)*, Curt Conway *(Judge)*, Robert Dowdell *(Blind Man)*, Cyril Delevanti, William Bryant, Bucklind Beery, Mike Masters.

A pretty vile western starring Janssen as a bitter, revenge-seeking Union soldier who escapes from prison to find Cobb, the rotten crook who put him there. Janssen sets himself up as a saloonkeeper in a small town and waits for Cobb to turn up. There he runs across one-armed Confederate Carradine who has just arrived in town and tried to steal a few bottles of Janssen's champagne. Unfortunately, Janssen has seen Cobb arrive on the same stage as Carradine and is in an irritable mood, so he kills the Confederate thief. This sends Carradine's wife Seberg into a tailspin. First she hates Janssen and hires Cobb to help her track him down, then she changes her mind and decides she loves him and tries to stop the assassins she has hired from doing their job. Meanshile, Janssen is after Cobb and soon they are all chasing their tails. Bloody, ludicrous, and inane.

p, Bernard L. Kowalski, Martin C. Schute; d, Kowalski; w, Clifford Newton Gould (based on a story by Richard Carr); ph, Gerald Fisher (Panavision, Movielab); m, Pat Williams; ed, Frank Mazzola, Fabian Tordjinann, Jerry Taylor; prod d, Ted Marshall; art d, Jose Rodriguez Granada; set d, Ernesto Carrasco; cos, Barbara Rosenquest.

Western **(PR:O MPAA:R)**

MACK, THE*1/2 (1973) 110m Cinerama c

Max Julien *(Goldie)*, Don Gordon *(Hank)*, Richard Pryor *(Slim)*, Carol Speed *(Lulu)*, Roger E. Mosley *(Olinga)*, Dick Williams *(Pretty Tony)*, William C. Watson *(Jed)*, George Murdock *(Fatman)*, Juanita Moore *(Mother)*, Paul Harris *(Blind Man)*, Kai Hernandez *(Chico)*, Annazette Chase *(China Doll)*, Junero Jennings *(Baltimore Bob)*, Lee Duncan *(Sgt. Duncan)*, Stu Gilliam *(Announcer)*, Sandra Brown *(Diane)*, Christopher Brooks *(Jesus Christ)*, Fritz Ford *(Desk Sergeant)*, John Vick *(Hotel Trick)*, Norma McClure *(Big Woman)*, David Mauro *(Laughing David)*, Allen Van, Willie Redman, Frank Ward, Ted Ward, Willie Ward, Andrew Ward, Roosevelt Taylor, Jay Payton, Terrible Tom, Bill Barnes, Jack Hunter.

Routine black exploitation violence starring Julien as a pimp (or "mack") whose rise to power—and the trouble he has keeping it—form the basis of this movie. While gathering all the materials necessary to get to the top rung of the ladder in prostitution (good-looking women, fancy cars) Julien must fight off rival "macks," a few crooked detectives (evil white men, of course), and the kingpin of drug dealers (an even more evil white man). Look for Richard Pryor as Julien's buddy. All right for fans of such stuff.

p, Harvey Bernhard; d, Michael Campus; w, Robert J. Poole; ph, Ralph Woolsey (CFI Color); m, Willie Hutch; ed, Frank C. Decot.

Crime **Cas.** **(PR:O MPAA:R)**

MACKENNA'S GOLD1/2** (1969) 128m Highroad/COL c

Gregory Peck *(Mackenna)*, Omar Sharif *(Colorado)*, Telly Savalas *(Sgt. Tibbs)*, Camilla Sparv *(Inga)*, Keenan Wynn *(Sanchez)*, Julie Newmar *(Heshke)*, Ted Cassidy *(Hachita)*, Lee J. Cobb *(The Editor)*, Raymond Massey *(The Preacher)*, Burgess Meredith *(The Storekeeper)*, Anthony Quayle *(Older Englishman)*, Edward G. Robinson *(Old Adams)*, Eli Wallach *(Ben Baker)*, Eduardo Ciannelli *(Prairie Dog)*, Richard "Dick" Peabody *(Avila)*, Rudy Diaz *(Besh)*, Robert Phillips *(Monkey)*, Shelly Morrison *(The Pima Squaw)*, J. Robert Porter *(Young Englishman)*, John Garfield, Jr. *(Adams Boy)*, Pepe Callahan *(Laguna)*, Madeleine Taylor Holmes *(Old Apache Woman)*, Duke Hobbie *(Lieutenant)*, Trevor Bardette *(Old Man)*, Victor Jory *(Narrator)*.

Overlong, overblown, and badly scripted western starring Peck as a sheriff who finds himself entrusted with a map (a dying Indian gave it to him) detailing the location of a mythical valley of gold. After memorizing and burning the map, Peck finds himself the target of every fortune seeker in the territory (they pop up in a seemingly endless parade of pointless guest shots including Massey, Meredith, Cobb, Robinson, Wallach, Wynn...). Peck's main rival, Sharif (a man who does not belong in westerns) eventually confronts him at the mouth of the canyon which leads to the gold, but a convenient avalanche closes off the entrance, leaving the two treasure hunters a bag of gold between them. Beautiful scenery and a surprisingly good score from Quincy Jones (composer Tiomkin was a co-producer) don't help sort out this mess.

p, Carl Foreman, Dimitri Tiomkin; d, J. Lee Thompson; w, Foreman (based on the novel by Will Henry); ph, Joseph MacDonald (Super Panavision, Technicolor); m, Quincy Jones; ed, Bill Lenny; prod d, Geoffrey Drake; art d, Drake, Gary Odell; set d, Alfred E. Spencer; cos, Norma Koch; spec eff, Drake, John Mackey, Bob Cuff, Willis Cook, Larry Butler; m/l, "Old Turkey Buzzard," Jones, Freddie Douglas (sung by Jose Feliciano); stunts, Buzz Henry.

Western **Cas.** **(PR:C MPAA:M)**

MACKINTOSH & T.J.** (1975) 96m Penland c

Roy Rogers *(Mackintosh)*, Clay O'Brien *(T.J.)*, Billy Green Bush *(Luke)*, Andrew Robinson *(Coley Phipps)*, Joan Hackett *(Maggie)*, James Hampton *(Cotton)*, Dennis Fimple *(Schuster)*, Luke Askew *(Cal)*, Larry Mahan, Walter Barnes, Edith Atwater, Ted Gehring, Jim Harrell, Dean Smith, Ron Hay, Guich Koock, Autry Ward, Steve Ward, Troy Ward.

Rogers came out of nearly twenty-five years of retirement—his last film was SON OF PALEFACE (1952) and he also had a brief bit in ALIAS JESSE JAMES (1959)—to star in this quiet, understated, but somewhat maudlin western about a hard-working, religious old cowboy and his rebellious teenage son O'Brien. Nothing special, except for a few questionable moments where O'Brien deals with a homosexual who makes a pass at him, and Robinson as a peeping-Tom sex maniac who, along with his redneck buddies Hampton and Fimple, tries to pin a murder rap on Rogers.

p, Tim Penland; d, Marvin J. Chomsky; w, Paul Savage; ph, Terry Mead (Technicolor); ed, Howard Smith; art d, Alan Smith; m/l, Waylon Jennings (performed by Jennings).

Western/Drama **(PR:C-O MPAA:PG)**

MACKINTOSH MAN, THE1/2** (1973, Brit.) 98m WB c

Paul Newman *(Rearden)*, Dominique Sanda *(Mrs. Smith)*, James Mason *(Sir George Wheeler)*, Harry Andrews *(Mackintosh)*, Ian Bannen *(Slade)*, Michael Hordern *(Brown)*, Nigel Patrick *(Soames-Trevelyan)*, Peter Vaughan *(Brunskill)*, Roland Culver *(Judge)*, Percy Herbert *(Taafe)*, Robert Lang *(Jack Summers)*, Jenny Runacre *(Gerda)*, John Bindon *(Buster)*, Hugh Manning *(Prosecutor)*, Wolfe Morris *(Malta Police Commissioner)*, Noel Purcell *(O'Donovan)*, Donald Webster *(Jervis)*, Keith Bell *(Palmer)*, Niall MacGinnis *(Warder)*, Leo Genn *(Rollins)*, Michael Poole *(Mr. Boyd)*, Eric Mason *(Postman)*, Ronald Clark *(Attendant)*, Antony Vicars *(Salesman)*, Dinny Powell *(Young)*, Douglas Robinson *(Danahoe)*, Jack Cooper *(1st Motorcyclist)*, Marc Boyle *(2nd Motorcyclist)*.

Surprisingly routine espionage film considering the talents of Huston as director and Hill as screenwriter. Newman stars as a man thrown into a world of danger, intrigue, and confusion by the mysterious Andrews, who furnishes him with a false identity as a thief and sends him on a daring diamond robbery. Due to an anonymous tip-off, Newman is arrested and sent to a top-security jail where he meets convicted Russian spy Patrick. Together they join in an escape organized by a group called the Scarperers and, after they reach the other side of the wall, they are drugged and sent to Ireland. The escape, of course, was organized by Andrews in the hope that Newman would be able to infiltrate the Scarperers and expose their leader, Mason (a powerful politician), as a criminal mastermind. Finding himself in an increasingly dangerous position, Newman escapes the Scarperers and contacts Andrews' daughter, Sanda, who informs him that her father has been seriously injured in a car crash. Deciding to continue the mission, Newman and Sanda board Mason's yacht to rescue Patrick. Soon after their arrival, Sanda is captured and drugged by Mason. Newman escapes and persuades the police to search the politician's boat, but Mason is able to bluff his way out of it. Newman returns alone and seeks a confrontation with Mason. Mason, however, holds Sanda and Patrick at gunpoint in a nearby church and forces Newman to agree to abandon his mission if all are allowed to go their separate ways. Newman reluctantly agrees, and as Patrick and Mason prepare to leave, Sanda draws a gun and kills them both, leaving Newman and the audience pretty confused at the fadeout. Huston has stated that Hill's script was vague and confusing, and that he himself participated in the project just to make some money. Apparently Huston, Newman, and producer Foreman debated on just how to end the film right up until the final day of shooting. THE MACKINTOSH MAN is by no means a bad film (as usual, even halfhearted direction by Huston is more professional than interested direction by most others) but it should have been better considering the names involved.

p, John Foreman; d, John Huston; w, Walter Hill (based on the novel *The Freedom Trap* by Desmond Bagley); ph, Oswald Morris (Technicolor); m, Maurice Jarre; ed, Russell Lloyd; prod d, Terry Marsh; art, d, Alan Tomkins; set d, Peter James.

Spy Drama **Cas.** **(PR:C MPAA:PG)**

MACOMBER AFFAIR, THE*1/2** (1947) 89m UA bw

Gregory Peck *(Robert Wilson)*, Robert Preston *(Francis Macomber)*, Joan Bennett *(Margaret Macomber)*, Reginald Denny *(Capt. Smollet)*, Carl Harbord *(Coroner)*, Earl Smith *(Kongoni)*, Jean Gillie *(Aimee)*, Vernon Downing *(Reporter Logan)*, Frederic Worlock *(Clerk)*, Hassan Said *(Abdullah)*, Martin Wilkins *(Bartender)*, Darby Jones *(Masai Warrior)*.

The tough, uncompromising Hemingway story, "The Short Happy Life of Francis Macomber" (a title too long for any marquee) was brought to the screen with vitality and invention by the eccentric and talented Zoltan Korda, brother of mogul Alexander, and it was surprisingly effective. Peck, Preston, and Bennett had more to do with that than the script. Preston is a wealthy playboy who, with wife Bennett at his side, hires a great white hunter, Peck, to guide them to the African hunting grounds. Bennett has little or no respect for Preston, knowing he is a weak-willed character with no courage at all, and she makes a play for Peck, whose honor will not permit him to dally with a married lady. It's a *menage a trois* without Peck's participation. At first, Preston shows his yellow streak on the dangerous safari, but he slowly emerges as a person discovering his manhood and courage. In a final hunt, he refuses to run from a charging animal but, before he can bring it down, he is shot by Bennett who claims she was trying to save his life. She is later tried for murder and acquitted, the jury deciding that her hapless spouse died from an accident. After her acquittal, Peck admits that he was in love with her but no longer has interest in her. It's left like that, ambiguous. Peck later stated that everyone in the production had a hand in adjusting the story to a film that would be acceptable to the censor. Hemingway, who had been paid $80,000 for the story, refused to help, ignoring cables for ideas from the studio. The film, except for background footage shot in Africa, was shot mostly on Hollywood sound stages. The script, though considerably changed from the original story, still retains the prosaic and direct prose style Hemingway made so famous. The hunting scenes were shot in the northern part of Baja, California. The cast and crew amused themselves by importing a marimba band to the campsite and later asked the band to come to Hollywood for a party but the band leader reported they could not play for their filmmaking friends as most of his players were wanted on murder charges in a recent shootout and had fled to the mountains. Korda was particularly vexed by producer Bogeaus who kept bursting onto the set in the middle of rehearsals to loudly announce a new title for the film. Finally, Bogeaus interrupted once too often, shouting: "I've got it, I've got it—We'll call it 'Congo!'" The volatile Korda took out a penknife and held it to Bogeaus' midsection, telling him that if he ever came onto his set again he would cut out his liver. The producer steered clear of the set thereafter. Many bizarre events and ideas clung to this strange but fascinating little film. One was an odd-looking machine created in the form of a charging buffalo which was to be shot by Preston and collapse at his feet just before striking him. The contraption cost $30,000 and never seemed to work right. It was made of rubber and hair and was driven by pistons. Writer Aldous Huxley appeared on the set one day while watching this strange machine and overhearing another conference on what to call the film. Suggested Huxley: "Why don't you call it 'The Rubba Buffalo'?"

p, Benedict Bogeaus, Casey Robinson; d, Zoltan Korda; w, Robinson, Seymour Bennett, Frank Arnold (based on the story "The Short Happy Life of Francis Macomber" by Ernest Hemingway); ph, O. H. Borradaile, John Wilcox, Fred Francis, Karl Struss; m, Miklos Rozsa; ed, James Smith, George Feld; md, Rozsa; art d, Erno Metzer; set d, Fred Widdowson; makeup, Otis Malcolm.

Adventure/Drama (PR:C MPAA:NR)

MACON COUNTY LINE** (1974) 87m AIP c

Alan Vint (*Chris Dixon*), Cheryl Waters (*Jenny*), Max Baer (*Deputy Reed Morgan*), Geoffrey Lewis (*Hamp*), Joan Blackman (*Carol Morgan*), Jesse Vint (*Wayne Dixon*), Sam Gilman (*Deputy Bill*), Timothy Scott (*Lon*), James Gammon (*Elisha*), Leif Garrett (*Luke*), Emile Meyer (*Gurney*), Doodles Weaver (*Augie*).

A Southern exploitation drama starring Baer (who also produced) as a redneck sheriff who assumes that outsiders Alan and Jesse Vint and their friend Waters are responsible for the murder of his wife Blackman. Baer sets out seeking revenge on the strangers, but in reality the killing was committed by Scott and Gammon. Eventually deputy Gilman learns the truth, but he is too late to prevent the inevitable disaster. RETURN TO MACON COUNTY, its sequel, soon followed.

p, Max Baer; d, Richard Compton; w, Baer, Compton (based on a story by Baer); ph, Daniel Lacambre (CFI color); m, Stu Phillips; ed, Tina Hirsch; art d, Roger Pancake; m/l, theme song, Bobbie Gentry (sung by Gentry).

Crime **Cas.** (PR:O MPAA:R)

MACUMBA LOVE* (1960) 86m UA c

Walter Reed (*Weils*), Ziva Rodann (*Venus de Viasa*), William Wellman, Jr. (*Sarah's Husband*), June Wilkinson (*Sarah*), Ruth de Souza (*Mama Rataloy*).

Fairly tedious programmer shot in Brazil starring Reed as a writer determined to unveil the evil rites of voodoo which he believes are responsible for a series of unsolved murders in the area. Much tribal dancing, garish photography, and bad acting, especially from *Playboy* "Playmate" June Wilkinson, who wanders around showing lots of cleavage. Directed and produced by actor Douglas Fowley, who played Doc Holliday in the popular "Wyatt Earp" TV series.

p&d, Douglas Fowley; w, Norman Graham (based on a story by Graham); ph, Rudolpho Lesey (Eastmancolor); m, Enrico Simonetti; m/l, Graham, Carlton S. Riggs, H. C. Donaldson; ch, Solano Trinidade.

Mystery (PR:A MPAA:NR)

MACUSHLA** (1937, Brit.) 59m FOX/Transatlantic bw

Pamela Wood (*Kathleen Muldoon*), Liam Gaffney (*Jim O'Grady*), Jimmy Mageean (*Pat Muldoon*), E. J. Kennedy (*Hugh Connolly*), Kitty Kirwan (*Bridget*), Brian Herbert (*Pat Rooney*), Edgar K. Bruce (*Dean McLaglen*), Max Adrian (*Kerry Muldoon*).

Policeman Gaffney meets and falls for Wood. It turns out that her brother and father (Adrian and Mageean) are nefarious characters operating a gunrunning and cattle smuggling outfit. After nearly killing a lawman, Adrian is forced to hide out in a cabin. The building catches fire in a battle between the law and the crooks, leaving Gaffney trapped by a fiery beam. However, his love's outlaw brother saves him, leaving him with Wood before taking off. The plot is simply one convention following another, but some realistic dialog gives this simplistic story a few added touches.

p, Victor M. Greene; d, Alex Bryce; w, David Evans (based on a story by Bryce); ph, Stanley Grant.

Drama (PR:A MPAA:NR)

MAD ABOUT MEN** (1954, Brit.) 90m GFD c

Glynis Johns (*Miranda/Caroline*), Anne Crawford (*Barbara*), Donald Sinden (*Jeff Saunders*), Margaret Rutherford (*Nurse Cary*), Dora Bryan (*Berengaria*), Nicholas Phipps (*Barclay Sutton*), Peter Martyn (*Ronald*), Noel Purcell (*Old Salt*), Joan Hickson (*Mrs. Forster*), Judith Furse (*Viola*), Irene Handl (*Mme. Blanche*), David Hurst (*Mantalini*), Martin Miller (*Dr. Fergus*), Deryck Guyler (*Editor*), Anthony Oliver (*Pawnbroker*), Harry Welchman (*Symes*), Meredith Edwards (*Police Constable*), Marianne Stone, Douglas Ives, George Woodbridge, Lawrence Ward, Dandy Nichols, Martin Boddey, Ken Richmond, Stringer Davis, Henry Longhurst, John Horsley.

Silly sequel to the equally silly MIRANDA, once again starring Johns as a mermaid who comes to the surface. This time she replaces a young schoolteacher who has gone on holiday and takes over her class (they have the same face, amazing!) in order to chase men.

p, Betty E. Box; d, Ralph Thomas; w, Peter Blackmore; ph, Ernest Steward (Technicolor); m, Benjamin Frankel; ed, Gerald Thomas.

Fantasy (PR:A MPAA:NR)

MAD ABOUT MONEY (SEE: HE LOVED AN ACTRESS, 1937, Brit.)

MAD ABOUT MUSIC*** (1938) 98m UNIV bw

Deanna Durbin (*Gloria Harkinson*), Herbert Marshall (*Richard Todd*), Arthur Treacher (*Tripps*), Gail Patrick (*Gwen Taylor*), William Frawley (*Dusty Rhodes*), Jackie Moran (*Tommy*), Helen Parrish (*Felice*), Marcia Mae Jones (*Olga*), Christian Rub (*Pierre*), Charles Peck (*Henry*), Elizabeth Risdon (*Louise Fusenot*), Nana Bryant (*Annette Fusenot*), Joan Tree (*Patricia*), Sid Grauman (*Himself*), Franklin Pangborn (*Hotel Manager*), Charles Judels (*Conductor*), Bert Roach (*Conductor*), Martha O'Driscoll (*Pretty Girl*), Cappy Barra's Harmonica Band, the Vienna Boys' Choir.

Charming Durbin vehicle (her third starring role) which sees the young singer as the daughter of vain and aging Hollywood actress Patrick. Durbin is sent to a Swiss boarding school by her mother so that Mom's public won't realize how old she's getting. Left abroad with no family, Durbin creates a fantasy father who is a world traveler and adventurer. When her doubting friends pressure her to produce this father, Durbin flies into a panic until she meets up with kindly British composer Marshall, who consents to play the role of her father and bail the overly imaginative girl out. Songs include: "I Love To Whistle" (sung by Durbin); "Chapel Bells," "Serenade To The Stars," "There Isn't A Day Goes By" (Harold Adamson, Jimmy McHugh). Remade in 1963 as THE TOY TIGER.

p, Joe Pasternak; d, Norman Taurog; w, Bruce Manning, Felix Jackson (based on a story by Marcella Burke, Frederick Kohner); ph, Joseph Valentine; ed, Philip Cahn.

Drama (PR:A MPAA:NR)

MAD ADVENTURES OF "RABBI" JACOB, THE
1974, Fr.(SEE: ADVENTURES OF RABBI JACOB, THE, 1973, Fr.)

MAD AT THE WORLD** (1955) 76m Filmakers bw

Frank Lovejoy (*Tom Lynn*), Keefe Brasselle (*Sam Bennett*), Cathy O'Donnell (*Anne Bennett*), Karen Sharpe (*Tess*), Stanley Clements (*Pete*), Paul Bryar (*Matt*), Paul Dobov (*Jamie*), James Delgado, Joseph Turkel, Sen. Estes Kefauver.

It's the seamy world of roving teenage punks that gets the quickie exploitation treatment in this minor trash number. After a prolog by the esteemed Sen. Kefauver, poor Brasselle goes through hell when his son is hit by a flying whiskey bottle. The infant is hospitalized on the verge of death and his angered father vows revenge. When the cops prove to be useless (as cops so often are in teenage punk films), Brasselle goes after the group of "trigger-happy teeners living for kicks!" (as the ads forewarned audiences). After catching up with the group of bad boys, Brasselle himself is in danger but the police finally get it together for a last minute rescue. Lawman Lovejoy overcomes earlier mishaps to capture the gang but it's all in vain, for the infant dies. Despite the downer ending the film is a pretty good exploitation film if watched with an eye for camp.

p, Collier Young; d&w, Harry Essex.

Teenage Exploitation (PR:C MPAA:NR)

MAD ATLANTIC, THE**½ (1967, Jap.) 103m Mifune/Toho bw (DOTO ICHIMAN KAIRI)

Toshiro Mifune, Makoto Sato, Mie Hama, Ryo Tamura, Tatsuya Mihashi, Tadao Nakamaru.

A drama built around a question of morality, as the captain of a Japanese fishing trawler is forced to decide between rescuing a fellow ship or hauling in an abundant catch. The film opens with the trawler returning from an unsuccessful outing. Unhappy with the output of this boat, the company that owns the trawler assigns one of its officials to supervise its next outing. At first the captain resents the newcomer but finally learns to respect him. But just as a huge school of fish is discovered and the nets lowered, a distress signal from a private yacht is picked up. The captain is then forced to choose between losing the nets and the big haul or letting the distress signal go unanswered.

p, Tomoyuki Tanaka, Koichi Sekizawa; d, Jun Fukuda; w, Hideo Ogawa, Shinichi Sekizawa; ph, Takao Saito (Tohoscope); m, Masaru Sato.

Drama (PR:O MPAA:NR)

MAD BOMBER, THE**

(1973) 91m Cinemation c (AKA: POLICE CONNECTION; DETECTIVE GERONIMO)

Vince Edwards (*Geronimo Minneli*), Chuck Connors (*William Dorn*), Neville Brand (*George Fromley*), Hank Brandt (*Blake*), Christina Hart (*Fromley's Victim*), Faith Quabius (*Martha*), Ilona Wilson (*Mrs. Fromley*), Nancy Honnold (*Anne Dorn*).

A bizarre crime film from Bert I. Gordon starring Edwards as the tough cop who must catch crazed rapist Brand (who watches pornographic footage of his wife to get himself in a frenzy) in order to find nutso bomber Connors, who blows up hospitals and schools with bombs he carries around in shopping bags. A must-see for Connors cultists.

p,d&w, Bert I. Gordon (based on a story by Marc Behm); ph, Gordon; m, Michel Mention; ed, Gene Ruggiero.

Crime   **Cas.**   **(PR:O MPAA:R)**

MAD CAGE, THE   (SEE: LA CAGE AUX FOLLES, 1978, Fr./Ital.)

MAD DOCTOR, THE** (1941) 90m PAR bw (GB: A DATE WITH DESTINY)

Basil Rathbone (*Dr. George Sebastien*), Ellen Drew (*Linda Boothe*), John Howard (*Gil Sawyer*), Barbara Allen [Vera Vague] (*Louise Watkins*), Ralph Morgan (*Dr. Charles Downer*), Martin Kosleck (*Maurice Gretz*), Kitty Kelly (*Winnie the House-keeper*), Hugh O'Connell (*Lawrence Watkin*), Hugh Sothern (*Hatch*), George Chandler (*Elevator Operator*), Douglas Kennedy (*Hotel Clerk*), Harry Hayden (*Ticket Agent*), Billy Benedict (*Copyboy*), Howard Mitchell, Charles McAvoy, Henry Victor.

Rathbone plays a Viennese psychiatrist who has come to New York City to continue his "hobby," which is marrying rich women and then making them disappear. He, along with his faithful assistant Kosleck, has managed to stay one step ahead of the law until they run into newspaper reporter Howard, who makes sure that their evil stops in the Big Apple.

p, George Arthur; d, Tim Whelan; w, Howard J. Green (based on a story by Green); ph, Ted Tetzlaff; ed, Archie Marshek.

Crime   **(PR:A MPAA:NR)**

MAD DOCTOR OF BLOOD ISLAND, THE*

(1969, Phil./U.S.) 86m Hemisphere c (AKA: BLOOD DOCTOR; TOMB OF THE LIVING DEAD)

John Ashley (*Bill Foster*), Angelique Pettyjohn [Heaven St. John] (*Sheila Willard*), Ronald Remy (*Dr. Lorca*), Alicia Alonso, Ronaldo Valdez, Tita Munoz, Tony Edmunds, Alfonso Carvajal, Bruno Punzalan, Edward Murphy, Johnny Long, Paquito Salcedo, Felisa Salcedo, Quiel Mendoza, Ricardo Hipolito, Cenon Gonzalez, Nadja.

Ashley's off to the mysterious Blood Island to investigate a story about a corpse with green blood. En route he meets a variety of people headed the same way, including the lovely Miss Pettyjohn, who's searching for her missing father. Once they arrive, they find the island under the control of the decidedly mad Remy, who's experimenting with a chlorophyll-based drug that is supposed to keep people young forever. Instead it creates living zombies with green blood that cause appropriate mayhem. After our heroes set Remy's laboratory ablaze, they leave the island believing the madman has been killed in the fire. But wait! He returns once more in a sequel film, BEAST OF BLOOD. This film was itself a sequel to the just as forgettable mess BRIDES OF BLOOD. When it was shown on its initial release with BRIDES OF BLOOD, the audiences were given green dyed water and told it was "green blood" that would serve as an aphrodisiac. Undoubtedly this helped many a teenager in the back aisles. The film itself is about what you'd expect, with hopelessly insipid dialog and a variety of zoom shots, presumably for dramatic effect. Pettyjohn ended up leaving the horror genre and changed her professional name to "Heaven St. John" when she later appeared in pornographic epics.

p, Eddie Romero; d, Romero, Geraldo de Leon; w, Reuben Candy; ph, Justo Paulino; m, Tito Arevalo.

Horror   **(PR:O MPAA:M)**

MAD DOCTOR OF MARKET STREET, THE*   (1942) 60m UNIV bw

Una Merkel (*Aunt Margaret*), Lionel Atwill (*Dr. Benson*), Nat Pendleton (*Red Hogan*), Claire Dodd (*Patricia Wentworth*), Richard Davies (*Jim*), John Eldredge (*Dwight*), Anne Nagel (*Mrs. Saunders*), Hardie Albright (*William Saunders*), Ray Mala (*Bareb*), Noble Johnson (*Elon*), Rosina Galli (*Tanao*), Al Kikume (*Kalo*), Milton Kibbee (*Hadley*), Byron Shores (*Crandall*), Tani Marsh, Billy Bunkley (*Tahitian Dancers*), Boyd Davis, Bess Flowers, Alan Bridge.

Pretty bad "Mad Doctor" movie starring Atwill as a quack who practices putting people into suspended animation and then reviving them until one day he makes an error and kills a man. He escapes on a ship, but the vessel sinks near a tropical island. Atwill and the survivors run into native chief Johnson (who almost *always* played native chiefs, including the one in KING KONG, 1933) and soon the nutty doctor stuns and amazes the locals with his suspended animation trick. Using their respect, Atwill soon sets himself up as king of the island, but his reign is shortlived because a rescue plane arrives and takes everyone but him back to civilization.

p, Paul Malvern; d, Joseph H. Lewis; w, Al Martin; ph, Jerry Ash; ed, Ralph Dixon.

Drama   **(PR:A MPAA:NR)**

MAD DOG   (SEE: MAD DOG MORGAN, 1976, Aus.)

MAD DOG COLL**   (1961) 88m COL bw

John Chandler (*Vincent Coll*), Neil Nephew (*Rocco*), Brooke Hayward (*Elizabeth*), Joy Harmon (*Caroline*), Jerry Orbach (*Joe*), Telly Savalas (*Lt. Dawson*), Glenn Cannon (*Harry*), Tom Castronova (*Ralphie*), Kay Doubleday (*Clio*), Vincent

Gardenia (*Dutch Schultz*), Ron Weyand (*Big Larry*), Peggy Furey (*Mother Coll*), Gilbert Leigh (*The Official*), Stephanie King (*The Official's Wife*), Gene Hackman (*Cop*), Leonardo Cimino, Joe Costa, Ronald Dawson, P. Barney Goodman, James Greene, Richard Velez, Jim Lester.

This shallow screen biography of one of the bloodiest killers of the 1920s, Vincent "Mad Dog" Coll, manages to detail several of his outrageous crimes, but fails to throw any light onto the man or the system that produced him. Chandler stars as the young gangster who grows up in a home marked by unhappiness and brutality. At the age of 17, he forms a small neighborhood gang and makes a desperate attempt to muscle his way into the mob. Chandler concentrates his efforts on the Dutch Schultz mob which controls all of the bootlegging in Harlem. As the months go by, the violence in the gang war escalates, culminating in a bloody fight on the waterfront where two children are killed. Dubbed "Mad Dog" by the press, Chandler and his only remaining gang member, Orbach, go into hiding. Now almost completely insane, Chandler kidnaps one of Gardenia's men whom he has come to believe is his hated dead father. In a rage, Chandler kills the man. Orbach, now realizing the extent of Chandler's insanity, informs the police of his former boss' whereabouts. The cops catch up to Chandler while he is making a phone call in a nearby drugstore, and machine-gun him to death. Not only does MAD DOG COLL fail as insightful drama, but most of the "facts," if not distorted beyond recognition, are completely fabricated. After committing several petty crimes with his brother Peter, and serving some time in reform school, the real-life Vincent Coll joined the Dutch Schultz mob as a gunman. After a few months on duty as a brutal enforcer, Coll began suffering from delusions of grandeur and decided he could take over the Dutchman's mob. Several brash moves and some bloodshed later, Shultz retaliated by having Coll's brother Peter shot down in the streets. Going completely wild, Coll snatched up large sections of Schultz's business and then began invading other mobsters' territories, including those of Owney Madden and Legs Diamond. Coll did kidnap a mob confidante, but it was one of Madden's men (George "Big Frenchy" DeMange), not Schultz's. Coll finally released the mobster and then repeated the deed on another one of Madden's mobsters a few months later. Schultz finally dispatched three of his best killers to get rid of Coll, but the crazy punk trapped them instead, spraying machine-gun bullets from a passing car. All three men escaped with their lives, but five children were shot (one was killed). It was this incident that got Coll dubbed "Mad Dog," not a waterfront brawl. Schultz's men caught up with Coll and it was they who machine-gunned him to death in a drugstore phone booth, not the police. In addition to the frustratingly fictitious script, the film is badly paced and held together with bothersome narration. One interesting aspect of it is that several actors and two crew members went on to bigger and better things. Telly Savalas plays a police lieutenant, Gene Hackman plays a cop, editor Ralph Rosenblum advanced to cutting such films as A THOUSAND CLOWNS (1965) and ANNIE HALL (1977), and assistant director Ulu Grosbard directed several notable films including STRAIGHT TIME (1978), TRUE CONFESSIONS (1981), and FALLING IN LOVE (1984).

p, Edward Schreiber; d, Burt Balaban; w, Schreiber (based on material by Leo Lieberman); ph, Gayne Reschner; m, Stu Phillips; ed, Ralph Rosenblum; art d, Richard Sylbert; set d, Gene Callahan; cos, Bill Walstrom; m/l, title song, Eddie D. Trush, Phillips; makeup, Bill Herman.

Crime/Biography   **(PR:C PMAA:NR)**

MAD DOG MORGAN***

(1976,Aus.) 102m Motion Picture Company/BEF c (AKA: MAD DOG)

Dennis Hopper (*Daniel Morgan*), Jack Thompson (*Detective Manwaring*), David Gulpilil (*Billy*), Frank Thring (*Superintendent Cobham*), Michael Pate (*Superintendent Winch*), Wallas Eaton (*Macpherson*), Bill Hunter (*Sgt. Smith*), John Hargreaves (*Baylis*), Martin Harris (*Wendlan*), Robin Ramsay (*Roget*).

An intelligent, extremely violent western set in the Australian outback of the mid-1800s. Hopper is a prospector who can't make a living at gold hunting, and thus turns to crime. He's captured and spends six years in prison. Upon his release he meets Gulpilil, a young Aborigine, and together they become infamous outlaws in New South Wales. Hopper slowly descends into self-destructive ways and finally walks into a rainstorm of gunfire after realizing that his hideout is surrounded. His performance is excellent, showing disturbing character changes with great subtlety. The direction captures the contrast between the hatefulness of the man and the beauty of the vast landscapes that surround him. The violence is particularly hard, though carefully created. Gulpilil is good in support as well. He also did fine work in such films as THE LAST WAVE (1977) and WALKABOUT (1971).

p, Jeremy Thomas; d&w, Philippe Mora (based on the book *Morgan the Bold Bushranger* by Margaret Carnegie); ph, Mike Molloy (Panavision); m, Patrick Flynn; ed, John Scott; art d, Bob Hilditch.

Crime/Biography   **Cas.**   **(PR:O MPAA:R)**

MAD EMPRESS, THE**

(1940) 72m WB bw (AKA: JUAREZ AND MAXIMILLIAN)

Medea Novara (*Empress Carlotta*), Lionel Atwill (*Bazaine*), Conrad Nagel (*Maximilian*), Guy Bates Post (*Napoleon*), Evelyn Brent (*Empress Eugenie*), Frank McGlynn, Sr. (*President Lincoln*), Nigel de Brulier (*Father Fisher*), Michael Visaroff (*Dr. Samuel Basch*), Earl Gunn (*Porfirio Diaz*), George Regas (*Mariano Escobedo*), Jason Robards, Sr. (*President Benito Juarez*), Rudolph Amendt (*Hertzfield*), Duncan Renaldo (*Col. Miguel Lopez*), Graciela Romero (*Mme. Bazaine*), Julian Rivero (*Tomas Mejia*), Claudia Dell, Gustav von Seyffertitz, Martin Garralaga, Rene de Luguro, Marin Sais, Edgar Norton, Franklin Murrel, Rolfe Sedan, Charles Bobett, Robert Frazer, Kort von Fuberg.

A somewhat tedious version of the Maximilian-and-Carlotta tale produced in Mexico and bought by Warner Bros. when producer Torres claimed he had made his movie before Warner Bros.' JUAREZ. Nagel and Novara star as the doomed figureheads of Mexico propped up by Napoleon III (played by Post). The political angles are clouded over to concentrate on the tragedy suffered by Nagel and Novara who are portrayed as innocent dupes who had no idea that the native population hated them. Novara goes mad on her return to Europe when she realizes that no aid will be sent to her husband who is trapped by an uprising in Mexico City. Overly melodramatic and trite, with a simplistic view of the events.

p&d, Miguel C. Torres; w, Jean Bart, Jerome Chodorov, Torres (based on a story by Torres); ph, Alex Phillips, Arthur Martinelli; ed, Carl Pierson; art d, F. Paul Sylos.

Historical Drama **(PR:A MPAA:NR)**

MAD EXECUTIONERS, THE**

(1965, Ger.) 92m CCC-Filmkunst/PAR bw (DER HENKER VON LONDON)

Hansjorg Felmy (Inspector John Hillier), Maria Perschy (Ann Barry), Dieter Borsche (Dr. MacFergusson), Rudolf Forster (Ann's Father), Harry Riebauer (Dr. Philip Trooper), Chris Howland (Cabby Pennypacker), Wolfgang Preiss (Morel Smith), Narziss Sokatscheff, Alexander Engel, Albert Besser, Stanislav Ledinek, Rudolf Fernau.

Felmy is a Scotland Yard inspector assigned to a very unusual case. A group of hooded vigilantes have taken it upon themselves to try to convict members of London's underworld in their own kangaroo court. Felmy is more interested in solving another crime. There is a sex maniac on the loose who decapitates women. One of his victims includes Felmy's sister so personal vengeance drives him to solve these murders. His fiancee Perschy agrees to be bait for the killer; she is abducted by Borsche, a crazed surgeon. He prepares to experiment on her when the vigilantes burst in and take him away. He is put on trial but the proceedings are interrupted by undercover agents who shoot the hooded judge. The face cover is removed, revealing the dead man to be none other than Felmy. Though it has an interesting premise, this film is far too confusing to follow. The ending itself is highly predictable.

p, Arthur Brauner; d, Edwin Zbonek; w, Robert A. Stemmle (based on the story "White Carpet" by Bryan Edgar Wallace); ph, Richard Angst; m, Raimund Rosenberger; ed, Walter Wischniewsky; prod d, Heinz Götze; art d, Hans Jurgen Kiebach, Ernst Schomer; cos, Trude Ulrich.

Mystery **(PR:O MPAA:NR)**

MAD GAME, THE**½

(1933) 73m FOX bw

Spencer Tracy (Edward Carson), Claire Trevor (Jane Lee), Ralph Morgan (Judge Penfield), J. Carrol Naish (Chopper Allen), John Miljan (William Bennett), Matt McHugh (Butts McGee), Kathleen Burke (Marilyn Kirk), Mary Mason (Lila Penfield), Harold Lally (Thomas Penfield), Willard Robertson (Warden), John Davidson (Doctor), Jerry Devine (Mike), Paul Fix.

Tracy stars as a bootlegger who is framed by his lawyer and sent to prison on an income tax-evasion rap. Once booze has been legalized, Tracy's gang turns to other criminal pursuits with special concentration on kidnaping. When the gang kidnaps Lally and Mason (the son-and daughter-in-law of Morgan, the judge who put Tracy behind bars) Tracy is paroled so that he may help capture his former partners, which he does, though he is mortally wounded in the process. Trevor is given a thankless role as the crusading lady reporter who has more than just a journalistic interest in Tracy. Fairly routine material elevated only by the presence of Tracy.

p, Sol Wurtzel; d, Irving Cummings; w, William Conselman, Henry Johnson; ph, Arthur Miller; md, Samuel Kaylin.

Crime **(PR:A MPAA:NR)**

MAD GENIUS, THE**½

(1931) 81m WB bw

John Barrymore (Ivan Tzarakov), Marian Marsh (Nana), Donald Cook (Fedor), Charles Butterworth (Karinsky), Luis Alberni (Serge Bankieff), Carmel Myers (Preskoya), Andre Luguet (Bartag), Frankie Darro (Fedor as a Boy), Boris Karloff (Fedor's Father), Mae Madison (Olga).

THE MAD GENIUS was an unsuccessful sequel to SVENGALI (1931). Not that it had the same characters, just that it had much the same story and the studio seemed to be attempting to fly on the coattails of the latter. Barrymore is a raving lunatic, a marionettist whose mother had been a Russian ballerina. His own club foot has kept him from following a career of pirouettes and pas de deux, so when he saves Darro from the abuse of his foster father, Karloff, he is heartened to see that the young boy is a natural dancer. He raises Darro until the boy grows into being Cook, then takes on the job of producing for a well-known ballet company, where his stars are Cook and Marsh (who was Trilby to Barrymore's Svengali). The man who stages the dancing is Alberni, a genius and a junkie. Cook and Marsh are attracted to each other and Barrymore attempts to keep them apart but it's too late. Cook and Marsh leave the ballet company and go to Paris where they are soon dancing in a Montmartre cafe until Marsh leaves him for a wealthy baron and Cook returns to the ballet company. One night, Cook spots Marsh in the audience and wants to see her, but Barrymore's grip on the youth is such that he can't bring himself to do it. (Earlier Barrymore had hypnotized Marsh into running off with the baron and it is with him she sits at the theater) Alberni goes mad from drugs and kills Barrymore with an axe and the body rolls onto the stage. Cook covers it, and, later, he and Marsh are reunited, now that Cook is out from under Barrymore's influence. There appears to have been some talk that part of this story was based on the life of Nijinsky, but that has not been confirmed. Orson Welles laid claim to having been the first director to shoot ceilings in films, yet this picture belies that as designer Grot had sets built with fabric ceilings that were clearly seen several times. The public stayed away from THE MAD GENIUS despite good direction by Curtiz and a wonderfully hammy star turn by Barrymore.

d, Michael Curtiz; w, J. Grubb Alexander, Harvey Thew (based on the play "The Idol" by Martin Brown); ph, Barney McGill; ed, Ralph Dawson; set d, Anton Grot; ch, Adolph Bolm.

Drama **(PR:A-C MPAA:NR)**

MAD GHOUL, THE**½ (1943) 64m UNIV bw

David Bruce (Ted Allison), Evelyn Ankers (Isabel Lewis), George Zucco (Dr. Alfred Morris), Robert Armstrong (Ken McClure), Turhan Bey (Eric Iverson), Milburn Stone (Sgt. Macklin), Andrew Tombes (Eagan), Rose Hobart (Della), Addison Richards (Gavigan), Charles McGraw (Detective Garrity), Gus Glassmire (Caretaker), Gene O'Connell (Radio Announcer), Isabelle Lamal (Maid), Lew Kelly (Stagehand), William Ruhl (Stagehand), Hans Herbert (Attendant), Bess Flowers, Cyril Ring (Extras in Audience), Lillian Cornell (Voice of Isabel Lewis).

Good, creepy fun starring Zucco as yet another mad scientist (he's a professor at a respected university), this time goofing around with an ancient Egyptian gas that turns anyone who sniffs it into a white-faced zombie who must drain living people's heart fluid to survive. Nasty doctor Zucco gives a dose to his unwitting assistant Bruce, who ends up shuffling around terrorizing the campus, including his lovely fiancee Ankers. Nosy reporter Armstrong figures out what's going on and gets killed for his trouble, but eventually Bruce turns on Zucco and gives him a whiff of his own ancient Egyptian medicine. Bey plays the love interest after Ankers dumps her zombie fiance, and the voice of Lillian Cornell handles "I Dreamt I Dwelt in Marble Halls" and "All for Love," the unnecessary musical numbers lip-synced by Ankers.

p, Ben Pivar; d, James Hogan; w, Brenda Weisberg, Paul Gangelin, Hans Kraly; ph, Milton Krasner; ed, Milton Carruth; art d, John Goodman.

Horror **(PR:C MPAA:NR)**

MAD HATTER, THE (SEE: BREAKFAST IN HOLLYWOOD, 1946)

MAD HATTERS, THE** (1935, Brit.) 68m British and Dominions-PAR bw

Chili Bouchier (Vicki), Sidney King (Tim Stanhope), Evelyn Foster (Ruth Stanhope), Kim Peacock (Joe), Grace Lane (Mrs. Stanhope), Bellenden Clarke (Gen. Stanhope), Toska von Bissing (Duchess), Vera Bogetti (Lady Felicity), H. Saxon-Snell, Roddy Hughes, Edgar Driver, Ralph Roberts.

When King decides to leave military school, his mother is furious. She has spent most of her money on the hope of a military career for her son and now that appears to be for naught. With the money left over, sister Foster is able to open a hat shop, though she really had hoped to become a nurse. But more problems arise when an exotic French lass (Bouchier) turns out to be the neighbor, attracting the attentions of Foster's fiance. Enter the ne'er-do-well King, who attracts the siren's attentions himself, giving a happy ending for all concerned. A minor comedy, with few laughs.

p, Anthony Havelock-Allan; d, Ivar Campbell; w, Christine Jope-Slade (based on the story "The Only Son" by James Stewart); ph, Francis Carver.

Comedy **(PR:A MPAA:NR)**

MAD HOLIDAY*½ (1936) 71m MGM bw

Edmund Lowe (Philip Trent), Elissa Landi (Peter Dean), ZaSu Pitts (Mrs. Kennedy), Ted Healy (Mert Morgan), Edmund Gwenn (Williams), Edgar Kennedy (Donovan), Soo Yong (Li Tai), Walter Kingsford (Ben Kelvin), Herbert Rawlinson (Capt. Bromley), Raymond Hatton ("Cokey Joe" Ferris), Rafaela Ottiano (Ning), Harlan Briggs (Kinney), Gustav von Seyffertitz (Hendrick Van Mier).

Dull mystery that tries to capture the flavor of THE THIN MAN but falls far from the mark. Lowe plays a frustrated Hollywood actor who goes on a cruise and refuses to return until the studio agrees to stop casting him in the endless number of murder mysteries he has been doing for them. Of course, on board Lowe finds himself embroiled in a real murder case when a stiff turns up in his cabin. Together with the lady writer, Landi, who has been penning the novels from which Lowe's career has been stifled, they trace the killers and eventually solve the mystery.

p, Harry Rapf; d, George B. Seitz; w, Florence Ryerson, Edgar Allan Woolf (based on the story "Murder in a Chinese Theatre" by Joseph Santley); ph, Joseph Ruttenberg; ed, George Boemler.

Mystery **(PR:A MPAA:NR)**

MAD LITTLE ISLAND**½

(1958, Brit.) 94m RANK c (AKA: ROCKETS GALORE)

Jeannie Carson (Janet McLeod), Donald Sinden (Hugh Mander), Roland Culver (Capt. Waggett), Catherine Lacey (Mrs. Waggett), Noel Purcell (Father James McAllister), Ian Hunter (Air Commodore Watchorn), Duncan Macrae (Duncan Ban), Jean Cadell (Mrs. Campbell), Gordon Jackson (George Campbell), Alex Mackenzie (Joseph McLeod), Carl Jaffe (Dr. Emile Hamburger), Nicholas Phipps (Andrew Wishart), Jameson Clark (Constable MacRae), Reginald Beckwith (Mumford), John Laurie (Capt. MacKechnie), Ronald Corbett (Drooby), James Copeland (Kenny MacLeod), John Stevenson Lang (Reverend Angus), Nell Ballantyne (Kirsty), Arthur Howard (Meeching), Jack Short (Roderick), Gabrielle Blunt (Catriona), Richard Dimbleby, Michael Foot, W.J. Brown, A.J.P. Taylor, Robert Boothby, Edgar Lustgarten, Daniel Farston.

Sinden is sent to the little island of Todday on a mission to scout the location for a possible missile site. With his okay, construction begins, and the angry cries of the islanders fall on deaf ears. Led by schoolteacher Carson, the natives make every attempt to sabotage the site, but are unsuccessful. Carson than hits on the idea of dying a local bird pink and complaining that the rare creature is endangered. This trick ruffles the public's feathers and construction is stopped. A less-comic sequel to TIGHT LITTLE ISLAND.

p, Basil Dearden; d, Michael Relph; w, Monja Danischewsky (based on the novel Rockets Galore by Compton Mackenzie); ph, Reginald Wyer (Eastmancolor); m, Cedric Thorpe Davie; ed, John Guthridge; md, Muir Mathieson; art d, Jack Maxsted; cos, Yvonne Caffin.

Comedy **(PR:A MPAA:NR)**

MAD LOVE**** (1935) 83m MGM bw (GB: THE HANDS OF ORLAC)

Peter Lorre *(Dr. Gogol)*, Colin Clive *(Stephen Orlac)*, Frances Drake *(Yvonne Orlac)*, Ted Healy *(Reagan)*, Edward Brophy *(Rollo)*, Sarah Haden *(Marie)*, Henry Kolker *(Prefect Rosset)*, May Beatty *(Francoise)*, Key Luke *(Dr. Wong)*, Isabel Jewell *(Marianne)*, Rollo Lloyd, Clarence H. Wilson, Sam Ash, Ian Wolfe, Sara Padden, Billy Gilbert, Charles Trowbridge, Frank Darien, Carl Stockdale, Robert Emmett Keane, Harold Huber, Hooper Atchley, Cora Sue Collins.

Peter Lorre was so good in this, his first American film, that Charlie Chaplin was quoted as saying, "He is the greatest living actor." A remake of the silent version that starred Conrad Veidt (it was remade poorly in 1960 as THE HANDS OF ORLAC), MAD LOVE combined Grand Guignol, surrealism, and a bit of comedy to great effect, and remains to this day a chilling film. Lorre is a doctor who adores Drake, star of the Parisian Horror Theatre. He finally works up the courage to tell her how he feels and she rebuffs him. There is a life-size replica of Drake in the theater's lobby and Lorre buys it, harboring a secret wish that, perhaps, he can bring it to life, as Pygmalion did with Galatea in the ancient Greek tale. Clive is Drake's husband, a famed pianist, and when he loses his hands in a railway accident, Drake goes to Lorre, a brilliant surgeon, and pleads with him to do something. Lorre grafts the hands of Brophy, a murderer who has just been executed, onto Clive's stumps. Clive is grateful and hopes he can play piano again, but all his knowledge doesn't help his manual dexterity. The dead man had been a knife thrower and, when Lorre kills Clive's stepfather, he uses psychological torture to make Clive think that he, Clive, did it. Now Brophy shows up and says that he had his head sewn back on by Lorre (revealing a neck brace and the stitches) and he wants his hands back. It's only when Brophy goes to Lorre's place that he unmasks, removes his makeup, and reveals himself to be Lorre playing the late murderer. Drake goes to Lorre's chamber and switches positions with the life-size replica, then pretends she has come to life. Lorre attempts to strangle her with her own long braids as Clive enters, throws a knife, and ends Lorre's life. There were three excellent cameramen on the film and that may have been a mistake. Director Freund had been the man behind the lens on many films and his addition of Toland and Lyons, who had different ideas from Freund and from each other, worked against the look of the film. Casting the likable Ed Brophy as the killer was also erroneous, but it may have been because Brophy was the only actor around who sort of resembled the odd-looking Lorre and was about the same diminutive size. The comedy relief, by Ted Healy (who used to headline with The Three Stooges) is unwelcome and only takes the edge off the scare tactics employed by everyone else. Mind you, Lorre is no mad scientist of the Lugosi-Karloff school. He is an excellent doctor who becomes obsessed with Drake and it is that love obsession that drives him to do the things he does. Through all of it, anyone who has ever been deeply in love will recognize his motivations, no matter how bizarre his activities.

p, John W. Considine, Jr.; d, Karl Freund; w, Guy Endore, P. J. Wolfson, John L. Balderston (based on the novel *Les Mains d'Orlac* by Maurice Renard); ph, Chester Lyons, Gregg Toland; m, Dimitri Tiomkin; ed, Hugh Wynn.

Horror **(PR:C MPAA:NR)**

MAD, MAD MOVIE MAKERS, THE
(SEE: LAST PORNO FLICK, THE, 1974)

MAD MAGAZINE PRESENTS UP THE ACADEMY
(SEE: UP THE ACADEMY, 1980)

MAD MAGICIAN, THE** (1954) 72m COL bw/c

Vincent Price *(Gallico)*, Mary Murphy *(Karen Lee)*, Eva Gabor *(Claire)*, John Emery *(Rinaldi)*, Donald Randolph *(Ross Ormond)*, Lenita Lane *(Alice Prentiss)*, Patrick O'Neal *(Bruce Allen)*, Jay Novello *(Mr. Prentiss)*.

Vastly inferior rip-off of Price's surprisingly successful 3-D shocker HOUSE OF WAX, also in 3-D with the star portraying a magician who goes berserk after his best kept magic secrets and his wife Gabor are stolen by rival magician Emery. This gives Price free rein to give his magic show a downright homicidal bent and kill his victims in bizarre ways including his famous buzz-saw trick. Highlight of the rather spotty 3-D was a few streams of water being shot at the audience. Price alone keeps this affair afloat.

p, Bryan Foy; d, John Brahm; w, Crane Wilbur; ph, Bert Glennon (3-D); m, Emil Newman, Arthur Lange; ed, Grant Whytock; art d, Frank Sylos.

Horror **(PR:C MPAA:NR)**

MAD MARTINDALES, THE** (1942) 65m Fox bw

Jane Withers *(Kathy Martindale)*, Marjorie Weaver *(Evelyn)*, Alan Mowbray *(Hugo Martindale)*, Jimmy Lydon *(Bobby)*, Byron Barr *(Peter Varney)*, George Reeves *(Julio)*, Charles Lane *(Virgil Hickling)*, Kathleen Howard *(Grandmother Varney)*, Robert Greig, Brandon Hurst *(Butlers)*, Steve Geray *(Van der Venne)*, Sen Yung *(Jefferson Gow)*, Emma Dunn *(Agnes)*, Hal K. Dawson *(Hotel Clerk)*, Don Dillaway *(Lawyer)*, Tom Yuen *(Chang Gow)*, Otto Hoffman *(Pawnbroker)*, Alec Craig *(Coachman)*, Harry Shannon *(Policeman)*, Dick French, Jack Chefe *(Barbers)*.

Withers hit the age of 16 and the end of her career in this one, set in 1900, which details her efforts to save her befuddled father from his increasingly strange business dealings and placate her sister Weaver when sis's boyfriend Barr turns his attentions toward her. Stilted and uninvolving.

p, Walter Morosco; d, Alfred Werker; w, Francis Edwards Faragoh (based on the play "Not for Children" by Wesley Towner, Ludwig Hirshfeld, Dr. Edmund Wolf); ph, Lucien Andriot; ed, Nick De Maggio; md, Emil Newman.

Drama **(PR:A MPAA:NR)**

MAD MASQUERADE (SEE: WASHINGTON MASQUERADE, THE, 1932)

MAD MAX ***1/2 (1979, Aus.) 90m Mad Max Pty/AIP-Filmways c

Mel Gibson *(Max)*; Joanne Samuel *(Jessie)*, Hugh Keays-Byrne *(The Toecutter)*, Steve Bisley *(Jim Goose)*, Roger Ward *(Fifi Macaffee)*, Vince Gil *(Nightrider)*, Tim Burns *(Johnny the Boy)*, Geoff Parry *(Bubba Zanetti)*, Paul Johnstone *(Cundalini)*, John Ley *(Charlie)*, Jonathon Hardy *(Labatoche)*, Sheila Florence *(May Swaisey)*, Reg Evans *(Station Master)*, Stephen Clark *(Sarse)*, Howard Eynon *(Diabando)*, John Farndale *(Grinner)*, Max Fairchild *(Benno)*, Jerry Day *(Ziggy)*, Peter Flemingham *(Senior Doctor)*, Phil Motherwell *(Junior Doctor)*, Mathew Constantine *(Toddler)*, Nic Gazzana *(Starbuck)*, Hunter Gibb *(Liar)*, David Cameron *(Underground Mechanic)*, Robina Chaffey *(Singer)*, Bertrand Cadart *(Clunk)*, David Bracks *(Mudguts)*, Brendan Heath *(Sprog)*, Steve Millicamp *(Roop)*, Lulu Pinkus *(Nightrider's Girl)*, George Novak *(Scuttle)*, Nick Lathouris *(Grease Rat)*, Lisa Aldenhoven *(Nurse)*, Andrew Gilmore *(Silvertongue)*, Nein Thompson *(TV Newsreader)*, Gil Tucker *(People's Overseer)*, Billy Tisdall *(Midge)*, Kim Sullivan *(Girl in Chevy)*.

Australia exported this creative, original, exciting, low-budget masterpiece which gave a young actor by the name of Mel Gibson his first starring role and a chance at becoming the heart-throb of the 1980's. Set in the near future, MAD MAX sees a society in chaos. "Law and order" is barely alive. The highways are filled with lunatic speed demons who run in packs like wolves. Gibson plays Max, a good cop who's fed up with his job. After chasing lunatic criminals for years and seeing his buddies killed in action with no end in sight, he would just like to retire and spend the rest of his days with his wife and child. His chief tries to bribe him with a new, faster police car ("the last of the V-8's") and by telling him that he's the last of the heroes. It doesn't work; Gibson is firm. The boss tells him to take a vacation and he does. Spending an idyllic week with his family on the beach, he decides to put away his badge and uniform for good. But this is not to be. A psychotic gang of road-rats kills Gibson's wife and child in revenge for the death of one of their members. Left with nothing to live for, Gibson turns avenger, dons his black leather uniform, fuels up his V-8, and goes off to kill those who killed his family. In the end, after he has killed off the whole gang, Gibson drives off to an uncertain future. Though the plot is that of a simple revenge western, director George Miller infuses the film with a kinetic combination of visual style, amazing stunt work, creative costume design and eccentric, detailed characterizations that practically jump out of the screen and grab the viewer by the throat. Miller, whose inspiration was comic books, serials and B westerns, has created some of the most stunning car-chase, crash-and-burn scenes ever put on film (the chase scenes in MAD MAX make films like BULLITT and THE FRENCH CONNECTION look dull in comparison). Miller is a filmmaker who seems to just have excitedly discovered the possibilities of composition, camera movement and editing and uses them to their fullest, most powerful effect, bringing *movement* back to the movies. Done independently with a laughably small budget (Miller edited most of the film in his bedroom), MAD MAX went on to make more money in Australia than George Lucas' STAR WARS. The American distributors, however, didn't quite know what to do with the film and stupidly dubbed lousy American-sounding voices over the Australians'. An even better sequel, THE ROAD WARRIOR (MAD MAX II in Australia), followed in 1981, and a third film, MAD MAX BEYOND THUNDERDOME, was released in the summer of 1985.

p, Byron Kennedy; d, George Miller; w, Miller, James McCausland (based on a story by Miller, Kennedy); ph, David Eggby (Todd-AO 35); m, Brian May; ed, Tony Paterson, Cliff Hayes; art d, Jon Dowding; cos, Clare Griffin; spec eff, Chris Murray; stunts, Grant Page; makeup, Viv Mephan.

Drama/Adventure **Cas.** **(PR:O MPAA:R)**

MAD MAX 2 (SEE: ROAD WARRIOR, THE, 1981)

MAD MEN OF EUROPE**
(1940, Brit.) 73m Aldwych/COL bw (GB: AN ENGLISHMAN'S HOME)

Edmund Gwenn *(Tom Brown)*, Mary Maguire *(Betty Brown)*, Paul von Hernried, [Paul Henreid] *(Victor Brandt)*, Geoffrey Toone *(Peter Templeton)*, Richard Ainley *(Geoffrey Brown)*, Desmond Tester *(Billy Brown)*, Carl Jaffe *(Martin)*, Meinhart Maur *(Waldo)*, Mavis Villers *(Dolly)*, Mark Lester *(Uncle Ben)*, Norah Howard *(Maggie)*, John Wood *(Jimmy)*.

Unabashed British wartime propaganda starring von Hernried as a Nazi spy who sneaks into England and is unknowingly taken in by the kindly Gwenn and his family. From there he is able to establish radio contact with the Nazis so that he can pinpoint British targets for German planes and paratroopers. To complicate matters, von Hernried starts a romance with Gwenn's unsuspecting daughter Maguire. Gwenn kills a German officer when the attack starts and is taken out and shot just as British bombers arrive to blow up the whole house.

p, Neville E. Neville; d, Albert de Courville; w, Ian Hay, Edward Knoblock (based on the play by Guy du Maurier, dialog by Rodney Ackland, Bob Edmunds); ph, Mutz Greenbaum, Henry Davis; ed, Lister Laurence; md, Louis Levy.

Spy Drama **(PR:A MPAA:NR)**

MAD MISS MANTON, THE1/2** (1938) 65m RKO bw

Barbara Stanwyck *(Melsa Manton)*, Henry Fonda *(Peter Ames)*, Sam Levene *(Lt. Mike Brent)*, Frances Mercer *(Helen Frayne)*, Stanley Ridges *(Eddie Norris)*, Whitney Bourne *(Pat James)*, Vicki Lester *(Kit Beverly)*, Ann Evers *(Lee Wilson)*, Catherine O'Quinn *(Dora Fenton)*, Linda Terry *(Myra Frost)*, Eleanor Hansen *(Jane)*, Hattie McDaniel *(Hilda)*, James Burke *(Sgt. Sullivan)*, Paul Guilfoyle *(Bat Regan)*, Penny Singleton *(Frances Glesk)*, Leona Maricle *(Sheila Lane)*, Kay Sutton *(Gloria Hamilton)*, Miles Mander *(Fred Thomas)*, John Qualen *(Subway Watchman)*, Grady Sutton *(District Attorney's Secretary)*, Olin Howland *(Mister X, Joe the Safecracker)*, Mary Jo Desmond *(Extra)*, Emory Parnell *(Doorman)*, Vinton Haworth *(Peter's Secretary)*, Irving Bacon *(Spengler the Process Server)*, Ted Oliver, Eddy Chandler *(Detectives)*, Jack Rice *(Doctor)*, Matt McHugh *(Waiter)*, Leonard Mudie *(Managing Editor)*, Robert Middlemass *(District Attorney)*, Walter Sande *(Investigator)*, Charles Halton *(Popsy the Lawyer)*, George Magrill *(Police-*

man), Buck Mack, Clarence H. Wilson, Otto Fries, Pierre Watkin, Charles Trowbridge.

Stanwyck is hardly mad, in the insane sense of the word. Rather, she is a madcap heiress given to outrageousness, like walking her dogs at four in the morning and teaming up with some of her feather-headed society debutante pals (among them Mercer, Lester, and Bourne) to have fun. Stanwyck finds a corpse on the street late one night and calls for her pals, but the body vanishes before the cops arrive. This gets Stanwyck's dander up and she and her friends function like so many Nancy Drews and become amateur detectives until they uncover Ridges as the villain. Along the way, Fonda, a newspaperman, says the whole thing is just one more of the mad Miss Manton's hoaxes and she sues for libel. Later, Fonda joins the cadre of cuties and they all solve the case together. It's a "screwball" comedy but with the added twist of a crime added. It doesn't come close to the classics of that genre for several reasons, not the least of which was that Fonda hated the script and didn't want to take the assignment, but he was shoehorned in by Walter Wanger, who had Fonda's personal services contract. Thus, when Wanger made the deal, Fonda dutifully arrived to do his job. Despite that, he was pro enough to turn in a good, if not outstanding, performance. Epstein, working without his brother on a rare occasion, turned in a witty enough script and THE MAD MISS MANTON should have been better, but it was like so many of the "madcap heiress meets newsman and sues for libel then winds up loving the big lug" stories that it blends into memory. Hal Yates' contribution to the screenplay was uncredited.

p, Pandro S. Berman, P. J. Wolfson; d, Leigh Jason; w, Philip G. Epstein, Hal Yates (based on a story by Wilson Collison); ph, Nicholas Musuraca; m, Roy Webb; ed, George Hively; art d, Van Nest Polglase, Carroll Clark; set d, Darrell Silvera; cos, Edward Stevenson; makeup, Jim Barker.

Comedy/Crime **Cas.** **(PR:A-C MPAA:NR)**

MAD MONSTER, THE* (1942) 77m PRC bw

Johnny Downs *(Tom Gregory)*, George Zucco *(Dr. Lorenzo Cameron)*, Anne Nagel *(Lenora)*, Sarah Padden *(Grandmother)*, Glenn Strange *(Petro)*, Gordon DeMain *(Prof. Fitzgerald)*, Mae Busch *(Susan)*, Reginald Barlow *(Prof. Warwick)*, Robert Strange *(Prof. Blaine)*, Henry Hall *(Country Doctor)*, Edward Cassidy *(Father)*, Eddie Holden *(Harper)*, John Elliott *(Prof. Hatfield)*, Charles Whitaker *(Policeman)*, Gil Patric *(Lieutenant Detective)*.

Low, low budget rip-off of THE WOLFMAN starring Zucco as yet another mad scientist. This time he turns large, dim-witted farmboy Strange into a large, dim-witted monster by injecting him with the blood of a wolf. This causes Strange to run amok across the countryside sinking his fangs into anything that moves until clever reporter Downs (who has a romantic attachment to Zucco's daughter Nagel) puts two-and-two together and traps the beast, who then turns on Zucco and kills him while perishing itself in the flaming laboratory. Good for laughs.

p, Sigmund Neufeld; d, Sam Newfield; w, Fred Myton; ph, Jack Greenhalgh; m, David Chudnow; ed, Holbook N. Todd; art d, Fred Preble.

Horror **Cas.** **(PR:A MPAA:NR)**

MAD MONSTER PARTY 1/2** (1967) 94m Videocraft International/AE c

The Voices of: Boris Karloff *(Baron Boris von Frankenstein)*, Phyllis Diller *(Frankenstein's Wife)*, Ethel Ennis, Gale Garnett, Allen Swift.

It's a monster of a convention as the new leader for the Worldwide Organization of Monsters must be chosen by the soon-to-be-retired Baron Boris von Frankenstein (the voice of Karloff). This is an animated feature using three-dimensional figures in a process called "Animagic," which is a stop-motion photography technique. All the biggies are there including The Werewolf, Dracula, the Creature From the Black Lagoon, King Kong, Dr. Jekyll and Mr. Hyde, The Mummy, and some parodies of Claude Rains (The Invisible Man), Charles Laughton (The Hunchback of Notre Dame) and Peter Lorre in an Igor-type being called "Yetch". Diller's, appropriately, is the voice of Karloff's ghoulish wife. Conflict between the major monsters erupts as well as some surprises for the Baron's normal nephew, a character by the name of Felix Flanken, who makes the mistake of falling for one of his uncle's mechanical creations. The Animagic technique works well, though it has a certain sort of eeriness to it. As with the majority of cheap animations, this was made strictly with a kiddie audience in mind, although animation buffs might want to watch for awhile.

p, Arthur Rankin, Jr.; d, Jules Bass; w, Len Korobkin, Harvey Kirtzman, Forrest J. Ackerman (based on a story by Rankin); ph, (Animagic, Eastmancolor); m/l, Maury Laws, Bass; puppet design, Jack Davis.

Animated Feature **Cas.** **(PR:AA MPAA:NR)**

MAD PARADE, THE**
(1931) 63m Liberty/PAR bw (AKA: FORGOTTEN WOMEN)

Evelyn Brent *(Monica Dale)*, Irene Rich *(Mrs. Schuyler)*, Louise Fazenda *(Fanny Smithers)*, Lilyan Tashman *(Lil Wheeler)*, Marceline Day *(Dorothy Quinlan)*, Fritzi Ridgeway *(Prudence Graham)*, June Clyde *(Janice Lee)*, Elizabeth Keating *(Bluebell Jones)*, Helen Keating *(Rosemary Jones)*.

A woman's version of THE BIG PARADE set during WW I and directed with slapdash, low-budget vigor by William "One Shot" Beaudine. Plot concerns the lives of nine women stationed in Europe during the war who serve with an ambulance patrol. Interesting premise suffers from typical plotting which details, among other things, the efforts of one of the women to steal the boy friend of another and a woman so hardened by the horrors of the battlefield that she turns bad and causes several breaches of conduct. Overly talky and dated, but historically interesting for its portrayal of strong women on the battlefield.

p, M. H. Hoffman; d, William Beaudine; w, Henry McCarthy, Frank R. Conklin, Gertrude Orr, Doris Malloy (based on the story "Women Like Men" by Orr, Malloy); ph, Charles Van Enger, Ernest Miller, Glenn Kerschner; ed, Richard Cahoon.

War **(PR:A MPAA:NR)**

MAD QUEEN, THE**
(1950, Span.) 115m Cifesa/Azteca bw (LOCURA DE AMOR)

Aurora Bautista *(Dona Juana)*, Fernando Rey *(Don Felipe)*, Sara Montiel *(Aldara)*, Jorge Mistral *(Capt. Don Alvar)*, Jesus Tordesillas *(Don Filiberto de Vere)*, Manuel Luna *(Don Juan Manuel)*, Juan Espantaleon *(Admiral)*, Ricardo Acero *(Charles 1st)*, Maria Canete *(Dona Elvira)*, Manuel Arbo *(Marliano)*, Felix Fernandez *(Inn Keeper)*, Arturo Marin *(Chievres)*, Luis Pena Sanchez *(Noble)*, Conrado S. Martin *(Hernan)*.

Convoluted historical melodrama starring Bautista as the daughter of Queen Isabel and King Ferdinand of Spain who is madly in love with her good-for-nothing husband Rey and fails to see the plot against her reign until it is too late. The members of her court scheme to have her declared insane and then install the easily manipulated Rey as the nation's figurehead in her place. Eventually all this plotting drives Bautista crazy and the villains get what they want. (In Spanish; English subtitles.)

d, Juan de Orduna; w, Manuel Tamayo y Baus, Alfredo Echegaray, Carlos Blanco (based on a story by Tamayo y Baus); ph, Jose F. Aguayo; English subtitles, Herman G. Weinberg.

Historical Drama **(PR:A MPAA:NR)**

MAD ROOM, THE** (1969) 93m COL c

Stella Stevens *(Ellen Hardy)*, Shelley Winters *(Mrs. Gladys Armstrong)*, Skip Ward *(Sam Aller)*, Carol Cole *(Chris)*, Severn Darden *(Nate)*, Beverly Garland *(Mrs. Racine)*, Michael Burns *(George)*, Barbara Sammeth *(Mandy)*, Jenifer Bishop *(Mrs. Ericson)*, Gloria Manon *(Edna)*, Lloyd Haynes *(Dr. Marion Kincaid)*, Lou Kane *(Armand Racine)*.

A remake of LADIES IN RETIREMENT starring Stevens as the companion of wealthy widow Winters who is about to marry Winters' stepson Ward. When Stevens learns that her teenage brother and sister are about to be released from a mental institution where they were kept after being suspected of killing their parents (it was never proved), she asks the reluctant Winters to take them in (Winters does not know about their past). Soon after, Winters discovers the truth about the pair and is found hacked to death. The children suspect each other, and Stevens buries Winters' body in the back yard. When the family dog is seen carrying one of Winters' severed hands in its mouth, Stevens, who has been the killer all along, goes completely berserk and butchers the dog in the basement, much to the horror of Ward who had no idea he was about to marry a psychopath.

p, Norman Maurer; d, Bernard Girard; w, Girard, A. Z. Martin (based on the play "Ladies in Retirement," by Reginald Denham, Edward Percy and the screenplay for the film, LADIES IN RETIREMENT, by Garrett Fort, Denham); ph, Harry Stradling, Jr. (Berkey Pathe Color); m, Dave Grusin; ed, Pat Somerset; art d, Sydney Z. Litwack; set d, Sidney Clifford; m/l, "Open My Eyes," "Wildwood Blues," NAZZ (sung by NAZZ); cos, Moss Mabry; makeup, Ben Lane.

Drama **(PR:O MPAA:M)**

MAD WEDNESDAY***
(1950) 79m California/RKO bw (AKA: THE SIN OF HAROLD DIDDLEBOCK)

Harold Lloyd *(Harold Diddlebock)*, Frances Ramsden *(Miss Otis)*, Jimmy Conlin *(Wormy)*, Raymond Walburn *(E.J. Waggleberry)*, Edgar Kennedy *(Jake the Bartender)*, Arline Judge *(Manicurist)*, Franklin Pangborn *(Formfit Franklin)*, Lionel Stander *(Max)*, Margaret Hamilton *(Flora)*, Al Bridge *(Wild Bill Hitchcock)*, Frank Moran *(Mike the Cop)*, Torben Meyer *(Barber)*, Victor Potel *(Prof. Potelle)*, Jack Norton *(James R. Smoke)*, Arthur Hoyt *(Jerimah P. Blackston)*, Georgia Caine *(Bearded Lady)*, Gladys Forrest *(Snake Charmer)*, Max Wagner *(Doorman)*, Rudy Vallee *(Banker Sargent)*, Julius Tannen *(Banker with Glasses)*, Robert Dudley *(Banker McDuff)*, Robert Grieg *(Coachman Thomas)*, Pat Harmon *(Coach in Scenes from THE FRESHMAN)*, Wilbur Mack *(Football Rooter)*, Charles R. Moore *(Bootblack)*, Dewey Robinson *(Lucky Leopold the Gambler)*, Harry Rosenthal *(A Reveler)*, Ethelreda Leopold *(Blonde Woman)*, Dot Farley *(Smoke's Secretary)*, Angelo Rossitto *(Midget)*, Tom McGuire *(Police Captain)*, J. Farrell MacDonald *(Desk Sergeant)*, Rob Reeves *(Ringling Bros. Representative)*, Franklyn Farnum *(Man Who Bumps into Harold on Street)*, Alice the Horse, Jackie the Lion.

When Preston Sturges was good (THE GREAT MCGINTY, SULLIVAN'S TRAVELS, etc.), he was wonderful. When he was bad (THE FRENCH THEY ARE A FUNNY RACE), he was awful. This film is somewhere in the middle and when it's good your sides will ache from laughter. It begins with a sequence from Lloyd's classic silent, THE FRESHMAN. Next, we learn that the football hero didn't go on to be a man of industry. Instead, he became a frumpy bookkeeper with no life other than at the office, with all his glory days behind him. When he's fired from his job after being faithful to the firm for two decades, he goes on a drunken spree, and, in as unlikely a series of events as you'll ever see, he wakes up the owner of a moth-eaten and bankrupt circus. Now he has to go out and raise the money to feed his animals and he winds up in a latter-day version of the scene for which he became so famous—hanging from a tall building. This time a huge lion is menacing him and the thrills and laughter intertwine so quickly that you'll be biting your nails through grinning teeth. Jimmy Conlin, whom Sturges used as a convict in SULLIVAN'S TRAVELS, plays the same kind of role he usually plays so well. MAD WEDNESDAY was financed by, of all people, Howard Hughes, a man not usually known for his sense of humor. It includes several excellent character bits by some of Hollywood's best second bananas: Kennedy (master of the slow burn), Stander (who left movies for years due to Red-baiting, then came back as a TV star), Hamilton (the ultimate witch), and Pangborn, who elevated prissiness to an art form. See if you can sit through the long, dead scenes and wait for Lloyd to get going. It'll be worth it. Lloyd was already in his middle fifties when he made this picture but hardly looked more than five years older than the scenes in THE FRESHMAN. He still moved like a stunt man and did his own dangerous exploits for this, his final film (other than a couple of documentaries). Controversy aplenty accompanied this film, which was the first one undertaken by California Pictures, the production company put together by Sturges and Howard Hughes. Sturges and Lloyd found each other difficult to work with, and at the beginning of the project were shooting scenes two different ways to satisfy both of them. Lloyd eventually relented, but the problems didn't stop there. The film was released through United Artists in 1947 with the title THE SIN OF HAROLD DIDDLEBOCK, but when it met with lukewarm box office results it was withdrawn and shelved. Hughes re-edited the picture, cut it from 89 minutes to 79 minutes, retitled it MAD WEDNESDAY, and released it through his own RKO organization in 1950.

p,d&w, Preston Sturges; ph, Robert Pittack; m, Werner Richard Heymann, Harry Rosenthal; ed, Thomas Neff; art d, Robert Usher; set d, Victor A. Gangelin: spec eff, John P. Fulton; m/l, "Auld Lang Syne" (sung by Harold Lloyd, Franklin Pangborn); makeup, Ted Larsen, Wally Westmore.

Comedy (PR:A MPAA:NR)

MAD YOUTH* (1940) 61m Atlas bw

Mary Ainslee, Betty Atkinson, Willy Castello, Betty Compson, Tommy Wonder, Lorelei Readoux, Margaret Fealy, Hal Price, Etheldra Leopold, Donald Kerr.

Inept low-budget picture starring Compson as the middle-aged gigolo-chasing mother of troubled teen Ainslee who falls in love with one of her mother's beaux. Padded with sub-standard rhumba acts and lengthy nightclub scenes, the film is overlong at 60 minutes and fails to hold even a modicum of interest.

p,d&w, Willis Kent; ph, Harvey Gould, Marcel Le Picard; ed, I. R. Johns.

Drama (PR:A MPAA:NR)

MADALENA½ (1965, Gr.) 95m Finos/Greek Motion Pictures bw

Aliki Vouyouklaki (Madalena), Dimitris Papamichael (Giorgas), Pantelis Zervos (Father), T. Morides, Thanassis Vengos.

Simplistic romance starring Vouyouklaki, a young woman who supports five sisters and one brother by running their late father's ferryboat. She meets Papamichael, the son of a man who owns a rival ferryboat company. She refuses to admit she has fallen in love with him but all is resolved when a priest manages to straighten things out and marry the couple. (In Greek; English subtitles.)

p, Th. A. Damaskinos, V. G. Michaelides; d, Dinos Dimopoulos; w, Georges Roussos; ph, Walter Lassally; m, Manos Hadjidakis; art d, Markos Zervas; English subtitles, Herman G. Weinberg.

Romance (PR:A MPAA:NR)

MADAM SATAN (SEE: MADAME SATAN, 1930)

MADAME½

(1963, Fr./Ital./Span.) 104m Cine Alliance-GESI Cinematografica-CC Champion-Agata/EM c (MADAME SANS-GENE)

Sophia Loren (Catherine Huebscher [Madame]), Robert Hossein (Lefevre), Julien Bertheau (Napoleon), Marina Berti (Elisa), Carlo Giuffere (Jerome), Gabriella Pallotta (Heloise), Annalis Gade (Caroline), Laura Valenzuela (Pauline), Gianrico Tedeschi (Roquet), Renaud Mary (Fouche), Celina Cely.

An ebullient, bawdy romp set in Napoleonic times that featured the sultry Loren as the outspoken laundress who washed the Little Corporal's shirts in 1792. She falls in love with Hossein, a sergeant, who has a cannon placed in her shop. There's a revolution on the horizon and she wants to join her lover at the front but he assures her the war will be over soon and she'll return to claim her. Time passes slowly during the war and four years go by. Hossein and Loren meet only once, in order to marry, and when she applies for a pass to the front from Napoleon (Bertheau), he doesn't recall her and sends her away. Loren jumps aboard a wagon full of "professional" women and locates her husband, now promoted on the battlefield to captain. They try to find a quiet place to celebrate their reunion but are soon caught and captured by the enemy Austrian troops. In their escape, they explode the Austrian ammo dump and when they return to French lines, Bertheau makes Hossein a full colonel for his bravery. Loren and Hossein fight side by side in the war and she is decorated for her efforts. When Berteau becomes Emperor, he dubs Hossein and Loren as the Duke and Duchess of Danzig, then considers elevating them again to King and Queen of Westphalia after Loren makes her court debut. Bertheau's sisters find Loren's manners unspeakable and prevail on him to not do as he planned. Bertheau is under their influence so he asks Hossein to shed Loren and wed a princess because the spectre of Loren as a Queen would make the Emperor look like a fool. Loren is livid, rushes into her leader's private quarters and reminds him of the days when he was a lowly soldier and could not afford to pay to keep his linen clean. Bertheau is taken by her logic and decides to allow her and Hossein to stay together and he will find someone else to be the rulers of Westphalia. Filmed on location in Spain and Italy, it's a light confection that falls pleasantly on the eyes and ears and is unmemorable moments later. The French title, MADAME SANS-GENE, means "free and easy" or "flippant" depending on which Berlitz teacher you ask. Lots of fun, MADAME had Peter Sellers tapped to play Napoleon and Gina Lollobrigida as Madame. The former would have been an asset, the latter a liablity. Period comedies, unless they are satires, are not easy to make happen. This worked only partially, but did have its share of amusement.

p, Maleno Malenotti; d, Christian-Jaque; w, Henri Jeanson, Ennio De Concini, Christian-Jaque, Franco Solinas, Jean Ferry (based on the play "Madame Sans Gene" by Emile Moreau, Victorien Sardou); ph, Robert Gerardi (Technirama, Technicolor); m, Angelo Francesco Lavagnino; ed, Jacques Desagneaux, Eraldo Da

Roma; art d, Jean d'Eaubonne, Mario Rappini; cos, Marcel Escoffier, Itala Scandariato.

Comedy (PR:A-C MPAA:NR)

MADAME AKI* (1963, Jap.) 114m Tokyo Eiga/Toho c (YUSHU HEIYA)

Hisaya Morishige (Katayuki), Fujiko Yamamoto (Aki), Michiyo Aratama (Misako), Tatsuya Nakadai (Tatsumi), Chieko Naniwa, Hiroyuki Nagato, Mayumi Ozora.

Morishige is a Japanese business executive who is harmlessly flirting with Aratama, the younger sister of a late friend. His wife, Yamamoto, after meeting with the girl suspects that her husband is cheating on her. When Morishige claims that he does indeed like Aratama, Yamamoto is convinced of his infidelity and has an affair with Nakadai, a young sculptor. Aratama spots the pair together and sees her chance to take her relationship with the older man a step further. He refuses her, realizing that she is young and idealistic, but finally sleeps with her as a consolation. Eventually Aratama and Nakadai fall in love. They decide to marry, leaving Yamamoto and Morishige to decide what they shall do with themselves.

p, Ichiro Sato; d, Shiro Toyoda; w, Toshio Yazumi (based on a story by Yasushi Inouye); ph, Kozo Okazaki (Tohoscope, Eastmancolor), m, Ikuma Dan.

Drama (PR:O MPAA:NR)

MADAME BOVARY* (1949) 115m MGM bw

Jennifer Jones (Emma Bovary), James Mason (Gustave Flaubert), Van Heflin (Charles Bovary), Louis Jourdan (Rodolphe Boulanger), Christopher Kent [Alf Kjellin] (Leon Dupuis), Gene Lockhart (J. Homais), Frank Allenby (Lhereux), Gladys Cooper (Mme. Dupuis), John Abbott (Mayor Tuvache), Henry [Harry] Morgan (Hyppolite), George Zucco (Dubocage), Ellen Corby (Felicite), Eduard Franz (Roualt), Henri Letondal (Guillaumin), Esther Somers (Mme. Lefrancois), Frederic Tozere (Pinard), Paul Cavanagh (Marquis D'Andervilliers), Larry Simms (Justin), Dawn Kinney (Berthe), Edith Evanson (Mother Superior), Edward Keane (Presiding Judge), Paul Bryar (Bailiff), Ted Infuhr (Boy), Florence Auer (Mme. Petree), Constance Purdy (Mme. Foulard), Harold Krueger (Harelip Youth), Karl Johnson (Drunken Guest), Bert Le Baron (Young Man), Phil Schumacher, Jack Stoney, Anne Kunde, Sailor Vincent, Dick Alexander, Helen Thurston, Lon Poff, Stuart Holmes, Fred Cordova (Guests), Eula Morgan, Gracille LaVinder (Women), Jeanine Caruso (Berthe at 15 Months), Ed Agresti, Charles Bancroft, Mayo Newhall, David Cavendish (Men), Andre Charisse (Young Man), Manuel Paris (Servant), Victor Kilian (Mons. Canivet), Angie O. Poulos (Porter), John Ardizoni (Lagandy), Dickie Derrel (Urchin), Charles De Ravenne (Pimply-Faced Youth), George Davis (Innkeeper), Jac George (Opera Conductor), Helen St. Rayner (Opera Singer), Vernon Steele (Priest).

Stunningly produced adaptation of Gustave Flaubert's controversial (at the time) novel, directed skillfully by Minelli. The film is structured with an odd (and only fairly successful) framing story that sees Mason as Flaubert on trial for indecency following publication of *Madame Bovary*. Mason proceeds to detail for the jury (and the viewer) his novel (this device harms the film somewhat because it distances the viewer from Jones' character by removing the events from a conventional filmic reality). Jones is a temperamental beauty who leaves a convent to help her father. Her boredom is suspended when Heflin, a young doctor, enters her life and proposes marriage. She accepts, but soon Heflin proves to be stodgy and dull, and her restlessness returns. Desperate for a change, she takes a rich lover, Jourdan, but the affair ends when he proves to be even shallower than Heflin. She enters into another affair with Kent, who resembles Jourdan, but this, too, soon ends. Desperation and panic take their toll on Jones and, unable to cope with her life's failures any longer, she commits suicide. While the script and structure of MADAME BOVARY is fairly poor (Mason's voice-over is particularly irritating and distracting), Minnelli triumphs over the material due to his confident handling of producer Berman's massive budget. The costumes, sets, and scale of the scenes are handled artfully, and the "Emma Bovary Waltz" sequence, with its large cast and complex choreography, stands as one of Minelli's finest sequences.

p, Pandro S. Berman; d, Vincente Minnelli; w, Robert Ardrey (based on the novel by Gustave Flaubert); ph, Robert Planck; m, Miklos Rozsa; ed, Ferris Webster; art d, Cedric Gibbons, Jack Martin Smith; set d, Edwin B. Willis, Richard A. Pefferle; cos, Walter Plunkett; spec eff, Warren Newcombe; ch, Jack Donohue; makeup, Jack Dawn.

Drama **Cas.** (PR:A MPAA:NR)

MADAME BUTTERFLY½ (1932) 86m PAR bw

Sylvia Sidney (Cho-Cho San), Cary Grant (Lt. B. F. Pinkerton), Charles Ruggles (Lt.Barton), Sandor Kallay (Goro), Irving Pichel (Yomadori), Helen Jerome Eddy (Cho-Cho's Mother), Edmund Breese (Cho-Cho's Grandfather), Judith Vosselli (Mme. Goro), Louise Carter (Suzuki), Dorothy Libaire (Peach Blossom), Sheila Terry (Mrs. Pinkerton), Wallis Clark (Cmdr. Anderson), Berton Churchill (American Counsul), Philip Horomato (Trouble).

Hopelessly dated film version of Puccini's opera sans the music. Grant stars as the dashing American Navy officer on leave in Japan where he meets and marries geisha girl Sidney despite the fact that he is engaged to an American girl back home. Sidney adapts to her husband's Western ways and when he returns to his fleet, she vows to remain faithful to him. Three years later Grant returns to Japan with his American wife (to whom he has confessed the previous marriage) and goes to the home of Sidney to break the news. Sidney, having made elaborate preparations for her husband's homecoming, answers the door with Grant's child (which she bore in his absence) in her arms. Met with an impossible situation, Sidney gives the child to her family and commits suicide. Remade in 1941 as THE DREAM OF BUTTERFLY.

p, B. P. Schulberg; d, Marion Gering; w, Josephine Lovett, Joseph Moncure March (based on the story by John Luther Long, and the play by David Belasco); ph, David Abel; m, Giacomo Puccini, W. Franke Harling.

Drama (PR:A MPAA:NR)

MADAME BUTTERFLY***

(1955 Ital./Jap.) 114m Toho-Rizzoli-Gallone/I.F.E. c

Karuo Yachigusa (*Cio-Cio-San, Sung by Orietta Moscucci*), Nicola Filacuridi (*Pinkerton, Sung by Giuseppe Campora*), Michiko Tanaka (*Suzuki, Sung by Anna Maria Canali*), Ferdinando Lidonni (*Sharpless*), Satoshi Nakamura (*Yamadori, Sung by Adelio Zagonara*), Kiyoshi Takagi (*Goro, Sung by Paolo Caroli*), Yoshio Kosugi (*Priest, Sung by Plinio Clabassi*), Josephine Corry (*Kate Pinkerton*), Takarazuka Kabuki Ballet of Tokyo (*Geishas*), Teatro Real Dell Opera Di Roma.

The first film version of Puccini's opera filmed as an opera. The sets were designed and built by Japanese art directors, the performers are mostly Japanese (with the singing dubbed by Italians), and the orchestrations were handled by the Italians. Though well done, with an eye for accuracy, MADAME BUTTERFLY is, nonetheless, a filmed opera and therefore somewhat dull.

p, Ivao Mori; d, Carmine Gallone; w, (based on the opera by Giacomo Puccini); ph, Claude Renoir (Technicolor); ed, Nicolo Lazzari; md, Oliviere de Fabritiis, Giuseppe Conca; cos, Takazo Raita; ch, Yoshio Aoyama.

Opera (PR:A MPAA:NR)

MADAME CURIE****

(1943) 124m MGM bw

Greer Garson (*Mme. Marie Curie*), Walter Pidgeon (*Pierre Curie*), Robert Walker (*David LeGros*), Dame May Whitty (*Mme. Eugene Curie*), Henry Travers (*Eugene Curie*), C. Aubrey Smith (*Lord Kelvin*), Albert Basserman (*Prof. Jean Perot*), Victor Francen (*President of University*), Reginald Owen (*Dr. Henri Becquerel*), Van Johnson (*Reporter*), Elsa Basserman (*Mme. Perot*), Lumsden Hare (*Prof. Reget*), James Hilton (*Narrator*), Charles Trowbridge, Edward Fielding, James Kirkwood, Nestor Eristoff (*Board Members*), Moroni Olsen (*President of Businessmen's Board*), Miles Mander, Arthur Shields, Frederic Worlock (*Businessmen*), Alan Napier (*Dr. Bladh*), Ray Collins (*Lecturer's Voice*), Almira Sessions (*Mme. Michaud*), Margaret O'Brien (*Irene at Age Five*), Dorothy Gilmore (*Nurse*), Gigi Perreau (*Eva at Age 18 Months*), Ruth Cherrington (*Swedish Queen*), Wyndham Standing (*King Oscar*), Harold de Becker, Guy D'Ennery (*Professors*), George Davis, William Edmunds (*Cart Drivers*), Michael Visaroff (*Proud Papa*), George Meader (*Singing Professor*), Franz Dorfler (*Assistant Seamstress*), Ray Teal (*Driver*), Noel Mills (*Wedding Guest*), Teddy Infuhr (*Son*), Mariska Aldrich (*Tall Woman*), Al Ferguson, Ben Gerien, Tony Carson, Maria Page, Isabelle Lamore, Justine Duney, Nita Pike (*People at Accident*), Leo Mostovoy (*Photographer*), Dickie Myers (*Master Michaud*), Francis Pierlot (*Mons. Michaud*), Howard Freeman (*Prof. Constant's Voice*), Ray Collins (*Lecturer's Voice*), Linda Lee Gates, Marie Louise Cates (*Perot Grandchildren*), Lisa Golm (*Lucille*), Marek Windheim (*Jewelry Salesman*), Eustace Wyatt (*Doctor*).

Warner Bros. had long been the home of film biographies and Louis B. Mayer wanted to change that. He tried first with Spencer Tracy as Edison, and despite the mild box-office returns, decided to take a chance with a film based on Eve Curie's book about her mother, which he'd acquired from Universal. Aldous Huxley and F. Scott Fitzgerald both took a crack at the screenplay, then it was abandoned when they couldn't get Greta Garbo to play the role. Sometime later, after Garson and Pidgeon had been successfully teamed in BLOSSOMS IN THE DUST and MRS. MINIVER, the studio decided to reactivate the project. It was a fine film that stirred many hearts and stayed fairly close to the truth, something that many biographies failed to do in the 1930s and 1940s. Garson is a poor Polish student studying in Paris around the turn of the century. She meets kindly Basserman, a professor, who gives her the chance to earn some francs while studying the magnetism of steel. Basserman notifies Pidgeon, a retiring scientist, that he wishes the man to share his small lab with Garson, and Pidgeon agrees. While working side by side, Pidgeon sees that she is a scientific whiz and soon falls in love with her, but is too shy to say anything about it. Garson plans to return to Poland and teach and Pidgeon can't bear the thought of losing her, so he finally screws up enough courage to ask for her hand in marriage and she readily accepts. In the meantime, they have been observing a piece of pitchblende which has been acting oddly due to some experiments. After returning from their brief honeymoon, Garson attacks the pitchblende problem and refuses to give up until, after five years of nonstop study, she discovers radium. As the years pass, they have children, O'Brien and Perreau, and go out hunting for money to finance their efforts. They eventually secure an old shed for their tests and more years of poverty and problems follow until they extract one tiny decogram of radium from thousands of pounds of pitchblende. They are honored and acclaimed and take a much-needed vacation in the country. On the day when they are to receive an award from the university, Pidgeon is killed in an auto accident. Garson continues her work and the film concludes. What is left out is that Curie may have had an affair with a married fellow worker a few years after her beloved husband died. Nominated for Best Picture, Best Actor, Best Actress, Best Cinematography, and Best Music, it won no awards against the competition of CASABLANCA, THE SONG OF BERNADETTE, WATCH ON THE RHINE, and THE MORE THE MERRIER. The script was intelligent and unusually interesting for a biography, and yet the best words in it came from Curie herself when she spoke to some of her colleagues in a university speech and said: "It is by these small candles that we shall see before us, little by little, the dim outlines of the great plan that shapes the universe, and I am among those who think that, for this reason, science has a great beauty, and, with its great spiritual strength, will in time cleanse the world of its evils, its ignorance, its poverty, diseases, wars, and heartaches."

p, Sidney Franklin; d, Mervyn LeRoy; w, Paul Osborn, Paul H. Rameau (based on the book by Eve Curie); ph, Joseph Ruttenberg; m, Herbert Stothart; ed, Harold F.

Kress; art d, Cedric Gibbons, Paul Groesse; set d, Edwin B. Willis, Hugh Hunt; cos, Irene Sharaff, Gile Steele; spec eff, Warren Newcombe, makeup, Jack Dawn.

Biography (PR:AAA MPAA:NR)

MADAME DE

(SEE: EARRINGS OF MADAME DE, THE, 1954, Ital.)

MADAME DEATH zero

(1968, Mex.) 85m Filmica Vergara bw (LA SENORA MUERTE)

John Carradine (*Dr. Diabolo*), Regina Torne, Elsa Cardenas, Miguel Angel Alvarez, Victor Junco, Nathanael Leon Frankenstein, Isela Vega, Alicia Ravel, Patricia Ferrer.

Torne is a disfigured woman who hires Carradine, a doctor, to help her regain her beauty. The experiments require Torne to find victims for skin transplants and blood transfusions. Director Salvador previously worked his limited talents with Viruta and Capulina, the "Mexican Abbott and Costello." His career also included EL MODERNO BARBA AZUL (1946), an obscure film that featured Buster Keaton.

p, Luis Enrique Vergara; d, Jaime Salvador; w, Ramon Obal, Jr.

Horror (PR:O MPAA:NR)

MADAME DU BARRY* 1/2

(1934) 79m WB bw

Dolores Del Rio (*Mme. Du Barry*), Reginald Owen (*King Louis XV*), Victor Jory (*Duke D'Aiguillon*), Osgood Perkins (*Richelieu*), Verree Teasdale (*Duchess De Granmont*), Henry O'Neill (*Duc De Choiseul*), Anita Louise (*Marie Antoinette*), Ferdinand Gottschalk (*Lebel*), Maynard Holmes (*Dauphin*), Dorothy Tree (*Adelaide*), Helen Howell (*Countess De Beam*), Joan Wheeler (*Florette*), Hobart Cavanaugh (*De La Vauguyon*), Jessie Scott (*Zamore*), Virginia Sale (*Sophie*), Camille Rouvelle (*Victoria*), Nella Walker (*Mme. De Noailles*), Halliwell Hobbes (*English Ambassador*), Arthur Treacher (*Master of the Bedroom*), Doris Lloyd (*Madame*), Mary Kornman (*Felice*), Robert Greig (*Chef*), Allan Cavan (*Nobleman*), Joan Barclay (*Bit*), Eula Guy, Victoria Vinton (*Young Girls*).

Another film version of the life of Louis XV's famous mistress, this time played by Del Rio as a conniving street waif whose rise to power in the decadent court of the king was given the treatment of a soap opera. Historically inaccurate and fairly pretentious.

p, Henry Blanke; d, William Dieterle; w, Edward Chodorov; ph, Sol Polito; ed, Bert Levy; art d, Jack Okey; ch, Albertina Rasch Dancers.

Historical Drama (PR:A MPAA:NR)

MADAME DU BARRY**

(1954 Fr./Ital.) 110m Ariane-Filmsonor-Francinex-Rizzoli/Cinedis c

Martine Carol (*Mme. Du Barry*), Andre Luguet (*Louis XV*), Daniel Ivernel (*Count Du Barry*), Gianna Maria Canale (*Mme. Gramont*), Massimo Serato (*Choisoul*), Dennis D'Ines (*Richilieu*), Jean Paredes (*Lebel*), Gabrielle Dorziat (*Madame*), Noel Roquevert (*Guillame*).

Slightly tongue-in-cheek historical drama starring Carol as the last mistress of Louis XV. The film details her beginnings as an obscure shop-girl who enters France's best bordello and eventually ends up in the bed of the doomed king, Luguet. Soon after his death, Carol is dragged to the streets and beheaded by the revolutionaries.

d, Christian-Jaque; w, Albert Valentin, Henri Jeanson, Christian-Jaque; ph, Christian Matras (Eastmancolor); ed, Jacques Desagneaux.

Drama (PR:C MPAA:NR)

MADAME FRANKENSTEIN

(SEE: LADY FRANKENSTEIN, 1971, Ital.)

MADAME GUILLOTINE* 1/2

(1931, Brit.) 75m W&F bw

Madeleine Carroll (*Lucille de Choisigne*), Brian Aherne (*Louis Dubois*), Henry Hewitt (*Vicomte d'Avennes*), Frederick Culley (*Marquis*), Hector Abbas (Le Blanc), Ian MacDonald (*Jacques*), H. Fisher White (*Le Farge*).

Against the backdrop of the French Revolution, a most unlikely (and unbelievable) romance takes place. Carroll is an aristocratic lady, loved by Aherne, a lawyer of the people. Though he is initially spurned, Carroll marries him after the revolution begins. When Aherne offers to go to the guillotine to save her life, the aristocrat turns herself in. However, goodness triumphs in the end as a forged pardon saves both their lives. At the time this film was released, Carroll and Aherne were two of England's leading stars. But, this trite material was well below both their talents. Supposedly director Fogwell's most ambitious film at the time, it rightly took a critical pounding.

p, Reginald Fogwell, Mansfield Markham; d, Fogwell; w, Harold Huth (based on a story by Fogwell); ph, Roy Overbaugh.

Drama (PR:A MPAA:NR)

MADAME JULIE

(SEE: WOMAN BETWEEN, THE, 1931)

MADAME LOUISE* 1/2

(1951, Brit.) 83m Nettlefold/BUT bw

Richard Hearne (*Mr. Pastry*), Petula Clark (*Miss Penny*), Garry Marsh (*Mr. Trout*), Richard Gale (*Lt. Edwards*), Doris Rogers (*Mrs. Trout*), Hilda Bayley (*Mme. Louise*), Charles Farrell (*Felling*), Vic Wise (*Curly*), Harry Fowler (*Clerk*), John Powe, Robert Adair, Doorn van Steyn, Anita [Sharp] Bolster, Pauline Goodwin, Mavis Greenaway, Pat Raphael, Mackenzie Ward, Gerald Rex.

After winning a dress boutique as part of a bet, a bookie throws himself into the enterprise and decides to modernize. After setting his new programs in place, the shop's old hands (led by Hearne) become incensed with the new developments. The bookmaker's plans backfire, leading to a variety of problems, and the shop is returned once more to its original owner. Though it showed promise, the material never lived up to its full comic potential.

p, Ernest G. Roy; d, Maclean Rogers; w, Michael Pertwee (based on the play by Vernon Sylvaine); ph, Wilkie Cooper.

Comedy **(PR:A MPAA:NR)**

MADAME PIMPERNEL (SEE: PARIS UNDERGROUND, 1945)

MADAME RACKETEER**

(1932) 72m PAR bw (GB: THE SPORTING WIDOW)

Alison Skipworth *("Countess von Claudwig"/Martha Hicks)*, Richard Bennett *(Elmer Hicks)*, George Raft *(Jack Houston)*, John Breeden *(David Butterworth)*, Evalyn Knapp *(Alice Hicks)*, Gertrude Messinger *(Patsy Hicks)*, Robert McWade *(James Butterworth)*, J. Farrell MacDonald *(John Adams)*, Walter Walker *(Arthur Gregory)*, George Barbier *(Warden Waddell)*, Cora Shumway *(Matron)*, Jessie Arnold *(Frankie)*, Anna Chandler *(Stella)*, Kate Morgan *(Maxine)*, Robert E. Homans *(Chief of Police)*, Arthur Hill *(Shanks)*, Eleanor Wesselhoeft *(Mrs. Donkenspeil)*, Ed Brady *(Taxi Driver)*, Frank Beal, Edgar Lewis, Scott Seaton, William Humphrey, Alf James *(Bank Directors)*, Irving Bacon *(Gus the Desk Clerk)*, Oscar Aptel, Arthur Hoyt.

Okay crime comedy starring Skipworth as a middle-aged thief who, upon her release from prison, immediately returns to a life of crime. She uses her criminal talents to ensure the happy futures of daughters Knapp and Messinger, who have been raised by their father, Bennett. When Skipworth spots racketeer Raft making overtures toward Messinger, she concocts a plan to expose him as a crook. She decides to align herself with Raft's gang to prove her point and, as a result, ends up back in jail.

d, Alexander Hall, Harry Wagstaff Gribble; w, Malcolm Stuart Boylan, Harvey Gates; ph, Henry Sharp.

Comedy/Crime **(PR:A MPAA:NR)**

MADAME ROSA* 1/2**

(1977, Fr.) 105m Lira/WB-COL-New Line c (LA VIE DEVANT SOI)

Simore Signoret *(Mme. Rosa)*, Claude Dauphin *(Dr. Katz)*, Samy Ben Youb *(Mohammed "Momo")*, Gabriel Jabbour *(Mr. Hamil)*, Michal Bat Adam *(Nadine)*, Costa Gavras *(Ramon)*, Stella Anicette *(Mme. Lola)*, Bernard La Jarrige *(Mr.Charmette)*, Mohammed Zineth *(Kadir Youssef)*, Genervievre Fontanel *(Maryse)*.

Signoret is an aging concentration camp survivor and ex-prostitute who cares for prostitutes' children in Paris' Arab-Jewish section. Though growing older and slowly losing her memory, she is still able to care for the children she loves, including Youb, an unruly, rebellious youth who cares deeply about her. She has delusions that the Gestapo is going to come for her, and makes the boy promise to hide her. When Dauphin, a doctor, shows up, Youb hides her in a secret room and claims she has gone to Israel. She dies, but he continues to keep her in the hideaway, until police make the discovery and take him away. The conflicts between Arabs and Jews and the ghosts of Nazism are well-handled, traveling through a racial and cultural milieu with grace and sensitivity to the different feelings therein. The film is a little talky, but the overall product is excellent. Mizrahi, the film's director and writer, is an Israeli of Moroccan origin who lived in France for 10 years before making this film. Costa Gavras, the famed director, had a starring role in MADAME ROSA, which won the Best Foreign Film Oscar in 1977. (In French; English subtitles).

p, Raymond Danon, Roland Girard, Jean Bolary; d, Moshe Mizrahi; w, Mizrahi (based on the novel *Momo* by Emile Ajar [Romain Gary]); ph, Nestor Almendros (Eastmancolor); m, Philippe Sarde, Dabket Loubna; ed, Sophie Coussein.

Drama **Cas.** **(PR:O MPAA:PG)**

MADAME SANS-GENE (SEE: MADAME, 1963, Fr./Ital./Span.)

MADAME SATAN 1/2** (1930) 80m DeMille/MGM bw

Kay Johnson *(Angela Brooks)*, Reginald Denny *(Bob Brooks)*, Lillian Roth *(Trixie)*, Roland Young *(Jimmy Wade)*, Elsa Peterson *(Martha)*, Boyd Irwin *(Captain)*, Wallace McDonald *(1st Mate)*, Wilfred Lucas *(A Roman Senator)*, Tyler Brooke *(Romeo)*, Lotus Thompson *(Eve)*, Vera Marsh *(Call of the Wild)*, Martha Sleeper *(Fish Girl)*, Doris McMahon *(Water)*, Marie Valli *(Confusion)*, Julianne Johnston *(Miss Conning Tower)*, Albert Conti *(Empire Officer)*, Earl Askam *(Pirate)*, Betty Francisco *(Little Rolls Riding Hood)*, Ynes Seabury *(Babo)*, Countess De Liguoro *(Spain)*, Katherine Irving *(Spider Girl)*, Aileen Ransom *(Victory)*, Theodore Kosloff *(Electricty, Ballet Mechanique)*, Jack King *(Herman)*, Edward Prinz *(Riff)*, Henry Stockbridge, June Nash, Mary Carlisle, Mary McAllister, Dorothy Dehn, Louis Netheaux, Ella Hall, Edwards Davis, Kasha Haroldi, Katherine DeMille, Verna Gordon, Natalie Storm, Elvira Lucianti, Marguerita Swope, Maine Geary, Allan Lane, Kenneth Gibson, Youcca Troubetskoy, Miss Vernon, Lorimer Johnson, John Byron, Natalie Visart, Abe Lyman and Band.

The appeal of this bizarre and nearly incomprehensible film, the only musical ever attempted by showman DeMille, is rooted in the macabre sense of humor on the part of certain viewers. For the humorless, this one is simply for the cuckoos. Johnson is a socialite who realizes she is losing her husband, Denny, who is paying too much attention to a fetching young Roth. To win back her husband's affections, Johnson turns herself into the mysterious "Madame Satan." Johnson changes from boring wife to sultry French tramp, wearing exaggerated costumes and makeup that disguises her appearance. She entices her husband Denny at a wild, elaborate costume party held inside a floating dirigible. Johnson's costume, with skull mask, is a cleverly revealing creation in the DeMille tradition; it's hardly there at all, a few strips of sequined cloth barely covering her breasts with the entire middle cut out. The cat-like costume is reprised by a host of other females in chorus lines, wearing cat suits with long black furry tails. These and other girls perform numerous exotic dance routines which, under LeRoy Prinz's direction, are nothing less than fantastic. During the dirigible's party flight a storm breaks loose and the airliner is struck by lightning and begins to burn, crashing earthward over New York City. Denny gives Johnson his own parachute and she jumps to safety, as do all the other strange party-goers. One girl, dressed as a Burmese idol with many arms, floats down upon a group of drunks, and Roth, dressed as a golden pheasant, swinging on a weather vane, lands on a church steeple. Denny rides the flaming dirigible to earth, jumping at the last second before impact, so that he dives into the Central Park reservoir. Young's escape is the most sensational as he parachutes into a zoo, landing in the lion's cages just as they're being fed, causing him to frantically take refuge in a tree until being rescued. Leisen's set of the dirigible is spectacular, as are the climactic scenes then in vogue with offbeat musicals. DeMille's famous temperament was in evidence during the producion. In one scene Natalie Visart, a bit player and friend of DeMille's adopted daughter Katherine, who debuted in this film, was standing near a short-circuiting fuse box and her costume caught fire, the flames eating away one layer after another of her thick taffeta gown. Visart did not move, being petrified with fear, and her lack of action probably saved her life. Dance director Prinz dove forward and doused the blaze just as it began to burn through the last layer. One dancer stood for hours on a high perch while DeMille took his time with an elaborate setup. The girl was about to faint and certainly fall to her death when Prinz called a halt to the scene and had the girl lowered to safety. DeMille exploded, saying that Prinz had ruined his scene. "The girl might have fallen and been killed," said Prinz. "Nonsense!" yelled DeMille before ordering the scene to proceed. The film amused DeMille, who produced it at the strong suggestion of MGM boss Louis B. Mayer but it failed to amuse the public and it lost money, unlike most of DeMille's films. (Between 1913 and 1931 DeMille's productions cost about $12 million overall but they returned a total gross of $28 million.) Songs include: "The Cat Walks," "We're Going Somewhere," "This Is Love" (Herbert Sothart, Clifford Grey), "Low Down," "All I Know Is You Are in My Arms," "Satan's Song," "Live and Love Today," "Auction Number" (Elsie Janis, Jack King).

p&d, Cecil B. DeMille; w, Jeanie Macpherson, Gladys Unger, Elsie Janis; ph, Harold Rosson; ed, Anne Bauchens; art d, Cedric Gibbons, Mitchell Leisen; cos, Adrian; ch, LeRoy Prinz.

Musical **(PR:A MPAA:NR)**

MADAME SPY** (1934) 70m UNIV bw

Fay Wray *(Maria)*, Nils Asther *(Capt. Franck)*, Edward Arnold *(Schultz)*, John Miljan *(Weber)* David Torrence *(Seerfeldt)*, Douglas Walton *(Karl)*, Oscar Apfel *(Pahlke)*, Vince Barnett *(Peter)*, Robert Ellis *(Sulkin)*, Stephen Alden Chase *(Petroskie)*, Rollo Lloyd *(Baum)*, Noah Beery, Sr. *(Gen. Philipow)*, A.S. Byron, Arthur Wanzer *(Chemists)*, Ferdinand Schumann-Heink *(Cafe Owner)*, Herbert Holcombe *(Orderly)*, Reginald Pasch *(Dumb Guy)*, Ruth Fallows *(Lulu)*, Robert Graves, Anders Van Haden *(Detectives)*, Edward Peil, Sr. *(Garage Proprietor)*, Werner Plack *(Conductor)*, Albert J. Smith *(Lackey)*, Philip Morris *(Russian Officer)*, Eddy Chandler *(Austrian Officer)*, Henry Grobel *(Austrian Aviator)*, Jerry Jerome *(Russian Aviator)*, Mabel Marden.

Totally implausible but beautifully shot film directed by former cameraman Karl Freund (he also directed the Karloff classic THE MUMMY), in which German captain Asther is hired by the Austrian secret service to capture a mysterious Russian agent known only as B-24. Unfortunately, agent B-24 happens to be Asther's own very Russian (well, as Russian as Fay Wray could get) wife. Remade from a German film entitled UNDER FALSE FLAGS (1932).

d, Karl Freund; w, William Hurlbut (based on the German film UNTER FALSCHE *FLAGGE* by Johannes Brandt, Joseph Than, Max Kimmich); ph, Norbert Brodine.

Spy Drama **(PR:A MPAA:NR)**

MADAME SPY* 1/2 (1942) 63M UNIV bw

Constance Bennett *(Joan Bannister)*, Don Porter *(David Bannister)*, John Litel *(Peter)*, Edward Brophy *(Mike Reese)*, John Eldredge *(Carl Gordon)*, Edmund MacDonald *(Bill Drake)*, Nana Bryant *(Alicia Rolf)*, Jimmy Conlin *(Winston)*, Selmer Jackson *(Harrison Woods)*, Nino Pipitone *(Miro)*, Cliff Clark *(Inspector Varden)*, John Dilson *(Martin, Proprietor)*, Johnny Berkes *(Hotel Clerk)*, Grace Hayle, Norma Drury, Mira McKinney *(Red Cross Women)*, Billy Wayne *(Driver's Helper)*, Pat West *(Driver)*, Reid Kilpatrick *(Announcer)*, William Gould *(Minister)*, Phil Warren *(Reporter)*, Anne O'Neal *(Woman)*, Thornton Edwards *(Foreign Cab Driver)*, Irving Mitchell *(Man)*, Sidney Miller *(Newsboy)*, Alexander Lockwood, Charles Sherlock, Pat Costello, Frank Marlowe *(Cab Drivers)*, Eddie Coke *(Attendant)*, Rico de Montez *(Filipino Servant)*, Gerald Pierce *(Page Boy)*, Eddie Coke, Jack Gardner *(Attendants)*.

Silly spy movie starring Bennett and Porter as a newlywed couple (he's a newspaper correspondent she met in Paris during a bombing raid) who travel throughout the war-torn world on their honeymoon. Upon their return to the States, Bennett starts having contact with Nazi spy leader Litel, and Porter gets suspicious. He follows the pair to Nazi spy headquarters, at a deserted New York State farmhouse, where a gun battle ensues. Bennett eventually is revealed as an American counterspy sent by the U.S. to foil the Nazis.

p, Marhshall Grant; d, Roy William Neill; w, Lynn Riggs, Clarence Upson Young (based on a story by Young); ph, George Robinson; ed, Ted J. Kent.

Spy Drama **(PR:A MPAA:NR)**

MADAME WHITE SNAKE 1/2**

(1963, Hong Kong) 105m Shaw Bros./Frank Lee International c (PAI-SHE CHUAN)

Lin Dai, Chao Lei, Margaret Tu Chuan.

A goddess who is actually a 1,000-year-old white snake falls in love with a drugstore clerk who had saved her in another lifetime. In order to repay him, she takes the form of a beautiful woman and marries him. Their life is idyllic until a Buddhist monk informs the clerk of his wife's true origin. He gives the man three amulets to reduce her power, but she overcomes the charms. One day the clerk sees her in her reptilian form and he dies from fright. The goddess revives her husband with a magic red mushroom obtained from the Holy Land. The monk returns and forces the man to magically fly to Mount Chin. There he pleads with Fa-hai, the God of All, to allow the marriage between the mortal and goddess. The god tries to kill the man by creating a flood, but he escapes. The god engages him in a battle once more and this time kills him. When the husband arrives in heaven, he finds his goddess spouse already there. This film, produced by the very successful Shaw Brothers, was based on a Chinese fairy tale.

p, Run Run Shaw; d, Yueh Feng; w, Ka Jui-fan (based on the Chinese fairy tale, "Pai She Chauan"); ph, T. Nishimoto (Shawscope, Eastmancolor); m, Wang Fu-ling.

Fantasy   (PR:C   MPAA:NR)

MADAME X**   (1929) 95m MGM bw (AKA: ABSINTHE)
Ruth Chatterton (Jacqueline), Lewis Stone (Floriot), Raymond Hackett (Raymond), Holmes Herbert (Noel), Eugenie Besserer (Rose), John P. Edington (Doctor), Mitchell Lewis (Col. Hanby), Ullrich Haupt (Laroque), Sidney Toler (Merivel), Richard Carle (Perissard), Carroll Nye (Darrell), Claude King (Valmorin), Chappell Dossett (Judge).

The first sound version of Frenchman Alexandre Bisson's classic tear-jerker starring Chatterton (whose appearance here launched her as one of the first major female stars of the talkies) as the bored wife of a diplomat whose affair with a playboy leads her on a path of self-destruction. Routine in most respects, and the first directing effort by actor Lionel Barrymore. His skill behind the camera is evident, but the overly histrionic material prevents any true sparks from flying. MGM's first two talkies, ALIAS JIMMY VALENTINE (1928), and BROADWAY MELODY (1928), were made using a stationary microphone. While MADAME X was being shot, Barrymore suggested putting the microphone on a fishing pole and following the characters around, which became for a time the established method of using the mike.

d, Lionel Barrymore; w, Willard Mack (based on the play by Alexandre Bisson); ph, Arthur Reed; ed, William S. Gray; art d, Cedric Gibbons; cos, David Cox.

Drama   (PR:A   MPAA:NR)

MADAME X**1/2   (1937) 75m MGM bw
Gladys George (Jacqueline Fleuriot), John Beal (Raymond Fleuriot), Warren William (Bernard Fleuriot), Reginald Owen (Maurice Dourel), William Henry (Hugh Fariman, Jr.), Henry Daniell (Lerocle), Philip Reed (Jean), Lynne Carver (Helene), Emma Dunn (Rose), Ruth Hussey (Annette), Luis Alberni (Scipio), George Zucco (Dr. LaFarge), Cora Witherspoon (Nora), Jonathan Hale (Hugh Fariman, Sr.), Adia Kuznetzoff (Capt. Dorcas).

Fourth version of the oft-filmed French weeper (other versions dated 1915, 1920 and 1929), this time starring George as the diplomat's wife whose brief fling with a playboy begins her long descent into prostitution, blackmail, and murder. Wood's direction of this trite material is standard and lends some credibility to the fairly ludicrous happenings.

p, James Kevin McGuinness; d, Sam Wood; w, John Meehan (based on the play by Alexandre Bisson); ph, John Seitz; m, David Snell; ed, Frank E. Hull; art d, Cedric Gibbons; m/l, "You're Setting Me on Fire," Walter Donaldson, Bob Wright, Chet Forrest.

Drama   (PR:A   MPAA:NR)

MADAME X***   (1966) 99m UNIV Eltee/UNIV c
Lana Turner (Holly Parker), John Forsythe (Clay Anderson), Ricardo Montalban (Phil Benton), Burgess Meredith (Dan Sullivan), Constance Bennett (Estelle Anderson), Keir Dullea (Clay Anderson, Jr.), John Van Dreelen (Christian Torben), Virginia Grey (Mimsy), Warren Stevens (Michael Spalding), Carl Benton Reid (Judge), Teddy Quinn (Clay, Jr. as a Boy), Frank Maxwell (Dr. Evans), Kaaren Verne (Nurse Riborg), Joe DeSantis (Carter), Frank Marth (Detective Combs), Bing Russell (Sgt. Riley), Teno Pollick (Manuel Lopez), Jeff Burton (Bromley), Jill Jackson (Police Matron), Neil Hamilton (Party Guest), Rodolfo Hoyos (Patron), Duncan McCleod (Official), Ruben Moreno, George Dega (Men), Mark Miranda (Mexican Boy), Byrd Holland (Cronyn the Butler), Kris Tel (Danish Woman), Brad Logan, Richard Tretter (Merchant Marines), Matilda Calhan (Miss Monteaux), Paul Bradley (Dancing Extra).

The seventh and best version of French playwright Bisson's overblown tear-jerker (other versions were filmed in 1915, 1920, 1929, 1937, 1948 as THE TRAIL OF MADAME X, 1960, and in 1981 as a made-for-TV picture) features a fine performance by Turner in the title role, and boasts handsome production by veteran "women's film" producer Hunter. The story sees Turner as the young wife of dull-but-rich diplomat Forsythe who seeks to quell her boredom by falling into an affair with playboy Montalban. When Montalban is accidentally killed in Turner's presence, the desperate woman turns to her nasty mother-in-law Bennett (in what was to be her last screen appearance) for help. The bitter, older woman (she never liked Turner) advises her to flee the country or face responsibility for ruining her husband's career. Turner says a tearful goodbye to her young son and disappears. As the years go by, Turner's fortunes go from bad to worse, and she soon finds herself forced into prostitution in Mexico. There she runs into slimy crook Meredith, who ensnares her into a clever blackmail scheme. When Turner learns the victim is to be Forsythe, she kills Meredith and is soon brought up on murder charges. Known only to the courts as Madame X, Turner is shocked to discover the young defense attorney (Dullea) assigned to defend her is her own son. Not wanting him or the jury to know the truth, Turner valiantly tries to suffer out the trial. Dullea, however, is strangely drawn to this mysterious woman. He defends her with youthful vigor and nearly wins the case, but the verdict is never heard. Turner

collapses from heart disease and tells Dullea her true identity before her death. The 1966 version of MADAME X succeeds despite its dated and somewhat maudlin plot line due to the total dedication of the principal participants. Turner used the material to rejuvenate her independent production company, thereby giving her a vested interest in the film's success. She chose producer Hunter for his experience with "women's pictures," and in the early stages of development, veteran melodrama director Douglas Sirk was slated to helm the ship. But it was Turner's heartfelt (and perhaps close-to-home, given her recent legal scandals) performance that gave this version of Bisson's classic weeper its real vitality.

p, Ross Hunter; d, David Lowell Rich; w, Jean Holloway (based on the play by Alexandre Bisson); ph, Russell Metty (Technicolor); m, Frank Skinner; ed, Milton Carruth; art d, Alexander Golitzen, George Webb; set d, John McCarthy, Howard Bristol; cos, Jean Louis; spec eff, Walter Hammond; m/l, "Swedish Rhapsody," Charles Wildman; makeup, Bud Westmore.

Drama   **Cas.**   (PR:A   MPAA:NR)

MADCAP   (SEE: TAMING THE WILD, 1937)

MADCAP OF THE HOUSE*1/2   (1950, Mex.) 89m Oro/Mier y Brooks bw
Pedro Armendariz, Susana Freyre, Julio Villarreal, Luis Beristain, Beatriz Aguirre.

Mexican comedy about a young convent girl whose stubborn ideas and bullish manner finally force the mother superior to take the girl home and allow her to choose between the order and the normal world.

d, Juan Bustillo Oro; w, Bustillo Oro, Paulino Masip.

Comedy   (PR:A   MPAA:NR)

MADCHEN FUR DIE MAMBO-BAR   (SEE: $100 A NIGHT, 1968, Ger.)

MADCHEN IN UNIFORM   (SEE: MAEDCHEN IN UNIFORM, 1965, Fr./Ger.)

MADDEST CAR IN THE WORLD, THE*
(1974, Ger.) 93m Barbara Film/WG (DAS VERRUECKTESTE AUTO DER WELT)
Robert Mark [Rudolf Zehetgruber], Kathrin Oginski, Sal Borgese, Evelyne Kraft, Walter Giller, Walter Roderer, Ruth Jecklin, Gerhard Frickhoefer, Walter Feuchtenberg.

The German version of THE LOVE BUG, a Volkswagon Beetle named "Dudu" enters a rally for its fourth and last film. The result is an unimaginative trans-European race showing the car going through various adventures with the help of such devices as helicopter blades. The intrepid vehicle can also drive up vertical cliffs, cross rivers and lakes, and fight back glaciers. A real snoozer, this was aimed at children, who will probably find it too inane for even their teddy bears to sit through. Star Mark was also known as Rudolf Zehetgruber, the man who produced, directed, and co-wrote the film.

p&d, Rudolf Zehetgruber; w, Zehetgruber, G. von Nazzani; ph, Ruediger Meichsner.

Comedy/Adventure   (PR:AAA MPAA:NR)

MADDEST STORY EVER TOLD, THE   (SEE: SPIDER BABY, 1968)

MADE*1/2   (1972, Brit.) 104m International C-Productions/Anglo-EMI c
Carol White (Valerie), John Castle (Father Dyson), Roy Harper (Mike), Margery Mason (Mrs. Marshall), Doremy Vernon (June), Sam Dastor (Mahdav), Richard Vanstone (Ray), Michael Cashman (Joe), Brian Croucher (Arthur), Ray Smith (1st Policeman), Carl Rigg (2nd Policeman), Bob Harris (Interviewer), Sean Hewitt (Andy), Michael Standing (Young Man on Train).

Dull and dated drama about a young woman, White, and her troubles coping with raising her child out of wedlock while contending with a terminally ill mother. The story follows White as she tries to sort out her messed-up life while juggling the influences of young priest Castle, and rock star Harper. Eventually she rejects both men's lifestyles and sets out on her own.

p, Joseph Janni; d, John Mackenzie; w, Howard Barker (based on his play "No One Was Saved"); ph, Ernest Day (Technicolor); m, John Cameron; ed, David Campling; prod d, Philip Harrison; md, Cameron; m/l, Roy Harper (sung by Harper).

Drama   (PR:C   MPAA:NR)

MADE FOR EACH OTHER***1/2   (1939) 85m UA bw
Carole Lombard (Jane Mason), James Stewart (Johnny Mason), Charles Coburn (Judge Joseph Doolittle), Lucile Watson (Mrs. Mason), Harry Davenport (Dr. Healy), Ruth Weston (Eunice Doolittle), Donald Briggs (Carter), Eddie Quillan (Conway), Esther Dale (Annie the Cook), Rene Orsell (Hilda), Louise Beavers (Lily the Cook), Alma Kruger (Sister Agnes), Fred Fuller (Doolittle's Brother), Edwin Maxwell (Messerschmidt), Harry Depp (Hutch), Michael Rentschler (Office Boy), Jackie Taylor (John, Jr. at Age 1), Robert Emmett O'Connor (Elevator Starter), Milburn Stone (Sam), Bonnie Belle Barber (John, Jr., Newly Born), Robert Strange, Perry Ivans, Gladden James (Doctors), Ward Bond (Jim Hatton), Jack Mulhall, Gary Owen, Carlisle Moore, Russ Clark, Mike Killian, John Austin, Arthur Gardner, (Radio Operators), Tom London, Lane Chandler (Rangers), Mary Field (Indianapolis Lab Assistant), Russell Hopton (Collins), Arthur Hoyt (Jury Foreman), Harlan Briggs (Judge), Wilhelmina Morris, Nella Walker, Marjory Wood, Ethel Marical (Nurses), Ivan Simpson (Simon), Betty Farrington (Hospital Cashier), Ruth Gillette (Blonde in Cafe), Olin Howland (Farmer), Fern Emmett (Farmer's Wife), Harry Worth (New York Chemist), Raymond Bailey (Salt Lake Hospital Chemist), J. M. Sullivan (John Hopkin's Chemist).

Amiable dramatic comedy that could have been mired in suds in another director's hands, but Cromwell emphasizes the lightness and smoothes over what might have jerked tears. Lombard proved here that she could move audiences with her dramatic prowess as well as she could make them laugh. Lombard and Stewart are just married and climbing aboard an ocean liner for their honeymoon. Stewart is an attorney and his boss, the somewhat deaf Coburn, calls him back to try a case. Watson is Stewart's mother and she is annoyed that her son has rushed into marriage with Lombard. Coburn would have liked it if Stewart had married his daughter, Weston. That failing, Weston marries another lawyer in the firm, Briggs. Later, Stewart and Lombard have Coburn, Weston, and Briggs over for dinner and it winds up to be comic and tragic simultaneously, as nothing works right. The evening is topped off when Coburn tells them all that his new son-in-law, Briggs, is now a partner in the company, something Stewart has been angling for. Lombard has a baby and the unpaid debts mount up. More hassles occur when Watson joins them in their tiny apartment, and then, on New Year's eve, the baby gets sick and needs medicine, but there is none available in New York. Stewart appeals to Coburn and does such a good job of it that Coburn realizes Stewart is a heck of a speaker when he's impassioned. The services of Quillan, a crackerjack pilot, are secured and he flies the needed serum from Salt Lake City to New York City in a blinding snowstorm. The baby recovers and the marital strife that had been suffered through by Stewart and Lombard is soon salved. A nice movie that leaves a "feel good" smile on one's face. Quillan began in movies in 1926 and was seen in 1986 on an episode of "Hell Town"—a cancelled NBC series starring Robert Blake. Sixty years in film and nary a performance that was less than excellent.

p, David O. Selznick; d, John Cromwell; w, Jo Swerling, Frank Ryan; ph, Leon Shamroy; m, Lou Forbes; ed, James E. Newcomb, Hal C. Kern; prod d, William Cameron Menzies; md, Forbes; art d, Lyle Wheeler; set d, Edward G. Boyle; cos, Travis Banton; spec eff, Jack Cosgrove.

Drama/Comedy **Cas.** **(PR:AA MPAA:NR)**

MADE FOR EACH OTHER*** (1971) 104m Fox c

Renee Taylor *(Pandora [Panda] Gold)*, Joseph Bologna *(Gig [Giggy] Pinimba)*, Paul Sorvino *(Gig's Father)*, Olympia Dukakis *(Gig's Mother)*, Helen Verbit *(Pandora's Mother)*, Louis Zorich *(Pandora's Father)*, Norman Shelly *(Dr. Furro)*, Ron Carey, Peggy Pope, Susan Brockman, Art Levy, Frieda Wexler, Barbara Levy, Despo *(The Group)*, Paul Dumont *(Byron)*, Reggie Baff *(Corrine)*, Candy Azzara *(Sheila)*, Fred Nassif *(TV Director)*, Connie Snow *(Ingrid)*, Carmel Altomare *(Aunt Josie)*, Ed Barth *(Ronnie)*, Armand de La Garza *(Sal)*, Dorothy de La Garza *(Dottie)*, Barbara Carson *(Bibi)*, Sammy Smith *(M.C.)*, Doreen Miller *(Teenage Pandora)*, Adam Arkin *(Teenage Gig)*, Mitchell Spera *(Gig as a Boy)*, Jeanne Kaplan *(Selma)*, Adam Apul *(Ned)*, Bobby Alto *(Al)*, Doyle Newberry *(Priest)*, Sully Boyar, Nancy Andrews *(Psychiatrists)*.

Charming, offbeat comedy written by Taylor and Bologna and starring them as two perennial losers who meet and fall in love at a group-therapy session. Semi-autobiographical (Taylor and Bologna are married in real life), the film is moving, human, and real, with a fine touch of romance. Shot in New York City.

p, Roy Townshend; d, Robert B. Bean; w, Renee Taylor, Joseph Bologna; ph, William Storz (DeLuxe Color); m, Trade Martin; ed, Sonny Mele; art d, Robert Ramsey; set d, Bill Canfield; cos, Elaine Mangel; makeup, Peter Garafola.

Comedy **(PR:C MPAA:GP)**

MADE IN HEAVEN** (1952, Brit.) 81m Fanfare/GFD c

David Tomlinson *(Basil Topham)*, Petula Clark *(Julie Topham)*, Sonja Ziemann *(Marta)*, A.E. Matthews *(Grandpa)*, Charles Victor *(Mr. Topham)*, Sophie Stewart *(Mrs. Topham)*, Richard Wattis *(The Vicar)*, Athene Seyler *(Miss Honeycroft)*, Philip Stainton *(Mr. Grimes)*, Ferdy Mayne *(Istfan)*, Alfie Bass *(Mr. Jenkins)*, Dora Bryan *(Mrs. Jenkins)*, Michael Brennan *(Sgt. Marne)*, Harold Kasket, George Bishop, Margot Lister, John Warren, Ronnie Stevens, Gilbert Davis, Stuart Latham.

Silly British comedy about a young married couple, Tomlinson and Clark, who are entered by his mother in the annual Dunmow Flitch (a contest in which a married couple can win a side of bacon if they can maintain connubial bliss for the judgement of the locals). Everything goes smoothly until an attractive Hungarian girl is hired to help out with the domestic chores.

p, George H. Brown; d, John Paddy Carstairs; w, William Douglas Home, Brown; ph, Geoffrey Unsworth (Technicolor); m, Ronald Hanmer; ed, John D. Guthridge.

Comedy **Cas.** **(PR:A MPAA:NR)**

MADE IN ITALY***

(1967, Fr./Ital.) 101m Documento-Orsay/Royal c (A L'ITALIENNE)

Marina Berti *(Bored Diner)*, Claudio Gora *(Her Husband)*, Lionello Pio Di Savola *(Another Diner)*, Lando Buzzanca *(Giulio)*, Iolanda Modio *(Rosalia)*, Walter Chiari *(Enrico)*, Lea Massari *(Monica)*, Virna Lisi *(Virginia)*, Giulio Bosetti *(Renato)*, Catherine Spaak *(Karol)*, Fabrizio Moroni *(Gianremo)*, Sylva Koscina *(Diana)*, Jean Sorel *(Orlando)*, Nino Manfredi *(Lamporecchi)*, Rossella Falk (Wronged Wife), Alberto Sordi *(Errant Husband)*, *Claudie Lange (Other Woman)*, Anna Magnani *(Anna)*, Andrea Checchi *(Father)*, Aldo Giuffre, Anita Durante, Tecla Scarano, Milena Vucotich, Giampiero Albertini, Aldo Bufi-Landi, Adelmo Di Fraia, Antonio Mazza.

A series of 32 vignettes that illustrates the ups and downs of life in modern-day Italy. Highlights include a very funny sequence starring Magnani as the tired mother of three children who tries to organize her clan *and* her unemployed husband to maneuver across a very busy street in order to buy some ice cream. By the time the hair-raising adventure is over, the store has run out of treats, but the shop owner recommends that the family try a nice drugstore that has just opened on the other side of the street. Other blackout sketches include: tourists having to ask other tourists the location of historical landmarks; a young Italian man who is relieved to hear that although his fiancee has been involved with robbery, kidnaping, and murder, she has remained a virgin; a dashing young man who goes to great lengths to seduce an attractive married woman, and then after he succeeds, loathing her presence because he cannot get rid of her...etc, etc. Some of the vignettes are stronger than others, but the film adds up to a fairly entertaining whole. (In Italian; English subtitles.)

p, Gianni Hecht Lucari; d, Nanni Loy; w, Ettore Scola, Ruggero Maccari, Loy (based on a story by Scola, Maccari); ph, Ennio Guarnieri (Techniscope, Technicolor); m, Carlo Rustichelli; ed, Ruggero Mastroianni; art d, Luciano Spadoni; cos, Pier Luigi Pizzi; makeup, Nilo Jacoponi.

Comedy **(PR:C MPAA:NR)**

MADE IN PARIS** (1966) 103m Euterpe/MGM c

Ann-Margret *(Maggie Scott)*, Louis Jourdan *(Marc Fontaine)*, Richard Crenna *(Herb Stone)*, Edie Adams *(Irene Chase)*, Chad Everett *(Ted Barclay)*, John McGiver *(Roger Barclay)*, Marcel Dalio *(Georges)*, Matilda Calnan *(Cecile)*, Jacqueline Beer *(Denise Marton)*, Marcel Hillaire *(Attendant)*, Michele Montau *(Elise)*, Reta Shaw *(American Bar Singer)*, Count Basie and His Octet, Mongo Santmaria and His Band *(Themselves)*.

Routine early Ann-Margret vehicle starring the buxom redhead as the sexy assistant of fashion buyer Adams who is sent to Paris to attend the fancy fashion shows. Adams' real motivation is to get Ann-Margret away from her son Everett who has been chasing the poor girl nonstop since he met her. In Paris, Ann-Margret meets up with the dashing Jourdan who happens to be a former lover of Adams. They begin a relationship of sorts, but the lovesick Everett flies to Paris in pursuit of Ann-Margret. To complicate matters, Ann-Margret meets and begins dating newspaperman Crenna, but upon Everett's arrival she realizes that it is he she truly loves, and she returns to America.

p, Joe Pasternak; d, Boris Sagal; w, Stanley Roberts; ph, Milton Krasner (Panavision, Metrocolor); m, George Stoll; ed, William McMillin; md, Stoll; art d, George W. Davis, Preston Ames; set d, Henry Grace, Keogh Gleason; cos, Helen Rose; ch, David Winters; m/l "Made in Paris," Burt Bacharach, Hal David (sung by Trini Lopez), "Paris Lullaby," Sammy Fain, Paul Francis Webster (sung by Ann-Margret, Louis Jourdan), "My True Love," Red Skelton, "Skol Sister," "Goof Proof," Quincy Jones (played by Count Basie and His Octet); makeup, Frank McCoy.

Comedy **(PR:A MPAA:NR)**

MADE IN U.S.A. 1/2**

(1966, Fr.) 90m Rome-Paris-Anouchka-S.E.P.I.C./Athos c

Anna Karina *(Paula Nelson)*, Laszlo Szabo *(Richard Widmark)*, Jean Pierre Leaud *(Donald Siegel)*, Yves Alfonso *(David Goodis)*, Ernest Menzer *(Edgar Typhus)*, Jean-Claude Bouillon *(Inspector Aldrich)*, Kyoko Kosaka *(Doris Mizoguchi)*, Marianne Faithful *(Herself)*, Claude Bakka *(Man with Marianne Faithful)*, Philippe Labro *(Himself)*, Remo Forlani *(Workman in Bar)*, Marc Dudicourt *(Barman)*, Jean-Pierre Biesse *(Richard Nixon)*, Sylvain Godet *(Robert MacNamara)*, Alexis Poliakoff *(Man with Notebook and Red Telephone)*, Eliane Giovagnoli *(Dentist's Assistant)*, Roger Scipion *(Dr. Korvo)*, Daniele Palmero *(Hotel Chambermaid)*, Rita Maiden *(Woman Who Gives Paula Information)*, Isabelle Pons *(Provincial Journalist)*, Philippe Pouzenc *(Policeman)*, Fernand Coquet *(Billposter)*, Miguel *(Dentist)*, Annie Guegan *(Girl in Bandages)*, Marika Perioli *(Girl with Dog)*, Jean-Philippe Nierman *(Note-Taking Policeman)*, Charles Bitsch *(Taxi Driver)*, Daniel Bart *(Policeman)*, Jean-Luc Godard *(Richard Politzer's Shadow and His Recorder Voice)*.

Karina ventures to a place in France called Atlantic City to find the killer of an ex-lover named Richard Politzer. Interested in her case, Menzer gets involved, dragging along his nephew Alfonso. When Menzer is found dead, Karina is arrested and eventually released into the custody of Szabo. His assistant, Leaud, accuses Karina of the crime. She kills him; Szabo tries to kill her, but ends up her victim, as does Alfonso. A crazy mosaic of a plot which, as is usually the case with Godard, is secondary to technique as he stretches the limits of the narrative form. This is a gangster film, of sorts, in which Godard pays homage to the films he knew as a youngster. He dedicated MADE IN U.S.A. to directors Sam Fuller and Nicolas Ray. What's more, he gives his characters such names as Richard Nixon, Aldrich, Widmark, Siegel, Mizoguchi, Goodis (the last being the pulp writer upon whose novel SHOOT THE PIANO PLAYER is based). The use of the gangster genre is merely a framework on which Godard can build his cinematic devices, experimenting here with innovative sound techniques and a vivid, comic book use of color. As Karina searches for answers she makes inquiries into the whereabouts of Richard Politzer, however, we never hear his last name, as it is always silenced by external sources (i.e. airplanes). There are also repeated instances when Politzer's voice (really Godard's) is barely audible as a tape recording of it supplies information on the kidnaping and murder of Ben Barka (a Moroccan leftist who became a news item). The logic being that since no real information was known about Barka's abduction, then none would be delivered in the tape recording. The film very clearly addresses the Americanization of French life—gangster films, pop music, and the bright billboardish settings—all of which were "made in U.S.A." Shot at the same time as 2 OR 3 THINGS I KNOW ABOUT HER, Godard felt it a challenge to in part make two films concurrently. He was inspired to make this movie in the interests of creating a female Humphrey Bogart character. Also of interest is the appearance of long-time Rolling Stones associate, Marianne Faithful, who sings "As Tears Go By." While not one of Godard's most watchable films, it certainly has it's moments, many of them comic—the absurd dialog in the bar scenes, for instance. Though MADE IN U.S.A. has been shown in the U.S., it never got an official release due to legal hassles over the novel upon which it was based.

p, Georges de Beauregard; d&w, Jean-Luc Godard (based on the novel *The Juggler* by Richard Stark [Donald Westlake]); ph, Raoul Coutard (Techniscope, Eastmancolor); m, Ludwig von Beethoven, Robert Schumann; ed, Agnes Guillemot.

Crime **(PR:C MPAA:NR)**

MADE ON BROADWAY** (1933) 68m MGM bw (AKA: THE GIRL I MADE)
Robert Montgomery (Jeff Bidwell), Sally Eilers (Mona Martine), Madge Evans (Claire Bidwell), Eugene Pallette (Terwilliger), C. Henry Gordon (Mayor Starling), Jean Parker (Adele), Ivan Lebedeff (Ramon), David Newell (Mayor's Secretary), Vince Barnett (Mr. Lepedis), Joseph Cawthorn (Schultz), Raymond Hatton, John Miljan.

Lightweight drama staring Montgomery as an ambitious publicity man who dumps his loyal wife, Evans, to rescue the nearly suicidal Eilers from taking the plunge, and then turns her into a society notable. From there he eventually learns that Eilers has used her new-found position to wriggle out of an involvement in a murder rap, and he slinks back to Evans, asking forgiveness. Underdeveloped and miscast.

p, Lucien Hubbard; d, Harry Beaumont; w, Courtenay Terrett (based on the story "Public Relations" by Terrett); ph, Norbert Brodine; ed, William S. Gray.

Drama (PR:A MPAA:NR)

MADELEINE*1/2
(1950, Brit.) 101m Pinewood-Cineguild-RANK/UNIV bw (AKA: STRANGE CASE OF MADELINE)

Ann Todd (Madeleine Smith), Norman Wooland (William Minnoch), Ivan Desny (Emile l'Angelier), Leslie Banks (James Smith), Edward Chapman (Dr. Thompson), Barbara Everest (Mrs. Smith), Andre Morell (Dean of Faculty), Barry Jones (Lord Advocate), Susan Stranks (Janet Smith), Elizabeth Sellars (Christina), Jean Cadell (Mrs. Jenkins), Ivor Barnard (Mr. Murdoch), David Morne (Lord Justice), Patricia Raine (Bessie Smith), Eugene Deckers (Mr. Thau), Amy Veness (Miss Aiken), John Laurie (Scots Divine), Irene Browne (Miss Grant), Henry Edwards (Clerk of the Court), Moira Fraser (Dancer), Kynaston Reeves (Dr. Penny), Cameron Hall (Dr. Yeoman), Douglas Barr (William the Boot Boy), Alfred Rodriguez, Moira Fraser (Highland Dancers), James McKechnie (Commentator), Anthony Newley (Bit), Eva Bartok (Girl).

Based on one of the most sensational murder cases of 19th-century Scotland, MADELEINE sees a bravura performance from Todd as the beautiful accused murderess. Todd is the attractive but reclusive and somewhat moody daughter of an upper-class family in Victorian Glasgow, Scotland, who meets Desny, a romantic social climber. The two carry on a brief clandestine affair, meeting in the maid's quarters in the basement of her father's mansion. Her father, Banks, a wealthy merchant, insists that Todd marry one of her own class, Wooland, but she is not attracted to the boring, rather stuffy young man and opts for the exciting Desny. Her lover, however, does not want to be kept in a closet and insists that Todd introduce him to her family so he can begin an open courtship; he fears that she will merely use him up and later discard him, eventually marrying one of her own caste. Todd asks Desny to take her away and marry her but he tells her he wants to be accepted by her social order. After viewing Todd dancing with Wooland at a fancy ball, Desny angrily and jealously threatens to show Todd's love letters to her father unless she formally introduces him to her family. Angered over these threats, Todd throws Desny over and becomes engaged to Wooland, yet she cannot forget her impetuous lover. Todd meets again with Desny several times but he is later found dead of arsenic poisoning. Todd is accused of killing Desny and is put on trial but her defense counsel makes one brilliant move after another, without putting Todd on the witness stand, and causes the jury to return a verdict of "Not Proven" (a verdict peculiar to Scotland; one, like this film, that judges Todd neither guilty nor innocent). The viewer is left to decide whether or not Todd is guilty at the chilling finale, but the director does allow this superb actress to climb into a carriage after her release, sit back, and let a small, knowing smile creep across her face. The script and direction are handled with amazing restraint, cleverly and carefully constructed, heightened by Todd's inherently enigmatic image. This was the last film produced by Cineguild, one that presents a fascinating criminal puzzle and excellent all-around performances. The real Madeleine Smith left Glasgow and settled in America, living a quiet, uncelebrated life. When she died at age 93, her friends and neighbors were shocked to learn that she was the notorious Glasgow lady who had turned Victorian England on its cultured head.

p, Stanley Haynes; d, David Lean; w, Haynes, Nicholas Phipps; ph, Guy Green; m, William Alwyn; ed, Geoffrey Foot; md, Muir Mathieson; set d, John Bryan; cos, Margaret Furse.

Crime Drama (PR:A MPAA:NR)

MADELEINE IS*1/2 (1971, Can.) 89m Spring-Glen-Warren/Alliance bw
Nicola Lipman (Madeleine), John Juliani (Toro), Wayne Specht (David/Clown), Gordon Robertson (John), Ronald Ulrich (Barry), Roxanne Irwin (Interviewer), Jim McQueen (Mr. G), Barry Cramer (Therapist), Margot Chapman (Lois), Bob Wood (Robin).

This self-indulgent account of a young woman trying to straighten out her life in the midst of confusing social pressures is a good-hearted effort, but fails to overcome handicaps in structure, technical factors, and performances. Lipman is the kind girl having an affair with a Marxist dropout, but really in love with a business type who is suffering from the same problems as she is. She eventually throws over the Marxist for the other fellow, but not before the audience gets a thorough dosage of how messed up her life really is, fantasy and all. A first feature directorial effort by Spring, Canada's first female producer-director.

p, Kenneth Specht; d, Sylvia Spring; w, Specht, Spring; ph, Doug McKay; m, Ross Barrett; ed, Luke Bennett.

Drama (PR:O MPAA:NR)

MADEMOISELLE1/2** (1966, Fr./Brit.) 103m Woodfall-Procinex/UA bw
Jeanne Moreau (Mademoiselle), Ettore Manni (Manou), Keith Skinner (Bruno), Umberto Orsini (Antonio), Jane Berretta (Annette), Mony Rey (Vievotte), Douking (The Priest), Rosine Luguet (Lisa), Gabriel Gobin (Police Sergeant), Pierre Collet

(Marcel), Jean Gras (Roger), Georges Aubert (Rene), Antoine Marin (Armand), Gerard Darrieu (Boulet), Charles Lavialle (Flood Farmer), Robert Larcebeau (2nd Fire Farmer), Rene Hell (Peasant), Jacques Chevalier (3rd Policeman), Claire Ifrane (Lucie), Denise Peronne (Maria), Annie-Savarin (Rose), Valerie Girodias (Josette), L. Chevallier (Old Peasant), Laure Paillette (Milk Woman), Catherine Parquier (Young Girl), Jacques Monod (Mayor), Paul Barge (Young Policeman).

Grim drama starring Moreau as a sexually repressed, psychopathic small-village schoolmarm who manages to disguise her psychosis until the arrival of good-looking Italian stud Manni. Manni, a woodcutter whose adolescent son Orsini is enrolled in Moreau's class, is a stranger in the farming village and distrusted by the locals. When the community suddenly is plagued by a series of floods, fires, and animal poisonings, the villagers immediately assume that Manni is responsible. In reality, it is Moreau who is committing the crimes. She seems to get an almost carnal pleasure from her misdeeds, which culminate in her seduction of Manni, who she then claims raped her. This pushes the villagers to the breaking point, and they seek the Italian out and stone him to death. Moreau, feigning a need to leave town due to her painful memories, packs her bags and moves on with only Orsini knowing the truth. (French and English versions.)

p, Oscar Lewenstein; d, Tony Richardson; w, Jean Genet (English Translation, Bernard Frechtman); ph, David Watkin (Panavision) [French Version, Philippe Brun]; ed, Anthony Gibbs [French Version, Sophie Coussein]; art d, Jacques Saulnier; set d, Charles Merangel, cos, Jocelyn Rickards.

Drama (PR:C MPAA:NR)

MADEMOISELLE DOCTEUR (SEE: UNDER SECRET ORDERS, 1943, Brit.)

MADEMOISELLE FIFI1/2** (1944) 69m RKO bw
Simone Simon (Elizabeth Rousset), John Emery (Jean Cornudet), Kurt Kreuger (Lt. von Eyrick), Alan Napier (Count de Breville), Helen Freeman (His Countess), Jason Robards, Sr. (Wholesaler in Wines), Norma Varden (His Wife), Romaine Callendar (Manufacturer), Fay Helm (His Wife), Edmund Glover (Young Priest), Charles Waldron (Cure of Cleresville), Mayo Newhall (Mons. Follenvie), Lillian Bronson (Mme. Follenvie), Alan Ward (Coach Driver), Daun Kennedy (Maid), William von Wymetal (Major), Max Willenz (Captain), Marc Cramer (Lieutenant), John Good (Fritz), Allan Lee (Hostler), Frank Mayo (Sergeant at Inn), Margaret Landry (Eva), Rosemary La Planche (Amanda), Marie Lund (Helene), Margie Stewart (Pamela), Violet Wilson (Aunt Marie), Paul Marion (Devoir), Ed Allen (Soldier), Richard Drumm (German Sentry), Victor Cutler (Soldier Waiter), Tom Burton, Steve Winston (Uhlans).

Disappointing Val Lewton production directed by Robert Wise and starring Simon as a brave French laundress who refuses to give in to her small town's Prussian oppressors, circa 1870. The title refers to the nickname given Prussian officer Kreuger, who proves to be the most brutal of the town's tormentors. Most of the action takes place on a claustrophobic stagecoach which carries a group of turncoat aristocrats to safety in England. There Simon, one of the passengers, takes her patriotic stand. The whole thing is a less-than-successful allegory for the horrors taking place in Europe during WW II.

p, Val Lewton; d, Robert Wise; w, Josef Mischel, Peter Ruric (based on stories by Guy de Maupassant); ph, Harry Wild; m, Werner Heymann; ed, J.R. Whittredge; md, Constantin Bakaleinikoff; art d, Albert D'Agostino, Walter E. Keller; set d, Darrell Silvera, Al Fields; cos, Edward Stevenson; spec. eff, Vernon L. Walker; songs, "Three Captains" (sung in French by Simon), "Drinking Song," (sung in German by men).

Drama (PR:A MPAA:NR)

MADEMOISELLE FRANCE (SEE: REUNION IN FRANCE, 1942)

MADHOUSE*1/2 (1974, Brit.) 89m Amicus/AIP c
Vincent Price (Paul Toombes), Peter Cushing (Herbert Flay), Robert Quarry (Oliver Quayle), Adrienne Corri (Faye Flay), Natasha Pyne (Julia), Michael Parkinson (TV Interviewer), Linda Hayden (Elizabeth Peters), Barry Dennen (Blount), Ellis Dayle (Alfred Peters), Catherine Willmer (Louise Peters), John Garrie (Inspector Harper), Ian Thompson (Bradshaw), Jenny Lee Wright (Carol), Julie Crosthwaite (Ellen), Peter Halliday (Psychiatrist).

Awful horror film starring Price as a washed-up horror film actor who, upon recovering from a nervous breakdown, agrees to do a TV series based on his character, "Dr. Death," which was popular in a series of films he had made. The shows are to be scripted by his old friend and former actor Cushing, and the producer of the TV series is played by Quarry. Soon after Price's arrival, the crew and cast of the show begin dying in ways incredibly similar to the deaths the characters suffered in Price's old movies. The mystery is simple-minded, the direction boring (the highlights being clips from Price's AIP classics), which leaves Price and Cushing struggling to bring some interest to a failed project.

p, Max J. Rosenberg, Milton Subotsky; d, Jim Clark; w, Greg Morrison, Ken Levison (based on the novel Devilday by Angus Hall); ph, Ray Parslow (Eastmancolor); m, Douglas Gamley; ed, Clive Smith; art d, Tony Curtis; spec eff, Kerss and Spencer; m/l, Gordon Clyde; makeup, George Blackler.

Horror **Cas.** (PR:C MPAA:PG)

MADIGAN*1/2** (1968) 101m UNIV c
Richard Widmark (Detective Daniel Madigan), Henry Fonda (Commissioner Anthony X. Russell), Inger Stevens (Julia Madigan), Harry Guardino (Detective Rocco Bonaro), James Whitmore (Chief Inspector Charles Kane), Susan Clark (Tricia Bentley), Michael Dunn (Midget Castiglione), Steve Ihnat (Barney Benesch), Don Stroud (Hughie), Sheree North (Jonesy), Warren Stevens (Capt. Ben Williams), Raymond St. Jacques (Dr. Taylor), Bert Freed (Chief of Detectives Hap Lynch), Harry Bellaver (Mickey Dunn), Frank Marth (Lt. James Price), Lloyd Gough

(Assistant Chief Inspector Earl Griffin), Virginia Gregg (Esther Newman), Henry Beckman (Patrolman Philip Downes), Woodrow Parfrey (Marvin), Dallas Mitchell (Detective Tom Gavin), Lloyd Haines (Patrolman Sam Woodley), Ray Montgomery (Detective O'Mara), Seth Allen (Subway Dispatcher), Kay Turner (Stella), Tonia Machinga (Rosita), Rita Lynn (Rita Bonaro), Robert Granere (Buster), Dallas Mitchell (Detective Tom Gavin), Conrad Bain (Hotel Clerk), Ed Crowley (Man at Precinct), John McLiam (Dunne), William Bramley (O'Brien), Scott Hale (Ambulance Driver), Philippa Bevans (Mrs. Hewitt), Diane Sayer (Doreen), Gloria Calomee (Policewoman Doris Hawkins), Albert Henderson (Lt. Strong), Abel Fernandez (Detective Rodriguez), Robert Ball (Prisoner), Paul Sorensen, Bob Biheller, Ollie O'Toole, Al Dunlap, Pepe Hern, Tom Rosqui, Sean Kennedy, Bob O'Connell (Men), Mina Martinez, Kathleen O'Malley, Elizabeth Fleming, Madeline Clive, Nina Varela, Kate Harrington (Women), Al Ruban (Kowalski), Lincoln Kilpatrick (Patrolman Grimes), Ralph Smiley (Captain).

Action-packed cops-and-robbers film co-written by longtime TV vet Howard Rodman, who evidently didn't like the way it turned out so he used his pseudonym of Henri Simoun. In the rough area known as Spanish Harlem in New York, detectives Widmark and Guardino arrest Ihnat, a wanted hoodlum who is hiding out in a tacky flat to avoid an indictment by the Brooklyn courts. Ihnat is in the sack with a nude woman and that distracts these two cops from their quarry long enough for Ihnat to pull a gun on them and order them to surrender their revolvers and permit him to escape. There is nothing more embarrassing for a cop than to lose his weapon, and they are lucky he didn't shoot them down, as he is already a murderer. Fonda, the police commissioner, dresses the two men down for allowing Ihnat to get away in such an inglorious manner and gives them 72 hours to nail the killer or they may wind up pounding beats in Staten Island, or suspended. Fonda has a lot of other woes as well; he's having an affair with Clark, who is married. Further, St. Jacques, a black minister, is in the midst of a row with the commissioner because his young activist son was badly beaten by racist cops. To compound matters, Fonda's pal Whitmore, an inspector for years, has been proven to have taken a bribe to keep a brothel in operation. So it's a hornet's nest that Widmark and Guardino walk into, and Fonda is livid that the two men broke rules to leave their own area to trail the missing Ihnat. Widmark is seen with his wife, Stevens, a woman who is in constant fear that her husband won't come home at night and who wishes he would give it up and spend some time with her. She also worries that Widmark may be seeing his old flame, North, once more. Stevens is a socialite type who finds the entire field of law enforcement repugnant to her sensibilities. While Widmark and Guardino search for Ihnat, he uses Widmark's service revolver to kill two other police officers. Through a lead given them by Dunn, a midget bookie, they meet Stroud, who works for Ihnat as a pimp. They finally trace Ihnat to an apartment on East 102nd Street back in Spanish Harlem, call for back-ups, and then ask the killer to give himself up. He refuses and there is a stand-off until Widmark, in a rage, goes into the building for the final shoot-out. Bullets fly and Ihnat is killed; Widmark is mortally wounded and dies in a local hospital. Stevens angrily confronts the cool Fonda, telling him that he is a heartless person who regarded her late husband as "just another lousy cop." This is as close to being a documentary as you'll ever see, in that, it's a painstaking look at real police work and sticks pins in the police department hierarchy. Co-writer Polonsky was (along with Rodman) a writer who had been blacklisted by the Red-baiters in the 1950s. Rodman took out a card in a construction union, and, long after he was readmitted to the Hollywood community, he maintained his status with the union until his death in December, 1985. Harry Bellaver may be remembered for his work in the TV series "Naked City" and his role as the barkeep to Spencer Tracy in THE OLD MAN AND THE SEA. All of the characters who lurked and worked in the background were excellent. It's unfortunate that many people inadvertently confused this picture with ELVIRA MADIGAN, the Swedish film that came out just before this one.

p, Frank P. Rosenberg; d, Donald Siegel; w, Henri Simoun [Howard Rodman], Abraham Polonsky, Harry Kleiner (based on the novel The Commissioner by Richard Dougherty); ph, Russell Metty (Techniscope, Technicolor); m, Don Costa; ed, Milton Shifman; art d, Alexander Golitzen, George C. Webb; set d, John McCarthy, John Austin; song, "You Don't Know What Love Is," sung by Sheree North; makeup, Bud Westmore.

Crime   (PR:C   MPAA:NR)

MADIGAN'S MILLIONS*

(1970, Span./Ital) 77m Westside International/AIP c (EL TESTAMENTO DE MADIGAN; UN DOLLARO PER 7 VIGLIACCHI)

Dustin Hoffman (Jason Fisher), Elsa Martinelli (Vicky Shaw), Cesar Romero (Mike Madigan), Gustavo Rojo, Franco Fabrizi, Fernando Hilbeck, Riccardo Garrone, Gerard Tichy, George Raft, Fernando Gilbert, Jose Maria Caffarel, Alfredo Mayo, Umberto Raho.

Dustin Hoffman's first appearance in films might have been his last if this film had been released before THE GRADUATE. He was lucky, in that this picture, though completed in 1967, languished in film vaults until it finally escaped. He showed bits and pieces of talent in this Madrid and Rome-locationed comedy, but it took a discerning eye to spot it. Hoffman is a young IRS snoop sent to Italy to locate millions stashed by Romero, a rackets czar who had been deported by the U.S. to his native land. Romero is killed by local hoods looking for the stash and Hoffman attempts to investigate, but is hampered in his work by the Roman police. Hoffman makes the acquaintance of Romero's daughter, Martinelli, although Hoffman doesn't know she is Romero's heiress and thinks she had been his lover. One night, Hoffman is being pursued and Martinelli allows him to crash on her couch. She has a young child (who Hoffman thinks is hers by Romero) and, upon waking, Hoffman finds all the money in the child's possession. When the local hoods attempt to steal the millions, the cops finally do something and nab the culprits. Hoffman learns that Martinelli was Romero's daughter and that clears the way for the two to have a relationship. Romero's role is tiny and was supposedly shot in a day or so. It was,

at one time, to be played by expatriate George Raft, but Raft was ill and Romero stepped in. The co-screenwriter was a longtime Hollywood trade-paper writer and critic, Henaghan, and he should have known better than to attempt to foist this kind of stale pasta on the public. They apparently shot this film in three languages, as the Italian version, UN DOLLARO PER 7 VIGLIACCHI, credits Dan Ash as the director, while the Spanish version, EL MILLON DE MADIGAN, credits Giorgio Gentili. In actuality, no one should take any credit for this and if they were smart they would all avoid having their names associated with it. Worth seeing if only to watch Hoffman in his earliest screen offering.

p, Sidney Pink; d, Stanley Prager, Girorgio Gentili, Dan Ash; w, James Henaghan, Jose Luis Bayonas; ph, Manola Rojas (Movielab Color); m, Gregorio Garcia Segura; ed, Antonio Ramirez; art d, Peiro Filippone.

Crime Comedy   (PR:A   MPAA:G)

MADISON AVENUE**

(1962) 94m FOX bw

Dana Andrews (Clint Lorimer), Eleanor Parker (Anne Tremaine), Jeanne Crain (Peggy Shannon), Eddie Albert (Harvey Ames), Howard St. John (J.D. Jocelyn), Henry Daniell (Stipe), Kathleen Freeman (Miss Haley), David White (Stevenson Brock), Betti Andrews (Miss Katie Olsen), Jack Orrison (Mayor of Bellefield), Yvonne Peattie (Miss Malloy), Arline Hunter (Miss Horn), Doris Fesette (Blonde), Grady Sutton (Dilbock), Leon Alton (Maitre d'), Michael Ford, The Sylte Sisters.

Failed expose of the high-powered world of advertising stars Andrews as an ad executive who is sudddenly fired from his job when his boss, St. John, senses he has become too cocky. To prove himself marketable, Andrews stops at nothing to muscle his way back into the business, including alienating his family, friends, and associates with his arrogant manner. He is hired back by St. John, but not before he realizes that to save his career he nearly lost what he really loves, his girl friend, Crain. Pat and uninvolving.

p&d, Bruce Humberstone; w, Norman Corwin (based on the novel The Build-Up Boys by Jeremy Kirk); ph, Charles G. Clarke (CinemaScope); m, Harry Sukman; ed, Betty Steinberg; md, Sukman; art d, Duncan Cramer, Leland Fuller; set d, Walter M. Scott, John Sturtevant; m/l, "Milk Song," Harry Harris; makeup, Ben Nye.

Drama   (PR:A   MPAA:NR)

MADISON SQUARE GARDEN**

(1932) 70m PAR bw

Jack Oakie (Eddie Burke), Marian Nixon (Bee), Thomas Meighan (Bill Carley) William Boyd (Sloane), ZaSu Pitts (Florrie), Lew Cody (Roarke), William Collier, Sr. (Doc Williams), Robert Elliott (Miller), Warren Hymer (Brassy Randall), Mushy Callahan (Kid McClune), Lou Magnolia (Referee), Jack Johnson Tom Sharkey, Tod Sloan, Mike Donlin, Billy Papke, Stanislaus Zybyszko, Tom Kennedy, Spike Robinson, Tammany Young, Damon Runyon, Jack Lait, Grantland Rice, Ed. W. Smith, Westbrook Pegler, Paul Gallico, Jack Kearns, Teddy Hayes.

Routine boxing picture starring Oakie as an honorable, though loud mouthed fighter who is set up by hoods Boyd and Cody during the big bout when they paint his opponent's hand bandages with cement, which enables the boxer to knock the stuffings out of Oakie. Though Oakie loses the bout, the trick is discovered and there is a massive showdown between the crooks and several old-time sports figures (Johnson, Sloan, Papke, and Zybyszko) who have minor roles as Madison Square Garden employees. Love interest is provided by Nixon as Oakie's faithful hotel telegraph operator girlfriend. Look for writer Damon Runyon in a bit part.

p, Charles R. Rogers; d, Harry Joe Brown; w, P.J. Wolfson, Allen Rivkin (based on a story by Thomas Burtis); ph, Henry Sharp.

Drama   (PR:A   MPAA:NR)

MADLY*½

(1970, Fr.) 85m Adel/New Line Cinema c (AKA: THE LOVE MATES)

Alain Delon (Julian), Mireille Darc (Agatha), Jane Davenport (Madly), Valentina Cortese (Woman), Pascale De Boisson (Lucienne).

Another French menage-a-trois romance starring Delon as a Frenchman who has more love than one woman, namely, Darc, can handle. Delon's hobbies are horseback riding, fast cars, dangerous kicks, and abusing Darc. Enter gorgeous American black girl Davenport who soon joins the fray which sees the three of them (Delon, Darc, and Davenport) horseback riding (on the same horse of course) and frolicking in bed. Strangely the sexual escapades are done separately (Delon/Darc, Delon/Davenport) which seems to cheat the audience out of what this was all leading up to.

p, Alain Delon; d, Roger Kahane; w, Pascal Jardin, Kahane, Mireille Airgoz; ph, Georges Barsky (Eastmancolor); m, Francis Lai; ed, Marcel Peulade; art d, Francois De Lamothe.

Romance   (PR:O   MPAA:NR)

MADMAN zero

(1982) 88m The Legend Lives/Farley c

Alexis Dubin (Betsy), Tony Fish (T.P.), Harriet Bass (Stacey), Seth Jones (Dave), Jan Claire (Ellie), Alex Murphy (Bill), Jimmy Steele (Richie), Paul Ehlers (Madman Marz), Carl Fredericks (Max), Michael Sullivan (Cook), Gaylen Ross.

Predictable, boring, and bloody horror film carrying on the FRIDAY THE 13TH tradition of a crazed killer terrorizing a secluded summer camp filled to the brim with young, nubile counselors. Bottom of the barrel.

p, Gary Sales; d&w, Joe Giannone; ph, James Momel (Cineffects Color); m, Sales, Stephen Horelick; ed, Dan Lowenthal; spec eff, Jo Hansen; cos, Paulette Aller; makeup, Hansen.

Horror   Cas.   (PR:O   MPAA:R)

MADMAN OF LAB 4, THE**   (1967, Fr.) 90m GAU (LE FOU DU LABO 4)

Jean Lefebvre (Fou), Maria Latour (Regina), Bernard Blier (Chief), Pierre Brasseur (Father), Margo Lion (Mother), Michel Serrault (Boss).

Lefebvre is a scientist on the run from spies, mobsters, the cops, and even his own boss after he invents a gas that makes people fall in love with each other. The film climaxes in a parody of a western film as a gangster boss comes to a Wild West town strangely located just outside of Paris, desperately seeking the gas for his own purposes. What could have been a cute little comedy is hampered severely by uneven direction. The pacing lags as the style alternates between the whimsical and the unnecessarily somber.

p&d, Jacques Besnard; w, Jean Halain; ph, Raymond Lemoigne.

Comedy   **(PR:A   MPAA:NR)**

MADMEN OF MANDORAS   (SEE: THEY SAVED HITLER'S BRAIN, 1963)

MADNESS OF THE HEART**   (1949, Brit.) 91m RANK-TC/UNIV bw

Margaret Lockwood (Lydia Garth), Paul Dupuis (Paul de Vandiere), Kathleen Byron (Verite Faimont), Maxwell Reed (Joseph Rondolet), Thora Hird (Rosa), Maurice Denham (Dr. Simon Blake), Raymond Lovell (Comte de Vandiere), Marie Burke (Comtesse de Vandiere), David Hutcheson (Max Ffoliott), Pamela Stirling (Felicite), Cathleen Nesbitt (Mother Superior), Joy Harrington (Sister Agnes), Peter Illing (Dr. Matthieu), Jack McNaughton (Attendant), Marie Autl (Nun), Kynaston Reeves (Sir Robert Hammond), Sheila Raynor, Marcel Poncin, Stafford Byrne, Patricia Cutts, Betty Blake, Cynthia Teale, Muriel Russell, Sam Lysons, Paul Anthony, George de Warfaz, Gordon Littman, Gillian Maude, Ann Hefferman, Arthur Reynolds, Fletcher Lightfoot, H.G. Stoker, Frank Ling, Peter Dunlop, Sam Kydd, Lionel Grose.

Average melodrama starring Lockwood as a young British girl who is suddenly struck blind soon after meeting and falling in love with young Frenchman Dupuis who had been visiting London. Convinced that her lust struck her blind, Lockwood enters a convent, but after six months the sisters persuade her to return to the secular life. Dupuis tracks her down and marries her soon after, taking her back to France with him. Unfortunately, the blind girl feels unwanted by Dupuis' parents and she becomes convinced that someone is trying to kill her. After a violent argument, Lockwood takes a nasty fall and loses the child she was carrying. Distraught over her husband's attitude toward the danger she feels, Lockwood returns to England and undergoes a dangerous operation to regain her sight. The surgery is a success and Lockwood returns to Dupuis to prove that her fears were real. Faking blindness to flush out her assailant, Lockwood finally succeeds. Their sexy, jealous young neighbor girl reveals herself as the evildoer. The villainess is killed in an amazingly timed car crash, allowing Lockwood and Dupuis to fall in love again.

p, Richard Wainwright; d&w, Charles Bennett (based on the novel by Flora Sandstrom); ph, Desmond Dickinson, Cecil Conney; m, Allan Gray; ed, Helga Cranston; md, Muir Mathieson; art d, Alexander Vetchinsky.

Drama   **(PR:A   MPAA:NR)**

MADONNA OF AVENUE A*½   (1929) 71m WB bw

Dolores Costello (Maria Morton), Grant Withers (Slim Shayne), Douglas Gerrard (Arch Duke), Louise Dresser (Georgia Morton), Otto Hoffman (Monk), Lee Moran (Gus), William Russell.

Typical melodrama starring Costello as a well-bred schoolgirl who breaks down when she learns that her mother, Dresser, whom she believed to be a high-society matron, is actually the hostess of a sleazy dance hall. It was all done before and would be done to death throughout the 1930s. Not even Curtiz's direction could pull anything extraordinary out of this cliched material.

d, Michael Curtiz; w, Ray Doyle, Bradley King, Francis Powers (based on a story by Leslie S. Barrows, Mark Canfield [Darryl F. Zanuck]); ph, Byron Haskin; ed, Doyle; m/l, "My Madonna," Fred Fisher, Louis Silvers.

Drama   **(PR:A   MPAA:NR)**

MADONNA OF THE DESERT**   (1948) 60m REP bw

Lynne Roberts (Monica Dale), Donald Barry (Tony French), Don Castle (Joe Salinas), Sheldon Leonard (Nick Julian), Paul Hurst (Pete Connors), Roy Barcroft (Buck Keaton), Paul E. Burns (Hank Davenport), Betty Blythe (Mrs. Brown), Grazia Narciso (Mama Baravelli), Martin Garralaga (Papa Baravelli), Frank Yaconnelli (Peppo), Maria Genardi (Mrs. Pasquale), Renee Donatt (Maria Baravelli), Vernon Cansino (Enrico).

Decent programmer starring Leonard, Roberts, and Barry as crooks out to steal a statue of the Madonna which is said to have miraculous powers. The statue is owned by rancher Castle and it is his duty to fend off the villains with the help of the icon. Silly, but well enough done.

p, Stephen Auer; d, George Blair; w, Albert DeMond (based on a story by Frank Wisbar); ph, John MacBurnie; ed, Harry Keller; md, Mort Glickman; art d, Frank Arrigo.

Western   **(PR:A   MPAA:NR)**

MADONNA OF THE SEVEN MOONS**½
                                  (1945, Brit.) 88m Gainsborough/UNIV bw

Phyllis Calvert (Maddalena Lambardi/Rosanna), Stewart Granger (Nino Barucci), Patricia Roc (Angela Lambardi), Peter Glenville (Sandro Barucci), John Stuart (Giuseppi), Jean Kent (Vittoria), Nancy Price (Mme. Barucci), Peter Murray Hill (Logan), Reginald Tate (Ackroyd), Dulcie Gray (Nesta), Amy Veness (Tessa), Hilda Bayley (Mrs. Fiske), Alan Haines (Evelyn), Evelyn Darvell (Millie), Danny Green, Eliot Makeham.

Bizarre romance starring Calvert as an Italian girl who has developed a split personality after being raped by a gypsy in her youth. Married to a rich wine merchant, Calvert has a nasty habit of disappearing for long periods of time and becoming the moll of Granger, a gypsy thief. The film was cut to 88 minutes for its U.S. release, thus eliminating Granger's rendition of "Rosanna," sung in honor of Calvert. It originally ran 105 minutes.

p, R.J. Minney; d, Arthur Crabtree; w, Roland Pertwee, Brock Williams (based on the novel by Margery Lawrence); ph, Jack Cox; m, Louis Levy; art d, Andrew Mazzei.

Crime/Romance   **(PR:C   MPAA:NR)**

MADONNA OF THE STREETS*½   (1930) 79m COL bw

Evelyn Brent (May), Robert Ames (Morton), Ivan Linow (Slumguillion), Josephine Dunn (Marion), J. Edwards Davis (Clark), Zack Williams (Blink), Ed Brady (Ramsey), Richard Tucker (Kingsley).

Boring melodrama, with minimal camera movement, set in San Francisco and starring Brent who looks forward to spending the fortune of her very rich companion. When her meal ticket is run over by a car, Brent desperately scrambles to find the male heir, his nephew, who happens to be a waterfront missionary. Once she locates the nephew, she does her best to get him to marry her. He does, but he spends the money on building a large home for the hoboes who populate the waterfront. In so doing, he "converts" Brent to his way of life.

p, Harry Cohn; d, John S. Robertson; w, Jo Swerling (based on "The Ragged Messenger" by William Babington Maxwell); ph, Sol Polito; ed, Gene Havlick; art d, Edward Jewell.

Drama   **(PR:A   MPAA:NR)**

MADONNA'S SECRET, THE**   (1946) 79m REP bw

Francis Lederer (James Harlan Corbin), Gail Patrick (Ella Randolph), Ann Rutherford (Linda "Morgan" North), Edward Ashley (John Earl), Linda Stirling (Helen North), John Litel (Lt. Roberts), Leona Roberts (Mrs. Corbin), Michael Hawks (Hunt Mason), Clifford Brooke (Mr. Hadley), Pierre Watkin (District Attorney), Will Wright (The Riverman), Geraldine Wall (Miss Joyce), John Hamilton (Lambert).

Low-budget programmer directly inspired by Edgar Ulmer's 1944 film BLUEBEARD. This time the story of a portrait painter linked to murder is updated and the action shifted from Ulmer's Paris to New York City. Lederer plays the mysterious painter who has fled Paris for the Big Apple due to controversy over his work. It seems that the model he used (whose face appears in all his work) turned up drowned in the Seine soon after he painted her. Pretty soon a model he uses in New York turns up dead, and then another, which spurs the sister of one of the dead girls to go undercover and pose as another one of his models to get the goods on him. Instead, she falls in love with the artist and eventually clears him of the crimes. (In Ulmer's film the artist is indeed the killer.)

p, Stephen Auer; d, William Thiele; w, Bradbury Foote, Thiele; ph, John Alton; m, Joseph Dubin; ed, Fred Allen; art d, Hilyard Brown; spec eff, Howard and Theodore Lydecker; m/l, Al Newman, Richard Cherwin, Ned Washington.

Mystery/Romance   **(PR:A   MPAA:NR)**

MADRON*   (1970, U.S./Israel) 93m GBC-Edric-Isracine/Four Star Excelsior c

Richard Boone (Madron), Leslie Caron (Sister Mary), Gabi Amrani (Angel), Chaim Banai (Sam Red), Paul Smith (Gabe Price), Aharon Ipale (Singer), Yaakov Banai (Sanchee), Sami Shmueli (Saba), Mosko Alkalay (Claude), Avraham Pelta (Drygulcher), Willy Gafni (Prospector).

Gross, bloody oater shot on location in Israel and starring Boone as a tough gunslinger who meets up with nun Caron, who was the sole surviving member of a convent slaughter by Apaches. Boone, who respects the kind nun, agrees to guide her through the desert to safety, which eventually calls for him to kill just about everything that moves. When accosted by outlaws, Boone stuns the bandits by ripping open Caron's habit and exposing her breasts. This distracts them enough for Boone to gun them down. One of the bandits, Amrani, survives and Caron makes him swear to be an ally. Eventually the former rivals develop a camaraderie, and Amrani makes the ultimate sacrifice by riding off alone to veer the attacking Apaches away from Caron and Boone. This leads to Boone making love to the distraught Caron, who sheds her habit the next morning. Learning that Amrani was captured by the Apaches, Boone sends Caron on her way and vows to enter the Indian camp alone and rescue his comrade against impossible odds. (If this sounds a bit like Sam Peckinpah's THE WILD BUNCH, consider that Amrani's character is even named Angel.) Boone enters the Apache stronghold and guns down most of the savages before being killed himself. Caron, meanwhile, makes her way back to civilization knowing that Boone sacrificed his life for her.

p, Emanuel Henigman, Eric Weaver; d, Jerry Hopper; w, Edward Chappell, Leo McMahon (based on a story by McMahon); ph, Marcel Grignon, Adam Greenberg (Eastmancolor); m, Riz Ortolani; ed, Renzo Lucidi; art d, Robert Ramsey; m/l, "Till Love Touches Your Life," Ortolani, Arthur Hamilton (sung by Richard Williams, Jan Daley).

Western   **(PR:O   MPAA:GP)**

MADWOMAN OF CHAILLOT, THE*
                                  (1969) 142m Commonwealth United/WB c

Katharine Hepburn (Countess Aurelia, the Madwoman of Chaillot), Charles Boyer (The Broker), Claude Dauphin (Dr. Jadin), Edith Evans (Josephine, the Madwoman of La Concorde), John Gavin (Reverend), Paul Henreid (General), Oscar Homolka (Commissar), Margaret Leighton (Constance, the Madwoman of Passy), Giulietta Masina (Gabrielle, the Madwoman of Sulpice), Nanette Newman (Irma), Richard

Chamberlain *(Roderick)*, Yul Brynner *(Chairman)*, Donald Pleasence *(Prospector)*, Danny Kaye *(Ragpicker)*, Fernand Gravet [Gravey] *(Police Sergeant)*, Gordon Heath *(Folksinger)*, Gerald Sim *(Julius)*, Manuella Von Oppen *(Newsgirl)*, Gilles Segal *(Deaf-mute)*, Gaston Palmer *(Juggler)*, Jacques Marin, Joellina Smalda, Henri Virjoleux, Harriett Ariel, Catherine Berg, Henri Cogan, Christian Duvaleix, Jackie Farley, George Hilsdon, Sabine Lods, Bernard Woringer.

What a shame to have wasted so many talents in this leaden update of Giraudoux's wonderful play. Anhalt's adaptation set it in the late 1960s and the whole thing seemed to fall flat, perhaps due to that. Hepburn was appearing in her thirty-seventh picture (only her eighth in color) as a woman living in Paris' Chaillot district who has three best girl friends, Masina, Leighton, and Evans, all of whom exist more in their memories than in the now. There is a conspiracy afoot and the meeting is taking place in a cafe near Hepburn's flat. Oil is thought to be lurking under Paris and these men aim to drill and find it. Chamberlain is related to one of these international brigands, Pleasence, and he tells Hepburn what's about to transpire. She is so dotty that she's not sure if Chamberlain is who he says he is or one of her long-dead lovers. The women get together and decide to foil the oillionaires with a plan of her own, so Hepburn approaches each of the conspirators separately and tells them that oil is beginning to bubble in her basement. Before the culprits arrive, she and her friends hold a mock trial of these men and they are sentenced to death. Later, she locks them in her basement. And that, friends, is that. John Huston had been slated to direct the film, then Forbes stepped in. It was logy, lukewarm, and lethargic despite the presence of a host of international stars, including Danny Kaye, as the ragpicker, who just about steals the show from everyone else. The villains, Brynner, Pleasence, Boyer, and Homolka are little more than cardboard, and even the radiant Masina seems stifled in the swamp of heavy-going. Further, the worst sin of all is that this comedy just isn't funny. Gravey, you may recall, once worked in the U.S., where the studio made him change his name to Gravet. Once he got back to France, he also took his real name again. Nice location shots in Paris and the south of France, but they are hardly enough to make this picture worth watching. Sigh . . . how can all of these famous movie actors agree to appear in such a slumgullion of a movie? Beats us.

p, Ely Landau; d, Bryan Forbes; w, Edward Anhalt (based on the play "La Folle de Chaillot" by Jean Giraudoux, translated by Maurice Valency); ph, Claude Renoir, Burnett Guffey (Technicolor); m, Michael J. Lewis; ed, Roger Dwyre; prod d, Ray Simm; md, Wally Scott; art d, Georges Petitot; set d, Dario Simone; cos, Rosine Delamare; makeup, Monique Archambault.

Comedy **(PR:A MPAA:NR)**

MAEDCHEN IN UNIFORM*****

(1932, Ger.) 110m Deutsche Film-Gemeinschaft bw (AKA: GIRLS IN UNIFORM)

Emilia Unda *(The Principal)*, Dorothea Wieck *(Fraulein von Bernburg)*, Hedwig Schlichter *(Fraulein von Kesten)*, Hertha Thiele *(Manuela von Meinhardie)*, Ellen Schwannecke *(Ilse von Westhagen)*.

In pre-Hitler Germany there were a number of excellent anti-authoritarian films which were up front and direct with their messages. This genre soon disappeared with the rise of the Nazis, because of the boldness of their stand for individual freedom. Perhaps the best of these films is MAEDCHEN IN UNIFORM, a sensitive film dealing with a young girl's experiences within the rigid structure of a girls' boarding school. Thiele is a new student in school, away from home for the first time. The shock of being away from her mother as well as her own introspective personality, causes her to withdraw from the other girls. The school's principal feels that Thiele's actions are inappropriate and not to be tolerated. Life is not meant to be easy and it is time the girl learned about hardships and the triumph in overcoming them. A woman of true Teutonic spirit, she declares to the girls, "Through discipline and hunger, hunger and discipline, we shall rise again." Many of the girls will leave the school to become soldiers' wives and mothers. They must learn to be stoic and face the world as it is. But Thiele cannot subscribe to this and becomes attached to Wieck, the one teacher who will listen to her. Fraulein Professor sees that the girl is frightened and high-strung. Unlike the others, it is not in her nature to conform. "I cannot stand the way you transform the children into frightened creatures," she tells the angered principal. Though at first she had been hesitant to help the newcomer, Wieck allows the girl emotionally close to her. Wieck herself is coming to the realization that her own will and as physical beauty are breaking down slowly under the oppressiveness and sees this sensitive girl as a way of achieving victory against authoritative rules and figures. But Thiele's emotional dependence on her mentor/teacher grows to an obsessive level. Unable to relate to anyone else, she finds herself falling in love with Wieck. When the principal has an anniversary celebration, highlighted by a class play, the sensitive young woman gives a fine, naturalistic performance which becomes symbolic of great personal triumph, both for her and for her teacher. At last she is able to be herself despite the conformity of the surroundings. But at a post-play celebration, buoyed by success and a little too much to drink, she publicly declares her love for Wieck. The principal is appalled by this and forbids Thiele from having any contact with Wieck. All pupils are ordered to stay away as well. Openly defying the principal and her dictatorial rules, Wieck attempts to speak with the girl, but this only increases Thiele's emotional burdens. In desperation she tries to throw herself over a balcony, but is stopped by a group of her fellow students. The principal, hearing a commotion, rushes to see what is the matter. But she is faced with the cold, hard stares of Wieck's classmates who tell what has happened. She slinks back into safety of the shadowed hallway, fearful and emotionally naked at this blow to her authority. MAEDCHEN IN UNIFORM is a film permeated with symbolism sometimes subtle, but often glaring. The principal, a hardline Prussian, is a haggard, mean-faced woman dressed in dark, semi-military garb with a ribbon and insignia constantly worn on the bosom. The girls themselves are dressed the same, wearing school uniforms that would suggest a prison more than the clothing of a young woman. It is a prophetic irony that the girls' black and white striped pajamas strongly resemble the uniforms worn by those imprisoned in Nazi concentration camps. As for Thiele, though she must dress the same as the others, the lighting used on her sets her apart from the other students, giving her an ethereal quality that makes her different. In summary, the film reflects an anti-authoritarian viewpoint. Interestingly enough, the film was both written and directed by women, and featured an all-female cast. Adapted from a well-known German play, the film has an assured quality. It knows what it wants to say and how to say it. Historically the film represents a finality. Within a few years the Nazis would control the film studios and the messages of films like MAEDCHEN IN UNIFORM were replaced by pro-Reich propaganda. MAEDCHEN IN UNIFORM was the first German sound film to be shown in America using subtitles. The titles were deliberately few so that the power of the film would tell the story, though synopses were printed and passed out to the audience. A remake in 1958, also made in Germany, does not come close to achieving the power of the original.

p, Carl Froelich; d, Leontine Sagan; w, Christa Winsloe, F. D. Andam (based on the play "Gestern und Heute" by Winsloe).

Drama **(PR:C MPAA:NR)**

MAEDCHEN IN UNIFORM**

(1965, Ger./Fr.) 91m Les Films Modernes-S.N-C.-CCC-Filmkunst/Seven Arts c (JEUNES FILLES EN UNIFORME)

Lilli Palmer*(Fraulein von Bernburg)*, Romy Schneider *(Manuela von Mainhardis)*, Therese Giehse *(Headmistress)*, Christine Kaufmann *(Mia)*, Danik Patisson *(Edelgard)*, Blandine Ebinger, Gina Albert, Sabine Sinjen, Marthe Mercadier, Paulette Dubost, Ginette Pigeon, Adelheid Seeck.

Acceptable remake of the classic German film of 1932. This time it's Schneider as the lonely girl at a strict boarding school falling in love with teacher Palmer, the only person to show her any kindness. When she confesses her feelings to her classmates in a drunken outburst, they ridicule her and the headmistress plans to expel her. Schneider attempts suicide but is prevented and then allowed to remain at school by the horrified headmistress. Palmer later resigns her position and leaves. Although slightly more explicit in its treatment, this version has nothing of the odd eroticism that made the earlier film so fascinating.

d, Geza Radvanyi; w, Franz Hollering, F.D. Andam (based on the play "Gestern und Heute" by Christa Winsloe); ph, Werner Krien (Eastmancolor); m, Peter Sandloff; ed, Ira Oberberg; set d, Emil Hasler, Walter Kutz; cos, Manon Hahn; makeup, Jupp Paschke, Anita Greil, Cilly Didzoneit, Heinz Stamm.

Drama **(PR:C MPAA:NR)**

MAEVA**

(1961) 90m Cascade-Victoria-Times c (AKA: WAHINE; TRUE DIARY OF A WAHINE; TRUE DIARY OF A VAHINE; TRUE STORY OF A WAHINE; PAGAN HELLCAT; MAEVA—PORTRAIT OF A TAHITIAN GIRL; CONFESSIONS OF A VAHINE)

Tumata Teuiau *(Maeva)*, Jean Kave *(Guido)*, Oscar Spitz *(Pierre)*, Poia *(Girl)*, Adienne de Joie *(Narrator)*, Lillian, Felicien.

A story of love, violence and lust features Teuiau as a beautiful young Tahitian native. She grows up in a small fishing town, working with a local native boy. She fantasizes about becoming his wife, but when the boy leaves, her dreams are dashed. After being raped by a sailor, Teuiau flees her homeland for Europe, where she becomes an artist's model. She meets Spitz and seduces him, but after they have an affair, Spitz leaves her for another. Once more her hopes are crushed, and she takes to frequenting local bars and picking up men for casual sexual encounters. Kave is a man she meets who appears to be different from the others, but he too leaves. Teuiau finally returns to her native village, and resumes her old job tending to the fishing boats. But at a native dance, a local man meets her and falls in love. At last Teuiau has found what she has been searching for—a man who loves her and will be steadfast. Filmed on location in Tahiti.

p&d, Umberto Bonsignori; w, Maya Deren; ph, Alberto Baldecchi (Eastmancolor); m, Teiji Ito; ed, Bonsignori; m/l, "Vahine Tahiti," "Paia" (performed by Drummers of Tahiti), "The White Ship" (sung by Augustine).

Drama **(PR:O MPAA:NR)**

MAEVA—PORTRAIT OF A TAHITIAN GIRL

(SEE: MAEVA, 1961)

MAFIA

**(1969, Fr./Ital.) 98m Panda-Corona/AIP c (LA MAFFIA FAIT LA LOI; IL GIORNO DELLA CIVETTA)

Claudia Cardinale *(Rosa Nicolosi)*, Franco Nero *(Capt. Bellodi)*, Lee J. Cobb *(Don Mariano Arena)*, Nehemiah Persoff *(Pizzuco)*, Serge Reggiani *(Parrinieddu)*, Rosanna Lopapero *(Caterina)*, Gaetano Cimarosa *(Zecchinetta)*.

An Italian police captain (Nero) investigates the murder of a construction supplier and encounters the force of Mafia silence, and the control it has over the people in the Sicilian town. He eventually discovers just how far the power of the Mafia reaches, including his own purview.

p, Ermanno Donati, Luigi Carpentieri; d, Damiano Damiani; w, Ugo Pirro, Damiani (based on the novel *Day Of The Owl* by Leonardo Sciascia); ph, Tonino Delli Colli (Berkey-Pathe Color) m, Giovanni Fusco; ed, Nino Baragli; art d, Sergio Canevari; cos, Marilu Carteny.

Crime Drama **(PR:C MPAA:M)**

MAFIA, THE**

(1972, Arg.) 120m Litoral c (LA MAFFIA)

Alfredo Alcon *(Luciano)*, Thelma Biral *(Ada)*, Jose Slavin *(Francesco Donato)*, China Zorilla *(Assunta)*, Hector Alterio *(Paolatti)*, Jose Maria Gutierrez *(Gallego)*.

Routine crime yarn from Argentina concerning a power struggle between Slavin, the boss of an old crime family, and Alcon, one of his young deputies. Alcon has designs on the old man's position and wants to expand the gang's activities. The kidnaping and murder of a young millionaire bring such a public outcry that the authorities unite to destroy the syndicate.

p&d, Leopoldo Torre-Nilsson; w, Beatriz Guido, Luis Pico Estrada, Rodolfo Mortola, Javier Torre, Torre-Nilsson (based on a story by Jose Dominiani, Osvaldo Bayer); ph, Anibal Di Salvo (Eastmancolor); m, Gustavo Beytelman; ed, Antonio Ripoll; makeup, Valentino.

Crime (PR:C MPAA:NR)

MAFIA GIRLS, THE* (1969) 74m Stage Four/RAF c

Anthony Allen (Capozzi), Marilyn Nordman (Millie), Cindy Stevens (Rita), Paul Stober (Stitch), Dolores Carlos (Sherri), Ruby Ross (Jan), Brenda Gibson (Sonia), Marcel De Lage (Dubois), Jack Spector (Lassiter).

Investigating the murders of several agents, INTERPOL man Allen and four other agents stumble upon a Miami-based criminal organization that blackmails politicians after setting them up with beautiful women. The gang self-destructs as ex-Nazi Stober uses a knife to remove his boss' eye, then gets pushed into the water by the boss' wife and eaten by sharks. Worthless exploitation.

p, Norman Senfield; d, Ed Ross; w, Bobby O'Donald; m, O'Donald.

Crime (PR:C-O MPAA:NR)

MAFIOSO**1/2** (1962, Ital.) 105m DD/Zenith International bw (IL MAFIOSO)

Alberto Sordi (Antonio Badalamenti), Norma Bengell (Martha Badalamenti), Cinzia Bruno (Donatella), Katiuscia Piretti (Patricia), Armando Thine (Dr. Zanchi), Lilly Bistrattin (Dr. Zanchi's Secretary), Gabriella Conti (Rosalia Badalamenti), Ugo Attanasio (Don Vincenzo), Carmelo Oliviero (Don Liborio), Francesco Lo Briglio (Don Calogero), Michèle Bally.

Depressing crime drama starring Sordi as an honest, hard-working factory foreman, who returns to his native Sicily with his family while on holiday. There he meets up with his old benefactor, Attanasio, who decides to make Sordi repay an old debt. He sends Sordi off to the United States, where he is forced by American gangsters to assassinate one of their rivals. Having no choice, Sordi fulfills the mafioso's wishes, and is just as quickly sent back to Italy. There he obeys the law of omerta (silence), and returns to his family to resume a normal life. MAFIOSO received the 1963 Golden Shell Award at the San Sebastian Film Festival.

p, Antonio Cervi; d, Alberto Lattuada; w, Rafael Azcona, Marco Ferreri, Age Scarpelli (based on a story by Bruno Caruso); ph, Armando Nannuzzi; m, Piero Piccioni, Nino Rota; ed, Nino Baragli; art d, Carlo Egidi; set d, Mario Ravasco.

Crime (PR:C MPAA:NR)

MAFU CAGE, THE** (1978) 102m Clouds c (AKA: MY SISTER, MY LOVE)

Lee Grant (Ellen), Carol Kane (Cissy), Will Geer (Zom), James Olson (David).

Bizarre, fairly engrossing film starring Grant and Kane as the strange daughters of a deceased anthropologist, who specialized in the study of wild primates. Grant, the more normal of the two, is a noted solar astronomist. Kane, however, is quite mad, and spends most of her time creating art pieces and torturing her father's apes in the huge Mafu cage. Grant keeps her sister at home rather than in an institution, and it becomes clear that the siblings share a sexual relationship. Eventually Kane's madness begins to overtake Grant, as her fears of men (Olson is her co-worker and lover for whom she feels no commitment) and dissatisfaction with heterosexual sex (the sex scenes between Olson and Grant are filmed in a distracted, cold manner, while those between Kane and Grant are given warmer, erotic visual treatment) boil to the surface. Olson makes the mistake of visiting Kane without Grant around, and allows her to chain him in the Mafu cage. He is then tortured and murdered by Kane and his body buried in the garden. This leaves Grant to discover the crime and soon she, too, meets the same fate. Kane's performance combined with an interesting (albeit manipulative) directing style saves this somewhat muddled film from being a total washout.

p, Diana Young; d, Karen Arthur; w, Don Chastain (based on a play by Eric Wespha); ph, John Bailey; m, Roger Kellaway; ed, Carol Littleton.

Drama Cas. (PR:O MPAA:R)

MAGGIE, THE (SEE; HIGH AND DRY, 1954, Brit.)

MAGIC** (1978) 106m FOX c

Anthony Hopkins (Corky/Voice of Fats), Ann-Margret (Peggy Ann Snow), Burgess Meredith (Ben Greene), Ed Lauter (Duke), E. J. Andre (Merlin), Jerry Houser (Cab Driver), David Ogden Stiers (George Hudson Todson), Lillian Randolph (Sadie), Joe Lowry (Club M.C.), Beverly Sanders (Laughing Lady), I. W. Klein (Maitre d'), Stephen Hart (Captain), Patrick McCullough (Doorman), Bob Hackman (Father), Mary Munday (Mother), Scott Garrett (Corky's Brother), Brad Beesley (Young Corky), Michael Harte (Minister).

Thanks to a brilliant and nervous performance from Hopkins, this film is an above-average thriller. Hopkins is a clever ventriloquist whose strangely realistic dummy, "Fats," is sharper and faster than his master, or so it seems, stealing scenes, dominating their ugly and insulting conversations on stage until the dummy appears to be taking over the act. To Hopkins, the dummy is also taking over his own psychic and intellectual personality. The ventriloquist's schizophrenia and paranoia become so acute that his mind is gripped in the terror of wholly losing his identity. Offstage he battles for his emotional life with "Fats," and, when his agent, Meredith, discovers the truth of the situation, Hopkins kills him, or believes that "Fats" has killed him. The killing is brought on when Meredith, ironically, tells Hopkins that he has put together a lucrative TV contract for him and "Fats." Hopkins believes by then that it will be seen over national TV that his dummy is really in control and he goes berserk. Hiding the body, the now utterly neurotic Hopkins flees to the mountain resorts of the Catskills in upper New York State, visiting a former lover, Ann-Margret. She, however, is married to Lauter, a husband who does not take

kindly to one-time boy friends cozying up to his voluptuous wife. Ann-Margret, an over-the-hill sexpot enthralled with the attention Hopkins lavishes upon her, encourages the near lunatic ventriloquist to hop into the hay, and a confrontation between Lauter and Hopkins explodes, with Hopkins killing the irate husband. From there on it's a quick ride down to disaster for Hopkins and Ann-Margret, with "Fats" giving a moving soliloquy at the end. Hopkins, who performed his own stunts and ventriloquism, is riveting as he delivers a high-voltage performance. Burgess is good as a Swifty Lazar type of super-agent and Lauter is almost as menacing as the weird-looking "Fats." Ann-Margret is a disappointment, her part reduced to prop status, a role calling for an ample bosom in a tight sweater. The first half hour is exceptional, but then the film becomes somewhat predictable, although Attenborough does bring forth the best from his actors. Goldman's script is too thin and, toward the end, sloppy and almost indifferent to the fate of his characters. Michael Redgrave's terrified ventriloquist in DEAD OF NIGHT (1946), from which Goldman certainly took his plot, is far superior to Hopkins' schizoid ventriloquist in MAGIC (albeit Redgrave's voice for his dummy was dubbed in DEAD OF NIGHT). The personality takeover of a dummy from master is not new and saw a variation on the theme in Lionel Barrymore's quirkish THE DEVIL DOLL (1936) role and an even more bizarre enactment of a tormented ventriloquist who loses his identity to his dummy by Erich von Stroheim in THE GREAT GABBO (1929).

p, Joseph E. Levine, Richard P. Levine; d, Richard Attenborough; w, William Goldman (based on his novel); ph, Victor J. Kemper (Panavision, Technicolor); m, Jerry Goldsmith; ed, John Bloom; prod d, Terence Marsh; art d, Richard Lawrence; set d, John Franco, Jr.; cos, Ruth Myers; spec eff, Robert MacDonald, Jr.; makeup, Lee Harman, Hallie Smith-Simmons.

Crime Drama Cas. (PR:O MPAA:R)

MAGIC BOW, THE**1/2** (1947, Brit.) 105m Gainsborough/UNIV bw

Stewart Granger (Paganini), Phyllis Calvert (Jeanne), Jean Kent (Blanchi), Dennis Price (Paul de la Roche), Cecil Parker (Germi), Felix Aylmer (Pasini), Frank Cellier (Antonio), Marie Lohr (Countess de Vermand), Henry Edwards (Count de Vermand), Mary Jerrold (Teresa), Betty Warren (Landlady), Antony Holles (Manager), David Horne (Rizzi), Charles Victor (Peasant), Eliot Makeham (Giuseppe), Yehudi Menuhin (Soloist), Stewart Rome, Robert Speaight, O.B. Clarence.

This biographical film is nothing more than a poorly strung series of cliches, that takes more than a few liberties with the true life story of violinist Paganini. Granger is the musician who falls for both a girl (Calvert) and his Stradivarius. She's a rich woman who gets him the beloved violin, after the plucky musician loses it gambling. After several love complications, including a duel with a Napoleonic soldier, Calvert arranges for her beloved to play before the Pope. Of course Granger's a success and it's happily ever after time. Despite some good performances, THE MAGIC BOW is drenched with its cliched situations and plot developments. Ultimately, the story ends up a dull, insignificant bit of tripe, though Menuhin's violin solos of Paganini's work do give the film some desperately needed class. Musical pieces include: "The Devil's Trill" (Giuseppe Tartini), "La Ronde des Lutins" (Brazzini), "Campanella," "Caprice Number 20," "Violin Concerto Number 1," "Introductions et Variations" (Nicolò Paganini), "Violin Concerto Opus 61," last movement (Ludwig Von Beethoven), "Romance" (Phil Greene, based on a theme by Paganini).

p, R. J. Minney; d, Bernard Knowles; w, Roland Pertwee, Norman Ginsbury (based on the novel The Magic Bow by Manuel Komroff); ph, Jack Cox, Jack Asher; ed, Alfred Roome; md, Basil Cameron; art d, A. Mezzei.

Biography (PR:A MPAA:NR)

MAGIC BOX, THE***** (1952, Brit.) 118m Festival/BL c

Renee Asherson (Miss Tagg), Richard Attenborough (Jack Carter), Robert Beatty (Lord Beaverbrook), Martin Boddey (Sitter in Bath Studio), Edward Chapman (Father in Family Group), John Charlesworth (Graham Friese-Greene), Maurice Colbourne (Bride's Father at Wedding), Roland Culver (1st Company Promoter), John Howard Davies (Maurice Friese-Greene), Michael Denison (Connaught Rooms Reporter), Robert Donat (William Friese-Greene), Joan Dowling (Friese-Green Maid), Henry Edwards (Butler at Fox Talbot's), Mary Ellis (Mrs. Collings), Marjorie Fielding (Elderly Viscountess), Robert Flemyng (Doctor in Surgery), Leo Genn (Maida Vale Doctor), Marius Goring (House Agent), Everly Gregg (Bridegroom's Mother at Wedding), Joyce Grenfell (Mrs. Clare), Robertson Hare (Sitter in Bath Studio), Kathleen Harrison (Mother in Family Group), William Hartnell (Recruiting Sergeant), Joan Hickson (Mrs. Stukely), Thora Hird (Doctor's Housekeeper), Stanley Holloway (Broker's Man), Patrick Holt (Sitter in Bath Studio), Michael Hordern (Official Receiver), Jack Hulbert (1st Holborn Policeman), Sidney James (Sergeant in Storeroom), Glynis Johns (May Jones), Mervyn Johns (Pawnbroker), Margaret Johnston (Edith Friese-Greene), Barry Jones (Bath Doctor), Peter Jones (Industry Man, Connaught Rooms), James Kenney (Kenneth Friese-Greene), Ann Lancaster (Bridesmaid in Wedding Group), Herbert Lomas (Warehouse Manager), John Longdon (Speaker in Connaught Rooms), Bessie Love (Bride's Mother, Wedding Group), Miles Malleson (Orchestra Conductor), Garry Marsh (2nd Company Promoter), Muir Mathieson (Sir Arthur Sullivan), A.E. Matthews (Old Gentleman, Bond St. Studio), John McCallum (Sitter in Bath Studio), Bernard Miles (Cousin Alfred), Richard Murdoch (Sitter in Bath Studio), David Oake (Claude Friese-Greene), Laurence Olivier (2nd Holborn Policeman), Cecil Parker (1st Platform Man at Connaught), Frank Pettingell (Bridegroom's Father at Wedding), Norman Pierce (Speaker in Connaught Rooms), Eric Portman (Arthur Collings), Dennis Price (assistant in Bond St. Studio), Michael Redgrave (Mr. Lege, Instrument Maker), Peter Reynolds (Bridegroom, Wedding Group), Margaret Rutherford (Lady Pond), Maria Schell (Helena Friese-Greene), Janette Scott (Ethel Friese-Greene), Ronald Shiner (Fairground Barker), Sheila Sim (Nursemaid), Madame Slobodskaya (Soloist at Bath Concert), John Stuart (2nd Platform Man at Connaught), Marianne Stone (Bride in Wedding Group), Basil Sydney (William Fox Talbot), Ernest Thesiger (Earl, Bond St.Studio), David Tomlinson (Assistant in Laboratory), Sybil

Thorndike *(Sitter in Bath Studio)*, Cecil Trouncer *(John Rudge)*, Michael Trubshawe *(Sitter in Bath Studio)*, Peter Ustinov *(Industry Man)*, Charles Victor *(Industry Man, Connaught Rooms)*, Kay Walsh *(Hotel Receptionist)*, Norman Watson *(Doctor in Connaught Rooms)*, Emlyn Williams *(Bank Manager)*, Harcourt Williams *(Tom, Workman at Lege & Co.)*, Googie Withers *(Sitter in Bath Studio)*, Joan Young *(Glove Shop "Dragon")*.

Just about everyone who ever appeared in British movies and was alive at the time worked in this feature. Donat plays William Friese-Greene, a pioneer in the film industry who patented the first motion picture camera. Opening in Bristol, where he was a photographer's assistant, he went on to become a successful society lenser in London and spent all of his time and money on his new invention (which he patented two years before Edison). His first wife, Schell, is his partner at the moment of his greatest success but she dies soon after. His second wife, Johnston, shares the failures, and Donat winds up broke and dies at a film industry meeting. In between, we are treated to the sight of at leat 50 of England's finest actors, all playing tiny bits (Olivier is a befuddled policeman dragged off his beat to look at Donat's invention; Ustinov, who worked one day on the film, is a film distributor et al.) to send the story hurdling along. Friese-Greene is barely recalled by anyone these days and had already been dead more than 30 years when this film was made, but there were those who felt his story had to be told and they convinced all of the actors that they had to give of themselves. Note the cast list and see that everyone agreed to take alphabetical billing so the not-well-known Asherson is seen at the top. It's a good-looking film and well directed by Boulting. Donat is excellent, and he has to be because he was working with the industry's finest.

p, Ronald Neame; d, John Boulting; w, Eric Ambler (based on *Friese-Greene,Close-up of an Inventor* by Ray Allister; ph, Jack Cardiff (Technicolor); m, Wiliam Alwyn; ed, Richard Best; prod d, John Bryan; art d, E. Hopewell Ash; set d, Dario Simoni; cos, Julia Squire; makeup, Harold Fletcher.

Biography **(PR:AA MPAA:NR)**

MAGIC BOX, THE, 1965

(SEE: GIRL WITH THE FABULOUS BOX, THE, 1965)

MAGIC BOY**

(1960, Jap.) 83m Toei/MGM c (SHONEN SARUTOBI SASUKE)

An evil witch disturbs the idyllic living a brother and sister enjoy in the countryside. The witch has done this by unleashing bandits, who terrorize local villagers and animals the brother and sister deeply care about. The young boy goes off to see a famous teacher of magic, and while he is gone, his sister is kidnaped. Eventually the boy returns, and joins forces with the master of magic and animals to save his sister and rid the countryside of the witch.

d, Akira Daikubara; w, Dohei Muramatsu (based on a story by Kazuo Dan); ph, Seigo Otsuka, Mitsuaki Ishikawa (Toeiscope, Magicolor); ed, Shinataro Miyamoto; md, Toru Funamura; art d, Seigo Shindo; m/l, "Magic Boy," Fred Spielman, Janice Torre (sung by Danny Valentino); animation d, Sanae Yamamoto; animators, Chikao Tera, Kazuko Nakamura, Shuji Konno, Masatake Kita, Daikichiro Kusube, Taku Sugiyama, Reiko Okuyama.

Animated Drama **(PR:A MPAA:NR)**

MAGIC CARPET, THE** (1951) 84m COL c

Lucille Ball *(Narah)*, John Agar *(Ramoth)*, Patricia Medina *(Lida)*, George Tobias *(Gazi)*, Raymond Burr *(Boreg)*, Gregory Gaye *(Ali)*, Rick Vallin *(Abdul)*, Jo Gilbert *(Maras)*, William Fawcett *(Ahkmid)*, Doretta Johnson *(Tanya)*, Linda Williams *(Estar)*, Perry Sheehan *(Copah)*, Eileen Howe *(Vernah)*, Minka Zorka *(Nedda)*, Winona Smith *(Ziela)*.

Routine "Arabian Nights"-type picture starring Agar as a deposed prince trying to free his people from the evil rule of the Caliph and his vizier, played by Burr. Agar enlists the aid of harem girl Ball (in her last film before "I Love Lucy" hit the airwaves) and together they win back the province, while zipping around on a flying carpet. Good cast and typically professional direction by veteran Landers make this one easy to sit through.

p, Sam Katzman; d, Lew Landers; w, David Matthews; ph, Ellis W. Carter (Supercinecolor); ed, Edwin Bryant; md, Mischa Bakaleinikoff; art d, Paul Palmentola.

Adventure **(PR:A MPAA:NR)**

MAGIC CHRISTIAN, THE* 1/2** (1970, Brit.) 95m Grand/COM c

Peter Sellers *(Sir Guy Grand)*, Ringo Starr *(Youngman Grand)*, Isabel Jeans *(Agnes)*, Caroline Blakiston *(Esther)*, Wilfrid Hyde-White *(Ship's Captain)*, Terence Alexander *(Mad Major)*, Peter Bayliss *(Pompous Toff)*, Joan Benham *(Socialite in Sotheby's)*, Patrick Cargill *(Auctioneer)*, Graham Chapman *(Oxford Stroke)*, John Cleese *(Director in Sotheby's)*, Clive Dunn *(Sommelier)*, Freddie Earlle *(Sol)*, Fred Emney *(Fitzgibbon)*, Kenneth Fortescue *(Irate Snob in Sotheby's)*, Peter Graves *(Interested Lord in Ship's Bar)*, Patrick Holt *(Duke in Sotheby's)*, David Hutcheson *(Lord Barry)*, Hattie Jacques *(Ginger Horton)*, John Le Mesurier *(Sir John)*, Jeremy Lloyd *(Lord Hampton)*, David Lodge *(Ship's Guide)*, C. Ferdy Mayne *(Edouard)*, Guy Middleton *(Duke of Mantisbriar)*, Peter Myers *(Lord Kilgallon)*, Dennis Price *(Winthrop)*, Robert Raglan *(Maltravers)*, Graham Stark *(Waiter)*, Leon Thau *(Engine Room Toff)*, Frank Thornton *(Police Inspector)*, Edward Underdown *(Prince Henry)*, Michael Trubshawe *(Sir Lionel)*, Michael Aspel, Michael Barrat, Harry Carpenter, W. Barrington Dalby, John Snagge, Alan Whicker *(TV Commentators)*, Richard Attenborough *(Oxford Coach)*, Leonard Frey *(Ship's Psychiatrist)*, Laurence Harvey *(Hamlet)*, Christopher Lee *(Dracula)*, Spike Milligan *(Traffic Warden)*, Roman Polanski *(Man Watching Cabaret)*, Raquel Welch *(Shipboard Galley Master)*, Tom Boyle *(My Man Jeff)*, Victor Maddern *(Hot Dog Vendor)*, Yul Brynner *(Lady Singer)*.

A brazen, irreverent, and wild satire that hits more often than it misses, THE MAGIC CHRISTIAN seeks to prove that people will do anything, absolutely *anything*, for money—if there's enough of it. Rich, bored Sellers adopts Starr as his son. Starr is a vagrant whom Sellers meets in the park; he seeks to show his new "son" the lengths that some folks will go to for the elusive pound. They go on a grouse hunt and Sellers uses a machine gun to nail the birds. He bribes the coxswain of the boat race at Henley; he pays the heavyweight champion of the world and his challenger to cease punching and start kissing during the title bout; he gives Harvey, the leading Shakespearean of the day, a sack full of money so the man will do a striptease during the most famous of all soliloquies. He goes to a posh restaurant and eats disgustingly enough so that anyone else would be thrown out, but since he lavishes money on everyone, they accept him. The episodes continue as Brynner, dressed outrageously as a transvestite, sings "Mad About The Boy" to Roman Polanski, whose eyes seem to be searching for the nearest exit. Sellers goes to Sotheby's auction house and bids the price high on a piece of junk, just to see some Americans attempt—and succeed— to outbid him. Now, as a final gesture, he invites scores of the British aristocracy aboard a huge yacht known as "The Magic Christian." Once there, the passengers are assaulted by Lee (as a vampire) and others who insult and harangue them, but they all remain aboard as they think they will be rewarded by the eccentric Sellers. Suddenly, it appears that the ship is about to sink, but when the passengers rush on deck, they see that they've never left the shore. To prove his point once and for all, Sellers dumps a fortune into a huge vat filled with unspeakable excreta, blood, goo, ooze, and sludge. The crowd dives into the yechh and Sellers and Starr leave for the park where they met in the first reel. There are so many funny episodes in the film and they go by so quickly that one seldom stops laughing. When Sellers' limo is ticketed by traffic warden Milligan, Sellers gives the man money enough to cause Milligan to eat the citation. The point that the authors are trying to make is made early and that's the major problem, as they continue to do variations on the theme until it gets totally out of hand and the bits begin to fall apart. Welch is seen briefly as a galley slave driver wielding a whip. Several others appear in cameo (see cast list), but the picture is Sellers' all the way as he does a neat job of underplaying the mad peer. Ringo Starr has little more to do than react by saying "yes, dad." He does that well, however, and cannot be faulted for his work. Chapman and Cleese, who helped with the screenplay, also appear briefly. Songs include: "Come and Get It" (Paul McCartney, performed by Badfinger), "Carry On to Tomorrow," "Rock of Ages" (performed by Badfinger), "Something in the Air" (John Keene, performed by Thunderclap Newman), "Mad About the Boy" (Noel Coward, sung by Yul Brynner).

p, Denis O'Dell; d, Joseph McGrath; w, McGrath, Terry Southern, Peter Sellers, Graham Chapman, Jon Cleese (based on the novel by Southern); ph, Geoffrey Unsworth (Technicolor); m, Ken Thorne; ed, Kevin Connor; prod d, Asheton Gorton; md, Thorne; art d, George Djurovic; set d, Peta Button; cos, Vangie Harrison; spec eff, Wally Veevers; ch, Lionel Blair; makeup, Harry G. Frampton.

Comedy **Cas.** **(PR:C-O MPAA:M)**

MAGIC CHRISTMAS TREE** (1964) 65m Holiday c

Chris Kroesen, Valerie Hobbs, Dick Parish, Charles Nix, Robert Maffei.

While trying to save the climbing cat of a witch he had just met, a young boy falls out of a tree and is rendered unconscious. While unconscious, he dreams of a magical ring and a tree which give him special powers. During his dream, he halts breakaway police cars and fire engines, controls a giant, and saves a kidnaped Santa Claus. Good Christmas fare but not likely to make it through eternity.

p, Diane Johnson, Chris Kroesen; d, Richard C. Parish; w, Harold Vaugn Taylor.

Fantasy **(PR:A MPAA:NR)**

MAGIC FACE, THE** (1951, Aust.) 88m COL bw

Luther Adler *(Janus the Great)*, Patricia Knight *(Vera Janus)*, William L. Shirer *(Himself)*, Ilka Windish *(Carla Harbach)*, Heinz Moog *(Hans Harbach)*, Peter Preses *(Warden)*, Manfred Inger *(Heinrich Wagner)*, Jasper Von Oertzen *(Major Weinrich)*, Charles Koenig *(Franz)*, Toni Mitterwurzer *(Hans)*, Annie Maiers *(Mariana)*, Sukman *(Himmler)*, Herman Ehrhardt *(Goering)*, R. Wanka *(General Rodenbusch)*, Willner *(General Von Schlossen)*, Michael Tellering *(General Heitmeier)*, Hans Sheel *(General Steig)*, Bell *(General Haldes)*, Eric Frey *(Colonel Raffenstein)*.

Offbeat tale set in wartime Germany starring Adler as a master impersonator, who tours the country with his wife, Knight. Hitler soon catches wind of the act, and wants to see it. Der Fuhrer is attracted to Knight, and Adler finds himself imprisoned and tortured by Nazi goons, while his wife plays with the leader of the Third Reich. Seeking revenge, Adler escapes his tormentors, kills Hitler and takes his place, doing the most realistic impersonation of his career. The thesis is that Germany lost the war because of Adler's sabotage. A nearly laughable premise pulled off due to Tuttle's crisp direction and Adler's credible performance.

p, Mort Briskin, Robert Smith; d, Frank Tuttle; w, Briskin, Smith; ph, Tony Braun; m, Herschel Burke Gilbert; ed, Henrietta Brunsch; art d, Eduard Stolba.

War/Drama **(PR:A MPAA:NR)**

MAGIC FIRE** (1956) 94m REP c

Yvonne De Carlo *(Minna)*, Carlos Thompson *(Franz Liszt)*, Rita Gam *(Cosima)*, Valentina Cortesa *(Mathilde)*, Alan Badel *(Richard Wagner)*, Peter Cushing *(Otto Wesendonk)*, Frederick Valk *(Minister von Moll)*, Gerhard Riedmann *(King Ludwig II)*, Eric Schumann *(Hans von Buelow)*, Robert Freytag *(August Roeckel)*, Heinz Klingenberg *(King of Saxonia)*, Charles Regnier *(Meyerbeer)*, Fritz Rasp *(Pfistermeister)*, Kurt Grosskurth *(Magdeburg)*, Hans Quest *(Robert Hubner)*, Jan Hendriks *(Michael Bakunin)*.

Tepid biography of brilliant German composer Richard Wagner, starring Badel (whose portrayal hardly lives up to Wagner's playboy reputation) as the title character and De Carlo as his first wife. The film concentrates on the composer's complicated love life, with only excerpts of his greatest works, produced under the steady supervision of Erich Wolfgang Korngold, to relieve the boredom. MAGIC FIRE fails to enlighten the viewer concerning Wagner or his music.

p&d, William Dieterle; w, Bertita Harding, E.A. Dupont, David Chantler (based on the novel by Harding); ph, Ernest Haller (Trucolor); m, Richard Wagner; ed, Stanley Johnson; md, Erich Wolfgang Korngold; art d, Robert Herlth; ch, Tatjana Gsovsky.

Biography   **(PR:A MPAA:NR)**

MAGIC FOUNTAIN, THE**   (1961) 82m Classic World-Davis Fil c

Peter Nestler (Prince Alfred), Helmo Kindermann (Prince Frederick), Josef Marz (Gustavo the Dwarf), Catherine Hansen (Princess Kathryn), Osman Ragheb (Prince Hans), Greear Wasson (Gregory the Boy), Erik Jelde (King Wilhelm), Cedric Hardwicke (King Wilhelm/Narrator), Rolf von Nauckhoff (Sir Phillip), Buddy Baer (Voice of Big Benjamin), Hans Conried (Voice of Otto the Owl).

Three young sons search for a magic fountain, for it has magical waters that will save their ailing father, the king. Two of the brothers take an evil turn, but the good brother (Nestler) comes upon the castle which holds the magic fountain. He removes a curse from the enchanted castle and gets his brothers returned to human form. But the brothers turn on Nestler, and make him look bad in the eyes of the king. However, he proves his worth to his father at the end. In 1964 Davis Films released subsequent versions of the film—one 85 minutes in length, the other 77 minutes in length—with Sir Cedric Hardwicke (the narrator in the original version) playing the king.

p&d, Allan David; w, John Lehmann (based on the story "Das Wasser des Lebens" by Jakob Grimm, Wilhelm Grimm); ph, Wolf Schneider (Ultrascope, Eastmancolor); m, Jacques Belasco; ed, Richard Hertel; spec eff, Weegee; m/l, "The Magic Fountain," Steve Allen, Don George.

Fantasy   **(PR:A MPAA:NR)**

MAGIC GARDEN, THE
              (SEE: PENNYWHISTLE BLUES, THE, 1952, South Africa)

MAGIC GARDEN OF STANLEY SWEETHART, THE*
                                        (1970) 112m MGM c

Don Johnson (Stanley Sweetheart), Linda Gillin (Shayne/Barbara), Michael Greer (Danny), Dianne Hull (Cathy), Holly Near (Fran), Victoria Racimo (Andrea), Brandon Maggart (Dr. Arthur Osgood/Man in Cafe).

Dated counterculture film starring Johnson (whose surprisingly long career didn't really take off until he starred as detective Crocket in NBC Television's "Miami Vice") as a dissatisfied college student who wanders through a series of sexual encounters of all types (one-on-one, menage-a-trois, etc.) and lots of drug abuse until he decides that there must be more to life and leaves it all behind. Johnson's vaguely likable performance and a decent collection of 1960s music on the soundtrack are the only bright spots in this otherwise laughable project. Songs include: "Nobody Knows," "Sweet Gingerbread Man" (Michel Legrand, Alan Bergman, Marilyn Bergman, sung by Richie Havens), "Time to Make a Turn" (Larry Wiegand, sung by The Crow), "Funny Now It Happens" (Jerry Styner), "Blood," "Tell Me a Story" (David Lucas), "Water" (Lucas, sung by Michael Greer), "Magic Mountain" (Jerry Goldsmith), "Keep on Keepin' That Man" (Dan Penn, Bobby Memmons, sung by Angeline Butler), "Sound of Love" (Barry Gibb, Maurice Gibb, Robin Gibb), "Peace on Earth" (Bernie Schwartz).

p, Martin Poll; d, Leonard Horn; w, Robert T. Westbrook (based on his novel); ph, Victor Kemper (Metrocolor); m, Jerry Styner; ed, Nick Archer, Ted Chapman, prod d, Gene Callahan; set d, Leif Pedersen, cos, Frank Thompson.

Drama   **(PR:O MPAA:R)**

MAGIC NIGHT**
              (1932, Brit.) 72m British & Dominion/UA bw (GB: GOODNIGHT VIENNA)

Jack Buchanan (Capt. Maximilian Schletoff), Clive Currie (Gen. Schletoff), William Kendell (Ernst), Herbert Carrick (Johann), Gibb McLaughlin (Max's Orderly), Clifford Heatherley (Donelli), O. B. Clarence (Theater Manager), Aubrey Fitzgerald (Waiter), Gina Malo (Frieda), Peggy Cartwright (Greta), Muriel Aked (Marya, Landlady), Joyce Bland (Countess Helga), Anna Neagle (Viki).

A predictable romance set in pre-WW I Austria starring Buchanan as a general's son who forsakes his engagement to countess Bland for the love of plain flower girl Neagle who blooms into an opera singer.

p&d, Herbert Wilcox; w, Holt Marvel, George Posford; ph, F. A. Young; m, Harry Ferritt, Tony Lowry; cos, Doris Zinkelsen.

Musical   **(PR:A MPAA:NR)**

MAGIC OF LASSIE, THE*   (1978) 99m International c

James Stewart, Mickey Rooney, Pernell Roberts, Stephanie Zimbalist, Michael Sharrett, Alice Faye, Gene Vans, The Mike Curb Congregation, Lassie.

A really lame attempt at resurrecting the "Lassie" series, which is nothing more than a badly scored tear-jerker that even children will find dim. The plot sees Lassie taken from her young owner by nasty guy Roberts, who uses the kid's whining to drive grandpa Stewart into selling his prize-winning California vineyards. When that fails, Roberts takes the collie to the Rockies, where she escapes, and makes a long and torturous (for the audience anyway) journey back to California and her master. As mentioned above, the musical score is downright hideous, with everyone from Stewart to Lassie (voice provided by none other than the "You Light Up My Life" girl, Debby Boone) singing at the drop of a hat. It's films like this that scare people away from sitting through anything with a "G" rating. Lame songs include: "A Rose

is Not a Rose" (sung by Alice Faye and on a jukebox by Pat Boone), "There'll Be Other Friday Nights," "Brass Rings and Daydreams," "Traveling Music," "Banjo Song," "That Hometown Feeling," "Thanksgiving Prayer," "When You're Loved," "Nobody's Property," "I Can't Say Goodbye" (Robert B. Sherman, Richard M. Sherman).

p, Bonita Granville Wrather, William Beaudine Jr.; d, Don Chaffey; w, Jean Holloway, Robert B. Sherman, Richard M. Sherman; m/l, Robert B. Sherman, Richard M. Sherman.

Drama   **(PR:AA MPAA:G)**

MAGIC SPECTACLES zero
                                        (1961) 74m Fairway International c
                    (AKA: TICKLED PINK; MAGICAL SPECTACLE)

Tommy Holden (Dr. Paul Ner De Nude/Angus L. Farnsworth), June Parr (Myra Farnsworth), Margo Mehling (The Secretary), Kay Cramer, Cindy Tyler, Danice Daniels, Jean Cartwright, Carla Olson (The Go Go Go Go Girls).

This brainless sex comedy has Holden playing a Parisian scientist who creates a pair of glasses that filter out the clothing of whomever the lenses are focused on. Centuries later, Holden's other characterization, a timid ad man with a shrewish wife, finds the glasses and takes off on a lark to secretly look at women in their underwear. Perfect viewing for sexists and misogynists everywhere.

p, Arch Hall, Sr.; d, Bob Wehling; w, Hall; ph, Vilis Lapenieks (Eastmancolor); ed, Alex Grasshoff.

Comedy   **(PR:O MPAA:NR)**

MAGIC SWORD, THE***   (1962) 80m UA c

Basil Rathbone (Lodac), Estelle Winwood (Sybil), Gary Lockwood (St. George), Anne Helm (Princess Helene), Liam Sullivan (Sir Branton), John Mauldin (Sir Patrick), Jacques Gallo (Sir Dennis), Leroy Johnson (Sir Ulrich), David Cross (Sir Pedro), Angus Duncan (Sir James), Taldo Kenyon (Sir Anthony), Maila Nurmi (Hag/Intruder), Jack Kosslyn (Ogre), Lorrie Richards (Anne), Ann Graves (Princess Laura), Marlene Callahan (Princess Grace), Merritt Stone (King), Danielle de Metz (French Girl), Nick Bon Tempi, Paul Bon Tempi (Siamese Twins), Ted Finn, Angelo Rossitto (Dwarfs), Richard Kiel (Pinhead).

A fun Bert I. Gordon sword-and-sorcery extravaganza starring Lockwood as a young knight who vows to rescue beautiful princess Helm from the evil clutches of wicked magician Rathbone. That's about all the plot there is, so sit back and enjoy the fairly decent special effects as Lockwood encounters a giant ogre, tiny people, Siamese twins, and a two-headed dragon.

p&d, Bert I. Gordon; w, Bernard Schoenfeld (based on a story by Gordon); ph, Paul C. Vogel (Eastmancolor); m, Richard Markowitz; ed, Harry Gerstad; art d, Franz Bachelin; set d, George R. Nelson; cos, Oscar Rodriguez; spec eff, Milt Rice; makeup, Dan Striepeke.

Fantasy   **Cas.**   **(PR:A MPAA:NR)**

MAGIC TOWN** 1/2   (1947) 103m RKO bw

James Stewart (Lawrence "Rip" Smith), Jane Wyman (Mary Peterman), Kent Smith (Hoopendecker), Ned Sparks (Ike Sloan), Wallace Ford (Lou Dicketts), Regis Toomey (Ed Weaver), Ann Doran (Mrs. Weaver), Donald Meek (Mr. Twiddle), E.J. Ballantine (Moody), Ann Shoemaker (Ma Peterman), Mickey Kuhn (Hank Nickleby), Howard Freeman (Richard Nickleby), Harry Holman (Mayor), Mickey Roth (Bob Peterman), Mary Currier (Mrs. Frisby), George Irving (Sen. Wilton), Selmer Jackson (Charlie Stringer), Robert Dudley (Dickey, the Reporter), Julia Dean (Mrs. Wilton), Joel Friedkin (Dingle), Paul Scardon (Hodges), George Chandler (Bus Driver), Frank Darien (Quincy), Larry Wheat (Sam Fuller), Jimmy Crane (Shorty), Richard Belding (Junior Dicketts), Danny Mummert (Benny), Griff Barnett (Henry), Edna Holland (Secretary), Eddie Parks (Bookkeeper), Paul Maxey (Fat Man in Hallway), Lee "Lasses" White (Old Timer), Snub Pollard (Townsman), Wheaton Chambers (Electrician), Edgar Dearing (Gray-Haired Man), Emmett Vogan (Reverend), Eddy Waller (Newcomer), Frank Fenton (Birch), Garry Owen (Man Smoking Offensive Cigar), William Haade, Dick Wessel (Moving Men), John Ince (Postman), Dick Elliott, Lee Phelps.

Producer Riskin wrote many of Frank Capra's best films and he could have used Capra's light touch to help this movie, which winds up flat and labored under Wellman. Stewart runs an opinion poll company but is having little success until he finds a small town that accurately reflects all of America. The people in the tiny burg are perfectly average and they think the way the experts think they should think. Stewart, Meek, and long-faced Sparks go to the town and pose as insurance men, but what they are actually doing is polling everyone on various matters. Wyman runs the local paper and Stewart falls for her, but that's erased when she discovers his real reason for being there and writes about him. The town booms when the truth gets out. Real estate values soar as the media pick up the story and the greedy villagers attempt to sell their property at inflated prices. The influx of radio, newspapers, tourists, and hucksters takes its toll on the town and it is soon ruined. Stewart appeals to the people to forget about their sudden fame and go back to the happy way they were before. Wyman takes him back and all ends well. Lots of terrific touches in the picture, especially the scene where Stewart and Wyman discover much about each other as they recite poems they learned in school. Stewart and Sparks have a drinking scene that's also a highlight, and there are two or three others that register, but the film lacks cohesiveness and eventually sputters.

p, Robert Riskin; d, William A. Wellman; w, Riskin (based on a story by Riskin, Joseph Krumgold); ph, Joseph F. Biroc; m, Roy Webb; ed, Sherman Todd, Richard C. Wray; md, C. Bakaleinikoff; art d, Lionel Banks; set d, George Sawley; m/l,

"My Book of Memory," "Magic Town," Mel Torme, Bob Wells, Webb and Edward Heyman.

Comedy/Drama   **Cas.**   **(PR:AA MPAA:NR)**

MAGIC VOYAGE OF SINBAD, THE**
(1962, USSR) 79m Mosfilm/Filmgroup c (SADKO)

Sergey Stolyarov (Sinbad), Alla Larionova (Luberia), Mark Troyanovskiy (Trifon), N. Malishyovskiy (Tanus), B. Surovtsev (Hadabad), Y. Leonidov (Cassim), M. Astangov (Prince Lal Bahari Day), I. Pereverzev (Abdalla), N. Kryuchkov (Old Merchant), S. Martinson (Moneylender), L. Fenin (Viking Leader), S. Kayukov (Neptune), O. Viklandt (Neptuna), Y. Myshkova (Princess Morgiana), L. Vertinskaya (The Phoenix).

This film was released in Russia in 1952 under the title of SADKO. It was released again in 1962 with a new title and anglicized names to appeal to U.S. audiences. The fantasy epic follows the adventures of Sinbad, who has promised the poverty-stricken people of Covasan that he will find the bird of happiness—the Phoenix. Sinbad uses his wits to get out of one predicament after another and eventually returns home to tell the people of Covasan the moral of the story—happiness is to be found right at home.

p, Art Diamond (U.S. version); d, James Landis (U.S. version), Aleksandr Ptushko (USSR version); w, Francis Ford Coppola (U.S. Version), K. Isayev (USSR version); ph, F. Provorov (Vistascope); m, V. Shebalin (Selections from the opera "Sadko" by Nikolai Andreevich Rimski-Korsakov); ed, George Stein; art d, Y. Kumankov; cos, O. Kruchinina; spec eff, S. Mukhin; ch, Sergey Koren; m/l, John Smich (U.S. version, sung by Gino Marsili); makeup, Jose Malar.

Fantasy   **(PR:A MPAA:NR)**

MAGIC WEAVER, THE**
(1965, USSR) 87m Gorky/AA c (MARYA-ISKUSNITSA; AKA: MARIA, THE WONDERFUL WEAVER)

Mikhail Kuznetsov (The Soldier), Ninel Myshkova (Maria), Vitya Perevalov (Ivanushka), Anatoliy Kubatskiy (Czar of the Water), Olya Khachapuridze (Alenushka), Georgiy Millyar (Kvak), Vera Altayskaya (Ttushka-Nepogodushka), I Troitskiy (Altyn Altynych), Aleksandr Khvylya (Mudrets-Molchanik), N. Kondratyev, A. Alyoshin, A. Baranov, Valentin Bryleyev, N. Kuznetsov, Konstantin Nemolyayev, V. Pitsek, K. Starostin, E. Traktovenko, M. Shcherbakov.

A good-natured soldier is making his way home after many years in the military, and along the way he makes animal friends. He encounters a little boy whose mother has been kidnaped by the evil czar of water. The mother, a weaver of exceptional skill, is being held in the underwater kingdom. The soldier and the little boy get help from the czar's kind granddaughter and rescue the weaver.

d, Aleksandr Rou; w, Yevgeniy Shvarts; ph, Dmitriy Surenskiy; m, A. Volkonskiy; art d, Y. Galey; set d, Anatoliy Dikan; spec eff, L. Akimov, Arseniy Klopotovskiy, V. Nikitchenko; m/l, Volkonskiy, V. Lifshits.

Fantasy   **(PR:A MPAA:NR)**

MAGIC WORLD OF TOPO GIGIO, THE** 1/2
(1961, Ital.) 75m Jolly Cinecidi-Compagnia Perego Telecast/COL c (LE AVVENTURE DI TOPO GIGIO; AKA: THE ITALIAN MOUSE)

Voices of: Peppino Mazzulo (Topo Gigio), Ermanno Roveri, Ignazio Colnaghi, Federica Milani, Armando Benetti, Ignazio Dolce, Milena Zini, Carlo Delfini.

An animated puppet film that has a mouse (Topo Gigio) and his two friends (one a cowardly worm) planning to take a rocket to the moon. But instead the flight takes them to an amusement park where they end up being the stars of the show with the help of a friendly puppeteer. A magician, whose show is next door, is angered by the attention the puppeteer is receiving and kidnaps one of Topo Gigio's friends. But the mouse outwits the magician and rescues his friend. The film has two endings. One has Topo Gigio finding the secret of the magician's tricks and humiliating him. The other has Topo convincing the magician to have a change of heart and join forces with the puppeteer for the children.

p, Richard Davis (U.S. version); d, Luca De Rico (U.S. version), Federico Caldura (Ital. version); w, Maria Perego, Mario Faustinelli, Guido Stagnaro (U.S. version), Caldura (Ital. version); ph, Giorgio Battilana (Eastmancolor); m, Armando Trovajoli; ed, Franco Alessandro; pro d, Franco Serino, set d, Mario Milani; cos, Sandro Negri; spec eff, Ettore Catallucci; m/l, "Topo of the King," "The Butterfly," Aldo Rossi; animation, Maria Perego (Topo Gigio), Annabella Spadon (Rosy), Grazia Curti (Giovannino), Emanuele Pagani, Emy Ricciotti.

Animation   **(PR:A MPAA:NR)**

MAGICAL SPECTACLES   (SEE: MAGIC SPECTACLES, 1961)

MAGICIAN, THE*** 1/2
(1959, Swed.) 102m Svensk Filmindustri/Janus bw (ANSIKTET; AKA: THE FACE)

Max von Sydow (Vogler), Ingrid Thulin (Manda Aman), Gunnar Bjornstrand (Vergerus), Naima Wifstrand (Grandmother), Bengt Ekerot (Spegel), Bibi Andersson (Sara), Gertrud Fridh (Ottilia), Lars Ekborg (Simson), Toivo Pawlo (Starbeck), Erland Josephson (Egerman), Ake Fridell (Tubal), Sif Ruud (Sofia), Oscar Ljung (Antonsson), Ulla Sjoblom (Henrietta), Axel Duberg (Rustan), Brigitta Pettersson (Sonna).

In THE MAGICIAN, Bergman takes this favorite theme and layers it on multiple planes. Von Sydow is a 19-century magician who heads a troupe of traveling illusionists. They come to a small Swedish town where the population doesn't believe in magic. Led by von Sydow, the troupe proceeds to play with the townspeople's minds, and Bergman, in turn, plays with the audience. Things are never quite what they seem, either narratively or cinematically. Through an imaginative use of the medium itself, Bergman plays with the audience's expecta-

tions by means of editing, lighting, and special effects. The mise-en-scene has a darkly rich gothic look that enhances the film's mysterious nature. Though at times the story is overwhelmed by the theme, THE MAGICIAN still holds great fascination. It challenges the intellect with a myriad of ideas about magic, reality, and the very nature of film itself. (In Swedish; English subtitles.)

p, Carl-Henry Cagarp; d&w, Ingmar Bergman; ph, Gunnar Fischer, Rolf Halmquist; m, Erik Nordgren; ed, Oscar Rosander; art d, P. A. Lundgren.

Drama   **Cas.**   **(PR:C MPAA:NR)**

MAGICIAN OF LUBLIN, THE** 1/2   (1979, Israel/Ger.) 115m Cannon c

Alan Arkin (Yasha Mazur), Louise Fletcher (Emilia), Valerie Perrine (Zeftel), Shelley Winters (Elizabeta), Lou Jacobi (Wolsky), Warren Berlinger (Herman), Shai K. Ophir (Shmul), Lisa Whelchel (Halina), Maia Danziger (Magda), Linda Bernstein (Esther), Lachi Nov (Bolek), Friedrich Schonfelder (Count Zaruski), Ophelia Stral (Rytza), Buddy Elias (Pan Kazarsky).

The unlikely blending of Israeli filmmakers and West German locations proved a financial bust in this more than $6 million picture that failed to get any notice from critics or audiences. Executive producer Harry N. Blum (OBSESSION, SKATEBOARD, AT THE EARTH'S CORE) said: "Had it come after YENTL, it might have had a different reaction." Perhaps. The fact that Singer won the Nobel Prize for literature as the picture was being made didn't help a bit. Also, it was at this time that producers Golan and Globus were in the midst of negotiating for Cannon Films so they could have a better outlet to distribute their films. There were many subtle nuances in the book that were glossed over by Golan in favor of more commercial factors or, perhaps, the screenplay did not know how to take an essentially spiritual and intellectual novel and turn it into a film. In place of the philosophical musings, Shelley Winters' breasts were seen. Arkin is a good magician who travels the back roads of Europe with his small act. He is never satisfied with his work and takes great pains to improve himself at every turn—a decidedly Jewish trait, and this is a decidedly Jewish movie. As he travels, we are treated to a fairly accurate look at the Eastern European customs of the era, which, when combined with the metaphysics and mysticism of the characters, serve to make the movie more than passingly interesting. We wonder if Singer, whose works revolve around this time in history and these complex subjects, could have been pleased with the outcome as the performances of Winters and many of the others are overboard as a K-Tel commercial. Jacobi, as the man who sponsors Arkin, is excellent, but veteran Berlinger is lost and Perrine is wasted. Arkin's performance is a curious mixture of subtle renderings and his patented hysterical shouting, and he never did find his characterization. Some excellent photography by Gurfinkel made the movie look its best when there were no actors on the screen.

p, Menahem Golan, Yoram Globus; d, Golan; w, Irving S. White, Golan (based on the novel by Isaac Bashevis Singer); ph, David Gurfinkel; m, Maurice Jarre; ed, Dov Henig; art d, Yurgent Kibach.

Drama   **(PR:C MPAA:R)**

MAGNET, THE**   (1950, Brit.) 79m EAL/GFD bw

Stephen Murray (Dr. Brent), Kay Walsh (Mrs. Brent), William [James] Fox (Johnny Brent), Meredith Edwards (Harper), Gladys Henson (Nannie), Thora Hird (Nannie's Friend), Michael Brooke, Jr. (Kit), Wylie Watson (Pickering), Julien Mitchell (The Mayor), Keith Robinson (Spike), Thomas Johnson (Perce), Bryan Michie (Announcer), Seamus Mor Na Feasag, [James Robertson Justice] (Tramp), Anthony Oliver (Policeman), Molly Hamley-Clifford (Mrs. Deas), Harold Goodwin (Pin-Table Attendant), Edward Davies (Delinquent Youth), Joan Hickson (Mrs. Ward), Grace Arnold (Mrs. Mercer), Joss Ambler (Businessman), Sam Kydd (Postman), David Boyd, Geoffrey Yin, Jane Bough, Russell Waters, Thea Gregson [Thea Gregory], Elsie Lowenthal.

British comedy starring Fox as the precocious son of psychiatrist Murray who steals a huge magnet and gets into all sorts of trouble. Most of the humor is derived from seeing the overly scholarly Murray seeking to analyze his son's normal juvenile behavior.

p, Michael Balcon; d, Charles Frend; w, T.E.B. Clarke; ph, Lionel Banes; m, William Alwyn; ed, Bernard Gribble, md, Ernest Irving; art d, Morahan.

Comedy   **(PR:A MPAA:NR)**

MAGNETIC MONSTER, THE***   (1953) 76m A-Men/UA bw

Richard Carlson (Dr. Jeffrey Stewart), King Donovan (Dr. Dan Forbes), Jean Byron (Connie Stewart), Harry Ellerbe (Dr. Allard), Leo Britt (Dr. Benton), Leonard Mudie (Dr. Denker), Byron Foulger (Simon), Michael Fox (Dr. Serny), John Zaremba (Chief Watson), Frank Gerstle (Colonel Willis), John Vosper (Captain Dyer), Michael Granger (Smith), Bill Benedict (Albert), Lee Phelps (City Engineer), Douglas Evans (Pilot), Strother Martin (Co-pilot), John Dodsworth (Cartwright), Kathleen Freeman (Nelly), Charlie Williams (Cabby), Jarma Lewis (Stewardess), Elizabeth Root (Joy), Watson Downs (Mayor).

Despite the fact that the stunning climax of this science-fiction film happens to be stock footage from the German film, GOLD, THE MAGNETIC MONSTER, it is actually a fairly interesting film in its own right. Carlson stars as a young scientist whose experiments with a new radioactive isotope get so out of hand that he accidentally creates a monster isotope which consumes energy. The monster lab experiment doubles its size every 12 hours by converting the absorbed energy into matter and emitting deadly radiation that threatens the existence of a nearby town. Eventually Carlson is able to lure the monster to an experimental Canadian power station (stolen from GOLD) where it is given an energy overdose of 900,000,000 volts. Sounds silly, but it plays better than it reads.

p, Ivan Tors; d, Curt Siodmak; w, Siodmak, Tors; ph, Charles Van Enger; m, Blaine Sanford; ed, Herbert L. Strock; prod d, George Van Marten; spec eff, Jack Glass.

Science Fiction   **(PR:C MPAA:NR)**

MAGNIFICENT AMBERSONS, THE*****

(1942) 88m Mercury Theatre Production/RKO bw

Joseph Cotten *(Eugene Morgan)*, Dolores Costello *(Isabel Amberson Minafer)*, Anne Baxter *(Lucy Morgan)*, Tim Holt *(George Amberson Minafer)*, Agnes Moorehead *(Fanny Amberson)*, Ray Collins *(Jack Amberson)*, Richard Bennett *(Maj. Amberson)*, Erskine Sanford *(Benson)*, J. Louis Johnson *(Sam the Butler)*, Don Dillaway *(Wilbur Minafer)*, Charles Phipps *(Uncle John)*, Dorothy Vaughn *(Woman at Funeral)*, Elmer Jerome *(Man at Funeral)*, John Elliott *(Guest)*, Nina Guilbert *(Guest)*, Sam Rice *(Man at Funeral)*, Olive Ball *(Mary)*, Kathryn Sheldon *(Matron)*, Anne O'Neal *(Mrs. Foster)*, Henry Roquemore *(Hardware Man)*, Mel Ford *(Fred Kinney)*, Lillian Nicholson *(Landlady)*, Bobby Cooper *(George as a Boy)*, Drew Roddy *(Elijah)*, Jack Baxley *(Rev. Smith)*, Nancy Gates *(Girl)*, James Westerfield *(Cop at Accident)*, Edwin August *(Man)*, Jack Santoro *(Barber)*, Orson Welles *(Narrator)*, Gus Schilling *(Drugstore Clerk)*, Georgia Backus *(Matron)*, Hilda Plowright *(Nurse)*, Bob Pittard *(Charlie Johnson)*, Billy Elmer *(House Servant)*, Maynard Holmes, Lew Kelly *(Citizens)*, John Maguire *(Young Man)*, Ed Howard *(Chauffeur/Citizen)*, William Blees *(Youth at Accident)*, Philip Morris *(Cop)*, Louis Hayward *(Ballroom Extra)*.

Though mutilated by studio cuts and wholly misunderstood at the time of its release, THE MAGNIFICENT AMBERSONS remains Welles' second great filmic masterpiece, one where his genius is stamped on every frame. Though the Tarkington novel upon whch Welles based his farewell to a gentler era is second rate, the film itself surpasses the original story, enhanced by a marvelous script and awe-inspiring techniques that, in many ways, go beyond CITIZEN KANE (1941). The look backward is fond, loving, sometimes clinical, always nostalgic as Welles profiles a wealthy Midwestern family whose members are close to American royalty in the town they dominate (Indianapolis, Indiana, most assuredly). The film is set during the final decade of the quaint, slow-paced and mannered 19th Century when conversation had nothing to do with expediency and was a learned grace, practiced and improved at the dinner table where words were chosen with decisive care. All in this film know which fork to use for salad and most, except for Holt, when to stop using it. Holt is the spoiled, insufferable, conceited, power-gluttonous son of the wealthy family, first seen whipping his buggy horse through town to the consternation of neighbors. Cotten is an inventor who loves Costello but loses her to wealthy Dillaway, one of the rich Ambersons. After some time away from the town, Cotten returns, now successful, having invented an automobile, an instrument of the future many of the old school find repulsive, especially the haughty Holt. Dillaway dies and Cotten, who is a widower with an attractive daughter, Baxter, attempts to rekindle his love affair with Costello. But Holt, who has been attracted to Baxter but rebuffed by her, suddenly steps between Cotten and his mother, denying Cotten access to the widow. Baxter, in turn, rejects Holt because he will not enter a profession, believing his family fortune should support his lifestyle of idle gentleman. Holt and Costello then go on an extended European tour to shed themselves of painful memories. Meanwhile, Cotten's auto factory prospers. Costello has a heart attack in Paris and is brought back to recuperate, but the old mansion and the family image has drastically changed. Now the Amberson mansion, once the center of high social activity, is dark, reduced to a mausoleum, and the family fortune has all but evaporated. The Amberson patriarch, Bennett, dies and it is soon learned, to Holt's horror, that there is no more family fortune. Cotten is rich but emotionally drained; Holt has still stubbornly refused him access to his dying mother, the surly youth's last revenge upon Cotten whom he envisions as a low-born usurper of the old life, an economic interloper whose dreadful machine has distorted and destroyed the old royal ways, and somehow brought the Amberson dynasty to ruin. He must close up the old house at the end and find employment so he can support himself and his spinster aunt, Moorehead, a tormented, lonely soul who has lived on the fringe of Amberson joy and sorrow, sharing the life of the family as would a dog getting the scraps of a magnificent dinner. Holt has mistreated her, too, and, in the end, she reveals his terrible nature to him. Holt does get his much deserved comeuppance. His collapse is complete at the end when he is almost killed in an accident but is visited by Cotten and Moorehead in the hospital and it is understood that he will be taken care of, that, despite his great deficiencies of character, Cotten will love him as if he were his own son, a love really carried over from Costello to her truculent offspring. The performances Welles draws forth from his cast are nothing less then superlative, particularly Cotten as the long-suffering but stalwart and noble gentleman caller, Moorehead as the embittered, peculiar, and loveless spinster aunt, and, surprisingly, Holt, who completely captured the despicable character of the utterly selfish son. Collins is a joy as the wise and kindly uncle and Baxter is radiant as the hopeful daughter. Costello, one-time silent screen goddess, is less effective but this is understandable since she is always shown as a fragile creature, half in shadow, almost as if she were an elusive romantic ghost Cotten must follow down the gaslit, expansive corridors of Amberson mansion. Sanford, an elderly bystander, waiting impatiently for Holt to get his due for the injuries he has visited upon others, is also appealing, and then there's that majestic, stentorian voice of Welles himself as he narrates this tragic tale of the passing of yesterday's quality. The film is so rich in innovative technique that it will take several viewings to note even the most essential elements. The "Welles sound" permeates every frame of the film, with his overlapping dialog giving a natural feel to the words spoken, the volume of the words diminishing as characters recede from the camera, speeches fading, others increasing in volume as the camera picks them up, other voices mixed with street sounds, and groups of citizens talking, their words meshing. Welles rehearsed his cast before each scene, then allowed them to improvise and add or delete his words, trusting to their ability to interpret what their distinct characters would or would not say. In crowd scenes he allows a host of gossips to function as a Greek chorus in estimating the worth of the Amberson and Morgan families. At times the voices of the characters boom and bellow, and, at others, they are so hushed that the words are barely discernible, all tailored to each carefully honed scene. The look of the film is duplicated by Welles from the low-key lighting used by photographers at the turn-of-the-century and Cortez's deep focus lensing is utterly arresting, dwelling upon set scenes only Welles could have framed. Notable are long 10-minute soliloquies that are saved from tedium by virtue of Welles' unique framing of a scene. Dolly and truck shots keep the film moving and fluid and some crane shots tower above the film and story to include not only its characters but the changing architecture from Victorian to modern, from resplendent to mundane, as Welles graphically shows the passing of an age, an almost mournful look at the face of America being revolutionized, from a plain, clean countenance to severe makeup, one age hiding another. To enhance his historical perspective, Welles uses the ancient iris up and down to open and close many scenes, a technique employed during the early silent era. In one sequence he uses this technique splendidly in showing Cotten adorning himself with the garments of the day, a charming sequence with Welles' voice-over describing the curious hats, spats, billowing trousers, with amusement but not sarcasm, for this is a film of extravagant respect for the past. Yet Welles does not ignore the many modern devices and photographic tricks he initally used in CITIZEN KANE and refined in THE MAGNIFICENT AMBERSONS, showing in split-second frames his people reflected in mirrors, highly glossed furniture, sometimes in a glare of light, most in half-shadow, as if the blackness of time were shutting out the light of the living. One of the most spectacularly joyous scenes is the sleigh-ride sequence; though realistic in every sense, Welles amazingly filmed this entire segment in a Los Angeles ice factory, taking 12 days to perfect the snow, the breaths from his actor's mouths. It is hard to believe that these scenes were not real exteriors. As part of his great visual gifts, Welles was able to show the true nature of the characters in their relevant actions—Moorehead peering over a railing to eavesdrop on those far below in the Amberson mansion's main foyer, or Holt methodically spooning down strawberry shortcake at the resplendent, enormous dining room table as he indifferently listens to aunt Moorehead pour out her heart, Cotten standing mute and stunned at the front door of the Amberson mansion which has been closed in his face by Holt who stands behind the frosted glass panes, a sinister shadow, the dolly shot down the main street at the opening, the photographically still shots of the drab modern structures at the end. Slowly, deliberately, Welles peels back the outward layers of the Amberson family members until all their imperfections are naked, piling vignette upon vignette to show their decline and destruction, not by his own hand but by that of time and change. Welles actually edited this film as he shot it, elliptically editing, scene by scene, foregoing the Moviola and sidestepping the cutting room floor. He was 26 when he sat down to write this screenplay which he finished in nine days. THE MAGNIFICENT AMBERSONS is really more controlled, more subtle and, even in his long long takes, presents more cinematic excitement than in his other masterpiece, CITIZEN KANE, though the story is less dynamic and sensational. So rich and lavishly spontaneous is this film that no fledgling filmmaker can learn without seeing it, studying it, absorbing it. Given the drastic overreaction of premiere audiences who failed to understand the film, it's a wonder that THE MAGNIFICENT AMBERSONS survived at all. When an audience in Pomona, California, first saw the film, viewers talked back to the screen characters, laughed, made jokes, and so terrified George J. Schaefer, President of RKO, that the studio boss left the theater red-faced and believing that Welles had presented him with a financial disaster. The studio had spent $1,125,000 on the film. The frightening premiere caused Schaefer to panic and he wrote Welles, then on location in Brazil for IT'S ALL TRUE (later aborted) that the waves of hooting and jeering from the Pomona audience were "like getting one sock in the jaw after another for two hours." In desperation to return money to RKO coffers, Schaeffer instructed Robert Wise to edit the film down drastically. Welles had already reduced the film from 148 minutes to 131 minutes but Wise cut the film down to 88 minutes and this even included adding a somewhat optimistic ending, the hospital scene at the end, a scene tacked on by a nameless studio writer and directed by Freddie Fleck with music added by Roy Webb. This presumptuous and dictatorial savaging of Welles' masterpiece, according to the great director-writer, destroyed " the whole heart of the picture really." Yet, THE MAGNIFICENT AMBERSONS survives as a masterpiece nevertheless. The cutting of more than 3,000 feet of Welles' film to provide the truncated version was not the final insult to Welles' genius. RKO president Shaeffer left the studio before the editing was completed and was himself later shocked to learn that THE MAGNIFICENT AMBERSONS was treated as a throw-away by his successors. It was sent out to second-run houses, as part of a twin bill with one of Lupe Velez's Mexican Spitfire films, a grade-B programmer. THE MAGNIFICENT AMBERSONS lost $625,000 and it would only recoup its investment after several more reissues. The Tarkington novel had been filmed as a silent in 1925 by Vitagraph, entitled PAMPERED YOUTH and starring Cullen Landis and Alice Calhoun.

p, Orson Welles; d, Welles, Freddie Fleck, Robert Wise; w, Welles (based on the novel by Booth Tarkington), ph, Stanley Cortez, Russell Metty, Harry J. Wild; m, Bernard Herrmann, Roy Webb; ed, Robert Wise, Jack Moss, Mark Robson; art d, Mark-Lee Kirk; set d, Al Fields; cos, Edward Stevenson; spec eff, Vernon L. Walker.

Drama **Cas.** **(PR:A MPAA:NR)**

MAGNIFICENT BANDITS, THE* 1/2

(1969, Ital./Span.) 102m Tritone-Medusa-D.I.A. c (O CANGACEIRO)

Thomas Milian, Ugo Pagliani, Eduardo Fajuardo, Howard Ross [Renato Rossini], Alfredo Santa Cruz, Jesus Guzman.

A peasant (Milian), to avenge the destruction of his farm by the Brazilian Army, starts organizing a group of guerrilla fighters. Pagliani is a mercenary who is hired to capture Milian, only to change sides and join him.

d, Giovanni Fago; w, Fago, Antonio Troisio, Bernardino Zapponi, Jose Luis Jerez; ph, Alejandro Ulloa.

Western **(PR:C MPAA:NR)**

MAGNIFICENT BRUTE, THE**

(1936) 77m UNIV bw

Victor McLaglen *(Big Steve Andrews)*, Binnie Barnes *(Della Lane)*, William Hall *(Bill*

Morgan), Jean Dixon *(Blossom Finney)*, Henry Armetta *(Bugati)*, Billy Burrud *(Pete Finney)*, Edward Norris *(Hal Howard)*, Ann Preston *(Mrs. Howard)*, Zeni Vatori *(Brains)*, Selmer Jackson *(Dr. Coleman)*, Adrian Rosley *(Papapolas)*, Etta McDaniel *(Lavolia)*, Esther Dale *(Mrs. Randolph)*, Joe Varga *(Wildcat)*, Tom Jackson *(Maxwell)*, Ray Brown *(Two-up Mooney)*, Charles Wilson *(Murphy)*.

Routine love triangle situation starring McLaglen, Barnes, and Hall as the parties in question whose paths cross in the steel mills. McLaglen plays a burly steelworker smitten with gold-digger Barnes, despite the longing glances of boardinghouse-owner Dixon. Hall is McLaglen's co-worker and buddy, until he is also taken with Barnes' vamp act. The conflict really heats up when a collection taken for the wife of a deceased mill worker is squandered by Hall in a stupid bet. This causes Hall to take it on the lam with Barnes, but the kindly Dixon persuades them to stay and face the music. Climax sees McLaglen rescue Dixon's son from being nearly boiled alive when the kid falls into a crucible about to be filled with molten metal. This act unites McLaglen and Dixon and everything is peachy at the end.

p, Charles R. Rogers; d, John G. Blystone; w, Owen Francis, Lewis R. Foster, Bertram Milhauser (based on a story by Francis and the story "Big" by Foster); ph, Merritt Gerstad; ed, Ted J. Kent.

Drama **(PR:A MPAA:NR)**

MAGNIFICENT CONCUBINE, THE **
(1964, Hong Kong) 97m Shaw Brothers/Frank Lee International c (YANG KWEI FEI)

Li Li-hua *(Yang Kwei Fei)*, Yen Chuan *(Emperor Ming Huang)*, Chao Lei *(Killer)*, Li Hsiang-chun *(Mei)*, Yang Chih-ching *(Yang Kuochung)*, Ku Wen-tsung, Ho Ping, Lin Ching, Weng Mu-lan, Lily Mo Chau.

A corrupt brother is appointed prime minister by the beloved emperor in 8th Century China only because he is related to the emperor's favorite concubine. But the concubine leaves and the emperor follows. The prime minister withholds this information until the court is forced to flee. The prime minister also has withheld wages from the faithful palace guard, who murder him and demand the death of his sister. They find the sister, who is discovered tending the sick emperor. She promises to kill herself once he is well and eventually honors her promise.

p, Runme Shaw; d, Li Han-hsiang; w, Wang Chih-po; ph, T. Nishimoto (Shaw-Scope, Eastmancolor); m, Wang Shun; ed, Chiang Hsing-ling.

Drama **(PR:A MPAA:NR)**

MAGNIFICENT CUCKOLD, THE 1/2**
(1965, Fr./Ital.) 117m Sancro-Copernic/CD bw (IL MAGNIFICO CORNUTO; LE COCU MAGNIFIQUE)

Claudia Cardinale *(Maria Grazia Artusi)*, Ugo Tognazzi *(Andrea Artusi)*, Bernard Blier *(Corna d'Oro)*, Michele Girardon *(Christiana)*, Salvo Randone *(Belisario)*, Jose-Luis de Vilallonga *(Presidente)*, Gian Maria Volonte *(Assessore)*, Paul Guers *(Gabriele)*, Philippe Nicaud *(Doctor)*, Susy Andersen *(Wanda)*, Alfonso Sansone, Ettore Mattia *(Guests)*, Brett Halsey, Jean Claudio.

A soap opera-type story about a successful businessman who has a beautiful and popular wife but still falls into an extramarital affair with a woman who is also married. This woman (Girardon) is so sharp at arranging her clandestine meetings that she starts to wonder if her lover's wife is doing the same. The husband (Tognazzi) also starts worrying, and when he confronts his wife about being unfaithful, she flippantly names an antique dealer. In anger, Tognazzi leaps from the car to challenge the innocent man, only to run into a stone wall and end up in the hospital. From there he monitors his wife's phone calls and finds out she was lying. So again he becomes a contented husband, but this time blissfully ignorant that his wife has now started a liaison with the doctor who treated him. (In Italian; English subtitles.)

p, Alfonso Sansone, Henryk Chroscicki; d, Antonio Pietrangeli; w, Diego Fabbri, Ruggero Maccari, Ettore Scola, Stefano Strucchi (based on the play "Le Cocu Magnifique" by Fernand Crommelynck); ph, Armando Nannuzzi; m, Armando Trovajoli; ed, Eraldo Da Roma; art d, Maurizio Chiari; cos, Nina Ricci, Chiari; English subtitles, Herman G. Weinberg.

Comedy **(PR:A MPAA:NR)**

MAGNIFICENT DOLL** (1946) 93m UNIV bw

Ginger Rogers *(Dolly Payne Madison)*, David Niven *(Aaron Burr)*, Burgess Meredith *(James Madison)*, Horace [Stephen] McNally *(John Todd)*, Peggy Wood *(Mrs. Payne)*, Frances Williams *(Amy)*, Robert H. Barrat *(Mr. Payne)*, Grandon Rhodes *(Thomas Jefferson)*, Henri Letondal *(Count D'Arignon)*, Joe Forte *(Sen. Ainsworth)*, Erville Alderson *(Darcy)*, George Barrows *(Jedson)*, Francis McDonald *(Barber Jenks)*, Emmett Vogan *(Mr. Gallentine)*, Arthur Space *(Alexander Hamilton)*, Byron Foulger *(Servant)*, Joseph Crehan *(Williams)*, Larry Blake *(Charles)*, Pierre Watkin *(Harper)*, John Sheehan *(Janitor)*, Ruth Lee *(Mrs. Gallentine)*, George Carleton *(Howard)*, Jack Ingram *(Lane, the Courier)*, Olaf Hytten *(Blennerhassett)*, Sam Flint *(Waters)*, Boyd Irwin *(Hathaway)*, Lee Phelps *(Hatch, a Bettor)*, Lois Austin *(Grace Phillips)*, Harlan Briggs *(Quinn)*, John Hines *(Dr. Ellis)*, Ferris Taylor *(Mr. Phillips)*, Eddy Waller *(Arthur, the Coachman)*, Stanley Blystone *(Bailiff)*, Stanley Price *(Man at Platform)*, Victor Zimmerman *(Martin)*, Ja George *(Gov. Stanley)*, Ethan Laidlaw *(Sanders, a Soldier)*, Mary Emery *(Woman)*, Carey Hamilton *(Sen. Mason)*, Dick Dickinson *(Man Who Falls)*, Larry Steers *(Lafayette)*, Frank Erickson *(Capt. White)*, Grace Cunard *(Woman with Baby)*, Tom Coleman *(Mr. Carroll)*, Pietro Sosso *(Mr. Anthony)*, Jack Curtis *(Edmond)*, Harry Denny *(Mr. Calot)*, Garnett Marks *(Justice Drake)*, Jerry Jerome *(Thomas)*, John Michael *(Ned)*, John Hamilton *(Mr. Witherspoon)*, Harlan Tucker *(Ralston)*, Vivien Oakland *(Mrs. Witherspoon)*, Al Hill *(Man)*, Joe King *(Jailer)*, Brandon Hurst *(Brown)*.

Dolly Madison's real life was fascinating. She helped the United States in the War of 1812 when she stole some important documents from the British; she had affairs; she was the woman behind one of our early presidents; and she was, perhaps, the most unique first lady of all time. Unfortunately, for history and for moviegoers, very little of that is seen in this boring film that bears as much resemblance to the truth as BLAZING SADDLES does to a western. Rogers loses her first husband, Quaker McNally, then opens a boarding house with her mother, Wood, in the Washington area. She is soon wooed by Niven, as the scoundrel Aaron Burr, and Meredith, as the quiet Madison, a philosopher at heart and not a man to seek high office. She has an affair with Burr, who later would kill Space (as Alexander Hamilton), but marries Madison and pushes him to the top of the political ladder when he becomes secretary of state to Rhodes (as Jefferson), and is just waiting in the wings to become president. Lavish production values are marred by Stone's dull screenplay. Rogers, Meredith, and Niven do what they can but are ultimately defeated by the words and the lethargic pace of Borzage's direction. The true story of this unusual woman has yet to be told. Famed milliner Lily Dache did the hats, most of which were more interesting than the dialog.

p, Jack H. Skirball, Bruce Manning; d, Frank Borzage; w, Irving Stone (based on the story by Stone); ph, Joseph Valentine; m, Harry J. Salter; ed, Ted J. Kent; md, David Tamkin; art d, Alexander Golitzen; set d, Russell A. Gausman, Ted Offenbecker; cos, Travis Banton, Vera West; makeup, Jack P. Pierce; hats, Lily Dache.

Biography **(PR:A MPAA:NR)**

MAGNIFICENT DOPE, THE** (1942) 84m FOX bw

Henry Fonda *(Tad Page)*, Lynn Bari *(Claire)*, Don Ameche *(Dawson)*, Edward Everett Horton *(Horace Hunter)*, George Barbier *(Barker)*, Frank Orth *(Messenger)*, Roseanne Murray *(Dawson's Secretary)*, Marietta Canty *(Jennie)*, Hal K. Dawson *(Charlie)*, Josephine Whittell *(Mrs. Hunter)*, Arthur Loft *(Fire Engine Salesman)*, Paul Stanton *(Peters)*, Harry Hayden *(Mitchell)*, Kitty McHugh *(Sadie)*, Hobart Cavanaugh *(Gowdy)*, Claire Du Brey *(Secretary)*, Pierre Watkin *(Carson)*, William Davidson *(Mr. Reindel)*, Byron Foulger, Harry Depp, Carey Harrison, Ralph Brooks, Jack Mower, Charles Meakim, Larry Wheat, Larry Williams, Ken Gibson, Frank Jaquet *(Men)*, Paul McVey *(John)*, Gladys Blake *(Another Secretary)*.

This picture misfires in an attempt to give Fonda the same kind of role as James Stewart in 1939's MR. SMITH GOES TO WASHINGTON or Gary Cooper in MR. DEEDS GOES TO TOWN (1936). Fonda, however, is not just a big, rawboned guy. No, he is a big, rawboned *lazy* guy from Vermont who works during the short New England summer renting boats, then settles in for the long winter and waits for summer again. He has no ambition and prides himself on that, so when aggressive Ameche, who heads a Dale Carnegie-type school, runs a contest to find the nation's biggest loser (in order to help his own failing business), Fonda is chosen to get the big $500 prize as well as a free course at Ameche's school. Ameche's girl friend is Bari, and Fonda is soon in love with her, but too timid to let her know so he asks her advice as to how to win the hand of a Vermont girl, who is totally nonexistent. Bari tells Fonda how to woo the woman and Fonda uses her suggestions on her. Ameche is no slouch and he spots this growing attraction, then encourages Fonda to make an effort to woo Bari, saying what really impresses her is a man of ambition, not one of sloth. Ameche, as high-powered in this as he was in CONFIRM OR DENY, gets Fonda employment as an insurance agent. Fonda, who moves at a snail's pace, is able to sell a huge policy to wealthy Barbier, a man who had shunned insurance men due to their hard tactics, and who had been turned down in the past because of high blood pressure. Fonda's laidback ways bring Barbier's blood pressure down and the man is able to pass the medical examination. Fonda makes a bundle on the deal and uses that to buy a new fire engine for his small Vermont town. Bari has learned that Ameche was willing to allow her to have a fling with Fonda just so he could publicize his school and the success of making the country's biggest loser into a winner. Bari goes back to Vermont with Fonda, but Ameche also prevails as he has learned a great deal from Fonda, and is now selling his school's services by using Fonda's calm technique. Ameche winds up with many more students than he's ever hoped for. The picture did well but Fonda didn't enjoy doing it. The most famous line in the picture was when Fonda stated his credo: "I've no respect for a man who was born lazy. It took me a long time to get where I am." For a man as industrious as Fonda, that was a stretch.

p, William Perlberg; d, Walter Lang; w, George Seaton (based on a story by Joseph Schrank); ph, Peverell Marley; ed, Barbara McLean; md, Emil Newman; art d, Richard Day, Wiard B. Ihnen.

Comedy/Drama **(PR:A MPAA:NR)**

MAGNIFICENT FRAUD, THE* 1/2 (1939) 74m PAR bw

Akim Tamiroff *(Jules LaCroix/President Alvarado)*, Lloyd Nolan *(Sam Barr)*, Mary Boland *(Mme. Geraldine Genet)*, Patricia Morison *(Claire Hill)*, Ralph Forbes *(Harrison Todd)*, Steffi Duna *(Carmelita)*, Ernest Cossart *(Duval)*, George Zucco *(Dr. Virgo)*, Robert Warwick *(Gen. Hernandez)*, Frank Reicher *(Garcia)*, Robert Middlemass *(Morales)*, Abner Biberman *(Ruiz)*, Donald Gallaher *(Dr. Diaz)*, Barbara Pepper *(June)*, Virginia Dabney *(2nd Blonde)*, Edward McWade *(Little Old Man)*, Julius Tannen *(American Business Man)*, Nestor Paiva *(Latin Business Man)*, Ernest Verebes.

Tamiroff stars as a skilled character actor who is called into service by confidence man Nolan to impersonate the assassinated dictator of a small South American country until the expected American aid arrives so they can take off with a large portion of the dough. Tamiroff, of course, plays the role to the hilt and begins to take his character seriously, while Nolan veers from his dishonest course, tranformed by the love of a good woman, Morison.

p, Harlan Thompson; d, Robert Florey; w, Gilbert Gabriel, Walter Ferris (based on a play by Charles G. Booth); ph, William Mellor; ed, James Smith.

Drama **(PR:A MPAA:NR)**

MAGNIFICENT LIE** (1931) 79m PAR bw

Ruth Chatterton *(Poll)*, Ralph Bellamy *(Bill)*, Stuart Erwin *(Elmer)*, Francoise Rosay *(Rosa Duchene)*, Sam Hardy *(Larry)*, Charles Boyer *(Jacques)*, Tyler Brooke *(Pierre)*, Tyrrell Davis *(Clarence)*, Jean Del Val *(Stage Manager)*.

Overwrought melodrama wherein Chatterton plays a famed French actress who visits the injured American troops during WW I. In the hospital she meets nearly blinded soldier Bellamy (in his first big role), who adores her. Thirteen years later, when Chatterton is touring New Orleans in a play, Bellamy shows up to see her again, but he loses his sight completely. Taking pity on the man, she arranges for a cafe singer, also played by Chatterton, to impersonate her so that Bellamy will not give up hope. Eventually the singer (who looks upon the assignment as just another job) falls in love with Bellamy, and when he regains his sight, he realizes that he loves her too, despite the deception. This film later proved to be an embarrassment for Boyer whose small role brought him little attention and some humiliation when the film was released in France where another actor dubbed his voice in French.

d, Berthold Viertel; w, Samuel Raphaelson, Vincent Lawrence, Leonard Merrick (based on the novel *Laurels and the Lady* by Merrick); ph, Charles Lang.

Drama (PR:A MPAA:NR)

MAGNIFICENT MATADOR, THE**
(1955) 94m FOX c (GB: THE BRAVE AND THE BEAUTIFUL)

Maureen O'Hara *(Karen Harrison)*, Anthony Quinn *(Luis Santos)*, Richard Denning *(Mark Russell)*, Thomas Gomez *(Don David)*, Lola Albright *(Mona Wilton)*, William Brooks Ching *(Jody Wilton)*, Eduardo Noriega *(Miguel)*, Lorraine Chanel *(Sarita Sebastian)*, Anthony Caruso *(Emiliano)*, Manuel Rojas *(Rafael Reyes)*, Jesus "Chucho" Solorzano, Rafael Rodriguez, Joaquin "Cagancho" Rodriguez, Antonio Velasquez, Felix Briones, Nacho Trevino, Jorge "Ranchero" Aguilar *(Themselves)*.

Lackluster outing for director Boetticher and star Quinn, who plays a famed matador whose reputation is ruined when he flees a bullfight after formally introducing his young rival Rojas to the bullfighting public. He seeks solace in the fancy hacienda of rich American admirer O'Hara, with whom he has an affair, which irritates her boy friend Denning no end. Seeking revenge, Denning attacks Quinn verbally, denouncing him as a coward. With O'Hara's help, Quinn overcomes his fear and returns to the ring to fight alongside Rojas, and together they defeat a ferocious bull. At the end of the match Quinn reveals that Rojas is actually his illegitimate son, thus explaining his initial reluctance to see him face death. Boetticher, as usual, makes the most of the fascinating Mexican locations, but the censors of the time prevented him from showing any details of actual bullfighting that might have saved the otherwise trite plot line from being a complete cliche.

p, Edward L. Alperson; d, Budd Boetticher; w, Charles Lang (based on a story by Boetticher); ph, Lucien Ballard (CinemaScope, Eastmancolor); m, Raoul Kraushaar, Alperson, Jr.; ed, Richard Cahoon; md, Kraushaar; m/l, title song, Alperson, Paul Herrick (sung by Kitty White); technical advisor, Carlos Arriya.

Drama Cas. (PR:A MPAA:NR)

MAGNIFICENT OBSESSION*** (1935) 112m UNIV bw

Irene Dunne *(Helen Hudson)*, Robert Taylor *(Bobby Merrick)*, Charles Butterworth *(Tommy Masterson)*, Betty Furness *(Joyce Hudson)*, Sara Haden *(Nancy Ashford)*, Ralph Morgan *(Randolph)*, Henry Armetta *(Tony)*, Gilbert Emery *(Dr. Ramsay)*, Arthur Hoyt *(Perry)*, Lowell Durham *(Junior Masterson)*, Alan Davis *(Dr. Justin)*, Crauford Kent *(Dr. Thomas)*, Edward Earle *(Mr. Miller)*, Inez Courtney *(May)*, Marion Clayton *(Amy)*, Beryl Mercer *(Mrs. Eden)*, Cora Sue Collins *(Ruth)*, Arthur Treacher *(Horace)*, Frank Reicher *(Dr. Rochard)*, Leonard Mudie *(Dr. Bardendreght)*, Walter Walker *(Nicholas Merrick)*, Purnell Pratt *(Hastings)*, Lucien Littlefield *(Breezy)*, Gino Corrado *(Antoine)*, Mickey Daniels *(Billy)*, Theodore Von Eltz *(Dr. Preston)*, William Arnold *(Chief Inspector)*, Leah Winslow, Ethel Sykes *(Women on Boat)*, Sherry Hall, Allen Connor, William Worthington, Louis LaVoie *(Men on Boat)*, Oscar Rudolph *(Western Union Boy)*, Eddy Chandler *(Mechanic)*, Sidney Bracey *(Butler)*, Alice Ardell *(Maid)*, Roy Brown, Gretta Gould, Frank Mayo, John M. Saint Polis, George Hackathorne, Beth Hazelton *(Ex-Patients)*, Sid Marion *(Sword Swallower)*, Arnold Korff, William Stack, Frederic Roland, Fredrik Vogeding *(Doctors)*, Walter Miller *(Chauffeur)*, Rollo Lloyd *(Tramp)*, Charles Coleman *(Butler)*, Joyce Compton, Georgette Rhodes, Helen Brown, Norma Drew *(Nurses)*, Vance Carroll, Henry Hale, Ray Johnson, Louis Natheau, Gladden James, Donald Kerr *(Reporters)*, Frank Maye *(John Stone)*, Sumner Getchell *(Jimmy)*.

This was the film that transported Robert Taylor from just another handsome face to superstardom. He was only 24 and already had such good looks that he was prettier than many of his female costars. But there were many handsome actors around who didn't have Taylor's ability and they soon fell by the wayside as Taylor continued to soar. Taylor plays a drunk whose reckless behavior causes the death of Dunne's husband. He has an accident and is taken to the hospital where the late physician was beloved. He tries to make his regrets known to Dunne and she walks away from him, then is hit by a car and blinded. This accident, compounded by the death of Dunne's husband, causes the wastrel to dedicate his life to becoming a doctor so he can operate on Dunne and restore her vision. Dunne's late husband had made a practice of selflessly aiding other people in complete anonymity. He was a wonderful person who did much to help humanity, according to Morgan, a close pal of the family. Taylor now begins to hang around the mansion where Dunne lives. She has no idea that he is the man who accidentally killed her husband and caused her impairment. They become great friends and later, in Paris, Dunne and stepdaughter Furness attempt to find a cure but it fails. Taylor is nearby and he and Dunne get closer and closer and love begins until she realizes who he is and that she cannot allow herself to fall for this man. She disappears and eludes Taylor's attempts at finding her. Taylor becomes a noted surgeon and the memory of the only woman he ever loved haunts him. Then he learns that Dunne is in a Virginia hospital, far from her area. Her condition is worse than ever and she desperately requires a most difficult and dangerous operation. At first, he is nervous about attempting it, but Morgan urges him on and Taylor uses every bit of his expert skill to perform the surgery. In the last scene, the one that sold millions of dollars in Kleenex, Dunne looks up at Taylor, blinks to clear the moisture from her eyes and we realize that she can see and she knows who it is who gave her that gift. Taylor smiles; he's paid his debt and can now spend the rest of his life with the woman he loves. Only the steeliest of hearts can resist being tugged by the story and the performance of the two stars. Dunne was 35 years old at the time, almost a generation more than Taylor, but his commanding voice and film presence could convince any viewer that he was far older than he was. The picture was remade in 1954, and shot Rock Hudson to the same heights Taylor once occupied.

p&d, John M. Stahl; w, George O'Neil, Sarah Y. Mason, Victor Heerman, Finley Peter Dunne (based on a novel by Lloyd C. Douglas); ph, John Mescall; ed, Milton Carruth.

Drama (PR:A MPAA:NR)

MAGNIFICENT OBSESSION** 1/2** (1954) 107m UNIV c

Jane Wyman *(Helen Phillips)*, Rock Hudson *(Bob Merrick)*, Barbara Rush *(Joyce Phillips)*, Agnes Moorehead *(Nancy Ashford)*, Otto Kruger *(Rudolph)*, Gregg Palmer *(Tom Masterson)*, Sara Shane *(Valerie)*, Paul Cavanagh *(Dr. Giraud)*, Judy Nugent *(Judy)*, George Lynn *(Williams)*, Richard H. Cutting *(Dr. Dodge)*, Will White *(Sgt. Ames)*, Helen Kleeb *(Mrs. Eden)*, Rudolph Anders *(Dr. Fuss)*, Fred Nurney *(Dr. Laradetti)*, John Mylong *(Dr. Hofer)*, Jack Kelly *(1st Mechanic)*, Lisa Gaye *(Switchboard Girl)*, William Leslie, Lance Fuller, Brad Johnson, Myrna Hansen *(Customers)*, Alexander Campbell *(Dr. Allan)*, Joe Mell *(Dan)*, Howard Dyrenforth *(Mr. Jouvet)*, Norman Schiller *(Mr. Long)*, Mae Clarke *(Mrs. Miller)*, Kathleen O'Malley *(Switchboard Girl)*, Joyce Hallward *(Maid)*, Lee Roberts *(2nd Mechanic)*, Harvey Grant *(Chris)*, Robert B. Williams *(Sgt. Burnham)*, Gail Bonney *(Phyllis)*, Lucille Lamar *(Nurse)*.

Not quite as heart-wrenching as the original version, this remake is still pretty good and does benefit from the colorization of the story. Blees wrote his screenplay based on the prior one and, more or less, did the same layout. Wyman is a blind woman and Hudson is the cad who becomes her savior. Hudson has been sort of responsible for Wyman's husband's accidental death, a man who was revered in the community as a combination of Dr. Kildare, Ben Casey, and every other angel of mercy ever seen. He had an obsession to do good things for people but with no recognition and Hudson takes up the flame. After the doctor's demise, Hudson attempts to apologize and Wyman, avoiding him, is blinded in an accident. With Kruger, a friend of the late, great physician, egging him on, Hudson forsakes his wastrel ways and decides to dedicate himself to medicine. Without revealing his true identity, he gets in touch with Wyman, and their relationship is soon a loving one. When she finds out who he is, she departs and, much later, he finds her in a terrible condition and performs the surgery that saves her life and restores her vision. Rather weepy at times, it is an unabashed appeal to the tear ducts and doesn't fail in the attempt. Director Douglas Sirk made only a few more films before retiring to Munich in 1959, just before he turned 60. Screenwriter Blees went into TV after the film was released and was responsible for producing and writing many hit shows, including "Combat."

p, Ross Hunter; d, Douglas Sirk; w, Robert Blees, Wells Root (based on the novel by Lloyd C. Douglas and the screenplay by Sarah Y. Mason, Finley Peter Dunne, Victor Heerman); ph, Russell Metty (Technicolor); m, Frank Skinner; ed, Milton Carruth; md, Joseph Gershenson; art d, Bernard Herzbrun, Emrich Nicholson; set d, Russell A. Gausman, Ruby R. Levitt; cos, Bill Thomas; spec eff, David S. Harsley.

Drama Cas. (PR:A MPAA:NR)

MAGNIFICENT ONE, THE** 1/2**
(1974, Fr./Ital.) 93m Ariane-Mondex-Cerito-Oceania-Rizzoli/Cine III c (LE MAGNIFIQUE)

Jean-Paul Belmondo *(Bob/Francois)*, Jacqueline Bisset *(Tatiana/Christine)*, Vittorio Capprioli *(Charron/Karpoff)*, Monique Tarbes *(Mme. Berger)*, Raymond Gerome *(Gen. Pontaubert)*, Hans Mayer *(Col. Collins)*, Jean Lefebvre *(Electrician)*, Andre Weber *(Plumber)*, Rodrigo Puebla *(Benson)*, Bruno Gargin *(Pilus)*, Rene Barrera *(The Chinese/The Bride)*, Etienne Assena *(Jean)*, Raoul Guilad *(The Albanian)*, Hubert Deschamps *(The Salesman)*, Jean-Pierre Rambal *(The Lecturer)*, Thalie Fruges *(Publishing House Hostess)*, Bernard Musson, Jack Berard, Louis Navarre *(Interpreters)*, Gaetan Noel *(Doctor)*, Charly Koubesserian *(Guard)*, Mario David.

Belmondo stars in this fairly likable comedy as an Ian Fleming-type writer whose real life becomes intertwined with that of his fictional character. The film shifts from Belmondo's somewhat dull existence which is only interrupted by next-door neighbor Bisset, to Belmondo's thriller character (also played by Belmondo) who, along with his helper (also played by Bisset), gets into all sorts of harrowing escapades. (In French; English subtitles.)

p, Alexandre Mnouchkine, Georges Danciger; d, Philippe de Broca; w, Francis Veber, de Broca; ph, Rene Mathelin (Panavision, Eastmancolor); m, Claude Bolling; ed, Henri Lanoe; art d, Francois de Lamothe; set d, Robert Christides; spec eff, Andre Pierdel, Leon Ortega, Georges Iaconelli.

Comedy (PR:A MPAA:NR)

MAGNIFICENT OUTCAST (SEE: ALMOST A GENTLEMAN, 1939)

MAGNIFICENT ROGUE, THE* 1/2 (1946) 74m REP bw

Lynne Roberts, Warren Douglas, Gerald Mohr, Stephanie Bachelor, Adele Mara, Grady Sutton,Donia Bussey, Ruth Lee, Charles Coleman, Dorothy Christy.

Roberts learns the rough side of her husband's business when the latter is sent off to WW II and she is forced to take over. Choppy goings for both Roberts and this film.

p, William J. O'Sullivan; d, Albert S. Rogell; w, Dane Lusier, Sherman L. Lowe (based on the story by Gerald Drayson Adams, Richard Sokolove); ph, John Alton; ed, Richard L. Van Enger; md, Mort Glickman; art d, Frank Hotaling; spec eff, Howard Lydecker, Theodore Lydecker.

Comedy/Drama (PR:A MPAA:NR)

MAGNIFICENT ROUGHNECKS*½ (1956) 73m AA bw

Jack Carson (Bix Decker), Mickey Rooney (Frank Sommers), Nancy Gates (Jane Rivers), Jeff Donnell (Julie), Myron Healey (Werner Jackson), Willis Bouchey (Ernie Biggers), Eric Feldary (Senor Ramon Serrano), Alan Wells (Danny), Frank Gerstle (Chuck Evans), Larry Carr (Guard), Matty Fain (Pepi), Joe Locke (Driver).

Carson and Rooney play the title characters whose tough work at South American oil wells is interrupted by the arrival of sexy oil expert Gates who shows up to take over Carson's job. His macho ego bruised, Carson stays on to show Gates the ropes and help bring in the first gusher. As can be expected, the two eventually fall in love. Typical programmer.

p, Herman Cohen; d, Sherman A. Rose; w, Stephen Kandel; ph, Charles Van Enger; m, Paul Dunlap; ed, Rose; md, Dunlap.

Drama/Romance (PR:A MPAA:NR)

MAGNIFICENT SEVEN, THE, 1954
(SEE: SEVEN SAMURAI, THE, 1954, Jap.)

MAGNIFICENT SEVEN, THE**** (1960) 128m Mirisch-Alpha/UA c

Yul Brynner (Chris), Eli Wallach (Calvera), Steve McQueen (Vin), Horst Buchholz (Chico), Charles Bronson (O'Reilly), Robert Vaughn (Lee), Brad Dexter (Harry Luck), James Coburn (Britt), Vladimir Sokoloff (Old Man), Rosenda Monteros (Petra), Jorge Martinez de Hoyos (Hilario), Whit Bissell (Chamlee), Val Avery (Henry), Bing Russell (Robert), Rico Alaniz (Sotero), Robert Wilke (Wallace).

THE MAGNIFICENT SEVEN comes thisclose (sic) to being a classic. It's the Americanization of the Akira Kurosawa film THE SEVEN SAMURAI (1954), and does a good job in mirroring the major themes and attitudes of the original in its attempt to re-create that monumental film in an occidental setting. Many who saw the original thought it might make a good western and it was just four years later that Sturges saw fit to do that. The core of the story is "protection for hire," something often seen in American films in the 1930s. The only department in which this film could not compete with Kurosawa's is in depicting the style, grace, and dignity of the samurai warrior. That kind of societal structure would not work in the western genre. Despite that, THE MAGNIFICENT SEVEN is an excellent film and deserved the accolades it has received through the years. Director Sturges and screenwriter Roberts had an awesome task because, until this time, Hollywood had often failed when attempting to adapt many of the foreign films that had achieved success. Rather than trying to re-create the subtleties of Kurosawa, they went ahead and made a rootin'-tootin' lots-o'-shootin' picture that could stand on its own. A small Mexican village is pillaged regularly by Wallach and his cutthroats. The quaking townsfolk don't have the courage or the ammo to take on Wallach and his desperadoes so they decide to hire seven of the toughest hombres that side of the Rio Grande. Brynner is the Seven's leader and he has recruited McQueen, Bronson, Vaughn, Dexter, Coburn, and Buchholz to help. They train the fearful townspeople to fight alongside them and set a snare for the wily Wallach and his group. A melee ensues and several of Wallach's men are killed but he gets new blood, returns, and captures the Seven, then re-establishes his hold over the village. The center of the film dips a bit as the actors begin to question what their mercenary lives are about. Wallach makes the fatal error of allowing the Seven to get away and they are soon back to rouse the villagers and haunt Wallach's plans for domination. The final battle takes place; Wallach is killed, four of the Seven also bite the dust, and Brynner and McQueen ride off into the sunset as Buchholz stays behind to live with Monteros. There's not a poor performance in the film but that's to be expected with this cast, although Brynner was the only "name" at the time the film was made. Five of the Seven would go on to become stars in the following years. Brynner had already won an Oscar for THE KING AND I and McQueen had made a splash in a TV series. The two men did not get along on the set. Coburn had less that 20 words to speak in the movie but it made no difference as his presence is what impressed everyone. The only actor who did not rise in the acting ranks was Dexter. He made a few films later, then gave it up to become a business associate of Frank Sinatra after he saved Old Blue Eyes from drowning while shooting NONE BUT THE BRAVE (1965). Sturges' direction is the key to the film. Just as he did in BAD DAY AT BLACK ROCK (1954) and THE GREAT ESCAPE (1963), Sturges assembled a flawless cast and put them through their paces. It's obvious that he studied Kurosawa's film before ever setting eye to eyepiece and that homage is appreciated. Bernstein's score has since become part of the fabric of American music and the main theme was used as the Marlboro cigarette signature. In the movie, everything worked once it was cleared. There were some incredible problems with the Mexican government censors as they felt that the script was not in keeping with their desires to make their country seem hospitable. Thus, the script had to be changed through philosophical, cultural, and societal sieves before the company was allowed to shoot. There were sequels (RETURN OF THE MAGNIFICENT SEVEN, GUNS OF THE MAGNIFICENT SEVEN, THE MAGNIFICENT SEVEN RIDE), but none approached the excellence of the original. Sturges received a ceremonial sword from Kurosawa after the Japanese director saw the film and enjoyed it. There have been many scholarly essays written about this movie and most should be discarded as it is what it appears to be and nothing more, a remake of a Japanese picture translated into a uniquely American film. The associate producer was veteran screenwriter-producer Lou Morheim who originally acquired the English language rights from Kurosawa for a paltry $250. Walter Bernstein and

Walter Newman did scripts, but the final credit went to Roberts after a Writer's Guild arbitration. Morheim had been set to produce but Sturges insisted that he produce as well as direct, so Morheim took the lesser credit although he functioned in the greater capacity. When interviewed, Morheim stated that Kurosawa had been asked why he made THE SEVEN SAMURAI and how it came to pass, and the Japanese master was quoted as having said, "All I was doing was trying to make a Japanese western." Morheim saw that and quickly nailed down the remake rights.

p&d, John Sturges; w, William Roberts, uncredited writing by Walter Newman, Walter Bernstein (based on the Japanese film THE SEVEN SAMURAI); ph, Charles Lang, Jr. (Panavision, DeLuxe Color); m, Elmer Bernstein; ed, Ferris Webster; art d, Edward Fitzgerald; set d, Rafael Suarez; spec eff, Milt Rice; makeup, Emile LaVigne, Daniel Striepke.

Western   **Cas.**   (PR:C MPAA:R)

MAGNIFICENT SEVEN DEADLY SINS, THE**½ (1971, Brit.) 107m Tigon c

Bruce Forsyth, Joan Sims, Roy Hudd, Harry Secombe, Leslie Phillips, Julie Ege, Harry H. Corbett, Ian Carmichael, Alfie Bass, Spike Milligan, Ronald Fraser.

That old staple of comedy, the sketch film, gets a workout in this collection of humor from England. Typical in British wit but—like many films of this nature—the jokes, as Groucho Marx once stated, have no age limit. Feldman and Chapman, two of Britain's funniest individuals, helped on the script.

p&d, Graham Stark; w, Bob Larbey, John Esmonde, Dave Freeman, Barry Cryer, Graham Chapman, Graham Stark, Marty Feldman, Alan Simpson, Ray Galton, Spike Milligan; ph, Harvey Harrison, Jr.; m, Roy Budd.

Comedy (PR:A-C MPAA:NR)

MAGNIFICENT SEVEN RIDE, THE** (1972) 100m Mirisch/UA c

Lee Van Cleef (Chris), Stefanie Powers (Laurie Gunn), Mariette Hartley (Arilla), Michael Callan (Noah Forbes), Luke Askew (Skinner), Pedro Armendariz, Jr. (Pepe Carral), William Lucking (Walt Drummond), James B. Sikking (Hayes), Ed Lauter (Scott Elliott), Melissa Murphy (Madge Buchanan), Darrell Larson (Shelly Donavan), Allyn Ann McLerie (Mrs. Donavan), Ralph Waite (Jim MacKay), Carolyn Conwell (Martha), Jason Wingreen (Warden), Elizabeth Thompson (Skinner's Woman), Rita Rogers (De Toro's Woman), Robert Jaffe (Bob Allan), Gary Busey (Hank Allan), Rodolfo Acosta (Juan De Toro).

Last and worst sequel to THE MAGNIFICENT SEVEN (1960) (the others were RETURN OF THE SEVEN, 1966, and GUNS OF THE MAGNIFICENT SEVEN, 1969) starring Van Cleef (who replaced Yul Brynner), now married and the marshal of a small town. When psycho-punk Larson robs a bank, shoots and wounds Van Cleef, and then kidnaps, rapes, and kills Van Cleef's wife Hartley, Van Cleef decides to accept an assignment that will require him to rescue some widowed white women from a band of vicious Mexican bandits. To do this he assembles eastern newspaper reporter Callan and five tough convicts (yeah, it adds up to seven) to ride in and mop up the Mexicans. Climactic shoot out is handled well enough to maintain some interest.

p, William A. Calihan; d, George McGowan; w, Arthur Rowe; ph, Fred Koenekamp (DeLuxe Color); m, Elmer Bernstein; ed, Walter Thompson; md, Bernstein; art d, Red McCormick, set d, Joe Stone; spec eff, Frank Brendel.

Western (PR:A MPAA:PG)

MAGNIFICENT SHOWMAN, THE (SEE: CIRCUS WORLD, 1964)

MAGNIFICENT SINNER**½
(1963, Fr.) 91m Speva/Film-Mart c (UNE JEUNE FILLE, UN SEUL AMOUR, KATIA)

Romy Schneider (Katia), Curt Jurgens (Alexander II), Pierre Blanchar (Koubaroff), Monique Melinand (Tsarina Maria), Antonine Balpetre (Kilbatchich), Francoise Brion (Sophie), Alain Saury (Revolutionary), Michel Bouquet (Bibesco), Jacqueline Marbaux, Bernard Dheran, Hubert Noel, Gabrielle Dorziat, Yves Barsacq.

A young girl from a poor family brags about knowing Tsar Alexander II. When the tsar visits the boarding school unexpectedly he confirms her story because he is taken in by her charm and beauty. He brings her to St. Petersburg and tells her of his plans for social reform. But a few days before the reforms are known to the public, revolutionaries bomb the tsar's carriage and he dies in her arms.

p, Michel Safra; d, Robert Siodmak; w, Charles Spaak, Georges Neveux; ph, Michel Kelber (Eastmancolor); m, Joseph Kosma; ed, Louisette Hautecoeur, Henri Tarerna; art d, Jean d'Eaubonne.

Drama (PR:A MPAA:NR)

MAGNIFICENT TRAMP, THE**
(1962, Fr./Ital.) 76m Filmsonor-Intermondia-Cinetel-Pretoria-Titanus/Cameo International bw (ARCHIMEDE, LE CLOCHARD)

Jean Gabin (Archimede), Darry Cowl (Arsene), Bernard Blier (Pichon), Julien Carette (Felix), Paul Frankeur (Gregoire), Jacqueline Maillan (Marjorie), Dora Doll (Mme. Pichon), Noel Roquevert (Retired Commandant), Albert Dinan (Restaurateur), Gaby Basset (Mme. Gregoire), Bernard Lajarrige.

A Paris hobo decides that jail would be a nice place to spend the upcoming cold winter. He keeps trying to create trouble, but fails to get arrested. A friend teaches him the fine art of stealing purebred dogs and getting them back to the owners for a reward. Then he decides to spend his winter at his dream spot— the Riviera. But first he has to figure out how to get out of trouble since another friend has exposed his scheme.

p, Jean-Paul Guibert; d, Gilles Grangier; w, Albert Valentin, Michel Audiard, Grangier (based on a story by Valentin from an idea of Jean [Gabin] Moncorge); ph,

Louis Page; m, Jean Prodromides; ed, Jacqueline Thiedot; art d, Jacques Colombier.

Comedy/Drama   (PR:A MPAA:NR)

MAGNIFICENT TWO, THE**   (1967, Brit.) 100m RANK c

Eric Morecambe (Eric), Ernie Wise (Ernie), Margit Saad (Carla), Virgilio Texeira (Carillo), Cecil Parker (British Ambassador), Isobel Black (Juanita), Martin Benson (President Diaz), Michael Godfrey (Manuelo), Sue Sylvaine, Henry Beltran, Tyler Butterworth (President's Children), Sandor Eles (Armandez), Andreas Malandrinos (Juan), Victor Maddern (Drunk Soldier), Michael Gover (Doctor), Charles Laurence (Assassin).

Fair comedy starring British zanies Morecambe and Wise as two gringo salesmen who travel to South America to sell their wares only to be caught up in a revolution. To save their necks, Morecambe is forced to pose as the deceased revolutionary's son, and when the uprising is over, he finds himself in control of the country.

p, Hugh Stewart; d, Cliff Owen; w, S.C. Green, R.M. Hills, Michael Pertwee (based on a story by, Peter Blackmore); ph, Ernest Steward (Eastmancolor); m, Ron Goodwin; ed, Pertwee, Gerald Hambling.

Comedy   (PR:A MPAA:NR)

MAGNIFICENT YANKEE, THE****
                (1950) 89m MGM bw (GB: THE MAN WITH THIRTY SONS)

Louis Calhern (Oliver Wendell Holmes, Jr.), Ann Harding (Fanny Bowditch Holmes), Eduard Franz (Judge Louis Brandeis), Philip Ober (Mr. Owen Wister), Ian Wolfe (Mr. Adams), Edith Evanson (Annie Gough), Richard Anderson (Reynolds), Guy Anderson (Baxter), James Lydon (Clinton), Robert Sherwood (Drake), Hugh Sanders (Parker), Harlan Warde (Norton), Charles Evans (Chief Justice Fuller), John R. Hamilton (Justice White), Dan Tobin (Dixon), Robert E. Griffin (Court Crier), Stapleton Kent (Court Clerk), Robert Malcolm (Marshall), Everett Glass (Justice Peckham), Hayden Rorke (Graham), Marshall Bradford (Head Waiter), Holmes Herbert (Justice McKenna), Selmer Jackson (Lawyer), George Spaulding (Justice Hughes), Todd Karns (Secretary), Freeman Lusk (Announcer), David McMahon (Workman), Sherry Hall, Jack Gargan, Dick Cogan, Tony Merrill (Reporters), Robert Board, Wilson Wood, James Horne, Gerald Pierce, Lyle Clark, David Alpert, Tommy Kelly, Bret Hamilton, Jim Drum (Secretaries), Wheaton Chambers, Gayne Whitman (Senators), William Johnstone (Lawyer).

An excellent cinematization of Emmet Lavery's long-running Broadway play in which Calhern also starred. THE MAGNIFICENT YANKEE is the story of Oliver Wendell Holmes and his rise to the top of American jurisprudence from Teddy Roosevelt to Franklin Roosevelt. In following his life, the movie also touches upon the history taking place all around, but never neglects the personal side of Holmes and his long and touching relationship with his wife, Harding. He is also seen with associate Franz, who plays Judge Brandeis (for whom the school is named). Also seen as one of Holmes' best friends is Ober, as author Owen Wister (THE VIRGINIAN among others), who bridges time gaps with a literate narration that never intrudes upon the drama. MGM production chief Dore Schary must have known that this would be more of a critical success than a popular one, but it did better at the wickets than anyone expected and turned a mild profit. There are many epigrams and bon mots attributed to Holmes in this picture but one is curiously missing. Holmes is reputed to have once said, after hearing a preposterous case in the Supreme Court, "The study of law is exquisite, but the practice of it is abominable." For those who like to spot mistakes, note the makeup of Holmes' long-time housekeeper, Evanson. While everyone else in the house ages well, she looks the same at the fade out as she did at the fade in. The question is did Evanson have an oil painting of her that was aging somewhere in an attic? The British title of the film referred to the number of Harvard lawyers sponsored by Holmes.

p, Armand Deutsch; d, John Sturges; w, Emmet Lavery (based on the book Mr. Justice Holmes by Francis Biddle and the play by Lavery); ph, Joseph Ruttenberg; m, David Raksin; ed, Ferris Webster; art d, Cedric Gibbons, Arthur Lonergan.

Biography   (PR:AA MPAA:NR)

MAGNUM FORCE***   (1973) 122m WB c

Clint Eastwood (Harry Callahan), Hal Holbrook (Lt. Briggs), Felton Perry (Early Smith), Mitchell Ryan (Charlie McCoy), David Soul (Davis), Tim Matheson (Sweet), Robert Urich (Grimes), Kip Niven (Astrachan), Christine White (Carol McCoy), Adele Yoshioka (Sunny), Albert Popwell (Sidney), Margaret Avery (Call Girl).

One of the most violent and graphically depicted movies ever made, MAGNUM FORCE is shatteringly effective. With the very successful DIRTY HARRY preceding it, MAGNUM FORCE takes cinematic violence to a crescendo as the sound of gunfire echoes across the screen. Eastwood is, as usual, a man of few, though often foul, words, who has drifted out of the high plains (in spirit) and planted his brogans somewhere in the vicinity of Powell and Mason streets in San Francisco. He is baffled, as is every other member of the San Francisco Police, by a series of killings of prominent Bay Area criminals. Somebody is knocking off the scumbuckets in town and there is absolutely no apparent motive that unifies the killings. (Charles Bronson is working out of New York so the thought of a DEATH WISH vigilante roaming the hills seems to be out!) Eastwood is fretting because his pal, Ryan, is on the verge of a nervous breakdown. His new partner, Perry, notes that all of the deaths were caused by the same weapon, a .357 Magnum, which, as any Eastwood fan can quote "is the most dangerous weapon in man's history." This is the gun that's widely used by members of the S.F.P.D. and the thought is that, perhaps, a cop is doing the erasing. Even though this is a semicomic moment in the film, Perry's suggestion is not lost on Eastwood who responds with his customary "uh." Eastwood ponders the murders and wonders if Ryan, who is teetering, might be the person responsible. Those thoughts go down the tubes when Ryan himself is dispatched in the same manner as the earlier hoods. Holbrook, Eastwood's boss,

suggests that the murders might be the work of a local criminal. Eastwood disagrees and wants to personally investigate the deaths, especially now that Ryan has also been killed, but Holbrook calls him off that case. At the training center, there's a shooting match between Eastwood and Soul, a young cop without much experience but who is a great marksman. Eastwood allows Soul to win the contest. He'd seen Soul and three others, Urich, Niven, and Matheson, practicing at the range in an earlier scene and the hint of suspicion begins to work its way up Eastwood's Mt. Rushmore face. After the match, Eastwood wants to try Soul's revolver and fires one round into a piece of wood. He collects the slug later, runs it down to ballistics, and learns that it matches the slug taken from Ryan's corpse. Things are all beginning to make sense now and Eastwood returns home where Soul and his brothers await him in the shadows. They now reveal that it was they who are ridding the city of "garbage." Eastwood doesn't see them as heroes, though, and he tells them that he thinks they are nothing less than killers. Soon afterwards, Perry is killed by a bomb in his mailbox and another one is planted in Eastwood's mailbox, which he disarms. Later, Holbrook asks Eastwood to take a ride with him as he has something he'd like to discuss with the taciturn cop. The ride begins and Holbrook pulls a gun on Eastwood, telling him that he is also part of the cabal and it is necessary to do this to keep the city clean. (Note: The story is based on the fact that a group of Brazilian cops were doing exactly the same thing until they were discovered.) Eastwood slams on the brakes and Holbrook's head is smashed on the dashboard. He pushes the man out the car door, then looks in the rear view mirror and sees that he's been trailed by the fearsome foursome on their cycles. Eastwood leads the quartet on a merry chase until they get to what must have been the same deserted ship that James Caan was on when he battled Arthur Hill in THE KILLER ELITE. Then, one by one, Eastwood knocks them off until he finally dispatches Soul as the man flies off the dock on his motorcycle in a remarkable bit of stuntsmanship. MAGNUM FORCE maintains the same dynamism as DIRTY HARRY, which was directed by Don Siegel. This picture was handled by Ted Post, who also did Eastwood's HANG 'EM HIGH. It's slightly more stylized than the original in cinematic techniques but the Milius/Cimino script has abated some of the excesses in violence. Eastwood takes a bit of time out for a brief love affair with a Japanese girl, Yoshioka, and he manages to sexually resist Ryan's widow, White. When Eastwood is on the case, very few women can get his mind away from his prey and that is part of his mythic charm because he mirrors the Old West, when heroes only kissed their horses and oiled their Colts. The four vigilantes are uniformly good and three of them went on to have TV series and movie success. Matheson played in ANIMAL HOUSE, Urich had two television series, and Soul was Starsky of "Starsky and Hutch" fame. MAGNUM FORCE grossed more that $20 million and spawned several more Harry tales by less talented people. The theme of the picture is summed up when Eastwood tells the four cops (who all look like over-aged Hitler Youth) "Shooting is all right, as long as the right people get shot." Essentially, it appeals to the vigilante-minded viewers who flocked to see all the DEATH WISH pictures, and it may be one of the best immoral films ever done. The second unit direction by Buddy Van Horn is superior, and Carey Loftin's action staging is a great contribution. The main problem is that there is so much gore that by the time Eastwood gets around to killing the other cops, we have been desensitized to all of it and just wish for a tender moment. There are almost none. MAGNUM FORCE did better than DIRTY HARRY and paved the way for THE ENFORCER, the third in the series. It's too bad that Eastwood has to make these movies to make money in order for him to do the kinds of movies he really wants to do, such as BRONCO BILLY, which keeled over at the box office. He is also a better director than most of the so-called "wonder boys" around and when he gets ready to hang up his holster, Eastwood will take his place in the directing ranks as a talent to be reckoned with. Holbrook has been seen in this sort of bureaucrat-turncoat role before, as in CAPRICORN ONE. He is best recalled for his magnificent portrayal of Mark Twain in his one-man show as well as the shadowy "Deep Throat" in ALL THE PRESIDENT'S MEN.

p, Robert Daley; d, Ted Post; w, John Milius, Michael Cimino (based on the story by Milius from original material by Harry Julian Fink, R.M. Fink); ph, Frank Stanley (Panavision, Technicolor); m, Lalo Schifrin; ed, Ferris Webster; art d, Jack Collis; set d, John Lamphear.

Crime   **Cas.**   (PR:C-O MPAA:R)

MAGOICHI SAGA, THE**
                (1970, Jap.) 95m Daiei c (SHIRIKURAE MAGOICHI)

Kinnosuke Nakamura (Magoichi Saika), Komaki Kurihara (Komichi), Kojiro Hongo (Priest Shin-so), Katsuo Nakamura (Tokichiro Kinoshita), Shintaro Katsu (Lord Nobunaga Oda), Yoko Namikawa (Princess Kano), Eiko Azusa.

Japanese lords battle for power during civil wars. Kinnosuke Nakamura and his 3,000 gunners are recruited to help Katsu, whose sister Nakamura thinks he loves. But Katsu has no sister and Nakamura is tricked. He swears revenge by vowing to help the priest-warriors of Honganji Temple. He then finds out he has been in love with one of the sisters of the priests all along.

d, Kenji Misumi; w, Ryuzo Kikushima (based on a story by Ryotaro Shiba); ph, Kazuo Miyagawa (Eastmancolor); m, Masaru Sato; art d, Yoshinobu Nishioka.

Action Drama   (PR:C MPAA:NR)

MAGUS, THE*   (1968, Brit.) 117m Blazer/FOX c

Michael Caine (Nicholas Urfe), Anthony Quinn (Maurice Conchis), Candice Bergen (Lily-[Julie Holmes]), Anna Karina (Anne), Paul Stassino (Meli), Julian Glover (Anton), Takis Emmanuel (Kapetan), George Pastell (Priest), Danielle Noel (Soula), Andreas Malandrinos (Goatherd), Corin Redgrave (Capt. Wimmel), Jerome Willis ("False" German Officer), Ethel Farrugia (Maria), George Kafkaris (2nd Partisan), Anthony Newlands (Party Host), Stack Constantino (3rd Partisan), Roger Lloyd Pack (Young Conchis).

THE MAGUS is a most confusing drama and, unlike many confusing films that ultimately find their way, this one never does and ends as fuzzily as it began. Caine is an English teacher who arrives on the Greek island of Phraxos where he has been engaged to teach the children. Once there, Caine meets Quinn, a wealthy man who apparently owns the island and who may be a mystic living a life of ease in a huge villa. On the other hand, he also might be a Quisling hiding out from avengers because he aided the Nazis during their assault on Europe. He could also be a movie producer making a picture. Whichever, he is an adroit gamesman who keeps everyone guessing about his true identity as well as his past history. Equally confounding is the identity of Quinn's companion, Bergen, about whom it is said that she died 50 years before and is a ghost, not a human. Either that, or she's an actress working for Quinn or, she is a paranoid schizophrenic. Nobody knows for sure about Quinn and Bergen, but Caine finds them fascinating. Caine has been called there to replace the former teacher who committed suicide, and one wonders if the same fate will befall him. While he was still in England, Caine dumped his former lover, Karina, in order to sever the relationship cleanly before coming to the island. Karina arrives and they reawaken their affair, but she is depressed because Caine seems more intrigued by Quinn and Bergen than with her. They spend a weekend in Athens and, after she flies back to England (she's a stewardess), he learns that she's taken her own life. Caine accuses Quinn of being responsible for Karina's death then Quinn admits he is treating Bergen for her mental illness and that he was the mayor of a town who personally beat three partisans to death rather than sacrifice nearly 100 villagers to the Nazis. Suddenly, Caine is on trial for egotism (seriously!) and is told that he must beat Bergen as part of his own punishment. He can't do it. Later, he awakens and is told by Quinn that he attempted suicide. He races to the villa and finds it now abandoned, as though no one had lived there for years. Parts of the film are spellbinding but the others are so cloaked in mystic lore and dizzying discrepancies that the audience is left blinking its eyes. Dead people come alive, live people no longer exist, etc.— it's like walking through a maze. Co-producer Kinberg is also a writer and was an executive at ABC Television for some years where he oversaw many films, none of which was as bad as this one.

p, John Kohn, Jud Kinberg; d, Guy Green; w, John Fowles (based on the novel by Fowles); ph, Billy Williams (Panavision, Deluxe Color); m, John Dankworth; ed, Max Benedict; prod d, Don Ashton; md, Dankworth; art d, William Hutchinson; cos, Anthony Mendelson; makeup, Charles Parker, Michael Morris.

Drama/Fantasy **(PR:C MPAA:R)**

MAHANAGAR (SEE: BIG CITY, THE, 1964, India)

MAHLER** ½** (1974, Brit.) 115m Mayfair/Visual Programme Systems c

Robert Powell *(Gustav Mahler)*, Georgina Hale *(Alma Mahler)*, Richard Morant *(Max)*, Lee Montague *(Bernhard Mahler)*, Rosalie Crutchley *(Marie Mahler)*, Benny Lee *(Uncle Arnold)*, Miriam Karlin *(Aunt Rosa)*, Angela Down *(Justine)*, David Collings *(Hugo Wolfe)*, Ronald Pickup *(Nick)*, Antonia Ellis *(Cosima Wagner)*, Ken Colley *(Krenek)*, Arnold Yarrow *(Grandfather)*, Dana Gillespie *(Anna von Mildenburg)*, Elaine Delmar *(Princess)*, Michael Southgate *(Alois Mahler)*, Otto Diamant *(Prof. Sladky)*, Gary Rich *(Young Mahler)*, Peter Eyre *(Otto)*, George Coulouris *(Dr. Roth)*, Andrew Faulds *(Doctor on Train)*, David Trevena *(Dr. Richter)*, Sarah McLellan *(Putzi)*, Claire McLellan *(Glucki)*, Oliver Reed *(Stationmaster)*.

MAHLER is one of the few Ken Russell films that does not offer drugs or religious overtones as the major theme. Instead, MAHLER is a slow biopic about the life of composer Gustav Mahler and, although Powell's portrayal of the tortured genius is a fine one, the story drags on like a politician's speech, and would have benefitted from Russell's infusion of imagery that has become his trademark. The film is a series of flashbacks on a train as Powell is returning to Vienna for the final coda of his life. The flashbacks concern the artist's rotten youth, his relationship with his wife, Hale (not a very good one), his conversion from Judaism (as he is elected to a high post and bows to the mounting anti-Semitism that overran Europe at the time), and his further obsession with his own mortality, a source of neurotic angst that plagued him until he expired in 1911. The film ends on an ironically hopeless note (D-flat, we think) as Mahler, who thinks he's getting better, is actually growing more ill and is doomed to his demise rather quickly. There are some stirring sequences, mostly concerning Mahler's music, which is treated like a character on its own. There are also several scenes which depict the composer's loneliness that are quietly as effective as the larger, rousing scenes. Characteristic of most of Russell's work, MAHLER looks exquisite and it's fortunate that his Baroque excesses have taken the place of his customary hallucinogenic ones. The sets, costumes, and all production values are first-rate, and Hale is excellent as Powell's wife, a woman who sacrificed a promising career in music for the sake of her husband. Oliver Reed, a favorite of Russell's, does an unbilled cameo as a stationmaster.

p, Roy Baird; d&w, Ken Russell; ph, Dick Bush (Technicolor); m, Bernard Haitink; ed, Michael Bradsell; art d, Ian Whittaker; cos, Shirley Russell; md, John Forsythe; ch, Gilliam Gregory.

Musical Biography **Cas.** **(PR:A-C MPAA:PG)**

MAHOGANY* ½ (1975) 109m PAR c

Diana Ross *(Tracy/Mahogany)*, Billy Dee Williams *(Brian)*, Anthony Perkins *(Sean)*, Jean-Pierre Aumont *(Christian Rosetti)*, Beah Richards *(Florence)*, Nina Foch *(Miss Evans)*, Marisa Mell *(Carlotta Gavin)*, Lenard Norris *(Wil)*, Ira Rogers *(Stalker)*, Kristine Cameron *(Instructress)*, Ted Liss *(Sweatshop Foreman)*, Marvin Corman *(Cab Driver)*, E. Rodney Jones *(Radio Announcer)*, Daniel Daniele *(Guiseppe)*, Princess Galitzine *(Herself)*, Jacques Stany *(Auctioneer)*, Bruce Vilanch, Don Howard, Albert Rosenberg *(Designers)*.

Begun under the direction of Tony Richardson and completed by director Berry Gordy, the film stars Ross as an aspiring black fashion designer who gets her big break from sleazy fashion photographer Perkins. During her rise to fame and fortune, Ross passes from the hands of Perkins to rich Italian Aumont, and eventually returns to poor but sincere Williams, who loved her before she was famous. The one redeeming aspect of this film is the theme song, sung by Ross.

p, Rob Cohen, Jack Ballard; d, Berry Gordy; w, John Byrum (based on a story by Toni Amber); ph, David Watkin (Panavision); m, Michael Masser; ed, Peter Zinner; md, Lee Holdridge; art d, Leon Erickson, Aurelio Crugnola; cos, Diana Ross; m/l, "Do You Know Where You're Going To?" Masser, Gerry Goffin (sung by Ross).

Drama/Romance **Cas.** **(PR:C MPAA:PG)**

MAID AND THE MARTIAN, THE (SEE: PAJAMA PARTY, 1964)

MAID FOR MURDER**

(1963, Brit.) 89m Anglo-Amalgamated/Janus bw (GB: SHE'LL HAVE TO GO)

Bob Monkhouse *(Francis Oberon)*, Alfred Marks *(Douglas Oberon)*, Hattie Jacques *(Miss Richards)*, Anna Karina *(Toni)*, Dennis Lotis *(Gilbert)*, Graham Stark *(Arnold)*, Clive Dunn *(Chemist)*, Hugh Lloyd *(Macdonald)*, Peter Butterworth *(Doctor)*, Harry Locke *(Stationmaster)*.

Monkhouse and Marks learn that their wealthy grandmother died and left her fortune to their cousin, Karina. The cousin visits and both men are more than willing to marry her. To avoid conflict, they decide that their best way to get the inheritance is to kill Karina. The brothers bungle every attempt and Karina catches on and goes off to marry her butler.

p, Jack Asher, Robert Asher; d, Robert Asher; w, John Waterhouse (based on a play, "We Must Kill Toni" by Ian Stuart Black); ph, Jack Asher; m, Philip Green; ed, Gerry Hambling; md, Green; art d, John Stoll; m/l, Green, Sonny Miller; makeup, Michael Morris.

Comedy **(PR:A MPAA:NR)**

MAID HAPPY** (1933, Brit.) 75m Bendar/Williams & Pritchard bw

Charlotte Ander *(Lena)*, Johannes Riemann *(Fritz)*, Dennis Hoey *(Sir Rudolph Bartlett)*, Marjory Mars *(Mary Loo)*, Sybil Grove *(Miss Warburton)*, Gerhard Damann *(Schmidt)*, Polly Luce *(Mudge)*, H. Saxon-Snell *(Bruckmann)*, Marie Ault *(Miss Woods)*.

In this Swiss-based musical Ander plays a young schoolgirl who's out to get a diplomat as the love of her life. In order to win his attention and thus his heart, Ander must pose as a socialite, which of course leads to the standard complications.

p&d, Mansfield Markham; w, Jack King (based on a story by Garrett Graham).

Musical **(PR:A MPAA:NR)**

MAID OF SALEM** (1937) 85m PAR bw

Claudette Colbert *(Barbara Clarke)*, Fred MacMurray *(Roger Coverman)*, Harvey Stephens *(Dr. John Harding)*, Gale Sondergaard *(Martha Harding)*, Louise Dresser *(Ellen Clarke)*, Bennie Bartlett *(Timothy Clarke)*, Edward Ellis *(Elder Goode)*, Beulah Bondi *(Abigail Goode)*, Bonita Granville *(Ann Goode)*, Virginia Weidler *(Nabby Goode)*, Donald Meek *(Ezra Cheeves)*, E. E. Clive *(Bilge)*, Halliwell Hobbes *(Jeremiah)*, Pedro de Cordoba *(Mr. Morse)*, Madame Sul-te-wan *(Tituba)*, Lucy Beaumont *(Rebecca)*, Henry Kolker *(Crown Chief Justice Laughton)*, William Farnum *(Crown Justice Sewall)*, Ivan F. Simpson *(Rev. Parris)*, Brandon Hurst *(Tithing Man)*, Sterling Holloway *(Miles Corbin)*, Babs Nelson *(Baby Mercy Cheeves)*, Mary Treen *(Suzy Abbott)*, Zeffie Tilbury *(Goody Hodgers)*, J. Farrell MacDonald *(Captain of Ship)*, Stanley Fields *(lst Mate)*, Lionel Belmore *(Tavern Keeper)*, Kathryn Sheldon *(Mrs. Deborah Cheeves)*, Rosita Butler *(Mary Watkins)*, Madge Collins *(Elizabeth)*, Amelia Falleur *(Sarah)*, Clarence Kolb *(Town Crier)*, Russell Simpson *(Village Marshal)*, Colin Tapley *(Roger's Friend)*, Tom Ricketts *(Giles Cory)*, Ricca K. Allen, Agnes Ayres, Wilson Benge, Sidney Bracy, Fritzi Brunett, Herbert Evans, Fryda Gagne, Edith Hallor, Frank E. Hammond, Carol Halloway, Harold Howard, Ward Lane, Stella Le Saint, Ralph Lewis, Vera Lewis, Anne O'Neal, Rita Owin, Audrey Reynolds, Allen D. Sewall, Walter Soderling, Al H. Stewart, William Wagner *(Bits)*, Chief Big Tree *(Indian)*, Harold Entwistle *(Court Clerk)*, Harold Nelson *(Judge)*, Hayden Stevenson *(Deputy Marshal)*, Thomas L. Brower *(Salem Town Marshal)*, James Marcus *(Sea Captain)*, John Power *(Minister)*, Jack Deery, Clive Morgan *(Non-Commissioned Officers)*, Colin Kenny, Sidney D'Albrook *(Hunters)*, J. R. Tozer *(Clergyman)*, Grace Kern *(Convict)*, Wally Albright *(Jaspar)*, Jack H. Richardson *(Sheriff)*, George Magrill *(Sailor)*, Charles McAvoy *(Father)*, Vangie Beilby *(Mother)*.

Casting MacMurray and Colbert in this talky epic of witch burning did nothing for any of the actors or 6 members of the creative force. It was a big bomb at the box office although the sets were incredibly authentic and there was nothing wrong with any of the acting. It's 1692 in Salem, Massachusetts. Colbert lives with her aunt, Dresser, and her cousin, Bartlett, and indicates a certain rebelliousness against the pinched society of New England. MacMurray, a man on the lam from Virginia, arrives in the small town and the two of them begin seeing each other although she must be careful because he is wanted. Granville, the troublemaking daughter of Bondi and Ellis, hates her family's black slave, Tituba, so she starts telling witch stories about the woman, saying that she has been possessed. This starts a wave of hysteria and Tituba, as well as many other innocents, are burned at the stake. Colbert is in total accord with the falsely accused and that puts her in a bad light as she may be the next one to get the final hot-foot. MacMurray realizes this and wants Colbert to flee with him. He goes to Boston to buy boat tickets but someone blows the whistle on him and he is tossed in the clink. Simultaneously, the madness has caught up to Colbert and she's accused and arrested of being a witch. On trial, Sondergaard, wife of the town doctor, Stephens, says that Colbert's mother had been burned in England for the same charge. Stephens had been attempting to aid Colbert, and Sondergaard became angry so it is unsure if what she says is real or induced by jealousy. Colbert gets the customary death sentence for matters of witchcraft, but is saved when MacMurray escapes from jail and comes back to Salem in time to disprove the charges against her. Granville, that little snit, confesses that she made the whole thing up and MacMurray and Colbert are left to spend the rest of their lives together. A brooding dark film about a dark subject and, in later years, Arthur Miller would use the same material to write his play "The Crucible," which did about as well as this picture. Granville did a similar role in THESE THREE and was almost typecast as an early Patti McCormack type (THE BAD SEED). In order to make the picture, the producers built an entire New England village in Santa Cruz, California.

p&d, Frank Lloyd; w, Walter Ferris, Bradley King, Durward Grinstead (based on the story by King); ph, Leo Tover; m, Victor Young; ed, Hugh Bennett; md, Boris Morros; art d, Hans Dreier, Bernard Herzbrun; set d, A. E. Freudeman; cos, Travis Banton.

Historical Epic (PR:A MPAA:NR)

MAID OF THE MOUNTAINS, THE*¹/₂ (1932, Brit.) 80m BIP/Wardour bw

Nancy Brown (*Teresa*), Harry Welchman (*Baldasarre*), Betty Stockfeld (*Angela Malona*), Albert Burdon (*Tonio*), Gus McNaughton (*Gen. Malona*), Garry Marsh (*Beppo*), Renee Gadd (*Vittoria*), Wallace Lupino (*Crumpet*), Dennis Hoey (*Orsino*), Alfredo and His Gypsy Orchestra.

Welchman plays a Robin Hood-type bandit in jolly old England robbing the wealthy to help the poor. But hell hath no fury like a woman scorned, and Welchman's career ends after his jealous girl friend turns him in after the bandit falls for Stockfeld, the governor's daughter. The production, unfortunately, is flat and lifeless, without any of the quick jauntiness needed for it to work.

p, John Maxwell; d, Lupino Lane; w, Lane, Douglas Furber, Frank Miller, Victor Kendall, Edwin Greenwood (based on the play by Frederick Lonsdale); ph, Claude Friese-Greene, Arthur Crabtree.

Musical/Adventure (PR:A MPAA:NR)

MAID TO ORDER*¹/₂ (1932) 65m Weil/Hollywood bw

Julian Eltinge, Jane Reid, Georgie Stone, Betty Boyd, Jack Richardson, Al Hill, Kernan Cripps, Charles Giblin.

Former vaudeville performer Eltinge, who has a penchant for detective work, finds himself aiding the cops in tracking down a ring of international smugglers who are running diamonds into the U.S. in coffee cans. Overseas, Scotland Yard arrests one of the gang members and Eltinge is called into service by impersonating her in order to trap the rest of the crooks. Lots of obvious gender jokes and not much else.

d, Elmer Clifton; w, Grace Elliott (based on a story by Doris Dembow, A. J. L. Parsons); m/l, Jack Stone, Fred Thompson, George Beauchamp.

Musical Comedy (PR:A MPAA:NR)

MAIDEN, THE**

(1961, Fr.) 90m Societe Francaise des Films/Green-Roth bw (LA MOME PIGALLE)

Claudine Dupuis (*Arlette*), Jean Gaven (*Michaud*), Dany Carrel (*Marie-Claude*), Philippe Nicaud (*Philippe*), Dora Doll (*Catherine*), Robert Berri (*Monsieur Jo*), Claude Godard (*Sonia*), Jean Tissier (*Albert*), Jacqueline Noelle (*Bigoudi*), Jacques Morel (*Mejean*), Jean Brochard (*Alfandari*), Julien Carette, Paul Demange, Colette Brumaire, Jose Lopez.

Dupuis is a nightclub singer who gets out of jail, returns to her nightlife, and discovers that three different groups are after her. The police, an insurance agency, and the underworld want to know where her former lover is. The mob sends Nicaud and he falls in love with her and decides to give up his criminal life. Dupuis ends up being poisoned by the underworld boss.

p&d, Alfred Rode; w, Jacques Companeez, Louis Martin; ph, Marc Fossard; m, Roger-Roger; ed, Louisette Hautecoeur; art d, Robert Bouladoux; makeup, Jean-Jacques Chanteau.

Drama (PR:A MPAA:NR)

MAIDEN FOR A PRINCE, A**

(1967, Fr./Ital.) 92m Fair-Orsay/Royal c (UNA VERGINE PER IL PRINCIPE; UNE VIERGE POUR LE PRINCE; AKA: A MAIDEN FOR THE PRINCE)

Vittorio Gassman (*Prince Don Vincenzo Gonzaga*), Virna Lisi (*Giulia*), Philippe Leroy (*Ippolito*), Tino Buazzelli (*Duke of Mantova*), Maria Grazia Buccella (*Marchesa of Pepara*), Vittorio Caprioli (*Marchese Liginio*), Paola Borboni (*The Matron*), Anna Maria Guarnieri (*Margherita Farnese*), Giusi Raspani Dandolo (*Duchess of Mantova*), Luciano Mandolfo (*Cardinal Farnese*), Esmeralda Ruspoli (*Bianca Cappello*), Mario Scaccia (*Cardinal Gonzaga*), Jose Luis de Vilallonga (*Alessandro dei Medici*), Anna Maria Polani (*Eleanora dei Medici*), Claudie Lange (*Marfisa*), Alfredo Bianchini (*Cavalier Vinta*), Leopoldo Trieste (*Marchese of Pepara*), Mariangela Giordano (*Lady Friend of the Prince*), Francesco Mule.

In 16th-Century Italy Gassman and Guarnieri marry, but there are rumors that their marriage hasn't been consummated. Gassman's father, Buazzelli, worries that he will have no heirs and demands the marriage be annulled. He wants his son to marry another princess, but her family won't agree until Gassman proves his manhood. The prince won't agree to the test until his father threatens to cut off his allowance. Gassman is paired with a virgin and after some setbacks proves his manhood.

p, Mario Cecchi Gori; d, Pasquale Festa Campanile; w, Giorgio Prosperi, Stefano Strucchi, Ugo Liberatore, Campanile; ph, Roberto Gerardi (Techniscope, Technicolor); m, Luis Enriquez Bacalov; ed, Otello Colangeli, Ruggero Mastroianni; art d, Pier Luigi Pizzi; cos, Pizzi; makeup, Nilo Jacoponi, Otello Sisi.

Comedy (PR:A MPAA:NR)

MAIDS, THE**   (1975, Brit.) 95m CineFilms/American Film Theatre c

Glenda Jackson (*Solange*), Susannah York (*Claire*), Vivien Merchant (*Madame*), Mark Burns (*Monsieur*).

Irritating, overly talky film adaptation of Jean Genet's stage play stars Jackson and York as two maids who despise their mistress Merchant and her life style. Much of the film centers around the deadly play-acting of the two women as they devise ways to bump off their boss, with each taking turns being "madame." By accident, York ends up getting the poison meant for Merchant. Aware of the potentially dull visual intrepretation from stage to screen, director Miles overcompensates and clutters his film with camera set-ups that distract from the material.

p, Robert Enders; d, Christopher Miles; w, Enders, Miles (based on Minos Volanakis' translation of a play by Jean Genet); ph, Douglas Slocombe (Technicolor); m, Laurie Johnson; ed, Peter Tanner; art d, Robert Jones.

Drama (PR:C MPAA:PG)

MAID'S NIGHT OUT¹/₂** (1938) 64m RKO bw

Joan Fontaine (*Sheila Harrison*), Allan Lane (*Bill Norman*), Hedda Hopper (*Mrs. Harrison*), George Irving (*Rufus Norman*), William Brisbane (*Wally Martin*), Billy Gilbert (*Popolopolis*), Cecil Kellaway (*Geoffrey*), Vicki Lester (*Adele*), Hilda Vaughn (*Mary*), Eddie Gribbon (*Hogan*), Frank M. Thomas (*McCarthy*), Solly Ward (*Mischa*), Lee Patrick (*Milk Route Customer*), Jack Carson (*Amusement Ride Operator*), Robert E. Homans (*Desk Sergeant*), Edgar Dearing (*Police Detective*), Paul Guilfoyle (*Bailbondsman*).

Lane bets his self-made millionaire father that he can't hold down a real job for one month. He becomes a milkman and on his route meets Fontaine, whom he mistakes as a servant. They get romantically involved and find themselves in a series of comical episodes. In the climactic chase scene, Fontaine throws a barrage of milk bottles at the pursuing police cars.

p, Robert Sisk; d, Ben Holmes; w, Bert Granet (based on a story by Willoughby Speyers); ph, Frank Redman; ed, Ted Cheesman.

Comedy (PR:A MPAA:NR)

MAIDSTONE zero (1970) 110m Supreme Mix c

Norman Mailer (*Norman T. Kingsley*), Rip Torn (*Raoul Rey O'Houlihan*), Beverly Bentley (*Chula Mae*), Joy Bang (*Joy Broom*), Jean Campbell (*Jeanne Cardigan*), Buzz Farber (*Luis*), Leo Garen (*Producer*), Robert Gardiner (*Secret Service Chief*), Luba Harrington (*Russian Delegate*), Ultra Violet (*Herself*), Lee Cook (*Lazarus*), Paul Austin, Ann Barry, Eddie Bonette, Steve Borton, Bob Byrne, Paul Carrol, Lang Clay, Harold Conrad, Billy Copley, Terry Crawford, John De Menil, Tony Duke, Tim Hickey, Ron Hobbs, Kahlil, Evelyn Larson, Robert Lucid, Mara Lynn, Diana MacKenzie, John Maloon, John Manazanet, Michael McClure, Carolyn Mc-Cullough, David McMullin, Penny Milford, Mitsou, Glenna Moore, Lenny Morris, Adeline Naiman, Ula Ness, Alfonso Ossorio, Noel E. Parmentel, Jr., Maggie Peach, Alice Raintree, Jack Richardson, Joe Roddy, Lee Roscoe, Bianca Rosoff, Peter Rosoff, Barney Rosset, Shari Rothe, Cliff Sager, Lucy Saroyan, Brenda Smiley, Lane Smith, Sally Sorrell, Carol Stevens, Greer St. John, Danae Torn, Jose Torres, Jan Pieter Welt, Bud Wirtschafter, Harris Yulin.

As good as he is a writer, that's how dreadful Mailer can be as a filmmaker. He shot this hodgepodge in five days, then took the next two years to edit the 45 hours of footage to 110 minutes. He also had to write a few books in order to pay the freight on what must be the most expensive home movie ever made. It was sort of improvised by more than 100 people and shot by a quintet of camera crews who attempted to film a film-within-a-film that plumbed new depths in pretentiousness. It's sometime in the future and Mailer plays a presidential candidate who is also a film director making a movie in Long Island in which he co-stars as the manager of a brothel for women that he runs with his half brother, Torn. All of the major political candidates have been killed and Mailer fears for his safety even though he's being protected by a group, which purports to be dedicated to saving the lives of candidates. Nevertheless, Mailer thinks they may be the killers. Mailer battles with some left wingers and some right wingers, fights with Bentley (his wife from whom he is separated), and there are several other incidents, none of which mean anything except to Mailer. In the end, Torn attacks him with a hammer, Mailer bites Torn's ear, and the incident is witnessed by the hysterical children and his screaming wife. It says nothing, means nothing, and is nothing. Mailer should stick to his typewriter and stay out from behind the camera. The only reason to see this is to gaze in wonderment at such tripe masquerading as drama. The movie might eventually make its money back if they cut it into 10 million little pieces and sell them as mandolin picks.

p, Buzz Farber, Norman Mailer; d&w, Mailer; ph, Jim Desmond, Richard Leacock, D. A. Pennebaker, Nicholas Proferes, Sheldon Rochlin, Diane Rochlin, Jan Pieter Welt (16mm, Eastmancolor); m, Isaac Hayes, Wes Montgomery and the Modern Jazz Quartet; ed, Welt, Mailer, Lana Jokel; m/l, theme song, Carol Stevens (sung by Stevens).

Drama (PR:C MPAA:NR)

MAIGRET LAYS A TRAP**

(1958, Fr.) 110m Inermondia-Jolly/RANK bw (MAIGRET TEND UN PIEGE; AKA: INSPECTOR MAIGRET)

Jean Gabin (*Maigret*), Annie Girardot (*Yvonne Maurin*), Olivier Hussenot (*Inspector Lagrume*), Jeanne Boitel (*Mme. Maigret*), Lucienne Bogaert (*Mme. Maurin*), Jean Desailly (*Marcel Maurin*), Jean Debucourt (*Guimart*), Guy Decomble (*Police Decoy*), Paulet Dubost (*Mauricette*), Gerard Sety (*Jo Jo*), Jacques Hilling (*The Butcher*).

Gabin is the famed police inspector from the series of popular novels, who here is on the case of four murdered women. Each was knifed and, though they had their clothes torn, they weren't molested. As Gabin pieces the clues together, everything points to Desailly as the murderer; even the sacrificial murder of Desailly's wife doesn't lead Gabin away from the young man.

d, Jean Delannoy; w, R. M. Arlaud, Michel Audiard, Delannoy (based on a novel by Georges Simenon); ed, Henri Taverna.

Murder Mystery   **(PR:C MPAA:NR)**

MAIL ORDER BRIDE   (1964) 83m MGM c (GB: WEST OF MONTANA)

Buddy Ebsen (*Will Lane*), Keir Dullea (*Lee Carey*), Lois Nettleton (*Annie Boley*), Warren Oates (*Jace*), Barbara Luna (*Marietta*), Paul Fix (*Jess Linley*), Marie Windsor (*Hanna*), Denver Pyle (*Preacher Pope*), Bill Smith (*Lank*), Kathleen Freeman (*Sister Sue*), Abigail Shelton (*Young Old Maid*), Jimmy Mathers (*Matt*), Doodles Weaver (*Charlie Mary*), Diane Sayer (*Lily*), Ted Ryan (*Bartender*).

Ebsen is a lawman who inherits the ranch of a dead buddy and along with that the man's troublemaking son, Dullea. The lawman figures he can get the kid settled down if he can get him married. Ebsen finds the perfect woman via mail order, and the young man is married to Nettleton. Problems still arise for Ebsen and the newlyweds, resulting in a few good chuckles. Director Kennedy went on to direct other western comedies, THE ROUNDERS and SUPPORT YOUR LOCAL SHER-IFF.

p, Richard E. Lyons; d&w, Burt Kennedy (based on a story by Van Cort); ph, Paul C. Vogel (Panavision, Metrocolor); m, George Bassman; ed, Frank Santillo, art d, George W. Davis, Stan Jolley; set d, Henry Grace, William Calvert; makeup, William Tuttle, Dick Hamilton.

Western   **(PR:A MPAA:NR)**

MAIL TRAIN**

(1941, Brit.) 87m FOX bw (GB: INSPECTOR HORNLEIGH GOES TO IT)

Gordon Harker (*Inspector Hornleigh*), Alastair Sim (*Sgt. Bingham*), Phyllis Calvert (*Mrs. Wilkinson*), Edward Chapman (*Mr. Blenkinsop*), Charles Oliver (*Dr. Wilkinson*), Percy Walsh (*Inspector Blow*), David Horne (*Commissioner*), Peter Gawthorne (*Colonel*), Wally Patch (*Sergeant Major*), Betty Jardine (*Daisy*), O. B. Clarence (*Prof. Mackenzie*), John Salew (*Mr. Tomboy*), Raymond Huntley (*Dr. Kerbishley*), Cyril Cusack, Bill Shine, Sylvia Cecil, Edward Underdown, E. Turner, Marie Makine, Richard Cooper.

Two Scotland Yard Inspectors accidentally discover an espionage ring and find themselves in a wide variety of predicaments because of it. One inspector is a comical blunderer while the other is only slightly more competent. Their misadventures include run-ins with a sexy female spy and her dangerous companions.

p, Edward Black; d, Walter Forde; w, Frank Launder, Val Guest, J. O. C. Orton (based on a character created by Hans Priwin); ph, Jack Cox, Arthur Crabtree; m, Louis Levy; ed, R. E. Dearing.

Crime Drama   **(PR:A MPAA:NR)**

MAILBAG ROBBERY***

(1957, Brit.) 70m Insignia/Tudor bw (GB: THE FLYING SCOT)

Lee Patterson (*Ronnie*), Kay Callard (*Jackie*), Alan Gifford (*Phil*), Margaret Withers (*Lady*), Mark Baker (*Gibbs*), Jeremy Bodkin (*Charlie*), Gerald Case (*Guard*), Kerry Jordan, John Dearth, Patsy Smart, John Lee, Geoffrey Bodkin.

A trio of thieves (Patterson, Callard, and Gifford) set out to rob "The Flying Scot" express train. They work out an elaborate plan and alter it in the face of unexpected obstacles. The suspense is well built in this finely constructed feature, right down to the overlooked detail that leads to the robbers' downfall.

p&d, Compton Bennett; w, Norman Hudis (based on a story by Ralph Smart, Jan Read); md, Stanley Black.

Suspense   **(PR:A-C MPAA:NR)**

MAIN ATTRACTION, THE* ½   (1962, Brit.) 90m Seven Arts/MGM c

Pat Boone (*Eddie*), Nancy Kwan (*Tessa*), Mai Zetterling (*Gina*), Yvonne Mitchell (*Elenora*), Kieron Moore (*Ricco*), John Le Mesurier (*Bozo*), Carl Duering (*Bus Driver*), Warren Mitchell (*Proprietor*), Lionel Murton (*Burton*), Golda Casimir (*Peasant Woman*), Lionel Blair (*Clown*), Frank Sieman (*Band Announcer*), Rios Brothers, Bill Picton.

Boone sheds his clean-cut image here as he plays a singer at an Italian cafe who's fired when he gets into a fight with a drunk. He meets Zetterling, an older woman, who invites him to join her circus ventriloquist act. Problems arise when Boone becomes attracted to the circus owner's daughter, Kwan. When Zetterling's ex-husband Blair (the clown) attacks Boone, Blair falls on a knife and Boone flees. He meets Kwan, who has also left the circus and the two spend the night in a mountain cabin. An avalanche hits and Boone saves the girl and returns to the circus to find Blair was not killed. Everyone reconciles and Boone pairs up with Kwan.

p, John Patrick; d, Daniel Petrie; w, Patrick and Marguerite Roberts; ph, Geoffrey Unsworth (Metroscope); m, Andrew Adorian; ed, Geoffrey Foot; md, Muir Mathieson; art d, Bill Hutchinson; ch, Lionel Blair; m/l, "The Main Attraction," Pat Boone, Jeff Corey, "Gondoli, Gondola," Carosone, Nisa, "Si, Si, Si," Domenico Modugno, Abel Baer, "Amore Baciami," C. A. Rossi, C. C. Testoni, Geoffrey Barnes, John Turner, Boone (All sung by Boone); makeup, Neville Smallwood.

Drama   **(PR:A MPAA:NR)**

MAIN CHANCE, THE*   (1966, Brit.) 60m EM bw

Gregoire Aslan (*Potter*), Edward De Souza (*Michael Blake*), Tracy Reed (*Christine*), Stanley Meadows (*Joe Hayes*), Jack Smethurst (*Ross*), Bernard Stone (*Miller*), Will Stampe (*Carter*), Julian Strange (*Butler*), Anthony Bailey (*Chauffeur*), Joyce Barbour (*Mme. Rozanne*).

De Souza is a ex-RAF pilot hired by Aslan to fly a mysterious package from France to England. The pilot figures to keep the package for himself, and this was anticipated by Aslan who's planted a bomb on the plane. But Reed, Aslan's secretary, saves De Souza from being blown out of the sky.

p, Jack Greenwood; d, John Knight; w, Richard Harris (based on the novel by Edgar Wallace); ph, James Wilson; m, Bernard Ebbinghouse; ed, Derek Holding.

Crime Drama   **(PR:A MPAA:NR)**

MAIN EVENT, THE zero   (1938) 55m COL bw

Robert Paige (*Mac Richards*), Jacqueline Wells [Julie Bishop] (*Helen Phillips*), Arthur Loft (*Jack Benson*), John Gallaudet (*Joe Carter*), Thurston Hall (*Capt. Phillips*), Gene Morgan (*Lefty*), Dick Curtis (*Sawyer*), Oscar O'Shea (*Capt. Rorty*), Pat Flaherty (*Moran*), John Tyrrell (*Steve*), Nick Copeland (*Jake*), Lester Dorr (*Buck*).

A textbook case of bad filmmaking in every sense, from the writing to the set design. Paige plays what is supposed to be a detective who goes after a fighter who has faked his own kidnaping before the big fight.

p, Ralph Cohn; d, Danny Dare; w, Lee Loeb (based on a story by Harold Shumate); ph, Allen G. Siegler; ed, Al Clark.

Action Drama   **(PR:A MPAA:NR)**

MAIN EVENT, THE**   (1979) 112m Barwood/WB c

Barbra Streisand (*Hillary Kramer*), Ryan O'Neal (*Eddie "Kid Natural" Scanlon*), Paul Sand (*David*), Whitman Mayo (*Percy*), Patti D'Arbanville (*Donna*), Chu Chu Malave (*Luis*), Richard Lawson (*Hector Mantilla*), James Gregory (*Gough*), Richard Altman (*Tour Guide*), Joe Amsler (*Stunt Double Kid*), Seth Banks (*Newsman*), Lindsay Bloom (*Girl in Bed*), Earl Boen (*Nose-Kline*), Roger Bowen (*Owner Sinthia Cosmetics*), Badja Medu Djola (*Heavyweight in Gym*), Rory Calhoun (*Fighter in Kid's Camp*), Sue Casey (*Brenda*), Kristine DeBell (*Lucy*), Alvin Childress, Al Denava, Rene Dijon, Shay Duffin, Murphy Dunne, Art Evans, Ron Henriques, Anthony Renya, Maurice Sneed, Lee Harman, Vic Heutschy, Ernie Hudson, Dave Ketchum, Jimmy Lennon, Len Lesser, Eddie "Animal" Lopez, Gilda Marx, Denver Mattson, Bill Murry, Brent Musburger, Robert Nadder, Harvey Parry, John Reilly, Tim Rossovich, Jack Somack, Richard S. Steele, Karen Wookey, Darrell Zwerling.

Streisand and O'Neal had a success with WHAT'S UP, DOC? and tried to capture the same sort of lightning in this film, but Zeiff's direction couldn't compare with Bogdanovich's and the result is as dull as watching paint dry. Streisand is a perfumer who is now bankrupt and owns the contract of down-and-out boxer O'Neal, whom she picked up as a tax loss while she still had a few bob. She spent several thousand on him when she had the money and she now means to get that cash back by pushing O'Neal into condition and having him win some bouts. D'Arbanville is O'Neal's girl friend and only the most unsophisticated moviegoers will believe that she'll occupy that same status by the picture's finale. Streisand plays her usual yenta who pushes everyone aside in her quest, totally ignores the truth about boxing, and gets her way when she and O'Neal marry in the most disappointing final scene since THE AMERICANIZATION OF EMILY. A yawn of a yarn. Zieff was a longtime television-commercial director, and one of his favorite actors, Jack Somack ("That's some spicy meatball" for Alka-Seltzer antiacid), has a small role. Writer-actor Dave Ketchum also has a tiny role and several members of the sports world are seen as themselves: sportscaster Brent Musburger and ring announcer Jimmy Lennon. Irish actor Shay Duffin has a bit, but doesn't show off the stuff that made his one-man tribute to Brendan Behan such a success on two continents. It's a shame that the male lead was prettier than the female but that's usually the case with Streisand. Songs include: "The Main Event," "Fight" (Paul Jabara, Bob Esty), "Angry Eyes" (Loggins and Messina), and "The Body Shop" (Michalski and Oosterveen), and all were as memorable as the film itself.

p, Jon Peters, Barbra Streisand; d, Howard Zieff; w, Gail Parent, Andrew Smith; ph, Mario Tosi (Technicolor); ed, Edward Warschilka; prod d, Charles Rosen; md, Gary LeMel; set d, James Payne; cos, Ruth Myers; stunts, Denver Mattson.

Comedy   **Cas.**   **(PR:A-C MPAA:PG)**

MAIN STREET, 1936   (SEE: I MARRIED A DOCTOR, 1936)

MAIN STREET**

(1956, Span.) 95m Cesareo Gonzales-Play Art/Trans-Lux bw (CALLE MAYOR; AKA: THE LOVEMAKER)

Betsy Blair (*Isabelle*), Jose Suarez (*Juan*), Yves Massard (*Jean*), Dora Doll (*Antonia*), Lila Kedrova (*Mme. Pepita*), Rene Blancard, Luis Pena, Jose Calvo, Alfonso Goda, Matilde M. Sampedro, Manuel Alexandre, Maria Gomez.

A group of older bachelors in a small village passes the time by pulling practical jokes. They decide to make Blair, a 35-year-old spinster, the butt of one of their jokes. Suarez is pushed into courting her and Blair falls deeply in love with him. Not wanting to hurt her any more, Suarez tells her the truth and Blair decides to stay and face the humiliation, rather than run away. This film was the Grand Prix winner at the Venice Film Festival. It was filmed in Spanish, and dubbed into English.

d&w, Juan Antonio Bardem; ph, Michel Kelber; m, Joseph Kosma; ed, Marguerite De Ochoa; md, Serge Baudo.

Drama   **(PR:A MPAA:NR)**

MAIN STREET AFTER DARK**   (1944) 57m MGM bw

Edward Arnold (*Lt. Lorrigan*), Selena Royle (*Ma Dibson*), Tom Trout (*Lefty*), Audrey Totter (*Jessie Belle*), Dan Duryea (*Posey*), Hume Cronyn (*Keller*), Dorothy Ruth Morris (*Rosalie*).

Royle heads a team of female pickpockets who prey on the soldiers and sailors waiting for their ships. Totter and Morris are her operatives and Arnold is the detective set out to nab them. Good cast and adequate direction make this a bearable trifle.

p, Jerry Bresler; d, Edward Cahn; w, Karl Kamb, John C. Higgins (based on a story by Higgins); ph, Jackson Rose; m, George Bassman; ed, Harry Komer; art d, Cedric Gibbons, Richard Duce.

Crime Drama (PR:A MPAA:NR)

MAIN STREET GIRL (SEE: PAROLED FROM THE BIG HOUSE, 1938)

MAIN STREET KID, THE** (1947) 64m REP bw

Al Pearce (Otis), Janet Martin (Jill), Alan Mowbray (Martine), Adele Mara (Gloria), Arlene Harris (Edie Jones), Emil Rameau (Max), Byron S. Barr (Bud Wheeling), Douglas Evans (Mark Howell), Roy Barcroft (Torrey), Phil Arnold (Riley), Sarah Edwards (Mrs. Clauson), Earle Hodgins (Judge Belin), Dick Elliott (Sam Trotter).

Pearce runs a print shop in a small town and has the ability to read minds due to a fortuitous blow on the head. Barr, the head of a publishing firm, gets involved with ex-showgirl Mara, who is in cahoots with Mowbray, a fake mindreader. Evans, an associate of Barr, wants the presidency of the company, and with Mara's and Mowbray's aid, they blackmail Barr. Pearce exposes the criminals before any damage can be done. A modest effort which gives then popular radio star Pearce a chance to do some film work.

p, Sidney Picker; d, R. G. Springsteen; w, Jerry Sackheim, John K. Butler (based on a radio play by Caryl Coleman); ph, John MacBurnie; ed, Tony Martinelli; md, Morton Scott; art d, Frank Hotaling.

Comedy/Drama (PR:A MPAA:NR)

MAIN STREET LAWYER*
(1939) 72m REP bw (GB: SMALL TOWN LAWYER)

Edward Ellis (Link), Anita Louise (Honey), Margaret Hamilton (Lucy), Harold Huber (Marco), Clem Bevans (Zeke), Robert Baldwin (Tom), Henry Kolker (Donnelly), Beverly Roberts (Flossie), Willard Robertson (Ralston), Richard Lane (Ballou), Ferris Taylor (Judge), Wallis Clark (Reynolds).

A silly courtroom drama with Ellis as a country lawyer who mishandles the prosecution of gangster Huber. Ellis throws the case because of his adopted daughter's involvement with the gangster. Ellis is fired as prosecutor, and then his daughter, Louise, is accused of murder, and father becomes her defense attorney. Unrealistic to say the least.

p, Robert North; d, Dudley Murphy; w, Joseph Krumgold, Devery Freeman (based on a story by Harry Hamilton); ph, Jack Marta; ed, William Morgan; md, Cy Feuer.

Drama (PR:A MPAA:NR)

MAIN STREET TO BROADWAY*½ (1953) 102m MGM bw

Tom Morton (Tony Monaco), Mary Murphy (Mary Craig), Agnes Moorehead (Mildred Waterbury), Herb Shriner (Frank Johnson), Rosemary de Camp (Mrs. Craig), Clinton Sundberg (Mr. Craig), Tallulah Bankhead, Ethel Barrymore, Lionel Barrymore, Gertrude Berg, Shirley Booth, Louis Calhern, Leo Durocher, Faye Emerson, Oscar Hammerstein II, Rex Harrison, Helen Hayes, Joshua Logan, Mary Martin, Lilli Palmer, Richard Rodgers, John Van Druten, Cornel Wilde, Bill Rigney, Chris Durocher, Arthur Shields (Themselves), Florence Bates, Madge Kennedy, Carl Benton Reid, Frank Ferguson, Robert Bray.

Morton is a young playwright who struggles to make it to the bright lights of Broadway and with no big surprise he makes it. A retread of so many breaking into show biz films that not even the walk-ons of many well-known stars can help breathe some fresh air into the story.

p, Lester Cowan; d, Tay Garnett; w, Samson Raphaelson (based on a story by Robert E. Sherwood); ph, James Wong Howe; ed, Gene Fowler, Jr.; md, Ann Ronell; m/l, "There's Music in You," Richard Rodgers, Oscar Hammerstein II; art d, Perry Ferguson.

Romantic Comedy Cas. (PR:A MPAA:NR)

MAIN THING IS TO LOVE, THE**½
(1975, Ital./Fr.) 110m Albina-Rizzoli-TIT/CFDC c (L'IMPORTANT C'EST D'AIMER)

Romy Schneider (Nadine), Fabio Testi (Servais), Jacques Dutronc (Jacques), Klaus Kinski (Karl), Claude Dauphin (Mazelli), Roger Blin (Father), Michel Robin (Lapade).

Testi is a photographer who sneaks on the set of a low-budget gangster film and begins to take pictures of the female star, Schneider. He wants to take cover pictures but she isn't very interested. They make a date anyway and start seeing each other on a regular basis. Her husband, Dutronc, watches all this happen from the sidelines, and when Testi puts up the money for a play to star Schneider he commits suicide, not wanting his wife to stay with him just because she pities him. Testi is beaten bloody by the thugs of the loan-shark and Schneider finds him and tells him she loves him.

d, Andrej Zulawski; w, Zulawski, Christopher Frank (based on a novel by Frank); ph, Ricardo Aronovitch (Eastmancolor); m, Georges Delerue; ed, Christiane Lack.

Drama (PR:C MPAA:NR)

MAIS OU ET DONC ORNICAR**½ (1979, Fr.) 110m Mallia c

Geraldine Chaplin (Isabelle), Brigitte Fossey (Anne), Jean-Francois Stevenin (Michel), Didier Flamand (Philippe), Jean-Jacques Biraud (Vincent).

Chaplin and Fossey break from the men in their lives to find their own identities. Chaplin directs a video production unit for sociological research while Fossey becomes a head garage mechanic, leaving little time for her husband and child. Through their work they find a lack of communication with the people they deal with. Chaplin becomes disappointed with the people she interviews and Fossey finds a growing gap between her and her husband which leaves him sad and

unhappy. The title is a schoolhouse device French children use to attempt to recall conjugations in their grammar classes, obviously, as the title, meant to convey the difficulty of communicating with others. A serious sensitive study of male and female emotional relationships.

p, Bertrand van Effenterre, Herbert de Zaltza; d, van Effenterre; w, van Effenterre, Dominique Woldon; ph, Nurith Aviv, Jean-Louis Melun, Thierry Jault; m, Antoine Duhamel; ed, Joele van Effenterre; art d, Max Berto.

Drama (PR:C MPAA:NR)

MAISIE ** (1939) 72m MGM bw

Robert Young (Slim Martin), Ann Sothern (Maisie Ravier), Ruth Hussey (Sybil Ames), Ian Hunter (Clifford Ames), Cliff Edwards (Shorty), Anthony [John Hubbard] Allan (Richard Raymond), Art Mix (Red), George Tobias (Rico), Richard Carle (Roger Bannerman), Minor Watson (Prosecuting Attorney), Harlan Briggs (Deputy Sheriff), Paul Everton (Judge), Joseph Crehan (Wilcox), Frank Puglia (Ernie), Willie Fung (Lee), Emmett Vogan (Court Clerk), Mary Foy (Sheriff's Wife), C.L. Sherwood (Drunk), Robert Middlemass.

Sothern is a small-time showgirl who takes the job as maid on Hunter's ranch. There she meets and begins a relationship with Young, and also attempts to smooth out Hunter's marital problems. She leaves the ranch after a fight with the manager, but returns when Young is accused of murdering Hunter. The first in the series of "Maisie" pictures starring Sothern. (See MAISIE series, Index.)

p, J. Walter Ruben; d, Edwin L. Marin; w, Mary C. McCall, Jr. (based on the novel Dark Dame by Wilson Collinson); ph, Leonard Smith; ed, Frederick Y. Smith; art d, Cedric Gibbons, Malcolm Brown; set d, Edwin B. Willis; cos, Valles, Dolly Tree.

Comedy (PR:A MPAA:NR)

MAISIE GETS HER MAN**
(1942) 85m MGM bw (GB: SHE GOT HER MAN)

Ann Sothern (Maisie Ravier), Red Skelton (Hap Hixby), Allen Jenkins (Pappy Goodring), Donald Meek (Mr. Stickwell), Lloyd Corrigan (Mr. Denningham), Fritz Feld (Prof. Orco), Walter Catlett (Jasper), Leo Gorcey (Cecil), Ben Welden (Percy Podd), Rags Ragland (Ears Cofflin), Frank Jenks (Art Giffman), Florence Shirley (Mrs. Taylor), Pamela Blake (Elsie).

Sothern is struggling to get on the Broadway stage when she meets Skelton, a stage-struck comedian, and a bundle of second-rate performers, producers, and agents. Sothern and Skelton are accused of swindling after the real criminal drops a bag full of money in their laps. The comedian is jailed and Sothern goes on the trail of the bad guy. The teaming of Sothern and Skelton works very well in this otherwise routine comedy. (See MAISIE series, Index.)

p, J. Walter Ruben; d, Roy Del Ruth; w, Betty Reinhardt, Mary C. McCall, Jr. (based on a story by Reinhardt and Ethel Hill from a character created by Wilson Collinson); ph, Harry Stradling; m, Lennie Hayton; ed, Frederick Y. Smith; art d, Cedric Gibbons; ch, Danny Dare; m/l, "Cookin' with Gas," Roger Edens.

Comedy (PR:A MPAA:NR)

MAISIE GOES TO RENO**
(1944) 90m MGM bw (GB: YOU CAN'T DO THAT TO ME)

Ann Sothern (Maisie Ravier), John Hodiak (Flip Hennahan), Tom Drake (Bill Fullerton), Marta Linden (Winifred Ashbourne), Paul Cavanagh (Roger Pelham), Ava Gardner (Gloria Fullerton), Bernard Nedell (J. E. Clave), Roland Dupree (Jerry), Chick Chandler (Tommy Cutter), Bunny Waters (Elaine), Donald Meek (Parsons), James Warren (Dr. Hanley Fleeson), Douglas Morrow (M.C.), William Tannen (Lead Man), Edward Earle (Clerk), Byron Foulger (Dr. Cummings), Leon Tyler (Boy), Noreen Nash (Goodlooking Girl), Dallas Worth, Lynn Arlen, Ethel Tobin, Elizabeth Dailey, Katharine [Karin] Booth (Girls at Party).

Sothern heads out to Reno for a deserved rest after working long hours in a defense plant. On the way a soldier gives her a note to deliver to his wife telling her that he wants a divorce. Sothern delivers the note, and becomes mixed up in a blackmail scheme when the woman she gave the note to turns out not to be the wife, but one of three people who want the real wife's money. In addition to being caught up in the mess, she romances card dealer Hodiak. (See MAISIE series, Index.)

p, George Haight; d, Harry Beaumont; w, Mary C. McCall, Jr. (based on a story by Harry Ruby, James O'Hanlon from a character created by Wilson Collinson); ph, Robert Planck; m, David Snell; ed, Frank E. Hull; art d, Cedric Gibbons, Howard Campbell; set d, Edwin B. Willis, Helen Conway; m/l, Sammy Fain, Ralph Freed.

Comedy (PR:A MPAA:NR)

MAISIE WAS A LADY**½ (1941) 76m MGM bw

Ann Sothern (Maisie Ravier), Lew Ayres (Bob Rawlston), Maureen O'Sullivan (Abigail Rawlston), C. Aubrey Smith (Walpole), Edward Ashley (Link Phillips), Joan Perry (Diana Webley), Paul Cavanagh (Cap Rawlston), William Wright (Judge), Edgar Dearing (Cop), Charles D. Brown (Doctor), Joe Yule (Barker), Hans Conried (Guest), Hillary Brooke (Guest).

Maisie (Sothern), the struggling showgirl, loses her carnival job because of an intoxicated Ayres. The judge decides that Sothern must be put on Ayres' payroll, who turns out to be a very wealthy man. She becomes the maid, but also helps solve the family's problems when she stops O'Sullivan from marrying a fortune hunter and gets Ayres off the booze. The film ends with Sothern engaged to her employer. (See MAISIE series, Index.)

p, J. Walter Ruben; d, Edwin L. Marin; w, Betty Reinhardt, Mary C. McCall, Jr. (based on a story by Reinhardt and Myles Connolly from a character created by Wilson Collinson); ph, Charles Lawton; ed, Frederick Y. Smith.

Comedy (PR:A MPAA:NR)

MAJIN**

(1968, Jap.) 86m Daiei c (DAIMAJIN; AKA: MAJIN, THE HIDEOUS IDOL; THE DEVIL GOT ANGRY; MAJIN, THE MONSTER OF TERROR)

Miwa Takada *(Kozasa Hanabusa)*, Yoshihiko Aoyama *(Tadafumi Hanabusa)*, Jun Fujimaki *(Kogenta)*, Ryutaro Gomi *(Samanosuke)*, Tatsuo Enzo *(Gunjuro)*.

The mixing of two of Japan's favorite genres, monsters and samurai, had to happen sooner or later. During a medieval civil war, the ruler and his wife are killed by the chamberlain, but the ruler's children are able to escape to the mountain. The chamberlain then becomes ruler and enslaves the inhabitants of the village. One of the children, the prince, and a servant are caught when they return to the village. The princess prays to the warrior god, Majin, and the god comes to life, saving the prince and killing the chamberlain. The monster Majin isn't as hokey as Godzilla, but the movie isn't THE SEVEN SAMURAI either.

p, Masaichi Nagata; d, Kimiyoshi Yasuda; w, Tetsuo Yoshida; ph, Fujio Morita (Daiei Scope, Eastmancolor); m, Akira Ifukube; ed, Hioshi Yamada; art d, Hisashi Okuda; spec eff, Kimiyoshi Kuroda.

Action/Adventure **(PR:A MPAA:NR)**

MAJIN, THE HIDEOUS IDOL (SEE: MAJIN, 1968, Jap.)

MAJIN, THE MONSTER OF TERROR (SEE: MAJIN, 1968, Jap.)

MAJOR AND THE MINOR, THE**** (1942) 100m PAR bw

Ginger Rogers *(Susan Applegate)*, Ray Milland *(Maj. Kirby)*, Rita Johnson *(Pamela Hill)*, Robert Benchley *(Mr. Osborne)*, Diana Lynn *(Lucy Hill)*, Edward Fielding *(Col. Hill)*, Frankie Thomas *(Cadet Osborne)*, Raymond Roe *(Cadet Wigton)*, Charles Smith *(Cadet Korner)*, Larry Nunn *(Cadet Babcock)*, Billy Dawson *(Cadet Miller)*, Lela Rogers *(Mrs. Applegate)*, Aldrich Bowker *(Rev. Doyle)*, Boyd Irwin *(Maj. Griscom)*, Byron Shores *(Cap. Durand)*, Richard Fiske *(Will Duffy)*, Norma Varden *(Mrs. Osborne)*, Gretl Dupont *(Mrs. Shackleford)*, Stanley Desmond *(Shumaker)*, Ethel Clayton, Gloria Williams *(Bit Women)*, Lynda Grey *(Bit Girl)*, Will Wright *(1st Ticket Agent)*, William Newell *(2nd Ticket Agent)*, Freddie Mercer *(Little Boy in Railroad Station)*, Carlotta Jelm *(Little Girl in Railroad Station)*, Tom McGuire *(News Vendor)*, George Anderson *(Man with Esquire)*, Stanley Andrews *(1st Conductor)*, Emory Parnell *(2nd Conductor)*, Guy Wilkerson *(Farmer Truck Driver)*, Milt Kibbee *(Station Agent)*, Archie Twitchell *(Sergeant)*, Alice Keating *(Nurse)*, Ralph Gilliam, Dick Chandlee, Buster Nichols, Stephen Kirchner, Kenneth Grant, Billy Clauson, John Bogden, Bradley Hail, Billy O'Kelly, Jack Lindquist, David McKim, Jim Pilcher, Don Wilmot *(Cadets)*, Billy Ray *(Cadet Summerville)*, Marie Blake *(Bertha)*, Mary Field *(Mother in Railroad Station)*, Dell Henderson *(Doorman)*, Ed Peil, Sr. *(Stationmaster)*, Ken Lundy *(Elevator Boy)*, Tom Dugan *(Deadbeat)*, Dickie Jones, Billy Cook.

A sparkling farce that marked Billy Wilder's directorial debut after years of writing witty screenplays for other directors to take credit for, THE MAJOR AND THE MINOR sails along breezily from the first scenes and never flags, due to scintillating dialog, potentially risque situations, and a pace that punches the laughs out in rapid-fire succession. Rogers is a working girl who has had it with New York City and is eager to return home to the Midwest. When she applies for a ticket at the station, she is shocked to learn that the prices have gone up and she doesn't have enough to cover the fare. When she learns that she does have enough for a half-fare, she dresses up as a 12-year-old child, and hopes to pull off the disguise until she reaches her home in Iowa. On board the train, she meets Milland, an Army major who is going to a boys' military school for a three day layover. Also on board are several young cadet officers who begin to make eyes at her. Milland, always the gentleman, finds his feelings stirred by this pre-teener and doesn't know how to handle it because she has been placed in his compartment to share the space for the journey. Once in Iowa, Milland's fiancee, Johnson, wants to keep him out of active service. Lela Rogers plays Ginger's mother and at one point, Ginger dresses up older to play Lela. Lela Rogers was Ginger's real mother so the resemblance was understandable. The masquerade is uncovered by Lynn, a teenager, but she keeps mum about it. The situations that Ginger Rogers is placed in were very sexy, even more than in many movies of today, but the censors turned a blind eye toward them as everything was in good fun and never sleazy. All the supporters were good and a special note for Benchley, who was making a name for himself as an actor (after years of writing for *The New Yorker* magazine and starring in a few shorts) before he died in 1945. The military school exteriors were filmed in Wisconsin at St. John's Military Academy in Delafield. This was Ginger Rogers' first film for Paramount since SITTING PRETTY. She had been toiling in the RKO vineyards for nine years. Producer Hornblow left Paramount after this to go on to a series of hits at MGM including GASLIGHT, THE HUCKSTERS, and THE ASPHALT JUNGLE. Remade as YOU'RE NEVER TOO YOUNG.

p, Arthur Hornblow, Jr.; d, Billy Wilder; w, Wilder, Charles Brackett, (based on the play "Connie Goes Home" by Edward Childs Carpenter and the story "Sunny Goes Home" by Fannie Kilbourne); ph, Leo Tover; m, Robert Emmett Dolan; ed, Doane Harrison; art d, Hans Dreier, Roland Anderson; cos, Edith Head; makeup, Wally Westmore.

Comedy **(PR:A MPAA:NR)**

MAJOR BARBARA***** (1941, Brit.) 121m Pascal-RANK/UA bw

Wendy Hiller *(Maj. Barbara Undershaft)*, Rex Harrison *(Adolphus Cusins)*, Robert Morley *(Andrew Undershaft)*, Emlyn Williams *(Snobby Price)*, Robert Newton *(Bill Walker)*, Sybil Thorndike *(The General)*, Deborah Kerr *(Jenny Hill)*, David Tree *(Charles Lomax)*, Penelope Dudley Ward *(Sarah Undershaft)*, Marie Lohr *(Lady Brittomart)*, Walter Hudd *(Stephen Undershaft)*, Marie Ault *(Rummy Mitchens)*, Donald Calthrop *(Peter Shirley)*, Cathleen Cordell *(Mog Habbijam)*, Torin Thatcher *(Todger Fairmile)*, Miles Malleson *(Morrison)*, Felix Aylmer *(James)*, Stanley Holloway *(Policeman)*, S. I. Hsiung *(Ling)*, Kathleen Harrison *(Mrs. Price)*, Mary Morris *(A Girl)*, Edward Rigby, Bombardier Billy Wells.

This is one of Shaw's most amusing and spritely comedies, excitingly enacted by Hiller and Harrison, although Shaw's monologs sometimes get boggy with verbiage. Hiller is an idealist and socialist, a major in the Salvation Army who busies herself with attacks on wealthy capitalists, chiefly her father, Morley, a munitions magnate. Harrison, a young professor of Greek history and literature, is hopelessly in love with Hiller but she resists his colorful advances; she's too busy saving the poor from the wealthy. Further complicating matters is Morley, a kind, calm, and benevolent tycoon who believes that the impoverished can be helped but only through the careful manipulation of funds. Hiller throws her father's ostensibly generous/ philosophy in his face and he responds by donating 50,000 pounds to the Salvation Army in its war against poverty. Thorndike, to Hiller's surprise, accepts the gift with gratitude. So disillusioned is Hiller that she quits her position with the Army. Then Harrison takes Hiller on a tour of her father's munitions factories and she quickly learns that the workers enjoy widespread benefits and are treated humanely. She is converted to a capitalistic viewpoint almost equal to that of her father who has proclaimed that "I am a millionaire. That is my religion." But her perspective is tempered with Shaw's own intrinsic belief that "the greatest of all our evils and the worst of our crimes is poverty." Hiller agrees with the pragmatic Harrison that money is a tool by which the poor can be aided. Shaw's 1905 social comedy was brought to the screen by Pascal, who had talked the curmudgeon playwright into allowing him to film PYGMALION, starring Leslie Howard and Hiller, in 1938, which had been a smash hit. MAJOR BARBARA, however, was not as well received, especially by American audiences which found it too, too sophisticated and could not relate at all to its socialist preachings. Hiller and Harrison are nevertheless brilliant and vibrant and Morley is wonderful as the tolerant father, even though he was only 32 at the time (playing the father of a 28-year-old Hiller). Newton, who plays an incorrigible money-grubbing slum dweller, is delightfully wicked. London's East End is well photographed by Neame and gives a picturesque view of the city.

p, Gabriel Pascal; d, Pascal, Harold French, David Lean; w, Anatole de Grunwald, George Bernard Shaw (based on the play by Shaw); ph, Ronald Neame; m, William Walton; ed, Charles Frend; prod d, Vincent Korda.

Comedy/Satire **Cas.** **(PR:A MPAA:NR)**

MAJOR DUNDEE*** (1965) 124m COL c

Charlton Heston *(Maj. Amos Charles Dundee)*, Richard Harris *(Capt. Benjamin Tyreen)*, Jim Hutton *(Lt. Graham)*, James Coburn *(Samuel Potts)*, Michael Anderson, Jr. *(Tim Ryan)*, Senta Berger *(Teresa Santiago)*, Mario Adorf *(Sgt. Gomez)*, Brock Peters *(Aesop)*, Warren Oates *(O. W. Hadley)*, Ben Johnson *(Sgt. Chillum)*, R. G. Armstrong *(Rev. Dhalstrom)*, L. Q. Jones *(Arthur Hadley)*, Slim Pickens *(Wiley)*, Karl Swenson *(Capt. Waller)*, Michael Pate *(Sierra Charriba)*, John Davis Chandler *(Jimmy Lee Benteen)*, Dub Taylor *(Priam)*, Albert Carrier *(Capt. Jacques Tremaine)*, Jose Carlos Ruiz *(Riago)*, Aurora Clavell *(Melinche)*, Begonia Palacios *(Linda)*, Enrique Lucero *(Dr. Aguilar)*, Francisco Reyguera *(Old Apache)*.

An offbeat and sometimes jumbled western adventure film sees Heston as a Union officer in charge of a jail in the Southwest. Among the prisoners is his boyhood friend, Harris, who has killed a Union guard and, along with Johnson, Oates, and others, is scheduled to hang. Renegade Apaches attack another Army outpost, killing everyone, and Heston decides to lead an expedition against them, asking for volunteers to follow the Indians into Mexico and track them down, killing or capturing them. Realizing he needs seasoned troops, Heston revokes the execution order for Harris and his men and they join a motley group of outcasts, misfits, and some Union troops. Harris and Heston battle all the way, especially after attacking a French garrison in a small Mexican village and taking along a voluptuous refugee, Berger, over whom they compete for affection. Heston is wounded by an Indian arrow while he enjoys a swim with the raven-haired Berger and he must be doctored in a village controlled by the French who are looking for the Americans. He recovers and, after the Americans skirmish with the renegade Apaches, collect their white hostage children, and send these back under escort, the ragged volunteers move back toward the U.S., followed hotly by a powerful French force of emperor Maximillian (later executed by Mexican patriots under the command of liberator Benito Juarez). Just as the Americans cross the river into the U.S., Harris, having nothing really to live for now that the Confederacy is smashed (at least that's the rationale), wheels his horse about and leads a solo charge into the French ranks and is killed. Heston and seven others return to the fort. The action is hot and heavy and Peckinpah does not spare the violence and gore, his specialty, The film seems to have been put together with director's paste and jumps erratically about, tearing the plot at the seams. But the leads are strong and convincing and solid character actors—Johnson, Oates, Taylor—do journeyman work. Coburn rides about as a scout with one arm, taking Heston's orders with a maniacal grin. Heston later regretted this film, complaining that production began without a completed script. The entire film was shot on location in Mexico.

p, Jerry Bresler; d, Sam Peckinpah; w, Harry Julian Fink, Oscar Saul, Peckinpah (based on a story by Fink); ph, Sam Leavitt (Panavision, Eastmancolor); m, Daniele Amfitheatrof; ed, William A. Lyon, Don Starling, Howard Kunin; art d, Al Ybarra; cos, Tom Dawson; spec eff, August Lohman.

Western/War **Cas.** **(PR:C-O MPAA:NR)**

MAJORITY OF ONE, A*** (1961) 156m WB c

Rosalind Russell *(Mrs. Jacoby)*, Alec Guinness *(Koichi Asano)*, Ray Danton *(Jerome Black)*, Madlyn Rhue *(Alice Black)*, Mae Questel *(Mrs. Rubin)*, Marc Marno *(Eddie)*, Gary Vinson *(Mr. McMillan)*, Sharon Hugueny *(Bride)*, Frank Wilcox *(Noah Putnam)*, Francis De Sales *(American Embassy Representative)*, Yuki Shimoda *(Mr. Asano's Secretary)*, Harriet MacGibbon *(Mrs. Putnam)*, Alan Mowbray *(Capt.

Norcross), Tsuruko Kobayashi (Mr. Asano's Daughter-in-Law), Lillian Adams (Mrs. Stein), Shirley Cytron, Arlen Stuart, Belle Mitchell (Neighbors), Bob Shield (Announcer), Dale Ishimoto (Taxi Driver).

Gertrude Berg and Cedric Hardwicke were the leads in the Broadway show that ran nearly 600 performances. Berg, who had been one of America's favorite radio and TV actresses in her creation "The Goldbergs" played a role she'd done many times before. Hardwicke, when seen across a theater's distance, could be believed as being Japanese. However, the casting of eminently WASPish Russell and "veddy" English Guinness works against the charm of the script because we see them in close-up on the screen, and Russell, despite being an excellent actress, fails to convince anyone she is a Jewish widow. Guinness fares a bit better as his job is to be inscrutable, which is much easier. Guinness also had studied Japanese ways and was able to convey the Asian attitudes with small gestures that contributed to his characterization. Russell is a Brooklyn widow whose one son was killed in WW II by the Japanese. So it is with great reluctance that she is taking a sea voyage to Japan with her daughter, Rhue, and her son-in-law, Danton, where he is to do some trade business as a diplomat. On board the ship, Russell meets Guinness, a wealthy Japanese man who was also tragically struck by the war and lost members of his family. Danton now learns that Guinness is a member of the negotiating group against whom Danton must deal and he wonders if Guinness is being particularly charming to Russell for that reason. Russell is taken with this man of such an opposite culture and she feels that Danton is too wary but she decides that it is better to be safe than sorry and so, on their last night on the ship, Russell will not dine with Guinness. In Japan, Danton makes a remark that is insulting to the sensitive oriental nature of Guinness and the trade meeting is called off. Russell will not let go of her new friend, though, so she travels to Guinness' home, a definite breach of etiquette, and they have an excellent time with each other. It is so much fun for both that Guinness decides to put his loss of face aside and begin negotiating with Danton again. A deal is struck and everything is hunky-dory until Guinness, in an unaccustomed moment of candor, admits that he adores Russell and wants to marry her. Russell is, at once, honored and stunned. She is also irked at the reaction of Rhue and Danton who have proven themselves to be prejudiced against Guinness by their reaction. Russell thinks it over, then gives him the answer of "no," and it isn't because she doesn't find him attractive or because there is such a wide gulf in their histories, it's simply that she feels that both of them continue to be controlled by their pasts and it will take a bit longer to be able to toss that aside and begin a new life. Time passes and Guinness has taken the honorable assignment of being a representative of Japan to the United Nations in New York. Russell is thrilled at his arrival and a new courtship begins, one that may, or may not, wind up in a marriage. Too bad they didn't have an actual Japanese-Jewish wedding as it might have had Guinness standing under the traditional Orthodox arbor and stepping on a sake cup to seal the union. Questel plays the same yenta neighbor she did on the stage and Marno repeats his Broadway role as the arrogant Japanese houseboy, Danton and Rhue are good in nonsympathetic parts and the whole film is amiable enough, but at a shade over two and a-half hours, it is far too long and, at times, trespassed on eternity.

p&d, Mervyn LeRoy; w, Leonard Spigelgass (based on the play by Spigelgass); ph, Harry Stradling, Sr. (Technicolor); ed, Philip W. Anderson; md, Murray Cutter; art d, John Beckman; set d, Ralph S. Hurst; cos, Orry-Kelly; makeup, Jean Burt Reilly; technical advisor, Takemo K. Shinohara.

Comedy/Drama (PR:A MPAA:NR)

MAKE A FACE** (1971) 90m Sperling c

Karen Sperling (Nina), Paolo Patti (Dr. Davis), Davis Bernstein (Stranger), Nicolas Surovy (Larry), Joe Horan (George), Jackie Doroshow (Pucci Lady), David Franciosi (2nd Stranger), John Chin (Delivery Boy).

A surrealistic character study featuring Sperling as a wealthy young woman who lives in a posh apartment in Manhattan. The story line bounces from reality to her dreams to her fantasies in no specific order. The film is hard to follow with its constant shifts of consciousness, and gets tedious at 90 minutes. Interestingly, actor-director Sperling is the granddaughter of Harry Warner and niece of Jack Warner (of Warner Bros.).

p, Karen Sperling; d, Sperling, Avraham Tau; w, Sperling, Barbara Connell (based on a screenplay by Tau); ph, Jeri Sopanen, Ken Van Sickle (DeLuxe Color); m, Tony Cohan; ed, Connell; set d, Tau; m/l, "When the Sun Comes Down," Cohan (sung by Lee Montgomery), "Truck Stop Rose," "11th Hour Hog Call," Cohan (sung by Cohan), "Fruit Song," "No Name Face," John Jacobs (sung by Jacobs).

Drama (PR:C MPAA:NR)

MAKE A MILLION*½ (1935) 64m MON/REP bw

Charles Starrett (Jones), Pauline Brooks (Irene), George E. Stone (Larkey), James Burke (Pete), Guy Asher (Corning), Norman Houston (Moxey), Monte Carter (Benny), Jimmy Aubrey (Soapy), George Cleveland (Blind Man).

Starrett is a college professor who is fired because of his radical economic theories. The college administration tells Starrett that he can have his job back when he makes a million dollars using his wild theories. Brooks is one of his students who also doesn't buy the professor's ideas. By panhandling and pulling a nationwide scam, Starrett becomes a multimillionare and wins Brooks.

p, Trem Carr; d, Lewis D. Collins; w, Charles Logue (based on a story by Emmett Anthony); ph, Milton Krasner; ed, Carl Pierson.

Comedy Cas. (PR:A MPAA:NR)

MAKE A WISH** (1937) 75m Principal/RKO bw

Bobby Breen (Chip), Basil Rathbone (Selden), Marion Claire (Irene), Henry Armetta (Moreta), Ralph Forbes (Mays), Leon Errol (Brennan), Billy Lee (Pee Wee), Donald Meek (Joseph), Herbert Rawlinson (Dr. Stevens), Leonid Kinskey (Moe),

Fred Scott (Minstrel), Charles Richman, Richard Tucker, Johnny Arthur, Barbara Barondess, Dorothy Appleby, Lillian Harmer, St. Luke's Choristers.

Young soprano Breen goes to summer camp and is befriended by composer Rathbone, who is suffering from a creative block. He gets new inspiration from letters by Breen's mother, Claire, an opera singer hoping for a comeback. The smart boy gets them together, resulting in the opera being finished, Mom becoming a star, and Breen getting a new father. Songs include: "Music in My Heart," "My Campfire Dreams," "Make a Wish," "Old Man Rip" (Oscar Straus, Louis Alter, Paul E. Webster).

p, Sol Lesser; d, Kurt Neumann; w, Gertude Berg, Bernard Schubert, Al Boasberg, Earle Snell, William Hurlbut (based on a story by Berg); ph, John Mescall; m, Oscar Straus; ed, Arthur Hilton; md, Dr. Hugo Riesenfeld; art d, Harry Oliver; ch, Larry Ceballos.

Musical Comedy Cas. (PR:A MPAA:NR)

MAKE AND BREAK (SEE: TELL ME LIES, 1968, Brit.)

MAKE BELIEVE BALLROOM** (1949) 79m COL bw

Jerome Courtland (Gene Thomas), Ruth Warrick (Liza Lee), Ron Randell (Leslie Todd), Virginia Welles (Josie Marlow), Al Jarvis (Himself), Adele Jergens (Herself), Paul Harvey (George Wilcox), Louis Jean Heydt (Jerskin Elliott), Frank Orth (Pop), Sid Tomack (Joe), Vernon Dent (Chef), Frankie Laine, Charlie Barnet, The King Cole Trio, Jimmy Dorsey, Toni Harper, Jan Garber, Jack Smith, Pee Wee Hunt, Kay Starr, Gene Krupa, The Sportsmen, Ray McKinley.

Courtland and Welles are carhops that enter a musical quiz show on Al Jarvis' radio program. They fall in love and win the grand prize, it's that simple. The best thing about this low-budget musical is the musical guest artists, which include Frankie Laine, The King Cole Trio, Kay Starr, Jimmy Dorsey, and Gene Krupa, among others. Musical numbers include, "Miss in Between Blues" (Allan Roberts, Lester Lee), "The Way the Twig Is Bent" (Roberts, Doris Fisher), "Make Believe Ballroom" (Leon Rene, Johnny Mercer, Al Jarvis), "I'm the Lonesomest Gal in Town" (Leon Brown, Albert von Tilzer), "On the Sunny Side of the Street" (Dorothy Fields, Jimmy McHugh), "It's a Blue World" (Bob Wright, Chet Forrest), "The Trouble with You Is Me" (Jack Segal, George Handy), "Hello Goodbye" (Alex Sullivan, Lew Pollack), "Disc Jockey Jump" (Gene Krupa, Gerry Mulligan), "Coming Out" (M. Christiance, Harry J. Cole).

p, Ted Richmond; d, Joseph Santley; w, Albert Duffy, Karen DeWolf (based on a story by Duffy from the radio programs of Al Jarvis and Martin Block); ph, Henry Freulich; ed, Jerome Thoms; art d, Paul Palmentola.

Musical (PR:A MPAA:NR)

MAKE HASTE TO LIVE** (1954) 90m REP bw

Dorothy McGuire (Crystal Benson), Stephen McNally (Steve), Mary Murphy (Randy Benson), Edgar Buchanan (Sheriff), John Howard (Josh), Ron Hagerthy (Hack), Pepe Hern (Rudolfo Gonzales), Eddy Waller (Spud Kelly), Carolyn Jones (Mary Rose).

McNally gets out of jail after serving an 18-year jail sentence for murdering his wife, McGuire. His wife, however, had not really been killed, but had left home with their baby daughter, and let her, husband be tried for a murder that never happened. McNally searches for her, seeking revenge. He finds McGuire and fully grown daughter Murphy in a small New Mexico town. He tries to use his daughter to get to McGuire. The film ends in a climactic chase through the ruins of an Indian cliff village where McNally falls to his death.

p, Herbert J. Yates; d, William A. Seiter; w, Warren Duff (based on a novel by Mildred and Gordon Gordon); ph, John L. Russell, Jr.; m, Elmer Bernstein; ed, Fred Allen.

Drama (PR:A MPAA:NR)

MAKE IT THREE* (1938, Brit.) 78m St. Margarets/MGM bw

Hugh Wakefield (Percy Higgin), Edmund Willard (Big Ed), Diana Beaumont (Annie), Sydney Fairbrother (Aunt Aggie), Jack Hobbs (Charlie), Olive Sloane (Kate), Alexander Field (Sam), C. Denier Warren (Mr. Cackleberry).

Henpecked bank clerk Wakefield is given a rather unusual choice: go to jail for three months in order to collect an inheritance, or marry his girl (Beaumont) who doesn't want to postpone marriage for that long. Wakefield opts for the money and deliberately messes up a burglary so he can land in jail, and thus collect the fortune. His cellmate forces the poor man to participate in a jailbreak, so that Beaumont is pacified by not having to wait for her nuptials after all as Wakefield marries her before he returns to jail. It's not much of an idea, and the results are a series of poorly constructed comic mishaps. Direction shows no flair for comedy.

p, Julius Hagen; d, David Macdonald; w, Vernon Sylvaine.

Comedy (PR:A MPAA:NR)

MAKE LIKE A THIEF**

(1966, Fin.) 79m Emerson c (AKA: RUN LIKE A THIEF)

Richard Long (Bart Lanigan), Ake Lindman (Arvo Maki), Pirkko Mannola (Marja), Rosemary Precht (Toini), Juhani Kumpulinen (Leonard Weston), Aulekki Tarnanen (Helvi), Esko Salamen (Gunman), Palmer Thompson (Detective), Uolevi Vahteristo, Seppo Wallin, Ismo Kallio, Sylva Rossi, Sirppa Sivori-Asp, Kyosti Kayhko, Aimo Paapio, Matti Lehtela, Seija Siikamaki, Kaarina Leskinen, Kauko Kokkonen, Nils Brandt, Martti Saarikivi, Annu Aarnela, Marita Tuhkunen, Inga-Lil Helin.

Long is left to take the blame for a large financial swindle and jumps bail to follow the men responsible. He tracks them down to Finland and hires mercenary Lindman to help him. Lindman turns Long over to police and gets $5,000, but Long escapes and offers Lindman much more to help him. Together they track down Kumpulinen, the man responsible for the swindle. Long decides not to kill Kumpulinen, and Long's name is cleared of all crimes.

p, Palmer Thompson, Veikko Laihanen; d, Thompson, Richard Long; w, Thompson; ph, Kalle Peronkoski, Reijo Hassinen (Eastmancolor); m, Erkki Meloski; ed, Kari Uusitalo; art d, Reino Helkesalo; set d, Haimi Oy.

Crime Drama **(PR:A MPAA:NR)**

MAKE ME A STAR*** (1932) 70m PAR bw

Stuart Erwin *(Merton Gill)*, Joan Blondell *(Flips Montague)*, ZaSu Pitts *(Mrs. Scudder)*, Ben Turpin *(Ben)*, Charles Sellon *(Mr. Gashwiler)*, Florence Roberts *(Mrs. Gashwiler)*, Helen Jerome Eddy *(Tessie Kearns)*, Arthur Hoyt *(Hardy Powell)*, Dink Templeton *(Buck Benson)*, Ruth Donnelly *(The Countess)*, Sam Hardy *(Jeff Baird)*, Oscar Apfel *(Henshaw)*, Frank Mills *(Chuck Collins)*, Polly Walters *(Doris Randall)*, Victor Potel, Bobby Vernon, Nick Thompson, Billy Bletcher, Snub Pollard, Bud Jamison *(Actors)*, Tallulah Bankhead, Clive Brook, Maurice Chevalier, Claudette Colbert, Gary Cooper, Phillips Holmes, Fredric March, Jack Oakie, Charlie Ruggles, Sylvia Sidney *(Guest Stars)*.

In this remake of the 1924 silent film MERTON OF THE MOVIES, Erwin plays a small-town grocery clerk who dreams of becoming a Hollywood star. He arrives in the city of dreams and quick-talks his way through the gates of a large movie studio. He meets Blondell, a movie extra, who gets him a part in a comedy western. He plays the role in total seriousness and at the preview realizes that he's been had. While he is packing his bags to go home, Blondell rushes over and explains the great future he can have as a comedian. Director Beaudine utilized much of the Paramount lot, including the studio restaurant, the cutting rooms, the entrance of the music building, and the sets of DR. JEKYLL AND MR. HYDE, MADAME RACKETEER, and DEVIL AND THE DEEP (stars of the latter film, Gary Cooper and Tallulah Bankhead, make cameo appearances in this film). An enjoyable comedy that gives a nostalgic look at Hollywood's golden age of the studio system.

d, William Beaudine; w, Sam Mintz, Walter DeLeon, Arthur Kober (based on the novel *Merton of the Movies* by Harry Leon Wilson and the play by George S. Kaufman and Marc Connelly); ph, Allen Siegler; ed, LeRoy Stone.

Comedy **(PR:A MPAA:NR)**

MAKE ME AN OFFER* 1/2 (1954, Brit.) 88m Group Three/BL c

Peter Finch *(Charlie)*, Adrienne Corri *(Nicky)*, Rosalie Crutchley *(Bella)*, Finlay Currie *(Abe Sparta)*, Meier Tzelniker *(Wendl)*, Ernest Thesiger *(Sir John)*, Wilfred Lawson *(Charlie's Father)*, Anthony Nicholls *(Auctioneer)*, Alfie Bass *(Fred Frames)*, Guy Middleton *(Armstrong)*, Vic Wise *(Sweeting)*, Mark Baker *(Mindel)*, Jane Wenham *(Dobbie)*, Richard O'Sullivan *(Charlie as a Boy)*, John Godden *(Charlie's Son)*, Eric Francis *(Auctioneer's Assistant)*, Juno.

Finch is an antique dealer who finds a valuable vase in the attic of an old man, and spends most of the film trying to raise the money to buy it. About as much fun as watching a grandfather clock.

p, W.P. Lipscomb; d, Cyril Frankel; w, Wolf Mankowitz, Lipscomb (based on the novel by Mankowitz); ph, Denny Densham (Eastmancolor); m, John Addison; ed, Bernard Gribble; art d, Denis Wreford.

Comedy **(PR:A MPAA:NR)**

MAKE MINE A DOUBLE**

(1962, Brit.) 86m Sydney Box-Four Star/Ellis bw (GB: THE NIGHT WE DROPPED A CLANGER)

Brian Rix *(Aircraftsman Arthur Atwood/Wing Comdr. Blenkinsop)*, Cecil Parker *(Air Vice-Marshal Sir Bertram Bukpasser)*, William Hartnell *(Sgt. Bright)*, Leslie Phillips *(Squadron Leader Thomas)*, Leo Franklyn *(Sgt. Belling)*, John Welsh *(Squadron Leader Grant)*, Toby Perkins *(Flight Lt. Spendal)*, Liz Fraser *(Lulu)*, Vera Pearce *(Mme. Grilby)*, Sarah Branch *(WAAF Hawkins)*, Oliver Johnston *(Air Commodore Turner)*, Hattie Jacques *(Ada)*, Larry Noble *(Farmer)*, John Chapman *(Wing Commander)*, Gilbert Harrison *(Corporal)*, Arnold Bell *(Wing Comdr. Jones)*, David Williams *(Wing Comdr. Priestly)*, Geoffrey Denys *(Monty's Double)*, Irene Handl *(Lulu's Mom)*, Charles Camerson *(Gen. Gimble)*, Denis Shaw *(Hammerstein)*, Peter Burton *(Pilot)*, Julian D'Albie, Arthur Brough, Ray Cooney, John Langham, Roland Bartrop, Julie Mendez, Harry Lane, Paul Bogdan, Victor Beaumont.

Rix plays both England's top secret service man and a look-alike airman. The airman poses as the agent to throw off the Germans so that the real agent can investigate the new buzz bombs in France. Orders get mixed up and the airman ends up in France and becomes a national hero when he is launched back to England inside one of the buzz bombs that he has accidentally defused. The secret service man tries in vain to prove that he's the real agent.

p, David Henley; d, Darcy Conyers; w, John Chapman; ph, Ernest Steward; m, Edwin Braden; ed, Sidney Stone, art d, Duncan Sutherland; m/l, "I Want a Man," Edwin Braden, Alan Reeve-Jones.

Comedy **(PR:A MPAA:NR)**

MAKE MINE A MILLION 1/2**

(1965, Brit.) 82m Jack Hylton/Schoenfeld bw (AKA: LOOK BEFORE YOU LAUGH)

Arthur Askey *(Arthur Ashton)*, Sidney James *(Sid Gibson)*, Dermot Walsh *(Martin Russell)*, Sally Barnes *(Sally)*, Olga Lindo *(Mrs. Burgess)*, Bernard Cribbins *(Jack)*, Bruce Seton *(Supt. James)*, Kenneth Connor *(Anxious Husband)*, Clive Morton *(National TV Director-General)*, Martin Benson *(Commercial TV Chairman)*, Lionel Murton *(Commercial TV Director)*, George Margo *(Assistant)*, David Nettheim *(Professor)*, Tommy Trinder, Dickie Henderson, Evelyn Laye, Dennis Lotis, Anthea Askey, Raymond Glendenning, Patricia Bredin, Leonard Weir, Gillian Lynne, Peter Noble, Sabrina, The Television Toppers, Penge Formation Dancers *(Guest Stars)*.

James is an ad promoter who persuades Askey, a makeup man for British TV, to help him sneak in a commercial for his product, Bonko Detergent, during a TV show. They pull it off, but Askey is fired. The two then set up a pirate station to broadcast their commercials at will. The van they use to broadcast from is hijacked by a gang of thieves who think there is gold in the van. Askey radios the police and the thieves are captured. Askey gets a new job with the TV network, and James interrupts the first show with his commercials.

p, John Baxter; d, Lance Comfort; w, Peter Blackmore, Talbot Rothwell, Arthur Askey (based on a story by Jack Francis); ph, Arthur Grant; ed, Peter Pitt; md, Stanley Black; art d, Denis Wreford.

Comedy **(PR:A MPAA:NR)**

MAKE MINE MINK*** (1960, Brit.) 101m Continental bw

Terry-Thomas *(Maj. Albert Rayne)*, Athene Seyler *(Dame Beatrice Appleby)*, Hattie Jacques *(Nanette Parry)*, Billie Whitelaw *(Lily)*, Elspeth Duxbury *(Elizabeth Pinkerton)*, Irene Handl *(Mme. Spolinski)*, Jack Hedley *(Jim Benham)*, Kenneth Williams *(Honorable Fred Warrington)*, Caroline Leigh *(Warrington's Secretary)*, Denis Shaw *(Cafe Proprietor)*, Michael Peake *(Thin Man)*, Derek Sydney *(Sinister Man)*, Steven Scott *(Fat Man)*, Sydney Tafler *(Lionel Spanager)*, Gordon Philpott *(1st Old Porter)*, Ron Moody *(Jelks, 2nd Old Porter)*, Penny Morrell *(Gertrude)*, Joan Heal *(Mrs. Dora Spanager)*, May Hallatt *(Old Mrs. Spanager)*, Claire Golding *(Ruby Golding)*, Felicity Young *(1st Shop Assistant)*, Dorinda Stevens *(Jean)*, Raymond Huntley *(Inspector Pape)*, Freddie Frinton *(Drunk)*, Michael Balfour *(Butler)*, Noel Purcell *(Burglar)*, Wensley Pithey *(Superintendent)*, Clement Freud *(Croupier)*.

A hilarious British comedy about a bumbling group of amateur thieves stealing furs. Seyler is a wealthy dame who discovers how easy it is to retrieve stolen merchandise and recruits Thomas (a retired military officer), Duxbury, and Jacques to make up a group of thieves to steal furs for charity. Their inept capers are an amusing blend of slapstick and subtle British humor, and it works very well.

p, Hugh Stewart; d, Robert Asher; w, Michael Pertwee, Peter Blackmore (based on the play "Breath of Spring" by Peter Coke); ph, Reg Wyer; m, Philip Green; ed, Roger Cherrill.

Comedy **Cas** **(PR:A MPAA:NR)**

MAKE MINE MUSIC*** (1946) 74m Disney/RKO c

Voices: Nelson Eddy, Dinah Shore, Benny Goodman and His Orchestra, The Andrews Sisters, Jerry Colonna, Andy Russell, Sterling Holloway, The Pied Pipers, The King's Men, The Ken Darby Chorus, Tatiana Riabouchinska, David Lichine.

A musical pastiche that's sort of the pop version of FANTASIA, MAKE MINE MUSIC has excellent animation and fine music, with 10 separate sequences unified by nothing at all beyond the fact that they're good entertainment. The segments include: "The Whale Who Wanted to Sing at the Met," with songs sung by Nelson Eddy as a whale whose one desire is to sing at the Metropolitan Opera; "The Martins and the Coys," a story about feuding mountain people; "A Jazz Interlude," with Benny Goodman featured on the number "All the Cats Join In," in which teenagers dance at the malt shop; "Peter and the Wolf," "A Ballad in Blue," and more and more and more. The picture took two years to make and the colors and animation are superb. Looking at Disney's work today, it is apparent how cheaply made the Saturday morning cartoons are and it is sad that the children don't know how good animation can be unless they are taken to a Disney retrospective that includes such movies as MAKE MINE MUSIC. Critics were less than kind to this movie when released and it disappeared quickly, which was a shame. The least the studio should do is put it on the Disney Channel to show people how animation should look. A particular highlight is Eddy's sequence as he sings bass, baritone, and tenor solo, which are then blended in a trio. Songs include: "Shortnin' Bread" (sung by Nelson Eddy), "Largo Al Factotum" from "The Barber of Seville" (Gioacchino Rossini, sung by Eddy), sextette from "Lucia di Lammermoor" (Gaetano Donizetti, sung by Eddy), Clown song from "Punchinello" (sung by Eddy), "Tristan Und Isolde" (Richard Wagner, sung by Eddy), "Devil's Song" from "Mephistopheles" (Arrigo Boito, sung by Eddy), Finale to Act III of "Martha" (Baron Friedrich von Flotow, sung by Eddy), "Johnny Fedora and Alice Blue Bonnet" (Allie Wrubel, Ray Gilbert, sung by The Andrews Sisters), "All the Cats Join In" (Alec Wilder, Eddie Sauter, Gilbert, performed by Benny Goodman and His Orchestra, sung by The Pied Pipers), "Without You" (Osvaldo Farres, Gilbert, sung by Andy Russell), "Two Silhouettes" (Charles Wolcott, Gilbert, sung by Dinah Shore), "Casey, the Pride of Them All" (Ken Darby, Eliot Daniel, Gilbert, sung by Jerry Colonna), "The Martins and the Coys" (Al Cameron, Ted Weems, sung by The King's Men), "Blue Bayou" (Bobby Worth, Gilbert, sung by The Ken Darby Chorus), "After You've Gone" (Henry Creamer, Turner Leighton, performed by Benny Goodman, Cozy Cole, Teddy Wilson, and Sid Weiss), "Peter and the Wolf" (Serge Prokofieff).

p, Joe Grant; d, Jack Kinney, Clyde Geronimi, Hamilton Luske, Robert Cormack, Joshua Meador; w, Homer Brightman, Dick Huemer, Dick Kinney, John Walbridge, Tom Oreb, Dick Shaw, Eric Gurney, Sylvia Holland, T. Hee, Dick Kelsey, Jesse Marsh, Roy Williams, Ed Penner, James Bodrero, Cap Palmer, Erwin Graham; md, Charles Wolcott; art d, Mary Blair, Elmer Plummer, John Hench; animators, Les Clark, Ward Kimball, Milt Kahl, John Sibley, Hal King, Eric Larson, John Lounsbery, Oliver M. Johnston, Jr., Fred Moore, Hugh Fraser, Judge Whitaker, Harvey Toombs, Tom Massey, Phil Duncan, Hal Ambro, Jack Campbell, Cliff Nordberg, Bill Justice, Al Bertino, John McManus, Ken O'Brien; backgrounds, Claude Coats, Art Riley, Ralph Hulett, Merle Cox, Ray Huffine, Albert Dempster, Thelma Witmer, Jim Trout; effects animation, George Rowley, Jack Boyd, Andy

Engman, Brad Case, Don Patterson; process effects, Ub Iwerks; color consultant, Mique Nelson.

Animation   (PR:AA MPAA:NR)

MAKE-UP*   (1937, Brit.) 72m Standard-International/ABF bw

Nils Asther (*Bux*), June Clyde (*Joy*), Judy Kelly (*Marion Hutton*), Kenneth Duncan (*Lorenzo*), John Turnbull (*Karo*), Lawrence Anderson (*Goro*), Johnnie Schofield (*Publicity Man*), Lawrence Grossmith (*Maj. Sir Edward Hutton*), Norma Varden (*Hostess*), Bombardier Billy Wells (*Ringmaster*), Jill Craigie (*Tania*), Roddy Hughes (*Mr. Greenswater*), Chapman's Circus (*Karo's Circus*).

Asther plays a former doctor, who is now a successful circus clown. He is able to use his medical skills on Kelly, a society girl, when she is rendered unconscious by an elephant. Kelly and Asther become romantically involved, much to the disliking of the clown's foster daughter, Clyde. When Clyde is accused of murdering the lion tamer, Asther comes to the rescue to prove her innocence.

p, K.C. Alexander, C.M. Origo; d, Alfred Zeisler; w, Reginald Long, Jeffrey Dell (based on the novel *Bux* by Hans Passendorf); ph, Phil Tannura, Eric Cross, Roy Day.

Drama   (PR:A MPAA:NR)

MAKE WAY FOR A LADY**   (1936) 65m RKO bw

Herbert Marshall (*Christopher Drew*), Anne Shirley (*June Drew*), Gertrude Michael (*Miss Eleanor Emerson*), Margot Grahame (*Valerie Broughton*), Clara Blandick (*Miss Dell*), Frank Coghlan, Jr. (*Billy Hopkins*), Mary Jo Ellis (*Mildred Jackson*), Maxine Jennings (*Miss Moore*), Taylor Holmes (*George Terry*), Helen Parrish (*Genevieve*), Willie Best (*Townley*), Maidel Turner (*Mrs. Jackson*), Murray Kinnell (*Dr. Barnes*), Grace Goodall (*Mrs. Hopkins*), Johnny Butler (*Briggs*), Alan Edwards (*Gregory*).

Shirley plays a young lady whose mother died, leaving just her and her father, Marshall. She overhears gossip that she is keeping her father from remarriage and sets out to find him a new wife. She chooses Grahame for him but, before the wedding bells ring, Shirley finds out that her father hates the woman. Marshall, on his own, finds the right woman in Michael.

p, Zion Myers; d, David Burton; w, Gertrude Purcell (based on the novel *Daddy and I* by Elizabeth Jordan); ph, David Abel; ed, George Crone.

Comedy   (PR:A MPAA:NR)

MAKE WAY FOR LILA**

(1962, Swed./Ger.) 90m Sandrews-Rhombus/Parade c (LAILA—LIEBE UNTER DER MITTERNACHTSSONNE; LAILA; AKA: LILA—LOVE UNDER THE MID-NIGHT SUN)

Erika Remberg (*Lila*), Joachim Hansen (*Anders*), Birger Malmsten (*Mellet*), Edvin Adolphson (*Aslak*), Alfred Maurstad (*Jompa*), Ann-Marie Gyllen (*Inger*), Isa Quensel (*Elli*), Sif Ruud, Bengt Blomgren, Anne Blomberg, Sonja Westerberg, Bengt Eklund.

A young Remberg is raised by a Lapland family after her real parents are killed by wolves. When she is older her foster father decides who she will marry and Remberg is happy with the man he picked until Hansen, a Norwegian merchant, shows up. Her chosen groom-to-be tries to kill the merchant but Hansen is able to stop the wedding at the last moment.

p, Rune Waldekranz, Georg M. Reuther; d, Rolf Husberg; w, Adolf Schutz, Husberg; ph, Sven Nykvist (Eastmancolor); m, Lars-Erik Larsson; ed, Lennart Wallen.

Drama   (PR:A MPAA:NR)

MAKE WAY FOR TOMORROW*½   (1937) 91m PAR bw

Victor Moore (*Barkley Cooper*), Beulah Bondi (*Lucy Cooper*), Fay Bainter (*Anita Cooper*), Thomas Mitchell (*George Cooper*), Porter Hall (*Harvey Chase*), Barbara Read (*Rhoda Cooper*), Maurice Moscovitch (*Max Rubens*), Elizabeth Risdon (*Cora Payne*), Minna Gombell (*Nellie Chase*), Ray Mayer (*Robert Cooper*), Ralph Remley (*Bill Payne*), Louise Beavers (*Mamie*), Louise Jean Heydt (*Doctor*), Gene Morgan (*Carlton Gorman*), Dell Henderson (*Auto Salesman*), Ruth Warren (*Secretary*), Paul Stanton (*Hotel Manager*), Ferike Boros (*Mrs. Rubens*), Granville Bates (*Mr. Hunter*), Nick Lukats (*Boy Friend*), George Offerman, Jr. (*Richard Payne*), Tommy Bupp (*Jack Payne*), Terry Ray (*Usherette*), Gene Lockhart (*Mr. Henning*), Byron Foulger (*Mr. Dale*), Averil Cameron (*Mrs. McKenzie*), Kitty McHugh (*Head Usherette*), Ralph Brooks (*Doorman*), Ethel Clayton (*Woman Customer*), Ralph Lewis, Phillips Smalley (*Businessmen*), Howard Mitchell (*Letter Carrier*), Don Brodie, Richard R. Neil (*Men*), William Newell (*Ticket Seller*), Rosemary Theby (*Woman*), Helen Dickson (*Bridge Player*), Leo McCarey (*Passerby/Man in Overcoat/Carpet Sweeper*).

This is a melancholy tear-jerker that never once goes over the edge into false or maudlin sentimentality. A sensitive script, flawless acting and direction didn't help at the box office because the saga of "what to do with the old folks" was not attractive to audiences that were still suffering from the aftermath of the Depression and were depressed enough. Give Paramount a lot of credit for attempting to bring this matter to the attention of audiences. Moore and Bondi are old and poor and the bank is about to take their home away. They tell this, at the last moment, to their children, Mitchell and his wife, Bainter, plus Read and Mayer. None of the kids has the space or the wherewithal to take both parents so Bondi and Moore must be split up. There are several scenes in both houses as the parents are seen attempting to live with their children and having difficulty. In the end, Moore and Bondi play a scene at the railway station from where they left on their honeymoon. They are to part again, perhaps forever, as Bondi must take refuge in an old woman's home and Moore, who is frail and can't take the cold of the Northeast, is to move to California.

This good-by scene is restrained, played for reality and tugs at the heart. Moore was already 60 when he accepted this unaccustomed dramatic role and he was simply brilliant. Bondi was only 46, but Wally Westmore's makeup did the job of convincing the eye that she was two decades older. Critics loved it and MAKE WAY FOR TOMORROW made many of the Best Film lists although it was nominated for no awards by the Academy. Mitchell and Bainter were born the same year, 1892, and were just 16 years younger than Moore although no one noticed. It was a timely motion picture then and the subject still lingers in the 1980s, now that people are living longer and it is becoming increasingly more expensive to tend one's parents. Bring several hankies or a box of tissues for this one. The one song was "Make Way For Tommorow", which had about as much acceptance as the film.

p&d, Leo McCarey; w, Vina Delmar (based on the novel *The Years Are So Long* by Josephine Lawrence and the play by Helen Leary, Nolan Leary); ph, William C. Mellor; m, Victor Young, George Antheil; ed, LeRoy Stone; md, Boris Morros; art d, Hans Dreier, Bernard Herzbrun; spec. eff., Gordon Jennings; m/l, "Make Way for Tomorrow," Leo Robin, Sam Coslow, Jean Schwartz; makeup, Wally Westmore.

Drama   (PR:A MPAA:NR)

MAKE YOUR OWN BED**   (1944) 82m WB bw

Jack Carson (*Jerry Curtis*), Jane Wyman (*Susan Courtney*), Alan Hale (*Walter Whirtle*), Irene Manning (*Vivian Whirtle*), George Tobias (*Boris Murphy*), Robert Shayne (*Lester Knight*), Tala Birell (*Marie Gruber*), Ricardo Cortez (*Fritz Alten*), Marjorie Hoshelle (*Elsa Wehmer*), Kurt Katch (*Paul Hassen*), Harry Bradley (*Mr. Brooking*), William Kennedy (*FBI Man*), Jack Mower (*Chauffeur*), Leah Baird (*John's Wife*), Jack Norton (*Drunk*), Joan Winfield (*Whirtle's Secretary*), Marie Blake (*Woman*), Ernest Hilliard, George Kirby (*Men in Waiting Room*).

Private investigator Carson is hired by Hale to pose as a butler to protect him from a group of Nazis. His fiancee, Wyman, is hired as a maid. It turns out that Hale hired them to be actual servants, not detectives. Carson and Wyman have no idea that Hale tricked them. When four actors from Hale's radio show arrive, the dim-witted couple think they have the Nazis. Carson fumbles his way into revealing the four as actual spies.

p, Alex Gottlieb; d, Peter Godfrey; w, Francis Swann, Edmund Joseph, Richard Weil (based on a play by Harvey J. O'Higgins, Harriet Ford); ph, Robert Burks; m, H. Roemheld; ed, Clarence Kolster; md, Leo F. Forbstein; art d, Stanley Fleischer; set d, Clarence Steensen; spec eff, Willard Van Enger.

Comedy   (PR:A MPAA:NR)

MAKER OF MEN*½   (1931) 71m COL bw

Jack Holt (*Dudley*), Richard Cromwell (*Bob*), Joan Marsh (*Dorothy*), Robert Alden (*Chick*), John Wayne (*Dusty*), Walter Catlett (*McNeill*), Natalie Moorhead (*Mrs. Rhodes*), Richard Tucker (*Mr. Rhodes*), Ethel Wales (*Aunt Martha*), Mike McKay.

An inferior football melodrama about a losing college team coached by Holt. The coach pushes son Cromwell into suiting up, but in the most important game, Cromwell's mistakes cause the team's defeat. He leaves school and is admitted to the rival college. He joins their football team and scores the winning touchdown against his father's team. Features John Wayne in an early supporting role as one of the players.

d, Edward Sedgwick; w, Howard J. Green (based on a story by Green, Sedgwick); ph, L. William O'Connell; ed, Gene Milford.

Drama   (PR:A MPAA:NR)

MAKING IT*½   (1971) 97m Alfran/FOX c

Kristoffer Tabori (*Phil Fuller*), Joyce Van Patten (*Betty Fuller*), Marlyn Mason (*Yvonne*), Bob Balaban (*Wilkie*), Lawrence Pressman (*Mallory*), Louise Latham (*Mrs. Wilson*), John Fiedler (*Ames*), Sherry Miles (*Debbie*), Denny Miller (*Skeeter*), Doro Merande (*Librarian*), Maxine Stuart (*Miss Schneider*), Tom Troupe (*Dr. Shurtleff*), David Doyle (*Mr. Fanning*), Dick Van Patten (*Warren*), Carol Arthur (*Mrs. Mallory*), Paul Appleby (*Ray*), Pamela Hensley (*Bar Girl*), Casey King (*Cafeteria Cashier*).

Tabori is a highschool senior who fools around with the physical education teacher's wife, Mason, as well as classmate Miles, who thinks she's pregnant. His widowed mother, Van Patten, loses her boy friend in a car crash, and later she discovers she is pregnant. When Tabori finds out that Miles isn't pregnant, he switches the abortion appointment for his mother. The doctor forces him to watch the operation in a very heavy-handed and melodramatic scene. As dated as REEFER MADNESS.

p, Albert S. Ruddy; d, John Erman; w, Peter Bart (based on the novel *What Can You Do?* by James Leigh); ph, Richard C. Glouner (DeLuxe Color); m, Charles Fox; ed, Allan Jacobs; m/l, "Morning Song," "The All-American," Fox, Norman Gimpel; makeup, Maurice Stein.

Drama   (PR:O MPAA:R)

MAKING LOVE*   (1982) 113m IndieProd/FOX c

Michael Ontkean (*Zack*), Kate Jackson (*Claire*), Harry Hamlin (*Bart*), Wendy Hiller (*Winnie*), Arthur Hill (*Henry*), Nancy Olson (*Christine*), John Dukakis (*Tim*),Terry Kiser (*Harrington*), Dennis Howard (*Larry*), Asher Brauner (*Ted*), John Calvin (*David*), Gwen Arner (*Arlene*), Gary Swanson (*Ken*), Ann Harvey (*Lila*), Stanley Kamel (*Charlie*), Chip Lucia (*Chip*), Doug Johnson (*Doug*), Ben Mittleman (*Ben*), Mickey Jones (*Cowboy Musician*), Joe Medalis (*Announcer*), Erica Hiller (*Lucie*), Michael Shannon (*Marty*), Arthur Taxier (*Don*), Phoebe Dorin (*Jenny*), Mark Schubb (*Josh*), Carol King (*Pam*), Camilla Carr (*Susan*), Lili Haydn (*Little Sister*), Paul Sanderson (*Bill*), David Knell (*Michael*), David Murphy, Michael Dudikoff, John Starr, Charles Zukow, Scott Ryder, Joanne Hicks, Stacey Kuhne, Stephanie Segal, Kedren Jones, Alexander Lockwood, Andrew Harris, Michael Harris, Robert Mikels, Jason Mikels.

Hollywood's attempt to deal with homosexual relationships falls flat and merely glosses over the subject. The familiar boy-meets-girl plot line is turned just a little here, which is supposed to then be provocative and ground-breaking filmmaking. Not by a long shot. The lame documentary-like talking heads cannot give this film even an ounce of credibility. The film could pass as a second-rate television movie, and some of the cast is better known on the small screen. Ontkean plays a California doctor married to TV executive Jackson, and seems happy until he meets gay novelist Hamlin. He is then confused. Hamlin and Ontkean have an affair, Jackson finds out, and the three of them come to an understanding. Simple and trite.

p, Allen Alder, Daniel Melnick; d, Arthur Hiller; w, Barry Sandler (based on a story by A. Scott Berg); ph, David M. Walsh (DeLuxe Color); m, Leonard Rosenman; ed, William H. Reynolds; prod d, James D. Vance; set d, Rick Simpson.

Drama **Cas.** **(PR:O MPAA:R)**

MAKING OF A LADY, THE (SEE: LADY HAMILTON, 1969 Ger./Ital./Fr.)

MAKING THE GRADE* ¹/₂ (1929) 63m FOX bw

Edmund Lowe (*Herbert Littell Dodsworth*), Lois Moran (*Lettie Ewing*), Albert Hart (*Lawyer*), Lucien Littlefield (*Silas Cooper*), James Ford (*Budd Davidson*), Sherman Ross (*Art Burdette*), John Alden (*Egbert Williamson*), Gino Conti (*Frank Dinwiddie*), Rolfe Sedan (*Valet*), Mary Ashley (*Lettie's Friend*), Lia Tora (*Another Girl Friend*).

Lowe plays a young man who comes back to his hometown and makes good. He tries hard to make his reputation as the strong type and win Moran. He succeeds as written. This was a mostly silent film with 10 percent dialog.

d, Alfred E. Green; w, Harry Brand, Edward Kaufman, Malcolm Stuart Boylan; ph, L.W. O'Connell, Norman Devol; m, Erno Rapee; ed, J. Edwin Robbins.

Drama **(PR:A MPAA:NR)**

MAKING THE HEADLINES* (1938) 60m COL bw

Jack Holt (*Nagel*), Beverly Roberts (*Jeane*), Craig Reynolds (*Withers*), Marjorie Gateson (*Muffin*), Dorothy Appleby (*Claire*), Gilbert Emery (*Edmund*), Tom Kennedy (*Handley*), Corbet Morris (*Ronald*), Sheila Bromley (*Grace*), John Wray (*Herb*), Maurice Cass (*Keer*), Tully Marshall (*Hackett*).

Holt is a cop and Reynolds is a reporter who join forces to bust gang activity. This gets Holt more press then his superiors and they send him to another district. There he gets involved in the case of a double murder. Uninteresting mystery and the culprits are obvious.

d, Lewis D. Collins, w, Howard J. Green, Jefferson Parker; ph, James S. Brown, Jr.; ed, Dwight Caldwell.

Mystery **(PR:A MPAA:NR)**

MAKO: THE JAWS OF DEATH* (1976) 93m Selected/Cannon c (AKA: THE JAWS OF DEATH)

Richard Jaeckel, Jennifer Bishop, Harold Sakata, John Davis Chandler, Buffy Dee, Ben Dronen, Paul Preston, Milton Smith, Robert Gordon, Jerry Albert, Luke Halpin, Marcie Knight.

With the success of JAWS in the summer of 1976, minor production companies were rushing to produce cheap shark movie imitations. This outing has Jaeckel making a living renting sharks. But he finds himself being abused by the local research facility and a roadhouse, so it's only natural that a little revenge is in order. From there on the film turns into a few set pieces on how the locals are done in by Jaeckel's sharks. Featured in the cast is Luke Halpin, a veteran of the "Flipper" movies and TV show, who apparently liked appearing in films relating to undersea creatures. Grefe, the producer and director, went on to become a second-unit director for numerous James Bond features.

p&d, William Grefe; w, Robert Madaris.

Drama **(PR:C MPAA:PG)**

MAKUCHI (SEE: IDIOT, THE, 1963, Jap.)

MALACHI'S COVE* ¹/₂ (1973, Brit.) 75m Penrith/Impact Quadrant c (AKA: THE SEAWEED CHILDREN)

Donald Pleasence, Dai Bradley, Veronica Quilligan, Arthur English, David Howe.

This family film chronicles the life of a 14-year-old girl living by herself in 1880 Cornwall. To make ends meet, the hardy young lass takes to selling seaweed. Simplistic though not simple-minded, making this an okay presentation for younger viewers.

p, Andrew Sinclair, Kent Walwin; d&w, Henry Herbert (based on a story by Anthony Trollope); ph, Walter Lassally; m, Brian Gascoigne.

Children's Drama **(PR:AAA MPAA:NR)**

MALAGA, 1954 (SEE: FIRE OVER AFRICA, 1954, Brit.)

MALAGA* (1962, Brit.) 95m Cavalcade-Douglas Fairbanks, Ltd/WB bw (AKA: MOMENT OF DANGER)

Trevor Howard (*John Bain*), Dorothy Dandridge (*Gianna*), Edmund Purdom (*Peter Carran*), Michael Hordern (*Inspector Farrell*), Paul Stassino (*Juan Montoya*), John Bailey (*Cecil*), Alfred Burke (*Shapley*), Peter Illing (*Pawnbroker*), Barry Keegan (*Corrigan*), Brian Worth (*Airport Guard*), Thelma D'Aguiar (*Spanish Woman*), Neville Becker (*Gigolo*), Martin Boddey (*Sir John Middleburgh*), Peter Elliott (*Waiter*), Helen Goss (*Lady Middleburgh*).

Howard, a jewel thief, gets out of jail and decides on one more caper. He wants to get money to go to the South Sea islands so he can retire. The job backfires and Howard's partners take off with the money. The jewel thief tracks them down. This was the final screen appearance for the very talented Dandridge, one of the few

black actresses of the 1950s to gain some reputation and star status. The material offered her here was a far cry from the greatness she revealed in her roles in CARMEN JONES and PORGY AND BESS. Dandridge died from a drug overdose in 1965, after having lost all her money in some very foolish investments.

p, Thomas Clyde; d, Laslo Benedek; w, David Osborn, Donald Ogden Stewart (based on *Scent of Danger* by Donald McKenzie); ph, Desmond Dickinson; m, Matayas Seiber; ed, Gerald Turney-Smith; md, Seiber; art d, Harry White, Pamela Cornell; makeup, Jim Hydes.

Crime Drama **(PR:A MPAA:NR)**

MALATESTA'S CARNIVAL* ¹/₂ (1973) 74m Windmill c

Herve Villechaize, Janine Carazo, Lenny Baker, Daniel Dietrich, Jerome Dempsey, William Preston, Elizabeth Henn, Paul Hostetler.

This odd horror-comedy boasted of a soundtrack specifically created to induce psychological terror. Otherwise, it's a fairly typical offbeat number featuring Villchaize (of television's "Fantasy Island") and an aggregation of monsters and ghouls who enjoy human snacks while watching old horror films on the boob tube. Strange stuff that undoubtedly will please fans of the truly bizarre.

p, Richard Grosser, Walker Stuart; d&w, Christopher Speeth.

Horror/Comedy **(PR:O MPAA:R)**

MALAY NIGHTS zero (1933) 63m Weeks/Mayfair bw (GB: SHADOWS OF SINGAPORE)

Johnnie Mack Brown, Dorothy Burgess, Ralph Ince, Raymond Hatton, Carmelita Geraghty, George Smith, Lionel Belmore, Mary Jane.

An unwatchable, low-budget independent film that has negative production values. From photography to direction, the level of incompetence is extreme. The story features families living on the waterfront involved in deep-sea diving. Brown is better known for his westerns, but most of those could not float any better than this clunker.

d, E. Mason Hopper; w, John Thomas Neville (based on a story by Glenn Ellis); ph, Jules Cronjager; ed, Byron Robinson.

Drama **(PR:A MPAA:NR)**

MALAYA* (1950) 98m MGM bw (GB: EAST OF THE RISING SUN)

Spencer Tracy (*Carnahan*), James Stewart (*John Royer*), Valentina Cortese (*Luana*), Sydney Greenstreet (*Dutchman*), John Hodiak (*Keller*), Lionel Barrymore (*John Manchester*), Gilbert Roland (*Romano*), Roland Winters (*Bruno Gruber*), Richard Loo (*Col. Tomura*), Lester Mathews (*Matisson*), Ian MacDonald (*Carlos Tassuma*), Charles Meredith (*Big Man*), James Todd (*Carson*), Paul Kruger (*Official*), Anna Q. Nilsson (*Secretary*), Herbert Heywood (*Bartender*), Carli Elinor (*Waiter*), Anthony Jochim (*Lean Man*), Joseph Crehan (*Fat Man*), Luther Crockett (*Navy Officer*), George Carleton (*Small Man*), Matt Moore (*Prison Official*), Ben Haggerty (*Sub Officer*), Spencer Chan (*Chinese Shipmaster*), Roque Espiritu (*Malay Servant*), Weaver Levy, Eddie Lee (*Japanese Aids to Tomura*), Leon Stewart (*Piano Player*), Leonard Strong (*Half-witted Malay*), David Fresco (*Barracuda Ed*), Jack Davis (*Captain*), DeForest Kelley (*Lt. Glenson*), Jack Shea (*Intern*), James Somers (*Army Transport Captain*), Victor Groves, Bismark Auelua, George Khoury, Peter Mamakos, James O'Gatty, Kula Tutiama, Carl Deloro, Uluao Letuli, Alex Pope, William Self (*Henchmen*), Robert Williams (*Army Sergeant*), Leon Lontoc, Paul Singh (*Servants*), Silan Chan (*Girl*), Joel Allen (*Federal Agent*).

The unlikely team of Tracy and Stewart embark on a secret mission during WW II. Their job is to smuggle a huge shipment of rubber out of Malaya without the Japanese detecting the operation. Stewart, a one-time reporter who knows the territory, and Tracy, a professional smuggler who is serving time in Alcatraz and is paroled for the mission, contact shifty Greenstreet who pinpoints the location of a rubber stockpile. More than 150,000 tons of rubber are smuggled through the Japanese lines to waiting U.S. ships but, on the last trip, patriot Stewart is killed; criminal Tracy proves his American mettle, however, and gets the shipment through while disposing of an insidious Japanese officer, Loo. It's all pretty hokey stuff and the script is soggy in the middle, but the story is based on real fact. Newsman Manchester Boddy suggested smuggling rubber out of Malaya to President Franklin D. Roosevelt in 1942 and his comments were taken seriously, with 300,000 tons of rubber taken out of that country. Boddy later wrote the screenplay for this film, citing what he knew about the operation. Greenstreet is good as the conniving plotter and so too is Hodiak as an FBI agent. Stewart and Tracy, however, seem to plod along under the weight of the unimaginative dialog. Thorpe's direction is uninspired and only the leads save this one from mediocrity.

p, Edwin H. Knopf; d, Richard Thorpe; w, Frank Fenton (based on a story by Manchester Boddy); ph, George Folsey; m, Bronislau Kaper; ed, Ben Lewis; md, Andre Previn; art d, Cedric Gibbons, Malcolm Brown; set d, Edwin B. Willis, Henry Grace; cos, Irene, Valles; spec eff, A. Arnold Gillespie.

Adventure/War **(PR:A MPAA:NR)**

MALE AND FEMALE (SEE: MALE AND FEMALE SINCE ADAM AND EVE, 1961, Arg.)

MALE AND FEMALE SINCE ADAM AND EVE* * (1961, Arg.) 74m All American/William Mishkin bw (AKA: MALE AND FEMALE; SOULS OF SIN)

Carol Cores (*Robert*), Nelly Meden (*Louise*), Goldie Flame (*Elsa*), Edward Cuitino (*Inspector Gomez*), Bill Kennedy (*Adam*), Alice Gardner (*Eve*).

Love and temptation are the main themes in the two tales in this film. The first, Adam and Eve, is well known, and the second concerns a man who gets involved with the mob to make enough money to impress his girl friend. After he commits a number of murders and robberies, she agrees to marry him, but he is killed when he tries to get out of the mob.

p, Alfredo Bedoya; d, Carlos Rinaldi.

Drama   (PR:A MPAA:NR)

MALE ANIMAL, THE****   (1942) 101m WB bw

Henry Fonda (*Tommy Turner*), Olivia de Havilland (*Ellen Turner*), Joan Leslie (*Patricia Stanley*), Jack Carson (*Joe Ferguson*), Eugene Pallette (*Ed Keller*), Herbert Anderson (*Michael Barnes*), Hattie McDaniel (*Cleota*), Ivan Simpson (*Dr. Damon*), Don Defore (*Wally*), Jean Ames ("*Hot Garters*" Garner), Minna Phillips (*Mrs. Blanche Lamon*), Regina Wallace (*Mrs. Myrtle Keller*), Frank Mayo (*Coach Sprague*), William Davidson (*Alumnus*), Bobby Barnes (*Nutsy Miller*), Albert Faulkner (*Boy*), Jane Randolph (*Secretary*), Spec O'Donnell, Ray Montgomery, David Willock, Don Phillips, Juanita Stark, Audrey Long, Marijo James, Charles Drake, Audra Lindley, Joan Winfield, Ann Edmonds, Ed Brian, Gig Young, Todd Andrews (*Students*), George Meeker, Will Morgan, Raymond Bailey, Walter Brooke, Hank Mann, William Hopper, Al Lloyd, Ed Graham, Cliff Saum, Glen Cavender, Creighton Hale (*Reporters*).

Charming comedic adaptation of the play by Thurber and Nugent (who also directed the film) about a stuffy midwestern college professor who plans to read a letter written by Vanzetti (of Sacco and Vanzetti infamy) to his students. The trustees, lead by Pallette, say that Fonda will be fired if he dares read the missive that was penned a few days before the alleged anarchists were executed. At the same time, Carson arrives in town. He's an old flame of Fonda's wife, de Havilland, and she is, once again, taken by his dubious charm. Carson has come home for "the big game" and Fonda thinks he's just a big, beefy bore. Anderson is the editor of the school paper who writes an editorial in which he applauds Fonda for his decision to read the controversial letter. The editorial also states that the school seems to have a bias against liberal teachers. Simpson, the dean, is irate and warns Fonda that his job is in jeopardy. Anderson loves Leslie, de Havilland's younger sister, but she likes Defore, a halfback on the football team. Matters come to a head when de Havilland suggests that Fonda forget about reading the letter. He refuses and cites the First Amendment. She gets angry, they quarrel, and she exits to join Carson at a cocktail party. Fonda and Anderson meet and get drunk together and this infusion of whiskey courage causes Fonda to say he will never let his wife be stolen by another man. Carson and de Havilland return to the Fonda home and he is smashed so badly that he attempts to fight the bigger Carson and only manages to knock himself unconscious. Carson lifts Fonda and puts him to bed and realizes that he may be in the middle of a separation. Although he likes de Havilland, that's as far as it goes and there's no way that he is about to steal her away. On the following day, Fonda has to read the letter in the school auditorium as there are so many who want to hear it. He's slightly hung over from the drinking the night before and, as he reads the real letter, the trustees and other members of the faculty are seen to visibly relax when they hear it as the letter contains no political words whatsoever. It's a lovely plea that calls for humanity to understand. Tears are seen at the corners of some eyes and de Havilland and Fonda are reunited. It was actually she who had slipped the letter into his pocket because he had forgotten it that morning due to his shaky condition. Fonda is acclaimed a hero by the school and Leslie also has a change of heart when she sees that Anderson is far deeper than the shallow Defore. Director Nugent not only co-wrote the play, he starred in it on Broadway and insisted that Fonda was the only person who could do it justice on screen. The remake, SHE'S WORKING HER WAY THROUGH COLLEGE (1952), was terrible. Fonda eventually played it on the stage in the 1950s when he accepted an offer from his one-time stock company to do the role. (One of the supporting parts in this stage version was essayed by an up-and-coming actress who had a hugging relationship with Fonda. It was his daughter, Jane.) This film is one of the best types of comedy, a funny story that actually has something to say instead of merely being satisfied to assault the ear with glib one-liners. In small roles, note Gig Young, David Willock, and Audra Lindley as students, as well as Raymond Bailey and William Hopper as reporters.

p, Hal B. Wallis; d, Elliott Nugent; w, Julius J. Epstein, Philip G. Epstein, Stephen Morehouse Avery (based on the play by James Thurber, Nugent); ph, Arthur Edeson; m, Heinz Roemheld; ed, Thomas Richards.

Comedy   (PR:A MPAA:NR)

MALE COMPANION**

(1965, Fr./Ital.) 92m P.E.C.F.-Ultra-Les Films du Siecle/International Classics c (UN MONSIEUR DE COMPAGNIE; POI TI SPOSERO)

Jean-Pierre Cassel (*Antoine*), Catherine Deneuve (*Isabelle*), Jean-Pierre Marielle (*Balthazar*), Irina Demick (*Nichole*), Annie Girardot (*Clara*), Sandra Milo (*Maria*), Marcel Dalio (*Krieg von Spiel*), Jean-Claude Brialy (*The Prince*), Andre Luguet (*Grandfather*), Valerie Lagrange (*Louisette*), Paolo Stoppa (*Prof. Gaetano*), Adolfo Celi (*Benvenuto*), Rosemarie Dexter (*Student*), Jacques Dynam (*Isabelle's Father*), Rosy Varte (*Isabelle's Mother*), Memmo Carotenuto (*Policeman*), Giustino Durano (*Baker*), Renee Passeur, Irene Chabrier, Sacha Briquet, Darius Socratos, Hubert Deschamps, Christian Lude.

Cassel is a young man whose philosophy is "laziness is the mother of all virtue." He spends all his time fishing with his rich grandfather. He falls asleep while they are fishing one day and dreams that his grandfather has died penniless. This forces Cassel to try to find a way to make money. He tries every dishonest way and the dream ends with him working as an iron smelter.

p, Julien Derode; d, Philippe de Broca; w, Henri Lanoe, de Broca (based on *Un Monsieur de Compagnie* by Andre Couteaux); ph, Raoul Coutard (Eastmancolor); m, Georges Delerue; ed, Francoise Javet; art d, Pierre Duquesne.

Comedy   (PR:A MPAA:NR)

MALE HUNT**

(1965, Fr./Ital.) 92m Filmsonor-Procinex-Mondex-Euro International/Pathe Contemporary bw (LA CHASSE A L'HOMME; CACCIA AL MASCHIO)

Jean-Paul Belmondo (*Fernand*), Jean-Claude Brialy (*Tony*), Catherine Deneuve (*Denise*), Francoise Dorleac (*Sandra*), Micheline Presle (*Isabelle*), Claude Rich (*Julien*), Marie LaForet (*Gisele*), Marie Dubois (*Sophie*), Bernard Blier (*Mons. Heurtin*), Helene Duc (*Mme. Armande*), Francis Blanche (*Papatakes*), Michel Serrault (*Prof. Lartois*), Bernadette Lafont (*Flora*), Mireille Darc (*Georgina*), Patrick Thevenon, Jacques Dynam, Tanya Lopert, Jacqueline Mille, Yvon Sarray.

Belmondo and Rich tell marriage horror stories to Brialy on his wedding day. This scares Brialy so much that he leaves his bride at the altar and takes off for Greece. He gives Belmondo his honeymoon cruise tickets and Belmondo meets a rich woman. Brialy falls in love with Dorleac, a swindler, and wants to marry her even though he knows it will not last.

p, Robert Amon, Claude Jaeger; d, Edouard Molinaro; w, France Roche, Michel Audiard (based on an idea by Yvon Guezel and stories by Albert Simonin, Michel Duran); ph, Andreas Winding; m, Michel Magne, Georges Zambetas; ed, Robert and Monique Isnardon; art d, Francois de Lamothe.

Comedy   (PR:A MPAA:NR)

MALE SERVICE zero   (1966) 63m Mitam bw

Jerry Harris, Karen Drake, Denine Martin.

A male prostitute proposes to one of his clients, but is spurned by the woman who finds him unworthy of her. Angered, he kills the woman, and fixes things so it appears her caretaker is guilty. However, another of his clients suspects his guilt and fools him into revealing his guilt. An ugly murder mystery with no worth whatsoever.

d, Arch Hudson.

Mystery/Crime   (PR:O MPAA:NR)

MALEFICES   (SEE: WHERE THE TRUTH LIES, 1962, Fr.)

MALENKA, THE VAMPIRE zero

(1972, Span./Ital.) 80m Europix c (LA NIPOTE DEL VAMPIRO; AKA: FANGS OF THE LIVING DEAD)

Anita Ekberg (*Malenka*), Rossana Yanni, Diana Lorys, Fernando Bilbao, Paul Muller, John Hamilton, Julian Ugarte, Adriana Ambesi.

Amateurish vampire film has Ekberg running around an ancient castle, pursued by the niece of a hapless witch-burning victim. There is plenty of bad dialog and cleavage, which seem to be a standard in cheap horror films.

p, Aubrey Ambert, Rossana Yanni; d&w, Armando De Ossorio

Horror   (PR:O MPAA:NR)

MALEVIL**

(1981, Fr./Ger.) 119m NEF-Diffusion-Stella Films-Antenne 2-Les Films Gibe Telecip/UGC c

Michel Serrault (*Emmanuel*), Jacques Dutronc (*Colin*), Robert Dhery (*Peyssou*), Jacques Villeret (*Momo*), Hanns Zischler (*Veterinarian*), Jean-Louis Trintignant (*Fulbert*), Penelope Palmer (*Evelyne*), Jacqueline Parent (*Cathy*).

A post-nuclear-holocaust story that slips into sappy melodrama about the future of mankind and the condition of the human animal. A group survives the blast by taking shelter in a wine cellar in a chateau named Malevil. They come out of the cellar to find a wasteland. They begin again by growing wheat in the nearby fields and rebuilding the chateau. Soon they discover a band of people living in train cars in a mountain tunnel led by an insane fascist, Trintignant, who is killed quickly. The train people join the survivors at the chateau. As things seem to be going well, helicopters from the new government arrive to take everyone to a *1984*-style city. Three people escape the government relocation, one being a pregnant young woman. The screenplay was adapted from the novel by Robert Merle, who withdrew his name from the film's credits.

p, Claude Nedjar; d, Christian de Chalonge; w, Chalonge, Pierre Dumayet (based on the novel by Robert Merle); ph, Jean Penzar (Panavision, CinemaScope); m, Gabriel Lared; ed, Henri Lanoe; art d, Max Douy; cos, Ghislain Uhry; makeup, Eric Muller, Catherine Demesmaeker.

Science Fiction   (PR:C MPAA:NR)

MALIBU   (SEE: SEQUOIA, 1934)

MALIBU BEACH*   (1978) 93m Marimark/Crown International c

Kim Lankford (*Dina*), James Daughton (*Bobby*), Susan Player Jarreau (*Sally*), Stephen Oliver (*Dugan*), Michael Luther (*Paul*), Flora Plumb (*Ms. Plickett*), Roger Lawrence Pierce (*Claude*), Sherry Lee Marks (*Margie*), Tara Strohmeier (*Glorianna*), Rory Stevens (*Charlie*), Parris Clifton Buckner, Bruce Kimball, Bill Adler, Jim Kester, Diana Herbert, Walter Maslow, Marty Rogalny, Tom Mahoney, James Oliver, David Clover, Nathan Roth, Jacqueline Jacobs.

A 1960s-style beach movie that takes full advantage of naked bodies, pot smoking, and foul language. Lankford is a lifeguard at the title beach who has muscle-head Oliver and beach bums Daughton and Luther chasing after her and friend Jarreau. A typical drive-in film, one where you can stop watching for 15 to 20 minutes and not miss a thing.

p, Marilyn J. Tenser; d, Robert J. Rosenthal; w, Celia Susan Cotelo, Rosenthal; ph, Jamie Anderson (DeLuxe Color); ed, Robert Barrere; art d, Fred Chriss; cos, Diana Daniels.

Comedy   Cas.   (PR:C MPAA:R)

MALIBU HIGH zero   (1979) 92m Crown International c

Jill Lansing (Kim), Stuart Taylor (Kevin), Katie Johnson (Lucy), Tammy Taylor (Annette), Garth Howard (Lance), Phyllis Benson (Mrs. Bentley), Al Mannino (Tony), John Grant (Donaldson), John Harmon (Elmhurst), Robert Gordon (Harry), Jim Devney (Wyngate), Cambra Zweigler (Valerie), Susan Gorton (Miss Primm), William Cohen (Jeweler), Bill Burke (Mr. H), Ken Layton (Mooney), Scott Walters (Paperboy).

A high school girl is a prostitute with a penchant for murder. One client is killed, which sets off the bloodletting that comprises the body of the film. This cheap exploitation movie makes some sordid attempts at psychoanalyzing the poor girl, which makes it all the more vile. The title implies a happy-go-lucky teen sex film, which just goes to show one cannot always categorize these lower market features by name alone.

p, Lawrence D. Foldes; d, Irv Berwick; w, John Buckley, Tom Singer (based on a story by Buckley); ph, William De Diego; ed, Dan Perry.

Crime   **Cas.**   **(PR:O   MPAA:R)**

MALICE   (SEE: MALICIOUS, 1974, Ital.)

MALICIOUS*   (1974, Ital.) 98m Cineriz/PAR c (MALIZIA; AKA: MALICE)

Laura Antonelli (Angela), Turi Ferro (Don Ignazio), Alessandro Momo (Nino), Tina Aumont (Luciana), Lilla Brignone (Nonna, Grandmother), Pino Caruso (Don Cirillo), Angela Luce (Widow Corallo), Gianluigi Chirzzi (Antonio), Massimilano Filoni (Enzino), Stefano Amato (Porcello), Grazia Di Marza (Adelina).

When his wife passes away, Sicilian Ferro hires Antonelli, a pretty young woman, to serve as housekeeper for himself and his three sons. Antonelli unknowingly charms the adolescent boys with her natural sensuality, which causes Momo to try to manipulate her. His blackmailing takes some cruel twists, but Antonelli outwits the boy with some seductions of her own. This Italian slice-of-life sex comedy works chiefly because of Antonelli. She brims with a fine combination of innocence and sensuality, carrying the story through its lesser developed moments of cheap sexual humiliation with intelligence and wit. There are also good satirical jabs at life in 1950s Sicily. Despite the occasional cruel humor, MALICIOUS works, an intriguing example of a popular Italian genre.

p, Silvio Clementelli; d, Salvatore Samperi; w, Samperi, Ottavio Jemma, Alessandro Parenzo (based on a story by Samperi); ph, Vittorio Storaro (Technicolor); m, Fred Bongusto; ed, Sergio Montanari; art d, Ezio Altieri.

Comedy   **Cas.**   **(PR:O   MPAA:R)**

MALIZIA   (SEE: MALICIOUS, 1974, Ital.)

MALOU*   (1983) 93m Quartet c

Ingrid Caven (Malou), Grischa Huber (Hannah), Helmut Griem (Martin), Ivan Desny (Paul), Marie Colbin (Lotte), Peter Chatel (Albert), Margarita Calahorra (Lucia), Lo Van Hensbergen (Paul's Father), Liane Saalborn (Paul's Mother), Cordula Riedel (Hannah at 12), Jim Kain (Uncle Max), Peer Raben, Winnetou Kampmann, Estrongo Nahama, Carl Duering, Antonio Skarmeta, Constanza Lira, Angela Villroel, Michael Boehme, Gerhard Hesse, Friedbert Rometsch, Reinhardt Vom Bauer, Friedhelm Lehmann, H.H. Muller, Annemarie Geyer.

Caven sets out from Germany to find out the truth about her mother. She travels to France and South America and learns that her mother's life was totally controlled by men. Caven decides that she will not trap herself by getting married in the traditional sense.

p, Regina Ziegler; d&w, Jeanine Meerapfel; ph, Michael Ballhaus; m, Peer Raben; ed, Dagmar Hirtz; art d, Rainer Schaper; cos, Anna Spaghetti.

Drama   **(PR:C   MPAA:R)**

MALPAS MYSTERY, THE**

        (1967, Brit.) 60m IA Merton Park-Langton/Schoenfeld bw

Maureen Swanson (Audrey Bedford), Allan Cuthbertson (Marshalt), Geoffrey Keen (Torrington), Ronald Howard (Dick Shannon), Sandra Dorne (Dora), Alan Tilvern (Gordon Seager), Leslie French (Wilkins), Catherine Feller (Ginette), Richard Shaw (Kornfeldt), Sheila Allen (Frau Kornfeldt), Edward Cast (Laker).

Swanson is released from prison after serving time for a crime she did not commit. Cuthbertson realizes she is the long-lost daughter of the wealthy Keen. Cuthbertson tries to disguise his mistress as Swanson but Keen is not fooled. Cuthbertson then abducts Swanson with the plan of forcing her to marry him. Scotland Yard investigator Howard arrives, kills Cuthbertson, and takes Swanson to Keen. This film was just one of more than 60 adaptations of Edgar Wallace's novels.

p, Julian Wintle, Leslie Parkyn; d, Sidney Hayers; w, Paul Tabori, Gordon Wellesley (based on Face In The Night by Edgar Wallace); ph, Michael Reed; m, Elisabeth Lutyens, Richard Carr; ed, Tristam Cones; md, Muir Mathieson; art d, Eric Saw.

Mystery   **(PR:A   MPAA:NR)**

MALPERTIUS* 1/2

        (1972, Bel./Fr.) 110m Societe D'Expansion du Spectacle/UA c

Orson Welles (Cassavius), Susan Hampshire (Nancy/Alice/Euryale), Mathieu Carriere (Yann), Jean-Pierre Cassel (Lampernisse), Sylvie Vartan (Bets), Michel Bouquet (Dideloo), Daniel Pilon (Mathias), Walter Rilla, Dora Van Der Groen.

A surrealistic horror film that is a sophomoric attempt to re-create the mood and style of films like THE CABINET OF DR. CALIGARI (1919). Welles is Carriere's uncle who heads a household full of strange relatives and crazed inhabitants. Carriere returns from sea to find that his uncle has captured dying Greek gods, sewn them into human flesh, and is holding one on an Ionian isle. The young man falls

in love with the Gorgon and she turns him into stone. The people involved with this production did not have a grasp of this genre.

d, Harry Kumel; w, Jean Ferry (based on the novel by Jean Ray); ph, Gerry Fisher (Eastmancolor); m, Georges Delerue; ed, Richard Marden; art d, Pierre Cadiou.

Horror   **(PR:C   MPAA:NR)**

MALTA STORY*   (1954, Brit.) 103m British Film Makers/UA bw

Alec Guinness (Peter Ross), Jack Hawkins (Air Commanding Officer), Anthony Steel (Bartlett), Muriel Pavlow (Maria), Flora Robson (Melita), Renee Asherson (Joan), Ralph Truman (Banks), Reginald Tate (Payne), Hugh Burden (Eden), Nigel Stock (Giuseppe), Harold Siddons (Matthews), Rosalie Crutchley (Carmella), Michael Medwin (Ramsay), Ronald Adam (Control Room Operator), Colin Loudan (O'Connor), Edward Chaffers (Stripey), Stuart Burge (Paolo), Noel William (Hobley), Jerry Desmonde (General), Ivor Barnard (Old Man), Peter Bull (Flying Officer), Richard Leven, Thomas Heathcote, Michael Craig, Lee Patterson, Maurice Denham (Voice Only).

Real newsreel footage, both Allied and Axis, is intercut with the story to give this action movie a lot more believability than most in the same genre. Guinness, who had been playing light comedy roles, does a straight dramatic part here as a reconnaisance pilot on his way to Egypt when he is forced to land in Malta after his plane has been disabled. His aerial photos have shown that the Germans are planning an attack on the island. Malta is vulnerable and being bombarded by Germans regularly. Further, all of the Allied carrier-based planes are nailed before they can fly into action. Malta is about to be decimated when some supplies manage to get through. Guinness falls in love with a local, Pavlow, but her brother Stock is in league with the Nazis. Pavlow likes her boss, Steel, so there is a bit of a love triangle to go with the action. Steel, however, is engaged to Asherson. Robson is Pavlow's and Stock's mother and she does a good job as a mother whose son is accused of treason. Guinness is preparing to lead the bombing of a German convoy when he is killed and Pavlow hears his last living words over the loudspeaker in the war room at British Headquarters in the emotional climax. Hawkins registers as Guinness' boss in much the same role we've seen him play before. The siege of Malta was an important chapter in the history of WW II but did not get the same coverage in the United States as the battles of Midway, The Coral Sea, or even The Bulge, so not that much was known about it in America. A fairly good war film that spent too much time on action and not enough in character development, MALTA STORY failed to make much of an impression once it left England.

p, Peter de Sarigny; d, Brian Desmond Hurst; w, William Fairchild, Nigel Balchin, Thorold Dickinson, de Sarigny; ph, Robert Krasker; m, William Alwyn; ed, Michael Gordon; md, Muir Mathieson.

War   **Cas.**   **(PR:A-C   MPAA:NR)**

MALTESE BIPPY, THE* 1/2   (1969) 92m MGM c

Dan Rowan (Sam Smith), Dick Martin (Ernest Grey), Carol Lynley (Robin Sherwood), Julie Newmar (Carlotta Ravenswood), Mildred Natwick (Molly Fletcher), Fritz Weaver (Mr. Ravenswood), Robert Reed (Lt. Tim Crane), David Hurst (Dr. Charles Strauss), Dana Elcar (Sgt. Kelvaney), Leon Askin (Axel Kronstadt), Alan Oppenheimer (Adolph Springer), Eddra Gale (Helga), Arthur Batanides (Tony), Pamela Rodgers (Saundra), Jenifer Bishop (Joanna Clay), Maudie Prickett (Mrs. Potter), Garry Walberg (Harold Fenster), Carol-Jean Thompson (Mona), Jerry Mann (Wesling), Charles Strauss, Mike Kellin.

Rowan and Martin, the stars of the late-1960s TV hit "Laugh-In," flop with this trite comedy. A mystery-comedy in the same vein as the Abbott and Costello vehicles with Rowan as the producer of skin flicks and Martin as his star who thinks he is turning into a werewolf. The two go to an old house on Long Island where they meet Newmar and Lynley and a bunch of murdered bodies. Turns out that Martin is not turning into a werewolf and everyone except for the comedy team is searching for a hidden diamond. In the end, everyone is killed and not happy with the film's ending Rowan and Martin offer their own ending as they walk off into the sunset.

p, Everett Freeman, Robert Enders; d, Norman Panama; w, Freeman, Ray Singer (based on a story by Freeman); ph, William H. Daniels (Panavision, Metrocolor); m, Nelson Riddle; ed, Ronald Sinclair, Homer Powell; md, Riddle; art d, George W. Davis, Edward Carfagno; set d, Robert R. Benton, Dick Pefferle; cos, Moss Mabry; makeup, William Tuttle.

Comedy   **(PR:A   MPAA:G)**

MALTESE FALCON, THE*

        (1931) 75m WB bw (AKA: DANGEROUS FEMALE)

Bebe Daniels (Ruth Wonderly), Ricardo Cortez (Sam Spade), Dudley Digges (Kaspar Gutman), Una Merkel (Effie Perine), Robert Elliott (Detective Dundy), J. Farrell MacDonald (Polhouse), Otto Matieson (Joel Cairo), Oscar Apfel (District Attorney), Walter Long (Miles Archer), Dwight Frye (Wilmer Cook), Thelma Todd (Iva Archer), Augustino Borgato (Captain Jacobi).

This is a slick, chic, and good-looking version, the first, of Hammett's classic crime tale and introduces that indefatigable private eye, Sam Spade, played with suave elan by Cortez. The basic mystery is kept intact with Daniels playing the shifty, untrustworthy lady who comes to Cortez and begs him to help her find a missing sister, setting up an accomplice who has stolen the Black Bird she, Digges (as Gutman, a role later made famous by Sydney Greenstreet) and others covet. Four murders later the jig is up and Cortez has solved the riddle and rounded up the culprits. Del Ruth's direction is smooth as good Scotch but the world he depicts is just too opulent, too polished for the seedy Sam Spade to occupy. Frye, who played the part of the nutty Renfield in DRACULA, released the same year, essays the role of the gunsel, Wilmer, like a man with permanent St. Vitus Dance.

d, Roy Del Ruth; w, Maude Fulton, Lucien Hubbard, Brown Holmes, (uncredited) Dashiell Hammett (based on the novel by Hammett); ph, William Rees; ed, George Marks.

Crime Drama/Mystery **(PR:A MPAA:NR)**

MALTESE FALCON, THE***** (1941) 100m WB bw

Humphrey Bogart *(Sam Spade)*, Mary Astor *(Brigid O'Shaughnessy)*, Gladys George *(Iva Archer)*, Peter Lorre *(Joel Cairo)*, Barton MacLane *(Detective Lt. Dundy)*, Lee Patrick *(Effie Perine)*, Sydney Greenstreet *(Kasper Gutman the Fat Man)*, Ward Bond *(Detective Tom Polhaus)*, Jerome Cowan *(Miles Archer)*, Elisha Cook, Jr. *(Wilmer Cook)*, James Burke *(Luke)*, Murray Alper *(Frank Richman)*, John Hamilton *(Bryan)*, Walter Huston *(Capt. Jacobi the Ship's Officer)*, Emory Parnell *(Mate of the La Paloma)*, Robert Homas *(Policeman)*, Creighton Hale *(Stenographer)*, Charles Drake, Bill Hopper, Hank Mann *(Reporters)*, Jack Mower *(Announcer)*.

Huston's first directorial production, one which proved to be a superlative *film noir* classic which set standards in the crime genre for decades to come. This was also Bogart's first significant role as the top-billed leading man and he is matchless as the inimitable Sam Spade. The film begins with a mystery inside a mystery, following the credits, a title roles up to reveal the words: "In 1539 the Knight Templars of Malta paid tribute to Charles V of Spain by sending him a Golden Falcon encrusted from beak to claw with rarest jewels—but pirates seized the galley carrying this priceless token and the fate of the Maltese Falcon remains a mystery to this day." Exterior shots of San Francisco next flood the scene; the Golden Gate Bridge, the Ferry Building, the skyscrapers (such as they were in that day), and a cut to an office window with the names "Spade and Archer" shown backward and then Bogart, sitting at his desk rolling a cigarette. (This bit of business shows Bogart's fierce independence; he creates his cigarettes by rolling his own from "the makings"—loose tobacco and a flat piece of paper he curls around the leaf, this in a day when cigarettes came prepacked.) Loyal secretary Lee Patrick announces a new client, Astor, who asks Spade to locate her missing sister, a helpless young thing who is somewhere in San Francisco with a mysterious man named Thursby. Astor says she has a date to meet Thursby that night and is hoping her errant sister will be with the rake. All of this Bogart quickly explains to his partner, Cowan, when he enters the office. After receiving a substantial retainer, Bogart assigns Cowan to follow Astor that night and help her free her sister from the clutches of Thursby. When Cowan shows up at the end of Bush Street he is startled to see someone holding a gun on him. The gun goes off and Cowan is blown backward over a street barrier and rolls down the hill, dead. Bogart gets a call and is told of his partner's sudden demise; he hurries to Bush and Stockton streets where plainclothes cop Bond shows him the murder weapon which Bogart identifies as "a Webley-Forsby, 45 automatic, eight shot. They don't make 'em anymore." Bogart tells Bond that Cowan was "tailing a guy named Thursby," but refuses to give him any more information. Bogart calls Astor's hotel but finds that she's checked out. He returns to his modest apartment but is soon visited by Bond and his superior, MacLane, a tough, uncompromising cop. They grill him about Cowan and the case he and his partner were working on. Bogart refuses to identify his client and flares up when they suggest he killed his partner. Then he learns that Thursby (never seen on camera) has been killed in front of his hotel. Bogart has an alibi and the cops back off. He pours them a drink and toasts: "Success, to crime!" The next morning Bogart is visited by George, Cowan's widow, who embraces him, suggesting that either they are having an affair or are about to begin one. Bogart brushes her off and he then receives a call from Astor, using still another name, asking him to come to see her. When Bogart confronts Astor, she asks him if he's told the police that she's his client. He tells her no, and then tells her he knows she made up the story about her sister and she tells him that Thursby was her companion and carried a gun and probably killed Cowan, but she has no idea who killed Thursby. Bogart agrees to find out who's behind the killings and threatening Astor's life but he makes sure she pays him most of the money she has on hand. When he returns to his office, Bogart finds a perfumed Lorre waiting for him, asking him to find a "black figure of a bird," offering him $5,000. Then, inexplicably, Lorre pulls a gun on Bogart, insisting upon searching his office. Bogart is too fast for him, knocking the gun out of his hand and cold-cocking Lorre. While Lorre is out Bogart goes through his things, inspecting his French and British passports, money, and an orchestra seat to the Geary Theatre. When Lorre comes to, he asks if Bogart has "the figure." Bogart doesn't know what he's talking about. They haggle for a while until Lorre gets his gun back and then insists upon searching Bogart's office. The amused detective tells him to go ahead. Later, Bogart sees that he is being followed but he loses the man and then visits Astor. He tells her that Lorre offered him $5,000 for "the black bird". He then kisses her but he demands she tell him what it's all about. Astor leaves with Bogart and they are later joined at Bogart's apartment by Lorre. Lorre and Astor grill each other as to "the black bird's" whereabouts and Lorre gets excited when Astor mentions that "the fat man" is in San Francisco. Astor and Lorre get into a fight and Bogart steps in and cuffs Lorre a few times, telling him: "When you're slapped you'll take it and like it." They are interrupted by a loud knock at the door and Bogart opens it to detectives Bond and MacLane, who barge inside where a facially gashed Lorre whines that Astor attacked him. They fall to arguing and MacLane says he is going to run them all into the police station but Bogart tells the cops they were merely pulling their legs and, rather than go to jail, Lorre and Astor back him up. The police leave empty-handed and disgusted. Lorre goes back to his hotel and Astor stays on as Bogart asks her: "What's this bird, this falcon, that everybody's all steamed up about?" Astor replies: "It's a black figure, as you know, smooth and shiny, of a bird, a hawk or falcon . . . " She then gives him a line about following the bird and he calls her a liar. "I am," she admits. "I've always been a liar." Astor reclines on a chaise lounge, holding her head dramatically and moaning: "I'm so tired, so tired of lying and making up lies . . . not knowing what is a lie and what's the truth." Bogart stares down at her for a moment, then kisses her, glancing out the window to see a man, the same man who had earlier followed him, watching his apartment. Later, Bogart goes to the Hotel Belvedere and asks to speak to Lorre on the desk phone. He spots the man who has been following him seated in the lobby. He puts down the phone and sits next to the gunman, Cook, and asks him where Lorre has gone but Cook pretends ignorance and tells him to "shove off." Bogart hails his friend, the house detective, Burke, who runs Cook out of the hotel. When Bogart returns to his office he learns that Greenstreet, the fat man, has been calling him. He meets with Astor and then sends her off with Patrick, to stay with his secretary for safekeeping. George shows up, vexed that Bogart hasn't called her, and he sends her on her way. He then gets a call from Greenstreet and goes to his hotel suite, greeted by gunsel Cook. Girthsome Greenstreet greets Bogart warmly, gives him a drink, and invites him to sit down. Bogart pumps him about the black bird. Greenstreet begins to tell Bogart about the bird but then gets evasive and Bogart explodes, smashing his glass and walking out, giving Greenstreet a deadline to explain the mystery. Later Cook stops Bogart on the street, telling him, with his hand in his pocket where a pistol obviously bulges, that Greenstreet wants to see him. Bogart gives Cook a wise remark and the gunsel snaps: "Keep on ridin' me. They're gonna be pickin' iron out of your liver!" Bogart snaps back: "The cheaper the crook, the gaudier the patter." Before they get to Greenstreet's suite, Bogart takes Cook's guns away from him and embarrasses the gunman in front of his boss by handing the guns over to Greenstreet, telling the fat man: "A crippled newsie took 'em away from him. I made him give 'em back." Greenstreet is in awe of the daring Bogart, saying: "By gad, you're a chap worth knowing. An amazing character." He and Bogart sit down to more drinks while Greenstreet relates the history of the Maltese Falcon, from the days of the "Order of the Hospital of Saint John of Jersusalem . . . We all know the Holy Wars to them were largely a matter of loot . . . " He explains how pirates stole the jewel-encrusted, priceless falcon being sent to King Charles and centuries later it was discovered in Paris where someone painted it with black enamel. Then, in 1923, a Greek antique dealer found the falcon, gave it another coat of enamel, and, explains Greenstreet, was murdered and the falcon stolen again. Greenstreet states that he traced the falcon to the home of a Russian general in Istanbul. He visited the Russian but the falcon was gone. He believes it is in San Francisco and may even be in Bogart's hands; Greenstreet offers Bogart $25,000 for the bird. He also promises to give Bogart one fourth of what he realizes on the sale of the falcon, once it is in his hands, of course. Bogart's vision begins to blur and he passes out after trying to leave the room; Greenstreet has obviously drugged his drink. Greenstreet leaves the room and returns wearing his jacket. Lorre comes out of another room and, after Cook kicks Bogart in the face, the sinister trio leave. Bogart regains consciousness and calls Patrick to learn that Astor is not with her. He searches Greenstreet's apartment and finds a newspaper. Under a column on ship arrivals he sees that one item has been encircled, the time of arrival of the *La Paloma* from Hong Kong. He is soon at the docks but finds that the ship is on fire. A dock officer, Parnell, tells him that all crew and passengers got off safely. Bogart returns to his office where Patrick gives him a shave. Then, bursting through the door, a man with a black hat pulled low over his face (Walter Huston, unbilled) staggers into the office clutching a package which he holds out to Bogart, then drops, murmuring: "You know . . . falcon." He collapses on the couch, dead. Bogart inspects his wallet and tells the panic-stricken Patrick that the dead man, who has been shot, is the captain of the *La Paloma*. Bogart inspects the package and grins, telling Patrick: "We've got it, angel. We've got it!" The phone rings and Patrick answers it and hears Astor screaming after giving the address of 26 Ancho Street; the line goes dead. Bogart tells Patrick to call the police after he's gone and explain how Huston died but not to mention the package. He takes the package to a baggage room and checks it, then mails the claim check to himself at a postal box. He takes a taxi ride to 26 Ancho Street but finds that it is an empty lot. He locates Astor at her old apartment building and he takes her to his apartment where Greenstreet, Lorre, and Cook are waiting in response to his call. Greenstreet gives Bogart $10,000 and asks him to get the falcon. Bogart tells the fat man that he expected more than $10,000. "Yes, sir," says Greenstreet: "But this is genuine coin of the realm. With a dollar of this you can buy ten dollars of talk." First, Bogart suggests that Greenstreet give his gunman Cook to the police as the fall guy for the murders already committed. This causes Cook to threaten Bogart but he makes a wrong move and Bogart knocks him cold. Cook later escapes while the plotters banter back and forth, over the price of the falcon. Finally, Bogart calls Patrick and tells her to pick up the package at the postal box and bring it to him. Bogart inspects the money Greenstreet has given him and discovers a $1,000 bill is missing and accuses Greenstreet of "palming" it, which the fat man jocularly admits to having done, turning over the bill. He is a crook to the marrow. Then Patrick appears and turns over the package to Bogart. Astor, Greenstreet, and Lorre jump up, grab the package, and tear away its wrappings, revealing a black statuette of a falcon. As Greenstreet inspects the bird, turning it around and around, he grows frantic, withdraws a penknife, and begins to cut away the black enamel. He cuts faster and faster, knicking, carving, slashing in a frenzy but finds no jewels encrusting its body, finally shouting: "It's a fake, it's a phony! It's lead! It's lead! It's a fake!" Bogart confronts Astor but she denies substituting the bird, insisting that this is the statuette she got from the Russian general. Greenstreet is close to nervous collapse while Lorre explodes at him, screaming: "You! It's you who bungled it! You and your stupid attempt to buy it! . . . You—you imbecile! You bloated idiot! You stupid fat-head, you!"Lorre breaks down and weeps while Greenstreet tries to regain control. Greenstreet then decides to go on the quest again for the elusive falcon and Lorre happily agrees to join him. Holding a gun on Bogart, Greenstreet demands he return the money; Bogart gives it back to the fat man but keeps $1,000 for his "time and expenses." Greenstreet shrugs and waddles out, Lorre trailing in his wake. Bogart calls the police and tells them to pick up Greenstreet, Lorre, and Cook. He next turns his attention to a frightened Astor, telling her he knows she killed his partner to implicate her unwanted lover and accomplice, Thursby, and then killed Thursby. "Well," he adds, "if you get a good break, you'll be out of Tahatchapi in 20 years and you can come back to me then . . . I hope they don't hang you, precious, by that sweet neck." Astor doesn't believe Bogart is going to turn her over to the police. "Yes, angel," he says solemnly, "I'm gonna send you over. The chances are you'll get off with life. That means if you're a good girl, you'll be out in 20 years. I'll be waiting for you. If they hang you, I'll always remember you." Still, Astor refuses to believe him, thinking he's joking. "Don't be silly," he reassures her, "you're taking the fall!" She appeals to him and the love she knows he has for her. Bogart doesn't argue. He sits down glumly, staring downward, saying: "Listen. This won't do any good. You'll never understand me, but I'll try once and then give it up. When a man's partner's killed he's supposed to do something about it. It doesn't make any difference what you thought of him. He was your partner and you're supposed to do something about it. And it happens we're in the detective business. Well, when one of your organization gets killed, it's bad business to let the killer get away with it, bad all around, bad for every detective everywhere." He goes on to tell Astor that if he lets her get away with murdering his partner, he would have something on her and "I couldn't be sure that you wouldn't put a hole in me some day." He admits he loves her but that doesn't change matters. Bogart kisses her and the doorbell rings. Bogart asks the police to come in. He turns over the falcon, the money Greenstreet left as a bribe for his silence, and then turns over Astor, telling them Astor killed his partner. Resigned, Astor goes out with MacLane. Bond picks up the statuette and says to Bogart: "It's heavy. What is it?" Bogart takes the falcon and begins carrying it out to the hallway. Replies Bogart: "The—er— stuff that dreams are made of." Puzzled, Bond can only grunt a "huh?" Bogart steps into the hallway to see Astor tearfully step into the elevator, the grate, looking like the bars on a cell, closing in front of her as she stares blankly ahead. The outer glass door of the elevator then closes, butting her off from Bogart's vision, and the light behind the glass begins to descend as Bogart, still carrying the falcon, walks down the stairs and out of sight. Jack Warner, head of Warner Bros., received a scene-for-scene breakdown from Huston and thought this was the final draft for THE MALTESE FALCON, approving it instantly. (Warner was never one to read anything but a contract too closely.) He believed that the flavor of the film had been retained completely by Huston and sanctioned the production but warned the novice director that his schedule was limited to six weeks and he dare not go over his $300,000 budget by a penny or he would be looking for a job. Producer Henry Blanke urged Huston to "make every shot count. No detail can be overlooked. Just remember that each scene, as you shoot it, is the most important scene in the picture." Producer Wallis, who directly oversaw this production, was impressed with Huston who lobbied desperately to direct the film for which he had written the screenplay. He had been a contract writer assigned to Warner's biographical film department. Wallis later claimed that "I decided to gamble with him." Following Blanke's advice to make every shot count, Huston took no chances, tailoring the screenplay with instructions to himself for a shot-for-shot setup, doing his own sketches for every scene, indicating the type of shot he intended to use, pan, dolly, truck, crab, boom, so that he would not take up time instructing the crew members and cast with last-minute, hurried directions. (This method is exactly how Alfred Hitchcock shot every one of his movies so that he was always on schedule and never went over budget.) Huston called a rehearsal and let his actors work out their scenes while he stood by, but he gave them no instructions; all they had to do was follow his minutely detailed script. "Only about 25 percent of the time would it be necessary to bring them around to conform with my original idea," he later recalled. Not a line of dialog from Huston's original screenplay was dropped and he cut only one brief scene when realizing that Bogart could achieve the same effect by making a quick phone call. Except for some exterior night shots, Huston shot the entire film in sequence, which greatly helped his actors. The shooting went so smoothly that there was actually extra time for the cast to enjoy themselves and Huston would lead Bogart, Astor, Bond, Lorre, and others to the Lakeside Golf Club near the Warner lot to frolic in the pool, dine and drink and talk until midnight, mostly about anything other than the black bird. One day's shooting was put aside for a difficult scene which Huston expedited by mounting two cameras on tracks and the cast got the scene down in two takes, a total of seven minutes before the cameras. Director and cast spent the rest of the day at the club. Huston was not hamstrung by his detailed script, however, and allowed for spontaneous technical ideas to take over a few scenes. In one scene he had specified many cutaways but then he allowed his brilliant cameraman, Edeson, to manipulate the dolly until the whole scene went fluid with about 26 dolly moves. The photography of the film is one of its great assets, shot with low-key lighting and employing inventive and arresting angles. Ceilings were used by Huston here to give the image of confinement, and sets, except for the hotel and the dock scene, are almost claustrophobic, suggesting that Bogart's investigation is extremely limited, that he has just so much space in which to search for that elusive black bird. And Huston coddled each scene with Edeson, to make sure the images blended with action and dialog, sometimes showing closeups of characters with other characters acting upon them or talking to them from a distance. The film begins leisurely but picks up speed as the involved plot unravels until it's going at a hectic pace that excites the viewer. Angle shots were invented to cleverly emphasize the nature of the characters. Some of the most arresting technical scenes involve the fat man, Greenstreet, especially when he is sitting down, slowly explaining the history of the falcon to Bogart, purposely drawing out his story so that one might think his monolog overlong but this, too, is by sinister design. He has been taking his time with Bogart so that the knockout drops he has slipped into Bogart's drink will take effect. As Greenstreet growls out his black tale of the bird the camera, from floor angle, shoots up at him, so that his gigantic girth fills the entire screen, dominates the scene so completely that it gives Greenstreet the evil authority he truly possesses, making him the leader of a conniving gang of greed-struck creatures. His expanse of belly, crossed by a gold watch chain, is marvelous to behold, for it tells the tale of the dark conspiracy about the falcon, one that is enormous, like the wealth the conspirators seek. Almost all of the scenes involving Astor suggest prison: In one scene she wears striped pajamas and the furniture in the room is stripped and the light coming through the windows cuts downward through venetian blinds, slivers of light suggesting bars, the bars on the elevator cage at the end when she takes her slow ride downward with the police, on her way to execution. (When Hammett wrote the original stories about the falcon and the eventual smash hit novel published in 1930, the state of California was still hanging condemned prisoners, but by 1941 when the story was filmed for the third time, the state had long been using the gas chamber, since December 2, 1935, when it claimed its first life, that of convicted murderer Albert Kessell, although some prisoners were executed by the rope in California as late as 1942. But these were condemned prisoners sentenced almost a decade earlier and such a fate would not have applied to Astor, after her certain conviction in 1941. So Bogart's line about how he hopes they "won't hang you by that pretty neck" is an anachronism.) Further increasing the film's tempo is Huston's incisive editing. The brilliant director also watched the film with composer Deutsch, suggesting just where and when music would help certain scenes. Huston was equally judicious in selecting his cast members. Bogart, however, was not the first choice to play the legendary Sam Spade. Wallis offered the role to George Raft who turned it down because he didn't want to work with Huston, an inexperienced director. Bogart accepted with alacrity and Huston was forever grateful; it was this film that cemented their lifelong friendship and wonderful in-tandem talents in future films such as THE TREASURE OF THE SIERRA MADRE (1947), KEY LARGO (1948), THE AFRICAN QUEEN (1951). Ironically, Raft had turned down another film, HIGH SIERRA, which Bogart took over, in 1941, one which made Bogart a star. Raft would go on turning down roles that Bogart would play and make famous, including the cynical and unforgettable hero of CASABLANCA (1942). The 42-year-old Bogart was delighted with Sam Spade, a character of honor and greed, a complex man who is both world-weary but ready for a new adventure and still capable of deep love. Bogart would later state: "I had a lot going for me in that one. First, there was Huston. He made the Dashiell Hammett novel into something you don't come across too often. It was practically a masterpiece. I don't have many things I'm proud of . . . but that's one." It was THE MALTESE FALCON that Ingrid Bergman would watch over and over again when preparing to make CASABLANCA so she would know how to interact with her co-star, Bogart. Huston's film version of THE MALTESE FALCON (the others being the 1931 version with Ricardo Cortez, the 1936 version with Bette Davis, entitled SATAN MET A LADY) was not seen by the author Hammett when it was first released. He saw it some six months after its first run and reported that it was "boring," but he was half drunk at the time. He saw it again sober some years later and told friends that it not only pleased him but that it was probably the best version of the work. Of course the wry, witty, anti-Establishment, anti-hero who drinks his whiskey neat, Sam Spade, is based upon Hammett himself, who, for many years in San Francisco was employed as a private detective for the Pinkerton Detective Agency. Hammett not only gave his identity to Sam Spade but his first name; the author's complete name was Samuel Dashiell Hammett but he discarded Samuel when launching his career as a writer. Hammett drew upon his detective years in creating many of the characters peopling THE MALTESE FALCON, the novel itself being pieced together from two of his stories published in *Black Mask* magazine in 1925, "The Whosis Kid," and "The Gutting of Couffignal." The novel itself was published in *Black Mask* in 1930 in five parts before being put into book form by Alfred A. Knopf. Lorre's role of Joel Cairo, who is decidedly effeminate, is based upon a criminal Hammett captured for the Pinkertons in 1920 in Pasco, Washington. Warner Bros. downplayed the homosexual image of Lorre's role in the film to avoid the censors, but they strongly hinted at it by having Lorre fuss about his clothes (he becomes hysterical when some blood from a scratch received from Astor ruins his shirt), and his calling cards and handkerchiefs have the overpowering smell of gardenias which Bogart makes a point of noting to Patrick before she shows him into his office. (In the novel, the secretary, Effie Perine, tells Spade before ushering Cairo into the office: "This guy is queer," a statement much too strong for films in 1942.) It is not by accident that Hammett applies the word "gunsel" to Wilmer, also thought to be homosexual as is Gutman; in fact, the whole bunch of greedy conspirators are decidedly homosexual. The word first appeared as "gunzel" in a crime novel published in 1914 called THE GAY CAT and means a passive male homosexual who is also too quick on the trigger. In the original 1931 version the Cairo character, Otto Matieson, is introduced to Ricardo Cortez by his secretary, Una Merkel, as if he were a lovely lady and the homosexual image all but vanishes in the second version, SATAN MET A LADY, in 1936, with the Cairo character transformed into an eccentric British killer, played by Arthur Treacher. Lorre, of course, is superb in his role as Cairo and was the only person selected for the role by Huston. The role of Wilmer, the gunsel, was also cast immediately, given to the strange but fascinating character actor, Cook. According to Huston, Cook "lived alone up in the High Sierra, tied flies, and caught golden trout between films. When he was wanted in Hollywood, they sent word up to his mountain cabin by courier. He would come down, do a picture, and then withdraw again to his retreat." The sinister fat man, Gutman, was another matter, but producer Wallis solved that casting dilemma, suggesting to Huston that he test a character actor who had had a long career in the legitimate theater, Greenstreet, who was then 61-years-old, weighed between 280 and 350 pounds (depending upon various reports at the time), a man who had never before made a film. In his test and film debut, Greenstreet was simply wonderful, waddling about with his penguin-like torso jutting forth, his soft, round features belying the sinister characters he would enact, his unique, hiccupy laugh, bulbous eyes glaring, a booming bass voice that roared orders or purred conspiracies. So well did Greenstreet enact Kaspar Gutman that he would be forever typecast as an overweight villain, but one of the first rank, in such films as THE VERDICT, THREE STRANGERS, and THE MASK OF DIMITRIOS. Though Greenstreet exudes confidence on screen, he was very nervous when making the film, especially during the early scenes where he had to deliver lengthy monologs. "Mary," he said to Astor, "hold my hand and tell me I won't make an ass of myself." To calm him down, Bogart, Astor, and Lorre would visit his dressing room, pouring him a few stiff shots of brandy which Greenstreet would wolf down, then smile, and waddle forth to shoot a scene. Greenstreet's many "by gads" uttered in the movie were purposely inserted by the censors, replacing the words "by God." Moreover, Huston was warned not to show excessive drinking by the characters but the director bristled at this, stating that Spade was a man who put away a half bottle of hard liquor a day and to show him abstaining would be to falsify his character. (Hammett himself was a heavy enough drinker as to be classified alcoholic.) The character Gutman, a deep-thinking rogue, was certainly based upon real life rascal A. Maundy Gregory, an overweight British detective who turned entrepreneur and was involved in many sophisticated intrigues known to Hammett, including a spectacular search for a long lost treasure not unlike the jewel-encrusted Maltese Falcon. Matching the sterling performances of other cast members was Astor as the lying Brigid. The role, originally intended for Geraldine Fitzgerald, who decided to appear in a play instead, went to Astor and she rendered a masterful performance. "I had a lovely pot to boil for Brigid," she later commented. "It was quite a bitches' cauldron." To achieve a character who is constantly lying, Astor purposely hyperventilated to capture a breath-catching look and she is so convincing that Bogart can only blurt admiration for her lies, which only *he* knows are lies: "You're good, you're real good." But she isn't good enough for Bogart "to play the sap" for her. Astor plays it breathless and helpless as a victim, to cover up her guilt as a murderess. She appears curiously matronly with a severe hairdo and sack-like dresses. But there are moments, when she appears most vulnerable but is really most dangerous, when her face turns sensuous, alluring, sultry, utterly enticing Bogart to apparent doom and corruption. Astor and Huston, along with the rest of the cast, had a lot of fun making THE MALTESE FALCON. To drive off visitors to the set, Huston devised a number system, one where he would call out a certain number and the actors would go into bizarre, volatile behavior. When a group of nuns were ushered onto the set by the studio publicity director, Huston called out a number and Astor stopped a scene with Bogart, lifted her dress unfashionably high and shouted: "Dammit, I've got another run in my stocking!" The nuns, all in shock, were hustled off the set. On another occasion some socially prominent Warner Bros. stockholders were watching a scene when the director called out: "Oh, Mr. Lorre, please, on the set, number 11!" Mary Astor's dressing room door burst open and a sheepish looking Lorre jumped out, adjusting his fly hurriedly. Another number signal would cause Bogart to step out of character and viciously lash out at either Greenstreet or Lorre, shouting: "Okay, I've had enough damned scene stealing from you! You jump one more line of mine and you're gonna be looking out of the back of your fat head!" He would growl, kick over furniture, and clench his fists menacingly until the visitors cleared out. THE MALTESE FALCON set became so notorious that the front office closed it from inspection, labeling it a "sealed production," which is exactly what Huston wanted so he could direct without interruption. The publicity director finally caught on and approached Huston, saying: "May I have your permission, *sir*, to bring over some very important visitors this afternoon? And without benefit of your goddamned gags?" Huston smiled and said: "You can try, my friend, you can certainly try." He didn't. The appearance of the great character actor Walter Huston, disguised in his small cameo role as the merchant marine captain who delivers the falcon to Bogart's office, unbilled, was done as a good luck gesture for his son. This was John's first movie as a director and Walter Huston wanted to seal it with his paternal presence. Walter Huston, by the way, had to promise Jack Warner that he would not demand a dime for his little role before he was allowed to stagger into the office and then fall backward, dead. The scene, of course, was done to perfection, but after it was shot, John thought to put into motion another of his practical jokes. That night, Astor, pretending to be the secretary of Hal Wallis, the producer, called Walter Huston at home. The veteran actor was still smarting because his son had asked him to perform many takes to "get it right," which was all a gag. When Astor called later she said Mr. Wallis wanted to talk to him. John Huston, disguising his voice, got on the line and pretended to be Wallis, saying: "Walter—I saw the rushes today and I thought you hammed it up a little too much. Really, a man of your experience. I think you had better come back tomorrow and redo that little scene until you get it right." Walter Huston exploded, shouting: "You tell my son to get another actor or go to hell! He made me take 20 falls today, and I'm sore all over, and I'm not about to take twenty more! Or even one!" He slammed down the phone and Huston and Astor broke into laughter. THE MALTESE FALCON was such an enormous critical and popular success that the studio immediately made plans to produce a sequel entitled THE FURTHER ADVENTURES OF THE MALTESE FALCON, which John Huston was to direct in early 1942 but he became involved in other directional chores, now that he was a hot property, and the cast members went into other productions so the sequel never became reality. (The sequel was to be based on three more Hammett stories, "Too Many Have Lived," "A Man Called Spade," and "They Can Only Hang You Once.") Radio claimed Sam Spade in a 30-minute adaptation of THE MALTESE FALCON on CBS' "The Lady Esther Screen Guild Players" on September 20, 1943, with Bogart, Astor, Greenstreet, and Lorre enacting their original roles. The story went over the airwaves again for CBS on July 3, 1946, when "Academy Award" presented Bogart, Astor, and Greenstreet. (The film did not win any Oscars but was nominated for Best Picture and Greenstreet won an Oscar nomination as Best Supporting Actor, so therefore the film qualified for the program.) Howard Duff played a more congenial detective in THE ADVENTURES OF SAM SPADE over the airwaves from 1946 to 1951, beginning on CBS and concluding on NBC. In 1975, Columbia produced a spoof on THE MALTESE FALCON called THE BLACK BIRD, starring George Segal as Sam Spade, Jr., with Patrick and Cook reprising their roles from the 1941 version. It was a less than sidesplitting experience. Seven plaster figurines of the falcon were used during the 1941 production. One of these was stolen from the Los Angeles County Museum of Art where it was on display with the others, in 1974, when the Segal production was underway. Some said the theft (or mislaying) of the figurine and the Segal film were designed to work in tandem, that the missing falcon was serving to hype the new film and that it was all a publicity stunt. If it was it backfired since news accounts on the missing falcon exceeded those of the anemic Segal film.

p, Hal Wallis, Henry Blanke; d, John Huston; w, Huston (based on the novel by Dashiell Hammett); ph, Arthur Edeson; m, Adolph Deutsch; ed, Thomas Richards; md, Leo B. Forbstein; art d, Robert Haas; cos, Orry-Kelly; makeup, Perc Westmore.

Crime Drama   Cas.   (PR:A MPAA:NR)

MAMA LOVES PAPA**   (1933) 70m PAR bw

Mary Boland (*Jessie Todd*), Charlie Ruggles (*Wilbur Todd*), Lilyan Tashman (*Mrs. McIntosh*), George Barbier (*Mr. Kirkwood*), Morgan Wallace (*Mr. McIntosh*), Walter Catlett (*Tom Walker*), Ruth Warren (*Sara Walker*), Andre Beranger (*Basil Pew*), Tom Ricketts (*Mr. Pierrepont*), Warner Richmond (*The Radical*), Frank Sheridan (*The Mayor*), Tom McGuire (*O'Leary*).

Boland and Ruggles are a middle-class couple and Boland decides it is time her husband becomes somebody. She dresses him up and sends him out and things begin to backfire. A pleasant comedy that seems to typify the early sound studio comedies.

d, Norman McLeod; w, Nunnally Johnson, Eddie Welch, Arthur Kober (based on a story by Douglas MacLean, Keene Thompson); ph, Gilbert Warrenton; ed, Richard Currier.

Comedy   (PR:A MPAA:NR)

MAMA LOVES PAPA*1/2   (1945) 61m RKO bw

Leon Errol (*Wilbur Todd*), Elisabeth Risdon (*Jessie Todd*), Edwin Maxwell (*Kirkwood*), Emory Parnell (*O'Leary*), Charles Halton (*Appleby*), Paul Harvey (*Mr. McIntosh*), Charlotte Wynters (*Mrs. McIntosh*), Ruth Lee (*Mabel*), Lawrence Tierney (*Sharpe*).

RKO bought the rights to Paramount's 1933 film for $85,000 and came out with a film worth about $5. Risdon buys a book on how to help her husband, Errol, succeed and ends up getting him into a number of messy situations. By mistake, Errol becomes park commissioner and gets involved with an underhanded recreational equipment manufacturer. He loses his job as commissioner, but luckily gets his old job back.

p, Ben Stoloff, Sid Rogell; d, Frank Strayer; w, Charles Roberts, Monte Brice; ph, Jack MacKenzie; m, Leigh Harline; ed, Edward W. Williams; art d, Albert S. D'Agostino, Lucius Croxton.

Comedy   (PR:A MPAA:NR)

MAMA RUNS WILD*   (1938) 67m REP bw

Mary Boland (*Alice Summers*), Ernest Truex (*Calvin Summers*), William Henry (*Paul*), Lynn Roberts (*Edith*), Max Terhune (*Applegate*), Joseph Crehan (*Tom Fowler*), Dorothy Page (*Mrs. Hayes*), Dewey Robinson (*Greengable*), Julius Tannen (*C. Preston Simms*), Sammy McKim (*Boy*), John Sheehan (*Snodey*), James C. Morton (*Adams*).

A lame comedy that becomes dumber with each passing moment. Boland and Truex move into the suburban Paradise Park, and when Boland stops a bank robber she runs for mayor. If elected, she plans to close the town bar. Her opposing candidate is her husband. She gets only two votes, hers and her husband's, and the film gets one star.

d, Ralph Staub; w, Gordon Kahn, Paul Gerard Smith, Frank Rowan, Hal Yates (based on a story by Kahn); ph, Ernest Miller; ed, Edward Mann; md, Alberto Colombo; art d, John Victor Mackay.

Comedy   (PR:A MPAA:NR)

MAMA STEPS OUT**   (1937) 63m MGM bw

Guy Kibbee (*Leonard Cuppy*), Alice Brady (*Ada Cuppy*), Betty Furness (*Leila Cuppy*), Stanley [Dennis Morgan] Morner (*Chuck Thompson*), Gene Lockhart (*Mr. Sims*), Edward Norris (*Ferdie Fisher*), Gregory Gaye (*Dmitri*), Ivan Lebedeff (*Coco*), Heather Thatcher (*Nadine*), Frank Puglia (*Priest*), Adrienne D'Ambricourt (*Jeanne*).

Brady goes to the Riviera with her new riches and becomes disillusioned with the phony people and their materialistic values. Brady takes her husband, Kibbee, and their children in search of a better life. A light comedy that works chiefly because of Brady's talents.

p, John Emerson; d, George R. Seitz; w, Anita Loos (based on the play "Ada Beats the Drum" by John Kirkpatrick); ph, Jackson Rose; ed, George Boemler; m/l, Edward Ward, Chet Forrest, Bob Wright.

Comedy   (PR:A MPAA:NR)

MAMBA*   (1930) 78m TIF c

Jean Hersholt (*August Bolte/Mamba*), Eleanor Boardman (*Helen von Linden*), Ralph Forbes (*Karl von Reiden*), Josef Swickard (*Count von Linden*), Claude Fleming (*Maj. Cromwell*), William Stanton (*Cockney Servant*), William von Brincken (*Maj. von Schultz*), Noble Johnson (*Hassim*), Hazel Jones (*Hassim's Daughter*), Andres de Segurola (*Guido*), Arthur Stone (*British Soldier*), Torben Meyer (*German Soldier*), Edward Martindel (*Fullerton*).

This film concerns Zulus in Africa, the end of WW I, and the tale of Hersholt. Hersholt takes his bride that he brought to Africa and gets entangled with warring tribes. A muddled independent film that was shot in Technicolor which is about as murky as the story. Shooting in the color process throughout the film was a formidable job at the time when even sound was a big deal.

d, Al Rogell; w, Tom Miranda, Winifred Dunn (based on a story by Ferdinand Schumann-Heink, John Reinhardt); ph, Charles Boyle (2-color Technicolor); m, James C. Bradford; art d, Andre Chautin.

Action Adventure   (PR:A MPAA:NR)

MAMBO** 1/2** (1955, Ital.) 94m PAR bw

Silvana Mangano *(Giovanna Masetti)*, Michael Rennie *(Count Enrico)*, Vittorio Gassmann *(Mario Rossi)*, Shelley Winters *(Tony Burns)*, Katherine Dunham *(Herself)*, Mary Clare, Eduardo Ciannelli, Julie Robinson, Walter Zappolini.

Sultry, voluptuous Mangano is a penniless young woman who is seen by a wealthy nobleman, Rennie, at a party when she does a sizzling mambo dance, and he helps further her ambitions as a dancer by enrolling her in a dance troupe run by Winters. She, meanwhile, is lusted after by sleazy, lascivious Gassmann who is all carnality and earth. Rennie, on the other hand, expresses ethereal love for Mangano and offers her a gentle and problem-free life if she will marry him. She defers to Gassmann whose greedy instincts are heightened when he learns that Rennie is terminally ill. He encourages Mangano to marry Rennie and wait until he dies so she can inherit his fortune and turn it over to him. She marries Rennie, who treats her with great kindness, and she returns his love before he dies. When she receives the inheritance, Mangano gives away the money and rejects the shocked Gassmann. Mangano returns to dance with Winters' troupe a wiser but sadder lady. Mangano sizzles the screen in her role of sensuous dancer and reveals a stunning figure during her slit-skirt routines. Rennie is princely and effective in his role of the gentleman and Gassmann is appropriately hateful as the conniving and repulsive lover. He and Mangano do a reprise of their roles in better films such as ANNA (1951) and BITTER RICE (1950). Winters is not impressive mostly due to a vaguely written role. The photography is poor, the sets murkily lit, and the film often offers eyestrain.

p, Dino de Laurentis, Carlo Ponti; d, Robert Rossen; w, Guido Piovene, Ivo Perilli, Ennio De Concini, Rossen; ph, Harold Rosson; m, Nino Rota, A. F. Lavagnino, Bernardo Noriega; ed, Adriana Novelli; md, Franco Ferrara; art d, Andre Andrejeff; cos, Jack Pratt, Guido Coltellacci; ch, Katherine Dunham.

Drama **(PR:C MPAA:NR)**

MAME** 1/2** (1974) 132m ABC/WB c

Lucille Ball *(Mame)*, Robert Preston *(Beauregard)*, Beatrice Arthur *(Vera)*, Bruce Davison *(Older Patrick)*, Joyce Van Patten *(Sally Cato)*, Don Porter *(Mr. Upson)*, Audrey Christie *(Mrs. Upson)*, Jane Connell *(Agnes Gooch)*, Kirby Furlong *(Young Patrick)*, John McGiver *(Mr. Babcock)*, Doria Cook *(Gloria Upson)*, Bobbi Jordan *(Pegeen)*, George Chiang *(Ito)*, Roger Price *(Teacher)*.

Some fictional characters are foolproof and can withstand even the most lumbering interpretation. One might have thought that would apply to Mame Dennis, the plucky heroine who captivated readers in Patrick Dennis' novel, then went to the stage in Lawrence and Lee's play, then came back as a musical with Angela Lansbury and finally came up short with this version that featured a miscast Lucille Ball. By adding the music (and excellent music it was, too, with a few hits) and larding it over with production values, the insouciance of the original Rosalind Russell film began by breathing heavily and continued from there until it lay exhausted under the heavy weight of Ball's frog-voiced performance. Add to that Bea Arthur sounding like a basso profundo, and the effect of their scenes is like hearing two gravelly radio announcers meeting on the street. The story remains the same with Ball, during Prohibition, taking nephew Furlong to a progressive education school, trying her hand at show business, and eventually marrying the incredibly wealthy Preston, a southerner who takes her down to the ol' plantation where everyone sings the title song, followed by the well-known scene where she attempts to ride a horse in the fox hunt and commits a serious breach of etiquette when she passes the Master of the Hounds, then the hounds, then the fox. In the last reel, Preston dies and Ball has to contend with her nephew, played by Davison, as he grows older, taking up with vapid debutante Cook and her bigoted parents, Porter and Christie. It all lies there like a bad Austrian meal. Onna White's choreography is just fair and not the best effort from the woman who staged some of the finest musical numbers ever seen in films, for OLIVER! (1968). Still, she did the best with whom she had and Ball, although once a Goldwyn Girl and a high-stepper, had barely enough energy to step low. The sets and costumes are good, and Saks' direction is as quick-paced and as fluffy as a roll of Charmin toilet tissue. The only problem is . . . you can't squeeze a movie. Jerry Herman's superior score included: "Mame," "We Need a Little Christmas," "If He Walked Into My Life," "Bosom Buddies," "It's Today," "Loving You," "My Best Girl," "What Do I Do Now? (Gooch's Song)," "Open a New Window," "The Man in the Moon," "St. Bridget," "The Letter." It is interesting to see how the musical came about by watching the Roz Russell version, then this one, and discovering that many of the songs derived from the dialog in the first, most notably "We Need a Little Christmas," which has since become a Christmas standard. Writer-publisher-raconteur Roger Price is very funny as the mad nudist teacher who runs Furlong's progressive school.

p, Robert Fryer, James Cresson; d, Gene Saks; w, Paul Zindel (based on the musical and straight play by Jerome Lawrence, Jerry Herman, Robert E. Lee from the novel *Auntie Mame* by Patrick Dennis); ph, Phil Lathrop (Panavision, Technicolor); ed, Maury Winetrobe; md, Ralph Burns, Billy Byers; art d, Harold Michelson; cos, Theadora van Runkle; ch, Onna White, Martin Allen.

Musical Comedy **Cas.** **(PR:A MPAA:PG)**

MAMI (SEE: MAMMY, 1937, Hung.)

MAMMA DRACULA* (1980, Bel./Fr.) 90m Valisa Films-SND/UGC c

Louise Fletcher *(Mamma Dracula/Countess Elizabeth Bathory)*, Maria Schneider *(Nancy Hawaii)*, Marc-Henri Wajnberg *(Vladimir)*, Alexander Wajnberg *(Ladislas)*, Jimmy Shuman *(Van Bloed)*, Michel Israel *(Rosa)*, Jess Hahn *(Superintendent)*.

A poor vampire spoof that has Fletcher (ONE FLEW OVER THE CUCKOO'S NEST, 1975) and Schneider (LAST TANGO IN PARIS, 1973) heading the cast. How two talented actresses can be found in a piece of junk like this is a puzzle. The film was directed by the man who did the X-rated cartoon SHAME OF THE JUNGLE and it seems he forgot he was directing humans instead of pieces of paper. Fletcher is Countess Elizabeth Bathory, who bathes in the blood of virgins to stay young. Virgins are in short supply these days and the Countess has a doctor developing synthetic blood while her sons kidnap young women from their fashion boutique.

p&d, Boris Szulzinger; w, Szulzinger, Pierre Sterckx, Marc-Henri Wajnberg; ph, Willy Kurant; m, Roy Budd; ed, Claude Cohen; cos, Mouchy Houblinne; makeup, Pascale Kellen.

Comedy **(PR:O MPAA:NR)**

MAMMA ROMA**** (1962, Ital.) 110m Arco/Cineriz bw

Anna Magnani *(Mamma Roma)*, Ettore Garofalo *(Ettore)*, Franco Citti *(Carmine)*, Silvana Corsini *(Bruna)*, Luisa Loiano *(Blancofiore)*.

Pasolini's second film after his debut film ACCATTONE! (1961) with Magnani as a prostitute who tries to start a new life. With her son, Garofalo, they move to a new part of town and she tries to make a living legitimately, but her past keeps popping up. She is forced occasionally to go back to the red-light district when money becomes scarce. Her son becomes a thief, and is caught and killed. The mood of the film is dismal and lingers long after the closing credits roll. Strongly realistic and one of Pasolini's best and most accessible films.

p, Alfredo Bini; d&w, Pier Paolo Pasolini; ph, Tonino delli Colli; m, Carlo Rustichelli; ed, Nino Baragli.

Drama **(PR:C MPAA:NR)**

MAMMY** 1/2** (1930) 83m WB bw-c

Al Jolson *(Al Fuller)*, Lois Moran *(Nora Meadows)*, Louise Dresser *(Mrs. Fuller)*, Lowell Sherman *(Westy)*, Hobart Bosworth *(Meadows)*, Tully Marshall *(Slats)*, Mitchell Lewis *(Tambo)*, Jack Curtis *(Sheriff)*, Stanley Fields *(Pig Eyes)*, Ray Cooke *(Props)*.

There's a bit of controversy about how this movie came to be. James Gleason, the actor-writer, is credited in some quarters with the original play but so is Irving Berlin. Be that as it may, the story concerns a minstrel show and all of the desperate attempts at keeping the presentation afloat. Jolson and Lewis are "end men" in the show and Sherman, playing Will West (who was the best emcee [interlocutor] of his day), is the leader of the pack. Moran's father, Bosworth, owns the show and she is in love with Sherman, who has a roving eye. Jolson, in order to help Moran get some sort of rise out of Sherman, makes a move on her but Sherman barely notices. Jolson is being fleeced at cards by some guys (and is drunk in the process. More about that later.) and Sherman drags him out of the game, then tells Lewis, the head fleecer, to make good the money or pay for his conniving. Lewis switches bullets in a prop gun and Sherman is wounded on stage when Jolson fires the weapon, not knowing that real ammunition has been substituted. Jolson is nabbed by the cops but escapes to see Dresser, his mother. She tells him to give himself up and he is on his way to doing that when Lewis admits he made the ammunition switch and Jolson is free. It's not a funny film, except when they do their minstrel routines. One interesting note is that part of the picture, the minstrel show, is done in bright Technicolor and pops out hard on the eyes after seeing the black and white. We do know that Berlin wrote most of the score that includes: "To My Mammy," "Across the Breakfast Table," "Looking at You," "Let Me Sing and I'm Happy," "Knight of the Road," and "Yes, We Have No Bananas" (with Frank Silver and Irving Cohn) which is sung to the music of Verdi's "Miserere " from "Il Trovatore." Van Winkle gets credit for "Who Paid the Rent?" and "The Albany Night Boat" appears to be a traditional number. Legend has it that Jolson actually drank two bottles of alcohol to add realism to his drunk scenes. Watching him play a sot, we can believe it.

p, Walter Morosco; d, Michael Curtiz; w, Joseph Jackson, Gordon Rigby (based on the play "Mr. Bones" by Irving Berlin and/or James Gleason); ph, Barney McGill (Technicolor); m, Berlin, Giuseppe Verdi.

Musical/Comedy **(PR:A MPAA:NR)**

MAN, THE** (1972) 93m ABC Circle/PAR c

James Earl Jones *(Douglas Dilman)*, Martin Balsam *(Jim Talley)*, Burgess Meredith *(Sen. Watson)*, Lew Ayres *(Noah Calvin)*, William Windom *(Arthur Eaton)*, Barbara Rush *(Kay Eaton)*, Georg Stanford Brown *(Robert Wheeler)*, Janet MacLachlan *(Wanda)*, Martin Brooks *(Wheeler's Lawyer)*, Jack Benny *(Himself)*, Simon Scott *(Hugh Gaynor)*, Patric Knowles *(South African Consul)*, Anne Seymour *(Ma Blore)*, Gilbert Green *(Congressman Hand)*, Lawrence Cook *(Congressman Streller)*, Vince Howard *(Congressman Eckworth)*, Leonard Stone *(Congressman Parmel)*, Philip Bourneuf *(Chief Justice Williams)*, Ted Hartley *(Press Secretary)*, Bob DoQui *(Webson)*, Elizabeth Ross *(Mrs. Smelker)*, Reginald Fenderson *(Rev. Otis Waldren)*, Edward Faulkner *(Secret Service Agent)*, Barry Russo *(Haley)*, Gary Walberg *(Pierce)*, Howard K. Smith *(Himself)*, William Lawrence *(Himself)*, Lew Brown *(Reporter Gilbert)*, Charles Lampkin *(Congressman Walding)*.

Jones becomes the first black President in this adaptation of Irving Wallace's bestseller. When the President and speaker of the house are killed by a collapsing building in Germany and the vice president is bedridden with a stroke, President Pro Tem of the Senate Jones becomes President. Jones attempts to prove that he is the top executive and deserves the respect of the office. Balsam is his chief advisor, Meridith the racist Southern senator, and Rush is Jones' over-ambitious wife. The screenplay was written by the creator of TV's "The Twilight Zone," Rod Serling.

p, Lee Rich; d, Joseph Sargent; w, Rod Serling (based on a novel by Irving Wallace); ph, Edward C. Rosson (Eastmancolor); m, Jerry Goldsmith; ed, George Nicholson; art d, James G. Hulsey; set d, James I. Berkey; cos, John Perry; makeup, Robert Sidell.

Drama **(PR:A MPAA:G)**

MAN, A WOMAN, AND A BANK, A ** 1/2
(1979, Can.) 100m Bennett Films/AE c (AKA: A VERY BIG WITHDRAWAL)

Donald Sutherland *(Reese)*, Brooke Adams *(Stacey)*, Paul Mazursky *(Norman)*, Allan Magicovsky *(Peter)*, Leigh Hamilton *(Marie)*, Nick Rice *(Gino)*, Peter Erlich *(Jerry)*, Paul Rothery *(Steve)*, Elizabeth Barclay *(Laura)*, Leanne Young *(Girl No.2)*, Sharon Spurrell, Tibbi Landers, Annette Dupuis *(Models)*, Jackson Davies, Walter Marsh *(Guards)*, Alex Willows *(Junior Shipping Clerk)*, Robert Forsythe *(Senior Shipping Clerk)*, Eunice Thompson *(Vault Lady)*, Bob Hughes *(Elevator Repair Guard)*, Alex Kliner *(Used Car Salesman)*, Cam Lane *(Citation Cop)*, Howard Hughes *(Van Cop)*, Fred Latremouille *(Duty Officer)*, David Glyn-Jones *(Locksmith)*.

Sutherland and Mazursky play an unlikely pair of bank robbers who use their computer expertise to pull a fast one that nets them millions. Adams plays the girl who falls head-over-heels for Sutherland, naive to his scheming. Enjoyment of this picture derives mainly from the lively performances of Sutherland and Mazursky (the director of AN UNMARRIED WOMAN, 1978, and NEXT STOP, GREENWICH VILLAGE, 1976), who seem interested in just having a good time. Director Black is sharp enough to recognize when to allow his actors a free hand.

p, Peter Samuelson, John B. Bennett; d, Noel Black; w, Raynold Gideon, Bruce A. Evans, Stuart Margolin (based on a story by Gideon, Evans); ph, Jack Cardiff; m, Bill Conti; ed, Carl Kress; prod d, Anne Pritchard.

Crime/Comedy **Cas.** **(PR:C MPAA:PG)**

MAN, A WOMAN AND A KILLER, A ** 1/2 (1975) 78m Schmidt c

Richard A. Richardson *(Dick)*, Edward Nylund *(Ed)*, Caroline Zaremba *(Z)*.

This offbeat independent feature from San Francisco has enough quirks and energy to overcome the hazards of low-budget filmmaking. Richardson is a paranoiac who believes someone is out to kill him. A real feeling for the city's atmosphere is nicely captured by the cast, as well as some original, highly inventive ideas. At one point San Franciscan dialog, complete with phrases indigenous to the city, is translated to the audience through subtitles. One of the co-directors, Wayne Wang, became a successful independent filmmaker later on with his Chinatown slices-of-life, including CHAN IS MISSING (1982) and DIM SUM.

p, Richard R. Schmidt; d, Schmidt, Wayne Wang; w, Richard A. Richardson, Schmidt, Wang; ph&ed, Schmidt.

Comedy-Drama **(PR:O MPAA:NR)**

MAN ABOUT THE HOUSE, A ** (1947, Brit.) 95m BL bw

Margaret Johnston *(Agnes Isit)*, Dulcie Gray *(Ellen Isit)*, Kieron Moore *(Salvatore)*, Guy Middleton *(Sir Benjamin Dench)*, Felix Aylmer *(Richard Sanctuary)*, Lilian Braithwaite *(Mrs. Armitage)*, Jone Salinas *(Maria)*, Maria Fimiani *(Assunta)*, Reginald Purdell *(Higgs)*, Fulvia de Priamo *(Gita)*, Nicola Esposito *(Antonina)*, Wilfred Caithness *(Solicitor)*, Victor Rietti, Andrea Malandrinos *(Peasants)*.

Johnston and Gray are two English spinsters who inherit a villa in Naples in the early 20th Century. When they arrive they find Moore, the handsome caretaker, and he marries Johnston. He poisons her because the villa and land had belonged to his family and he wants them back. Gray brings in Middleton, an English doctor, who uncovers the murder. When the doctor confronts Moore with the facts the two fight and Moore plunges to his death from a clifftop.

p, Edward Black; d, Leslie Arliss; w, Arliss, J.B. Williams (based on the novel by Francis Brett Young and play by John Perry); ph, Georges Perinal; m, Nicholas Brodsky; ed, Russell Lloyd; md, Philip Green; art d, Andre Andrejew; set d, Alex Waugh; cos, G.K. Benda; spec eff, W. Percy Day; makeup, Charles Parker.

Mystery Thriller **(PR:A MPAA:NR)**

MAN ABOUT TOWN * 1/2 (1932) 71m FOX bw

Warner Baxter *(Stephen Morrow)*, Karen Morley *(Helena)*, Conway Tearle *(Bob Ashley)*, Leni Stengel *(Countess Vonesse)*, Lawrence Grant *(Count Vonesse)*, Alan Mowbray *(Ivan Boris)*, Lillian Bond *(Carlotta Cortez)*, Halliwell Hobbes *(Hilton)*, Noel Madison *(Tony)*, Noel Francis *(Hazel)*.

Baxter is an American secret service agent and Tearle is the British ambassador to the U.S. in this confused drama. They both fall in love with Morley and it ruins their friendship. Morley marries Tearle even though she loves Baxter. Throw in blackmail and a murder, and you have a B picture that holds no interest.

d, John Francis Dillon; w, Leon Gordon (based on the novel by Denison Clift); ph, James Wong Howe.

Spy/Romance **(PR:A MPAA:NR)**

MAN ABOUT TOWN ** 1/2 (1939) 85m PAR bw

Jack Benny *(Bob Temple)*, Dorothy Lamour *(Diana Wilson)*, Edward Arnold *(Sir John Arlington)*, Binnie Barnes *(Lady Arlington)*, Monty Woolley *(Dubois)*, Isabel Jeans *(Mme. Dubois)*, Phil Harris *(Ted Nash)*, Betty Grable *(Susan)*, E.E. Clive *(Hotchkiss)*, Eddie Anderson *(Rochester)*, Leonard Mudie *(Gibson)*, Pina Troupe *(Themselves)*, Peggy Steward *(Mary)*, Patti Sacks *(Jane)*, Matty Malneck Orchestra, the Merriel Abbott Dancers *(Themselves)*, Herbert Evans *(Englishman)*, Clifford Severn *(English Bellboy)*, Cyril Thornton *(Walter)*, Kay Linaker *(Receptionist)*.

Not one of Jack Benny's best but there's enough good fun and belly laughs to satisfy all but the most finicky. Benny is a Broadway producer on a trip to London. He yearns for *l'amour* with singer Lamour but she finds him a bore with no sex appeal. In order to make her jealous, he begins to flirt with Barnes. Barnes and Jeans have husbands, Arnold and Woolley, who are not paying enough attention to them so the women use Benny to arouse their husbands' ire and jealousy. The two men go after Benny but he is saved by the intervention of Anderson, his long-suffering valet. In the end, Lamour falls for Benny and the picture concludes. It was the kind of movie that you watch, laugh at, and don't recall the next day. Betty Grable was to have the Lamour role but she had to have an emergency appendectomy. She returned before the end of shooting to do one of the musical numbers. The songs are undistinguished. They include: "Strange Enchantment" (Frank Loesser, Frederick Hollander, sung by Dorothy Lamour), "Bluebirds in the Moonlight" (Ralph Rainger, Leo Robin), "Fidgety Joe" (Loesser, Matty Malneck, sung by Betty Grable), and "That Sentimental Sandwich" (Loesser, Hollander, sung by Lamour and Phil Harris). Benny tapped Harris and Anderson from his popular radio show and didn't play his usual persona of the penny-pinching, epicene radio star. The very best scenes were between Anderson and Benny. They had developed their timing to such a fine edge that there was never a dull moment when they were on screen in any movie. Several variety bits including the Merriel Abbott Dancers, and as neat a group of pulchritudinous Petty Girls as anyone will ever lay eyes upon. Benny was one of the country's top radio stars and audiences who had been listening to him for years couldn't get enough of him on screen. He, Bob Hope, and George Burns probably lasted longer than any other comedians in show business. Hope is funny when he gets good material from his army of writers, Burns is the ultimate straight man, but Benny was funny without saying a word or moving a muscle. Now *that's* funny.

p, Arthur Hornblow, Jr.; d, Mark Sandrich; w, Morrie Ryskind (based on the story by Ryskind, Allan Scott, Zion Meyers); ph, Ted Tetzlaff; ed, LeRoy Stone; md, Victor Young; art d, Hans Dreier, Robert Usher; ch, LeRoy Prinz.

Comedy/Musical **(PR:AA MPAA:NR)**

MAN ABOUT TOWN **
(1947, Fr.) 89m Pathe/RKO bw (LE SILENCE EST D'OR)

Maurice Chevalier *(Emile)*, Francois Perier *(Jacques)*, Marcelle Derrien *(Madeleine)*, Dany Robin *(Lucette)*, Robert Pizani *(Duperrier)*, Raymond Cordy *(Curly)*, Paul Olivier *(The Cashier)*, Roland Armontel *(Celestin)*, Gaston Modot *(Cameraman)*, Bernard La Jarrige *(Paolo)*, Paul Demange *(Sultan)*.

A light, frothy farce that marked the return of Chevalier to the screen after seven years and was Clair's first French movie after a dozen years. Although the picture took some awards (Grand Prize at Brussels and the Critic's Circle Award at Locarno), it wasn't all that good and surely fell far below Clair's best works. Shot at the Joinville Studios in Paris, MAN ABOUT TOWN used Chevalier's narration to bridge story gaps and it was a clunky decision. It's 1906 Paris. Derrien, a naive country girl, comes to town to find her missing father, an actor. In order to locate him she asks for help from sixtyish producer-director Chevalier, who had once courted her mother in days of yore. Derrien learns that her dad is on the road in a show so she will stay in Paris and await his return. Chevalier offers her the opportunity to observe the new film medium and asks if she'd like to play in his latest effort. She agrees to do that and Chevalier, upon noting the crew's lust, warns them to stay away from this *naif*. When the crew adheres to Chevalier's command, Derrien is perplexed because she usually has to fend men off. That bewilderment turns to tears when she feels that no one loves her. Chevalier, by this time, has fallen for Derrien, but he cannot bring himself to voice that. Later, Derrien meets Perier, a handsome young actor, and he is also taken by her but doesn't know how to handle the situation, so he asks Chevalier for his advice. Chevalier is now in a Cyrano position as he aids Perier but still can't tell Derrien how he feels. Meanwhile, he is professionally puzzled as he can't come up with an ending for the film he is shooting. When Derrien confesses that she loves Perier, Chevalier realizes he must step aside for youth and that also gives him the idea for his film's ending, as he rewrites it so the hero, not the villain, gets the girl at the fadeout. There's only one song in the film, "Place Pigalle," and the plot would surely have been aided by music, but they chose to make it a straight comedy and it barely succeeded on that level. The most fun was had when they burlesqued the fledgeling film industry and had several Gallic equivalents of the Keystone Studios crowd. (In French; English commentary.)

p&d, Rene Clair; w, Clair, Robert Pirosh (based on a story by Clair); ph, Armand Thirard; md, Georges Van Parys; art d, Leon Barsacq; cos, Christian Dior; m/l, "Place Pigalle," M. Alstone, Maurice Chevalier (sung by Chevalier).

Comedy **(PR:A MPAA:NR)**

MAN ACCUSED * (1959) 58m Danziger/UA bw

Ronald Howard *(Bob Jenson)*, Carol Marsh *(Kathy Riddle)*, Ian Fleming *(Sir Thomas)*, Catherina Ferraz *(Anna)*, Brian Nissen *(Derek)*, Robert Dorning *(Beckett)*, Stuart Saunders *(Curran)*, Colin Tapley *(Inspector)*, Howard Lang, Gordon Needham, Graham Ashley, Diana Chesney, Kenneth Edwardes.

Howard becomes engaged to Marsh, a baronet's daughter, and his future looks good. But that would not make much of a film, so a hackneyed, formula plot involving his frameup on a murder charge is introduced. Howard manages to break out of jail and, to no one's surprise, finds the real killers. He hands them over to the law and can then marry his girl. This poorly made work follows each convention of a wronged-man plot and ultimately offers nothing at all.

p, Edward J. Danziger, Harry Lee Danziger; d, Montgomery Tully; w, Mark Grantham; ph, Jimmy Wilson.

Crime **(PR:C MPAA:NR)**

MAN AFRAID ** (1957) 83m UNIV bw

George Nader *(Rev. David Collins)*, Phyllis Thaxter *(Lisa Collins)*, Tim Hovey *(Michael Collins)*, Eduard Franz *(Carl Simmons)*, Harold J. Stone *(Lt. Marlin)*, Judson Pratt *(Wilbur Fletcher)*, Reta Shaw *(Nurse Willis)*, Butch Bernard *(Ronnie Fletcher)*, Mabel Albertson *(Maggie)*, Martin Milner *(Ship Hamilton)*.

An average melodrama about Nader, who shoots and kills a teenage burglar who broke into his family's house. Nader's wife, he and his son fear for their lives when the boy's father, Franz, vows revenge. The angered father corners Nader's son, Hovey, under a pier and Nader persuades the grief-crazed father not to kill his son and asks Franz to forgive him.

p, Gordon Kay; d, Harry Keller; w, Herb Meadow (based on a story by Daniel B. Ullman); ph, Russell Metty (CinemaScope); m, Henry Mancini; ed, Ted J. Kent; art d, Alexander Golitzen, Philip Barber; cos, Bill Thomas.

Drama (PR:A MPAA:NR)

MAN AGAINST MAN** (1961, Jap.) 116m Toho c (OTOKO TAI OTOKO)

Toshiro Mifune, Ryo Ikebe, Takashi Shimura, Ymui Shirakawa, Akemi Kita, Yuriko Hoshi, Yuzo Kayama, Jun Tazaki, Akihiko Hirata, Yutaka Sada.

Two men, who were friends during the war, set up their own businesses and find their lives crossing again. Gangsters want the one man's shipping business and they plan to meet at the other man's nightclub. Things do not work out and the men join forces to fight the mobsters.

d, Senkichi Taniguchi; w, Ichiro Ikeda, Ei Ogawa; ph, Rokuro Nishigaki (Tohoscope, Eastmancolor).

Crime Drama (PR:C MPAA:NR)

MAN AGAINST WOMAN*½ (1932) 70m COL bw

Jack Holt (Johnny McCloud), Lillian Miles (Lola Parker), Walter Connolly (Mossie Ennis), Gavin Gordon (Georgie Perry), Arthur Vinton (Happy O'Neill), Emmett Corrigan (Christy), Clarence Muse (Smoke Johnson), Harry Seymour (Brodie), Jack LaRue (Alberti), Katherine Claire Ward (Landlady).

Holt is a detective in love with torch singer Miles. She hooks up with criminal Connolly and they go off to Bermuda. Holt is suckered into capturing the crook and bringing him back to his gang (he had double-crossed them). When Holt delivers Connolly the gang decides to kill both of them, but a squad of motorcycle police officers prevent it. This leaves Holt open to start a relationship with Miles.

d, Irving Cummings; w, Jo Swerling (based on a story by Keene Thompson); ph, Teddy Tetzlaff.

Crime (PR:A MPAA:NR)

MAN ALIVE*½ (1945) 70m RKO bw

Pat O'Brien (Speed), Adolphe Menjou (Kismat), Ellen Drew (Connie), Rudy Vallee (Gordon Tolliver), Fortunio Bonanova (Prof. Zorado), Joseph Crehan (Doc Whitney), Jonathan Hale (Osborne), Minna Gombell (Aunt Sophie), Jason Robards (Fletcher), Jack Norton (Willie the Wino), Donn Gift (Messenger Boy), Myrna Dell (Sister), Carl "Alfalfa" Switzer (Ignatius), Gertrude Short (Frowsy Dame), Robert Clarke (Cabby), Robert E. Homans (Uncle Barney).

O'Brien is Drew's husband who drinks too much when he finds out that she has invited one of her old admirers for a visit. On the drive home, he gets into a car accident and is reported dead although he is alive. O'Brien's friend Menjou, who is a magician, advises him to dress like a ghost and haunt his wife and her ex-beau, Vallee. The film cost $738,000, but the humor is only worth about $3.

p, Robert Fellows; d, Ray Enright; w, Edwin Harvey Blum (based on a story by Jerry Cady, John Tucker Battle); ph, Frank Redman; m, Leigh Harline; ed, Marvin Coil; md, C. Bakaleinikoff; art d, Albert D'Agostino, Al Herman; set d, Darrell Silvera, Victor Gangelin; spec eff, Vernon L. Walker.

Comedy (PR:A MPAA:NR)

MAN ALONE, A*** (1955) 95m REP c

Ray Milland (Wes Steele), Mary Murphy (Nadine Corrigan), Ward Bond (Gil Corrigan), Raymond Burr (Stanley), Arthur Space (Dr. Mason), Lee Van Cleef (Clantin), Alan Hale, Jr. (Anderson), Douglas Spencer (Henry Slocum), Thomas B. Henry (Maybanks), Grandon Rhodes (Luke Joiner), Martin Garralaga (Ortega), Kim Spalding (Sam Hall), Howard J. Negley (Wilson), Julian Rivero (Tio Rubio), Lee Roberts (Higgs), Minerva Urecal (Mrs. Maule), Thorpe Whiteman (Boy), Dick Rich (Kincaid), Frank Hagney (Dorfman).

Milland makes his directorial debut in this excellent western. Milland is a gunfighter who hides out in the house of sheriff Bond when a lynch mob wants to hang him for two murders. The sheriff has yellow fever and his daughter, Murphy, helps Milland prove that banker Burr is the one behind the murders and the robbery of the stagecoach. Bond has also been in collaboration with Burr, but comes to Milland's defense in the end. After Burr and his gang are taken care of, Milland settles down in the town with Murphy because he figures the next town will be just as bad.

p, Herbert J. Yates; d, Ray Milland; w, John Tucker Battle (based on a story by Mort Briskin); ph, Lionel Lindon (Trucolor); m, Victor Young; ed, Richard L. Van Enger; md, Young; art d, Walter Keller; cos, Adele Palmer.

Western **Cas.** (PR:A MPAA:NR)

MAN AND A WOMAN, A***½

(1966, Fr.) 102m Les Films 13/AA c & tinted bw (UN HOMME ET UNE FEMME)

Anouk Aimée (Anne Gauthier), Jean-Louis Trintignant (Jean-Louis Duroc), Pierre Barouh (Pierre Gauthier), Valerie Lagrange (Valerie Duroc), Simone Paris (Head Mistress), Antoine Sire (Antoine Duroc), Souad Amidou (Francoise Gauthier), Yane Barry (Mistress of Jean-Louis), Paul Le Person (Garage Man), Henri Chemin (Jean-Louis Codriver), Gerard Sire (Announcer).

Tres, tres French, undeniably romantic, intensely visual, A MAN AND A WOMAN won two Oscars: one for Best Story/Screenplay, the other for Best Foreign Film. When first released, many critics felt the picture was conspicuously artsy and lacking in any true story content, but time appears to have improved the perception of the movie and Lelouch's artful (rather than artsy) handling of the love story has now been acknowledged as an important contribution to the films of the 1960s. A man, Trintignant, and a woman, Aimée, meet at the boarding school where both have children in attendance. Aimée misses her train ride to Paris and Trintignant offers to drive her home. As they drive, they learn about each other. She is an actress and a widow and he is a race car driver. When they meet again the following weekend

with their children, Sire and Amidou, they share a picnic and a beautiful day of sailing. He now admits that his late wife committed suicide because she couldn't handle the anxiety she felt each time he went out to race. He'd had a near-fatal accident some years before but refused to give up racing, and her reaction was to take her own life. They part and he goes to Monaco for a race and receives a telegram from Aimée stating that she loves him. He responds by driving all night to see her, but when they finally get together, she cannot totally give herself to him, as the memory of her late husband haunts her. He is disappointed and thinks that their brief relationship is now over. She gets on the train to Paris and he is driving back, then changes his mind about going home and races for the station, where he is waiting when her train arrives. She disembarks, he runs to her, picks her up in his arms, swings her around and fin, it's over. A MAN AND A WOMAN was probably responsible for more love affairs in 1966 than any other movie. Young couples could hardly wait to leave the theater and get to their bedrooms after seeing the movie. Francis Lai's catchy score aided matters greatly and the major thematic music is still recognizable two decades later. Many of Lelouch's techniques (switching from color to black-and-white and tinted film, as well as his use of slow motion) are studied in film schools today and quite rightly so, as he has always been a forerunner in the realm of French film blanc.

p&d, Claude Lelouch; w, Lelouch, Pierre Uytterhoeven (based on a story by Lelouch); ph, Lelouch (Eastmancolor); m, Francis Lai; ed, Lelouch, G. Boisser, Claude Barrois; art d, Robert Luchaire; m/l, Lai, Pierre Barouh, "Samba Saravah," Baden Powell, Vincius de Moraes (sung by Nicole Croisille, Jean-Claude Briodin, Barouh).

Drama **Cas.** (PR:A-C MPAA:NR)

MAN AND BOY*½ (1972) 98m Jemmin/Levitt-Pickman c

Bill Cosby (Caleb Revers), Gloria Foster (Ivy Revers), Leif Erickson (Sheriff Mossman), George Spell (Billy Revers), Doublas Turner Ward (Lee Christmas), John Anderson (Stretch), Henry Silva (Caine), Dub Taylor (Atkins), Shelley Morrison (Rosita), Yaphet Kotto (Nate Hodges).

A boring western with Cosby chasing horse thieves in the old West. Cosby is a homesteader who has his horses stolen by Ward. Kotto sets out with his son, Spell, to get them back. Their Odyssey across the Southwest is a total yawn.

p, Marvin Miller; d, E.W. Swackhamer; w, Harry Essex, Oscar Saul; ph, Arnold Rich (CFI Lab); m, J. J. Johnson; ed, John A. Martinelli; art d, Rolland Brooks; set d, Anthony Mondello; cos, Glenn Wright; m/l, "Better Days," Johnson (sung by Bill Withers).

Western (PR:A MPAA:G)

MAN AND HIS MATE (SEE: ONE MILLION B.C., 1940)

MAN AND THE BEAST, THE**½

(1951, Arg.) 80m Sono bw (EL HOMBRE Y LA BESTIA; EL EXTRANO CASO DEL HOMBRE Y LA BESTIA; EL SENSACIONAL Y EXTRANO CASO DEL HOMBRE Y LA BESTIA; AKA: THE STRANGE CASE OF THE MAN AND THE BEAST)

Mario Soffici, Olga Zubarry, Jose Cibrian, Rafael Frontura.

An adaptation of Robert Louis Stevenson's Dr. Jekyll And Mr. Hyde that comes off rather well. Hyde is made up to look more like a vampire-like creature than a werewolf as in most of the Hollywood versions.

p&d, Mario Soffici; w, Soffici, Ulises Petit de Murat, Carlos Marin; ph, Antonio Merayo, Alberto Munoz.

Horror (PR:A MPAA:NR)

MAN AND THE MOMENT, THE** (1929) 75m FN-WB bw

Billie Dove (Joan), Rod LaRocque (Michel), Gwen Lee (Viola), Robert. Schable (Skippy), Charles Sellon (Joan's Guardian), George Bunny (Butler), Doris Dawson.

Dove and LaRocque are two young, wealthy adults who decide to get married to escape from their problems. Dove wants to get rid of her guardian and LaRocque wants to ditch the gold-digging blonde who is after him. They go through the ceremony and then they spend their wedding night on a yacht. Dove disappears the next day through a porthole with the blonde following her on the yacht and planning to ruin her reputation. Chase after chase with cars and planes and finally Dove and LaRocque end up staying together for good.

d, George Fitzmaurice; w, Agnes Christine Johnston, Paul Perez (based on a story by Elinor Glyn); ph, Sol Polito; cos, Max Ree.

Comedy/Drama (PR:A MPAA:NR)

MAN AND THE MONSTER, THE*

(1965, Mex.) 78m Cinematografica/Transinternational bw (EL HOMBRE Y EL MONSTRUO)

Enrique Rambal, Abel Salazar, Martha Roth, Ofelia Guilmain, Anita Blanch, Jose Chavez, Carlos Suarez, Maricarmen Vela.

A concert pianist sells his soul to the devil to become successful. The one drawback is when a certain piece of music is played he turns into a murdering monster. A concert manager suspects the pianist of a series of murders and proves it by playing that tune.

p, Abel Salazar; d, Rafael Baledon; w, Salazar; ph, Raul Martinez Solares; m, Gustavo Cesar Carrion; ed, Carlos Savage.

Horror (PR:A MPAA:NR)

MAN AT LARGE*½ (1941) 70m FOX bw

Marjorie Weaver (Dallas Davis), George Reeves (Bob Grayson), Richard Derr (Max), Steve Geray (Botany), Milton Parsons (Mr. Sartoris), Spencer Charters (Mr.

Gallon), Lucien Littlefield *(Mr. Jones),* Elisha Cook, Jr. *(Hotel Clerk),* Minerva Urecal *(Mrs. Jonas),* Bodil Ann Rosing *(Housekeeper),* Richard Lane *(Mr. Grundy),* Barbara Pepper *(Blonde),* William Edmunds *(Kisling),* George Cleveland *(Sheriff),* Kurt Katch *(Hans Brinker).*

Weaver is a newspaper reporter who is sent out to find an escaped Nazi flier. Reeves, an FBI man posing as a rival newsman, is also on the trail. Weaver causes some comical interference for Reeves as he tracks down the spy ring the flier is to meet up with.

p, Ralph Dietrich; d, Eugene Forde; w, John Larkin; ph, Virgil Miller; ed, John Brady; md, Emil Newman.

Spy **(PR:A MPAA:NR)**

MAN AT SIX (SEE: GABLES MYSTERY, THE, 1931, Brit.)

MAN AT THE CARLTON TOWER**

(1961, Brit.) 57m Merton Park/Anglo Amalgamated bw

Maxine Audley *(Lydia Daney),* Lee Montague *(Tim Jordan),* Allan Cuthbertson *(Supt. Cowley),* Terence Alexander *(Johnny Time),* Alfred Burke *(Harry Stone),* Nigel Green *(Lew Daney),* Nyree Dawn Porter *(Mary Greer),* Geoffrey Frederick *(Sgt. Pepper).*

When a Rhodesian jewel thief kills a policeman, the authorities just can't seem to locate the man. Enter an ex-cop turned sleuth, who gets on the trail and solves the crime. There are a few entertaining moments in this minor mystery, but not enough to make it anything special.

p, Jack Greenwood; d, Robert Tronson; w, Philip Mackie (based on the novel *The Man At The Carlton* by Edgar Wallace).

Crime/Mystery **(PR:C MPAA:NR)**

MAN AT THE TOP** (1973, Brit.) 87m Hammer-Dufton/Anglo-EMI c

Kenneth Haigh *(Joe Lampton),* Nanette Newman *(Lady Ackerman),* Harry Andrews *(Lord Ackerman),* William Lucas *(Marshall),* Clive Swift *(Massey),* Paul Williamson *(Tarrant),* John Collin *(Wisbech),* John Quentin *(Digby),* Danny Sewell *(Weston),* Charlie Williams *(George Harvey),* Anne Cunningham *(Mrs. Harvey),* Angela Bruce *(Joyce),* Margaret Heald *(Eileen),* Norma West *(Sarah Tarrant),* Jaron Yaltan *(Taranath),* Nell Brennan *(Waitress),* Verne Morgan *(Records Clerk),* Tim Brinton *(Newsreader),* Mary Maude *(Robin),* John Conteh *(Black Boxer),* Patrick McCann *(White Boxer).*

Adapted from a popular British TV show of the same title and with the same star, Haigh. He's worked his way up from his lower class beginnings to a good job in the business world. Haigh is still aiming his sights higher, and problems arise when his boss, Andrews, tries to put the blame for a bad business move on him.

p, Peter Charlesworth, Jock Jacobsen; d, Mike Vardy; w, Hugh Whitemore, John Junkin (based on characters created by John Braine); ph, Brian Probyn (Eastmancolor); m, Roy Budd; ed, Chris Barnes; art d, Don Picton.

Drama **(PR:A MPAA:NR)**

MAN BAIT** (1952, Brit.) 78m Lippert bw (GB: THE LAST PAGE)

George Brent *(John Harman),* Marguerite Chapman *(Stella),* Raymond Huntley *(Clive),* Peter Reynolds *(Jeff),* Diana Dors *(Ruby),* Eleanor Summerfield *(Vi),* Meredith Edwards *(Dale),* Harry Fowler *(Joe),* Conrad Phillips *(Todd),* Isabel Dean *(May).*

Brent is a bookstore owner who is blackmailed when his clerk, Dors, gets him to embrace her. Blackmail is the goal, and Reynolds persuades her to help him get money from Brent. They send a letter to Brent's invalid wife, which brings about her death. Brent pays the money and then Reynolds kills Dors. Brent is suspected of the murder, but is cleared when his secretary, Chapman, traps the killer. Pretty lightweight stuff for Hollywood veterans Brent and Chapman.

p, Anthony Hinds; d, Terence Fisher; w, Frederick Knott (based on a story by James Hadley Chase); ph, Walter Harvey; ed, Maurice Rootes.

Crime **(PR:A MPAA:NR)**

MAN BEAST*1/2 (1956) 67m Associated Producers bw

Rock Madison *(Lon Raynon),* Virginia Maynor *(Connie Hayward),* Tom Maruzzi *(Steve Cameron),* Lloyd Nelson *(Trevor Hudson),* George Wells Lewis *(Dr. Erickson),* George Skaff *(Varga),* Jack Haffner *(Kheon),* Wong Sing *(Trader).*

Maynor and Nelson put together an expedition to find Maynor's missing brother, who was lost in the Himalayas. They don't find Maynor's sibling, but find instead the Abominable Snowman who kills everyone in the expedition except Maynor and Nelson. A low budget exploitation film that was double-billed in the theaters with GODZILLA.

p&d, Jerry Warren; w, Arthur Cassidy; ph, Victor Fisher; m, Josef Zimanich; ed, James R. Sweeney.

Adventure **Cas.** **(PR:A MPAA:NR)**

MAN BEHIND THE GUN, THE** (1952) 82m WB c

Randolph Scott *(Maj. Callicut),* Patrice Wymore *(Lora Roberts),* Dick Wesson *("Monk"),* Philip Carey *(Capt. Roy Giles),* Lina Romay *(Chona Degnon),* Roy Roberts *(Mark Sheldon),* Morris Ankrum *(Bram Creegan),* Katharine Warren *(Phoebe Sheldon),* Alan Hale, Jr. *(Olof),* Douglas Fowley *(Buckley),* Tony Caruso *(Vic Sutro),* Clancy Cooper *("Kansas" Collins),* Robert Cabal *(Joaquin Murietta),* James Brown, Reed Howes, Rory Mallinson, John Logan, Vickie Raaf, Lee Morgan, Ray Spiker, Edward Hearn, Terry Frost, Charles Horvath, Art Millian, Rex Lease, Jack Parker, James Bellah, Billy Vincent, Albert Morin, Edward Colemans, Herbert Deans.

Scott is an undercover cavalry officer who goes out to Los Angeles to break a gang that wants to make Southern California a separate state. As he tries to track down the leader of the gang he falls in love with school teacher Wymore. Scott finally exposes senator Roberts who wants to build his own empire. Action is always in the forefront of this typical western.

p, Robert Sisk; d, Felix Feist; w, John Twist (based on a story by Robert Buckner); ph, Bert Glennon (Technicolor); m, David Buttolph; ed, Owen Marks.

Western **(PR:A MPAA:NR)**

MAN BEHIND THE MASK, THE**1/2

(1936, Brit.) 79m Joe Rock/MGM bw

Hugh Williams *(Nick Barclay),* Jane Baxter *(June Slade),* Maurice Schwartz *(The Master),* Donald Calthrop *(Dr. Walpole),* Henry Oscar *(Officer),* Peter Gawthorne *(Lord Slade),* Kitty Kelly *(Miss Weeks),* Ronald Ward *(Jimmy Slade),* George Merritt *(Mallory),* Reginald Tate *(Hayden),* Ivor Barnard *(Hewitt),* Hal Gordon *(Sergeant),* Barbara Everest, Wilfred Caithness, Moyna Fagan, Henry Caine, Syd Crossley, Gerald Fielding.

Baxter and Williams attend a masked ball, intending to elope at the night's end. What they don't count on is a madman who attacks the couple and takes Baxter hostage. The kidnaper takes on Williams' identity, using his guise to steal the golden Shield of Kahm (one of those mysterious icons only found in museums and movies) from Baxter's father. Williams and Baxter's father go looking for the kidnaper, and after a last minute rescue by authorities, the madman is revealed to be a crazed astronomer. This is pretty hokey stuff, but a spirited direction (an early effort from the director of THE RED SHOES and PEEPING TOM) manages to make this better than the material probably deserved.

p, Joe Rock; d, Michael Powell; w, Ian Hay, Syd Courtenay, Jack Byrd, Stanley Haynes (based on the novel *The Chase of the Golden Plate* by Jacques Futrelle); ph, Francis Carver.

Crime **(PR:A MPAA:NR)**

MAN BETRAYED, A* (1937) 58m REP bw

Eddie Nugent, Kay Hughes, Lloyd Hughes, John Wray, Edwin Maxwell, Theodore Von Eltz, Thomas E. Jackson, William Newell, Smiley Burnette, Christine Maple, John Hamilton, Ralf Harolde, Grace Durkin, Carleton Young, Mary Bovard, Sam Ash, Pat Gleason.

When Nugent is framed, Wray's hoodlums help prove his innocence. Lloyd Hughes is a young minister just back from Africa who also gets mixed up in this convoluted tale.

p, William Berke; d, John H. Auer; w, Dorrell McGowan, Stuart McGowan; ph, Ernest Miller.

Crime Drama **(PR:A MPAA:NR)**

MAN BETRAYED, A*1/2

(1941) 83m REP bw (GB: CITADEL OF CRIME; AKA: WHEEL OF FORTUNE)

John Wayne *(Lynn Hollister),* Frances Dee *(Sabra Cameron),* Edward Ellis *(Tom Cameron),* Wallace Ford *(Casey),* Ward Bond *(Floyd),* Harold Huber *(Morris Slade),* Alexander Granach *(T. Amato),* Barnett Parker *(George the Butler),* Ed Stanley *(Prosecutor),* Tim Ryan *(Mr. Wilson),* Harry Hayden *(Langworthy),* Russell Hicks *(Pringle),* Pierre Watkin *(Governor),* Ferris Taylor *(Mayor),* Joseph Crehan *(Newspaper Editor),* Robert E. Homans *(Traffic Cop),* Tristram Coffin *(Night Club Patron),* Dick Elliott *(Ward Heeler),* Joe Devlin *(Tramp),* Minerval Urecal *(Librarian).*

Wayne is a young small-town lawyer who arrives in the big city to prove that the death of a basketball player was actually a murder, not suicide. Meanwhile, he falls in love with Dee, the daughter of a corrupt politician (Ellis), and works to keep the girl without sacrificing his own principles.

p, Armand Schaefer; d, John Auer; w, Isabel Dawn, Tom Kilpatrick (based on a story by Jack Moffitt); ph, Jack Marta; ed, Charles Craft; md, Cy Feuer; art d, John Victor Mackay.

Drama **(PR:A MPAA:NR)**

MAN BETWEEN, THE*** (1953, Brit.) 100m London/UA bw

James Mason *(Ivo Kern),* Claire Bloom *(Susanne Mallison),* Hildegarde Neff *(Bettina),* Geoffrey Toone *(Martin),* Aribert Waescher *(Halendar),* Ernst Schroeder *(Kastner),* Dieter Krause *(Horst),* Hilde Sessak *(Lizzi),* Karl John *(Inspector Kleiber).*

A suspense thriller set during the days of the cold war, director Reed mines territory gone over already in THE THIRD MAN but changes the locale to Berlin. Bloom, a British miss, arrives in Berlin to holiday with her doctor brother, Toone, and his wife, Neff, a German national. Bloom finds mystery when Neff is tailed by Krause (who follows her on a bicycle), and is threatened on the phone. Neff and Bloom take a short day trip to East Berlin where they meet Mason, a one-time attorney who now deals in black market items as well as luring people wanted by the Communists across the line into the Eastern sector. Neff balks when Bloom decides to go ice skating with Mason, then, liking him and his charming ways, Bloom invites Mason to come to Toone's home for dinner. Later, Neff admits that she had once been married to Mason, a good man until Nazism made him a cynic. Neff has thought Mason died during the war, but since he's alive, that makes her a bigamist. Mason is using that to get Neff to help lure Schroeder back to the waiting guns of the Communists. Toone informs the West German police of Mason's plan and a trap is set that is ruined when Krause tells Mason about it. Bloom is kidnaped by the East Germans, who think she is Neff. Mason is struck by Bloom's naive ways and her belief that he can be saved from himself, so he aids her escape and a chase begins that takes them across rooftops, then driving through various sections of the city. They are about to flee successfully when Mason sees there is no way out, jumps from the vehicle, and is gunned down by the police as the van crosses the border to freedom. Stark, dingy, and dark, THE MAN BETWEEN never really catches fire, as it's hard to picture the craggy Mason and the radiant Bloom as potential lovers. The depressing backgrounds of Berlin must have kept many people from telling their travel agents that they wanted to go there on vacation. Lots of atmosphere but virtually no appeal to the emotions, which makes it similar to a latter-day film that covered some of the same ground, THE SPY WHO CAME IN FROM THE COLD.

p&d, Carol Reed; w, Harry Kurnitz, Eric Linklater (based on the novel *Susanne in Berlin* by Walter Ebert); ph, Desmond Dickinson; m, John Addison; ed, A.S. Bates; md, Muir Mathieson; art d, Andre Andrejew; cos, Bridget Sellers.

Spy Drama **(PR:A MPAA:NR)**

MAN CALLED ADAM, A** (1966) 103m Trace-Mark/EM bw

Sammy Davis, Jr. *(Adam Johnson)*, Ossie Davis *(Nelson Davis)*, Cicely Tyson *(Claudia Ferguson)*, Louis Armstrong *(Willie "Sweet Daddy" Ferguson)*, Frank Sinatra, Jr. *(Vincent)*, Peter Lawford *(Manny)*, Mel Torme *(Himself)*, Lola Falana *(Theo)*, Jeanette DuBois *(Martha)*, Johnny Brown *(Les)*, George Rhodes *(Leroy)*, Michael Silva *(George)*, Michael Lipton *(Bobby Gales)*, Kai Winding, Kenneth Tobey, Gerald S. O'Loughlin, Morris Erby, Michael V. Gazzo, Matt Russo, Will Hussing, Ted Beniades, Roy Glenn, Donald Crabtree, Elvera Davis, Brunetta Bernstein.

In this downbeat drama, Davis is a guilt-ridden jazz musician who blames himself for the car accident in which his family is killed. His bitterness and others' prejudices get in the way of his career, and when he walks off stage at a Cincinnati club, his gigs dry up. He meets Tyson, a civil right activist, but she rejects his advances. Lawford is an uncaring agent who sets up a tour for Davis and his band in the segregated south, where the white member of his troupe, Sinatra, Jr., is badly beaten by three white men. Stunned by the violence, Davis joins Armstrong on stage at a casino. He collapses, however, and dies backstage. Ike Jones was the first black to get producer credit in a major Hollywood movie. Songs include "All That Jazz," "Whisper To One," (Benny Carter), "Muskrat Ramble" (Edward Ory, Ray Gilbert), "I Want to Be Wanted"; "Playboy Theme"; "Back O'Town Blues"; "Someday Sweetheart." Davis' trumpet playing in the film was dubbed by Nat Adderly.

p, Ike Jones, James Waters, d, Leo Penn; w, Les Pine, Tina Rome; ph, Jack Priestly; m, Benny Carter; ed, Carl Lerner; art d, Charles Rosen; set d, Sam Robert.

Drama **(PR:C MPAA:NR)**

MAN CALLED BACK, THE* (1932) 79m TIF/Worldwide bw

Conrad Nagel *(Dr. David Yorke)*, Doris Kenyon *(Dianna St. Clair)*, John Halliday *(St. Clair)*, Juliette Compton *(Vivien Lawrence)*, Reginald Owen *(Dr. Atkins)*, Mona Maris *(Lilaya)*, Alan Mowbray *(King's Counsel)*, Gilbert Emery *(Defense Counsel)*, Mae Busch *(Rosie)*, John T. Murray *(Corlis)*.

Halliday commits suicide but attempts to frame his wife, Kenyon, by making it look like a murder. Nagel comes to the rescue, and Kenyon helps him overcome his drinking problem. A laughable piece of melodrama.

d, Robert Florey; w, Robert Presnell, Andrew Soutar (based on the book *Silent Thunder* by Soutar); ph, Henry Sharpe; ed, Martin G. Cohn.

Drama **(PR:C MPAA:NR)**

MAN CALLED DAGGER, A* (1967) 86m Global Screen Associates/MGM c

Paul Mantee *(Dick Dagger)*, Terry Moore *(Harper Davis)*, Jan Murray *(Rudolph Koffman/SS Obergruppenfuhrer Hans Leitel)*, Sue Anne Langdon *(Ingrid)*, Eileen O'Neill *(Erica)*, Maureen Arthur *(Joy)*, Leonard Stone *(Karl Rainer)*, Richard Kiel *(Otto)*, Mimi Dillard *(Girl in Auto)*, Bruno Ve Sota *(Dr. Grulik)*, Margie Nelson, Lenore Waring, Diane Neff, Martha Luttrell, Virginia Wood *(Ingrid's Girls)*.

With the popularity of the James Bond films and the spy spoof IN LIKE FLINT, spy spoofs surged. A MAN CALLED DAGGER, like most of the bunch, was a lesser effort. Mantee, the secret agent with a laser-beam wrist watch and other far-out and implausible gadgets, chases after ex-Nazi concentration camp commandant Murray. The agent is helped by female co-agent Moore, and together they prevent the former SS colonel's plot to brainwash world leaders.

p, Lewis M. Horwitz; d, Richard Rush; w, James Peatman, Robert S. Weekley (based on an idea by W.L. Riffs); ph, Laszlo [Leslie] Kovacs (Movielab Color); m, Steve Allen; ed, Len Miller, Tom Boutross, md, Ronald Stein; art d, Mike McCloskey, Glen Holse; cos, Vana Carroll; spec eff, Gary Kent; m/l, "A Man Called Dagger," Allen, Buddy Kaye, "Don't Rock the Boat" (sung by Maureen Arthur); makeup, Rafaelle Patterson.

Spy/Comedy **(PR:A MPAA:NR)**

MAN CALLED FLINTSTONE, THE½** (1966) 90m COL c (AKA: THAT MAN FLINTSTONE)

Voices: Alan Reed, Sr. *(Fred Flintstone)*, Mel Blanc *(Barney Rubble)*, Jean Vander Pyl *(Wilma Flintstone)*, Gerry Johnson *(Betty Rubble)*, Don Messick, Janet Waldo, Paul Frees, Harvey Korman, John Stephenson, June Foray.

The Flintstones started out as a popular prime-time television show on ABC-TV. This full-length cartoon featuring the stone-age family was brought into the theaters during the TV show's sixth season. The Flintstones live a contemporary life in prehistoric time (garbage disposal is a bird, a stone car is started by the people inside giving a running start). The film, another in the spy spoof sweepstakes, has a better sense of humor and orginality even though it's aimed at the younger set. Fred is an exact double of master spy Rock Slag, and when Slag is put out of commission, the Stone Age Secret Service puts Fred in his place. Fred, his wife Wilma, and neighbors Barney and Betty Rubble go to Paris on a supposed vacation. Fred is to find the Green Goose, the head of SMIRK and his accomplice Tanya. From Paris, Fred and group go to Rome, where he and Barney are taken prisoners by the Goose. Rock Slag arrives at the last moment to save Fred, Barney, and Eu-rock. An enjoyable animated film for the kids. Mel Blanc, the man behind the voices of Bugs Bunny, Daffy Duck, and other Warner Bros. cartoon characters, does the voice of Barney Rubble. Songs include: "Pensate Amore" (John McCarthy, Doug Goodwin, sung by Louis Prima), "Team Mates," "Spy Type Guy," "The Happy Sounds of Paree," "The Man Called Flintstone," "When I'm Grown Up," "Tickle Toddle" (McCarthy, Goodwin).

p&d, Joseph Barbera, William Hanna; w, Harvey Bullock, R.S. Allen (based on a story by Bullock, Allen, and story material by Barbera, Hanna, Warren Foster, Alex Lovy); ph, Charles Flekal, Roy Wade, Gene Borghi, Bill Kotler, Norman Stainback, Dick Blundell, Frank Parrish, Hal Shiffman, John Pratt (Eastmancolor); m, Marty Paich, Ted Nichols; ed, Warner Leighton, Milton Krear, Pat Foley, Larry Cowan, Dave Horton; art d, William Peresz; animation director, Charles A. Nichols; animation, Irv Spence, George Goepper, George Nicholas, Edward Barge, Edwin Aardal, Jerry Hathcock, Don Lusk, Kenneth Muse, Richard Lundy, Bill Keil, Ed Parks, John Sparey, Allen Wilzbach, George Kreisl, George Germanetti, Carlo Vinci, Hugh Fraser, Hicks Lokey; spec eff, Brooke Linden.

Animation **(PR:AAA MPAA:NR)**

MAN CALLED GANNON, A** (1969) 105m UNIV c

Tony Franciosa *(Gannon)*, Michael Sarrazin *(Jess Washburn)*, Judi West *(Beth)*, Susan Oliver *(Matty)*, John Anderson *(Capper)*, David Sheiner *(Sheriff Polaski)*, James Westerfield *(Amos)*, Gavin MacLeod *(Lou)*, Eddie Firestone *(Maz)*, Ed Peck *(Delivery Rider)*, Harry Davis *(Harry)*, Robert Sorrells *(Goff)*, Terry Wilson *(Cass)*, Eddra Gale *(Louisa)*, Harry Basch *(Ben)*, James Callahan *(Bo)*, Cliff Potter *(Ike)*, Jason Evers *(Mills)*, Jack Perkins *(Railroad Lineman)*.

A remake of MAN WITHOUT A STAR that falls miles short of the original directed by King Vidor in 1955. Franciosa is a drifter who takes a job on West's ranch during a local range war. He takes Easterner Sarrazin under his guidance to make the city slicker into a cow puncher. Their friendship is torn when they find themselves pitted against each other in the range war. Nothing outstanding; another routine western that didn't take any chances.

p, Howard Christie; d, James Goldstone; w, Gene Kearney, Borden Chase, D.D. Beauchamp (based on the novel *Man Without a Star* by Dee Linford); ph, William Margulies (Techniscope, Technicolor); m, Dave Grusin; ed, Gene Palmer, Richard M. Sprague; art d, Alexander Golitzen, Henry Bumstead; set d, John McCarthy, George Milo; cos, Helen Colvig; m/l, "A Smile, A Mem'ry and an Extra Shirt," Grusin, Marilyn Bergman, Alan Bergman (sung by Grusin); stunts, John Daheim; makeup, Bud Westmore, Vincent Romaine.

Western **(PR:A MPAA:PG)**

MAN CALLED HORSE, A½** (1970) 114m NGP c

Richard Harris *(Lord John Morgan)*, Judith Anderson *(Buffalo Cow Head)*, Jean Gascon *(Batise)*, Manu Tupou *(Yellow Hand)*, Corinna Tsopei *(Running Deer)*, Dub Taylor *(Joe)*, William Jordan *(Bent)*, James Gammon *(Ed)*, Edward Little Sky *(Black Eagle)*, Lina Marin *(Thorn Rose)*, Tamara Garina *(Elk Woman)*, Michael Baseleon *(He-Wolf)*, Manuel Padilla *(Leaping Buck)*, Iron Eyes Cody *(Medicine Man, Sun Vow Ritual)*, Tom Tyon, Jackson Tail, Richard Fools Bull, Ben Eagleman *(Medicine Men, Singers)*, Terry Leonard *(Striking Bear)*, Lloyd One Star, Frank Rabbit, Jr., Justin Thin Elk, Ardene Turning Bear, Ross Kills Enemy, James Never Miss A Shot, Samuel White Horse, Lawrence Old Cross, Ben Black Bear, Bruce Pretty Bird *(Warriors)*, Sioux Indians of the Rosebud Reservation.

Harris stars as an aristocratic Englishman captured by Sioux Indians and integrated into their culture in this gory western that became inexplicably popular and spawned two sequels (the first sequel, THE RETURN OF A MAN CALLED HORSE, is better than the original). Basically a detailed examination of Sioux tribal life, the film tends to be a bit long-winded in spots. The highlight, a scene *still* talked about, depicts Harris proving his manhood in a Sun Vow Initiation ceremony that requires him to be strung up in a teepee with ropes hooked through his pectorals (this sequence was supervised by veteran stuntman Yakima Canutt). By all accounts, the events depicted are historically accurate, but historical accuracy does not always guarantee a well-paced, interesting film. The third sequel was titled TRIUMPH OF A MAN CALLED HORSE.

p, Sandy Howard; d, Elliot Silverstein; w, Jack DeWitt (based on the story by Dorothy M. Johnson); ph, Robert Hauser (Panavision, Technicolor); m, Leonard Rosenman, Lloyd One Star; ed, Philip W. Anderson, Gene Fowler, Jr.; prod d, Dennis Lynton Clark; art d, Phil Barber; set d, Raul Serrano; cos, Edward Marks, Jack Martell, Ted Parvin; spec eff, Federico Farfan, Tim Smythe; makeup, Richard Cobos, Frank Griffin, Keester Sweeney; stunts, Terry Leonard.

Western **Cas.** **(PR:O MPAA:GP)**

MAN CALLED NOON, THE** (1973, Brit.) 94m Frontier Films/NG c

Richard Crenna *(Noon)*, Stephen Boyd *(Rimes)*, Rosanna Schiaffino *(Fan)*, Farley Granger *(Judge Niland)*, Patty Shepard *(Peg)*, Angel del Pozo *(Janish)*, Howard Ross *(Bayles)*, Aldo Sambrell *(Kissling)*, Jose Jaspe *(Henneker)*, Charley Bravo *(Lang)*, Ricardo Palacios *(Brakeman)*, Fernando Hilbeck *(Ford)*, Joe Canalejas *(Cherry)*, Cesar Burner *(Charlie)*, Julian Ugarte *(Cristobal)*, Barta Barri *(Mexican)*, Adolfo Thous *(Old Mexican)*, Bruce Fischer *(Ranch Hand)*.

Crenna is a gunslinger who's afflicted with amnesia after he's struck by a bullet. He struggles to find his identity, and also seeks revenge for his dead wife and child. He's aided by Schiaffino, who unknowingly operates the bandits' hideout, and outlaw Boyd in his attempt to reap justice from the murdering thieves headed by Granger. A British production shot in Spain.

p, Euan Lloyd; d, Peter Collinson; w, Scot Finch (based on a novel by Louis L'Amour); ph, John Cabrera (Technicolor); m, Luis Bacalov; ed, Alan Pattillo; art d, Jose Maria Tapiador.

Western **(PR:C MPAA:R)**

MAN CALLED PETER, THE*1/2** (1955) 119m FOX c

Richard Todd *(Peter Marshall)*, Jean Peters *(Catherine Marshall)*, Marjorie Rambeau *(Miss Fowler)*, Jill Esmond *(Mrs. Findlay)*, Les Tremayne *(Sen. Harvey)*, Robert Burton *(Mr. Peyton)*, Gladys Hurlburt *(Mrs. Peyton)*, Gloria Gordon *(Barbara)*, Billy Chapin *(Peter John Marshall)*, Sally Corner *(Mrs. Whiting)*, Voltaire Perkins *(Sen. Wiley)*, Betty Caulfield *(Jane Whitney)*, Marietta Canty *(Emma)*, Edward Earle *(Sen. Prescott)*, Mimi Hutson *(College Girl)*, Agnes Bartholomew *(Grandmother)*, Peter Votrian *(Peter Marshall, Ages 7 to 14)*, Janet Stewart *(Nancy)*, Ann Davis *(Ruby Coleman)*, Arthur Tovay *(Usher)*, Sam McDaniel *(Maitre d')*, Betty Caulfield *(Jane Whitney)*, Dorothy Neumann *(Miss Crilly)*, Oliver Hartwell *(Janitor)*, Doris Lloyd *(Miss Hopkins)*, William Forrest *(President)*, Barbara Morrison *(Miss Standish)*, Carlyle Mitchell *(Dr. Black)*, Amanda Randolph *(Willie)*, Rick Kelman *(Peter, Age 5 1/2)*, Louis Torres, Jr. *(Peter, Age 6 1/2)*, Emmett Lynn *(Mr. Briscoe)*, William Walker *(Butler)*, Charles Evans *(President of Senate)*, Alexander Campbell, Jonathan Hole *(Elders)*, Larry Kent *(Chaplain)*, Roy Glenn, Jr. *(Holden)*, Ruth Clifford *(Nurse)*, Ben Wright *(Mr. Findlay)*, Florence MacAfee *(Mrs. Ferguson)*, Christopher Cook *(Bon Hunter)*, Winston Severn *(David Weed)*, Maudie Prickett *(Mrs. Pike)*, Richard Garrick *(Col. Whiting)*.

A MAN CALLED PETER is a fine film about the life of Peter Marshall, the Scotsman who became the chaplain for the U.S. Senate, a man revered and respected for his ventures into the human spirit. Marshall appealed to the young and the old in his sermons, as this picture will if you are at all interested in watching a good yarn with solid ideals and equally solid production values. The movie is mainly concerned with Marshall's sermons. Now, while that might sound as inspiring as a snore-filled Sunday, it is much more than that. Todd is captivating as Marshall, as is Peters as his wife. She must deal with his tuberculosis and derives her strength from his sermons, as do many of his parishioners, including one senator, Tremayne, who rises up to right the political machine in his home state. There are struggles along the way, to be sure, most of which deal with the traditional types who don't like Todd's straying from the stodgy ways of the past. In the end, Todd wins out and proves to the doubting Thomases and Thomasinas that religion is a living thing, not merely there to resurrect the past. The message is never blatant and the performances are uniformly excellent under Koster's direction. The sermons are fascinating and never less than honest. Based on a book by the preacher's wife, it lovingly retraces their lives together up to his death, when she is able to sustain herself and assuage her grief through the memory of his teachings. Shot in and around Washington, D.C., the movie looks as good as it sounds and any attempt at a stilted religioso movie has been put aside in favor of the very human story of two people who dearly love each other.

p, Samuel G. Engel; d, Henry Koster; w, Eleanore Griffin (based on the book by Catherine Marshall); ph, Harold Lipstein (CinemaScope, DeLuxe Color); m, Alfred Newman; ed, Robert Simpson; md, Newman; art d, Lyle Wheeler, Maurice Ransford; cos, Renie; spec eff, Ray Kellogg.

Drama **(PR:AA MPAA:NR)**

MAN CALLED SLEDGE, A1/2** (1971, Ital.) 93m COL c

James Garner *(Luther Sledge)*, Dennis Weaver *(Ward)*, Claude Akins *(Hooker)*, John Marley *(The Old Man)*, Laura Antonelli *(Ria)*, Wade Preston *(Ripley)*, Ken Clark *(Floyd)*, Tony Young *(Mallory)*, Paola Barbara *(Jade)*, Mario Valgoi *(Beetle)*, Lorenzo Piani *(Guthrie)*, Franco Giomelli *(Joyce)*, Bruno Corazzari *(Bice)*, Altiero Di Giovanni *(Kehoe)*, Laura Betti *(Sister)*, Lorenzo Fineschi *(Toby)*, Didi Perego *(Elizabeth)*, Remo De Angelis *(Poker Player)*, Fausto Tozzi, Riccardo Garrone, Allan Jones, Herman Reynoso, Steffen Zacharias.

Garner is a bandit who robs a gold shipment with the help of his crony Weaver and a band of outlaws. The group has a falling out over how the shipment should be split and the gold is stolen from Garner and Weaver by the rest of the group. The two friends track them down to a Mexican town, resulting in a bloody shootout during a religious festival. The film was directed by film and TV actor Vic Morrow, who brings a distinctive American flair to this Italian production. He tosses in a large dose of religious symbolism, which is typical of spaghetti westerns (the troops guarding the gold shipment travel in a cross formation, the gold is hidden behind the church altar during the climactic gunfight, Garner uses a cross as a splint for his broken arm so he can shoot his gun, Antonelli is tortured in a church by the band of outlaws). There are no heroes in this film making it hard to identify with anyone, but the film moves at a good pace with a mood that will linger after the ending credits. (In English.)

p, Dino De Laurentiis; d, Vic Morrow; w, Morrow and Frank Kowalski; ph, Luigi Kuveiller (Technicolor); m, Gianni Ferrio; ed, Renzo Lucidi; prod d, Mario Chirai; art d, Mario Scisci; set d, Enzo Eusepi; cos, Elio Micheli; spec eff, Pasquino Benesanti; m/l, "Other Men's Gold," Bill Martin, Phil Coulter (sung by Stefan Grossman); stunts, Remo De Angelis; makeup, Giuliano Laurenti.

Western **(PR:O MPAA:R)**

MAN CALLED SULLIVAN, A (SEE: GREAT JOHN L., THE, 1945)

MAN COULD GET KILLED, A**

(1966) 97m UNIV c (AKA: WELCOME, MR. BEDDOES)

James Garner *(William Beddoes)*, Melina Mercouri *(Aurora-Celeste da Costa)*, Sandra Dee *(Amy Franklin)*, Tony Franciosa *(Steve-Antonio)*, Robert Coote *(Hatton-Jones)*, Roland Culver *(Dr. Mathieson)*, Gregoire Aslan *(Florian)*, Cecil Parker *(Sir Huntley Frazier)*, Dulcie Gray *(Mrs. Mathieson)*, Martin Benson *(Politanu)*, Peter Illing *(Zarik)*, Niall MacGinnis *(Ship's Captain)*, Virgilio Teixeira *(Inspector Rodrigues)*, Isabel Dean *(Miss Bannister)*, Daniele Vargas *(Osman)*, Nello Pazzafini *(Abdul)*, George Pastell *(Lazlo)*, Arnold Diamond *(Milo)*, Conrad Anderson *(Heinrich)*, Eric Domain *(Max)*, Pasquale Fasciano *(Carmo)*, Ann Firbank *(Miss Nolan)*, Nora Swinburne *(Lady Frazier)*, Jenny Agutter *(Linda Frazier)*, Builiano Raffael *(Ludmar)*, Yamilli Humar *(Rosa)*, Pontifex, Jonas Braimer, D. A. Segurd, E. Cianfelli, M. Bevilacqua, M. R. Caldas, O. Acursio, J. Paixio, A. Costa, L. Pinhao, G. Dusmatas, C. DiMaggio, C. Calisti, C. Perone, P. Solvay, M. Tempesta, S. Minoi, R. Castelli, R. Alessandri, G. Lipari, K. Goncalves.

Garner is an American businessman in Lisbon who's mistaken for a British secret agent. The agent was on a mission to recover missing industrial diamonds and Garner is chased by Mercouri, Franciosa, and many others for the diamonds he doesn't have. A slapstick spy spoof that blurs into the other secret agent comedies that saturated the theaters in the 1960s.

p, Robert Arthur; d, Ronald Neame; w, Richard Breen, T. E. B. Clarke (based on the novel *Diamonds for Danger* by David Esdaile Walker); ph, Gabor Pogany (Panavision, Technicolor); m, Bert Kaempfert; ed, Alma Macrorie; art d, John De Cuir; set d, Giuseppe Chevalier; stunts, John Daheim.

Comedy/Action **(PR:A MPAA:NR)**

MAN CRAZY** (1953) 79m FOX bw

Neville Brand *(Paul Wocynski)*, Christine White *(Georgia Daniels)*, Irene Anders *(Millie Pickett)*, Colleen Miller *(Judy Bassett)*, John Brown *(Mr. Duncan)*, Joe Turkel *(Ray)*, Karen Steele *(Marge)*, Jack Larsen *(Bob)*, Bill Lundmark *(Steve)*, John Crawford *(Farmer)*, Ottola Nesmith *(Mrs. Becker)*, Charles Victor *(Mechanic)*, Frances Osborne *(Woman Customer)*.

White, Anders, and Miller are three restless teenagers from Minnesota who steal $28,000 from their local drugstore and head for Hollywood. They have fun in the sun, get into some problems with men, and the druggist tracks them down. The girls are caught, but not before White marries Brand and starts a farm with the stolen money.

p, Sidney Harmon, Philip Yordan; d, Irving Lerner; w, Harmon, Yordan; ph, Floyd Crosby; m, Ernest Gold; ed, Marjorie Fowler.

Drama **(PR:A MPAA:NR)**

MAN DETAINED1/2** (1961, Brit.) 59m Merton Park/Anglo-Amalgamated bw

Bernard Archard *(Inspector Verity)*, Elvi Hale *(Kay Simpson)*, Paul Stassino *(James Helder)*, Michael Coles *(Frank Murray)*, Ann Sears *(Stella Maple)*, Victor Platt *(Thomas Maple)*, Patrick Jordon *(Brand)*, Jean Aubrey *(Gillian Murray)*.

A photographer is killed and a secretary is kidnaped. To rescue the woman an unusual scheme is concocted. The police use a burglar, caught with stolen counterfeit money, to bait a trap which eventually snares the killer. Based on a novel by the popular British mystery writer Edgar Wallace.

p, Jack Greenwood; d, Robert Tronson; w, Richard Harris (based on the Novel *A Debt Discharged* by Edgar Wallace).

Crime **(PR:C MPAA:NR)**

MAN EATER OF HYDRA

(SEE: ISLAND OF THE DOOMED, 1968, Span./Ger.)

MAN ESCAPED, A****

(1957, Fr.) 102m GAU/New Yorker bw (UN CONDAMNE A MORT S'EST ECHAPPE; LE VENT SOUFFLE OU IL VEUT; AKA: THE WIND BLOWETH WHERE IT LISTETH)

Francois Leterrier *(Lt. Fontaine)*, Charles Le Clainche *(Francois Jost)*, Roland Monod *(De Leiris the Pastor)*, Maurice Beerblock *(Blanchet)*, Jacques Ertaud *(Orsini)*, Roger Treherne *(Terry)*, Jean-Paul Delhumeau *(Hebrard)*, Jean-Philippe Delamare *(Prisoner No. 110)*, Jacques Oerlemans *(Chief Warder)*, Klaus Detlef Grevenhorst *(German Intelligence Officer)*, Leonard Schmidt *(German Escort)*.

Leterrier is a Resistance hero captured by the Nazis and imprisoned in Fort Montluc. From there, he carefully and meticulously plans his escape. He is joined by cell mate Le Clainche and together they successfully scale the walls. Based on a published account of Andre Devigny, a Resistance fighter who was to be executed in 1943, A MAN ESCAPED is one of Bresson's finest works. Even after the success of THE DIARY OF A COUNTRY PRIEST, Bresson had to wait five years to get this project underway. The two films have in common a faith in God. Faith is most obvious in the picture's alternate title, THE WIND BLOWETH WHERE IT LISTETH (one of the working titles was HELP YOURSELF, as in "heaven helps those who . . ."), and in the use of music (Mozart's "Mass in C Minor"). As in many of Bresson's films, the cast is made up of non-professionals such as Leterrier who was a philosophy graduate and a lieutenant in the military. This, and the fact that Bresson was a POW at the start of WW II, makes for an authentic, detailed account of the spirit of the Resistance movement. Also contributing was Devigny's contribution as a technical adviser, and the use of his actual cell for the location. Bresson received the "Best Director" prize from the Cannes Film Festival in 1957 for the movie, a unanimous decision. In a similar, but less successful manner, Don Siegel detailed a prison break in 1979's ESCAPE FROM ALCATRAZ with Clint Eastwood in the starring role.

p, Jean Thuiller, Alaine Poire; d&w, Robert Bresson (based on articles by Andre Devigny); ph, Leonce-Henry Burel; m, Wolfgang Amadeus Mozart ("Kyrie" from "Mass in C Minor"); ed, Raymond Lamy; art d, Pierre Charbonnier.

Drama **(PR:A MPAA:NR)**

MAN FOLLOWING THE SUN

(SEE: SANDU FOLLOWS THE SUN, 1965, USSR)

MAN FOR ALL SEASONS, A***** (1966, Brit.) 120m Highland/COL c

Paul Scofield *(Sir Thomas More)*, Wendy Hiller *(Alice More)*, Leo McKern *(Thomas Cromwell)*, Robert Shaw *(King Henry VIII)*, Orson Welles *(Cardinal Wolsey)*, Susannah York *(Margaret More)*, Nigel Davenport *(Duke of Norfolk)*, John Hurt *(Richard Rich)*, Corin Redgrave *(William Roper)*, Colin Blakely *(Matthew)*, Yootha Joyce *(Averil Machin)*, Anthony Nichols *(King's Representative)*, John Nettleton *(Jailer)*, Eira Heath *(Matthew's Wife)*, Molly Urquhart *(Maid)*, Paul Hardwick

(Courtier), Michael Latimer *(Norfolk's Aide)*, Philip Brack *(Captain of Guard)*, Martin Boddey *(Governor of Tower)*, Eric Mason *(Executioner)*, Matt Zinnerman *(Messenger)*, Vanessa Redgrave *(Anne Boleyn)*, Cyril Luckham *(Archbishop Cranmer)*, Jack Gwillim *(Chief Justice)*, Thomas Heathcote *(Boatman)*.

A MAN FOR ALL SEASONS is one of those unique films that is, at once, prestigious and commercial. The studio took a large gamble when they agreed to film Bolt's play, even though it had been a hit with the cognescenti of London and New York. There was a large question as to whether or not the heartland folks would care about the story of Sir Thomas More, a Catholic statesman in England, who rebelled against Henry VIII's self-proclaimed status as the head of the Church of England and paid for his religious beliefs by having his head exhibited on London Bridge. It took six years to get on the screen and the wait was worth it. Scofield is More and appointed to be the Cardinal's (Welles) successor as Lord Chancellor. More is a highly religious man and devoted to his beliefs and comes to grips with Shaw, as Henry VIII, who wants to divorce his wife and take a new bride. Since the sacrament of marriage is to be upheld at all costs, Scofield objects to Shaw's plan. Shaw can objectively appreciate Scofield's beliefs, but he will not allow them to stand in the way of shedding his barren wife to marry Redgrave (Boleyn), who was dispatched in a different fashion and in a different film (ANNE OF THE THOUSAND DAYS). Scofield is bound to serve his king but makes no bones about his feelings regarding the divorce. The Pope also refuses Shaw's request, so Shaw, believing himself to be as infallible in his way as the Popes have declared themselves to be in their ways, makes himself the spiritual leader of his country, in addition to his duties as sovereign. The bishops of England soon acquiesce in the founding of the new church and Scofield hands in his resignation, wanting to be put out to pasture and live his life in peace. Scofield makes no public comment on Shaw's actions and Shaw is irked by his one-time friend's silence. Prodded by McKern (Thomas Cromwell, not Oliver) and a corps of lackeys, Shaw demands that Scofield sign a writ of allegiance to Shaw as the head of church and state. Since Scofield feels that the pope is his religious leader, he refuses and is quickly penned in the Tower of London for his denial. McKern and Hurt falsify some charges against Scofield, as they believe he must be executed quickly or his imprisonment might prove a thorn in their sides. Scofield is accused and tried for high treason (is anyone ever convicted of low treason?) and is taken to meet the executioner, who lops off his head. He is tranquil and forgiving of the hooded man who takes his life, but he makes an impassioned speech against the actions of Shaw and his cronies, whom he feels are acting in the worst interests of God. Scofield won the Oscar in this, his first major role (He'd been in four other films before) on screen, after having played the part on stage in London and on Broadway. The decision to keep him, rather than cast some big name like Burton or O'Toole, was a wise and brave one. Hurt showed some of the talent he was to demonstrate in later years when he stepped out to become a star and Shaw also scored in a multi-dimensional performance as the most outrageous monarch in British history. At two hours, it's a perfect length and the film neither drags nor races. Inventive camera work and all technical credits were superb. The film won Oscars for Best Picture, Best Actor, Best Director, Best Screenplay (from another medium), Best Color Cinematography, Best Color Costume Design, and seven awards from the British Film Academy for all the aforementioned categories as well as Best British Film. Not once did Zinneman succumb to allowing any emoting. Scofield was strong, restrained, and could show his inner fortitude with the smallest facial expression, not an easy task for a stage actor who had always faced the problem of playing to the far reaches of the theater. Hiller is good as Scofield's wife, as is York as their daughter. In real life, the head of More was stuck on a pole on London Bridge for quite some time until one of his daughter's friends climbed the pole and tossed the head to her as she waited in a boat under the bridge. She then took the rotting head and united it with the body that had been buried some time before. The movie excited audiences in the 1960s for many reasons other than the fact that it was so good. More's stand against authority, at the loss of his life, was something the rebels of that era could identify with as they marched against the policies of the government's waging a no-win war in Southeast Asia.

p&d, Fred Zinneman; w, Robert Bolt, Constance Willis (based on the play by Bolt); ph, Ted Moore (Technicolor); m, Georges Delerue; ed, Ralph Kemplen; prod d, John Box; md, Delerue; art d, Terence Marsh; set d, Josie MacAvin; cos, Elizabeth Haffenden, Joan Bridge; makeup, George Frost, Eric Allwright.

Drama **Cas.** **(PR:A MPAA:NR)**

MAN FRIDAY 1/2** (1975, Brit.) 115m Keep-ABC Entertainment-ITC/AE c

Peter O'Toole *(Robinson Crusoe)*, Richard Roundtree *(Friday)*, Peter Cellier *(Carey)*, Christopher Cabot *(McBain)*, Sam Seabrook *(Young Girl)*, Stanley Clay *(Young Boy)*, Joel Fluellen.

Yet another variation of Defoe's classic *Robinson Crusoe*, MAN FRIDAY doesn't compare with the 1954 film, THE ADVENTURES OF ROBINSON CRUSOE, which earned Dan O'Herlihy an Oscar nomination (that he lost to Marlon Brando for ON THE WATERFRONT). O'Toole is Crusoe and has already spent a dozen years stranded on an island when five natives arrive from a nearby island. Four of them are burying the fifth in an elaborate native ceremony, and O'Toole arrives with a loaded pistol and shoots three of them. He spares Roundtree and names him Friday (because that's what day it is) after Roundtree bows and darn near rolls over like a whipped dog. O'Toole feels it is his job in life to make Roundtree a Christian, or kill him in the attempt. Roundtree is wise and soon realizes that his captor is whacked out, so he does everything O'Toole wants, including the burial of his compatriates. O'Toole teaches Roundtree English, how to play various sports and allows himself to be "civilized" or, at least, pretends that. Roundtree is beaten regularly, even though he does his best to please O'Toole. Eventually, Roundtree feels so put upon that he volunteers to be executed rather than continue this servile situation. O'Toole hates the thought of being alone again, so he eases off and puts Roundtree on a salary by paying him gold coins he keeps in a large chest. Roundtree has no idea what these are worth and wonders. O'Toole gives him a comparison and says that 2,000 of the coins would be about right to buy all of O'Toole's goods and his hut. A ship appears on the horizon and O'Toole rejoices until he learns it's a slave trader. Cellier and Cabot come off the ship to meet O'Toole and he overhears that they mean to kill him and take Roundtree on the ship and later sell him as a slave. O'Toole and Roundtree get together to kill the two men and drive their crew out to sea. Now O'Toole and Roundtree try to leave the island by means of a crude raft, but they are soon tossed ashore again. Roundtree shows O'Toole something very interesting; he has found the ship O'Toole arrived on, dived deeply underwater, and has brought up with him the requisite 2,000 coins to buy all of O'Toole's possessions. Now the tide turns and O'Toole becomes the slave. He must sleep on the sand, do all of Roundtree's bidding, and must help build another raft. The construction of the raft is finished and the two men sail to Roundtree's island where a great reunion celebration takes place. O'Toole, seeing this rush of warmth, indicates that he might like to become part of Roundtree's tribe and that request is considered at a council meeting. But as Roundtree recounts all the indignities that O'Toole put him through, it is soon clear that the tribe will not accept O'Toole because his presence could prove to be a perilous force to the tribe. O'Toole pleads with the tribe but all of his words fall on deaf ears and he is taken back to his lonely island and left on the beach to sit and read from the Bible. In the original ending (cut from the print), O'Toole's last scene shows him about to blow his head off with his musket, but that was deemed as too much of a down ending and excised. The true-life story is supposed to have happened to a Scots sailor who was abandoned for four years on a small island off the coast of Chile, then rescued. His journal was published in 1712 and served as the inspiration for Defoe's novel. The island was Juan Fernandez, although the people who live on the island of Tobago (part of the two-island country of Trinidad and Tobago) claim that it was their land upon which Selkirk, the Scotsman, landed and lived for those four years. MAN FRIDAY is often too glib for its own good and it appears that much of the script was constructed to hear the sound of O'Toole's voice as he prates on and on. Two men on an island was better seen in HELL IN THE PACIFIC, in which Toshiro Mifune and Lee Marvin faced off against each other.

p, David Korda; d, Jack Gold; w, Adrian Mitchell (based on his play from the novel *The Life and Strange Surprising Adventures of Robinson Crusoe, of York, Mariner* by Daniel Defoe); ph, Alex Phillips (Panavision, Eastmancolor); m, Carl Davis; ed, Anne V. Coates; prod d, Peter Murton; art d, Agustin Ytuarte; set d, Enrique Esteves; spec eff, Leon Ortega, Michael Merchan; ch, Tino Rodriguez; m/l, Davis; makeup, Bill Lodge.

Drama **Cas.** **(PR:A-C MPAA:PG)**

MAN FROM BITTER RIDGE, THE 1/2** (1955) 80m UNIV c

Lex Barker *(Jeff Carr)*, Mara Corday *(Holly Kenton)*, Stephen McNally *(Alec Black)*, John Dehner *(Ranse Jackman)*, Trevor Bardette *(Walter Dunham)*, Ray Teal *(Shep Bascom)*, Warren Stevens *(Linc Jackman)*, Myron Healey *(Clem Jackman)*, John Harmon *(Norman Roberts)*, John Cliff *(Wolf Landers)*, Richard Garland *(Jace Gordon)*, Jennings Miles.

Barker is a special investigator who goes to the town of Tomahawk to bring to justice the men responsible for a series of stagecoach holdups and killings. The main suspects are McNally and his group of sheepherders. Barker, along with sheriff Bardette, suspects that aspiring politician Dehner and his gunmen are the guilty parties. This was the first western directed by Jack Arnold, a master of such science fiction classics as THE INCREDIBLE SHRINKING MAN and THE CREATURE FROM THE BLACK LAGOON.

p, Howard Pine; d, Jack Arnold; w, Lawrence Roman, Teddi Sherman (based on the novel by William MacLeod Raine); ph, Russell Metty (Eastmancolor); ed, Milton Carruth; md, Joseph Gershenson; art d, Alexander Golitzen, Bill Newberry; cos, Jay Morley, Jr.

Western **(PR:A MPAA:NR)**

MAN FROM BLACK HILLS, THE** (1952) 58m Silvermine/MON bw

Johnny Mack Brown *(Johnny)*, James Ellison *(Jim Fallon)*, Randy Brooks *(Jimmy Fallon)*, Lane Bradford *(Sheriff Moran)*, I. Stanford Jolley *(Pete Ingram)*, Robert Bray *(Ed Roper)*, Stanley Price *(Shealey)*, Denver Pyle *(Hartley)*, Ray Bennett *(Hugh Delaney)*, Joel Allen *(Bates)*, Stanley Andrews *(Pop Fallon)*, Florence Lake *(Martha)*, Bud Osborne, Merrill McCormack, Roy Bucko, Ralph Bucko.

This Brown western has the cowboy riding with Ellison, who is to be reunited with his long-lost parents. When the two arrive in town they discover that Brooks is masquerading as the lost son in order to inherit the title of a gold mine. Brown makes sure that the right heir to the mine is united with his parents.

p, Vincent M. Fennelly; d, Thomas Carr; w, Joseph O'Donnell; ph, Ernest Miller; m, Raoul Kraushaar; ed, Sam Fields.

Western **(PR:A MPAA:NR)**

MAN FROM BLANKLEY'S, THE*** (1930) 67m WB bw

John Barrymore *(Lord Strathpeffer)*, Loretta Young *(Margery Seaton)*, William Austin *(Mr. Poffley)*, Albert Gran *(Uncle Gabriel Gilwattle)*, Emily Fitzroy *(Mrs. Tidmarsh)*, Dick Henderson *(Mr. Tidmarsh)*, Edgar Norton *(Dawes)*, Yorke Sherwood *(Mr. Bodfish)*, Dale Fuller *(Miss Flanders)*, D'Arcy Corrigan *(Mr. Ditchwater)*, Louise Carver *(Mrs. Gilwattle)*, Mary Milloy *(Mrs. Ditchwater)*, Diana Hope *(Mrs. Bodfish)*, Tiny Jones *(Miss Bugle)*, Gwendolen Logan *(Maid)*, Angella Mawby *(Gwennie)*, Sybil Grove *(Maid)*.

A short, funny film that pokes great fun at the difference in the classes. Barrymore was rarely seen during these early days in anything less than doublet and hose, so it was a surprise when he decided he wanted to try his hand and face at a modern-day comedy. Although the cast is American, someone must have worked very closely with them to firm up their British accents, as they are virtually without flaws. Barrymore is a muddle-headed peer who wanders into the wrong house when he drinks a bit too much. The hostess of the home has planned a gala dinner and only had 13 guests, so she's hired a professional company, Blankley's, to supply her with someone befitting the other attendees at the dinner. She thinks it's Barrymore and invites him in. The film makes sport of the American guests and is a sharp satire with some fine slapstick scenes as well. Barrymore dominates the proceedings as the pomposity of parvenus is punctured. Fitzroy is the hostess and Carver is hilarious as a noisy Chicago matron who alternately slaps back and hoots, then settles down in a vain attempt to act as a classy dowager instead of another version of The Unsinkable Molly Brown. The picture is sort of stagy, for good reason, as it was a stage play to start with. The short running time makes one wonder how much was cut out. This was Young's thirteenth feature film and she was not yet 18 years of age.

d, Alfred E. Green; w, Harvey Thew, Joseph Jackson (based on the play by F. Anstey [Thomas Anstey Guthrie]); ph, James Van Trees.

Comedy (PR:A MPAA:NR)

MAN FROM BUTTON WILLOW, THE** (1965) 87m United Screen Arts c

Voices of: Dale Robertson (*Justin Eagle*), Edgar Buchanan (*Sorry*), Barbara Jean Wong (*Stormy*), Howard Keel, Herschel Bernardi, Ross Martin, Verna Felton, Shep Menken, Pinto Colvig, Cliff Edwards, Thurl Ravenscroft, John Hiestand, Clarence Nash, Edward Platt, Buck Buchanan.

An animated western for the young ones with Robertson doing the voice of the hero, Justin Eagle. He's an undercover agent for the government who lives on a farm with a number of animals, his Chinese ward, and an old friend named Sorry. The agent/rancher is called upon to save Senator Freeman, who has been kidnaped. This he does, aided by his horse, Rebel, and the hero rides back to his ranch as the sun sets. Kid's stuff. This was the first film distributed through Robertson's company, United Screen Arts.

p, Phyllis Bounds Detiege; d&w, David Detiege; ph, Max Morgan; m, George Stoll, Robert Van Eps; ed, Ted Baker, Sam Horta; prod d, Ernie Nordli; md, Stoll; m/l, Dale Robertson, George Bruns, Mel Henke, Phil Bounds (sung by Robertson, Howard Keel, Edgar Buchanan).

Western **Cas.** (PR:AA MPAA:NR)

MAN FROM CAIRO, THE*¹/₂ (1953) 81m LIPPERT bw

George Raft (*Mike Canelli*), Gianna Maria Canale (*Lorraine*), Massimo Serato (*Basil Constantine*), Guido Celano (*Emile Touchard*), Irene Papas (*Yvonne*), Alfredo Varelli (*Prof. Crespi, "Gen. Dumont"*), Leon Lenoir (*Akhim Bey*), Mino Doro (*Maj. Blanc*), Angelo Dessy (*Pockmark*), Richard McNamara (*Stark*), Franco Silva (*Armeno*).

Typical Raft crime story that had a chance to impress but the dull direction did it in. Raft is in Algeria where someone mistakenly thinks he's an American who has been engaged by French Intelligence to help find $100 million in gold that was secreted in the North African desert nine years before, during the war. Raft goes with the flow and meets Papas, whom he thinks will help, but she is soon killed. The cops, headed by Lenoir, can't arrest Raft as they have no evidence, but they do keep a sharp eye on him. Raft meets nightclub thrush Canale and induces her to admit that she and club owner Serato own a recording that purportedly gives the location of the cache. Serato is slain and Raft finds Varelli and uncovers the fact that he was the commanding officer who hid the gold. Canale is kidnaped and Raft discovers that the local intelligence boss, Doro, has another business. He's made a fortune in transportation and is getting the gold out of Algeria through a smuggling operation. Lenoir and his men kill Doro, and a reward for the missing gold is split between Raft and Varelli. Raft plans to use his share of the loot to make an honest woman out of Canale, something the picture failed to do. In a career that saw him make many B films, this one must rank with the B-est of them all. Even Papas, a Greek actress of striking beauty and classical training, failed to show any of her stuff here. Ho-hum and hokum.

p, Bernard Luber; d, Ray H. Enright; w, Eugene Ling, Philip and Janet Stevenson (based on a story by Ladislas Fodor); ph, Mario Abutelli; m, Renzo Rossellini; ed, Mario Berandrei; md, Franco Ferrare.

Crime Drama (PR:A MPAA:NR)

MAN FROM CHEYENNE** (1942) 60m REP bw

Roy Rogers (*Roy*), George "Gabby" Hayes (*Gabby*), Sally Payne (*Sally*), Lynne Carver (*Marian*), William Haade (*Ed*), James Seay (*Jim*), Gale Storm (*Judy*), Jack Ingram (*Jack*), Jack Kirk, Fred Burns, Jack Rockwell, Sons of the Pioneers, Al Taylor, Chick Hannon, Art Dillard, Frank Brownlee, Bob Nolan, Pat Brady, Trigger the Horse.

Roy is a government agent who's out in Wyoming tracking down modern cattle rustlers. The rustlers are led by Carver, an Eastern girl who wants to go back and live in style. She coaxes info from the ranchers with her good looks, and uses the info to rustle their herds. When Rogers uncovers the workings of the gang, Payne and Storm drag Carver into jail by her hair. This was the first film in which Rogers didn't use his real name, Leonard Slye (smart career move).

p&d, Joseph Kane; w, Winston Miller; ph, Reggie Lanning; ed, William Thompson; md, Cy Feuer.

Western **Cas.** (PR:A MPAA:NR)

MAN FROM CHICAGO, THE*¹/₂ (1931, Brit.) 74m BIP/COL bw

Bernard Nedell (*Nick Dugan*), Dodo Watts (*Cherry Henderson*), Joyce Kennedy (*Irma Russell*), Morris Harvey (*Rossi*), Albert Whelan (*Sgt. Mostyn*), Austin Trevor (*Inspector Drew*), Billy Milton (*Barry Larwood*), O. B. Clarence (*John Larwood*), Dennis Hoey (*Jimmy Donovan*), Ben Welden (*Ted*), Leonard Dainton, Matthew Boulton, Syd Crossley, Fred Lloyd.

Nedell is an American criminal who uses the son of a garage owner as his alibi when he robs a bank and kills a policeman. Trevor is a Scotland Yard detective who trails Nedell only to be shot dead by the American in a night club. Nedell is cornered by police, but escapes when his girl friend holds up detective Clarence with a gun. The murderer is finally killed when he is run over by a car driven by his girl friend.

p, John Maxwell; d, Walter Summers; w, Summers, Walter C. Mycroft (based on the play "Speed" by Reginald Berkeley); ph, James Wilson, Walter Harvey; ed, Leslie Norman.

Crime Drama (PR:A MPAA:NR)

MAN FROM COCODY*¹/₂
(1966, Fr./Ital.) 84m Euro France -S.N.E. Gaumont-P.C.M/AIP c (LE GENTLEMAN DE COCODY; DONNE, MITRA E DIAMANTI)

Jean Marais (*Jean-Luc Herve de la Tommeraye*), Liselotte Pulver (*Baby*), Philippe Clay (*Renaud Lefranc*), Nancy Holloway (*Nancy*), Maria Grazia Buccella (*Angelina*), Jacques Morel (*Rouffignac*), Robert Dalban (*Pepe*).

An idiotic adventure film about a secret society called the Sons of the Panther which works on the side of justice. The group stops a band of jewel thieves from stealing a cargo of diamonds off a downed plane.

p, Roger Duchet, Alain Poire; d, Christian-Jaque; w, Jean Ferry, Jacques Emmanuel, Christian-Jaque (based on a story by Claude Rank); ph, Pierre Petit (Franscope, Eastmancolor); m, Michel Magne; ed, Jacques Desagneau; spec eff, Gil Delamare. song, "Man from Cocody," sung by Nancy Holloway.

Action Adventure (PR:A MPAA:NR)

MAN FROM COLORADO, THE** (1948) 99m COL c

Glenn Ford (*Col. Owen Devereaux*), William Holden (*Capt. Del Stewart*), Ellen Drew (*Caroline Emmett*), Ray Collins (*Big Ed Carter*), Edgar Buchanan (*Doc Merriam*), Jerome Courtland (*Johnny Howard*), James Millican (*Sgt. Jericho Howard*), Jim Bannon (*Nagel*), William "Bill" Phillips (*York*), Denver Pyle (*Easy Jarrett*), James Bush (*Dickson*), Mikel Conrad (*Morris*), David Clark (*Mutton McGuire*), Ian MacDonald (*Jack Rawson*), Clarence Chase (*Charlie Trumbull*), Stanley Andrews (*Roger MacDonald*), Myron Healey (*Powers*), Craig Reynolds (*Parry*), David York (*Rebel Major*), Ben Corbett (*Deputy*), Fred Graff (*Parks*), Phin Holder (*Sandes*), Fred Coby, Ray Hyke (*Veterans*), Eddie Fetherston (*Jones*), Pat O'Malley (*Citizen*), Symona Boniface (*Matron*), Walter Baldwin (*Tom Barton*).

One of the earliest of the "psychological westerns," this one went beyond psychology and psychiatry and into the realm of psychoses as Ford stars as a sadistic Civil War veteran who has been killing for the sheer joy of it, even after the official battles cease. His mind was unbalanced by the terrors of the war and he manages somehow to secure a job as a judge in Colorado. His former army pal, Holden, knows that Ford is teetering on the brink of insanity, so he obtains a job as Ford's marshal in an attempt to keep his one-time crony from getting out of hand. Ford kills criminals who have raised the flag of surrender, he is far too liberal with his sentences of death, and the town is ready to rebel against him. Holden stalwartly tries to calm Ford down but the man is in a constant rage. When Ford removes the mining concessions of several ex-soldiers, Holden joins them and they become outlaws. Drew is Ford's wife, but she can do nothing to staunch his blood lust and finally leaves him in favor of Holden. As you might imagine, there is a violent battle between the two former friends, Holden and Ford. They are battling with their fists in a burning building when the roof caves in and kills Ford, thus relieving Holden of the task. No question that the producers were attempting to draw a parallel between the returning Civil War men in the film and the real veterans who were coming home from WW II and carrying both mental and physical scars on their beings. This was a strange juxtaposition of themes and it ultimately failed, but they must be commended for trying to unravel the twisted knots in a man's mind when he is assaulted by death from all sides.

p, Jules Schermer; d, Henry Levin; w, Robert D. Andrews, Ben Maddow (story by Borden Chase); ph, William Snyder (Technicolor), m, George Duning; ed, Charles Nelson; md, Morris W. Stoloff; art d, Stephen Goosson, A. Leslie Thomas; set d, Wilbur Menefee, Sidney Clifford; cos, Jean Louis.

Western (PR:A-C MPAA:NR)

MAN FROM C.O.T.T.O.N. (SEE: GONE ARE THE DAYS, 1963)

MAN FROM DAKOTA, THE**
(1940) 74m MGM bw (AKA: AROUSE AND BEWARE)

Wallace Beery (*Sgt. Barstow*), John Howard (*Oliver Clark*), Dolores Del Rio (*Eugenia, "Jenny"*), Donald Meek (*Mr. Vestry*), Robert Barrat (*Parson Summers*), Addison Richards (*Provost Marshal*), Frederick Burton (*Leader*), John Wray (*Carpenter*), Gregory Gaye (*Col. Borodin*), Frank Hagney (*Guard*), William Royle (*Supervisor*), Ted Oliver, Buddy Roosevelt (*Officers*), Hugh Sothern (*General*), Edward Hearn (*Captain*), John Butler (*Voss*), Tom Fadden (*Driver*), Francis Ford (*Horseman*), William Haade (*Union Soldier*).

Beery and Howard are Union soldiers during the Civil War who escape from a Confederate prison and head back to friendly ground. Along the way they pick up Del Rio, a Russian emigre who's killed a Confederate officer. From the dead officer they take a map of Confederate positions, which aids their travels through enemy lines. Beery gets the map to Grant's headquarters, becomes a hero, and wins Del Rio. This was Del Rio's first film for MGM in twelve years and her first screen appearance in two.

p, Edward Chodorov; d, Leslie Fenton; w, Laurence Stallings (based on the novel *Arouse and Beware* by MacKinlay Kantor); ph, Ray June; ed, Conrad A. Nervig; art d, Cedric Gibbons, Malcolm Brown; set d, Edwin B. Willis; cos, Gile Steele, Dolly Tree; makeup, Jack Dawn.

Western (PR:A MPAA:NR)

MAN FROM DEATH VALLEY, THE* ¹/₂ (1931) 61m MON bw

Tom Tyler, John Oscar, Gino Corrado, Stanley Blystone, Betty Mack, Hank Bell, Si Jenks.

Tyler is a secret service agent who rides into town where old flame Mack is now engaged to the sheriff. Tyler robs the bank to expose a scheme by the sheriff and his group of Mexican bandits to pull off the bank heist themselves. Tyler then wins back the affections of Mack.

d, Lloyd Nosler; w, George Arthur Durlam, Nosler (based on a story by Durlam and Nosler); ph, Archie Stout.

Western (PR:A MPAA:NR)

MAN FROM DEL RIO** (1956) 82m UA bw

Anthony Quinn (Dave Robles), Katy Jurado (Estella), Peter Whitney (Ed Bannister), Douglas Fowley (Doc Adams), John Larch (Bill Dawson), Whit Bissell (Breezy Morgan), Douglas Spencer (Jack Tillman), Guinn "Big Boy" Williams (Fred Jasper), Marc Hamilton (George Dawson), Adrienne Marden (Mrs. Tillman), Barry Atwater (Dan Ritchy), Carl Thayler (The Kid), William Erwin (Roy Higgens), Otto Waldis (Tom Jordan), Paul Harber (Mr. Brown), Jack Hogan (Boy), Frank Richards (Stableman), Katherine DeMille (Woman).

Quinn is an uneducated Mexican gunfighter who is hired as the sheriff of Mesa. Believing that the job gives him the dignity and respect he needed, Quinn buys new clothes and attempts to join in the town's activities only to find that the townspeople look down upon him—they just want his quick gun when it's needed. Whitney, the saloon owner, figures that he can use Quinn to gain control of the town. When the sheriff breaks his wrist in a brawl, Whitney makes his move. He calls Quinn out for a showdown, but when Quinn removes the bandage from his wrist, Whitney backs down. Shown to be a coward, the saloon owner is thrown out of town. Quinn also wins the affections of Jurado. Quinn's performance, which added an extra dimension to the character, raises this western above the standard fare.

p, Robert L. Jacks; d, Harry Horner; w, Richard Carr; ph, Stanley Cortez; m, Frederick Steiner; ed, Robert Golden; art d, William Glasgow; cos, Frank Beetson, Opal Vils.

Western (PR:A MPAA:NR)

MAN FROM DOWN UNDER, THE** (1943) 103m MGM bw

Charles Laughton (Jocko Wilson), Binnie Barnes (Aggie Dawlins), Richard Carlson ("Nipper" Wilson), Donna Reed (Mary Wilson), Christopher Severn ("Nipper" as a Child), Clyde Cook (Ginger Gaffney), Horace [Stephen] McNally ("Dusty" Rhodes), Arthur Shields (Father Polycarp), Evelyn Falke (Mary as a Child), Hobart Cavanaugh ("Boots"), Andre Charlot (Father Antoine).

Laughton was far too, shall we say, epicene to ever convince anyone that he'd been a professional boxer, but that's what the producers attempt to make us believe in this otherwise okay film. WW I is ending and ex-pugilist Laughton, an Aussie sarge, picks up two Belgian orphans, Severn and Falke, before leaving England for his home in Australia. He leaves Barnes, a singer, at the dock and departs. Laughton raises the kids, and Severn grows into being Carlson, a boxer who wins the lightweight title and then has to quit due to injuries. Falke grows up to be Reed and is sent off to a private boarding school. Carlson has won some money in the ring and Laughton uses it to buy a large estate which he converts into a hotel. Years have passed and Barnes arrives, now a rich widow, at the inn which is having a tough time. Barnes gambles with Laughton and vengefully takes the hotel away from him with her prowess at cards and craps. Reed and Carlson don't know that they are not blood relations and are attracted to each other but must sublimate that. McNally, a reporter from the U.S., is after Reed but she rejects him. WW II is upon them and a Japanese attack forces them all under the same roof. Laughton reveals that Reed and Carlson are not related and he and Barnes wind up rekindling the fire that they once had. The co-producer's name was Dull, and, unfortunately, so is much of the movie. An added highlight is that the famous revue producer, Andre Charlot took an acting job as the priest. Thank heaven that they didn't lay the Aussie accent on too thickly or we never would have heard any of the dialog, inane as it might be.

p, Robert Z. Leonard, Orville O. Dull; d, Leonard; w, Wells Root, Thomas Seller (based on a story by Bogart Rogers, Mark Kelly); ph, Sidney Wagner; m, David Snell; ed, George White; art d, Cedric Gibbons; spec eff, A. Arnold Gillespie; m/l, Earl Brent.

Drama (PR:A-C MPAA:NR)

MAN FROM FRISCO** (1944) 91m REP bw

Michael O'Shea (Matt Braddock), Anne Shirley (Diana Kennedy), Gene Lockhart (Joel Kennedy), Dan Duryea (Jim Benson), Ray Walker (Johnny Rogers), Robert Warwick (Bruce McRae), Forbes Murray (Maritime Commissioner), Ann Shoemaker (Martha Kennedy), Tommy Bond (Russ Kennedy), Charles Wilson, Ed Peil, Sr., William Nestell, Roy Barcroft (Key Men), Russell Simpson (Dr. Hershey), Erville Alderson (Judge McLain), Olin Howlin (Eben Whelock), Stanley Andrews (Chief Campbell), Martin Garralaga (Mexican), Ira "Buck" Woods (Black Worker), Stephanie Bachelor (Ruth Warnecke), Charles Sullivan (Irishman), William Haade (Brooklyn), Sid Gould (Russian), Tom London (Old Salt), George Cleveland (Mayor Winter), Nolan Leary, Hal Price, Jack Low, Harry Tenbrook, Dick Alexander, Sam Bernard, Lee Shumway, George Lloyd (Workmen), Judy Cook (Worker), Eddy Waller (Older Worker), Tom Chatterton (Doctor), Minerva Urecal (Widow Allison), Jack Gardner, Rex Lease, Roy Darmour (Men), Effie Laird (Mrs. Hanson), Virginia Carroll, Marjorie Kane (Girls), Patricia Knox (Girl Welder), Gino

Corrado (Tony D'Agostino), Frank Moran (Mr. Hanson), Norman Nesbitt (Announcer), H. Michael Barnitz (Ruth Warnecke's Baby), Chester Conklin (Baggage Man), Rosina Galli (Mrs. Palaski), George Neise (Narrator), Monte Montana (Montana), Frank Marlowe (Tough Guy), Ben Taggart (Superintendent), Sam Flint (Chief of Police), Grace Lenard, Weldon Heyburn (Couple in Trailer), Jimmy Conlin (Mayor's Secretary), Harrison Greene (Politician), John Hamilton (Governor), Bud Geary (Bit Man), Kenne Duncan, Jack Kirk (Foremen), Larry Williams (Sam), Maxine Doyle (Woman), John Sheehan (Gang Boss).

This simple-minded programmer from Republic starts off well but quickly gets bogged down in stereotypes and clichéd storytelling. O'Shea, in an unbelievable performance, is an engineer in a shipyard. Thanks to his savvy, the yard is able to produce ships using a new, revolutionary building technique, which makes for better, cheaper ships. This leads to an inevitable romance in the form of Shirley.

p, Albert J. Cohn; d, Robert Florey; w, Ethel Hill, Arnold Manoff (based on a story by George Worthing Yates, George Carlton Brown); ph, Jack Marta; m, Marlin Skiles; ed, Ernest Nims; art d, Russell Kimball.

Drama (PR:A MPAA:NR)

MAN FROM GALVESTON, THE* (1964) 57m WB bw

Jeffrey Hunter (Timothy Higgins), Preston Foster (Judge Homer Black), James Coburn (Boyd Palmer), Joanna Moore (Rita Dillard), Edward Andrews (Hyde), Kevin Hagen (John Dillard), Martin West (Stonewall Grey), Ed Nelson (Cole Marteen), Karl Swenson (Sheriff), Grace Lee Whitney (Texas Rose), Claude Stroud (Harvey Sprager), Sherwood Price (George Taggart), Arthur Malet (Barney), Marjorie Bennett (Mrs. Warren).

The pilot film for the T.V. series "Temple Houston," which was originally to be shown on the tube. Warner Bros. felt that the series would get an extra pump if released as a feature film. The story is a simple-minded courtroom drama with Hunter as a frontier lawyer defending former girl friend Moore, who's accused of murder. Hunter sleepwalks through this undramatic waste of time, perhaps the fault of executive producer Jack Webb who is known for films and television shows that rival sleeping pills. Directed by actor William Conrad, Webb, at the time of this film, was head of Warner Bros. television production.

p, Michael Meshekoff; d, William Conrad; w, Dean Riesner, Michael Zagor (based on the story "Galahad of Cactus City" by Philip Lonergan); ph, Bert Glennon; m, David Buttolph; ed, Bill Wiard; art d, Carl Macauley; set d, William L. Kuehl.

Western (PR:A MPAA:NR)

MAN FROM GOD'S COUNTRY** (1958) 72m AA c

George Montgomery (Dan Beattie), Randy Stuart (Nancy Dawson), Gregg Barton (Colonel), Kim Charney (Stony Warren), Susan Cummings (Mary Jo Ellis), James Griffith (Mark Faber), House Peters, Jr. (Curt Warren), Phillip Terry (Sheriff), Frank Wilcox (Beau Santee), Al Wyatt (Henchman).

Montgomery is a quick-drawing sheriff who's asked to resign from his post. The townspeople want a quieter town and the only gun that is blazing is the sheriff's. Montgomery goes to the town of Sundown where he and Civil War buddy Peters join forces to clean up the town. With justice served, Montgomery hooks up with Stuart, a dance hall hostess, and Peters with Cummings.

p, Scott R. Dunlap; d, Paul Landres; w, George Waggner; ph, Harry Neumann (CinemaScope, Deluxe Color); m, Marlin Skiles; ed, George White; art d, David Milton; m/l, "New Day at Sundown," Jack Brooks, Gerald Fried.

Western (PR:A MPAA:NR)

MAN FROM GUN TOWN, THE** (1936) 58m Puritan bw

Tim McCoy (Tim Hanlon), Billie Seward (Ruth McArthur), Rex Lease (Alan McArthur), Jack Clifford (Sheriff), Wheeler Oakman (De Long), Bob McKenzie (Gillis), Jack Rockwell (Slater), George Chesebro (Carnes), George Pearce (Wells), Ella McKenzie (Aunt Sarah), Horace B. Carpenter (Gillespie), Hank Bell.

McCoy comes to the rescue of rancher Seward, who's being harassed by Chesebro, Oakman, and their gang. When McCoy arrives, the outlaws have framed Seward for the murder of her brother. McCoy sends the lead flying, but in the end he doesn't stay with Seward, which would have been the typical ending. Instead he rides off alone to forget the killing he was forced into.

p, Nat Ross; d, Ford Beebe; w, Beebe, Thomas H. Ince, Jr. (based on a story by Beebe); ph, James Diamond; ed, Robert Johns.

Western (PR:A MPAA:NR)

MAN FROM HEADQUARTERS** (1942) 64m MON bw

Frank Albertson (Larry Doyle), Joan Woodbury (Ann), John Maxwell (Marvin), Max Hoffman, Jr. (Padroni), Dick Elliott (Jones), Byron Foulger (Hotel Manager), Robert Kellard (Hotel Clerk), Arthur O'Connell (Goldie), Paul Bryar (Knucks), Irving Mitchell (Nate), George O'Hanlon (Weeks), Christine McIntyre (Telegraph Girl), Mel Ruick, Gwen Kenyon, Jack Mulhall, Maynard Holmes, Charles Hall.

Albertson is a Chicago police reporter who solves a gangland murder. He's then kidnaped by gangsters from St. Louis in order to keep him from testifying against their boss. Albertson escapes, meets up with Woodbury, and together they pin a robbery on the crime boss.

p, Lindsley Parsons; d, Jean Yarbrough; w, John Krafft and Rollo Lloyd; ph, William Strohbach; ed, Jack Ogilvie; md, Edward Kay.

Crime Drama (PR:A MPAA:NR)

MAN FROM HELL, THE* (1934) 55m Marcey/Cristo bw

Reb Russell (Clint Mason), Fred Kohler (Anse McCloud), Ann Darcy (Nancy Campbell), George Hayes (Col. Campbell), Jack Rockwell (Lon Kelly), Charles French (Sandy), Murdock MacQuarrie (Sheriff Jake), Charles "Slim" Whitaker

(Tom Hosford), Tommy Bupp (Timmy McCarroll), Tracy Lane (Gillis), Yakima Canutt (Yak), Mary Gordon (Mrs. Frank McCarroll), Roy D'Arcy.

A cheap western, from a small-time production company, starring former football hero Russell. Russell is a sheriff who goes undercover as an outlaw to unmask the mayor, Kohler, as the head of a gang of bandits. Director Collins became very successful in directing series westerns in the 1940s.

p, Willis Kent; d, Lew Collins; w, Melville Shyer (based on a story by Ed Earl Repp); ph, William Nobles; ed, Roy Luby.

Western   **(PR:A   MPAA:NR)**

MAN FROM HELL'S EDGES*   (1932) 63m Sono Art/World Wide bw

Bob Steele (Bob Williams), Nancy Drexel (Betty), Julian Rivero (Lobo), Robert E. Homans (Sheriff), George Hayes (Shamrock), Peewee Holmes (Half Pint), Earl Dwire (Morgan), Dick Dickinson, Perry Murdock (Drake Bros.), Gilbert Holmes, Blackie Whiteford.

Cowboy Steele in another B-production western with familiar story and action. Steele is wrongly arrested for murder, escapes from jail, gets the real criminal, and gets the girl.

p, Trem Carr; d, Robert N. Bradbury; w, Bradbury; ph, Wilfrid Cline; ed, Carl Pierson.

Western   **(PR:A   MPAA:NR)**

MAN FROM HONG KONG*¹/₂
(1975) 102m FOX c (AKA: THE DRAGON FLIES)

Jimmy Wang Yu (Fang), George Lazenby (Wilton), Hugh Keays-Byrne (Morrie), Roger Ward (Bob), Ros Spiers (Caroline), Grant Page (Assassin), Rebecca Gilling (Angelica), Frank Thring (Willard), Hung Kam Po, Deryk Barnes, Bill Hunter, Ian Jamieson.

The martial arts antics take place this time down under in Sydney, Australia. Police officer Yu is assigned to hunt down drug dealer Lazenby (James Bond in ON HER MAJESTY'S SECRET SERVICE) who is a kung fu expert. Not much story but a lot of kicks, punches, and blood.

p, Raymond Chow, John Fraser; d&w, Brian Trenchard Smith; ph, Russell Boyd; m, Noel Quinlan; ed, Ron Williams.

Martial Arts   **(PR:O   MPAA:R)**

MAN FROM LARAMIE, THE****   (1955) 104m COL c

James Stewart (Will Lockhart), Arthur Kennedy (Vic Hansbro), Donald Crisp (Alec Waggoman), Cathy O'Donnell (Barbara Waggoman), Alex Nicol (Dave Waggoman), Aline MacMahon (Kate Canaday), Wallace Ford (Charley O'Leary), Jack Elam (Chris Boldt), John War Eagle (Frank Darrah), James Millican (Tom Quigby), Gregg Barton (Fritz), Boyd Stockman (Spud Oxton), Frank de Kova (Padre), Frank Cordell, Jack Carry, William Catching, Frosty Royse (Mule Drivers), Eddy Waller (Dr. Selden).

The westerns of director Anthony Mann revitalized the genre in the 1950s because they were derived from classic struggles inspired by such works as the Bible and Shakespeare. His westerns weren't just action-packed chases, they were adult dramas which illustrated the psychological and moral dilemmas regarding the family, hatred, revenge, the land, and the nature of savagery versus civilization. In addition to being skillfully shot, acted, and scripted, Mann brought an intelligence to the western only surpassed by John Ford. THE MAN FROM LARAMIE introduces us to another Mann-Stewart character driven by an obsession. Stewart leaves his home in Laramie, Wyoming, on a mission to uncover the men responsible for selling automatic rifles to the Apaches who had slaughtered his brother while serving in the cavalry. He enters the town of Coronado, New Mexico, and soon learns that most of the territory is ruled by Crisp, an aging, almost blind, megalomanical rancher who has been waging a long war against rival female rancher MacMahon, a former lover. While riding through some salt flats owned by Crisp, Stewart is confronted by the powerful rancher's psychotic son, Nicol. Unaware that he has done anything wrong, Stewart finds himself beaten and dragged through his bonfire, while Nicol's henchmen burn his wagons and shoot his mules. It looks as though Nicol is going to beat Stewart to death until the violence is interrupted by Kennedy, the foreman of the ranch and Crisp's adopted son. Stewart is brought back to the ranch where Crisp pays for the damages and advises the stranger to leave town. Determined to find the men responsible for his brother's death, Stewart ventures to MacMahon's ranch and is hired by the woman rancher. He learns that Crisp has become increasingly concerned with who will take over his empire, and although Kennedy has been running things smoothly for years, the rancher is likely to pick Nicol, his blood heir. Finally Crisp, blind to his adopted son's failings, chooses Nicol to take over the ranch, enraging Kennedy. Stewart continues digging for clues regarding the sale of the guns. He is once again caught by Nicol and his men. After a brutal fight where Stewart stomps on Nicol's hand, the crazed cowboy has his men subdue the stranger while he fires a bullet through Stewart's hand at point blank range. Nicol's men, disgusted by their participation in this cowardly act, help the crippled Stewart onto his horse and send him on his way. Still angry over the inheritance of the ranch, Kennedy starts an argument with Nicol regarding the guns and kills him. Stewart, of course, is blamed for the murder. Soon after, Crisp discovers that his sons have been selling rifles to the Apaches. He confronts Kennedy on the trail and a fight ensues. To keep their evil deeds a secret, Kennedy pushes the old man off a jagged cliff. Stewart learns the truth about the guns and confronts Kennedy. Cornered on a cliff with Stewart on one side and Apaches below, an unarmed Kennedy awaits his fate. Stewart trains his Winchester on the gun-runner, but at the moment he finally can enact his revenge, his hands begin to shake and he finds himself unable to kill. Instead, he pushes the cart of rifles over the edge of the cliff. The Apaches see their guns destroyed and retaliate by shooting Kennedy dead. An emotionally drained Stewart mounts his horse and returns to Laramie. At the time of his death in 1967,

director Mann had announced his plan to adapt Shakespeare's King Lear as a western (much the same way Japanese director Akira Kurosawa would years later with RAN in 1985). One can see that THE MAN FROM LARAMIE was something of a dress rehearsal for this project. Crisp, as Lear, frets over the continuation of his empire and is blind to the fact that it is Kennedy who loves him most. His guilt feelings regarding his ruthless life (and having turned his former lover into an enemy) cloud his mind and move him to make bad decisions that ensure his downfall. This is the stuff of tragedy, and it does not often surface in westerns. THE MAN FROM LARAMIE came at the end of a cycle of collaboration between director Mann and actor Stewart which produced some of the greatest westerns ever made, WINCHESTER '73 (1950), BEND OF THE RIVER, THE NAKED SPUR (both in 1952), and THE FAR COUNTRY (1954). Their creative teamwork stands equal to those of John Ford-John Wayne and Budd Boetticher-Randolph Scott collaborations which helped establish the western genre as a true American art form. Not to be missed.

p, William Goetz; d, Anthony Mann; w, Philip Yordan, Frank Burt (based on a Saturday Evening Post story by Thomas T. Flynn); ph, Charles Lang (Technicolor); m, George Duning; ed, William Lyon; md, Morris W. Stoloff, Arthur Morton; art d, Cary Odell; set d, James Crowe; m/l, "Man from Laramie," Lester Lee, Ned Washington; makeup, Clay Campbell.

Western   **(PR:C   MPAA:NR)**

MAN FROM MONTANA*¹/₂
(1941) 59m UNIV bw (GB: MONTANA JUSTICE)

Johnny Mack Brown (Bob Dawson), Fuzzy Knight (Grubby), Billy Lenhart (Butch), Kenneth Brown (Buddy), Jeanne Kelly [Jean Brooks] (Linda), Nell O'Day (Sally), William Gould (Thompson), James Blaine (Dunham), Dick Alexander (Kohler), Karl Hackett (Trig), Edmund Cobb (Dakota), Frank Ellis (Decker), Kermit Maynard (Chris), Jack Shannon (Tex), Murdock MacQuarrie (Preston), Charles McMurphy (Dugan), The King's Men.

Brown is a sheriff who defends the homesteaders from a band of invading outlaws. The outlaws try to stir up trouble between the ranchers and homesteaders, but Brown does some fast talking and shooting. Below par for a western from one of Brown's series. Songs include: "Call of the Range," "Western Trail," "Bananas Make Me Tough," "Little Joe."

p, Will Cowan; d, Ray Taylor; w, Bennett Cohen; ph, Charles Van Enger.

Western   **(PR:A   MPAA:NR)**

MAN FROM MONTEREY, THE**   (1933) 59m WB bw

John Wayne (Capt. John Holmes), Ruth Hall (Dolores), Luis Alberni (Felipe), Francis Ford (Don Pablo), Nina Quartaro (Anita Garcia), Lafayette [Lafe] McKee (Don Jose Castanares), Donald Reed (Don Luis Gonzales), Lillian Leighton (Juanita), Charles Whitaker (Jake Morgan), Jim Corey, Duke, the Devil Horse.

Wayne is a U.S. Army captain who is sent to Monterey to get Mexican landowners to register their property under Spanish land grants or lose them to public domain. Reed is the perpetrator of the land swindles, who is trying to kill Spanish landowner McKee. Wayne not only stops the swindler, but also the marriage of Hall to villain Reed. This was Wayne's last series western for Warner Bros.

p, Leon Schlesinger; d, Mack V. Wright; w, Lesley Mason; ph, Ted McCord; ed, William Clemens.

Western   **(PR:A   MPAA:NR)**

MAN FROM MONTREAL, THE**   (1940) 61m UNIV bw

Richard Arlen (Clark Manning), Andy Devine (Constable Bones Blair), Kay Sutton (Myrna Montgomery), Anne Gwynne (Doris Blair), Reed Hadley (Ross Montgomery), Addison Richards (Capt. Owens), Joseph Sawyer (Biff Anders), Jerry Marlowe (Jim Morris), Tommy Whitten (Brad Owens), Eddy C. Waller (Old Jacques), Eddy Conrad (Marcel Bircheaux), William Royle (Luther St. Paul), Lane Chandler (Constable Rankin), Don Brodie (Pete), Karl Hackett (McLennon), Pat Flaherty (Tom).

Arlen is a trapper accused of stealing pelts who sets out to prove his innocence, pitting the fur trappers against the Mounties headed by Devine. Things are finally squared away when Arlen shows that he didn't commit the crime. Gwynne plays Arlen's girl friend and Sutton plays the vamp.

p, Ben Pivar; d, Christy Cabanne; w, Owen Francis (based on a story by Pivar); ph, Milton Krasner.

Action/Adventure   **(PR:A   MPAA:NR)**

MAN FROM MOROCCO, THE*¹/₂   (1946, Brit.) 89m ABP/Pathe bw

Anton Walbrook (Karel Langer), Margaretta Scott (Manuela), Mary Morris (Sarah Duboste), Reginald Tate (Ricardi), Peter Sinclair (Jock Sinclair), David Horne (Dr. Duboste), Hartley Power (Col. Bagley), Sybilla Binder (Erna), Charles Victor (Bourdille), Josef Almas (Franz), John McLaren (Pete), Dennis Arundell (Galzini), Andre Randall (French General), Carl Jaffe (German General), Orlando Martins (Jeremiah), Paul Demel, David Baxter, Margaret Emden, Jan van Loewen, Paul Sheridan, Gwen Bateman, Henry Morrell, Stuart Lindsell, Roger Snowden, Robert Arden, Harold Berens, Glyn Rowland, Marie Ault, Paul Bonitas.

British war movie dealing with a group of men of different nationalities fighting fascism in Spain. The freedom fighters encounter a sadistic Vichy officer, a murdering female spy in disguise as a nurse, and other fascists as the volunteers struggle to get vital information to England.

p, Warwick Ward; d, Max Greene; w, Edward Dryhurst, Margaret Steen, Ward (based on a story by Rudolph Cartier); ph, Basil Emmott; m, Mischa Spoliansky.

Action/Adventure   **(PR:A   MPAA:NR)**

MAN FROM MUSIC MOUNTAIN** ¹/₂   (1938) 58m REP bw

Gene Autry (Gene), Smiley Burnette (Frog), Carol Hughes (Helen), Sally Payne (Patsy), Ivan Miller (Scanlon), Edward Cassidy (Brady), Lew Kelly (Bowdie Bill), Howard Chase (Abbott), Albert Terry (Buddy), Frankie Marvin (Larry), Earl Dwire (Martin), Lloyd Ingraham (Harmon), Lillian Drew (Mrs. Chris), Al Taylor (Hank), Joe Yrigoyen (Pete), Polly Jenkins and Her Plowboys, Dick Elliott, Hal Price, Cactus Mack, Gordon Hart, Rudy Sooter, Harry Harvey, Meredith McCormack, Chris Allen, Champion the Horse.

Autry, the singing, punching cowboy, rides high in this effort, which includes enjoyable songs and quick-paced action that covers the holes in the standard story. Autry puts a quick halt to unscrupulous land developers trying to fleece ranchers, whose land is full of gold. Songs include "Love, Burning Love" (Autry, Johnny Marvin, and Fred Rose).

p, Charles E. Ford; d, Joseph Kane; w, Betty Burbridge, Luci Ward (based on a story by Bernard McConville); ph, Jack Marta; ed, Lester Orlebeck; m/l, Peter Tinturin, Jack Lawrence, Eddie Cherkose, Smiley Burnette, Gene Autry, Johnny Marvin, Fred Rose.

Western   **Cas.**   **(PR:A MPAA:NR)**

MAN FROM MUSIC MOUNTAIN** ¹/₂   (1943) 71m REP bw

Roy Rogers (Roy), Ruth Terry (Laramie Winters), Paul Kelly (Victor Marsh), Ann Gillis (Penny Winters), George Cleveland (Sheriff Joe Darcey), Pat Brady (Pat), Renie Riano (Christina Kellog), Paul Harvey (Arthur Davis), Hank Bell (Dobe Joe), Jay Novello (Barker), Hal Taliaferro (Wally Wales) (Slade), Bob Nolan and the Sons of the Pioneers (Themselves), I. Stanford Jolley, Jack O'Shea, Tom Smith, Charles Morton, Trigger the Horse.

Roy returns to his hometown to make a radio show appearance and gets mixed up in a feud between the cattlemen and sheepherders. He takes on the role of deputy sheriff long enough to solve the dispute. Enough time is left at the finale, however, for some "good ol' hometown music-makin'" by Roy along with Bob Nolan's Sons of the Pioneers.

p, Harry Grey; d, Joseph Kane; w, Bradford Ropes, J. Benton Chaney; ph, William Bradford; ed, Tony Martinelli; md, Morton Scott; art d, Russell Kimball.

Western   **(PR:A MPAA:NR)**

MAN FROM NEVADA, THE   (SEE: NEVADAN, THE, 1950)

MAN FROM NEW MEXICO, THE**   (1932) 54m MON bw

Tom Tyler, Caryl Lincoln, Robert Walker, Jack Richardson, Lafe McKee, Frank Ball, Lewis Sargent, Blackie Whiteford, Slim Whitaker, Frederick Ryter, Jack Long, William Nolte, C. V. Bussey, Lee Tinn.

A gang of outlaws comes up with the idea of injecting snake poison into cattle herds instead of the expected serum. Their intention is to deplete a rancher's stock and force him into selling. Tyler buddies up to the outlaws, but then admits to his working for the Cattleman's Association. Lincoln turns in a fine performance as the skillful rider who lends Tyler a hand.

p, Trem Carr; d, J. P. McGowan; w, Harry Hoyt (based on the story "Fang Branded" by Frederick Ryter); ph, Edward Kull.

Western   **(PR:A MPAA:NR)**

MAN FROM NOWHERE, THE (SEE: ARIZONA COLT, 1965, Fr./Ital./Span.)

MAN FROM OKLAHOMA, THE**   (1945) 68m REP bw

Roy Rogers (Himself), George "Gabby" Hayes (Gabby Whittaker), Dale Evans (Peggy Lane), Roger Pryor (Jim Gardner), Arthur Loft (J.J. Cardigan), Maude Eburne (Grandma Lane), Sam Flint (Mayor), Si Jenks (Jeff Whittaker), June Bryde (Little Bird on the Wing), Elaine Lange (Vera Graham), Charles Soldani (Chief Red Feather), Edmund Cobb (Ferguson), George Sherwood (Slade), Eddie Kane (Club Manager), George Chandler, Wally West, Tex Terry, Bob Wilke, Bobbie Priest, Dorothy Bailer, Rosamond James, Melva Anstead, Beverly Reedy, Geraldine Farnum, Bob Nolan and the Sons of the Pioneers, Trigger the Horse.

Roy does his thing in the open territory country of Oklahoma, saving Evans from some prairie undesirables. The standout in this typical oater is Eburne, a granny who packs a six-gun and raises some dust when she has to. Songs include "I'm Beginning To See The Light" (Harry James, Duke Ellington, Johnny Hodges, Don George) and "The Martins And The McCoys."

p, Louis Gray; d, Frank McDonald; w, John K. Butler; ph, William Bradford; ed, Tony Martinelli; md, Morton Scott; art d, Fred A. Ritter; spec eff, Howard and Theodore Lydecker.

Western   **(PR:AAA MPAA:NR)**

MAN FROM O.R.G.Y., THE zero

(1970) 75m United Hemisphere-Delta/Cinemation Industries c (AKA: THE REAL GONE GIRLS)

Robert Walker [Jr.] (Steve Victor), Steve Rossi (Luigi), Slappy White (Vito), Louisa Moritz (Gina Moretti), Lynn Carter (Madam), Mike Dailey (Lucky Pierre), Shannon O'Shea, Mimi Dillard, Mark Hannibal, Michel Stany, Mary Marx, Jan Bank.

Walker, the head of a sexual research organization, sets out to locate three prostitutes who are the benefactors of a recently deceased madam's fortune. The women are identifiable thanks to a tattoo of a gopher on their behinds. Two of the hookers are murdered and the third is too rich to care, so a midget (Dailey) ends up with the dough. Lots of T-and-A; better suited for an "X" rating but somehow got an "R".

p, Sidney Pink; d, James A. Hill; w, Ted Mark (based on the novel by Mark); ph, Jose F. Aguayo Jr. (Movielab Color); m, Charles Bernstein; ed, Evan Lottman.

Comedy/Crime   **(PR:O MPAA:R)**

MAN FROM PLANET X, THE** ¹/₂   (1951) 70m Mid-Century/UA bw

Robert Clarke (Lawrence), Margaret Field (Enid Elliot), Raymond Bond (Prof. Elliot), William Schallert (Mears), Roy Engel (Constable), Charles Davis (Geordie), Gilbert Fallman (Dr. Blane), David Ormont (Inspector).

One of the staples of science fiction, this Edgar G. Ulmer film is a fine example of what can be done on a low budget. Shot in six days on the sets left over from JOAN OF ARC (1948), it features Clarke as a reporter in foggy Scotland who is confronted by a friendly alien. The alien's plea for aid for its freezing planet is met with obliteration by the British Army's bazookas. The failure of humanity and the cold-hearted emotions of the Earth's inhabitants are carefully depicted in the bleak ending. One of Ulmer's better efforts from the latter half of his career, the film also boasts one-time Screen Actors' Guild president Schallert among its lead players.

p, Aubrey Wisberg, Jack Pollexfen; d, Edgar G. Ulmer; w, Wisberg, Pollexfen; ph, John L. Russell; m, Charles Koff; ed, Fred C. Feitshans, Jr.; art d, Angelo Scibetti; spec eff, Andy Anderson, Howard Weeks, Jack Rabin.

Science-Fiction   **Cas.**   **(PR:A MPAA:NR)**

MAN FROM RAINBOW VALLEY, THE** ¹/₂   (1946) 56m REP c

Monte Hale (Monte), Adrian Booth (Kay North), Jo Ann Marlowe (Ginny Hale), Ferris Taylor (Col. Winthrop), Emmett Lynn (Locoweed), Tom London (Healey), Bud Geary (Tracy), Kenne Duncan (Lafe), Doyle O'Dell (Jim), Bert Roach (Mayor), The Sagebrush Serenaders: Enright Busse, John Scott, Frank Wilder.

Hale is on the hunt for Outlaw, a stolen stallion which is supposed to be used in a promotional stunt publicizing a cartoon strip. Since it has never been branded the owner cannot make a legal claim, so the thief is tricked into returning it. Photographed in Trucolor, an offshoot of Magnacolor, which Republic was fond of using. The Sagebrush Serenaders and Hale provide the singing. The songs include "Ridin' Down the Trail" and "The Man in the Moon Is a Cowhand."

p, Louis Gray; d, Robert Springsteen; w, Betty Burbridge; ph, Bud Thackery (Trucolor); ed, Edward Mann; md, Mort Glickman; art d, Hilyard Brown; m/l, Eddie Cherkose, Cy Feuer, Roy Rogers, Glen Spencer.

Western   **(PR:A MPAA:NR)**

MAN FROM SNOWY RIVER, THE***

                (1983, Aus.) 102m Hoyts Distribution Cambridge/FOX c

Kirk Douglas (Harrison/Spur), Jack Thompson (Clancy), Tom Burlinson (Jim Craig), Terence Donovan (Henry Craig), Tommy Dysart (Mountain Man), Bruce Kerr (Man in Street), David Bradshaw (A. B. "Banjo" Paterson), Sigrid Thornton (Jessica), Tony Bonner (Kane), June Jago (Mrs. Bailey), Chris Haywood (Curly), Kristopher Steele (Moss), Gus Mercurio (Frew), Howard Eynon (Short Man), Lorraine Bayly (Rosemary), John Nash (Tall Man).

Douglas plays a dual role as two brothers, one an aristocratic landowner (Harrison), the other a one-legged scraggly prospector (Spur). The pair experience a falling out which is not even addressed until the latter half of the picture. More important are the characterizations by Douglas, which are based on an age-old Australian legend which is drummed into the heads of students there in much the same way as Tom Sawyer and Huck Finn in the U.S. The film was one of Australia's top-grossing pictures, though the producers took a chance in casting the American Douglas in the role. (Robert Mitchum and Burt Lancaster also were considered.) A fine directorial debut from George Miller who, not surprisingly, is easily confused with the director of MAD MAX (1979) and THE ROAD WARRIOR (1982), also named George Miller.

p, Geoff Burrowes; d, George Miller; w, John Dixon, Fred Cullen (based on the poem by A. B. "Banjo" Paterson); ph, Keith Wagstaff (Panavision, Eastmancolor); m, Bruce Rowland; ed, Adrian Carr; art d, Leslie Binns; cos, Robin Hall; makeup, Vivien Mephan.

Adventure   **Cas.**   **(PR:C MPAA:R)**

MAN FROM SUNDOWN, THE* ¹/₂

                (1939) 58m COL bw (GB: A WOMAN'S VENGEANCE)

Charles Starrett (Larry Whalen), Iris Meredith (Barbara Kellogg), Richard Fiske (Tom Kellogg), Jack Rockwell (Hank Austin), Alan Bridge (Slick Larson), Richard Botiller (Rio Mason), Ernie Adams (Shorty Bates), Bob Nolan (Bob), Pat Brady (Pat), Robert Fiske (Capt. Prescott), Edward Piel, Sr. (Sheriff Wiley), Clem Horton (Bat), Forrest H. Dillon (Kirk), Edmund Cobb (Roper), Tex Cooper, Al Haskell, Edward J. LeSaint, Kit Guard, George Chesebro, Oscar Gahan, Frank Ellis, Sons of the Pioneers.

A weak horse opry which has Starrett in the saddle cleaning up after a Texas outlaw who ruthlessly kills anyone who gets in his way. Meredith, who gets in just about everyone's way, manages to escape danger when Starrett helps her out.

d, Sam Nelson; w, Paul Franklin; ph, Benjamin Kline; ed, William Lyon; m/l, Bob Nolan, Tim Spencer.

Western   **(PR:A MPAA:NR)**

MAN FROM TANGIER   (SEE: THUNDER OVER TANGIER, 1957, Brit.)

MAN FROM TEXAS, THE** ¹/₂   (1939) 56m MON bw

Tex Ritter (Tex Allen), Hal Price (Sheriff Missouri), Charles B. Wood (Shooting Kid), Vic Demourelle, Jr. (Jeff Hall), Roy Barcroft (Drifter), Frank Wayne (Longhorn), Kenne Duncan (Speed Dennison), Ruth Rogers (Laddie), Tom London (Slim), Charles King, Nelson McDowell, Sherry Tansey, Chick Hannon, White Flash The Horse.

Ritter, in one of his best entries, goes undercover to help out a hurting rancher. He finds out that Barcroft is behind a plot to buy up valuable railroad land at less than generous prices. Ritter does a good turn for Wood, but is let down by the ungrateful punk. He comes around in the end, however, to aid in Barcroft's defeat amidst some gutsy and hard-hitting gunplay.

p, Edward Finney; d, Al Herman; w, Robert Emmett [Tansey]; ph, Marcel Le Picard; ed, Fred Bain; m/l "Prairie Lights," "Men Who Wear the Stars" (sung by Tex Ritter).

Western **(PR:A MPAA:NR)**

MAN FROM TEXAS, THE* (1948) 71m EL bw

James Craig (El Paso Kid), Lynn Bari (Lee Bixbee), Johnnie Johnston (Billy Taylor), Una Merkel (Widow Weeks), Wally Ford (Jed), Harry Davenport (Pop Hickey), Sara Allgood (Aunt Belle), Vic Cutler (Charles Jackson), Reed Hadley (U.S. Marshal), Clancy Cooper (Jim Walsh), Bert Conway (Bob Jackson), King Donovan (Sam), Glen Arthur, Susan O'Connor.

There's not much to this minor B western, which has Craig helping the poor widowed Merkel but, in the meantime, doing some bank robbing. Not much sympathy can be given to Craig who spends more time riding the fence between lawfulness and lawlessness than he does riding a horse.

p, Joseph Fields; d, Leigh Jason; w, Fields, Jerome Chodorov (based on a play by E. B. McGinty); ph, Jackson J. Rose; ed, Alfred DeGaetano, Norman Colbert; md, Irving Friedman; art d, Edward Ilou; m/l, Earl Robinson, Fields.

Western **(PR:A MPAA:NR)**

MAN FROM THE ALAMO, THE*** (1953) 79m UNIV c

Glenn Ford (John Stoud), Julia Adams (Beth Anders), Chill Wills (John Gage), Victor Jory (Jess Wade), Hugh O'Brian (Lt. Lamar), John Day (Cavish), Myra Marsh (Ma Anders), Mark Cavell (Carlos), Jeanne Cooper (Kate Lamar), Neville Brand (Dawes), Edward Norris (Mapes), Guy Williams (Sergeant), George Eldredge, Ward Negley, Dan Poore.

Ford stars in this taut western as one of the soldiers defending the Alamo against Santa Ana's forces. When it is decided that the men will draw straws and the winner will try to escape and warn the soldiers' families of the impending danger, Ford is chosen and becomes the sole survivor of the massacre. When he reaches his family's home he finds that they, too, have been slaughtered, as have all the other families. Ford is labeled a coward, having run out on the brave soldiers who gave their lives at the Alamo. Rather than defend himself, Ford remains stoical until he can find out who is responsible for the deaths of the families. He discovers that Jory, together with a group of men disguised as Mexican soldiers, did the killings. Ford has trouble finding support, especially from rigid Army lieutenant O'Brian. The only person who believes in him is Adams, who does her best to comfort Ford after the loss of his wife. Bent on revenge, Ford hunts down Jory and his men and deals them a just sentence. THE MAN FROM THE ALAMO, while less interesting than Boetticher's "Ranown" films (scripted by Arthur Kennedy and starring Randolph Scott from 1956–60), is notable as a precursor to those pictures. Ford, while less rugged than Scott, shows early signs of the typical Boetticher hero. "The essence of the hero," according to Jim Kitses in his study of Boetticher in Horizons West, "is the knowledge that action is both gratuitous and essential. Revenge is meaningless since the wife is dead; yet it is necessary because it is evidence of a way of life that the hero embodies." This description also bears resemblance to another character Ford played in 1953—the tough policeman in THE BIG HEAT bent on avenging the murder of his wife.

p, Aaron Rosenberg; d, Budd Boetticher; w, Steve Fisher, D. D. Beauchamp (based on a story by Niven Busch, Oliver Crawford); ph, Russell Metty (Technicolor); m, Frank Skinner; ed, Virgil Vogel; art d, Alexander Golitzen, Emrich Nicholson; cos, Bill Thomas.

Western **(PR:A MPAA:NR)**

MAN FROM THE BIG CITY, THE (SEE: IT HAPPENED OUT WEST, 1937)

MAN FROM THE DINERS' CLUB, THE*** (1963) 96m Dena Pictures-Ampersand/COL bw

Danny Kaye (Ernie Klenk), Cara Williams (Sugar Pye), Martha Hyer (Lucy), Telly Savalas (Foots Pulardos), Everett Sloane (Martindale), Kay Stevens (Bea Frampton), Howard Caine (Bassanio), George Kennedy (George), Jay Novello (Mooseghian), Ann Morgan Guilbert (Ella Trask), Ronald Long (Minister), Mark Tobin (Quas), Cliff Carnell (Buzzy), Edmund Williams (Jerry Markus), [Harry] Dean Stanton (1st Beatnik), Carol Dixon (Little Girl), John Newton (Father), Dorothy Neumann (Spinster).

Kaye is a clerk at the Diners' Club offices who inadvertently approves an application for gangster Savalas. He tries to correct his mistake by paying Savalas a visit at the health club which he uses as a front. It is then that the mobster notices a physical characteristic that he shares with Kaye—two different size feet. Savalas hits on the idea of burning down the health club with Kaye inside in the hope that the police would mistake Kaye's charred remains as his own. Savalas prepares his scheme and then makes for the airport, but Kaye escapes. The finale has Savalas captured after Kaye creates a traffic jam. A sub-standard film for Tashlin, but still better than most comedies of the period. Scriptwriter Bill Blatty later became William Peter Blatty and published the novel The Exorcist, which was funny in its own way. Cast as the 1st Beatnik is Dean Stanton, the fine character actor who is perhaps better known as Harry Dean Stanton.

p, Bill Bloom; d, Frank Tashlin; w, Bill Blatty (based on a story by Blatty, John Fenton Murray); ph, Hal Mohr; m, Stu Phillips; ed, William A. Lyon; art d, Don Ament; set d, William Kiernan; cos, Pat Barto; spec eff, Richard Albain; m/l "The

Man From the Diners' Club," Johnny Lehmann, Steve Lawrence (sung by Lawrence); makeup, Ben Lane.

Comedy **(PR:A MPAA:NR)**

MAN FROM THE EAST, THE** (1961, Jap.) 103m Toho c (HIGASHI KARA KITA OTOKO)

Yuzo Kayama, Yuriko Hoshi, Shiro Osaka, Makoto Sato, Jun Funato, Kazuo Yashiro, Kokinji Katsura, Shin Morikawa, Sahara Kenji, Toru Abe.

Kayama is a young minstrel who is beaten up by a gang of thugs without putting up a fight. He is helped by a poet and moves in with him in the slums. Gangsters are trying to get rid of all the slum inhabitants and slum dwellers turn to Kayama, but he will not fight. He had been a prizefighter who killed his best friend in the ring. When he finds the poet murdered by the gangsters, he aids the slum people in driving out the thugs.

d, Umeji Inoue; w, Katsuya Suzaki, Yoshio Hasuike; ph, Kozo Okazaki (Tohoscope, Eastmancolor); m, Hajime Kaburagi.

Drama **(PR:A MPAA:NR)**

MAN FROM THE EAST, A*** (1974, Ital./Fr.) 122m P.E.A.-Les Productions Artistes Associes/UA c(E PRI LO CHIAMAVONO IL MAGNIFICO)

Terence Hill [Mario Girotti] (Tom), Gregory Walcott (Bull), Harry Carey, Jr. (Holy Joe), Dominic Barto (Monkey), Yanti Somer (Candida), Riccardo Pizzuti.

Hill is a Bostonian who takes a job at his father's out-West ranch. He eventually puts down his books and his bicycle and learns the ropes of the Western way of living. A comic bookish piece of mass entertainment which takes from the Hollywood riches of old westerns and gives to the Italian public. A bit too heavy on the violence and language for the youngsters.

p, Alberto Grimaldi; d&w, E. B. Clucher [Enzo Barboni]; ph, Aldo Giordani (Technicolor); m, Guido de Angelis, Maurizio de Angelis; ed, Eugenio Alabiso; art d, Enzo Bulgarelli.

Western/Comedy **(PR:C-O MPAA:PG)**

MAN FROM THE FIRST CENTURY, THE* (1961, Czech.) 95 m Czechoslovensky Film/Czech bw (MUZ Z PRVNIHO STOLETI; AKA: THE MAN FROM THE PAST; MAN IN OUTER SPACE)

Milos Kopecky (Joseph), Radovan Lukavsky (Adam), Anita Kajlichova, Otomar Krejca, Vit Olmer, Lubomir Lipsky, Vladimir Hlavaty, Josef Hlinomatz, Zdenek Rehor, Anna Pitasova.

A science fiction comedy with Kopecky accidentally blasting himself off in a spaceship. He returns to earth in the year 2447 with an alien, Lukavsky, and finds the world ruled by automation. A heavy-handed comedy with poor acting.

d&w, Oldrich Lipsky; ph, Vladimir Novotny.

Science Fiction/Comedy **(PR:A MPAA:NR)**

MAN FROM THE FOLIES BERGERE, THE (SEE: FOLIES BERGERE, 1935)

MAN FROM THE PAST, THE (SEE: MAN FROM THE FIRST CENTURY, THE, 1961, Czech.)

MAN FROM THE RIO GRANDE, THE*1/2 (1943) 55m REP bw

Don "Red" Barry (Lee Grant), Wally Vernon (Jimpson Simpson), Twinkle Watts (Herself), Harry Cording (John King), Nancy Gay (Doris King), Kirk Alyn (Tom Traynor), Paul Scardon (Two-way Hanlon), Roy Barcroft (Ace Holden), Kenne Duncan (Chick Benton), Jack Kirk (Curly Wells), Kansas Moehring (Art Thomas), LeRoy Mason, Earle Hodgins, Ken Terrell, Robert Homans, Tom London, Bud Geary, Jack O'Shea.

This Barry film miraculously combines the old West with ice-skating. Yes, ice-skating! Twinkle Watts is an 8-year-old skater who nearly loses her million-dollar inheritance to a scheming outlaw, until six-shootin' Barry saves the day.

p, Eddy White; d, Howard Bretherton; w, Norman S. Hall; ph, John MacBurnie; m, Mort Glickman; ed, Ralph Dixon; art d, Russell Kimball.

Western **(PR:A MPAA:NR)**

MAN FROM THUNDER RIVER, THE**1/2 (1943) 57m REP bw

Wild Bill [William] Elliott, George ["Gabby"] Hayes, Anne Jeffreys, Ian Keith, John James, Georgia Cooper, Jack Ingram, Eddie Lee, Charles King, Bud Geary, Jack Rockwell, Ed Cassidy, Roy Brent, Al Taylor, Al Bridge, Edmund Cobb, Robert Barron, Jack O'Shea, Curley Dresden, Frank McCarroll.

Rip-snorting western has Elliott and his comrades discovering a plot by some outlaws to nab a cache of gold ore. The bad guys are stopped before the hour is up, with a young woman being saved as well. The action rarely lets up in this entertaining, action-packed outing.

p, Harry Grey; d, John English; w, J. Benton Cheney; ph, Bud Thackery; m, Mort Glickman; ed, Harry Keller; art d, Russell Kimball.

Western **Cas.** **(PR:A MPAA:NR)**

MAN FROM TORONTO, THE** (1933, Brit.) 77m Gainsborough/GAU bw

Jessie Matthews (Leila Farrar), Ian Hunter (Fergus Wimbush), Fred Kerr (Bunston), Ben Field (Jonathan), Margarde Yarde (Mrs. Hubbard), Kathleen Harrison (Martha), George Turner (Povey), Herbert Lomas (Jake), Lawrence Hanray (Duncan), Kenneth Kove (Vicar), Sybil Grove (Vicar's Wife), Percy Parsons (Hogbin), George Zucco (Squire), Diana Cotton, Bob Abel, Billy Shine, Sam Wilkinson.

A little charmer about a couple, Matthews and Hunter, who will inherit a million bucks providing they wed. The catch is they have never met. Neither of them goes for the idea, but after Matthews poses as a maid, Hunter falls in love anyway. Kerr, as the lawyer, does his best to pair the two off and carries the weight of the picture while doing so.

p, Michael Balcon; d, Sinclair Hill; w, W. P. Lipscomb (based on the play by Douglas Murray); ph, Leslie Rowson.

Comedy (PR:A MPAA:NR)

MAN FROM TUMBLEWEEDS, THE** 1/2 (1940) 59m COL bw

Bill Elliott (Sounders), Iris Meredith (Spunky), Dub Taylor (Cannonball), Raphael Bennett (Kilgore), Francis Walker (Lightning), Ernie Adams (Shifty), Al Hill (Honest John), Stanley Brown (Slash), Richard Fiske (Dixon), Edward J. LeSaint (Cameron), Don Beddoe (Governor), Eddie Laughton, John Tyrrell, Ed Cecil, Jack Lowe, Buel Bryant, Olin Francis, Jay Lawrence.

Elliott is hired to head a group of rangers who are given the authority to pursue outlaws over the county lines. Because of a lack of funds, Elliott turns to the local penitentiary to gather his bunch. In return for a top-notch showing, they are offered full pardons. Meredith, on leave from the Charles Starrett pictures, serves as the female entertainment. Director Lewis gives a decent showing of the talents that would later emerge in his 1950s B westerns.

p, Leon Barsha; d, Joseph H. Lewis; w, Charles Francis Royal; ph, George Meehan; ed, Charles Nelson.

Western (PR:A MPAA:NR)

MAN FROM UTAH, THE* (1934) 55m Lone Star/MON bw

John Wayne (John Weston), Polly Ann Young (Marjorie Carter), George Hayes (George Higgins), Yakima Canutt (Cheyenne Kent), Edward Peil, Sr. (Barton), Anita Campillo (Dolores), Lafe McKee (Judge Carter), George Cleveland (Sheriff), Earl Dwire, Artie Ortego.

Wayne joins the rodeo and breaks up a gang of rodeo racketeers. Like most of Lone Star's productions the western opens with a fistfight with the Duke in the middle of the melee.

p, Paul Malvern; d, Robert N. Bradbury; w, Lindsley Parsons; ph, A. J. Stout; ed, Carl Pierson.

Western **Cas.** (PR:A MPAA:NR)

MAN FROM WYOMING, A* (1930) 71m PAR bw

Gary Cooper (Jim Baker), June Collyer (Patricia Hunter), Regis Toomey (Jersey), Morgan Farley (Lt. Lee), E. H. Calvert (Maj. Gen. Hunter), Mary Foy (Inspector), Emile Chautard (French Mayor), Ed Deering (Sergeant), William B. Davidson (Major), Ben Hall (Orderly), Hall Parker.

A poor WW I melodrama stars Cooper as captain in the Army Engineer Corps who marries AWOL ambulance driver Collyer. She is a society girl who became bored with the war, ran away and drew enemy fire to Cooper's company. He must arrest her and grows to admire her stamina when she marches like one of his men in their trek back from the front. They marry in a small town. Coop and his company are sent back to the front and he is reported dead. She becomes an officers' party girl. When Cooper, who was only wounded, finds her, he will not have anything to do with her. In the end, the war is over and the couple make up. Boring, poorly written, and unbelievable.

d, Rowland V. Lee; w, John V. A. Weaver, Albert Shelby Le Vino (based on a story by Joseph Moncure March, Lew Lipton); ph, Harry Fischbeck; ed, Robert Bassler.

Drama (PR:A MPAA:NR)

MAN FROM YESTERDAY, THE*** (1932) 71m PAR bw

Claudette Colbert (Sylvia Suffolk), Clive Brook (Capt. Tony Clyde), Charles Boyer (Rene Goudin), Andy Devine (Steve Hand), Alan Mowbray (Dr. Waite), Ronald Cosbey (Baby Tony), Emil Chautard (Priest), George Davis (Taxi Driver), Reginald Pasch (Hotel Clerk), Christian Rub (Terrace Waiter), Boyd Irwin (British Colonel), Donald Stuart (Private Atkins), Barry Winton (Cpl. Simpkins), Yola d'Avril (Tony's Girl), Barbara Leonard (Steve's Girl), Greta Meyer (Inn Proprietress).

Colbert marries Brook during WW II while Paris is in the midst of a fictitious air raid. She later receives word that he has been killed in combat, but she refuses to marry Boyer, the army surgeon whom she assisted. Brook resurfaces after the war's end and, finding Colbert in love with Boyer, goes off to die. Fine performances from a fine cast which include Devine in a shining role.

d, Berthold Viertel; w, Oliver H. P. Garrett (based on the play by Nell Blackwell, Rowland G. Edwards); ph, Karl Struss.

War/Drama/Romance (PR:A MPAA:NR)

MAN FROM YESTERDAY, THE* 1/2

(1949, Brit.) 68m International Motion Pictures/REN bw

John Stuart (Gerald Amersley), Henry Oscar (Julius Rickman), Gwyneth Vaughan (Doreen Amersley), Marie Burke (Doris Amersley), Laurence Harvey (John Matthews), Grace Arnold, Cherry Davis.

In order to contact her late fiance's spirit Burke uses the spiritual powers of Oscar, a stranger from India who has mysteriously arrived at her household. But she too is soon dead, so Oscar accuses Stuart of killing both Burke and the fiance. The angered Stuart pushes his accuser out of a window, killing the man. From there the story takes an odd twist, showing the preceding events to be a dream. But word arrives at the household that Oscar, who was en route to their home from India, has passed away himself. Though this was full of potential as a good creepy psychological drama, the story is given only a perfunctory treatment that ultimately results in nothing of great interest. Harvey acquits himself well in this film, made during the

year he first achieved leading-man roles in feature films. He went on to greater things, including ROOM AT THE TOP (1958).

p, Harry Reynolds; d, Oswald Mitchell; w, John Gilling; ph, Cyril Bristow.

Drama (PR:O MPAA:NR)

MAN GOES THROUGH THE WALL, A
(SEE: MAN WHO WALKED THROUGH THE WALL, 1964, Ger.)

MAN HE FOUND, THE (SEE: WHIP HAND, THE, 1951)

MAN HUNT** (1933) 64m King/RKO bw

Junior Durkin (Junior), Charlotte V. Henry (Josie), Dorothy Reid [Mrs. Wallace Reid] (Mrs. Scott), Arthur Vinton (Wilkie), Edward Le Saint (Woodward), Richard Carle (Sheriff), Carl Gross, Jr. (Abraham).

Durkin and Henry are two young boys who set out to solve the case of stolen diamonds. Their clues lead them to the adult detective who is handling the case. Seems he is the one who stole the diamonds and committed murder along the way. Strictly for the little ones.

p, J. G. Bachman; d, Irving Cummings; w, Sam Mintz, Leonard Praskins; ph, Joseph Valentine.

Mystery (PR:A MPAA:NR)

MAN HUNT** (1936) 65m WB bw

Marguerite Churchill (Jane Carpenter), Ricardo Cortez (Frank Kingman), Chic Sale (Ed Hoggins), Maude Eburne (Mrs. Hoggins), Don Barclay (Waffles), Frederic Blanchard (Bill Taylor), Larry Kent (Jim Buinter), Cy Kendall (Sheriff at Hackett), Billy Wayne (Dunk), George E. Stone (Silk), Milt Kibbee (Sam), William Gargan (Hank Dawson), Richard Purcell (Skip McHenry), Anita Kerry (Babe), Kenneth Harlan (Jim Davis), Russell Simpson (Parkington), Olin Howland (Starrett), Addison Richards (Mel Purdue), George Ernest (Jackie), Nick Copeland (Blackie), Eddie Shubert (Joe).

Gargan is a young rookie reporter who is trying to hunt down bank robber Cortez and succeeds with the help of an army of G-men. He also ends up hooking schoolteacher Churchill, who is fired from her classroom post. You have seen it all before.

p, Bryan Foy; d, William Clemens; w, Roy Chanslor (based on the story by Earl Felton); ph, Joseph Ruttenberg; ed, Louis Haase; art d, Esdras Hartley.

Crime (PR:A MPAA:NR)

MAN HUNT**** (1941) 105m FOX bw

Walter Pidgeon (Capt. Thorndike), Joan Bennett (Jerry), George Sanders (Quive-Smith), John Carradine (Mr. Jones), Roddy McDowall (Vaner the Cabin Boy), Ludwig Stossel (Doctor), Heather Thatcher (Lady Risborough), Frederic Worlock (Lord Risborough), Roger Imhof (Capt. Jensen), Egon Brecher (Whiskers), Holmes Herbert (Farnsworthy), Fredrik Vogeding (Ambassador), Lucien Prival (Umbrella Man), Herbert Evans (Reeves), Edgar Licho (Little Fat Man), Eily Malyon (Postmistress), John Rogers (Cockney), Lester Mathews (Major), Arno Frey (Police Lieutenant), Keith Hitchcock (London Bobby), Otto Reichow, Bob Stephenson, William Haade (Sentries), Adolph Milar (Pigeon Man), Sven Borg (1st Mate), Hans Joby (Tracker), Douglas Gerrard (Policeman), Clifford Severn (Cockney Boy), Charles Bennett, Bobbie Hale (Costermongers), Frank Benson, Cyril Delevanti (Cab Drivers), Walter Bonn, Carl Ottmar (Harbor Police), Carl Ekberg (Hitler), Olaf Hytten (Secretary), William Vaughn (Chief of Harbor Police), Virginia McDowall (Postmistress' Daughter), Bruce Lester (Co-Pilot), Richard Fraser (Navigator), Kurt Krueger (German Attache).

One of the best-loved of Lang's spy dramas, MAN HUNT is an exciting, tightly constructed, atmospheric picture which stars Pidgeon as a big-game hunter who packs up his rifle for a vacation in the Bavarian Alps. While walking through a forest near Adolf Hitler's Berchtesgaden retreat in the aftermath of the Munich Pact, Pidgeon spots the dictator in his gun sight. As a sportsman, he curiously pulls the trigger but only a click is heard. Then he puts a bullet in the empty chamber and prepares to shoot, but is apprehended by the Gestapo. Gestapo leader Sanders pressures him into signing a confession and when he refuses he is mercilessly beaten. His body is dumped into an abyss in order to make the beating look like an accident. Stumbling through the forest and wading through murky swamps, Pidgeon makes his way to a rowboat in the harbor. With the help of a friendly youngster, McDowall, he stows away on a Danish steamer. Also on board, however, is the mysterious Carradine who has found Pidgeon's passport and has taken his identity. Hiding in the shadows of London streets, Pidgeon tries to reach safety while being pursued by Sanders and his thugs. Pidgeon meets Bennett, a friendly cockney prostitute, who helps him find a hiding place. Pidgeon becomes enamored of Bennett and buys her a handsome arrow-shaped hatpin for her tam-o'-shanter, claiming that "every soldier needs a crest for his cap." A confrontation finally occurs between Pidgeon and Carradine, resulting in a furious chase through London's underground. The darkness obscures their hand-to-hand battle, which climaxes when one of them is pushed into the path of an oncoming train. The following day, Bennett reads a newspaper story which reports that a body, mangled beyond recognition, was found and could be identified as Pidgeon only by his passport. The passport, of course, was being held by Carradine. Bennett and Pidgeon are reunited, but not for long. Their teary parting takes place on London Bridge and is interrupted by a bobby. Fearing that Pidgeon may be identified by the bobby, Bennett plays the prostitute and is taken away, creating the necessary diversion. Returning to her flat, Bennett is met by Sanders and his men and killed when she fails to cooperate with them. Pidgeon's countryside cave hideout proves ineffective and he is discovered by Sanders. He is trapped inside with only a single small air shaft and Sanders informs him of Bennett's murder, producing the arrow hatpin as evidence. Being a resourceful hunter, Pidgeon constructs a makeshift bow-and-arrow and kills Sanders through the airshaft. After a series of newsreel shots depicting the advancement of the war and the raging battles between the Germans and the Royal Air Force, Pidgeon is seen parachuting into Germany with a rifle slung over his back as a narrator says: "And from now on somewhere within Germany is a man with a precision rifle and the high degree of intelligence and training that is required to use it. It may be days, months, or even years—but this time he clearly knows his purpose." Based on the best-selling novel, *Rogue Male*, MAN HUNT was scripted by the immensely talented Dudley Nichols and intended as a John Ford picture. Ford, however, disliked the subject matter and the film was offered, by Darryl Zanuck, to Lang. Lang encountered, as he often did, some problems on the set involving both the Hays Code and financial restraints by Zanuck. Lang, a great lover of complex female characters, had cast Bennett as a compassionate, honest girl who happened to be a prostitute. The Hays Code, however, disagreed with the idea of casting prostitutes in a "glamorous light" and forced some scenes to be amended. According to Lang, "We had to prominently show a sewing machine in her apartment, thus she was not a whore, she was a 'seamstress.' Talk about authenticity." Most objectionable to Zanuck was the parting scene between Pidgeon and Bennett which was to take place on London Bridge. Zanuck was distressed by the fact that a "decent" girl (such as Bennett's character) had to play the whore in front of Pidgeon, the man she loved. Zanuck refused to allow any money in the budget for this scene—a scene which Lang felt essential. Regardless of Zanuck's sentiments, Lang, his cameraman, Miller, and unit manager Benny Silvi planned to go ahead with the scene. Digging among the studio's props, they found a single bridge railing. Two were needed, however, so Lang dug into his pockets, pulled out $40, and paid to have a second one constructed. Without the aid of studio workers (whose unions would not allow such defiance), Lang, Miller, and Silvi stole into the studio at 4 a.m. They painted the backdrop, hung light bulbs in a manner of diminishing perspective to create depth, and then obscured the whole thing in a blanket of fog. The result was a beautifully atmospheric set. When Zanuck finally saw that day's "rushes," he barked, "Where the hell's that set? I want to talk to Silvi! You keep that set and we'll shoot a whole picture on it." There was no set, however, and Lang had successfully pulled one over on Zanuck. "Naturally," Lang added, "I didn't rub it in."

p, Kenneth McGowan; d, Fritz Lang; w, Dudley Nichols (based on the novel *Rogue Male* by Geoffrey Household); ph, Arthur Miller; m, Alfred Newman; ed, Allan McNeil; art d, Richard Day, Wiard B. Ihnen; set d, Thomas Little; cos, Travis Banton.

Espionage (PR:A MPAA:NR)

MAN HUNTER, THE* (1930) 60m WB bw

John Loder (*George Castle*), Nora Lane (*Lady Jane Winston*), Charles Delaney (*Jim Clayton*), Pat Hartigan (*Crosby*), Christiane Yves (*Maid*), Floyd Shackleford (*Simba*), Billy Bletcher (*Buggs*), John Kelly (*Charlie*), Joe Bordeaux (*Dennis*), Rin Tin Tin (*Rinty*).

It should be pretty shameful to all involved that a dog (Rin Tin Tin) is the only thing of value in this picture. Businesswoman Lane heads for Africa after wondering why her ivory investments are yielding such little profit. While in the Dark Continent, she discovers that an employee of hers is skimming off the top. Things get hairy, but Rinty saves the day, and the film.

d, Ross Lederman; w, James A. Starr (based on a story by Lillian Hayward); ph, James Van Trees.

Adventure (PR:A MPAA:NR)

MAN I KILLED (SEE: BROKEN LULLABY, 1932)

MAN I LOVE, THE (1929) 70m PAR bw

Richard Arlen (*Dum-Dum Brooks*), Mary Brian (*Celia Fields*), Olga Baclanova (*Sonia Barondoff*), Harry Green (*Curly Bloom*), Jack Oakie (*Lew Layton*), Pat O'Malley (*D. J. McCarthy*), Leslie Fenton (*Carlo Vesper*), Charles Sullivan (*Champ Mahoney*), Sailor Vincent (*K. O. O'Hearn*), Robert Perry (*Gateman*).

Arlen takes to the ring as a small-town boxer who heads to Manhattan with wife Brian. Once in the Big Apple, Arlen batters the champ in an exhibition bout. He gets a real chance at the title later in the film and sends the champ to the mat a number of times before emerging victorious.

p, David O. Selznick; d, William A. Wellman; w, Herman J. Mankiewicz, Percy Heath; ph, Harry Gerard; ed, Allyson Shaffer.

Sports Drama (PR:A MPAA:NR)

MAN I LOVE, THE* (1946) 96m WB bw

Ida Lupino (*Petey Brown*), Robert Alda (*Nicky Toresca*), Andrea King (*Sally Otis*), Martha Vickers (*Virginia Brown*), Bruce Bennett (*Sam Thomas*), Alan Hale (*Riley*), Dolores Moran (*Gloria O'Connor*), John Ridgely (*Roy Otis*), Don McGuire (*Johnny O'Connor*), Warren Douglas (*Joe Brown*), Craig Stevens (*Johnson*), William Edmunds (*Tony Toresca*), James Dobbs (*Jimmy*), Patrick Griffin (*Buddy Otis*), Florence Bates (*Mrs. Thorpe*), Eddie Bruce, Tom Quinn (*Drunks*), Barbara Brown (*Maggie*), Janet Barrett (*Cashier*), Robin Raymond (*Lee, the Waitress*), Frank Ferguson (*Army Doctor*), Jack Wise (*Waiter*), Jack Mower (*Desk Sergeant*), Monte Blue (*Cop*), Jack Daley (*Flynn, the Bartender*), Ben Welden (*Jack Atlas*), John Vosper (*Man with Gloria*), Peg LaCentra (*Singing Voice for Lupino*), Tony Romano.

Lupino heads west to Long Beach, Calif., where she gets a job in Alda's nightclub as a singer. She gets involved with Alda, a tough mug with mob ties, but eventually snubs him and peddles her affections to piano player Bennett. Some nice atmosphere which does not fully compensate for a weak script. The dandy selection of tunes includes: "Body and Soul" (Edward Heyman, Johnny Green), "Why Was I Born?" (Jerome Kern, Oscar Hammerstein II), "Bill" (Kern, Hammerstein, P. G.

Wodehouse), "The Man I Love," "Liza" (George Gershwin, Ira Gershwin), "If I Could Be With You (One Hour Tonight)" (Henry Creamer, Jimmy Johnson).

p, Arnold Albert; d, Raoul Walsh, John Maxwell; w, Catherine Turney, Jo Pagano (based on the novel *Night Shift* by Maritta Wolff); ph, Sid Hickox; m, Max Steiner; ed, Owen Marks; md, Leo F. Forbstein; art d, Stanley Fleischer; set d, Eddie Edwards; spec eff, Harry Barndoller, Edwin DuPar.

Musical/Drama (PR:A MPAA:NR)

MAN I MARRIED, THE* (1940) 77m Zanuck/FOX bw (AKA: I MARRIED A NAZI)

Joan Bennett (*Carol*), Francis Lederer (*Eric Hoffman*), Lloyd Nolan (*Kenneth Delane*), Anna Sten (*Freda Heinkel*), Otto Kruger (*Heinrich Hoffman*), Maria Ouspenskaya (*Frau Gerhardt*), Ludwig Stossel (*Dr. Hugo Gerhardt*), Johnny Russell (*Ricky*), Lionel Royce (*Herr Deckhart*), Fredrik Vogeding (*Traveler*), Ernst Deutsch (*Otto*), Egon Brecher (*Czech*), William Kaufman (*Conductor*), Frank Reicher (*Freihof*), Charles Irwin (*English Newspaperman*), Lillian Porter (*Receptionist*), Lillian West (*Secretary*), Harry Depp (*Man*), Walter Bonn (*Customs Official*), Glen Cavender (*Petty Official*), Hans Von Morhart, William Yetter (*Gestapo Officers*), Ragnar Quale (*Freihof's Older Son*), Rudy Frolich (*Freihof's Son*), John Stark, Tom Mizer, Hans Schumm, Rudolph Anders (*Storm Troopers*), Carl Freybe (*Gestapo Official*), Greta Meyer (*Hausfrau*), Albert Geigel (*Boy*), Eleanor Wesselhoeft (*Old Lady*), Diane Fisher (*Young Girl*), John Hiestand, Leyland Hodgson, Arno Frey, Eugene Borden (*Announcers*).

A gripping anti-Nazi tale which has Bennett and her German-American husband paying a visit to Deutschland in 1938. While there, husband Lederer becomes brainwashed into the Nazi way of thought and joins the party. He falls in love with Sten, another Hitler fanatic, and demands a divorce. He insists on retaining custody of their son, however. Bennett allies with Lederer's dad, who tells his son that his own mother was Jewish and that it is only fair to allow his son to return to America with Bennett. No mercy is given to the Nazi philosophy, resorting instead to well-directed jabs at the swastika-donned men.

p, Raymond Griffith; d, Irving Pichel; w, Oliver H. P. Garrett (based on the *Liberty* magazine series "I Married a Nazi" by Oscar Schisgall); ph, Peverell Marley; ed, Robert Simpson; md, David Buttolph.

War/Drama (PR:A MPAA:NR)

MAN I MARRY, THE (1936) 79m UNIV bw

Doris Nolan (*Rena Allen*), Michael Whalen (*Ken Durkin*), Marjorie Gateson (*Eloise Hartley*), Gerald Oliver Smith (*Throckton Van Courtland*), Nigel Bruce (*Robert Hartley*), Richard "Skeets" Gallagher (*Jack Gordon*), Cliff Edwards (*Jerry Ridgeway*), Ferdinand Gottschalk (*Organist*), Harry Barris (*Piano Player*), Chic Sale (*Sheriff*), Edward McWade (*Druggist*), Harry Hayden (*Minister*), Rollo Lloyd (*Woody Ryan*), Peggy Shannon (*Margot Potts*), Richard Carle (*Storekeeper*), Lew Kelly (*Counterman*), Harry Tyler (*Man*), Arthur Aylesworth, Harry Stubbs.

Nolan falls in love with Whalen, who makes a living writing plays. He suddenly becomes a success and correctly attributes his rise to Nolan, who runs a play-reading agency and has an uncle who is a Broadway producer. He begins fuming when he realizes that he did not make it on his own, but romance blooms in the end. Standard stuff with some funny moments.

p, Val Paul; d, Ralph Murphy; w, Harry Clork (based on a story by M. Coates Webster); ph, Joseph Valentine, John P. Fulton; ed, Bernard W. Burton.

Drama (PR:A MPAA:NR)

MAN I WANT, THE (1934, Brit.) 68m BL/MGM bw

Henry Kendall (*Peter Mason*), Wendy Barrie (*Marion Round*), Betty Astell (*Prue Darrell*), Davy Burnaby (*Sir George Round*), Hal Walters (*Haddock*), Wally Patch (*Ernie*).

Another of the innumerable 1930s British farces which are generally lifeless and very, very forgettable. The story revolves around a cooked-up premise of Kendall finally gaining a vote of confidence from Burnaby so he can marry his daughter. To do this he first apprehends those responsible for the theft of Burnaby's costly jewels, a feat that Kendall achieves without knowing that he is solving a crime. It's difficult to find anything amusing in this tired situation.

p, Herbert Smith; d, Leslie Hiscott; w, Michael Barringer.

Comedy (PR:A MPAA:NR)

MAN IN A COCKED HAT (1960, Bri.) 87m Boulting Bros./Show bw (GB: CARLTON-BROWNE OF THE F.O.)

Terry-Thomas (*Cadogen de Vere Carlton-Browne*), Peter Sellers (*Prime Minister*), Luciana Paoluzzi (*Princess Ilyena*), Thorley Walters (*Col. Bellingham*), Ian Bannon (*Young King*), Miles Malleson (*British Resident*), Raymond Huntley (*Foreign Office Minister*), John Le Mesurier (*Grand Duke*), Kynaston Reeves (*Sir Arthur Carlton-Browne*), Marie Lohr (*Lady Carlton-Browne*), Marne Maitland (*Archipelagos*), John Van Eyssen (*Hewitt*), Nicholas Parsons (*Rodgers*), Basil Dignam (*Security Officer*), Ronald Adam (*Sir John Farthing*), Sam Kydd (*Signaller*), Michael Ward (*Hotel Receptionist*), Irene Handl (*Mother in Newsreel*), John Glyn Jones (*Interviewer*), Harry Locke (*Commentator*), James Dyrenforth (*Admiral*).

Minor British comedy outing featuring Terry-Thomas as an ambassador assigned to sort out the problems on the tiny British-ruled island of Gallardia after a rich mineral deposit is discovered and other major world powers are seen hunting around for a piece of the action. These events instigate a revolution led by Prime Minister Sellers who tries to overthrow the British. Typical British farce.

p, John Boulting; d&w, Jeffery Dell, Roy Boulting; ph, Max Greene; m, John Addison; ed, Anthony Harvey.

Comedy   **(PR:A MPAA:NR)**

MAN IN BLACK, THE*   (1950, Brit.) 75m Hammer/Exclusive bw

Betty Anne Davies (*Bertha Clavering*), Sidney James (*Henry Clavering*), Anthony Forwood (*Victor Harrington*), Sheila Burrell (*Janice*), Hazel Penwarden (*Joan*), Courtney Hope (*Mrs. Carter*), Lawrence Baskcomb (*Sandford*), Valentine Dyall (*Storyteller*), Molly Palmer (*Gerald Case*).

James is a wealthy man married to the shrewish Davies. She wants to inherit every last pence he owns, and begins a plan to drive James' daughter mad in order to fulfill her dream. But James catches on to his wife and, using yoga, fakes his own death. He then poses as a gardener to spy on Davies. The story is drivel, with some unintentionally campy plot developments. The story was adapted from a British radio series, perhaps proving that some dramas are better heard than seen.

p, Anthony Hinds; d, Francis Searle; w, John Gilling, Searle (based on the radio series "Appointment with Fear" by John Dickson Carr); ph, Cedric Williams.

Crime   **(PR:C-O MPAA:NR)**

14902
MAN IN BLUE, THE**¹/₂   (1937) 64m UNIV bw

Robert Wilcox (*Frankie Dunne*), Edward Ellis (*Martin Dunne*), Nan Grey (*June Hanson*), Richard Carle (*Willie Loomis*), Ralph Morgan (*Professor*), Alma Kruger (*Mrs. Dunne*), Billy Burrud (*Frankie, as a Boy*), Aggie Herring (*Aggie*), Frederick Burton (*Parke Lewis*), Herbert Corthell (*Pat Casey*), Selmer Jackson (*District Attorney*), Milburn Stone ("*Dutch*"), Florence Bates (*Woman*).

Wilcox is an honest bank teller who is raised by Ellis, a cop who feels guilty for shooting down the boy's petty thief dad. The youngster (played by Burrud) grows up to respect the law and turns his back on an illegit offer from his shady uncle. An interesting melodrama.

p, Kubec Glasmon; d, Milton Carruth; w, Lester Cole (based on the story "The Cop" by Glasmon); ph, George Robinson; ed, Paul Landres; md, Charles Previn.

Drama   **(PR:A MPAA:NR)**

MAN IN GREY, THE***   (1943, Brit.) 93m Gainsborough-GAU/UNIV bw

Margaret Lockwood (*Hesther Snow*), James Mason (*Marquis of Rohan*), Phyllis Calvert (*Clarissa Rohan*), Stewart Granger (*Peter Rokeby*), Helen Haye (*Lady Rohan*), Raymond Lovell (*Prince Regent*), Nora Swinburne (*Mrs. Fitzherbert*), Martita Hunt (*Miss Patchett*), Jane Gill-Davis (*Lady Marr*), Amy Veness (*Mrs. Armstrong*), Stuart Lindsell (*Lawrence*), Diana King (*Jane Seymour*), Ann Wilton (*Miss Edge*), Celia Lamb (*Louisa*), Lupe Maguire (*Sally Campbell*), Beatrice Varley (*Gypsy*), Harry Scott, Jr. (*Toby*), Drusilla Wills (*Cook*), Gertrude Maesmore Morris (*Lady Bessborough*), Hargrave Pawson (*Lord Craven*), James Carson (*Gervaise*), Roy Emmerton (*Gamekeeper*), Babs Valerie (*Molly*), Wally Kingston (*Old Porter*), Glynn Rowland (*Lord Mildmay*), Patrick Curwen (*Doctor*), Lola Hunt (*Nurse*), Mary Naylor (*Blennerhasset*), Ruth Woodman (*Polly*), A. E. Matthews (*Auctioneer*), Kathleen Boutall (*Amelia*).

In 1943, bombs were falling on London, yet the British kept making movies, and some very good ones at that. Granger, a young pilot, meets Calvert, a peeress, as the ancestral home of her family is being sold. They begin to compare notes about their pasts and learn that his mother's forebear was madly in love with the ancestor from whom Calvert took her name. Flashback to the 19th Century where we meet Lockwood, a very poor young girl who was abandoned by her father. She meets and is befriended by Calvert (as her own ancestor) at their school. Calvert is very wealthy and becomes wealthier when she marries Mason, a marquis. But their marriage is loveless. Lockwood falls for a young ensign and elopes. Mason doesn't want a wife but he does want an heir. Calvert has a child and years pass. She attends the theater one night and sees Lockwood. Calvert hires her old pal as a governess for the child and also finds that she is more than passingly intrigued by Granger, as the young leading man who has been playing in the role opposite Lockwood. Once inside the mansion, Lockwood becomes Mason's mistress and deviously plans to get Calvert out of her life by pushing her and Granger closer together. Calvert and Granger are getting ready to move to Jamaica, where he is a rich man, but Lovell, the prince regent, prevails on her to stay so as to avoid a huge, juicy scandal. Calvert becomes ill and Lockwood, angered by the fact that her best-laid plans have gang aglay, allows her friend to die. Granger hears of this and becomes enraged, so much so that he beats Lockwood into a pulp and she dies. As the film ends, we have returned to modern times and Granger and Calvert leave the house sale smiling. We can only presume that they have found something in each other that should have been consummated years before and they mean to do just that now. England had been making war movies to help the patriotic effort and small comedies to take the mind off the buzz-bombs. Then this one came along and did so well at the box office that a series of "Gainsborough Gothics" followed. The public, if not the critics, ate them up and it was soon the "wicked lady of the month" time as the pictures flowed freely. Lockwood and Mason, who had been making movies for almost 10 years each, both became superstars due to this one. Granger (whose real name is James Stewart) was appearing in his first large role after eight small ones, and he took the audience's fancy. They could re-release the novel today and it would score very well with the "romance" crowd who flock to their newsstands for the latest by Danielle Steele or Cynthia Freeman. Arliss, a one-time screenwriter, went on to make many of the more popular costume dramas released by Gainsborough.

p, Edward Black; d, Leslie Arliss; w, Margaret Kennedy, Doreen Montgomery, Arliss (based on the novel by Lady Eleanor Smith); ph, Arthur Crabtree; m, Cedric Mallabey; ed, R. E. Dearing; md, Louis Levy; art d, Walter Murton; cos, Elizbeth Haffenden.

Costume Drama   **Cas.**   **(PR:A-C MPAA:NR)**

MAN IN HALF-MOON STREET, THE***   (1944) 92m PAR bw

Nils Asther (*Julian Karell*), Helen Walker (*Eve Brandon*), Reinhold Schunzel (*Dr. Kurt Van Bruecken*), Paul Cavanagh (*Dr. Henry Latimer*), Edmond Breon (*Sir Humphrey Brandon*), Morton Lowry (*Allen Guthrie*), Matthew Boulton (*Inspector Garth*), Brandon Hurst (*Simpson, Butler*), Aminta Dyne (*Lady Minerva Aldergate*), Arthur Mulliner (*Sir John Aldergate*), Edward Fielding (*Col. Ashley*), Reginald Sheffield (*Mr. Taper*), Eustace Wyatt (*Inspector Lawson*), Forrester Harvey (*Harris, a Cabby*), Konstantin Shayne (*Dr. Vishanoff*), Gerald Oliver Smith (*Clerk*), Leyland Hodgson (*Dr. Albertson*), Harry Cording (*1st Bobby*), Clive Morgan (*Plainclothesman*), Arthur Blake (*Man*), Ernie Adams (*Porter*), Norman Ainsley (*Butler*), Edward Cooper (*Liveried Servant*), John Sheehan (*Expressman*), Frank Baker (*Plainclothesman*), T. Arthur Hughes (*Plainclothesman*), Frank Moran (*Skipper*), John Power (*Guard*), Don Gallaher (*Ticket Agent*), Bob Stevenson (*Guard*), Bobby Hale (*Deck Hand*), Cy Ring (*O'Hara*), Wilson Benge (*Official*), George Broughton (*Morgue Official*), Robert Cory, Frank Hagney, Al Ferguson (*Bobbies*).

A skillfully scripted and atypically intelligent B movie which blends horror and unconditional love in believable unity. Asther is an artist and scientist who falls in love with Walker after painting her portrait. He fails to tell her, however, that he is actually well into his elderly years and is staying young by unnatural scientific methods. It turns out that, with the collaboration of endocrinologist Schunzel, Asther has been receiving gland transplants every decade. Schunzel accuses Asther of disregarding his original humanitarian intentions in favor of ruthless killing, and refuses to perform any more operations. Asther resorts to enlisting the aid of another doctor, but after the murder of a med student Scotland Yard starts to snoop. Walker, who has not failed to show her love for Asther, professes that she "shares his madness because there's grandeur in it." An example of true love if there ever was one. Asther, by the picture's finale, rapidly begins to age at a train station and dies a gray-haired old man. Well-handled on all fronts, this ageless film was remade in 1959 by Hammer Films as THE MAN WHO COULD CHEAT DEATH.

p, Walter MacEwan; d, Ralph M. Murphy; w, Charles Kenyon, Garrett Fort (based on the play by Barre Lyndon); ph, Henry Sharp; m, Miklos Rozsa; ed, Tom Neff; art d, Hans Dreier, Walter Tyler.

Horror/Romance   **(PR:A MPAA:NR)**

MAN IN HIDING   (SEE: MAN-TRAP, 1961)

MAN IN OUTER SPACE
              (SEE: MAN FROM THE FIRST CENTURY, THE, 1961, Czech.)

MAN IN POSSESSION, THE**   (1931) 79m MGM bw

Robert Montgomery (*Raymond Dabney*), Charlotte Greenwood (*Clara*), Irene Purcell (*Crystal Wetherby*), C. Aubrey Smith (*Mr. Dabney*), Beryl Mercer (*Mrs. Dabney*), Reginald Owen (*Claude Dabney*), Alan Mowbray (*Sir Charles Cartwright*), Maude Eburne (*Esther*), Forrester Harvey (*Sheriff*), Yorke Sherwood (*Butcher*).

Montgomery poses as a butler to help the wealthy Purcell out of a jam and falls in love with her. The film's main selling point obviously was not the simple plot, but its casually steamy treatment of the Montgomery-Purcell relationship. Co-scripted by author P. G. Wodehouse.

d, Sam Wood; w, Sarah Y. Mason, P. G. Wodehouse (based on the play by H. M. Harwood); ph, Oliver T. Marsh; ed, Ben Lewis; art d, Cedric Gibbons.

Comedy   **(PR:A-C MPAA:NR)**

MAN IN POSSESSION, THE   (SEE: PERSONAL PROPERTY, 1937)

MAN IN THE ATTIC**¹/₂   (1953) 82m Panoramic/FOX bw

Jack Palance (*Slade*), Constance Smith (*Lily Bonner*), Byron Palmer (*Paul Warwick*), Frances Bavier (*Helen Harley*), Rhys Williams (*William Harley*), Sean McClory (*1st Constable*), Leslie Bradley (*2nd Constable*), Tita Phillips (*Daisy*), Lester Matthews (*Inspector Melville*), Harry Cording (*Sgt. Bates*), Lillian Bond (*Annie Rowley*), Lisa Daniels (*Mary Lenihan*), Isabel Jewell (*Katy*).

Palance is perfectly cast in the Jack the Ripper role of Slade, a psychotic pathologist who boards in a house in foggy London. It is there that he falls in love with the proprietor's daughter, Smith, who rejects him. Unfortunately there's a long list of femmes who've previously spurned Palance, and they've all ended up on the wrong end of the knife. Smith comes close to experiencing the same fate, but Scotland Yard inspector Palmer comes to the rescue. He gives Palance a good chase which ends as the Ripper takes a suicide leap into the Thames. A well-done but inferior remake of THE LODGER (1944).

p, Robert L. Jacks; d, Hugo Fregonese; w, Robert Presnell, Jr., Barre Lyndon (based on the book *The Lodger* by Marie Belloc Lowndes); ph, Leo Tover; ed, Marjorie Fowler; md, Lionel Newman; art d, Lyle Wheeler, Leland Fuller.

Drama/Horror   **(PR:C MPAA:NR)**

MAN IN THE BACK SEAT, THE**
              (1961, Brit.) 57m Independent Artists/Anglo Amalgamated bw

Derren Nesbitt (*Tony*), Keith Faulkner (*Frank*), Carol White (*Jean*), Harry Locke (*Joe Carter*).

Fairly good film adaptation of an Edgar Wallace novel centers on two young crooks' attempts to rob a bookmaker as he leaves the racetrack with the day's winnings. The overanxious youths discover, however, that their victim has chained the bag of money to his wrist so it can't be removed. This forces them to take the man with them as they try to find a way to retrieve the money.

p, Julian Wintle, Leslie Parkyn; d, Vernon Sewell; w, Malcolm Hulke, Eric Paice (based on the novel by Edgar Wallace).

Crime   **(PR:A MPAA:NR)**

MAN IN THE DARK** ½ (1953) 70m COL bw

Edmond O'Brien *(Steve Rawley/James Blake)*, Audrey Totter *(Peg Benedict)*, Ted de Corsia *(Lefty)*, Horace McMahon *(Arnie)*, Nick Dennis *(Cookie)*, Dayton Lummis *(Dr. Marston)*, Dan Riss *(Jawald)*, Shepard Menken *(Intern)*, John Harmon *(Herman)*, Ruth Warren *(Mayme)*.

O'Brien is a mobster who goes under the knife to have his memory altered and make him forget his past. His former gangster pals kidnap him and try to force him to locate $130,000 in stashed cash. He gets the money back, and, after a hair-raising rollercoaster chase, returns it to the wronged insurance company. A remake of THE MAN WHO LIVED TWICE, this film was the first shot in 3-D by a major studio. The original prints are in sepia tone.

p, Wallace MacDonald; d, Lew Landers; w, George Bricker, Jack Leonard, William Sackheim (based on the story by Tom Van Dycke, Henry Altimus); ph, Floyd Crosby; ed, Viola Lawrence; md, Ross DiMaggio; art d, John Meehan; set d, Robert Priestley.

Crime **(PR:A MPAA:NR)**

MAN IN THE DARK*

(1963, Brit.) 80m Mancunian/UNIV bw (GB: BLIND CORNER)

William Sylvester *(Paul Gregory)*, Barbara Shelley *(Anne Gregory)*, Elizabeth Shepherd *(Joan Marshall)*, Alexander Davion *(Rickie Seldon)*, Mark Eden *(Mike Williams)*, Ronnie Carroll *(Ronnie)*, Barry Aldis *(Compere)*, Edward Evans *(Chauffeur)*, Frank Forsyth *(Policeman)*, Joy Allen, Unity Greenwood, Wendy Martin *(Dancers)*.

Conniving woman talks her artist lover into murdering her husband, a blind pop music composer. A routine, however, brutal, programmer.

p, Tom Blakeley; d, Lance Comfort; w, James Kelly, Peter Miller (based on a story by Vivian Kemble); ph, Basil Emmott; m, Peter Hart, Brian Fahey; ed, John Trumper; md, Fahey; m/l "Blind Corner," "Where Ya Going?" Stan Butcher, Syd Cordell, "Princess," "Disk Jockey Bounce," Fahey, "Concerto" Hart.

Crime Drama **(PR:A MPAA:NR)**

MAN IN THE DINGHY, THE**

(1951, Brit.) 83m Imperadio/Snader bw (GB: INTO THE BLUE)

Michael Wilding *(Nicholas Foster)*, Odile Versois *(Jackie)*, Jack Hulbert *(John Fergusson)*, Constance Cummings *(Mrs. Kate Fergusson)*, Edward Rigby *(Bill, the Skipper)*.

Husband and wife, Hulbert and Cummings, are surprised to find that Wilding has stowed away on a Norway-bound yacht. They try to send him ashore in a number of French ports and have no luck, due to the fact he has fallen in love with the ship's cook, Versois. There's nothing new about this film, but it's ample entertainment.

p, Michael Wilding, Herbert Wilcox; d, Wilcox; w, Pamela Wilcox [Bower], Donald Taylor, Nicholas Phipps; ph, Max Green [Mutz Greenbaum]; m, Mischa Spoliansky; ed, Bill Lewthwaite.

Comedy **(PR:A MPAA:NR)**

MAN IN THE GLASS BOOTH, THE*** ½

(1975) 117m American Film Theatre c

Maximilian Schell *(Arthur Goldman)*, Lois Nettleton *(Miriam Rosen)*, Luther Adler *(Presiding Judge)*, Lawrence Pressman *(Charlie Cohn)*, Henry Brown *(Jack Arnold)*, Richard Rasof *(Moshe)*, David Nash *(Rami)*, Martin Berman *(Uri)*, Sy Kramer *(Rudin)*, Robert H. Harris *(Dr. Weisberg)*, Leonidas Ossetynski *(Samuel)*, Lloyd Bochner *(Churchill)*, Norbert Schiller *(Schmidt)*.

Originally done as a stage play by actor-writer Robert Shaw (who was so good as Quint in JAWS), THE MAN IN THE GLASS BOOTH is a *roman a clef* about Adolf Eichmann and is an excellent and graphic portrait of the beast that was the Nazi war machine. Schell is a wealthy Jewish businessman living in New York City, or is he? He's captured by Israelis and brought to trial for the torture and murder of millions of victims, Jews and otherwise, during WW II. As the film unspools, we are even more confused about Schell's true identity, as he denies everything. All of the accusatory and anecdotal material is delivered by the witnesses, as opposed to flashbacks, which is what is usually the case. Director Hiller felt that the material was strong enough to stand on its own and didn't need the cinematic "opening up" that would have been done in the hands of many other directors. So he elected to stay close to the play's text in form and style and lets the actors play and be the stars, rather than enlisting any camera tricks. Schell is riveting as the impostor living a life of ease and comfort until the benign mask is stripped from his face. Eichmann had been seated in a glass booth for the duration of his trial and that is the meaning of the title. The picture raises many questions which deal with the guilt that those who have oppressed others might feel long after their ugly deeds have become bitter memories. Although the truth is that when many Nazis have been captured, they have shown almost no regrets for what they did. Adler as the presiding judge and Nettleton as the prosecutor are among the fine supporting cast, but it is Schell who radiates the evil of the Nazi so well that his is the performance one recalls. He was nominated for an Oscar that year but lost in the sweep of ONE FLEW OVER THE CUCKOO'S NEST.

p, Ely Landau; d, Arthur Hiller; w, Edward Anhalt (based on the play by Robert Shaw); ph, Sam Leavitt; ed, David Bretherton; prod d, Joel Schiller; cos, John A. Anderson; makeup, Stan Winston.

Drama **(PR:A MPAA:PG)**

MAN IN THE GREY FLANNEL SUIT, THE*** ½ (1956) 152m FOX c

Gregory Peck *(Tom Rath)*, Jennifer Jones *(Betsy Rath)*, Fredric March *(Ralph Hopkins)*, Marisa Pavan *(Maria)*, Ann Harding *(Mrs. Hopkins)*, Lee J. Cobb *(Judge Bernstein)*, Keenan Wynn *(Caesar Gardella)*, Gene Lockhart *(Hawthorne)*, Gigi Perreau *(Susan Hopkins)*, Portland Mason *(Janie)*, Arthur O'Connell *(Walker)*, Henry Daniell *(Bill Ogden)*, Connie Gilchrist *(Mrs. Manter)*, Joseph Sweeney *(Edward Schultz)*, Sandy Descher *(Barbara)*, Mickey Maga *(Pete)*, Kenneth Tobey *(Mahoney)*, Ruth Clifford *(Florence)*, Geraldine Wall *(Miriam)*, Alex Campbell *(Johnson)*, Jerry Hall *(Freddie)*, Jack Mather *(Police Sergeant)*, Frank Wilcox *(Dr. Pearce)*, Nan Martin *(Miss Lawrence)*, Tris Coffin *(Byron Holgate)*, William Phillips *(Bugala)*, Leon Alton *(Cliff)*, Phyllis Graffeo *(Gina)*, Dorothy Adams *(Mrs. Hopkins' Maid)*, Dorothy Phillips *(Maid)*, Mary Benoit *(Secretary)*, King Lockwood *(Business Executive)*, Lomax Study *(Elevator Operator)*, John Breen *(Waiter)*, Renato Vanni *(Italian Farm Wife)*, Mario Siletti *(Carriage Driver)*, Lee Graham *(Crew Chief)*, Michael Jeffrey *(Mr. Sims)*, Roy Glenn *(Master Sergeant Matthews)*, Otto Reichow, Jim Brandt, Robert Boon *(German Soldiers)*, Harry Lauter, Paul Glass, William Phipps *(Soldiers)*, DeForrest Kelley *(Medic)*, Alfred Caiazza, Raymond Winston, John Crawford *(Italian Boys)*.

This is a story of middle-class, middle-America seen through the eyes of one young businessman, Peck, who had served with distinction in WW II and is now in a mortgaged house (for $10,000) and has a wife, Jones, and three children whose futures are uncertain if he does not land a better job. Moreover, there is a claim on the house Peck inherited from his grandmother, made by Sweeney, a vicious old and greedy caretaker who, as events later prove, falsifies his claims to the old estate. While commuting back and forth to his job in New York City, Peck remembers vividly his days in the service. A man sits in front of him wearing a heavy winter coat with a fur-lined collar. He recalls how, when freezing, he knifed a youthful German soldier to death to steal his coat during WW II. On another occasion he recalls how, fighting the Japanese, he had thrown a grenade and accidentally killed his best friend. He also remembers Pavan, a beautiful girl he loved but never returned to after the war. Instead, he is married to Jones, who is anything but a forward-looking, vibrant helpmate. She is a spoiled, nagging, neurotic woman who never seems to be pleased with her better-than-average lot in life. Lockhart, one of Peck's fellow commutors, tells Peck of a new, well-paying job at UBC and he applies as a speechwriter for its dynamic president, March. First he is interviewed by dry, clinical O'Connell, who does everything to discourage his application, as does his superior, Daniell, a soft-spoken but insidious character who revels in his position as top aide to March. Meanwhile, trying to solve the claims against Peck's small estate is Cobb, a Jewish judge in Westport, Connecticut, where Peck and Jones reside. Peck finally gets the job at UBC and meets March, the man at the top, an impeccable, brilliant, and well-meaning man who has sacrificed his personal life, as he explains to Peck in a moment of candor, for the respected role of tycoon. Peck later learns what that sacrifice entails: a wife who has no use for March and a daughter, Perreau, who is utterly spoiled and has no respect for her father as she squanders her life with a wastrel who, in the words of her mother, "is right out of the F. Scott Fitzgerald era." March relies more and more on Peck, insisting he help him with an important speech, even if it consumes his off hours. The extra time Peck spends at work causes stress with his wife and Jones really gets hysterical after Peck confesses to her that he has just learned that he has an illegitimate child in Italy, and that Pavan has written to him asking for some minimum support. Jones tells him she wants a divorce and he is to leave the house. When Peck tries to reason with her, Jones gets hysterical. Peck is on the brink of getting promoted to a top position at UBC but, at the last minute, refuses to work on March's speech over a weekend, telling the boss that he's "one of those nine-to-five" men. He risks his position but the understanding March respects him for his stand and it appears he will get that top job anyway. By this time, Jones has calmed down and goes with Peck to Cobb. They ask the humanitarian judge, who has dismissed a suit by the avaricious Sweeney, to help them out with Peck's sexual faux pas. Cobb admires the couple, particularly Jones, who suggests that they send money to Pavan regularly and asks him to arrange the payments. "This is a day, I'm sure," intones Cobb, "that inspired the poet to say that God is in His heaven and all is right with the world." Peck does a fine job with a rather shallow story, as does that consummate actor March. All the supporting players play well their Madison Avenue stereotypes. Wynn is particularly effective as the elevator operator who spots Peck going to work and gives him the information about Pavan and their child. Cobb, though registering his typical hysterics, is very effective as the emotional judge. Jones, however, misreads her role and does a job of flagrant overacting, turning her part into pure soap, an unbelievable and embarrassing performance accented by the obvious fact that Jones is much too old for her part. Johnson's script and direction have some flair but bog down midway. Peck, always the professional, researched his role by going to New York City and immersing himself in the advertising world, commuting with countless others wearing ubiquitous grey flannel suits. He was never recognized. The actor felt that the film "was spotted," but that it "had some good sequences," particularly those flashbacks depicting the war and his time with Pavan. This was Zanuck's last personally produced film before he left Fox, one he felt was superior and, in production values, it was. When Peck and Jones had appeared together in DUEL IN THE SUN a decade earlier the reserved Peck was simply overwhelmed by the flamboyant, raven-haired actress, vowing never to act with her again. He nevertheless holds his own in THE MAN IN THE GREY FLANNEL SUIT, despite the fact that Jones' husband, mogul David O. Selznick, bombarded director Johnson with memos on how to shoot his wife, how to dress her, how to have her makeup done. Finally, Zanuck called Selznick and said: "Listen you ———, keep your fingers out of my film!" From Selznick came a rare response—silence.

p, Darryl F. Zanuck; d&w, Nunnally Johnson (based on the novel by Sloan Wilson); ph, Charles G. Clarke (CinemaScope, DeLuxe Color); m, Bernard Herrman; ed, Dorothy Spencer; art d, Lyle Wheeler, Jack Martin Smith; set d, Walter M. Scott, Stuart A. Reiss; cos, Charles LeMaire; makeup, Ben Nye.

Drama **(PR:A MPAA:NR)**

MAN IN THE IRON MASK, THE*** (1939) 110m UA bw

Louis Hayward *(Louis XIV/Philippe)*, Joan Bennett (Maria Theresa), Warren William *(D'Artagnan)*, Joseph Schildkraut *(Fouquet)*, Alan Hale *(Porthos)*, Miles

Mander *(Aramis)*, Bert Roach *(Athos)*, Walter Kingsford *(Colbert)*, Marian Martin *(Mlle. de la Valliere)*, Montagu Love *(Spanish Ambassador)*, Doris Kenyon *(Queen Anne)*, Albert Dekker *(Louis XIII)*, William Royle *(Commandant of Bastille)*, Fred Cavens *(Francois)*, Boyd Irwin *(Royal High Constable)*, Howard Brooks *(Cardinal)*, Ian MacLaren *(Valet de Chambre)*, Dorothy Vaughan *(Woman)*, Harry Woods *(King's Officer)*, Lane Chandler *(Palace Guard)*, Peter Cushing, Reginald Barlow, Wyndham Standing, Sheila Darcy, Robert E. Milash, D'Arcy Corrigan, Emmett King, Dwight Frye, Nigel de Brulier.

James Whale's quality version of Dumas' classic tale of two twin brothers, one being the King of France and the other a prisoner at Isle St. Marguerite (Hayward in a dual role). William, as musketeer D'Artagnan, comes to the imprisoned brother, who is mercilessly forced to wear an iron mask to prevent anyone from realizing he is heir to the throne. Whale directed this elaborately costumed adventure with the greatest of verve, though his career came to a halt in 1941. He died mysteriously in his swimming pool 16 years later. This film also marked the first screen appearance of Peter Cushing.

p, Edward Small; d, James Whale; w, George Bruce (based on the novel by Alexandre Dumas); ph, Robert Planck; m, Lucien Moraweck; ed, Grant Whytock; md, Lud Gluskin; art d, John DuCasse Schulze; spec eff, Howard Anderson.

Adventure Cas. (PR:A MPAA:NR)

MAN IN THE MIDDLE***

(1964, U.S./Brit.) 94m Talbot-Pennebaker-Belmont/FOX bw (AKA: THE WINSTON AFFAIR)

Robert Mitchum *(Lt. Col. Barney Adams)*, France Nuyen *(Kate Davray)*, Barry Sullivan *(Gen. Kempton)*, Trevor Howard *(Maj. Kensington)*, Keenan Wynn *(Lt. Winston)*, Sam Wanamaker *(Maj. Kaufman)*, Alexander Knox *(Col. Burton)*, Gary Cockrell *(Lt. Morse)*, Robert Nicholls *(Lt. Bender)*, Michael Goodliffe *(Col. Shaw)*, Errol John *(Sgt. Jackson)*, Paul Maxwell *(Maj. Smith)*, Lionel Murton *(Capt. Gunther)*, Russell Napier *(Col. Thompson)*, Jared Allen *(Capt. Dwyer)*, David Bauer *(Col. Mayburt)*, Edward Underdown *(Maj. Wyclif)*, Howard Marion Crawford *(Maj. Poole)*, William Mitchell *(Staff Sgt. Quinn)*, Al Waxman *(Cpl. Zimmerman)*, Glenn Beck *(Cpl. Burke)*, Frank Killibrew *(Cpl. Baxter)*, Edward Bishop *(Lieutenant at Sikri)*, Terence Cooper *(Maj. Clement)*, Graham Skidmore *(Maj. Hennessy)*, Terry Skelton *(Col. Burnside)*, Paul Blomley *(Col. Winovich)*, Alistair Barr *(Col. Kelly)*, Brian Vaughan *(Maj. McCabe)*, Julian Burton *(Maj. Cummings)*.

Military courtroom dramas have always made for crackling good films. From THE CAINE MUTINY COURT MARTIAL to CONDUCT UNBECOMING to BREAKER MORANT, we have always been engrossed by the workings of the court-martial. So it is with MAN IN THE MIDDLE. It's WW II and a large problem looms between the British and American troops stationed in India. Wynn, an American lieutenant, shoots and kills Mitchell, a British staff sergeant, in front of nearly a dozen witnesses. Mitchum is asked to defend Wynn by his general, Sullivan, and agrees after having been told that Wynn is sane and fit for trial. Then Mitchum learns through nurse Nuyen (a member of the Lunacy Commission) that the head of the Commission, Knox, discounted the psychiatric evidence prepared by physician Wanamaker, the hospital's chief of such matters. Wanamaker has closely examined Wynn and believes him to be a psychopath who is not fit to stand trial. The British and the Americans are at odds over this case and Knox wants it all tied up neatly and quickly so the relations between the factions can be soldered. Mitchum contacts Wanamaker and asks that the doctor come to the trial and bring along with him his report on Wynn's mental state. Knox, in an attempt to push the matter through, makes certain that Wanamaker won't be there by having him shipped off to a hospital some distance away. Mitchum now approaches a British psychiatrist-major, Howard, who also believes that Wynn is dangerously mentally ill, but he will not testify to that as he fears the wrath of Knox. Howard's theory is that Wynn murdered Mitchell because, although Wynn was an officer and Mitchell an NCO, both had the exact same duties and Howard opines that Wynn did it because he fancies himself a victim and was determined to, at last, make someone else a victim. That's just so much hogwash, as Mitchum soon learns when he interviews Wynn and sees that the man is a staunch bigot and killed Mitchell because he had been going out with a black woman. Wynn (marvelous in the role) feels that Mitchell was mixing the purity of the races by consorting with the dark-hued woman. This attitude causes Mitchum to hate his client, but he has a job to do and means to do it. Mitchum realizes that Wynn is nuts, yet he conducts the trial as though Wynn were sane and keeps his surprise witness for the last moment. He has called for Wanamaker to make an appearance at the trial, then is shattered to hear that Wanamaker has been killed in an accident. Howard is called to testify and admits that none of the Lunacy Commission members could be deemed as qualified to judge Wynn's sanity. Under Mitchum's probing cross-examination, Howard discusses Wynn's madness and Wynn breaks and begins to rant. This convinces the court that Mitchum was right and Wynn is sent to a hospital rather than a gallows. Mitchum and Nuyen have a brief vacation together before he leaves. The arguing factions are united and the British and Americans prepare to go to battle side by side. Music was by OLIVER's Lionel Bart and lent a good undertone. With such a situation, there should have been more fireworks, but Mitchum's sleepy way negated that, and the picture, which might have been a powerhouse, fizzles somewhat but still has enough innate drama to make it worth your watching. The brief love story between Mitchum and Nuyen seems to have been pasted on as an afterthought.

p, Walter Seltzer; d, Guy Hamilton; w, Keith Waterhouse, Willis Hall (based on the novel *The Winston Affair* by Howard Fast); ph, Wilkie Cooper (CinemaScope); m, Lionel Bart, John Barry; ed, John Bloom; md, John Barry; art d, John Howell; cos, Ivy Baker; makeup, Sydney Turner.

Drama (PR:A-C MPAA:NR)

MAN IN THE MIRROR, THE** (1936, Brit.) 83m Twickenham/Wardour bw

Edward Everett Horton *(Jeremy Dike)*, Genevieve Tobin *(Helen)*, Garry Marsh *(Tarkington)*, Ursula Jeans *(Veronica)*, Alastair Sim *(Interpreter)*, Aubrey Mather *(Bogus of Bokhara)*, Renee Gadd *(Miss Blake)*, Viola Compton *(Mrs. Massiter)*, Felix Aylmer *(Earl of Wigan)*, Stafford Hilliard *(Dr. Graves)*.

The man in the mirror is actually the alter ego of timid businessman Horton. The apparition one day appears and tells the meek little man he has the courage Horton lacks. The film is pretty much a one-line joke, as the alter ego fights the fearful fellow's battles.

p, Julius Hagen; d, Maurice Elvey; w, F. McGrew Willis, Hugh Mills (based on the novel by William Garrett); ph, Curt Courant.

Fantasy/Drama (PR:A MPAA:NR)

MAN IN THE MOON***

(1961, Brit.) 99m Excalibur-Allied Film Makers/TransLux bw

Kenneth More *(William Blood)*, Shirley Ann Field *(Polly)*, Norman Bird *(Herbert)*, Michael Hordern *(Dr. Davidson)*, John Glyn-Jones *(Dr. Wilmot)*, John Phillips *(Prof. Stephens)*, Charles Gray *(Leo)*, Bernard Horsfall *(Rex)*, Bruce Boa *(Roy)*, Noel Purcell *(Prosecutor)*, Ed Devereaux *(Storekeeper)*, Newton Blick *(Dr. Hollis)*, Richard Pearson, Lionel Gamlin *(Doctors)*, Russell Waters *(Woomera Director)*, Danny Green *(Lorry Driver)*, Jeremy Lloyd *(Jaguar Driver)*.

More gets fired as a professional guinea pig for the Common Cold Research Center because he can't catch a cold. He quickly gets hired for testing by the National Atomic Research Center, which is looking for a physically fit chap to send to the moon. When a contest to land the first man on the moon is held and a $280,000 prize is offered, More takes the bait. The blastoff is a failure, however, and he lands back on Earth.

p, Michael Relph; d, Basil Dearden; w, Relph, Bryan Forbes; ph, Harry Waxman; m, Philip Green; ed, John Guthbridge; prod d, Don Ashton; art d, Jack Maxsted; set d, Peter Murton; cos, Anthony Mendelson; makeup, William Partleton, John Webber.

Comedy (PR:A MPAA:NR)

MAN IN THE MOONLIGHT MASK, THE* 1/2

(1958, Jap.) 102m Toei bw (GEKKO KAMEN; AKA: THE MOONBEAM MAN)

Fumitake Omura, Junya Usami, Hiroko Mine, Mitsue Komiya, Yaeko Wakamizu, Yasushi Nagata.

The evil Skull Mask battles it out with the good Moonlight Mask over plans for a new weapon. The Moonlight Mask turns out to be a policeman and the bad guy is revealed as the weapon inventor's assistant. This Japanese action-adventure film combines two superhero films, DAIICHIBU and DAINIBU. It's very pleasing to the eye, but the story is worthless.

d, Tsuneo Kobayashi; w, Yarunori Kawauchi; ph, Ichiro Hoshijima.

Action/Adventure (PR:A MPAA:NR)

MAN IN THE NET, THE* 1/2 (1959) 97m Mirisch-Jaguar/UA bw

Alan Ladd *(John Hamilton)*, Carolyn Jones *(Linda Hamilton)*, Diane Brewster *(Vickie Carey)*, John Lupton *(Brad Carey)*, Charles McGraw *(Steve Ritter)*, Tom Helmore *(Gordon Moreland)*, Betty Lou Holland *(Roz Moreland)*, John Alexander *(Mr. Carey)*, Edward Binns *(Capt. Green)*, Kathryn Givney *(Mrs. Carey)*, Barbara Beaird *(Emily Jones)*, Susan Gordon *(Angel Jones)*, Charles Herbert *(Timmie Moreland)*, Mike McGreevy *(Buck Ritter)*, Steven Perry *(Leroy)*, Alvin Childress *(Alonzo)*, Douglas Evans *(Charlie Raines)*, Natalie Masterson *(Mrs. Jones)*, Pat Miller, Bill Cassidy *(State Troopers)*.

Far below par for the talents involved (Curtiz and Ladd), this crime mystery has painter Ladd trying to resolve his differences with Jones, his mentally disturbed, alcoholic wife. She wants to leave their cozy New England quarters and return to New York, where she thinks Ladd should work as an advertising artist. He prefers to sit outside and capture the liveliness of neighborhood children on his canvas. After visiting a psychiatrist friend in New York, he returns home to find his house ransacked, his paintings slashed, and Jones missing. The film takes an illogical turn when his neighbors place the blame on him and form a lynch mob. It's the children, however, that come to his aid and prove his innocence. There are too many unfulfilled promises and plot holes for this one to add up to much. The re-release of SHANE at the same time (fortunately for Ladd) drew audiences to that film instead of this one.

p, Walter Mirisch; d, Michael Curtiz; w, Reginald Rose (based on the novel *Man in a Net* by Patrick Quentin); ph, John Seitz; m, Hans J. Salter; ed, Harold LaVelle, Richard Heermance; art d, Hilyard Brown.

Drama (PR:A MPAA:NR)

MAN IN THE ROAD, THE** (1957, Brit.) 83m Gibraltar/REP bw

Derek Farr *(Ivan Mason)*, Ella Raines *(Rhona Ellison)*, Donald Wolfit *(Professor Cattrell)*, Lisa Daniely *(Mitzi)*, Karel Stepanek *(Dmitri Palenkov)*, Cyril Cusack *(Dr. Kelly)*, Olive Sloane *(Mrs. Lemming)*, Bruce Beeby *(Dr. Manning)*, Russell Napier *(Supt. Davidson)*, Frederick Piper *(Inspector Hayman)*, John Welsh, Alfred Maron.

Farr plays a scientist suffering from amnesia who is told by the Communists that he is an accountant bound for Russia. The complicated plot never really amounts to anything more than predictable propaganda, though a capable cast handles the material in a professional and convincing manner.

p, Charles A. Leeds; d, Lance Comfort; w, Guy Morgan (based on the novel *He Was Found in the Road* by Anthony Armstrong); ph, Stan Pavey; m, Bruce Campbell; ed, Jim Connock; md, Philip Martell; art d, Eric Shaw.

Crime/Mystery (PR:A MPAA:NR)

MAN IN THE SADDLE 1/2**

(1951) 87m Ranown/COL c (GB: THE OUTCAST)

Randolph Scott *(Owen Merritt)*, Joan Leslie *(Laure Bidwell)*, Ellen Drew *(Nan*

Melotte), Alexander Knox *(Will Isham)*, Richard Rober *(Fay Dutcher)*, John Russell *(Hugh Clagg)*, Alfonso Bedoya *(Cultus Charley)*, Guinn "Big Boy" Williams *(Bourke Prine)*, Clem Bevans *(Pay Lankershim)*, Cameron Mitchell *(George Virk)*, Richard Crane *(Juke Virk)*, Frank Sully *(Lee Repp)*, George Lloyd *(Tom Croker)*, James Kirkwood *(Sheriff Medary)*, Frank Hagney *(Ned Bale)*, Don Beddoe *(Love Bidwell)*, Tennessee Ernie Ford.

Scott gets run off the range by Knox, who doesn't want him hanging around because he's afraid Scott may steal his wife, Leslie. Scott takes to the mountains with schoolteacher Drew, though Leslie's in love with him too. Drifter Russell shows up and tries to take Drew away from Scott, and both become engaged in a wonderfully exciting brawl. Scott heads back into town to settle his score with Knox, and after a good deal of gunplay leaves with Drew by his side. Leslie is left at Knox's ranch, a widow. Some excellent photography during the nighttime raids and De Toth's skillful direction make for one heck of a western.

p, Harry Joe Brown; d, Andre De Toth; w, Kenneth Gamet (based on the novel by Ernest Haycox); ph, Charles Lawton, Jr. (Technicolor); ed, Charles Nelson; art d, George Brooks; m/l, Ralph Murphy, Harold Lewis.

Western   **(PR:A MPAA:NR)**

MAN IN THE SHADOW** 1/2   (1957) 80m UNIV bw (GB: PAY THE DEVIL)

Jeff Chandler *(Sheriff Ben Sadler)*, Orson Welles *(Virgil Renchler)*, Colleen Miller *(Skippy Renchler)*, Ben Alexander *(Ab Begley)*, Barbara Lawrence *(Helen Sadler)*, John Larch *(Ed Yates)*, James Gleason *(Hank James)*, Royal Dano *(Aiken Clay)*, Paul Fix *(Herb Parker)*, Leo Gordon *(Chet Huneker)*, Martin Garralaga *(Jesus Cisneros)*, Mario Siletti *(Tony Santoro)*, Charles Horvath *(Len Bookman)*, William Schallert *(Jim Shaney)*, Joseph J. Greene *(Harry Youngquist)*, Forrest Lewis *(Jake Kelley)*, Harry Harvey, Sr. *(Dr. Creighton)*, Joe Schneider *(Juan Martin)*, Mort Mills *(Gateman)*.

Orson Welles is cast in his only western as a powerful rancher who runs his Texas Xanadu with an iron fist. When one of his Mexican laborers is brutally beaten to death, sheriff Chandler starts applying pressure. He gets no support from the townsfolk, however, who fear that Welles will leave town and take his wealth with him. Chandler goes too far and ends up tied to the back of a pickup truck and dragged through town by a couple of Welles' henchmen. The finale has ranch foreman Larch emerging as the murderer, ending the inquiries into Welles' affairs. An average western elevated solely by Welles' excellent performance as a sort of Kane of the West.

p, Albert Zugsmith; d, Jack Arnold; w, Gene L. Coon; ph, Arthur E. Arling (CinemaScope); m, Joseph Gershenson; ed, Edward Curtiss; art d, Alexander Golitzen, Alfred Sweeney; set d, Russell A. Gausman, John P. Austin; cos, Bill Thomas; makeup, Bud Westmore.

Western   **(PR:A MPAA:NR)**

MAN IN THE SHADOW, 1957   (SEE: VIOLENT STRANGER, 1957, Brit.)

MAN IN THE SKY   (SEE: DECISION AGAINST TIME, 1957, Brit.)

MAN IN THE STORM, THE**

       (1969, Jap.) 95m Toho bw (ARASHI NO NAKA NO OTOKO)

Toshiro Mifune *(Saburo Watari)*, Kyoko Kagawa *(Akiko)*, Akio Kobori *(Tsujido)*, Jun Tazaki *(Karate Expert)*, Akemi Negishi *(Okon)*.

Mifune is the new judo instructor at the Shimoda police station who becomes involved with Kagawa, the daughter of the instructor he's replacing. Kobori, a jealous pupil, unsuccessfully challenges Mifune to a duel. When Mifune loses his job after a fight with some naval officers, Kobori challenges him again. Mifune beats him and wins Kagawa's hand.

p, Tomoyuki Tonaka; d, Senkichi Taniguchi; w, Taniguchi, Takero Matsuura, Takeo Murata; m, Urato Watanabe; art d, Yasuhide Kato.

Drama   **(PR:A MPAA:NR)**

MAN IN THE TRUNK, THE*   (1942) 71m FOX bw

Lynne Roberts *(Peggy)*, George Holmes *(Dick Burke)*, Raymond Walburn *(Jim Cheevers)*, J. Carroll Naish *(Reginald DeWinters)*, Dorothy Peterson *(Lola DeWinters)*, Eily Malyon *(Abbie Addison)*, Arthur Loft *(Sam Kohler)*, Milton Parsons *(Dr. Pluma)*, Matt McHugh *(Detective Murtha)*, Charles Cane *(Lt. Braley)*, Theodore Von Eltz *(Swann)*, Joan Marsh *(Yvonne)*, Syd Saylor *(Joe)*, Douglas Fowley *(Ed Mygatt)*, Tim Ryan *(Auctioneer)*, Vivian Oakland *(Mrs. Kohler)*.

Holmes is a young attorney who comes to the assistance of a bookie who is wrongly accused of murder. The murdered man is found in an old trunk 10 years after the crime. When the trunk is opened, the corpse's ghost pops out and helps prove the bookie's innocence. A boring attempt at suspense.

p, Walter Morosco; d, Malcolm St. Clair; w, John Larkin; ph, Glen MacWilliams; m, Cyril J. Mockridge; ed, Alexander Troffey; art d, Richard Day, Albert Hogsett.

Crime   **(PR:A MPAA:NR)**

MAN IN THE VAULT* 1/2   (1956) 73m Batjac/RKO bw

William Campbell *(Tommy Dancer)*, Karen Sharpe *(Betty Turner)*, Anita Ekberg *(Flo Randall)*, Berry Kroeger *(Willis Trent)*, Paul Fix *(Herbie)*, James Seay *(Paul De Camp)*, Mike Mazurki *(Louie)*, Robert Keys *(Earl Farraday)*, Gonzales Gonzales *(Pedro)*, Nancy Duke *(Trent's Girl Friend)*, Vivianne Lloyd *(Singer)*.

A less-than-eventful crime thriller that has the mob forcing locksmith Campbell to make keys for a safe-deposit box that holds $200,000. Standard stuff with Ekberg, the sexy gang moll, bringing in most of the customers. Includes the song "Let the Chips Fall Where They May" (Henry Vars, By Dunham). Produced by Robert E. Morrison for Batjac Productions, John Wayne's company.

p, Robert E. Morrison; d, Andrew V. McLagen; w, Burt Kennedy (based on the novel *The Lock and the Key* by Frank Gruber); ph, William H. Clothier; m, Henry Vars; ed, Everett Sutherland.

Crime   **(PR:A MPAA:NR)**

MAN IN THE WATER, THE* 1/2

(1963) 80m Key West/Crown International bw (AKA: ESCAPE FROM HELL ISLAND)

Mark Stevens *(Capt. James)*, Jack Donner *(Lyle Dennison)*, Linda Scott [Ann Rouzer] *(Linda Dennison)*, David Aldrich *(Pete Sands)*, Louis Oquendo *(Senor Rios)*, Russell Smith, Jr. *(Coast Guard Officer)*, Mercedes Marlowe *(Mrs. Pete Sands)*, Jack Clarke *(Bartender at Sloppy Joe's)*, Bern Martin, Alexander Panas, Edmund Reed.

Stevens, a charter boat captain in Key West, Florida, smuggles a group of refugees from Cuba. On the way back to the States, the boat is spotted by Cuban gun ships and Marlowe is killed. U.S. authorities take his boat and pull his license. Stevens then becomes involved with Scott, who is married to Donner. Donner has Stevens charter his sloop to Bermuda and tries to kill him. Donner is killed, and Stevens rekindles his relationship with Scott.

p, T. L. P. Swicegood; d, Mark Stevens; w, Swicegood (based on the book by Robert Sheckley); ph, Meredith M. Nicholson; m, William Loose, Nat Aldeen; ed, Betty Steinberg; spec eff, Thol O. Simonson.

Drama   **(PR:A MPAA:NR)**

MAN IN THE WHITE SUIT, THE****   (1952) 85m Ealing/RANK-UNIV bw

Alec Guinness *(Sidney Stratton)*, Joan Greenwood *(Daphne Birnley)*, Cecil Parker *(Alan Birnley)*, Michael Gough *(Michael Corland)*, Ernest Thesiger *(Sir John Kierlaw)*, Vida Hope *(Bertha)*, Howard Marion Crawford *(Cranford)*, Duncan Lamont *(Harry)*, Henry Mollison *(Hoskins)*, Vida Hope *(Bertha)*, Patric Doonan *(Frank)*, Harold Goodwin *(Wilkins)*, Olaf Olsen *(Knudsen)*, Colin Gordan *(Hill)*, Joan Harben *(Miss Johnson)*, Miles Malleson *(Tailor)*, Arthur Howard *(Roberts)*, Roddy Hughes *(Green)*, Edie Martin *(Mrs. Watson)*, George Benson *(The Lodger)*, Judith Furse *(Nurse Gamage)*, Mandy Miller *(Little Girl)*, Frank Atkinson *(Baker)*, Billy Russell *(Night Watchman)*, John Rudling *(Wilson)*, Desmond Roberts *(Mannering)*, Stuart Latham *(Harrison)*, Mandy Miller *(Gladdie)*, Brian Worth *(King)*, Roddy Hughes *(Roberts)*, Charlotte Mitchell, Ewan Roberts, Charles Saynor, Russel Waters, Charles Cullum, F. B. J. Sharp, Scott Harold, Jack Howard, Jack McNaughton.

A sharp satirical comedy with serious undertones that indicted the British industrial system, THE MAN IN THE WHITE SUIT offers a tour de force by master comic Guinness. He is an eccentric inventor, crazy most believe, except Greenwood, daughter of millionaire textile king Parker. Chemist Guinness is allowed access to Parker's elaborate development laboratory, supplied with all the chemicals and equipment he requires. Guinness bars all other employees except one aide, although Parker and others can't help but peek inside to see where their considerable investment is going. On one occasion, they injudiciously enter the lab just when one of Guinness' many experiments goes awry, causing an explosion that leaves them smoldering and black-faced. Throughout the expensive process the noise from the lab is a consistent bubbling and gurgling sound that nearly drives Parker and his fellow textile moguls crazy. Meanwhile, Greenwood, patient and vaguely in love with the obsessed Guinness, constantly allays Parker's fears and remains supportive of Guinness while fending off her stuffy fiance, Gough. Finally Guinness comes through, creating a miracle fabric of pristine white. It cannot be destroyed. It will not tear and resists all stains. He makes a suit of this fabulous new material, dosed with his formula, and is heralded by Parker as a great inventor. But, before the fabric is put on the market, its drawbacks become fearfully evident. The fabric cannot be dyed any color, and its eternal existence without damage or aging threatens to put thousands of workers out of jobs. The tycoons gather, under Thesiger's direction, and agree to obtain the formula and the suit and destroy both. Thus begins a wild chase with Guinness flitting to and fro, dodging a bevy of textile magnates and their minions. He is ultimately cornered on a street during a rainstorm and, as he is caught and the pursuers begin grabbing at the fabulous suit, the fabric comes to pieces in their hands, the simple rain water having destroyed an otherwise indestructible fabric. Guinness is left pathetically standing in the middle of a street in his underwear until a kind soul gives him a raincoat. He begins walking dejectedly away, the camera showing a glum, defeated look on his face. Then he stops and stands rigid for a moment, a look of enlightenment spreading across his face, along with a knowing smile as if to suggest he knows what went wrong. That he intends to set matters right and go back to the laboratory to create his superfabric is evident when the sound of the bubbling and gurgling rises dramatically as he marches solemnly forward to his new task. THE MAN IN THE WHITE SUIT, besides offering consistent humor and often hilarious scenes, is another minor masterpiece of acting on Guinness' part, one where he showed marvelous restraint that gives way to brief hysteria, emphasizing again the complete versatility of this astounding actor, one of the greatest to ever grace the screen. Greenwood is fetching and empathic, and Parker, as her vacillating father is a jewel. Thesiger, who had essayed the mad, fruity scientist in THE BRIDE OF FRANKENSTEIN two decades earlier, is wonderful as the decrepit but all-powerful industrial czar who decrees Guinness' fate for the sake of business. In addition to the laughs, this film also indicts the ruthless and manipulative ways of businessmen. The acerbic social criticism lacing the film does not exclude union representatives, vitally embodied in burly Hope, a female organizer radiating considerable intimidation. Producer Balcon did much to raise the quality level of Ealing Studios with comedy-satires such as THE MAN IN THE WHITE SUIT. He was also responsible for such delightful films as PASSPORT TO PIMLICO (1949), WHISKEY GALORE (1949), and THE LAVENDER HILL MOB (1951), also starring the inimitable Guinness. The actor had some difficulty doing one stunt in this film; he was supposed to lower himself from a building during the chase, and complained that the wire holding him was inadequate. Director Mackendrick still asked him to do it and the actor fell when only four feet off the ground. Reported Guinness dryly: "No one apologized; they rarely do in films, as very few people care to take responsibility."

p, Michael Balcon; d, Alexander Mackendrick; w, Roger MacDougall, John Dighton, Mackendrick (based on the play by MacDougall); ph, Douglas Slocombe; m, Benjamin Frankel; ed, Bernard Gribble; md, Ernest Irving; art d, Jim Morahan; cos, Anthony Mendleson; spec eff, Sidney Pearson, Geoffrey Dickinson; makeup, Ernest Taylor, Harry Frampton.

Comedy/Satire   **Cas.**   **(PR:A MPAA:NR)**

MAN IN THE WILDERNESS**1/2

(1971, U.S./Span.) 105m Wilderness Film/WB c

Richard Harris (Zachary Bass), John Huston (Capt. Filmore Henry), Henry Wilcoxon (Indian Chief), Percy Herbert (Fogarty), Dennis Waterman (Lowrie), Prunella Ransome (Grace), Norman Rossington (Ferris), James Doohan (Benoit), Bryan Marshall (Potts), Ben Carruthers (Longbow), Robert Russell (Smith), John Bindon (Coulter), Bruce M. Fischer (Wiser), Dean Selmier (Russell), Rudy Althoff, Sheila Raynor, Manolo Landau, William Layton, Judith Furse, Tamara Sie, Joaquin Solis, Martha Tuck, Peggy the Bear.

Star Harris and producer Howard team up again for another wilderness struggle picture after the success of their A MAN CALLED HORSE. Harris, part of an expedition group, while traveling through the Northwest Territory, is mauled by a grizzly and left for dead by crew leader Huston. While regaining his strength and contemplating revenge against Huston, Harris looks back, in flashback, at the events leading up to his present state. The sadism that was so prevalent in A MAN CALLED HORSE is diminished here, but there is still more than enough blood and violence. The gruff and embittered Huston is up to par and succeeds in holding the weak script together, and Harris' performance is also commendable.

p, Sanford Howard; d, Richard C. Sarafian; w, Jack DeWitt; ph, Gerry Fisher (Panavision Technicolor); m, Johnny Harris; ed, Geoffrey Foot; prod d, Dennis Lynton Clark; art d, Gumersindo Andres; cos, Clark; spec eff, Richard M. Parker; m/l, "Zach Bass Theme," Harris, John Bromley; makeup, William Lodge.

Adventure   **(PR:O MPAA:GP)**

MAN INSIDE, THE**1/2

(1958, Brit.) 90m Warwick/COL bw

Jack Palance (Milo March), Anita Ekberg (Trudie Hall), Nigel Patrick (Sam Carter), Anthony Newley (Ernesto), Bonar Colleano (Martin Lomer), Sean Kelly (Rizzio), Sidney James (Franklin), Donald Pleasence (Organ Grinder), Eric Pohlmann (Tristao), Josephine Brown (Mrs. Frazur), Gerard Heinz (Stone), Alec Mango (Lopez), Anne Aubrey (Girl on Train), Bill Shine (English Husband), Joan Ingram (English Wife), Naomi Chance (Jane Leyton), Maxwell Shaw (Desk Clerk, Lisbon), Mary Laura Wood, Angela White, Alfred Burke, Mark Baker, Alex Gallier, Walter Gotell, Richard Golding.

Fast-moving action-adventure film features Patrick as a mild clerk who has been ogling a famous diamond for 15 years, then decides to steal it (this character and motivation is similar to Alec Guinness' in THE LAVENDER HILL MOB). He commits a murder in order to rob the gem, then is soon seen as a dapper, dashing man-about-town in various European cities. Palance has been privately hired to track down the diamond and, within minutes, a corps of different folks is after the jewel, including Ekberg, who falsely claims that the diamond belongs to her family. Kelly and Colleano, two hoodlums, also give chase. The rest of the film is a chase that flies between New York, Madrid, London, and Paris. It predictably ends with Palance winding up with Ekberg who returns the diamond to the real owners. Along the way, there are some good comic interludes to counterpoint the tension of the action, which has Patrick, Colleano, and Kelly all dead by film's end. Newley plays a Spanish cab driver with a penchant for pulchritude and he works his bushy eyebrows for good advantage, providing the best humor of the film, sublimating his usual over-acting. So much goes on in the film that we forget the plot from time to time. There are two songs; "The Man Inside" and "Trudie," neither of which dented the charts. Newley, who was 10 times the songwriter that he was the actor, should have written the tunes and something might have happened to this movie with a hit song to publicize it. This was Colleano's last movie before dying in a car crash at the age of 34. Co-producer Broccoli and co-writer Maibaum would team again for many of the "James Bond" movies.

p, Irving Allen, Albert Broccoli, Harold Huth; d, John Gilling; w, Richard Maibaum, Gilling, David Shaw (based on a novel by M. E. Chaber); ph, Ted Moore (CinemaScope); m, Richard Bennett; ed, Bert Rule; md, Muir Mathieson; art d, Ray Simms; cos, Elsa Fennell; m/l, "The Man Inside," "Trudie," Len Praverman, Joe Henderson.

Crime   **(PR:C MPAA:NR)**

MAN IS ARMED, THE*

(1956) 70m REP bw

Dane Clark, William Talman, May Wynn, Robert Horton, Barton MacLane, Fredd Wayne, Richard Benedict, Richard Reeves, Harry Lewis, Bob Jordan, Larry J. Blake, Darlene Fields, John Mitchum.

Haphazardly plotted and produced crime drama in which a man unknowingly helps a gang pull off a big heist. The gang discovers that the man is more trouble than he is worth and, as a result, things don't go as smoothly as planned. This attempt to add tension to the suspenseless drama looks incredibly phony and keeps the cast under too tight a rein.

p, Edward J. White; d, Franklin Adreon; w, Richard Landau, Robert C. Dennis (based on the story by Don Martin); ph, Bud Thackery; m, R. Dale Butts; ed, Tony Martinelli; art d, Walter Keller.

Crime   **(PR:A MPAA:NR)**

MAN IS TEN FEET TALL, A	(SEE: EDGE OF THE CITY, 1956)
MAN KILLER	(SEE: PRIVATE DETECTIVE 62, 1933)
MAN MAD	(SEE: NO PLACE TO LAND, 1958)

MAN MADE MONSTER***

(1941) 59m UNIV bw (GB: THE ELECTRIC MAN; AKA: THE ATOMIC MONSTER)

Lionel Atwill (Dr. Rigas), Lon Chaney, Jr. (Dan McCormick), Anne Nagel (June Lawrence), Frank Albertson (Mark Adams), Samuel S. Hinds (Dr. Lawrence), William Davidson (District Attorney), Ben Taggart (Detective Sergeant), Connie Bergen (Nurse), Ivan Miller (Doctor), Chester Gan (Chinese Boy), George Meader (Dr. Bruno), Frank O'Connor (Detective), John Dilson (Medical Examiner), Byron Foulger (2nd Alien), Russell Hicks (Warden), Douglas Evans (Alien).

A classic "B" horror-science fiction film that represented Lon Chaney Jr.'s first foray into the genre (Universal considered this his trial run and its success led to roles in THE WOLFMAN and THE GHOST OF FRANKENSTEIN). Fresh from his triumph as Lenny in OF MICE AND MEN, Chaney plays a carnival sideshow performer whose act involves amazing displays of electrical wizardry. One night, when the carny bus crashes into an electrical pole during a storm, Chaney finds himself the only survivor. After a series of medical tests, it is discovered that he has somehow built up an immunity to electricity. Crazed scientist Atwill (who steals the movie from Chaney) latches on to Chaney and uses him in experiments to develop a race of supermen. Atwill slowly drains Chaney of energy and transforms him into a weak-willed zombie who will obey his command. As Chaney's face becomes more gaunt and haunted looking, his friends begin to suspect something's wrong (especially after he electrocutes a bowlful of pet goldfish). Eventually, Atwill's boss, Hinds, begins to suspect the truth and Chaney, acting on Atwill's orders, kills him. Chaney is caught, tried and sentenced to death in the electric chair, a fate that Atwill awaits with unbridled scientific glee. When the executioner throws the switch, prison officials are taken by surprise when Chaney absorbs every volt, breaks out of the chair wreaking havoc on the prison and kills the warden. Atwill takes his now-glowing (literally, in a simple and very effective optical trick) guinea pig back to the lab and clothes him in an insulated rubber suit that conserves his overabundant energy. Things go awry for Atwill, however, when he decides to try out his theories on the heroine, Nagel, whom Chaney had fallen for earlier in the picture. The glowing monster flies into a rage, kills Atwill with a few thousand volts and runs off into the night. He runs afoul of a barbed-wire fence, tearing his suit and draining him of his energy. Short, fast-paced and economical, MAN MADE MONSTER sports two fine central performances (Atwill and Chaney) and a fairly intelligent script, which keeps the inherent silliness of the material well under control.

p, Jack Bernard; d, George Waggner; w, Joseph West (based on the story "The Electric Man" by H. J. Essex, Sid Schwartz, Len Golos); ph, Elwood Bredell; m, Charles Previn; ed, Arthur Hilton; md, Hans J. Salter; spec eff, John P. Fulton.

Science Fiction   **(PR:A MPAA:NR)**

MAN MISSING   (SEE: YOU HAVE TO RUN FAST, 1961)

MAN OF A THOUSAND FACES***1/2

(1957) 122m UNIV bw

James Cagney (Lon Chaney), Dorothy Malone (Cleva Creighton Chaney), Jane Greer (Hazel Bennet), Marjorie Rambeau (Gert), Jim Backus (Clarence Logan), Robert J. Evans (Irving Thalberg), Celia Lovsky (Mrs. Chaney), Jeanne Cagney (Carrie Chaney), Jack Albertson (Dr. J. Wilson Shields), Roger Smith (Creighton Chaney at Age 21), Robert Lyden (Creighton Chaney at Age 13), Rickie Sorensen (Creighton Chaney at Age 8), Dennis Rush (Creighton Chaney at Age 4), Nolan Leary (Pa Chaney), Simon Scott (Carl Hastings), Clarence Kolb (Himself), Danny Beck (Max Dill), Phil Van Zandt (George Loane Tucker), Hank Mann, Snub Pollard (Comedy Waiters), Marjorie Bennett (Maid).

Other than Douglas Fairbanks, Jr., Rudolph Valentino, and Charlie Chaplin there were few who approached the star status in the silent film era of Lon Chaney, the master of disguise, a makeup genius who specialized in roles embodying terror. He was the heart of horror during the glorious days of the silents, and Cagney's essaying this great artist is nothing less than spectacular. Cagney is shown as the son of deaf-mute parents who himself is free of afflictions. He becomes a successful vaudeville entertainer, offering magical performances as a mime (knowing full well what it means to be without sound), a juggler, and a man of many routines and characters, all creatively constructed through inventive makeup. Cagney meets beautiful but neurotic Malone and makes her his assistant. They fall in love and marry, but when Malone is taken home by Cagney to meet his gentle but wordless parents she becomes hysterical and then glumly resigned to the ugly belief that any children they might have will be congenitally afflicted. Nothing Cagney can say or do will convince her otherwise. Malone remains terrified of having a deaf-and-dumb baby. When their child is born, she will not even look at him, until Cagney brings the child to her and loudly claps his hands close to the boy's ears, causing him to scream and Malone to become overjoyed. But Malone begins to resent her husband's rising popularity and, when he becomes a headliner, she competes with his fame by taking on a lover, then abandoning him and their son, Creighton (later Lon Chaney, Jr.). Hurt and embittered, his boy put into a home because he lacks funds to support him, Cagney goes to Hollywood in 1913 to become a film extra. He works like a man possessed, answering every call for actors, his makeup box constantly at his side. Rambeau, who plays noble ladies in bit parts, becomes his friend but she is puzzled by his whirlwind work schedule. One hour he is playing a spear-holder, the next a pirate, changing his face constantly into a whole new character. When Rambeau quizzes him about his frantic schedule, Cagney replies: "I've got to get my kid out of hock." Cagney becomes so much in demand as a versatile character actor that he soon begins to earn substantial money in the movies and is able to have his little boy join him, especially after he meets and falls in love with Greer, a loving and generous woman who supports him and treats his son as her own. Cagney goes on to superstardom, enacting horrific figures such as THE HUNCHBACK OF NOTRE DAME, THE PHANTOM OF THE OPERA, and strange, compelling, but mostly always sinister characters in such films as WEST OF ZANZIBAR, THE PENALTY, THE UNHOLY THREE, and LONDON AFTER MIDNIGHT, all Chaney smash hits. Cagney, Greer, and the boy live a tranquil life, the star enjoying his mountain retreat where he fishes and teaches his son his life style and principles. One of the many great little scenes involves Cagney trying to get his son to sleep, making his face up to resemble a funny little grandmotherly type who stitches her fingers together. Then Malone comes back into Cagney's life, having lost her voice, ironically, from illness, and demanding to have the boy returned to her. Cagney is adamant, refusing to even allow her to visit the child, but persuaded by the compassionate Greer, he allows the boy to visit his mother. Malone's utter helplessness causes the teenage Creighton to stay with her and, in young manhood, as Smith, he continues to live with Malone, supporting her with his own acting work. Cagney disowns Smith for his loyalty to a woman who had earlier deserted both of them but, when dying of throat cancer at the height of his fantastic career, Cagney reconciles with his son. Cagney is riveting as Chaney, who died in 1930 at the age of 47, enacting the many great roles the silent star made famous in startling cameo performances. Some of the facts in Chaney's life were altered, but this did not affect a top-notch production. Cagney was ever-mindful of Chaney's credo: "Unless I suffer, how can I make the public believe me?" when making this film. He acts with serene dignity, plumbing the tortuous life of a great artist, showing restraint when not acting and fully developing the sensitive, withdrawn character that was Lon Chaney. When on camera, fully understanding the tormented man he was playing, Cagney gives vent to his agony, such as slobbering mindlessly in the bell tower as the deformed hunchback, or weeping unconsolably as the phantom over his hideous appearance. Cagney studied the actor's life and came to a deep understanding about why Chaney chose to play misfits and freaks; it was a way of expiating his own remorse over a miserable personal life. (Oddly, Cagney had, in these years, played a number of characters who were physically or psychologically crippled, like Martin "The Gimp" Snyder in LOVE ME OR LEAVE ME, and the unbalanced Arthur Cody Jarrett in WHITE HEAT.) Chaney's unforgettable makeup tricks could not be exactly duplicated since the actor's secrets of disguise died with him, but makeup artists Bud Westmore and Jack Kevan did a great job in coming close. "In doing the life story of such a great screen artist as Lon Chaney it belabors the obvious to say that I found it a challenge," Cagney later said. He acted his heart out in this film and certainly deserved an Oscar nomination which he did not receive. (The film was captioned for the deaf by the U.S. Department of Health, Education, and Welfare.) Malone gives a strong but strange performance as the weird first Mrs. Chaney and Greer is outstanding as the second wife. Lovsky, as Cagney's deaf-mute mother, is superb and also deserved an Oscar nomination for supporting actress. MGM mogul Irving Thalberg is played unconvincingly by Evans, who was "discovered" sitting at poolside by Thalberg's widow, Norma Shearer, but, as an actor, he proved to be just another pretty boy without a tad of talent. Ironically, Evans later became a real-life mogul, heading Paramount from 1966 to 1976. Pevney's direction lags in spots and he sometimes overplays the tearjerking scenes but is mostly effective. Smith, playing the 21-year-old Creighton Chaney, is rather stoical. The real Creighton, who became Lon Chaney, Jr., and gleaned some fame in enacting horror roles for Universal (THE WOLF MAN in particular), was himself a rather pathetic figure. The battle between his mother and father scarred his memories and troubled him throughout his own tormented life. As a teenager, Creighton Chaney searched widely for the mother who had abandoned him, finally tracking her down to a small ranch in the desert. He knocked on the door and a thin woman with haunted, hollow eyes answered. "My name is Creighton Chaney and I'm looking for Mrs. Cleva Fletcher," he said. "I'm sorry," she said, "no one here by that name," and the woman began to close the door. Then someone inside the house shouted out, like a stabbing knife, no doubt, into the heart of the inquiring youth: "Who is it, Cleva?"

p, Robert Arthur; d, Joseph Pevney; w, Ivan Goff (based on a story by Ralph Wheelwright); ph, Russell Metty; m, Frank Skinner; ed, Ted Kent; md, Joseph Gershenson; art d, Alexander Golitzen, Eric Orbom; cos, Bill Thomas; spec eff, Clifford Stine; makeup, Bud Westmore, Jack Kevan.

Drama (PR:A MPAA:NR)

MAN OF AFFAIRS* (1937, Brit.) 70m GAU bw (GB: HIS LORDSHIP)

George Arliss (Richard/Lord Dunchester), Romilly Lunge (Bill Howard), Rene Ray (Vera), Jessie Winter (Lady Dunchester), John Ford (Ibrahim), Allan Jeayes (Barak), Lawrence Anderson (Nahil), Bernard Merefield (Phillpotts), John Turnbull (Stevenson), Basil Gill (Abdullah).

Arliss is cast in a dual role as a detective who tries to uncover the kidnaping plot of his brother, the Foreign Secretary of Britain. He impersonates the brother in order to solve a mysterious murder which could bring the Brits into a war. Of course he's successful, but allows his brother to take the kudos. The best thing about it is some nice split screen work which has detective Arliss shaking the hand of Secretary Arliss.

p, S. C. Balcon; d, Herbert Mason; w, Maude T. Howell, L. du Garde Peach, Edwin Greenwood (based on the play "The Nelson Touch" by Neil Grant); ph, Gunther Krampf; ed, M. Gordon.

Crime/Drama (PR:A MPAA:NR)

MAN OF AFRICA* (1956, Brit.) 73m Group 3/Eden c

Violet Mukabuerza (Violet), Frederick Bijuerenda (Jonathan), Members of The Bakiga and Batwa Tribes.

Life among the pygmies of the remote sections of Uganda is explored in this fictionalized documentary, produced by Grierson, the director of DRIFTERS and THE FISHING BANKS OF SKYE. The style of the film is similar to the great

filmmaker's, taking a look at the life styles of a native people and grafting a simple story to give the work a human element. However, MAN OF AFRICA shows none of Grierson's flair for this specialized genre. Though the lives of the tribes are well documented in the footage, the film moves at a deadening pace that bores more than educates. An unnecessary love story between Mukabuerza and Bijuerenda simply gets in the way of the real life stories. Still, for all its problems, MAN OF AFRICA (a title no doubt attempting to capitalize on Robert Flaherty's well known MAN OF ARAN) does look good, particularly in capturing the more intimate moments in the pygmies' lives.

p, John Grierson; d, Cyril Frankel; w, Montagu Slater (based on a story by Frankel); ph, (Ferraniacolor); m, Malcolm Arnold.

Drama (PR:A MPAA:NR)

MAN OF BRONZE (SEE: JIM THORPE—ALL AMERICAN, 1951)

MAN OF CONFLICT* (1953) 72m Atlas bw

Edward Arnold (J. R. Compton), John Agar (Ray Compton), Susan Morrow (Jane Jenks), Fay Roope (Ed Jenks), Herbert Heyes (Evans), Dorothy Patrick (Betty), Bob Carson (Official), Russell Hicks (Murdock), John Hamilton (Cornwall), Lovyss Bradley (Miss Garner), Leslie O'Pace (Preston), Frank O'Connor (Watchman), Lee Phelps (Police Captain), Allan Schute (Butler), John Holland (Doctor).

Arnold is a wealthy, tyrannical industrialist who tries to force his son, Agar, to follow in his insensitive footsteps. Agar instead sides with the company's employees and holds tight to the morals and values his father has forgotten.

p&d, Hal R. Makelim; w, Hal Richards; ph, Harold Stine; m, Albert Glasser; ed, William Shea, Chandler House; art d, Ralph Berger.

Drama (PR:A MPAA:NR)

MAN OF CONQUEST* (1939) 105m REP bw

Richard Dix (Sam Houston), Gail Patrick (Margaret Lea), Edward Ellis (Andrew Jackson), Joan Fontaine (Eliza Allen), Victor Jory (William Travis), Robert Barrat (Davy Crockett), George Hayes (Lannie Upchurch), Ralph Morgan (Stephen Austin), Robert Armstrong (Jim Bowie), C. Henry Gordon (Santa Ana), Janet Beecher (Mrs. Lea), Pedro de Cordoba (Oolooteko), Max Terhune ("Deaf" Smith), Ferris Taylor (Jonas Lea), Kathleen Lockhart (Mrs. Allen), Leon Ames (John Hoskins), Charles Stevens (Zavola), Lane Chandler (Bonham), Sarah Padden (Mrs. Houston).

Republic Studios was never known as a substantial movie-making organization. Its rag-tag sound stages and skimpy back lot offered little to viewers other than a seemingly endless stream of B westerns. But on occasions Republic put forth a film of some importance and this is one of them, made significant by Dix's powerful performance as frontier fighter Sam Houston, who, more than anyone, brought Texas into existence as a sovereign entity and later as a state of the union. The film faithfully follows this man of destiny through his greatest days, his beginning in Tennessee where Ellis, playing Andrew Jackson, teaches him the ways of clever politics and how he becomes twice governor of the state, touching upon his first marriage. Dix then travels to Arkansas where he is adopted by the Cherokee Indians and his second marriage is depicted. The last part of this stirring film, directed with great energy by Nichols, details Dix's involvement with the Texas fight for freedom against Mexico and the battle scenes here, briefly of the Alamo and at San Jacinto, are outstanding. Dix is terrific as Houston, playing the great man with few histrionics and considerable restraint. He first wife is played by Fontaine and she registers weakly, while Patrick, as the second wife, is more believable. Ellis is very good as Old Hickory. Gordon plays a wicked Santa Ana, while the men at the Alamo—Barrett, Jory, Armstrong—are well essayed. The production values are startlingly good.

p, Sol C. Siegel; d, George Nichols, Jr.; w, Wells Root, E. E. Paramore, Jr. (based on a story by Root, Harold Shumate); ph, Joseph H. August; m, Victor Young; ed, Edward Mann; art d, John Victor Mackay; cos, Adele Palmer, Edith Head; spec eff, Howard Lydecker.

Western (PR:A MPAA:NR)

MAN OF COURAGE* (1943) 66m PRC bw

Barton MacLane (John Wallace), Charlotte Wynters (Joyce Griffith), Lyle Talbot (George Dickson), Dorothy Burgess (Sally Dickson), Patsy Nash (Mary Ann), Forrest Taylor (Crandall), John Ince (Tom Haines), Jane Novak (Mrs. Black), Erskine Johnson (Himself), Claire Grey (Alice), Steve Clark (Judge Roberts), Billy Gray (Mike Wilson), Frank Yaconelli (Pete).

After some crooked political dealings, a murderous and kidnaping mobster is brought to trial by MacLane, the hard-working and honest district attorney.

p, Lester Cutler; d, Alexis Thurn-Taxis; w, Arthur St. Claire, Barton MacLane, John Vlahos (based on a story by MacLane, Herman Ruby, Lew Pollack); ph, Marcel LePicard; ed, Fred Bain; md, Lee Zahler; m/l, "Now and Then," Lew Pollack.

Crime/Drama (PR:A MPAA:NR)

MAN OF EVIL½ (1948, Brit.) 90m Gainsborough/UA bw (GB: FANNY BY GASLIGHT)

Phyllis Calvert (Fanny Hopwood), James Mason (Lord Manderstoke), Wilfrid Lawson (Chunks), Stewart Granger (Harry Somerford), Margaretta Scott (Alicia), Jean Kent (Lucy Beckett), John Laurie (William Hopwood), Stuart Lindsell (Clive Seymore), Nora Swinburne (Mrs. Hopwood), Amy Veness (Mrs. Heaviside), Ann Wilton (Carver), Helen Haye (Mrs. Somerford), Cathleen Nesbitt (Kate Somerford), Ann Stephens (Fanny as a Child), Gloria Sydney (Lucy as a Child), Guy le Feuvre (Dr. Lowenthall), John Turnbull, Helen Goss, Peter Jones, Maureen O'Brien, Beryl Laverick, Virginia Keiley, Guy Gy-Mas, Beresford Egan, Joan Rees.

Loosely based on the 1940s best-seller *Fanny By Gaslight*, this English production's U.S. release was held up for four years. A tale of love, peddled passions, bastardy, and the clash of social classes, the film has youthful, innocent Calvert in more perils than Pauline, though of a different order. Calvert is the illegitimate child of a turn-of-the-century Member of Parliament; her foster parents keep a bordello. When her foster dad is killed by villain Mason, whose social standing prohibits his prosecution for the crime, Calvert leaves the bawdyhouse of her childhood to live with her real father. Deeply resented by her new stepmother and an object of desire to the evil Mason, who has been sleeping with said new stepmother, Calvert's torments are allayed only by her friendship with kindly, sympathetic butler Lawson, and by her romantic involvement with her real father's socially prominent secretary, Granger. When her new stepmother threatens a scandal over her unfortunate childhood history, her dad kills himself. Granger's family interferes with the romance. The prurient Mason challenges Granger to a duel; Mason is killed. The litany of mortifications seems endless, and the film is ultimately a dreary melodrama, despite a fine cast. This was one of the films of the mid-1940s to catapult Granger to his position as one of Britain's two top leading men (along with co-star Mason).

p, Edward Black; d, Anthony Asquith; w, Doreen Montgomery, Aimee Stuart (based on the novel *Fanny By Gaslight* by Michael Sadleir); ph, Arthur Crabtree; m, Cedric Mallabey; ed, R. E. Dearing; md, Louis Levy; art d, John Bryan; cos, Elizabeth Haffenden.

Drama **(PR:A MPAA:NR)**

MAN OF IRON* (1935) 62m FN-WB bw

Barton MacLane *(Chris Bennett)*, Mary Astor *(Vida)*, John Eldredge *(Tanahill)*, Dorothy Peterson *(Bessie)*, Joseph Crehan *(Tom Martin)*, Craig Reynolds *(Adams)*, Joseph King *(Balding)*, John Qualen *(Collins)*, Joseph Sawyer *(Crawford)*, Florence Fair *(Mrs. Balding)*, Edward Keene *(Mortgage Man)*, Joseph Pogue, Gordon Elliott.

MacLane is a fast-rising factory worker who makes it to vice president. On the way to the top, however, he loses the friendship and trust of his former co-workers. Workers stage a strike at the end of the picture. Poorly constructed and implausibly acted.

p, Bryan Foy; d, William McGann; w, William Wister Haines (based on a story by Dawn Powell); ph, L. W. O'Connell; ed, Terry Morse; md, Leo F. Forbstein; art d, Hugh Reticker.

Drama **(PR:A MPAA:NR)**

MAN OF IRON (SEE: RAILROAD MAN, THE, 1965, Ital.)

MAN OF IRON****

(1981, Pol.) 140m Film Polski-Film Unit X/UA c (CZLOWIEK Z ZELAZA)

Jerzy Radziwilowicz *(Tomczyk)*, Krystyna Janda *(Agnieszka)*, Marian Opania *(Winkiel)*, Irene Byrska *(Anna Hulewicz' Mother)*, Boguslaw Linda *(Radio/TV Technician Dzidek)*, Wieslawa Kosmalska *(Anna)*, Andrzej Seweryn *(Capt. Wirski)*, Krzysztof Janczar *(Kryszka)*, Boguslaw Sobczuk *(TV Editor)*, Frantiszek Trzeciak *(Badecki)*, Jan Tesarz *(Szef)*, Anna Walentynowicz, Lech Walesa, Janusz Gajos, Marek Kondrat, Jerzy Trela, Krystyna Zachwatowicz-Wajda, Wojciech Alaborski, Halina Labonarska, Bozena Dykiel.

A sequel to Andrzej Wajda's MAN OF MARBLE, MAN OF IRON employs the same techniques of interviewing, as well as the same scriptwriter and lead players. It is a realistic portrayal of Gdansk from the student reform movement of 1968 to the Solidarity strikes in 1980. Radziwilowicz is a strike leader who is harassed by the government and news reporter Opania. While trying to conduct a smear campaign against the young laborer, Opania is faced with deciding where his loyalties lie in the strike. Wajda presents the audience with a superb amalgam of fictional characters and a real-life situation. The film not only entertains, but acts as historical documentation of this tense period in Polish history. The legendary labor leader Lech Walesa also makes an appearance. Targeted with the expected political pressures, MAN OF IRON was finished only hours before its premiere at the Cannes Film Festival, where it won top honors. (In Polish; English subtitles.)

d, Andrzej Wajda; w, Aleksander Scibor-Rylski; ph, Edward Klosinski, Janusz Kalicinski; m, Andrzej Korzynski; ed, Halina Prugar; art d, Allan Starski, Maja Chrolowska; cos, Wieslawa Starska.

Historical Drama **(PR:C MPAA:PG)**

MAN OF LA MANCHA*½ (1972) 135m Produzioni Europee Associate/UA c

Peter O'Toole *(Miguel de Cervantes/Don Quixote/Alonso Quijana)*, Sophia Loren *(Dulcinea/Aldonza)*, James Coco *(Manservant/Sancho Panza)*, Harry Andrews *(Governor/Innkeeper)*, John Castle *(Duke/Dr. Carrasco/Black Knight/Knight of the Mirrors)*, Brian Blessed *(Pedro)*, Ian Richardson *(Padre)*, Julie Gregg *(Antonio/Lady in White)*, Rosalee Crutchley *(Housekeeper)*, Gino Conforti *(Barber)*, Marne Maitland *(Captain of the Guard)*, Dorothy Sinclair *(Maria/Innkeeper's Wife)*, Miriam Acevedo *(Fermina)*, Dominic Barto, Poldo Bendandi, Peppi Borza, Mario Donen, Fred Evans, Francesco Ferrini, Paolo Gozlino, Teddy Green, Peter Johnston, Roy Jones, Connel Miles, Steffen Zacharias, Lou Zamprogna, Calogero Caruana, Rolando De Santis *(Muleteers)*.

This smash musical saw 2,329 performances in New York City, but bringing it to the screen proved an expensive disaster where $12 million was squandered on the belief that the leading players didn't have to sing effectively to make the movie a hit, an idiotic notion at best since the music is the only worthwhile thing about this historical opus. Thrown into a 17th Century dungeon for having offended the Spanish Inquisition with his supposedly heretical writings, Cervantes, O'Toole, busies himself by writing the outlandish, delightful tale of knight errant Don Quixote, which O'Toole proceeds to enact, tilting at windmills and followed by his lapdog servant, Coco, playing Sancho Panza. Loren, playing a sluttish serving wench, Aldonza, becomes the virginal Dulcinea, the wonderful dream lady of Cervantes/Quixote's hopes. A group of muleteers enters the village where O'Toole and Coco are resting, gang-raping Loren who taunts them into ravishing her. Castle and Gregg then arrive; Quixote's niece, Gregg, begs him to go home but he insists upon staying in the woebegone village and driving off the pesky muleteers to restore the golden age of chivalry. O'Toole is successful but is ultimately defeated by the Black Knight, also played by Castle. The old knight is dying but Loren gives him solace at the end, coming to his deathbed to remind him of all the virtues he has taught her to uphold. O'Toole regains his faith through Loren's courageous beliefs and he dies happy. His story finished, Cervantes climbs the dungeon stairs to hear his fate from the Inquisition, with his fellow prisoners so moved by his tale that they lift their voices in song to him. The critics lambasted this film and rightly so because of the producer's presumptuous stance that pleasing voices, which none of the leads have, were not important in making a good musical. Loren shrieks out her songs and Coco is a monotone. Too bad. The songs are wonderful and this film does a vast disservice to Leigh and Darion who wrote the music and lyrics, although Wasserman's book was never much good. Where the whopping $12 million went is anybody's guess since the film was shot on two miserable sound stages with sets that are slapdash at best. O'Toole called them "the most depressing sets that ever existed." It was believed that O'Toole sang his own tunes but his voice was dubbed by Simon Gilbert and even that voice was awful! Loren insisted she sing her own songs without dubbing and she got her way. She was later quoted as saying: "This is a challenge. I never have appeared in a musical before. I sing a little but I don't know yet if they will use my voice . . . I hope I can, as it's very personal to me. To tell something by singing, to portray emotions in a song, this is very beautiful to me." Well, Loren couldn't sing even a little and the only emotion she portrayed in her songs was that of a bleating cow being led to the slaughter, or in a hayloft scene where she not too convincingly resists a group of lust-crazed rapists, a shabby reprise of her scenes in TWO WOMEN. O'Toole, as the pixilated Quixote, seems to stumble through the role and Coco appears glad to be getting a paycheck for his overacting. Producer-director Hiller used an iron hand on this dismal production which rarely shows a spark of life. Songs and musical numbers include (all by Leigh and Darion): "It's All the Same," "The Impossible Dream," "Barber's Song," "Man of La Mancha," "Dulcinea," "I'm Only Thinking of Him," "Little Bird, Little Bird," "Life as It Really Is," "The Dubbing," "A Little Gossip," "Aldonza," "Golden Helmet of Mambrino," and "The Psalm."

p&d, Arthur Hiller; w, Dale Wasserman (based on the play by Wasserman, suggested by Cervantes' "Don Quixote"); ph, Giuseppe Rotunno (DeLuxe Color); m, Mitch Leigh; ed, Robert C. Jones, Folmar Blangsted; md, Laurence Rosenthal; art d, Luciano Damiani; set d, Arrigo Breschi; cos, Damiani; spec eff, Adriano Pischiutta; ch, Gillian Lynne; m/l, Leigh, Joe Darion; makeup, Charles Parker, Euclide Santoli, Guisse Giuseppe Annunziata.

Musical **Cas.** **(PR:C MPAA:NR)**

MAN OF MARBLE*½**

(1979, Pol.) 160m Enterprise de Realization de Films-Ensembles Cinematographiques-Ensemble X/Film Polski c (CZLOWIEK Z MARMURU)

Jerzy Radziwilowicz *(Mateusz Birkut/His Son Maciek Tomcyzyk)*, Michal Tarkowski *(Wincenty Witek)*, Krystyna Zachwatowicz *(Hanka Tomcyzk)*, Piotr Cieslak *(Michalak)*, Wieslaw Wojick *(Jodia)*, Krystyna Janda *(Agnieszka)*, Tadeusz Lomnicki *(Jerzy Burski)*, Jacek Lomnicki *(Young Burski)*, Leonard Zajaczkowski *(Leonard Frybos)*, Jacek Domanski *(Sound Man)*, Grzegorz Skurski *(Chauffeur/Lighting Man)*, Magda Teresa Wojcik *(Editor)*, Boguslaw Sobczyk *(TV Writer)*, Zdsilaw Kozien *(Agnieska's Father)*, Irena Laskowska *(Museum Employee)*, Jerzy Moniak *(Moniak)*, Wieslaw Drzewicz *(Manager of the Restaurant)*, Kazmierz Kaczor *(Security Man)*, Eva Zietek *(Secretary)*, B. Fronczkowiak *(Official from the Ministry of the Interior)*.

The post-WW II Polish regimes have been plagued with political problems and inconsistencies which culminated in the workers' revolt and eventual martial law crackdown in 1982. The situations which led to these troubles were foreshadowed by one of Poland's highest-ranking directors in this black satire. He follows a film student (Janda) who wants to make a documentary about a former worker as her graduation requirement. Radziwilowicz is to be her subject, a man who had been lauded for his brick-laying skills before vanishing into total obscurity. Previously the subject of a film which showed what a great worker he was, Radziwilowicz became something of a star. But problems arose when he began believing the publicity himself and thus started interfering in worker politics. The government quickly covered him up, disgracing the man's name, and banishing him into historical obscurity. This is the story Janda discovers, through interviews with Radziwilowicz's contemporaries and family, and through old newsreels. Similar to CITIZEN KANE in exposition style, Wajda has fashioned a sophisticated indictment of the Stalinist rule, with all of its warts clearly exposed. Wajda followed this with MAN OF IRON, using similar storytelling methods to portray the rise of Poland's Solidarity movement and its leader Lech Walesa.

p&d, Andrzej Wajda; w, Aleksander Scibor-Rylski; ph, Edward Klosinski (Eastmancolor); m, Andrzej Korzynski; ed, Halina Pugarowa, Maria Kalinciska, prod d, Allan Starski, Wojciech Majda, Maria Osiecka-Kuminek; cos, Lidia Rzeszewska, Wieslawa Konopelska.

Drama **(PR:C-O MPAA:NR)**

MAN OF MAYFAIR*½ (1931, Brit.) 83m PAR bw

Jack Buchanan *(Lord William)*, Joan Barry *(Grace Irving)*, Warwick Ward *(Ferdinand Barclay)*, Nora Swinburne *(Elaine Barclay)*, Ellaline Terriss *(Old Grace)*, Lilian Braithwaite *(Lady Kingsland)*, Cyril Raymond *(Charles)*, Charles Quartermaine *(Dalton)*, Sebastian Smith *(Macpherson)*, J. Fisher White *(Wilson)*, The Francis Mangan Girls.

Buchanan stars as an aristocrat with a crush on showgirl Barry. He continues his pursuit by posing as a stagehand, at the same time hoping to make an impression on Barry's prudish mother, who is unaware of her daughter's profession. Mainly a vehicle to show off Buchanan's comic skills, which are mostly unmemorable.

p, Walter Morosco; d, Louis Mercanton; w, Eliot Crawshay Williams, Hugh Perceval (based on the novel *A Child in Their Midst* by May Edginton).

Comedy   **(PR:A   MPAA:NR)**

MAN OF MUSIC**   (1953, USSR) 100m Mosfilm/Artkino c

Boris Smirnov (*Mikhail Glinka*), Lyubov Orlova (*Ludmilla*), L. Durasov (*Alexander Pushkin*), Svyatoslav Richter (*Franz Liszt*), B. Vinogradova (*Giuditta Pasta*), M. Nazvanov (*Nicholas I*).

Smirnov, appearing in his first film after a successful stage career, plays composer Mikhail Glinka in this colorful biography. The composer's operas ''Ivan Susanin'' and ''Russian and Ludmilla'' are prominently featured in the film, and excerpts from both are performed. The Bolshoi Opera chorus and orchestra also perform a rendition of ''Glory to Thee.'' A sprinkling of Soviet propaganda weighs the picture down in parts, but otherwise it is enjoyable and entertaining. Excellent photography by the near-legendary Edouard Tisse. (In Russian; English subtitles.)

d, Gregory Alexandrov; w, P. Pavlenko, N. Treneva, Alexandrov; ph, Edouard Tisse (Magicolor); m, V. Shcherbachev, V. Shebalin; set d, A. Utkin.

Biography   **(PR:A   MPAA:NR)**

MAN OF SENTIMENT, A*½   (1933) 62m CHES/FD bw

Marian Marsh (*Julia Wilkens*), Owen Moore (*Stanley Colton*), Christian Rub (*Herman Heupelkossel*), William Bakewell (*John Russell*), Emma Dunn (*Mrs. Russell*), Edmund Breese (*Mr. Russell*), Geneva Mitchell (*Doris Russell*), Jack Pennick, Pat O'Malley, Syd Saylor, Lucille Ward, Cornelius Keefe, Sam Adams, Otto Hoffman.

This slow-moving film tells the story of Marsh, a career-oriented gal who is set to marry the wealthy Moore. After an auto accident, she meets the not-so-wealthy Bakewell and falls in love with him. She chooses love over money and rejects Moore. It then turns out that Bakewell is the black-sheep son of rich parents. Through a turn of events the parents accept Bakewell and his beloved back into the family, and all is well.

d, Richard Thorpe; w, Robert Ellis (based on the story by Frederick Hazlitt Brennan); ph, M. A. Anderson.

Drama/Romance   **(PR:A   MPAA:NR)**

MAN OF THE FAMILY   (SEE: TOP MAN, 1943)

MAN OF THE FOREST**½   (1933) 59m PAR bw

Randolph Scott (*Brett Dale*), Verna Hillie (*Alice Gaynor*), Harry Carey (*Jim Gaynor*), Noah Beery, Sr. (*Clint Beasley*), Barton MacLane (*Mulvey*), Buster Crabbe (*Yegg*), Guinn ''Big Boy'' Williams (*Big Casino*), Vince Barnett (*Little Casino*), Blanche Frederici (*Mrs. Forney*), Tempe Pigott, Tom Kennedy, Frank McGlynn, Jr., Duke Lee, Lew Kelly, Merrill McCormack.

Scott comes to the aid of the helpless Hillie, who is about to be bullied by Beery. Beery tries to frame Scott for the murder of Hillie's father, but justice gets its way in the end. A little hokey at times, but still well worth it. Based on the novel by Zane Grey, the film also features lions in some of the action scenes.

p, Harold Hurley; d, Henry Hathaway; w, Jack Cunningham, Harold Shumate (based on the novel by Zane Grey); ph, Ben Reynolds; art d, Earl Hedrick.

Western   **(PR:A   MPAA:NR)**

MAN OF THE HOUR, THE***

       (1940, Fr.) 93m Les Films Marquis/Trio bw (L'HOMME DU JUOR)

Maurice Chevalier (*Himself/Alfred Boulard*), Elvire Popesco (*Mona Talia*), Alerme (*Cormier de la Creuse*), Josette Day (*Suzanne Petit*), Marcelle Geniat (*Mother Boulard*), Robert Lynen (*Milo*), Paulette Elambert (*Suzanne's Sister*), Marguerite Deval (*The Grand Old Lady*), Pizani (*The Poet*), Fernand Fabre (*The Painter*), Renee Devillers (*The Flower Girl*), Aimos (*An Old Actor*).

Chevalier is cast as an electrician who wants to be a singer like Maurice Chevalier. While walking down the street he sees actress Popesco involved in a near-fatal accident. He volunteers himself as a blood-donor and saves her life. The newspapers publicize this act of valor and he receives a bundle of money for the rights to his story. When the electrician is invited to Popesco's chateau, his girl friend, Day, implores him not to go, but he doesn't pay attention. Eventually, he gets a chance to sing alongside the real Chevalier, thanks to some trick photography. In the finale, the electrician realizes he is out of his class and returns to Day. Originally released in France in 1936. (In French; English subtitles.)

p&d, Julien Duvivier; w, Charles Spaak, Maurice Chevalier, Charles Vidiac, Duvivier; ph, Roger Hubert; m/l, Jean Weiner, Borel-Clerk, Michel Emer, Vincent Scotto.

Musical   **(PR:A   MPAA:NR)**

MAN OF THE HOUR   (SEE: COLONEL EFFINGHAM'S RAID, 1945)

MAN OF THE MOMENT**½   (1935, Brit.) 82m FN-WB bw

Douglas Fairbanks, Jr. (*Tony*), Laura La Plante (*Mary*), Claude Hulbert (*Rufus*), Margaret Lockwood (*Vera*), Donald Calthrop (*Butler*), Peter Gawthorne (*Father*), Monty Banks (*Doctor*).

Hard-up Fairbanks saves La Plante from drowning herself and, after offering her shelter, ends up falling in love with her. Unfortunately, this ruins his chance to marry an heiress but, in this case, true love defeats the toughest of odds. With a lucky roll

of the dice, La Plante and Fairbanks manage to break the bank at a Monte Carlo casino and get back on their feet again. Good performances by Fairbanks and La Plante, and some witty dialog make this an enjoyable piece of mindless entertainment.

p, Irving Asher; d, Monty Banks; w, Roland Pertwee, Guy Bolton, A. R. Rawlinson (based on the play ''Water Nymph'' by Yves Mirande); ph, Basil Emmott, Leslie Rowson.

Comedy   **(PR:A   MPAA:NR)**

MAN OF THE MOMENT**½   (1955, Brit.) 95m Group bw

Norman Wisdom (*Norman*), Lana Morris (*Penny*), Belinda Lee (*Sonia*), Jerry Desmonde (*Jackson*), Karel Stepanek (*Lom*), Garry Marsh (*British Delegate*), Inia te Wiata (*Toki*), Evelyn Roberts (*Sir Kenneth*), Violet Farebrother (*Queen of Tawaki*), Martin Miller (*Swiss Tailor*), Eugene Deckers (*Day Lift Man*), Hugh Morton (*Mitchell*), Cyril Chamberlain (*British Delegate*), Lisa Gastoni (*Chambermaid*), Harold Kasket (*Enrico*), Beverly Brooks (*Air Hostess*), Charles Hawtrey (*Producer*), A. J. ''Man Mountain'' Dean (*Bodyguard*), The Beverley Sisters, Macdonald Hobley, Phillip Harben, Ronnie Waldman, Bruce Seton, ''The Grove Family,'' Philip Gilbert, Julia Arnall, Doreen Dawne, Edward Evans, Ruth Dunning, Sheila Sweet, Peter Bryant, Margaret Downs, Susan Beaumont, Michael Ward, Derek Sydney, Peter Taylor, Peggyann Clifford, Ivan Craig, Joseph Behrman.

Wisdom is a British ministry clerk who ends up sitting in for an injured delegate at a Geneva conference. When he uses his veto power to assist a small Pacific nation, he is knighted by his home country but threatened by foreign powers. Some fine slapstick moments, including a television studio chase that interrupts several programs. Songs, all sung by the Beverley Sisters, include: ''Dreams for Sale'' (Arthur Groves, Peter Carroll), ''Beware'' (Norman Wisdom), ''Yodelee Yodelay'' and ''Man of the Moment'' (Jack Fishman).

p, Hugh Stewart; d, John Paddy Carstairs; w, Vernon Sylvaine, Carstairs (based on a story by Maurice Cowan); ph, Jack Cox.

Comedy   **(PR:A   MPAA:NR)**

MAN OF THE PEOPLE**   (1937) 80m MGM bw

Joseph Calleia (*Jack Moreno*), Florence Rice (*Abbey*), Thomas Mitchell (*Grady*), Ted Healy (*Joe the Glut*), Catherine Doucet (*Mrs. Reid*), Paul Stanton (*Stringer*), Robert Emmett Keane (*Murphy*), Jonathan Hale (*Carter Spetner*), Jane Barnes (*Marie Rossetti*), William Ricciardi (*Pop Rossetti*), Noel Madison (*Dopey Benny*), Soledad Jiminez (*Mrs. Rossetti*), Edward Nugent (*Edward Spetner*), Donald Briggs (*Baldwin*).

Calleia is the son of an Italian immigrant who makes good and gets a law degree. He soon finds, however, that he can't get anywhere in politics without the help of the crooked political organization. He goes along with what is expected in crooked politics, until he makes district attorney. But when he tries to free himself of his ties to the crooks, he finds himself harassed and forced to run as an independent in order to straighten out his career.

p, Lucien Hubbard; d, Edwin L. Marin; w, Frank Dolan (based on a story by Dolan); ph, Charles Clarke; m, Edward Ward; ed, William S. Gray.

Drama   **(PR:A   MPAA:NR)**

MAN OF THE WEST*****   (1958) 100m UA c

Gary Cooper (*Link Jones*), Julie London (*Billie Ellis*), Lee J. Cobb (*Dock Tobin*), Arthur O'Connell (*Sam Beasley*), Jack Lord (*Coaley*), John Dehner (*Claude*), Royal Dano (*Trout*), Robert Wilke (*Ponch*), Jack Williams (*Alcutt*), Guy Wilkerson (*Conductor*), Chuck Roberson (*Rifleman*), Frank Ferguson (*Marshal*), Emory Parnell (*Gribble*), Tina Menard (*Mexican Woman*), Joe Dominguez (*Mexican Man*).

This is the last western directed by Anthony Mann and it is his most powerful and disturbing foray into the genre. Working this time with Cooper instead of Jimmy Stewart, Mann once again tells a tale of Shakespearian proportions where the heroes are complicated men struggling against their own worst instincts. The film opens as Cooper, a seemingly pleasant and somewhat guileless bumpkin, leaves his wife and two children and boards a train. He has been entrusted by the people of his small Texas town to travel to Ft. Worth and hire a new schoolteacher with the large sum of money he has been given. On the train he meets O'Connell, a nervous con man who enlists beautiful saloon singer London in a scheme to fleece Cooper, though she is rather hesitant. Telling Cooper that London is a schoolteacher, O'Connell almost succeeds in his con, but the train is halted by bandits before the transaction takes place. The robbers turn out to be the notorious Tobin gang, a psychotic band of thieves prone to extreme violence. After the robbery, Cooper, London, and O'Connell are stranded when the train leaves without them. Luckily, Cooper grew up in the area and takes his companions to a nearby cabin. There they find the Tobin gang, led by the grizzled and cruel Cobb. Surprisingly, it is revealed that Cobb is Cooper's uncle and that this unassuming man from a small Texas town used to be a member of the brutal gang. Cooper's unplanned homecoming is somewhat strained. Although Cobb is very glad to see his favorite nephew, Cooper's sadistic cousins, Lord, Dano (who is a mute), and Wilke resent and distrust him. Thinking that Cooper has returned to rejoin the gang, Cobb happily relates a few bone-chilling reminiscences about the old days when he and his nephew would kill and rob. Lord, meanwhile, has become very excited by the presence of London, and he forces her to strip naked while holding a knife to Cooper's throat. The tension builds as London disrobes. Though it is obvious she has probably worked as a prostitute in the past, Cooper cannot stand to see this woman degraded in this way. Before she removes her undergarments, Cobb stops the depraved Lord by yelling at him for ruining the train robbery. To ensure that no further sexual molestations occur, Cooper tells Cobb that London is his woman. Cobb promises to enforce Cooper's request, but then takes the money intended to pay for the schoolteacher. He then allows his ''guests'' to stay in the barn. London begins to fall in love with Cooper, and in a scene charged with sexuality, a tempted Cooper begins telling the singer of his wife and family in a herculean effort to suppress his desire for her. Soon after, Cooper's cousin Dehner, the smartest of the gang, rides up to the cabin. Dehner replaced Cooper as second-in-command of the gang and the two men have a grudging respect for one another, perhaps because they recognize that they are two sides of the same coin. Cobb declares that there is a bank to rob in Lassoo, a town which represents the glory days of the gang, and the robbers pack up and ride off, accompanied by their guests. At their first encampment, Cooper has it out with Lord and there is a brutal fight. Cooper wins the battle and then strips Lord of his clothes in front of London. The crazed Lord grabs his pistol and tries to shoot Cooper, but O'Connell takes the bullet instead. Disgusted by his son's cowardly act, Cobb shoots Lord dead. Depressed over the incident, Cobb agrees to let Cooper ride into Lassoo to scout the bank. Accompanied by the mute Dano, Cooper discovers that Lassoo is now a ghost town. The only thing in the bank is a lone Mexican woman. In an inexplicable fit of rage, Dano shoots the woman. Shocked, Cooper kills Dano. Worried when Cooper and Dano haven't returned, Cobb sends Dehner and Wilke to Lassoo to search for them. When they arrive, Cooper manages to kill Wilke easily, but he and Dehner have a long and brutal gun battle. Eventually, Cooper kills Dehner, but he does so regretfully, because it is like shooting a mirror image of himself. Before he leaves, Cooper sadly folds Dehner's arms to cover his chest as a sign of respect. Cooper rides back to the camp to fetch London and settle things with Cobb. Upon his return he discovers that Cobb has raped London and run off into the mountains. Cobb stands atop the rocks and watches as his favorite nephew comes to serve justice. Cooper tells Cobb that he has killed all his sons. His madness now completely out of control, Cobb taunts Cooper ("Kill me . . . you've lost your taste for it.") and fires wildly in the air, forcing his nephew to shoot him. Cobb tumbles down the rocks and falls dead in a crumpled heap. Cooper takes his money from Cobb's corpse and, accompanied by London, rides out of the wilderness. As in Mann's other westerns with Stewart, there is an air of epic tragedy to MAN OF THE WEST. Cooper, a man whose past is as vicious and sordid as the other members of the Tobin gang, somehow managed to reject that life and start anew as a respectable man of the community. He wandered out of the savage wilderness and was able to adapt to the new civilization by repressing his brutal instincts. His accidental reentry into the gang causes his base instincts to once again boil to the surface. After years of conformity, Cooper is again able to be cold, hard, brutal, and lethal. He also understands that Cobb and the gang's time is up. The Old West they once knew is now a ghost town. These savages no longer have a place. Dehner and Cobb understand this. Cobb, in his raving madness, realizes that his time is up and that Cooper, who represents the new world, must kill him. He forces Cooper to shoot by violating what he believed to be his nephew's woman. Offering only token resistance, the true "Man of the West" dies in a crumpled heap after falling from a great height. Mann ended his stunning series of westerns most appropriately. His western heroes and villains do not wear white and black hats to tell good from evil. They are real people who suffer from anxiety, guilt, hatred, and self-doubt. Some succumb to these savage impulses and are destroyed after having outlived their epoch. The others (Stewart's characters, Cooper), all who have sinned, manage to overcome their dark sides and attain some sort of grace. MAN OF THE WEST was Mann's last western, and his importance to the genre cannot be overstated. While others would come to test the same waters and make significant contributions to the western (most notably Sam Peckinpah, Sergio Leone, and Clint Eastwood), Mann was one of the last consistently superior directors to leave his unique stamp on the genre.

p, Walter M. Mirisch; d, Anthony Mann; w, Reginald Rose (based on the novel *The Border Jumpers* by Will C. Brown); ph, Ernest Haller (CinemaScope, DeLuxe Color); m, Leigh Harline; ed, Richard Heermance; art d, Hillyard Brown; set d, Ed Boyle; cos, Yvonne Wood; m/l, title song, Bobby Troup.

Western **(PR:C-O MPAA:NR)**

MAN OF THE WORLD** (1931) 71m PAR bw

William Powell *(Michael Trevor)*, Carole Lombard *(Mary Kendall)*, Wynne Gibson *(Irene Hoffa)*, Guy Kibbee *(Harold Taylor)*, Lawrence Gray *(Frank Thompson)*, Andre Cheron *(Victor)*, George Chandler *(Fred)*, Thomas Costello *(Spade Henderson)*, Maud Truax *(Mrs. Jowitt)*, Tom Ricketts *(Mr. Bradkin)*.

Powell is an outcast American journalist living in Paris, who runs a scandal sheet and blackmails visiting wealthy Americans. Together with his girl friend, Gibson, they milk thousands of dollars out of unsuspecting Americans as a means for Powell to get back at the society that rejected him. He hits upon the idea of bilking debutante Lombard out of her money, but when he falls in love with her, Powell decides not to go through with it. He attempts to break off with Gibson, but she threatens to inform on him to the police if he does, and convinces him that he'll never be free of his past. Instead, Powell agrees to her plan to extort Lombard's uncle, Kibbee, out of $10,000. Lombard, believing Powell to be a crook, flees to the states with her fiance. Powell and Gibson sail for South Africa, and on ship Powell tears up Kibbee's check.

d, Richard Wallace, Edward Goodman; w, Herman J. Mankiewicz (based on a story by Mankiewicz); ph, Victor Milner.

Drama **(PR:A MPAA:NR)**

MAN OF TWO WORLDS* (1934) 92m RKO bw

Francis Lederer *(Aigo)*, Elissa Landi *(Joan Pemberton)*, Henry Stephenson *(Sir Basil Pemberton)*, J. Farrell MacDonald *(Michael)*, Walter Byron *(Eric Pager)*, Forrester Harvey *(Tim)*, Ivan Simpson *(Dr. Lott)*, Lumsden Hare *(Capt. Swan)*, Christian Rub *(Knudson)*, Emil Chautard *(Natkusiak)*, Steffi Duna *(Guinana)*, Sarah Padden *(Olago)*, Gertrude Wise.

Czech actor Lederer makes his U.S. screen debut as an Eskimo who is brought to England by Stephenson. He is exposed to culture and the lovely Landi whom he mistakenly believes is in love with him. He ends up back with his iglooed tribe, however, by the film's end, returning to his primitive ways and his role as his tribe's premier hunter. Captain Frank E. Kleinschmidt served as technical advisor.

p, Pandro S. Berman; d, J. Walter Ruben; w, Howard J. Green, Ainsworth Morgan (based on the novel by Morgan); ph, Henry W. Gerrard; ed, Jack Hively; md, Max Steiner.

Drama **(PR:A MPAA:NR)**

MAN OF VIOLENCE zero
(1970, Brit.) 107m Miracle c (AKA: THE SEX RACKETEERS)

Michael Latimer *(Moon)*, Luan Peters *(Angel)*, Derek Aylward *(Nixon)*, Maurice Kaufmann *(Charles Grayson)*, Derek Francis *(Sam Bryant)*, Kenneth Hendel *(Hunt)*, George Belbin *(Burgess)*, Sidney Conabere *(Alec Powell)*, Virginia Wetherell *(Gale)*, Steve Emerson *(Steve)*, Erika Raffael *(Goose)*, Peter Thornton *(Mike)*, Andreas Malandrinos *(Pergolesi)*, Michael Balfour *(Cafe Owner)*, Patrick Jordan *(Mentobar Captain)*, Jessica Spencer *(Joyce)*, Sheila Babbage *(Caroline)*, John Keston *(Girling)*, Mark Allington *(Choiken)*.

An unduly complicated crime picture which centers on a group of Londoners who try to get $90,000,000 in gold bullion from a revolution-torn Arab country. Mixed in with this is an excessive amount of violence and sex.

p&d, Peter Walker; w, Bruce Comport, Walker; ph, Norman Langley (Eastmancolor); m, Cyril Ornadel; ed, Peter Austen-Hunt.

Crime **(PR:O MPAA:NR)**

MAN ON A STRING**
(1960) 92m COL bw (GB: CONFESSIONS OF A COUNTERSPY)

Ernest Borgnine *(Boris Mitrov)*, Kerwin Mathews *(Bob Avery)*, Colleen Dewhurst *(Helen Benson)*, Alexander Scourby *(Vadja Kubelov)*, Glenn Corbett *(Frank Sanford)*, Vladimir Sokoloff *(Papa)*, Friedrich Joloff *(Nikolai Chapayev)*, Richard Kendrick *(Inspector Jenkins)*, Ed Prentiss *(Adrian Benson)*, Holger Hagen *(Hans Gruenwald)*, Robert Iller *(Hartmann)*, Reginald Pasch *(Otto Bergman)*, Carl Jaffe *(People's Judge)*, Eva Pflug *(Rosnova)*, Michael Mellinger *(Detective)*, Clete Roberts *(Narrator)*.

Borgnine is a Moscow-born U.S. citizen who makes a living by aiding Soviet spy rings. When he is pressured by the U.S. intelligence, Borgnine begins to spy for the U.S. government. Loosely based on the life of Soviet agent Boris Morros, the picture benefits from its fine documentary-style location photography.

p, Louis de Rochemont; d, Andre de Toth; w, John Kafka, Virginia Shaler (based on the book *Ten Years a Counterspy* by Boris Morros, Charles Samuels); ph, Charles Lawton, Jr., Albert Benitz, Gayne Rescher, Pierre Poincarde; m, George Duning; ed, Al Clark; art d, Carl Anderson; set d, James M. Crowe.

Spy Drama **(PR:A MPAA:NR)**

MAN ON A SWING*** (1974) 108m Jaffilms/PAR c

Cliff Robertson *(Police Chief Lee Tucker)*, Joel Grey *(Franklin Wills)*, Dorothy Tristan *(Janet Tucker)*, Peter Masterson *(Willie Younger)*, Elizabeth Wilson *(Dr. Anna Wilson)*, George Voskovec *(Dr. Nicholas Holmar)*, Ron Weyand *(Dr. Philip Fusco)*, Lane Smith *(Ted Ronan)*, Joe Ponazecki *(Dan Lloyd)*, Christopher Allport *(Richie Tom Keating)*, Patricia Hawkins *(Diana Spenser)*, Richard Venture *(Man in Motel)*, Dianne Hull *(Maggie Dawson)*, Gil Gerard *(Donald Forbes)*, Richard Dryden *(Mr. Dawson)*, Alice Drummond *(Mrs. Dawson)*, Richard McKenzie *(Sam Gallagher)*, Brendan Fay *(Father Connally)*, Clarice Blackburn *(Mrs. Brennan)*, Nicholas Pryor *(Paul Kearney)*, Josef Sommer *(Peter Russell)*, Shawn Campbell *(Steve Barron)*, Clarence Felder *(Coach)*, Benjamin Slack *(Ronnie)*, Penelope Milford *(Evelyn Moore)*, Bruce French *(Check-out Man)*, Loretta Fury *(Mrs. Segretta)*, Roy Mason *(Plant Manager)*, James Galvin *(Man in Plant)*.

A puzzling crime thriller starring Grey as a clairvoyant who helps Robertson solve a case involving a demented sex murderer. Robertson, however, thinks Grey is the guilty one. Robertson is less than impressive, leaving the picture's top performance to Grey, who is superb. The film starts out as a top-notch murder mystery but deteriorates as it gets more involved. The score by Lalo Schifrin tries to hold it all together.

p, Howard P. Jaffe; d, Frank Perry; w, David Zelag Goodman; ph, Adam Holender (Technicolor); m, Lalo Schifrin; ed, Sidney Katz; prod d, Joel Schiller; set d, Hubert Oates; cos, Ruth Morley.

Crime **(PR:C MPAA:PG)**

MAN ON A TIGHTROPE, 1949 (SEE: MAN ON A TIGHTROPE, 1953)

MAN ON A TIGHTROPE**** (1953) 105m FOX bw

Fredric March *(Karel Cernik)*, Terry Moore *(Tereza Cernik)*, Gloria Grahame *(Zama Cernik)*, Cameron Mitchell *(Joe Vosdek)*, Adolphe Menjou *(Fesker)*, Robert Beatty *(Barovic)*, Alex D'Arcy *(Rudolph)*, Richard Boone *(Krofta)*, Pat Henning *(Konradin)*, Paul Hartman *(Jaromir)*, John Dehner *(The Chief)*, Mme. Brumbach *(Mme. Cernik)*, Hansi *(Kalka)*, Birnbach Circus *(Cirkus Cernik)*, Dorothea Wieck *(Duchess)*, Philip Kenneally *(Sergeant)*, Edelweiss Malchin *(Vina Konradin)*, William Castello *(Captain)*, Margaret Slezak *(Mrs. Jaromir)*, Peter Beauvais *(S.N.B. Captain)*, Robert Charlebois *(S.C.B. Lieutenant)*, Gert Frobe, Rolf Naukhoff *(Police Agents)*.

March, in another powerful role, is the manager of a little Czech circus that is trying to get across the border through the Iron Curtain to freedom. March's family has owned the circus for generations and, when the Communists take over Czechoslovakia, his young performers are drafted into the service and his equipment sadly goes to seed without proper repair and parts replacement which the new regime denies him. Moreover, he is told he no longer owns the circus, but operates it for the benefit of the state. His troupers are instructed to perform their routines so that the

Communist credo is emphasized, which rankles the fiercely independent March. He nevertheless plays a waiting game, waiting until his circus nears the Bavarian border. Meanwhile, he tries to keep his willful daughter Moore from becoming entangled with a worthless, shiftless, lion tamer, Mitchell. Grahame, his young wife, believes March is a coward, especially after she sees him cowering under instructions from Communist cop Menjou. March learns that there is a spy in the circus and suspects Mitchell, but he later learns that it's the brawny Boone, the man in charge of the equipment. At the border, March parades his circus in full regalia, distracting guards, then unleashes dogs the guards believe to be wolves and stampedes his elephants while the performers race pell mell across a bridge in their wagons and into free Germany. March is shot to death by Boone who, in turn, is killed by a circus dwarf. With March dead, Grahame, now proud of her dead husband, vows to carry on in his shoes. Kazan's direction is flawless and the story, written with great style and sharp dialog by Sherwood, is superb. Shot on location in Bavaria, Germany, authentic acts were used and the entire Birnbach Circus was employed for this excellent production.

p, Robert L. Jacks; d, Elia Kazan; w, Robert Sherwood (based on the story "International Incident" by Neil Paterson); ph, Georg Kraus; m, Franz Waxman; ed, Dorothy Spencer; md, Earle Hagen; art d, Hans E. Kerhnert, Theodore Zwirsky; cos, Ursula Maes; makeup, Arthur Schramm, Fritz Seyfried.

Drama **(PR:A MPAA:NR)**

MAN ON AMERICA'S CONSCIENCE, THE

(SEE: TENNESSEE JOHNSON, 1942)

MAN ON FIRE*** (1957) 95m MGM bw

Bing Crosby *(Earl Carleton)*, Inger Stevens *(Nina Wylie)*, Mary Pickett *(Gwen Seward)*, E.G. Marshall *(Sam Dunstock)*, Malcolm Brodrick *(Ted Carleton)*, Richard Eastham *(Bryan Seward)*, Anne Seymour *(Judge Randolph)*, Dan Riss *(Mack)*.

In one of his finer dramatic roles, Crosby plays a divorced father who fights his wife and the courts in an effort to retain custody of his son. After a split which is far from amiable, Crosby refuses to allow his ex-wife to see their son. She takes him to court and the judge sides with her, granting her and her new husband custody. Crosby then unsuccessfully tries to get his son back by force, but finally his angers are quelled by his friend and lawyer Stevens.

p, Sol C. Siegel; d&w, Ranald MacDougall (based on a story by Malvin Wald, Jack Jacobs); ph, Joseph Ruttenberg; m, David Raksin; ed, Ralph E. Winters; art d, William A. Horning, Hans Peters; m/l, "Man on Fire," Sammy Fain, Paul Francis Webster (sung by the Ames Brothers).

Drama **(PR:A MPAA:NR)**

MAN ON THE EIFFEL TOWER, THE**** (1949) 97m RKO c

Charles Laughton *(Inspector Maigret)*, Franchot Tone *(Radek)*, Burgess Meredith *(Huertin)*, Robert Hutton *(Bill Kirby)*, Jean Wallace *(Edna Wallace)*, Patricia Roc *(Helen Kirby)*, Belita *(Gisella)*, George Thorpe *(Comelieu)*, William Phipps *(Janvier)*, William Cottrell *(Moers)*, Chaz Chase *(Waiter)*, Wilfrid Hyde-White *(Prof. Grollet)*.

Simenon's seminal sleuth, Maigret, was never better enacted than by the shrewd, slow and sure Laughton who is after a thrill killer-for-hire, Tone, in a superb *film noir* production. The nephew of a rich woman hires Tone to kill his aunt and Laughton investigates. At first Laughton suspects Meredith (who also directed the film), a blind knife-grinder, but he dismisses this obvious choice. He unearths Tone, a psychopathic murderer who enjoys killing, the act feeding a warped ego in that he can get away with killing and bait the police at the same time. Laughton learns that Hutton has hired Tone to kill his wife Roc allowing him to go off with alluring, sensual Wallace. Through learning the plot, Laughton also identifies the real murderer, Tone, and the two play a cat-and-mouse game until Tone cracks under the psychological strain and makes a break for it. During his escape he is trapped and must retreat up the Eiffel Tower, Laughton and his police squads climbing up, up, up after Tone who is finally killed when realizing there is no way out. The acting is outstanding in this film, Tone actually overcoming Laughton's masterful mannerisms in their scenes together, while Meredith adroitly performs his red-herring role. The lensing by Cortez in rich Ansco color, lovingly shows a majestic Paris while sharply capturing the thrilling story and, especially at the end, the superb chase on the Eiffel Tower. Michelet's score is also exceptional. Meredith directs with a sure and measured hand.

p, Irving Allen; d, Burgess Meredith; w, Harry Brown (based on the story "A Battle of Nerves" by Georges Simenon); ph, Stanley Cortez (Ansco Color); m, Michel Michelet; ed, Louis H. Sacken; md, C. Bakaleinikoff; art d, Rene Renoux.

Crime Drama **Cas.** **(PR:A MPAA:NR)**

MAN ON THE FLYING TRAPEZE, THE****

(1935) 65m PAR bw (GB: THE MEMORY EXPERT)

W.C. Fields *(Ambrose Wolfinger)*, Mary Brian *(Hope Wolfinger)*, Kathleen Howard *(Leona Wolfinger)*, Grady Sutton *(Claude Neselrode)*, Vera Lewis *(Mrs. Cordelia Neselrode)*, Lucien Littlefield *(Mr. Peabody)*, Oscar Apfel *(President Malloy)*, Lew Kelly *(Adolph Berg)*, Tammany Young *("Willie" the Weasel)*, Walter Brennan *("Legs" Garnett)*, Arthur Aylesworth *(Night Court Judge)*, Harry Ekezian *(Hookallockah Mishabbob)*, Tor Johnson *(Tosoff)*, David Clyde *(J. Farnsworth Wallaby)*, Ed Gargan *(1st Patrolman)*, Eddie Chandler *(2nd Patrolman)*, James Burke *(3rd Patrolman)*, James Flavin *(Henry the Chauffeur)*, Sarah Edwards *(Car Owner)*, Carlotta Monti *(Ambrose's Secretary)*, Sam Lufkin *(Ticket Taker)*, Helen Dickson *(Miss Dickson)*, Lorin Raker *(Ring Announcer)*, Heinie Conklin *(Street Cleaner)*, Michael S. Visaroff *(Homicidal Maniac)*, Harry C. Bradley *(Peeved Driver)*, Rosemary Theby *(Helpful Pedestrian)*, Jack Baxley *(Night Court Officer)*, George French *(Clerk)*, Billy Bletcher *(Timekeeper)*, Robert Littlefield *(Neighbor with Correct Time)*, Minerva Urecal *(Italian Woman in Ambulance)*, Mickey Bennett *(Office Employee)*, Dorothy Thompson *(Information Girl)*, Albert Taylor *(Clerk)*, Mickey McMasters *(Referee)*, Charles Morris *(Turnkey)*, Eddie Sturgis *(Bystander at Arena Gate)*, Pat O'Malley *(Officer)*, Keith Daniels *(Ticket Seller)*, Joseph Sawyer *(Ambulance Driver)*.

Another Fields gem reprises his prisoner of middleclass life routine so expertly and hilariously profiled in IT'S A GIFT. Here Fields is seen brushing his teeth four times late at night, gargling from a flask in the bathroom, until his wife Howard complains about the noise. He trundles to bed and snores off in the batting of a gnat's eyelash. He is awakened by Howard who has heard noises coming from the vent. "There are burglars singing in the cellar!" Howard tells him. "What are they singing?" replies Fields groggily. After he complains about the quality of the singing, Howard insists that Fields go downstairs to investigate, taking his gun. He passes his wife and tells her not to be afraid, that the gun isn't even loaded. "No," she snaps, "but you are." But the gun goes off by accident and Howard faints. Fields looks down on her remorsefully, sees her coming around, and says without much enthusiasm: "Oh good, I didn't kill you." The shot brings Howard's mother, Lewis, and son, Sutton, on the run. Then Fields' daughter Brian comes in and chastises her stepbrother Sutton for refusing to go downstairs to face the burglars with her father. Fields goes alone, tripping at the head of the basement stairs and sailing downward, landing on his backside. The two burglars, Brennan and Young, are tipsy, having broken into Fields' barrel of applejack. After he introduces himself, they genially offer him a drink. Soon they are all drinking together and singing "On the Banks of the Wabash." A cop shows up, but instead of arresting Young and Brennan, he takes a noggin and joins the group to make a singing quartet. Fields asks the cop to let the burglars go but he explains that he must perform his duty so the four go down to the courthouse where the intruders are released but Fields is charged with manufacturing spirits without a license and thrown into jail. Fields appeals to his wife but Howard, Sutton, and Lewis refuse to bail him out, laughing hysterically at his plight. Brian saves her father by bailing him out with the last of her savings. Fields assumes that Brian was sent by Howard and the daughter does not correct his error. The next morning at breakfast, Howard refuses to kiss him and Sutton smugly calls him a "jailbird." Most of the food goes to the pompous Sutton, with Howard spearing the last piece of sausage. Fields is left to eat cold toast and he says pathetically: "I've been eating cold toast for eight years now . . . I kinda like it." It's obvious from the sour look on his face as he crunches into it that he hates it. Then Howard becomes elated to find one of her avant-garde poems is in the morning paper. She begins reading it word for meaningless word, while Fields suffers through every posturing phrase, responding only with loud bites of his brick-hard toast. Howard ends her recitation with "and the beautiful part of it is there's no punctuation!" Then Sutton exclaims that he has just "found" a $15 front-row ticket to a wrestling match; it's Fields' ticket and he has been looking forward to the match for months but cannot admit that he spent such a large amount of money on such an extravagance and grins and bears Sutton's obvious theft of his prized possession. Fields is late for work and is greeted affably by his secretary, Monti (who was Fields' real life secretary and mistress and wound up writing a book about the master comedian, *W.C. and Me)*. His boss Apfel, is annoyed at his being late but tolerates such conduct because Fields has a photographic memory which is needed by his firm. Apfel has an important client arriving and asks Fields about him. Memory expert Fields gives him a detailed background. Fields later asks for a day off and suggests that his mother-in-law, Lewis, has just passed away. "It must be very hard to lose your mother-in-law," commiserates Apfel. "Yes," Fields responds, "it is very hard . . . Almost impossible." Fields takes off for the wrestling match but not before getting four tickets in the same parking place and trying to fix a flat on a steep hill which results in his spare rolling down the hill away from him, Fields in hot pursuit, dodging cars. Funeral flowers arrive at Fields' home and Howard thinks they are for her husband who has been killed. Then office employee Littlefield, who hates Fields, calls and asks how Lewis has died. Howard tells him that her mother is very much alive. Fields arrives at the wrestling arena to find the place sold out; in fact, he is the last customer to arrive and the ticket window is slammed in his face just as be begins to pay for a ticket. He views the fierce match through a knothole, watching one wrestler toss the other out of the ring and the arena. Fields rushes to the door, smashed open by the wrestler's flying body which strikes Fields and sends him flat to the gutter. The crowd pours out of the arena, including secretary Monti who helps her boss to his feet. Sutton also emerges and believes Fields is drunk and having an affair with Monti; he rushes home to gleefully break the news. When Fields arrives home he is met by Howard, Lewis, and Sutton, who lambast him for lying about Lewis' premature death, losing his job over the lie, and having an affair while drunk. He denies the latter charge but admits he was wrong about reporting Lewis dead (although it's clear he relished doing it). Then, when Brian defends her father and Sutton threatens to hit her, Fields finally explodes and knocks Sutton cold, leaving with his daughter. They get an apartment. Apfel, meanwhile, is looking for his memory expert but Littlefield tells him he fired Fields for lying about Lewis. Apfel demands that he get him back; another important client is coming to town and he needs information about him. Littlefield calls Fields who is at that moment searching through want ads for jobs with his daughter. Brian answers and hears that Fields' old job is again available. She thinks fast and tells Littlefield that her father has just been offered a great position with "Moe Litvak at the Irish Linen Mills," making twice his old salary. Littlefield consults quickly with Apfel who tells him to double Fields' salary. This is done, but Brian also insists that her father's vacation begin that day and at full salary. Littlefield, utterly squelched, agrees. Now Fields is in the driver's seat, literally; Howard returns to him but living under his terms and lifestyle. He takes the family out for a drive in his new luxury roadster, Fields at the wheel and his daughter and wife beside him. In the rumble seat are the obnoxious Sutton and Lewis. A sudden rainstorm breaks loose and Fields puts up the top, handing a thermos of hot coffee around to wife and child. In the rumble seat, Sutton and Lewis get the drenching of their rotten lives, the much desired comeuppance. THE MAN

ON THE FLYING TRAPEZE had nothing to do with circuses except the circus of life as Fields so humorously saw it. Howard was his favorite on-screen wife and he was glad to tell reporters what an accomplished actress she was. Howard, who had been a singer with the Metropolitan Opera before becoming a fashion writer, was asked to take a part in the movie DEATH TAKES A HOLIDAY while visiting the set. She did, and stayed on in Hollywood to become a regular character actress. Brian got the part in this movie in an offhanded way. She was Fields' neighbor, living nearby at Toluca Lake. One day, she recalled, Fields called to her across the lake, shouting: "I've got a script and you've got to be my daughter!" Here Fields wrote a story that mirrors his life and, in particular, his career at Paramount where he had been fired, then hired back at a fabulous salary after IT'S A GIFT and other films skyrocketed the comedian to his much deserved fame. Fields never cued his fellow actors, which caused his directors no end of confusion. He liked a loose set and told favorites like Sutton to "butt in" whenever they thought he had said enough. The film's title has no bearing to the story; it was simply a title Fields liked and kept trying to use until Paramount allowed it for this film, rather than let him use EVERYTHING HAPPENS AT ONCE or LO, THE POOR INDIAN. Fields was reported seriously ill after the completion of THE MAN ON THE FLYING TRAPEZE and some said he was deathly ill of the grippe or pneumonia. It was booze, of course, and he dried out in a sanitarium, then prepared for another film.

p, William LeBaron; d, Clyde Bruckman; w, Ray Harris, Sam Hardy, Jack Cunningham, Bobby Vernon (based on a story by Hardy, Charles Bogle [W.C. Fields]); ph, Al Gilks; ed, Richard Currier.

Comedy   **(PR:A MPAA:NR)**

MAN ON THE PROWL*   (1957) 86m Jana/UA bw

Mala Powers (*Marlan Wood*), James Best (*Doug Gerhardt*), Ted De Corsia (*Detective*), Jerry Paris (*Woody*), Vivi Jannis (*Mrs. Gerhardt*), Josh Freeman (*Josh Wood*), Jeff Freeman (*Jeff Wood*), Peggy Maley (*Alma Doran*), Eugenia Paul (*Dorothy Pierce*), Bob Yeakel (*Himself*).

A failed attempt to draw a psychological sketch of a maniacal killer. Best prowls around Powers, a married mother of two who owns a garage catering to sports cars. Best sets his twisted mind on her and won't give up until he gets her. The last girl he wanted who resisted him was violently killed. He tries to kill Powers' husband and eventually takes her children as hostages. His plan is to trick Powers into coming to him, but instead the cops come along and the mad killer is shot to death.

p, Jo Napoleon, Art Napoleon; d, Art Napoleon; w, Jo Napoleon, Art Napoleon; ph, Nick Musuraca; m, Ernest Gold; ed, Paul Weatherwax; art d, Howard Richmond.

Crime Drama   **(PR:A MPAA:NR)**

MAN ON THE RUN*½   (1949, Brit.) 82m ABF-Pathe bw

Derek Farr (*Peter Burdon*), Joan Hopkins (*Jean Adams*), Edward Chapman (*Inspector Mitchell*), Laurence Harvey (*Detective Sgt. Lawson*), Howard Marion Crawford (*First Paratrooper*), Alfie Bass (*Bargee's Mate*), John Bailey (*Dan Underwood*), John Stuart (*Inspector McBain*), Edward Underdown (*Slim*), Leslie Perrins (*Charlie*), Kenneth More (*Cpl. Newman*), Martin Miller (*Proprietor*), Eleanor Summerfield (*May Baker*), Anthony Nicholls (*Inspector*), Cameron Hall, Valentine Dyall, Howard Douglas, Laurence Ray, Bruce Belfrage, Robert Adair, Charles Paton, Basil Cunard, Jack McNaughton, Margaret Goodman, Virginia Winter, Lalage Lewis, Patrick Barr, Gerald Case, John Boxer, Roy Russell, R. Stuart Lindsell.

Farr is an Army deserter who tries to sell his revolver, but while in the store a robbery occurs. Naturally Farr is the one who is arrested. Hopkins comes along, however, and helps him prove his innocence.

p,d,&w, Lawrence Huntington; ph, Wilkie Cooper, Arthur Graham; m, Philip Green; ed, Monica Kimick.

Crime   **(PR:A MPAA:NR)**

MAN ON THE RUN, 1964   (SEE: KIDNAPPERS, THE, 1964, US/Phil.)

MAN OR GUN*½   (1958) 79m REP bw

MacDonald Carey (*Maybe Smith*), Audrey Totter (*Fran Dare*), James Craig (*Pinch Corley*), James Gleason (*Sheriff Jackson*), Warren Stevens (*Mike Ferris*), Harry Shannon (*Justine Corley*), Jil Jarmyn (*Mrs. Pinch Corley*), Robert Burton (*Burt Burton*), Ken Lynch (*Buckstorm*), Karl Davis (*Swede*), Julian Burton (*Billy Corley*), Carl York (*Jack Corley*), Harry Klekas (*Dodd*), Mel Gaines (*Diego*), Ron McNeil (*Nick*), Larry Grant (*Rough*).

An uninteresting treatment of the classic western story line about the drifter who rides into a town that is held under the tyrannical grip of a power-hungry family and liberates the well-meaning, but cowardly townsfolk. Carey plays the part of the man whose gun does all the talking.

p, Vance Skarstedt; d, Albert C. Gannaway; w, Skarstedt, James C. Cassity; ph, Jack Marta (Naturama); m, Gene Garf, Ramez Idriss; ed, Merrill White; art d, Ralph Oberg; cos, Alexis Davidoff.

Western   **(PR:A MPAA:NR)**

MAN OUTSIDE, THE*½   (1933, Brit.) 50m REA/RKO bw

Henry Kendall (*Harry Wainwright*), Gillian Lind (*Ann*), Joan Gardner (*Peggy Fordyce*), Michael Hogan (*Shiner Talbot*), Cyril Raymond (*Capt. Fordyce*), John Turnbull (*Inspector Jukes*), Louis Hayward (*Frank Elford*), Ethel Warwick (*Georgina Yapp*).

Kendall is a blundering private detective trying to uncover stolen jewels. Instead of finding an ordinary crook, he discovers that the police inspector is the guilty one.

p, Julius Hagen; d, George A. Cooper; w, H. Fowler Mear (based on the story by Donald Stuart).

Crime   **(PR:A MPAA:NR)**

MAN OUTSIDE, THE**   (1968, Brit.) 97m Trio-Group W/AA c

Van Heflin (*Bill Maclean*), Heidelinde Weis (*Kay Sebastian*), Pinkas Braun (*Rafe Machek*), Peter Vaughan (*Nikolai Volkov*), Charles Gray (*Charles Griddon*), Paul Maxwell (*Judson Murphy*), Ronnie Barker (*George Venaxas*), Linda Marlowe (*Dorothy*), Gary Cockrell (*Brune Parry*), Bill Nagy (*Morehouse*), Larry Cross (*Austen*), Rita Webb (*Landlady*), Christopher Denham (*Detective Sergeant*), Willoughby Gray (*Detective Inspector*), Archie Duncan (*Detective Superintendent Barnes*), Carole Ann Ford (*Cindy*), Carmel McSharry (*Olga*), John Sterland (*Spencer*), Alex Marchevsky (*Mikhail*), Paul Armstrong (*Gerod*), Hugh Elton (*Vadim*), Derek Baker (*Gerod's Assistant*), Frank Crawshaw (*Drunken Hick*), Roy Stone (*Albert*), Harry Hutchinson (*Caretaker*), Gabrielle Drake (*B.E.A. Girl*), Carol Kingsley (*Barmaid*), Martin Terry (*Gambling Club Barman*), Anna Willoughby (*Boutique Attendant*), Suzanne Owens (*Attendant*).

Heflin is an ex-CIA agent who was dismissed for helping a fellow agent defect to East Berlin. He inadvertently gets mixed up in another defection, this time of a top Soviet agent, Braun, to the U.S. He is then framed by the Russians for the murder of a nightclub hostess for his part in the defection. He learns that Braun is in hiding but won't come forward without a guarantee of safety. Braun comes out, but the Russians kidnap Heflin's friend, Weis, and threaten to torture her unless Braun is returned. After a barrage of gunplay, Heflin helps Braun and Weis escape without harm. It is then revealed that the American agent Heflin had supposedly helped defect to East Berlin was actually kidnaped by the Russians. Heflin is offered his CIA job back, but declines.

p, William Gell; d, Samuel Gallu; w, Gallu, Julian Bond, Roger Marshall (based on the novel *Double Agent* by Gene Stackleborg); ph, Gil Taylor (Techniscope, Technicolor); m, Richard Arnell; ed, Tom Noble; art d, Peter Mullins.

Spy Drama   **(PR:A MPAA:M)**

MAN-PROOF*½   (1938) 74m MGM bw

Myrna Loy (*Mimi Swift*), Franchot Tone (*Jimmy Kilmartin*), Rosalind Russell (*Elizabeth Kent*), Walter Pidgeon (*Alan Wythe*), Rita Johnson (*Florence*), Nana Bryant (*Meg Swift*), Ruth Hussey (*Jane*), Leonard Penn (*Bob*), John Miljan (*Tommy Gaunt*), William Stack (*Minister*), Oscar O'Shea (*Gus the Bartender*), Marie Blake (*Telephone Girl*), Dan Tuby (*Flight Announcer*), Aileen Pringle, Grace Hayle, Laura Treadwell (*Women*), Mary Howard, Frances Reid (*Girls*), Betty Blythe (*Country Club Woman*), Dorothy Vaughan (*Matron*), Claude King (*Man at Party*), Joyce Compton (*Guest*), Francis X. Bushman, Jr. (*Young Man at Fight*), Gwen Lee (*Girl at Fight*), Jack Norton (*Drunk at Fight*), May Beatty (*Landlady*), Irving Bacon (*Drug Clerk*). No actor can defeat a lousy script, and four fine talents are done in by a lackluster screenplay and some slow direction in this paltry attempt at comedy. Loy is in love with the dapper Pidgeon but he's more interested in money, so he marries wealthy Russell, a pal of Loy's, and she is more than shocked when she's invited to be a bridesmaid. Stunned, but still a class act, she goes to the wedding. But seeing her Pidgeon in the nest of Russell causes her to drink too much, and, in the comedy highlight of the film, she plays a drunk scene and lets Pidgeon know that she's unwilling to step out of his life and will be patiently waiting when he and Russell come back from their wedding trip. Loy is on the rebound, has a brief fling with Tone, a cynical newspaperman-artist, but she can't get Pidgeon out of her mind. When Russell and Pidgeon come back to New York, Loy seems to be resigned to the fact that they will be wed forever. They all go out for an evening at the fights at Madison Square Garden; Loy can't keep her eyes off Pidgeon and realizes she's still in love with him. She serves notice on Russell, and later, when Loy and Pidgeon are having a talk, Russell enters and is irked. She says that Pidgeon can have a divorce because she has since learned that he only married her for her wealth. It all works out when Russell takes Pidgeon back and Loy suddenly finds something interesting in Tone that she, and we, hadn't seen in the earlier sequences. Tired, dull, and with no real motivation other than to put four stars in the stew and see what they could cook up.

p, Louis D. Lighton; d, Richard Thorpe; w, George Oppenheimer, Vincent Lawrence, Waldemar Young (based on the novel *The Four Marys* by Fanny Heaslip Lea); ph, Karl Freund; m, Franz Waxman; ed, George Boemler; spec eff, John Hoffman.

Comedy/Drama   **(PR:A MPAA:NR)**

MAN STOLEN**½   (1934, Fr.) 90m FOX-Europa/FOX bw (FR: ON A VOLE UN HOMME)

Lili Damita (*Annette*), Charles Fallot (*Victor*), Pierre Labry (*Balafre*), Raoul Marco (*Inspector*), Henry Garat (*Jean de Lafaye*), Nina Myral (*Old Lady*), Robert Goupil (*Legros*), Pierre Pierade (*Remy*), Fernand Fabre (*Robert*).

Damita is the representative for a group of businessmen who are at odds with youthful banker Garat. After he is kidnaped by his enemies, the lovely Damita falls in love with Garat. The film is blessed by some wonderful shots of the French Riviera and an entertaining sequence on a train trip southbound from Paris. Interesting mainly as an early work by director Max Ophuls, as well as actress Damita.

p, Erich Pommer; d, Max Ophuls; w, Rene Pujol, Hans Wilhelm; ph, Rens Colas; m, Bronislaw Kaper, Walter Jurmann.

Drama   **(PR:A MPAA:NR)**

MAN THEY COULD NOT HANG, THE**½   (1939) 64m COL bw

Boris Karloff (*Dr. Henryk Savaard*), Lorna Gray (*Janet Saavard*), Robert Wilcox (*Scoop Foley*), Roger Pryor (*District Attorney Drake*), Don Beddoe (*Lt. Shane*), Ann Doran (*Betty Crawford*), Joseph de Stephani (*Dr. Stoddard*), Dick Curtis

(Kearney), Byron Foulger (Lang), James Craig (Watkins), John Tyrrell (Sutton), Charles Trowbridge (Judge Bowman).

Karloff plays a scientist who experiments with bringing the dead back to life through the use of an artificial heart. He performs his experiment on a willing young student but is stopped when his girl friend rushes in with the police. Karloff is consequently hung. His assistant, Foulger, revives Karloff via the heart device, but the scientist has changed. He no longer is the noble man he once was. He traps the judge, jury, and witnesses that convicted him in his house, and kills them off one by one. His daughter, Gray, begs him to have mercy and attempts to open the electronically shielded prison cells. Karloff fails to shut off the power in time and Gray is electrocuted. The police apprehend Karloff and he begs them to allow one final operation. He successfully revives his daughter, then destroys his scientific secret by destroying himself. This picture is the first of three similar films Karloff made under the direction of Nick Grinde, the others being THE MAN WITH NINE LIVES and BEFORE I HANG. The story seems far-fetched but was actually based on the real-life experiments of Dr. Robert Cornish who, during the 1930s, was reviving dead dogs. Cornish tried to further his theories by testing them on executed prisoners, but his request was denied.

p, Wallace MacDonald; d, Nick Grinde; w, Karl Brown (based on a story by Leslie T. White, George W. Sayre); ph, Benjamin Kline; ed, William Lyon; md, M. W. Stoloff; art d, Lionel Banks.

Horror   Cas.   (PR:C   MPAA:NR)

MAN THEY COULDN'T ARREST, THE*

(1933, Brit.) 72m Gainsborough/Gaumont bw

Hugh Wakefield (John Dain), Gordon Harker (Tansey), Renee Clama (Marcia), Nicholas Hannen (Lyall), Garry Marsh (Delbury), Robert Farquharson (Count Lazard), Dennis Wyndham (Shaughnessy).

An amateur private eye shows off an invention to Scotland Yard that allows him to tune in criminal conversations. He listens in on a scheme organized by the Black Pearl gang, only to discover his fiancee's father is a member. He overhears a murder and spends the majority of the film trying to find the culprit. An implausible plot made worse by lame performances hampered by the dubbing of the voices with American actors.

p, Michael Balcon; d, T. Hayes Hunter; w, Hunter, Arthur Wimperis, Angus Macphail (based on the novel by "Seamark" [Albert J. Small]); ph, Leslie Rowson; ed, Ian Dalrymple.

Crime   (PR:A   MPAA:NR)

MAN TO MAN½**

(1931) 68m WB bw

Grant Mitchell (Barber John Bolton), Lucille Powers (Emily), Phillips Holmes (Michael Bolton), George Marion, Sr. (Jim McCord), Otis Harlan (Rip Henry), Russell Simpson (Uncle Cal Bolton), Dwight Frye (Vint Glade), Bill Banker (Tom), Robert Emmett O'Connor (Sheriff), Paul Nicholson (Ryan), Barbara Weeks (Alice), Charles Sellon (Judge), Johnny Larkins (Bildad), James Neill (B. B. Beecham), James Hall.

Holmes is a teenager who is shocked to learn that his barber father (Mitchell) is doing time for murder. When Mitchell is pardoned, a reunion is a long time coming, but finally occurs when Holmes, whose bank account is faltering, is bailed out by Mitchell. A well-paced picture directed with an adroit hand by Allan Dwan and featuring Dwight Frye (FRANKENSTEIN, DRACULA) in a bit part.

d, Allan Dwan; w, Joseph Jackson (based on the story "Barber John's Boy" by Ben Ames Williams); ph, Ira Morgan; ed, George Marks.

Drama   (PR:A   MPAA:NR)

MAN TO REMEMBER, A*

(1938) 79m RKO bw

Anne Shirley (Jean), Edward Ellis (Dr. John Abbott), Lee Bowman (Dick Abbott), William Henry (Howard Sykes), Granville Bates (George Sykes), Harlan Briggs (Homer Ramsey), Frank M. Thomas (Jode Harkness), Charles Halton (Perkins), John Wray (Johnson), Gilbert Emery (Dr. Robinson), Dickie Jones (Dick as a Child), Carole Leete (Jean as a Child), Joseph de Stephani (Jorgensen).

Ellis is cast as a country doctor who is a kind-hearted, giving, community man. The film is structured in a series of flashbacks which episodically relate the doctor's career. For example, kindness is bestowed on a poor man who cannot afford his $100 medical bill when Ellis reduces it to only $2. He is also instrumental in getting a banker to provide funds for a local hospital. Without any box-office names, A MAN TO REMEMBER reached a wide audience through word-of-mouth and because of the talents of first-time director Garson Kanin and second-time scripter Dalton Trumbo. This picture's success was followed by a half-hearted sequel called CAREER, which was again scripted by Trumbo, and starred Ellis and Shirley.

p, Robert Sisk; d, Garson Kanin; w, Dalton Trumbo (based on the story "Failure" by Katharine Haviland-Taylor); ph, J. Roy Hunt; m, Roy Webb; ed, Jack Hively; art d, Van Nest Polglase; spec eff, Douglas Travers.

Drama   (PR:A   MPAA:NR)

MAN TRAILER, THE½**

(1934) 59m COL bw

Buck Jones (Dan Lee), Cecilia Parker (Sally Ryan), Arthur Vinton (Burk), Clarence Geldert (Sheriff Ryan), Steve Clark (Bishop), Charles West (Gorman), Lew Meehan, Dick Botiller, Artie Ortego, Tom Forman, Silver the Horse.

Jones, wrongly accused of being an outlaw, saves Parker in a stagecoach robbery and prevents the bandits from taking the money. He soon falls for Parker and becomes marshal of the small town. There's a plot to expose his spotted past, but Jones emerges clean. A remake of the William S. Hart silent THE RETURN OF DRAW EGAN (1916) and of director Hillyer's own THE LONE RIDER (1930). The

latter was Buck Jones' first Columbia western, while THE MAN TRAILER was his last.

p, Irving Briskin; d&w, Lambert Hillyer; ph, Benjamine Kline, Wilbur McGaugh; ed, Gene Milford.

Western   (PR:A   MPAA:NR)

MAN-TRAP**

(1961) 93m Tiger/PAR bw (GB: MAN IN HIDING)

Jeffrey Hunter (Matt Jameson), David Janssen (Vince Biskay), Stella Stevens (Nina Jameson), Elaine Devry (Liz Adams), Arthur Batanides (Cortez), Perry Lopez (Puerco), Bernard Fein (Fat Man), Virginia Gregg (Ruth), Mike Vandever (Bobby-Joe), Hugh Sanders (E.J. Malden), Tol Avery (Lt. Heissen), Bob Crane, Dorothy Green, Jack Albertson.

Hunter and Stevens play a suburban couple whose marriage is disintegrating through boredom and booze, when Hunter's old war buddy Janssen shows up with a scheme to get $3 million. The money has been stolen from a Latin American dictator, and is due at the San Francisco airport. Janssen is wounded during the take, so the two must hide out at Hunter's home. In a drunken encounter with her maid, Stevens falls to her death. Hunter finds the body, panics, and buries it in a slab of cement. On his return home, he is beaten by Latin thugs looking for the money. This opens an old war injury, forcing a loss of memory. Good performances are wasted in a script filled with absurd situations.

p, Edmond O'Brien, Stanley Frazen; d, O'Brien; w, Ed Waters (based on the novelette Taint of the Tiger by John D. MacDonald); ph, Loyal Griggs (Panavision); m, Leith Stevens; ed, Jack Lippiatt; art d, Al Roelofs; cos, Edith Head.

Drama   (PR:A   MPAA:NR)

MAN TROUBLE**

(1930) 85m FOX bw

Milton Sills (Mac), Dorothy Mackaill (Joan), Kenneth MacKenna (Graham), Sharon Lynn (Trixie), Roscoe Karns (Scott), Oscar Apfel (Eddie), James Bradbury, Jr. (Goofy), Lew Harvey (Chris), Harvey Clark (Uncle Joe), Edythe Chapman (Aunt Maggie).

Sills is a tough cabaret owner who falls in love with songbird Mackaill. She, however, falls for singing newspaperman Karns. Consistently average from start to finish, and includes the following tunes: "You Got Nobody to Love," "Now I Ask You," "You Do, Don't You?," and "Pick Yourself Up—Brush Yourself Off" (James F. Hanley, Joseph McCarthy).

d, Berthold Viertel; w, George Manker Watters, Marion Orth, Edwin Burke (based on a story by Ben Ames Williams); ph, Joseph August; ed, J. Edwin Robbins; set d, William S. Darling; cos, Sophie Wachner.

Musical   (PR:A   MPAA:NR)

MAN UPSTAIRS, THE**

(1959, Brit.) 88m ACT/BL bw

Richard Attenborough (Peter Watson, the Man), Bernard Lee (Inspector Thompson), Donald Houston (Sanderson), Dorothy Alison (Mrs. Barnes), Virginia Maskell (Helen Grey), Maureen Connell (Eunice Blair), Kenneth Griffith (Pollen), Charles Houston (Nicholas), Patricia Jessel (Mrs. Lawrence), Walter Hudd (Superintendent), Amy Dalby (Miss Acres), Edward Judd (P.C. Stevens), Polly Clark (Dulcie), Graham Stewart (Sgt. Morris), Alfred Burke (Mr. Barnes), Patrick Jordan (Injured Sergeant), John Charlesworth, Raymond Ray, Arthur Gross, David Griffith, Dan Cressy, Victor Brookes.

A superb performance from Attenborough is at the core of this character study. He is cast as a former scientist who accidently causes the death of his fiancee's brother. Stricken with an overbearing guilt, Attenborough assumes a false identity and holes up in a seedy boarding house. One night he locks himself in his room and begins to crack up. The police are called in and a variety of sentiments are elicited from among the tenants.

p, Robert Dunbar; d, Don Chaffey; w, Alun Falconer, Dunbar, Chaffey (based on a story by Falconer); ph, Gerald Massie-Collier; ed, John Trumper.

Drama   (PR:A   MPAA:NR)

MAN WANTED*½**

(1932) 63m WB bw

Kay Francis (Lois Ames), David Manners (Tom Sheridan), Andy Devine (Andy Doyle), Una Merkel (Ruth Holman), Kenneth Thomson (Fred), Claire Dodd (Ann Le Maire), Charlotte Merriam (Miss Smith), Edward Van Sloan (Manager), Robert Greig (Harper), Guy Kibbee, Virginia Sale.

Francis tires of her husband, fires her secretary, and hires Manners to replace her. She takes Manners with her everywhere, even dictating to him in her hotel bedroom. After Francis divorces her husband and Manners breaks off his engagement to Merkel, the loving pair get together. Director Dieterle's average direction is overshadowed by the rising talent of a young cameraman named Gregg Toland, who would go on to achieve fame as the man who shot CITIZEN KANE, as well as an endless series of successful films for William Wyler.

p, Hal Wallis; d, William Dieterle; w, Charles Kenyon (based on a story by Robert Lord); ph, Gregg Toland; ed, James Gibbon.

Romantic Comedy   (PR:A   MPAA:NR)

MAN WHO BROKE THE BANK AT MONTE CARLO, THE**

(1935) 70m FOX bw

Ronald Colman (Paul Gallard), Joan Bennett (Helen Berkeley), Colin Clive (Bertrand Berkeley), Nigel Bruce (Ivan), Montagu Love (Director), Ferdinand Gottschalk (Office Man), Frank Reicher (2nd Assistant Director), Lionel Pape (3rd Assistant Director), Leonid Snegoff (Nick the Chef), Sam Ash (Guard), Charles Coleman (Headwaiter), Vladimir Bykoff (Helen's Guide), John Pecora (Patron), Lynn Bari (Flower Girl), Charles Fallon (Croupier), Georgette Rhodes (Check Room Girl), Alphonse Du Bois (Taxi Driver), Andre Dheron (Dealer), Ramsay Hill,

Milton Royce *(Ushers)*, Harold Minjir *(Man with Girl)*, Bruce Wyndham *(Excited Man)*, George Beranger, Arthur Stuart Hull *(Casino Assistants)*, Dora Clement, Cecil Weston *(Women)*, Rudolf Myzet *(Changeur)*, Frederic Sullivan *(Pompous Man)*, Anya Taranda *(Girl at Bar)*, Francisco Maran *(Doorman)*, Eva Dennison *(Indignant Woman)*, Alphonse Martel *(Chasseur)*, William Stack, John Spacey *(Directors)*, Don Brody *(Photographer)*, John Miltern *(1st Assistant Director)*, Leonard Carey *(Captain of Waiters)*, E.E. Clive, Bob De Coudic, Joseph De Stefani *(Waiters)*, Gino Corrado *(Desk Clerk)*, Ferdinand Munier *(Maitre d' Hotel)*, Maurice Cass *(Assistant Maitre d' Hotel)*, John George *(Hunchback)*, Manuel Paris *(Doorman)*, George Sorel *(Hotel Clerk)*, Frank Dunn *(Steward)*, Shirley Anderson *(Telephone Girl)*, Frank Thornton *(Guard)*, Jacques Vanaire, General Theodore Lodi *(Captains of Waiters)*, Will Stanton *(Drunk Waiter)*, Christian Rub *(Gallard's Guide)*, Nicholas Soussanin, Alexander Melesh *(Cooks)*, I. Miraeva *(Singing and Dancing Cook)*, Joseph Marievsky, Norman Stengel *(Singers)*, Art Miles, Gaston Glass *(Bits)*, Regina Rambeau *(Girl)*, Walter Bonn *(Doorman)*, J. Vlaskin, V, Sabot, N. Mohoff *(Dancers)*, A. Trevor Bland *(Dancer)*, Tom Herbert *(Man at Table)*, Torben Meyer.

This was the shortest film and the longest title for Colman and although the idea has great possibilities, most of them were flubbed by the people behind the scenes. It's just after WW I and the Russian Revolution, and Colman, an expatriate White Russian prince, has been forced to take a job driving a cab in order to buy his blinis. He is one of several emigres who now live in Paris and talk of nothing but the good old days when the Czar reigned supreme. After he demonstrates a silly gambling "system," a bunch of his old Russian pals give him enough money to try his luck at the gaming tables of the famed Monaco casino. He proceeds to win millions of francs after an incredible run of luck at that most expensive of all games, baccarat. He returns to Paris, pays off the investors in his scheme, and goes to Switzerland for a well-earned vacation. He has given interviews telling the press that the average bettor should be wary about attempting the same ploy because, in the end, the casino, by dint of their house percentage, will always win. The management of the casino wants to get what they can of their money back, so they hire Bennett, and her brother, Clive, to again lure Colman to the tables. While on holiday in Yodel-land, Bennett falls for the romantic Colman, who is soon back at Monte Carlo where he loses everything he's won. Bennett feels awful about what she's done and tears up her paycheck, then tries to find Colman. In Paris, Colman sees Bennett working at a cabaret, borrows money to rent some evening duds, goes in to see her, rejects her, and leaves. Bennett races after him to learn that he is a mere cab driver, a fact that will make it much easier for her to wind up with him. In the final scene, Colman is again seated at the "Russian Table" of his favorite cafe and holding court. This picture may have been one of the first to have derived its heritage from a song, "I'm the Man Who Broke the Bank At Monte Carlo," which was a hit many years before the movie. Bruce does a good comic turn as Colman's pal and masquerading valet. The movie was the first joint venture between the newly merged companies of Twentieth Century and Fox.

p, Darryl F. Zanuck, Nunnally Johnson; d, Stephen Roberts; w, Howard Ellis Smith, Johnson (based on the play "Monsieur Alexandre, Igra, Lepy and the Gamble" by Illia Surgutchoff, Frederick Albert Swann); ph, Ernest Palmer; md, Oscar Bradley; m/l Bert Kalmar, Harry Ruby.

Comedy **(PR:A MPAA:NR)**

MAN WHO CAME BACK, THE* (1931) 74m FOX bw

Janet Gaynor *(Angie)*, Charles Farrell *(Stephen Randolph)*, Kenneth MacKenna *(Capt. Trevelyan)*, William Holden *(Thomas Randolph)*, Mary Forbes *(Mrs. Gaynes)*, Ulrich Haupt *(Charles Reisling)*, William Worthington *(Capt. Gallon)*, Peter Gawthorne *(Griggs)*, Leslie Fenton *(Baron Le Duc)*.

THE MAN WHO CAME BACK should have stayed away. Only the most dedicated Gaynor and Farrell fans will find anything at all in this terrible adaptation of a Broadway hit that had lots going for it on the stage and hardly anything at all on the screen. Farrell is the scion of New York wealth and enjoys his dissolute existence. Holden, Farrell's father, forces the rakehell to go to California in order to escape his old ways and make a life for himself. Farrell responds by hitting all the fleshpots in San Francisco and drinking away his allowance. While there, Farrell meets Gaynor, a singer, and they fall in love. Holden has his son shanghaied and sent to, of course, Shanghai, in another attempt to set the boy straight. In the Open City, Farrell heads right for the opium dens and finds Gaynor already there, now hopelessly addicted to the juice of the poppy. She tells him that since he left San Francisco with no notice, she thought he was either dead or didn't care about her any more. Farrell tells her what happened and the two marry, then sail to Hawaii where they shed their vice-ridden ways and become solid citizens. After a year or so, Farrell hears his father is ill, so he travels to New York to patch up the rent of the family fabric. When Holden talks poorly about Farrell's new wife, Farrell is angered, but it's only a feeble joke on Holden's part, as he has brought Gaynor to the city via a faster route and they have already established themselves in a loving father-in-law and daughter-in-law relationship. Whereas the play showed the degradation of alcohol and drugs, all of that is whitewashed in favor of a sappy romantic story as the studio tried their fifth consecutive Farrell-Gaynor duet. Squeaky-clean Gaynor and Farrell as dope fiends did not sit well with audiences who had come to love their pairings in SEVENTH HEAVEN and STREET ANGEL. Holden died shortly after the film and was not related to the later William Holden, whose real name was William Franklin Beedle, Jr. THE MAN WHO CAME BACK was a remake of 1924 Fox film which had George O'Brien and Dorothy Mackaill in the lead roles.

d, Raoul Walsh; w, Edwin J. Burke (based on the play by Jules Eckert Goodman, from the novel by John Fleming Wilson); ph, Arthur Edeson; ed, Harold Schuster; set d, Joseph Urban.

Drama **(PR:C MPAA:NR)**

MAN WHO CAME FOR COFFEE, THE***

(1970, Ital.) 98m Mars/CIC c (VENGA A PRENDERO IL CAFFE DA NOI)

Ugo Tognazzi *(Emerenziano)*, Francesca Romana Coluzzi *(Tarsilla)*, Milena Vukotic *(Camilla)*, Angela Goodwin *(Fortunata)*, Jean Jacques Fourgeaud *(Paolino)*, Valentine *(Caterina)*, Francesco Rissone *(Mansueto)*.

Tognazzi stars as a lust-driven tax inspector who retires to a household run by three church-going maidens. Before long he is married to one of them (Goodwin) but carrying on in the other two's bedrooms. All goes well until he tries to add a fourth woman to his collection. Good fun mixed nicely with social commentary. (In Italian; English subtitles.)

p, Maurizio Lodi-Fe; d, Alberto Lattuada; w, Adriano Baracco, Tullio Kezich, Lattuada, Piero Chiara (based on the novel *La Spartizione* by Chiara); ph, Lamberto Caimi (Eastmancolor); m, Fred Bongusto; ed, Sergio Montanari; art d, Vincenzo Del Prato.

Comedy **(PR:O MPAA:NR)**

MAN WHO CAME TO DINNER, THE**** (1942) 112m WB bw

Bette Davis *(Maggie Cutler)*, Ann Sheridan *(Lorraine Sheldon)*, Monty Woolley *(Sheridan Whiteside)*, Richard "Dick" Travis *(Bert Jefferson)*, Jimmy Durante *(Banjo)*, Reginald Gardiner *(Beverly Carlton)*, Billie Burke *(Mrs. Stanley)*, Elisabeth Fraser *(June Stanley)*, Grant Mitchell *(Ernest Stanley)*, George Barbier *(Dr. Bradley)*, Mary Wickes *(Miss Preen)*, Russell Arms *(Richard Stanley)*, Ruth Vivian *(Harriett Stanley)*, Edwin Stanley *(John)*, Betty Roadman *(Sarah)*, Charles Drake *(Sandy)*, Nanette Vallon *(Cosette)*, John Ridgely, Herbert Gunn, Creighton Hale *(Radio Men)*, Pat McVey *(Harry)*, Laura Hope Crews *(Mrs. Gibbons)*, Frank Coghlan, Jr. *(Telegram Boy)*, Vera Lewis *(Woman)*, Frank Moran *(Michaelson)*, Chester Clute *(Mr. Gibbons)*, Roland Drew *(Newspaperman)*, Sam Hayes *(Announcer)*, Ernie Adams *(Haggerty)*, Eddy Chandler *(Guard)*, Hank Mann, Cliff Saum *(Expressmen)*, Billy Wayne *(Vendor)*, Dudley Dickerson *(Porter)*, Jack Mower, Frank Mayo *(Plainclothesmen)*, Fred Kelsey *(Man)*, Georgia Carroll, Lorraine Gettman [Leslie Brooks], Peggy Diggins, Alix Talton *(Girls)*.

This smash hit Broadway comedy became a smash hit movie due to a superb adaptation and the retention of Woolley, who played the lead on the stage. Davis had seen the play and wanted to take the secondary role as the "Great Man's" secretary. It was to originally star John Barrymore, but he had trouble with the lines and Woolley was paged to repeat his role. The studio paid the then-unheard-of price of a quarter of a million dollars for the rights and their investment paid off many times. It's a very thinly veiled account of some real people in an unlikely situation. Alexander Woollcott and Harpo Marx and Noel Coward were all part of the Algonquin Hotel crowd who met for regular lunches. Others in that group included Benchley, Dorothy Parker, and Franklin P. Adams. Hart and Kaufman took what they knew of the lunchers and placed them into a "fish-out-of-water" situation and the result was a funny, acerbic, and successful play and film. Woolley (as Woollcott) is on a lecture tour across the U.S. when he arrives in Ohio and accepts a dinner invite from one of the leading families of the small town. He is traveling with Davis, his tolerant secretary, and slips on the ice outside the home. He is carried inside as he shouts insults and says he will sue them for everything they have. Mitchell and Burke, who own the house and are the essence of Midwest respectability (which makes them everything Woolley dislikes), are frightened by the thought of the lawsuit and attempt to make Woolley comfortable as he waits for Barbier, the family doctor, to complete the examination which concludes that Woolley has been hurt badly and must stay in a wheelchair until he is well enough to leave. This throws the Mitchell-Burke household into chaos as Woolley malevolently decides to have a bit of amusement by making everyone around conform to his wishes. He charms the servants and advises the home's children, Arms and Fraser, to flee immediately and seek to make their own ways apart from this stifling Ohio existence. Meanwhile, Davis is falling for local newsman-playwright Travis, and Woolley sees that he may lose her services, so he calls Sheridan, a sexy actress who is living in Palm Beach luxury as the mistress of a titled Englishman, and persuades her to come to cold Ohio with the promise of a leading role in a new play by Travis. His plan is to have Sheridan vamp Travis and get him away from Davis. Sheridan arrives and Davis is hip to Woolley's plan, so she threatens to leave his employ. Woolley gets rid of Sheridan by packing her inside a mummy case to Philadelphia. Four penguins arrive from Admiral Byrd, as well as a live octopus from another admirer. Now Woolley finds out that his leg isn't badly hurt at all, as Barbier admits he diagnosed the injury incorrectly. But by this time, Woolley has laid many plans and he can't leave, so he convinces Barbier to keep mum with the promise that he can have the man's memoirs published and they will surely be a best-seller. Woolley is to make his annual Christmas radio broadcast from the Ohio location, so a full boys' choir and a large radio crew descend upon the house. In the meantime, he is also visited by Durante (as Harpo Marx) and Gardiner, as a Noel Coward-type. Mitchell finally learns that Woolley is faking it and orders him out of the house in an attempt to quash the children's dreams of escaping. Now Woolley recognizes Mitchell's oddball sister, Vivian, as an alleged axe murderess who was tried and acquitted of killing her parents. With this fodder for his cannon, Woolley remains in the house, fixes up Davis' romance with Travis, and sends Arms and Fraser out into the world. His work done, Woolley stands and exits the home and truly breaks his leg on the ice. As he is carried bodily for the second time, a call from Eleanor Roosevelt comes in and the picture ends. Witty lines, wonderful performances, and topnotch characterizations from all concerned. Clute and Crews, although having billing as Mr. and Mrs. Gibbons, never appear in the final print. There was no mistaking the originals upon whom the story was based. Any other people might have sued, but Woolley and the others were apparently delighted at having been enshrined in the Comedy Hall of Fame by Kaufman and Hart's writing.

p, Hal B. Wallis, Jerry Wald, Jack Saper; d, William Keighley; w, Julius J. and Philip G. Epstein (based on the play by George S. Kaufman, Moss Hart); ph, Tony

Gaudio; m, Frederick Hollander; ed, Jack Killifer; md, Leo F. Forbstein; art d, Robert Haas; cos, Orry-Kelly.

Comedy **(PR:A MPAA:NR)**

MAN WHO CHANGED, THE
(SEE: MAN WHO CHANGED HIS NAME, 1934, Brit.)

MAN WHO CHANGED HIS MIND
(SEE: MAN WHO LIVED AGAIN, THE, 1936)

MAN WHO CHANGED HIS NAME, THE*
(1934, Brit.) 71m Twickenham/DuWorld bw (AKA: THE MAN WHO CHANGED)

Lyn Harding *(Selby Clive)*, Betty Stockfeld *(Nita Clive)*, Leslie Perrins *(Frank Ryan)*, Ben Welden *(Jerry Muller)*, Aubrey Mather *(Sir Ralph Whitcomb)*, Richard Dolman *(John Boscombe)*, Stanley Vine.

Harding is the man who changed, or actually shortened, his name, which was the same as that of a wife-murderer. Through present wife Clive, Harding tries to buy some property in Canada owned by a wealthy Englishman. She, however, gets edgy after a couple of supposed accidents and explains to her former beau Perrins that her husband is trying to kill her. Harding, however, is actually trying to prove that Perrins is a cad for encouraging Clive to leave him. A very talky mystery with little action.

p, Julius Hagen; d, Henry Edwards; w, H. Fowler Mear, Edgar Wallace (based on the play by Wallace); ph, Sydney Blythe.

Crime/Drama **(PR:A MPAA:NR)**

MAN WHO CHEATED HIMSELF, THE** ½** (1951) 86m FOX bw

Lee J. Cobb *(Ed Cullen)*, John Dall *(Andy Cullen)*, Jane Wyatt *(Lois Frazer)*, Lisa Howard *(Janet)*, Alan Wells *(Nito Capa)*, Harlan Warde *(Howard Frazer)*, Tito Vuolo *(Pietro Capa)*, Mimi Aguglia *(Mrs. Capa)*, Charles Arnt *(Mr. Quimby)*, Marjorie Bennett *(Mrs. Quimby)*, Bud Wolfe *(Blair)*, Morgan Farley *(Rushton)*, Howard Negley *(Olson)*, William Gould *(Medical Examiner)*, Art Milan *(Airport Clerk)*, Gordon Richards *(Butler)*, Terry Frost *(Detective)*, Mario Siletti *(Machetti)*, Charles Victor *(Attorney)*.

A murky plot mars this otherwise interesting *film noir* which oddly casts Wyatt as the *femme fatale* who is having an affair with police lieutenant Cobb. She is in the process of divorcing Warde when he attempts to rob his own house. He is shot by Wyatt, who calls on Cobb to help get rid of the body. They decide to take the corpse to the airport, and deposit it there. They are seen, however, and policeman Dall, who is Cobb's brother, discovers that Cobb is involved in the cover up. Cobb and Wyatt hide out at the base of the Golden Gate Bridge, but are discovered by Dall, who unknowingly has been trailed by the police. Cobb is brought to trial and in the courtroom sees Wyatt with her new paramour, a lawyer.

p, Jack M. Warner; d, Felix E. Feist; w, Seton I. Miller, Philip MacDonald (based on a story by Miller); ph, Russell Harlan; m, Louis Forbes; ed, David Weisbart; prod d, Van Nest Polglase; cos, Elois Janssen; spec eff, Rex Wimpy; makeup, Abe Haberman.

Crime **(PR:A MPAA:NR)**

MAN WHO COULD CHEAT DEATH, THE** ½**
(1959, Brit.) 83m Hammer/PAR c

Anton Diffring *(Dr. Georges Bonner)*, Hazel Court *(Janine Dubois)*, Christopher Lee *(Dr. Pierre Gerard)*, Arnold Marle *(Dr. Ludwig Weisz)*, Delphi Lawrence *(Margo Philippe)*, Francis De Wolff *(Inspector Legris)*, Gerda Larsen *(Street Girl)*, Middleton Woods, Michael Ripper, Denis Shaw, Ian Hewitson, Frederick Rawlings, Marie Burke, Charles Lloyd-Pack, John Harrison, Lockwood West, Ronald Adam, Barry Shawzin.

This Hammer horror film is as intelligent and well crafted as the rest of their productions, this time casting Diffring as a 104-year-old man who looks to be in his mid-30s. Set at the turn of the century, Diffring removes the "uter parathyroid" gland from living victims and uses it to rejuvenate his living self. Lee stars as his less-than-willing aide in this remake of THE MAN IN HALF MOON STREET.

p, Michael Carreras; d, Terence Fisher; w, Jimmy Sangster (based on the play "The Man in Half Moon Street" by Barre Lyndon); ph, Jack Asher (Technicolor); m, Richard Bennett; ed, James Needs; md, John Hollingsworth; makeup, Roy Ashton.

Horror **(PR:C MPAA:NR)**

MAN WHO COULD WORK MIRACLES, THE*** ½**
(1937, Brit.) 82m LFP/UA bw

Roland Young *(George McWhirter Fotheringay)*, Ralph Richardson *(Col. Winstanley)*, Edward Chapman *(Maj. Grigsby)*, Ernest Thesiger *(Mr. Maydig)*, Joan Gardner *(Ada Price)*, Sophie Stewart *(Maggie Hooper)*, Robert Cochran *(Bill Stoker)*, Lawrence Hanray *(Mr. Bamfylde)*, George Zucco *(Moody)*, Wallace Lupino *(Police Constable Winch)*, Lady Tree *(Housekeeper)*, Joan Hickson, Gertrude Musgrove *(Effie Brickman)*, Wally Patch *(Supt. Smithelle)*, Bernard Nedell *(Reporter)*, Bruce Winston *(Cox, Landlord)*, George Sanders *(Indifference, a God)*, Ivan Brandt *(Player, a God)*, Torin Thatcher *(Observer, a God)*, Mark Daly *(Toddy Beamish)*, Jane Baxter.

Although billed as a comedy, this followup to THINGS TO COME (although filmed earlier, it was released afterward) is more of a whimsical social drama without many laughs. Three gods look down on Earth and try to decide if the place is worth keeping in the celestial solar system. Sanders, Thatcher, and Brandt argue about the relative merits of the tiny planet, and so they pick the most unlikely Earthling and bestow upon him miraculous powers to see if absolute power will corrupt absolutely. Young, a mild, meek draper's assistant in Essex, England, is tapped by the gods and is soon doing what appears to be little magic tricks, making items appear and disappear, turning a lamp over in mid-air, etc. As he comes to the realization that his powers are limitless, Young wants to alter the course of humanity, to stop wars and illness, and to make the world into Utopia. Richardson, a somewhat deranged ex-colonel, thinks that would be a mistake and goes after Young with a gun, only to find that the man has made himself bullet-proof and safe from death. Despite his abilities, Young can't use them to change people's emotions and is unable to get shopgirl Gardner to love him. He causes a policeman to go to Hell, then to San Francisco. He cures a young woman of freckles, et al. He eventually creates a great palace where he will be the ruler of the Earth. He brings all the people to that palace and tells them of his plan, but they don't believe he has the power to do what he says he can, despite their being in this odd building with this odd man and having no previous knowledge of how they got there. To demonstrate how strong he is, Young orders the Earth to stop rotating and the result is that the crowd flies off the Earth and begins tumbling in space. Since Young is impervious, he is able to shout his final wish, that he be returned to the little pub where this all began and that matters go back to where they were with no knowledge of what happened. That is what transpires and Young is left with the feeling that it may have all been a figment of his imagination. The going gets sort of heavy as Wells makes his point that Utopia can never be achieved because the world is not ready for it. The film features exceptional special effects that would cost millions today if attempted. The whimsy wears a bit thin after a while. The film is fondly recalled by those who haven't seen it lately. Lajos Biro was not credited for his contribution to the screen play. Sources conflict on the actress who played the role of Effie Brickman; some credit Joan Hickson, others credit Gertrude Musgrove.

p, Alexander Korda; d, Lothar Mendes; w, H.G. Wells, Lajos Biro (based on the short story by Wells); ph, Harold Rosson; m, Michael [Mischa] Spoliansky; ed, William Hornbeck, Philip Charlot; prod d, Vincent Korda; md, Muir Mathieson; spec eff, Ned Mann, Lawrence Butler, Edward Cohen.

Comedy/Fantasy **(PR:A MPAA:NR)**

MAN WHO COULDN'T WALK, THE** ½**
(1964, Brit.) 63m Falcon-Taurus bw

Eric Pohlmann *(The Consul)*, Peter Reynolds *(Keefe Brand)*, Pat Clavin *(Carol)*, Reed De Rouen *(Luigi)*, Bernadette Milnes *(Cora)*, Richard Shaw *(Enrico)*, Martin Cass *(Beppo)*, Margot van der Burgh *(Maria)*, Maurice Bannister *(Joey)*, Martin Gordon *(Lou)*, Andre Muller *(Johnny)*, Owen Berry *(Watchman, No. 1)*, John Baker *(Watchman, No. 2)*.

A bizarre crime thriller from England with Pohlmann heading a gang of jewel thieves from his wheelchair. He acquires the services of top safecracker Reynolds and sets up a risky heist during an international exposition. The job is nearly successful, but one of the men gets gunned down by the police and Reynolds is captured by a rival gang leader. He then learns that the leader is responsible for his father's death years ago in Chicago. He sets out to confront Pohlmann, but before he can do so, the trigger-happy mother of one of the gang members guns the leader down.

p, Jock MacGregor, Umesh Mallick; d, Henry Cass; w, Mallick; ph, James Harvey; m, Wilfred Burns; ed, Robert Hill; art d, John Earl; makeup, Jimmy Evans.

Crime Drama **(PR:A MPAA:NR)**

MAN WHO CRIED WOLF, THE** ½** (1937) 66m UNIV bw

Lewis Stone *(Lawrence Fontaine)*, Tom Brown *(Tommy Bradley)*, Barbara Read *(Nan)*, Marjorie Main *(Amelia Bradley)*, Robert Spencer *(Reporter)*, Robert Gleckler *(Capt. Walter Reid)*, Forrester Harvey *(Jocko)*, Billy Wayne *(Halligan)*, Jameson Thomas *(George Bradley)*, Pierre Watkin *(Governor)*, Russell Hicks *(Prosecuting Attorney)*, Selmer Jackson *(Defense Attorney)*, Howard Hickman *(Doctor on Stage)*, Stanley Andrews, John Hamilton *(Judges)*, Matt McHugh *(Desk Sergeant)*, Fredrik Vogeding *(Resident Doctor)*, Ben Taggart *(Plain Clothes Officer)*, Anne O'Neal *(Landlady)*, Reverend Neal Dodd *(Priest)*, Sherry Hall *(Ballistic Expert)*, Jack Daley *(Policeman)*, Jason Robards, Sr. *(Doctor)*, Walter Miller *(Killer)*, William Castle, Hal Cooke *(Customers at Box Office)*, Eddie Fetherston *(Box Office Cashier)*, Ernie Adams *(Reporter)*, Russ Clark *(Prison Guard)*, Charles Bennett *(Taxi Manager)*, James Blaine *(Doorman)*, Wilson Benge *(Butler)*, Arthur Yeoman *(Court Clerk)*, Gertrude Astor *(Landlady)*, Henry Boman *(Lodger)*.

A low-budgeter which is blessed with a plot similar to "The Twilight Zone" about an old actor (Stone) who habitually confesses to murders which he didn't commit. The police think he's a nut case, but he's really been planning a murder for years. When he finally does commit the crime, his son is accused, forcing Stone to beg the police to believe his story. It's all very routine from direction to performance, but the surprise-filled script makes it watchable.

p, E.M. Asher; d, Lewis R. Foster; w, Charles Grayson, Cy Bartlett (based on the story "Too Clever To Live" by Arthur Rolhsfel); ph, George Robinson; ed, Frank Gross.

Crime/Drama **(PR:A MPAA:NR)**

MAN WHO DARED, THE** (1933) 72m FOX bw

Preston Foster *(Jan Novak)*, Zita Johann *(Teena Pavelic)*, Joan Marsh *(Joan)*, Irene Biller *(Tereza Novak)*, Clifford Jones *(Dick)*, June Vlasek *(Barbara)*, Leon Waycoff [Ames] *(Yosef Novak)*, Douglas Cosgrove *(Dan Foley)*, Douglas Dumbrille *(Judge Collier)*, Frank Sheridan *(Sen. McGuiness)*, Leonid Snegoff *(Posilipo)*, Matt McHugh *(Karel)*, Jay Ward *(Jan as a Boy)*, Elsie Larson, Lita Chevret, Vivian Reid.

Billed as "an imaginative biography" this film takes glorious liberties with the life of Chicago Mayor Anton Cermak, who was inadvertently gunned down on Feb. 15, 1933, by a bullet intended for President-elect Franklin Roosevelt. Foster, in the title role (though his character name is different), plays a Polish immigrant who rises to the top of Chicago's political ranks, paving the way for a Democratic party which may never cease. He is seen against the backdrop of a city feeling the industrial advancements of a modern age in which the horse-and-buggy bowed to the gasoline engine. The sugary, angelic treatment of Cermak certainly could not offend anyone involved, but seems to be more of a reaction to his recent death than his actual life.

d, Hamilton McFadden; w, Dudley Nichols, Lamar Trotti; ph, Arthur Miller; ed, Al DeGaetano.

Biography   **(PR:AA MPAA:NR)**

MAN WHO DARED, THE**

(1939) 60m FN/WB bw

Charles Grapewin, Henry O'Neill, Dickie Jones, Jane Bryan, Elisabeth Risdon, James McCallion, John Russell, Fred Tozere, John Gallaudet, Grace Stafford, Emmett Vogan.

An innocent family becomes the object of obtuse malice from a gang of hoods when they witness events that could send one of gangland's leaders to the electric chair. Overcoming the bodyguards provided by the law, the hoods easily kidnap one family member, prompting grandpa Grapewin to rescue his grandson from an almost certain death. This remake of the 1931 STAR WITNESS lacks the strength of its predecessor; mainly because William Wellman was not at the helm as in the earlier version.

p, Bryan Foy; d, Crane Wilbur; w, Lee Katz (based on the story "Star Witness" by Lucien Hubbard); ph, Arthur L. Todd; ed, Harold McLernon.

Crime/Drama   **(PR:A MPAA:NR)**

MAN WHO DARED, THE**½

(1946) 66m COL bw

Leslie Brooks, George Macready, Forrest Tucker, Charles D. Brown, Warren Mills, Richard Hale, Charles Evans, Trevor Bardette, William Newell, Brooks Benedict, Tom Kingston, Doris Houck.

Fairly engaging drama in which a crusading reporter is out to expose some of the errors in the judicial system, specifically the concept of "circumstantial evidence." To do so he makes himself look like the prime suspect in a murder case. Though not a mover of social issues, the film is entertaining nonetheless. THE MAN WHO DARED represents the feature-film debut of director Sturges, who later became well-known for his action-oriented westerns, including THE MAGNIFICENT SEVEN and GUNFIGHT AT THE O.K. CORRAL.

p, Leonard S. Picker; d, John Sturges; w, Edward Bock, Malcolm Boylan (based on the story by Maxwell Shane, Alex Gottlieb); ph, Philip Tannura; ed, Charles Nelson; md, Mischa Bakaleinikoff; art d, George Brooks.

Crime/Drama   **(PR:A MPAA:NR)**

MAN WHO DIED TWICE, THE*½

(1958) 70m REP bw

Rod Cameron (Bill Brennon), Vera Ralston (Lynn Brennon), Mike Mazurki (Rak), Gerald Milton (Hart), Richard Karlan (Santoni), Louis Jean Heydt (Hampton), Don Megowan (T. J. Brennon), John Maxwell (Chief Hampton), Bob Anderson (Sgt. Williams), Paul Picerni (George), Don Haggerty (Frank), Luana Anders (Young Girl Addict), Jesslyn Fax (Sally Hemphill).

The final screen appearance for the skating-champ-turned-actress, Ralston, THE MAN WHO DIED TWICE was quite similar to many of her other outings which all seemed to prove that she never should have left the ice. She plays a nightclub singer whose husband burned to death. When she sees two men murdered she loses all control. Story is not all that bad, but the acting, particularly Ralston's, and overall handling left much to be desired.

p, Rudy Ralston; d, Joe Kane; w, Richard C. Sarafian; ph, Jack Marta (Naturama); ed, Fred Knudtson; md, Gerald Roberts; art d, Ralph Oberg; set d, John McCarthy Jr.; cos, Alexis Davidoff; m/l, Jerry Gladstone, Al DeLory; makeup, Bob Mark.

Drama   **(PR:A MPAA:NR)**

MAN WHO FELL TO EARTH, THE***½

(1976, Brit.) 140m BL/Cinema 5 c

David Bowie (Thomas Jerome Newton), Rip Torn (Nathan Bryce), Candy Clark (Mary-Lou), Buck Henry (Oliver Farnsworth), Bernie Casey (Peters), Jackson D. Kane (Prof. Canutti), Rick Riccardo (Trevor), Tony Mascia (Arthur), Linda Hutton (Elaine), Hilary Holland (Jill), Adrienne Larussa (Helen), Lilybell Crawford (Jewelry Story Owner), Richard Breeding (Receptionist), Peter Prouse (Peter's Associate), Capt. James Lovell (Himself), Albert Nelson (Waiter), Preacher and Congregation of Presbyterian Church, Artesia, N. M. (Themselves).

Nicolas Roeg's cult classic about an alien, Bowie, who arrives on Earth in search of water for his drought-ridden planet where his wife and children are dying of thirst. Bowie takes an Earth name and arrives at the office of homosexual patent attorney Henry and offers him a number of invention designs with which they can make a great deal of money, enough for Bowie to build a vehicle for him to return to his home planet. In hardly any time, Bowie and Henry are running a huge financial empire, one of the world's largest corporations. Torn is a professor of chemistry who spends his off-hours seducing his students. He wants to know more about Bowie's company and how they can do all of these fabulous inventions and now they have become a $300 million company in three years. Bowie is hiding out in New Mexico when he meets hotel clerk Clark and she encourages him to drink gin and watch TV. Not a person to do things halfway, Bowie is soon guzzling the booze and watching several TV sets simultaneously as he continues his plan to start his own space project. Torn is hired by Henry to help on the secret space exploration and uses his nearness to X-ray Bowie. When he sees that Bowie is not human, Torn questions him. Bowie admits he is an extraterrestrial, but he means no harm to Earth's population. Bowie continues to drink and watch TV and becomes more and more human in his life style, if not his being. Clark is annoyed by Bowie's indifference and when he shows her his alien form, she is repulsed. Henry realizes that Clark may be a distraction for Bowie, so he offers her money to leave, but the cash means nothing to her; she loves Bowie and that's all that matters. Large companies begin to pressure Bowie and Henry to sell the patents but they refuse. Henry and his lover,

Riccardo, are mysteriously killed when they fall out of a high hotel window. Casey is the villain behind this and arranges for Bowie to be taken prisoner. Years pass as Bowie is held in a deserted hotel and many torturous tests are made on him. The huge company goes belly up and Torn goes into Casey's employ, then marries Clark. Bowie finally escapes his captors but he is no longer news. He records an album called "The Visitor" in the vain hope that the radio waves will carry out into the universe and his wife, if she is still alive, may hear it. Bowie begins to wander the Earth as a drunk. He has failed in his mission and realizes he can never get back to his home planet. The film looks wonderful and cultists have named it one of their favorites. The soundtrack also helps establish the near-future mood although Bowie doesn't sing much at all. Roeg began his career as a cameraman (and worked on LAWRENCE OF ARABIA) and it is clear he is in charge of the imagery all the way. The sets are very stylish and all technical credits are firstquality. Bowie proves he isn't just another ugly face with his performance in this film and should have a continuing career as an actor. There is no question that E.T. has the same premise: i.e., an alien who wants to go back to the home planet. The way Roeg handles it is far different than Steven Spielberg's method (E.T.) and, in some ways, more satisfying because it is nowhere near as calculating. There are many changes from the Tevis novel, not all of them for the better. Roeg enjoys using singers as actors and cast Art Garfunkel and Mick Jagger in films that also became cult classics but never made that much noise in the popular world. It's essentially a science-fiction movie with a touch of social commentary and modern music tossed in to add to the stew. Eddy Arnold sings "Make the World Go Away" in addition to the rock tunes. Executive producer Litvinoff, an American, lived in England for many years and also served as exec on BARRY LYNDON. The Preacher and congregation of the Artesia, New Mexico, Presbyterian Church appear in the film as themselves. In England, where the censorship laws are somewhat more restrictive, this movie received an "X" rating due to nudity and soft-core sexual matter. Originally released at 140 minutes, the U.S. distributor, Cinema 5, edited the film down to versions of 117, 120, and 125 minutes, before restoring it to its original length in 1980.

p, Michael Deeley, Barry Spikings; d, Nicolas Roeg; w, Paul Mayersberg (based on the novel by Walter Tevis); ph, Anthony Richmond (Panavision); ed, Graeme Clifford; md, John Phillips; spec eff, Paul Ellenshaw.

Science-Fiction   **Cas.**   **(PR:C-O MPAA:R)**

MAN WHO FINALLY DIED, THE*½

(1967, Brit.) 98m White Cross/Goldstone bw

Stanley Baker (Joe Newman), Peter Cushing (Dr. von Brecht), Mai Zetterling (Lisa), Eric Portman (Inspector Hofmeister), Niall MacGinnis (Brenner), Nigel Green (Hirsch), Barbara Everest (Martha), Georgina Ward (Maria), Harold Scott (Professor), James Ottaway (Rahn), Alfred Burke (Heinrich), Mela White (Helga), Maya Sorell (Minna).

After WW II, Baker goes back to the small Bavarian village where his father lived. He is told that his father died after escaping from the Communists and had married Zetterling. Baker feels that certain facts are being kept from him and when he begins to do some investigating he finds that an important scientist switched places with his father. Cushing and Zetterling plan to take the doctor to the East, but Baker stops them and gets the scientist out of the country.

p, Norman Williams; d, Quentin Lawrence; w, Lewis Greifer, Louis Marks (based on a story by Greifer); ph, Stephen Dade; m, Philip Green; ed, John Jympson; art d, Scott MacGregor.

Drama   **(PR:A MPAA:NR)**

MAN WHO FOUND HIMSELF, THE**

(1937) 67m RKO bw

John Beal (Jim Stanton), Joan Fontaine (Doris King), Philip Huston (Dick Miller), Jane Walsh (Barbara Reed), George Irving (Dr. Stanton), James "Jimmy" Conlin (Nosey Watson), Frank M. Thomas (Roberts), Diana Gibson (Helen), Dwight Frye (Patient), Billy Gilbert (Fat Hobo), Stanley Andrews (Department of Commerce Official), Jonathan Hale (Dr. Tom Smythe), Douglas Wood, Edward Van Sloan (Doctors), Edward Gargan (Cop), George Meeker (Howard Dennis).

Young surgeon Beal turns his back on his medical career and takes up the life of a hobo. Fontaine, however, gets him back into the ranks of social acceptance as he performs some delicate surgery in a flying hospital. Fontaine's performance was a nice hint of the things to come, but the rest of the case is shadowed by two notable bit performers, Frye (Renfield to Bela Lugosi's DRACULA) and the lovably hysterical Gilbert.

p, Cliff Reid; d, Lew Landers; w, J. Robert Bren, Edmund L. Hartmann, G. V. Atwater, Thomas Lennon (based on the story "Wings of Mercy" by Alice F. Curtis); ph, J. Roy Hunt; ed, Jack Hively; spec eff, Vernon L. Walker.

Drama   **(PR:A MPAA:NR)**

MAN WHO HAD POWER OVER WOMEN, THE**

(1970, Brit.) 89m Kettledrum/AE c

Rod Taylor (Peter Reaney), Carol White (Jody Pringle), James Booth (Val Pringle), Penelope Horner (Angela Reaney), Charles Korvin (Alfred Felix), Alexandra Stewart (Frances), Keith Barron (Jake Braid), Clive Francis (Barry Black), Marie-France Boyer (Maggie), Magali Noel (Mrs. Franchetti), Geraldine Moffat (Lydia Blake), Wendy Hamilton (Mary Gray), Ellis Dale (Norman), Philip Stone (Angela's Father), Sara Booth (Sarah Pringle), Matthew Booth (Mark Pringle), Jimmy Jewel (Mr. Pringle), Virginia Clay (Mrs. Pringle), Patrick Durkin (Herbie), Diana Chance (Stripper), Ruth Trouncer (Mrs. Gray), Paul Farrell (Reaney's father).

A British comedy which mixes sex with social satire as Taylor plays a talent agency public relations man who represents pop singer Francis. After a fiasco involving the singer and a girl whom he allegedly bedded turns into an abortion scandal, Taylor leaves the agency. He goes on a drinking binge and splits with his wife. He turns to friend Booth, but sleazily seduces the fellow's wife, White. Eventually, Booth is killed in a car accident and the singer's past is publicized. Taylor turns his back on it all and departs with White. Entertaining in spots, but overall it's a pretty dated and heavy-handed attempt.

p. Judd Bernard; d, John Krish; w, Allan Scott, Cris Bryant, Andrew Meredith (based on the novel by Gordon M. Williams); ph, Gerry Turpin (Eastmancolor); ed, Thom Noble; art d, Colin Grimes; cos, Brian Cox; m/l, "Bend Over Backwards," Johnny Mandell, Hal David (sung by Bill and Buster); makeup, George Partleton.

Comedy/Satire **(PR:C MPAA:R)**

MAN WHO HAUNTED HIMSELF, THE**

(1970, Brit.) 94m Associated British/Levitt-Pickman c

Roger Moore *(Harold Pelham)*, Hildegard Neil *(Eva Pelham)*, Alastair Mackenzie *(Michael)*, Hugh Mackenzie *(James)*, Kevork Malikyan *(Luigi)*, Thorley Walters *(Bellamy)*, Anton Rodgers *(Tony Alexander)*, Olga Georges-Picot *(Julie)*, Freddie Jones *(Dr. Harris)*, John Welsh *(Sir Charles Freeman)*, Edward Chapman *(Barton)*, Laurence Hardy *(Mason)*, Charles Lloyd Pack *(Jameson)*, Gerald Sim *(Morrison)*, Ruth Trouncer *(Pelham's Secretary)*, Aubrey Richards *(Research Scientist)*, Anthony Nicholls *(Sir Arthur Richardson)*, John Carson *(Ashton)*, John Dawson *(Barber)*, Terence Sewards *(Jeweler's Assistant)*.

Implausible but well-done treatment which mixes fantasy with some standard thriller techniques. After suffering a nasty car accident in which business executive Moore momentarily "dies" on the operating table, an alter ego escapes and raises hell without Moore's knowledge. Soon Moore discovers that he is having an affair with a woman he met only once and his business career seems to have a mind of its own. Moore does a decent job making the transition from his TV series "The Saint" to the big screen, a switch that would be irreversible after his subsequent Bond pictures. Based on an episode from TV's "Alfred Hitchcock Presents." Dearden's final film before dying in a car accident the following year.

p, Michael Relph; d, Basil Dearden; w, Relph, Dearden (based on *The Case of Mr. Pelham* by Anthony Armstrong); ph, Tony Spratling (Technicolor); m, Michael J. Lewis; ed, Teddy Darvas; md, Lewis; art d, Albert Witherick; cos, Beatrice Dawson; spec eff, Tommy Howard, Charles Staffel.

Drama/Fantasy **Cas.** **(PR:A MPAA:GP)**

MAN WHO KILLED BILLY THE KID, THE*

(1967, Span./Ital.) 86m Aitor/Kinesis bw (EL HOMBRE QUE MATAO BILLY EL NINO)

Peter Lee Lawrence [Karl Hirenbach] *(Billy)*, Fausto Tozzi *(Pat Garrett)*, Dianik Zurakowska, Gloria Milland, Luis Prendes, Barta Barry.

A dull Italian western that tells the story of Billy the Kid and Pat Garrett like an old Hollywood B western. The film is a far cry from the stylized Italian westerns that were coming out at the same time.

p, Silvio Battistini; d, Julio Buchs; w, Buchs, Federico de Urrutia; ph, Miguel Mila.

Western **(PR:A MPAA:NR)**

MAN WHO KNEW TOO MUCH, THE****

(1935, Brit.) 75m GAU bw

Leslie Banks *(Bob Lawrence)*, Edna Best *(Jill Lawrence)*, Peter Lorre *(Abbott)*, Frank Vosper *(Ramon Levine)*, Hugh Wakefield *(Clive)*, Nova Pilbeam *(Betty Lawrence)*, Pierre Fresnay *(Louis Bernard)*, Cicely Oates *(Nurse Agnes)*, D. A. Clarke Smith *(Binstead)*, George Curzon *(Gibson)*, Henry Oscar *(Dentist)*, Celia Lovsky.

Hitchcock's career was in doubt when he made this film after having delivered a few questionable movies but THE MAN WHO KNEW TOO MUCH reestablished him as a pantheon director. Married couple Banks and Best are vacationing in Switzerland with daughter Pilbeam. Frenchman Fresnay befriends them but is later killed. Before dying, Fresnay whispers a secret—that a diplomat will be assassinated at great embarrassment to the British Government. But, to keep Banks' lips sealed, Pilbeam is kidnaped, to be held until after the assassination by hired killer Lorre, scheduled to take place during a concert at the Albert Hall in London. After several harrowing adventures, Banks rescues his child, and Best, while standing in an aisle at the Albert Hall, spots Lorre as he is about to shoot the diplomat and screams at the appropriate moment, alerting the victim who moves and is only wounded. Lorre and the other culprits in the conspiracy are rounded up and the family is reunited at the end. Hitchcock handles the story with swift and sure decision, his scenes quickly paced and full of inventive setups. The final scenes of the famous shoot-out, where Banks discovers the hideout where Pilbeam is being kept and rescues her while Lorre and others fire on police, are based on the infamous 1911 siege of Sidney Street where bobbies and anarchists shot it out in a bloody battle. It is in this film that Hitchcock develops for the first time many a theme he would repeat in films to come, the innocent victims suddenly caught up in a terrifying situation with apparently no way out, breathless chases in popular public places, and death appearing in an instant when least expected. Here death first appears during a nightclub act when Banks, Pilbeam, and Best are laughing while they hold the ends of an unraveling sweater being stripped from a dancer. And the suspense is constant, then accelerated toward the fearful conclusion with a bullet tearing into the heart of Fresnay. This was Lorre's first English-speaking part; he had been brought to England at Hitchcock's request after the director saw him in Fritz Lang's impressive M. Lorre, a weird person who always did the unpredictable, appealed to Hitchcock's sense of humor and his own eccentric behavior. When not shooting during the 10-week production, the director and the Hungarian actor told off-color stories to each other and played practical jokes on each other, sending strange deliveries to the other's door in the middle of the night. Lorre won at this game, having 300 singing canaries sent to Hitchcock's home at three in the morning. Hitchcock achieved an expensive look to this film when he really worked with a limited budget. For the Albert Hall scene, the most sumptuous scene in the film, he masked the huge audience by having Fortunino Matania paint most of the audience and then Hitchcock reflected the painting in a mirror to the camera lens and thus realistically staged an ambitious scene that really wasn't there. As with all his films, the masterful Hitchcock did sketches of each of his scenes and planned his setups down to the last detail before the cast and crew members ever assembled on the set. Playwright Williams was asked to spruce up some of the dialog and he did give it some zing but he was disappointed during the production. He looked forward to meeting Hitchcock but the director never appeared; Williams did all his writing at home and missed meeting England's most brilliant filmic helmsman. Hitchcock's cameraman, Courant, a German who spoke no English, pretended to understand Hitchcock's elaborate setups but then did as he pleased, which enraged the director. He upbraided Courant, speaking perfect German, before the entire crew and the admonished cinematographer became immediately submissive, shooting the scenes exactly as Hitchcock wanted them. During the production, Hitchcock happened to see Mervyn LeRoy's masterpiece, I AM A FUGITIVE FROM A CHAIN GANG, and noticed a harrowing scene in a barber chair where Paul Muni's face is hidden from police by a hot towel. He had planned on using that very scene in THE MAN WHO KNEW TOO MUCH but changed it so as not to be accused of copying and reworked the scene into a much more frightening chair, that of a dentist, a scene where Banks gives knockout gas to a pursuer. (This same ploy was used in an Errol Flynn film, FOOTSTEPS IN THE DARK, a direct lift from Hitchcock.) Hitchcock did not like child actors but he got along so well with Pilbeam that he gave her her first adult leading role in his film, YOUNG AND INNOCENT, three years later.

p, Michael Balcon; d, Alfred Hitchcock; w, A. R. Rawlinson, Charles Bennett, D. B. Wyndham-Lewis, Emlyn Williams, Edwin Greenwood (based on a story by Bennett, Wyndham-Lewis); ph, Curt Courant; m, Arthur Benjamin; ed, H. St. C. Stewart; md, Louis Levy; art d & set d, Alfred Junge, Peter Proud.

Crime Drama **Cas.** **(PR:C MPAA:NR)**

MAN WHO KNEW TOO MUCH, THE****

(1956) 120m PAR c

James Stewart *(Dr. Ben McKenna)*, Doris Day *(Jo McKenna)*, Brenda de Banzie *(Mrs. Drayton)*, Bernard Miles *(Mr. Drayton)*, Ralph Truman *(Buchanan)*, Daniel Gelin *(Louis Bernard)*, Mogens Wieth *(Ambassador)*, Alan Mowbray *(Val Parnell)*, Hillary Brooke *(Jan Peterson)*, Christopher Olsen *(Hank McKenna)*, Reggie Nalder *(Rien the Assassin)*, Richard Wattis *(Assistant Manager)*, Noel Willman *(Woburn)*, Alix Talton *(Helen Parnell)*, Yves Brainville *(Police Inspector)*, Carolyn Jones *(Cindy Fontaine)*, Abdelhaq Chraibi, Lou Krugman *(Arabs)*, Betty Baskcomb *(Edna)*, Leo Gordon *(Chauffeur)*, Patrick Aherne *(English Handyman)*, Louis Mercier, Anthony Warde *(French Police)*, Lewis Martin *(Detective)*, Gladys Holland *(Bernard's Girl Friend)*, John O'Malley *(Uniformed Attendant)*, Peter Camlin *(Headwaiter)*, Albert Carrier *(French Policeman)*, Ralph Heff *(Henchman)*, John Marshall *(Butler)*, Eric Snowden *(Special Branch Officer)*, Edward Manouk *(French Waiter)*, Donald Lawton *(Desk Clerk)*, Patrick Whyte *(Special Branch Officer)*, Mahin S. Shahrivar *(Arab Woman)*, Alex Frazer *(Man)*, Allen Zeidman *(Assistant Manager)*, Milton Frome, Walter Gotell *(Guards)*, Frank Atkinson, Liddell Peddieson, Mayne Lynton, John Barrard *(Workmen in Taxidermist Shop)*, Alexis Bobrinsky *(Foreign Prime Minister)*, Janet Bruce *(Box Office Woman)*, Naida Buckingham *(Lady in the Audience)*, Clifford Buckton *(Sir Kenneth Clarke)*, Barbara Burke *(Girl Friend of the Assassin)*, Pauline Farr *(Ambassador's Wife)*, Harry Fine *(Edington)*, Wolf Priess *(Aide to Foreign Prime Minister)*, George Howe *(Ambrose Chappell, Sr.)*, Harold Kasket *(Butler)*, Barry Keegan *(Patterson)*, Lloyd Lamble *(General Manager of Albert Hall)*, Enid Lindsey *(Lady Clarke)*, Janet Macfarlane *(Lady in Audience)*, Leslie Newport *(Inspector at Albert Hall)*, Elsa Palmer *(Woman Cook)*, Arthur Ridley *(Ticket Collector)*, Alma Taylor *(Box Office Woman)*, Guy Verney *(Footman)*, Peter Williams *(Police Sergeant)*, Richard Wordsworth *(Ambrose Chappell, Jr.)*.

The original version of this film so appealed to Hitchcock that he felt it could take a remake and survive. He also felt he could improve upon it which is still in debate. Though the director altered some locales, he kept the original story fairly much intact and heightened the tale with a much more lavish production than his 1935 film received. Further intensifying this topflight thriller is Stewart's performance, and that of songbird Day, both sweetly innocent and unsuspecting tourists whose vacation in French Morocco turns into a nightmare. Stewart, a doctor, and Day, a former musical star, and their son, Olsen, are enjoying their holiday when they meet a friendly British couple, de Banzie and Miles. Frenchman Gelin also befriends them and asks them to dinner. They show up at the restaurant where they run into de Banzie and Miles, dining with them when Gelin fails to show up. Halfway through the dinner, Gelin does appear but he ignores them, dining with someone else, an act which infuriates Stewart. The following day, while Stewart and Day are shopping in the bazaar, an Arab runs frantically up to them after having been stabbed in the back. Stewart grabs the man as he falls and finds, to his horror, a dye coming off on his hands. Beneath the dark coloring is the Frenchman Gelin, who is in disguise. Before he dies, Gelin whispers something to Stewart. When returning to the hotel, Stewart finds that his son, Olsen, who was being taken care of by the kindly de Banzie, is gone and so too are the boy's babysitters, de Banzie and Miles, gone to England as kidnapers. He receives a call telling him that if he keeps his mouth shut about Gelin's secret, the boy will not be harmed. Stewart is concerned about telling his emotional wife so he gives Day an injection, a sedative to allay her fears, after he tells her the dreadful news about their son. After injecting Day, Stewart breaks the news to her and she still becomes hysterical before passing out. Then it's a race back to England with the authorities willing to cooperate but they know Stewart is holding back information. He is fearful of relaying Gelin's information that an important foreign diplomat is scheduled to be assassinated at the Albert Hall during a concert. Stewart, with a thin clue, decides to hunt for his boy on his own, much to the chagrin of Scotland Yard. He loses trailing Yard detectives and goes to a small manufacturing company. Before dying, Gelin had named Ambrose Chapel as one of the conspirators. Stewart confronts Chappel (Howe), an old man, and accuses him of kidnaping his son. The old man, his son, and workers then gang up on Stewart and he barely escapes with his life. He and Day later realize that Ambrose Chapel is not a person but a place and they find a little chapel where de Banzie and Miles are holding Olsen. But the kidnapers escape with the boy and Stewart barely manages to survive an attack by a group of chair-throwing thugs while his wife Day stands outside in the street at a pay phone frantically calling police. Stewart escapes the small church just as police arrive. Later, Day goes to the Albert Hall and spots the killer, Nalder, but he warns her that if she utters a word, her son will be killed instantly. But Day, standing in the aisle in the middle of the performance and seeing the assassin aiming his weapon at the diplomat in a box high above, cannot allow an innocent person to be killed. Just at the climactic musical moment, with cymbals crashing, she screams. The diplomat moves and is shot but is only wounded and the assassin is apprehended. Still, Stewart and Day do not have their son back. They are led to believe that Olsen is being held in the embassy of the wounded dignitary and accept an invitation to a party in their honor as the embassy wishes to show its gratitude for saving the diplomat's life. During the party Stewart tells his wife to sing their son's favorite tune, "Que Sera, Sera" ("Whatever Will Be, Will Be" by Jay Livingston and Ray Evans), and loudly so the boy, if he is in the embassy, will take heart and perhaps let Stewart know where he is. Day sits down at the piano and begins to sing, louder and louder, to the puzzlement of the guests. Stewart sneaks up the stairs and begins searching the long hallways, finally going up to the third floor. Day's voice is booming now, echoing upward to a room where Olsen is being held by de Banzie who knows the child is to be killed and has argued with her husband against such brutality. Olsen yells out and Stewart bursts through the door but Miles appears and holds onto the boy, threatening to shoot him. Stewart tells the boy to come to him, that he won't be harmed and, at the last minute, his wife pleading for the boy's life, Miles relents and Stewart takes his son into his arms and downstairs where Day sees the boy and runs to him. The family, once more united, leaves in safety while the diplomat in the embassy, a man wishing to usurp the chief dignitary who was wounded, is unmasked, along with his henchmen. Though there is obviously more polish and a lavish budget in this remake, the Stewart version of THE MAN WHO KNEW TOO MUCH is no more and no less impactful than the first version. Again, Hitchcock's scenes are beautifully framed and tautly directed, the pace of the child hunt accelerated gradually until suspense reaches fever pitch, in two climaxes, the assassination attempt at the Albert Hall and in the embassy search. Stewart is excellent as the hapless victim, a favorite Hitchcock hero who perfectly fit the mold of everyman. (In VERTIGO he is a victimized cop with a psychological problem dealing with heights, in other Hitchcock films, such as ROPE and REAR WINDOW, he gets involved as a curious bystander who begins to act upon the situation instead of being utterly victimized by it but nevertheless brings himself into jeopardy.) Day is surprisingly good and the "Que Sera, Sera" song was good enough to win an Oscar as Best Song, becoming a smash hit on record. The script was updated from the original and, except for the changing of the vacation locale, from Switzerland to Morocco, and the song as a code bit, the story pretty much remained intact. Hitchcock shot the film on location in Marrakesh, Morocco, and in England and Hollywood. He did use the actual Albert Hall this time (in the original version it was a set), but much of the audience was a fake as in the original. Here he employed the anxious "Storm Cloud Cantata" leading up to the assassination attempt. Hitchcock had longtime collaborator Hayes work on the script but he later brought in his old friend Angus McPhail, one-time intelligence expert, to sit in on scenes and advise the director on the bits of espionage pattering through the script. McPhail contributed little or nothing to the script and could hardly sit still on the set without shaking to pieces, such was his condition due to the advanced alcoholism that would shortly kill him. Hitchcock nevertheless insisted that McPhail get screen credit, causing Hayes to seek arbitration from the Screenwriters' Guild which decided that McPhail should receive no credit. The action caused a rupture between Hitchcock and Hayes who had written three other films for him. All four Hayes scripts, including THE MAN WHO KNEW TOO MUCH, according to the writer, brought him only $75,000 before taxes, over a three-year period of time. Hitchcock told him he had gotten valuable experience writing the films and let it go at that. The murder scene in the Marrakesh marketplace almost turned into a riot. Somehow the natives, hundreds of them, used as extras, got the word that unless they were on camera they would not get paid, so they milled and shoved and pushed their ways about so they could see the camera, almost knocking down Stewart and Day, jockeying for position. Grumbling turned to shouting, then a few fights broke out. Police had to restore order by calling in backup squads. All the while Hitchcock, wearing his traditional dark blue suit, white shirt, and nondescript tie, sat under a huge umbrella, waiting wordlessly for the crowds to tire themselves and take his soft-spoken direction.

p&d, Alfred Hitchcock; w, John Michael Hayes, Angus McPhail (based on a story by Charles Bennett, D. B. Wyndham-Lewis); ph, Richard Mueller (VistaVision, Technicolor); m, Bernard Herrmann; ed, George Tomasini; md, Herrmann; art d, Hal Pereira, Henry Bumstead; set d, Sam Comer, Arthur Krams; cos, Edith Head; spec eff, John P. Fulton; m/l, "Que Sera, Sera," "We'll Love Again," Jay Livingston, Ray Evans, "Storm Cloud Cantata," Arthur Benjamin, Wyndham-Lewis.

Crime Drama **Cas.** **(PR:A MPAA:PG)**

MAN WHO LAUGHS, THE*

(1966, Ital.) 94m Sanson/MGM c (L'UOMO CHE RIDE)

Lisa Gastoni *(Lucrezia Borgia)*, Edmund Purdom *(Cesare Borgia)*, Jean Sorel *(Astorre/Angelo)*, Ilaria Occhini *(Dea)*, Linda Sini.

Yet another tale of Lucrezia and Cesare Borgia, the infamous sex-crazed Romans of the 1500s. Sorel in a dual role plays two youngsters, Astorre and Angelo, the latter of whom is seduced by Lucrezia (Gastoni) and after an operation, replaces Astorre for political reasons. Weird Italian film which is heavy on the exploitation.

p, Joseph Fryd; d, Sergio Corbucci; w, Corbucci, E. Sanjust, A. Issaverdens, A. Bertolotto, L. Ronconi, F. Bosetti; ph, Enzo Barboni (Eastmancolor); m, Piero Piccioni; ed, Mario Serandrei.

Drama **(PR:O MPAA:NR)**

MAN WHO LIES, THE** 1/2

(1970, Czech./Fr.) 95m Como Films-C.C.F. Lux-Ceskoslovensky Film/Grove Press bw (L'HOMME QUI MENT)

Jean-Louis Trintignant *(Boris Varissa)*, Ivan Mistrik *(Jean)*, Sylvie Breal *(Maria)*, Sylvia Turbova *(Sylvia)*, Suzana Kocurikova *(Laura)*, Dominique Prado *(Lisa)*, Josef Kroner *(Frantz)*, Julius Vasek *(Man)*, Catherine Robbe-Grillet.

Trintignant is an alleged fighter with the resistance who escapes from the German forces, stumbles across his own grave, then ends up in a town where freedom fighter Mistrik is being honored. He tells everyone that he had fought with the man, but no one remembers him. He weaves his way into Mistrik's family and tries to seduce his wife. The supposedly dead freedom fighter enters and shoots Trintignant dead. Trintignant arises and begins telling his story again.

p, Jan Tomaskovic; d&w, Alain Robbe-Grillet; ph, Igor Luther; ed, Bob Wade.

Drama **(PR:C MPAA:NR)**

MAN WHO LIKED FUNERALS, THE* 1/2

(1959, Brit.) 60m Pennington-Eady/RANK bw

Leslie Phillips *(Simon Hurd)*, Susan Beaumont *(Stella)*, Bill Fraser *(Jeremy Bentham)*, Mary Mackenzie *(Hester Waring)*, Jimmy Thompson *(Lt. Hunter)*, Anita Sharp Bolster *(Lady Hunter)*, Lily Lapidus *(Ma Morelli)*, Charles Clay, Alastair Hunter, Hester Paton-Brown, Thelma Ruby, Shaun O'Riordan, Paul Stassino, Etain O'Dell, James Ottaway, Arthur Mullard, Laurence Taylor, Paul Bogdan, Marianne Stone, Michael Bird, Anthony Green, Brian Tyler.

Inane premise for a film has Phillips trying to help a boys' club by threatening to publish nasty material on people who have recently passed away. By accosting the bereaved right after the funeral, he hopes to blackmail these relatives and thus raise the needed funds for the boys' home. But he runs into problems when tangling with a gangster's family. A few good laughs are offered, but not enough to carry the film. Film also tends a bit too much toward the sentimental side in a manner that is totally unnecessary.

p, Jon Penington; d, David Eady; w, Margot Bennett (based on the story by Cicely Finn, Joan O'Connor); ph, Eric Cross.

Comedy **(PR:A MPAA:NR)**

MAN WHO LIVED AGAIN, THE***

(1936, Brit.) 61m GAU bw (GB: THE MAN WHO CHANGED HIS MIND; AKA: THE BRAINSNATCHERS; DR. MANIAC)

Boris Karloff *(Dr. Laurience)*, Anna Lee *(Dr. Claire Wyatt)*, John Loder *(Dick Haslewood)*, Frank Cellier *(Lord Haslewood)*, Donald Calthrop *(Clayton)*, Cecil Parker *(Dr. Gratton)*, Lyn Harding *(Prof. Holloway)*, Clive Morton, D. J. Williams, Brian Pawley.

Rarely seen Karloff film (as are *all* the early British Karloff films: THE GHOUL and JUGGERNAUT) shot in England in which he once again plays a mad scientist with another earth-shattering invention. This time in the lab Karloff perfects a matter-transfer device (taking one item, scrambling the atoms in the air, then reassembling them in a different location) which concentrates on shifting *brains* from one body to another. When his theories are laughed out of the scientific community and his financial supporter, Cellier, backs out, Karloff gets his revenge by transferring his former benefactor's brain into the crippled and dying body of his faithful assistant Calthrop. Unfortunately the mind-transfer is a failure and both men die. Undaunted and suddenly in love with his female assistant (Lee), Karloff decides to seduce her by promising eternal youth (wherein they would just keep transferring their minds to younger bodies through the ages). Upset when she rejects him in favor of Cellier's son Loder (who has gotten a bit suspicious about father's disappearance), Karloff forces Loder into a mind-transfer and the operation is a success. Things go bad, however, when the cops burst in and Karloff (with Loder's brain) falls out an open window during a botched escape attempt. The enraged Lee forces Karloff to submit to a re-transfer of his mind back into his now-broken and dying body (which she performs). When the transfer proves successful, a now-sane (and much nobler) Karloff decides that his secrets should die with him. Perhaps Karloff's best mad doctor role (a part which would plague his career), THE MAN WHO LIVED AGAIN also benefits from a typically fine British production with lush sets, crisp cinematography, and a literate script (the matter-transfer device would rise again, 20 years later, in THE FLY).

p, Michael Balcon; d, Robert Stevenson; w, L. DuGarde Peach, Sidney Gilliat, John L. Balderston; ph, Jack Cox; ed, R. E. Dearing, Alfred Roome; art d, Alex Vetchinsky; makeup, Roy Ashton.

Science Fiction **(PR:A MPAA:NR)**

MAN WHO LIVED TWICE** 1/2

(1936) 73m COL bw

Ralph Bellamy *(James Blake/Slick Rawley)*, Marian Marsh *(Janet Haydon)*, Thurston Hall *(Dr. Schuyler)*, Isabel Jewell *(Peggy Russell)*, Nana Bryant *(Mrs. Margaret Schuyler)*, Ward Bond *(Gloves Baker)*, Henry Kolker *(Judge Treacher)*, Willard Robertson *(Logan)*, Ed Keane.

Bellamy is a scarred murderer on the run who takes refuge in a hospital where he overhears a doctor's new scientific theories. He has the doctor perform a type of surgery which will alter Bellamy's brain and face, making him into a newer, better person. With a new name (James Blake), Bellamy rises to the top of the medical profession, but soon his past resurfaces sending him before a judge. He is convicted for his crime, but soon afterwards pardoned by the governor. Remade as MAN IN THE DARK with Edmond O'Brien in the lead.

p, Ben Pivar; d, Harry Lachman; w, Tom Van Dycke, Fred Niblo, Jr., Arthur Strawn (based on the story by Van Dycke, Henry Altimus); ph, James Van Trees; ed, Byron Robinson.

Crime/Drama **Cas.** **(PR:A MPAA:NR)**

MAN WHO LOST HIMSELF, THE**   (1941) 72m UNIV bw

Brian Aherne (John Evans/Malcolm Scott), Kay Francis (Adrienne Scott), Henry Stephenson (Frederick Collins), S. Z. Sakall (Paul), Eden Gray (Venetia Scott), Nils Asther (Peter Ransome), Sig Rumann (Dr. Simms), Dorothy Tree (Mrs. Van Avery), Janet Beecher (Mrs. Milford), Marc Lawrence (Frank DeSoto), Henry Kolker (T. J. Mulhausen), Sarah Padden (Mrs. Cummings, the Maid), Henry Roquemore (Bartender), Frederick Burton (Mr. Milford), Margaret Armstrong (Mrs. Van der Girt), Russell Hicks (Mr. Van der Girt), Selmer Jackson (Mr. Green), William Gould (Mr. Ryan), Ethel Clifton (Maid), Paul Bryar (Bar Waiter), Irene Colman (Office Girl), Cyril Ring (Relative), Frank O'Connor (Cab Driver), Lloyd Whitlock (Attendant), Billy Benedict (Messenger Boy), Billy Engel (Newsboy), Wilson Benge (Butler).

Aherne in a dual role plays a Puerto Rican adventurer who is drinking with an eccentric millionaire look-alike. They end up in each other's homes, but the millionaire dies in a car accident which leads to a case of mistaken identity. His wife does not know that he is alive as he tries to untangle the mess he is in. Sort of a version of THE PASSENGER, but with a sense of humor.

p, Lawrence W. Fox, Jr.; d, Edward Ludwig; w, Eddie Moran (based on the novel by H. DeVere Stacpoole); ph, Victor Milner; ed, Milton Carruth; md, Charles Previn.

Comedy   (PR:A   MPAA:NR)

MAN WHO LOST HIS WAY, THE   (SEE: CROSSROADS, 1942)

MAN WHO LOVED CAT DANCING, THE**   (1973) 114m MGM c

Burt Reynolds (Jay Grobart), Sarah Miles (Catherine Crocker), Lee J. Cobb (Lapchance), Jack Warden (Dawes), George Hamilton (Crocker), Bo Hopkins (Billy), Robert Donner (Dub), Sandy Kevin (Ben), Larry Littlebird (Iron Knife), Nancy Malone (Sudie), Jay Silverheels (The Chief), Jay Varela (Charlie), Sutero Garcia, Jr. (Grobart's Son), Larry Finley (Bartender), Owen Bush (Conductor).

In this new twist of an Old West story, Reynolds plays an outlaw on the run for murdering his wife's killer and rapist, and from a robbery committed with outlaw pals Warden and Hopkins. Miles is a woman on the run from her abusive husband, Hamilton. She's attracted to Reynolds' strength, his quiet, reflective manner, and his devoted love of the memory of his Indian wife, Cat Dancing. She spends a good part of the movie being dragged, beaten, and almost raped by Warden and Hopkins, but slowly she and Reynolds fall in love and she travels across country with him to the Indian village where his son lives. Cobb plays the bounty hunter after Reynolds, who is joined in the search by Hamilton. This was Reynolds' first big role, based on the first novel of an Indiana housewife, and it won him the recognition he had spent years in bit parts trying to achieve. It was a box office hit, and opened the door to his successful career. He went on to make several other films with Hopkins, including a movie with a similar, though modern-day tale, SMOKEY AND THE BANDIT.

p, Martin Poll, Eleanor Perry; d, Richard G. Sarafian; w, Perry (based on the novel by Marilyn Durham); ph, Harry Stradling, Jr. (Metrocolor, Panavision); m, John Williams; ed, Tom Rolf; art d, Edward C. Carfagno; set d, Ralph C. Hurst; cos, Frank Thompson.

Western   **Cas.**   (PR:C-O   MPAA:PG)

MAN WHO LOVED REDHEADS, THE***   (1955, Brit.) 89m LFP/UA c

Moira Shearer (Sylvia/Daphne/Olga/Colette), John Justin (Mark St. Neots), Roland Culver (Oscar), Gladys Cooper (Caroline), Denholm Elliott (Denis), Harry Andrews (Williams), Patricia Cutts (Bubbles), John Hart (Sergei), Moyra Fraser (Ethel), Joan Benham (Chloe), Jeremy Spencer (Young Mark), Melvyn Hayes (Sidney).

An engaging British comedy that follows the romantic escapades of Justin, who as a young boy falls eternally in love with a redhead. As he sexually ripens, his desire for carrot-tops does not decrease. The object of his passion is ballerina Shearer who fills four pairs of shoes—his first love, a cockney lass, a Russian dancer, and a mannequin. In the end, Justin's wife, Cooper, reveals to him that she has known about his redhead affairs all along. The film leaves us with an ironic twist, when Justin doesn't recognize his aged first love among his dinner guests.

p, Josef Somlo; d, Harold French; w, Terence Rattigan (based on the play "Who Is Sylvia?" by Rattigan); ph, Georges Perinal (Eastmancolor); m, Benjamin Frankel; ed, Bert Bates; set d, Paul Sheriff; ch, Alan Carter (with excerpts from Tchaikovsky's "The Sleeping Beauty"); cos, Loudon Sainthill.

Comedy   (PR:A   MPAA:NR)

MAN WHO LOVED WOMEN, THE***
(1977, Fr.) 119m Les Films du Carrosse-Les Productions Artistes Associes/Cinema
                                  5 c (L'HOMME QUI AIMAIT LES FEMMES)

Charles Denner (Bertrand Morane), Brigitte Fossey (Genevieve Bigey), Nelly Borgeaud (Delphine Grezel), Leslie Caron (Vera), Genevieve Fontanel (Helene), Nathalie Baye (Martine Desdoits), Sabine Glaser (Bernadette), Valerie Bonnier (Fabienne), Martine Chassing (Denise), Roselyne Puyo (Nicole), Anna Perrier (Uta), Monique Dury (Mme. Duteil), Nella Barbier (Lilliane), Anonymous (Aurore), Frederique Jamet (Juliette), M. J. Montfaion (Christine Morane), Jean Daste (Doctor), Roger Leenhardt (Mons. Betany), Henri Agel (Lecturer), Jean Servat (Lecturer), Michel Marti (Bertrand as a Child).

This swiftly paced, light-hearted exercise in obsessive passion by Truffaut is filled with subtle insights into what creates such extreme desires as those depicted by Denner, the "man" of the title. A well-off researcher, Denner is the most woman crazy man ever to appear on film. He can't keep his mind off women, with the mere glance at a woman in black silk stockings sending him on a long journey to find the rest of the person who possesses such a fine set of gams. All the while that Denner is chasing skirts, he remains charming and innocent, never feeling as if he is doing anything wrong, just attempting to satisfy his desire. None of the numerous women

whom he seduces ever have any grudges about the way Denner carries on with other women, and all seem to gain a needed satisfaction through these affairs. It is Denner's obsession that leads to his eventual death; chasing the pair of legs he caught sight of at the beginning of the film, he is run over by a car. Then in the hospital, a pretty nurse walks by his bed, forcing Denner to reach after her behind and disconnecting his life-support system. His funeral, where the film also began, is peopled with what appears to be dozens of his conquests, all mourning at the loss of this dearly loved man. At one point, Denner sits down to write his memoirs, working all night long to get his various amours down on paper. It would seem that his obsessive nature lay in his unfulfilling relationship with his mother, a woman who really had no room for a child, and carried on a number of affairs with men. Fossey, the editor who has been reading these writings, is also one of Denner's affairs, and is herself obsessed with what it was that made this man need women so much. THE MAN WHO LOVED WOMEN is filled with Truffaut's sense of ironic humor, is always charming, and never in any way offending. Like all of Truffaut's romantic comedies, what appears as flippant and sugary is actually a cover for some very complex statements about the nature of love, Truffaut himself, and the cinema. A Hollywood remake of this film was made in 1983 directed by Blake Edwards and starring Burt Reynolds; it possessed quite a bit of merit in its own right. (In French; English subtitles.)

d, Francois Truffaut; w, Truffaut, Michel Fermaud, Suzanne Schiffman; ph, Nestor Almendros; m, Maurice Jaubert; ed, Martine Barraque-Curie.

Drama/Comedy   **Cas.**   (PR:O   MPAA:NR)

MAN WHO LOVED WOMEN, THE* 1/2   (1983) 118m COL c

Burt Reynolds (David), Julie Andrews (Marianna), Kim Basinger (Louise), Marilu Henner (Agnes), Cynthia Sikes (Courtney), Jennifer Edwards (Nancy), Sela Ward (Janet), Ellen Bauer (Svetlana), Denise Crosby (Enid), Tracy Vaccaro (Legs), Barry Corbin (Roy), Ben Powers (Al), Jill Carroll (Sue), Schweitzer Tanney (Doctor), Regis Philbin (Regis Philbin), Joseph Bernard (Dr. Simon Abrams), John J. Flynn, Jr. (Henry), Jim Knaub (Carl), Jim Lewis (Lt. Cranzano), Roger Rose (Sgt. Stone), Jennifer Ashley (David's Mother), Tony Brown (David at 16), Philip Alexander (David at 12), Jonathan Rogal (David at 8), Margie Denecke (Aerobics Instructor), Jerry Martin (Man at Barbeque), Sharon Hughes, Nanci Rogers (Nurses), Cindi Dietrich (Darla), Kai J. Wong, Walter Soo Hoo, Marilyn Child, Arnie Moore, Lisa Blake Richards, Noni White, Lynn Webb, Jason Ross, Alisa Lee, Shelly Manne, Don Menza, James G. Rowles, Andrew Simpkins, Los Angeles Ballet.

Edwards' remake of Truffaut's 1977 comedy falls miles short of the original and what we've seen Edwards capable of creating. Reynolds plays a sculptor who is an incurable womanizer. He pays a visit to psychiatrist Andrews in the hopes of removing a creative block he's been experiencing, and instead falls for her and she for him. Although Edwards may have been attempting a humorous study of man's fragilities, this clumsilydone comedy fails with its unoriginal story line, comedy routines, and pat answers. One co-writer credited is none other than Edwards' own psychiatrist.

p, Blake Edwards, Tony Adams; d, Edwards; w, Edwards, Milton Wexler, Geoffrey Edwards (based on a comedy by Francois Truffaut); ph, Haskell Wexler (Metrocolor); m, Henry Mancini; ed, Ralph E. Winters; prod d, Roger Maus; art d, Jack Senter; set d, Dianne I. Wager, Jacques Valin; cos, Ann Roth; m/l, Mancini, Alan Bergman, Marilyn Bergman (theme song sung by Helen Reddy).

Comedy   **Cas.**   (PR:O   MPAA:R)

MAN WHO MADE DIAMONDS, THE** 1/2   (1937, Brit.) 73m WB-FN bw

Noel Madison (Joseph), James Stephenson (Ben), Lesley Brook (Helen Calthrop), George Galleon (Tony), Renee Gadd (Marianne), Wilfrid Lawson (Gallanie), Philip Ray (Tompkins), J. Fisher White (Prof. Calthrop), Hector Abbas (Nichols), Jim Regan, Dino Galvani.

Professor White develops a formula for manufacturing diamonds and is murdered for it by assistant Madison. Brook, White's daughter, investigates the case and almost pays for it with her life before she is rescued by detective Galleon. Better than average for this kind of thing.

p, Irving Asher; d, Ralph Ince; w, Michael Barringer, Anthony Hankey (based on a story by Frank A. Richardson); ph, Basil Emmott.

Crime   (PR:A   MPAA:NR)

MAN WHO NEVER WAS, THE***   (1956, Brit.) 103m Sumar/FOX c

Clifton Webb (Lt. Cmdr. Ewen Montagu), Gloria Grahame (Lucy), Robert Flemyng (George Acres), Josephine Griffin (Pam), Stephen Boyd (O'Reilly), Andre Morell (Sir Bernard Spilsbury), Laurence Naismith (Adm. Cross), Geoffrey Keen (Gen. Nye), Michael Hordern (Gen. Coburn), Moultrie Kelsall (The Father), Cyril Cusack (Taxi Driver), Joan Hickson (Landlady), William Russell (Joe), Richard Wattis (Shop Assistant), Allan Cuthbertson (Vice-Admiral), Terence Longden (Larry), Brian Oulton (Wills Officer), William Squire (Lt. Jewell), Ronald Adam (Adams), Miles Malleson (Scientist), Gibb McLaughlin (Club Porter), Peter Williams (Adm. Mountbatten), Michael Brill (Doctor), John Welsh (Bank Manager), Cecily Paget-Bowman (Secretary), Robert Brown (French), Everly Gregg (Club Matron), Lloyd Lamble (Passport Officer), Gordon Bell (Customs Officer), Wolf Frees (Adm. Canaris), Gerhard Puritz (German Colonel), D. A. Clarke-Smith (Laurence, a Consul), Peter Sellers (Voice of Winston Churchill), Ewen Montagu.

Based on fact, stupendous fact and ruse that is, THE MAN WHO NEVER WAS provides marvelous entertainment and not too few thrills. Webb is a British intelligence officer who conceives an elaborate, even outlandish hoax to outwit the Germans in WW II, gulling them into believing that the Allies intend to invade Greece, not Sicily, in 1943. He suggests to superior Naismith and others that a body be put adrift to float ashore so that German intelligence will find it and believe the tale that it tells—that the Allies do not plan to invade Sicily as expected, but Greece, in order that German reserve units may be shifted to that locale and away from the heart of the attack, Sicily. After receiving permission to go ahead with what the high command skeptically considers an impractical plan, Webb, his assistant Flemyng, and others locate the body of a young man, Kelsall's son, and preserve it while a fake identity is created. The dead man becomes "Major Martin," an intelligence officer who carries not only military identification but other papers that establish the fact that he is a club member and has a bank account. Moreover—thanks to a suggestion of Griffin, another Webb aide—he has a fiancee and carries a love letter written to him by Griffin. Inside a briefcase handcuffed to him is information that clearly spells out the details of an Allied invasion of Greece. To make the finding of this body less suspicious, Webb accompanies the preserved-in-dry-ice body on a submarine which surfaces off the coast of Spain; the body is left adrift to float in with the tide near Huelva. Rightfully concluding that the Fascist regime would allow its German allies to inspect the corpse, the British soon learn that German intelligence has examined and copied everything found on the body, then returned every document to its rightful place before the Spanish turn the effects over to the British, along with the body. At first the British are uncertain as to whether or not the Germans will take the bait. They soon learn that Nazi intelligence is cautious but considering "Major Martin" to have been a real entity. The Germans send one of their top agents operating in England to check on the dead man. This clever spy is Irishman Boyd who arrives in London and checks with the dead man's bank; the bank official contacts Webb and other British agents and Boyd is closely watched. He is seen going to the dead man's private club and inquiring about his membership. When he learns that the dead man is a member he is almost persuaded, but he goes one bold step further, contacting the dead man's "girl friend." Here, however, he makes a mistake and meets the wrong girl, Grahame. She is really the right girl, since Griffin used her name in writing the letter but, when Griffin tries to impersonate her, things get mixed up and Grahame returns home just when Boyd appears. Ironically, Grahame has just lost her fiancee in the war and is distraught to the point of hysteria. Boyd believes she truly has lost her fiance, "Major Martin," and goes to his short-wave radio to report the dead man as "genuine" to his German masters. The Germans transfer whole divisions to the inactive Greek front, which allows the Allies to make a "soft" landing on Sicily. The fabulous ruse saves countless lives and, following the war, Webb visits the dead man's grave, placing a medal there. The final scene repeats the first scene shown, a body washing ashore and an echoing voice saying: "Last night, I dreamt a dead man won the fight." Neame's direction is faultless and the tension is maintained throughout this splendid film. Webb, who could often slip into super-sophistication or silly comedy, held a tight reign on his histrionics here and performed admirably. Boyd is a convincing spy, filled with guile and suspicion and, in his bit part as the father of the dead man, Kelsall is excellent. Griffin is effective as Webb's aide, as is Flemyng, but Grahame—normally a superb actress—goes awry here, overacting to the point of embarrassment.

p, Andre Hakim; d, Ronald Neame; w, Nigel Balchin (based on the book by Ewen Montagu); ph, Oswald Morris (CinemaScope, DeLuxe Color); m, Muir Mathieson.

Spy Drama **(PR:A MPAA:NR)**

MAN WHO PAWNED HIS SOUL (SEE: UNKNOWN BLOND, 1934)

MAN WHO PLAYED GOD, THE 1/2**
(1932) 81m WB bw (GB: THE SILENT VOICE)

George Arliss *(Montgomery Royale)*, Violet Heming *(Mildred Miller)*, Ivan Simpson *(Battle)*, Louise Closser Hale *(Florence Royale)*, Bette Davis *(Grace Blair)*, Andre Luguet *(The King)*, Donald Cook *(Harold Van Adam)*, Charles E. Evans *(The Doctor)*, Oscar Apfel *(The Lip Reader)*, Paul Porcasi *(French Concert Manager)*, Raymond Milland *(Eddie)*, Dorothy Libaire *(Jenny)*, William Janney *(First Boy)*, Grace Durkin *(First Girl)*, Russell Hopton *(Reporter)*, Murray Kinnell *(King's Aide)*, Harry Stubbs *(Chittendon)*, Hedda Hopper *(Alice Chittendon, His Wife)*, Wade Boteler *(Detective)*, Alexander Ikonikoff, Michael Visaroff, Paul Panzer *(Russian Officers)*, Fred Howard.

Concert pianist Arliss performs a private concert for king Luguet but loses his hearing when an anarchist throws a bomb into the palace in an assassination attempt. Depressed and at the end of his career, Arliss returns to his home town of New York with his fiancee Davis. After a suicide attempt, Arliss discovers that he can read lips. He spends all of his time staring into nearby Central Park, eavesdropping on people's conversations. He becomes generous, bestowing upon the unfortunates various gifts. When he "overhears" a conversation between Davis and Cook, the man she really loves, Arliss allows her to break off the engagement, knowing that she is staying only to serve him. He then donates a pipe organ to a church where he proceeds to play hymns which he cannot hear, but feel. The religious overtones are excessive, but the subject matter allows for them and diminishes any feeling of intrusion. Arliss does a fine job, returning to the roles he first played in the 1922 silent version. Davis makes her first Warner Brothers appearance, and there are also bits from Hedda Hopper and a young Ray Milland. Remade in 1955 as SINCERELY YOURS with Liberace.

p, Jack L. Warner; d, John G. Adolfi; w, Julien Josephson, Maude Howell (based on a short story by Gouverneur Morris, and the play "The Silent Voice" by Jules Eckert Goodman); ph, James Van Trees; m, Salvatore Santaella; ed, William Holmes.

Drama **(PR:A MPAA:NR)**

MAN WHO RECLAIMED HIS HEAD, THE*** (1935) 82m UNIV bw

Claude Rains *(Paul Verin)*, Joan Bennett *(Adele Verin)*, Lionel Atwill *(Henri Dumont)*, Juanity [Baby Jane] Quigley *(Linette Verin)*, Bessie Barriscale *(Louise, Maid)*, Henry O'Neill *(Fernand DeMarney)*, Lawrence Grant *(Marchand)*, William B. Davidson *(Charlus)*, G. P. Huntley, Jr. *(Pierre)*, Valerie Hobson *(Mimi, Carnival Girl)*, Wallace Ford *(Curly)*, Ferdinand Gottschalk *(Baron)*, Hugh O'Connell *(Danglas)*, Henry Armetta *(Laurent)*, Doris Lloyd *(Lulu)*, Noel Francis *(Chon-Chon, Curly's Girl)*, Carol Coombe *(Clerk)*, Phyllis Brooks *(Secretary)*, Gilbert Emery *(His Excellency)*, Walter Walker, Edward Martindel, Crauford Kent, Montague Shaw *(Dignitaries)*, Purnell Pratt, Jameson Thomas, Edward Van Sloan *(Munitions Board Directors)*, Judith Wood *(Margot)*, James Donlan *(Man in Theater Box)*, Rollo Lloyd *(Jean)*, Lloyd Hughes *(Andre, Dumont's Secretary)*, Bryant Washburn, Sr. *(Antoine)*, Boyd Irwin *(Petty Officer)*, Anderson Lawler *(Jack)*, Will Stanton *(Drunk Soldier)*, George Davis *(Lorry Driver)*, Lionel Belmore *(Train Conductor)*, Emerson Treacy *(French Student/Attacked Pacifist)*, John Rutherford, Hyram A. Hoover, Lee Phelps *(Soldiers)*, Rudy Cameron *(Maitre D')*, Norman Ainsley *(Steward)*, Russ Powell *(Station Master)*, Harry Cording *(French Mechanic)*, Lilyan Irene *(Woman Shopper)*, William Ruhl *(Shopper's Husband)*, Rolfe Sedan *(Waiter)*, Ben F. Hendricks *(Chauffeur)*, Maurice Murphy *(Leon)*, William Gould *(Man)*, Carl Stockdale *(Tradesman)*, Tom Ricketts, Joseph Swickard, William West, Colin Kenny *(Citizens)*, Ted Billings *(Newsboy)*, William Worthington *(Attendant)*, Nell Craig, Grace Cunard *(Women)*, Wilfred North *(Bit)*, Russ Clark *(French Truck Driver)*, John Ince *(Speaker)*, Margaret Mann *(Granny)*.

An odd one about a ghost writer, Rains, who turns out brilliantly inspiring pieces on the evils of war and the immorality of the warmongers. He is sent by his publisher, Atwill, into the most dangerous WW I fronts, so the latter can court Rains' wife. While on the front he continues to preach peace, but when he suddenly decides to head home, he finds Atwill with his wife and proceeds to behead his boss. A strong anti-war statement which details the effects that constant, widespread killing can have on the peaceful individual. Bennett turns in a fine performance, as does Quigley, better known as Baby Jane, who can't help but steal all the scenes she is in.

p, Carl Laemmle, Jr.; d, Edward Ludwig; w, Jean Bart [Marie Antoinette Sarlabous], Samuel Ornitz (based on the play by Bart); ph, Merritt Gerstad; ed, Murray Seldeen.

Drama **(PR:A MPAA:NR)**

MAN WHO RETURNED TO LIFE, THE** (1942) 61m COL bw

John Howard *(David Jameson)*, Lucile Fairbanks *(Jane Bishop)*, Ruth Ford *(Beth Beebe)*, Marcelle Martin *(Daphne Turner)*, Roger Clark *(Harland Walker)*, Elizabeth Risdon *(Minerva Sunday)*, Paul Guilfoyle *(Clyde Beebe)*, Clancy Cooper *(Clem Beebe)*, Helen MacKellar *(Ma Beebe)*, Kenneth MacDonald *(Constable Foster)*, Carol Coombs *(Marjorie Bishop)*.

Howard stars here in a good idea which just doesn't deliver. After leaving a Southern town without a trace and resettling in California with a wife, Howard reads in the paper that a man is about to be hanged for his murder. He returns to his home town, thereby saving the victim who is really the recipient of the locals' anti-Yankee sentiments.

p, Wallace MacDonald; d, Lew Landers; w, Gordon Rigby (based on the story by Samuel W. Taylor); ph, Philip Tannura; ed, Arthur Seid; md, M. W. Stoloff; art d, Lionel Banks.

Drama **(PR:A MPAA:NR)**

MAN WHO SHOT LIBERTY VALANCE, THE***
(1962) 123m Ford/PAR bw

James Stewart *(Ransom Stoddard)*, John Wayne *(Tom Doniphon)*, Vera Miles *(Hallie Stoddard)*, Lee Marvin *(Liberty Valance)*, Edmond O'Brien *(Dutton Peabody)*, Andy Devine *(Link Appleyard)*, Ken Murray *(Doc Willoughby)*, John Carradine *(Maj. Cassius Starbuckle)*, Jeanette Nolan *(Nora Ericson)*, John Qualen *(Peter Ericson)*, Willis Bouchey *(Jason Tully)*, Carleton Young *(Maxwell Scott)*, Woody Strode *(Pompey)*, Denver Pyle *(Amos Carruthers)*, O. Z. Whitehead *(Ben Carruthers)*, Paul Birch *(Mayor Winder)*, Joseph Hoover *(Hasbrouck)*, Anna Lee *(Passenger)*, Charles Seel *(President, Election Council)*, Leonard Baker *(Man)*, Larry Finley *(Bar X Man)*, Daniel Borzage, Ralph Volkie *(Townsmen)*, Charles Morton, Mike Edward Jaurequi *(Drummers)*, Brian "Slim" Hightower *(Shotgun)*, Jack Williams, Charles Hayward, Chuck Roberson, Mario Arteaga *(Henchmen)*, George "Shug" Fisher *(Kaintuck the Drunk)*, Ted Mapes *(Highpockets)*, Ronald "Jack" Pennick *(Jack the Bartender)*, Bob Morgan *(Roughrider)*, Earle Hodgins *(Clue Dumfries)*, Monty Montana *(Politician on Horseback)*, Strother Martin *(Floyd)*, Lee Van Cleef *(Reese)*, Robert F. Simon *(Handy Strong)*, Stuart Holmes, Dorothy Phillips, Buddy Roosevelt, Gertrude Astor, Eva Novak, Slim Talbot, Bill Henry, John B. Whiteford, Helen Gibson, Major Sam Harris, Jack Kenny.

This is a solid, if overrated, Ford western, one which has its share of cliches and predictability, but it's still fascinating to watch Wayne and Stewart deal with hellion Marvin in a fast-changing West. The movie opens after the story is all over, in 1910, when Stewart, a U.S. senator, and his wife, Miles, return to the western town of Shinbone. They have come unannounced and unexpected to attend Wayne's funeral, which piques the interest of a local reporter who quizzes them about their interest in this obscure dead rancher. Stewart, with Miles' approval, begins to tell the reporter exactly how he came to know Wayne and the movie goes into flashback to a time when Shinbone was in its wild and woolly days. At that time Stewart is a fledgling lawyer who has no place to practice and no clients interested in any kind of law other than what comes out of a six-gun. The man with the most deadly gun is Marvin, the dreaded Liberty Valance, who goes nowhere without two killer nitwits, Van Cleef and Martin. Stewart is waylaid by Valance and his men just as he enters Shinbone territory; they believe he is an agitator for statehood, exactly what a group of powerful businessmen do not want. Valance, of course, is the western thug working for this clique and he brutally beats up Stewart and leaves him for dead. Wayne finds him on the trail and takes him to town, finding him a restaurant where he can take shelter and recuperate. When Stewart goes to work in the restaurant owned by Qualen, where Miles is the cook, he is ridiculed for his awkward efforts as a waiter, Marvin and his boys tripping and insulting him at every turn. Stewart sleeps in the kitchen and continues to practice law by lamplight, ignoring challenges from the drunken cowboys who vex him. Miles is attracted to him but it's obvious to everyone, especially Wayne, that she will be his wife. Wayne and a drunken editor of a little newspaper, O'Brien, are the only people who have ever stood up to Marvin. He fears Wayne and hates O'Brien, who is constantly printing unkind remarks about him. In one scene inside the restaurant, Wayne orders a steak and when Stewart tries to serve it, Marvin trips him and the steak goes flying onto the floor. Marvin and Van Cleef guffaw like the cretinous goons they are, and Marvin revels in Stewart's refusal to face him with a gun over the repeated insults, calling the lawyer "yellow." Wayne stands all the way up and marches over to Marvin and tells him to pick up the steak, *his* steak. Marvin sneers and stands up, his hand twitching toward his gun, but he thinks twice about it. He picks up the steak but intends to deal with Wayne later. Stewart lobbies for statehood and wins an election, with Wayne's help, as a delegate to the convention to ratify statehood. This causes Marvin to explode and he tells Stewart he will return to Shinbone and kill him. Stewart tries to learn how to use a six-gun but even Wayne cannot teach him the finer arts of gunfighting and Stewart puts his trust in his lawyer's shingle, hanging it out in O'Brien's newspaper office. O'Brien prints one editorial too many and Marvin and his goons pay him a visit, pistol-whipping him and wrecking his press. Marvin also orders Stewart to face him that night in the streets of Shinbone and the enraged Stewart gets his gun. It is dark when the two men meet and several shots are fired. Marvin falls dead and Stewart is hailed as a hero and, on the strength of his shootout with outlaw Marvin, he is elected U.S. senator, marrying Miles who has always loved him. When Wayne hears that his girl, or the girl he has always taken for granted as his girl, Miles, will be Stewart's wife, he returns to his ranch and sets it on fire, almost burning with it, but is saved at the last moment by his trusty friend and worker, Strode. Stewart cannot stand the fact that he is being elected to office for killing a man and is about to walk out on the nomination when Wayne takes him aside and tells him that he, not Stewart, shot the outlaw from the shadows, that he did it because Miles came to him and asked him to save Stewart's life, and that he did it only for Miles. Stewart now must continue to take the credit for the killing for Miles' sake, Wayne tells him, and he does. Later, Stewart is about to become governor of the state he helped to create and begins to back down from the undeserved reputation he has earned in the Valance shooting as a law-and-order candidate. And again, Wayne appears, as Stewart's conscience, and tells him he must go on fighting for the right and for the belief Miles has in him. Stewart goes on to become governor and later serves with great distinction in Washington. Wayne lives in obscurity until passing on, which brings the film fully around to the present again. The reporter listening to the story begins to tear up the notes he has taken. Stewart says: "You're not going to use the story?" Replies the reporter, quoting his late but great editor, O'Brien: "It ain't news. This is the West. When the legend becomes the fact, print the legend!" Starkly photographed and often heavily screened for nighttime shots, Ford's picture of the West here is a gloomy one, murky and often pitch black when the only thing that comes out of it is beast Marvin. He allows many cliches and stereotypes to people the film. The crusading newspaper editor beaten to pulp is not new and had been used in many an earlier western, notably DODGE CITY. Oddly Ford, the master of great western exterior scenes, shot the entire film on two Paramount sound stages. Auteur critics and others read much into this rather routine Ford film where the insights and value judgments existed only in their inventive and superlative-clutching minds. The movie is certainly above average, thanks to the performances by Stewart and Wayne, but Marvin is so flamboyant a badman that he is simply a caricature, more than his outlandish Oscar-winning performance in CAT BALLOU. The script was slightly above average; on the whole, this was simply a quick reworking of a standard western yarn.

p, Willis Goldbeck; d, John Ford; w, Goldbeck, James Warner Bellah (based on a story by Dorothy M. Johnson); ph, William H. Clothier; m. Cyril J. Mockridge, Alfred Newman; ed, Otho Lovering; art d, Hal Pereira, Eddie Imazu; set d, Sam Comer, Darrell Silvera; cos, Edith Head; makeup, Wally Westmore.

Western **Cas.** **(PR:A MPAA:NR)**

MAN WHO STOLE THE SUN, THE**
(1980, Jap.) 130m Kitty bw (TAIYO O NUSUNDA OTOKO)

Kenji Sawada *(Makoto Kido)*, Bunta Sugawara *(Yamashita)*, Kimiko Ikegami, Yutaka Mizutani, Toshiyuki Nishida, Yonosuke Ito.

In this black comedy idea, Japanese pop idol Sawada is a science teacher who builds an atomic bomb in his apartment and threatens to use it if the government doesn't meet his strange demands. He wants the rock band The Rolling Stones to be allowed to give a concert, even though they aren't allowed in Japan because of their drug arrest records. He also demands that the TV networks broadcast baseball games to their end, rather than have them cut off at the strict Japanese closedown times. The teacher doesn't get his demands and he is pursued throughout the movie by detective Sugawara. In the process, he falls in love with a crazy disc jockey. Unfortunately, this New Wave Japanese picture runs out of steam before the finale, allowing for ridiculous plot turns and a curt ending. (In Japanese; English subtitles.)

d, Kazuhiko Hasegawa; w, Hasegawa, Leonard Schrader; ph, Tatsuo Suzuki; m, Takayuki Inoue.

Comedy **(PR:C MPAA:NR)**

MAN WHO TALKED TOO MUCH, THE* ½ (1940) 76m WB bw

George Brent *(Stephen Forbes)*, Virginia Bruce *(Joan Reed)*, Brenda Marshall *(Celia Farraday)*, Richard Barthelmess *(J. B. Roscoe)*, William Lundigan *(Johnny Forbes)*, John Litel *(District Attorney Dixon)*, George Tobias *(Slug McNutt)*, Henry Armetta *(Tony Spirella)*, Alan Baxter *(Garland)*, Marc Lawrence *(Lofty Kyler)*, Clarence Kolb *(E. A. Smith)*, John Ridgely *(District Attorney Brooks)*, David Bruce *(Gerald Wilson)*, Louis Jean Heydt *(Barton)*, Ed Stanley *(District Attorney Nelson)*, Paul Phillips *(Trigger)*, Elliott Sullivan *(Bill)*, Dick Rich *(Butch)*, William Forrest *(Federal District Attorney Greene)*, William Gould *(Chief Kendall)*, Kay Sutton *(Mrs. Knight)*, William Hopper, George Haywood, Creighton Hale *(Reporters)*, Lottie Williams *(Wilson's Mother)*, Frank Mayo *(Keeper)*, Cliff Saum, Glen Cavender, Jack Richardson *(Prisoners)*, Rosina Galli *(Mrs. Spirella)*, Maris Wrixon, Phyllis Hamilton *(Secretaries)*, Harry Seymour *(Painter)*, Vera Lewis *(Woman)*, Susan Peters *(Girl)*, George Reeves *(Hotel Clerk)*, Sam McDaniel *(Porter)*, James Blaine *(Guard)*, Dana Dale *(Governor's Secretary)*.

Brent is a lawyer who, with the help of some hard cash, is talked into defending gangster Barthelmess. He takes the job because he is practically penniless after giving up prosecution law after he sent an innocent kid to the chair, and uses the money to send his younger brother through law school. But Lundigan, as the brother, is an idealist and angrily doublecrosses Brent, whom he sees as crooked for defending gangsters, by turning in evidence to the FBI which convicts Brent. Shocked at what he sees as his brother's betrayal, Brent frames Lundigan on a murder charge. But blood is thicker than cash, and he then proceeds to save his younger sibling from the chair by getting the real killer to confess. This film was a remake of THE MOUTHPIECE, which was again remade as the Edward G. Robinson vehicle ILLEGAL.

p, Edmund Grainger; d, Vincent Sherman; w, Walter DeLeon, Tom Reed (based on the play "The Mouthpiece" by Frank J. Collins); ph, Sid Hickox; ed, Thomas Pratt.

Crime/Drama **(PR:A MPAA:NR)**

MAN WHO THOUGHT LIFE, THE* ½
(1969, Den.) 96m ASA bw (MANDEN DER TAENKTE TING)

Preben Neergaard, John Price, Lotte Tarp.

Price can make things materialize by mere thought and he wants Neergaard, a surgeon, to help him create an artificial human. The doctor won't have anything to do with it, so Price slowly thinks out a new doctor. This poorly paced and extremely static film is the second Danish science fiction movie ever. (HIMMELSKIIBET, 1917, was the first.)

d, Janes Ravn; w, Ravn, Henrik Stangerup; ph, Witold Leszczynski.

Science Fiction **(PR:A MPAA:NR)**

MAN WHO TURNED TO STONE, THE zero (1957) 80m Clover/COL bw

Victor Jory *(Dr. Murdock)*, Ann Doran *(Mrs. Ford)*, Charlotte Austin *(Carol Adams)*, William Hudson *(Dr. Jess Rogers)*, Paul Cavanagh *(Cooper)*, Tina Carver *(Big Marge)*, Jean Willes *(Tracy)*, Victor Varconi *(Myer)*, Frederick Ledebur *(Eric)*, George Lynn *(Freneau)*, Barbara Wilson *(Anna)*.

Jory and his fellow scientists have devised a way to live forever. They harness the energy of young girls by putting them into a bathtub full of chemicals with wires attached to their heads. If they don't get the necessary charge, they begin to turn to stone. To solve their problem of the shortage of available females, they head a reformatory for women. But when the prisoners start showing up dead at an alarming rate, prison psychiatrist Hudson exposes their wicked scheme. In the end, the reformatory is burnt to cinders, and Jory and his gang turn to solid rock. Written by blacklisted screenwriter Bernard Gordon, who used the pseudonym Raymond T. Marcus for this picture.

p, Sam Katzman; d, Leslie Kardos; w, Raymond, T. Marcus [Bernard Gordon]; ph, Benjamin H. Kline; m, Ross Di Maggio; ed, Charles Nelson; md, Di Maggio; art d, Paul Palmentola.

Horror **(PR:C MPAA;NR)**

MAN WHO UNDERSTOOD WOMEN, THE ½** (1959) 135m FOX c

Leslie Caron *(Ann Garantier)*, Henry Fonda *(Willie Bauche)*, Cesare Danova *(Marco Ranieri)*, Myron McCormick *(Preacher)*, Marcel Dalio *(Le Marne)*, Conrad Nagel *(G.K.)*, Edwin Jerome *(The Baron)*, Bern Hoffman *(Soprano)*, Harry Ellerbe *(Kress)*, Frank Cady *(Milstead)*, Ben Astar *(French Doctor)*.

This is a divided movie that spends the first half being witty and satiric and very "inside" on the subject of Hollywood, then falls apart when it goes into farce and then into drama. Fonda is an aging motion picture *wunderkind* who has made a lot of films which have won many Oscars but failed to ignite much audience approval. (The character is based on any of several movie types from Orson Welles to Preston Sturges to choose your own prototype.) We see his life in Tinseltown and all the silly things movie people do. Fonda meets Caron, a young actress, and decides to Galatea-ize her and make her into the next reigning screen star. He writes, produces, directs, and acts in a film with Caron that finally achieves the success everyone knew he was capable of. Until then, his films had won countless awards but failed at the box office. Caron feels that he cares more for her as a vehicle for his writing and directing than as a flesh-and-blood Frenchwoman. While in Nice, Caron is charmed by Danova, a good-looking pilot, who knows his way around women as well as he knows how to fly blind. Fonda learns of their attraction and hires killers to erase the Gallic Romeo. The assassin, Hoffman, is persuaded by his partner, Jerome, that love must triumph and to kill Danova would be an error. So it's either let them both live or knock them both off. Once Fonda hears that, he changes his mind and tries to save Caron. By this time, Caron and Danova are planning to part company as Hoffman, gun in hand, nears the duo. Jerome, a sentimental old coot, shoots Hoffman as he is about to dispatch the lovers. This action takes place at a sylvan spot high atop a mountain overlooking the Mediterranean and Fonda, rushing to save Caron, falls off the cliff and winds up in a hospital swathed in bandages as he and Caron reconcile. Fonda was so disappointed in the results of this film that he did not make another for nearly three years. Johnson and Fonda had been pals for more than two decades and Fonda just could not say no to a man with such a long history of tasteful films, but Johnson, wearing three hats, was too near the project to see the faults that everyone else must have seen, especially the audience when it finally came out.

p,d&w, Nunnally Johnson (based on the novel *The Colors of Day* by Romain Gary); ph, Milton Krasner (CinemaScope, DeLuxe Color); m, Robert Emmett

Dolan; ed, Marjorie Fowler; md, Earle Hagen; art d, Lyle Wheeler, Maurice Ransford; set d, Walter M. Scott, Paul S. Fox; cos, Charles LeMaire; spec eff, L. B. Abbott; m/l, "A Paris Valentine," Dolan, Paul Francis Webster.

Comedy   (PR:A-C MPAA:NR)

MAN WHO WAGGED HIS TAIL, THE**½
(1961, Ital./Span.) 91m Chamartin-Falco/Continental bw (UN ANGELO E SCESO A BROOKLYN; UN ANGEL PASO POR BROOKLYN; AKA: AN ANGEL PASSED OVER BROOKLYN)

Peter Ustinov (*Mr. Bossi*), Pablito Calvo (*Tonino*), Aroldo Tieri (*Bruno*), Silvia Marco (*Giulia*), Maurizio Arena (*Alfonso*), Jose Isbert (*Pietrino*), Isabel de Pomes (*Paulina*), Caligola (*Dog*), Franca Tamantini, Carlos Casaravilla, Lola Bremon, Renato Chiantoni, Juan de Landa, Jose Marco Davo, Enrique A. Diosdado.

Ustinov is a cruel slum landlord who has a curse put on him by a man who sells fairy tales. He becomes a dog and the curse will only be broken when someone loves him. He is befriended by Calvo, and when the dog sees one of his tenants being swindled of her inheritance he eats the money. Calvo can't forgive the dog, but the dog makes up for his action when he saves Calvo from a group of thugs. The young boy professes his love for the dog, the spell is broken, and Ustinov turns over a new leaf.

d, Ladislao Vajda; w, Istvan Bekeffi, Gian Luigi Rondi, Ugo Guerra, Ottavio Alessi, Jose Santugini, Vajda; ph, Enrique Guerner; m, Bruno Canfora; ed, Juan Penas; art d, Juan Antonio Simont.

Fantasy   (PR:A MPAA:NR)

MAN WHO WALKED ALONE, THE*   (1945) 70m PRC bw
David O'Brien (*Cpl. Marion Scott*), Kay Aldridge (*Wilhelmina Hammond*), Walter Catlett (*Wiggins*), Guinn "Big Boy" Williams (*Champ*), Isabel Randolph (*Mrs. Hammond*), Smith Ballew (*Alvin Baily*), Nancy June Robinson (*Patricia Hammond*), Ruth Lee (*Aunt Harriet*), Chester Clute (*Mr. Monroe*), Vivian Oakland (*Mrs. Monroe*), Vicki Saunders, Robert Hartzell, Charles Williams, Frank Melton, Donald Kerr, Eddy Waller, Don Brodie, Tom Dugan, William B. Davidson, Dick Elliott, Jack Raymond, Jack Mulhall, Charles Jordan, Tom Kennedy, Paul Newlan, Lloyd Ingraham, Elmo Lincoln.

O'Brien is a returning soldier, dismissed for medical reasons, who settles in the town of his dead friend. He soon meets a rich socialite who is in her fiance's stolen car. She gives him a lift and explains that she's just left the man she's supposed to marry. The police nab them for driving a hot car and O'Brien is suspected of being a deserter. The finale, complete with a police band, mayor and governor, reveals that he is actually a war hero.

p, Leon Fromkess; d&w, Christy Cabanne; w, Robert Lee Johnson (based on a story by Cabanne); ph, James Brown; m, Karl Hajos; ed, W. Donn Hayes; art d, Paul Palmentola.

Drama   (PR:A MPAA:NR)

MAN WHO WALKED THROUGH THE WALL, THE**
(1964, Ger.) 99m Pen/Shawn International bw (EIN MANN GEHT DURCH DIE WAND, AKA: A MAN GOES THROUGH THE WALL)

Heinz Ruhmann (*Herr Buchsbaum*), Nicole Courcel (*Yvonne Steiner*), Rudolf Rhomberg (*Painter*), Rudolf Vogel (*Fuchs*), Peter Vogel (*Hirschfield*), Hubert von Meyerinck (*Pickler*), Hans Leibelt (*Holtzheimer*), Anita von Ow, Michael Burk, Hans Poessenbacher, Gunter Graewert, Max Haufler, Karl Lieffen, Richard Bohne, Elfie Pertramer, Henry Vahl, Eduard Loibner, Karl Michael Vogler, Lina Carstens, Dietrich Thoms, Fritz Eckhardt, Werner Hessenland, Georg Lehn, Ernst Fritz Furbringer, Friedrich Domin.

Ruhmann is a revenue officer who finds his peaceful world disturbed by both his supervisor and a new neighbor who teaches piano lessons. He takes the advice of an old professor literally when he advises that "when your back is up against the wall, walk through it," and finds that he really can walk through walls. His new-found power helps him become department head at work and discover that his neighbor is an attractive widow. He falls in love with her, and resigns himself to his new-found happiness when he loses his power because he no longer needs it.

p, Kurt Ulrich; d, Ladislao Vajda; w, Istvan Bekeffi, Hans Jacoby (based on the novel *Le Passe-Muraille* by Marcel Ayme); ph, Bruno Mondi; m, Franz Grothe; prod d, Uors van Planta, art d, Rolf Zehetbauer, Gottfried Will.

Comedy   (PR:A MPAA:NR)

MAN WHO WAS NOBODY, THE**
(1960, Brit.) 58m Merton Park/Anglo Amalgamated bw

Hazel Court (*Marjorie Stedman*), John Crawford (*South Africa Smith*), Lisa Daniely (*Alma Weston*), Paul Eddington (*Franz Reuter*), Robert Dorning (*Vance*), Kevin Stoney (*Joe*), Jack Watson (*Inspector*), Vanda Godsell (*Mrs. Ferber*).

When a jewel thief is murdered by an unknown assailant, his brother from far-away places solicits the help of female detective Court. Romance blossoms as the killer is found; a gambler is the guilty party. A minor thriller.

p, Jack Greenwood; d, Montgomery Tully; w, James Eastwood (based on a novel by Edgar Wallace).

Crime   (PR:C MPAA:NR)

MAN WHO WAS SHERLOCK HOLMES, THE***
(1937, Ger.) 80m UFA bw (DER MANN, DER SHERLOCK HOLMES WAR)
Hans Albers (*Sherlock Holmes*), Heinz Ruhmann (*Dr. Watson*), Marieluise Claudius (*Mary Berry*), Hansi Knoteck (*Jane Berry*), Hilde Weissner (*Madame Ganymar*), Siegfried Schurenberg (*Mon. Lepin*), Paul Bildt (*The Man Who Laughed*).

Albers does not play Conan Doyle's character, but a man who is mistaken for the great sleuth and decides to go along with the impersonation. His friend, Ruhmann, is assumed to be Watson, and the pair get involved in tracking down rare and counterfeit stamps during the 1936 World Exposition in Paris. While searching for the real stamps, Albers is arrested for impersonating Sherlock Holmes, but always in the background is a chuckling man who looks like the real Holmes. He turns out to be none other than Conan Doyle (Bildt) and he helps overturn Albers' conviction at the trial by declaring Sherlock Holmes to be his fictitious character and by giving Albers the right to be called "the man who was Sherlock Holmes." Albers was one of Germany's biggest movie stars, often called the German Gable, and Sherlock Holmes movies were big hits with German audiences in the 1930s.

d, Karl Hartl; w, R. A. Stemmle, Hartl.

Comedy   (PR:A MPAA:NR)

MAN WHO WASN'T THERE, THE zero   (1983) 111m PAR c
Steve Guttenberg (*Sam*), Lisa Langlois (*Cindy*), Jeffrey Tambor (*Boris*), Art Hindle (*Ted*), Morgan Hart, Bill Forsythe, Bruce Malmuth, Ivan Naranjo, Clement St. George, Vincent Baggetta, Charlie Brill, Michael Ensign, Richard Paul.

In this 3-D comedy, Guttenberg plays a detective who gets hold of a dying scientist's formula that turns people invisible. U.S. and Russian agents, afraid of the formula getting into the wrong person's hands and upsetting the balance of world power, pursue Guttenberg throughout the film.

p, Frank Mancuso, Jr.; d, Bruce Malmuth; w, Stanford Sherman; ph, Frederick Moore (Movielab); m, Miles Goodman; ed, Harry Keller; art d, Charles Hughes; spec eff, Martin Becker.

Comedy   Cas.   (PR:C MPAA:R)

MAN WHO WATCHED TRAINS GO BY, THE
(SEE: PARIS EXPRESS, 1952, Brit.)

MAN WHO WON, THE*
(1933, Brit.) 70m BIP/Powers bw (GB: MR. BILL THE CONQUEROR)

Henry Kendall (*Sir William Normand*), Heather Angel (*Rosemary Lannick*), Nora Swinburne (*Diana Trenchard*), Sam Livesey (*Dave Lannick*), Louis Tinsley (*Deborah Turtle*), Moore Marriott (*Tom Turtle*), Sam Wilkinson (*Noah*), A. Bromley Davenport (*Lord Blagden*), Tonie Edgar Bruce (*Lady Blagden*), David Hawthorne (*George Jelby*), Helen Ferrers (*Mrs. Priddy*).

Kendall plays an idle aristocrat who takes to farming under the romantic notion of becoming William the Conqueror. His thinking goes like this: his farm, though not worked for several years, is near the spot where William once staged his great battle. Kendall decides he will conquer England through his hard work on the farm. He falls in love with Angel, one of the local farm girls. But a dispute arises over her father's desire to control Kendall's land. He resorts to setting the heir's crops ablaze. Then Kendall is invited to a party where he runs into an old flame, Swinburne, who has been after him for some time. She manages to get Kendall a job so that he can be near her. However, Kendall discovers that he really loves Angel and he returns to the farm to marry her.

p&d, Normal Walker; w, Dion Titheradge (based on the novel *Mr. Bill the Conqueror* by Titheradge); ph, Claude Friese Greene; ed, S. Simmonds.

Romance   (PR:A MPAA:NR)

MAN WHO WOULD BE KING, THE*****   (1975, Brit.) 129m AA c
Sean Connery (*Daniel Dravot*), Michael Caine (*Peachy Carnehan*), Christopher Plummer (*Rudyard Kipling*), Saeed Jaffrey (*Billy Fish*), Karroum Ben Bouih (*Kafu-Selim*), Jack May (*District Commissioner*), Doghmi Larbi (*Ootah*), Shakira Caine (*Roxanne*), Mohammed Shamsi (*Babu*), Paul Antrim (*Mulvaney*), Albert Moses (*Ghulam*), Kimat Singh, Gurmuks Singh (*Sikh Soldiers*), Yvonne Ocampo, Nadia Atbib (*Dancers*).

That this picture did not win one Oscar is a rebuke to the shortsightedness and chauvinism of the Motion Picture Academy. It was nominated for Direction, Editing, Production Design, Art Direction, and Costumes but was trampled by ONE FLEW OVER THE CUCKOO'S NEST. THE MAN WHO WOULD BE KING is the movie that answers the question: "Why don't they make films like that anymore?" by being exactly that, a film they don't make anymore. The director is John Huston, a man who made many pictures "like they don't make anymore" and this must rank as one of his greatest achievements in a career chock-a-block with brilliant work. It was originally a 12,000-word short story by Rudyard Kipling which Huston read when but a lad and he meant to make it for years, first with Clark Gable and Humphrey Bogart, then with Richard Burton and Peter O'Toole. It did not work out until Foreman got $8 million from Manny Wolf at the struggling Allied Artists company and the picture was launched. In later years, both Caine and Connery sued Allied Artists for a share in the profits. It's a vast parable that vaguely and metaphorically intimates some of the colonial injustices visited upon the various natives by the avaricious British Empire of the era. Kipling appears to be saying: "If you walk into another man's land and look only to take what is rightfully his, you will pay a mortal price." Plummer is Kipling and he is in his Lahore, India, office one night when an aged beggar, Caine, enters. The unrecognizable man is old, a bit mad, and his voice sounds like couscous mixed with gravel. Caine begins to spin an incredible yarn that Plummer can hardly believe and we flashback to another Kipling office. Connery and Caine, now young and vibrant and a bit of a boorish braggart, ask Plummer to witness a document attesting to what they have told him. They are British Army officers in India who have supplemented their service incomes by engaging in various cons and schemes. At this point, they have very little left of their booty, having lavished it all on high-living and low women. They are undaunted by their empty pockets and have concocted a new plan; they will sojourn into the hills of Kafiristan (a province in eastern Afghanistan now called Nurestan) where they intend to set themselves up as rulers. Plummer is taken by these two brash explorers-to-be and secures an appointment for them with the man in charge of the district, May. He is not at all impressed with them and goes so far as to call the pair "detriments" to the British cause in India. Caine and Connery respond by duck-walking out the door of May's office. They return to Plummer's office, not the least bit daunted by May's rejection. Plummer believes in them, despite the fact that Caine had once stolen his pocket watch and returned it later when he saw the Masonic sign on the timepiece and, being a Mason as well, Caine felt duty bound to return it. Caine and Connery endure several hardships as they trek over hill and dale, through the storied Khyber Pass and down into the glorious valley of Kafiristan. With the aid of a few renegades, they attack the city of Sikandergul, a holy ancient place once ruled by Alexander the Great. In the course of events, Connery is struck in the chest by an arrow and is surprised when he is not killed. In full view of the amazed battlers, he does not fall mortally wounded. Instead, he blithely pulls the arrow out of his chest. The natives think he is a god who cannot be killed by the weapons of mere humans. What they do not know is that the arrow hit his Freemason pendant and failed to penetrate his flesh. The natives immediately throw down their arms and prostrate themselves before Connery because they believe, as had been prophesied in their rituals, that he is the incarnation of Alexander who has come back to lead them. Connery is somewhat jolted by this. He had meant to steal a lot of gems and gold and get the heck out of there but the prospect of being a living god appeals to him. Caine says it might be best for them to take the money and run but Connery is rapidly becoming corrupted by all this adulation and thinks he might just stay a while. (One wonders how the story would have turned if Caine's character would have been the lucky so-and-so.) Connery accepts all of the plaudits and begins to think that, perhaps, he *is* the second coming of Alexander. Caine wants no part of it and decides to leave before what he feels is a tragedy. Connery has decided to take himself a wife (Shakira Caine, Michael's real-life spouse at the time), but Connery urges his old friend to remain for the nuptials. Shakira shows up at the wedding and is terrified at the prospect of marrying a god which causes her to bite Connery's face and draw blood. The natives, who do know that gods have no blood, begin to advance on the men because they now understand that Connery is human. Connery and Caine make a run for it but Connery is killed when he falls into a deep gorge and Caine is caught, crucified and left for dead. Back to the present in Plummer's office and Caine reveals himself to be Connery's partner and the tale he is telling is not a fiction, it is a memory. The picture ends in the office and we have been treated to slightly more than two hours of high adventure in the genre of GUNGA DIN and BEAU GESTE. It is a love story between two men, the kind of stuff Huston and John Ford and Howard Hawks did so well so long ago. Plummer was amazing in his portrayal of Kipling and took great pains and a long time to prepare for his brief, though important role. This was his best acting work since SOUND OF MUSIC and may have been better than that. In order to achieve reality, Plummer secured a tape of Kipling's voice from the British Broadcasting offices and several photographs of the late story-teller and thoroughly immersed himself into the persona of Kipling. What came out was worth all the effort. Made on location in Morocco because of the costs and dangers of shooting in Afghanistan, the picture had niggling flaws. Caine might have gone over the top a bit for some tastes but we feel that was necessary in order to separate the nature of the two men. Jarre's music was, surprisingly, not an asset to the film as it did not have the feeling of the area. Still, it did not detract from what was happening on screen and we can be thankful the score was not cleffed by some barbarian looking for a hit tune. Jaffrey plays Connery's and Caine's interpreter in the early scenes and sacrifices himself for the men. It was a small role in which Jaffrey registered well. Connery also appeared in another adventure film in 1975, the pretentious THE WIND AND THE LION that was a midget compared to the grandeur of THE MAN WHO WOULD BE KING. There was an underlying message in the movie that was never stated, only hinted at. Britain had been a most imperialistic country and it was about this time that the sun began to set on the Empire. Connery and Caine were the last remnants of the explorers who left that tight little island and stepped into other worlds. At one point, Caine says to Kipling: " . . . we're going away to another place where a man isn't crowded and can come into his own. We're not little men and there's nothing we're afraid of." A remarkable movie with more adventure than all of Steven Spielberg's and George Lucas's films put together and with characterizations that make those latter-day *wunderkinds'* works look like what they are; cinematic comic strips and bubble gum for the eyes.

p, John Foreman; d, John Huston; w, Huston, Gladys Hill (based on the story by Rudyard Kipling); ph, Oswald Morris (Panavision, Technicolor); m, Maurice Jarre; ed, Russell Lloyd; prod d, Alexander Trauner; art d, Tony Inglis; set d, Inglis; cos, Edith Head.

Adventure **Cas.** **(PR:A-C MPAA:PG)**

MAN WHO WOULD NOT DIE, THE* 1/2

(1975) 83m Sun Target/Centaur-Dandrea c (AKA: TARGET IN THE SUN)

Dorothy Malone *(Paula Stafford)*, Keenan Wynn *(Victor Slidell)*, Aldo Ray *(Frank Keefer)*, Alex Sheafe *(Marc Rogers)*, Joyce Ingalls *(Pat Reagan)*, Fred Scollay *(Lt. Willetts)*, James Monks *(Mr. Reagan)*, Jess Osuna *(Agent Soames)*, Dennis McMullen *(Harry Bonner)*, Hal Lasky *(News Reporter)*, Kathy Triffon *(Jackie)*, Valerie Shorr *(Girl Friend)*, Rick Lede *(Ramirez)*, Barry Simco *(C.P.O. Murthy)*, John Peters *(Yardman)*.

After a series of mysterious deaths Sheafe finds himself being harrassed by Wynn's goons. Sheafe begins conducting an investigation of his own and comes to suspect that the three men killed were all the same person. He meets Ingalls, whose father was one of the dead men. An investigation proves that Ingalls' father was indeed all three of the men killed, staging elaborate accidents in order to cover the million-and-a-half dollars he stole in bonds. However, Wynn is also after the money and suspects Sheafe of being in on the scam with Ingalls' father. The mystery winds down to its eventual conclusion, but not before throwing the audience into total confusion. The various lines of the mystery overwhelm themselves in emotionless, unfeeling performances by the cast. Despite the excellent photography, there is little to recommend in the film. It gives the pretense of being a thriller, when in actuality nothing much goes on in the process. Two of the three top-billed players get killed early on.

p, Lawrence M. Dick, Robert Arkless; d, Arkless; w, Arkless, George Chesbro, Stephen Taylor (based on the novel *The Sailcloth Shroud* by Charles Williams); ph, Lowell McFarland (Movielab Color); m, Art Harris; ed, Arline Garson; spec eff, Roblan; m/l, "Somehow," Sammy Cahn; makeup, Peter Wrona.

Mystery/Thriller **(PR:C MPAA:PG)**

MAN WHO WOULDN'T DIE, THE**

(1942) 65m FOX bw

Lloyd Nolan *(Michael Shayne)*, Marjorie Weaver *(Catherine Wolff)*, Helene Reynolds *(Anne Wolff)*, Henry Wilcoxon *(Dr. Haggard)*, Richard Derr *(Roger Blake)*, Paul Harvey *(Dudley Wolff)*, Olin Howland *(Chief Meek)*, Billy Bevan *(Phillips, the Butler)*, Robert Emmett Keane *(Alfred Dunning)*, LeRoy Mason *(Zorah Bey)*, Jeff Corey *(Coroner Larson)*, Francis Ford *(Caretaker)*.

Nolan is a private eye who is hired by millionaire Harvey to find out who is trying to kill him and his daughter. He goes undercover as the daughter's husband and discovers that wife Reynolds is in cahoots with a crazed Hindu, whom everyone believes to be dead. (See: MICHAEL SHAYNE Series, Index.)

p, Sol M. Wurtzel; d, Herbert I. Leeds; w, Arnaud d'Usseau (based on the novel *No Coffin for the Corpse* by Clayton Rawson, and the character created by Brett Halliday); ph, Joseph P. MacDonald; ed, Fred Allen; md, Emil Newman; art d, Richard Day, Lewis Creber.

Crime **(PR:A MPAA:NR)**

MAN WHO WOULDN'T TALK, THE**

(1940) 72m FOX bw

Lloyd Nolan *(Joe Monday)*, Jean Rogers *(Alice Stetson)*, Richard Clarke *(Steve Phillips)*, Onslow Stevens *(Frederick Keller)*, Eric Blore *(Horace Parker)*, Joan Valerie *(Miss Norton)*, Mae Marsh *(Mrs. Stetson)*, Paul Stanton *(Attorney Cluett)*, Douglas Wood *(Walker)*, Irving Bacon *(Paul Gillis)*, Lester Scharff *(Henri Picot)*, Harlan Briggs *(Foreman of Jury)*, Elizabeth Risdon *(Woman Juror)*, Renie Riano *(Lilly Wigham)*.

Nolan assumes a new identity after murdering a wealthy miner, and in an act of martyrdom refuses to defend himself rather than expose others, instead resigning himself to death. The law won't allow that, however, and they gather enough facts to prove his innocence. A remake of Paul Muni's debut film THE VALIANT.

p, Sol M. Wurtzel; d, David Burton; w, Robert Ellis, Helen Logan, Lester Ziffren, Edward Ettinger (based on the play "The Valiant" by Holworthy Hall, Robert M. Middlemass); ph, Virgil Miller; ed, Alexander Troffey; md, Samuel Kaylin.

Crime/Drama **(PR:A MPAA:NR)**

MAN WHO WOULDN'T TALK, THE** 1/2

(1958, Brit.) 97m Wilcox-Neagle/BL bw

Anna Neagle *(Mary Randall Q.C.)*, Anthony Quayle *(Dr. Frank Smith)*, Zsa Zsa Gabor *(Eve Trent)*, Katherine Kath *(Miss Yvonne Delbeau)*, Dora Bryan *(Telephonist)*, Patrick Allen *(Kennedy)*, Hugh McDermott *(Bernie)*, Leonard Sachs *(Prof. Harvard)*, Edward Lexy *(Hobbs)*, John Paul *(John Castle)*, John Le Mesurier *(Judge)*, Anthony Sharp *(Baker)*, Anthony Pendrell *(Jury Foreman)*, Cyril Chamberlain *(Liftman)*, John Welsh *(George Fraser)*, David Aylmer *(Cross)*, Ballard Berkeley *(Court Clerk)*, Lloyd Lamble *(Bellamy)*, Gordon Whiting, Jan Conrad, Diana King, Jennifer Jayne, Graham Stewart, Anthony Woodruff, John Harvey, Norman Mitchell, Alice Gachet, Neal Arden, Keith Banks, Lorraine Clewes, Jeff Shane, Middleton Woods.

Quayle and Gabor are an American couple in London posing as honeymooners, when in reality they are secret agents out to get top secret information. Gabor turns up dead with all the accusations pointing toward Quayle. Neagle plays the counsel appointed to defend Quayle, who runs into difficulty because Quayle is unable to disclose certain information. The screenplay was written by writers well versed in litigation, so the courtroom scenes have a strong sense of realism. The performances are convincing, though marred by several characters who don't fit in the plot.

p&d, Herbert Wilcox; w, Edgar Lustgarten (based on the book by Stanley Jackson); ph, Gordon Dines; m, Stanley Black; ed, Bunny Warren.

Drama **(PR:A MPAA:NR)**

MAN WITH A CLOAK, THE***

(1951) 81m MGM bw

Joseph Cotten *(Dupin)*, Barbara Stanwyck *(Lorna Bounty)*, Louis Calhern *(Thevenet)*, Leslie Caron *(Madeline Minot)*, Joe De Santis *(Martin)*, Jim Backus *(Flaherty)*, Margaret Wycherly *(Mrs. Flynn)*, Richard Hale *(Durand)*, Nicholas Joy *(Dr. Roland)*, Roy Roberts *(Policeman)*, Mitchell Lewis *(Waiter)*, Jean Inness *(Landlady)*, Hank Worden *(Driver)*, Francis Pierlot *(Pharmacist)*, Helen Eby-Rock *(Angry Woman)*, Charles Watts, Phil Dunham, James Logan, Cameron Grant *(Quartet)*, Robin Winans, Rudy Lee, Lynette Bryant *(Children)*, Dan Foster *(Clerk)*, Duke Johnson *(Juggler)*, James Gonzalez *(Bit Man)*, Melba Snowden, Janet Lavis, Charlotte Hunter, Carmen Clifford, Miriam Hendry, Ernie Flatt *(Specialty Dancers)*, Jonathan Cott.

Caron arrives in New York from France to talk Calhern, a crippled, dying, and alcoholic former marshal under Napoleon, into restoring his estranged grandson, her lover, into his will to boost the funds of the fledgling French Republic. In America, though, she runs afoul of Stanwyck and De Santis, Calhern's housekeeper and butler, respectively, who are planning to murder the old man to secure the inheritance for themselves. Caron enlists the help of Cotten, a mysterious drunken, poetry-reciting stranger who persuades Calhern to change his will in his grandson's favor. Unfortunately, Calhern's lawyer is poisoned and a pet raven hides the new will. Calhern sees the hiding place, but at that instant is paralyzed by a stroke. With his eyes, though, he guides Cotten to the spot and virtue triumphs. The finale reveals Cotten to be none other than Edgar Allan Poe, a fact that most of the audience should have guessed long ago. An unconvincing melodrama that never generates any tension or suspense, mostly due to slack direction and lackluster writing. Jim Backus, who had a minor role, once described the film as a "pretentious piece of *merde*." Stanwyck's first film after her much publicized breakup with Robert Taylor; her coworkers were amazed at her composure and professionalism in the face of heartbreak. Director Markle had previously gained attention with tight, low budget efforts like JIGSAW (1949) and NIGHT INTO MORNING (1951), and on the strength of those he was given a contract with MGM and bigger budgets. He tried to secure Marlene Dietrich for the Stanwyck role and Lionel Barrymore for the Calhern part. Neither was available, and although Stanwyck is more than adequate as the murderous housekeeper, the film lacks the spark that Dietrich could have brought to it. A critical and popular failure, the film crippled Markle's budding career and he would not direct another feature for 12 years.

p, Stephen Ames; d, Fletcher Markle; w, Frank Fenton (based on a story by John Dickson Carr); ph, George J. Folsey; m, David Raksin; ed, Newell P. Kimlin; art d, Cedric Gibbons, Arthur Lonergan; set d, Edwin B. Willis, Arthur Krams; cos, Walter Plunkett, Gile Steele; makeup, William Tuttle.

Drama **(PR:A MPAA:NR)**

MAN WITH A GUN** (1958, Brit.) 60m Merton Park/Anglo-Amalgamated bw

Lee Patterson *(Mike Davies)*, Rona Anderson *(Stella)*, John le Mesurier *(Harry Drayson)*, Warren Mitchell *(Joe Harris)*, Glen Mason *(Steve Riley)*, Carlo Borelli *(Carlo)*, Harold Lang *(John Drayson)*, Cyril Chamberlain *(Superintendent Wood)*, Jack Taylor, Richard Shaw, Alec Finter, Joe Gibbons, Peter Thornton.

When a nightclub burns to the ground Patterson is assigned by an insurance company to find the cause. Initially the detective suspects le Mesurier, the club's owner, of torching the place. But Patterson meets le Mesurier's niece Anderson, who helps the investigator uncover a mob protection scheme that was reponsible for the fire. With the help of the police, Patterson is able to break up the ring in this so-so crime story. Despite some fast pacing in the direction, the script is too simplistic for the fare.

p, Jack Greenwood; d, Montgomery Tully; w, Michael Winner; ph, John Wiles.

Crime **(PR:C MPAA:NR)**

MAN WITH A MILLION***
(1954, Brit.) 92m Group/UA c (GB: THE MILLION POUND NOTE)

Gregory Peck *(Jerry Adams)*, Jane Griffiths *(Portia Landsdowne)*, Ronald Squire *(Oliver Montpelier)*, A. E. Matthews *(Duke of Frognall)*, Wilfrid Hyde-White *(Roderick Montpelier)*, Joyce Grenfell *(Duchess of Cromarty)*, Maurice Denham *(Reid)*, Reginald Beckwith *(Rock)*, Brian Oulton *(Lloyd)*, John Slater *(Parsons)*, Wilbur Evans *(American Ambassador)*, Hartley Power *(Hastings)*, George Devine *(Chop House Proprietor)*, Bryan Forbes *(Todd)*, Ann Gudrun *(Renie)*, Hugh Wakefield *(Duke of Cromarty)*, Ronald Adam *(Samuel Clements)*, Ernest Thesiger *(Bank Director)*, Hugh Latimer *(Bumbles Receptionist)*, Eliot Makeham *(Consulate Official)*, Richard Caldicott *(James)*, Jack McNaughton *(Williams)*, Joan Hickson, John Kelly, Harold Goodwin.

This is a delightful comedy, happily and convincingly enacted by Peck. He is a penniless seaman stranded in London when he is literally called in from the street by two eccentric multi-millionaires, Squire and Hyde-White. These filthy rich brothers have made a bet about a man being able to live like a king if he had a million pound note and without ever spending a dime. Peck is given the note and, at first, he thinks it's all a joke and that the note is worthless, but when he produces it to pay for a small charge, pandemonium sets in. He is suddenly hailed as an eccentric American millionaire and he is soon living in the most luxurious hotel suite, wearing Savile Row clothes, and dining in the most fashionable restaurants. No one asks that he pay a bill, these are forwarded for later payment. In fact, when Peck buys some comparatively worthless stock, no payment is demanded, the brokers not wishing to offend the tycoon by asking that he transact business upon demand. In fact, Peck's considerable purchase causes a run on the stock so that its value shoots skyward. Griffiths falls in love with Peck and he plans to wed the fetching young lady when disaster strikes. The note is stolen and then word gets out that Peck is no longer in possession of the note. The gracious creditors now turn savage and swarm all over Peck, making his life miserable. His friends, except for Griffiths and his loyal butler, Beckwith, all desert him. Just when Peck is about to be thrown into debtor's prison, the note is returned and Peck further learns that the once worthless stock he has purchased has made him a wealthy man. He returns the note to the brothers and goes off to marry Griffiths, his future assured. Neame's direction is full of vitality and the movie provides consistent humor and delightful situations with a script faithful to the original Twain story. The film is beautifully photographed by Unsworth and the Victorian-era sets are impressive. Though Peck was better served with such films as ROMAN HOLIDAY, this film is still a rewarding satire on human greed and British traditions.

p, John Bryan; d, Ronald Neame; w, Jill Craigie (based on the story "The Million Pound Note" by Mark Twain); ph, Geoffrey Unsworth (Technicolor); m, William Alwyn; ed, Clive Donner; art d, Jack Maxsted; set d, Ario Simoni; cos, Margaret Furse; makeup, George Blackler.

Comedy/Satire **(PR:A MPAA:NR)**

MAN WITH BOGART'S FACE, THE* 1/2**
(1980) 106m FOX c (AKA: SAM MARLOW, PRIVATE EYE)

Robert Sacchi *(Sam Marlow)*, Franco Nero *(Hakim)*, Michelle Phillips *(Gena Anastas)*, Olivia Hussey *(Elsa Borsht)*, Misty Rowe *(Duchess)*, Victor Buono *(Commodore Anastas)*, Herbert Lom *(Mr. Zebra)*, Sybil Danning *(Cynthia)*, Dick Bakalyan *(Lt. Bumbera)*, Gregg Palmer *(Sgt. Hacksaw)*, Jay Robinson *(Wolf Zinderneuf)*, George Raft *(Petey Cane)*, Yvonne DeCarlo *(Theresa Anastas)*, Mike Mazurki *(Himself)*, Victor Sen Yung *(Mr. Wing)*, Henry Wilcoxon *(Chevalier)*, A'Leshia Brevard *(Mother)*, Peter Mamakos *(Spoony Singh)*, Joe Theismann *(Jock)*, Buck Kartalian *(Nicky)*, Martin Kosleck *(Horst Borsht)*, Philip Baker Hall *(Dr. Inman)*, Mike Masters *(Ralph)*, Kathleen Bracken *(Mona)*, Larry Pennell *(George)*, Ed McCready *(Garbage Man)*, Rozelle Gayle *(Mastodon)*, Everett Creach *(Buster)*, Bill Catching *(Nero's Uncle)*, Alan Foster *(Driver)*, Wally Rose, Ralph Carpenter *(Gunmen)*, Jerry Somers *(Catalina Driver)*, James Bacon, Marilyn Beck, Frank Barron, Dick Whittington, Robert Osborne, Will Tusher *(Reporters)*.

A rollicking sendup of mystery movies that is totally explained by the title. Sacchi is an actor who, when he does his hair a certain way and curls his lip, is so much like Humphrey Bogart that it is uncanny. In 1985 he would co-write, produce, and star in a play about Bogart where he received excellent reviews and big business in Los Angeles. Looking that much like Bogart has been a boon and a bane to Sacchi who is a talented enough actor to play other roles but the type-casting may be a problem. TV veteran Fenady wrote the novel, the screenplay, and produced this picture under Indianapolis real estate czar Mel Simon's banner. Simon also was executive producer for THE STUNT MAN two years before and neither that nor this film made much money. Too bad, as THE MAN WITH BOGART'S FACE is funny, exciting, and deliciously satiric for movie buffs who will recognize the prototypes. Sacchi plays a man who had plastic surgery to look like his favorite star, Bogart. He opens a small detective agency (that was actually shot in producer-writer Fenady's office in a building he owned on the corner of Larchmont and Beverly Boulevard in Los Angeles) and hires Rowe to be his blonde, dingbat secretary. After a shooting, Sacchi's face is in the papers and he is called upon by several clients, all of whom want him to find The Eyes of Alexander, jewels stolen from a famous statue of Alexander the Great. The baubles are sought by Nero, a Turkish mogul, whose secretary is Danning (before she became a "Rambette" and started shooting people in the RAMBO films of the mid-1980s). Buono, in a parody of Sidney Greenstreet, is a Greek shipping millionaire who also craves the gems and Lom, doing Peter Lorre, is another brigand. Nazi Robinson has just come out of a Greek jail after being convicted as a war criminal and he too is involved. (Robinson's name in the film is Zinderneuf, the same name as the fort in BEAU GESTE.) Add to this Hussey, whose father, Kosleck (Horst Borsht), wants the goods. Kosleck, who played Nazis in so many films, is killed early on. Phillips is the Astor-type, a mysterious woman who also wants the jewels. Action, murder, and laughs follow as the film goes from yachts to mansions and winds up on a boat docked at the Island of Santa Catalina where Nero and Buono attempt to outbid each other for the gems and have to strip down to their underwear while Lom is being tossed to waiting sharks. If that sounds silly, it is, wonderfully silly, but played totally straight by everyone and therein lies the fun. Phillips, whom Sacchi keeps remarking looks a great deal like Gene Tierney, is good and so is Hussey, but Rowe steals the distaff plaudits with her bewildered impression of the ultimate dizzy blonde. Sacchi's film name is Sam Marlow, a cross between Sam Spade and Philip Marlowe, the two most famous private eyes in filmdom. Six well-known radio and newspaper reporters play themselves in the picture, including one-time *Hollywood Reporter* editor Frank Barron. Mazurki, in a spoof on his own role in an early mystery, also plays himself. Football player Joe Theismann is seen briefly as a strong-armer. Theismann's name had been pronounced "Theezeman" until he was touted for the famed Heisman trophy and his college press department altered the pronunciation of his name to conform with that of the award. It has remained that way throughout his playing career. In small roles, note Raft and DeCarlo.

p, Andrew J. Fenady; d, Robert Day; w, Fenady (based on the novel by Fenady); ph, Richard C. Glouner (CFI Color); m, George Duning; ed, Eddie Saeta; prod d, Robert Kinoshita; set d, Richard McKenzie; cos, Oscar Rodriguez, Jack Splangler, Voulee Giokaris; m/l, "The Man with Bogart's Face," "Looking at You," Fenady, Duning (sung by Armando Compean).

Comedy/Mystery **Cas.** **(PR:A-C MPAA:PG)**

MAN WITH CONNECTIONS, THE**
(1970, Fr.) 91m COL-Renn/Royal c (LE PISTONNE)

Guy Bedos *(Claude Langmann)*, Yves Robert *(The Father)*, Rosy Varte *(The Mother)*, Georges Geret *(Corsican Adjutant)*, Jean-Pierre Marielle *(The Lieutenant)*, Zorica Lozic *(Tania)*, Claude Pieplu *(The Major)*, Claude Melki *(Kudierman)*, Nina Demestre *(Arlette)*.

Bedos is an actor who is drafted into the French army, and must leave his ballerina girl friend, Lozic. He swings himself a Paris assignment, but then is quickly transferred to a different French province. The actor gets special privileges because he tells everyone that he knows Brigitte Bardot. He becomes a medic and is sent to Morocco and there he declares all his friends to be unfit for duty because of faked illnesses. A broad comedy that is quickly forgotten.

p,d&w, Claude Berri; ph, Alain Derobe (Eastmancolor); m, Georges Moustaki; ed, Sophie Coussein; art d, Jacques d'Ovidio; cos, Andree Demarez; makeup, Genevieve Monteil.

Comedy **(PR:C MPAA:R)**

MAN WITH MY FACE, THE** (1951) 86m UA bw

Barry Nelson *(Chick Graham/Albert Rand)*, Lynn Ainley *(Cora Graham)*, John Harvey *(Buster Cox)*, Carole Mathews *(Mary Davis)*, Jim Boles *(Meadows)*, Jack Warden *(Walt Davis)*, Henry Lascoe *(Martinez)*, Johnny Kane *(Al Grant)*.

Another case of mistaken identity is the basis for this slow-moving crime drama. Nelson is the hard-working accountant who is innocently involved in a $1 million caper because he exactly resembles one of the real crooks. Several killings by trained dogs, though, manage to convince the police of Nelson's innocence. In his dual role, Nelson does a formidable job, but the rest of the performances are below standard, severely marring the project.

p, Edward F. Gardner; d, Edward J. Montaigne; w, Samuel W. Taylor, T. J. McGowan (based on a novel by Taylor); ph, Fred Jackman, Jr.

Crime   (PR:A MPAA:NR)

MAN WITH NINE LIVES, THE***

(1940) 73m COL bw (GB: BEHIND THE DOOR)

Boris Karloff (*Dr. Leon Kravaal*), Roger Pryor (*Dr. Tim Mason*), Jo Ann Sayers (*Judith Blair*), Stanley Brown (*Bob Adams*), Hal Taliaferro (*Sheriff Stanton*), Byron Foulger (*Dr. Bassett*), Charles Trowbridge (*Dr. Harvey*), Ernie Adams (*Pete Daggett*), Lee Willard (*Jasper Adams*), Ivan Miller (*Sheriff Haley*), Bruce Bennett (*State Trooper*), John Dilson (*John Hawthorne*).

Karloff plays a near-crazed scientist searching for a cure for cancer. He freezes patients in a state of suspended animation. When the family of a man Karloff has frozen comes snooping around, Karloff accidentally drugs them along with himself, but they are revived ten years later by a researcher, Pryor. Karloff goes at it with renewed fervor, knowing he is close to finding the cure. Karloff is a gem in his role as the scientist, and the rest of the cast well supports the Karloff character. The director keeps the suspense going throughout.

p, Wallace MacDonald; d, Nick Grinde; w, Karl Brown (based on a story by Harold Shumate); ph, Benjamin Kline; ed, Al Clark; md, Morris W. Stoloff; art d, Lionel Banks.

Mystery/Science Fiction   (PR:A MPAA:NR)

MAN WITH 100 FACES, THE**

(1938, Brit.) 72m GAU bw (GB: CRACKERJACK)

Tom Walls (*Jack Drake*), Lilli Palmer (*Baroness von Haltse*), Noel Madison (*Sculpie*), Edmond Breon (*Tony Davenport*), Leon M. Lion (*Hambro Golding*), Charles Heslop (*Burge*), Ethel Griffies (*Annie*), H. G. Stoker (*Inspector Benting*), Michael Shepley (*Wally Astill*), Henry B. Longhurst (*Inspector Lunt*), Edmund Dalby (*Lug*), Tarver Penna (*Morella*), Muriel George (*Mrs. Humbold*), Fewlass Llewellyn, Tony de Lungo, Robert Nainby, Jack Lester, Andrea Malandrinos, Jack Vyvyan, Victor Fairley, Margaret Davidge, Hal Walters, Bobby Gail, Charles Hiller.

The standard theme of a crook who robs the rich to give to the poor serves as the story line for this low-budget picture. In this one, the hero takes his goods to the local hospitals. Story suffers from stereotypical characters and situations, but this is glossed over by a fast-paced plot. Direction hampers the movement of the story by placing too much importance on the love theme.

p, Edward Black; d, Albert de Courville; w, A. R. Rawlinson, Michael Pertwee, Basil Mason (based on the novel by W. B. Ferguson); ph, Jack Cox; ed, A. C. O'Doneghue; md, Louis Levy.

Drama   (PR:A MPAA:NR)

MAN WITH THE BALLOONS, THE**

(1968, Ital./Fr.) 85m CHAM-CON/Sigma III bw-c (L'UOMO DAI CINQUE PALLONI; L'UOMO DAI PALLONCINI)

Marcello Mastroianni (*Mario*), Catherine Spaak (*Giovanna*), Ugo Tognazzi (*Man with Car*), William Berger, Sonia Romanoff, Antonio Altoviti, Igi Polidoro, Charlotte Folcher.

Originally produced in black and white in 1964, then cut and added to the film OGGI, DOMANI E DOPODOMANI (TODAY, TOMORROW, AND THE DAY AFTER THAT), a Carlo Ponti production. Ferreri reclaimed his portion, and it was released as a feature after original scenes were tinted and color footage was added. The result is a somewhat confusing spoof about a rich industrialist, overplayed by Mastroianni, who is driven crazy by the mystery of how a balloon works. As his girl friend, Spaak manages to convey a strong sense of eroticism while remaining totally clad. Songs are: "Barefoot" (sung by Orietta Berti), and two instrumentals, "Where Have You Been" and "Black-White" (performed by the Gep and Gep combo).

p, Carlo Ponti; d, Marco Ferreri; w, Ferreri, Rafael Azcona; ph, Aldo Tonti; m, Teo Usuelli; art d, Carlo Egidi

Comedy   (PR:A MPAA:NR)

MAN WITH THE DEADLY LENS, THE   (SEE: WRONG IS RIGHT, 1982)

MAN WITH THE ELECTRIC VOICE, THE   (SEE: FIFTEEN WIVES, 1934)

MAN WITH THE GOLDEN ARM, THE**1/2   (1955) 119m Carlyle/UA bw

Frank Sinatra (*Frankie Machine*), Kim Novak (*Molly*), Eleanor Parker (*Zosch Machine*), Arnold Stang (*Sparrow*), Darren McGavin (*Louie*), Robert Strauss (*Schwiefka*), George Mathews (*Williams*), John Conte (*Drunky*), Doro Merande (*Vi*), George E. Stone (*Sam Markette*), Emil Meyer (*Inspector Bednar*), Shorty Rogers (*Himself*), Shelly Manne (*Himself*), Leonid Kinskey (*Dr. Dominowski*), Frank Richards (*Piggy*), Ralph Neff (*Chester*), Ernest Raboff (*Bird-Dog*), Martha Wentworth (*Vangie*), Jerry Barclay (*Junkie*), Leonard Bremen (*Taxi Driver*), Paul E. Burns (*Suspenders*), Charles Seel (*Proprietor*), Will Wright (*Lane*), Tommy Hart (*Kvorka*), Frank Marlowe (*Antek*), Joe McTurk (*Meter Reader*).

This was a pioneering film in that it defied the Production Code with some of the depictions of dope addiction. There had been other dope operas before but none had gone so far in showing the pain and despair of heroin addiction. In any of several other directors' hands, this might have been a classic, but Preminger does not know when to let well enough alone and lays it on thicker than shlag on Viennese coffee. Knowing Preminger's penchant for endless "takes" and Sinatra's feelings about getting it right the first time and refusing to do more than one "take," the screaming on the set must have been loud enough to be heard in Sweden. Nelson Algren's book was deservedly a best seller and the film made a few dollars,

mostly because of Sinatra's excellent acting in the lead, as a professional card dealer struggling with the torment of drugs. Sinatra's just come home from half a year in Kentucky, where he was supposedly cured of his addiction. He arrives in his old Chicago neighborhood where he is welcomed by Stang, a slightly retarded street goniff whom he loves and McGavin, a drug pusher who happily offers Sinatra a fix, just for old times' sake. Sinatra says "no thanks" and goes home to his wife, Parker, an angry woman confined to a wheelchair. Sinatra has great plans to become a jazz drummer but Parker wants him to return to his old job, dealing cards at Strauss' illegal poker game. Sinatra does not want to but she appeals to his guilt by pointing out it was he who crippled her when he crashed a car while drunk. Laden by this onus, Sinatra does what Parker wants and moves into his old slot with Strauss. At Strauss' club, Sinatra meets Novak, a professional B-girl who gets the men to buy her drinks at inflated prices and then does not come across. Sinatra falls hard for Novak but cannot bring himself to leave his helpless wife. Still desiring a new career as a drummer, he attempts to practice at home but Parker keeps carping about all that noise so he stops and begins practicing at Novak's apartment. It pays off and he is rewarded by an audition so he quits his job at Strauss'. But there is a big poker game coming up and Strauss prevails on him for one last deal. It is a two-day poker game and Sinatra succumbs to McGavin's offer of a fix. The game goes on and Sinatra pushes the audition off but when he is caught cheating, he is beaten up. By the time he gets to the audition, he is totally strung out on drugs and in need of a shot so badly that he cannot perform. Meanwhile, McGavin walks into Sinatra's apartment and finds Parker standing up and walking around. Now he knows that she had been using her "crippled" status to hold on to him. McGavin means to tell Sinatra about this but Parker, in desperation, pushes McGavin down the long, dark stairwell and he dies in the fall. Sinatra learns from Novak that he is McGavin's suspected killer and he knows that he must talk to the police but he will not do it on drugs so he agrees to go "cold turkey" in Novak's apartment. It's a brutal sequence as he screams, cries, pounds walls, etc. until he rises, three days later, weak but clean. He goes to his apartment to tell Parker that he is going away with Novak but he will continue to support her. She jumps up from the wheelchair and follows him after he walks out the door. Then she sees cops in the hall and leaps out the window to her death. Sinatra is at her side when she dies as Novak watches in the background. The movie had a slickness to it that worked against the grittiness of the story. Stang stood out in his role, a rare dramatic outing for a man who spent most of his life as a comic flunky, beginning with his work on Henry Morgan's radio show in the 1940s. Novak did not have much to do except look pretty and act concerned. Parker never hit the right mixture of self-hate and pity. It was Sinatra's movie all the way despite the clumsy script, the obvious sets, and Preminger's hammering direction. Although ostensibly set in Chicago, there is absolutely no feeling of the Windy City and it might as well have taken place in Fresno.

p&d, Otto Preminger; w, Walter Newman, Lewis Meltzer (based on the novel by Nelson Algren); ph, Sam Leavitt; m, Elmer Bernstein; ed, Louis R. Loeffler; md, Bernstein; art d, Joseph Wright; set d, Darrell Silvera; cos, Joe King, Adele Parmenter; makeup, Jack Stone, Bernard Ponedel, Ben Lane.

Drama   Cas.   (PR:O MPAA:NR)

MAN WITH THE GOLDEN GUN, THE**   (1974, Brit.) 123m EON/UA c

Roger Moore (*James Bond*), Christopher Lee (*Scaramanga*), Britt Ekland (*Mary Goodnight*), Maud Adams (*Andrea*), Herve Villechaize (*Nick Nack*), Clifton James (*Sheriff J. W. Pepper*), Soon Taik Oh (*Hip*), Richard Loo (*Hai Fat*), Marc Lawrence (*Rodney*), Bernard Lee ("*M*"), Lois Maxwell (*Miss Moneypenny*), Marne Maitland (*Lazar*), Desmond Llewellyn ("*Q*"), James Cossins (*Colthorpe*), Chan Yiu Lam (*Chula*), Carmen Sautoy (*Saida*), Gerald James (*Frazier*), Michael Osborne (*Naval Lieutenant*), Michael Fleming (*Communications Officer*).

This ninth entry in the James Bond series is Moore's second turn as the super-sleuth. This time his mission is to uncover a solar energy device, leading him to Hong Kong and international hit man Lee. Ekland plays his assistant from British intelligence. Efforts of the screenwriters to add more humor is a hindrance to the plot development, with the pace lagging until the climactic finale. The cast gives convincing performances in some eccentric roles. (See JAMES BOND series, Index)

p, Albert R. Broccoli, Harry Saltzman; d, Guy Hamilton; w, Richard Maibaum, Tom Mankiewicz (based on the novel by Ian Fleming); ph, Ted Moore, Oswald Morris (DeLuxe Color); m, John Barry; ed, John Shirley, Raymond Poulton; prod d, Peter Murton; art d, Peter Lamont, John Graysmark; spec eff, John Stears; m/l, Barry, Don Black; stunts, W. J. Milligan, Jr.

Spy/Fantasy   Cas.   (PR:A MPAA:PG)

MAN WITH THE GREEN CARNATION, THE

(SEE: GREEN BUDDHA, THE, 1954, Brit.)

MAN WITH THE GREEN CARNATION, THE***

(1960, Brit.) 123 m Warwick-Viceroy/Kingsley c (GB: THE TRIALS OF OSCAR WILDE; AKA: THE GREEN CARNATION)

Peter Finch (*Oscar Wilde*), John Fraser (*Lord Alfred Douglas*), Yvonne Mitchell (*Constance Wilde*), Lionel Jeffries (*Marquis of Queensberry*), Nigel Patrick (*Sir Edward Clarke*), James Mason (*Sir Edward Carson*), Emrys Jones (*Robbie Ross*), Maxine Audley (*Ada Leverson*), James Booth (*Alfred Wood*), Paul Rogers (*Frank Harris*), Lloyd Lamble (*Charles Humphries*), Sonia Dresdel (*Lady Wilde*), Ian Fleming (*Arthur*), Laurence Naismith (*Prince of Wales*), Naomi Chance (*Lily Langtry*), Michael Goodliffe (*Charles Gill*), Liam Gaffney (*Willie Wilde*), Gladys Henson (*Landlady*), Cecily Paget-Bowman (*Lady Queensberry*), Meredith Edwards (*Auctioneer*), Derek Aylward (*Lord Percy Douglas*), A. J. Brown (*Justice Collins*), David Ensor (*Justice Wills*), William Kendall, Ronald Cardew, Anthony Newlands, Robert Percival.

Finch plays the famous English playwright and wit who sues the Marquis of Queensberry (Jeffries) for libel when Jeffries accuses Finch of being a sodomite.

Finch has had a relationship with Jeffries' son, Fraser, even though he has strong feelings for his wife and children. Mason, the defense counsel, proves that Finch is a practicing homosexual and Jeffries is acquitted. The ill-starred playwright suffers through two trials for gross indecency and must spend two years in jail. On his release, a friend advises him to leave the country, and at the train station he says goodbye to his wife but ignores his former youthful lover Fraser, who remains in the background. Praise is due for the film's concentration more on Oscar Wilde's personality and way of life than on the actual trial, which suffers from a weak performance in thrust and parry by Mason and by Patrick, as Wilde's counsel.

p, Harold Huth; d&w, Ken Hughes (based on the play "The Stringed Lute" by John Furnell and the book *The Trials of Oscar Wilde* by Montgomery Hyde); ph, Ted Moore (Technirama, Technicolor); m, Ron Goodwin; ed, Geoffrey Foot; art d, Ken Adam, Bill Constable.

Drama (PR:A MPAA:NR)

MAN WITH THE GUN***
(1955) 83m UA bw (GB: THE TROUBLE SHOOTER; AKA: MAN WITHOUT A GUN)

Robert Mitchum (*Clint Tollinger*), Jan Sterling (*Nelly Bain*), Karen Sharpe (*Stella Atkins*), Henry Hull (*Marshal Sims*), Emile Meyer (*Saul Atkins*), John Lupton (*Jeff Castle*), Barbara Lawrence (*Ann Wakefield*), Ted De Corsia (*Rex Stang*), Leo Gordon (*Ed Pinchot*), James Westerfield (*Drummer*), Florenz Ames (*Doc Hughes*), Robert Osterloh (*Virg Trotter*), Jay Adler (*Cal*), Amzie Strickland (*Mary Atkins*), Stafford Repp (*Arthur Jackson*), Thom Conroy (*Bill Emory*), Maudie Prickett (*Mrs. Elderhorn*), Mara McAfee (*Mable*), Angie Dickinson (*Kitty*), Norma Calderon (*Luz*), Joe Barry (*Dade Holman*).

This is a fine little western, which takes a basic plot out of a countless number of programmers, and uses it to advantage with intelligent dialog and characters. Mitchum is a sort of good guy-for hire. He'll take any town that pays him to fight off outlaws. His wife Sterling leaves him, tired of the life her man leads. While out in search of her, Mitchum is hired by a town under the thumb of a land-grabber. He does in the bad man and his henchman, winning back the affections of Sterling in the process. A well-cast film, with an ensemble that perfectly supports Mitchum. Coupled with good direction that knows the material, with some crisp photography and editing, the result is an overall good action western which rises above so many of the genre. Look for Dickinson in one of her earlier film roles. An auspicious debut for producer Goldwyn, Jr., a crown prince of Hollywood-mogul royalty.

p, Samuel Goldwyn, Jr.; d, Richard Wilson; w, N. B. Stone, Jr., Wilson; ph, Lee Garmes; m, Alex North; ed, Gene Milford; md, Emil Newman; art d, Hilyard Brown; cos, Jerry Bos, Evelyn Carruth.

Western (PR:C MPAA:NR)

MAN WITH THE MAGNETIC EYES, THE*1/2
(1945, Brit.) 52m British Foundation bw

Robert Bradfield (*Inspector Norman Wade*), Henry Norman (*Van Deerman*), Joan Carter (*Diana Wilbur*), Peter Lilley (*Harry Wilbur*), Charles Penrose (*Roberts*), Mabel Twemlow (*Mrs. Morton Rose*), Andrew Belhomme (*Count Arno*).

A ridiculous hodgepodge of pseudo-thriller plot elements is hashed together in this effort. Lilley is arrested on charges of stealing the plans for a secret weapon. However, Bradfield, who is in love with Lilley's sister Carter, suspects there is someone else behind the crime. Carter is then kidnaped, and Norman is suspected as the criminal mastermind. The mindless plot takes another twist down its spy cliche path, as Belhomme, a phony count, is shot by Bradfield. The dead man proves to have been the bad guy all along, using the very handy B-film convention of hypnotism to mesmerize people into carrying out nefarious schemes. Of course it's all unconvincing. This film was typical, though, for a post-WW II thriller in England.

p,d&w, Ronald Haines (based on the novel by Roland Daniel); ph, Stanley Fletcher.

Crime/Thriller (PR:C MPAA:NR)

MAN WITH THE SYNTHETIC BRAIN (SEE: PSYCHO A GO-GO, 1965)

MAN WITH THE TRANSPLANTED BRAIN, THE**1/2
(1972, Fr./Ital./Ger.) 72m Parc-Mag Bodard-Marianne-UGC-Mars/PAR-Orion bw (L'HOMME AU CERVEAU GREFFE)

Mathieu Carriere (*Franz*), Jean-Pierre Aumont (*Marcilly*), Nicoletta Machiavelli (*Helena*), Michel Duchaussoy (*Degangac*), Marianne Eggerikx (*Mariane*), Martine Sarcey (*Ponson*), Monique Melinand.

Aumont, a noted surgeon, is dying from heart disease. His brain is transplanted into the body of Carriere, a German race car driver, who is dying of brain injuries. The transplant is a success, but things get complicated when it's discovered that the surgeon's daughter, Machiavelli, was the racer's lover. The film focuses on the moral and incestual themes and lets the horror aspects fall away.

p, Philippe Dussart, Maurice Urban; d&w, Jacques Doniol-Valcroze (based on a book by Victor Vicas and Alain Franck); ph, Etienne Becker (Eastmancolor); ed, Nicole Berckmans; art d, Claude Pignot.

Science Fiction (PR:A MPAA:NR)

MAN WITH THE X-RAY EYES, THE (SEE: "X"—THE MAN WITH THE X-RAY EYES, 1963)

MAN WITH THE YELLOW EYES (SEE: PLANETS AGAINST US, THE, 1961, Ital./Fr.)

MAN WITH THIRTY SONS, THE (SEE: MAGNIFICENT YANKEE, THE, 1950)

MAN WITH TWO BRAINS, THE** (1983) 93m Aspen/WB c

Steve Martin (*Dr. Michael Hfuhruhurr*), Kathleen Turner (*Dolores Benedict*), David Warner (*Dr. Necessiter*), Paul Benedict (*Butler*), Richard Brestoff (*Dr. Pasteur*), James Cromwell (*Realtor*), George Furth (*Timon*), Peter Hobbs (*Dr. Brandon*), Earl Boen (*Dr. Conrad*), Bernie Hern (*Gun Seller*), Frank McCarthy (*Olsen*), William Traylor (*Inspector*), Randi Brooks (*Fran*), Don McLeod (*Gorilla*), Merv Griffin (*Elevator Killer*), Bernard Behrens (*Gladstone*), Russell Orozco (*Juan*), Natividad Vacio (*Ramon*), David Byrd (*Desk Clerk*), Adrian Ricard, Sparky Marcus, Perla Walter, Mya Akerling, Peter Elbling, Diane Peterson, Kate Sarchet, Wendy Sherman, Warwick Sims, Breck Costin, Tom Spratley, Estelle Reiner, Art Holliday, Jeffrey Combs, Jenny Gago, Elma V. Jackson, Oceana Marr, John Easton Stuart, Haunani Minn, Mel Gold, Stephanie Kramer, George Fisher.

Scientist Martin tries to transplant the brain of a very sweet woman into the body of his "unpleasant" wife, Turner. The premise of this comedy sounds good on paper, but is lost somewhere in the translation to the screen. Martin and director Reiner need better reins on their wacky style of humor. Better than Martin's debut film THE JERK, but it falls short of Martin's potential. Martin can be respected for taking giant risks with each of his film projects. The brain's voice was provided by Oscar winning actress Sissy Spacek.

p, David V. Picker, William E. McEuen; D, Carl Reiner; w, Reiner, Steve Martin, George Gipe; ph, Michael Chapman (Technicolor); m, Joel Goldsmith; ed, Bud Molin; prod d, Polly Platt; art d, Mark Mansbridge; set d, Robert Sessa; cos, Kevin Brennan; spec eff, Allen Hall, Clay Pinney, Robert Willard; makeup, Lance Anderson.

Comedy Cas. (PR:O MPAA:R)

MAN WITH TWO FACES, THE*** (1934) 72m FN/WB bw

Edward G. Robinson (*Damon Wells*), Mary Astor (*Jessica Wells*), Ricardo Cortez (*Ben Weston*), Mae Clarke (*Daphne Martin*), Louis Calhern (*Stanley Vance*), John Eldredge (*Barry Jones*), Arthur Byron (*Dr. Kendall*), Henry O'Neill (*Inspector Crane*), David Landau (*Detective William Curtis*), Emily Fitzroy (*Hattie*), Margaret Dale (*Martha Temple*), Dorothy Tree (*Patsy Dowling*), Arthur Aylesworth (*Morgue Keeper*), Virginia Sale (*Peabody*), Mary Russell (*Debutante*), Mrs. Wilfred North (*Matron*), Howard Hickman (*Mr. Jones*), Maude Turner Gordon (*Mrs. Jones*), Dick Winslow (*Call Boy*), Frank Darien (*Doorman*), Bert Moorhouse (*Driver*), Ray Cooke (*Bell Boy*), Jack McHugh (*Newsboy*), Douglas Cosgrove (*Lieutenant of Detectives*), Wade Boteler (*Detective*), Guy Usher (*Weeks*), Milton Kibbee (*Rewrite Man*), Joseph Crehan (*Editor*).

Tight, tense mystery finds Robinson portraying a famous egotistical New York stage actor whose sister, Astor, is the reigning queen of the same Broadway domain until she suddenly has a downward mental spiral and cannot seem to function. Astor is under the undue influence of her husband, Calhern. When Calhern vanishes with no trace and without reason, Astor's mental state returns to normal and she is back on top of her game. Calhern reappears (he had been in jail) and Astor starts to crumble once more. Calhern takes Astor to the hotel suite of a producer. He wants her to sell her rights in the show so he can have some money with which to operate. Later, Calhern is found murdered in the suite and Astor is home, a blithering idiot with no memory of how this came to pass. The producer, a man named Chautard, is nowhere to be found and the police are stymied. One detective, Landau, sticks with the case and he uncovers some interesting facts; Calhern may have murdered his first wife and was involved in various illegal activities. Landau searches the room in which Calhern died and finds a false mustache secreted in a Gideon Bible. Landau recalls once seeing a stage play that had a character not unlike the vanished Chautard in it so he starts looking at actors around town and settles into a suspicion of Astor's brother, Robinson. Landau does not hide his thoughts of Robinson's guilt and eventually hands the actor the mustache and tells him that he should pay more attention to details if the matter should ever rise again. Robinson, who is obviously the killer, is taken aback by this benign comment. Landau indicates that the earth is a better place for Calhern's passing and now he will close the case and mark it "unsolved." The only other person who knows Robinson is guilty is producer Cortez, but he will not talk because he is in love with Astor and has been waiting for her to get out from under Calhern's thumb. Robinson had to enlist Cortez's aid when he used the producer's office in which to make the change of clothes and disguise in order to become the mythical Chautard. Astor is happy, starring in a hit play and her good feelings are compounded when Cortez proposes and she accepts. Hard to believe that the censors allowed this to get past them as Robinson got away with murder and there was no retribution given to the character. EGR had a good time hamming it up and the entire cast seemed to be enjoying the proceedings.

p, Robert Lord; d, Archie Mayo; w, Tom Reed, Niven Busch (based on the play "Dark Tower" by George S. Kaufman, Alexander Woollcott); ph, Tony Gaudio; ed, William Holmes; art d, John Hughes.

Mystery (PR:A-C MPAA:NR)

MAN WITH TWO HEADS, THE zero (1972) 80m Mishkin c

Denis De Marne (*Dr. William Jekyll/Mr. Blood*), Julia Stratton (*April Conners*), Gay Feld (*Mary Ann Marsden*), Jacqueline Lawrence (*Carla*), Berwick Kaler (*Smithers*), Bryan Southcombe (*Oliver Marsden*), Jennifer Summerfield (*Vicky*).

Little did Robert Louis Stevenson realize when he penned the classic tale of Dr. Jekyll and Mr. Hyde that it would serve as inspiration to all-too-many bad filmmakers. This ranks as one of the worst renditions of the story. De Marne is the good doctor, this time experimenting on the brain of a late mass murderer. He manages to locate and isolate the portion of the brain that causes evil impulses, creating a special solution with the material. He experiments on little animals but before long we know what's coming. As the nasty, serum-induced "Mr. Blood," De Marne roams the streets, killing his laboratory assistant and a saloon singer. He's about to do in his fiancee Feld (a prerequisite for films of this ilk) but to no one's surprise is shot by police before completing the killing. There's no quality at all in this inane garbage, just some pseudo-science and plenty of cheap thrills for those who enjoy such fare. Staten Island moviemaker Milligan journeyed all the way to England to manufacture this bomb.

p, William Mishkin; d&w, Andy Milligan (based on the story "The Strange Case of Dr. Jekyll and Mr. Hyde" by Robert Louis Stevenson); ph, Milligan; art d, Elaine; cos, Rafine; m/l, David Tike; makeup, Lois Marsh.

Horror   (PR:O MPAA:PG)

MAN WITH TWO LIVES, THE* ½   (1942) 67m MON bw

Edward Norris (Phillip Bennett), Frederick Burton (Hobart Bennett), Addison Richards (Lt. Bradley), Edward Keane (Dr. Clarke), Hugh Sothern (Prof. Toller), Eleanor Lawson (Louise Hammond), Wilma Francis (Helen Lengel), Tom Seidel (Reginald Bennett), Elliot Sullivan (Eric), Anthony Warde (Hugo), Ernie Adams (Gimpy), Kenne Duncan (Jess), Marlo Dwyer, George Kirby, Jack Ingraham, Jack Buckley, Lois Landon, Francis Richards, George Dobbs.

A new twist on the Frankenstein story portrays a youth, seriously injured in a car accident, whose life is restored through the transfiguration of an electrocuted criminal's soul. It all turns out to be a dream.

p, A. W. Hackel; d, Phil Rosen; w, Joseph Hoffman; ph, Harry Neumann; ed, Martin G. Cohn.

Horror   (PR:A MPAA:NR)

MAN WITH X-RAY EYES, THE
                    (SEE: "X"—THE MAN WITH THE X-RAY EYES, 1963)

MAN WITHIN, THE, 1948   (SEE: SMUGGLERS, THE, 1948, Brit.)

MAN WITHIN, THE, 1975   (SEE: SMUGGLERS, THE, 1975, Brit.)

MAN WITHOUT A BODY, THE* (1957, Brit.) 80m British Filmplays/Eros bw

Robert Hutton (Dr. Phil Merritt), George Couloris (Karl Brussard), Julia Arnall (Jean Kramer), Nadja Regin (Odette Vernay), Sheldon Lawrence (Dr. Lew Waldenhaus), Michael Golden (Nostradamus), Peter Copley (Leslie), Kim Parker (Maid), Tony Quinn (Dr. Brandon), Maurice Kauffman (Chauffeur), Frank Forsyth (Detective), Norman Shelley (Dr. Alexander), Stanley Van Beers (Mme. Tussaud's Guide), Edwin Ellis (Publican), William Sherwood (Dr. Charot), Donald Morley (Stockbroker), Ernest Bale (Customs Officer).

Couloris, a financier, with the help of Hutton, a scientist, revives the head of Nostradamus. Couloris wants to use Nostradamus' power of prediction to help run his business and thereby gain more power. Hutton gets the head of a new body as Couloris tries to make the head's powers his own. A very absurd film which was co-directed by Billy Wilder's brother, Lee.

p, Guido Coen, W. Lee Wilder; d, Wilder, Charles Saunders; w, William Grote; ph, Brendan Stafford.

Science Fiction   **Cas.**   (PR:A MPAA:NR)

MAN WITHOUT A FACE, THE*   (1935, Brit.) 62m EM/RKO bw

Carol Coombe (Joan Ellis), Cyril Chosack (Billy Desmond), Moore Marriott (Tinker John), Ronald Ritchie (Paul Keefe), Billy Holland (Detective), Ben Williams (Warder), Vi Kaley (Landlady), Fred Withers.

Chosack is suspected of murder after finding money belonging to a murder victim. He's taken to prison but en route the train Chosack is aboard crashes. He takes a body from the wreckage, substituting the badly hurt person for himself. After settling down and marrying his sweetheart, Chosack learns the man he substituted is to be hanged for the crime. Wrought with guilt, Chosack decides to turn himself in, but it turns out the man was the real killer all along. How's that for contrived coincidence? The body of the film matches its unbelievable ending, with poor treatment on the part of both the production staff and the incompetent cast.

p, George King, Randall Faye; d, King; w, Faye (based on a story by St. John Irvine).

Crime Drama   (PR:A MPAA:NR)

MAN WITHOUT A FACE, 1964   (SEE: PYRO, 1964, U.S./Span.)

MAN WITHOUT A FACE, THE, 1975 (SEE: SHADOWMAN, 1975, Fr./Ital.)

MAN WITHOUT A GUN   (SEE: MAN WITH THE GUN, 1955)

MAN WITHOUT A STAR* ½   (1955) 89m UNIV c

Kirk Douglas (Dempsey Rae), Jeanne Crain (Reed Bowman), Claire Trevor (Idonee), William Campbell (Jeff Jimson), Richard Boone (Steve Miles), Mara Corday (Moccasin Mary), Myrna Hansen (Tess Cassidy), Jay C. Flippen (Strap Davis), George Wallace (Tom Carter), Paul Birch (Mark Tolliver), William Phipps (Cookie), Jack Elam (Drifter), Myron Healey (Mogollon), Eddy C. Waller (Bill Cassidy), Frank Chase (Little Waco), Roy Barcroft (Sheriff Olson), Millicent Patrick (Box Car Alice), Casey MacGregor (Hammer), Jack Ingram (Jessup), Ewing Mitchell (Johnson), William Challee, Sheb Wooley, William Philips, James Hayward, Malcolm Atterbury, Mark Hanna, Lee Roberts.

An intelligent and often tense western about the end of an era. Douglas is a wandering cowboy trying to keep ahead of the barbed wire encroaching the plains. He meets Campbell, a farmboy eager to learn the ways of a two-fisted cowboy. Douglas takes the lad under his wing, teaching him everything from gunhandling to the unspoken laws of the West. Both are hired by Crain as ranch hands, not realizing that the woman is a conniving manipulator. She is intent on making herself a fortune by expanding her cattle herds at any cost—including range wars. Crain attempts to

seduce Douglas into helping her with this plot but when she brings in some hired guns the old-time cowboy up and leaves. Douglas' brother had been killed in range wars and he wants no part in Crain's battle. He ends up in a nearby town and renews a friendship with Trevor, a good-spirited dance hall owner. Douglas begins to enjoy himself at the establishment and even sings a little ditty called "And the Moon Grew Brighter and Brighter" (penned by Jimmy Kennedy and Lou Singer) to the amused clientele. Meanwhile, Crain has hired Boone to do her bidding, holding him under a seductive spell. The sadistic man will do anything for his employer and goes after Douglas. After receiving a savage beating, Douglas realizes that the time for action has arrived. He organizes area ranches into a confrontation with Crain. Though successful in battle Douglas also hands himself a significant loss. He has stopped Crain's land-grabbing but he also has done his part in closing off the open lands he so dearly loves. Leaving Campbell with a rancher's daughter the young man has fallen for, Douglas heads out West to continue his endless search for the wide-open spaces. This was Vidor's last western and the eminent director combined his elements with excellent results. Though the story remains traditional for the genre, underlying tensions and themes are weaved in throughout. Crain's sensuality is a tempting siren, calling and devouring victims without mercy in an unspoken battle between the sexes. Douglas is forced to confront his various feelings head-on in a tough decision as to what must succumb to reality. This is one of his liveliest roles. He handles the part with a good mixture of bravado and humor as he struggles with his confused loyalties. His skills as a cowboy ring true and even his banjo playing (a talent he learned specifically for the number) works. Vidor was quite impressed with Douglas' ability to throw himself completely into the character. "Kirk comes across with aggressive strength," he wrote. "It is rather difficult, I imagine, to project an aggressive image in scene after scene all day from nine to six and not have some of it rub off on yourself." Douglas would later play a modern age cowboy undergoing similar internal struggles in LONELY ARE THE BRAVE. This was remade in 1968 as A MAN CALLED GANNON.

p, Aaron Rosenberg; d, King Vidor; w, Bordon Chase, D. D. Beauchamp (based on the novel by Dee Linford); ph, Russell Metty (Technicolor); m, Joseph Gershenson; ed, Virgil Vogel; md, Gershenson; art d, Alexander Golitzen, Richard H. Reidel; cos, Rosemary Odell; m/l, Arnold Hughes, Frederick Herbert, Jimmy Kennedy, Lou Singer.

Western   **Cas.**   (PR:C MPAA:NR)

MAN, WOMAN AND CHILD**   (1983) 99m Gaylord/PAR c

Martin Sheen (Bob Beckwith), Blythe Danner (Sheila Beckwith), Craig T. Nelson (Bernie Ackerman), David Hemmings (Gavin Wilson), Nathalie Nell (Nicole Guerin), Maureen Anderman (Margo), Sebastian Dungan (Jean-Claude Guerin), Arlene McIntyre (Jessica Beckwith), Missy Francis (Paula Beckwith), Billy Jacoby (Davey Ackerman), Ruth Silveira (Nancy Ackerman), Jacques Francois (Louis), Randy Dreyfus (Shakespeare Student), Dennis Redfield (TWA Clerk), Frederick Cintron (TWA Host), Anne Bruner, Eve Douglas (TWA Stewardesses), Lorraine Williams (Woman at Bar-B-Que), Mark E. Boucher, David E. Boucher (Soccer Players), Homer Taylor (Basketball Player), Lisa Figueroa, Frank Koppola, David O. Thomas (Students), Jan Stratton, John Wyler, Gwil Richards, Lila Waters, James Beach, Richard McGonagle, Grace Woodard, Louis Plante (Faculty).

Sheen stars as a happily married man whose family life is interrupted by the news that he has an illegitimate son. When the former lover, Nell, dies, the son is sent to live with the father and the father's legitimate family. This causes tension in the until-now happy family at having to adapt to the intruder, ending in a lot of overdramatized sobbing. Sheen and Danner manage to deliver competent performances in roles which are low on believability.

p, Elmo Williams, Elliot Kastner; d, Dick Richards; w, Erich Segal, David Z. Goodman (based on the novel by Segal); ph, Richard H. Kline, Jean Tournier (Deluxe Color); m, Georges Delerue; ed, David Bretherton; prod d, Dean Edward Mitzner; cos, Joseph G. Aulisi.

Drama   **Cas.**   (PR:A MPAA:PG)

MAN-EATER   (SEE: SHARK!, 1970, U.S./Mex.)

MAN-EATER OF HYDRA
                    (SEE: ISLAND OF THE DOOMED, 1968, Ger./Span.)

MAN-EATER OF KUMAON***   (1948) 79m UNIV bw

Sabu (Narain), Wendell Corey (Dr. John Collins), Joanne Page (Lali), Morris Carnovsky (Ganga Ram), James Moss (Panwah), Ted Hecht (Native Doctor), Argentina Brunetti (Sita), John Mansfield (Bearer), Eddie Das (Ox-Cart Driver), Charles Wagenheim (Panwah's Father), Estelle Dodge (Mother), Lal Chand Mehra, Phirose Nazir, Virginia Wave (Farmers), Frank Lackteen, Jerry Riggin, Noyle Morrow, Ralph Moody, Alan Foster (Villagers).

Jungle adventure has Corey as a doctor tracking down a man-eating tiger that has been laying seige to a native village. In the process the doctor undergoes a change as he learns to accept and appreciate the villagers' perspectives. Footage is a combination of studio and actual jungle shots. Performances are believable, even those of the natives. Direction is paced to keep the tension mounting.

p, Monty Shaff, Frank P. Rosenberg; d, Byron Haskin; w, Jeanne Bartlett, Lewis Meltzer, Richard Q. Hubler, Alden Nash (based on the book by Jim Corbett); ph, William C. Mellor; m, Hans J. Salter; ed, George Arthur; art d, Arthur Lonegan.

Adventure   (PR:A MPAA:NR)

MAN-KILLER   (SEE: OTHER LOVE, THE, 1947)

MAN'S AFFAIR, A**   (1949, Brit.) 62m Concord/Exclusive bw

Hamish Menzies (Jim), Cliff Gordon (Ted), Diana Decker (Sheila), Joan Dowling (Joan), Wallas Eaton (Leonard), Joyce Linden, Bruce Walker.

Menzies and Gordon are miners who vacation at the seashore. There they meet Decker and Dowling, and the quartet hits it off nicely. However, a playboy pal of the men comes along; with the ensuing quarrel, he starts breaking up the four. Fortunately, the younger sister of one of the men is able to use her charms, managing to get everyone back together. The premise is silly and the result isn't much better in the far-fetched comedy.

p&d, Jay Gardner Lewis; w, Lewis, Harold Stewart; ph, Douglas Ransome, Norman Johnson.

Comedy   **(PR:A   MPAA:NR)**

MAN'S CASTLE, A***   (1933) 70m COL bw

Spencer Tracy (Bill), Loretta Young (Trina), Glenda Farrell (Fay LaRue), Walter Connolly (Ira), Arthur Hohl (Bragg), Marjorie Rambeau (Flossie), Dickie Moore (Joie the Crippled Boy), Harvey Clark (Cafe Manager), Henry Roquemore (Man in Audience), Hector V. Sarno (Grocer), Helen Jerome Eddy, Robert Grey, Tony Merlo, Kendall McComas, Harry Watson.

Tracy plays a roughneck living in a shantytown who takes in desperate and homeless Young. She makes his forsaken shack into something of a home, while he manages to make some money doing odd jobs. Tracy meets up with a showgirl, Farrell, who is willing to support him and give him a taste of the better life. However, he discovers Young is pregnant and, in an effort to support her, commits a robbery. The robbery is foiled and Tracy is wounded. Realizing how much he needs Young, Tracy runs off with her to start a new life. Cast gives efficient performances despite a script that lapses a bit too much into sentimentality. Considering the times, A MAN'S CASTLE contains some pretty racy material (out-of-wedlock pregnancy, cohabitation) and even gives the audience a brief glance at Tracy diving nude into a river. The Production Code was put into place the year after this film was released, putting an end to such candid film-making for a while.

d, Frank Borzage; w, Jo Swerling (based on a play by Lawrence Hazard); ph, Joseph August; m, Frank Harling, Constantin Bakaleinikoff; ed, Viola Lawrence.

Drama   **(PR:A   MPAA:NR)**

MAN'S COUNTRY**   (1938) 53m MON bw

Jack Randall (Jack), Ralph Peters (Snappy), Marjorie Reynolds (Madge), Walter Long (Lex/Buck), Bud Osborne (Jed), Dave O'Brien (Bert), Ernie Adams (Caleb Hart), Charles King (Guard), David Sharpe, Forrest Taylor, Harry Harvey, Sherry Tansey.

Routine western casts Randall as a ranger out to do in a band of cutthroats led by Long. Cast gives believable performances, and Long capably handles a dual role as twin brothers with opposite temperaments. Direction drags in parts but keeps the suspense going.

p, Robert Tansey; d, Robert Hill; w, Robert Emmett [Tansey]; ph, Bert Longenecker; ed, Howard Dillinger.

Western   **(PR:A   MPAA:NR)**

MAN'S FAVORITE SPORT (?)**1/2   (1964) 120m UNIV c

Rock Hudson (Roger Willoughby), Paula Prentiss (Abigail Page), Maria Perschy (Isolde "Easy" Mueller), Charlene Holt (Tex Connors), John McGiver (William Cadwalader), Roscoe Karns (Maj. Phipps), Forrest Lewis (Skaggs), Regis Toomey (Bagley), Norman Alden (John Screaming Eagle), Don Allen (Tom), James Westerfield (Policeman), Tyler McVey (Customer Bush), Kathie Browne (Marcia), Joan Tewksbury, Betty Hanna (Women in Elevator), Dianne Simpson (Elevator Operator), Joan Boston (Joan), Holger Bendixen (Fisherman), Ed Stoddard (Escort), Paul Bryar (Policeman), Jim Bannon (Forest Ranger), Lincoln Demyan (Scoutmaster), Edmund Williams (Desk Clerk), Christopher White (Boy Scout), Elise Kraal (Girl on Motorbike), Ollie O'Toole (Waiter), Margaret Sheridan (Cadwalader's Secretary), Paul Langton (Mr. Stern), Med Flory (Tucker), John Zaremba, Chuck Courtney, Edy Williams.

Director-producer Hawks returned to the comic formulas that worked so well for him in BRINGING UP BABY and I WAS A MALE WAR BRIDE, but achieved only limited success. Cary Grant was able to carry the earlier films with a characteristic charm that leading man Hudson was unable to match. Hudson is cast as the star fishing supplies salesman at a large sporting goods store who knows nothing about fishing. Publicity agent Prentiss convinces Hudson's boss, McGiver, that Hudson should enter a fishing contest. With a little luck and assistance from a bear, Hudson wins. Knowing he's a fake, he forfeits the prize and subsequently gets fired. In the end, Hudson gets his job back and lands Prentiss as well. Hawks delivers his usual job of heavy-handed direction, but the film's premise is too flimsy to spread over two hours. Script is marred by tired comic routines and slow pacing. The cast, with the execption of Hudson, offers very good performances, Prentiss in particular.

p&d, Howard Hawks; w, John Fenton Murray, Steve McNeil (based on the story "The Girl Who Almost Got Away" by Pat Frank); ph, Russell Harlan (Technicolor); m, Henry Mancini; ed, Stuart Gilmore; art d, Alexander Golitzen, Tambi Larsen; set d, Robert Priestly; cos, Edith Head; spec eff, Ben McMahon; m/l, title song, Mancini, Johnny Mercer; makup, Bud Westmore.

Comedy   **(PR:A   MPAA:NR)**

MAN'S GAME, A*1/2   (1934) 59m COL bw

Tim McCoy (Tim), Evalyn Knapp (Judy), Ward Bond (Dave), DeWitt Jennings (Chief Jordan), Alden Chase, Wade Boteler, Nick Copeland, Bob Kortman.

McCoy and Bond are two buddies with nothing better to do but to become firemen. Bond, the hero in every fire he fights, joins forces with McCoy to get Knapp off an embezzlement rap. Production techniques are below standard, and all the fires look like they occur in the same building.

d, D. Ross Lederman; w, Harold Shumate; ph, All Siegler.

Action   **(PR:A   MPAA:NR)**

MAN'S HERITAGE   (SEE: SPIRIT OF CULVER, 1939)

MAN'S HOPE****

                                  (1947, Span.) 78m Lopert Films bw (SIERRA DE TERUEL)

Majuto (Capt. Munoz), Nicolas Rodriguez (Pilot Marquez), Jose Lado (The Peasant), Members of the International Brigade, Spanish Peasants.

This film was shot in Spain during the Spanish Civil War and later smuggled into occupied France, where screening was postponed until after the liberation in WW II. As a result, it was eight years before the public was allowed to view MAN'S HOPE. When it finally was screened it received the Louis Delluc Award, one of the highest honors the French could bestow on a film. It is a filmic representation of Malraux's own novel, in which a sense of realism is gained through actual footage of the sounds of real gunfire and bombing which are frightening and provide the basis for a powerful film. The story focuses on the efforts of a Loyalist Squadron to destroy a bridge. To do so, the squadron must neutralize a new airfield, and the only one who can tell them where it is is a peasant who can't read a map. The peasant is then taken on the air raid so that he can locate the target. The story is void of common plot progression, and the action is discontinuous. But, the project's realism makes it possible to overlook these minor flaws. (In Spanish; English subtitles.)

p,d&w, Andre Malraux (based on the novel Espoir by Malraux); ph, Louis Page; m, Darius Milhaud.

War   **(PR:A   MPAA:NR)**

MAN'S LAND, A**   (1932) 65m AA bw

Hoot Gibson, Marion Shilling, Skeeter Bill Robbins, Al Bridge, Charles King, Ethel Wales, Hal Burney, Robert Ellis, William Nye, Merrill MacCormack, Slim Whitaker.

In this routine western, Shilling travels west to set up a ranch and runs into trouble when the cattle start stampeding. Gibson is the foreman who saves the day and wins the girl.

p, M. H. Hoffman, Jr.; d, Phil Rosen; w, Adele Buffington; ph, Harry Neumann, Tom Galligan; ed, Mildred Johnson.

Western   **(PR:A   MPAA:NR)**

MAN'S WORLD, A**   (1942) 60m COL bw

William Wright (Dan O'Driscoll), Marguerite Chapman (Mona Jackson), Larry Parks (Chick O'Driscoll), Wynne Gibson (Blossom Donovan), Roger Pryor (Bugsy Nelson), Frank Sully (Sammy Collins), Ferris Taylor ("Chief" DeShon), Edward Van Sloan (Doc Stone), Clancy Cooper (John Black), James Millican (Parks), Lloyd Bridges (Brown), Al Hill (Eddie Bartlett), Ralph Peters (Vince Carrol), Alan Bridges (Capt. Peterson), Eddie Kane (Doc Drake), Beaulah Parkington, Grace Lenard, Diana Snyder, Thelma White (Girls), Frank Richards (Thomas), Shirley Patterson (Nurse Bentley).

The amusing tale has Chapman playing a well-meaning nurse who finds herself falling under the spell of a gangster. Before long this pretty woman is dancing the jig for the entertainment of miners, but her strong will gets her out of this ill-suited situation and back on the right track.

p, Wallace MacDonald; d, Charles Barton; w, Edward T. Lowe, Jack Roberts (based on the story by Roberts, Jack Buckner); ph, George Meehan; ed, Richard Fantl; md, M. W. Stoloff.

Drama   **(PR:A   MPAA:NR)**

MANCHU EAGLE MURDER CAPER MYSTERY, THE*1/2

                                             (1975) 80m UA c

Gabriel Dell (Malcolm), Will Geer (Dr. Simpson), Joyce Van Patten (Ida Mae), Anjanette Comer (Arlevia), Vincent Gardenia (Big Daddy), Barbara Harris (Miss Fredericks), Jackie Coogan (Sheriff), Huntz Hall (Deputy), Sorrel Booke (Dr. Melon), Dick Gautier (Oscar), Nita Talbot (Jasmine), Howard Storm (Freddie), Nick Colasanto (Bert).

Comic spoof on film noirish detective movies has Dell as a novice private eye trying to solve the murder of his eccentric milkman. There are some genuinely funny moments and some good performances in this otherwise cliche-filled attempt at parody. Made in 1973, it was shelved for two years and had limited appeal upon release.

p, Edward K. Dodds; d, Dean Hargrove; w, Hargrove, Gabriel Dell; ph, Wilmer Butler (CFI Color); m, Dick DeBenedictus; ed, Bud Small; art d, Arch Bacon.

Comedy   **(PR:A   MPAA:PG)**

MANCHURIAN CANDIDATE, THE***1/2   (1962) 126m M.C.-Essex/UA bw

Frank Sinatra (Bennett Marco), Laurence Harvey (Raymond Shaw), Janet Leigh (Rosie), Angela Lansbury (Raymond's Mother), Henry Silva (Chunjim), James Gregory (Sen. John Iselin), Leslie Parrish (Jocie Jordon), John McGiver (Sen. Thomas Jordon), Khigh Dhiegh (Yen Lo), James Edwards (Cpl. Melvin), Douglas Henderson (Colonel), Albert Paulsen (Zilkov), Barry Kelley (Secretary of Defense), Lloyd Corrigan (Holborn Gaines), Madame Spivy (Berezovo's Lady Counterpart), Joe Adams (Psychiatrist), Whit Bissell (Medical Officer), Mimi Dillard (Melvin's Wife), Anton von Stralen (Officer), John Laurence (Gossfeld), Tom Lowell (Lembeck), Richard La Pore (Mavole), Nicky Blair (Silvers), William Thourlby (Little), Irving Steinberg (Freeman), John Francis (Haiken), Robert Riordan (Nominee), Reggie Nalder (Gomel), Harry Holcombe (General), Miyoshi Jingu (Miss Gertrude), Anna Shin (Korean Girl), Bess Flowers (Gomel's Lady Counterpart), Helen Kleeb, Maye Henderson (Chairladies), Mickey Finn, Richard Norris, Johnny Indrisano (Reporters), Lou Krugg (Manager), Mike Masters, Tom Harris (FBI Men), Mariquita Moll (Soprano), Robert Burton (Convention Chairman), Karen Norris (Secretary), Jean Vaughn (Nurse), Ray Spiker (Policeman), Merritt Bohn (Jilly),

Frank Basso *(Photographer)*, Julia Payne, Lana Crawford, Evelyn Byrd *(Guests at Party)*, Ray Dailey *(Page Boy)*, Estelle Etterre, Mary Benoit, Rita Kenaston, Maggie Hathaway, Joan Douglas, Frances Nealy, Ralph Gambina, Sam "Kid" Hogan *(People in Hotel Lobby)*, James Yagi, Lee Tung Foo, Raynum Tsukamoto *(Chinese Men in Hotel Lobby)*, Nick Bolin.

This now somewhat dated melodrama pitting the ideals of the U.S. against the Soviets early in the Cold War still has some startling and fascinating moments and—by virtue of stellar acting by Harvey and, to some lesser degree, Sinatra—this film has some historic significance, and provides many memorable scenes. Brainwashing has been dealt with in films concerned with Korea where Communists applied psychological persuasian on captured American troops. Here, the process is taken one terrible step further, the programming of an American soldier into a robot who will act, once given the prearranged codes, in any fashion indicated by his control force. Harvey returns from the Korean War a super hero, holder of the Congressional Medal of Honor, but those in his platoon—including his own commanding officer, Sinatra—are vague about how Harvey actually won the medal, just stating that he is a great hero. Sinatra and another soldier, however, begin to have recurring nightmares about Korea and, when this is reported, an investigation into Harvey and his present activities takes place, conducted by Sinatra. Piece by sinister piece, Sinatra and others put it together. He, Harvey, and the entire platoon received mass brainwashing until all came to believe Harvey was a hero when, in truth, he had been programmed as a killer. But whom is he to kill? Upon his return from service Harvey leaves his overly protective mother (Lansbury) and her husband (Gregory), a dominated fascist-oriented senator. Harvey goes to work as a journalist but, when his control contacts him with the code, Harvey becomes a robot, killing without guilt or memory of his crime. He shoots and kills a liberal columnist-publisher. The brainwashing wears off with Sinatra and he is able to determine just how Harvey is controlled. Harvey, now married, is sent to kill his own wife and his father-in-law, a liberal senator, and the controller turns out to be Harvey's own mother, Lansbury, the top Communist spy in the U.S.! She also orders her robot-like son to kill the presidential nominee; her husband, who is the vice-presidential running mate, will then take over the control of the White House. Harvey climbs to a small room at the top of Madison Square Garden with a rifle—he's a crack shot—and, under the influence of his mother, aims at the presidential nominee on the stage where his mother and Gregory also sit. But, at the last moment, Harvey's clouded mind clears and he is able to see reality and the truth. With that realization, all the brutal murders he has committed come flooding with guilt into Harvey's mind as he stands there wearing the Congressional Medal of Honor around his neck and holding a long-range rifle in his hands. He nevertheless fires his weapon twice, killing not the presidential nominee, but his own mother and Gregory, who slump forward dead on the Garden stage. Abruptly he ameliorates "the disgrace" he has created for the medal and himself, and he turns the gun on himself and fires, committing suicide. THE MANCHURIAN CANDIDATE played fast and loose with the concept of brainwashing but Harvey's performance is so obsessive that he fascinates from beginning to brutal end. Sinatra, as the puzzled commander, is also top drawer but Gregory as the hen-pecked McCarthy-type politician, and the fanatical Communist mother Lansbury, are not much more than flamboyant cliches. Frankenheimer's direction has that usual stark and jolting quality, half real, half surreal, but it falters in the so-called "dream sequences" in that these scenes are forced and as blatant as the worst WW II propaganda film. There was never any doubt that the Communist menace was and is real; the question is how sophisticated were their military intelligence people just behind the Korean front lines where all those brains were scrubbed. But Frankenheimer became a real force in American cinema by virtue of this powerful film, being one of the first to indict the illogical and tyrannical witch-hunting of the McCarthyites. THE MANCHURIAN CANDIDATE is political fiction if not at its finest, certainly at its most forceful on the screen, and earned distinction as one of the first of a genre that mixed reality, symbolism, and the fantastic, alternating caprice and grim fact so that the view is jarred from one scene to the next, like riding on a speeding train constantly being rerouted. Frankenheimer reportedly created the brainwashing scenes on the spot, having no specifications in the script for such sequences. He is only partially effective here in that he allows his cameras—with weird angles, fluid dolly and truck shots—to achieve what is not spoken, let alone explained, as the GIs are put through their paces by an unctuous Chinese military psychiatrist (if you can call him that). Sinatra reportedly invested considerable money in this production, which saw a huge box-office return.

p, George Axelrod, John Frankenheimer; d, Frankenheimer; w, Axelrod, Frankenheimer (based on the novel by Richard Condon); ph, Lionel Lindon; m, David Amram; ed, Ferris Webster; prod d, Richard Sylbert; md, Amram; art d, Richard Sylbert, Phil Jeffries; set d, George R. Nelson; cos, Moss Mabry; spec eff, Paul Pollard; makeup, Bernard Ponedel, Jack Freeman, Ron Berkeley, Dorothy Parkinson.

Drama/War **(PR:C-O MPAA:NR)**

MANDABI**

(1970, Fr./Senegal) 90m Les Films Domireve-Comptoir Francais du Film/Grove c (LE MANDAT; AKA: THE MONEY ORDER)

Mamadou Gueye *(Ibrahim Dieng)*, Ynousse N'Diaye *(1st Wife)*, Issa Niang *(2nd Wife)*, Serigne N'Diayes *(Imam)*, Serigne Sow *(Maissa)*, Moustapha Toure *(Shopkeeper)*, Farba Sarr *(Businessman)*, Moudoun Faye *(Mailman)*, Moussa Diouf *(Nephew)*, Christophe M'Doulabia [Christophe Colomb] *(Water Seller)*, Therese Bas *(Dieng's Sister)*, Mamadou Cisoko.

Gueye tries to cash a money order from his nephew, but finds he can't because he doesn't have an identity card. He can't get an identity card without a birth certificate, and he can't get a certificate without a photograph. Everywhere he goes he must have something else—either identification or money. After a series of misfortunes and setbacks, Gueye realizes his nephew is ripping him off.

p, Jean Maumy; d&w, Ousmane Sembene (based on a story by L. S. Senghor); ph, Paul Soulignac (Eastmancolor); ed, Gilou Kikoine.

Comedy **(PR:A MPAA:NR)**

MANDALAY* 1/2 (1934) 65m WB bw

Kay Francis *(Tanya Borisoff/Spot White)*, Ricardo Cortez *(Tony Evans)*, Warner Oland *(Nick)*, Lyle Talbot *(Dr. Gregory Burton)*, Ruth Donnelly *(Mrs. Peters)*, Reginald Owen *(Police Commissioner)*, Hobart Cavanaugh *(Purser)*, David Torrence *(Captain)*, Rafaela Ottiano *(The Countess)*, Halliwell Hobbes *(Col. Dawson Ames)*, Etienne Girardot *(Mr. Abernathie)*, Lucien Littlefield *(Mr. Peters)*, Bodil Rosing *(Mrs. Kleinschmidt)*, Herman Bing *(Prof. Kleinschmidt)*, Harry C. Bradley *(Henry P. Warren)*, James B. Leong *(Ram Singh)*, Shirley Temple *(Betty Shaw)*, Lillian Harmer *(Louisa Mae Harrington)*, Torben Meyer *(Mr. Van Brinker)*, Leonard Mudie *(Lieutenant)*, Frank Baker *(1st Mate)*, Olaf Hytten *(Cockney Purser)*, Eric Wilton *(English Agent)*, Otto Frisco *(Fakir)*, George Huerrera *(Steward)*, Desmond Roberts *(Sergeant)*.

Lithe, lean Kay Francis looks wonderful in clothes because she had very little bust to break the lines of the Orry-Kelly creations. She also has great difficulty pronouncing her "r's" and her screenwriters knew that so they attempted to write her speeches with as few of those offending letters as they could. In this piece of fluff, Francis is the lover of Cortez, a shadowy munitions smuggler, who dumps her in steamy Rangoon where she gets a job at a local nightspot run by Oland (in another of his bogus Oriental impressions). She soon becomes the kind of star Marlene Dietrich used to be when dumped in places by her various screen lovers. Later, she gets together with drunken doctor Talbot and they are soon in love. Cortez walks back into the picture and gets his. He fakes a suicide by leaving the porthole in his cabin open and an empty poison bottle on the table. But Francis eventually puts some poison in his drink and he falls overboard and no one seems to notice or care. Everybody drinks and smokes and makes witty small talk and the film's short length is its main asset. Francis is lovely to look at and dreadful (or is it dweadful?) to listen to. An escapist film for everyone who was suffering the ills of the Depression, MANDALAY is a curious film because it allowed the lady to get away with murder (or so it seemed), something that was usually frowned (or is it fwowned?) upon. Sammy Fain and Irving Kahal wrote the song "When Tomorrow Comes."

p, Robert Presnell; d, Michael Curtiz; w, Austin Parker, Charles Kenyon (based on a story by Paul Hervey Fox); ph, Tony Gaudio; ed, Thomas Pratt; art d, Anton Grot; cos, Orry-Kelly; m/l, Irving Kahal, Sammy Fain.

Comedy/Drama **(PR:A-C MPAA:NR)**

MANDARIN MYSTERY, THE* 1/2 (1937) 65m REP bw

Eddie Quillan *(Ellery Queen)*, Charlotte Henry *(Josephine Temple)*, Rita La Roy *(Martha Kirk)*, Wade Boteler *(Inspector)*, Franklin Pangborn *(Mellish)*, George Irving *(Dr. Alexander Kirk)*, Kay Hughes *(Irene Kirk)*, William Newell *(Guffy)*, George Walcott *(Donald Trent)*, Edwin Stanley *(Bronson)*, Edgar Allen *(Reporter)*, Anthony Merrill *(Craig)*, Richard Beach *(Reporter)*, Monte Vandegrift *(1st Detective)*.

Quillan is the detective trying to recover a valuable Chinese Mandarin stamp who uncovers a ring of counterfeiters, and manages to fall in love. Strong, believable performances are severely marred by a cliched script and weak direction, with the film unfortunately mostly played for laughs. Republic dropped the Ellery Queen programmers after this, its second attempt to make a series out of the detective, and Ellery Queen was not picked up again until 1940, when Columbia resumed the format for seven more features. (See ELLERY QUEEN series, Index.)

p, Nat Levine; d, Ralph Staub; w, John F. Larkin, Rex Taylor, Gertrude Orr, Cortland Fitzsimmons (based on a story by Ellery Queen); ph, Jack Marta; m, Harry Grey; ed, Grace Goddard.

Crime/Comedy **Cas.** **(PR:A MPAA:NR)**

MANDINGO** (1975) 126m PAR c

James Mason *(Maxwell)*, Susan George *(Blanche)*, Perry King *(Hammond)*, Richard Ward *(Agamemnon)*, Brenda Sykes *(Ellen)*, Ken Norton *(Mede)*, Lillian Hayman *(Lucrezia Borgia)*, Roy Poole *(Doc Redfield)*, Ji-Tu Cumbuka *(Cicero)*, Ben Masters *(Charles)*, Paul Benedict *(Brownlee)*, Ray Spruell *(Wallace)*, Louis Turenne *(De Veve)*, Duane Allen *(Topaz)*, Earl Maynard *(Babouin)*, Beatrice Winde *(Lucy)*, Debbie Morgan *(Dite)*, Irene Tedrow *(Mrs. Redfield)*, Reda Wyatt *(Big Pearl)*, Simon McQueen *(Madame Caroline)*, Evelyn Hendrickson *(Beatrix)*, Stanley Reyes *(Major Woodford)*, John Barber *(Le Toscan)*, Durwyn Robinson *(Meg)*, Kerwin Robinson *(Alph)*, Deborah Ann Young *(Tense)*, Debra Blackwell *(Blonde Girl)*, Kuumba *(Black Mother)*, Stocker Fontelieu *(Wilson)*.

Dreary dramatization of a popular novel has Mason as a slave owner with a firm belief in master-slave relations. King is the heir son who learns of a new type of existence in master-slave relations through his affair with a pretty slave, and his gambling with her husband. Performances are overdramatized and unbelievable in a script which suffers from the same weaknesses. Heavyweight boxer Ken Norton debuted in this role as King's favorite fighting slave.

p, Dino DeLaurentiis; d, Richard Fleischer; w, Norman Wexler (based on the novel by Kyle Onstott and the play by Jack Kirkland); ph, Richard H. Kline (Technicolor); m, Maurice Jarre; ed, Frank Bracht; prod d, Boris Leven; set d, John Austin; cos, Ann Roth; m/l, "Born in This Time," Jarre, Hi Tide Harris (sung by Muddy Waters).

Drama **Cas.** **(PR:O MPAA:R)**

MANDRAGOLA**

(1966 Fr./Ital.) 97m Arco Film-CCFC-Lux/Europix-Consolidated bw (LA MANDRAGOLA; AKA: MANDRAGOLA/THE LOVE ROOT; THE LOVE ROOT)

Rosanna Schiaffino *(Lucrezia)*, Philippe Leroy *(Callimaco)*, Jean-Claude Brialy *(Ligurio)*, Totò *(Fra Timoteo)*, Romolo Valli *(Nicia)*, Nilla Pizzi *(Sostrata, Lucrezia's*

Mother), Armando Bandini *(Siro)*, Pia Fioretti, Mimo Billi, Donato Castellaneta, Ugo Attanasio, Luigi Leoni, Renato Montalbano.

Subtle adaptation of the long-banned Machiavelli classic has Valli as the husband desperate for his faithful wife to have a baby. Leroy poses as a doctor, convincing the wife, Schiaffino, to take a potion made of the Mandrake weed, which will cause the first man to lay with her to die, but will cure her sterility. Leroy disguises himself in order to become the intended victim, revealing himself to Schiaffino. The two fall in love proving the husband to be more concerned with making money than with his wife's needs. Performances, dubbed in English, are good, aided by a well-polished direction.

p, Alfred Bini; d, Alberto Lattuada; w, Lattuada, Luigi Magni, Stefano Strucchi (based on a story by Niccolo Machiavelli); ph, Tonino Delli Colli; m, Gino Marinuzzi Jr.; ed, Nino Baragli; cos, Danilo Donati.

Drama/Comedy **(PR:A MPAA:NR)**

MANDRAGOLA/THE LOVE ROOT (SEE: MANDRAGOLA, 1966, Fr./Ital.)

MANDY (SEE: CRASH OF SILENCE, 1952, Brit.)

MANFISH* ½ (1956) 78m UA c

John Bromfield *(Brannigan)*, Lon Chaney, Jr. *("Swede")*, Victor Jory *("Professor")*, Barbara Nichols *(Mimi)*, Tessa Prendergast *(Alita)*, Eric Coverly *(Chavez)*, Vincent Chang *(Domingo)*, Theodore Purcell *("Big Boy")*, Vere Johns *(Bianco)*, Arnold Shanks *(Aleppo)*, Clyde Hoyte *(Calypso)*, Jack Lewis *(Warren)*.

Loosely based on two Edgar Allan Poe short stories, "The Gold Bug" and "The Tell-tale Heart," this picture teams up Jory and Bromfield to find a hidden pirate treasure. After they find the treasure—and Jory has made good use of the Manfish, Bromfield's boat—Jory kills Bromfield, tying the body to an oxygen tank. Picture was actually shot off the coast of Jamaica, lending a picturesque background. Otherwise, the film fails to captivate interest for too long a period, with performances void of believability. Barbara Nichols in her first film role, a tough songstress. Calypso numbers include: "Big Fish" and "Goodbye" sung by Clyde Hoyte, and "Beware the Caribbean" by Albert Elms.

p&d, W. Lee Wilder; w, Joel Murcott, Myles Wilder (based on "The Tell-tale Heart" and "The Gold Bug" by Edgar Allan Poe); ph, Charles S. Wellborn (De Luxe Color); m, Albert Elms; ed, G. Turney Smith; m/l, Richard Koerner, Clyde Hoyte, Elms.

Adventure **(PR:A MPAA:NR)**

MANGANINNIE ½** (1982, Aus.) 91m Tasmanian/Contemporary c

Mawuyul Yathalawuy *(Manganinnie)*, Anna Ralph *(Joanna Waterman)*, Phillip Hinton *(Edward Waterman)*, Elaine Mangan *(Margaret Waterman)*, Buruminy Dhamarrandji *(Meenopeekameena)*, Reg Evans *(Quinn)*, Jonathan Elliott *(Simon Waterman)*, Timothy Latham *(William Waterman)*, Barry Pierce, Tony Tapp, Paddy Garritty, Brian Duhig, Barrie Muir, Lex Clark, Peter Thompson, Brian Young, Allen Harvey, Don Evans, Bill McCluskey, Leone Dickson, Tas Burns.

Director John Honey's first feature is a slow-moving tale from Australia in which a girl lost in the desert, Ralph, meets up with an aborigine woman looking for her lost tribe. The two cannot speak each other's language but manage to create a system of communication, enabling them to search together. The film lacks any real sense of pace or dramatic content, but concentrates much too heavily on the scenery and the aborigine going through her rituals. The picture can be commended for approaching the problems with the way the white man has abused the aborigines.

p, Gilda Baracchi; d, John Honey; w, Ken Kelso (based on the novel by Beth Roberts); ph, Gary Hansen (Eastmancolor); m, Peter Sculthorpe; ed, Mike Woolveridge; art d, Neil Angwin.

Adventure **(PR:A MPAA:G)**

MANGO TREE, THE ½** (1981, Aus.) 93m Pisces/Satori c

Geraldine Fitzgerald *(Grandma Carr)*, Robert Helpmann *(The Professor)*, Christopher Pate *(Jamie Carr)*, Gerald Kennedy *(Preacher Jones)*, Gloria Dawn *(Pearl)*, Carol Burns *(Maudie Plover)*, Barry Pierce *(Angus McDonald)*, Diane Craig *(Miss Pringle)*, Ben Gabriel *(Wilkenshaw)*, Gerry Duggan *(Scanlon)*, Jonathan Atherton *("Stinker" Hatch)*, Tony Bonner *(Capt. Hinkler)*.

Set in Queensland during WW I, Pate plays a teenage boy whose relation to his environment and the local inhabitants changes as he becomes more aware of his society and his sexuality. Film is crucially marred by the miscasting of Pate (the producer's son) as the lead figure; he just doesn't look like a teenage kid. Otherwise the performances are all topnotch, with good production values.

p, Michael Pate; d, Kevin Dobson; w, Pate (based on the novel by Ronald McKie); ph, Brian Probyn; m, Marc Wilkinson; ed, John Scott; art d, Leslie Binns; cos, Pat Forster.

Drama **Cas.** **(PR:O MPAA:NR)**

MANHANDLED** (1949) 96m PAR bw

Dorothy Lamour *(Merl Kramer)*, Don Duryea *(Karl Benson)*, Sterling Hayden *(Joe Cooper)*, Irene Hervey *(Ruth Bennett)*, Philip Reed *(Guy Bayard)*, Harold Vermilyea *(Dr. Redman)*, Alan Napier *(Alton Bennett)*, Art Smith *(Detective Lt. Dawson)*, Irving Bacon *(Sgt. Fayle)*.

Not quite a *film noir*, MANHANDLED is a little lighter than that, perhaps a *film gris*. Napier tells his psychiatrist, Vermilyea, that he has been suffering from a nightmare. He dreams that he has murdered his wife, Hervey, when he found out that she was sneaking around with a lover behind his back. In no time at all, Hervey is found dead and her best gems are missing. Napier is immediately suspected by detective Smith and by the insurance investigator on the case, Hayden. Napier, as you might imagine, is innocent. (Nobody accused of a crime in the first reel is ever guilty. Otherwise there wouldn't be a film. One notable exception is 1985's THE JAGGED EDGE in which Jeff Bridges is accused of killing his wife and. . .oh, but we should not be telling you that, should we?) Lamour, who might have helped the film if there had been a scene in which she could have worn a sarong, is Vermilyea's secretary and she types up all the cases, so she knew about the dream and the jewels. She had told her nogoodnick boy friend, Duryea, about it and that rat, a lowlife private eye, managed to get a duplicate key to the Napier apartment. He intended to steal the gems but when he got there, Vermilyea had already murdered Hervey and was stealing the baubles. Duryea subdued Vermilyea and took the jewels away. Vermilyea tells Duryea that he knows it was Duryea and the two men cook up a plan to frame Lamour for the murder so they can share the booty and get off untouched. Vermilyea seems to go along with Duryea's plan but it is a ruse and he locks Duryea in a closet, then runs off with the gems. Duryea cannot be held in check very long, crashes out of the closet and runs Vermilyea down with his car. Now he has the gems and he wants to get rid of Lamour so he goes to her place and is about to kill her because he knows she may blow the whistle on him. That attempt is stymied when Smith and Bacon arrive and keep Duryea from tossing Lamour off the roof. A couple of jokes liven things up and Duryea does a good job in the role of the underhanded private eye. He was the epitome of the cynical and sneering evil soul for whom women always fall. In later years, he became well-known in that type of role but his earliest success came when he played the weak-willed son in the Broadway play (and the later film of) Lillian Hellman's "The Little Foxes."

p, William H. Pine, William C. Thomas; d, Lewis R. Foster; w, Foster, Whitman Chambers (based on the story "The Man Who Stole a Dream" by L. S. Goldsmith); ph, Ernest Laszlo; m, Darryl Calker; ed, Howard Smith; md, David Chudnow; art d, Lewis H. Creber; set d, Alfred Keggeris; cos, Edith Head, Odette Myrtil; makeup, Paul Stanhope, Emil Lavigne.

Crime **(PR:A MPAA:NR)**

MANHATTAN***** (1979) 96m UA bw

Woody Allen *(Isaac Davis)*, Diane Keaton *(Mary Wilke)*, Michael Murphy *(Yale)*, Mariel Hemingway *(Tracy)*, Meryl Streep *(Jill)*, Anne Byrne *(Emily)*, Karen Ludwig *(Connie)*, Michael O'Donoghue *(Dennis)*, Victor Truro, Tisa Farrow, Helen Hanft *(Party Guests)*, Bella Abzug *(Guest of Honor)*, Gary Weis *(Television Director)*, Kenny Vance *(Television Producer)*, Charles Levin, Karen Allen, David Rasche *(TV Actors)*, Damion Sheller *(Isaac's Son, Willie)*, Wallace Shawn *(Jeremiah)*, Mark Linn Baker, Frances Conroy *(Shakespearean Actors)*, Bill Anthony *(Porsche Owner #1)*, John Doumanian *(Porsche Owner #2)*, Ray Serra *(Pizzeria Waiter)*.

People may argue about the relative merits of ANNIE HALL (which took Oscars for Best Picture, Best Direction, Best Actress, and Best Screenplay) vis-a-vis MANHATTAN, which won nothing but is a better and more realized film. By this time, Allen had forsworn the glib one-liner and spent more time developing rich, round characters about whom we could care. As the title indicates, the action takes place on that small island that the Dutch bilked out of the Manhattan Indians for a pittance. Allen is a well-known and wealthy television scribe who has had it with the medium and wants to use his talent to amuse in another fashion, perhaps even with something serious. He knows how to make people laugh but can he move them? A study in New York neuroses (if there's one he does not have, it is only because he has not heard of it yet, but give him time), Allen sometimes lives with the teen-age Hemingway, who is studying drama at her high school and may still be growing. He is more than twice her age and it weighs on his mind and contributes to his already full capacity for guilt. Hemingway adores him and wants nothing more than to please him but he begins pushing her away and opting for an end to their relationship. He talks about his dreams of becoming an important writer and shares his angst about Hemingway with his best friend, Murphy, who admits that he is not having an easy time of it in his domestic relationship with his wife, Byrne (who had been married to Dustin Hoffman off-screen). Ennui has set into the Murphy-Byrne marriage and he has taken up with Keaton, a bright but apparently pseudo-intellectual woman. Murphy is also suffering in his work and would like to toss aside his frippery in favor of something more challenging. Murphy introduces Keaton to Allen and Allen finds her annoying, aggressive, and, underneath that, fascinating. In a while, Allen realizes that her behavior is all a sham and she is, in truth, a lovely person who is acting the way she thinks people should act in Manhattan. They become friends, though not lovers. Not yet. Allen visits his ex-wife, Streep, who has taken their young son, Sheller, and moved in with a lesbian, Ludwig, with whom she is deliriously happy. Streep is writing a book about her life with Allen, her divorce, and her ultimate happiness as a lesbian. The book is called *Marriage, Divorce and Selfhood* and Allen tries to persuade her not to publish it. But she does and it's a huge hit and everyone in America now knows how weird Allen is. Meanwhile, Hemingway is growing closer to Allen and he continues to discourage the attachment, insisting that their age differential is too vast to overcome. Murphy and Keaton decide to terminate their affair and Murphy, who knows that Allen and Keaton do like each other, suggests that they begin a relationship. When Keaton and Allen commence their affair, Allen seriously brushes Hemingway off by saying that it would be better if she went to London for her dramatic school education. Deeper into his affair with Keaton, Allen understands that she still adores Murphy and could never be that passionate about him. Allen knows that Murphy loves Keaton, but does not have the courage to leave his wife to enjoy some mid-life happiness with Keaton. He chastizes Murphy for being weak and breaks off with Keaton. Later, Allen works up the courage to quit his writing job in television and begins work on his novel, a huge, sprawling work on the city he loves—if he can ever get past the first page which he rewrites several times during the movie. Later, Allen lies down on his couch and turns on his small tape recorder so he can list all the things he loves: "Let's see, there's Willy Mays, the crabs at Sam Wo's. . .Tracy's face" . . .Hemingway plays Tracy and with that, he leaps off the couch and runs into the streets looking for a taxi. Naturally, there's none to be found and he races along the avenues of his beloved borough until he finally gets to the apartment building where

Hemingway lives. She is about to leave for her six-month term in London and Allen finally understands the depth of his love for her but it is too late, she's already committed to the trip and there is no way she can stop. Allen attempts to persuade her to stay but no, she feels it's important for her to leave Manhattan, to stretch her legs, spread her wings, and see what life is like east of First Avenue. Allen fears that she will change, she will not be the same person, perhaps she will even forget his name. She assures him that she will be back in half a year and says, before getting into the waiting cab: "You have to have a little faith in people." And the look in Allen's eyes is as exquisite a moment as the smile on Charlie Chaplin's face when recognized by the once-blind girl in CITY LIGHTS. MANHATTAN is funny, though not as funny as some of Allen's earlier work. But it has such insight, such depth, that the other films seem as shallow as pie plates by comparison. The music, by that most Manhattan of all composers, George Gershwin, is the perfect accompaniment for the film. Allen's camera direction is as unobtrusive as a British butler and as he grows more mature, he seems to feel that the least direction is the best. And he is right. With faith in the script and the actors, why mess around with rack focus and lenses and shots that get in the way of the story? Shooting it in black and white was also a benefit as Manhattan is a black and white city (as opposed to Los Angeles, which looks as good as it's going to look in color) and the grime and grit have never seemed more inviting. Hemingway is breathtakingly beautiful and acts as well as she looks. In a small role, note Wallace Shawn, who has since distinguished himself as a writer for the stage and screen (MY DINNER WITH ANDRE) as well as an actor in several other films (ATLANTIC CITY). The producers petitioned to change the "R" rating to a "PG" but were turned down, mostly because of the content concerning the older man and the teen-age girl. If he never made another movie, this would be Woody Allen's masterpiece. The music is performed by the New York Philharmonic conducted by Zubin Mehta and the Buffalo Philharmonic conducted by Michael Tilson Thomas.

p, Charles H. Joffe; d, Woody Allen; w, Allen, Marshall Brickman; ph, Gordon Willis (Panavision); m, George Gershwin; ed, Susan E. Morse; prod d, Mel Bourne; set d, Robert Drumheller; cos, Albert Wolsky, Ralph Lauren; makeup, Fern Buchner.

Comedy/Drama **Cas.** **(PR:C MPAA:R)**

MANHATTAN ANGEL*½ (1948) 68m COL bw

Gloria Jean *(Gloria Cole)*, Ross Ford *(Eddie Swenson)*, Patricia White *(Maggie Graham)*, Thurston Hall *(Everett H. Burton)*, Alice Tyrrell *("Queenie" Walters)*, Benny Baker *(Aloysius Duff)*, Russell Hicks *(J. C. Rayland)*, Fay Baker *(Vi Langdon)*, Toni Harper *(Toni)*, Jimmy Lloyd *(Elmer)*, Leonard Sues *(Lester)*, Ralph Hodges *(Harry)*, Dorothy Vaughan *(Mrs. Cole)*, Isabel Withers *(Miss Shelton)*, Peggy Wynne *(Esther)*, Barbara Brier *(Virginia Schuyler)*, Ida Moore *(Priscilla Lund)*, Robert Cherry *(Gus Davis)*.

Dull, predictable yarn has Jean as an advertising copywriter fighting to raise money to keep a factory from being built over a youth center on the Lower East Side. She has a face-off with the tightwad owner of the factory, and her own agency's chief account. Direction is slack and ill-paced, with varied performances. High points: Jean's singing powers. Songs include: "I'll Take Romance" (Oscar Hammerstein II and Ben Oakland), "Candy Store Blues" (Nick Castle, Herb Jeffries, Eddie Beal), "Naughty Aloysius" (Robert Wilder), and "It's a Wonderful, Wonderful Feeling" (Jack Segal, Dewey Bergman).

p, Sam Katzman; d, Arthur Dreifuss; w, Albert Derr (based on the story by George H. Plympton, Derr); ph, Ira H. Morgan; ed, Richard Fantl; md, Mischa Bakaleinikoff; art d, Paul Palmentola.

Musical **(PR:A MPAA:NR)**

MANHATTAN COCKTAIL** (1928) 72m PAR bw

Nancy Carroll *(Babs)*, Richard Arlen *(Fred)*, Danny O'Shea *(Bob)*, Paul Lukas *(Renov)*, Lilyan Tashman *(Mrs. Renov)*.

Early sound picture is without dialog, only using the sound to produce two vocal numbers sung by Carroll. Story opens with a symbolic prologue of the Greek myth in which Theseus slays the Minotaur, then flees with Ariadne from the Isle of Crete. The actual story opens with two guys and a gal, recent college graduates, out to pursue their careers on Broadway. They meet up with a merciless producer, Lukas, who forces the kids to lose any desire to continue with the stage. Despite the unsympathetic role of the producer created by the writers, Lukas turns in a fine performance.

d, Dorothy Arzner; w, Ethel Doherty (based on a story by Ernest Vajda); ph, Harry Fischbeck; ed, Doris Drought; m/l, "Another Kiss" and "Gotta Be Good" Victor Schertzinger.

Drama **(PR:A MPAA:NR)**

MANHATTAN HEARTBEAT** (1940) 72m FOX bw

Robert Sterling *(Johnny Farrell)*, Virginia Gilmore *(Dottie)*, Joan Davis *(Edna)*, Edmund MacDonald *(Spike)*, Don Beddoe *(Preston)*, Paul Harvey *(Dr. Bentley)*, Irving Bacon *(Sweeney)*, Mary Carr *(Lady In Music Store)*, Ann Doran *(Shop Girl's Friend)*, Jill Bennett *(Shop Girl)*, James Flavin *(Truck Driver)*, Edgar Dearing *(Policeman)*, Jan Duggan *(Wife)*, Harry Tyler *(Husband)*, Gaylord Pendleton *(Tony)*, Edward Earle *(Official)*, Murray Alper *(Mechanic)*, Dick Winslow *(Bus Driver)*, George Reed *(Porter)*, Louise Lorimer, Ruth Warren *(Nurses)*, Emmett Vogan *(Doctor)*, Lenita Lane *(Bentley's Nurse)*.

Remake of BAD GIRL released nine years previously, but lacking the comic quality of the earlier film. This one concentrates on the romance and marriage of a young couple, Sterling and Gilmore, and their troubles adapting to responsibilities. Sterling is an airplane mechanic, who must make some extra money to pay for doctor bills, and to keep his nagging, expectant wife off his back. Scripting is slowly paced, with a weak and novice-like direction. Performances are adequate, with Davis managing to generate some humor.

p, Sol M. Wurtzel; d, David Burton; w, Harold Buchman, Clark Andrews, Jack Jungmeyer, Jr., Edith Skouras (based on the play by Vina Delmar and Brian Marlow, from the novel by Delmar); ph, Virgil Miller; ed, Alexander Troffey; md, Cyril J. Mockridge.

Drama **(PR:A MPAA:NR)**

MANHATTAN LOVE SONG** (1934) 72m MON/FD bw

Robert Armstrong *(Williams)*, Dixie Lee *(Jerry Stewart)*, Helen Flint *(Carol Stewart)*, Franklin Pangborn *(Garrett Weatherby)*, Nydia Westman *(Annette)*, Harold Waldridge *(Phineas Jones)*, Cecil Cunningham *(Pancake Annie)*, Harrison Green *(Joe Thomas)*, Herman Bing *(Gustave)*, Edward Dean.

Lee and Flint are two wealthy, carefree sisters who suddenly find themselves penniless when their financial advisor commits suicide. Their chauffeur and maid have saved up enough money to take over the rent of the house, the two sisters taking up the household duties. Fine performances are marred by miscasting. Script has many amusing twists, but direction is off-paced and weak.

p, Trem Carr; d, Leonard Fields; w, Fields, David Silverstein (based on the novel by Cornell Woolrich); ph, Robert Planck; ed, Carl Pierson; m/l, Bernie Grossman, Edward Ward, Silverstein.

Comedy **(PR:A MPAA:NR)**

MANHATTAN MADNESS, 1936

(SEE: ADVENTURE IN MANHATTAN, 1936)

MANHATTAN MADNESS, 1943, Brit.

(SEE: ADVENTURE IN BLACKMAIL, 1943, Brit.)

MANHATTAN MELODRAMA**** (1934) 93m COS/MGM bw

Clark Gable *(Blackie Gallagher)*, William Powell *(Jim Wade)*, Myrna Loy *(Eleanor)*, Leo Carrillo *(Father Joe)*, Nat Pendleton *(Spud)*, George Sidney *(Poppa Rosen)*, Isabel Jewell *(Anabelle)*, Muriel Evans *(Tootsie Malone)*, Claudelle Kaye *(Miss Adams)*, Frank Conroy *(Blackie's Attorney)*, Jimmy Butler *(Jim as a Boy)*, Mickey Rooney *(Blackie as a Boy)*, Landers Stevens *(Inspector of Police)*, Harry Seymour *(Piano Player)*, William N. Bailey, King Mojave, W. R. Walsh *(Croupiers)*, Charles R. Moore *(Black Boy in Speakeasy)*, Thomas Jackson *(Snow)*, John Marston *(Coates)*, Lew Harvey *(Crap Dealer)*, Billy Arnold *(Black Jack Dealer)*, Jim James *(Chemin De Fer Dealer)*, Stanley Taylor *(Police Interne)*, James Curtis *(Party Leader)*, Herman Bing *(German Proprietor)*, Edward Van Sloan *(Yacht Skipper)*, Jay Eaton *(Drunk)*, Harrison Greene *(Eleanor's Dance Partner)*, Leslie Preston *(Jim's Dance Partner)*, William Stack *(Judge)*, Emmett Vogan, Sherry Hall *(Assistant District Attorneys)*, Lee Phelps *(Bailiff)*, Charles Dunbar *(Panhandler)*, John M. Bleifer *(Chauffeur)*, Allen Thompson *(Spectator on Street)*, G. Pat Collins *(Miller in Prison)*, Wade Boteler *(Guard in Prison)*, Sam McDaniel *(Black Man in Prison)*, James C. Eagles *(Boy in Prison)*, Samuel S. Hinds *(Warden)*, Don Brodie, Ralph McCullough, Eddie Hart *(Reporters)*, George Irving *(Campaign Manager)*, Garry Owen *(Campaign Manager)*, Bert Russell *(Blind Beggar)*, Lee Shumway, Carl Stockdale, Jack Kenny *(Policemen)*, Curtis Benton *(Announcer)*, Dixie Lonton *(Irish Woman)*, Pepi Sinoff *(Jewish Woman)*, Donald Haynes *(Stud)*, Bert Sprotte, William Irving *(German Note Holders)*, Alexander Melesh *(Master of Ceremonies)*, Vernon Dent *(Old German Man)*, Henry Roquemore *(Band Leader)*, Jack Lipson *(Uncle Angus)*, William Augustin, Stanley Blystone *(Detectives)*, Oscar Apfel *(Assembly Speaker)*, Leo Lance *(Trotsky)*, Leonid Kinskey *(Trotsky Aide)*, Shirley Ross *(Cotton Club Singer)*, Noel Madison *(Mannie Arnold)*, Pat Moriarity *(Heckler)*.

Gable, when he made this film, was king of the MGM lot and had just finished the sleeper of 1934, IT HAPPENED ONE NIGHT. Just as he was believable as the down-to-earth reporter in the Capra classic, he was most memorable in MANHATTAN MELODRAMA as the tough, callous, and fatalistic gangster whose only soft spot is for his boyhood friend. It's a splendid film, packed with action and the kind of tuxedo sophistication hallmarking the 1930s. Van Dyke, who had created the wonderful, awesome SAN FRANCISCO, one of the great disaster films of the decade, begins this slick opus with another real-life disaster, the awful burning of the *General Slocum,* a tourist tub which caught fire on June 15, 1904, burning in the middle of the East River and killing 1,021 persons before being beached. (Its captain, Van Schaick, later went to prison for negligence.) Two boys, Rooney and Butler, are on the boat with their families, heading for a picnic, and with them is priest Carrillo. When the ship begins to burn, both boys lose their families but are rescued in the water by Carrillo. Sidney, a kindly Jewish merchant who has lost his family in the catastrophe, takes both boys as his own and raises them. One, Butler, is a fine student and upstanding youth; Rooney, on the other hand, is a ne'er-do-well who spends his time shooting craps and cutting school. The youths, nevertheless, share a deep affection for each other, as would brothers. They grow up to be Gable, one of New York City's slickest and wealthiest gamblers and racketeers, and Powell, a noble prosecuting attorney who can't be bullied, bribed, or bought. Slinky, sultry Loy is Gable's girl, but she doesn't care too much for her lover's manners, morals, or general outlook. Loy is no common gangster's moll; she is educated, refined, beautiful, and full of wit. She abhors Gable's racketeering ways, believing he is decent at heart. She asks him to give up the rackets, but he only smiles. Lucky beyond belief, Gable wins against all comers, his tables always packed with more compulsive "suckers." Quips Loy: "You'll win somebody's mother some night." To him, everyone is on the take. "Everyone can be paid off with chips," he tells her. When Gable wins a yacht, he takes Loy aboard, promising that he will name the ship after her. She's more interested in marriage, children, and a home and tells him so. Gable turns a deaf ear to this understandable plea, wanting to keep things as they are. He asks her what's wrong with her that night. "It isn't tonight," she replies. "It's every night. Worrying about you, hating what you do, hating who you meet." It's clear that they are close to breaking up. Then Powell, Gable's boyhood friend, is elected to the powerful position of New York City prosecutor.

Gable intends to celebrate with him but business interferes and he sends Loy to entertain Powell. She gets into a taxi with the startled Powell, telling him: "Pardon me if I intrude," explaining that Gable has sent her as a substitute. They go to the Cotton Club where they keep tempo with the band by using little wooden mallets provided by the club, and enter into a bantering conversation that was to be the hallmark of the Loy-Powell love team for the next two decades, this being their first film together. "Nothing like a district attorney to keep a girl in shape," she tells him. "We must have a good wrestle some day." The urbane and smooth-talking Powell then gives her a glossy account of his life, opening with the line: "I was born at home because I wanted to be near mother." Meanwhile, Gable is having trouble with Madison, a high-stepping gambler who has welched on a wager. After getting his last excuse from Madison, Gable pays him a visit with his sidekick Pendleton. Gable shoots Madison when he goes for a gun and flees with Pendleton. But Pendleton leaves behind a coat he has picked up at Gable's apartment, one left by Powell when depositing Loy. The coat is found by police and Powell puts the coat and Gable together, although he can't believe his pal would murder someone in cold blood and leave his coat behind; Powell tells his assistant, Jackson, that Gable is innocent but Jackson insists that the coat belongs to Powell and that Gable is responsible for the Madison killing (Madison being a loose prototype of Arnold Rothstein, the infamous Manhattan gambler murdered in 1928, a killing never solved). When Gable hears what Pendleton has done, he has his sidekick rush to his tailor and make an exact copy of Powell's coat, planting the wooden mallet from the Cotton Club Powell had left behind in the coat pocket. Then, just as Powell is about to reluctantly indict Gable for the Madison killing, the new coat is delivered to Powell with a note from Gable, telling him that he had left this behind when taking Loy out on the town. Hurriedly, Powell tries on the coat and it fits perfectly. He compares it to the coat found in the murder room and is still puzzled. Then he reaches into the pocket of the coat he is wearing and finds the wooden mallet from the Cotton Club and proudly tells Jackson: "This is *my* coat!" He dismisses the notion that Gable was responsible for killing Madison. A short time later Loy breaks up with Gable and begins to see Powell. They marry and she settles down to the life she's always wanted. But during the campaign for governor, Jackson, who has been fired by Powell for his bribe-taking habits, tries to blackmail Powell, telling him that if he doesn't pay him off, he'll make it public that his wife was once Gable's lover and thus prove collusion in the Madison killing. Loy overhears this threat and goes to Gable, begging him to help. Gable helps by cornering Jackson in the men's room of Madison Square Garden where he shoots the blackmailer to death without batting an eyelash. He steps outside to see a blind beggar squatting on the floor. Gable smiles, tosses a dollar into the blind man's hat and walks away. The beggar lifts his dark glasses and looks after him. (This scene duplicates one appearing in Fritz Lang's M.) Some time later, with the blind man testifying, Gable is indicted for Jackson's killing, prosecuted ironically by Powell. Gable mutely sits in court while Powell attacks him as the corrupt product of Prohibition. When Gable's lawyer attempts to put up some sort of defense, Gable stops him, publicly admiring his friend. ("Class, it's written all over him," he tells his lawyer.) Powell, torn between his duty and his love for Gable, follows the dictates of the law. Loy, meanwhile, is beside herself; she has already visited Gable and begged him to tell Powell that it was she who put him up to confronting Jackson. He refuses to sully her marriage or destroy Powell's chance to be governor. In fact, Powell's brilliant prosecution of Gable will assure him of the governorship. The summation Powell makes to the jury is impassioned and eloquent: "For years men and women in this country tolerated racketeers and murderers. Because of their own hatred of Prohibition they felt in sympathy with those who broke a law they felt to be oppressive. Crime and criminals became popular. Killers became heroes. But, gentlemen—Prohibition has gone! And the gangsters and killers who came with it must go with it! In finding Blackie Gallagher guilty of murder we are faced with more than the avenging of one death. We are faced with a choice which we must make. Either we can surrender to an epidemic of crime and violence which would destroy our homes and our community or we can give warning to the gangsters and murderers that they are—through! In 1904, when the *General Slocum* burned, I made a boyish effort to save Blackie Gallagher's life. Today, I demand from you. . .his death!" Gable, hearing this, still loves his friend. Powell writes him a note in court which is passed to his table and reads: "Sorry, I had to do it." Gable writes back. "It's okay, kid. I can take it. Can you?" Gable is found guilty and is sentenced to the electric chair. Powell is elected governor on the strength of the conviction. As Gable's death date nears, Loy grows frantic. She begs Powell to commute Gable's sentence to life imprisonment but he refuses to show favoritism. Then she tells him that it was she who went to Gable and told him about Jackson's blackmailing of Powell and that he killed Jackson out of love for him. Powell, in shock, goes to the prison and tells Gable that he can't allow him to go to the chair, knowing what he knows. Gable tells him to forget it. He is resigned to death, as he has already let the prison population know, going from the main cell block into the death house with a swagger (while a prisoner plays music for him on a windup Victrola, "Blue Moon"), stopping at one cell and telling another condemned prisoner with bravado: "Keep your chin up and your nose clean, kid. Forget about that commutation. You don't want it anyway. Die the way you lived, all of a sudden, that's the way to go. Don't drag it out—living like that doesn't mean a thing." To Powell he repeats the same short, sweet philosophy, refusing to live out his life in prison: "If I can't live the way I want, let me die the way I want." He refuses clemency and swaggers to the electric chair. Later, in an anti-climactic scene, Powell resigns his position as governor, telling the New York state legislature that Gable killed a man for his benefit, even though he had no knowledge of the crime. Loy is waiting for him when he leaves the chamber. "What are you going to do," she asks him. "I don't know," Powell replies, "try again from the start. Something else." She begins walking with him, saying: "Let me try with you." Gable is hard as nails in this one—reflecting an inner core wrapped in granite, playing a man willing to kill for a friend and die for the deed, upholding his own strange code of ethics—where Powell, the sleek and polished pal, seems less attractive as the regular guy, one whose own ethics are so lofty as to tower beyond

the humanity of his friends and the woman he loves. So noble (and unbelievable) is Powell that he will give away his governorship and future over a principle. Gable and Powell are excellent as the polarized pals, even though they appear on screen together in only a few scenes. For Loy, this was her first significant role, after having appeared as vamps and Orientals since the silent days, her first film being PRETTY LADIES for MGM in 1925, although she did ease out of her stereotyped roles with substantial parts in THE ANIMAL KINGDOM (1932) and TOPAZE (1933). For Gable this was a candy-dance and he is fascinating as the hard-boiled cookie rushing toward death, impervious to law, society, and even manners. (Gable has some lines in this film that would never be allowed today. On his way to the electric chair he stops at a cell and tells a black prisoner: "Don't eat any wooden pork chops!" His crude manner is infectious; when one of his high-rolling customers wins big in Gable's casino, the man turns to Gable's black porter, handing him his winnings and saying: "Here, buy yourself a pair of yeller shoes!") The film, shot in Van Dyke's whirlwind style, completed in twenty-four days at a budget of $355,000, was very popular and earned more than $400,000 its first time around. The theme of two close friends going separate ways would be used countless times over in movies, notably in ANGELS WITH DIRTY FACES (1938) with James Cagney and Pat O'Brien. The teaming of Powell and Loy for the first time was electric and they would do thirteen more films together, most of them in the delightful THIN MAN series (see Index). Said Loy to a reporter about her first screen appearance with Powell: "From the very first scene we did together in MANHATTAN MELODRAMA we felt that particular magic there was between us. There was this feeling of rhythm, of complete understanding and an instinct of how each of us could bring out the best in the other." Future mogul Selznick produced this film and, despite protests from MGM executives, insisted upon using Powell, who had been a matinee idol since 1922 in the silent era. It was thought that Powell was "all washed up," but his appearance here as the dapper prosecutor and his teaming with Loy not only saved his career but made him a superstar all over again. This was the film that John Dillinger was reportedly watching on the night the FBI claimed he was killed in Chicago. (At the Biograph Theater, July 22, 1934, but evidence unearthed by Jay Robert Nash in two books, *Dillinger: Dead or Alive?* and *The Dillinger Dossier* clearly indicates otherwise.) MANHATTAN MELODRAMA was reprised on "Lux Radio Theatre," with Don Ameche playing Gable's role (!) on September 9, 1940.

p, David O. Selznick; d, W. S. Van Dyke II; w, Oliver H. P. Garrett, Joseph L. Mankiewicz (based on the story "Three Men" by Arthur Caesar); ph, James Wong Howe; ed, Ben Lewis; art d, Cedric Gibbons, Joseph Wright; set d, Edwin B. Willis; cos, Dolly Tree; spec eff, Slavko Vorkapich; m/l, Richard Rodgers, Lorenz Hart.

Crime Drama (PR:A MPAA:NR)

MANHATTAN MERRY-GO-ROUND*

(1937) 82m REP bw

Phil Regan *(Jerry Hart)*, Leo Carrillo *(Gordoni)*, Ann Dvorak *(Ann Rogers)*, Tamara Geva *(Charlizzini)*, James Gleason *(Danny the Duck)*, Henry Armetta *(Spadoni)*, Luis Alberni *(Martinetti)*, Smiley Burnette *(Frog)*, Selmer Jackson *(J. Henry Thorne)*, Eddie Kane *(McMurray)*, Moroni Olsen *(Jonathan)*, Nellie V. Nichols *(Momma Gordoni)*, Gennaro Curci *(Michael Angelo)*, Sam Finn *(Speed)*, Al Herman *(Blackie)*, Robert E. Perry *(Baldy)*, Jack Adair *(Eddie)*, Thelma Wunder *(Dorothy)*, Joe DiMaggio, Max Terhune, Gene Autry, The Lathrops, Rosalean and Seville *(Themselves)*, Ted Lewis, Cab Calloway, Jack Jenny and Their Orchestras, Louis Prima and His Band, Kay Thompson Ensemble.

The guest appearances by the many performers serve as the only strong point in this mish-mash collection of talent. It also hinders the story from developing. The story that does exist centers around a group of hoods, headed by Carrillo, who take over a sound recording company, using strong-arm methods of coercing disagreeable performers. Songs include: "Mamma I Wanna Make Rhythm" (Jerome Jerome, Richard Bryon, Walter Kent), "Manhattan Merry-Go-Round" (Pinky Herman [Herman Pinkus], Gustave Haenschen), "Heaven?" "I Owe You," "It's Round-up Time in Reno" (Gene Autry).

p, Harry Sauber; d, Charles F. Riesner; w, Sauber (based on a musical revue by Frank Hummert); ph, Jack Marta; ed, Murray Seldeen, Ernest Nims; md, Alberto Colombo.

Musical **Cas.** (PR:A MPAA:NR)

MANHATTAN MOON**

(1935) 67m UNIV bw (GB: SING ME A LOVE SONG)

Ricardo Cortez *(Dan Moore)*, Dorothy Page *(Yvonne/Toots Malloy)*, Henry Mollison *(Reggie Van Dorset)*, Hugh O'Connell *(Speed)*, Luis Alberni *(Luigi)*, Henry Armetta *(Tony)*, Regis Toomey *(Eddie)*, L'Estrange Millman *(Secretary)*, Irving Bacon *(Lunch Man)*, Jean Rogers.

Lighthearted fare, if not predictable, stars Page as a French nightclub singing sensation, with a double, also played by Page, who takes the singing star's place at all social engagements. Cortez is the rags-to-riches nightclub owner determined to seduce the singer, but who unintentionally falls for her double. Highlights of the picture are the songs sung by Page, which include: "Manhattan Moon," "My Other Me," "First Kiss" (Arthur Morton, Betty Trivers).

p, Stanley Bergerman; d, Stuart Walker; w, Robert Presnell, Barry Trivers, Ben Grauman Kohn, Aben Kandel (based on a story by Robert Harris); ph, Charles Stumar; m, Karl Hajos; ed, Phil Cahn.

Comedy (PR:A MPAA:NR)

MANHATTAN MUSIC BOX

(SEE: MANHATTAN MERRY-GO-ROUND, 1938)

MANHATTAN PARADE*1/2

(1931) 78m WB c

Winnie Lightner *(Doris)*, Charles Butterworth *(Herbert)*, Walter Miller *(John)*, Joe Smith *(Lou Delman)*, Charles Dale *(Jake Delman)*, Greta Grandstedt *(Charlotte)*,

Bobby Watson (Paisley), Dickie Moore (Junior), Luis Alberni (Vassiloff), Polly Walters (Phone Girl), Charles Middleton (Sheriff), Claire McDowell (Nancy), Douglas Gerard (Toreador), Nat Pendleton (Lady Godiva's Husband), Bill Irving (The Suit of Armor), Harold Waldridge (1st Page Boy), Frank Conroy (Brighton), William Humphries (Napoleon), Edward Van Sloan (Lawyer), Ethel Griffies (Mrs. Beacon).

Satire of backstage life on Broadway loses its effect as it falls into slapstick routines. Smith and Dale are two producers who are victims of the whims of an eccentric and demanding foreign director in their attempts to stage a costly costume production. Performances are varied, with Lightner suffering from miscasting, which indicates the position she was in with Warner Brothers at the time. Script manages to generate some laughs, but otherwise falls flat. Songs include: "I Love a Parade," "Temporarily Blue" (Ted Koehler, Harold Arlen), "I'm Happy When You're Jealous" (Bert Kalmar, Harry Ruby).

d, Lloyd Bacon; w, Robert Lord, Houston Branch (based on the play "She Means Business" by Samuel Shipman); ph, Dev Jennings (Technicolor); ed, Bill Holmes.

Musical   (PR:A MPAA:NR)

MANHATTAN SHAKEDOWN*   (1939) 56m Warwick bw

John Gallaudet (Jerry Tracey), Rosalind Keith (Gloria Stoner), George McKay (Brains), Reginald Hincks (Dr. Stoner), Bob Rideout (Mike Orell), Phyllis Clare (Peggy Orell), Donald Douglas (Hadley Brown), Micael Heppell.

Low-budget routine story stars Gallaudet as the crusading columnist out to destroy a blackmailing doctor, Hincks. Performances are unimpressive, and the production suffers from lapses in continuity, e.g., a clock in the background is out of sync.

p, Kenneth J. Bishop; d, Leon Barsha; w, Edgar Edwards (based on a story by Theodore Tinsley); ph, George Meehan; ed, William Austin.

Drama   (PR:A MPAA:NR)

MANHATTAN TOWER*½   (1932) 67m Remington bw

Mary Brian, Irene Rich, James Hall, Hale Hamilton, Noel Francis, Nydia Westman, Clay Clement, Billy Dooley, Jed Prouty, Wade Boteler.

Mish-mash of stories taking place inside a large office building, reportedly the Empire State Building. Stories range from bank failures to love scenes to eccentric clerks. Story has good potential, with a fitting cast and an interesting plot, but all this was never fulfilled in production.

d, Frank Strayer; w, Norman Houston (based on a story by David Hempstead, Jr.; ph, Ira Morgan; ed, Harry Reynolds.

Drama   (PR:A MPAA:NR)

MANHUNT   (SEE: FROM HELL TO TEXAS, 1958)

MANHUNT   (SEE: ITALIAN CONNECTION, THE, 1973, U.S./Ital./Ger.)

MANHUNT IN THE JUNGLE**   (1958) 79m WB c

Robin Hughes (Cmdr. George M. Dyott), Luis Alvarez (Aloique), James Wilson (Col. P. H. Fawcett), Jorge Montoro (Carissimo), Natalia Manzuelas (Pedro's Wife), James Ryan (Wilbur Harris), John B. Symmes (Himself), Richard McCloskey (Dr. Emmett Wilson), Harry Knapp (Portuguese Explorer), Emilio Meiners (Pedro), Enrique Gonzales (Bernadino), M. Torres Acho (Juan), Alfonso Santilla (Julio).

Routine jungle adventure, shot entirely in the Amazon jungle, is based on the true story of the search for an explorer who mysteriously disappeared while trying to find a lost city. Performances are adequate if not realistic, with a story, though cliched, that manages to keep a thread of suspense going. Color photography of the jungle is stunning.

p, Cedric Francis; d, Tom McGowan; w, Sam Merwin, Jr., Owen Crump (based on the book Man Hunting in the Jungle by George M. Dyott); ph, Robert Brooker (Warner Color); m, Howard Jackson; ed, Robert Warwick; art d, William Jersey.

Adventure   (PR:A MPAA:NR)

MAN HUNTERS OF THE CARIBBEAN zero
(1938) 51m Inter-Continent bw

Andre Roosevelt, Capt. E. Erskine Loch, Carol Jeffries.

Group searching for hidden treasure comes into contact with warring natives, exotic animals, and other tropical items. Unbelievable performances in unrealistic situations, further marred by the lack of any sense of pacing, keep this picture from ever taking off. Instead it lapses into the ridiculous position of being unintentionally funny.

p, Luis Rojas de la Torres; d, Andre Roosevelt, Ewing Scott; w, Ethel La Blanche, Paul Franklin (based on a story by J. Hoffman, M. Shaff).

Adventure   (PR:A MPAA:NR)

MANIA**
(1961, Brit.) 87m Triad/Valiant-Pacemaker bw (GB: THE FLESH AND THE FIENDS; AKA: PSYCHO KILLERS; THE FIENDISH GHOULS)

Peter Cushing (Dr. Robert Knox), June Laverick (Martha), Donald Pleasence (William Hare), George Rose (William Burke), Dermot Walsh (Dr. Geoffrey Mitchell), Renee Houston (Helen Burke), Billie Whitelaw (Mary Patterson), John Cairney (Chris Jackson), Melvyn Hayes (Daft Jamie), June Powell (Maggie O'Hara), Geoffrey Tyrrell (Old Davey), Beckett Bould (Old Angus), George Bishop (Blind Man), Philip Leaver (Dr. Elliott), George Woodbridge (Dr. Ferguson), John Rae (Rev. Lincoln), Andrew Faulds (Inspector McCulloch), Esma Cannon (Aggie), Raf De La Torre (Baxter), Michael Balfour (Drunken Sailor), George Street (Barman), Michael Mulcaster (Undertaker), Jack McNaughton (Stallholder).

Sleazy 19th-Century Edinburgh is the backdrop for respectable doctor Cushing's immoral manner of medical research. A couple of hoods, Rose and Pleasence, aid Cushing by murdering townsfolk and letting him study the bodies. Their killing spree goes too far when they make corpses out of one of the doctor's pupils, his girl friend, and a well-liked community member. The duo is caught, and Rose goes to the gallows while Pleasence is grabbed by an angry mob that burns out his eyes. Cushing, meanwhile, maintains his community standing in an admirable dramatic role. Some excessive gore adds even more texture to the dreary atmosphere. Story is based on actual events that occurred in Scotland in the early 19th Century involving Burke and Hare.

p, Robert S. Baker, Monty Berman; d, John Gilling; w, Gilling, Leon Griffiths (based on a story by Gilling); ph, Berman (Dyaliscope); m, Stanley Black; ed, Jack Slade; art d, John Elphick.

Horror   (PR:O MPAA:NR)

MANIAC zero
(1934) 67m Roadshow Attractions/Hollywood Producers & Distributors bw

Bill Woods (Don Maxwell), Horace Carpenter (Dr. Meirschultz), Ted Edwards (Buckley), Phyllis Diller (Mrs. Buckley), Thea Ramsey (Alice Maxwell), Jennie Dark (Maizie), Marvel Andre (Marvel), Celia McGann (Jo), J. P. Wade (Mike the Morgue Attendant), Marion Blackton (Neighbor).

Just as every popular film genre had an early forebear, so has the mindless exploitation horror film. Before FRIDAY THE THIRTEENTH there was MANIAC, a racy (for its time) exploitation feature from the same people who gave the film world such camp classic shorts as MARIJUANA, WEED WITH ROOTS IN HELL, and HOW TO UNDRESS IN FRONT OF YOUR HUSBAND. Carpenter, a former member of Cecil B. DeMille's ensemble (and thus starting a trend of fine actors being reduced to quick exploitation features), is a mad scientist who wants to revive the dead. His assistant, Woods, is an ex-vaudevillian who does his master's bidding before going mad and killing Carpenter. Some of the better moments include a rather bizarre rapist who thinks he's Edgar Allan Poe's killer orangutan from "Murders in the Rue Morgue," the munching of a cat's eye, and two women battling it out in a locked chamber, using syringes as weapons. Director Esper and his wife Stadie operated off Hollywood's poverty row, and did quite good business. While they didn't get bookings in quality theaters, the majority of their films were booked in burlesque houses and the forerunners of the modern "adult" theaters. But Esper apparently had no shame, taking out an ad in "Modern Motherhood" magazine with his platform for decent, wholesome film fare. In its own way, MANIAC is something of a classic with a delightfully campy style. Footage from two silent features—the Swedish WITCHCRAFT THROUGH THE AGES (1920) and the German SIEGFRIED (1923) were also incorporated into the footage, superimposed over Woods' face to symbolize his deepening madness. Some editions of the film contained footage explaining the nature of mental illness, thus giving Esper the excuse to claim this was an educational feature. A final note: the Phyllis Diller listed in the cast is not the better known comedienne of the same name.

p&d, Dwain Esper; w, Hildegarde Stadie; ph, William Thompson; ed, William Austin.

Horror   Cas.   (PR:O MPAA:NR)

MANIAC**   (1963, Brit.) 87m Hammer/COL bw

Kerwin Mathews (Geoff Farrell), Nadia Gray (Eve Beynat), Donald Houston (Georges Beynat), Liliane Brousse (Annette Beynat), George Pastell (Inspector Etienne), Arnold Diamond (Janiello), Norman Bird (Salon), Justine Lord (Grace), Jerold Wells (Giles), Leon Peers (Blanchard).

Confusing plot has Houston sentenced to life imprisonment in an insane asylum after torching to death the man who raped his daughter Gray. Several years later, Mathews, a traveling American artist, wanders upon the girl and her stepmother, Brousse. He falls in love with Gray, and then is seduced by Brousse, who also convinces Mathews to help with her husband's escape. While her husband was in the asylum, Brousse had grown attached to his guard, who is willing to help the husband escape. After the escape, the husband is found dead in the trunk of a car, with a new torch killer on the loose. What could have been an interesting thriller is marred by a plot that is hard to follow, and lapses into a routine ending.

p, Jimmy Sangster; d, Michael Carreras; w, Sangster; ph, Wilkie Cooper (Megascope); m, Stanley Black; ed, Tom Simpson; md, Black; art d, Edward Carrick; makeup, Basil Newall.

Thriller   Cas.   (PR:C MPAA:NR)

MANIAC! zero
(1977) 90m New World c (AKA: RANSOM; ASSAULT ON PARADISE; THE TOWN THAT CRIED TERROR)

Oliver Reed, Deborah Raffin, Stuart Whitman, Jim Mitchum, John Ireland, Paul Koslo (Victor).

Whitman is a corrupt millionaire who is threatened by a Vietnam vet who dresses like an Indian. The vet threatens to kill all the important people in a resort town if he isn't given 5 million dollars. Whitman calls hit man Reed to take care of the situation. Raffin plays a reporter in this film, which degrades the image of Vietnam veterans.

p, James V. Hart; d, Richard Compton; w, John C. Broderick, Ron Silkosky; ph, Charles Correll; m, Don Ellis.

Drama   (PR:C MPAA:PG)

MANIAC, 1978, Ital.   (SEE: MANIAC MANSION, 1978, Ital.)

MANIAC* (1980) 87m Magnum/Analysis Film Corp. c

Joe Spinell *(Frank Zito)*, Caroline Munro *(Ann D'Antoni)*, Gail Lawrence *(Rita)*, Kelly Piper *(Nurse)*, Rita Montone *(Hooker)*, Tom Savini *(Disco Boy)*, Hyla Marrow *(Disco Girl)*, James Brewster *(Beach Boy)*, Linda Lee Walter *(Beach Girl)*, Tracie Evans *(Street Hooker)*, Sharon Mitchell *(2nd Nurse)*, Carol Henry *(Deadbeat)*, Nella Bacmeister *(Carmen Zito)*, Louis Jawitz *(Art Director)*, Denise Spagnuolo *(Denise)*, Billy Spagnuolo *(Billy)*, Frank Pesce *(TV Reporter)*, Candice Clements, Diane Spagnuolo *(Park Mothers)*, Kim Hudson *(Lobby Hooker)*, Terry Gagnon *(Woman in Alley)*, Joan Baldwin, Jeni Paz *(Models)*, Janelle Winston *(Waitress)*, Randy Jurgensen, Jimmy Aurichio *(Cops)*.

Exploitation slasher film, shot on location in New York City, has little to offer beyond blood and guts. Spinell plays a man, mistreated by his mother as a child, who takes it out on beautiful young women. He scalps his intended victims, placing the hair on mannequins in his apartment. An attempt at viewer identification has Spinell crying himself to sleep in the midst of the mannequins he considers his friends. He also manages to romance a young fashion photographer, Munro. Spinell is convincing in his role as the madman, but the script and direction are unable to balance the terror scenes with the rest of the story. Music performed by Gino Braniere, Don Armando's 2nd Avenue Rhumba Band.

p, Andrew Garroni, William Lustig; d, Lustig; w, C. A. Rosenberg, Joe Spinell (based on a story by Spinell); ph, Robert Lindsay (TVC Labs Color); m, Jay Chattaway; ed, Lorenzo Marinelli; makeup, Tom Savini.

Horror Cas. (PR:O MPAA:R)

MANIAC MANSION zero
(1978, Ital.) 85m Group I c (AKA: AMUCK; MANIAC; REPLICA OF A CRIME)

Farley Granger, Barbara Bouchet, Rosalba Neri, Silvio Amadio.

Surely there must be some sort of logical reason why actors with great roles to their names end up doing garbage like MANIAC MANSION. Granger, who is best remembered for his fine performance in Alfred Hitchcock's classic STRANGERS ON A TRAIN (1951), is reduced to playing a mystery writer turned sexual lunatic in this wretched exercise. When his secretary is missing, Bouchet (the woman's sister) goes out looking for her. It was originally produced in 1972, but the American release was held off for six years.

p&d, Jurgen Goslar.

Thriller (PR:O MPAA:R)

MANIACS ARE LOOSE, THE (SEE: THRILL KILLERS, THE, 1965)

MANIACS ON WHEELS**
(1951, Brit.) 76m Rank-Wessex/International Releasing bw (GB: ONCE A JOLLY SWAGMAN)

Dirk Bogarde *(Bill Fox)*, Bonar Colleano *(Tommy Possey)*, Renee Asherson *(Pat Gibbon)*, Bill Owen *(Lag Gibbon)*, Cyril Cusack *(Duggie Lewis)*, Thora Hird *(Ma Fox)*, James Hayter *(Pa Fox)*, Pauline Jameson *(Mrs. Lewis)*, Stuart Lindsell *(Mr. Yates)*, Moira Lister *(Dotty Liz)*, Sandra Dorne *(Kay Fox)*, Sidney James *(Rowton)*, Anthony Oliver *(Derek)*, Dudley Jones *(Taffy)*, Russell Waters *(Mr. Possey)*, Frederick Knight *(Chick)*, Michael Kent *(Solicitor)*, June Bardsley *(WAAF Sergeant)*, Cyril Chamberlain *(Reporter)*, Jennifer Jayne *(Autograph Hunter)*, Graham Doody *(Dr. MacKenzie)*, Joyce Tyler *(WAAF Officer)*, Patric Doonan *(Dick Fox)*, Jill Allan *(2nd WAAF Officer)*, Betty Cooper *(Solicitor's Secretary)*, Edward Judd.

Bogarde plays a young factory worker in the 1930s who quits his job to become a motorbike racer. He becomes successful, but falls victim to his own ego. He stops racing after his wife, who has insisted that he give it up, decides to leave him. Performances are lifeless, and plot development burdensome. Racing sequences, however, are well-handled.

p, Ian Dalrymple; d, Jack Lee, R. Q. McNaughton; w, Lee, William Rose, Cliff Gordon (based on the novel by Montagu Slater); ph, H. E. Fowle, L. Cave-Chinn; m, Bernard Stevens; ed, Jack Harris; art d, Fred Pusey.

Drama (PR:A MPAA:NR)

MANILA CALLING*** (1942) 81m FOX bw

Lloyd Nolan *(Lucky Matthews)*, Carole Landis *(Edna Fraser)*, Cornel Wilde *(Jeff Bailey)*, James Gleason *(Tom O'Rourke)*, Martin Kosleck *(Heller)*, Ralph Byrd *(Corbett)*, Charles Tannen *(Fillmore)*, Ted [Michael] North *(Jamison)*, Elisha Cook, Jr. *(Gillman)*, Harold Huber *(Santoro)*, Lester Matthews *(Wayne Ralston)*, Louis Jean Heydt *(Watson)*, Victor Sen Yung *(Amando)*, Rudy Robles, Angel Cruz, Carlos Carrido *(Moro Soldiers)*, Ken Christy *(Logan)*, Leonard Strong *(Japanese Officer)*, Richard Loo, Charles Stevens *(Filipinos)*, Ted Hecht *(Japanese Announcer)*.

Propagandistic war drama is set in the jungles of the Philippines. Nolan organizes a group of soldiers into a guerrilla unit after the Japanese invasion of the island has left them stranded. They are aided through the efforts of radio operator Wilde to relay information. The movie's message is that if everyone sticks together, regardless of the situation, the enemy can be outdone. Cast gives fitting performances, and good direction keeps the pace moving, despite a weak script.

p, Sol M. Wurtzel; d, Herbert I. Leeds; w, John Larkin; ph, Lucien Andriot; ed, Alfred Day; md, Cyril J. Mockridge, Emil Newman; art d, Richard Day, Lewis Creber.

War (PR:A MPAA:NR)

MANINA (SEE: GIRL IN THE BIKINI, 1958, Fr.)

MANITOU, THE** (1978) 104m Weist-Simon/AE c

Tony Curtis *(Harry Erskine)*, Michael Ansara *(Singing Rock)*, Susan Strasberg *(Karen Tandy)*, Stella Stevens *(Amelia Crusoe)*, Jon Cedar *(Dr. Jack Hughes)*, Ann Sothern *(Mrs. Karmann)*, Burgess Meredith *(Dr. Ernest Snow)*, Paul Mantee *(Dr. Robert McEvoy)*, Jeanette Nolan *(Mrs. Winconis)*, Lurene Tuttle *(Mrs. Hertz)*, Ann Mantee *(Floor Nurse)*, Hugh Corcoran *(MacArthur)*, Tenaya *(Singing Rock's Wife)*, Carole Hemingway *(Prostitute)*, Beverly Kushida *(2nd Floor Nurse)*, Jan Heininger *(Wolf)*, Michael Laren *(Michael)*, Joe Gieb *(Misquamacas)*.

In this shocker, Strasberg discovers a 400-year-old medicine man growing on her back. Former lover and phony spiritualist Curtis can't help in any way, nor can the local medics. Ansara, a modern-day medicine man, is enlisted to confront the evil spirit. This picture tries to shock the audience through the special effects, but it comes off looking pretty silly.

p&d, William Girdler; w, Girdler, Jon Cedar, Tom Pope (based on the novel by Graham Masterson); ph, Michel Hugo (Panavision, CFI Color); m, Lalo Schifrin; ed, Bub Asman; prod d, Walter Scott Herndon; set d, Cheryal Kearney; cos, Michael Faeth, Agnes Lyon.

Horror Cas. (PR:C MPAA:PG)

MANJI (SEE: PASSION, 1968, Jap.)

MANNEQUIN* (1933, Brit.) 54m REA/RKO bw

Harold French *(Peter Tattersall)*, Judy Kelly *(Heather Trent)*, Diana Beaumont *(Lady Diana Savage)*, Whitmore Humphries *(Billy Armstrong)*, Richard Cooper *(Lord Bunny Carstairs)*, Ben Welden *(Chris Dempson)*, Faith Bennett *(Queenie)*, Vera Boggetti *(Nancy)*, Anna Lee *(Babette)*, William Pardue, Carol Lees, Tonie Edgar Bruce.

After meeting society girl Beaumont, boxer Humphries dumps his girl friend Kelly. But he soon discovers that Beaumont views him as no more than a plaything, and has even bet against him in an upcoming match. The angered pug proves her wrong by winning the fight, and the spurned Kelly's heart back as well. There's not an honest moment in this bit of mindless tripe. The boxing sequences are equally phony, and in some instances this film induces moments of unintended laughter.

p, Julius Hagen; d, George A. Cooper; w, Charles Bennett.

Drama (PR:A MPAA:NR)

MANNEQUIN 1/2** (1937) 92m MGM bw

Joan Crawford *(Jessie Cassidy)*, Spencer Tracy *(John L. Hennessey)*, Alan Curtis *(Eddie Miller)*, Ralph Morgan *(Briggs)*, Mary Phillips *(Beryl)*, Oscar O'Shea *(Pa Cassidy)*, Elizabeth Risdon *(Mrs. Cassidy)*, Leo Gorcey *(Clifford Cassidy)*, George Chandler *(Swing Magoo)*, Bert Roach *(Schwartz)*, Marie Blake *(Mrs. Schwartz)*, Matt McHugh *(Mike)*, Paul Fix *(Smooch)*, Helen Troy *(Bubbles Adair)*, Phillip Terry *(Man at Stage Door)*, Gwen Lee *(Girl Worker)*, Donald Kirke *(Dave McIntyre)*, Virginia Blair, Jim Baker, Ruth Dwyer *(Wedding Guests)*, Jimmy Conlin *(Elevator Operator)*, Frank Jaquet *(Stage Doorman)*.

Crawford and Tracy only made this one film together. Too bad they did not have better material for their solo effort. Crawford is a Hester Street girl (New York's Lower East Side) who loves Curtis, a two-bit con artist. They do not have much money but they are in love so she agrees to marry him when he pops the question. They have a small wedding dinner in a restaurant and are congratulated by shipping magnate Tracy, at the next table. Tracy is instantly taken by Crawford, something that his assistant, Morgan, sees clearly. The Crawford-Curtis marriage is rocky from the start and gets rockier when she becomes increasingly aware of his small-time schemes which will probably put him in jail if they become more brazen. Crawford leaves Curtis and gets a job as a model for expensive clothes (what they used to call "mannequins" in those days) where she meets Tracy again. Her heart still belongs to Curtis, or so she thinks, so she does not encourage the smitten Tracy. But Tracy's warm, winning way soon melts her reserve so she divorces Curtis and marries Tracy. Curtis has conveniently disappeared, for a while. They take a long and happy honeymoon abroad and when they return, Tracy's business is having labor problems. Enter Curtis again with a scheme to blackmail Crawford and Tracy. Crawford tells Curtis to buzz off but Tracy misunderstands their relationship and thinks that his wife still may love her ex-husband. Tracy is under serious pressure at his business and is now feeling mighty low in his domestic life but plucky Crawford makes certain that Tracy knows she will not desert him and they will face the future together. It's an old rags-to-riches plot and Crawford could never persuade anyone she came from downtrodden Hester Street (immortalized in the movie of the same name by Joan Micklin Silver, for which she won an Oscar nomination for her script), an area that was almost totally Eastern European Jewish and Crawford, as good as she could be, was as Eastern European as Sabu. Leo Gorcey, as her kid brother, is far more believable in the role because that is the area from whence he came. Curtis was excellent in his film debut (he did a tiny bit in WINTERSET) and would have had a long career were it not cut short by his death following a kidney operation. Though it was rumored that Crawford and Tracy argued during this film, the flamboyant actress dispelled such notions in her autobiography: "It was inspiring to play opposite Tracy. His is such simplicity of performance, such naturalness and humor. He walks through a scene just as he walks through life. He makes it seem so easy, and working with him I had to learn to underplay. We worked together as a unit, as if we'd worked together for years. . .*Slug* I called him, from the day he was clowning around and took the stance of a boxer. In the most serious scene, Slug could break me up. . .From Slug I learned to keep my own identity in a scene, not to be distracted by anything, including Tracy. Columnists insisted we were feuding. We never had a moment's disharmony." Crawford suffered a bout with pneumonia during the production and her physicians urged her to take up sports; she and Tracy played polo until the actor took a nasty spill and promised that he would stay away from such dangerous activities. To the studio he was too valuable to break his neck while socking a ball with a mallet while leaning from a racing horse.

p, Joseph L. Mankiewicz; d, Frank Borzage; w, Lawrence Hazard (based on the story "Marry for Money" by Katherine Brush); ph, George Folsey; m, Edward Ward; ed, Frederick Y. Smith; art d, Cedric Gibbons, Paul Groesse; set d, Edwin B.

Willis; cos, Adrian; m/l, "Always and Always," Ward, Robert Wright, Chet Forrest (sung by Joan Crawford).

Drama   (PR:A   MPAA:NR)

MANNER MUSSEN SO SIEN   (SEE: HIPPODROME, 1961, Ger.)

MANNISKOR MOTS OCH LJUV MUSIK UPPSTAR I HJARTAT
(SEE: PEOPLE MEET AND SWEET MUSIC FILLS THE HEART, 1964, Den./Swed.)

MANNY'S ORPHANS   (SEE: HERE COME THE TIGERS, 1978)

MANOLETE**   (1950, Span.) 80m Hercules bw

Jose Greco (Rafael), Paquito Rico (Dolores), Pedro Ortega (Manolete), Juanita Manso (Soledad), Manolo Moran (Favier), Ava Adamaz.

Film biography of Spanish bullfighter Manolete combines actual newsreel footage with staged footage. Some exciting moments, though performances are a bit overplayed and the direction is shaky. Greco's flamenco dancing is fine, however.

d, Florian Rey; w, Llovety Manzano; ph, Enrique Guerner; ed, Ropence.

Drama   (PR:A   MPAA:NR)

MANOLIS**   (1962, Brit.) 52m Witanhurst/Bargate bw

Michali Maridalis (Manolis), Paul Homer (Puppet Man).

In this Greek-based drama, Maridalis is a teenager who ends up in trouble with a gang. He's nearly drowned but is saved by Homer, a puppeteer who helps the lad get a new start with his life. The kids might enjoy it.

p&d, Paul H. Crosfield; w, Rex Berry.

Drama   (PR:A   MPAA:NR)

MANON**   (1950, Fr.) 91m Alcina-DIF/Discina bw

Cecile Aubry (Manon Lescaut), Michel Auclair (Robert Des Grieux), Serge Reggiani (Leon Lescaut), Henri Vilbert (Ship's Captain), Gabrielle Dorziat (Mme. Agnes), Raymond Souplex (Mons. Paul), Andre Valmy (Bandit Chief), Helena Manson (Normandy Peasant), Andrex (Marseilles Black Marketeer), Daniel Ivernel (American Officer).

A film made during the "Tradition of Quality" period in France, popular after WW II. The story opens with a flashback of Aubry being condemned by the local villagers for her affair with Resistance fighter Auclair. They escape to Paris and take refuge with her brother who takes advantage of the girl by forcing her to become a prostitute. The young pair attempts an escape again, this time to Israel, but is attacked by a group of Arabs while tracking across the desert. In a sappy finish, the boy buries the girl he tried to save.

p, Paul-Edmond Decharme; d, Henri-Georges Clouzot; w, Clouzot, Jean Ferry (based on the novel Manon Lescaut by Abbe Antoine-Francois Prevost); ph, Armand Thirard; m, Paul Misraki; ed, Monique Kirsanoff; set d, Max Douy.

Drama   (PR:A   MPAA:NR)

MANON 70**   (1968, Fr.) 105m Corona-Transinter-Roxy-Panda/Valoria c

Catherine Deneuve (Manon), Jean-Claude Brialy (Jean-Paul), Sami Frey (Des Grieux), Elsa Martinelli (Annie), Robert Webber (Ravaggi), Paul Hubschmid (Simon), Claude Genia (Wife), Jean Martin (Hotelman).

Remake of earlier French film stars Deneuve as a prostitute who caters to the rich. She meets and falls in love with Frey, a radio reporter, but continues to take on customers to support her expensive tastes. Film suffers from an ambiguity in its purpose, failing to penetrate the surface for any insight into the sexual questions raised. Performances are adequate.

d, Jean Aurel; w, Cecil St. Laurent, Aurel (based on the novel Manon Lescaut by Abbe Prevost); ph, Edmond Richard (Eastmancolor); ed, Anne-Marie Cotret.

Drama   (PR:O   MPAA:NR)

MANOS, THE HANDS OF FATE zero   (1966) 74m Sun City/Emerson c

Tom Neyman, Diane Mahree, Hal Warren, John Reynolds.

A putrid horror film made by a good ol' fertilizer salesman from El Paso, Texas. Warren and his family stumble across a cult of "night people," and their presence causes arguments to erupt among cult members. The master gets tired of the fighting and has the face of a female member disfigured by a burning hand. A fun vacation for the whole family.

p,d&w, Hal P. Warren; ph, (Eastmancolor).

Horror   (PR:C   MPAA:NR)

MANPOWER***   (1941) 105m WB bw

Edward G. Robinson (Hank McHenry), Marlene Dietrich (Fay Duval), George Raft (Johnny Marshall), Alan Hale (Jumbo Wells), Frank McHugh (Omaha), Eve Arden (Dolly), Barton MacLane (Smiley Quinn), Walter Catlett (Sidney Whipple), Joyce Compton (Scarlett), Lucia Carroll (Flo), Ward Bond (Eddie Adams), Egon Brecher (Pop Duval), Cliff Clark (Cully), Joseph Crehan (Sweeney), Ben Welden (Al Hurst), Carl Harbaugh (Noisy Nash), Barbara Land (Marilyn), Barbara Pepper (Polly), Dorothy Appleby (Wilma), Roland Drew (Man), Eddie Fetherston, Charles Sherlock, Jeffrey Sayre, De Wolfe Hopper, William Hopper, Al Herman, Cliff Saum (Men), Ralph Dunn (Man at Phone), Harry Strang (Foreman), Nat Carr (Waiter), John Kelly (Bouncer), Isabel Withers (Floor Nurse), Joan Winfield, Faye Emerson (Nurses), James Flavin (Orderly), Chester Clute (Clerk), Nella Walker (Floorlady), Harry Holman (Justice of the Peace), Dorothy Vaughan (Mrs. Boyle), Beal Wong (Chinese Singer), Jane Randolph (Hat Check Girl), Eddy Chandler, Lee Phelps (Detectives), Robert Strange (Bondsman), Billy Wayne (Taxi Driver), Brenda Fowler (Saleslady), Joyce Bryant (Miss Brewster), Gayle Mellott, Muriel Barr (Models), Joe Devlin (Bartender), Pat McKee (Bouncer), Georgia Caine (Head Nurse), Charles Sullivan, Fred Graham, Elliott Sullivan, William Newell, Murray Alper, Dick Wessel (Linemen), Harry Seymour (Piano Player), Vera Lewis (Wife), Drew Roddy, Peter Caldwell, Harry Harvey, Jr., Bobby Robb (Boys), John Harmon (Benny), Jean Ames (Thelma), Frank Mayo (Doorman), William Gould (Desk Sergeant), Leah Baird (Matron), Herbert Heywood (Watchman), William Royle (Cop), Lynn Baggett.

Robinson and Raft are two-fisted, hard-drinking linemen who compete for the affections of hostess Dietrich in this no-holds-barred melodrama. Both brawlers are close friends and, during a storm, work desperately to repair some damaged lines. Robinson brushes against a high-voltage live wire and one of his legs becomes paralyzed. Later, during another crisis, Brecher, another veteran lineman, is killed and Robinson and Raft break the sad news to his daughter, Dietrich, who works as a hostess in a dingy nightclub. Both roommates are interested in her, Raft knowing her past. He had earlier accompanied Brecher to a jail when she was released for her sinful ways. Robinson is smitten by the blonde bombshell but Raft, attempting to save his friend from being hurt, tries to convince his pal that Dietrich is no good. Robinson won't hear of it; he believes Dietrich got a bad break. He hangs around the club where she warbles out her sad songs, cadging drinks for the house from suckers, not the least of whom is Robinson. So enamored is he of her that he asks her to marry him, even knowing she's more attracted to Raft. Dietrich wants to escape her miserable honky-tonk life and accepts. Just after the marriage Raft is injured on the job and Robinson insists he stay with him and Dietrich to recuperate. Dietrich takes this opportunity to tell Raft she loves him but he rejects her, reminding her that she's married to his pal Robinson. Dietrich decides to leave town, but stops off at her old club to say goodbye to the girls—Arden, Compton, and others—and gets caught in a police raid. When Raft hears that Dietrich has been arrested, he goes to the jail and bails her out. Dietrich again declares her love for him, but this time, to make his point, he slugs her. Raft then goes off to help a repair crew in trouble during a storm. Dietrich locates a roadshow where she finds Robinson and tells him that she's in love with his best friend. Robinson explodes and dashes outside into the storm. He confronts Raft and the two have a terrific fight with Robinson falling to his death. This leaves Raft and Dietrich to pursue happiness together. Though loaded with cliches, action director Walsh helms this film with such vigor that it has a dynamic virility hard to ignore. Robinson and Raft are compelling as the feuding pals and Dietrich is her unique and alluring self, here playing the barroom floozy belting out her clip-joint songs: "I'm in No Mood for Music Tonight," " He Lied and I Listened" (Frederick Hollander, Frank Loesser). Solid support is given by rough and tumble fellow linemen Hale and McHugh. Director Walsh had his hands full with this temperamental cast. Both Robinson and Raft were quite taken with Dietrich, particularly Raft. The tough, slick-haired actor refused to appear a weakling in front of the actress. One scene called for Raft to lose his grip on a strap being held by Robinson so that Robinson would fall to his death. Raft marched into Jack Warner's office and demanded that the scene be cut, that he would appear unmanly if he let Robinson slip from his hold. "Couldn't the strap break?" asked Raft. Warner shrugged his approval and said yes, scratching his head in puzzlement as Raft went off happily. But there was no joy on the set between the two tough guys. Robinson was very patronizing to Raft, telling him how to deliver his lines, and Raft responded by loudly telling Robinson to keep his advice to himself. Both men began shouting at each other and, before director Walsh could step in, several punches were thrown, with Robinson getting the worst of it. When the men were separated, Robinson walked off the set, refusing to finish the film. The argument had to be settled by the Screen Actor's Guild. When the two did resume work, their attitude toward each other was ice cold. Dietrich kept aloof and made no comment about her battling costars bur she was involved with a real sock on the jaw nevertheless. Raft had balked at having to hit a lady, Dietrich, as called for in the script, and when he did throw the punch, it accidentally connected and sent her sailing down a flight of stairs, causing her to break her ankle. Raft himself had his share of mishaps, falling 38 feet from a telephone pole to land unconscious; he was sent to the hospital in shock and with three broken ribs. The Raft-Robinson feud ended some years later when the two met on stage at a benefit. They snarled at each other, Robinson pointed a finger at Raft and told him "to get out of town." Raft took out the famous coin he had flipped in SCARFACE and told Robinson that Hollywood wasn't "big enough for the both of us." The two then rushed each other, embraced, and danced off the stage together. By then, the feud had turned into a gag. Years later, hospitalized in his old age, Robinson received a telegram reading: "Get well, your pal, George Raft."

p, Mark Hellinger; d, Raoul Walsh; w, Richard Macaulay, Jerry Wald; ph, Ernest Haller; m, Adolph Deutsch; ed, Ralph Dawson; md, Leo B. Forbstein; art d, Max Parker; cos, Milo Anderson; spec eff, Byron Haskin, H. F. Koenekamp; makeup, Perc Westmore.

Drama   (PR:A   MPAA:NR)

MANSION OF THE DOOMED zero
(1976) 89m Group I c (AKA: THE TERROR OF DR. CHANEY)

Richard Basehart (Dr. Leonard Chaney), Gloria Grahame (Nurse Katherine), Trish Stewart (Nancy Chaney), Lance Henriksen (Dr. Dan Bryan), Libbie Chase (Girl), Vic Tayback (Detective), Al Ferrara, Arthur Space.

Basehart is a doctor who feels guilty about the auto accident that left his daughter, Stewart, blind and so he tries to restore her sight. He kidnaps people and removes their eyes and tries to place them into his daughter. None of the operations works, and Basehart has a large collection of eyeless people in his dungeon who eventually escape and rip out the doctor's eyes. The audience should keep its collective eyes closed during this terrible remake of Georges Franju's LES YEUX SANS VISAGE. Producer Charles Band was 21 at the time he made this film, and apparently had much to learn.

p, Charles Band; d, Michael Pataki; w, Frank Ray Perilli; ph, Andrew Davis (Deluxe Color); m, Robert O. Ragland.

Horror (PR:O MPAA:R)

MANSLAUGHTER** (1930) 85m PAR bw

Claudette Colbert (*Lydia Thorne*), Fredric March (*Dan O'Bannon*), Emma Dunn (*Miss Bennett*), Natalie Moorhead (*Eleanor*), Richard Tucker (*Albee*), Hilda Vaughn (*Evans*), G. Pat Collins (*Drummond*), Gaylord Pendleton (*Bobby*), Arnold Lucy (*Piers*), Ivan Simpson (*Morson*), Irving Mitchell (*Foster*), George Chandler (*Roadside Observer*), Bess Flowers (*Party Guest*), Louise Beavers (*Inmate at Prison*), Stanley Fields (*Peters*).

A remake of the 1922 version that starred Leatrice Joy and Thomas Meighan, producer-writer-director Abbott did some considerable adaptation on this story and brought it up to date as well as removing much of the cloying sentiment. Colbert is an heiress with little regard for people or property. When she accidentally kills a motorcycle cop with her car, March, the zealous district attorney, is determined that there not be one law for the rich and one for the poor so he pounds that home to the jury and Colbert is sent to jail. Once inside, she begins to learn about the other classes and is shocked to find her one time maid also in prison, a woman whose first name she never knew. Colbert spends two years inside the gray walls and comes out a better woman for it. She was supposed to be there much longer but strings were pulled and old favors called in by her family and she manages to do the stint in a much shorter time. March has fallen in love with her and regrets what he did but his feeling for the law outstrips his affection for Colbert. He comes back to a private practice and wants to have a relationship with Colbert but she will have nothing to do with him at first, even going so far as to plan revenge. In the end, she will probably join March in marriage, if we can believe the final scene in which she chases him down a street with affection, not anger, in her eyes. The best scenes are in the courtroom and at the prison where Colbert is, at first, shunned and then accepted by the other inmates as an equal. In a small role, note Louise Beavers as one of the inmates. Abbott was in his forties when he worked on this film and while other creators were thinking about retiring, he was just beginning and continued working well into his late nineties.

p,d&w, George Abbott (based on the story by Alice Duer Miller); ph, A. J. Stout; ed, Otho Lovering.

Drama (PR:A MPAA:NR)

MANSTER, THE zero
(1962, Jap.) 72m UA/Lopert bw (AKA: THE MANSTER—HALF MAN, HALF MONSTER; THE SPLIT)

Peter Dyneley (*Larry Stanford*), Jane Hylton (*Linda Stanford*), Satoshi Nakamura (*Dr. Suzuki*), Terri Zimmern (*Tara*), Toyoko Takechi (*Emiko*), Jerry Ito (*Supt. Aida*), Norman Van Hawley (*Ian Matthews*), Alan Tarlton (*Jennsen*).

Stanford is an American reporter who is given a mysterious injection by Nakamura. The reporter discovers that he has a third eye on his shoulder and soon it develops into a head. The two-headed monster begins killing people and then splits into Stanford and an ape man. The reporter throws the monster into a volcano.

p, George P. Breakston; d, Kenneth B. Crane, Breakston; w, Walter J. Sheldon (based on the story "Nightmare" by Breakston); ph, David Mason; m, Hirooki Ogawa; ed, Kenneth Crane; art d, Nobori Miyakuni.

Science Fiction Cas. (PR:A MPAA:NR)

MANSTER—HALF MAN, HALF MONSTER, THE
(SEE: MANSTER, THE, 1962, Jap.)

MANTIS IN LACE*½ (1968) 80m Boxoffice International c (AKA: LILA)

Susan Stewart (*Lila*), Steve Vincent (*Sgt. Collins*), M. K. Evans (*Lt. Ryan*), Vic Lance (*Tiger*), Pat Barrington (*Cathy*), Janu White (*Angel*), Stuart Lancaster (*Frank*), John Caroll (*Ben*), John LaSalle (*Fred*), Hinton Pope (*Chief Barnes*), Bethel Buckalew (*Bartender*), Lyn Armondo (*R. E. Woman*), Norton Holper (*Tenant*), Judith Crane, Cheryl Trepton (*Dancers*).

Stewart is a topless go-go dancer who takes up killing men while tripping on LSD. She picks up customers at the club and takes them to a warehouse where she kills them. She hallucinates that one man has a bunch of bananas as a head and kills him with a screwdriver, and she sees another with a hypodermic needle. She also kills a truck driver who plans to rape her, and the police kill her boy friend, thinking he's the mass murderer when he pulls a gun which Stewart thinks is a giant insect. When she begins to hack up his body, the police realize they have killed an innocent man. The film was shot in New York City by cinematographer Laszlo Kovacs who would go on to shoot EASY RIDER the next year.

p, Sanford White; d, William Rotsler; w, White; ph, Laszlo [Leslie] Kovacs (Eastmancolor); m, Frank Coe; ed, Peter Perry; set d, Frank Borass; m/l, "Lila," Vic Lance (sung by Lynn Harper); spec eff, Ed DePriest; makeup, Mike Weldon.

Drama (PR:O MPAA:R)

MANTRAP, THE*½ (1943) 57m REP bw

Henry Stephenson (*Sir Humphrey Quilp*), Lloyd Corrigan (*Anatol Duprez*), Joseph Allen, Jr. (*Eddie Regan*), Dorothy Lovett (*Jane Mason*), Edmund MacDonald (*Assistant District Attorney Knox*), Alice Fleming (*Miss Mason*), Tom Stevenson (*Robert Berwick*), Frederick Worlock (*Patrick Thomas Berwick*), Jane Weeks (*Miss Woolcott*).

This lifeless picture features Stephenson as a retired Scotland Yard man who writes books on criminology. The D.A.'s office calls him in to aid them in a case as a tribute to his 70th birthday. The police are certain they have the case solved, but Stephenson comes up with a brilliant solution, making their modern calculations

look worthless. Action is much too slowly paced, and the script fails to hold any suspense.

p&d, George Sherman; w, Curt Siodmak; ph, William Bradford; ed, Arthur Roberts; md, Morton Scott; art d, Russell Kimball.

Mystery (PR:A MPAA:NR)

MANTRAP, 1953 (SEE: WOMAN IN HIDING, 1953, Brit.)

MANTRAP, 1961 (SEE: MAN-TRAP, 1961)

MANUELA (SEE: STOWAWAY GIRL, 1957, Brit.)

MANULESCU**½ (1933, Ger.) 78m Hisa bw

Ivan Petrovicz, Ellen Richter, Mady Christians, Olly Gebauer, H. Hildebrandt, Hubert von Meyerinck, V. Fritz Kampers.

Petrovicz stars as the famous jewel thief and lady-killer Manulescu, who goes about his antics until caught and placed in jail. He escapes, and goes to the Riveria to continue his game. But he manages to get caught again. Well-paced direction keeps the story interesting.

p, Ellen Richter; d, Dr. W. Wolff; w, G. Klaren, Rameau.

Drama/Comedy (PR:A MPAA:NR)

MANUSCRIPT FOUND IN SARAGOSSA
(SEE: SARAGOSSA MANUSCRIPT, THE, 1972, Pol.)

MANY A SLIP* (1931) 64m UNIV bw

Joan Bennett (*Pat Coster*), Lew Ayres (*Jerry Brooks*), Slim Summerville (*Hopkins*), Ben Alexander (*Ted Coster*), Virginia Sale (*Smitty*), Roscoe Karns (*Stan Price*), Vivien Oakland (*Emily Coster*), J. C. Nugent (*William Coster*).

Bennett plays a wealthy society girl who can't hook a beau. She finally sinks her claws into Ayres when the two fall in a lake. At their second meeting, he proposes because he thinks she's pregnant. After they're married and settled down, she discloses that the pregnancy was a scam. Ayres leaves, only this time Bennett really is pregnant. The cast delivers an adequate performance for an unbelievable script, further marred by lax production.

p, Carl Laemmle, Jr.; d, Vin Moore; w, Gladys Lehman (based on the play by Edith Fitzgerald, Robert Riskin); ph, Jerome Ash; ed, Maurice Pivar, Harry W. Lieb; art d, Wallace Koessler.

Comedy (PR:A MPAA:NR)

MANY HAPPY RETURNS*½ (1934) 62m PAR bw

Guy Lombardo (*Guy Lombardo*), Gracie Allen (*Gracie*), George Burns (*Burns*), Joan Marsh (*Florence Allen*), George Barbier (*Horatio Allen*), Franklin Pangborn (*Allen's Secretary*), Ray Milland (*Ted Lambert*), Egon Brecher (*Dr. Otto von Strudel*), Stanley Fields (*Joe*), John Kelly (*Mike*), William Demarest (*Brinker*), John Arthur (*Davies*), Morgan Wallace (*Nathan Silas*), Kenneth Thompson (*Motion Picture Director*), Larry Adler (*Harmonica Player*), Veloz and Yolanda (*Dance Team*), John Taylor, Clark Rutledge (*Tap Dancers*), Kent Taylor (*Actor*).

This film provided an excuse to bring the famed radio personalities of Burns and Allen to the screen, as well as Guy Lombardo. This was a sure-fire box-office combination. All that was needed was a story to go around it, which, unfortunately, MANY HAPPY RETURNS failed to provide. The story revolves around Burns being bribed by Allen's father to marry the girl and keep her as far away as possible. Allen has the habit of destroying everything she gets her hands on, so the father pays Burns $10 for every mile they drive. This premise is not enough to keep the movie going; the laughs, more often than not, are predictable, and the whole thing drags. Surprisingly, the direction managed to keep some form of pace. Songs include: "Fare Thee Well," "I Don't Wanna Play," "Bogey Man" (Arthur Johnston, Sam Coslow), "The Sweetest Music This Side of Heaven" (Carmen Lombardo, Cliff Friend).

d, Norman McLeod; w, Keene Thompson, Ray Harris, J. P. McEvoy, Claude Binyon (based on the story by Lady Mary Cameron); ph, Henry Sharp; ed, Richard Currier.

Comedy (PR:A MPAA:NR)

MANY RIVERS TO CROSS**½ (1955) 92m MGM c

Robert Taylor (*Bushrod Gentry*), Eleanor Parker (*Mary Stuart Cherne*), Victor McLaglen (*Cadmus Cherne*), Jeff Richards (*Fremont*), Russ Tamblyn (*Shields*), James Arness (*Esau Hamilton*), Alan Hale, Jr. (*Luke Radford*), John Hudson (*Hugh*), Rhys Williams (*Lige Blake*), Josephine Hutchinson (*Mrs. Cherne*), Sig Rumann (*Spectacle Man*), Rosemary DeCamp (*Lucy Hamilton*), Russell Johnson (*Banks*), Abel Fernandez (*Slangoh*), Ralph Moody (*Sandak*).

Taylor plays a Kentucky frontiersman, whose only desire is to find a northwest passage until Parker decides she wants him to marry her, and persistently pursues him, despite rebuffs. It even goes so far as a shotgun wedding, with McLaglen, as Parker's father, holding the gun to Taylor. Eventually the bow is tied, and Parker follows Taylor to the northwest, only to be held up by Indians. Taylor rescues the girl, retiring to his fate. The script is well-balanced, tying comedy in with drama and featuring a cast that gives entertaining caricatures of backwoods types.

p, Jack Cummings; d, Roy Rowland; w, Harry Brown, Guy Trosper (based on a story by Steve Frazee); ph, John Seitz (CinemaScope, Eastmancolor); m, Cyril J. Mockridge; ed, Ben Lewis; md, Mockridge; art d, Cedric Gibbons, Hans Peters; cos, Walter Plunkett.

Comedy (PR:A MPAA:NR)

MANY TANKS MR. ATKINS** ½ (1938, Brit.) 68m WB-FN bw

Reginald Purdell *(Pvt. Nutter)*, Claude Hulbert *(Claude Fishlock)*, Barbara Greene *(Rosemary Edghill)*, Davy Burnaby *(Lord Fishlock)*, Frederick Burtwell *(Col. Edghill)*, Jack Melford *(Capt. Torrent)*, Arthur Hambling *(Sgt.-Maj. Hornett)*, Edward Lexy *(Sgt. Butterworth)*, Edmond Breon *(Colonel)*, Ralph Truman *(Zanner)*, Dorothy Seacombe *(Mrs. Hornett)*, Robb Wilton, Andre Morell.

The British have always had a knack for farce, with good frenzied action that can give otherwise minor material a few deserved laughs. This pre-WW II example has Purdell (who also was the film's co-writer) playing a soldier who's just invented a tank supercharger. He's eager to try out the new device, doing so at the expense of military hardware. Soon the Germans learn of the device and spies are dispatched to fetch it for their own uses. Because of Purdell's combined bumbling with fellow soldier Hulbert, the plans are almost lost to the enemy, but all turns out well. The energy within the film gives the material added zest, making for an enjoyable time.

p, Jerome Jackson; d, Roy William Neill; w, Austin Melford, Reginald Purdell, John Dighton, J. O. C. Orton; ph, Basil Emmott.

Comedy (PR:A MPAA:NR)

MANY WATERS** (1931, Brit.) 76m Associated Metropolitan/Pathe bw

Lilian Hall-Davis *(Mabel Barcaldine)*, Arthur Margetson *(Jim Barcaldine)*, Elizabeth Allan *(Freda Barcaldine)*, Donald Calthrop *(Compton Hardcastle)*, Sam Livesey *(Stanley Rosel)*, Mary Clare *(Mrs. Rosel)*, Robert Douglas *(Godfrey Marvin)*, Charles Carson *(Henry Delauney)*, Ivan Samson *(Philip Sales)*, Renee Macready *(Dolly Sales)*, Herbert Lomas *(Everett)*, D. Hay Petrie *(Director)*, J. Fisher White *(Gentleman)*, Monckton Hoffe *(Registrar)*, Clare Greet, S. A. Cookson, Paul Gill, E. R. Reeves, David Miller, Philip Hewland, Cecily Oates, Billy Shine.

This soapsuds drama is a backward look at the shared lives of longtime married couple Davis and Margetson. They remember the good times, as well as the major tragedy of their marriage when their daughter was impregnated by an already-wed neighbor, then subsequently died in childbirth. The story is a routine break-out-the-handkerchiefs sort of film, typical of lower-caste dramas.

p, J. A. Thorpe; d, Milton Rosmer; w, Monckton Hoffe (based on the play by Leon M. Lion); ph, Henry Gerrard, Hal Young.

Drama (PR:A MPAA:NR)

MAOS SANGRENTAS

(SEE: VIOLENT AND THE DAMNED, THE, 1962, Braz.)

MARA MARU** ½ (1952) 98m WB bw

Errol Flynn *(Gregory Mason)*, Ruth Roman *(Stella Callahan)*, Raymond Burr *(Brock Benedict)*, Paul Picerni *(Steven Ranier)*, Richard Webb *(Andy Callahan)*, Dan Seymour *(Lt. Zuenon)*, Georges Renavent *(Ortega)*, Robert Cabal *(Manuelo)*, Henry Marco *(Perol)*, Nestor Paiva *(Capt. Van Hoten)*, Howard Chuman *(Fortuno)*, Michael Ross *(Big China)*, Paul McGuire *(1st Mate)*, Ben Chavez, Leon Lontoc, Alfredo Santos *(Policemen)*, Don Harvey *(Larry)*, Ralph Sancuyo *(Harbor Policeman)*, Leo Richmond, Ted Laurence *(Motor Cops)*.

This production was made toward the end of Flynn's explosive career and it proved a lesser entry in the adventure genre but nevertheless provided a fair share of thrills. Flynn is a deep sea diver who knows where a jewel-encrusted cross lies buried in the deeps of the China Sea, on a sunken PT boat. Burr, wealthy, greedy, and venal, hires Flynn to navigate his yacht to the treasure spot and during the voyage plots abound through the ranks of greedy crew members. Meanwhile, Roman, who is in love with Flynn, tries to talk him out of the diving scheme. The great adventurer nevertheless makes his perilous dives, battles Burr and his henchmen, and retrieves the holy relic. At the last minute, he regains his scruples and returns the cross to its rightful owners, taking it to a small native church, in Manila, in the Philippines. There's plenty of action and Flynn is exceptional in the last third of the film where he regains his conscience. Location shooting took place on Catalina Island and in Los Angeles and Newport Beach Harbors. The San Fernando Mission doubled as the filipino church.

p, David Weisbart; d, Gordon Douglas; w, N. Richard Nash (based on a story by Philip Yordan, Sidney Harmon, Hollister Noble); ph, Robert Burks; m, Max Steiner; ed, Robert Swanson; md, Murray Cutter; Art d, Stanley Fleischer; set d, Lyle B. Reifsnider; cos, Milo Anderson; spec eff, H.F. Koenekamp; makeup, Gordon Bau.

Adventure (PR:A MPAA:NR)

MARA OF THE WILDERNESS** ½

(1966) 90m Unicorn/AA c (AKA: VALLEY OF THE WHITE WOLVES)

Adam West *(Ken Williams)*, Linda Saunders *(Mara Wade)*, Theo Marcuse *(Jarnagan)*, Denver Pyle *(Kelly)*, Sean McClory *(Dr. Frank Wade)*, Eve Brent *(Mrs. Wade)*, Roberto Contreras *("Friday")*, Ed Kemmer *(1st Pilot)*, Stuart Walsh *(2nd Pilot)*, Lelia Walsh *(Mara Wade, age 7)*.

Alaska serves as the setting for the story of a young girl abandoned in the wilderness after her parents are killed by a bear. She is taken in by wolves, who raise the child to adulthood. Researcher West is caught in a trap, and the girl saves his life. From this point on, West attempts to keep the girl from Marcuse, who wants to sell her to a freak show. West's motivation is to ease the girl back into civilization. Performances are satisfactory, with the color photography of the Alaskan wilderness an added feature.

p, Brice Mack; d, Frank McDonald; w, Tom Blackburn (based on a story by Rod Scott); ph, Robert Wyckoff (Eastmancolor); m, Harry Bluestone; ed, Harold M. Gordon; art d, Michael Haller; makeup, Louis La Cava.

Adventure (PR:A MPAA:NR)

MARACAIBO** ½ (1958) 88m Theodora/PAR c

Cornel Wilde *(Vic Scott)*, Jean Wallace *(Laura Kingsley)*, Abbe Lane *(Elena Holbrook)*, Francis Lederer *(Miguel Orlando)*, Michael Landon *(Lago Orlando)*, Joe E. Ross *(Milt Karger)*, Jack Kosslyn *(Raoul Palma)*, Lillian Buyeff *(Mrs. Montera)*, George Ramsey *(Mr. Montera)*, Martin Vargas, Lydia Goya, Carmen D'Antonio *(Dancers)*, Ampola del Vando *(Amelia)*, Manuel Lopez *(Boatman)*, George Navarro *(Waiter)*, Frank Leyva *(Bartender)* Gregory Irvin *(Boy Tourist)*.

Set and filmed off the coast of Venezuela, the story centers around the efforts to put out the nasty fire of an offshore oil well. Wilde is the only man with the know-how to handle the blaze, which he brings under control before Maracaibo is blown off the map. In the interlude he romances Wallace, a visiting novelist who, although at first aloof to the amorous Wilde, quickly gives in. Wallace was Wilde's real-life wife at the time the picture was made. Performances are convincing, with a balance maintained between the drama of the fire and the drama of the romance.

p&d, Cornel Wilde; w, Ted Sherdeman (based on a novel by Stirling Silliphant); ph, Ellsworth Fredricks (VistaVision, Technicolor); m, Laurindo Almeida; ed, Everett Douglas; art d, Hal Pereira, Joseph MacMillan Johnson; set d, Sam Comer, Grace Gregory; cos, Edith Head, Sydney LaVine; spec eff, John P. Fulton.

Drama (PR:A MPAA:NR)

MARAT/SADE

(SEE: PERSECUTION AND ASSASSINATION OF JEAN-PAUL MARAT AS PERFORMED BY THE INMATES OF THE ASYLUM OF CHARENTON UNDER THE DIRECTION OF THE MARQUIS DE SADE, 1967, Brit.)

MARATHON MAN**** (1976) 125m PAR c

Dustin Hoffman *(Babe Levy)*, Laurence Olivier *(Szell)*, Roy Scheider *(Doc Levy)*, William Devane *(Janeway)*, Marthe Keller *(Elsa)*, Fritz Weaver *(Prof. Biesenthal)*, Richard Bright *(Karl)*, Marc Lawrence *(Erhard)*, Allen Joseph *(Babe's Father)*, Tito Goya *(Melendez)*, Ben Dova *(Szell's Brother)*, Lou Gilbert *(Rosenbaum)*, Jacques Marin *(LeClerc)*, James Wing Woo *(Chen)*, Nicole Deslauriers *(Nicole)*, Lotta Andor-Palfi *(Old Lady on 47th Street)*, Lionel Pina, Church, Tricoche, Jaime Tirelli, Wilfredo Hernandez *(Street Gang)*, Harry Goz, Michael Vale, Fred Stuthman, Lee Steele *(Jewelry Salesmen)*, William Martel *(Bank Guard)*, Glenn Robards, Ric Carrott *(Plainclothesmen)*, Alma Beltran *(Laundress)*, Billy Kearns, Sally Wilson *(Tourists)*, Tom Ellis *(TV Announcer)*, Bryant Fraser *(Young Photographer)*, George Dega *(Hotel Valet)*, Gene Bori *(French Doctor)*, Annette Claudier *(Nurse)*, Roger Etienne *(Headwaiter)*, Ray Serra *(Truck Driver)*, Madge Kennedy *(Lady in Bank)*, Jeff Palladini *(Young Babe)*, Scott Price *(Young Doc)*.

A truly harrowing film, MARATHON MAN is a clever series of accidents that produce a nightmare thriller with an unrelenting attack on the viewer's nerves. Hoffman is a naive Columbia University student in New York who runs whenever possible to prepare himself for the Olympic marathon. A history student, Hoffman is haunted by the memory of his father's suicide, brought about during the McCarthy witch-hunts, his father being a liberal teacher accused of un-Americanism. Hoffman's brother, Scheider, an American secret agent who is involved with old Nazi Olivier, is attacked and almost piano-wired to death in his Paris apartment by Woo, a hired killer, but he surprisingly manages to survive. He returns to the U.S. to find Hoffman involved with another student, Keller, and the two brothers are observed meeting and staying together. Scheider is aware that Olivier's brother, keeper of his gems, has died of a stroke during a traffic accident in New York City and that Olivier must now leave his hiding place in South America to retrieve a horde of priceless diamonds taken from Jewish victims of concentration camps during WW II. Scheider and fellow American agent Devane have been control agents for Olivier, getting information from him in his South American hideaway in exchange for his safety and certain emoluments, on behalf of the U.S. government. Olivier, known in his halcyon days as "Die Weisse Engele" because of his long white locks, cuts his hair and escapes from his jungle hideout, taking a plane to New York. Once Olivier is in America, Scheider meets with him again. Suspecting that Scheider is after the gems, Olivier stabs Scheider, then disappears with his crony Nazis. The mortally wounded Scheider staggers back to his brother's apartment and dies in Hoffman's arms, but he cannot utter a word. Olivier's goons break into the apartment, seize Hoffman, and take him to an abandoned warehouse. Here Hoffman is strapped into a chair and Olivier appears with a set of dental tools, similar to those he employed when removing gold from the mouths of concentration camp prisoners. He begins to drill open an oral cavity in Hoffman's mouth, periodically asking the perplexed youth: "Is it safe?" This is obviously a code question which Hoffman, totally in the dark about his brother's intrigues, cannot possibly answer. Olivier sadistically continues to probe Hoffman's mouth, inflicting excruciating pain on the youth by drilling into an exposed nerve. Hoffman passes out and Olivier concludes that he knows nothing. Hoffman suddenly breaks away and runs madly through Manhattan, outdistancing his pursuers, Devane and the Nazis, and returning to his apartment where—with the help of a street gang—he gets his father's gun. He is no longer the liberal non-violent student. Now he wants revenge for his brother and for himself. Meanwhile, Olivier goes to a New York City bank and empties a safe deposit box full of diamonds into his briefcase. To better grasp the market value of the diamonds, Olivier takes some of them to a pawnshop where he is told they are priceless. When the pawnbroker recognizes him, Olivier quickly departs. As he scurries through the predominantly Jewish neighborhood, several people recognize the infamous Nazi as the one who persecuted them in the concentration camps, one elderly woman hysterically crying out: "The human monster on the streets of Manhattan!" But though she follows after him, passersby think her senile and Olivier escapes in the crowd. Later Hoffman captures Olivier and takes him and the briefcase full of diamonds to a deserted indoor city reservoir where he compels Olivier to endure a worse torture than Olivier inflicted upon him, allowing him to keep all the diamonds he can swallow. Olivier painfully swallows several diamonds, then lunges forward when Hoffman tosses the diamonds into the sewage system, attempting to save them, turning to stab Hoffman but falling on his own knife and dying. Coupled to this sweet revenge is the fact that Hoffman shoots it out with agent Devane, who has killed Keller, learning that both are in the conspiracy. The shy, gullible, trusting college student, by the end of this twisting and turning film, is transformed into a worldly, tough opponent, one who, the viewer is left assured, will not be running mindlessly through the world. Hoffman is excellent as Olivier's crazed victim and Olivier is the essence of evil, his sadistic acts so expertly enacted that the film has a deeply disturbing factor. Schlesinger's direction is highly stylized and more than effective, jammed with action and offering unforgettably terrifying scenes. Scheider is good as the errant older brother. Devane is his usual tricky self as the double-dealing intelligence chief, but Keller is too enigmatic a plant. Goldman's script, based on his novel, is literate and full of surprises, as it should be. This was a heavy grosser in its initial release, gleaning more than $16 million at the box office.

p, Robert Evans, Sidney Beckerman; d, John Schlesinger; w, William Goldman (based on his novel); ph, Conrad Hall (Panavision, Metrocolor); m, Michael Small; ed, Jim Clark; md, Small; prod d, Richard MacDonald; art d, Jack DeShields; set d, George Gaines; cos, Robert De Mora; spec eff, Richard E. Johnson, Charles Spurgeon; makeup, Ben Nye, Dick Smith.

Spy Drama/Thriller Cas. (PR:O MPAA:R)

MARAUDERS, THE*** (1947) 63m Hopalong Cassidy/UA bw

William Boyd *(Hopalong Cassidy)*, Andy Clyde *(California Carlson)*, Rand Brooks *(Lucky Jenkins)*, Ian Wolfe *(Black)*, Dorinda Clifton *(Susan)*, Mary Newton *(Mrs. Crowell)*, Harry Cording *(Black)*, Earle Hodgins *(Clerk)*, Richard Bailey *(Oil Driller)*, Dick Alexander, Herman Hack.

Boyd plays the legendary western hero, after a gang of outlaws responsible for a number of murders. Wolfe is the leader of the gang which has driven all the inhabitants out of a small town to give the bandits free access to the oil under the land. Action is well paced, with well-placed comic injections on the part of Clyde. Performances are convincing. (See HOPALONG CASSIDY series, Index).

p, Lewis J. Rachmil; d, George Archainbaud; w, Charles Belden (based on characters created by Clarence E. Mulford); ph, Mack Stengler; m, David Chudnow; ed, McLure Capps, Fred W. Berger.

Western (PR:A MPAA:NR)

MARAUDERS, THE** (1955) 81m MGM c

Dan Duryea *(Mr. Avery)*, Jeff Richards *(Corey Everett)*, Keenan Wynn *(Hook)*, Jarma Lewis *(Hannah Ferber)*, John Hudson *(Roy Rutherford)*, Harry Shannon *(John Rutherford)*, David Kasday *(Albie Ferber)*, James Anderson *(Louis Ferber)*, Richard Lupino *(Perc Kettering)*, Peter Mamakos *(Ramos)*, Mort Mills *(Carmack)*, John Damler *(Cooper)*, Michael Dugan *(Sal)*, Ken Carlton *(Thumbo)*.

This routine western features Richards as a lone homesteader in cattle country. Rancher Shannon throws a number of his gunmen at Richards only to have them shot down in Richards' determination to stay put. Performances are varied with over-acting in several cases hurting the believability of the project.

p, Arthur M. Loew, Jr.; d, Gerald Mayer; w, Jack Leonard, Earl Felton (based on a novel by Alan Marcus); ph, Harold Marzorati (Eastmancolor); m, Paul Sawtell; ed, Russell Selwyn; art d, Cedric Gibbons, Eddie Imazu.

Western (PR:A MPAA:NR)

MARAUDERS, THE, 1962 (SEE: MERRILL'S MARAUDERS, 1962)

MARCH HARE, THE*** (1956, Brit.) 85m B&A-Achilles/BL c

Peggy Cummins *(Pat Mcguire)*, Terence Morgan *(Sir Charles Hare)*, Martita Hunt *(Lady Anne)*, Cyril Cusack *(Lazy Mangan)*, Wilfrid Hyde-White *(Col. Keene)*, Derrick De Marney *(Capt. Marlow)*, Charles Hawtrey *(Fisher)*, Maureen Delaney *(Bridget)*, Ivan Samson *(Hardwicke)*, Macdonald Parke *(Maguire)*, Peter Swanwick *(Nils Svenson)*, Charles Wade *(Tim Doughty)*, John Gilbert *(Connor)*, Fred Johnson *(Joe Duffy)*, Bernard Rook *(Slater)*, Reginald Beckwith *(Insurance Broker)*, Stringer Davis *(Doctor)*, Clem Lister *(Commissionaire)*.

Ireland serves as the background for this story of a reckless young baron, Morgan, who loses the ancestral home and lands at the gambling table. The new owner's daughter, Cummins, an American, mistakes Morgan for a horse groom, and keeps him on in that position. A romance between the two begins to develop, set against the breeding of a young colt given to the boy by his aunt. The colt grows up to be an ace racing horse, winning the Derby. The CinemaScope photography creates a postcard impression of the Irish countryside. The cast exhibits a wide range of personalities, handled well through the direction.

p, Bertram Ostrer, Albert Fennell; d, George More O'Ferrall; w, Gordon Wellesley, Paul Vincent Carroll, Allan MacKinnon (based on the novel *Gamblers Sometimes Win* by T. H. Bird); ph, Jack Hildyard (CinemaScope, Eastmancolor); m, Philip Green; ed, Gordon Pilkington.

Drama (PR:A MPAA:NR)

MARCH OF THE SPRING HARE*1/2
(1969) 97m Gulliver/Pantages c (AKA: ROOMMATES)

Dan Mason *(Henry)*, Harvey Marks *(Solly)*, Barbara Press *(Sandy)*, Theon Banos *(Rhoda)*, Allen Garfield *(Martin Axborough)*, Rick Wessler *(Bookmaster)*, Stanley Brock *(Madison)*, The Pageant Players *(Performers in Play)*.

A muddled comedy-drama about a file clerk, Mason, who daydreams about a life of Buddhist meditation. He asks his girl friend, Press, to move in with him and his roommate, Marks. As his girl friend moves in, Mason sleeps with his co-worker Banos and Marks starts an affair with Press. Mason discovers that his boss is a swindler, makes up with his girl friend, and his roommate moves out.

p, Leo Baran, Harvey Bernstein; d&w, Jack Baran; ph, Bruce Sparks; m, Earth Opera; ed, David Wilson.

Comedy/Drama (PR:O MPAA:R)

MARCH OF THE WOODEN SOLDIERS, THE
(SEE: BABES IN TOYLAND, 1934)

MARCH ON PARIS 1914—OF GENERALOBERST ALEXANDER VON KLUCK—AND HIS MEMORY OF JESSIE HOLLADAY*1/2** (1977) 75m Hawk Serpant c

AND HIS MEMORY OF JESSIE HOLLADAY***1/2

Wulf Gunther Brandes *(Young Von Kluck/Narrator)*, Jessie Holladay Duane *(Jessie Holladay)*, Barrows Mussey *(Old Von Kluck)*, Frau Barrows Mussey *(Baroness Von Dohup)*, Walter Gutman *(2nd Narrator)*.

An unusual, witty, and delightful film fantasy based partly on the memoirs of a German general who tried to invade Paris in 1914 and partly on the visions of its director. Brandes is the general who attempts the ill-fated invasion and is turned back at the Paris suburbs by a group even more motley than his own. Interspersed throughout this story is a fantasy suggesting that the reason for the failure was Duane, a young woman whom the general had an affair with years before. Using narration derived from the real general's memoirs, battle plans, and photographs, amidst contempory scenes, Gutman spins an unusual tale brimming with imagination. The director doesn't just tend to the main story, but adds ruminations that seemingly have nothing to do with the matters at hand. Gutman himself was one of the more unlikely candidates to become a filmmaker. At age 74 he had already worked as a stock market analyst, art critic, and painter before turning to cinema. Gutman claimed the only reason to make the film was to take the beautiful Mrs. Duane on a trip to France where the film was shot. She was, he wrote, "a beautiful young woman who, curse the fates, is a half century younger than me."

p,d&w, Walter Gutman; ph, Gutman, Mike Cuchar; m, Jessie Holladay Duane; ed, Gutman, Shirley Clarke.

Comedy/Fantasy (PR:C MPAA:NR)

MARCH OR DIE*** (1977, Brit.) 107m ITC-Associated General/COL c

Gene Hackman *(Maj. William Sherman Foster)*, Terence Hill *(Marco Segrain)*, Max von Sydow *(Francois Marneau)*, Catherine Deneuve *(Simone Picard)*, Ian Holm *(El Krim)*, Rufus *(Sgt. Triand)*, Jack O'Halloran *(Ivan)*, Marcel Bozzuffi *(Lt. Fontaine)*, Andre Penvern *("Top Hat" Francois Gilbert)*, Paul Sherman *(Fred Hastings)*, Vernon Dobtcheff *(Mean Corporal)*, Marne Maitland *(Leon)*, Gigi Bonds *(Andre)*, Wolf Kahler, Mathias Hell *(Germans)*, Jean Champion *(Minister)*, Walter Gotell *(Col. Lamont)*, Paul Antrim *(Mollard)*, Catherine Willmer, Arnold Diamond *(Petite Lady and Her Husband)*, Maurice Arden *(Pierre Lahoud)*, Albert Woods *(Henri Delacorte)*, Liliane Rovere *(Lola)*, Elisabeth Mortensen *(French Street Girl)*, Leila Shenna *(Arab Street Girl)*, Francois Valorbe *(Detective)*, Villena *(Gendarme)*, Guy Deghy *(Ship's Captain)*, Jean Rougerie, Guy Mairesse *(Legionnaires at Station)*, Eve Brenner *(Singing Girl)*, Guy Marly *(Singing Legionnaire)*, Margaret Modlin *(Lady in Black)*, Ernest Misko *(Aide in Minister's Office)*.

The French Foreign Legion has been the subject of countless films, some accurate, some romanticized, some outright ridiculous. This one is a little bit of each, but is one of the more realistic. Hackman, an American who had been kicked out of West Point, heads a contingent of French Foreign Legionnaires who are pulled out of the front lines in 1918 during WW I. Battle weary, decimated by the war, the group nevertheless accepts its new posting to Morocco, picking up new recruits for the dangerous assignment of guarding Von Sydow, a Louvre curator intent upon excavating a sacred tomb. Hackman protests, stating that an earlier expedition was massacred attempting to take away the same archaeological treasures. Yet he obeys his superiors and sets out for Morocco. The new recruits include Hill, a cat burglar fleeing arrest, O'Halloran, a giant one-time Imperial Guardsman of the Russian Court, Sherman, an aristocrat seeking adventure, and Penvern, a talented musician who wears a top hat. During the voyage to Morocco, Hill attempts to woo beautiful Deneuve, whose father was one of the archaeologists lost on the previous expedition and who is traveling to Africa to find him. Hackman catches Hill out of steerage and forces him to drink one bottle of liquor after another, getting him drunk on the spot and embarrassing him in front of Deneuve. Later, as the troops travel by train, Arabs block the tracks and their leader, Holm, warns Hackman—an old adversary he respects—not to attempt to return to the sacred ruins. He then brings forth two of the archaeologists captured earlier, one being Deneuve's father; they are in rags, squatting in cages, their tongues cut out, blinded. Before Holm can make another move, Hackman whips out his pistol and kills both men, depriving Holm of his hostages. The train is allowed to proceed to the fort at Bousaada where the recruits undergo rigorous training under the command of sadistic officer Bozzuffi (who smashes his fist through Penvern's cherished top hat and slugs Hill in the face, drawing blood, when the burglar gives him a smart remark). The troops are then ordered to march with full packs through the desert as the blistering sun mercilessly beats down on them. Stragglers, they are warned, will be left behind; it is "march or die," they are told. The sensitive but fragile Penvern, his boots causing his feet to bleed, falls out and the troop marches away over a sand dune, leaving him to perish but the humane Hill drops out of line and goes back for him. He later appears at the fort, dragging the musician with him. Though Hackman admires his courage, he vows to discipline Hill for his disobedience and chains him to a post in the middle of the compound, a choker causing him to slowly strangle. Deneuve persuades Hackman to stop the punishment, promising Hackman that she will not return Hill's love for her (Hackman is in love with her and part of his animosity toward upstart Hill involves competing for her affection). Penvern, meanwhile, goes off with a whore but proves to be impotent and, ridiculed by the troops, commits suicide. The Legionnaires then march to the excavation site where Holm and his thousands of Arabs attack, even after Hackman has turned over Von Sydow's find, the coffin of

"The Angel of the Desert," to Holm. The desert leader cannot be pacified, since he is using the archaeological digs as an excuse to unite all the tribes to drive out the foreigners. The massive attack against the Legionnaires sees the Arabs slaughtered but their sheer numbers overwhelm the defenders and Hackman is killed. Hill and a few others are left to take the tale of the Arab victory back to civilization to impress the foreigners with Holm's power. Hill bids Deneuve goodbye once back at Bousaada, wishing her a happy life. He has decided to stay in the Legion and at the end he lectures new recruits about the rigors and discipline they will face. This is a hardboiled movie, replete with excessive violence, sadism, torture, gratuitous bloodletting, and savage fury from all quarters. Hackman is compelling as the war-scarred leader and Hill fascinating as the weird but brave burglar adapting to army life. Deneuve has little to do but look pretty and the supporting players are lost inside the traditions and protocol of the Legion's activities. The film is still well-made, offering an interesting if offbeat and incomplete story. Alcott's lensing is superior as he captures the exotic settings of the Sahara Desert where the film was shot on location. (Alcott won an Oscar for his photography in BARRY LYNDON.) The film, with a $9 million price tag, returned only $1 million at the box office, proving to be a larger financial bath than the bloodbath spilled in the last and riveting battle scene. Richards' direction is up and down, even though he intended to make the most realistic French Foreign Legion film on record. It still doesn't compare with the 1939 production of BEAU GESTE or the more comedic, campy TEN TALL MEN, and yet it is unfair to compare MARCH OR DIE with Marty Feldman's inept comedy THE LAST REMAKE OF BEAU GESTE, as have some reaching critics. The title of the film comes from the French motto "Marche ou Creve" which was often tattooed on the feet of Legionnaires.

p, Dick Richards, Jerry Bruckheimer; d, Richards; w, David Zelag Goodman (based on a story by Goodman and Richards); ph, John Alcott; m, Maurice Jarre; ed, John C. Howard, Stanford C. Allen, O. Nicholas Brown; md, Jarre; prod d, Gil Parrondo; art d, Jose Maria Tapiador; set d, Julian Mateos, Dennis Parrish; cos, Gitt Magrini, Tony Scarano; spec eff, Robert MacDonald; m/l, "La Marseillaise," Claude Joseph Rouget de Lisle (performed by Andre Previn), "Plaisir d'Amour," Jules Massenet (performed by Previn); makeup, Jose Antonio Sanchez; Stunts, Glenn Wilder, Chuck Hayward, Juan Majan

Adventure   Cas.   (PR:C-O MPAA:PG)

MARCHA O MUERE   (SEE: COMMANDO, 1964, Bel./Ital./Span./Ger.)

MARCHANDES D'ILLUSIONS   (SEE: NIGHTS OF SHAME, 1961, Fr.)

MARCHANDS DE FILLES   (SEE: SELLERS OF GIRLS, 1967, Fr.)

MARCIA O CREPA   (SEE: COMMANDO, 1964, Bel./Ital./Span./Ger.)

MARCO***   (1973) 109m Tomorrow Entertainment/Cinerama c

Desi Arnaz, Jr, (Marco Polo), Zero Mostel (Kublai Khan), Jack Weston (Maffio Polo), Cie Cie Win (Aigiarm), Aimee Eccles (Kuklatoi), Fred Sadoff (Niccolo Polo), Mafumi Sakamoto (Letanpoing), Tetsu Nakamura (Sea Captain), Van Christie (Chontosai), Osamu Ohkawa (Ling Su), Masumi Okada (Ti Wai), Romeo Muller (Pitai Brahmas), Yuka Kamebuchi (Mme. Tung), Ikio Sawamura (Lomar).

This lighthearted musical adaptation of the legendary Marco Polo journey to the Orient was filmed partially in the Toho studios and partially in locations in the Orient, giving the picture an exotic quality accented by lavish sets and costume designs. Mostel plays the powerful Kublai Khan who has taken a great liking to the young adventurer, Arnaz. He selects a daughter for Arnaz to marry, as well as appointing him special emissary to Madagascar. Some of the songs include: "By Damn" (sung by Win, Arnaz, Weston), "Walls" (sung by Mostel), "A Family Man" (sung by Mostel), "Spaghetti" (sung by Weston, Arnaz). The picture may not be accurate in its depiction of the famous journey, but it makes for pleasant viewing. In one of the better sequences, filmmakers used Animagic, a process that combines animation with live action, for Arnaz to relate his adventure to the palace children.

p, Arthur Rankin, Jr., Jules Bass; d, Seymour Robbie; w, Romeo Muller; ph, Richard R. Nishigaki (Eastmancolor); m, Maury Laws; art d, Shinobu Muraki; cos, Emi Wada; ch, Ron Field; m/l, Laws, Muller.

Musical   Cas.   (PR:A MPAA:G)

MARCO POLO**   (1962, Fr./Ital.) 95m Panda-Transfilmorsa/AIP c (L'AVVENTURA DI UN ITALIANO IN CINA; AKA: GRAND KHAN)

Rory Calhoun (Marco Polo), Yoko Tani (Princess Amuroy), Robert Hundar [Claudio Undari] (Mongka), Camillo Pilotto (Grand Khan), Pierre Cressoy (Cuday), Michael Chow (Ciu-Lin), Thien-Huong (Tai-au), Poing Ping.

Calhoun is the famous explorer who saves Tani, the daughter of the Grand Khan, from bandits. When Calhoun is jailed in Peking, Kahn frees him. Calhoun helps repel rebels with a special cannon he builds using the gunpowder made by an old hermit and then Tani offers her hand in marriage to him. He declines and continues his exploration of the Far East.

p, Ermanno Donati, Luigi Carpentieri; d, Hugo Fregonese, Piero Peirotti; w, Carpentieri, Oreste Biancoli, Duccio Tessari, Pierotti, Antoinette Pellevant, Ennio De Concini, Eliana De Sabata (based on a story by Biancoli, Pierotti); ph, Riccardo Pallottini (CinemaScope, Technicolor); m, Angelo Lavagnino, Les Baxter; ed, Ornella Micheli; art d, Aurelio Crugnola, Franco Fumagalli; cos, Mario Giorsi.

Adventure/Drama   (PR:A MPAA:NR)

MARCO POLO JUNIOR*   (1973, Aus.) 90m Premore c

Voices of: Bobby Rydell, Arnold Stang, Corie Sims, Kevin Golsby, Larry Best.

It seems there are only two kinds of children's films, good or bad. And since children can often be the harshest of critics, one might think that filmmakers become a bit

more particular when working in this genre. However, such is not the case with the people behind this poorly animated nonsense. The story involves a lad who is generation number 49 behind the famous explorer Marco Polo. He's in possession of one-half of his great forebear's golden medallion of friendship. The plucky youngster is determined to return it to Xanadu, meeting up with an assortment of pirates, dragons, and other nasties before uniting his half with that of the predictably beautiful (and woefully helpless) princess. Junior also helps her Royal Highness get back to her rightful place on the throne. Everyone gets an equal share of blame for the film's ineptitudes. The animation is no better than that of most Saturday morning cartoons, and the songs that fill the soundtrack are unmemorable. Rydell, a minor pop star best known for his appearance as Ann-Margret's boy friend in BYE BYE BIRDIE, provides the hero's voice and used his own limited singing talents occasionally.

p&d, Eric Porter; w, Sheldon Maldoff; ph, Joe Dugonics, John Cummings (Eastmancolor); md, Joel Herron; m/l, Herron, Maldoff, Jack Grimsley, Julian Lee, Larry Pontius.

Children's Film   Cas.   (PR:A MPAA:G)

MARCO THE MAGNIFICENT***   (1966, Ital./Fr./Yugo./Egypt/Afghanistan) 100m ITTAC-S.N.C.-Prodi Cinematografica-Avala Film-Mounir Rafla-Italf Kaboul-Cinecustodia/MGM c (LE MERAVIGLIOSE AVVENTURE DI MARCO POLO; LA FABULEUSE AVENTURE DE MARCO POLO; MARKO POLO)

Horst Buchholz (Marco Polo), Anthony Quinn (Kublai Khan), Orson Welles (Ackerman), Omar Sharif (Emir Alaou), Elsa Martinelli (Woman with the Whip), Akim Tamiroff (Old Man of the Mountain), Gregoire Aslan (Achmed Abdullah), Robert Hossein (Prince Nayam), Massimo Girotti (Marco's Father, Nicolo), Folco Lulli (Spinello), Lee Sue Moon (Gogatine), Bruno Cremer (Guillaume de Tripolis), Jacques Monod (Nicolo de Vicenza), Mica Orlovic (Marco's Uncle Matteo), Mansoureh Rihai (Taha), Guido Alberti (Pope Gregory X), Virginia Onorato.

This film took forever to make, was beset by all sorts of financial and production problems, and still wound up looking well and making a few lire, marks, francs, and rials overseas. Gary Cooper once starred as the great Polo, as did Rory Calhoun (in a film that was shooting at about the same time) and the original intention was to star Alain Delon with Christian-Jaque as director (matter of fact, C-J did begin shooting in 1962, then was replaced or quit). They wound up with Buchholz (who, at one time, used the name Henry Bookholt in THE CONFESSIONS OF FELIX KRULL) in the lead as the man who brought pasta and gunpowder back from the Orient. It was Pope Gregory X, Alberti, who sent the sailor to Asia to offer Catholic civilization to the Mongol hordes, lead by Quinn as Kublai Khan. Buchholz takes off on a trek that brings him through Jerusalem, across the Himalayas and through the Gobi Desert to China. On the trip, they are captured by Tamiroff who executes one of Buchholz's men in a glass bell torture chamber (not a pretty sight). Sheik Sharif helps Polo and his men get away to Samarkand where he is united with Girotti, his father. They are beset by Mongolian bandits and helped by Martinelli, who wields a whip, and lays down her life to save his. After many travails, all of them well-photographed and filled with action, Buchholz is attacked by Quinn's enemies and escapes aboard the barge of Moon, who is a princess on her way to Quinn's palace where the old man will choose a new bride. In China, Buchholz learns that the docile Quinn is at odds with his warlike son, Hossein, whose men are eventually overcome in a battle that features the first use of gunpowder. Narration states that Buchholz remained in China for 17 years before returning to Italy where he was promptly tossed in jail for staying away too long. Shot in Yugoslavia, France, Egypt, Italy, and Afghanistan, with lots of money lavished on sets and costumes, MARCO THE MAGNIFICENT suffers from too much production and not enough script. Welles has a small role as Buchholz's teacher and is barely recognizable under all his makeup. Tamiroff is terrifically comic as the "old man of the mountain" and Sharif does his usual good work. Much splicing from the various false starts of the movie and a difference of styles on the part of the four directors is evident. Filled with inconsistencies and yet, underneath the errors, there's enough action and adventure to satisfy all but the most bloodthirsty.

p, Raoul J. Levy; d, Denys de La Patelliere, Noel Howard, Christian-Jaque, Cliff Lyons; w, de La Patelliere, Raoul J. Levy, Jacques Remy, Jean-Paul Rappeneau; ph, Armand Thirard (Franscope, Eastmancolor); m, Georges Garvarentz; ed, Jacqueline Thiedot, Noelle Balenci, Albert Jurgenson; art d, Jacques Saulnier; cos, Jacques Fonteray; spec eff, Roscoe Cline.

Historical Adventure   (PR:C MPAA:NR)

MARDI GRAS* 1/2**   (1958) 107m FOX c

Pat Boone (Pat Newell), Christine Carere (Michelle Marton), Tommy Sands (Barry Denton), Sheree North (Eadie), Gary Crosby (Tony Runkle), Fred Clark (Curtis), Richard Sargent (Dick Saglon), Barrie Chase (Torchy), Jennifer West (Sylvia), Geraldine Wall (Ann Harris), King Calder (Lt. Col. Vaupell), Robert Burton (Comdr. Tydings), Alfred Tonkel (Indian), Earle Hodgins (Doorman), Robert Wagner, Jeffrey Hunter, Corps of Cadets of the Virginia Military Institute.

A thin plot doesn't hurt this film that features a lot of fairly good song and dance numbers with the New Orleans Mardi Gras as a backdrop. Several cadets of the Virginia Military Institute conduct a raffle to win a date with the French movie star, Carere, who is queen of the Mardi Gras. Boone meets Carere even before he knows who she is, and the two fall in love immediately. Studio publicity catches hold of the romance and blows it way out of proportion for commercial reasons, but the two eventually get away from it all and spend some serious time romancing. Performances are adequate, with director Goulding nicely blending narrative, music, and New Orleans stock footage. Songs include: "That Man" (sung by Sheree North), "Bigger Than Texas," "I'll Remember Tonight," "Mardi Gras March," "Bourbon Street Blues," "Loyalty," "A Fiddle, a Rifle," and "Stonewall Jackson."

p, Jerry Wald; d, Edmund Goulding; w, Winston Miller, Hal Kanter (based on a story by Curtis Harrington); ph, Wilfred M. Cline (CinemaScope, DeLuxe Color); m, Lionel Newman; ed, Robert Simpson; md, Newman; ch, Bill Foster; cos, Charles LeMaire; m/1, Sammy Fain, Paul Francis Webster.

Musical (PR:A MPAA:NR)

MARDI GRAS MASSACRE zero
(1978) 97m Weis c (AKA: CRYPT OF DARK SECRETS)
Curt Dawson, Gwen Arment, Laura Misch, Wayne Mack, Ronald Tanet, Cathryn Lacey, Nancy Dancer.

How they managed to stretch this squalid material into a full 97 minutes is perhaps one of the biggest mysteries of movie history. A single photograph would have been plenty to tell the entire story, and would supply about the same amount of gore. An Aztec priest travels to various festivals throughout the world to find prostitutes to sacrifice to his goddess, Coatla—God of the Four Directions and Queen of Evil in the Universe. No reason to cancel plans for Mardi Gras next year.

p,d&w, Jack Weis; ph, Weis, Don Piel, Jack McGowan; m, Dennis Coffey, Mike Theodore; spec eff, Mike Nahay; makeup, Albert Brown, Jr.

Horror Cas. (PR:O MPAA:NR)

MARGEM, A (SEE: MARGIN, THE, 1969, Braz.)

MARGIE** (1940) 59m UNIV bw
Tom Brown (Bret), Nan Grey (Margie), Mischa Auer (Gomez), Edgar Kennedy (Chauncey), Allen Jenkins (Kenneth), Eddie Quillan (Joe), Wally Vernon (Al), Joy Hodges (Ruth), Richard Lane (Mr. Dixon), Emmett Vogan (Mr. White), Pauline Haddon (Miss Walters), David Oliver (Waiter), Frank Faylen (Mr. Leffingwell), John Sheehan (Mr. Caldwell), Effie Parnell (Mrs. Horstenwalder), Horace MacMahon, Ralph Peters (Detectives), Aileen Carlyle (Mrs. Gypsum-Weed), Edward McWade (Pinwinkle), Gene Collins (Ethridge), Mary Kelly (Mme. Hogan), Natalie Moorhead (Mrs. Dixon), Jack Arnold (Young Man), Grace Stafford (Miss Bradley), Anne O'Neal (Maid), Heinie Conklin (Vendor), Andy Devine (Unbilled Guest Bit).

The picture got its title from a former pop tune, a title tactic Universal was using quite a bit during this period. This one centers on a young couple, Brown and Grey; he's trying to make it as a songwriter, and she as a radio scriptwriter. Their frustration ignites marital strife, leading to a temporary separation. A series of screwball events gets the two back together. The script lacks believability, but is a showcase for comic routines and a couple of songs, which are performed well. Songs include: "Margie" (Con Conrad, Benny Davis, J. Russell Robinson), "When Banana Blossoms Bloom" (Sam Lerner, Charles Previn), and "Oh Fly with Me" (Paul Gerard Smith, Previn).

p, Joseph G. Sanford; d, Otis Garrett, Paul Gerard Smith; w, Erna Lazarus, W. Scott Darling, Smith (based on a story by Lazarus, Darling); ph, Stanley Cortez; ed, Ted Kent; md, H. J. Salter; art d, Jack Otterson.

Comedy/Musical (PR:A MPAA:NR)

MARGIE**** (1946) 94m FOX c
Jeanne Crain (Margie McDuff), Glenn Langan (Prof. Ralph Fontayne), Lynn Bari (Miss Isabelle Palmer), Alan Young (Roy Hornsdale), Barbara Lawrence (Marybelle Tenor), Conrad Janis (Johnny Green), Esther Dale (Grandma McSweeney), Hobart Cavanaugh (Angus McDuff), Ann Todd (Joyce), Hattie McDaniel (Cynthia), Don Hayden (Boy Charlie), Hazel Dawn (Vi), Vanessa Brown (Wanda), Diana Herbert (Senior), Milton Parsons (Jefferson), Margaret Wells (Matron), Warren Mills (Arnold), Richard Kelton (Debater), Tom Stevenson (Salesman), Cecil Weston (School Teacher), Robert Ford, Herbert Kelt, Robert Scheerer, Basil Walker.

MARGIE is a sweet and very lovely nostalgia piece that never falls flat as it evokes memories of the 1920s. The entire movie is told in flashback when Crain tells her teenage daughter, Todd, the way it was way back when. Crain is a typical flapper who is pursued by boy friend Young but she has her eyes on Langan, the handsome young French teacher who has captured the fluttering hearts of all the coeds. Crain's rival at the school is Lawrence but they are friendly, rather than bitter, enemies. In the end, Crain winds up with Langan who is now Todd's father. Along the way, the script shows us the way life was for the teens of the 1920s and the madness of raccoon coats, Charleston dancing, putting rouge on the knees and pouring peroxide on the hair. In other words, it's the same thing now except that kids adopt different fashions, and follow different fads. There have been high school movies in almost every generation as audiences have been treated to productions from BEACH PARTY to FOOTLOOSE. MARGIE is another high school movie but aims for the heart and the funny bone with none of the smarminess seen in later years. Not much of a plot beyond Crain's crush on Langan and a brief sequence showing her on the school's debating team but it's filled with humorous situations which almost all pay off, except for the one that has Crain's underwear elastic breaking once too often and almost putting that gag over the edge. Co-author of the story McKinney also was responsible for MY SISTER EILEEN. The story for MARGIE would have been sufficient but the film also is laced with some of the best tunes of the era including: "Three O'Clock in the Morning" (by Dorothy Terriss and Julian Robledo), "A Cup of Coffee, a Sandwich and You" (by Billy Rose, Al Dublin, and Joseph Meyer, sung by Barbara Lawrence), "I'll See You in My Dreams" (by Gus Kahn and Isham Jones), "Margie" (by Benny Davis, Con Conrad, and J. Russel Robinson), "At Sundown" (by Walter Donaldson), "My Time Is Your Time" (by Eric Little and Leo Dance), "Avalon" (by Al Jolson and Vincent Rose), "Collegiate" (by Mo Jaffe and Nat Bronx), "Charmaine," "Diane" (by Erno Rapee and Lew Pollack), "April Showers" (by Buddy De Sylva and Louis Silvers), "Charleston" (by Cecil Mack and James P. Johnson), "Wonderful One" (by Terriss, Paul Whiteman, and Ferde Grofe from a theme by Marshall Neilan), and "Ain't She Sweet?" (by Jack Yellen and Milton Ager).

p, Walter Morosco; d, Henry King; w, F. Hugh Herbert (based on stories by Ruth McKinney, Richard Bransten); ph, Charles Clarke (Technicolor); m, Alfred Newman; ed, Barbara McLean; md, Newman; art d, James Basevi, J. Russell Spencer, Lyle Wheeler; spec eff, Fred Sersen.

Musical/Comedy (PR:AAA MPAA:NR)

MARGIN, THE,**
(1969, Braz.) 66m Film-Maker's Distribution Center, Film-Makers' Cooperative bw
(A MARGEM)
Mario Benvenuti, Valeria Vidal, Bentinho, Lucy Rangel, Tele, Kare, Paula Ramos, Brigitte, Ana F. Mendonca, Paulo Gaeta, Nelson Gaspari, Virgilio Sampaio, Dantas Filho, Luiz Alberto Luciano Pessoa, Jose Licneraki.

The lives of four people—two men and two women—are changed when a white barge carrying a beautiful woman comes down the Tiete river. The two men and two women begin relationships and die. The barge returns and takes them aboard.

p, Ozualdo R. Candeias, Michel Saddi; d&w, Candeias; ph, Belarmino Mancini; m, Luiz Chaves.

Drama (PR:A MPAA:NR)

MARGIN FOR ERROR** (1943) 74m FOX bw
Joan Bennett (Sophie Baumer), Milton Berle (Moe Finkelstein), Otto Preminger (Karl Baumer), Carl Esmond (Baron Max von Alvenstor), Howard Freeman (Otto Horst), Poldy Dur (Frieda Schmidt), Clyde Fillmore (Dr. Jennings), Ferike Boros (Mrs. Finkelstein), Joseph Kirk (Officer Solomon), Hans Von Twardowski (Fritz), Ted [Michael] North, Elmer Jack Semple, J. Norton Dunn (Saboteurs), Hans Schumm (Kurt Muller), Ed McNamara (Mulrooney), Selmer Jackson (Coroner), Eddie Dunn (Desk Sergeant), Barney Ruditsky (Policeman), Don Dillaway (Reporter), Dick French (Photographer), Ruth Cherrington (Dowager), Byron Foulger (Drug Store Clerk), Emmett Vogan (Fingerprint Expert), David Alison (Jacoby), Wolfgang Zilzer (Man), Allan Nixon, Malcolm McTaggart, Tom Seidel (Soldiers), John Wald, Gary Breckner (American Announcers), Ludwig Donath (Hitler's Voice), Bill O'Brien (Waiter), Ralph Byrd (Pete, the Dice-Playing Soldier).

The film is an adaptation of the popular Broadway hit, which didn't take to the screen as well as expected. The spoof features Preminger as a Nazi German consul prior to the war, guarded by Jewish police officers. Bennett is the consul's wife, a position she takes only to keep her father in Czechoslovakia free from harm. Esmond is the assistant, forced into taking the rap for Preminger's illegal use of funds, and Freeman is an aide in the process of getting the brush-off. When Preminger turns up dead from a gunshot wound, stabbing, and poison, Berle, who plays a policeman, determines that the cause is suicide. The story is told in flashback by Berle as he's on a boat, going overseas to fight in World War II. The script manages to emote a few well-placed laughs, but the dialog is better suited for the stage. Further harm is done by Preminger's heavy-handed direction, not at all appropriate for something of this nature. Performances are varied.

p, Ralph Dietrich; d, Otto Preminger; w, Lillie Hayward (based on the play by Clare Boothe); ph, Edward Cronjager; m, Leigh Harline; ed, Louis Loeffler; md, Emil Newman; art d, Richard Day, Lewis Creber; set d, Thomas Little, Al Orenbach.

Comedy (PR:A MPAA:NR)

MARIA CANDELARIA (SEE: PORTRAIT OF MARIA, 1944, Mex.)

MARIA CHAPDELAINE (SEE: THE NAKED HEART, 1955, Brit.)

MARIA ELENA (SEE: SHE-DEVIL ISLAND, 1936, Mex.)

MARIA MARTEN (SEE: MURDER IN THE OLD RED BARN, 1936, Brit.)

MARIA, THE WONDERFUL WEAVER
(SEE: MAGIC WEAVER, THE, 1965, USSR)

MARIAGE A L'ITALIENNE
(SEE: MARRIAGE ITALIAN STYLE, 1964, Fr./Ital.)

MARIANNE** (1929) 84m COS-MGM bw
Marion Davies (Marianne), Cliff Edwards (Soapy), Lawrence Gray (Stagg), Benny Rubin (Sam), Scott Kolk (Lt. Frane), George Baxter (Andre), Robert Edeson (General), Emil Chautard (Pere Joseph), Oscar Apfel.

Davies stars as a French girl in love with an American doughboy, but she can't run off with him because she is betrothed to a French soldier. When the betrothed turns up blind, and takes to the priesthood, Davies is free to follow her American. Davies managed a believable performance, even faking a French accent. Other performers played well off Davies. Songs include: "When I See My Sugar," "Marianne," "Oo-La-La" (Roy Turk, Fred Ahlert), "Hang On To Me," "Just You, Just Me" (Raymond Klages, Jesse Greer), and "Blondy" (Arthur Freed, Nacio Herb Brown). A silent version of the film also was shot with Oscar Shaw, Robert Castle, Robert Ames, Mack Swain featured in roles played in the sound version by Gray, Baxter, Edwards, and Edeson.

d, Robert Z. Leonard; w, Dale Van Every, Joe Farnham, Laurence Stallings, Gladys Unger (based on a story by Van Every); ph, Oliver Marsh; ed, Basil Wrangell, James McKay; art d, Cedric Gibbons; cos, Adrian.

Musical (PR:A MPAA:NR)

MARIE-ANN** (1978, Can.) 90m Canadian Film Production c
Andrea Pelletier (Marie-Ann), John Juliani (Jean Baptiste), Tantoo Martin (Tantoo), Gordon Tootoosie (Chief of the Indian Tribe), Bill Dowson (Steward), Linda Kupecek (Luise), David Schurman.

Filmed against lush Canadian wilderness, this is a rather simplified story of a young woman, Pelletier, whose husband really doesn't want her around. To satisfy her husband, who has an Indian mistress, and to keep herself from being sent back to the farm, Pelletier allows herself to be adopted by an Indian tribe. Script and direction are generally weak, but the charm of the story keeps the picture interesting.

d, R. Martin Walters; w, Marjorie Morgan; ph, Reginald Morris; m, Maurice Marshall.

Western   **(PR:A   MPAA:NR)**

MARIE ANTOINETTE****   (1938) 160m MGM bw

Norma Shearer (*Marie Antoinette*), Tyrone Power (*Count Axel de Fersen*), John Barrymore (*King Louis XV*), Gladys George (*Mme. DuBarry*), Robert Morley (*King Louis XVI*), Anita Louise (*Princess DeLamballe*), Joseph Schildkraut (*Duke of Orleans*), Henry Stephenson (*Count Mercey*), Reginald Gardiner (*Artois*), Peter Bull (*Gamin*), Albert Dekker (*Count de Provence*), Joseph Calleia (*Drouet*), Barnett Parker (*Prince de Rohan*), Cora Witherspoon (*Mme. de Noailles*), Holmes Herbert (*Herald*), Walter Walker (*Benjamin Franklin*), Henry Kolker (*Court Aide*), Horace MacMahon (*Rabblerouser*), Robert Barrat (*Citizen*), Scotty Beckett (*Dauphin*), Alma Kruger (*Empress Marie Theresa*), Henry Daniell (*LaMotte*), George Meeker (*Robespierre*), Ivan F. Simpson (*Sauce*), Marilyn Knowlden (*Princess Theresa*), Leonard Penn (*Toulan*), George Zucco (*Governor of Conciergerie*), Theodore Von Eltz (*Officer in Entrance Hall*), Hugh Huntley (*Man in Opera Hall*), Guy D'Emmery (*Minister*), Ian Wolfe (*Herbert the Jailer*), John Burton (*LaFayette*), Mae Busch (*Mme. LaMotte*), Cecil Cunningham (*Mme. de Lerchenfeld*), Ruth Hussey (*Mme. De LePolignac*), Victor Kilian (*Guard in Louis' Cell*), Claude King (*Choisell*), Herbert Rawlinson (*Goguelot*), Barry Fitzgerald (*Peddler*), Lionel Royce (*Guillaume*), Kathryn Sheldon (*Mme. Tilson*), Lawrence Grant (*Old Nobleman*), Harry Davenport (*Mons. de Cosse*), Dick Alexander (*Man with Pike*), George Houston (*Marquis de St. Priest*), Wade Crosby (*Danton*), Moroni Olsen (*Bearded Man*), Dorothy Christy (*Lady in Waiting to Mme. DuBarry*), Anthony Warde (*Marat*), Olaf Hytten (*Boehmer the Jeweler*), Rafaela Ottiano (*Louise*), Buddy Roosevelt, Lane Chandler (*Revolutionary Officers*), Brent Sargent (*St. Pre*), Tom Rutherford (*St. Clair*), Charles Waldron (*Swedish Ambassador*), Zeffie Tilbury (*Dowager at Birth of Dauphin*), Frank Elliott (*King's Chamberlain*), Lyons Wickland (*Laclos*), Guy Bates Post (*Convention President*), Gustav von Seyffertitz (*King's Confessor*), Nigel DeBrulier (*Archbishop*), Howard Lang (*Franz*), Mary Howard (*Olivia*), Ramsay Hill (*Major Domo*), Jack George (*Orchestra Leader*), Thomas Braidon (*Lackey*), Denis d'Auburn (*Beuregaard*), Frank Campeau (*Lemonade Vendor*), Harts Lind (*Nurse*), Frank Jaquet (*Keeper of the Seal*), Jacques Lory (*French Peasant*), Bea Nigro (*Woman at the Opera*), Harold Entwistle (*Old Aristocrat at Opera*), Edward Keane (*General*), Frank McGlynn, Jr. (*Soldier with Rude Laugh*), Esther Howard (*Streetwalker*), Inez Palange (*Fish Wife*), Frank Arthur Swales (*Chimney Sweep*), Billy Engle (*Man with Goblet*), Alonzo Price (*2nd Guardsman*), Erville Alderson (*Passport Official*), Duke R. Lee (*Coach Driver*), Ben Hall (*Young Man with Lantern*), Neil Fitzgerald (*1st Councilor*), Harry Stubbs (*2nd Councilor*), Ben Hendricks (*National Guard*), George Kirby (*Priest*), Corbet Morris (*La Rue*), Trevor Bardette (*1st Municipal*), John Butler (*2nd Municipal*), Alan Bridge (*Official in Passport Office*), William Steele (*Footman*), Helene Millard, Dorothy Christy, Frances Millen, Mimi Olivera (*Ladies in Waiting to DuBarry*), Luana Walters, Greta Granstedt, Ann Evers, Ocean Claypoole, Claire Owen, Roger Converse, Phillip Terry, Vernon Downing (*Bits in Gaming House*), Carl Stockdale (*National Guard*).

This massive, opulent, even extravagant production was done in the grand Hollywood manner and was designed exclusively for the queen of MGM's lot, Shearer, and put into motion as early as 1933 by her husband, the famous Irving Thalberg, boy genius of the studio. But Thalberg died and, while Shearer was away from the silver screen for two years, every craftsman and creative person at MGM labored to create this romantic opus for her triumphant return. Shearer, playing the last and tragic queen of France, is married off to Morley, Louis Auguste, the Dauphin of France, by her calculating mother, Kruger, playing the Empress of Austria. Shearer is repelled at her first meeting with her new husband, who is dullwitted, fat, and ungainly, a royal stick-in-the-mud. Adding further insult to her throne room plight are Barrymore, the sneering, jeering Louis XV, Morley's father, his scheming cousin, Schildkraut, playing the Duke of Orleans, and George, the conspiratorial Madame Du Barry, Barrymore's notorious mistress. Shearer is alone in her bed on her wedding night, Morley admitting he is incapable of performing his sexual duties. George, who considers Shearer a competitor for the lustful eye of Barrymore, also forms intrigues against her; Shearer quickly becomes a pariah at the Versailles court. She seeks solace in lavish parties and in wearing the most expensive gowns ever made. She tosses away fortunes at the gaming tables and, in one sumptuous casino, Shearer meets the dashing, handsome Power, Count Axel de Fersen, a rich Swedish nobleman, beginning a quiet love affair with him. Austrian ambassador Stephenson begs Shearer to strengthen his country's alliance with France by giving a huge ball and recognizing George as a "woman of royal position," but Shearer winds up insulting George and enraging Barrymore who threatens to annul her marriage and send her back to Austria in disgrace. Alone and frightened, Shearer is comforted by her lover, Power. Then Barrymore suddenly dies and Morley becomes king. Power tells Shearer that he can secretly love a dauphine but not the Queen of France. He wishes her well and then sails for America, seeking a new life. Shearer vows to be a good if not great queen and remain loyal to portly Morley; she bears him two children. Schildkraut, who had refused to help Shearer in her time of need, is now an outcast at court and, in vengeance, becomes the leader of the Revolution, financing the radicals attempting to destroy the monarchy. When the revolutionaries overthrow Versailles, Schildkraut has Morley and Shearer thrown into prison. Power, hearing of his lover's plight, arranges an escape but the royal couple are recognized by Calleia, a revolutionary, and they are recaptured at Varennes when attempting to cross the border. Power still won't give up. He sneaks into the prison where Shearer is held and plots another escape, but this time it's too late. The gracious queen goes to her death on the guillotine. (Marie Antoinette had to be the coolest condemned prisoner in French history. When mounting the scaffold she accidentally stepped on the executioner's foot and then spoke her last words, an

apology: "Pardon me, monsieur.") On a French rooftop, Power stands, head bowed as he hears the roll of drums announcing the death of the woman he loves, on his finger a ring given to him by Shearer, one which bears the inscription: "Everything leads me to thee." MARIE ANTOINETTE was exclusively a Shearer picture, although MGM boss Louis B. Mayer would have preferred not to have made the film and worked secretly and vindictively to destroy his star's nerves if not her sanity, attempting sabotage at every turn. When Thalberg died in 1936, Shearer's lawyers went into battle with MGM, insisting that, as part of Thalberg's $4 million estate and studio contracts, Shearer and her children were entitled to a share of the profits Mayer and his partners were gleaning. Mayer bristled at the thought of sharing his millions and began to express a long and deep-seated resentment he had for Thalberg who had taken the bows for all the superlative films MGM had made for a decade. When the legal battle turned decidedly ugly, Loew's president, Nicholas Schenck, Mayer's boss, grew angry, telling Mayer that he was abusing Shearer, the widow of a man who had greatly helped to make MGM the fine studio it was. He insisted the widow get her just inheritance. This put Mayer in his place but he went on with his intrigues all the same. He rankled at the fact that the settlement worked out allowed Shearer and her children four percent profit on all MGM films produced during the time of her husband's contract, 1924 through 1938, the year in which the production genius intended to branch out with his own independent production company, distributing his films like Selznick, and using Loew's as his distributing arm. Moreover, Shearer was given, at Schenck's insistence, a six-film contract at $150,000 per film. Shearer's problems were increased when William Randolph Hearst and his mistress-actress Marion Davies got into the act, or almost got into it. Hearst had once before attempted to snag a Shearer project for Davies from MGM where his own production company, Cosmopolitan Pictures, was headquartered, THE BARRETTS OF WIMPOLE STREET (1934). His agents had gone after the MARIE ANTOINETTE property but Thalberg's people got to author Stefan Zweig first to secure the novel for a Shearer film. According to Davies, it was Mayer who quashed the Hearst effort to obtain the property. "If Marion wants it [the MARIE ANTOINETTE film], she can have it!" Shearer reportedly stated at a Hearst party, but it was a different story when Davies later confronted Mayer. The mogul told her that, as envisioned by Hearst, the production would be enormously expensive: "I've no hopes for a production of that size and certainly you are supposed to be a comedienne— I can't visualize you as Marie Antoinette, so I don't want to spend that much money on a production of yours." Davies was outright insulted, later commenting: "That last part got me burned up. I called W.R. in San Francisco and he was furious. When we saw that MGM wouldn't let me make the picture, we decided to leave the lot." Some later reported that the grab for the film by Hearst was merely a ploy so he could divest himself of MGM and move to the Warner Bros. lot, and still others probing these incredible studio intrigues believed that it was Mayer who used the clash over the film as a way of getting rid of Hearst and his heavy-handed production ways. When Hearst left the MGM lot he did so in his usual extravagant manner, having the lavish bungalow reserved for mistress Davies sliced up into huge sections and trucked away in a long caravan to its new home in Burbank at Warner Bros. Still, Mayer made life unpleasant for Shearer, first by removing her favored director, Sidney Franklin, and replacing him with Van Dyke, the latter being a quick, no-nonsense helmsman who didn't like to make more than one or two takes for each scene, and was much loved by the cost-conscious Mayer. According to Morley, writing in his memoirs, *Robert Morley: A Reluctant Autobiography:* "Franklin had worked on the picture for two years. Van Dyke had never seen the script before he started shooting and knew apparently nothing whatever about the French or their revolution." Morley was not Thalberg's original choice for the role of Louis XVI; the production chief wanted Charles Laughton for the role but Laughton, and his wife Elsa Lanchester, whom Thalberg also wanted to play the role of Princess De Lamballe, were unavailable when the film finally went into production. (Maureen O'Sullivan was the next candidate to play Princess DeLamballe, but she was pregnant when the film finally got underway and the part went to Anita Louise who had herself played Marie Antoinette in MADAME DU BARRY, produced by Warner Bros. in 1934.) Morley disliked the whole production and referred to it as "MARIE AND TOILETTE." Shearer had more reason than Morley to dislike the treatment she received. Van Dyke refused to accord her the status of reigning queen of the lot and balked at her request for more takes. In one instance, where Van Dyke had already shot several takes of a scene, Shearer demanded it be reshot and he adamantly refused. Shearer walked off the set but returned the next day and apologized. The technicians, aware now that, with Thalberg dead, Shearer's power at MGM was declining fast, showed her no special respect and, when she tripped over a wire and fell flat on her backside, the hoops of her magnificent dress billowing upward, they roared with laughter, something that would never have happened in the Thalberg era. Shearer surprised them, however, by laughing along with them. Shearer was nominated for an Oscar for her exceptional performance but lost out to Bette Davis for JEZEBEL and Morley lost out as Best Supporting Actor to Walter Brennan for KENTUCKY. (Shearer would later reenact her role as Marie Antoinette on radio for the "Maxwell House Coffee Hour" in September 1938.) Almost totally ignored throughout the lavish production was Power, then the reigning king of Twentieth Century-Fox. His part was almost that of a supporting player, which caused Fox's boss, Darryl Zanuck, to explode. Mayer had loaned out Spencer Tracy to Fox for the making of STANLEY AND LIVINGSTON. In return, Zanuck gave Mayer his prized star, Power. When seeing that all the publicity and major scenes went to Shearer and that Power was treated like a handsome prop, Zanuck vowed he would never again loan out his studio's top box-office draw and Power would not again be available for any films made outside of Fox for another 15 years. Yet everything about MARIE ANTOINETTE was so awesome that, despite its whopping $1.8 million cost, it turned into a huge money-maker for MGM. Its budget showed in every stunning scene. Gibbon's sets were nothing less than magnificent and were crammed with authentic French artifacts of the period, looted from Parisian antique stores by set designer Willis, who spent three months and a fortune abroad in his foraging expedition for MGM.

Costumers Adrian and Steele designed period gowns and male attire for thousands of extras, and particularly for the 152 actors with lines. More than 500 yards of white satin were used for gowns worn by leading actresses, most of this going into a stunning wedding gown worn by Shearer. Gibbons' sets were glorious—sweeping halls, expansive ballrooms, royal chambers that dripped the authenticity of Versailles; Gibbons would win an Oscar nomination but lose out to Carl J. Weyl for THE ADVENTURES OF ROBIN HOOD. No less than 200 dancers were choreographed by Rasch for the ballroom scenes and Stothart's score is both tender and rousing, perfectly suited to the scenes and the period. Daniels' camera work is exceptional and Van Dyke makes this long film move like a short one, presenting swift and decisive scenes without any real lags. Shearer was never better but the flamboyant Barrymore and the sly and unctuous Schildkraut steal almost all her scenes when present. This was truly MGM at its production zenith, a rich, ornate, and wholly satisfying film.

p, Hunt Stromberg; d, W. S. Van Dyke II, (uncredited) Julien Duvivier; w, Claudine West, Donald Ogden Stewart, Ernest Vajda, F. Scott Fitzgerald (based on a book by Stefan Zweig); ph, William Daniels; m, Herbert Stothart; ed, Robert J. Kern; art d, Cedric Gibbons, William A. Horning; set d, Edwin B. Willis; cos, Adrian, Gile Steele; ch, Albertina Rasch; spec eff, Slavo Vorkapich; m/1, "Amour Eternal Amour," Bob Wright, Stothart, Chet Forrest; makeup, Jack Dawn.

Historical Epic/Romance   **(PR:A   MPAA:NR)**

MARIE DES ILES   (SEE: MARIE OF THE ISLES, 1960, Fr.)

MARIE GALANTE***   (1934) 88m FOX bw

Spencer Tracy (Crawbett), Ketti Gallian (Marie Galante), Ned Sparks (Plosser), Helen Morgan (Tapia), Siegfried Rumann (Brogard), Leslie Fenton (Tenoki), Arthur Byron (Gen. Phillips), Robert Lorraine (Ratcliff), Jay C. Flippen (Sailor), Frank Darien (Ellsworth), Stepin Fetchit (Bartender), Tito Coral (Tito).

Intriguing story with lots of interesting twists has Gallian kidnaped by a drunken sailor. He later claims her to be a stowaway, and throws her off the ship near the Panama Canal Zone. She earns a living by working in dance halls, until she runs into Tracy, an American detective investigating a plot to blow up the canal. Gallian becomes involved in counterespionage to stop the culprit from going through with his plan and in the process falls in love with Tracy. Complications in the attempts to catch the culprit arise out of the presence of Japanese, English, and U.S. undercover agents all unaware of the aim or purpose of the others. Slow-paced direction is made up for by an intriguing plot and first-rate performances.

p, Winfield Sheehan; d, Henry King; w, Reginald Berkeley (based on a novel by Jacques Deval); ph, John Seitz; md, Arthur Lange.

Spy Drama   **(PR:A   MPAA:NR)**

MARIE OF THE ISLES**   (1960, Fr.) 105m Radius c (MARIE DES ILES)

Belinda Lee (Marie), Magali Noel (Julie), Alain Saury (Duparquier), Folco Lulli (Lefort), Jacques Castelot (Saint Andre), Noel Roquevert (Baracuda), Jean Tissier (Fauvel).

17th-Century pirate tale has the governor of an island kidnaped by pirates, giving an unscrupulous nobleman the chance to go through with his evil plans unhampered. But the governor escapes in time to save everyone. Picture has lax production values, and performances not quite up to par.

d, Georges Combret; w, Pierre Maudru, Combret (based on the novel by Robert Gaillard); ph, Pierre Petit (Eastmancolor); ed, C. Laboreur.

Adventure/Drama   **(PR:A   MPAA:NR)**

MARIE WALEWSKA   (SEE: CONQUEST, 1937)

MARIGOLD**1/2   (1938, Brit.) 74m ABF bw

Sophie Stewart (Marigold Sellar), Patrick Barr (Lt. Archie Forsyth), Phyllis Dare (Mme. Marly), Edward Chapman (Mordan), Nicholas Hannen (Maj. Sellar), Hugh Dempster (Bobbie Townsend), Pamela Stanley (Queen Victoria), Ian Maclean (James Paton), Elliot Mason (Beenie), Katie Johnson (Sarita Dunlop), James Hayter (Peter Cloag), Jean Clyde, Mary Barton, Jack Lambert.

Stewart is a young, independent woman living with a minister and his wife in 1842 England. When her guardians deny her a chance to see Queen Victoria's appearance at Edinburgh, Stewart defiantly packs her things and travels there alone. While at Edinburgh she falls in love with a lieutenant, and eventually meets an actress who proves to be her mother. This comes as a surprise to Stewart, for her guardians had caused her to believe her mother was long dead. The feminist ideologies in the film were certainly ahead of their time, but well captured in the drama. Stewart is excellent as the feisty woman. Young actress Stewart made a sufficient impression in this and other films to receive a Hollywood offer. She went to the U. S. after this film, where she appeared in NURSE EDITH CAVELL (1939) and MY SON, MY SON (1940). Disaffected by the business in the U.S., she returned to England in 1943, where she appeared in more films and also resumed her stage career.

p, Walter C. Mycroft; d, Thomas Bentley; w, Dudley Leslie (based on the play by Charles Garvice, Allen Harker, F. Prior); ph, Gunther Krampf.

Drama   **(PR:A   MPAA:NR)**

MARIGOLD MAN zero   (1970) 90m Golden Age/Emerson c

Greg Mullavey (Harry), Harry Cohn (George), Joan Lemmo (Landlady), Pearl Shear (Dowager), Lew Horn (Neighbor), Elaine Partnow (Harry's Girl Friend), James Tartan (Policeman).

Mullavey and Cohn are unemployed, living in Hollywood, and broke. They don't have to worry about paying their rent because the landlady is in love with Mullavey,

who passes the time by daydreaming about planting marigolds from Los Angeles to New York. He thinks that will help mankind.

p, William Norton, Paul Leder; d, Leder; w, Norton; ph, Arch Archambault, Norton (Eastmancolor); art d, Kathy O'Toole.

Comedy   **(PR:C   MPAA:NR)**

MARIGOLDS IN AUGUST***   (1980, South Africa) 87m Serpent-R.M. c

Winston Ntshona (Daan), John Kani (Melton), Athol Fugard (Paulus).

With the apartheid situation of the South African government, an intelligent drama from that country dealing with the plight of blacks is an all too rare commodity. Thus, a feature like MARIGOLDS IN AUGUST is something to be treasured. Written by Fugard, South Africa's best known playwright, it tells a simple story about a black gardener (Ntshona) who must travel a long distance by foot into the white district in order to look for work. He fears that the job will disappear when another black (Kani) shows up. Ntshona thinks that this new man wants to rob a local supermarket and forces him out of the area. Together the two end up with a white poacher (played by Fugard) and the three come to realize that only by working together and sharing will anything be accomplished. Though this is a simplistic theme, it's played with a sincerity that takes the drama to heart. The ensemble is honest in their portraits of men fighting uncontrollable circumstances, carrying the story's allegorical elements well. The film itself was a subject of controversy when the Soviet Union objected to it being shown at the Berlin Film Festival. Only after it was learned that many of Fugard's plays had been staged in Soviet-controlled Eastern European countries was the protest dropped.

d, Ross Devenish; w, Athol Fugard; ph, Michael Davis, ed, Lionel Selwyn.

Drama   **(PR:C   MPAA:NR)**

MARILYN*   (1953, Brit.) 70m Nettlefold/BUT bw (AKA: ROADHOUSE GIRL)

Maxwell Reed (Tom Price), Sandra Dorne (Marilyn Saunders), Leslie Dwyer (George Saunders), Vida Hope (Rosie), Ferdy Mayne (Nicky Everton), Hugh Pryse (Coroner), Kenneth Connor (Driver), Ben Williams (Foreman).

Reed is a garage mechanic enraptured with his boss's seductive wife, Dorne. Boss Dwyer doesn't care for the attention this mechanic pays to his wife, but Maxwell ends up killing his boss in a fight. With Dorne's help, the murder is covered up and together the pair open a roadhouse. Mayne is a rich man who helps out Dorne with some needed money but gradually learns what happened to her husband. Dorne switches her fleeting affections back to Reed as the police close in on the murderous pair. The plot is a sort of poor man's THE POSTMAN ALWAYS RINGS TWICE without any of that story's steamy heart. Both production values and the ensemble are faltering in this inconsequential story of love and murder.

p, Ernest G. Roy; d&w, Wolf Rilla (based on the play "Marian" by Peter Jones); ph, Geoffrey Faithfull.

Crime   **(PR:O   MPAA:NR)**

MARINE BATTLEGROUND*1/2 (1966, U.S./S.K.) 88m Paul Mart/Manson bw

Jock Mahoney (Nick Rawlins), Pat Yi (Nurse Young Hi Park), Youngson Chon (Young Hi as a Child), Tong-hui Chang (Squad Leader), Tae-yop Yi (PFC Ku), Pong-su Ku (PFC Bong Ku), David Lowe (1st Patient), Lloyd Kino (2nd Patient), George Zaima.

Yi is an American nurse during the Vietnam War who tells her story to reporter Mahoney in flashbacks. She grew up in Korea during the war there in the early 1950s. She lost her mother during the battle at Inchon and she was adopted by Marines. All but two of the Marines were killed during the battle and Yi became a nurse in her memory.

p, Paul Mart; d, Manli Lee, Milton Mann; w, Mann, Han-chul Yu, Burton Moore, Tom Morrison (based on a story by Kook-jin Jang); ph, William Hines, Jingmin Su (CinemaScope); m, Jaime Mendoza-Nava; ed, Mann; art d, Wally Moon, Sungchil Hong, Tod Jonson.

War/Drama   **(PR:A   MPAA:NR)**

MARINE RAIDERS*1/2   (1944) 91m RKO bw

Pat O'Brien (Maj. Steven Lockhard), Robert Ryan (Capt. Dan Craig), Ruth Hussey (Ellen Foster), Frank McHugh (Sgt. Louis Leary), Barton MacLane (Sgt. Maguire), Richard Martin (Jimmy), Edmund Glover (Miller), Russell Wade (Tony Hewitt), Robert Anderson (Lt. Harrigan), Michael St. Angel (Lt. Sherwood), Martha MacVicar [Vickers] (Sally), Harry Brown (Cook), Sammy Stein (Sergeant), William Forrest (Col. Carter), Mike Kilian (Shoe Gag Soldier), Audrey Manners (Aussie WAAF), Harry Clay (Wounded Marine), Eddie Woods (Officer on Ship), Blake Edwards (Marine), John Elliott (Admiral), Barry Macollum (Innkeeper).

Routine Hollywood propaganda has Ryan and O'Brien as two officers in the Marines during the Guadalcanal invasion. When the Army takes over, their company is given a short leave in Australia, allowing Hussey and Ryan a chance to meet and fall in love. Fearing that his good buddy is falling into the clutches of a woman, O'Brien gets orders to have him and Ryan sent back to the States to train recruits. Angered at his friend's actions, Ryan refuses to speak to O'Brien. A new mission allows a stopover in Australia, where Ryan and Hussey wed before the men go off into battle. Performances and technical aspects are all up to standard. Picture effectively uses stock footage of plane attacks on Guadalcanal. Note producer-writer-director Blake Edwards in a small part.

p, Robert Fellows; d, Harold Schuster; w, Warren Duff (based on a story by Martin Rackin, Duff); ph, Nicholas Musuraca; m, Roy Webb; ed, Philip Martin, Jr.; md, Constantin Bakaleinikoff; art d, Albert D'Agostino, Walter E. Keller; set d, Darrell Silvera, Harley Miller; spec eff, Vernon L. Walker.

War/Drama   **(PR:A   MPAA:NR)**

MARINES ARE COMING, THE**   (1935) 68m Mascot bw

William Haines (*Bill Taylor*), Esther Ralston (*Dorothy*), Conrad Nagel (*Capt. Benton*), Armida (*Rosita*), Edgar Kennedy (*Buck Martin*), Hale Hamilton (*Col. Gilroy*), George Regas (*The Torch*), Michael Visaroff (*Laredo*), Dell Henderson (*Admiral*), Broderick O'Farrell.

Set in the jungles of Central America, the picture stars Haines and Nagel as a couple of Marines out for the same girl, Ralston. The girl can't make up her mind, but winds up going for Haines. This proves to be a mistake when Mexican spitfire Armida comes into the picture claiming to be Haines' girl.

p, Nat Levine; d, David Howard; w, James Gruen, (based on a story by John Rathmell, Colbert Clark); ph, Ernie Miller, William Nobles; ed, Thomas Scott; m/l, "My Brazilian Baby," Gus Edwards. (sung by Armida).

War   (PR:A MPAA:NR)

MARINES ARE HERE, THE**   (1938) 61m MON bw

Gordon Oliver (*Jones*), June Travis (*Terry*), Ray Walker (*Hogan*), Guinn "Big Boy" Williams (*Sgt. Gibbons*), Ronnie Cosbey (*Tommy*), Billy Dooley (*Muggsy*), Pat Gleason (*One Step*), Edward Earle (*Lt. Drake*), Wade Boteler (*Sgt. Foster*).

Immature picture which idolizes the Marines by having a group of them trying to do in a gang of bandits. Oliver plays a misanthrope who has a change of heart after seeing the light. Performances are varied, with the supporting cast lending some good characterizations.

p, Scott R. Dunlap; d, Phil Rosen; w, Jack Knapp, J. Benton Cheney (based on a story by Edwin C. Parsons, Charles Logue); ph, Gilbert Warrenton; ed, Russell Schoengarth; md, Abe Meyers.

War Drama   (PR:A MPAA:NR)

MARINES COME THROUGH, THE*   (1943) 60m Astor bw

Wallace Ford (*Singapore*), Toby Wing (*Linda Dale*), Grant Withers (*Jack*), Sheila Lynch (*Maisie*), Michael Doyle (*Lt. Landers*), Don Lanning (*Dick Weber*), Frank Rasmussen (*Beckstrom*), Roy Elkins (*Charles*), James Neary (*Top Sergeant*), Thomas McKeon (*Col. Dale*).

Weak picture about the efforts to stop some Nazis from stealing the plans for a newly invented bombsight. Film suffers from a story line that doesn't hold the viewer's interest, as well as unconvincing performances, unrealistic sets, and messy dialog.

p, George Hirliman; d, Louis Gasnier; w, D. S. Leslie (based on a story by Lawrence Meade); ph, J. Burgi Contner.

War   (PR:A MPAA:NR)

MARINES FLY HIGH, THE*1/2   (1940) 68m RKO bw

Richard Dix (*Lt. Darrick*), Chester Morris (*Lt. Malone*), Lucille Ball (*Joan Grant*), Steffi Duna (*Teresa*), John Eldredge (*John Henderson*), Paul Harvey (*Col. Hill*), Horace MacMahon (*Monk O'Hara*), Robert Stanton (*Lt. Hobbs*), Ann Shoemaker (*Mrs. Hill*), Nestor Paiva (*Fernandez*), Ethan Laidlaw (*Barnes*), Dick Hogan (*Cpl. Haines*).

Predictable yarn has Ball as the owner of a cocoa plantation at a Central American site, also the outpost for a Marine platoon. Dix and Morris are the uniformed men fighting for Ball's affection. The two men get a chance to prove themselves when Ball is kidnaped by bandits who have been terrorizing her plantation. Even though outnumbered 10 to one, the small group of Marines manages to hold on. Acceptable performances are marred by an unbelievable plot line and plodding dialog. The original director, Nicholls, was killed in an auto accident in mid-production.

p, Robert Sisk; d, George Nicholls, Jr., Ben Stoloff; w, Jerry Cady, Lt. Comdr. A. J. Bolton (based on a story by A. C. Edington); ph, Frank Redman; ed, Frederic Knudtson; md, Roy Webb.

War   (PR:A MPAA:NR)

MARINES, LET'S GO**1/2   (1961) 103m FOX c

Tom Tryon (*Skip Roth*), David Hedison (*David Chatfield*), Tom Reese (*McCaffrey*), Linda Hutchins (*Grace Blake*), William Tyler (*Russ Waller*), Barbara Stuart (*Ina Baxter*), David Brandon (*Newt Levells*), Steve Baylor (*Chase*), Peter Miller (*Hawkins*), Adoree Evans (*Ellen Hawkins*), Hideo Inamura (*Pete Kono*), Vince Williams (*Hank Dyer*), Fumiyo Fujimoto (*Song Do*), Henry Okawa (*Yoshida*).

Purely an exploitation picture, this film follows a Marine platoon from the battlefields of Korea to regimental reserve status in Japan and back to Korea, giving the men a chance to prove themselves. Reese plays the overbearing sergeant who's busted down to private, but still proves to be the real leader of these men. Characters are all the stereotypes which could possibly be imagined, but the cast handles these caricatures well. Walsh does his usual adequate job in handling the action sequences. Look for some location scenes filmed in Japan.

p&d, Raoul Walsh; w, John Twist (based on a story by Walsh); ph, Lucien Ballard (CinemaScope, DeLuxe Color); m, Irving Gertz; ed, Robert Simpson; art d, Jack Martin Smith, Alfred Ybarra; m/l, title song, Mike Phillips, George Watson (sung by Rex Allen); makeup, Ben Nye.

War   (PR:A MPAA:NR)

MARIUS***1/2   (1933, Fr.) 103m Joinville-PAR/PAR bw

Jules Raimu (*Cesar Olivier*), Orane Demazis (*Fanny*), Pierre Fresnay (*Marius*), Fernand Charpin (*Honore Panisse*), Alida Rouffe (*Honorine Cabanis*), Robert Vattier (*Mon. Brun*), Paul Dullac (*Felix Escartefigue*), Alexandre Mihalesco (*Piquoiseau*), Edouard Delmont (*2nd Mate*), Milly Mathis (*Aunt Claudine Foulon*), Callamand (*Le Goelec*), Maupi (*Stoker*), V. Ribe (*Customer*), Oueret (*Felicie*), Vassy (*Arab*).

MARIUS is the first of the *Marseilles Trilogy* penned by Marcel Pagnol. The next two were FANNY (1932), and CESAR (1936). It was later condensed as a stage musical for Broadway, then, inexplicably, the songs were deleted for a boring 1960 film. The same actors appearing in MARIUS also worked in the sequels. Fresnay, in the title role, toils at a bar in Marseilles and yearns for the sea. Raimu, his father, is a widower, who prates about Fresnay's lack of drive but truly adores his boy. Raimu spends his time consorting with the wealthy Charpin (who was to be featured in the next film when he marries Demazis), ferry captain Dullac and customs inspector Vattier. Fresnay loves Demazis, daughter of rotund Rouffe, a local fishwife, although he is unable to make a lasting commitment to her because the call of the sea is too strong. Charpin asks for Demazis's hand and Fresnay flies off the handle although Demazis is delighted by this turn of events because she hopes Fresnay's jealousy will cause him to propose. It does not work because Fresnay learns from Mihalesco that there's a spot on a boat leaving the port that night. Rouffe is depressed because Demazis loves Fresnay and has no intention of marrying the rich Charpin. Rouffe meets with Raimu and they talk about a possible dowry if Fresnay and Demazis can ever get together. The young woman enters the bar that night and confesses that she loves Fresnay and that she has spurned Charpin. Fresnay admits he loves her as well and she is the only reason why he has stayed in town. Mihalesco enters and informs Fresnay that the man who was to leave the departing ship has returned so that seaman's slot is now again filled. Demazis and Fresnay go to his small room to make love. Time passes and Raimu senses that Fresnay is attached to some woman but cannot figure out who. All this time, Demazis is planning to marry Fresnay although he is avoiding the issue. Mihalesco, a local waterfront man, tells Fresnay that another boat is about to leave and there is a spot to be filled aboard. When Fresnay declines, Mihalesco retorts that Fresnay's relationship with Demazis may well spell the end of any hopes for getting out of Marseilles for the adventurous young man. Demazis overhears the conversation and frets because she does not ever want to be accused of not allowing Fresnay to have his career at sea. Rouffe is enraged when she finds Fresnay and Demazis in bed in the girl's room and she rushes to Raimu and demands that the two children marry at once. Raimu confronts Fresnay across the breakfast table and suggests the boy make an honest woman out of the girl. Mihalesco comes by to say that the boat is leaving and Demazis hears that and selflessly tells Fresnay that she had planned to accept Charpin's proposal because he is a rich man and would settle a sum on her poor mother. Fresnay grabs his already-packed suitcase and races to the dock as Demazis keeps Raimu busy until his son has made it to the boat. Raimu takes Demazis to his room and begins to explain that the two parents have made the right decision and they are urging the lovebirds to marry. Demazis's face turns white upon hearing this, then she turns to look out the window, sees Fresnay's ship sailing out to sea and she faints in Raimu's arms as the picture ends. A touching and deeply affecting movie that was snubbed by the British until 1949 because it presented premarital sex in such a natural fashion and without recriminations. Raimu, a stage actor as well as a silent screen comedian, is wonderful as Cesar and carried that role to even higher levels in the sequels. Fresnay, in order to prepare for his role as a waterfront bartender, took a job as a bartender in a waterfront bar. The results are evident. The no-nonsense, no-tricks direction of Korda made this feel real, with none of the camera techniques that were the vogue at the time. Korda wisely concentrated on the humanity of the people and bypassed any attempts at saying: "Look at me directing!" It was also shot in Swedish and German simultaneously. Pagnol stayed on the set and watched carefully, then allowed Marc Allegret to direct FANNY and took over those chores himself for CESAR. This film was rereleased in 1948 with English subtitles and 25 minutes added to the running length.

p, Marcel Pagnol; d, Alexander Korda; w, Pagnol (based on the play by Pagnol); ph, Ted Pahle; m, Francis Gromon; ed, Roger Spiri Mercanton; prod d, Alfred Junge, Vincent Korda.

Drama   **Cas**   (PR:C MPAA:NR)

MARIZINIA*1/2

(1962, U.S./Braz.) 82m International Film Enterprises/International Film Enterprises-Diamond-Golden Eagle c (AKA: MARIZINIA, THE WITCH BENEATH THE SEA; THE WITCH BENEATH THE SEA)

John Sutton (*John Morgan*), Gina Albert, Zygmunt Sulistrowski, Celeneh Costa, Eugenio Carlos.

South American fishermen save a woman from drowning, but want to throw her back into the sea when the fish become scarce. She escapes and joins two explorers on a journey through the Amazon jungle. They have a number of adventures and she falls in love with Sutton. Title song is sung by Johnny Starr.

p&d, Zygmunt Sulistrowski; w, Anita Manville, Austin Green (based on a story by Sulistrowski).

Adventure   (PR:A MPAA:NR)

MARIZINIA, THE WITCH BENEATH THE SEA
(SEE: MARIZINIA, 1962, U.S./Braz.)

MARJORIE MORNINGSTAR**1/2   (1958) 125m Beachwold/WB c

Gene Kelly (*Noel Airman*), Natalie Wood (*Marjorie Morgenstern*), Claire Trevor (*Rose Morgenstern*), Everett Sloane (*Arnold Morgenstern*), Martin Milner (*Wally*), Ed Wynn (*Uncle Samson*), Carolyn Jones (*Marsha Zelenko*), George Tobias (*Greech*), Martin Balsam (*Dr. David Harris*), Jesse White (*Lou Michaelson*), Edward [Edd] Byrnes (*Sandy Lamm*), Paul Picerni (*Phillip Berman*), Alan Reed (*Puddles Podell*), Ruta Lee (*Imogene*), Edward Foster (*Carlos*), Patricia Denise (*Karen*), Howard Best (*Seth*), Lester Dorr (*Elevator Operator*), Carl Sklover (*Leon Lamm*), Jean Vachon (*Mary Lamm*), Elizabeth Harrower (*Miss Kimble*), Guy Raymond (*Mr. Klabber*), Leslie Bradley (*Blair*), Maida Severn (*Tonia Zelenko*), Fay Nuell (*Helen Harris*), Fred Rapport (*Nate*), Harry Seymour (*Frank*), Shelley Fabares (*Seth's Girl Friend*), Walter Clinton (*Mr. Zelenko*), Pierre Watkin (*Civil Official*), Reginald

Sheffield (Clerk), Sandy Livingston (Betsy), Peter Brown (Alec), Gail Ganley (Wally's Girl Friend), Russell Ash (Harry Morgenstern), Rad Fulton (Romeo).

Herman Wouk wrote a very Jewish novel and the producers felt that it just might have been too ethnic for the general public so they cast Irish-as-Paddy's-Pig Kelly in the male lead and Russian-French Wood as the heroine. Danny Kaye was originally penciled in to play the role and declined, so Kelly got the nod. There was a lot of flack from the studio and writer Freeman almost took his name off the credits but changed his mind at the last minute. Wood changes her name from Morgenstern to Morningstar, which signals her desire to bury her cultural background. At the bar mitzvah of her brother, Best, she questions the stern religious rule of her father, Sloane, and mother, Trevor. When they will not hear of any rebellion, she confides in her uncle, Wynn, an eccentric old geezer with a winsome charm. Wood scores as Juliet in her Hunter College show, then travels to upstate New York where she has taken a job as drama counselor at a camp. With best pal, Jones, they visit South Wind, a resort complex not unlike the famed Tamamint where many stars first got their breaks under camp director Max Liebman. Wood meets Kelly, a big fish in that little pond. Kelly is the actor, director, singer, and choreographer of the South Wind shows. He dazzles her so that she is hardly aware his aide, Milner, is smitten by her. Kelly likes Wood although there is no chance for any lasting relationship because he is too busy being the idol of many other women. Sloane and Trevor come upstate and meet Kelly and make it clear to Wood that they do not approve of her cavorting with an older man who has no business prospects other than in the unstable entertainment world. Wynn accompanies them and does a comic turn as a matador for the guests and then has a fatal heart attack. Wood is shattered, then decides to end the affair with Kelly who understands and is relieved. Her legacy from the liaison is the name that he has chosen for her, Morningstar, just as he changed his name from Ehreman to Airman. Wood returns to Hunter College after the summer and her parents are thrilled when it appears that she will marry Balsam, a doctor. Kelly calls and tells her that he is now working at a respectable job at an advertising agency because he knew her parents wanted him to give up show business if they were to continue their affair. This sacrifice on Kelly's part makes Wood love him even more than she did before. Milner has written a hit play and Kelly and Wood attend the show. Kelly is consumed by jealousy over the success of his former flunky and he vanishes until Wood finds him in the room of a flaxen floozy in Greenwich Village. She whacks him across his face and exits. Jones now is engaged to producer White and when Kelly and Wood meet at the White-Jones wedding, Kelly attempts to salve matters, says he is contrite and that he is hard at work on a new revue. Wood cannot turn her back on Kelly and persuades White to produce Kelly's show. In the interim, Sloane and Trevor are now resigned that they cannot talk Wood out of Kelly's grasp so they shrug and give their O.K. to the duo. Kelly's show bombs and he vanishes again. This time to London where Milner explains to Wood that Kelly does not want to be found. Kelly is soon back at the scene of his greatest triumphs, South Wind, and Wood travels there and sees Kelly is in his element, surrounded by a battalion of pretty young girls. She finally understands Kelly's need to be adored, but not intimately touched. Wood goes off with Milner, who has been waiting for her since the first reel. The picture was about as Jewish as SEVEN SAMURAI and spent most of its time dwelling on show business, which was hardly Wouk's intent in the massive novel. Kelly was supposed to be a second-rate musical talent but could not resist giving it his all and when he danced and sang the Oscar-nominated tune "A Very Special Love," it worked against the theory that he was not a good enough performer to make it in the real world. Sloane and Trevor are excellent as the parents and manage to convey the ethnic quality without ever crossing into kvetchiness and burlesque. The "Catskill Mountain Life" has been seen in a few films and plays like "Having a Wonderful Time" and "Wish You Were Here" but they have never been truly and totally depicted and the same goes for this version of the Borscht Belt. Kelly was 46 and Wood was just 20 when they made the picture and the feelings of the parents, upon seeing the wrinkled Kelly, were sincere, especially since Sloane was only three years older.

p, Milton Sperling; d, Irving Rapper; w, Everett Freeman (based on the novel by Herman Wouk); ph, Harry Stradling (Warner Color); m, Max Steiner; ed, Folmar Blangsted; md, Ray Heindorf; art d, Malcolm Bert; cos, Howard Shoup; ch, Jack Baker; m/l, "A Very Special Love," Sammy Fain, Paul Francis Webster.

Drama   **(PR:A-C   MPAA:NR)**

MARK, THE*½   (1961, Brit.) 127m FOX bw

Maria Schell (Mrs. Ruth Leighton), Stuart Whitman (Jim Fuller), Rod Steiger (Dr. Edmund McNally), Brenda De Banzie (Mrs. Cartwright), Donald Houston (Austin, Reporter), Donald Wolfit (Mr. Clive), Paul Rogers (Milne), Maurice Denham (Arnold Cartwright), Amanda Black (Janie), Marie Devereaux (Ellen) Bill Foley (Mr. Fuller), Anne Monaghan (Mrs. Fuller), Josephine Frayne (Patricia), Eddie Byrne (Acker), Bandana Das Gupta (Inez), Harry Baird (Cole), John Welsh (1st Officer), Russell Napier (2nd Officer).

Poignant story has Whitman, the child of a domineering but pampering mother and an ineffectual father, growing into manhood confused about his manliness. An unhappy affair leaves him only more bewildered, and he becomes more and more attracted to young girls, whom he does not feel threatened by. This leads to his being convicted of abducting a 10-year-old girl with the intention of molesting her. Whitman is sentenced to three years in prison under the care of psychiatrist Steiger. After learning to understand and cope with his situation, Whitman is released ready to start anew. He manages to find a decent job and becomes engaged to Schell, a widow with a 10-year-old girl. When a nosy reporter spots Whitman after a child has been molested, Whitman's past is brought out into the open, ruining his marriage plans as well as the career he has been pursuing. Whitman is convincing in his role, with added flavor by Steiger as the eccentric psychiatrist. There is a nice warm feeling between Whitman, Schell, and Black in the family-like scenes. Script lapses into unbelievable situations at times, such as the reporter's inquisitiveness, but

overall it flows well. The flashbacks used to explain Whitman's problems growing up are overly intrusive.

p, Raymond Stross; d, Guy Green; w, Sidney Buchman, Stanley Mann (based on the novel by Charles Israel); ph, Douglas Slocombe (CinemaScope); m, Richard Rodney Bennett; ed, Peter Taylor; md, John Hollingsworth; art d, Ray Simm; set d, Josie MacAvin; makeup, Charles Nash.

Drama   **(PR:A   MPAA:NR)**

MARK IT PAID**   (1933) 69m COL bw

William Collier, Jr., Joan Marsh.

Collier plays an honest speedboat driver who refuses to throw a race and is framed for his convictions. Picture has some nice action sequences in the racing scenes.

d, D. Ross Lederman; w, Charles Condon.

Drama   **(PR:A   MPAA:NR)**

MARK OF CAIN, THE**   (1948, Brit.) 88m RANK-TC/GFD bw

Sally Gray (Sarah Bonheur), Eric Portman (Richard Howard), Patrick Holt (John Howard), Dermot Walsh (Jerome Thorn), Dennis O'Dea (Sir William Godfrey), Edward Lexy (Lord Rochford), Theresa Giehse (Sister Seraphine), Maureen Delaney (Daisy Cobb), Helen Cherry (Mary), Vida Hope (Jennie), Dora Sevening (Mme. Bonheur), Janet Kay (Sylvia The Tweenie, Maid), James Hayter (Dr. White), Andrew Cruickshank (Sir Jonathon Dockwra), Marjorie Gresley (Lady Rochford), Beryl Measor (Nurse Brand), May MacDonald (Mrs. White), Susan English (Sally Howard), Johnny Schofield (Chemist), Helen Goss (Lizzie Burt), John Warren (Mr. Wilkins), Rose Howlett (Mrs. Wilkins), Miles Malleson (Mr. Burden), William Mervyn (Mr. Bonnington), Noel Howlett (Judge), Arthur Howard (Clerk of the Court), Hope Matthews (Foreman of the Jury), Olwen Brookes (Mrs. Fisher), Sidney Bromley (Martin, Richard's Man), Fred Johnson (Prison Chaplain), Albert Ferber (Pianist), John Hollingsworth (Conductor), George Opoka (Mons. Vernier), Jacqueline Robert (Mme. Vernier), Tony Etienne (Jean, Chateau Footman), Willoughby Gray (Photographer), Adrian Wallet (Reporter), James Carson (Opera House Attendant), Mary Daniels, Jean Bowler (Program Sellers), Wensley Pithey (Police Inspector), Michael Logan (Police Sergeant), Norah Gordon, Christiana Forbes, Colleen Nolan, Sheila Raynor (Wardresses), Jean Anderson.

Lavish costume drama has Gray loved by two brothers, Portman and Holt, with Portman exceedingly jealous of his suave brother. Holt and Gray marry, but after a couple of years their marriage is marred by Gray's inability to play the role of proper hostess. Taking Portman as her confidant, she tells him her troubles. Portman attempts to convince her to divorce his brother and run off with him. When the couple has a reconciliation, jealous Portman poisons his brother, making all the evidence point to Gray. Story drags as the direction fails to maintain a level of suspense, and is further marred by the cast overplaying their roles.

p, W. P. Lipscomb; d, Brian Desmond Hurst; w, Lipscomb, Francis Crowdy, Christianna Brand (based on the novel Airing in a Closed Carriage by Joseph Shearing); ph, Erwin Hillier; m, Bernard Stevens; ed, Sydney Stone; md, Muir Mathieson; art d, Vetchinsky; cos, Eleanor Abbey; makeup, G. Rodway.

Drama   **(PR:A   MPAA:NR)**

MARK OF THE APACHE   (SEE: TOMAHAWK TRAIL, 1957)

MARK OF THE AVENGER   (SEE: MYSTERIOUS RIDER, THE, 1938)

MARK OF THE CLAW   (SEE: DICK TRACY'S DILEMMA, 1947)

MARK OF THE DEVIL*
(1970, Ger./Brit.) 90m c (BRENN, HEXE, BRENN; HEXEN BIS AUFS BLUT GEQUALT; AKA: BURN, WITCH, BURN)

Herbert Lom (Count Cumberland), Udo Kier (Baron Christian von Meru), Olivera Vuco (Vanessa), Reggie Nalder (Albino), Herbert Fux (Chief Executioner), Gaby Fuchs, Michael Maien, Ingeborg Schoener, Doris von Danwitz, Dorothea Carrera, Marlies Peterson, Gunther Clemens, Johannes Buzalski, Adrian Hoven.

Lom is a witch trial judge in 18th-Century Austria. He has the pleasure of ordering witches to have their tongues ripped out, to be burned at the stake, to be stretched on the rack, and other exciting punishments. A very sadistic horror film that is full of gore but has no redeeming scares.

p, Adrian Hoven; d, Michael Armstrong; w, Sergio Cassner, Percy Parker; ph, Ernst W. Kalinke (Eastmancolor); m, Michael Holm; art d, Max Melin.

Horror   **(PR:O   MPAA:NR)**

MARK OF THE DEVIL II*
(1975, Ger./Brit.) 90m Hallmark c (HEXEN-GESCHANDET UND TODE GEQUALT; AKA: WITCHES: VIOLATED AND TORTURED TO DEATH)

Erica Blanc, Anton Diffring, Reggie Nalder, Percy Hoven, Lukas Ammann, Jean Pierre Zola, Astrid Kilian, Ellen Umlaud, Rosy-Rosy, Johannes Buzalski, Harry Hardt.

The sequel to MARK OF THE DEVIL. Just more witches being tortured and killed in as many ways as humanly possible.

d, Adrian Hoven; w, Hoven, Fred Denger.

Horror   **(PR:O   MPAA:R)**

MARK OF THE GORILLA**   (1950) 68m COL bw

Johnny Weissmuller (Jungle Jim), Trudy Marshall (Barbara Bentley), Suzanne Dalbert (Nyobi), Onslow Stevens (Brandt), Robert Purcell (Kramer), Pierce Lyden (Gibbs), Neyle Morrow (Head Ranger), Selmer Jackson (Warden Bentley).

Stevens plays the head of a gang in search of Nazi loot buried in the jungle. The gang disguise themselves as gorillas to scare away natives so they can look for the loot without arousing suspicion, but Weissmuller, the white man who has adopted the ways of the apes, uncovers their plot. Performances are convincing, with good production considering the modest budget. (See JUNGLE JIM series, Index.)

p, Sam Katzman; d, William Berke; w, Carroll Young (based on the comic strip); ph, Ira S. Morgan; ed, Henry Batista; md, Mischa Bakaleinikoff; art d, Paul Palmentola.

Adventure **(PR:A MPAA:NR)**

MARK OF THE HAWK, THE*** (1958) 83m UNIV c (GB: ACCUSED)

Eartha Kitt (Renee), Sidney Poitier (Oban), Juano Hernandez (Amugu), John McIntire (Craig), Helen Horton (Barbara), Marne Maitland (Sandar Lal), Gerard Heinz (Govenor General), Earl Cameron (Prosecutor), Patrick Allen (Gregory), Clifton Macklin (Kanda), Ewen Solon (Inspector), Lockwood West (Magistrate), Francis Matthews (Overholt), Phillip Vickers (Ben), Bill Nagy (Fred), N. C. Doo (Dr. Lin), David Goh (Ming Tao), Harold Siddons (1st Officer), Frederick Treves (2nd Officer), Lionel Ngakane (African Doctor), Andy Ho (Chinese Officer), John A. Tinn (Chinese Soldier).

Political-racial strife on the Dark Continent serves as the thematic background for Poitier to be torn between two loyalties. Poitier plays an educated African who comes back home to work as a legislator. When his brother, Macklin, heads a revolt against the existing white regime, Poitier is confused as to where his loyalties lie. Direction is well paced, though lapsing into too much dialog at times. Performances are good, with Poitier convincing as the confused native son.

p, Lloyd Young; d, Michael Audley, Gilbert Gunn; w, H. Kenn Carmichael (based on a story by Young); ph, Edwin Hillier, Toge Fujihira (SuperScope, Technicolor); m, Matyas Seiber; ed, Edward Jarvis; md, Louis Levy; art d, Terence Verity; m/1, "This Man Is Mine," Ken Darby (sung by Eartha Kitt).

Drama **(PR:A MPAA:NR)**

MARK OF THE LASH* 1/2 (1948) 60m Western Adventure/Screen Guild bw

Al "Lash" LaRue, Al "Fuzzy" St. John, Suzi Crandall, Marshall Reed, John Cason, Jimmy Martin, Tom London, Lee Roberts, Steve Darrell, Jack Hendricks, Cliff Taylor, Harry Cody, Britt Wood.

LaRue, along with his whip, impersonates a land investigator who has died in order to prevent local ranchers from losing their water. Bad guy Reed dams the river in hopes the ranchers will leave so he can have their land, however, LaRue puts some giant holes in his scheme.

p, Ron Ormond; d, Ray Taylor; w, Ormand, Ira Webb; ph, Ernest Miller; m, Walter Greene; ed, Hugh Winn; art d, Vincent Taylor.

Western **(PR:A MPAA:NR)**

MARK OF THE PHOENIX* 1/2 (1958, Brit.) 64m BUT bw

Julia Arnall (Petra), Sheldon Lawrence (Chuck Martin), Anton Diffring (Inspector Schell), Eric Pohlmann (Duser), George Margo (Emilson), Michael Peake (Koos), Martin Miller (Brunet), Roger Delgado, Bernard Rebel, Frederick Schrecker, Pierre Chaminade, Corinne Grey, Jennifer Jayne, Edouard Assaly, Victor Beaumont, Norma Parnell, Howard Green, Tom Clegg.

After a Belgian metallurgist invents an alloy that can withstand nuclear radiation, he's murdered by an international gang of thieves. A quantity of the alloy is taken and made into a cigarette case. This is planted on Lawrence, a jewel thief himself, who the gang hopes will unknowingly smuggle the case into East Germany. Instead, Lawrence tries to sell the case back to the gang's leader, nearly getting killed in the process. He escapes death, handing the cigarette case over to authorities as the film ends. The plot takes twist after twist, but the results are barely satisfactory. Rather than being a complicated thriller, this is a confusing mess with an ensemble that can't do much with the material.

p, W. G. Chalmers; d, Maclean Rogers; w, Norman Hudis (based on a story by Desmond Cory); ph, Geoffrey Faithfull.

Crime/Thriller **(PR:C MPAA:NR)**

MARK OF THE RENEGADE** (1951) 81m UNIV c

Ricardo Montalban (Marcos), Cyd Charisse (Manuella), J. Carrol Naish (Luis), Gilbert Roland (Don Pedro Garcia), Andrea King (Anita Gonzales), George Tobias (Bardosa), Antonio Moreno (Jose De Vasquez), Georgia Backus (Duenna Concepcion), Robert Warwick (Col. Vega), Armando Silvestre (Miguel De Gandara), Bridget Carr (Rosa), Alberto Morin (Cervera), Renzo Cesana (Father Juan), Roberto Cornthwaite (Innkeeper), Edward C. Rios (Paco), Dave Wolfe (Landlord).

Escapist entertainment set in the early days of California has Montalban, an undercover agent for the Republic of Mexico, out to spoil a plot by Roland to create a separate Republic of California. Montalban disguises himself as one of a gang of pirates, led by Tobias, out to sack Los Angeles for Roland's cause. This is just a ploy to enable Montalban to get the information he needs. While disguised as a pirate, he is forced to wed Roland's daughter Charisse. Postcard-like photography and lavish costuming and sets are a plus in this actioner, which lacks story development but has plenty of well-paced action to make up for it. Performances are good.

p, Jack Gross; d, Hugo Fregonese; w, Louis Solomon, Robert Hardy Andrews (based on a story by Johnston McCulley); ph, Charles P. Boyle (Technicolor); m, Frank Skinner; ed, Frank Gross; art d, Bernard Herzbrun, Robert Boyle; ch, Eugene Loring.

Adventure **(PR:A MPAA:NR)**

MARK OF THE VAMPIRE*** (1935) 60m MGM bw

Bela Lugosi (Count Mora), Lionel Barrymore (Prof. Zelen), Lionel Atwill (Inspector Neumann), Elizabeth Allan (Irena Borotyn), Holmes Herbert (Sir Karell Borotyn), Jean Hersholt (Baron Otto von Zinden), Carol Borland (Luna Mora), Donald Meek

(Dr. Doskil), Ivan Simpson (Jan), Egon Brecher (Coroner), Henry Wadsworth (Count Feodor Vincenty), Eily Malyon (Sick Woman), Christian Rub (Deaf Man), Torbin Meyer (Card Player), Zeffie Tilbury (Grandmother), Rosemary Glosz (Innkeeper's Wife), Claire Vedara (English Woman), Guy Bellis (English Man), Baron Hesse (Bus Driver), Mrs. Lesovosky (Old Woman in Inn), Robert Greig (Fat Man), James Bradbury, Jr., Leila Bennett, June Gittelson, Michael Visaroff, Franklin Ardell.

After having dropped out of the genre following FREAKS in 1932, horror director Tod Browning made his comeback with this pseudo-vampire opus which is a virtual scene-for-scene remake of his own silent film LONDON AFTER MIDNIGHT (little seen since 1927 and feared lost). MGM gave Browning a class production and provided him with an exceptional cast. The striking Carol Borland, a 21-year-old protege of Lugosi who worked with him on the stage in "Dracula," was given her big break and managed to create one of the most recognizable characters in horror movies on the basis of one film. Set in Czechoslovakia, the action takes place in a spooky, cobweb-filled castle recently inhabited by Herbert and his daughter, Allan. Rumor has it that the previous owner, Lugosi, had murdered his daughter, Borland, and then shot himself. It is said that their undead spirits haunt the castle and are determined to kill off any new residents (originally the relationship between Lugosi and Borland was portrayed to be incestuous, but all those references were cut). When the dead body of Herbert is found drained of all blood with two puncture holes in the neck, police inspector Atwill, doctor Meek, and baron Hersholt vow to solve the crime. Not wanting her to remain alone in the castle, Hersholt offers his home to Allan. As the months pass, Allan and her handsome young count, Wadsworth, make plans to marry. Meanwhile, Barrymore, a vampire hunter, arrives to rid the castle of the undead. A curious Atwill and Hersholt sneak up to the castle windows at night and watch as the recently murdered Herbert sits playing the organ for Lugosi as Borland flies across the room like a bat. Later that evening, Hersholt is confronted by the vampires and the terrified man rushes back to Barrymore convinced he is the next victim. Barrymore hypnotizes Hersholt and takes him back to the night of Herbert's murder. Deep in hypnosis, Hersholt reveals that he murdered Herbert to stop Allan's arranged marriage to Wadsworth because he wanted her for himself. Hersholt then describes how he drugged Herbert and drained his blood into a wine glass. Having solved the murder, Barrymore awakens Hersholt and turns him over to the police. In a dressing room, we see that Lugosi and Borland were merely actors hired to scare the killer out into the open. Though the film does manage to convey an appropriately eerie mood through some fabulous set design and superior cinematography by James Wong Howe, MARK OF THE VAMPIRE is disappointing due to its "twist" ending. Armed with the knowledge that all the spooky hocus-pocus was just an elaborate ruse by police to catch a killer (in an investigation that takes well over a year), the illogic of the action becomes annoyingly manipulative. Did the police persuade the townsfolk to act like they believe in vampires? Even the cast was dismayed by the red-herring ending. Browning shot the film as straight horror without informing his players how the film was to end. Therefore, all the principals, including Lugosi and Borland, actually believed themselves to be participants in a true vampire movie. When the twist ending was revealed, the cast urged Browning to reject it and stay within the horror premise. When he refused, Lugosi and Borland compromised and offered an alternative which left the possibility that their characters were actually vampires pretending to be actors. Browning refused to give in and the hokey ending remained. Lugosi, Borland, and most horror fans took this as a slap in the face from Browning, as if he were saying they were silly for allowing themselves to believe in such nonsense. Not only does the ending turn the vampires into fakes, but the script leaves Lugosi speechless until the final scene when he reveals that he's an actor. Despite its shortcomings, MARK OF THE VAMPIRE does contain some effective moments and became the last time (with the exception of ABBOTT AND COSTELLO MEET FRANKENSTEIN, which was a self-conscious parody) that Lugosi would play a vampire without embarrassing himself.

p, E.J. Mannix; d, Tod Browning; w, Guy Endore, Bernard Schubert; ph, James Wong Howe; ed, Ben Lewis; art d, Cedric Gibbons; makeup, Jack Dawn.

Horror/Crime **(PR:C MPAA:G)**

MARK OF THE VAMPIRE, 1957 (SEE: VAMPIRE, THE, 1957)

MARK OF THE WHISTLER, THE** 1/2 (1944) 60m COL bw (GB: THE MARKED MAN)

Richard Dix (Lee Nugent), Janis Carter (Patricia Henley), Porter Hall (Joe Sorsby), Paul Guilfoyle (Limpy Smith), John Calvert (Eddie Donnelly), Matt Willis (Perry Donnelly), Matt McHugh, Howard Freeman.

Based on the CBS radio story, this film features Dix as a drifter ready to lay claim to an old bank account only to find himself the target of two men out for revenge. It seems that Dix had a run-in with the men's father over the money, and as a result, the father ended up in jail. Dix gets out of this mess and befriends a crippled peddler who, as it turns out, is the real owner of the nest egg. Direction is evenly paced and performances are up to par. (See: THE WHISTLER series, Index.)

p, Rudolph C. Flothow; d, William Castle; w, George Bricker (based on a story from the radio program "The Whistler" by Cornell Woolrich); ph, George Meehan; m, Wilbur Hatch; ed, Reg Brown; art d, John Datul.

Drama **(PR:A MPAA:NR)**

MARK OF THE WITCH* 1/2 (1970) 84m Presidio/Lone Star c

Robert Elston (Mac Stuart), Anitra Walsh (Jill), Darryl Wells (Alan), Marie Santell (Margery of Jourdemain), Barbara Brownell (Sharon), Jack Gardner (Harry), Sande Drewes (Marybeth), Gary Brockette (Howard), Lori Taylor (Alice), John Figlmiller (Ricky), Lawrence DuPont (Dr. Quimby).

Walsh is taking a class on superstition and accidentally becomes possessed by a witch who was hanged in 1648. The witch persuades Walsh's teacher and her boy friend to teach her the ways of modern society. Walsh begins to kill people, and the instructor, Elston, tries to stop her, but he is seduced by the witch. He kisses her and finds himself transported back to 17th-Century England just in time for his own execution.

p, Mary Davis, Tom Moore; d, Moore; w, Davis, Martha Peters; ph, Robert E. Bethard (Eastmancolor); m, Whitey Thomas; ed, Ken Harrison; set d, Jim Carver; m/l, title song, Anitra Walsh (sung by Trella Hart); makeup, Lynn Brooks.

Horror   **(PR:C MPAA:GP)**

MARK OF ZORRO, THE****   (1940) 93m FOX bw

Tyrone Power (*Don Diego Vega*), Linda Darnell (*Lolita Quintero*), Basil Rathbone (*Capt. Esteban Pasquale*), Gale Sondergaard (*Inez Quintero*), Eugene Pallette (*Fra Felipe*), J. Edward Bromberg (*Don Luis Quintero*), Montagu Love (*Don Alejandro Vega*), Janet Beecher (*Senora Isabella Vega*), Robert Lowery (*Rodrigo*), Chris-Pin Martin (*Turnkey*), George Regas (*Sgt. Gonzales*), Belle Mitchell (*Maria*), John Bleifer (*Pedro*), Frank Puglia (*Cafe Proprietor*), Pedro De Cordoba (*Don Miguel*), Guy d'Ennery (*Don Jose*), Eugene Borden (*Officer of the Day*), Fred Malatesta, Fortunio Bonanova (*Sentries*), Harry Worth, Gino Corrado, Lucio Vellegas (*Caballeros*), Paul Sutton (*Soldier*), Michael [Ted] North (*Bit*), Ralph Byrd (*Student/Officer*), Franco Corsaro (*Orderly*), Hector Sarno (*Peon at Inn*), Stanley Andrews (*Commanding Officer*), Victor Kilian (*Boatman*), Raphael Curio (*Manservant*), Charles Stevens (*Jose, a Peon*), William Edmunds (*Peon*), Jean Del Val (*Sentry*), Frank Yaconelli (*Servant*).

A smashing swashbuckler, the finest of the many Zorro films, this remarkable film owes everything to its inventive and action-minded director Mamoulian. This was Fox's answer to Warner Bros.' THE ADVENTURES OF ROBIN HOOD. Power is marvelous as the fop by day and brave avenger by night. He is the son of Love, the one-time Alcalde of early 19th-Century Los Angeles who returns from Europe at his father's request to find that Bromberg has replaced his benevolent father and that the people are now energetically oppressed by the new Alcalde's tax collectors, led by cruel captain Rathbone. The area nobles, the caballeros, are powerless to resist the newly appointed governor Bromberg, whose rule is studded with torture, humiliation, and death. Bromberg is himself without compassion, obsessed with the accumulation of gold. His vain and pompous wife, Sondergaard, longs only for the glories of the European courts. Into this shaky world struts Power, a perfumed and boorish aristocrat full of little magic tricks, gossip,and a disdainful air—or, at least, that is what he appears to be. Rathbone, Bromberg, and their minions consider him a harmless popinjay. Then, to the surprise of the tyrants and the relief of the peons and caballeros, a masked rider appears, demanding in proclamations that Bromberg either resign his post or face his vengeance, carving his signature with a Z, slashed with a sword, to signify his name: Zorro. The avenger, dressed all in black, proves to be an amazing swordsman, attacking and defeating Rathbone's soldiers, stealing tax money, and upsetting Bromberg's plans at every turn. He even visits Bromberg in his lodgings, terrifying him before disappearing through a secret panel. Rathbone persuades Bromberg to hold onto his power and he begins to investigate the identity of the masked intruder. No one but the viewer realizes that Zorro and Love's foppish son are one and the same. Still playing the repulsive fop, Power visits Bromberg and meets his wife Sondergaard, flattering her mercilessly. He also meets Bromberg's ravishingly beautiful niece, Darnell, and utterly charms her while they dance. Sondergaard, who is having an affair with Rathbone, goes riding with the young caballero to learn of social events in Spain; Power ingratiates himself to her only to learn more of Bromberg's plans. Rathbone, ever the intriguer, advises the rather dull-witted Bromberg that a marriage between Power and his niece Darnell would help unite the caballeros and his tyrannical government. Power agrees since he is really in love with the beautiful girl but Darnell is glum over the prospect of marrying an ineffectual idler. She quickly changes her mind when Power reveals his identity as the daring Zorro. The masked avenger continues to steal back the tax money squeezed from the peons, giving this to a courageous priest, Pallette, who in turn distributes the money to the starving people. Rathbone finds some of the money in the priest's mission and imprisons Pallette. Meanwhile, Power visits Bromberg in the office of his Alcalde mansion, terrifying the man. Just before Bromberg is about to put a shaky signature to his resignation, his protector, the evil Rathbone, bursts into the office and he and Power duel to the death, Rathbone being killed. Bromberg is not a complete fool, however, and realizes that only a former occupant of the mansion would know its secret passageways. He rightfully deduces that Power is Zorro and has him thrown into jail. Love arrives and protests, telling Bromberg that his "worthless son," whom he has all but disinherited, could never be the daring Zorro. He is quickly convinced by Power, however, that he is indeed the legendary Zorro, and the two lead the caballeros in open revolt against Bromberg. With the help of the peons, they overthrow the cruel regime and Love is reinstated as the governor. Power and Darnell plan to marry and raise a large family, according to Power's last charming remarks at the fadeout. Power cuts a stylish and convincing Zorro, vigorously playing the brilliant swordsman, although his more strenuous routines are performed by stunt double Albert Cavens. Mamoulian cleverly cuts in and out of his terse scenes to suggest more action than really occurs, maintaining an exciting pace. The final deadly confrontation between Rathbone and Power is a magnificent and thrilling duel no less exciting than the final contretemps between Errol Flynn and Rathbone in THE ADVENTURES OF ROBIN HOOD. Rathbone is terrific as the villain, always fondling his sword, prepared at any moment to draw blood for sport or sadistic amusement. "Most men have objects they play with," Rathbone remarks in one scene. "Churchmen have their beads . . . I toy with a sword!" He gestures with a sword when he talks and, in most of his scenes, when a sword is not convenient, Rathbone has a symbolic replacement. At one dinner, he jabs relentlessly at an orange on a table with a knife to make his point. It is at this juncture that one of the movie's inside jokes is blurted. Power, playing the light-footed fop at dinner, notices Rathbones' persecution of the orange and remarks: "Captain, you seem to regard that poor fruit as an enemy." Rathbone

snaps back: "A rival!" When this film was released much comparison went on between the Power movie and the 1921 Zorro production directed by Fred Niblo and starring the amazingly energetic Douglas Fairbanks, Sr., but the silent film pales before the lavish, elegant, and intelligent Mamoulian production. Power would go on to more swashbuckling films, THE BLACK SWAN, CAPTAIN FROM CASTILE, PRINCE OF FOXES, THE BLACK ROSE, but none ever seemed to quite equal the early and electric impression he made with the public in THE MARK OF ZORRO, much enhanced by a dynamic and memorable score from Newman. Though he did not perform all his swordplay stunts, his filmic adversary Rathbone paid Power a supreme compliment: "Power was the most agile man with a sword I've ever faced before a camera. Tyrone could have fenced Errol Flynn into a cocked hat." This was high praise and generous at that since Rathbone received two fairly severe cuts in the forehead during his riveting duel with Power. Ironically, Power himself did much, while pretending to be the weak-willed, spineless fop, to promote his image of intrepid swashbuckler, remarking while daubing his mouth with a lace handkerchief in one scene: "Swordplay is such a *violent* business." On another occasion he states: "Dashing about with a cutlass is quite out of fashion—hasn't been done since the Middle Ages." And yet he becomes the personification of the man of daring who saves his people and brings forth justice through his slashing sword. His mark is his memory, the Z slashed onto walls (and even the uniforms of the soldiers he defeats), coupled to his warning to Bromberg after visiting his inner sanctum: "I have been here once and I can return." There were other Zorros, even Yakima Canutt, the great stuntman, playing the role in 1937 in ZORRO RIDES AGAIN. Frank Langella had a swipe at the dashing role in 1974, but none would ever equal Power's role; he looked and acted like a man who could, with bold acts and brave heart, change the course of history. And, of course, for the burgeoning coffers of Fox, he did.

p, Raymond Griffith; d, Rouben Mamoulian; w, John Tainton Foote, Garrett Fort, Bess Meredyth (based on the novel *The Curse of Capistrano* by Johnston McCulley); ph, Arthur Miller; m, Alfred Newman; ed, Robert Bischoff; md, Newman; art d, Richard Day, Joseph C. Wright; set d, Thomas Little; cos, Travis Banton.

Adventure   **(PR:A MPAA:NR)**

MARKED BULLET, THE   (SEE: PRAIRIE STRANGER, 1941)

MARKED FOR MURDER**   (1945) 58m PRC bw

Tex Ritter, Dave O'Brien, Guy Wilkerson, Marilyn McConnell, Henry Hall, Edward Cassidy, Jack Ingram, Charles King, Robert Kortman, Wen Wright, The Milo Twins, Kermit Maynard.

There's a feud brewing between sheep ranchers and cattle ranchers in this entry of the TEXAS RANGERS series. Ritter and company discover the local banker is behind it all, exposing the man so the feud comes to a peaceful conclusion. A typical Western outing. (See: TEXAS RANGERS series, Index)

p, Arthur Alexander; d&w Elmer Clifton; ph, Edward Kull; ed, Holbrook N. Todd; md, Lee Zahler.

Western   **(PR:A MPAA:NR)**

MARKED GIRLS*1/2   (1949, Fr.) 102m Siritzky bw

Viviane Romance (*Regine*), Georges Flament (*Dede*), Renee Saint-Cyr (*Juliette*), Jean Worms (*Regent*), Marguerite Deval (*Gaby*), Francis de Carco (*Francis Carco*).

This attempt to transfer De Carco's novel *Prison de Femmes* to the screen doesn't take very well. Story evolves around an orphan girl, Saint-Cyr, who is sent to jail for three years. She is able to wed a wealthy businessman through the underworld connections she's made in prison. Story lacks believability; the blatant direction doesn't help matters any. Performances are routine. (In French; English subtitles.)

p, Roger Richebe; d&w, Francis de Carco (based on his novel *Prison de Femmes*).

Drama   **(PR:A MPAA:NR)**

MARKED MAN, THE   (SEE: MARK OF THE WHISTLER, THE, 1944)

MARKED MEN*   (1940) 66m PRC bw

Warren Hull (*Bill Carver*), Isabel Jewell (*Linda Harkness*), John Dilson (*Dr. Harkness*), Paul Bryar (*Joe Mallon*), Charles Williams (*Charlie Sloane*), Lyle Clement (*Marshal Tait*), Budd L. Buster (*Marvin*), Al St. John (*Gimpy*), Eddie Featherstone (*Marty*), Ted Erwin (*Mike*), Art Miles (*Blimp*), The Dog Wolf (*Gray Shadow*).

Disappointing effort has Hull as a man wrongly accused of planning a prison break, after being set up by a bunch of gangsters. He manages to get his revenge by taking the gangsters on a long trek through the deserts of Arizona, where the men eventually collapse. What could have been a good story is marred by lax production values, weak direction, and unrealistic performances.

p, Sigmund Neufeld; d, Sherman Scott; w, George Bricker (based on a story by Harold Greene); ph, Jack Greenhalgh; ed, Holbrook N. Todd.

Crime   **(PR:A MPAA:NR)**

MARKED ONE, THE*1/2   (1963, Brit.) 65m Planet bw

William Lucas (*Don Mason*), Zena Walker (*Kay Mason*), Patrick Jordan (*Inspector Mayne*), Laurie Leigh (*Maisie*), David Gregory (*Ed Jones*), Edward Ogden (*Nevil*), Arthur Lovegrove (*Benson*), Brian Nissen (*Charles Warren*).

A child is kidnaped and the police are unable to make a break in the case. However, a truck driver, who had done some time in prison before reforming, discovers the getaway vehicle carried counterfeit plates. He is able to trace the number which facilitates the victim's rescue.

p, Tom Blakeley; d, Francis Searle; w, Paul Erickson.

Crime/Drama   **(PR:A MPAA:NR)**

MARKED TRAILS** (1944) 59m MON bw

Hoot Gibson *(Parkford)*, Bob Steele *(Bob Stevens)*, Veda Ann Borg *(Blanche)*, Mauritz Hugo *(Slade)*, Steve Clark *(Harry Stevens)*, Charles Stevens *(Denver)*, Ralph Lewis *(Jed)*, Lynton Brent *(Tex)*, Bud Osborne *(Sheriff)*, George Morrell *(Liveryman)*, Allen B. Sewell *(Mr. Bradley)*, Benny Corbett *(Blackie)*.

Routine western has Gibson and Steele tracking down a band of cohorts over oil they've been trying to swindle. Gang is lead by Borg. Having a woman as the head of a gang is at least something original.

p, William Strohbach; d, J.P. McCarthy; w, McCarthy, Victor Hammond (based on a story by McCarthy, Hammond); ph, Harry Neumann; ed, John C. Fuller.

Western **(PR:A MPAA:NR)**

MARKED WOMAN*** 1/2** (1937) 96m WB bw

Bette Davis *(Mary Dwight)*, Humphrey Bogart *(David Graham)*, Jane Bryan *(Betty Strauber)*, Eduardo Ciannelli *(Johnny Vanning)*, Isabel Jewell *(Emmy Lou Egan)*, Allen Jenkins *(Louie)*, Mayo Methot *(Estelle Porter)*, Lola Lane *(Gabby Marvin)*, Ben Welden *(Charley Delaney)*, Henry O'Neill *(District Atty. Sheldon)*, Rosalind Marquis *(Florrie Liggett)*, John Litel *(Gordon)*, Damian O'Flynn *(Ralph Krawford)*, Robert Strange *(George Beler)*, James Robbins *(Bell Captain)*, William B. Davidson *(Bob Crandall)*, John Sheehan *(Vincent, a Sugar Daddy)*, Sam Wren *(Mac)*, Kenneth Harlan *(Eddie, a Sugar Daddy)*, Raymond Hatton *(Lawyer at Jail)*, Frank Faylen *(Taxi Driver)*, Harlan Briggs *(Man in Phone Booth)*, Guy Usher *(Ferguson, the Detective)*, Milton Kibbee *(Male Secretary at D.A.'s Office)*, Jeffrey Sayre *(Assistant to Graham)*, Herman Marks *(Little Joe)*, Emmett Vogan *(Court Clerk)*, Pierre Watkin *(Judge)*, Mary Doyle *(Nurse)*, Carlos San Martin *(Headwaiter)*, Allen Matthews *(Henchman)*, Alan Davis *(Henchman)*, Arthur Aylesworth *(John Truble)*, Edwin Stanley *(Detective Casey)*, John Harron *(Taxi Driver)*, Alphonse Martel *(Doorman)*, Philip G. Sleeman *(Crap Table Attendant)*, Mark Strong *(Bartender)*, Jack Mower *(Foreman)*, Wendell Niles *(News Commentator)*.

This hard-hitting crime film, based upon the notorious career of Charles "Lucky" Luciano, New York City vice lord, was a tour de force for Davis who had just battled her studio, Warner Bros., into a standstill over contract disputes. Repulsive hoodlum Ciannelli, essaying Luciano, gathers his so-called hostesses (then a euphemism for prostitute) to announce that he is opening a swanky nightspot, the Club Intime, and that the girls must make sure that customers are steered to the bar to drink and to his crooked gambling tables. Davis tells him that the new place will be nothing more than a clip joint and Ciannelli gives her a wicked smile, telling her that that's exactly what it will be and anyone who doesn't want to cooperate can quit. Davis and her girl friends, Methot, Lane, Jewell, and Marquis, are resigned to working in the high-class whorehouse and gambling den. Then O'Flynn, a customer who loses more money to Ciannelli than he can pay, is warned to leave town by Davis. He is nevertheless murdered and Davis swears she will tell what she knows to crusading district attorney Bogart. But when she is brought into court, Davis clams up, threatened with death by Ciannelli's goons. Later, her unsuspecting sister, Bryan, goes to Ciannelli's club and is killed by Ciannelli when she resists the advances of his associate, Davidson. Enraged, Davis vows this time to send Ciannelli to prison for life. Welden and other Ciannelli goons barge into Davis' apartment and beat her senseless, scarring her face for life, making her a "marked woman." From her hospital bed, however, Davis implores her fellow prostitutes—Methot, Marquis, Jewell, and Lane—to testify with her in court to put the monster Ciannelli away. They agree and, thanks to Davis and company's scathing courtroom testimony drawn forth by a crusading Bogart, Ciannelli is convicted and sent to prison. In the end, Davis and her friends are given the thanks of the authorities and walk solemnly into the night to face an uncertain future. (Luciano, one of the sleaziest, most vicious hoodlums to operate in New York, earned more than $10,000 a week from the toils of 1,000 prostitutes; it was Luciano who made prostitution into a bargain-basement nationwide syndicate operation. Bogart, who plays the role of the prosecuting attorney, is really essaying Thomas E. Dewey, who put Luciano away after getting five of his most notorious prostitutes to testify against him.) Davis, though grateful that Jack Warner had not given her a poor script in retaliation for her stand against his dictatorial contract policies, was nevertheless her feisty self when returning to the studio after many months to perform marvelously as the spirited prostitute. She didn't like the way she was bandaged for her courtroom scene after having been mutilated, so she went to her own doctor who applied realistic bandages, then drove through the front gate at Warner Bros. where gate guards frantically called the front office to report that Davis had been in a horrible accident, so realistically was she made up. Producer Wallis ran down to see his star and was relieved to find out that Davis' bandages covered no real lacerations. But Davis cut him off before he could object to her self-styled makeup, stipulating to Wallis: "We film this makeup or we don't film *me* today!" The bandages, with the inimitable Davis beneath them, went before the cameras without protest. This was Davis' best performance since her appearance in THE PETRIFIED FOREST (1936) and OF HUMAN BONDAGE (1934). The fetching Bryan was thought by some to be Davis' intended replacement at Warner's, but the star shocked one and all by adopting the newcomer as a protege, encouraging her to assert herself before the cameras. Davis later said of Bryan: "The last time I played with her [in MARKED WOMAN], I had to hide her face in a pillow to keep her from stealing my scenes!"

p, Lou Edelman; d, Lloyd Bacon; w, Robert Rossen, Abem Finkel, Seton I. Miller; ph, George Barnes; m, Bernard Kaum, Heinz Roehmheld; ed, Jack Killifer; md, Leo F. Forbstein; art d, Max Parker; cos, Orry-Kelly; spec eff, James Gibbons, Robert Burks, m/l, "My Silver Dollar Man," Harry Warren, Al Dubin, "Mr. and Mrs. Doaks," M.K. Jerome, Jack Scholl.

Crime Drama **(PR:C MPAA:NR)**

MARKETA LAZAROVA**** (1968, Czech.) 180m Barrandov bw

Magda Vasaryova *(Marketa Lazarova)*, Frantisek Velicky *(Mikolas)*, Michal Kozuch *(Lazar)*, Pavla Polaskova *(Alexandria)*, Josef Kemr *(Kozlik)*, Ivo Paluch *(Adam/Jednorucka)*, Harry Studt *(Old Count Christian)*, Vlastimil Harapes *(Young Count Christian)*, Vladimir Mensik *(Wandering Monk Bernard)*, Karla Chadimova *(Prioress)*.

Based on 13th Century Czechoslovakian legend, this epic follows the adventures of a clan of feudal lords, who apply robbery and kidnaping to meet their desired goals. This film is a convincing portrayal of a people fearful of mystic power and whose lives are controlled by superstition. The clans are shown as cruel and barbarian, thinking nothing of raping a woman or beheading a man in grotesque fashion; this being the only existence they know. Director Vlacil does not try to romanticize medieval knighthood, but creates an atmosphere of mysticism and superstition. This is accomplished in an excellent fashion. (In Czechoslovakian; English subtitles.)

d, Frantisek Vlacil; w, Vlacil, Frantisek Pavicek (based on the novel, *Marketa Lazarova*, by Vladislav Vancura); ph, Bedich Batka; m, Zdenek Liska; ed, Mirslav Hajek; set d, Oldrich Okac.

Adventure **(PR:O MPAA:NR)**

MARKO POLO

(SEE: MARCO THE MAGNIFICENT, 1966, Afghanistan/Egypt/Fr./Ital.)

MARKOPOULOS PASSION, THE (SEE: ILLIAC PASSION, THE, 1968)

MARKSMAN, THE** (1953) 62m MON/Westwood-AA bw

Wayne Morris, Elena Verdugo, Frank Ferguson, Rick Vallin, I. Stanford Jolley, Tom Powers, Robert Bice, Stanley Price, Russ Whiteman, Brad Johnson, William Fawcett, Jack Rice, Tim Ryan.

A band of outlaws terrorizes a community with cattle rustling and murder. The town leaders turn to a local marksman, an expert with a telescopic rifle, in an effort to save the people from the nefarious gang. After being appointed deputy marshal, the marksman takes to his new task to stop the outlaws.

p, Vincent M. Fennelly; d, Lewis D. Collins; w, Dan Ullman; ph, Ernest Miller; m, Raoul Kraushaar; ed, Sam Fields; art d, David Milton.

Western **(PR:C MPAA:NR)**

MARLOWE*** (1969) 95m MGM c

James Garner *(Philip Marlowe)*, Gayle Hunnicutt *(Mavis Wald)*, Carroll O'Connor *(Lt. Christy French)*, Rita Moreno *(Dolores Gonzales)*, Sharon Farrell *(Orfamay Quest)*, William Daniels *(Mr. Crowell)*, H.M. Wynant *(Sonny Steelgrave)*, Jackie Coogan *(Grant W. Hicks)*, Kenneth Tobey *(Sgt. Fred Beifus)*, Nate Esformes *(Paleface)*, Bruce Lee *(Winslow Wong)*, Christopher Cary *(Chuck)*, George Tyne *(Oliver Hady)*, Corinne Comacho *(Julie)*, Paul Stevens *(Dr. Vincent Lagardie)*, Roger Newman *(Orrin Quest)*, Read Morgan *(Gumpshaw)*, Warren Finnerty *(Manager)*, Bartless Robinson *(Munsey)*, Ted Derby *(Tiger Man)*, Carolan Daniels, Marlain Kallevig *(Women)*, Chet Stratton *(Harold Munsey)*, Hoke Howell *(Intern)*, Mark Allen *(Attendant)*, Jason Wingreen *(Clerk)*, Ann Carroll *(Mona)*, Emil Alegata *(Waiter)*, Isabel Colley *(Receptionist)*, Bert L. Bantle, Tony Conkle *(Pilots)*, Dee Carroll *(Nurse)*, Jack English *(Director)*, Lou Whitehill *(Assistant Director)*, Mary Wilcox *(YWCA Clerk)*, Tom Monroe *(Policeman)*, Nicole Jaffe *(Lilly)*, Camille Grant *(Belly Dancer)*, Fay Wilkie *(Psychologist)*, Buddy Garion *(Maitre d')*, Paul Micale *(Waiter)*, Angus Duncan *(TV Actor)*.

Garner is a Los Angeles private detective hired by Farrell to find her missing brother. He traces him to a hotel where he asks the manager and the man now occupying the brother's room his whereabouts. Both deny knowing anything but both are murdered with ice picks shortly thereafter. Garner follows a lead and ends up with photographs of noted television star Hunnicutt in compromising clinches with gangster Wynant. Wynant sends henchman Lee to Garner's office to warn him off the case, and detective O'Connor harasses the private eye, believing him guilty of the hotel manager's murder. Garner eventually tracks Farrell's brother, Newman, to doctor Stevens, where he is dying of an ice pick wound, He travels to Wynant's house and finds the gangster dead, Hunnicutt beside the body volunteering her guilt. Garner fixes the evidence to look like suicide and learns that Hunnicutt and Farrell are sisters. He further learns that Moreno, a stripper friend of Hunnicutt's, was Wynant's former lover. He accuses her of killing the gangster, but before he can do anything else, Stevens, Moreno's ex-husband, shows up and shoots her before turning the gun on himself. Transposition of Raymond Chandler's detective hero of the 1940s into the 1960s fails mostly in Garner's portrayal. He's too relaxed and lacking in the cynical edge Marlowe has in the original stories and that Humphrey Bogart and Alan Ladd successfully brought to the screen. Other elements found in the originals are more successfully seen, like the tangled plot that never does neatly resolve all its loose ends, and strange secondary characters with odd names. The movie is best remembered now for a scene in which Lee, in his first screen appearance, destroys Garner's office as the helpless detective can only sit and watch.

p, Gabriel Katzka, Sidney Beckerman; d, Paul Bogart; w, Stirling Silliphant (based on the novel *The Little Sister* by Raymond Chandler); ph, William H. Daniels (Metrocolor); m, Peter Matz; ed, Gene Ruggiero; md, Matz; art d, George W. Davis, Addison Hehr; set d, Henry Grace, Hugh Hunt; cos, Jimmy Taylor, Florence Hackett; spec eff, Virgil Beck; stunts, Bruce Lee; makeup, Phil Rhodes.

Crime **(PR:A MPAA:M)**

MARNIE** 1/2** (1964) 120m UNIV c

Tippi Hedren *(Marnie Edgar)*, Sean Connery *(Mark Rutland)*, Diane Baker *(Lil Mainwaring)*, Martin Gabel *(Sidney Strutt)*, Louise Latham *(Bernice Edgar)*, Bob Sweeney *(Cousin Bob)*, Milton Selzer *(Man at the Track)*, Alan Napier *(Mr. Rutland)*, Henry Beckman *(1st Detective)*, Edith Evanson *(Rita)*, Mariette Hartley

(Susan Clabon), Bruce Dern *(Sailor)*, S. John Launer *(Sam Ward)*, Meg Wyllie *(Mrs. Turpin)*, Louise Lorimer *(Mrs. Strutt)*.

MARNIE commits that most uncharacteristic of sins from such a cinemaster as Hitchcock, it never shuts up. Grace Kelly had already been princess of all she surveyed in Monaco for six years and Hitchcock hoped this script would lure her back into motion pictures. When that prospect created a stir among the Monagasques (which is what the people of Monaco are called), Kelly declined and the role went to Hedren who had just finished THE BIRDS a year before. It's a psychological mystery in that Hedren is seen as a cold, neurotic man-hater who uses her kleptomania to overcome her sexual frustrations. Gabel is a businessman who discovers that his secretary has rifled his safe. Further investigation shows that this same woman, under different aliases and using different wigs, has been guilty of several such robberies. Hedren is tortured by what she does, has bad dreams, and goes berserk when she sees the color red or hears thunder. She has a pet horse whom she visits after each theft and a good deal of her ill-gotten gains go toward supporting the animal. The rest of the money she sends to her crippled mother, Latham, a religious fanatic who hates men and has spent a lifetime warning her daughter against them. Hedren loves her mother dearly but the old woman, who lives in Baltimore, never offers Hedren anything in return. Hedren gets a new job in Connery's company and he, having heard Gabel describe the woman who robbed him, is hip to Hedren from the start but does not let on that he knows who she is and what she does. There is a thunderstorm and Hedren reacts as before, with total hysteria. Connery seeks to soothe her and recognizes that she is in an unbalanced mental state. Despite that, he finds her attractive, much more so than Baker, who is the sister of Connery's late wife, and eager to become his wife. Just as suspected, Hedren steals the contents of Connery's safe but he nabs her and says he will turn her over to the authorities if she does not agree to marry him. Faced with no choice, she agrees but insists that Connery not attempt to force himself on her sexually until she is mentally ready to acquiesce. On their shipboard honeymoon, he promises but goes back on his word and rapes his wife. She responds by attempting suicide and is barely rescued by Connery from the liner's swimming pool. (If she had really wanted to drown her sorrows, she would have jumped overboard.) Connery uses his small psychological knowledge to play word games with Hedren and she begins to respond when she realizes that he does love her and is attempting to help her. They return to the wealthy Connery's home, and she says they must have separate sleeping quarters, which he allows. There is a large party which Gabel attends. When he thinks Hedren looks familiar, she insists they have never met before and is backed up by Connery who knows full well from where Gabel knows Hedren. Baker is also wary as Hedren had claimed that she had no family and now speaks of a mother in Maryland. Connery has fallen deeply for Hedren and wants to pay back all of her robbery debts. In a fox hunt, Hedren seens a red hunting coat, gets crazy and takes her precious animal on a wild ride that culminates when the horse does not clear a fence, breaks a leg, and she must destroy the one living creature which she loved totally and without question. She returns to the house and is in the process of robbing the safe when Connery stops her and says he will give her the money. She cannot take it. Connery feels he must get to the bottom of this, so he and Hedren drive to Baltimore to see Latham. There is another thunderstorm which lays Hedren low and causes her to begin to recall all the reasons why she is the way she is. Her mother had been a prostitute and when Hedren responded to the apparent comforting by sailor-customer Dern (or was it molestation?), Latham hit the sailor with a fireplace poker. Dern fell on Latham, rendering her lame. Then the child killed the sailor with the poker. So it all tied neatly up in one package; hatred of men, the bloody color red, thunderstorms, etc. Hedren has a gigantic realization scene and now understands everything. Connery gives her another choice: life with him or jail. You have one guess as to which path she treads. Hitchcock is seen in a hotel lobby as his customary cameo. It was Connery's U.S. debut (after playing the redoubtable Bond in British films) and the box office results were negligible. Obvious rear screen projection, weak leading lady, and a verbose script all contributed to MARNIE's box-office downfall.

p&d, Alfred Hitchcock; w, Jay Presson Allen (based on the novel by Winston Graham); ph, Robert Burks (Technicolor); m, Bernard Herrmann; ed, George Tomasini; prod d, Robert Boyle; set d, George Milo; cos, Edith Head; makeup, Jack Barron, Howard Smith, Bob Dawn.

Psychological Mystery **(PR:C MPAA:PG)**

MAROC 7*** (1967, Brit.) 91m Cyclone/PAR c

Gene Barry *(Simon Grant)*, Elsa Martinelli *(Claudia)*, Cyd Charisse *(Louise Henderson)*, Leslie Phillips *(Raymond Lowe)*, Denholm Elliott *(Inspector Barrada)*, Alexandra Stewart *(Michele Craig)*, Eric Barker *(Prof. Bannen)*, Angela Douglas *(Freddie)*, Tracy Reed *(Vivienne)*, Maggie London *(Suzie)*, Penny Riley *(Penny)*, Ann Norman *(Alexa)*, Lionel Blair *(Hotel Receptionist)*, Paul Danquah *(Police Officer)*, Tom Lee *(Abdullah)*, Anne Padwick *(Consuela)*, Richard Montez *(Pablo)*, Roger Good *(Hotel Manager)*, Anthony Bygraves *(Young Photographer)*, Robert Mill *(Tony)*, George Selway, Diane Bester, Michael Mundell, Vivienne Burgess, Michael Haynes, Jonathon Hanson, John Wreford, Mark Elwes, Pamela Abbott, Colette Wilde.

Charisse plays the editor for a fashion magazine, whose frequent trips abroad are a good front for the jewel-smuggling operation she runs on the side. Her photographer and top model join her in the racket. Secret agent Barry is on to Charisse. Posing as a safecracker, he convinces Charisse to let him in on a scheme to smuggle an expensive diamond out of Morocco. Working with the local chief of police, Barry attempts to catch Charisse and her gang redhanded. Aided by the scenic photography of the Moroccan landscape this entertaining story is filled with enough twists to keep the audience guessing throughout. Performances are varied, with Charisse failing to project the type of authority her role calls for. Barry is slick and smooth as ever. Direction is well paced, but the script is hampered by uneasy dialog.

p, John Gale, Leslie Phillips; d, Gerry O'Hara; w, David Osborn (based on the story by Osborn); ph, Kenneth Talbot (Panavision, Technicolor); m, Kenneth K.V. Jones; ed, John Jympson; art d, Seamus Flannery; spec eff, Ernie Sullivan; m/l, party music and theme song, Paul Ferris, Nicky Henson; makeup, Bill Lodge.

Crime **(PR:A MPAA:NR)**

MAROONED* ½ (1933, Brit.) 67m BL/FOX bw

Edmund Gwenn *(Tom Roberts)*, Viola Lyel *(Sarah Roberts)*, Iris March *(Mary Roberts)*, Victor Garland *(Norman Bristowe)*, Hal Walters *(Joe)*, Griffith Humphreys *(Convict)*, Wally Patch *(Wilson)*, Philip Hewland *(Jacob)*, Wilfred Shine *(Maille)*, Frances Davey, George Manship, Frederick Ross.

Gwenn and Lyel are a married couple raising March as a foster daughter. March is unaware that her real father is in prison serving a life sentence. Soon a convict arrives at the secluded lighthouse, claiming to be the girl's father. Gwenn hides the man from authorities, but gradually it's revealed March's real father had died a year ago. The impersonator meets his doom, though, when he falls from the lighthouse. An unrealistic, simple-minded British programmer with no real imagination to it.

p, Herbert Smith; d, Leslie Hiscott; w, Michael Barringer.

Drama **(PR:C MPAA:NR)**

MAROONED*** (1969) 134m COL c

Gregory Peck *(Charles Keith)*, Richard Crenna *(Jim Pruett)*, David Janssen *(Ted Dougherty)*, James Franciscus *(Clayton Stone)*, Gene Hackman *(Buzz Lloyd)*, Lee Grant *(Celia Pruett)*, Nancy Kovack *(Teresa Stone)*, Mariette Hartley *(Betty Lloyd)*, Scott Brady *(Public Affairs Officer)*, Craig Huebing *(Flight Director)*, John Carter *(Flight Surgeon)*, George Gaynes *(Mission Director)*, Tom Stewart *(Houston Cape-Commander)*, Frank Marth *(Space Systems Manager)*, Duke Hobbie *(Titan Systems Specialist)*, Dennis Robertson *(Launch Director)*, George Smith *(Cape Weather Officer)*, Vincent Van Lynn *(Cannon, Journalist)*, Walter Brooke *(Radin, Network Commentator)*, Mauritz Hugo *(Hardy)*, Bill Couch *(Russian Cosmonaut)*, Mary-Linda Rapelye *(Priscilla Keith)*.

Gripping, yet starkly realistic portrayal of three astronauts, Crenna, Hackman, and Franciscus, on an extended special mission, finding themselves unable to re-enter the Earth's atmosphere. Peck plays the commander at the Houston base, trying to call the right shots from the ground. As the oxygen supply lessens, the stranded astronauts are more assured of eventual death. Hackman breaks down into a fit of tears while talking to his wife over intercommunications television. When Peck suggests one of the men commit suicide to allow enough oxygen for the remaining two, nobody takes him up on it. But soon after, the commander, Crenna, on the pretext of going outside to repair something, detaches himself from the ship, floating to his death in outer space. Just as the two remaining men have given up any hope of surviving, Russian cosmonauts come to their rescue with a new supply of oxygen. Film offers a combination of highly technical jargon and emotional suspense in a well-balanced effort. The technical effects are extremely realistic, making the impact of the film much more powerful. The tension and suspense delivered through the performances and the development of the plot are almost ruined by an unrealistic and unbelievable ending.

p, M. J. Frankovich, John Sturges; d, Sturges; w, Mayo Simon (based on the novel by Martin Caidin); ph, Daniel Fapp (Panavision, Technicolor); ed, Walter Thompson; prod d, Lyle R. Wheeler; set d, Frank Tuttle; cos, Seth Banks; spec eff, Lawrence W. Butler, Donald C. Glouner, Robie Robinson.

Adventure/Science Fiction **Cas.** **(PR:A MPAA:G)**

MARQUIS DE SADE: JUSTINE (SEE: JUSTINE, 1969, Ital./Span.)

MARRIAGE, A*** (1983) 90m Filmco/Cinecom c

Ric Gitlin *(Ted)*, Isabel Glasser *(Nancy)*, Jane Darby *(Jane)*, Jack Rose *(Mark)*.

Low budget independent feature traces the development of a long love affair between two high school sweethearts, which leads to marriage. It then traces the disintegration and eventual divorce of the same couple. The film is structured entirely in flashbacks from the husband's point of view, as he is preparing to sign the divorce papers. This is the first feature production for writer-director Tung, who manages to provide a sensitive and realistic story combined with touches of humor.

p, David Greene; d&w, Sandy Tung; ph, Benjamin Davis (Technicolor); ed, Michael R. Miller; m, Jack Waldman; art d, Farrel Levy Duffy.

Drama **(PR:C MPAA:NR)**

MARRIAGE BOND, THE** (1932, Brit.) 82m Twickenham/RKO bw

Mary Newcombe *(Jacqueline Heron)*, Guy Newall *(Toby Heron)*, Stewart Rome *(Sir Paul Swaythling)*, Ann Casson *(Binnie Heron)*, Florence Desmond *(Elsie)*, Denys Blakelock *(Alfred Dreisler)*, Lewis Shaw *(Frere Heron)*, Humberston Wright *(Jenkins)*, Amy Veness *(Mrs. Crust)*, A. Bromley Davenport *(MFH)*.

Newcombe is convinced by her children to leave Newall, her alcoholic husband. Newcombe is then romanced by Rome, a wealthy baronet, as her children grow up to be angry, embittered adults. Meanwhile, Newall recovers from his addiction to the bottle, reconciling with Newcombe at the film's end. The drama is a touch trite, but the overall sincerity of the cast gives the film some benefits.

p, Julius Hagen; d, Maurice Elvey; w, H. Fowler Mear (based on a story by Muriel Stewart); ph, Basil Emmott.

Drama **(PR:A MPAA:NR)**

MARRIAGE BY CONTRACT*** (1928) 70m TS bw

Patsy Ruth Miller *(Margaret)*, Lawrence Gray *(Don)*, Robert Edeson *(Winters)*, Ralph Emerson *(Arthur)*, Shirley Palmer *(Molly)*, John St. Polis *(Father)*, Claire

McDowell *(Mother)*, Ruby Lafayette *(Grandma)*, Duke Martin *(Dirke)*, Raymond Keane *(Drury)*.

Early sound picture has Miller playing a young girl who marries a boy her age under the conditions of a contract. When the boy comes home stewed and admits to being with another girl, Miller runs home to her mother and tears up the contract, crying herself to sleep. She goes through three more marriages, the last one to a gigolo who marries her for money she obtained from her previous husband. When she winds up broke, the gigolo decides it's time to split. At this point Miller threatens suicide with a gun, but accidentally kills the gigolo in a scuffle. Fortunately everything past the time when she fell asleep, after tearing up the original contract, turns out to be just a bad dream. Miller runs back to her original husband, asking him to marry her in church. Miller gives a stunning performance, realistically portraying a young girl and maturing to an elderly lady, and looking the part in each role. The rest of the performances are weak in comparison to hers.

p, John M. Stahl; d, James Flood; w, Frances Hyland; ph, Ernest Miller; m, Manny Baer; ed, L. R. Brown; m/l "When the Right One Comes Along," L. Wolfe Gilbert, Mabel Wayne, "Come Back to Me," Dave Goldberg, A. E. Joffe.

Drama **(PR:A MPAA:NR)**

MARRIAGE CAME TUMBLING DOWN, THE**
(1968, Fr.) 88m Champs Elysees-Isabelle/Royal c (CE SACRE GRAND-PERE)

Michel Simon *(Grandfather Jericho)*, Marie Dubois *(Marie)*, Yves Lefebvre *(Jacques)*, Thalie Fruges *(Agathe)*, Serge Gainsbourg *(Remy)*, Mary Marquet *(La Duchesse)*, Jeanne Helia *(Jeanne)*.

Dubois and Lefebvre, a couple whose marriage is failing, go on a three-week holiday. They stay with Lefebvre's grandfather, Simon, who soon realizes how bad his son's marriage is. One day, Lefebvre returns from visiting his mistress and spots a stunning woman sunbathing. The woman turns out to be his wife, and slowly their relationship is rekindled.

p, Jules Borkon; d, Jacques Poitrenaud; w, Albert Cossery, Poitrenaud (based on the novel *I Am Called Jericho* by Catherine Paysan); ph, Jean-Marc Ripart (Eastmancolor); m, Serge Gainsbourg.

Comedy Drama **(PR:A MPAA:G)**

MARRIAGE FORBIDDEN (SEE: DAMAGED GOODS, 1937)

MARRIAGE-GO-ROUND, THE*½ (1960) 98m FOX c

Susan Hayward *(Content Delville)*, James Mason *(Paul Delville)*, Julie Newmar *(Katrin Sveg)*, Robert Paige *(Dr. Ross Barnett)*, June Clayworth *(Flo Granger)*, Joe Kirkwood, Jr. *(Henry)*, Mary Patton *(Mamie)*, Trax Colton *(Crew Cut)*, Everett Glass *(Professor)*, Ben Astar *(Sultan)*, Bruce Tegner *(Judo Man at Pool)*, Mark Bailey *(Boy)*, Ann Benton *(Girl)*, John Bryant *(Young Professor)*.

Tasteless remake of popular Broadway hit which didn't take to the screen very well. Mason is an anthropology professor, faithful to his wife, Hayward, through their entire 16 years of marriage. When the daughter of an acquaintance of Mason's comes to stay with the couple, Mason and Hayward have the first real test of their marriage. The guest is Newmar, a six-foot-tall, athletic, ravishing Swede, who has one thought on her mind—to have a baby by Mason. She reasons that the combination of her looks and his brains would produce a genetically perfect child. Hayward doesn't take too well to this, with the expected results. Though the performances are believable, the material just isn't funny. The director tries to help things out by quickening the pace, but to no avail.

p, Leslie Stevens; d, Walter Lang; w, Stevens (based on his own play); ph, Leo Tover (CinemaScope, DeLuxe Color); m, Dominic Frontiere; ed, Jack W. Holmes; art d, Duncan Cramer, Maurice Ransford; cos, Charles LeMaire; m/l, "Marriage-Go-Round," Alan Bergman, Marilyn Keith, Lew Spence (sung by Tony Bennett).

Comedy **(PR:A MPAA:NR)**

MARRIAGE IN THE SHADOWS** (1948, Ger.) 89m Defa/Gramercy bw

Paul Klinger *(Hans Wieland)*, Ilse Steppat *(Elisabeth)*, Alfred Balthoff *(Kurt Bernstein)*, Claus Holm *(Dr. Herbert Blohm)*, Willi Prager *(Dr. Louis Silbermann)*, Hans Leibelt *(Fehrenbach)*, Lothar Firmans *(State Secretary)*, Karl Hellmer *(Gallenkamp)*.

Predictable story from Germany that deals with anti-Semitism during the Nazi regime. The major drawback to this feature is the dependence upon stereotypes provided by American features, instead of first-hand perspectives from the filmmakers. Story revolves around an Aryan actor who marries a Jewish girl despite the severe laws against such marriages. The couple become the recipients of some horrible treatment by neighbors and members of the Nazi Party. The lead performances are genuinely moving, but the supporting cast falls into stereotypical roles. (In German; English subtitles.)

d&w, Kurt Maetzig (based on the novel by Hans Scheikart); ph, Friedel Behn-Grund, Eugen Klagemann; m, Wolfgang Zeller; ed, Alice Ludwig; English titles, Charles Clement.

Drama **(PR:A MPAA:NR)**

MARRIAGE IS A PRIVATE AFFAIR** (1944) 116m MGM bw

Lana Turner *(Theo Scofield West)*, James Craig *(Capt. Miles Lancing)*, John Hodiak *(Lt. Tom West)*, Frances Gifford *(Sissy Mortimer)*, Hugh Marlowe *(Joseph I. Murdock)*, Natalie Schafer *(Mrs. Selworth)*, Herbert Rudley *(Ted Mortimer)*, Paul Cavanagh *(Mr. Selworth)*, Morris Ankrum *(Ed Scofield)*, Jane Green *(Martha)*, John Warburton *(Chris)*, Byron Foulger *(Ned Bolton)*, Tom Drake *(Bill Rice)*, Shirley Patterson *(Mary Saunders)*, Rev. Neal Dodd *(Minister)*, Nana Bryant *(Nurse)*, Cecilia Callejo *(Senora Guizman)*, Virginia Brissac *(Mrs. Courtland West)*, Addison Richards *(Col. Ryder)*, Keenan Wynn *(Maj. Bob Wilton)*, Eve Whitney *(Maid of Honor)*, Hazel Brooks, Ann Lundeen, Linda Deane, Lynn Arlen, Beryl McCutcheon, Elizabeth Daily *(Bridesmaids)*, Sam McDaniel *(Black Porter)*, Bruce Kellogg *(Young Lieutenant)*, George Meeker *(Josie)*, Douglas Morrow *(Lieutenant Colonel)*, Ann Codee *(Saleswoman)*, Eula Guy *(Maid)*, Charles Coleman *(Butler)*, Arthur Space *(Drunk)*, Alexander D'Arcy *(Mr. Garby)*, Jody Gilbert *(Girl Taxi Driver)*, Kay Williams *(Pretty Girl)*, Katherine [Karin] Booth *(Girl with Miles)*.

This marked Turner's return to the screen after having her daughter, Cheryl, by restaurateur Steve Crane. To mark the moment, they gave her a role that kept her on screen for almost every frame of the nearly-two hour film, dressed her in several gorgeous gowns by Irene, and coiffed her beautifully by Sydney Guilaroff. Turner is a New York City social butterfly who winters in Florida and summers in Reno, as she waits for her flighty mother, Schafer (in her film debut), to shed her latest husband and marry a new one. Schafer is the distaff equivalent of Tommy Manville and has been married so many times that she has rice marks on her face. Turner marries Hodiak (whom Schafer thinks will make an adorable first husband for any girl) and tries hard to be a devoted wife and mother. Hodiak is a pilot who later takes to the ground to oversee a wartime laboratory position. Turner finds it difficult to give up her carefree life of nighteries and various lovers, although she does make an attempt at settling down. Later, she runs into a former lover, Craig, and when he is only diffident about seeing her, she decides to reawaken the old flame by wearing a revealing outfit and going to the Officer's Club where Craig is. Later, upon her return home, she finds Hodiak waiting up for her and angered that she had forgotten this was their baby's first birthday and they were to celebrate it together. Things settle down and the middle of the movie concerns the many facets of a couple's second year of marriage. Craig's presence is also a thorn in Hodiak's side and Turner has a few moments when she considers divorcing Hodiak, but that's over when Hodiak is sent to New Guinea and he and Turner reconcile via a short wave radio. There was a bomber group stationed overseas that called themselves "The Lana Turner Squadron" and they wanted to be the first to see her latest movie. So MGM arranged to show the film in September 1944, at a Naples theater where the pilots in her squadron whooped and whistled and cheered. Hodiak replaced Gene Kelly in the role, and Schafer, who was to achieve dubious fame as Jim Backus' wife in "Gilligan's Island," played Turner's mother a quarter of a century later in TV's "The Survivors," a series that didn't.

p, Pandro S. Berman; d, Robert Z. Leonard; w, David Hertz, Lenore Coffee (based on the novel by Judith Kelly); ph, Ray June; m, Bronislau Kaper; ed, George White; art d, Cedric Gibbons, Hubert B. Hobson; set d, Edwin B. Willis, Richard Pefferle; cos, Irene; makeup, Jack Dawn.

War/Comedy **(PR:A MPAA:NR)**

MARRIAGE—ITALIAN STYLE*** (1964, Fr./Ital.) 102m EM c

Sophia Loren *(Filomena Marturano)*, Marcello Mastroianni *(Domenico Soriano)*, Aldo Puglisi *(Alfredo)*, Tecla Scarano *(Rosalie)*, Marilu Tolo *(Diane)*, Pia Lindstrom *(Cashier)*, Giovanni Ridolfi *(Umberto)*, Vito Moriconi *(Riccardo)*, Generoso Cortini *(Michele)*, Raffaello Rossi Bussola *(Lawyer)*, Vincenza Di Capua *(Mother)*, Vincenzo Aita *(Priest)*.

Mastroianni and Loren, as a pair of on-and-off lovers, are funny and sad in this Italian farce which owes much of its appeal to director De Sica's inventiveness and natural caprice. The film opens in 1964 while Mastroianni is admiring the wedding dress his fiancee is going to wear at upcoming nuptials. He suddenly hears that his long-time mistress, Loren, is on her deathbed with a priest at her side. He goes to her and then remembers how he first met her in 1943 during a Naples air raid while she was hiding in the closet of a bordello. In flashback he becomes her first patron and the true love of her life. Following the war, Mastroianni again meets the busty whore and is so enamored of her that he takes her from the brothel and gets her an apartment of her own. Loren manages his bar and restaurant while he continues playing the field. Later, he installs the hefty Loren as his housekeeper in his mother's home where she slaves to clean, cook, and look after his elderly, ailing mother, slipping into Mastroianni's bed late at night like a sex sneak. She is reduced to servant status, having to stay in the maid's room when Mastroianni is not at home. Then the story flashes forward to show Loren deathly ill and Mastroianni promising to marry her (in front of a priest) as a deathbed gesture. She miraculously recovers and holds her ex-lover to his promise. Though he rashly marries Loren, Mastroianni explodes when Loren tells him that she has three grown sons who will come to live with them. He has the marriage annulled, saying he has been tricked and that Loren has perpetrated a fraud. But then he is told that one of the boys is his own son. After meeting the youths, Mastroianni is convinced that they are all his sons and he accepts Loren and the boys as his real family. Loren cries tears of happiness at the fadeout. It's all pretty silly but De Sica's surprising twists and turns and his deft direction lift this fluffy farce above the average. Loren doesn't have to act, merely steam the screen with her voluptuous body; in one brothel scene her Amazonian body is so skimpily clad that she shows every curve and cranny, but Mastroianni is very funny as the hoodwinked Lothario. There is, however, something grotesquely erotic about the whole thing where the humor is bogged down in seedy brothel scenes. Loren jiggling about in a spider costume that is almost not there presents bad taste at its most extravagant.

p, Carlo Ponti; d, Vittorio De Sica; w, Eduardo De Filippo, Renato Castellani, Antonino Guerra, Leo Benvenuti, Piero De Bernardi (based on the play "Filumena Marturano by De Filippo"); ph, Roberto Gerardi (Eastmancolor); m, Armando Trovajoli; ed, Adriana Novelli; art d, Carlo Egidi; set d, Dario Micheli; cos, Piero Tosi, Vera Marzot, Annamode; makeup, Giuseppe Annunziata, Giuseppe Banchelli.

Comedy **(PR:O MPAA:NR)**

MARRIAGE OF A YOUNG STOCKBROKER, THE*½**
(1971) 95m FOX c

Richard Benjamin *(William Alren)*, Joanna Shimkus *(Lisa Alren)*, Elizabeth Ashley *(Nan)*, Adam West *(Chester)*, Patricia Barry *(Dr. Sadler)*, Tiffany Bolling *(Girl in the*

Rain), Ed Prentiss (*Mr. Franklin*), William Forrest (*Mr. Wylie*), Johnny Scott Lee (*Mark*), Bill McConnell (*Charlie McGuire*), Alma Beltran (*Raquel*), Norman Leavitt (*Mr. Van Meter*), Ron Masak (*1st Baseball Fan*), Bob Hastings (*2nd Baseball Fan*), Ken Snell (*Cab Driver*).

Benjamin plays a happily married but bored husband who takes to innocent voyeurism for kicks. His wife Shimkus is upset and confused by her husband's behavior. Spurred on by her overbearing sister, Ashley, who recently dropped her alcoholic husband, Shimkus heads for the west coast. The couple discover how much they mean to each other, and are quickly reunited. Benjamin and Shimkus deliver fair performances, supported by a cast who keep the story interesting. What the script lacks in its approach to story construction, it makes up for in well-structured direction.

p&d, Lawrence Turman; w, Lorenzo Semple, Jr. (based on the novel by Charles Webb); ph, Laszlo Kovacs (DeLuxe Color); m, Fred Karlin; ed, Fred Steinkamp; prod d, Pato Guzman; set d, Walter M. Scott, Audrey A. Blasdel; cos, Doris Rambeau, Ed Wynigear; spec eff, Howard A. Anderson Company; m/l, "Can It Be True," Karlin, Tylwyth Kymry (sung by Linda Ronstadt); makeup, Alan Snyder.

Comedy   Cas.   **(PR:A MPAA:R)**

MARRIAGE OF BALZAMINOV, THE**½
(1966, USSR) 90m Mosfilm/Artkino c (ZHENITBA BALZAMINOVA)

Georgiy Vitsin (*Balzaminov*), Lyudmila Shagalova (*His Mother*), Lidiya Smirnova (*Matchmaker*), Ye. Savinova (*Matryona*), Zhanna Prokhorenko (*Kapochka*), Lyudmila Gurchenko (*Ustinka*), Tamara Nosova (*Nichkina*), Nikolay Kryuchkov (*Neuyedenov*), Rolan Bykov (*Chebakov*), Inna Makarova (*Anfisa*), Nadezhda Rumyantseva (*Raisa*), Tatyana Konyukhova (*Khimka*), Nonna Mordyukova (*Belotelova*), G. Shpigel, B. Baybakov, Sh. Baron, I. Bykov, A. Vlasov, V. Gerasin, G. Donyagin, S. Yefimov, V. Zavyalov, V. Kiryanov, A. Konyashin, V. Korotkov, V. Lazarev, M. Krivova, Al Larionov, Yu. Rodnoy, F. Sergeyev, M. Suvorov, V. Tatarinov.

Vitsin is a meek clerk who daydreams about becoming an heroic general, a czar, or great lover. His life doesn't even approach his dreams, and he has no luck finding a beautiful, rich wife. Finally, he does marry an obese, old, albeit rich widow, who doesn't come close to the bride of his fantasies.

d&w, Konstantin Voinov (based on the novel *Prazdnichnyy Son Do Obeda* by Aleksandr Nikolayevich Ostrovskiy); ph, G. Kupriyanov (Moscolor); m, Boris Chaykovskiy; art d, F. Yasyukevich.

Comedy   **(PR:A MPAA:NR)**

MARRIAGE OF CONVENIENCE, 1934   (SEE: HIRED WIFE, 1934)

MARRIAGE OF CONVENIENCE**
(1970, Brit.) 58m Merton Park/Schoenfeld bw

John Cairney (*Larry Wilson*), Harry H. Corbett (*Inspector Jock Bruce*), Jennifer Daniel (*Barbara Blatr*), Russell Waters (*Sam Spencer*), Trevor Maskell (*Detective Sgt. Collins*), Trevor Reid (*Supt. Carver*), John Van Eyssen (*John Mandle*), Moira Redmond (*Tina*), Patricia Burke (*Woman in Flat*), Alex Scott (*Vic Ellis*), Pauline Shepherd (*Evie Martin*), Duncan Burns (*Garage Apprentice*), Howard Goorney (*Onion Seller*), Alexander Archdale (*Prison Governor*), Leila Williams (*Secretary*).

Cairney escapes from prison and finds that his partner, Redmond, has married the former Scotland Yard inspector (Van Eyssen) who arrested him. The couple has used the money from the robbery that Cairney was convicted of to open a seaside resort. Inspector Corbett follows the escaped con to the resort and arrests the couple and Cairney.

p, Jack Greenwood; d, Clive Donner; w, Robert Stewart (based on the novel *The Three Oak Mystery* by Edgar Wallace); ph, Brian Rhodes; m, Francis Chagrin; ed, Bernard Gribble; art d, Wilfred Arnold.

Crime Drama   **(PR:A MPAA:NR)**

MARRIAGE OF CORBAL   (SEE: PRISONER OF CORBAL, 1939, Brit.)

MARRIAGE OF FIGARO, THE**
(1963, Fr.) 105m Les Productions Cinematographiques/Union c (LE MARIAGE DE FIGARO)

Georges Descrieres (*Count Almaviva*), Yvonne Gaudeau (*Countess Almaviva*), Jean Piat (*Figaro*), Micheline Boudet (*Suzanne*), Louis Seigner (*Bartholo*), Denise Gence (*Marceline*), Jean Meyer (*Bazile*), Michele Grellier (*Cherubin*), Georges Chamarat (*Antonio*), Maurice Porterat (*Doublemain*), Georges Baconnet (*Brid'oison*), Madame Bonnefoux (*Fanchette*), Jean-Paul Roussillon (*Grippe-Soleil*), Henri Tisot (*Pedrille*), Louis Eymont (*Bailiff*), Members and Students of the Comedie-Francaise.

This is the film version of Pierre-Augustin Caron de Beaumarchais' play, "La Folle Journee, Ou Le Mariage De Figaro," a production put on by the Comedie-Francaise. Includes selections from "Le Nozze di Figaro" by Wolfgang Amadeus Mozart.

p, Pierre Gerin; d, Jean Meyer; w, (based on the play "La Folle Journee, Ou Le Mariage De Figaro" by Pierre-Augustin Caron de Beaumarchais); ph, Henri Alekan (Eastmancolor); ed, Claude Durand; art d, Robert Clavel; set d&cos, Suzanne Lalique; m/l, de Beaumarchais.

Comedy   **(PR:A MPAA:NR)**

MARRIAGE OF FIGARO, THE**
(1970, Ger.) 189m Polyphon and TV Productions/Polytel International c (DIE HOCHZEIT DES FIGARO)

Tom Krause (*Count Almaviva*), Arlene Saunders (*Countess*), Heinz Blankenburg

(*Figaro*), Edith Mathis (*Susanna*), Elisabeth Steiner (*Cherubino*), Kurt Marschner (*Basilio*), Maria von Ilosvay (*Marzelline*), Noel Mangin (*Bartolo*), Jurgen Forster (*Don Curzio*), Karl Otto (*Antonio*), Natalie Usselmann (*Barbarina*).

Enjoyable adaptation of the popular Mozart opera was originally made for German television and released theatrically in the U.S. The three-hour-plus length is a bit tiresome, but sitting through the entire performance is a worthwhile experience.

p, Rolf Liebermann; d, Joachim Hess; w, Wolfgang Amadeus Mozart, Lorenzo Da Ponte, "Le Nozze di Figaro"; ph, Hannes Schindler (Eastmancolor); m, Mozart; art d, Ita Maximovna; md, Hans Schmidt-Isserstedt (conducting the Hamburg State Orchestra, Choir of Hamburg State Opera).

Opera   **(PR:A MPAA:NR)**

MARRIAGE OF MARIA BRAUN, THE****
(1979, Ger.) 120m Albatros-Trio-Westdeutscher Rundfunk- Filmerlog der Autoren /New Yorker c (DIE EHE DER MARIA BRAUN)

Hanna Schygulla (*Maria Braun*), Klaus Lowitsch (*Hermann Braun*), Ivan Desny (*Oswald*), Gottfried John (*Willi*), Gisela Uhlen (*Mother*), Gunter Lamprecht (*Hans*), Hark Bohm (*Senkenberg*), George Byrd (*Bill*), Elisabeth Trissenaar (*Betti*), Rainer Werner Fassbinder (*Peddler*), Isolde Barth (*Vevi*), Peter Berling (*Bronski*), Sonja Neudorfer (*Red Cross Nurse*), Lieselotte Eder (*Frau Ehmcke*), Volker Spengler (*Conductor*), Karl-Heinz von Hassel (*Lawyer*), Michael Ballhaus (*Anwalt*), Christine Hopf de Loup (*Notary*), Dr. Horst-Dieter Klock (*Gentleman With Car*), Gunther Kaufmann, Bruce Low (*American G.I.s*), Claus Holm (*Doctor*), Anton Schirsner (*Grandpa Berger*), Hannes Kaetner (*Justice of the Peace*), Martin Haussler (*Reporter*), Norbert Scherer, Rolf Buhrmann, Arthur Glogau (*Wardens*).

The first in Fassbinder's trilogy about women in post-WW II Germany, which also includes VERONICA VOSS and LOLA, this was the film which solidified Fassbinder's reputation both abroad and in Germany. The opening sequence shows a German city being torn apart by Allied bombs, while Schygulla, in the title role, is about to be married to her soldier fiance Lowitsch. The priest performing the ceremony attempts to run for cover before the marriage is completed, but Lowitsch tackles him, forcing him to finish. Right after this Lowitsch is sent to the Russian Front, and Schygulla stays in her poverty-stricken home with her mother and sister, dedicated to waiting for her husband to arrive. Every day she goes to the train station with a sign on her back asking for information about her husband, but none comes. Finally her brother-in-law says that he is positive that Lowitsch has died. Schygulla becomes a barmaid in a cafe which caters to American soldiers; it is here where she meets Byrd, the black soldier who becomes her lover, helps supply her family with food items in low supply, and, most importantly, teaches Schygulla English. When she has nearly forgotten about her husband, he pops up, starving and emasculated, just as Schygulla and Byrd are preparing to make love. When the two men start to scuffle, Schygulla knocks Byrd over the head with a bottle. Lowitsch takes the blame for this crime, being sent to jail for a number of years while Schygulla undertakes her own prosperous career for importer Desny. In a cold and manipulative manner, she makes herself totally indispensable to this man who has become her lover and her boss. In the process she becomes a very wealthy woman, yet all the time she refuses to relinquish the romantic notion of the love she has for her imprisoned husband. Working in a maniacal fashion, she refuses to allow her cold exterior to be penetrated, even by Desny, who has declared his love for her over and over, and is driven nearly insane by the woman's rejections. Desny allows Schygulla more and more control over his company, but when Lowitsch is due to be let out of jail, the two men make a deal behind Schygulla's back which gives Lowitsch a large part of Desny's fortune, on condition that he go to Canada until the businessman's death. The film's end finally has Schygulla and Lowitsch reunited, ready to consummate their marriage. Returning from Desny's funeral, Schygulla finds her man waiting for her. Schygulla is stripped to nothing but her black lingerie showing an emotional excitability absent throughout the film, but her long awaited reunion is destroyed through one of the few instances of carelessness she reveals. Having left the gas running on the stove, she prepares to light a cigarette, blowing the posh home, her husband, and herself into oblivion. The highly stylized, deliberate structure of THE MARRIAGE OF MARIA BRAUN owes much to the same style of Douglas Sirk's 1950s Hollywood melodramas, such as IMITATION OF LIFE and WRITTEN ON THE WIND. As in these films, the director remains distanced from the heart-wrenching dramatics that are taking place, making MARRIAGE OF MARIA BRAUN a study of German society in its postwar rebuilding process. Fassbinder remains even more removed from the material than does Sirk—a product of the alienating atmosphere that is prominent in a Germany striving to make itself one of the industrial powers, yet failing to account for the human bonds that make a society healthy. The effect of this upon the heroine, Schygulla, is of great pity at seeing a young beautiful woman placing herself in an emotional vacuum. A statement made even more powerful when her aging mother, a remnant of prewar Germany, takes on a lover and pursues an emotionally fulfilling life while her daughter is unable to do so. Schygulla is quite powerful in this role, probably the best of her career, remaining cold and aloof, yet evoking a strong sense of pity. Though THE MARRIAGE OF MARIA BRAUN is not always an easy film to understand, the stark atmosphere, icy performances, and poignant revelations make it one of the most important films to emerge from Germany in the 1970s, and one of the best of Fassbinder's shortened career. (In German; English subtitles.)

p, Michael Fengler; d, Rainer Werner Fassbinder; w, Peter Marthesheimer, Pia Frohlich, Fassbinder (based on an idea by Fassbinder); ph, Michael Ballhaus; m, Peer Raben; ed, Juliane Lorenz, Franz Walsch [Fassbinder]; art d, Norbert Scherer, Helga Ballhaus, Claud Kottmann, Georg Borgel; set d, Andreas Willim, Arno Mathes, Hans Sandmeier; cos, Barbara Baum, Susi Reichel, George Kuhn, Ingeborg Proller.

Drama   **(PR:O MPAA:R)**

MARRIAGE ON APPROVAL*

(1934) 67m Monarch bw (GB: MARRIED IN HASTE)

Barbara Kent, Donald Dillaway, Phyllis Barry, William Farnum, Leila McIntyre, Edward Woods, Dorothy Grainger, Otis Harlan, Lucille Ward, Clarence Geldert.

Weak picture has a couple getting married while drunk, with the girl not even realizing what is happening. Story moves too slowly to hold much attention.

d, Howard Higgin; w, Olga Printzlau, Edward Sinclair, Higgin (based on the novel by Priscilla Wayne); ph, Edward Kull; ed, Fred Bain.

Comedy (PR:A MPAA:NR)

MARRIAGE ON THE ROCKS**

(1965) 109m WB c

Frank Sinatra (Dan Edwards), Deborah Kerr (Valerie Edwards), Dean Martin (Ernie Brewer), Cesar Romero (Miguel Santos), Hermione Baddeley (Jeannie MacPherson), Tony Bill (Jim Blake), John McGiver (Shad Nathan), Nancy Sinatra (Tracy Edwards), Davey Davison (Lisa Sterling), Michel Petit (David Edwards), Trini Lopez (Himself), Joi Lansing (Lola), Tara Ashton (Bunny), Kathleen Freeman (Miss Blight), Flip Mark (Rollo), DeForest Kelley (Mr. Turner), Sigrid Valdis (Kitty), Byron Foulger (Mr. Bruno), Parley Baer (Dr. Newman), Reta Shaw (Saleslady at Saks), Nacho Galindo (Mayor), Hedley Mattingly (Mr. Smythe).

A faintly amusing comedy that did not amuse the Mexican authorities who objected to Romero's portrayal as a quickie divorce lawyer south of the border. Sinatra and Kerr have been married nearly 20 years and he runs a successful advertising agency. He thinks he is happily married but Kerr does not and is in the process of divorcing him as she meets with family attorney McGiver, a booze-swilling, woman-chasing bachelor. Kerr's complaint is that she married an exciting swinger but the years have made him boring. McGiver wants to keep them together so he suggests she doff her flannel nightwear, buy a sexy negligee, and take Sinatra off for a second honeymoon. Martin has the same idea. Martin had also been in love with Kerr before Sinatra popped the question and Martin has never found another woman. Kerr and Sinatra take off for a holiday in Mexico and are mistakenly divorced by lawyer Romero, a man who runs faster than the ambulances he chases. Undaunted, Kerr and Sinatra decide to have a gala re-marriage but Sinatra has to fly back to the States on business then must leave the home office and go to Detroit to repair a problem with the agency's largest client. Not wishing to strand Kerr alone, Sinatra asks Martin to go to Mexico and keep her company and explain why he is delayed. Martin arrives in Mexico and Romero mistakenly marries the two of them! Rather than get a quickie divorce from Martin, Kerr thinks she can use this marriage to make Sinatra jealous and get her old hubby back. But Sinatra, upon discovering he's single, will not fall for it and begins to live his one-time swinging life in Martin's pad at Malibu, Calif. Despite the hot and cold running blondes, Sinatra is unhappy. Kerr now learns that she is pregnant because of that short but passionate trip to Mexico. On Thanksgiving, Sinatra and Kerr reconcile and plan to have a large church wedding once she can shed Martin in a real court of law. Nancy Sinatra plays Frank's daughter, a role she was born to play. Trini Lopez sings "There Was a Sinner Man" which took five writers to compose. Tony Bill, now a producer-director, plays Nancy's boy friend, three years after having played Sinatra's younger brother in COME BLOW YOUR HORN.

p, William H. Daniels; d, Jack Donohue; w, Cy Howard (based on the story "Community Property" by Howard); ph, Daniels (Panavision, Technicolor); m, Nelson Riddle; ed, Sam O'Steen; md, Riddle; art d, LeRoy Deane; set d, Arthur Krams, William L. Kuehl; cos, Walter Plunkett, Carroll and Company; ch, Jonathan Lucas; m/l, "There Was a Sinner Man," Trini Lopez, Bobby Weinstein, Bobby Hart, Billy Barberis, Teddy Randazzo (sung by Lopez); makeup, Gordon Bau.

Comedy (PR:A-C MPAA:NR)

MARRIAGE PLAYGROUND, THE***

(1929) 70m PAR bw

Fredric March (Martin Boyne), Mary Brian (Judith Wheater), Lilyan Tashman (Joyce Wheater), Huntley Gordon (Cliff Wheater), Kay Francis (Lady Wrench), William Austin (Lord Wrench), Seena Owen (Rose Sellers), Philippe De Lacy (Terry Wheater), Anita Louise (Blanca Wheater), Little Mitzi Green (Zinnie), Billie Seay (Astorre [Bun] Wheater), Ruby Parsley (Beatrice "Beechy"), Donald Smith (Chipstone "Chip" Wheater), Jocelyn Lee (Sybil Lullmer), Maude Turner Gordon (Aunt Julia Langley), David Newell (Gerald Omerod), Armand Kaliz (Prince Matriano), Joan Standing (Miss Scopey), Gordon De Main (Mr. Delafield).

Touching, yet absorbing tale of 18-year-old Brian, forced to be the mother to a horde of brothers and sisters and half-brothers and sisters, while her rich parents are out playing. March, an American traveling in Italy, befriends Brian, who takes an immediate liking to him, as do the brood of children. This attraction on Brian's part eventually leads to love, but March has a fiancee in Switzerland. He leaves, only to return after dropping his fiancee. March and Brian both deliver moving performances, aided by a good supporting cast. The production on the technical level is all top notch.

d, Lothar Mendes; w, J. Walter Ruben, Doris Anderson (based on the novel The Children by Edith Wharton); ph, Victor Milner.

Drama (PR:A MPAA:NR)

MARRIAGE SYMPHONY

(SEE: LET'S TRY AGAIN, 1934)

MARRIED AND IN LOVE**

(1940) 58m RKO bw

Alan Marshal (Leslie Yates), Barbara Read (Helen Yates), Patric Knowles (Paul Wilding), Helen Vinson (Doris Wilding), Hattie Noel (Hildegard), Frank Faylen (Man in Bar), Carol Hughes (Woman in Bar).

Common theme about former lovers, now happily married, who meet and start up their romance again. Vinson is married to an independently wealthy man when she bumps into her old lover Marshal, sparking long-hidden desires. Marshal, who has

since become a successful doctor, has a wife who has devoted everything to him. Performances are stifled behind a dreary script.

p, Robert Sisk; d, John Farrow; w, S.K. Lauren; ph, J. Roy Hunt; m, Arthur Lange; ed, Harry Marker; art d, Van Nest Polglase; cos, Renie.

Drama (PR:A MPAA:NR)

MARRIED BACHELOR***

(1941) 87m MGM bw

Robert Young (Randolf Haven), Ruth Hussey (Norma Haven), Felix Bressart (Dr. Ladislaus Milio), Lee Bowman (Eric Santley), Sheldon Leonard (Johnny Branigan), Sam Levene (Cookie Farrar), Roy Gordon (Hudkins), Douglass Newlin (Devlin), Murray Alper (Sleeper), Charlotte Wynters (Margaret Johns), Hillary Brooke (Connie Gordon), Joe Yule, Sr. (Waiter), Connie Gilchrist (Mother with Baby), Charles Ray (Man in Lounge Room), Bess Flowers (Salesgirl), Inez Cooper (Customer), Natalie Thompson (Santley's Secretary), Mimi Doyle (Stenographer).

Delightful comedy has Young in desperate need of $1,000 to pay off a racetrack bet made with a gangster. To raise money, he gets hold of a manuscript based on a bachelor's view of married life, publishes it under his own name, and becomes an immediate hit. The situation forces Young to separate from his wife, Hussey, which puts a strain on their once happy marriage. Adequate performances to a well-paced script.

p, John W. Considine, Jr.; d, Edward Buzzell; w, Dore Schary (based on a story by Manuel Seff); ph, George Folsey; m, Lennie Hayton; ed, Ben Lewis; art d, Cedric Gibbons.

Comedy (PR:A MPAA:NR)

MARRIED BEFORE BREAKFAST**

(1937) 70m MGM bw

Robert Young (Tom Wakefield), Florence Rice (Kitty Brent), June Clayworth (June Baylin), Barnett Parker (Tweed), Warren Hymer (Harry), Helen Flint (Miss Fleeter), Hugh Marlowe (Kenneth), Tom Kennedy (Mr. Baglipp), Edgar Dearing (Police Sergeant), Irene Franklin (Mrs. Baglipp), Mary Gordon (Mrs. Nevins), Harlan Briggs (Mr. Moriarity), Richard Carle (Colonel), Josephine Whittell (Miss Willis), Leonid Kinskey (Lapidoff), Pierre Watkin (Mr. Potter), Paul Stanton (Mr. Dow), Douglas Wood (Mr. Camden), Eddie Dunn (Lester O'Brien), Edward LeSaint (Judge Rafferty), Si Jenks (Janitor), Boyd Irwin, Sr. (Mr. Baylin), Bea Nigro (Mrs. Baylin), Tom Dugan (Cop), Tommy Bond (Baglipp's Kid), Jack Norton (Drunk), Henry Taylor (Moreno), Luke Cosgrave (Peddler), Spencer Charters (Fireman), Dennis O'Keefe (Salesman), Joseph Crehan (Dalton), Joe Caits, Warren Hymer, George Taylor (Gangsters).

Spoof has Young inventing a shaving cream which doesn't need razors, and then getting paid a quarter of a million dollars by a razor blade company to forget it. With the money he takes his fiancee, a society girl, on a trip around the world. This leads to a whole mess of escapades and ends with Young losing his fiancee, but gaining a new girl. Script and direction are too slow-paced for this type of material which hinders the otherwise good performances.

p, Sam Zimbalist; d, Edwin L. Marin; w, George Oppenheimer, Everett Freeman (based on the story by Harry Ruskin); ph, Leonard Smith; ed, William S. Gray.

Comedy (PR:A MPAA:NR)

MARRIED BUT SINGLE

(SEE: THIS THING CALLED LOVE, 1940)

MARRIED COUPLE, A***

(1969, Can.) 96m Aquaris/Fode c

Billy and Antoinette Edwards, Bogart Edwards.

A film crew entered the house of copywriter Edwards and filmed 70 hours of the family's life together when their marriage was at a crisis point. Picture concentrates on the bitter arguments between the couple and, at times, shows some of the lighter moments. There is little dramatic structure, so a sense of flow is lost. Film displays some beautiful color photography.

p&d, Allan King; ph, Richard Leiterman (Technicolor); m, Zal Yanovsky, Doug Bush; ed, Arla Saare.

Drama (PR:O MPAA:NR)

MARRIED IN HASTE, 1931

(SEE: CONSOLATION MARRIAGE, 1931)

MARRIED IN HASTE, 1934

(SEE: MARRIAGE ON APPROVAL, 1934)

MARRIED IN HOLLYWOOD**

(1929) 110m FOX bw-c

J. Harold Murray (Prince Nicholai), Norma Terris (Mitzi Hofman/Mary Lou Hopkins), Walter Catlett (Joe Glitner), Irene Palasty (Annushka), Lennox Pawle (King Alexander), Tom Patricola (Mahai), Evelyn Hall (Queen Louise), John Garrick (Stage Prince), Douglas Gilmore (Adjutant Octavian), Gloria Grey (Charlotte), Jack Stambaugh (Capt. Jacobi), Bert Sprotte (Herr von Herzen), Lelia Karnelly (Mrs. von Herzen), Herman Bing (Herr Director), Paul Ralli (Namari), Donald Gallaher (Film Director), Carey Harrison, Roy Seegar (Detectives)

Thin plot line has Terris as a showgirl touring in Europe, where she meets and falls in love with a Balkan prince, Murray. This is something his parents won't stand for, but a revolution allows the prince to escape to Hollywood where he and his true love are married. Murray and Terris show very little acting ability, but these recently borrowed musical stage stars were mainly recruited to display their vocal talents, which they did marvelously. The final Hollywood sequences to this film were reproduced in color. Allegedly this was the first Hollywood musical which actually used Hollywood as the setting for the story. Songs include: "Dance Away the Night," "Peasant Love Song," "A Man, a Maid," "Deep in Love," "Bridal Chorus," "National Anthem," and "Once Upon a Time."

d, Marcel Silver; w, Leopold Jacobson, Bruno Hardt-Warden (based on the story by Harlan Thompson); ph, Charles Van Enger, Sol Halperin; m, Oscar Straus; ed,

Dorothy Spencer; cos, Sophie Wachner, Alice O'Neill; m/l, Thompson, Dave Stamper, Arthur Kay.

Musical   (PR:A MPAA:NR)

MARRIED TOO YOUNG**

(1962) 80m Headliner bw (AKA: I MARRIED TOO YOUNG)

Harold Lloyd, Jr. (Tommy Blaine), Jana Lund (Helen Newton), Anthony Dexter (Grimes), Marianna Hill (Marla), Trudy Marshall (Susan Newton), Brian O'Hara (George Newton), Nita Loveless (Grace Blaine), Lincoln Demyan (George Blaine), David Bond (Justice of the Peace), Cedric Jordan (Mike), Richard Davies (Judge), Joel Mondeaux (Felton), George Cisar (Miltie), Irene Ross (Phyllis), Frank Harding (Daddy-O), Tom Fransden (Sportscaster).

Lloyd and Lund are high school students who elope and then have a second ceremony to please their parents. Lloyd drops his dreams of becoming a doctor and takes a job as a mechanic. The couple moves into Lund's parents' home where her father, O'Hara, sets up rules that Lloyd must follow. Their problems mount when Lloyd unknowingly gets involved in a car theft ring. Both sets of parents finally join together and send the young man to college.

d, George Moskov; w, Nathaniel Tanchuck; ph, Ernest Haller; m, Manuel Francisco; ed, Maurice Wright; set d, Ted Driscoll; makeup, Fred Phillips.

Drama   (PR:A MPAA:NR)

MARRIED WOMAN, THE***1/2

(1965, Fr.) 94m Anouchka-Orsay/Royal bw (UNE FEMME MARIEE; GB: A MARRIED WOMAN)

Macha Meril (Charlotte), Bernard Noel (Robert, the Lover), Philippe Leroy (Pierre, the Husband), Rita Maiden (Mme. Celine), Margaret Le Van, Veronique Duval (Girls in Swimming Pool), Chris Tophe (Nicolas), Georges Liron (The Physician), Roger Leenhardt (Himself), Jean-Luc Godard (Narrator).

Meril plays a Parisian housewife married to airplane pilot Leroy, and with a lover, Noel, on the side. When she turns up pregnant, she realizes either man could be the father. The decision of whether to leave her husband for Noel is not given any assistance by either man, both of whom seem able to communicate with Meril only on a physical level. By the end of the film, she is still undecided and the viewer must imagine what she finally does. The original title, LA FEMME MARIEE (A MARRIED WOMAN), was changed by request of the French censors, who considered it a reference to all married French women. Includes extracts from Beethoven String Quartets 7, 9, 10, 14, and 15. (In French; English subtitles.)

d&w, Jean-Luc Godard; ph, Raoul Coutard; m, Claude Nougaro; ed, Agnes Guillemot, Francoise Collin; art d, Henri Nogaret; cos, Laurence Clairval; m/l, "Java," Nougaro, "Quand le Film est Triste," John D. Loudermilk, G. Aber, L. Morisse (sung by Sylvie Vartan).

Drama   **Cas.**   (PR:C MPAA:NR)

MARRY ME*1/2

(1932, Brit.) 75m Gainsborough/ID-GAU bw

Renate Muller (Ann Linden), Harry Green (Sigurd Bernstein), George Robey (Aloysius Novak), Ian Hunter (Robert Hart), Maurice Evans (Paul Hart), Billy Caryll (Meyer), Charles Hawtrey, Jr. (Billy Hart), Charles Carson (Korten), Viola Lyel (Frau Krause), Sunday Wilshin (Ida Brun).

Muller falls in love with a member of Berlin society and finally wins his heart after becoming his housekeeper. The story tries hard to be convincing but somehow falls short.

p, Michael Balcon; d, William Thiele; w, Angus Macphail, Anthony Asquith (based on a story by Stephen Zador, Franz Schulz, Ernst Angel).

Musical/Comedy   (PR:A MPAA:NR)

MARRY ME!**

(1949, Brit.) 97m Gainsborough/GFD bw

Derek Bond (Andrew Scott), Susan Shaw (Pat), Patrick Holt (Martin Roberts), Carol Marsh (Doris), David Tomlinson (David Haig), Zena Marshall (Marcelle), Guy Middleton (Sir Gordon Blake), Nora Swinburne (Enid Lawson), Brenda Bruce (Brenda), Denis O'Dea (Sanders), Jean Cadell (Hestor Parsons), Mary Jerrold (Emily Parsons), Yvonne Owen (Sue Carson), Alison Leggatt (Miss Beamish), Beatrice Varley (Mrs. Perrins), Anthony Steel (Jack Harris), Anthony Neville, George Merritt, Sandra Dorne, Judith Furse, Tamara Lees, Esma Cannon, Mary [Marianne] Stone, Everley Gregg, J. H. Roberts, Lyn Evans, Hal Osmond, Cyril Chamberlain, John Warren, Ann Valery, John Boxer, Herbert C. Walton, Dan Yarranton, Jill Allen.

The adventures of four couples are portrayed in this episodic film about a marriage bureau. The acting and production are efficient, though the characters are stereotyped into predictable situations.

p, Betty Box; d, Terence Fisher; w, Denis Waldock, Lewis Gilbert; ph, Ray Elton, David Harcourt; m, Clifton Parker; ed, Gordon Pilkington.

Comedy/Romance   (PR:A MPAA:NR)

MARRY ME AGAIN**1/2

(1953) 73m RKO bw

Robert Cummings (Bill), Marie Wilson (Doris), Ray Walker (Mac), Mary Costa (Joan), Jess Barker (Jenkins), Lloyd Corrigan (Mr. Taylor), June Vincent (Miss Craig), Richard Gaines (Dr. Pepperdine), Moroni Olsen (Mr. Courtney), Frank Cady (Dr. Day), Joanne Arnold (Wac), Bob Thomas (Himself).

Cummings and Wilson are about to be married when he is called to serve as a fighter pilot in the Korean War. While he's gone Wilson inherits a million dollars from an eccentric aunt. When Cummings returns home he is bewildered at his fiancee's new status. Unwilling to accept a less-than-breadwinner role in the family, he calls off the marriage and re-enlists in the Air Force, only to be submitted to intensive psychiatric testing on the grounds that anyone who would turn down the assets of Miss Wilson

(both physical and financial) must be crazy. In a terrifically funny sequence, Cummings is interviewed by doctors trying to figure out whether or not he "likes girls." Finally Wilson, in order to pacify her man, gives the money to a veterans' housing project, and the film ends happily. Don't miss a satirical highlight where a movie house usher confuses actual onscreen action for a real fight, only to be reassured by her manager that the brawl is just a part of the current 3-D attraction. This film was a sort of family affair with Robert Fallon, Wilson's real-life husband, serving as associate producer and Tashlin's wife, Costa, in a good characterization as a Wac.

p, Alex Gottlieb; d&w, Frank Tashlin (based on a story by Gottlieb); ph, Robert de Grasse; m, Raoul Kraushaar; ed, Edward Mann; art d, Daniel Hall.

Comedy   (PR:A MPAA:NR)

MARRY ME! MARRY ME!**

(1969, Fr.) 87m Renn-Parafrance-Madeleine/AA c (MAZEL TOV OU LE MARIAGE)

Claude Berri (Claude Avram), Elisabeth Wiener (Isabelle Schmoll), Regine (Marthe), Louisa Colpeyn (Mme. Schmoll), Gregoire Aslan (Schmoll), Prudence Harrington (Helen), Betsy Blair (2nd English Teacher), Gabriel Jabbour (Mons. Avram), Estera Galion (Mme. Avram).

Berri is an encyclopedia salesman who gets Wiener, the daughter of a Belgian diamond merchant, pregnant and dutifully agrees to marry her. Before meeting the rest of her family, Berri takes English lessons and falls in love with his tutor, Harrington. After a dreadful weekend with Wiener's family he asks his tutor to marry him. She agrees and the salesman breaks the news to Wiener. Then he discovers that Harrington has changed her mind and has married an airline pilot. Berri marries Wiener and, a few years later, decides he's a happy man.

p,d,&w, Claude Berri; ph, Ghislain Cloquet (DeLuxe Color); m, Emile Stern; ed, Sophie Coussein; cos, Paola Pilla.

Comedy/Drama   (PR:A MPAA:M)

MARRY THE BOSS' DAUGHTER*1/2

(1941) 60m FOX bw

Brenda Joyce (Fredericka Barrett), Bruce Edwards (Jefferson Cole), George Barbier (J. W. Barrett), Hardie Albright (Putnam Palmer), Ludwig Stossel (Franz Polgar), Bodil Rosing (Mrs. Polgar), Brandon Tynan (Mr. Dawson), Charles Arnt (Blodgett), George Meeker (Snavely), Frank McGlynn (Hoffman), Edward Cooper (Jenkins), Eula Guy (Miss Simpson), Paul McGrath (Taylor), Marek Windheim (Faranelli), Matt McHugh (Leiber), Jeebee (Nicholas).

Edwards is a naive young man who arrives in New York City, determined to make something of himself. He finds a dog, the lost pet of Joyce, and returns it to her. She's overwhelmed by his act of kindness and talks her father (Barbier) into giving the young man a job in his Manhattan business. Edwards soon discovers potentially damaging errors in the company files, shows the boss, gets a fat promotion and Joyce's hand in marriage. It's just one cliche after another in this insepid production, which served as the lower half of B features in the 1940s.

p, Lou Ostrow; d, Thorton Freeland; w, Jack Andrews (based on the story "The Boy" by Sandor Farago, Alexander G. Kenedi); ph, Charles Clarke; ed, Louis Loeffler.

Drama   (PR:A MPAA:NR)

MARRY THE GIRL*1/2

(1935, Brit.) 69m BL bw

Sonnie Hale (Wally Gibbs), Winifred Shotter (Doris Chattaway), Hugh Wakefield (Hugh Delafield), Judy Kelly (Jane Elliott), C. Denier Warren (Banks), Kenneth Kove (Cyril Chattaway), Maidie Hope (Mrs. Elliott), Wally Patch (Bookmaker), John Deverell (Judge), Lawrence Anderson.

After rich fellow Hale becomes engaged to Kelly, Shotter's mother forces her to sue Hale for breach of promise. Kelly enlists the help of her pal Wakefield, a lawyer, to catch Shotter in a compromising position, thus ruining any chance she might have in court. However, the plot backfires, as Hale is blamed for the incident. His fiancee leaves him for the lawyer, so Hale finally decides that Shotter just may be the girl for him after all. The idea is fresh and chock full of farcical potential but never is developed as well as one might hope. The cast does its best to make up for that, though, with light comic performances.

p, Herbert Smith; d, P. Maclean Rogers; w, Rogers, Kathleen Butler (based on a play by Arthur Miller [British], George Arthurs).

Comedy   (PR:A MPAA:NR)

MARRY THE GIRL*1/2

(1937) 66m WB bw

Mary Boland (Ollie Radway), Frank McHugh (David Partridge), Hugh Herbert (John B. Radway), Carol Hughes (Virginia Radway), Allen Jenkins (Specs), Mischa Auer (Dimitri), Alan Mowbray (Dr. Stryker), Hugh O'Connell (Michael Forrester), Teddy Hart (Bill), Tom Kennedy (Jasper), Dewey Robinson (Buster), Olin Howland (1st Southerner), Arthur Aylesworth (2nd Southerner), William B. Davidson (Drake), Charles Judels (Andre Victor Antoine Descate), Irving Bacon, Louis Mason, Louise Stanley, Bess Flowers.

A group of zany family members, headed by siblings Herbert and Boland, runs a news syndicate. The office is populated with a variety of crazies, including Mowbray as a dubious psychiatrist and O'Connell, the inebriated cartoonist. The main body of the story involves the love affair between Hughes, the niece of Herbert and Boland, and Auer, the paper's looney-tune caption writer. The oldsters are against the relationship and set out to nip the romance in the bud. Despite three screen writers and a fairly good comedic cast, this film goes nowhere. The situations are tired and the characters, though well played, are hampered by the script which leaves them little room to play around in—a necessary element for something with the pretensions of "zaniness." Evidently no one told the production team.

p, Hal B. Wallis; d, William McGann; w, Sig Herzig, Pat C. Flick, Tom Reed (based on the novel by Edward Hope); ph, Arthur Todd; ed, Warren Low; art d, Max Parker.

Comedy   **(PR:A MPAA:NR)**

MARRYING KIND, THE** ½   (1952) 92m COL bw

Judy Holliday (*Florence Keefer*), Aldo Ray (*Chet Keefer*), Madge Kennedy (*Judge Carroll*), Sheila Bond (*Joan Shipley*), John Alexander (*Howard Shipley*), Rex Williams (*George Bastian*), Phyllis Povah (*Mrs. Derringer*), Peggy Cass (*Emily Bundy*), Mickey Shaughnessy (*Pat Bundy*), Griff Barnett (*Charley*), Susan Hallaran (*Ellen*), Barry Curtis (*Joey, Age 4*), Christie Olsen (*Joey, Age 6*), Wallace Acton (*Newhouse*), Elsie Holmes (*Marian*), Joan Shawlee (*Dancer*), Thomas B. Henry (*Mr. Jenner*), Frank Ferguson (*Mr. Quinn*), Don Mahin (*Roy*), Larry Blake (*Benny*), Tom Farrell (*Cliff*), Gordon Jones (*Steve*), John Eliott (*Minister*), Joe McGuinn (*Bus Driver*), Richard Gordon (*Lawyer*), Patrick Butler (*Child*), Malan Mills (*Charlotte*), Charles [Bronson] Buchinski (*Eddie*), Nancy Kulp (*Edie*), Robert Hartley, Charles Brewer, Johnnie Kiado (*Musicians*).

A sort of comedy with some heavy drama, THE MARRYING KIND had two of the most recognizable voices around in it: Holliday's high, squeaky, sometimes shrill sound and newcomer Ray's raspy growl. The film begins in the divorce court run by Kennedy (the silent screen star in a rare talking appearance) as Ray and Holliday vent their spleens and explain why they want to split. The picture flashes back as the couple goes through their disagreements and misunderstandings. They meet in a public park, marry, have children (one of whom dies in a drowning accident) and eventually desire to call it quits. After they have discussed their points of view, they realize that they do love each other and will reconcile. Along the way, there are some very funny scenes (and excellent dialog by Kanin and Gordon) as well as a few dramatic moments that tug at the heart—particularly the one in which their child dies. Cukor directs stylishly and Holliday is obviously confident about Cukor's work, having taken the Oscar for her last film with him and the Kanins, BORN YESTERDAY. Ray makes an auspicious entrance on the movie scene (this was his second film but his first huge role) and Charles Bronson is seen briefly as Ray's post office buddy. Bond, Shaughnessy, and Cass play far too broadly and the picture descends into a situation comedy whenever any of them come on screen. Location shots are at Stuyvesant Town, an apartment complex on the East Side of Manhattan.

p, Bert Granet; d, George Cukor; w, Ruth Gordon, Garson Kanin; ph, Joseph Walker; m, Hugo Friedhofer; ed, Charles Nelson; md, Morris W. Stoloff; art d, John Meehan; set d, William Kiernan; cos, Jean Louis; makeup, Clay Campbell.

Comedy/Drama   **(PR:A MPAA:NR)**

MARRYING WIDOWS*   (1934) 65m Tower bw

Judith Allen, Minna Gombell, Lucien Littlefield, Johnny Mack Brown, Bert Roach, Sarah Padden, Virginia Sales, Nat Carr, Arthur Hoyt, Otto Hoffman, Syd Saylor, Gladys Blake, George Grandee.

As a favor to a friend, Gombell tries to shake down Littlefield for his money. Aside from Gombell's fairly good performance this one is a real loser. The plot barely exists and the actors behave like a bunch of walk-ons. The photography is far below the standards of the day, even for cheapies like this one. Utterly forgettable.

d, Sam Newfield; w, Adele Buffington; ph, Harry Forbes.

Drama   **(PR:C MPAA:NR)**

MARS NEEDS WOMEN zero   (1966) 80m Azalea bw

Tommy Kirk (*Dop*), Yvonne Craig (*Dr. Marjorie Bolen*), Byron Lord (*Col. Page*), Anthony Houston, Larry Tanner, Warren Hammack, Cal Duggan (*Martians*), Bill Thurman, Pat Delaney, Donna Lindberg, Sherry Roberts, Bubbles Cash, Roger Ready, Neil Fletcher, George Edgley, Dick Simpson, Barnett Shaw, Chet Davis, Ron Scott, Don Campbell, Gordon Buloe, Claude Earls, Bob Lorenz, David Englund, Ann Palmer, Pat Cranshaw, Sally Casey, Sylvia Rundell, Terry Davis.

Martians, led by Kirk, come to Earth in search of females to help repopulate Mars. Cheap, amateurish, and dull, do not even come close to defining this sci-fi mess. Listed as one of those films that represents Hollywood filmmaking at its worst.

p,d&w, Larry Buchanan; ph, Robert C. Jessup.

Science Fiction   **(PR:A MPAA:NR)**

MARSCHIER ODER KREIPER

     (SEE: COMMANDO, 1964, Bel./Ital./Span./Ger.)

MARSEILLAISE   (SEE: LA MARSEILLAISE, 1939, Fr.)

MARSEILLES CONTRACT, THE   (SEE: DESTRUCTORS, THE, 1974, Brit.)

MARSHAL OF AMARILLO** ½   (1948) 60m REP bw

Allan "Rocky" Lane (*Himself*), Eddy Waller (*Nugget Clark*), Mildred Cole (*Marjorie Underwood*), Clayton Moore (*Art Crandall*), Roy Barcroft (*Ben*), Trevor Bardette (*Frank Welch*), Minerva Urecal (*Mrs. Pettigrew*), Denver Pyle (*Night Clerk*), Charles Williams (*Hiram Short*), Tom Chatterton (*James Underwood*), Peter Perkins (*Sam*), Tom London (*Snodgrass*), Lynn Castile (*Matilda*), Black Jack the Horse.

Lane's comic sidekick, Waller, finds some unusual goings-on at a seemingly deserted hotel. It seems a group of outlaws led by Moore (who went on to become a good guy as television's "Lone Ranger") are holding rich easterner Chatterton hostage and are after his daughter Cole as well. The story ends in an exciting stagecoach chase with Lane in hot pursuit of Moore. Fast-paced direction makes this a better-than-average western, with an exciting climax.

p, Gordon Kay; d, Phillip Ford; w, Bob Williams; ph, John MacBurnie; ed, Harold Minter; md, Morton Scott; art d, Frank Arrigo.

Western   **(PR:A MPAA:NR)**

MARSHAL OF CEDAR ROCK** ½   (1953) 54m REP bw

Allan "Rocky" Lane (*Himself*), Eddy Waller (*Nugget Clark*), Phyllis Coates (*Martha Clark*), Roy Barcroft (*Henry Mason*), Bill Henry (*Bill Anderson*), Robert Shayne (*Paul Jackson*), John Crawford (*Chris Peters*), John Hamilton (*Prison Warden*), Kenneth MacDonald (*Sheriff*), Herbert Lytton (*John Harper*), Black Jack the Horse.

The railroad is coming to town and everyone wants a piece of the action. Barcroft appears to be a model citizen but is really buying up ranchers' land cheaply so he can make a large profit when the train finally arrives. Henry is a convicted bank robber wrongly sent up the river by Barcroft. Of course Lane rides in on his mighty horse "Black Jack" and saves the day. A standard programmer with a wonderfully comic performance by Barcroft. This was directed by Keller, who took over the Lane series for its last few pictures.

p, Rudy Ralston; d, Harry Keller; w, Albert DeMond (based on a story by M. Coates Webster); ph, John MacBurnie; m, Stanley Wilson; ed, Tony Martinelli; art d, Frank Hotaling.

Western   **Cas.**   **(PR:A MPAA:NR)**

MARSHAL OF CRIPPLE CREEK, THE**   (1947) 58m REP bw

Allan Lane (*Red Ryder*), Bobby Blake (*Little Beaver*), Martha Wentworth (*The Duchess*), Trevor Bardette (*Tom Lambert*), Tom London (*Baker*), Roy Barcroft (*Link*), Gene Stutenroth (*Long John Case*), William Self (*Dick Lambert*), Helen Wallace (*Mrs. Lambert*).

An outlaw is hijacking gold shipments out of a Colorado mining town. The sheriff hasn't a clue but leaves it to Lane and his little pal Blake to solve the mystery. Bardette is a reformed outlaw, now a cook, who helps solve the crime. This was the last of the RED RYDER films for the Republic series and was not much of an effort. The budget and screenplay were both stripped to the bare minimum. Bardette is the only interesting character in the film. Blake was one of the few child actors who was able to carry on his career to adulthood, making some notable features, including IN COLD BLOOD. (See RED RYDER series, Index.)

p, Sidney Picker; d, R. G. Springsteen; w, Earle Snell (based on the comic strip by Fred Harman); ph, William Bradford; ed, Harold R. Minter; md, Mort Glickman; art d, Frank Arrigo.

Western   **(PR:A MPAA:NR)**

MARSHAL OF GUNSMOKE   (1944) 58m UNIV bw

Tex Ritter (*Ward*), Russell Hayden (*Tom*), Fuzzy Knight (*Glow-Worm*), Jennifer Holt (*Ellen*), Harry Woods (*Curtis*), Herbert Rawlinson (*Garrett*), Ethan Laidlaw (*Larkin*), Ray Bennett (*Spike*), Michael Vallon (*Ezra Peters*), Ernie Adams (*Nugget*), Slim Whitaker (*Nevada*), George Chesebro, James Farley, William Desmond, Dan White, Roy Brent, Bud Osborne, Johnny Bond and His Red River Valley Boys.

Ritter is a U.S. marshal who arrives in a frontier town to stop a gang of outlaws from fixing the local elections. Action-packed, as are all of Ritter's films, with, of course, music.

p, Oliver Drake; d, Vernon Keays; w, William Lively; ph, Harry Neumann; ed, Al Todd; md, H.J. Salter; art d, John B. Goodman, Abraham Grossman.

Western   **(PR:A MPAA:NR)**

MARSHAL OF HELDORADO**   (1950) 53m Lippert bw

Jimmy Ellison (*Shamrock*), Russ Hayden (*Lucky*), Raymond Hatton (*Colonel*), Fuzzy Knight (*Mayor Deacon*), Betty [Julie] Adams (*Ann*), Tom Tyler (*Mike*), George Lewis (*Nate*), John Cason (*Jake*), Stanley Price (*Marshal*), Stephen Carr (*Razor*), Dennis Moore (*Doc*), George Chesebro (*Stanton*), Bud Osborne (*Brad*), Jimmy Martin (*Ben*), Cliff Taylor (*Doctor*), Ned Roberts (*Bartender*), Jack Hendricks (*Zero*), Wally West (*Bagen*), James van Horn (*Townsman*), Jack Geddes (*Customer*), Carl Mathews.

A stock western about a town so full of bad guys that no one wants to be the sheriff. Knight, the town's mayor, tricks Hayden into the job. With the help of marshal Ellison he brings the outlaws to justice and cleans up the town. This could have been exceptionally boring but is saved thanks to the comic characterizations of Hayden and Ellison. The rest of the film is about as standard as the plot.

p, Ron Ormond, Murray Lerner; d, Thomas Carr; w, Ormond, Maurice Tombragel; ph, Ernest Miller; ed, Hugh Winn; md, Walter Greene; art d, Fred Preble.

Western   **Cas.**   **(PR:A MPAA:NR)**

MARSHAL OF LAREDO**   (1945) 56m REP bw

Bill Elliott (*Red Ryder*), Bobby Blake (*Little Beaver*), Alice Fleming (*The Duchess*), Peggy Stewart, Roy Barcroft, Tom London, George Carleton, Wheaton Chambers, Tom Chatterton, George Chesebro, Don Costello, Bud Geary, Robert Grady, Sarah Padden, Jack O'Shea, Lane Bradford, Ken Terrell, Dorothy Granger, Dick Scott.

A lawyer becomes involved with outlaws, gets framed, and is nearly hanged for his troubles. Fortunately for him, this is a RED RYDER film, so hero Elliott and his sidekick Blake manage to save him in the nick of time, teaching him a thing or two along the way. (See RED RYDER series, Index.)

p, Sidney Picker; d, R. G. Springsteen; w, Bob Williams (based on comic strip characters created by Fred Harman); ph, Bud Thackery; ed, Charles Craft; md, Richard Cherwin; art d, Hilyard Brown.

Western   **(PR:A MPAA:NR)**

MARSHAL OF MESA CITY, THE*** (1939) 62m RKO bw

George O'Brien (Mason), Virginia Vale (Virginia), Leon Ames (Sheriff), Henry Brandon (Allison), Lloyd Ingraham (Mayor), Slim Whitaker (Butch), Mary Gordon (Ma), Harry Cording (Henderson), Joe McGuinn (Joe), Frank Ellis (Harry), Wilfred Lucas, Carl Stockdale, Cactus Mack, Richard Hunter, Sid Jordan.

After a group of outlaws takes over the political offices of a frontier town, former marshal O'Brien is brought in to clean them out. This is one of O'Brien's best films and, despite the cliched plot, he's completely natural. He worked with his longtime director, Howard, and the two knew each other so well at this point that the chemistry translated into the finished project. The film featured Vale as the love interest, who got the part after winning the second annual RKO "Gateway to Hollywood" contest (this despite the fact that she had been a starlet under the name "Dorothy Howe" at Paramount!). A remake of the 1935 picture THE ARIZONIAN.

p, Bert Gilroy; d, David Howard; w, Jack Lait, Jr.; ph, Harry Wild; ed, Frederick Knudtson; art d, Van Nest Polglase.

Western (PR:A MPAA:NR)

MARSHAL OF RENO*** (1944) 54m REP bw

Bill Elliott (Red Ryder), Bobby Blake (Little Beaver), Alice Fleming (The Duchess), George Hayes, Herbert Rawlinson, Tom London, Jay Kirby, Charles King, Jack Kirk, Kenne Duncan, LeRoy Mason, Bob Wilke, Fred Burns, Tom Steele, Edmund Cobb, Fred Graham, Blake Edwards, Hal Price, Bud Geary, Jack O'Shea, Al Taylor, Marshall Reed, Tom Chatterton, Carl Sepulveda, Ken Terrell, Horace B. Carpenter, Charles Sullivan, Roy Barcroft (Voice Only).

On the Western frontier, a battle rages between two municipalities as to which will be named the county seat. Enter Elliott and his faithful companion Blake (did he ever put this role on his resume when trying to find acting jobs as an adult?). Everything is smoothed over in the typical wholesome fashion that differed little from any of the other RED RYDER films. This was one of four in the series starring "Wild Bill" Elliott (Donald Barry had played Red Ryder in an earlier serial) cranked out during the year. It was the last to feature George "Gabby" Hayes as co-sidekick along with Blake. (See RED RYDER series, Index.)

p, Louis Gray; d, Wallace Grissell; w, Anthony Coldeway (based on a story by Coldeway, Taylor Cavan and on comic strip characters created by Fred Harman); ph, Reggie Lanning; m, Joseph Dubin; ed, Charles Craft; art d, Gano Chittenden.

Western (PR:A MPAA:NR)

MARSHAL'S DAUGHTER, THE*1/2 (1953) 71m UA bw

Laurie Anders (Laurie Dawson), Hoot Gibson (Ben Dawson), Ken Murray (Sliding Bill Murray), Harry Lauter (Russ Mason), Bob [Robert] Bray (Anderson), Bob Duncan (Trigger Gans), Forrest Taylor (Uncle Jed), Tom London (Sheriff Flynn), Bruce Norman (Little Boy), Cecil Elliott (Miss Tiddleford), Bette Lou Walters (Miss Bolton), Francis Ford (Gramps), Julian Upton (Brad), Ted Jordan (Augie), Lee Phelps (Sheriff Barnes), Harry Harvey (Bartender), Danny Duncan (Drunk), Bob Gross (Frenchie), Preston Foster (Himself), Johnny Mack Brown (Himself), Jimmy Wakely (Himself), Buddy Baer (Himself).

A loosely strung episodic film features Anders (known for her television cry, "Ah luv those wide open spaces!") in the title role. Her father, Gibson, is a former marshal and together they track down outlaw Duncan. Producer Murray plays the comic relief. This was Gibson's first film in nearly 10 years and hardly worth the effort. Every time the action gets going, things stop so Anders can sing a cowboy song, while Gibson just seems to be going through the motions. Foster, Wakely, Baer, and Brown make cameo appearances in a poker game, and famed cowboy-singer Tex Ritter sings the title tune.

p, Ken Murray; d, William Berke; w, Bob Duncan; ph, Jack MacKenzie; m, Darrell Calker; ed, Reg Browne; m/l, Marjorie Thrasher, Jimmy Wakely, Jack Rivers, Stan Jones, Murray.

Western (PR:A MPAA:NR)

MARSHMALLOW MOON
(SEE: AARON SLICK FROM PUNKIN CRICK, 1952)

MARTIAN IN PARIS, A* (1961, Fr.) 87m Les Films Univers bw (UN MARTIEN A PARIS)

Darry Cowl, Nicole Mirel, Henri Vilbert, Gisele Grandre, Michele Verez, Pierre Louis, Roland Segur.

Cowl is a Martian who is sent to Earth to find out about the planet's mysterious sickness "love." He arrives and falls victim to the disease himself with a variety of women. A poorly written farce with Cowl obviously imitating the like of Jerry Lewis very unconvincingly.

p, Jacques Vilfrid; d, Jean-Daniel Daninos; w, Vilfrid, Daninos; ph, Marcel Combes.

Science Fiction (PR:A MPAA:NR)

MARTIN***1/2 (1979) 95m Laurel Group/Libra c

John Amplas (Martin), Lincoln Maazel (Cuda), Christine Forrest (Christina), Elayne Nadeau (Mrs. Santini), Tom Savini (Arthur), Sarah Venable (Housewife Victim), Fran Middleton (Train Victim), Al Levitsky (Lewis).

An interesting mixture of horror and social satire from the king of modern gore films, Romero. His NIGHT OF THE LIVING DEAD, a gross yet funny horror film, set new standards for the independent film maker which Romero maintained throughout his career. Amplas plays a 17-year-old convinced he's an 84-year-old vampire. Lacking fangs, he resorts to crude forms of bloodletting, employing razor blades and syringes to get the task done. Maazel is his grandfather, determined to rid the family of its vampire curse by destroying his "Nosferatu" grandson. Amplas is egged on by a local radio talk-show, to which he is a regular caller, after explaining why he does

what he does. Romero himself appears as a priest, and gore makeup artist Savini is the fiance of Amplas' cousin Forrest. Though extremely bloody, this is a neatly made and fun little satire. Amplas' conversations with the radio talk-show host give some real insight into the nature of fame, the media, and manipulation. Despite some technical problems due to the limited budget, Romero's direction is excellent. He builds his suspense nicely and there's a fine use of sepiatone flashbacks to show Amplas in Rumania. Not for the faint of heart or the weak of stomach but definitely worth seeing.

p, Richard Rubinstein; d&w, George A. Romero; ph, Michael Gornick; m, Donald Rubinstein; ed, Romero; spec eff & makeup, Tom Savini.

Horror Cas. (PR:O MPAA:R)

MARTIN LUTHER**1/2 (1953) 105m De Rochemont bw

Niall MacGinnis (Martin Luther), John Ruddock (Vicar von Staupitz), Pierre Lefevre (Spalatin), Guy Verney (Melanchthon), Alastair Hunter (Carlstadt), David Horne (Duke Frederick), Fred Johnson (Prior), Philip Leaver (Pope Leo X), Dr. Egon Strohm (Cardinal Aleander), Alexander Gauge (Tetzel), Irving Pichel (Brueck), Leonard White (Emissary), Hans Lefebre (Charles V), Annette Carell (Katherine von Bora).

Cinematographer Brun was nominated for an Oscar and it was his work that elevated this from a religious documentary into a full-fledged picture. The title reveals the nature of the movie; it's an accurate depiction of the life of the first Protestant as he broke with the Catholic church and started the Reformation that would cause rumbles in the church's hierarchy which still are often felt. It is not "entertainment" in the usual sense of the word but it did have a large audience among Lutherans, and may be one of the better religious biographies made. Old Vic veteran MacGinnis is believable as Luther and a fine cast of British actors has been assembled under Pichel's leisurely direction. Pichel took a role in the film as well. It was financed by six church groups and filmed in Germany, where many of the events actually took place. Although not widely released, the picture continues to be shown to church groups and has had a life long beyond the customary release schedules. All of the history of the man is revealed, beginning with his studies of the law, his decision to leave the laity and enter the priesthood, his years of devotion to his monastery, and his eventual demand that the church reform itself. His trial at the Diet of Worms is highly dramatic and the film concludes when Luther leaves the priesthood to marry and to further the cause of protestation against the Catholic Church, which is how the word Protestant came about. In reality, it might have been pronounced "Pro-test-ant" but that did not fall lightly on the ears. Mark Lothar's music is a plus but one wishes there might have been some leavening humor in it, or the script, to make the man look more human. It was made with such respect that the subject matter seems gloomy when it should have been uplifting. Compare this to the life of Sir Thomas More in A MAN FOR ALL SEASONS and see the difference.

p, Louis de Rochemont, Lothar Wolff; d, Irving Pichel; w, Allen Sloane, Wolff; ph, Joseph C. Brun; m, Mark Lothar; art d, Fritz Maurischat, Paul Markwitz; consultants, Pastor Peter Heinemann, Dr. Johannes Stuhlmacher.

Historical Biography (PR:AA MPAA:NR)

MARTIN ROUMAGNAC (SEE: ROOM UPSTAIRS, THE, 1946, Fr.)

MARTY**** (1955) 91m UA bw

Ernest Borgnine (Marty), Betsy Blair (Clara), Esther Minciotti (Mrs. Pilletti), Karen Steele (Virginia), Jerry Paris (Thomas), Frank Sutton (Ralph), Walter Kelley (The Kid), Robin Morse (Joe), Augusta Ciolli (Catherine), Joe Mantell (Angie).

If any film deserves to be called "heartwarming" this one does, along with providing a poignant and utterly memorable performance by Borgnine, one he found impossible to equal and, of course, that has to do with the part he made into magic. Borgnine is a burly, lonely, good-natured man living with his mother with no prospects for any other kind of future. The heavy-set Bronx butcher lives in a small world populated by his Italian relatives and fast-aging male friends, chiefly Mantell. When Borgnine and Mantell meet after work they stand about mindlessly thinking of ways to fill their lives with something interesting to do. Their soon predictable, groping interchange never varies each eve: "So, what do you wanna do tonight, Marty?" "I dunno, Angie. What do you wanna do?" At home, Borgnine is totally dominated by his love-smothering mother, Minciotti, who fusses and worries over him. When Borgnine attempts to step outside of his world he's roundly rejected as a bumbling, unattractive person. He attends a dance with Mantell and others and tries to pick up some girls but strikes out. Then he later spots homely Blair, a schoolteacher whose life is excruciatingly similar to his, dull, hopeless, one inching into loveless middle-age. Borgnine asks Blair to dance and they are soon talking and begin to date. But Borgnine runs into a brick wall when he introduces Blair to his mother and male friends. His pals call her a "dog" and Minciotti is downright hostile to her, considering Blair a threat to her son and her own life with her son. Borgnine, not a courageous man, backs away from Blair, not calling her as promised, leaving her to sit miserably at home alone, watching TV. Borgnine agonizes over ignoring the woman he has grown to love and finally revolts against his family, friends, and environment, calling Blair and, in his simple way, telling her he loves her, proposing. She accepts him for a happy fadeout. MARTY, coming in the mid-1950s, in an era of epics and extravagant films designed to stifle upstart television, was all the more startling in that it was a movie expanded from an original TV drama, written brilliantly by Chayefsky, one of the leaders of what came to be known as "kitchen dramas" or "clothesline dramas." Borgnine's virtuoso performance is enthralling and won for him a well-deserved Oscar. Oscars also went to Chayefsky for Best Screenplay and to Mann for Best Direction. Before doing this film Borgnine was nothing more than an uninteresting heavy but he showed the world the great depths of his own character. Mantell also gives a superb performance as the pal addicted to the more bloody passages of Mickey Spillane, constantly asserting: "Boy, he sure can write!" Blair is less effective and Minciotti is more of a prop mother. UA executives were not enthusiastic about the production and almost cancelled the movie; they, along with the rest of Hollywood's elite, were amazed at the movie's universal success and MARTY soon set a trend toward the small-budgeted, prosaic films to come.

p, Harold Hecht; d, Delbert Mann; w, Paddy Chayefsky (based on a television play by Chayefsky); ph, Joseph La Shelle; m, Roy Webb; ed, Alan Grosland, Jr.; art d, Edward S. Haworth, Walter Simonds; cos, Norma; m/l, Harry Warren.

Drama **Cas.** **(PR:A MPAA:NR)**

MARTYR, THE***
(1976, Ger./Israel) 90m Corman-Israel-Produktion CCC/Spiegel-Joseph Green c (DER MARTYRER)

Leo Genn *(Dr. Korczak)*, Orna Porat *(Stofa)*, Efrat Pavi *(Ruth)*, Chad Kaplan *(Yakov)*, Benjamin Volz *(Michael)*, Charles Werner *(Adam)*.

Genn is a doctor in the Warsaw ghetto who takes care of children orphaned by the war and manages to keep a children's hospital running inside the ghetto. When the Nazis clear out the area, he opts to remain with the children he loves and is sent to a concentration camp. Though Genn is a bit overdramatic, the children are completely natural throughout. The scenes of ghetto life are painfully realistic and nicely handled. The political implications behind this film are just as interesting as the final product. Director Ford was once a big name in Polish filmmaking but left for Israel after anti-Semitic reaction of the Polish government to the 1967 Seven Days War between Israel and Egypt. More importantly, this Holocaust-themed story (based on a true account) was the first co-production of West Germany and Israel, signifying a sort of artistic reconciliation between Jews and Germans for the atrocities of WW II.

p, Artur Brauner; d, Aleksander Ford; w, Josef Gross (based on a scenario by Alexander Ramati); ph, Jerzy Lipman (Eastmancolor); m, Moshe Wilensky; ed, C. O. Bartning.

Drama **(PR:C MPAA:NR)**

MARTYRS OF LOVE**
(1968, Czech.) 73m Barrandov/New Line Cinema bw (MUCEDNICI LASKY)

"The Junior Clerk's Temptation": Petr Kopriva *(Junior Clerk)*, Marta Kubisova *(Girl)*, Jitka Cerhova *(1st Girl in Nightclub)*, Ivana Karbanova *(2nd Girl in Nightclub)*, Lindsay Anderson *(Himself)*; "Anastasia's Dream": Hana Kuberova *(Anastasia)*, Karel Gott *(Singer)*, Jan Klusak *(Captain)*, Vladimir Preclik *(Tramp)*; "Orphan Rudolph's Adventure": Josef Konicek *(Orphan Rudolph)*, Denisa Kvorakova *(Girl)*.

A trilogy of romance stories; the first is a temptation, the second a dream, and the third an adventure. The temptation has a shy clerk who spends all his savings on a night on the town and ends up with a woman in his bed, but she only wants to sleep. The dream is about a maid who chases after a singer. When he rejects her, she falls in love with a medical officer who wants to marry her. She panics and jumps on a train where a gypsy then begins to flirt with her. She awakens to the reality of her job as a waitress on a train. The third story has an orphan who is invited to a garden party. The rich guests give him a suit and treat him like an old friend. He also meets a woman, and when he returns to see her the next day he can't find the girl, his friends, or the garden.

p&d, Jan Nemec; w, Nemec, Ester Krumbachova; ph, Miroslav Ondricek; m, Jan Klusak, Karel Mares; ed, Miroslav Hajek; art d, Olin Bosak.

Comedy/Drama **(PR:A MPAA:NR)**

MARVIN AND TIGE** (1983) 104m Marvin Film Partners/Major c

John Cassavetes *(Marvin Stewart)*, Billy Dee Williams *(Richard Davis)*, Denise Nicholas-Hill *(Vanessa Jackson)*, Gibran Brown *(Tige Jackson)*, Fay Hauser *(Brenda Davis)*, Georgia Allen *(Carrie Carter)*.

Brown is an Atlanta street kid, left alone after his mother dies. The 11-year-old black youth attempts suicide but is rescued by a failed middle-aged white man (Cassavetes). Gradually a bond forms between the two. When Brown becomes ill, Cassavetes searches for the boy's father. He finds the man in due time, as Williams, the man who deserted the boy's mother years before, turns up as the father of three additional children in a nifty little nuclear family. He doesn't want the responsibilities of his past catching up with him, but anyone with a sense of film cliches knows what the outcome is going to be. This isn't a bad film, just an untruthful one. Though the three leads give sincerity to their roles, the initial premise is wholly dishonest, with a simplistic telling that well telegraphs the unfolding action. This is a classic example of why well-meaning ideas need much more than perfunctory shaping to work. The film was further hampered by the unforeseen horror of a series of child murders in Atlanta, where the production was shot. Released shortly after the killer of many young black children was arrested and convicted, the idea of a black child alone in the company of a white stranger simply didn't wash.

p, Wanda Dell; d, Erick Weston; w, Weston, Dell (based on a novel by Frankcina Glass); ph, Brian West (DeLuxe Color); m, Patrick Williams; ed, Fabien Dahlen Tordjmann; art d, Paul Rhudy, Frank Blair; set d, Scott Stevens, Tanya Moontaro; cos, Cheryl Kilborn, Christine Goluding.

Drama **(PR:C MPAA:PG)**

MARX BROTHERS AT THE CIRCUS (SEE: AT THE CIRCUS, 1939)

MARX BROTHERS GO WEST (SEE: GO WEST, 1940)

MARY (SEE: MURDER, 1930, Brit.)

MARY BURNS, FUGITIVE*** (1935) 84m PAR bw

Sylvia Sidney *(Mary Burns)*, Melvyn Douglas *(Barton Powell)*, Alan Baxter *("Babe" Wilson)*, Pert Kelton *(Goldie Gordon)*, Wallace Ford *(Harper)*, Brian Donlevy *(Spike)*, Esther Dale *(Kate)*, Frank Sully *(Steve)*, Boothe Howard *(Red Martin)*, Norman Willis *(Joe)*, Frances Gregg *(Matron)*, Charles Waldron *(District Attorney)*, William Ingersoll *(Judge)*, Rita Stanwood Werner *(Nurse Agnes)*, Grace Hayle *(Nurse Jennie)*, Daniel Haynes *(Jeremiah)*, Joe Twerp *(Willie)*, William Pawley *(Mike)*, James Mack, Walter Downing *(Farmers)*, Isabel Carlisle, Henry Hall *(Tourists)*, Dorothy Vaughan *(Irish Matron)*, Esther Howard *(Landlady)*, Morgan Wallace *(Managing Editor)*, Phil Tead *(Reporter)*, Ann Doran *(Newspaper Girl)*, Fuzzy Knight *(Dance Hall Attendant)*, Max Wagner *(Sailor)*, Gertrude Walker, Treva Lawler *(Hostesses)*, Charles Wilson *(G-Man in Dance Hall)*, George Chandler *(Cashier)*, Sammy Finn *(Dapper Mobster)*, Richard Pawley *(Slim Fergus)*, Bert Hanlon *(Hymie)*, Dan Merman *(Man)*, Cora Sue Collins *(Little Girl)*, Otto Fries *(Clerk at Employment Agency)*, Earl Ebbe *(Photographer)*, Gus Reed *(Manager)*, Tom Ford *(Orderly)*, Patricia Royale *(Scullery Maid)*, Beverly King, Virginia George *(Nurses)*, Bob Reeves, Bob Walker, Walter Shumway, Jack Mower, Ivan Miller, Kernan Cripps *(G-Men)*.

A routine story about a woman who unknowingly gets involved with a killer transcends its formula roots, thanks to the fine ensemble performance and some good direction. Sidney plays newcomer Baxter's lover. Through circumstantial evidence she is arrested and sent to prison on trumped up charges. She soon escapes and meets a new love, Douglas, who helps hide her from the law until her name is cleared. Although Sidney's role is probably the most stereotyped, she gives an effective and realistic performance. Baxter, a veteran of Broadway's Group Theater, makes a fine screen debut as her cold-blooded lover. Howard uses his actors well, and shows a good hand with his direction, making the film a good deal better than its script. In lesser hands this would have been just another B gangster film, but Howard and his cast turn it into something fresh and out of the ordinary.

p, Walter Wanger; d, William K. Howard; w, Gene Towne, Graham Baker, Louis Stevens (based on a story by Towne, Baker); ph, Leon Shamroy; ed, Pete Fritsch; cos, Helen Taylor.

Crime/Romance **(PR:A MPAA:NR)**

MARY HAD A LITTLE** (1961, Brit.) 83m Caralan-Dador/Lopert-UA bw

Agnes Laurent *(Mary Kirk)*, John Bentley *(Dr. Malcolm Nettel)*, Jack Watling *(Scott Raymond)*, Hazel Court *(Laurel Clive)*, John Maxim *(Burly Shavely)*, Rose Alba *(Duchess of Addlecombe)*, Patricia Marmont *(Angie)*, Noel Howlett *(Pottle)*, Michael Ward *(Hunter)*, Trevor Reid *(Dr. Liversidge)*, Charles Saynor *(Taxi Driver)*, Sidney Vivian *(Grimmick)*, Mark Hardy *(Hawkes)*, Michael Madden *(Tigg)*, Margaret Bull *(1st Woman)*, Yvonne Ball *(2nd Woman)*, Raymond Ray *(Park Keeper)*, Clifford Mollison *(Watkins)*, Frances Bennett *(Esther)*, Vincent Harding *(Carney)*, John Cazabon *(Fitchett)*, Tony Thawnton *(Shakespeare)*, Terry Scott *(Police Sergeant)*, John Ronane *(1st Intern)*, Stephen John *(2nd Intern)*.

Struggling British theater producer Watling overhears a conversation by Bentley, a psychiatrist who is convinced that by hypnotizing a pregnant woman he can create the perfect child. Watling, who is trying to raise funds for his new production, bets the doctor 5,000 pounds that his theory has more holes than Swiss cheese. He then talks his friend Laurent, a struggling actress in her own right, to pose as the pregnant woman and guarantee that he will win. Bentley agrees she is the perfect candidate and begins treatment, but complications arise when doctor and client fall in love. Soon Bentley and his theory are the subject of ridicule, so Laurent decides to help him out by really becoming pregnant. After getting good and soused she storms over to Watling's apartment and demands he have sex with her. Who should arrive at that moment but the good doctor and Watling's fiancee Court. The scam is then brought out into the open, but all ends happily as Laurent and Bentley decide to tie the knot and really try the experiment. Though there is plenty of room within this framework for some pretty witty and farcical situations, nothing ever really pans out to expectations. Jokes and set-ups are formula and old hat. Watling is fun to watch though—his wonderfully comic performance really carries the film.

p, George Fowler, David E. Rose; d, Edward Buzzell; w, Robert E. Kent, Jameson Brewer, Peter Miller, James Kelly (based on the play by Arthur Herzog, Jr., Al Rosen, Muriel Herman); ph, Desmond Dickinson; m, Bruce Campbell; ed, Bernard Gribble; md, Philip Martell; art d, John Blezard, Jim Morahan; m/l, title song, Buzzell, Campbell (sung by Dick James); makeup, Gerry Fletcher.

Comedy **(PR:C MPAA:NR)**

MARY JANE'S PA½** (1935) 70m FN-WB bw (GB: WANDERLUST)

Aline MacMahon *(Ellen Preston)*, Guy Kibbee *(Sam Preston)*, Tom Brown *(King Wagner)*, Robert McWade *(John Wagner)*, Minor Watson *(Kenneth Marvin)*, Nan Gray *(Lucille)*, Johnny Arledge *(Linc Overman)*, Robert Light *(Fred)*, Betty Jean Haney *(Mary Jane)*, Oscar Apfel *(Bailey)*, DeWitt Jennings *(Sheriff)*, Carl Stockdale, Edward McWade, Jack Kennedy, John Hyams, Louis Mason.

After working hard as a printer for most of his life, Kibbee leaves his wife and children to satisfy his urge for wandering. Ten years go by and his wife (MacMahon) has become a powerful local figure, running a large newspaper. She is very bitter towards Kibbee but allows him a job as a household servant so he can be closer to his daughters. In the meantime, local gangsters, out to ruin her, destroy her printing press. Using a hand press, Kibbee helps MacMahon by getting out a special edition of her paper and also manages to melt the hate built up by his absence. Though nothing special, the film has a nice folksy feel to it with naturalistic dialog and some realistic feeling to the characters. The American title was completely misleading as to the nature of the film.

p, Robert Presnell; d, William Keighley; w, Tom Reed, Peter Milne (based on the play by Edith Ellis Furness and the novel by Norman Way); ph, Ernest Haller; ed, Clarence Kolster; art d, Esdras Hartley.

Drama **(PR:A MPAA:NR)**

MARY LOU** (1948) 65m COL bw

Robert Lowery *(Steve Roberts)*, Joan Barton *(Ann Parker)*, Glenda Farrell *(Winnie Winford)*, Abigail Adams *(Mary Lou)*, Frank Jenks *(Mike Connors)*, Emmett Vogan *(Murry Harris)*, Thelma White *(Eve Summers)*, Pierre Watkin *(Airline President)*, Charles Jordan *(Mortimer Cripps)*, Leslie Turner *(Mrs. Harris)*, Chester Clute *(Cheever Chesney)*, Frankie Carle and His Orchestra.

Light post-WW II entertainment features Barton as an airline hostess who wants to be a singer for a band. Problems arise when she and another singer argue over which of them has the rights to the moniker "Mary Lou." Through the usual movie cliches Barton comes out on top. This is simplistic, though aptly acted and directed. Like many features of the day, it was merely a showcase for some big band numbers and musical set pieces. Songs include: "Mary Lou" (J.R. Robinson, Abe Lyman, George Waggner), "Don't Mind My Troubles," "I'm Sorry I Didn't Say I'm Sorry" (Allan Roberts, Lester Lee), "That's Good Enough for Me," "Wasn't It Swell Last Night?" (Roberts, Doris Fisher), "Carle's Boogie" (Frankie Carle), "Learning to Speak English" (Facundo Rivero, Ben Blossner).

p, Sam Katzman; d, Arthur Dreifuss; w, M. Coates Webster; ph, Ira H. Morgan; ed, Viola Lawrence; md, Mischa Bakaleinikoff; art d, Paul Palmentola.

Musical **(PR:A MPAA:NR)**

MARY, MARY ½** (1963) 125m WB c

Debbie Reynolds *(Mary McKellaway)*, Barry Nelson *(Bob McKellaway)*, Diane McBain *(Tiffany Richards)*, Hiram Sherman *(Oscar Nelson)*, Michael Rennie *(Dirk Winston)*.

MARY, MARY is so-so. At over two hours, it's been padded out and there is nothing slower than a comedy where the jokes don't play. Breen's adaptation should have sliced some of the excesses, instead of adding to them. It wasn't much more than a movie of the play and that would have been all right except that the actors seemed to be waiting for laughs. The editing was awful (do we blame LeRoy or Wages?) and they even cut from one person to another in the *middle* of a punch line, a definite no-no. The picture was released while Kerr's play was still making money on the New York stage as well as on tour, and it's a fairly foolproof work in the mouths of the right actors. Nelson is a newly divorced book publisher who is in trouble with the IRS. His attorney, Sherman, states that Nelson has to go through his files and justify some of his expenses or he is going to pay a whopping fee to the government, as he is being audited. Since Nelson has no idea what all the cancelled checks mean, he must call upon his ex-wife, Reynolds, to come back to their home and help him go through the pile of checks. Nelson feels antsy about getting together with Reynolds, but his fiancee, McBain, would like to meet the woman who shed the man she is about to marry. Reynolds arrives and Nelson's wartime pal, Rennie, a waning Hollywood actor, finds her attractive. Reynolds can't get a hotel room in New York, so she must use Nelson's apartment, which is okay because Nelson and McBain are out of town briefly to visit her parents, who want to meet their son-in-law to be. There's a violent snowstorm and Nelson returns unexpectedly to his New York flat where he finds Reynolds and Rennie in a clinch. Rennie exits and Nelson and Reynolds stay up all night talking (and doing one-liner after one-liner) because the weather is so lousy that neither can leave the apartment. After a reconciliation seems hinted at, they fall back into the arguing that caused the divorce in the first place and she announces that she is going down to New Orleans with Rennie. By this time, Nelson realizes that he dearly loves Reynolds and he won't allow her to run off with Rennie, so he locks her in a closet and Rennie leaves for the Crescent City without her. McBain sees that Nelson still loves Reynolds and she graciously departs to allow the two former spouses to work it out. Lots of sexy talk about life, love, and marriage, with rafts of jokes, sometimes a few too many. Anyone not familiar with the publishing and literary establishments won't appreciate all of the inside jokes and the generous salting of real names in the script. Reynolds' character can't resist the wise bon mot, even when faced with a situation that calls for real emotion. The picture made some money, but those wishing to get the full benefit of the story should see the play. It's running *somewhere* at all times.

p&d, Mervyn LeRoy; w, Richard Breen (based on the play by Jean Kerr); ph, Harry Stradling (Technicolor); m, Frank Perkins; ed, David Wages; art d, John Beckman; set d, Ralph S. Hurst; cos, Travilla; makeup, Gordon Bau.

Comedy **(PR:A-C MPAA:NR)**

MARY, MARY, BLOODY MARY* (1975, U.S./Mex.) 101m Translor-Proa c

Cristina Ferrare *(Mary)*, David Young *(Ben Ryder)*, Helena Rojo *(Greta)*, John Carradine *(Mary's Father)*, Arthur Hansel *(U.S. Agent)*, Enrique Lucero *(Mexican Police Lieutenant)*, Susan Kamini *(Hitchhiker)*.

Cover-girl Ferrare (better known as the ex-wife of millionaire John DeLorean) plays a lesbian vampiress who is an artist by day and a neck-stabbing blood drinker by night. Among her victims are an embassy official and both male and female lovers. Carradine, who plays her father, wisely left the picture before production was finished. He was replaced by an extremely unconvincing double. As for Ferrare, her performance at the DeLorean trial was far and away better than the so-called acting she does here. The one saving grace in this film is some imaginative editing and interesting camera work. Otherwise, it's a forgettable bore.

p, Robert Yamin, Henri Bollinger; d, Juan Lopez Moctezuma; w, Malcolm Marmorstein (based on a story by Don Rico, Don Henderson); ph, Miguel Garzon; m, Tom Bahler; ed, Federico Landeras.

Horror **(PR:O MPAA:R)**

MARY NAMES THE DAY (SEE: DR. KILDARE'S WEDDING DAY, 1941)

MARY OF SCOTLAND ½** (1936) 123m RKO bw

Katharine Hepburn *(Mary Stuart)*, Fredric March *(Earl of Bothwell)*, Florence Eldridge *(Elizabeth Tudor)*, Douglas Walton *(Darnley)*, John Carradine *(David Rizzio)*, Robert Barrat *(Morton)*, Gavin Muir *(Leicester)*, Ian Keith *(James Stuart Moray)*, Moroni Olsen *(John Knox)*, William Stack *(Ruthven)*, Ralph Forbes *(Randolph)*, Alan Mowbray *(Throckmorton)*, Frieda Inescort *(Mary Beaton)*, Donald Crisp *(Huntley)*, David Torrence *(Lindsay)*, Molly Lamont *(Mary Livingston)*, Anita Colby *(Mary Fleming)*, *Jean Fenwick (Mary Seton)*, Lionel Pape *(Burghley)*, Alec Craig *(Donal)*, Mary Gordon *(Nurse)*, Monte Blue *(Messenger)*, Leonard Mudie *(Maitland)*, Brandon Hurst *(Arian)*, Wilfred Lucas *(Lexington)*, D'Arcy Corrigan *(Kirkcaldy)*, Frank Baker *(Douglas)*, Cyril McLaglen *(Faudoncide)*, Lionel Belmore *(English Fisherman)*, Doris Lloyd *(Fisherman's Wife)*, Bobby Watson *(His Son)*, Robert Warwick *(Sir Francis Knollys)*, Ivan Simpson, Murray Kinnell, Lawrence Grant, Nigel De Brulier, Barlowe Borland *(Judges)*, Walter Byron *(Sir Francis Walsingham)*, Wyndham Standing *(Sergeant-at-Arms)*, Earle Foxe *(Earl of Kent)*, Paul McAllister *(Du Croche)*, Gaston Glass *(Chatelard)*, Neil Fitzgerald *(Nobleman)*, Jean Kircher, Judith Kircher *(Prince James)*, Robert H. Homans *(Jailer)*.

This version of the well-known story is just slightly better than the remake, mainly because of Hepburn's radiance and March's work as her second husband. Hepburn is Mary and she returns from having grown up and married the late King of France. She is now ready to assume her throne as Queen of Scotland but her arrival sparks fears in the heart of Eldridge, Queen Elizabeth, who is worried that Hepburn might make a claim to her throne. Hepburn marries Walton and takes on March, the Earl of Bothwell, as her protector. Hepburn has a son, James (played by twins Jean and Judith Kircher), and her long-time aide, Carradine, is murdered. Walton sells Hepburn down the river to the Scottish nobles and is, himself, then killed. She marries March amid a wave of angry public comment. March leaves Scotland to keep down a rebellion and Hepburn rules alone until the Scottish peers renege on their vows of protection and Hepburn is put in jail. She escapes, makes her way south to England, and asks Eldridge for help but is tossed in jail and languishes there for 18 years. March dies abroad and Hepburn is sentenced to death for treason. Eldridge will pardon Hepburn if Hepburn signs away her claims to the throne but Hepburn refuses and is executed. They never revealed March's family name in the film because it was Hepburn and the actress is a direct descendant of that family. Helen Hayes played the role on the stage to great success but the film was a financial dud. Ford, who had better luck with male-oriented films, may have been the wrong choice for this basically female movie as it is only March who produces any sort of fire at all. Eldridge and March were married at the time and stayed married for almost 50 years. Ford's direction was interesting and experimental in that he shot Hepburn and Eldridge very differently, with different lighting and widely varying camera angles and a sharp delineation of the background score so we soon know where we are supposed to place our sympathies. Didn't help.

p, Pandro S. Berman; d, John Ford; w, Dudley Nichols (based on the play by Maxwell Anderson); ph, Joseph H. August; m, Max Steiner; ed, Jane Loring; md, Nathaniel Shilkret; art d, Van Nest Polglase, Carroll Clark; set d, Darrell Silvera; cos, Walter Plunkett; spec eff, Vernon L. Walker; makeup, Mel Burns.

Historical Drama **Cas.** **(PR:A MPAA:NR)**

MARY POPPINS***** (1964) 140m Disney/BV c

Julie Andrews *(Mary Poppins)*, Dick Van Dyke *(Bert/Mr. Dawes, Sr.)*, David Tomlinson *(Mr. Banks)*, Glynis Johns *(Mrs. Banks)*, Hermione Baddeley *(Ellen)*, Reta Shaw *(Mrs. Brill)*, Karen Dotrice *(Jane Banks)*, Matthew Garber *(Michael Banks)*, Elsa Lanchester *(Katie Nanna)*, Arthur Treacher *(Constable Jones)*, Reginald Owen *(Adm. Boom)*, Ed Wynn *(Uncle Albert)*, Jane Darwell *(The Bird Woman)*, Arthur Malet *(Mr. Dawes, Jr.)*, Cyril Delevanti *(Mr. Grubbs)*, Lester Matthews *(Mr. Tomes)*, Clive L. Halliday *(Mr. Mousely)*, Donald Barclay *(Mr. Binnacle)*, Marjorie Bennett *(Miss Lark)*, Alma Lawton *(Mrs. Corry)*, Marjorie Eaton *(Miss Persimmon)*, Doris Lloyd *(Depositor)*, Maj. Sam Harris *(Citizen)*, James Logan.

MARY POPPINS is as perfect a film musical as anyone would ever care to see. It was also the most inventive musical written for the screen in the 1960s and the timelessness of the story and the excellence of the performance will assure the Disney studio of re-releases well into the next century. The blend of live action and animation is flawless and the tunes by the Sherman brothers are each, in their own way, gems that never stop the story for their own sake. It's a magical film and, at 2 hours and 20 minutes, one would think that little tykes would tire of it but that is not the case at all because it is unceasingly charming and whimsical. Based on the books by P. L. Travers, screenwriters Walsh and DaGradi have concocted a superb script that captures all the charm of those books and condenses several incidents into one cohesive screenplay. Tomlinson is a London banker who takes out an advertisement in the *London Times* newspaper for a nanny. Johns, Tomlinson's wife, an early advocate of women's rights, cannot seem to find anyone who is disciplinarian enough to take care of their two obstreperous children, Garber and Dotrice. The Tomlinson children have differing ideas as to the kind of nanny they wish and so they write their own ad but their father finds it, tears it up, and burns it in the fireplace. However, the pieces miraculously come together and go up the flue. Next day, many prospective nannies arrive but a mysterious wind blows them all away before they can interview. Enter Andrews, who glides down from on high with a magical umbrella as her parachute. She meets Tomlinson and agrees to take the job. Garber and Dotrice are incurably messy and Andrews uses her magical abilities (and a song) to get them to straighten up their quarters. Next, she takes them for a walk where they meet Van Dyke, a chimney sweep with a penchant for art. Van Dyke has drawn a picture on the sidewalk and it becomes real as the four of them enter that world, play and dance with animated penguins who serve them tea, leap aboard a carousel where the horses seem to have minds of their own, dash across the countryside and, in general, have a wonderful time. Then the rain begins to fall and they must get out of the picture Van Dyke drew or be stuck in that land forever.

They barely make it and get home, flushed with the excitement of a beautiful experience. Next day, Andrews takes Garber and Dotrice to meet her eccentric uncle, Wynn, who loves nothing more than laughing and when he guffaws, he becomes lighter-than-air and floats to the ceiling. He invites Andrews, Garber, and Dotrice to join him up there; they begin laughing and rise like human balloons. When the children tell their father these incredible tales, it goes without saying that he will not believe one syllable of them. He would like to sack Andrews but she charms him out of those thoughts, then suggests that his children might enjoy knowing exactly what it is he does for a living so Tomlinson agrees to take the children to the bank. That night, Andrews sings to Garber and Dotrice about the bird woman who sits outside the institution selling bird feed for two pence a bag. At the bank in the morning, Tomlinson wants Garber to start his thrift pattern by opening an account with his tuppence but the boy, impressed by bird woman Darwell, would prefer to feed the birds with his money. There's a disagreement with Malet, the bank's chairman, and suddenly, a run on the tellers' windows begins. Crowds start to race for their money and the children run out. Later, they are in a dark and dreary section of the city where they are found by Van Dyke, covered in soot. He takes them across the London rooftops and explains to them, in song and dance, about the life he happily leads. Tomlinson is fired that night for what happened earlier and he undergoes a transformation as he realizes that he had run his household like a martinet and his family may have suffered for his preciseness and detached air. He tells the bank's directors where to go and exits. The next day, he comes out of the house's basement where he has spent the entire night mending a kite the children had broken a few days before. Garber and Dotrice are thrilled by his new attitude and they all run to the local park to fly the repaired kite. Satisfied that she had united the family, Andrews leaves to find some other family that needs her services. The picture ends as Andrews flies away. There is so much fun in this movie that one hardly knows where to begin detailing it. Johns, as the suffragette mother, is delicious and some of the sight gags are priceless. When Tomlinson is stripped of his rank at the bank, he slams a hole in his bowler, then turns his umbrella inside out, both symbols of his position and status in the banking world. The production design and the animation-live action sequences are nothing short of breathtaking. There are those carpers who say it was MY FAIR LADY for tiny tots and that the Sherman score sounded derivative of that play, both of which took place in roughly the same time frame in the same locale. Don't believe it. Whereas MY FAIR LADY (the film) was sometimes laborious, MARY POPPINS flies like the wind and never flags for an instant. There is much technical wizardry in the film but that never gets in the way of the essential humanity of the story. It could have been a sticky sweet goo if someone else had gotten his mitts on it, but Disney oversaw the production and director Stevenson handled the multi-faceted story so well that it never became cutesy for the sake of cutesiness. MARY POPPINS was nominated for 13 Academy Awards and won in only five categories. Best Actress, Best Film Editing, Best Original Score, Best Song ("Chim Chim Cheree"), and Best Special Visual Effects. A fitting and ironic twist came when Audrey Hepburn, who was chosen over Andrews to play the MY FAIR LADY film role that Andrews originated on Broadway, was not even nominated for the Best Actress award, although MY FAIR LADY did get eight Oscars that year. MARY POPPINS was Disney's crowning achievement in a life that had already seen him win more Oscars than any other person in the history of films. There are many set-pieces in the film which could stand on their own as superb shorts, without ever knowing what the rest of the movie was about. Cases in point are the dance on the London rooftops, the "Feed The Birds" segment and, of course, the sequence of the quartet walking into a sidewalk drawing. Be aware that you need not be a child to appreciate this. It's always nice to have a youngster at your side, just to see the face light up. But your face may also light up as you watch this movie. Special plaudits to the people who cast the film as there is not a mistake in it. Treacher plays a constable (nice to see him out of his butler uniform), Baddeley is the Cockney maid, and Owen is very funny as the retired admiral who lives in a "ship-shape" house that is furnished like a ship. Despite being on land, he continues to fire a cannon to signify the hour of 6 p.m., an old sea tradition that he will not shed. When they make the list of the greatest children's movies ever made, this will probably tie with THE WIZARD OF OZ for the top spot. One major element that makes this film hum is the songs. The Sherman brothers had been longtime Disney contract writers and they reached their pinnacle with this score. Songs by the brothers include: "Supercalifragilistic-expialidocious" (the longest one-word title tune is sung by Andrews and Van Dyke), "Chim Chim Cheree" (sung by Van Dyke), "A Spoonful of Sugar" (sung by Andrews) "The Perfect Nanny" (sung by Dotrice and Garber), "Sister Suffragette" (sung by Johns), "The Life I Lead" (sung by Tomlinson), "Stay Awake" (sung by Andrews, Van Dyke, and Wynn), "Feed the Birds" (sung by Andrews), "Fidelity, Feduciary Bank" (sung by Van Dyke and Tomlinson), "Let's Go Fly a Kite" (sung by Johns and Tomlinson), "Jolly Holliday" (sung by Van Dyke and Andrews), "I Love to Laugh" (sung by Van Dyke, Andrews, and Wynn), "Step in Time" (sung by Van Dyke), and "A Man Has Dreams" (sung by Van Dyke and Tomlinson). Many, many years have passed since this film was first released and we think it's time for a sequel because Andrews is in her middle years, about the age the novelist saw the original Mary Poppins.

p, Walt Disney, Bill Walsh; d, Robert Stevenson; w, Walsh, Don DaGradi (based on the *Mary Poppins* books by P. L. Travers); ph, Edward Colman (Technicolor); m, Irwin Kostal: ed, Cotton Warburton; art d, Carroll Clark, William H. Tuntke; set d, Emile Kuri, Hal Gausman; cos, Tony Walton; spec eff, Peter Ellenshaw, Eustace Lycett, Robert A. Mattey; ch, Marc Breaux, Dee Dee Woods; makeup, Pat McNalley; animation d, Hamilton S. Luske; animation art d, McLaren Stewart; animators, Milt Kahl, Ollie Johnston, John Lounsbery, Hal Ambro, Frank Thomas, Ward Kimball, Eric Larson, Cliff Nordberg, Jack Boyd.

Musical/Comedy **Cas.** **(PR:AAA MPAA:NR)**

MARY, QUEEN OF SCOTS** (1971, Brit.) 128m UNIV c

Vanessa Redgrave *(Mary, Queen of Scots)*, Glenda Jackson *(Queen Elizabeth)*, Patrick McGoohan *(James Stuart)*, Timothy Dalton *(Henry, Lord Darnley)*, Nigel Davenport *(Lord Bothwell)*, Trevor Howard *(William Cecil)*, Daniel Massey *(Robert Dudley, Earl of Leicester)*, Ian Holm *(David Riccio)*, Andrew Keir *(Ruthven)*, Tom Fleming *(Father Ballard)*, Katherine Kath *(Catherine de Medici)*, Beth Harris *(Mary Seton)*, Frances White *(Mary Fleming)*, Bruce Purchase *(Morton)*, Brian Coburn *(Huntly)*, Vernon Dobtcheff *(Duc de Guise)*, Raf De La Terre *(Cardinal de Guise)*, Richard Warner *(Walsingham)*, Maria Aitken *(Lady Bothwell)*, Jeremy Bulloch *(Andrew)*, Robert James *(John Knox)*, Richard Denning *(Francis, King of France)*.

Everyone who enjoyed Hal Wallis' production of ANNE OF THE THOUSAND DAYS and, to a greater extent, his BECKET, eagerly awaited this film and was disappointed by the results of another look backward at British history. Although Queen Elizabeth and Queen Mary never did meet in real life, the decision was made to give them some confrontations in the picture (art was not only imitating life, it was replacing and rewriting it). The story had been told before in a 1936 RKO film, MARY OF SCOTLAND, that starred Katharine Hepburn, was directed by John Ford, and adapted by Dudley Nichols from Maxwell Anderson's play. They should have left it there for, although this was sumptuous and opulent, it was essentially empty. When but 9 months old the child is named queen, then raised in France by her mother's Catholic family in the middle 1500s. At 16, Redgrave marries Denning, the boy King of France, but he dies soon afterwards and her mother-in-law, Kath, thinks she is responsible for the young king's demise. Just as Kath is about to banish Redgrave, her royal emissary, Davenport, arrives with the news that her half-brother, McGoohan (a Protestant), has asked for her to return and take the mantle as Queen of Scotland since her mother has died. McGoohan, however, wants the crown for himself and is in cahoots with the British Queen Elizabeth (Jackson). Redgrave decides to take the position as Queen of Scotland and sails over from France. Jackson will not allow the group in England and will not guarantee them a safe journey so Redgrave, et al., must go directly to Scotland. There they are greeted by religious prejudice from the Calvinists, led by James, and a barrage of hostility from all the other Protestants, for Redgrave is, after all, a Catholic. Redgrave is quickly ensconced on the throne and shows herself to be a sober and intelligent queen, something that Jackson and McGoohan never expected. They must act fast before she solidifies her hold on the people of Scotland. Jackson sends Massey, a charming commoner who is in great favor at court, to woo Redgrave. Jackson agrees to sign a succession document to the British throne if Redgrave marries Massey. Just in case Redgrave finds the Protestant Massey not to her liking, Jackson includes dissolute and apparently bisexual Dalton, a Catholic, in the traveling party. Things go awry when she chooses the debauched Dalton over the dashing Massey and marries him, in total disagreement with her advisors. Dalton's plans include taking over as king but Redgrave is too smart for her husband so Dalton contacts McGoohan and they conspire to take the life of the one man who has Redgrave's ear, her aide, Holm. Redgrave is now pregnant by Dalton and she manages to escape, with the help of Davenport, after Holm is murdered. Davenport leads a force against the rebels and defeats them, then Dalton, who is suffering from syphilis, is killed by angry Protestant nobles who hope to pin the rap for the murder on Davenport, already a suspect in Dalton's death because it is obvious that he is in love with Redgrave and has recently annulled his own marriage to marry her. Davenport eventually is cleared of suspicion but he has to leave Scotland to go to Europe where he dies, insane, in a prison in Denmark. Now without her husband, Davenport, Redgrave is forced to abdicate in favor of her baby son. Redgrave goes to England and meets with Jackson, asking for help. She is betrayed by Jackson and tossed into jail where she spends the next 18 years. Redgrave continues trying to escape and rally her Catholic supporters, who would like to see Jackson dead, and this causes Jackson to insist that Redgrave renounce her actions and her followers or be executed. Redgrave will not and she is rewarded for her stand by having her head separated from her body on Feb. 8, 1587, at Fotheringay Castle. (Note . . . Fotheringay is the name H. G. Wells gave to his lead character in THE MAN WHO COULD WORK MIRACLES.) The film was nominated for five Oscars: Best Actress (Redgrave), Best Sound, Best Costumes, Best Score, and Best Art Direction, but it won none of those. The picture is long, beautiful, and dull.

p, Hal B. Wallis; d, Charles Jarrott; w, John Hale; ph, Christopher Challis (Panavision, Technicolor); m, John Barry; ed, Richard Marden; prod d, Terence Marsh; md, Barry; art d, Robert Cartwright; set d, Peter Howitt, Pamela Cornell; cos, Margaret Furse; makeup, George Frost.

Historical Drama **(PR:A-C MPAA:GP)**

MARY RYAN, DETECTIVE** (1949) 68m COL bw

Marsha Hunt *(Mary Ryan)*, John Litel *(Capt. Billings)*, June Vincent *(Estelle Byron)*, Harry Shannon *(Sawyer)*, William "Bill" Phillips *(Joey Gunney)*, Katharine Warren *(Mrs. Sawyer)*, Victoria Horne *(Wilma Hall)*, Arthur Space *(Mike Faber)*, John Dehner *(Belden)*, Kernan Cripps *(Riley)*, Chester Clute *(Chester Wiggin)*, Clancy Cooper *(McBride)*, Robert B. Williams *(Tom Cooper)*, Doreen McCann *(Patsy Hall)*, Ben Welden *(Sammy)*, Paul Bryar *(Chuck)*, Jim Nolan *(Johnson)*, Charles Russell *(Baker)*, Isabel Randolph *(Mrs. Simpson)*, Robert Emmett Keane *(Munsell)*, Jimmy Lloyd *(Gordon)*, Ralph Dunn *(Parker)*, Edward F. Dunn *(MacDougal)*.

A routine detective story with the female sleuth as a plot twist. Hunt is on the trail of a fencer of stolen goods. She gets herself arrested in order to gain the confidence of a notorious shoplifter and is then able to obtain the address of the top man's hideout and puts him under arrest. The plot is strictly formula with standard acting and production values. Hunt is a little too perky for her role and it's difficult to swallow her as a hard-boiled detective.

p, Rudolph C. Flothow; d, Abby Berlin; w, George Bricker (based on a story by Harry Fried); ph, Vincent Farrar; m, Mischa Bakaleinikoff; ed, James Sweeney; md, Bakaleinikoff; art d, George Brooks.

Crime **(PR:C MPAA:NR)**

MARY STEVENS, M.D.**

(1933) 72m WB bw

Kay Francis (Mary Stevens, M.D.), Lyle Talbot (Don Andrews), Glenda Farrell (Glenda), Thelma Todd (Lois Rising), Una O'Connor (Mrs. Simmons), Charles Wilson (Walter Rising), Hobart Cavanaugh (Alf Simmons), Harold Huber (Tony), George Cooper (Pete), John Marston (Dr. Lane), Christian Rub (Gus), Reginald Mason (Hospital Superintendent), Walter Walker (Dr. Clark), Ann Hovey (Miss Gordon), Constantine Romanoff (Dynamite Schultz), Wilfred Lucas (Barry), Lloyd Ingraham (Ship's Captain), Harry Seymour (Ship's Officer), Wallace MacDonald (Purser), Harry C. Myers (Nervous Patient), Grace Hayle (Wealthy Lady), Ed Gargan (Cop), Sid Miller (Nussbaum).

Francis is a woman physician having an affair with her alcoholic colleague, Talbot. She becomes pregnant and goes to Paris to have her baby and avoid a scandal, but on her way back to America, the baby dies of infantile paralysis. She manages, however, to save the lives of two other children on the same ocean liner she's aboard and, upon returning, finds that Talbot has divorced his wife so that he can marry her. A real soaper and fairly lurid but, for its time, quite bold. The death of her illegitimate child and the marriage between Francis and Talbot were both undoubtedly devices aimed at pleasing the censors of the day. The film is an interesting reflection on the Hollywood attitudes and the studio attempts to be daring within censorable reason. Production values were adequate, though the direction tended to emphasize the "juicier" aspects of the screenplay.

p, Hal B. Wallis; d, Lloyd Bacon; w, Rian James, Robert Lord (based on the novel by Virginia Kellogg); ph, Sid Hickox; ed, Ray Curtiss; md, Leo F. Forbstein; cos, Orry-Kelly.

Drama (PR:A MPAA:NR)

MARYA-ISKUSNITSA

(SEE: MAGIC WEAVER, THE, 1965, USSR)

MARYJANE*

(1968) 95m AIP c

Fabian (Phil Blake), Diane McBain (Ellie Holden), Kevin Coughlin (Jordan Bates), Michael Margotta (Jerry Blackburn), Patty McCormack (Susan Hoffman), Russ Bender (Harry Braxton), Booth Colman (Maynard Parlow), Baynes Barron (Police Chief Otis Mosley), Henry Hunter (Mayor Arthur Ford), Phil Vandervort (Herbie Mueller), Ivan Bonar (Roger Campbell), Robert Lipton (Dick Marsh), Byron Morrow (Judge), Ward Ramsey (Mr. Blackburn), Frank Alesia (Frenchy), Bruce Mars (Toby), Steve Cory (Chuck Poe), Harold Ayer (Minister), Linda Cooper (Linda), Ronnie Dayton (George), Terri Garr (Terri), Jo Ann Harris (Jo Ann), Hilaric Thompson (Tillurie), David Meo (Ben), Wayne Heffley (Ice Cream Company Manager), Dodie Warren (Angela), Carl Gottlieb (Larry Kane), Peter Madsen (Kirby), Garry Marshall (Service Station Attendant), Joe E. Ross (Mr. Reardon), Floyd Mutrux (Ollie), Helen Steussloff (Waitress), Perry Cook (Shop Owner), Linda Sue Risk (Little Girl), Dick Gautier, Peter Marshall.

In this attempt to make a sort of REEFER MADNESS for the 1960s, washed-up pop star Fabian plays a high school art teacher who discovers that some of his students are actually "turning on" with the demon weed! Since he himself admitted to "trying" marijuana once in college, he knows what dangers the kids are in for. Margotta is a sensitive student lured into a "maryjane" party by bad kid Coughlin. McBain is another teacher at the school that Fabian is attracted to until she is discovered as the main dope supplier for the school. She's also a firm believer in extended learning, and has given some of the male students first-hand lessons in their sex education. Ultimately the good are rewarded and the bad are punished in this classic example of the "so-bad-it's-good" genre. The hokey and socially backward script is by the unlikely team of "Hollywood Squares" host Marshall, and Gautier, the C.O.N.T.R.O.L. robot of TV's "Get Smart." They both have bit parts as well. Don't miss an early screen appearance by Garr as one of the turned-on school kids. McCormack, who played the little girl in the BAD SEED, is all grown up here as the girl friend of the tough drug pusher. Although Alesia receives screen credit for the role of "Frenchy" some sources claim the role was played by Tom Nolan. It is interesting to note that the producers took themselves very seriously in this poorly made camp piece. Material sent out to theaters suggested special screenings for local clergymen, so as to inspire some anti-drug sermons.

p&d, Maury Dexter; w, Richard Gautier, Peter Marshall (based on a story by Dexter); ph, Richard Moore (Pathecolor); m, Mike Curb, Lawrence Brown; ed, Sidney Levin; art d, Paul Sylos; set d, Harry Reif; makeup, Bob Mark.

Drama (PR:O MPAA:NR)

MARYLAND**

(1940) 92m FOX c

Walter Brennan (William Stewart), Fay Bainter (Charlotte Danfield), Brenda Joyce (Linda), John Payne (Lee Danfield), Charles Ruggles (Dick Piper), Hattie McDaniel (Hattie), Marjorie Weaver (Georgie Tomlin), Sidney Blackmer (Spencer Danfield), Ben Carter (Shadrach), Ernest Whitman (Dogface), Paul Harvey (Buckman), Robert Lowery (Tom Bolton), Spencer Charters (Judge), Ed Thorgersen (Announcer), Stanley Andrews (Doctor), Erville Alderson (Diggs), Frank Thomas (Veterinarian), Cliff Clark (Sheriff), Grace Hayle (Mrs. Carrington), William B. Davidson (John Addison), Clarence Muse (Rev. Bitters), Mme. Sultewan (Naomi), Bobby Anderson (Lee Danfield, Age 7), Dickie Jones (Lee Danfield, Age 11), Patsy Lou Barber (Linda, Age 5), George Reed (Uncle Henry), Zack Williams (Fields), Darby Jones (Aleck), Mildred Gover (Polly), Thaddeus Jones (Brother Moses), Arie Lee Branche (Maybelle), Clinton Rosemond (Brother Dickey), Gladden James (Court Clerk), Edward Fielding (Chairman), E. E. Olive, Helen Koford [Terry Moore], Jesse Graves, Floyd Shackelford, Olive Ball, Charles Moore.

After her husband is killed during a fox hunt, Bainter sends her son off to school in Europe and sells the family stables. When son Payne returns, he meets Brennan, his father's former trainer, and falls in love with his two horses as well as Brennan's daughter Joyce. After entering and winning the Maryland Hunt, Payne succeeds in melting his mother's prejudices and phobias towards horses. Though a formula plot,

the film is lushly photographed in Technicolor and tells some factual information about Maryland's history. The acting is fine, despite the weaknesses in the script. Carter plays a comic black stable groom in a rousing revival meeting that is one of the film's highlights. Though this was considered entertaining and insightful in its time, today the scene reflects the prejudices of racism of Hollywood during the 1930s and 40s.

p, Darryl F. Zanuck, Gene Markey; d, Henry King; w, Ethel Hill, Jack Andrews; ph, George Barnes, Ray Rennahan, Natalie Kalmus; m, Alfred Newman; ed, Barbara McLean; md, Newman; art d, Richard Day, Wiard Ihnen.

Drama (PR:A MPAA:NR)

MAS ALLA DE LAS MONTANAS

(SEE: DESPERATE ONES, THE, 1968, U.S./Span.)

MASCULINE FEMININE****

(1966, Fr./Swed.) 103m Anouchka-Argos-Svensk-Sandrews/Royal bw (MASCULIN FEMININ)

Jean-Pierre Leaud (Paul), Chantal Goya (Madeleine), Marlene Jobert (Elisabeth), Michel Deborb (Robert), Catherine-Isabelle Duport (Catherine), Eva-Britt Strandberg (Lavinia), Birger Malmsten (Actor), Elsa Leroy (Miss 19), Francoise Hardy (Woman with the American Officer), Chantal Darget (Woman on Metro), Brigitte Bardot, Antoine Bourseiller (Themselves).

This was Godard's inquiry into the generation he refers to as the "children of Marx and Coca-Cola," the 1960s youth culture. Leaud is a confused young romantic in search of perfect love. He meets pop singer Goya in a cafe, and eventually they move in together. Leaud deals with his changing attitudes by taking a job for a market research firm, gathering data, and interviewing people such as a young woman voted "Miss 19." While Goya pursues her singing career, Leaud tries to co-exist with her and her two roommates, Jobert and Duport. Eventually Goya becomes pregnant and Leaud, in what appears to be an accident, falls from an apartment window. Leaud's character is practically an extension of the Antoine Doinel character created by Francois Truffaut. He even adopts the name Doinel at one point in the film. Here Leaud's reason for living is love, but this notion becomes difficult in a detached and increasingly consumer-oriented society. With MASCULINE FEMININE Godard began a steady string of political pictures which led to his eventually self-imposed exile from commercial cinema. His interest in the synthesis of fiction and documentary is in full gear with this picture, often devoting long static shots of people being interviewed, his method of bringing to the screen a chronicle of Parisian youth in the winter of 1965. Ironically, however, the picture was banned in France for those under 18, striking somewhat of a blow to Godard's intentions. The final product bore so little resemblance to the originals by de Maupassant that his publishers dissolved the contract they had made with Argos. The only trace of de Maupassant is in a short scene in which his material takes the form of the film the characters are seeing. This is one of Godard's most masterful pictures, which is simultaneously charming and innovative.

d&w, Jean-Luc Godard (based on the stories "The Signal" and "Paul's Mistress" by Guy de Maupassant); ph, Willy Kurant; m, Francis Lai, Jean-Jacques Debout; ed, Agnes Guillemot, Marguerite Renoir.

Drama Cas. (PR:C-O MPAA:NR)

MASK, THE* 1/2

(1961, Can.) 83m Taylor-Roffman/WB (AKA: EYES OF HELL; THE SPOOKY MOVIE SHOW) bw

Paul Stevens (Dr. Allan Barnes), Claudette Nevins (Pamela Albright), Bill Walker (Lt. Martin), Anne Collings (Jill Goodrich), Martin Lavut (Michael Randin), Leo Leyden (Dr. Soames), Eleanor Beecroft (Mrs. Kelly), William Bryden (Anderson), Norman Ettlinger (Prof. Quincy), Stephen Appleby (Museum Guide), Ray Lawlor (Lab Technician), Jim Moran (Himself), Nancy Island (Girl Who Is Killed), Rudy Linschoten (Dr. Barnes' Alter Ego), Paul Nevins (Demon of the Mask).

Archeologist Lavut pays a visit to psychiatrist Stevens and explains that he's found a ceremonial mask inhabited by evil spirits that force the wearer to commit murder. Stevens laughs off his guest who leaves and commits suicide. Shortly thereafter, Stevens receives the mask in his mail, and then the fun really begins. This not-so-scary horror film has one great gimmick going for it. After Stevens dons his mask, viewers are told to "Put the mask on—now!" An obedient audience member would then put on a pair of 3-D glasses and watch special "Depth Dimension 3-D" sequences where the unspeakable acts occur. Among the hallucinations are assorted ghouls sacrificing a beautiful woman on an altar, and another creature rowing a coffin-like boat through a sea of mist. After Stevens attempts to attack his fiancee the mask is finally restored to its rightful place in a museum, only to attract the attention of another museum visitor. Is this the end? We can only hope so. Despite the unique audience-participation gimmick, this is a fairly uninspired horror film. The plot is full of gaping holes that simply can't be covered and a lot of loose ends are never explained at the climax. Lot's of gore in the 3-D sequences, and there's no suspenseful buildup. Despite its poor box office returns, this somehow gets re-released periodically.

p&d, Julian Roffman; w, Frank Taubes, Sandy Haber, Slavko Vorkapich; ph, Herbert S. Alpert; m, Louis Applebaum; ed, Stephen Timar, Robert Schulte; art d, David S. Ballou, Hugo Wuehtrich; spec eff, Herman Townsley, James Gordon; ch, Don Gillies.

Horror (PR:O MPAA:NR)

MASK OF DIIJON, THE* 1/2

(1946) 73m PRC bw

Erich von Stroheim (Diijon), Jeanne Bates (Victoria), William Wright (Tony Holiday), Edward Van Sloan (Sheffield), Mauritz Hugo (Danton), Denise Vernac

(Denise), Robert Malcolm *(Fleming)*, Hope Landin *(Mrs. McGaffey)*, Shimen Ruskin *(Guzzo)*, Roy Darmour *(Mark Lindsay)*, Antonio Filauri *(Alex)*.

Erich von Stroheim was one of the most gifted directors in the early days of movies, but after spending more money than anyone in his quest for authenticity, he could not get any directorial assignments, and so he earned what little living he could as an actor. He was an imposing performer, solid, stolid, with a "presence" that jumped off the screen even in the most minor films, such as this. He's a mad magician who lives in a sleazy boarding house that caters to acts who can only aspire to be third-rate as they are someplace around sixth-rate. Bates is married to von Stroheim and works as his assistant. Wright is a pianist who adores Bates, although he won't make an overt move on her. Van Sloan owns a magic store and he and Bates have concocted an interesting guillotine act which they show to von Stroheim, who disdains it and says that he is now about to try something new, hypnosis. Wright and Bates have been "friends" long before she married von Stroheim and he's come back to the boarding house run by Landin. The couple have no money, so they take a job at Filauri's tacky nightclub, but von Stroheim, who is out of practice, goofs and his wife falls when he attempts to place her, rigid, between two chairs. Wright is blamed for this and von Stroheim becomes insanely jealous and wrongly believes Bates and Wright are having an affair. After practicing his hypnosis, von Stroheim tests out his theories by making Hugo, a dancer, kill himself. Bates gets a job singing at the club and von Stroheim arrives one night to watch her, then hypnotizes her into killing Wright, which she almost does while singing a song to his accompaniment. But she's taken the wrong gun and the several shots she fires at Wright are all blanks. Cops snare von Stroheim in Van Sloan's cellar magic store, toss a few tear gas cannisters in, and the bald Teuton trips and is decapitated by the trick guillotine seen earlier when the house cat unties the cords that let the blade fall on von Stroheim's bull neck. Except for von Stroheim, the acting was barely adequate. Anyone familiar with von Stroheim's directorial work (and the films of Lew Landers, who specialized in these Poverty Row pictures) will recognize the German's touch in several of the scenes—an attempt to elevate a somber story into something with style. Vernac was von Stroheim's longtime live-in lover during his waning years and he, no doubt, used some influence to get her the job of Hugo's wife. One could always sense the seething under von Stroheim's sour countenance. It was either due to a bad stomach or the hatred of a town that turned against him.

p, Max Alexander, Alfred Stern; d, Lew Landers; w, Arthur St. Claire, Griffin Jay (based on a story by St. Claire); ph, Jack Greenhalgh; ed, Roy Livingston; md, Lee Zahler; art d, Edward Jewell; m/l, "White Roses," Carroll K. Cooper, Zahler (sung by Jeanne Bates), "Disillusion," Lou E. Zoeller, Billy Austin (sung by Bates).

Drama **(PR:A-C MPAA:NR)**

MASK OF DIMITRIOS, THE***** (1944) 95m WB bw

Sydney Greenstreet *(Mr. Peters)*, Zachary Scott *(Dimitrios)*, Faye Emerson *(Irana Preveza)*, Peter Lorre *(Cornelius Latimer Leyden)*, George Tobias *(Fedor Muishkin)*, Victor Francen *(Wladislaw Grodek)*, Steven Geray *(Bulic)*, Florence Bates *(Mme. Chavez)*, Eduardo Ciannelli *(Marukakis)*, Kurt Katch *(Col. Haki)*, Marjorie Hoshelle *(Anna Bulic)*, Georges Metaxa *(Hans Werner)*, John Abbott *(Mr. Pappas)*, Monte Blue *(Dhris Abdul)*, David Hoffman *(Konrad)*, Philip Rock, Rita Holland, Rola Stewart *(People on Beach)*, Georges Renavent *(Fisherman)*, Peter Helmers *(Reporter)*, Lal Chand Mehra, Jules Molnar, Walter Palm *(Servants)*, Pedro Regas *(Morgue Attendant)*, Nino Pipitone *(Hotel Clerk)*, Eddie Hyans, Antonio Filauri, Alfred Paix, Saul Gorss *(Men)*, Frank Lackteen *(Officer in Smyrna)*, Nick Thompson *(Porter)*, Hella Crossley *(Hostess)*, Carmen D'Antonio *(Nightclub Dancer)*, Fred Essler *(Bostoff)*, John Bleifer *(Coach Driver)*, Albert Van Antwerp *(Landlord)*, Edgar Licho *(Cafe Proprietor)*, Michael Visaroff, Louis Mercier *(Policemen)*, Felix Basch *(Vaxoff)*, Leonid Snegoff *(Stambulisky)*, Gregory Golubeff *(Doorkeeper)*, Carl Neubert *(Secretary)*, Lotte Palfi *(Receptionist)*, John Mylong *(Druhar)*, May Landa *(Flower Girl)*, Alphonse Martell *(Croupier)*, Ray de Ravenne *(Taxi Driver)*, Marek Windheim *(Hotel Clerk)*, Charles Andre *(Conductor)*, Vince Barnett *(Cafe Customer)*.

One of the great *film noir* classics to come out of the 1940s, THE MASK OF DIMITRIOS boasts no superstars, just uniformly fine talents, a stupendous script full of intrigue, surprises, and subtle turns, and Negulesco's exciting and innovative direction. It's an edge-of-the-seat thriller all the way. Lorre, who really stars here, though he received fourth billing, even after Scott whose film debut this was, is a Dutch mystery writer vacationing in Istanbul. At a party he meets one of his most ardent fans, Katch, head of the secret police, who tells him that the body of arch criminal Dimitrios Makropoulous (Scott), a man he has sought for years, has washed up on the nearby beach, murdered, stabbed to death. What fascinates Lorre about the dead man is Katch's obsession with Scott, a man who practiced "murder, treason, and betrayal" as a way of life, one Katch has never seen until dead. Katch piques Lorre's morbid curiosity to the point where the writer accompanies the police chief to the morgue to view the body. Following this grim visit, Lorre decides to write a novel about the sinister Scott and begins to delve into the criminal's sordid past. In his search for the real Scott, Lorre travels through the Balkans—through Smyrna, Athens, Sofia, Belgrade, and finally to Paris. "What is it about a man like that?" Lorre asks Katch at the beginning of his quest. "Why does anyone trust him in the first place?" While Lorre books passage, portly, calculating Greenstreet enters Lorre's Istanbul hotel, picks up a paper announcing the discovery of Scott's body, and crushes the newspaper angrily. On the train to Sofia, Greenstreet suddenly joins Lorre in his compartment. The fat man ingratiates himself to Lorre, telling him as he settles back on the train couch opposite the pensive Lorre: "There's not enough kindness in the world. If only men would live as brothers without hatred, seeing only the beautiful things, but no, there are always people who look on the black side." Lorre goes to sleep while Greenstreet eyes him over a book he is reading, one entitled: *Pearls of Everyday Wisdom.* When the train reaches Sofia, Greenstreet recommends a hotel where Lorre will be comfortable. In Sofia, Ciannelli, a journalist friend of Lorre's, takes him to a murky, smoky cabaret run by Emerson, once Scott's lover. She tells him, after some reluctance, about how Scott, down and out in Sofia, starving in an apartment next to hers without being able to pay the rent, observed her as she alighted from a carriage with a wealthy merchant at her side. Shown in flashback to 1923, Scott begs some food from Emerson and also borrows some money. He promises to pay her back and does, with interest. Scott is now well-dressed and admits that he blackmailed Emerson's merchant-lover for the money. She falls in love with Scott who promises her jewels and furs, a fine apartment. At dinner, police pick Scott up for questioning when they identify him as a member of a Bulgarian patriotic society. Later he is shown with a rich patron from whom he seeks more money, and is turned down, for an unspecified chore. Later, a diplomat is assassinated (in a rainy scene reminiscent of the assassination shown in Alfred Hitchcock's FOREIGN CORRESPONDENT). Scott takes refuge in Emerson's apartment, telling his lover to lie to police should they come, that she is to say he's been with her all day. She does. Then he leaves, after taking almost all her money, promising to pay her back. He vanishes and she never again sees him or the money. It's back to the present and Lorre departs the club, returning to his hotel room which he finds ransacked. The fat man is present; Greenstreet holds a gun on him and asks him to close the door. Alarmed, Lorre tells him: "I can only conclude that you're a thief or you're drunk." Greenstreet sits down with a smug smile on his face and tells him that he is interested in Scott and wants to know what Lorre has learned about the evildoer. When he learns that Lorre has seen the body of Scott in the Turkish mortuary, Greenstreet becomes confused. He tells Lorre that he should not go to Belgrade, that he will find out nothing and will get into trouble with the authorities. He tells him that Francen, a rich and powerful political intriguer in Geneva, will help him and he proposes an alliance to determine the reality of Scott's death. He tells Lorre that, after he sees Francen, he should travel to Paris to see him and promises some spoils, a half million French francs, which "will buy a lot of good things." Lorre goes to Geneva where Francen, a retired master spy, tells him how Scott was employed by him to obtain military secrets in Yugoslavia for Italy in 1926. In a flashback to Belgrade Scott is shown befriending Geray, a clerk in the government. He allows Geray to win large amounts in fixed games but then arranges for him to lose an enormous amount of money. Scott tells Geray that he will make good his debts only if he steals the new secret plans for the minefields of the Otranto Strait. To stave off ruination and save his sluttish wife disgrace, Geray complies but later commits suicide. Scott, moreover, steals the plans from Francen and sells them elsewhere. In another flash forward, Lorre, now thoroughly disgusted with the truth about the conniving Scott, goes to Paris to see Greenstreet who is living in a lavish apartment hidden away in a deserted building. There Greenstreet tells Lorre exactly what piece of information he possesses that is worth a half million French francs, his own memory of what the dead man in Istanbul looked like. Greenstreet tells Lorre that he was part of a smuggling ring which Scott betrayed and that the dead man found in Instanbul was another member of the ring, Konstantin Gollos, and Scott is very much alive. Greenstreet intends to blackmail Scott, who murdered Gollos and passed the body off as his own, using Lorre as the man who can identify the dead man and Scott as not being one and the same. The price tag is one million francs. Scott later delivers the money but attempts to kill both Greenstreet and Lorre. He wounds Greenstreet but Lorre knocks the gun out of his hands and Greenstreet picks it up. Lorre, at Greenstreet's request, steps outside, while Scott begs: Come back! Or do you want this carrion to kill me?" A shot rings out and Scott is killed. Police arrive at Lorre's summons, and Greenstreet steps outside, helped down the stairs by gendarmes. As the police take the bulky smuggler away, he turns to Lorre and tells him to send him a copy of the novel he will write about Scott, saying: "I'll have a lot of time to read it where I'm going." He adds at the fadeout: "You see, there's not enough kindness in the world." Other than Ambler's American title for his novel and the fact that the mystery-detective writer in it is English, almost nothing was changed from the original novel; the character of the writer was changed from English to Dutch to account for Lorre's accent. Though Lorre performs one of his few sympathetic roles, and does it with fascinating aplomb, his scenes with Greenstreet are dominated by what Lorre affectionately called "the old man" who had become his close personal friend after their appearance together in THE MALTESE FALCON. The entire film fits with the murky intrigue of the era, its stylized sets, its low-key lighting, and a literate, witty script to enchance the wonderful character actors in their segmented roles. Francen is particularly effective as the suave master spy. Greenstreet matches Lorre's enigmatic character with his own girthsome mystique and newcomer Scott is a properly loathsome creature without remorse or compassion for his myriad victims. Emerson as the deserted tart is also very good as is the hapless, trusting Geray. This film, under Negulesco's superb guidance, remains a superlative espionage yarn that mixes fact with fiction, Ambler's despicable anti-hero is most certainly based upon one of the world's greatest intriguers, Basil Zaharoff, billionaire munitions king whose early career is unmistakably that of the scheming Dimitrios Makropoulos.

p, Henry Blanke; d, Jean Negulesco; w, Frank Gruber (based on the novel *A Coffin For Dimitrios* by Eric Ambler); ph, Arthur Edeson; m, Adolph Deutsch; ed, Frederick Richards; md, Leo F. Forbstein; art d, Ted Smith; set d, Walter Tilford; makeup, Perc Westmore.

Crime/Spy Drama **(PR:A MPAA:NR)**

MASK OF DUST (SEE: RACE FOR LIFE, 1954, Brit.)

MASK OF FU MANCHU, THE*** (1932) 72m MGM bw

Boris Karloff *(Dr. Fu Manchu)*, Lewis Stone *(Nayland Smith)*, Karen Morley *(Sheila Barton)*, Charles Starrett *(Terence Granville)*, Myrna Loy *(Fah Lo See)*, Jean Hersholt *(Prof. Von Berg)*, Lawrence Grant *(Sir Lionel Barton)*, David Torrence *(McLeod)*, Herbert Bunston, Gertrude Michael, Ferdinand Gottschalk, C. Montague Shaw, Willie Fung.

Karloff, on loan to MGM after his smash success with Universal Studio's FRANKENSTEIN, plays the evil doctor with twitching mustache and 3-inch fingernails. He and daughter Loy are off to fetch the scimitar and golden mask of Genghis Khan. Once obtaining these artifacts from the tomb of the great warlord, Karloff will be able to destroy the white man and become conquerer of all the world. Stone, in his pre-Judge Hardy days, is a Scotland Yard detective trying to stop Karloff, but he is too late. Karloff gets the mask and sword and proceeds to carry out his wicked plans. With the aid of Loy, he conducts a series of bizarre, yet gleefully sadistic sets of torture on his victims. Hersholt is a British museum official who is done away by enclosing walls decorated with sharp spikes. Morley is cut into pieces and her fiance, Starrett (who became famous for his DURANGO KID series), is injected with a concoction of the better parts of spiders, snakes, and scorpions. Finally Stone, who is being lowered head first into a pool of crocodiles, manages to escape and turns Karloff's evil death ray onto its creator and his offspring. Originally directed by Vidor, replaced after a few weeks by Brabin, this is the Fu Manchu fan's ultimate movie. Superior to the Christopher Lee films in the 1960s, Karloff's characterization is the personification of evil, the right combination of cruelty and sadism. Loy's support is equally fine, with her performance as the depraved woman who is drawn to Starrett. The combined direction of Vidor and Brabin was well meshed, glossing over some holes in the story and wisely emphasizing the camp nature with a fast-paced style. Loy said, in fact, that she and Karloff decided early on that the only way this bizarre story could be handled was to play it tongue-in-cheek all the way through, which they did. It was Loy's last oriental role after 10 years of typecasting as a mysterious, almost always oriental, vamp. (See FU MANCHU series, Index.)

p, Irving Thalberg; d, Charles Brabin, King Vidor; w, Irene Kuhn, Edgar Allan Woolf, John Willard (based on the novel by Sax Rohmer); ph, Tony Gaudio; ed, Ben Lewis; art d, Cedric Gibbons; cos, Adrian; spec eff, Kenneth Strickfaden.

Adventure/Horror **(PR:C MPAA:NR)**

MASK OF FURY (SEE: FIRST YANK INTO TOKYO, 1945)

MASK OF KOREA* 1/2
(1950, Fr.) 61m Ellis Films bw (AKA: GAMBLING HELL)

Erich von Stroheim *(Werner Krali)*, Sessue Hayakawa *(Ying Tchai)*, Mireille Balin *(Marie)*, Roland Toutain *(Peter Malone)*, Louise Carletti *(Jasmina)*, Henry Guisol *(Ahneido)*, George Lannes *(Captain)*, Jimmy Gerald *(Steward)*.

Von Stroheim plays a gun runner, readying himself to ship $250,000 worth of munitions to revolutionaries in Korea. He's having an affair with Frenchwoman Balin, while trying to keep both his business and love life a secret from daughter Carletti, who herself is romantically involved with Toutain, a British journalist who exposes von Stroheim, along with a gambling operation operated by Hayakawa. Poorly made with a trite script, this was clearly below the talents of von Stroheim, who was also a great director. Bad dubbing doesn't help the picture, though the explosive action-filled climax does hold some interest.

p, Jean Delannoy; d, John Rossi; w, Roger Vitrac (based on a story by Maurice Dekobra).

Drama **(PR:A MPAA:NR)**

MASK OF THE AVENGER 1/2** (1951) 83m COL c

Anthony Quinn *(Viovanni Larocca)*, John Derek *(Capt. Renato Dimorna)*, Jody Lawrance *(Maria D'Orsini)*, Arnold Moss *(Colardi)*, Eugene Iglesias *(Rollo D'Anterras)*, Dickie LeRoy *(Jacopo)*, Harry Cording *(Zio)*, Ian Wolfe *(Signor Donner)*, Carlo Tricoli *(Baron Marchese)*, David Bond *(Marco)*, Wilton Graff *(Count Dimorna)*, Tristram Coffin *(Noncommissioned Officer)*, Ric Roman *(lst Guard)*, Philip Van Zandt *(Artillery Major)*, Chuck Hamilton *(Officer)*, Mickey Simpson *(Rudolpho)*, Belle Mitchell *(Woman Busybody)*, Minerva Urecal *(Market Woman)*, Trevor Bardette *(Farmer)*, Lester Sharpe *(Majordomo)*, Gregory Gay *(Col. Von Falker)*.

This is an entertaining swashbuckler with all the proper elements intact: horses, intrigue, fancy costumes, and colorful sets. Derek plays a soldier home from the Austrian-Italian war of 1848. He finds his father has been killed as a traitor. The townspeople turn on him as well and he swears revenge. Quinn, the local military governor, rescues Derek from the mob, and althrough the young man is grateful he remains suspicious of his benefactor and the man's assistant (Moss). After Iglesias' family is killed and Iglesias is imprisoned by Quinn, Derek dons a black mask and saves his girl friend Lawrance from Quinn's guards, then frees Iglesias. Banding together a group of loyalists, Derek leads a party to expose Quinn. But Quinn is one step ahead of the avenger and surrenders his town to the Austrian enemy. Undaunted, Derek and company fight back and recapture the town. However, Iglesias is killed in the battle and Quinn captures Lawrance as he escapes. Derek catches up with Quinn but is stunned in a fall from his horse. Lawrance keeps the evil Quinn at bay with a large sword until Derek recovers and has his revenge at last. Though the complicated story is full of plot holes, this is a fairly handsome production that moves right along, having a good time with the different set pieces the genre calls for. Derek is appropriately dashing as the hero, with Quinn the definitive evil governor type. The music and editing help the film's flow, and though the story is fairly routine this ends up being a good time at the movies.

p, Hunt Stromberg; d, Phil Karlson; w, Jesse L. Lasky, Jr., Ralph Bettinson, Philip MacDonald (based on a story by George Bruce from Alexandre Dumas' novel "The Count of Monte Cristo"); ph, Charles Lawton, Jr. (Technicolor); m, Mario Castelnuovo-Tedesco; ed, Jerome Thoms; md, M.W. Stoloff; art d, Harold MacArthur; cos, Jean Louis.

Adventure **(PR:A MPAA:NR)**

MASK OF THE DRAGON* 1/2 (1951) 51m Lippert bw

Richard Travis *(Phil Ramsey)*, Sheila Ryan *(Ginny O'Donnell)*, Sid Melton *(Manchu Murphy)*, Michael Whalen *(Maj. Clinton)*, Lyle Talbot *(Lt. McLaughlin)*, Richard Emory *(Dan Oliver)*, Dee Tatum *(Terry Newell)*, Jack Reitzen *(Kim Ho)*, Mr. Moto *(Simo)*, Karl Davis *(Kingpin)*, John Grant *(Announcer)*, Curt Barrett's Trailsmen *(Three Stars)*, Eddie Lee *(Chen Koo)*, Ray Singer *(Grantland)*, Carla Martin *(Sarah)*, Dick Paxton, Barbara Atkins.

A poor attempt at combining comedy and mystery against the story of a GI returning from the Korean conflict that has little to say. After the vet is found stabbed in the back, his civilian buddy, Travis, along with female interest, Ryan, tracks down the murderer. There are dealings with an oriental curio shop owner, a mysterious jade dragon, some TV studio intrigue, and a walk through Chinatown, all hashed up in the same standard form with an ineffectual Travis leading the way. The weak script doesn't help much, giving the actors little to do other than spout uninspired lines. The other production values are adequate, though restricted by the film's low budget.

p, Sigmund Neufeld; d, Samuel Newfield; w, Orville Hampton; ph, Jack Greenhalgh; m, Dudley Chambers; ed, Carl Pierson.

Mystery **(PR:A MPAA:NR)**

MASK OF THE HIMALAYAS (SEE: STORM OVER TIBET, 1952)

MASKED PIRATE, THE (SEE: PIRATES OF CAPRI, THE, 1949)

MASKED RAIDERS 1/2** (1949) 60m RKO bw

Tim Holt *(Tim)*, Richard Martin *(Chito)*, Marjorie Lord *(Gale)*, Gary Gray *(Artie)*, Frank Wilcox *(Corthell)*, Charles Arnt *(Doc)*, Tom Tyler *(Trig)*, Harry Woods *(Marshal Barlow)*, Houseley Stevenson *(Uncle Henry)*, Clayton Moore *(Matt)*, Bill George *(Luke)*.

Holt and Martin are a pair of marshals out to stop a Robin Hood-style gang of masked outlaws. The gang is using stolen loot to help innocent ranchers help pay off their mortgages to bad guy banker Wilcox. The surprise twist is that the "Diablo Kid," the gang's leader, turns out to be the stunning Miss Lord. Holt and Martin cure her of her vigilante ways and together they bring in the bad guys. An average western outing with the standard amount of gunplay, horse riding, and background scenery.

p, Herman Schlom; d, Lesley Selander; w, Norman Houston; ph, George E. Diskant; ed, Les Millbrook, art d, Albert S. D'Agostino, Feild Gray.

Western **(PR:A MPAA:NR)**

MASKED RIDER, THE 1/2** (1941) 57m UNIV bw

Johnny Mack Brown *(Larry)*, Fuzzy Knight *(Patches)*, Nell O'Day *(Jean)*, Grant Withers *(Douglas)*, Virginia Carroll *(Margarita)*, Guy D'Ennery *(Don Sebastian)*, Carmela Cansino *(Carmencita)*, Roy Barcroft *(Luke)*, Dick Botiller *(Pedro)*, Fred Cordova *(Pablo)*, Al Haskell *(Jose)*, Rico De Montez *(Manuel)*, Bob O'Connor *(Guard)*, The Guadalajara Trio, The Jose Cansino Dancers.

A better than average western thanks to the use of Latin American dancers and singers rather than the same ordinary cowpoke musical relief. Brown and Knight are a pair of drifters who head south of the border for some employment. They get jobs at a silver mine and soon find themselves trying to solve crimes committed by a mysterious masked rider. The standard plot is helped by dialog that is unusually witty for the genre and by Beebe's crisp direction. Songs include "La Golondrina," "Carmelita," "Casenoble," "Cancanita," and "Chiapanacas."

p, Will Cowan; d, Ford Beebe; w, Sherman Lowe, Victor I. McLeod (based on a story by Sam Robins); ph, Charles Van Enger, Milton Rosen, Everett Carter.

Western **(PR:A MPAA:NR)**

MASKED STRANGER (SEE: DURANGO KID, THE, 1940)

MASOCH* 1/2** (1980, Ital.) 109m Difilm c

Paolo Malco, Francesca De Sapio, Fabrizio Bentivoglio, Inga Alexandrova, Dario Mazzoli, Remo Remotti, Valeria D'Obici, Stefano Calanchi, Franca Lumachi, Claudio Sorrentino, Stefano Stefanelli, Farris Fabio.

This well done biographical drama is a re-telling of the life of writer Sacher-Masoch, from whose name the word "masochism" was derived. Though this certainly has its kinkier moments, it is hardly a pornographic picture. Dealing with the writer's marriage to a lower-class woman (well played by De Sapio), the story tells the difficulties in their dominant-submissive marriage. Malco is the slave to his wife's demands and urges her to take lovers, which leads to the collapse of their marriage. She beats and humiliates her husband, all at his suggestion. Quite easily this could have drifted off into a Penthouse Forum fantasy but Taviani wisely uses the inherent dramatic tones of the story to make the characters' behavior realistic and believable. There's a nice use of screen dissolves to close scenes on an abrupt and effective note. Backed with a good musical score and period costumes and set design, this may not be for everyone, but is certainly worth looking at.

p, Franco Brogi Taviani, Giancarlo di Fonzo, Tonino Paoletti; d&w, Taviani; ph, Angelo Bevilacqua (Eastmancolor); m, Gianfranco Plenizio.

Drama **(PR:O MPAA:NR)**

MASON OF THE MOUNTED** (1932) 58m MON bw

Bill Cody, Andy Shuford, Nancy Drexel, Art Smith [Art Mix], Jack Carlisle, Blackie Whiteford, Nelson McDowell, James Marcus, Joe Dominguez, LeRoy Mason, Dick Dickinson, Frank Hall Crane, Jack Long, Earl Dwire, Gordon McGee.

Average film that unlike many other westerns of the day told its story in only 58 minutes without throwing in any padding. A young Royal Canadian Mounted Policeman heads into the U.S. to hunt a murderer. He finds his man running a horse stealing ring and with the help of the U.S. marshal does his job in that bold Mountie manner. Good acting and production values made this suitable little program piece that filled out double bills in 1932.

p, Trem Carr; d&w, Harry Fraser; ph, Archie Stout.

Western **Cas.** **(PR:A MPAA:NR)**

MASQUE OF THE RED DEATH, THE*1/2** (1964, U.S./Brit.) 86m Alta Vista-Anglo Amalgamated/AIP c

Vincent Price *(Prince Prospero)*, Hazel Court *(Juliana)*, Jane Asher *(Francesca)*, David Weston *(Gino)*, Patrick Magee *(Alfredo)*, Nigel Green *(Ludovico)*, Skip Martin *(Hop Toad)*, John Westbrook *(Man in Red)*, Gaye Brown *(Senora Escobar)*, Julian Burton *(Senor Veronese)*, Doreen Dawn *(Anna-Marie)*, Paul Whitsun-Jones *(Scarlatti)*, Jean Lodge *(His Wife)*, Verina Greenlaw *(Esmeralda)*, Brian Hewlett *(Lampredi)*, Harvey Hall *(Clistor)*, Robert Brown *(Guard)*, David Davies, Sarah Brackett.

This is probably one of the best Corman-produced features, a wondrous symphony of the macabre and color, loosely based on two Edgar Allan Poe stories. Price is at his evil quintessence, playing a 12th-Century Italian prince who lives for his one true love, Satan. Using peasants to satisfy his sadistic desires, Price jails two locals for defying his harsh tax laws. Asher, the daughter of one and the fiancee of the other, pleads for mercy. He tells her that only one will be spared and uses her emotions for his private amusements. Court is a woman who brands her breast and makes a pact with the devil, but Price shows no interest in her. Later she helps Asher in aiding her father, Green, and fiance, Weston, to escape. But Price recaptures the pair and orders them to cut themselves up using five knives, one of which is poisoned. Green lunges for the evil prince but is impaled on a sword. Weston, finally allowed to go free, is sent to a village that is being burned as its population is overrun with the "Red Death," a terrible plague sweeping the land. But on his way to the town, Weston is greeted by a mysterious figure who tells him to return to the castle and wait for Asher. The stranger enters the town and Price dies of the plague. Weston and Asher are allowed to go free in an eerie finish. A subplot, involving Martin as a court dwarf, has the little man burning alive Magee, a nobleman clad in a gorilla suit. Weird and extremely downbeat, this undoubtedly is the most serious film ever to come from Corman. Any hint of camp is quickly squelched, making the terror all the more frightening. The use of colors is brilliant and is a nice complement to Price's inspired performance. The entire project was shot in just five weeks, a long shooting schedule when one considers most Corman projects took only two to three weeks.

p&d, Roger Corman; w, Charles Beaumont, R. Wright Campbell (based on "The Masque of the Red Death" and "Hop-Frog, or the Eight Chained Orang-outangs" by Edgar Allan Poe); ph, Nicolas Roeg (Panavision/Pathecolor); m, David Lee; ed, Ann Chegwidden; prod d, Daniel Haller; md, Lee; art d, Robert Jones; set d, Colin Southcott; cos, Laura Nightingale; spec eff, George Blackwell; ch, Jack Carter; makeup, George Partleton.

Horror **(PR:C MPAA:NR)**

MASQUERADE zero (1929) 65m FOX bw

Leila Hyams *(Sylvia Graeme)*, Alan Birmingham *(Dan Anisty/Dan Maitland)*, Clyde Cook *(Blodgett)*, J. Farrell MacDonald *(Joe Hickey)*, Arnold Lucy *(Bannerman)*, George Pierce *(Andrew Graeme)*, John Breeden *(1st Reporter)*, Jack Pierce *(2nd Reporter)*, Pat Moriarity *(3rd Reporter)*, Jack Carlisle *(4th Reporter)*, Lumsden Hare.

With the advent of talkies, the studios became fascinated with the new medium and began cranking out film after film that was visually simplistic and had nonstop chatter. Often the dialog was so overwhelming that it drained all life from the story. This is such a picture, a yarn about some crooks being chased by a bumbling detective (Cook). Adding to the confusion is the fact that Birmingham, while playing two roles, pretends he is the other character which confuses the heroine who is trying to locate some papers which she hopes will clear her father of a criminal charge that has landed him in jail. While such a story would probably have been a great comic two-reeler, the added length and long speeches don't add up to much of anything here.

d, Russell J. Birdwell, Lumsden Hare; w, Frederick Hazlitt Brennan, Malcolm Stuart Boylan (based on a story by Louis Joseph Vance); ph, Charles Clarke, Don Anderson; ed, Ralph Dietrich.

Crime/Comedy **(PR:A MPAA:NR)**

MASQUERADE***
(1965, Brit.) 101m Novus/UA c (AKA: OPERATION MASQUERADE; THE SHABBY TIGER)

Cliff Robertson *(David Frazer)*, Jack Hawkins *(Col. Drexel)*, Marisa Mell *(Sophie)*, Michel Piccoli *(Sarrassin)*, Bill Fraser *(Dunwoody)*, Christopher Witty *(Prince Jamil)*, Tutte Lemkow *(Paviot)*, Keith Pyott *(Gustave)*, Jose Burgos *(El Mono)*, Charles Gray *(Benson)*, John Le Mesurier *(Sir Robert)*, Roger Delgado *(Ahmed Ben Fa'id)*, Jerold Wells *(Brindle)*, Felix Aylmer *(Henrickson)*, Denis Bernard *(King Ahmed)*, Ernest Clark *(Minister)*, David Nettheim *(Photographer)*, Anthony Singleton *(His Assistant)*, Norman Fisher *(Bishop)*, Eric Blyth *(General)*, James Mossman *(Himself)*.

With picturesque scenes filmed in the Middle East and Spain, MASQUERADE looks better than it is. The only shortcoming in the otherwise all-British cast is Robertson in the lead. Great Britain and the mythical Arab country of Ramaut have been negotiating an oil lease deal, but it's fallen apart so Hawkins, a colonel who had saved the Arab country during WW II, is called in on a strange assignment. His job is to kidnap Witty, the youthful heir to the throne, and keep him under wraps until it's time for him to assume the mantle of king, then have him sign the agreement favorable to the English. To aid him in their nefarious scheme, Hawkins calls upon old pal Robertson, who is sent to Spain to meet Hawkins and Witty at a fabulous villa. Once there, he meets Mell and her cadre of criminals, then is knocked senseless and awakens to find that Witty is gone. The powers-that-be think that Robertson is part of the cabal, but Hawkins, knowing better, comes to Robertson's side. Now Robertson learns that Hawkins is behind the whole plot and is planning to give Witty back to his uncle, Bernard, in return for a huge sum. Hawkins had become disenchanted by his bosses' greed and decided that he wanted some of that money for himself. Robertson confronts Hawkins with the knowledge and Hawkins immediately wants to cut the American in on the deal, but jut-jawed Robertson refuses. Hawkins leaves with Witty and Robertson goes after him. While crossing a rope bridge, the ropes break and Witty and Hawkins' lives are saved by Robertson in a daring bit of derring-do. The whole thing has been witnessed by the British toppers and they mistake what Hawkins' motives were, rewarding him with a citation and a good job with the oil company. Witty is returned to his country and Robertson gets a bit of money for his troubles. Along the way, we've been treated to some high adventure in a traveling circus, a mysterious castle, and several gun battles. It's all done with tongue in cheek and Hawkins is excellent as he parodies the stiff-upper-lip roles he's done so many times for real. There are more predicaments in this than RAIDERS OF THE LOST ARK, though not as well done. Robertson underplays to the point of somnambulism.

p, Michael Relph; d, Basil Dearden; w, Relph, William Goldman (based on the novel *Castle Minerva* by Victor Canning), ph, Otto Heller (Eastmancolor); m, Philip Green; ed, John D. Guthridge; prod d, Don Ashton; md, Green; art d, Jack Stephens; cos, Beatrice Dawson; m/l, "Masquerade," Green, Norman Newell; makeup, Harry Frampton.

Adventure/Comedy **(PR:A MPAA:NR)**

MASQUERADE IN MEXICO** (1945) 96m PAR bw

Dorothy Lamour *(Angel O'Reilly)*, Arturo de Cordova *(Manolo Segovia)*, Patric Knowles *(Thomas Grant)*, Ann Dvorak *(Helen Grant)*, George Rigaud *(Boris Cassall)*, Natalie Schafer *(Irene Denny)*, Mikhail Rasumny *(Paolo)*, Billy Daniels *(Rico Fenway)*, The Guadalajara Trio *(Themselves)*, Martin Garralaga *(Jose)*, Lester Luther *(Felipe Diaz)*, Dina Smirnova *(Friedo Diaz)*, Enrique Valadez, Rita Lupino *(Specialty Dancers)*, Mimi Doyle *(Stewardess)*, Lucille Porcett *(Woman at Airport)*, Al Haskell, Leo Murtin, Art Felix, Ray Beltram *(Taxi Drivers)*, Eddie Laughton, William Newell, James Flavin, Charles A. Hughes, *(FBI Men)*, Robert Middlemass, George Anderson, Perc Launders *(Customs Officials)*, Don Avalier *(Headwaiter)*, Frank Faylen *(Brooklyn)*, Pepito Perez *(Angel's Chauffeur)*, Frank Leyva *(Newspaperman)*, Mae Bush, Julia Faye, Ernest Hilliard, Miriam Franklin, Stan Johnson, Roberta Jonay, Jean Acker, John Marlowe, Gordon Arnold, Allen Pinson, Charles Teske *(Guests)*, Ted Rand, Guy Zanette *(Servants)*.

While on vacation in Mexico City, nightclub entertainer Lamour finds herself being hunted as a suspected jewel thief. De Cordova is a woman-chasing bullfighter who's after Dvorak, wife of banker Knowles. Knowles rescues Lamour from the police and gets her to entice de Cordova away from his wife. An expensively made bit of fluff, this was a Mexican based version of the 1939 Parisian set picture MIDNIGHT, also by the same director. The set pieces in this version are all right though nothing special. Lamour has a few good numbers such as "Forever Mine," but this is a minor film at best.

p, Karl Tunberg; d, Mitchell Leisen; w, Tunberg (based on a story by Edwin Justus Mayer, Franz Spencer); ph, Lionel Lindon; m, Victor Young; ed, Alma Macrorie; md, Young; art d, Hans Dreier, Roland Anderson; spec eff, Gordon Jennings; ch, Billy Daniels; m/l, Bob Russell, Eddie Lisbona, Maria T. Lara, Ben Raleigh, Bernie Wayne.

Musical **(PR:C MPAA:NR)**

MASQUERADER, THE1/2** (1933) 84m Goldwyn/UA bw

Ronald Colman *(Sir John Chilcote/John Loder)*, Elissa Landi *(Eve Chilcote)*, Juliette Compton *(Lady Joyce)*, Halliwell Hobbes *(Brock)*, David Torrence *(Fraser)*, Creighton Hale *(Lakely)*, Helen Jerome Eddy *(Robbins)*, Eric Wilton *(Alston)*, C. Montague Shaw *(Speaker of the House)*.

This was Coleman's eighteenth and final film for Goldwyn. Based on a 1905 best-seller, then a play, then a silent film which starred Guy Bates Post in 1922, THE MASQUERADER puts Colman, once again, in a dual role. (He probably played more dual roles than anyone, a practice that culminated, sort of, with A DOUBLE LIFE, for which he won an Oscar. Prior to that, he'd done THE MAGIC FLAME and later THE PRISONER OF ZENDA in the two lead parts.) There's an angry session at England's Parliament and Colman (as Sir John) is having a tough time handling his chores—mostly due to the fact that he is a dope addict. He attempts to make a speech, but the words don't come out right. Afterward, he pushes past his pals, including his mistress, Compton, and staggers into the dank streets where he runs into his identical cousin (also Colman). They pass the time of night for a few moments, then Colman (Loder) tells Colman (Sir John) that if he ever needs someone to fill in for him, just call. Colman (Sir John) stumbles to Compton's residence with that thought in his mind. Later, Colman (Sir John) goes back to his own home, which he shares with his estranged wife, Landi. She's freshly returned from France and he asks her if she's come home because she's run out of Parisian gigolos. He goes to his own room where his valet, Hobbes, helps him to bed. Hobbes is the only person who is aware that the peer is a junkie. The following day Colman (Sir John) goes to Colman's (Loder) house and collapses, unable to move. Hobbes has been on his master's trail and pleads with Colman (Loder) to take the other's place at Parliament to make the speech that all of the other peers have been expecting. Colman (Loder) doesn't think he can handle it, but Hobbes spends some time teaching him about his master's mannerisms until confidence arrives and the speech is a sensation. Colman (Loder) has sent the peers into wild applause. Later, he goes to the mansion of the man he is pretending to be and must be careful to appear as though he knows exactly what he's doing because Hale and Torrence, leaders of his party, are with him. There's a gala party that night and Colman (Loder) makes the error of believing that Compton is his wife. Hobbes stays close to Colman to help avoid errors and assures the man that this masquerade won't have to be continued for much longer. Hobbes tells Colman (Loder) that Colman (Sir John) is civil to his own wife, Landi, but little more. Landi knows about Compton and tolerates the situation for the sake of propriety. Colman (Loder) finds himself attracted to Landi and she, faced with a very different person, begins to love her "husband" all over again. Compton can't believe the way Colman (Loder) has changed, so she hires a man to investigate this new attitude because she suspects that a double may have been employed. Meanwhile, Colman (Sir John) is recovering at his look-a-like's apartment with Hobbes keeping tabs on him. The lord is rapidly becoming disenchanted with the masquerade, so, despite Hobbes' pleadings, he gets himself in shape to attend a party. Compton is about to expose Colman (Loder) as a phony when Colman (Sir John) arrives and saves the day. She'd noticed that Colman (Loder) had a scar that she knew her lover did not have. Colman (Sir John) returns to the other flat and Colman (Loder) decides that he has to give up his dream of loving Landi and come clean. Then Hobbes arrives and says that won't be necessary, Colman (Sir John) has died and Colman (Loder) must now walk in his cousin's shoes forever. Faced with the deliciousness of Landi, that's no problem for Colman (Loder) and he heartily agrees. Landi had become ill just before the picture began and plans were made to replace her with Benita Hume (whom Colman married five years later), but she recovered in time for the job. Colman and producer Goldwyn were at odds while this picture was being planned, as Goldwyn had been quoted as saying that Colman was a better actor when he drank and looked more interesting when he was debauched then when he was in good shape. This caused Colman to sue the producer for $2 million in libel charges. After this movie came out, the suit apparently just sort of went away.

p, Samuel Goldwyn; d, Richard Wallace; w, Howard Estabrook, Moss Hart (based on the play by John Hunter Booth and the novel by Katherine Cecil Thurston); ph, Gregg Toland; m, Alfred Newman; ed, Stuart Heisler; art d, Richard Day.

Drama (PR:A MPAA:NR)

MASSACRE★★ (1934) 74m FN-WB bw

Richard Barthelmess *(Joe Thunder Horse)*, Ann Dvorak *(Lydia)*, Dudley Digges *(Elihu P. Quissenberry)*, Claire Dodd *(Norma)*, Henry O'Neill *(Dickinson)*, Robert Barrat *(Dawson)*, Arthur Hohl *(Dr. Turner)*, Sidney Toler *(Thomas Shanks)*, Clarence Muse *(Sam)*, William V. Mong *(Grandy)*, Agnes Narcha *(Jennie)*, Douglas Dumbrille *(Chairman)*, Wallis Clark *(Cochran)*, DeWitt Jennings *(Sheriff Jennings)*, Frank McGlynn, Sr. *(Missionary)*, Philip Faversham, George Blackwood, Charles Middleton, Tully Marshall, Juliet Ware, James Eagles, Samuel S. Hinds.

Hollywood has always mistreated native Americans in both story and character. This film is better than most in that regard. Though the studio saw MASSACRE as a standard action melodrama, the maltreatment of Indians by white men in America's history is clearly shown in a rare programmer where the Indians are not bloodthirsty heathens. Barthelmess is woefully miscast as a Sioux, away from his home reservation for a number of years. After becoming a star in a Wild West show, he hears that his father is dying. Returning to his homeland, he is appalled by the treatment his people have received at the hands of the whites. There's a good deal of fighting and rioting in his quest for justice in what eventually winds down to a standard happy ending. Barthelmess does not look like what his role calls for, but he plays with some degree of believability. At times the film actually overcomes its action set pieces to make a statement about the treatment of Indians in this country. On the whole, though, this is a standard action picture without any real social commitment.

p, Robert Presnell; d, Alan Crosland; w, Ralph Block, Sheridan Gibney (based on a story by Block, Robert Gessner); ph, George Barnes; ed, Terry Morse; art d, John Hughes.

Western (PR:A MPAA:NR)

MASSACRE★ (1956) 76m FOX c

Dane Clark *(Ramon)*, James Craig *(Ezparza)*, Marta Roth *(Angelica)*, Jaime Fernandez *(Juan Pedro)*, Ferrusquilla *(Vincent)*, Miguel Torruco *(Chavez)*, Jose Munoz *(Macario)*, Enrique Zambrano *(Munez)*, Victor Jordan, Luci Aura Gonzales, Jose Luis Rojas, Jose Palido, Rudolfo Toledo Rivera, Angel Maldonado, Cuauatemoc Ortega, Juan Yanes, Augusto Yanes, Mario Yanes, Sergio Yanes, Ramon Chavez Perez.

This tired, trite Western has a saving grace in a unique ending. Otherwise it's a boring tale of gunrunners driving the Yacqui Indians to war so whites can make a profit. The dialog is bland and not much is done with the production values. The twist ending has the secret cache of arms being blown up and the Indians wiping out the gunrunners, but by then the film has lost what little interest the ending could make up for.

p, Robert L. Lippert, Jr., Olallo Rubio, Jr.; d, Louis King; w, D. D. Beauchamp (based on a story by Fred Freiberger, William Tunberg); ph, Gilbert Warrenton (Ansco Color); m, Gonzalo Curiel; ed, Carl Pierson; md, Curiel.

Western (PR:A MPAA:NR)

MASSACRE AT CENTRAL HIGH★★★ (1976) 85m Evan/Brian-New Line c

Derrel Maury *(David)*, Andrew Stevens *(Mark)*, Robert Carradine *(Spoony)*, Kimberly Beck *(Teresa)*, Roy Underwood *(Bruce)*, Steve Bond *(Craig)*, Damon Douglas *(Paul)*, [Cheryl] Rainbeaux Smith *(Mary)*, Lani O'Grady *(Jane)*, Steve Sikes *(Rodney)*, Dennis Court *(Arthur)*, Jeffrey Winner *(Oscar)*, Thomas Logan *(Harvey)*.

After being assigned to write and direct a high school exploitation feature, writer-director Daalder surprised his bosses by delivering not only the sex and violence picture they had expected, but by also creating what probably ranks as the only intellectual film in the genre. Maury is the new kid in school who finds it run by three brutes (Underwood, Bond, and Douglas). His long-time buddy, Stevens, tells the newcomer to get in good with this trio and Central High will be at his disposal. But the bullies dismiss him as a troublemaker and won't allow him in their circle. Meanwhile, they continue to terrorize students, attacking the student librarian while wrecking another student's beloved jalopy. When Maury offers to help fight back,

the librarian tells him "We lose our own battles." The ruling three question Stevens about his friend and he promises to straighten out the newcomer. But when Maury stops them from raping Smith and O'Grady (with the classic exploitation film names "Mary" and "Jane") Underwood, Bond, and Douglas warn Stevens for the last time: get Maury to knuckle under or there'll be severe penalties. Stevens has a fight with girl friend Beck and she goes off with Maury. When Stevens sees the two skinny-dipping he lies and tells his three superiors that he tried to talk sense into Maury but he wouldn't listen. While Maury is fixing the jalopy they destroyed, the three drop it on him, crushing his leg. Maury lives but can no longer continue his beloved jogging. The time has come for direct action. While Underwood is hang gliding, a cable on his craft snaps. Bond is tricked into performing a dive into an empty swimming pool. Douglas' van goes over a cliff. To his horror Stevens realizes that his old pal is behind the murders. Confronting his one-time friend, Maury announces that he is indeed responsible and dares Stevens to do something about it. But Stevens loves his friend too much and refuses to raise a hand. Since Maury also cares for Beck, he refuses to fight as well in deference to her feelings. But soon Maury finds himself in the position he has loathed as the weaklings he tried to defend attempt to court favors from their new hero. Fights break out and a series of pipe bombs begin eliminating students once more. Maury again challenges his old friend to stop him, knowing full well what the answer will be. He locks Stevens and Beck in his workshop and goes to the school where a big dance is being held. He plants a bomb and prepares to watch the blast. But Beck and Stevens have escaped and are now at the gym. Maury tries to get them to leave but they refuse. Panic-stricken, he retrieves the bomb and hurries it outside, where he is killed in an explosion. The two survivors tell the authorities that another student (earlier killed in Maury's second wave of murders) had planted the bomb and Maury gave his life to save the people gathered at the dance. Shot in only three weeks on a minimal budget, MASSACRE AT CENTRAL HIGH was heralded by critics everywhere. Most compared it to an allegory for the rise and fall of Nazi Germany, with Underwood, Bond, and Douglas as the ruling Fascists, the student body as the frightened masses, and Maury as the lone freedom fighter. While this may be carrying things to an extreme, this certainly was no ordinary violent teen picture. We are subjected to a world run entirely by adolescents, with hardly any adults present. Daalder understood the average American teenager's view of high school: it is a highly structured social caste system where differences are not tolerated. Adults, though present, are of little consequence. It is one's peers that ultimately decide what happens and woe be to the fool who attempts to change this rigid system. Go into any high school in America and you'll find characters not unlike those in MASSACRE AT CENTRAL HIGH . Daalder's use of disorienting cinematography, high-angle shots, and dream-like blackouts help push his message through to the audience. Granted, this is no masterpiece: there is enough gratuitous nudity and gore to satisfy someone looking for a far less challenging film experience. But the average exploitation-viewer didn't understand the film and it died an unfair box office death. Beck was the stepdaughter of Leonetti, who wrote the film's unusual and haunting score. He was better known as the host of TV's "Your Hit Parade" and one of the few people who dared to testify in public against the Mafia.

p, Harold Sobel (Bill Lange, uncredited); d&w, Renee Daalder; ph, Burt Van Munster; m, Tommy Leonetti; ed, Harry Keramidas; art d, Russell Tune; spec eff, Roger George; m/l, "You're At the Crossroads of Your Life," Leonetti; makeup, Peter Deyell.

Drama Cas. (PR:O MPAA:R)

MASSACRE AT FORT HOLMAN
(SEE: REASON TO LIVE, A REASON TO DIE, A, 1974, Ital./Fr./Ger./Span.)

MASSACRE AT THE ROSEBUD
(SEE: GREAT SIOUX MASSACRE, THE, 1965)

MASSACRE CANYON★ (1954) 66m COL bw

Phil Carey *(Lt. Richard Faraday)*, Audrey Totter *(Flaxy)*, Douglas Kennedy *(Sgt. James Marlowe)*, Jeff Donnell *(Cora)*, Guinn "Big Boy" Williams *(Peaceful)*, Charlita *(Gita)*, Ross Elliott *(George Davis)*, Ralph Dumke *("Parson" Canfield)*, Mel Welles *(Gonzales)*, Chris Alcaide *(Running Horse)*, Steve Ritch *(Black Eagle)*, John Pickard *(Lt. Ridgeford)*, James Flavin *(Col. Joseph Tarant)*, Bill Hale *(Lt. Farnum)*.

Carey has to lead a wagon train full of rifles through hostile Indian territory. Ritch is the renegade leader of the Indians, attacking the party as it goes through a canyon. But a secret tunnel is found and the train rides off to safety. The insipid story is saved only by the action-packed finale; otherwise the acting is bland and the direction is as inspired and creative as the script.

p, Wallace MacDonald; d, Fred F. Sears; w, David Lang; ph, Lester H. White (Sepiatone); m, Mischa Bakaleinikoff; ed, Aaron Stell.

Western (PR:A MPAA:NR)

MASSACRE HILL★★
(1949, Brit.) 103m Ealing/GFD bw (GB: EUREKA STOCKADE)

Chips Rafferty *(Peter Lalor)*, Jane Barrett *(Alicia Dunne)*, Jack Lambert *(Commissioner Rede)*, Peter Illing *(Raffaello)*, Gordon Jackson *(Tom Kennedy)*, Ralph Truman *(Gov. Hotham)*, Sydney Loder *(Vern)*, John Fernside *(Sly Grog Seller)*, Grant Tyler *(Sgt. Maj. Milne)*, Peter Finch *(Humffray)*, Kevin Brennan *(Black)*, John Fegan *(Hayes)*, Al Thomas *(Scobie)*, Ron Whelan *(Bentley)*, Dorothy Allison *(Mrs. Bentley)*, Reg Wykeham *(Dr. Moore)*, Betty Ross *(Mary O'Rourke)*, John Wiltshire *(Father Smythe)*, Nigel Lovell *(Capt. Wise)*, Charles Tasman *(Gov. Latrobe)*, Frederick Vern, John Cazabon.

During the Australian gold rush of 1851, the colonial authorities become alarmed that men are abandoning the land to hunt for gold. They attempt to harass the miners but the men organize and build a stockade. Government troops, much better armed and trained, have little difficulty in routing the miners out of their pathetic fortress, but public opinion turns away from the government and they are forced to concede to the miners' demands. Eventually Rafferty, the leader of the miners who lost an arm in the battle, is elected to Parliament. Not bad action story with a lesson in Australian history thrown in gratis.

p, Leslie Norman; d, Harry Watt; w, Watt, Walter Greenwood (based on a story by Watt); ph, George Heath; m, John Greenwood; ed, Norman; art d, Charles Woolveridge.

Adventure   **(PR:A   MPAA:NR)**

MASSACRE IN ROME*   (1973, Ital.) 103m CHAM/NG c

Richard Burton (Col. Kappler), Marcello Mastroianni (Don Antonelli), Leo McKern (Gen. Kurt Maelzer), John Steiner (Col. Dollmann), Della Boccardo (Elena), Renzo Montagnani (Police Chief Caruso), Gian Carlo Prete (Paolo), Robert Harris (Father Pancrazio).

An interesting war drama that was based on the controversial book Death in Rome, which suggested that Pope Pius XII was aware of Hitler's plan to kill ten Italians for every German lost in a partisan attack, then either ignored the edict or could do nothing about it. Burton is the German colonel caught between his duty to the Fuehrer and his love for the city of Rome and its people. McKern is his alcoholic superior officer, determined to carry out the orders. Mastroianni is a Vatican priest who choses to die with the Romans rather than live the cowardly existence he had as the liaison between the Romans and Germans. Filmed in a documentary style, the film has a number of well-crafted sequences. The film is in two parts: first the partisan attack of the Italians and Germans; then the second half involving the fate of 300 Italian hostages whose fate hangs between the Vatican and Germany. The film is keenly edited, nicely balancing the two very different halves. Burton gives what was probably one of the best of his later performances.

p, Carlo Ponti; d, George Pan Cosmatos; w, Cosmatos, Robert Katz (based on the book Death in Rome by Katz); ph, Marcello Gatti (Technicolor); m, Ennio Morricone; ed, Francoise Bonnot, Roberto Silvi; art d, Arrigo Berschi.

War   **(PR:C   MPAA:PG)**

MASSACRE RIVER*¹/₂   (1949) 77m Windsor/AA-MON bw

Guy Madison (Larry Knight), Rory Calhoun (Phil Acton), Carole Mathews (Laura Jordan), Cathy Downs (Kitty Reid), Johnny Sands (Randy Reid), Steve Brodie (Burke Kimber), Art Baker (Col. James Reid), Iron Eyes Cody (Chief Yellowstone), Emory Parnell (Sgt. Johanssen), Queenie Smith (Mrs. Johanssen), Eddy Waller (Joe), James Bush (Eddie), John Holland (Roberts), Douglas Fowley (Simms), Harry Brown (Piano Player), Kermit Maynard (Scout), Gregg Barton (Frank).

Below average Western action piece finds Madison and Calhoun as two Army officers who are both in love with Downs, a colonel's daughter. She prefers Madison but he ends up falling for shady lady Mathews. There's also some fighting with the Indians but this is downplayed, with the romantic problems being the centerpiece of the story. This was an unusual move for B Westerns and it just doesn't work. The players aren't talented enough to make the love story believable and the action scenes are poorly done. This was Madison's second Western, the genre that he ended up making his name in.

p, Julian Lesser, Frank Melford; d, John Rawlins; w, Louis Stevens; ph, Jack MacKenzie; m, Lucien Moraweck, John Leipold; ed, Richard Cahoon, W. J. Murphy; md, Lud Gluskin; art d, Lucius Croxton.

Western   **(PR:A   MPAA:NR)**

MASTER AND MAN*¹/₂   (1934, Brit.) 54m BIP/Pathe bw

Wallace Lupino (Wally), Barry Lupino (Barry), Gus McNaughton (Blackmailer), Faith Bennett (Lady Sinden), Syd Crossley (Coffee Stall Keeper), Hal Gordon (Gamekeeper), Harry Terry (Tiny), George Humphries (Slim).

The Lupino brothers play a pair of tramps who use a location along the Thames River for their home. The two ne'er-do-wells end up being mistaken for cultured gentlemen. They attend a party thrown by society woman Bennett, and end up stopping some arsonists from torching her mansion. Wallace Lupino wrote the comedy specifically to fit his and his brother's talents, but the humor is unoriginal. The film pushes for laughs, but the idea is rooted in silent two-reel comedy, a more practicable forum for the material. Imagine the scenario as a Charlie Chaplin vehicle!

p, Walter C. Mycroft; d, John Harlow; w, Wallace Lupino.

Comedy   **(PR:A   MPAA:NR)**

MASTER GUNFIGHTER, THE zero
                                        (1975) 121m Taylor-Laughlin/Billy Jack c

Tom Laughlin (Finley), Ron O'Neal (Paulo), Lincoln Kilpatrick (Jacques), GeoAnn Sosa (Chorika), Barbara Carrera (Eula), Victor Campos (Maltese), Hector Elias (Juan), Michael Lane (Frewen), Richard Angarola (Don Santiago), Patti Clifton.

After playing a violence-prone peace lover in BILLY JACK, THE TRIAL OF BILLY JACK, and BILLY JACK GOES TO WASHINGTON, Laughlin decided to try something new and daring. Taking the plot from an old Japanese samurai picture (GOYOKIN, 1966), Laughlin had it reworked into a plot dealing with—surprise!— a violence-prone, Old West peace lover. This poorly plotted and extremely violent piece (considering its PG rating) finds Laughlin a moralist cowboy in 1836. He spends most of the picture spouting liberal social rhetoric before proving his point by bashing heads. Angarola is Laughlin's father-in-law, a stereotypical bad guy. He's behind some Indian massacres and land grabbing that doesn't make his son-in-law too happy. The film is a rambling mess, but what can you expect when the director credited (Frank Laughlin) is the star's nine-year-old son? Laughlin sank $3.5 million of his BILLY JACK kitty into this ego-fest and the results were promptly and rightfully derided by critics. Angered, Laughlin spent an additional $3.75 million on

ads which boldly stated that critics were "frustrated writers who failed to make it in show business."

p, Philip L. Parslow; d, Frank [Tom] Laughlin; w, Harold Lapland; ph, Jack A. Marta (Panavision, Metrocolor); m, Lalo Schifrin; ed, William Reynolds, Danford Greene; prod d, Albert Brenner; set d, Ira Bates; stunts, Henry Wills.

Western   **(PR:C   MPAA:PG)**

MASTER MINDS*   (1949) 64m MON bw

Leo Gorcey (Slip Mahoney), Huntz Hall (Sach Debussy Jones), Billy Benedict (Whitey), Bennie Bartlett (Butch), David Gorcey (Chuck), Gabriel Dell (Gabe Moreno), Bernard Gorcey (Louie Dumbrowsky), Glenn Strange (Atlas), Alan Napier (Dr. Druzik), William Yetter (Otto), Kit Guard (Benny), Skelton Knaggs (Hugo), Jane Adams (Nancy Marlowe), Whitey Roberts (Juggler), Harry Tyler (Constable Isaih Hoskins), Anna Chandler (Woman), Chester Clute (Mike Barton), Minerva Urecal (Mrs. Hoskins), Stanley Blystone (Henchman), Robert Coogan (Young Man), Pat Goldin (Father), Tim Connor (Hoskins Boy), Kent O'Dell (Second Hoskins Boy).

The Boys run into some trouble when Hall gets a toothache and is suddenly able to predict the future. He starts working a carnival side-show and meets up with Napier, a mad scientist who wants to transplant Hall's mind into that of a monster ape man. How will anyone know the difference? Another in the insipid "Bowery Boys" series, the monster makeup was done by Pierce, who apparently had fallen from the grace he had when he created the great monsters for Universal Studios. (See BOWERY BOYS series, Index.)

p, Jan Grippo; d, Jean Yarbrough; w, Charles R. Marion, Bert Lawrence; ph, Marcel LePicard; m, Edward J. Kay; ed, William Austin; md, Kay; art d, David Milton; set d, Raymond Boltz, Jr.; makeup, Jack P. Pierce.

Comedy   **(PR:A   MPAA:NR)**

MASTER OF BALLANTRAE, THE*   (1953, U.S./Brit.) 88m WB c

Errol Flynn (James Durrisdeer), Roger Livesey (Col. Francis Burke), Anthony Steel (Henry Durrisdeer), Beatrice Campbell (Lady Alison), Yvonne Furneaux (Jessie Brown), Jacques Berthier (Arnaud), Felix Aylmer (Lord Durrisdeer), Mervyn Johns (MacKellar), Charles Goldner (Mendoza), Ralph Truman (Maj. Clarendon), Francis De Wolff (Matthew Bull), Moultrie Kelsall (MacCauley), Charles Carson (Col. Banks), Gillian Lynne (Marianne), Jack Taylor, Stephen Vercoe.

Flynn's last picture for Warner Bros., under the long-time contract, was a moderately successful swashbuckler that took so many liberties with Stevenson's massive book that it was almost unrecognizable by the time it was completed. Flynn was in some financial trouble in the U.S. with unpaid alimony and IRS problems and he had always been popular in Europe so when this picture came up, he was all for doing it. Many of the film companies had money in various foreign countries which they were not allowed to take out so the cash had to be used for productions that would give employment to the local populace. This film was beautifully shot in the Scottish Highlands, along the Cornwall coast and in Palermo, Sicily, and the story has been considerably simplified. Flynn is the heir to a Scottish title who becomes part of a rebellion against the King of England. The rebels are soon defeated and the authorities are after Flynn so he departs to the West Indies with Livesey, an Irish soldier of fortune. Flynn thinks that he may have been betrayed by his brother, Steel, who remained loyal to his king. Down in the Indies, Flynn and Livesey have several adventures including scrapes with pirates. The two men eventually amass enough wealth to return to Scotland where Flynn wants to marry his longtime amour, Campbell. But she thought he was dead so she is now engaged to Steel, another rankle in Flynn's plans for revenge. It takes a while for the family squabble to be assuaged and when Flynn learns that blood is thicker than loyalty to the Crown, he forgives Steel but he does take Campbell away with him and he and Livesey escape the British forces and sail off for further adventures on the other side of the Atlantic. In the mammoth novel, both brothers die and Flynn's character is hardly the most likeable chap. All of that vanished in this script and if you have not read the novel, you might well enjoy the movie. Flynn was already showing signs of his hell-raising and did not leap and thrust and parry with the same verve he showed in CAPTAIN BLOOD and other films. He was only 44 when the picture was made and the tooth was getting somewhat long for this type of glamorous acrobatics.

d, William Keighley; w, Herb Meadow, Harold Medford (based on the novel by Robert Louis Stevenson); ph, Jack Cardiff (Technicolor); m, William Alwyn; ed, Jack Harris; md, Muir Mathieson; art d, Ralph Brinton; cos, Margaret Furse; makeup, George Frost; ch, Patrick Crean.

Adventure   **(PR:A   MPAA:NR)**

MASTER OF BANKDAM, THE*   (1947, Brit.) 105m Holbein/GFD bw

Anne Crawford (Annie Pickersgill), Dennis Price (Joshua Crowther), Tom Walls (Simeon Crowther, Sr.), Stephen Murray (Zebediah Crowther), Linden Travers (Clara Baker), Jimmy Hanley (Simeon Crowther, Jr.), Nancy Price (Lydia Crowther), David Tomlinson (Lancelot Handel Crowther), Patrick Holt (Lemuel Pickersgill), Herbert Lomas (Tom France), Frederick Piper (Ben Pickersgill), Beatrice Varley (Mrs. Pickersgill), Raymond Rollett (Handel Baker), April Stride (Sophie Teresa Crowther), Avis Scott (Mary Crowther), Nicholas Parsons (Edgar Hoylehouse), Maria Var (The Singer), Shelagh Fraser (Alice France), Edgar K. Bruce (Ezra Hoylehouse), Frank Henderson (Dr. Clough), Aubrey Mallalieu (Dr. Bouviere), Kenneth Buckley (Brough), Lyn Evans (Beaumont), Bertram Shuttlesworth (Shires).

A well-told, if slightly longer than necessary epic dealing with three generations in an English mill family. Murray and Price are two rival brothers in a Yorkshire town, fighting for the control of their father's wool mill. Murray marries a local socialite and becomes the town's mayor after building a new hospital. He does this at the expense of the family business, which widens the gap between the siblings. Price dies in a building cave-in at the mill. Walls, the father, is suspicious but Murray assures him it was an accident. Before he dies Walls finds out that it was, indeed, an accident, though one Murray could have prevented. But the old man dies before he can write his son out of the will and Murray inherits the property. He and his wife have a son, who is a rich pampered brat. He sees Price's son Hanley is clearly made to run the mill, but puts his ne'er do well offspring in charge. After returning from Vienna for treatment of a heart ailment Murray finds that his nephew has faced an angry mob of strikers after his son turned coward. Seeing this causes the man to realize who the mill is truly destined for and turns Hanley into the master of the mill. Though the British accents may be a little much for American audiences, this is generally a well acted film throughout. Based on a popular novel of the day, it has a good sense of historical accuracy for its 36-year time span (1854–1900). The direction never falters with the different characters, keeping the film compelling throughout. Var sings "The Fire Of Your Love."

p, Nat Bronsten, Walter Forde, Edward Dryhurst; d, Forde; w, Dryhurst, Moie Charles (based on the novel *The Crowthers of Bankdam* by Thomas Armstrong); ph, Basil Emmott, Arthur Grant; m, Arthur Benjamin; ed, Terence Fisher; md, Muir Mathieson; art d, George Patterson; cos, Doris Lee; makeup, Gerry Fletcher.

Drama   **(PR:C MPAA:NR)**

MASTER OF HORROR* 1/2
(1965, Arg.) 61m Gates-Torres-Vicente Marco/U.S. Films bw (OBRAS MAESTRAS DEL TERROR; AKA: MASTERWORKS OF TERROR)

Narciso Ibanez Menta, Carlos Estrada, Inez Moreno, Narciso Ibanez Serrador, Mercedes Carreras, Lillian Valmar.

Two of Edgar Allan Poe's short stories are adapted for the screen, "The Facts In M. Valdemar's Case" and "The Cask of Amontillado." They don't compare to Roger Corman's versions in TALES OF TERROR (1962). The third story, "The Telltale Heart," was cut for the U.S. release.

p, Nicolas Carreras; d, Enrique Carreras; w, Louis Penafiel (based on stories by Edgar Allan Poe); ph, Americo Hoss; m, Victor Schlichter; ed, Jose Gallego; art d, Mario Vanarelli.

Horror   **(PR:C-O MPAA:NR)**

MASTER OF LASSIE
(SEE: HILLS OF HOME, 1948)

MASTER OF MEN*
(1933) 65m COL bw

Jack Holt (*Buck Garrott*), Fay Wray (*Kay Walling*), Theodore von Eltz (*Grenuker*), Walter Connolly (*Sam Parker*), Berton Churchill (*Mr. Walling*).

An idiotic story set just before the great stock market crash of 1929. Holt is a financial wizard, the head of a steel mill. He goes to New York and wheels some big deals bringing in lots of dough. But wife Wray gets jealous of her husband's love for work and lets one of his enemies know his every move. This results in bankruptcy for Holt the night before Wall Street lays an egg. Finding themselves broke, Holt and Wray kiss and make up, readying themselves for a life of proverty. Slow, poorly directed and as bankrupt as the stock market was on November 1, 1929.

d, Lambert Hillyer; w, Edward Paramore, Seton I. Miller (based on a story by Chester Erskine, Eugene Solow); ph, Joseph August; ed, Gene Havlick.

Drama   **(PR:A MPAA:NR)**

MASTER OF TERROR
(SEE: 4D MAN, THE, 1959)

MASTER OF THE ISLANDS
(SEE: HAWAIIANS, THE, 1970)

MASTER OF THE WORLD* 1/2
(1935, Ger.) 109m Ariel bw (DER HERR DER WELT; AKA: RULER OF THE WORLD)

Walter Janssen (*Dr. Heller*), Sybille Schmitz (*Vilma, his Wife*), Walter Franck (*Wolf, his Assistant*), Siegfried Schurenberg (*Baumann, Mining Engineer*), Klaus Pohl, Aribert Waesher, Willi Schur, Otto Wernicke, Karl Platen, Ernst Behmer.

A crazed scientist creates an army of robots which are controlled by human workers pushing buttons. This was director Piel's fourth and last science fiction film (DIE GROSSE WETTE—1915, EIN UNSICHTBARER GEHT DURCH DIE STADT—1933 and DIE WELT OHNE MASKE—1934).

d, Harry Piel; w, George Muehlen-Schute; ph, Ewald Daub.

Science Fiction   **(PR:A MPAA:NR)**

MASTER OF THE WORLD**
(1961) 104m Alta Vista/AIP c

Vincent Price (*Robur*), Charles Bronson (*Strock*), Henry Hull (*Prudent*), Mary Webster (*Dorothy*), David Frankham (*Philip*), Richard Harrison (*Alistair*), Vito Scotti (*Topage*), Wally Campo (*Turner*), Steve Masino (*Weaver*), Ken Terrell (*Shanks*), Peter Besbas (*Wilson*).

In an unlikely role, Bronson plays a peaceful government agent of the late 19th century. He takes his daughter Webster, her fiance Frankham, and munitions expert Hull on a balloon voyage over a mysterious Pennsylvania crater. It has been the cause of several strange eruptions and Bronson's job is to find out what's been happening. They are shot down and discover that the crater is the secret headquarters of Price. He is a scientist putting the finishing touches on "the Albatross" an enormous flying ship. He intends to use the craft to fly around the world and destroy all instruments of destruction, eliminating war from the face of the Earth. Taking his prisoners along, Price proceeds in a frenzied glee, destroying not only the munitions but innocent people as well. Bronson decides to destroy the ship, even at the risk of the hostages' lives. But an emergency repair landing on a Mediterranean island affords a chance to escape and Bronson destroys the "Albatross" with the evil Price and his crew being killed. This was one of AIP's more expensive outings. Despite some good special effects, the film is surprisingly bland.

Though Bronson is better in this than most of his other films, he still has a hard time expressing more than three or four emotions. Price is a complete disappointment, giving a restrained performance where a more outrageous parody would have been in order. The film does employ stock footage of man's early attempts at powered flight and the effect is both comical and intelligent.

p, James H. Nicholson; d, William Witney; w, Richard Matheson (based on the novels *Master of the World* and *Robur, the Conqueror* by Jules Verne); ph, Gil Warrenton, Kay Norton (Magnacolor); m, Les Baxter; ed, Anthony Carras; prod d, Daniel Haller; art d, Haller; set d, Harry Reif; spec eff, Tim Barr, Wah Chang, Gene Warren, Ray Mercer; m/l, Baxter, Lenny Addelson, "Master of the World," (sung by Darrye Stevens); makeup, Fred Phillips.

Fantasy/Adventure   **Cas.**   **(PR:A MPAA:NR)**

MASTER PLAN, THE**
(1955, Brit.) 78m Gibraltar/GN bw

Wayne Morris (*Maj. Brent*), Tilda Thamar (*Helen*), Norman Wooland (*Col. Cleaver*), Mary Mackenzie (*Miss Gray*), Arnold Bell (*Gen. Goulding*), Marjorie Stewart (*Yvonne*), Laurie Main (*Johnny Orwell*), Frederick Schrecker (*Dr. Morgan Stem*), Seymour Green, Lucienne Hill, Alan Tilvern, John Gabriel, Richard Marner.

Set in Germany after WW II, Morris is the American major given the assignment of stopping information leakage to the Communists. He winds up actually working for the enemy, a result of blackouts he suffers which allow for the spies to hypnotize him and then have him photograph valuable documents. Intriguing story suffers from inefficient production techniques. Morris, a legitimate war hero who had shot down seven Japanese aircraft and sunk three ships, was in a career decline at the time; he went to England for this one as a result.

p, Steven Pallos, Charles A. Leeds; d, Hugh Raker [Cy Endfield]; w, Raker, Donald Bull (based on the TV play "Operation North Star" by Harold Bratt); ph, Jonah Jones; m, De Wolfe; ed, Jim Connock; art d, Scott Macgregor.

Spy Drama   **(PR:A MPAA:NR)**

MASTER RACE, THE**
(1944) 96m RKO bw

George Coulouris (*Von Beck*), Stanley Ridges (*Phil Carson*), Osa Massen (*Helena*), Carl Esmond (*Andrei*), Nancy Gates (*Nina*), Morris Carnovsky (*Old Man Bartoc*), Lloyd Bridges (*Frank*), Eric Feldary (*Altmeier*), Helen Beverly (*Mrs. Varin*), Gavin Muir (*William Forsythe*), Paul Guilfoyle (*Katry*), Richard Nugent (*Sgt. O'Farrell*), Louis [Ludwig] Donath (*Schmidt*), Herbert Rudley (*John*), Ghislaine [Gigi] Perreau (*Baby*), Jason Robards, Sr. (*Jacob Weiner*), Merrill Roden (*George Rudan*).

This fairly well-done tale deals with Coulouris as a German officer, loyal to Hitler's ideals. Disguised as a Belgian patriot, he comes to a small village and spreads Nazi hatred in an effort to make the town vulnerable for a coming Nazi blitzkrieg. Released towards the end of WW II, the film opened with stock footage of the D-Day invasion of Normandy then cut to Nazi headquarters, where Coulouris and his fellow officers are given the assignment to weaken the outlying areas of the Empire for preparation of a new Nazi rise. Though it did fairly well at the box office, the film was not nearly as successful as the same production team's film HITLER'S CHILDREN from the previous year. Coulouris did an efficient job as the Nazi officer making a last attempt to save his ideology, and the supporting cast worked well in ensemble. One of many exploitation movies made to show how good the allies were and how awful the Nazis were, it had some fairly good moments. The sets which were supposedly depicting a bombarded, northern European town were the same sets as had been used for THE HUNCHBACK OF NOTRE DAME where they served as medieval Paris.

p, Robert Golden; d, Herbert J. Biberman, Madeleine Dmytryk; w, Biberman, Anne Froelick, Rowland Leigh (based on a story by Biberman); ph, Russell Metty; m, Roy Webb; ed, Ernie Leadley; md, Constantin Bakaleinikoff; art d, Albert D'Agostino, Jack Okey; cos, Renie.

Drama   **Cas.**   **(PR:C MPAA:NR)**

MASTER SPY**
(1964, Brit.) 71m Eternal/AA bw

Stephen Murray (*Boris Turganev*), June Thorburn (*Leila*), Alan Wheatley (*Paul Skelton*), John Carson (*Richard Colman*), John Brown (*John Baxter*), Jack Watson (*Capt. Foster*), Ernest Clark (*Dr. Pembury*), Peter Gilmore (*Tom Masters*), Marne Maitland (*Dr. Asafu*), Ellen Pollock (*Dr. Morrell*), Hugh Morton (*Sir Gilbert Saunders*), Basil Dignam (*Richard Horton*), Victor Beaumont (*Petrov*), Derek Francis (*Police Inspector*), Hamilton Dyce (*Airport Controller*).

Murray is a Russian scientist who defects to England and is assigned a top-secret job with a government nuclear research lab. But he's an agent for the Russkies and passes information to Wheatley, a wealthy landowner who gives the goods to Moscow. Lab assistant Thorburn catches on but it turns out that Murray is really a British spy passing phony information to traitor Wheatley. Murray goes through the motions of a trial and is finally sent back to Moscow where he will be a mole for the Brits, leaving the audience with a nagging question: if Murray was an Englishman working as a spy in Russia in the first place, why the elaborate plan to trip him up in Great Britain? The picture is often darkly lit to the point of distraction in an otherwise routine production.

p, Maurice J. Wilson; d, Montgomery Tully; w, Wilson, Tully (based on the story "They Also Serve" by Gerald Anstruther and Paul White); ph, Geoffrey Faithfull; m, Ken Thorne; ed, Eric Boyd-Perkins; md, Philip Martell; art d, Harry White.

Spy Drama   **(PR:A MPAA:NR)**

MASTER TOUCH, THE*
(1974, Ital./Ger.) 96m Verona/WB c (UN UOMO DA RISPETTARE; AKA: HEARTS AND MINDS)

Kirk Douglas (*Wallace*), Florinda Bolkan (*Anna*), Giuliano Gemma (*Marco*), Rene Koldehoff (*Police Detective*), Wolfgang Preiss (*Miller*).

Douglas is a safe-cracker fresh out of jail. His wife (Bolkan) doesn't want him to go back to his old job but he can't help himself and with the aid of trapeze artist Gemma, he's soon up to his old tricks. This formula time-waster was saved from the National General Pictures dust-shelf after Warner Brothers took over First Artists Productions releasing commitments.

p, Marina Cicogna; d, Michele Lupo; w, Mino Roli, Franco Bucceri, Roberto Leoni, Lupo; ph, Tonino Delli Colli (Eastmancolor); m, Ennio Morricone; ed, Antonietta Zitta; art d, Francesco Bronzi; cos, Enrico Sabbatini.

Crime   **Cas.**   **(PR:C MPAA:PG)**

MASTERMIND**½   (1977) 131m Master/Goldstone c

Zero Mostel (*Inspector Hoku*), Bradford Dillman, Gawn Grainger, Keiko Kishi, Frankie Sakai, Herbert Berghof, Jules Munshin, Sorrell Booke.

A fairly good spoof of CHARLIE CHAN films features Mostel as an oriental detective assigned to protect a special robot from various foreign governments. It is full of good comic slapstick that Mostel was a master of, but surprisingly this 1969 production was withheld from release for years before seeing a few limited engagements. Comedy fans might want to try and find it, as this is worth a look.

p, Malcolm Stuart; d, Alex March; ph, (Eastmancolor).

Comedy   **Cas.**   **(PR:A MPAA:G)**

MASTERSON OF KANSAS**½   (1954) 72m COL c

George Montgomery (*Bat Masterson*), Nancy Gates (*Amy Merrick*), James Griffith (*Doc Holliday*), Jean Willes (*Dallas Corey*), Benny Rubin (*Coroner*), William A. Henry (*Charlie Fry*), David Bruce (*Clay Bennett*), Bruce Cowling (*Wyatt Earp*), Gregg Barton (*Sutton*), Donald Murphy (*Virgil Earp*), Gregg Martell (*Mitch*), Sandy Sanders (*Tyler*), Jay Silverheels (*Yellow Hawk*), John Maxwell (*Merrick*), Wesley Hudman (*Gage*), Leonard Geer (*Lt. Post*).

Montgomery, Griffith and Cowling are three of the West's most famous lawmen out to stop bad guy Henry from inciting an Indian war. The angry Indian chief is played by Silverheels, who gained his fame as Tonto on the TV series "The Lone Ranger." The slight script concentrates on wall-to-wall action. Gates is a fairly appealing love interest and Maxwell is fine as her hapless rancher father.

p, Sam Katzman; d, William Castle; w, Douglas Heyes; ph, Henry Freulich (Technicolor); ed, Henry Batista.

Western   **(PR:A MPAA:NR)**

MATA HARI***½   (1931) 91m MGM bw

Greta Garbo (*Mata Hari*), Ramon Novarro (*Lt. Alexis Rosanoff*), Lionel Barrymore (*Gen. Serge Shubin*), Lewis Stone (*Andriani*), C. Henry Gordon (*Dubois*), Karen Morley (*Carlotta*), Alec B. Francis (*Caron*), Blanche Frederici (*Sister Angelica*), Edmund Breese (*Warden*), Helen Jerome Eddy (*Sister Genevieve*), Frank Reicher (*The Cook, a Spy*), Sarah Padden (*Sister Theresa*), Harry Cording (*Ivan*), Gordon De Main (*Aide*), Mischa Auer (*Executed Man*), Michael Visaroff (*Orderly*), Cecil Cunningham (*Gambler*).

The subject of the Javanese-Dutch spy of WW I, Mata Hari, was not new to films, but when Garbo essayed the role of the beautiful exotic dancer who bedded for secret information, it was not only news but caused MGM to produce a lavish and memorable film. We first see the German spy in Paris, posing as a dancer. Her spymaster, Stone, directs her to intercept certain Russian messages involving Allied troop movements. For some time Garbo has been having an affair with Barrymore, an indiscreet general, but she meets Novarro, a lowly lieutenant, and truly falls in love with him. Then she learns that Novarro has the messages she is seeking and she forsakes her love for him to serve her country, taking him to bed while her associates copy his messages. Barrymore learns of the tryst and explodes, threatening to turn Garbo in as an agent and implicate Novarro. To save herself and her unwitting lover, Garbo shoots and kills Barrymore. When Novarro begins to seek out Barrymore, Garbo compels him to leave. The pilot flies to Russia where he is shot down and blinded in the crash. Learning of this, Garbo follows her instincts of love rather than her military orders and goes to Novarro to tell him of her devotion to him. Stone orders an agent to kill her but the man is foiled by local police. Garbo is then unmasked and is brought to trial. Rather than involve Novarro in testimony that will expose her black past to him, she pleads guilty so that his memory of her will be pure. Just before her execution, Novarro is brought to her—Garbo's last request—thinking her prison is a hospital and that she is dying of an illness. They meet briefly, declare their love, and then she is led from her cell, accompanied by nuns, to the firing squad. Garbo is stunning and full of her special mystique as the exotic dancer-spy, doing one number wearing a sort of bikini-like costume, snaking her body about a lascivious-looking, many-armed Buddha-like statue, an odd, interpretive dance which reveals more of the great star's gorgeous body then ever before displayed. Fitzmaurice directs with great style here and uses exquisite production values to the fullest. Both Garbo and Novarro had accents that later caused some sneering critics to ridicule some of their lines in MATA HARI, particularly one of Novarro's which sounded like "what's the mata, Mata?" Of course, little shown here is based on real events. Gertrud Margarete Zelle MacLeod, 1876–1917, danced in Paris and stole secrets from the French for the Germans, low-level secrets at that, until she was uncovered as a spy and shot, not in Russia, but at Saint-Lazare in France on October 15, 1917, smilingly facing a firing squad that proved to be made up of either bad marksmen or men loathe to kill a woman, only four bullets finding their marks. Mata Hari was in love with a blind Russian aviator but he was nowhere near her when she died. It would have been impossible for Garbo to simulate the real Mata Hari's dance since she cavorted before drooling audiences, mostly all male, naked except for breastplates. No mention is made of the spy's little girl, who was being raised in a Dutch convent at the time of her execution. Mata Hari gave a French journalist a locket containing a miniature picture of herself ringed with tiny pearls to give to her daughter an hour before her execution. Mata Hari, a Dutch

pseudonym meaning "Eye of the Dawn," was profiled in films by Asta Nielsen in a German production, DIE SPIONIN (1921), by Magda Sonja in MATA HARI, DIE ROTE TANZERIN (1927), and by Jeanne Moreau in MATA HARI (1965), but none compared with the fabulous Garbo interpretation. Although this film lacked the violence that permeated the spy's real world, it captures momentarily the actual hazards awaiting any agent who faltered, particularly in the scene where Morley, a hesitant German spy, is murdered by agents. British censors insisted that the actual execution scene be cut and it was, not appearing in any American prints after the film's initial release. Also softened were two love scenes where Novarro and Garbo clinch and then turn out the lights. Of particular annoyance to the British was one scene where Garbo reclines on a couch and Novarro stands over her, looking up to an icon of The Virgin Mary, and then sinking into the arms of the alluring spy, as if to indicate that Garbo's seductive power was stronger than any religious symbol. In the British version, the icon was changed to a portrait of somebody's mother with a vigil light beneath it. The finish of Garbo's weird, undulating dance before the Malaysian idol shows her naked back, hips gyrating as she does a subtle strip and some of these scenes may have been performed by one of Garbo's many uncredited doubles, maybe Elizabeth Taylor-Martin or perhaps the most used double, Sigrun Salvason, a woman possessing her own brand of mystique, she being found mysteriously killed in 1934. This was Garbo's 18th movie, the second with Barrymore, the fifth with Stone, and the one and only with Novarro, then Hollywood's greatest heartthrob and matinee idol. Garbo had earlier played a spy in THE MYSTERIOUS LADY but with a lesser impact.

p, Irving Thalberg; d, George Fitzmaurice; w, Benjamin Glazer, Leo Birinski, Doris Anderson, Gilbert Emery; ph, William Daniels; ed, Frank Sullivan.

Spy Drama   **(PR:A MPAA:NR)**

MATA HARI***

(1965, Fr./Ital.) 95m Filmel Films Du Carrose-Simar-Films Fida Cinematografica/Magna Pictures bw (MATA HARI AGENT H-21; MATA HARI, AGENTE SEGRETO H 21)

Jeanne Moreau (*Mata Hari*), Jean-Louis Trintignant (*Capt. Francois Lassalle*), Claude Rich (*Julien, The Chauffeur*), Frank Villard (*Colonel Pelletier*), Albert Remy (*Adam Zelle*), Georges Riquier (*Ludovic*), Henri Garcin (*Gaston*), Hella Petri (*Baronne du Maine*), Marie Dubois (*Soldier's Fiancee*), Nicole Desailly (*Mata Hari's Maid*), Carla Marlier (*Chambermaid*), Jean-Marie Drot (*German Spy Chief*), Marcel Berbert (*Plainsclothesman Following Mata Hari*), Georges Geret, Charles Denner.

This neat version of the famous spy's adventures takes a different approach than one might suspect. Rather than play up the romantic end of the spy life, we are shown the portrait of a woman who happens to be a spy. Nicely portrayed by Moreau, the script is co-written by Truffaut, whose own work often reflected the fascination with the characters of his leading women. The story follows Moreau as she carries on her activities during WW I. Ordered by her German superiors to seduce the French captain Trintignant, she does so, stealing needed papers but inadvertently falling in love with her victim. This eventually leads to her downfall and she is finally shot after being found guilty of espionage. Moureau gives a nicely understated performance, letting all the paradoxes of the woman flow naturally. At times her performance carries an improvisational feeling. The film's direction is straightforward, telling the story well, but never quite capturing its romantic nature.

p, Eugene Lepicier; d, Jean-Louis Richard; w, Richard, Francois Truffaut; ph, Michel Kelber; m, Georges Delerue; ed, Kenout Peltier; art d, Claude Pignot; cos, Pierre Cardin.

Biography   **(PR:C MPAA:NR)**

MATA HARI'S DAUGHTER**

(1954, Fr./Ital) 92m Regent bw (LA FILLE DE MATA HARI; AKA: DAUGHTER OF MATA HARI)

Ludmilla Tcherina (*Elyne*), Erno Crisa (*Prince Anak*), Frank Latimore (*Douglas Kent*), Milly Vitale (*Angela*), Enzo Bilotti (*Von Hopen*), V. Inkyinoff (*Naos*).

Ballerina Tcherina manages to get a few dance numbers in as she plays the title spy. In Indonesia in 1941, she attempts to help the Dutch stop the relentless Japanese onslaught, but for her troubles is placed against a wall and shot. Mediocre espionage thriller suffers from bad dubbing.

d, Carmine Gallone, Renzo Merusi; w, Merusi, Jean Aurel, Piccini Vitali (based on the novel by Cecil Saint-Laurent); ph, Gabor Pogany; m, Alessandro Casagrande; ed, Borys Levine; art d, Virgilio Marchi; ch, Ludmilla Tcherina.

Spy Drama   **(PR:A MPAA:NR)**

MATALOS Y VUELVE

(SEE: KILL THEM ALL AND COME BACK ALONE, 1970, Ital./Span.)

MATCH KING, THE***½   (1932) 70m FN/WB-FN bw

Warren William (*Paul Kroll*), Lili Damita (*Marta Molnar*), Glenda Farrell (*Babe*), Harold Huber (*Scarlatti*), Spencer Charters (*Oscar*), John Wray (*Foreman*), Murray Kinnell (*Nyberg*), Hardie Albright (*Eric Borg*), Juliette Compton (*Sonia*), Claire Dodd (*Ilse Wagner*), Alan Hale (*Borglund*), Edmund Breese (*Christofsen*), Harry Beresford (*Hobe*), George Meeker (*Erickson*), DeWitt Jennings (*Rodensky*), Alphonse Ethier (*Uncle*), Robert McWade (*Larsen*), Greta Meyer, Bodil Rosing.

This is an unabashed biography of one of the most spectacular world-wide swindlers of all time, Ivar Kreuger, made hot on the heels of Kreuger's suicide in Paris after he was exposed as a giant fraud, having bilked tens of thousands of investors out of countless millions by selling worthless stock in his many bogus European companies. The film begins in Paris just as William, playing Kroll/Kreuger, realizes he is about to be revealed as a swindler and contemplates suicide. He thinks back to his earliest beginnings and, in flashback, he is shown as a street cleaner in Chicago, where he plans a murder in his fantastic scheme to monopolize something used repeatedly every day, the common kitchen match. He swindles bankers into pumping tons of money into his phony firms, using and discarding women along the way as if they were burned-out matches. On his rise to ill-gotten riches, the suave William attracts a famous European film star, played by Damita, who dresses, acts, and talks like Greta Garbo, and for good reason. Garbo was one of Kreuger's real-life victims, reportedly duped into investing substantial funds in his bogus schemes. The film comes very close to reality, even detailing the method by which William/Kreuger negotiated a $40 million loan from Wall Street financiers (which actually happened). Director Bretherton deftly, and with startling pace, details a sinister career of murder, blackmail, and forgery that is no less fanciful than Kreuger's actual machinations. (Kreuger built his fortune by offering some Italian bonds, which he had masterfully forged, as collateral for his multi-million-dollar loans and only when these bonds were determined to be fake did his career end.) The overall production of this film is superior and William is a wonder to behold as he handles his conniving role with marvelous restraint. Damita is a bit campy as the Garbo-like actress who dumps her lover-entrepreneur after suspecting his empire is about to collapse. All in all, THE MATCH KING is an intriguing artifact of the early talkie era.

p, Hal Wallis; d, Howard Bretherton; w, Houston Branch, Sidney Sutherland (based on the novel by Einar Thorvaldson); ph, Robert Kurrle; ed, Jack Killifer.

Crime Drama   **(PR:C MPAA:NR)**

MATCHLESS**   (1967, Ital.) 104m Dino de Laurentiis/UA c

Patrick O'Neal (Perry "Matchless" Liston), Ira von Furstenberg (Arabella), Donald Pleasence (Andreanu), Henry Silva (Hank Norris), Nicoletta Machiavelli (Tipsy), Howard St. John (Gen. Shapiro), Sorrell Booke (Col. Coolpepper), Tiziano Cortini (Hogdon), Valery Inkijinoff (Hypnotizer), Andy Ho (O-Chin), Elizabeth Wu (O-Lan), M. Mishiku (Li-Huang), Jacques Herlin (O-Chin's Doctor), Giulio Donnini (Professor), Lewis Jordon, Alfredo Martinelli, Ennio Antonelli.

Spy spoof features O'Neal as a journalist mistaken for a spy by Chinese Communists. He's tortured in an effort to get some information about a secret chemical and then thrown into a cell. There he encounters an ancient Oriental who gives him a magic ring that when rubbed will temporarily turn its wearer invisible. He uses it to escape from a firing squad but ends up being tortured by Americans for the same reasons as he was in the film's beginning. He finally agrees to help obtain the formula for the U.S., with the aid of von Furstenberg. After tussles with another spy (Machiavelli) and an American traitor (Silva) he uses the magic ring to get the formula. But realizing how dangerous this chemical is he throws it into a Hamburg harbor. The film has an oddball sense of fun, poking its elbow into the ribs of the military and spy films in general. But the effect is hampered by the poor quality filmmaking. Though filmed in English, von Furstenberg's dialog is clearly a bad dubbing job. The director has a good feel for comedy pacing but there is little talent shown in the amateur photography job, which is far too grainy. O'Neal is a good character actor but the supporting cast is too uneven in talent to make this work.

p, Ermanno Donati, Luigi Carpentieri; d, Alberto Lattuada; w, Lattuada, Dean Craig [Mario Pierotti], Luigi Malerba, Jack Pulman (based on a story by Donati); ph, Sandro D'Eva (Technicolor); m, Ennio Morricone, Piero Piccioni, Gino Marinuzzi, Jr.; ed, Franco Fraticelli; md, Bruno Nicolai; art d, Enzo del Prato; set d, Gisella Longo; cos, Piero Tosi, Cesare Rovatti, Forquet; spec eff, Guy Delecluse.

Spy/Comedy   **(PR:C MPAA:NR)**

MATCHLESS½   (1974, Aus.) 55m Australian Film Institute bw

Sally Blake (Cynthia), Denise Otto (Annie), Allan Penney (Victor).

An interesting effort, produced in part by the Experimental Film and Television Fund of the Australian Film Institute. The story deals with two women living together. One is mentally disturbed and the other epileptic. They take in an alcoholic boarder to help make ends meet but the film ends tragically with his death on a park bench. Told somewhat surrealistically, what appears to be flashbacks are often scenes in "real" time. First-time director Popadopoulos shows some talent and keeps the film interesting despite its depressing and meandering story. The trio of actors, all unknowns, give fairly accomplished performances.

p&d, John Papadopoulos; w, Sally Blake; ph, Russell Boyd; ed, Kit Guyatt.

Drama   **(PR:O MPAA:NR)**

MATCHMAKER, THE*½   (1958) 101m PAR bw

Shirley Booth (Dolly Levi), Anthony Perkins (Cornelius), Shirley MacLaine (Irene Molloy), Paul Ford (Horace Vandergelder), Robert Morse (Barnaby Tucker), Perry Wilson (Minnie Fay), Wallace Ford (Malachi Stack), Russell Collins (Joe Scanlon), Rex Evans (August), Gavin Gordon (Rudolph), Torben Meyer (Maitre D'), Joe Forte, Jon Lormer, Arthur Lovejoy, Sandra Giles, Loraine Crawford, Fred Somers.

A long, long time ago, John Oxenford wrote a British farce called "A Day Well Spent." That served as the "inspiration" for Johann Nestroy, a Viennese playwright who penned a work using the same subject matter. While on a trip to Austria, Thornton Wilder happened to see a revival of Nestroy's play (or so the legend goes as related by Viennese Otto Preminger who saw that play in the 1920s) and appropriated it as the 1938 flop "The Merchant Of Yonkers." It was then revised and presented as "The Matchmaker" in 1955 and became a hit with Robert Morse repeating his original Broadway role in the film. The picture was made later as the musical play and movie, HELLO DOLLY. It is 1884 and Yonkers matchmaker Booth (in just about her only comedy film role) is trying to unite Ford, a shopkeeper/merchant and MacLaine, a Manhattan hatmaker. Her plan is actually to nab Ford for herself but she must first pretend to be doing a job for him. Ford and Booth venture to the city and leave his two clerks, Perkins and Morse, behind to watch the store. Both young men are very naive and, with the boss gone, they make a pact to go to New York and kiss a pretty girl, any pretty girl. In a weird turn of events, Morse and Perkins meet MacLaine and her pal, Wilson, and squire them to

one of the city's poshest restaurants. They then discover that they do not have enough money to pay the bill. That is overcome as Perkins conveniently finds the wallet of Ford, who is in the next private dining room, with Booth. Ford discovers this and fires the hapless youths. Booth is about to lose a commission and, worse than that, lose Ford. She helps Perkins open a shop across the road from Ford's and he must acquiesce; he'll marry Booth and take Perkins in as a partner. There were some changes in Hayes' script from the play, none of which improved the piece. The actors had the annoying task of speaking directly at the camera with their comments, something that works on the stage from time to time but breaks the mood in a film. The one weak link in the excellent ensemble was the casting of Wilson as MacLaine's friend. Further investigation of that flaw uncovered the fact that she was married to the director. Nuf said.

p, Don Hartman; d, Joseph Anthony; w, John Michael Hayes (based on the play by Thornton Wilder); ph, Charles Lang (VistaVision); m, Adolph Deutsch; ed, Howard Smith; art d, Hal Pereira, Roland Anderson; cos, Edith Head.

Comedy   **(PR:A MPAA:NR)**

MATCHMAKING OF ANNA, THE**

                    (1972, Gr.) 87m Katsourides c (TO PROXENIO TIS ANNAS)

Anna Vaguena (Anna), Stavros Kalarogiou (Kosmas), Smaro Veaki (Anna's Mistress), Ketty Panou (The Mistress' Daughter), Costas Regopoulos (Mistress' Son-in-law).

A simple and well-told story of love among the working class features Vaguena as the long-time maid of Veaki. A marriage between Kalarogiou and Vaguena is arranged by Veaki's daughter Panou. The young couple goes out for a walk and though they feel awkward, they gradually get to know one another and feel the beginnings of love. Not realizing the time Vaguena returns to her mistress' home quite late. Kalarogiou is blamed and considered to be not good enough for the young girl. In addition, the family realizes they cannot do without her maid services and try to break up the marriage. Even the girl's mother agrees, as she needs the money her daughter gives her. Reluctantly Vaguena subordinates her feelings to practicality and accepts her fate. This is an especially sensitive and well-made film. The direction is straight-forward, nicely portraying the maid's boring existence and giving a magical quality to her brief love affair. Vaguena is marvelous, giving a fine performance that is natural and effective. The supporting cast is equally fine, and the overall production values are excellent. An impressive, humanistic tale.

p, Dinos Katsourides; d, Pantelis Voulgaris; w, Menis Koumantareas, Voulgaris; ph, Nicos Kavoukides.

Drama   **(PR:O MPAA:NR)**

MATE DOMA IVA?

                    (SEE: DO YOU KEEP A LION AT HOME?, 1966, Czech.)

MATHIAS SANDORF**   (1963, Fr.) 105m SFC-DIC-Procusa/UGC c

Louis Jourdan (Mathias), Serena Vergano (Elizabeth), Renaud Mary (Sarcany), Bernard Blier (Torenthal), Francisco Rabal (Rotenborg).

This was one of the few Jules Verne novels never adapted by American studios. The story is the simple tale of a nobleman, played by Jourdan, who sides with revolutionaries in a fictional 19th Century country. His daughter (Mary), is involved with the head of the country's army and has her father arrested. However his underground friends help him escape and together they rise up to overthrow the evil government. The story and dialog are simplistic and cartoonish at best, but there's some well-done action sequences that carry the film along to its climax.

d, Georges Lampin; w, Gerard Cartier, Charles Spaak, Lampin (based on the novel by Jules Verne); ph, C. Paniagua (Eastmancolor); ed, Henri Taverna.

Adventure   **(PR:A MPAA:NR)**

MATILDA*½   (1978) 105m AIP c

Elliott Gould (Bernie Bonnelli), Robert Mitchum (Duke Parkhurst), Harry Guardino (Uncle Nono), Clive Revill (Billy Baker), Karen Carlson (Kathleen Smith), Roy Clark (Wild Bill Wildman), Lionel Stander (Pinky Schwab), Art Metrano (Gordon Baum), Larry Pennell (Lee Dockerty), Roberta Collins (Tanya Six), Lenny Montana (Mercanti), Frank Avianca (Renato), Jimmy Lennon (Ring Announcer), Don Dunphy (Ringside Announcer), George Latka (Referee), Mike Willesee (Australian Announcer).

MATILDA is a G-Rated picture that bounces along as happily as the kangaroo it concerns. Gould is a two-bit promoter who occupies a tiny office with his brother-in-law, Stander, manager of heavyweight champ Pennell. The real manager is Guardino, a gangland chief who hides behind Stander. Mitchum is a latter-day Grantland Rice-type sports columnist who would like to expose Guardino as the power behind the heavyweight division champ. Revill is a former welterweight champ who is in financial trouble and Karen Carlson is the animal lover who objects when a kangaroo is put up against a human in a boxing match. The plot wafts along, exposes the characters, and culminates in a Nevada title crack for a kangaroo against the champion. It's all as believable as a politician's promise, but lots more fun, as producer Ruddy (of GODFATHER fame) and director Mann allow Gould to play a hustling theatrical agent who goes from holes in his shoes to cashmere jackets when he takes on a kangaroo client. Roy Clark is miscast as the boxing commissioner, but lovely Roberta Collins is delightful as always. Several real ring announcers are seen as themselves, including the dean of them all, Don Dunphy. Comic actor Art Metrano does well in a tiny part. The picture came and went like a Santa Ana wind and disappeared from sight, despite fairly good notices. It's the kind of picture Disney used to make and deserved a better fate. Old fashioned, sometimes hokey, but good fun through and through and only marred by too many product plugs that annoyed the eyes. The same blatant plugging was seen to terrible advantage in SUPERMAN where it seemed every other scene had a Marlboro ad in it.

p, Albert S. Ruddy; d, Daniel Mann; w, Ruddy, Timothy Galfas (based on the book by Paul Gallico); ph, Jack Woolf (Movielab Color); ed, Allan A. Jacobs; prod d, Boris Levin; cos, Jack Martell, Donna Roberts Orme; spec eff, Jerry Endler; m/l, "When I'm With You I'm Feeling Good," Carol Connors, Ernie Sheldon (sung by Pat and Debbie Boone).

Comedy **Cas.** **(PR:A MPAA:G)**

MATINEE IDOL* ¹/₂ (1933, Brit.) 75m Wyndham/UA bw

Camilla Horn (Sonia Vance), Miles Mander (Harley Travers), Marguerite Allan (Christine Vance), Viola Keats (Gladys Wheeler), Anthony Hankey (Sir Brian Greville), Hay Petrie (Mr. Clappit), Margaret Yarde (Mrs. Clappit), Albert Whelan (Barlow).

The stage serves as the background for this moderately intriguing murder mystery which has German actress-dancer Horn turning detective as the blonde charmer attempts to clear her sister (Allan) from a murder charge. Theater atmosphere adds a touch of glamour to the mundane plotting.

p, Bray Wyndham; d, George King; w, Charles Bennett.

Mystery **(PR:A MPAA:NR)**

MATING GAME, THE*** (1959) 96m MGM c

Debbie Reynolds (Mariette Larkin), Tony Randall (Lorenzo Charlton), Paul Douglas (Pop Larkin), Fred Clark (Oliver Kelsey), Una Merkel (Ma Larkin), Philip Ober (Wendell Burnshaw), Philip Coolidge (Reverend Osgood), Charles Lane (Bigelow), Trevor Bardette (Chief Guthrie), Bill Smith (Barney), Addison Powell (DeGroot), Rickey Murray (Lee Larkin), Donald Losby (Grant Larkin), Cheryl Bailey (Victoria Larkin), Caryl Bailey (Susan Larkin).

This fun farce stars Randall as a tax examiner out to investigate farmer Douglas and his wife Merkel. Upon his arrival, he discovers this couple has never paid taxes, nor do they use money. A typical transaction involves a ton of manure traded for some hogs which are swapped for a refrigerator, which in turn is traded in on an organ that ends up being a donation to the church. This confusing system, along with Douglas' conniving ways, cause Randall to quaff one too many. He's then enraptured with the lovely, earthy farm girl Reynolds and decides to help the family. His superior discovers his improprieties and presents Douglas with a bill for $50,000. But Randall comes to the rescue, finding a claim for an ancestor of Douglas that dates to the Civil War. According to his calculations, the government owes Douglas $14,000,000. But Douglas agrees to forget the whole thing if the government will agree to forgive his past transgressions as well as future tax bills. The direction maintains a furious screwball pace, and the laughs come easily and often. Reynolds is a delight, nearly stealing the picture. Though Randall is a bit stiff in his straight scenes, his comic turns are terrific, especially his marvelous drunken scene and the resulting hangover. Some nice camera work and a snappy script.

p, Philip Barry, Jr.; d, George Marshall; w, William Roberts (based on the novel The Darling Buds of May by H. E. Bates); ph, Robert Bronner (CinemaScope, Metrocolor); m, Jeff Alexander; ed, John McSweeney, Jr.; art d, William A. Horning, Malcolm Brown; cos, Helen Rose; m/l, title song, Charles Strouse, Lee Adams (sung by Reynolds).

Comedy **(PR:A MPAA:NR)**

MATING OF MILLIE, THE** ¹/₂ (1948) 87m COL bw

Glenn Ford (Doug Andrews), Evelyn Keyes (Millie McGonigle), Ron Randell (Ralph Galloway), Willard Parker (Phil Jones), Virginia Hunter (Madge), Jimmy Hunt (Tommy Bassett), Mabel Paige (Mrs. Hanson), Virginia Brissac (Mrs. Thomas), Patsy Creighton (Cookie), Tom Stevenson (Harvey Willoughby).

Keyes is a business woman with her heart set on adopting an orphan. Since regulations state she must be married in order to adopt, she reluctantly goes out looking for a husband. She enlists the help of her pal Ford—a free-wheeling type who has similar feelings towards marriage—to help her find a mate. You'd have to be dead not to figure out what happens next in this amusing comedy. Ford and Keyes work well as a team, playing with and against each other nicely. Hunt is a little too cute as the orphan that Keyes falls for. The dialog is witty, and the film is well directed in a good comedic style.

p, Casey Robinson; d, Henry Levin; w, Louella MacFarlane, St. Clair McKelway (based on a story by Adele Comandini); ph, Joseph Walker; m, Werner R. Heymann; ed, Richard Fantl; md, M.W. Stoloff; art d, Stephen Goosson, Walter Holscher; cos, Jean Louis.

Comedy **(PR:A MPAA:NR)**

MATING OF THE SABINE WOMEN, THE
(SEE: SHAME OF THE SABINE WOMEN, THE, 1962, Mex.)

MATING SEASON, THE** ¹/₂ (1951) 101m PAR bw

Gene Tierney (Maggie Carleton), John Lund (Van McNulty), Miriam Hopkins (Fran Carleton), Thelma Ritter (Ellen McNulty), Jan Sterling (Betsy), Larry Keating (Mr. Kallinger, Sr.), James Lorimer (George C. Kallinger, Jr.), Gladys Hurlbut (Mrs. Conger), Cora Witherspoon (Mrs. Williamson), Malcolm Keen (Mr. Williamson), Ellen Corby (Annie), Billie Bird (Mugsy), Samuel Colt (Col. Conger), Grayce Hampton (Mrs. Fahnstock), Stapleton Kent (Dr. Chorley), Bob Kortman (Janitor), Jimmy Hunt (Boy), Bess Flowers (Friend at Wedding), Gordon Arnold, John Bryant (Ushers at Wedding), Jean Ruth, Laura Elliott (Bridesmaids), Charles Dayton (Best Man at Wedding), Beth Hartman (Receptionist), Mary Young (Spinster), Martin Doric (Maitre D'), Tito Vuolo (Industrialist), Gilda Oliva (Telephone Girl), Baker Sichol (Cashier), Willa Pearl Curtis (Goldie), Franklyn Farnum, Richard Neill, Sam Ash, Jack Richardson (Board of Directors), Beulah Christian, Kathryn Wilson, Beulah Parkington, Margaret B. Farrell (Board of Directors' Wives), William Welsh

(Mr. Paget), William Fawcett (Mr. Tuttle), Carol Coombs (Susie), Jean Acker, Sally Rawlinson, Tex Brodux, Bob Rich (Party Guests).

The main reason to see this film is to marvel at the superior comedy timing of Thelma Ritter in a role that earned her the second of an unprecedented six nominations as Best Supporting Actress. Lund is a wage slave at a factory when he meets Tierney, a wealthy young woman who knows everyone and who feels equally at home dancing with an ambassador or with Lund, the man she falls for and marries. Ritter is Lund's mother, a no-nonsense woman who runs a hamburger stand until the bank forecloses on her. She hitchhikes to see her son and his new wife and arrives the night that the young couple are having their first party. Mistaken as a domestic sent to help, she quickly sizes up the situation and pretends to be a maid, despite Lund's protests. He is somewhat embarrassed by his humble beginnings and Hopkins, as Tierney's mother, is shown up to be a snob under Ritter's relentless good sense. There's a gaggle of giggles as Ritter shows her son and daughter-in-law that the lower classes have just as much wit as the upper classes, plus 50 percent. Ritter succeeds in winning over Tierney, getting her son to acknowledge his origins, and meriting the attention of Lund's superiors as he goes up the ladder to success. Ritter had a way with a line that socked it over without ever seeming to underline anything. Her underplaying is what makes the comedy work and when she is on screen, it lights up. Otherwise, the picture looks like any of the TV network shows you watch, smile at occasionally, then forget the moment the news comes on.

p, Charles Brackett; d, Mitchell Leisen; w, Brackett, Walter Reisch, Richard Breen; ph, Charles B. Lang, Jr.; m, Joseph J. Lilley; ed, Frank Bracht; art d, Hal Pereira, Roland Anderson; cos, Oleg Cassini.

Comedy **(PR:A MPAA:NR)**

MATKA JOANNA OD ANIOLOW
(SEE: JOAN OF THE ANGELS, 1962, Pol.)

MATRIMONIAL BED, THE*
(1930) 98m FN-WB (GB: A MATRIMONIAL PROBLEM)

Frank Fay (Adolphe Noblet/Leopold), Lilyan Tashman (Sylvaine), James Gleason (Gustave Corton), Beryl Mercer (Corinne), Florence Eldridge (Juliette), Marion Byron (Marianne), Arthur Edmund Carewe (Dr. Friedland), Vivian Oakland (Suzanne Trebel), James Bradbury, Sr. (Chabonnais).

Fay gets amnesia and disappears. His wife, Eldridge, believes her husband to be dead and marries Gleason. Five years later she passes by a barber shop and who should be the man with the shears but her presumably dead husband! Though cute in parts, the leading players aren't much to speak of. Fay overacts while Eldridge predates Charles Bronson using one facial expression and a monotone voice throughout. Some cheap homosexual jokes are made between Fay and husband No. 2, Gleason, which were probably daring for the day. The action takes place on only two sets! Remade in 1941 as KISSES FOR BREAKFAST.

d, Michael Curtiz, w, Harvey Thew, Seymour Hicks (based on a play by Yves Mirande, Andre Mouezy-Eon); ph, Dev Jennings.

Comedy **(PR:A MPAA:NR)**

MATRIMONIAL PROBLEM, A (SEE: MATRIMONIAL BED, THE, 1930)

MATRIMONIO ALL'ITALIANA
(SEE: MARRIAGE, ITALIAN STYLE, 1964, Fr./Ital.)

MATTER OF CHOICE, A** (1963, Brit.) 79m Holmwood/Bry bw

Anthony Steel (John Crighton), Jeanne Moody (Lisa Grant), Ballard Berkeley (Charles Grant), Malcolm Gerard (Mike), Michael Davis (Tony), Penny Morrell (Jackie), Lisa Peake (Jane), James Bree (Alfred), George Moon (Spiek).

Moody plays a woman whose extramarital affair ends in tragedy when her lover, a man who also suffers from diabetes, is killed. This event causes problems for the gang of kids who accidentally killed the man, a deed they had no intention of actually committing.

p, George Maynard; d, Vernon Sewell; w, Paul Ryder (based on the story by Sewell, Derren Nesbitt).

Crime/Drama **(PR:A MPAA:NR)**

MATTER OF CONVICTION, A (SEE: YOUNG SAVAGES, THE, 1961)

MATTER OF DAYS, A***
(1969, Fr./Czech.) 98m Telcia Films-CFD/Royal c (A QUELQUES JOURS PRES)

Thalie Fruges (Francoise), Vit Olmer (Pavel), Philippe Baronnet (Jean-Louis), Jana Sulcova (Vladena), Milan Mach (The Father), Michel Ducrocq (Philippe), Josef Cap (Stasek), Valerie Vienne (Maite), Raduz Chmelik (Conservative Professor), Ota Ornest (Kotas), Petr Svojtka (Kotalik), Daniele Garnier (Virginie), Pascal Fardoulis (Elder Student), Alexandre Klimenko (Director), Jean-Pierre Marichal (Gruber), Jeanne Heuclin (Cook), Dorothee Blank (Concubine), Shoshana Seguev (Goddess), Ladislav Jansky (Honza), Lenka Termer (Radka), Hana Brejchova (Kueta), Karel Pavlik (Policeman).

Fruges is a French sociology student, married to Baronnet, a drama student. She falls in love with one of her professors (Olmer), a French language teacher who shares her love of political activism. Set against the political student turmoil in Prague during 1967–68, the two become involved until Olmer discovers that she is married. Returning to Paris for the winter holidays, she asks Baronnet for a divorce. He is deeply hurt by her infidelity and refuses. Fruges returns to Prague, only to find her relationship with Olmer has changed. He is beginning to show support for the Dubcek government which she is vehemently opposed to. Fruges calls Baronnet back in Paris, hoping for a reconciliation but he has achieved some success as an actor and no longer wants a wife to hold him back. In May comes word of the student revolts in Paris and Fruges, realizing that Olmer will never live up to her ideals, leaves to join her fellow students in France. This film is really just another well-told love story of people's lives somehow dictated by unplanned circumstances. The real story of the student unrest in Europe is nicely woven into the framework, never giving the feeling of being merely a contemporary gimmick. Scenes are nicely built and there's some interesing usage of flashback as well. Acting is fresh and natural by a cast of relative unknowns.

p&d, Yves Ciampi; w, Ciampi, Rodolphe M. Arlaud, Valdimir Kalina, Alena Vostra (based on a story by Ciampi); ph, Vladimir Novotny, Claude Saunier; m, Svata Havelka, Jean-Jacques Debout, Christian Gaubert; ed, Georges Alepee; art d, Jan Zavorka; set d, Karel Lukas, Jacques Preisach; cos, La Gaminerie; makeup, V. Hamr, Chantal Godaert.

Drama (PR:O MPAA:R)

MATTER OF INNOCENCE, A** (1968, Brit.) 102m Mariana/UNIV c (GB: PRETTY POLLY)

Hayley Mills *(Polly Barlow)*, Trevor Howard *(Robert Hook)*, Shashi Kapoor *(Amaz)*, Brenda De Banzie *(Mrs. Innes-Hook)*, Dick Patterson *(Rick Preston)*, Kalen Liu *(Lorelei)*, Patricia Routledge *(Miss Gudgeon)*, Peter Bayliss *(Critch)*, Dorothy Alison *(Mrs. Barlow)*, David Prosser *(Ambrose)*, Toni Murphy *(Lady Tourist)*, Eric Young *(Lim Kee)*, Sarah Abdullah *(Bad Girl)*, Anthony Chin *(Japanese Proprietor)*, S. Y. Han *(Oculist)*, Colonel Fairbanks *(Minister)*, Fred Bryant, Lorne Polanski, Peter Martin, Paul Fagg *(Sailors)*, Edward Johnson *(Gunther)*, Ong Ah Lock *(Noughts & Crosses Boy)*, Palham Groom, Norman Grant *(Planters)*, Peter Honri *(Cabin Steward)*.

Mills is a very plain young woman who escorts her rich aunt, De Banzie, to Singapore. De Banzie drowns at the hotel swimming pool and Mills finds herself in possession of her aunt's money and jewels. The young woman buys new clothes and discovers how good looking she can be. Mills is chased after by many men including Kapoor, who is a gigolo. She leaves for England with a parrot from Kapoor and newly found confidence.

p, George W. George, Frank Granat; d, Guy Green; w, Keith Waterhouse, Willis Hall (based on the story *Pretty Polly Barlow* by Noel Coward); ph, Arthur Ibbetson (Techniscope, Technicolor); m, Michel Legrand; ed, Frank Clarke; art d, Peter Mullins; cos, Anthony Mendleson; m/l, "Pretty Polly," Legrand, Don Black (sung by Matt Munro); makeup, Trevor Crole-Rees.

Comedy/Drama (PR:A MPAA:NR)

MATTER OF LIFE AND DEATH, A (SEE: STAIRWAY TO HEAVEN, 1946, Brit.)

MATTER OF MORALS, A 1/2** (1961, U.S./Swed.) 98m Fortress/UA bw (DE SISTA STEGEN)

Patrick O'Neal *(Alan Kennebeck)*, Maj-Britt Nilsson *(Anita Andersson)*, Mogens Wieth *(Erik Walderman)*, Eva Dahlbeck *(Eva, His Wife)*, Claes Thelander *(Bjornson)*, Lennart Lindberg *(Sven Arborg)*, Vernon Young *(Henderson)*, Gosta Cederlund *(Eklund)*, Hampe Faustman *(Kronstad)*.

A story of murder and embezzlement features O'Neal as the representative of a Milwaukee bank who goes to Stockholm to oversee the final details of a $1 million loan to a Swedish factory. There he meets Wieth, the factory manager who has secretly been embezzling money from absentee owner Cederlund. O'Neal falls in love with Nilsson, Wieth's sister-in-law. Although she tries to discourage the American, O'Neal returns home to divorce his wife and once more flies to Stockholm. She again tries to reject him, but to prove his love he joins Wieth in his schemes and makes him the beneficiary of the loan, which was also a partial insurance policy for Cederlund. The boss unexpectedly returns and the pair plot to kill him. But their plans are foiled when Cederlund commits suicide. Still wanting the money, O'Neal tries to make it look like a murder. The police catch him in the act but he escapes and kills Wieth before being apprehended once more. Nicely photographed by Ingmar Bergman's photographer Nykvist, the film gives the Stockholm locations the feel of a crime film within the *mise-en-scene*. However the plot is too slowly built. Nilsson is a standout as the object of O'Neal's affections, doing a fine job in her supporting role. O'Neal and Wieth play nicely off one another in their uneasy partnership. Though this was a Swedish/American coproduction, the dominant language is English.

p, Steven Hopkins, John D. Hess; d, John Cromwell; w, Hess; ph, Sven Nykvist; m, Dag Wiren; ed, Eric Norden; md, Torbjorn Lundquist; set d, Bibi Lindstrom.

Crime (PR:O MPAA:NR)

MATTER OF MURDER, A* (1949, Brit.) 59m Vandyke/GN bw

Maureen Riscoe *(Julie McKelvin)*, John Barry *(Geoffrey Dent)*, Charles Clapham *(Col. Peabody)*, Ivan Craig *(Tony)*, Ian Fleming *(Inspector McKelvin)*, John Le Mesurier *(Ginter)*, Peter Madden *(Sgt. Bex)*, Sonya O'Shea, Blanche Fothergill.

Dull crime drama in which a henpecked bank clerk is driven to embezzlement to obtain the money needed to keep his girl friend happy. When she turns up dead he flees the city to keep from being blamed. With the actual murderer and a detective on his trail, the man takes cover in a boarding-house run by a detective and his daughter where he becomes the killer's next intended victim. Extreme situations make absolutely no sense and are presented in an incoherent manner, much to the discredit of director Gilling, who usually is associated with brisk low-budget thrillers.

p, Roger Proudlock, Sam Lee; d&w, John Gilling; ph, S. D. Onions.

Crime (PR:A MPAA:NR)

MATTER OF RESISTANCE, A (SEE: LA VIE DE CHATEAU, 1966, Fr.)

MATTER OF TIME, A* (1976, Ital./U.S.) 99m AIP c

Liza Minnelli *(Nina)*, Ingrid Bergman *(Contessa)*, Charles Boyer *(Count Sanziani)*, Spiros Andros *(Mario Morello)*, Tina Aumont *(Valentina)*, Gabriele Ferzetti *(Antonio Vicari)*, Orso Maria Guerrini *(Gabriele d'Orazio)*, Amedeo Nazzari *(Tewfik)*, Fernando Rey *(Charles Van Maar)*, Isabella Rossellini *(Sister Pia)*, Geoffrey Coppleston *(Hotel Manager)*, Dominot *(Hotel Porter)*, Jean Mas *(Kaiser)*, Anna Proclemer *(Jeanne Blasto)*, Arnoldo Foa *(Pavelli)*.

Just about everyone associated with this awkward, choppy film would rather forget they made it, but we can't let them or we would not be doing our jobs as the most complete guide to motion pictures ever assembled, so here goes.. . . Minnelli is a hot new movie star in the middle of a press conference where she recalls her past and the time when she and cousin, Aumont, went to work in a tacky Roman hotel as maids. One of the guests is Bergman, looking frightful as an aged kook who flees back in memory. Minnelli pictures herself in the long-winded stories that Bergman, a contessa, relates. The film is a series of flashbacks (within a flashback) that culminates when Minnelli is discovered by a producer and Bergman dies. Next to the old woman at her death is a nurse who looks oddly like the deceased must have looked in her youth. That's for good reason; the role was played by Bergman's daughter, Isabella Rossellini, her child by Italian director Roberto Rossellini. It was the birth of her two children by Rossellini which caused Bergman to be chastized by the blue-noses in the U.S. Compare that with today when Steven Spielberg and Amy Irving have a child and finally get around to marriage a few months later and no one cares at all. Times do change. Minnelli's father, Vincente, directed this mishmash but there was apparently so much interference in the editing that he publicly disclaimed any responsibility. The film takes place in 1949 and the locations were wisely chosen to make that work. Coproducer Skirball, a one-time rabbi, had already made his fortune in films and real estate and was busily giving away millions to charity, something he continued until his death, in his nineties, in December, 1985. The two songs by Kander and Ebb (who wrote CABARET for Minnelli as well as her play "The Rink") are as forgettable as everything else about this movie.

p, Jack H. Skirball, J. Edmund Grainger; d, Vincente Minnelli; w, John Gay (based on the novel *Film of Memory* by Maurice Druon); ph, Geoffrey Unsworth (Movielab Color); m, Nino Oliviero; prod d, Veniero Colasanti, John Moore; ed, Peter Taylor; set d, Arrigo Breschi; m/l, Fred Ebb, John Kander, George Gershwin, B. G. De Sylva.

Comedy/Drama Cas. (PR:A-C MPAA:PG)

MATTER OF WHO, A** (1962, Brit.) 92m Foray/MGM bw

Terry-Thomas *(Archibald Bannister)*, Alex Nicol *(Edward Kennedy)*, Sonja Ziemann *(Michele Cooper)*, Richard Briers *(Jamieson)*, Clive Morton *(Hatfield)*, Vincent Ball *(Doctor Blake)*, Honor Blackman *(Sister Bryan)*, Cyril Wheeler *(Steven Cooper)*, Carol White *(Beryl)*, Jacqueline Jones *(Miss Forsythe)*, Guy Deghy *(Nick Ivanovitch)*, Martin Benson *(Rahman)*, Bruce Beeby *(Captain Brook)*, Geoffrey Keen *(Foster)*, Eduard Linkers *(Linkers)*, Andrew Faulds *(Ralph)*, Barbara Hicks *(Margery)*, Michael Ripper *(Skipper)*, George Cormack *(Henry)*, Julie Alexander, Chulam Mohammed, Roland Branel, Meekah.

A strange idea for a comedy finds the always charming Thomas fighting a smallpox epidemic. He's a "germ detective" for WHO (World Health Organization) who finds evidence of the disease after a passenger on a plane from the Middle East has died. Along with partner Nicol, he sets out for the oil fields. Wheeler is an American oilman detained for possible exposure to the smallpox. After two more cases pop up, Thomas links the outbreak to Deghy, an unscrupulous oilman who will do anything to control the lucrative oil business. It is revealed in a climactic ending that he infected an important document that Wheeler had been carrying. After Wheeler's death, Thomas is hot on another trail that could be equally as dangerous—namely the romancing of the American's widow played by Ziemann. The laughs are uneasy at best—the story is too dramatic to be a successful comedy and ultimately the laughs harm the overall theme. The plot gets somewhat intricate though the direction never gets caught up with all the varied elements.

p, Walter Shenson, Milton Holmes; d, Don Chaffey; w, Holmes, Patricia Lee (based on a story by Lee and Paul Dickson); ph, Erwin Hillier; m, Edwin Astley; ed, Frank Clarke; art d, Elliot Scott; spec eff, Tom Howard.

Comedy/Mystery (PR:A MPAA:NR)

MAURIE* 1/2 (1973) 113m Ausable/NG c (AKA: BIG MO)

Bernie Casey *(Maurice Stokes)*, Bo Swenson *(Jack Twyman)*, Janet MacLachlan *(Dorothy)*, Stephanie Edwards *(Carol)*, Paulene Myers *(Rosie)*, Bill Walker *(Stokes)*, Maidie Norman *(Mrs. Stokes)*, Curt Conway *(Dr. Stewart)*, Jitu Cumbuka *(Oscar)*, Lori Busk *(Lida)*, Tol Avery *(Milton)*, Chris Schenkel.

Based on the true ordeal of a professional basketball player for the Cincinnati Royals after a head injury forced him to remain hospitalized for 10 years until his death. Casey plays the player who is not only faced with the loss of his career but of his life as well, with Swenson as the teammate-buddy who goes to extremes to help his pal. Director Mann (THE ROSE TATOO, BUTTERFIELD 8) obtained fine performances in the manner that marked his more successful projects, but the script is so laden with obtuse sentimentalism that all the work by Mann and his actors seems totally wasted.

p, Frank Ross, Douglas Morrow; d, Daniel Mann; w, Morrow; ph, John Hora (Technicolor); ed, Walter A. Hannemann; art d, Wally Berns.

Drama (PR:A MPAA:G)

MAUSOLEUM zero (1983) 96m Western International/Motion Picture Marketing c

Marjoe Gortner *(Oliver)*, Bobbie Bresee *(Susan)*, Norman Burton *(Dr. Andrews)*, Maurice Sherbanee *(Ben)*, Laura Hippe (Aunt Cora), LaWanda Page *(Elsie)*, Sheri Mann *(Dr. Logan)*, Julie Christy Murray *(Susan at Age 10)*, Bill Vail *(Final Demon)*.

An ancient curse has the sweet, pretty Bresee doing some nasty stuff, via telekinesis, in the effort to return a demon back to the hell from which it came. Special effects are of the cheapest kind providing the only reason to find enjoyment in this sloppy horror film. A few flashes of skin also characterize this would-be shocker, which had a near-clone film, ONE DARK NIGHT, released at about the same time. One-time child revivalist Gortner continues his religious pursuits on a different level than formerly in this demonic-possession laugh riot.

p, Robert Barich, Robert Madero; d, Michael Dugan; w, Barich, Madero (based on the screenplay and story by Katherine Rosenwink); ph, Barich; m, Jaime Mendoza-Nava; ed, Richard C. Bock; art d, Robert Burns; spec eff, Roger George.

Horror   **Cas.**   **(PR:O MPAA:R)**

MAVERICK, THE*¹/₂   (1952) 71m Silvermine/AA bw

Wild Bill Elliott (Lt. Devlin), Myron Healey (Sergeant Frick), Phyllis Coates (Della Watson), Richard Reeves (Frank Bullitt), Terry Frost (Trooper Westman), Rand Brooks (Trooper Barnham), Russell Hicks (Major Hook), Robert Bray (Corp. Johnson), Florence Lake (Grandma Watson), Gregg Barton (George Pane), Denver Pyle (Bud Karnes), Robert Wilke (William Massey), Eugene Roth (Fred Nixon), Joel Allen (John Rowe).

Elliott, Healey, and Bray have to bring three prisoners to the stockade. They reluctantly agree to bring Coates and her grandmother Lake along the trail. Healey defects and joins ranks with the bad guys and a gun battle ensues with Elliott winning and the ladies safely escorted to their destination. The film moves far too slowly to be of much interest until Healey joins the badmen. From then on it's all action. This was the first of three films for Elliott and director Carr.

p, Vincent M. Fennelly; d, Thomas Carr; w, Sid Theil; ph, Ernest Miller (Sepiatone); m, Raoul Kraushaar; ed, Sam Fields; art d, David Milton.

Western   **(PR:A MPAA:NR)**

MAVERICK QUEEN, THE***   (1956) 92m REP c

Barbara Stanwyck (Kit Banion), Barry Sullivan (Jeff), Scott Brady (Sundance), Mary Murphy (Lucy Lee), Wallace Ford (Jamie), Howard Petrie (Butch Cassidy), Jim Davis (A Stranger), Emile Meyer (Malone), Walter Sande (Sheriff Wilson), George Keymas (Muncie), John Doucette (Loudmouth), Taylor Holmes (Pete Callaher), Pierre Watkin (McMillan), Karen Scott, Carol Brewster (Girls), William Loftos (Guard), Jack Harden (Logan), Herbert Jones (Little Boy), Robert Swan, Tristram Coffin (Card Players), Jack O'Shea (Waiter).

Stanwyck plays a Southern gal who comes west and opens up a hotel/saloon called "The Maverick Queen." Her partners include famed outlaws Brady and Petrie, leaders of the Wild Bunch Gang. Sullivan enters the scene as a supposed outlaw who is actually an undercover Pinkerton detective out to break up and arrest the Wild Bunch. He is posing as the infamous gunman Cole Younger and Stanwyck falls in love with him. She ends up dying when the real Younger (Davis) shows up. She takes the bullets so Sullivan might live and settle down with Murphy, the owner of a struggling ranch. This interesting little western was a well-told piece and nicely acted throughout. It was adapted from an unfinished story by Zane Grey, completed by his son, Romer. Unlike the Newman-Redford film BUTCH CASSIDY AND THE SUNDANCE KID, Brady and Petrie play the famed outlaws for the criminals they really were, rather than the comic portrayals of the 1969 film. Photographed on location in Colorado, THE MAVERICK QUEEN was Republic's first film shot in "Naturama," the studio's own wide-screen process. More honest in its realism than many movie westerns.

p. Herbert J. Yates; d, Joe Kane; w, Kenneth Gamet, DeVallon Scott (based on the novel by Zane Grey, completed by Romer Grey); ph, Jack Marta (Naturama, Trucolor); m, Victor Young; ed, Richard L. Van Enger; art d, Walter Keller; set d, John McCarthy, Jr., Fay Babcock; cos, Adele Palmer, Olive Koenitz, Ted Towey; spec eff, Howard Lydecker, Theodore Lydecker, Glen Delamare; makeup, Jack Dusick.

Western   **Cas.**   **(PR:A MPAA:NR)**

MAX DUGAN RETURNS**   (1983) 98m FOX c

Marsha Mason (Nora), Jason Robards, Jr. (Max Dugan), Donald Sutherland (Brian), Matthew Broderick (Michael), Dody Goodman (Mrs. Litke), Sal Viscuso (Coach), Panchito Gomez (Luis), Charley Lau (Himself), Mari Gorman (Pat), Brian Part (Kevin), Billie Bird (Older Woman), Tessa Richarde (Blonde in Shoe Store), James Staahl (Man in Shoe Store), Duke Stroud, Sondra Blake (Teachers), David Morse (Shoe Store Cop), Santos Morales (Grocer), Irene Olga Lopez (His Wife), Tom Rosales, Jr. (Tommy) Tom Fridley (Steve), Kiefer Sutherland (Bill), Bill Aylesworth (Chris), Lydia Nicole (Celia), Elisa Dolenko (Maria), Marc Jefferson (Wendall), Tom Spratley (Truck Washer), Ray Girardin (Umpire), Joey Coleman (3rd Baseman), Pop Attmore (Baseball Player), Grace Woodard (Maitre D'), Ken Neumeyer (Waiter), Robert D'Arcy (Cabbie), Shelley Morrison (Mother), Frank D'Annibale (Bears' Coach), John Corvello (Basketball Coach), Howard Himelstein (Shoe Store Cop), Carmen Silveroli, Sr. (Shoe Store Manager).

Sentimental fluff written by Neil Simon with Mason as a single parent trying to raise her son, Broderick. Up pops her father, Robards, who's a gangster type that showers money and gifts on the daughter he hasn't seen for years. At first, Mason doesn't want anything to do with his gifts or him, but by the end of the film daughter loves father and father escapes the snooping cop, Sutherland, who is dating Mason.

p, Neil Simon, Herbert Ross; d, Ross; w, Simon; ph, David M. Walsh (DeLuxe Color); m, David Shire; ed, Richard Marks; prod d, Albert Brenner; art d, David Haber; set d, Kandy Stern.

Comedy   **Cas.**   **(PR:A MPAA:PG)**

MAXIME**

(1962, Fr.) 94m Films Raoul Ploquin-Cocinor/Interworld Film Distributors bw

Charles Boyer (Maxime), Michele Morgan (Jacqueline Monneron), Arletty (Gazelle), Felix Marten (Hubert Treffujean), Jacques Dufilho (Flick), Micheline Luccioni (Liliane), Jane Marken, Meg Lemonnier, Andre Brunot, Jean-Marie Proslier, Yvonne Constant, Genevieve Morel, Odette Barancay, Van Doude, Fernand Fabre, Lud Germain, Richard Larke, Liliane Patrick.

Boyer is an old aristocrat who helps Marten, a dull, drunk millionaire, win over Morgan. She has never met Marten but has heard plenty and sets her sights on Boyer. When she discovers that the old man is poor, her interest wanes and when she does meet Marten, who has taken Boyer's advice, she falls in love with him.

p, Raoul Ploquin; d, Henri Verneuil; w, Albert Valentin, Henri Jeanson, Verneuil (based on a novel by Henri Duvernois); ph, Christian Matras; m, Georges Van Parys; ed, Gabriel Rongier; art d, Robert Clavel; cos, Rosine Delamare.

Drama   **(PR:A MPAA:NR)**

MAXWELL ARCHER, DETECTIVE*

(1942, Brit.) 73m MON bw (GB: MEET MAXWELL ARCHER)

John Loder (Maxwell Archer), Leueen MacGrath (Sarah), Athole Stewart (Superintendent Gordon), Marta Labarr (Nina), George Merritt (Inspector Cornell), Ronald Adam (Nicolides), Peter Halliwell Hobbes (George Gull), Ralph Roberts (George Gull, Sr.), Syd Crossley (Perkins), Barbara Everest (Miss Duke), John Lothar.

Loder is a private detective who, much to the chagrin of all the boys down at Scotland Yard, solves a seemingly impossible mystery. Oh, where is Sherlock Holmes when you need him? Poorly made with a dopey script that gives the actors little room to breathe, let alone act.

p, William Sistrom; d, John Paddy Carstairs; w, Katherine Strueby (based on the novel by Hugh Clevely); ph, Claude Friese Greene; ed, Alan Jaggs; md, W.L. Trytel; art d, Ian White.

Mystery   **(PR:C MPAA:NR)**

MAYA*¹/₂   (1966) 91m MGM c

Clint Walker (Hugh Bowen), Jay North (Terry Bowen), I. S. Johar (One-Eye), Sajid Kahn (Raji), Jairaj (Gammu Ghat), Sonia Sahni (Sheela), Ullas (Village Spokesman), Nan Palshikar (Raji's Father), Uma Rao (One-Eye's Daughter), Madhusdan Pathak (Station Master).

After the death of his mother North (from TV's "Dennis the Menace" series) goes off to India to join Walker, the father he idolizes. But the lad is disillusioned when he discovers that his big-game hunting pop is now a coward after a nasty encounter with a tiger. When Walker kills a cheetah that North was domesticating it's all a little much for the boy and he runs off. He meets Kahn, an Indian boy who promised his dying father that he would deliver a sacred white elephant to a jungle temple. After battling various jungle tigers and the evil Johar, the two boys are surprised to find Walker. Apparently he's been to the Wizard of Oz for now he has some courage. Together they deliver the baby elephant and all ends happily. The dopey story and ham-bone acting was salvaged by a nice job with the photography, which used the India locales to their best advantage. Otherwise this one is best left for the kids, who undoubtedly will delight in seeing the baby elephant. MAYA was later adapted into a short-lived television series.

p, Frank King, Maurice King; d, John Berry; w, John Fante (based on Gilbert Wright's adaptation of a story by Jalal Din, Lois Roth); ph, Gunter Senftleben (Technicolor); m, Riz Ortolani; ed, Richard V. Heermance; art d, Edward S. Haworth, Ram Yedekar; spec eff, Milt Rice; makeup, Reudiger von Sperl.

Adventure   **(PR:A MPAA:NR)**

MAYA zero   (1982) 114m Wing & a Prayer/Claridge c

Berta Dominguez D. (Maya Murillo), Joseph D. Rosevich (Martin Kirkman), Luis Manuel (Juan Dominguez), Valeria Riccardo (Valeria), Mario Rabaglia (Hollywood).

Hopelessly amateurish effort dealing with the faculty and staff of a FAME-type school for kids who want to be fashion designers and models. The episodic story line shows Dominguez D. as she bravely conquers racial conflicts and hatred resulting in peace, happiness and love for the cast and an overdose of saccharin for the audience. A bad synching job doesn't help any of the hammy performances. Originally shot in 16mm and blown up to 35mm.

p, Antiqua Domsa; d, Agust Agustsson, Ruth Schell; w, Berta Dominguez D., Joseph D. Rosevich; ph, Oliver Wood (Du Art Color); m, Bika Reed, Don Salmon, Guacaran; ed, Ruth Schell.

Drama   **(PR:C MPAA:NR)**

MAYBE IT'S LOVE**   (1930) 74m WB bw

Joan Bennett (Nan Sheffield), Joe. E. Brown (Speed Hanson), James Hall (Tommy Nelson), Laura Lee (Betty), Anders Randolf (Mr. Nelson), Sumner Getchell (Whiskers), George Irving (President Sheffield), George Bickel (Professor), Howard Jones (Coach Bob Brown), Bill Banker (Bill), Russell Saunders (Racehorse Russell), Tim Moynihan (Tim), W.K. Schoonover (Schoony), E. N. Sleight (Elmer), George Gibson (George), Ray Montgomery (Ray), Otto Pommerening (Otto), Kenneth Haycraft (Ken), Howard Harpster (Howard), Paul Scull (Paul), Stuart Erwin (Brown of Harvard), Tom Hanlon (Tony).

Bennett is the daughter of college president Irving. They don't have much of a football team, so she doffs her glasses and bats her eyes in an effort to bring 11 of the best All-Americans to the school. Hall is the love interest for the girl, a bad boy turned good. Brown is comic relief, using his great big mouth in his protests about being replaced on the team. Cute but dumb and similar to many college football programmers of the early 1930s. Cast included the members of the 1929 All-American football team.

d, William Wellman; w, Joseph Jackson (based on a story by Mark Canfield [Darryl F. Zanuck]; ph, Robert Kurrle; ed, Edward McDermott; m/l, "Maybe It's Love," "All American," Sidney Mitchell, Archie Gottler, George W. Meyer; cos, Orry-Kelly.

Comedy **(PR:A MPAA:NR)**

MAYBE IT'S LOVE* (1935) 62m FN-WB bw

Gloria Stuart *(Bobby Halevy)*, Ross Alexander *(Rims O'Neil)*, Frank McHugh *(Willie Sands)*, Helen Lowell *(Mrs. Halevy)*, Philip Reed *(Adolph Mengle, Jr.)*, Joseph Cawthorn *(Adolph Mengle, Sr.)*, Dorothy Dare *(Lila)*, Ruth Donnelly *(Florrie Sands)*, Henry Travers *(Mr. Halevy)*, J. Farrell MacDonald *(The Cop)*, Maude Eburne *(Landlady)*.

Stuart is secretary to company boss Cawthorn. She's got a thing for office boy Alexander but the boss' son Reed has it in for her. He can't make headway so he gets Reed jealous and the rival calls off the romance. But he realizes the error of his ways and decides to marry Stuart after all. He gets fired and her family picks on his faults. He tells them to get lost and Stuart takes another job and leaves Alexander. He finds out where she works and begs forgiveness. After getting back his old job, all is resolved. Witless, with fairly sappy dialog. You'd never guess that this was adapted from a play by the very talented playwright Anderson. Overlong at 62 minutes and a real waste of acting talents.

p, Harry Joe Brown; d, William McGann; w, Jerry Wald, Harry Sauber, Lawrence Hazard, Daniel Reed (based on the play "Saturday's Children" by Maxwell Anderson); ph, Arthur Edeson; ed, James Gibbon; art d, John Hughes.

Comedy **(PR:A MPAA:NR)**

MAYERLING***** (1937, Fr.) 96m Concordea/Cinematographique/Nero bw

Charles Boyer *(Archduke Rudolph of Austria)*, Danielle Darrieux *(Marie Vetsera)*, Suzy Prim *(Countess Larisch)*, Jean Dax *(Emperor Franz Joseph)*, Gabrielle Dorziat *(Empress Elizabeth)*, Jean Debucourt *(Count Taafe)*, Marthe Regnier *(Baroness Vetsera [Helene])*, Yolande Laffron *(Stephanie)*, Vladimir Sokoloff *(Chief of Police)*, Andre Dubosc *(Loschek the Valet)*, Gina Manes *(Marinka)*, Rene Bergeron *(Szeps)*.

Here is one of the greatest love stories ever brought to the screen, the bittersweet, painfully poignant romance between the star-crossed Crown Prince Rudolph of Austria and his adoring mistress, Marie Vetsera. Boyer, in a riveting performance, essays the role of Rudolph, son of the powerful Franz Joseph, Emperor of Austria-Hungary. In the opening scene, students protesting the tyrannical rule of Franz Joseph are rounded up by police and among their number is Boyer. He is brought before his father, Dax, playing Franz Joseph, who compels Boyer to renounce his radical position for the sake of his royal blood and the throne. Further, Dax forces his son into a marriage of blue-blood alliance, to a woman he does not love. Everywhere there are court spies assigned to track and trail the errant Boyer but he manages to elude his followers at a fair. There he meets 17-year-old Marie Vetsera, Darrieux, and it's love at first sight, although she has no idea that he is Prince Rudolph. The couple enjoy little pleasures such as tossing rings around a swan's neck and watching a puppet show. The following night Darrieux attends the opera and looks up, startled, to see the handsome young man from the fair sitting in the royal box next to Dax and other members of the royal family. Though she comes from an aristocratic family, there is no hope that Darrieux can reach as high as the throne. Yet Boyer reaches out for her, meeting secretly with the beautiful young woman. They rendezvous in private rooms of the Imperial Palace, the Hofburg itself, and elsewhere. Only in the presence of Darrieux does Boyer find joy and peace of mind. She responds to his generous love with an open innocence Boyer has never before experienced. All the jaded intrigues, the world-weary politicking fade in the little warm world of these two lovers. The snooping Debucourt, Count Taafe, Dax's adviser, discovers the love affair and contacts Darrieux's mother, Regnier, who suddenly takes her daughter on a forced vacation to Trieste, vowing she will "cure her of this madness." With Darrieux gone, Boyer drowns his depression with heavy drinking, partying joylessly from eve to dawn. When Darrieux does come back, he faces her with a sneer, raving: "Haven't you ever seen a man drunk before?" That he has been with other women since her departure seems to cause him no remorse. "I'll love all the women in Vienna if I want," he shouts at her, "and you can do nothing! Nothing!" Darrieux gives him back his own painful stare and says tenderly: "Oh, my love, how you suffer." In this moment their love is cemented, their innermost fears and thoughts and emotions intertwined. They decide that they will never be separated again. Boyer gives Darrieux a wedding ring bearing the inscription "United in Love Unto Death." He then writes the Pope, asking for an annulment of his marriage to Laffron. Dax receives the Pope's reply, a firm refusal. The angry emperor calls his son before him, tongue-lashing him and ordering Boyer to blot Darrieux out of his mind. "You have 24 hours to end the affair," decrees Dax. A brilliant court ball that night is attended by a pensive Boyer and the wife he does not love, Laffron. Suddenly, Boyer spots Darrieux and, ignoring his startled wife, goes to her and asks that she dance with him to lead off the grand ball. Shocking everyone, the two whirl about the enormous ballroom. Later, as Laffron leaves the ball, Darrieux and Laffron glare at each other and Darrieux refuses to bow to the archduchess. That night, while the snow gently falls, the lovers flee to Boyer's remote hunting lodge, Mayerling, nestled in the deep Vienna Woods. For one grand and glorious day the lovers savor the minutes with deep affection for each other. As night falls they make a death pact. Earlier Darrieux had asked that Boyer grant her only one wish, that she die before he does. When Darrieux goes to bed, Boyer sits quietly by the fire, thinking through the night. Just as dawn breaks, on January 30, 1889, Boyer gets a pistol and, looking down at the sleeping Darrieux, sends a bullet into her head. His faithful old servant, Dubosc, comes to the chamber door and Boyer tells him the shot he heard was undoubtedly from the hunters nearby. Boyer lies down next to Darrieux on the bed; there is a trickle of blood from her forehead but she appears to be sleeping in deep peace. His soulful look at his lover is Boyer's last. Another shot rings out and the camera only shows his quivering hand, reaching desperately for her hand, and, at the last second of life, clutching it. MAYERLING is a touching masterpiece and a great tragic love story written with poetic strength that is hard to match. Litvak's carefully constructed scenes emphasize the ill-starred love affair without making it tawdry; there are sensitivities in every frame which recall a haunting line from Keats' "The Eve of St. Agnes:" "And they are gone, aye ages long ago, these lovers fled away into the storm." Only Boyer could have played the doomed Rudolph so expertly and with such incisive understanding; he became the part wholly, giving a majestic performance. Darrieux counters his fascinating role with one so tender and electric that she embodies that beautifully sad young woman who chose death with the man of her heart rather than a long and uneventful life. Boyer and Darrieux became internationally famous after the release of MAYERLING. Boyer, who had made some unsuccessful films in Hollywood earlier, returned to the movie mecca a great star and he would remain so for years to come, a romantic idol of millions of adoring female viewers who thought of him as *the* continental lover. His triumphs as such were many: ALGIERS (1938), where he played the unforgettable Pepe Le Moko, ALL THIS AND HEAVEN, TOO (1940) (also directed by Litvak), ARCH OF TRIUMPH, as the idealistic surgeon Ravic without passport or future. (Boyer would sadly emulate Rudolph, and the character he made so famous, on August 16, 1978, committing suicide a few days after his ailing wife of 44 years died. He chose not the pistol but barbituates.) MGM quickly signed Darrieux to a long-term contract, paying her a fortune and billing her as "the world's greatest actress." But her Hollywood career would be short-lived and she would star in only one film under her MGM contract, THE RAGE OF PARIS (1938), before returning to Europe. She would enjoy a resurgence of fame in the 1950s, appearing in LA RONDE (1950), FIVE FINGERS (1952) with James Mason, and LADY CHATTERLEY'S LOVER (1955). This was also the film that brought Litvak to Hollywood and earned him a rich contract, which is what the director sought when he put together the cast for this international hit, insisting that Darrieux and Boyer play the lead roles, knowing Boyer's name would mean much in America. Oddly, Boyer was offered the role but did not jump at it, though he wanted it. He even suggested to Litvak that the renowned French actor Pierre Fresnay play Rudolph. Replied Litvak: "Fresnay could play Rudolph if there were no Charles Boyer. But for Charles Boyer there can be no substitute. I will not make the picture without you." Boyer agreed and the film soon went into production. The great matinee idol was always perplexed at the popularity he enjoyed with millions of women who thought "the great lover" the most attractive male in films. Boyer once remarked: "I do not know when I became so nice looking as they all say. I suppose it was when I lost my hair and began experimenting with toupees. In silent films, I looked like a bandit who eats little children." The story of MAYERLING, though based on Anet's stirring novel, is rooted in reality. The 31-year-old Rudolph, found with his 17-year-old mistress Marie Vetsera dead in the royal hunting lodge, caused the Austrian court to misrepresent the facts, such as they were known. Here was the heir to the Hapsburg throne of the sprawling and powerful Austro-Hungarian empire, then more powerful than France and Germany put together, found a suicide. At first the court, through a mortified Franz Joseph, declared that Rudolph had died of an apoplectic attack. Royal reports quickly changed the story to say that the heir apparent had died of a heart attack, when no such condition ever existed. The royal family eventually had to admit that Rudolph had committed suicide but they emphasized that he had gone insane. Through this position, the Hapsburgs were able to persuade the Catholic Church, which dominates Austria, to allow the prince to be buried in hallowed ground, his remains given holy rites before being entombed inside the imperial crypt at the Kaisergruft, which is now located beneath the Capuchin Church in Vienna. Marie Vetsera was not talked about after the double deaths; in fact, little or nothing was immediately known about her presence at Mayerling. One report had it that Austrian officers of the Imperial Guard removed her body in such a way as to suggest that she was still alive, propping up her body in the back with a large broadsword, and making it appear that she was actually walking and alive between the two huge officers who carried her forth from Mayerling. Another report had it that the escorts of the dead girl were her uncles. Not until the girl was secretly buried in a small cemetery next to the Abbey of Heiligenkreuz, a few miles from Mayerling, did the story of the suicide pact emerge. But by then many stories were blurted, some even invented by the royal household, to confuse the reasons for the deaths. Radicals had it that Franz Joseph himself had his son assassinated, believing that if Rudolph assumed the throne he would dissolve the monarchy and create a democracy. Anti-monarchists insisted that Rudolph was a morbid, mentally deranged and dissolute prince who was fascinated with death and that he had several times earlier asked women to join him in a suicide pact. Court sponsored gossip tried to establish murder, that Marie killed Rudolph by poison or blew out his brains when he fell asleep after he informed her that their romance was over. Still another report had it that the naive, innocent, and emotionally gullible girl was flattered into the suicide pact, thrilling to the thought that her body would be found next to that of a great Hapsburg. The official records of the deaths have long since vanished, hidden, then destroyed before the turn of the century, leaving the most positive of the stories to persist, that Rudolph and Marie did join in a death pact, dedicated to dying together since they could not live together, creating one of the world's great love tragedies. Mayerling, now the site of a Carmelite convent where nuns pray in a small chapel on the spot where the lovers met their sad end, has become the symbol of a great young love denied, crushed, stilled, in the tainted name of empire. And it was the empire that killed these two that would perish when Rudolph's successor, Francis Ferdinand, was assassinated in 1914 at Sarajevo by low-born Gabriel Princip, a member of a radical group not dissimilar to that which Rudolph once reportedly joined, an assassination that began WW I and ended forever the old Hapsburg dynasty. All of it, somehow—this great, sorrowful tale of love—is capsulated on the tombstone of Marie Vetsera. Beneath her name, "Marie Freiin ["baroness"] v. Vetsera," is the inscription: "He cometh forth like a flower, and is cut down." Another version of this story was the French-made MAYERLING TO SARAJEVO (1940) and a full remake appeared in 1968, directed and written by

Terence Young and starring Omar Sharif and Catherine Deneuve, a poor imitation of the original.

d, Anatole Litvak; w, Joseph Kessel, Irma Von Cube (based on the novel *Idyl's End* by Claude Anet); ph, Armand Thirard; m, Arthur Honegger; ed, Henri Rust; m/l, H. May, Serge Veber.

Romance   **Cas.**   **(PR:C-O MPAA:NR)**

MAYERLING**   (1968, Brit./Fr.) 140m Corona-Winchester/MGM c

Omar Sharif (*Crown Prince Rudolf*), Catherine Deneuve (*Baroness Maria Vetsera*), James Mason (*Emperor Franz Josef*), Ava Gardner (*Empress Elizabeth*), James Robertson-Justice (*Edward Prince of Wales*), Genevieve Page (*Countess Larisch*), Ivan Desny (*Count Josef Hoyos*), Andrea Parisy (*Crown Princess Stephanie*), Fabienne Dali (*Mizzi Kaspar*), Maurice Teynac (*Mortiz Szeps*), Moustache (*Bratfisch*), Bernard Lajarrige (*Loschek*), Veronique Vendell (*Lisl Stockau*), Charles Millot (*Count Taafe*), Roger Pigaut (*Count Karolyi*), Mony Dalmes (*Baroness Helen Vetsera*), Lyne Chardonnet (*Hannah Vetsera*), Alain Saury (*Baltazzi*), Irene von Meyendorff (*Countess Stockau*), Jean-Claude Bercq (*Duke Michael of Braganza*), Jacques Berthier (*Prince John Salvator*), Howard Vernon (*Prince Montenuevo*), Jean-Michel Rouziere (*Police Superintendent*), Roger Lumont (*Inspector Losch*), Jacqueline Lavielle (*Marinka*), Jacques Dorfmann (*Rioting Student*), Anthony Stuart (*Head Gardener*), Pierre Vernet (*Court Tailor*), Richard Larke (*McTavish*), Fred Vellaca (*Lawson*), Liane Dayde, James Urbain, Genia Melikova, Michel Nunes (*Dancers in "Giselle"*).

Despite a fine performance by Sharif and an opulent setting, this is a disappointing film. Sharif plays the real life Prince of Hapsburg, circa 1888. Disgusted with the royal life, he joins his fellow students in demonstrations for the liberation of Hungary, in an open defiance of his father (Mason). A politically arranged marriage to Parisy only drives Sharif to morphine and a series of affairs. But when he meets Deneuve, the 17-year-old daughter of a *nouveau riche* family, Sharif falls in love. However the family is unacceptable to his father because of their commoner background and Mason forbids Sharif to see the girl. She is sent off to Venice while Sharif is forced to go on an inspection tour. He tries to get his unhappy marriage annulled but to no avail. Gardner, playing Sharif's mother, suggests that he meet Deneuve at a family hunting lodge near Vienna. While there, word comes that the Hungarian revolt is successful and Mason knows of Sharif's part in the plans. Knowing they will never be happy the lovers kills themselves by pistol. The grand scope of the film often overruns the story and unlike other historical epics such as DOCTOR ZHIVAGO or REDS, the human element is lost beneath the historical events. Overlong, the film also has poorly written dialog. The acting is fairly good by the principals though Gardner is a little young to be believed as the mother. Had the film been shortened in both length and scope it might have been an interesting work. As it is, MAYERLING hopscotches its way through people and history, never really doing as much as it could with the strong source material. A far better version with the same title was made in France in 1936. The Grand Ballet Classique de France, under the direction of Claude Giraud, performs "Giselle."

p, Robert Dorfmann; d, Terence Young; w, Young, Denis Cannan, Joseph Kessel (based on the novels *Mayerling* by Claude Anet and *The Archduke* by Michael Arnold, and historical documentation); ph, Henri Alekhan (Panavision, Technicolor); m, Francis Lai; ed, Ben Rayner; prod d, Georges Wakhevitch; art d, Maurice Colasson, Tony Roman; cos, Marcel Escoffier.

Historical Epic   **(PR:C MPAA:NR)**

MAYFAIR GIRL*   (1933, Brit.) 67m WB bw

Sally Blane (*Brenda Mason*), John Stuart (*Robert Blair*), D. A. Clarke-Smith (*Capt. Merrow*), Glen Alyn (*Santa*), Roland Culver (*Dick Porter*), James Carew, Charles Hickman, Winifred Oughton, Philip Strange, Anna Lee, Lawrence Anderson.

Yankee-in-London Blane starts hanging out with some of the less desirable elements of London society and soon gets herself accused of murder. Luckily her old beau, lawyer Stuart, has not lost total interest in the girl, and uses his courtroom expertise to set her free. Blane (the sister of Loretta Young) momentarily left Hollywood to appear in this lame production. The trip was a total waste as far as this film is concerned.

p, Irving Asher; d, George King; w, Brandon Fleming.

Crime/Drama   **(PR:A MPAA:NR)**

MAYFAIR MELODY**   (1937, Brit.) 83m Teddington/WB bw

Keith Falkner (*Mark*), Joyce Kirby (*Brenda*), Bruce Lister (*Dickie*), Glen Alyn (*Daphne*), George Galleon (*Lord Chester*), Louis Goodrich (*Ludborough*), Ian McLean (*Collecchi*), Vivienne Chatterton (*Mme. Collecchi*), Chili Bouchier (*Carmen*), Aubrey Mallalieu (*Dighton*).

Nonsense involving Kirby as the daughter of an automobile magnate. She's as spoiled as a girl can be but when she hears Falkner sing, her entire demeanor changes. Working hard, she helps this auto mechanic become a great operatic baritone. Well known for his radio appearances at the time, Falkner is stiff and unnatural in his role though Kirby does a fairly good job. The story is extremely trite and unbelievable. Too many unnecessary details are packed in, making the film overlong and more than a little dull. The cast comes through reasonably well however.

p, Irving Asher; d, Arthur Woods; w, James Dyrenforth; ph, Basil Emmott; m, Kenneth Leslie Smith; ch, Jack Donohue; m/l, Smith, Dyrenforth.

Musical/Comedy   **(PR:A MPAA:NR)**

MAYHEM   (SEE: SCREAM, BABY, SCREAM, 1969)

MAYOR OF 44TH STREET, THE*   (1942) 85m RKO bw

George Murphy (*Joe Jonathan*), Anne Shirley (*Jessie Lee*), William Gargan (*Tommy Fallon*), Richard Barthelmess (*Ed Kirby*), Joan Merrill (*Vicki Lane*), Freddy Martin (*Freddy Martin*), Rex Downing (*Bitz McCarg*), Millard Mitchell (*Herman*), Mary Wickes (*Mamie*), Eddie Hart (*Gromm*), Roberta Smith (*Red*), Marten Lamont (*Shoemaker, Kirby's Attorney*), Walter Reed (*Lew Luddy*), Robert Smith (*Eddie, the House Manager*), Lee Bonnell (*Head Waiter*), Kenneth Lundy (*Dude*), Esther Muir (*Hilda, Switchboard Operator*), John H. Dilson (*Carter, General Manager*), Monty Collins (*Piano Player*), Pete Theodore (*Dancer*), Jack Byron (*Bandleader*), Jane Patten (*Girl at Office*), Gerald Pierce (*Mickey, the Messenger Boy*), David Kirkland (*Petey*), Rosemary Coleman, Wayne McCoy, Richard Martin (*Office Clerks*), Jane Woodworth, Linda Rivas (*Actresses*), John McGuire (*Curley Sharp*), Reginald Barlow (*Watchman*), Jack Gardner, Clarence Hennecke, Johnny Tryon (*Photographers*), James Mena (*Filipino Servant*), Matt Moore (*Jerry, the Office Worker*), Ken Christy (*District Attorney*), George Ford (*Phil the Dancer*), Lola Jensen (*Phil's Partner*), Norman Mayes (*Rathskeller*), Barbara Clark (*Dancing Girl*), Frank O'Connor (*Cop*), Donald Kerr, Mike Lally (*Mugs*), The Freddy Martin Orchestra.

After retiring from vaudeville, ex-hoofer Murphy opens up an agency for dance bands. He decides to play social worker as well, hiring a group of street kids so they'll have something to do besides hang out on the corner. But after he hires the kids' leader Downing, he finds nothing but trouble. A former convict that Murphy helped to parole, Barthelmess, tries to muscle in on the agency so he'll have a base for his blackmail operations. Martin's real-life dance band provided much of the music. "When There's a Breeze on Lake Louise" was nominated for an Oscar as Best Song. Unfortunately that was about it for highlights in what amounted to a mean-spirited picture that had nothing good to say about kids. The performances are okay with Murphy and Shirley having a love story somewhere in the middle of this mess. But the overriding mood of the film is too downbeat to make it worth watching. Songs included "Your Face Looks Familiar," "Heavenly, Isn't He?" "Let's Forget It," "You're Bad For Me," "A Million Miles From Manhattan" "When There's A Breeze On Lake Louise" (Mort Greene, Harry Revel).

p, Cliff Reid; d, Alfred E. Green; w, Lewis R. Foster, Frank Ryan (based on a story by Robert D. Andrews suggested by a "*Collier's*" magazine article by Luther Davis, John Cleveland); ph, Robert de Grasse; ed, Irene Morra; md, C. Bakaleinikoff; cos, Renie; ch, Nick Castle.

Drama/Musical   **(PR:A MPAA:NR)**

MAYOR OF HELL, THE***   (1933) 85m WB bw

James Cagney (*Patsy Gargan*), Madge Evans (*Dorothy Griffith*), Allen Jenkins (*Mike*), Dudley Digges (*Mr. Thompson*), Frankie Darro (*Jimmy Smith*), Farina (*Smoke*), Dorothy Peterson (*Mrs. Smith*), John Marston (*Hopkins*), Charles Wilson (*Guard*), Hobart Cavanaugh (*Tommy's Father*), Raymond Borzage (*Johnny Stone*), Robert Barrat (*Mr. Smith*), George Pat Collins (*Brandon*), Mickey Bennett (*Butch Kilgore*), Arthur Byron (*Judge Gilbert*), Sheila Terry (*The Girl*), Harold Huber (*Joe*), Edwin Maxwell (*Louis Johnston*), William V. Mong (*Walters*), Sidney Miller (*Izzy Horowitz*), George Humbert (*Tony's Father*), George Offerman, Jr. (*Charlie Burns*), Charles Cane (*Tommy Groman*), Wallace MacDonald (*Johnson's Assistant*), Adrian Morris (*Car Owner*), Snowflake (*Hemingway*), Wilfred Lucas (*Guard*), Bob Perry, Charles Sullivan (*Collectors*), Ben Taggart (*Sheriff*).

Feisty, sassy Cagney flits about in this social-comment film like a banty rooster. He's a smart talking gangster with friends in high political places who get him appointed as a "deputy inspector" to the state reform school. Upon arrival, he sees how the youngsters are mistreated by sadistic warden Digges and some of his brutal guards. Evans, the nurse on duty, complains of the inhuman treatment to Cagney and asks him to change things. Touched by the plight of Darro and others, and in love with Evans, Cagney reforms, and gets Digges kicked out, replacing him. He works with the boys and allows them to establish a system of self-government and an honor code. Conditions improve as does the morale of the youthful inmates. But Cagney's experiment ceases when he hears that a rival gang is making inroads into his rackets. He returns to the city and kills a rival mobster, then goes into hiding. The boys feel deserted and betrayed by Cagney when the cruel Digges returns to persecute them. When Cagney hears of the harsh treatment again put in place at the reformatory, he risks all, returns, and runs Digges and his henchmen out once and for all, setting matters straight and winning Evans' hand. Countering Cagney's cocky magnanimity is Digges' chilling portrait of evil. The role of the nurse was originally intended for Joan Blondell, then Glenda Farrell, but both actresses had other commitments and it went to Evans who is rather anemic as a whining crusader. Darro is solid as one of the oppressed inmates and Mayo's direction has a kick in it. This film, remade as CRIME SCHOOL in 1938, starring Humphrey Bogart, was one of the many films Cagney made in the early 1930s, produced in a schedule that was nonstop in the Warner Bros. grind mill. Said Cagney later: "MAYOR OF HELL . . . was the old mixture . . . I was kept pretty busy . . . we worked until three or four in the morning. I'd look over and there'd be the director, Archie Mayo, sitting with his head thrown back, sawing away. He was tired, we were all tired. This kind of pressure the studio put on us because the studio wanted to get the thing done as cheaply as possible."

p, Lucien Hubbard; d, Archie Mayo; w, Edward Chodorov (based on a story by Islin Auster); ph, Barney "Chick" McGill; ed, Jack Killifer; md, Leo F. Forbstein; art d, Esdras Hartley; cos, Orry-Kelly; makeup, Perc Westmore.

Crime Drama   **(PR:C MPAA:NR)**

MAYOR'S NEST, THE*½

(1932, Brit.) 74m British and Dominions/Wolf and Friedman Film Service bw

Sydney Howard (*Joe Pilgrim*), Claude Hulbert (*Algernon Ashcroft*), Al Bowlly (*George*), Muriel Aked (*Mrs. Ashcroft*), Frank Harvey (*Councillor Blackett*), Michael

Hogan *(Tom Ackroyd)*, Miles Malleson *(Clerk)*, Cyril Smith *(Magistrate)*, Syd Crossley *(Milkman)*.

Aked is a rich social worker who finds an unemployed trombonist (Howard) and persuades him to run for mayor with her financial support. Comic Howard wins the election and helps raze the slums owned by the defeated candidate. Howard's bizarre antics and a couple of mediocre songs don't do anything to make this programmer any more memorable.

p, Herbert Wilcox, d&w, Maclean Rogers (based on a story by R.P. Weston, Bert Lee, Jack Marks); ph, F.A. Young.

Comedy **(PR:A MPAA:NR)**

MAYOR'S NEST, THE, 1941
(SEE: RETURN OF DANIEL BOONE, THE, 1941)

MAYTIME**** (1937) 132m MGM bw

Jeanette MacDonald *(Marcia Morney/Miss Morrison)*, Nelson Eddy *(Paul Allison)*, John Barrymore *(Nicolai Nazaroff)*, Herman Bing *(August Archipenko)*, Tom Brown *(Kip Stuart)*, Lynne Carver *(Barbara Roberts)*, Rafaela Ottiano *(Ellen)*, Charles Judels *(Cabby)*, Paul Porcasi *(Composer Trentini)*, Sig Rumann *(Fanchon)*, Walter Kingsford *(Rudyard)*, Edgar Norton *(Secretary)*, Guy Bates Post *(Emperor Louis Napoleon)*, Iphigenie Castiglioni *(Empress Eugenie)*, Anna Demetrio *(Mme. Fanchon)*, Frank Puglia *(Orchestra Conductor)*, Adia Kuznetzoff *(Dubrovsky, Czaritza's Minister/Student in Cafe)*, Joan Le Sueur *(Maypole Dancer)*, Russell Hicks *(M. Bulliet, Voice Teacher)*, Harry Davenport, Harry Hayden, Howard Hickman, Robert C. Fischer *(Opera Directors)*, Harlan Briggs *(Bearded Director)*, Frank Sheridan *(O'Brien, a Director)*, Billy Gilbert *(Drunk in Cafe)*, Ivan Lebedeff *(Empress' Dinner Companion)*, Leonid Kinskey *(Student in Bar)*, Clarence Wilson *(Waiter)*, Maurice Cass *(Opera House Manager)*, Douglas Wood *(Massilon, Hotel Manager)*, Bernard Suss *(Assistant Manager)*, Henry Roquemore *(Publicity Man)*, Alexander Schonberg *(French Proprietor)*, Mariska Aldrich *(Opera Contralto)*, Paul Weigel *(Prompter)*, Ben Welden, Jose Rubio, Jack Murphy, Blair Davies, Agostino Borgato, Alberto Morin *(Students)*, Delmar Watson, Buster Slavens, Grace Hayle, Luke Cosgrave, Diana Dean, Allen Cavan, Sarah Edwards *(Bits)*, Christian Frank *(Gendarme)*, George Davis *(Usher)*, Pat Somerset *(Gossiper)*, Ian Wolfe *(Court Official)*, Gus Leonard *(Concierge)*, Brandon Hurst *(Master of Ceremonies)*, Eric Lonsdale, Guy D'Ennery *(Aides)*, Claude King *(Noble)*, Forbes Murray *(Aide)*, Fred Graham, Frank O'Connor *(Servants)*, Barlowe Borland *(Stage Doorman)*, Charles Requa *(Stage Manager)*, Arthur Stuart Hull, Harold Entwhistle *(Roues)*, Frank Elliott *(Aide)*, Jacques Lory *(Drunk)*, Belle Mitchell *(Maid)*, Hans Joby *(Doctor)*, Christian Rub *(Sleeper Outside Cafe)*, Genaro Spagnoli *(Chef)*, Paul Cremonesi *(Opera Critic)*, Oscar Rudolph, Herta Lind *(Peasants)*, Jolly Lee Harvey *(Fat Woman)*, Armand "Curley" Wright *(Bow-and-Arrow Stand Man)*, Sidney Jarvis, Albert Pollet *(Cabbies)*, Francisco Maran *(Gendarme)*, Ed Goddard *(Juggling Clown)*, Bob Watson, Helen Parrish *("Merry Month of May" Singers)*, Joan Breslaw *(Queen of the May)*, Nan Merriman, George London *("Les Huguenots" Chorus)*, The Don Cossack Chorus *(Chorus for "Le Regiment de Sambre et Meuse")*.

The play upon which this is based was so popular that *two* productions ran simultaneously on Broadway in 1917. A few years later, they made it as a silent film but it boggles the mind to think that B. P. Schulberg could have thought such a story, where music is such an integral part, made any sense with no sound. In 1937, MGM was the reigning studio in Hollywood and released several excellent movies: THE GOOD EARTH, CAPTAINS COURAGEOUS, ROSALIE, and SARATOGA and yet this musical topped them all at the box office and remains popular to this day and many TV stations still broadcast it during the month of May. Thalberg himself was producer with Ed Goulding as director but when the frail mogul died at age 37, everything was suspended and the Technicolor footage that had already been shot was scrapped. Two of the original cast, Frank Morgan and Paul Lukas, moved on to other roles and Barrymore replaced Lukas, while Bing stood in for Morgan. This was the third Eddy-MacDonald duet and it was her personal favorite because they had so much more to do and sing and proved they had more depth as actors than had previously been noted. The picture cost the incredible sum of $1.5 million and more than quintupled its investment, although there is some talk that the cost also included the discarded footage that never illuminated any screen. MAYTIME is truly an operetta in that it uses some superior classical music with popular songs, and, somehow, they made it so palatable to the 1930s audiences that the cash register chimed merrily for months. MacDonald is an aged woman in 1906. She goes to a May Day celebration and meets Brown who confides that his fiancee, Carver, yearns for a big-time singing career. MacDonald talks to Carver and tells her that she, too, once had those ambitions and was, in fact, a famous opera star. Forty years before (in flashback), she had been a student of Barrymore's when Louis Napoleon was running France and, after achieving a huge success, she accepts Barrymore's marriage proposal, more out of gratitude for her career than passion. Later that night, she travels to the Left Bank, enters a bistro and hears the magnificent voice of Eddy, as he leads the students in song. Later, she and Eddy meet, and when he learns that she is from the U.S. he takes her out to dine and then to a May Day festival. MacDonald wonders why she is doing this with such a handsome young man when she has just agreed to marry her teacher, Barrymore, but emotion prevails over logic and the day turns out to be a wonderful experience for both of them. As the afternoon wanes and evening draws near, MacDonald must tell Eddy the truth about her upcoming marriage. The two go off in different directions. She stays in Europe where she finds fame and he travels back to the U.S. where he achieves equal success. Several years go by and MacDonald is to make her U.S. debut and her co-star is Eddy, in a turn of events that startled no one. Their love is rekindled and Eddy insists that they can never be separated again. MacDonald asks Barrymore for a divorce and he responds by going to Eddy's residence and killing him. Flash forward as the old MacDonald is finishing her tale to Carver and recommends that the girl forget about her career and concentrate on something longer lasting—the love of a good man. Carver sees the wisdom of MacDonald's words and agrees to toss aside her dreams of singing and accept the proposal of Brown. MacDonald dies and the picture ends as the ghostly figures of MacDonald and Eddy reprise, for the umpteenth time, the great and stirring hit song, "Will You Remember?" (by Rida Johnson Young and Sigmund Romberg). Eddy and MacDonald made many films together, eight in all, and their admiration for each other's talents was never more evident than in this one, which they reprised several years later on the "Lux Radio Theatre" in September 1944. For the record, the origination of the plot came from a 1914 play in German titled "Wei Einst Im Mai." The silent version of the story starred Ethel Shannon and Harrison Ford who was not related to the actor who was born 10 years after the first Ford retired. Actor Herman Bing began his career as assistant to director F. W. Murnau but he turned to performing when Murnau died in a 1931 traffic accident. Songwriters Bob Wright and Chet Forrest were just 20 or so when they wrote for this film. In later years, they would do new lyrics to Borodin's music for KISMET as well as revise Greig for SONG OF NORWAY. One other interesting sidelight was the bogus opera "Czaritza" which was written from Tschaikovsky's music with French lyrics by Giles Guilbert. Orson Welles also had a false opera done for CITIZEN KANE, "Salammbo," and the device was originally used when "Carnival" was written for CHARLIE CHAN AT THE OPERA in 1936. Other music includes: "Maytime Finale" (by Young and Romberg), "Virginia Ham and Eggs" (sung by Nelson Eddy), "Vive l'Opera" (by Herbert Stothart, Bob Wright, and Chet Forrest), "Student Drinking Song" (by Stothart), "Carry Me Back to Old Virginny" (by James A. Bland; sung by Eddy and Jeanette MacDonald), "Reverie" (based on Romberg airs), "Jump Jim Crow," "Road to Paradise," "Dancing Will Keep You Young" (by Young, Cyrus Wood, and Romberg), "Page's Aria" (from "Les Huguenots" by Meyerbeer), "Les Filles de Cadiz" (by Leo Delibes), "Street Singer" (by Forrest, Wright, and Stothart), "Now is the Month of Maying" (traditional with lyrics by Thomas Morley), "Chi Me Frena" (from "Lucia di Lammermoor" by Gaetano Donizetti), "William Tell Overture" (by Giacchino Antonio Rossini), "Soldiers' Chorus" (from "Faust" by Charles Gounod), "Anvil Chorus," "Miserere" (from "Il Trovatore" by Giuseppe Verdi), "Largo Al Factotum" (from "The Barber of Seville" by Rossini), "Caro Nome," "La Donna E Mobile" (from "Rigoletto" by Verdi), "O, Du Mein Holder Abendstern" (from "Tannhauser" by Richard Wagner), "Liebestod" (from "Tristan And Isolde" by Wagner), "Sempre Libera" (from "La Traviata" by Verdi), "Sumer Is Icumen In," "Mazurka," "Napoleonic Waltz," "Plantons La Vigne," "The Last Rose of Summer," "I Dreamt I Dwelt in Marble Halls," "Santa Lucia," "Nobles Seigneurs," "Une Dame Noble Et Sage," "Road to Paradise," "Sidewalks of New York," and "Columbia, The Gem of the Ocean." Despite all the praise and all the business the movie generated, MAYTIME made very few of the "Ten Best" lists for 1937 and only received one Oscar nomination for Stothart's excellent musical direction.

p, Hunt Stromberg; d, Robert Z. Leonard, William Von Wymetal; w, Noel Langley (based on the operetta by Rida Johnson Young, Sigmund Romberg); ph, Oliver T. Marsh; ed, Conrad A. Nervig; md, Herbert Stothart; art d, Cedric Gibbons, Frederic Hope; set d, Edwin B. Willis; cos, Adrian; ch, Val Raset.

Musical **(PR:A MPAA:NR)**

MAYTIME IN MAYFAIR** (1952, Brit.) 94m Imperadio/REA c

Anna Neagle *(Eileen Grahame)*, Michael Wilding *(Michael Gore-Brown)*, Peter Graves *(D'Arcy Davenport)*, Nicholas Phipps *(Sir Henry Hazelrigg)*, Thora Hird *(Janet)*, Michael Shepley *(Shepherd)*, Tom Walls *(Inspector)*, Max Kirby *(Mr. Keats)*, Desmond Walter-Ellis *(Mr. Shelley)*, Tom Walls, Jr. *(Policeman)*, Doris Rogers *(Lady Manbury-Logan-Manbury)*, Mona Washbourne *(Lady Leveson)*, Mignon O'Doherty, Glen Alyn, Pauline Johnson, Alan Reid, Trevor Dennis, Richard West, Bob Hawes, Teddy Lane, David Ellis, David Gardiner, Pat Clare, Sabina Gordon, Cynthia Williams, Eugenie Sivyer, Paddy Johnston, Pam Kail, Monica Francis, Pat Dare, Josephine Ingram.

Wilding inherits a dress shop run by Neagle. For some reason a rival shop keeps getting the new fashions until some detective work proves that Wilding's cousin Phipps is providing the information to rival shop owner Graves. Neagle, who has been angry with her new boss over this development, forgives him as the two head off on a romantic junket to the south of France. The plot is about as simple as they come but it's told so nicely that you can't help but be charmed. Wilding and Neagle are a sort of British Astaire and Rogers, playing well off one another in this lighthearted romp. The beautiful fashion designs, as well as glorious set decor, are well captured in the Technicolor photography.

p, Anna Neagle, Herbert Wilcox; d, Wilcox; w, Nicholas Phipps; ph, Max Greene [Mutz Greenbaum], Austin Dempster; m, Robert Farnon; ed, Raymond Poulton.

Romance/Musical **(PR:A MPAA:NR)**

MAZE, THE 1/2** (1953) 81m AA bw

Richard Carlson *(Gerald McTeam)*, Veronica Hurst *(Kitty Murray)*, Katherine Emery *(Mrs. Murray)*, Michael Pate *(William)*, John Dodsworth *(Dr. Bert Dilling)*, Hillary Brooke *(Peggy Lord)*, Stanley Fraser *(Robert)*, Lillian Bond *(Mrs. Dilling)*, Owen McGiveney *(Simon)*, Robin Hughes *(Richard Roblar)*, Clyde Cook *(Cab Driver)*.

A strange piece features Carlson and Hurst as a couple about to be married. He is summoned back to his ancestral home in Scotland and does not return. Worried, Hurst follows her love, accompanied by Emery, her aunt and constant chaperone. They find Carlson at his family's castle but are shocked to find him prematurely grey and refusing to speak to them. They walk about the castle until coming onto an outdoor hedge maze. Entering, Emery spots something unusual at the center. Closer investigation proves the unusual thing to be a hideous man-frog. It is revealed that the amphibious humanoid is Carlson's 200-year-old ancestor. Its climactic death frees the man from a curse and the once-more youthful man marries Hurst. Though somewhat hampered by its minuscule budget, this 3-D nightmare is fascinating to look at. The direction moves the story suspensefully through its eerie sets (also designed by the director). The man-frog practically leaps out at the audience with the 3-D effects. The actors take their roles seriously, making this a cut above average.

p, Richard Heermance; d, William Cameron Menzies; w, Dan Ullman (based on a story by Maurice Sandoz); ph, Harry Neumann (3-D); m, Marlin Skiles; ed, John Fuller; prod d, Menzies; art d, David Milton.

Horror **(PR:C MPAA:NR)**

MAZEL TOV OU LE MARIAGE (SEE: MARRY ME! MARRY ME!, 1969, Fr.)

M'BLIMEY zero (1931, Brit.) 72m Associated Sound Film Industries/UA bw

Sam Blake, Eddie Martin, Kenneth Kove, Arthur Sinclair, Marie O'Neill, Bernard Ansell.

An obscure little comedy about a group of Africans who travel to England to film a travelog. This one is probably still locked in a vault because it never got a major release in the U.S.—or Britain.

d, J. Elder Wills; w, Wills, C. H. Dand (based on a story by Hans Neiter, Fred Swann).

Comedy **(PR:A MPAA:NR)**

MC CABE AND MRS. MILLER* (1971) 120m WB c

Warren Beatty *(John McCabe)*, Rene Auberjonois *(Sheehan)*, John Schuck *(Smalley)*, Bert Remsen *(Bart Coyle)*, Keith Carradine *(Cowboy)*, Julie Christie *(Constance Miller)*, William Devane *(The Lawyer)*, Corey Fischer *(Mr. Elliott)*, Shelley Duvall *(Ida Coyle)*, Michael Murphy *(Sears)*, Anthony Holland *(Hollander)*, Tom Hill *(Archer)*, Don Francks *(Buffalo)*, Rodney Gage *(Summer Washington)*, Lili Francks *(Mrs. Washington)*, Hugh Millais *(Dog Butler)*, Manfred Schulz *(Kid)*, Jace Vander Veen *(Breed)*, Jackie Crossland *(Lily)*, Elizabeth Murphy *(Kate)*, Carey Lee McKenzie *(Alma)*, Linda Sorensen *(Blanche)*, Elisabeth Knight *(Birdie)*, Janet Wright *(Eunice)*, Maysie Hoy *(Maisie)*, Linda Kupecek *(Ruth)*, Jeremy Newsom *(Jeremy Berg)*, Wayne Robson *(Bartender)*, Jack Riley *(Riley Quinn)*, Robert Fortier *(Town Drunk)*, Wayne Grace *(Bartender)*, Wesley Taylor *(Shorty Dunn)*, Anne Cameron *(Mrs. Dunn)*, Graeme Campbell *(Bill Cubbs)*, J. S. Johnson *(J. J.)*, Joe Clarke *(Joe Shortreed)*, Harry Frazier *(Andy Anderson)*, Edwin Collier *(Gilchrist)*, Terence Kelly *(Quigley)*, Brantley F. Kearns *(Fiddler)*, Joan Maguire, Harvey Lowe, Eric Schneider, Milos Zatovic, Claudine Melgrave, Derek Deurvorst, Alexander Daikun, Gordon Robertson *(Townspeople)*.

This jumbled, mumbling, fumbling film is a cult production with those who identify with failure and back stabbing and those with no redeeming virtues whatsoever. Thanks to director Altman's almost non-presence, the actors do as they please, including swallowing, snorting, and whispering their lines in such a fashion that fully half this film cannot be understood, which is just as well. From the other half the viewer can grasp a weird Beatty, circa 1902, ambling into a raw northwestern wilderness town called Presbyterian Church where he gambles his way to some winnings and then establishes a whorehouse with his surly lover Christie as the madam and chief prostitute. She is about as alluring as dead herring in a hothouse. Miners nevertheless pour into the brothel-bathhouse and Beatty's success does not go unnoticed by the local mining operators who offer him $6250 to sell out. Beatty—cocky with commercial triumph—refuses, holding out for $15,000. Christie warns her smart-talking partner that the company employs hired guns to get its way but he tells her will handle the goons with reason. While Christie is sucking on an opium pipe which frizzles her hair, gunmen come to town and, in a shootout, Beatty is mortally wounded. He crawls about town mumbling and leaking from Altman's specially designed blood blisters and then dies in a snowdrift. Excessively violent, lacking any human ethics, and portraying love as a five-dollar fee in a whore's bed, MC CABE AND MRS. MILLER is one of the most overrated so-called westerns on record. It's dull, poorly written, directed with indifference (at best), and Zsigmond's limp soft focus gives mushy, murky hues to almost every scene, guaranteeing eyestrain and migraine. Technically shoddy, this film typifies Altman at his trashiest. Christie—capable of better—is about the laziest whore imaginable, certainly one who would never have made a dime in the Old West where such women had to work as hard as any cowboy. Beatty grunts, grins, and garbles his witless remarks like a cretin looking for a mind. At best, the film is wholly incompetent and so undisciplined that certain critics mistook this outstanding inadequacy as intended art of some kind (which it never was). Shot on location in Canada (the snowdrifts could have been shot anywhere), Altman went over budget by $600,000 for a total cost of $4 million and the film barely made that amount back at the box office. Altman apparently sought to create the crude look achieved so masterfully by George Stevens in SHANE but his town, which cost more than $200,000 to build in the Canadian wilderness, is a clapboard pile of buildings in which no self-respecting hobo would rest for an hour. The cast members, other than Beatty and Christie, stroll and bounce around the icy little town thinking up lines to say and movements to make. Devane is a grumble and Duvall—whom Altman met at a party and decided to make into an actress (and this has to be the classic case of one too many)—squeaks her way through a bordello on the verge of momentary collapse. Altman later stated that he made this idiotic western because he wanted "to destroy all the myths of heroism." Only a rank, two-bit, punk director would ignore the fact that the West and heroes are synonymous and make a film that had nothing to do with the West, only the disinteresting, amateur creations of his on-set actors. It's a pretty silly way to make films, sort of saying: "You actors make up the film as we go along, and move whichever way you like and maybe the camera will photograph you or an egg lying about and if this catches on, I'll take the credit for it as the enigmatic genius I am. If it fails, well, you dumped this mess on the public, not me. I'm only the director!"

p, David Foster, Mitchell Brower; d, Robert Altman; w, Altman, Brian McKay (based on the novel *McCabe* by Edmund Naughton); ph, Vilmos Zsigmond (Panavision, Technicolor); m, Leonard Cohen; ed, Louis Lombardo; prod d, Leon Ericksen; art d, Phillip Thomas, Al Locatelli; cos, Erickson; spec eff, Marcel Vercoutere; m/l, Cohen; makeup, Robert Jiras, Ed Butterworth, Phyllis Newman.

Western **Cas.** **(PR:O MPAA:R)**

MC CONNELL STORY, THE** 1/2** (1955) 107m WB c (GB: TIGER IN THE SKY)

Alan Ladd *(Joseph C. "Mac" McConnell, Jr.)*, June Allyson *(Pearl "Butch" McConnell)*, James Whitmore *(Ty Whitman)*, Frank Faylen *(Sgt. Sykes)*, Robert Ellis *(Bob)*, Willis Bouchey *(Newton Bass)*, Sarah Selby *(Mom)*, Gregory Walcott *(1st M.P.)*, John Pickard *(2nd M.P.)*, Frank Ferguson *(Mechanic)*, Perry Lopez *(Red)*, Dabbs Greer *(Pilot Instructor)*, Edward Platt *(Medical Corps Instructor)*, Vera Marshe *(Blonde)*.

This true-life story of a real American hero was marred when the subject of the film, Capt. Joseph McConnell, Jr., died while testing a Sabre jet just a few weeks before this picture was set to roll. McConnell had shot down 15 enemy planes during the Korean War and arrived in the United States to great accolades. he'd hoped to return for another tour of duty but his superiors felt he was more important to the war effort stateside and they forbade his desire to get back to Korea; then fate took matters and McConnell's plane crashed at Edwards Air Force Base in California. Ladd is the lead, a private from a small town in New England in the early days of WW II. He's assigned to medical duty but he wants to fly so he takes private lessons in order to qualify. Meanwhile, he falls in love with Allyson and they are sent to Texas where she becomes pregnant. Before they can settle in the Lone Star State, Ladd is sent to Washington for pilot training. Allyson goes back to Massuchusetts to bear their daughter and Ladd becomes a bomber navigator where he serves out his war duty. There's a new kind of fighter plane being developed, a jet-engined demon. Whitmore, an old pal of Ladd's, is in charge of the program and gets Ladd assigned to it. Ladd and Allyson move from base to base, have two more children, and finally settle in the Apple Valley area of California. War breaks out in Korea and Ladd, now a full-fledged jet pilot, downs several planes, then is sent home to Apple Valley where he discovers that his neighbors have built him the house of which he'd only dreamed. He becomes a test pilot over the tears of Allyson (and could anyone cry as well as she could?), who wishes he'd ground himself but she knows that she can never keep him earthbound. Ladd takes off for his last flight and soars into real-life history and film lore. An unabashedly patriotic story with good performances by all, the picture also had the benefit of technical advice from some of the pilots who had actually been there, including Capt. Manuel J. Fernandez (see credit list), one of the top aces in the service at that time. Co-screenwriter Rolfe later created the TV series "The Man From U.N.C.L.E." He foreshadowed his later success with some excellent bits of humor in what could have been a syrupy script. The picture had action, romance, and lots of good fun until the tragic and true conclusion.

p, Henry Blanke; d, Gordon Douglas; w, Ted Sherdeman, Sam Rolfe (based on a story by Sherdeman); ph, John Seitz (CinemaScope, Warner Color); m, Max Steiner; ed, Owen Marks; art d, John Beckman; cos, Howard Shoup; technical advisor, Col. William L. Orris, USAF, Capt. Manuel J. Fernandez, USAF.

Biography **(PR:A MPAA:NR)**

MC CORD (SEE: MINUTE TO PRAY, A SECOND TO DIE, A, 1968, U.S./Ital.)

MC CULLOCHS, THE (SEE: WILD MCCULLOCHS, THE, 1975)

MC FADDEN'S FLATS* 1/2 (1935) 64m PAR bw

Walter C. Kelly *(Dan McFadden)*, Andy Clyde *(Jock McTavish)*, Richard Cromwell *(Sandy McTavish)*, Jane Darwell *(Nora McFadden)*, Betty Furness *(Molly McFadden)*, George Barbier *(Mr. Hall)*, Phyllis Brooks *(Mary Ellis Hall)*, Howard Wilson *(Robert Hall)*, Nella Walker *(Mrs. Hall)*, Frederick Burton *(Jefferson)*, Patrick Moriarty *(Pat Malone)*, Esther Michelson *(Mrs. Bernstein)*, Anna Demetrio *(Mrs. Bono)*, Jerry Mandy *(Tony Bono)*, Joe Barton *(Bernstein)*, Mary Forbes, Lee Kohlmar.

The old story of boy meets girl while their parents fight it out. Kelly and Clyde are the adults, the best of friends when they're not at war with one another. Furness and Cromwell are the young couple. Some funny moments, but mostly a string of comic cliches in this programmer.

p, Charles R. Rogers; d, Ralph Murphy; w, Arthur Caesar, Edward Kaufman, Andy Rice, Casey Robinson (based on a play by Gus Hill); ph, Ben Reynolds; ed, Joseph Kane.

Comedy **(PR:A MPAA:NR)**

MC GUIRE, GO HOME!** (1966, Brit.) 101m RANK/CD c (GB: THE HIGH BRIGHT SUN)

Dirk Bogarde *(Maj. McGuire)*, George Chakiris *(Haghios)*, Susan Strasberg *(Juno Kozani)*, Denholm Elliott *(Baker)*, Gregoire Aslan *(Gen. Skyros)*, Colin Campbell *(Emile Andros)*, Joseph Furst *(Dr. Andros)*, Katherine Kath *(Mrs. Andros)*, George Pastell *(Prinos)*, Paul Stassino *(Alkis)*, Nigel Stock *(Col. Park)*.

Set against a backdrop of Britain's troubles with Cyprus in the late 1950s, Bogarde is a British intelligence agent tracking down a terrorist leader. Strasberg is an American archeology student visiting friends whom she unwittingly discovers are hiding the terrorist, Chakiris. Bogarde believes she knows where Chakiris is hiding, but she refuses to tell. However, Chakiris presumes she has revealed his whereabouts and threatens to kill her. Fearing for her life, Strasberg hides out in Bogarde's apartment where the pair fall in love. But when British intelligence finds out he is hiding her, they relieve him of his duties and transfer him to Greece. Strasberg follows him there, where they discover that a mysterious man who has been following them is none other than a private detective hired to gather evidence for a divorce by Bogarde's wife. Although this film attempts to show the Cypriot struggle for independence during this time, the plot is too simplistic and never goes deep enough for the audience to analyze the troubles, causes, or attitudes that plagued Cyprus in the late 1950s.

p, Betty E. Box; d, Ralph Thomas; w, Ian Stuart Black, Bryan Forbes (based on the novel by Black); ph, Ernest Steward (Eastmancolor); m, Angelo Francesco Lavagnino; ed, Alfred Roome; prod d, Charles Orme; md, Muir Matheson; art d, Syd Cain, Franco Fontana; cos, Yvonne Caffin.

Adventure (PR:A MPAA:NR)

MC GLUSKY THE SEA ROVER (SEE: HELL'S CARGO, 1935, Brit.)

MC HALE'S NAVY**½ (1964) 93m UNIV c

Ernest Borgnine (Lt. Comdr. Quinton McHale), Tim Conway (Ensign Charles Parker), Joe Flynn (Capt. Wallace Burton Binghamton), Bob Hastings (Lt. LeRoy Carpenter), Gary Vinson (Q. M. George "Christy" Christopher), John Wright (Radioman Willy Moss), Carl Ballantine (Torpedoman Lester Gruber), Billy Sands (Motor Machinist Mate Harrison "Tinker" Bell), Edson Stroll (Gunner's Mate Virgil Edwards), Gavin MacLeod (Seaman Joseph "Happy" Hanes), Yoshio Yoda (Takeo "Fuji" Fujiwara), Jean Willes (Margo Monet), Claudine Longet (Andrea Bouchard), George Kennedy (Henri Le Clerc), Marcel Hillaire (Chef de Gendarmes), Dale Ishimoto (Japanese Captain), John Mamo (Japanese J.G.), Sandy Slavik (French Girl).

Moving from the small screen to the big time, this comedy, inspired by the ABC sit-com, finds Borgnine and company trying to make some fast wartime cash by setting up a delayed-result racing parlor aboard their P.T. boat. The scheme fails and they find themselves in debt to a bunch of marines. Through a series of various mishaps, the crew members find themselves going in and out of debt like a yo-yo on a string. They acquire a race horse which causes a Japanese submarine to run aground, among other things. Lots of shtick and hokum abounds in what was little more than an expansion of the popular television show.

p&d, Edward J. Montagne; w, Frank Gill, Jr., G. Carleton Brown (based on a story by Si Rose); ph, William Margulies (Pathecolor); m, Jerry Fielding; ed, Sam E. Waxman; art d, Alexander Golitzen, Russell Kimball; set d, John McCarthy, James S. Redd; cos, Helen Colvig; spec eff, Roland Skeete; makeup, Bud Westmore.

Comedy (PR:A MPAA:NR)

MC HALE'S NAVY JOINS THE AIR FORCE**½ (1965) 92m UNIV c

Joe Flynn (Capt. Wallace Burton Binghamton), Tim Conway (Ensign Charles Parker), Bob Hastings (Lt. Carpenter), Gary Vinson (Q. M. George "Christy" Christopher), Billy Sands (Motor Machinist Mate Harrison "Tinker" Bell), Edson Stroll (Gunner's Mate Virgil Edwards), John Wright (Radioman Willy Moss), Gavin MacLeod (Seaman Joseph "Happy" Haines), Yoshio Yoda (Takeo "Fuji" Fujiwara), Tom Tully (Gen. Harkness), Susan Silo (Smitty), Henry Beckman (Col. Platt), Ted Bessell (Lt. Wilbur Harkness), Jean Hale (Madge), Cliff Norton (Maj. Grady), Willis Bouchey (Adm. Doyle), Berkeley Harris (Vogel), Jacques Aubuchon (Dimitri), Len Lesser (NKVD Commissar), Henry Corden (NKVD Deputy), Jack Bernardi (1st Russian Seaman), Norman Leavitt (2nd Russian Seaman), Andy Albin (3rd Russian Seaman), Joe Ploski (4th Russian Seaman), Tony Franke (Tresh), Clay Tanner (Lt. Wilson).

The further adventures of WW II's most unlikely patrol boat. But this time it's without Borgnine, who declined to do the role he had played on TV and in the first MC HALE'S NAVY film after a salary dispute with Universal. This time out, Conway ends up in charge of the ship and inadvertently gets promoted time after time, thanks to some strange mishaps. After a drunken bout, he ends up in an Air Force uniform, gets involved with some Russians, and eventually is honored for bravery by no less than the President of the U.S. Somewhat funnier than the first film, with a similar reliance on slapstick gags, well visualized by director Montagne.

p&d, Edward J. Montagne; w, John Fenton Murray (based on a story by William J. Lederer); ph, Lionel Lindon (Technicolor); m, Jerry Fielding; ed, Sam E. Waxman; art d, Alexander Golitzen, Russell Kimball; set d, John McCarthy, James S. Redd; spec eff, Roland Skeete; makeup, Bud Westmore, Rolf Miller.

Comedy (PR:A MPAA:NR)

MC KENNA OF THE MOUNTED*½ (1932) 66m COL bw

Buck Jones, Greta Granstedt, James Flavin, Walter McGrail, Niles Welch, Mitchell Lewis, Claude King, Glenn Strange, Bud Osborne, Edmund Cobb, Silver the Horse.

Depite his cowboy garb, Jones plays a mountie who gets kicked out of the elite brigade after he's framed and publicly disgraced. But the unusually melodramatic plot does not quite work in this film where background scenes are reused over and over, as when Jones and others pass the same river again and again, and the usual routines are involved in this attempt at a complicated mystery, love story, and western all rolled into one.

d, D. Ross Lederman; w, Stuart Anthony (based on a story by Randall Faye); ph, Benjamin Kline; ed, Gene Milford.

Western (PR:A MPAA:NR)

MC KENZIE BREAK, THE***½ (1970) 108m UA c

Brian Keith (Capt. Jack Connor), Helmut Griem (Kapitan Schluetter), Ian Hendry (Maj. Perry), Jack Watson (Gen. Kerr), Patrick O'Connell (Sgt. Maj. Cox), Horst Janson (Neuchl), Alexander Allerson (Von Sperrle), John Abineri (Kranz), Constantin De Goguel (Lt. Hall), Tom Kempinski (Schmidt), Eric Allan (Hochbauer), Caroline Mortimer (Sgt. Bell), Mary Larkin (Cpl. Watt), Gregg Palmer (Berger), Michael Sheard (Unger), Ingo Mogendorf (Fullgrabe), Franz van Norde (Dichter), Desmond Perry (Accomplice), Jim Mooney (Guard Foss), Vernon

Hayden (Scottish Dispatcher), Maura Kelly (Scots Lassie), Noel Purcell (Ferry Captain), Paul Murphy (Weber), Frank Hayden (Holtz), Paddy Robinson (Pilot), Robert Somerset (Guard), Des Keogh (Guard), Barry Cassin (Guard Jones), Denis Latimer (Lt. Everett), Conor Evans (Orderly Joss), Stephen Good (Paisley), Brendan Mathews (Guard), Emmet Bergin (Orderly Johnston), John Kavanagh (Police Inspector), Joe Pilkington (Police Communications Sergeant), Dave Kelly (Adjutant), Mark Mulholland (Skipper), Martin Dempsey (Colonel), Alec Doran (Police Official).

Well executed, taut drama dealing with German prisoners in an Allied POW camp, a rare subject in American films. Keith is an Irish intelligence agent sent to Camp McKenzie in Scotland. After a prison riot is quelled with fire hoses, Keith suspects it was merely a ruse to distract attention from an escape plot. This theory is proven to be true after Janson, a homosexual prisoner ostracized by his fellow inmates and severely beaten during the riot, mumbles something about an escape. But Janson is myseriously strangled before regaining consciousness and Keith is forced into a cat-and-mouse game with Griem, a captured U-Boat captain the Irishman suspects is behind the plan. He allows the prisoners to break free in hopes of capturing the U-Boat sent to pick up the men, but his plans go awry, and all but two of the Germans escape. Keith is left facing disciplinary action for his failure. Suspense is nicely sustained throughout the film thanks to the particularly strong characterizations by Keith and Griem. Though the character played by the former is a hard drinking, unorthodox soldier, he is highly intelligent, a nice complement to Griem's more calculating but equally brainy character.

p, Jules Levy, Arthur Gardner, Arnold Laven; d, Lamont Johnson; w, William Norton (based on the novel The Bowmanville Break by Sidney Shelley); ph, Michael Reed (DeLuxe Color); m, Riz Ortolani; ed, Tom Rolf; prod d, Frank White; set d, Keith Liddiard; cos, Tiny Nicholls; spec eff, Thomas "Knobby" Clark; makeup, Alan Brownie.

War/Suspense (PR:C MPAA:PG)

MC LINTOCK!**½ (1963) 127m Batjac/UA c

John Wayne (George Washington McLintock), Maureen O'Hara (Katherine McLintock), Yvonne De Carlo (Louise Warren), Patrick Wayne (Devlin Warren), Stefanie Powers (Becky McLintock), Jack Kruschen (Birnbaum), Chill Wills (Drago), Jerry Van Dyke (Matt Douglas, Jr.), Edgar Buchanan (Bunny Dull), Bruce Cabot (Ben Sage), Perry Lopez (Davey Elk), Michael Pate (Puma), Strother Martin (Agard), Gordon Jones (Matt Douglas), Robert Lowery (Gov. Cuthbert H. Humphrey), Ed Faulkner (Young Ben Sage), H.W. Gim (Ching), Aissa Wayne (Alice Warren), Chuck Roberson (Sheriff Lord), Hal Needham (Carter), Pedro Gonzales, Jr. (Carlos), Hank Worden (Jeth), Leo Gordon (Jones), Mary Patterson (Beth), "Big" John Hamilton (Fauntleroy), Ralph Volkie, Dan Borzage (Loafers), John Stanley (Running Buffalo), Kari Noven (Millie), Mari Blanchard (Camille), Frank Hagney (Bartender), Bob Steele (Railroad Engineer).

A western "Taming of the Shrew" for the Duke finds Wayne hiring local widow De Carlo as his cook. She brings along her two children, a 7-year-old daughter and a teenaged son who is hired as a ranch hand (both played by Wayne's real-life kids). All seems well until his estranged wife, O'Hara, returns from the East with divorce on her mind. She also wants custody of their 17-year-old daughter, Powers, a college girl. Powers returns from school and is immediately courted by the younger Wayne and a Harvard beau, Van Dyke. The two suitors take to fighting it out, and it's revealed that Van Dyke is the son of one of Wayne's worst enemies. Wayne's problems are compounded by Indian raids, as well as his never-ending arguments with O'Hara. Finally out of patience with his wife, he publicly spanks her, which gathers an appreciative audience. He then tells her to get the divorce if she really wants it, only to have her throw herself into his arms, proclaiming her love. Loud and brassy, Wayne does a good job in his broad comedy role, although it is doubted that the picture could have gotten away with the spanking scene if it were made today. High points of the film are O'Hara being chased by Wayne all over town in her white pantaloons and practically the whole cast sliding down a hill into a big mud hole.

p, Michael Wayne; d, Andrew V. McLaglen; w, James Edward Grant; ph, William H. Clothier (Panavision, Technicolor); m, Frank De Vol; ed, Otho Lovering; prod d, Richard Kuhn; art d, Hal Pereira, Eddie Imazu; set d, Sam Comer, Darrell Silvera; cos, Frank Beetson, Jr., Ann B. Peck; m/l, "Love in the Country," De Vol, "By" Dunham (sung by The Limelighters), "Just Right for Me," "Cakewalk," "When We Dance," Dunham; makeup, Web Overlander.

Comedy/Western (PR:A MPAA:NR)

MC MASTERS, THE**

(1970) 90m Jayjen/Chevron c (AKA: THE BLOOD CROWD; THE MCMASTERS...TOUGHER THAN THE WEST ITSELF)

Brock Peters (Benjie), Burl Ives (Neal McMasters), David Carradine (White Feather), Nancy Kwan (Robin), Jack Palance (Kolby), Dane Clark (Spencer), John Carradine (Preacher), L. Q. Jones (Russell), R. G. Armstrong (Watson), Frank Raiter (Grant), Alan Vint (Hank), Marion Brash (Mrs. Watson), Neil Davis (Sylvester), Paul Eichenberg (Jud), Richard Alden (Lester), Lonnie Samuel (Bull), Albert Hockmeister (Sheriff), Rev. David Strong (Otis), Dumas Slade (Cullen), Joan Howard (Mrs. Spencer), William Kiernan (Bartender), Jose Maranio (Indian Joe), Leo Dillenschneider (Watson's Son), Richard Martinez (Black Fox), Joseph Duran (Black Cloud), Bill Alexander (Barber), Frank Nanoia (Rancher), David Welty (Kolby's Son).

This bleak, realistic-looking western is notable for being one of the first in the genre to deal with the racial prejudice of whites against blacks and native Americans. Unfortunately, its goals were ultimately undermined by the producers, who released the film with two different endings. Peters plays the black soldier returning home to the South after fighting for the North in the Civil War, only to find himself the victim of prejudice. Ives, the white rancher who raised him, offers him half of his land, which Peters accepts. But no one will work for a black man, so the land is about to be sold when the younger Carradine, an Indian befriended by Peters, leads his tribe to help Peters with the roundup. However, the local whites don't take to this, and trouble ensues. One ending has the local bad guys, led by Palance, win out. The other finds Peters defeating Palance. This wishy-washy attitude of the producers, who couldn't decide whether to go for morality or box office gross, undermined what could have been an important statement about racial prejudices.

p, Monro Sachson; d, Alf Kjellin; w, Harold Jacob Smith; ph, Lester Shorr (Movielab Color); m, Coleridge-Taylor Perkinson; ed, Melvin Shapiro; prod d, Joel Schiller; md, Perkinson; art d, Schiller; set d, George R. Nelson; spec eff, Herman Townsley, Ted Alires.

Western **(PR:O MPAA:GP)**

MC Q** (1974) 116m Batjac/WB c

John Wayne *(Detective Lt. Lon McQ)*, Eddie Albert *(Capt. Ed Kosterman)*, Diana Muldaur *(Lois Boyle)*, Colleen Dewhurst *(Myra)*, Clu Gulager *(Franklin Toms)*, David Huddleston *(Edward M. "Pinky" Farrow)*, Jim Watkins *(J. C. Davis)*, Al Lettieri *(Manny Santiago)*, Julie Adams *(Elaine Forrester)*, Rogert E. Mosley *(Rosey)*, William Bryant *(Sgt. Stan Boyle)*, Joe Tornatore *(LaSalle)*, Kim Sanford *(Ginger)*, Richard Kelton *(Radical)*, Richard Eastham *(Walter Forrester)*, Dick Friel *(Bob Mahoney)*, Fred Waugh, Chuck Roberson *(Bodyguards)*.

Wayne trades in his saddle for a seat in a sports car and his six-shooter for a snubnose .38 in this disappointing crime picture set in the streets of Seattle. Wayne, a veteran officer, quits the police force after the murder of his best friend, Bryant, a fellow cop. He refuses to believe that Bryant was involved in drug-trafficking, nor does he believe that his death was the work of radical student hippies. His superior, Albert, forbids him to investigate the murder, causing Wayne to turn in his badge. Wayne persists and nearly gets involved with Muldaur, the dead cop's widow, who displays an acceptable amount of grief but is really working with a corrupt cop, Gulager, in a scheme to get hold of a priceless cache of drugs. Unknowingly, Wayne has the drugs hidden in his car, which explains Muldaur's interest. The loss of a best friend is only the first of Wayne's problems. Having divorced his wife, the attractive Adams, Wayne also loses his daughter, whose life has become too busy to spend any more Sundays with him. Wayne then turns to Dewhurst, a cocktail waitress and former prostitute whose life has as little meaning as Wayne's. The two find a mutual bond in their loneliness and spend the night together. Soon afterwards, Dewhurst is killed, filling Wayne with the inextinguishable desire for vengeance. He sets his sights on local drug kingpin Lettieri (who was equally mean in THE GODFATHER and THE GETAWAY), and beats him into oblivion when he corners him in a bathroom. Lettieri, however, isn't the mastermind behind the drug-trafficking—it's the police themselves who have pinned their crimes on the mob. After a jarring chase scene which ends on a deserted beach, Wayne emerges victorious but still resigns himself to the fate of being a policeman. He makes peace with Albert, whom he originally suspected of being corrupt, accepts his badge, and returns to the force. After turning down the lead role in DIRTY HARRY (1971), a role which was also offered to Frank Sinatra, Wayne admitted that he was aiming for that Clint Eastwood audience with MC Q. Unfortunately, however, director Sturges (BAD DAY AT BLACK ROCK, THE MAGNIFICENT SEVEN) couldn't bring the same excitement to his film that Don Siegel did with DIRTY HARRY. The result was just another nail in the western coffin—the last great western hero, John Wayne, had transformed into your average angry cop. Wayne took another stab at police work in the following years, BRANNIGAN, before returning to solid western ground in his last two pictures—ROOSTER COGBURN and THE SHOOTIST. MC Q made it into the news in 1986 during the overthrow of Philippine president Ferdinand Marcos. After an anti-Marcos military group seized control of the national television station, MC Q, for some unknown reason, was shown in place of the regular programming. A strange move for the Filipinos, to which one can attach absolutely no significance.

p, Jules Levy, Arthur Gardner, Lawrence Roman; d, John Sturges; w, Roman; ph, Harry Stradling, Jr. (Panavision, Technicolor); m, Elmer Bernstein; ed, Bill Ziegler; prod d, Walter Simonds; spec eff, Howard Jensen.

Crime **Cas.** **(PR:O MPAA:PG)**

MC VICAR 1/2** (1982, Brit.) 111m Crown International c

Rogert Daltrey *(McVicar)*, Adam Faith *(Probyn)*, Cheryl Campbell *(Sheila)*, Steven Berkoff *(Harrison)*, Brian Hall *(Stokes)*, Jeremy Blake *(Johnson)*, Leonard Gregory *(Collins)*, Peter Jonfield *(Harris)*, Anthony Trent *(Tate)*, Matthew Scurfield *(Jeffries)*, Joe Turner *(Panda)*, Terence Stuart *(Sid)*, Charlie Cork *(Martin)*, Ronald Herdman *(Nobby)*, Tony Haygarth *(Rabies)*, Tony Rohr *(Bootsie)*, Ralph Watson *(Principal Officer E Wing)*, Richard Simpson *(Douglas)*, Allan Mitchell *(Jackson)*, Stanley Lloyd *(Magistrate)*, Mikki Margorian *(Secretary)*, James Marcus *(Sewell)*, Georgina Hale *(Kate)*, Anthony May *(Billy)*, Malcolm Tierney *(Frank)*, Raymond Skipp *(Bimbo)*, Billy Murray *(Joey)*, John Rolfe *(Graham)*, Ricky Parkinson *(Russell)*, David Beames *(Policeman)*, Robert Walker *(Co-driver)*, Jamie Foreman *(Driver)*, Ian Hendry *(Hitchens)*, Malcolm Terris *(Principal Officer)*, Charles Cork, Paul Kember, Stephen Bent *(Warders)*, Harry Fielder *(Harry)*, Michael Feast *(Cody)*.

Daltrey is a convict who escapes prison, pulls a few jobs, and is rearrested in this intriguing crime drama. Based on an autobiography by John McVicar (who wrote the script, as well), the film shows a picture of the British underworld not often seen on film. Daltrey, the former singer with the rock group The Who, does a competent if uninspired job in the lead, though Campbell and former British teen idol Faith are better. Daltrey sings the soundtrack, including "Free Me" (which became a hit single), "Just A Dream Away," "Waiting for a Friend," "Without Your Love," "McVicar," "White City Lights," and "I'm Not Going Home."

p, Bill Curbishley, Roy Baird, Roger Daltrey; d, Tom Clegg; w, John McVicar (based on the book *McVicar By Himself* by McVicar); ph, Vernon Layton; m, Jeff Wayne; ed, Peter Boyle; art d, Brian Ackland-Snow.

Crime **Cas.** **(PR:C MPAA:R)**

ME 1/2**

(1970, Fr.) 83m Athos-Parc-Stephan-Renn-Films du Carrosse/Altura c (L'ENFANCE NUE; AKA: NAKED CHILDHOOD)

Michel Terrazon *(Francois)*, Marie-Louise Thierry *(Mme. Minguet)*, Rene Thierry *(Minguet)*, Marie Marc *(Meme)*, Henri Puff *(Raoul)*, Pierrette Deplanque *(Josette)*, Linda Gutemberg *(Simone)*, Raoul Billery *(Roby)*, Maurice Coussoneau *(Letillon)*.

Terrazon is a 10-year-old boy who is abandoned by his mother and goes through a number of foster parents before he is taken in by one family he becomes close to. He develops a special relationship with the family's grandmother, but when she dies, he has a hard time adjusting. He drops a cat down a flight of stairs in order to prove that cats land on their feet, and then nurses the cat back to health. Then he causes a serious accident when he drops bars from a bridge. This results in the young boy being sent to a special school, but he knows that upon his release he can return to the family. (In French; English subtitles.)

p, Francois Truffaut, Claude Berri, Mag Bodard, Guy Benier; d, Maurice Pialat; w, Pialat, Arlette Langman; ph, Calude Beausoleil (Eastmancolor); English titles, Gwendolyn Wright.

Drama **(PR:A MPAA:NR)**

ME AND MARLBOROUGH 1/2** (1935, Brit.) 78m GAU bw

Cicely Courtneidge *(Kit Ross)*, Tom Walls *(Duke of Marlborough)*, Barry Mackay *(Dick Welch)*, Alfred Drayton *(Sgt. Bull)*, Iris Ashley *(Josephine)*, Ivor McLaren *(Sgt. Cummings)*, Gibb McLaughlin *(Old Soldier)*, Peter Gawthorne *(Staff Colonel)*, Cecil Parker *(Colonel of the Greys)*, George Merritt *(Harley)*, Cyril Smith *(Cpl. Fox)*, Mickey Brantford *(Ens. Coke)*, Randle Ayrton *(King Louis XIV)*, Henry Oscar *(Goultier)*, Percy Walsh *(Naylor)*.

Amusing farce features Courtneidge as the proprietress of a country pub who has just gotten married. On the night of the wedding, someone offers her husband a shilling. It turns out to be the local recruiting officer, who has tricked the poor man into accepting the Queen's bounty for enlistment, so off he goes. Courtneidge dresses up in soldier's garb and follows her husband, during the course of which she saves Walls (Malborough) from capture by the French (supposedly based on a real incident), eventually saving him from a spy trial. Walls and Courtneidge make an interesting pair, for he is subdued and she falls just short of pie-in-the-face comedy. The romance is sometimes sacrificed for unnecessary gags, but overall this is a fairly enjoyable little programmer.

p, Michael Balcon; d, Victor Saville; w, W. P. Lipscomb, Reginald Pound, Ian Hay, Marjorie Gaffney; ph, Charles Van Enger, C. Courant; m/l, Noel Gay, Clifford Grey.

Comedy **(PR:A MPAA:NR)**

ME AND MY BROTHER zero (1969) 95m Two Faces/New Yorker bw-c

Julius Orlovsky *(Himself)*, Joseph Chaikin *(Julius Orlovsky)*, John Coe *(Psychiatrist)*, Allen Ginsberg, Peter Orlovsky *(Themselves)*, Virginia Kiser *(Social Worker)*, Nancy Fish *(Herself)*, Cynthia McAdams *(Actress)*, Roscoe Lee Browne *(Photographer)*, Seth Allen, Maria Tucci, Jack Greenbaum, Christopher Walken, Beth Porter, Fred Ainsworth, Richard Orzel, Philippe La Prelle, Otis Young, Gregory Corso, Sully Boyar, Joel Press, Louis Waldon.

Strange and ugly film about a catatonic schizophrenic released from the hospital. The film starts with Orlovsky playing himself but because of his condition he is eventually replaced by Chaikin. The film incorporates the subject's brother and a few of the Beat Generation poets (Ginsberg and Corso the most notable) as it meanders about, looking at the subject's life. He is recruited for a film about homosexuals, gets lost in San Francisco and is finally re-institutionalized. Subjected to Thorazine and electro-shock he is finally released once more to his brother Peter. Using a variety of film techniques including split screens, double exposure, freeze frame and just about anything else imaginable, the film plays around with fantasy and reality with the same apparent ease with which it plays with its subject's life. Made over a three and one-half year period, the film reeks of cruelty and disrespect to Julius Orlovsky. It was banned from public screening at the Venice Film Festival. This classic example of garbage wrapped in the protective cloak of "art" contains some surprisingly talented names such as Browne and Walken, well before they were appearing in high-quality projects. Even more surprising is the appearance of Shepard's name in the writing credits. Though his work certainly shows an unusual and bizarre imagination, it never has matched the cruelty of ME AND MY BROTHER.

p, Helen Silverstein; d, Robert Frank; w, Frank, Sam Shepard; ph, Frank; ed, Frank, Silverstein, Lynn Ratener, Bob Easton.

Drama **(PR:O MPAA:NR)**

ME AND MY GAL** (1932) 78m FOX bw (GB: PIER 13)

Spencer Tracy *(Dan Dolan)*, Joan Bennett *(Helen Riley)*, Marion Burns *(Kate Riley)*, George Walsh *(Duke Castege)*, J. Farrell MacDonald *(Pat "Pop" Riley)*, Noel Madison *(Baby Face Castenega)*, Henry B. Walthall *(Sgt. Collins)*, Bert Hanlon *(Jake the Tailor)*, Adrian Morris *(Detective Al Allen)*, George Chandler *(Eddie Collins)*, Will Stanton *(Drunken Fisherman)*, Frank Moran *(Frank, a Dock Worker/Wedding Guest)*, Roger Imhof *(Down and Outer)*, Pat Moriarity *(Priest)*, James Marcus *(Tugboat Capt. Mike Ryan)*, Russ Powell *(Burper)*, Billy Bevan *(Ashley)*, Ralph Sipperly *(English Drunk)*, Phil Tead *(Radio Salesman)*, Heinie Conklin *(Worker)*, Eleanor Wesselhoeft *(Wife)*.

Not a great effort on the part of anyone involved, ME AND MY GAL is a wisecracking attempt at comedy that falls like a two-day-old souffle because the jokes come so quickly and are cornier than a podiatrist's office. Tracy is a young policeman who patrols the waterfront area of downtown New York City. Bennett is a waitress at a local hash house with a hard attitude and lots of cynicism in her dialog. Burns is Bennett's sister and a much more naive type as proven by the fact that she falls hard for Walsh, a no-goodnik gangster of the lowest level. Burns is fascinated by Walsh and has been totally taken in by his snakelike charm, but Tracy sees through the malfeasant and nabs the crook, just before he is about to commit the greatest crime of all—capturing Burns' heart. With the little sister saved from that fate, Bennett is free to marry the cop of her dreams, Tracy. It's a padded 79-minute picture and the only effective comedy scene is a parody of STRANGE INTERLUDE done by Tracy and Bennett. That movie was out just ahead of this one and created such a sensation that Fox must have thought they'd have some fun at MGM's expense and called it "Strange Inner-tube" in the satire. The villain, Walsh, had been a silent screen star with a large following, who did some Douglas Fairbanks-type roles. At one point, he was to be the star of BEN-HUR (the silent version) but backstage politics caused him to be replaced by Ramon Novarro. Walsh's brother was Raoul Walsh, the famed director, and the two of them worked together here as well as a number of other times.

d, Raoul Walsh; w, Arthur Kober (based on a story by Barry Connors, Philip Klein); ph, Arthur Miller; ed, Jack Murray; art d, Gordon Wiles; cos, Rita Kaufman.

Comedy **(PR:A MPAA:NR)**

ME AND MY PAL** (1939, Brit.) 74m Welwyn/Pathe bw

Dave Willis *(Dave Craig)*, Pat Kirkwood *(Peggy)*, George Moon *(Hal Thomson)*, A. Giovanni *(Giovanni)*, John Warwick *(Charlie)*, Arthur Margetson *(Andrews)*, Aubrey Mallalieu *(Governor)*, Eliot Makeham *(Cripps)*, O. B. Clarence *(Judge)*, Ernest Butcher *(Webb)*, Hugh Dempster *(Joe)*, Gerry Fitzgerald *(Singing Convict)*, Ian Fleming, Robert Adair, Joe Mott, Agnes Laughlan, C. Denier Warren.

Willis and Moon are a pair of van drivers duped by a smooth-talking con man into thinking that they are working with the police while they are actually helping him defraud an insurance company. Eventually they team with the police to catch the man. Fast but not very good late career outing for director Bentley, who began his career in the very early silents.

p, Warwick Ward; d, Thomas Bentley; ph, Ernest Palmer.

Comedy **(PR:A MPAA:NR)**

ME AND THE COLONEL** (1958) 109m COL bw

Danny Kaye *(S. I. Jacobowsky)*, Curt Jurgens *(Col. Prokoszny)*, Nicole Maurey *(Suzanne Roualet)*, Francoise Rosay *(Mme. Bouffier)*, Akim Tamiroff *(Szabuniewcz)*, Martita Hunt *(Mother Superior)*, Alexander Scourby *(Maj. Von Bergen)*, Liliane Montevecchi *(Cosette)*, Ludwig Stossel *(Dr. Szicki)*, Gerard Buhr *(German Captain)*, Franz Roehn *(Mons. Girardin)*, Celia Lovsky *(Mme. Arle)*, Clement Harari *(Gestapo Man)*, Alain Bouvette *(Rothschild's Chauffeur)*, Albert Godderis *(Mons. Gravat)*, Karen Lenay *(Denise)*, Eugene Borden *(Pierre Michel)*, Maurice Marsac *(French Lieutenant)*.

Despite the fine performances by the two leads, this film never quite delivers the satirical punch it thinks it does. Kaye is a Jewish refugee stuck in Paris shortly before the Nazis arrive. He manages to get hold of a car and takes along one passenger, an anti-Semetic Polish colonel played by Jurgens. Putting his prejudice on hold to save his skin, Jurgens has his driver stop and pick up girl friend Maurey. But Kaye's wit and charm appeal to her and she switches her affections to him, much to the chagrin of Jurgens. The trio hide in a castle to escape the Germans but are captured anyway. Kaye pretends that Jurgens is a long lost cousin and they work their way out of the situation. Slowly the anti-Semite's feelings change and he grows fond of Kaye and forgets his prejudices. Kaye and Jurgens play well off each other and really carry the film, for sequences are poorly linked and the story never quite knows where to go. It becomes highly predictable and far too sentimental for it's own good.

p, William Goetz; d, Peter Glenville; w, S. N. Behrman, George Froeschel (based on the play "Jacobowsky and the Colonel" by Franz Werfel); ph, Burnett Guffey; m, George Duning; ed, William A. Lyon, Charles Nelson; art d, George Wakerich, Walter Holscher.

Comedy **(PR:A MPAA:NR)**

ME, NATALIE** (1969) 110m Cinema Center-Nob Hill/NG c

Patty Duke *(Natalie Miller)*, James Farentino *(David Harris)*, Martin Balsam *(Uncle Harold)*, Elsa Lanchester *(Miss Dennison)*, Salome Jens *(Shirley Norton)*, Nancy Marchand *(Mrs. Miller)*, Phil Sterling *(Mr. Miller)*, Deborah Winters *(Betty Simon)*, Roland Hale *(Stanley Dexter)*, Bob Balaban *(Morris)*, Matthew Cowles *(Harvey Belman)*, Ann Thomas *(Mrs. Schroder)*, Al Pacino *(Tony)*, Catherine Burns *(Hester)*, Robyn Morgan *(Natalie age 7)*, Daniel Keyes *(Surviving Brother)*, Peter Turgeon *(Attorney)*, Milt Kamen *(Plastic Surgeon)*, Ross Charap *(Arnold)*, Dorothea Duckworth *(Mrs. Simon)*, Milo Boulton *(Mr. Simon)*, Dennis Allen *(Max)*, Robert Frink *(Freddie)*, Melinda Blachley *(Betty Simon Age 10)*.

Duke is a wonder in this fairly bland, episodic tale of a young girl's adventures in New York City's Greenwich Village. After suffering numerous disappointments in her adolescent life, Duke goes to college and becomes involved with political activists. Her parents bribe an optometry student to date their daughter, hoping she will come to her senses. But Duke discovers what's going on and runs off to the Village like so many others before her "to find herself." She gets a job as a cocktail waitress in a place called "the Topless-Bottomless Club" and meets a young artist, played by Farentino. She rides from her apartment to his studio in the building dumb-waiter and eventually they become lovers. Invited to an old school pal's wedding, Duke takes great delight in learning that the wedding is out of necessity because the bride is pregnant. To top things off, her new husband's a drunk. Duke heads back to the Village and goes to her lover's apartment. But after discovering a woman in his bed she comes to the traumatic discovery that Farentino is married. When confronted, he admits this is true, but offers to divorce his wife and live with Duke. She rejects this offer and gives up on the Village, returning once more to her parents' home. Despite some of the cliches about Duke's "free" life (her riding the dumb-waiter; a moosehead on her wall) this is a good character study. Had it been handled by a lesser actress, the results may have been closer to a stereotype, but Duke overcomes this and makes the character three dimensional and realistic. We believe and care about this person. Coe's direction is straightforward, but not nearly as well paced as A THOUSAND CLOWNS, a better directoral effort about another free spirit fighting back. Don't miss Al Pacino playing a minor role in his first screen appearance.

p, Stanley Shapiro; d, Fred Coe; w, A. Martin Zweiback (based on a story by Shapiro); ph, Arthur J. Ornitz (DeLuxe Color); m, Henry Mancini; ed, Sheila Bakerman, Jack McSweeney; art d, George Jenkins; m/l, title song, Mancini, Rod McKuen; makeup, Dick Smith.

Comedy/Drama **(PR:C MPAA:M)**

MEAL, THE*** (1975) 90m Ambassador c

Dina Merrill, Carl Betz, Leon Ames, Susan Logan, Vici Powers, Steve Potter, Corinne Bustad, Mike Rasmussen, Bill Dunnagan.

A surprise sleeper from Florida, beautifully photographed and an interesting look at some unusual things. The setting is simple: a group of people have gathered together for a dinner party. Before the night is through they will have devoured not only the meal, but each other as well, both psychologically and sexually. Brutal in its candor and often quite funny, THE MEAL features Merrill as the evening's hostess. She has gathered together a group of local rich folk who want to liquidate her holdings. An interesting and compelling work.

p,d&w, R. John Hugh; m, Stu Phillips.

Drama **(PR:O MPAA:R)**

MEAN DOG BLUES*½ (1978) 108m Crosby/AIP c

Gregg Henry *(Paul Ramsey)*, Kay Lenz *(Linda Ramsey)*, George Kennedy *(Capt. Omar Kinsman)*, Scatman Crothers *(Mudcat)*, Tina Louise *(Donna Lacey)*, Felton Perry *(Jake Turner)*, Gregory Sierra *(Jesus Gonzales)*, James Wainwright *(Sgt. Hubbell Wacker)*, William Windom *(Victor Lacey)*, John Daniels *(Yakima Jones)*, Marc Alaimo *(Guard)*, Edith Atwater *(Linda's Mother)*, James Boyd *(Sonny)*, Edward Call *(Road Gang Guard)*, Christina Hart *(Gloria)*.

Second-rate combination of I AM A FUGITIVE FROM A CHAIN GANG and COOL HAND LUKE finds Henry as a country western musician mistakenly implicated in a crime and sentenced to five years on a chain gang. From there on, it's a long and predictable turn of events. Kennedy is the prison guard with an odd fascination for Dobermans, but with surprisingly little to do. Windom and Louise are a married couple who get Henry into trouble in the first place. Windom certainly deserved better than this and Louise's role makes you wonder why the movie star ever left "Gilligan's Island." Surprisingly, Henry overcomes the script to give a fairly decent performance. Direction and cinematography are at a par with the modest demands of the film.

p, Charles A. Pratt, George Lefferts; d, Mel Stuart; w, Lefferts; ph, Robert B. Hauser (DeLuxe Color); m, Fred Karlin; ed, Houseley Stevenson; art d, J. S. Poplin; set d, Don Sullivan; cos, Bill Milton, Chris Zamiara; stunts, Bill Couch.

Prison **Cas.** **(PR:O MPAA:R)**

MEAN FRANK AND CRAZY TONY** (1976, Ital.) 85m Aquarius c

Lee Van Cleef, Tony LoBianco, Edwige Fenech, Jess Hahn, Jean Rochefort, Joe Scedi.

LoBianco is a groupie who begins tagging after his idol, gangster Van Cleef. This lightweight spoof of the genre has some enjoyable moments. The U.S. prints were heavily reworked by Simon Nuchtern before release here.

p, Dino deLaurentiis; d, Michele Lupo; ph, (Technicolor); m, Riz Ortolani.

Crime **(PR:O MPAA:R)**

MEAN JOHNNY BARROWS** (1976) 90m Po-Boy/Atlas c

Fred Williamson *(Johnny Barrows)*, Roddy McDowall *(Tony Da Vinci)*, Stuart Whitman *(Mario Racconi)*, Luther Adler *(Don Racconi)*, Jenny Sherman *(Nancy)*, Aaron Banks *(Capt. O'Malley)*, Anthony Caruso *(Don Da Vinci)*, Mike Henry *(Carlo Da Vinci)*, Elliott Gould *(The Professor)*, R. G. Armstrong *(Richard)*, Bob Phillips, James Brown.

Vietnam vet Williamson returns home from the Army after being dishonorably discharged for striking an officer. Unable to find work, he hangs around a restaurant owned by a Mafia family, headed by Adler. He turns down a trigger job to kill members of a rival family but continues to hang around the restaurant because of his attraction to Sherman, an employee of the family. She is having an affair with McDowall and they conspire to provoke a gang war that will leave everyone dead, while they escape with all the money. The rival family attacks and kills most of Adler's family, while Sherman pretends to have been kidnaped and raped by McDowell. Angered now, Williamson goes to the rival headquarters and kills everyone. When he meets Sherman later she is enraged that he has survived and ruined her plans and despite his pleas of love she kills him. Running away from the scene she steps on a land mine she had planted as a trap for him. Williamson's second attempt at directing is a slow, obvious film, though his performance is good.

p&d, Fred Williamson; w, Charles Walker; ph, Bob Caramico (Panavision, Movielab Color).

Crime **Cas.** **(PR:O MPAA:R)**

MEAN STREETS**** (1973) 110m TPS/WB c

Harvey Keitel *(Charlie)*, Robert De Niro *(Johnny Boy)*, Amy Robinson *(Teresa)*, David Proval *(Tony)*, Richard Romanus *(Michael)*, Cesare Danova *(Giovanni)*, Victor Argo *(Mario)*, George Memmoli *(Joey Catucci)*, Lenny Scaletta *(Jimmy)*, Jeannie Bell *(Diane)*, Murray Mosten *(Oscar)*, David Carradine *(Drunk)*, Robert Carradine *(The Young Assassin)*, Lois Walden *(Jewish Girl)*, Harry Northup *(Vietnam Veteran)*, Dino Seragusa *(Old Man)*, D'Mitch Davis *(Black Cop)*, Peter Fain *(George)*, Julie Andelman *(Girl at Party)*, Robert Wilder *(Benton)*, Ken Sinclair *(Sammy)*, Catherine Scorsese *(Woman on the Landing)*, Martin Scorsese *(Shorty the Killer in the Car)*.

MEAN STREETS is so authentically New York Italian that you can almost smell the garlic coming off the screen. This was Scorcese's third film (after WHO'S THAT KNOCKING AT MY DOOR? and BOXCAR BERTHA) and, arguably, his best. In later years he would get involved in the studio system and never have the same kind of freedom although some of his later works did have more success at the box office. To someone from, let's say, Sioux City, New York's Little Italy area is as foreign as Oslo and it may be that the viewer should be conversant with the neighborhood to appreciate all the subtleties and nuances in the movie. Made on a pittance budget of under $600,000 (much of which was deferred), with less than two weeks of rehearsal and only six days of actual shooting in New York (the rest was done in Los Angeles because it was cheaper to shoot out West and make it look like the East), MEAN STREETS is the story of Keitel, DeNiro, and Robinson and their relationships with each other and with the various members of the cast who inhabit the area just north of Canal Street from Chinatown. Keitel is a dandy who seldom leaves the house unless he's dressed flawlessly. He still lives at home (it was a tradition that a young Italian not leave the family residence until he is ready to marry) and hangs out with a group of middle-twenties Italian hoodlums at Proval's bar. Keitel has been having an affair with Robinson, an epileptic girl who lives next door, but he must keep that quiet. She's the cousin of DeNiro, who is a mercurial type of loner, forever in financial trouble and currently in heavy debt to Romanus, the slick, epicene loan shark who is rapidly losing patience as the "vigorish" (interest) mounts. There are several episodes (and not much of a single propelling story), all of which are indicative of the lives of these Lower East Siders: Northup comes home from Vietnam and the boys throw him a party, but he explodes and can't handle it; Carradine gets drunk and falls asleep on the bar; the Italians harass Jewish girl Waldon and beat up the man she's with; Keitel and Company sell bogus fireworks (totally illegal in New York) to some kids who have come in from the suburbs and are taken by the con; there's a battle at a pool hall over an alleged slur, but it's a word that none of them has ever heard, so they just assume it's bad (more about that later); and several other sequences. DeNiro's life is in danger because Romanus has been insulted by DeNiro in front of the other guys at the bar, so Keitel decides he'd better get his pal to a place where no one will ever look for him, Brooklyn. Before that, DeNiro pleads with Keitel to get him "in" with Keitel's uncle (Danova), a "man of respect" (read "Mafia") in the area who can call off Romanus and, perhaps, even get DeNiro some work. Keitel won't do that, as he doesn't want to involve his big-time uncle in any of DeNiro's small-time problems. This decided, Keitel will take DeNiro to hide out in Brooklyn until the heat is off and they are about to leave when Robinson joins them in Proval's borrowed automobile. They don't realize it, but they are being followed by Romanus and two shooters in another car. Once they get into Brooklyn, the gunmen open fire and blood begins to flow in the lead car. It careens off the street, smashes into walls, and knocks over a hydrant. Robinson may be dead, Keitel is bleeding, DeNiro is . . . we never know. The picture ends as the criminals have gotten away with it. Since the picture is mainly comprised of incidents, it's a bit lax in story content, in the usual sense of the word, but by the time it's over, you have been presented with as graphic and honest an indication of the lifestyles of these people as you'll ever care to see. These young men are strictly two-bit kids, nothing like the Corleones, and their world is circumscribed by the limitations of Little Italy. In the Bronx, just a generation before, we saw the Italians of MARTY and company and these guys are nothing like those guys. Keitel's character is rich with complexity. He fancies himself a saint and is always testing his religiousness. He also goes out of his way to help DeNiro when others might have turned aside from someone as flaky. Despite his attempts at saintliness, he also gets drunk, picks up women, and beats up men. The relationship of Keitel to DeNiro is not unlike George and Lenny in OF MICE AND MEN, for DeNiro may be somewhat mentally off and Keitel looks upon DeNiro as his benefactor and protector. Robinson is an angry young woman who is on edge because of her epilepsy and her inability to get Keitel to commit to anything beyond sex with her. The lives of all the cast are intertwined in a tale that is sometimes deliberately dull, often exciting, and always interesting. When Keitel was attending Lincoln High School in Coney Island, there were several words that were unique to that place. Someone who was "Gropo" was thought to be dense, a person who was "Harvey" was automatically good at everything, and if you were a "Mook" that meant you were even stupider than a "Gropo." In MEAN STREETS, a bloody battle takes place in Memmoli's pool hall over the word "Mook," although they never explain why it occasions such an insult. When interviewed on that, Scorcese said that he put it in the movie when he heard about an argument in Brooklyn over that word and he thought it was funny. They pronounce it "mooook," although the correct pronunciation is "mook" as in "book." Louis Gossett, Jr., a near-contemporary of Keitel's, is acknowledged as having created the expression "Harvey Mookie" which designates a person as being good at being stupid. All the roles are wonderfully cast with special plaudits to DeNiro and Romanus in the difficult role of the greasy loan shark. Romanus, a Greek, is an excellent blues pianist, although he didn't have the opportunity to show that side of his talents in this picture. It took seven years from the time Martin and Scorcese completed the first draft to raise the money to make the film. Memmoli had been one of the comedians with The Ace Trucking Company, but dropped out of show business to pursue a career in home renovation before his death in 1985, the result of having been more than 500 pounds in weight. Very harsh (but very true) language makes this film a poor choice for young people but "Glen Garry Glen Ross" was even fouler and it won the Pulitzer Prize, so who are we to judge?

p, Jonathan T. Taplin; d, Martin Scorsese; w, Scorsese, Mardik Martin; ph, Kent Wakeford (Technicolor); ed, Sid Levin.

Drama **Cas.** **(PR:O MPAA:R)**

MEANEST GAL IN TOWN, THE* (1934) 62m RKO bw

ZaSu Pitts, El Brendel, Pert Kelton, James Gleason, Skeets Gallagher, Barney Furrey, Bud Geary, Harry Holman, Robert McKenzie, Arthur Hoyt, Edward McWade, Morgan Wallace, Wallis Clark.

Pitts, the owner of a dry goods store, is having a wonderful romance with barber Brendel until a traveling show gets stranded in the town. Then title character Kelton does what she can to bust up the romance until she finally ends up with Gleason. Former vaudevillian Gallagher is a fast-talking salesman. Some minor amusements are few and far between during the course of this overlong, poorly executed programmer.

d, Russell Mack; w, Richard Schayer, Mack, H. W. Hanemann (based on a story by Arthur Horman); ph, J. Roy Hunt; ed, James B. Morley; md, Max Steiner.

Comedy **(PR:A MPAA:NR)**

MEANEST MAN IN THE WORLD, THE** (1943) 57m FOX bw

Jack Benny *(Richard Clark)*, Priscilla Lane *(Janie Brown)*, Eddie "Rochester" Anderson *(Shufro)*, Edmund Gwenn *(Frederick P. Leggitt)*, Matt Briggs *(Mr. Brown)*, Anne Revere *(Kitty Crockett)*, Margaret Seddon *(Mrs. Leggitt)*, Helene Reynolds *(Wife)*, Don Douglas *(Husband)*, Harry Hayden *(Mr. Chambers)*, Arthur Loft *(Mr. Billings)*, Andrew Tombes *(Judge)*, Paul Burns *(Farmer)*; Hobart Cavanaugh *(Mr. Throckmorton)*, Jan Duggan *(Mrs. Throckmorton)*.

Writers Seaton and House just about rewrote this play to fit the talents of comedian Benny. A friendly lawyer with a tightwad image, he is convinced by his valet, Rochester, to become meaner and business will boom. Benny agrees and soon the bucks start rolling in. But his girl, Lane, doesn't like the new Benny personality and dumps him. After a highly publicized photo of Benny taking candy from a baby he's dubbed "The Meanest Man in the World" by the New York City papers. But all is righted thanks to Lane's father, Briggs. It is refreshing to see Rochester play a black role that was equal to, if not better than that of his white boss. Considering Hollywood's treatment of blacks in the movies of the era, Rochester was a notable and talented exception.

p, William Perlberg; d, Sidney Lanfield; w, George Seaton, Allan House (based on a play by Augustin MacHugh, George M. Cohan); ph, Peverell Marley; m, Cyril J. Mockridge; ed, Robert Bischoff; md, Emil Newman; art d, Richard Day, Albert Hogsett.

Comedy **(PR:A MPAA:NR)**

MEANWHILE BACK AT THE RANCH

(SEE: BALLAD OF JOSIE, THE, 1968)

MEANWHILE, FAR FROM THE FRONT

(SEE: SECRET WAR OF HARRY FRIGG, THE, 1968)

MEAT CLEAVER MASSACRE zero

(1977) 82m Group I c (AKA: THE HOLLYWOOD MEAT CLEAVER MASSACRE)

Larry Justin, Bob Mead, Bob Clark, Jim Habif, Sandra Crane, Evelyn Ellis, Jonathan Grant, Christopher Lee *(Narrator)*.

The title tells it all in this low-budget splatter film. When the family of a professor of the occult is murdered by hoodlums, the professor goes after them, with all the powers at his disposal, not to mention kitchen implements. Christopher Lee usually shows better judgment than to appear in a sleazy item such as this.

p, Steven L. Singer; d, Evan Lee.

Horror **(PR: MPAA:R)**

MEATBALLS*1/2 (1979, Can.) 92m PAR c

Bill Murray *(Tripper)*, Harvey Atkin *(Morty)*, Russ Banham *(Crockett)*, Ron Barry *(Lance)*, Jack Blum *(Spaz)*, Matt Craven *(Hardware)*, Kristine DeBell *(A. L.)*, Norma Dell'Agnese *(Brenda)*, Cindy Girling *(Wendy)*, Todd Hoffman *(Wheels)*, Keith Knight *(Fink)*, Kate Lynch *(Roxanne)*, Margot Pinvidic *(Jackie)*, Paul Boyle *(Ace)*, Alison Diver *(Carla)*, Valerie Fersht *(Liza)*, Vince Guerriero *(Rhino)*, Patrick Hynes *(Andrew)*, Hadley Kay *(Bradley)*, Billie Kishonti *(Jeffrey)*, Allan Levson *(Peter DeWitt)*, Chris Makepeace *(Rudy)*, James McLarty *(Horse)*, Heather Preece *(Patti)*, Ruth Rennie *(Jodi)*, Sarah Torgov *(Candace)*, Michael Kirby *(Eddy)*, Greg Swangon, Peter Hume.

Bill Murray is the only reason to see this film. His high energy and sensitive acting abilities, when called for, take this cliche film out of the ordinary and give it the style that did not appear in the script or the direction. It's little more than a typical TV movie of the week (with some rough language and a bit of sex tossed in), but it appealed to the kids who had actually been to a summer camp in their lives and the result was a box-office hit that earned more than $20 million. Other than Murray, you may not recognize many of the actors, as this was a Canadian film which utilized actors from north of the border who are unfamiliar to most Americans. Murray is the head counselor at Camp North Star, where the management and staff are as inept a group as can be imagined. The campers are comprised of the usual stereotypes: the disturbed kid, the fat nerd, the Romeo, and several nubile young women. There's no real "story" in the film, just a lot of incidents, some of them admittedly funny, but many which fall flat. If you liked camp, you may like this film. If you hated camp, you may also like this film. If you like good comedies, you probably won't like this film. It's really more pre-teen than teenage comedy because: by the time kids reach thirteen, they've seen most of these sight gags on TV several times. Murray's personal appeal and elan push the picture to heights that it doesn't deserve. Murray also demonstrates another side of his talent in the scenes with Makepeace, the young man who doesn't seem to be able to fit in. Bernstein's score is a definite plus to a picture that was mostly minuses.

p, Dan Goldberg; d, Ivan Reitman; w, Len Blum, Goldberg, Janis Allen, Harold Ramis; ph, Don Wilder (Sonolab Color); m, Elmer Bernstein; ed, Debra Karen; art d, David Charles; cos, Judy Gellman; m/l, Bernstein, Norman Gimbel.

Comedy **Cas.** **(PR:C MPAA:PG)**

MECHANIC, THE** (1972) 100m UA c (AKA: KILLER OF KILLERS)

Charles Bronson *(Arthur Bishop)*, Jan-Michael Vincent *(Steve McKenna)*, Keenan Wynn *(Harry McKenna)*, Jill Ireland *(Prostitute)*, Linda Ridgeway *(Louise)*, Frank de Kova *(Syndicate Head)*, Lindsay H. Crosby *(Policeman)*, Takayuki Kubota *(Yamoto, Karate Master)*, Martin Gordon *(American Tourist)*, James Davidson *(Intern)*, Steve Cory *(Messenger)*, Patrick O'Moore *(Old Man)*, Kevin O'Neal *(Cam)*, Linda Grant *(Bathtub Girl)*, Louis Fitch *(Librarian)*, Hank Hamilton *(Kori)*, Hiroyasu Fujishima *(Aikido Master)*, Michael Hinn *(Rifle Range Attendant)*, Christine Forbes *(Bikini Waitress)*, Father Amando de Vincenzo *(Priest)*, Gerald Saunderson Peters *(Butler)*, Ernie Orsatti *(Chickin Lickin' Driver)*, J. N. Roberts *(Gang Leader)*, Sara Taft *(Garden Party Woman)*, John Barclay *(Garden Party Man)*, Allan Gibbs *(Bodyguard No. 1)*, Frank Orsatti *(Bodyguard No. 2)*, Celeste Yarnall *(The Mark's Girl)*, Athena Lorde *(Old Woman)*, Howard Morton *(Car Polish Man)*, Ken Wolger *(1st Hippie)*, Allison Rose *(Young Girl)*, Enzo Fiermonte *(The Mark)*, Stephen Vinovich *(5th Hippie)*, Trina Mitchum *(3rd Hippie)*.

"Murder is only killing without a license and everybody kills— the Army, the police . . . " This sums up the philosophy of anti-hero Bronson, a hired assassin or "mechanic," known for his cold-blooded and efficient work. Vincent plays the young apprentice, eager to learn the business from its best practitioner. Told episodically, the pair go on a series of Bondian-type adventures, leading up to a trick ending where Bronson and Vincent manage to cheat some killers who are trying to get at them. Though extremely violent, the film is surprisingly boring in spots. Bronson gives his usual Mt. Rushmore performance, paralleled by Vincent's almost gee-whiz adulation of his mentor. At times the relationship between the two borders on homosexuality though Ireland (the real-life Mrs. Bronson) is brought in for a few minor, time-consuming scenes as a call-girl. Many critics saw through the ploy and commented on the unusually close nature of Vincent's worship of the older man. The routine and terse script is by Carlino, who could write better films than THE MECHANIC indicates. Some nice location photography in downtown Los Angeles and Naples, Italy. Directed by Winner (Bronson's choice) who had previously worked with the star in CHATO'S LAND and would team with him again in DEATH WISH.

p, Robert Chartoff, Irwin Winkler, Lewis John Carlino; d, Michael Winner; w, Carlino; ph, Richard Kline, Robert Paynter (Deluxe Color); m, Jerry Fielding; ed, Frederick Wilson; md, Fielding; art d, Roger E. Maus, Herbert Westbrook; cos, Lambert Marks; spec eff, Richard F. Albain; makeup, Phillip Rhodes; stunts, Alan R. Gibbs.

Action/Thriller **Cas.** **(PR:O MPAA:PG)**

MED MORD I BAGAGET (SEE: NO TIME TO KILL, 1963, Brit./Swed./Ger.)

MEDAL FOR THE GENERAL (SEE: GAY INTRUDERS, THE, 1946, Brit.)

MEDAL FOR BENNY, A ½** (1945) 77m PAR bw

Dorothy Lamour *(Lolita Sierra)*, Arturo de Cordova *(Joe Morales)*, J. Carrol Naish *(Charley Martin)*, Mikhail Rasumny *(Raphael Catalina)*, Fernando Alvarado *(Chito Sierra)*, Charles Dingle *(Zach Mibbe)*, Frank McHugh *(Edgar Lovekin)*, Rosita Moreno *(Toodles Castro)*, Grant Mitchell *(Mayor of Pantera)*, Douglas Dumbrille *(General)*, Nestor Paiva *(Frank Alviso)*, Eva Puig *(Mrs. Catalina)*, Pepito Perez *(Pamfilo Chaves)*, Minerva Urecal *(Mrs. Chavez)*, Frank Reicher *(Father Bly)*, Robert E. L. Homans *(Chief of Police)*, Edward Fielding *(Governor)*, Max Wagner *(Jake)*, Isabelita Castro *(Luz)*, Oliver Blake, Victor Potel, Harry Hayden, *(Pepsters)*, Jack Gardner *(Cameraman/Red)*, Eddy Chandler *(Bank Guard)*, Tom Fadden *(Eddie Krinch)*, Alice Fleming *(Dowager)*, Chico Sandoval *(Paisano)*, Maxine Fife *(Telephone Operator)*, Jimmie Dundee *(Cop)*.

Off-beat satire features Naish as the father of "Benny," an off-screen character who was considered a bad kid in the small Southern California fishing town he lived in. Word comes that he has been posthumously awarded a Congressional Medal of Honor for wiping out 100 Japanese soldiers before taking a sniper's bullet himself. Naturally, everyone in the town falls all over each other to praise the local kid. Lamour plays the woman Benny was engaged to, and De Cordova is her new fiance. In order not to destroy the town's illusions, De Cordova joins the Army instead of marrying the girl. Lamour and Naish are standouts in this funny and well-scripted piece. Naish's speech at the end is particularly memorable. Naish, the Irish-American who practically made a career in the movies by portraying Latin types, won an Academy Award nomination for his meaty role of a *paisano* in the little town. The story by Steinbeck and Wagner also was a nominee. A good little sleeper that says a lot on the nature of heroes and heroism in America.

p, Paul Jones; d, Irving Pichel; w, Frank Butler, Jack Wagner (based on a story by Wagner, John Steinbeck); ph, Lionel Lindon; m, Victor Young; ed, Arthur Schmidt; art d, Hans Dreier, Hal Pereira; spec eff, Gordon Jennings.

Satire **(PR:A MPAA:NR)**

MEDALS (SEE: SEVEN DAYS LEAVE, 1930)

MEDEA***

(1971, Ital./Fr./Ger.) 100m San Marco-Rosima Anstaldt-Les Films Number One-Janus-Fernsehen/New Line Cinema c

Maria Callas *(Medea)*, Massimo Girotti *(Creon)*, Laurent Terzieff *(The Centaur)*, Giuseppe Gentili *(Jason)*, Margareth Clementi *(Glauce)*, Anna Maria Chio *(Nurse)*, Paul Jabor, Luigi Urbini, Gerard Weiss, Giorgio Trombetti, Franco Jacobbi, Gian Paolo Durgar.

Fascinating if not entirely successful adaptation of the Euripedes play has opera diva Callas in her sole screen appearance as the sorceress queen. Gentili is Jason, come to Colchis to retrieve the golden fleece. Callas, daughter of the king and high priestess of a human-sacrificing sun cult, falls in love with Gentili and with her younger brother steals the fleece from the temple. When they are pursued she chops her brother into pieces and throws him off the cart. The pursuing soldiers, bound by tradition, stop to bury the pieces. Callas escapes back to Greece with Gentili and becomes his queen, although she is not comfortable in civilized Corinth. After 10 years and two sons, Gentili tells Callas that he is going to marry princess Clementi, and that Callas is to be banished. Callas accepts the news calmly and later sends Clementi a cloak and headpiece as gifts. When Clementi puts them on they erupt in flames and the girl plunges over a cliff. Callas takes her two sons and after bathing them and putting them to bed, silently murders each with a dagger. Gentili comes to her to beg for the bodies of his sons, but she conjures up a wall of flame and, screaming at him, allows herself to be consumed by the fire. Callas is a commanding presence and Pasolini is clearly obsessed with her profile. For the most part, though, he doesn't let her acting carry the film, relying on his own purely visual methods to do the job. (In Italian; English subtitles.)

p, Franco Rossellini, Marina Cicogna; d&w, Pier Paolo Pasolini (based on the play by Euripides); ph, Ennio Guarnieri (Eastmancolor); ed, Nino Baragli; md, Pasolini, Elsa Morante; art d, Dante Ferretti, Nicola Tamburro; cos, Piero Tosi.

Drama **(PR:O MPAA:NR)**

MEDICINE MAN, THE* (1930) 65m TIF bw

Jack Benny *(Dr. John Harvey)*, Betty Bronson *(Mamie Goltz)*, Eva Novak *(Hulda)*, E. Alyn Warren *(Goltz)*, Billy Butts *(Buddy)*, Adolph Milar *(Peter)*, Georgie [George E.] Stone *(Steve)*, Tommy [Tom] Dugan *(Charley)*, Vadim Uraneff *(Gus)*, Caroline Rankin *(Hattie)*, Dorothea Wolbert *(Sister Wilson)*.

Benny plays the title role, a traveling huckster who uses and abandons women as he goes from town to town. He meets Bronson, a waif who's been abused by her father, and his demeanor changes completely. Only slightly amusing, Benny's fans might want to take a look but otherwise it's forgettable.

d, Scott Pembroke; w, Ladye Horton, Eva Unsell (based on the play by Elliott Lester); ph, Max Dupont, Art Reeves; ed, Russell Schoengarth.

Comedy **(PR:A MPAA:NR)**

MEDICINE MAN, THE* (1933, Brit.) 52m REA/Radio bw

Claud Allister *(Hon. Freddie Wiltshire)*, Frank Pettingell *(Amos Wells)*, Pat Paterson *(Gwendoline Wells)*, Ben Welden *(Garbel)*, Jeanne Stuart *(Flossie)*, Viola Compton *(Mrs. Wells)*, Drusilla Wills *(Boadicea Briggs)*, Ronald Simpson *(Dr. Wesley Primus)*, S. Victor Stanley *(Bitoff)*, Betty Astell *(Patient)*, John Turnbull, Andrea Malandrinos, William Home, Syd Crossley.

Allister is persuaded to trade places with a doctor friend but gets into trouble when gangsters come looking for him to amputate the leg of a wounded robber. Luckily, a chloroform bottle falls and breaks and the sweetish, colorless liquid knocks everyone out. A couple of okay laughs, but basically just another British programmer by veteran comedy director Davis. Paterson one year later would become the wife of great screen "lover" Charles Boyer.

p, Julius Hagen; d, Redd Davis; w, Michael Barringer, Robert Edmunds.

Comedy **(PR:A MPAA:NR)**

MEDICO OF PAINTED SPRINGS, THE**

(1941) 58m COL bw (AKA: DOCTOR'S ALIBI)

Charles Starrett *(Steven Monroe)*, Terry Walker *(Nancy Richards)*, Ben Taggart *(John Richards)*, Ray Bennett *(Ed Gordon)*, Wheeler Oakman *(Fred Burns)*, Richard Fiske *(Kentucky Lane)*, Edmund Cobb *(Sheriff)*, Edythe Elliott *(Maw Blaine)*, Bud Osborne *(Karns)*, Steve Clark *(Ellis)*, Charles Hamilton *(Pete)*, George Chesebro *(Joe)*, Lloyd Bridges, Jim Corey, The Simp-Phonies, Raider the Horse.

The first of three westerns which cast Starrett as Dr. Steven Monroe, a traveling medic who is as devoted to health as to justice. Here he makes a stop in the title town to examine Rough Rider recruits, and ends up settling a dispute between some cattlemen and sheep ranchers.

p, Jack Fier; d, Lambert Hillyer; w, Winston Miller, Wyndham Gittens (based on the book by James L. Rubel); ph, Benjamin Kline; ed, Mel Thorsen.

Western **(PR:A MPAA:NR)**

MEDIUM, THE*** (1951) 84m Transfilm bw

Marie Powers *(Mme. Flora)*, Anna Maria Alberghetti *(Monica)*, Leo Coleman *(Toby)*, Belva Kibler *(Mrs. Nolan)*, Beverly Dame *(Mrs. Gobineau)*, Donald Morgan *(Mr. Gobineau)*.

The film version of the Gian-Carlo Menotti opera, which he himself directed. Powers is a deceptive medium who fakes supernatural effects with the help of the young Alberghetti (in her first role) and mute Coleman, who manipulate the surroundings from behind curtains. During one seance, Powers feels a hand clutching her throat. She accuses her customers, but then convinces herself that Coleman did it. Though she believes it may have been a supernatural power punishing her, she still takes her anger out on the boy. He is thrown out of the house during a downpour, but sneaks back in to visit Alberghetti, whom he loves. Powers sees something moving behind a curtain and asks who is there. She gets no response, and, not realising it is Coleman, fires a gun, killing the boy. The music is top-notch, and the special effects and camerawork nicely illustrate the libretto, which is sung in English.

p, Walter Lowendahl; d&w, Gian-Carlo Menotti (based on his opera); ph, Enzo Serafin; m, Menotti; ed, Alexander Hammid; md, Thomas Schippers; art d, Georges Wakhevitch.

Opera **(PR:A MPAA:NR)**

MEDIUM COOL**** (1969) 110m H and J/PAR c

Robert Forster *(John Cassellis)*, Verna Bloom *(Eileen Horton)*, Peter Bonerz *(Gus)*, Marianna Hill *(Ruth)*, Harold Blankenship *(Harold Horton)*, Sid McCoy *(Frank Baker)*, Christine Bergstrom *(Dede)*, Robert McAndrew *(Pennybaker)*, William Sickinger *(News Director Karlin)*, Beverly Younger *(Rich Lady)*, Marrian Walters *(Social Worker)*, Edward Croke *(Plainclothesman)*, Sandra Ann Roberts *(Blonde in Car)*, Doug Kimball *(Newscaster)*, Peter Boyle *(Gun Clinic Manager)*, Georgia Tadda *(Secretary)*, Charles Geary *(Buddy, Harold's Father)*, Jeff Donaldson, Richard Abrams, Felton Perry, Val Grey, Bill Sharp, Robert Paige, Walter Bradford, Russell Davis, Livingston Lewis, Barbara Jones, John Jackson *(Black Militants)*, Simone Zorn, Madeleine Maroou, Mickey Pallas, Lynn Erlich, Lester Brownlee, Morris Bleckman, Wally Wright, Sam Ventury, George Boulet *(Reporters and Photographers)*, James Jacobs, Spence Jackson, Dorien Suhr, Kenneth Whitener, Connie Fleischauer, Mary Smith, Nancy Lee Noble *(Kennedy Students)*, Linda Handelman, Maria Friedman, Kathryn Schubert, Barbara Brydenthal, Elizabeth Moisant, Rose Bormacher *(Gun Clinic Ladies)*, Janet Langhart *(Maid)*, Roger Phillips, Robert Blankenship, China Lee, Sirri Murad.

Does life imitate art or is it the other way around? In the case of skyjacking, there was never any until after Rod Serling wrote a story for TV. In the matter of a helicopter used to break someone out of jail, it was done in Mexico, then a film (BREAKOUT) was made on the subject, and then it was done again in real life in December of 1985. In MEDIUM COOL, life and art imitate each other, as Haskell Wexler deftly blends real riot footage with staged shots, and then mixes his own actors into actual fracases on the streets until they are no longer playing roles—they are living them. The title is a none-too-subtle pun of media critic Marshall McLuhan's description of TV when he called it the "cool medium." (McLuhan, by the way, appeared in the film ANNIE HALL, in answer to Woody Allen's plea when Allen was in a movie line with a pseudo-intellectual prattling on about McLuhan with an inane way of interpreting him. McLuhan appears, by magic, tells the fraud he doesn't know what he's talking about, then leaves with Allen's thanks.) Forster is a news cameraman for a local Windy City TV station. He works in tandem with Bonerz and the two of them are hard-shelled to the events of the day, so much so that when they come across a car accident, they calmly get their footage before calling for an ambulance. Forster comes across a black cab driver (McCoy) who finds several thousand dollars in his cab and he attempts to persuade the driver to turn in the cash so he, Forster, can get some additional material for the story. When the man refuses, all of his militant friends harass Forster and Bonerz until they leave. (Note: This is based on an actual occurrence and in real life the driver did return the money. The incident so intrigued Wexler that, at one time, he planned to make a film about it. Failing that, he put the situation into MEDIUM COOL as a secondary plot line.) Later, the driver does return the money and is thought to be a fool by everyone. At a parking lot, Forster finds young Blankenship and thinks the boy is attempting to break into his car. He chases Blankenship who drops a box in which resides his pet pigeon. Forster sees that the boy wasn't trying to steal anything and travels to the poor neighborhood where Blankenship lives with his mother, Bloom, in a run-down apartment. Bloom is on welfare and came to Chicago from the hills of West Virginia. Since it's 1968, the city of Chicago is in turmoil. Thousands of anti-war protesters horde into the city to speak out against Vietnam for the benefit of the Democratic conventioneers who are there to choose a new candidate now that Lyndon Johnson has declared himself out of the race. Mayor Richard Daley rallies his police force and calls for back-up units from the National Guard to help quell any possible disturbances. Forster turns on his camera and sees some of the brutality taking place and is chastized by his bosses at the station for spending too much time covering the action. When he learns that much of his footage has been handed over to the Federal Bureau of Investigation (presumably so they can make a case against the protesters), Forster is enraged and lets his superiors know in no uncertain terms. For his efforts, he is fired. Until now, he's been having an affair with nurse Hill, but the forced vacation from work causes him to spend most of his time with Bloom and Blankenship and he finds himself attracted to her. The Democrats convene and Forster secures a free-lance job to shoot it. Blankenship spies his mother and Forster in a clinch and is so hurt by this that he runs away. This is the afternoon and evening of the first meeting of the convention and the streets are no safe place to be. Bloom looks for Blankenship and winds up in Grant Park in the midst of a battle between police and protesters. Forster locates her there, while tear gas shells are exploding everywhere and heads are being cracked by police batons. Neither of them know that Blankenship is already on his way home safely. Forster and Bloom get into his car and cruise the city looking for the boy. Forster's mind is whirling with the events of the day and he is not paying attention to driving and he crashes into a tree. Bloom is killed and Forster is badly hurt. He looks around the area to see if anyone can help. A driver comes by, sees the carnage, stops to photograph the accident, then drives off without being of any assistance, thus, "framing" the movie with an ending similar to the beginning, except that the observer at the start is the victim at the conclusion. Filmed on location in Chicago, Minnesota, Washington, and Kentucky, MEDIUM COOL got only a medium reception from audiences, perhaps because the news events that were seen on the air every night were even more bizarre than the ones in the film. It's hard to say where the script left off and the improvisation began as so much was happening in actuality that Wexler must have kept one eye on his script and one ear on the police radio so he could race to locations, shoot sequences, and edit them into the finished product. The original "X" rating (later lowered to an "R") was mainly due to a nude bedroom sequence with Forster and Hill as well as the graphic language and the violence. It's odd that the sight of a woman's nude body caused such a furor, but no one seems to mind when violence is done to it. Bonerz, who later became a foil to Bob Newhart in his TV show, is an adroit actor, a good comedian, and, lately, a director. He is like Mel Tillis in that he stutters when he speaks but not when he acts. Wexler, the scion of a wealthy Chicago family, likes to take chances and use his own money. In 1985 he would make only his second feature film, a story of the revolution in Nicaragua, LATINO. MEDIUM COOL was praised by critics and shunned by crowds and no one can figure out why. Perhaps the events of the day eclipsed whatever fiction Wexler could manufacture. Blankenship was a real mountain boy living with his family in the Appalachian neighborhood of Chicago. Many of the actors were non-pros who were impressed into the film and never did anything else in show business. An exception to that was Peter Boyle, in a small role as the manager of a gun clinic. His next role shot him into the stratosphere when he played the title in JOE. In many of the larger scenes, the public never knew they were being filmed for a movie, so the blend of fiction and documentary goes more than halfway on each side. Of particular note is an off-screen shout by someone who says "Watch out, Haskell, it's real!" and Wexler chose to leave that on the soundtrack to demonstrate that the chaos had not been staged.

p, Jerrold and Haskell Wexler, Tully Friedman; d&w, Haskell Wexler (based on the novel *The Concrete Wilderness* by Jack Couffer); ph, Haskell Wexler (Technicolor); m, Mike Bloomfield; ed, Verna Fields; art d, Leon Erickson; m/l, "Merry-Go-Round" (sung by Wild Man Fisher).

Drama **Cas.** **(PR:O MPAA:R)**

MEDJU JASTREBOVIMA

(SEE: FRONTIER HELLCAT, 1966, Fr./Ital./Ger./Yugo.)

MEDUSA TOUCH, THE* (1978, Brit.) 110m ITC/WB c

Richard Burton *(John Morlar), Lino Ventura (Brunel)*, Lee Remick *(Dr. Zonfeld)*, Harry Andrews *(Assistant Commissioner)*, Marie-Christine Barrault *(Patricia)*, Michael Hordern *(Atropos the Fortune Teller)*, Derek Jacobi *(Townley the Publisher)*, Robert Lang *(Pennington)*, Jeremy Brett *(Parrish)*, Alan Badel *(Barrister)*, Michael Byrne *(Duff)*, Gordon Jackson *(Dr. Johnson)*, Robert Flemyng *(Judge McKinley)*, Norman Bird *(Father)*, Jennifer Jayne *(Mother)*, Philip Stone *(Dean)*, Maurice O'Connell *(Sgt. Robbins)*, Avril Elgar *(Mrs. Pennington)*, John Normington *(Schoolmaster)*, Malcolm Tierney *(Deacon)*, James Hazeldine *(Lovelass)*, Mark Jones *(Sgt. Hughes)*, Wendy Gifford *(Receptionist)*, Gordon Honeycombe *(TV Newscaster)*, Frances Tomelty *(Nanny)*, Brooks Williams *(Male Nurse)*, Victor Winding *(Senior Police Officer)*, Anthony Blackett *(Mounted Police Officer)*, John Flanagan *(Police Constable)*, Denyse Alexander *(Hospital Doctor)*, Stanley Lebor *(Police Doctor)*, George Innes *(Van Driver)*, Ian Marter *(Detective in Street)*, Cornelius Bowe *(Young Morlar)*, Adam Bridges *(Morlar at Age 10)*, Joseph Clark *(Morlar at Age 14)*, Christopher Burgess *(Pilot)*, Matthew Long *(Copilot)*, Earl Rhodes *(Parson)*, Colin Rix *(Engineer)*.

Another one of those movies that was more of a "deal" than it was a picture. Lino Ventura makes his English film debut (probably due to the fact that there was some financing from French sources) and he comes off better than anyone else. Burton is whacked on the head by an unseen assailant and no one can figure out why. He is virtually dead, but his brain continues to function. Ventura enters and attempts to decipher the riddle. He interviews Remick, Burton's psychiatrist, and learns that Burton is possessed of an unusual mental facility. He is a telekinetic who can cause things to happen. So as Burton lies in the hospital attached to life-support systems, a London church implodes, a jetliner smashes into a skyscraper, etc. Ventura continues to investigate and learns that Burton's brain may have been the reason for several unexplained disasters. Burton is an ogre who can wreak physical havoc on anything he thinks about and Ventura ploddingly assesses the facts, then puts a stop to all the chaos. This was Burton's follow-up to EXORCIST II, THE HERETIC and that picture was such tripe that people stayed away in droves from this one. THE MEDUSA TOUCH is so bad you'll have to sit through it 10 times to get your money's worth. Believe it or not, if Irwin Allen had made this movie, it might have been better. Instead, it was "presented" by Sir Lew Grade, a ubiquitous presence in the financing of British films in the 1970s and 1980s.

p, Anne V. Coates, Jack Gold; d, Gold; w, Gold, John Briley (based on a novel by Peter Van Greenaway); ph, Arthur Ibbetson (Panavision, Technicolor); m, Michael J. Lewis; ed, Coates; art d, Peter Mullins.

Disaster **Cas.** **(PR:C MPAA:PG)**

MEET BOSTON BLACKIE 1/2** (1941) 61m COL bw

Chester Morris *(Boston Blackie)*, Rochelle Hudson *(Cecelia Bradley)*, Richard Lane *(Inspector Faraday)*, Charles Wagenheim *(The Runt)*, Constance Worth *(Marilyn Howard)*, Jack O'Malley *(Monk)*, George Magrill *(Georgie)*, Michael Rand *(Mechanical Man)*, Eddie Laughton *(Freak Show Barker)*, John Tyrrell *(Freak Show Doorman)*, Harry Anderson *(Dart Game Barker)*, Byron Foulger *(Blind Man)*.

Slick-haired, hard-eyed Morris debuts as Boston Blackie, an ex-con who turns to the side of the law after a corpse shows up in his cabin en route by ocean liner to the U.S. from Europe. Of course he is accused and must escape from the cops to gather enough evidence to prove his innocence. He discovers that a giant spy ring is being fronted by an oceanside carnival and, by uncovering it, saves his skin. This became the groundwork for a series of 13 more episodes, each with similar plots. (See BOSTON BLACKIE series, Index).

p, Ralph Cohn; d, Robert Florey; w, Jay Dratler (based on characters created by Jack Boyle); ph, Franz F. Planer; ed, James Sweeney.

Crime **(PR:A MPAA:NR)**

MEET DANNY WILSON***   (1952) 86m UNIV bw

Frank Sinatra (Danny Wilson), Shelley Winters (Joy Carroll), Alex Nicol (Mike Ryan), Raymond Burr (Nick Driscoll), Tommy Farrell (Tommy Wells), Vaughn Taylor (T. W. Thatcher), Donald MacBride (Sergeant), Barbara Knudsen (Marie), Carl Sklover (Taxi Driver), John Day (Gus), Jack Kruschen (Heckler), Tom Dugan (Turnkey), Danny Welton (Joey Thompson), Pat Flaherty (Mother Murphy), Carlos Molina (Bandleader), George Eldredge (Lt. Kelly), Bob Donnelly (Emerson), John Indrisano (Truck Driver), Tony Curtis (Man in Nightclub).

A combination musical and crime story, MEET DANNY WILSON is not unlike the story of the singer in THE GODFATHER, who goes from being a nobody to a star and gets involved with criminals along the way. Sinatra is the singer and Nicol is his pianist and they are barely making enough for coffee and Danish as they work some sleazy clubs. They meet Winters, a nitery thrush, who introduces them to Burr, a boite owner. Burr thinks Sinatra may have something so they make an oral contract for Burr to manage Sinatra in return for half the singer's income. Sinatra becomes a hit on stage but a flop in his love life. He adores Winters, as does Nicol, but she prefers the pianist to the crooner. Burr gets into trouble with the cops and has to hide out but he continues hounding Sinatra for his half of the money. There's a lot of money involved and Burr becomes threatening and eventually pulls a gun. Nicol steps in front of the weapon and takes the bullet meant for Sinatra. Now Sinatra goes after Burr and the two have a confrontation in Wrigley Field after the sun has gone down. There's a gun battle and Sinatra kills Burr. Lest you think there's a mistake by having the final scene in a floodlit Wrigley Field, be aware that it's not the one in Chicago. The finale takes place in the one-time home of the California Angels in downtown Los Angeles. There was some true material from Sinatra's life here, but everyone denied it. Some of the best songs in Ol' Blue Eyes' repertoire were dotted throughout the film. They include: "I've Got a Crush on You" (George Gershwin, Ira Gershwin), "How Deep Is the Ocean?" (Irving Berlin), "When You're Smiling" (Mark Fisher, Joe Goodwin, Larry Shay), "All of Me" (Seymour Simons, Gerald Marks), "She's Funny That Way" (Richard Whiting, Richard Moret), "That Old Black Magic" (Harold Arlen, Johnny Mercer), "You're a Sweetheart" (Jimmy McHugh, Harold Adamson), "Lonesome Man Blues" (Sy Oliver), "A Good Man Is Hard to Find" (Eddie Green, sung with Shelley Winters). Sinatra's acting is excellent (Why not? He was playing himself and who can do that better than he can?), and Winters displays a pleasant voice on her few opportunities to chirp.

p, Leonard Goldstein; d, Joseph Pevney; w, Don McGuire; ph, Maury Gertsman; ed, Virgil Vogel; md, Joseph Gershenson; art d, Bernard Herzbrun, Nathan Juran; set d, Russell A. Gausman, Julia Heron; cos, Bill Thomas; spec eff, David S. Horsley; ch, Hal Belfer; makeup, Bud Westmore.

Musical/Drama   **(PR:A   MPAA:NR)**

MEET DR. CHRISTIAN**1/2   (1939) 68m RKO bw

Jean Hersholt (Dr. Christian), Dorothy Lovett (Judy Price), Robert Baldwin (Roy Davis), Enid Bennett (Anne Hewitt), Paul Harvey (John Hewitt), Marcia Mae Jones (Marilee), Maude Eburne (Mrs. Hastings), Frank Coghlan, Jr. (Bud), Patsy Lee Parsons (Patsy Hewitt), Sarah Edwards (Mrs. Minnows), John Kelly (Cass), Eddie Acuff (Benson). Jackie Moran (Don Hewitt).

A pleasant down-home entry which casts Hersholt as the title doctor in the mythical town of Rivers End, Minnesota, who for years had been a CBS radio favorite. He's a humble, friendly country doctor ("If anything goes wrong, don't hesitate to call me") who is more concerned with the health of the townspeople than financial rewards. His chief goal is to get a hospital built, but he has to deal with the stubborn mayor (Harvey) who is more concerned with new roads than the voters' well-being. Harvey whistles a different tune after his daughter's life is saved by the gentle physician with the Danish accent in his voice and a name borrowed from Hersholt's favorite author, Hans Christian Andersen. (See DR. CHRISTIAN series, Index)

p, William Stephens; d, Bernard Vorhaus; w, Ian McLellan Hunter, Ring Lardner, Jr., Harvey Gates (based on a story by Gates); ph, Robert Pittack; ed, Edward Mann; md, Constantin Bakaleinikoff; art d, Bernard Herzbrun.

Drama   **Cas.**   **(PR:A   MPAA:NR)**

MEET JOHN DOE*****   (1941) 135m WB bw

Gary Cooper ("John Doe"/Long John Willoughby), Barbara Stanwyck (Ann Mitchell), Edward Arnold (D. B. Norton), Walter Brennan (Colonel), James Gleason (Henry Connell), Spring Byington (Mrs. Mitchell), Gene Lockhart (Mayor Lovett), Rod LaRocque (Ted Sheldon), Irving Bacon (Beany), Regis Toomey (Bert Hansen), Warren Hymer (Angelface), Aldrich Bowker (Pop Dwyer), Ann Doran (Mrs. Hansen), Sterling Holloway (Dan), Mrs. Gardner Crane (Mrs. Brewster), J. Farrell MacDonald (Sourpuss Smithers), Pat Flaherty (Mike), Carlotta Jelm, Tina Thayer (Ann's Sisters), Bennie Bartlett (Red, the Office Boy), Sarah Edwards (Mrs. Hawkins), Stanley Andrews (Weston), Andrew Tombes (Spencer), Pierre Watkin (Hammett), Garry Owen (Sign Painter), Charlie Wilson (Charlie Dawson), Gene Morgan (Mug), Cyril Thornton (Butler), Edward Earle (Radio M.C.), Mike Frankovich (Radio Announcer), Harry Holman (Mayor Hawkins), Bess Flowers (Newspaper Secretary), Emma Tansey (Mrs. Delaney), Mitchell Lewis (Bennett), Billy Curtis, Johnny Fern (Midgets), Vernon Dent (Man), Vaughn Glaser (Governor), Selmer Jackson, Knox Manning, John B. Hughes (Radio Announcers at Convention), Hall Johnson Choir, Lucia Carroll (Themselves), James McNamara (Sheriff), Frank Austin (Grubbel), Edward Keane (Relief Administrator), Lafe McKee (Mr. Delaney), Edward McWade (Joe, Newsman), Guy Usher (Bixler), Walter Soderling (Barrington), John Hamilton (Jim, Governor's Associate), William Forrest (Governor's Associate), Charles K. French (Fired Reporter), Edward Hearn (Mayor's Secretary), Hank Man (Ed, a Photographer), James Millican (Photographer), Harry Davenport (Ex-owner of Bulletin), Paul Everton (G.O.P. Man), Forrester Harvey (Bum), Mary Benoit, Mildred Coles (Secretaries), Ed Kane (Tycoon), Melvin

Lang, Alphonse Martel (Foreign Dignitary), Wyndham Standing, Ed Stanley (Democrat), Isabelle La Mal, Alfred Hall, George Melford, Henry Roquemore (Chamber of Commerce Members), John Ince (Doctor), Gail Newbray (Telephone Operator), Earl Bunn, Eddie Cobb, Jack Cheatham (Policemen), Lew Davis, Howard Chase, Floyd Criswell, (Electricians), Carl Ekberg, Frank Fanning, Eddie Fetherston (Reporters), Walter Finden, Jack Gardner (Photographers), William Gould (Sergeant), Kenneth Harlan (Publicity Man), Richard Kipling (Police Commissioner), Frank Meredith, Jack Mower, Cliff Saum, Don Turner (Guards), Forbes Murray (Legislator), Maris Wrixon, Suzanne Carnhan (Autograph Hounds), Frank Mayor (Attendant), Wedgwood Nowell, Evelyn Barlowe, Fritzi Brunette, Lucie Carroll, Florence Lawler, E. Dockson, Ethel Gilstrom, Claire Mead, Mrs. Wilfrid North, Elsa Petersen, Sada Simmons, Bessie Wade, Lillian West, Mack Gray, Jay Guedillio, Donald Hall, Jimmy Harrison, Max Hoffman, Frank Jaquet, Charles McAvoy, Larry McGrath, Joe McGuinn, Tom McGuire, Frank Moran, Clark Morgan, George Pembroke, Bob Perry, Ed Piel, Sr., Hal Price, Stanley Price, Don Roberts, Thomas W. Ross, Bernard Wheeler, Ed Williams, Max Blum, Sidney Bracy, Glen Cavender, Inez Gay, Bess Meyers, Sally Sage, Lottie Williams, Ed Graham, Stuart Holmes, Al Lloyd, Paul Panzer, Jack Richardson, Leo White, Tom Wilson, Charles Trowbridge, Henry Frederick Vogeding, Jack Wise.

Sentimental, optimistic, moralistic, with a message for the good of the common man, MEET JOHN DOE is another Capra good-will film and it's superb on every level, even though its ending is a tail wagging the dog. The film opens as Stanwyck, a struggling journalist, is fired from her job when a new managing editor, Gleason, takes over her newspaper. She angrily writes her last piece about a mythical idealist she calls John Doe and through him rants about the little guy being punished and mistreated by tycoons, moguls, magnates, and captains of industry. To make good his protest, Doe states, in Stanwyck's fabricated letter to the paper, that he will leap off the top of City Hall on Christmas Eve. The public response is enormous and Gleason demands that Stanwyck turn over the letter she has received from this so-called John Doe. She confesses that there is no letter, that she made up the whole story but then, to keep the job she values above all else, Stanwyck suggests they find a phony hero from the ranks of the great unemployed and continue the story to sell more papers. Another paper jeeringly labels the story a fraud and Gleason, to save his newspaper's image, orders Stanwyck to pick out a stewbum and make him into her real life John Doe. The man selected is Cooper, called Long John Willoughby, a one-time minor league pitcher whose arm has gone bad and put him out of work and on the bum. He wolfs down a free meal and is persuaded to play the John Doe role for money that will go toward an operation to heal his arm. Cooper and sidekick Brennan, who thinks the whole thing is exactly what it is, a lot of baloney, live in a luxurious hotel, their meals and board paid by the paper, while Stanwyck writes story after story about her idealistic John Doe. He becomes so popular that her readers demand to see the man of the people in the flesh. Gleason has finally had enough of the hoax but Stanwyck intends to milk the tale for all it's worth, going to publisher Arnold, a grandiose, vain, and politically ambitious creature who thinks just like Stanwyck. Says Stanwyck to her boss: "If he made a hit around here, he can do it every place else in the country. And you'd be pulling the strings!" The scheme appeals to Arnold who envisions himself in the White House. Now he has a national celebrity to champion his causes, mouth his ideas, Cooper. Arnold is a Huey Long type, controlling his state with a private army of goons, state police, and local politicians all in his hip pocket. All the media channels are controlled by him, newspapers and radio, and Arnold quickly puts the naive Cooper on the airways to spout everyday generalities of good will, but, coming out of his mouth, a man with down-home sincerity, countless thousands find new meaning in his phrases. Cooper reads a speech prepared by Stanwyck, saying: "To most of you, your neighbor is a stranger, a guy with a barking dog and a fence around him. Now you can't be a stranger to any guy who's on your own team. So tear down the fence that separates you . . . You'll tear down a lot of hates and prejudices . . . I know a lot of you are saying to yourself: 'He's asking for a miracle'. . . . Well, you're wrong. It's no miracle . . . I see it happen once every year . . . at Christmastime . . . . Why can't that spirit last the whole year round? Gosh, if it ever did—we'd develop such a strength that no human force could stand against us." The radio speech is so effective that thousands of John Doe fan clubs spring up overnight and Cooper becomes one of the nation's great celebrities. But the bush-league pitcher has no intention of carrying the gentle fraud further. Despite Stanwyck's pleadings that he is doing good for everyone, Cooper takes a walk with his friend Brennan, who considers all people who want to control other people "helots." But, to Cooper's amazement, he is turned back by the very people he has influenced. Recognized in one small town, he is swamped by his admirers. Soda jerk Toomey and scores of other John Doe Club members swarm about him and Toomey tells him how his inspirational words have changed their lives, how he and his wife Doran have, after many years of mistreating their seemingly grouchy neighbor, made friends with J. Farrell MacDonald. Toomey explains that MacDonald was not unfriendly at all, not the "sourpuss" everyone calls him, but that he is merely hard of hearing which is why he never returned a friendly greeting. Cooper is overwhelmed by his supporters and soon agrees to Stanwyck's proposal to stump the country in setting up a national John Doe movement. This of course is exactly what the scheming Arnold wants. He informs his henchmen that the upcoming national convention of the John Doe Club will really act as his own launching pad for the presidency. "That practically means 90 percent of the voters," he smiles wickedly. But Gleason, who is an honest newsman, gets drunk and tells Cooper what evil Arnold really intends to do with the John Doe movement. Bursting into Arnold's enormous mansion unannounced, Cooper finds Stanwyck and Arnold meeting with political bigwigs. He denounces his sponsor and then informs him that "I'm going down to that convention and I'm going to tell those people exactly what you and your fine-feathered friends are trying to cook up for them." Arnold shouts back that if he makes that kind of move, he will expose Cooper as a fraud and wreck the John Doe movement. Cooper, after bopping a henchman in the beezer, storms out, daring Arnold to try to stop the movement. At the outdoor convention site, where thousands are gathered, Cooper mounts the podium and begins to expose Arnold but Arnold's goons pull him back and Arnold himself addresses the crowd, telling one and all that Cooper is not only a fake but that he stole all the money from the donations and dues to the John Doe clubs and that he never even wrote the original letter. Moreover, Arnold tells the now incensed and disillusioned club members, Cooper never had any intention of jumping off the top of City Hall! When Cooper again tries to speak to the masses assembled beneath a sea of umbrellas during a rainstorm, he is jeered, called a phony, and pelted with rotten fruit and vegetables, the latter supplied by Arnold's minions planted in the crowd. The movement dissolves on the spot, its thoroughly disheartened members going off into their own separate, lonely worlds. The John Doe movement has been smashed. As Cooper has prophetically said earlier to Arnold: "If you can't control it, you'll kill it!" Cooper decides to revive the movement the only way he knows how; he will actually throw himself off the top of City Hall to prove that he is genuine. On Christmas Eve, Arnold and his bigwigs stand bundled on top of the tall building, waiting to see if Cooper will show up. He does, but Stanwyck is there to beg him not to kill himself. She tells him that "the first John Doe already died to keep the good will movement alive, and He has kept that idea alive for more than two thousand years . . . It's [an idea] worth dying for, it's an idea worth living for . . . . This is no time to give up." She faints into Cooper's arms. Still, he is determined to jump but suddenly Toomey, Doran, and other diehard John Doe Club members appear and plead with him not to commit suicide. "We need you," Doran says. "There were a lot of us who didn't believe what that man [Arnold] said. We were going to start our own John Doe Club again whether we saw you or not . . . . And there were a lot of others going to do the same thing . . . . Only it would be a lot easier with you. Please . . . please come with us, Mr. Doe." Cooper pauses for a moment, glancing to the edge of the roof, then, with Stanwyck in his arms, he joins his followers and leaves the roof. Arnold and his people are left to glare after the man who has defeated them. Gleason, who has joined the "little people," turns to Arnold and says triumphantly before walking away: "There you are, Norton, the people! Try and lick that!" As the snow continues to fall and the victorious "little people" exit, the choral finale of Beethoven's Ninth Symphony dominates the fadeout. The ending of MEET JOHN DOE has been accused by some critics of being tacked on, to provide a happy ending. Actually, Capra added the scene with the club members when he realized that just Stanwyck's plea would not alter Cooper's suicidal intent, that Cooper needed to be reassured that those who had followed his idealistic beliefs from the beginning were there to continue to believe in him. But it's a small compromise in an otherwise brilliant masterpiece. Cooper, who starred in Capra's MR. DEEDS GOES TO TOWN, also the story of a small town rube who faces seemingly insurmountable odds, is perfect as the direct, uncomplicated, and decent man of the people who is manipulated by anti-democratic forces until he rebels against the tyrants who seek to mislead and use the people. He is Everyman and Capra could not have chosen a more believable John Doe. Stanwyck, the ambitious news lady who sacrifices her own scruples to get ahead only to learn the great lesson of humility and honor from her own creation is outstanding, as is Arnold, who essays his portrait in degenerate power with great and convincing polish. (Ann Sheridan was originally sought to play Stanwyck's role.) All the marvelous character actors, the mainstay of any Capra production, Gleason, Brennan, Toomey, Doran, La Rocque, Byington, Lockhart, Holloway, MacDonald, are touching and superlative. MEET JOHN DOE, developed by Riskin and Capra in story form, stems from a Harry Langdon comedy, LONG PANTS, which Capra directed in 1927, but it is much more in message and content. Next to MR. SMITH GOES TO WASHINGTON, and IT'S A WONDERFUL LIFE, this film personifies Capra's democratic principles. He would later state: "My whole philosophy is in my films. People are basically good or can be made good. Sentimental? Of course, but so what? Let's not be hard-boiled about this. Happy endings—life is full of them." This film really comes down to accepting (or rejecting) the Golden Rule: "Love thy neighbor." But Capra never presents such platitudes in broad and sweeping terms, shrewdly showing how simple honesty and generosity come from simple acts, a handshake, a smile, a closeup of a couple facing fear and/or threat. Cooper's personality is early on established after he and his sidekick Brennan finish the first good meal they've eaten in months. To celebrate Cooper pulls out his harmonica and Brennan his ocarina ("sweet potato") and they play a little duet. MEET JOHN DOE was Capra's first independent film production done away from his home studio Columbia and beyond the tryannical reach of its boss, Harry Cohn. It's basically an answer to the fascist elements then in America, notably the German-American Bund which was pro-Nazi. Capra wanted to warn Americans about the powerful fascist influences in their midst and did so mightily with this film. Though MEET JOHN DOE reportedly profited Capra and Riskin's independent company $900,000 on its initial release, Capra later reported that the tax bite was so heavy that he dissolved the company after a few months. So great had Capra's reputation become that all the leading players in MEET JOHN DOE agreed to do the film without reading the script. Actually, they had no script to read since Capra, Riskin, and others were just putting the idea together. It mattered not to Barbara Stanwyck who is quoted in *Stanwyck* by Jane Ellen Wayne as saying about her feet-first appearance in MEET JOHN DOE: "There is no one like Frank Capra. He is in a class all by himself. It is a joy watching him work every day. You make other pictures to live, but you live to make a Capra picture."

p&d, Frank Capra; w, Robert Riskin (based on a story "The Life and Death of John Doe" by Robert Presnell, Richard Connell); ph, George Barnes; m, Dimitri Tiomkin; ed, Daniel Mandell; md, Leo F. Forbstein; art d, Stephen Goosson; cos, Natalie Visart; spec eff, Jack Cosgrove.

Drama **Cas.** **(PR:A MPAA:NR)**

MEET MAXWELL ARCHER

(SEE: MAXWELL ARCHER, DETECTIVE, 1939, Brit.)

MEET ME AFTER THE SHOW*** (1951) 86m FOX c

Betty Grable *(Delilah)*, Macdonald Carey *(Jeff)*, Rory Calhoun *(David Hemingway)*, Eddie Albert *(Christopher Leeds)*, Fred Clark *(Tim)*, Lois Andrews *(Gloria Carstairs)*, Irene Ryan *(Tillie)*, Steve Condos, Jerry Brandow *(Specialty Dancers)*, Arthur Walge *(Joe)*, Edwin Max *(Charlie)*, Robert Nash *(Barney)*, Don Kohler *(Airline Clerk)*, Rodney Bell *(Dr. Wheaton)*, Harry Antrim *(Judge)*, Lovyss Bradley *(Wardrobe Mistress)*, Jewel Rose *(Hairdresser)*, Carol Savage *(Secretary)*, Michael Darrin *(Orchestra Leader)*, Joe Haworth *(George)*, Perc Launders *(Turnkey)*, Gwen Verdon *(Dancer)*, Max Wagner *(Doorman)*, Al Murphy *(Process Server)*, Lick Cogan *(Man)*, Billy Newell *(Stage Manager)*.

The story is trite but the musical numbers are outstanding in this frothy film. Broadway star Grable learns that husband-producer Carey is fooling around with other women and she quits Carey's show. Angry and seeking satisfaction, Grable pretends to lose her memory and returns to Miami where she began her career years earlier. Taking her old name and doing her old act, Grable proceeds to relive her early years while inviting the leering attentions of playboy Calhoun. Her faked amnesia, of course, is to bring her errant husband Carey around. Jealous and believing he is about to lose his sexy wife, Carey professes his love to Grable and, equally important to her, convinces the leggy singer-dancer that he will never again stray from their marital bed. She confesses faking her loss of memory and she and Carey are reunited. Typical of the vacuous musicals of this period and the type of corn popped by producer Jessel, there's little substance to the tale but the production numbers give this one an above-average status. Cole's and Verdon's choreography is excellent; they provide one show-stopping number after another. Song and dance numbers include: "It's a Hot Night in Alaska," "I Feel Like Dancing" (which also features, with Grable, co-choreographer Gwen Verdon), "No Talent Joe," "Bettin' On a Man" (Jule Styne, Leo Robin).

p, George Jessel; d, Richard Sale; w, Mary Loos, Sale (based on a story by Erna Lazarus, W. Scott Darling); ph, Arthur E. Arling (Technicolor); ed, J. Watson Webb, Jr.; md, Lionel Newman; art d, Lyle Wheeler, Joseph C. Wright; ch, Jack Cole, Gwen Verdon; spec eff, Fred Sersen.

Musical **(PR:A MPAA:NR)**

MEET ME AT DAWN**

(1947, Brit.) 99m FOX bw (AKA: THE GAY DUELIST)

William Eythe *(Charles Morton)*, Stanley Holloway *(Emile)*, Hazel Court *(Gabrielle Vermorel)*, George Thorpe *(Sen. Philipe Renault)*, Irene Browne *(Mme. Renault)*, Beatrice Campbell *(Margot)*, Basil Sydney *(Georges Vermorel)*, Margaret Rutherford *(Mme. Vermorel)*, Ada Reeve *(Concierge)*, Graeme Muir *(Count de Brissac)*, Wilfrid Hyde-White *(News Editor)*, John Ruddock *(Doctor)*, O. B. Clarence *(Ambassador)*, Aubrey Mallalieu *(Prefect of Police)*, James Harcourt *(Butler)*, Charles Victor *(1st Client)*, John Salew *(2nd Client)*, Percy Walsh *(Shooting Gallery Man)*, Hy Hazell *(1st Girl in Restaurant)*, Joan Seton *(Vermorel's Secretary)*, Katie Johnson *(Mme. Vermorel's Housekeeper)*, Diana Decker *(2nd Girl in Restaurant)*, Lind Joyce *(Yvonne Jadin)*, Guy Rolfe, Charles Hawtrey.

Turn of the century Paris is the backdrop for this romantic comedy which has Eythe supporting himself by working as a professional duelist. He is hired by a group of politicians to insult and challenge a prominent senator. He feigns a dispute over Court, a young lovely whose father happens to operate the local newspaper and who, without knowing his daughter is involved, brands the woman "Madame X." The finale has Eythe and Court falling in love, and her father becoming the local hero when he is challenged to a duel by Eythe, whom he has insulted, when Eythe allows him to nick him and win the match.

p, Marcel Hellman; d, Thornton Freeland, Peter Cresswell; w, Lesley Storm, James Seymour (based on the play "La Tueur" by Marcel Achard, Anatole Litvak); ph, Gunther Krampf; m, Mischa Spoliansky; ed, E. B. Jarvis; art d, Norman Arnold; cos, R. Gower Parks, Nathan; ch, Dimitri Vladimiroff, Leon Paul; m/l, "I Guess I'm Not the Type," Robert Musel (sung by Lind Joyce); makeup, George Claff.

Comedy/Romance **(PR:A MPAA:NR)**

MEET ME AT THE FAIR 1/2** (1952) 87m UNIV c

Dan Dailey *("Doc" Tilbee)*, Diana Lynn *(Zerelda Wing)*, Chet Allen *("Tad" Bayliss)*, "Scatman" Crothers *(Enoch Jones)*, Hugh O'Brian *(Chilton Corr)*, Carole Mathews *(Clara Brink)*, Rhys Williams *(Pete McCoy)*, Thomas E. Jackson *(Billy Gray)*, Russell Simpson *(Sheriff Evans)*, George Chandler *(Deputy Sheriff Leach)*, Virginia Brissac *(Mrs. Spooner)*, Doris Packer *(Mrs. Swaile)*, Edna Holland *(Miss Burghey)*, George L. Spaulding *(Governor)*, Paul Gordon *(Cyclist)*, Johnson & Diehl *(Juggling Act)*, The Black Brothers *(Acrobatic Comedy Act)*, John Maxwell *(Mr. Spooner)*, George Riley *(M.C.)*, Iron Eyes Cody *(Chief Rain-in-the-Face)*, Donald Kerr *(Stage Manager)*, Franklyn Farnum, Harte Wayne, Roger Moore *(Wall Street Tycoons)*, Robert Shafto *(Prime Minister Disraeli)*, Dante Dipaolo *(Specialty Dancer)*, George Arglen *(Howie)*, Jon Gardner *(Ed)*, Sam Pierce *(Party Stooge)*, Max Wagner *(Iceman)*, Jack Gargan *(District Attorney's Secretary)*, Brick Sullivan *(Policeman)*, Butch the Dog *(Spook)*.

While not one of the most interesting Douglas Sirk films, MEET ME AT THE FAIR does entertain. Dailey is a crooked medicine show operator who befriends the young Allen, a runaway from the local orphanage. With the help of social worker Lynn and medicine show assistant Crothers, Dailey exposes the orphanage which is badly in need of reform. It turns out that the district attorney who is defending the orphanage and trying to prosecute Dailey for kidnaping is also Lynn's fiance. A fine slice of Americana set in 1904. One of the fair to middling screenplays scripted by Irving Wallace before he became a best-selling novelist. Songs include: "Meet Me at the Fair" (Milton Rosen, Frederick Herbert, sung by Carole Mathews), "I Was There" (F. E. Miller, Benjamin "Scatman" Crothers, sung by Dan Dailey, Crothers, Chet Allen), "Remember the Time" (Kenny Williams, Marvin Wright, sung by Dailey and Mathews), "Ave Maria" (Franz Schubert, sung by Allen), "Ezekiel Saw de Wheel" (sung by Crothers), "Sweet Genevieve" (George Cooper, Henry Tucker, sung by the Quartette), "All God's Chillun Got Wings" (sung by Crothers, Allen), "I Got the Shiniest Mouth in Town" (Stan Freberg, sung by Crothers), "O Susannah!" (Stephen Foster, sung by Dailey, Crothers, and Allen), "Bill Bailey, Won't You Please Come Home?" (Hughie Cannon, sung by Carole Mathews).

p, Albert J. Cohen; d, Douglas Sirk, Jack Daniels; w, Irving Wallace, Martin Berkeley (based on Gene Markey's novel *The Great Companions*); ph, Maury Gertsman (Technicolor); ed, Russell Schoengarth; md, Joseph Gershenson; art d, Bernard Herzbrun, Eric Orbom; set d, Russell A. Gausman, Ruby R. Levitt; cos, Rosemary Odell; ch, Kenny Williams.

Drama/Musical **(PR:A MPAA:NR)**

MEET ME IN LAS VEGAS*** (1956) 112m MGM c (GB: VIVA LAS VEGAS)

Dan Dailey *(Chuck Rodwell)*, Cyd Charisse *(Maria Corvier)*, Agnes Moorhead *(Miss Hattie)*, Lili Darvas *(Sari Hatvani)*, Jim Backus *(Tom Culdane)*, Oscar Karlweis *(Loisi)*, Liliane Montevecchi *(Lilli)*, Cara Williams *(Kelly Donavan)*, George Kerris *(Young Groom)*, Betty Lynn *(Young Bride)*, The Slate Brothers *(Themselves)*, Peter Rugolo *(Conductor)*, John Brascia *(Specialty Dancer)*, John Harding *(Worried Boss)*, Benny Rubin *(Croupier)*, Jack Daly *(Meek Husband)*, Henny Backus *(Bossy Wife)*, Jerry Colonna *(MC at Silver Slipper)*, Paul Henreid *(Maria's Manager)*, Frankie Laine *(Guest Star at Sands)*, Mitsuko Sawamura *(Japanese Girl)*, Marc Wilder *(Prince Charming)*, Frank Sinatra, Debbie Reynolds, Tony Martin, Peter Lorre, Vic Damone, Elaine Stewart.

Producer Pasternak does here what he always did well (or badly), presenting a platter full of sizzle and a few well-done sausages, but he peoples this film with a bevy of real-life stars who bring class and entertainment of high order. The story isn't much. Dailey is a gambling fool of a rancher who is addicted to roulette, a game where nobody should win after one lucky turn. Yet he wins and wins, because Charisse, a lovely, leggy ballerina, becomes his good luck charm. Every time he holds Charisse's hand the numbers come up for Dailey. Between the spins of the notorious wheel, a bevy of great tunes and dance numbers is presented. The center of most of the activity is The Sands casino, but Dailey and Charisse, who form a 50-50 percentage partnership in their luck-and-toss routine against Las Vegas roulette wheels, saunter through most of the other glamour spots almost as an advertisement for America's foremost gaming gulch. Charisse's hand is lucky for more than just gambling. Every time Dailey clutches her five fingers the chickens on his ranch lay eggs in record-breaking numbers. This girl is too good to let go and Dailey proposes, saying that he'll follow Charisse about on her dancing circuit for six months out of the year but she must spend the other six months down on the farm with him. She accepts. The guest stars pop up in clever scenes. As Charisse and Dailey pass a man with his back turned to the camera, pulling the arm of a slot machine, the slot pays off with a cascade of money. The man turns about without expression on his face. It's Sinatra. Quick cuts show Reynolds sipping coke with Damone, Angeli dining with Martin, and a wonderful 10-second shot of Peter Lorre sitting at a blackjack table and snapping to dealer Karlweis: "Hit me, you creep!" Songs by Nicholas Brodszky and Sammy Cahn include: "The Girl with the Yaller Shoes" (sung and danced by Dailey and Charisse), "If You Can Dream" (sung over the credits by The Four Aces, reprised by Lena Horne), "Hell Hath No Fury" (sung by Frankie Laine), "Lucky Charm" (sung by Jerry Colonna in a nightclub routine), "I Refuse to Rock 'n' Roll" (sung by Cara Williams), "Rehearsal Ballet" and "Sleeping Beauty Ballet" (danced by Charisse) and the big number, "Frankie and Johnny" (danced with slinky, hip-grinding moves by Charisse with new lyrics by Sammy Cahn, sung during the number by Sammy Davis, Jr., with Charisse as Frankie, John Brascia as Johnny, and Liliane Montevecchi as Nelly Bly).

p, Joe Pasternak; d, Roy Rowland; w, Isobel Lennart; ph, Robert Bronner (CinemaScope, Eastmancolor); m, Georgie Stoll; ed, Albert Akst; art d, Cedric Gibbons, Urie McCleary; set d, Edwin B. Willis, Richard Pefferle; cos, Helen Rose; spec eff, Warren Newcombe; ch, Hermes Pan, Eugene Loring; makeup, William Tuttle.

Musical **(PR:A MPAA:NR)**

MEET ME IN MOSCOW**

(1966, USSR) 73m Mosfilm/Accord-Cinemasters bw (YA SHAGAYU PO MOSKVE)

Nikita Mikhalkov *(Kolka)*, Aleksey Loktev *(Volodya)*, Galina Polskikh *(Alena)*, Yevgeniy Steblov *(Sasha)*, V. Basov *(Floor Polisher)*, Rolan Bykov *(Man in Park)*, A. Aleynikova, V. Ananina, S. Besedina, V. Vasilyeva, N. Vinogradova, N. Likhobabina, Ye. Melnikova, I. Miroshnichenko, A. Pavlova, A. Rumyantseva, Irina Skobtseva, L. Sokolova, D. Stolyarskaya, I. Titova, V. Babenko, B. Balakin, B. Bityukov, A. Bogolyubov, V. Volkov, G. Guskov, P. Dolzhanov, L. Durov, Ye. Kazakov, Uno Masaaki, K. Novikov, A. Smirnov, V. Sorokovov, V. Shilov, V. Shkurkin, V. Shurupov, G. Yalovich.

On a stopover in Moscow, Siberia-bound Loktev befriends Mikhalkov and Steblov. Steblov prepares to marry and Mikhalkov takes off with Loktev to meet a famous writer who admires a short story Loktev has penned. After meeting an attractive store clerk, Polskikh, they begin feuding over her, but after she gets Loktev out of jail the three remain friendly. They return home to attend a wedding party, but find that Steblov and his new bride have had an argument. Everything works out in the end as Loktev continues on his way to Kamchatka. A Russian comedy which follows the Hollywood format of cramming a 24-hour period in a character's life full of zany adventures.

d, Georgiy Daneliya; w, Gennadiy Shpalikov; ph, Vadim Yusov; m, Andrey Petrov; ed, L. Lysenkova; art d, A. Myagkov; cos, D. Ozerova, spec eff, B. Pluzhnikov, A. Rudachenko; makeup, T. Panteleyeva.

Comedy **(PR:A MPAA:NR)**

MEET ME IN ST. LOUIS***** (1944) 113m MGM c

Judy Garland *(Esther Smith)*, Margaret O'Brien *("Tootie" Smith)*, Mary Astor *(Mrs. Anne Smith)*, Lucille Bremer *(Rose Smith)*, June Lockhart *(Lucille Ballard)*, Tom Drake *(John Truett)*, Marjorie Main *(Katie)*, Harry Davenport *(Grandpa)*, Leon Ames *(Mr. Alonzo Smith)*, Hank Daniels *(Lon Smith, Jr.)*, Joan Carroll *(Agnes Smith)*, Hugh Marlowe *(Col. Darly)*, Robert Sully *(Warren Sheffield)*, Chill Wills *(Mr. Neely)*, Donald Curtis *(Dr. Terry)*, Mary Jo Ellis *(Ida Boothby)*, Ken Wilson *(Quentin)*, Robert Emmett O'Connor *(Motorman)*, Darryl Hickman *(Johnny Tevis)*, Leonard Walker *(Conductor)*, Victor Kilian *(Baggage Man)*, John Phipps *(Mailman)*, Maj. Sam Harris *(Mr. March)*, Mayo Newhall *(Mr. Braukoff)*, Belle Mitchell *(Mrs. Braukoff)*, Sidney Barnes *(Hugo Borvis)*, Myron Tobias *(George)*, Victor Cox *(Driver)*, Kenneth Donner, Buddy Gorman, Joe Cobbs *(Clinton Badgers)*, Helen Gilbert *(Girl on Trolley)*.

The deep-seated love for Americana by the viewing public was never better served than in this beautiful musical about a time no more. In this heart-tugging, nostalgic look at turn-of-the-century Americans, Garland shines and shines under the stylish direction of her future husband, Minnelli. She is backed up by a terrific cast and the music is romantic, glowing, and as memorable as the Washington Monument. This may be the best period musical ever made. There weren't many that came as good as MEET ME IN ST. LOUIS. The film opens in 1903 and ends the following year. The heart of the story is a single family with Ames and Astor as the parents of daughters Garland, Bremer, Carroll, O'Brien, and son Daniels. There is also capricious grandpa Davenport and family maid Main. Ames is a well-to-do businessman in St. Louis who maintains his family in a stylish Edwardian home. Bremer is courted by a beau at home and carries on a romantic correspondence with another beau away at college. Garland develops a crush on the new boy who moves next door, Drake, and they eventually fall in love and plan to marry. Flitting in and out of almost every scene is O'Brien in the finest role of her childhood career. As "Tootie," the precocious, imaginative youngest daughter, O'Brien steals the film in one precious scene after another. In one scene she sneaks downstairs to a party hosted by her big sisters, Garland, Bremer, and Carroll. Here she joins Garland in a funny little song, "I Was Drunk Last Night." She also sings and does a cakewalk with Garland in giving a wonderful rendition of "Under the Bamboo Tree" (Bob Cole and J. Rosamond Johnson). The family is emotionally disrupted when Ames proudly announces that his company has promoted him and he will be working in the New York office which means the family will be moving. No one but Ames wants to move. The children are upset, especially O'Brien, who buries her dolls in the back yard and, during Christmastime, destroys a snowman on the lawn as a way of showing her despair at having to leave St. Louis, this just after Garland sweetly warbles "Have Yourself a Merry Little Christmas" (Hugh Martin, Ralph Blane). O'Brien's Halloween scenes are equally touching as fright and humor are boiled to a delicious mixture by Minnelli. Here the little girl is goaded by neighbor children to confront the grouches of the community and daringly faces down Newhall, who takes it all good-humoredly while O'Brien, at fever-pitch, races back to her awed friends to announce that "I *killed* him!" Wistful and memorable tunes kept coming in this exquisite film, particularly "The Boy Next Door" and the big production number, a grand five-minutes of great song and choreography, "The Trolley Song" (both by Martin and Blane). The travail of relocating to New York is settled when, rather than make his loving family miserable, Ames refuses the company promotion and decides to stay in St. Louis. He and his family—daughters with fiances, his son with his intended, Lockhart, O'Brien bubbling joy, and Main and Davenport sighing relief—attend the opening of the World's Fair in St. Louis, 1904, swelling with pride over the fact that their city is the center of the world's attention. Minnelli proves his keen eye for period detail as well as an affectionate perspective for the past and its simple ways and values; he rightly glorifies the family and presents old-fashioned sentiment without being banal or mawkish, displaying a startling balance of emotions from scene to scene, from song to song. Said Minnelli: "The picture was divided into four seasons. I decided to introduce each segment of the film by using the Smith's American Gothic house at 5135 Kensington Avenue as a lovely filigreed illustration, like the greeting cards of the era. Each card would dissolve into the live action of the Smith family." At first, Garland didn't want to make the film; after reading the script she believed that it's lack of plot and story line would mean disaster but Minnelli convinced her that the music and production numbers would more than hold the movie together. O'Brien, who apparently could gush rivers of tears on cue, could not bring herself to shed one tear for a vital scene. Her mother then told the director what secret it was that would always turn on the tears and asked the director to tell her daughter that her pet dog was going to be shot and die. Minnelli reluctantly did so and O'Brien suddenly burst into the tears he sought. The cameras caught the tearful scene and, when finished, O'Brien halted her crying abruptly and, according to Minnelli "went skipping happily off the set. I went home feeling like a monster." This was Minnelli's first color film and he made great use of the process, offering rich, deep colors that gave the overall look of the film soft, gentle images which reflected the era and setting. The 22-year-old Garland never looked more beautiful than in MEET ME IN ST. LOUIS, much to the credit of her eccentric makeup lady, Dotty Ponedel, who had created Marlene Dietrich's "look" at Paramount. Ponedel made a few simple changes in Garland's appearance. She raised her eyebrows, tweezed her hairline, and gave her a fuller lower lip by arranging her lipstick, applying white liner to her lower eyelids so that her large eyes would look even larger. In his selection of music, most of what appears in the film later becoming standards, Minnelli chose well, the tunes perfectly suited to the era and the characters. Only one, "Boys and Girls Like You and Me" by Richard Rodgers and Oscar Hammerstein (not used in OKLAHOMA) was later dropped. The movie was based upon a series of tales entitled "The Kensington Stories," by Sally Benson, which appeared in *The New Yorker* in 1941–42. MGM official Fred Finklehoffe bought the stories for a reported $40,000 and producer Freed took over the project, one which became so dear to his heart that he actually dubbed Ames' voice for the song "You and I." The sets, designed by Ayers, who had staged

"Oklahoma" on Broadway, were replete with broad streets, gabled, gothic homes, large lawns, bay windows, and filigreed woodwork and cost MGM more than $200,000, then a staggering amount, but the studio would use the resplendent MEET ME IN ST. LOUIS set many times over. This was Bremer's film debut; she had been a Radio City Rockette and had some success with a nightclub act before making this film. Van Johnson was originally slated to play Garland's beau but he was canceled at the last moment and replaced by Drake. Astor, playing Garland's mother, essayed the same kind of role with Garland in LISTEN, DARLING in 1938. It was Astor who helped to snap Garland out of her doldrums and worries which caused her to hide out in her dressing trailer, working up her courage to go back onto the set while she kept the entire cast and crew waiting. Astor finally had enough and marched into Garland's dressing room, telling her: "Either get the hell on the set or I'm going home!" The no-nonsense Astor knew little of the deep anxieties that would later consume one of America's greatest talents. Other songs included in this masterpiece of Americana include: "Skip to My Lou" (Martin, Blane, sung by Garland, Bremer, Drake, Daniels, Jr.), "Over the Bannister" (sung by Garland, Drake), "Meet Me in St. Louis" (Andrew B. Sterling, Kerry Mills), "Brighten the Corner" (Gabriel), "Summer in St. Louis," "The Invitation" (Edens), "All Hallow's Eve," "Ah, Love," "The Horrible One" (Salinger), "Goodbye My Lady Love" (Howard), "Under the Anheuser Bush" (Von Tilzer), "Little Brown Jug" (Eastburn), "The Fair" (Hayton).

p, Arthur Freed; d, Vincente Minnelli; w, Irving Brecher, Fred F. Finklehoffe (based on the stories by Sally Benson); ph, George Folsey (Technicolor); ed, Albert Akst; md, Georgie Stoll; art d, Cedric Gibbons, Lemuel Ayers; set d, Edwin B. Willis, Paul Huldschinsky; cos, Irene Sharaff; ch, Charles Walters.

Musical   Cas.   (PR:AAA MPAA:NR)

MEET ME ON BROADWAY**   (1946) 78m COL bw

Marjorie Reynolds (Ann Stallings), Fred Brady (Eddie Dolan), Jinx Falkenburg (Maxine Whittaker), Spring Byington (Sylvia Storm), Loren Tindall (Bob Storm), Gene Lockhart (John Whittaker), Allen Jenkins (Deacon McGill), William Forrest (Dwight Ferris), Jack Rice (Grannis).

Brady is an arrogant young director with aspirations of making it big on Broadway. His attitude, however, leaves him with nothing to stage but an amateur country club show. Brady gets a boost in the right direction after falling for Reynolds, whose dad is the rich owner of the country club. Musical numbers include: "I Never Had a Chance," "Fifth Avenue," "Is It Worth It?," "Only for Me" (Saul Chaplin, Edgar De Lange), "She Was a Good Girl" (Allan Roberts, Doris Fisher).

p, Burt Kelly; d, Leigh Jason; w, George Bricker, Jack Henley (based on the story by Bricker); ph, Burnett Guffey; ed, James Sweeney; md, M. W. Stoloff; art d, Stephen Goosson, Walter Holscher.

Musical   (PR:A MPAA:NR)

MEET ME TONIGHT   (SEE: TONIGHT AT 8:30, 1953, Brit.)

MEET MISS BOBBY SOCKS*   (1944) 68m COL bw

Bob Crosby (Don Collins), Lynn Merrick (Helen Tyler), Louise Erickson (Susan Tyler), Robert White (Howard Barnes), Howard Freeman (Mr. Tyler), Mary Currier (Mrs. Tyler), Pat Parrish (Gloria), Sally Bliss (Pillow), John Hamilton (Swanson), Douglas Wood (Whitaker), Pierre Watkin (Quinlan), Louis Jordan and the Tympany Five, The Kim Loo Sisters.

Crosby returns from the war to become a nightclub singer. With the help of his fans and love interest Merrick, he rises to the top. This film was made to ride along on the Frank Sinatra craze, which was just then beginning to take off in spectacular fashion after four movies. Includes the songs: "Fellow On A Furlough" (Bobby Worth), "I'm Not Afraid" (Kim Gannon, Walter Kent), "Come With Me, My Honey" (Mack David, Joan Whitney, Alex Kramer), "Two Heavens" (Don George, Ted Grouya), "Deacon Jones" (Johnny Lange, Hy Heath, Charles Loring).

p, Ted Richmond; d, Glenn Tryon; w, Muriel Roy Bolton; ph, George Meehan; ed, Jerome Thoms; md, Marlin Skiles; art d, Lionel Banks, Carl Anderson.

Musical   (PR:A MPAA:NR)

MEET MISS MARPLE   (SEE: MURDER SHE SAID, 1961, Brit.)

MEET MR. CALLAGHAN**   (1954, Brit.) 88m Pinnacle/Eros bw

Derrick de Marney (Slim Callaghan), Harriette Johns (Cynthia Meraulton), Peter Neil (William Meraulton), Adrienne Corri (Mayola), Delphi Lawrence (Effie), Belinda Lee (Jenny Appleby), Larry Burns (Darkey), Trevor Reid (Inspector Gringall), John Longden (Jeremy Meraulton), Roger Williams (Bellamy Meraulton), Frank Henderson, Michael Partridge, Howard Douglas, Frank Sieman, Robert Adair, Michael Balfour.

Johns hires detective de Marney after her rich uncle changes his will in her favor. When he finds out the old man is already dead, he suspects her, but eventually unmasks her fiance as the killer. Mystery programmer has a couple of good moments, but little else.

p, Guido Coen, Derrick de Marney; d, Charles Saunders; w, Brock Williams (based on the play by Gerald Verner and the novel The Urgent Hangman by Peter Cheyney); ph, Harry Waxman.

Crime   (PR:A MPAA:NR)

MEET MR. LUCIFER**   (1953, Brit.) 81m EAL/GFD bw

Stanley Holloway (Mr. Sam Hollingsworth/Mr. Lucifer), Peggy Cummins (Kitty Norton), Jack Watling (Jim Norton), Barbara Murray (Patricia Pedelty), Joseph Tomelty (Mr. Pedelty), Kay Kendall (Lonely Hearts Singer), Gordon Jackson (Hector McPhee), Charles Victor (Mr. Elder), Humphrey Lestocq (Arthur Simmonds), Ernest Thesiger (Mr. Macdonald), Jean Cadell (Mrs. Macdonald), Frank

Pettingell (Mr. Roberts), Olive Sloane (Mrs. Stannard), Joan Sims (Fairy Queen), Raymond Huntley (Mr. Patterson), Ian Carmichael (Man Friday), Olga Gwynne (Principal Boy), Irene Handl (Lady with Dog), Gladys Henson (Lady in Bus), Edie Martin (Deaf Woman), Roddy Hughes (Billings), Eliot Makeham (Edwards), Dandy Nichols (Mrs. Clarke), Bill Fraser (Band Leader), Geoffrey Keen (Voice of Mr. Lucifer), Gilbert Harding, MacDonald Hobley, Philip Harben, David Miller (TV Personalities, Themselves), Eddie Leslie, Molly Hamley-Clifford, Toke Townley, Fred Griffiths, Herbert C. Walton, Diane Cilento.

Holloway, one of Satan's employees, causes some problems for a couple of people by introducing a new television set into their lives. Tomelty is given the set as a retirement gift, but soon finds himself in debt from all the liquor he's been serving to his curious viewer-neighbors. He sells the set to his upstairs boarders, newlyweds who end up arguing over it. A satire on the evils of television, which becomes an unintentional satire on the evils of careless filmmaking. If Ealing had devoted a little more effort to this picture, it could have been very funny.

p, Monja Danischewsky; d, Anthony Pelissier; w, Danischewsky, Peter Myers, Alec Graham (based on the play "Beggar My Neighbour" by Arnold Ridley); ph, Desmond Dickinson; m, Eric Rogers; ed, Bernard Gribble; art d, Wilfred Shingleton.

Comedy/Fantasy   (PR:A MPAA:NR)

MEET MR. MALCOLM*½   (1954, Brit.) 65m Corsair/ABF-Pathe bw

Adrianne Allen (Mrs. Durant), Sarah Lawson (Louie Knowles), Richard Gale (Colin Knowles), Duncan Lamont (Superintendent Simmons), Meredith Edwards (Whistler Grant), Pamela Galloway (Andria Durant), John Horsley (Tony Barlow), John Blythe (Carrington-Phelps), Claude Dampier (Joe Tutt), Nigel Green, Simone Lovell, Jean St. Clair, Derek Prentice.

Slow-moving mystery concerned with a body found at the base of a cliff with two cigarette butts and an empty pack. Gale is a mystery writer who helps the police solve the case. Not very interesting.

p, Theo Lageard; d, Daniel Birt; w, Brock Williams; ph, Hone Glendinning.

Crime   (PR:A MPAA:NR)

MEET MR. PENNY*½   (1938, Brit.) 70m BN/ABF bw

Richard Goolden (Henry Penny), Vic Oliver (Allgood), Fabia Drake (Annie Penny), Kay Walsh (Peggy Allgood), Patrick Barr (Clive Roberts), Hermione Gingold (Mrs. Wilson), Wilfrid Hyde-White (Mr. Wilson), Charles Farrell (Jackson), Hal Walters (Cecil), Joss Ambler (Gridley), Jack Raine (Preston), Renee Gadd (Mrs. Brown), Tom Gill, Daphne Raglan, Gilbert Davis.

Community residents, enraged that their allotments are going to have a warehouse built on them, hold a produce show, but drunk Goolden ruins the affair. Later he redeems himself and saves the allotments. Adapted from a popular radio series, the story should have stayed there.

p, John Corfield; d, David Macdonald; w, Victor Kendall, Doreen Montgomery (based on the radio series "Mr. Penny" by Maurice Moisiewitsch); ph, Bryan Langley.

Comedy   (PR:A MPAA:NR)

MEET MY SISTER*½   (1933, Brit.) 70m Pathe bw

Clifford Mollison (Lord Victor Wilby), Constance Shotter (Joan Lynton), Enid Stamp-Taylor (Lulu Marsac), Fred Duprez (Hiram Sowerby), Frances Dean (Helen Sowerby), Jimmy Godden (Pogson), Helen Ferrers (Hon. Christine Wilby), Patrick Barr (Bob Seymour), Syd Crossley (Butler), Frou-Frou.

Mollison plays a bankrupt lord who tries to break off with his mistress in order to marry the daughter of an American millionaire. Duprez, a master of farce, is outstanding. A well-acted and keenly directed picture.

p, Fred Watts; d, John Daumery; ph, Jack Parker, Gerald Gibbs.

Comedy   (PR:A MPAA:NR)

MEET NERO WOLFE***   (1936) 73m COL bw

Edward Arnold (Nero Wolfe), Joan Perry (Ellen Barstow), Lionel Stander (Archie Goodwin), Victor Jory (Claude Roberts), Nana Bryant (Sarah Barstow), Dennie Moore (Mazie Gray), Russell Hardie (Manuel Kimball), Walter Kingsford (E. J. Kimball), Boyd Irwin, Sr. (Prof. Barstow), John Qualen (Olaf), Gene Morgan (O'Grady), Rita Cansino [Hayworth] (Maria Maringola), Frank Conroy (Dr. Bradford), Juan Toreno (Carlo Maringola), Martha Tibbetts (Anna), Eddy Waller (Golf Starter), George Offerman, Jr. (Mike), William Benedict (Johnny), Raymond Borzage (Tommy), William Anderson (Bill), Eric Wilton (Butler), Al Matthews (Attendant), David Worth (Kimball's Chauffeur), Roy Bliss (Messenger Boy), Arthur Stewart Hull, Jay Owen, Henry Roquemore, Arthur Rankin.

Arnold is outstanding as the beer-gulping, orchid-growing sleuth who masterfully unravels baffling murder mysteries without ever leaving his comfortable home. A college president is suddenly murdered while playing golf and, with Stander doing the legwork, Arnold discovers that a young mechanic with an inventive flair had been forced to create a weird but effective blow-gun for shooting poisoned darts. The killer of the college president also disposes of the mechanic. Meanwhile, Arnold indulges in his culinary delights, working the pants off his personal chef, Qualen, and nurturing his orchids in his steamy hothouse. The tension and mystery are well conceived and sustained by director Biberman, and the script is taut and true to Stout's novel. Columbia intended to produce a long series of films based on Stout's girthsome character but Arnold bowed out, wanting more expansive roles and finding them with THE TOAST OF NEW YORK and COME AND GET IT. Next, with Stander still playing the loyal Archie, Columbia cast Walter Connolly in the detective role, but Connolly's severe asthmatic attacks would not permit him to continue the series. Connolly's only appearance as the indefatigable Nero Wolfe was in THE LEAGUE OF FRIGHTENED MEN (1937), which ended Columbia's once-hopeful series. Fledgling actress Rita Cansino, later Hayworth, appears briefly in this film, seeking the whereabouts of her missing brother; this was one of five films she made for Columbia as a freelancer until signing on as a contract player and later becoming the studio's top film goddess. Joan Perry, playing the female lead, later became the wife of Harry Cohn, Columbia's tyrannical boss, better known to his persecuted employees as "White Fang."

p, B. P. Schulberg; d, Herbert Biberman; w, Howard J. Green, Bruce Manning, Joseph Anthony (based on the novel *Fer de Lance* by Rex Stout); ph, Henry Freulich; ed, Otto Meyer; md, Howard Jackson; cos, Lon Anthony.

Mystery   **(PR:A MPAA:NR)**

MEET SEXTON BLAKE**   (1944, Brit.) 80m BN-Strand/Anglo American bw

David Farrar *(Sexton Blake)*, John Varley *(Tinker)*, Magda Kun *(Yvonne)*, Gordon McLeod *(Inspector Venner)*, Manning Whiley *(Raoul Sudd)*, Kathleen Harrison *(Mrs. Bardell)*, Dennis Arundell *(Johann Sudd)*, Cyril Smith *(Belford)*, Ferdy Mayne *(Slant-eyes)*, Betty Huntley-Wright *(Nobby)*, Jean Simmons *(Eva Watkins)*, Roddy Hughes, Charles Farrell, Tony Arpino, Charles Rolfe, Philip Godfrey, Billy Howard, John Powe, Mark Jones, Jack Vyvyan, Henry Wolston, David Keir, Elsie Wagstaff, Brookes Turner, Alfred Harris, Margo Johns, Olive Walter.

Detective Farrar is hired to find a ring and some photographs allegedly taken off the body of a man killed in an air raid. He learns that the objects are clues to the formula for a revolutionary new alloy for airplanes and that the villain is the stepbrother of the man who hired him. Overblown melodrama, but quite entertaining in an unintended way.

p, Louis H. Jackson; d&w, John Harlow (based on characters created by Harry Blyth); ph, Geoffrey Faithfull.

Crime   **(PR:A MPAA:NR)**

MEET SIMON CHERRY**   (1949, Brit.) 67m Hammer/Exclusive bw

Zena Marshall *(Lisa Colville)*, John Bailey *(Henry Dantry)*, Hugh Moxey *(Rev. Simon Cherry)*, Anthony Forwood *(Alan Colville)*, Ernest Butcher *(Young)*, Jeanette Tregarthen *(Monica Harling)*, Courtney Hope *(Lady Harling)*, Arthur Lovegrove *(Charlie)*, Gerald Case.

Moxey is an Anglican parson and amateur detective who clears Marshall of a murder charge when he proves that Tregarthen died of a heart attack. This low-budget adaptation of a radio series is competent enough.

p, Anthony Hinds; d, Godfrey Grayson; w, Gale Pedrick, Grayson, A. R. Rawlinson (based on the radio series "Meet the Rev" by Pedrick); ph, Cedric Williams.

Crime   **(PR:A MPAA:NR)**

MEET THE BARON**1/2   (1933) 67m MGM bw

Jack Pearl *(The Baron)*, Jimmy Durante *(Joe McGoo)*, ZaSu Pitts *(Zasu)*, Ted Healy *(Ted)*, Edna May Oliver *(Dean Primrose)*, Ben Bard *("Sharlie")*, Henry Kolker *(Real Baron)*, William B. Davidson *(Radio Man)*, Moe Howard, Jerry Howard, Larry Fine *(Stooges)*, Greta Meyer.

Pearl and Durante start in the African jungles, work their way to a ticker tape-lined Broadway, and end up at a girl's college where they stage a few production numbers. Pearl as the phony baron is lucky enough to be hounded by Pitts, who mistakes him for the real baron. It's a free-for-all where comedy bits are concerned, but the plot is too weak to add the needed support. An early appearance from The Three Stooges, before they were called that, adds some camp value.

p, David O. Selznick; d, Walter Lang; w, Arthur Kober, William K. Wells, Allen Rivkin, P. J. Wolfson (based on the story by Herman J. Mankiewicz, Norman Krasna); ph, Allen Siegler; ed, James E. Newcom; m/l, Dorothy Fields, Jimmy McHugh.

Comedy   **(PR:A MPAA:NR)**

MEET THE BOY FRIEND*   (1937) 63m REP bw

David Carlyle [Robert Paige] *(Tony Page)*, Carol Hughes *(June Delaney)*, Warren Hymer *("Bugs" Corrigan)*, Pert Kelton *(Beulah Potts)*, Andrew Tombes *(J. Ardmore Potts)*, Gwili Andre *(Vilma Vlare)*, Oscar and Elmer *(Themselves)*, Smiley Burnette *(Orchestra Leader)*, Syd Saylor *(Buddy)*, Leonid Kinskey *(Dr. Sokoloff)*, Selmer Jackson *(Madison)*, Cy Kendall *(Walters)*, Robert Middlemass *(McGrath)*, Mary Gordon *(Mrs. Grimes)*, Beverly Hillbillies *(Themselves)*.

Carlyle is America's top crooner, known as "America's Boy Friend," a title he hates as much as all the fame which surrounds him. When a shady actress tries to marry him, the niece of an insurance executive (who has taken a $300,000 antimarriage policy on the singer) succeeds in winning him over. She is, however, kidnaped in the process, forcing him to rescue her before the ceremony can take place. Nothing here to hold the interest, except (maybe) for a glimpse of Burnette out of his usual western garb.

p, Colbert Clark; d, Ralph Staub; w, Bradford Ropes (based on the story by Jack Raymond, Robert Arthur); ph, Ernest Miller; ed, William Morgan; m/l, Harry Tobias, Roy Ingraham, Smiley Burnette, Alberto Colombo.

Comedy/Romance   **(PR:A MPAA:NR)**

MEET THE CHUMP**   (1941) 60m UNIV bw

Hugh Herbert *(Hugh Mansfield)*, Lewis Howard *(John Mansfield)*, Jeanne Kelly [Jean Brooks] *(Madge Reilly)*, Anne Nagel *(Miss Burke)*, Kathryn Adams *(Gloria Mitchell)*, Shemp Howard *(Stinky Fink)*, Richard Lane *(Slugs)*, Andrew Tombes *(Revello)*, Hobart Cavanaugh *(Juniper)*, Charles Halton *(Dr. Stephanowsky)*, Martin Spellman *(Champ)*, Ed Gargan *(Muldoon)*, Iris Adrian *(Blonde)*, Michael Gaddis *(Man)*.

Herbert is an absent-minded executor of a $10 million estate which his nephew (Lewis Howard) will take control of on his 25th birthday. As that age approaches,

Herbert panics because he has allowed the trust funds to dwindle to almost nothing. Rather than admit he's botched up his nephew's finances he tries suicide, and finally decides to commit the nephew to a mental asylum to keep him from finding out the truth about the money. After a run-in with some gangsters everything gets straightened out. Jeanne Kelly later became known as Jean Brooks, appearing in some episodes of the FALCON series.

p, Ken Goldsmith; d, Edward F. Cline; w, Alex Gottlieb (based on the story by Hal Hudson, Otis Garrett); ph, Elwood Bredell; ed, Milton Carruth.

Comedy   **(PR:A MPAA:NR)**

MEET THE DUKE*1/2   (1949, Brit.) 64m New Park/ABF bw

Farnham Baxter *(Duke Hogan)*, Heather Chasen *(Carol)*, Gale Douglas *(Van Gard)*.

American boxer Baxter inherits a dukedom and a castle. When he goes to take up residence, he finds a group of suspicious-looking servants who turn out to be crooks searching for a treasure hidden in the house. Tolerable programmer with nothing to recommend it.

p, Link Neale; d, James Corbett; w, Farnham Baxter (based on the play "Ice on the Coffin" by Temple Saxe); ph, Ernest Palmer.

Comedy   **(PR:A MPAA:NR)**

MEET THE GIRLS*1/2   (1938) 66m FOX bw

June Lang *(Judy Davis)*, Lynn Bari *(Terry Wilson)*, Robert Allen *(Charles Tucker)*, Ruth Donnelly *(Daisy Watson)*, Gene Lockhart *(Homer Watson)*, Erik Rhodes *(Maurice Leon)*, Wally Vernon *(Delbert Jones)*, Constantine Romanoff *(Tiny)*, Jack Norton *(Fletcher)*, Emmett Vogan *(Mr. Brady)*, Paul McVey *(Collins)*, Harlan Briggs *(Captain)*.

Entertainers Lang and Bari lose their jobs in Honolulu and stow away on a San Francisco-bound liner. They get mixed up with a gang of jewel thieves and have to prove their innocence before they can safely land on their home shores. An ocean liner caper that failed to make many waves.

p, Howard J. Green; d, Eugene Forde; w, Marguerite Roberts; ph, Edward Snyder; ed, Fred Allen; md, Samuel Kaylin.

Comedy/Crime   **(PR:A MPAA:NR)**

MEET THE MAYOR*   (1938) 62m Times bw

Frank Fay *(Spencer Brown)*, Ruth Hall *(Norma Baker)*, Hale Hamilton *(George Diamond)*, George Meeker *(Harry Bayliss)*, Berton Churchill *(Martin Sloan)*, Eddie Nugent *(Steve)*, Esther Howard *(Mrs. Prescott)*, Franklin Pangborn *(Hotel Clerk)*, Nat Pendleton *(Kelly)*, Nick Copeland *(Copeland)*, Eddie Borden *(Catlett)*.

A vehicle for the vaudeville and radio act of Fay, who not only acts in this one but also wrote and produced it. He plays a small-town hotel elevator operator who gets drawn into a battle for town mayor. A weak script and poor camerawork don't do much for Fay's material.

p, Frank Fay; d, Ralph Cedar; w, Walter DeLeon, Charles Belden (based on the story by Fay); ph, William Rees; m, Edward Ward; ed, Don Hayes.

Comedy   **(PR:A MPAA:NR)**

MEET THE MISSUS**   (1937) 65m RKO bw

Victor Moore *(Otis Foster)*, Helen Broderick *(Emma Foster)*, Anne Shirley *(Louise Foster)*, Alan Bruce *(Steve Walton)*, Edward H. Robins *(Gordon Cutting)*, William Brisbane *(Prentiss)*, Frank M. Thomas *(Barney Lott)*, Ray Mayer *(Mr. White)*, Ada Leonard *(Princess Zarina)*, George Irving *(Magistrate)*, Alec Craig *(College President)*, Willie Best *(Mose)*, Virginia Sale *(Mrs. Moseby)*, Jack Norton *(Mr. Norton)*, Valerie Bergere *(Mrs. North-West)*, Frederic Santley *(Mr. Corn Belt)*, Don Wilson *(Radio Announcer)*.

A tired comedy which misses the mark as far as laughs are concerned. Broderick is the domineering wife of Moore, who stays home and tends to the housework while his wife goes about her day. She spends all her time clipping newspaper coupons and entering a wide array of contests. When she enters the "Happy Noodles Housewives' Competition" she is beaten by Moore, who's had more than enough practice.

p, Albert Lewis; d, Joseph Santley; w, Jack Townley, Bert Granet, Joel Sayre (based on the novel *Lady Average* by Jack Goodman, Albert Rice); ph, Jack Mackenzie; ed, Frederic Knudtson; md, Roy Webb; art d, Van Nest Polglase.

Comedy   **(PR:A MPAA:NR)**

MEET THE MISSUS**1/2   (1940) 64m REP bw

Roscoe Karns *(Joe Higgins)*, Ruth Donnelly *(Lil Higgins)*, Spencer Charters *(Grandpa)*, George Ernest *(Sidney Higgins)*, Lois Ranson *(Betty Higgins)*, Polly Moran *(Widow Jones)*, Astrid Allwyn *(Violet)*, Alan Ladd *(Johnny Williams)*, Harry Woods *(Shillingford)*, Dorothy Ann Seese *(Millie Lou)*, Harry Tyler *(Mr. Godfrey)*.

An enjoyable Higgins family tale which has Ernest losing $5,000 worth of bonds he was delivering. His dad, Karns, comes up with the idea of marrying their grandpa, Charters, to a wealthy old widow. Charters sends the old dame a letter stating his intentions, but Karns succeeds in getting a bank loan. Charters is left in a jam, and finally has to decide not to marry the woman, but she sues for breach of promise. The madcap adventures of this crazy family are all straightened out by the finale. (See HIGGINS FAMILY series, Index.)

p, Robert North; d, Mal St. Clair; w, Val Burton, Ewart Adamson, Taylor Cavan; ph, Ernest Miller; ed, Ernest Nims.

Comedy   **(PR:A MPAA:NR)**

MEET THE MOB**   (1942) 62m MON bw

ZaSu Pitts *(Aunt Emma)*, Roger Pryor *(Terry)*, Warren Hymer *(Joe)*, Gwen Kenyon *(Maris)*, Douglas Fowley *(Gus Hammond)*, Elizabeth Russell *(Zelda)*, Tristram Coffin

(Henderson), Lester Dorr (Duke), Wheeler Oakman (Blackie), Gene O'Donnell (Steve), Irving Mitchell (Crenshaw), Bud McTaggart (Mickey).

Pitts is a spinster from the country who, after reading in the paper of her son's notoriety, visits the city. She finds the boy involved with some gangsters who mistake her for a feared murderess. They lay out the red carpet for Pitts, who works to keep her kid honest. A nifty idea that, unfortunately, doesn't work as well as it could have.

p, Lindsley Parsons; d, Jean Yarbrough; w, George Bricker, Edmond Kelso (based on the story by Harry Hervey); ph, Mack Stengler; ed, Jack Ogilvie; md, Edward Kay.

Comedy/Crime (PR:A MPAA:NR)

MEET THE NAVY**½ (1946, Brit.) 85m BN/Anglo-American bw-c

Lionel Murton (Johnny), Margaret Hurst (Midge), John Pratt (Horace), Robert Goodier (Tommy), Phyllis Hudson (Jenny), Percy Haynes (Cook), Bill Oliver (C.P.O. Oliver), Jeanette de Hueck (Gracie), Oscar Natzke (Fisherman), Alan Lund, Mae Richards (Dancers).

An entertaining British musical that takes a behind-the-scenes look at the Royal Canadian Navy revue which entertains Allied troops before arriving in London to perform for the Royal Family.

p, Louis H. Jackson; d, Alfred Travers; w, Lester Cooper, James Seymour (based on a story by Cooper); ph, Ernest Palmer, Moray Grant (Technicolor sequence); m, Louis Silvers, Larry Ceballos; md, Eric Wilde, Bonnie Munro.

Musical Cas. (PR:A MPAA:NR)

MEET THE NELSONS (SEE: HERE COME THE NELSONS, 1952)

MEET THE PEOPLE** (1944) 99m MGM bw

Lucille Ball (Julie Hampton), Dick Powell (William "Swanee" Swanson), Virginia O'Brien ("Woodpecker" Peg), Bert Lahr ("The Commander"), Rags Ragland (Mr. Smith), June Allyson (Annie), Steve Geray (Uncle Felix), Paul Regan ("Buck"), Howard Freeman (Mr. Peetwick), Betty Jaynes (Steffi), John Craven (John Swanson), Morris Ankrum (Monte Rowland), Miriam LaVelle (Miriam), Ziggie Talent (Ziggie), Mata & Hari (Oriental Dancers), Vaughn Monroe and his Orchestra, The King Sisters, Spike Jones and His City Slickers, Kay Medford (Mrs. Smith), Joey Ray (Dance Director), Patsy Moran (Homely Girl), Pat West (Man), Roger Moore (Chauffeur), Celia Travers (Secretary), Robert Emmett O'Connor (Attendant), Fred "Snowflake" Toones (Pullman Porter), Bobby Blake (Jimmy-Age 7), Dickie Hall (Billy-Age 5), Russell Gleason (Bill), Myron Healey (Marine), Creighton Hale (Hotel Clerk), Leon Belasco (Dress Designer), Thelma Joel, Barbara Bedford, Mary Ganley, Katharine Booth, Mary McLeod (Girls), Lucille Casey, Natalie Draper, Alice Eyland, Noreen Nash, Linda Deane, Hazel Brooks, Eve Whitney, Erin O'Kelly, Peggy Maley, Kay Williams, Florence Lundeen (Show Girls).

Ball is a Broadway performer who finds herself attracted to playwright/welder Powell. When she gains the rights to his play and takes the lead role, Powell dismisses her from the cast because she is too snobbish. To prove him wrong, she takes a job at a Maryland shipyard to "meet the people" and ends up winning over her fellow workers, as well as Powell. Some fine tunes offset the routine script. Included are "Meet the People" (Ralph Freed, Sammy Fain; sung by Dick Powell), "In Times Like These" (Freed, Fain; sung by Powell, Lucille Ball, Vaughn Monroe), "Schickelgruber" (Freed, Fain; sung by Spike Jones and His City Slickers); "I Like to Recognize the Tune" (Richard Rodgers, Lorenz Hart; sung by June Allyson, Monroe, Ziggy Talent, Virginia O'Brien), "It's Smart to Be People" (E. Y. Harburg, Burton Lane), and "Say That It's Sweethearts Again" (Earl Brent; sung by O'Brien).

p, E. Y. Harburg; d, Charles Reisner; w, S. M. Herzig, Fred Saidy (based on a story by Sol Barzman, Ben Barzman, Louis Lantz); ph, Robert Surtees; ed, Alexander Troffey; md, Lennie Hayton; art d, Cedric Gibbons; ch, Sammy Lee, Charles Walters, Jack Donohue.

Musical (PR:A MPAA:NR)

MEET THE STEWARTS**½ (1942) 72m COL bw

William Holden (Michael Stewart), Frances Dee (Candace Goodwin), Grant Mitchell (Mr. Goodwin), Marjorie Gateson (Mrs. Goodwin), Anne Revere (Geraldine Stewart), Roger Clark (Ted Graham), Danny Mummert (John Goodwin), Ann Gillis (Jane Goodwin), Margaret Hamilton (Willametta), Don Beddoe (Taxi Driver), Mary Gordon (Mrs. Stewart), Edward Gargan, Tom Dugan (Moving Men), Marguerite Chapman (Ann), William Wright (Winkie), Arthur Loft (Man), Ed Thomas (Waiter), Barbara Brown (Woman), Ralph Sanford (Cop), Boyd Davis (Mr. Brighton), Willie Fung (Wong), Chester Clute (Mr. Hamilton).

A pleasant marital comedy in which 24-year-old Holden agrees to marry the wealthy Dee if she will live within his modest means. She is able to meet the challenge initially, but she eventually sends Holden spinning with a nasty country club bill, and the pair splits. A comic reunion brings them together by the finale. The story is routine, but the fine supporting cast—Gateson, Mitchell, Hamilton, Beddoe—does a commendable job.

p, Robert Sparks; d, Alfred E. Green; w, Karen DeWolf (based on the story "Something Borrowed" from the "Candy and Mike Stewart" magazine story series by Elizabeth Dunn), ph, Henry Freulich; m, Leo Shuken; ed, Al Clark; md, M. W. Stoloff; art d, Lionel Banks.

Comedy (PR:A MPAA:NR)

MEET THE WIFE** (1931) 76m CC/COL bw

Laura LaPlante (Gertrude Lennox), Lew Cody (Philip Lord), Joan Marsh (Doris Bellamy), Harry Myers (Harvey Lennox), Claude Allister (Victor Staunton), William Janney (Gregory Brown), Edgar Norton.

In this tired comedy, LaPlante finds herself in a bind. Already married to Myers, she is thrown into a state of confusion when her supposedly dead husband, Cody, turns up. There are a few funny bits, but not enough to sustain interest.

d, A. Leslie Pearce; w, F. McGrew Willis, Walter DeLeon (based on the play by Lynn Starling); ph, Charles Van Enger, Glen Kershner; ed, Jack English.

Comedy (PR:A MPAA:NR)

MEET THE WILDCAT* (1940) 65m UNIV bw

Ralph Bellamy (Brod William), Margaret Lindsay (Ann Larkin), Joseph Schildkraut (Leon Dumeray), Allen Jenkins (Max, Cab Driver), Jerome Cowan (Digby Vanderhood), Robert O. Davis (Feral), Frank Puglia (Chief of Police), Guy D'Ennery (Mordaunt), Hans Herbert (Marco), Juan De La Cruz (Director), Reed Hadley (Basso), Gloria Franklin (Annabelle Lee), Iris Adrian (Blande).

Bellamy is a New York cop on the trail of an art thief known as "The Wildcat." Also trailing the thief is reporter Lindsay, who mistakes Bellamy for the real culprit. They both land in jail, and Bellamy plans to escape by dressing up in Lindsay's clothes. Set in Mexico City, the picture lacks a sure directorial hand and a plausible script.

p, Joseph G. Sanford; d, Arthur Lubin; w, Alex Gottlieb; ph, Stanley Cortez; ed, Arthur Hilton.

Crime/Comedy (PR:A MPAA:NR)

MEET WHIPLASH WILLIE (SEE: FORTUNE COOKIE, THE, 1966)

MEETING AT MIDNIGHT (SEE: CHARLIE CHAN IN BLACK MAGIC, 1944)

MEETINGS WITH REMARKABLE MEN** (1979, Brit.) 110m Remar/Libra c

Dragan Maksimovic (G.I. Gurdjieff), Terence Stamp (Prince Lubovedsky), Athol Fugard (Professor Skridlov), Gerry Sundquist (Karpenko), Bruce Myers (Yelov), Warren Mitchell (Gurdjieff's Father), Mikica Dimitrijevic (Young Gurdjieff), Donald Sumpter (Pogossian), Natasha Parry (Vitvitskaia), Fahro Konjhodzic (Soloviev), Tom Fleming (Father Giovanni), David Markham (Dean Borsh), Fabijan Sovagovic (Dervish), Bruce Purchase (Father Maxim), Martin Benson (Dr. Ivanov), Roger Lloyd Pack (Pavlov), Sami Tahasuni (Bogga Eddin), Malcolm Hayes (Teacher), Constantin De Goguel (Captain), Colin Blakeley (Tamil), Jeremy Wilkin (Artillery Officer), Alan Tilvern, Tony Vogel, Ian Hogg, Ben Zimet, Ahmet Kutbay, Abbas Moayeri, Cimenli Fahrettin, Gregoire Aslan, Oscar Peck, Mitchell Horner, Nigel Greaves, Paul Henley.

This film is based on the memoirs of G.I. Gurdjieff, the inspirational and meditative cult figure who set out across Asia to discover the essence of life. He begins his search as a questioning youngster, and develops into a knowledgeable teacher who mixes dance and meditation. Directed by the theatrical experimentalist Peter Brook, the film is never quite as remarkable as the men Gurdjieff meets.

p, Stuart Lyons; d, Peter Brook; w, Jeanne de Salzmann, Brook (based on the book by G. I. Gurdjieff); ph, Gilbert Taylor (Eastmancolor); m, Thomas De Hartmann, Laurence Rosenthal; ed, John Jympson; prod d, George Wakhevitch; set d, Malak Khazai.

Biography (PR:A MPAA:G)

MEGAFORCE zero (1982) 99m Golden Harvest/FOX c

Barry Bostwick (Ace Hunter), Persis Khambatta (Zara), Michael Beck (Dallas), Edward Mulhare (Byrne-White), George Furth (Professor Eggstrum), Henry Silva (Guerera), Michael Kulcsar (Ivan), Ralph Wilcox (Zac), Evan Kim (Suki), Anthony Penya (Sixkiller), J. Victor Lopez (Lopez), Michael Carven (Anton), Bobby Bass (Motorcyclist), Samir Kamour (Aide), Youssef Merhi (Radio Operator), Roger Lowe (Chauffeur), Robert Fuller (Pilot), Ray Hill, Jr. (Tank Commander).

A smash-'em-up futuristic fantasy about a near-defenseless little country being invaded by a technologically advanced superpower. In an inexplicable bit of casting, Bostwick stars as Ace Hunter, a jump-suited rider/pilot of a flying motorcycle. This film cost well over $20 million, and it looks like every cent of the budget was spent without an inkling of intelligence. Former stuntman Hal Needham, who also is responsible for several action pictures starring Burt Reynolds, directed this megaflop. At least he's consistent.

p, Albert S. Ruddy; d, Hal Needham; w, James Whittaker, Ruddy, Needham, Andre Morgan (based on a story by Robert Kachler); ph, Michael Butler (Panavision, Technicolor); m, Jerrold Immel; ed, Patrick Roark, S. Skip Schoolnik; prod d, Joel Schiller; art d, Carlo Wenger; spec eff, Cliff Wenger, Sr.; m/l, Kevin Russell, Tod Howarth, Jonathan Cain, James McClarty (performed by 707).

Science Fiction Cas. (PR:C MPAA:PG)

MEGLIO VEDOVA (SEE: BETTER A WIDOW, 1969, Fr./Ital.)

MEIN KAMPF—MY CRIMES** (1940, Brit.) 75m ABF bw

Herbert Lom, Robert Beatty, Peter Ustinov.

With WW II raging over in Europe, anti-German propaganda was a popular subject for British filmgoers. This work was no exception. The pseudo-documentary took its title from Hitler's treatise, portraying his rise to power in Germany. One moment has a traitorous young man turning his father over to the Gestapo for speaking out against Hitler. This was a remake of sorts of the similar French film APRES MEIN KAMPF—MES CRIMES.

p, Walter C. Mycroft; d, Norman Lee; w, Alec Dyer; ph, Walter James Harvey.

Drama (PR:C MPAA:NR)

MELANIE** (1982, Can.) 109m Simcom/EM c

Glynnis O'Connor (Melanie Daniel), Burton Cummings (Rick Manning), Paul Sorvino (Walter Greer), Trudy Young (Rondo Colton), Don Johnson (Carl Daniel),

Jamie Dick (*Tyler Daniel*), Donann Caven (*Ginny*), Jodie Drake (*Eula Gibson*), L. Q. Jones (*Buford*), Lisa Dal Bello (*Marcie*), Yvonne Murray (*Brandy*), David Willis (*Darryl Adrian*).

Though overrun with cliches, MELANIE is still an entertaining tale about an illiterate Arkansas woman (O'Connor), who loses custody of her young son to her husband (Johnson). Hoping to find her son, she takes off for the California army base where her husband is stationed. She drops in on her friend, Young, who is living with a has been rock star struggling to make a comeback (Cummings, formerly of the Guess Who, in a semi-autobiographical role). Eventually, O'Connor and Cummings fall in love to the dismay of Sorvino, the lawyer who has asked for O'Connor's hand. Their romance is the catalyst Cummings needs, sending him back to the top of the charts. The film is riddled with formulas from start to finish, some of which work. Some strong performances (especially Sorvino's) hold it together.

p, Peter Simpson; d, Rex Bromfield; w, Robert Guza, Jr., Richard Paluck (based on the story by Michael Green); ph, Richard Ciupka; m, Paul Zaza; ed, Brian Rovak; prod d, Roy Forge Smith; m/l, Burton Cummings.

Drama   **Cas.**   **(PR:A MPAA:NR)**

MELBA**¹/₂   (1953, Brit.) 113m Horizon/UA c

Patrice Munsel (*Nellie Melba*), Robert Morley (*Oscar Hammerstein*), John McCallum (*Charles Armstrong*), John Justin (*Eric Walton*), Alec Clunes (*Cesar Carlton*), Sybil Thorndike (*Queen Victoria*), Joseph Tomelty (*Thomas Mitchell*), Martita Hunt (*Mme. Marchesi*), Beatrice Varley (*Aunt Catherine*), Marcel Poncin (*Roger*), Theodore Bikel (*Paul Brotha*), Violetta Elvin (*Prima Ballerina*), Cecile Chevreau (*Annette*), Charles Craig, the Orchestra and Chorus of the Covent Garden Opera, the Sadler's Wells Ballet.

One of Milestone's two British films of the 1950s, MELBA was a misfired attempt to ride the coattails of a recently filmed Gilbert and Sullivan biography. It's the story of opera singer Nellie Melba (Munsel) who, in flashback, details her rise to fame from her humble Australian farm girl beginnings. Opera fans will enjoy the singing, but there's not much else here. Musical numbers include the mad scene from Gaetano Donizetti's opera "Lucia Di Lammermoor," excerpts from Giuseppe Verdi's "La Traviata," and "Is This the Beginning Of Love?" (Norman Newell, Mischa Spoliansky).

p, S. P. Eagle [Sam Spiegel]; d, Lewis Milestone; w, Harry Kurnitz; ph, Ted Scaife, Arthur Ibbetson (Technicolor); ed, W. J. Lewthwaite; md, Muir Mathieson, Dennis Arundel; art d, Andre Andrejew; ch, Pauline Grant.

Musical/Biography   **(PR:A MPAA:NR)**

MELINDA*¹/₂   (1972) 109m MGM c

Calvin Lockhart (*Frankie J. Parker*), Rosalind Cash (*Terry Davis*), Vonetta McGee (*Melinda*), Paul Stevens (*Mitch*), Rockne Tarkington (*Tank*), Ross Hagen (*Gregg Van*), Renny Roker (*Dennis Smith*), Judyann Elder (*Gloria*), Jim Kelly (*Charles Atkins*), Jan Tice (*Marcia*), Lonne Elder (*Lt. Daniels*), Edmund Cambridge (*Detective*), George Fisher (*Young Man*), Allen Pinson (*Rome*), Joe Hooker (*Rome's Servant*), Jack Manning (*Bank Man*), Gene LeBell (*Hood*), Gary Pagett (*Sgt. Adams*), Khalil Bezaleel (*Washington*), Nina Roman (*Bank Woman*), Jeanie Bell (*Jean*), Earl Maynard, Dori Dixon, Douglas C. Lawrence, Evelyne Cuffee, Peaches Jones (*Karate Group*).

A black-exploitation film that attempts to treat the characters with intelligence, but fails in terms of a working script. Lockhart is a hip, narcissistic deejay who plots revenge after his girl friend (McGee) is brutally murdered in his apartment. With the help of Cash, Lockhart tries to learn why McGee was killed and who was behind it. He discovers a tape recording that ties mobster Stevens to the assassination of a union leader. McGee was in possession of the tape and paid for it with her life. There is an excess of violence (which goes hand-in-hand with the genre) and some fine karate work by Kelly, a businessman who comes to Lockhart's aid. There is also an attempt, however weak, at romance between Lockhart and Cash—unusual for this genre.

p, Pervis Atkins; d, Hugh A. Robertson; w, Lonne Elder III (based on the story by Raymond Cistheri); ph, Wilmer C. Butler (Metrocolor); m, Jerry Butler, Jerry Peters; ed, Paul L. Evans; art d, Edward C. Carfagno; set d, Sal Blydenburgh; stunts, George Fisher; makeup, Ray Brooks.

Action/Crime   **(PR:O MPAA:R)**

MELODIE EN SOUS-SOL   (SEE: ANY NUMBER CAN WIN, 1963, Fr.)

MELODY***

     (1971, Brit.) 103m Hemdale-Sagittarius/Levitt-Pickman c (AKA: S.W.A.L.K.)

Jack Wild (*Ornshaw*), Mark Lester (*Daniel Latimer*), Tracy Hyde (*Melody Perkins*), Colin Barrie (*Chambers*), Billy Franks (*Burgess*), Ashley Knight (*Stacey*), Craig Marriott (*Dadds*), William Vanderpuye (*O'Leary*), Peter Walton (*Fensham*), Camille Davies (*Muriel*), Dawn Hope (*Maureen*), Kay Skinner (*Peggy*), Sheila Steafel (*Mrs. Latimer*), Kate Williams (*Mrs. Perkins*), Roy Kinnear (*Mr. Perkins*), Hilda Barry (*Grandma Perkins*), James Cossins (*Headmaster*), Ken Jones (*Mr. Dicks*), June Jago (*Miss Fairfax*), June Ellis (*Miss Dimkins*), Tim Wylton (*Mr. Fellows*), John Gorman (*Boys' Brigade Captain*), Petal Young (*Betty*), Robin Hunter (*George*), Neil Hallett, Tracy Reed (*Man and Woman in Hospital, TV Film*), Deborah Childs, Heather Gibson, Susan Hassell, Sara Maddern, Stephanie Muldenhall, Jacqueline Pullen, Leslie Roach, Caroline Stratford, Gill Wain, Karen Williams (*Girls' Group*), Leonard Brockwell, Billy Ferguson, Robin Hopwood, Nigel Kingsley, Peter Lewis, Stephen Mallett, Kenny Robson, Tommy Skipp, Wayne Thistleton, Roy Wain, Ricky Wales (*Boys' Group*).

OLIVER! star Lester is a pre-teen who falls in love with and plans to marry Hyde, a young cutie his own age. They inform their parents of their desire to wed, despite the pleas of their older friend Wild (another OLIVER! veteran). While the picture

isn't very convincing, the actors' unrelenting innocence more than makes up for it. A plus for Bee-Gees fans is a fine score which is worlds apart from SATURDAY NIGHT FEVER. Songs include: "Teach Your Children" (Crosby, Stills, Nash and Young), "In the Morning of My Life," "Spicks and Specks" (Barry Gibb), "Melody Fair," "Give Your Best to the First of May," "To Love Somebody" (Bee Gees), "Working on it Night and Day" (Richard Hewson, Gordon Gray, sung by the Bee Gees). Scriptwriter Parker would go on to direct MIDNIGHT EXPRESS and PINK FLOYD—THE WALL, and producer Puttnam would later deliver CHARIOTS OF FIRE.

p, David Puttnam; d, Waris Hussein, Andrew Birkin; w, Alan Parker; ph, Peter Suschitzky (Technicolor); m, The Bee-Gees, Richard Hewson; ed, John Victor Smith; art d, Roy Stannard; makeup, Betty Blattner.

Drama   **Cas.**   **(PR:AAA MPAA:G)**

MELODY AND MOONLIGHT*¹/₂   (1940) 72m REP bw

Johnny Downs (*Danny O'Brian*), Barbara Jo Allen [Vera Vague] (*Adelaide*), Jerry Colonna (*Abner Kellogg*), Mary Lee (*Ginger*), Frank Jenks (*Butch Reilly*), Claire Carleton (*Gloria*), Jonathan Hale (*Otis Barnett*), Martin Lamont (*Standish Prescott*), Jane Frazee (*Kay Barnett*), The Kidoodlers.

Downs is a bellhop with high hopes of starting a tap dance routine with Frazee, whose millionaire father doesn't care for the idea. Eventually he comes around and sponsors the radio show that they appear on. It is a less than average musical entry, but in comparison with most of Republic's earlier musicals, it's a gem. It does feature a couple of near look-alikes with Frazee bearing more than a passing resemblance to Lana Turner, and Lee reminding one of a young Judy Garland. The chatty Allen was previously known to radio listeners as Vera Vague. Musical numbers include: "Rooftop Serenade," "Tahiti Honey," "Top O' The Mornin'," "I Close My Eyes," "Melody And Moonlight" (Jule Styne, Sol Meyer, George Brown).

p, Robert North; d, Joseph Santley; w, Bradford Ropes (based on a story by David Silverstein); ph, Ernest Miller; ed, Ernest Nims; md, Cy Feuer; art d, John Victor Mackey; Aida Broadbent.

Musical   **(PR:A MPAA:NR)**

MELODY AND ROMANCE**   (1937, Brit.) 71m BL bw

Hughie Green (*Hughie Hawkins*), Margaret Lockwood (*Margaret Williams*), Jane Carr (*Kay Williams*), Alastair Sim (*Prof. Williams*), Garry Marsh (*Warwick Mortimer*), C. Denier Warren (*Capt. Hawkins*), Julien Vedey (*Jacob*), Margaret Scudamore (*Mrs. Hawkins*), Joyce Cannon and Geraldine, Rex Roper and Maisie, Bobby Price, Audrey Foster, Joey Hopkinson, Mary Kelly, Connie Russell, Hughie Green's Gang.

Silly musical has Green trying to become a radio star. He meets and falls in love with Lockwood, the daughter of a scientist. Unable to get anywhere in his career, he brings a group of his friends into the act and becomes a success. On the night of their big radio show, the studio catches fire and Green saves Lockwood from death. Some talented cast members provide whatever reason there is for watching this one. This was Sim's sixteenth film after only two years in the business.

p, Herbert Smith; d, Maurice Elvey; w, L. duGarde Peach (based on a story by Leslie Howard Gordon, Elvey); ph, George Stretton.

Musical/Comedy   **(PR:A MPAA:NR)**

MELODY CLUB*   (1949, Brit.) 63m Tempean/Eros bw

Terry-Thomas (*Freddy Forrester*), Gwyneth Vaughan (*Jean*), Len Lowe (*Tony*), Bill Lowe (*Birdie*), Michael Balfour (*Max*), Lilian Grey, Arthur Gomez, Anthony Shaw, Sylvia Clark, Jack Mayne, Ida Patlanski.

Terry-Thomas, in one of his earliest starring roles, is a bumbling detective who manages to catch a gang of crooks at a nightclub despite his stupidity. Not an original joke to be found anywhere in this filler item.

p, Robert Baker, Monty Berman; d, Berman; w, Carl Nystrom; ph, Peter Newbrook.

Comedy   **(PR:A MPAA:NR)**

MELODY CRUISE**   (1933) 76m RKO bw

Charles Ruggles (*Pete Wells*), Phil Harris (*Alan Chandler*), Greta Nissen (*Ann Von Rader*), Helen Mack (*Laurie Marlowe*), Chick Chandler (*Hickey, Steward*), June Brewster (*Zoe*), Shirley Chambers (*Vera*), Florence Roberts (*Miss Potts*), Marjorie Gateson (*Mrs. Wells*), Betty Grable (*Stewardess*).

Ruggles and Harris are on a California-bound steamship full of desirable young gals. As much as Ruggles tries to keep millionaire Harris from ending up a husband, Harris finds himself a gal anyway. Before long, however, an argument between the two lovers results in the gal running away, causing Ruggles to hunt her down. This was the debut film for Academy Award winning short film director Sandrich (SO THIS IS HARRIS), and it was also the first feature for associate producer Brock, the one-time head of RKO's short film department, who insisted on Sandrich as director. Betty Grable makes a bit appearance as one of the anxious-to-wed ladies. Songs include: "I Met Her at a Party," "He's Not the Marrying Kind," "Isn't This a Night for Love," "This is the Hour" (Val Burton, Will Jason).

p, Merian C. Cooper; d, Mark Sandrich; w, Sandrich, Ben Holmes, Allen Rivkin, R. G. Wolfson (based on a story by Sandrich and Holmes); ph, Bert Glennon; ed, Jack Kitchen; art d, Van Nest Polglase, Carroll Clark.

Musical   **(PR:A MPAA:NR)**

MELODY FOR THREE**¹/₂   (1941) 67m RKO bw

Jean Hersholt (*Dr. Paul Christian*), Fay Wray (*Mary Stanley*), Walter Woolf King (*Antoine Pirelle*), Schuyler Standish (*Billy Stanley*), Patsy Lee Parsons (*Nancy Higby*), Maude Eburne (*Mrs. Hastings*), Astrid Allwyn (*Gladys McClelland*), Irene Ryan (*Mrs. Higby*), Donnie Allen (*Red Bates*), Leon Tyler (*Clarence*), Andrew

Tombes (*Mickey*), Irene Shirley (*Mrs. Mitchell*), Alexander Leftwich (*Mr. Simpson*), Toscha Seidel, Elvia Allman, Cliff Nazarro.

A change of pace for the Dr. Christian series has the medico (Hersholt) letting up on his practice and concentrating, instead, on trying to reunite a divorced couple. Wray is a music teacher with a violin virtuoso son (Standish) who takes a job as a nurse for Hersholt to supplement her income. When her ex-husband, orchestral conductor King, is identified as a plane crash victim, Hersholt calls Wray to assist on the case. An emotional reunion follows, with King joyfully discovering his son's talents. (See DR. CHRISTIAN series, Index.)

p, William Stephens; d, Erle C. Kenton; w, Leo Loeb, Walter Ferris; ph, John Alton; m, C. Bakaleinikoff; ed, Edward Mann; md, Bakaleinikoff; art d, Bernard Herzbrun.

Drama   **Cas.**   **(PR:A MPAA:NR)**

MELODY FOR TWO*1/2   (1937) 60m WB bw

James Melton (*Tod Weaver*), Patricia Ellis (*Gale Starr*), Marie Wilson (*Camille Casey*), Fred Keating (*"Remorse" Rumson*), Winifred Shaw (*Lorna Wray*), Craig Reynolds (*Bill Hallam*), Gordon Elliott (*Wilson*), Charles Foy (*"Scoop" Trotter*), Eddie "Rochester" Anderson (*Exodus Johnson*), Eddie Kane (*Alex Montrose*), Gordon Hart (*Woodruff*), Harry Hayden (*Armstrong*), Dick Purcell (*Mel Lynch*), Billie, Jack, and Donald O'Connor.

Unhappy with the arrangements he is given, band leader Melton leaves his group and his vocalist girl friend Ellis. The duo eventually reunite and together become a success over the airwaves. This was the last of three contracted pictures for Melton, whose career fizzled to nothingness after this effort. A list of fine tunes starting with the Al Dubin-Harry Warren composition "September in the Rain" also includes "A Flat in Manhattan," "An Excuse for Dancing," "Jose O'Neill, the Cuban Heel," "Dangerous Rhythm" (M. K. Jerome, Jack Scholl), "Melody for Two" (Dubin, Warren).

p, Bryan Foy; d, Louis King; w, George Bricker, Luci Ward, Joseph K. Watson (based on the story "Special Arrangements" by Richard Macaulay); ph, Arthur Todd; ed, Jack Saper; md, Leo F. Forbstein; cos, Milo Anderson; ch, Bobby Connolly, Richard Vreeland.

Musical   **(PR:A MPAA:NR)**

MELODY GIRL   (SEE: SING, DANCE, PLENTY HOT, 1940)

MELODY IN SPRING**   (1934) 75m PAR bw

Lanny Ross (*John Craddock*), Charlie Ruggles (*Warren Blodgett*), Mary Boland (*Mary Blodgett*), Ann Sothern (*Jane Blodgett*), George Meeker (*Wesley Prebble*), Herman Bing (*Wirt*), Joan Gale (*Suzan*), June Gale (*Suzette*), Jane Gale (*Suzanna*), Wade Boteler (*Anton*), William J. Irving (*2nd Guide*), Helen Lynd (*Blonde*), Thomas Jackson (*House Detective*), Wilfred Hari (*Suzuki*).

A minor film with some exquisite silliness from director McLeod. Ruggles is an eccentric collector who gathers such useless things as trophies and bedposts. He also does his darnedest to keep his daughter (Sothern) from falling into the clutches of energetic radio crooner Ross. Things look dim for the couple when Ruggles drags his daughter off to the Swiss Alps, but a happy ending follows. Tunes include: "Melody in Spring," "The Open Road," "It's Psychological," "Ending with a Kiss" (Harlan Thompson, Lewis Gensler).

p, Douglas MacLean; d, Norman Z. McLeod; w, Benn W. Levy (based on a story by Frank Leon Smith); ph, Henry Sharp; ed, Richard Currier.

Musical   **(PR:A MPAA:NR)**

MELODY IN THE DARK*   (1948, Brit.) 68m Advent/Adelphi bw

Ben Wrigley (*Ben*), Eunice Gayson (*Pat*), Richard Thorp (*Dick*), Dawn Lesley (*Dawn*), Myrette Morven, Russell Westwood, Lionel Newbold, Ida Patlanski, Neville Sidney, Alan Dean, Carl Carlisle, Maisie Weldon, The Keynotes, The Stardusters, The London Lovelies.

An actress inherits a spooky old mansion from her uncle and takes her company with her to take up residence. Beset by ghosts, they eventually find out that they are the victims of a hoax perpetrated by the servants, who have the uncle locked up, believing that they will inherit the house. Not much worthwhile, though Wrigley does his best.

p&d, Robert Jordan Hill; w, John Guillermin; ph, Jo Jago.

Musical/Comedy   **(PR:A MPAA:NR)**

MELODY INN   (SEE: RIDING HIGH, 1943)

MELODY LANE*1/2   (1929) 76m UNIV bw

Eddie Leonard (*Des Dupree*), Josephine Dunn (*Dolores Dupree*), Huntley Gordon (*Juan Rinaldi*), George E. Stone (*Danny Kay*), Jane La Verne, Rose Coe (*Constance Dupree*), Blanche Carter (*Nurse*), Jake Kern (*Orchestra Leader*), Monte Carter (*Stage Manager*).

A husband-and-wife vaudeville dance team, Leonard and Dunn, split up when the latter lands a legit acting role. After a couple of years the pair reunite—Dunn, a successful starlet, and Leonard, a struggling prop man. The unlikely event which brings them together is the injury of their young daughter. She miraculously recovers when dad literally sings her back to health. Being Universal's first all-talkie musical doesn't help the fact that the script and dialog are rather poorly conceived. Universal apparently felt, in the infancy of sound, that nothing mattered but the songs, which are, in fact, quite hummable. They include: "The Song of the Islands" (Charles King), "Here I Am," "There's Sugar Cane Round My Door," "The Boogy Man Is Here" (Eddie Leonard, Grace Stern, Jack Stern), "Roly Boly Eyes" (Leonard).

d, Robert F. Hill; w, Hill, J. G. Hawks (based on the play "The Understander" by Jo Swerling); ph, Joseph Brotherton; ed, Daniel Mandell; cos, Johanna Mathieson.

Musical   **(PR:A MPAA:NR)**

MELODY LANE*   (1941) 60m UNIV bw

Judd McMichael, Ted McMichael, Joe McMichael, Mary Lou Cook (*The Merry Macs*), Leon Errol (*McKenzie*), Anne Gwynne (*Patricia Reynolds*), Robert Paige (*Gabe Morgan*), Billy Lenhart (*Butch*), Kenneth Brown (*Buddy*), Don Douglas (*J. Roy Thomas*), Louis Da Pron (*Louis*), Clifford "Red" Stanley (*Slim*), Charles Coleman (*Mr. Abercrombis*), Will Lee (*Mr. Russo*), Tim Ryan (*Police Sergeant*), Barbara Brown (*Mrs. Stuart*), Baby Sandy.

The Merry Macs are cast as a foursome of Iowa entertainers who head for New York but get involved in some trouble when a radio sponsor interferes with the show. Tunes include: "Septimus Winner," "Peaceful Ends the Day," "Cherokee Charlie," "Let's Go to Calicabu," "Swing-a-Bye My Baby," "Changeable Heart," "If It's a Dream Don't Wake Me," "Since the Farmer in the Dell," "Caliacau" (Norman Berens, Jack Brooks), "Listen to the Mockingbird."

p, Ken Goldsmith; d, Charles Lamont; w, Hugh Wedlock, Jr., Howard Snyder, Morton Grant, George Rony (based on a story by Bernard Feins); ph, Jerome Ash; m, Roy Chamberlain; ed, Otto Ludwig; art d, Jack Otterson.

Musical   **(PR:A MPAA:NR)**

MELODY LINGERS ON, THE**   (1935) 65m Reliance/UA bw

Josephine Hutchinson (*Ann Prescott*), George Houston (*Salvini*), John Halliday (*Marco Turina*), Mona Barrie (*Sylvia Turina*), Helen Westley (*Manzoni*), Laura Hope Crews (*Mother Superior*), William Harrigan (*Jonesy*), David Scott (*Guido*), Walter Kingsford (*Croce*), Ferdinand Gottschalk (*Da Vigna*), Grace Poggi (*Carmen*), Inez Palange (*Louisa*), Frank Puglia (*Giuseppe*), Francesco Maran (*Lt. Zetti*), Adele St. Maur (*Celeste*), Eddie Conrad (*Fruit Vendor*), Gennaro Curci (*Innkeeper*), Eily Malyon (*Sister Maria*), Marion Ballou (*Sister Agnes*), Nina Campana, William von Brincken.

Hutchinson is the piano virtuosa mother of a war baby (Scott), fathered by Italian captain and opera singer Houston, who is subsequently killed while trying to save Hutchinson and Westley. Hutchinson commendably sacrifices her piano career in an attempt to locate the child she abandoned years earlier in a church. Houston competently performs several selections from Bizet's "Carmen."

p, Edward Small; d, David Burton; w, Ralph Block, Philip Dunne (based on a novel by Lowell Brentano); ph, Robert Planck; m, Georges Bizet; md, Alfred Newman; ch, Reginald LeBorg.

Musical/Drama   **(PR:A MPAA:NR)**

MELODY MAKER, THE*1/2   (1933, Brit.) 56m WB/FN bw

Lester Matthews (*Tony Borrodaile*), Joan Marion (*Mary*), Evelyn Roberts (*Reggie Bumblethorpe*), Wallace Lupino (*Clamart*), A. Bromley Davenport (*Jenks*), Vera Gerald (*Grandma*), Joan White (*Jerry*), Charles Hawtrey (*Tom*), Tonie Edgar Bruce (*Donna Lola*).

Matthews is a composer who falls in love with Marion, an aspiring composer. He takes the sonata she is entering in a competition and rewrites it as a musical comedy. Rejected from the competition for not being a proper sonata, it is later bought by a theatrical producer and Marion forgives Matthews. A weak programmer, all but forgotten.

p, Irving Asher; d, Leslie Hiscott.

Comedy   **(PR:A MPAA:NR)**

MELODY MAKER, 1946   (SEE: DING DONG WILLIAMS, 1946)

MELODY MAN**   (1930) 75m COL bw-c

William Collier, Jr. (*Al Tyler*), Alice Day (*Elsa*), John St. Polis (*Earl Von Kemper*), Johnny Walker (*Joe Yates*), Mildred Harris (*Martha*), Albert Conti (*Crown Prince Friedrich*), Tenen Holtz (*Gustav*), Lee Kohlmar (*Adolph*), Bertram Marburgh (*Van Baden, Austrian Minister of Police*), Anton Vaverka (*Emperor Franz Josef of Austria*), Major Nichols (*Bachman*).

St. Polis plays a murderous Viennese composer who kills his adulterous wife and her lover. He packs his bags and, with his young daughter, flees for the States. 18 years pass and the composer is earning his living as a Broadway restaurant musician. His daughter (Day) also has an interest in music and lands a job as an arranger with a jazz combo. She and her beau, one of the jazz players, rearrange an old composition of St. Polis'. The Austrian authorities take notice and bring the composer to justice. Loosely based on the play of the same name, this pic briefly employed the Technicolor process with a 12-minute opening sequence, and featured the tune "Broken Dreams" (Ballard McDonald, Arthur Johnston, Dave Dreyer; sung by Buster Collier).

d, R. William Neill; w, Howard J. Green (based on the play "Melody Man" by Richard Rodgers, Lorenz Hart); ph, Ted Tetzlaff; ed, Leonard Wheeler; art d, Harrison Wiley.

Musical/Drama   **(PR:A MPAA:NR)**

MELODY OF LIFE   (SEE: SYMPHONY OF SIX MILLION, 1932)

MELODY OF LOVE, THE**   (1928) 83m UNIV bw

Walter Pidgeon (*Jack Clark*), Mildred Harris (*Madelon*), Jane Winton (*Flo Thompson*), Tommy [Tom] Dugan (*Lefty*), Jack Richardson (*Music Publisher*), Victor Potel (*The Gawk*), Flynn O'Malley.

Songwriter Pidgeon enlists in the Army at the urging of his buddy, Dugan, and soon finds himself at the front. He leaves his gal behind and falls in love with French cabaret singer Harris. He is wounded by an enemy shell and loses the use of his right arm, so he is sent home. He tries to cuddle up to his jilted girl friend, but she sends him packing. Luckily for him, Harris loves him enough to make the transatlantic trip to the States, and by the hand of fate (or the scriptwriter) they meet. Naturally Pidgeon regains the use of his arm, and even more naturally composes a little tune for Harris. A pleasant picture which wouldn't be remembered if it weren't for its being Universal's first all-talkie. As with THE LIGHTS OF NEW YORK (the first all-talkie, released by Warner's three months earlier) this picture is full of the cinematic evils that accompanied the new sound technology. The camera was not allowed to move (a far cry from what one could see in the German expressionist cinema) out of fear that it would be audible on the soundtrack, and the actors' blocking was dictated by microphone placement. One of the real joys of these early talkies is trying to guess where the soundman hid the microphone. Carl Laemmle had to do some wheelin' and dealin' to get this picture made. He had asked William Fox if he could borrow some of Fox's Movietone sound equipment, ostensibly to perform some tests. After a week, the equipment was returned and THE MELODY OF LOVE was "in the can." The Fox Movietone system, with its optical sound stripe directly on the film, would become the standard method of synchronous sound recording, surpassing Warner's Vitaphone system of recording on discs.

d, A. B. Heath; w, Robert Arch, Robert Welsh (based on a story by Heath); ph, Walter Scott; ed, B. W. Burton.

Musical **(PR:A MPAA:NR)**

MELODY OF LOVE* (1954, Ital.) 96m IFE bw

Giacomo Rondinella *(Giacomo)*, Maria Fiore *(Maria)*, Giovanni Grasso *(Don Salvatore)*, Giuseppe Porelli *(Don Raffaele)*, Mirko Ellis *(Renato)*, Tina Pica *(Concetta)*, Carlo Romano *(Mr. Ferrario)*, Dante and Beniamino Maggio *(Dante and Beniamino)*, Nadia Gray *(Nadia)*.

Rondinella and childhood sweetheart Fiore are in love and want to marry, but Fiore's dad (Grasso) has other plans. He picks out a mate for the girl who's ready and willing to rise to the top of the business world. In the meantime, Rondinella heads for the stage, where he's chosen a career as an actor. Grasso's hand-picked mate turns out to be a drug-smuggler and the lovers wind up in each other's arms for the finale. Nothing of interest, though there is some fine singing by Rondinella, a pop singer with Radio-Rome. (In Italian; English subtitles.)

p, Roberto Amoroso; d, Mario Costa; w, A. G. Maiano, Amoroso, Costa; ph, Francesco Izzarelli; m, Gino Filippini.

Musical **(PR:A MPAA:NR)**

MELODY OF MY HEART* 1/2 (1936, Brit.) 82m Incorporated Talking Films/BUT bw

Derek Oldham *(Joe Montfort)*, Lorraine La Fosse *(Carmel)*, Bruce Seton *(Jim Brent)*, Hughes Macklin *(Mr. Smith)*, Dorothy Vernon *(Mrs. Dearwell)*, Macarthur Gordon *(Manager)*, Colin Cunningham *(Ramenado/Jose)*, Joe Velitch *(Pastias)*, Joyce St. Clair *(Mercedes)*, Clelia Matania, Adriana Otero, Robert Gilbert, Wensley Russell, Mabel Twemlow, Bobbie Slater, Clarissa Selwynne, Pearl Beresford, Doris Mortlock, Mignon Marchland, Ian Wilson, Stanley Radcliffe, James Carroll, Phil Sturgess, Jack Morris, Johnnie Schofield, Jack Jarman, Bombardier Billy Wells, Eleanor Hallam, Covent Garden Chorus, Horace Sheldon's Orchestra.

Odd musical thriller has La Fosse leaving her lover for a boxer. When the factory where she and her ex-lover work stages an amateur production of "Carmen", he sees his chance to do her in, but she is saved in the nick of time by the boxer. Justifiably forgotten today.

p, Brandon Fleming, George Barclay; d, Wilfred Noy; w, Fleming.

Musical **(PR:A MPAA:NR)**

MELODY OF THE PLAINS* (1937) 53m Spectrum bw

Fred Scott, Louise Small, Al St. John, David Sharpe, Lafe McKee, Bud Jamieson, Slim Whitaker, Hal Price, Lew Meehan, Carl Matthews, Billy Lenhart, George Morrell, George Fiske, White King the Horse.

A substandard cattle-rustlin' horse opry with Scott as the singing plainsman who pals up with little Lenhart, a fiddlin', singin', and dancin' 4-year-old. Harmed by some unusually sloppy direction from Newfield and haphazard lensing by Kline.

p, Ray Callaghan, Jed Buell; d, Sam Newfield; w, Bennett Cohen; ph, Robert Kline; ed, William Hess; m/l, Don Swander, June Hershey.

Western **(PR:A MPAA:NR)**

MELODY OF YOUTH (SEE: THEY SHALL HAVE MUSIC, 1939)

MELODY PARADE** (1943) 73m MON bw

Mary Beth Hughes *(Anne O'Rourke)*, Eddie Quillan *(Jimmy Tracy)*, Tim Ryan *(Happy Harrington)*, Irene Ryan *(Gloria Brewster)*, Mantan Moreland *(Skidmore)*, Andre Charlot *(Carroll White)*, Kenneth Harlan *(Jedson)*, Cy Ring *(Adams)*, Armida, Jerry Cooper, Anson Weeks and His Orchestra, Ted Fio Rito and His Orchestra, Loumel Morgan Trio, Ruloff, Follette and Lunard, Ramon Ros, Ruby Dandridge, Paul Porcasi.

Quillan is an ambitious busboy in a nightclub run by Tim Ryan, who is teetering on the brink of bankruptcy. Quillan repeatedly tries his hand at auditioning girls to sing in the club and one day Irene Ryan shows up. Quillan and owner Ryan mistake her for a wealthy heiress who can help get the club back on its feet. The business gets some new blood when hat-check girl Hughes gets a chance to deliver a few tunes. A confused, but fairly entertaining picture, which includes "I Don't Know," "Woman Behind the Man Behind the Gun," "Amigo," "Whatever Possessed Me," "Mr. and Mrs. Commando," "Don't Fall in Love," and "Speechless" (Eddie Cherkose, Edward Kay).

p, Lindsley Parsons; d, Arthur Dreifuss; w, Tim Ryan, Charles Marion; ph, Mack Stengler; m, Eddie Cherkose, Edward Kay; ed, Dick Currier; md, Kay; ch, Jack Boyle.

Musical **(PR:A MPAA:NR)**

MELODY RANCH** (1940) 84m REP bw

Gene Autry *(Gene)*, Jimmy Durante *(Cornelius J. Courtney)*, Ann Miller *(Julie Shelton)*, Barton MacLane *(Mark Wildhack)*, Barbara Jo Allen [Vera Vague] *(Veronica Whipple)*, George "Gabby" Hayes *(Pop)*, Jerome Cowan *(Tommy Summerville)*, Mary Lee *(Penny)*, Joseph Sawyer *(Jasper Wildhack)*, Horace MacMahon *(Bud Wildhack)*, Clarence Wilson *(Judge Henderson)*, William Benedict *(Slim)*, Ruth Gifford, Maxine Ardell, Veda Ann Borg, George Chandler, Jack Ingram, Lloyd Ingraham, John Merton, Horace Murphy, Tom London, Edmund Cobb, Slim Whitaker, Curley Dresden, Dick Elliott, Billy Bletcher, Art Mix, George Chesebro, Tiny Jones, Herman Hack, Jack Kirk, Merrill McCormack, Wally West, Bob Wills and the Texas Playboys, Frankie Marvin, Carl Cotner, Tex Cooper, Chick Hannon, Tom Smith, Champion the Horse.

Autry is invited to pay a visit to his hometown of Torpedo, Arizona, and makes honorary sheriff for the Frontier Days Celebration. When MacLane and his outlaw gang start raising a ruckus, Autry decides to wear the badge just as long as it takes to rid the town of the gang. Durante is at his best as the announcer of Autry's radio show. Advertised more as a musical than a Western, MELODY RANCH (the name of Autry's radio show) was helmed by Joseph Santley, who was better known on the sound stage. The film also featured an early role for Ann Miller, and radio comedienne Vera Vague (Barbara Joe Allen). Songs, all by Jule Styne and Eddie Cherkose, include, "Melody Ranch," "Call of the Canyon" (sung by Autry), "We Never Dream the Same Dream Twice" (Autry, Miller), "Vote for Autry" (Durante), "My Gal Sal" (Miller), "Torpedo Joe," "What Are Cowboys Made Of?" "Rodeo Rose," "Back in the Saddle Again," "Go Back to the City Again."

p, Sol C. Siegel; d, Joseph Santley; w, Jack Moffitt, F. Hugh Herbert, Sid Culler, Ray Golden; ph, Joseph August; ed, Murray Seldeen; md, Raoul Kraushaar, art d, Joseph Victor Mackay.

Musical/Western **Cas.** **(PR:A MPAA:NR)**

MELODY TIME* 1/2** (1948) 75m Disney/RKO c

Roy Rogers, Luana Patten, Bobby Driscoll, Ethel Smith, Bob Nolan, Sons of the Pioneers, and the voices of Buddy Clark, The Andrews Sisters, Fred Waring and his Pennsylvanians, Frances Langford, Dennis Day, Freddy Martin and His Orchestra, Jack Fina, The Dinning Sisters.

This was the last musical compilation film from the Disney studios and one of the best. It allowed Disney's animators to use their entire gamut of creative abilities, ranging from the irrepressible comedy of Donald Duck to the more refined work reminiscent of FANTASIA. After Clark is introduced as a linking narrator via a magical paint brush, the first sequence begins. A young couple out for an afternoon of ice-skating begin to argue. Their quarrel comes to an abrupt end when the boy saves the girl from a near drowning. Two rabbits witness the scene and re-enact all the business before it's finally revealed the story is a flashback memory of a long-married couple. Next is a marvelously surreal piece, dubbed "an instrumental nightmare." Using Rimski-Korsakov's "Flight of the Bumble Bee" jazzed up with the accompaniment of Freddy Martin and His Orchestra, we see a much befuddled honey-making insect buzzing about in a frenzied effort to escape a variety of musical perils. The third story is a re-telling of the Johnny Appleseed folktales with Day providing the voices. In the end, Appleseed is brought to heaven by an angel only to discover there are no apple trees there. But, the narrator tells us, there are apple blossoms to be found in the sky every time we see a group of clouds. "Little Toot" is a real treat. The title tugboat is constantly getting into trouble in his attempts to emulate its father. He is finally reprimanded by being sent out past the 12-mile limit but Little Toot redeems himself by saving a ship on a stormy night. Narration is provided in song by the Andrews Sisters. "Trees," an animated version of the Joyce Kilmer poem, is the most self-conscious work in the film. With Fred Waring and His Pennsylvanians providing the soundtrack music, this is Disney animation at it's best. A myriad of pictures with a connecting theme of trees is portrayed using color, light, and shadow to achieve its effects. "Blame It on the Samba" once more teams Donald Duck up with his pal Joe Carcioca from the popular cartoon "The Three Caballeros." The two sit bored and blue (no exaggeration!) until a cocktail with Ethel Smith as a sort of secret ingredient manages to perk up their spirits. They engage in a marvelous dance until at last the pair returns to Cafe Samba for a big finish. Also making a return from "The Three Caballeros" is an off-the-wall fowl which serves as a sort of samba-inclined bartender. The final segment features King of the Cowboys Roy Rogers and the Sons of the Pioneers. In their live-action sequence they croon the song "Blue Shadows" against a series of desert night scenes. Rogers then tells Driscoll and Patten the story of Pecos Bill, a boy raised by coyotes. Bill is able to out-howl any animal around but eventually returns to civilization. He meets a horse named Widowmaker and the two become best of friends. Romance comes between them though when Bill meets Slue Foot Sue. He and the cowgirl decide to tie the knot, which makes Widowmaker jealous. On their wedding day Sue decides to ride the beast who throws off the fiesty gal. She lands on her bustle and starts bouncing until she ends up heading towards the moon. In his sorrow, Bill returns to the coyotes and howls for his beloved every night. And that, Rogers explains to the youngsters, is why coyotes howl at the moon. MELODY TIME as a whole is particularly interesting to animation buffs. The visual styles are as varied as the segments, ranging from the complicated detail work of "Trees" to the more simplistic stylizations of "Johnny Appleseed." There is a lack of cohesiveness between segments and when "Pecos Bill" ends, the film comes to a sudden, unnatural conclusion. MELODY TIME comes off as exactly as Disney intented: a compendium of unrelated shorts. The bumble bee's nightmare "Bumble Boogie" and "Trees" were later edited together as a short film called CONTRASTS IN

RHYTHM. Some of the stories here were also combined with a few of the cartoons from MAKE MINE MUSIC for the 1955 feature release MUSICLAND. Songs include: "Melody Time" (George Weiss, Bennie Benjamin), "Little Toot" (Allie Wrubel), "The Lord Is Good to Me," "The Apple Song," "The Pioneer Song" (Kim Gannon, Walter Kent), "Once Upon a Wintertime" (Bobby Worth, Ray Gilbert), "Blame It on the Samba" (Ernesto Nazareth, Gilbert), "Blue Shadows on the Trail," "Pecos Bill" (Eliot Daniel, Johnny Lange).

p, Walt Disney; d, Clyde Geronimi, Wilfred Jackson, Hamilton Luske, Jack Kinney; w, Winston Hibler, Erdman Penner, Harry Reeves, Homer Brightman, Ken Anderson, Ted Sears, Joe Rinaldi, Art Scott, Bill Cottrell, Bob Moore, Jesse Marsh, John Walbridge, Hardie Gramatky; animators, Harvey Toombs, Ed Aardal, Cliff Nordberg, John Sibley, Ken O'Brien, Judge Whitaker, Marvin Woodward, Hal King, Don Lusk, Rudy Larriva, Bob Cannon, Hal Ambro; ph, Winton Hoch (Technicolor); ed, Donald Halliday, Thomas Scott; md, Eliot Daniel, Ken Darby; m/l, Kim Gannon, Walter Kent, Ray Gilbert, Johnny Lunge, Allie Wrubel, Bobby Worth, Benny Benjamin, George Weiss.

Animation/Musical   **(PR:AAA   MPAA:NR)**

MELODY TRAIL**   (1935) 60m REP bw

Gene Autry (Himself), Smiley Burnette (Frog Millhouse), Ann Rutherford (Millicent Thomas), Wade Boteler (Timothy), Al Bridge (Matt Kirby), Willy Castello (Frantz), Marie Quillen (Perdita), Fern Emmett (Nell), Gertrude Messinger (Cuddles), Tracy Lane (Slim), George De Normand (Pete), Marion Dowling (Sally), Ione Reed (Mamie), Jane Barnes (Helen), Abe Lefton, Buck the Wonder Dog, Champion the Horse.

An early vehicle for singing cowboy Autry which has him taking some outlaws to task for kidnaping a baby which he's supposed to be watching. The top tune is Gene's own classic "Hold On, Little Doggie, Hold On." The finale has seven cowgals marrying seven cowguys, which may sound a little familiar to fans of SEVEN BRIDES FOR SEVEN BROTHERS. Other songs: "On the Prairie," "Lookin' for the Lost Chord," "The Hurdy Gurdy Man," "My Prayer for Tonight," "End of the Trail," "I'd Love a Home in the Mountains."

p, Nat Levine; d, Joseph Kane; w, Sherman Lowe (based on a story by Lowe, Elizabeth Burbridge); ph, Ernest Miller; ed, Lester Orlebeck.

Western/Musical   **Cas.**   **(PR:AA   MPAA:NR)**

MELTING POT, THE   (SEE: BETTY CO-ED, 1946)

MELVIN AND HOWARD***½   (1980) 93m UNIV c

Jason Robards (Howard Hughes), Paul LeMat (Melvin Dummar), Elizabeth Cheshire (Darcy Dummar), Mary Steenburgen (Lynda Dummar), Chip Taylor (Clark Taylor), Melvin E. Dummar (Bus Depot Counterman), Michael J. Pollard (Little Red), Denise Galik (Lucy), Gloria Grahame (Mrs. Sisk), Pamela Reed (Bonnie Dummar), Dabney Coleman (Judge Keith Hayes), Joseph Ragno (Attorney Maxwell), John Glover (Attorney Freese), Jack Kehoe (Jim Delgado), Charles Napier (Ventura), Robert Ridgely (TV Master of Ceremonies), Susan Peretz (Chapel Owner), Charlene Holt (Mrs. Worth), Melissa Williams (Sherry Dummar), Rick Lenz (Melvin's Lawyer), Danny Dark ("Easy Street" Announcer), Martine Beswick (Real Estate Woman), Gene Borkan, Lesley Margret Burton, Wendy Lee Couch, Marguerite Baierski, Janice King, Deborah Ann Klein, Theodora Thomas, Elise Hudson, Robert Wentz, Hal Marshall, Naida Reynolds, Herbie Faye, Sonny Davis, Brendan Kelly, Danny Tucker, Shirley Washington, Cheryl Smith, John Thundercloud, Antony Alda, Gary Goetzman, Kathleen Sullivan.

Steenburgen and screenwriter Goldman won Oscars for their work in this often amusing comedy-drama that was more interesting than it was emotionally arresting. The real-life man upon whom it is based, Melvin Dummar, made some claims and was rejected by the Howard Hughes estate and the court, and he wound up with hardly any fame and surely no fortune for his alleged encounter with the reclusive billionaire. LeMat (a much underrated and underused actor) is milkman Dummar. He's driving along a Nevada highway and picks up an old tramp whom he thinks may be drunk. He's nice to the old bearded guy, Robards (in an excellent performance that got him an oscar nomination, though he lost to Tim Hutton for ORDINARY PEOPLE), and even gives him two bits at the end of the ride. LeMat is one of the people who always seem to have a dark cloud over their heads, with an inability to keep a job or satisfy his wife, Steenburgen, who has already shed him a couple of times. They remarry and she goes on a TV show, "Easy Street," where she tap dances and answers some questions and wins $10,000 in as neat a parody of the stupidity of game shows as has ever been seen on the screen. LeMat is shocked to find that the bum he gave a quarter to was Howard Hughes and, when the man dies, he leaves LeMat over $150 million! When the news gets out, LeMat is besieged by well-wishers, and all of the people who put him down in the past are now his best friends. In the end, the only thing Dummar got out of it was a fee for his story, a small appearance in the picture as a bus depot counterman, and a brief glimpse of the fame that Andy Warhol says we all will have at least 15 minutes worth of in our lives. It's a pleasant film, often funny, sometimes touching and well-photographed, but we are never totally involved with the lives of LeMat and Steenburgen and, least of all, Robards, in a very brief appearance. Pollard, who has been missing from the screen for too long, does a good job as LeMat's pal, and the comedy highlight of the film is Bob Ridgely as the all-teeth game show host. It's a satire so telling that you'll nearly fall off your seat. Ridgely, who is one of the busiest commercial actors and cartoon voices around, hit the nail dead center with his performance. Some have compared this film with a few of the earlier pictures of Preston Sturges, but we feel it only comes close to the admixture of comedy and drama in such classics as THE GREAT McGINTY and SULLIVAN'S TRAVELS. Director Demme took chances by making this movie in a "small" way and featuring the little people and the little things they do. The risk was admirable, but he might have had more success by lengthening the scenes between LeMat and Robards, for

that is when the picture works best. Good editing, fine music, and noteworthy production design by Toby Rafelson, the wife of director Bob Rafelson. As the "Easy Street" announcer, watch Danny Dark, one of the most successful "voices" in the history of TV and radio. He has been the sound of NBC, Budweiser, and so many other products that it's impossible to list his credits.

p, Art Linson, Don Phillips; d, Jonathan Demme; w, Bo Goldman; ph, Tak Fujimoto (Technicolor); m, Bruce Langhorne; ed, Craig McKay; prod d, Toby Rafelson; art d, Richard Sawyer; set d, Bob Gould.

Comedy/Drama   **Cas.**   **(PR:C-O   MPAA:R)**

MEMBER OF THE JURY*   (1937, Brit.) 61m FOX bw

Ellis Irving (Walter Maitland), Marjorie Hume (Mary Maitland), Franklyn Bellamy (Sir John Sloane), Arnold Lucy (Uncle), Roy Russell (Attorney General), Aubrey Pollock (Defense), W. E. Holloway (Judge).

Ellis is a clerk assigned to a jury hearing the case of his employer (Bellamy), to whom he feels indebted. Despite much evidence, he refuses to find him guilty and later proves his innocence. Worthless programmer.

p, John Findlay; d, Bernard Mainwaring; w, David Evans (based on a novel by John Millard); ph, Stanley Grant.

Crime   **(PR:A   MPAA:NR)**

MEMBER OF THE WEDDING, THE***   (1952) 91m COL bw

Ethel Waters (Berenice Sadie Brown), Julie Harris (Frankie Addams), Brandon De Wilde (John Henry), Arthur Franz (Jarvis), Nancy Gates (Janice), William Hansen (Mr. Addams), James Edwards (Honey Camden Brown), Harry Bolden (T. T. Williams), Dick Moore (Soldier), Danny Mummert (Barney MacKean), June Hedin (Helen), Ann Carter (Doris).

Harris is a 12-year-old girl who is quickly approaching that awkward time known as adolescence. She imagines herself a member of her brother's wedding party, and then tries to tag along for the honeymoon. Dejected at being refused, she runs away, but returns home after a near-sexual brush with a drunken soldier pushes her further toward womanhood. Upon her return home, she receives the tragic word that her next-door cousin De Wilde has died suddenly. After a passage of time, the picture ends with her entering the dating stage of teenhood. Director Fred Zinnemann would follow this up with SHANE, making the wide-eyed De Wilde a household name. The photography is obviously the work of a master, and it adds a certain atmosphere, which becomes a life-support for the film's sometimes slow-moving drama. Cameraman Mohr, approaching the end of his long career, had previously shot such films as THE JAZZ SINGER, THE WEDDING MARCH, A MIDSUMMER NIGHT'S DREAM, and RANCHO NOTORIOUS. Five people from the award-winning Broadway play (Harris, Waters, De Wilde, Hansen, and Bolden) repeat their roles in this film. The stage role of the 12-year old girl made Julie Harris (she was 25 years old at the time) a Broadway leading light. De Wilde won the stage's Donaldson Award for his debut effort (492 performances).

p, Stanley Kramer; d, Fred Zinnemann; w, Edna Anhalt, Edward Anhalt (based on the novel and play by Carson McCullers); ph, Hal Mohr; m, Alex North; ed, William Lyon; md, Morris Stoloff; art d, Cary Odell; set d, Frank Tuttle.

Drama   **(PR:A   MPAA:NR)**

MEMENTO MEI*   (1963) 70m Martin Charlot bw-c

Patrick Silva (Pat), Don Tescher (Doctor), Edward Mulvaney (Old Man), Cecilia Souza (Girl), Robert D. Browne, Edward Stasack (Men), Richard Drake (Masked Man/Giant), Juliette May Fraser (Old Lady), David Asherman (Hunchback), Cor Mulder (Barber), Wright Esser (Artist), Jean Charlot (Client).

An old, hospitalized man (Silva) has a dreamy flashback to his youth in which he gets carried into a surrealistic fantasy involving his girl friend, a man in a white mask whose face Silva falls through, a bearded giant, and a dancing hunchback. Silva is thrown into a stream which makes his beard grow to unheard-of proportions. His forehead is cut while he is alone in a forest and he pulls out of the wound a three-leaf fern. He then finds himself in an artist's studio where his face becomes the abstract portrait that is on the canvas. Maybe it all makes sense, but it's probably not worth the effort. Photographed on location in Hawaii in 16mm, this novelty silent was a one-man show for Martin Charlot.

p,d,ph&ed, Martin Charlot.

Fantasy   **(PR:C   MPAA:NR)**

MEMOIRS OF A SURVIVOR*½
                    (1981, Brit.) 115m Memorial-National Film Finance/EMI c

Julie Christie ("D"), Christopher Guard (Gerald), Leonie Mellinger (Emily Mary Cartwright), Debbie Hutchings (June), Nigel Hawthorne (Victorian Father), Pat Keen (Victorian Mother), Georgina Griffiths (Victorian Emily), Christopher Tsangarides (Victorian Son), Mark Dignam (Newsvendor/Gardener), Alison Dowling (Janet White), John Franklyn-Robbins (Prof. White), Rowena Cooper (Mrs. White), Barbara Hicks (Woman on Waste Ground), John Cromer (Man Delivering Emily), Adrienne Byrne (Maureen), Marion Owen Smith (Sandra), Tara MacGowran (Jill), Jeanne Watts, Pamela Cundell, Bryan Matheson (Neighbors), Ann Tirard (Victorian Nurse), Jeilo Edwards (Woman at Newstand), Arthur Lovegrove, John Rutland (Men at Newstand), Mark Farmer, John Altman, David Squire.

Christie is a character in the post-nuclear holocaust future torn between the social decay she sees around her and her Victorian fantasy world. The climax has her walking through her wall into the past in this feeble attempt at adapting Doris Lessing's overly-symbolic science-fiction novel. As fine an actress as Christie is, she just can't overcome the silliness of some of this film's scenes. Hopefully she will soon find a role which serves her as well as PETULIA or DON'T LOOK NOW.

p, Michael Medwin, Penny Clark; d, David Gladwell; w, Gladwell, Kerry Crabbe (based on the novel by Doris Lessing); ph, Walter Lassally (Technicolor); m, Mike Thorn; ed, William Shapter; prod d, Keith Wilson; spec eff, Effects Associates.

Drama/Fantasy **(PR:C MPAA:NR)**

MEMORY EXPERT, THE (SEE: MAN ON THE FLYING TRAPEZE, 1935)

MEMORY FOR TWO (SEE: I LOVE A BANDLEADER, 1945)

MEMORY OF US** (1974) 93m Cinema Financial of America c

Ellen Geer *(Betty)*, Will Geer *(Motel Manager)*, Jon Cypher *(Brad)*, Barbara Colby *(Iris)*, Robert Hogan *(John)*, Charlene Polite *(Stella)*, Joyce Easton *(Lisa)*, Rose Marie *(Housekeeper)*, Robbie Rist, Ann Elizabeth Beesley *(Betty's Children)*, Peter Brown *(Winston)*.

Geer is a typical upper-class, middle-aged housewife of the early 1970s. Her husband is openly sleeping around, her kids are weighing her down, and she's getting edgy. She tries swapping mates, but not surprisingly is left unsatisfied. She also frequents a motel every day in an attempt to find herself, and to get her husband jealous. Geer, who also scripted, has made a picture which effectively deals with a predominantly women's issue of the 1970s, but now it looks a bit dated and out of place. Her father, Will Geer, makes a small appearance as the dirty-minded manager of the motel.

p, James P. Polakof; d, H. Kaye Dyal; w, Ellen Geer; ph, Hiro Morikawa (DeLuxe Color); m, Ed Bogas; ed, Robert Estrin, Verna Fields, Harry Keramidas; art d, Joe Guerena; m/l, Bogas, Geer.

Drama **(PR:A MPAA:PG)**

MEN, THE**** (1950) 85m Kramer/UA bw (AKA: BATTLE STRIPE)

Marlon Brando *(Ken)*, Teresa Wright *(Ellen)*, Everett Sloane *(Dr. Brock)*, Jack Webb *(Norm)*, Richard Erdman *(Leo)*, Arthur Jurado *(Angel)*, Virginia Farmer *(Nurse Robbins)*, Dorothy Tree *(Ellen's Mother)*, Howard St. John *(Ellen's Father)*, Nita Hunter *(Dolores)*, Patricia Joiner *(Laverne)*, John Miller *(Mr. Doolin)*, Cliff Clark *(Dr. Kameran)*, Ray Teal *(Man at Bar)*, Marguerite Martin *(Angel's Mother)*, Obie Parker *(The Lookout)*, Ray Mitchell *(Thompson)*, Pete Simon *(Mullin)*, Paul Peltz *(Hopkins)*, Tom Gillick *(Fine)*, Randall Updyke III *(Baker)*, Marshall Ball *(Romano)*, Carlo Lewis *(Gunderson)*, William Lea, Jr. *(Walter)*.

This was Brando's film debut and, as such, he set standards not only for his fellow actors but for himself, giving a traumatic performance as a WW II veteran whose wounds have made him a paraplegic. Brando is shown at the beginning as a lieutenant leading a platoon of men into the square of a small European village. Suddenly, a sniper's bullet rings out and Brando, hit in the lower back, falls, paralyzed for life. He is shown next in the hospital, angry, resentful, and uncooperative with his doctors and nurses. His girl friend, Wright, visits him but the embittered Brando turns her away. He resists treatment but doctor Sloane slowly breaks through Brando's mental wall, convincing him to begin his exercise program. He builds up his upper torso through strenuous exercises and learns to expertly manipulate his wheelchair, later learning how to drive a specially equipped auto. Wright will not give up on him and soon Brando accepts *her* proposal and agrees to marry her. Brando, despite his determined ambition to stand during the wedding ceremony, is disappointed by his body and gets drunk on his wedding night and cracks up the car. He winds up back in the hospital, again feeling sorry for himself. The other paralyzed veterans in the ward hold a meeting and decide that Brando must go; he rages against their decision and even Sloane, to whom he appeals, sides with the other men. They order him to go to his home and take up wedded life with Wright. Brando finally sees the light and goes to the brave woman who loves him despite his affliction. Kramer had earlier produced such message-filled films as CHAMPION and HOME OF THE BRAVE, the first dealing with the corruption of the blood sport of prizefighting, the second dealing with racism and bigotry. Here Kramer, through the expert direction of Zinnemann, dealt with the adjustment of severely wounded men without much hope of complete recovery. Zinnemann never steps over the line into mawkishness or bathos, and Foreman's witty, sensitive script is excellent and is the reason Brando agreed to appear in this film. He had, while enjoying widespread kudos for his Broadway roles—chiefly in "A Streetcar Named Desire"—stated that Hollywood producers "never made an honest picture in their lives and probably never will." He backed down from this position with THE MEN, which was a critical if not a commercial success. Brando worked hard at his role, actually moving into a 32-bed ward with real paraplegics, observing their day-to-day agonies and struggles and working their ordeals into his role. He did not ignore the pranks for which he was known at the time. He loved to wheel himself outside with the others and, while visitors stood by in shock, suddenly jump out of his wheelchair and run madly across the hospital lawns. On another occasion, Brando and several paraplegics went to a bar and drank heavily. A woman possessed of God's word suddenly approached them and began sermonizing, telling them that if they put their trust in the Lord they would be cured. Brando, pretending to respond to her zealot's diatribe, stood up shakily from his wheelchair, walked wobbly-legged toward her, and after a few steps—a tortured look on his face and an expression of shock on hers—he broke into a frantic tap dance which caused the woman to faint on the spot.

p, Stanley Kramer; d, Fred Zinnemann; w, Carl Foreman; ph, Robert De Grasse; m, Dimitri Tiomkin; ed, Harry Gerstad; md, Tiomkin; prod d, Rudolph Sternad.

Drama **Cas.** **(PR:C MPAA:NR)**

MEN AGAINST THE SKY** (1940) 75m RKO bw

Richard Dix *(Phil Mercedes)*, Kent Taylor *(Martin Ames)*, Edmund Lowe *(Dan McLean)*, Wendy Barrie *(Kay Mercedes)*, Granville Bates *(Burdett)*, Grant Withers *(Grant)*, Donald Briggs *(Dick Allerton)*, Charles Quigley *(Flynn)*, Selmer Jackson *(Capt. Sanders)*, Terry Belmont [Lee Bonnell] *(Capt. Wallen)*, Jane Woodworth *(Miss LeClair)*, Pamela Blake *(Nurse)*, Chester Tallman, Joe Bordeaux, Ted O'Shea, M. G. McConnell, Jack Gray, Douglas Spencer, Ray Johnson *(Mechanics)*, Lee Phelps *(Shop Foreman)*, Harry Harvey *(Reception Clerk)*, Thornton Edwards *(Court Clerk)*, Roy Gordon *(Judge)*, Paul Everton, Forbes Murray *(Bankers)*, Jan Buckingham *(Secretary)*, Helene Millard *(Mrs. McLean)*, John Sheehan *(Bartender)*, Max Wagner *(Electrician)*, Denis Green *(Col. Kolbec)*, George Lewis *(Lt. Norval)*, Harry Tyler *(Passenger)*, Earle Hodgins *(Barker)*, Eddie Dunn *(Cop)*.

Richard Dix had already made his mark in the sky with his films ACE OF ACES and THE LOST SQUADRON (as well as many others), so it was no surprise when he was cast for this high-in-the-firmament picture. This time, he's a once-famous flier who has fallen from popular favor and now earns his living doing stunt flying at various little air shows and county fairs. He drinks too much and you wouldn't want to be standing under him, but his heart is pure and when his sister, Barrie, hires on at Lowe's airplane factory as a designer, Dix does what he can to help her. Lowe is one of those early seat-of-the-pants plane manufacturers who is always close to having his business crash, but he has a new design on the board, a high-speed plane that will decimate the competition. Dix helps Barrie in her designs, the plane passes the rigid governmental tests, and she gets the credit for the work, thus enabling her to marry Taylor, her amour, who is the chief designer. There was a bit of real footage mixed in with the other reels and we have a chance to see the Howard Hughes' airplane that broke the cross-America record with a flight that took just under seven and one half hours from Burbank, California to Newark, New Jersey. A few laughs, lots of fine aerial camerawork, and tip-top production values throughout. Belmont's name was changed in later years to Lee Bonnell. It's not a great picture and not even a good one, just a fair programmer that could take its place on the second half of the long-dead double bills. The screenplay was by a man who died shortly thereafter in a car crash with his wife, the "Eileen" of MY SISTER EILEEN. Nathaniel "Pep" West had already been acknowledged as a novelist for *Miss Lonelyhearts* and, perhaps the most biting Hollywood story of them all, *The Day Of The Locust*, both of which were made into movies. He was only 36 at the time of his demise, a great loss to anyone who appreciated literature.

p, Howard Benedict; d, Leslie Goodwins; w, Nathaniel West (based on a story by John Twist); ph, Frank Redman; ed, Desmond Marguette; md, Frank Tours; spec eff, Vernon L. Walker.

Air Drama **(PR:A MPAA:NR)**

MEN AGAINST THE SUN** $^{1}/_{2}$ (1953, Brit.) 65m Kenya Films/Monarch bw

John Bentley *(Hawker)*, Zena Marshall, Alan Tarlton, Liam O'Laoghaire, Edward Johnson, Ambrose, Shanti Pandit, Flavia Andrade, K. A. Kolhatker.

When Bentley is assigned to supervise the first Mombasa-to-Uganda railroad construction project, he finds the job riddled with hazards. Not only must he deal with the threat of lions, but he must also put up with Marshall, a missionary doctor who demands to be taken along. The project is finished by film's end, and Bentley and Marshall decide to marry. This film was the first co-production of Kenya and Britain.

p, Alastair Scobie; d, Brendan J. Stafford; w, Scobie; ph, Stafford.

Drama **(PR:A MPAA:NR)**

MEN ARE CHILDREN TWICE***

(1953, Brit.) 74m ABF-Pathe bw (GB: VALLEY OF SONG)

Mervyn Johns *(Minister Griffiths)*, Clifford Evans *(Geraint Llewellyn)*, Maureen Swanson *(Olwen Davies)*, John Fraser *(Cliff Lloyd)*, Rachel Thomas *(Mrs. Lloyd)*, Betty Cooper *(Mrs. Davies)*, Rachel Roberts *(Bessie Lewis)*, Hugh Pryse *(Lloyd, Undertaker)*, Edward Evans *(Davies, Shop)*, Kenneth Williams *(Lloyd, Haulage)*, Alun Owen *(Pritchard)*, Kenneth Evans, Howell Davis, Emrys Leyshon, Prysor Williams, Desmond Llewellyn, Ronnie Harries, John Wynn, Dudley Jones, John Glyn Jones, Madoline Thomas, Olwen Brookes, Ben Williams, Ann Elsden, Sarah Davies, Valentine Dunn, Eric Francis, Denys Graham, Lane Meddick.

A Welsh village's annual production of Handel's "Messiah" is the cause of a feud between the community's two leading families when the choirmaster decides that Cooper will sing the contralto part, although Thomas has sung the part for the last 15 years. Fraser and Davies put off their elopement to try to reconcile the families, but it is not until Evans decides that both women will sing the part that peace returns to the village. A likable comedy, very well done by all concerned. Reminiscent of the Ealing comedies of the same period.

p, Vaughan N. Dean; d, Gilbert Gunn; w, Cliff Gordon, Phil Park (based on the radio play "Choir Practice" by Gordon); ph, Lionel Banes; m, Robert Gill; ed, Richard Best.

Comedy **(PR:A MPAA:NR)**

MEN ARE LIKE THAT* $^{1}/_{2}$ (1930) 105m PAR bw

Hal Skelly *(Aubrey Piper)*, Doris Hill *(Amy Fisher)*, Charles Sellon *(Pa Fisher)*, Clara Blandick *(Ma Fisher)*, Morgan Farley *(Joe Fisher)*, Helene Chadwick *(Clara Hyland)*, William B. Davidson *(Frank Hyland)*, Eugene Pallette *(Traffic Cop)*, George Fawcett *(Judge)*, Gordon DeMain *(Rogers)*, E. H. Calvert *(Superintendent)*.

An uneventful and tiresome adaptation of the long-running Broadway play of 1924 entitled "The Show-Off." Skelly is in the lead role as a mouthy and obnoxious fellow who manages to get on everyone's bad side except for his darling wife. While the script by Herman J. Mankiewicz and Marion Dix is overly literal it is not as problematic as Skelly's lame performance, shining only for the song-and-dance numbers.

d, Frank Tuttle; w, Marion Dix, Herman J. Mankiewicz (based on the play "The Show-Off" by George Kelly); ph, A. J. Stout; ed, Verna Willis.

Comedy **(PR:A MPAA:NR)**

MEN ARE LIKE THAT* 1/2

(1931) 70m COL bw (GB: THE VIRTUOUS WIFE; AKA: ARIZONA)

Laura La Plante (Evelyn Palmer), John Wayne (Lt. Bob Benton), June Clyde (Bonita Palmer), Forrest Stanley (Col. Bonham), Nena Quartaro (Conchita), Susan Fleming (Dot), Loretta Sayers (Peggy), Hugh Cummings (Hank).

Of interest only to catch an early glimpse of John Wayne, who stars as a West Point graduate. Upon receiving his degree, Wayne drops his girl, but after a transfer to an Arizona Army post meets up with her, only to find her married to his best friend-commanding officer. Film sticks unfailingly to the play on which it is based, which also made it to the screen as a 1918 Douglas Fairbanks silent.

d, George B. Seitz; w, Robert Riskin, Dorothy Howell (based on the play "Arizona" by Augustus Thomas); ph, Teddy Tetzlaff; ed, Gene Milford.

Drama   (PR:A MPAA:NR)

MEN ARE NOT GODS*

(1937, Brit.) 82m LFP/UA bw

Miriam Hopkins (Ann Williams), Gertrude Lawrence (Barbara Halford), Sebastian Shaw (Edmund Davey), Rex Harrison (Tommy Stapleton), A. E. Matthews (Skeates), Val Gielgud (Producer), Laura Smithson (Katherine), Lawrence Grossmith (Stanley), Sybil Grove (Painter), Winifred Willard (Mrs. Williams), Wally Patch (Gallery Attendant), James Harcourt (Porter), Noel Howlett (Cashier), Rosamund Greenwood (Piano Player), Paddy Morgan (Kelly), Nicholas Nadejin (Iago), Michael Hogarth (Cassio).

The title comes from a a line in "Othello," but that is about the last time anything literary happens (except for scenes from that Shakespeare play). Men are not gods and this is not much of a movie. Matter of fact, it gets downright embarrassing at times. The first release was eight minutes longer but lay there like a dead smelt, so the decision was made to snip a bit. They should have snipped more. Lawrence is the wife of Shaw, a classical actor. She appeals to Hopkins, secretary to theatrical critic Matthews, who has written a scathing review of Shaw's performance. Lawrence wants Hopkins to alter the review so the play becomes a hit. The amended review is printed and people flock to the theater, but Hopkins is fired. She is rehired when people seem to like the version of "Othello," then other complications ensue. Hopkins meets Shaw and falls for him, and Lawrence, a very jealous woman and Shaw's costar in the play, sees that she must put a stop to this right away. She asks Hopkins to cease and desist and allow their marriage to continue. Shaw is just as nuts over Hopkins as she is over him and has other plans for his wife. The two actors are on stage and Hopkins is in the audience when Shaw, as the Moor, begins to choke Lawrence, as Desdemona, but this time it's for real. Hopkins realizes what Shaw is up to and lets out a shriek that would raise Marlowe from the grave to argue the authorship of the play. Shaw, who may or may not have been thinking about actually killing his wife (or was it the throes of the scene that caused the extra clench around Lawrence's neck?), stops throttling her, and later we learn that Lawrence is pregnant. That news is enough to get Hopkins out of their lives and she exits as Shaw and Lawrence clasp each other. Very hokey and totally unbelievable, it's amazing that someone had the nerve to make this picture and not transform it into a comedy, as the situations are often funnier than many mirthful movies. Harrison is wasted (in his 6th screen appearance) and so is our time. They attempted suspense here, but it's as tense as a Perry Como medley.

p, Alexander Korda; d, Walter Reisch; w, G. B. Stern, Iris Wright, Reisch; ph, Charles Rosher; m, Geoffrey Toye; ed, William Hornbeck, Henry Cornelius; md, Muir Mathieson; prod d, Vincent Korda; cos, Rene Hubert; spec eff, Ned Mann.

Drama   **Cas.**   (PR:A-C MPAA:NR)

MEN ARE SUCH FOOLS*

(1933) 64m Jefferson/RKO bw

Leo Carrillo (Tony Mello), Vivienne Osborne (Lilli Arno), Una Merkel (Molly), Joseph Cawthorn (Werner), Tom Moore (Tom Hyland), Earle Foxe (Joe Darrow), Paul Hurst (Stiles), Paul Porcasi (Klepak), Eddie Nugent (Eddie), Albert Conti (Spinelli), Edward Le Saint (Warden), J. Farrell MacDonald, Lester Lee.

Carrillo isn't given much to work with this time out. He's cast as an unlucky Italian who, after bringing his German wife to America, finds that she's sleeping around with cabaret owner Foxe. Carrillo beats him up and is sent to San Quentin. Before long he gets out on parole, but finds his wife dead—a suicide over an unhappy affair. He kills Foxe and is promptly booted back into prison—for life. He becomes the victim of amnesia and only regains his memory by composing a march that is performed by his cellmates. Jefferson Pictures was a production company (though not for long) begun by Joseph I. Schnitzer, who had resigned as RKO studio head.

p, Joseph I. Schnitzer; d, William Nigh; w, Viola Brothers Shore, Ethel Doherty (based on the story by Thomas Lloyd Lennon); ph, Charles Schoenbaum; art d, Ed C. Jewel.

Drama   (PR:A MPAA:NR)

MEN ARE SUCH FOOLS**

(1938) 66m WB bw

Wayne Morris (Jimmy Hall), Priscilla Lane (Linda Lawrence), Humphrey Bogart (Harry Galleon), Hugh Herbert (Harvey Bates), Penny Singleton (Nancy), Johnnie Davis (Tad), Mona Barrie (Beatrice Harris), Marcia Ralston (Wanda Townsend), Gene Lockhart (Bill Dalton), Kathleen Lockhart (Mrs. Dalton), Donald Briggs (George Onslow), Renie Riano (Mrs. Pinkel), Claude Allister (Rudolf), Nedda Harrigan (Mrs. Nelson), Eric Stanley (Mr. Nelson), James Nolan (Bill Collyer), Carole Landis (June Cooper).

Just an okay second feature that wastes the talents of all the actors, MEN ARE SUCH FOOLS tells the story of Lane, the executive secretary of Herbert, an ad agency executive in New York, and her romantic travails. Lane lives with Singleton, who is engaged to Davis. Singleton is ecstatically happy about her impending marriage and continues to tell Lane how wonderful matrimony is, but Lane has her eyes set on success in the advertising business with no current room in her heart for

love. Morris is mad for Lane, but she thinks that he'll never get anywhere in the world and so she keeps him at arm's length. At the agency, Lane comes up with a hangover cure that is a hit for one of their clients and keeps the account when it had been about to depart for another company. Lane gets in tight with Herbert, who has her meet Briggs and Barrie, the aggressive and assertive business brains behind the agency. Morris watches Lane rise quickly in her position but pleads with her to quit and marry him rather than follow a career. Barrie invites Lane and Morris to her house in the country and while there, Morris convinces Lane to become affianced. Then Lane meets Bogart, a heavyweight at the agency. He's sort of engaged to Ralston, but has been conducting a surreptitious affair with Barrie all the while. Lane decides to charm Bogart and get him to help her up the ladder of success. Time goes by and Bogart is attempting to bed Lane. In order to get on her good side, he toys with her vanity and subtly moves Morris out of the picture. Then Lane has an argument with Morris, but they reconcile and he talks her into quitting her position. Now she tries to inspire him to ambition, though it's to no avail and she eventually resumes her work at the agency. Morris hears a story over the radio to the effect that Lane and Bogart are sailing for Europe. Morris responds by going to the radio studio, finding Bogart, and knocking him soundly about the head and shoulders. Then Morris races for the dock, but the ship has sailed. He's distraught until he learns that Lane did not go with the ocean liner. She arranged for the item on the radio to see if Morris was really serious about his love for her. Bogart is on the ship and is shocked when he finds Ralston in his cabin, not Lane. Lane had sent Ralston a wire asking her to be there and the picture ends as Bogart and Ralston sail away. Nothing much to recommend this other than seeing Bogart in a light part. Nedda Harrigan (Mrs. Nelson) met and married Josh Logan, the stage director, and stopped doing these kinds of roles.

p, David Lewis; d, Busby Berkeley; w, Norman Reilly Raine, Horace Jackson, (based on the novel by Faith Baldwin [Faith Cuthrell]); ph, Sid Hickox; m, Heinz Roemheld; ed, Jack Killifer; art d, Max Parker; cos, Howard Shoup.

Comedy/Drama   (PR:A MPAA:NR)

MEN BEHIND BARS

(SEE: DUFFY OF SAN QUENTIN, 1954)

MEN CALL IT LOVE*

(1931) 72m MGM bw

Adolphe Menjou (Tony Minot), Leila Hyams (Connie), Norman Foster (Jack), Mary Duncan (Helen), Hedda Hopper (Callie), Robert Emmett Keane (Joe), Harry Northrup (Brandt).

Menjou's sophistication couldn't cover for the lack of a dramatic element in this talky talkie. A dissatisfied wife is in love with the single Menjou, who is in love with a happily wed woman. When the second wife's husband is caught with another woman things get rocky, but the two reunite by the film's end. High society fluff with unusual naughtiness for the era.

d, Edgar Selwyn; w, Doris Anderson (based on the play "Among the Married" by Vincent Lawrence); ph, Harold Rosson; ed, Frank Sullivan.

Drama   (PR:C MPAA:NR)

MEN IN EXILE**

(1937) 58m FN-WB bw

Dick Purcell (James Carmody), June Travis (Sally Haines), Alan Baxter (Danny), Margaret Irving (Mother Haines), Victor Varconi (Col. Gomez), Olin Howland (Jones), Veda Ann Borg (Rita), Norman Willis (Rocky Crane), Carlos De Valdez (Gen. Alcatraz), Alec Harford (Limey), John Alexander (Winterspoon), Demitris Emanuel (Gomez's Aide).

Purcell is the exiled man living with a gang of criminals on an island called Caribo. He ends up in the middle of a conflict between the iron-willed island commandant and a gang of gun runners, and romances the hardened Travis. Though the plot is thin, the action is fast-paced and the performances notable.

d, John Farrow; w, Roy Chanslor (based on a story by Marie Baumer, Houston Branch); ph, Arthur Todd; ed, Terry Morse.

Action/Drama   (PR:A MPAA:NR)

MEN IN HER DIARY** 1/2

(1945) 73m UNIV bw

Peggy Ryan (Doris Mann), Jon Hall (Randolph Glenning), Louise Allbritton (Isabel Glenning), Ernest Truex (Williams), Virginia Grey (Diana Lee), William W. Terry (Tommy Burton), Alan Mowbray (Douglas Crane), Eric Blore (Florist), Samuel S. Hinds (Judge Morgan), Jacqueline de Wit (Marjorie), Maxie Rosenbloom (Moxie), Sig Rumann (Mme. Irene), Addison Richards (Cavanaugh), Lorraine Miller (Pat Mann), Robin Raymond (Stella), Minerva Urecal (Mrs. Braun), Arthur Loft (Attorney Reynolds), Vivian Austin (Linda), Lorin Raker (Whitman).

Ryan gets herself into a comical mess after keeping imaginary writings of romantic encounters with a number of men. One of them happens to be her boss, and when his wife gets her hands on the diary she sues for divorce. A lot of fun.

p, Howard Welsch; d, Charles Barton; w, F. Hugh Herbert, Ellwood Ullman, Lester Cole (based on a story by Kerry Shaw); ph, Paul Ivano; m, Milton Rosen; ed, Paul Landres; art d, John B. Goodman, Richard H. Riedel; ch, Carlos Romero; m/l, "Makin' a Million," "Keep Your Chin Up," Everett Carter, Rosen (sung by Grey).

Comedy   (PR:A MPAA:NR)

MEN IN HER LIFE**

(1931) 70m COL bw

Lois Moran (Julia Cavanaugh), Charles Bickford (Flashy Madden), Victor Varconi (Count Ivan), Donald Dilloway (Dick Webster), Luis Alberni (Anton), Adrienne D'Ambricourt (Maria), Barbara Weeks (Miss Mulholland), Wilson Benge (Wilton), Oscar Apfel (Blake), Hooper Atchley (District Attorney).

Moran plays a woman with a shady past who is being blackmailed by Varconi as she makes plans to marry a senator's son. She meets and becomes friendly with bootlegger Bickford, who offers to put a stop to Varconi's scheming. His methods are a little strong as he ends up killing the count and goes on trial for murder. Moran must decide whether to risk her reputation by testifying on Bickford's behalf, giving the real story of what happened, or letting her savior go to the chair. She saves him and they end up a happy couple. Good acting and some nice shots of Paris and New York make this a worthy drama.

d, William Beaudine; w, Robert Riskin, Dorothy Howell (based on the novel by Warner Fabian); ph, Ted Tetzlaff; ed, Richard Cahoon.

Drama **(PR:A MPAA:NR)**

MEN IN HER LIFE, THE*** (1941) 89m COL bw

Loretta Young *(Lina Varsavina)*, Conrad Veidt *(Stanislas Rosing)*, Dean Jagger *(David Gibson)*, Eugenie Leonovich *(Marie)*, John Shepperd [Shepperd Strudwick] *(Roger Chevis)*, Otto Kruger *(Victor)*, Paul Baratoff *(Manilov)*, Ann Todd *(Rose)*, Billy Rayes *(Nurdo)*, Ludmila Toretzka *(Mme. Olenkova)*, Tom Ladd *(Lina's Dance Partner)*.

Young is an accomplished ballerina who reaches great heights thanks to the disciplined hand of her instructor, Veidt. She marries him more out of respect than love, but before long he dies. She then weds shipping tycoon Jagger and leaves with him for Europe, temporarily abandoning her dancing career. When she decides to resume her career, she and Jagger separate. When she gives birth to a daughter, Jagger takes the child to New York and Young soon follows for a happy reconciliation. This was Ratoff's first independent venture, and it was a handsomely mounted and well-acted tale.

p&d, Gregory Ratoff; w, Frederick Kohner, Michael Wilson, Paul Trivers (based on the novel *Ballerina* by Lady Eleanor Smith); ph, Harry Stradling, Arthur Miller; ed, Francis D. Lyon; md, David Raksin; ch, Adolph Bohm.

Drama **(PR:A MPAA:NR)**

MEN IN WAR* 1/2** (1957) 104m Security/UA bw

Robert Ryan *(Lt. Benson)*, Aldo Ray *(Montana)*, Robert Keith *(Colonel)*, Philip Pine *(Riordan)*, Vic Morrow *(Zwickley)*, Nehemiah Persoff *(Lewis)*, James Edwards *(Killian)*, L. Q. Jones *(Sam Davis)*, Adam Kennedy *(Maslow)*, Scott Marlowe *(Meredith)*, Walter Kelley *(Ackerman)*, Robert Normand *(Christensen)*, Anthony Ray *(Penelli)*, Michael Miller *(Lynch)*, Victor Sen Yung *(Korean Sniper)*, Race Gentry *(Haines)*.

The Korean War, like the fracas in Vietnam, was never popular with the American public, despite all the waving of flags by the politicos in Washington who tried to convince the country that both wars really meant something. Because the moviegoers were hip to the duplicity, hardly any of the movies about either conflict were embraced, a direct contrast to the movies about WW II, when we all knew who the enemy was and we knew why we had to hate them. Such was the case with this film, as good a movie as one can make about an unpopular chapter in U.S. history. Ryan is the tough, grizzled lieutenant who is attempting to save his weary platoon and Ray is a sergeant whose job is to squire his shell-shocked colonel, Keith, back to a field hospital where the man can be treated. Ryan's transportation is wrecked, so he takes over Ray's jeep, with Keith in it, to carry the needed ammo and other equipment to help his stranded platoon fend off the enemy. Ray is totally against this, as he knows what his job is and he makes Ryan aware that this is darn close to a kidnaping. The men make their way through hostile territory, amidst several skirmishes, and get to Ryan's group, only to discover that Ryan's men are mostly dead and that the Koreans now occupy the hill where Ryan had left the platoon. Ray and Ryan heroically take the high ground in as realistic a battle as ever limned, then stand on the hill and pay homage to their deceased fellow warriors at the fadeout. It's a little film, in that it doesn't show vast numbers of men taking huge acreage, but this microcosm of heroism is much more effective because we see the dirty dogfaces, the men who shed blood, rather than the generals who sip brandy and smoke cigars while their men "die well" (to quote a line from Stanley Kubrick's antiwar film, PATHS OF GLORY).The fear in the eyes of the soldiers has seldom been better shown. One of the more effective scores by Elmer Bernstein also helps to make the point that war stinks.

p, Sidney Harmon; d, Anthony Mann; w, Philip Yordan (based on the novel *Combat* by Van Van Praag); ph, Ernest Haller; m, Elmer Bernstein; ed, Richard C. Meyer; md, Bernstein; art d, Frank Sylos.

War Drama **Cas.** **(PR:A-C MPAA:NR)**

MEN IN WHITE*** (1934) 80m COS/MGM bw

Clark Gable *(Dr. Ferguson)*, Myrna Loy *(Laura)*, Jean Hersholt *(Dr. Hochberg)*, Elizabeth Allan *(Barbara)*, Otto Kruger *(Dr. Levine)*, C. Henry Gordon *(Dr. Cunningham)*, Russell Hardie *(Dr. Michaelson)*, Henry B. Walthall *(Dr. McCabe)*, Wallace Ford *(Shorty)*, Russell Hopton *(Pete)*, Samuel S. Hinds *(Dr. Gordon)*, Frank Puglia *(Dr. Vitale)*, Leo Chalzel *(Dr. Wren)*, Donald Douglas *(Mac)*.

Gable emerges as good actor—much to the surprise of his MGM bosses—in this film, where he had earlier played mediocre roles in gangster programmers. Here he is a dedicated, brilliant physician being guided by veteran doctor Hersholt. He meets and falls in love with playgirl Loy, whose only interest is having a good time. Forget medical science and research and helping humanity, she tells Gable, and take up a society practice where you can make big money. He does, forsaking Hersholt and the girl who loves him, Allan, whom he had impregnated. Allan has an abortion but develops peritonitis and, while Gable stands by helplessly, she dies. The death affects both Gable and Loy and she realizes that he should be devoting himself to the elimination of disease rather than living the good life. This theme was to see much usage in many films to come, but here it was fresh and original, and this film proved a big box-office success, as well as establishing Gable as a substantial actor and furthering the long career of Loy. Boleslawski's direction is meticulous and impressive. This was the first of seven films Gable would make with Loy and she later stated that "it seems incredible that we were never lovers." But this was not the case with Allan, the other woman of the film. During the production Gable and Allan had a brief affair which later caused writer Anita Loos to say of him: "Clark had a Babbitt mentality about sex in those days. That old, early American male idea that you must take on any girl that comes your way."

p, Monta Bell; d, Richard Boleslawski; w, Waldemar Young (based on the play by Sidney Kingsley); ph, George Folsey; m, William Axt; ed, Frank Sullivan; art d, Cedric Gibbons.

Drama **(PR:A MPAA:NR)**

MEN LIKE THESE (SEE: TRAPPED IN A SUBMARINE, 1931, Brit.)

MEN MUST FIGHT* (1933) 72m MGM bw

Diana Wynyard *(Laura Seward)*, Lewis Stone *(Edward Seward)*, Phillips Holmes *(Bob Seward)*, Ruth Selwyn *(Peggy Chase)*, Robert Grieg *(Albert, Butler)*, Robert Young *(Geoffrey)*, Hedda Hopper *(Mrs. Chase)*, Donald Dillaway *(Steve)*, Mary Carlisle *(Evelyn)*, Luis Alberni *(Soto)*, May Robson *(Maman Seward)*.

Wynyard is the pacifist mother of Holmes and wife of Secretary of State Stone who is entirely opposed to war, chiefly because her first lover was shot down over France in WW I. Prophetically, the screenwriters created a second world war which began in 1940. Stone, as expected, turns into the pro-U.S. warmonger, while Wynyard makes every effort to keep her son from enlisting. Holmes breaks her hold, however, and goes off to fight. The spectacular finale has a New York City air strike topple the Empire State Building. While the predictions of the film did not completely come true, Holmes was an unfortunate victim of fate, a real-life victim of WW II.

p&d, Edgar Selwyn; w, C. Gardner Sullivan (based on a play by Reginald Lawrence, S. K. Lauren); ph, George Folsey; ed, William Gray.

War Drama **(PR:A MPAA:NR)**

MEN OF AMERICA* (1933) 57m RKO bw (GB: THE GREAT DECISION)

Bill [William] Boyd *(Jim Parker)*, Charles "Chic" Sale *(Smokey Joe)*, Dorothy Wilson *(Annabelle)*, Ralph Ince *(Cicero)*, Henry Armetta *(Tony Garboni)*, Inez Palange *(Mrs. Garboni)*, Theresa Maxwell Conover *(Postmistress)*, Alphonse Ethier *(Oley Jensen)*, Ling *(Chinese Joe)*, Eugene Strong, Fatty Layman, Fred Lindstrand, Frank Mills.

Boyd is new to a small western town and quickly becomes a suspect in a rash of crime which hits the community like a brickbat. He teams up with Sale, the owner of the general store, to squelch the gang of culprits that is behind the mayhem. Slow-moving, talky, and poorly-scripted. RKO had intentions of building an action series around Boyd, but this film convinced the studio not to. Two years later he would move over to Paramount to make HOPALONG CASSIDY, the first in a series which would eventually include more than 60 films.

d, Ralph Ince; w, Samuel Ornitz, Jack Jungmeyer (based on a story by Humphrey Pearson, Henry McCarty); ph, J. Roy Hunt; ed, Edward Schroeder.

Western **(PR:A MPAA:NR)**

MEN OF BOYS TOWN 1/2** (1941) 106m MGM bw

Spencer Tracy *(Father Flanagan)*, Mickey Rooney *(Whitey Marsh)*, Bobs Watson *(Pee Wee)*, Larry Nunn *(Ted Martley)*, Darryl Hickman *(Flip)*, Henry O'Neill *(Mr. Maitland)*, Mary Nash *(Mrs. Maitland)*, Lee J. Cobb *(Dave Morris)*, Sidney Miller *(Mo Kahn)*, Addison Richards *(The Judge)*, Lloyd Corrigan *(Roger Gorton)*, George Lessey *(Bradford Stone)*, Robert Emmet Keane *(Burton)*, Arthur Hohl *(Guard)*, Ben Welden *(Superintendent)*, Anne Revere *(Mrs. Fenely)*.

Somewhat sentimentalized sequel to BOYS TOWN, which took three Oscars and several other nominations. Many of the earlier actors have returned for this one and if there hadn't been a previous story, this might have done better, but as it is with so many sequels, it doesn't reach the heights of the original. Cobb is the pawnbroker who helped to establish the place where boys can go and he is called upon by Tracy, reprising his Father Flanagan role, to raise some more money. In the two years since we saw the first picture, the Town has been driven deeply into debt and Cobb can't see how they can get out of the financial barrel they're in. Nunn is a boy who has been crippled by a vicious beating in a reform school. He arrives at Boys Town with a serious attitude problem and hates everyone and everything around him. Rooney and some of the other boys attempt to bring Nunn back to his senses, but the bitter boy resists. O'Neill and Nash are an older couple who want to adopt a boy. They have the money to provide any youth with a wonderful life and they think it might be better if they get a mature lad, rather than an infant. Meanwhile, Tracy helps find Nunn a dog upon whom the frustrated boy can lavish whatever affection is in his heart. The animal has been provided by O'Neill and Nash, but they choose Rooney to be the object of their affection and affluence and he goes home with them. Despite all of their love and the luxury they lavish on him, Rooney misses his life at Boys Town and the camaraderie of all his pals. Rooney goes to visit a friend at the local reform school, but they won't let him in. While driving away, Rooney discovers that Hickman, an inmate, has hidden in the car to escape the brutality of the institution. Rooney feels for Hickman and won't blow the whistle on him, but when Hickman robbs $200, both Rooney and Hickman are tossed into the reform school. Rooney's pal commits suicide and his mother, Revere, appeals to Tracy to expose the treatment at the institution. Tracy bulls his way into the school, successfully demonstrates to the powers-that-be that this is no place to keep young men, and takes Rooney and Hickman out of the reform school and back to Boys Town. Meanwhile, Nunn has agreed to an operation to cure him and even though it's successful, he is not motivated to walk until his beloved dog is accidentally killed. At the pet's funeral on the Boys Town grounds, Nunn stands and walks to the grave. O'Neill and Nash come up with the needed cash to keep the place in business and the film is over. Good acting from all and a special nod to young Sidney Miller, who grew up to be the successful writer-director-performer who worked for many years with Donald O'Connor in a nightclub act.

p, John Considine, Jr.; d, Norman Taurog; w, James Kevin McGuinness; ph, Harold Rosson; m, Herbert Stothart; ed, Frederick Y. Smith; art d, Cedric Gibbons, Henry McAfee; set d, Edwin B. Willis.

Drama   **(PR:AA   MPAA:NR)**

MEN OF CHANCE* 1/2   (1932) 65m RKO bw

Mary Astor (*Marthe*), Ricardo Cortez (*Johnny Silk*), John Halliday (*Dorval*), Ralph Ince (*Farley*), Kitty Kelly (*Gertie*), James Donlan, George Davis.

Cortez plays a man with an uncanny knack for picking winning horses. Two rival gamblers want to get information out of Cortez, and they enlist the aid of Astor. The scheme works until Astor falls for Cortez and marries him. In the race which ends the film, Cortez is a big winner and his rivals are big losers. Some good race footage and competent performances are undone by improbable dialog. Interestingly, the film received its first booking only after Universal canceled its FRANKENSTEIN premiere due to a contract dispute.

d, George Archainbaud; w, Louis Stevens, Wallace Smith (based on the story by Louis Weitzenkorn); ph, Nick Musuraca; ed, Archie Marshek.

Drama   **(PR:A   MPAA:NR)**

MEN OF DESTINY   (SEE: MEN OF TEXAS, 1942)

MEN OF IRELAND**

(1938, Ireland) 64m Irish National/J. H. Hoffberg (GB: ISLAND MAN; WEST OF KERRY)

Cecil Ford (*Neal O'Moore*), Eileen Curran (*Eileen Guheen*), Brian O'Sullivan (*Liam*), Gabriel Fallon (*Father O'Sullivan*), Daisy Murphy (*Peg*), Gerald Duffy (*The Boy*), Eugene Leahy, Paddy Carey.

Ford is a medical student in Dublin who spends a holiday on the Blasket Islands, situated off the west coast of Ireland. He falls for Curran, which creates tension since she's the love of O'Sullivan. During a fishing trip, O'Sullivan goes overboard and Ford's attempts to save him prove futile, but O'Sullivan approves the Ford-Curran union before he dies. An apparent attempt to duplicate Robert Flaherty's excellent documentary MAN OF ARAN (1934), MEN OF IRELAND fails to fully capture life on the Blasket Islands, and its melodramatic story slows things down.

p, Victor Taylor; d, Dick Bird; w, Patrick Keenan Heale (based on a story by John Duffy, Donal O'Cahil); ph, Sidney Eaton.

Drama   **(PR:A   MPAA:NR)**

MEN OF SAN QUENTIN*   (1942) 80m PRC bw

J. Anthony Hughes (*Jack Holden*), Eleanor Stewart (*Anne Holden*), Dick Curtis (*Butch Mason*), Charles Middleton (*Saunderson*), Jeffrey Sayre (*Jimmy*), George Breakston (*Louis*), Art Mills (*Big Al*), John Ince (*Board Chairman*), Michael Mark (*Convict in Ravine*), Joe Whitehead (*Joe Williams*), Skins Miller (*Himself*), Jack Shay (*Phone Guard*), Jack Cheatham (*Court Gate Guard*), Drew Demarest (*Guard Gaines*), Nancy Evans (*Mrs. Doakes*).

A feeble prison drama about a guard (Hughes) who becomes warden and his attempts to implement reforms. The climax occurs when he alone prevents a break attempt.

p, Martin Mooney, Max M. King; d, William Beaudine; w, Ernest Booth (based on the story by Mooney); ph, Clark Ramsey; ed, Dan Miller.

Drama   **(PR:A   MPAA:NR)**

MEN OF SHERWOOD FOREST** 1/2   (1957, Brit.) 77m Hammer/Astor c

Don Taylor (*Robin Hood*), Reginald Beckwith (*Friar Tuck*), Eileen Moore (*Lady Alys*), David King-Wood (*Sir Guy Belton*), Patrick Holt (*King Richard*), John Van Eyssen (*Will Scarlett*), Douglas Wilmer (*Sir Nigel Saltire*), Harold Lang (*Hubert*), Leslie Linder (*Little John*), Vera Pearce (*Elvira*), John Kerr (*Brian of Eskdale*), John Stuart (*Moraine*), Raymond Rollett (*Abbot St. Jude*), Leonard Sachs (*Sheriff of Nottingham*), Bernard Bresslaw (*Outlaw*), Ballard Berkeley (*Walter*), Wensley Pithey (*Hugo*), Toke Townley, Jackie Lane, Tom Bowman, Edward Hardwicke, Michael Godfrey, Robert Hunter, Dennis Wyndham, Peter Arne, Jack McNaughton.

Taylor, following in the very large footprints of Douglas Fairbanks and Errol Flynn, portrays the legendary bandit. Duped by two disloyal noblemen into undertaking a suicidal mission to retrieve plans to free King Richard from a German castle, he goes to Germany disguised as a troubador but is captured. The Merrie Men free him and save the king from an ambush. Low-budget swashbuckler is good fun for the undiscriminating.

p, Michael Carreras; d, Val Guest; w, Allan MacKinnon; ph, Jimmy Harvey (Eastmancolor).

Adventure   **(PR:A   MPAA:NR)**

MEN OF STEEL* 1/2   (1932, Brit.) 71m Langham/UA bw

John Stuart (*James "Iron" Harg*), Benita Hume (*Audrey Paxton*), Franklin Dyall (*Charles Paxton*), Heather Angel (*Ann Ford*), Alexander Field (*Sweepy Ford*), Sydney Benson (*Lodger*), Mary Merrall (*Mrs. Harg*), Edward Ashley Cooper (*Sylvano*), Sydney Benson, Gerard Clifton, Ian Braested.

Stuart is a steel mill foreman who rises up to head of the company. He ignores machinery he knows to be unsafe until his secretary is almost killed in an accident and he makes needed changes. Routine drama hardly worth staying awake through.

p, Bray Wyndham; d, George King; w, Edward Knoblock, Billie Bristow (based on a novel by Douglas Newton); ph, Geoffrey Faithfull.

Drama   **(PR:A   MPAA:NR)**

MEN OF STEEL, 1937   (SEE: BILL CRACKS DOWN, 1937)

MEN OF STEEL, 1980   (SEE: STEEL, 1980)

MEN OF TEXAS** 1/2   (1942) 82m UNIV bw (GB: MEN OF DESTINY)

Robert Stack (*Barry Conovan*), Broderick Crawford (*Henry Clay Jackson*), Jackie Cooper (*Robert Houston Scott*), Anne Gwynne (*Jane Baxter Scott*), Ralph Bellamy (*Major Lamphere*), Jane Darwell (*Mrs. Scott*), Leo Carrillo (*Sam Sawyer*), John Litel (*Col. Scott*), William Farnum (*Gen. Sam Houston*), Janet Beecher (*Mrs. Sam Houston*), J. Frank Hamilton (*Dwight Douglass*), Kay Linaker (*Mrs. Olsen*), Joseph Crehan (*Crittenden*), Addison Richards (*Silas Hurlbert*), Frank Hagney.

"Chicago Herald" reporter Stack ventures to Texas with photographer Carrillo to get the real, untold story of post-Civil War Texas. Immediately after the war's end, Stack captures the feelings of the Confederate soldiers returning home to territories occupied by Union militia. The Chicagoans visit Gen. Sam Houston in his Huntsville home and meet Crawford and his band of rebels, who refuse to accept the South's defeat. A fine cast from top to bottom provides for some above-average entertainment.

p, George Waggner; d, Ray Enright; w, Harold Shumate, Richard Brooks (based on the story "Frontier" by Shumate); ph, Milton Krasner; ed, Clarence Kolster; art d, Jack Ottersen.

War Drama   **(PR:A   MPAA:NR)**

MEN OF THE DEEP   (SEE: ROUGH, TOUGH, AND READY, 1945)

MEN OF THE FIGHTING LADY****   (1954) 79m MGM c

Van Johnson (*Lt. Howard Thayer*), Walter Pidgeon (*Comdr. Kent Dowling*), Louis Calhern (*James A. Michener*), Dewey Martin (*Ensign Kenneth Schechter*), Keenan Wynn (*Lt. Comdr. Ted Dodson*), Frank Lovejoy (*Lt. Comdr. Paul Grayson*), Robert Horton (*Ensign Neil Conovan*), Bert Freed (*Lt. Andrew Szymanski*), Lewis Martin (*Comdr. Michael Coughlin*), George Cooper (*Cyril Roberts*), Dick Simmons (*Lt. Wayne Kimbrell*), Chris Warfield (*Pilot White*), Steve Rowland (*Pilot Johnson*), Ed Tracy (*Pilot Brown*), Paul Smith (*Ensign Dispatcher*), John Rosser (*Officer*), Ronald Lisa (*Replacement*), Teddy Infuhr (*Szymanski's Son*), Sarah Selby (*Mrs. Szymanski*), Jerry Mather, Ronald Stafford, Joseph "Bucko" Stafford (*Dodson's Sons*), Ann Baker (*Mary Reynolds*), Jonathan Hale (*Announcer*), Dorothy Patrick (*Mrs. Dodson*).

This top flight action film records an all-male cast of aircraft carrier pilots during the Korean War, their heroic flights, and tragic deaths. Johnson is the lead pilot around whom the stories revolve, all told to Calhern, playing the role of writer James A. Michener, by Martin, Wynn, Lovejoy, and others. There are a lot of landings and take-offs from the carrier and some thrilling dogfights between American and Russian-made jets but the most exciting sequence, which was based on a story by another writer, Burns, is where Johnson "talks down" a blinded Martin, so that he can land on the deck of their carrier. Here the whistling wind and the talk between the pilots would have sufficed to heighten the drama but it is almost drowned out by Rosza's overwhelming, rich score. Marton's direction is swift and economical and Ruggiero's editing is adroit and clever as he intercuts the dramatic and action scenes. (Ruggiero went to Washington and gleaned a great deal of black and white footage with some color stock footage shot during WW II and the Korean War, to be used in the film. He found one spectacular scene of a plane crashing on a carrier in 16mm black and white and, when returning to Hollywood, had backdrop specialist Warren Newcomb paint this sequence, no more than 30 feet of film, in color for a $5,000 fee, then spliced this scene to some live action footage. When Ruggiero returned to Washington to get and receive approval of the film, Pentagon experts asked him where he got the color footage for the crash and he replied: "I had it made." The Washington experts refused to believe this could be done until Ruggiero sent them the two cuts of expertly doctored film.) Pidgeon, as the ship's surgeon, is a standout, as are Johnson, Martin, and, in particular, Lovejoy, the commander who advocates low-level bombing to achieve his objectives. Freed provides some burly laughs as a much harassed repair officer putting together the broken pieces of the jets aboard the carrier. This was a heavy box office winner for MGM at the time of its release, coming just as the Korean War ended.

p, Henry Berman; d, Andrew Marton; w, Art Cohn (based on stories appearing in *The Saturday Evening Post* entitled "The Forgotten Heroes of Korea" by James A. Michener and "The Case of the Blind Pilot" by Comdr. Harry A. Burns, USN); ph, George Folsey (Ansco Color); m, Miklos Rozsa; ed, Gene Ruggiero; art d, Cedric Gibbons; tech adv, Comdr. Paul N. Gray, USN.

War Drama   **(PR:A   MPAA:NR)**

MEN OF THE HOUR*   (1935) 61m COL bw

Richard Cromwell (*Dave Durkin*), Billie Seward (*Ann Jordan*), Wallace Ford (*Andy Blane*), Jack LaRue (*Nick Thomas*), Wesley Barry (*Dick Williams*), Charles Wilson (*Harper*), Pat O'Malley (*Police Captain*), Ernie Adams, Eddie Hart, Marc Lawrence, Gene Morgan, Stanley Taylor.

The adventures of newsreel cameramen Cromwell and Ford are brought to the screen along with their passions for Miss Seward. The climax has the pair photographing a killing and then going on a chase after the culprits. Filled with newsreel and stock footage.

d, Lambert Hillyer; w, Anthony Coldeway; ph, Benjamin Kline; ed, John Rawlins.

Drama/Action   **(PR:A   MPAA:NR)**

MEN OF THE NIGHT**   (1934) 58m COL bw

Bruce Cabot (*Kelly*), Judith Allen (*Mary*), Ward Bond (*Connors*), Charles Sabin (*Davis*), John Kelly (*Chuck*), Matthew Betz (*Schmidt*), Walter McGrail (*Louie*), Maidel Turner (*Mrs. Webley*), Arthur Rankin (*Pat*), Charles C. Wilson (*Benson*), Frank Darien (*Mr. Webley*), Harry Holman (*Fat Man at Pig Stand*), James Wang (*Chop Suey Parlor Owner*), Al Hill, Louis Natheau (*Holdup Men*), Eddie Foster

(Pedro), Frank Marlowe (Gas Station Attendant), Gladys Gale (Mrs. Everett), Robert Graves (Mr. Everett), Pearl Eaton (Ethel), Frank Meredith (Motorcycle Officer), Jack Mack (Bill), Tom London (Dave Burns), Dick Rush (Conductor), Lucille Ball (Peggy), Frank O'Connor (Boss Painter), Lee Shumway (Detective), Mitchell Ingraham (Telegraph Operator), Jack King, Matty Roubert (Newsboys), Ernie Adams (Sandy), Charles McMurphy (Policeman), Bruce Randall (Police Car Driver), Herman Marks (Crook), Dutch Hendrian (Henchman), Jeanne Lawrence, Isabel Vecki, Peggy Leon, Phyllis Crane, Nell Baldwin, Louise Dean, Lucille De Never (Women).

Detective Cabot is assigned to capture a gang of thieves in Hollywood. Bond provides comic relief and Allen provides the love interest as Cabot gets his men. A lot of car chases and gunplay, though it's pretty repetitious.

d&w, Lambert Hillyer (based on his story); ph, Henry Freulich; ed, Al Clark.

Crime Drama (PR:A MPAA:NR)

MEN OF THE NORTH* (1930) 60m MGM bw

Gilbert Roland (Louis LeBey), Barbara Leonard (Nedra), Arnold Korff (John Ruskin), Robert Elliott (Sgt. Mooney), George Davis (Cpl. Smith), Nena Quartaro (Woolie Woolie), Robert Graves, Jr. (Priest).

Roland is a Canadian trapper in the Northwest Territory who falls in love with Leonard, the daughter of a wealthy mine owner. He is at first suspected of robbing gold messengers, but proves his innocence by rescuing Leonard and her father from a deadly snowstorm. The first and last MGM talkie to be shot in five (rather than three) versions: English, French, German, Italian, and Spanish.

d, Hal Roach; w, Richard Schayer (based on a story by Willard Mack); ph, Ray Binger; ed, Tom Held; art d, Cedric Gibbons; ch, Sammy Lee.

Drama (PR:A MPAA:NR)

MEN OF THE PLAINS*1/2 (1936) 62m Colony/GN bw

Rex Bell (Jim Dean), Joan Barclay (Laura), George Ball (Billy), Charles King (Johnson), Forrest Taylor (Travis), Roger Williams (Cole), Ed Cassidy (Gray), Lafe McKee (Dad Baxter), Jack Cowell (Lucky Gordon).

G-man cowboy Bell tracks and apprehends a gang of old west outlaws with a metropolitan gangster for a leader. Barclay is his romantic interrerst as the childhood sweetheart who has ties with the bad guys.

p, Arthur Alexander, Max Alexander; d, Robert Hill; w, Robert Emmett; ph, Robert Cline; ed, Charles Henkel.

Western (PR:A MPAA:NR)

MEN OF THE SEA*1/2 (1938, USSR) 83m Belogskino/Amkino bw

Boris Livanov (Commissar Vikhoriev), L. Viven (Comdr. Rostovtsev), V. Safranov (Vavilov), Leonid Smit (Signal Man Kolessov), V. Kriuger (Gunner Zheslov), G. Iniutina (Glafira), P. Gofman (Pilot Bezenchuk), V. Uralski (Machinist Kharitonich), K. Sorokin (Orderly), P. Kirillov (Dietrich), K. Matrossov (Lavretski).

Set in 1918, this picture has the Bolshevik fleet successfully defending the Baltic and Petrograd against invading forces. A husband and wife romance is tossed in for good measure, but essentially the film is concerned with the spirit of the war. (In Russian; English titles.)

d, Alexander Feinzimmer; w, Alexander Zenovin, Alexander Sthein; ph, Sviatoslav; m, V. Sherbachev.

War (PR:A MPAA:NR)

MEN OF THE SEA***

(1951, Brit.) 70m ATP/Astor bw (GB: MIDSHIPMAN EASY)

Hughie Green (Jack Easy), Margaret Lockwood (Donna Agnes), Harry Tate (Mr. Biggs), W. Robert Adams (Mesty), Roger Livesey (Capt. Wilson), Dennis Wyndham (Don Silvio), Lewis Casson (Mr. Easy), Tom Gill (Gascoine), Frederick Burtwell (Mr. Easthupp), Desmond Tester (Gossett), Dorothy Holmes-Gore (Mrs. Easy), Norman Walker, Arthur Hambling, Arnold Lucy, Esme Church, Anthony Rogers, Jacky Green, Roy Sharpe, Arthur Gomez, Andrea Malandrinos, Gladys Gordon, Christine Keir.

Good adventure movie has Green a youth in the late 18th Century who enlists in the British navy and becomes involved in a number of exciting exploits, among them, rescuing Lockwood from pirates, capturing an enemy frigate, and locating a lost treasure. Carol Reed's first solo feature (he had previously co-directed IT HAPPENED IN PARIS with Robert Wyler) shows some indication of the classics such as THE THIRD MAN (1949) and OUTCAST OF THE ISLANDS (1951) that he would later produce. (Filmed in 1935).

p, Basil Dean, Thorold Dickinson; d, Carol Reed; w, Anthony Kimmins, Peggy Thompson (based on the novel Midshipman Easy by Captain Marryat); ph, John W. Boyle; m, Frederic Austin; ed, Sidney Cole; md, Ernest Irving; art d, Edward Carrick.

Adventure (PR:A MPAA:NR)

MEN OF THE SKY* (1931) 71m FN-WB bw

Irene Delroy (Madeleine), Jack Whiting (Jack Ames), Bramwell Fletcher (Eric), John St. Polis (Madeleine's Father), Edwin Maxwell (Count), Otto Harbach (French Major), Armand Kaliz (Senor Mendoca), Frank McHugh, Lotti Loder, Otto Matieson.

A fine musical score by Jerome Kern and Otto Harbach (who also scripted) adds life to this tale of WW I French spy Delroy, her American pilot lover Whiting, and her spying father St. Polis. The lightness of tone that fills the opening is darkened when all three face a firing squad at the film's finale. Songs include: "Every Little While," "Boys March," "Stolen Dreams," "You Ought To See Sweet Marguerite."

d, Alfred E. Green; w, Jerome Kern, Otto Harbach (based on their story); ph, John Seitz; ed, Desmond O'Brien; md, Erno Rapee.

Musical/Drama (PR:A MPAA:NR)

MEN OF THE TENTH (SEE: RED, WHITE, AND BLACK, THE, 1970)

MEN OF THE TIMBERLAND*1/2 (1941) 61m UNIV bw

Richard Arlen, Andy Devine, Linda Hayes, Francis McDonald, Willard Robertson, Paul E. Burns, Gaylord [Steve] Pendleton, Hardie Albright, Roy Harris [Riley Hill], John Ellis, Jack Rice.

When a wealthy young woman takes over the ownership of valuable timberlands, she becomes the easy prey of a mischievous lumber operator who is only too willing to see that all her land is cleared of its trees. Luckily Arlen and Devine interfere to see that such a project is never carried through. Worthwhile as a chance to see Devine in another of his humorous sidekick roles.

p, Ben Pivar; d, John Rawlins; w, Maurice Tombragel, Griffin Jay (based on the story by Paul Jarrico); ph, John W. Boyle; ed, Milton Carruth; md, Maurice Wright, H. J. Salter; art d, Jack Otterson.

Western (PR:A MPAA:NR)

MEN OF TOMORROW* (1935, Brit.) 59m LFP/Mundus bw

Robert Donat (Julien Angell), Merle Oberon (Ysobel d'Aunay), Joan Gardner (Jane Anderson), Maurice Bradell (Allan Shepherd), Emlyn Williams ("Horners"), Annie Esmond (Mrs. Oliphant), Charles Carson (Senior Proctor), Gerald Cooper (Tutor), John Traynor (Mr. Waters), Esther Kiss (Maggie), Patric Knowles.

Originally released in 1932 at 88 minutes, this British film was re-released due to the rising popularity of Donat and Oberon, though they were not the film's headliners. The story belongs to Bradell, a college lad who becomes a successful novelist after being expelled from Oxford. His romance with Gardner hits the skids when she accepts a job in Oxford's chemistry lab, bringing the relationship to an end. There's a cheery reunion by the finale, however. Directed and edited by Sagan, certainly one of the few women behind the camera in the early 1930s. Sagan in 1931 directed the highly successful German picture MADCHEN IN UNIFORM (MAIDENS IN UNIFORM) which featured an all-female cast.

p, Alexander Korda; d, Leontine Sagan, Zoltan Korda; w, Arthur Wimperis, Anthony Gibbs (based on the novel The Young Apollo by Gibbs); ph, Bernard Browne; ed, Sagan; set d, Vincent Korda.

Drama (PR:A MPAA:NR)

MEN OF TWO WORLDS (SEE: KISENGA, MAN OF AFRICA, 1952, Brit.)

MEN OF YESTERDAY1/2** (1936, Brit.) 82m UK Films/AP&D bw

Stewart Rome (Maj. Radford), Sam Livesey, Hay Petrie, Eve Lister, Cecil Parker, Roddy Hughes, Ian Colin, George Robey, Will Fyffe, Ella Shields, Dick Henderson, Edgar Norfolk, Dick Francis, Edgar Driver, Frederick Culley, Freddie Watts, Patric Curwen, Stanley Kirby, Vi Kaley, Ernest Jay, John Hepworth, Henry Hepworth, J. Neil More, Gustave Ferrari, Denis Hayden, Terry Doyle, Barbara Everest.

An unusual and interesting plea for peace set during Depression years in England. Rome, a demobilized WW I major, attempts to organize a reunion of veterans of that war which will include not only British troops, but French and German, as well. Losing his job—and his income—Rome becomes dispirited and loses interest in his pacifistic quest; he even considers suicide for a time. His old army orderly, Livesey, a streetwise non-commissioned officer, rallies to him and helps to see him through his depression. The reunion of one-time enemies takes place after all. Clips from this film were released as a short subject, CAMP CONCERT, in 1941, in the second year of WW II.

p, John Barter; d, John Baxter; w, Gerald Elliott, Jack Francis.

Drama (PR:A MPAA:NR)

MEN ON CALL* (1931) 60m FOX bw

Edmund Lowe, Mae Clarke, William Harrigan, Warren Hymer, Joe Brown, Ruth Warren, Sharon Lynn, George Corcoran.

An unimpressive and extremely low-budget romancer which casts Lowe as a train engineer who falls in love with dancer Clarke. It's not long before he discovers that she has a spotted past, which caused her to change her name. He promptly walks away. Wandering carelessly in the train yard he is smacked by a train, but only injured. In a state of depression Lowe takes to the life of a park bench bum. A coast guard captain befriends him and takes him to sea where (yes, you guessed it) a young girl is drowning. He jumps in to save Clarke (whom he hasn't seen in years) and instantly they close the gap that stood between them. A laughable effort.

d, John Blystone; w, James K. McGuiness, Basil Woon (based on a story by McGuiness); ph, Charles Clarke; ed, Paul Weatherwax.

Drama/Romance (PR:A MPAA:NR)

MEN ON HER MIND, 1935 (SEE: GIRL FROM TENTH AVENUE, THE, 1935)

MEN ON HER MIND* (1944) 67m PRC bw

Mary Beth Hughes (Lily Durrell), Edward Norris (Jeffrey Wingate), Ted North (Jim Lacey), Alan Edwards (Roland Palmer), Luis Alberni (Alberti Verdi), Kay Linaker (Eloise Palmer), Claire Rochelle (Mayme Munson), Lyle Latell ("Big Joe" Munroe), Eva Hamill (Gracie Tuttle), Isabel La Mal (Miss Wiggins), Jane Chandler (Frank Tuttle).

Hughes is an ambitious girl who sets the goal of becoming a popular radio and nightclub vocalist. She refuses to let romance deter her from her career, but finally relents and walks down the aisle. Includes the tune "Heaven On Earth" (Lee Zahler, Pat O'Dea).

p, Alfred Stern; d, Wallace W. Fox; w, Raymond I. Schrock; ph, Robert Cline; ed, Charles Henkel, Jr.; md, Lee Zahler; art d, Paul Palmentola.

Musical   **(PR:A MPAA:NR)**

MEN PREFER FAT GIRLS**

(1981, Fr.) 86m Groupement des Editeurs de Films-SFP/CCFC c (LES HOMMES PREFERENT LES GROSSES)

Josiane Balasko (Lydie), Ariane Larteguy (Eva), Luis Rego (Gerard), Dominique Lavanant (Arlette), Daniel Auteuil (Jean-Yves), Xavier Saint-Macary (Ronald), Thierry Lhermitte (Herve).

A comical tale of a beefy young French gal (Balasko, who also co-scripted) who shares a room with an air-headed model after being abandoned by her fiance. Includes a fine cast of tasteful cabaret comics from France.

p, Lise Fayolle, Giorgio Silvagni, Dominique Harispuru; d, Jean-Marie Poire; w, Poire, Josiane Balasko; ph, Bernard Lutic; m, Catherine Lara; ed, Noelle Boisson; art d, Nicole Rachline.

Comedy   **(PR:C MPAA:NR)**

MEN WITH WINGS** 1/2

(1938) 105m PAR c

Fred MacMurray (Pat Falconer), Ray Milland (Scott Barnes), Louise Campbell (Peggy Ranson), Andy Devine (Joe Gibbs), Lynne Overman (Hank Rinebow), Walter Abel (Nick Ranson), Porter Hall (Hiram F. Jenkins), Kitty Kelly (Martha Ranson), Virginia Weidler (Peggy Ranson at Age 8), Donald O'Connor (Pat Falconer at Age 10), Billy Cook (Scott Barnes at Age 10), James Burke (J. A. Nolan), Willard Robertson (Col. Hadley), Dennis Morgan (Galton), Charles Trowbridge (Alcott), Jonathan Hale (Long), Juanita Quigley (Patricia Falconer at Age 6), Joan Leslie (Patricia Falconer at Age 11), Mary Brodel (Patricia Falconer at Age 17), Marilyn Knowlden (Patricia Falconer at Age 18), Archie Twitchell (Nelson), Dorothy Tennant (Mrs. Hill), Helen Dickson, Lillian West, Ethel Clayton (Women), Grace Goodall (Matron), Charles Williams (Telegraph Operator), Harry Woods (Baker), Jack Chapin (Sentry), Pat West, Lee Phelps, David Newell, Charles Hamilton (Photographers), Ronnie Rondell, Frank Mills (Mechanics), Art Rowlands, Garry Owen, Bobby Tracy, James Burtis, Paul Kruger, Ralph McCullough, Jerry Storm (Reporters), Norah Gale, Dorothy White, Dorlores Casey, Evelyn Keyes, Sheila Darcy, Cheryl Walker, Jane Dewey, Jean Fenwick, Kitty McHugh (Nurses), George Chandler (Cody), Al Hill (Mail Driver), Syd Saylor (Jimmy), Billy Bletcher (Red Cross Man), Franklin Parker (Mail Truck Driver), Sherry Hall (Field Official), Frank Clark (Burke), Robert E. Perry (Waiter), Russell Hicks (Gen. Marlin), Ruth Rogers (Girl), Jack Hubbard (Attendant), Dell Henderson (Chairman), Edward Earle (Officer), Paul Mantz (Pilot), Claire Du Brey (Edith).

Director Wellman had been a daredevil flier during WW I, had made the film WINGS, and had just come off winning the Oscar for his story on A STAR IS BORN (with Robert Carson, who wrote the story for this film), so he and Carson seemed to be the logical choices to make MEN WITH WINGS. Despite that and the lush color photography, the movie failed to ignite imaginations, as it was more of a cavalcade of flight rather than a solid story. The picture opens with three young kids, O'Connor, Weidler, and Cook, who fly a kite. Then we hear about the Wright Brothers and their successful flight at Kitty Hawk, followed by a scene with Abel, a reporter, as he attempts to fly and becomes the first air casualty, perishing in a fiery crash. Time passes and the three children grow up to become MacMurray, Campbell, and Milland. MacMurray marries Campbell, they have a child, and Milland, despite the fact that he has always loved Campbell, remains a pal to the two. With Devine around as an airplane mechanic (and to provide whatever laughs there are in the film), the careers of the three are traced until MacMurray takes off to help the Chinese in their war with the Japanese. The love story between MacMurray and Campbell takes up too much time when more emphasis on the early days of flight might have made better cinema. In the end, MacMurray loses his life in his desire to help the Chinese, and Milland moves in to take his place. Some superb aerial shots, including a dog fight, the testing of planes, and lots of other high-in-the-sky shots. But if you were to cut the excellent action, it's sort of a dull love story and falls into the mold of a cliche "two guys and a gal" tale. Ever since planes caught the public's fancy, Hollywood began making movies about them and this film was an attempt to get the same large audiences which had been attracted to TEST PILOT with Gable. In a small role, you may recognize Paul Mantz, who went on to head his own company with Frank Tallman—called "Tallmantz"—until he lost his life in an accident while shooting FLIGHT OF THE PHOENIX. Both Mantz and Tallman had been acknowledged as the best movie stunt pilots in the business and yet both lost their lives in planes. Tallman's death occured on what appeared to be a routine flight between two small airports in Southern California. He ran into thunderheads and crashed. Bad weather has always been the major problem with small airplanes and the movie community suffered a great loss with the deaths of these two air pioneers. In a small role as the pre-teen Campbell, look for Joan Leslie in her second film.

p&d, William A. Wellman; w, Robert Carson; ph, W. Howard Greene (Technicolor); ed, Tommy Scott; aerial ph, Charles Marshall.

Drama   **(PR:A MPAA:NR)**

MEN WITHOUT HONOUR*

(1939, Brit.) 59m Smith & Newman/EPC British bw

Ian Fleming (Frank Hardy), Grace Arnold (Mrs. Hardy), Howard Douglas (Fayne), W. T. Hodge (Vigor), Charles Paton (Vicar).

Poorly produced crime drama in which lawyer Fleming goes undercover to try to trap a couple of crooks for the police. The lawyer temporarily loses his wife and son when they think his honest nature has turned sour. Fleming helps to resolve the

worthless-stock swindle organized by Douglas and Hodge, saving myriad capitalists from potential ruin. Bad acting and poor plotting make this British entry a loser.

p, Bernard Smith; d, Widgey R. Newman; w, George A. Cooper (based on a story by Newman).

Crime/Drama   **(PR:A MPAA:NR)**

MEN WITHOUT LAW**

(1930) 65m Beverly/COL bw

Buck Jones (Buck Healy), Carmelita Geraghty (Juanita), Tom Carr (Tom Healy), Harry Woods (Murdock), Fred Burns (Sheriff Jim), Lydia Knott (Mrs. Healy), Victor Sarno (Senor Del Rey), Syd Saylor (Hank), Fred Kelsey (Deputy Sheriff), Lafe McKee, Ben Corbett, Art Mix [George Kesterson], Silver the Horse.

A fine Buck Jones outing which has the hero returning to Arizona after the war and seeking out the sister of a war buddy. The girl, Geraghty, has joined up with an outlaw gang which has own brother is also a member of. Everything is cleared up by the finish with the gang boss defeated and Geraghty in Jones' arms.

p, Sol Lesser; d, Louis King; w, Dorothy Howell (based on a story by Lew Seiler); ph, Ted McCord; ed, Roy Snyder; art d, Edward Jewell.

Western   **(PR:A MPAA:NR)**

MEN WITHOUT NAMES**

(1935) 66m PAR bw

Fred MacMurray (Richard Hood/Dick Grant), Madge Evans (Helen Sherwood), Lynne Overman (Gabby Lambert), David Holt (David Sherwood), J. C. Nugent (Maj. Newcomb), Leslie Fenton (Monk), Herbert Rawlinson (Crawford), Dean Jagger (Jones), Grant Mitchell (Andrew Webster), Clyde Dilson (Butch), Arthur Aylesworth (Drew), Helen Shipman (Becky), Hary Tyler (Steve), Elizabeth Patterson (Aunt Ella), Russ Clark (Adams), Frank Shannon (Leahy), Paul Fix (The Kid), George Lloyd (Louie), Hilda Vaughn (Nurse Simpson), Helen Brown (Dorothy Lambert), Creighton Hale (Groom), Oliver Eckhardt (Usher), Irving Bacon (Town Character), Caroline "Spike" Rankin (Miss Alice Withers), Ricca Allen (Lucy Withers), Ben Hall (Mr. Youngblood), Frank Sheridan (Police Captain), Jack Mulhall, Samuel Godfrey, Phil Tead (Reporters), Ben Taggart (Police Lieutenant), Arthur "Pop" Byron (The Yap), Ivan "Dusty" Miller, Buddy Roosevelt (Agents), Stanley Andrews (Jim the Fingerprint Man), John Wray (Sam "Red" Hammond), Henry Roquemore (Mr. Hines).

An early Fred MacMurray outing which has him working as a government detective in pursuit of a bank robbing gang. He finally tracks them to a small town and emerges victorious from a factory shootout which is undeniably a copy of THE MAN WHO KNEW TOO MUCH. There's not nearly enough story here to hold one's interest for long, but then again the film's barely an hour long.

p, Albert Lewis; d, Ralph Murphy; w, Howard J. Green, Kubec Glasmon (based on a story by Dale Van Every, Marguerite Roberts); ph, Ben Reynolds; ed, Stuart Heisler.

Crime   **(PR:A MPAA:NR)**

MEN WITHOUT SOULS**

(1940) 62m COL bw

John Litel (Rev. Thomas Storm), Barton MacLane (Blackie Drew), Rochelle Hudson (Suzan Leonard), Glenn Ford (Johnny Adams), Don Beddoe (Warden Schafer), Cy Kendall (Capt. White), Eddie Laughton (Lefty), Dick Curtis (Duke), Richard Fiske (Crowley), Walter Soderling (Old Mack).

An average copy of previous prison dramas with Litel as the tough chaplain who saves the life of Ford (in one of his first roles). Entering prison to avenge his father's death, Ford gets involved with a murderous gang and a jailbreak. Litel comes to Ford's rescue in a formula ending. Interesting mainly to see a baby-faced Ford.

d, Nick Grinde; w, Robert D. Andrews, Joseph Carole (from the story by Harvey Gates); ph, Benjamin Kline; m, M. W. Stoloff; ed, James Sweeney.

Crime Drama   **(PR:A MPAA:NR)**

MEN WITHOUT WOMEN***

(1930) 77m FOX bw

Kenneth MacKenna (Chief Torpedoman Burke), Frank Albertson (Ens. Price), Paul Page (Handsome), Walter McGrail (Cobb), Warren Hymer (Kaufman), J. Farrell MacDonald (Costello), Stuart Erwin (Jenkins the Radio Operator), George LeGuere (Pollock), Ben Hendricks, Jr. (Murphy), Harry Tenbrook (Dutch Winkler), Warner Richmond (Lt. Comdr. Bridewell), Roy Stewart (Capt. Carson), Charles Gerard (Comdr. Weymouth), Pat Somerset (Lt. Digby), John Wayne, Robert Parrish.

Hard-hitting suspenseful story that will leave you wrung out by the gripping drama. The picture begins in Shanghai where a bunch of U.S. sailors are having a wild time in a huge night spot that features anything at all a person might want in the way of liquid or fleshy entertainment. The crew is called for duty and has to say bye-bye to the girls of the club. They return to their submarine carrying various artifacts as well as bottles of hooch. Once on the submarine, they head out to sea, are involved in a collision, and go straight to the bottom. There is no way for them to escape as the sea water damages various parts of the ship, including the wireless equipment, so there is just a little time before the "S.O.S." ceases. A few other ships have heard the weak signal and the rest of the film is a race with death as the vessels steam toward the stricken sub. Air is rapidly getting foul and we see the men reveal themselves under the pressure of their approaching deaths. Divers arrive and go down 90 feet where they attempt to communicate with the trapped men by rapping on the hull. The picture intercuts between the rescuers and the trapped submariners. One by one, the men go through the torpedo tube and now a problem arises; the captain, Stewart, feels he must stay with the ship, as one man is needed to remain there to pull the levers which free the next to last man. McKenna, however, has a back story; he is a British officer who was cashiered from his service in disgrace and everyone thought he was dead. If he is discovered to be alive, it would be an embarrassment for the woman he loves and left behind. So McKenna whacks Stewart unconscious and sends him through the torpedo tube and stays in the sub, where he will perish. The sailors bob to the surface one by one and when Stewart comes up and realizes what's happened, he keeps McKenna's secret. While a bugler plays "Taps," the crew stand at attention for the heroism of McKenna, who is still at the bottom of the sea. There have been several "men-under-the-sea" films since, none of which compares with the tension of this, which may have been the first of the "trapped" genre. This was the first collaboration between Ford and Nichols, a partnership that lasted for years and resulted in several of the most memorable of the macho pictures. Look for John Wayne in a small role. Actor Robert Parrish later became an editor (winning the Oscar for BODY AND SOUL with Francis Lyons), then a director of many films.

d, John Ford; w, Dudley Nichols (based on a story by Ford, James Kevin McGuinness); ph, Joseph August; m, Peter Brunelli, Glen Knight; ed, Paul Weatherwax; art d, William Darling.

Sea Drama   **(PR:A   MPAA:NR)**

MEN WOMEN LOVE   (SEE: SALVATION NELL, 1931)

MENACE, THE*½   (1932) 71m COL bw

H. B. Warner (Tracy), Bette Davis (Peggy), Walter Byron (Ronald), Natalie Moorhead (Caroline), William B. Davidson (Utterson), Crauford Kent (Lewis), Halliwell Hobbes (Phillips), Charles Gerrard (Bailiff), Murray Kinnell (Carr).

Strictly a routine programmer despite the presence of blonde Davis and Warner, THE MENACE was one of those bottom-of-the-bill films that failed to excite anyone except the relatives of the people associated with the movie. Byron is a handsome Englishman who is sent to prison for killing his father. But it's all a ruse, as the poor lad is innocent and has been condemned due to the testimony of his stepmother, Moorhead, who wants the estate for herself. Byron escapes penal servitude and comes to the U.S. where he gets a job as a roughneck in the oilfields. While working there bringing in a gusher, his face is burned and he must have a total remake on his phiz with an excellent plastic surgeon. Now looking like someone else entirely, he decides to return to England and clear his name. He arrives at the estate to learn that Moorhead is offering it for sale. He insinuates himself into the family and neither Moorhead nor Davis, his one-time fiancee, spots him for who he is. Byron senses that Moorhead is behind his late father's demise, so he soon works his way into her heart and feigns a romantic attachment. When he gives her a precious necklace, she happily shows it to her apparently permanent house guests, Kent and Davidson, who are the killers of Byron's father. Byron decides to see if there is honor among thieves, so he steals the necklace and deliberately makes it look as though Davidson is the crook. Kent learns that Davidson "stole" the bauble and promptly kills his partner and when Davis discovers the body, she faints dead away. In walks the top-billed Warner, a representative of Scotland Yard, to clear up this second murder at the estate. Warner is apparently much smarter than anyone else because he soon spies the fact that Byron is the man who was sent to jail for the murder of his father. Warner is about to take Byron in, but the young man is too quick and adroitly sets a snare which causes Kent to admit that he killed Davidson and aided Moorhead in killing Byron's father. That out of the way, Davis and Byron are free to live happily in the ancestral mansion. This film meant little to anyone except Davis, for it was here that she met character actor Kinnell, who was a great pal of George Arliss. Kinnell arranged a meeting between Davis and Arliss and he decided to use her in his film THE MAN WHO PLAYED GOD, which, in turn, led to several important jobs and Davis' career went skyward.

p, Sam Nelson; d, Roy William Neill; w, Dorothy Howell, Charles Logue, Roy Chanslor (based on The Feathered Serpent by Edgar Wallace); ph, L. William O'Connell; ed, Gene Havlick.

Crime Drama   **(PR:A-C   MPAA:NR)**

MENACE**   (1934) 57m PAR bw

Gertrude Michael (Helen Chalmers), Paul Cavanagh (Colonel Crecy), Henrietta Crosman (Mrs. Thornton), John Lodge (Ronald Cavendish), Robert Allen (Andrew Forsythe), Raymond Milland (Freddie Bastion), Berton Churchill (Norman Bellamy), Desmond Roberts (Underwood), Halliwell Hobbes (Skinner), Forrester Harvey (Wilcox), Montagu Love (Police Inspector), Doris Llewellyn (Cynthia Bastion), Arletta Duncan (Gloria Chambers), Gwenllian Gill (Alison Bastion), Arthur Clayton (Police Officer), Rita Carlyle (English Landlady), A. S. Byron (English Police Sergeant).

A mysterious maniac threatens Michael, Cavanagh, and Churchill and follows them from Africa to California. He has it in his head that the trio is responsible for the death of his brother. He gets to Churchill, but before he can kill again he is captured. Standard suspenser.

d, Ralph Murphy; w, Anthony Veiller, Chandler Sprague (based on a story by Philip MacDonald); ph, Benjamin Reynolds.

Drama   **(PR:A   MPAA:NR)**

MENACE, 1934, Brit.   (SEE: WHEN LONDON SLEEPS, 1934, Brit.)

MENACE IN THE NIGHT**
(1958, Brit.) 78m Gibraltar/UA bw (GB: FACE IN THE NIGHT)

Griffith Jones (Rapson), Lisa Gastoni (Jean Francis), Vincent Ball (Bob Meredith), Eddie Byrne (Art), Victor Maddern (Ted), Clifford Evans (Inspector Ford), Joan Miller (Victor's Wife), Leonard Sachs (Victor), Leslie Dwyer (Toby), Jenny Laird (Postman's Widow), Angela White (Betty Francis), Barbara Couper (Mrs. Francis), Marie Burke (Auntie), Andre Van Gyseghem (Bank Manager).

Robbers led by Jones plan a near perfect heist of 250 pounds sterling from a van on its way to an incinerator. They steal the withered notes, but are seen by a lovely blonde witness (Gastoni), who cooperates with the police. Also on their trail is an energetic young reporter. In-fighting tears the gang apart, however, resulting in the death of one member. The remaining three end up in the Thames after the driver

hurls the getaway car off of a rising London Bridge. Hampered by some less-than-impressive camerawork.

p, Charles Leeds; d, Lance Comfort; w, Norman Hudis, John Sherman (based on the novel Suspense by Bruce Graeme); ph, Arthur Graham; m, Richard Bennett; ed, Peter Pitt; md, Philip Martell; art d, John Stoll.

Crime   **(PR:A   MPAA:NR)**

MENNESKER MODES OG SOD MUSIK OPSTAR I HJERTET
(SEE: PEOPLE MEET AND SWEET MUSIC FILLS THE HEART, 1969, Swed.)

MENSCHEN IM NETZ   (SEE: UNWILLING AGENT, 1968, Ger.)

MEPHISTO**   (1981, Ger.) 144m Mafilm-Durniok/Cinegate-Analysis c

Klaus Maria Brandauer (Hendrik Hofgen), Krystyna Janda (Barbara Bruckner), Ildiko Bansagi (Nicoletta Von Niebuhr), Karin Boyd (Juliette Martens), Rolf Hoppe (The General), Christine Harbort (Lotte Lindenthal), Gyorgy Cserhalmi (Hans Miklas), Christiane Graskoff (Cesar Von Muck), Peter Andorai (Otto Ulrichs), Ildiko Kishonti (Dora Martin), Tamas Major (Oskar H. Kroge), Maria Bisztrai, Sandor Lukacs, Agnes Banfalvi, Judit Hernadi, Vilmos Kun, Ida Versenyi, Istvan Komlos, Sari Gencsy, Zdzislaw Mrozewski, Stanislava Strobachova, Karoly Ujlaky, Professor Martin Hellberg, Katalin Solyom, Gyorgy Banffy, Josef Csor, Hedi Temessy, David Robinson, Geza Kovacs, Teri Tordai, Hans Ulrich Laufer, Margrid Hellberg, Kerstin Hellberg.

The winner of 1982's Academy Award for "Best Foreign Film," MEPHISTO is an inspired update of the "Faust" legend with a paramount performance by Klaus Maria Brandauer. A critically acclaimed stage actor, Brandauer tires of the usual entertainment forms of theater and attempts something more revolutionary, a la Bertolt Brecht. He does not rise to fame, however, occassionally having to deal with such nuisances as having his name spelled wrong on a poster. Brandauer sells his soul, not to the devil but to the Nazis—his desire for fame more urgent than his dislike for the oppressor. It is only later, after he is indebted to the Third Reich, that he realizes his mistake. Based on a novel by Klaus Mann, son of Thomas, and exquisitely photographed, MEPHISTO is bubbling over with energy. It is Brandauer's bravura performance that deserves the most credit for this energy. He went on to grace American screens with his villainous role in the James Bond thriller NEVER SAY NEVER AGAIN. (In German; English titles.)

p, Manfred Durniok; d, Istvan Szabo; w, Szabo, Peter Dobai (based on the novel by Klaus Mann); ph, Lajos Koltai (Eastmancolor); m, Zdenko Tamassy; ed, Zsuzsa Csekany; art d, Jozsef Romvari.

Drama   **Cas.**   **(PR:O   MPAA:NR)**

MEPHISTO WALTZ, THE*   (1971) 115m FOX c

Alan Alda (Myles Clarkson), Jacqueline Bisset (Paula Clarkson), Curt Jurgens (Duncan Ely), Barbara Parkins (Roxanne), Bradford Dillman (Bill Delancey), William Windom (Dr. West), Kathleen Widdoes (Maggie West), Pamelyn Ferdin (Abby Clarkson), Curt Lowens (Agency Head), Gregory Morton (Conductor), Janee Michelle (Agency Head's Girl), Lilyan Chauvin (Woman Writer), Khigh Dhiegh (Zanc Theun), Alberto Morin (Bennet), Berry Kroeger (Raymont), Terence Scammell (Richard).

When an aging piano player (Jurgens) grants Alda an interview, strange things happen. Jurgens, a practicing Satanist, takes over Alda's body to continue living after he dies of leukemia. Bisset, Alda's wife, eventually notices the change (though it takes a bit too long) and also becomes possessed after making a pact with the devil. Bisset then kills Jurgens' daughter, Parkins (with whom Jurgens is carrying on an incestuous affair), assuming her body, and ending up with Jurgens/Alda. There are some genuinely chilling scenes (as in most Satanic films), but it is still a made-for-TV-ish ROSEMARY'S BABY rip-off. A creepy score by Goldsmith is nearly as frightening as the subject matter. Jakob Gimpel does a piano rendition of Franz Liszt's "The Mephisto Waltz".

p, Quinn Martin; d, Paul Wendkos; w, Ben Maddow (based on the novel by Fred Mustard Stewart); ph, William W. Spencer (DeLuxe Color); m, Jerry Goldsmith; ed, Richard Brockway; art d, Richard Y. Haman; set d, Walter M. Scott, Raphael Bretton; cos, Moss Mabry; spec eff, Howard A. Anderson; makeup, Dan Striepeke.

Horror/Drama   **(PR:C-O   MPAA:R)**

MERCENARIES, THE   (SEE: DARK OF THE SUN, 1968, Brit.)

MERCENARY, THE*½
(1970, Ital./Span.) 105m P.E.A.-Produzioni Associate Delphos-Profilms 21/UA c (IL MERCENARIO; SALARIO PARA MATAR)

Franco Nero (Bill Douglas), Tony Musante (Eufemio), Jack Palance (Ricciolo), Giovanna Ralli (Columba), Eduardo Fajardo (Alfonso Garcia), Bruno Corazzari (Studs), Remo De Angelis (Hudo), Joe Camel (Larkin), Franco Giacobini (Pepote), Vicente Roca (Elias Garcia), Jose Riesgo (2nd Mexican), Angel Ortiz (3rd Mexican), Fernando Villena (Sergeant), Tito Garcia (Vigilante), Angel Alvarez (Notary), Juan Cazalilla (Mayor), Guillermo Mendez (Captain), Jose Zalde (Innkeeper), Alvaro de Luna (Ramon), Jose Antonio Lopez (Juan), Milo Quesada (Marco), Raf Baldassarre (Mateo), Jose Canalejas (Pablo), Simon Arriaga (Simon), Paco Nieto (Antonio), Jose Ma Aguinaco (Ramirez), Franco Ressel, Ugo Adinolfi.

A better than average spaghetti oater has Nero in the title role as the hired hand assigned to help a mine owner transport silver across the border to Texas during the Mexican Revolution. He finds himself up against a troop of Mexican soldiers, killing them with the aid of a machinegun after they try to claim the mine. Nero teams with Musante and together they travel around, rob banks, and free revolutionaries. Eventually, after a fair amount of fighting and back-stabbing, the pair go their separate ways. The highlight, however, is when a naked Palance (also a mercenary) is left by Nero in the desert. Morricone's score, again, is as atmospheric as the setting.

MERCHANT OF SLAVES

p, Alberto Grimaldi; d, Sergio Corbucci; w, Luciano Vincenzoni, Sergio Spina, Corbucci (based on a story by Franco Solinas, Giorgio Arlorio); ph, Alejandro Ulloa (Techniscope, Technicolor); m, Ennio Morricone, Bruno Nicolai; ed, Eugenio Alabiso; art d, Luis Vazquez, Piero Filippone; cos, Jurgen Henze; spec eff, Manuel Baquero, C. Battistelli; makeup, Raoul Ranieri.

Western (PR:C MPAA:NR)

MERCHANT OF SLAVES*

(1949, Ital.) 68m Colosseum/Lux bw

Annette Back (*Fiamma*), Enzo Fiermonte (*Ali*), Mara Ciukleva (*Marta*), Augusto Di Giovanni (*Marco*), Dino Di Luca (*Andrea*), Augusto Marcacci (*Ahmed*), Elena Zareschi (*Francesca*).

A slave ship captained by Fiermonte picks up a number of half-clad women along the coast of Italy. Back is the unfortunate one who falls in love with the captain and soon ends up with child. Her family is far from happy and plots to kill her and the newborn. She makes a getaway, however, on board the ship with Fiermonte. Confused and exploitative. (In Italian; English subtitles).

d, Duilio Coletti; w, Nicola Manzari, Cesare Vico Ludovici; ph, Aldo Tonti; m, Piero Giorgi; English titles, Clare Catalano.

Drama (PR:C MPAA:NR)

MERCY ISLAND**

(1941) 72m REP bw

Ray Middleton (*Warren Ramsey*), Gloria Dickson (*Leslie Ramsey*), Otto Kruger (*Dr. Sanderson*), Don Douglas (*Clay Foster*), Forrester Harvey (*Capt. Lowe*), Terry Kilburn (*Wiccy*).

Set in the Florida Keys (a pleasant change of scenery) this picture centers around a fishing outing led by Middleton. In pursuit of an elusive fish, the afternoon at sea turns into a nightmarish adventure. The group ends up shipwrecked on a remote island, with only a minimum of provisions. An island recluse comes to their aid, but not before Middleton has gone completely mad and has been eaten by an alligator. Some favorable island photography and underwater camerawork.

p, Armand Schaefer; d, William Morgan; w, Malcolm Stuart Boylan (based on the novel by Theodore Pratt); ph, Reggie Lanning; ed, Ernest Nims.

Adventure (PR:A MPAA:NR)

MERCY PLANE**

(1940) 72m PRC bw (GB: WONDER PLANE)

James Dunn (*Speed Leslie*), Frances Gifford (*Brenda Gordon*), Matty Fain (*Rocco Wolf*), William Pawley (*Jim Gordon*), Harry Harvey (*Curly*), Forbes Murray (*Benson*), Edwin Miller, Duke York.

Dunn plays a pilot who's hired to test a new, specially equipped medical plane. When the plane is stolen, he's the chief suspect and is grounded. Gifford is an ace female pilot who convinces her brother, Pawley, to give Dunn a job. It turns out that Pawley runs a gang which steals planes and sells them to other nations, and he was behind the theft of the medical plane. Pawley is devoted to his sister, and Dunn kidnaps her in an effort to trap Pawley and prove his innocence. The plot works, and Dunn gets the plane and the girl.

p, Sigmund Neufeld; d, Richard Harlan; w, William Lively; ph, Jack Greenhalgh; ed, Holbrook N. Todd.

Action (PR:A MPAA:NR)

MERELY MARY ANN** 1/2

(1931) 72m FOX bw

Janet Gaynor (*Mary Ann*), Charles Farrell (*John Lonsdale*), Beryl Mercer (*Mrs. Leadbatter*), J. M. Kerrigan, Tom Whitely (*Draymen*), Lorna Balfour (*Rosie Leadbatter*), Arnold Lucy (*Vicar Smedge*), G. P. Huntley, Jr. (*Peter Brooke*), Harry Rosenthal.

Cleaning girl Gaynor meets pianist-composer Farrell one day while cleaning his boardinghouse room. She is attracted to him, and he eventually falls for her. Because he refuses to compose popular songs he doesn't make enough cash to cover the rent. He gets his big break when asked to write an opera. She inherits a great fortune, which scares Farrell off. He refuses to marry her because of his fear that people will think he wed her for her wealth. Unhappy, though a success, he returns to the cottage where they first met, and unexpectedly is reunited with Gaynor. Silent versions of the film were made in 1916 and 1920 in the U.S., with Michael Curtiz directing a European version in his native Hungary in 1916.

d, Henry King; w, Jules Furthman (based on the play by Israel Zangwill); ph, John Seitz, Arthur Arling; ed, Frank Hull; m/l, James F. Hanley.

Romance (PR:A MPAA:NR)

MERELY MR. HAWKINS*

(1938, Brit.) 71m RKO bw

Eliot Makeham (*Alfred Hawkins*), Sybil Grove (*Charlotte Hawkins*), Dinah Sheridan (*Betty Hawkins*), George Pembroke (*John Fuller*), Jonathan Field (*Richard*), Jack Vyvyan (*Harry*), Max Adrian (*Mr. Fletcher*), Michael Ripper, Ann Wilton.

Another of those early British farces having a ridiculous premise. A man, Makeham, is made president of The Henpecked Husbands' League (believe it or not). He saves his daughter Sheridan from a disastrous marriage to a crook posing as a rich man. It is through this feat that Makeham is able to prove to his wife who wears the pants in the family; it was his wife who tried marrying the daughter off to this crook in the first place. Had they had anything to work with, the actors might have created some genuinely funny moments, but it would be hard to find the slightest thing to laugh about except the thought that someone actually had the naivete to make this milktoast myth into a film.

p, George Smith; d, Maclean Rogers; w, John Hunter; ph, Geoffrey Faithfull.

Comedy (PR:A MPAA:NR)

MERMAID, THE**

(1966, Hong Kong) 99m Shaw Brothers/Frank Lee c

Ivy Ling Po (*Chang Chen*), Li Ching (*Fairy Marina/Peony Chin*), Ching Miao (*Lord Pao*), Au-yang Sha-fei (*Madam Wang*), Yang Tse-ching (*Chin*), Chiang Kuang-chao (*Turtle Fairy*), Tung Di (*Lobster Fairy*), Li Yuen-chung (*Sorcerer*), Yeh Ching, Feng I, Yueh Hua.

An operatic fairy tale which has a young peasant trying to become a learned man in order to become worthy enough to wed the woman he is betrothed to. A fairy comes to his aid and eventually the pair fall in love. The Goddess of Mercy lends her wand so the fairy can shed her alternate form, that of a 1,000-year-old carp, and happily wed the now-wiser peasant.

p, Runme Shaw; d, Kao Li; w, Chang Chein; ph, Tung Shao-yung (Shawscope, Eastmancolor); m, Wang Fu-ling; ed, Chiang Hsing-lung; art d, Chen Chi-jui.

Operatic Film/Fantasy (PR:A MPAA:NR)

MERMAIDS OF TIBURON, THE*

(1962) 77m Aquarex-Pacifica/Filmgroup-Art Films c (AKA: THE AQUA SEX)

Diane Webber (*Mermaid Queen*), George Rowe (*Dr. Samuel Jamison*), Timothy Carey (*Milo Sangster*), Jose Gonzalez-Gonzalez (*Pepe Gallardo*), John Mylong (*Ernst Steinhauer*), Gil Baretto (*Senor Barquero*), Vicki Kantenwine, Nani Morrissey, Judy Edwards, Jean Carroll, Diana Cook, Karen Goodman, Nancy Burns (*Mermaids*).

Rowe is a marine biologist and Carey is a murderer. Both are on the trail of elusive "fire pearls" which are reputed to be somewhere near Tiburon, an obscure island off the coast of Mexico. While tracking the gems, Carey kills Mexican sea captain Gonzalez-Gonzalez and Rowe meets up with a school of mermaids. (What other collective noun could there be for them? A bevy of? A convey of? If they were mermaids with loose morals, we might call them "a blare of strumpets.") Most of the above-water narrative is dull and laced with pseudo-science. The picture takes a turn for the better (but not much) when it dives beneath the surface. Mermaids have been seen before (MR. PEABODY AND THE MERMAID) and after (SPLASH) but seldom less engagingly than in this film. Made in something called Aquascope.

p,d&w, John Lamb; ph, Lamb, Hal McAlpin, Brydon Baker (Aquascope, Eastmancolor); m, Richard La Salle; ed, Bert Honey.

Drama (PR:A-C MPAA:NR)

MERRILL'S MARAUDERS*** 1/2

(1962) 98m United States Productions/WB c

Jeff Chandler (*Brig. Gen. Merrill*), Ty Hardin (*Stock*), Peter Brown (*Bullseye*), Andrew Duggan (*Maj. [Doc] Nemeny*), Will Hutchins (*Chowhound*), Claude Akins (*Sgt. Kolowicz*), Luz Valdez (*Burmese Girl*), John Hoyt (*Gen. Stilwell*), Charles Briggs (*Muley*), Jack C. Williams (*Medic*), Chuck Hicks (*Cpl. Doskis*), Vaughan Wilson (*Lt. Col. Bannister*), Pancho Magolona (*Taggy*), Chuck Roberson, Chuck Hayward (*Officers*), Peter Brown (*Bullseye*).

In Burma in 1944, Chandler commands a regiment deep behind Japanese lines. Though exhausted by their long trek through the jungle, the men capture their objective like the well-trained, experienced fighting men they are. As they sit resting, expecting to be relieved, Chandler receives orders to march them several hundred more miles to capture a rail yard at Shadzup and then on to Myitkina. He tells the men about Shadzup but doesn't tell them about the second objective. The men manage to drag themselves along, growing disoriented as hunger, disease, and fatigue take their toll. Finally they reach Shadzup and a confused, bloody battle ensues among a labyrinth of concrete pillars. After the battle the men again collapse exhausted only to have Chandler exhort them to get on their feet and move on to Myitkina. They don't move and Chandler collapses, dead of a heart attack. Lieutenant Hardin takes over and gets them moving on to the next objective. An excellent study of the burden of command as Chandler is forced by orders from his superiors to push his men onward when they clearly are unable to move. And yet move they do, out of personal loyalty to Chandler and because they're the infantry and that's what they've been trained to do. The film's centerpiece is the assault on Shadzup. The cutting is quick and confusing, as the men twist and scramble around the concrete megaliths, killing and dying (Fuller originally intended to show the number of men killed accidentally by their own side in the confusion of the battle, but this was rejected as too depressing). When the battle is over, a crane shot reveals just how small the battlefield was, and the ground is covered with hundreds of dead Americans and Japanese. One of Fuller's most successful films, it is also quite accurate in its historical details, and the film boasts well-written dialog, excellent cinematography, and terrific performances, including Chandler in his last role. He died of blood poisoning following surgery before the film was released.

p, Milton Sperling; d, Samuel Fuller; w, Fuller, Milton Sperling (based on the novel by Charlton Ogburn, Jr.); ph, William Clothier (Technicolor); m, Howard Jackson; ed, Folmar Blangsted; art d, William Magginetti; spec eff, Ralph Ayres; makeup, Gordon Bau.

War (PR:C-O MPAA:NR)

MERRILY WE GO TO HELL* 1/2

(1932) 78m PAR bw (GB: MERRILY WE GO TO. . .)

Sylvia Sidney (*Joan Prentice*), Fredric March (*Jerry Corbett*), Adrienne Allen (*Claire Hempstead*), Richard "Skeets" Gallagher (*Buck*), Florence Britton (*Charlcie*), Esther Howard (*Vi*), George Irving (*Mr. Prentice*), Kent Taylor (*Dick Taylor*), Charles Coleman (*Damery*), Leonard Carey (*Butler*), Milla Davenport (*Housekeeper*), Robert Greig (*Baritone*), Rev. Neal Dodd (*Minister*), Mildred Boyd (*June*), Cary Grant (*Stage Leading Man*), Gordon Westcott, Jay Eaton, Pat Somerset (*Friends*), Theresa Harris (*Powder Room Attendant*), LeRoy Mason (*Guest*), Dennis O'Keefe (*Usher*), Tom Ricketts (*Guest at Wedding*), Edwin Maxwell (*Jake Symonds, Agent*), Bill Elliott (*Dance Extra*), Ernie S. Adams (*Reporter*).

In England, the bluenoses decided that the title would never do so it had to be amended to MERRILY WE GO TO. . . . That decision is almost, but not quite, as inane as the movie. Everyone drank and smoked in the movies of the early 1930s and this is a prime example. March is a mostly tipsy newpaperman who has aspirations to the theater and is on the verge of having a play of his produced. He is about to attend his own engagement party, but goes out on a toot and leaves his fiancee, Sidney, fuming. She's a wealthy heiress and very concerned about status. Gallagher, a friend of March's, has been assigned to keep an eye on the newsman but doesn't live up to his promise. March's play opens and he celebrates by getting even drunker than the time before. Sidney and March are married and he manages to misplace the wedding ring, so they have to replace it with a can opener in order to seal the marriage. March keeps tossing 'em down and Sidney gets disenchanted and leaves him, returning to Chicago and her father, Irving. But the short marriage has produced a pregnancy and several complications. Sidney goes to the hospital and her life is threatened. Irving is totally against March, but he finally relents somewhat and March goes to see Sidney in the hospital where he promises to swear off the hooch so they can make a new life together as a family. One of the very earliest female directors, Dorothy Arzner, does her best with the bogus sophistication, but it's to no avail and the picture of March trying to emulate Jack Norton (the world's best screen drinker) is not a pretty one. A lot of drinking jokes in the padded story take up too much time and are no substitute for content. In a small role, you'll spot Cary Grant in his third screen assignment.

d, Dorothy Arzner; w, Edwin Justus Mayer (based on the novel *I, Jerry Take Thee, Joan* by Cleo Lucas); ph, David Abel.

Comedy **(PR:A-C MPAA:NR)**

MERRILY WE LIVE*** (1938) 90m MGM bw

Constance Bennett *(Jerry Kilbourne)*, Brian Aherne *(Wade Rawlins)*, Billie Burke *(Mrs. Emily Kilbourne)*, Alan Mowbray *(Grosvenor, the Butler)*, Patsy Kelly *(Rosa, the Cook)*, Ann Dvorak *(Minerva Harlan)*, Bonita Granville *(Marion Kilbourne)*, Tom Brown *(Kane Kilbourne)*, Clarence Kolb *(Mr. Kilbourne)*, Marjorie Rambeau *(Senator Harlan's Wife)*, Philip Reed *(Herbert Wheeler)*, Willie Best *(George W. Jones)*, Sidney Bracey *(2nd Butler)*, Paul Everton *(Senator Harlan)*, Marjorie Kane *(Rose, the Maid)*.

A vibrant quick-moving farce from Hal Roach and Norman Z. McLeod, which casts Burke as the harebrained mother of an equally daffy family. She is obsessed with doing a good turn and allows bums to come in off the street and live with the family. When an unshaven writer (Aherne) asks to use the phone he is mistaken for another tramp and invited in. He accepts and soon gets accustomed to her hospitality. He brings a sense of order to the household and inevitably falls in love with Bennett, Burke's eldest daughter. A sterling example of screwball comedy under the seasoned hands of a fine producer and director.

p, Hal Roach; d, Norman Z. McLeod; w, Eddie Moran, Jack Jevne; ph, Norbert Brodine; ed, William Terhune; md, Marvin Hatley; art d, Charles D. Hall; spec eff, Ray Seawright; m/l, title song, Phil Charig, Arthur Quenzer.

Comedy **(PR:A MPAA:NR)**

MERRY ANDREW ½** (1958) 103m MGM c

Danny Kaye *(Andrew Larabee)*, Pier Angeli *(Selena)*, Baccaloni *(Antonio Gallini)*, Noel Purcell *(Matthew Larabee)*, Robert Coote *(Dudley Larabee)*, Patricia Cutts *(Letitia Fairchild)*, Rex Evans *(Gregory Larabee)*, Walter Kingsford *(Mr. Fairchild)*, Peter Mamakos *(Vittorio Gallini)*, Rhys Williams *(Constable)*, Tommy Rall *(Giacomo Gallini)*.

Kaye, an instructor at a stuffy boys' school in England, sets out on an archaeological dig and finds himself befriended by a circus performer. He travels with the girl (Angeli) to the big top where he dons some clown makeup and gets into the act. Pretty tame in comparison to Kaye's early efforts, but still enjoyable. Includes the tunes: "Pipes of Pan," "Salud," "Chin Up Stout Fellows," "Everything Is Tickety Boo," "You Can't Always Have What You Want," "Square of the Hypotenuse," and "Here's Cheers" (Saul Chaplin, Johnny Mercer).

p, Sol C. Siegel; d, Michael Kidd; w, Isobel Lennart, I. A. L. Diamond (based on the story "The Romance of Henry Menafee" by Paul Gallico); ph, Robert Surtees (CinemaScope, Metrocolor); m, Saul Chaplin; ed, Harold F. Kress; md, Nelson Riddle; art d, William Horning, Gene Allen; cos, Walter Plunkett; ch, Kidd.

Musical/Comedy **(PR:AA MPAA:NR)**

MERRY CHRISTMAS MR. LAWRENCE****

(1983, Jap./Brit.) 124m Recorded Picture-Cineventure TV, Asahi-Oshima/UNIV c

David Bowie *(Celliers)*, Tom Conti *(Col. John Lawrence)*, Ryuichi Sakamoto *(Capt. Yoni)*, Takeshi *(Sgt. Hara)*, Jack Thompson *(Hicksley-Ellis)*, Johnny Okura *(Kanemoto)*, Alistair Browning *(DeJong)*, James Malcolm *(Celliers' Brother)*, Chris Brown *(Celliers at Age 12)*, Yuya Uchida, Ryunosuke Kaneda, Takashi Naito, Tamio Ishikura, Rokko Toura, Kan Mikami, Yuji Honma, Daisuke Iijima, Hideo Murota, Barry Dorking, Geoff Clendon, Grant Bridger, Richard Adams, Marcus Campbell, Colin Francis, Richard Hoare, Martin Ibbertson, Marc Berg, Rob Jayne, Richard Mills, Mark Penrose.

Conti, a British officer in a POW camp in Java during WW II, is awakened by Takeshi to witness the hara-kiri of a Korean guard. The guard has sodomized a Dutch prisoner and to regain his dignity he will be allowed to commit suicide. Conti tries to intervene in this brutal game, but he is beaten back. The camp commandant, Sakamoto arrives as the guard takes a bayonet and plunges into himself, but suffers only a wound. Sakamoto demands a report be filed by the time he returns from the trial of a British soldier. Bowie is the defiant soldier on trial for spying. Sakamoto is taken by Bowie's strength and after a faked firing squad the British soldier is delivered to Sakamoto's camp. There, Bowie is reunited with Conti, whom he had fought with in Libya. Conti finds Sakamoto's concern over Bowie's health and past strange and soon discovers that the captain plans to make Bowie the prisoners' commanding officer, replacing Thompson. Sakamoto finds Thompson's reciting of the Geneva Convention rules and refusal to honor the Dutch soldier's death at the offical hara-kiri of the guard signs of weakness. With the Dutchman's death, the camp is put on a 48-hour fast for spiritual laziness. Bowie defies the Japanese by bringing in food and leading the men in a memorial for the dead soldier. Sakamoto throws Bowie into the cells and Conti is also placed there when a radio is found in the sick bay. After Sakamoto's butler tries to kill Bowie for being a demon, the British soldier backs down from Sakamoto's challenge to fight him. Bowie confesses to Conti the terrible burden of guilt he has been carrying. As a young man, Bowie allowed a group of schoolmates, to humiliate his hunchbacked younger brother in an initiation rite. The incident causes his brother never to sing again (he had a beautiful voice and would create his own songs). On Christmas, Conti and Bowie are released from the cells by a drunk Takeshi, who explains to the two men that he's Father Christmas. Sakamoto calls in all POW officers and after Takeshi explains why he set Conti and Bowie free he asks Thompson how many men in their ranks are experts in weapons and ammunitions. This has been a running question that Thompson refuses to answer. Sakamoto calls all prisoners out and announces plans to execute Thompson. Bowie breaks rank and kisses the Japanese commander on both cheeks which causes Sakamoto to collapse. For his actions, Bowie is buried up to his neck in a lime pit, Thompson and a group of prisoners are lead by Takeshi to build an airstrip, Sakamoto is relieved of duty and Bowie dies just as the war ends. Four years later Conti visits Takeshi. Conti tells him that he had taken a lock of Bowie's hair to Sakamoto's shrine (Sakamoto had taken the lock of hair when Bowie was buried in the pit) and the Japanese sergeant tells him he had dreamt of Bowie. In a powerfully emotional ending, Takeshi calls out to his friend as he leaves. "Merry Christmas, Merry Christmas Mr. Lawrence." This was Oshima's first English film (the director of IN THE REALM OF THE SENSES-1976) and it's a highly ambitious film that has its problems, but those are overshadowed by the film's emotional power. The scene of brutality and masochism are counterbalanced by the small gestures of kindness. Takeshi's releasing of Conti and Bowie and his final scene are extremely powerful. Even though these are small moments, they achieve monumental proportions in light of the brutality of the same man. Some scenes will make viewers uncomfortable, but every act of violence and brutality is an important part of the plot. The film might be hard to comprehend for a viewer with no knowledge of Japanese or English codes of honor and behavior. Many reasons for the characters actions are not outwardly explained, but the reasons can be found buried in Oshima's complex story. The attraction of Sakamoto to Bowie seems somewhat forced and Oshima's reasoning hasn't transferred well from paper to screen. Sakamoto appears to see in Bowie the strength and iron will that he strives for in himself and his men (including the prisoners). There are also indications that the Japanese commander has a suppressed homoerotic attraction to the British officer. Bowie recognizes this and uses it to his advantage (he kisses Sakamoto knowing it will prevent Thompson's execution). This is all inferred, but never clearly developed. The relationship between Conti and Takeshi is, on the other hand, well developed and takes the forefront because we are given a better understanding of these two men. Takeshi is sadistic, but we have an understanding why. He clings wholeheartedly to the Samurai code of honor and sees no wrong in his action. He is also a kind man in a off-handed way—he reports the Korean guard's suicide as an accident so his family will receive a pension. Releasing Conti and Bowie on Christmas also exposes the human side of the bamboo wielding guard. Takeshi's performance is brilliant and it's surprising to discover that this was the first dramatic role for Japan's popular comedian. His complex and layered performance and Oshima's isolation of Takeshi's expressive face at the right moments help create the strongest and best developed character in the film. Another newcomer to the motion picture screen is Sakamoto. He is one of Japan's most popular pop artists and his highly original score for the film complements and strengthens Oshima's story. Rock star Bowie's performance proves his talent and Conti, as the bilingual officer, offers a strong and balanced portrayal.

p, Jeremy Thomas; d, Nagisa Oshima; w, Oshima, Paul Mayersberg (based on the novel *The Seed And The Sower* by Laurens Van Der Post); ph, Toichiro Narushima (Eastmancolor); m, Ryuichi Sakamoto; ed, Tomoyo Oshima; prod d, Shigemasa Toda; art d, Andrew Sanders.

War Drama **Cas.** **(PR:O MPAA:R)**

MERRY COMES TO STAY**

(1937, Brit.) 79m EM/Sound City bw (GB: MERRY COMES TO TOWN)

ZaSu Pitts *(Winnie Oatfield)*, Guy Newall *(Prof. John Stafford)*, Betty Ann Davies *(Marjorie Stafford)*, Stella Arbenina *(Mme. Saroni)*, Bernard Clifton *(Dennis Stafford)*, Margaret Watson *(Grandmother Stafford)*, Basil Langton *(Noel Slater)*, Muriel George *(Cook)*, Tom Helmore *(Peter Bell)*, Cecil Mannering *(Horace Bell)*, George Sims *(Sales Manager)*, W. T. Elwanger *(Mr. Ramp)*, Arthur Finn *(Mr. Walheimer)*, Sybil Grove *(Zoe)*, Dorothy Bush *(Winnie)*, Hermione Gingold *(Ida Witherspoon)*, Mabel Twemlow *(Mrs. C. Wriggle)*, Janet Fitzpatrick *(Rosie Fish)*, George Sims, Jack Hellier, Margeret Yarde.

Pitts, a Detroit secretary at a small school, is left $500 by the recently deceased principal and plans a London vacation. Her new boss, however, fires her when she insists upon getting some time off. In England she finds her relatives living barely above the poverty level. Thinking she has received a hefty inheritance, they are angered at her apparent stinginess, but all turns out well as she, by pure chance, patches up their financial matters.

p&d, George King; w, Brock Williams (based on a story by Evadne Price); ph, Hone Glendinning.

Comedy **(PR:A MPAA:NR)**

MERRY COMES TO TOWN (SEE: MERRY COMES TO STAY, 1937, Brit.)

MERRY FRINKS, THE**(1934) 67m FN-WB bw (GB: THE HAPPY FAMILY)

Aline MacMahon (Mom Frink), Guy Kibbee (Uncle Newt), Hugh Herbert (Joe), Allen Jenkins (Emmett), Helen Howell (Grandma), Joan Wheeler (Lucille), Frankie Darro (Norman), Ivan Lebedeff (Ramon), James Burke, Harold Huber, Louise Beavers, Maidel Turner, Harry Beresford, Harry C. Bradley, James Bush, Charles Coleman, Joan Sheldon, Ethel Wales, Ed Keane, Ivan Linow, Michael Visaroff.

A grotesquely obnoxious family headed by unselfish mother MacMahon steers itself through a variety of incidents which border on humor. Mom is as loony as her offspring—two sons, one a communist, the other an aspiring prizefighter, and one daughter who is making a play for a married booking agent in hopes of getting herself a radio gig. She spends most of her time trying to find work for her husband. When his brother dies of chronic indigestion after a lavish Oriental dinner, she is left a $500,000 inheritance, providing she leave the family behind. She takes the money and runs, but finds herself returning to the nest. It's not especially funny, nor is the storytelling technique very polished, but it is sure an oddity.

d, Alfred E. Green; w, Gene Markey, Kathryn Scola; ph, Arthur Edeson; ed, James Gibbon; art d, Jack Okey.

Comedy   **(PR:A MPAA:NR)**

MERRY-GO-ROUND zero   (1948, Brit.) 53m Federated bw

Bonar Colleano, Jr., Beryl Davis, Leon Sherkot.

This corny story—in which a film producer is on a search for ideas for his new film—is actually an excuse to present something resembling music and comedy. The problem is that the jokes aren't funny and the music is of such poor quality that it's not worth listening to.

p, Margaret Cordin; d, Josh Binney; ph, Jo Jago.

Comedy   **(PR:A MPAA:NR)**

MERRY-GO-ROUND OF 1938**   (1937) 90m UNIV bw

Bert Lahr (Bert), Jimmy Savo (Jimmy), Billy House (Billy), Alice Brady (Aunt Hortense), Mischa Auer (Mischa), Joy Hodges (Sally Brown), Louise Fazenda (Mrs. Penelope Updike), John King (Tony Townsend), Barbara Read (Clarice Stockbridge), Richard Carle (Col. Frooks), Howard Cantonwine (Hector), Charles Williams (Dave Clark), Charles Coleman (Butler), Joyce Kay (Sally, Young Girl), Fay Helm ("Dainty Doris"), John Kelly (Bus Driver), Beverly Ann Welch (Trap Drummer), Dave Apollon and His Orchestra.

A vaudeville quartet cares for the orphaned daughter of a high-wire performer killed in the act. Twenty years later the girl is in the music business, heading for the top. She meets a fellow whom she plans to marry, but his parents refuse to allow him to wed an entertainer. The quartet comes to the lovers' aid and finally persuades the stubborn folks to give their consent. Splendid musical numbers include: "I'm In My Glory," "More Power to You," "You're My Dish," (Harold Adamson, Jimmy McHugh); "The Woodman's Song" (E. Y. Harburg, Harold Arlen); "River Stay 'Way from My Door" (Mort Dixon, Harry Woods).

p, B. G. DeSylva; d, Irving Cummings; w, Monte Brice, A. Dorian Otvos (based on a story by Brice, Henry Myers); ph, Joseph Valentine; ed, Ted Kent, Charles Maynard; md, Charles Previn; ch, Carl Randall.

Musical   **(PR:A MPAA:NR)**

MERRY MONAHANS, THE**½   (1944) 91m UNIV bw

Donald O'Connor (Jimmy Monahan), Peggy Ryan (Patsy Monahan), Jack Oakie (Pete Monahan), Ann Blyth (Sheila De Royce), Rosemary De Camp (Lillian De Royce), John Miljan (Arnold Pembroke), Gavin Muir (Weldon Laydon), Isabel Jewell (Rose), Ian Wolfe (Clerk), Robert E. Homans (Policeman), Marion Martin (Soubrette), Lloyd Ingraham (Judge), The Hollywood Lovelies.

Aging vaudeville vet Oakie turns out a dandy dose of song-and-dance numbers along with his two kids, O'Connor and Ryan. While Oakie is trying to get De Camp into his arms, O'Connor's trying the same act on singer Blyth. Songs: "Lovely," "Beautiful to Look At," "We're Having a Wonderful Time," "Impersonations," and "Stop Foolin" (Irving Bibo, Don George). Hits from previous years included: "Isle d'Amour" (Earl Carroll, Leo Edwards); "When You Wore a Tulip" (Jack Mahoney, Percy Wenrich); "What Do You Want to Make Those Eyes at Me For?" (Howard Johnson, Joseph McCarthy, James V. Monaco); "Rock-A-Bye Your Baby with a Dixie Melody" (Sam Lewis, Joe Young, Jean Schwartz); "Rose Room" (Harry Williams, Art Hickman); "I'm Always Chasing Rainbows" (Joseph McCarthy, Harry Carroll); "In My Merry Oldsmobile" (Vincent Bryan, Gus Edwards); "I Hate to Lose You" (Grant Clarke, Archie Gottler).

p, Michael Fessier, Ernest Pagano; d, Charles Lamont; w, Fessier, Pagano; ph, Charles Van Enger, John P. Fulton; ed, Charles Maynard; md, Hans J. Salter; art d, John B. Goodman, Martin Obzina; ch, Louis Da Pron, Carlos Romero.

Musical   **(PR:A MPAA:NR)**

MERRY WIDOW, THE*****

                (1934) 99m MGM bw (AKA: THE LADY DANCES)

Maurice Chevalier (Prince Danilo), Jeanette MacDonald (Sonia), Edward Everett Horton (Ambassador Popoff), Una Merkel (Queen Dolores), George Barbier (King Achmed), Minna Gombell (Marcelle), Ruth Channing (Lulu), Sterling Holloway (Mischka), Henry Armetta (Turk), Barbara Leonard (Maid), Donald Meek (Valet), Akim Tamiroff (Maxim's Manager), Herman Bing (Zizipoff), Lucien Prival (Adamovitch), Luana Walters, Sheila Mannors [Sheila Bromley], Caryl Lincoln, Edna Waldron, Lona Andre (Sonia's Maids), Patricia Farley, Shirley Chambers, Maria Troubetskoy, Eleanor Hunt, Jean Hart, Dorothy Wilson, Barbara Barondess, Dorothy Granger, Jill Dennett, Mary Jane Halsey, Peggy Watts, Dorothy Dehn, Connie Lamont (Maxim Girls), Charles Requa, George Lewis, Tyler Brooke, John

Merkyl, Cosmo Kyrle Bellew (Escorts), Roger Gray, Christian J. Frank, Otto Fries, George Magrill, John Roach (Policemen), Gino Corrado, Perry Ivins (Waiters), Katherine Burke [Virginia Field] (Prisoner), George Baxter (Ambassador), Paul Ellis (Dancer), Leonid Kinskey (Shepherd), Evelyn Selbie (Newspaper Woman), Wedgewood Nowell (Lackey), Richard Carle (Defense Attorney), Morgan Wallace (Prosecuting Attorney), Frank Sheridan (Judge), Arthur "Pop" Byron (Doorman), Claudia Coleman (Wardrobe Mistress), Lee Tin (Excited Chinese Man), Nora Cecil (Animal Woman), Tom Frances (Orthodox Priest), Winter Hall (Priest), Matty Roubert (Newsboy), Ferdinand Munier (Jailer), Dewey Robinson, Russell Powell, Billy Gilbert (Fat Lackeys), Arthur Housman, Johnny "Skins" Miller (Drunks), Hector Sarno (Gypsy Leader), Bella Loblov (Gypsy Violinist), Jan Rubini (Violinist), Jason Robards, Sr. (Arresting Officer), Albert Pollet (Head Waiter), Rolfe Sedan (Gabrielovitsch), Jacques Lory (Goatman), Lane Chandler (Soldier).

THE MERRY WIDOW, one of 30 operettas by Franz Lehar, began life in Vienna at the end of 1905 and was an instant smash. It was brought to the U.S. in 1907 and starred Donald Brian and Ethel Jackson, then became a silent two-reeler in 1912 with Wallace Reid and Alma Rubens in the leads. In 1925, Erich von Stroheim directed Mae Murray and John Gilbert in a silent version that made as many enemies among bluenoses as it made friends in the audience. Clark Gable was seen as an extra in that one and the production was opulent and excessive, although somewhat orgiastic (one of the leads was a foot fetishist), and the battles between Murray and "the heavy Hun" (which is what she called von Stroheim) were heard from Culver City to Caracas. Since music was such an important part of the story, the silent version gave us only the plot (a pretty good one) and was saved by the overwhelming performance by Gilbert, who was to have only a bit more success when the sound era came in. Gilbert's voice, by today's standards, would have been more than acceptable as it was a light baritone. But movie audiences of the 1920s had imagined Gilbert to have a deep basso and when it came up in the middle-to-high range, his career was over. This film version of THE MERRY WIDOW is the best of the lot (including the ho-hum remake in 1952). MacDonald is the immensely wealthy widow who lives in the small country of Marshovia and controls more than half the wealth. The tiny land depends on her spending her money there and when she can't find a suitable husband, she decides to move to Paris and seek another liaison. (Note: Grace Moore was originally set for the role but film lore has it that she wouldn't take second position to Chevalier, so MacDonald was tapped for the title role.) The King, Barbier, finds Chevalier in his wife's chambers (Merkel) and punishes the Prince (although the relationship is never quite explained how Barbier could be King, Chevalier the Prince, and Merkel the woman they share), and sends him off to Paris where he is to woo MacDonald and bring her back to her native land. He must succeed in this or he will be court-martialed upon his return. Chevalier is a playboy with an eye for women and he has apparently slept with all of the young girls in Paris and a number of the older ones. He leaves for Paris, attended by Meek, his valet, and meets MacDonald at Maxim's, where she is pretending to be one of the many "B-girls" who work the club and cause the stuffed shirts to order too much champagne. MacDonald and Chevalier are both taken with each other, dance and sing together, and find themselves attracted, but he doesn't know her true identity at first. When they encounter each other at the embassy party tossed by Horton, the ambassador, she finally understands what his assignment entails. (One of the funniest lines in the picture comes when Horton asks Clevalier at Maxim's, "Have you ever had diplomatic relations with a woman?") Chevalier has a huge hangover, the result of the party at Maxim's, and is shocked when he meets MacDonald, whom he thought was named "Fifi," when he had fallen for her earlier. MacDonald is as stiff as an iceberg as Chevalier tries to win her back and to let her know that he really does love her and it is not a result of his job. They have a magnificent dance number and all seems well until Horton makes a public announcement that Chevalier and MacDonald are to be married. She responds by shouting at Chevalier. She has been embarassed publicly and will never believe another word he speaks! A failure, Chevalier is arrested and taken back to Marshovia. Barbier and Merkel are packing their things because they feel the country will fall, now that Chevalier has not brought MacDonald home. There's a huge trial and every comely woman in the land is there to see their heartthrob who is to be tried for treason. MacDonald arrives from Paris to say that Chevalier did the best he could with her; he lied, he deceived, and he tried every which way to win her heart in the service of his country. Chevalier attempts to appeal to MacDonald and explain that he truly loves her but she won't listen. Chevalier makes a speech saying that any man who has been with hundreds of women and is willing to spend the rest of his life with only one should be hanged. He is applauded by the men in the courtroom. Later, MacDonald visits him in his cell and the two get into an argument, then find that they are locked in. Outside the cell, Barbier, Horton, and his cabinet are listening. To heighten the mood, they have a gypsy orchestra play music, spray cologne through the bars, and have champagne sent through the revolving food-hole in the door. Needless to say it all ends happily as a minister's face is seen at the cell door and he marries the two at the finale. Oliver Marsh, who handled the photography in the 1925 version, came back to lens this one beautifully, and Merkel went from this one to the 1952 remake where she played the widow's secretary. Lehar's music was given new lyrics by Lorenz Hart, Gus Kahn, and an uncredited Richard Rodgers, with main themes that included: "Girls, Girls, Girls," "Vilia," "Tonight Will Teach Me to Forget," "Melody of Laughter," "Maxim's," "The Girls at Maxim's," "The Merry Widow Waltz," "If Widows Are Rich," "Russian Dance" (done in a gibberish lyric to represent the Marshovian language), and several reprises as well as bits and pieces of the original score used as background music. Cedric Gibbons and Frederic Hope took the only Oscar for this $1,600,000 picture that lost more than $100,000 when all the tickets were counted. It was frothy, funny, tuneful, and MacDonald more than held her own in the comedy department as she snapped off the lines with Carole Lombard-like expertise. The dancing, choreographed by Albertina Rasch, was as good as you could get and the huge waltz at the embassy ball must rank among one of the best large ensemble pieces ever filmed. The genesis of how the film came to pass began when Lehar, Stein, and Leon sold the rights to Herman Tausky, who then sold it to Henry Savage, who sold it to MGM. After the silent version, a real Prince by the name of Danilo sued MGM because of the use of his name and they paid him $4,000 in "nuisance money" to get him out of their hair. Another version had been planned by MGM in 1930 (as a sound film) with Sidney Franklin to direct, but von Stroheim said that many of the plot turns in his version were his (and co-author Ben Glazer's), so the studio passed on that one. Three years later, after countless lawyers took their fees, it was all straightened out and this film was made. MacDonald was a newcomer (Chevalier was a huge star), and this was her first experience in lip-syncing. That practice was soon the custom and much of the excitement of "live" performances from early musicals was lost in later years. The picture was filmed simultaneously in French for the European market, with MacDonald and Chevalier appearing in both films. Tamiroff also appeared in the French version but in a different role. Chevalier had played with MacDonald at Paramount where she was a supporting actress. He never really liked her, but everyone else did, and this pairing was near perfection.

p, Irving Thalberg; d, Ernst Lubitsch; w, Samson Raphaelson, Ernest Vajda (based on the operetta "Die Lustique Witwe" by Franz Lehar, Victor Leon, Leo Stein); ph, Oliver T. Marsh; m, Lehar; ed, Frances March; md, Herbert Stothart; art d, Cedric Gibbons, Frederic Hope; set d, Edwin B. Willis, Gabriel Scognamillo; cos, Adrian, Ali Hubert; ch, Albertina Rasch.

Musical/Comedy   **(PR:A-C   MPAA:NR)**

MERRY WIDOW, THE**   (1952) 105m MGM c

Lana Turner (Crystal Radek), Fernando Lamas (Count Danilo), Una Merkel (Kitty Riley), Richard Haydn (Baron Popoff), Thomas Gomez (King of Marshovia), John Abbott (Marshovian Ambassador), Marcel Dalio (Police Sergeant), King Donovan (Nitki), Robert Coote (Marquis De Crillon), Sujata (Gypsy Girl), Lisa Ferraday (Marcella), Shepard Menken (Kunjany), Ludwig Stossel (Major Domo), Dave Willock (Attache), Wanda McKay (1st Girl), Anne Kimbell (2nd Girl), Edward Earle (Chestnut Vendor), Gwen Verdon (Specialty Dancer), Gregg Sherwood, Joi Lansing (Maxim Girls).

Though shot in glorious color, this version paled when compared with the 1934 black-and-white version. New lyrics by Paul Francis Webster and a reworked screenplay did nothing to enhance the story, though lots of money was spent on the production and it did garner two Oscars: for Best Art Direction/Set Decoration and for Best Costumes. Turner is the widow of a Marshovian blacksmith who went to the U.S. and amassed a huge fortune in industry. She has almost $100 million and the tiny country is in heavy financial trouble, so they invite her there to dedicate a statue to her late husband, but it's a ploy on the part of Gomez, the King, who assigns Lamas to court her and, hopefully, marry her in order to get her money. Lamas is against the whole idea and thinks that Turner's secretary, Merkel (who played the queen in 1934), is the woman in question. When Turner discovers what Lamas is up to, she goes to Paris and pretends to be a poor dancer at Maxim's. Lamas, who has not seen her, meets her at Maxim's and falls in love, not knowing that she is his target. He is in a pickle, as he really loves Turner and doesn't know if he can give her up to marry the rich American woman he's supposed to wed for his country. Lamas prefers to be court-martialed over relinquishing Turner. There's an embassy ball and Turner ceases her masquerade, then gives Ambassador Abbott a check for 800 million "drankas" to help pay off the country's debts. Lamas thinks that she is now broke and rushes to embrace her, not knowing that the exchange rate puts the "dranka" way down and all she's donated to Marshovia is the paltry sum of $1 million, not enough to put a dent into her considerable fortune. Songs include: "Vilia," (sung by Lamas this time, not the Widow) "Girls, Girls, Girls," "Night," "I'm Going to Maxim's," "Can-Can," and "The Merry Widow Waltz." Turner was looped by singer Trudy Erwin and Cole's dance creations didn't come near the ones by Albertina Rasch. Gwen Verdon is one of the dancers and all of the secondary comedy roles are handled well. Lamas is very charming, but the big hole in the piece is Turner's work. She never had the bubbly insouciance needed for the role. Lamas and Turner had an off-stage romance that culminated in her divorce from Bob Topping. She never married Lamas and took Lex Barker as her fourth of seven different husbands.

p, Joe Pasternak; d, Curtis Bernhardt; w, Sonya Levien, William Ludwig (based on the operetta by Franz Lehar, Victor Leon, Leo Stein); ph, Robert Surtees (Technicolor); m, Lehar; ed, Conrad A. Nervig; md, Jay Blackton; art d, Cedric Gibbons, Paul Groesse; set d, Edwin B. Willis, Arthur Krams; cos, Helen Rose, Gile Steele; spec eff, A. Arnold Gillespie, Warren Newcombe; ch, Jack Cole; m/l, Lehar, Paul Francis Webster; makeup, William Tuttle.

Musical/Comedy   **(PR:A   MPAA:NR)**

MERRY WIVES, THE**   (1940, Czech.) 80m A-B Films/Lloyd bw

Zdenek Stepanek (Count Nicholas), Ladislav Pesek (Ocko), Hana Vitova (Elisabeth), Adina Mandlova (Rose), Vaclav Vydra (William of Vresovice), Helena Friedlova (Ludmila), Frantisek Smolik (Triska), Jirina Shejbalova (Sofia), Theodor Pistek (Vodnansky), Antonie Nedosinska (His Wife), Elen Halkova (Eve), Bedrich Karen (David Wolfram), Frantisek Kreuzman (Felix of Hasenburg), Zvonimir Rogoz (Secretary), Nezilavela Nikolska (Gypsy), Anna Steimarova (Lena).

The tale of a wine-guzzling Czech count whose penchant for love affairs takes a back seat to his driving out of some local criminals. His adventures with the town prostitutes were, no doubt, considerably saucier before the censor board started clipping. Made in Czechoslovakia before Hitler's invasion, the film didn't make it to the U.S. until a few years later, then was held up while censors removed the sequences considered to be too racy for American audiences. (In Czech; English subtitles.)

d&w, Otakar Vavra (based on a story by Zdenek Stepanek); ph, Jan Roth; m, Jaroslav Kricka.

Drama   **(PR:C   MPAA:NR)**

MERRY WIVES OF RENO, THE* 1/2   (1934) 64m WB bw

Margaret Lindsay (Madge), Daondl Woods (Frank), Guy Kibbee (Tom), Glenda Farrell (Bunny), Hugh Herbert (Col. Fitch), Frank McHugh (Al), Roscoe Ates (The Trapper), Ruth Donnelly (Lois), Hobart Cavanaugh (Derwent).

Lack of direction hampers this spotty comedy which gets a few kicks in at Reno's slack divorce laws. When the husband of a cheating wife comes home to find the overcoats of two men, his marriage, and the marriages of the other two men, go progressively downhill.

p, Robert Lord; d, H. Bruce Humberstone; w, Lord, Joe Traub (based on a story by Lord); ph, Ernest Haller; ed, Thomas Pratt; art d, Jack Okey; cos, Orry-Kelly.

Comedy   **(PR:A   MPAA:NR)**

MERRY WIVES OF TOBIAS ROUKE, THE*

(1972, Can.) 95m Anytim/Astral c

Michael Magee (Narrator), Paul Bradley (Laslow), Henry Beckman (Tobias), Judy Gault (Fancy), Linda Sorenson (Holly), Earl Pomerantz (Harper), Ratch Wallace (Jed), Monica Parker (Fat Girl), Samuel Jephcott (Privates).

A con man and his girl friend devise a plot which has her getting married to a wealthy fellow at the turn of the century. When the rich man's wife returns she is told that the girl is really his daughter, and the con man her brother-in-law. Weighed down by an excessively twisty script which neither the cast nor crew can pull off.

p, Stan Feldman, John Board; d, Board; w, George Mendeluk, Arthur Slabotsky; ph, Paul Van Der Linden; m, Terry Bush; ed, Alan Collins; art d, Lillian Sarafinchen.

Comedy   **(PR:A   MPAA:NR)**

MERRY WIVES OF WINDSOR, THE**

(1952, Ger.) Deutsche Film/Central Cinema bw

Sonja Ziemann (Frau Fluth), Camilla Spira (Frau Reich), Paul Esser (Sir John Falstaff), Calus Holm (Herr Fluth), Alexander Engel (Herr Reich), Eckart Dux (Fenton), Ina Halley (Anna Reich), Joachim Teege (Herr Spaerlich), Gerhard Frickhoffer (Dr. Cajus).

A German version of Shakespeare's play and Nicolai's opera, which tells the familiar tale of the drinking and womanizing Falstaff, who becomes the victim of two of Windsor's merry wives. The Berlin State Opera provides the music, with the dubbed-in voices of German singers Rita Streich, Martha Modl, Hans Kramer, and Helmut Krebs. (In German; English subtitles.)

p, Walter Lehmann; d, Georg Wildhagen; w, Wolff von Gordon, Wildhagen (based on William Shakespeare's play and Otto Nicolai's opera); ph, Eugen Klagemann, Kurt Herlth.

Opera   **(PR:A   MPAA:NR)**

MERRY WIVES OF WINDSOR, THE** 1/2

(1966, Aust.) 97m Wien/Sigma III c

Norman Foster (Sir John Falstaff), Colette Boky (Frau Fluth [Mistress Ford]), Igor Gorin (Herr Fluth [Mr. Ford]), Mildred Miler (Frau Reich [Mistress Page]), Edmond Hurshell (Herr Reich [Master Page]), Lucia Popp (Anna), Ernst Shutz (Fenton), John Gittings (Cajus), Marshall Raynor (Sparlich), Rosella Hightower (Ballerina).

The tale of Falstaff is told in dazzling Technicolor in this Austrian version of the classic Shakespeare play. Two of Windsor's fun-loving wives, Boky and Miler, turn down Falstaff's advances and instead play a couple of practical jokes on the aging fellow. Finally, with the help of their husbands, the wives get back at Falstaff by scaring the dickens out of him in a forest. Blessed with some fine operatic voices. The Zagreb Symphony Orchestra provides the music.

p, Norman Foster; d, George Tressler; w, Foster (based on the play by William Shakespeare and the opera by Otto Nicolai); ph, Hannes Staudinger (Technicolor); m, Nicolai; ed, Paula Dvorak; md, Milan Howath; art d, Hugo Halbig; set d, Gerd Krauss; cos, Helga Pinnow; ch, Rosella Hightower; makeup, Arthur Schramm.

Opera   **(PR:A   MPAA:NR)**

MERTON OF THE MOVIES***   (1947) 83m MGM bw

Red Skelton (Merton Gill), Virginia O'Brien (Phyllis Montague), Gloria Grahame (Beulah Baxter), Leon Ames (Lawrence Rupert), Alan Mowbray (Frank Mulvaney), Charles D. Brown (Jeff Baird), Hugo Haas (Von Strutt), Harry Hayden (Mr. Gashwiler), Tom Trout (Marty), Douglas Fowley (Phil), Dick Wessell (Chick).

The third time around as a film for the popular George S. Kaufman and Marc Connelly play, the first being a silent version in 1924 and then another in 1932 under the title MAKE ME A STAR. Skelton is the star in this version, playing a dreamy theater usher who gets a trip to Hollywood as part of a publicity stunt to boost the plunging career of Ames. O'Brien's keen sense of spotting possible talent makes her realize the potential of Skelton; she does her bit to push the man along until he makes it to star status. The thrust in this version was to recapture the atmosphere present in the early days of Hollywood; the producers even employed Buster Keaton to give Skelton lessons in slapstick technique. As a whole this film exhumes the aura of one good time for all the people involved, stacking up as solid Hollywood entertainment.

p, Albert Lewis; d, Robert Alton; w, George Wells, Lou Breslow (based on the play by George S. Kaufman, Marc Connelly and the novel by Harry Leon Wilson); ph, Paul C. Vogel; m, David Snell; ed, Frank E. Hull; art d, Cedric Gibbons, Howard E. Hull.

Comedy   **(PR:A   MPAA:NR)**

MES FEMMES AMERICAINES(SEE: RUN FOR YOUR WIFE, 1966, Fr./Ital.)

MESDAMES ET MESSIEURS
     (SEE: BIRDS, THE BEES, AND THE ITALIANS, THE, 1967, Fr./Ital.)

MESA OF LOST WOMEN, THE zero
(1956) 70m A. J. Frances White-Joy Houck bw (AKA: LOST WOMEN; LOST WOMEN OF ZARPA)

Jackie Coogan (*Dr. Arana*), Richard Travis (*Don Mulcahey*), Allan Nixon (*Doc Tucker*), Mary Hill (*Doreen*), Robert Knapp (*Grant Phillips*), Tandra Quinn (*Tarantella*), Harmon Stevens (*Masterson*), Samuel Wu (*Wu*), Geroge Barrows (*George*), Lyle Talbot (*Narrator*), Katena Vea [Katherine Victor], Chris-Pin Martin, John Martin, Angelo Rossitto, Fred Kelsey.

Coogan is a mad scientist a la Uncle Fester (the role he played on TV's "Addams Family")who spends his time in the Mexican desert tinkering around and enlarging tarantulas to gigantic proportions. Another pet project is creating a race of savage superwomen with extra-long fingernails. When a plane is forced down in Coogan's vicinity, the reign of terror begins. Two folks do escape, however, before the mesa is bombed into oblivion. It's a toss-up as to which is worse—the script or the direction. The eccentric guitar-piano score was reused by Edward D. Wood, Jr. in JAIL BAIT (1954). Made in 1952, MESA OF LOST WOMEN was released in 1956 to take advantage of the shortage of new movies at that time.

p, Melvin Gale, William Perkins; d, Herbert Tevos, Ron Ormond; w, Tevos; ph, Karl Struss, Gilbert Warrenton; ed, Hugh Winn, Ray Lockert.

Science-Fiction   **(PR:A MPAA:NR)**

MESQUITE BUCKAROO*   (1939) 59m Metropolitan bw
Bob Steele (*Bob*), Carolyn Curtis (*Betty*), Frank LaRue (*Bond*), Juanita Fletcher (*Sarah*), Charles King (*Trigger*), Gordon Roberts (*Sands*), Ted Adams (*Luke*), James Whitehead (*Mort*), Ed Brady (*Hank*), Bruce Bane (*Cookie*), Snub Pollard (*Suds*), John Elliott (*Hawks*), Jimmy Aubrey, Carleton Young.

Steele and Adams place a bet on which one of them is a better bronc buster. Before the competition can take place, however, Steele is kidnaped, but makes it back to the rodeo in the nick of time to win the prize. Whatever you do, don't judge all oaters by this one. It must have been made to feed the cast.

p&d, Harry S. Webb; w, George Plympton (based on his story); ph, Edward Kull; ed, Fred Bain; md, Frank Sannucci.

Western   **(PR:A MPAA:NR)**

MESSAGE, THE   (SEE: MOHAMMAD, MESSENGER OF GOD, 1977)

MESSAGE FROM SPACE** 1/2
(1978, Jap.) 105m Toei-Tohokushinsha Eiga/UA c (UCHU KARA NO MESSEJI; UCHU NO MESSEJI)

Vic Morrow (*Gen. Garuda*), Sonny [Shinichi] Chiba (*Hans*), Philip Casnoff (*Aaron*), Peggy Lee Brennan (*Meia*), Sue Shiomi (*Esmeralida*), Tetsuro Tamba (*Noguchi*), Mikio Narita (*Rockseia XII*), Makoto Sato (*Urocco*), Hiroyuki Sandada (*Shiro*), Isamu Shimuzu (*Robot Beba 2*), Masazumi Okabe (*Jack*), Noburo Mitani (*Kamesasa*), Hideyo Amamoto (*Dark*), Junkichi Orimoto (*Kido*), Harumi Sone (*Lazari*).

An admirable offspring of the science-fiction stylings of STAR WARS and the devices of THE SEVEN SAMURAI. A group of eight hired soldiers protect a small planet which is on the edge of doom. The script comes complete with small, talking robots and some better-than-average effects. A great debt is also paid to the spirit of Jules Verne by including a spaceship modeled after 19th-Century sailing vessels. With a $5 million budget it was, at the time, the most expensive Japanese film ever. Director Fukasaku is no stranger to high price tags, having co-directed TORA, TORA, TORA.

p, Banjiro Uemura, Yoshinori Watanabe, Tan Takaiwa; d, Kinji Fukasaku, Nobuo Yajim; w, Hiroo Matsuda; ph, Toro Nakajima; m, Ken-Ichiro Morioka; art d, Tetsuzo Osawa; spec eff, Nobuo Yajima, Masahiro Noda, Shotaro Ishinori, Minoru Nakano, Noboru Takanashi.

Science-Fiction   **(PR:A MPAA:PG)**

MESSAGE TO GARCIA, A* 1/2   (1936) 77m FOX bw
Wallace Beery (*Sgt. Dory*), John Boles (*Lt. Andrew Rowan*), Barbara Stanwyck (*Raphaelita Maderos*), Herbert Mundin (*Henry Piper*), Martin Garralaga (*Rodriquez*), Juan Torena (*Luis Maderos*), Alan Hale (*Dr. Krug*), Enrique Acosta (*Gen. Garcia*), Jose Luis Tortosa (*Pasquale Castova*), Mona Barrie (*Spanish Spy*), Warren Hymer (*Sailor*), Andre Cuyas, John Duval (*Sentries*), Count Stefanelli (*Raphaelita's Father*), Frederick Vogeding (*German Stoker*), Philip Morris (*Army Officer*), Voice of John Carradine (*President McKinley*), Rosita Harlan (*Girl*), Fred Goday (*Citizen*), Pedro Vinas (*Servant*), Octavio J. Giraud (*Spanish Commandant*), Patrick Moriarity (*Irish Stoker*), Augustine Guzman (*Sentry*), Lucio Villegas (*Commandant*), Art Dupuis (*Waiter*), Blanca Vischer (*Chiquita*), Dell Henderson (*President McKinley*), Manuel Paris (*Lieutenant*), George Irving (*Col. Wagner*), Davison Clark (*Admiral*), Sam Appel, M. Pelufa, David Clyde, Carlos Montalban, Iris Adrian, Si Jenks, J. Betancourt.

If you can accept Stanwyck doing a Spanish accent over her own Brooklyn accent, then you might find this film passably interesting. Then again, perhaps not, because there is so much wrong with this rewriting of history that one hardly knows where to begin. The true incident upon which it was based was more than enough to make a movie about, but the studio nabobs at Fox must have thought it needed something more, so they toyed with facts and combined them with more than a little fiction. It's Cuba, during the Spanish-American War and Boles, a U.S. soldier, is assigned the task of bringing a message from President McKinley to the leader of the Cuban

insurgents, Acosta, to the effect that the U.S. will back him in his desire to rid the island nation of the Spanish yoke. It's not that easy to find the leader, as he is hiding in the same mountains Castro used before taking over from Batista. In order to locate Acosta, Boles teams up with Beery, a Marine renegade, and they begin their trek through the underbrush. Next, they encounter Stanwyck, the daughter of a Cuban patriot who was martyred by the enemy. Their hegira takes them through dangerous territory, with spies and cutthroats lurking behind every stand of sugar cane. They face crocodiles and torture, and Boles is personally manhandled by spy Hale. Beery double-crosses Boles, then changes his mind and saves the young soldier and eventually dies so Boles can deliver the missive. At the conclusion, Cuban rebels save Boles and Stanwyck. The story was based on the book by the man who actually did the deed, Rowan, and an essay by Elbert Hubbard that popularized the feat and made the expression "A Message To Garcia" part of the lexicon of the English language. Stanwyck seems ill-at-ease all the way through and her accent wobbles from scene to scene as if she couldn't make up her mind about how to play the role. Some snappy dialog doesn't overpower the basic falseness of the film.

p, Darryl F. Zanuck; d, George Marshall; w, W. P. Lipscomb, Gene Fowler; Sam Hellman, Gladys Lehman (based on the book by Lt. Andrew S. Rowan and an essay by Elbert Hubbard); ph, Rudolph Mate; ed, Herbert Levy; md, Louis Silvers; art d, William Darling, Rudolph Sternad; set d, Thomas Little; technical advisor, Francois B. DeValdes.

Historical Adventure   **(PR:A MPAA:NR)**

MESSALINE** 1/2   (1952, Fr./Ital.) 111m FS bw
Maria Felix (*Messaline*), Jean Chevrier (*Valere*), Georges Marechal (*Cassius*), Jean Tissier (*Nestor*), Michel Vitold (*Narcisse*), Delia Scala (*Cynthia*), Memo Bessami (*Augustus*).

A spectacle which aptly deals with the decadence of ancient Rome. Mexican actress Felix portrays the lusty Messaline with vigorous sensuality as she leaves her husband, the Emperor Augustus, to search for perfect love. The search takes her into the streets as a prostitute. Directed by Carmine Gallone, a prolific director from the silent days whose best work can be seen in his musicals.

d&w, Carmine Gallone; ph, Andre Brizzi; ed, Nicolo Lazarri.

Historical Drama   **(PR:A MPAA:NR)**

MESSENGER OF PEACE* 1/2   (1950) 87m Astor bw
John Beal (*Pastor Armin Ritter*), Peggy Stewart (*Evangeline Lockley*), William Bakewell (*Pastor Willie Von Adel*), Paul Guilfoyle (*Peter Kerl*), Fred Essler (*Hans Dache*), Raphael Bennett (*Gus Frommel*), Maude Prickett (*Matty Frommel*), Al Bridge (*Harry Franzmeirer*), Elizabeth Kerr (*Lottie Franzmeirer*), William Gould (*Jacob Torgel*), Edythe Elliott (*Hilda Torgel*), Brook Shayne (*Magda Torgel*), Joe Brown, Jr. (*Ted Horner*).

Low-budgeter which follows a young seminary student from his school days to his days as an elderly pastor. A preachy film, heavy on religious propaganda, which undermines the simple story.

p, Roland Reed; d, Frank Strayer; w, Glenn Tryon (based on a story by Henry Rische); ph, Walter Strenge; ed, Jack Oglivie; md, Al Columbo.

Drama   **(PR:A MPAA:NR)**

MESSIAH OF EVIL   (SEE: DEAD PEOPLE, 1974)

METALSTORM: THE DESTRUCTION OF JARED-SYN zero
                (1983) 84m Albert Band/UNIV c
Jeffrey Byron (*Dogen*), Mike Preston (*Jared-Syn*), Tim Thomerson (*Rhodes*), Kelly Preston (*Dhyana*), Richard Moll (*Hurok*), R. David Smith (*Baal*), Larry Pennell (*Alx*), Marty Zagon (*Zax*), Mickey Fox (*Poker Annie*), J. Bill Jones (*Baal's Lieutenant*), Winston Jones (*Chimera*), Mike Jones, Mike Walter, Rick Militi, Speed Stearns, Lou Joseph, Rush Adams, Mike Cassidy, Tony Cecere, Larry Howe, Tom Jacobs.

Byron is a space ranger who is sent on an intergallactic mission to save a planet from a madman's evil and destructive ways. Fortunately (or maybe not) Byron is successful and the audience isn't even treated to the obligatory destruction that the title promises. A poor exploitation of the renewed 3-D craze, which can waste 84 minutes of any viewer's life. A ripoff of a number of fine pictures, including STAR WARS (1977) and ROAD WARRIOR (1981).

p, Charles Band, Alan J. Adler; d, Band; w, Adler; ph, Mac Ahlberg (Stereovision 3-D, Movielab Color); m, Richard Band; ed, Brad Arensman; art d, Pamela B. Warner; set d, Jay Wertz, James Thornton; spec eff, Joe Quinlan, Gregory Van Der Veer; cos, Kathie Clark; makeup, D. J. White, A. Apone, Kenny Myers, F. H. Isaacs.

Science-Fiction/Adventure   **Cas.**   **(PR:C MPAA:PG)**

METAMORPHOSES* 1/2   (1978) 89m Sanrio c
This was the first production from Sanrio Films, an animated feature which is uneven at best. Director and writer Takashi has adapted tales from Greek and Roman mythology. One of the main problems of the film is that if you don't know Greek and Roman mythology you'll never be able to follow the stories. The stories include the creation; Actaeon the hunter being turned into a stag by the goddess Diana; Orpheus and Eurydice; Mercury and the House of Envy; Perseus and Medusa; and the final tale of Phaeton and the sun chariot. The film was three years in the making, but it's crippled by the script and spotty animation. Some sequences can rival Disney animation, but the animation as a whole is inconsistent.

p, Terry Ogisu, Hiro Tsugawa, Takashi; d&w, Takashi (based on Ovid's *Metamorphoses*); ph, Bill Millar (Technicolor); ed, Barbara Ottinger; prod d, Paul Julian, Ray Aragon, Kuni Fukai, Rebecca Ortega Mills, Akira Uno; md, Bob Randles.

Animated Fantasy **(PR:A MPAA:PG)**

METEMPSYCO (SEE: TOMB OF TORTURE, 1966, Ital.)

METEOR* (1979) 103m AIP c

Sean Connery (*Dr. Paul Bradley, Astrophysicist*), Natalie Wood (*Tatiana Nikolaevna Donskaya*), Brian Keith (*Dr. Alexei Dubov, Russian Astrophysicist*), Martin Landau (*Gen. Barry Adlon, Hercules Project Director*), Trevor Howard (*Sir Michael Hughes, Chief of Jodrell Bank Observatory in Great Britain*), Joseph Campanella (*Gen. Easton, Air Force Chief of Staff*), Roger Robinson (*Hunter*), Karl Malden (*Harry Sherwood, Director of NASA*), Richard A. Dysart (*Secretary of Defense*), Henry Fonda (*The President of the United States*), Katherine De Hetre (*Jan Watkins, Trajectory Analysis Officer*), James G. Richardson (*Alan Marshall, Assistant Trojectory Analysis Officer*), Michael Zaslow (*Sam Mason*), John McKinney (*Peter Watson*), John Findlater (*Astronaut Tom Easton*), Paul Tulley (*Astronaut Bill Frager*), Allen Williams (*Astronaut Michael McKendrick*), Bibi Besch (*Helen Bradley*), Gregory Gay (*Russian Premier*), Clyde Kusatsu (*Yamashiro*), Burke Burns (*Coast Guard Officer*), Joe Medalis (*Bartender*), Charles Bartlett, Raymond O'Keefe (*Guards*), Henry Olek (*Army Translator*), Peter Bourne (*United Nations President*), Bo Brundin (*Manheim*), Stately Mann (*Canadian Representative*), Ronald Neame (*British Representative*), Philip Sterling (*Russian Representative*), Arthur Adams (*Zambian Representative*), Fred Carney (*United States Representative*), Sybil Danning (*Girl Skier*), Meschino Paterlini (*Boy Skier*), Jon Yune (*Siberian Man*), Eileen Saki (*Siberian Woman*), Carole Hemingway (*Sherwood's Secretary*), Clete Roberts (*Network Newscaster*), Osman Ragheb (*Swiss TV Newscaster*), Yu Wing (*Chinese Fisherman*), Yai Tsui Ling (*Chinese Fisherman's Wife*), Rick Slaven (*Canteen Worker*), Selma Archerd (*Woman in Subway*), Domingo Ambriz (*Boy with Radio*), Chris Baur, Paul Camen, Dorothy Catching, Bill Couch, William Darr, Joan Foley, Paul Laurence, Johnny Moio, Read Morgan, Conrad Palmisano, Tony Rocco, Jesse Wayne (*Communications Center Technicians*), Ted Duncan, Larry Duran, Ken Endoso, Martha Garza, Len Glasgow, Marilyn Jones, Valerie Kelly, Jack Lilley, Nick Palmisano, George Robotham, Sonny Shields, Al Wyatt (*Stunts*).

An $18 million star-studded disaster film, which in itself is a major disaster. The title rock is hurtling toward the Earth and scientists from the U. S. and U.S.S.R. try to avert a collision by using missiles to demolish the asteroid. Some accompanying smaller meteors cause widespread damage, such as a tidal wave against Hong Kong and the destruction of a large part of New York City, trapping some of the stars underneath the city. Connery is the American scientist, Keith is his Russian counterpart, and Wood (she speaks Russian in real life as she came from immigrant parents) is Keith's assistant who falls in love with Connery. The missiles destroy the oncoming orb.

p, Arnold Orgolini, Theodore Parvin; d, Ronald Neame; w, Stanely Mann, Edmund H. North (based on a story by North); ph, Paul Lohmann (Panavision); m, Laurence Rosenthal; ed, Carl Kress; prod d, Edward Carfagno; art d, David Constable; set d, Barbara Krieger; spec eff, Glen Robinson, Robert Steaples; cos, Albert Wolsky.

Science-Fiction **Cas.** **(PR:C MPAA:PG)**

METEOR MONSTER (SEE: TEENAGE MONSTER, 1957)

METROPOLITAN* (1935) 80m FOX bw

Lawrence Tibbett (*Thomas Renwick*), Virginia Bruce (*Anne Merrill*), Alice Brady (*Ghita Galin*), Cesar Romero (*Niki Baroni*), Thurston Hall (*T. Simon Hunter*), Luis Alberni (*Ugo Pizzi*), George Marion, Sr. (*Perontelli*), Ruth Donnelly (*Marina*), Franklyn Ardell (*Marco*), Adrian Rosley (*Mr. Tolentino*), Christian Rub (*Weidel*), Etienne Girardot (*Nello*), Jessie Ralph (*Charwoman*).

Brady is an operatic prima donna who walks out on the Metropolitan Opera to form her own company. She pulls together promising young talent and baritone Tibbett as her leading man. When Brady leaves her own company, Tibbett takes charge and the opera company becomes a big success. This was the first film from newly formed 20th Century-Fox and did rather poorly at the box office. Songs include: "De Glory Road" (Clement Wood, J. Russell Bodley), "On the Road to Mandalay" (Rudyard Kipling, Oley Speaks), arias from Gounod's "Faust," Rossini's "The Barber of Seville," the prolog to Leoncavallo's "Pagliacci," "The Toreador Song" and "Micaela's Aria" from Bizet's "Carmen," "Last Night When We Were Young," an original song by Harold Arlen and E. Y. Harburg was cut from the film before its release, a fate it was to suffer two more times in films with Judy Garland and Frank Sinatra. In each case, it was felt the song was too sad.

p, Darryl F. Zanuck; d, Richard Boleslawski; w, Bess Meredyth, George Marion, Jr. (based on a story by Meredyth); ph, Rudolph Mate; ed, Barbara McLean; md, Alfred Newman.

Musical **(PR:A MPAA:NR)**

MEURTRE EN 45 TOURS (SEE: MURDER AT 45 RPM, 1965, Fr.)

MEXICALI KID, THE* 1/2 (1938) 57m MON bw

Jack Randall (*Jack*), Wesley Barry (*Mexicali Kid*), Eleanor Stewart (*Jean*), Baron William von Brincken (*Gorson*), Ed Cassidy (*Sheriff*), Bud Osborne (*Chris*), George Chesebro (*Joe*), Ernie Adams (*Carl*), Frank LaRue, Sherry Tansey.

Randall is out to get revenge for the murder of his bank cashier brother and with his guns loaded, rides off into the desert. There he finds the title character, Barry, and rescues him from a desert death. Barry is a criminal, but Randall reforms him and together they keep Stewart from losing her ranch. Barry is killed in the final shoot-out in a burning town. Randall's star was dimming and this was the first

western in which he didn't sing. Producer Tansey wrote the screenplay under the pseudonym Robert Emmett.

p, Robert Tansey; d, Wallace Fox; w, Robert Emmett [Tansey]; ph, Bert Longenecker.

Western **Cas.** **(PR:A MPAA:NR)**

MEXICALI ROSE* 1/2 (1929) 60m COL bw (GB: THE GIRL FROM MEXICO)

Barbara Stanwyck (*Mexicali Rose*), Sam Hardy (*Happy Manning*), William Janney (*Bob Manning*), Louis Natheaux (*Joe the Croupier*), Arthur Rankin (*Loco the Halfwit*), Harry Vejar (*Ortiz*), Louis King (*Dad the Drunk*), Julia Beharano (*Manuela*), Jerry Miley, Claude Gillingwater, Jr.

Hardy is a gambling saloon owner on the Mexican border who falls in love with boy-crazy Stanwyck. When Stanwyck has an affair with another man, Hardy has her kicked out of town. In revenge, she marries Hardy's kid brother, Janney. The couple honeymoons in the Mexican town in which Hardy's saloon is located and he doesn't let on that he knows Stanwyck. Satisfied that she has gotten her revenge, Stanwyck begins fooling around with men around town. This brings on her death when she woos the town crazy, Rankin, who kills her.

p, Harry Cohn; d, Erle C. Kenton; w, Gladys Lehman, Norman Houston; ph, Ted Tetzlaff; ed, Leon Barsha.

Drama **(PR:A MPAA:NR)**

MEXICALI ROSE** 1/2 (1939) 60m REP bw

Gene Autry (*Gene*), Smiley Burnette (*Frog*), Noah Beery (*Valdes*), Luana Walters (*Anita Loredo*), William Farnum (*Padre Dominic*), William Royle (*Carruthers*), LeRoy Mason (*Blythe*), Wally Albright (*Tommy*), Kathryn Frye (*Chalita*), Roy Barcroft (*McElroy*), Dick Botiller (*Manuel*), Vic Demourelle (*Hollister*), John Beach (*Brown*), Henry Otho (*Alcalde*), Joe Dominguez, Al Haskell, Merrill McCormack, Fred "Snowflake" Toones, Sherry Hall, Al Taylor, Josef Swickard, Tom London, Jack Ingram, Eddie Parker, Champion the Horse.

Autry was rapidly becoming the top singing cowboy and this film held the formula that made him a Saturday matinee star. Autry and his sidekick Burnette protect a mission for poor Mexican children from oil swindlers. Autry is helped by Mexican bandit Beery, who styles himself after the Robin Hood character in one of Autry's songs. Songs include: "You're the Only Star in My Blue Heaven" which was a favorite with Autry fans, and "Mexicali Rose" (Autry).

p, Harry Grey; d, George Sherman; w, Gerald Geraghty (based on a story by Luci Ward, Connie Lee); ph, William Nobles; ed, Tony Martinelli.

Western **(PR:A MPAA:NR)**

MEXICAN, THE (SEE: HURRICANE HORSEMAN, 1931)

MEXICAN HAYRIDE* 1/2 (1948) 77m UNIV bw

Bud Abbott (*Harry Lambert*), Lou Costello (*Joe Bascom/Humphrey Fish*), Virginia Grey (*Montana*), Luba Malina (*Dagmar*), John Hubbard (*David Winthrop*), Pedro de Cordoba (*Senor Martinez*), Fritz Feld (*Prof. Ganzmeyer*), Tom Powers (*Ed Mason*), Pat Costello (*Tim Williams*), Frank Fenton (*Gus Adamson*), Sid Fields (*Reporter*), Chris Pin Martin (*Mariachi Leader*), Flores Brothers Trio (*Trio*), Argentina Brunetti (*Indian Woman*), Mary Brewer, Marjorie L. Carver, Karen Randle, Kippee Valez, Yolanda Gonzalez, Lucille Casey, Toni [Mary] Castle, Lorraine Crawford, Donna de Mario (*Martell*) (*Girls*), Eddie Kane (*Mr. Clarke*), Ben Chavez (*Magician*), Pedro Regas (*Proprietor*), Charles Miller (*Mr. Lewis*), Harry Brown (*Businessman*), Joe Kirk (*2nd Businessman*), Julian Rivero (*Ticket Seller*), Tony Roux (*Blanket Weaver*), Roque Ybarra (*Basket Weaver*), Joe Dominguez (*Artist*), Felipe Turich (*Silversmith Dealer*), Julia Montoya (*Woman*), George Mendoza (*Photographer*), Robert Elias (*Mexican Boy*), Rose Marie Lopez (*Mexican Child*), Earl Spainard (*Bellboy*), Suzanne Ridgway (*Artist's Model*), Cosmo Sardo (*Headwaiter*), Caroline Lopez (*Mexican Girl*), Fred Hoose (*Businessman*), Charles Rivero (*Ticket Taker*), Alfonso Pedroza (*Mexican Man*), Alex Montoya, Reed Howes, Robert Lugo, Lalo Encinas, John L. Sylvester, Sol Murgi, Rudy German, Hans Moebus (*Men*).

Not much more then a typical Abbott and Costello vehicle, the film is filled with jokes and situations similar to those in any of their other films. Abbott heads a gang of stock swindlers and makes Costello its fall guy. When things become too hot they go south of the border and start a fake mining outfit with Costello again the patsy. The threadbare story allows Costello to perform increasingly worn antics. Best sequence is when Costello steps into the bullring and subdues the bull with his clowning. Luba Malina delivers one mediocre song, "Is It Yes, Or Is It No?" (Scharf, Jack Brooks). (*See:* ABBOTT AND COSTELLO series, Index.)

p, Robert Arthur; d, Charles T. Barton; w, Oscar Brodney, John Grant (based on a musical play by Herbert and Dorothy Fields, Cole Porter); ph, Charles Van Enger; m, Walter Scharf; ed, John Gross; md, Scharf; art d, Bernard Herzbrun, John F. De Cuir; set d, Russell A. Gausman, John Austin; ch, Eugene Loring.

Comedy **(PR:A MPAA:NR)**

MEXICAN MANHUNT* (1953) 71m AA bw

George Brent (*Dave Brady*), Hillary Brooke (*Eve Carter*), Morris Ankrum (*Tip Morgan*), Karen Sharpe (*Linda Morgan*), Marjorie Lord (*Sheila Barton*), Douglas Kennedy (*Dan McCracken*), Alberto Morin (*Pablo*), Carleton Young (*Caruthers*), Stuart Randall (*Lucky Gato*), Marvin Press (*Cookie*).

Lame thriller set in Mexico about a writer who turns detective to try to solve a murder that occurred fifteen years earlier. Exotic background does nothing to add to the intrigue of the plot, with a decent cast that is totally wasted. Suave leading man Brent effectively retired after this one, settling down to raise horses except for brief bits and a small featured role in another film in 1978, BORN AGAIN.

p, Lindsley Parsons; d, Rex Bailey; w, George Bricker; ph, William Sickner; ed, Leonard W. Herman; md, Edward J. Kay; art d, Dave Milton; set d, Ben Bone; makeup, Ted Larsen.

Mystery   **(PR:A MPAA:NR)**

MEXICAN SPITFIRE**¹/₂   (1939) 67m RKO bw

Lupe Velez (*Carmelita Lindsay*), Leon Errol (*Uncle Matt Lindsay/Lord Basil Epping*), Donald Woods (*Dennis Lindsay*), Linda Hayes (*Elizabeth*), Cecil Kellaway (*Chumley*), Elizabeth Risdon (*Aunt Della Lindsay*), Charles Coleman (*Butler*).

Velez is a Mexican entertainer who elopes with young businessman Woods. His ex-fiancee is out to break up the marriage and what ensues is an enjoyable Mack Sennett-type comedy. Errol plays the dual role as Woods' uncle and an English whiskey baron who is one of Woods' clients in this light, but energetic comedy. Even though the film was not profitable, RKO continued the Spitfire films as a series. (See MEXICAN SPITFIRE series, Index.)

p, Cliff Reid; d, Leslie Goodwins; w, Joseph A. Fields, Charles E. Roberts (based on a story by Fields); ph, Jack MacKenzie; ed, Desmond Marquette; md, Paul Sawtell; art d, Van Nest Polglase.

Comedy   **Cas.**   **(PR:A MPAA:NR)**

MEXICAN SPITFIRE AT SEA*¹/₂   (1942) 73m RKO bw

Lupe Velez (*Carmelita Lindsay*), Leon Errol (*Uncle Matt Lindsay/Lord Basil Epping*), Charles "Buddy" Rogers (*Dennis Lindsay*), ZaSu Pitts (*Miss Pepper*), Elizabeth Risdon (*Aunt Della Lindsay*), Florence Bates (*Mrs. Baldwin*), Marion Martin (*Flo*), Lydia Bilbrook (*Lady Epping*), Eddie Dunn (*Mr. Skinner*), Harry Holman (*Mr. Baldwin*), Marten Lamont (*Purser*), John Maguire (*Ship's Officer*), Ferris Taylor (*Capt. Nelson*), Richard Martin, Wayne McCoy (*Stewards*), Warren Jackson (*Shipboard Reporter*), Julie Warren (*Maid*), Lou Davis (*Ship's Waiter*), Mary Field (*Maid*).

None from the Spitfire series could match the first film, MEXICAN SPITFIRE, and this one is no exception. Velez goes off to Hawaii to get an advertising contract for her husband. Errol goes off with her, impersonating an influential lord to help the sales pitch. Most of the action happens on the ship taking them to the islands. The story line is too thin to keep up laughs and interest for 73 minutes. (See MEXICAN SPITFIRE series, Index.)

p, Cliff Reid; d, Leslie Goodwins; w, Jerry Cady, Charles E. Roberts; ph, Jack MacKenzie; ed, Theron Warth.

Comedy   **(PR:A MPAA:NR)**

MEXICAN SPITFIRE OUT WEST**   (1940) 76m RKO bw

Lupe Velez (*Carmelita Lindsay*), Leon Errol (*Uncle Matt Lindsay/Lord Basil Epping*), Donald Woods (*Dennis Lindsay*), Elizabeth Risdon (*Aunt Della Lindsay*), Cecil Kellaway (*Chumley*), Linda Hayes (*Elizabeth*), Lydia Billbrook (*Lady Ada Epping*), Charles Coleman (*Ponsby*), Charles Quigley (*Roberts*), Eddie Dunn (*Skinner*), Grant Withers (*Withers*), Tom Kennedy (*Taxi Driver*), Gus Schilling (*Desk Clerk*), Ferris Taylor (*Thorne*), Dick Hogan (*Bellhop*), Vinton Haworth (*Brown*), Charles Hall (*Elevator Boy*), Youda Hays (*Maid*), Frank Orth (*Window Cleaner*), Rafael Storm (*Travel Clerk*), Rita Owin (*Public Stenographer*), Ted Mangean (*Page Boy*), Lester Dorr (*Harry*), Warren Jackson (*Stranger*), Carl Freemanson (*Bartender*), Sammy Stein (*Cowboy*), Paul Everton (*Dignitary*), Herta Margot (*Beauty Contest Winner*), Jane Woodworth (*Bit*), John Sheehan (*Janitor*), Fred Kalsey, Kernan Cripps (*Cops*).

Velez doesn't feel that husband Woods is paying enough attention to her and decides to fake a divorce to get things back on the right track. She takes off to Reno with her husband and uncle, played by Errol, in tow. There's a subplot about Errol who masquerades as Lord Epping and the situations he gets into when the real lord shows up. (See MEXICAN SPITFIRE series, Index.)

p, Cliff Reid, Lee Marcus; d, Leslie Goodwins; w, Charles E. Roberts, Jack Townley (based on a story by Roberts); ph, Jack MacKenzie; m, Roy Webb; ed, Desmond Marquette; art d, Van Nest Polglase; spec eff, Vernon L. Walker.

Comedy   **(PR:A MPAA:NR)**

MEXICAN SPITFIRE SEES A GHOST*   (1942) 70m RKO bw

Lupe Velez (*Carmelita Lindsay*), Leon Errol (*Uncle Matt Lindsay/Lord Basil Epping/Hubbell*), Charles "Buddy" Rogers (*Dennis Lindsay*), Elizabeth Risdon (*Aunt Della Lindsay*), Donald MacBride (*Percy FitzPatten*), Minna Gombell (*Edith FitzPatten*), Don Barclay (*Fingers O'Toole*), John McGuire (*Luders*), Lillian Randolph (*Hyacinth*), Mantan Moreland (*Lightnin'*), Harry Tyler (*Bascombe*), Marten Lamont (*Harcourt*), Jane Woodworth, Julie Warren (*Secretaries*), Richard Martin (*Chauffeur*), Linda Rivas, Sally Wadsworth, (*Bits*).

One of the weakest entries in the MEXICAN SPITFIRE series, the film is interesting only thanks to Errol's antics. A haunted house turns out to be inhabited by enemy agents making nitroglycerin. This takes a back seat to Errol impersonating Lord Epping to keep Rogers from losing potential business. (See MEXICAN SPITFIRE series, Index.)

p, Cliff Reid; d, Leslie Goodwins; w, Charles E. Roberts, Monte Brice; ph, Russell Metty; ed, Theron Warth; md, C. Bakaleinikoff; art d, Albert D'Agostino, Carroll Clark.

Comedy   **(PR:A MPAA:NR)**

MEXICAN SPITFIRE'S BABY*¹/₂   (1941) 69m RKO bw

Lupe Velez (*Carmelita Lindsay*), Leon Errol (*Uncle Matt Lindsay/Lord Basil Epping*), Charles "Buddy" Rogers (*Dennis Lindsay*), Elizabeth Risdon (*Aunt Della*

Lindsay), Lydia Bilbrook (*Lady Ada Epping*), ZaSu Pitts (*Miss Pepper*), Fritz Feld(*Pierre*), Marion Martin (*Suzanne*), Lloyd Corrigan (*Chumley*), Vinton Haworth (*Hotel Clerk*), Tom Kennedy (*Sheriff*), Max Wagner (*Bartender*), Jane Patten (*Dennis' Stenographer*), Jack Briggs (*Orchestra Leader*), Jane Woodworth (*Cashier*), Ted O'Shea (*Manager*), Dick Rush (*Cop*), Chester Tallman (*Photographer*), Jack Grey, Buddy Messinger, Jack Gardner, Jimmy Harrison, Don Kerr (*Reporters*).

Another zany Spitfire "B" picture. Velez and her family are staying in an Arizona inn and a baby cub starts a series of routine situations. Errol's performance is the best thing in the movie. (See MEXICAN SPITFIRE series, Index.)

p. Cliff Reid; d, Leslie Goodwins; w, Charles E. Roberts, Jerry Cady, James Casey (based on a story by Roberts); ph, Jack MacKenzie; ed, Harry Marker.

Comedy   **(PR:A MPAA:NR)**

MEXICAN SPITFIRE'S BLESSED EVENT*¹/₂   (1943) 63m RKO bw

Lupe Velez (*Carmelita Lindsay*), Leon Errol (*Uncle Matt Lindsay/Lord Basil Epping*), Walter Reed (*Dennis Lindsay*), Elizabeth Risdon (*Aunt Della Lindsay*), Lydia Bilbrook (*Lady Ada Epping*), Hugh Beaumont (*Mr. Sharpe*), Aileen Carlyle (*Mrs. Pettibone*), Alan Carney (*Bartender*), Marietta Canty (*Verbena*), Ruth Lee (*Mrs. Walters*), Wally Brown (*Desk Clerk*), Robert Anderson (*Capt. Rogers*), George Plues (*Driver*), Eddie Dew (*Sheriff Walters*), Billy Edward Reed (*Attendant*), Charles Coleman (*Parker*), Eddie Borden (*Messenger Boy*), June Booth (*Nurse*), Anne O'Neal (*Matron at Orphanage*), George Rogers, Dorothy Rogers, Don Kramer (*Dancers*), Joan Barclay, Patti Brill, Margaret Landry, Margie Stewart, Barbara Hale, Rita Corday, Mary Halsey, Ann Summers, Rosemary LaPlanche.

The eighth and final segment of the "Mexican Spitfire" series, and one of the last films of Velez' career, has her borrowing someone's baby when a wealthy man indicates the desire to do business with her baby's father. This is all prompted by the mistake of the rich man's in hearing that Velez has given birth to a baby. What he did not understand was that the baby was an ocelot kitten. Scripters worked hard to generate humor but failed miserably, finally relying on routines used earlier in the series. (See MEXICAN SPITFIRE series, Index.)

p, Bert Gilroy; d, Leslie Goodwins; w, Charles E. Roberts, Dane Lussier (based on the story by Roberts); ph, Jack MacKenzie; ed, Harry Marker; md, C. Bakaleinikoff; art d, Albert S. D'Agostino, Walter E. Keller.

Comedy   **(PR:A MPAA:NR)**

MEXICAN SPITFIRE'S ELEPHANT**   (1942) 63m RKO bw

Lupe Valez (*Carmelita Lindsay*), Leon Errol (*Lord Basil Epping/Uncle Matt Lindsay*), Walter Reed (*Dennis Lindsay*), Elizabeth Risdon (*Aunt Della Lindsay*), Lydia Bilbrook (*Lady Ada Epping*), Marion Martin (*Diana*), Lyle Talbot (*Reddy*), Luis Alberni (*Luigi*), George Cleveland (*Chief Inspector*), Marten Lamont (*Arnold*), Jack Briggs (*Lewis*), Arnold Kent (*Don Jose Adamos*), Max Wagner (*Headwaiter*), Keye Luke (*Lao Lee, Chinese Magician*), Tom Kennedy (*Joe, Cafe Bartender*), Neely Edwards (*Ship Bartender*), Harry Harvey (*Ship Steward*), Lloyd Ingraham (*Stage Doorman*), Jack Arnold [Vinton Haworth] (*Hotel Manager*), Don Barclay (*Mr. Smith*), Ann Summers (*Lindsay's Maid*), Mary Stuart (*Maid*), Ronnie Rondell (*MC*), Ralph Brooks, Bess Flowers (*Diners*), Eddie Borden (*Waiter*).

Velez, husband Reed, and Reed's uncle Errol board an ocean liner heading for the U.S., and smugglers Talbot and Martin plant a glass elephant full of stolen gems on Errol. He loses the elephant and once in the States the crooks scramble to recover it. This is the one film in the series that came closest to the first film. (See MEXICAN SPITFIRE series, Index.)

p, Bert Gilroy; d, Leslie Goodwins; w, Charles E. Roberts (based on a story by Goodwins, Roberts); ph, Jack MacKenzie; ed, Harry Marker; md, C. Bakaleinikoff; art d, Albert D'Agostino, Feild M. Gray.

Comedy   **(PR:A MPAA:NR)**

MEXICANA**   (1945) 83m REP bw

Tito Guizar ("*Pepe*" *Villarreal*), Constance Moore (*Alison Calvert*), Leo Carrillo (*Esteban Guzman*), Estelita Rodriquez (*Lupita*), Howard Freeman (*Beagle*), Steven Geray (*Laredo*), Jean Stevens (*Bunny*), St. Luke's Choristers, Peter Meremblum Junior Orchestra.

Guizar, Mexico's version of Frank Sinatra, gets tired of his fans ripping his clothes off and goes looking for someone to pose as his wife. He figures if the teeny-boppers think he's married, they'll be a little easier on his wardrobe. He chooses Moore, but they don't see eye to eye and things build to some fair comic situations. Songs include, "Mexicana," "Lupita," "See Mexico," "Heartlessness," "Time Out For Dreaming," "De Corazon A Corazon" (Gabriel Ruiz, Ned Washington), "Somewhere There's A Rainbow" (Walter Scharf, Washington), "The Children's Song" (sung by St. Luke's Choristers).

p&d, Alfred Santell; w, Frank Gill, Jr.; ph, Jack Marta; ed, Arthur Roberts; md, Walter Scharf; art d, Russell Kimball, James Sullivan; spec eff, Howard and Theodore Lydecker; ch, Nick Castle.

Musical   **(PR:A MPAA:NR)**

MEXICO IN FLAMES*¹/₂

       (1982, USSR/Mex./Ital.) 131m Mosfilm-Conacitez-Vides International c

Franco Nero (*John Reed*), Ursula Andress (*Mabel Dodge*).

The USSR wouldn't let Warren Beatty outdo them on the life of writer John Reed, and that is why we have MEXICO IN FLAMES. This is the first in a three-part film epic covering the journalist's life, but it falls far short of Beatty's REDS. Nero is Reed and Andress is his rich patron and lover and they carry on a torrid romance as he covers labor riots and revolutions during the years 1910–1915. Most of the film takes place in Mexico where Nero follows the Mexican revolution. The script is so stiff and full of poetic and political rhetoric that it's hard to keep from laughing at the most serious moments.

d, Sergei Bondarchuk; w, Bondarchuk, V. Ezhov; ph, V. Jusov; m, Jorges Eras.

Drama   (PR:O   MPAA:NR)

MI MUJER ES DOCTOR (SEE: LADY DOCTOR, THE, 1963, Fr./Ital./Span.)

MIAMI EXPOSE**   (1956) 73m Clover/COL bw

Lee J. Cobb (*Bart Scott*), Patricia Medina (*Lila Hodges*), Edward Arnold (*Oliver Tubbs*), Michael Granger (*Louis Ascot*), Eleanore Tanin (*Anne Easton*), Alan Napier (*Raymond Sheridan*), Harry Lauter (*Tim Grogan*), Chris Alcaide (*Morrie Pell*), Hugh Sanders (*Chief Charlie Landon*), Barry L. Connors (*Stevie*).

Cut from the same mold as producer Katzman's THE HOUSTON STORY and THE MIAMI STORY, MIAMI EXPOSE is a fair low-budget crime picture helped tremendously by the presence of Cobb. He is a police lieutenant whose partner is killed while investigating a mob murder. Rival gangs are battling over the gambling action in Florida. Cobb hides witness Medina in an Everglade cabin and waits for the gangster to come after her. Veteran character actor Edward Arnold, who played a lobbyist, died during production of this film at the age of 66.

p, Sam Katzman; d, Fred F. Sears; w, James B. Gordon; ph, Benjamin H. Kline; m, Mischa Bakaleinikoff; ed, Al Clark; md, Bakaleinikoff; art d, Paul Palmentola.

Crime   (PR:A   MPAA:NR)

MIAMI RENDEZVOUS   (SEE: PASSION HOLIDAY, 1963)

MIAMI STORY, THE**   (1954) 75m COL bw

Barry Sullivan (*Mick Flagg*), Luther Adler (*Tony Brill*), John Baer (*Ted Delacorte*), Adele Jergens (*Gwen Abbott*), Beverly Garland (*Holly Abbott*), Dan Riss (*Frank Alton*), Damian O'Flynn (*Chief Martin Belman*), Chris Alcaide (*Robert Bishop*), Gene D'Arcy (*Johnny Loker*), George E. Stone (*Louie Mott*), David Kasday (*Gil Flagg*), Tom Greenway (*Charles Earnshaw*), George A. Smathers.

A documentary-styled crime melodrama with Sullivan as an ex-gangster who is hired by a citizen's committee to compile evidence against Miami crime boss Adler. There have already been two gang killings and the people want to put an end to the violence and vice. Sullivan masquerades as a rival Cuban gangster to get the goods on Adler and solve his own son's kidnaping. Apparently inspired by the U.S. Senate's crime investigations of the time, an introduction by Florida Sen. George Smathers lends credibility to the gritty story.

p, Sam Katzman; d, Fred F. Sears; w, Robert E. Kent; ph, Henry Freulich; m, Mischa Bakaleinikoff; ed, Viola Lawrence; art d, Paul Palmentola; spec eff, Jack Erickson.

Crime   (PR:A   MPAA:NR)

MICHAEL AND MARY**   (1932, Brit.) 76m Gainsborough/UNIV bw

Herbert Marshall (*Michael Rowe*), Edna Best (*Mary Rowe*), Frank Lawton (*David Rowe*), Elizabeth Allan (*Romo*), D. A. Clarke-Smith (*Harry Price*), Ben Field (*Tullivant*), Margaret Yarde (*Mrs. Tullivant*), Sunday Wilshin (*Violet Cunliffe*).

Marshall is a writer who marries Best, his typist, even though she is married to a man who has disappeared and is believed to be dead. Marshall becomes famous and he and Best have a son. Years later, the son is about to get married and Best's first husband shows up. Marshall hits him and the man falls dead from a heart attack. The family concocts a story to keep Marshall from going to jail. A slender story of true love which made a charming play but fails to stand up on the screen.

p, Michael Balcon; d, Victor Saville; w, Angus Macphail, Robert Stevenson, Lajos Biro (based on a play by A. A. Milne); ph, Leslie Rowson; ed, Ian Dalrymple, John Goldman.

Drama   (PR:A   MPAA:NR)

MICHAEL O'HALLORAN **   (1937) 68m REP bw

Wynne Gibson, Warren Hull, Jackie Moran, Charlene Wyatt, Sidney Blackmer, Hope Manning, G. P. Huntley, Jr., Robert Greig, Helen Howell, Vera Gordon, Pierre Watkin, Dorothy Vaughan, Bodil Rosing, Guy Usher.

A misty-eyed story involving the adventures of a 10-year-old newsboy who is eternally devoted to his disabled sister. The two are orphaned, which makes them a convenient charity case for a local woman going through a sticky divorce. She takes in the pair to prove her worth to the courts but ends up falling for the moppets. The kids love her in turn, and all is neatly resolved when her husband sees this touching trio and decides to cancel the divorce proceedings. As they say "only in the movies . . . "

p, Herman Schlom; d, Karl Brown; w, Adele Buffington (based on a story by Gene Stratton-Porter); ph, Jack Marta; ed, Edward Mann.

Drama   (PR:A   MPAA:NR)

MICHAEL O'HALLORAN**   (1948) 76m Windsor/MON bw

Scotty Beckett (*Michael O'Halloran*), Allene Roberts (*Lily Nelson*), Tommy Cook (*Joey*), Isabel Jewell (*Mrs. Nelson*), Charles Arnt (*Doc Bruce, Druggist*), Jonathan Hale (*Judge*), Gladys Blake (*Saleslady*), Roy Gordon (*Dr. Carrell*), Florence Auer (*Mrs. Crawford*), William Haade (*Detective*), Dorothy Granger (*Ward Nurse*), Douglas Evans (*Dr. Johnson*), Beverly Jons (*Student Nurse*), Greg Barton (*Officer Barker*), Lee Phelps (*Lounergan*), Harry Strang (*Officer Martin*), Bob Scott (*Pete*), Ethyl Halls (*Woman*), Ralph Brooks (*Interne*), Rob Haines (*Court Clerk*).

A tear-jerker about an orphaned newsboy, Beckett, who takes in a crippled young girl, Roberts, when her alcoholic mother is injured. He gets a doctor to examine the girl and finds that her affliction is a mental state caused by her mother's actions. Beckett is arrested for helping the girl, but when Roberts walks, seemingly cured of her affliction, Beckett is released.

p, Julian Lesser, Frank Melford; d, John Rawlins; w, Erna Lazarus (based on a novel by Gene Stratton-Porter); ph, Jack McKenzie; ed, John Sheets; md, Lud Gluskin; art d, Lucius O. Croxton.

Drama   (PR:A   MPAA:NR)

MICHAEL SHAYNE, PRIVATE DETECTIVE** 1/2   (1940) 77m FOX bw

Lloyd Nolan (*Michael Shayne*), Marjorie Weaver (*Phyllis Brighton*), Joan Valerie (*Marsha Gordon*), Walter Abel (*Elliott Thomas*), Elizabeth Patterson (*Aunt Olivia*), Donald MacBride (*Chief Painter*), Douglas Dumbrille (*Gordon*), Clarence Kolb (*Brighton*), George Meeker (*Harry Grange*), Charles Coleman (*Ponsby*), Michael Morris (*Al*), Robert Emmett Keane (*Larry Kincaid*), Frank Orth (*Steve*), Irving Bacon (*Fisherman*).

This is the first in the Michael Shayne series with Nolan as a private detective of Irish descent. He's hired by Kolb to a be a bodyguard for his gambling daughter Weaver. Because of a series of crooked gambling setups, Weaver's boy friend is killed and Nolan becomes a suspect. With ease the detective solves the murder and wins Weaver. (See MICHAEL SHAYNE series, Index.)

p, Sol M. Wurtzel; d, Eugene Forde; w, Stanley Rauh, Manning O'Connor (based on a novel by Brett Halliday); ph, George Schneiderman; ed, Al De Gaetano; md, Emil Newman.

Mystery   (PR:A   MPAA:NR)

MICHAEL STROGOFF, 1937
                                            (SEE: SOLDIER AND THE LADY, THE, 1937)

MICHAEL STROGOFF* 1/2
        (1960, Fr./Ital./Yugo.) 111m Emil Natan-Hakim/CD c (MICHAEL STROGOFF)

Curt [Curd] Jurgens (*Michael Strogoff*), Genevieve Page (*Nadia Fedorovna*), Silva Koscina (*Santarre, Gypsy*), Francoise Fabian (*Natko*), Jean Paredes (*Jolivet, Journalist*), Gerard Buhr (*Blount, Journalist*), Henri Nassiet (*Ivan Ogareff*), Jacques Dacqmine (*The Grand Duke*), V. Inkijinoff (*Feofar Khan*), Sylvie (*Marfa Strogoff*), Officers and Men of the Yugoslav Cavalry.

Jurgens is the Russian Czar's special courier who must get a message to the Czar's troops in the 19th Century. Since he must travel through Tartar-held land, he takes Page with him to avoid suspicion. They're captured by the Tartars and a slave girl saves Jurgens from being blinded. Through the plodding storyline of this dubbed picture, Jurgens finally gets his message to the troops and so ends the boredom.

p, Emile Natan; d, Carmine Gallone; w, Marc-Gilbert Sauvajon (based on a novel by Jules Verne); ph, Robert Le Febvre (Eastmancolor); m, Norbert Glanzberg; ed, Nicolo Lizzari; cos, Marcel Escoffier.

Drama   (PR:A   MPAA:NR)

MICHELLE *
(1970, Fr.) 87m Paris Inter/Audubon bw (ADORABLES CANAILLES; AKA: SEXY GANG)

Linda Veras, Agnes Datin, Karine Ker, Sylvain Corthay, Jean-Louis Tristan, Pascal Oge, Kim Camba, Sandrine.

Veras as the title character escapes from prison, falls in love with a painter, and gets herself involved in a murder. Veras ends up back in the slammer but not before receiving a marriage proposal. Originally released in 1967.

d, Henry Jacques; w, Jacques, Claude Sandron; ph, Jean-Michel Boussaguet; m, Armand Seggian; ed, Charles Nobel.

Crime Drama   (PR:C   MPAA:NR)

MICHIGAN KID, THE**   (1947) 69m UNIV c

Jon Hall (*Michigan Kid*), Victor McLaglen (*Curley*), Rita Johnson (*Sue*), Andy Devine (*Buster*), Byron Foulger (*Mr. Porter*), Stanley Andrews (*Sheriff*), Milburn Stone (*Lanny*), William Brooks (*Steve*), Joan Fulton [Shawlee] (*Soubrette*), Leonard East (*Dave*), Ray Teal (*Sergeant*), Guy Wilkerson (*Shotgun Messenger*), Eddy C. Waller (*Post Office Clerk*), Karl Hackett (*Sam*), Tom Quinn (*Hank*), Bert Le Baron (*Rifleman*), Edmund Cobb (*Joe*), William Ching, Griff Barnett, George Chandler, Robert J. Wilke.

Hall is an ex-U.S. marshal who heads to Arizona to start a ranch. On the way, he foils a stagecoach robbery led by McLaglen. The bandit wants revenge on Hall and both men chase each other as they hunt for the 50 grand belonging to Johnson. A fast-moving western that swells with action. The photography by Virgil Miller is topnotch, and Devine, as a cruel outlaw, plays against his usual western character.

p, Howard Welsch; d, Ray Taylor; w, Roy Chanslor, Robert Presnell (based on the novel *Michigan Kid* by Rex Beach); ph, Virgil Miller (Cinecolor); m, Hans J. Salter; ed, Paul Landres; art d, Jack Otterson, Abraham Grossman; m/l, "Whoops My Dear," Jack Brooks, H. J. Salter.

Western   (PR:A   MPAA:NR)

MICKEY*   (1948) 87m EL c

Lois Butler (*Mickey*), Bill Goodwin (*George Kelly*), Irene Hervey (*Louise Williams*), John Sutton (*Ted Whitney*), Rose Hobart (*Lydia Matthews*), Hattie McDaniel (*Bertha*), Skippy Homeier (*Hank Evans*), Beverly Wills (*Cathy Williams*), Leon Tyler (*Robbie Matthews*).

Butler plays a tomboy who becomes a young woman and finds the transition very hard going. The viewer will find this poorly scripted and directed film a dismal prospect. Goodwin is Butler's widowed father and Harvey is the pretty next-door neighbor. Butler even sings several forgettable tunes.

p, Aubrey Schenck; d, Ralph Murphy; w, Muriel Roy Bolton, Agnes Christine Johnston (based on the novel *Clementine* by Peggy Goodin); ph, John W. Boyle

(Cinecolor); m, Marlin Skiles; ed, Norman Colbert; md, Irving Friedman; m/l, Mario Silva, Randolph Van Scoyk.

Drama (PR:A MPAA:NR)

MICKEY ONE**¹/₂ (1965) 93m Florin-Tatira/COL bw

Warren Beatty (*Mickey One*), Alexandra Stewart (*Jenny*), Hurd Hatfield (*Castle*), Franchot Tone (*Ruby Lopp*), Teddy Hart (*Berson*), Jeff Corey (*Fryer*), Kamatari Fujiwara (*The Artist*), Donna Michelle (*The Girl*), Ralph Foody (*Police Captain*), Norman Gottschalk (*The Evangelist*), Dick Lucas (*Employment Agent*), Jack Goodman (*Cafeteria Manager*), Jeri Jensen (*Helen*), Charlene Lee (*The singer*), Benny Dunn (*Nightclub Comic*), Denise Darnell (*Stripper*), Dick Baker (*Boss at Shaley's*), Helen Witkowski (*Landlady*), William Koza, David Crane (*Art Gallery Patrons*), Mike Fish (*Italian Restaurant Owner*), Greg Louis, Gus Christy (*Bartenders*), David Eisen (*Desk Clerk*), Robert Sickinger (*Policeman*), Lew Prentiss (*Kismet Boss*), Grace Colette (*B-Girl*), Boris Gregurevitch (*Kismet Comic*), James Middleton (*Iggie*), Dink Freeman (*Xanadu M.C.*), Tom Erhardt.

Paranoia is the chief problem Beatty suffers from in this moody, murky, and often frightening movie about nighclub entertainers and Chicago mobsters. Beatty is a standup comic, not very good, who runs up a lot of gambling debts and then, believing he is about to be beaten for nonpayment, runs away. He hides out on the West Side of Chicago, using an assumed name and getting a janitorial job where he spends most of his waking hours hauling garbage. Then Beatty's ego, not unlike that of Lenny Bruce's, yearns to again be edified; he must go back on the stage and make people laugh and win applause at all costs. He contacts his agent, Hart, who books him into Hatfield's club. Before resuming his career, Beatty is almost evicted from his apartment for nonpayment of rent but he falls in love with the tenant scheduled to replace him, Stewart, who pays his way. Then Beatty shows up at Hatfield's nightclub but freezes when he learns that Hatfield has arranged for him to perform before only one man who ostensibly will get him jobs in many nightclubs throughout the Midwest. Beatty assumes that the man is a member of the syndicate who is looking to punish him and cuts his act short in panic, fleeing. Guilt-ridden, Beatty runs madly about town looking for the mob's floating crap game so he can square things but he is beaten senseless for his efforts by a group of doormen all dressed in different uniforms. He returns to an incensed Hatfield who tells him he is more or less in bondage to him for the rest of his life. Beatty is convinced when he hears that his agent Hart has vanished and presumes him a murder victim of the mob, Hart having paid for Beatty's welching. He opens at the Hatfield club, resigned to his dismal fate. This is a bleak underworld opus erratically directed by Penn and filled with too many neurotics, in addition to the jumpy Beatty, to be wholly believable. The only person of real substance here is Stewart and she obviously loses out to Hatfield for sexual control of the comic Beatty, the fey actor possessing Beatty in the end. Hatfield's homosexual posture in MICKEY ONE is savage and repugnant, his blathering emotions presenting the aura of mob violence and inhumanity. To say that this film is in the Hitchcockian tradition is to commit, as several critics in the past have done, filmic heresy. Beatty's haunted character is nevertheless obsessive and fascinating as he runs about the on-location sites in Chicago where the production was centered. The unmistakable stamp made upon the film by Penn and Beatty, who later teamed to make the impressive BONNIE AND CLYDE, is a capital "A" for art and that meant commercial doom, as they knew it did. The story is basically pretentious and lags long in spots, jolted into action by sophomoric motivations. Everyone except Stewart seems distorted and grotesque; Hatfield, the gnome-like Hart, and the pasty-faced, manic-eyed Tone who seems as if he has one foot in the grave and hisses his line. (Tone was 61 when he made this film and shows the ravages of a merciless beating he took from another actor, Tom Neal, who pulverized him when finding him with his ex-lover, actress Barbara Payton, herself later skidding down to check fraud and prostitution.) Stan Getz's frenetic jazz renditions, composed by Eddie Sauter, are too loud and irritating to make for the proper mood.

p&d, Arthur Penn; w, Alan M. Surgal; ph, Ghislain Cloquet; m, Jack Shaindlin, Eddie Sauter; ed, Aram Avakian; prod d, George Jenkins; cos, Domingo Rodriguez; makeup, Robert Jiras.

Crime Drama (PR:C-O MPAA:NR)

MICKEY, THE KID*¹/₂ (1939) 68m REP bw

Bruce Cabot (*Jim Larch*), Ralph Byrd (*Dr. Cameron*), ZaSu Pitts (*Lil*), Tommy Ryan (*Mickey*), Jessie Ralph (*Mrs. Hudson*), June Storey (*Sheila*), J. Farrell MacDonald (*Sheriff*), John Qualen (*Mailman*), Robert Elliott (*Farrow*), Scotty Beckett (*Bobby*), James Flavin, Archie Twitchell.

Cabot is a criminal raising his young son, Ryan, in the slums until he kills a bank teller in a robbery. The outlaw sends his son to his grandmother, but when the G-men close in on the boy, father and son go on the run together. They hijack a bus full of school kids and end up running into a snowdrift. Ryan won't let his father leave the kids to freeze to death, so Cabot goes for help and is shot in the process. Ryan becomes a hero when he builds a fire for the kids to keep warm.

p, Herman Schlom; d, Arthur Lubin; w, Doris Malloy, Gordon Kahn (based on a story by Alice Altschuler); ph, Jack Marta; m, Cy Feuer; ed, Murray Seldeen, William Morgan; md, Feuer; art d, John Victor Mackay.

Crime Drama (PR:A MPAA:NR)

MICROSCOPIA (SEE: FANTASTIC VOYAGE, 1966)

MICROWAVE MASSACRE zero (1983) 76m Reel Life c

Jackie Vernon (*Donald*), Loren Schein (*Roosevelt*), Al Troupe (*Philip*), Claire Ginsberg (*May*), Lou Ann Webber (*Dee Dee Dee*), Anna Marlowe (*Chick*), Sarah Alt (*Evelyn*), Cindy Grant (*Susie*), Karen Marshall (*Neighbor*), Marla Simon (*Knothole Girl*), Phil de Carlo (*Sam*).

This bottom-of-the-barrel production is an incompetent and grotesque black comedy about a construction worker, Vernon, who cooks up women in his microwave. He starts with his wife, Ginsberg, and accidentally finds the taste pleasing to his palate. He brings home women, kills them when he's having sex with them, and then pops them into the microwave. The humor is forced and cheap and everyone is mugging it up in front of the camera. The film was made about five to six years before the release date above and was only distributed as a home video.

p, Thomas Singer, Craig Muckler; d, Wayne Berwick; w, Singer (based on a story by Muckler); ph, Karen Grossman; m, Leif Horvath; ed, Steven Nielson; art d, Robert Burns.

Horror Cas. (PR:O MPAA:NR)

MID-DAY MISTRESS zero

(1968) 74m Camelot/Distribpix bw (AKA: THE BUSINESSMAN'S LUNCH; MID-DAY MISS)

Tekla Anderson (*Lauri Blaine*), Stan Howard (*Harry*), Sam Stewart (*Groovy*), Lino Desmond (*Rico*), Alou Mitsou.

Anderson plays a hooker who falls in love with Stewart, a street sleaze who doles out drugs to his Greenwich Village pals with great generosity (he gets the cash from his sister who lives with a film director on the French Riviera). The mob, noticing a drop in business, tries to get Stewart to stop giving away the drugs. They accidentally kill Stewart and rape Anderson. Anderson eventually becomes the mob boss's mistress, but soon learns that he is responsible for Stewart's death and her rape by the gang. To get back at him she has sex with men in front of the mobster who subsequently has become paralyzed. It's amazing to see the way drugs and the 1960s subculture made some filmmakers falsely believe they had talent. There is a fine score by Sly and the Family Stone, however.

p, Henrik Emyl; d, Rolf Emyl; w, Nils Emyl; m, Sly and the Family Stone.

Drama (PR:O MPAA:NR)

MIDAREGUMO (SEE: TWO IN THE SHADOW, 1968, Jap.)

MIDARERU (SEE: YEARNING, 1964, Jap.)

MIDAS RUN**

(1969) 106m Selmur-Motion Pictures/Cinerama c (AKA: A RUN ON GOLD)

Richard Crenna (*Mike Warden*), Anne Heywood (*Sylvia Giroux*), Fred Astaire (*John Pedley*), Roddy McDowall (*Wister*), Ralph Richardson (*Henshaw*), Cesar Romero (*Dodero*), Adolfo Celi (*Aldo Ferranti*), Maurice Denham (*Crittenden*), John LeMesurier (*Wells*), Aldo Bufi-Landi (*Carabiniere*), Fred Astaire, Jr. (*Co-Pilot*), Jacques Sernas (*Giroux*), Karl Otto Alberty (*Dietrich*), George Hartman (*Pfeiffer*), Caroline De Fonseca (*Mrs. Pfeiffer*), Stanley Baugh (*Pilot*), Bruce Beeby (*Gordon*), Robert Henderson (*The Dean*).

Astaire is an officer in the British Secret Service who decides to steal a large gold shipment after being passed over for knighthood. He tricks Crenna, a college professor who was fired for his war protests, into helping him make off with the $15 million gold shipment from a commerical jet. Also involved in the scheme are Heywood and Celi, an ex-Luftwaffe pilot who forces the jet liner down with his Messerschmidt. Once the heist is pulled off, Astaire has Celi arrested. It turns out he wasn't really after the gold, but wanted to capture the German and earn his knighthood. Crenna gets away with some of the gold and marries Heywood, and Astaire gets the reward money from Lloyd's of London along with his knighthood.

p, Raymond Stross; d, Alf Kjellin; w, James Buchanan, Ronald Austin, Berne Giler (based on a story by Giler); ph, Ken Higgins; m, Elmer Bernstein; ed, Frederic Steinkamp; art d, Arthur Lawson, Ezio Cescotti; set d, Massimo Tavazzi; m/l, title song, Don Black, Bernstein (sung by Anne Heywood); makeup, Pino Capogrosso.

Crime Mystery (PR:C MPAA:M)

MIDAS TOUCH, THE*¹/₂ (1940, Brit.) 70m FN-WB bw

Barry K. Barnes (*Evan Jones*), Judy Kelly (*Lydia Brenton*), Frank Cellier (*Corris Morgan*), Bertha Belmore (*Mrs. Carter-Blake*), Iris Hoey (*Ellie Morgan*), Philip Friend (*David Morgan*), Anna Konstam (*Mamie*), Evelyn Roberts (*Maj. Arnold*), Scott Harrold (*Harkness, Chauffeur*), Eileen Erskine (*Rosalie*), Mervyn Johns, Clayton Greene.

A dull melodrama about a wealthy businessman, Cellier, who is reunited with his long-lost son, Barnes. Barnes is now a fast-talking salesman working for his father's company when Dad realizes who he is. Kelly is Barnes' love interest and Belmore is a clairvoyant who predicts that Cellier will die in a car wreck involving Barnes. Cellier does die in a car crash, but his son is saved. After a promising beginning, the film moves quickly.

p, Sam Sax; d, David MacDonald; w, Cy Wood, Brock Williams (based on a novel by Margaret Kennedy); ph, Basil Emmott.

Thriller (PR:A MPAA:NR)

MIDDLE AGE CRAZY**¹/₂ (1980, Can.) 89m Tormont/FOX c

Bruce Dern (*Bobby Lee*), Ann-Margret (*Sue Ann*), Graham Jarvis (*J. D.*), Eric Christmas (*Tommy*), Helen Hughes (*Ruth*), Geoffrey Bowes (*Greg*), Michael Kane (*Abe Titus*), Diane Dewey (*Wanda Jean*), Vivian Reis (*Becky*), Patricia Hamilton (*Barbara Pickett*), Anni Lantuch (*Janet*), Deborah Wakeham (*Nancy*), Gina Dick (*Linda*), Thomas Baird (*Porsche Salesman*), Norma Dell'Agnesi (*Valedictorian*), Shirley Solomon (*Condo Salesman*), Elias Zarou (*Priest*), Michele Chiponski (*Topless Dancer*), Victor Sutton (*Limo Driver*), Jack Mather (*Minister*), Jim Montgomery (*Nancy's Boy Friend*), John Facenda (*Sportscaster's Voice*).

Dern is a Houston building contractor who hits his 40th birthday and the mid-life crisis. Ann-Margret is his wife and she throws a surprise birthday that turns into a comic nightmare for Dern. He also has a daydream of speaking in front of his son's high school graduating class and making a mockery of the typical commencement address. Things change drastically when Dern's father dies and everyone then comes to him with their problems. He takes off to Dallas on a job where he starts an affair with a Dallas Cowboy cheerleader, Wakeham, and loses an important contract. Eventually, Dern turns back to his wife and family in a trite and sentimental ending. The film, on the whole, works well and has some hilarious moments and Dern and Ann-Margret are well cast. Dern proves that he can handle romantic leads as well as he does crazed characters. Shot in its entirety in Toronto.

p, Robert Cooper, Ronald Cohen; d, John Trent; w, Carl Kleinschmitt (based on a song by Jerry Lee Lewis); ph, Reginald Morris (DeLuxe Color); m, Matthew McCauley; ed, John Kelly; art d, Karen Bromley.

Comedy/Drama **(PR:O MPAA:R)**

MIDDLE AGE SPREAD***

(1979, New Zealand) 94m Endeavour/New Zealand Film Commission c

Grant Tilly (Colin), Dorothy McKegg (Elizabeth), Peter Sumner (Reg), Bridget Armstrong (Isobel), Donna Akersten (Judy), Bevan Wilson (Robert).

Tilly is a middle-aged college teacher who is promoted to principal at the time he is experiencing a number of personal crises. He starts jogging to reduce his growing girth and begins an affair with a young female teacher, moist-lipped man killer Akersten. Everything comes to a head when Tilly hosts a dinner party with his bored wife, McKegg. The evening becomes a comic confessional. The finely scripted film was adapted from a hit New Zealand stage play by Roger Hall.

p, John Barnett; d, John Reid; w, Keith Aberdein (based on a play by Roger Hall); ph, Alun Bollinger; m, Stephen McCurdy; ed, Michael Horton.

Comedy/Drama **(PR:O MPAA:NR)**

MIDDLE COURSE, THE*1/2

(1961, Brit.) 60m Danzinger/UA bw

Vincent Ball (Cliff Wilton), Lisa Daniely (Anna), Peter Illing (Gromik), Roland Bartrop (Paul), Marne Maitland (Renard), Robert Rietty (Jacques), Andre Maranne (Franz), Yvonne Andre (Martine).

It's WW II in France, where the inhabitants of a small village are forced to adopt the most ingenious methods to cope with the occupying German forces. A Canadian pilot crashes nearby and plays an essential part in helping the villagers in their own little battle. Predictable type of war drama that went out of fashion in the U.S. 10 years before this was made, but probably will always be resurrected in a nation that suffered so much at the time.

p, Brian Taylor; d, Montgomery Tully; w, Brian Clemens.

War **(PR:A MPAA:NR)**

MIDDLE OF THE NIGHT***1/2

(1959) 118m Sudan/COL bw

Kim Novak (Betty Preisser), Glenda Farrell (Mrs. Mueller, Betty's Mother), Fredric March (Jerry Kingsley), Jan Norris (Alice Mueller), Lee Grant (Marilyn), Effie Afton (Mrs. Carroll, Neighbor), Lee Philips (George Preisser), Edith Meiser (Evelyn Kingsley), Joan Copeland (Lillian Kingsley), Martin Balsam (Jack), David Ford (Paul Kingsley), Audrey Peters (Elizabeth Kingsley), Betty Walker (Rosalind Neiman, the Widow), Albert Dekker (Walter Lockman), Rudy Bond (Gould), Lou Gilbert (Sherman), Dora Weissman (Lucy, Lockman's Wife), Lee Richardson (Joey, Lockman's Son), Anna Berger (Caroline), Alfred Leberfeld (Ellman), Nelson Olmsted (Erskine).

Paddy Chayefsky always had a wonderful way with words and sometimes he was seduced by his own ability to recreate naturalistic conversation. Such was the case in MIDDLE OF THE NIGHT because the dialog is quite real, albeit often thick, and some of the meat was obscured by fat. It began life as a TV drama which starred E. G. Marshall and Eva Marie Saint. Then Chayefsky expanded the 1954 version into a 1956 play which featured Edward G. Robinson and a very young Gena Rowlands. For the film, March returned to the screen after a three year holiday and Novak took the femme lead. As good as March was, he had some trouble playing a Jewish businessman (although ethnicity was somewhat sacrificed to make the story palatable to middle America), and Novak, who was still maturing as an actress, was in a bit over her head. March is a wealthy garment center manufacturer in New York. He is in his indeterminate 60s and has been a widower for quite a while. Novak is the firm's receptionist and just getting over a divorce. She was deeply hurt by her flighty first husband and finds March a comfort in many ways. He, on the other hand, has been resisting a second marriage with a woman near his age, as he is still sprightly and doesn't want to spend the rest of his life watching TV and planning cruises. The two of them find their needs fulfilled in each other and are soon in love. There's no question that Novak truly cares for March and this is because of his money. There is much to like in the March character, as he is thoughtful and charming, and the affair has an advantageous effect on his outlook and health, as he seems to get younger with each passing day under Novak's revitalization. Everybody, but everybody, is against this affair, which is about to culminate in a marriage. Farrell and Norris (Novak's mother and sister) are dumb and crude and don't mask their feelings on the matter. Dekker, an aging roue, is March's partner and fears that March may not survive that kind of sexual stimulation. Copeland is March's possessive daughter and resents the thought of Novak occupying the same place in her father's heart as her late mother. Despite that, plans go ahead for the marriage. Novak is perplexed by all of the disputes and she makes the mistake of having a one-night stand with her ex-husband, jazz musician Phillips. March is hurt by that and wonders if the others may be right—that Novak doesn't know what she wants. The union is called off but both parties are so unhappy apart that they eventually reunite, say "the hell with everything," and are gloriously happy. The difference in age may mean a short marriage and leave Novak a widow, but their joy transcends any logic and the emotion takes over. All the smaller roles were cast with exquisite precison and Balsam, Grant, and particularly Walker (from the Broadway show), are excellent. May-December marriages have

been seen many times in films and will continue to be seen as long as movies are made. Very few of them will be as good as this one. Lots of laughs, a few tears, and Chayefsky's unerring ear for naturalistic dialog are what makes MIDDLE OF THE NIGHT as human as it is. Mann and Chayefsky worked well together before in MARTY and THE BACHELOR PARTY and their respect for each other's talents is evident in every frame. Mann opened up the stage piece just enough to make it cinematic and not enough to make the audience feel that it was merely an artifice. The brownstones, the streets, Central Park, and, most of all, the people of New York, are wonderfully romanticized. Best of all, the story works and we can believe that these two unlikely people can find happiness together. Four people (Walker, Afton, Philips, Balsam) from the original Broadway play that starred Edward G. Robinson and Gena Rowlands appeared in this movie version.

p, George Justin; d, Delbert Mann; w, Paddy Chayefsky (based on his play); ph, Joseph Brun; m, George Bassman; ed, Carl Lerner; md, Bassman; art d, Edward S. Haworth; set d, Jack Wright, Jr.; cos, Frank L. Thompson, Jean Louis; makeup, George Newman.

Drama **(PR:A-C MPAA:NR)**

MIDDLE WATCH, THE**

(1930, Brit.) 100m BIP bw

Owen Nares (Capt. Maitland, R. N.), Jacqueline Logan (Mary Carlton), Jack Raine (Cmdr. Baddeley), Dodo Watts (Fay Eaton), Fred Volpe (Adm. Sir Herbert Hewitt), Henry Wenman (Marine Ogg), Reginald Purdell (Cpl. Duckett), Margaret Halstan (Lady Agatha Hewitt), Phyllis Loring (Nancy Hewitt), Hamilton Keene (Capt. Randall, R. M.), Muriel Aked (Charlotte Hopkinson), George Carr (Ah Fong), Syd Crossley (Sentry).

Nares is a ship captain who finds that two females didn't get off his battleship before it sailed and he hides them in his quarters. The women, Logan and Watts, are found by the admiral, Volpe. The film is stagey, thanks mainly to the cumbersome audio recording equipment used at that time, but contains some humorous moments.

p, John Maxwell; d, Norman Walker; w, Walker, Frank Launder (based on a play by Ian Hay, Stephen King-Hall); ph, Jack J. Cox, Claude Friese-Greene; ed, S. Simmons, Emil De Rulle.

Comedy **(PR:A MPAA:NR)**

MIDDLE WATCH, THE*1/2

(1939, Brit.) 87m ABF bw

Jack Buchanan (Capt. Maitland), Greta Gynt (Mary Carlton), Fred Emney (Adm. Sir Reginald Hewitt), Kay Walsh (Fay Eaton), David Hutcheson (Cmdr. Baddeley), Leslie Fuller (Marine Ogg), Bruce Seton (Capt. Randall), Martita Hunt (Lady Elizabeth Hewitt), Louise Hampton (Charlotte Hopkinson), Romney Brent (Ah Fong), Ronald Shiner (Engineer), Jean Gillie, Reginald Purdell.

The zany antics that were uproarious on the stage fell flat in this uneven screen presentation. Dashing, worldly Buchanan plays the captain of a battleship on which there is a party on the eve of its departure. Two women who took part in the festivities, glamorous Gynt and Walsh, wake up the next morning to discover themselves still aboard ship, and the ship well out to sea. The rest of the film consists of the sailors trying to hide these two stowaways from the woman-hating Buchanan and the admiral. First filmed in 1930.

p, Walter C. Mycroft; d, Thomas Bentley; w, Clifford Grey, J. Lee-Thompson (based on the play by Ian Hay, Stephen King-Hall); ph, Claude Friese-Greene.

Comedy **(PR:A MPAA:NR)**

MIDDLETON FAMILY AT THE N.Y. WORLD'S FAIR*1/2

(1939) 50m Audio/Modern Talking Picture c

Marjorie Lord (Babs), James Lydon (Bud), Ruth Lee (Mother), Harry Shannon (Father), Adora Andrews (Grandma), Douglas Stark (Jim Treadway), George J. Lewis (Nicholas Makaroff), Georgette Harvey (Maid), Ray Perkins, Helen Bennett.

A thinly veiled promotional film for the N.Y. World's Fair and Westinghouse, the company that financed the movie, for the stated purpose of telling the public about the wonderful opportunities for America's youth in the industrial world. To drive home the point, the film has the Middleton family visit the Fair, spending most of their time at the Westinghouse exhibit. Commercial films such as this were fairly common in the 1930s, but this one was unique in that it had a semblance of a plot and characters involved in a story not directly related to the promotional message. The film was offered free to exhibitors.

d, Robert R. Snody; w, Snody (based on a story by G. R. Hunter, Reed Drummond); ph, William Steiner; md, Edwin E. Ludig; ed, Sol E. Feuerman.

Drama **(PR:A MPAA:NR)**

MIDNIGHT*1/2

(1934) 76m All-Star/UNIV c (AKA: CALL IT MURDER)

Sidney Fox (Stella Weldon), O. P. Heggie (Edward Weldon), Henry Hull (Nolan), Margaret Wycherly (Mrs. Weldon), Lynne Overman (Joe Biggers), Katherine Wilson (Ada Biggers), Richard Whorf (Arthur Weldon), Humphrey Bogart (Garboni), Granville Bates (Henry McGrath), Cora Witherspoon (Elizabeth McGrath), Moffat Johnson (District Attorney Plunkett), Henry O'Neill (Mr. Ingersoll), Helen Flint (Ethel Saxon).

Heggie is a jury foreman at the trial of a woman accused of murdering her lover. Since the act could be considered a crime of passion, acquittal is possible until Heggie asks her if she took the dead man's money after the murder. She admits she did, which leads to her conviction and a death sentence. Heggie is considered to be responsible for the verdict, and is hounded by reporters after the trial. He steadfastly maintains that the woman is a murderess and must pay the price. On the evening of her execution, Heggie's own daughter, Fox, kills her lover, Bogart, a gangster whom she believes has betrayed her. Heggie believes his daughter must also be tried, but the district attorney, who has benefited from the publicity generated by the earlier trial, convinces him that prosecution is unnecessary since Bogart was a criminal himself. An interesting story is hampered by stagey direction and weak dialog.

p,d&w, Chester Erskin (based on the play by Paul Sifton, Claire Sifton).

Drama   **Cas.**   **(PR:A MPAA:NR)**

MIDNIGHT**1/2   (1939) 94m PAR bw

Claudette Colbert (Eve Peabody/"Baroness Czerny"), Don Ameche (Tibor Czerny), John Barrymore (George Flammarion), Francis Lederer (Jacques Picot), Mary Astor (Helene Flammarion), Elaine Barrie (Simone), Hedda Hopper (Stephanie), Rex O'Malley (Marcel), Monty Woolley (Judge), Armand Kaliz (Lebon), Lionel Pape (Edouart), Ferdinand Munier, Gennaro Curci (Major Domos), Leander de Cordova, William Eddritt, Michael Visaroff, Joseph Romantini (Footmen), Carlos de Valdez (Butler), Joseph De Stefani (Head Porter), Arno Frey (Room Clerk), Eugene Borden, Paul Bryar (Porters), Leonard Sues (Bellboy), Eddy Conrad (Prince Potopienko), Billy Daniels (Roger), Bryant Washburn (Guest), Nestor Paiva (Woman's Escort), Judith King, Joyce Mathews (Girls), Harry Semels (Policeman).

Story is set in Paris where Colbert is a struggling showgirl. Wealthy Barrymore believes gigolo Lederer is paying too much attention to his wife, Astor, and he hires Colbert to keep Lederer occupied. Ameche plays a taxi driver who has fallen in love with Colbert. When the group goes to Barrymore's chateau in Versailles, Colbert is constantly in danger of being exposed, and the plot is further complicated when Ameche arrives, posing as her husband. Eventually, Barrymore and Astor solve their problems and Ameche and Colbert plan to wed. A witty, well-paced comedy. Astor's appearance here was cleverly designed to hide a thickening body. The actress' waistline was hidden from view by costumer Head who encased her in furs. She was shown seated behind tables having lunch or playing bridge and in a scene where Astor was to lead a conga line, she was unexpectedly called to the phone. It was also a sad reunion with Barrymore who had been her lover 20 years earlier when they appeared on the stage. "He was sick and old," she remembered in A Life on Film. "He was vague and quiet and sat on the set barely talking to anyone." Barrymore could not remember his lines so he worked off cue cards, "but even with cue cards," added Astor, "and only a faint idea of what the picture was all about, he had enough years of experience behind him to be able to act rings around anyone else." Oddly, another woman in Barrymore's life, Barrie, his then wife, was also in the cast. At one point Astor, sitting next to Barrymore on the set, reached over to touch his hand and he pulled away, saying "don't . . . My wife—ah—Miss Barrie—is very jealous." She watched the Great Profile then brush away tears, then laugh at his brimming emotions.

p, Arthur Hornblow, Jr.; d, Mitchell Leisen; w, Charles Brackett, Billy Wilder (based on a story by Edwin Justus Mayer, Franz Shulz); ph, Charles Lang; ed, Doane Harrison; m/l, Ralph Freed, Frederick Hollander.

Comedy   **(PR:A MPAA:NR)**

MIDNIGHT**   (1983) 91m Congregation/Independent-International c

Lawrence Tierney (Bert Johnson), Melanie Verlin (Nancy Johnson), John Hall (Tom), Charles Jackson (Hank), Doris Hackney (Harriet Johnson), John Amplos (Abraham), Robin Walsh (Cynthia), David Marchick (Cyrus), Greg Besnak (Luke).

Verlin runs away from home after her cop father, 1940s movie star Tierney, tries to rape her. She is picked up by two young men as she heads for California and finds that she's the captive of a devil worshiping family. They plan to sacrifice the young woman at midnight on Easter Sunday, but Tierney shows up to save his daughter. Written by John Russo, who wrote the script for George A. Romero's NIGHT OF THE LIVING DEAD. The low-budget horror film was shot in Pittsburgh and finished by 1980, but wasn't distributed until 1983. The script has enough twists and variations from the usual horror story lines that it's refreshing and the special effects are well done, but there's little else to recommend it.

p, Donald Redinger; d&w, John A. Russo (based on his novel); ph, Paul McCollough (Eastmancolor); m, The Sand Castle; ed, McCollough; cos, Irene; songs, "One Man's Family," The Sand Castle; makeup, Tom Savini.

Horror   **(PR:O MPAA:R)**

MIDNIGHT ALIBI**1/2   (1934) 60m FN-WB bw

Richard Barthelmess (Lance McGowan), Ann Dvorak (Joan Morley), Helen Lowell (Abigail Ardsley), Helen Chandler (Abigail Ardsley, as a Girl), Harry Tyler (Hughie), Henry O'Neill (Mr. Ardsley), Robert Barrat (Angie McGowan), Vincent Sherman ("Black" Mike), Eric Wilton (Watts), Robert McWade (Senator), Paul Hurst (Babe), Boothe Howard (Slim), Purnell Pratt, Arthur Aylesworth.

Barthelmess is a gambler who gets entangled with the mob and hides out in the apartment of Lowell. Lowell is an old spinster who has lived in seclusion most of her life because of a failed romance as a young woman. The mob boss, his big brother, is killed and Barthelmess is arrested for the crime. Lowell comes to court and perjures herself, telling the judge that the gambler was with her the night of the crime.

d, Alan Crosland; w, Warren Duff (based on "The Old Doll's House" by Damon Runyon); ph, William Rees; ed, Jack Killifer; cos, Orry-Kelly.

Crime   **(PR:A MPAA:NR)**

MIDNIGHT ANGEL**1/2   (1941) PAR bw (AKA: PACIFIC BLACKOUT)

Robert Preston (Robert Draper), Martha O'Driscoll (Mary), Phillip Merivale (John Ronnel), Eva Gabor (Marie Duval), Louis Jean Heydt (Kermin), Thurston Hall (Williams), Mary Treen (Irene), J. Edward Bromberg (Pickpocket), Spencer Charters (Night Watchman), Cy Kendall (Hotel Clerk), Russell Hicks (Commanding Officer), Paul Stanton (Judge), Clem Bevans (Night Watchman), Robert Emmett Keane (Defense Attorney), Edwin Maxwell (District Attorney), Rod Cameron (Pilot).

Preston, the inventor of an anti-aircraft device, is framed for a murder, convicted, and sentenced to death. As he's being taken to the prison there is a city wide blackout and the handcuffed Preston escapes. He meets O'Driscoll, who helps him find the enemy agents who set him up. A well-paced B action melodrama.

p, Burt Kelly; d, Ralph Murphy; w, Lester Cole, W. P. Lipscomb (based on a story by Franz Spencer, Curt Siodmak); ph, Theodor Sparkuhl; ed, Thomas Scott; m/l, Hoagy Carmichael, Helen Meinardi; art d, Hans Dreier, Franz Bachelin.

Thriller   **(PR:A MPAA:NR)**

MIDNIGHT AT MADAME TUSSAUD'S
                    (SEE: MIDNIGHT AT THE WAX MUSEUM, 1936, Brit.)

MIDNIGHT AT THE WAX MUSEUM*
(1936, Brit.) 66m Premier Sound/PAR bw (GB: MIDNIGHT AT MADAME TUSSAUD'S)

Lucille Lisle (Carol Cheyne), James Carew (Sir Clive Cheyne), Charles Oliver (Harry Newton), Kim Peacock (Nick Frome), Patrick Barr (Gerry Melville), Billy [William] Hartnell (Stubbs), Lydia Sherwood (Brenda), Bernard Miles (Modeller).

A financier bets that he can spend the night in the Chamber of Horrors section in London's wax museum and finds himself the intended murder victim of the man who plans to wed his daughter. Actual scenes shot inside Madame Tussaud's Museum do nothing to add believability to this project, ill-conceived by former-composer-turned-screenwriter Macdougall and cowriter Peacock. One of the last films directed by Pearson, rated England's top director of silent films in the period 1915–1925.

p, J. Steven Edwards; d, George Pearson; w, Roger Macdougall, Kim Peacock (based on the story by Edwards, Macdougall); ph, Jan Stallich.

Crime   **(PR:A MPAA:NR)**

MIDNIGHT AUTO SUPPLY
                    (SEE: LOVE AND MIDNIGHT AUTO SUPPLY, 1978)

MIDNIGHT CLUB**1/2   (1933) 64m PAR bw

Clive Brook (Colin Grant), George Raft (Nick Mason), Helen Vinson (Iris Whitney), Alison Skipworth (Lady Barrett-Smythe), Sir Guy Standing (Commissioner Hope), Alan Mowbray (Arthur Bradley), Ferdinand Gottschalk (George Rubens), Ethel Griffies (The Duchess), Forrester Harvey (Thomas Roberts), Billy Bevan, Charles McNaughton (Detectives), Paul Perry (Grant's Double), Celeste Ford (Iris' Double), Pat Somerset (Bradley's Double), Rita Carlyle (Nick's Landlady), Jean de Briac (Headwaiter), Leo White (Waiter), Teru Shimada, Charles Coleman.

Casting against type, they gave Raft the hero's role and made Brook the villain. It didn't work. Brook leads a pack of chic jewel thieves who have an interesting twist to their machinations; they all have "doubles" who stand in for them at various posh locations so they have perfect alibis while they go out and purloin the baubles. Standing is the Scotland Yard chief and he is confused by the situation, so he imports American Raft, a cop, to help in cracking this befuddlement. (This same plot was used, after a fashion, in the John Wayne-Richard Attenborough picture BRANNIGAN.) Raft meets Vinson, one of the crooks, and is soon flipping his coin about her. After solving the case, Raft can't bear turning Vinson over to the authorities, and she feels terrible that Brook is going to jail. Brook, in as neat a bit of martyrdom as Joan of Arc, makes a deal to take all the blame on the provision that Vinson goes free. Once that's accomplished, the film is over. Raft does okay in his role, an unaccustomed one as a policeman (although he did do that in later years), but he was always more of a stereotype than an actor. There are some funny moments, especially when Raft, speaking in a New York dialect that would be hard to understand for anyone west of the Hudson River, decries Vinson's manner of speech and the fact that she doesn't know how to talk what he considers to be English. The main problem with the movie is the obliteration of any suspense early on when the revelation about the "doubles" is explained. Had they kept that from the audience for a while longer, there might have been some tension or interest on the part of the viewers. As it was, MIDNIGHT CLUB became "an open mystery" and fizzled like a dud firecracker. Co-screenwriter Charteris will be mainly remembered for having created "The Saint," a character who was variously played by Louis Hayward, George Sanders, Jean Marais, Hugh Sinclair and, on TV, by Roger Moore.

d, Alexander Hall, George Somnes; w, Seton I. Miller, Leslie Charteris (based on a story by E. Phillips Oppenheim); ph, Theodor Sparkuhl; ed, Eda Warren.

Crime Drama   **(PR:A MPAA:NR)**

MIDNIGHT COURT**1/2   (1937) 64m WB bw

Ann Dvorak (Carol O'Neil), John Litel (Victor Shanley), Carlyle Moore, Jr. (Bob Terrill), Joseph Crehan (Judge Thompson), Walter Miller (Lt. Jerry Burke), William B. Davidson (Al Kruger), John Sheehan ("Clouter" Hoag), Stanley Fields ("Slim" Jacobs), Gordon Elliott (City Attorney Seabrook), Gordon Hart (Superior Court Judge), Harrison Green (Bailiff Turner), Charles Foy (Dutch), Eddie Foster (Louie), Lyle Moraine (Harry Jills), George Offerman, Jr. (Adolph Nodle), Joan Woodbury (Chiquita).

Litel is an attorney who loses in his bid for the D.A. spot and then gets involved with a car theft ring. He represents the crooks in court and keeps them out of jail until Moore, a mechanic, is murdered. With some persuading from his former wife, Dvorak, Litel turns to prosecuting the gang.

p, Bryan Foy; d, Frank McDonald; w, Don Ryan, Kenneth Gamet (based on their story "Justice after Dark"); ph, Warren Lynch; ed, Frank Magee.

Crime   **(PR:A MPAA:NR)**

MIDNIGHT COWBOY**** (1969) 119m UA c

Dustin Hoffman *(Enrico "Ratso" Rizzo)*, Jon Voight *(Joe Buck)*, Sylvia Miles *(Cass)*, John McGiver *(Mr. O'Daniel)*, Brenda Vaccaro *(Shirley)*, Barnard Hughes *(Towny)*, Ruth White *(Sally Buck)*, Jennifer Salt *(Annie)*, Gil Rankin *(Woodsy Niles)*, Gary Owens, T. Tom Marlow *(Little Joe)*, George Eppersen *(Ralph)*, Al Scott *(Cafeteria Manager)*, Linda Davis *(Mother on Bus)*, J. T. Masters *(Old Cowhand)*, Arlene Reeder *(Old Lady)*, Georgann Johnson *(Rich Lady)*, Jonathan Kramer *(Jackie)*, Bob Balaban *(Young Student)*, Anthony Holland *(TV Bishop)*, Jan Tice *(Freaked-Out Lady)*, Paul Benjamin *(Bartender)*, Peter Scalia, Vito Siracusa *(Vegetable Grocers)*, Peter Zamaglias *(Hat Shop Owner)*, Arthur Anderson *(Hotel Clerk)*, Tina Scala, Alma Felix *(Laundromat Ladies)*, Richard Clarke *(Escort Service Man)*, Ann Thomas *(Frantic Lady)*, Viva *(Gretel McAlbertson)*, Gastone Rossilli *(Hansel McAlbertson)*, Joan Murphy *(Waitress)*, Al Stetson *(Bus Driver)*, Ultra Violet, Paul Jabara, International Velvet, William Door, Cecelia Lipson, Taylor Mead, Paul Morrissey, Paul Jasmin *(Party Guests)*.

MIDNIGHT COWBOY was the only "X"-rated picture to ever win the Oscar as Best Movie of the year. They lowered the rating to an "R" later and, by today's standards, it's almost a "PG-13". Director Schlesinger also took an Academy Award as did screenwriter Salt. Hoffman, Voight, and Miles had nominations but lost to John Wayne for TRUE GRIT and Goldie Hawn in CACTUS FLOWER. It's a seamy look at the vile side of New York and some of the denizens who haunt the streets and abandoned houses of Manhattan. The picture goes to the high spots and lowlifes of the city with one very funny parody of the Andy Warhol crowd in there for comic relief, but it is essentially depressing, almost to the point of being unbearable. Voight is a restless and frustrated dishwasher in a tiny Texas burg and he is a walking stud who feels he can use his sexual abilities to satisfy all of the rich New York women who don't know what real loving is like from a real man. He bids farewell to his Lone Star pals (including Jennifer Salt, the screenwriter's daughter) and heads for the Big Apple. On the trip, he waxes reminiscent about his past and we flashback to see his history: the uncaring father who deserted his slatternly mother; his grandmother, White, and all of her "gentlemen callers,"; and a past history of apparently every sexual experience he ever had. Voight arrives in New York and checks into a second-rate hotel, then cruises the streets until he meets Miles, a blowsy blonde. Voight makes love to the loudmouthed woman in her expensive apartment, but when the time comes for him to extract his fee, she has no money and he has to give her a few bob for a taxi. Voight wanders into a tacky bar and meets Hoffman, a street hustler who steals for a living, when he isn't coughing, due to a tubercular condition. When Hoffman learns why Voight is in town he offers to be the Texan's "manager" and sends him on a job to the room of McGiver, a homosexual who is deeply involved with Jesus. Voight and Hoffman argue over that assignment, then smooth over their differences and Hoffman invites Voight to crash with him in an abandoned building where Hoffman makes his drafty home. The two men become George and Lenny (from OF MICE AND MEN) as they get closer and talk about how it's going to be when they make their big score. They want to settle in the warmth of south Florida and never have to face a New York winter again. But Voight finds that life in the big city is not what he'd expected and he has a series of encounters that never seem to pan out, including one with a young homosexual in a 42nd Street theater. Voight allows the youth to have his way with him then learns that the boy has no money. Voight and Hoffman go to the Warholish party in the Village and Voight meets Vaccaro, a hot number, who gives him a double sawbuck for his passionate efforts. The cold is setting in and Hoffman is frightened because he is rapidly becoming immobile and knows that he is prey for the muggers and other predators who monitor Manhattan's streets. Realizing that Hoffman must be taken out of the city to a warmer climate if he is to survive, Voight beats up a male customer and takes enough money for the two of them to have bus fare to Miami. The two men sit on the bus as they go south and talk of the way things are going to be, but Hoffman dies before he can see the palm trees and the clean wide streets of Miami. Voight holds the body of the best friend he ever had as the picture concludes. Based on the novel by James Leo Herlihy, the screenplay is an excellent example of how a novel can be realized for the screen and merited the Oscar it received. After the success of THE GRADUATE and the disaster of MADIGAN'S MILLIONS (which was made prior to THE GRADUATE but released afterwards), Hoffman was very picky about his roles and refused several parts that were not unlike the young man who was seduced by Mrs. Robinson. He wanted something completely unique and surely found that in the part of Ratso Rizzo. Voight had appeared on Broadway in "The Sound of Music" and a couple of less-than-memorable films (HOUR OF THE GUN, FEARLESS FRANK, OUT OF IT) before soaring to the heights with this role. Englishman Schlesinger had an unerring eye for capturing the grime and slime and reality of New York; sometimes it takes a foreigner to see the U.S. in a new light, just as Czech Milos Forman did with RAGTIME and Britisher Michael Apted did with COAL MINER'S DAUGHTER. The subject matter was such a downer that no one thought this would be the hit that it became. So much for the insiders in Hollywood. The location shots were in Texas, Florida, and, of course, New York, and cinematographer Holender wrung the last bit of atmosphere from each area. In a small role as one of the partygoers, note songwriter Paul Jabara, who later won an Oscar for writing "The Last Dance" for the forgettable THANK GOD IT'S FRIDAY. Good work by jazz harmonicist Jean "Toots" Theilemans helps the mood immensely. MIDNIGHT COWBOY was as close to being a great movie as you can come without getting there. There were several songs used as background music and one of them, "Everybody's Talking" (Fred Neil, sung by Harry Nilsson), was a hit. Other tunes included: "A Famous Myth," "Tears and Toys" (Jeffrey Comanor, sung by The Group), "He Quit Me" (Warren Zevon, sung by Lesley Miller), "Old Man Willow," (Stan Bronstein, Michael Shapiro, Myron Yules, Richard Sussman, sung by Elephants Memory), "Jungle Jim at the Zoo" (Bronstein, Sussman, Richard Frank, sung by Elephants Memory), "Crossroads of the Stepping Stones" (Shapiro, Bronstein, sung by Elephants Memory).

p, Jerome Hellman; d, John Schlesinger; w, Waldo Salt (based on the novel by James Leo Herlihy); ph, Adam Holender (DeLuxe Color); m, John Barry; prod d, John Robert Lloyd; set d, Philip Smith; ed, Hugh A. Robertson; cos, Ann Roth; makeup, Dick Smith, Irving Buchman.

Drama **Cas.** **(PR:O MPAA:R)**

MIDNIGHT DADDIES* (1929) 59m Sono Art-World Wide bw

Harry Gribbon *(Charlie Mason)*, Andy Clyde *(Wilbur Louder)*, Alma Bennett *(A Vamp)*, Addie McPhail *(Charlie's Sweetheart)*, Rosemary Theby *(Wilbur's Wife)*, Katherine Ward *(Wilbur's Mother-in-Law)*, Jack Cooper *(Modiste Shop Owner)*, Vernon Dent, Natalie Joyce.

Mack Sennett's first talkie production falls short of his silent slapstick comedies. The script is stretched to extremes to cover 59 munutes and most of the gags are repeated. The slight story involves an Iowa boy setting up his own business and the problems that arise. His cousin shows up so a few more jokes could be written in. You'll be hard pressed to find the humorous moments in this one.

p&d, Mack Sennett; w, John A. Waldron, Earle Rodney, Hampton Del Ruth, Harry McCoy; ph, John W. Boyle; ed, William Hornbeck.

Comedy **(PR:A MPAA:NR)**

MIDNIGHT EPISODE** (1951, Brit.) 78m Triangle/COL bw

Stanley Holloway *(Prof. Prince)*, Leslie Dwyer *(Albert)*, Reginald Tate *(Inspector Lucas)*, Meredith Edwards *(Detective Sgt. Taylor)*, Wilfrid Hyde-White *(Mr. Knight)*, Joy Shelton *(Mrs. Arnold)*, Raymond Young *(Miller)*, Leslie Perrins *(Charles Mason)*, Sebastian Cabot *(Benno)*, Campbell Copelin *(The General)*, Natasha Parry *(Jill Harris)*.

Holloway is down-and-out actor who recites Shakespeare and opens the car doors of theater patrons to earn some money. In one of the cars is a dead body and Holloway runs off, then returns to find that the body has disappeared and a wallet full of money is lying in the gutter. He turns some of the money over to the police and then hides the wallet and the rest of the cash in a seat in a cheap Italian cafe. The wallet holds vital clues to the identity of the dead man and his murderers. The owner of the restaurant finds the wallet, turns it in to the police, and the murderers are arrested. The film was reissued in 1955 with 11 minutes cut out.

p, Theo Lageard; d, Gordon Parry; w, Rita Barisse, Reeve Taylor, Paul Vincent Carroll, David Evans, William Templeton (based on the novel *Monsieur La Souris* by Georges Simenon); ph, Hone Glendining; m, Mischa Spoliansky; ed, Charles Hasse.

Mystery **(PR:A MPAA:NR)**

MIDNIGHT EXPRESS**** (1978, Brit.) 120m Casablanca/COL c

Brad Davis *(Billy Hayes)*, Randy Quaid *(Jimmy Booth)*, Bo Hopkins *(Tex)*, John Hurt *(Max)*, Paul Smith *(Hamidou)*, Mike Kellin *(Mr. Hayes)*, Norbert Weisser *(Erich)*, Irene Miracle *(Susan)*, Paolo Bonacelli *(Rifki)*, Michael Ensign *(Stanley Daniels)*, Franco Diogene *(Yesil)*, Kevork Malikyan *(Prosecutor)*, Mihalis Yannatos *(Translator)*, Gigi Ballista *(Chief Judge)*, Tony Boyd *(Aslan)*, Peter Jeffrey *(Ahmet)*, Ahmed El Shenawi *(Negdir)*, Zanninos Zanninou *(Turkish Detective)*, Dimos Starenios *(Ticket Seller)*.

MIDNIGHT EXPRESS is a powerful film that will rivet the viewer from the first instant it flashes on screen. So deep and so powerful is the message that it is not easy to grasp it fully until after the doors to the theater have been closed for the night or the video tape has been returned to the rental store. The acting is superb, the direction is excellent, and Moroder's score is exhilarating and may be one of the best in modern films. The picture received five Oscar nominations, for Best Movie, Best Direction, Best Supporting actor (Hurt), and won for Best Music and Best Script From Another Source. Alfred Hitchcock used to make films about innocent people being thrust into situations beyond their control. In the cast of MIDNIGHT EXPRESS, the lead is a guilty man and that's immediately stated. Based on the true-life story of Billy Hayes (now working as an actor in Hollywood), it begins as Davis and girl friend, Miracle, are about to leave for home after a trip to Turkey. Davis is seen taping blocks of hashish to his body before climbing aboard the airplane. Miracle is totally unaware of his attempt at smuggling, and when Davis is caught with the goods at the airport, she is bypassed and allowed to leave Turkey. The Turkish government was on the alert for drug smugglers and we never know if this was a tipoff or just a coincidence that Davis was caught. In a brilliantly tense scene, Davis is herded at gunpoint to a room where he is stripped and interrogated. From here, he is taken to a fierce Turkish prison, a place that makes Sing Sing look like a Beverly Hills country club. It's a jail where the prisoners must fend for themselves and the notion of human rights is an alien as a JDL member at a PLO meeting. Comfort means a night when someone isn't brutally raped, beaten, or otherwise abused. Davis meets many of the other inmates, including a few Westerners who are all in there for the same drug raps. Quaid is the American, Hurt is the dope-smoking Englishman, and Weisser is a gay Scandinavian with whom Davis has a brief sexual liason. (How much of what is truth and what is fiction can not be discerned unless one has read the book by Hayes and Hoffer.) The prisoners are shown to be wayward sheep rather than the smugglers and criminals they are, and that sort of stacks the deck in favor of eliciting sympathy from the audience. In the first half of the film, Davis' father, Kellin, attempts to get his son out of jail by hiring a local attorney, Jeffrey, to defend him. But the Turkish legal system is like a court filled with kangaroos and they are bent on making Davis an example to others who may have the same idea. In a sensational courtroom moment, Davis berates his captors with an obscene lambasting of the judges, most of whom don't speak English and have no idea what he's saying. He is sentenced to more years than he thought he'd get, and, once remanded to the jail, he makes plans to take the "Midnight Express" out of there (the euphemism for escape). Davis and Quaid try to get out by burrowing, but are caught and beaten badly by Paul Smith, the behemoth sadist who runs the security department for the jail. Davis is shipped to the insane ward, which makes the previous incarceration look like a Hilton Hotel. Miracle comes to visit him and they are separated by a wall of glass in the small visitor's cell. Miracle opens her blouse so Davis can see her breasts in what may be his last look at a near-naked woman. While doing this, he masturbates. One of the prisoners, Diogene, is a fink for the guards who sells goods to the other prisoners. When he is to be released, he is beaten by the others, and Davis bites the man's tongue out! Now Davis is taken to the torture room by Smith and is about to be whacked around again, probably until he dies. There is a clothes spike attached to the wall and Davis fights back, sending the 300-pound Smith up against the wall, where the spike impales Smith and kills him. Davis puts on some guard's clothing and walks out the door of the jail into the dusk. The final sequence is a series of snapshots chronicling the happy reunion of Davis and family, not an altogether prudent choice on the part of the creators, but the film was so dour and downbeat that they must have felt the audience needed their hearts to be lightened before strolling up the aisles. There's not a bad performance in the picture, not even a mediocre one. Quaid's portrayal of the slightly deranged American is perfection; Hurt, as the addicted Englishman, is a study in understatement; Weisser is totally believable; and Smith must rank a close second to Hume Cronyn's Capt. Munsey in BRUTE FORCE for sheer evil in a prison official. The standout is Davis, who is given the task of displaying just about every emotion known to man and succeeds. MIDNIGHT EXPRESS is often a bit too stylish for its own good, something that may have been an indulgence on the part of Parker, who also showed the same zealous adherence to style over substance with BUGSY MALONE and BIRDY. It is, however, most effective, Parker and editor Hambling both won British Film Academy Awards for their work. The picture was shot in Greece and on the island of Malta, where they used Fort St. Elmo to double as the Turkish prison. This movie, more than all the warnings from the U.S. government, probably did more to discourage amateur dope smugglers than any other medium of communication. Extremely violent and sadistic; not for youngsters.

p, David Puttnam, Alan Marshall; d, Alan Parker; w, Oliver Stone (based on the book by Billy Hayes, William Hoffer); ph, Michael Seresin (Eastmancolor); m, Giorgio Moroder; ed, Gerry Hambling; prod d, Geoffrey Kirkland; art d, Evan Hercules; cos, Milena Canonero, Bobby Lavender; m/l, "Istanbul Blues," David Castle; makeup, Mary Hillman, Penny Steyne; stunts, Roy Scammell.

True Drama **Cas.** **(PR:O MPAA:R)**

MIDNIGHT FOLLY**

(1962, Fr.) Groupement des Editeurs de Films-Unidex/Unidex bw (LES DEMONS DE MINUIT)

Charles Boyer *(Pierre)*, Pascale Petit *(Daniele)*, Maria Mauben *(Katherine)*, Charles Belmont *(Claude)*, Berthe Grandval *(Sophie)*.

Boyer stars in this broad view of the French upper class. He's a governmental minister who gets a call from a married woman. She tells him she's going to commit suicide because of his son. Boyer takes off on a search for his son and is aided by an unhappy rich girl. Boyer is exposed to strip poker games and other decadent pastimes. He finds his son, he returns to the woman he had rejected, and has an affair with the helpful young lady.

d, Marc Allegret, Charles Gerard; w, Bernard Revon, Serge Friedman, Pascal Jardin; ph, Gilbert Sarthre; ed, Suzanne De Troeye.

Drama **(PR:C MPAA:NR)**

MIDNIGHT INTRUDER** (1938) 66m UNIV bw

Louis Hayward *(Gilbert)*, Eric Linden *(Rogers Ridder, Jr.)*, J. C. Nugent *(Doc)*, Barbara Read *(Patricia)*, Irving Bacon *(Evans)*, Robert Greig *(Willets)*, Pierre Watkin *(Winslow)*, Sheila Bromley *(Peggy)*, Paul Everton *(Mr. Ridder)*, Nana Bryant *(Mrs. Ridder)*, Joe Crehan *(Harwood)*, Selmer Jackson *(Judge Hammond)*, Jan Duggan *(Mrs. Randolph)*, Guy Usher *(Mike Kelly)*, Theodore Osborn *(Joe Dillon)*, Matty Fain *(Romano)*, Fay Helm *(Marion Loree)*, Ruth Robinson *(Mrs. Winslow)*, Charley Foy, Billy Wayne *(Taxi Drivers)*, Aileen Carlyle *(Maid)*, Lee Phelps *(Deputy)*, Alexander Leftwich *(Cashier)*, Jimmie Lucas *(Waiter)*, Polly Vann *(Cook)*, Jack Gardner *(Messenger)*, Allen Fox *(Radio Operator)*, Charlie Sullivan *(Cop)*, Billy Engle *(Race Track Tout)*, Charles Murphy *(Truck Driver)*.

Hayward and Nugent are two horse betters who lose all their money on a long shot. Trying to hitch a ride to the next racetrack, they take shelter in what they think is an abandoned mansion. They find clothes and put them on and are discovered by servants who mistake the two as the owner's son and friend. The mistaken identities creat a number of complications.

p, Trem Carr; d, Arthur Lubin; w, George Waggner, Lester Cole (based on the novel *Welcome Imposter* by Channing Pollock); ph, Milton Krasner; ed, Bernard W. Burton; md, Charles Previn; art d, Jack Otterson.

Comedy **(PR:A MPAA:NR)**

MIDNIGHT LACE*** (1960) 108m UNIV c

Doris Day *(Kit Preston)*, Rex Harrison *(Tony Preston)*, John Gavin *(Brian Younger)*, Myrna Loy *(Aunt Bea)*, Roddy McDowall *(Malcolm)*, Herbert Marshall *(Charles Manning)*, Natasha Parry *(Peggy Thompson)*, John Williams *(Inspector Byrnes)*, Hermione Baddeley *(Dora)*, Richard Ney *(Daniel Graham)*, Rhys Williams *(Victor Elliott)*, Doris Lloyd *(Nora)*, Richard Lupino *(Simon Foster)*, Anthony Dawson *(Ash)*, Anna Cheselka, Vladimir Oukhtomsky *(Ballet Dancers)*, Rex Evans *(Basil Stafford)*, Jim Hyland *(Policeman)*, Mary Flynn *(Nurse)*, Tom Toner, Donald Journeau *(Porters)*, Paul Collins *(Kevin)*, Jimmy Fairfax *(Bus Driver)*, John Sheffield *(Attendant)*, Joan Staley *(Blonde)*, Peter Fontaine *(Workman)*, Leon Charles *(Man)*, Richard Peel *(Tommy)*, Roy Dean *(Harry)*, Pamela Light *(Beautician)*, Jack Livesey *(MP)*, Anthony Eustrel *(Salesman)*, Gage Clarke *(Salesman in Gun Shop)*, Terence DeMarney *(Tim)*, Keith McConnell *(Policeman)*, Elspeth March *(Woman)*, Hayden Rorke *(Dr. Garver)*.

Day is an American woman married to wealthy London businessman Harrison. Her life suddenly becomes fraught with terror when a mysterious voice begins trailing her through the thick London fog. Soon the voice threatens Day over the telephone, vowing to murder the frightened woman. While on a shopping spree, Day is nearly killed when someone pushes her under a bus. Harrison, along with Day's visiting aunt Loy and even Scotland Yard, dismiss the growing evidence as fantasies of an unbalanced mind if not outright lies. Day can find sympathy only in Gavin, a construction foreman, but his occasional strange behavior suggests that he may be the secret tormentor. Also suspect is McDowall, the pesty son of Day's servant, who worships his father's employer. Eventually (and to no one's surprise) it develops that Harrison and his mistress Parry are behind the goings-on in an attempt to make Day's death appear to be a suicide. Gavin catches onto the plot before the police and in the climax saves Day from a chase atop a towering scaffolding. The plotting is simple for a thriller, introducing the characters, then inviting the audience to guess "whodunnit." Despite an ad campaign that told audiences not to reveal the "unique plot developments," there's nothing "unique" in the suspense and any genre fan can easily spot Harrison as the culprit long before it's revealed. While nothing to rival Hitchcock, the film's *mise-en-scene* and direction make up for the easy intrigues. MIDNIGHT LACE has a handsome style and look that give a much-needed boost to the proceedings. Miller's directoral pacing also helps, infusing suspense with subtle touches here and there. Day makes a switch from light comedy to suspense fairly well, creating a believable victim with her perfomance, while Harrison, his usual debonair self, adopts a sinister air. Loy's role is disappointing as Day's eccentric aunt, giving an occasional humorous touch to a part clearly below her abilities. Day undergoes no less than 17 costume changes, for which designer Irene received a well-earned Oscar nomination. Harrison's life was at a low ebb when he agreed to take his role in MIDNIGHT LACE. He was still hurting from the loss of his wife, Kay Kendall, to leukemia the year before. After appearing in a less-than-successful play satirizing Charles de Gaulle, he reluctantly accepted the part of Tony Preston, dreading the thought of the lonely Hollywood life. On set he struck up a friendship with Day who was a devout Christian Scientist. In his autobiography, *Rex*, Harrison recalled, "We used to hold what amounted to Christian Science sessions on the set (or so it seemed to me), when all the lights would be put out and the director could be heard telling Doris, *sotto voce*, 'God is in the studio, God is in the flowers, God is on the set . . . ' At which point I would wander away and sit down to ponder life and death." Day lent Harrison some books on Christian Science but during the course of the shooting the actor somehow managed to lose them. " . . . When at the end of the film she asked for them back, and I had to own up, I felt I was growing horns," Harrison recalled.

p, Ross Hunter, Martin Melcher; d, David Miller; w, Ivan Goff, Ben Roberts (based on the play *Matilda Shouted Fire* by Janet Green); ph, Russell Metty (Eastmancolor); m, Frank Skinner; ed, Russell F. Schoengarth, Leon Barsha; md, Joseph Gershenson; art d, Alexander Golitzen, Robert Clatworthy; set d, Oliver Emert; cos, Irene; m/l, "Midnight Lace," Joe Lubin, Jerome Howard, "What Does a Woman Do?" Allie Wrubel, Maxwell Anderson.

Suspense **(PR:C MPAA:NR)**

MIDNIGHT LADY* (1932) 65m CHES bw

Sarah Padden *(Nita St. George)*, John Darrow *(Bert)*, Claudia Dell *(Jean Austin)*, Theodore Von Eltz *(Byron Crosby)*, Montagu Love *(Harvey Austin)*, Lucy Beaumont *(Grandma Austin)*, Lina Basquette *(Mona)*, Donald Keith *(Don Austin)*, Brandon Hurst *(District Attorney)*, B. Wayne Lamont *(Tony)*.

Padden is the owner of a speakeasy who had left her family years before to escape a domineering mother-in-law. Her children think she is dead, but when daughter Dell is accused of murder, her mother comes forward and takes the rap. Eventually, the real killer is identified and Padden and Dell reunited. A decent cast can't overcome the weak script and silly dialog, and the picture is further hampered by substandard production credits.

d, Richard Thorpe; w, Edward T. Lowe; ph, M. A. Anderson.

Drama **(PR:A MPAA:NR)**

MIDNIGHT LIMITED** (1940) 61m MON bw

John King *(Val)*, Marjorie Reynolds *(Joan)*, George Cleveland *(Professor)*, Edward Keane *(Harrigan)*, Pat Flaherty *(Conductor)*, Monte Collins *(Kranz)*, Herb Ashley *(Trainman)*, I. Stanford Jolley *(Frenchie)*, Buck Woods *(Willy)*, Lita Chevret.

King is a private detective out to foil the criminals attempting to rob the "Midnight Limited" train from N.Y. to Montreal. King is helped by Reynolds, a victim of the robbers, and the film moves smoothly to an enjoyable payoff.

p, T. R. Williams; d, Haward Bretherton; w, Harrison Carter, C. H. Williams; ph, Harry Neumann; ed, Karl Zint.

Crime/Mystery **(PR:A MPAA:NR)**

MIDNIGHT MADNESS* (1980) 110m BV c

David Naughton *(Adam)*, Debra Clinger *(Laura)*, Eddie Deezen *(Wesley)*, Brad Wilkin *(Lavitas)*, Maggie Roswell *(Donna)*, Stephen Furst *(Harold)*, Irene Tedrow *(Mrs. Grimhaus)*, Michael J. Fox *(Scott)*, Joel P. Kenney *(Flynch)*, Alan Solomon *(Leon)*.

The only thing special about this teenage piece of junk is that it's the first film produced by Walt Disney that doesn't carry the Disney name. Guess they realized what a dud they had. The film is minus the usual juvenile raunch, but it's also minus any brains. A grad student sets up an all-night scavenger hunt which leads to a lot of dumb jokes and predicatable situations.

p, Ron Miller; d&w, David Wechter, Michael Nankin; ph, Frank Phillips (Technicolor); m, Julius Wechter; ed, Norman R. Palmer, Jack Sekely; art d, John B. Mansbridge, Richard Lawrence; set d, R. Chris Westlund, Roger M. Shook; spec eff, Danny Lee.

Comedy   **Cas.**   **(PR:C   MPAA:PG)**

MIDNIGHT MADONNA***1/2**   (1937) 56m PAR bw

Warren William (*Blackie Denbo*), Mady Correll (*Kay Barrie*), Kitty Clancy (*Penelope "Penny" Long*), Edward Ellis (*Judge Clark*), Robert Baldwin (*Vinny Long*), Jonathan Hale (*Stuart Kirkland*), Frank Reicher (*Vincent Long II*), Joseph Crehan (*Moe Grinnell*), May Wallace (*Mrs. Withers*), Irene Franklin (*Cafe Proprietor*), Jack Clifford, Ruth Robinson, Mildred Gover, Donald Kirke, Nick Copeland, Alonzo Price, Clyde Dilson, Harry Tyler, Brooks Benedict, Matty Fain, Hymie Miller, George Magrill, Duke York.

A highly sentimental, sugar-coated film about the custody battle for Clancy. Her father, William, is a gambler who left his wife and daughter, and now wants Clancy because she's inherited a large sum of money from her grandfather. Correll, the mother, is found to be an unfit mother because she's an entertainer, and Clancy joins her ruthless father. Jurist Ellis proves that William bought witnesses and Clancy and Correll are reunited.

p, Emanuel Cohen; d, James Flood; w, Doris Malloy, Gladys Lehman (based on a story by David Boehm); ph, Robert Pittack; ed, Ray F. Curtiss; art d, Wiard Ihnen; m/l, Arthur Johnson, John Burke.

Drama   **(PR:A   MPAA:NR)**

MIDNIGHT MAN, THE****1/2**   (1974) 117m UNIV c

Burt Lancaster (*Jim Slade*), Susan Clark (*Linda*), Cameron Mitchell (*Quartz*), Morgan Woodward (*Clayborn*), Harris Yulin (*Casey*), Robert Quarry (*Dr. Pritchet*), Joan Lorring (*Judy*), Lawrence Dobkin (*Mason*), Ed Lauter (*Leroy*), Mills Watson (*Cash*), Charles Tyner (*Ewing*), Catherine Bach (*Natalie*), William Lancaster (*King*), Quinn Redeker (*Swanson*), Eleanor Ross (*Noll*), Richard Winterstein (*Virgil*), William T. Hicks (*Charlie*), Peter Dane (*Metterman*), Linda Kelsey (*Betty*), William Splawn (*Lamar*), Susan MacDonald (*Elaine*), Joel Gordon Kravitz (*Pearlman*), Nick Cravat (*Gardener*), Rodney Stevens (*Jimmy*), Weems Oliver Baskin III (*Bartender*), Jean Perkins (*Nurse*), Harold N. Cooledge, Jr. (*Collins*), Gene Lehfeldt (*Casey's Driver*), William Clark (*Deputy*), Elizabeth Black (*Bus Dispatcher*), Rachel Ray (*Parolee*), David Garrison (*Photographer*), Hugh Parsons (*Grocery Clerk*), Lonnie Kay (*Hostess*), G. Warren Smith (*Director*), Lucille Meredith (*Radio Evangelist*), Mal Alberts (*Basketball Announcer*), Alan Gibbs, Jim Burke, Frank Orsatti, Julie Johnson (*Stunts*).

A convoluted crime meller which stars Lancaster as a former police detective imprisoned for the murder of his wife's lover. After his stretch behind bars, Lancaster is released into the custody of sexy parole officer Clark. He is given a place to stay by friends Mitchell and Lorring, and finds a job at a nearby university as a night watchman. He again finds himself surrounded by murder, however, when a student, Bach, is found dead. Suspicion falls on Tyner, a janitor with an uneasy religious fervor. Lancaster is unconvinced by the hasty accusations made by sheriff Yulin and sets out to find the real killer. He digs deeper and deeper, opening up a complex can of blackmail, politics, and rape. It seems that Bach had admitted, on audio cassette, to her psychologist that she had relations with her father, Woodward, a powerful state senator. Woodward and his henchmen, Lauter, Watson, and Hicks, turn up as the most likely suspects and are eventually taken care of by Lancaster. Unfortunately, THE MIDNIGHT MAN doesn't deliver what is promised and succeeds only in swallowing up the characters in favor of the plot. THE MIDNIGHT MAN did mark Lancaster's first venture into the director's chair, a task he shared with Kibbee along with producing and writing. For some time before beginning THE MIDNIGHT MAN Lancaster professed an urge to get behind the camera: "When you reach my sort of age, and have done so much acting-wise, you begin to look around and wonder what to do next. I feel it's about time I made a move towards directing again. I'm always trying to tell directors what to do, so I really ought to go away and do it myself." Having satisfied his curiosity Lancaster decided to remain in his actor's shoes and as a result turned in a number of superb performances including ATLANTIC CITY (1981) and LOCAL HERO (1983).

p,d&w, Roland Kibbee, Burt Lancaster (based on the novel *The Midnight Lady and the Mourning Man* by David Anthony); ph, Jack Priestley (Panavision, Technicolor); m, Dave Grusin; ed, Frank Morriss; prod d, James D. Vance; set d, Joe Stone; m/l, Grusin, Morgan Ames (sung by Yvonne Elliman).

Crime   **(PR:O   MPAA:R)**

MIDNIGHT MANHUNT   (SEE: ONE EXCITING NIGHT, 1945)

MIDNIGHT MARY**   (1933) 71m MGM bw

Loretta Young (*Mary Martin*), Ricardo Cortez (*Leo Darcy*), Franchot Tone (*Tom Mannering*), Andy Devine (*Sam Travers*), Una Merkel (*Bunny*), Frank Conroy (*District Attorney*), Warren Hymer (*Angelo Ricci*), Ivan Simpson (*Tindle*), Harold Huber (*Puggy*), Sandy Roth (*Blimp*), Martha Sleeper (*Barbara*), Charles Grapewin (*Clerk*), Halliwell Hobbes (*Churchill*), Robert Emmett O'Connor (*Cop*).

Young is on trail for her life and flashes back to the ways and means by which she came to be in this spot. Her police blotter shows the chronicle of a woman gone wrong and how she got there. She's a 10-year-old orphan who falls into bad company, and gets mixed up with villain Cortez and his gang, Hymer, Huber, Merkel, and Roth (a one-time MGM assistant director who took a job as an actor on this one). They plot to rob a posh private club where gambling and alcohol vie for popularity. Tone is the wealthy son of even wealthier parents and he and Young are tossed together as Young tries to go straight, then goes crooked, and ends up in Tone's arms at the end to forsake her evil ways. MIDNIGHT MARY was a hit in

1933, although, other than Young's performance, there is not much reason to see this film. Cortez is almost a parody of the bad guy and Tone is namby-pamby to the point of being annoying. Devine, in one of his earliest efforts, already showed that he had a large career in front of him, as he provides the few good laughs in the picture. The story was by a woman who made her name, Anita Loos, writing about interesting females. Loos also wrote or collaborated on such women-oriented movies as GENTLEMEN PREFER BLONDES, THE FALL OF EVE, THE RED-HEADED WOMAN, BLONDIE OF THE FOLLIES, THE GIRL FROM MISSOURI, THE WOMEN, and on and on. Not one of Wellman's best when you consider that he also directed PUBLIC ENEMY, BEAU GESTE, A STAR IS BORN, and THE OX-BOW INCIDENT. Still, even Ty Cobb, who had the highest career batting average in the history of baseball, made an out almost six and a half times out of every 10 at-bats. And he was a Hall-of-Fame player. So was Wellman.

p, Lucien Hubbard; d, William A. Wellman; w, Gene Markey, Kathryn Scola (based on the story by Anita Loos); ph, James Van Trees; ed, William S. Gray; cos, Adrian.

Crime Drama   **(PR:A-C   MPAA:NR)**

MIDNIGHT MEETING**

(1962, Fr.) 90m Editions Cinegraphiques-Argos Films/Lux bw (LE RENDEZ-VOUS DE MINUIT)

Lilli Palmer (*Anne/Eva*), Maurice Ronet (*Pierre*), Michel Auclair (*Jacques*).

The second film from film critic Roger Leenhardt (first was THE LAST VACATION) is the story of a film critic who becomes interested in a woman who leaves a film in tears. He follows her and asks why she's crying. The woman tells him that she's seen the movie many times and that the heroine, a rich woman who can't find meaning in her life, reminds her of herself. In the film, the heroine kills herself and that is what the woman plans to do. The film is intercut with scenes of the movie the two have watched. The heroine of the movie kills herself by jumping from a Paris bridge, but the woman doesn't go through with the suicide because of the concern the film critic has for her.

d, Roger Leenhardt; w, Jean-Pierre Vivet, Leenhardt; ph, Jean Badal; ed, Henri Lanoe.

Drama   **(PR:A   MPAA:NR)**

MIDNIGHT MELODY   (SEE: MURDER IN THE MUSIC HALL, 1946)

MIDNIGHT MENACE   (SEE: BOMBS OVER LONDON, 1937, Brit.)

MIDNIGHT MORALS*   (1932) 61m Mayfair bw

Beryl Mercer (*Prison Matron*), De Witt Jennings, Charles Delaney, Alberta Vaughn, Gwen Lee, Rex Lease.

Delaney is a rookie cop who falls in love with dancer Vaughn, but his father, Jennings, disapproves. When the dancer is framed with stealing some jewels, she gets six months in jail and thinks Delaney's father is responsible. When she gets out of jail the couple continue their romance and Delaney quits the police force. Everything works out as Vaughn solves a murder and that gets her in good with pop and the rest of the family.

p, Cliff Broughton; d, E. Mason Hooper; w, Norman Houston; ph, Jules Cronjager; ed, Byron Robinson.

Crime Drama   **(PR:A   MPAA:NR)**

MIDNIGHT MYSTERY**   (1930) 69m RKO bw

Betty Compson (*Sally Wayne*), Hugh Trevor (*Gregory Sloane*), Lowell Sherman (*Tom Austen*), Rita LaRoy (*Madeline Austen*), Ivan Lebedeff (*Mischa Kawelin*), Raymond Hatton (*Paul Cooper*), Marcelle Corday (*Harriet Cooper*), June Clyde (*Louise Hollister*), Sidney D'Albrook (*Barker*), William Fresley Burt (*Rogers*).

A large party is held on an island off the New England coast and the host decides to brighten up the evening by acting out a murder and having the guests try to solve the crime. The man who's supposed to be killed goes off and when he comes back he finds everyone gone except the husband of the woman with whom he's been having an affair. The husband kills the man thinking that the game will hide his tracks. Mystery writer Compson takes on the role as sleuth and gets the husband to confess.

p, William LeBaron; d, George B. Seitz; w, Beulah Marie Dix (based on the play "Hawk Island" by Howard Irving Young); ph, Joseph Walker.

Murder Mystery   **(PR:A   MPAA:NR)**

MIDNIGHT PATROL, THE***1/2**   (1932) 67m MON bw

Regis Toomey (*John Martin*), Betty Bronson (*Ellen Gray*), Edwina Booth (*Joyce Greeley*), Mary Nolan (*Miss Willing*), Earle Foxe (*Judson*), Robert Elliott (*Howard Brady*), Edward Kane (*Stuart*), William Norton Bailey (*Powers*), Mischa Auer (*Dummy Black*), Mack Swain, Tod Sloan, Jim Jeffries, Jack Mower, Barry Oliver, Wilfred Lucas, J. C. Fowler, Ray Cooke, Snub Pollard.

Ambitious, and very naive, newshound Toomey will stop at nothing to get the biggest and best scoop, even if it kills him. He smuggles himself into prison to interview mute murderer Auer, which he is able to do as he knows the sign language that mute/deaf people use. It is quite amazing that Toomey managed to stay alive throughout the course of this hard-to-take film. Somehow he did, and his adventures are at least delivered in a fashion that keeps an audience interested.

d, Christy Cabanne; w, George Jeske, Barry Barringer, C. E. Roberts (based on the story by Arthur Hoerl); ph, Lou Physioc.

Crime   **(PR:A   MPAA:NR)**

MIDNIGHT PLEASURES**

(1975, Ital.) 90m Delfo Cinematografica-Rizzoli/Film Ventures c (A MEZZANOTTE VA LA RONDA DEL PIACERE)

Claudia Cardinale (Gabriella Sansoni), Vittorio Gassman (Andrea Sansoni), Giancarlo Giannini (Gino Benacio), Monica Vitti (Tina Candela), Renato Pozzetto (Fulvio).

A masochistic Italian comedy about male attitudes toward women. Vitti is on trial for murder of Giannini and Cardinale is one of the jury members. Cardinale becomes fascinated with Vitti telling of her love affair with Giannini, who likes to slap Vitti into sexual excitement and adoration. Cardinale believes Vitti's testimony offers insights into the nature of true love, and she begins to reshape her relationship with husband Gassman. When Giannini appears, quite alive, charges are dropped against Vitti and the film indicates both couples have been enriched by the experience.

p, Elio Scardamaglia; d, Marcello Fondato; w, Fondato, Francesco Scardamaglia; ph, Pasquale DeSantis (Technicolor); m, Guido and Maurizio De Angelis; ed, Sergio Montanari; art d, Luciano Ricceri.

Comedy   (PR:O MPAA:NR)

MIDNIGHT RAIDERS   (SEE: OKLAHOMA RAIDERS, 1944)

MIDNIGHT SPECIAL*   (1931) 60m Chesterfield bw

Glenn Tryon (Gerald Boone), Merna Kennedy (Ellen Harboard), Tom O'Brien (Dan Padden), Mary Carr (Mrs. Boone), Norman Phillips, Jr. (Billy), Jimmy Aubrey (Joe), Phillips Smalley (Mr. Harboard).

Tryon is a railroad telegraph dispatcher who is in love with wealthy Kennedy. One night he is tied up by a gang of crooks so he can't switch the "Midnight Special" onto the right track. The train crashes and Tryon is fired. Along with his kid brother Phillips, Tryon discovers that the chief dispatcher is the leader of the gang and wanted to discredit the hero so he could have Kennedy. Uninspired treatment of an old story.

p, George R. Batchelor; d, Duke Worne; w, Arthur Hoerl, Ehren Johns (based on a story by Arthur Hoerl); ph, M. A. Anderson; ed, Tom Persons.

Drama   (PR:A MPAA:NR)

MIDNIGHT STORY, THE***

(1957) 89m UNIV bw (GB: APPOINTMENT WITH A SHADOW)

Tony Curtis (Joe Martini), Marisa Pavan (Anna Malatesta), Gilbert Roland (Sylvio Malatesta), Jay C. Flippen (Sgt. Jack Gillen), Argentina Brunetti (Mama Malatesta), Ted de Corsia (Lt. Kilrain), Richard Monda (Peanuts Malatesta), Kathleen Freeman (Rosa Cuneo), Herbert Vigran (Charlie Cuneo), Peggy June Maley (Veda Pinelli), John Cliff (Giuseppe), Russ Conway (Sgt. Sommers), Chico Vejar (Frankie Pellatrini), Tito Vuolo (Grocer), Helen Wallace (Mother Catherine), James Hyland (Frank Wilkins).

Curtis is a San Francisco traffic cop who dedicates himself to finding the murderer of the priest who had raised him. He's denied a homicide assignment, so he resigns from the force to find the killer. Everything seems to point to Roland, a close friend of the slain priest. Roland asks Curtis to move in with him and his cousin, Pavan, and Curtis accepts hoping he'll find Roland is not the killer. The ex-cop discovers that Roland has an alibi for the night of the murder, and falls in love with Pavan. On the day the two are to be married it's revealed that Roland's alibi was a lie. The murderer is run over by a truck before police can get to him. A taut and suspenseful mystery.

p, Robert Arthur; d, Joseph Pevney; w, Edwin Blum, John Robinson (based on a story by Blum); ph, Russell Metty (CinemaScope); m, Joseph Gershenson; ed, Ted J. Kent; art d, Alexander Golitzen, Eric Orbom.

Crime Mystery   (PR:A MPAA:NR)

MIDNIGHT TAXI, THE*1/2   (1928) 62m WB bw

Antonio Moreno ("Taxi" Driscoll), Helene Costello (Nan Parker), Tommy Dugan ("Mile-Away" Morgan), William Russell (Joe Brant), Myrna Loy (Mrs. Joe Brant), Bobbie Agnew (Jack Madison), Pat Hartigan (Detective Blake), Jack Santoro (Lefty), William Hauber (Squint), Paul Kreuger (Dutch), Spencer Bell (Rastus).

A run-of-the-mill story of bootleggers double-crossing each other, stolen bonds, really nice good guys and very mean bad men. The title is taken from the taxis that transport the bootleg liquor. Dugan steals the show with his stuttering and clowning which had audiences howling. (Remember, sound movies were a new experience.)

d, John G. Adolfi; w, Freddie Foy, Joseph Jackson, Harvey Gates (based on a story by Gregory Rogers [Darryl F. Zanuck]); ph, Frank Kesson; ed, Owen Marks.

Crime   (PR:A MPAA:NR)

MIDNIGHT TAXI*1/2   (1937) 69m FOX bw

Brian Donlevy (Chick Gardner), Frances Drake (Gilda Lee), Alan Dinehart (Philip Strickland), Sig Rumann (John Rudd), Gilbert Roland (Flash Dillon), Harold Huber (Lucky Todd), Paul Stanton (J. W. McNeary), Lon Chaney, Jr. (Erickson), Russell Hicks (Barney Flagg), Regis Toomey (Hilton).

FBI man Donlevy goes undercover as a taxi driver and gets a job with a company that is suspected of running a counterfeit ring. He falls in love with Drake who works for the taxi company and befriends the counterfeiter-taxi drivers and quickly gets to the leader. This B action picture contains nothing that stands out.

p, Milton H. Feld; d, Eugene Forde; w, Lou Breslow, John Patrick (based on a story by Borden Chase); ph, Barney McGill; ed, Al De Gaetano; md, Samuel Kaylin.

Crime   (PR:A MPAA:NR)

MIDNIGHT WARNING, THE**1/2   (1932) 63m Weeks/Mayfair bw

William [Stage] Boyd (William Cornish), Claudia Dell (Enid Van Buren), Henry Hall (Dr. Barris), John Harron (Erich), Hooper Atchley (Dr. Stephen Walcott), Huntley Gordon (Mr. Gordon), Phillips Smalley (Dr. Brown), Lloyd Ingraham (Adolph Klein), Lloyd Whitlock (Rankin), Art Winkler, Lon Poff.

After returning from a lengthy visit to the Orient, Dell goes to the hotel where she and her brother had checked in only hours before. He has disappeared, hotel personnel claim not to remember seeing him and the register shows Dell checked in alone. Doctors tell her she is suffering from delusions and never really had a brother, and she starts to believe she is going insane. Detective Boyd gets on the case and his careful investigation reveals that Dell's brother had died from the bubonic plague and the hotel engaged in an elaborate coverup so as not to alarm other guests. The story was one which had been around for awhile, and seems to have first arisen during the 1893 Columbian Exposition in Chicago, where it was alleged that a local hotel had attempted a similar scheme following the death of a guest. The story would be used again in SO LONG AT THE FAIR (1952). Here, it is given a suspenseful treatment, with Boyd turning a good performance as a masterful sleuth.

d, Spenser Gordon Bennet; w, John Thomas Neville (based on a story by Norman Battle); ph, Jules Cronjager; ed, Byron Robinson; md, Lee Zahler.

Mystery   Cas.   (PR:A MPAA:NR)

MIDSHIPMAN, THE   (SEE: MIDSHIPMAN GOB, THE, 1932, Brit.)

MIDSHIPMAID GOB*1/2

(1932, Brit.) 84m GAU/Woolf and Freedman Film Service bw (GB: THE MIDSHIPMAID)

Jessie Matthews (Celia Newbiggin), Fred Kerr (Sir Percy Newbiggin), Basil Sydney (Cmdr. Ffosberry), A. W. Baskcomb (AB Pook), Claud Allister (Chinley), Anthony Bushell (Lt. Valentine), Edwin Lawrence (Tappett), Nigel Bruce (Maj. Spink), Archie Glen (Bundy), Albert Rebla (Robbins), John Mills (Golightly), Antony Holles (Lt. Kingsford), George Zucco (Lord Dore), Joyce Kirby (Dora), Condos Brothers (Horse).

Kerr is an economy expert trying to find ways to cut costs during a visit to the fleet in Malta. Matthews is his beautiful daughter who accompanies him and the plot involves crew members attempting to woo her. A concert on board a ship provides a few songs and a few comedy bits.

p, Michael Balcon; d, Albert de Courville; w, Stafford Dickens (based on a play by Ian Hay, Stephen King-Hall); ph, Mutz Greenbaum.

Comedy   (PR:A MPAA:NR)

MIDSHIPMAN EASY   (SEE: MEN OF THE SEA, 1935, Brit.)

MIDSHIPMAN JACK*1/2   (1933) 73m RKO bw

Bruce Cabot (Jack Austin), Betty Furness (Ruth Rogers), Frank Albertson (Russell Burns), Arthur Lake (Allan), Purnell Pratt (Capt. Rogers), Florence Lake (Sally), Margaret Seddon (Mrs. Burns), John Darrow (Clark).

Cabot enrolls at the US Naval Academy and has a hard time adjusting to the rules and regulations. Quickly he becomes naval material and teaches the freshmen about pride and loyalty. Cabot also gets to marry the commander's daughter, Furness. RKO did the story in 1937 under the title ANNAPOLIS SALUTE.

d, Christy Cabanne; w, Frank Wead, F. McGrew Willis; ph, Alfred Gilks; ed, Basil Wrangell.

Drama   (PR:A MPAA:NR)

MIDSTREAM*1/2   (1929) 85m TIF-Stahl bw

Ricardo Cortez (James Stanwood), Claire Windsor (Helen Craig), Montagu Love (Dr. Nelson), Larry Kent (Martin Baker), Helen Jerome Eddy (Mary Mason), Leslie Brigham (Mephistopheles), Genevieve Schrader (Marguerite), Louis Alvarez (Faust), Florence Foyer (Marthe).

Cortez is a wealthy, aging Wall Street financier who falls in love with the much younger Windsor. He travels to Europe for an operation which will restore his youth and then, after faking his own death, returns to the U.S., posing as his nephew. He begins a relationship with Windsor and all goes well until they attend a performance of "Faust." Cortez is thoroughly shaken by Windsor's comments about the play, and the stress causes him to revert to his actual age. Windsor leaves and a wiser Cortez marries his secretary, who has loved him for years. A major portion of the film is silent, but it does include about 20 munutes of a performance of "Faust."

d, James Flood; w, Frances Guihan, Frederick Hatton, Fanny Hatton (based on a story by Bernice Boone); ph, Jackson Rose; m, Hugo Riesenfeld; ed, Desmond O'Brien; m/l, title song, L. Wolfe Gilbert, Abel Baer.

Drama   (PR:A MPAA:NR)

MIDSUMMER'S NIGHT'S DREAM, A***1/2   (1935) 132m WB bw

James Cagney (Bottom), Dick Powell (Lysander), Joe E. Brown (Flute), Jean Muir (Helena), Hugh Herbert (Snout), Ian Hunter (Theseus), Frank McHugh (Quince), Victor Jory (Oberon), Olivia de Havilland (Hermia), Ross Alexander (Demetrius), Grant Mitchell (Egeus), Nini Theilade (Prima Ballerina Fairy), Verree Teasdale (Hippolyta, Queen of the Amazons), Anita Louise (Titania), Mickey Rooney (Puck), Dewey Robinson (Snug), Hobart Cavanaugh (Philostrate), Otis Harlan (Starveling), Arthur Treacher (Ninny's Tomb), Katherine Frey (Pease-Blossom), Helen Westcott (Cobweb), Fred Sale (Moth), Billy Barty (Mustard Seed).

This was Warner Bros.' great plunge into "culture" despite the fact that the organization was always known as "the working class" studio. All of Hollywood was amazed when Jack Warner suddenly and inexplicably put aside $1.5 million for the Reinhardt production of the Immortal Bard's fantasy. A MIDSUMMER'S NIGHT

DREAM, believed to have been performed at London's Globe Theatre, circa 1595, involves creatures of the forest, chiefly fairies, and artisans who plan to put on a play to amuse the royal court. Mitchell demands that de Havilland (Hermia) marry Alexander (Demetrius), despite the fact that she is in love with Powell (Lysander), and, unless she goes through with the nuptials, Hunter (Theseus, Duke of Athens), will severely punish her. Hunter himself is also preparing to marry Teasdale (Hippolyta, Queen of the Amazons). De Havilland and Powell elope, escaping to the forest, and Alexander pursues them, he, in turn, pursued by Muir (Helena) who is crazy in love with Alexander. Meanwhile the local artisans, Cagney, McHugh, Herbert, Brown, and others, enter the forest to rehearse the play they intend to perform for Hunter's wedding. The rulers of the forest, the supernatural fairies, come to life. Their monarchs, Jory (Oberon) and Louise (Titania), are quarreling and Jory, in a fit of pique during the lover's squabble, orders the mischievous Rooney (Puck) to squeeze the juice of a passion flower into Louise's eyes so that she will fall madly in love with the first creature she sees when awakening. Rooney, to complicate matters, playfully turns Cagney (Bottom) into part animal, changing his head into that of an ass. This is the creature Louise first spots and instantly adores. Rooney also uses the magic potion to alter the affections of the four lovers, so that de Havilland and Powell begin to hate each other. Not until Jory, Louise, Puck, and the scores of fairies in their netherworld kingdom depart the forest do things get back to normal, Cagney regaining his head, and the lovers being reunited. Cagney and company go on to perform an awkward play for the edification of Hunter and his court. This film was all Reinhardt (1873–1943), who had successfully staged the play in Europe and was thought to be one of the great theatrical geniuses of the early 20th Century, being the most esteemed impresario in Berlin from 1903 to 1932 when he immigrated to Hollywood to escape Nazi persecution. Though he had successfully staged great productions of Moliere, Strindberg, Ibsen, and Shaw, Reinhardt insisted that the greatest play to be turned into a film was A MIDSUMMER'S NIGHT DREAM since the fairy sequences offered the proper magic for celluloid. He demanded that Korngold, with whom he had worked in Europe, be brought in to do the score, based on the music Mendelssohn created in 1843 for the play. That Warners undertook this elaborate and involved Shakespearean project is still a mystery. The studio threw all of its best talent into the film, even crooner Powell, whose southern accent (born in Arkansas) was still somewhat pronounced. In later years, Powell would state that he never really understood the lines he mouthed in the film. Cagney overcomes a background deficient in Shakespeare by turning his role of Bottom into an energy-packed performance that is more acrobatic than theatrical. Only Hunter and a few others with deep classical backgrounds in theater were comfortable with their roles but it all come off as convincing, especially the manic Rooney. The hoarse-voiced child actor during a production break went tobogganing at a winter resort and broke his leg midway during shooting and had to be wheeled quickly through the forest's foliage by stagehands as he rode an unseen bicycle. Reinhardt was assisted by Dieterle, one of his most ardent admirers. Reinhardt had no idea of how to film his masterpiece and it soon became apparent that he would lead the production to doom if steps weren't taken. Cinematographer Ernest Haller, following Reinhardt's obtuse instructions, filmed the forest scenes so that most of these were blurs and the foliage was so dense that the actors could not be distinguished from the trees. Haller was fired and Mohr brought in to replace him. Mohr had half the forest cut down and Grot's elaborate sets thinned out, but the forest still appeared dense, with each leaf glued onto branches and painted silver to give that gossamer effect. The photography emerged as stunning and visually exciting, perhaps the best thing about this strange film. (Mohr won an Oscar for his work and one went to editor Dawson.) The delicate ballet sequences by Nijinska and Theilade (the latter playing the leading ballerina in the film) were thought to be ineffective and were rechoreographed in the Busby Berkeley mold. Cagney's lightning movements and piping delivery pleased Reinhardt who later stated: "The part of Bottom has always been played by a stout, middle-aged man. Why? James Cagney's type is perfect and his performance delights me." But, though Cagney thought Reinhardt "a nice man" he and the rest of the cast realized that the aging impresario didn't know what he was doing. "I did not want to play Bottom," Cagney said in 1936, "I fought against it. The first news that I was cast for the role came to me accidentally. Somebody told me Mr. Reinhardt had seen me in LADY KILLER ages ago and remembered my performance. From that, he wanted me to do Bottom." Korngold, who composed his score by watching every scene as it was made, returned from the screening room after viewing the dance of the fairies. Cagney asked him what he thought of the scene and Korngold blurted: "Ah, *wunderbar*! Terrific—tremendous— stupendous—but *bad*!" Brown, who gives one of the best performances in the group of artisans as Flute later stated in his autobiography, *Laughter is a Wonderful Thing*: "Some of us were certainly not Shakespearean actors. Besides myself from the circus and burlesque, there was Jimmy Cagney from the chorus and Hugh Herbert from burlesque. At the beginning we went into a huddle and decided to follow the classic traditions in which Herbert and I were brought up. I really believe Shakespeare would have liked the way we handled his low comedy and I'm sure the Minsky Brothers did. The Bard's words have been spoken better but never bigger or louder."

p, Max Reinhardt; d, Reinhardt, William Dieterle; w, Charles Kenyon, Mary McCall, Jr. (based on the play by William Shakespeare); ph, Hal Mohr; m, Felix Mendelssohn; ed, Ralph Dawson; md, Leo F. Forbstein, Erich Wolfgang Korngold; art d, Anton Grot; cos, Max Ree; ch, Bronislava Nijinska, Nina Theilade; spec eff, Fred Jackman, Byron Haskin, H. E. Koenekamp; makeup, Perc Westmore.

Comedy **Cas.** **(PR:A MPAA:NR)**

MIDSUMMERS NIGHT'S DREAM, A****

(1961, Czech) 74m Ceskoslovensky/Showcorporation c

Voices of: Richard Burton *(Narrator)*, Tom Criddle *(Lysander)*, Ann Bell *(Hermia)*, Michael Meacham *(Demetrius)*, John Warner *(Egeus)*, Barbara Leigh-Hunt *(Helena)*, Hugh Manning *(Theseus)*, Joss Ackland *(Quince)*, Alec McCowen *(Bottom)*, Stephen Moore *(Flute)*, Barbara Jefford *(Titania)*, Jack Gwillim *(Oberon)*, Roger Shepherd *(Puck)*, Laura Graham *(Hippolyta)*.

A wonderfully executed and beautifully photographed version of Shakespeare's famous play with a cast of puppets. Winner of the Grand Prix at the Cannes Film Festival. A great way to expose this classic play to a wider audience.

p, Jiri Trnka; d, Trnka, Howard Sackler; w, Trnka, Jiri Brdecka, Sackler (based on the play by William Shakespeare); ph, Jiri Vojta (CinemaScope, Eastmancolor); m, Vaclav Trojan; ed, Hana Walachova; art d, Trnka; anim, Jan Karpas, Stanislav Latal, Vlasta Jurajdova, Bretislav Pojar, Jan Adam, Bohumil Sramek.

Puppet Film **(PR:AAA MPAA:NR)**

MIDSUMMER NIGHT'S DREAM, A***

(1966) 93m Oberon/Showcorporation c

Suzanne Farrell *(Titania)*, Edward Villella *(Oberon)*, Arthur Mitchell *(Puck)*, Mimi Paul *(Helena)*, Nicholas Magallanes *(Lysander)*, Patricia McBride *(Hermia)*, Roland Vazquez *(Demetrius)*, Francisco Moncion *(Theseus)*, Gloria Govrin *(Hippolyta)*, Richard Rapp *(Bottom)*, Jacques D'Amboise *(Court Danseur)*, Allegra Kent *(Court Danseuse)*, Members of the New York City Ballet Company.

The Shakespeare play done as a ballet translates surprisingly well to the screen without alteration of the stage production. George Balanchine's choreography makes full use of the film's visual advantages and works around the framing limitations. All dancers are from the New York City Ballet Company and their performances are flawless.

p, Richard Davis; d, George Balanchine; w, William Shakespeare; ph, Arthur J. Ornitz (Panavision, Eastmancolor); m, Felix Mendelssohn; ed, Armond Lebowitz; art d, Albert Brenner; cos, Karinska; ch, Balanchine.

Fantasy **(PR:A MPAA:NR)**

MIDSUMMER NIGHT'S DREAM, A 1/2**

(1969, Brit.) 124m Shakespeare-Filmways/Eagle c

Derek Godfrey *(Theseus)*, Barbara Jefford *(Hippolyta)*, Hugh Sullivan *(Philostrato)*, Nicholas Selby *(Egeus)*, David Warner *(Lysander)*, Michael Jayston *(Demetrius)*, Diana Rigg *(Helena)*, Helen Mirren *(Hermia)*, Ian Richardson *(Oberon)*, Judi Dench *(Titania)*, Ian Holm *(Puck)*, Paul Rogers *(Bottom)*, Sebastian Shaw *(Quince)*, Bill Travers *(Snout)*, John Normington *(Flute)*, Clive Swift *(Snug)*, Donald Eccles *(Starveling)*.

This film adaptation of Shakespeare's play uses the Royal Shakespeare Company for the cast and needless to say that the acting is first-rate. This version is rather stiff since it is basically a filmed play performance. There is barely any movement or utilization of the Athens' landscape. The film was financed by the Columbia Broadcasting System.

p, Martin Ransohoff, Michael Birkett; d, Peter Hall; w, William Shakespeare; ph, Peter Suschitzky (Eastmancolor); m, Guy Woolfenden; ed, Jack Harris; cos, Ann Curtis; makeup, Neville Smallwood.

Fantasy **(PR:A MPAA:NR)**

MIDSUMMER NIGHT'S SEX COMEDY, A 1/2** (1982) 88m Orion/WB c

Woody Allen *(Andrew)*, Mia Farrow *(Ariel)*, Jose Ferrer *(Leopold)*, Julie Hagerty *(Dulcy)*, Tony Roberts *(Maxwell)*, Mary Steenburgen *(Adrian)*, Adam Redfield *(Student Foxx)*, Moishe Rosenfeld *(Mr. Hayes)*, Timothy Jenkins *(Mr. Thompson)*, Michael Higgins *(Reynolds)*, Sol Frieder *(Carstairs)*, Boris Zoubok *(Purvis)*, Thomas Barbour *(Blint)*, Kate McGregor-Stewart *(Mrs. Baker)*, J. David Copeland, Tony Farentino.

Woody Allen is a very funny man. For some, he has transcended mere mortal status and risen into the hallowed and lofty aerie of comic divinity. Few people in modern times have provided intelligent audiences with humor that makes one think. But many idols have feet of clay and never more obviously have Allen's plaster toes been demonstrated. A MIDSUMMER NIGHT'S SEX COMEDY is a trifle that owes much to Bergman in style and to Groucho Marx in content. It's the turn of the century in America and Allen, a stock broker and sometime inventor, is spending a weekend at a farmhouse in upstate New York with his wife, Steenburgen. Allen's primary concern at this point is wooing his own wife and getting her to climb into bed with him, a practice she seems to have abandoned. Steenburgen's cousin, Ferrer, and his fiancee, Farrow, arrive. He is a pretentious intellectual and she a relentless nymphomaniac. They are planning to be married right away and it is obvious that she is enamoured of his brain rather than his body. Roberts and his girl friend, Hagerty, also arrive. He is a womanizing doctor and she is apparently his current short-time fling. The stage is set for Allen's version of SMILES OF A SUMMER NIGHT, or is it? Allen is terribly frustrated by Steenburgen's unwillingness to make whoopee and that is further exacerbated by Farrow's presence. Some years before, Allen had an unconsummated affair with Farrow, but he never laid a hand on her. He now knows that Farrow is a wanton trollop and he could kick himself for having respected her because no one else did. Farrow flirts shamelessly with Roberts, who falls hard for her. Ferrer, on the other hand, wants to spend his last few hours of bachelorhood in bed with Hagerty. She is not averse to this, although she's been spending much of her time advising Steenburgen how to put some excitement back into the marriage with Allen. It's a pastoral setting, beautifully photographed by Willis, and the pace ambles snail-like from one farcical episode to the next without much drive. Several bon mots pepper the screenplay, but Allen is hamstrung by his inability to make comments on modern life or to risk being anachronistic. In the end, it's unfulfilling and doesn't have the wallop, the belly laughs, or the wry comments usually found in an Allen film. What must have begun as a frothy sex romp eventually turns a bit flat, like a beer that has sat too long. Many grins and chortles, very few guffaws.

p, Robert Greenhut; d&w, Woody Allen; ph, Gordon Willis (Technicolor); m, Felix Mendelssohn; ed, Susan E. Morse; prod d, Mel Bourne; art d, Speed Hopkins; cos, Santo Loquasto.

Comedy **Cas.** **(PR:C-O MPAA:PG)**

MIDWAY** (1976) 132m UNIV c (GB: THE BATTLE OF MIDWAY)

Charlton Heston (*Capt. Matt Garth*), Henry Fonda (*Adm. Chester W. Nimitz*), James Coburn (*Capt. Vinton Maddox*), Glenn Ford (*Rear Adm. Raymond A. Spruance*), Hal Holbrook (*Cmdr. Joseph Rochefort*), Toshiro Mifune (*Adm. Isoroku Yamamoto*), Robert Mitchum (*Adm. William F. Halsey*), Cliff Robertson (*Cmdr. Carl Jessop*), Robert Wagner (*Lt. Cmdr. Ernest L. Blake*), Robert Webber (*Rear Adm. Frank J. "Jack" Fletcher*), Ed. Nelson (*Adm. Harry Pearson*), James Shigeta (*Vice Adm. Chuichi Nagumo*), Christina Kokubo (*Haruko Sakura*), Monte Markham (*Cmdr. Max Leslie*), Biff McGuire (*Capt. Miles Browning*), Kevin Dobson (*Ens. George Gay*), Christopher George (*Lt. Cmdr. C. Wade McClusky*), Glenn Corbett (*Lt. Cmdr. John Waldron*), Gregory Walcott (*Capt. Elliott Buckmaster*), Edward Albert (*Lt. Tom Garth*), Dabney Coleman (*Capt. Murray Arnold*), Conrad Yama (*Adm. Nobutake Kondo*), Dale Ishimoto (*Vice Adm. Moshiro Hosogaya*), Larry Csonka (*Cmdr. Delaney*), Dennis Rucker (*Ens. Mansen*), Pat Morita, Lloyd Kino, Michael Richardson, John Fujioka, Bennett Ohta, Clyde Kusatsu, Erik Estrada, Ken Pennell, Kip Niven, Kurt Grayson, James Ingersoll, David Macklin, Richard Sarradet, Robert Ito, Phillip R. Allen, Sab Shimono, Steve Kanaly.

Despite a crowded cast of famous actors, this WW II drama falls flat from claustrophobic sets, cliched lines, and a hackneyed story. The best action sequence of the film is the bombing run on Tokyo at the opening credits, which is lifted wholly from the black-and-white film, THIRTY SECONDS OVER TOKYO, tinted in red to conform to this color production. This overlong film deals with the events leading up to and including the decisive naval battle of WW II, Midway, fought in June 1942, where planes from U.S. carriers utterly destroyed a Japanese invasion fleet, sinking four enemy carriers and sending to the bottom Japan's vision of world supremacy. A corny subplot deals with Heston as a navy commander whose ensign son, Albert, wants to marry a Hawaiian girl with Japanese blood and his attempts to get the Navy to approve of the marriage. He fails, and his son will not forgive him as they both go into battle, Albert to survive the slaughter of the U.S. plane crews attacking the Japanese carrier force. Fonda does an admirable job essaying the role of the stoic Admiral Nimitz and Ford is above average as Admiral Spruance, the man who led the American carriers to victory. Holbrook is probably the most likable and intriguing in this production bloated with "cameo appearances." He is the unorthodox Navy officer who breaks the Japanese code, which allows the Americans to know exactly what the enemy has in store for the invasion of Midway Island. Mitchum appears in only two scenes, as the ill, bedridden Admiral Halsey, who suggests Ford replace him. Mitchum refused to get a Halsey crew cut for his two day's shooting schedule and "told them they could send my salary to charity." The battle scenes were shot in miniature and the cost-cutting on the production is evident. The "Sensurround" system provided nothing more than exaggerated battle noises that annoyed viewers rather than enhancing the production. Technical achievements were at a minimum with many scenes borrowed from TORA, TORA, TORA and other Japanese films. Mifune's lines were badly dubbed by American announcer Paul Frees and delivered with such stentorian overplay that viewers laughed at almost every line.

p, Walter Mirisch; d, Jack Smight; w, Donald S. Sanford; ph, Harry Stradling, Jr. (Sensurround, Panavision, Technicolor); m, John Williams; ed, Robert Swink, Frank J. Urioste; art d, Walter Tyler; set d, John Dwyer; spec eff, Jack McMaster; technical advisor, Vice Adm. Bernard M. Strean, U.S.N.(Ret.).

War Drama **Cas.** **(PR:A MPAA:PG)**

MIDWIFE, THE* (1961, Greece) 80m Finos/Greek Motion Pictures bw

Orestis Makris (*Dr. Lycourgos*), Georgia Vassiliadou (*The Midwife*), Xenie Kalogeropoulos (*Kathy Lycourgos*), Dimitris Papamichael (*Dimitrios*), Eleni Zaferiou (*Mrs. Lycourgos*).

A long-standing rivalry between village doctor Makris and local midwife Vassiliadou is amicably resolved when his daughter falls in love with her son. Boring comedy-drama of interest only to Greek-speaking audiences.

d&w, Alekos Sakellarios.

Comedy-Drama **(PR:A MPAA:NR)**

MIGHT MAKES RIGHT (SEE: FOX AND HIS FRIENDS, 1975, Ger.)

MIGHTY, THE*¹/₂ (1929) 74m PAR bw

George Bancroft (*Blake Greeson*), Esther Ralston (*Louise Patterson*), Warner Oland ("*Shiv*" *Sterky*), Raymond Hatton (*Dogey Franks*), Dorothy Revier (*Mayme*), Morgan Farley (*Jerry Patterson*), O. P. Heggie (*J. K. Patterson*), Charles Sellon (*The Mayor*), E. H. Calvert (*Major General*), John Cromwell (*Mr. Jameison*).

A WW I melodrama with Bancroft as a gangster who goes to war and rises to the rank of major. He returns from the battlefields of Europe to break the news to a family that their son, a young officer, had died in his arms during a battle. When Bancroft falls in love with the soldier's sister, he decides to stick around and accept a job as the town's police commissioner.

d, John Cromwell; w, Nellie Revell, William Slavens McNutt, Grover Jones, Herman Mankiewicz (based on a story by Robert N. Lee); ph, J. Roy Hunt; ed, George Nichols, Jr., Otho Lovering.

Drama **(PR:A MPAA:NR)**

MIGHTY BARNUM, THE**¹/₂ (1934) 87m 20th Century/UA bw

Wallace Beery (*Phineas T. Barnum*), Adolphe Menjou (*Mr. Bailey Walsh*), Virginia Bruce (*Jenny Lind*), Rochelle Hudson (*Ellen*), Janet Beecher (*Nancy Barnum*), Tammany Young (*Todd*), Lucille La Verne (*Joyce Heth*), George Brasno (*Gen.*

Tom Thumb), Olive Brasno (*Lavinia Thumb*), Richard Brasno (*Gilbert*), May Boley (*Zorro the Bearded Lady*), John Hyams (*J. P. Skiff*), Herman Bing (*Man with Frog*), Davison Clark (*Horace Greeley*), George MacQuarrie (*Daniel Webster*), Tex Madsen (*Cardiff Giant*), Ian Wolfe (*Swedish Consul*), Sam Adams, Sam Godfrey, Milton Wallace (*Collectors*), Franklyn Ardell (*Sam*), Brenda Fowler, Theresa Maxwell Conovor, Ethel Wales (*Matrons*), Capt. E. H. Calvert (*House Detective*), Charles Judels (*Maitre d'*), Frank McGlynn, Sr. (*Barnum's Butler*), Christian Rub (*Ole the Masseur*), Frank Morgan (*Joe*), Greta Meyer (*Jennie Lind's Maid*), Gertrude Astor, Maude Ogle, Alice Lake, Naomi Childers (*Women in Museum*), John Lester Johnson (*Black Attendant*), Billy McClain (*Barnum's Footman*).

The life of the great showman receives a less effective treatment than one might expect with Beery in the title role, but there are moments that recapture that golden era of color and panache when Barnum excited the world with his spectacular attractions. Beery is disarming and prosaic in his antics to enhance his general goods New York City store by populating it with sideshow freaks, much to the disgust of his New England wife Beecher. The store grows into an emporium of freaks and curiosities but trouble arises when La Verne, playing the reported 100-year-old nursemaid to George Washington, is exposed as a fraud, as is Boley, the Bearded Lady. Undaunted, Beery goes after bigger and bigger attractions, signing British singer Jenny Lind (Bruce) and bringing her to New York where she becomes the rage. Next the great showman signs on Brasno, playing the role of the inimitable midget, Tom Thumb, and his fortunes soar. But the bumbling Beery soon alienates Lind by giving a party in her honor and then disgracing her through his awkward fumbling. Through his romancing of Bruce, Beery loses the affections of Beecher, who leaves him and returns to New England. He has also lost the friendship of his dearest pal, Menjou, playing Bailey Walsh, who has taken to drink over Barnum's follies. Then he loses Lind, and finally his museum. But the very people he has supported for years, the freaks, come to his rescue, providing money for Beery to continue his museum. Beecher also returns to stay by his side. Disaster again strikes when the museum is burned down by competitors. But Beery cannot be licked. Menjou shows up, a reformed drunk full of plans. With him is a gigantic elephant, Jumbo, a present from Lind to Beery. As Beery, Menjou, and the elephant head a Manhattan parade, Beery excitedly outlines his plans to start a circus, "the greatest show on earth," which will be known as Barnum and Bailey. (Walsh used his first name for the liaison as it sounded more alliterative.) The rest, as they say, is history. Beery holds this one together and Menjou is effective in the few scenes where he appears. The wonderful collection of colorful characters makes the film special, but Beecher is limp in her role of the long-suffering wife and Bruce is less than believable as songstress Lind, her voice being dubbed.

p, Darryl F. Zanuck; d, Walter Lang; w, Gene Fowler, Bess Meredyth; ph, Peverell Marley; m, Alfred Newman; ed, Allen McNeill, Bobby McLean.

Biography **(PR:A MPAA:NR)**

MIGHTY CRUSADERS, THE* (1961, Ital.) 87m Max/Falcon c (LA GERUSALEMME LIBERATA)

Francisco Rabal (*Tancrid*), Sylva Koscina (*Clorinda*), Gianna Maria Canale (*Armida*), Rik Battaglia (*Renaldo*), Philippe Hersent (*Geoffrey of Bouillon*), Livia Contardi, Andrea Aureli.

Another of Italy's costume spectaculars with poor dubbing and scantily dressed women. Rabal is one of the knights of the Crusade who, during an attack on Jerusalem, falls in love with Koscina, daughter of the king of Persia. Unbeknown to Rabal, she throws on some armor and enters the battle and, in what is supposed to be an ironic ending, he kills his lover. How did he know it was she under all that steel dressing?

p, Octavio Poggi; d, Carlo Ludovicio Bragaglia; w, Frederica Nutter (based on the poem "Gerusalemme Liberata" (Jerusalem Delivered) by Torquato Tasso); ph, Rodolfo Lombardi (Supercinescope); m, Roberto Nicolosi; ed, Renato Cinquini; cos, Giancarlo Salimbeni.

Action/Adventure **(PR:A MPAA:NR)**

MIGHTY GORGA, THE zero (1969) 83m Borealis/American General-Western International

Anthony Eisley (*Mark Remington*), Megan Timothy (*April Adams*), Kent Taylor (*Bwana Jack*), Scott Brady (*Morgan*), Lee Parrish (*George*), Bruce Kemp (*Witch Doctor*), Sheldon Lee (*Kabula*).

Eisley, an American circus manager, treks to Africa to capture a 50-ton gorilla for show under the big top. He and his expedition are about to be sacrificed by a native tribe when Gorga causes a disruption. They escape to a nearby cave, where they unearth a fortune in jewels. The big gorilla survives, a couple of greedy expedition members are killed, and the surviving folks return to U.S. soil. All that's missing from this film are the Empire State Building and some semblance of talent.

p, Robert V. O'Neil, David L. Hewitt; d, Hewitt; w, Jean Hewitt, David Prentiss; ph, Gary Cramer (DeLuxe Color); m, Charles Walden.

Adventure **(PR:A MPAA:G)**

MIGHTY JOE YOUNG** (1949) 94m Arko/RKO bw

Terry Moore (*Jill Young*), Ben Johnson (*Gregg*), Robert Armstrong (*Max O'Hara*), Frank McHugh (*Windy*), Douglas Fowley (*Jones*), Denis Green (*Crawford*), Paul Guilfoyle (*Smith*), Nestor Paiva (*Brown*), Regis Toomey (*John Young*), Lora Lee Michel (*Jill as a Girl*), James Flavin (*Schultz*), Joseph Young (*the Gorilla*), Dale Van Sickel (*Stuntman*), Primo Carnera, Wee Willie Davis, Henry "Bomber Kulkavich" Kulky, Sammy Stein, Karl David, Ian "Iron Man" Batchelor, Phil "Swedish Angel" Olafsson, Frank "Man Mountain Dean" Leavitt, Ivan Rasputin, Sammy Menacker (*Strongmen*), Selmer Jackson, Ellen Corby, Addison Richards, Iris Adrian.

Though produced by the same people responsible for the classic KING KONG, MIGHTY JOE YOUNG is a pale imitation. Moore lives in the jungles of Africa and raises the extremely large gorilla. Up pops Broadway producer Armstrong (a star in KING KONG) who is looking for a "knock 'em dead" act for his new nightclub in Hollywood. Armstrong and his bunch bring Moore and Joe to the city of dreams and build an act around the beast. As part of the act, Moore plays "Beautiful Dreamer" on a piano while the gorilla holds her above his head, and Joe is pitted against 10 wrestlers in a game of tug o' war. Some drunk patrons give Joe some drinks which spurs him to go on a rampage. The gorilla makes up for his folly, however, by rescuing children from a burning orphanage. He then goes back to live peacefully in Africa. While the nightclub sequence is great camp and the special effects by Willis O'Brien (KING KONG) and Ray Harryhausen are topnotch, the film doesn't capture the magic of KING KONG. The orphanage fire had originally been tinted.

p, John Ford, Merian C. Cooper; d, Ernest B. Schoedsack; w, Ruth Rose (based on a story by Cooper); ph, J. Roy Hunt; ed, Ted Cheesman; md, C. Bakaleinikoff; cos, Adele Balkan; spec eff, Willis O'Brien, Ray Harryhausen, Harold Stine, Bert Willis, Linwood Dunn, Peter Peterson, George Lofgren, Marcel Delgado, Fitch Fulton.

Fantasy Cas. (PR:A MPAA:NR)

MIGHTY JUNGLE, THE* (1965, U.S./Mex.) 88m Mexico Films/Parade c

Marshall Thompson *(Marsh Conners)*, David DaLie *(Dave Reardon)*, Antonio Gutierrez *(Tony)*, Rosenda Monteros *(Orica)*, Andres Soler, Jose Jasso, Jose Chavez, Lou Krugman *(Narrator)*.

This disjointed adventure tale follows Thompson off to the Congo, where he meets up with elephants, Pygmies, and the Congo River rapids. Meanwhile, DaLie joins an Amazonian expedition during which he becomes a meal for a crocodile. The entire Amazonian sequence, lifted from a 1959 Mexican picture entitled LA CIUDAD SAGRADA, looks as cheap as the Congo footage.

p, Robert Patrick; d, David DaLie, Arnold Belgard; w, DaLie, Belgard; ph, Augustin Martinez Solares, Laurie Friedman; m, Les Baxter; ed, Norman Suffern, Erma Levin; art d, Edward Fitzgerald.

Adventure Cas. (PR:A MPAA:NR)

MIGHTY MCGURK, THE** (1946) 83m MGM bw

Wallace Beery *(Roy "Slag" McGurk)*, Dean Stockwell *(Nipper)*, Edward Arnold *(Mike Glenson)*, Aline MacMahon *(Mamie Steeple)*, Cameron Mitchell *(Johnny Burden)*, Dorothy Patrick *(Caroline Glenson)*, Aubrey Mather *(Milbane)*, Morris Ankrum *(Fowles)*, Clinton Sundberg *(Flexter)*, Charles Judels *(First Brewer)*, Torben Meyer *(Second Brewer)*, Stuart Holmes *(Sightseer)*, Edward Earle *(Martin)*, Tom Kennedy *(Man at Punching Machine)*, Trevor Tremaine *(Cockney)*, Lee Phelps *(Cop)*, Joe Yule *(Irish Immigrant)*, Skeets Noyes *(Panhandler)*, Jimmy Dundee, Frank Marlowe *(Mugs)*, Fred Gilman, Frank Mayo, Lew Smith *(Agents)*, Harry Tyler, James Flavin, Dewey Robinson, Slim Summerville.

Beery is a down-and-out boxer who hangs out at Arnold's saloon. The boxer takes in young Stockwell, hoping that the boy's rich uncle will reward him. Beery straightens out and takes on Arnold in an effort to protect the Salvation Army from being kicked out of its building. A sappy melodrama that features Beery in his usual role as the lovable slob.

p, Nat Perrin; d, John Waters; w, William R. Lipman, Grant Garrett, Harry Clark; ph, Charles Schoenbaum; m, David Snell; ed, Ben Lewis; art d, Cedric Gibbons, Hubert Hobson; set d, Edwin B. Willis, Alfred Spencer; cos, Howard Shoup, Irene.

Drama (PR:A MPAA:NR)

MIGHTY MOUSE IN THE GREAT SPACE CHASE*** (1983) 87m Filmation-Viacom/Miracle c

An entertaining animated feature starring the Superman of mice. In this film, Mighty saves the entire universe from certain destruction at the hands of the malevolent cat, Harry the Heartless. Good kid stuff.

p, Lou Scheimer, Norm Prescott, Don Christensen; d, Ed Friedman, Lou Kachivas, Marsh Lamore, Gwen Wetzler, Kay Wright, Lou Zukor; ph, R. W. Pope (Technicolor); m, Yvette Blais, Jeff Michael; ed, James Blodgett, Ann Hagerman, Earl Biddle; art d, Alberto De Mello, James Fletcher.

Animated Feature Cas. (PR:AAA MPAA:NR)

MIGHTY TREVE, THE ½** (1937) 68m UNIV bw

Noah Beery, Jr. *("Bud" McClelland)*, Barbara Read *(Aileen Fenno)*, Samuel S. Hinds *(Uncle Joel Fenno)*, Hobart Cavanaugh *(Mr. Davis)*, Alma Kruger *(Mrs. Davis)*, Julian Rivero *(Pepe)*, Edmund Cobb *(Slego)*, Erville Alderson *(Hibbens)*, Guy Usher *(Wilton)*, Tuffy the Dog *(Treve)*, Spencer Charters.

Tearjerking boy and his dog movie with Beery, Jr., as the young lad whose best friend is Tuffy, a German Shepherd. The two are hired to watch and control a flock of sheep on a ranch. Hinds, the boy's uncle, blames Tuffy for attacking his sheep and tries to get rid of him. Enjoyable pre-Lassie children's fare that will probably bring a tear to adult's eyes, too.

p, Val Paul; d, Lewis D. Collins; w, Albert R. Perkins, Marcus Goodrich, Charles Grayson (based on the novel by Albert Payson Terhune); ph, Jerome Ash; ed, Philip Cahn.

Drama (PR:AAA MPAA:NR)

MIGHTY TUNDRA, THE (SEE: TUNDRA, 1936)

MIGHTY URSUS* ½ (1962, Ital./Span.) 92m Cine Italia-Atenea/UA c (AKA: URSUS)

Ed Fury *(Ursus)*, Luis Prendes *(Setas)*, Moira Orfei *(Attea)*, Cristina Gajoni *(Magali)*, Mary Marlon [Maria Luisa Merlo] *(Doreide)*, Mario Scaccia, Roberto Camardiel, Rafael Luis Calvo, Mariangela Giordano, Soledad Miranda.

Fury sets out to reclaim his betrothed (Orfei) from a sect of pagan priests who've kidnaped her. He reaches her, only to discover she is under the evil spell of the high priest. Orfei tries to kill Fury by throwing him into an arena with a giant bull. He kills the animal, which causes a revolt among the natives. In the violence that follows, the girl is killed, and Fury leaves with his new love, a blind slave girl whose vision has been restored.

d, Carlo Campogalliani; w, Giuliano Carmineo, Giuseppe Mangione, Sergio Sollima (based on a story by Mangione); ph, Eloy Mella (Totalscope, Eastmancolor); m, Roman Vlad; art d, Antonio Simont.

Drama (PR:A MPAA:NR)

MIGHTY WARRIOR, THE (SEE: TROJAN HORSE, THE, 1962, Fr./Ital.)

MIKADO, THE ½** (1939, Brit.) 93m UNIV bw

Kenny Baker *(Nanki-Poo)*, Martyn Green *(Ko-Ko)*, Sydney Granville *(Pooh-Bah)*, John Barclay *(The Mikado)*, Gregory Stroud *(Pish-Tush)*, Jean Colin *(Yum-Yum)*, Constance Willis *(Katisha)*, Elizabeth Paynter *(Pitti-Sing)*, Kathleen Naylor *(Peep-Bo)*.

A nicely produced film version of the Gilbert and Sullivan operetta. The Japanese Emperor's son masquerades as a poor minstrel in his search for a woman to fall in love with. The music was recorded by the London Symphony Orchestra and the D'Oyly Carte Opera Company. Songs include "Three Little Maids," "The Flowers that Bloom in the Spring Tra La," "Tit-Willow," "A Wandering Minstrel, I" "For He's Going to Marry Yum, Yum," "I've Got a Little List," "Behold the Lord High Executioner." Bernard Knowles' camera work won him an Academy Award.

p, Geoffrey Toye, Josef Somlo; d, Victor Schertzinger; w, Toye (based on the opera by W. S. Gilbert, Arthur Sullivan); ph, Bernard Knowles, William Skall (Technicolor); cos, Marcel Vertes.

Musical (PR:A MPAA:NR)

MIKADO, THE ½** (1967, Brit.) 125m B.H.E./WB c

Donald Adams *(The Mikado)*, Philip Potter *(Nanki-Poo)*, John Reed *(Ko-Ko)*, Kenneth Sandford *(Pooh-Bah)*, Thomas Lawlor *(Pish-Tush)*, George Cook *(Go-To)*, Valerie Masterson *(Yum-Yum)*, Peggy Ann Jones *(Pitti-Sing)*, Pauline Wales *(Peep-Bo)*, Christene Palmer *(Katisha)*, Katherine Dyson, Abby Hadfield, Susan Maisey, Marian Martin, Alison Parker, Vera Ryan, Anna Vincent, Mercia Glossop, Beti Lloyd-Jones, Jennifer Marks, Norma Millar, Abigail Ryan, Anne Sessions *(Ladies' Chorus)*, Glyn Adams, John Hugill, Gordon Mackenzie, Ralph Mason, Clifford Parkes, David Rayson, Howard Williamson, Neville Grave, Peter Lodwick, James Marsland, Alfred Oldridge, Anthony Raffell, John Webley *(Men's Chorus)*.

THE MIKADO was arguably Gilbert and Sullivan's greatest work. Shortly after its production, the two men fought with each other over the price of a new carpet for their Savoy Theatre (which they co-owned with D'Oyly Carte) and the rest of their output never came near the standards of their earlier operettas. This one had been filmed before, in 1939, with Kenny Baker as Nanki-Poo. Here, we have a chance to see the famed D'Oyly Carte Opera Company in action. They had been the official delineators of G&S until going out of business in the early 1980s. Their benefactress, Miss Bridget D'Oyly Carte, died in 1985, and with her went the last vestiges of the company. The story of how THE MIKADO came to be written bears mentioning. Gilbert, the book and lyric writer, used to come up with the original ideas and he couldn't find any notion to excite his composer partner, Sullivan. Gilbert had a notion about a magical lozenge that he attempted to cram down Sullivan's good senses several times, but the composer resisted. It was about this time that there was a Japanese exposition around London and everyone was going to see it. At the same moment, Gilbert had purchased a Japanese ceremonial sword a while before, and one night, while walking heavily around the house in search of a thought, the sword fell off the wall where it had been hung. Gilbert had a bulb light up over his head as he looked at the weapon and he began to write the book for THE MIKADO. On stage, this is one of the best and happiest musicals you'll see, but the film version isn't fried fish or sushi, it's somewhere in between and so it looks like a photographed stage play (though one given widescreen treatment) that's been only slightly opened from the Savoy Theatre stage to make it palatable for movie-watchers. The time is somewhere way back when in old Japan. The most powerful person in all of the land is the Mikado (Adams) and he rules with iron chopsticks. His son, Potter, flees from his father's influence, rather than marry the ugly and older woman to whom he has been promised by Adams, Palmer. He is now working his way across the country as a singer-of-songs and arrives in a town called Titipu where he meets and falls in love with Masterson, and then learns that she must marry the local nabob, Reed, who is her guardian as well as the Lord High Executioner. Reed has a bit of a problem, as the Mikado has decreed that at least one execution must take place every month, but he can't find anyone to execute. Potter offers his services as the victim, but only on the condition that he be allowed to marry Masterson, thereby having one glorious month of happiness. Reed has to think about that a moment but there are additional woes: It seems there is a law that states a man's wife must be buried next to him if he is the recipient of the executioner's sword across his neck. That's taken care of when Sandford, the Grand Poo-Bah (if you ever wondered where that expression came from), agrees to forge a death certificate. Sandford holds about 10 titles in the town and can officially witness his own signature. The Mikado arrives with his ugly daughter-in-law elect, Palmer, in tow. He is delighted that there has been an execution but enraged to find out that it was his own son. When that's explained, Palmer wants Potter as her husband, but the young lad says that he intends to stay dead unless he can marry the love of his life, Masterson. Adams thinks about that, gives his blessing to Potter and Masterson, and then turns to the carping Palmer, who is still single and still ugly. In order to save his own skin, Reed woos and wins Palmer and the two of them will live in nagging happiness forever. The songs were glorious and included: "The Mikado," "Three Little Maids from School," "I've Got a Little List," "Titwillow,"

Titwillow," "He's Going to Marry Yum-Yum," "A Wandering Minstrel, I," "The Mighty Troops of Titipu," "The Lord High Executioner," "I Would Kiss You Fondly Thus," "A Short Chop-Chop on a Big Black Block," "Here's a Howdy-Doo," "The Emperor of Japan and His Daughter-In-Law Elect," "Let the Punishment Fit the Crime (His Object All Sublime)," "The Flowers that Bloom in the Spring," and several unnamed arias. In THE MIKADO, there are no stars other than the plot and the songs. All of the actors are from the D'Oyly Carte Company (whose stage production was directed by Anthony Besch) and may be heard on the official albums. There was an attempt to tell the story of Gilbert and Sullivan in a 1953 movie, but it bore very little resemblance to the facts. Sullivan was the son of an Irish father and an Italian mother (who it is said was half-Jewish) to whom he was devoted until she died. Sullivan never married and the combination of his bachelorhood and his relationship with his mother set tongues to wagging, but what the Londoners of the era didn't know was that Sullivan was an incurable rakehell who specialized in having affairs with married women, so he had to be discreet. Sullivan was a star in his early twenties and was knighted by Queen Victoria long before his partner, who was miffed at the slight, even though the knighthood was not for their shows as much as it was for Sullivan's more serious work, which included "Onward, Christian Soldiers" and "The Lost Chord." Gilbert was a failed attorney who turned to poetry to pick up some extra money. When that became playwriting, he happily forsook the bar in favor of the quill. He married but his wife had no children and Gilbert was as much of a run-around as Sullivan and kept falling for young girls who looked like his wife. He died while attempting to save one of them as she struggled in a pond at his home. The shock of jumping into the water caused Gilbert to have a fatal heart attack.

p, Anthony Havelock-Allan, John Brabourne; d, Stuart Burge; w, William Schwenk Gilbert, Arthur Sullivan; ph, Gerry Fisher (Technicolor); ed, Alma Godfrey; md, Isidore Godfrey; art d, Peter Howitt; set d, Disley Jones; cos, Charles Ricketts, Jones; m/l, W. S. Gilbert, Arthur Sullivan; makeup, Colin Garde, Tony Sforzini.

Musical **(PR:AAA MPAA:NR)**

MIKEY AND NICKY 1/2** (1976) 119m PAR c

Peter Falk *(Mikey)*, John Cassavetes *(Nicky)*, Ned Beatty *(Kinney)*, Rose Arrick *(Annie)*, Carol Grace *(Nell)*, William Hickey *(Sid Fine)*, Sanford Meisner *(Dave Resnick)*, Joyce Van Patten *(Jan)*, M. Emmet Walsh *(Bus Driver)*, Sy Travers *(Hotel Clerk)*, Peter Scoppa *(Counter Man)*, Virginia Smith *(Jan's Mother)*, Jean Shevlin *(Lady on Bus)*, Danny Klein *(Harry)*, Martin Wolfson *(Candy Store Man)*, Eugene Hobgood *(Mel)*, David Pendleton *(Bar Patron)*, William Gill *(Bartender)*, Marilyn Randall *(Shirley)*, Reuben Greene *(Franklyn)*.

This movie is sort of like pickled herring; you either love it or hate it. We, however, stand right in the middle because there is much to enjoy in the movie and just as much to yawn over. One has the feeling that this was a play that was never produced on stage and went directly to the screen from the typewriter. Since so much of it is dialog with very little cinematic action, it just feels stage-bound. Cassavetes and Falk are two small-time thugs who have been friends since their youth. Cassavetes is going to be killed by Beatty, the unlikely hit man in the service of boss Meisner (who was just about everyone's acting coach in New York at one time). Cassavetes gets in touch with Falk after trying to get help from his estranged wife, Van Patten, and his current amour, Grace. Falk is apparently going to help Cassavetes get away from the potential assassin, though we are often struck by Falk's words and his actions and not sure if he is friend or foe. Some very touching scenes punctuate the camaraderie, but the film is essentially far too long and self-indulgent and talky to elicit much emotional response. It's a character study that's more like something seen in a drafty East Village theater that holds 65 people. It's hard to say where the script ends and the improvisation begins, as it looks very much like many of Cassavetes' films we've seen before. The only person missing is Gazzara. The executive producer was veteran TV executive Bud Austin, who had run Paramount Television before moving into feature production. Very foul language and some painful sequences make this hardly fit for anyone with a priggish attitude. This was the third film directed by May and the most experimental. Her first two were A NEW LEAF (which she also wrote and costarred in) and THE HEARTBREAK KID, with a script by Neil Simon and some terrific performances by her daughter, Jeannie Berlin, Charles Grodin, and Cybill Shepherd.

p, Michael Hausman; d&w, Elaine May; ph, Victor J. Kemper (Panavision, Movielab Color); m, John Strauss; ed, John Carter, Sheldon Kahn; prod d, Paul Sylbert; set d, John P. Austin.

Drama **(PR:C-O MPAA:R)**

MILCZACA GWIAZDA

(SEE: FIRST SPACESHIP ON VENUS, 1962, E. Ger./Pol.)

MILDRED PIERCE***** (1945) 111m WB bw

Joan Crawford *(Mildred Pierce)*, Jack Carson *(Wally Fay)*, Zachary Scott *(Monte Beragon)*, Eve Arden *(Ida)*, Ann Blyth *(Veda Pierce)*, Bruce Bennett *(Bert Pierce)*, George Tobias *(Mr. Chris)*, Lee Patrick *(Maggie Binderhof)*, Moroni Olson *(Inspector Peterson)*, Jo Ann Marlowe *(Kay Pierce)*, Barbara Brown *(Mrs. Forrester)*, Charles Trowbridge *(Mr. Williams)*, John Compton *(Ted Forrester)*, Butterfly McQueen *(Lottie)*, Garry Owen, Clancy Cooper, Tom Dillon, Charles Jordan *(Policemen)*, James Flavin, Jack O'Connor *(Detectives)*, Larry Rio *(Reporter)*, George Anderson *(Peterson's Assistant)*, Johnny Walsh *(Delivery Man)*, Robert Arthur *(High School Boy)*, Joyce Compton, Lynne Baggett, Marion Lessing, Doria Caron, Marjorie Kane, Elyse Brown *(Waitresses)*, Manart Kippin *(Dr. Gale)*, David Cota *(Pancho)*, George Meader, Harold Miller, Robert Lorraine *(Men)*, Joan Wardley *(Wife)*, Don Grant *(Bartender)*, Chester Clute *(Mr. Jones)*, Robert Evans *(Sailor)*, Wallis Clark *(Wally's Lawyer)*, Perk Lazello *(Attorney's Clerk)*, Angela Green, Betty Alexander, Ramsay Ames, Helen Pender *(Party Guests)*, Joan Winfield *(Piano Teacher)*, John Christian *(Singing Teacher)*, Leah Baird *(Police Matron)*, Paul Panzer *(Waiter)*, William Alcorn *(Soldier)*, John Sheridan *(Clerk)*, Dick Kipling, Wheaton Chambers, William Ruhl *(Personnel Men)*, Mary Ellen Meyran, Jean Lorraine *(Women)*, Jimmy Lono *(Houseboy)*, Mary Servoss *(Nurse)*.

Here is one of the great soap operas ever made with the queen of pathos, Crawford, making so much out of her persecuted female role that she walked away with an Oscar. Both Barbara Stanwyck and Bette Davis turned down the lead part but producer Jerry Wald prevailed upon Crawford and the film swept the 1945 box offices, returning $5 million to Warner Bros. and putting Crawford back on top as *the* leading lady of films. Crawford is married to Bennett in a marriage that has gone sour. While she dotes on their two daughters, chiefly the oldest, Blyth, Bennett finds pleasant company with another woman. As the marriage breaks up, Crawford takes penny ante jobs to keep Blyth in good schools and nice clothes. Then she gets a job as a waitress, with the help of wise-cracking Arden. She becomes so good at the job and is so full of ideas on how to provide better service and good but inexpensive food that real estate man Carson agrees to help her open her own restaurant. Playboy Scott, who is rich in real estate but poor in cash, gives her the property on which she builds her new place. The restaurant not only prospers but Crawford soon branches out until she has a lucrative chain of eateries and is in the big money. She marries Scott so that his social prestige and position will rub off on her daughter Blyth, but this plan backfires when Scott begins to pay more attention to Blyth than to Crawford. He also goes through Crawford's hard-earned fortune like a plague of locusts and she is soon forced into bankruptcy, this after she has made him a partner in her business. The crushing blow comes when Crawford learns that Scott has been having an affair with Blyth behind her back. She confronts him with this dirty affair and he promises to cease and desist but they don't take into account rotten Blyth, who is about as spoiled a brat as ever tongued cavier from a silver spoon. Blyth kills Scott for rebuffing her and the ever-sacrificing Crawford tells police that she, not her daughter, murdered the bounder. The cops soon discover the real truth and take Blyth away to a well-deserved cell while Bennett shows up, weary of playing the field and vowing his eternal love for good-hearted Crawford, begging her to take him back. She does and they start a new life. Everything about MILDRED PIERCE is top rate, from stellar production values to Curtiz's marvelously paced direction where he refuses to allow sentiment to rule the story. The script itself is sharp, literate, and innovative, with plenty of snappy dialog. Steiner's score is exceptional and Haller's photography is outstanding. This was a real tour de force for Crawford who, many believed, was finished in films. She had been with MGM for 18 years as one of the studio's queens but had been let go in 1943 by Louis B. Mayer, who felt her box office appeal was waning. She signed with Warner Bros. but sat around for a year doing nothing until Wald brought the MILDRED PIERCE script to her. She quickly read it and called the producer, exclaiming: "I love it! I love it! It's exactly what I've been waiting for." But Curtiz, Jack Warner's choice to direct the film, the hottest helmsman on the studio lot, was not in love with directing Joan Crawford. When told of Warner's wishes, Curtiz exploded to Wald: "Me direct that tempermental bitch! Not on your goddamn life! She comes over here with her highhat airs and her goddamn shoulder pads! I won't work with her. She's through, washed up. Why should I waste my time directing a has-been?" Crawford was told about Curtiz' reluctance to direct her, Wald, of course, softening the volatile director's words. So eager was Crawford to make the film that she stooped to asking to do a screen test for Curtiz. He agreed and, after seeing Crawford as Mildred, he told Wald: "Okay, I'll work with her, but she better know who's boss!" Universal contract player Blyth, then only 16 years old, was also rejected by the picky Curtiz, but Crawford took the youngster aside and worked over her lines with her and then did a screen test with her, as she did with most of the other character actors, amazing one and all at Warners that such a luminous star would deign to perform such mundane chores. Curtiz accepted Blyth and her career was assured. The first day on the set proved near disastrous. Curtiz, sitting high up on a boom chair, looked down to see Crawford come forth with an elaborate hairdo and lip makeup which he said was overdone. Then her private dress designer showed up with a handful of expensive new gowns and Curtiz took one look at them and yelled: "No, you sonofabitch! I told you—no shoulder pads!" Crawford appeared and Curtiz ran up to her, tearing at her dress and shouting: "You and your damned Adrian shoulder pads! This stinks!" Tears came to Crawford's eyes as she said: "Mr. Curtiz, I happened to buy this dress at Sears, Roebuck. There are no shoulder pads!" Crawford took Curtiz's abuse until the director realized that she would suffer humiliation to make a good film and he began to appreciate her devotion and slavish work habits connected to MILDRED PIERCE. Moreover, she astounded the Warner Bros. technical people who had never before worked with her by shining in every scene, delivering what she knew would be the greatest role of her career. The front office knew it, too, and began to lobby for the Best Actress Oscar. Hedda Hopper, the powerful Hollywood gossip columnist, then wrote an article in which she stated: "Insiders say that Joan Crawford is delivering such a terrific performance on MILDRED PIERCE that she's a cinch for the Academy Award." Other columnists and publicists jumped on the bandwagon. When the film was completed, Crawford and Curtiz met at a post-production party where the actress jokingly gave the director a gargantuan pair of shoulder pads designed by Adrian. Curtiz smiled and then told the cast and crew that he had an announcement to make. Boomed the director: "When I agreed to direct Miss Crawford, I felt she was going to be stubborn as a mule, and I made up my mind to be plenty hard on her. Now that I have learned how sweet she is and how professional and talented she is, I take back even thinking those things about her." When the film opened, the critics raved about her performance and millions poured into the theaters to see the great movie queen, believing she had just given the finest performance of her life. Crawford was on top again, bigger than ever. The hard-boiled writer of the novel, James M. Cain, sent her a leather-bound copy of *Mildred Pierce*, enscribed thusly: "To Joan Crawford, who brought Mildred to life as I had always hoped she would be and who has my lifelong gratitude." Crawford's bravura performance in the film was not matched by her attendance at the Academy Awards ceremonies. She called Wald and other studio bosses and told them she could not appear, that she felt she would not win and, if she did, she would make "an ass" of herself if she had to make a speech. On the night of the Oscars she was physically ill, according to her personal physician, who reported that she had a temperature of 104, that she could not attend. Her home was filled with photographers who poured into her lavish bedroom where, on the bed, she listened to the ceremonies being announced on radio. When Charles Boyer announced she had won the Oscar, the photographers had a field day, the bedroom exploding in a sea of blinding flashbulbs. Wald called from the ceremonies to congratulate Crawford, and Blyth appeared to embrace her. Celebrities, headed by Van Johnson, her most ardent fan, poured into the Crawford home to pay homage. The great star had regained her regal status. Exhausted, she was asked to pose for one more shot, lying on her bed, her eyes closed as if asleep, clutching the Oscar that had been delivered to her. She did, and the crowd left her to her quiet glory. Arden, who is a joy to watch as Crawford's pal in MILDRED PIERCE, and who remained the leading lady's friend long after the film, was also nominated for an Academy Award for Best Supporting Actress but lost out to Anne Revere, who played Elizabeth Taylor's mother in NATIONAL VELVET. Arden thought the script for MILDRED PIERCE was "fairly interesting," but, as she stated in her autobiography, *Three Phases of Eve*: "I would never have guessed that it would bring Crawford her only Oscar and me a nomination in the supporting category, and become a classic."

p, Jerry Wald; d, Michael Curtiz; w, Ranald MacDougall (based on the novel by James M. Cain); ph, Ernest Haller; m, Max Steiner; ed, David Weisbart; md, Leo F. Forbstein; art d, Anton Grot; set d, George James Hopkins; cos, Milo Anderson; spec eff, Willard Van Enger; makeup, Perc Westmore.

Drama   **Cas.**   **(PR:A MPAA:NR)**

MILE A MINUTE   (SEE: RIDERS OF THE SANTA FE, 1944)

MILE A MINUTE LOVE*   (1937) 70m Ace bw

William Bakewell, Arletta Duncan, Duncan Renaldo, Vivien Oakland, Wilfred Lucas, Earle Douglas, Etta McDaniel.

Low-budget production that attempts to tell the story of an idealistic inventor who finds that his work interests a gang of hoods involved in a motorboat race. How the young man handles this awkward situation is always predictable. Renaldo, better known as the "Cisco Kid," wrote the story, proving that a cowboy should remain in the saddle.

p, Fanchon Royer; d, Elmer Clifton; w, Edwin Anthony (based on a story by Duncan Renaldo); ph, Arthur Martinelli; ed, Edward Schroeder.

Crime/Drama   **Cas.**   **(PR:A MPAA:NR)**

MILESTONES***   (1975) 195m Stone bw/c

Grace Paley (*Helen*), David C. Stone (*Joe*), John Douglas (*John*), Laurel Berger (*Laurel*), Mary Chapelle (*Mama*), Bobby Buechler (*Jamie*), Liz Dear (*Liz*), Jay Foley (*Terry*), Suey Hagadorn (*Suey*), Harvey Quintal (*Harvey*), Kalaho (*Erika*), Lou Ho (*Lou*), Tina Shepherd (*Elizabeth*), Paul Zimet (*Peter*).

A huge independent undertaking by Robert Kramer and John Douglas. The film takes the audience on a journey across the United States, with characters interwoven through the film via their interrelationships. One couple travels state to state, fighting all the way. Another man tries to relate to his son, now on his own. The film also focuses on a group of Vietnam vets and ex-radicals, and their attempts to adjust to the changing times. The film works well because the directors avoid heavy-handedness and allow the audience to judge the characters. An insightful examination of the transition from the 1960s to the 1970s.

p, David C. Stone, Barbara Stone; d,w&ed, Robert Kramer, John Douglas; ph, Douglas, Kramer.

Drama   **(PR:C MPAA:NR)**

MILITARY ACADEMY**   (1940) 66m COL bw

Tommy Kelly (*Tommy Lewis*), Bobby Jordan (*Dick Hill*), David Holt (*Sandy Blake*), Jackie Searl (*Prentiss Dover*), Don Beddoe ((*Marty Lewis*), Jimmy Butler (*Cadet Dewey*), Walter Tetley (*Cadet Blackburn*), Earle Foxe (*Maj. Dover*), Edward Dew (*Capt. Kendall*), Warren Ashe (*Capt. Banning*), Joan Brodel [Leslie] (*Marjorie Blake*).

Out of the same mold as BOY'S TOWN, MILITARY ACADEMY focuses on boys who, in the course of 66 minutes, become young men. Kelly is a gangster's son who rises above his father's name, and Jordan, one of the Dead End Kids, is the big man at the academy.

d, D. Ross Lederman; w, Karl Brown, David Silverstein (based on a story by Richard English); ph, Allen G. Siegler; ed, Gene Milford.

Drama   **(PR:A MPAA:NR)**

MILITARY ACADEMY WITH THAT TENTH AVENUE GANG*
(1950) 64m COL bw (GB: SENTENCE SUSPENDED; AKA: MILITARY ACADEMY)

Stanley Clements (*Stash*), Myron Welton (*Danny*), Gene Collins (*Mac*), Leon Tyler (*Specs*), James Millican (*Maj. Tony Thomas*), William Johnstone (*Col. Jamison*), James Seay (*Maj. Norcross*), John R. Hamilton (*Judge Townsend*), Dick Jones (*Richard Reilly*), Buddy Swan (*Williams*), Conrad Binyon (*Yost*), John Michaels (*Calhoun*), Buddy Burroughs (*Walker*), John McGuire (*Lt. Waverly*), Jack Reynolds (*Lt. Jones*), Russ Conway (*Capt. Bagby*), Tim Ryan (*Specs' Father*).

A judge sends four juvenile delinquents to a military academy in an attempt to mold them into good citizens. A familiar story line with stock characters and a cliched ending.

p, Wallace MacDonald; d, D. Ross Lederman; w, Howard J. Green; ph, William Bradford; ed, James Sweeney; art d, Victor Green.

Drama   **(PR:A MPAA:NR)**

MILITARY POLICEMAN   (SEE: OFF LIMITS, 1952)

MILITARY SECRET½**   (1945, USSR) 73m Soyuzdet/Artkino bw

Sergei Lukianov (*Col. Lartsev*), Ivan Malishevsky (*Capt. Bakhmetiev*), Alexei Gribov (*Secret Service Commissar*), Andrei Tutishkin (*Engineer Leontiev*), Victor Byelokurov (*Weininger*), Omar Abdulov (*Gestapo Col. Krasehke*), Natasha Borskaya (*Maria Zubova*), Natalia Alisova (*Natalia Ossenina*).

Gribov is a Soviet counterespionage agent sent to prevent Nazi Gestapo agent Byelokurov from capturing a Soviet inventor who has developed a secret weapon the Nazis want. An engaging thriller with a little romance thrown in to keep things interesting. Superb camera work by Sergei Uruseysky. (In Russian; English subtitles.)

d, Vladimir Legoshin; w, Leonid Tur, Peter Tur, Leo Sheynin; ph, Sergei Uruseysky; m, Konstantin Korchmarev; English titles, Charles Clement.

Thriller   **(PR:A MPAA:NR)**

MILKMAN, THE**   (1950) 87m UNIV bw

Donald O'Connor (*Roger Bradley*), Jimmy Durante (*Breezy Albright*), Joyce Holden (*Ginger Burton*), William Conrad (*Mike Morrel*), Piper Laurie (*Chris Abbott*), Henry O'Neill (*Roger Bradley, Sr.*), Paul Harvey (*District Attorney Abbott*), Jess Barker (*John Carter*), Elisabeth Risdon (*Mrs. Carter*), Frank Nelson (*Mr. Green*), Charles Flynn (*Sgt. Larkin*), Garry Owen (*Irving*), John Cliff (*Joe*), Bill Nelson (*Duke*), Eddie Acuff (*Herman Schultz*), Lucille Barkley (*Nurse*), Minerva Urecal (*Mrs. Dillon*), Howard Negley (*Herman*), John Skins Miller (*Harry*), Richard Powers [Tom Keene] (*Duzik*), Norman Field (*Bradley Butler*), Ruth Brady (*Miss Williams*), Therese Lyons (*Bradley Maid*), Joe Kerr (*Man in Window*), Edward Clark (*Old Man*), Bob Stephenson (*Cop*), Charmienne Harker (*Lana*), Hal Smith (*Milkman*), Ralph Montgomery (*Brown*), David Newell (*Fireman*), Perc Launders (*Police Sergeant*), Vesey O'Davoren (*Carter's Butler*), Kippee Valez (*Carmen*), Hazel Keener (*Woman*), Jerry Lewis (*Milkman*), Marilyn Mercer (*Telephone Operator*), Dave Dunbar (*Bill*), Larry McGrath (*Danny*), Charles Hall (*Ed*), Audrey Betz (*Plump Girl*), Marian Dennish (*Pretty Girl*), John McKee, Donald Kerr, Frank Malet, Doug Carter, Wally Walker, Pat Combs, Bob Garvin (*Milkmen*), Jewel Rose (*Secretary*), Paul Power (*Butler*), Parke MacGregor (*Photographer*), John O'Connor, Chester Conklin (*Men*), Paul Palmer (*Policeman*), Carey Loftin, Dick Crockett, Eddie Parker, Frank McGrath, Frank McMahon, Tom Steele, Gordon Carveth, Jimmy Dundee, Wes Hopper, Wally Rose, Chick Collins, Cliff Lyons.

THE MILKMAN did not deliver the cream in this picture, a silly vehicle for O'Connor and Durante in which they strut what little stuff is given them by the quartet of writers. That it took four authors to make this film is a mystery and proof that too many cows spoil the milk. O'Connor is an addled war veteran whose father, O'Neill, owns a large dairy. O'Neill's old pal, Durante, works for a different milk company and is about to retire from his job. O'Neill would like O'Connor to rest from his war rigors, as the boy has a speech affliction that causes him to speak like one of Ross Bagdasarian's chipmunks when he is under tension, which is often. O'Connor wants to follow in O'Neill's footsteps, but when his own father won't give him a job, O'Connor goes to work with Durante. But he is a terrible milkman, nervous and unable to follow the advice of the 1940s song, "Milkman, Keep Those Bottles Quiet." Risdon owns the rival milk company and her ne'er-do-well nephew, Barker, is in hock to a gang of gamblers led by William Conrad, before he got *really* fat. There's a bit of menace, some nice comedy work by Durante (and far too much mugging by O'Connor), and a few songs that never went anywhere. The best acting in the picture is turned in by Piper Laurie as the girl who wins O'Connor. Screenwriter Stern became very successful in TV, writing "The Honeymooners," and producing "Get Smart," and "MacMillan and Wife," and other shows. Ragaway became a best-selling author of small, very funny books which he published through Stern's book company, Price-Stern-Sloan. All four writers would do far better in years to come on their own, proving once more that, when it comes to writing a script, in unity there is mediocrity. Songs include: "Girls Don't Want My Money" (Jimmy Durante, Jack Barnett, sung by Durante), "That's My Boy" (Durante, Barnett, sung by Durante, Donald O'Connor), "It's Bigger Than Both of Us" (Sammy Fain, Barnett, sung by Durante, O'Connor), "Early Morning Song" (Fain, Barnett, sung by O'Connor).

p, Ted Richmond; d, Charles T. Barton; w, Albert Beich, James O'Hanlon, Martin Ragaway, Leonard Stern (based on a story by Ragaway, Stern); ph, Clifford Stine; m, Milton Rosen; ed, Russell Schoengarth; art d, Bernard Herzbrun, Robert Boyle; set d, Russell Gausman, Roland Fields; cos, Rosemary Odell.

Comedy   **(PR:A MPAA:NR)**

MILKY WAY, THE*½**   (1936) 83m PAR bw

Harold Lloyd (*Burleigh "Tiger" Sullivan*), Adolphe Menjou (*Gabby Sloan*), Verree Teasdale (*Ann Westley*), Helen Mack (*Mae Sullivan*), William Gargan (*Elwood "Speed" MacFarland*), George Barbier (*Wilbur Austin*), Dorothy Wilson (*Polly Pringle*), Lionel Stander (*Spider Schultz*), Charles Lane (*Willard, Reporter*), Marjorie Gateson (*Mrs. E. Winthrop LeMoyne*), Bull Anderson (*Oblitsky*), Jim Marples (*O'Rourke*), Larry McGrath (*Referee*), Bonita (*Landlady*), Milburn Stone (*1st Reporter*), Paddy O'Flynn (*2nd Reporter*), Henry Roquemore (*Doctor*), Arthur S. "Pop" Byron (*Cop*), Eddie Dunn (*Barber*), Larry McGrath (*Referee, Todd Fight*), Jack Clifford (*Announcer, Todd Fight*), Jack Perry ("*Tornado*" *Todd*), Phil Tead (*Radio Announcer, Todd Fight*), Jack Murphy (*Newsboy*), Bob Callahan (*Onion*), Eddie Fetherston (*Cameraman*), Leonard Carey (*Butler*), Antrim Short (*Photographer*), Melville Ruick (*Austin's Secretary*), Harry Bowen (*Bartender*), James Farley (*Fight Promoter*), Harry Bernard (*Cop-Tenant*), Morrie Cohan (*Referee, Polo*

Grounds), Dan Tobey *(Announcer, Polo Grounds)*, Sam Hayes *(Radio Announcer, Polo Grounds)*, Gertrude Astor, Ethel May Halls *(Women)*, Victor Potel, Ray Cooper, Thomas A. Curran *(Men)*, Marty Martin *(Ticket Seller)*, Lloyd Ingraham *(Barber Shop Customer)*, Oscar Smith *(Barber Shop Porter)*, Hazel Laughton *(Woman in Coupe)*, Jay Belasco *(Man in Car)*, Wally Howe *(Dr. O. O. White, Veterinary)*, Murray Alper *(2nd Taxi Driver)*, Harry C. Myers *(Photographer at Apartment)*, Charles K. French *(Guest at Mrs. LeMoyne's)*, Gus Leonard *(Musician in Band, Title Fight)*, Anthony Quinn *(Extra)*, Eugene Barry, Charles McMurphy, Earl M. Pingree *(Policemen)*, Broderick O'Farrell, James Ford *(Extras at Fight)*, Frank Mills, Bruce Mitchell *(Todd Fight Extras)*, Tom Hanlon *(La Grue Fight Announcer)*, Agnes the Horse.

A very funny film that showed Lloyd making the transition from silent to sound films with no problems. It was later remade with Danny Kaye as THE KID FROM BROOKLYN, but this one is far funnier, mainly due to Lloyd's abilities. Lloyd is a milquetoast milkman who happens to be in the right place at the right time, and when middleweight champion Gargan throws a punch and Lloyd ducks, that punch is returned by bruiser Stander. The champ is knocked senseless and Lloyd gets the credit. Menjou is the insomniac manager of Gargan and he and girl friend Teasdale are at a loss as to what to do now that their champ is getting thwacked in the press. Menjou decides to take on Lloyd as a boxer-client and the rest is as predictable as the sun rising in the east. Lloyd stepped aside from producing chores and only acted in THE MILKY WAY, and the result was that he could concentrate on his comedy without worrying about finances and other woes. He was superb in his patented role, another variation of the bespectacled, naive everyman who triumphs over the forces of irony every time. It was only when Lloyd departed from this customary role that his movies suffered. An astute businessman who kept ownership of many of his films, Lloyd became enormously rich and lived in baronial splendor in a mansion with more than 40 rooms. Next time you watch a Harold Lloyd film, realize that he lost his right thumb and forefinger in an accident on a 1920 silent, HAUNTED SPOOKS, but he never used stunt men or doubles on any of the death-defying high altitude gags he devised. Lloyd had been released by Mack Sennett who didn't think Lloyd was funny. At one point, Lloyd was the highest-paid actor in the world, so even Mack Sennett was wrong. Songs include "She's Got a Brother," "The Blue Danube Waltz," "For He's a Jolly Good Fellow," "Yankee Doodle Dandy," "The Bear Went Over the Mountain," "The Skaters' Waltz," "A Hot Time in the Old Town Tonight."

p, E. Lloyd Sheldon; d, Leo McCarey; w, Grover Jones, Frank Butler, Richard Connell (based on the play by Lynn Root, Harry Clork); ph, Alfred Gilks; ed, LeRoy Stone; art d, Hans Dreier, Bernard Herzbrun; set d, A. E. Freudeman.

Comedy **Cas.** **(PR:AA MPAA:NR)**

MILKY WAY, THE* 1/2**
(1969, Fr./Ital.) 105m Greenwich-Fraia/U-M c (LA VOIE LACTEE, LA VIA LATTEA)

Paul Frankeur *(Pierre)*, Laurent Terzieff *(Jean)*, Alain Cuny *(Man with Cape)*, Edith Scob *(Virgin Mary)*, Bernard Verley *(Jesus)*, Francois Maistre *(French Priest)*, Claude Cerval *(Brigadier)*, Muni *(Mother Superior)*, Julien Bertheau *(Maitre d'Hotel)*, Ellen Bahl *(Mme. Garnier)*, Michel Piccoli *(The Marquis)*, Agnes Capri *(Lamartine Institution Directress)*, Michel Etcheverry *(The Inquisitor)*, Pierre Clementi *(The Devil [Angel of Death])*, Georges Marchal *(The Jesuit)*, Jean Piat *(The Jansenist)*, Denis Manuel *(Rodolphe)*, Daniel Pilon *(Francois)*, Claudio Brook *(Bishop)*, Julien Guiomar *(Spanish Priest)*, Marcel Peres *(Spanish Innkeeper)*, Delphine Seyrig *(Prostitute)*, Jean-Claude Carriere *(Priscillian)*, Christine Simon *(Therese)*, Augusta Carriere *(Sister Francoise)*, Jean-Daniel Ehrmann *(Condemned Man)*, Pierre Lary *(Young Monk)*, Bernard Musson *(French Innkeeper)*, Michel Dacquin *(Mons. Garnier)*, Gabriel Gobin *(Father)*, Pierre Maguelon *(Civil Guard Corporal)*, Marius Laurey *(Blind Man)*, Jean Clarieux *(Apostle Peter)*, Christian Van Cau *(Apostle Andrew)*, Claudine Berg *(Mother)*, Rita Maiden, Beatrice Constantini *(Priscillian's Daughters)*, Claude Jetter *(Virgin in Spanish Inn)*, Jacqueline Rouillard *(Restaurant Maid)*, Jose Bergosa *(Priscillian's First Deacon)*, Douking *(Shepherd)*, Jean-Louis Broust, Stephane Bouy, Michel Creton, Raoul Delfosse, Jean Dhermay, Pascal Fardoulis, Paul Pavel, Douglas Read, Jacques Rispal, Cesar Torres.

Frankeur and Terzieff are travelers en route to a Spanish shrine. On the way they meet a collection of characters who symbolize the principle heresies of modern culture. Wonderful religious allegory from brilliant director Luis Bunuel that examines the relationships between man and that which is sacred. While Bunuel's works are generally described as "art films," THE MILKY WAY drew a rather unlikely audience in Copenhagen. One day a caravan of gypsies pulled up in front of the theater, bought tickets, and watched the film. They returned several days in a row, and the manager, who spoke a different language, tried to find out why. Not surprisingly, he received no reply, but from then on allowed the caravan to see the film for free.

p, Serge Silberman; d, Luis Bunuel; w, Bunuel, Jean-Claude Carriere; ph, Christian Matras (Eastmancolor); m, Bunuel; ed, Louisette Hautecoeur; art d, Pierre Guffroy; cos, Jacqueline Guyot, Francoise Tournafond; makeup, Jacqueline Pipard.

Religious Drama **(PR:C MPAA:PG)**

MILL OF THE STONE WOMEN**
(1963, Fr./Ital.) 94m Wanguard-Faro-Explorer-C.E.C./Parade c (IL MULINO DELLE DONNE DI PIETRA, LE MOULIN DES SUPPLICES; AKA: HORROR OF THE STONE WOMEN, THE HORRIBLE MILL WOMEN)

Pierre Brice *(Hans)*, Scilla Gabel *(Helfy)*, Dany Carrel *(Lisolette)*, Wolfgang Preiss *(Professor Wahl)*, Herbert Boehme *(Bohlem)*, Marco Guglielmi *(Raab)*, Liana Orfei, Olga Solbelli.

A bizarre little horror film set in Amsterdam around 1912. Brice, a young art student, is researching an 18th-century windmill-driven carousel decorated not with horses, but statues of women in a variety of death poses. He discovers the bodies are mummified corpses of women killed by a mad scientist to supply his dying daughter with blood.

p, Gianpaolo Bigazzi; d, Giorgio Ferroni; w, Remigio Del Grosso, Ugo Liberatore, Giorgio Stegani, Ferroni (based on a story by Ferroni, Del Grosso, from a short story by Peter Van Weigen); ph, Pierludovico Pavoni (Dyaliscope, Eastmancolor); m, Carlo Innocenzi; ed, Antonietta Zita; art d, Arrigo Equini.

Horror **(PR:O MPAA:NR)**

MILL ON THE FLOSS 1/2** (1939, Brit.) 82m Morgan/Standard bw

Frank Lawton *(Philip Wakem)*, Victoria Hopper *(Lucy Deane)*, Fay Compton *(Mrs. Tulliver)*, Geraldine Fitzgerald *(Maggie Tulliver)*, Griffith Jones *(Stephen Guest)*, Mary Clare *(Mrs. Moss)*, James Mason *(Tom Tulliver)*, Athene Seyler *(Mrs. Pullet)*, Sam Livesey *(Mr. Tulliver)*, Amy Veness *(Mrs. Deane)*, Felix Aylmer *(Mr. Wakem)*, Eliot Makeham *(Mr. Pullet)*, William Devlin *(Bob Jakin)*, Ivor Barnard *(Mr. Moss)*, David Horne *(Mr. Deane)*, O. B. Clarence *(Mr. Gore)*, Cecil Ramage *(Luke)*, Pauline de Chalus *(Maggie as a Child)*, Martita Hunt *(Mrs. Glegg)*, James Roberts *(Mr. Glegg)*, Philip Frost *(Philip Wakem as a Child)*, A. W. Payne *(Bob Jakin as a Child)*, William Holloway *(D. Stelling)*, Eldon Gorst *(Tom as a Child)*, Anna Murrell, Hilary Pritchard, Beatrice Marsden, Fred Withers, A.E. Johnson, Sidney Monckton, Cynthia Stock, Geraldine Wilton, Edmund Willard.

There's a bit of "Romeo and Juliet" in here, a trace of the Hatfields and the McCoys, and little pieces of several other stories. Livesey owns a mill on the Floss River in Lincolnshire in England. An irrigation scheme is planned by the lord who runs the area, but Livesey intends to maintain his water rights, despite the legal machinations of Aylmer, who represents the estate. There's a lawsuit and an angry trial, and Livesey loses everything he's worked for. Meanwhile, his son, Mason, is trying to raise some money to pay off Livesey's debts or else the old fellow may wind up in servitude. Livesey's daughter, Fitzgerald, falls in love with Aylmer's crippled son, Lawton. Livesey is so enraged by Aylmer's lawsuit that he takes a horsewhip to the barrister, but a stroke lays him dead in the process. Fitzgerald winds up in an embarrassing romantic situation with Jones, a pal of Lawton's, and the current fiance of her childhood buddy, Hopper. It's a trick to ruin her name and that it does, so she is shunned by one and by all, even her brother, Mason, who should know better. No one in the small town will talk to the young girl except Lawton, who knows that her heart is pure. The two of them are reunited and both die when a dam breaks and a huge flood inundates the tiny town and takes their lives. Presumably, the feud between families ends with the loss of the two lovers. There was a similar denoument in HURRY SUNDOWN, but that picture was so bad that when shown in a single theater at a fourplex, the stench of it caused people to leave in the other three theaters. Not so with THE MILL ON THE FLOSS. This was merely unsatisfying, although it did have enough good acting to cover the 82 minutes.

p, John Clein; d, Tim Whelan; w, John Drinkwater, Garnett Weston, Austin Melford, Whelan (based on the novel by George Eliot); ph, John Stumar; ed, John Datlowe.

Drama **(PR:A MPAA:NR)**

MILLER'S WIFE, THE* 1/2
(1957, Ital.) 95m Titanus/Distributors Corporation of America c (AKA: THE MILLER'S BEAUTIFUL WIFE)

Sophia Loren *(Carmela)*, Vittorio De Sica *(The Governor)*, Marcello Mastroianni *(Luca, the Miller)*, Paolo Stoppa *(Gardunia)*, Yvonne Sanson *(Governor's Wife)*, Carletto Sposito, Virgilio Riento.

A remake of De Sica's THREE CORNERED HAT (1934), this sex farce is nothing more than an amusing piffle but is so forced and labored in production that it bores within minutes. Loren is the busty, sexy wife of miller Mastroianni, coveted by the lusty new Spanish governor of Naples in the year 1860. The governor, De Sica, arrests Mastroianni on trumped-up charges, then, with the miller languishing in a cell, he goes after his sensuous wife Loren, offering a pardon for her husband if she will hop into bed. Loren outwits De Sica by drugging his drink, then skipping off to prison with the pardon where she intends to free her husband. Mastroianni, however, has already escaped and returns home to find De Sica in deshabille, believing he has had his way with his wife. Incensed, the miller goes to the governor's mansion where he almost rapes De Sica's wife, but Loren stops him and convinces him that she has not bartered her ample favors for his release. It's all a bit Neapolitan, too much for the average viewer to swallow and the film is so haphazardly directed by Camerini and so broadly acted by all, especially the hopelessly inept Loren, that only a few burlesque laughs are available. A poor entry from abroad.

p, Carlo Ponti, Dino De Laurentiis; d, Mario Camerini; w, Mario Camerini, Ennio De Concini, Augusto Camerini, Alessandro Continenza, Ivo Perilli (based on the play by Pedro de Alacon); ph, Enzo Serafin (CinemaScope, Eastmancolor); m, A. F. Lavagnino; art d, Guido Fiorini; English subtitles, Herman G. Weinberg.

Comedy **(PR:O MPAA:NR)**

MILLERSON CASE, THE* 1/2 (1947) 72m COL bw

Warner Baxter *(Dr. Robert Ordway)*, Nancy Saunders *(Belle Englehart)*, Clem Bevans *(Sheriff Akers)*, Griff Barnett *(Doc Sam Millerson)*, Paul Guilfoyle *(Jud Rookstool)*, James Bell *(Ezra Minnich)*, Addison Richards *(Dr. Wickersham)*, Mark Dennis *(Bye Minnich)*, Robert Stevens *(Dr. Prescott)*, Eddie Parker *(Lt. Callahan)*, Vic Potel *(Hank Nixon)*, Eddy Waller *(Jeremiah Dobbs)*, Russell Simpson *(Squire Tuttle)*, Sarah Padden *(Emma Millerson)*, Barbara Pepper *(Eadie Rookstool)*, Frances Morris *(Ella Minnich)*.

Sophisticated Baxter once again plays the popular Crime Doctor, a one-time criminal himself who suffers from amnesia after having received a knock on the head and who then devotes himself to solving crimes of a psychological nature. Here, Baxter attempts to get away for a brief vacation, but is driven by his compassionate nature to take part in the investigation of a murder. This is one of the three pictures in the 10-film series in which dark and mature Baxter is taking a vacation when the story opens, perhaps harkening back to the fact that he was not in top shape when the series began. After suffering a nervous breakdown in the early 1940s, he resumed performing in the Crime Doctor series, which gave him the chance to continue working at age 51 at a pace no more demanding than two films a year, each shot in only one month. A gradual fading out for the resonant voiced leading man who once received as much fan mail as Clark Gable or Robert Taylor. (See CRIME DOCTOR series, Index.)

p, Rudolph C. Flothow; d, George Archainbaud; w, Raymond L. Schrock (based on the story by Gordon Rigby, Carlton Sand); ph, Philip Tannura; ed, Dwight Caldwell; md, Mischa Bakaleinikoff; art d, Harold MacArthur.

Crime/Drama (PR:A MPAA:NR)

MILLIE* 1/2 (1931) 85m RKO bw

Helen Twelvetrees (Millie), Robert Ames (Tommy Roche), Lilyan Tashman (Helen Riley), Joan Blondell (Angie), John Halliday (Jimmy Daimer), James Hall (Jack Maitland), Anita Louise (Connie), Edmund Breese (Attorney), Frank McHugh (Holmes), Franklin Parker (Spring), Charlotte Walker (Mrs. Maitland), Harry Stubbs (Mark), Harvey Clark (Hawksworth), Charles Delaney (Mike), Carmelita Geraghty (Miss Vail), Geneva Mitchell (Clara Roscoe), Otis Harlan (Luke), Marie Astaire (Bobby), Aggie Herring (Landlady).

Twelvetrees can't seem to settle down; she ends her first marriage and jumps from one love affair to another. The only man she will have nothing to do with is a wealthy broker, Halliday, who begins to romance the woman's 16-year-old daughter. When he ignores her warnings to leave the girl alone, Twelvetrees kills him. During the murder trial, daughter comes to mom's rescue at the last moment to tell what had happened the night of the killing. A worn melodrama that creaks from rust and cliches.

p, Charles R. Rogers; d, John Francis Dillon; w, Charles Kenyon, Ralph Murphy (based on the novel by Donald Henderson Clarke); ph, Ernest Haller.

Drama (PR:A MPAA:NR)

MILLIE'S DAUGHTER* 1/2 (1947) 70m COL bw

Gladys George, Gay Nelson, Paul Campbell, Norma Varden, Arthur Space, Nana Bryant, Ethel Griffies, Harry Hayden, Paul Maxey, Robert Emmett Keane.

Well-meaning but ultimately hokey picture about a woman who goes overboard attempting to steer her daughter away from a life of crime. The daughter is restless and is showing the usual signs of growing up, so the mother makes herself an example in hopes that the girl won't go bad. Characters and plot never escape the overly sentimental premise.

p, William Bloom; d, Sidney Salkow; w, Edward Huebsch (based on a story by Donald Henderson Clarke); ph, Allen Siegler; ed, Aaron Stell; art d, Charles Clague.

Drama (PR:A MPAA:NR)

MILLION, THE*** (1931, Fr.) 83m Tobis bw (LE MILLION)

Annabella (Beatrice), Rene Lefebvre (Michel), Paul Olivier ("Father Tulipe" Crochard, a Gangster), Louis Allibert (Prosper), Constantin Stroesco (Sopranelli), Odetta Talazac (La Chanteuse), Vanda Greville (Vanda), Raymond Cordy (Taxi Driver).

An entertaining French farce about two starving artists winning the lottery. They win a million florins but the winning ticket ends up in an old coat that is stolen. The two men frantically chase down the thief to find that he's sold the coat to an opera singer. They head for the opera house as do a group of crooks who have discovered the contents of the coat. The opera house is turned into a three-ring circus as possession of the coat is fought over by all involved. Director Clair masterfully uses music to accentuate the comic situations.

d&w, Rene Clair (based on a musical play by Georges Berr, M. Guillemaud); ph, Georges Perinal, Georges Raulet; m, Armand Bernard, Philippe Pares, Georges Van Parys; art d&set d, Lazare Meerson.

Comedy (PR:A MPAA:NR)

MILLION DOLLAR BABY* 1/2 (1935) 67m MON bw

Jimmy Fay (Pat Sweeney), Arline Judge (Grace Sweeney), Ray Walker (Terry Sweeney), George E. Stone (Joe Lewis), Eddie Kane (Bill Donovan), Willard Robertson (Doctor), Ralf Harolde (Mac), Lee Shumway (Tony), Ed Peil, Sr. (Louie), Paul Porcasi (Marvelo No. 1), Wilbur Mack (Freeman), Jeanette Loff (Rita Ray).

Walker and Judge are a husband and wife vaudeville team who dress their son, Fay, like Shirley Temple to enter the poor kid in a contest. Fay wins the contest and finds himself on a train in his Shirley outfit heading for Hollywood. The boy doesn't like what possible fate awaits him so he jumps off the train. He meets a helpful hobo, and a gang of bank robbers who see financial possibilities with the young boy. Things get even more outlandish from there.

p, Ben Verschleiser; d, Joseph Santley; w, Santley, John W. Krafft (based on a story by Santley); ph, Harry Neumann; ed, Carl Pierson; m/l, Santley.

Comedy (PR:A MPAA:NR)

MILLION DOLLAR BABY** (1941) 100m WB bw

Priscilla Lane (Pamela McAllister), Jeffrey Lynn (James Amory), Ronald Reagan (Peter Rowan), May Robson (Cornelia Wheelwright), Lee Patrick (Josie LaRue), Helen Westley (Mrs. Galloway), Walter Catlett (Simpson), Richard Carle (George the Butler), George Barbier (Marlin), John Qualen (Dr. Patterson), Fay Helm (Mrs. Grayson), Nan Wynn (Flo), John Ridgley (Ollie Ward), Maris Wrixon (Diana Bennett), John Sheffield (Alvie Grayson), George Humbert (Tony), James Burke (Callahan), Greta Meyer (Anna), Jean Ames (Phyllis), Charles Drake (Crew

Haircut), George Davis (Swiss Taxi Driver), Ed Gargan (Customs Officer), William Forrest, Ted Thompson, Gaylord "Steve" Pendleton, Tony Hughes, David Oliver, David Clarke, Herbert Vigran, Frank Otto, George Campeau, Garrett Craig, Charles Marsh, Kenneth Harlan, Billy Wayne (Reporters), Inez Gay, Paulette Evans (Women), Eddie Graham, Jack Wise, Stuart Holmes, Nat Carr (Men), Pedro De Cordoba (Conductor), Will Morgan (Member of Orchestra), Irving Bacon (Income Tax Man).

Robson is a millionairess living in Europe who is contacted by lawyer Lynn. He tells her that her father had made his millions by defrauding his own partner. Robson returns to the States and meets with Lane, the granddaughter of the partner. The millionairess moves into the same boarding house as Lane and gives her a million dollars. The money causes her more problems than it's worth. Her musician boy friend, Reagan, won't marry into money so Lane gives it all to charity. Robson's performance is worth watching in this otherwise lightweight film.

p, Hal B. Wallis; d, Curtis Bernhardt; w, Casey Robinson, Richard Macaulay, Jerry Wald (based on "Miss Wheelwright Discovers America" by Leonard Spigelgass); ph, Charles Rosher; m, Frederick Hollander; ed, Rudi Fehr; cos, Orry-Kelly.

Drama (PR:A MPAA:NR)

MILLION DOLLAR COLLAR, THE** (1929) 61m WB bw

Rin-Tin-Tin (Rinty, a Dog), Matty Kemp (Bill Holmes), Evelyn Pierce (Mary French), Philo McCullough (Joe French), Tommy Dugan (Ed Mack), Allan Cavan (The Chief), Grover Liggon (Scar).

After nearly being killed in a car crash, Rin-Tin-Tin is pulled from the wreckage by Kemp. The dog has a stolen diamond necklace hidden in his collar, but Kemp is unaware of this until the robbers kidnap him. Pierce, a gang moll, grows disenchanted with the hoodlums and she helps the marvelous German Shepherd rescue Kemp. Exciting entertainment with Rin-Tin-Tin performing a number of amazing stunts.

d, D. Ross Lederman; w, Robert Lord; ph, Nelson Laraby; ed, William Holmes.

Crime (PR:A MPAA:NR)

MILLION DOLLAR DUCK (SEE: $1,000,000 DUCK, 1971)

MILLION DOLLAR KID** (1944) 66m MON bw

Leo Gorcey (Muggs McGinnis), Huntz Hall (Glimpy McClasky), Gabriel Dell (Lefty), Billy Benedict (Skinny), Louise Currie (Louise Cortland), Noah Beery, Sr. (Capt. Matthews), Iris Adrian (Maisie Dunbar), Herbert Heyes (John Cortland), Robert Greig (Spevin), Johnny Duncan (Roy Cortland), Stanley Brown (Lt. Andre Dupree), Patsy Moran (Mrs. McClasky), Mary Gordon (Mrs. McGinnis), Al Stone (Herbie), Bobby Stone (Rocky), Dave Durand (Danny), Bud Gorman (Pinkie), Jimmy Strand (Stinkie), Pat Costello (Spike), Bernard Gorcey (Messenger).

The East Side Kids, earlier known as the Dead End Kids in another film series, aid wealthy Heyes in ridding the neighborhood of a gang of punks. The rich man's son, Duncan, is actually one of these ruffians, but when his brother is killed in the war, Duncan helps Gorcey and the boys round up the punks. (See BOWERY BOYS series, Index.)

p, Sam Katzman, Jack Dietz; d, Wallace Fox; w, Frank Young; ph, Marcel Le Picard; ed, Carl Pierson; md, Edward Kay; art d, Ernest Hickerson.

Comedy Drama Cas. (PR:A MPAA:NR)

MILLION DOLLAR LEGS*** (1932) 64m PAR bw

Jack Oakie (Migg Tweeny, American Brush Salesman), W.C. Fields (The President of Klopstokia), Andy Clyde (The Major-Domo), Lyda Roberti (Mata Machree), Susan Fleming (Angela), Ben Turpin (Mysterious Man), Hugh Herbert (Secretary of Treasury), George Barbier (Mr. Baldwin), Dickie Moore (Willie, Angela's Brother), Billy Gilbert (Secretary of the Interior), Vernon Dent (Secretary of Agriculture), Teddy Hart (Secretary of War), John Sinclair (Secretary of Labor), Sam Adams (Secretary of State), Irving Bacon (Secretary of the Navy), Ben Taggart (Ship's Captain), Hank Mann (Customs Inspector), Chick Collins (Jumper), Syd Saylor (Starter at the Games), Ernie Adams (Contestant), Eddie Dunn (Coachman), Al Bridge, Heinie Conklin (Spies in Capes), Herbert Evans (Butler), Lew Kelly (Conductor), Don Wilson (Stationmaster), Tyler Brooke (Olympics Announcer), Hobart Bosworth (Olympics Official Starter), Eddie Baker, Edgar Dearing (Train Officials), Charles Hall, Bobby Dunn, Herman Brix [Bruce Bennett], Billy Engle (Klopstokian Athletes).

Silly, funny, satiric, and surrealistic, MILLION DOLLAR LEGS was a satire of the 1932 Olympic Games (held in Los Angeles) made before the fact! It was released to coincide with the Summer Games and may have been too funny and barbed for the take-sports-seriously crowd. There is a mythical country known as Klopstokia (not unlike the Marx Brothers' Fredonia or Grand Fenwick, site of THE MOUSE THAT ROARED) with an odd way of doing things. They elect their president by pulling arms, there is a spy hiding behind each tree, and the man who heads the country must also be the strongest person. Further, there is something about the air or the food of Klopstokia that causes everyone in the land to be incredibly good at sports; thus, little tykes can jump six feet in the air and a mile run for a Klopstokian is like a 440-yard dash. In order to get on the map, Klopstokia enters the Olympics. The rest of the film is a melange of intrigue, slapstick, barbed parody, chases, and darned near a laugh every minute. Cline called in several of the best silent-film gagsters (Turpin, Mann, et al.), and the result was a look back at some of the best silent gags ever devised, with the addition of some sharp dialog. This picture was close to being a superior one, but the script and the direction held back from going that one extra step that moves humor up to the realm of art. The gags, by themselves, were excellent, but when strung together, the story faded in favor of the jokes and there was not one moment when anyone could take anything seriously. It could have been delicious but all it became was flavorful satire.

p, Herman J. Mankiewicz; d, Edward Cline; w, Henry Myers, Nick Barrows (based on a story by Joseph L. Mankiewcz); ph, Arthur Todd.

Comedy (PR:A MPAA:NR)

MILLION DOLLAR LEGS**½ (1939) 59m PAR bw

Betty Grable (*Carol Parker*), John Hartley (*Greg Melton*), Donald O'Connor (*Sticky Boone*), Jackie Coogan (*Russ Simpson*), Larry "Buster" Crabbe (*Coach Baxter*), Peter Lind Hayes (*Freddie Fry*), Dorothea Kent (*Susie Quinn*), Richard Denning (*Hunk Jordan*), Philip Warren (*Buck Hogan*), Edward Arnold, Jr. (*Blimp Garrett*), Thurston Hall (*Gregory Melton, Sr.*), Roy Gordon (*Dean Wixby*), Matty Kemp (*Ed Riggs*), William Tracy (*Egghead Jackson*), Joyce Mathews (*Bunny*), Russ Clark (*Referee*), Wallace Rairden (*Crandall*), John Hart (*Haldeman*), Bill Boggess (*Wells*), Ken Nolan (*Thurston*), Billy Wilkerson (*Rich*), Jim Kelso (*Carpenter*), Si Jenks (*Bus Driver*), Pat West (*George*), Billy Gilbert (*Dick Schultz*), Eve Carlton (*Girl*), Charles Regan, Allen Fox (*Men*), Tom Dugan (*Man Behind*), George Anderson (*President Greene*), Eleanor Counts (*Co-Ed*), William Holden (*Graduate Who Says "Thank You"*), Byron Foulger (*Mr. Day*), Anthony Marsh (*MacDonald*), Rob Ireland (*Hall*), Roger Laswell (*Alden*), Bill Conselman, Jr. (*Husky Student*).

A minor B-level comedy notable for some talents that would go on to bigger things. Hartley is a rich kid trying to stay out of his father's wealthy shadow while away at school. The college rowing team needs new equipment to replace the leaky boats they're unfortunately equipped with. Rather than go to dad for the money, Hartley takes up a collection from his teammates, then bets the wad on a racehorse dubbed "Million Dollar Legs." Though the nag is a long shot, Hartley's gamble pays off. He buys the needed rowing equipment for the team, which goes on to beat a rival crew in the climax. As comedies go this is about average with a standard plot and characters. Paramount and the other major studios often used these B features as testing grounds for up-and-coming talent. Notable among this cast is Grable, then a still struggling starlet trying to find her niche. She's passable enough here in a role that doesn't require her to do much more than look pretty. The film's title had nothing to do with her physical attributes, though ironically her gams would later be insured for $1 million with Lloyds of London. At the time she was married to costar Coogan, whose days as a child star were long gone. Also in the cast was a peppy 14-year-old by the name of Donald O'Connor. This was one of the many programmers he appeared in as a youth before making his mark as an adult performer. Those with a quick eye will also be able to spot Holden in a one-line role. His next film would be GOLDEN BOY, a part that launched him to stardom. Featured as a coach is Crabbe, popular then with his FLASH GORDON serial. In an uncredited codirector position was Dmytryk who would later become a fine director in his own right and would also be cited for contempt of Congress and convicted as one of the Hollywood Ten during the movie industry's Communist blacklisting period in the late 1940s.

d, Nick Grinde, Edward Dmytryk; w, Lewis Foster, Richard English (based on a story by Foster); ph, Harry Fischbeck; ed, Stuart Gilmore.

Comedy (PR:A MPAA:NR)

MILLION DOLLAR MANHUNT* (1962, Brit.) 67m BUT/Anglo Amalgamated bw (GB: ASSIGNMENT REDHEAD)

Richard Denning (*Keen*), Carole Mathews (*Hedy*), Ronald Adam (*Scammel/Dumetrius*), Danny Green (*Yottie*), Brian Worth (*Ridgeway*), Jan Holden (*Sally*), Hugh Moxey (*Sgt. Coutts*), Elwyn Brook-Jones (*Mitchell*), Peter Swanwick (*Bonnet*).

Denning is a secret agent on the trail of an international gang of thieves who plot to heist $12 million in counterfeit Nazi money. He falls in love, however, with Mathews, a cabaret singer who is part of the gang. When gang leader Adam commits murder, Mathews comes to Denning's side in the hope of convicting Adam. In the final scenes, Mathews is killed by Adam, who in turn is killed by Denning. A tedious crime melodrama.

p, William G. Chalmers; d&w, Maclean Rogers (based on the novel *Requiem for a Redhead* by Al Bocca); ph, Ernest Palmer; m, Wilfred Burns; ed, Peter Mayhew; art d, John Stoll.

Crime (PR:A MPAA:NR)

MILLION DOLLAR MERMAID*** (1952) 115m MGM c (GB: THE ONE-PIECE BATHING SUIT)

Esther Williams (*Annette Kellerman*), Victor Mature (*James Sullivan*), Walter Pidgeon (*Frederick Kellerman*), David Brian (*Alfred Harper*), Donna Corcoran (*Annette at Age 10*), Jesse White (*Doc Cronnel*), Maria Tallchief (*Pavlova*), Howard Freeman (*Aldrich*), Charles Watts (*Policeman*), Wilton Graff (*Garvey*), Frank Ferguson (*Prosecutor*), James Bell (*Judge*), James Flavin (*Conductor*), Willis Bouchey (*Director*), Adrienne D'Ambricourt (*Marie the Housekeeper*), Charles Heard (*Official*), Clive Morgan (*Judge*), Queenie Leonard (*Mrs. Graves*), Stuart Torres (*Son*), Leslie Denison (*Purser*), Wilson Benge (*Caretaker*), Elisabeth Slifer (*Soprano*), Al Ferguson (*London Bobby*), Vernon Downing (*Newspaper Man*), Creighton Hale (*Husband*), James L. "Tiny" Kelly, Pat Flaherty (*Policemen*), Paul Bradley (*Defense Attorney*), James Aubrey (*Pawnbroker*), Patrick O'Moore (*Master of Ceremonies*), George Wallace (*Bud Williams*), Paul Frees (*Band Leader*), Louis Manley (*Fire-eater*), Edward Clark (*Elderly Man*), Gordon Richards (*Casey*), Benny Burt (*Bum*), Rod Rogers (*Marcellino the Clown*), Harry Hines (*Watchman*), Clarence Hennecke (*Newsboy*), Genevieve Pasques (*Maid*), Thomas Dillon (*Process Server*), Louise Lorimer (*Nurse*), Mack Chandler (*Robbie the Prop Man*), Mary Earle, Bobby Hale, T. Arthur Hughes, Percy Lennon, Kay Wiley, Gail Bonney, Rosemarie Bowe.

Esther Williams was truly a one-of-a-kind in the movie business. By her own admission, she couldn't sing, dance, or even act very well and being a swimmer was hardly enough to make movies about. Still, she did 25 films for MGM and in only

a few did they justify her diving and swimming. In MILLION DOLLAR MERMAID, there was a reason for the lovely Esther to get into a swimsuit, as she was playing a real-life heroine of the water, Annette Kellerman. Liberties were taken with the true story (but that is almost always the rule, not the exception) by writer Freeman, who usually wrote in collaboration but took a solo screen credit on this. It's the early 1890s in Australia and Corcoran is the 10-year-old daughter of Pidgeon, a music teacher. Corcoran has been born with a leg disorder and she regains her strength by swimming. Years pass and Corcoran becomes Williams, a beautiful, self-assured woman who is acknowledged across the world as being the best female swimmer. Pidgeon can't handle some business problems, so he takes a position in London at a music school and Williams accompanies him on the sea voyage from Down Under to Blighty. Aboard the ship, Williams and Pidgeon meet Mature and White, who own a boxing kangaroo which they intend to show off in England. (See the film MATILDA for the further adventures of a boxing kangaroo.) Mature has already heard of Williams' watery ways and suggests that she might need management in order to make a few pounds. Pidgeon is totally against it and Williams, who is planning to study ballet, is not all that interested in professional swimming, but she does find some attraction in Mature. They all arrive in London and Pidgeon is nonplused to discover that the job he thought he had no longer exists. Williams attempts to find some dancing work, but it's as scarce as sincerity in a game show host's smile, so she contacts Mature and agrees to be part of the big ballyhoo for his kangaroo stunt. She swims nearly 30 miles down the River Thames and ignites the press of England, soon becoming a celebrity for what she thought was a simple task. Mature sees that Williams may have a large career looming, so he goes to New York to see if he can get Williams a booking at the reigning king of Broadway's showcases, the Hippodrome. Brian manages the huge theater and feels that he can't use Williams in any way, so Mature decides to stir up some publicity and hies her north to Boston where she will try another long swim. But Mature has another card up his sleeve and makes sure Williams dresses in a revealing (for the time), one-piece suit that leaves little to the imagination. Then he arranges to have her arrested for wearing the shocking swimwear (after first notifying the press), and she is eventually released by a judge who sees through the publicity ploy. But all the hoopla is heard across the land and Mature uses the ink to make Williams a nationwide figure and a draw at the turnstiles. Williams and Mature work closely with each other and that results in a love affair that is briefly ceased after a disagreement. (As Cecily says in THE IMPORTANCE OF BEING EARNEST when she tells Algernon of their affair—which only exists in her diary—"No engagement is worth anything unless it has not been broken at least once.") Williams is hired by Brian to be the star of a new water ballet at the Hippodrome and Mature leaves to promote the career of a reckless pilot. Brian and Williams get closer until he pops the question and she accepts. But when pressed to name the day, Williams continues to postpone matters for one reason or another and eventually agrees to marry Brian when she finishes a movie she's been working on. On the final day of the picture, Williams is hurt badly in an accident. The glass on the water tank shatters and she is taken to the hospital to recover. While there, both Brian and Mature come to visit her, and when Brian sees how she responds to Mature's presence, he realizes that she was merely agreeing to marry him on the rebound and he reaches for his hat and departs, leaving the two lovebirds cooing. The underwater choreography by Brier is only topped by some spectacular above-water work by Busby Berkeley that stands out far above the general nature of the movie. Berkeley used more than 100 swimmers, 55-foot-high streams of yellow and red smoke, and ramps upon which the swimmers slid into the water while carrying lit torches. Then Williams dove from a 50-foot-high swing into the mass of swimmers, who immediately went into one of Berkeley's ferris-wheel effects (shot from an overhead camera), with the finale being several hundred lit sparklers coming *out* of the water and becoming a backdrop to the ensemble. It surely ranks as one of the best water-ballet sequences ever. The small comedic touches were aptly handled by Jesse White, who has been doing that since the 1940s and continues well into the 1980s. Ballerina Maria Tallchief is seen as Pavlova, but none of the other famed performers of the era is depicted. LeRoy's direction is apparently nonexistent and what might have made this into a super film would have been a good musical score with tunes by Harry Warren or Richard Rodgers or Cole Porter. They opted to do it straight, though, and blew the chance to do another great MGMusical. Williams made three other big movies after this, DANGEROUS WHEN WET, EASY TO LOVE, and JUPITER'S DARLING, but none came close to the panache of MILLION DOLLAR MERMAID. The only tune we hear completely is "Let Me Call You Sweetheart" (Leo Friedman, Beth Slater Whitson).

p, Arthur Hornblow, Jr.; d, Mervyn LeRoy; w, Everett Freeman; ph, George J. Folsey (Technicolor); ed, John McSweeney, Jr.; md, Adolph Deutsch; art d, Cedric Gibbons, Jack Martin Smith; set d, Edwin R. Willis, Richard Pefferle; ch, Busby Berkeley; underwater ch, Audrene Brier.

Biography (PR:A MPAA:NR)

MILLION DOLLAR PURSUIT** (1951) 59m REP bw

Penny Edwards (*Ronnie LaVerne*), Grant Withers (*Carlo Petrov*), Norman Budd (*Monte Norris*), Steve Flagg (*Lt. Whitcomb*), Rhys Williams (*Waxey Wilk*), Mikel Conrad (*Louie Palino*), Paul Hurst (*Ray Harvey*), Denver Pyle (*Nick Algren*), Ted Pavelec (*Muller*), John de Simone (*Speed Nelson*), Don Beddoe (*Bowen*), Edward Cassidy (*Deputy Sheriff*), Edward Clark (*Holcomb*), John Hamilton (*Inspector Morgan*), George Brand (*Parker*), Jack Shea (*Lt. Spears*).

Budd is a small-time hoodlum who decides to rob a department store. He plans to get $500,000 and then make himself known as a mastermind of robbery, but his big mouth ruins those plans. Withers and his mob move in to take control, and Budd is handed a lesser role in the heist. Edwards plays a nightclub singer and Flagg is the police lieutenant who's in love with her.

p, Herbert J. Yates; d, R. G. Springsteen; w, Albert DeMond, Bradbury Foote (based on a story by DeMond); ph, Walter Strenge; m, Stanley Wilson; ed, Robert M. Leeds; art d, Frank Hotaling; cos, Adele Palmer.

Crime Drama **(PR:A MPAA:NR)**

MILLION DOLLAR RACKET (SEE: $1,000,000 RACKET, 1937)

MILLION DOLLAR RANSOM* ½ (1934) 78m UNIV bw

Phillips Holmes (*Stanton Casserly*), Edward Arnold (*Vincent Shelton*), Mary Carlisle (*Francesca Shelton*), Wini Shaw (*Babe*), Andy Devine (*Careful*), Robert Gleckler (*Doc*), Marjorie Gateson (*Elita Casserly*), Edgar Norton (*Meigs*), Bradley Page (*Easy*), Hughey White (*Innocence*), Charles Coleman (*Towers*), Henry Kolker (*Dr. Davis*), Jane Darwell, Jay C. Flippen, Spencer Charters.

Arnold is a bootlegger who, upon release from prison, finds he's out of a job because Prohibition has ended. He meets the wealthy Holmes, who makes the penniless crook an offer—if he helps fake the rich man's kidnaping, Holmes will pay him a hefty sum of money. Holmes hopes that the publicity of his kidnaping will stop his mother's marriage to a gold-digging man. A gang of hoodlums wants a cut of the ransom, not knowing it's all a put-on. Holmes falls in love with Arnold's daughter, Carlisle; and Arnold sacrifices himself so the two love birds can escape the clutches of the gang.

d, Murray Roth; w, William R. Lipman, Ben Ryan (based on the story "Ransom, One Million Dollars" by Damon Runyon); ph, George Robinson; ed, Murray Selden; m/l, Walter Donaldson.

Crime Drama **(PR:A MPAA:NR)**

MILLION DOLLAR WEEKEND* ½ (1948) 73m Masque/EL bw

Gene Raymond (*Nicholas Lawrence*), Stephanie Paull (*Cynthia Strong*), Francis Lederer (*Alan Marker*), Robert Warwick (*Dave Dietrich*), Patricia Shay (*Sally*), James Craven (*Dr. George Strong*), Royal Hawaiian Serenaders.

Raymond swindles $1 million from the company he works for and heads for Shanghai. On the plane to Honolulu he meets Paull and Lederer. Lederer is trying to blackmail Paull, and Raymond falls in love with her while the blackmailer takes off with the briefcase full of money. Raymond chases him back to San Francisco and regains the loot after a chase and fist fight. With briefcase in hand, Raymond returns to his office, quietly puts the money back, and returns to Paull waiting for him in Hawaii.

p, Matty Kemp; d, Gene Raymond; w, Charles S. Belden (based on a story by Kemp, Raymond); ph, Paul Ivano; m, Phil Ohman, Howard Jackson; art d, Lewis Creber; m/l, "My Destiny," "Where Have You Been," Dorothy Daniels, Dorothy Roberts, "Heaven in Blue Hawaii," Paul Key.

Comedy **(PR:A MPAA:NR)**

MILLION EYES OF SU-MURU, THE*
(1967, Brit.) 95m Sumuru/AIP c (GB: SUMURU; AKA: THE 1,000,000 EYES OF SU-MURU)

Frankie Avalon (*Tommy Carter*), George Nader (*Nick West*), Shirley Eaton (*Su-Muru*), Wilfrid Hyde-White (*Col. Baisbrook*), Klaus Kinski (*President Boong*), Patti Chandler (*Louise*), Salli Sachse (*Mikki*), Ursula Rank (*Erna*), Krista Nell (*Zoe*), Marie Rohm (*Helga*), Paul Chang (*Inspector Koo*), Essie Huang (*Kitty*), Jon Fong (*Col. Medika*), Denise Davreux, Mary Cheng, Jill Hamilton, Lisa Gray, Christine Lok, Margaret Cheung, Louise Lee (*The Su-Muru Guard*).

Avalon and Nader are an ill-equipped pair of American agents who assist British Intelligence in stopping the sexy, but sadistic Eaton. Cast as Su-Muru, Eaton plans to rule the world by enslaving everyone with her army of women (hence, the million eyes). Her plan is foiled thanks to the unfaltering wit of Avalon and Nader who pose as aides to Kinski, who is turned into stone at the end. After tossing the agents in her torture chamber, Su-Muru finds herself up against the Hong Kong police, who eventually obliterate her island with explosives. RIO 70 is the equally lame sequel.

p, Harry Alan Towers; d, Lindsay Shonteff; w, Kevon Kavanagh (based on the story by Peter Welbeck [Harry Alan Towers] from the books and characters created by Sax Rohmer); ph, John Kotze (Techniscope, Technicolor); m, Johnny Scott; ed, Allan Morrison; md, Scott; art d, Scott MacGregor.

Adventure **(PR:A MPAA:NR)**

MILLION POUND NOTE (SEE: MAN WITH A MILLION, 1954, Brit.)

MILLION TO ONE, A* (1938) 59m Puritan bw

Herman Brix [Bruce Bennett] (*Johnny Kent*), Joan Fontaine (*Joan Stevens*), Monte Blue (*John Kent, Sr.*), Kenneth Harlan (*William Stevens*), Suzanne Kaaren (*Pat Stanley*), Reed Howes (*Duke Hale*), Ed Piel (*Mac, the Editor*), Ben Hall (*Joe, a Reporter*), Dick Simmons (*A Friend*).

A dull Olympics film with Brix and Howes battling it out for the gold medal in the decathlon. Fontaine, a society girl, wants to make the athletic Brix her husband. Blue plays Brix's father and trainer; Harlan plays Fontaine's father.

p, Fanchon Royer; d, Lynn Shores; w, John T. Neville; ph, James Diamond; ed, Edward Schroeder.

Drama **(PR:A MPAA:NR)**

MILLIONAIRE, THE*** (1931) 82m WB bw

George Arliss (*James Alden*), Evalyn Knapp (*Barbara Alden*), David Manners (*Bill Merrick*), James Cagney (*Schofield, Insurance Salesman*), Bramwell Fletcher (*Carter Andrews*), Florence Arliss (*Mrs. Alden*), Noah Beery, Sr. (*Peterson*), Ivan Simpson (*Dr. Harvey*), Sam Hardy (*McCoy*), J. Farrell MacDonald (*Dan Lewis*), Tully Marshall (*Briggs*), J. C. Nugent (*Doctor*), Charles Grapewin, Charles E. Evans, Ethel Griffies, Ben Hall.

An interesting comedy-drama that was remade 16 years later (and not nearly as well) as THAT WAY WITH WOMEN. Arliss is a Henry Ford type, the immensely wealthy and overworked head of his own enormous automobile company. His wife, Arliss (his real wife as well), wishes he'd slow down. Cagney, a brash, fast-talking insurance man, makes a pitch in one scene for Arliss' business. The old fella is just this side of total exhaustion and considering the advice of his doctor, Nugent. to take off a half year or find himself pushing up daisies. Cagney tells Arliss that if he stays inactive and has no reason to get up in the morning, one day he just won't get up. Arliss can't stand not doing anything, so he masquerades as a poor man and buys a half interest in a gas station with Manners, who just happens to be in love with the Arliss' daughter, Knapp, but doesn't know that his crotchety partner is one of the richest men around. Manners works at the station while studying architecture. Later, when Manners comes to call and asks for the hand of Knapp, he is shocked to see that his partner is her father. It's all improbable, but so what? The young lovers get together, the old man realizes that he can be happy *despite* being rich, everyone winds up smiling, and, after all, how much more can be asked of a movie? The screenplay is sharp and pointed and may have sired the TV show of the same name, although no credit seems to have been given to Biggers on the program which starred Marvin Miller. Biggers is the same man who invented Charlie Chan, who first appeared in films in 1926. Simpson, a long-time pal of Arliss, usually worked in the same movies with him and this time plays the magnate's valet.

d, John G. Adolfi; w, Julien Josephson, Maude T. Powell, Booth Tarkington (based on the story "Idle Hands" by Earl Derr Biggers); ph, James Van Trees; ed, Owen Marks; md, Leo F. Forbstein; makeup, Perc Westmore.

Comedy/Drama **(PR:A MPAA:NR)**

MILLIONAIRE FOR A DAY (SEE: LET'S BE RITZY, 1934)

MILLIONAIRE FOR CHRISTY, A** (1951) 91m Thor/FOX bw

Fred MacMurray (*Peter Ulysses Lockwood*), Eleanor Parker (*Christy Sloane*), Richard Carlson (*Dr. Roland Cook*), Kay Buckley (*June Chandler*), Una Merkel (*Patsy*), Douglas Dumbrille (*A. K. Thompson*), Raymond Greenleaf (*Benjamin Chandler*), Nestor Paiva (*Mr. Rupello*), Chris-Pin Martin (*Galan, Fat Mexican*), Julian Rivero (*Thin Mexican*), Everett Glass (*Dr. Whipple*), Almira Sessions (*Myrtle*), Sam Flint (*Mayor*), Ralph Peters (*Collector*), Ralph Hodges (*Bud*), Byron Foulger (*Sam*), Walter Baldwin (*Mr. Sloane*), Lane Chandler (*Tall Reporter*), Charles Williams (*Reporter with Glasses*), Emmett Vogan (*Fat Reporter*), Robert Bice (*Reporter with Tape Recorder*), Billy Snyder (*Herald Photographer*), Al Hill (*Cab Driver*), Emmett Lynn (*Hermit*), Gene Gericko (*Office Joker*), Jo Carroll Dennison (*Nurse Jackson*), John Indriasano (*Mechanic*).

A 1950s version of a 1930s screwball comedy, this falls a bit short, but has enough laughs to make it seem shorter than it is. MacMurray is a radio commentator with a honey voice and lots of sugary philosophy; Parker is the secretary to a large legal firm who is dispatched to California to tell MacMurray that he has been left a $2 million fortune. MacMurray is about to marry Buckley and has no idea of his good fortune, so Parker is going to use her knowledge to win MacMurray away from Buckley, who is secretly admired by MacMurray's pal, Carlson, a doctor. The marriage is about to transpire when best man Carlson ankles the place and MacMurray races after the doctor to La Jolla, down the coast from Los Angeles. On the way, he and secretary Parker are moored in a fog bank along the shore and hit by a semi-tidal wave. They are also taken in by rotund Martin, who is throwing a tequila party for his Mexican pals and thinks that MacMurray and Parker are on their honeymoon. In the end, Carlson is teamed with Buckley (whom he's wanted from reel one), and MacMurray's fortune is donated to charity, but by that time, Parker loves him for being good old Fred and doesn't need the addition of all that cash to cement her affections. It's a cute romantic-comedy without much taxing of the brain cells. In other words, when you've had too much coffee and you can't fall asleep, this should do it.

p, Bert E. Friedlob; d, George Marshall; w, Ken Englund (based on a story by Robert Harari); ph, Harry Stradling; m, Victor Young; ed, Daniel Mandell; md, Young; art d, Boris Leven; m/l, "I Don't Stand a Ghost of a Chance with You."

Comedy/Romance **(PR:A MPAA:NR)**

MILLIONAIRE KID* ½ (1936) 50m Reliable bw

Betty Compson, Bryant Washburn, Charles Delaney, Lois Wilde, Creighton Hale, Bradley Metcalfe, Eddie Gribbon, Al St. John, Josef Swickard, John Elliott, Earl Dwire, Ed Cassidy, Arthur Thalasso, Roger Williams.

Rich kid turns to crime when his parents get divorced. In this way he stays out of a family feud and away from the possibility of hurting either his mother's or father's feelings. Sheds little realistic light on the problem of divorce, but at least it tries. Once-popular star Compson made this cheapie when her career was in decline.

p&d, Bernard B. Ray; w, Jack Natteford, Blanch Church; ph, William Hyer; ed, Fred Bain.

Drama/Crime **(PR:A MPAA:NR)**

MILLIONAIRE MERRY-GO-ROUND (SEE: PLAYBOY, THE, 1942, Brit.)

MILLIONAIRE PLAYBOY, 1937 (SEE: PARK AVENUE LOGGER, 1937)

MILLIONAIRE PLAYBOY** (1940) 64m RKO bw (GB: GLAMOUR BOY)

Joe Penner (*Joe Zany*), Linda Hayes (*Lois*), Russ Brown (*Bob*), Fritz Feld (*Gorta*), Tom Kennedy (*Murph*), Granville Bates (*Stafford*), Arthur Q. Bryan (*J. B. Zany*), Adele Pearce (*Eleanor*), Diane Hunter (*Hattie*), Mary Milford (*Bertha*), Mantan Moreland (*Bellhop*).

Penner has a stumbling block in his relationships with women every time he kisses a woman he gets a bad case of hiccups. Penner's rich father, Bryan, pays psychologist Brown $5,000 to cure his son. The doctor takes the young man to a summer resort which is filled with stunning young ladies. In the midst of his treatment, Penner discovers that his father wants to buy the resort to build a dam and is using his men, Kennedy and Bates, to try to scare away the guests. The young man comes to the aid of the owner, Hayes, and foils his father's plans.

p, Robert Sisk; d, Leslie Goodwins; w, Bert Granet, Charles E. Roberts (based on a story by Granet); ph, Jack MacKenzie; m, Paul Sawtell; ed, Desmond Marquette; art d, Van Nest Polglase; spec eff, Vernon L. Walker.

Comedy   **(PR:A MPAA:NR)**

MILLIONAIRES IN PRISON*¹/₂   (1940) 63m RKO bw

Lee Tracy (*Nick Burton*), Linda Hayes (*Helen Hewitt*), Raymond Walburn (*Bruce Vander*), Morgan Conway (*James Brent*), Truman Bradley (*Dr. Wm. Collins*), Virginia Vale (*May Thomas*), Cliff Edwards (*Happy*), Paul Guilfoyle (*Ox*), Thurston Hall (*Harold Kellogg*), Chester Clute (*Sidney Keats*), Shemp Howard (*Professor*), Horace MacMahon (*S.O.S.*), Thomas E. Jackson (*Warden Hammond*), Elliott Sullivan (*Brody*), Selmer Jackson (*Dr. Lindsay*), Jack Arnold (*Windsor*).

A comedy about two millionaire stockbrokers (Conway and Clute), sent to prison for setting up a phony stock deal. The prison is run like a country club and headed by kind convict Tracy. The main thrust of the film concerns the prison doctor, Bradley, who is searching for a cure for Malta fever. The doctor finds a cure thanks to four inmates who volunteer to serve as guinea pigs.

p, Howard Benedict; d, Ray McCarey; w, Lynn Root, Frank Fenton (based on a story by Martin Mooney); ph, Harry Wild; m, Roy Webb; ed, Theron B. Warth; art d, Van Nest Polglase; spec eff, Vernon L. Walker.

Comedy   **(PR:A MPAA:NR)**

MILLIONAIRESS, THE***

(1960, Brit.) 90m Anatole de Grunwald, Ltd./FOX c

Sophia Loren (*Epifania Parerga*), Peter Sellers (*Dr. Ahmed el Kabir*), Alastair Sim (*Sagamore*), Vittorio De Sica (*Joe*), Dennis Price (*Dr. Adrian Bond*), Gary Raymond (*Alastair*), Alfie Bass (*Fish Curer*), Miriam Karlin (*Mrs. Joe*), Noel Purcell (*Prof. Merton*), Virginia Vernon (*Polly*), Basil Hoskins (*1st Secretary*), Diana Coupland (*Nurse*), Willoughby Goddard (*President*), Pauline Jameson (*Muriel Pilkington*), Graham Stark (*Butler*), Wally Patch (*Whelk-Seller*), Tempe Adam (*Gloria*), Charles Hill (*Corelli*), Eleanor Summerfield (*Mrs. Willoughby*), Gordon Sterne (*2nd Secretary*), Davy Kaye (*Tommy True*).

A spritely romp for Sellers who really makes this film zig and zag, THE MILLIONAIRESS, a Shaw comedy that opened in 1937 in Vienna, features sultry, Amazonian Loren as the richest woman in the world whose only ambition is to be happily married. She has had an unhappy marriage with Raymond, and her solicitor, Sim, suggests she see a psychiatrist to help straighten out her thinking, sending her to Price who sees dollar signs and makes advances which Loren encourages until Price passes some critical remarks about her father. Loren cannot accept anything critical about her domineering father and suddenly breaks off her relationship with Price. Later, the sexy heiress meets a shy Indian doctor, Sellers, a dedicated physician who is utterly devoted to his clinic for the poor. He appears indifferent to her beauty and wealth and Loren then and there decides that he's the man for her and she will somehow compel him to marry her. She asks that he examine her for any possible illness and by the time he turns around, Loren has stripped to girdle, garters, nylons, and heels, her heaving bosom, displayed as much as discretion will allow, beckoning. Sellers just about has a heart attack as Loren advances upon him. He insists that she dress and that she is too healthy to be sick. Loren intends to help the inadequately equipped clinic; she has all the buildings around the clinic destroyed and begins to build a mammoth medical complex around it, intending for Sellers to run it. He is terrified by the dominating Loren and challenges her to live three months without benefit of her riches and make a living on her own. Loren counters that she will do it if Sellers will triple the income he presently takes in from his clinic. He agrees and they both go about their tasks, except that Sellers has no intention of enacting his share of what he considers a mad plan. Loren succeeds in supporting herself but Sellers loses money instead of making it and then happily admits his failure, telling Loren that since he has done so miserably it is obvious that he is not the man for her and marriage is out of the question. Loren is crushed and announces that she will enter a Tibetan convent. Just at the last moment, Sellers realizes he loves Loren and the two are united. Asquith's direction is brisk and sure and Sellers is a funny marvel to behold as he twists and turns in his little schemes to evade the pursuing Loren. As the love-seeking heiress, Loren displays a rare figure and gives an unusually good performance, as does Purcell, who essays the role of an inebriated physician, one of the most convincing drunks ever seen on screen. Sim is also good as the sly, corrupt solicitor who directs Loren to friend Price, expecting to share in the fortune he will snare if Loren goes to the altar with him. De Sica, long a personal director for Loren, appears briefly and amusingly as a spaghetti-maker who has no interest in having a bank account. Scriptwriter Mankowitz and adapter Aragno played fast and loose with Shaw's original play, changing the idealistic doctor to an Indian physician, obviously to allow for Sellers' pet Indian imitation, and much of Shaw's verbiage was discarded for the sake of situations better filmed in action than spoken. All in all, THE MILLIONAIRESS is amusing and provides some outright laughs thanks to Sellers' buffoon-like caricature.

p, Pierre Rouve; d, Anthony Asquith; w, Wolf Mankowitz, Riccardo Aragno (based on the play by George Bernard Shaw); ph, Jack Hildyard (CinemaScope, Eastmancolor); m, Georges van Parys; ed, Anthony Harvey; prod d, Paul Sheriff; art d, Harry White; set d, Pamela Cornell; cos, Pierre Balmain; makeup, Dave Aylott.

Comedy   **(PR:A MPAA:NR)**

MILLIONS*¹/₂   (1936, Brit.) 70m Wilcox/GFD bw

Gordon Harker (*Otto Forbes*), Frank Pettingell (*Sir Charles Rimmer*), Richard Hearne (*Jimmy Forbes*), Jane Carr (*Jane Rimmer*), Stuart Robertson (*Bastian*), Antony Holles (*Billy Todd*), Ellen Pollock (*Janet Mason*), Jack Hobbs (*Parsons*), Ernest Sefton (*Naseby*), Queenie Leonard.

Versatile British comedian Harker (cop or crook, it never mattered) does his bit here as a millionaire with an unruly son, one-time boy clown Hearne. Passing himself off as a composer, Hearne tries to impress his father, thus getting back in his good graces and ensuring an inheritance. However, Harker's business rival, Pettingell, gets wind of the deception and attempts to use this knowledge to his own advantage. Harker works overtime to keep his son out of jail and his own reputation clean. Laughs are few and far between.

p, Herbert Wilcox; d, Leslie Hiscott; w, Michael Barringer; ph, Frederick A. Young.

Comedy   **(PR:A MPAA:NR)**

MILLIONS IN THE AIR**   (1935) 71m PAR bw

John Howard (*Eddie Warren*), Wendy Barrie (*Marion Keller*), Willie Howard (*Tony Pagano*), George Barbier (*Calvin Keller*), Benny Baker (*Benny*), Eleanore Whitney (*Bubbles*), Robert Cummings (*Jimmy*), Catharine Doucet (*Mrs. Waldo-Walker*), Samuel S. Hinds (*Colonel Edwards*), Halliwell Hobbes (*Theodore*), Dave Chasen (*Dave*), Alden [Stephen] Chase (*Gordon Rogers III*), Bennie Bartlett (*Kid Pianist*), Billy Gilbert (*Nick Popadopolis*), Ralph Spence (*Jason*), Marion Ladd (*Sally*), Irving Bacon (*Mr. Perkins*), Inez Courtney (*Miss Waterbury*), Harry C. Bradley (*Mr. Waldo-Walker*), Russell Hicks (*Davis*), Harry Tenbrook (*Mike*), Paul Fix (*Hank, the Drunk*), Marion Hargrove (*Blonde*), Joan Davis (*Singer*), Adrienne Marden (*Girl*), Frances Robinson (*Blonde Drunk*), Paul Newlan (*Charles Haines, the Mechanic, Voice of Bing Crosby*), Elba Evans (*Mary Flynn*), Barbara Ray (*Gum-Chewing Girl*), Lillianne Leighton (*Fat Lady*), Marina Schubert (*Blonde*), Paddy O'Flynn (*Attendant*), Bess Wade (*Tough Girl*), Harry Semels (*Greek*), Florence Dudley (*Wise-Cracking Girl*), Jack Hill, Al Burke (*Motor Cops*), Sam Ash (*Headwaiter*), Donald Kerr (*Andy*), Jack Raymond (*Kibitzer*), Lillian Drew (*Woman on Street*).

MILLIONS IN THE AIR uses the thin story line of a daughter, Barrie, who tries to get on her father's radio amateur hour. Barrie disguises herself, performs on the show with singing ice-cream salesman John Howard, and together they win the big prize. Comic contributions come from Baker and Chasen, but Willie Howard gets the biggest laughs as the amateur opera singer. Songs include: "Laughing at the Weather," "A Penny in My Pocket," Ralph Rainger, Leo Robin, "You Tell Her—I Stutter," Billy Rose, Cliff Friend, "Love Is Just Around the Corner," Robin, Lewis Gensler. Other songs are by Frederick Hollander, Arthur Johnston, and Sam Coslow.

p, Harold Hurley; d, Ray McCarey; w, Sig Herzig, Jane Storm; ph, Harry Fishbeck; ed, Ellsworth Hoagland.

Musical/Comedy   **(PR:A MPAA:NR)**

MILLIONS LIKE US***   (1943, Brit.) 103m Gainsborough/GFD bw

Eric Portman (*Charlie Forbes*), Patricia Roc (*Celia Crowson*), Gordon Jackson (*Fred Blake*), Anne Crawford (*Jennifer Knowles*), Joy Shelton (*Phyllis Crowson*), Megs Jenkins (*Gwen Price*), Terry Randall (*Annie Earnshaw*), Basil Radford (*Charters*), Naunton Wayne (*Caldicott*), Moore Marriott (*Jim Crowson*), John Boxer (*Tom Crowson*), Valentine Dunn (*Elsie Crowson*), John Salew (*Dr. Gill*), Hilda Davies (*Miss Hodge*), Beatrice Varley (*Miss Wells*), Amy Veness (*Mrs. Blythe*), Irene Handl (*Landlady*), Angela Foulds, Terence Rhodes, Paul Drake, John Wynn, Albert Chevalier, Frank Webster, Courtney Luck, Amy Dalby, Johnnie Schofield, Jack Vyvyan, Arthur Denton, Jonathan Field, Avis Scott, Clifford Cobbe, Grace Allardyce, Barry Steele, Gordon Edwards, Brenda Bruce, Stanley Paskin, Bertha Willmott, John Slater, Hugh Cross, Alan Haines, George Hirste.

Roc is an aircraft factory worker during WW II who falls in love with and marries air gunner Jackson. Though Jackson is killed in action, the film never becomes melodramatic. Everything is staged and acted so simply and to the point that the action seems realistic, perhaps because the film was shot at the height of the war when everyone involved in the production was directly connected to the conflict raging around them in a way their American counterparts were not. The film was reissued in 1947.

p, Edward Black; d&w, Frank Launder, Sidney Gilliat; ph, Jack Cox, Roy Fogwell.

Drama   **(PR:A MPAA:NR)**

MILLS OF THE GODS*¹/₂   (1935) 67m COL bw

May Robson (*Mary Hastings*), Fay Wray (*Jean*), Victor Jory (*Jim Devlin*), Raymond Walburn (*Willard*), James Blakely (*Alex*), Josephine Whittell (*Henrietta*), Mayo Methot (*Sarah*), Albert Conti, Samuel S. Hinds, Willard Robertson, Edward Van Sloan, Frank Reicher, Fredrik Vogeding, Edward Keane.

Robson has taken over the family business after her husband has died. She is getting on in years and would like to turn the company over to her children, but none of them is responsible enough. Instead she turns the plant over to a committee of executives, just before the stock market crashes in 1929. Robson's company is forced to work at only 10% of capacity and the mother pleads with her children to help her out, but they won't put a cent into the company. The son starts a riot among the workers in which Robson's grandson is killed. Meanwhile, the granddaughter becomes romantically involved with one of the company agitators, and the film ends with a suggestion that the two will marry.

p, Robert North; d, Roy W. McNeill; w, Garret Fort (based on a story by Melville Baker, John S. Kirkland); ph, Allen Seigler; ed, Jack Rawlins.

Drama   **(PR:A MPAA:NR)**

MILOSC DWUDZIESTOLATKOW

(SEE: LOVE AT TWENTY, 1963, Fr./Ital./Jap./Pol./Ger.)

MIMI** (1935, Brit.) 98m Alliance/First Division bw

Douglas Fairbanks, Jr. *(Rodolphe)*, Gertrude Lawrence *(Mimi)*, Diana Napier *(Mme. Sidonie)*, Harold Warrender *(Marcel)*, Carol Goodner *(Musette)*, Richard Bird *(Colline)*, Martin Walker *(Schaunard)*, Austin Trevor *(Lamotte)*, Lawrence Hanray *(Barbemouche)*, Paul Graetz *(Durand)*, Jack Raine *(Duke)*.

Fairbanks is a playwright struggling to create a salable play and Lawrence is a poor waif who becomes an inspiration for him. They fall in love, and begin planning a life together. Fairbanks writes a winning play, but then Lawrence falls ill. She dies shortly after Fairbanks becomes successful. Loosely based on the novel *La Vie de Boheme* by Henri Murger.

p, Walter C. Mycroft; d, Paul L. Stein; w, Clifford Grey, Paul Merzbach, Denis Waldock, Jack Davies, Jr. (based on the novel *La Vie de Boheme* by Henri Murger); ph, Jack Cox; m, G. H. Clutsam, Giacomo Puccini; ed, Leslie Norman.

Drama (PR:A MPAA:NR)

MIN AND BILL**** (1930) 66m MGM bw

Marie Dressler *(Min Divot)*, Wallace Beery *(Bill)*, Dorothy Jordan *(Nancy Smith)*, Marjorie Rambeau *(Bella Pringle)*, Donald Dillaway *(Dick Cameron)*, DeWitt Jennings *(Groot)*, Russell Hopton *(Alec Johnson)*, Frank McGlynn *(Mr. Southard)*, Greta Gould *(Mrs. Southard)*, Jack Pennick *(Merchant Seaman)*, Hank Bell *(Sailor)*, Henry Roquemore *(Bella's Stateroom Lover)*, Miss Vanessi *(Woman)*.

One of the most unlikely romantic duos to ever stroll across a screen was the pairing of 62-year-old Marie Dressler and big-bellied 55-year-old Wallace Beery. And yet they were such a lovable couple that they came back in a sequel to this three years later, TUGBOAT ANNIE, and played in DINNER AT EIGHT that same year, but not as husband and wife. Dressler won an Oscar for her role in MIN AND BILL over such sexpots as Marlene Dietrich for MOROCCO, Irene Dunne for the first CIMARRON, Ann Harding in HOLIDAY, and Norma Shearer for her work in A FREE SOUL. Shearer had won the year before for THE DIVORCEE and presented Dressler with the statuette. Although MIN AND BILL was a drama and even had a slightly heart-tugging plot, what most viewers recall are the hilarious comedy sequences and the noisy relationship between Dressler and Beery. Dressler is the rough-and-tumble owner of a cheap waterfront hotel on the California coast. Beery is the local fisherman who is the object of her affections when she isn't doting on Jordan, a sweet young girl whose mother, Rambeau, deserted her several years ago. Dressler works Jordan very hard, minces no words with the girl and treats her roughly, but Jordan loves Dressler and realizes that the lady is all bluster and is the only person who has ever cared that deeply about her. The truant officers want Jordan out of there and living in a better environment as well as going to school regularly. Furthermore, the local Prohibition officers have been observing the cafe and may soon close it up. Jordan is sent to live with the school's principal, McGlynn, and his wife, Gould. Dressler gives her up reluctantly and it's a tearful scene because Jordan would much prefer to stay with Dressler. Rambeau, a drunken slut, returns. She is Jordan's mother and, until now, has wanted nothing to do with her daughter and had left her in Dressler's hands. Dressler talks Rambeau into going to San Francisco and staying away from this area, as it's going to be better for Jordan if she doesn't see her mother or even know the woman is alive. Dressler scrapes up some money, takes Jordan out of the principal's home and sends her to an exclusive boarding school where Jordan meets Dillaway (making his film debut in this movie) and they fall in love. Soon enough, Jordan and Dillaway are planning to be married and, as Dillaway is from a very rich family, this is a most advantageous wedding for Jordan. He doesn't care a whit about her history; all he does is love her madly. Coincidence rears its head when Jordan comes back to the waterfront hotel on the same boat as Rambeau, who is caught in a compromising position with a man in her room, Roquemore. Upon arriving, Rambeau learns of Jordan's good luck in snaring a wealthy fella, and she tells Dressler that she wants her share of the booty and intends to blackmail whomever she can blackmail in order to get some money. Dressler and Rambeau get into an argument that leads to violence. Rambeau burns Dressler's face with a hot iron and Dressler pulls a rod and drills the lady on the spot. Bell, a sailor who dislikes Dressler, finks to the cops, and Dressler is taken by the local police as Jordan and Dillaway sail off on their honeymoon. Dressler had been a huge star in the silent era, but her career waned until she made a triumphant return in ANNA CHRISTIE earlier that year. Then came MIN AND BILL and she was to spend her last years as the biggest star at the biggest studio, MGM. She was best friends with screenwriter Marion, who was married to director Hill. There was a foreign version made but Dressler and the others did not appear in it. She died in 1934. Six years later the studio attempted another sequel, TUGBOAT ANNIE RIDES AGAIN, and used the woman whom Annie had shot in the first version, Marjorie Rambeau. That same year, Rambeau won an Oscar nomination as Best Supporting Actress for PRIMROSE PATH.

d, George Hill; w, Frances Marion, Marion Jackson (based on the novel *Dark Star* by Lorna Moon); ph, Harold Wenstrom; ed, Basil Wrangell; art d, Cedric Gibbons.

Drama/Comedy (PR:A MPAA:NR)

MIN VAN BALTHAZAR (SEE: AU HASARD, BALTHAZAR, 1970, Fr.)

MINAMI NO SHIMA NI YUKI GA FURA
(SEE: SNOW IN THE SOUTH SEAS, 1963, Jap.)

MIND BENDERS, THE*** (1963, Brit.) 99m Novus/AIP bw

Dirk Bogarde *(Dr. Henry Longman)*, Mary Ure *(Oonagh Longman)*, John Clements *(Maj. Hall)*, Michael Bryant *(Dr. Tate)*, Wendy Craig *(Annabelle)*, Harold Goldblatt *(Prof. Sharpey)*, Geoffrey Keen *(Calder)*, Terry Palmer *(Norman)*, Norman Bird *(Aubrey)*, Roger Delgado *(Dr. Jean Bonvoulois)*, Edward Fox *(Stewart)*, Terence Alexander *(Coach)*, Georgina Moon *(Persephone)*, Teresa Van Hoorn *(Penny)*, Timothy Beaton *(Paul)*, Christopher Ellis *(Peers)*, Edward Palmer *(Porter)*, Elizabeth Counsell *(Girl Student on Station)*, Anthony Singleton *(Boy Student on Station)*, Pauline Winter *(Mother)*, Philip Ray *(Father)*, Rene Setan *(1st Indian Student)*, Ashik Devello *(2nd Indian Student)*, Robin Hawdon *(Student in Oxford)*, Terence Edmond *(1st Student at Party)*, Ian Dewar *(Crowd Ringleader)*, Saggy *(The Dog)*.

A strange movie that leaves a deeper impression than one might think it should, due to the originality of the plot and the tense direction. It is the direct predecessor of ALTERED STATES, a picture that screenwriter Paddy Chayefsky took his name off after seeing the excesses of director Ken Russell. In this film, director Dearden was not as excessive and the result is a frighteningly believable treatment of a science-fiction idea. Bogarde is a young scientist seeking to clear the name of his colleague, Goldblatt, who commits suicide early in the film. Because a briefcase with 1000 pounds was found near Goldblatt's body (he'd thrown himself under a train at Oxford Station), it is assumed that he was doing it out of guilt for having betrayed the British government, for which he worked as a research professor in the very specific field of sensory deprivation. Bogarde is Goldblatt's friend and contends that it was the pressure of the work that caused the man to kill himself, not real or even imagined guilt at having betrayed his Queen and Country. The security man on the case, Clements, shows Goldblatt's boss, Keen, some dubious evidence of the dead man's guilt, then goes to Bogarde and wonders what he has to say in defense of his former pal. Bogarde thinks that Goldblatt was a patriot and if he did give away any secrets, it was not voluntary, rather, it was because he was brainwashed. Clements doubts the reality of brainwashing and Bogarde says it is a fact and decides to demonstrate the techniques. Bogarde claims that if a man is placed in a water-filled tank of a certain temperature, he will be stripped of his senses and fair game for any psychological attacks. Bogarde gets into the tank for many hours and comes out of it on the brink of a nervous breakdown. Bogarde is madly in love with his wife, Ure, and his aide, Bryant, seeks to show Clements that even that kind of love can be undermined by these techniques. They tape the session but Clements is still unconvinced that it worked. As time passes, Ure tells Bogarde that she is pregnant and his reaction is, to say the least, diffident, which is hardly the way one would think he'd respond. Now Bogarde begins cavorting around the college area with Craig, a local tramp and that is, again, an uncommon manner of behavior for a man of Bogarde's sensibilities. Clements now realizes that Bogarde's mind has been bent by the experiment of a few months before and tries to convince Bogarde of what happened (Bogarde can't recall it) by playing him the tape recording, but Bogarde remains indifferent and leaves the area with Craig to go live on her houseboat. When Ure, who is near the end of her pregnancy, falls and must be prepared for the start of early labor, Bogarde is there and helps with the baby's delivery. It is this act which brings him back to his senses and the picture ends happily as Bogarde is, once again, whole. Bogarde is excellent and his scenes with the prying Clements are particularly good examples of cat versus mouse. The locations at Oxford are a bit stilted, as is much of the dialog, but the photography and the sincerity of the players make this a better bet than ALTERED STATES as an example of the brainwashing techniques. The same sort of thing was briefly seen in THE IPCRESS FILE, two years after this. In a small role, note Edward Fox, before he became famous. Goldblatt, a much-underused actor, is one of the famed Abbey Players of Ireland. The baby's birth sequence is so graphic that children (or adults) with weak stomachs must be warned that it comes near the end of the film and may upset some dinners.

p, Michael Relph; d, Basil Dearden; w, James Kennaway; ph, Denys Coop; m, Georges Auric; ed, John D. Guthridge; md, Muir Mathieson; art d, James Morahan; cos, Anthony Mendleson; makeup, Harry Frampton.

Science Fiction Drama (PR:C-O MPAA:NR)

MIND OF MR. REEDER, THE
(SEE: MYSTERIOUS MR. REEDER, THE, 1939, Brit.)

MIND OF MR. SOAMES, THE*** (1970, Brit.) 97m Amicus/COL c

Terence Stamp *(John Soames)*, Robert Vaughn *(Dr. Michael Bergen)*, Nigel Davenport *(Dr. Maitland)*, Donal Donnelly *(Dr. Joe Allen)*, Christian Roberts *(Thomas Fleming)*, Vickery Turner *(Naomi)*, Scott Forbes *(Richard Bannerman)*, Judy Parfitt *(Jenny Bannerman)*, Norman Jones *(Davis)*, Dan Jackson *(Nicholls)*, Joe McPartland *(Inspector Moore)*, Pamela Moseiwitsch *(Girl on Train)*, Eric Brooks *(TV Floor Manager)*, Billy Cornelius *(Sgt. Clifford)*, Jon Croft *(Guard)*, Esmond Webb *(Ticket Seller)*, Bill Pilkington *(Pub Owner)*, Kate Bimchy *(Barmaid)*, Joe Gladwin *(Old Man in Car)*, Tony Caunter *(Schoolteacher)*.

Stamp is a 30-year-old man who has been in a coma since birth. American neurosurgeon Vaughan brings him to consciousness and Davenport begins to put the man-child through an accelerated education program. Stamp becomes a media sensation when a TV crew tapes his progress for a television special. Vaughan and Davenport clash over the educational technique, with Davenport feeling a program of harsh discipline to be the most beneficial, while the U.S. surgeon wants Stamp to be brought up as a baby with all the love one needs to grow. Stamp runs away and, because of his childlike manner finds the outside world hostile. This pushes Stamp to violent behavior and he kills Vaughan while the television cameras are running. Similar to the 1968 film CHARLY without the sentimentality.

p, Max Rosenberg, Milton Subotsky; d, Alan Cooke; w, John Hale, Edward Simpson (based on the novel by Charles Eric Maine); ph, Billy Williams (Technicolor); m, Michael Dress; ed, Bill Blunden; md, Dress; prod d, Bill Constable; art d, Don Mingaye; set d, Andrew Low; makeup, Jill Carpenter.

Science Fiction (PR:A MPAA:GP)

MIND READER, THE*½ (1933) 69m FN bw

Warren William *(Chandra Chandler)*, Constance Cummings *(Sylvia)*, Allen Jenkins *(Frank)*, Donald Dillaway *(Jack)*, Mayo Methot *(Sonny)*, Clarence Muse *(Sam)*, Natalie Moorhead *(Mrs. Austin)*, Clara Blandick *(Auntie)*, Harry Beresford *(Blaney)*, Harry Stubbs *(Thompson)*, Robert Greig *(Swami)*, Earle Foxe *(Don)*, Ruthelma Stevens *(Ann)*.

William is an unsuccessful carnival grifter who becomes a phony clairvoyant, a ruse that works out better for him thanks to the help of Jenkins and Muse. The fake mind reader marries Cummings, who thinks William's act is authentic. When she finds out the truth, William goes straight and tries his hand as a door-to-door salesman. As this doesn't pay too well, William again joins up with Jenkins in a scheme to tip off society folks when their mates are cheating on them. After the death of an irate husband, William is sent to jail, but Cummings promises to wait for him.

p, Hal Wallis; d, Roy Del Ruth; w, Wilson Mizner, Robert Lord (based on a play by Vivian Cosby); ph, Sol Polito; ed, James Gibbons.

Drama   **(PR:A   MPAA:NR)**

MIND SNATCHERS, THE   (SEE: HAPPINESS CAGE, THE, 1972)

MIND YOUR OWN BUSINESS*½   (1937) 76m PAR bw

Charlie Ruggles (Orville), Alice Brady (Melba), Lyle Talbot (Crane), Benny Baker (Sparrow), Jack LaRue (Cruger), William Demarest (Droopy), Frankie Darro (Bob), Robert Baldwin (Jeeper), Lloyd Crane [Jon Hall], Horace Stewart, Gene Lockhart, Charles C. Wilson, William B. Davidson, Paul Harvey, Duke York, Theodore Von Eltz, David Sharpe, Los Angeles Troop No. 107, Boy Scouts of America.

Ruggles is a Boy Scout master with a radio gossip show. When he predicts the murder of a politician minutes before it happens, problems arise quickly. First the district attorney has him arrested, and then he's kidnaped by the gangsters who killed the man. To the rescue comes Ruggles' Boy Scouts who take care of the gangster and save their leader.

p, Emanuel Cohen; d, Norman McLeod; w, Dore Schary (based on a story by John Francis Larkin); ph, Robert Pittack; ed, George McGuire; md, George Stoll.

Comedy   **(PR:A   MPAA:NR)**

MINDWARP: AN INFINITY OF TERROR*   (SEE: GALAXY OF TERROR)

MINE OWN EXECUTIONER***

(1948, Brit.) 103m London-Harefield/FOX bw

Burgess Meredith (Felix Milne), Dulcie Gray (Patricia Milne), Kieron Moore (Adam Lucian), Barbara White (Molly Lucian), Christine Norden (Barbara Edge), John Laurie (Dr. James Garsten), Michael Shepley (Peter Edge), Lawrence Hanray (Dr. Lefage), Walter Fitzgerald (Dr. Norris Pile), Martin Miller (Dr. Hans Tautz), Jack Raine (Inspector Pierce), Helen Haye (Lady Maresfield), John Stuart (Dr. John Hayling), Edgar Norfolk (Sir George Freethorne), Clive Morton (Robert Paston), Joss Ambler (Julian Briant), Ronald Simpson (Mr. Grandison), Gwynne Whitby (Miss English), Malcolm Dalmayne (Charlie Oakes), Michael Hordern.

A disturbing but powerful film, Meredith gives a virtuoso performance in MINE OWN EXECUTIONER as a psychiatrist who takes on too much without enough background information and the results are disastrous. Meredith accepts as a patient ex-RAF pilot Moore, who has suffered terribly in a jungle crash in Burma and has spent years as an inmate in a Japanese prison camp. He has undergone unspeakable torture and has become a total schizophrenic, one who has already abused his wife, White, threatening to kill her. Meredith applies his psychology with intensive treatments, unraveling the layers of Moore's mind, as it were. But when he begins to slacken his psychological application, Moore becomes more and more irresponsible, beginning a senseless affair with a sexy married woman, Norden, and later murdering his wife. Meredith learns that his patient has taken refuge on the ledge of a towering building and he goes to the spot, crawling out on the ledge and bravely trying to talk Moore back inside. He loses the argument, with Moore taking a suicide dive. At a later inquest Meredith is pilloried as a malpracticing physician but his reputation is saved by a medical colleague, Laurie, and his loyal wife, Gray, helps Meredith to maintain his own sanity during the trying time. Omitted from the script is the fact that Meredith is playing the part of a third-year medical student who dropped out of school and became a self-styled psychiatrist, lacking the proper credentials and experience to undertake his hazardous treatment of Moore, background that would have clarified the story for the viewer. Kimmins' direction is adroit and well paced and Meredith and Moore carry the film from one nightmare scene to another with great talent and no little conviction. An oddball film, MINE OWN EXECUTIONER is nevertheless absorbing.

p, Anthony Kimmins, Jack Kitchin; d, Kimmins; w, Nigel Balchin (based on his novel); ph, Wilkie Cooper; m, Benjamin Frankel; ed, Richard Best; prod d, Kenneth Horne; md, Dr. Hubert Clifford; art d, William C. Andrews; set d, Anne Head; cos, Alan Haines; spec eff, W. Percy Day; makeup, John O'Gorman.

Drama   **(PR:C-O   MPAA:NR)**

MINE WITH THE IRON DOOR, THE**   (1936) 64m Principal/COL bw

Richard Arlen (Bob Harvey), Cecilia Parker (Marta Hill), Henry B. Walthall (David Burton), Stanley Fields (Dempsey), Spencer Charters (Thad Hill), Charles Wilson (Pitkins), Barbara Bedford (Secretary), Horace Murphy (Garage Man).

Arlen is a tenderfoot salesman who heads west to find buried treasure in the famed Mine with the Iron Door. Things become difficult for him when eccentric villain Walthall tries to stop him from digging up the cache. Arlen and Parker fall in love along the way.

p, Sol Lesser; d, David Howard; w, Don Swift, Daniel Jarrett (based on a novel by Harold Bell Wright); ph, Frank B. Good; ed, Arthur Hilton; md, Abe Meyer; art d, Ben Carre, Lewis J. Rachmil.

Western   **(PR:A   MPAA:NR)**

MINESWEEPER**   (1943) 67m PAR bw

Richard Arlen (Lt. Jim Smith), Jean Parker (Mary Smith), Russell Hayden (Elliot), Guinn "Big Boy" Williams (Fixit), Emma Dunn (Moms), Charles D. Brown (Commander), Frank Fenton (Lt. Gilpin), Chick Chandler (Comey Welch), Douglas

Fowley (Lt. Wells), Ralph Sanford (Cox), Billy Nelson (Boatswain Helms), Robert Mitchum (Chuck).

Arlen is a graduate from Annapolis who deserted the Navy because of his gambling habit. When WW II breaks out, he re-enlists under an alias and is assigned to the title vessel. He gives up his life to defuse a new type of enemy mine endangering approaching ships. Another morale-building film made during WW II, which is second rate in every way. Robert Mitchum appears in a small role as a crew member, but was unbilled, and is frequently uncredited for this bit part.

p, William Pine, William Thomas; d, William Berke; w, Edward T. Lowe, Maxwell Shane; ph, Fred Jackman, Jr.; ed, William Ziegler; art d, F. Paul Sylos.

Drama   **(PR:A   MPAA:NR)**

MINI-AFFAIR, THE*   (1968, Brit.) 92m United Screen Arts c

Georgie Fame (Georgie Hart), Rosemary Nicols (Charlotte), John Clive (Joe), Bernard Archard (Sir Basil Grinling), Lucille Soong (Lucille), Rick Dane (Mike Maroon), Julian Curry (Ronnie), Gretchen Regan (Marianne), Madeline Smith (Samantha), Clement Freud (Stephen Catchpole), Totti Truman-Taylor (Aunt Grace), Clive Dunn (Tyson), Roy Kinnear (Fire Extinguisher Salesman), Eric Pohlmann (World Banker), William Rushton (Chancellor of the Exchequer), Irene Handl (Chinese-Restaurant Cook).

Three lonely girls concoct a plan to kidnap their idols—a pop singer, the Minister of Popular Culture, and a disc jockey. At first the abductees try to get away, but grow to like the girls. The deejay escapes and calls the police. The girls, however, persuade him to drop the charges. The finale has the group paired off into three loving couples. A forgettable picture that includes a hit song by the Bee Gees, "Words."

p, Richard A. Herland; d&w, Robert G. Amram (based on an idea by Herland); ph, Derek Waterman (Techniscope, Technicolor); m, The Bee Gees; ed, John Ireland; md, Bill Shepherd; art d, Edwin Florence; m/l, "The Mini-Affair," Howard Blaikley, "Words," Barry Gibb, Maurice Gibb, Robin Gibb (sung by Georgie Fame); makeup, Renee Claff.

Romantic Comedy   **(PR:A   MPAA:NR)**

MINI-SKIRT MOB, THE*½   (1968) 82m AIP c

Jeremy Slate (Lon), Diane McBain (Shayne), Sherry Jackson (Connie Logan), Patty McCormack (Edie), Ross Hagen (Jeff Logan), Harry Dean Stanton (Spook), Ronnie Rondell (L. G.).

McBain stars as the head of a female biker gang seeking revenge on old boy friend Hagan, who is now newly married to Jackson. The cyclists terrorize the couple on their honeymoon, but only succeed in causing the death of McBain's sister, McCormack. Even more embittered, McBain tries to run over the newlyweds, who attempt to escape on foot. In the ensuing scuffle, McBain falls over a cliff, hanging onto life with only one hand. Jackson holds onto McBain while her husband goes for the police, but the enraged bride decides to deal out her own justice and lets McBain fall to her death.

p&d, Maury Dexter; w, James Gordon White; ph, Arch R. Dalzell (Perfectcolor); m, Les Baxter; ed, Sidney Levin; m/l, "The Mini-Skirt Mob," Valjean Johns, Guy Hemric (sung by The American Revolution, Patty McCormack).

Action   **(PR:O   MPAA:NR)**

MINI WEEKEND   (SEE: TOMCAT, THE, 1968, Brit.)

MINISTRY OF FEAR****   (1945) 84m PAR bw

Ray Milland (Stephen Neale), Marjorie Reynolds (Carla Hilfe), Carl Esmond (Willi Hilfe), Hillary Brooke (Mrs. Bellane), Percy Waram (Inspector Prentice), Dan Duryea (Cost/Travers), Alan Napier (Dr. Forrester), Erskine Sanford (Mr. Rennit), Thomas Louden (Mr. Newland), Aminta Dyne (1st Mrs. Bellaire), Rita Johnson (2nd Mrs. Bellaire), Eustace Wyatt (Blind Man), Mary Field (Miss Penteel), Byron Foulger (Mr. Newby), Lester Matthews (Dr. Morton), Helena Grant (Mrs. Merrick), Connie Leon (Lady Purchaser of Cake), Evelyn Beresford (Fat Lady), Frank Dawson (Vicar), Eric Wilton, Boyd Irwin, Frank Baker, Colin Kenny (Scotland Yard Men), Wilson Benge (Air Raid Warden), Leonard Carey (Porter), Olaf Hytten (Clerk in Tailor Shop), Cyril Delavanti (Railway Ticket Agent), Matthew Boulton (Government Official), David Clyde (English Bobby), Bruce Carruthers (Police Clerk), Clive Morgan, George Broughton (Men in Tailor's Shop), Grayce Hampton (Lady with Floppy Hat), Ottola Nesmith (Woman at Admission Gate), Jessica Newcombe (Cake Booth Lady), Anne Curson (Lady with Children), Hilda Plowright (Maid), Harry Allen (Delivery Man), Frank Leigh, Francis Sayles, Edmond Russell (Men), Arthur Blake (Officer), Edward Fielding (Executive).

Uncertainty and fear of the unknown are the hallmarks of this classic film noir by master director Lang, one that—until the last revelations of the mystery—is guaranteed to puzzle and chill the viewer. Milland gives a spellbinding performance as a man recently released from an insane asylum who finds that the real madness is all around him in the outside world. Milland has been an asylum inmate for two years for ostensibly murdering his wife. She was ill and he brought poison home to perform euthanasia but could not bring himself to go through with it; while his back was turned she took the fatal dose and he was convicted nevertheless. But the terrors of the asylum are nothing compared to the wartime England into which Milland steps. He waits for a train to London and then follows a crowd to a local carnival which is sponsored by a Nazi front organization called "Mothers of the Free Nations." He is mistaken for a Nazi agent and it is arranged for him to win a large cake which he carries back to the depot. As he turns to get onto the train, he hears the ominous sound of a tapping cane and then, through the thick cloud of steam from the train's engines emerges a blind man, Wyatt, who joins Milland in his compartment. Milland offers him a piece of cake which he takes with groping fingers. (The camera shows in close-up the vacant stare of Wyatt but the so-called blind man suddenly focuses, for a brief, chilling moment, on Milland, then resumes his sightless look.) Wyatt begins to crumble the cake in his hands, until it goes to little pieces. He suddenly grabs the cake, leaves the compartment, and runs wildly across a marsh where he is blown to pieces by a bomb planted in the cake. Milland, who has been mechanically chasing the man, stands staring in horror. Once in London, Milland goes to the "Mothers of the Free Nations" organization where he is met by sympathetic Reynolds and Esmond, brother and sister. Esmond takes Milland to see Brooke, one of the sponsors of the carnival where he received the strange, exploding cake to see if she can offer some kind of explanation. Dyne, a medium, who told Milland's fortune at the carnival, is about to hold a seance at this time and Milland is asked to participate. He does but is instantly accused by a so-called spirit voice of killing his wife. Before he can protest, a shot rings out and when the lights go on, another guest, Duryea, is found dead on the floor. Police arrive and accuse Milland of murdering the man. The medium in the room is not really the woman he first met at the fair, although she insists she is. She is Johnson, not Dyne, which will perplex the viewer even further, as it does Milland. Before he can be arrested, Milland escapes. He briefly employs a seedy, middle-aged private detective, Sanford, a weird little man who drinks alcohol out of teacups and puffs on a stubby cigar. The eccentric detective is more trouble than help, especially when he gets himself killed. Fleeing the seance murder, Milland goes to the only person he knows, Reynolds. She takes him to a small London bookshop where the owner agrees to hide him. In return, he asks that Milland deliver a suitcase full of books to Napier, but the hotel room to which he is directed is empty and the phone is dead. The hallway outside is strangely deserted. Milland begins to open the suitcase but his instincts suddenly tell him to leap aside. As he does, the suitcase goes off with a terrific explosion. Milland awakens in a hospital. He hears the creaking of a rocking chair and sees a man from the back all dressed in black. The man, Waram, is a Scotland Yard inspector, and he tells Milland he's wanted for murder. Milland tells him he doesn't know how the man at the seance was shot and Waram tells him he doesn't know what he's talking about, that he's a suspect in the murder of private detective Sanford, adding: "They shouldn't have let you out of that asylum." Now Milland doubts even his memory, as well as the soundness of his own mind. Milland persuades police to go to the marsh where the blind man was blown up and they accompany him to the site, where Milland finds—in a ruined shed in the marsh—some fragments of the cake and inside this a piece of microfilm. Upon examining this, police realize that it shows part of some important minefield charts. Now Milland and the police realize that they are dealing with enemy agents and they soon trace the Nazis to a haberdashery store. Milland and Waram pretend to be fitted for new suits and spot tailor Duryea, the man Milland was accused of murdering at the seance. Duryea goes to a phone and dials a number with a pair of lethal-looking scissors, telling his customer: "I think you'll find that when you've worn it once the shoulders will settle." Next, knowing he is exposed, Duryea goes into a fitting room and drives the scissors into his stomach while standing before three mirrors. The telephone call is traced, however, to Esmond, and Duryea's message becomes clear to police: a suit delivered to Esmond contains microfilm in its lining. Milland gets to Esmond before the police and he struggles with the Nazi agent who is about to kill him when Reynolds, who really loves Milland, shoots her brother. But Nazi agents then attack the pair and drive them up onto the roof where they hide in the darkness. The door leading to the roof is open, but Milland and Reynolds can see nothing but blackness on the stairway. They wait for their own grim ends. All is silence; then some slight movement is heard as the Nazi agents start to approach. There is a blaze of gunfire, then more silence. Suddenly, appearing on the roof are Scotland Yard detectives, not Nazis. Milland and Reynolds are saved. The suspense in this thriller espionage yarn is terrific as Lang, ever the careful craftsman, shows only what is necessary to the confusing plot; the viewer sees only what Milland sees and is as perplexed as the hero. Like the fragments of an intricate crossword puzzle, Lang puts together one piece after another until the riddle is solved, but almost at the cost of Milland's life. The low-key lighting and moody cinematography by Sharp are perfectly suited to the chilling tale. Never before did Lang present such an elaborate structure in any film, using a Kafka-like approach where shadow, silence, and normally pedestrian movements—shown out of context and with an off-key perspective—take on images of the sinister. There is a pervasive, almost doomed atmosphere to the entire film, which the director attempted to relieve with a brief epilog showing Milland and Reynolds driving to their honeymoon in a world bright with sunshine: a countryside at peace, ripe with summer. Reynolds talks about their wedding and mentions a wedding cake. Milland shudders and says: "Cake? No! No cake!" Milland is excellent as the victimized man who endures the tortures of most of the film before he realizes that he's been sane all along. Lang's imprint is everywhere on the film, which remains one of his *film noir* classics. He had accepted the directorial chore of this film before reading the script. He received a call from his agent and, as soon as he learned the film would be based upon Graham Greene's novel, he accepted this assignment. But he did not like the script written by producer Miller and was much pained years later when he viewed the film on TV "where it was cut to pieces."

p, Seton I. Miller; d, Fritz Lang; w, Miller (based on the novel by Graham Greene); ph, Henry Sharp; m, Victor Young; ed, Archie Marshek; art d, Hans Dreier, Hal Pereira; set d, Bert Granger.

Spy Drama **(PR:C MPAA:NR)**

MINIVER STORY, THE** (1950, Brit./U.S.) 104m MGM bw

Greer Garson *(Kay Miniver)*, Walter Pidgeon *(Clem Miniver)*, John Hodiak *(Spike Romway)*, Leo Genn *(Steve Brunswick)*, Cathy O'Donnell *(Judy Miniver)*, Reginald Owen *(Mr. Foley)*, Anthony Bushell *(Dr. Kanesley)*, Richard Gale *(Tom Foley)*, Peter Finch *(Polish Officer)*, William [James] Fox *(Toby Miniver)*, Cicely Paget-Bowman *(Mrs. Kanesley)*, Ann Wilton *(Jeanette)*, Henry Wilcoxon *(Vicar)*, Eliot Makeham *(Mr. Farraday)*, Brian Roper *(Richard)*, Paul Demel *(Jose Antonio Campos)*, Alison Leggatt *(Mrs. Foley)*.

THE MINIVER STORY was too late to be a sequel and not good enough to catch the kind of business at the box office that the original did. There's none of the inspiration of the former; instead, it's been replaced by a dour, glum attitude that only succeeds in causing bottoms to squirm. Garson is again Mrs. Miniver and she is suffering from a never-named fatal disease, one of the famed "Hollywood" ailments that cause actors to waste away for the length of the picture and only show their debilitation by the addition of paler and paler makeup as the movie continues. She has been having a kind of romance with Hodiak, an American colonel stationed in England. The war is over in London and Garson is with Hodiak who declares his love for her, but now that her husband, Pidgeon, is due to come back, she has to put a stop to Hodiak's attitude. The doctor has told Garson that she doesn't have much longer to live, so she is determined to make her remaining days happy ones. Daughter O'Donnell is returning from service in Egypt and son Fox, who had been sheltered in the U.S., is also coming back to England. Garson doesn't tell them of her medical condition. Gale, the boy who used to bring them groceries, is now in love with O'Donnell but she has a crush on middle-aged Genn, a married man. Pidgeon, an architect, sees the devastation of London and, rather than look at it as an opportunity to rebuild, he decides that he might prefer to take another job in Brazil. Garson is determined to straighten out her family's problems before being called by the Grim Reaper, so she visits Genn and persuades him to forego obtaining a divorce in order to marry O'Donnell. She works on his nostalgia and his guilt and, in the end, Genn is convinced that he still loves his mate, something that sends O'Donnell up the wall, as she never thought her mother would interfere in her love life. O'Donnell never wants to talk to Garson again and thinks that her mother "doesn't understand" what real love is, even with a married man. Then Garson reveals a letter written by Hodiak. In it, he states that he is now once again thrilled to be with his wife and that any feelings he may have felt for Garson were real, but they were also, no doubt, influenced by the conditions of war—moments when people grabbed for whatever happiness they could find because they didn't know if the next buzz bomb overhead had their names stenciled on the side. After O'Donnell sees the folly of her ways and decides to waltz into Gale's arms, Garson tells the family of her time clock ticking. Pidgeon is stunned by the news and will now stay in England and ease Garson's final moments. Garson dies on the day when O'Donnell and Gale are married and the film concludes on a totally depressing note (D-Flat, probably). The characterizations were somewhat altered in this sequel. Garson was no longer plucky, she was downright Joan of Arc-ish. Pidgeon went from being a fun-loving Father-Who-Knows-Best to almost a twit. The young son was played by William Fox, who changed his name to James Fox and appeared in many films until he gave up acting in favor of religion in 1973. In MRS. MINIVER, her oldest son was played by Richard Ney, whom Garson married for the four years from 1943 through 1947. Since they were already divorced in 1950, there was no way Ney would get work in this picture. She was only 10 years older than Ney but her superior acting and his youthful appearance made that credibility-stretch work. THE MINIVER STORY would have been better off unfilmed, as the spine of the original story had the war raging around them, people doing things for patriotism, and just about everything being motivated by the conflagration. In this case, the war is over and, with that removed, it denigrates into a very ordinary soap opera. Owen and Wilcoxon reprised their original roles, as did one of the screenwriters, Froeschel.

p, Sidney Franklin; d, H. C. Potter; w, Ronald Millar, George Froeschel (based on characters created by Jan Struther); ph, Joseph Ruttenberg; m, Herbert Stothart, Miklos Rosza; ed, Harold F. Kress, Frank Clarke; md, Muir Mathieson; art d, Alfred Junge; cos, Walter Plunkett, Gaston Malletti; spec eff, Tom Howard.

Drama **(PR:A MPAA:NR)**

MINNESOTA CLAY 1/2**

(1966, Ital./Fr./Span.) 95m Ultra-Jaguar-Franco London/Harlequin c (L'HOMME DU MINNESOTA)

Cameron Mitchell *(Minnesota Clay)*, Georges Riviere *(Fox)*, Ethel Rojo *(Estella)*, Diana Martin *(Nancy)*, Anthony Ross *(Scratchy)*, Fernando Sancho *(Ortiz)*, Alberto Cevenini *(Andy)*, Antonio Casas *(Jonathan)*, Julio Pena *(Lt. Evans)*, Nando Poggi *(Tubbs)*, Joe Kamel *(Millicet)*, Gino Pernice, Madelaine Deheco, Jose Manuel Martin, Patricia del Frate.

The first western by the director of DJANGO, made during the same time as Sergio Leone's A FISTFUL OF DOLLARS. Corbucci's style is more in keeping with traditional American westerns, which varies greatly from Leone's approach. Mitchell plays a gunfighter who is imprisoned for a crime he didn't commit and he escapes from jail to seek revenge. He goes to a Mexican village where Riviere, the man who withheld evidence from Mitchell's trial, is living. Even though he's going blind, Mitchell guns down almost every outlaw in town. Riviere, the man Mitchell really wants, is the last left to die. Mitchell, now completely blind, leads Riviere down to a dark basement and uses sound to defeat him in a gunfight.

p, Danilo Marciani; d, Sergio Corbucci; w, Corbucci, Adriano Bolzoni (based on a story by Bolzoni); ph, Jose Fernandez Aguayo (Eastmancolor); m, Piero Piccioni; ed, Franco Fraticelli; art d, Carlo Simi; set d, Francisco Canet.

Western **(PR:C MPAA:NR)**

MINNIE AND MOSKOWITZ** (1971) 114m UNIV c

Gena Rowlands *(Minnie Moore)*, Seymour Cassel *(Seymour Moskowitz)*, Val Avery *(Zelmo Swift)*, Tom Carey *(Morgan Morgan)*, Katherine Cassavetes *(Sheba Moskowitz)*, Elizabeth Deering *(Girl)*, Elsie Adams *(Florence)*, Lady Rowlands *(Georgia Moore)*, Holly Near *(Irish)*, Judith Roberts *(Wife)*, Jack Danskin *(Dick Henderson)*, Eleanor Zee *(Mrs. Grass)*, Sean Joyce *(Ned)*, David Rowlands *(Minister)*, John Cassavetes *(Jim)*, Kathleen O'Malley, Jimmy Joyce, Santos Morales, Chuck Wells.

This is the sixth of Cassavetes's home movies that have found distribution by some strange quirk of fate. It is also the most nepotistic of his works, with his wife in the lead, his mother as the male lead's mother, his mother-in-law as the female lead's mother, his brother-in-law as the minister, his three children in a party sequence, two of his best pals, Avery and Cassel, in important roles, plus Cassel's wife, Deering, and mother-in-law, Ames, as well as the two Cassel kids. Oddly enough, despite all of that blatant pork-barreling, the picture still manages to be . . . only adequate. It's a two person play that matches (or mismatches) a pair of characters with backgrounds as different as Fiddler on The Roof Tevye from Auntie Mame. Cassavetes admits that he was greatly influenced by Frank Capra, but this looks more like overblown Paul Mazursky. Rowlands is a former prom-queen about to turn 40. She's been having an affair with married man Cassavetes and wants out. Meanwhile, thirtyish Cassel, an aging hippy, is giving up his job parking cars in New York and moving to Los Angeles and a job parking cars. He actually likes the work because he enjoys automobiles and likes driving the various models he comes into contact with on a daily basis. He also finds L.A. more amenable to his lifestyle than the harshness of New York City. Rowlands is a lonely woman who spends whatever time she can with her married boy friend and the rest of her spare moments with Ames, her best pal and movie-going companion. Cassavetes is cruel to Rowlands but she puts up with it, desperate for some male companionship, until Cassavetes's wife threatens suicide and he has to call off the affair. They meet for a last time at a local museum. (He has brought his two kids with him. They are there at the request of Cassavetes's wife and will corroborate the cessation of the affair.) That done, Rowlands accepts a blind date with Avery, a noisy boor who never once notices Rowland's delicate condition. They have a bite of lunch at a restaurant and Avery proposes marriage. She sees that this guy is nuts and wants to get away. In the parking lot, Avery begins to harass Rowlands but this is espied by Cassel who comes to her rescue. He gets Avery out of the picture, then gets Rowlands into his pickup truck and rides away with her. In less than a minute, Cassel decides that he is madly in love with Rowlands. She thinks there must be something weird in the air, as she has now had two enamored suitors within minutes. She leaps out of the pickup truck and Cassel follows her until she agrees to go on a date with him. What the hell, she has nothing to lose, her old beau has gone back to his wife, what the hell? The two of them, as different as chalk from cheese, have a lengthy series of scenes as they go from hotdog stand to hotdog stand and he begins to break down her resolve. These scenes are touching, sometimes funny, and usually violent because it seems that Cassel is a "victim" who is always being beaten up. They plan a wedding over the objections of everyone (most of all Cassel's mother, wonderfully played by Cassavetes's mother, who can't believe that someone actually wants to marry her son and not even pregnant). At the wedding, minister David Rowlands forgets his lines but it doesn't make a difference to Cassel and Rowlands, who have made up their minds to live happily ever after. Cassavetes moves away from his usual somber and sour mood with this "kitchen sink" comedy, but just about every role was overwritten and overplayed. As is usually the case in Cassavetes films, it's hard to tell where the script ends and the improvising on a theme begins. Cassel is a very good actor and always believable. It's a shame that he only seems to be highlighted in films by Cassavetes, such as FACES (Best Supporting Actor Nomination) and THE KILLING OF A CHINESE BOOKIE. The rest of his career is a mystery.

p, Al Ruban; d&w, John Cassavetes; ph, Arthur J. Ornitz, Alric Edens, Michael Margulies (Technicolor); ed, Robert Heffernan, Fred Knudtson; md, Bo Harwood; cos, Helen Colvig.

Drama/Comedy   **(PR:C   MPAA:PG)**

MINOTAUR, 1955   (SEE: LAND OF THE MINOTAUR, 1955)

MINOTAUR, THE*
(1961, Ital.) 96m UA c (TESEO CONRO IL MINOTAURO) (AKA: THE MINOTAUR-THE WILD BEAST OF CRETE; THESEUS AGAINST THE MINOTAUR; THE WARLORD OF CRETE)

Bob Mathias (Theseus, Prince of Athens), Rosanna Schiaffino (Ariane/Phaedra), Alberto Lupo (Chrysone), Rick Battaglia (Demetrius), Nico Pepe (Gerione), Carlo Tamerlani (King Minos), Nerio Bernardi (King Egeo [Aegeus]), Tina Lattanzi (Queen Pasiphae), Paul Muller (Doctor), Tiziana Casetti (Elea), Alberto Plebani (Xanto), Susanne Loret (Amphitrite), Milo Malagoli (The Minotaur), Adriano Micantoni (Sunis), Amedeo Trilli (Ctesiphorus), Andrea Scott (Alcmene), Vittorio Vaser (Timon), Vladimiro Picciafuochi (Jailer).

Another exploitative Greek mythology film from Italy, with Olympic decathlon gold-medal winner Bob Mathias in the starring role. Mathias as Prince Theseus saves Schiaffino from being sacrificed to the Minotaur, a half-man, half-bull creature. The Prince, to keep the beast happy, throws Schiaffino's wicked sister (also played by Schiaffino) into the Minotaur's labyrinth.

p, Giorgio Agliani, Dino Mordini, Rudolphe Solmsen; d, Silvio Amadio; w, Sandro Continenza, Gian Paolo Callegari, Daniel Mainwaring; ph, Aldo Giordani (Totalscope, Technicolor); m, Carlo Rustichelli; ed, Nella Nannuzzi; art d, Piero Poletto; cos, Perruzzi; ch, Adriano Vitale.

Action   **(PR:A   MPAA:NR)**

MINOTAUR, 1976   (SEE: LAND OF THE MINOTAUR, 1976, Gr.)

MINOTAUR, WILD BEAST OF CRETE
                          (SEE: MINOTAUR, THE, 1961, Ital.)

MINSTREL BOY, THE*   (1937, Brit.) 79m Dreadnought/BUT bw

Fred Conyngham (Mike), Chili [Dorothy] Bouchier (Dee Dawn), Lucille Lisle (Angela), Kenneth Buckley (Austin Ravensbourne), Basil Langton (Ed), Marjorie Chard (Lady Ravensbourne), Mabel Twemlow (Lady Pont), Granville Darling (Pat), Ronald Walters, Pat Kavanagh, Dorothy Vernon, Xenia and Boyer.

Poor attempt to create a musical features Lisle in a sizzling romance when she runs off with musician Conyngham (Britain's B-picture Fred Astaire) to get away from her overbearing fiance. She is all set on leaving her new beau as well when she thinks he's got a thing going with hot brunette singer Bouchier. But Lisle's fears prove to be nothing more than an overworked imagination, paving the way for a drearily sentimental ending in which she rescues Conyngham from certain death. Dreary offering from former child actress Wood [Joan Morgan] the scenarist, who, incidentally, is the daughter of the producer.

p&d, Sydney Morgan; w, Joan Wentworth Wood [Morgan].

Musical/Drama   **(PR:A   MPAA:NR)**

MINSTREL MAN*   (1944) 69m PRC bw

Benny Fields (Dixie Boy Johnson), Gladys George (Mae White), Alan Dinehart (Lew Dunn), Roscoe Karns (Lasses White), Judy Clark (Caroline, Age 16), Gloria Petroff (Caroline, Age 5), Molly Lamont (Caroline's Mother), Jerome Carson (Bill Evans), John Raitt (John Raitt), Eddie Kane (Booking Agent), Lee White, The Ernestos.

Fields is a minstrel singer who gives his daughter to another couple (George and Karns) to raise when his wife (Lamont) dies in childbirth. Meanwhile, Fields continues on tour with his career. When his daughter, Clark, grows up she becomes a performer. Fields returns home and joins his daughter onstage to sing a tune he wrote. Songs include, "Remember Me to Carolina" (Paul Francis, Webster, Harry Revel), "My Melancholy Baby" (George A. Norton, Ernie Burnett), "Cindy," "I Don't Care if the World Knows About It," "Shakin' Hands With the Sun," and "The Bamboo Cane," (Webster, Revel).

p, Leon Fromkess; d, Joseph H. Lewis; w, Irwin Franklin, Pierre Gendron (based on a story by Martin Mooney, Raymond L. Schrock); ph, Marcel Le Picard; m, Ferde Grofe; ed, Carl Pierson; md, Leo Erdody; prod d, Edgar G. Ulmer; art d, Paul Palmentola; ch, Johnny Boyle.

Musical   **Cas.**   **(PR:A   MPAA:NR)**

MINUTE TO PRAY, A SECOND TO DIE, A*
(1968, Ital.) 103m Documento-Selmur/Cinerama c (UN MINUTO PER PREGARE, UN ISTANTE PER MORIRE; AKA: DEAD OR ALIVE)

Alex Cord (Clay McCord), Arthur Kennedy (Roy Colby), Robert Ryan (Gov. Lem Carter), Nicoletta Machiavelli (Laurinda), Mario Brega (Kraut), Renato Romano (Cheap Charley), Gian Pier Albertini (Fred Duskin), Daniel Martin (Father Santana), Enzo Fiermonte (Dr. Chase), Pedro Canalejas (Seminole), Franco Lantieri (Butler), Osiride Pevarelli (Fuzzy), Jose Manuel Martin (El Bailarin), Antonio Molino Rojo (Sein), Rosita Palomar (Ruby), Paco Sanz (Barber), Paolo Magalotti (Sid), Massimo Sarchielli (Zack), Ottaviano Dell'Acqua (Clay, as a Boy), Alberto Del'Acqua (Ruby's Son), Antonio Vico (Jonas), Aldo Sambrell (Jesus Maria), Ivan Scratuglia, Silla Bettini.

McCord is an 1870s gunslinger who has a $10,000 bounty on his head. He goes to the town of Escondido which is full of outlaws waiting for the governor (Ryan) to grant them amnesty. McCord has several run-ins with the town crime boss, Brega. After he is forced to kill Brega's henchmen, he rides to Tuscona to receive amnesty from the governor. In the American version, the film ends there; in the foreign version, McCord is killed by bounty hunters who don't know about his amnesty.

p, Albert Band; d, Franco Giraldi; w, Ugo Liberatore, Louis Garfinkle (based on a story by Band and Liberatore); ph, Aiace Parolin (Eastmancolor); m, Carlo Rustichelli; ed, Alberto Gillitti; md, Bruno Nicolai; art d, Massimiliano Capriccioli; set d, Guido Josia; cos, Luciana Fortini; spec eff, Erasmo Bacciucchi, Giovanni Corridoni; makeup, Michele Trimarchi.

Western   **(PR:C   MPAA:R)**

MINX, THE* 1/2   (1969) 84m Jara/Cambist c

Jan Sterling (Louise Baxter), Robert Rodan (Henry Baxter), Shirley Parker (Terry), Adrienne Jalbert (Nicole), Robbie Heywood (Susan), Michael Beirne (John Lawson), Ned Cary (Benjamin Thayer), Allan Dellay (Walter Harris), Philip Faversham (Charles Brennan), William Gleason (Sam Burke), Russell Baker (Oppenheimer), Teal Traina (Himself), The Cyrkle.

Rodan is the president of a large company who tries to take over another company, Eastern Devices, by using Parker, Jalbert, and Heywood to blackmail two board members from that company. He obtains compromising pictures of the board members, but private detective Gleason, hired by Rodan's wife (Sterling) to blackmail Rodan, foils the scheme. The film was finished a year earlier in 1967, but couldn't get a distributor until 10 minutes of sexually explicit scenes were edited in.

p, Herbert Jaffey, Raymond Jacobs; d, Jacobs; w, Jacobs, Jaffey; ph, Victor Petrashevic; m, Tom Dawes, Don Dannemann; ed, Larry Marinelli; spec eff, Jacobs.

Drama   **(PR:O   MPAA:R)**

MIO FIGILIO NERONE   (SEE: NERO'S MISTRESS, 1962, Fr./Ital.)

MIR VKHODYASHCHEMU
                    (SEE: PEACE TO HIM WHO ENTERS, 1963, USSR)

MIRACLE, THE, 1948   (SEE: WAYS OF LOVE, 1948, Ital.)

MIRACLE, THE*   (1959) 121m WB c

Carroll Baker (Teresa), Roger Moore (Capt. Michael Stuart), Walter Slezak (Flaco), Vittorio Gassman (Guido), Katina Paxinou (La Roca), Dennis King (Casimir), Gustavo Rojo (Cordoba), Isobel Elsom (Reverend Mother), Carlos Rivas (Carlitos), Torin Thatcher (Duke of Wellington), Elspeth March (Sister Dominica), Daria Massey (Gata), Lester Matthews (Capt. John Bolting).

Baker plays a nun in a Spanish convent who falls in love with Moore, a soldier battling the Napoleonic army in Spain. When Baker leaves the convent to pursue Moore, a statue of the Virgin Mary comes to life, assuming the position of the absent nun. Believing Moore to be dead, Baker marries gypsy Gassman, who is killed by his jealous brother. Baker then becomes involved with bullfighter Rojo, who is killed in the bull ring. She finally meets Moore again just prior to the battle of Waterloo, but decides to return to her convent. The statue then returns to its place on the pedestal. Supposedly a religious theme, the story fails to delve deeply into spiritual experiences, or anything religious for that matter. Baker's performance lacks any warmth needed for this role, while the men she plays opposite depict stereotypical macho types. The film's highpoint is the Technicolor photography.

p, Hanry Blanke; d, Irving Rapper; w, Frank Butler (based on the play by Karl Vollmoeller); ph, Ernest Haller (Technirama, Technicolor); m, Elmer Bernstein; ed, Frank Bracht; md, Ray Heindorf; art d, Hans Peters; cos, Marjorie Best.

Drama **(PR:A MPAA:NR)**

MIRACLE CAN HAPPEN, A (SEE: ON OUR MERRY WAY, 1948)

MIRACLE IN HARLEM** (1948) 69m Herald/Screen Guild bw

Sheila Guyse *(Julie Weston)*, Stepin Fetchit *(Swifty)*, Hilda Offley *(Aunt Hattie)*, Creighton Thompson *(Rev. Jackson)*, Kenneth Freeman *(Jim Marshall)*, William Greaves *(Bert Haltam)*, Sybil Lewis *(Alice Adams)*, Lawrence Criner *(Albert Marshal)*, Jack Carter *(Phillip Manley)*, Milton Williams *(Wilkinson)*, Monte Hawley *(Lt. Renard)*, Ruble Blakey, Alfred Chester *(Detectives)*, Savannah Churchill, Juanita Hall Choir, Lavada Carter, Norma Shepherd, Lynn Proctor Trio.

By the time MIRACLE IN HARLEM was released, Herald Pictures had already released a number of other pictures with all-Black casts, but the one-time original idea had begun to wear thin and the genre needed new developments to remain fresh. The story here revolves around the syndicate taking over the candy shop of an elderly widow. When the head of the syndicate turns up dead, the finger is pointed at the widow's foster daughter, Guyse. Script suffers from unbelievable situations and cliched dialog, but the cast still manages some worthwhile performances.

p, Jack Goldberg; d, Jack Kemp; w, Vincent Valentini; ph, Don Malkames; m, John Gluskin; art d, Frank Namezy.

Drama **(PR:A MPAA:NR)**

MIRACLE IN MILAN****
(1951, Ital.) 100m ENIC/Joseph Burstyn bw (MIRACOLO A MILANO)

Branduani Gianni *(Little Toto at Age 11)*, Francesco Golisano *(Good Toto)*, Paolo Stoppa *(Bad Rappi)*, Emma Gramatica *(Old Lolatta)*, Guglielmo Barnabo *(Mobbi the Rich Man)*, Brunella Bovo *(Little Edvige)*, Anna Carena *(Signora Marta Altezzosa)*, Alba Arnova *(The Statue)*, Flora Cambi *(Unhappy Sweetheart)*, Virgilio Riento *(Sergeant)*, Arturo Bragaglia *(Alfredo)*, Ermino Spalla *(Gaetano)*, Riccardo Bertazzolo *(Wrestler)*, Angelo Prioli *(1st Commander)*, Francesco Rissone *(2nd Commander)*.

The writing-directing team of Zavattini and De Sica produced this picture shortly after the international acclaim they received with THE BICYCLE THIEF. Though failing to receive the recognition of the earlier film, MIRACLE IN MILAN is an equally touching look into human nature. Concentrating on the plight of the poor in post-WW II Italy, the story is essentially a fairy tale, and like all good fairy tales, it is packed with a strong moralistic overtone. Golisano is an orphaned youth who finds refuge in a colony of beggars. He helps to organize the poor colony, and generates a new sense of happiness among the otherwise distraught members of the group. When a wealthy landowner decides to kick the beggars off the land so he can dig for oil, Golisano is given a magic dove by a fairy. Not only are the landowner's attempts thwarted, but the magical powers of the dove also allows Golisano to grant wishes to the beggars. Unable to deny them anything, he grants the greedy wishes of all the beggars, until someone eventually steals the dove. The landowner is now able to take over the land, with the inhabitants forced into jail. The dove returns to Golisano while he's in jail, allowing him to free all the prisoners. As in the other Neo-Realism films, the performers are a combination of actors and the actual denizens of the street. Here, all the players manage to capture realistic and humane portrayals, with only Barnabo being a bit overbearing as the rich industrialist. What might otherwise have been lost in implausibility, is handled in a subtle manner through the direction of De Sica, resulting in a sharp satire. (In Italian; English subtitles.)

p&d, Vittorio De Sica; w, Cesare Zavattini, De Sica, Suso Cechi D'Amico, Mario Chiari, Adolfo Franci (based on the story "Toto Il Buono" by Zavattini); ph, Aldo Graziati; m, Alessandro Cicognini; ed, Eraldo Da Roma; art d, Guido Fiorini; spec eff, Ned Mann; English titles, Herman G. Weinbert.

Drama/Fantasy **(PR:A MPAA:NR)**

MIRACLE IN SOHO** ½ (1957, Brit.) 98m Rank c

John Gregson *(Michael Morgan)*, Belinda Lee *(Julia Gozzi)*, Cyril Cusack *(Sam Bishop)*, Rosalie Crutchley *(Mafalda Gozzi)*, Peter Illing *(Papa Gozzi)*, Marie Burke *(Mama Gozzi)*, Ian Bannen *(Filippo Gozzi)*, Brian Bedford *(Johnny)*, Barbara Archer *(Gwladys)*, John Cairney *(Tom)*, Lane Meddick *(Steve)*, Billie Whitelaw *(Maggie)*, Julian Somers *(Potter)*, Harry Brunning *(Ernie)*, Douglas Ives *(Old Bill)*, George Cooper *(Foreman)*, Cyril Shaps *(Mr. Swoboda)*, Richard Marner *(Karl)*, Gordon Humphris *(Buddy Brown)*, Betty Shale *(Mrs. Coleman)*, Junia Crawford *(Delia)*, Michael Collins *(Lorry Driver)*, Wilfrid Lawson *(Mr. Morgan)*, Colin Douglas *(Supervisor)*, George Eugeniou *(Espresso Owner)*, Lucia Guillon *(Dolores)*, Fred Johnson *(Priest)*, Freda Bamford *(Mrs. Mop)*, Paul Stassino *(Paulo)*, Lynn Tracey *(Tall Girl)*, Eileen Forbes *(Staff Nurse)*.

Gregson plays a member of a road repair team, fixing a street in London's Soho district, where he gains the acquaintance of an Italian family on the verge of migrating to Canada. Despite the efforts of the mother and father to keep the family together, the eldest son and daughter desire to stay behind to pursue their love interests. The son becomes disillusioned, however, when Gregson, an acknowledged ladies' man, tells the boy about his girl friend's easy virtue. The oldest daughter is reluctant to go because of her chance to marry a wealthy cafe owner she does not really love, but to whom she is attracted for the financial security he has to offer. The youngest daughter, though at first the most vehement about keeping the family together, changes her mind as she grows infatuated with Gregson, becoming the only member of the family to remain behind. When Gregson abandons her as soon as his job in Soho is finished, she goes to a local cathedral and prays for his return. The miracle occurs when a broken water main requires the return of the road crew. Though the picture is well directed and the performances are sufficient, the production is marred by a slow-moving script that lapses into awkward sentimentalism.

p, Emeric Pressburger; d, Julian Amyes; w, Pressburger; ph, Christopher Challis (Eastmancolor); m, Brian Easdale; ed, Arthur Stevens; cos, Julie Harris.

Drama **(PR:A MPAA:NR)**

MIRACLE IN THE RAIN** (1956) 107m WB bw

Jane Wyman *(Ruth Wood)*, Van Johnson *(Arthur Hugenon)*, Peggie Castle *(Millie Kranz)*, Fred Clark *(Stephen Jalonkik)*, Eileen Heckart *(Grace Ullman)*, Josephine Hutchinson *(Agnes Wood)*, William Gargan *(Harry Wood)*, Marcel Dalio *(Waiter)*, George Givot *(Headwaiter)*, Barbara Nichols *(Arleene Witchy)*, Halliwell Hobbes *(Eli B. Windgate)*, Paul Picerni *(Young Priest)*, Alan King *(Sgt. Gil Parker)*, Irene Seidner *(Mrs. Hamer)*, Arte Johnson *(Monty)*, Marian Holmes *(Mrs. Rickles)*, Minerva Urecal *(Mrs. Canelli)*, Frank Scannell *(Auctioneer)*, Walter Kingson *(Narrator)*, Anna Dewey *(Elderly Woman)*, Lucita *(Accordionist)*, Rose Allen *(Elderly Woman)*, Jess Kirkpatrick *(Andy the Bartender)*, Allen Ray *(40-Year-Old Man)*, Diana Dawson *(25-Year-Old Woman)*.

Ben Hecht was usually a lot more cynical than what he showed in his novel and screenplay for this hankie-grabber. Wyman is a plain secretary who works in an office headed by Clark. Her best friend is old maid Heckart and she spends most of her time trying to bring her mother, Hutchinson, out of the depression the woman went into when her husband, Gargan, left her years before. Wyman meets Johnson in New York's Central Park during a rainstorm. He's a Tennessee boy and the two of them, though from very diverse backgrounds, fall in love. Johnson goes overseas with his service unit, dies in action, and Wyman begins to physically disintegrate. Her health, never very strong, disappears and she goes deeper and deeper into herself. When it looks as though she won't be able to last much longer, she makes her way to St. Patrick's Church, on Fifth Avenue, and Johnson materializes, sees her for a moment, and leaves her with a coin he'd taken to war with him. That coin is proof to Wyman that this miracle was not merely a figment of her fevered brow. A bit of comedy from comic King and Nichols, as a stripper, but it's otherwise heavy-going. A very young Arte Johnson is seen briefly. Too many secondary stories and not enough on-screen time between Wyman and a living, breathing Johnson, are what detract from the picture.

p, Frank P. Rosenberg; d, Rudolph Mate; w, Ben Hecht (based on his novel); ph, Russell Metty; m, Franz Waxman; ed, Thomas Reilly; md, Waxman; art d, Leo K. Kuter; cos, Milo Anderson; m/l, "I'll Always Believe in You," Ray Heindorf, M.K. Jerome, Ned Washington.

Drama **(PR:A MPAA:NR)**

MIRACLE IN THE SAND (SEE: THREE GODFATHERS, 1936)

MIRACLE KID* (1942) 66m PRC bw

Tom Neal *(Jimmy)*, Carol Hughes *(Pat)*, Vicki Lester *(Helen)*, Betty Blythe *(Gloria)*, Ben Taggart *(Gibbs)*, Alex Callam *(Bolger)*, Thornton Edwards *(Pedro)*, Minta Durfee *(Pheney)*, Gertrude Messinger *(Marge)*, Adele Smith *(Lorraine)*, Frank Otto *(Shady)*, Paul Bryar *(Rocco)*, Pat Gleasch *(Reporter)*, Billy McGown *(Tiger)*, Joe Gray *(Kayo Kane)*, Gene O'Donnell *(Usher)*, Warren Jackson *(Headwaiter)*, John Ince *(Commissioner)*, Larry McGrath, Sam Lufkin *(Referees)*.

Weak re-enactment of the tired story about the boy forced into boxing against his better wishes. Here Neal and Hughes play a couple about to become engaged, but are separated when he proves to be an able boxer. He wins a number of bouts and a bit of publicity, but goes back to Hughes in the end. Everything about this effort, except for one or two performances, are below standard, resulting in a film which never manages to deliver.

p, John T. Coyle; d, William Beaudine; w, Gerald Drayson Adams, Henry Sucher, Coyle; ph, Arthur Martinelli; ed, Guy V. Thayer, Jr.; md, Clarence Wheeler.

Drama **(PR:A MPAA:NR)**

MIRACLE MAN, THE** ½ (1932) 85m PAR bw

Sylvia Sidney *(Helen Smith)*, Chester Morris *(John Madison)*, Robert Coogan *(Bobbie Holmes)*, John Wray *(The Frog)*, Ned A. Sparks *(Harry Evans)*, Hobart Bosworth *(The Patriarch)*, Lloyd Hughes *(Thornton)*, Virginia Bruce *(Margaret Thornton)*, Boris Karloff *(Nikko)*, Irving Pichel *(Henry Holmes)*, Frank Darien *(Hiram Higgins)*, Florine McKinney *(Betty)*, Lew Kelly *(Parker)*, Jackie Searle.

This was a controversial story when originally written as a play by George M. Cohan, Frank Packard, and Robert Davis. It stayed a hot subject as a silent in 1919 and raised a lot of hackles when it came out in 1932. Even in the 1980s, there is much to recognize in this story. There are a gang of thugs working the Chinatown area in San Francisco. When one of them is knocked off, Morris (their leader) thinks he'd better flee until the heat is off and he goes to hide out in a small town on the windswept California coast. Once there, he learns of the powers of Bosworth, a local faith healer who seems to be able to make the lame and halt walk. Morris concocts a plan to bilk wealthy invalids out of their money by using Bosworth's ability on the air waves. Sydney poses as Bosworth's distant relative and brings in another of the gang members, Wray, to pose as a cripple who is healed by Bosworth. Wray is, in fact, a contortionist who can twist his body into knots and can convulse at will. The scheme backfires when the gang members note that Bosworth's powers are real and people are actually healed. Then, one by one, they reform and, in the end, the money that Morris and company had hoped to use for high living is put to work to build a chapel after Bosworth dies. Karloff is seen briefly as a Chinese tavern owner and it's interesting to note that Wray and not Karloff was touted as "the new Lon Chaney" in this film, and it's Wray who takes the role played in the silent film by "The Man Of A Thousand Faces" and does it to perfection. Karloff's career had been sputtering and he attempted to jump-start it with this part. Bosworth is superb as the faith healer, a role originally set for Tyrone Power, Sr., but given to Bosworth when that actor died before shooting began. Times have changed and television has replaced radio, but you can still see scenes similar to this film's on any Sunday night's TV fare in the U.S. The practitioners maintain that faith healing is not a fraud; if you have enough faith, you can be healed. If it doesn't work, you must look inside yourself as not having enough faith. That kind of logic has created many evangelical millionaires who live very well on the donations and gifts sent in by their viewers. The 1919 silent version of this film was one of the films that brought Lon Chaney, Sr. to prominence. (He originated the John Wray-contortionist part.)

d, Norman Z. McLeod; w, Waldemar Young, Samuel Hoffenstein (based on the story by Frank L. Packard, Robert H. Davis and the play by George M. Cohan); ph, David Abel; art d, Hans Dreier.

Crime/Drama (PR:A MPAA:NR)

MIRACLE OF FATIMA
(SEE: MIRACLE OF OUR LADY OF FATIMA, THE, 1952)

MIRACLE OF LIFE (SEE: OUR DAILY BREAD, 1934)

MIRACLE OF MORGAN'S CREEK, THE***** (1944) 99m PAR bw

Eddie Bracken (Norval Jones), Betty Hutton (Trudy Kockenlocker), Diana Lynn (Emmy Kockenlocker), Brian Donlevy (Governor McGinty), Akim Tamiroff (The Boss), Porter Hall (Justice of the Peace), Emory Parnell (Mr. Tuerck), Alan Bridge (Mr. Johnson), Julius Tannen (Mr. Rafferty), Victor Potel (Newspaper Editor), Almira Sessions (Justice's Wife), Esther Howard (Sally), J. Farrell MacDonald (Sheriff), Connie Tompkins (Cecilia), Georgia Caine (Mrs. Johnson), Torben Meyer (Doctor), George Melford (U.S. Marshal), Jimmy Conlin (The Mayor), Harry Rosenthal (Mr. Schwartz), Chester Conklin (Pete), Frank Moran (1st M.P.), Budd Fine (2nd M.P.), Byron Foulger, Arthur Hoyt (McGinty's Secretaries), Nora Cecil (Head Nurse), Jack Norton (Man Opening Champagne), Joe Devlin (Mussolini), Bobby Watson (Hitler), William Demarest (Officer Kockenlocker), Kenneth Gibson, Keith Richards (Secret Service Men), Hal Craig, Roger Creed (State Police), Jan Buckingham, Judith Lowry (Nurses), Freddie Steele (Soldier), Robert Dudley (Man).

The "miracle" of THE MIRACLE OF MORGAN'S CREEK is how they ever got it made in the first place. This onslaught against American morals in small towns, against the wartime romances of servicemen, against just about everything that the country held sacrosanct during WW II was reckless, exaggerated and, perhaps, one of the funniest movies ever. Sturges was at his irreverent best with his screenplay and direction of this most unlikely story that he makes one totally believe could happen. Hutton is a man-crazy blonde who lives in the tiny town of Morgan's Creek with her bitchy sister, Lynn, and her policeman father, Demarest. She allows herself to get just a tad careless during one wild and passionate night with a soldier whom she *thinks* she may have married, and becomes pregnant. The soldier, who she recalls is named something like "Ratsky-Watsky," vanishes and since being pregnant in a small town without being married is the worst thing that can happen in a girl's life, Hutton's sometime bank clerk boy friend, Bracken, is tapped to be the father of whatever she's carrying. Bracken would love to be in the service but he is too nervous to be inducted and sees spots before his eyes whenever he is under too much stress. Bracken dresses in a uniform (from WW I) to marry Hutton under another name, the one she opines belongs to the sire of whatever is cooking inside her. In one mix-up after another, Bracken winds up being sought by authorities for impersonating a soldier, corrupting the morals of a minor, kidnaping, forgery, and bank robbery and he has to get out of town in a hurry. It looks mighty bad for the young couple and the only thing that can save them is a miracle. It's provided when Hutton gives birth to the first set of sextuplets ever and all is forgiven as the news races across the country and makes Hutton and Bracken into national celebrities. Every single tiny role is handled with deftness and Sturges even gets in a few holdovers from an earlier success, THE GREAT McGINTY, by having Brian Donlevy and Akim Tamiroff stop by for a few well-chosen words. The idea of having squeaky-clean Hutton shown as a, shudder, girl with loose morals was a sensation that somehow eluded the censor's scissors. Some say that the plot managed to escape snipping because the picture was so funny that no one could take it seriously, but the truth is that this movie kept a tight grasp on reality and that's what made it so hilarious. Hutton's enormous energy radiated in every frame and Bracken was a marvel as the befuddled swain. Later that same year, he was to repeat his comedic success under Sturges's baton with his work in HAIL THE CONQUERING HERO, another satirical barb at the mores of the day. He never even came close to either film in any of his subsequent work. There's no question that some latter-day producer will find this story and think that it will be wonderful to remake. They'll do it and the result will pall and bore by comparison. Hutton went on to make several sensational musicals, including ANNIE GET YOUR GUN, before suffering an injury to her shoulder, then a series of personal problems. She was only 23 years old in THE MIRACLE OF MORGAN'S CREEK and her youthful exuberance leaped off the screen and grabbed audiences by their hearts. As early as 1942 Hutton was a Sturges groupie, begging him to write a role for her. He did, this one, which was perfect for the boisterous blonde. Moreover, when Sturges got around to finishing this side-splitting comedy epic (he began toying with the idea as early as 1937), he heard that Paramount intended to destroy an attractive small town set and advised

studio executives to preserve it since this would be the locale of Morgan's Creek. Bracken at first refused to play in another Hutton film since he felt he was being used to build up her career at the expense of his own, that every time he went to see a film in which he appeared with Hutton, there were four or five of her singing numbers that had been inserted in the film without his knowledge. When Sturges reassured Bracken that there would be no singing numbers for Hutton in THE MIRACLE OF MORGAN'S CREEK, he finally agreed to appear in the film. Sturges, who had begun his movie career as a screenwriter, was one of the most influential director-writers of the 1940s, with one hit after another, including: THE GREAT McGINTY, CHRISTMAS IN JULY, THE LADY EVE, SULLIVAN'S TRAVELS, THE PALM BEACH STORY, this film, HAIL THE CONQUERING HERO, THE GREAT MOMENT, MAD WEDNESDAY (not a smash but still fairly funny), UNFAITHFULLY YOURS, and THE BEAUTIFUL BLONDE FROM BASHFUL BEND, which starred Betty Grable but would have been better served if Hutton took the role. Sturges was nominated for a writing Oscar, but that's all the notice the movie academy gave this comedy masterpiece. It was remade by Paramount in 1958 as ROCK-A-BYE BABY.

d&w, Preston Sturges; ph, John F. Seitz; m, Leo Shuken, Charles Bradshaw; ed, Stuart Gilmore; art d, Hans Dreier, Ernst Fegte; set d, Stephen Seymour; cos, Edith Head; m/l, "The Bell in the Bay," Sturges; makeup, Wally Westmore.

Comedy (PR:C MPAA:NR)

MIRACLE OF OUR LADY OF FATIMA, THE***
(1952) 102m WB c (GB: MIRACLE OF FATIMA, THE)

Gilbert Roland (Hugo Da Silva), Angela Clark (Maria Rosa), Frank Silvera (Arturo Dos Santos), Jay Novello (Antonio), Richard Hale (Father Ferreira), Norman Rice (Manuel Marto), Frances Morris (Olimpia), Carl Millitaire (Magistrate), Susan Whitney (Lucia Dos Santos), Sherry Jackson (Jacinta Marto), Sammy Ogg (Francisco Marto).

In 1917, the Virgin Mary appeared before three children near the village of Fatima in Portugal and commanded them to return to the spot on the 13th of each month. Despite the efforts of the Portuguese government and the Catholic Church, huge throngs of the faithful would gather and on October 13 the sun was seen to lurch toward the Earth and several in the crowd reported miraculous cures. These historical facts are depicted more or less accurately in this film, although being a Hollywood product, certain liberties are taken with the characters, but the film does work on an entertainment level. Whitney, Jackson, and Ogg are the children who see the apparition, and Roland is their adult friend, himself a dropout from the Church, who counsels the children to keep their visions to themselves because he knows the troubles the Church and government will give them. It was the swarms of pilgrims who descended on Fatima during the holy year of 1951 that inspired Warner Bros. to produce the film.

p, Bryan Foy; d, John Brahm; w, Cran Wilbur, James O'Hanlon; ph, Edwin DuPar (Warner Color); m, Max Steiner; ed, Thomas Reilly; art d, Edward Carrere; set d, G. W. Berntsen; spec eff, Robert Burks.

Religious Drama (PR:A MPAA:NR)

MIRACLE OF SAN SEBASTIAN
(SEE: GUNS FOR SAN SEBASTIAN, 1968, U.S./Fr./Ital./Mex.)

MIRACLE OF SANTA'S WHITE REINDEER, THE*
(1963) 60m Fantasy bw (AKA: THE MIRACLE OF THE WHITE REINDEER)

Charles Winninger, Fritz Feld, Ruthy Robinson, Dennis Holmes, Hal Smith.

Veteran actors Winninger and Feld make a weak attempt to add life to this obscure fantasy tale. Feld, who has been in films as early as 1929, had a small role in BRINGING UP BABY, and continued on with his career to play a minor part in 1967's BAREFOOT IN THE PARK and 1977's THE WORLD'S GREATEST LOVER. As for genial Winninger, who started in films in 1915, it was his last picture.

Fantasy (PR:A MPAA:NR)

MIRACLE OF THE BELLS, THE***1/2 (1948) 120m RKO bw

Fred MacMurray (Bill Dunnigan), Valli (Olga Treskovna), Frank Sinatra (Father Paul), Lee J. Cobb (Marcus Harris), Harold Vermilyea (Nick Orloff), Charles Meredith (Father Spinsky), Jim Nolan (Ted Jones), Veronica Pataky (Anna Klovna), Philip Ahn (Ming Gow), Frank Ferguson (Dolan the Director), Frank Wilcox (Dr. Jennings), Ray Teal (Koslick), Dorothy Sebastian (Katie), Billy Wayne (Tom Elmore), Syd Saylor (Freddy Evans), Thayer Roberts (Earl of Warwick), Herbert Evans (Nobleman), Franz Roehn (Cauchon), Pat Davis (Assistant Director), Ned Davenport, Charles Miller (Priests), Tom Stevenson (Milton Wild), Jim Pierce, Roger Creed (Soldiers), Eula Guy (Woman), Franklyn Farnum, Snub Pollard, Beth Taylor (Worshipers), Bill Clauson (Bellringer's Son), Art Dupuis (Man), Maxwell Hamilton (Ray Tanner), Bert Davidson (Bob Briggs), George Chandler (Max the Telegraph Operator), Max Wagner (Baggage Man), Oliver Blake (Slenzka), Regina Wallace (Martha).

The sentimentality runs over a bit in this inspirational film but THE MIRACLE OF THE BELLS is also a fine film with outstanding performances from all. Press agent and hard guy MacMurray arrives in Coaltown, Pennsylvania, with the body of a young actress. The coffin is taken to a small church, St. Michael's, where MacMurray tells youthful priest Sinatra his mission. It was the dying wish of the dead woman, Valli, that she be buried in the family churchyard and that all the bells of her home town, which she had left many years earlier to seek fame, ring for the three days of her funeral. The press agent then begins to tell Sinatra the brief history of the once vibrant and promising actress. We see in flashback how MacMurray, strolling down the aisle of a burlesque house, spots a young chorus girl so inept at dance routines that she is fired. "Give the kid a break," he asks the stage manager, and his friend complies, saving Valli's budding career. MacMurray then strolls out of the theater as

Valli looks after him gratefully. They meet later as Valli climbs the ladder of acting successes, getting one role after another with no little help from MacMurray. She tells him in one scene that she must become a great actress because she comes from a town without hope, without a belief in the future and if she, product of that depressed and forlorn community, can become a success on the screen, the people of Coaltown can look up at her and see something shining for them, that they will grasp hope, knowing that one of their own is able to climb out of the coal pits and a life without promise to become someone. So in love with her is MacMurray that he devotes his energies to promoting her into bigger and bigger parts until Valli is given by movie mogul Cobb the lead role of Joan of Arc. She exhausts herself in the part, so much so that her health fails but she struggles to complete the film which all consider a masterpiece. Shortly after the production is finished, Valli dies. MacMurray is shocked and angry to learn that Cobb refuses to release the film, even though he knows it to be great. Cobb's reasoning is that he cannot distribute a film with a dead girl as a star, especially one whom no one has ever seen before, that the public will either not respond to an unknown dead woman on the silver screen, no matter how great her talents, or he fears that viewers will love her so much that they will be angry and resentful when they realize they will never see her in another film. MacMurray tells Cobb he's crazy, that Valli died to make a brilliant film for him, and he is repaying her sacrifice by ignoring it, by shelving the film. But nothing can budge Cobb and his decision goes unchanged. MacMurray, with his last few dollars, keeps faith with the dead girl he still loves and takes her home to Coaltown, asking Sinatra to ring the bells of his church for three days. Sinatra agrees but when MacMurray asks about the other churches in town, Sinatra tells him that it will cost a great deal of money, especially for the huge churches in the better part of town. MacMurray nevertheless makes the rounds of the churches, talking to priests, deacons, and pastors of all faiths, giving them checks to make sure their bells ring around the clock for three days. Thousands of dollars are written on MacMurray's checks, all rubber and he knows it, but it's a weekend and, before the banks open on Monday, well, perhaps a miracle will happen. It does, but not in a way MacMurray or anyone else would expect. The bells alert the town and draw the curious to the funeral at Sinatra's little church, all coming to the services for a dead girl none of them know. As the bells continue hour by hour, the press picks up the story and MacMurray pumps up the reporters with tales about Valli, retelling her brief life story. The wire services pick up the story and soon Valli's life is front page news. Readers of papers and radio listeners hearing the story begin to pour into tiny St. Michael's until it is packed night and day. Then, on the last day of the ringing of the bells, churchgoers gasp in shock, as do MacMurray and Sinatra who are present, when they see the statues of the Blessed Virgin and St. Michael, both large statuaries flanking the coffin of Valli, turn slowly, grinding loudly on their granite pedestals, as they uniformly come to face and look down on the coffin. The faithful swoon, faint, cross themselves, and proclaim it a miracle. Reporters race to phones to report the phenomenon while Sinatra grabs a flashlight and goes to the basement of the church. There he investigates the underpinnings of the old church and later reports to MacMurray that the beams holding up the floor were placed under too much stress by the crowds in the church and these shifting beams put strain on the pillars on which the statues rested, causing them to turn. MacMurray begs the priest not to announce that story to the worshipers and the world, to let the dead Valli have her miracle, reminding him how such a marvelous event will bring a glow to the hearts of everyone in miserable Coaltown and make of their community something they never thought they or Valli would be—special and blessed. But Sinatra tells him he cannot perpetuate a hoax. In his announcement he points out the moving beams and pillars and then states that higher authorities must determine whether or not a miracle occurred. For the believers, however, there is no doubt. The statues moved to turn and look down on tragic Valli of their own accord. A miracle has happened in their eyes and soon thousands stream into the town and the press spreads the story. Cobb, irritated but impressed by the publicity campaign MacMurray has mounted, appears and, although he has fought the campaign all along, decides to release Valli's film as well as cover MacMurray's debts. The battle has been won; Valli's great performance will be seen and loved by the world at film's end. Pichel, normally a program director, excels here with a quickly constructed story, inventively conceived, and shot with great care. The Hecht-Reynolds script is terrific, full of great lines and touching scenes which never get syrupy or sloppy, thanks to MacMurray's sharp projection of a cynical press agent who opens his heart to Valli and Valli's deeply sincere portrayal of the immigrant actress. She is exceptional and her small reading of the Joan of Arc scenes are stunning. De Grasse's lensing is also outstanding, as is Harline's score. Sinatra sings one simple song, "Ever Homeward" (Kasimierz Lubomirski, Jule Styne, Sammy Cahn), in his understated and very effective performance as an empathetic priest who wants to believe more than most in the miracle he can too easily explain.

p, Jesse L. Lasky, Walter MacEwen; d, Irving Pichel; w, Ben Hecht, Quentin Reynolds, DeWitt Bodeen (based on the novel by Russell Janney); ph, Robert de Grasse; m, Leigh Harline; ed, Elmo Williams; md, C. Bakaleinikoff; art d, Ralph Berger; cos, Renie; ch, Charles O'Curran; m/l, Jule Styne, Sammy Cahn; makeup, Karl H. Herlinger.

Drama   **Cas.**   **(PR:A MPAA:NR)**

MIRACLE OF THE HILLS, THE**½   (1959) 73m AP/FOX bw

Rex Reason (Scott Macauley), Theona Bryant (Alison Wingate), Jay North (Davey Leonard), Gilbert Smith (Mark Leonard), Tracy Stratford (Laurie Leonard), Gene Roth (Sheriff Crane), I. Stanford Jolley (Dr. Tuttle), Gene Collins (Silas Jones), Kelton Garwood (Seth Jones), Paul Wexler (Sam Jones), Kenneth Mayer (Milo Estes), June Vincent (Mrs. Leonard), Pat O'Hara (Lucky), Tom Daly (Mike), Cecil Elliott (Miss Willowbird), Charles Arnt (Fuzzy), Claire Carleton (Sally), Nan Leslie (Joanne Tashman), Betty Lou Gerson (Kate Peacock), Vincent Townsend, Jr. (Harry).

Relatively low-budget, though well-crafted, picture that uses a western setting to deliver a moralistic message. Reason plays a rugged minister who takes over the church in a broken-down town. The main source of income for its inhabitants stems from a mine owned by a former prostitute, Gerson, who is bitter over the way the townspeople treated her in the past. She changes when three innocent children are trapped in a mine because of Gerson's neglect. The chidren are saved through a miraculous earthquake, motivating Gerson (encouraged by the ever-faithful Reason) to clean up the town. The inspirational theme of the script, though a bit corny, is kept alive by interesting subplots. The film is aided by realistic performances and effective direction.

p, Richard E. Lyons; d, Paul Landres; w, Charles Hoffman; ph, Floyd Crosby (CinemaScope); m, Paul Sawtell, Bert Shefter; ed, Betty Steinberg; art d, Lyle R. Wheeler, John Mansbridge.

Western   **(PR:A MPAA:NR)**

MIRACLE OF THE WHITE REINDEER, THE
         (SEE: MIRACLE OF SANTA'S WHITE REINDEER, THE, 1963)

MIRACLE OF THE WHITE STALLIONS**
(1963) 117m Disney/BV c (AKA: FLIGHT OF THE WHITE STALLIONS, THE)

Robert Taylor (Col. Podhajsky), Lilli Palmer (Verena Podhajsky), Curt Jergens (Gen. Tellheim), Eddie Albert (Rider Otto), James Franciscus (Maj. Hoffman), John Larch (Gen. Patton), Brigitte Horney (Countess Arco-Valley), Philip Abbott (Col. Reed), Douglas Fowley (U.S. General), Charles Regnier (Gen. Stryker), Fritz Wepper (Rider Hans), Gunther Haenel (Groom Sascha), Hans Habietinek (Innkeeper Hager), Philo Hauser (Dispatcher), Michael Janisch (Refugee Leader), Margarethe Dux (Woman Railroad Official), Max Haufler (Engineer), Robert Dietl (German M.P. Captain), Josef Krastel (Attendant Carl), Peter Jost (Kreisleiter), Kurt Jager (2nd Rider), Olaf Tschierschke (3rd Rider), Herbert Prikopa (Orderly Tellheim), Erik Schumann (German Capt. Danhoff), Helmut Janatsch (Intruder), Michael Tellering (Stryker's Adjutant), Hal Galili (Brooklyn G.I.), Harry Hornisch (1st Rider), Hugo Lindinger, Larry Billman, Fritz Eckhardt.

A film based on the true story of the efforts to save the valued Lipizzan horses during WW II, which served as a comeback for Taylor, who had been absent from the screen for over three years. Taylor in the lead role also proved to be the film's major drawback. Taylor plays the head of the Spanish Riding School in Vienna, fearful for the future of the famed and gallant Lipizzan horses during the bombardment of the city. He appeals to Jurgens, a German general, for aid in transferring the horses to a safe place in the advent of the approaching Allied forces. Jurgens is able to transfer the horses under a proclamation allowing art treasures, to be moved for safety's sake. However, during the transfer, the mares are separated from the stallions, forcing Taylor to worry that the breed will die out. With the American forces in Vienna, Taylor appeals to Gen. Patton (Larch) for help by putting on a performance of the magnificent animals. Awed by their performance, Larch enables the mares to be transported back to Vienna. Script suffers from characters that lack depth, with most of the cast falling victim to this weakness, though some performances manage a bit of sparkle, particularly Jurgens in the role of the German general. Taylor is especially flat, probably as the result of the material offered by this script.

p, Walt Disney, Peter V. Herald; d, Arthur Hiller; w, A.J. Carothers (based on the book The Dancing White Stallions of Vienna by Col. Alois Podhajsky), ph, Gunther Anders (Technicolor); m, Paul Smith; ed, Alfred Srp, Cotton Warburton; art d, Werner Schlichting, Isabella Schlichting; cos, Leo Bei; spec eff, Paul Waldherr; m/l, "Just Say, Auf Wiedersehen," Richard M. Sherman, Robert B. Sherman; makeup, Rudolf Ohlschmidt, Leopold Kuhnert; Tech supv (Vienna), Col. Alois Podhajsky.

Drama   **(PR:AA MPAA:NR)**

MIRACLE ON MAIN STREET, A**   (1940) 78m COL bw

Margo, Walter Abel, Lyle Talbot, Wynne Gibson, Veda Ann Borg, William Collier, Sr., Jane Darwell, Pat Flaherty, George Humbert, Jeanne Kelly, Susan Miller.

Touching Christmas story in which a dance hall girl happens upon a baby left to die in the alleys of Los Angeles. Taking the baby in with the intention of providing some type of home, the girl runs into minor complications when her brute of a husband decides to make an appearance after a long absence. Story has plenty of character to make it interesting, but lacks the directorial skill to make it a winner.

p, Jack Skirball; d, Steven Sekely; w, Frederick Jackson (based on a story by Samuel Ornitz, Boris Ingster); ph, Charles Van Enger; ed, Barney Rogan.

Drama   **(PR:A MPAA:NR)**

MIRACLE ON 34TH STREET, THE*****
(1947) 96m FOX bw (GB: THE BIG HEART)

Maureen O'Hara (Doris Walker), John Payne (Fred Gailey), Edmund Gwenn (Kris Kringle), Gene Lockhart (Judge Henry X. Harper), Natalie Wood (Susan Walker), Porter Hall (Mr. Sawyer), William Frawley (Charles Halloran), Jerome Cowan (Thomas Mara), Philip Tonge (Mr. Shellhammer), James Seay (Dr. Pierce), Harry Antrim (Mr. Macy), Thelma Ritter, Mary Field (Mothers), Theresa Harris (Cleo), Alvin Greenman (Albert), Anne Staunton (Mrs. Mara), Robert Hyatt (Thomas Mara, Jr.), Richard Irving, Jeff Corey (Reporters), Anne O'Neal (Secretary), Lela Bliss (Mrs. Shellhammer), Anthony Sydes (Peter), William Forrest (Dr. Rogers), Alvin Hammer (Mara's Assistant), Joseph McInerney (Bailiff), Ida McGuire (Drum Majorette), Percy Helton (Santa Claus), Jane Green (Mrs. Harper), Marlene Lyden (Dutch Girl), Jack Albertson, Guy Thomajan (Post Office Employees), Robert Lynn (Macy's Salesman), Jean O'Donnell (Secretary), Snub Pollard (Mail-Bearing Court Officer), Robert Karnes, Basil Walker (Interns), Herbert Heyes (Mr. Gimbel), Stephen Roberts (Guard), Teddy Driver (Terry), Robert Gist (Window Dresser), Patty Smith (Alice).

Here is a beloved and heart-warming film that is shown regularly, and rightly so, every Christmas, a tale for young and old, even the cynical who won't stand a chance resisting the message and accepting the glowing image. Gwenn walks away with this film as *the* man who spreads the true meaning of Christmas and embodies the spirit of Yuletide. The film opens during the Christmas Parade in Manhattan with O'Hara, an advertising executive for Macy's Department Store, aghast at finding the Santa Claus (the marvelous wheezing character actor Helton) for the store's float so drunk he can't stand up and wave at the kiddies waiting to see him. Chastising O'Hara for employing such a derelict and disgracing the image of Santa Claus is Gwenn, a twinkly-eyed, white-bearded elderly gentleman. Desperate, O'Hara asks Gwenn his name and he tells her it's "Kris Kringle." She ignores the name and pleads with him to replace the drunken Helton. He accepts with alacrity and dons the Santa Claus suit, leading the parade and becoming the hit of the event, the most memorable Santa Claus on record. So delighted are Macy's executives with Gwenn that they encourage O'Hara to hire him as their resident Santa Claus during the Christmas rush. O'Hara's daughter, raised to face what O'Hara terms "reality" at an early age, meets Gwenn when her mother brings the genial gentleman home for dinner after she hires him. There he also meets young idealistic lawyer Payne, O'Hara's fiance. Payne does not believe in O'Hara's modern viewpoint that her child must have no illusions, dreams, or a belief in "fairy tales." Wood, a sweet, intelligent, and prematurely sophisticated child, tells Gwenn that she does not believe in Santa Claus, even though he intimates that *he* might be that very gentlemen, in the flesh. Gwenn's conduct further upsets some punctilious and self-ordained authorities on human behavior such as the stuffy, lying, and manipulating personnel director, Hall. The old gentleman startles Macy's customers when he hears that children are asking for certain toys that the store might not have or toys that are inferior, suggesting to parents that they go to other stores for better products. At first, the Macy staff panics but customers are so overwhelmed with "this new policy full of the Christmas spirit," praising the goodwill attitude of the management, that Gwenn is lauded and praised by Antrim, playing Mr. Macy. The store's sales soar and Macy's is known quickly as the "store with a heart." The press gets hold of the story and Gwenn poses for photographs not only with Antrim-Macy but with Heyes, playing Mr. Gimbel, whose store has also adopted a similar friendly policy. Slowly, the little cynic Wood comes to believe that Gwenn is the real Santa Claus, her belief reinforced by the magical little things Gwenn does. Wood watches in amazement as a small girl climbs on Gwenn's lap to talk to him in Dutch, she being a recent immigrant. Her mother explains that she cannot speak English but Gwenn merely smiles and then carries on a fluent conversation with the little girl in her native language. Jealous of Gwenn and his growing popularity and resenting the fact that a mere stock boy, Greenman, has been promoted to the august position of Gwenn's costumed helper, personnel director Hall has Greenman demoted and labels him an "incompetent." Upon hearing this, Gwenn goes to Hall and tells him he is cruel and heartless to label the gentle youth with his pseudo-psychological phrases. Hall sneers and jeers at him and Gwenn bops him on the forehead with his cane. It's a slight blow but Hall, seeing O'Hara and other department heads approaching, pretends he has been severely attacked. He insists that Gwenn is unbalanced and demands a sanity hearing. When examined, Gwenn refuses to play an evasive game, as Payne cautions him to do, but openly admits that he is the one and only Santa Claus. Even O'Hara and Wood plead with the old gentleman to avoid declaring himself, but he cannot ignore his identity. Gwenn is institutionalized pending a legal hearing. His defense counsel is Payne and it looks bleak for Gwenn when he is brought into court with judge Lockhart pretty much convinced at the start that he must commit Gwenn to permanent confinement. Cowan, the prosecuting attorney, takes the case and his winning for granted but he does not count on the mysterious forces that always seem to surround Gwenn. Cowan's own wife and young son turn on him for prosecuting Santa Claus and Payne shrewdly calls Cowan's son to testify that there is, indeed, a Santa Claus, since "daddy told me so." Cowan backs away from this self-defeating cross-examination but he hammers away at the fact that Gwenn cannot prove he is Santa Claus, a line of reasoning obviously supported by judge Lockhart. But in his chambers during a recess, political boss Frawley meets with Lockhart and teaches him the political facts of life, pointing out that mothers and fathers and merchants everywhere, not to mention every child in the world, will think him a monster if he judges Gwenn to be insane, and, Frawley ruefully points out before departing, "that means votes." Lockhart then begins bending over backward to help Gwenn and Payne in their seemingly hopeless cause. Then a postal employee, Albertson, gets the idea of sending all the thousands of letters sent to Santa Claus in the dead letter bins to the courtroom where Gwenn is being tried. The following day Payne asks judge Lockhart if he will accept the U.S. Post Office as an authority with impeccable judgment. Lockhart says he does but that he doesn't get the point. "You will, your Honor," says Payne, and asks a score of guards to carry into the court dozens of bags of mail which are opened and dumped on Lockhart's bench, a mountain of mail all addressed to Santa Claus. Lockhart chooses the better part of this happy accident to get off the hook and accepts the U.S. Post Office as the authority which has decreed Gwenn as the genuine Father Christmas and declares the old man "the one and only Santa Claus." Gwenn is edified, Payne triumphant, and O'Hare and Wood jubilant. By the end of the film O'Hara has come around to encouraging her daughter to nurture her dreams and beliefs. She and Payne, with Wood in the back seat, drive around a new subdivision, planning their wedding. Wood screams for them to stop and spots a house she had earlier asked Gwenn to get for her. To the amazement of O'Hara and Payne, the house is the exact duplicate of a photo Wood has shown to her mother earlier. Wood runs into the house, ecstatic, believing Gwenn has delivered as promised. O'Hara and Payne follow her into the house which is empty. "The sign outside says it's for sale," Payne says to O'Hara, as a way of telling her that he'll buy it if they wed. They embrace, then Payne spots something out of the corner of his eye that makes his eyebrow arch in wonder. "Oh, no." he says. O'Hara follows his gaze, and is equally startled. The camera shows a cane leaning against the wall, Gwenn's cane, and it zooms in to capture the cane in a close-up to make the point for the fade-out. Gwenn (1875–1959) gives one of the most charming, endearing performances in the history of films, an image so appealing that his gentle personality has been indelibly identified with the spirit of Santa Claus and Christmas ever since the completion of this superb production. He won an Oscar for this role, and there was never any doubt that he would. Christmas has been profiled in dozens of films but seldom, if ever, has the Yuletide been so wonderfully presented. Only a few films covering this greatest of seasons approach THE MIRACLE ON 34TH STREET (IT'S A WONDERFUL WORLD, A CHRISTMAS CAROL, 1938, to name two). The story was the brainchild of director Seaton and writer Davies, who had been discussing the possibility of developing a story that kept alive the real meaning of Christmas right in the middle of its commercialism. Fox mogul Zanuck was not too impressed with the proposed story and allowed Seaton only a minimal budget to make the film, a rare misjudgment on the part of the super producer; this film would be one of the studio's all-time money makers. Seaton, who shot most of the film on location in New York during the 1946 Christmas season, persuaded Macy's Department Store officials to allow his cameras to roam through its busy confines to authentically capture the shopping hustle and bustle. When Zanuck viewed the film he predicted such a lukewarm public response that he didn't even wait to release the film at Christmastime, distributing it during the summer of 1947. It was still running six months later when millions of children were posting letters to Santa and has been running somewhere in the world ever since as one of the great fantasy classics. The movie was later subjected to a coloring process for TV with the belief that if a film is not in color it has no present marketability, which is about as logical as saying that any film without a happy ending is not worth seeing. The color process was a dismal failure, the texture and hues badly off the mark, appearing washed out, drab, and forced, particularly unsuccessful in that it fails to capture the bright, happy colors of the season.

p, William Perlberg; d, George Seaton; w, Seaton (based on a story by Valentine Davies); ph, Charles Clarke, Lloyd Ahern; m, Cyril Mockridge; ed, Robert Simpson; art d, Richard Day, Richard Irvine; set d, Thomas Little, Ernest Lansing; spec eff, Fred Sersen.

Fantasy **Cas.** **(PR:AAA MPAA:NR)**

MIRACLE WOMAN, THE*** 1/2

(1931) 90m COL bw

Barbara Stanwyck *(Florence "Faith" Fallon)*, David Manners *(John Carson)*, Sam Hardy *(Bob Hornsby)*, Beryl Mercer *(Mrs. Higgins)*, Russell Hopton *(Sam Welford)*, Charles Middleton *(Simpson)*, Eddie Boland *(Collins)*, Thelma Hill *(Gussie)*, Aileen Carlyle *(Violet)*, Al Stewart *(Brown)*, Harry Todd *(Briggs)*, Ed Le Saint *(Parishioner)*, Ivan Linow *(Gunboat)*, John Kelley *(Stagehand)*, Bud Flanagan [Dennis O'Keefe] *(Man in Audience)*, Fred Warren *(Pianist)*, Mary Doran *(Party Guest)*, Lorraine Hubbell *(Child)*, Mary Bracken *(Girl)*.

John Meehan and Robert Riskin wrote a play for Broadway that starred Alice Brady and was as close to the truth about Aimee Semple MacPherson as one could get without being sued. Sinclair Lewis had already written *Elmer Gantry* but that was such hot stuff that the censors would not allow it to be filmed. The subject of phony evangelists was a tricky one, as there were (and still are) many who believed in the words these people were saying and contributed mightily to their coffers in the hopes of securing a better pew at the Church of the Great Beyond. Stanwyck is most believable as the daughter of a pastor who has just been released from his parish and that discharge has caused the old man to die of a broken heart. Stanwyck goes in front of the congregation and delivers a stinging denunciation of the hypocrisy of the parishioners to their faces. These words are heard by Hardy, a two-bit promoter and conman who realizes that Stanwyck is mighty handy with her mouth, so he talks her into becoming an evangelist and she is soon one of the most important pulpit pounders in the land. Phony cripples are hired to be "healed" and make their testimony heard by the pigeons (a practice that continues to this day) and Stanwyck is caught up in the furor and becomes too successful to stop. Manners is a blind ex-pilot who is about to kill himself by leaping out a window when he hears Stanwyck preaching on the radio and decides that she might be able to cure him by faith. He goes to the tent and volunteers to step inside a cage with a huge lion. That faith brings him closer to Stanwyck and she is soon in love with him. Hopton is the press agent for the group and he wants a larger piece of the spoils, but Hardy won't hear of it and knocks off the ink-grabber rather than cut him in. Manners is helped by his love for Stanwyck and overcomes his shyness by declaring himself through his ventriloquist's dummy, rather than speaking out for himself. When Hardy sees that Manners and Stanwyck are getting too close for his comfort, he arranges a trip to the Holy Land to get her away from the blind lad. Stanwyck is beginning to understand that her faith healing is just a lot of nonsense and that the people whom she has really healed just needed something, anything to believe in. (Sort of like the "true believer" of whom Eric Hoffer wrote in his epic book on the subject of people who will follow any flag or cause and need something to die for.) All of her ravings don't help Manners recover his sight and, to the authors' and director's credit, there is no miracle recovery for Manners, even when Hardy whacks him hard on the head and it seems that the boy just might have one of those amazing recoveries in time for the fade-out. Hardy sets the tent ablaze as Stanwyck is about to confess to all that she is a sham. Later, Stanwyck is a member of the Salvation Army when she gets a wire from Manners and it is to be hoped that the two young people will get together. Riskin later became Capra's favorite screenwriter and wrote such classics as IT HAPPENED ONE NIGHT, MR. DEEDS GOES TO TOWN, LOST HORIZON, YOU CAN'T TAKE IT WITH YOU, and MEET JOHN DOE. This was an expensive film for its day and every penny shows on the screen. There's not a wasted word or frame of film in the movie. Capra thought it was corny and filled with claptrap but he was wrong; it was a much finer picture than that. It would have been even better if Capra and the writers would have had the freedom to use sabers instead of pins on their subjects. More than 50 years later, there are still several evangelists using the exact same techniques, except that now they are doing it for millions of dollars per week on television.

p, Harry Cohn; d, Frank Capra; w, Dorothy Howell, Jo Swerling (based on the play "Bless You Sister" by John Meehan, Robert Riskin); ph, Joseph Walker; ed, Maurice Wright; art d, Mack Parker.

Drama (PR:A-C MPAA:NR)

MIRACLE WORKER, THE*** (1962) 106m Playfilms/UA bw

Anne Bancroft *(Annie Sullivan)*, Patty Duke *(Helen Keller)*, Victor Jory *(Capt. Keller)*, Inga Swenson *(Kate Keller)*, Andrew Prine *(James Keller)*, Kathleen Comegys *(Aunt Ev)*, Beah Richards *(Viney)*, Jack Hollander *(Mr. Anagnos)*, Peggy Burke *(Helen at Age 7)*, Mindy Sherwood *(Helen at Age 5)*, Grant Code *(Doctor)*, Michael Darden *(Percy at Age 10)*, Dale Ellen Bethea *(Martha at Age 10)*, Walter Wright, Jr. *(Percy at Age 8)*, Donna Bryan *(Martha at Age 7)*, Diane Bryan *(Martha at Age 5)*, Keith Moore *(Percy at Age 6)*, Michele Farr *(Young Annie at Age 10)*, Allan Howard *(Young Jimmie at Age 8)*, Judith Lowry *(1st Crone)*, William F. Haddock *(2nd Crone)*, Helen Ludlum *(3rd Crone)*, Belle the Dog.

This endearing story of one of the 20th Century's greatest women began as a book by Keller, then became a play on Broadway in October, 1959, which starred Bancroft and Duke and was directed by Penn from the words of William Gibson. When the time came to make the film, Penn, Gibson, and producer Coe insisted that Bancroft and Duke be retained for the movie and the results were an Oscar for both female leads and nominations for the screenplay and direction. Both leads were born with the name Anna Marie (an odd coincidence) 15 years apart in New York. Bancroft went into films early in life and made a series of dumb movies like TREASURE OF THE GOLDEN CONDOR, GORILLA AT LARGE, NEW YORK CONFIDENTIAL, etc., before she went back to New York and secured the role of Gittel in "Two for the Seesaw," another Gibson play. After her success in that, there was no other choice for the part of Keller's teacher as far as Gibson, Penn, and Coe were concerned. When the time came to film TWO FOR THE SEESAW, Bancroft was bypassed in favor of Shirley MacLaine, despite her wonderful notices, or it might have been that she was busy making THE MIRACLE WORKER, a better picture with much more to say. Duke's career began very early when her older brother Raymond, was acting at a club and she was in attendance and was spotted by John and Ethel Ross, a married couple who specialized in managing moppets. They were taken by her and spent the next few years working with young Ann (which is the name she is still called by old friends) until she began appearing regularly on New York television in various soap operas as well as many stage performances. She was not yet a teenager when she riveted audiences with the role as Keller on Broadway and her Best Supporting Actress Oscar had been the award given to the youngest performer before Tatum O'Neal eclipsed that achievement by winning one before she turned 10 for PAPER MOON. THE MIRACLE WORKER is a powerful picture, even as the credits roll. Duke is groping and ogling in her silent world when Bancroft arrives in Tuscumbia, Alabama, on a mission to teach the girl how to communicate through sign language. But Duke is not just deaf; she's also blind and the task seems impossible. Bancroft, we learn, was blind at birth and still must wear very thick glasses in order to see images. Her own life had been brutalized by many years in institutions and the loss of the one person she cared about, a crippled brother who died young. Bancroft senses that the only way she can make any progress with Duke is to separate the child from the doting influence of her mother, Swenson, and the shrill, overbearing ways of her father, Jory. Duke's parents see the intelligence in that demand and Duke and Bancroft move into a small out-building on the property for a trial run of a few weeks. It is harrowing as Duke claws, kicks, scratches, and bites her way around Bancroft, but there is a glimmer of hope after the fortnight concludes, as Duke has learned to dress herself and can now recite the alphabet by touch. Duke has made some progress but cannot put the alphabet letters together with the notion that these symbols represent items, feelings, et cetera. Bancroft requests another week alone with Duke but Jory and Swenson want their child back in the house and, once that takes place, Duke regresses to her formerly wild state. This time, however, Bancroft is there to counter Duke's moves with loving, though firm, discipline. She will not let Duke get away with anything near the chaos she'd been wreaking on her guilty parents. At the dinner table one night, Duke tips over the water pitcher and Bancroft drags her outside to the water pump and forces her to refill it. And that's where the revelation occurs; when the liquid drenches Duke, she "signs" the word for water on Bancroft's hand. Bancroft indicates her happiness at the breakthrough and Duke excitedly runs around the front yard spelling out the words for everything she can touch. The connection has been made and the audience is magnetized by the scene as the film ends. Everyone is to be congratulated for their work on this film. Penn and cinematographer Caparros use short dissolves to great advantage and the score, by Rosenthal, heightens every nuance of the drama. Years later, Gibson wrote a sequel which Penn directed for the stage. It was called "Monday After the Miracle" and starred Jane Alexander as Annie and Karen Allen as Helen. The play was a dismal flop. In it, Allen spoke the lines the way she must have thought a deaf person would speak but she was in and out of vocal character. There was a sexual overlay placed on the story with an affair between Keller and . . . never mind. It failed deservedly and lost several hundred thousand for producers Ray Katz and Sandy Gallin, two show business managers (they handled Dolly Parton, Cher, Joan Rivers, and others) who thought they knew theater. The sequel took place many years hence and had none of the fire and drama of the original. Some things are better left unsequelized. THE MIRACLE WORKER was based on Keller's own book, then was an unproduced ballet in 1953, came to TV on "Playhouse 90" (CBS) in 1957, and eventually to the stage in 1959. The interiors were shot in New York and the exteriors in New Jersey, which doubled for Alabama. The eight-minute sequence that featured a physical fight between Bancroft and Duke as the teacher attempts to teach the pupil some manners will long be remembered as one of the most electrifying ever staged or filmed. In real life, Keller had lost her sight and hearing at the age of 19 months. Alexander Graham Bell asked the Perkins Institution (founded in 1829) to send someone to work with the child and they assigned

26-year-old Sullivan, who arrived in Alabama and began her teaching on March 2, 1887. After the first breakthrough, the child began to read by feeling the words on raised cardboard and then made her own sentences by arranging the letters in a frame. In 1904, Keller graduated magna cum laude from Radcliffe College. She learned how to speak at the Horace Mann School for the Deaf in Boston by feeling the position of the tongue and lips of others with her fingers. She began to lip-read by putting her fingers on the lips of others while the words were being tapped out on her hand by an interpreter. In 1902, her book, *The Story Of My Life*, was published, followed by another book, *Optimism*. Keller began lecturing in 1913 to raise funds for the American Foundation for the Blind and Sullivan stayed with Keller until the teacher died in 1936. In 1920, Keller would join with Clarence Darrow, Upton Sinclair, Jane Addams, Norman Thomas, Felix Frankfurter, and others to form the American Civil Liberties Union (ACLU). She spent the rest of her life in the service of the handicapped and died in 1968. The rest of her life would make a wonderful movie. One of the assistant directors was Ulu Grosbard, who later directed THE SUBJECT WAS ROSES and STRAIGHT TIME.

p, Fred Coe; d, Arthur Penn; w, William Gibson (based on his play and Helen Keller's book, *The Story Of My Life*); ph, Ernesto Caparros; m, Laurence Rosenthal; ed, Aram Avakian; art d, George Jenkins, Mel Bourne; cos, Ruth Morley.

Drama Cas. (PR:A MPAA:NR)

MIRACLES DO HAPPEN* (1938, Brit.) 59m New Realm bw

Jack Hobbs *(Barry Strangeways)*, Bruce Seton *(Rodney)*, Marjorie Taylor *(Peggy)*, Aubrey Mallalieu *(Prof. Gilmore)*, George Carney *(Greenlaw)*, Molly Hamley-Clifford *(Mrs. Greenlaw)*, Antony Holles *(Proctor)*, Michael Ripper.

The producers of this farce were really stretching it when they came up with the premise for this inexcusable mess. Hobbs is the devoted nephew of Mallalieu, an inventor who has discovered a method to create artificial milk. Only funds are lacking to market this new creamy invention, so Hobbs takes it upon himself to play the role of business wizard. About as funny as it sounds, and little credit to former scripter Rogers.

p, George Smith; d, Maclean Rogers; w, Kathleen Butler (based on the story by Con West, Jack Marks); ph, Geoffrey Faithfull.

Comedy (PR:A MPAA:NR)

MIRACLES FOR SALE* (1939) 71m MGM bw

Robert Young *(Michael Morgan)*, Florence Rice *(Judy Barclay)*, Frank Craven *(Dad Morgan)*, Henry Hull *(Dave Duvallo)*, Lee Bowman *(La Clair)*, Cliff Clark *(Inspector Gavigan)*, Astrid Allwyn *(Mrs. Zelma La Clair)*, Walter Kingsford *(Col. Watrous)*, Frederic Worlock *(Dr. Sabbatt)*, Gloria Holden *(Mme. Rapport)*, William Demarest *(Quinn)*, Charles Lane *(Hotel Clerk)*, John Piccori *(Colonel)*, Edward Earle *(Man)*, Richard Loo *(Chinese Soldier)*, Frank Sully *(Bus Driver)*, Eddie Acuff *(Taxi Driver)*, Phillip Terry *(Master of Ceremonies)*, Chester Clute *(Waiter)*, Harold Minjir *(Tauro)*, Harry Tyler *(Taxi Driver)*, Truman Bradley *(Master of Ceremonies)*, E. Allyn Warren *(Dr. Mendricks)*, James C. Morton *(Electrician)*, Paul Sutton *(Capt. R Z. Storm)*, Armand Kaliz *(Francois)*, Fred Warren *(Police Surgeon)*, Suzanne Kaaren *(Girl)*, John Davidson *(Weird Voice)*, Claire McDowall *(Woman)*, Alphonse Martell *(Head-waiter)*, Monte Vandegrift *(Bergin)*, Edward Kilroy *(Attendant)*, Harry Vejar *(Citizen)*, Manuel Paris *(Sinister Man)*, Margaret Bert *(Mary)*, Frances McInerney *(Magician's Assistant)*, William Norton Bailey *(Man in Box)*, Cyril Ring *(Numbers' Man)*, Amelia Stone.

Young plays an illusionist trying to protect Rice after two of her wealthy friends are murdered while involved in some innocent dabblings into the occult. During the course of the film, Young reveals the tricks behind the supernatural effects. The story keeps the suspense going to the very end, aided by well-paced direction in Browning's last screen effort.

d, Tod Browning; w, Harry Ruskin, Marion Parsonnet, James Edward Grant (based on the book *Death from a Top Hat* by Clayton Rawson); ph, Charles Lawton; ed, Frederick Y. Smith; art d, Cedric Gibbons, Gabriel Scognamillo; set d, Edwin B. Willis; cos, Dolly Tree; makeup, Jack Dawn.

Mystery (PR:A MPAA:NR)

MIRACOLO A MILANO (SEE: MIRACLE IN MILAN, 1951 Ital.)

MIRACULOUS JOURNEY* (1948) 83m FC c

Rory Calhoun *(Larry)*, Audrey Long *(Mary)*, Virginia Grey *(Patricia)*, George Cleveland *(Hermit)*, Jim Bannon *(Nick)*, June Storey *(Rene)*, Thurston Hall *(Kendricks)*, Carole Donne *(Jane)*, Tom Lane *(Copilot)*, Flame the Dog, Jimmy the Crow.

The African jungle serves as the backdrop for a collection of characters who survive a plane's crash landing. Learning to survive in the jungle, aided by a man who had been marooned there several years earlier, teaches the eccentric group of characters a bit of humility. The group is eventually saved when pilot Calhoun manages to find his way out of the jungle and to a helicopter. What could have been an interesting film loses force because of the filmmakers' inability to decide whether the story should concentrate on the moral aspects or the action. Direction does little to solve this problem; performances are standard.

p, Sigmund Neufeld; d, Peter Stewart; w, Fred Myton; ph, Jack Greenhalgh (Cinecolor); ed, Holbrook N. Todd; set d, Elias Reif; m/l, Lew Porter, Leo Erody.

Adventure/Drama (PR:A MPAA:NR)

MIRAGE ** 1/2 (1965) 108m UNIV bw

Gregory Peck *(David Stillwell)*, Diane Baker *(Sheila)*, Walter Matthau *(Ted Caselle)*, Kevin McCarthy *(Josephson)*, Jack Weston *(Lester)*, Leif Erickson *(Maj. Crawford)*, Walter Abel *(Charles Calvin)*, George Kennedy *(Willard)*, Robert H. Harris *(Dr. Broden)*, Anne Seymour *(Frances Calvin)*, House Jameson *(Bo)*, Hari Rhodes *(Lt.

Franken), Syl Lamont *(Benny)*, Eileen Baral *(Irene)*, Neil Fitzgerald *(Joe Turtle)*, Franklin E. Cover *(Group Leader)*.

MIRAGE is a mystery in the truest sense because it is just as baffling at the fade out as it was at the fade in. The film is held together by the firm direction of Dmytryk and a good performance by Peck. It was lensed on location in New York City, so it was a visual repast, if not an intellectual one. During an unexplained blackout at a major Gotham skyscraper, a prominent "man of peace," Abel, falls out of a 27th story to his death. Peck races down the stairwells (the elevators are out of commission) to the street below. When he emerges, he is met by several people who know him, including Baker. When he reenters the building, he is stunned to find that the offices and business he recalled were there, aren't there at all! He is confused, goes to his apartment, and is met by Weston, who holds a gun on him, insisting that they must see a man Weston refers to as "the Major." Peck knocks out Weston and goes straight to the police to explain his plight. They listen but don't believe a word of it, as he cannot provide them with even the most mundane information about his own life, like his birthday. Peck thinks he may be going mad, visits psychiatrist Harris who listens, then refuses to get involved because the story sounds fishy and might involve the frightened shrink with the cops, something he'd like to avoid. One detective, Matthau, believes Peck is telling the truth but he is soon murdered by unknown killers. Further, Peck is now being tailed by Weston and Kennedy, two gunmen who are intent on finding out what Peck is up to, even though Peck himself has no idea of that. Peck returns to psychiatrist Harris and they begin to work out Peck's problem together. The conclusion reached is that Peck is a physiochemist who lost his memory after he saw his friend, Abel, fall to his death. They also deduce that Peck has discovered a new way to neutralize radiation, and that he had taken the findings to Abel, who had wanted to bring it to his "associate," Erickson, a tycoon. When Peck refused to give the discovery to anyone for business reasons (preferring to give it to the world as a donation), Abel attempted to take the formula away from Peck by force as Peck was burning the paper on which it was written. In his zealousness to get the formula, Abel slipped and went out the window. It all comes back to Peck in a flash and he goes to Erickson's office to confront him. When Peck's life is threatened by the shadowy businessman (Erickson's alliance with the supposedly peaceful Abel is also not firmly demonstrated), Peck is saved by Baker, who walks in and out of scenes with aplomb and no rhyme or reason. Though the picture flits around like a tsetse fly in Upper Volta, it is still fun to watch, most of the time. Screenwriter Stone (who also wrote CHARADE and cowrote FATHER GOOSE just before this assignment) may have bitten off more than he could spew with this adaptation from Ericson's original material. There are no questions answered and no cogent arguments to drive the film forward from scene to scene. This is in sharp contrast to the Hitchcock-type stories they were certainly attempting to emulate. Peck is good as the enigmatic protagonist who is seldom actually threatened, except by his own self-doubt. Matthau does well in his brief bit as the detective but he isn't around long enough to be appreciated. During the production, director Dmytryk took Matthau aside and told him: "You should have a great career in films. You can be one of our top character actors." Matthau bristled and replied: "Charactor actor, hell! I'm going to be one of the top leading men." Dmytryk, a vastly underrated director, brought forth another one of his inventive techniques with this film. To show flashbacks he discarded the usual oil dissolves where the effect is an undulating, out-of-focus image to suggest dream or memory sequences. He went to straight cuts touched off with a short lead-in line and audiences still grasped the sequence of events. The technique has been used ever since, although not always with effectiveness. Remade in 1968 as JIGSAW.

p, Harry Keller; d, Edward Dmytryk; w, Peter Stone (based on the novel *Fallen Angel* by Walter Ericson); ph, Joseph MacDonald; m, Quincy Jones; ed, Ted J. Kent; art d, Alexander Golitzen, Frank Arrigo; set d, John McCarthy, John Austin; cos, Jean Louis; makeup, Bud Westmore.

Mystery **(PR:A-C MPAA:NR)**

MIRAGE**** (1972, Peru) 82m Bernardo Batievsky c

Helena Rojo, Miguel Angel Flores, Oriando Sach, Hernan Romero, Gabrial Figueroa, Romulo Leon, Raquel Meneses, Enrique Cox, Enrique Flores, Cesar Elias, Hernan Bejar.

Complex story about a young man who inherits a broken down estate at the edge of the Peruvian desert, with no explanation about the former owners or what had become of the once thriving house. By searching through the rocks and sands for relics, he discovers the answers to the mystery, told in flashback. The film combines the boy's search with other socio-economic issues relevant to Peru in a confusing, but insightful manner. The photography of the desert is stunning.

d&w, Armando Robles Godoy; ph, Mario Robles Godoy; m, Enrique Pinella; set d, Mario Pozzi.

Drama **(PR:C MPAA:NR)**

MIRANDA*** (1949, Brit.) 80m Gainsborough/EL bw

Glynis Johns *(Miranda)*, Googie Withers *(Clare Marten)*, Griffith Jones *(Paul Marten)*, John McCallum *(Nigel Hood)*, Margaret Rutherford *(Nurse Cary)*, David Tomlinson *(Charles)*, Yvonne Owen *(Betty)*, Sonia Holm *(Isobel)*, Lyn Evans *(Inn Landlord)*, Maurice Denham *(Cockle Vendor)*, Brian Oulton *(Manell)*, Zena Marshall *(Secretary)*, Howard Douglas *(Fisherman)*, Charles Penrose *(Stage Manager)*, Stringer Davis *(Museum Attendant)*, Hal Osmond *(Railway Carman)*, Anthony Drake, Charles Rolfe, Charles Paton, Frank Webster, Toni McMillan, Thelma Rea, Joan Ingram, Gerald Campion.

Jones is a wealthy doctor on a fishing trip to the ocean when mermaid Johns forces him to take her to London. Her lower body is wrapped up and she confines herself to a wheelchair to make her appear as an invalid. In London her unusual beauty and charm cause men to fall in love with her, while the women are jealous, leading to disaster in several households. Johns soon becomes homesick for the sea, returning to care for her new baby. Script and direction are well paced, creating a succession of well-placed laughs. Johns is believable in a role that would normally be hard to accept. Followed by the sequel MAD ABOUT MEN.

p, Betty E. Box; d, Ken Annakin; w, Peter Blackmore, Denis Waldock (based on the play by Blackmore); ph, Raymond Elton; m, Temple Abady; ed, Gordon Hales; art d, George Patterson; cos, Yvonne Caffin; makeup, Len Garde.

Comedy **(PR:A MPAA:NR)**

MIRIAM (SEE: TRILOGY, 1969)

MIRROR CRACK'D, THE***

(1980, Brit.) 105m EMI/Associated Film Distribution c

Angela Lansbury *(Miss Marple)*, Wendy Morgan *(Cherry)*, Margaret Courtenay *(Mrs. Bantry)*, Charles Gray *(Bates the Butler)*, Maureen Bennett *(Heather Babcock)*, Carolyn Pickles *(Miss Giles)*, Eric Dodson *(The Major)*, Charles Lloyd-Pack *(Vicar)*, Richard Pearson *(Dr. Haydock)*, Thick Wilson *(Mayor)*, Pat Nye *(Mayoress)*, Peter Woodthorpe *(Scoutmaster)*, Geraldine Chaplin *(Ella Zielinsky)*, Tony Curtis *(Marty N. Fenn)*, Edward Fox *(Inspector Craddock)*, Rock Hudson *(Jason Rudd)*, Kim Novak *(Lola Brewster)*, Elizabeth Taylor *(Marina Rudd)*, Marella Oppenheim *(Margot Bence)*, Anthony Steel *(Sir Derek Ridgeley)*, Dinah Sheridan *(Lady Amanda Ridgeley)*, Oriana Grieve *(Kate Ridgeley)*, Kenneth Fortescue *(Charles Foxwell)*, Hildegard Neil *(Lady Foxcroft)*, Allan Cuthbertson *(Peter Montrose)*, George Silver *(DaSilva)*, John Bennett *(Barnsby)*, Nigel Stock *(Inspector Gates)*.

Anyone who recalls Margaret Rutherford's version of Agatha Christie's Miss Marple may be a trifle disappointed by Lansbury's portrayal of the redoubtable spinster-detective, but they have surrounded her with so many cameos that it matters little. This is not the average mystery, as it bears all the trademarks of its renowned creator: sly dialog, cagey characters, and unexpected plot twists. Based on her novel *The Mirror Crack'd from Side to Side*, screenwriters Sandler and Hales stuck close to the premise and that faithfulness is both the charm and the undoing of the movie. Most of the stars are nostalgic throwbacks to the 1950s and this movie marks a number of reunions. Taylor and Hudson had been in GIANT together and she'd worked with Lansbury in NATIONAL VELVET. In this film, Taylor is excellent in a role she was living at the time, an aging actress bent on making a comeback. Taylor is the victim of a painful mental breakdown as well as being several years away from her beloved career. The breakdown was caused by a tragedy that may or may not have been accidental (and was, in fact, a true occurrence which took place in the life of Gene Tierney), and the person who is suspected as having caused it now lives in the small hamlet where Taylor and the others have come to make a film. Two murders sully the quiet village and Taylor's nephew arrives. This is Fox, an inspector with Scotland Yard. The movie company is making their version of "Mary, Queen of Scots" and Novak has been cast in the lead by her producer husband Curtis. Lots of inside jokes for movie buffs as Taylor and Novak pelt each other with verbal abuse. Hudson is the film's director and Taylor's husband, though carrying on an affair with his secretary, Chaplin. Amid the murders is a satire of a film company on location, but it is nowhere near as honest as the brilliant DAY FOR NIGHT which handled the same plot (sans the deaths). Lansbury, who went on to play a similar role in TV's "Murder, She Wrote," is a no-nonsense Marple as opposed to the deliciously daft but irresistible quality of Rutherford. Once Lansbury and Fox come on the scene, the picture begins to get murky, in sharp contrast to the lightness of the earlier exchanges. The major problem is that the casting seems to be divided in two camps: the subdued English and the loudmouthed Americans, who become caricatures. Fox's character is outstanding, using his knowledge of film lore to solve the mystery. There is, as usual, the explanation denoument in the last reel, but it would be unfair to any lover of Christie to explain it here. If you know the true Tierney story, that should be enough of a clue to help solve the puzzle. The actors are all allowed to play somewhere over the top and that is good fun . . . for a while. Too much of it can become as tedious as a geometry exam.

p, John Brabourne, Richard Goodwin; d, Guy Hamilton; w, Jonathan Hales, Barry Sandler (based on the novel *The Mirror Crack'd from Side to Side* by Agatha Christie); ph, Christopher Challis (Technicolor); m, John Cameron; ed, Richard Marden; prod d, Michael Stinger; art d, John Roberts; cos, Phyllis Dalton; m/l, Irving Berlin.

Mystery **Cas.** **(PR:A-C MPAA:PG)**

MIRROR HAS TWO FACES, THE 1/2**

(1959, Fr.) 105m Franco-London/Continental bw (LE MIROIR A DEUX FACES)

Michele Morgan *(Marie-Jose)*, Bourvil *(Tardivet)*, Ivan Desny *(Gerard)*, Elisabeth Manet *(Veronique)*, Gerard Oury *(Dr. Bosc)*, Sandra Milo *(Ariane)*, Sylvie *(Mme. Tardivet)*, George Chamaret *(Mons. Vauzanges)*, Jane Marken *(Mme. Vauzanges)*, Carette *(Mons. Benoit)*, Georgette Anys *(Mme. Benoit)*.

A twist on the Pygmalion theme has Morgan as a homely, but sensitive and intelligent girl. She marries an oafish school teacher, though she is really in love with her brother-in-law. When her husband is involved in an auto accident with a plastic surgeon, the doctor agrees to redo Morgan's face as compensation, giving Morgan the face she really deserves. With her new looks, she is able to find true love, but her husband is driven to killing the doctor who performed the surgery. The filmmakers do a fine job of delving into the problems people face when a fairy tale like transformation takes place, though the film suffers from an over-analysis of the situation. Also, Morgan is too glamorous to pull off the type of physical transformation that occurs. (In French; English subtitles.)

p, Alain Poire; d, Andre Cayatte; w, Cayatte, Gerard Oury; ph, Christian Matras; ed, Paul Cayatte; m, Louiguy; English titles, Herman C. Weinberg.

Drama **(PR:A MPAA:NR)**

MIRTH AND MELODY (SEE: LET'S GO PLACES, 1929)

MISADVENTURES OF MERLIN JONES, THE ** 1/2

(1964) 88m Disney/BV c

Tommy Kirk (Merlin Jones), Annette Funicello (Jennifer), Leon Ames (Judge Holmby), Stuart Erwin (Police Capt. Loomis), Alan Hewitt (Prof. Shattuck), Connie Gilchrist (Mrs. Gossett), Dal McKennon (Detective Hutchins), Norman Grabowski (Norman), Kelly Thordsen (Muller), Michael Fox (Kohner), Bert Mustin (Bailiff), June Ellis (Stanley the Chimp).

Unappealing attempt from the Disney studios which is more deserving of treatment as a TV movie than a feature. The story revolves around Kirk as a brainy college student who invents an apparatus which allows him to read minds. When he is brought before a judge for a traffic violation, he discovers that the judge is planning a robbery. As it happens, the judge, Ames, is actually a mystery writer incognito and the robbery plan was the plot for his next novel. As an experiment, Kirk later hypnotizes the judge into stealing a mistreated chimpanzee. Corny plot fails to generate any solid comedy. Funicello, as Kirk's coed girl friend, is fairly bland, as is the rest of the cast. Followed by a sequel, THE MONKEY'S UNCLE.

p, Ron Miller; d, Robert Stevenson; w, Tom August, Helen August (based on a story by Bill Walsh); ph, Edward Colman (Technicolor); m, Buddy Baker; ed, Cotton Warburton; art d, Carroll Clark, William Tuntke; set d, Emile Kuri, Hal Gausman; cos, Chuck Keehne, Gertrude Casey; m/l, "Merlin Jones," Richard M. Sherman, Robert B. Sherman; makeup, Pat McNalley.

Comedy   **(PR:AAA   MPAA:NR)**

MISBEHAVING HUSBANDS * 1/2   (1941) 65m PRC bw

Ralph Byrd (Bob Grant), Esther Muir (Grace Norman), Harry Langdon (Henry Butler), Gayne Whitman (Gilbert Wayne), Luana Walters (Jane Forbes), Florence Wright (Nan Blake), Frank Hagney (Gooch), Byron Barr (Floor Walker), Vernon Dent (Sgt. Murphy), Billy Mitchell (Memphis), Hennie Brown (Opal), Betty Blythe (Mrs. Butler), Frank Jacquet, Charlotte Treadway, Mary McLaren, Gertrude Astor.

Overworn theme has unhappy wives seeking divorce and finding consolation in the arms of handsome but treacherous lawyers. Here the wife is too suspicious of her store-owner husband, whose only fault is in assisting the selection of the window models. Haphazard direction does little to help this implausible story.

p, Jed Buell; d, William Beaudine; w, Claire Parrish, Charles A. Rogers (based on a story by Sea Sabin, Vernon Smith); ph, Art Read; ed, Robert Crandall.

Comedy   **(PR:A   MPAA:NR)**

MISBEHAVING LADIES * 1/2   (1931) 65m WB/FN bw

Lila Lee, Ben Lyon, Louise Fazenda, Lucien Littlefield, Julia Swayne Gordon, Emily Fitzroy, Martha Mattox, Virginia Grey, Oscar Apfel.

Forgotten little comedy has Lee a European princess who returns to the small midwestern hometown she left as a child. Mistaken by the town residents for a seamstress, she encourages the error, with mostly predictable results.

d, William Beaudine; w, Julian Josephson (based on the story "Once There Was a Princess" by Juliet Wilbur Tompkins); ph, John Seitz; ed, Terrill Morse.

Comedy   **(PR:A   MPAA:NR)**

MISCHIEF ***   (1931, Brit.) 67m British and Dominions/GAU bw

Ralph Lynn (Arthur Gordon), Winifred Shotter (Diana Birkett), Jeanne Stuart (Eleanor Bingham), James Carew (Reginald Bingham), Jack Hobbs (Tom Birkett), Maud Gill (Louise Piper), Kenneth Kove (Bertie Pitts), Louie Emery (Mrs. Easy), A. Bromley Davenport.

This British farce is a nice combination of slapstick and verbal comedy, with Stuart as a loyal wife thinking about having an affair. When her husband, Carew, goes to Paris for business, she leaves for a cottage with her boy friend. Her husband's friends are in pursuit of the would-be lovers, who are turned out by the cottage's owner. Carew's pal Lynn arrives and starts his own romantic encounters. An above-average production for British features of this period.

p, Herbert Wilcox; d, Jack Raymond; w, W.P. Lipscomb, Maclean Rogers (based on the play by Ben Travers); ph, F. A. Young.

Comedy   **(PR:A   MPAA:NR)**

MISCHIEF *   (1969, Brit.) 57m Shand/Children's Film Foundation c

Paul Fraser (Davy), Iain Burton (Harry), Adrienne Byrne (Jenny), Michael Newport (Sam), Gina Malcolm (Pat Crawford), Gerald Sim (Jim), Colin Gordon (Mr. Crawford), Bill Owen (Quarryman).

A retired circus pony throws little Byrne, but helps a boy rescue her. Boring children's film that few children will sit still through.

p, Ian Shand, Jack Grossman; d, Shand; w, Grossman.

Children   **(PR:A   MPAA:NR)**

MISFITS, THE ***   (1961) 124m Seven Arts/UA bw

Clark Gable (Gay Langland), Marilyn Monroe (Roslyn Taber), Montgomery Clift (Perce Howland), Thelma Ritter (Isabelle Steers), Eli Wallach (Guido), James Barton (Old Man in the Bar), Estelle Winwood (Church Lady), Kevin McCarthy (Raymond Taber), Dennis Shaw (Young Boy in Bar), Philip Mitchell (Charles Steers), Walter Ramage (Old Groom), Peggy Barton (Young Bride), J. Lewis Smith (Fresh Cowboy in Bar), Marietta Tree (Susan), Bobby La Salle (Bartender), Ryall Bowker (Man in Bar), Ralph Roberts (Ambulance Driver).

A disturbing but captivating film of modern cowboys who have lost their purpose and simple ethics in a world that has robbed them of the West into which they were born. THE MISFITS was Gable's last film. That the strenuous stunts and bronc-busting feats he performed killed Gable is still in debate but it is certain that he gave one of the finest performances of his career for the fade-out. This was also Monroe's

last film, one that ended a glittering but torturous career. Gable and sidekicks Wallach and Clift are cowboys without saddles, driving a pickup about the West in search of odd jobs, but mostly following the rodeo circuits, living on the fringe of the rope-and-tie action. Their talk is laced with thin bravado and they have more of the past to discuss than the future. In Reno, they meet recently divorced blond voluptuary Monroe who left her successful businessman husband. She is a one-time stripper who is seeking truth and a meaningful relationship (as they say) with anyone who can relate to her idealistic notions. Gable is twice Monroe's age, has no noble purpose, and intends to round up "misfit" horses, those wild mustangs too small for rodeo or ranch work, so they can be ground up for dog food. His partners are Wallach, a one-time bombardier, and Clift, a troubled rodeo rider who hates his stepfather. Both men take a liking to the neurotic Monroe and try to persuade her to leave Gable, and go with either of them, but she remains steadfast to the old cowboy, believing he has a heart of gold if she can only discover the shaft leading to it. When Monroe learns the truth of the trio's horse-catching mission, she denounces Gable and his buddies, which incenses Gable. After all, he's only trying to make a living. The group traps a small herd of horses and Monroe pleads with Clift and Wallach to let the feisty leader go, but Gable is adamant. No woman will tell him his business, even though it's a business he knows is rotten to the core. He breaks the wild stallion and then, showing the compassion Monroe always knew was there, lets the horse go. He and Monroe drive off to make some sort of life together, Gable saying: "Just head for that big star. It will take you home." This is an awkward film, even though it has many fine moments, most of them Gable's—when he gets drunk and begins calling for his long-lost children, his spirited horse-breaking scenes (he did not employ a double and the strain undoubtedly caused him to have a fatal heart attack shortly thereafter), and some of his nostalgic scenes with Monroe. The actress is weak and directionless in her part, trying to adopt Actor's Studio methods and deadpanning her scenes while belying her altruistic lines with a jiggling, tight-skirted image. She's unbelievable and hardly the Monroe of old. Miller's presence at the on-location scenes in Reno and Dayton, Nevada, undoubtedly inhibited director Huston who fails to develop anyone's character except Gable's. Huston could not control the actress who seemed to be on the verge of a nervous breakdown; she did not show up in time for her scenes and, when she did show up, she could not remember a line of dialog until heavy coaching jarred her memory. Miller's dialog is sprinkled with his self-styled poetry which sounds good but means little. "We've all got to go sometime," Gable says, "dying's as natural as living." Wallach the flier moans: "I can't make a landing and I can't get up to God." Much has been said about this film being a brilliant mood piece of a dying Old West but that is not enough to make it a masterpiece. It's good because the cast is brilliant and so too is most of Miller's script and Huston's direction, but that's the problem. The separate brilliance of the leading players, the writer, and the director all pull in different directions. Gable had misgivings about performing the part and suspected Miller's script of being too arty, but he took on the introspective role and did much more with it than even Miller expected, the playwright-screenwriter initially believing that the one-time matinee idol was unsuitable for the part. Gable received $750,000 for his part, plus ten percent of the gross and an overtime rate of $48,000-a-week. Gable, instead of being upset with the drug-taking, sick-to-the-stomach Monroe, treated her with great consideration and kindness, working with her and never complaining when she appeared late for scenes. He was the same with Clift, but resented Wallach and his "method" school of acting, often quipping to Wallach that they would be having "boiled ham" for lunch after their scenes. Wallach would retort with: "Hey, king, can you lower my taxes?" Huston and Gable got along, although the director unnerved the actor by losing great amounts of money at the Reno gambling dens and then bragging about it. Miller grew to admire Gable greatly, later stating: "He was, of course, more glamorous than the real Gay, the one I wrote—any actor would be, the acting dimension does this. But the gallant essence, he did not enlarge on or overdo. He was a gent." Clift was also on the razor's edge when the film was made, drinking heavily and never fully recovering from a car accident that had scarred him. He does have one poignant scene in a phone booth where he tries to communicate with an indifferent mother but for the most part he is merely hanging on to his neurotic role. Early in the film technicians made the mistake of having Clift bare-hand the ropes he used in handling the horses and, since much footage had been shot without gloves, the actor had to go on using his bare hands until they were completely raw and rope-burned. Clift received $200,000 for his performance. The film was begun on July 18, 1960 and was completed on November 24, 1960; Gable had died eight days earlier and the following March his wife Kay gave birth to his one and only child. The picture was also Monroe's last completed feature film. After filming was finished, Monroe went into production with SOMETHING'S GOT TO GIVE, a comedy costarring Dean Martin. Her death from a sleeping-pill overdose occurred in the middle of the production.

p, Frank E. Taylor; d, John Huston; w, Arthur Miller; ph, Russell Metty; m, Alex North; ed, George Tomasini; md, North; art d, Stephen Grimes, William Newberry; set d, Frank McKelvy; cos, Jesse Munden; spec eff, Cline Jones; stunts, John Day, Jim Palen, Richard Pasco, Chuck Roberson; makeup, Frank LaRue, Frank Prehoda, Allan Snyder, Bunny Gardel.

Western   **Cas.**   **(PR:C   MPAA:NR)**

MISHPACHAT SIMCHON   (SEE: SIMCHON FAMILY, THE, 1969, Israel)

MISLEADING LADY, THE **   (1932) 70m PAR bw

Claudette Colbert (Helen Steele), Edmund Lowe (Jack Craigen), Stuart Erwin (Boney), Robert Strange (Sydney Parker), George Meeker (Tracy), Selena Royle (Alice Cannell), Curtis Cooksey (Bob Cannell), William Gargan (Fitzpatrick), Nina Walker (Jane Weatherly), Edgar Nelson (Steve), Fred Stewart (Babe), Harry Ellerbe (Spider), Will Geer (McMahon), Donald MacBride (Bill).

Unexceptional picture stars Colbert as a social butterfly trying to find some purpose to her meaningless life by turning to the stage. But theater director Strange proves a barrier to her plans, as does explorer Lowe, who kidnaps Colbert for his own romantic purposes. Except for the appearance of Erwin as an escapee from a mental institution, there is little here to maintain much interest.

d, Stuart Walker; w, Adelaide Heilbron, Caroline Francke (based on a play by Charles W. Goddard, Paul Dickey); ph, George Folsey; cos, Lucille [Lady Duff Gordon].

Comedy   **(PR:A MPAA:NR)**

MISS ANNIE ROONEY**   (1942) 84m UA bw

Shirley Temple (*Annie Rooney*), William Gargan (*Tim Rooney*), Guy Kibbee (*Grandpop Rooney*), Dickie Moore (*Marty White*), Peggy Ryan (*Myrtle*), Roland DuPree (*Joey*), Jonathan Hale (*Mr. White*), Gloria Holden (*Mrs. White*), Mary Field (*Mrs. Metz*), George Lloyd (*Burns*), Jan Buckingham (*Madam Sylvia*), Selmer Jackson (*Mr. Thomas*), June Lockhart (*Stella Bainbridge*), Charles Coleman (*Sidney*), Edgar Dearing (*Policeman*), Virginia Sale (*Myrtle's Mother*), Shirley Mills (*Audrey Hollis*), Noel Neill (*Marty's Friend*), Byron Foulger (*Randall*), Wilson Benge (*Butler*).

Temple had problems finding a good film that would allow her to make the transition to more adult roles and help her recapture the success she had as a child star. MISS ANNIE ROONEY proved to be no exception, as it depends too heavily on the overworn story line about the poor girl falling for the rich boy, though the rich boy's father disapproves. In this case, everything is smoothed over when Temple's father pursues Moore's father with his idea for synthetic rubber. When the idea proves fruitful, Moore's father begins to see Temple in a new light. Temple is unable to do much with the script's burdensome dialog, which is the film's major drawback.

p, Edward Small; d, Edwin L. Marin; w, George Bruce; ph, Lester White; ed, Fred Feitshans, Jr.; md, Edward Paul; art d, John DuCasse Schulze; cos, Royer; ch, Nick Castle.

Drama   **Cas.**   **(PR:A MPAA:NR)**

MISS FANE'S BABY IS STOLEN***
(1934) 70m PAR bw (GB: KIDNAPPED; AKA: MISS FANE'S BABY)

Dorothea Wieck (*Madeline Fane*), Alice Brady (*Mrs. Molly Prentiss*), Baby LeRoy (*Michael Fane*), William Frawley (*Capt. Murphy*), George Barbier (*MacCready*), Alan Hale (*Sam*), Jack LaRue (*Bert*), Dorothy Burgess (*Dotty*), Irving Bacon (*Joel Prentiss*), George "Spanky" McFarland (*Johnny Prentiss*), Cullen Johnson (*Billie Prentiss*), Carmencita Johnson (*Minnie Prentiss*), Kay Lou Barnes (*Baby Prentiss*), Florence Roberts (*Agnes*), Edwin Maxwell (*Judge*), Charles Wilson (*Chief of Police*), Adrian Rosley, Charles McAvoy, Harrison Greene, Leslie Palmer, Marcelle Corday, Louis Natheaux.

This story of kidnaping was the first of its sort to follow the famous Lindbergh case. Baby LeRoy plays the child of a famous movie star, kidnaped from his luxurious Beverly Hills home. After frantic attempts on the part of the police and the mother, the baby is finally found by a farmer's wife, Brady, who drives to town pursued by the kidnapers. One memorable scene has the mother's voice pleading for her baby over the radio; LeRoy hears the familiar voice through the radio, and searches for the body that goes with it. Though the plot suffers from some implausible situations, as a whole the film delivers a sensitive and touching message. George McFarland played "Spanky" in the "Our Gang" series, known on television as "The Little Rascals."

d, Alexander Hall; w, Jane Storm, Adela Rogers St. John (based on the story by Rupert Hughes); ph, Alfred Gilks; ed, James Smith.

Drama   **(PR:A MPAA:NR)**

MISS FIX-IT   (SEE: KEEP SMILING, 1938)

MISS GRANT TAKES RICHMOND***1/2
(1949) 87m COL bw (GB: INNOCENCE IS BLISS)

Lucille Ball (*Ellen Grant*), William Holden (*Dick Richmond*), Janis Carter (*Peggy Donato*), James Gleason (*J. Hobart Gleason*), Gloria Henry (*Helen White*), Frank McHugh (*Kilcoyne*), George Cleveland (*Judge Ben Grant*), Stephen Dunne (*Ralph Winton*), Arthur Space (*Willacombe*), Will Wright (*Roscoe Johnson*), Jimmy Lloyd (*Homer White*), Loren Tindall (*Charles Meyers*), Ola Lorraine (*Jeanie Meyers*), Claire Meade (*Aunt Mae*), Roy Roberts (*Foreman*), Charles Lane (*Woodruff*), Harry Harvey (*Councilman Reed*), Harry Cheshire (*Leo Hopkins*), Nita Mathews (*Ruth*), Glen Thompson (*Carpenter*), Peter Brocco, Toni Newman, Marjorie Stapp, Don Hayden, Bradley Johnson, Robert Strong, Bret Hamilton, Tom Kingston (*Bits*), Syd Saylor (*Surveyor*), Michael Cisney (*Lawyer*), Eddie Acuff (*Bus Driver*), Bill Lechner (*Soda Clerk*), Charles L. Marsh (*Court Clerk*), Charles "Chuck" Hamilton (*Cop*), Wanda Cantlon (*Maid*), Stanley Waxman (*Sig Davis*), Cosmo Sardo (*Maitre D'*), Cliff Clark (*Job Boss*), Wanda Perry (*Ruth*), Charles Sullivan (*Worker*), Ted Jordan, Jerry Jerome, Jack Overman, Paul Newlan, Michael Ross (*Hoods*).

A charming, literate comedy that foreshadowed Ball's talents to amuse. It was one of Holden's first starring attempts at funnybone-tickling after several dramatic roles. Ball is a seemingly addle-brained secretary who is hired by Holden, a young sharpster who runs a bookmaking ring, to run the office. She has no idea that the company she works for is engaged in illegal doings and thinks that it's a real estate office. McHugh is the mental whiz who remembers all the bets and has no need to write anything down, and Gleason is an old-time bookie who doesn't like the fact that they are using such an elaborate front. There was a huge housing shortage in 1949 and Ball is soon involved with the plights of the homeless who call the office for accommodations. To keep from being discovered, Holden goes along with the gag and winds up promoting a low-cost housing scheme. Holden is in a bit of trouble and owes many thousands to a huge gambling syndicate, so he decides to use the

housing ploy to extract the cash needed to pay off the hoods. Money comes in from potential homebuyers and Holden and his cohorts engage in what might be called "Byzantine bookkeeping" and take the money out of the company. The money has soon vanished and Ball is left holding the bag for all the investors' capital. All this time, the syndicate that owns Holden's note has been run by Carter, who would willingly tear up the marker if Holden paid some romantic attention to her. Instead, Holden sells his small bookmaking operation to Carter to get the 50 grand that he's stolen. He uses that to repay the investors. Ball breaks into Carter's house and pretends to be a tough broad and frightens Carter into relinquishing her claim on Holden. Ball and Holden fall predictably in love and will spend the rest of their lives holding hands and doing good things for people who have no place to live. Holden was about 31 at the time the film was made and in fast comedic company with Ball and veterans McHugh, Gleason, and the others. He more than held his own in the laugh department and that may have been one of the reasons why he was engaged to be in one of the best comedies ever, BORN YESTERDAY, a year or so later, after having appeared in one of the best dramas ever, SUNSET BOULEVARD. Although the story credit goes to Everett Freeman (whose older brother, Devery, collaborated on the screenplay), it felt very much like a Damon Runyon yarn, right down to the girl who is smarter than you think and the bookie who turns out to have a heart of gold. Good comedy work from a veritable stalk of excellent "second bananas."

p, S. Sylvan Simon; d, Lloyd Bacon; w, Nat Perrin, Devery Freeman, Frank Tashlin (based on a story by Everett Freeman); ph, Charles Lawton, Jr.; m, Heinz Roemheld; ed, Jerome Thoms; md, Morris Stoloff; art d, Walter Holscher; set d, James Crowe; cos, Jean Louis; makeup, Clay Campbell.

Crime/Comedy   **(PR:A MPAA:NR)**

MISS JESSICA IS PREGNANT**
(1970) 82m Triskele/Joseph Brenner bw (AKA: SPRING NIGHT, SUMMER NIGHT; JESSICA)

Larue Hall (*Jessica*), Ted Heim [Ted Garrotte] (*Carl*), Marj Johnson (*Mother*), John Crawford (*Father*), Tracy Smith (*Jessica's Sister*), David Ayres (*Gas Station Owner*).

Hall, the daughter of hillbilly parents, is impregnated by her half-brother. Hall's father is filled with rage, causing the boy to flee. He returns, however, to take Hall away from the decadent environment. First shown at the Pesaro Film Festival in 1967.

p, Franklin Miller, J.L. Anderson; d, Anderson; w, Doug Rapp, Miller, Anderson; ph, David Prince, Brian Blauser, Art Stifel; ed, Anderson, Miller.

Drama   **(PR:O MPAA:R)**

MISS JUDE   (SEE: TRUTH ABOUT SPRING, THE, 1965, Brit.)

MISS LONDON LTD.**   (1943, Brit.) 99m Gainsborough/GFD bw

Arthur Askey (*Arthur Bowman*), Evelyn Dall (*Terry Arden*), Anne Shelton (*Gail Martin*), Richard Hearne (*Commodore*), Max Bacon (*Romeo*), Jack Train (*Joe Nelson*), Peter Graves (*Capt. Rory O'More*), Jean Kent (*The Encyclopedia*), Ronald Shiner (*Sailor*), Iris Lang, Virginia Keiley, Una Shepherd, Sheila Bligh, Noni Brooke, Patricia Owens.

Dall is the daughter of an American, the owner of an escort agency, who discovers that business is bad despite WW II. She teams with Askey in a series of schemes to raise some military customers. Good songs and some funny comedy bits break up this overlong film. Dall was an American nightclub singer who turned up in several British wartime musicals.

p, Edward Black; d, Val Guest; w, Guest, Marriott Edgar; ph, Basil Emmott; l, Guest.

Musical Comedy   **(PR:A MPAA:NR)**

MISS MINK OF 1949**   (1949) 69m FOX bw

Jimmy Lydon (*Joe Forrester*), Lois Collier (*Alice Forrester*), Richard Lane (*Herbert Pendelton*), Barbara Brown (*Mrs. Marshall*), Paul Guilfoyle (*Uncle Newton*), June Storey (*Rose Pendelton*), Grandon Rhodes (*Nietsche*), Walter Sande (*O'Mulvaney*), Don Kohler (*Skeet Price*), Vera Marsh (*Hortense*), Dorothy Granger (*Mrs. O'Mulvaney*), Iris Adrian (*Mrs. McKelvey*).

Lydon and Collier are a young married couple of relatively modest circumstances, when Collier wins a mink coat in a contest. Changes in their lives occur as they try to live up to the extravagance of the coat; further complications arise from mooching relations and a boss' wife, who wants the coat for herself. The mink is eventually stolen, with everyone ending up at the courthouse. The well-paced direction manages to keep the proper amount of laughs going.

p, Sol M. Wurtzel; d, Glenn Tryon; w, Arnold Belgard; ph, Benjamin Kline; m, Mahlon Merrick; ed, William Claxton; md, David Chudnow; art d, Eddie Imazu.

Comedy   **(PR:A MPAA:NR)**

MISS MUERTE   (SEE: DIABOLICAL DR. Z, THE, 1967, Fr./Span.)

MISS PACIFIC FLEET*1/2   (1935) 66m WB bw

Joan Blondell (*Gloria Fay*), Glenda Farrell (*Mae O'Brien*), Warren Hull (*Sgt. Tom Foster*), Allen Jenkins (*Kewpie Wiggins*), Hugh Herbert (*Mr. August Freitag, President, Better Business Bureau*), Minna Gombell (*Sadie Freitag*), Eddie Acuff (*Clarence*), Marie Wilson (*Virgie Matthews*), Guinn "Big Boy" Williams (*Nick*), Anita Kerry (*Annie*), Mary Green (*Violet*), Marie Astaire, Lucille Collins (*Girls*), Eddy Chandler (*Chief Petty Officer*), Paul Irving (*Mr. Winch*), Mary Doran (*Miss LaMay*), Sam Rice (*Proprietor*), Ben Hendricks (*Cop*), Paul Fix, James Burtis (*Sailors*), Louis Natheaux, Nick Copeland, Joe Bordeaux (*Mugs*), Harrison Greene (*Jackson*), Douglas Fowley (*Second*), Allen Wood (*Hay*), Emmett Vogan, Harry Seymour (*Announcers*), Jack Norton (*Radio Official*), Tom Manning (*Judge*), Stuart Holmes (*Conductor*), Claude Peyton (*Caretaker*).

Pointless farce has Blondell and Farrell as two stranded show girls trying to make their way back to New York. They devise the scheme of a popularity contest among the sailors, with Blondell taking the prize. Except for a couple of well-placed laughs the picture falls flat, with the talented cast given nothing to work with.

p, Earl Baldwin; d, Ray Enright; w, Lucille Newmark, Patsy Flick, Peter Milne (based on a story by Frederick Hazlitt Brennan); ph, Arthur Todd; ed, Clarence Kolster; md, Leo F. Forbstein; art d, Esdras Hartley; cos, Orry-Kelly.

Comedy   **(PR:A MPAA:NR)**

MISS PILGRIM'S PROGRESS**   (1950, Brit.) 82m Angel/GN bw

Michael Rennie (*Bob Thane*), Yolande Donlan (*Laramie Pilgrim*), Garry Marsh (*Mayor*), Emrys Jones (*Vicar*), Reginald Beckwith (*Mr. Jenkins*), Helena Pickard (*Mrs. Jenkins*), Jon Pertwee (*Postman Perkins*), Richard Littledale (*Mr. Thane*), Bruce Belfrage (*Manager*), Valentine Dyall (*Superintendent*), Peter Butterworth (*Jonathan*), Avril Angers (*Factory Girl*), Barry Faber, Arthur Hill, Ivan Craig, Trevor Hill, Marianne Stone, Mary Vallange, Terry Randall, Frances Marsden, Frederick Bradshaw, Basil Lord, Raymond Waters.

Formula plot has Donlan as a factory girl who exchanges jobs with an English girl, and lands in the small village of Whitehall. She is so taken by the quiet, simple lifestyle that when government planners intend to destroy the village to use the land, Donlan rallies the normally sedate townspeople against this new plan. The script relies on the sure-fire technique of cultural differences for humor, with the English countryside providing a pleasant background.

p, Daniel M. Angel, Nat Cohen; d, Val Guest; w, Guest; ph, Bert Mason; m, Philip Martell; ed, Douglas Myers.

Comedy   **(PR:A MPAA:NR)**

MISS PINKERTON* 1/2   (1932) 66m FN bw

Joan Blondell (*Miss Adams/Miss Pinkerton*), George Brent (*Inspector Patten*), Mae Madison (*2nd Nurse*), John Wray (*Hugo*), Ruth Hall (*Paula Brent*), Allan Lane (*Herbert Wynne*), C. Henry Gordon (*Dr. Stewart*), Donald Dillaway (*Charles Elliott*), Elizabeth Patterson (*Aunt Juliet*), Blanche Frederici (*Mary*), Mary Doran (*Florence Lenz*), Holmes Herbert (*Arthur Glenn*), Eulalie Jensen (*Miss Gibbons*), Treva Lawler (*3rd Nurse*), Luana Walter (*1st Nurse*), Lucien Littlefield (*Henderson*), Nigel de Brulier (*Coroner*), Walter Brennan (*Police Broadcaster*), Lyle Talbot (*Editor*).

Routine whodunit has Blondell and Brent as the leads in this overly confusing tale of a murder mystery with a number of possible culprits. By trying to maintain a fast pace, the direction loses much of the suspense. The vast array of characters and situations also makes it next to impossible to follow what is going on. Blondell and Brent do the best they can with the material given, but all in a vain attempt.

p, Hal Wallis; d, Lloyd Bacon; w, Nevin Busch, Lillian Hayward (based on the novel by Mary Roberts Rinehart); ph, Barney McGill; ed, Ray Curtis.

Mystery   **(PR:A MPAA:NR)**

MISS PRESIDENT** 1/2
(1935, Hung.) 90m Reflektor/Hungarian bw (ELNOK KISASSZONY)

Lilly Murati (*Zsuzsi Vazsonyi*), Pal Javor (*Istvan Torok*), Ella Gombaszogi (*Miss Berta*), Gyula Kabos (*Odon Vas*), Jenoe Toerzs (*Kollar*), Marta Naday (*Kato*), Sandor Pethes (*Peter Galdy*), G. Partos (*Mr. White*).

Murati plays the fiery heiress of a large factory, who refuses to marry her guardian, Toerzs, on the grounds that she is in love with someone else. At Toerzs' insistence to name her beloved, Murati gives the name of a man she had seen in the newspaper. Toerzs searches out the man, Javor, and gives him a job in the factory. The script manages to maintain a balance between the romantic story line and the slapstick comedy, but the editing slows down the action. Some nice photography of the Hungarian countryside.

d, Andre Marton; w, Miklos Vitez, Istvan Bekeffy.

Comedy   **(PR:A MPAA:NR)**

MISS ROBIN CRUSOE**   (1954) 74m FOX c

Amanda Blake, George Nader, Rosalind Hayes.

Blake is a shipwrecked girl in this female version of the classic Daniel Defoe tale of Robinson Crusoe. She comes to the aid of Hayes, who is nearly killed by natives. Nader, a seaman who washes up to shore, rounds out the cast in this brainless adventure.

p&d, Eugene Frenke; w, Harold Nebenzal, Richard Yriondo (based on a story by Al Zimbalist); ph, Virgil Miller (Eastmancolor); m, Elmer Bernstein; ed, Thomas Pratt; art d, Frank P. Sylos.

Adventure   **(PR:A MPAA:NR)**

MISS ROBIN HOOD*   (1952, Brit.) 78m Group 3/Union bw

Margaret Rutherford (*Miss Honey*), Richard Hearne (*Henry Wrigley*), Michael Medwin (*Ernest*), Peter Jones (*Lidstone*), James Robertson Justice (*McAllister*), Sidney James (*Sidney*), Dora Bryan (*Pearl*), Frances Rowe (*Marion*), Eunice Gayson (*Pam*), Edward Lexy (*Wilson*), Eric Berry (*Lord Otterbourne*), Russell Waters (*Bunyan*), Reg Varney (*Dennis*), Suzanne Gibbs (*Sue*), Francis de Wolff (*Accident Policeman*).

Hearne is the meek, neat author of wild adventure novels for girls who is accosted by Rutherford's eccentric devotee. She involves him in a scheme to steal a whiskey formula from the distillers who stole it from her ancestors long ago. Once they have the recipe they are offered partnerships in the distillery and—thanks to Rutherford's assault on the publisher with a swarm of schoolgirls—Hearne gets to keep writing novels for his fans. A very bad comedy, right in the middle of a period when nearby

Ealing Studios were making some of the best comedies ever done. Group 3 was a company set up by the government so they could give money to filmmakers other than Rank and Associated British. Michael Balcon was made chairman of the company and Grierson, the founder of the modern documentary movement, was made one of the executive producers. Almost all their films were commercial failures and the company was soon disbanded.

p, John Grierson, Donald Wilson; d, John Guillermin; w, Val Valentine, Patrick Campbell (based on a story by Reed de Rouen); ph, Arthur Grant.

Comedy   **(PR:A MPAA:NR)**

MISS SADIE THOMPSON***   (1953) 91m COL c

Rita Hayworth (*Sadie Thompson*), Jose Ferrer (*Alfred Davidson*), Aldo Ray (*Sgt. Phil O'Hara*), Russell Collins (*Dr. Robert MacPhail*), Diosa Costello (*Ameena Horn*), Harry Bellaver (*Joe Horn*), Wilton Graff (*Governor*), Peggy Converse (*Mrs. Margaret Davidson*), Henry Slate (*Griggs*), Rudy Bond (*Hodges*), Charles Bronson (*Edwards*), Frances Morris (*Mrs. MacPhail*), Peter Chong (*Chung*), John Grossett (*Reverend*), Billy Varga, Teddy Pavelec, Frank Stanlow, Harold Tommy Hart, Charles Horvath, Ben Harris, Ted Jordan, Eduardo Cansino, Jr., John Duncan (*Marines*), Erlynn Mary Botelho, Elizabeth Bartilet, Dennis Medieros (*Children*), Joe McCabe (*Native*), Robert G. Anderson (*Dispatcher*), Al Kikume (*Native Secretary*), Fred Letuli (*Native Messenger*).

Every actress of note has longed to play a prostitute on screen, considering such an ignoble part a real challenge, and no script delved more deeply or significantly into the sluttish heart than Maugham's "Rain." Jeanne Eagels made the role of Sadie legendary, as did Gloria Swanson and myriad others, not the least of whom was Joan Crawford in RAIN. Hayworth, who had specialized in vamps for decades—as Dona Sol in BLOOD AND SAND and in the title role of SALOME, to name two—made a memorable Miss Thompson. The tropical tramp shows up on a Pacific island just after WW II, to be greeted by salivating Marines, chiefly sergeant Ray who falls in love with Hayworth and proposes. She almost accepts but is thwarted by religious zealot Ferrer who condemns her and insists she return to San Francisco where she is wanted on a morals charge. She begs to be sent somewhere, anywhere else. Meanwhile, Hayworth, to while the steamy nights away, joins the Marines in their makeshift saloon to shake her hips about with such tunes as "The Heat is On," "Hear No Evil, See No Evil," and "Blue Pacific Blues" ("Sadie Thompson's Song" by Lester Lee and Ned Washington). Ferrer, however, is like a terrier and won't let go of Hayworth, insisting she embrace religion. She does, genuinely atoning for her past sins, but it's all for naught. Ferrer's real reason for persecuting her is that he wants that slightly overweight and sweating body for himself. He rapes her and commits suicide the next day. Hayworth, a little wiser but no longer interested in having her soul saved, leaves the island, apparently intending to return to San Francisco anyway and pay her dues. Filmed in Hawaii, this was an oddball film in that it was originally intended to be a musical but it lacked a consistent score with only three songs performed by Hayworth (dubbed). One song, "The Heat is On," offers a display of erotic dancing seldom seen on the screen, as Rita gyrates a busty, hippy body while dripping sweat, and driving the ogling Marines to near frenzy. She gives a fiery performance and carries the film. Ferrer, who later stated that he took on the role of the religious nut only to offset criticism about his supposed un-American activities, is trapped in a one-dimensional role. Ray is wholly inept, playing the role of the sergeant as a big, dumb, gullible guy where he was savvy and a sharp character in the original script (much better played by William Gargan in RAIN). Hayworth weighed about 10 pounds more than her usual weight but here, stuffed into a dress so tight her body threatens to escape from it at any moment, she is right for the role of the bawdy lady she is playing. Filmed originally in 3-D.

p, Jerry Wald; d, Curtis Bernhardt; w, Harry Kleiner (based on the story "Rain" by W. Somerset Maugham); ph, Charles Lawton, Jr. (3-D; Technicolor); m, George Duning; ed, Viola Lawrence; md, M. W. Stoloff; art d, Carl Anderson; set d, Louis Diage; cos, Jean Louis; ch, Lee Scott; m/l, Lester Lee, Ned Washington, Allan Roberts; makeup, Caly Campbell.

Drama   **Cas.**   **(PR:O MPAA:NR)**

MISS SUSIE SLAGLE'S** 1/2   (1945) 88m PAR bw

Veronica Lake (*Nan Rogers*), Sonny Tufts (*Pug Prentiss*), Joan Caulfield (*Margaretta Howe*), Ray Collins (*Dr. Elijah Howe*), Billy De Wolfe (*Ben Mead*), Bill Edwards (*Elijah Howe, Jr.*), Pat Phelan (*Elbert Riggs*), Lillian Gish (*Miss Susie Slagle*), Roman Bohnen (*Dean Wingate*), Morris Carnovsky (*Dr. Fletcher*), Renny McEvoy (*Clayton Abernathy*), Lloyd Bridges (*Silas Holmes*), Michael Sage (*Irving Asrom*), E. J. Ballantine (*Dr. Metz*), Theodore Newton (*Dr. Boyd*), J. Lewis Johnson (*Hizer*), Ludwig Stossel (*Otto*), Charles E. Arnt (*Mr. Johnson*), Isabel Randolph (*Mrs. Howe*), Kathleen Howard (*Miss Wingate*), Frederick Burton (*Dr. Bowen*), Chester Morrison (*Paul*), William Meader, Albert Ruiz, Stan Johnson, Jerry James, Harold Bernadi (*Students*), Cyril Ring (*Instrumental Man*), Pierre Watkin (*Superintendent*), Alan Bridge (*Taxi Driver*), Byron Poindexter (*Orderly*), Milton Kibbee (*Little Man*), Mary Herriot (*Gwen*), William Challee (*Intern*), Connie Thompkin (*Alice*), Dorothy Adams (*Mrs. Johnson*).

Gish runs a boarding house at a medical school, giving the boys studying to become doctors the needed inspiration. Tufts is one of her boarders who is trying to romance Caulfield, but runs into trouble because he lacks funds and needs to devote a lot of time to studying. The story concentrates heavily upon the institutionalism of the boarding house. What would otherwise be a pretty drab subject is illuminated by the problems of various students. However, this also leads to the inability to keep a consistent plot going throughout; the various stories needing to be blended better. Camera work is good, as are the rest of the production techniques.

p, John Houseman; d, John Berry; w, Anne Froelick, Hugo Butler, Theodore Strauss, Adrian Scott (based on the novel by Augusta Tucker); ph, Charles Lang,

Jr.; m, Daniele Amfitheatrof; ed, Archie Marshek; art d, Hans Dreier, Earl Hedrick; m/l, Ben Raleigh, Bennie Wayne.

Drama   (PR:A   MPAA:NR)

MISS TATLOCK'S MILLIONS***   (1948) 101m PAR bw

John Lund (Burke), Wanda Hendrix (Nan Tatlock), Barry Fitzgerald (Denno Noonan), Monty Woolley (Miles Tatlock), Ilka Chase (Cassie Van Alen), Robert Stack (Nickey Van Alen), Dorothy Stickney (Emily Tatlock), Elizabeth Patterson (Cora), Leif Erickson (Dr. Mason), Dan Tobin (Clifford Tatlock), Hilo Hattie (Kamamamaluas), Richard Rancyd [Haydn] (Fergel), Clifford Brooke (Pete), Howard Joslin (Assistant Director), Bill Neff (The Real Schuyler), Ray Milland (Himself), Mitchell Leisen (Director), Hugh Allen (Bartender), Beulah Christian (Upstairs Maid).

A lightning-fast screwball comedy about a family full of lunatics whose only sane member is Hendrix. When a rich relative dies and leaves a multi-million dollar will, the entire family's presence is requested, including Hendrix's irresponsible nitwit brother. The big problem, however, is finding him. Unfortunately he slipped away from his keeper, Fitzgerald, while vacationing in Hawaii, leaving no signs of his whereabouts. Fitzgerald's feeble solution is to hire Lund, a Hollywood stunt man, to impersonate the brother in order for Hendrix to receive her inheritance. Their scam seems easy enough until Lund falls in love with his "sister," Hendrix. In the meantime, everyone in the family is trying to get a piece of the inheritance and Lund must work overtime in order to protect Hendrix from their greedy clutches. The manic pace continues full steam ahead until it nearly hits the breaking point. Hendrix is saved when her real brother resurfaces with a Hawaiian wife and a brood of kiddies. Hendrix gets her rightful inheritance and is allowed to go public with her love for Lund. A crisp script with a barrage of snappy dialog keeps this one moving along with nary a dull moment. Director Haydn—a British comedian known for his neurotic character roles— successfully displayed his talents in this, his first directorial assignment, as well as making a small appearance under the pseudonym of Richard Rancyd.

p, Charles Brackett; d, Richard Haydn; w, Brackett, Richard L. Breen (based on the play "Oh! Brother" by Jacques Deval); ph, Charles B. Lang, Jr.; m, Victor Young; ed, Everett Douglas; art d, Hans Dreier, Franz Bachelin; set d, Sam Comer, Ross Dowd; cos, Edith Head; spec eff, Gordon Jennings; makeup, Wally Westmore.

Comedy   (PR:A   MPAA:NR)

MISS TULIP STAYS THE NIGHT*   (1955, Brit.) 68m Jaywell/Adelphi bw

Diana Dors (Kate Dax), Patrick Holt (Andrew Dax), Jack Hulbert (Police Constable Feathers), Cicely Courtneidge (Millicent Tulip/Angela Tulip), A. E. Matthews (Mr. Potts), Joss Ambler (Inspector Thorne), Pat Terry-Thomas (Judith Gale), George Roderick, Brian Oulton.

Novelist Holt and wife Dors are awakened one night by Courtneidge. She hands Holt a gun and some jewels and asks for a bed. In the morning they find her shot dead; Holt faces arrest for the crime. Courtneidge's twin sister (also Courtneidge) shows up and Holt manages to deduce that she is the killer. Badly done on all counts. Director Arliss is the son of famed character actor George Arliss, whose many biographical movies made him the Paul Muni of early British talkies.

p, John O. Douglas; Bill Luckwell; d, Leslie Arliss; w, Douglas, Luckwell, Jack Hulbert; ph, Kent Talbot.

Crime   (PR:A   MPAA:NR)

MISS V FROM MOSCOW*¹/₂
            (1942) 68m M&H/PRC bw (AKA: INTRIGUE IN PARIS)

Lola Lane (Vera Marova), Noel Madison (Capt. Anton Kleis), Howard Banks (Steve Worth), Paul Weigel (Henri Devallier), John Vosper (Col. Wolfgang Heinrich), Anna Demetrio (Mme. Finchon), William Vaughn (Capt. Richter), Juan De La Cruz (Pierre), Kathryn Sheldon (Minna), Victor Kendell (Gerald Naughton), Richard Kipling (Dr. Suchevsky).

Less-than-thrilling espionage tale has Lane as an undercover agent for the Soviets sent to Paris to uncover information on Nazi submarine movements. Because of her close resemblance to a Nazi spy, she is able to infiltrate the Gestapo with little difficulty; her identifying feature is a special coin. The coin is also what tips off the Nazis, forcing her to flee France, aided by the American Banks. What could have been a good thriller is marred by an incredibly slackened pace. Stock footage of Nazi marches and warships is used to heighten realism, but comes off as cliched. Cast does a decent job, with the personalities of the characters coming through, but to little avail.

p, George W. Merrick; d, Albert Herman; w, Arthur St. Clair, Sherman Lowe; ph, Marcel LePicard; ed, W. L. Brown; md, Lee Zahler.

Spy Drama   (PR:A   MPAA:NR)

MISSILE FROM HELL**¹/₂
(1960, Brit.) 104m Criterion/Eros-NTA bw (AKA: UNSEEN HEROES; BATTLE OF THE V1; V1)

Michael Rennie (Stefan), Patricia Medina (Zofia), Milly Vitale (Anna), David Knight (Tadek), Esmond Knight (Stricker), Christopher Lee (Brunner), Carl Jaffe (General), John G. Heller (Fritz), Peter Madden (Stanislaw), Gordon Stearne (Margraaf), George Pravda (Karewski), Julian Somers (Himmler), Carl Duering (Scientist), Harold Siddons (Wing Commander Searby), George Pastell (Eryck), Henry Vidom (Konim), Stanley Zevic (Kubula), Gregory Dark (Franus), Jan Conrad (Wlodek), Tom Clegg (Anton), Robert Raikes (Dakota Pilot), Valerie White (German Forewoman), Geoffrey Chater (Minister of Defense).

Rennie and Knight are Polish resistance fighters during WW II who become forced laborers at Peenemunde, the location of the secret Nazi V1 factory. They gather

information which is smuggled back to England and even try to ambush a truck carrying one of the rockets. The attack fails but later they find an unexploded missile from a failed test out in a field. They carry it off and have it flown back to England, where it is instrumental in helping the Allies defeat the onslaught. Fairly good WW II drama enacted by a talented cast shows an aspect of the war not often seen.

p, George Maynard, John Bash; d, Vernon Sewell; w, Jack Hanley, Eryk Wlodek (based on the book They Saved London by Bernard Newman); ph, Basil Emmott; m, Robert Sharples; ed, Lito Carruthers.

War   (PR:A   MPAA:NR)

MISSILE TO THE MOON*   (1959) 78m Astor bw

Gary Clarke (Lon), Cathy Downs (June Saxton), K. T. Stevens (Queen Lido), Laurie Mitchell (Lambda), Michael Whalen (Dirk Green), Nina Bara (Alpha), Richard Travis (Arnold Dayton), Tommy Cook (Gary), Marjorie Hellen (Zeema), Lee Roberts (Henry Hunter); International Beauty Contest winners: Sandra Wirth (Florida), Pat Mowry (New Hampshire), Tania Velia (Yugoslavia), Sanita Pelkey (New York), Lisa Simone (France), Marianne Gaba (Illinois), Renate Hoy (Germany), Mary Ford (Minnesota).

A third-rate science fiction picture which has an expedition landing on the moon and battling the by now standard race of sexy but aggressive women. They are also pitted against some rockmen who emerge from the lunar subsoil, and a giant hairy spider. Bad, very bad, but good for a laugh.

p, Marc Frederic; d, Richard Cunha; w, H. E. Barrie, Vincent Fotre; ph, Meredith Nicholson; m, Nicholas Carras; ed, Everett Dodd; set d, Harry Reif; cos, Marjorie Corso; spec eff, Ira Anderson, Harold Banks, Harold Wooley; makeup, Harry Thomas.

Science Fiction   (PR:A   MPAA:NR)

MISSING****   (1982) 122m Polygram/UNIV c

Jack Lemmon (Ed Horman), Sissy Spacek (Beth Horman), Melanie Mayron (Terry Simon), John Shea (Charles Horman), Charles Cioffi (Capt. Ray Tower), David Clennon (Consul Phil Putnam), Richard Venture (U.S. Ambassador), Jerry Hardin (Col. Sean Patrick), Richard Bradford (Carter Babcock), Joe Regalbuto (Frank Teruggi), Keith Szarabajka (David Holloway), John Doolittle (David McGeary), Janice Rule (Kate Newman), Ward Costello (Congressman), Hansford Rowe (Senator), Tina Romero (Maria), Richard Whiting (Statesman), Martin Lasalle (Paris), Terry Nelson (Col. Clay), Robert Hitt (Peter Chernin), Felix Gonzalez (Rojas), M. E. Rios (Mrs. Duran), Jorge Russek (Espinoza), Edna Nochoechea (Pia), Alan Penwrith (Samuel Roth), Alex Camacho (Silvio), M. Avilla Comacho (Doctor), Kimberly Farr (Young Woman), Elizabeth Cross (Ann), Piero Cross (Hotel Manager), Gary Richardson (Embassy Operator), Josefina Echanove (Doctor), Robert Johnstreet (Bob), Lynda Spheeris (Woman in U.S. Embassy), Jorge Mancilla (Airport Captain), Gerardo Vigil (Sexy Soldier), Mario Valdez (Laundry Officer), Jaime Garza (Young Man at Stadium), Joe Tompkins (Marine Officer), John Fenton (Carlos), Jacqueline Evans, Jorge Santoyo, Juan Vazquez, Antonio Medellin, Albert Cates.

Co-executive producer Peter Guber likes taking shots at authority, as he proved with MIDNIGHT EXPRESS. This time, he joins forces with Costa-Gavras, who has made a career out of politically oriented films, and the result is a stunning denunciation of the U.S. government and how it conspired to keep the truth of the death of a U.S. citizen from exposure. Costa-Gavras toned down his usual hard-hitting attack and offered a more human view of the moral dilemma of a man searching for his son in a hostile environment where even the man's own embassy offers nothing but blind alleys and vague promises. Rather than focus in on the evil men behind the scenes, Costa-Gavras looked at the violent injustices and pain forced upon a downtrodden populace. In this case, it is the people of Chile (although the country is never named) and their lives during the first days of the Pinochet regime. It's a slightly fictionalized true story of a Christian Scientist father, Lemmon, who is a staunch supporter of the American Way. His son, Shea, is a left-winger and currently living in the capital city of the anonymous country with his wife, Spacek. Shea has a habit of being nosy, perhaps too much so for the government's pleasure, and one day he disappears. His only crime has been curiosity. Spacek attempts to find Shea but doors slam on her left and right. Lemmon flies to the country and attempts to put some pressure on the American officials. He and Spacek are politically at odds and bicker constantly, as he is a firm believer in his country, right or wrong. The arguing gets so intense that they sometimes forget their common quest. Bits of information come to them from various sources and as the picture rolls on, they see something in what the other says and become closer. They are enraged by the casual slaughter of the country's people as they relentlessly search for the missing Shea. In one harrowing sequence, Spacek's life is almost ended when she has to dodge a hail of bullets on her way back to where she is staying; this is a direct result of her ignoring the curfew imposed by the dictator. In an equally powerful and somewhat surrealistic scene, a white horse gallops down a side street, symbolizing the out-of-control nature that freedom has come to in such a ruthless setting. Lemmon finally cracks and takes his anger out on the emasculated American officials when he finds out they are conspiring with the crooked government. In a room full of bodies, Shea's friend, Regalbuto, is found dead. Lemmon is gut-wrenching as the father of the missing youth. His performance transcends the realm of believability and goes straight to actuality, with never a sense of "acting!" (which is, of course, the height of acting as an art). Spacek is equal to the task as the young woman who's followed her liberal husband on his misguided fact-finding mission, only to endure the terrible results of their political naivete. Greek-born Costa-Gavras (he never uses his first name, Constantin) has made a series of such films. After his 1968 film, SHOCK TROOPS, was chopped brutally by his American distributor, Costa-Gavras insisted on the "final cut" and the next picture he made was Z, an examination of the Lambrakis case. In 1970, he directed THE CONFESSION, which showed the purges wrought by Stalin in Czechoslovakia, then STATE OF SIEGE, in 1972, which concerned the CIA's meddling in Uruguay. In 1975, SPECIAL SECTION demonstrated the French government's helpfulness in persecuting the Jews in the early 1940s. Lemmon got to know the man upon whom MISSING was based, Ed Horman, and they became friends. Alexander Haig denounced the picture before it was released, but subsequent facts have proven the essential honesty of the story. The film was made very quietly in Mexico, with such a lid on the proceedings that no one knew what the story was about while it was being shot. The music by Vangelis supported the bold filming by Costa-Gavras and everyone must be lauded for their work. It was a "committed" film and the first English-language work by Costa-Gavras.

p, Edward and Mildred Lewis; d, Costa-Gavras; w, Donald Stewart, Costa-Gavras (based on *The Execution of Charles Horman* by Thomas Hauser); ph, Ricardo Aronovich; m, Vangelis; ed, Francoise Bonnot; prod d, Peter Jamison; art d, Augustin Ytuarte, Luceoro Isaac; set d, Linda Spheeris; cos, Joe I. Tompkins; spec eff, (matte paintings) Albert Whitlock.

Drama **Cas.** **(PR:A-C MPAA:PG)**

MISSING, BELIEVED MARRIED* (1937, Brit.) 66m British and Dominions/PAR bw

Wally Patch (*Flatiron Stubbs*), Julien Vedey (*Mario Maroni*), Hazel Terry (*Hermione Blakiston*), Emilio Cargher (*Emilio Graffia*), Peter Coke (*Peter*), Margaret Rutherford (*Lady Parke*), Charles Paton (*Mr. Horton*), Irene Handl (*Chambermaid*), George Turner, Sheila Young.

Heiress Terry flees her engagement when she finds that the count she was about to wed is a fortune-hunting fraud. A blow to the head during a street brawl leaves her with amnesia, and she is taken in by Patch and Vedey, a pair of street vendors. The spurious count turns up again and convinces Terry to go to Paris with him, but Patch and Vedey follow and rescue her again. Weak comedy doesn't provide the laughs.

p, Anthony Havelock-Allan; d, John Paddy Carstairs; w, A. R. Rawlinson; ph, Francis Carver.

Comedy **(PR:A MPAA:NR)**

MISSING CORPSE, THE* (1945) 62m PRC bw

J. Edward Bromberg (*Henry Kruger*), Isabel Randolph (*Mrs. Kruger*), Eric Sinclair (*James Kruger*), Frank Jenks (*Hogan*), Paul Guilfoyle (*McDonald*), John Shay (*Jeffry Dodd*), Lorell Sheldon (*Phyllis Kruger*), Ben Welden (*Jon Clary*), Charles Coleman (*Egbert*), Michael Branden (*Trigg*), Eddy Waller (*Desmond*), Elayne Adams (*Miss Ames*), Mary Arden (*Madge*), Charles Jordan (*Draper*), Anne O'Neal (*Mrs. Swanaker*), Jean Ransome (*Marie*), Ken Terrell (*Motor Cop*), Isabel Withers (*Miss Patterson*).

Bromberg plays a publisher in a bitter feud with his rival Guilfoyle. When Guilfoyle is found dead, Bromberg fears all the evidence will point to him, so with the aid of his wisecracking chauffeur, Jenks, Bromberg does everything possible to hide the corpse. Direction keeps a well-paced balance between the comic and suspense elements. This is aided by worthwhile performances.

p, Leon Fromkess, Martin Mooney; d, Albert Herman; w, Raymond L. Schrock (based on a story by Harry O. Hoyt); ph, James Brown; m, Karl Hajos; ed, W. Donn Hayes; art d, Paul Palmentola.

Comedy/Mystery **(PR:A MPAA:NR)**

MISSING DAUGHTERS* (1939) 63m COL bw

Richard Arlen (*Wally King*), Rochelle Hudson (*Kay Roberts*), Marian Marsh (*Josie Lamonte*), Isabel Jewell (*Peggy*), Edward Raquello (*Lucky Rogers*), Dick Wessel (*Brick McGirk*), Eddie Kane (*Nick*), Wade Boteler (*Capt. McGraw*), Don Beddoe (*Al Farrow*), Claire Rochelle (*Doris*).

Routine story about girls being tricked into becoming dance hall hostesses by phony talent agents. Hudson is the sister of one of the victims out to uncover the scam with the aid of a newspaper reporter. Unusually stiff depiction of a worn-out subject.

d, C. C. Coleman, Jr.; w, Michael Simmons, George Bricker; ph, Henry Freulich; m, M. W. Stoloff; ed, Gene Havlick.

Crime **(PR:A MPAA:NR)**

MISSING EVIDENCE ** 1/2** (1939) 64m UNIV bw

Preston Foster (*Bill Collins*), Irene Hervey (*Linda Parker*), Inez Courtney (*Nellie Conrad*), Chick Chandler (*Jerry Howard*), Noel Madison (*Duncan*), Joseph Downing (*Marty Peters*), Oscar O'Shea (*"Pop" Andrews*), Tom Dugan (*"Blinkey" Cullen*), Ray Walker (*McBride*), Cliff Clark (*Allen Jennings*).

Foster plays an FBI agent out to smash a sweepstake counterfeiting racket. He falls in love with Hervey, the girl he is investigating. She leads him to the bosses responsible for originating the counterfeiting operation. The director gives the material a realistic bent. An example is the opening sequence of newsreel-type footage of lottery ticket buyers describing what they plan to do with their winnings. Rosen directs with a high degree of care, to a cast that plays little more than stereotypes.

p&d, Phil Rosen; w, Arthur T. Horman (based on a story by Dorrell and Stuart E. McGowan); ph, Milton Krasner; ed, Ted Kent.

Crime **(PR:A MPAA:NR)**

MISSING GIRLS* (1936) 66m CHES bw (GB: WHEN GIRLS LEAVE HOME)

Roger Pryor (*Jimmie Dugan*), Muriel Evans (*Dorothy Benson*), Sidney Blackmer (*Dan Collins*), Noel Madison (*Ben Davis*), Ann Doran (*Ann Jason*), George Cooper (*Zig*), Dewey Robinson (*Harry Wilson*).

Thriller concentrates on several girls leaving home, their reasons for doing so, and what becomes of them in the big city. The principal girl becomes a housemaid, only to be kidnaped. Pryor is the reporter trying to get some inside stories. The script, by journalist Mooney, is filled with the type of sensationalism common to newspapers in the 1930s.

p, George R. Batcheller; d, Phil Rosen; w, Martin Mooney, John W. Krafft; ph, M. A. Anderson; ed, Roland Read.

Drama/Crime **(PR:A MPAA:NR)**

MISSING GUEST, THE* (1938) 68m UNIV bw

Paul Kelly (*Scoop Hanlon*), Constance Moore (*Stephanie Kirkland*), William Lundigan (*Larry Dearden*), Edwin Stanley (*Dr. Carroll*), Selmer Jackson (*Frank Baldrich*), Billy Wayne (*Vic*), George Cooper (*Jake*), Patrick J. Kelly (*Edwards, the Butler*), Florence Wix (*Linda Baldrich*), Harlan Briggs (*Frank Kendall, Editor*), Pat C. Flick (*Inventor*), John Harmon (*Baldrich's Guard*).

Feeble attempt at mystery has Kelly as a newspaper reporter forced to spend the night in a haunted house where two murders have occurred. The director attempts to move the story along by relying on cliched and overused items, common to this sort of genre. Problem is that what is supposed to be scary comes off as funny. Cast does its best with the poor material.

p, Barney A. Sarecky; d, John Rawlins; w, Charles Martin, Paul Perez (based on "Secrets of the Blue Room" by Erich Philippi); ph, Milton Krasner; ed, Frank Gross.

Mystery **(PR:A MPAA:NR)**

MISSING JUROR, THE* (1944) 66m COL bw

Jim Bannon (*Joe Keats*), Janis Carter (*Alice Hill*), George Macready (*Harry Wharton/Jerome Bentley*), Jean Stevens (*Tex*), Joseph Crehan (*Willard Apple*), Carole Mathews (*Marcy*), Cliff Clark (*Inspector Davis*), Edmund Cobb (*Cahan*), Mike Mazurki (*Cullie*), George Lloyd (*George Sasbo*).

Bannon plays a newspaper reporter investigating six mysterious deaths; the six dead men were members of a jury that convicted a man to a death sentence. Because the convicted man had already been sent to the electric chair, the police are baffled as to the possible causes of vengeance. But Bannon, going on a hunch, follows the remaining jurors, discovering that the convicted man is alive and out to get his vengeance on the rest of the jury. Well-balanced direction keeps the suspense going up to the very end.

p, Wallace MacDonald; d, Oscar "Budd" Boetticher, Jr.; w, Charles O'Neal (based on the story by Leon Abrams, Richard Hill Wilkinson); ph, L. W. O'Connell; ed, Paul Borofsky; md, Mischa Bakaleinikoff; art d, George Brooks.

Mystery **(PR:A MPAA:NR)**

MISSING LADY, THE* (1946) 60m MON bw (AKA: THE SHADOW AND THE MISSING LADY)

Kane Richmond, Barbara Reed, George Chandler, James Flavin, Pierre Watkin, Dorothea Kent, Jack Overman, George Lewis, James Cardwell, Bert Roach, Gary Owen, Ray Teal, Jo-Carroll Dennison, Ralph Dunn, Dewey Robinson, Anthony Warde, Claire Carleton, Almira Sessions, Nora Cecil, Douglas Wood.

The third of three SHADOW pictures filmed in 1946 by Monogram, THE MISSING LADY stars Richmond as the famous cloaked crime solver. This time he is on the trail of the mysterious murderer of an art dealer. The Shadow's only tangible piece of evidence is a stolen jade statuette of a woman. As usual, he shakes up the underworld and fishes out the evil culprit.

p, Joe Kaufman; d, Phil Karlson; w, George Callahan; ph, William Sickner; ed, Ace Herman; art d, David Milton.

Crime **(PR:A MPAA:NR)**

MISSING MILLION, THE* 1/2 (1942, Brit.) 84m Signet/ABF bw

Linden Travers (*Joan Walton*), John Warwick (*Bennett*), Patricia Hilliard (*Dora Coleman*), John Stuart (*Inspector Dicker*), Ivan Brandt (*Rex Walton*), Brefni O'Rorke (*Coleman*), Charles Victor (*Nobb Knowles*), Marie Ault (*Mrs. Tweedle*), James Donald.

When a millionaire disappears just before his wedding, his sister (Travers) hires detective Stuart to find him. Stuart follows a trail of corpses to a gang headed by The Panda, who has kidnaped the millionaire with help from the man's fiancee. The latter is conscience-stricken and leads Stuart to The Panda, who proves to be an endangered species and ends the encounter dead. Routine second feature inevitably based on an Edgar Wallace novel.

p, Hugh Perceval; d, Phil Brandon; w, James Seymour (based on the novel by Edgar Wallace); ph, Stephen Dade.

Crime **(PR:A MPAA:NR)**

MISSING NOTE, THE* (1961, Brit.) 56m Walton/Children's Film Foundation bw

Heather Bennett (*Joan*), Hennie Scott (*Tom*), John Moulder-Brown (*Willie*), Toke Townley (*Mr. Parker*), Vivian Lacey (*Suzie*), Tommy Godfrey (*Sam*), Edgar Driver (*Mr. Newbolt*), Patricia Leslie (*Mrs. Harris*), Regimental Sergeant Major Brittain (*Commissionaire*).

A battered old piano is sought by a group of children and a jewel thief who has hidden his loot inside. Strictly for kiddie consumption.

p, Henry Passmore; d, Michael Brandt; w, Mary Cathcart Borer (based on a story by Frank Wells).

Children **(PR:AA MPAA:NR)**

MISSING PEOPLE, THE* (1940, Brit.) 73m GN/MON bw

Will Fyffe (*J. G. Reeder*), Kay Walsh (*Peggy Gillette*), Lyn Harding (*Joseph Branstone*), Ronald Shiner (*Sam Hackett*), Ronald Adam (*Surtees*), Patricia Roc (*Doris Bevan*), Anthony Holles (*Ernest Branstone*), Reginald Purdell (*Harry Morgan*), Maire O'Neill (*Housekeeper*), Lawrence Hanray, O. B. Clarence.

Another in the "Mr. Reeder" series has Fyffe as the aging detective who comes out of retirement to help Scotland Yard uncover the reasons behind the mysterious disappearances of 27 elderly women. Fyffe adds a great deal of charm to his role as he pieces the puzzle together in a manner baffling to the younger detectives. Otherwise, the plot is unbelievable but makes for some light-hearted fun.

p, Charles Q. Steele; d, Jack Raymond; w, Lydia Hayward (based on the novel "The Mind of Mr. Reeder" by Edgar Wallace); ph, George Stretton.

Mystery (PR:A MPAA:NR)

MISSING PERSONS (SEE: BUREAU OF MISSING PERSONS, 1933)

MISSING REMBRANDT, THE* 1/2 (1932, Brit.) 78m Twickenham/FD bw

Arthur Wontner (*Sherlock Holmes*), Ian Fleming (*Dr. Watson*), Minnie Raynor (*Mrs. Hudson*), Francis L. Sullivan (*Baron von Guntermann*), Dino Galvani (*Carlo Ravelli*), Miles Mander (*Claude Holford*), Jane Welsh (*Lady Violet Lumsden*), Philip Hewland (*Inspector Lestrade*), Anthony Hollis (*Marquis de Chaminade*), Herbert Lomas (*Maning*), Ben Welden (*Pinkerton Agent*), Kenji Takase (*Chang Wu*).

Inferior adaptation of Sir Arthur Conan Doyle's tale, has Wontner portraying the super-sleuth as he tries to uncover the whereabouts of a Rembrandt that has been stolen from the Louvre. His searches lead him to the home of Sullivan, a wealthy baron who will do anything to get what he wants. One of these dastardly deeds leads to his eventual capture; that is, the blackmailing of Welsh with her letters. Mander is the desperate, drug-addicted artist who performs the incredible task of stealing the Rembrandt, yet cannot seem to overcome the powers of Sullivan, who eventually kills him. As a contrast to the prowess of Wontner, an American detective is thrown into the case but he cannot seem to match wits with the diabolical Sullivan. Wontner is unconvincing in his role as Holmes, coming off more as a clown than a great detective. The rest of the cast give adequate, though shallow, performances. Plot is unable to keep enough suspense going to maintain any level of interest; this is further marred by an inadequate production. (See SHERLOCK HOLMES series, Index.)

p, Julius Hagen; d, Leslie Hiscott; w, Cyril Twyford, H. Fowler Mear (based on the story "Charles August Milverton" by Sir Arthur Conan Doyle); ph, Sydney Blythe, Basil Emmott; ed, Jack Harris.

Mystery (PR:A MPAA:NR)

MISSING TEN DAYS** 1/2 (1941, Brit.) 77m bw (GB: TEN DAYS IN PARIS; AKA: SPY IN THE PANTRY)

Rex Harrison (*Bob Stevens*), Karen Verne (*Diane de Guermantes*), C. V. France (*Gen. de Guermantes*), Leo Genn (*Lanson*), Joan Marion (*Denise*), Antony Holles (*Francois*), John Abbott (*Andre*), Robert Rendel (*Sir James Stevens*), Mavis Clair (*Marie*), Andre Morell (*Victor*), Hay Petrie (*Benoit*), Frank Atkinson (*Pierre*), Mai Bacon, Donald McLeod, Percy Walsh.

Intricate and fast-moving spy picture has Harrison as a devil-may-care roue who has a plane accident in which his flying companion is killed in France. He wakes up in Paris and is told about the crash, but he doesn't recall what's happened to him in the 10 days from the plane accident to the moment he awakens. Turns out that he'd put on his downed pal's clothes; chauffeured a pretty girl, Verne; and gotten involved with spies, Marion and Genn, who are enemies of the English-French Alliance and doing everything to subvert it. There are some secret fortifications and the villains have the plans and will blow up the redoubts if Harrison and Verne don't get there in time to stop them. A time bomb has been placed on a train carrying ammunition and it is set to go off when the train enters the fortified area. Need we tell you that they get there in time? Since there was a war going on at the time and this was made in Europe, there is a lot of believability in the script. The screenplay is based on a popular mystery of the time that fills in some of the holes left in the film. Not much to recommend this movie other than a look at Harrison when he was only 33 years old and already in his 14th film.

p, Irving Asher; d, Tim Whelan; w, John Meehan, Jr., James Curtis (based on the novel *The Disappearance of Roger Tremayne* by Bruce Graeme); ph, Otto Kanturek; ed, Hugh Stewart.

Spy Drama (PR:A MPAA:NR)

MISSING WITNESS (SEE: LOVE'S OLD SWEET SONG, 1933, Brit.)

MISSING WITNESSES*** (1937) 60m FN-WB bw

John Litel (*Inspector Lane*), Dick Purcell (*Bull Regan*), Jean Dale (*Mary Norton*), Sheila Bromley (*Gladys Wagner*), William Haade (*Emmet White*), Ben Welden (*Wagner*), Raymond Hatton ("*Little Joe*" *Macey*), Harland Tucker (*Ward Sturgis*), Jack Mower (*Butler*), John Harron (*Harris*), Michael Mark (*Hartman*), Earl Gunn (*Chivvy Predo*), Louis Natheaux (*Heinie Dodds*).

Fictionalized account of Thomas Dewey's fight to clean up the rackets in New York City has Litel as the detective appointed to investigate racketeering. Purcell plays his bumbling sidekick who falls in love with Dale, the secretary who gives Litel the information he needs to pin down the rackets boss. Screenwriters Gamet and Ryan are former newspaper people and manage to give a fairly accurate account of what the racketeering conditions were in New York at the time. Though the picture is a bit heavy-handed on the crime-doesn't-pay aspect, it still produces a lot of well-paced, believable action.

p, Bryan Foy; d, William Clemens; w, Kenneth Gamet, Don Ryan; ph, Sid Hickox; ed, Fred Richards, cos, N'Was Mackenzie.

Crime (PR:A MPAA:NR)

MISSING WOMEN* 1/2 (1951) 60m REP bw

Penny Edwards (*Claudia Rankin*), James Millican (*Hans Soderling*), John Gallaudet

(*Lt. Kellcher*), John Alvin (*Eddie Ennis*), Fritz Feld (*Pierre*), James Brown (*Mike Purnell*), Robert Shayne (*Mr. Cincotta*), Marlo Dwyer (*Mae Berringer*), William Forrest (*Capt. E. W. Willis*), John Hedloe (*Phillip Rankin*), Mary Alan Hokanson (*Saleswoman*), Patricia Joiner (*Waitress*).

Unimaginative story features Edwards as a newlywed whose husband, Hedloe, is killed by a gang of car thieves. Edwards plans her revenge by getting into jail by manufacturing a prison record. There she learns about the car theft racket, which leads to the murderers. When her true identity finally is revealed, she is saved by the police. Script and performances lack believability and this is further hampered by careless direction.

p, Stephen Auer; d, Philip Ford; w, John K. Butler; ph, John Macburnie; m, Stanley Wilson; ed, Harold Minter; art d, Frank Hotaling; cos, Adele Palmer.

Crime (PR:A MPAA:NR)

MISSION BATANGAS* 1/2 (1968) 100m Batangas-Diba/Manson c

Dennis Weaver (*Chip Corbett*), Vera Miles (*Joan Barnes*), Keith Larsen (*Col. Turner*), Leopoldo Salcedo, Helen Thompson, Vic Diaz, Bruno Punzalan, Fred Galang, Tony Dungan, Ernesto La Guardia.

Weaver plays a pilot out for himself who crash-lands in the Philippines and has a change of heart as he meets and falls in love with Miles. Nurse Miles and Army officer Larsen are trying to hide the Phillipine supply of gold bullion from the invading Japanese armies by smuggling it aboard a waiting submarine. When the ship is damaged beyond repair, their new plan of attack is to sink the ship, with the gold aboard, to the bottom of the ocean. Invading Japanese soldiers kill Larsen and mortally wound Miles. This gives Weaver the motivation to go through with the suicidal sinking of the boat. Shot in the Philippines, and other than some interesting scenery, the picture has little else to offer. The story and performances fall into a stereotype, with the direction offering no sense of balance to move the story.

p&d, Keith Larsen; w, Lew Antonio (based on a story by Larsen); ph, Herbert Theis (Technicolor); ed, Tony Di Marco, George Schrader; spec eff, Santos Hilario; makeup, Lily Joaquino.

War Cas. (PR:A MPAA:NR)

MISSION BLOODY MARY** (1967, Fr./Ital./Span.) 102m Fida-Jacques Roitfeld-Epoca-Estela/Telefilm c (OPERATION LOTUS BLEU; AGENT 077—MISSIONE BLOODY MARY; LA MUERTE ESPERA EN ATENAS; AGENTE 077; MISION BLOODY MARY; OPERACION LOTO AZUL)

Ken Clark (*Dick Malloy*), Helga Line (*Elsa Freeman*), Mitsouko (*Kuan*), Philippe Hersent (*Lester*), Umberto Raho (*Prof. Betz*), Susan Terry (*Juanita*), Antonio Gradoli, Andrea Scotti, Brand Lyonell, Peter Blades, Peter Bosch, Franca Polesello, Pulloa Coy, Mirko Ellis, Dario Michaelis, Erik Bianchi, Alfredo Mayo, Ignazio Leone, Tomas Blanco, John Fordan, Felix Fernandez.

"Bloody Mary" is a nuclear bomb stolen by an international spy ring and CIA agent 077 (Clark) is assigned to get it back. His mission takes him to an Athens-bound freighter on which he is up against both Russian and Chinese agents. He eventually discovers the bomb and captures the guilty pair, Line and Raho, in Monte Carlo.

d, Terence Hathaway [Sergio Grieco]; w, Sandro Continenza, Marcello Coscia, Leonardo Martin; ph, Juan Julio Baena (Techniscope, Technicolor); m, Angelo Francesco Lavagnino; ed, Enzo Alfonsi, Petra Nieva; md, Lavagnino; art d, Franco Lolli, Nedo Azzini, Ramiro Gomez Garcia.

Adventure/Spy Drama (PR:A MPAA:NR)

MISSION GALACTICA: THE CYLON ATTACK* (1979) 107m Glen A. Larson/UNIV c

Richard Hatch, Dirk Benedict, Lorne Greene, Lloyd Bridges, Herbert Jefferson, Jr.

This is a couple of more television episodes strung together as in this picture's predecessor, BATTLESTAR GALACTICA. The space crew is still trying to find Earth, but in the meantime have to destroy the Cylons, a villainous army of robots. An emotionless void in which special effects try to cover for the horrid writing.

p, David J. O'Connell; d, Vince Edwards, Christian I. Nyby II; w, Glen A. Larson, Jim Carlson, Terrence McDonnell; ph, Frank Thackery, H. John Penner; spec eff, David H. Garber, Wayne Smith.

Science Fiction (PR:A MPAA:NR)

MISSION MARS* (1968) 87m Sagittarius/AA c

Darren McGavin (*Mike Blaiswick*), Nick Adams (*Nick Grant*), George DeVries (*Duncan*), Heather Hewitt (*Edith Blaiswick*), Michael DeBeausset (*Cliff Lawson*), Shirley Parker (*Alice Grant*), Bill E. Kelly (*Russian Astronaut*), Chuck Zink (*Chuck, Radio Operator*), Ralph Miller (*Simpson*), Art Barker (*Doctor*), Monroe Myers (*Lawson's Aide*).

Dull depiction of the first mission to Mars by an American flight team is a plodding tale which offers no action until the end. McGavin and Adams are the two astronauts on the dangerous mission, who encounter two dead Russian cosmonauts as they approach the planet. A third cosmonaut is found on the planet in an apparent state of suspended animation. They manage to revive the cosmonaut, but are attacked by a strange force activated by the sun's rays. The filmmakers can be commended for portraying an alien as something other than a humanoid, but for little else, with the cast as lifeless as the story. This was the first feature to be made at Miami's Studio City Complex, which explains the poor technical aspects. Stock footage of Cape Kennedy is inserted, acting more as an obstruction than in lending a sense of realism.

p, Everett Rosenthal; d, Nicholas Webster; w, Mike St. Clair (based on a story by Aubrey Wisberg); ph, Cliff Poland (Berkey Technical Laboratory); ed, Paul Jordan;

prod d, Hank Aldrich; spec eff, Haberstroh Studios; cos, Grover Cole; m/l, Berge Kalajian, Gus Pardalis (sung by The Forum Quorum).

Science Fiction **(PR:A MPAA:G)**

MISSION OVER KOREA** (1953) 85m COL bw

John Hodiak *(Capt. George Slocum)*, John Derek *(Lt. Pete Barker)*, Audrey Totter *(Kate)*, Maureen O'Sullivan *(Nancy Slocum)*, Harvey Lembeck *(Sgt. Maxie Steiner)*, Richard Erdman *(Cpl. Swenson)*, William Chun *(Clancy)*, Rex Reason *(Maj. Hacker)*, Richard Bowers *(Singing Soldier)*, Todd Karns *(Lt. Jerry Barker)*, Al Choi *(Maj. Kung)*.

Heroic pilots fight the Chinese "volunteer" pilots in the sky during the early days of the Korean conflict. Derek is a headstrong rookie out to avenge his brother's death, while Hodiak is his commanding officer trying to keep him in line. Some talented cast members are wasted, while some untalented ones are much too heavily relied on. Released subsequent to the armistice agreement, this embarrassing film contained every war-film cliche ever invented. Actor Rex Reason, who later did remarkably good work in low-budget B westerns, was the best thing in the film as the sensible, pragmatic commanding officer in this trite story.

p, Robert Cohn; d, Fred F. Sears; w, Jesse L. Lasky, Jr., Eugene Ling, Martin M. Goldsmith (based on a story by Richard Tregaskis); ph, Sam Leavitt; ed, Henry Batista; art d, George Brooks.

War **(PR:A MPAA:NR)**

MISSION STARDUST*

(1968, Ital./Span./Ger.) 95m P.E.A.-Aitor-Tefi/Times c (4. . .3. . .2. . .1.. MORTE; ORBITA MORTAL; PERRY RHODAN—SOS AUS DEM WELTALL)

Lang Jeffries *(Maj. Perry Rhodan)*, Essy Persson *(Thora)*, Gianni Rizzo *(Criminal Leader)*, John Karlsen *(Kress)*, Pinkas Braun *(Rotkin)*, Luis Davila *(Capt. Bull)*, Daniel Martin, Joachim Hansen, Ann Smyrner, Stefano Sibaldi, Janos Bartha, Giuseppe Addobbati, Jose Jaspe.

European cult-hero and pulp novel character Perry Rhodan (Jeffries) travels to the moon and returns to Earth (East Africa, to be precise) with a couple of stranded, sickly astronauts from some advanced civilization. A spy ring tries to kidnap the alien duo by posing as doctors, but their plan fails. A cure is found for the astronaut's ailments and they return home. Stick to the novel, since the film is so poorly done.

p, E. Von Theumer; d, Primo Zeglio; w, Karlheinz Vogelmann, Karlheinz Scheer, Sergio Donati, Frederico de Urrutia, Zeglio (based on the story by Vogelmann and the novels in the "Perry Rhodan" series by Clark Dalton [Walter Enstine]); ph, Riccardo Pallottini, Manuel Merino (Techniscope, Technicolor); m, Anton Garcia Abril; ed, Renato Cinquini; art d, Jaime Perez Cubero; m/l, Marcello Giombini.

Science Fiction/Drama **(PR:A MPAA:G)**

MISSION TO HELL (SEE: SAVAGE! 1962)

MISSION TO HONG KONG (SEE: RED-DRAGON, 1967, Ital./Ger.)

MISSION TO MOSCOW*** (1943) 123m WB bw

Walter Huston *(Ambassador Joseph E. Davies)*, Ann Harding *(Mrs. Davies)*, Oscar Homolka *(Maxim Litvinov)*, George Tobias *(Freddie)*, Gene Lockhart *(Vyacheslav Molotov)*, Frieda Inescort *(Mme. Molotov)*, Eleanor Parker *(Emlen Davies)*, Richard Travis *(Paul Grosjean)*, Helmut Dantine *(Maj. Kamenev)*, Victor Francen *(Vyshinsky)*, Henry Daniell *(Minister Joachim Von Ribbentrop)*, Barbara Everest *(Mrs. Ivy Litvinov)*, Dudley Field Malone *(Prime Minister Winston Churchill)*, Roman Bohnen *(Krestinsky)*, Maria Palmer *(Tanya Litvinov)*, Moroni Olsen *(Col. Faymonville)*, Minor Watson *(Loy Henderson)*, Vladimir Sokoloff *(Mikhail Kalinin)*, Maurice Schwartz *(Dr. Botkin)*, Jerome Cowan *(Spendler)*, Konstantin Shayne *(Nikolai Bukharin)*, Manart Kippen *(Joseph Stalin)*, Kathleen Lockhart *(Lady Chilston)*, Kurt Katch *(Semer Timoshenko)*, Felix Basch *(Dr. Hjalmar Schacht)*, Frank Puglia *(Judge Ulrich)*, John Abbott *(Grinko)*, Charles Trowbridge *(Secretary of State Cordell Hull)*, Leigh Whipper *(Haile Selassie)*, Georges Renavent *(President Paul Van Zeeland)*, Clive Morgan *(Anthony Eden)*, Alex Chirva *(Pierre Laval)*, Doris Lloyd *(Mrs. Churchill)*, Olaf Hytten *(Parliament Member)*, Art Gilmore *(Commentator)*, Don Clayton *(Vincent Massey)*, Duncan Renaldo, Mino Bellini *(Italian Reporters)*, Fred Schumann-Heinck, Rolf Lindau, Peter Michael *(German Reporters)*, George Davis, Jean Del Val *(French Reporters)*, Emory Parnell *(Speaker of House)*, Pat O'Malley *(Irish-American)*, Mark Strong *(Englishman)*, Albert D'Arno *(Frenchman)*, Rudolf Steinbeck *(German)*, Gino Corrado *(Italian)*, Glenn Strange *(Southerner)*, Frank Faylen, Joseph Crehan *(Reporters)*, Pierre Watkin *(Naval Attache)*, Edward Van Sloan *(German Diplomat)*, Tanya Samova *(Flower Girl)*, Elizabeth Archer [Scherbachova] *(Elderly Woman)*, Lumsden Hare *(Lord Chilston)*, Robert C. Fischer *(Von Schulenberg)*, Alex Caze [Rene Plaissetty] *(Coulendre)*, Leonid Snegoff *(Kommodov)*, Edgar Licho *(Bookseller)*, Victor Wong, Luke Chan, Allen Jung *(Japanese Diplomats)*, Louis Jean Heydt, John Hamilton, Frank Ferguson, Bill Kennedy, William Forrest *(American Newsmen)*, Alexander Granach *(Russian Air Force Officer)*, Francis Pierlot *(Doctor)*, Forbes Murray, Edward Keane, William Gould *(Isolationists)*, Harry Cording *(Blacksmith)*, Betty Roadman *(Mother)*, Hooper Atchley *(Father)*, Eugene Eberly *(Son)*, Arthur Loft *(Man with Microphone)*, Mike Mazurki *(Workman)*, Tom Tully *(Engineer)*, Lionel Royce *(Dr. Schmitt)*, Eugene Borden *(French Minister)*, Oliver Blake, Monte Blue, Ernie Adams, Eddie Kane, Edmund Cobb, Howard Mitchell, Frank Wayne, Jack Kenny, Ben Erway, Mauritz Hugo *(Hecklers)*, Gene Gary *(Russian Foreman)*, Cyd Charisse, Michel Panaieff *(Specialty Dancers)*, Al Kunde *(Father)*, Evelynne Smith *(Daughter)*, Frank Hemphill *(Grandfather)*, Isabel Withers *(Woman)*, Tamara Shayne *(Russian Nurse)*, Frank Reicher, Daniel Ocko, Ivan Tresault, Peter Goo Chong, George Lessey, Wallis Clark, Oliver Cross, Ray Walker, Capt. Jack Young, Ernest Hauserman, Ross Ford, Warren Douglas, Barbara Brown, Hans Schumm, Dr. Ernest Golm, Lisa Golm, Henry Victor, Louis Arco, Alfred Ziesler, Richard Ryan, Erwin Kalser, Esther Zeitlin, Nina Biagio, Nikolai Celikhovsky, Michael Visaroff, Nick Kobliansky, Gabriel Lenoff, Alex Akimoff, Sam Savitsky, George Glebeff, Mike Tulligan, Adia Kuznetzoff, Dimitris Alexis, Henry Guttman, Robert Balkoff, Mischa Westfall, Rosa Margot, Valya Terry, Virgina Christine, Sandor Szabo, David Hoffman, Charles La Torre, Marie Melesch, Michael Mark, Martin Noble, Lee Tung Foo, John Dilson, Jean de Braic, George Sorel, Ted E. Jacques, Billie Louie, Loulette Sablon, Marian Lessing, Joan Winfield, Tiana Menard, Peggy Watts, Irene Pedrini, Alex Melesh, Marek Windheim, Ivan Lebedeff, Gregory Golubeff, Jack Gardner, Sam Goldenberg, Egon Brecher, Zina Torchina, Vera Richkova, Jean Wong, Irina Semochenko, Christine Gordon, Joseph Kamaryt, Baroness Yvonne Hendricks, Olga Uljanovskaja, Patrica Fung, Igorde Navrotsky, James Flavin, William B. Davidson, Herbert Heyes, George Carleton, Zoia Karabanova, Alec Campbell, Nicco Romoff, Noel Cravat, Emile Rameau, Feodor Chaliapin, John Maxwell, Jacqueline Dalya, Herbert Ashley, Frank Penny, Frank Jacquet, Fred Essler, John Wengraf, Robert Shayne, Lily Norwood.

A controversial and blatant propaganda film that attempted to show how smart Ambassador Davies was in his book of the same name and how the Russians were our friends. After removing the case for the U.S.S.R. and the critical cannons fired against American isolationism, this must be measured on its own terms as a movie and it is a well-done picture with the almost impossible task of depicting history nearly as fast as it was happening. Huston is Davies and he and his family (Harding and Parker) are seen leaving the U.S. for Russia, stopping off in Germany on their way to the Soviet Union where they meet all the heavyweight Communists. Some of the makeup jobs on Kippen (Stalin), Lockhart (Molotov), and the others are sensational; some are weak. It's almost a travelog of Russia, as we are treated to scenes of Soviet life which border on the ludicrous (and were heartily laughed at by Moscow moviegoers) and include factory sequences and various other tries at humanizing the people behind the Iron Curtain. The oddest section is a re-creation of the 1937 purge trials, supposedly culled from the actual testimony and purporting to show that the leaders knew of Germany and Japan's Axis plot. It's very pro-Russian and Jack Warner, who later became a hard conservative spokesman, must have been embarrassed every time he looked at the movie in later years. Curtiz had a difficult task directing all of these speaking roles (see cast list) and making an interesting movie. He succeeded on that level, but, knowing what we know now, it's a combination curiosity piece and fairy tale. It also gave work to just about every actor with an accent in Hollywood at the time. Left-wingers hailed it, right-wingers hated it, we only appreciated the filming techniques that went into making it.

p, Robert Buckner; d, Michael Curtiz; w, Howard Koch (based on the book by Joseph E. Davies); ph, Bert Glennon; ed, Owen Marks; art d, Carl Jules Heyl; ch, LeRoy Prinz; montages, Don Siegel; technical advisor, Jay Leyda.

Drama **(PR:A MPAA:NR)**

MISSIONARY, THE** ½ (1982) 90m HandMade Film/COL c

Michael Palin *(Rev. Charles Fortescue)*, Maggie Smith *(Lady Ames)*, Trevor Howard *(Lord Ames)*, Denholm Elliott *(The Bishop)*, Michael Hordern *(Slatterthwaite)*, Graham Crowden *(Rev. Fitzbanks)*, Phoebe Nicholls *(Deborah)*, Tricia George *(Ada)*, Valerie Whittington *(Emmeline)*, John Barrett *(Limping Old Man)*, Peter Vaughan *(McEvoy)*, Rosamund Greenwood *(Lady Fermly)*, Roland Culver *(Lord Fermly)*, David Suchet *(Corbett)*, Derrick O'Connor *(Gym Trainer)*, Timothy Spall *(Parswell)*, Anne-Marie Marriott *(Emily)*, Janine Dutivitski *(Millicent)*, Julian Curry *(Portland)*, Charles McKeown *(Leicester)*, Ishaq Bux *(Maharajah)*, Tony Steedman *(Lord Quimby)*, Damaris Hayman *(Lady Quimby)*, Frank Mills *(Sir Cyril Everidge)*, Dawn Archibald, Frances Barber, Debbie Bishop, Ceri Jackson, Janine Lesley, Sasha Mitchell, Francine Morgan, Sophie Thompson, Sally Watkins *(Mission Girls)*, Tony Fawcett, Jaime Barr, Edward Bumstead *(Boys at Mudflats)*, Neil Innes *(Singer)*, David Leland, Hugh Fraser, Peter Bourke, Tilly Vosburgh, Arthur Howard, Hugh Walters, David Dixon, Anton Lesser, Yuseef Shah.

Palin, of Monty Python fame, plays a missionary who has spent 10 years teaching European history to native kids in an African village. But he has stayed in contact with his hometown sweetheart via numerous letters. He is called back to London and assigned the new duties of running a slum mission for "fallen women." To get the finances to support the project, Palin appeals to Smith, a wealthy aristocrat he met on the boat from Africa. She will only help if Palin will add a bit of romance to her empty love life. Story makes for a great deal of ironic situations, but as a whole it is too weak and fragmented to really hold together. This is somewhat made up for by a brilliant and lively cast, which manages to take full advantage of the numerous laughs.

p, Neville C. Thompson, Michael Palin; d, Richard Loncraine; w, Palin; ph, Peter Hannan (Panavision, Rank Film Lab Color); m, Mike Moran; ed, Paul Green; art d, Norman Garwood; cos, Shuna Harwood.

Comedy **Cas.** **(PR:O MPAA:R)**

MISSISSIPPI, 1931 (SEE: HEAVEN ON EARTH, 1931)

MISSISSIPPI** ½ (1935) 73m PAR bw

Bing Crosby *(Tom Grayson/Col. Steele)*, W. C. Fields *(Commodore Orlando Jackson)*, Joan Bennett *(Lucy Rumford)*, Queenie Smith *(Alabam)*, Gail Patrick *(Elvira Rumford)*, Claude Gillingwater, Sr. *(Gen. Rumford)*, John Miljan *(Maj. Patterson)*, Edward Pawley *(Joe Patterson)*, Fred Kohler, Sr. *(Capt. Blackie)*, John Larkin *(Rumbo)*, Libby Taylor *(Lavinia Washington)*, Harry Myers *(Joe, Stage Manager)*, Paul Hurst *(Hefty)*, Theresa Maxwell Conover *(Miss Markham)*, Al Richmond, Francis McDonald, Stanley Andrews, Eddie Sturgis, George Lloyd *(Gamblers)*, Bruce Covington *(Colonel)*, Jules Cowles *(Bartender)*, Harry Cody *(Abner, Bartender)*, Lew Kelly, Matthew Betz *(Men at Bar)*, Jack Mulhall *(Duelist)*, Victor Potel *(Guest)*, Bill Howard *(Man in Auditorium)*, Jack Carlyle *(Referee)*, Richard Scott *(Second)*, Jan Duggan *(Passenger on Boat)*, James Burke *(Passenger in Pilot House)*, Helene Chadwick, Jerome Storm *(Extras at Opening)*, The Cabin

Kids, Molasses, January *(Themselves)*, King Baggott *(1st Gambler)*, Mahlon Hamilton *(2nd Gambler)*, Charles L. King *(Desk Clerk)*, Jean Rouverol *(Friend of Lucy)*, Mildred Stone, Mary Ellen Brown, Mabel Van Buren, Bill Harwood *(Party Guests)*, J. P. McGowan *(Dealer)*, Clarence Geldert *(Hotel Proprietor)*, Fred "Snowflake" Toones *(Valet)*, Forrest Taylor *(Man at Bar Who Orders Sarsaparilla)*, Warner Richmond *(Man at Bar Who Pulls a Gun)*, Oscar Smith *(Valet)*, Robert McKenzie *(Show Patron)*, Ann Sheridan *(Extra at Engagement Party and Girls' School)*, Dennis O'Keefe, Arthur Millett, Clarence L. Sherwood, Bert Lindley, Roy Bailey, Warren Rogers, Jean Clarendon, Dan Crimmins, William Howard Gould.

There's not enough music in MISSISSIPPI to call it a musical and the only comedy provided is when Fields waddles on screen in another of his amusing characterizations, so it's a stretch to call it a "musical comedy," but that's about as close as can be, so that's what it is. This was the third go-around for Tarkington's play "Magnolia," with the first being a silent entitled THE FIGHTING COWARD and the second, an early Buddy Rogers sound film, RIVER OF ROMANCE. Crosby is a mustachioed young swain who is attending an engagement party to celebrate his union with Patrick. Miljan, a major in the Southern army, picks a fight with Crosby and demands "satisfaction"—in other words, a duel. Since it's a totally imaginary slight that Miljan is suffering from, Crosby sees no reason to engage in a fight to the death and he refuses to duel, thus embarrassing his in-laws-to-be, led by Gillingwater and seconded by Patrick. They brand him with the "White Feather" and Crosby departs the area to join Fields on a showboat that runs up and down "ol' man ribber." As he leaves, Crosby's exit is noted with a bit of wistfulness by Patrick's younger sister, Bennett, who sees Crosby's actions as far more heroic than yellow. Once aboard the showboat, Fields spots Crosby as a comer and makes him the traveling show's number one attraction. It isn't long before Crosby is crooning away and setting hearts fluttering. Now, snarling Kohler enters. He's a scoundrelly sleazeball who challenges Crosby to a battle in a local saloon. But the man is so hyper that he accidentally shoots himself dead with his own gun during the melee and Crosby is soon heralded as the man who rid the Mississippi of one of the worst scourges ever known in those parts. His billing aboard the ship changes to that of "the Singing Killer" and business booms. Bennett, who had found Crosby's pacificism so attractive, is not thrilled by this dubious designation and he has to explain to her that it's something Fields has named him and surely not an indication of his bloodthirstiness. This is compounded when we learn that Kohler was a cousin of Bennett's and Patrick's. Crosby is determined not to lose the love of Bennett, whom he has come to adore far more than his previous fiancee, so he goes to the Gillingwater plantation, knocks out Miljan and his hulking brother, Pawley, and shows them that he's not a coward at all. Now he bounds to Bennett's room, breaks down the door and claims her as his own, takes her to the showboat, and only then, with Fields backing him up, does Bennett learn that Crosby's reputation as a tough guy is all a mistake and he is gentleness personified (although you couldn't tell by the way he trounced Pawley and Miljan). The picture ends with Crosby and Bennett in a clinch. One hilarious sequence involves Fields in a poker game: he deals himself five aces, then notices that his four opponents are looking at him like vultures to a carcass, so he attempts to change the hand and is mystified when he keeps dealing aces to himself, much as he'd like to lose the hand in order to save his skin. Crosby replaced singer Lanny Ross in the role when the studio saw a few day's worth of the rushes and decreed that Ross didn't have enough excitement in his performance. They were right and Ross wasn't seen much in films after that. Three tunes became hits: "Down by the River," "Soon," and "Easy to Remember but So Hard to Forget" (Richard Rogers, Lorenz Hart, sung by Bing Crosby). The single song by Stephen Foster already had been a hit, "Swanee River" (sung by Crosby).

p, Arthur Hornblow, Jr.; d, A. Edward Sutherland; w, Francis Martin, Jack Cunningham, Claude Binyon, Herbert Fields (based on the play "Magnolia" by Booth Tarkington); ph, Charles Lang; ed, Chandler House; art d, Hans Dreier, Bernard Herzbrun.

Musical Comedy **(PR:A MPAA:NR)**

MISSISSIPPI GAMBLER** (1929) 57m UNIV bw

Joseph Schildkraut *(Jack Morgan)*, Joan Bennett *(Lucy Blackburn)*, Carmelita Geraghty *(Suzette Richards)*, Alec B. Francis *(Junius Blackburn)*, Otis Harlan *(Tiny Beardsley)*, William Welsh *(Capt. Weathers)*.

Overly predictable yarn about gambling on a steamboat on the Mississippi has Schildkraut as the card shark who underneath it all is not such a bad guy. He played this part just after the success he had with SHOW BOAT, which shares the same subject matter with MISSISSIPPI GAMBLER. Bennett is the object of Schildkraut's affections. She is the daughter of Francis, the man, Schildkraut just demolished at the table. But Schildkraut throws a game to Bennett to allow her to get her father's money back, the stakes of the game being Bennett's honor against her father's money. Bennett and Schildkraut look nice, but that is about it, as they plod their way through this one.

p, Carl Laemmle; d, Reginald Barker; w, Edward T. Lowe Jr., Winifred Reeve, H. H. Van Loan (based on the story by Karl Brown, Leonard Fields); ph, Gilbert Warrenton; ed, R. B. Wilcox; m/l, L. Wolfe Gilbert, Harry Akst.

Drama **(PR:A MPAA:NR)**

MISSISSIPPI GAMBLER* 1/2 (1942) 60m UNIV bw

Kent Taylor *(Johnny Forbes)*, Frances Langford *(Beth Cornell)*, John Litel *(Francis Carvel/Jim Hadley)*, Shemp Howard *(Milton Davis)*, Claire Dodd *(Gladys La Verne)*, Wade Boteler *(Brandon)*, Douglas Fowley *(Chet Matthews)*, Aldrich Bowker *(Editor)*, Eddie Dunn *(Dexter)*, Dave Oliver *(Croupier)*.

Taylor plays a reporter on the trail of an underworld killer, which leads him to the hideout of a former rackets boss. The mobster has had plastic surgery, and is posing as a respectable plantation owner, but Taylor sees through all this, leading to the mob boss' arrests. One of the few bright spots in this otherwise routine story is the appearance of Howard as a zany taxi driver. The songs serve no purpose.

p, Paul Malvern; d, John Rawlins; w, Al Martin, Roy Chanslor (based on a story by Martin, Marion Orth); ph, John W. Boyle; ed, Arthur Hilton; md, Charles Previn; art d, Jack Otterson; cos, Vera West; m/l, "I'm Hitting the Hot Spots," Jimmy McHugh Harold Adamson (sung by Claire Dodd), "There Goes My Romance," "Got Love," Everett Carter, Milton Rosen (sung by Frances Langford).

Crime/Drama **(PR:A MPAA:NR)**

MISSISSIPPI GAMBLER, THE*** (1953) 99m UNIV c

Tyrone Power *(Mark Fallon)*, Piper Laurie *(Angelique Duroux)*, Julia Adams *(Ann Conant)*, John McIntire *(Kansas John Polly)*, William Reynolds *(Pierre)*, Paul Cavanagh *(Edmund Duroux)*, John Baer *(Laurent Duroux)*, Ron Randell *(George Elwood)*, Robert Warwick *(Gov. Paul O'Monet)*, Guy Williams *(Andre)*, Ralph Dumke *(Caldwell)*, Hugh Beaumont *(Kennerly)*, King Donovan *(Spud)*, Gwen Verdon *(Voodoo Dancer)*, Alan Dexter *(Man)*, Al Wyatt, Dale Van Sickel, Michael Dale, Bert LeBaron *(Henchmen)*, Dennis Weaver *(Julian Conant)*, Marcel de la Brosse *(Maitre d')*, Frank Wilcox *(Judge)*, Edward Earle *(Duroux Lawyer)*, Andre Chariot *(Keith)*, William Vedder *(Minister)*, Frank Wilcox *(Judge)*, Larry Thor *(Captain)*, Bill Walker *(Duroux Butler)*, Roy Engel *(Captain of the Cultana)*, Dayton Lummis *(Sanford)*, Dorothy Bruce, Angela Stevens *(Girls)*, Rolfe Sedan, Saul Martell *(Tailors)*, Maya Van Horn *(Mme. Lesanne)*, Tony Hughes *(Teller)*, Fred Cravens *(Emile)*, George Hamilton *(Elwood Butler)*, David Newell *(Helmsman)*, Paul Bradley *(Gambler)*, LeRoi Antienne *(Singer)*, Anita Ekberg, Renate Hoy, Jackie Loughery, Jeanne Thompson *(Bridesmaids)*, Eduardo Cansino, Jr., John O'Connor, Paul Kruger, Robert Strong, Jack Del Rio, Buddy Roosevelt, Jon Shepord.

A robust, exciting tale, MISSISSIPPI GAMBLER has dashing Power in the title role, playing the son of a renowned New York fencing master. En route to New Orleans from St. Louis, Power gets into a poker game with Baer, snobbish son of a wealthy Southern family. When Baer loses a fortune he pays off by giving Power an expensive necklace belonging to his haughty sister Laurie. The gallant Power offers to return the necklace to Laurie but arrogant Laurie refuses, telling him he can put on all the airs of a cavalier he wishes but he's still a low life. Power teams up with veteran gambler McIntire on board ship and makes plans to open a lavish but honest gambling casino in New Orleans. He does, winning many friends who admire his chivalric manners, including Cavanagh, father of Baer and Laurie, who accepts the necklace and returns it to a daughter who continues to treat Power as dirt. Though she loves Power, Laurie cannot bring herself to show it. Power later meets improverished belle Adams and becomes her protector after her brother, Weaver, commits suicide over gambling losses. Laurie becomes bitterly jealous when seeing Power escorting Adams about New Orleans but her brother Baer falls in love with Adams who lets him down gently for she, too, is in love with Power. Baer, incensed at being rejected and blaming Power for his romantic plight, challenges the successful gambler to a duel. He cheats on the dueling ground but Power does not use his shot to kill his opponent and Baer is sent away in disgrace. Now Laurie really hates (and continues to love) Power for bringing her brother to social ruin and she spitefully marries banker Randall, even though she doesn't love him. Randall, meanwhile, to satiate his wife's appetite for expensive things, embezzles bank funds, and Baer, who runs into Power on a riverboat, attempts to kill his rival but falls on his own knife and dies. Power then learns that his friend Cavanagh is dying from wounds he received in a duel while defending Power's honor and the gambler rushes back to New Orleans to be at his deathbed. Randall's crooked ways are discovered and a run on his bank causes Power and McIntire to lose their fortune. Out of money, Power returns to the river and is about to sail north to gamble his way into another fortune when Laurie arrives to tell him that Randall has deserted her and that she has loved him and only him all along. He embraces her and they leave for a new life together. This costumer is handsomely mounted and Power is commanding as the suave, noble gambler. Mate directs with great vigor and the production values are superior in every sense. Laurie plays the petulant belle with a little too much venom, although she is ravishing and appealing. McIntire is excellent as the seasoned gambler, a role he had earlier played with much more sinister overtones in THE FAR COUNTRY. The theme of this film has been worked and reworked many times and much of the story content, plot, and even the characters, chiefly the roles essayed by Power and Laurie, owes a great debt to THE FOXES OF HARROW and, to a lesser degree, THE GAMBLER FROM NATCHEZ, starring Dale Robertson. Jeff Chandler, one of Universal's top leading men at the time, was originally slated to play the lead role here, but other commitments kept him from the chore. Rock Hudson was also considered for the part but then Power was brought in at a whopping salary in his first production away from his home studio, Fox, since his disastrous loanout to MGM for MARIE ANTOINETTE, and the only other time he did a non-Fox film since 1936. Power and producer Richmond became fast friends while working on this film and the two later formed a production company, Copa Productions, for independent filmmaking.

p, Ted Richmond; d, Rudolph Mate; w, Seton I. Miller; ph, Irving Glassberg (Technicolor); m, Frank Skinner; ed, Edward Curtiss; art d, Alexander Golitzen, Richard Riedel; set d, Russell A. Gausman, Julia Heron; cos, Bill Thomas; ch, Gwen Verdon.

Adventure **(PR:C MPAA:NR)**

MISSISSIPPI MERMAID* 1/2**

(1970, Fr./Ital.) 123m Films Du Carrosse-Les Productions Artistes Associes-Delphos/Lopert-UA c (LA SIRENE DU MISSISSIPPI; LA MIA DROGA SI CHIAMA JULIE)

Jean-Paul Belmondo *(Louis Mahe)*, Catherine Deneuve *(Julie Roussel/Marion)*, Michel Bouquet *(Comolli)*, Nelly Borgeaud *(Berthe Roussel)*, Marcel Berbert *(Jardine)*, Martine Ferriere *(Landlady)*, Roland Thenot *(Richard)*, Yves Drouhet.

Belmondo is a millionaire tobacco planter who becomes engaged to Deneuve through a personal column. He is taken by her beauty and they soon marry, but she leaves him with his bank account. He hires a private detective to find her, but eventually finds her himself, or so he thinks. The girl he finds is not his wife, but bears an uncanny resemblance to her (not surprising since Deneuve plays both roles). Eventually Belmondo learns that his new companion is trying to kill him. As he is about to be poisoned, he professes his love for Deneuve, who promptly knocks the cup from his hand and shamefully vows to love him forever. This is Truffaut's most successful attempt to blend a complex, Hitchcockian genre film with his own personality. It was also his first chance to work with superstars, a fact which brought people to the theaters in droves. The film is full of references to cinema—a clip from LA MARSEILLAISE (the picture is dedicated to Jean Renoir, whose film LA CARROSSE D'OR [THE GOLDEN COACH] was the inspiration for the name of Truffaut's production company), and homages to Humphrey Bogart, Nick Ray, Honore de Balzac, Jean Cocteau, and a *Cahiers Du Cinema* editor who bore the same name as this film's detective, Comolli.

p, Marcel Berbert; d&w, Francois Truffaut (based on the novel *Waltz into Darkness* by William Irish [Cornell Woolrich]); ph, Denys Clerval (Dyaliscope, DeLuxe Color); m, Antoine Duhamel; ed, Agnes Guillemot; art d, Claude Pignot; makeup, Michel Deruelle.

Mystery/Drama   **(PR:A MPAA:GP)**

MISSISSIPPI RHYTHM* 1/2   (1949) 68m MON bw

Jimmie Davis (*Himself*), Veda Ann Borg (*Jeanette*), Lee "Lasses" White (*Dixie Dalrymple*), Sue England (*Dorothy Kenworthy*), James Flavin (*Stan Caldwell*), Paul Maxey (*Judge Kenworthy*), Paul Bryar (*Sad Sam Beale*), Joel Marston (*Duke McCall*), Guy Beach (*Pop Lassiter*), Peeme Elmo, Duke York, Jim Dill, Lyle Talbot, Lillian Lindsco, Wheaton Chambers, Charles Jordan, Aileen Dixon, Bill Burt, Larry Rio, The Sunshine Band.

Story serves as little more than a vehicle for the performance of a few songs by former Louisiana governor Davis. In this one, he is on his way to claim an inheritance when he discovers that his new partner is actually a crook who has been keeping the town under his control. Davis rallies the surrounding farmers to the election polls through the use of his songs, something Davis did in real life during his own campaigns. Songs sung by Davis include: "You Are My Sunshine," "I Can't Say Good Bye," "No One Will Ever Know," and "It Makes No Difference Now."

p, Lindsley Parsons; d, Derwin Abrahams; w, Gretchen Darling (based on a story by Louise Rousseau); ph, William Sickner; ed, Ace Herman; art d, David Milton.

Drama   **(PR:A MPAA:NR)**

MISSISSIPPI SUMMER*   (1971) 88m New Line c

J. A. Preston, Lisle Wilson, Jared Martin, Robert Earl Jones.

In the American South of 1964, a troupe of actors, some black, some white, travel in a bus from town to town performing a play about voter registration. They meet opposition everywhere, and gradually the group disintegrates, the blacks going their way, and the whites theirs. Simplistic and badly acted, the film barely made a ripple when released. Funding from the American Film Institute helped get this waste of a film to the screen.

p, William Bayer, Eric Peniston; d&w, Bayer; ph, Bruce Torbet.

Drama   **(PR:C MPAA:NR)**

MISSOURI BREAKS, THE***   (1976) 126m UA c

Marlon Brando (*Lee Clayton*), Jack Nicholson (*Tom Logan*), Randy Quaid (*Little Tod*), Kathleen Lloyd (*Jane Braxton*), Frederic Forrest (*Cary*), Harry Dean Stanton (*Calvin*), John McLiam (*David Braxton*), John Ryan (*Si*), Sam Gilman (*Hank Rate*), Steve Franken (*Lonesome Kid*), Richard Bradford (*Pete Marker*), James Greene (*Hellsgate Rancher*), Luana Anders (*Rancher's Wife*), Danny Goldman (*Baggage Clerk*), Hunter Von Leer (*Sandy*), Virgil Frye (*Woody*), R. L. Armstrong (*Bob*), Dan Ades (*John Quinn*), Dorothy Newman (*Madame*), Charles Wagenheim (*Freighter*), Vern Chandler (*Vern*).

In the 1970s westerns started to come a little weird and this one was downright eccentric, although Brando, as a nutty gunfighter, and Nicholson, as a leader of rustlers, are fascinating to watch if not believable in their disjointed roles. The film opens as a rustler, on ranch baron McLiam's orders, is hanged, no little example for Nicholson, who heads a gang of vicious horse thieves. The hanged man, Von Leer, was Nicholson's friend and he intends to avenge the death, but he falls for Lloyd—daughter of the cattle baron—and somehow gets persuaded into settling down to the mundane chores of farming, much to the disgust of his gang. The rustlers nevertheless—without Nicholson's help—keep raiding McLiam's herds, which drives the cattle baron half crazy. He sends for a top gun bounty hunter, Brando, who turns out to be the most unpredictable and outright strangest creature to ever visit a western movie. To capture one outlaw he takes to wearing a bonnet and dress and when Nicholson goes to kill him he finds Brando taking a bubble bath, a sight that so jars him that he misses his opportunity to kill him. Brando continues his rampage, destroying all the rustlers except Nicholson who manages to finish off the weirdo in the end. The whole thing, script, acting, and especially Penn's heavy-handed direction, is bizarre and about as real a slice of the Old West as a grenade launcher. Yet there's a perverse joy in watching Brando and Nicholson try to compete with each other in mugging, switching accents (Brando), and mannerisms that could only be found elsewhere in institutions like Bellevue Insane Asylum (or those wards devoted to certifiable lunatics). The erratic and exotic behavior of the stars is infectious, with Quaid, Forrest, Stanton, and others mimicking them with slavish devotion.

p, Elliott Kastner, Robert M. Sherman; d, Arthur Penn; w, Thomas McGuane; ph, Michael Butler (DeLuxe Color); m, John Williams; ed, Jerry Greenberg, Stephen

Rotter, Dede Allen; prod d, Albert Brenner; art d, Stephen Berger; set d, Marvin March; cos, Patricia Norris.

Western   **Cas.**   **(PR:C-O MPAA:PG)**

MISSOURI OUTLAW, A**   (1942) 58m REP bw

Don "Red" Barry (*Cliff Dixon*), Lynn Merrick (*Virginia Randall*), Noah Beery (*Sheriff Dixon*), Paul Fix (*Mark Roberts*), Al St. John (*Willoughby*), Frank LaRue (*Randell*), Kenne Duncan (*Chandler*), John Merton (*Bancroft*), Carleton Young (*Allen*), Frank Brownlee (*Jensen*), Fred "Snowflake" Toones, Karl Hackett, Lee Shumway, Ray Bennett, Bob McKenzie, Kermit Maynard, Frank McCarroll, Curley Dresden, Herman Hack.

Routine western has Barry as a misjudged youth who helps banish a gang which has been coercing the ranchers and storeowners out of money. Some worthwhile performances and top-notch riding keep this one from being overly typical.

p&d, George Sherman; w, Doris Schroeder, Jack Lait, Jr.; ph, Jack Marta; ed, William Thompson.

Western   **(PR:A MPAA:NR)**

MISSOURI TRAVELER, THE***   (1958) 103m BV c

Brandon de Wilde (*Brian Turner*), Lee Marvin (*Tobias Brown*), Gary Merrill (*Doyle Magee*), Paul Ford (*Finas Daugherty*), Mary Hosford (*Anna Love Price*), Ken Curtis (*Fred Mueller*), Cal Tinney (*Clyde Hamilton*), Frank Cady (*Willie Poole*), Mary Field (*Nelda Hamilton*), Kathleen Freeman (*Serena Poole*), Will Wright (*Sheriff Peavy*), Tom Tiner (*Rev. Thorndyke*), Billy Bryant (*Henry Craig*), Barry Curtis (*Jimmy Price*), Eddie Little (*Red Poole*), Rodney Bell (*Herb Davis*), Helen Brown (*Hattie Neely*), Billy Newell (*Pos Neely*), Roy Jensen (*Simpson*), Earle Hodgins (*Old Sharecropper*).

Heartwarming story has de Wilde as a 15-year-old runaway orphan, out to make it on his own as a farmer. His determination has a strong effect upon the entire rural community. Merrill is the newspaper editor who takes him under his wing, with Marvin acting as the boy's nemesis, treating de Wilde with a gruffness that will help prepare him for the battles he will have to face. Young de Wilde gives a realistic portrayal, with Marvin and Merrill filling their roles to a tee.

p, Patrick Ford; d, Jerry Hopper; w, Norman Shannon Hall (based on a novel by John Burress); ph, Winton C. Hoch (Technicolor); m, Jack Marshall; ed, Tom McAdoo; art d, Jack Okey; cos, Frank Beetson, Ann Peck.

Drama   **(PR:A MPAA:NR)**

MISSOURIANS, THE** 1/2   (1950) 60m REP bw

Monte Hale (*Bill Blades*), Paul Hurst (*John X. Finn*), Roy Barcroft (*Nick Kovacs*), Lyn Thomas (*Peg*), Howard J. Negley (*Lucius Valentine*), Robert Neil (*Steve Kovacs*), Lane Bradford (*Stash*), John Hamilton (*McDowell*), Sarah Padden (*Mother*), Charles Williams (*Postmaster*), Perry Ivins (*Judge*).

Action-filled western features Hale as a sheriff in a small town which treats Neil with malice because of his Polish descent and relationship to the desperado Barcroft. When Barcroft comes to the town to hide out, he attempts to steal the church fund, but Hale nabs him and puts him behind bars. Well-paced direction keeps the abundant amount of action steady.

p, Melville Tucker; d, George Blair; w, Arthur E. Orloff; ph, John MacBurnie; m, Stanley Wilson; ed, Robert M. Leeds; art d, Frank Arrigo; m/l, "Roll Along Wagon Wheels" (sung by Monte Hale).

Western   **Cas.**   **(PR:A MPAA:NR)**

MR. ACE**   (1946) 84m UA bw

George Raft (*Eddie Ace*), Sylvia Sidney (*Margaret Wyndham Chase*), Stanley Ridges (*Toomey*), Sara Haden (*Alma Rhodes*), Jerome Cowan (*Peter Craig*), Sid Silvers (*Pencil*), Alan Edwards (*Chase*), Roman Bohnen (*Prof. Adams*), Joyce Bryant, The Flennoy Trio.

An ordinary political drama with little to recommend it other than Sidney's performance as an early-day Geraldine Ferraro. Raft is a political kingmaker (or, as in this instance, a queen-maker) who runs a club not unlike Tammany Hall in New York. He has fixed feelings about how to manipulate the populace and has used them to great advantage in rising to the top of a dirty field. Along comes Sidney, a well-to-do congresswoman who wants to run for governor of this unnamed state (the way Ella Grasso did in Connecticut), and she needs the help of Raft and his associates to win. He is the ultimate male chauvinist who believes a woman's place is under the heel of a man and he will have nothing to do with her or her candidacy. Sidney is married to Edwards but it's just for show and there's no love lost (or found) between them. Sidney and Raft have a meeting at her country home where she pleads her case and says she is willing to make some "adjustments" in her platform in order to secure his aid. Raft is so anti-Sidney that he sides with her opponents and is willing to say in court that he spent the night with her so Edwards and her enemies can use that to besmirch her good name. Sidney is hip to their machinations and sneaks into Reno for a quickie split before they can mount their campaign against her. Now Raft meets Bohnen, a solid citizen whom Raft respects. Bohnen has been helping Sidney all along and swears by her honesty, thus convincing Raft that he might have to amend his feelings about women in politics. Bohnen and Raft start a new organization to help Sidney (one totally separate from Raft's other affiliation). They do this on the sly and swing many of the independent voters off the fence and into Sidney's camp. The election takes place and Sidney wins. However, Raft and his cronies (from the other club) are accused of election fraud. Sidney, by this time, has fallen for the slow-talking Raft and tells him that she loves him. But it looks bad for Raft and she promises to help. He refuses that assistance, says that he'll go it alone, and that he expects to go up the river for about the same amount of time as she'll serve in the state house, but that he'll be back and they can make lifetime plans. There are two other twists in the plot, but they make about as much sense as most of the postwar B movie scripts. There is one song, "Now and Then," but whoever sings it is so out of focus in the background that we can't tell you who it was. Nice work from the always-reliable Cowan as Sidney's press agent and some humor is contributed by Silvers as Raft's number one flunkey.

p, Benedict Bogeaus; d, Edwin L. Marin; w, Fred Finklehoffe; ph, Karl Struss; m, Heinz Roemheld; ed, James Smith; md, David Chudnow; prod d, Ernst Fegte; set d, Fred Widdowson; cos, Greta; spec eff, Robert Moreland; m/l, "Now and Then," Sid Silvers, Finklehoffe.

Drama **(PR:A MPAA:NR)**

MR. AND MRS. NORTH 1/2** (1941) 68m MGM bw

Gracie Allen *(Pamela North)*, William Post, Jr. *(Gerald P. North)*, Paul Kelly *(Lt. Weigand)*, Rose Hobart *(Carol Brent)*, Virginia Grey *(Jane Wilson)*, Tom Conway *(Louis Berex)*, Porter Hall *(George Reyler)*, Millard Mitchell *(Mullins)*, Lucien Littlefield *(Barnes, Postman)*, Inez Cooper *(Mabel Harris)*, Keye Luke *(Kumi)*, Jerome Cowan *(Ben Wilson)*, Stuart Crawford *(Stuart Blanton)*, Fortunio Bonanova *(Buano)*, Felix Bressart *(Arthur Talbot)*, Harry Strang *(Cop)*, Tim Ryan, James Flavin, Lee Phelps.

Mystery spoof has Allen and Post as a married couple who come home to their apartment after a weekend absence to find a corpse in the closet. The couple wind up all their friends as suspects and try to solve the crime. Script is overly talky, but Allen, who carries the majority of the lines, and without George Burns for a change, gives the script some life. Direction does a good job in keeping a level of suspense going in the midst of all the comedy.

p, Irving Asher; d, Robert B. Sinclair; w, S. K. Lauren (based on the play by Owen Davis, from a story by Richard and Frances Lockridge); ph, Harry Stradling; ed, Ralph Winters.

Comedy/Mystery **(PR:A MPAA:NR)**

MR. AND MRS. SMITH*** (1941) 95m RKO/RKO-Films Incorporated bw

Carole Lombard *(Ann Smith/Ann Krausheimer)*, Robert Montgomery *(David Smith)*, Gene Raymond *(Jeff Custer)*, Jack Carson *(Chuck Benson)*, Philip Merivale *(Mr. Custer)*, Lucile Watson *(Mrs. Custer)*, William Tracy *(Sammy)*, Charles Halton *(Mr. Deever)*, Esther Dale *(Mrs. Krausheimer)*, Emma Dunn *(Martha)*, William Edmunds *(Proprietor of Lucy's)*, Betty Compson *(Gertie)*, Patricia Farr *(Gloria)*, Adele Pearce [Pamela Blake] *(Lily)*, Frank Mills *(Taxi Driver)*, Alec Craig *(Thomas the Clerk)*, Robert Emmett Keane *(Section Manager)*, Jack Gardner *(Elevator Boy)*, Ralph Sanford *(Store Checker)*, Murray Alper *(Harold the Driver)*, Georgia Carroll *(Pretty Girl)*, Ralph Dunn *(Clerk)*, James Flavin *(Escort)*, Ralph Brooks *(Waiter Captain)*, Ronnie Rondell *(Waiter)*, Jim Pierce *(Doorman)*, Barbara Wooddell *(Secretary to David)*, Beatrice Maude *(Secretary to Jeff)*, Allen Wood, Ernie Alexander *(Bellhops)*, Emory Parnell *(Conway)*, Stan Taylor *(Clerk)*, Francis Compton *(Mr. Flugle)*, D. Johnson, Sam Harris.

This was Hitchcock's only full-out American comedy (if we discount the black humor of THE TROUBLE WITH HARRY) and is not entirely satisfying. He agreed to direct it because Lombard was a close friend and felt that his style might widen the thin material and make it something better than it was. Lombard would film only one more movie after this, the wonderful TO BE OR NOT TO BE, before dying in 1942 in a small plane. She was on her way to California from a war-bond selling trip to the Midwest. Since this movie was released, the basic idea of the plot seems to have been used on every sit-com in TV. Lombard and Montgomery are a happy, if always-battling, couple. Their love is strong and they respect each other so much that they are willing to listen to the brittle dialog each hurls. When first married, they agreed that they would never walk out on the other while having an argument and since they are totally opposite in so many ways, that forces them to stay together for periods up to a week. As the picture begins, they have been quarreling side by side for three days. Once that's over, Lombard sweetly asks Montgomery if he would marry her again, given the opportunity. He thinks a moment, shrugs, and says he wouldn't, even though we know that he is mad about her. It's just Montgomery's way of teasing his bride but she doesn't find it at all funny. Montgomery goes to his office and is met by lawyer Halton, who explains that Lombard and Montgomery really aren't married because the state in which they married had shifted boundary lines just before the service. There's no problem, though, as all the couple has to do is remarry. Montgomery goes home for dinner and doesn't know that Halton has also visited Lombard at their residence. She eagerly awaits Montgomery's suggestion that they get married again but he says nothing about it. She suggests they return to the Italian restaurant where they spent so much of their courtship time but the dinner turns out to be a shambles. The restaurant has a new owner, Edmunds, and nothing is as they remember it. The soup they order is so vile that the scruffy restaurant cat even refuses it. The couple return home and Lombard, who has been waiting for her husband's proposal, realizes that he has no desire for another wedding, becomes enraged, and locks Montgomery out of the bedroom. She announces that she is going to retake her maiden name (Krausheimer) and since they are not married, there will be no need for a messy divorce. Montgomery moves to his men's club, has a few scenes with Carson in the steam room, and is totally perplexed about how to win back his wife. Raymond is Montgomery's law partner and he has been mad about Lombard for years, so he thinks the time is ripe for him to declare his affection for the sultry blonde. Raymond moves in and begins to woo Lombard, who is using that ploy as a tool in her effort to win back Montgomery (even though she may not realize that). Lombard and Raymond go to a Lake Placid lodge and Montgomery won't let them alone. His attentions eventually convince Lombard that he does indeed love her and she willingly tosses Raymond aside for Montgomery. It's a cute film, not nearly as funny as most of Lombard's other comedies, but there's enough good humor in MR. AND MRS. SMITH to make it a pleasant hour and a half. Hitchcock's direction is flawless, but with no chance for suspense or thrills. Hitchcock went out of his way to hire Compson for her role in this film; she had been kind to him when he was a lowly set designer in the 1920s and he was never a man to forget. The director knew that her star had faded considerably and she was down to acting in small roles so he made sure she had a substantial part in MR. AND MRS. SMITH. With the leading players he was genial, particularly with the often ribald Lombard who had long wanted to work with him. Hitchcock's remark about all actors being cattle (the printed source of this remark has never been pinpointed) brought about an elaborate joke. When he appeared on the set to begin shooting, Hitchcock found a small pen with three calves. Around the neck of each hung a sign with the name of the three leading actors' names on them. Hitchcock countered this Lombard jest by having assistants suddenly hold up cue cards during her important scenes which caused Lombard's perfect delivery to go awry so that she muffed her lines. She retaliated when it came time for Hitchcock to make his cameo appearance, this time as a bum cadging money from Montgomery for a drink. Lombard herself directed the bit, making Hitchcock do the tiny scene over and over again, insisting that more and more powder from the makeup people be added to his slowly reddening face. Sources conflict on the credit for the musical score, citing both Ward and Webb; however, it is likely that Ward contributed the score, while Webb acted as the musical director.

p, Harry E. Edington; d, Alfred Hitchcock; w, Norman Krasna; ph, Harry Stradling; m, Edward Ward, Roy Webb; ed, William Hamilton; art d, Van Nest Polglase, L. P. Williams; spec eff, Vernon L. Walker.

Comedy **Cas.** **(PR:A MPAA:NR)**

MISTER ANTONIO** (1929) 71m TIF bw

Leo Carrillo *(Antonio Camaradino)*, Gareth Hughes *(Joe)*, Frank Reicher *(Milton Jorny)*, Eugenie Besserer *(Mrs. Jorny)*, Virginia Valli *(June Ramsey)*, Franklin Lewis *(Earl Jorny)*.

Carrillo plays an organ grinder who falls for the daughter of a corrupt politician. Because Carrillo knows of some of the mayor's illegal doings, the mayor tries to persuade him into thinking that the girl has no interest in him. But this proves to be false, as the girl straps herself to his donkey, begging to be taken away. Hughes gives an entertaining performance as the organ grinder's sidekick.

d, James Flood, Frank Reicher; w, Frederick Hatton, Fanny Hatton (based on the story by Booth Tarkington); ph, Ernest Miller; ed, Arthur Roberts.

Drama **(PR:A MPAA:NR)**

MR. ARKADIN 1/2**
(1962, Brit./Fr./Span.) 93m Cervantes-Filmorsa-Sevilla-Mercury/Talbot-Cari bw
(GB: CONFIDENTIAL REPORT)

Orson Welles *(Gregory Arkadin)*, Robert Arden *(Guy Van Stratten)*, Paola Mori *(Raina Arkadin)*, Michael Redgrave *(Burgomil Trebitsch)*, Patricia Medina *(Mily)*, Akim Tamiroff *(Jakob Zouk)*, Mischa Auer *(The Professor)*, Katina Paxinou *(Sophie)*, Jack Watling *(Marquis of Rutleigh)*, Gregoire Aslan *(Bracco)*, Peter Van Eyck *(Thaddeus)*, Suzanne Flon *(Baroness Nagel)*, Frederic O'Brady *(Oskar)*, Tamara Shane *(The Blonde in the Apartment)*, Gordon Heath *(Pianist)*.

A very strange motion picture shot in Spain, Germany, Italy, and France in 1954 and 1955, it took almost seven years to edit, complete, and find distribution. Welles wrote the novel and the screenplay, starred and directed, a feat not unlike his monumental CITIZEN KANE. The results here are, unfortunately, not as monumental. Welles enjoyed examining the lives of unique men. He did so with KANE, Harry Lime in THE THIRD MAN, Cagliostro in BLACK MAGIC, Cesare Borgia in PRINCE OF FOXES, and MACBETH. In the instance of MR. ARKADIN, Welles presents a European financial jackal who will stop at nothing to achieve his goals. The movie is shot in the Welles style of dialog overlaps, off-angles, and constant attempts to keep the viewer's eyes and ears out of balance. It gets off to a fast start with a gun battle along the docks at Naples. Aslan is dying and the mortally wounded fellow's last words have to do with Arkadin (Welles) and his wife, Sophie (Paxinou). Arden's girl friend, Medina, hears the words and Arden, knowing that Welles is one of the richest men in creation, thinks he might be able to cadge a few lire out of the industrialist. Arden goes to Spain where he turns up at an elaborate party and gets to Welles through the man's young daughter, Mori (whom Welles married the following year), but Welles is too sharp and spots Arden as a two-bit fraud. There is something troubling Welles, though, for he claims he has no idea of his own past and is suffering from a form of amnesia. He engages Arden to investigate his own life and to report on what he finds. The only recall Welles has of his life is that he woke up one day with his pockets filled with money while wandering on a European street. As Arden goes deeper into Welles' background and gathers information, he notes that every person he speaks with who can give him information is being systematically killed. Arden discovers that Welles made his first bundle as a white slaver who used and abused women and sold them into bondage to anyone who could afford the tariff. It isn't long before Arden understands that he is a dupe and is being manipulated by Welles in order to find and erase anyone who might have dangerous information on the financier. Soon enough, Arden understands that Welles is doing this in order to quash anything that might lower his esteem in the eyes of his daughter. Since there is only one person who knows it all, Arden realizes that his life is hanging by a thread. In order to forestall his own death, Arden approaches Mori and tells her to get in touch with Welles, who is flying home in a single-engine plane. When Mori radios him, Welles thinks that she knows his entire history and becomes so emotionally distraught that he takes his own life by leaping from the plane to his death, a totally unexpected turn of events. Welles began planning this film in 1951 and it took four years to get financing. The weakest link in the story is Arden, who is not convincing in his role as the investigator. Some of the cameo appearances almost, but not quite, made up for Arden. Paxinou was Welles' estranged wife, Redgrave was a gay fence who claimed to be an antique dealer, Auer was the proprietor of a flea circus (and got all the funny lines in the script), and Tamiroff was a tailor. Welles tested the story by making it the plot of one of his radio shows a few years before shooting. It's a movie that could have been terrific but, like so much of Welles' later work, it suffered from being too arch, too concerned with style, and forgot that a story must be told. In CITIZEN KANE, despite all the man's excesses, we saw why he was the way he was and we ultimately sympathized with him and understood his motivations. Here, Arkadin is a rotter from the start and we couldn't care less about his life or death.

p, Louis Dolivet; d, Orson Welles; w, Welles (based on his novel); ph, Jean Bourgoin; m, Paul Misraki; ed, Renzo Lucidi; art d, Welles; set d, Luis Perez Espinosa, Gil Parrondo, Francisco Prosper; cos, Welles.

Drama (PR:C MPAA:NR)

MR. ASHTON WAS INDISCREET
(SEE: SENATOR WAS INDISCREET, THE, 1948)

MR. BELVEDERE GOES TO COLLEGE*** (1949) 82m FOX bw

Clifton Webb (Lynn Belvedere), Shirley Temple (Ellen Baker), Tom Drake (Bill Chase), Alan Young (Avery Brubaker), Jessie Royce Landis (Mrs. Chase), Kathleen Hughes (Kay Nelson), Taylor Holmes (Dr. Gibbs), Alvin Greenman (Corny Whittaker), Paul Harvey (Dr. Keating), Barry Kelley (Griggs), Bob Patten (Joe Fisher), Lee MacGregor (Hickey), Helen Westcott (Marian), Jeff Chandler (Pratt), Clancy Cooper (McCarthy), Evelynn Eaton (Sally), Judy Brubaker (Barbara), Kathleen Freeman (Babe), Lotte Stein (Marta), Peggy Call (Jean Auchincloss), Ruth Tobey (Nancy), Elaine Ryan (Peggy), Pattee Chapman (Isabelle), Joyce Otis (Fluffy), Lonnie Thomas (Davy), Reginald Sheffield (Prof. Ives), Colin Campbell (Prof. Lindley), Katherine Lang (Miss Cadwaller), Isabel Withers (Mrs. Myrtle), Arthur Space (Instructor), Gil Stratton, Jr.

Slick piece of comedy has Webb as a famous writer who decides to attend college in order to receive a distinguished literary award. He figures he can complete the four year program in just a year without too much problem. But a pushy journalism major, played by Temple, sees Webb's presence as a chance to write a dynamite article, and continually pesters the writer. Webb's performance, aided by the well-paced direction, manages to generate a steady flow of laughter. Temple, in the shadow of Webb, has better material with which to work than the majority of her later roles.

p, Samuel G. Engel; d, Elliott Nugent; w, Richard Sale, Mary Loos, Mary McCall, Jr. (based on the character from "Sitting Pretty" created by Gwen Davenport); ph, Lloyd Ahern; m, Alfred Newman; ed, Harmon Jones; art d, Lyle Wheeler, Richard Irvine; cos, Bonnie Cashin.

Comedy (PR:A MPAA:NR)

MR. BELVEDERE RINGS THE BELL*** (1951) 87m FOX bw

Clifton Webb (Lynn Belvedere/Oliver Erwenter), Joanne Dru (Miss Tripp), Hugh Marlowe (Rev. Watson), Zero Mostel (Emmett), William Lynn (Mr. Beebe), Doro Merande (Mrs. Hammer), Frances Brandt (Miss Hoadley), Kathleen Comegys (Mrs. Sampler), Jane Marbury (Mrs. Gross), Harry Hines (Mr. Cherry), Warren Stevens (Reporter), William and Ludwig Provaznik (Stahmer Twins), Cora Shannon (Mrs. Petit), J. Farrell MacDonald (Kroeger), Cecil Weston (Martha), Thomas Browne Henry (Father Shea), Hugh Beaumont (Policeman), Ray Montgomery, Don Kohler (Reporters), Edward Clark (Mailman), Norman Leavitt (Pharmacist), Dorothy Neumann (Librarian), Harry Antrim (Bishop), Harris Brown (Hotel Manager), Guy Wilkerson (Kramer), Ferris Taylor (Curtis), Luther Crockett (Harris), Ted Stanhope (Beach), Kathryn Sheldon (Housekeeper), Ted Pearson (Desk Sergeant), Robert Malcolm (Mr. Holmes).

Webb plays an admirable lecturer on tour, when he comes across an old people's home whose inhabitants act as if they were already dead. Acting on the belief that old age is more a mental than physical state, he gets admitted to the old age home pretending to be a man in his seventies. His youthful spirit begins to spread to the other guests, so that when his true age is discovered, everyone is so active, no one cares that they were taken in. Webb also manages to spark some life into a romance between the minister of the home, Marlowe, and his fiancee, Dru, by making Marlowe jealous. Direction keeps a well-paced flow going, handling the changes in the elderly characters smoothly. Webb, though not the center of all the comedy as in most of the Belvedere films, gives a charming performance without becoming overly righteous.

p, Andre Hakim; d, Henry Koster; w, Ranald MacDougall (based on the play "The Silver Whistle" by Robert C. McEnroe and the character "Belvedere" created by Gwen Davenport); ph, Joseph LaShelle; m, Cyril J. Mockridge; ed, William B. Murphy; md, Lionel Newman; art d, Lyle Wheeler, John DeClair; cos, Renie.

Comedy (PR:A MPAA:NR)

MR. BIG** (1943) 73m UNIV bw

Gloria Jean (Patricia), Donald O'Connor (Donald), Peggy Ryan (Peggy), Robert Paige (Johnny Hanley), Elyse Knox (Alice Taswell), Samuel S. Hinds (Jeremy Taswell), Bobby Scheerer (Bobby), Richard Stewart (Genius), Mary Eleanor [Elinor] Donahue (Muggsy), Florence Bates (Mrs. Davis), Ray Eberle.

Though not much of a story, this film about a group of drama students who stage a lively show, does offer an abundance of song and dance routines to make up for its lack of plot. The students at a ritzy type of drama school are at odds with the owner's belief in teaching nothing but the classics. The kids would rather concentrate on swing-type entertainment, so when the owner goes away they decide to try and stage their own show. Though the difficulties seem insurmountable, the kids manage to pull it off in time to prove to the owner the worth of the new types of music and dance. Songs include: "This Must Be a Dream," "Kittens with Their Mittens Laced," "Things I Want to Say," "Spirit Is in Me," "Rude, Crude, and

Unattractive," "Thee and Me," "We're Not Obvious" (Inez James, Buddy Pepper); "Moonlight and Roses" (Ben Black, Neil Moret).

p, Ken Goldsmith; d, Charles Lamont; w, Jack Pollexfen, Dorothy Bennett (based on the story "School for Jive" by Virginia Rooks); ph, George Robinson; m, Charles Previn; ed, Frank Gross; md, Previn; art d, John B. Goodman, Harold MacArthur; cos, Vera West; ch, Louis da Pron.

Musical (PR:A MPAA:NR)

MR. BILL THE CONQUEROR (SEE: MAN WHO WON, THE, 1932, Brit.)

MR. BILLION** (1977) 91m Pantheon/FOX c

Terence Hill (Guido Falcone), Valerie Perrine (Rosi Jones), Jackie Gleason (John Cutler), Slim Pickens (Duane Hawkins), William Redfield (Leopold Lacy) Chill Wills (Col. Clayton T. Winkle), Dick Miller (Bernie), R.G. Armstrong (Sheriff T. C. Bishop), Dave Cass (Boss Kidnaper), Sam Laws (Pops Dinwitty), John Ray McGhee (Carnell Dinwitty), Kate Heflin (Lucy), Leo Rossi (Italian Kidnaper), Frances Heflin (Mrs. Apple Pie), Ralph Chesse (Anthony Falcon), Bob Minor (Black Kidnaper), Bob Herron (Moose), Helen Bentley (TV Reporter), Martin Kove (Texas Gambler), Laurence Somma (Dealer), Robert Statts (Conductor), Frank Barone (Casino Manager), Mary Woronov (Actress), Paul Bartel (Agent), Eric Barnes, Earl Boen (Col. Winkle's Aides), Julia Hare (Nancy, Newscaster), Clay Braden (Airline Stewardess), Stan Ritchie (Bartender), Dan Lee Gant (Bus Clerk), Neil Summers (Deputy Hank), Henry Kinji (Indian), Denver Mattson (Deputy Joe), Walt Davis (Chauffeur), Gavin James (Airplane Pilot), George W. Cumming (Cable Car Conductor), Aldo Rendine (Restaurant Owner), Gianna Dauro (Owner's Wife), Maurizio Fiori, Massimiliano Filoni (Owner's Children), Marco Tulli (Translator), Cesare Nizzica (Head Mechanic), Vicky George (Lady Waiting for a Car).

A return to the type of philosophy behind Frank Capra's MR. DEEDS GOES TO TOWN has Hill as an Italian auto mechanic who has inherited his rich uncle's estate. The only stipulation is that he must claim his inheritance in San Francisco within 20 days. Gleason, as a sneaky executor of the estate, does everything in his power to keep Hill from achieving his goal, so that Gleason can handle the money. This includes a seduction of Perrine, which fails as she falls in love with Hill, plus numerous chase scenes, fight scenes, and kidnap attempts. When Hill finally makes it, with minutes to spare, he doles out important positions and money to the people who helped him retrieve his inheritance. Other than Capra, the picture also borrows heavily from Hitchcock in the development of the chase scenes across country.

p, Steven Bach, Ken Friedman; d, Jonathan Kaplan; w, Friedman, Kaplan; ph, Matthew F. Leonetti (DeLuxe Color); m, Dave Grusin; ed, O. Nicholas Brown; art d, Richard Berger; set d, Sam Jones, Joe Chavalier; cos, Seth King, Stephanie Colin, Bill Jobe, Mal Pape; spec eff, Paul Stewart.

Drama (PR:A MPAA:PG)

MR. BLANDINGS BUILDS HIS DREAM HOUSE*** (1948) 94m RKO/Selznick bw

Cary Grant (Jim Blandings), Myrna Loy (Muriel Blandings), Melvyn Douglas (Bill Cole), Reginald Denny (Simms), Sharyn Moffett (Joan Blandings), Connie Marshall (Betsy Blandings), Louise Beavers (Gussie), Harry Shannon (W. D. Tesander), Ian Wolfe (Smith), Tito Vuolo (Mr. Zucca), Nestor Paiva (Joe Appollonio), Jason Robards, Sr. (John Retch), Lurene Tuttle (Mary), Lex Barker (Carpenter Foreman), Emory Parnell (Mr. Delford), Will Wright (Eph Hackett), Frank Darien (Judge Quarles), Stanley Andrews (Murphy), Cliff Clark (Jones), Franklin Parker (Simpson), Charles Middleton (Wrecker), Cy Slocum (Man), Jack Jahries (Elevator Operator), Robert Bray, Frederich Ledebur (Workmen), Don Brodie (Charlie), Hal K. Dawson (Mr. Selby), Kernan Cripps (Cop), Ralph Stein (Proprietor), Mike Lally, Bud Wiser (Customers), Gene Leslie (Taxi Driver), Dan Tobin (Bunny Funkhauser).

The novel upon which this film was based was very funny and timely. This movie suffered in the translation to the screen, although it did have enough humor to make it a hit. The years have not been gentle to MR. BLANDINGS BUILDS HIS DREAM HOUSE and there are many tedious stretches in the film that feel leaden. This was the third duet for Grant and Loy and they added a weak triangular plot-turn with Douglas in order to add some spice to a one-joke premise. Grant and Loy are married Manhattanites who must give up their apartment and find new lodgings for themselves and their daughters, Moffett and Marshall. As in the Kaufman and Hart play "George Washington Slept Here," the leads are seduced by the dream of having their own suburban home in the greenery of the country. A sharp realtor, Wolfe, sells them an ancient house that's nearly 200 years old and they pay an incredible sum for the privilege of living in a drafty, dilapidated home. The rest of the movie is a series of incidents (somewhat interminable) that looks like just another segment of TV's "Green Acres." Grant tries to deal with architect Denny as he decides to raze the old house and start from scratch. There are several gags we've all seen (or heard) before, such as the jam-packed hall closet that disgorges everything each time the door is opened (a running joke on the old "Fibber McGee and Molly" radio series), water rising in the cellar, windows that don't fit flush and allow the elements to invade, and all of the expected jokes that come with the territory. Whatever fun one gets is in watching Grant's frustration as he deals with the problems of being a home builder. Douglas' comedic talents are totally wasted as the couple's attorney, who is their close friend and upon whom the screenwriters have attempted to place the mantle of "other man". In a small role, note Lex Barker, one-time movie TARZAN.

p, Norman Panama, Melvin Frank; d, H. C. Potter; w, Panama, Frank (based on the novel by Eric Hodgins); ph, James Wong Howe; m, Leigh Harline; ed, Harry Marker; md, Constantin Bakaleinikoff; art d, Albert S. D'Agostino, Carroll Clark; set d, Darrell Silvera, Harley Miller; cos, Robert Kalloch; spec eff, Russell A. Cully.

Comedy Cas. (PR:A MPAA:NR)

MR. BOGGS STEPS OUT*1/2 (1938) 68m GN bw

Stuart Erwin (Oliver Boggs), Helen Chandler (Oleander), Toby Wing (Irene), Tully Marshall (Ross), Spencer Charters (Angus Tubbs), Otis Harlan (Katz), Walter Byron (Andrews), William Moore (DeBrette), Harry Tyler (Mason), Eddie Kane (Manager), Milburn Stone, Nora Cecil, Harrison Green, Elliott Fisher, Wilson Benge, Mike Jeffries, Isabel LaMal, Betty Mack, Otto Hoffman.

Dull situation-type comedy has Erwin as a statistician who wins a bundle of money by coming closest in his guess of the number of beans in a barrel. With the money he decides to do something other than his usual line of work, and buys a barrel factory. Problems arise with keeping Marshall's pickle factory open when slickster Byron tries to keep this from happening. The usual type of romantic situations develop with small town girl Chandler getting a crush on Erwin, while he gets the hots for Wing. Picture never manages to keep much interest going.

p, Ben Pivar; d, Gordon Wiles; w, Richard English (based on the story by Clarence Buddington Kelland); ph, John Stumar; ed, Gene Milford.

Comedy (PR:A MPAA:NR)

MISTER BROWN**1/2 (1972) 85m Andrieux c

Al Stevenson (George Brown), Judith Elliotte (Clarissa Brown), Tyrone Fulton (Mike Brown), Nancy Goddard, Bert Kramer (Their Voices), Pauline Chew Morgan, Ted Harris, Peggy Toy, Jeannine Altobelli, Chuckie Bradley, Billy Green Bush, Bert Kramer, Charles Mott, Christopher Cannon, Charles Douglas, Cheryl Carter, Charles Jackson, Johnny Jingles, Christopher Mock, Michael Elliotte, Wednesday Lea Packer.

Low budget independent feature has Stevenson as a black man moving his family from Louisiana to Los Angeles in the hopes of starting his own business. Though he has no credit, he manages to open the bakery he has always dreamed about. However, the business never does well enough to maintain itself, forcing Stevenson to abandon his bakery and acquire a sanitation job. Cast is all black, but picture keeps away from this aspect, instead concentrating on the story about the hardships all people face when trying to pursue their dreams. Plots like this one can easily become overly sentimental, but Andrieux manages to keep everything at a fairly level tempo; his only weakness is his occasional loss of control in direction, when he gives the actors free reign and they take it too far.

p,d,w&ph, Roger Andrieux; m, John Lee Hooker; ed, Andrieux.

Drama (PR:C MPAA:NR)

MR. BROWN COMES DOWN THE HILL** (1966, Brit.) 88m WEST/MRA bw

Eric Flynn (Mr. Brown), Mark Heath (Black Man), Lillias Walker (Harlot), John Richmond (Bishop), Richard Warner (Doctor), Bryan Coleman (Bishop), Alan White (Andy), Donald Simpson (Bishop).

Weird religious allegory, film has Flynn a mysterious preacher who restores the faith in the hearts of Heath, Walker, and Richmond before the inevitable persecutors arrive to make a martyr out of him. Not the sort of thing that will turn up on the late movie.

p,d&w, Henry Cass (based on a play by Peter Howard).

Religious Drama (PR:A MPAA:NR)

MISTER BUDDWING** (1966) 99m MGM bw (GB: WOMAN WITHOUT A FACE)

James Garner (Mister Buddwing), Jean Simmons (The Blonde), Suzanne Pleshette (Fiddle), Katharine Ross (Janet), Angela Lansbury (Gloria), George Voskovec (Shabby Old Man), Jack Gilford (Mr. Schwartz), Joe Mantell (1st Cab Driver), Raymond St. Jacques (Hank), Ken Lynch (Dan), Beeson Carroll (Policeman), Billy Halop (2nd Cab Driver), Michael Hadge (Counterman), Charles Seel (Printer), John Tracy (Tony), Bart Conrad (Chauffeur), Wesley Addy, Kam Tong, Romo Vincent, James O'Rear, Nichelle Nichols, Rafael Campos, John Dennis, Pat Li, Rikki Stevens, (Dice Players), Paul Andor (Man on Street).

Garner plays an amnesiac who wakes up on a bench in Central Park, unable to remember anything about himself. He decides to take the name "Buddwing," based on a beer ad and a plane that he sights when he first awakens. He then has several encounters which slowly lodge his past back into his memory. Ross is the college girl who reminds him of his ex-fiancee from college. Pleshette is an actress who plays several records for Garner, forcing him to remember that he forsook a career as a composer when he was younger, due to poverty. Simmons is a socialite who takes Garner along to a crap game in Harlem. There he recalls that his wife is recovering from a suicide attempt after Garner's unpleasant reaction to her pregnancy, and he rushes to the hospital where she's been taken. The various subplots offer some interest in and of themselves, but they are not blended well enough to keep the entire story going. Garner is easily forgettable in his role as the amnesiac, being outshone by the three women he meets in search of his identity.

p, Delbert Mann, Douglas Laurence, Dale Wasserman; d, Mann; w, Wasserman (based on the novel Buddwing by Evan Hunter); ph, Ellsworth Fredricks, m, Kenyon Hopkins; ed, Fredric Steinkamp; art d, George W. Davis, Paul Groesse; set d, Henry Grace; Hugh Hunt; cos, Helen Rose; makeup, William Tuttle.

Drama (PR:C MPAA:NR)

MR. BUG GOES TO TOWN*** (1941) 78m PAR c (AKA: HOPPITY GOES TO TOWN)

Voices: Kenny Gardner, Gwen Williams, Jack Mercer, Ted Pierce, Mike Meyer, Stan Freed, Pauline Loth.

This was the last cartoon feature that the Fleischer brothers, Max and Dave, released before going their separate ways. Story concerns an insect community faced with problems inside their group, coupled with pressures due to the encroachment of the human race. Unfortunately, this expensive production was a financial failure, causing the animators, who had been the chief rival of Walt Disney studios, to fold up shop. MR. BUG GOES TO TOWN did not have the success of the earlier features, such as GULLIVER'S TRAVELS, due to a weak story development that never focuses on any single cartoon character, further marred by voices which evoke no sense of personality behind the drawings. Animation, however, is quite good, well ahead of its time, with the possible exception of flawed human characters. Songs include: "We're the Couple in the Castle," "I'll Dance at Your Wedding," "Boy Oh Boy."

p, Max Fleischer; d, Dave Fleischer; w, D. Fleisher, Dan Gordon, Ted Pierce, Isidore Sparber, William Turner, Mike Meyer, Graham Place, Bob Wickersham, Cal Howard; ph, Charles Schnettler (Technicolor); md, Leigh Harline; m/l, Hoagy Carmichael, Frank Loesser, Herman Timberg, Four Marshals and Royal Guards.

Cartoon (PR:AAA MPAA:NR)

MR. CELEBRITY** (1942) 68m PRC bw

Buzzy Henry (Danny Mason), James Seay (Jim Kane), Doris Day (Carol Carter), William Halligan (Mr. Mason), Gavin Gordon (Travers), Johnny Berkes (Johnny Martin), Jack Baxley (Judge Culpepper), Larry Grey (Cardo the Great), John E. Ince (Joe Farrell), Frank Hagney (Dugan), Jack Richardson (Geraghty), Alfred Hall (Scanlon), Smokey Saunders (Smokey), William Whitman, Ruth Clifford, Henry Hastings, Billy Mitchell, William Pagan, Francis X. Bushman, Clara Kimball Young, James Jeffries.

Routine racetrack story centers around uncle Seay, a young veterinarian, and his kid nephew, Henry, both of whom love horse racing. When the rich grandfather demands custody of the youngster, however, the two run off to a farm that serves as a resting place for former celebrities. The farm owns an old nag, "Mr. Celebrity," whom Seay conditions to run in a large race. The horse wins, of course, thus granting the two enough money to stay together. Performances are satisfactory, but the story is too overly predictable to hold much interest.

p, Martin Mooney; d, William Beaudine; w, Mooney (based on the story by Charles Samuels, Mooney); ph, Arthur Martinelli; ed, Robert Crandall.

Drama (PR:A MPAA:NR)

MR. CHEDWORTH STEPS OUT**1/2 (1939, Aus.) 92m Cinesound/Associated British Empire bw

Cecil Kellaway, James Raglan, Joan Deering, Rita Pauncefort, Peter Finch, Jean Hatton, Sydney Wheeler.

Kellaway plays a down-and-out clerk who happens upon a bag of money. Unknown to him the money is all counterfeit, forcing the innocent man to become involved with gangland members, as well as federal agents. Overall, the performances are topnotch and the direction well-paced, but the storyline is weak.

d, Ken G. Hall; w, Frank Harvey; ph, George Heath; md, Hamilton Webber; songs, "Lo, Hear the Gentle Lark," "If It Rains Who Cares?" sung by Jean Hatton.

Crime/Drama (PR:A MPAA:NR)

MR. CHUMP** (1938) 60m WB bw

Johnnie Davis (Bill Small), Lola Lane (Jane Mason), Penny Singleton (Betty Martin), Donald Briggs (Jim Belden), Chester Clute (Ed Mason), Frank Orth (Sheriff), Granville Bates (Mr. Sprague), Spencer Charters (Mr. Koeper), Clem Bevans (Pop), Sidney Bracy (Theater Manager).

Lighthearted fun has Davis as a trumpet player who spends little time working, but has developed his own system of making millions on paper in the stock market. When two bank officers use Davis' system with the banks' money, they lose heavily, landing themselves in jail. But Davis manages to save the day. A bit too predictable and unbelievable, but no one takes themselves too seriously, making for a bit of fun. Davis sings "As Long As You Live."

p, Bryan Foy; d, William Clemens; w, George Bricker; ph, Arthur Edeson; ed, Harold McLernon; m/l, Johnny Mercer, Bernie Hanighen, Charles Henderson.

Comedy (PR:A MPAA:NR)

MISTER CINDERELLA*1/2 (1936) 75m MGM bw

Jack Haley (Joe Jenkins), Betty Furness (Patricia Randolph), Arthur Treacher (Watkins), Raymond Walburn (Peter Randolph), Robert McWade (Gates), Rosina Lawrence (Mazie), Monroe Owsley (Aloysius Merriweather), Kathleen Lockhart (Aunt Penelope), Edward Brophy (Detective McNutt), Charlotte Wynters (Martha), Tom Dugan (Spike Nolan), Iris Adrian (Lil), Toby Wing (Lulu), Morgan Wallace (Fawcett), Arthur Aylesworth (Simpson), John Hyams (Mr. Wilberforce), Leila McIntyre (Mrs. Wilberforce).

Lackluster comedy that uses just about every cliche slapstick routine known to film. Story revolves around an ordinary barber who poses as a millionaire. Familiar gags include tripping socialites at a party, the accidental fire started in a cabin where a lady is disrobing, the mistaken identity joke, the hero losing his swimming trunks, and races up the beach and back, to name just a few of the tiresome comedy routines filling this picture.

p, Hal Roach; d, Edward Sedgwick; w, Arthur Vernon Jones, Richard Flournoy (based on the story by Jack Jevne); ph, Milton Krasner; ed, Jack Ogilvie.

Comedy (PR:A MPAA:NR)

MISTER CINDERS** (1934, Brit.) 72m BIP/Wardour bw

Clifford Mollison (Jim Lancaster), Zelma O'Neal (Jill Kemp), Kenneth Western (Lumley Lancaster), George Western (Guy Lancaster), W. H. Berry (Police Constable Merks), Renee Houston (Mrs. Phipps), Edward Chapman (Mr. Gaunt), Edmond Breon (Sir George Lancaster), Finlay Currie (Henry Kemp), Lorna Storm

(Minerva Kemp), Esme Church *(Lady Agatha Lancaster)*, Henry Mollison *(Cross)*, Ellen Pollock *(Donna Lucia)*, Sybil Grove, Julian Royce, Mabelle George.

Mollison is the poor relative of a wealthy family who is mistreated by all as they try to marry either of the two other sons to American heiress O'Neal. She poses as a servant in the household and ends up marrying Mollison after she saves him from a charge of robbery. Odd musical gender-variation of Cinderella has some good songs and a spirited cast, despite technical limitations.

p, Walter C. Mycroft; d, Fred Zelnik; w, Clifford Grey, Frank Miller, Jack Davies, Kenneth Western, George Western (based on a play by Grey, Miller, Greatrex Newman); ph, Otto Kanturek; m, Vivian Ellis.

Musical **(PR:A MPAA:NR)**

MR. COHEN TAKES A WALK** ½** (1936, Brit.) 81m WB bw

Paul Graetz *(Jake Cohen)*, Violet Farebrother *(Rachel Cohen)*, Chili Bouchier *(Julia Levine)*, Mickey Brantford *(Jack Cohen)*, Ralph Truman *(Sam Cohen)*, Barry Livesey *(Joe Levine)*, Kenneth Villiers *(Bob West)*, Meriel Forbes *(Sally O'Connor)*, George Merritt *(Pat O'Connor)*, Sam Springson *(Abraham Levy)*.

Charming story about a self-made Jewish businessman who creates a successful large business from his meager beginnings as a peddler. His sons adapt a number of modern methods in running the business, which leaves the old man feeling left out in the cold. He longs for the old simple way of doing things, so when his wife dies of a heart attack, he takes to a life of wandering, leaving his business in the hands of his sons. He travels to America, where he reads in the paper that all the workers of his store have gone on strike. He returns with his youngest son, and takes over the store again, this time insisting on his own methods of management. His youngest boy also shuns the new way of doing business, but shocks his father when he announces that he intends to marry a Gentile girl. Story ends with the bride and groom getting married in a dual religious ceremony with the father's blessing.

p, Irving Asher; d, William Beaudine; w, Brock Williams (based on the novel by Mary Roberts Rinehart); ph, Basil Emmott; ed, A. Bates.

Drama **(PR:A MPAA:NR)**

MISTER CORY*** (1957) 92m UNIV c

Tony Curtis *(Cory)*, Martha Hyer *(Abby Vollard)*, Charles Bickford *(Biloxi)*, Kathryn Grant *(Jen Vollard)*, William Reynolds *(Alex Wyncott)*, Russ Morgan *(Ruby Matrobe)*, Henry Daniell *(Earnshaw)*, Willis Bouchey *(Mr. Vollard)*, Joan Banks *(Lola)*, Louise Lorimer *(Mrs. Vollard)*, Harry Landers *(Andy)*, Dick Crockett *(The Cook)*, Hylton Socher *(Bellboy)*, Glen Kramer *(Ronnie Chambers)*, Paul Bryar *(Dealer)*, George Eldredge *(Guest)*, Charles Horvath *(Truck Driver)*, Jack Gargan *(Golfer)*, Dick Monda *(Boy)*, Billy Eagle *(Vendor)*, Anna Stein.

Curtis plays a youth from the slums of Chicago who betters himself through gambling, eventually becoming a partner with Bickford of a fashionable gambling casino. Story spans a period of several years, beginning with his job as a bus boy at a summer resort, where he meets two society girls, Hyer and Grant. Curtis meets up with the two girls later on, Hyer having an affair with him, but not seeing him worthy for anything else. Her younger sister, Grant, has a genuine affection for Curtis, eventually marrying him, at which point Curtis decides to go legitimate. Curtis is convincing in the title role, with Edwards' direction blending the cast in a well-paced effort.

p, Robert Arthur; d, Blake Edwards; w, Edwards (based on the story by Leo Rosten); ph, Russell Metty (CinemaScope, Eastmancolor); ed, Edward Curtiss; md, Joseph Gershenson; art d, Alexander Golitzen, Ernie Orbom; cos, Bill Thomas.

Drama **(PR:A MPAA:NR)**

MR. DEEDS GOES TO TOWN***** (1936) 115m COL bw

Gary Cooper *(Longfellow Deeds)*, Jean Arthur *(Babe Bennett)*, George Bancroft *(MacWade)*, Lionel Stander *(Cornelius Cobb)*, Douglas Dumbrille *(John Cedar)*, Raymond Walburn *(Walter)*, Margaret Matzenauer *(Madame Pomponi)*, H. B. Warner *(Judge Walker)*, Warren Hymer *(Bodyguard)*, Muriel Evans *(Theresa)*, Ruth Donnelly *(Mabel Dawson)*, Spencer Charters *(Mal)*, Emma Dunn *(Mrs. Meredith)*, Wryley Birch *(Psychiatrist)*, Arthur Hoyt *(Budington)*, Stanley Andrews *(James Cedar)*, Pierre Watkin *(Arthur Cedar)*, John Wray *(Farmer)*, Christian Rub *(Swenson)*, Jameson Thomas *(Mr. Semple)*, Mayo Methot *(Mrs. Semple)*, Margaret Seddon *(Jane Faulkner)*, Margaret McWade *(Amy Faulkner)*, Russell Hicks *(Dr. Malcolm)*, Gustav von Seyffertitz *(Dr. Frazier)*, Edward Le Saint *(Dr. Fosdick)*, Charles [Levison] Lane *(Hallor)*, Irving Bacon *(Frank)*, George Cooper *(Bob)*, Gene Morgan *(Waiter)*, Walter Catlett *(Morrow)*, Edward Gargan *(2nd Bodyguard)*, Paul Hurst *(1st Deputy)*, Paul Porcasi *(Italian)*, Franklin Pangborn *(Tailor)*, George F. ["Gabby"] Hayes *(Farmers' Spokesman)*, Mary Lou Dix *(Shop Girl)*, George Meeker *(Brookfield)*, Barnett Parker *(Butler)*, Patricia Monroe, Lillian Ross *(Hat Check Girls)*, Peggy Page *(Cigarette Girl)*, Janet Eastman *(Shop Girl)*, Bud Flannigan [Dennis O'Keefe] *(Reporter)*, Dale Van Sickel *(Lawyer)*, Harry C. Bradley *(Anderson)*, Edwin Maxwell *(Douglas)*, Billy Bevan *(Cabby)*, Ann Doran *(Girl on Bus)*, Cecil Cunningham, Bess Flowers, Beatrice Curtis, Beatrice Blinn, Pauline Wagner, Frank Hammond, Charles Sullivan, Flo Wix, Hal Budlong, Ethel Palmer, Juanita Crosland, Vacey O'Davoren.

This is a devastatingly simple story with a populist point of view but it is shown with such charm and charisma and acted so well by Cooper and Arthur that it has become another Capra classic. Cooper is a rural rube from Vermont who inherits his uncle's vast fortune and becomes national news overnight. He plays the tuba and is the local poet. The whole town turns out to see Cooper off to New York at the train station; he will assume the responsibilities of his uncle's business and move into an enormous mansion. But cynical news editor Bancroft does not fall for Cooper's image of a simple, honest man, calling him a "cornfed bohunk." He assigns Arthur to interview Cooper, with instructions to not spare the ridicule, but the aggressive and devious reporter cannot corral Cooper. She fakes a faint in front of his residence and the gallant Cooper picks her up and takes care of her. She tells him she's unemployed and begins wheedling information from him. Cooper's sincerity and decency, however, turn Arthur's derision of the new multimillionaire into affection, then love. Cooper also falls for Arthur and, while escorting her home to her shabby tenement building, he pauses at the steps and withdraws a poem which he has written for her, really a proposal, and she reads it with a breaking, almost choking whisper: "I've tramped the earth with hopeless beat/Searching in vain for a glimpse of you./Then heaven thrust you at my very feet./A lovely angel, too lovely to woo./My dream has been answered, but my life's just as bleak./I'm handcuffed, I'm speechless, in your presence divine./My heart wants to cry out, if it only could speak./I love you, my angel, be mine, be mine." Cooper is no sap, however, even though he's gone mushy for Arthur. He knows that the $20 million he's inherited is being sought piecemeal and wholesale from petty moochers to his conniving lawyer, Dumbrille, and high-positioned associates. Yet he craves only the simple joys, such as visiting Grant's Tomb with Arthur, one of the real reasons he has decided to live in New York. In the misty evening, the pair stand before the tomb and Arthur asks him what he sees. Cooper replies lyrically: "I see a small Ohio farm boy becoming a great soldier. I see thousands of marching men. I see General Lee with a broken heart surrendering. And I can see the beginning of a new nation, like Abraham Lincoln said. And I can see that Ohio farm boy being inaugurated as President. Things like that can only happen in a country like America." Arthur, meanwhile, is having conscience problems. She has been secretly writing articles about Cooper, whom she has dubbed "Cinderella Man," in which she points out his eccentric spending habits. Further, she resents the way the sophisticated New York writers treat Cooper when he and Arthur dine in a posh restaurant where such successful poets and scribes gather. They goad him into reciting a few lines of his homespun poetry, then wildly and viciously lampoon and ridicule him. Cooper's initial response is not a fist to some pugnacious jaws, but a little speech that stuns them: "I know I must look funny to you. Maybe if you came to Mandrake Falls, you'd look funny to us . . . But nobody'd laugh at you and make you ridiculous—'cause that wouldn't be good manners." Only after making the statement does Cooper smack a few of the more insulting writers. New York is not Cooper's kind of place and he tells Arthur so, that wealthy New Yorkers "work so hard at living, they forget how to live. . . . They've created a lot of grand palaces here, but they forgot about the noblemen to put in them." Bancroft sees Arthur is going soft on her subject when he hears her exclaim that Cooper is "either the dumbest, silliest idiot . . . or he's the grandest guy alive." She goes on recording Cooper's antics, how he feeds doughnuts to delivery horses, tickles the feet of statues, slides down bannisters, and chases fire engines. Then Cooper finds out Arthur has been the source of the articles ridiculing him and he gives her up, along with deciding to give away his entire fortune, advertising for needy farmers to come to see him, that he will finance their failing farms. He is swamped with hordes of moochers, as well as genuine applicants. Dumbrille and his host of lawyers, along with two of Cooper's relations, bring a suit, labeling Cooper insane. He is put in a cell pending an insanity hearing where he is charged with playing the tuba to think, feeding a horse doughnuts, irresponsibly offering to spend his money in financing failed farms, and being "pixilated" as testified to by two old maids from his home town of Mandrake Falls. During the hearing Cooper remains silent throughout Dumbrille's relentless attack and it soon appears that he will be certified and institutionalized. Arthur goes to him, begging him to defend himself and declaring her love for him. Cooper's spirits soar and he takes up the challenge. He tells judge Warner that playing the tuba is nothing unusual, that it relaxes him and aids him in solving his problems, that others, like the judge, he has noticed, do similar things like "doodling." He explains that he fed doughnuts to horses because he was drunk, a condition that many young men sometimes find themselves in. He adds that he intended to help farmers and, in so doing, help the country and as far as the two old maids are concerned, he has them testify that *everyone* in Mandrake Falls, according to them, is "pixilated." Then Cooper lands a solid blow to the arrogant Dumbrille's jaw, which draws loud cheers from the farmers present in the courtroom. Warner beams and states: "In my opinion, you are not only sane, you are the sanest man who ever walked into this courtroom." Cooper is lifted onto the shoulders of the farmers and, amidst cheers, is carried triumphantly from the courtroom. Cooper is shown huddling with Arthur momentarily to secure their bond before going on to spread his populist philosophy and money among the waiting farmers. Capra directs flawlessly as he captures the whole prosaic character essayed by Cooper and the actor is tailor-made for the role. Cooper is completely natural and believable in his role, as is Arthur, whose heart is much larger than her ambitions. Both remained favorites of Capra and he would use Cooper again in MEET JOHN DOE and Arthur, one of the director's special heroines, in MR. SMITH GOES TO WASHINGTON and YOU CAN'T TAKE IT WITH YOU. Cooper received his first Oscar nomination with this touching film, his first done at Columbia. Capra took home an Oscar for Best Director. Capra never had any doubt in casting Cooper for the role of Longfellow Deeds—his first, last, and only choice—but he was in a quandary over the female lead until he spotted Arthur in a minor western. He asked Columbia chief Cohn to sign her up for the film but Cohn resisted, telling the director that "she has no name." Capra countered by saying: "She's got a great voice, Harry." Sneered Cohn: "Great voice! Did you see her face? Half of it's angel and the other half horse!" But the mogul relented as Capra persisted. The director was at his high-water mark at Columbia, with Cohn allowing Capra to function as he pleased without front-office interference. Capra insisted that only Cooper play the lead in the film and this caused the production to be delayed for six months while Cooper fulfilled other duties, costing Columbia $100,000. Cohn did not want any more postponements so he okayed Arthur and the production got under way. Arthur literally shook with the jitters before each scene, believing she could not pull it off. According to Capra, she vomited in her dressing room before and after each scene and, while waiting to go on the set, she walked about nervously swearing at herself. Yet she was flawless once before the cameras. The supporting cast is extraordinary, notably Dumbrille, Bancroft, Stander, and that venerable character player Warner, who appeared in many a

Capra film and had played Christ in DeMille's classic, KING OF KINGS. Yet the film—which was nominated but lost out in the Oscar race for Best Picture, Best Actor, Best Screenplay, and Best Sound—reached immense popularity and gleaned a fortune for Columbia chiefly because of the gangling, rumpled, taciturn Cooper, a man to whom all American men could relate. As Cooper himself once said: "I think it's because I look like the guy down the street. I'm just an ordinary Joe who became a movie star." But nothing about Cooper was really ordinary; he was mostly spectacular and was one of the most durable film stars in history, ranking in the top-10 list for 15 years. In 1939 he made almost $500,000, becoming the highest paid American citizen that year and he would earn more than $10 million throughout his long and stunning career.

p&d, Frank Capra; w, Robert Riskin (based on the story "Opera Hat" by Clarence Budington Kelland); ph, Joseph Walker; ed, Gene Havlick; md, Howard Jackson; art d, Stephen Goosson; cos, Samuel Lange; spec eff, E. Roy Davidson.

Comedy (PR:A MPAA:NR)

MR. DENNING DRIVES NORTH** 1/2

(1953, Brit.) 93m LFP/Carroll Pictures bw

John Mills (Tom Denning), Phyllis Calvert (Kay Denning), Sam Wanamaker (Chick Eddowes), Herbert Lom (Mados), Eileen Moore (Liz Denning), Raymond Huntley (Wright), Bernard Lee (Inspector Dodds), Wilfrid Hyde-White (Woods), Freda Jackson (Ma Smith), Sheila Shand Gibbs (Matilda), Trader Faulkner (Ted Smith), Russell Waters (Harry Stopes), Michael Shepley (Chairman), John Stuart (Wilson), Ronald Adam (Coroner), Ambrosine Phillpotts (Mrs. Blades), Hugh Morton (Inspector Shell), David Davies (Chauffer), Herbert Walton (Yardley), John Stevens, Edward Evans (Policemen), Lyn Evans (Mr. Fisher), John Warren (Mr. Ash), Raymond Francis (Clerk of the Court).

Comedic thriller has Mills visiting an international crook with whom his daughter is having an affair. He tries to buy the man off, but in the process accidentally kills him. Panicking, he plans to come back later for the body, drive north and dump it in a ditch. But when he returns to recover the corpse, he finds it has disappeared. The rest of the film involves his desperate attempts at covering up the death of his daughter's lover, and at the same time trying to locate the missing corpse before anyone else does.

p, Anthony Kimmins, Stephen Mitchell; d, Kimmins; w, Alec Coppel (based on the novel by Coppel); ph, John Wilcox; m, Benjamin Frankel; ed, Gerald Turney-Smith.

Crime (PR:A MPAA:NR)

MR. DISTRICT ATTORNEY* 1/2

(1941) 69m REP bw

Dennis O'Keefe (P. Cadwallader Jones), Florence Rice (Terry Parker), Peter Lorre (Paul Hyde), Stanley Ridges (District Attorney Winton), Minor Watson (Arthur Barrett), Charles Arnt (Herman Winkle), Joan Blair (Betty Paradise), Charles Halton (Hazelton), Alan Edwards (Grew), George Watts (Judge White), Sarah Edwards (Miss Petherby), Helen Brown (Mrs. Hyde), Ben Welden (Monk Westman).

Based on a popular radio program, O'Keefe plays a novice D.A. fresh out of law school. When he botches up the case, O'Keefe is assigned to tracking down a former politician, Lorre, who had vanished four years earlier with a large payoff. He is assisted by newspaper reporter Rice, who traces the money to a showgirl. Aware of the threat to his safety, Lorre contacts Watson for assistance, but is double-crossed by Watson, who fears for his own reputation. Except for Lorre's brief appearance, this picture has little going for it; the direction is ill-paced, and the script bumbling. (See MR. DISTRICT ATTORNEY series, Index)

p, Leonard Fields; d, William Morgan; w, Karl Brown, Malcolm Stuart Boylan (based on the radio program by Phillips H. Lord); ph, Reggie Lanning; m, Cy Feuer; ed, Edward Mann; art d, John Victor Mackay.

Crime (PR:A MPAA:NR)

MR. DISTRICT ATTORNEY**

(1946) 81m COL bw

Dennis O'Keefe (Steve Bennett), Adolphe Menjou (District Attorney Craig Warren), Marguerite Chapman (Marcia Manning), Michael O'Shea (Harrington), George Coulouris (James Randolph), Jeff Donnell (Miss Miller), Steven Geray (Berotti), Ralph Morgan (Ed Jamison), John Kellogg (Franzen), Charles Trowbridge (Longfield), Frank Reicher (Peter Lantz).

Confusing screen adaptation from the popular radio program has O'Keefe as a young assistant D.A. who falls hopelessly in love with a vicious vamp, Chapman. Menjou, as the D.A., is onto the girl, but only offends O'Keefe by delving into his private life. When the greedy Chapman kills two men and is about to do in O'Keefe, he finally returns to his senses. Decent performances and good production, unfortunately, are lost in a haphazard script. (See MR. DISTRICT ATTORNEY series, Index.)

p, Samuel Bischoff; d, Robert B. Sinclair; w, Ian McLellan Hunter (based on the story by Sidney Marshall from the radio program "Mr. District Attorney" by Phillips H. Lord); ph, Bert Glennon; m, Herschel "Burke" Gilbert; ed, William Lyon; md, M. W. Stoloff; art d, Stephen Goosson, George Brooks; set d, Earl Teass; cos, Jean Louis.

Crime (PR:A MPAA:NR)

MR. DISTRICT ATTORNEY IN THE CARTER CASE

(SEE: CARTER CASE, THE, 1947)

MR. DODD TAKES THE AIR**

(1937) 85m FN-WB bw

Kenny Baker (Claude Dodd), Alice Brady (Mme. Sonia Moro), Jane Wyman (Marjorie Day), Henry O'Neill (Gateway), Ferris Taylor (Hiram P. Doremus), Frank McHugh ("Sniffer" Hurst), Gertrude Michael (Jessica Stafford), John Eldredge (Jim Lidin), Harry Davenport (Doc Quinn), Linda Perry (Information Desk Girl), Maidel

Turner (Lil Doremus), Addison Richards (Doctor), Clifford Soubier (Ben Kidder), Sibyl Harris (Mrs. Kidder), Florence Gill (Miss Carrie Bowers), Anderson Lawler (Production Manager), Claudia Simmons (Phone Girl), Paul Regan Maxey (Fred, Substitute Singer), James Ford (Guest), Frank Faylen (Reporter), Eric Wilton (Butler), John Spacey (Headwaiter), Elliott Sullivan (Taxi Driver), Owen King (Announcer), William Hopper (2nd Production Manager), Luis Alberni, Al Herman.

An attempt at satire has Baker as a small town electrician whose strong voice impresses a New York sponsor. When Baker is taken to New York, however, he suffers an attack of bronchitis and his voice changes from a baritone to a tenor. He goes on the air, but is accused of being a fake. Unwittingly, however, he is a hit with the audience, but is kept by his manager from ever appearing in public. He spends his spare time tinkering with an old radio gadget that revitalizes old sets. But when it appears that his invention might be stolen, Wyman takes out a patent in her own name and marries Baker too. Songs include: "Am I in Love," "If I Were a Little Pond Lilly," "The Girl You Used to Be," "Here Comes the Sandman," "Remember Me."

p, Mervyn LeRoy; d, Alfred E. Green; w, William Wister Haines, Elaine Ryan (based on the story "The Great Crooner" by Clarence Budington Kelland); ph, Arthur Edeson; m, Adolph Deutsch; ed, Thomas Richards; md, Leo F. Forbstein; art d, Robert Haas; cos, Milo Anderson; m/l, Harry Warren, Al Dubin.

Musical (PR:A MPAA:NR)

MR. DOODLE KICKS OFF* 1/2

(1938) 75m RKO bw

Joe Penner (Doodle Bugs), June Travis (Janice), Richard Lane ("Offside," Assistant Coach), Ben Alexander (Larry), Billy Gilbert (Prof. Minorous), Jack Carson (Rochet), Alan Bruce (Mickey), George Irving (President Martin), William B. Davidson (Mr. Bugs), Pierre Watkin (Mr. Wondel), Frank M. Thomas (Coach Hammond), Wesley Barry (1st Sophomore), Bob Parrish (2nd Sophomore), Steve Putnam, Jack Arnold, Bob Nash, Edward Arnold, Jr., Bill Corson.

Ridiculous farce has Penner as the son of a wealthy merchant, Davidson, who wants his son to graduate from his alma mater as a star athlete. To accomplish this, Davidson offers a generous contribution to the school if Penner proves himself on the football field. Picture offers some interesting comic routines on the field, but otherwise falls flat in its all too familiar approach.

p, Robert Sisk; d, Leslie Goodwins; w, Bert Granet (based on the story by Mark Kelly); ph, Russell Metty; ed, Ted Cheesman; md, Roy Webb; m/l, "My All American Band," "It's a Mystery to Me," Hal Raynor.

Comedy (PR:A MPAA:NR)

MR. DRAKE'S DUCK** 1/2

(1951, Brit.) 76m Eros/UA bw

Douglas Fairbanks, Jr. (Don Drake), Yolande Donlan (Penny Drake), Howard Marion-Crawford (Maj. Trevers), Reginald Beckwith (Mr. Boothby), Wilfrid Hyde-White (Mr. May), John Boxer (The Sergeant), Jon Pertwee (Reuben), Peter Butterworth (Higgins), Tom Gill (Capt. White), A. E. Matthews (Brigadier).

Early satire on nuclear arms, with an added poke at the military, has Fairbanks and Donlan as American newlyweds who move to England to live on a farm Fairbanks has inherited. Because of a mistaken nod of the head, Donlan unwittingly purchases five dozen ducks at an auction, one of which lays radioactive eggs. Soon the British army is called in and they quarantine the entire farm. Then the navy, and finally the air force, force their way into the act, each branch of service laying claim to the duck. In the end, they wind up capturing the wrong duck, but nobody knows the better. Clever idea with an added twist to the old fairy tale, "The Goose Who Laid the Golden Egg."

p, Daniel M. Angel, Douglas Fairbanks, Jr.; d&w, Val Guest (based on the play by Ian Messiter); ph, Jack Cox, Harry Gillam; m, Bruce Campbell; ed, Sam Simmonds; md, Phillip Martelli; art d, Maurice Carter; cos, Julie Harris.

Comedy (PR:A MPAA:NR)

MR. DREW (SEE: FOR THEM THAT TRESPASS, 1949, Brit.)

MR. DYNAMITE**

(1935) 75m UNIV bw

Edmund Lowe ("Mr. Dynamite" T. N. Thompson), Jean Dixon (Lynn), Esther Ralston (Charmion), Victor Varconi (Jarl Dvorjak), Verna Hillie (Mona), Minor Watson (Lewis), Robert Gleckler (King), Jameson Thomas (Williams), Matt McHugh (Sunshine), G. Pat Collins (Rod), Greta Meyer (Jans), Bradley Page (Felix), James Burtis (Joe).

Detective thriller, with a touch of comedy, has Lowe as a witty private detective whose smart-aleckness makes him unpopular with the law. After cracking a murder case, Lowe's methods land him in trouble with the police, forcing him to leave town. Lowe adds some color to the Hammett detective.

p, E. M. Asher; d, Alan Crosland; w, Doris Malloy, Harry Clork (based on the story "On the Make" by Dashiell Hammett); ph, George Robinson.

Crime (PR:A MPAA:NR)

MR. DYNAMITE**

(1941) 63m UNIV bw

Lloyd Nolan (Tommy N. Thornton), Irene Hervey (Vicki Martin), J. Carroll Naish (The Professor), Robert Armstrong (Paul), Ann Gillis (Joey), Frank Gaby (Valla), Elisabeth Risdon (Achilles), Shemp Howard (Abdullah), Cliff Nazarro (Man), Monte "Sonny" Brewer (Skinnay).

Nolan plays a star baseball pitcher who becomes involved with a murder after falling for British spy Hervey at a carnival. The two try to keep one step ahead of the law as they uncover a ring of Nazi spies. Plot eventually falls into predictability, with the cast pulling off their performances in a standard manner.

p, Marshall Grant; d, John Rawlins; w, Stanley Crea Rubin; ph, John Boyle; ed, Ted Kent.

Spy **(PR:A MPAA:NR)**

MISTER 880*½** (1950) 90m FOX bw

Burt Lancaster *(Steve Buchanan)*, Dorothy McGuire *(Ann Winslow)*, Edmund Gwenn *(Skipper Miller)*, Millard Mitchell *(Mac)*, Minor Watson *(Judge O'Neil)*, Howard St. John *(Chief)*, Hugh Sanders *(Thad Mitchell)*, James Millican *(Olie Johnson)*, Howland Chamberlin *(Duff)*, Larry Keating *(Lee)*, Kathleen Hughes *(Secretary)*, Geraldine Wall *(Miss Gallagher)*, Mervin Williams *(U.S. Attorney)*, Norman Field *(Bailiff)*, Helen Hatch *(Maggie)*, Robert B. Williams *(Sergeant)*, Ed Max *(Mousie)*, Frank Wilcox *(Mr. Beddington)*, George Adrian *(Carlos)*, Michael Lally *(George)*, Joe McTurk *(Gus)*, Minerva Urecal *(Rosie)*, George Gastine *(Waiter)*, Ray De Ravenne, Paul Bradley, Arthur Dulac *(Men)*, Curt Furberg *(German)*, Joan Valerie *(Cashier)*, Jack Daly *(Court Clerk)*, Dick Ryan *(U.S. Marshal)*, William J. O'Leary *(Junk Man)*, Billy Gray *(Mickey)*, Billy Nelson *(Taxi Driver)*, Bill McKenzie *(Jimmy)*, Herbert Vigran *(Barker)*, Mischa Novy *(Violinist)*, Erik Neilsen, Michael Little, Patrick Miller, Whitey Haupt, Timmie Hawkins, Tommie Mann Menzies, Gary Pagett, Peter Roman *(Boys)*, Ronnie Ralph *(High School Boy)*, Rico Alaniz *(Spanish Interpreter)*, Eddie Lee, George Lee *(Chinese Interpreters)*, Victor Desny *(Russian Interpreter)*, Sherry Hall *(Clerk in Cigar Store)*, John Hiestand *(Narrator)*, Bessie Wade, Polly Bailey *(Women)*, Robert Boon, Dr. D. W. De Roos *(Dutchmen)*.

An enchanting comedy which stars the cheery Gwenn as an aging counterfeiter who prints $1 bills as needed in order to support himself. Although he is breaking the law, he does so in such a harmless, whimsical way that one can hardly condemn him. He counterfeits bills not only because he needs money to live, but because he loves and respects his old-fashioned printing press, which he dearly refers to as "Cousin Henry." Gwenn proves an embarrassment for the Federal agents who have been trying to track him for 10 years. A new addition to the Secret Service, Lancaster, gets assigned to the case and comes closer than any other agent. He traces one of the bills to an apartment where he meets McGuire, a pretty translator for the United Nations. They fall in love and soon afterwards Lancaster discovers that the elusive counterfeiter is McGuire's neighbor. It becomes as difficult for Lancaster to turn Gwenn in as it is for the judge to sentence him. Gwenn's honest charm elicits sympathy from all concerned and he is let off with a reduced sentence. While Lancaster and McGuire perform admirably, it is Gwenn who steals the show. This performance is one of his most memorable (lined up beside his Oscar-winning MIRACLE ON 34TH STREET performance in 1947 and his endearing role in 1955's THE TROUBLE WITH HARRY) and earned him a Best Supporting Actor nomination. Unfortunately, Gwenn is on screen even less than Lancaster and his title role is reduced to the support of an average romance plot between Lancaster and McGuire.

p, Julian Blaustein; d, Edmund Goulding; w, Robert Riskin (based on the *New Yorker* article "Old Eight Eighty" by St. Clair McKelway); ph, Joseph LaShelle; m, Sol Kaplan; ed, Robert Fritch; md, Lionel Newman; art d, Lyle Wheeler, George W. Davis; spec eff, Fred Sersen.

Drama/Comedy **(PR:AA MPAA:NR)**

MR. EMMANUEL** (1945, Brit.) 92m TC/EL bw

Felix Aylmer *(Mr. Emmanuel)*, Greta Gynt *(Elsie Silver)*, Walter Rilla *(Willi Brockenburg)*, Peter Mullins *(Bruno)*, Ursula Jeans *(Frau Heinkes)*, Elspeth March *(Rose Cooper)*, Frederick Richter *(Heinkes)*, Frederick Schiller *(Examiner)*, Charles Goldner *(Committee Secretary)* Yvan DeLay *(Klaus)*, Irene Handl *(Trude)*, Meier Tzelniker *(Mr. Silver)*, Arnold Marle *(Kahn)*, Maria Berger *(Frau Kahn)*, David Baxter *(Otto)*, Norman Pierce *(John Cooper)*, Guy Deghy *(Police Lieutenant)*, Neil Ballantyne *(Cameron)*, Oscar Ebelsbacher *(Professor)*, Eric Freund *(Lawyer)*, Milo Sperber *(Student)*, Lyonel Watts *(Headmaster)*, Margaret Vyner *(Frau Lindstroem)*, Louis de Wohl, Jean Simmons.

Film adaptation of the novel results in being an unevenly paced story of an old Jew, Aylmer, who has lived his entire life in the ghetto of Manchester. He befriends a young refugee from Nazi Germany and promises the boy that he will go to Germany and find his mother. Once in the Third Reich, he is captured and tortured by the Gestapo, finally released because of the efforts of an old friend, Gynt, who is now the mistress of a high Nazi official. Story concludes with Aylmer finding the woman he seeks, but she rejects her son in favor of her new husband, a Nazi. Note 15-year-old Jean Simmons in her second screen role.

p, William Sistrom; d, Harold French; w, Louis Golding, Gordon Wellesley, Norman Ginsburg (based on the novel by Golding); ph, Otto Heller, Gus Drisse; m, Mischa Spoliansky; ed, Alan Jaggs; art d, Norman Arnold.

Drama **(PR:A MPAA:NR)**

MR. FAINTHEART (SEE: $10 RAISE, 1935)

MR. FORBUSH AND THE PENGUINS (SEE: CRY OF THE PENGUINS, 1971, Brit.)

MR. FOX OF VENICE (SEE: HONEY POT, THE, 1967, Brit.)

MISTER FREEDOM**
(1970, Fr.) 95m Les Films du Rond-Point-O.P.E.R.A./Grove c

Donald Pleasence *(Dr. Freedom)*, Delphine Seyrig *(Marie-Madeleine)*, John Abbey *(Mister Freedom)*, Philippe Noiret *(Moujik Man)*, Catherine Rouvel *(Marie Rouge)*, Sami Frey *(Christ Man)*, Jean-Claude Drouot *(Dick)*, Serge Gainsbourg *(Mr. Drugstore)*, Yves Montand *(Capt. Formidable)*, Rufus *(Freddie Fric)*, Simone Signoret, Daniel Cohn-Bendit, Yves Lefebvre, Michel Creton, Rita Maiden, Sabine Sun, Colin Drake, Henry Pillsbury.

Heavy-handed political satire, delivered in the form of a comic strip, has Abbey as an American super hero in a uniform that is a combination of a space suit and football uniform, fighting for the continuation of democracy. His mission is to keep France from the communists. He offers the French a type of freedom dependent upon adaptation to Abbey's own restrictions, such as keeping blacks in their place and buying only American goods. However, Abbey has confrontations with similar types of comic strip characters which represent opposing ideals: namely Red China Man, Christ Man, and Moujik (Russian) Man. In the end, Abbey decides that France is not worthy of his freedom, so he blows it up with an atom bomb. Picture manages some genuinely interesting caricatures and situations, but the entire approach by William Klein is too redundant and it fails to offer any true insights into the politics of France.

p, Guy Belfond; Michel Zemer, Christian Thivat; d&w, William Klein; ph, Pierre Lhomme (Eastmancolor); m, Serge Gainsbourg; ed, Anne-Marie Cotret; art d, Jacques Dugied, Andre Piltant; cos, Janine Klein.

Fantasy **(PR:A MPAA:NR)**

MR. GRIGGS RETURNS (SEE: COCKEYED MIRACLE, THE, 1946)

MR. H. C. ANDERSEN* (1950, Brit.) 62m British Foundation bw

Ashley Glynne *(Hans Christian Andersen)*, Constance Lewis *(Mrs. Andersen)*, Terence Noble *(Mr. Andersen)*, Stuart Sanders *(Bailiff)*, June Elvin *(Jenny Lind)*, Edward Sullivan *(Charles Dickens)*, Victor Rietty *(King Frederick)*, Kenyon Jervis, Eric Kemp, Dafydd Havard, Mercedes Desmore, Nan Kearns, Madam van Deerbeck, Barbara Madock, Doreen Hughes, Billy Stuart, Frank Crawshaw, Jennifer Dearman, Kitty Kenehan, Charles Cooper, Charles Reynolds, Denise Hurst, Catherina Ferray, Zoe Monteanu, Marcus Innesley, Helen Hill, Eileen Cleveland.

Highly fictionalized biography of children's story-writer Andersen, interspersed with animated versions of his stories and, for some odd reason, "Ali Baba and the Forty Thieves." Ineptly done, abysmally acted, and best avoided.

p&d, Ronald Haines; w, Ronald and Jean Haines (based on the book *The True Story Of My Life* by Hans Christian Andersen); ph, W. R. Hutchinson; animation director, Leon Boje.

Biography **(PR:A MPAA:NR)**

MR. HEX** (1946) 63m MON bw (GB: THE PRIDE OF THE BOWERY)

Leo Gorcey *(Slip)*, Huntz Hall *(Sach)*, Bobby Jordan *(Bobby)*, Gabriel Dell *(Gabe Moreno)*, Billy Benedict *(Whitey)*, David Gorcey *(Chuck)*, Gale Robbins *(Gloria Williams)*, Ben Welden *(Bull Laguna)*, Ian Keith *(Raymond The Hypnotist)*, Sammy Cohen *(Evil Eyes Fagin)*, Bernard Gorcey *(Louie)*, William Ruhl *(Mob Leader)*, Danny Beck *(Danny the Dip)*, Rita Lynn *(Margie)*, Joe Gray *(Ray Teasdale/"Billy Butterworth")*, Eddie Gribbon *(Blackie)*, John Indresano *(Referee Joe McGowan)*, Gene Stutenroth *(Bill, Henchman)*, Jimmy Aubrey *(Waiter)*, Dewey Robinson *(Truck Driver)*, Meyer Grace *(Spud, Henchman)*.

Sach is a boxer who gains strength while under hypnosis in this Bowery Boys entry. He gets in the ring against a one-time champ (who took an alias after a face-lift made him unrecognizable) who also is under a spell. The shady champ's manager has Sach's secret hypnotizing coin stolen, but Slip finds a replacement just minutes before the fight. The champ's real identity comes out and justice is served. Producer-writer Grippo had a special interest in the subject of hexes and magic, being a one-time magician himself. (See BOWERY BOYS series, Index).

p, Jan Grippo; d, William Beaudine; w, Cyril Endfield (based on a story by Grippo); ph, James Brown; ed, Richard Currier, Seth Larson; md, Edward J. Kay; art d, David Milton; set d, Raymond Boltz, Jr.; m/l, "One Star-Kissed Night," "A Love Song To Remember," Louis Herscher (sung by Gale Robbins); makeup, Milburn Morante.

Comedy **(PR:A MPAA:NR)**

MR. HOBBS TAKES A VACATION*** (1962) 115m FOX c

James Stewart *(Mr. Hobbs)*, Maureen O'Hara *(Peggy Hobbs)*, Fabian *(Joe)*, Lauri Peters *(Katey)*, Lili Gentle *(Janie)*, John Saxon *(Byron)*, John McGiver *(Martin Turner)*, Marie Wilson *(Emily Turner)*, Reginald Gardiner *(Reggie McHugh)*, Valerie Varda *(Marika)*, Natalie Trundy *(Susan Carver)*, Josh Peine *(Stan Carver)*, Michael Burns *(Danny Hobbs)*, Minerva Urecal *(Brenda)*, Richard Collier *(Mr. Kagle)*, Peter Oliphant *(Peter Carver)*, Thomas Lowell *(Freddie)*, Stephen Mines *(Carl)*, Dennis Whitcomb *(Dick)*, Michael Sean *(Phil)*, Sherry Alberoni, True Ellison *(Girls in Dormitory)*, Ernie Gutierrez *(Pizza Maker)*, Barbara Mansell *(Receptionist)*, Maida Severn *(Secretary)*, Darryl Duke *(Boy)*, Doris Packer *(Hostess)*.

Stewart is a St. Louis banker who is looking forward to a serene vacation on the West Coast. He and his family take a cottage at the seashore for 30 days of rest and relaxation but it hardly turns out that way. Their rental is a weird old place that is so ramshackle that their live-in cook, Urecal, will have none of it and flees. There is a lovely beach just outside the home, but Stewart and O'Hara's son Burns typically falls in front of the television set and becomes a "couch potato," unwilling to move. Peters, their young daughter, has just had new braces put on her teeth and is so embarrassed by the metal in her mouth that she absolutely refuses to be seen in public. Daughter Trundy comes to the house with her unemployed husband, Peine, and they are joined by other daughter, Gentle, who is furious when her husband, Saxon, begins to eye the body of local vamp Varda, who wears a bikini to great advantage. O'Hara, still a handsome woman, has to fend off Gardiner, a member of the local yacht club who fancies her as a summer fling. Disaster piles upon disaster in Johnson's inventive adaptation of Streeter's novel, and Stewart shows himself to be a good, solid father in this satire of "togetherness." He gets Peters out of her doldrums by introducing her to Fabian, he steers a small boat through an impossible fog, and he aids McGiver and Wilson, two besotted guests, in their hobby of bird-watching. Saxon is paying too much attention to Varda, and Stewart manages to destroy that, as well as sabotage Gardiner's onslaught of O'Hara. Just about every rotten thing that can happen on a vacation happens to Stewart and family, and he is thrilled when the 30 days is over and he can now safely go back to work. That joy is tempered when he learns that O'Hara had such a good time that she's leased the house again for the following summer vacation. It's a fairly predictable story and the direction is a whirlwind, sometimes a bit too fast. Johnson's witty quips and the likeability of the seasoned Stewart insure a raft of laughs where tedium might have set in. The main set is magnificent and resembles a stage setting. Huzzahs for Smith, Brown, Scott, and Reiss.

p, Jerry Wald; d, Henry Koster; w, Nunnally Johnson (based on the book *Hobbs' Vacation* by Edward Streeter); ph, William C. Mellor (CinemaScope, DeLuxe Color); m, Henry Mancini; ed, Marjorie Fowler; art d, Jack Martin Smith, Malcolm Brown; set d, Walter M. Scott, Stuart A. Reiss; cos, Don Feld; spec eff, L. B. Abbott; m/l, "Cream Puff," Mancini, Johnny Mercer (sung by Fabian); makeup, Ben Nye.

Comedy **(PR:AA MPAA:NR)**

MISTER HOBO*** (1936, Brit.) 80m GAU/GB bw (GB: GUV'NOR, THE)

George Arliss *(Francis Rothschild/Spike/The Guv'nor)*, Gene Gerrard *(Flit)*, Frank Cellier, *(Barsac)*, Patric Knowles *(Paul)*, Viola Keats *(Madelaine)*, Henrietta Watson *(Mrs. Granville)*, George Hayes *(Dubois)*, Mary Clare *(Mme. Barsac)*, [Howard] Marion Crawford, Mervyn Johns.

Fine little comedy finds Arliss and Gerrard in France under arrest for a minor offense. Arliss gives his name as Rothschild and the cops check with the famous family to see if he's really one of theirs. Of course he's not but they give him 2,000 francs from their charity fund. Arliss deposits it and the banker, thinking that his customer is a member of that wealthy bunch, suggests that his new client may draw against that account. It seems the bank is on the verge of going broke and the banker sees this as a new lease on life. Gerrard is made a secretary and accidentally saves the fortune of a young girl from a crooked dealer. All is discovered but forgiven by film's end. Though the situation is contrived, the script is quite good and completely believable. It's all helped by a terrific ensemble effort handled with grace and style. It's a smoothly directed, witty little piece.

p, Michael Balcon; d, Milton Rosmer; w, Maude Howell, Guy Bolton (based on the story "Rothschild" by Paul Lafitte); ph, Mutz Greenbaum [Max Greene]; m, Arthur Benjamin; ed, Charles Saunders; md, Louis Levy.

Comedy **(PR:A MPAA:NR)**

MR. HULOT'S HOLIDAY*****

(1954, Fr.) 85m Cady/GAU-Images bw (LES VACANCES DE MONSIEUR HULOT) (AKA: MONSIEUR HULOT'S HOLIDAY)

Jacques Tati *(Mr. Hulot)*, Nathalie Pascaud *(Martine)*, Louis Perrault *(Fred)*, Michelle Rolla *(The Aunt)*, Andre Dubois *(Commandant)*, Suzy Willy *(Commandant's Wife)*, Valentine Camax *(Englishwoman)*, Lucien Fregis *(Hotel Proprietor)*, Marguerite Gerard *(Strolling Woman)*, Rene Lacourt *(Strolling Man)*, Raymond Carl *(Waiter)*, Jean-Pierre Zola *(Businessman)*, Michele Brabo *(Holidaymaker)*, Georges Adlin *(South American)*.

Winner of the Grand Prize at the Cannes Film Festival, MR. HULOT'S HOLIDAY did not win the Best Foreign Language Film at the Oscars because there was no such award at the time. Instead, they gave Tati the Oscar in 1958 for MY UNCLE, a far less funny film, but they may have done that because this one couldn't take an Oscar four years before. Tati, born Jacques Tatischeff, was France's Chaplin. He doesn't say much in this movie which he also co-wrote and directed. He doesn't have to say much, as Tati was the last great film mime. Richmond Shepard, who was the official mime at the 1984 Olympics, insists that Tati was one of the best there ever was, as good as Chaplin and Marceau. The only problem is that Tati's output was so tiny: five shorts in the 1930s, a bit in SYLVIE AND THE PHANTOM, a small role in DEVIL IN THE FLESH, another short called THE SCHOOL FOR POSTMEN, and then his first feature, THE BIG DAY. Then he made this film and followed that with MY UNCLE, PLAYTIME, TRAFFIC, and PARADE. Before his death in 1982, he won the Grand Prix National du Cinema, the highest award that can be given by France's film community. If he made nothing but MR. HULOT'S HOLIDAY, it would stand as Tati's CITIZEN KANE. Tati is a loose-limbed bachelor who is oblivious to everything around him. He comes to a resort on the coast of Brittany for a small vacation and chaos follows him wherever he strolls. Other guests at the hotel are comely Pascaud, whom Tati would like to get to know better, but his shyness hampers him from making a direct assault on her sensibilities. Also in residence at the hotel are various familiar types one sees, including the workaholic who can't stop doing business (Zola), the burly British old maid (Camax), the muscular beach boy, the besieged waiter (Carl), the former military man who still thinks he's leading a battalion (Dubois), the couple who takes walks to collect sea shells (Lacourt and Gerard), the henpecked husband with the shrewish wife. In short, everyone you may have ever met on holiday. Hulot prances into a somber funeral, his sports car is driven off the road by a large American automobile, and a breakneck series of incidents come one after the other, all hilarious. He rents a kayak and the boat snaps in half and appears to be a shark in the water. He chases a ping-pong ball and pushes a cardplayer's chair to another table where another game is being played. The cardplayer lays his card on the second table and the result is that a huge argument begins. By this time, you must have realized that there is no plot. And yet there is a method to Tati's madness as he lets the separate incidents build up until one's sides are aching. Although there is very little dialog, there is a great deal of sound, and this is used brilliantly in many off-screen gags that Tati appears to never notice. He's the man who can walk into a 300 foot-long room on the south end and when he closes the door, a Ming vase falls off the table on the north end. Whereas many directors might go for all the various shots (long shot, closeups, etc.), Tati sets up his camera and lets the action happen in the frame, something Woody Allen has taken to doing with great success in the last few years. People run in and out of the frame and there are many things happening in the same shot. Tati asks the viewer to make the choice of what to watch and one's eyes automatically go to the funniest part. In the finale, Tati finds himself in a fireworks factory, casually reaches for a match to light his pipe, which is always going out, and tosses the match away, still lit. The fireworks explode and the entire coastline of Brittany lights up. Next morning, Tati gets ready to leave the area, and the other guests all give him the air, with his only pals being a couple of the adults and all the children. He climbs into his wheezing auto, a 1924 Amilcar, and drives off, unaware of the disasters he has spawned and looking forward to his next vacation. Tati is a comedian in the deadpan tradition of Keaton and with the innocence of Langdon, with a bit of Lloyd's derring-do and physicality. Most of the other actors in the film were non-pros and the results achieved belied that, but Tati felt it would be more believable with unrecognizable people in the parts. He was, of course, correct.

p, Jacques Tati, Fred Orain; d, Tati; w, Tati, Henri Marquet, Pierre Aubert, Jacques Lagrange; ph, Jacques Mercanton, Jean Mousselle; m, Alain Romans; ed, Suzanne Baron, Charles Bretoneiche, Jacques Grassi; prod d, Henri Schmitt; art d, R. Brian Court, Schmitt.

Comedy **Cas.** **(PR:AAA MPAA:NR)**

MR. IMPERIUM** (1951) 87m MGM c (GB: YOU BELONG TO MY HEART)

Lana Turner *(Fredda Barlo)*, Ezio Pinza *(Mr. Imperium)*, Marjorie Main *(Mrs. Cabot)*, Barry Sullivan *(Paul Hunter)*, Sir Cedric Hardwicke *(Prime Minister Bernand)*, Keenan Wynn *(Motor Cop)*, Debbie Reynolds *(Gwen)*, Ann Codee *(Anna Pelan)*, Wilton Graff *(Andrew Bolton)*, Giacomo Spadoni *(Giovanni)*, Chick Chandler *(George Hoskins)*, Joseph Vitale *(Bearded Man)*, Mae Clarke *(Secretary)*, Don Haggerty *(Director)*, Jimmy Cross *(Assistant Director)*, Tony Marlo *(Lackey)*, Cliff Clark *(Restaurant Proprietor)*, Matt Moore *(Gateman)*, Mitchell Lewis *(Old Watchman)*, Arthur Walsh, Allan Ray, Wilson Wood, Bobby Troup *(Specialties in Band)*, Dick Simmons *(Air Corps Colonel)*.

There are some stage actors who never could have the same kind of charisma on screen. Alfred Drake, Alfred Lunt and Lynn Fontanne are the first that come to mind and the same goes for Ezio Pinza, who was the toast of the Great White Way in "South Pacific" but whose career never took off on celluloid. This is another one of those PRINCE AND THE SHOWGIRL stories. Pinza is the prince from *Mitteleuropa* who falls for nitery chirp Turner while he is on holiday in Italy. They are mad for each other until he gets the call to move up one notch to be the king of his land and departs. A dozen years pass in a twinkling and Turner has become a huge Hollywood star and he strolls back in her life, which is currently (and conveniently) free of male companionship at the time. They go off to Palm Springs for a couple of days of sun and lust (with some good comedy provided by Main and Reynolds as the Palm Springs landlady and her niece), but Pinza is no Prince of Wales and he cannot give up his throne for the woman he loves. Hardwicke, the prime minister of the country, reminds Pinza of his duties and he reluctantly leaves Turner, but with the promise that he will come back again. Audiences had been waiting for this movie, but the studio saw it as more of a Thanksgiving entree than a picture, so they held it back until after another Pinza picture, STRICTLY DISHONORABLE, was issued, hoping it would be a hit and people would flock to see the great singer's next one. Neither picture made a dent in the audience's pocketbooks and Pinza's movie fortunes went plummeting. Singer Trudy Erwin again supplied Turner's singing voice. The songs included: "My Love and My Mule" (Harold Arlen, Dorothy Fields, sung by Trudy Erwin), "Andiamo," "Let Me Look at You" (Arlen, Fields, sung by Ezio Pinza), and the hit "You Belong to My Heart" (Ray Gilbert, Augustin Lara, sung by Pinza).

p, Edwin H. Knopf; d, Don Hartman; w, Hartman, Knopf (based on a play by Knopf); ph, George J. Folsey (Technicolor); m, Bronislau Kaper; ed, George White, William Gulick; md, Johnny Green; art d, Cedric Gibbons, Paul Groesse; set d, Edwin B. Willis, Richard A. Pefferle; cos, Walter Plunkett; makeup, William Tuttle.

Drama **(PR:A MPAA:NR)**

MR. INNOCENT (SEE: HAPPENING, THE, 1967)

MR. INVISIBLE (SEE: MR. SUPERINVISIBLE, 1974, Ital./Span./Ger.)

MR. JIM—AMERICAN, SOLDIER, AND GENTLEMAN
(SEE: SERGEANT JIM, 1962, Yugo.)

MR. KLEIN1/2** (1976, Fr.) 122m FOX-Lira-Quartet c

Alain Delon *(Mr. Klein)*, Jeanne Moreau *(Florence)*, Suzanne Flon *(Concierge)*, Michel Lonsdale *(Pierre)*, Juliet Berto *(Janine)*, Jean Bouise *(Man)*, Francine Berge *(Nicole)*, Massimo Girotti *(Mr. Charles)*.

Delon plays a school principal who becomes involved in the search for a missing Jew during the German occupation of France. Losey shows he is still able to maintain a level of suspense, but the plot falters in its ambiguities and other weaknesses.

p, Raymond Danon, Alain Delon, Jean Pierre Labrande, Robert Kupferberg; d, Joseph Losey; w, Franco Solinas; ph, Gerry Fisher (Eastmancolor); m, Egisto Macchi, Pierre Porte; ed, Henri Lanoe; art d, Alexander Trauner.

Drama **Cas.** **(PR:C MPAA:PG)**

MR. LEMON OF ORANGE*1/2 (1931) 70m FOX bw

El Brendel *(Mr. Lemon/Silent McGee)*, Fifi Dorsay *(Julie La Rue)*, William Collier, Sr. *(Mr. Blake)*, Ruth Warren *(Mrs. Blake)*, Joan Castle *(June Blake)*, Donald Dillaway *(Jerry)*, Eddie Gribbon *(Walter)*, Nat Pendleton *(Gangster)*, Jack Rutherford.

An attempt to combine comedy with a crime drama has Brendel as an innocent man having the exact same features as a notorious gangland figure. Brendel has to spend the rest of the time dodging the police and enemies of the gangster. The picture is filled with countless gags, all of which have been used before. Otherwise the story is too weak to hold water, lapsing into predictable situations. Brendel manages to pull off a few good laughs.

d, John G. Blystone; w, Eddie Cantor, Edwin Burke, Jack Hayes (based on a story by Hayes); ph, Joseph August; ed, Ralph Dixon.

Comedy/Crime (PR:A MPAA:NR)

MR. LIMPET (SEE: INCREDIBLE MR. LIMPET, THE, 1964)

MR. LORD SAYS NO** 1/2**

(1952, Brit.) 76m London Independent/Souvaine bw (GB: THE HAPPY FAMILY)

Stanley Holloway *(Henry Lord)*, Kathleen Harrison *(Lillian Lord)*, Naunton Wayne *(Mr. Filch)*, Dandy Nichols *(Ada)*, John Stratton *(David)*, Eileen Moore *(Joan)*, Shirley Mitchell *(Marina)*, Margaret Barton *(Anne)*, George Cole *(Cyril)*, Tom Gill *(Maurice Hennessey)*, Miles Malleson *(Mr. Thwaites)*, Geoffrey Sumner *(Sir Charles Spanniell)*, Laurence Naismith *(Councillor)*, Edward Lexy, Cameron Hall, Hal Osmond, John Salew, Ernest Butcher, Lyn Evans, Michael Ward, Richard Wattis, David Keir, Anthony Oliver, Campbell Singer, Peter Martyn, Arthur Hambling, Eileen Way.

British satire has Holloway and Harrison as a married couple who refuse to give up their property when the government wants their land for a festival site. The picture offers a lot of subtle humor in its depiction of the British as stubborn people and the government as clumsy and ineffectual.

p, William MacQuitty, Sydney Box; d, Muriel Box; w, Muriel and Sydney Box (based on the play by Michael Clayton Hutton); ph, Reginald H. Wyer.

Comedy (PR:A MPAA:NR)

MR. LUCKY*** (1943) 100m RKO bw

Cary Grant *(Joe Adams)*, Laraine Day *(Dorothy Bryant)*, Charles Bickford *(Hard Swede)*, Gladys Cooper, *(Capt. Steadman)*, Alan Carney *(Crunk)*, Henry Stephenson *(Mr. Bryant)*, Paul Stewart *(Zepp)*, Ray Johnson *(Mrs. Ostrander)*, Erford Gage *(Gaffer)*, Walter Kingsford *(Convoy Commissioner Hargraves)*, J. M. Kerrigan *(McDougal)*, Edward Fielding *(Foster)*, Vladimir Sokoloff *(Greek Priest)*, Florence Bates *(Mrs. Van Every)*, John Bleifer *(Siga)*, Juan Varro *(Joe Bascopolus)*, Frank Mills *(Workman at Slot Machine)*, Mary Forbes *(Dowager)*, Don Brodie *(Dealer)*, Joseph Crehan, Kernan Cripps *(Plainclothesmen)*, Art Yeoman, Jack Gargan *(Reporters)*, Isabel Withers, Daphne Moore *(Nurses)*, Emory Parnell *(Dock Watchman)*, Lloyd Ingraham *(Taxi Driver)*, Hilda Plowright *(Maid)*, Ray Flynn *(Cop)*, Budd Fine *(Stevedore)*, Charles Lane *(Comstock)*, Frank Henry *(Reporter on Street)*, Robert Strange *(Captain Costello)*, Hal K. Dawson *(Draft Board Director)*, Al Rhein, Sammy Finn, Al Murphy, Fred Rapport *(Gamblers)*, Major Sam Harris *(Gambling Extra)*, Mary Stuart, Rita Corday, Ariel Heath *(Girls)*.

Co-screenwriter Milton Holmes had been the tennis pro at the Beverly Hills Tennis Club and, in that capacity, met many of the stars and moguls who made the movies. He cooked up a story and showed it to Cary Grant who thought it had some merit. Holmes was paid a fee, then went on salary as he teamed with veteran Adrian Scott to write the screenplay. At first glance, it's not an easy tale to swallow because Grant is shown as a rogue gambler who takes great pleasure in dodging the draft and is not above bilking a charity out of money earmarked for the war effort. Despite that, the picture turned a neat profit that neared $2 million (chicken feed by the standards of the 1980s, but that was back when $1 million was a lot of money). Grant owns a gambling ship and needs a bundle to outfit the craft for a trip to Cuba. The draft board sends "greetings" and Grant's associates, Stewart and Carney, also get the word from the government. Bickford skippers the gambling ship and is awaiting orders. Grant's pal is dying and holds a 4-F card, so Grant appropriates it and takes the identity of the dead man. Meanwhile, the American Relief Society, a group of wealthy women who are raising money to transport medical supplies, appears on the scene. Day (on loan from MGM) is an heiress who is interested in Grant's scheme. He thinks that he might be able to raise a bit of loot for her group, which is also supported by Cooper and Johnson, by running a gambling concession at a charity ball. His intention is, of course, to bilk the society out of the money so he can use it to refurbish his ship and to make millions on the high seas. At the ball, Grant sees the money pile up when Stewart arrives and wants his cut of the take. To further complicate matters, Grant is now operating with a phony I.D. and his dead pal was a two-time loser and the next conviction means a life term. It all works out, of course, and Grant and Day fall for each other and Grant is redeemed through the love of a good woman. It's almost a takeoff on a gangster movie but takes itself seriously too often and, in the end, is not a particularly tasteful story. It was made again in 1950 as GAMBLING HOUSE and also inspired a TV series in 1959. Putting aside any moralizing, it's a well-made movie with some fun attached. Stewart, the heavy, was appearing in his third movie after having made his debut as Welles' valet in CITIZEN KANE at the age of 33 after nearly 20 years of stage acting. MR. LUCKY was blessed with a good cast and a sensational title, but it was not a terrific film.

p, David Hempstead; d, H.C.Potter; w, Milton Holmes, Adrian Scott (from the story "Bundles for Freedom" by Holmes); ph, George Barnes; m, Roy Webb; ed, Theron Warth; prod d, William Cameron Menzies; md, Constantin Bakaleinikoff; art d, Albert S. d'Agostino, Mark-Lee Kirk; set d, Darrell Silvera, Claude Carpenter; cos, Renie; spec eff, Vernon L. Walker; song, "Something to Remember You By."

Crime/Drama Cas. (PR:A MPAA:NR)

MR. MAGOO'S HOLIDAY FESTIVAL*** (1970) 104m UPA/Maron c

"Mr. Magoo's Christmas Carol": voices of Jim Backus *(Mr. Magoo/Ebenezer Scrooge)*, Jack Cassidy *(Bob Cratchit)*, Joan Gardner *(Tiny Tim/Christmas Past)*, Jane Kean *(Belle Fezziwig)*, Royal Dano *(Marley's Ghost)*, Morey Amsterdam *(Brandy/James)*, Les Tremayne *(Christmas Present)*, Marie Matthews *(Young Scrooge)*, Laura Olsher *(Mrs. Cratchit)*, Paul Frees *(Old Fezziwig/Undertaker)*, John Hart; "Mr. Magoo's Snow White": voices of Jim Backus *(Mr. Magoo/7 Dwarfs)*, Julie Bennett *(Snow White)*, Howard Morris *(Prince)*, Joan Gardner *(Queen)*, Everett Sloane.

A pair of familiar animated tales with Mr. Magoo "acting" in both. "Mr. Magoo's Christmas Carol" originally aired on television in 1962, while "Mr. Magoo's Snow White" was on TV in 1965. Well-done with a fine cast of familiar voices. "Mr. Magoo's Christmas Carol" includes the songs "Alone in the World," "It's Great To Be Back on Broadway," "The Lord's Bright Blessing," "Ringle, Ringle," "We're Despicable," and "Winter Is Warm" (Jule Styne, Bob Merrill).

p, Lee Orgel; d, Abe Levitow; w, Barbara Chain (based on the book *A Christmas Carol* by Charles Dickens and the fairy tale "Schneewittchen und die Sieben Zwerge" by Jakob and Wilhelm Grimm); m, Carl Brandt ("Mr. Magoo's Snow White"), Walter Scharf ("Mr. Magoo's Christmas Carol"); ed, Sam Horta, Earl Bennett, George Probert, Wayne Hughes; prod d, Lee Mishkin, Robert Singer, Richard Ung, Corny Cole, Shirley Silvey, Tony Rivera, Marty Murphy, Sam Weiss; md, Scharf ("Mr. Magoo's Christmas Carol); Animation, John Walker, Hank Smith, Xenia, Ed Solomon, Tom McDonald, Casey Onaitis.

Animated Film (PR:AAA MPAA:G)

MR. MAJESTYK*** (1974) 104m UA c

Charles Bronson *(Vince Majestyk)*, Al Lettieri *(Frank Renda)*, Linda Cristal *(Nancy Chavez)*, Lee Purcell *(Wiley)*, Paul Koslo *(Bobby Kopas)*, Taylor Lacher *(Gene Lundy)*, Frank Maxwell *(Detective Lt. McAllen)*, Alejandro Rey *(Larry Mendoza)*, Jordon Rhodes *(Deputy Sheriff Harold Ritchie)*, Vern Porter *(Gas Station Attendant)*, Julio Tomaz *(Bert Santos)*, Allan Pinson, Robert Templeton *(Kopas Muscle Men)*, Bill Morris *(Police Officer)*, Jim Reynolds *(Black Prisoner)*, Eddy Reyes, Larry Cortinez *(Chicano Prisoners)*, Howard Beasley *(TV Reporter Ron Malone)*, Bus Gindhart, Tom Hickman *(TV Camera Crew)*, Kenny Bell, Max Reed *(Press Photographers)*, Luis Ramirez *(Labor Contractor)*, Alma Lawrentz *(Mrs. Mendoza)*.

Somehow they managed to take the subject of the mistreatment of migrant workers and turned it into a vehicle for displaying Bronson's violent heroics. In this one he's a farmer who is exemplary for his fairness but he lands in jail anyway. During an attempted jailbreak by Lettieri, Bronson foils the mafioso's attempts, and offers to return the chieftain for his own freedom. This done, Lettieri threatens to get even with Bronson. First, one of Bronson's workers has his legs pinned into a loading dock by a slow-moving car. The result is bloodless but painful to think about. When Bronson still refuses to back off, Lettieri's men locate his watermelon stock and machine-gun it into oblivion. The rest of the film shows Bronson battling the hitmen of Lettieri from his Colorado ranch and, of course, emerging victorious. Based on a novel by Elmore Leonard, whose crime fiction has slowly creeped into movies. HOMBRE (1967) is based on a work of his, as is STICK (1985), which unfortunately received a miserable screen treatment.

p, Walter Mirisch; d, Richard Fleischer; w, Elmore Leonard; ph, Richard H. Kline (DeLuxe Color); m, Charles Bernstein; ed, Ralph E. Winters; art d, Cary Odell; spec eff, Robert N. Dawson.

Adventure Cas. (PR:C MPAA:PG)

MR. MOM** 1/2** (1983) 91m Sherwood/FOX c (GB: MR. MUM)

Michael Keaton *(Jack)*, Teri Garr *(Caroline)*, Frederick Koehler *(Alex)*, Taliesin Jaffe *(Kenny)*, Courtney White, Brittany White *(Megan)*, Martin Mull *(Ron)*, Ann Jillian *(Joan)*, Jeffrey Tambor *(Jinx)*, Christopher Lloyd *(Larry)*, Tom Leopold *(Stan)*, Graham Jarvis *(Humphries)*, Carolyn Seymour *(Eve)*, Michael Alaimo *(Bert)*, Valri Bromfield *(Doris)*, Charles Woolf *(Phil)*, Miriam Flynn *(Annette)*, Derek McGrath, Michael Ensign, Ken Olfson, Frank Birney, Hilary Beane, Edie McClurg, Patti Deutsch, Estelle Omens, Patty Dworkin, Bernadette Birkett, James Gallery, Tom Rayhall, Danny Mora, Maurice Sneed, Phil Simms, Bruce French, Henry Flores, Roger Menache, Dennis Landry, Lisa Freeman, Marley Simms, Kay Dingle, Robert Lussier, Jacque Lynn Colton, Mandy Ingber.

MR. MOM was presented by television mogul Aaron Spelling and looks it. Not that the movie is bad, it's just more like an elongated sit-com or, at the best, an ABC TV Movie Of The Week. It also shows us why situation comedies are 24 minutes and 25 seconds in length (after all the commercials, promos, and titles). We've seen the issue of role reversal many times in TV comedy and often on the talk shows, so there is no reason why we should be pestered with it at the movie theater, especially in view of the fact that it offers no new insights on the subject. Despite this, MR. MOM did well at the box office, due, in part, to the meteoric rise of Keaton, who was so good in NIGHT SHIFT, co-starring with TV's Henry Winkler and directed by TV's Ron Howard. MR. MOM is the story of how Keaton loses his position in a Detroit auto plant and must take over at home while his wife, Garr, goes out to earn their daily bread. She is excellent at bringing home the bacon and he is thrust into a satirical look at all the problems of being a house-husband with all the attendant troubles with the kids, supermarket coupons (Keaton and a bunch of women play poker with coupons instead of money), and the rest of the predictable farce-making material. There is little we haven't seen before as handled by Hugh Beaumont or Robert Young or Carl Betz, except for the overtones of the bored housewives with whom Keaton comes in contact. While Keaton is suffering from sexual harassment at home, Garr is going through the same stuff at her advertising job. It could have been a caustic and telling look at the plight of the middle class during a minor depression in the nation's economy, but it soon becomes just another ordinary comedy that is only saved by the superior work of the actors. Screenwriter John Hughes (now also a director) was so annoyed at the final outcome of the film that he has, more or less, washed his hands of the project, although it was too late for him to have his name removed when he saw the print. Hughes writes well for younger performers (THE BREAKFAST CLUB, et al.) and it might be interesting to see what the original script looked like before shooting. Dragoti, who directed the very funny LOVE AT FIRST BITE, knows his way around the advertising business, the result of having spent many years making many of the nation's best commercials as a director. Several of today's directors have come from that world, including Howard Zieff and John Schlesinger. Rounding out the cast are a host of other television players such as Martin Mull ("Fernwood Tonight"), Ann Jillian ("It's A Living"), Chris Lloyd ("Taxi"), Graham Jarvis ("Mary Hartman [2]"), Edie McClurg ("The Kallikaks"), Patti Deutsch ("Laugh-In") and others. MR. MOM was produced by former TV actress Lynn Loring (married to TV actor Roy Thinnes) and TV producer Lauren Shuler. It goes without saying that MR. MOM was later sold to cable and syndication TV and did quite well. There are companies who charge fees for getting clients named in movies. Look at MR. MOM with that in mind and note how many "plugs" there are in the picture, particularly in the poker-playing sequence, to see how that is done. There may be 10 different companies named in that scene and when you consider that the picture will have been seen by millions (with the TV showings), you'll realize just how valuable those kind of mentions can be.

p, Lynn Loring, Lauren Shuler; d, Stan Dragoti; w, John Hughes; ph, Victor J. Kemper (Metrocolor); m, Lee Holdridge; ed, Patrick Kennedy; prod d, Alfred Sweeney; cos, Nolan Miller.

Comedy **Cas.** **(PR:A-C MPAA:PG)**

MISTER MOSES 1/2** (1965) 113m Talbot-Belmont/UA c

Robert Mitchum *(Joe Moses)*, Carroll Baker *(Julie Anderson)*, Ian Bannen *(Robert)*, Alexander Knox *(Rev. Anderson)*, Raymond St. Jacques *(Ubi)*, Orlando Martins *(Chief)*, Reginald Beckwith *(Parkhurst)*, "Susie" of Nairobi *(Emily the Elephant)*.

This is a light-hearted attempted at making a modern-day story of Moses with Mitchum as the star. It only works partially, as Mitchum doesn't have the wherewithal to carry such a heavy load. He's an American conman, phony doctor, and sometime diamond smuggler operating in Africa. He is tossed into a river by a group of irate Africans who were wiser than he gave them credit for. Floating downstream, he lands in the bulrushes (is this literal enough for you?) next to a village that is about to be flooded as part of a government dam project. He's rescued by Baker, the daughter of the resident missionary, Knox, who is trying to convince the natives that they have to leave, but the locals are reluctant to go because they will not be allowed to take their animals with them. Since the natives feel that their animals are like family, they elect to die with them rather than separate. Mitchum puts on a magic show for the natives and sets fire to a bush—a little trick he learned while working in a circus a while back. At the same time, the local commissioner, Bannen, is about to use force to move the recalcitrant villagers. However, Martins, the chief, has heard about Moses in the Bible and announces that Mitchum is a reincarnation of that hero and that he has been chosen by Fate to lead them out of the wilderness. Mitchum is less than thrilled at that designation and would like to get out of it, but Baker knows all about his illegal dealings and threatens to report him to the authorities unless he agrees to head the column across the wastelands. Along the way, Mitchum is at odds with St. Jacques, an African who was educated in the U.S., and who resents Mitchum's influence over the tribesmen, especially since St. Jacques thinks he's something special because his daddy is the local witch doctor. Mitchum opens the gates to the dam so the water runs off and he can lead the Africans across (again the parallel). St. Jacques knows that Mitchum is a fraud and not the spirit of Moses, so he attempts to unmask Mitchum and begins a wild dance that results in Bannen's helicopter being destroyed and St. Jacques being burned to death in a fire. The trek continues until Mitchum gets the villagers to the appointed place. Bannen has known about Mitchum's crooked background but needed him to lead the natives. Now that that's over, Bannen gives Mitchum the chance to exit, which he does into the jungle. Baker decides that she would enjoy being a smuggler's girl rather than a missionary's daughter and she chases after him as the picture ends. If the story of a trip across Africa with a conman and a relative of a missionary sounds familiar, we refer you to THE AFRICAN QUEEN, which did it earlier and far better. The acting was okay but St. Jacques was too loathesome to be believable. Good camera work and lots of panoramic vistas for those who enjoy travelogs. Filmed in Kenya, at Lake Naivasha and in the game reserve at Amboselli.

p, Frank Ross; d, Ronald Neame; w, Charles Beaumont, Monja Danischewsky (based on the novel by Max Catto); ph, Oswald Morris (Panavision, Technicolor); m, John Barry; ed, Peter Weatherley, Philip W. Anderson; md, Barry; art d, Syd Cain; makeup, George Frost.

Adventure **(PR:A MPAA:NR)**

MR. MOTO AND THE PERSIAN OIL CASE

(SEE: RETURN OF MR. MOTO, THE, 1965, Brit.)

MR. MOTO IN DANGER ISLAND 1/2**

(1939) 63m FOX bw (GB: MR. MOTO ON DANGER ISLAND; AKA: DANGER ISLAND)

Peter Lorre *(Mr. Moto)*, Jean Hersholt *(Sutter)*, Amanda Duff *(Joan Castle)*, Warren Hymer *(Twister McGurk)*, Richard Lane *(Commissioner Gordon)*, Leon Ames *(Commissioner Madero)*, Douglas Dumbrille *(Comdr. La Costa)*, Charles D. Brown *(Col. Tom Castle)*, Robert Lowery *(Lt. George Bentley)*, Don Douglas *(Petty Officer)*, Ward Bond *(Sailor Sam The Wrestler)*, Eddie Marr *(Capt. Dahlen)*, Harry Woods *(Grant)*, Paul Harvey *(Governor John Bentley)*, Harry Strang *(Smuggler)*.

Lorre plays the famous detective as he is asked by the U.S. government to uncover a diamond smuggling ring in Puerto Rico. He gets assistance from wrestler Hymer, and Lorre proves that his small size is no indication of his superior abilities. The picture maintains a constant sense of intrigue and suspense, keeping one guessing as to who of the many suspects is responsible for the smuggling operation. Lorre outwits everybody in his ingenius solution. (See MR. MOTO series, Index.) One in the series of "Mr. Moto" films.

p, John Stone; d, Herbert I. Leeds; w, Peter Milne (based on story ideas by John Reinhardt, George Bricker, from the novel *Murder in Trinidad* by John W. Vandercook, based on a character created by J. P. Marquand); ph, Lucien Andriot; ed, Harry Reynolds; md, Samuel Kaylin; art d, Richard Day, Chester Gore; cos, Herschel.

Crime **(PR:A MPAA:NR)**

MR. MOTO ON DANGER ISLAND

(SEE: MR. MOTO IN DANGER ISLAND, 1939)

MR. MOTO TAKES A CHANCE** (1938) 63m FOX bw

Peter Lorre *(Mr. Moto)*, Rochelle Hudson *(Victoria Mason)*, Robert Kent *(Marty Weston)*, J. Edward Bromberg *(Rajah Ali)*, Chick Chandler *(Chick Davis)* George Regas *(Boker, High Priest)*, Fredrik Vogeding *(Capt. Zimmerman)*, Al Kikume *(Yao)*, Gloria Roy *(Wife)*, James B. Leong *(Bit Man)*.

A disappointing effort in the series of "Mr. Moto" thrillers, mainly because of the attempt to put too much into too short a time slot, without generating the type of suspense common to the earlier pictures. In this one Lorre poses as an archaeologist in Southeast Asia, but is actually interested in a nearby province where a fanatical priest, Regas, is planning to rid the entire area of its white population. Aided by agent Hudson and the legitimate ruler (Bromberg), Lorre, disguised as an ancient guru, sneaks into the cave where the ammunition is hidden. He then uses it against Regas and his forces. Many of the performances seem overly forced, as does the plot, which is further marred by studio settings that look anything but realistic. But Lorre still manages to give an intriguing performance. (See MR. MOTO series, Index.)

p, Sol M. Wurtzel; d, Norman Foster; w, Lou Breslow, John Patrick (based on a story by Willis Cooper, Foster, based on a character created by J. P. Marquand); ph, Virgil Miller; ed, Nick De Maggio; md, Samuel Kaylin; cos, Herschel.

Adventure/Mystery **(PR:A MPAA:NR)**

MR. MOTO TAKES A VACATION** (1938) 65m FOX bw

Peter Lorre *(Mr. Moto)*, Joseph Schildkraut *(Hendrik Manderson)*, Lionel Atwill *(Prof. Hildebrand)*, Virginia Field *(Eleanor Kirke)*, John King *(Howard Stevens)*, Iva Stewart *(Susan French)*, Victor Varconi *(Paul Borodoff)*, John Bleifer *(Wendling)*, Honorable Wu *(Wong)*, Morgan Wallace *(David Perez)*, Anthony Warde *(Joe Rubla)*, Harry Strang *(O'Hara)*, John Davidson *(Prince Suleid)*, Willie Best *(Driver)*, George P. Huntley, Jr. *(Archie Featherstone)*, Leyland Hodgson *(Ship's Waiter)*, George Chandler *(Reporter)*, William Gould *(Police Cmdr.)*, Ralph Dunn *(Police Guard)*.

The last of the "Mr. Moto" series to star Lorre, who admitted dissatisfaction with the role, this picture doesn't have the appeal of the earlier films. Lorre is out to safeguard a priceless gem, recently excavated from an Egyptian site. Under the premise of being on vacation, Lorre makes his way to San Francisco, where the gem is to be on display. His fears turn out to be correct when a notorious international criminal, Schildkraut, whom Lorre figured would try and steal the gem, does so. Schildkraut, a master of disguises, poses as a philanthropist and backer of the expedition. Overall the story is weak and unconvincing, with little or no suspense. Lorre and the rest of the cast have difficulty in presenting the poor material. (See MR. MOTO series, Index.)

p, Sol M. Wurtzel; d, Norman Foster; w, Foster, Philip MacDonald (based on the character created by J. P. Marquand); ph, Charles Clarke; ed, Norman Colbert; md, Samuel Kaylin; cos, Herschel.

Mystery **(PR:A MPAA:NR)**

MR. MOTO'S GAMBLE 1/2** (1938) 71m FOX bw

Peter Lorre *(Mr. Moto)*, Keye Luke *(Lee Chan)*, Dick Baldwin *(Bill Steele)*, Lynn Bari *(Penny Kendall)*, Douglas Fowley *(Nick Crowder)*, Jayne Regan *(Linda Benton)*, Harold Huber *(Lt. Riggs)*, Maxie Rosenbloom *("Knock-out" Wellington)*, John Hamilton *(Philip Benton)*, George E. Stone *(Jerry Connors)*, Ward Bond *(Biff Moran)*, Lon Chaney Jr. *(Joey)*, Paul Fix *(Gangster)*, Edward Marr *(Sammy)*, Pierre Watkin *(District Attorney)*, Charles D. Brown *(Editor "Scotty")*, Bernard Nedell *(Clipper McCoy)*, Charles Williams *(Gabby Marden)*, Cliff Clark *(Tom McGuire)*, Russ Clark *(Frankie Stanton)*, Fred Kelsey *(Mahoney)*, Frank McGlynn, Jr., Ralph Dunn, David Newell *(Detectives)*, George Magrill, Adrian Morris, Bob Ryan *(Policemen)*, Jack Stoney *(Kid Grant)*, Frank Fanning *(Turnkey)*, Edward Earle *(Medical Examiner)*, Emmett Vogan *(Fingerprint Man)*, Irving Bacon *(Sheriff)*, Olin Howland *(Deputy Sheriff)*.

Originally meant to be a "Charlie Chan" episode, but when Warner Oland became ill the studio decided to salvage what they could of the already begun project, so it became MR. MOTO'S GAMBLE. Lorre is the teacher of a class for future sleuths, whose students include Luke, the son of Charlie Chan, and Rosenbloom, a hopeless kleptomaniac. Lorre receives the assistance of both pupils as he solves the ring murder of a boxer. Lorre pins it on the owner of the auditorium where the bout is being held. The script is a well-blended combination of mystery and comedy, with Luke and Rosenbloom carrying most of the comedy. (See MISTER MOTO series, Index.)

p, Sol M. Wurtzel, John Stone; d, James Tinling; w, Charles Belden, Jerry Cady (based on the character created by John P. Marquand); ph, Lucien Andriot; ed, Nick DiMaggio; md, Samuel Kaylin; art d, Bernard Herzbrun, Haldane Douglas; cos, Helen A. Myron.

Mystery/Comedy **(PR:A MPAA:NR)**

MR. MOTO'S LAST WARNING 1/2** (1939) 71m FOX bw

Peter Lorre *(Mr. Moto)*, Richard Cortez *(Fabian, Ventriloquist)*, Virginia Field *(Connie Porter)*, John Carradine *(Danforth/Richard Burke)*, George Sanders *(Eric Norvel)*, Joan Carol *(Mary Delacour)*, Robert Coote *(Rollo Venables)*, Margaret Irving *(Mme. Delacour)*, Leyland Hodgson *(Capt. Hawkins)*, John Davidson

(Hakim), Teru Shimada *(Fake Mr. Moto)*, Georges Renavent *(Adm. Delacour)*, E. E. Clive *(Commandant)*, Holmes Herbert *(Bentham)*, C. Montague Shaw *(First Lord of Admiralty)*.

The setting for this Moto adventure is Port Said, where a gang of criminals, headed by Cortez and Sanders and sponsored by an unnamed country, are attempting to instigate a war between England and France. Their plan of attack is to sink the French fleet as it enters the Suez canal. Carradine, an agent for Britain, infiltrates the gang, only to be discovered and forced to the bottom of the ocean. At which point Lorre makes his appearance, posing as the Japanese shopkeeper of the store located across from the hangout of Cortez. He manages to intercept the gang's efforts just in the nick of time. Evenly paced suspense, with a cast, in addition to Lorre, who manage some very convincing portrayals. (See MR. MOTO series, Index.)

p, Sol M. Wurtzel; d, Norman Foster; w, Philip MacDonald, Foster (based on the character created by J. P. Marquand); ph, Virgil Miller; ed, Norman Colbert; md, Samuel Kaylin; cos, Helen A. Myron.

Mystery **Cas.** **(PR:A MPAA:NR)**

MR. MUGGS RIDES AGAIN** (1945) 63m Banner/MON bw

Leo Gorcey *(Ethelbert Aloysius "Muggs" McGinnis)*, Huntz Hall *(Glimpy)*, Billy Benedict *(Skinny)*, Johnny Duncan *(Squeegie Robinson)*, Bud Gorman *(Danny)*, Mende Koenig *(Sam)*, Minerva Urecal *(Nora "Ma" Brown)*, Nancy Brinkman *(Elsie)*, Bernard B. Brown *(Gaby O'Neill)*, George Meeker *(Dollar Davis)*, John H. Allen *(Scruno)*, Pierre Watkin *(Dr. Fletcher)*, Milton Kibbee *(Veterinarian)*, Frank Jacquet *(Steward Farnsworth)*, Bernard Gorcey *(Meyer)*, I. Stanford Jolley *(Mike Hanlin)*, Michael Owen *(Joe English)*, Betty Sinclair *(Nurse)*.

Gorcey is suspended from the racetrack after a gang of betters submit false evidence against him. When one of the gamblers falls for the stable owner's daughter, he confesses to taking part in the wrongdoings and comes to the aid of Gorcey. His men shoot him because of his betrayal and drug the owner's horses. However, the culprits are foiled before their horse can claim the prize money. A bit less fun than we've come to expect from Gorcey and company. (See BOWERY BOYS series, Index.)

p, Sam Katzman, Jack Dietz; d, Wallace Fox; w, Harvey H. Gates; ph, Ira Morgan; ed, William Austin; md, Edward Kay; art d, David Milton; spec eff, Ray Mercer.

Comedy **(PR:A MPAA:NR)**

MR. MUGGS STEPS OUT 1/2** (1943) 63m Banner/MON bw

Leo Gorcey *(Ethelbert "Muggs" McGinnis)*, Huntz Hall *(Glimpy)*, Billy Benedict *(Pinky, "Skinny")*, Bobby Stone *(Speed)*, Bud Gorman *(Skinny)*, Dave Durand *(Danny)*, Jimmy Strand *(Rocky)*, Joan Marsh *(Brenda Murray)*, Patsy Moran *(Maisie O'Donnell)*, Gabriel Dell *(Dips Nolan)*, Eddie Gribbon *(Butch Grogan)*, Halliwell Hobbes *(Charney)*, Stanley Brown *(Virgil Wellington III)*, Betty Blythe *(Margaret Murray)*, Emmett Vogan *(John Aldredge Murray)*, Nick Stuart *(Diamonds Hamilton)*, Noah Beery, Sr. *(Judge)*, Lottie Harrison *(Elizabeth, The Dowager)*, Kay Marvis Gorcey *(Dancer)*.

Bowery Boys' picture from the time when they were known as the "East End Kids" has Gorcey avoiding reform school by being hired as a chauffeur for Fifth Avenue socialite Blythe, much to her husband's consternation. When the couple have a fancy dinner to announce their daughter's engagement, Gorcey gets the rest of the gang to act as servants. This turns out to be a wise move, as the boys solve the theft of a valuable necklace, after originally being accused of the crime. Lots of humor in the contrast between the "Kids" and the wealthy snobs, though some of the boys are beginning to look a bit old to be playing teenagers. The direction is smooth, though the photography is below par. (See BOWERY BOYS series, Index.)

p, Sam Katzman, Jack Dietz; d, William Beaudine; w, William X. Crowley, Beryl Sachs; ph, Marcel le Picard; ed, Carl Pierson; md, Edward Kay, set d, Ernest Hickerson.

Comedy **(PR:A MPAA:NR)**

MR. MUSIC 1/2** (1950) 113m PAR bw

Bing Crosby *(Paul Merrick)*, Nancy Olson *(Katherine Holbrook)*, Charles Coburn *(Alex Conway)*, Robert Stack *(Jefferson Blake)*, Tom Ewell *(Haggerty)*, Ruth Hussey *(Lorna Marvis)*, Ida Moore *(Aunt Amy)*, Charles Kemper *(Danforth)*, Donald Woods *(Tippy Carpenter)*, Gower Champion *(Himself)*, Marge Champion *(Herself)*, Groucho Marx *(Himself)*, Peggy Lee *(Herself)*, Dorothy Kirsten *(Herself)*, The Merry Macs *(Themselves)*, Claude Curdle [Richard Haydn] *(Jerome Thisby)*.

Richard Haydn, who played the gladiola-sniffing, pince-nez-wearing prig in so many movies, does a cameo in the film which he also directed with the same professionalism he showed as an actor. It's a cotton-candy story that merely serves to give the audience an opportunity to be regaled by several tunes from the pen and piano of Burke and Van Heusen. Crosby is a successful songwriter who would rather play golf (with his butler, Ewell, as his caddy) than write. He's already made a bundle with his work and would now like to have a little fun on the links. Coburn is an old-time producer who has fallen from favor and is looking for a score for his new show, one that'll get him back in the big-time on Broadway. Olson is Crosby's secretary and she prevails on her boss to go back to work. He's dating Hussey at the time, but it's easy to see that Olson will soon replace Hussey in his affections as the picture unreels. Olson is still in college and some of the undergrads pledge to help raise the 300 grand which is eventually donated by Haydn. The rest of the movie is the show they write and produce with a few cameos by well-knowns to help the marquee value. The story was sort of based on Sam Raphelson's play "Accent on Youth" (which had already been filmed in 1935 as a romance and was made again in 1959 as BUT NOT FOR ME) and it's as thin as a dedicated anorexic but that has little to do with all the fun engendered by the goings-on. It's more of a 1930s film than one of the 1950s and suffers from being long on time and short on plot. Haydn directed it well enough, but couldn't overcome the shortcomings of a mild script from the usually excellent Smith-Corona of Sheekman, who wrote so well for the Brothers Marx as well as many others. Haydn didn't use his own name in his acting role and was billed as "Claude Curdle." Songs include: "Life is So Peculiar" (James Van Heusen, Johnny Burke, sung by Bing Crosby, Peggy Lee, The Merry Macs, reprised by Crosby, Groucho Marx), "Accidents Will Happen" (Van Heusen, Burke, sung by Crosby, Dorothy Kirsten), "High on the List," "Wouldn't It Be Funny," "Wasn't I There?" "Mr. Music," "Once More the Blue and White," "Milady," and "Then You'll Be Home" (Van Heusen, Burke).

p, Robert L. Welch; d, Richard Haydn; w, Arthur Sheekman (based on the play "Accent on Youth" by Samson Raphaelson); ph, George Barnes; m, Joseph J. Lilley, Troy Sanders; ed, Doane Harrison, Everett Douglas; md, Lilley, Van Cleave; art d, Hans Dreier, Earl Hedrick; spec eff, Farciot Edouart; ch, Gower Champion; m/l, James Van Heusen, Johnny Burke.

Musical/Comedy **(PR:A MPAA:NR)**

MR. ORCHID 1/2** (1948, Fr.) 100m BCM/Lopert bw (LE PERE TRANQUILLE)

Noel-Noel *(Mr. Edouard Martin)*, Nadine Alari *(Monique Martin)*, Jose Arthur *(Pierre Martin)*, Claire Olivier *(Mme. Martin)*, Jean Varas *(Peitier)*, Paul Frankeur *(Simon)*, Delaitre *(Charrat)*, Lemontier *(Father Charles)*.

This character study of a French patriot during the Nazi Occupation has comedian Noel as the chief of the underground who uses his hobby of growing orchids to hide his radio equipment. Even, though leisurely, paced effort, which keeps up a good level of suspense.

d, Rene Clement; w, Noel-Noel, Rene Cloeree.

Drama **(PR:A MPAA:NR)**

MR. PATMAN* 1/2 (1980, Can.) 105m Film Consortium of Canada c

James Coburn *(Mr. Patman)*, Kate Nelligan *(Peabody)*, Fionnula Flanagan *(Abadaba)*, Les Carlson *(Abernathy)*, Candy Kane *(Mrs. Beckman)*, Michael Kirby *(Dr. Turley)*, Alan McRae *(Dr. Bloom)*, Jan Rubes *(Vrakatas)*, Hugh Webster *(Wolfe)*, Lyn Griffin *(Monica)*, Tabitha Herrington *(Montgomery)*, Lois Maxwell *(The Director)*.

The only reason they may have made this was to take advantage of the Canadian tax money that was being tossed about at that time. In order to do that, the producers have to use either Canadians or Britons in many of the on-screen or behind-the-camera jobs and such was the case with this film. Coburn is a weird Irish male-nurse (sort of) who works in a psychiatric ward of a Canadian hospital where he is beloved by one and all, in part due to his charm, in part due to his caring about the inmates. He is being shadowed by a mysterious tracker and he worries that it might be the husband of his landlady, Flanagan, with whom he is conducting some hanky-panky. He is also hoping to do the same thing with another hospital staffer, Nelligan, with whom he works the late shift. As the picture continues, one of Coburn's patients commits suicide, another is released as "cured" but is still nuts, and a third perishes of a coronary upon being released. Now we see that Coburn is as whacko as the patients and that his tracker only exists in his own mind and that his mind is playing tricks on him and he thinks Nelligan has died in an auto accident. Coburn battles with Kirby, a pompous doctor, and makes sport with the man so that Kirby becomes the laughing stock of the hospital. That gets Coburn his walking papers and he leaves with Nelligan, after first helping another patient flee the hospital against regulations. Things don't work out for Nelligan and Coburn and they eventually come back to the area where Coburn attempts to take up again with Flanagan but she won't have any of it. In a funk, Coburn kills his cat (thereby losing all the cat fanciers in the audience who may have liked the picture up until now), goes totally mad and thinks that he is being chased by a dead patient, and ends up inside the hospital as a patient himself. In a way, it's a bit like LILITH, the Warren Beatty-Jean Seberg film in which Beatty is also a psychiatric employee who winds up nuts. That was depressing, this is just dumb. Guillermin's direction here is on a par with his work in SHEENA, slow and stupid, with no pacing whatsoever. The movie was made in Vancouver, Canada, and that lovely city never looked worse.

p, Bill Marshall, Alexander MacDonald; d, John Guillermin; w, Thomas Hedley; ph, John Coquillon; m, Paul Hoffert; ed, Max Benedict, Vince Hatherly; prod d, Trevor Williams.

Drama **(PR:C MPAA:NR)**

MR. PEABODY AND THE MERMAID 1/2** (1948) 89m UNIV bw

William Powell *(Mr. Peabody)*, Ann Blyth *(Mermaid)*, Irene Hervey *(Mrs. Polly Peabody)*, Andrea King *(Cathy Livingston)*, Clinton Sundberg *(Mike Fitzgerald)*, Art Smith *(Dr. Harvey)*, Hugh French *(Maj. Hadley)*, Lumsden Hare *(Col. Mandrake)*, Fred Clark *(Basil)*, James Logan *(Lieutenant)*, Mary Field *(Wee Shop Clerk)*, Beatrice Roberts *(Mother)*, Cynthia Corley *(Nurse)*, Tom Stevenson, Richard Ryan *(Waiters)*, Mary Somerville *(Lady Trebshaw)*, Bobby Hyatt *(Boy)*, Ivan H. Browning *(Sidney)*, Carol Savage *(Daphne)*, Ola Lorraine *(Receptionist)*, Winifred Harris, Lydia Bilbrook *(Voices)*.

Nunnally Johnson, the man who wrote the action-packed script for THE DIRTY DOZEN (with Lukas Heller), is the producer-writer of this film, a motion picture that could not be more different in content and intent from the Heller collaboration. Based on a novel by Guy and Constance Jones, this is the story of a man turning 50, Powell, who is suffering from a middle-age crisis and is sent by his doctor, Smith, on a holiday in the Caribbean where he is told to rest up until the crisis clears. While out fishing for his dinner, the proper Bostonian hooks something a little larger than his pole can handle, Blyth, a voluptuous mermaid. Powell takes her back to his beach cottage and places her in the fish pond, where she can be comfortable. Now a series of friends come to visit Powell, and although Powell tells them about his prize catch, all they ever see of her is her tail, thus raising the question that Powell's brain may have been fried by the tropical sun. His wife, Hervey, leaves temporarily, his pals desert him, and Blyth is his only friend, and she never says a word. In the course of events, Powell falls in love with the mute mermaid, but she finally goes back to Davey Jones and Powell must live the rest of his life with the memory of her. Hervey returns and Powell sighs. Along the way, there is one very funny scene where Powell buys the top half of a two piece swim suit from clerk Field, then tries to explain why a bra is important to Blyth. Andrea King drops by as a sexpot wench with eyes for Powell; then she sings a tune by Johnny Mercer and Robert Emmett Dolan called "The Caribbees" which makes little sense to the plot and was probably in there to attempt an Oscar award for Best Song. Two better mermaid films were MIRANDA and SPLASH, but this is the one most people recall fondly. An oddity about the picture is that nine out of 10 who saw it think it was in color, but it wasn't. It plays well for the 55 minutes, then starts to sink, and eventually goes belly up.

p, Nunnally Johnson; d, Irving Pichel; w, Johnson (based on the novel *Peabody's Mermaid* by Guy Jones, Constance Jones); ph, Russell Metty, David S. Horsley; m, Robert Emmett Dolan; ed, Marjorie Fowler; art d, Bernard Herzbrun, Boris Leven; set d, Russell A. Gausman, Rubey R. Levitt; cos, Grace Houston.

Comedy/Fantasy **Cas.** **(PR:AA MPAA:NR)**

MR. PEEK-A-BOO**

(1951, Fr.) 74m Cite-Arthur Sachson/UA bw (GAROU GAROU LE PASSE MURAILLE; LE PASSE MURAILLE)

Joan Greenwood *(Susan)*, Bourvil *(Leon Dutilleul)*, Marcelle Arnold *(Germaine)*, Roger Treville *(Burdin)*, Henri Cremieux *(Lecuyer)*, O'Brady *(Doctor)*, Craddock C. Monroe *(Elmer)*, Payne Williams *(Jean-Paul)*, Charles Jarell *(Maurice)*, Raymond Souplex, Gerard Oury, Jacques Erwin.

Bourvil stars as a government clerk who discovers he can walk through walls. He is coaxed by a friend to try his hand at thievery, but he finds he is not overly fond of it, until he spots a beautiful English girl, Greenwood, who has been forced into robbery through blackmail. Bourvil immediately falls in love with her, but she is unimpressed by him. Eventually he alllows himself to be caught, ending up in jail, and having some fun with the police by repeatedly escaping. French comedian Bourvil adds a lot of charm to his role as the scapegoat clerk in a performance reminiscent of Chaplin. The film was shot in France with the dialog spoken in English in an attempt to capture the American market.

p, Jacques Bar; d, Jean Boyer; w, Boyer, Michel Audiard (based on the novel *The Man Who Walked Through Walls* by Marcel Ayme); ph, Charles Suin; m, George Van Parys; art d, Robert Giordani; spec eff, Henry Harris, Paul Raibaud.

Comedy **(PR:A MPAA:NR)**

MR. PERRIN AND MR. TRAILL*** (1948, Brit.) 92m TC/EL bw

David Farrar *(David Traill)*, Marius Goring *(Vincent Perrin)*, Greta Gynt *(Isobel Lester)*, Raymond Huntley *(Moy-Thompson)*, Edward Chapman *(Birkland)*, Mary Jerrold *(Mrs. Perrin)*, Ralph Truman *(Comber)*, Finlay Currie *(Sir Joshua Varley)*, Maurice Jones *(Clinton)*, Lloyd Pearson *(Dormer)*, May MacDonald *(Mrs. Dormer)*, Viola Lyel *(Mrs. Comber)*, Archie Harradine *(White)*, Donald Barclay *(Rogers)*, Pat Nye *(Matron)*, Howard Douglas *(Jenkins)*, John Campbell *(Garden)*, Donald Barclay *(Rogers)*, Brendan Clegg *(Dodge)*, Cavan Malone *(Benson)*, David Spencer, Roddy Hughes, David Lines, Brian McDermott, Roy Sargent, Johnnie Schofield, John Warren, Sheila Huntington, Majorie Gresley, Lavender Lee.

Sharp attack on the British social system has Goring as a private school teacher whose position is threatened by Farrar, a young, lively teacher straight from the commandos. Goring has spent 21 years as a teacher at the school, making him feel as if he is more deserving of respect than the youthful Farrar. His jealousy almost leads to murder when Farrar also gains the affections of the girl Goring has doted on. The story is built mainly on characterizations, making the movement seem to lapse a bit. Both Goring and Farrar are excellent in their portrayals.

p, Alexander Galperson; d, Lawrence Huntington; w, L. A. G. Strong, T. J. Morrison (based on the novel by Hugh Walpole); ph, Erwin Hillier; m, Alan Gray; ed, Ralph Kemplen; md, Muir Mathieson; art d, Tom Morahan.

Drama **(PR:A MPAA:NR)**

MR. POTTS GOES TO MOSCOW***

(1953, Brit.) 93m Transocean/Stratford bw (GB: TOP SECRET)

George Cole *(George Potts)*, Oscar Homolka *(Zekov)*, Nadia Gray *(Tania Ivanova)*, Frederick Valk *(Rakov)*, Geoffrey Sumner *(Pike)*, Wilfrid Hyde-White *(Sir Hurbert Wells)*, Ronald Adam *(Barworth Controller)*, Edwin Styles *(Barworth Superintendent)*, Kynaston Reeves *(Barworth Director)*, Ernest Jay *(Prof. Layton)*, Richard Wattis *(Barnes)*, Michael Medwin *(Smedley)*, Frederick Leister *(Prime Minister)*, Henry Hewitt *(Minister of Health)*, Walter Horsbrugh *(1st Cabinet Minister)*, Anthony Shaw *(2nd Cabinet Minister)*, Tim Turner *(1st Reporter)*, Gibb McLaughlin *(Schoolmaster)*, Michael Balfour *(Jersey Sailor)*, Hal Osmond *(Jersey Waiter)*, David Hurst *(Prof. Deutsch)*, Charles Goldner *(Gaston)*, Irene Handl *(Mrs. Tidmarsh)*, Gerard Heinz *(Director)*, Olaf Pooley *(Prof. Roblottski)*, Eleanor Summerfield *(Cecilia)*, Phyllis Morris *(Mrs. Tweedy)*, Myrtle Reed *(Air Hostess)*, David Hurst *(Prof. Deutsch)*, Bernard Rebel *(Prof. Trubiev)*, Ronnie Stevens *(Aubrey)*, Guido Lorraine, Terence Alexander, Richard Marner, Martin Boddey, Fred Berger, Victor Maddern, Reed de Rouen, Johnny Catcher, Willoughby Gray, Stanislaus Zienciakiewicz, Christopher Lee, Ina De La Haye.

Well-paced British satire on the cold war has Cole as a sanitary engineer suddenly involved in espionage, when he mistakenly finds himself the possessor of British atom bomb plans. This makes him an immediate hit with the Russian government, while Cole never seems to understand what all the fuss is about. Picture manages to poke fun at both sides in an innocent and charming manner. Homolka and White are excellent in their caricatures as a bungling Russian and a scientist, respectively.

p&d, Mario Zampi; w, Jack Davis, Michael Pertwee; ph, Stanley Pavey; m, Stanley Black; ed, Giulio Zampi.

Comedy **(PR:A MPAA:NR)**

MR. PULVER AND THE CAPTAIN (SEE: ENSIGN PULVER, 1964)

MR. QUILP* 1/2**

(1975, Brit.) 120m AE c (AKA: OLD CURIOSITY SHOP, THE)

Anthony Newley *(Daniel Quilp)*, David Hemmings *(Richard Swiveller)*, David Warner *(Sampson Brass)*, Michael Hordern *(Grandfather/Edward Trent)*, Paul Rogers *(Single Gent/Henry Trent)*, Jill Bennett *(Sally Brass)*, Mona Washbourne *(Mrs. Jarley)*, Peter Duncan *(Kit Nubbles)*, Yvonne Antrobus *(Betsy Quilp)*, Sarah Jane Varley *(Nell)*, Sarah Webb *(Duchess)*, Windsor Davies *(George, Mrs. Jarley's Assistant)*, Philip Davis *(Tom Scott)*, David Battley *(Codlin)*, Ronald Lacey *(Harris)*, Margaret Whiting *(Mrs. Jiniwin)*, Maxwell Shaw *(Isaac List)*, Tony Caunter *(Joe Jowl)*, Bryan Pringle *(Mr. Garland)*, Rosalind Knight *(Mrs. George)*, Jenny Tomasin *(Mrs. Simmons)*, Fred Evans *(Jerry)*, Eddie Davies *(Mr. Grinder)*, Norman Warwick *(Vuffin)*, Graham Weston, Bernard Taylor *(Policemen)*, Brian Glover *(Furnaceman)*, Desmond Cullum-Jones *(Jailer)*, Harry Markham *(Sexton)*, Johnny and Suma Lamonte *(Jugglers)*, The Barbours *(Stiltwalkers)*, Sadie Corre *(Midget)*, Christopher Greener *(Giant)*, Malcolm Weaver *(Acrobat)*.

Charles Dickens spun some wonderful yarns and a number of them were made into good musicals (OLIVER!, "Pickwick!" for the stage, and, most recently in 1985, "The Mystery of Edwin Drood"), but some of them will never be able to serve as musical books, something that should have been realized by the Readers Digest Group, who financed this movie and chose Newley to star and write the score. When two long-time collaborators part after success, one wonders which was the strong partner? (This question can be raised in the case of partners Norman Panama and Melvin Frank. On his own, Frank did BUONA SERA, MRS. CAMPBELL, A TOUCH OF CLASS, and other hits, while Panama penned or helmed NOT WITH MY WIFE YOU DON'T, THE MALTESE BIPPY, and I WILL, I WILL . . . FOR NOW.) Newley and Leslie Bricusse had sensations with "Stop the World, I Want to Get Off" and "The Roar of the Greasepaint, the Smell of the Crowd" for both the British and the American stage and when they found they could no longer work with each other, each went a separate way. Bricusse wrote the score for DR. DOOLITTLE (winning an Oscar) as well as GOODBYE MR. CHIPS and SCROOGE. Newley wrote CAN HIERONYMUS MERKIN EVER FORGET MERCY HUMPPE AND FIND TRUE HAPPINESS? and MR. QUILP. They teamed again in 1971 to do the delightful score for WILLIE WONKA AND THE CHOCOLATE FACTORY. Newley plays the title role, a hunchbacked Shylock and he does it as though he were Quasimodo singing baritone. He is in cahoots with shyster Warner and his sister, Bennett, and most of the film concerns their relationship with storekeeper Hordern and his granddaughter, Varley. The "Old Curiosity Shop" is about to be foreclosed when Rogers arrives. He's the long-missing (and quite wealthy) brother of Hordern and is there to make sure the store is not shuttered. Duncan is the young swain who pants after Varley, Webb is a cute child of the streets, Hemmings (looking very slim and young) is an amiable cad, and Davis plays Newley's long-suffering assistant. Antrobus has the unenviable task of being Newley's wife. The photography and the period sets are excellent, but the G-rated story does go downhill at the end when Varley passes away, followed quickly by Newley (who was the villain of the piece anyhow and hardly mourned). In an attempt to make this a family picture, most of the bite has been taken out of the story and the result is sheer pap, made difficult to chew by the casting. The Newley-written tunes include "When a Felon Needs a Friend" (which may or may not have been a parody of the old pipe tobacco slogan, "when a fellow needs a friend"), "Somewhere," "Love Has the Longest Memory," "Happiness Pie," "The Sport of Kings," "What Shouldn't Happen to a Dog," and "Quilp." Elmer Bernstein did the scoring and managed to get some good sounds out of the material. Newley doesn't read music nor can he play an instrument, so he composes by humming into a tape recorder and usually gives the tape to award-winning arranger Ian Fraser, who puts it down on paper, enhances it by chords, and makes the song sometimes better than it deserves to be, but Fraser was unavailable at the time. This was not a good choice for a musical and they might have been wiser to do Dickens' *Martin Chuzzlewit* or *Our Mutual Friend* or even *Barnaby Rudge*.

p, Helen M. Strauss; d, Michael Tuchner; w, Louis and Irene Kamp (based on the book *The Old Curiosity Shop* by Charles Dickens); ph, Christopher Challis (Panavision, Technicolor); ed, John Jympson; prod d, Elliot Scott; art d, Norman Reynolds; cos, Anthony Mendleson; ch, Gillian Lynne; m/l, Newley.

Musical **(PR:A MPAA:G)**

MR. QUINCEY OF MONTE CARLO 1/2** (1933, Brit.) 53m WB-FN bw

John Stuart *(Mr. Quincey)*, Rosemary Ames *(Norma McLeod)*, Ben Welden *(Grover Jones)*, George Merritt *(Inspector)*, Victor Fairley *(Manager)*.

Stuart, a timid bank clerk, inherits a fortune and goes on a spree in Monte Carlo. Eventually he invests the remainder of his money in a film company. Not bad, though all but forgotten today.

p, Irving Asher; d, John Daumery; w, Brock Williams.

Comedy **(PR:A MPAA:NR)**

MR. RADISH AND MR. CARROT (SEE: TWILIGHT PATH, 1965, Jap.)

MR. RECKLESS* 1/2** (1948) 66m Pine-Thomas/PAR bw

William Eythe *(Jeff Lundy)*, Barbara Britton *(Betty Denton)*, Walter Catlett *(Joel Hawkins)*, Minna Gombell *(Ma Hawkins)*, Nestor Paiva *(Gus)*, Lloyd Corrigan *(Hugo Denton)*, James Millican *(Pete)*, Ian MacDonald *(Jim Halsey)*.

Talky and predictable look at oil rig workers, with Eythe as one of the heartier members of the crew involved in a romantic bind. When he wanders into a town where his old love Britton resides, he discovers that she has become engaged to someone else. Eythe then sets about romancing the girl back, which doesn't take all that much work.

p, William Pine, William Thomas; d, Frank McDonald; w, Maxwell Shane, Milton Raison; ph, Ellis W. Carter; m, Harry Lubin; ed, Howard Smith; art d, Lewis W. Creber.

Drama/Adventure (PR:A MPAA:NR)

MR. REEDER IN ROOM 13 (SEE: MYSTERY OF ROOM 13, 1938, Brit.)

MR. RICCO *1/2 (1975) 98m MGM/UA c

Dean Martin (Joe Ricco), Eugene Roche (Detective Cronyn), Thalmus Rasulala (Frankie Steele), Denise Nicholas (Irene Mapes), Cindy Williams (Jamison), Geraldine Brooks (Katherine Fremont), Philip Thomas (Purvis Mapes), George Tyne (Detective Barrett), Robert Sampson (Justin), Michael Gregory (Detective Tanner), Joseph Hacker (Markham), Jay Fletcher (Detective Jackson), Oliver Givins (Calvin Mapes), Frank Puglia (Uncle Enzo), Ella Edwards (Sally), H. B. Barnum III (Luther).

Lackluster crime drama has Martin (interestingly but woefully miscast) as a San Francisco criminal lawyer who gets client Rasulala freed, only to realize that he has apparently embarked on a series of nasty murders of policemen and the like. Martin hardly seems aware that he's acting, possibly because he's not. The film was made to fulfill a contract that specified Martin must appear in three MGM films in addition to headlining at the MGM Grand Hotel in Las Vegas. After this disaster they apparently decided to skip the other two.

p, Douglas Netter; d, Paul Bogart; w, Robert Hoban (based on a story by Ed Harvey, Francis Kiernan); ph, Frank Stanley (Metrocolor); m, Chico Hamilton; ed, Michael McLean; art d, Herman A. Blumenthal; set d, Don Sullivan; ch, George Fisher.

Crime (PR:C MPAA:PG)

MISTER ROBERTS***   (1955) 123m Orange/WB c

Henry Fonda (Lt. (jg) Doug Roberts), James Cagney (Captain), Jack Lemmon (Ens. Frank Thurlowe Pulver), William Powell (Doc), Ward Bond (C.P.O. Dowdy), Betsy Palmer (Lt. Ann Girard) Phil Carey (Mannion), Nick Adams (Reber), Harry Carey, Jr. (Stefanowski), Ken Curtis (Dolan), Frank Aletter (Gerhart), Fritz Ford (Lidstrom), Buck Kartalian (Mason), William Henry (Lt. Billings), William Hudson (Olson), Stubby Kruger (Schlemmer), Harry Tenbrook (Cookie), Perry Lopez (Rodrigues), Robert Roark (Insignia), Pat Wayne (Bookser), Tige Andrews (Wiley), Jim Moloney (Kennedy), Denny Niles (Gilbert), Francis Conner (Johnson), Shug Fisher (Cochran), Danny Borzage (Jonesey), Jim Murphy (Taylor), Martin Milner (Shore Patrol Officer), Gregory Walcott (Shore Patrolman), James Flavin (M.P.), Jack Pennick (Marine Sergeant), Duke Kahanamoko (Native Chief), George Brangier (French Colonial Officer), Clarence E. Frank (Naval Officer), Carolyn Tong (Chinese Girl), Kathleen O'Malley Maura Murphy, Mimi Doyle, Jeanne Murray-Vanderbilt, Lonnie Pierce (Nurses).

Joshua Logan, who wrote the play with novelist Tom Heggen, and wrote the screenplay with Frank Nugent, never did like this movie. He desperately wanted to direct it and was swayed from his desire by being paid more money *not* to direct it than if he had. He still carps over the way Ford and LeRoy joined forces to make it, perhaps, more slapsticky than originally intended and, because of that, Logan has refused to allow anyone to do anything else with the property. He feels he made a mistake in not directing it and in allowing the forgettable TV series to be made that may have been detrimental to the memory of the American literature's most fascinating characters. Fonda had been out of movies for years and the studio bosses felt he no longer had the power to bring in the customers despite his having played the role on Broadway from the start. Fonda had been self-exiled from Hollywood and was enjoying a fine stage career in New York (where he preferred to live) in three plays, "Mr. Roberts," "Point Of No Return," and "The Caine Mutiny Court Martial." Holden and Brando were suggested by producer Hayward but director Ford said he would have nothing to do with the movie unless Fonda got the role, so that became a fait accompli. However, it wasn't long before Ford and Fonda clashed, mostly due to the fact that the Fonda had some fixed ideas as to how to play Roberts, the result of doing it so many times before. The arguments between star and director became so bitter that a fistfight erupted and the tension on the set was thicker than an agent's hide. Actually, according to Fonda in *Fonda, My Life*, after the first day's shooting where Powell faltered on some of his lines, Ford summoned Fonda to his quarters where he lay on a couch. He had been drinking heavily (and would openly drink two cases of cold beer during each day's filming until he almost passed out, his chores taken over by Ward Bond, his old friend). "I understand you're not happy with the work," Ford said to Fonda. The actor said that he was "not happy with that first scene with Powell." Ford suddenly shot upward and hit Fonda so hard he sent him sprawling against a door. The actor had no intention of fighting the older man and left. Ford later came to him to apologize but Fonda wanted none of it. Ford then had a gall-bladder attack and went into the hospital to dry out and was replaced by Warner's veteran LeRoy, who finished the picture. Ford is reported to have denied responsibility for some of the heavy-handed humor shoehorned into the film. Heggen had written a hit novel while in his early twenties and teamed with Logan to write the play, but he couldn't handle all the success (or so it seems) and took his own life while still a young man, with his share in the play and picture going to his sister in the Midwest. By this time, the story of MR. ROBERTS is fairly well-known. Fonda is the cargo officer of the U.S.S. Reluctant, a toothpaste-and-toilet paper supply-ship aimlessly sailing in the South Pacific. He feels that the war is going on around him and he yearns to be a part of it. The captain, Cagney, is a small-time Hitler who is forever making his crew unhappy by his assinine orders. Fonda is a calm man who is only driven to outrage by Cagney and retaliates by tossing the man's pet palm tree over the side in order

to get even. Powell is the ship's physician, a kind, quiet man who teams with Fonda in lacerating Cagney. Lemmon, in an Oscar-winning Best-Supporting-Actor performance, is the sex-crazed ensign (a TV series about his character was also attempted, as well as a sequel in 1964) who supplies most of the frenetic action and countless punch lines. There are several episodes along the way: the hilarious scene where Powell makes ersatz Scotch whiskey out of grain alcohol, Coca-Cola, hair tonic, and iodine; Lemmon puts a firecracker in the ship's laundry (he is the laundry officer) and a billion soapsuds invade the ship; and a bevy of nurses are smuggled aboard ship, led by Betsy Palmer. (In the play, only one nurse was seen, but they must have felt there was strength in numbers, so they upped it to half dozen for the movie.) Cagney takes away shore leave from the men and uses that as a wedge against Fonda, who must then shed his rebellious ways in order to get some liberty for the men, though he cannot tell them why he now appears to be mealy-mouthed. Further, Fonda must promise to respect the Captain's palm tree and to cease and desist in asking for transfer from the ship. Eventually, Fonda does get his transfer and the final scene tugs the heart as Fonda's last letter is read to the men after they learn that he's been killed in a freak accident aboard his new ship. Lemmon is now the men's leader and he marches straight to Cagney's cabin, tosses the palm tree overboard, and demands to know why Cagney is doing some of the things he's been doing. Besides the humor, there are many touching moments, notably the one where the crew makes a home-made medal for Fonda before he leaves, the Order of the Palm Leaf, which means more to Fonda than any Distinguished Service Cross or Congressional Medal of Honor. Much of the harsh language was deleted from the film, which marked Cagney's forty-fourth movie for Warner Brothers. MR. ROBERTS received nominations for Best Sound and Best Picture but lost to MARTY. Logan was called in near the end of shooting to help with the direction on a few crucial scenes but his stamp is hardly noticeable. It made nearly $10 million and was shot aboard the U.S.S. Hewell at the South Pacific island of Midway, before moving to Kaneoke Bay in Hawaii for the final filming. Although Ford only directed for a brief time before becoming ill, he gets top billing over LeRoy, an odd circumstance but probably contractual rather than having been determined by arbitration. MR. ROBERTS is a fine movie and just misses being the classic screen story that it might have been. It's too long, has a few flat stretches, and suffers a bit by comparison to the stage play. The character of Roberts is the quintessential American: fun-loving; sacrificing; warm and heroic, without tooting his own horn. If he ever existed in real life, it would have been an honor to have been his friend. The film was followed by the sequel ENSIGN PULVER.

p, Leland Hayward; d, John Ford, Mervyn LeRoy; w, Joshua Logan, Frank S. Nugent (based on the play by Logan and Thomas Heggen and the novel by Heggen); ph, Winton C. Hoch (CinemaScope, WarnerColor); m, Franz Waxman; ed, Jack Murray; art d, Art Loel; set d, William L. Kuehl; cos, Moss Mabry; Song, "If I Could Be with You One Hour Tonight" (sung by Jack Lemmon); makeup, Gordon Bau; technical advisers, Adm. John Dale Price, USN, Cmdr. Merle MacBain, USN.

Comedy/Drama Cas. (PR:A MPAA:NR)

MR. ROBINSON CRUSOE* (1932) 70m UA bw

Douglas Fairbanks, Sr. (Steve Drewel), William Farnum (William Belmont), Earle Browne (Prof. Carmichale), Maria Alba (Saturday).

Fairbanks stars as a wealthy hunter on his way to Sumatra for a tiger hunt. He comes to a small deserted island, and decides to take it easy there for a while, building himself an abode which resembles a Park Avenue Penthouse. The exaggeration of details and the forced direction make this an unbelievable effort. The scenic photography and the score by Alfred Newman are the two high points in the picture.

p, Douglas Fairbanks; d, Edward Sutherland; w, Tom Geraghty (based on the story by Elton Thomas); ph, Max Dupont; m, Alfred Newman; ed, Robert Kern.

Comedy Cas. (PR:A MPAA:NR)

MISTER ROCK AND ROLL* (1957) 86m PAR bw

Alan Freed (Himself), Rocky Graziano (Himself), Teddy Randazzo (Himself), Lois O'Brien (Carol Hendricks), Jay Barney (Joe Prentiss), Al Fisher and Lou Marks (Larry and Lou), Earl George (Leo), Ralph Stantly (Station Rep), Lionel Hampton and his Band, Frankie Lymon and The Teenagers, Chuck Berry, LaVern Baker, Clyde McPhatter, Brook Benton, Little Richard, Ferlin Husky, The Moonglows, Shaye Cogan.

When reporter O'Brien writes an article praising rocker Randazzo, her stuffed-shirt editor rewrites it as an attack on the musical genre. Disc jockey Freed takes up the challenge and—after explaining the history of Rock and its development from Blues, Jazz, and Country-and-Western (with the examples of LaVerne Baker, Lionel Hampton and his Band, and Ferlin Husky illustrating each)—he calls on his young listeners to prove they're not a bunch of hoodlums by raising money for the heart fund. The plot isn't much and none of the leads could act their way out of a paper bag, but with this much great music (over thirty songs!) in one film, such considerations fade into insignificance. Freed, Randazzo, Berry, Lymon, Baker, and The Moonglows had all appeared in ROCK, ROCK, ROCK the year before.

p, Ralph Serpe, Howard B. Kreitsek; d, Charles Dubin; w, James Blumgarten; ph, Morris Hartzband; ed, Angie Ross; md, Robert Rolontz.

Drama (PR:A MPAA:NR)

MR. SARDONICUS* (1961) 89m COL bw (AKA: SARDONICUS)

Ronald Lewis (Sir Robert Cargrave), Audrey Dalton (Maude Sardonicus), Guy Rolfe (Sardonicus), Oscar Homolka (Krull), Vladimar Sokoloff (Father), Erika Peters (Elenka), Tina Woodward (The Girl), Constance Cavendish (Mrs. Higgins), Mavis Neal (Head Nurse), Charles H. Radilac (Stationmaster), David Janti (Janku), Franz Roehn (Gravedigger), Annalena Lund (1st Girl), Ilse Burkert (2nd Girl), Albert

D'Arno (Gatekeeper), William Castle (Narrator), Lorna Hanson (Anna), James Forrest (Wainwright).

A tidy horror-thriller, which is more effective through its power of suggestion than it is through any shocking visuals, though there are a couple of incidents to satisfy those looking to be shocked. The story revolves around a rich baron, Rolfe, whose face has been permanently frozen into a wide grin after uncovering his father's corpse to get at a winning lottery ticket. This source of his great wealth has also become his lifelong misery. Rolfe insists upon having Lewis, a famous neurosurgeon and former lover of Rolfe's wife, attempt a solution for his problem. Rolfe himself had been experimenting on possible solutions, though more disagreeable than those of medical doctors, such as having Homolka, the one-eyed servant, attach leeches to pretty girls' faces. Lewis succeeds, but in doing so leaves Rolfe without the ability to eat or speak. The picture is filled with atmosphere, and keeps the suspense going throughout. Homolka gives a startling performance as the sinister servant.

p&d, William Castle; w, Ray Russell (based on a short story by Russell); ph, Burnett Guffey; m, Von Dexter; ed, Edwin Bryant; art d, Cary Odell; set d, James M. Crowe; makeup, Ben Lane.

Horror   (PR:C MPAA:NR)

MR. SATAN   (1938, Brit.) 79m WB-FN bw

Skeets Gallagher (Connelly), James Stephenson (Tim Garnett), Chili Bouchier (Jacqueline Manet), Franklin Dyall (Zubova), Betty Lynne (Conchita), Mary Cole (Billy), Robert Rendel (Seymour), Eric Clavering (Wilson), Dino Galvani (Scipio), Cot d'Ordan, Bryan Powley, Victor Fairley.

Stephenson is a war correspondent who locates Bouchier, the agent of unscrupulous armament monger Dyall, only to fall in love with her. Dyall fakes a suicide to throw off pursuers, then sinks a ship in an attempt to provoke a war. Bouchier kills her employer, but is herself mortally wounded. She dies in Stephenson's arms as the movie fades. Predictable action film at least keeps moving.

p, William Collier; d, Arthur Woods; w, John Meehan, Jr.; J.O.C. Orton; ph, Robert La Presle.

Crime   (PR:A MPAA:NR)

MR. SCOUTMASTER½   (1953) 87m FOX bw

Clifton Webb (Robert Jordan), Edmund Gwenn (Dr. Stone), George "Foghorn" Winslow (Mike), Frances Dee (Helen Jordan), Orley Lindgren (Ace), Veda Ann Borg (Blonde), Jimmy Moss (Vernon), Sammy Ogg (Harold Johnson), Jimmy Hawkins (Herbie), Skip Torgerson (Christy Kerns), Dee Aaker (Arthur), Mickey Little (Chick), Jon Gardner (Larry), Sarah Selby (Mrs. Weber), Amanda Randolph (Savannah), Otis Garth (Swanson), Teddy Infuhr (Lew Blodges), Harry Seymour (Customer), Bill McKenzie (Andy), Steve Brent (Sammy), Robert B. Williams (Motorcycle Policeman), Bob Sweeney (Hackett), Tina Thompson (Little Sister), Billy Nelson (Chauffeur), Stan Malotte (Mr. Weber), Gordon Nelson (Scout Executive), Dabbs Greer (Fireman), Dee Pollock (Scout No. 1), Martin Dean (Scout No. 2), Robert Winans (Bookworm Scout), Dick Fortune (Page Boy), Ralph Gamble (Executive), Tom Greenway (Doorman), Ned Glass (News Dealer), Mary Alan Hokanson, Kay Stewart, and Elizabeth Flournoy (Den Mothers).

Webb plays a television star whose show is being sponsored by the makers of a breakfast cereal. In order to find out something about boys and thus get more juvenile interest in his show, Webb becomes involved with the Boy Scouts. He goes through a change of heart, as he spends his time camping and hiking with the boys. The fatherless Webb becomes so attached to one boy, who has been living with a careless aunt, that he winds up adopting him. Webb adds a good humorous touch to the material, which, except for its lapses into sentiment, is well paced and convincing.

p, Leonard Goldstein; d, Henry Levin; w, Leonard Praskins, Barney Slater (based on the book by Rice E. Cochran); ph, Joseph La Shelle; m, Cyril Mockridge; ed, William B. Murphy; md, Lionel Newman; art d, Lyle Wheeler, Albert Hogsett; cos, Renie.

Comedy/Drama   (PR:A MPAA:NR)

MR. SEBASTIAN   (SEE: SEBASTIAN, 1968, Brit.)

MR. SKEFFINGTON*   (1944) 146m WB-FN bw

Bette Davis ("Fanny" Beatrice Trellis Skeffington), Claude Rains (Job Skeffington) Walter Abel (George Trellis), Richard Waring (Trippy Trellis), George Coulouris (Dr. Byles), Marjorie Riordan (Young Fanny), Robert Shayne (MacMahon), John Alexander (Jim Conderley), Jerome Cowan (Edward Morrison), Charles Drake (Johnny Mitchell), Dorothy Peterson (Manby), Peter Whitney (Chester Forbish), Bill Kennedy (Thatcher), Tom Stevenson (Rev. Hyslup), Halliwell Hobbes (Soames, Fanny's 1st Butler), Walter Kingsford (Dr. Melton), Gigi Perreau (Young Fanny at Age 2-5), Bunny Sunshine (Young Fanny at 5), Dolores Gray (Singer), Molly Lamont (Miss Morris, Secretary), Sylvia Arslan (Young Fanny at Age 10), Harry Bradley (The Rector), Creighton Hale (Casey, Employee), Ann Doran (Marie, Nursemaid), Georgia Caine (Mrs. Newton), Lelah Tyler (Mrs. Forbish), Mary Field (Mrs. Hyslup), Regina Wallace (Mrs. Conderly), Bess Flowers (Mrs. Thatcher), Edward Fielding (Justice of the Peace), Vera Lewis (Justice's Wife), Erskine Sanford (Dr. Fawcette), Cyril Ring (Perry Lanks), Crane Whitley (Louie, Speakeasy Owner), Matt McHugh, Will Stanton (Drunks), Saul Gorss (Plainclothesman), Ann Codee (French Modiste), Jac George (Henri), Dagmar Oakland (Woman), William Forrest (Clinton, Fanny's 2nd Butler), John Vosper (Artist), Janet Barrett (Witness), Frances Sage (Skeffington's First Secretary), Minerval Urecal (Woman in Beauty Shop), Joe Devlin (Boat Employee), Richard Erdman (Western Union Boy).

A long deluxe soap opera that follows Davis and Rains for 26 years and gives the audience the opportunity to watch Davis age (through some brilliant makeup by

Perc Westmore) and wind up looking not unlike she looked when she reached the age of the character in the film. Davis and Rains were nominated for Oscars but lost that year to Ingrid Bergman and Barry Fitzgerald (Best Supporting Actor) and rightly so. Both Davis and Rains had done far better work in other films before and would do so again. Davis is a gorgeous New York socialite who learns that her brother, Waring, is guilty of stealing money from Rains' bank in order to make up his gambling losses. She's informed of this by Rains himself, a bright financial Merlin who seems to be able to turn anything into profits. Rains is on the brink of prosecuting Waring, whom Davis dearly loves, but she persuades him not to and agrees to marry Rains in a loveless, but friendly union. Waring is outraged that his sister sacrificed her life because of him and he leaves town to join the British air corps and fight in the Great War that the U.S. had not yet entered. Waring is killed in the service and Davis is shattered, blaming her husband for her brother's death, as he never would have joined the service if she hadn't have married him (sort of a convoluted shifting of guilt, but necessary to motivate the rest of the plot). Davis is now pregnant by Rains, but that doesn't stop her from separating from him when the war ends. A divorce follows and Rains settles a lot of cash on Davis. Rains takes their daughter (who ages from Perreau [2] to Sunshine [5] to Arslan [10] and moves to Europe, while Davis continues to sleep with just about anyone in the U.S. who asks. Her marriage to Rains didn't stop her extramarital affairs and now that she's single, she increases the bedroom activity. WWII begins and Rains sends their daughter, now played by Riordan at 18, back to the States. Davis is currently dallying with Drake, a handsome engineer, and when they go on a sailing trip, Davis contracts the dread diptheria and barely manages to survive, but the disease causes her hair to fall out and her formerly beautiful face to be ravaged. Davis tries everything to look better, all the tricks of the makeup trade, but it's to no avail and she remains creased and crinkled. Davis is then stunned when Drake marries Riordan and they move to California. Davis is now totally on her own, almost disfigured, and there's not a man who would take her to bed unless she put two bags over her face. Abel, Davis' cousin, enters and tells her than Rains has returned from Europe. He's been the target of anti-Semitism, spent time in a Nazi concentration camp, and has come home without a sou, a deutsch mark, or a shilling in his threadbare pockets. Davis goes to visit Rains and discovers that he's now totally blind. Rains remembers Davis as being the most beautiful woman in the world, so when she says she would like nothing better than to spend the rest of her life taking care of him, Rains forgives all of her previous behavior and they embrace at the fade-out. The novel was by "Elizabeth." Davis had a tough job in going from girlish glee to churlish bitterness and she helped accomplish that by pitching her normally deep voice about eight notes higher when playing the younger role. Then, as the picture progressed, she lowered the tone until, by the time she reaches 50 or so (and looks 80), her voice is back to her normal bass-baritone. In essence, it's a morality play that says, "No matter what you do, your husband will be there when you need him." Maybe. If he's blind.

p, Philip G. Epstein, Julius J. Epstein, James Leicester (based on the novel by "Elizabeth" [Mary Annette Beauchamp Russell]); ph, Ernest Haller; m, Franz Waxman; ed, Ralph Dawson; md, Leo F. Forbstein; art d, Robert Haas; set d, Fred MacLean; cos, Orry-Kelly; makeup, Perc Westmore.

Drama   (PR:C MPAA:NR)

MR. SKITCH*½   (1933) 70m Fox bw

Will Rogers (Mr. Skitch), ZaSu Pitts (Mrs. Skitch), Rochelle Hudson (Emily Skitch), Florence Desmond (Flo), Harry Green (Cohen), Charles Starrett (Harvey Denby), Eugene Pallette (Cliff Merriweather).

Flawed picture has Rogers and Pitts as a hard-working farm couple from Missouri forced off their land and out of their home when they can't pay the mortgage. They take their family on a cross-country tour to Yellowstone Park and the Grand Canyon, where they meet more mishaps. All works out for the best in the end when their daughter Hudson meets and falls in love with an Army cadet. Plot suffers from loose ends and other unbelievable events, but the picture manages to deliver a few laughs.

d, James Cruze; w, Ralph Spence, Sonya Levien (based on the novel Green Dice by Anne Cameron); ph, John Seitz; md, Louis DeFrancesco; art d, William Darling; cos, Rita Kaufman.

Comedy   (PR:A MPAA:NR)

MR. SMITH CARRIES ON**

                    (1937, Brit.) 68m British and Dominions/PAR bw

Edward Rigby (Mr. Smith), Julien Mitchell (Mr. Minos), H. F. Maltby (Sir Felix), Dorothy Oldfield (Hilary Smith), Basil Langton (Jerry Stone), Franklyn Bellamy (Mr. Williams), Margaret Emden (Mrs. Smith), Frederick Culley (Mr. Fane), Dorothy Dewhurst, Jo Monkhouse.

Mitchell is a financier who tries to force clerk Rigby to help him defraud a group of investors. Rigby refuses and Mitchell threatens suicide. They struggle for the gun and, of course, it goes off, killing Mitchell. Rigby hides the body and takes over the company, making a deal that saves the company and everyone's money. The body is discovered and Rigby is arrested, but the police figure out the truth and he is freed. Routine melodrama indistinguishable from dozens like it.

p, Anthony Havelock-Allan; d, Lister Laurance; w, Ronald Gow (based on a story by John Cousins and Stephen Clarkson); ph, Francis Carver.

Crime   (PR:A MPAA:NR)

MR. SMITH GOES TO WASHINGTON***   (1939) 125m COL bw

Jean Arthur (Saunders), James Stewart (Jefferson Smith), Claude Rains (Sen. Joseph Paine), Edward Arnold (Jim Taylor), Guy Kibbee (Gov. Hubert Hopper), Thomas Mitchell (Diz Moore), Eugene Pallette (Chick McGann), Beulah Bondi (Ma Smith), H. B. Warner (Sen. Fuller), Harry Carey (President of the Senate), Astrid

Allwyn *(Susan Paine)*, Ruth Donnelly *(Mrs. Emma Hopper)*, Grant Mitchell *(Sen. MacPherson)*, Porter Hall *(Sen. Monroe)*, Pierre Watkin *(Sen. Barnes)*, Charles Lane *(Nosey)*, William Demarest *(Bill Griffith)*, Dick Elliott *(Carl Cook)*, H. V. Kaltenborn *(Broadcaster)*, Kenneth Carpenter *(Announcer)*, Jack Carson *(Sweeney)*, Maurice Costello *(Diggs)*, Allan Cavan *(Ragner)*, Frederick Hoose *(Senator)*, Joe King *(Summers)*, Paul Stanton *(Flood)*, Russell Simpson *(Allen)*, Stanley Andrews *(Sen. Hodges)*, Walter Soderling *(Sen. Pickett)*, Frank Jaquet *(Sen. Byron)*, Ferris Taylor *(Sen. Carlisle)*, Carl Stockdale *(Sen. Burdette)*, Alan Bridge *(Sen. Dwight)*, Edmund Cobb *(Sen. Gower)*, Frederick Burton *(Sen. Dearhorn)*, Vera Lewis *(Mrs. Edwards)*, Dora Clemant *(Mrs. McGann)*, Laura Treadwell *(Mrs. Taylor)*, Ann Doran *(Paine's Secretary)*, Douglas Evans *(Francis Scott Key)*, Lloyd Whitlock *(Schultz)*, Myonne Walsh *(Jane Hopper)*, Billy Watson, Delmar Watson, John Russell, Harry Watson, Garry Watson, Baby Dumpling *[Larry Simms], (The Hopper Boys)*, Clyde Dilson, William Newell, George Chandler, Evelyn Knapp, Dub Taylor, Jack Gardner, Donald Kerr, Eddie Kane, George McKay, Gene Morgan, Matt McHugh, William Arnold, Hal Cooke, James McNamara, Jack Egan, Eddy Chandler *(Reporters)*, Eddie Fetherston, Ed Randolph, Milton Kibbee, Vernon Dent, Craig Stevens, Ed Brewer, Anne Cornwall, James Millican, Mabel Forrest, Nick Copeland, Dulce Daye *(Senate Reporters)*, Byron Foulger *(Hopper's Secretary)*, Margaret Mann *(Nun)*, Fred "Snowflake" Toone, Charles Moore *(Porters)*, Frances Gifford, Adrian Booth, Linda Winters, [Dorothy Comingore] *(Girls)*, Mary Gordon, June Gittelson, Lorna Gray *(Women)*.

The essence of this great and wonderful film is best summarized in the thought that the only necessity for the triumph of evil is that good men do nothing. Stewart gives the performance of his career, matched only in another Capra classic seven years later, IT'S A WONDERFUL LIFE. Here Capra goes to the deepest roots of his beliefs, showing American democratic ideals in peril with only the naive, the gullible, the pure of spirit to lead the nation back to its principles. Stewart, just as Gary Cooper was the guy down the block, was the boy next door, hard-working, honest, decent in every respect, someone to be counted on, no matter the crisis, no matter the lurking doom. Here he is a rural bumpkin who heads the Boy Rangers in his state and, when the incumbent U.S. senator for that state dies, the governor, Kibee, and political bigwig Arnold decide that he would be the ideal fill-in senator since he is wholly naive and will take orders from the state's esteemed senior senator, Rains. It's all a dream come true for Stewart who goes to Washington with the aim of improving his state. Arnold and Rains, of course, expect Stewart to be nothing more than a rubber stamp to their crooked legislation, chiefly a pork-barreling scheme to finance a new dam in the state that will enrich their real estate holdings. The Washington press corps greeting Stewart when he gets off the train quickly realize that he's a gullible novice and they quickly wisecrack him into performing bird calls and posing like the native Indians of his state, photos which later appear in the local press and hold Stewart up to ridicule. He meets beautiful Allwyn, Rains' daughter, and is agog. Before going to his duties, Stewart rubbernecks the capital, culminating in a moving scene before the Lincoln Monument where an old black man standing with his grandson reads the spine-tingling inscription at the base of the statue while Stewart beams with pride and patriotism. Going to his office, Stewart meets Arthur, a Washington-wise, cynical secretary assigned to him, a woman so fed up with political back-stabbing and intrigues—as she has told press secretary Mitchell—that she wants to quit. Stewart's innocent ways, however, immediately captivate her and she stays on to see what this unpredictable young man will do next. When Stewart reads the stories about himself which describe him as an "incompetent clown" he fumes and rages and quickly indicts himself as having brought disgrace upon his state, its people, and mostly his idol, Rains. "The Silver Knight" of the Senate, as Rains is called, soothes the young man by telling him he can still do good by sponsoring a bill for a national boy's camp, Stewart's pet project, that he must stay on to complete that job. Stewart enthusiastically and tirelessly begins drafting the bill with Arthur at his side. She at first thinks he's a bit too idealistic but he quickly sets her straight by pointing out what kind of spirit the bill must entail, while gesturing out a window to the floodlit capitol dome: "Liberty is too precious a thing to be buried in books, Miss Saunders. Men should hold it up in front of them every single day of their lives and say, 'I'm free, to think and to speak.' My ancestors couldn't. I can. And my children will." Later, when Stewart describes his western state with its "lazy streams" and "tall grasses," she falls in love with the image and with Stewart himself, defending him to cynics like Mitchell and others. Then Arthur learns that Arnold, Kibbee, and Rains are in a conspiracy to use the very site of the boy's camp for a useless dam which will enhance their own fortunes. She explains the grim facts of life to naive Stewart but the apprentice senator will not believe the boondoggle. He goes to Rains who not only confirms Arthur's discovery but gently, firmly, tells Stewart where he really stands: "You've been living in a boy's world . . . You have to check your ideals outside the door like you do your rubbers. I've had to compromise. I've had to play ball. That's how states and empires have been built since time began." The blow is devastating to Stewart since Rains is not only his boyhood idol but one of the best friends of his idealistic father, a newspaper editor who had been killed in championing freedom. Stewart challenges Rains and angrily tells him that he won't sacrifice his principles for some cheap, shoddy deal to make money. He tells Rains that he will expose the corrupt scheme, but Rains is too fast for him, announcing in the Senate that Stewart is the crook, that he owns the very land upon which the boy's camp was to be built, and that he is only enriching himself with his ostensibly noble bill. To compound this vicious lie, Rains even produces a deed to the land with Stewart's name forged on it, and offers this up as evidence to his fellow senators who, in turn, explode in wrath and demand Stewart be impeached and kicked out of their august body. Stewart is crushed, admitting to Arthur that he is finished. She won't have it, she tells him, tossing aside her jaded perspective and opting for optimistic battle. Fight, she tells him, and outlines how he can filibuster until he finds enough evidence through his friends in his own state to prove his case. The next morning Stewart arrives at his desk in the Senate, armed for battle, bringing food and books. He tells the Senate how Rains, Arnold, and others are really using the Willet Creek site to establish a fake dam and line their own pockets. Meanwhile, Stewart's mother, Bondi, and others organize an army of young boys who print up the truth, put up banners, and lead parades, distributing handbills to support Stewart's claim. The children are roughed up, their materials destroyed by an army of goons under Arnold's orders; the newspaper magnate has directed that all information about Stewart's heroic fight in the Senate be censored. The voters of Stewart's state only know the lies he, Arnold, spreads through his newspapers and radio stations. Yet, Stewart plunges on hour after hour, holding the floor, lambasting the corrupt political powers who rob the citizens of their birthright, working on Rains and his softening conscience. There are few in the Senate who sympathize with Stewart, most believing him to be an adventurer and a crook. But the President of the Senate, Carey, knowingly shows his empathy, helping the young man when he can. For 23 hours (in one of the great virtuoso performances in the history of film) Stewart battles off one challenge after another until, exhausted, he is suddenly confronted with stacks and stacks of letters and telegrams, reportedly from people from his state but all manufactured by Arnold and his army of stooges, which demand he quit his position. Stewart staggers forth and inspects the baskets full of phony wires and letters, grabbing two handfuls and holding them up (resembling the image of the crucifixion) and hoarsely states to his one-time benefactor, Rains: "I guess this is just another lost cause, Mr. Paine. All you people don't know about the lost causes. Mr. Paine does. He said once they were the only causes worth fighting for. And he fought for them once, for the only reason that any man ever fights for them. Because of just one plain simple rule: 'Love thy neighbor.' And in this world today, full of hatred, a man who knows that one rule has a great trust." Stewart knows his own strength is now failing and he cannot go on but his spirit is indomitable: "You all think I'm licked. Well, I'm not licked and I'm going to stay right here and fight for this lost cause even if this room gets filled with lies like these and the Taylors [Arnold] and all their armies come marching into this place. Somebody'll listen to me . . . some . . . " Stewart collapses as Arthur screams from the gallery where she has been watching, in anguish over his plight. But the strain of witnessing Stewart also shows on Rains, whose guilt now is overwhelming. He goes to the cloak room and a shot rings out. He is next seen struggling with other senators who prevent him from taking his own life; he breaks away from those holding him and bursts into the Senate to loudly confess before his peers that Stewart is innocent and that he and others are the crooks, but "not that boy!" A miracle has happened, a Frank Capra miracle, but a miracle nevertheless. The enemies of democracy and freedom have collapsed from within and Stewart is not only vindicated but has triumphed along with Arthur, his lady love, and all the young boys and those who have not lost their faith in mankind. Capra's masterpiece is about all that and more, even reaffirming the ugly fact that the Arnolds of the world with their private police forces, their seemingly limitless power and money to buy and force public opinion to their will, are very much with us. The film is all style and each scene is emotion-packed, sapping the viewer but in a healthy, invigorating way. And it is moral without being hortatory or academic; this is no civic lesson but one of the most important filmic documents ever made, for it chronicles through the eyes and speech of the magnificent Stewart the true human values that make up the heart, muscle, and soul of America. Capra uses every technique available, long shots, quick cuts in closeup, montages that convey an accelerated story line without disrupting it. Here every move has a meaning, even those of the great supporting players, all endorsing Capra's credo of "one man, one film." Though Stewart is naive to begin with, the film is sophisticated in its relentless showing of raw power and yet the sophistication withers under the emotional blast of truth. Oscar nominations for this film reached 11, including one for Best Actor, Stewart, Best Director, Best Picture and Rains and Carey for Best Supporting Player, but the single Oscar won was for Best Original Story by Foster. This was Stewart's first Oscar nomination but he was eased out by Robert Donat for GOODBYE, MR. CHIPS in a stellar year of acting and production. Yet the film served to really launch Stewart's career and he became a major star because of it, soon appearing in such films as DESTRY RIDES AGAIN with Marlene Dietrich and THE SHOP AROUND THE CORNER with Margaret Sullavan. The Foster story upon which the film is based was purchased by director Rouben Mamoulian, but when Columbia chief Harry Cohn went to buy it for Capra, offering Mamoulian $75,000 for it, the director mysteriously rejected the bid. Only when Cohn allowed Mamoulian to direct a film he wanted desperately to helm, GOLDEN BOY, did the director sell the rights to the Foster story, amazing the dollar-conscious Cohn by accepting not $75,000, but only what he had paid for it, $1,500. Once Capra got hold of the story, it was suggested that Gary Cooper, star of Capra's MR. DEEDS GOES TO TOWN, play in the film that was tentatively entitled MR. DEEDS GOES TO WASHINGTON but Capra wanted someone utterly naive, an actor almost boyish, and he immediately seized upon Stewart, retaining Arthur, his first choice, as the cynical secretary. His erstwhile assistant director, Art Black, shot all the background film in Washington, D.C., capturing the monuments and busy streets and this was rear-projected on the Hollywood set where the film was made. Capra himself went to Washington and hired Senate expert Jim Preston who showed him the Senate Chamber when empty. Said Capra to Preston when viewing the most august political chamber in America, one housing the country's most exclusive club: "First thing, I want you to arrange for our crew to come in here and photograph all the details—inkwells, pencils, stationery, everything down to the hole the Union soldier kicked in Jeff Davis' desk the day Jeff walked out to join the Confederacy. Later on you will come to Hollywood to help me select 96 actors to fill those desks—that look like real senators." Art director Banks reproduced the Senate Chamber down to the last detail. Capra picked Carey to play the Vice President and President of the Senate because of his "strong American face." The great cowboy star, who had been in films since 1908, raced to see Capra when the part was offered but he doubted he could present the required image. During the first takes when he was supposed to administer the oath of office to Stewart the veteran horse opera star muffed his lines repeatedly. Not wishing to further embarrass Carey, Capra called a lunch break and when the cast returned he took Carey aside and told him: "Harry, while the cameras are still set up, let's try the scene again. This time, remember this. The people of America have elected you as their Vice President. You are just one heart tick away from the White House. Forget Harry Carey the cowboy actor. Swear this new senator in as Harry Carey the Vice President of the United States." Carey squared his shoulders and delivered his lines perfectly. There was no element of the production that Capra did not personally supervise in detail. He met with temperamental score composer Tiomkin and told him to forget the music of European composers, to think only about native American themes and folk music. Replied the thick-accented Tiomkin: " . . . in my head is notes like apple pie so American." While shooting the end of Stewart's filibuster, Capra realized that his voice was not hoarse enough for a man who had been supposedly talking for 23 hours and he called in a physician who induced the hoarseness by swabbing Stewart's throat with a mercury solution so that his vocal cords would swell and when struggling to speak in this condition Stewart achieved what Capra had been looking for. When the film was completed the Washington Press Club sponsored a premier showing at the DAR's huge Constitution Hall on October 16, 1939. Choruses sang, bands played patriotic hymns and marches, and the hall filled up with senators, congressmen, Supreme Court justices, all of the Georgetown political aristocracy, more than 4,000 viewers. Harry Cohn and other studio executives occupied a box reserved for Columbia; this was the greatest publicity coup ever gleaned by any Hollywood studio and Cohn was swelling with pride. Capra was introduced and was met with deafening applause. Then the film was run. Two-thirds of the way through people began walking out, others grumbling and making thumbs-down gestures. The political bigwigs began to shout: "Outrage!" and "Insult!" It was turning into a nightmare for Capra who froze in his seat. He glanced to the Cohn box and it was empty; the mogul had fled at the first grumble. Later, Capra courageously sat through a dinner at the Press Club where its members assaulted him verbally, calling him every name in the book for even daring to show graft lifting its hideous head in the Senate and for showing Mitchell, one of their number, as a heavy drinker. The newsmen protested too much; one editor of a Washington daily protested Capra's showing Washington reporters as imbibers, and, while thoroughly himself drunk, tried to hit the director and fell flat on his face. Capra and his wife escaped the carnage when sympathetic film critics from New York who had loved and praised the film, ran physical interference for the couple as they fled the Press Club. The Washington press corps, however, continued the attacks in its newspapers, vilifying Capra as being so presumptuous as to even suggest anything bad could happen in the Senate. Capra rightly assumed they were jealous and fearful that their "private preserve" of news and their ability to manipulate public opinion had been transgressed and trespassed by Hollywood. Several politicians angrily spoke against MR. SMITH GOES TO WASHINGTON, not the least of whom was Sen. Alben W. Barkley, later Vice President of the U.S. Barkley told a reporter for *The Christian Science Monitor* that the film was a "grotesque distortion" of how the Senate was run, "as grotesque as anything ever seen! Imagine the Vice President of the United States winking at a pretty girl in the gallery in order to encourage a filibuster! Can you visualize Jack Garner winking up at Hedy Lamarr in order to egg her on? . . . And it showed the Senate as the biggest aggregation of nincompoops on record! At one place the picture shows the senators walking out on Mr. Smith as a body when he is attacked by a corrupt member. The very idea of the Senate walking out at the behest of that old crook! It was so grotesque it was funny. It showed the Senate made up of crooks, led by crooks, listening to a crook . . . It was so vicious an idea it was a source of disgust and hilarity to every member of Congress who saw it." When asked if any of his fellows liked the film, Barkley fumed: "I did not hear a single senator praise it . . . I speak for the whole body. The vote was 96 to 0 and no filibuster." Other politicians chimed in, echoing Barkley's sentiments, but they gave Capra that suspicious feeling that they were protecting not a governmental entity but a very private club which had been invaded by the interloping director. Sen. James F. Byrnes, a Democrat from South Carolina, labeled the film "outrageous . . . exactly the kind of picture that dictators of totalitarian governments would like to have their subjects believe exists in a democracy." Here Byrnes was heralding the possibility of governmental action against the film and films like it. Certain newsmen mounted a similar attack, saying that foreigners might get the distinct idea that elected officials were recruited from jails. Another report, this one printed by Hollywood columnist Jimmy Fidler, had it that Columbia had been offered $2 million to scrap MR. SMITH GOES TO WASHINGTON, a payment to be made by several other movie studios fearful of government censorships. Harry Cohn of Columbia nevertheless released the film and where Barkley and the U.S. Senate may have universally condemned the film, the American public flocked to see it, endorsed it, loved it for the masterpiece that it was and still is. Yet pressures kept coming in the film's first few months of release for it to be suppressed. Even Joseph P. Kennedy, ambassador to Britain, sent Cohn a telegram, telling him that it was a blow to American prestige and weakened the morale of America's allies; Kennedy urged Cohn to withdraw the film from European release. Cohn nervously showed the telegram to Capra who told his boss, as quoted from the director's autobiography, *The Name Above the Title*: "Harry, no ambassador has the right to censor films. Besides, he's mistaken . . . we are what we are and Mr. Smith is what he is—a shot in the arm for all the Joes in the world that resent being bought and sold and pushed around by all the Hitlers in the world." Cohn, egotist and swaggering mogul that he was, was ever mindful of powers greater than he that could reach out and hurt if not destroy little Columbia Studio. Yet he stood firm with Capra. The film was not withdrawn from any theater in any part of the world lucky enough to book it. It was and is one of Capra's greatest films. And for Harry Cohn, the so-called insensitive, money-grubbing, wheeler-dealer, it was his finest hour.

p&d, Frank Capra; w, Sidney Buchman (based on the book *The Gentleman from Montana* by Lewis R. Foster); ph, Joseph Walker; m, Dimitri Tiomkin; ed, Gene Havlick, Al Clark; md, Morris Stoloff; art d, Lionel Banks; cos, Kalloch; tech adv, Jim Preston.

Drama **Cas.** **(PR:AAA MPAA:NR)**

MR. SOFT TOUCH** (1949) 92m COL bw (GB: HOUSE OF SETTLEMENT)

Glen Ford *(Joe Miracle)*, Evelyn Keyes *(Jenny Jones)*, John Ireland *("Early" Byrd)*, Beulah Bondi *(Mrs. Hangale)*, Percy Kilbride *(Rickle)*, Clara Blandick *(Susan Balmuss)*, Ted de Corsia *(Rainey)*, Stanley Clements *(Yonzi)*, Roman Bohnen *(Barney Teener)*, Harry Shannon *(Sgt. Garret)*, Gordon Jones *(Muggles)*, Jack Gordon *(Fanner)*, Ray Mayer *(Victor Christopher)*, Angela Clarke *(Clara Christopher)*, Mikel Conrad *(Officer Miller)*, Charles Trowbridge *(Judge Fuller)*, Lora Lee Michel *(Sonya)*, William Rhinehart *(Al)*, Leon Tyler *(Percentage)*, William Edmunds *(Alex)*.

Ford stars as a hunted gambler who has robbed a gambling institution of money he considers rightfully his. He takes refuge in a settlement house run by social worker Keyes, who mistakes Ford for a wife beater. The two eventually fall in love, with Ford devoting himself to helping the underprivileged. The use of two directors, Levin and Douglas, shows in the uneven pace and the stereotyped performances.

p, Milton Holmes; d, Henry Levin, Gordon Douglas; w, Orin Jannings (based on a story by Holmes); ph, Joseph Walker, Charles Lawton, Jr.; m, M.W. Stoloff; ed, Richard Fantl; md, Stoloff; art d, George Brooks; cos, Jean Louis.

Drama **(PR:A MPAA:NR)**

MR. STRINGFELLOW SAYS NO**

(1937, Brit.) 76m Incorporated Talking Films/National Provincial bw (AKA: ACCIDENTAL SPY)

Neil Hamilton *(Jeremy Stringfellow)*, Claude Dampier *(Mr. Piper)*, Muriel Aked *(Mrs. Piper)*, Kathleen Gibson *(Miss Piper)*, Marcelle Rogez *(Marta)*, Franklin Dyall *(Count Hokana)*, Peter Gawthorne *(Prime Minister)*.

Hamilton is a mild-mannered church youth group leader who becomes entangled in international intrigue when a car driven by a spy crashes through his house. The spy tries to tell Hamilton an important secret, but dies before he can finish. Soon everyone is after Hamilton, and after escaping both an airplane and the Tower of London, he is knighted and elected to Parliament. The material could have been handled better, but a good romp nonetheless.

p, Brandon Fleming, Reginald Gottwitz, d, Randall Faye; w, Faye, Fleming.

Comedy **(PR:A MPAA:NR)**

MR. SUPERINVISIBLE**

(1974, Ital./Span./Ger.) 90m Edo-Producciones Cinematographica Dia-Peter Carsten/K-Tel c (L'INAFFERRABILE INVINCIBLE; EL INVENCIBLE HOMBRE INVISIBLE; AKA: MR. INVISIBLE)

Dean Jones, Gastone Moschin, Ingeborg Schoener, Peter Carsten, Amalia de Isaura, Roberto Camardiel.

A European attempt to duplicate Disney's successful family comedy format. They thought by placing Dean Jones in a starring role and employing the gimmick of invisibility they would produce a hit. Jones is a scientist who invents a new virus which is a valuable tool in fighting germ warfare. He and his sheepdog spend half of their screen time invisible and unseen while trying to recover the lost drug. K-Tel, the masters of a number of useless TV-advertised products, tried to sell this one by offering a free trip to Disneyland.

p, Peter Carsten; d, Anthony Dawson [Antonio Margheriti]; w, Mary Eller, Oscar Saul [Luis Marquina]; ph, Allejandro Ulloa (Technicolor).

Fantasy/Children's Comedy **(PR:AAA MPAA:G)**

MR. SYCAMORE* (1975) 87m Capricorn/Film Venture c

Jason Robards, Jr. *(John Gwilt)*, Sandy Dennis *(Jane Gwilt)*, Jean Simmons *(Estelle Benbow)*, Robert Easton *(Fred Staines)*, Brenda Smith *(Daisy)*, Mark Miller *(Rev. Fletcher)*, Richard Bull *(Dr. Ferfield)*, Ian Wolfe *(Abner/Arnie)*, Lou Picetti *(Humphrey)*, David Osterhout *(Officer Kelly)*, Jerome Thor *(Higgins)*, Curtis Taylor *(Harry)*, Paul Berini, Eddie Lewis *(Milkmen)*, Darby Hinton *(Frank)*, Synda Scott *(Clubwoman)*, Ron D'Ippolito. Richard Redd *(Attendants)*, Hall Brock *(Albert)*, Twana Nugent *(Albert's Sister)*, Don Spector, Wayne Smith *(Workmen)*, Walter Scott *(Truck Driver)*, Janine Johnson *(Piano Student)*, Everet Smith *(Officer)*, Lance Cremer *(Newsboy)*.

A strange curiosity piece that might have made some sense if whimsy had been injected, but failed to make any noise because it lay there like a lump of clay on the eyes. Robards is a weak-willed postman married to an all-time shrew, Dennis, who is so overbearing that Robards decides the only way to escape her is to metamorphosize into a tree (hence the title)! In passing, Robards has a fantasy romance with the town librarian, Simmons, but that's all in his head. Along the way, Robards goes from a sympathetic to a self-centered man and we lose any feeling of caring about him, something we never have for the preposterous, posturing Dennis, whose acting tricks pall very quickly. When she first came on the screen in SPLENDOR IN THE GRASS, her nervous and quirky mannerisms were thought to be a breakthrough in realistic acting. But she's done that same sort of irritating thing throughout her career and it came to a head in THE THREE SISTERS, after a career that had her in some excellent films like WHO'S AFRAID OF VIRGINIA WOOLF? UP THE DOWN STAIRCASE, and THE OUT OF TOWNERS, and audiences saw that's just about *all* she does. Easton is better known off-screen in Hollywood where he is acknowledged as the best dialect teacher in the industry. Simmons might as well as have phoned her role in for all the impact she has and Robards should be ashamed of himself for ever getting involved with such tripe. There is a story here, somewhere under all the embarrassing dialog, but it's too much trouble to find it. The one song, "Time Goes By," has nothing to do with Herman Hupfeld's classic, "As Time Goes By," which was a hit many years before Dooley Wilson faked it at the piano in CASABLANCA.

p&d, Pancho Kohner; w, Kohner, Ketti Frings (based on a story by Robert Ayre and a play by Frings); ph, John Morrill (CFI Color); m, Maurice Jarre; ed, George Van Noy, Andrew Herbert; art d, Charles French; m/l, "Time Goes By," Paul Francis Webster.

Comedy/Drama   (PR:A   MPAA:NR)

MISTER TEN PERCENT* 1/2   (1967, Brit.) 84m AB/WPD c

Charlie Drake (Percy Pointer), Derek Nimmo (Tony), Wanda Ventham (Kathy), John Le Mesurier (Jocelyn Macauley), Anthony Nicholls (Casey), Noel Dyson (Mrs. Gorman), John Hewer (Townsend), Anthony Gardner (Claude Crepe), Ronald Radd (Publicist), John Laurie (Scotsman), Annette Andre (Muriel), Justine Lord (Lady Dorothea), George Baker (Lord Edward), Joyce Blair (Lady Dorothea), Una Stubbs (Lady Dorothea).

Terrible comedy about a builder with artistic pretensions who writes a serious drama, only to have it taken as a comedy and become a great success. Fortunately the British didn't export this one.

p, W.A. Whittaker; d, Peter Graham Scott; w, Norman Hudis, Charlie Drake (based on a story by Mira Avrech).

Comedy   (PR:A   MPAA:NR)

MR. TOPAZE   (SEE: I LIKE MONEY, 1961, Brit.)

MR. UNIVERSE**   (1951) 79m Laurel/EL bw

Jack Carson (Jeff Clayton), Janis Paige (Lorraine), Vincent Edwards (Tommy Tomkins), Bert Lahr (Joe Pulaski), Robert Alda (Fingers Maroni), Dennis James, Maxie Rosenbloom, Joyce Matthews, Harry Landers, Donald Novis, Murray Rothenberg.

Low budget take-off on professional wrestling has Carson and Lahr trying to promote their new wonder Edwards. The honest and hard-working Edwards proves to be better than the managers had expected, as he wins a bout they were trying to prep him to lose, thus winning the bet they had made against him. Outside the wrestling ring the plot falters, but otherwise the picture offers some well-rounded humor, especially in its caricatures of wrestlers and other types who hang around the ring.

p&d, Joseph Lerner; w, Searle Kramer; ph, Gerald Hirschfield; m, Dimitri Tiomkin; ed, Geraldine Lerner; md, Tiomkin.

Comedy   (PR:A   MPAA:NR)

MISTER V   (SEE: PIMPERNEL SMITH, 1941, Brit.)

MR. WALKIE TALKIE**   (1952) 65m Rockingham/Lippert bw

William Tracy (Sgt. Doubleday), Joe Sawyer (Sgt. Ames), Margia Dean (Entertainer), Russell Hicks (Col. Lockwood), Robert Shayne (Capt. Burke), Frank Jenks (Jackson), Alan Hale, Jr. (Tiny), Wong Artarne (Lt. Kim).

Sawyer plays a soldier during the Korean War who asks for a transfer to the front lines in order to get away from Tracy, a sergeant with a photographic mind who never shuts up. But his peace doesn't last for long as Tracy is among the first set of new recruits to the front line, forcing the two to start up their feud again. Loose story offers some genuinely funny antics, with Sawyer and Tracy taking the whole show. Margia Dean sings one song, "I Love the Men" (Leon Klatzkin, Tom Adair).

p, Hal Roach, Jr.; d, Fred L. Guiol; w, Edward Seabrook, George Carleton Brown; ph, Walter Strenge; m, Leon Klatzkin; ed, Roy Luby.

Comedy   (PR:A   MPAA:NR)

MR. WASHINGTON GOES TO TOWN**   (1941) 64m Dixie National bw

F. E. [Flournoy E.] Miller (Wallingford), Mantan Moreland (Schenectady), Maceo B. Sheffield (Brutus), Arthur Ray (Blackstone), Marguerite Whitten (Lady Queenie), Clarence Morehouse (Gorilla), Monty Hawley (Stilletto), Zoreta Steptoe (Mrs. Brutus), Florence O'Brien (Chambermaid).

The competition between two black men, Moreland and Miller, to obtain possession of a hotel serves as the backdrop for some crazy antics and absurd situations. Well-paced direction and witty script keep this all-black comedy zesty, despite its rather weak plot.

p&d, Jed Bruell; w, Walter Weems, Lex Neal (based on a story by Weems); ph, Jack Greenhalgh; m, Harvey Brooks; ed, William Faris.

Comedy   (PR:A   MPAA:NR)

MR. WHAT'S-HIS-NAME** 1/2   (1935, Brit.) 67m WB/FN bw

Seymour Hicks (Alfred Henfield/Mons. Herbert Herbert), Olive Blakeney (Ann Henfield), Enid Stamp-Taylor (Corinne Henfield), Garry Marsh (Yates), Tonie Edgar Bruce (Sylvia), Martita Hunt (Mrs. Davies), Henry Longhurst (Mr. Bullen), Louis Broughton (Mr. Holt), Margaret Damer, Arthur Metcalfe, Dorothy Hammond, Eric Hales, Reg Marcus, Bombardier Billy Wells, Gunner Moir.

Hicks is a millionaire pickle entrepreneur who loses his memory in a train crash. He eventually opens a beauty salon and marries one of the hairdressers. He finds himself through circumstances in his old home, where his wife has remarried, believing herself a widow. His amnesia clears up and he forgets about the years between. Clever script competently rendered.

p, Irving Asher; d, Ralph Ince; w, Tom Geraghty, Frank Launder (based on a play by Yves Mirande, Seymour Hicks); ph, Basil Emmott.

Comedy   (PR:A   MPAA:NR)

MR. WINKLE GOES TO WAR**

(1944) 80m COL bw (GB: ARMS AND THE WOMAN)

Edward G. Robinson (Wilbert George Winkle), Ruth Warrick (Amy Winkle), Ted Donaldson (Barry), Bob Haymes (Jack Pettigrew), Richard Lane (Sgt. "Alphabet"), Robert Armstrong (Joe Tinker), Richard Gaines (Ralph Wescott), Walter Baldwin (Plummer), Art Smith (McDavid), Ann Shoemaker (Martha Pettigrew), Paul Stanton (A.B. Simkins), Buddy Yarus (Johnson), William Forrest (Captain), Bernadine Hayes (Gladys), Jeff Donnell (Hostess No. 1), Howard Freeman (Mayor), Nancy Evans, Ann Loos (Girls), Larry Thompson (M.P.), Warren Ashe (Captain), James Flavin (Sergeant No. 1), Bob [Robert] Mitchum (Corporal), Herbert Hayes (Doctor), Fred Kohler, Jr. (Sergeant No. 2), Fred Lord (Draftee No. 1), Cecil Ballerino (Draftee No. 2), Ted Holley (Draftee No. 3), Ben Taggart, Sam Flint, Nelson Leigh, Forbes Murray, Ernest Hilliard (Doctors), Les Sketchley, Ed Jenkins, Paul Stupin (Draftees), Terry Frost (M.P.), Hugh Beaumont (Range Officer), Dennis Moore (Sergeant), Emmett Vogan (Barber), Tommy Cook (4th Kid).

It's hard to say "Mr. Winkle Goes to War" without adding "ee-eye-ee-eye-oh!" With a title like that, one would expect a war comedy, but this film was made and released at the height of WW II and the country was taking matters rather seriously. Robinson stars in a role that required a serious imagination-stretch to accept because he's seen as a wimpy bank clerk who is approaching the age when men are no longer drafted into the service. He's been at the same financial institution for almost 15 years and has had it up to here, so he quits and decides to spend his time making a living with his avocation, a repair shop he's built next to his house. When wife Warrick won't put up with his behavior, she tells him that he must either return to his job at the bank or leave the house and move into the fix-it shop. He is now cowed by her ultimatum and chooses to ensconce himself next to his repair tools. A draft notice comes in the mail and Robinson is certain he'll never be able to pass the physical. He goes to the induction center and meets Haymes, the son of a pal, and both pass the physical and are sent to basic training, where they meet Lane and Armstrong. At the age of 44, Robinson has to battle to get through training, but when he does, he is justifiably proud and refuses to leave the service, even when the maximum age is lowered to 38. The quartet is shipped to the Far East. A bulldozer needs repair and Robinson is the only man with the know-how to do it, so he races across fields strafed by Japanese guns, fixes the bulldozer, then, as guns blaze, rides it into a foxhole where the Japanese are crushed by its weight. He is wounded in the fracas and is taken to a hospital where he learns that Lane and Armstrong are dead. Robinson is honorably discharged with several awards given for heroism and goes home to his small town where a huge welcome home celebration has been planned for him. Still a modest man, he avoids the hoopla and goes straight to his repair shack where Warrick awaits him. They embrace and he is invited to come back into the house. There is some humor in the film, but it's not easy to take tough guy Robinson as a mild-mannered nerd, even though he tries mightily. Note Robert Mitchum in a small role as a corporal. They mixed in real war footage with the staged scenes and it looked fairly authentic.

p, Jack Moss; d, Alfred E. Green; w, Waldo Salt, George Corey, Louis Solomon (based on the novel by Theodore Pratt); ph, Joseph Walker; m, Carmen Dragon, Paul Sawtell; ed, Richard Fantl; md, M.W. Stoloff; art d, Lionel Banks, Rudolph Sternad; m/l, "Sweet Genevieve" (sung by Bob Haymes).

War   (PR:A   MPAA:NR)

MR. WISE GUY**   (1942) 70m Banner/MON bw

Leo Gorcey (Ethelbert "Muggs" McGinnis), Bobby Jordan (Danny Collins), Huntz Hall (Glimpy Stone), Billy Gilbert (Knobby), Guinn "Big Boy" Williams (Luke Manning), Warren Hymer (Dratler), Gabriel Dell (Rice Pudding Charlie), Joan Barclay (Ann Mitchell), Douglas Fowley (Bill Collins), "Sunshine Sammy" Morrison (Scruno), David Gorcey (Peewee), Bobby Stone (Chalky Jones), Ann Doran (Dorothy Melton), Benny Rubin (Waiter), Bill Lawrence (Skinny), Jack Mulhall (Jim Barnes), Dick Ryan (Jed Miller) Sidney Miller ("Charlie Horse"), Joe Kirk.

East Side Kids are wrongly accused of stealing a truck and sent off to reform school. One of the brothers of the boys has been accused of murder and is sentenced to death. But when the boys notice on a newsreel that a trucker they earlier helped is picking up a lottery ticket, they put two and two together and solve the crime. They break out of reform school just in time to save the condemned brother. Story suffers from lapses in plot, weak character development, and overlooked plot situations. Boys still manage to give their usual entertaining performances. (See BOWERY BOYS series, Index.)

p, Sam Katzman, Jack Dietz; d, William Nigh; w, Sam Robins, Harvey Gates, Jack Henley (based on a story by Martin Mooney); ph, Art Reed; ed, Carl Pierson; md, Johnny Lange, Lew Porter; art d, G.C. Van Marter.

Drama/Comedy   Cas.   (PR:A   MPAA:NR)

MR. WONG AT HEADQUARTERS   (SEE: FATAL HOUR, 1940)

MR. WONG, DETECTIVE**   (1938) 70m MON bw

Boris Karloff (James Lee Wong), Grant Withers (Capt. Sam Street), Maxine Jennings (Myra, Dayton's Secretary), Evelyn Brent (Olga), Lucien Prival (Mohl), John St. Polis (Karl Roemer), William Gould (Meisel), Hooper Atchley (Wilk), John Hamilton (Dayton), Frank Bruno (Lascari), Lee Tong Fu (Tchain), George Lloyd (Devlin), Wilbur Mack, Grace Wood, Lynton Brent.

The first detective film that Karloff made in the CHARLIE CHAN-MR. MOTO vein, which of course had him speaking with his British tone of voice. A chemical manufacturer, Hamilton has purchased the rights to a deadly but odorless poisonous gas, bringing anonymous death threats against him. He seeks the help of Karloff, but the following day, Hamilton is gassed to death, as are two of his business partners. Karloff and San Francisco police captain Withers encounter a gang of international spies, who want the gas formula to give to a foreign government. Karloff discovers that the deadly gas has been sealed in a glass bulb which ends up shattering from the shrill sounds of a police siren. Karloff reveals that the real murderer is the inventor, who thought he was being taken by his partners. This film was remade as the CHARLIE CHAN film DOCKS OF NEW ORLEANS. (See MR WONG series, Index.)

p, Scott R. Dunlap; d, William Nigh; w, Houston Branch (based on Hugh Wiley's stories); ph, Harry Neumann; ed, Russell Schoengarth; md, Art Meyer; makeup, Gordon Bau.

Mystery/Crime   **Cas.**   **(PR:A   MPAA:NR)**

MR. WONG IN CHINATOWN**   (1939) 70m MON bw

Boris Karloff (James Lee Wong), Grant Withers (Inspector Sam Street), Marjorie Reynolds (Bobby Logan), Peter George Lynn (Capt. Jackson), William Royle (Capt. Jaime, "Orient Maid"), Huntley Gordon (Davidson, Bank Manager), James Flavin (Sgt. Jerry), Lotus Long (Princess Lin Hwa), Richard Loo (Aged Chinese), Bessie Loo (Lilly May), Lee Tong Foo (Willie), "Little Angelo" Rositto (Dwarf), Guy Usher (Commissioner).

Karloff returns for the third time as the Chinese detective, Mr. Wong, investigating the death of Chinese princess Long, who is killed in Karloff's house by a poison dart. Karloff and policeman Withers are aided by Reynolds, Withers' reporter fiancee, following a trail which leads them to Long's apartment, where they discover the body of her maid. The only witness is a mute Chinese dwarf, who later disappears. It is eventually discovered that Long was murdered by Gordon, the bank manager, who wanted to forge her signature, withdraw the large amount of her cash, and subvert her plan to buy American planes for China's fight against Japan. Karloff is nearly killed in the process, but he eventually captures the culprit. Remade as THE CHINESE RING. (See MR. WONG series, Index.)

p, Scott R. Dunlap; d, William Nigh; w, W. Scott Darling (based on a story by Hugh Wiley); ph, Harry Neumann; ed, Russell Schoengarth; makeup, Gordon Bau.

Mystery/Crime   **Cas.**   **(PR:A   MPAA:NR)**

MISTER, YOU ARE A WIDOWER
                    (SEE: SIR, YOU ARE A WIDOWER, 1971, Czech.)

MISTERIOUS DE ULTRATUMBA
                    (SEE: BLACK PIT OF DR. M, 1961, Mex.)

MRS. BROWN, YOU'VE GOT A LOVELY DAUGHTER*1/2
                    (1968, Brit.) 95m MGM c

Peter Noone (Herman Tulley), Karl Green (Karl), Keith Hopwood (Keith), Derek Leckenby (Derek), Barry Whitwam (Barry), Stanley Holloway (George Brown), Mona Washbourne (Mrs. Brown), Lance Percival (Percy Sutton), Marjorie Rhodes (Gloria), Sheila White (Tulip), Sarah Caldwell (Judy Brown), Hugh Futcher (Swothard), Drewe Henley (Clive Wingate), Avis Bunnage (Tulip's Mother), John Sharp (Oakshot), Nat Jackley (Pub Singer), Rita Webb (Woman in Pub), Billy Milton (Landlord), Dermot Kelly (Con Man), Tom Kempinski (Vince Hobart), Lynda Baron (Miss Fisher), Joan Hickson (Landlady), Iris Salder (Stewpot Iris), Nan Munro (Mother at Station), Pamela Cundell (Woman on Embankment), Paul Farrell (White City Clerk), Michelle Cook (Hippie Girl), James Myers (Page Boy), Margery Manners (Pub Singer).

An energetic and chaotic musical comedy starring Peter Noone and his Herman's Hermits, the popular British pop group of the 1960s, who also had a top tune of the same name. Noone inherits a prize greyhound named Mrs. Brown and decides to make his fortune by racing the dog and eventually winning a national derby. The other Mrs. Brown's daughter is Caldwell, whose mother is the wealthy Washbourne. Noone and the boys eventually land a singing job in the nightclub, and both the dog and Caldwell disappear for a while. Later, the dog is found and wins a big race plus gives birth to puppies. Noone gives up on Caldwell and notices that his neighbor has grown into a lovely woman. Producer Klein managed the Beatles for a while. All the songs are sung by Herman's Hermits and include: "It's Nice to Be Out in the Morning," "Ooh, She's Done It Again," "Lemon and Lime," "The World Is for the Young," "Holiday Inn" (Graham Gouldman), "The Most Beautiful Thing in My Life" (Kenny Young), "Daisy Chain" (Peter Noone, Keith Hopwood, Karl Green, Derek Leckenby), "Mrs. Brown, You've Got a Lovely Daughter" (Trevor Peacock), and "There's a Kind of Hush" (Les Reed, Geoff Stephens).

p, Allen Klein; d, Saul Swimmer; w, Thaddeus Vane; ph, Jack Hildyard (Panavision, Metrocolor); m, Ron Goodwin; ed, Tristam Cones; art d, David Provis; cos, Beatrice Dawson; makeup, Eddie Knight.

Musical/Comedy   **Cas.**   **(PR:A   MPAA:NR)**

MRS. DANE'S DEFENCE*   (1933, Brit.) 67m National Talkies/PAR bw

Joan Barry (Felicia/Mrs. Dane), Basil Gil (Sir Daniel Carteret), Francis James (Lionel Carteret), Ben Field (Mr. Bulsom-Porter), Clare Greet (Mrs. Bulsom-Porter), Evan Thomas (James Risby), Evelyn Walsh-Hall (Lady Eastney), Tony Paynter, John H. Vyvyan.

Boring melodrama has Barry—not the Joan Barry responsible for the scandalous paternity suit against Charles Chaplin in 1944—fleeing scandal in Monte Carlo by coming to England and adopting the name of a dead cousin. She falls in love with James, the son of Judge Gill, who refuses permission for them to marry until finally he takes pity on her and lets the marriage proceed. The end of the road for Barry's career, after starring in Hitchcock's RICH AND STRANGE only the year before.

p, Harry Rowson; d, A.V. Bramble; w, Lydia Hayward, Kenelm Foss (based on a play by Henry Arthur Jones).

Drama   **(PR:A   MPAA:NR)**

MRS. FITZHERBERT**   (1950, Brit.) 99m BN/Stratford bw

Peter Graves (Prince of Wales), Joyce Howard (Maria Fitzherbert), Leslie Banks (Charles James Fox), Margaretta Scott (Lady Jersey), Wanda Rotha (Princess Caroline of Brunswick), Mary Clare (Duchess of Devonshire), Frederick Valk (King George III), Ralph Truman (Richard Brinsley Sheridan), John Stuart (Duke of Bedford), Helen Haye (Lady Sefton), Chili Bouchier (Norris, Maid), Lily Kann (Queen Charlotte), Lawrence O'Madden (Lord Southampton), Frederick Leister (Henry Errington), Julian Dallas (Prince William), Barry Morse (Beau Brummell), Eugene Deckers (Philippe), Ivor Barnard (Rev. Burt), Henry Oscar (William Pitt), Arthur Dulay (Franz Joseph Haydn), Moira Lister.

Class differences and romance in 1783 are brought to the screen when Graves, the prince regent, falls in love with a Catholic widow, Howard. She laughs off his romantic overtures, realizing that nothing will ever come of the relationship. The jilted Graves resorts to a suicide attempt and when Howard sees the state he is in, gives in to a secret marriage. Rumors of the marriage spread throughout the country causing a split between Howard and Kann. Graves denies his marriage, Howard runs away, and he soon weds Rotha.

p, Louis H. Jackson; d, Montgomery Tully; w, Tully (based on the novel, Princess Fitz, by Winifred Carter); ph, James Wilson, Gerald Moss; m, Stanley Black; ed, Charles Hasse; md, Hans May; art d, R. Holmes Paul; cos, Eva Melova; makeup, Henry Hayward.

Drama   **(PR:A   MPAA:NR)**

MRS. GIBBONS' BOYS**   (1962, Brit.) 82m Byron/BL bw

Kathleen Harrison (Mrs. Gibbons), Lionel Jeffries (Lester Gibbons), Diana Dors (Myra), John Le Mesurier (Coles), Frederick Bartman (Mike Gibbons), David Lodge (Frank Gibbons), Dick Emery (Woodrow), Eric Pohlmann (Morelli), Milo O'Shea (Horse), Peter Hempson (Ronnie).

Harrison is an aged widow whose new romance is disrupted when her two sons (Bartman and Lodge) break out of jail and come home to hide out. Harrison, one of the best examples of the British tradition of slightly batty old woman characters, is just about the only reason for watching this otherwise stale comedy.

p, Harry Halstead; d, Max Varnel; w, Varnel, Peter Blackmore (based on a play by Will Glickman, Joseph Stein).

Comedy   **(PR:A   MPAA:NR)**

MRS. LORING'S SECRET   (SEE: IMPERFECT LADY, THE, 1947)

MRS. MIKE* 1/2   (1949) 98m Regal/UA bw

Dick Powell (Sgt. Mike Flannigan), Evelyn Keyes (Kathy O'Fallon), J.M. Kerrigan (Uncle John), Angela Clarke (Sarah Carpentier), John Miljan (Mr. Howard), Nan Boardman (Georgette Beauclaire), Will Wright (Dr. McIntosh), Frances Morris (Mrs. Howard), Joel Nestler (Pierre Carpenter), Jean Inness (Mrs. Mathers), Chief Yowlachie (Atenou), Fred Aldrich (Louis Beauclaire), Clarence Straight (Cameron), Gary Lee Jackson (Tommy Henderson), Romere Darling (Mrs. Henderson), Archie Leonard (Trader Henderson), James Fairfax (Danny Hawkins), Robin Camp (Tommy Howard), Donald Pietro (Joe Howard), Janet Sackett (Madeleine Beauclaire), Judith Sackett (Barbette Beauclaire).

Keyes stars as a girl from Boston who falls in love with and marries a Canadian Mountie, Powell, after venturing into the Northwest woods. Set at the turn-of-the-century, the picture is most concerned with Keyes' ability to adapt her urban outlook to a more rugged way of life.

p, Samuel Bischoff; d, Louis King; w, Alfred Lewis Levitt, DeWitt Bodeen (based on the novel by Benedict and Nancy Freedman); ph, Joseph Biroc; ed, Paul Weatherwax; md, Louis Forbes; art d, Arthur Lonegan; set d, Robert Priestley; m/l, "Kathy," Max Steiner, Ned Washington (sung by Dick Powell).

Drama   **(PR:A   MPAA:NR)**

MRS. MINIVER***   (1942) 134m MGM bw

Greer Garson (Mrs. Kay Miniver), Walter Pidgeon (Clem Miniver), Teresa Wright (Carol Beldon), Dame May Whitty (Lady Beldon), Henry Travers (Mr. Ballard), Reginald Owen (Foley), Miles Mander (German Agent's Voice), Henry Wilcoxon (Vicar), Richard Ney (Vin Miniver), Clare Sandars (Judy Miniver), Christopher Severn (Toby Miniver), Brenda Forbes (Gladys the Housemaid), Rhys Williams (Horace Perkins), Marie De Becker (Ada the Cook), Helmut Dantine (German Flier), Mary Field (Miss Spriggins), Tom Conway (Man), St. Luke's Choristers (Choral Voices), Paul Scardon (Nobby), Ben Webster (Ginger), Aubrey Mather (George the Innkeeper), Forrester Harvey (Huggins), John Abbott (Fred the Porter), Connie Leon (Simpson the Maid), Billy Bevan (Conductor), Florence Wix (Woman with Dog), Bobby Hale (Old Man), Alice Monk (Lady Passenger), Ottola Nesmith (Saleslady), Douglas Gordon (Porter), Gerald Oliver Smith (Car Dealer), Alec Craig (Joe), Clara Reid (Mrs. Huggins), Harry Allen (William), Leslie Vincent (Dancing Partner), John Burton (Halliday), Leonard Carey (Haldon's Butler), Eric Lonsdale (Marston), Guy Bellis (Barman), Charles Irwin (Mac), Ian Wolfe (Dentist), Dave Thursby (Farmer), Charles Bennett (Milkman), Arthur Wimperis (Sir Henry), David Clyde (Carruthers), Colin Campbell (Bickles), Herbert Clifton, Leslie Francis (Doctors), Dave Dunbar, Art Berry, Sr., Sid D'Albrook (Men in Store), Gene Byram, Virginia Bassett, Aileen Carlyle, Irene Denny, Herbert Evans, Eula Morgan, Vernon Steele, Vivie Steele, Marek Windheim, Tudor Williams (Glee Club Members), Kitty Watson, Hugh Greenwood, Sybil Bacon, Flo Benson (Contestants), Harold Howard (Judge), Billy Engle (Townsman), John Burton, Louise Bates (Miniver Guests), Edward Cooper (Waiter), Walter Byron, Ted Billings, Dan Maxwell, Frank Atkinson, Henry King, Gil Perkins, John Power (Men in Tavern), Thomas Louden (Mr. Verger), Peter Lawford (Pilot), Stanley Mann (Workman), Leslie Sketchley, Emerson Fisher-Smith, Frank Baker, Colin Kenny (Policemen).

MGM's mighty mogul Louis B. Mayer bowed to no man but he was forever tipping his hat to England and was noted as Hollywood's most slavish Anglophile. And this touching, often wonderful film, a classic of its day, was Mayer's tribute to the indefatigable spirit of the British people at their finest hour during WW II. It's a simple story—invariably the best kind for movies—which profiles a charming, gentle family that lives in the small village of Belham outside of London. It is the summer of 1939 and the beautiful Garson is about to return home after buying an expensive hat in London. At the train station she is met by railroad supervisor Travers who so appreciates this lovely, charming lady that he asks if he can name his new species of hybrid rose "Mrs. Miniver" which he plans on entering in a local flower contest. Garson happily agrees and then returns to her country home a bit sheepish, not wanting to admit her extravagance. Then her husband, kind and thoughtful Pidgeon, tells her with some fair amount of guilt that he has purchased a new car. *Then* she freely admits buying a new hat. In a series of vignettes, the Miniver family is shown to be a happy, well-adjusted cluster of humans. Garson's son, Ney, answers the door one day to greet Wright, who has a request. She asks Ney to persuade his mother to ask Travers to withdraw his spectacular rose from the flower contest so that her grandmother, Lady Beldon (Whitty), can win the grand prize, which she has done for decades. Ney instead falls in love with Wright and their courtship begins. Wright and Ney become engaged just as WW II begins and Garson, Pidgeon, and their family—like the rest of the civilized world—are caught up in a cataclysmic war. Family members do their bit on the home front. Then Pidgeon goes off with the other men of the village in little boats to help take off hundreds of thousands of retreating British soldiers stranded on the beaches of Dunkirk. In his absence Garson holds her family together and then suddenly discovers a wounded German pilot, Dantine, outside her house. He attempts to smooth-talk her into letting him get away but Garson, holding a gun on him, is too shrewd for him and turns him over to authorities. When Pidgeon returns, his son Ney and Wright are married. When they return they attend the quaint flower show where Whitty, as usual, wins, but she is gracious and realizes that the uncomplaining Travers really has the prize rose and she turns the award over to the grateful old gentleman. During an air raid, Wright is machine-gunned to death by a low-flying Nazi plane and Ney later flies with his RAF squadron against the enemy, Garson vainly trying to pick out his plane above. But to her, all the young men flying overhead are her sons. At the end, with tragedy struck deep like a knife into her own family, Garson gathers her young children and husband about her and attends church, now a near ruin from the incessant German bombing (not unlike the ruins of the destroyed cathedral at Coventry). There the local vicar, Wilcoxon, delivers a powerful and moving speech, one of the most patriotic in film record. Says Wilcoxon with great fervor: "We, in this quiet corner of England, have suffered the loss of friends very dear to us. Some—close to the church. And our hearts to go out in sympathy to the two families who share the cruel loss of a young girl who was married at this altar only two weeks ago. The homes of many of us have been destroyed, and the lives of young and old have been taken. There is scarcely a household that hasn't been struck to the heart. And why? Surely you must have asked yourself this question. Why, in all conscience, should these be the ones to suffer? Children, old people, a young girl at the height of her loveliness. Why these? Are these our soldiers? Are these our fighters? Why should they be sacrificed? I shall tell you why. Because this is not only a war of soldiers in uniform. It is a war of the people—all of the people, and it must be fought not only on the battlefield, but in the cities and in the villages, in the factories and on the farms, in the home and in the heart of every man, woman, and child who loves freedom. Well, we have buried our dead but we shall not forget them. Instead they will inspire us with an unbreakable determination to free ourselves and those who come after us from the tyranny and terror that threatens to strike us down. This is the people's war! It is our war! We are the fighters! Fight it then! Fight it with all that is in us! And may God defend the right!" When Winston Churchill saw the film he brimmed with pride and publicly announced that MRS. MINIVER would prove to be more valuable than the combined efforts of six divisions. The Wilcoxon speech was reprinted in tens of thousands of leaflets and these were dropped over Allied-enemy positions during the remainder of the war. But there are so many poignant scenes and delicate little touches that bear the masterwork of director Wyler that this film deserves a permanent classic status, not the least of which is the scene where Garson—while her small children clutch Pidgeon and herself—reads heroically inside a makeshift bomb shelter the story of "Alice in Wonderland" while the Nazis methodically bomb her village and kill her friends and relatives. Her performance is magnificent and won her an Oscar for Best Actress, an award she never believed she would win. In fact, Garson tried hard not to take the role for the very reason that MGM queen Norma Shearer and Ann Harding had turned down the role; none wanted to have a grown son on screen with them, a visual reminder of their ages. First Mayer reminded his favorite star that she owed her considerable career to him; he and MGM had made her famous and rich. The Irish-born redhead still said no. She would not take the role under any circumstances. Then Mayer tried his begging routine, altering his cajoling and wheedling. Next he became hardheaded and threatened to cancel Garson's contract. Garson only gave him her best winning smile and said no. In desperation, Mayer grabbed the script and acted out all the parts, having Garson interject her lines, reading in a frenzy with her, telling her breathlessly that she would become the most famous actress in the world if she undertook the part. In a dizzy swirl of what she later described as confusion, Garson finally accepted the Mrs. Miniver role, walked out of Mayer's office, and promptly fainted when she realized what she had done. Later, Wilcoxon, one of her supporting players, stopped the still-dazed Garson and said: "May I congratulate you in advance?" Replied Garson: "What for?" "This picture," said Wilcoxon. "I think you'll win an Academy Award for your role." Snapped Garson: "Mr. Wilcoxon, I have admired you in the past, but now I can no longer admire you." "I finally played it," she later said, "but Louis Mayer did it better than I did." She would gush out the longest acceptance speech (five and a half minutes) in the history of the Academy Awards when receiving her Oscar for Best Actress,

beginning with the words, "I'm practically unprepared." Commented some wag at the ceremonies held at the Coconut Grove in the Ambassador Hotel in Los Angeles: "Her acceptance speech was longer than her part." Mary Pickford was only one of those attending who felt the ceremonies were insufferable, later stating with some bitterness "No one person could arrange anything so boring." Pickford was the founder of the Academy and winner of its first Best Actress Award. She had been put at the rear of the hall with her husband, Charles "Buddy" Rogers. Pickford resigned from the Academy that night. Pidgeon was also nominated as Best Actor but he lost out to everyone's favorite that year, James Cagney, for YANKEE DOODLE DANDY. MRS. MINIVER swept the awards that year, however, with Wright winning for Best Supporting Actress (she had also been nominated for Best Actress for her stunning portrayal of Gary Cooper's wife in PRIDE OF THE YANKEES), Wyler for Best Director (he was awarded the statuette in absentia, flying over Germany on a bombing mission at the very time he was announced the winner), Ruttenberg for Best Cinematography, and Froeschel, Hilton, West, and Wimperis for Best Screenplay, with producer Franklin getting the Irving G. Thalberg Memorial Award. The movie did unexpectedly well with the American public, becoming a favorite for years with an entire generation of moviegoers and establishing Garson as a superstar. It returned more than $5.5 million to MGM from its first release in domestic sales alone and much more in foreign distribution. Garson continued to vex Mayer with regard to the film even after it was completed. She planned to marry her onscreen son, Ney, who was 27 at that time (and she was 34, having been born in 1908). Mayer asked her not to announce the marriage until after the film's first run through the theaters, believing that her marriage to a younger man might cause some concern among moviegoers. She agreed and waited, and while she waited Ney, whom she finally wedded, was drafted into the U.S. Navy. Producer Franklin was originally given a limited budget for the film, so small that it was decided to shoot it in black-and-white instead of color to save money. He felt that the story line was somewhat fragmentary with several of the popular Struther essays strung together in the quickly written script (finished by the four writers in three weeks); Franklin even predicted that the film would lose $100,000 and no one was more surprised than he when it went on to make box office legend. MRS. MINIVER opened at the giant Radio City Music Hall where 558,000 people flocked to see it in 25 days. Many associated with the film later denounced it, particularly in the 1970s when it became fashionable to be cynical about anything patriotic. Garson was among them, apologizing to a 1970 Annapolis, Maryland, audience before its screening by saying: "You have to understand, we really thought we were doing something important at the time." Wyler himself off-handedly labeled the movie that brought him an Oscar "synthetic," and these rather chic remarks were echoed by so-called film critics whose egos cannot abide the space occupied by films made outside of their own time, those feeling that their own shabby little prestige among academic or cult cliques is jeopardized by any movie with a cast larger than the ultra-boring MY DINNER WITH ANDRE. During WW II the enemy saw MRS. MINIVER as a powerful weapon being used aginst them. Nazi propaganda minister Joseph Goebbels called the movie an "exemplary propaganda film for German industry to copy." Director Wyler realized the potent propaganda he was creating with MRS. MINIVER. He later stated, as quoted from *William Wyler* by Axel Madsen: "The most satisfaction I get out of a film, aside from its critical and financial success, is its contribution to the thinking of people, socially or politically. In this sense, every film is propaganda . . . MRS. MINIVER was perfect as propaganda *for* the British because it was a story about a family, about the kind of people audiences would care about." When he began directing the film, Wyler was reminded by Mayer that America was not at war with Germany and that he was directing Dantine to play a fanatical Nazi. Mayer pointed out that the film should not be directed against the Germans. Wyler countered by saying that if he had several Germans in the film he might make *one* of them sympathetic, adding "but I've got only one German and as long as I only have one, he's going to be one of Goering's little monsters." Mayer reluctantly told Wyler to go ahead but not to "overdo" it. Wyler knew what to do with the limited budget he was given and he cleverly masked the Dunkirk evacuation scenes, shooting them all in the studio tank, which is where aquatic star Esther Williams would later make almost all her films. The battleships and little sailing vessels used in the Dunkirk scenes were all miniatures. By the time Wyler finished the film, America was at war with Germany and Louis B. Mayer was ready to do battle. He looked at the final scene, listened to Wilcoxon's speech, and concluded it was too conciliatory, not strong enough. Wilcoxon, already in service, was given a day off and spent one night with Wyler rewriting the last speech, and drawing heavily on Churchillian style, going to the studio the following morning at 9 a.m., and finishing the final take within an hour, rendering one of the most dynamic statements made on film to that date. The teaming of Garson and Pidgeon proved effective, as it had in an earlier tear-jerker, BLOSSOMS IN THE DUST, but when the pair were brought back in 1950 to do THE MINIVER STORY where Garson dies, the public backed off and the film all but flopped.

p, Sidney Franklin; d, William Wyler; w, Arthur Wimperis, George Froeschel, James Hilton, Claudine West (based on the novel by Jan Struther); ph, Joseph Ruttenberg; m, Herbert Stothart; ed, Harold F. Kress; art d, Cedric Gibbons, Urie McCleary; set d, Edwin B. Willis; cos, Kalloch; spec eff, Arnold Gillespie, Warren Newcombe; m/l, "Midsummer's Day," Gene Lockhart (performed by St. Luke's Choristers).

War Drama   **(PR:A MPAA:NR)**

MRS. O'MALLEY AND MR. MALONE**   (1950) 69m MGM bw

Marjorie Main (*Hattie O'Malley*), James Whitmore (*John J. Malone*), Ann Dvorak (*Connie Kepplar*), Phyllis Kirk (*Kay*), Fred Clark (*Tim Marino*), Dorothy Malone (*Lola Gillway*), Clinton Sundberg (*Donald*), Douglas Fowley (*Steve Kepplar*), Willard Waterman (*Mrs. Ogle*), Don Porter (*Myron Brynk*), Jack Bailey (*Announcer*), Nancy Saunders (*Joanie*), Basil Tellou (*The Greek*), James Burke (*Conductor*), Eddie Walter (*Rigger*), Regis Toomey, Herbert Vigran (*Reporters*), Fred Brady (*Orchestra Leader*), Henry Corden (*Sascha*), Edward Earle (*Mr. Fillion*),

Elizabeth Flournoy *(Mrs. Fillion)*, Noreen Mortensen *(Margie)*, Mae Clarke, Thelma Rigdon, Stanley Blystone, Bette Arlen, Lisa Lowry, Philo McCullough, Jerry Lacoe, Jr. *(Passengers)*, Pat Williams *(Pirate Girl)*, Jeffrey Sayre, J. Lewis Smith *(Photographers)*, Diana Norris *(Jessie)*, Donna Norris *(Bessie)*.

A buzzing, witty comedy mystery which stars Whitmore as a sly lawyer and Main as a sharp-tongued Montana widow. They meet on a train traveling from Chicago to New York. Whitmore is trying to catch up with a client who owes him $10,000 and Main has to collect a radio jackpot prize. The two get mixed up in a mystery when the client is found dead in Whitmore's compartment. They humorously try to get to the bottom of the mystery, but before they can accomplish the task, another corpse shows up. Songs include the title number and "Possum Up a Gum Stump," rasped out by Main.

p, William H. Wright; d, Norman Taurog; w, William Bowers (based on the story by Craig Rice, Stuart Palmer); ph, Ray June; m, Adolph Deutsch; ed, Gene Ruggiero; art d, Cedric Gibbons, Daniel B. Cathcart.

Comedy/Mystery **(PR:A MPAA:NR)**

MRS. PARKINGTON**½ (1944) 124m MGM bw

Greer Garson *(Susie Parkington)*, Walter Pidgeon *(Maj. Augustus Parkington)*, Edward Arnold *(Amory Stilham)*, Frances Rafferty *(Jane Stilham)*, Agnes Moorehead *(Aspasia Conti)*, Selena Royle *(Mattie Trounsen)*, Gladys Cooper *(Alice, Duchess de Brancourt)*, Lee Patrick *(Madeleine)*, Dan Duryea *(Jack Stilham)*, Rod Cameron *(Al Swann)*, Tom Drake *(Ned Talbot)*, Helen Freeman *(Helen Stilham)*, Cecil Kellaway *(Edward, Prince of Wales)*, Hugh Marlowe *(John Marbey)*, Tala Birell *(Lady Nora Ebbsworth)* Peter Lawford *(Lord Thornley)*, Fortunio Bonanova *(Signor Cellini)*, Mary Servoss *(Mrs. Graham)*, Gerald Oliver Smith *(Taylor)*, Ruth Brady *(Bridgett)*, Howard Hickman *(Dr. Herrick)*, Marcelle Corday *(Mme. de Thebes)*, Bryon Foulger *(Vance)*, Wallis Clark *(Capt. McTavish)*, Ann Codee *(Mme. Dupont)*, Frank Reicher *(French Doctor)*, George Davis *(French Policeman)*, Harry Cording *(Humphrey)*, Celia Travers *(Belle)*, Kay Medford *(Minnie)*, Hans Conried *(Mr. Ernst)*, Edward Fielding *(Rev. Pilbridge)*, Alma Kruger *(Mrs. Jacob Livingston)*, Rhea Mitchell *(Mrs. Humphrey)*, Ivo Henderson *(Albert)*, Charles Pecora *(Headwaiter)*, Mary Zavian, Erin O'Kelley *(Can-Can Girls)*, Myron Tobias *(Boy)*, Eugene Borden *(Drunk)*, Charles Cane, Al Hill, Bert Le Baron, Al Ferguson, Richard Thorne *(Miners)*, Lee Tung-Foo *(Sam)*, Marek Windheim *(Gaston)*, Johnny Berkes *(Beggar)*, Franco Corsaro *(Gypsy Fiddler)*, Anna Marie Stewart *(Mme. De Thebes)*, Bertha Feducha, Symona Boniface *(Fitters)*, Robert Greig *(Mr. Orlando)*, Maurice Cass *(Shopkeeper)*, Gordon Richards *(James the Butler)*, Guy Bellis *(Footman)*, Rex Evans *(Fat Man)*, Doodles Weaver, Bobby Barber *(Caterers)*, Chef Milani *(Maitre d'Hotel)*, Grace Hayle *(Fat Lady)*, Billy Bletcher, Harry Tyler, Vernon Dent, Bud Jamison *(Quartette)*, Warren Farlan *(Herbert Parkington at Age 2½)*, Betty Bricker, Dorothy Phillips, Jessie Arnold *(Pedestrians in Mining Town)*, Margaret Bert, Naomi Childers *(Nurses)*, Harry Adams, Nolan Leary, John Bohn, Leonard Mellin, John Phipps, Billy Engle, Fred Rapport, Maurice Briere *(Waiters at Ball)*, Tiff Payne *(Billiard Expert)*, Maj. Douglas Francis, Harvey Shepherd *(Grooms)*, Wyndham Standing *(Butler)*, Brandon Hurst *(Footman)*, Saint Luke's Choristers.

Garson and Moorehead both received Oscar nominations for their roles in this overblown saga and they both deservedly lost. This was the fifth pairing of Garson and Pidgeon, but it didn't come off nearly as well as the others, although the picture, which cost $2 million or so, did make lots of money for the studio. Based on Louis Bromfield's best seller, it's a chronicle of a woman from 1875 through 1938, as she goes from a maid in a boarding house to a grande dame in grandeur. It's the night before Christmas and all through the house of Garson, a woman in her eighties, there are reverberations of trouble as she discovers that her pompous son-in-law, Arnold, has been involved in dubious financial dealings and now needs money from Garson in order to extricate himself or else face a trial. Garson calls in all the members of the family, as the decision must be theirs. In order to forestall Arnold's trip to Sing Sing, they must kick in part or all of the inheritances. The children and grandchildren bitch about what might happen and Garson flashes back to her earlier life when she met Pidgeon, a wealthy mine owner who had come to a tiny town in Nevada to look over his silver holdings. Garson and Pidgeon meet, then wed after his mother dies in a mine cave-in. (Why the old lady was down there is a perplexing thing.) He takes her back to Manhattan and hires his ex-mistress, Moorehead, to teach the unsinkable Garson (for she is rather like the Unsinkable Molly Brown) the proper etiquette to use when mixing with the upper crust. Pidgeon builds a huge house and sends out invitations to "the 400" to attend a soiree, but his invites are spurned by Park Avenue's upturned noses. Pidgeon is infuriated by the snub and begins a campaign to wreck the financial situations of the snubbers by playing havoc with the stock market and cornering certain stocks. When their son Farlan dies, Garson stays in New York while Pidgeon goes to Europe. She joins him when she learns he's taken Birell, a titled lady, as his London mistress. Garson uses her friendship with Kellaway (the Prince of Wales) to break up the amour her husband is having. Then Pidgeon is conveniently killed in a car crash and we flash forward to 1938 where Garson's family informs her that they will not back son-in-law Arnold. Garson is adamant and says that she will help Arnold with all of her money and, if the need arises, all of theirs. In the movie, Pidgeon is portrayed as a womanizer who goes so far as to leave Garson on their wedding night to carouse around the city. Moorehead, who usually played very different roles, is seen as a sexpot who had been one of Pidgeon's many women. The unfaithful playboy was also a character seldom portrayed by Pidgeon. Garson's bright red hair was covered by a black wig (a concession to the black-and-white film), and it made her look odd. All in all, an attempt at grandeur that is as empty as a football stadium in April. In the version released in England, Hugo Haas played a king (replacing Kellaway as the Prince of Wales) and Birell's role was changed to a countess. This was done to assuage any problems that may have been due to a portrayal of British royalty.

p, Leon Gordon; d, Tay Garnett; w, Robert Thoeren, Polly James (based on the novel by Louis Bromfield); ph, Joseph Ruttenberg; m, Bronislau Kaper; ed, George Boemler; art d, Cedric Gibbons, Randall Duell; set d, Edwin B. Willis, McLean Nisbet; spec eff, A. Arnold Gillespie, Warren Newcombe, Danny Hall.

Drama **(PR:A MPAA:NR)**

MRS. POLLIFAX–SPY* (1971) 110m UA c

Rosalind Russell *(Mrs. Emily Pollifax)*, Darren McGavin *(Johnny Farrell)*, Nehemiah Persoff *(Gen. Berisha)*, Harold Gould *(Col. Nexdhet)*, Albert Paulsen *(Gen. Perdido)*, John Beck *(Sgt. Lulash)*, Dana Elcar *(Carstairs)*, James Wellman *(Mason)*, Dennis Cross *(Bishop)*, Nick Katurich *(Stefan)*, Don Diamond *(DeGamez, Book Shop Proprietor)*, Robert Donner *(Larrabee)*, Tom Hallick *(Roger)*, Vassily Sulich *(Albanian Private)*, Patrick Dennis *(Tourist)*.

Russell plays a bored housewife looking for excitement—and finds it when she begins working for the CIA. Unfortunately, Russell ended her fine career (HIS GIRL FRIDAY, PICNIC) with this tired picture, which she also wrote under a pseudonym.

p, Frederick Brisson; d, Leslie Martinson; w, C.A. McKnight [Rosalind Russell] (based on the novel *The Unexpected Mrs. Pollifax* by Dorothy Gilman); ph, Joseph Biroc (DeLuxe Color); m, Lalo Schifrin, Andre Previn; ed, Stefan Arnsten, Philip W. Anderson; md, Schifrin; art d, Jack Poplin; set d, William Kuehl; cos, Noel Taylor; m/l, "Merdita," Previn; makeup, Fred Williams.

Spy Comedy **(PR:A MPAA:G)**

MRS. PYM OF SCOTLAND YARD*** (1939, Brit.) 65m Hurley/GN bw

Mary Clare *(Mrs. Pym)*, Edward Lexy *(Inspector Shott)*, Nigel Patrick *(Richard Loddon)*, Janet Johnson *(Maraday Wood)*, Anthony Ireland *(Henry Menchen)*, Irene Handl *(Miss Bell)*, Vernon Kelso *(Frank Wood)*, Robert English *(Commissioner)*, Lionel Dymoke, Arthur Ridley, Ben Williams, Arthur Owen, Jack Jameson, Joan Halliday.

Clare is a detective investigating the murders of two women who were members of a psychic club. This is Pym's cup of tea. She exposes the killer as the medium (a fake) and saves an heiress from becoming the next victim. Well written, eerily atmospheric, and benefiting greatly by a wonderful performance by Clare. One of the best of the thousands of British drawing room mysteries.

p, Victor Katona; d, Fred Elles; w, Elles, Nigel Morland, Peggy Barwell (based on the novel by Morland); ph, Bryan Langley.

Crime **(PR:A MPAA:NR)**

MRS. WARREN'S PROFESSION**
(1960, Ger.) 103m Real-Film/Europa bw (FRAU WARREN'S GEWERBE)

Lilli Palmer *(Mrs. Warren)*, O.E. Hasse *(Sir Crofts)*, Johanna Matz *(Vivie)*, Helmut Lohner *(Frank Gardner)*, Rudolf Vogel *(Samuel Gardner)*, E.F. Fuerbringer *(Pread)*, Elisabeth Flickenschildt *(Mother Warren)*, Ernie Mangold *(Liz)*.

Made 60 years after it was put on the stage, this German adaptation of a George Bernard Shaw play comes across as well as an ancient Shaw vehicle might. Being nothing more than filmed theater, the play concerns a woman, Palmer, who lives comfortably off the profits of her many European brothels. She has kept this fact from her daughter, Matz, who lives in England. When Matz discovers the truth, it causes a major rift in their relationship.

d, Akos von Rathony; w, Eberhard Keinforff, Johanna Sibelius (based on a play by George Bernard Shaw); ph, Albert Benitz; m, Siegfried Franz.

Drama **(PR:A MPAA:NR)**

MRS. WIGGS OF THE CABBAGE PATCH*** (1934) 80m PAR bw

Pauline Lord *(Mrs. Elvira Wiggs)*, W.C. Fields *(Mr. C. Ensworth Stubbins)*, ZaSu Pitts *(Miss Tabitha Hazy)*, Evelyn Venable *(Lucy Olcott)*, Kent Taylor *(Bob Redding)*, Charles Middleton *(Mr. Bagby)*, Donald Meek *(Mr. Hiram Wiggs)*, Jimmy Butler *(Bill Wiggs)*, George Breakston *(Jimmy Wiggs)*, Edith Fellows *(Australia Wiggs)*, Virginia Weidler *(Europena Wiggs)*, Carmencita Johnson *(Asia Wiggs)*, George Reed *(Julius, Servant)*, Mildred Gover *(Priscilla, Maid)*, Arthur Housman *(Dick Harris, Drunk)*, Sam Flint *(Railroad Agent Jenkins)*, James Robinson *(Mose)*, Bentley Hewlett *(Box Office Man)*, Edward Tamblyn *(Eddie, Usher)*, Clara Lou [Ann] Sheridan *(Girl)*, Lillian Elliott *(Mrs. Bagby)*, Earl Pingree *(Brakeman)*, George Pearce *(Minister)*, Del Henderson *(House Manager)*, Al Shaw, Sam Lee *(Comedians)*, Walter Walker *(Dr. Barton)*, Tyler Brooks *(Ticket Taker)*.

This story began way back at the turn of the century as a novel by Alice Hegan Rice. It was then adapted for the stage by Anne Crawford Flexner in 1904, made as a silent in 1919, and then became a film in 1934. The 1942 remake was a disappointment. Produced by silent screen star Douglas MacLean, this version was, by far, the best of the lot, mostly due to the presence of two superior *farceurs*, Fields and Pitts. Lord lives in a shantytown shack with her quintet of children, Butler, Fellows, Johnson, Weidler, and Breakston (check the cast names for her daughters) and their dog. Butler finds an old horse that's about to be put to pasture (or to sleep) and the animal is immediately adopted by the kind family. It's Thanksgiving and they are offering their prayers for the meager meal of stew which the good Lord has bestowed upon them. Venable, a wealthy young lass who lives in one of the town's mansions, arrives with a proper Thanksgiving meal and the family has their neighbor, Pitts, join them. Despite the abject poverty of the "Cabbage Patch" in which they live, there is an almost Dickens-like hope about the inhabitants. The only sad note is that Lord's husband disappeared several years before and no one has been able to locate him since. On the surface, Venable seems to have everything going for her, but even the rich have problems. Her fiance, Taylor, arrives. He is a handsome, young newspaperman and he and Venable are having a premarital spat. While at the house, Taylor hears Breakston's hacking cough and realizes that the boy needs medical care at a hospital. The boy is sent to be cured and the other brother, Butler, is now the main support of the family. He has the old horse tethered to a wagon and he sells firewood to people in the area and makes enough money to support the clan. In lieu of money on one delivery, he trades the wood for five tickets to a show. Lord and the kids go to the theater and are having a grand time when she is called to the hospital where Butler perishes in her presence as she arrives. That kind of loss would lay any family low, but this group is made of sterner stuff and take it in their stride. Pitts, who is only a friend but has been accepted into the family as a member, is a spinster and Lord is determined to find her a husband, so enter Fields. Pitts and Fields are hilarious in their passionate wooing and he agrees to take her hand, but only after sampling her cooking. Pitts cooks about as well as horses ride motorcycles, so Lord whips up a few dishes and Fields tastes them, pronounces them scrumptious, and the marriage is on. Meanwhile, Venable and Taylor want to do something special for the family and invest a few bucks to place ads in newspapers across the U.S. in order to find Lord's missing husband. At the same time, the villain who holds the mortgage on the house, Middleton, is about to foreclose. Now Lord's husband, the missing Meek, returns home. He's just as muddled and tacky as he was the day he left. His seedy appearance shatters Lord's hopes for getting the $25 needed to pay the mortgage; then she goes through the pockets of his threadbare suit and miraculously finds the money there. The mortgage is paid and the family all turn out for the marriage of Taylor and Venable. It's essentially a very old-fashioned drama, but the comedy between Fields and Pitts, which occurs in the second half of the film, is worth the wait. Lord never falls into the bathetic as Mrs. Wiggs and manages to keep her kids together with spice and humor. Lots of tears, lots of laughs, and a good feeling at the end of the film. A sequel, LOVEY MARY, was made to the silent version by MGM in 1926.

p, Douglas MacLean; d, Norman Taurog; w, William Slavens McNutt, Jane Storm (based on the novel by Alice Hegan Rice and the play by Anne Crawford Flexner); ph, Charles Lang, ed, Anne Bauchens; art d, Hans Dreier, Robert Odell.

Drama/Comedy (PR:A MPAA:NR)

MRS. WIGGS OF THE CABBAGE PATCH*¹/₂ (1942) 80m PAR bw

Fay Bainter (Mrs. Elvira Wiggs), Carolyn Lee (Europena Wiggs), Hugh Herbert (Marcus Throckmorton), Vera Vague [Barbara Jo Allen] (Tabitha Hazy), John Archer (Dr. Robert Redmond), Betty Brewer (Asia Wiggs), Barbara Britton (Lucy Olcott), Moroni Olsen (Dr. Olcott), Carl "Alfalfa" Switzer (Billy Wiggs), Mary Thomas (Australia Wiggs), Billy Lee (Jimmy Wiggs), Betty Farrington (Mrs. Prescott), Ethel Griffies (Mrs. Graham), Janet Beecher (Mrs. Olcott), Harry Shannon (Mr. Wiggs), Olin Howlin (Jacob Diezal), John Sheehan (Box Office Man), Clem Bevans (Postman).

The third and, hopefully, the final version of the 1901 book, this picture didn't come up to the standards of the 1934 movie which featured W.C. Fields and ZaSu Pitts in the roles that Herbert and Vague took here. The story remains essentially the same with very little deviation from the earlier script. Bainter is the redoubtable Mrs. Wiggs, living in the poverty-stricken area known as "The Cabbage Patch" with her five children, Carolyn Lee, Switzer, Brewer, Thomas, and Billy Lee. Vague is the next door neighbor who meets Herbert through an ad in a matrimonial magazine. The family suffers greatly from the loss of the missing husband and Switzer supports them all by selling firewood, with an old horse that was destined for the glue factory pulling the wagon. Two of the kids are going to be taken away for adoption, Billy Lee dies in the hospital, young doctor Archer takes a liking to the family, meets Britton and has a subplot romance with her and, in the end, the father, Shannon, returns home after a fruitless search for gold in Alaska. The picture ultimately fails because honey is ladled on so heavily that we know our tear ducts are meant to be tugged at and not enough of the pluckiness of the family remains from the 1934 picture. Herbert and Vague try hard to match the comedy antics of Pitts and Fields, but there's no comparison between the abilities of the former and the latter.

p, Sol C. Siegel, Ralph Murphy; d, Murphy; w, Doris Anderson (based on a screenplay by William Slavens McNutt, Jane Storm, from the play by Anne Crawford Flexner and the book by Alice Hegan Rice); ph, Leo Tover; ed, Anne Bauchens; art d, Hans Dreier, William Flannery.

Drama/Comedy (PR:AA MPAA:NR)

MISTRESS FOR THE SUMMER, A** (1964, Fr./Ital.) 80m Boreal-FS-SPA/AM c (UNE FILLE POUR L'ETE; UNA RAGAZZA PER L'ESTATE; AKA: A LOVER FOR THE SUMMER)

Pascale Petit (Manette), Micheline Presle (Paule), Michel Auclair (Philippe), Georges Poujouly (Michel), Antoine Balpetre (Poet), Aime Clariond (Rosenkrantz), Henri Vidon (The King), Claire Maurier (Viviane), Bernard Lajarrige (Bartender), Eva Linkova, Geo Harry, Georges Meister, Sylvie Coste, Nicole Nantheuil, Ariana Galli, Giuseppe Porelli, Marina Malfatti.

A painter is invited to spend the summer at a wealthy friend's home, and on the way there picks up a young woman traveler. He falls in love with the girl, but his friend's son begins to move in on her. She realizes by the summer's end that she is in love with the painter, but she dies in a boating accident, shattering the painter's hopes. Includes a fine score by Georges Delerue, whose soundtracks have become a staple of French cinema. Released in Paris and Rome in 1960.

p, Pierre Meyrat; d, Edouard Molinaro; w, Molinaro, Maurice Clavel (based on the novel Une Fille Pour L'Ete by Clavel); ph, Jean Bourgoin (Dyaliscope, Eastmancolor); m, Georges Delerue; ed, Robert Isnardon; art d, George Levy.

Drama (PR:C MPAA:NR)

MISTRESS OF ATLANTIS, THE**¹/₂ (1932, Ger.) 87m Nero bw (DIE HERRIN VON ATLANTIS; L'ATLANTIDE; AKA: LOST ATLANTIS)

English-language cast: Brigitte Helm (Antinea), John Stuart (Capt. Morhange), Gibb McLaughlin (Capt. de Saint Avil), Odette Florelle (Clementine), Vladimir Sokoloff (Count Bielowsky/Jitomir Chieftain), Georges Tourreil (Lt. Ferrieres), Mathias Wiemann (The Norwegian), Gustav Diesal.

One of the classic versions of the legend of Atlantis—the mythic culture that sank to the bottom of the sea during the height of its power. Brigitte Helm (METROPOLIS) plays the island queen whose palace halls are filled with evil and the mummified bodies of her many lovers. Filmed simultaneously in three versions (English, French, German—all with moderately different casts), it marked the beginning of the end for the great German director of the silent era (PANDORA'S BOX), G.W. Pabst. For a seven-year period Pabst turned out an unbroken string of successes, but with the change of governments in Germany his probing into the social and erotic predictions of the audience wasn't well received. Based on Pierre Benoit's novel, which also inspired Jacques Feyder's superior Atlantis tale (L'ATLANTIDE), Pabst's film was blessed with the unsurpassed art direction of Erno Metzner.

p, Seymour Nebenzahl; d, Georg Wilhelm Pabst; w, Ladislaus Vajda, Hermann Oberlaender (based on the novel by Pierre Benoit); ph, Eugen Schuftan [Schuefftan], Joseph Barth, Ernest Koerner; m, Wolgang Zeller; ed, Hans Oser; prod d, Erno Metzner.

Drama/Fantasy (PR:A MPAA:NR)

MISTRESS OF THE APES* (1981) CineWorld c

Jenny Neumann, Barbara Leigh.

The missing link (or creatures that are supposed to pass as such things) lose their last woman member, but adopt another in the person of a modern woman searching for her long-lost husband who comes to prefer these creatures to the monstrous males back home. Hard-to-swallow premise makes for some pretty entertaining moments, including trite philosophical meandering.

p, John F. Rickert; d&w, Larry Buchanan; ph, Nicholas Josef Von Sternberg.

Horror Cas. (PR:O MPAA:R)

MISTRESS OF THE WORLD** (1959, Ital./Fr./Ger.) 107m CCC-Franco London Film-Continental/UFA bw (HERRIN DER WELT; LES MYSTERES D'ANGKOR; IL MISTERO DEI TRE CONTINENTI)

Martha Hyer, Carlos Thompson, Micheline Presle, Gino Cervi, Lino Ventura, Sabu, Wolfgang Preiss.

Based, in part, on a silent German serial of the same name, this picture is rooted in science fiction. When a scientist (Cervi) discovers a formula that allows him to control gravity, he becomes the subject of a plot by Chinese agents. Thompson and Ventura are agents for Swedish intelligence and come to the scientist's rescue. The first of director William Dieterle's (THE DEVIL AND DANIEL WEBSTER, THE HUNCHBACK OF NOTRE DAME) films after returning to his native Germany. Unfortunately, this film is nothing more than a fine serial, which originally was shown in two parts—one at 100 minutes, the other at 90 minutes.

p&d, William Dieterle; w, Jo Esinger, M.G. Petersson; ph, Richard Angst, Richard Oelers, Peter Homfield.

Science-Fiction/Crime (PR:A MPAA:NR)

MISTY*** (1961) 93m FOX c

David Ladd (Paul Beebe), Arthur O'Connell (Grandpa Beebe), Pam Smith (Maureen Beebe), Anne Seymour (Grandma Beebe), Duke Farley (Eba Jones), People of Chincoteaque, Virginia.

Set on an island off the coast of Virginia, this charming children's film stars 12-year-old Ladd and his young sister Smith as an orphaned pair living with their grandparents. When the locals engage in their annual Pony-Penning Day activities, the children joyfully go along. They travel to a nearby island and round up a herd of wild ponies which are then put up for auction. The children are able to capture a mare named Phantom, which has eluded the pony-penners for some time, as well as snaring its colt, which they tag Misty. They've saved $100 in order to purchase a pony, but when Phantom and Misty are put up at auction a stranger ends up as the owner. Some of the townsfolk come to the aid of the heartbroken youngsters, and eventually they get the pony they wanted. Phantom returns to the wild, but Misty decides to remain with her new owners.

p, Robert B. Radnitz; d, James B. Clark; w, Ted Sherdeman (based on the novel Misty of Chincoteague by Marguerite Henry); ph, Leo Tover, Lee Garmes (CinemaScope, DeLuxe Color); m, Paul Sawtell, Bert Shefter; ed, Frederick Y. Smith; art d, Duncan Cramer, Maurice Ransford; set d, Walter M. Scott, Stuart A. Reiss; makeup, Ben Nye.

Children's Adventure (PR:AAA MPAA:NR)

MIT EVA DIE SUNDE AN
(SEE: PLAYGIRLS AND THE BELLBOY, THE, 1962, Fr.)

MITCHELL** (1975) 97m Essex/AA c

Joe Don Baker (Mitchell), Martin Balsam (James Arthur Cummins), John Saxon (Walter Deaney), Linda Evans (Greta), Merlin Olsen (Benton), Morgan Paull (Salvatore Mistretta), Harold J. Stone (Tony Gallano), Robert Phillips (Chief Albert Pallin), Buck Young (Detective Aldridge), Rayford Barnes (Detective Tyzack), Todd Bass (Child), Jerry Hardin (Desk Sergeant), Lilyan MacBride (Rich Lady), Robin Narke (Customs Officer), Sidney Clute (Rudy Moran), Duffy Hambleton (Edmondo Bocca), Carole Estes (Prudence Lang), Vicky Peters (Helena Jackman), John Ashby (Burglar), Bill Sullivan (Don Townsend), Jim B. Smith (Sgt. O'Hagen), Charles Glover (Officer Danziger), Charles Tamburro (Helicopter Pilot), Gary M. Combs (Helicopter Officer), Stan Stone (Sergeant), Tom Lawrence (Bel Air Patrolman), Alan Gibbs (Mustang Hood), Dick Ziker, Phil Altman (Alley Hoods), Bob Orrison, Gary McLarty, Paul Nuckles (Mistretta Hoods).

An over-familiar crime film that stars Baker as a tough, no-holds-barred cop who is on the trail of drug traffickers Balsam and Saxon. You've seen it all before . . . on TV.

p, R. Ben Efraim; d, Andrew V. McLaglen; w, Ian Kennedy Martin; ph, Harry Stradling (Technicolor); m, Larry Brown; ed, Fred A. Chulack; md, Jerry Styner; set d, Fred Price; cos, Dave Grayson; spec eff, Chuck Gaspar.

Crime   (PR:O   MPAA:R)

MIVTZA KAHIR   (SEE: TRUNK TO CAIRO, 1966, Israel/Ger.)

MIX ME A PERSON*1/2   (1962, Brit.) 116m Wessex-BL/BLC bw

Anne Baxter (*Dr. Anne Dyson*), Donald Sinden (*Philip Bellamy, Q.C.*), Adam Faith (*Harry Jukes*), David Kernan (*Socko*), Frank Jarvis (*Nobby*), Peter Kriss (*Dirty Neck*), Carole Ann Ford (*Jenny*), Anthony Booth (*Gravy*), Topsy Jane (*Mona*), Jack MacGowran (*Terence*), Walter Brown (*Max Taplow*), Glyn Houston (*Sam*), Dilys Hamlett (*Doris*), Meredith Edwards (*Johnson*), Alfred Burke (*Lumley*), Russell Napier (*P.C. Jarrold*), Barbara Barnet (*Receptionist*), Julie Milton (*Lorna*), Tim Pearce (*Tough*), Ed Devereaux (*Superintendent Malley*), Ray Barrett (*Inspector Wagstaffe*), Donald Morley (*Prison Governor*), Lawrence James (*Patrol Officer*), Gilbert Wynne (*1st Prison Officer*), Norman Johns (*2nd Prison Officer*).

A psychiatric crime melodrama about a young man, Faith, who is accused of killing a policeman. No one believes Faith's innocence except his lawyer's wife, Baxter, who is also a shrink. She visits Faith in prison and with the help of flashbacks we learn the real events. To impress his girlfriend, Faith steals a Bentley and gets a flat tire which a cop helps him to change. The cop tries to hail a passing truck, but a shot rings out from the cab of the truck, killing the cop. Later, Faith is found in shock beside the gun and the dead policeman. Baxter discovers that the Bentley Faith "borrowed" belonged to a man who supplied guns to the I.R.A., and that the policeman was offed by rival gun-runners.

p, Victor Saville, Sergei Nolbandov; d, Leslie Norman; w, Ian Dalrymple, Roy Kerridge (based on the novel by Jack Trevor Story); ph, Ted Moore; m, Johnny Worth; ed, Ernie Hosler; m/l, Worth.

Mystery/Drama   (PR:C   MPAA:NR)

MIXED COMPANY**1/2   (1974) 109m Llenroc/UA c

Barbara Harris (*Kathy*), Joseph Bologna (*Pete*), Lisa Gerritsen (*Liz*), Arianne Heller (*Mary*), Stephen Honanie (*Joe*), Haywood Nelson (*Freddie*), Eric Olson (*Rob*), Jina Tan (*Quan*), Tom Bosley (*Al*), Dorothy Shay (*Marge*), Ruth McDevitt (*Miss Bergguist*), Bob G. Anthony (*Krause*), Ron McIlwain (*Walt Johnson*), Roger Price (*The Doctor*), Keith Hamilton (*Milton*), Jason Clark (*Police Sergeant*), Charles J. Samsill (*Police Officer*), Jophery Clifford Brown (*Basketball Player*), Rodney Hundley (*Announcer*), Darell L. Garretson (*Referee*), Calvin Brown (*Santa Claus*), Al McCoy and The Phoenix Suns (*Voice of Phoenix Suns*), The Phoenix Suns.

Director Shavelson (YOURS, MINE AND OURS) brings the colorful problems of an oversized family to the screen once again. Struggling basketball coach Bologna is rendered sterile after a late-life bout with the mumps, so he and his wife, Harris, already with three kids, decide to adopt, taking into their home a young black child. The racial fears and bigotries of their neighbors are ripped open by the sight of the youngster on the same block as their own precious kiddies. To ease his insecurities, Bologna and Harris adopt another minority. The adoption agency tosses in an extra kid, bringing the total of adoptees equal to the number of natural offspring. The additional household members—an American Indian and a Vietnamese—partici- pate in the string of crazy, mixed-up happenings that follow. A sub-plot about Bologna's losing basketball team is only worth mention because the players are, in real life, the Phoenix Suns.

p&d, Melville Shavelson; w, Shavelson, Mort Lachman; ph, Stan Lazan; m, Fred Karlin; ed, Walter Thompson, Ralph James Hall; prod d, Stan Jolley; set d, Raphel Bretton.

Drama   (PR:C   MPAA:PG)

MIXED DOUBLES*   (1933, Brit.) 69m British and Dominions/PAR bw

Jeanne de Casalis (*Betty Irvine*), Frederick Lloyd (*Sir John Doyle*), Molly Johnson (*Lady Audrey*), Cyril Raymond (*Reggie Irvine*), Athol Fleming (*Ian MacConochie*), Rani Waller (*Rose MacConochie*), Quinton McPherson (*Reverend Arthur Escott*), Gordon McLeod (*Consul*), George Bellamy (*Barrett*).

Lame domestic farce which attempts to make something of the inane premise of a couple who believe themselves to have been divorced at one time, who meet years later, who fall in love all over again, and—deciding to take wedding vows again— discover that they were never divorced in the first place. Not the type of material from which entertaining films are created.

p, Herbert Wilcox; d, Sidney Morgan; w, Joan Wentworth Wood [Morgan] (based on the play by Frank Stayton).

Comedy   (PR:A   MPAA:NR)

M'LISS**   (1936) 66m RKO bw

Anne Shirley (*M'liss Smith*), John Beal (*Stephen Thorne*), Guy Kibbee (*Washoe Smith*), Douglas Dumbrille (*Lou Ellis*), Moroni Olsen (*Jake*), Frank M. Thomas (*Alf Edwards*), Arthur Hoyt (*Mayor Morpher*), Barbara Pepper (*Clytie Morpher*), Margaret Armstrong (*Mrs. Morpher*), Esther Howard (*Rose*), James Bush (*Jack Farlan*), Ray Mayer, William Benedict, Louis Mason, Arthur Loft, Fern Emmett.

Shirley shines as the most naive, wide-eyed woman in the West in this loose adaptation of Bret Harte's mining-camp saga. The lissome miss skips and hops through the saloons and bordellos, lithely leaping over the manure that fills the streets, fetching her besotted father Kibbee home from his forays of drunken depravity, pouting prettily after being startled by the all-too-frequent gunplay. Innocently bussed by Beal, the sunny sweetheart assumes that she is affianced and hastens to the whorehouse seeking the sage counsel of a senior resident anent the caveats of connubial arrangements. Innocence triumphs over improvidence, of

course. The film was originally made in 1918 with Mary Pickford and in 1922 as THE GIRL WHO RAN WILD.

p, Robert Sisk; d, George Nicholls, Jr.; w, Dorothy Yost (based on the novel by Bret Harte); ph, Robert de Grasse; ed, William Morgan; md, Alberti Columbo; art d, Van Nest Polglase, Perry Ferguson.

Romance   (PR:A   MPAA:NR)

MOB, THE***   (1951) 87m COL bw

Broderick Crawford (*Johnny Damico*), Betty Buehler (*Mary Kiernan*), Richard Kiley (*Thomas Clancy*), Otto Hulett (*Lt. Banks*), Matt Crowley (*Smoothie*), Neville Brand (*Gunner*), Ernest Borgnine (*Joe Castro*), Walter Klavun (*Sgt. Bennion*), Lynne Baggett (*Peggy*), Jean Alexander (*Doris*), Ralph Dumke (*Police Commissioner*), John Marley (*Tony*), Frank de Kova (*Culio*), Jay Adler (*Russell*), Duke Watson (*Radford*), Emile Meyer (*Gas Station Attendant*), Carleton Young (*District Attor- ney*), Fred Coby (*Plainclothesman*), Ric Roman (*Police Officer*), Art Millan, Paul Bryar (*Officers*), Michael McHale (*Talbert*), Kenneth Harvey (*Paul*), Don Megowan (*Bruiser*), Richard Irving (*Prowl Cop Driver*), Robert Fould, Tom Greenway, Dick Pinner, Jack Finley (*Men*), Al Mellon (*Joe*), Don De Leo (*Cigar Store Proprietor*), Peter Prouse (*Fred*), Sidney Mason, David McMahon (*Cops*), Ernie Venneri (*Crew Member*), Robert Anderson (*Mate*), Jess Kirkpatrick (*Mason*), Charles Marsh (*Waiter*), Charles [Bronson] Buchinski (*Jack*), Mary Alan Hokanson, Virginia Chapman (*Nurses*), William Pullen (*Plotter*), Peter Virgo (*Bakery Truck Driver*), Larry Dobkin (*Doctor*), Harry Lauter (*Daniels*), Paul Dubov (*Johnson*).

A brutal little crime film which stars Crawford as an undercover cop who poses as a corrupt dock worker in order to get the goods on the mobsters who run the wharf. Disturbed by this hard-case newcomer, the mob dispatches enforcers Brand and Borgnine to persuade Crawford to cool his jets. The undercover cop manages to convince the gangsters that his talents could be valuable to their operation, and he is given a low-level position in the mob organization. Once inside the gang, Crawford is surprised to find another undercover agent, Kiley. Kiley has been assigned to uncover the identity of the mob leader who is known only as "Smoothie." Together the cops employ a number of devices to ferret out the information—everything from brutalizing informants to using glow-in-the-dark liquid in order to follow the mob kingpin's car (hardly a novel device; a smoother sleuth, Sherlock Holmes—as played by Basil Rathbone—had used the same trick nine years before in SHERLOCK HOLMES AND THE SECRET WEAPON). Eventually Crawford manages to force "Smoothie" to reveal himself, and he is gunned down by police in a hospital while trying to put the kibosh on Crawford and his girl friend Buehler. Corruption is found in every dark corner of THE MOB, from dock workers to the police department itself. The film's view of society is bleak and depressing, with the lines between good and bad frequently blurred. Crawford and Kiley are often shown to be just as brutal as the men they are trying to put behind bars in this interesting precursor of brutal-cop crime films to come (such as the DIRTY HARRY series). THE MOB boasts a veritable who's who of urban tough guys with Neville Brand, Ernest Borgnine, and even Charles Bronson (billed "Buchinski" here) in a small role, lending their brutish talents to the dark proceedings. While not at all a pleasant film, THE MOB is a gripping, violent drama which will satisfy fans of the crime genre.

p, Jerry Bresler; d, Robert Parrish; w, William Bowers (based on the novel *Waterfront* by Ferguson Findley); ph, Joseph Walker; m, George Duning; ed, Charles Nelson; md, Morris Stoloff; art d, Cary Odell; set d, Frank Tuttle; makeup, Clay Campbell.

Crime   ·   (PR:C-O   MPAA:NR)

MOB TOWN zero   (1941) 59m UNIV bw

Billy Halop (*Tom Barker*), Huntz Hall (*Pig*), Bernard Punsley (*Ape*), Gabriel Dell (*String*), Dick Foran (*Sgt. Frank Conroy*), Anne Gwynne (*Marion Barker*), Darryl Hickman (*Butch/"Shrimp"*), Samuel S. Hinds (*Judge Luther Bryson*), Victor Kilian (*Uncle Lon Barker*), Truman Bradley (*Cutler, Cop*), John Butler (*Rummel, Auto Junker*), John Sheehan (*Mr. Loomis*), Roy Harris, Peter Sullivan (*Boys*), Dorothy Darrell, Elaine Morley, Beverly Roberts (*Girls*), Cliff Clark (*Police Chief*), Paul Fix (*Monk Bangor*), Will Wright (*Pawnbroker*), Eva Puig (*Mrs. Minch*), Dorothy Vaughan (*Mrs. Flynn*), Edward Emerson (*Nutsy*), Rosina Galli, Mary Kelly (*Women*), Dick Rich (*Manager*), Bob Gregory (*Police Officer*), Claire Whitney (*Mrs. Simpson*), Terry Frost (*Henderson*), John Kellogg (*Brick*), Clara Blore (*Woman*), Harris Berger (*Charlie, Paper Boy*), Duke York (*Burly Man*), Hally Chester, Joe Recht (*Boys*), Ed Dew (*Court Clerk*), Pat Costello (*Man*).

One of the worst entries in the Bowery Boys series, MOB TOWN has a kind-hearted cop (Foran) trying to reform the young thugs, but running into an obstacle with Halop. It turns out that Foran is the copper who sent Halop's brother up the river. Halop associates with a gang of hoodlums for a while, but eventually comes back to the fold. The film offers a great deal of exposition, but never seems to get anywhere, and before you know it (but not soon enough) the end credits pop up. (See BOWERY BOYS Series, Index)

p, Ken Goldsmith; d, William Nigh; w, Brenda Weisberg, Walter Doniger; ph, Elwood Bredell; ed, Arthur Hilton; md, Hans J. Salter; art d, Jack Otterson; set d, R. A. Gausman; cos, Vera West.

Comedy   (PR:A   MPAA:NR)

MOBS INC*   (1956) 62m Premier bw (GB: MOBS INCORPORATED)

Reed Hadley, Douglas Dumbrille, Don Hagerty, Will Geer, Marjorie Reynolds.

Under the influence of the television series RACKET SQUAD, three vignettes concerning swindle operations are presented. The first shows how a hoodlum and his dance-hall companion enter a wealthy home under the guise of wanting to take pictures. The next has a woman using a stock-market scheme to raise a sizable sum of money for herself. The final sequence is about the ways in which a young man takes advantage of the kindness and generosity of the inhabitants of a small town by posing as an arthritis victim in need of funds to fix up his farm. This man convinces the people that miraculous waters are spouting underneath the land, getting them to fork over thousands to buy it back. Lecturing by Hadley and the meekest of efforts put into production make these short lectures look as if they should have never left TV.

p, Hal Roach, Jr.; d, William Asher; w, Will Gould, Lee Loeb.

Crime   **(PR:A   MPAA:NR)**

MOBY DICK***½   (1930) 75m WB bw

John Barrymore *(Capt. Ahab)*, Joan Bennett *(Faith)*, Lloyd Hughes *(Derek)*, May Boley *(Whale Oil Rosie)*, Walter Long *(Stubbs)*, Tom O'Brien *(Starbuck)*, Nigel de Brulier *(Elijah)*, Noble Johnson *(Queequeg)*, William Walling *(Blacksmith)*, Virginia Sale *(Old Maid)*, Jack Curtis *(1st Mate)*, John Ince *(Rev. Mapple)*.

Barrymore reprises the Ahab role he played in the silent THE SEA BEAST (1926) in this film, differing mightily from Melville's novel. The story has Barrymore and evil stepbrother Hughes battling over the affections of preacher's daughter Bennett. On a whaling voyage Hughes shoves Barrymore overboard into the maw of the great white title whale, which bites his leg off. The stump is cauterized on the deck as Barrymore screams and several men sit on him to hold him down. Twisted by pain and the loss of his leg, Barrymore returns home. When Bennett sees the frightening figure, she naturally recoils in shock and runs away. Barrymore takes this as proof of what his brother has been hinting, that Bennett doesn't love him anymore. The peg-legged sea captain leaves home again, obsessed with killing Moby Dick. After seven years of searching the whale is located and killed, Barrymore driving home the harpoon. Hughes gets his comeuppance, leaving Barrymore free to return to New Bedford and Bennett. In many ways the film does not hold up today, owing to its ludicrous plot complete with evil stepbrother right out of 19th-Century melodrama and a fake whale that won't fool anyone (although the life-sized rubber model is more convincing than that used in the 1926 version, a bar of carved soap with buttons for eyes a technician hurriedly knocked out after the expensive mechanical whale that was built sank like a stone on its first trial). It is Barrymore who makes the film worth watching today. His acting is more subtle than it was in the silent version, but he still conveys the basic madness of Ahab's obsessive hunt for the whale that took his leg. Although Barrymore wanted his wife of the time, Dolores Costello, to take the female lead, her pregnancy prevented it. Barrymore picked Bennett, the daughter of an old friend from the New York stage, to play the role. She was worried at first; Barrymore's alcoholic excesses were already the stuff of legend, and although she had known him since her childhood, she still felt intimidated by his awesome talent. She needn't have worried, "He couldn't have been sweeter or more considerate," she said later.

d, Lloyd Bacon; w, J. Grubb Alexander (based on the novel by Herman Melville); ph, Robert Kurrle.

MOBY DICK*****   (1956, Brit.) 116m Moulin/WB c

Gregory Peck *(Capt. Ahab)*, Richard Basehart *(Ishmael)*, Leo Genn *(Starbuck)*, Harry Andrews *(Stubb)*, Bernard Miles *(Man of Man)*, Orson Welles *(Father Mapple)*, Mervyn Johns *(Peleg)*, Noel Purcell *(Carpenter)*, Friedrich Ledebur *(Queequeg)*, James Robertson Justice *(Capt. Boomer)*, Edric Connor *(Daggoo)*, Seamus Kelly *(Flask)*, Philip Stainton *(Bildad)*, Joseph Tomelty *(Peter Coffin)*, Royal Dano *(Elijah)*, Francis De Wolff *(Capt. Gardiner)*, Tamba Alleney *(Pip)*, Ted Howard *(Blacksmith)*, Tom Clegg *(Tashtego)*, Iris Tree *(Lady with Bibles)*.

Herman Melville's works are as difficult to translate to the screen as a condensation of the Bible (and that was attempted and failed miserably). Yet Huston manages to make a superb, powerful, and obsessive film of Melville's greatest work in MOBY DICK, with a stellar cast and a dogged faithfulness to the original story that is no less fanatical than Captain Ahab's insane quest for the great white whale. The film opens to show—at a distance—Basehart making his way toward the whaling village of New Bedford in the year 1840, his voiceover uttering the three most famous words in great literature: "Call me Ishmael. . . ." Once at the village inn, Basehart shares a room with Ledebur, a strangely tattooed West Indian harpooner whose mystical antics cause him to be apprehensive. Basehart's fears are reinforced by Welles, as the local parson, who mounts his pulpit—shaped in the form of a ship's prow—and illustrates a frightening picture of hazards and dangers at sea and how easily mortal man might lose his soul when in such perils. Then Basehart and Ledebur sign on board the *Pequod*, commanded by peg-legged Peck (Captain Ahab), a wild-eyed, stone-hearted captain whose face is horribly scarred, a jagged line running into his hairline where it continues as a streak of white. Before the ship leaves port, Dano, a ragged stranger, shouts out an ominous prediction to the alarmed crew. Once at sea, Peck brings his crew together to tell its members that this voyage is no routine hunt for whales but a vengeance mission wherein he seeks the monster whale of lore, Moby Dick, the very creature that ripped his leg from him and scarred his body and soul for life. He whips them into a frenzy, compelling them to swear allegiance to him and his mission, to die first before giving up the hunt, even if it takes the *Pequod* around the world. Peck nails a gold coin to the main mast and tells one and all that this will belong to the one who first spots the whale. They then all drink a strange toast, dipping their harpoons, heated to white-hot points, into their grog. The ship sails on while Genn unsuccessfully tries to persuade Peck to give up his mad plan. When Moby Dick is finally sighted, the crew members become as obsessed with killing the great sea beast as is Peck, and all row crazily after the whale, harpooning it again and again, only to die as the mammoth whale drags each boat beneath the sea in its dives. Basehart—in the sea, his longboat wrecked—looks up to see Peck entangled in the many harpoon ropes covering the body of the much-sought beast, riding the creature, holding a harpoon which he plunges again and again into the whale's body, screaming out his years of wrath: " . . . to the last I grapple with thee! From hell's heart I stab at thee! For hate's sake I spit my last breath at thee!" The whale takes another deep dive and Peck, emerging sometime

later still entangled in the ropes, appears dead but his arm flops back and forth with the whale's movements, as if beckoning Basehart and others to join him in death. The whale then turns toward the *Pequod*, ramming and sinking it. Basehart floats on alone, holding onto a coffin crafted for Ledebur's use, to state in voiceover that "only I survived to tell thee. . . ." MOBY DICK, under Huston's superb direction, is one of the most authentic looking and powerful historical adventure/drama films ever produced, even though the director later stated that the film was "the most difficult picture I ever made." Huston had looked forward to making the film for twenty years—hoping to direct his father, Walter Huston, in the lead role of the mad captain Ahab—but the senior Huston died in 1950, six years before Huston completed his masterpiece. Huston first asked screen historian James Agee to write the script with him, but Agee opted to commit himself to directing a film, his first, and thereby lost the opportunity to work on MOBY DICK. (Agee lost out both ways since the film he was to direct was never produced.) For the next-to-impossible role of mad captain Ahab, Huston selected Peck, oddly suggesting the part to the actor at a party when they met. Peck was surprised that the director would select him for such a part, stating that he thought he'd be better suited to the role of Starbuck. The actor later commented that he thought that Huston himself would have been the ideal candidate to enact Ahab: "His intense desire to make this picture without any compromise is certainly comparable to Ahab's relentless quest to kill the whale." Though Peck attacked the difficult role with enthusiasm he felt, at production's end, that he disliked himself as the obsessed Ahab. "I thought I was miscast in it, but I've never regretted having done it. It was a try, a risk." There were many risks involved in making this incredible film. Huston's penchant for realism caused him to order a world-wide search for the vessel that most conformed to the specifications of the *Pequod*, as outlined by Melville. In Scarborough, an English port town, the *Hispanola* was found, a perfectly outfitted sailing ship used earlier by Walt Disney in filming TREASURE ISLAND. This ship was originally called the *Rylands*, a 100-year-old wooden-hulled three master which had been used as a museum. It was made seaworthy and re-christened the *Pequod* for the film. Then Huston located Youghal, another small port town on the south Irish coast, and this became his New Bedford. The making of the whale itself took many months; Moby Dick was 90 feet long and had a weight of several tons. Its skin was made of plastic and rubber stretched over a steel frame and it was controlled electronically. Actually, two more whales were made as back-ups. But these make-believe whales were so heavy that they almost disappeared in the ocean waters when towing cables broke several times as they were being towed into open seas. When the sea battle between the *Pequod's* crew and Moby-Dick occurred, Huston, cast, and crew were all in the middle of St. George's Channel in the South Irish Sea. Between the unpredictable stormy weather and numerous mishaps, Huston later stated, "we were lucky that nobody got killed." Genn, playing Starbuck, fell twenty feet into an open boat that was supposed to be elevated to the deck of the *Pequod* but had suddenly dropped to sea level. He was taken to the hospital and put into a cast, out of production for several weeks. Basehart was injured and Peck almost killed. In the final scene where Peck is lashed to the side of the fake whale, a fog bank enshrouded the area and the actor "lost sight of the motor launch that was towing the whale with an underwater line. The towline snapped and I was in the fog in a squall in waves that were 10-15 feet high, along on a slippery rubber whale. And I thought 'What a way to go!' But I yelled and they were able to find me in the fog. I got off that whale in a hurry." The three whales were constructed at a cost of between $25,000 and $30,000 each. Two were lost in the sea when towlines broke and for years were seen bobbing about the high seas, mistaken for the real thing. The whale that was used in the last climactic scenes was driven, alone, by Huston himself. He was taking no chances of losing his last replica of Moby Dick. The director later paid tribute to the heroic work performed by Peck: "The last shot of the picture was Ahab lashed to the back of Moby Dick by harpoon lines. This had to be done by Greg Peck himself. A stunt man could not fill in because of the closeups. . . . Greg was underwater for a good long time." Peck, as challenged by making a masterpiece as was Huston, insisted that these hazardous shots be re-taken just to make sure they had captured the intended scene. Huston concentrated most of the film on Peck as Ahab, masterfully showing how he slips into insanity and violent death. "I always thought that *Moby Dick* was a great blasphemy," stated Huston. "Here was a man who shook his fist at God. The thematic line in *Moby Dick* seemed to me always to have been: 'Who's the judge when the judge himself is dragged to the bar? Who's to condemn but he, Ahab!' This was, to me, the point at which I tried to aim the whole picture, because I think that's what Melville was essentially concerned with, and this is, at the same time, the point which makes *Moby Dick* so extremely timely in our age." For Peck, it was a different interpretation altogether: "I got to thinking Ahab was just a damned old fool . . . screaming that if there is a God he's a malevolent God and he's chasing the whale because to him it signifies a fate and a destiny he cannot control." One of the film's finest attributes is its beautiful muted colors which give a feeling of the era. Huston and cameraman Morris created a "desaturation" process which meshed color and monochrome photography, involving three color imbibitions superimposed on a low-contrast black-and-white silver image. A golden aquatint tone which replicated old whaling prints was thus achieved, much like the vivid colors Huston had created for the wonderful MOULIN ROUGE, proving him to be—as well as one of the finest dramatic directors—a master of cinema coloring. Although many critics speared Peck as playing Ahab wrongly—and this was expected since Huston was dealing with a mystic literary work that caused critics to protect their own fierce notions—the film is nevertheless splendid on all counts. Peck and the supporting players, notably Genn, Basehart, Andrews, Purcell, and Ledebur, are superb as the crew mesmerized by the hypnotic Ahab. Huston received the New York Film Critics Award as Best Director but the film suffered needlessly because of the possessive preconceived prejudices of certain critics who really wanted to make their own film of *Moby Dick*. The film Huston made is certainly the best to date, a great film that captures the significance of Melville's marvelous novel. The first two films starred John Barrymore, in 1926 in THE SEA BEAST, a silent, and MOBY DICK in 1930, both pictures taking excessive liberties with the story. Shot on location in Ireland, Portugal, the Azores, the Canary Islands, and Wales.

p, John Huston, Vaughan N. Dean; d, Huston; w, Huston, Ray Bradbury (based on the novel by Herman Melville); ph, Oswald Morris (Technicolor); m, Philip Stainton; ed, Russell Lloyd; md, Louis Levy; art d, Ralph Brinton; cos, Elizabeth Haffenden; spec eff, Gus Lohman.

Adventure/Drama **Cas.** **(PR:C MPAA:NR)**

MODEL AND THE MARRIAGE BROKER, THE*** (1951) 103m FOX bw

Jeanne Crain *(Kitty Bennett)*, Scott Brady *(Matt Hornbeck)*, Thelma Ritter *(Mae Swazey)*, Zero Mostel *(Wixted)*, Michael O'Shea *(Doberman)*, Helen Ford *(Emmy Swazey)*, Frank Fontaine *(Johannson)*, Dennie Moore *(Mrs. Gingras)*, John Alexander *(Mr. Perry)*, Jay C. Flippen *(Dan Chancellor)*, Nancy Kulp *(Hazel)*, Bunny Bishop *(Alice)*, Kathryn Card *(Mrs. Kuschner)*, Maude Prickett *(Delia Seaton)*, Athalie Daniell *(Trudy)*, Dennis Ross *(Joe)*, Ken Christy *(Mr. Kuschner)*, Shirley Mills *(Ina Kuschner)*, Eve March *(Miss Eddy)*, Tommy Noonan *(Young Clerk)*, Jacqueline French *(Miss Perry)*, Edna May Wonacott *(Miss Perry)*, June Hedin *(Miss Perry)*, Frank Ferguson, Harris Brown *(Conventioneers)*, Mae Marsh *(Bit)*, Joyce MacKenzie *(Doris)*.

A sparkling, heart-warming comedy which stars Crain as the model and Ritter as the marriage broker. Ritter runs a dating service on the side, and when she discovers that Crain is having an affair with a married man, she gets to work. Ritter makes Crain go to see an unmarried X-ray technician she knows, on the pretext of looking for a missing earring, hoping the two will start to date and Crain will forget about the married man. Ritter's involvement goes a bit far, but the two eventually end up falling in love. To return the favor, Crain fixes up Ritter with a prospective husband.

p, Charles Brackett; d, George Cukor; w, Brackett, Walter Reisch, Richard Breen; ph, Milton Krasner; m, Cyril J. Mockridge; ed, Robert Simpson; md, Lionel Newman; art d, Lyle Wheeler, Don DeCuir.

Comedy **(PR:A MPAA:NR)**

MODEL FOR MURDER* 1/2 (1960, Brit.) 73m Parroch/Cinema Associates bw

Keith Andes *(David Martens)*, Hazel Court *(Sally Meadows)*, Jean Aubrey *(Annabelle Meadows)*, Michael Gough *(Kingsley Beauchamp)*, Julia Arnall *(Diana Leigh)*, Patricia Jessel *(Mme. Dupont)*, Peter Hammond *(George)*, Edwin Richfield *(Costard, Chauffeur)*, Alfred Burke *(Podd)*, Richard Pearson *(Bullock)*, George Benson *(Freddie)*, Diane Bester *(Tessa)*, Howard Marion-Crawford *(Inspector Duncan)*, Neil Hallett *(Sgt. Anderson)*, Barbara Archer *(Betty Costard)*, Annabel Maule *(Hospital Sister)*, Charles Lamb *(Lock Keeper)*.

Mundane thriller with Andes an American Merchant Marine officer in London finding himself as the accused in a jewelry heist, a result of being in the wrong place at the wrong time. Looking for the model girl friend of his deceased brother, he stumbles into the heist being carried off by Gough. With the aid of Court, and a bit of his training, Andes manages to keep himself out of jail to track down the real crooks. Old plot is given nothing new as treated here.

p, C. Jack Parsons, Robert Dunbar; d, Terry Bishop; w, Bishop, Dunbar (based on the story by Peter Fraser); ph, Petter Hennessy.

Crime **(PR:A MPAA:NR)**

MODEL MURDER CASE, THE**
(1964, Brit.) 90m Viewfinder-BL-Bryanston/Cinema V bw (GB: GIRL IN THE HEADLINES)

Ian Hendry *(Inspector Birkett)*, Ronald Fraser *(Sgt. Saunders)*, Margaret Johnston *(Mrs. Gray)*, Natasha Parry *(Perlita Barker)*, Jeremy Brett *(Jordan Barker)*, Kieron Moore *(Herter)*, Peter Arne *(Hammond Barker)*, Jane Asher *(Lindy Birkett)*, Rosalie Crutchley *(Maude Klein)*, Robert Harris *(William Lamotte)*, Duncan MacRae *(Barney)*, Zena Walker *(Mildred Birkett)*, James Villiers *(David Dane)*, Alan White *(Inspector Blackwell)*, Martin Boddey *(Superintendent)*, Marie Burke *(Madame Lavalle)*, Patrick Holt *(Walbrook)*, Griffith Davies *(Teddy Boy)*, Gabrielle Brune *(Lamotte's Secretary)*, Peter Elliott *(Waiter)*, Terence Brook *(Detective Sgt. Carter)*, David Randall *(P.C. Jackson)*, Douglas Robinson *(Harrison)*, John Forbes-Robertson *(Porter)*, Hugh Latimer *(Man in Club)*, Amanda Bowman *(Receptionist)*, Neville Becker *(Steward)*, Peter Forbes-Robertson *(Police Doctor)*.

The unimaginative title tells it all. A model is found shot to death in her apartment and police investigators Hendry and Fraser are assigned to the case. A television star is first suspected of the crime, then the investigation turns to a gang of narcotics smugglers. The guilty party turns out to be the girl's mother, who was jealous of her husband's attention for the girl. About as exciting as its title.

p, John Davis; d, Michael Truman; w, Vivienne Knight, Patrick Campbell (based on the novel *The Nose On My Face* by Laurence Payne); ph, Stanley Pavey; m, John Addison; ed, Frederick Wilson; md, Addison; art d, Alan Withy; set d, Peter James; m/l, "Casta Diva," sung by Elizabeth Vaughan; makeup, Wally Schneiderman.

Crime **(PR:A MPAA:NR)**

MODEL SHOP, THE*** (1969) 90m COL c

Anouk Aimee *(Lola)*, Gary Lockwood *(George Matthews)*, Alexandra Hay *(Gloria)*, Carol Cole *(Barbara)*, Severn Darden *(Portly Man)*, Tom Fielding *(Gerry)*, Neil Elliot *(Fred)*, Jacqueline Miller *(1st Model)*, Anne Randall *(2nd Model)*, Duke Hobbie *(David)*, Craig Littler *(Rob)*, Hilarie Thompson *(Girl Hippie)*, Jeanne Sorel *(Secretary)*, Jon Lawson *(Tony)*, David Mink *(Bearded Hippie)*, Jay Ferguson *(Jay)*, Jon Hill *(Allan)*, Fred Willard *(Gas Station Attendant)*, Ken Prymus *(Short-Order Cook)*.

The first American film from French director Demy is an interesting look at 24 hours in a young man's life. Lockwood is a 26-year-old Los Angeles architect. He knows he is about to be drafted, so he quits his dull job designing gas pipes, and marks his limited time. His girl friend Hay is an ambitious actress who doesn't understand his temporal trepidations. A finance company wants to repossess his car, so he borrows money from a musician friend to pay it off. Lockwood sees a beautiful woman in a big car and becomes obsessed with her. He follows her to a model shop, where men pay large sums of money to photograph nude women. He spends part of his money to photograph and make contact with the woman, Aimee, who is French. After a second photo session, Lockwood learns that Aimee's husband ran off with another woman, leaving her stranded in the United States, and that posing in the model shop is the only work she could get without a permit. She invites Lockwood home, and he tells her of his fears of going to Vietnam, his uncertain future, and his love for her. They spend the night together and Lockwood gives her the rest of his car money, so she can get back to France. Lockwood returns home and finds that both Hay and his car are gone. He calls Aimee, but she has already left for France. Lockwood gets his draft notice and realizes that he can cope with and face his future. Like so many *auteurs*, Demy is constructing a continuing body of work with this film, which uses situations and characters—and actors—from several of his previous pictures, notably LOLA (1961), BAY OF THE ANGELS (1963) and THE UMBRELLAS OF CHERBOURG (1964). Songs and musical numbers include "Nothing to Do and Little to Say" (Spirit), selections from "Scheherezade" (Nikolai Andreevich Rimsky-Korsakov), and selections from the works of Johann Sebastian Bach and Robert Schumann.

p,d, Jacques Demy; w, Demy, Adrien Joyce; ph, Michel Hugo (Perfect Color); m, Spirit; ed, Walter Thompson; prod d, Kenneth A. Reid; md, Marty Paich; set d, Anthony Mondell; cos, Rita Riggs; m/l, Spirit; makeup, Ben Lane.

Drama **PR:C-O MPAA:M)**

MODEL WIFE 1/2** (1941) 78m UNIV bw

Dick Powell *(Fred Chambers)*, Joan Blondell *(Joan Keating Chambers)*, Ruth Donnelly *(Mrs. Milo Everett)*, Charles Ruggles *(Mr. Milo Everett)*, Lucile Watson *(J. J. Benson)*, Lee Bowman *(Ralph Benson)*, Kathryn Adams *(Salesgirl)*, John Qualen *(Janitor)*, Frank Faylen *(Master of Ceremonies)*, Dale Winter *(Anna)*, Mary Kelly *(Miss Kendall)*, Ferdinand Munier *(Mr. Howard)*, George Chandler *(Joe)*, Henry Roquemore *(Perry)*, Vera Lewis *(Mrs. Leahy)*, Gloria Blondell *(Gloria)*, Grace Stafford *(Miss Manahan)*, Virginia Carroll, Catherine Lewis *(Salesgirls)*, Jack Gwynne *(Prestidigitator)*, Billy Gilbert *(Dominic)*, Charles Sherlock, Mervin Williams *(Players)*, Tom Seidel *(Stage Door Johnnie)*, Irene Colman *(Miss Smith)*, Ray Cooke *(Mailman)*, Dick Wessel *(Laundry Man)*, Mary Carr *(Servant)*, Sunnie O'Dea *(Fired Salesgirl)*, Lorraine Kruger, Glen Turnbull.

Powell and Blondell, who teamed successfully in so many musicals for Warner Bros., shifted studios for this cute comedy. The two are secret spouses employed in a snobbish salon. Their couturier employer, Watson, has a strict rule: she employs only the unmarried. The undercover couple develop a passion for progeny, but are unable to afford the associated expenses, particularly when their jobs are at hazard. Blondell's proposed pregnancy would certainly come to the fore; the shop does not deal with maternity clothes which she might model. Complications ensue when Watson's playboy son Bowman comes to work in the salon and gets a yen for model Blondell. Irate, Powell discloses the hideous secret: he and Blondell are *wed*. Fired, Powell separates from Blondell and accepts a job in China. All ends well as Watson repents her harsh policy and the happy pair reunite. The picture was put together by agent Charles K. Feldman, who bought the rights to the story from producer/director Jason and engaged his major talents, including Powell, Blondell, and the screenwriters, for a percentage of the gross (an unusual arrangement in the contract-player era).

p&d, Leigh Jason; w, Charles Kaufman, Horace Jackson, Grant Grarrett (based on a story by Jason); ph, Norbert Brodine; ed, Arthur Hilton; md, H.J. Salter.

Comedy **(PR:A MPAA:NR)**

MODELS, INC.* (1952) 73m Mutual bw (GB: THAT KIND OF GIRL)

Howard Duff *(Lennie Stone)*, Coleen Gray *(Rusty Faraday)*, John Howard *(John Stafford)*, Marjorie Reynolds *(Peggy Howard)*, Louis Jean Heydt *(Cronin)*, Ed Max *(Looie)*, Benny Baker *(Freddy)*, James Seay *(Detective Sgt. Mooney)*, Charles Cane *(Big Jim)*, Sue Carlton *(Ann)*, Lou Lubin *(Max)*, Mary Hill *(Millie)*, Frank Ferguson *(Banker Reynolds)*.

This limp crime drama has Howard, a respected entrepreneur, operating a modeling agency and training school. He falls hard for gold-digger Gray whom he bejewels and be-minks. Gray's one-time sweetheart, Duff, released from prison, re-enters her life with an obnoxious proposition. He suggests that Howard's prestigious parlor of pulchritude might be turned into a lucrative if somewhat sleazy peep-show operation, with filmless "amateur photographers" invited to film the damsels in their flimsies. Gray, attempting to evade this noxious notion, marries Howard to escape the ex-convict's importunities. Too late: she and Duff are both killed in a shoot-out with the police who have hunted him because he violated parole. This was the first filmic offering of Mutual Pictures, an independent production and releasing company, and it portended doom. The company disappeared from view shortly afterward. Actor Duff, on the other hand—with wife Ida Lupino—went on to many successful production ventures.

p, Hal E. Chester; d, Reginald LeBorg; w, Harry Essex, Paul Yawitz (based on an original story and adaptation by Alyce Canfield); ph, Stanley Cortez; ed, Bernard W. Burton; md, Herschel Burke Gilbert; art d, Ernest Fegte.

Crime **(PR:C MPAA:NR)**

MODERATO CANTABILE 1/2**
(1964, Fr./Ital.) 95m Iena-Jacques Companeez-Documento/Royal bw

Jeanne Moreau *(Ann Desbaredes)*, Jean-Paul Belmondo *(Chauvin)*, Didier Haudepin *(Pierre Desbaredes)*, Valerie Dobuzinsky *(Assassin)*, Pascale de Boysson *(Patronne)*, Collette Regis *(Miss Giraud)*.

Moreau is a wealthy but bored industrialist's wife who, while waiting for her son's (Haudepin) music lesson to finish, hears the scream of a woman in a nearby cafe. She sees a man being taken away from the body of a dead woman. Fascinated by the incident, she begins to frequent the cafe and soon meets Belmondo, an employee of her husband. For a number of days they meet and discuss the murder. Belmondo, however, realizes that she has her own death wish and leaves her. Directed by ocean-hopping theatrical director Peter Brook (LORD OF THE FLIES), it features an interesting amalgam of the French New Wave at that point in time (the film was released in France in 1960)—Moreau was just about to appear in Truffaut's masterpiece JULES AND JIM, Belmondo was to star in Godard's classic BREATH-LESS, and co-writer Duras had just scripted Resnais' HIROSHIMA, MON AMOUR. It was co-produced by screenwriter Jacques Companeez's (THE LOWER DEPTHS, CASQUE D'OR) company.

p, Raoul J. Levy; d, Peter Brook; w, Marguerite Duras, Gerard Jarlot, Brook (based on the novel by Duras); ph, Armand Thirard (CinemaScope); m, Antonio Diabelli (Sonata No. 4 in B-flat, opus 168); ed, Albert Jurgenson; art d, Jean Andre.

Drama (PR:C MPAA:NR)

MODERN HERO, A** (1934) 70m WB bw

Richard Barthelmess (Pierre Radler), Jean Muir (Joanna Ryan), Marjorie Rambeau (Mme. Azais), Verree Teasdale (Lady Claire Benson), Florence Eldridge (Leah), Dorothy Burgess (Hazel Radler), Hobart Cavanaugh (Mueller), William Janney (Young Pierre), Theodore Newton (Elmer), J.M. Kerrigan (Ryan), Arthur Hohl (Homer Flint), Maidel Turner (Aunt Clara), Mickey Rentschler (Peter), Richard Tucker (Eggelson), Judith Vosselli (Mrs. Eggelson).

The only film made in the U. S. by the brilliant Austrian Pabst (who worked first in Germany and then, concurrent with Hitler's rise to power there, in France) was a disappointment to its creator, to his admirers, and to the public. Critics of the time laid the blame on the unfamiliar language Pabst was forced to accommodate—thus the need for dialog director Collins—but Pabst was accustomed to polylingual filming; his L'ATLANTIDE (1932) was simultaneously shot in three languages, including English. The story deals with the rise and subsequent fall of the ruthless, ambitious Barthelmess who, starting as a trick bicycle rider in a circus, engineers his way to wealth and power in the industrial U. S. of the 1920s. His methods are those espoused by the many writers of the Horatio Alger novels that were popular at the time. No, not honesty and prudence, but the methods the Alger heroes actually used: getting chummy with the daughter of the boss. Through womanizing, Barthelmess becomes a tycoon, sitting atop the world. Sadly, that world crumbles as the Great Depression strikes. Wiped out financially, Barthelmess' last female conquest deserts him. Long thought to be an uncompromising social reformer, Pabst left an anomalous message with this film, which seems to say simply: don't get caught in a Great Depression. Following this foray to the New World, Pabst returned to France, then made his blitzkrieg run for Hitler's Germany, the one-time apparent socialist making National Socialist movies for the duration of WW II.

p, James Seymour; d, G.W. Pabst, Arthur Greville Collins; w, Gene Markey, Kathryn Scola (based on the novel by Louis Bromfield); ph, William Rees; ed, James Gibson; art d, Robert Haas; cos, Orry-Kelly.

Drama (PR:A MPAA:NR)

MODERN HERO, A 1941 (SEE: KNUTE ROCKNE-ALL AMERICAN, 1941)

MODERN LOVE** 1/2 (1929) 71m UNIV bw

Charley Chase (John Jones), Kathryn Crawford (Patricia Brown), Jean Hersholt (Renault), Edward Martindel (Weston), Anita Garvin (Brunette), Betty Montgomery.

A partial talkie, with Crawford as a designer for an exclusive dressmaking shop, who in order to keep her estate, must keep her marriage to Chase a secret. Chase poses as the butler and sneaks in and out of Crawford's house before the waking neighbors notice. A well-directed and witty romantic comedy.

d, Arch Heath; w, Albert DeMond, Beatrice Van (based on a story by Van); ph, Jerry Ash.

Comedy (PR:A MPAA:NR)

MODERN MADNESS (SEE: BIG NOISE, THE, 1936)

MODERN MARRIAGE, A* 1/2 (1962) Ken/MON bw (AKA: FRIGID WIFE)

Prolog: Jean Neher (Ruth Turner), Sondra Fisher (Barbara Reed), Sid Noel (Bill Turner), Bob Carr (Larry Reed), Ken Elliott (Dr. Foster); Story: Reed Hadley (Dr. Donald Andrews), Margaret Field (Evelyn Brown), Robert Clarke (Bill Burke), Nana Bryant (Mrs. Brown), Charles Smith (Jimmy Watson), Dick Elliott (Mr. Burke), Lelah Tyler (Mrs. Burke), Pattee Chapman (Mary), Frank Fenton (Mr. Brown), Edward Keane (Dr. Connors), Bert Wenland (Porter), Christine McIntyre (Nurse), Buddy Gorman (Messenger boy), Buddy Swan (Spike), Sherry Jackson (Evelyn, 5 years old), Dian Fauntelle (Secretary's Voice), Peggy Wynne (Nurse), Bret Hamilton (Delivery Man).

Impotence and frigidity in a clinical setting. Originally released in 1950, but re-released in 1961 with a tacked-on prolog, making the picture a film within a film. In the prolog, Neher and Fisher confer in a group-therapy setting with physician Elliott. Neher is unable to relate to her husband sexually; Fisher's husband is unable to relate to her in that very way. Demonstrating therapy by analogy, Elliott recounts the case history (segue into the 1950 release) of the frigid Field, who broke the bond of matrimony immediately after her elopement with Clarke. Following a suicide attempt, Field is seen by psychiatrist Hadley, who spots the natural culprit, her domineering mom. Presumably, this fable helps the prolog pair get it, respectively, off and up.

Prolog: p, John Kenlo [Julius Weinstein]; d, Ben Parker; w, Kenlo; Story: p, David Diamond; d, Paul Landres; w, Sam Roeca, George Wallace Sayre, Paul Popenoe,;

ph, William Sickner; m, Edward J. Kay; ed, Otho Lovering, Philip Cahn; md, Kay; art d, David Milton; set d, Raymond G. Boltz.

Drama (PR:O MPAA:NR)

MODERN MIRACLE, THE
(SEE: STORY OF ALEXANDER GRAHAM BELL, THE, 1939)

MODERN PROBLEMS* 1/2 (1981) 91m FOX c

Chevy Chase (Max), Patty D'Arbanville (Darcy), Mary Kay Place (Lorraine), Nell Carter (Dorita), Brian Doyle-Murray (Brian), Mitch Kreindel (Barry), Dabney Coleman (Mark), Arthur Sellers (Mobile Supervisor), Sandy Helberg (Pete), Neil Thompson, Carl Irwin (Controllers), Ron House (Vendor), Buzzy Linhart (Tile Man), Henry Corden (Dubrovnik), Christine Nazareth (Redhead), Luke Andreas (Tough Guy), Jan Speck (Brunette), Vincenzo Gagliardi (Singer), Francois Cartier (Pianist), Pat Proft (Maitre d'), Jim Hudson (Doctor), Tom Sherohman (Waiter), Frank Birney (Man in Lobby), Reid Olson (Principal Dancer).

Chase is an overworked air-traffic controller who, after being exposed to nuclear waste, discovers he has telekinetic powers. He begins to use his powers to get back at the people who have tried to darken his life. An unfunny but well-cast picture, which assumed that people were still interested in telekinesis. It's the supporting roles that keep this picture from falling completely flat—Place (ex of TV's "Mary Hartman, Mary Hartman"), Coleman (of the same, and of TOOTSIE), and Doyle-Murray (TV's "Saturday Night Live" and brother of actor Bill Murray). Despite its forced humor, the picture grossed more than $15 million on first release.

p, Alan Greisman, Michael Shamberg; d, Ken Shapiro; w, Shapiro, Tom Sherohman, Arthur Sellers; ph, Edmund Koons (DeLuxe Color); m, Dominic Frontiere; ed, Michael Jablow; prod d, Jack Senter; spec eff, Ira Anderson, Jr., Triplane Films; makeup, Jack Wilson.

Comedy **Cas.** (PR:A-C MPAA:PG)

MODERN ROMANCE*** 1/2 (1981) 93m COL c

Albert Brooks (Robert Cole), Kathryn Harrold (Mary Harvard), Tyann Means (Waitress), Bruno Kirby (Jay), Jane Hallaren (Ellen), Karen Chandler (Neighbor), Dennis Kort (Health Food Salesman), Bob Einstein (Sporting Goods Salesman), Virginia Feingold (Bank Receptionist), Thelma Leeds (Mother), Candy Castillo (Drugstore Manager), James L. Brooks (David), George Kennedy (Himself/Zeron), Rick Beckner (Zeon), Jerry Belson (Jerry), Harvey Skolnik (Harvey), Ed Weinberger (Ed), Meadowlark Lemon (Himself), Albert Henderson (Head Mixer), Cliff Einstein (Music Mixer), Gene Garvin (Sound Effects Mixer), Hugh Warden (Bank Dick), Kelly Ann Nakano (Hostess), Joe Bratcher (Jim), George Sasaki, Victor Toyota, Roger Ito (Japanese Businessmen).

Brilliant, hysterically funny, and at times uncomfortably insightful comedy directed by and starring Brooks as a film editor desperately trying to commit himself to his girl friend Harrold. Brooks allows himself torture through all the pain and joy of being in love throughout the course of the film. From the opening scene, where he announces that he no longer wishes to see Harrold (an event, we gather, that has taken place more than once in their relationship), Brooks is a man torn between freedom and dependence. Immediately after the breakup, Brooks throws himself into a routine that he feels will allow him to forget her. He buys hundreds of dollars worth of jogging clothes and vitamins. He goes through his Rotofile of friends and old dates. He avoids talking to his mother. He tries to become absorbed in his work (editing a really bad science-fiction film for an exploitation studio). None of these cures take, and soon Brooks is leaving gifts on Harrold's doorstep in an effort to win her back. He does win her back, but soon all the concern, paranoia, and doubt return and threaten to ruin the relationship once again. Eventually, after a less-than-romantic evening in the mountains, Brooks and Harrold decide to marry. An end title tells us that they were divorced only days later, and then remarried, and then divorced. . . . Not only does MODERN ROMANCE contain some of the most insightful perceptions regarding realistic love relationships ever put on screen, but it also offers an uproarious glimpse into the technical side of the movie business, one never before shown in such detail. Brooks shows the viewer how scenes in a film are edited while advancing the narrative because he's chattering away to his best friend and assistant editor Kirby while doing it. The scene where Brooks and Kirby must dub some sound effects in a mixing studio before a disinterested group of union technicians is fascinating, and yet at the same time, incredibly funny. Brooks is a progressive, innovative comic filmmaker (see also REAL LIFE and LOST IN AMERICA) whose films deserve a wider audience. A Hollywood brat—he's the son of the actor who used a Greek accent and the soubriquet Parkyakarkus to good effect in such films as THE LIFE OF THE PARTY (1937) and EARL CARROLL VANITIES (1945)—Brooks knows the business.

p, Andrew Scheinman, Martin Shafer; d, Albert Brooks; w, Brooks, Monica Johnson; ph, Eric Saarinen (Metrocolor); m, Lance Rubin; ed, David Finfer; prod d, Edward Richardson.

Comedy **Cas.** (PR:C MPAA:R)

MODERN TIMES**** (1936) 85m Chaplin/UA bw

Charles Chaplin (A Worker), Paulette Goddard (Gamine), Henry Bergman (Cafe Owner), Stanley J. Sanford (Big Bill/Worker), Chester Conklin (Mechanic), Hank Mann, Louis Natheaux (Burglars), Stanley Blystone (Sheriff Couler), Allan Garcia (Company Boss), Sam Stein (Foreman), Juana Sutton (Woman with Buttoned Bosom), Jack Low, Walter James (Workers), Dick Alexander (Convict), Dr. Cecil Reynolds (Prison Chaplain), Myra McKinney (Chaplain's Wife), Lloyd Ingraham (Prison Governor), Heinie Conklon (Workman), John Rand, Frank Moran (Convicts), Murdock McQuarrie, Wilfred Lucas, Edward le Saint, Fred Maltesta, Ted Oliver, Edward Kimball.

Sometimes known as "the last of the great silent feature comedies," this picture reflects holdout Chaplin's resistance to the times, which were a-changin'; synchronous dialog was everywhere ascendant by the time of the film's release, yet MODERN TIMES contains mostly sound effects, synchronous music, and a pattern song with nonsense syllables. The film's opening has a shot of a seemingly endless number of sheep racing across the screen and then its corollary, factory-bound workers streaming from a subway train. Chaplin, numbered among the laborers, tightens hexagonal nuts on a seemingly endless stream of steel plates coursing along a conveyor belt. Armed with two wrenches, he nips spasmodically at the bolts as they speed on their way. Momentarily diverted, Chaplin pursues a plate he has missed down the conveyor line, inexorable in his singleness of purpose, decking his coworkers in his frantic flight to tighten the fastenings that have evaded him. Finally catching the errant hardware, Chaplin returns to his normal tempo, only to have boss Garcia, bored, decide to speed up the assembly section. Chaplin's labors become a mad, sporadic jazz ballet. Sneezing, he misses a bolt, then frantically dives onto the conveyor line, hoping to catch it. As his coworkers attempt to hold him back, Chaplin is borne by the moving belt into a chute, to emerge among great cogs and gears, actually at one with the machinery, tightening every available nut in his transit. A worker operates the mechanism that reverses the belt's direction and Chaplin emerges, still madly tightening. Taking a brief break, Chaplin sneaks a cigarette in the washroom. Suddenly, one entire wall of the room becomes a giant TV screen bearing the image of boss Garcia, screaming at the little man to get back to work, a "Big Brother" portent later realized in George Orwell's novel *1984*. Chaplin is next selected to "volunteer" as the test subject for a new automatic feeding machine, by means of which boss Garcia hopes to keep his laborers toiling during what would otherwise be their lunch period. Strapped into the huge mechanized nursemaid, Chaplin faces a turntable with arms that push food into his waiting mouth (including a rotating ear of corn), neatly following each course with a swipe of his soiled mouth by a huge buffer "napkin." A malfunction causes the mechanical feeding station to speed up; it spews shaken-loose hardware, which it shoves into Chaplin's mouth; spills scalding soup in his lap; and grinds his teeth with the rapidly whirling corncob before it flies apart. Returning to the conveyor line after his lunchtime experiment, Chaplin resumes his frenetic labors, which finally drive him as mad as the machinery. Spotting a secretary with nutlike buttons on the back of her clothing, he chases her from the building, pausing in his pursuit only to give a few twists of his wrenches to a fire hydrant outside. Diverted again, he encounters a matronly passerby with nutlike decorations on the bosom of her dress. Again he gives chase, only to be intercepted by a policeman, who reverses the race. Running back into the factory, the berserk little laborer wreaks havoc, using a squirting oil can as a weapon before he is finally captured and led away for treatment at a mental hospital. Cured and released from confinement, Chaplin wanders the city seeking another job. A truck with an overlong load whizzes past him, and its red warning flag flies off. Ever helpful, the little job-seeker picks it up and, waving it in the air to attract attention, follows after the truck. A group of indigent Communists gathers in his wake, trailing the red banner. Arrested as their leader, Chaplin is jailed, finally finding peace and respite in his comfortable cell. A fellow prisoner—a drug addict—conceals some cocaine in a salt cellar, which Chaplin inadvertently uses. Possessed of the sense of enormous strength afforded by the drug, he foils a proposed jailbreak and, all against his will, is given his freedom in reward. Simultaneously, Goddard the gamine—who has stolen food to save her starving sisters—escapes from juvenile officers after her father has been killed in a labor dispute. She and Chaplin meet and enjoy one another's company. When she is caught and taken to a juvenile detention center, he decides to return to a comfortable jail cell and orders a huge meal in a posh restaurant. Unable to pay for the meal, the minuscule mendicant is hastened into a patrol wagon by the police, where he encounters fellow passenger Goddard. Overjoyed at the reunion, the two escape and segue into a dream of suburban bliss in a vine-covered cottage. Substituting the accessible for the fantasy, they move into a deserted waterfront shack—he bedding down in an adjacent outbuilding—and enjoy a simulation of their mutual dream. To further the fantasy, Chaplin finds employment as night watchman in a large department store. He surreptitiously gets the gorgeous gamine into the store, where she may wallow in the luxuries intended for sale to the well-to-do: an ermine bedspread on a down-filled mattress, for one. Seeking to spend as much time as possible with his love, the resourceful watchman has found a way to minimize the time he must spend at his duties; he dons roller skates to speed his way to the time-clock stations within the store. He demonstrates his proficiency on the wheels to his admiring enamorata, performing a remarkable roller ballet, skating perilously close to an atrium ledge with a broken safety railing. When his one-time factory colleagues, discharged from their jobs, break into the store, Chaplin offers them all the hospitality the emporium can afford. Charged with the crime come the dawning, he finds himself once more consigned to the slammer. Her companion in the calaboose, Goddard must seek work; she finds a job as a cabaret singer. When Chaplin is released from prison, she prevails upon the cabaret owner to give him a job as a waiter. One evening, a celebrated singer misses his booking at the cabaret, and Chaplin is pressed into service as his hurried replacement. His featured number is "Je Cherche Apres Titine" (Leo Daniderff). Unable to memorize the lyrics to the tune in so short a time, Chaplin writes them on his celluloid cuffs, planning to peek at them during his rendition. When he strides out on stage, Chaplin shoots his cuffs in a preliminary bit of posturing; they fly from his wrists, landing among the audience, losing him his prompter notes. Unfazed, the clever comedian extemporizes, vamping gibberish lyrics in no known language as he carries the story in pantomime, singing such nonsense phrases as: "Se bella pew satore, je notre so katore/je notre qui kavore, je la ku la qui la kwa!" as all the while his body eloquently speaks of a flirtation with a shy miss who finally succumbs to his amorous advances. At the song's conclusion, the cabaret crowd applauds wildly, and Chaplin's success as a singer seems assured. However, the police are onto the runaway gamine; the two must leave hurriedly to follow a different destiny. Dejected at first by the loss of their close approach to the realization of their mutual dream, they gaze at one another. Seeing what they still have in each other, they perk up; clasping hands, they say "We'll get along," and continue down the road. This remarkable picture—three years in the making, like most of Chaplin's feature pictures (although shooting itself took only $10^1/_2$ months, the shortest shooting schedule on any of his feature films since A WOMAN OF PARIS in 1923)—was hardly novel in its theme of Luddite disaffection with the mechanized society of the times. Following the film's release, Chaplin was sued for plagiarism by the French production company Films Sonores Tobis, producer of Rene Clair's A NOUS LA LIBERTE (1932), representatives of which cited similarities in the conveyor-belt sequences of the two films. The lawsuit was dropped after director Clair pointed out that he would be honored and flattered to find that he had been able to render such assistance to the wonderful "Charlot." "God knows," Clair is reported to have said, "I have certainly borrowed enough from *him*." There seems little doubt that Chaplin's social consciousness had been formed years before, during his impoverished London childhood. The man-eaten-by-machine theme reportedly came to the 12-year-old Chaplin in 1901, when he was apprenticed as a printer's devil and found himself dwarfed by an enormous Wharfedale printing press, which "I thought . . . was going to devour me." Further ideas for the factory sequence of the film came from verbal reports of the Detroit automotive assembly lines and from an enormous automatic dishwashing machine—complete with conveyor belt—Chaplin saw in a Los Angeles restaurant. As early as 1931, two years before production started, Chaplin expressed his concern with the social issues of the Great Depression, stating, "Machinery should benefit mankind. It should not spell tragedy and throw it out of work. . . . Something is wrong. Things have been badly managed when five million men are out of work in the richest country in the world. . . ." And again, speaking of his own adulation by an adoring public, " . . . what kind of a filthy world is this—that makes people lead such wretched lives that if anybody makes 'em laugh they want to kneel down and touch his overcoat, as though he was Jesus Christ raising 'em from the dead. . . ." Chaplin's resistance to synchronous dialog was legend, even though this picture is the first to contain such dialog by the comic master himself (in a sort of parody, a patter song in gibberish). Chaplin *had* spoken for the cinema before, actually—in a newsreel filmed in Vienna in 1931 during a world tour, when he said "*Gute tag, gute tag*" into the microphone—but dialog simply was not his way to go, even as late as 1936. For one thing, he was accustomed to the silent-screen technique of cranking the camera at different rates of speed to modify the tempo of the picture; synchronous dialog had to be shot at a fixed rate of 24 frames per second. For another, he felt that he had no need of dialog, nor, apparently did he; five days after the premiere of MODERN TIMES, Chaplin—with his protege Goddard and her mother—sailed for Honolulu and a well-deserved vacation on the *SS Coolidge*, aboard which he met poet-painter-filmmaker Jean Cocteau. Though neither artist could speak the other's language, Cocteau was to say, "Yet we talked without the slightest difficulty. . . . What is this language? It is a *living* language . . . the language of mime, the language of poets . . . " As early as 1922, Chaplin had compared sound in films with painting statues: "I would as soon rouge marble cheeks," he said, and in 1931, "I give the talkies six months more, at the most a year. Then they're done." Part of the problem in Chaplin's view echoed the anti-mechanistic theme of the film; sadly observing the mountain of equipment gathered together for transport to a location site during shooting, he said, "We used to go to the park with a stepladder, a bucket of whitewash, and Mabel Normand, and make a picture." Still, with all his reservations about the talkies, Chaplin fudged the issue, viewing synchronized dialog as, perhaps, " . . . an addition, not as a substitute" for the vixuals on the screen. Indeed, in November of 1934, Chaplin and Goddard made sound tests at the studio to hear how they might sound should dialog be decided on for the film. Both had good voices, and Chaplin ordered a dialog script prepared. The script was choppy and failed to follow the tempo Chaplin wanted for the film, so he trashed it, going with his first instinct instead. Music and sound effects were a different matter altogether; Chaplin felt that these *belonged*, and he took infinite pains with them. He handled many of the sound effects for MODERN TIMES personally; the stomach-rumbling sounds made by the hungry job-seeker in the film were created by Chaplin blowing bubbles in a pail of water. Work on the musical score took months, with Chaplin and his musical collaborators screening and re-screening sequences of the film. Chaplin was a hard musical taskmaster; during a recording session, he insulted the musicians. Conductor Newman, enraged by Chaplin's rudeness, hurled his baton away and stormed off the stage, cursing as he departed. Newman telephoned mogul Samuel Goldwyn, stating that he would never work with Chaplin again (he didn't, ending a long association). Arranger David Raksin, loyal to Newman, rejected Chaplin's request that he take up the baton, and the task went to co-arranger Edward Powell. MODERN TIMES was costar Goddard's first big break in pictures. Chaplin had met the actress aboard cinemogul Joseph Schenck's yacht when she was doing bit parts in Hal Roach comedies. He formed a close personal relationship with the young actress–22 years his junior—who was to live with him as his wife (some sources cite an undocumented marriage between the two that reportedly took place in China after this film's release). Goddard is a perfect gamine in the picture, as she was in life—a charmer, lovely, vibrant, and active, with a fine sense of humor and a compassionate nature. Many of Chaplin's features had him similarly befriending a homeless girl, including THE VAGABOND (1916), THE CIRCUS (1928), CITY LIGHTS (1931), and, later, LIMELIGHT (1952). He never befriended a more appealing waif than Goddard. Chaplin had originally planned a less happy ending for the two in MODERN TIMES, thinking to reprise the pathos of his previous success, CITY LIGHTS. As originally plotted, the dispirited hero—discharged from the mental hospital following his breakdown—sees his beautiful gamine, who has come to visit him, now a nun. They say their goodbyes, and as she stares after his retreating form, her gamine spirit leaves her black-clad body and dances after him, all unseen. Her kindly old Mother Superior touches her arm, breaking the vision, and she turns away, retreating to her convent. This script—which still exists—might, if followed, have served as a sop to moralists who would otherwise object to the quasi-romantic relationship implicit in the picture between the mature (though ever childlike) protagonist and the gamine, whose indeterminate age was certainly below that of consent. Goddard's gamine character was unique among Chaplin's adoptive waifs in many ways. It was less distanced from him than most of the other orphans of a stormy, unsettled society. Indeed, the gamine is very like her protector; their stories parallel one another in many ways even prior to their first meeting. This might have reflected Chaplin's close relationship with his likable costar, who served as mother to his children, whom even Chaplin's ex-wife Lita liked enormously. Chaplin enjoyed a considerable advantage over his previous films with this one; he was able to do the planning and much of the scripting in privacy, away from his hectic, acolyte-ridden home, aboard the *Panacea*, the 38-foot Chris-Craft motor cruiser he purchased in 1933. MODERN TIMES was enormously successful in the U.S. It was less so in the USSR (where the Stakhanovites were interested in speeding up production, not slowing it) and was banned completely as Communist propaganda in Fascist Italy and in Nazi Germany (whose Fuhrer was to be so cruelly parodied in Chaplin's next film, THE GREAT DICTATOR, in 1940). Still, the film was not a novel departure into social criticism for Chaplin; all his pictures had their share of that, even the old two-reelers. Indeed, one critic said of MODERN TIMES that it was really just four two-reelers strung together: "The Shop," "The Jailbird," The Watchman," and "The Singing Waiter." It is true enough that each of the four sequences can stand on its own; its creator inflexibly followed the muse that had served him so well in his earlier work. This is the film that truly marked the passing of an era; despite its sound-on-film technology, it is the last of the great silent feature pictures. Although he retained much of his silent style—and all of his talent—when he created his future films, the master of mime was finally forced to adapt to modern times. Other songs and musical numbers used in the film include "Hallelujah, I'm a Bum," "Prisoner's Song" (C. Massey), "How Dry Am I" and "In the Evening By the Moonlight" (Bland).

p,d&w, Charles Chaplin; ph, Roland Totheroh, Ira Morgan; m, Chaplin; md, Alfred Newman (uncredited, Edward Powell); art d, Charles D. Hall, Russell Spencer.

Comedy **(PR:A MPAA:NR)**

MODESTY BLAISE** 1/2 (1966, Brit.) 118m FOX c

Monica Vitti *(Modesty Blaise)*, Terence Stamp *(Willie Garvin)*, Dirk Bogarde *(Gabriel)*, Harry Andrews *(Sir Gerald Tarrant)*, Michael Craig *(Paul Hagan)*, Clive Revill *(McWhirter/Sheik Abu Tahir)*, Alexander Knox *(Minister)*, Rossella Falk *(Mrs. Fothergill)*, Scilla Gabel *(Melina)*, Michael Chow *(Weng)*, Joe Melia *(Crevier)*, Saro Urzi *(Basilio)*, Tina Marquand *(Nicole)*, Oliver MacGreevy *(Tattooed Man)*, Jon Bluming *(Hans)*, Lex Schoorel *(Walter)*, Marcello Turilli *(Strauss)*, Giuseppe Paganelli *(Friar)*, Wolfgang Hillinger *(Handsome)*, Roberto Bisacco *(Enrico)*, John Karlsen *(Oleg)*, Silvan *(The Great Pacco)*, John Stacy *(Tyboria Captain)*, Robin Hunter *(Pilot)*, Denys Graham *(Copilot)*, Patrick Ludlow *(Under Secretary)*, Robin Fox *(Man Who Pushes the Doorbell)*, George Fisher.

In her first English-speaking role Vitti, one of Italy's finest actresses, takes the role of popular British comic strip detective Modesty Blaise. She is a super-agent (a la James Bond) who is called upon by the British Secret Service to keep an eye on a Mid-east-bound diamond shipment. Bogarde, in an unlikely but effective piece of casting, plays her archrival, who she mistakenly thought was dead. He's very much alive and, with his gang of sadistic thugs, pursues her and the gems. Eventually she is captured by Bogarde, who forces her assistant, Stamp, to steal the jewels. Vitti escapes (disguised as a monk!) and safely delivers the diamonds to their rightful owner, who in turn presents them to her for her troubles. Well, what do you expect? . . . it's based on a comic strip. Vitti is superbly camp (as is everything else about the picture), making this one of those "fine wine" pictures that get better with age. An ample amount of pop culture, mod clothes, and colorful characters. Bogarde's delicate flower of a villain is wonderfully effete in this, director Losey's closest approach to pure comedy. Songs include "Modesty" (John Dankworth, Benny Green, sung by David and Jonathan), "We Should've" (Dankworth, Green, Evan Jones).

p, Joseph Janni; d, Joseph Losey; w, Evan Jones (based on a story by Peter O'Donnell, Stanley Dubens and the comic strip created by O'Donnell, Jim Holdaway); ph, Jack Hildyard (DeLuxe Color); m, John Dankworth; ed, Reginald Beck; prod d, Richard MacDonald; md, Dankworth; art d, Jack Shampan; cos, Beatrice Dawson, Douglas Hayward, Marissa Martelli; makeup, Neville Smallwood, Martelli.

Spy/Adventure **(PR:A MPAA:NR)**

MODIGLIANI OF MONTPARNASSE***

(1961, Fr./Ital.) 110m Franco London Films-Astra-Pallavicini/CD bw (MONTPARNASSE 19; MONTPARNASSE; AKA: THE LOVERS OF MONTPARNASSE)

Gerard Philipe *(Amedeo Modigliani)*, Lilli Palmer *(Beatrice Hastings)*, Anouk Aimee *(Jeanne Hebuterne)*, Gerard Sety *(Sborowski)*, Lila Kedrova *(Mme. Sborowski)*, Lea Padovani *(Rosalie)*, Jean Lanier *(Hebuterne)*, Denise Vernac *(Mme. Hebuterne)*, Lino Ventura *(Morel)*, Marianne Oswald *(Berthe Weil)*, Antoine Tudal *(Cendrars)*, Francois Jone *(Commissaire of Police)*, Paquerette *(Mme. Salomon)*, Daniel Mendaille *(Professor)*, Harry Max *(Doctor)*, Arlette Poirier *(Lulu)*, Robert Ripa *(Marcel)*, Frank Edwards *(Mr. Dickson)*, Carol Sands *(Mrs. Dickson)*, Judith Magre, Cynda Glenn.

The biography of the alcoholic genius painter Amedeo Modigliani, which was first released in Paris in 1958. Philipe, in the title role, is encouraged to lead a life of wild drinking by his mistress, writer Beatrice Hastings (Palmer). He neglects his health until he meets a young art student, Aimee, with whom he falls in love. Her father soon takes her away, and the painter is told to move to the south of France to improve his tuberculosis. The pair meet again in Nice, where the long-necked lady becomes both his lover and his model. After a failed exhibition of his work, the painter falls to the ground and later dies. As a whole, the film is somewhat of a failure for Becker, but there are enough fine moments to recommend it. It is also interesting as a historical look at an artistically alive period of French life. Originally, Max Ophuls was to have directed (he prepared a script with Henri Jeanson), but with his death in 1957 the project was handed over to Becker (who died shortly afterward, in 1960). Becker's quarrels with Jeanson and the presence of Modigliani's daughter on the set only added to Becker's problems, but in the end he was still able to produce an interesting, though faulted film. Includes a foreword by Jean Cocteau.

p, Ralph Baum; d, Jacques Becker; w, Becker, Max Ophuls, Henri Jeanson (based on the novel *Les Montparnos* by Georges Michel Michel); ph, Christian Matras; m, Georges Van Parys, Paul Misraki, Johann Sebastian Bach; ed, Marguerite Renoir; art d, Jean d' Eaubonne; set d, Maurice Bourbotte; cos, Georges Annenkov; makeup, Yvonne Fortuna.

Biographical Drama **(PR:A MPAA:NR)**

MOGAMBO**** (1953) 115m MGM c

Clark Gable *(Victor Marswell)*, Ava Gardner *(Eloise Y. Kelly)*, Grace Kelly *(Linda Nordley)*, Donald Sinden *(Donald Nordley)*, Philip Stainton *(John Brown Pryce)*, Eric Polhmann *(Leon Boltchak)*, Laurence Naismith *(Skipper)*, Denis O'Dea *(Father Josef)*, Asa Etula *(Young Native Girl)*, Wagenia Tribe of Belgian Congo, Samburu Tribe of Kenya Colony, Bahaya Tribe of Tanganyika, M'Beti Tribe of French Equatorial Africa.

A remarkable and action-packed remake of RED DUST (1932, directed by Victor Fleming), this is one of Ford's more stylish yet unpredictable films, lacking his stock company and the so-called "Fordian elements" that go to make up the director's unmistakable signature. Yet MOGAMBO is solid and exciting, dealing subtly with a love triangle involving white safari leader Gable, showgirl Gardner, and cool, married Kelly. Gardner visits Gable in his African quarters; he learns that she has arrived to be the guest of a rich maharaja who never appears. She must wait for the steamer to arrive to take her away and spends her time with Gable, exchanging barbs and mild insults but falling in love with the virile, self-confident white hunter. She betrays the fact that she's pleased when hearing that the steamer has broken down and her visit must be prolonged. Then Sinden and Kelly arrive, representatives of various zoos. Sinden is an anthropologist who is seeking to capture gorillas in order to study their habits. He hires Gable to lead a safari to capture gorillas and Gardner goes along. Gardner sees that Gable is attracted to beautiful blonde Kelly and she tries to persuade him not to tamper with her. Gable, however, believes he is in love with Kelly and takes Sinden aside to tell him the truth but he stops short when he realizes how deeply he will hurt the kind and faithful husband. Gable has the opportunity to see Sinden killed so he can have Kelly all to himself but, again, he is too noble, and saves the Englishman. To shut off the affection flowing from Kelly, Gable meets with Gardner, drinking with her in her tent and when Kelly comes to investigate the noise, she sees them embracing and kissing. Kelly raises a pistol and shoots Gable in the shoulder. When Sinden comes on the run, Gardner proves she is noble, too, and tells the anthropologist that she, Gardner, shot Gable for making improper advances. Sinden and Kelly leave and Gable is left with Gardner, a woman he realizes he truly loves. He asks her to stay with him and she does. MOGAMBO lacks the lusty story of the original RED DUST, and the wild banter between Gable and his then costar Jean Harlow, who had been dead 16 years when this film was made. Gable is no longer the rough-and-tumble young plantation manager, but a seasoned, somewhat weary white safari guide and hunter. But his female costars, Kelly and Gardner, here exchange the verbal sparring, being diametric opposites. Gardner is the sensual, earthy, and often vulgar type while Kelly is refined, distant, and even prudish. Yet it is Kelly who smoulders with repressed desires that explode at the finale and prove her the lesser person, allowing Gardner to win the pure heart of Gable. Ford provides action all the way, trekking his cameras through Kenya, Tanganyika, and Uganda. Instead of using a traditional bravura score for the film, Ford insisted that the sounds of Africa would be more effective on the sound track. He had scores of animal and bird sounds and dozens of native shouts recorded and interspersed on the sound track, punctuating the dialog and action to lend authenticity to the exotic locales his cameras profiled. The absence of the lush sound track was a rarity for an MGM production; executives thought such devices too experimental for their "family" audience but they deferred to the great Ford. There are scenes reminiscent of Ford's great westerns as he visually exploits the lavish African landscape. In one scene, Gable stoically marches through a gauntlet of spear-holding tribesmen—coming resolutely toward the camera, facing danger—while the horizon spreads to infinity beyond him, a scene not unlike the finale of MY DARLING CLEMENTINE where Henry Fonda (as Wyatt Earp) rides away from the camera, down a road stretching into infinity. Ford does not ignore the torrid scene of the outdoor shower which was one of the highlights of RED DUST, one where bombshell Harlow bathed in the altogether. Here it's Gardner behind the wooden stall with Gable handing her the towel. Where RED DUST was bawdy and brawling and unsophisticated, MOGAMBO (meaning "to speak" in native idiom) is cultured, despite the primitive surroundings, and its characters operate on a more educated, literate level. Their emotions, however, are as earthbound as those in RED DUST. Ford spoke little of this taut production, commenting: "I never saw the original picture. I liked the script and the story. I liked the setup and I'd never been to that part of Africa—so I just did it." With the enormous success of its 1950 production of KING SOLOMON'S MINES, MGM was only too happy to allow Ford a free hand in producing another super adventure-romance film on the Dark Continent. Gable disliked flying and his plane was forced down on a rough plain in East Africa during a hailstorm with hail the size of a man's fists, but then he flew with Ford and other cast and crew members every day from Nairobi to a game preserve in Kenya for location shots. Gardner arrived in Africa with her secretary and then-husband, Frank Sinatra, on hand. The Gardner-Sinatra romance was falling apart as the singer was on the career skids. While in Africa, Sinatra got wind of the fact that Columbia was about to cast FROM HERE TO ETERNITY and he pleaded with his wife to ask her friend, Columbia chief Harry Cohn, to give him a part. She did and Sinatra left to secure the role with a screen test. Meanwhile, according to later reports, Gardner left for London midway during the production to have Sinatra's child but lost the baby in a miscarriage. The actress reportedly told Joe Hyams, "All my life I had wanted a baby and the news that I lost him (I'm sure it was a boy) was the cruelest blow I had ever received. Even though my marriage to Frank was getting shakier every day, I didn't care. I wanted a baby by him." Sinatra had given Gardner a mink coat to celebrate their one-year anniversary as man and wife. The actress took one look at it and then tossed it aside. Gable witnessed the act and later told a friend: "I'd never let a woman treat me like that." Gardner felt that director Ford was ignoring her, that he had nothing but contempt for her as a sex goddess as touted by MGM, but he finally took her aside and told her: "You're damned good. Just take it easy." They then got along famously on and off the set. Ford reported later that "she was a real trouper. She was unhappy over Sinatra but she worked . . . I loved her." Gardner caused more than one set of eyebrows to arch among local officials who came to Ford to complain that she was purposely exhibiting her naked body to the natives when taking open-air baths in her canvas tub. When this was brought up to the actress she laughed and later ran through the camp completely naked for all the cast, crew, and natives to see. Gable's life was altered much by this film. He became an ardent flier and even halted the production so he could fly back to the U.S. to have his teeth fixed (trusting only his American dentist), an ongoing problem with the star. The actor enjoyed hunting and, when the production was stalled for one technical reason or another, he went on hunting expeditions by himself and, before their falling out, sometimes with Ford. He killed a crocodile that had been menacing a river tribe and became a local hero; the natives thereafter called Gable "Bwana." Kelly, however, called Gable "Ba" which was Swahili for "father." Gable liked Gardner but he was emotionally drawn to Kelly, giving her a party on location when the beautiful blonde actress celebrated her 24th birthday. They swam in jungle lakes together and Gable read the poetry Kelly wrote for him. The budding romance ended when Kelly decided that the relationship was impossible since Gable was twice her age. Gable was then suffering from some slight palsy and his hands shook during some takes which Ford patiently reshot. But the director lost his patience with Gable when the actor asked for another take with Gardner when he felt the scene was not right. Ford ignored him, walking away, causing a breach between the actor and director which was not patched up until the cast and crew went to England to finish some interior scenes. MOGAMBO proved to be a box office bonanza for MGM, returning almost $5 million from its initial release. Gable finished BETRAYED for the studio the next year and then departed forever as executives wrung their hands in financial anguish. They had wanted to get rid of the salary-heavy star but MOGAMBO and BETRAYED so shored up Gable's image and box office appeal that he was again rising to mainstream popularity. He refused to discuss another contract and went off to make films elsewhere, taking with him his $400,000 in pension money. The story was used one other time, when Gable reprised his RED DUST role in 1940 for a "Gulf Screen Guild" radio production, also featuring Ann Sothern (playing the Harlow role) and Jeffrey Lynn.

p, Sam Zimbalist; d, John Ford; w, John Lee Mahin (based on the play "Red Dust" by Wilson Collison); ph, Robert Surtees, F. A. Young (Technicolor); ed, Frank Clarke; art d, Alfred Junge; cos, Helen Rose.

Adventure/Romance   Cas.   (PR:A   MPAA:NR)

MOGLIAMANTE   (SEE: WIFEMISTRESS, 1977, Ital.)

MOHAMMAD, MESSENGER OF GOD**¹/₂**
(1976, Lebanon/Brit.) 179m Filmco International/Tarik-Irwin Yablans c (AL-RIS-ALAH; AKA: THE MESSAGE)

Anthony Quinn (*Hamza*), Irene Papas (*Hind*), Michael Ansara (*Abu-Sofyan*), Johnny Sekka (*Bilal*), Michael Forest (*Khalid*), Damien Thomas (*Zaid*), Garrick Hagon (*Ammar*), Ronald Chenery (*Mosaab*), Michael Godfrey (*Barra*), Peter Madden (*Toothless Man*), Habib Ageli (*Hudayfa*), Ahmed Abdelhalim (*Uriqat*), George Camiller (*Waleed*), Neville Jason (*Jaafar*), Martin Benson (*Abu-Jahal*), Robert Brown (*Otba*), Wolfe Morris (*Bu-Lahab*), Bruno Barnabe (*Umaya*), John Humphry (*Ubada*), John Bennett (*Salool*), Donald Burton (*Amr*), Andre Morell (*Abu-Talib*), Rosalie Crutchley (*Somaya*), Ewen Solon (*Yasser*), Elaine Ives Cameron (*Arwa*), Nicholas Amer (*Suheil*), Gerard Hely (*Sinan*), Hassan Joundi (*Kisra*), Earl Cameron (*Annajashi*), Ronald Leigh-Hunt (*Heraclius*), Leonard Trolley (*Silk Merchant*), Salem Gedara (*Wahshi*), Mohammad Al Gaddary (*Money Lender*); Richard Johnson (*Narrator*).

Though the film is really just your run-of-the-mill, multimillion-dollar religious spectacle, MOHAMMAD, MESSENGER OF GOD became notorious for the controversy surrounding its production and release, the dramatic climax of which came when black Muslim terrorists held a Washington, D.C., B'nai B'rith building and its employees hostage, threatening to kill everyone unless the American premiere of the film was canceled. It hardly seemed worth all the fuss because this religious epic, which dramatically illustrates the beginnings of the Muslim faith, is not very good. The main problem with the film is that though the sacred Mohammad's name is in the title, the holy man himself was not allowed to appear on screen due to the Muslims' fanatical belief that he should never be visually represented. Presented with this seemingly fatal drawback, first-time producer-director Moustapha Akkad decided to go for the next best thing and have the film concentrate on Mohammad's Uncle Hamza, a brave warrior. When rumors flew that everyone from Charlton Heston to Peter O'Toole was to play the role (some sects misunderstood and assumed that these bastions of white-bread Western culture were to play *Mohammad*) several fanatical Muslim sects threatened to blow up the production. After a lot of fancy talking, Akkad convinced the Muslims that the film would be done in good taste and even hired a group of Muslim religious scholars to approve every page of the screenplay. This seemed to calm everyone down, but then, inexplicably, after the film was in production the religious experts changed their minds and *condemned* the whole production. After the company constructed a massive set duplicating Mecca in Morocco, an angry King Faisal of Saudi Arabia put the screws to Morocco's King Hassan and forced him to kick the filmmakers out, using the excuse that Akkad's expensive and very realistic set of Mecca might confuse true believers traveling to pray in the real Holy City and cause them to mistakenly venture into the bogus Mecca. Left without a set—or, in fact, a country in which to shoot—Akkad eventually turned to none other than the psycho-ruler of Libya, Muammar Qaddafi, for support. Eventually, after having bounced around in every major Muslim nation and spending millions upon millions of dollars, MOHAMMAD, MESSENGER OF GOD was released, much to the chagrin of the terrorists who ensured that the film got some bad word-of-mouth and it promptly bombed.

p&d, Moustapha Akkad; w, H.A.L. Craig, A.B. Jawdat Al-Sahhar, Tawfik Al-Hakim, A.B. Rahman Al-Sharkawi, Mohammad Ali Maher; ph, Jack Hildyard, Said Baker, Ibrahim Salem (Panavision, Eastmancolor); m, Maurice Jarre; ed, John Bloom; prod d, Tambi Larsen, Maurice Fowler; md, Jarre; art d, Terry Parr, Nejib Khoury; cos, Phyllis Dalton; makeup, Neville Smallwood, Alan Boyle; stunts, Ken Buckle.

Religious Drama   (PR:C-O   MPAA:PG)

MOHAWK**¹/₂   (1956) 79m FOX c

Scott Brady (*Jonathan Adams*), Rita Gam (*Onida*), Neville Brand (*Rokhawah*), Lori Nelson (*Cynthia Stanhope*), Allison Hayes (*Greta*), John Hoyt (*Butler*), Vera Vague [Barbara Jo Allen] (*Aunt Agatha*), Rhys Williams (*Clem Jones*), Ted De Corsia (*Indian Chief Kowanen*), Mae Clarke (*Minikah His Wife*), John Hudson (*Capt. Langley*), Tommy Cook (*Keoga*), Michael Granger (*Priest*), James Lilburn (*Sergeant*), Chabon Jadi (*Dancer*).

Set along the east coast before this country won its independence, this "eastern" western casts Brady as the heroic Boston artist who is more than popular with the ladies. He's got Mohawk princess Gam after him, as well as Bostonian Nelson and barmaid Hayes. When he's commissioned to paint some landscapes for a Massachusetts Indian society, he gets entangled in a conflict between the redskins and the settlers of Mohawk Valley. The trouble stems from greedy land-grabber Hoyt, who killed the son of a Mohawk chief. It takes the death of Indian warrior Brand, at the hands of Brady, to put an end to the conflict. Brady returns to his palette and ties the knot with hometown girl Nelson.

p, Edward L. Alperson; d, Kurt Neumann; w, Maurice Geraghty, Milton Krims; ph, Karl Struss (Widevision, Eastmancolor); m, Edward L. Alperson, Jr.; ed, William B. Murphy; md, Raoul Kraushaar; m/l "Mohawk," "Love Plays the Strings of My Banjo," Alperson, Jr., Paul Herrick.

Western   (PR:A   MPAA:NR)

MOJAVE FIREBRAND*¹/₂   (1944) 55m REP bw

Bill Elliott, George "Gabby" Hayes, Anne Jeffreys, LeRoy Mason, Jack Ingram, Harry McKim, Karl Hackett, Forrest Taylor, Hal Price, Marshall Reed, Kenne Duncan, Bud Geary, Jack Kirk, Fred Graham, Tom London, Frank Ellis, Tom Steele, Bob Burns, Jess Cavan, Art Dillard, Bud Osborne, Larry Steers.

A quintessential Hayes role has him as a crotchety old prospector whose years of struggle finally pay off with a large silver find. A gang of thugs get wind of this news and are quick to impose themselves onto Hayes, leaving ample opportunity for Elliott to come to the rescue.

p, Eddy White; d, Spencer G. Bennett; w, Norman S. Hall; ph, Ernest Miller; m, Mort Glickman; ed, Harry Keller; art d, Fred Ritter.

Western   (PR:A   MPAA:NR)

MOKEY*¹/₂   (1942) 88m MGM bw

Dan Dailey, Jr. (*Herbert Delano*), Donna Reed (*Anthea Delano*), Bobby "Robert" Blake [Mickey Gubitosi] (*Mokey Delano*), Cordell Hickman (*Booker T. Cumby*), William "Buckwheat" Thomas (*Brother Cumby*), Etta McDaniel (*Cindy Molishus*), Marcella Moreland (*Begonia Cumby*), George Lloyd (*Pat Esel*), Matt Moore (*Mr. Pennington*), Cleo Desmond (*Aunt Deedy*), Cliff Clark (*Mr. Graham*), Mary Field (*Mrs. Graham*), Bobby Stebbins (*Brickley Autry*), Sam McDaniel (*Uncle Ben*).

One of the many B pictures cranked out by MGM during its contract-player years to showcase new talent, this little film had a lot of talent in the showcase. Reed received an Academy Award as Best Supporting Actress for FROM HERE TO ETERNITY; Dailey (he soon dropped the "Jr." from his name) became one of the most celebrated song-and-dance men in the movies; Blake (who, when even younger, appeared in "Our Gang" comedies as Mickey Gubitosi) went on to become a TV superstar. The thin plot deals with the difficulties Blake experiences in dealing with his new stepmother, Reed. Basically a chronicle of malicious mischief with a final happy ending.

p, J. Walter Ruben; d, Wells Root; w, Root, Jan Fortune (based on stories by Jennie Harris Oliver); ph, Charles Rosher; ed, Frank Sullivan.

Drama   (PR:A   MPAA:NR)

MOLE, THE   (SEE: EL TOPO, 1971, Span.)

MOLE PEOPLE, THE*   (1956) 77m UNIV bw

John Agar (*Dr. Roger Bentley*), Cynthia Patrick (*Adad Gizelle*), Hugh Beaumont (*Dr. Jud Bellamin*), Alan Napier (*Elinu High Priest*), Nestor Paiva (*Prof. Etienne Lafarge*), Phil Chambers (*Dr. Paul Stuart*), Rodd Redwing (*Nazer*), Robin Hughes (*First Officer*), Arthur D. Gilmour (*Sharu*), Dr. Frank Baxter (*Himself*), Yvonne De Lavallade (*Dancer*), James Logan (*Officer*), Kay Kuter, John Dodsworth, Marc Hamilton (*Priests*), Pat Whyte (*Guard*), Joseph Abdullah (*Arab Foreman*), Billy Miller (*Arab Boy*), Eddie Parker (*Moleman*).

A setting of scientific hullabaloo surrounds this terrible tale of a team of explorers headed by Agar and Beaumont, who descend into an Asian mountain's depths and discover a race of albinos living in complete darkness. They also find a race of mole people who are the slaves of the albinos. When the albinos give Agar and Beaumont a hard time, the mole folks emerge and lend a helping hand. The weapon used by our heroes in their thankfully unbloody combat with the albinos is a flashlight, which serves them well until the batteries fail. Heroine Patrick, unlike her pallid mountain-dwelling brethren, has a touch of melanin in her makeup, and thus seems not to have been within the mountain for as long as the rest of her race. Includes a hysterical (however unintentionally so) prolog from a University of Southern California professor (Baxter) who comments on the scientific nature of the film's subject matter. If only the theater were as dark as the mole people's pitch-black living quarters.

p, William Alland; d, Virgil Vogel; w, Laszlo Gorog; ph, Ellis Carter; m, Hans J. Salter; ed, Irving Birnbaum; md, Joseph Gershenson; art d, Alexander Golitzen, Robert E. Smith; cos, Jay A. Morley, Jr; spec eff, Clifford Stine; makeup, Bud Westmore.

Science Fiction **(PR:A MPAA:NR)**

MOLESTER, THE
(SEE: NEVER TAKE CANDY FROM A STRANGER, 1961, Brit.)

MOLLY (SEE: GOLDBERGS, THE, 1950)

MOLLY AND LAWLESS JOHN** (1972) 97m Malibu/PDC c

Vera Miles *(Molly Parker)*, Sam Elliott *(Johnny Lawler)*, Clu Gulager *(Deputy)*, John Anderson *(Sheriff Parker)*, Cynthia Myers *(Dolly)*, Charles A. Pinney, Robert Westmoreland, Melinda Chavaria, Pasqualita Baca, George LeBow, Dave Burleson, Grady Hill, Dick Bullock, Terry Kingsley-Smith.

Outlaw Elliot cons his way out of jail by befriending sheriff's wife Miles. After the pair run off together, however, Miles gets fed up with his macho behavior and kills him. She returns to her husband (Anderson), makes up a kidnaping story, and demands her reward money. A heavy supply of cliches weighs down this feminist joke beyond the repair of Nelson's apt direction.

p, Dennis Durney; d, Gary Nelson; w, Terry Kingsley-Smith; ph, Charles Wheeler (DeLuxe Color); m, Johnny Mandel; ed, Gene Fowler, Jr.; prod d, Mort Rabinowitz; set d, Ray Paul; m/l, Mandel, Marilyn and Alan Bergman.

Western **(PR:A MPAA:PG)**

MOLLY AND ME** (1929) 87m TS bw

Belle Bennett *(Molly Wilson)*, Joseph E. Brown [Joe E. Brown] *(Jim Wilson)*, Alberta Vaughn *(Peggy McCoy)*, Charles Byer *(Dan Kingsley)*.

This very early talkie, like many of its time, had only about 17 minutes of sound, with the rest of the narrative carried by titles. The story concerns a burlesque team, Bennett and the irrepressible Brown (who went on to greater things), who play mostly to the hicks in the sticks. When Brown gets a lucrative offer to play the big-city Frolics as a solo, he accepts the engagement and Bennett, forced to play it single, resumes her rustic rounds. Vamped by Vaughn during his stint on the New York stage, Brown pens a missive to Bennett attesting his plans to stay solo until he lands the lovely novelty act. On learning that vixen Vaughn was simply demonstrating friendliness, Brown tries to recover his letter to Bennett. Too late! The disconsolate Bennett, heartbroken but a trouper to the last, continues her theatrical engagement. Brown, having entrained to town, takes a box in her theater and from it croons one of their old duets. She joins in the refrain and once again the troupers are twain.

d, Albert Ray; w, Lois Leeson, Fred and Fannie Hatton; ph, Frank Zucker, Ernest Miller; m, Hugo Riesenfeld; ed, Russell Shields; md, Joseph Littau; m/l, "In the Land of Make Believe," by L. Wolfe Gilbert and Abel Baer.

Musical/Drama **(PR:A MPAA:NR)**

MOLLY AND ME*** (1945) 76m FOX bw

Gracie Fields *(Molly)*, Monty Woolley *(Graham)*, Roddy McDowall *(Jimmy Graham)*, Reginald Gardiner *(Peabody)*, Natalie Schafer *(Kitty)*, Edith Barrett *(Julia)*, Clifford Brooke *(Pops)*, Aminta Dyne *(Musette)*, Queenie Leonard *(Lily)*, Doris Lloyd *(Mrs. Graham)*, Patrick O'Moore *(Ronnie)*, Lewis L. Russell *(Sir Arthur Burroughs)*, Ethel Griffies *(Mrs. Lamb)*, Eric Wilton *(George)*, Jean Del Val *(Pierre)*, Leyland Hodgson *(Manager)*, Lillian Bronson *(Perkins)*, David Clyde *(Angus)*, Jerry Shane *(Messenger Boy)*, Boyd Irwin *(Lord Alexander)*, Ottola Nesmith *(Lady Alexander)*, Tony Ellis *(Flower Boy)*, Walter Tetley *(Grocery Boy)*, Gordon Richards *(McDougall)*, Matthew Boulton *(Sergeant)*, Leslie Denison *(Policeman)*, Jean Prescott *(Barmaid)*.

Fields is charming as an unemployed entertainer who undertakes the task of housekeeping for autocratic English aristocrat Woolley, a retired Member of Parliament who has alienated the scion of his noble house, McDowall. Discharging Woolley's disgruntled domestics, who have been stealing from him, she replaces them with her show-business friends. Her personality and understanding handling of his affairs charm the lion-like lord, whom she reconciles with his heir. When Woolley's ex-wife Lloyd appears with a scheme to blackmail the bearded bully, Fields enlists the aid of her theatrical co-workers to simulate a situation in which the would-be extortionist appears to have committed murder. Fields sings several songs, including "Bring Back My Bonnie," "The Awfulness, the Sinfulness, the Wickedness of Men," and "Christopher Robin."

p, Robert Bassler; d, Lewis Seiler; w, Leonard Praskins, Roger Burford (based on the novel by Frances Marion); ph, Charles Clarke; m, Cyril J. Mockridge; ed, John McCafferty; md, Emil Newman; art d, Lyle Wheeler, Albert Hogsett; cos, Yvonne Wood; spec eff, Fred Sersen.

Musical/Comedy **(PR:A MPAA:NR)**

MOLLY LOUVAIN
(SEE: STRANGE LOVE OF MOLLY LOUVAIN, THE, 1932)

MOLLY MAGUIRES, THE*** (1970) 124m Tamm Productions/PAR c

Richard Harris *(James McParlan/McKenna)*, Sean Connery *(Jack Kehoe)*, Samantha Eggar *(Mary Raines)*, Frank Finlay *(Davies)*, Anthony Zerbe *(Dougherty)*, Bethel Leslie *(Mrs. Kehoe)*, Art Lund *(Frazier)*, Anthony Costello *(Frank McAndrew)*, Philip Bourneuf *(Father O'Connor)*, Brendan Dillon *(Mr. Raines)*, Frances Heflin *(Mrs. Frazier)*, John Alderson *(Jenkins)*, Malachy McCourt *(Bartender)*, Susan Goodman *(Mrs. McAndrew)*, Peter Rogan *(Gomer James)*, William Clune *(Franklin Gowen)*, Phillip Richards *(Gen. Charles Albright)*, Karen Machon *(Girl at Football Game)*, Tom Jones *(Football Player)*.

The Molly Maguires were members of a secret union organization made up of malcontent anthracite miners of eastern Pennsylvania, circa 1876. In order to improve working conditions and correct the inhuman treatment members received from flinty, cruel mine owners, the Mollies dynamited and sabotaged mines, killed bosses, and made up a large lethal underground force that struck terror into the heart of the government itself. At least that's what this absorbing movie relates, whether it be fiction or fact. The leader, Jack Kehoe (Connery) is a tough, shrewd adversary to the owners and his iron hand runs the Mollies. The owners hire Harris, a Pinkerton detective, to infiltrate the Mollies and report their activities back to them so they can eradicate the Irish menace. Harris rents a room in the home of a disabled miner and promptly begins to court his daughter, Eggar, while he lets it be known that he is wanted for murder. Connery, though he is given in-depth reports about Harris which confirm that he is an enemy of the owners, is skeptical about Harris and delays recruiting him into the Mollies. Then Harris helps Connery's football team defeat a Welsh group on the field and later administers a savage beating to a brutal policeman. He is tentatively taken into the secret society and, to further convince Connery of his sincerity, he votes to murder a mine boss and even rescues one of the Mollies involved in the killing. When Eggar's father dies, Connery and Harris—now fast allies—break into a company store to steal a suit for the burial, then set fire to the place. Later, Connery and Costello plan to blow up a mine, but when Harris gets wind of the plan he turns them over to police. Raids are led against the society's leaders; many of them are shot to death while in their beds with their wives by private policemen. Connery is captured and thrown into prison, with Harris testifying against him. Harris meets with Connery in his prison cell as Connery waits to be hanged, seeking absolution from the Irish leader. None is forthcoming, only hate and Connery's branding of traitor. Moreover, Harris is wholly rejected by Eggar as being a Judas. The Pinkerton detective, as in real life, goes off to head the Denver department of the agency while Connery goes to his death. This was a costly film to make, more than $11 million going into a production that was shot almost wholly on location in eastern Pennsylvania in Eckley, Llewelyn, Wilkes-Barre, Bloomsburg, and Hazelton, with additional scenes shot in Chunk, Weatherly, Mauch, and Ashland. Much of the early period is suberbly captured in the crude mining town sets, the homes, and the music which includes such traditional Irish songs as "Gary Owen," "Eileen Aroon," and "Cockles and Mussels." Ritt's direction, however, is airless and sluggish and, when scenes are set in the mines, outright claustrophobic with camerman Howe—normally an outstanding cinematographer—dwelling on long shots, and such dim lighting that it's next to impossible to discern many of the scenes in the mine shafts. In his attempt to reach authenticity and use only available torch and helmet light (the weak candles affixed to the miner's helmets), Howe pitched the production into dismal darkness. Connery is good, as is Harris, but Ritt allows them to sink into dialects that almost make them inarticulate. The story is all Pinkerton and highly prejudiced as such. The awful plight of the miners at the time—with no job protection whatsoever, putting them wholly at the mercy of the owners—receives short shrift; they are portrayed as savage, murderous, and unfeeling creatures, not worthy of empathy or understanding. The film cannot compare with John Ford's masterpiece about coal miners, HOW GREEN WAS MY VALLEY (1941), but it has moments of quality and passion that are memorable. It failed miserably at the box office, returning only $1.5 million from its initial release.

p, Martin Ritt, Walter Bernstein; d, Ritt; w, Bernstein (based on the book *Lament for the Molly Maguires* by Arthur H. Lewis); ph, James Wong Howe (Panavision, Technicolor); m, Henry Mancini; ed, Frank Bracht; art d, Tambi Larsen; set d, Darrell Silvera; cos, Dorothy Jeakins; spec eff, Willis Cook; makeup, Wally Westmore; stunts, Roger Creed.

Historical Drama **(PR:C-O MPAA:PG)**

MOM AND DAD* (1948) 87m Hallmark/Hygienic bw

Hardie Albright *(Carl Blackburn)*, Sarah Blake *(Lois Austin)*, George Eldridge *(Dan Blake)*, June Carlson *(Joan Blake)*, Jimmy Clark *(Dave Blake)*, Bob Lowell *(Jack Griffin)*.

An exploitation picture disguised as a morality play, MOM AND DAD has a legal history much more interesting than its story. The plot deals with a girl whose mother doesn't tell her about the birds and the bees, so she's easy prey to the first Lothario to come along. When she turns up pregnant, her mother blames herself and with her daughter leaves town. Concluding scenes are documentary footage of the birth of a baby, followed by some lurid demonstrations of the effects of syphillis. When first released in 1948, the Director of Public Safety for Newark, New Jersey, tried to revoke the license of the exhibitor, claiming that the film was suitable only for educational purposes; a re-release in 1956 was denied licensing as indecent by the New York state censorship board, although the film was licensed on appeal. In Chicago in 1958 the film was banned as obscene and immoral if shown for entertainment—as an educational film it was allright. It is hard now to see what was so offensive about the film. Its low budget look and flat acting would probably put most people to sleep before they'd see anything offensive.

p, Kroger Babb, Jack Hossey; d, William Beaudine; w, Mildred Horn; ph, Barney Saracky.

Drama   **(PR:O MPAA:NR)**

MOMENT BY MOMENT zero   (1978) 105m UNIV c

Lily Tomlin *(Trisha)*, John Travolta *(Strip)*, Andra Akers *(Naomi)*, Bert Kramer *(Stu)*, Shelley R. Bonus *(Peg)*, Debra Feuer *(Stacie)*, James Luisi *(Dan Santini)*, John O'Leary *(Pharmacist)*, Neil Flanagan *(Storekeeper)*, Jarvais Hudson *(Gas Station Attendant)*, Tom Slocum *(Band Leader)*, Michael Consoldane *(Hotel Desk Clerk)*, Jo Jordan *(Bookstore Lady)*, Joseph Schwab *(Druggist)*.

A well-meant but poorly executed love story involving the attraction of an older woman (Tomlin) for a younger man (Travolta). Tomlin is separated from her husband and lives in a beach house, when along comes beach boy-bum Travolta, who begins pursuing her with almost adolescent passion. Hackneyed scripting makes Travolta's earnest and likeable efforts in the role a waste of talent. Too bad. The subject needs exploring, considering the rash of stories about older men falling for younger women.

p, Robert Stigwood; d&w, Jane Wagner; ph, Phillip Lathrop (Panavision); m, Lee Holdridge; prod d, Harry Horner; ed, John F. Burnett; cos, Albert Wolsky.

Romance/Drama   **(PR:O MPAA:R)**

MOMENT OF DANGER   (SEE: MALGA, 1960, Brit.)

MOMENT OF INDISCRETION*   (1958, Brit.) 71m Danzigers/UA bw

Ronald Howard *(John Miller)*, Lana Morris *(Janet Miller)*, John Van Eyssen *(Corby)*, John Witty *(Bryan)*, Denis Shaw *(Inspector Marsh)*, Ann Lynn *(Pauline)*, John Stone *(Eric)*, Arnold Bell *(Surgeon)*, Judy Bruce, Piers Keelan, Mark Singleton, Totti Truman Taylor, Walter Horsbrugh, Stuart Saunders, Robert Dorning, Brian Haines.

Reluctant to disclose her whereabouts on the night of the murder of her one-time fiance's mistress—she had gone to wish her old friend bon voyage on the eve of his departure from the country—married-woman Morris is accused of the murder. Police have traced to her a handkerchief she inadvertently dropped at the scene of the crime. Her ever-loyal husband Howard leaps to her defense and runs down the real killer in this ineptly written thriller.

p, Edward J. and Harry Lee Danziger; d, Max Varnel; w, Brian Clemens, Eldon Howard; ph, Jimmy Wilson.

Crime/Drama   **(PR:A MPAA:NR)**

MOMENT OF TERROR***   (1969, Jap.) 100m Toho bw (JAP: HIKINIGE)

Hideko Takamine *(The Mother)*, Yoko Tsukasa, Eitaro Ozawa, Hisashi Nakayama, Toshio Kurosawa, Daisuke Kato, Natsuko Kahara, Yutaka Sada.

A dark melodrama about a woman whose child is run over by a car driven by the wife of an executive. The mother gets a job in the woman's house with the intention of killing her son, who is the same age as the dead boy. A depressing idea, which falls in line with the body of Naruse' work. Naruse made one more picture after this one before his death in 1969. Originally released in Japan in 1966.

p, Masumi Fujimoto; d, Mikio Naruse; w, Zenzo Matsuyama; ph, Rokuro Nishigaki (Tohoscope); m, Masaru Sato.

Drama   **(PR:C MPAA:NR)**

MOMENT OF TRUTH, THE**

(1965, Ital./Span.) 105m Federiz-A.S/Rizzoli c (VIVIR DESVIVIENDOSE; EL MOMENTO DE LA VERDAD; IL MOMENTO DELLA VERITA)

Miguel "Miguelin" Mateo *(Miguel)*, Pedro Basauri *(Maestro Pedrucho)*, Jose Gomez Sevillano *(Impresario)*, Linda Christian *(American Woman)*.

Farm boy Mateo heads for the bullrings of Barcelona and quickly becomes a subject of the press as he rises to the top of the toreador pantheon. His downfall is just as abrupt, however, as he dies in the ring while facing a killer bull. Rosi, a fine director in the neorealist tradition, seems to contradict his goals by dubbing this otherwise truthful study of Spanish bullfighting into Italian.

p, Antonio Cervi, Francesco Rosi; d, Rosi; w, Rosi, Pedro Portabella, Ricardo Munoz Suay, Pedro Beltran, Raffaele La Capria (based on a story by Rosi); ph, Gianni Di Venanzo, Aiace Parolin, Pasquale De Santis (Techniscope, Technicolor); m, Piero Piccioni; ed, Mario Serandrei; set d, Jose Antonio de la Guerra.

Drama   **(PR:A MPAA:NR)**

MOMENT OF TRUTH   (SEE: NEVER LET GO, 1962, Brit.)

MOMENT TO MOMENT**   (1966) 108m UNIV c

Jean Seberg *(Kay Stanton)*, Honor Blackman *(Daphne Fields)*, Sean Garrison *(Mark Dominic)*, Arthur Hill *(Neil Stanton)*, Gregoire Aslan *(Inspector DeFargo)*, Peter Robbins *(Timmy Stanton)*, Donald Woods *(Mr. Singer)*, Walter Reed *(Hendricks)*, Albert Carrier *(Travel Agent)*, Lomax Study *(Albie)*, Richard Angarola *(Givet)*, Georgette Anys *(Louise)*.

A standard suspenser from Mervyn LeRoy which casts the pixied Seberg as the lonely wife of Hill, who is always away giving psychiatric lectures. While he's away, Seberg starts to play, choosing young naval officer Garrison as her lover. A quarrel between the two ends in the accidental shooting to death of Garrison, with panic-stricken Seberg, trying to hide the body, calling upon her trustworthy neighbor, Blackman, to help. They toss the body in a ravine and anonymously call the police, but when the cops show up—no body. Surprise—Garrison was only wounded and is suffering from amnesia in a nearby hospital. The ending has all the mess cleaned up, with Garrison quietly returning to his post after being treated by the cuckolded husband and Seberg and Hill living happily ever after. Unfortunately, LeRoy starts off with an intriguing premise, but takes the easy way out by resorting

to the familiar "amnesia" excuse. Seberg looks wonderful, especially against the background of the French Riviera, recalling her days of BONJOUR TRISTESSE.

p&d, Mervyn LeRoy; w, John Lee Mahin, Alec Coppel (based on Coppel's story "Laughs With a Stranger"); ph, Harry Stradling (Technicolor); m, Henry Mancini; ed, Philip W. Anderson; art d, Alexander Golitzen, Alfred Sweeney; set d, John McCarthy, John Austin; makeup, Bud Westmore; hairstyles, Larry Germain; cos, Rosemary Odell, Yves Saint Laurent; m/l, "Moment to Moment," Johnny Mercer, Mancini.

Drama   **(PR:A MPAA:NR)**

MOMENTS**1/2   (1974, Brit.) 102m Pemini Organisation c

Keith Michell, Angharad Rees, Bill Fraser, Jeannette Sterke, Donald Hewlett, Keith Bell, Val Minifie, Paul and Helena Michell.

A depressing picture about a middle-aged British accountant who barely makes it through his daily routine. After 20 years of the same, boring job, and the death of his wife and child in an automobile accident, he packs his bags and heads for a resort where he and his family shared many unforgettable moments. He has a meaningless affair with a shapely young woman, but eventually commits suicide. Take a pass on this one.

p, Peter Crane, Michael Sloan, David M. Jackson; d, Crane; w, Sloan; ph, Wolfgang Suschitzky (Eastmancolor); m, John Cameron; ed, Roy Watts; set d, Bruce Atkins.

Drama   **(PR:O MPAA:NR)**

MOMMAN, LITTLE JUNGLE BOY

(SEE: LITTLE JUNGLE BOY, 1969, Aust.)

MOMMIE DEAREST zero   (1981) 129m PAR c

Faye Dunaway *(Joan Crawford)*, Diana Scarwid *(Christina Crawford as an Adult)*, Steve Forrest *(Greg Savitt)*, Howard Da Silva *(Louis B. Mayer)*, Mara Hobel *(Christina as a Child)*, Rutanya Alda *(Carol Ann)*, Harry Goz *(Al Steele)*, Michael Edwards *(Ted Gelber)*, Jocelyn Brando *(Barbara Bennett)*, Priscilla Pointer *(Mrs. Chadwick)*, Joe Abdullah *(Captain)*, Gary Allen *(Jimmy the Photographer)*, Selma Archerd *(Connie)*, Adrian Aron *(Woman Guest)*, Xander Berkeley *(Christopher Crawford as an Adult)*, Matthew Campion *(Bruce, Actor in Soap)*, Carolyn Coates *(Mother Superior)*, Jerry Douglas *(Interviewer)*, Margaret Fairchild *(Mother Superior at Orphanage)*, Ellen Feldman *(Ginny)*, James Kirkwood *(Master of Ceremonies)*, Virginia Kiser *(Beth Simpson)*, Phillip R. Allen, Michael D. Gainsborough, Matthew Faison *(Executives)*, Robert Harper *(David)*, Cathy Lind Hayes *(Nurse)*, Victoria James *(Photographer)*, Dawn Jeffory *(Vera)*, S. John Launer *(Chairman of Board)*, Russ Marin *(Funeral Director)*, Nicholas Mele *(Assistant Director)*, Belita Moreno *(Belinda Rosenberg)*, Warren Munson *(Lawyer)*, Alice Nunn *(Helga)*, Norman Palmer *(Male Guest)*, David F. Price *(Tony)*, Jeremy Scott Reinbolt *(Christopher Crawford at Age 5)*, Michael Talbott *(Driver)*, Arthur Taxier *(Decorator)*, Joseph Warren *(Mr. Dodd)*, Erica Wexler *(Susan)*.

With the possible exception of Adolph Hitler, nobody deserves the kind of axe-murderer's work done on Joan Crawford in MOMMIE DEAREST. The book sold 4 million copies, a tribute to the public's desire to see dirty linen, and producer Yablans thought he could get the same kind of business at the theaters. Crawford is portrayed as a combination of Medea and Medusa, although the picture was so poorly done that no one cared and her legend and work will live far longer than the memory of this abortion. It begins in 1939, after Crawford had already been married to Douglas Fairbanks, Jr. and Franchot Tone. She is a huge star but is not happy living in her huge home (more about that place later) with her secretary, Alda, a long-suffering assistant. Dunaway, in a remarkable makeup job, talks to her lawyer-lover, Forrest, and he handles all the paper work necessary for Dunaway to adopt a female child, Hobel. Dunaway names the child Christina and swears to give it all the things that she never had. Hobel is an ordinary tyke and finds it difficult living with a perfectionist mother who is a cross between CRAIG'S WIFE (which Crawford played to perfection in HARRIET CRAIG) and Lucretia Borgia. Dunaway's business life begins to flag and she takes out her frustrations on the person nearest (though not dearest) to her with a wave of child abuse. She spanks her, cuts off her hair, and berates the child by the second. Forrest can't take the beast Dunaway has become and exits. After that, Dunaway becomes "the Los Angeles Open" as she takes on a series of lovers with the speed of a Gatling gun. Hobel never gets their names and refers to all of them as "uncle," as it's much easier. Da Silva (Mayer) lets Dunaway know that he is losing money on her movies and that her tenure at MGM is finito. Dunaway is shocked by her dismissal. Alda wakes up Hobel and her adopted brother, Reinbolt, and the kids are forced to help Dunaway pull up all the rose bushes in the garden, a totally mad act. Dunaway makes MILDRED PIERCE and wins the Oscar, which also signals a rebirth of her film career. But her domestic life remains a nightmare. When her daughter makes the terrible error of hanging up her clothes on a wire, rather than a wooden, hanger, she is punished by being beaten with the hanger, then sentenced to clean her already-shining room. The child is sent to an exclusive school and comes home, now a teenager played by Scarwid, and is told that there is no further money in the coffers to pay for education, so the girl has to go to work to make the needed cash for her expensive tuition. The excuse is that Warner Bros. studio has cancelled her acting contract, but Scarwid soon learns that Dunaway is spending great sums of money on her own pleasures. Scarwid is nailed by Dunaway as she is beginning to discover sex and Dunaway pulls her out of school, then tells the press that Scarwid was expelled. Now Scarwid is sent to a strict school run by nuns where Dunaway hopes all the "evil" will be purged from her. Later, Scarwid returns home and meets Dunaway's last husband, Goz, the chairman of the board of Pepsi-Cola. (In life, Crawford had been married to actor Phil Terry from 1942 through 1946 but that, along with many other facts, is bypassed.) Dunaway and Goz move to New York City and she helps prove that Pepsi hits the spot. Goz (who was one of the many actors to play Tevya in "Fiddler On The Roof" on stage) dies and Dunaway resists a movement to get her tossed off the board of the huge company. Scarwid becomes an actress on a soap opera, Dunaway goes downhill until she dies and Alda contends to Scarwid that her mother always loved her. Scarwid wonders why she and her brother, now played by Berkeley, were cut out of the will. The exact quote from the will stated "for reasons which are well known to them." And so ends one of the vilest abberations ever committed to the screen. The real truth is that Crawford adopted four children including twins she named Cathy and Cindy. They are never mentioned in the picture. Crawford loved the letter "c" and even had dogs named Cliquot, Camille, and Chiffon. It can only be presumed that all the children's clothes must have been monogrammed "C.C." and that this enabled Crawford to make the kids wear hand-me-downs. The house in which all of this allegedly took place was not in Hollywood; it was on North Bristol in Brentwood and it has an eerie life of its own insofar as most of the residents have had some sort of woe. Donald O'Connor lived there unhappily for years and turned to drinking (he's since stopped and has never been happier or healthier). Anthony Newley lived there later and his career fell apart, and the owners after that allegedly had some domestic problems. There is a comic poster of Crawford that says "I Never Laid A Hand On Those———-Kids!" The movie is downright laughable and Dunaway doesn't chew the scenery, she grinds it into baby food by her relentless gnawing. It has garnered a large cult audience since it first dirtied the silver screen, in much the same way as THE ATTACK OF THE KILLER TOMATOES (a far superior picture) did. People go to see the film dressed as Crawford and carrying wire hangers and shouting things at the actors. Dunaway looked a great deal like Crawford due to the amazing makeup by Schram and Harman, but so would Eddie Murphy look like Crawford if he was caked with the same glop. This picture goes beyond "camp" into a new ionosphere of tastelessness until it becoems inadvertently funny. Unfortunately, Yablans took this (as well as another misfire he made, MONSIGNOR) seriously and went so far as to get a one-fourth writing credit. The author, Christina Crawford, is not shown to good advantage, as she is seen first as a brat, then as a snotty teenager, and, finally, as a vengeful, jealous bitch. Perry's direction is appalling and overdone and the whole affair is blown so out of proportion that there's not a realistic moment in it. The picture failed to get much action at the box office. Nobody deserves this kind of treatment, particularly someone who is dead and can't answer the charges. There are enough people in Hollywood who knew Crawford and dispute the material to make us believe that not all of it was totally without exaggeration. Dunaway likes doing bios and made pictures about Eva Peron, The Duchess Of Windsor, Aimee Semple McPherson, and Marilyn Monroe. She would be wise to stop parodying others and to create her own memorable character (with the right script) as she showed she could in Chayefsky's scathing portrait of a real-life TV executive in NETWORK, for which she deservedly won the Oscar. The part had also been offered to Anne Bancroft who turned it down. Scarwid, a native Georgian, has a southern accent so thick that you could spread it on a waffle. How a Californian could come up with such a molasses-and-pone sound is beyond human ken and stands out like a pink sheet at a KKK meeting. Daily Variety columnist Army Archerd's wife, Selma, plays a small role and Brando's sister, Jocelyn, is also briefly seen. Many years later, comedian John Byner, appearing on Cable TV's "Bizarre" did an immensely funny satire called "Adolph Dearest" where he played the dictator's son, Sammy, and apologized for his father's behavior while trying to hawk a book on a TV talk show. Other than the makeup men, the only people in Hollywood to be congratulated are those who refused to work on MOMMIE DEAREST.

p, Frank Yablans; d, Frank Perry; w, Yablans, Perry, Tracy Hotchner, Robert Getchell (based on the book by Christina Crawford); ph, Paul Lohmann (Metrocolor); m, Henry Mancini; ed, Peter E. Berger; prod d, Bill Malley; art d, Harold Michelson; cos, Irene Sharaff; makeup, Charles H. Schram, Lee C. Harman.

Biography   **Cas.**   **(PR:C-O MPAA:PG)**

MON ONCLE   (SEE: MY UNCLE, 1958, Fr.)

MON ONCLE ANTOINE   (SEE: MY UNCLE ANTOINE, 1971, Can.)

MON ONCLE D'AMERIQUE**
(1980, Fr.) 125m Andrea-T.F. 1/New World c (AKA: LES SOMNAMBULES)

Gerard Depardieu (Rene Ragueneau), Nicole Garcia (Janine Garnier), Roger-Pierre (Jean Le Gall), Nelly Borgeaud (Arlette Le Gall), Marie Dubois (Therese Ragueneau), Pierre Arditi (Zambeaux), Gerard Darrieu (Leon Veestrate), Phillippe Laudenbach (Michael Aubert), Alexandre Rignault (Jean's Grandfather), Guillaume Boisseau (Jean as a Child), Jean Daste (Mons. Louis), Laurence Badie (Mme. Veestrate), Helena Manson (Mme. Crozet), Dorothee (Narrator), Prof. Henri Laborit (Himself).

Alain Resnais' greatest commercial success is an offbeat, humorous case study of three characters—manager Depardieu, actress Garcia, and executive Roger-Pierre. Their pasts are quickly accounted for, allowing the focus to be placed on the pursuit of their careers. This is intercut with segments of a lecture from Prof. Henri Laborit, a behavioral scientist speaking in a pure documentary fashion (Resnais had, in fact, attempted to do a short documentary project with Laborit), contributing his theories on memory. Resnais also intercuts footage from other movies, ones which serve as inspiration for the three main characters—for Depardieu it is Jean Gabin's films; for Garcia it is Jean Marais; for Roger-Pierre it is Danielle Darrieux. The success of this film experiment was phenomenal in both commercial and critical terms (and somewhat unexplainable). It won numerous awards, including six French Cesars and an Academy Award nomination for screenwriter Jean Gruault, who also penned Resnais' previous picture, STAVISKY, and his next film, L'AMOUR A MORT. The title refers to the French joke that everyone has a distant relative who went to America, made a fortune, and would someday return home to solve their problems. (In French.)

p, Philippe Dussart; d, Alain Resnais; w, Jean Gruault (inspired by the works of Prof. Henri Laborit); ph, Sacha Vierny (Eastmancolor); m, Arie Dzierlatka; ed, Albert Jurgenson; set d, Jacques Saulnier.

Drama/Comedy   **(PR:C MPAA:PG)**

MON PREMIER AMOUR   (SEE: MY FIRST LOVE, 1978, Fr.)

MONA KENT   (SEE: SIN OF MONA KENT, 1961)

MONASTERY GARDEN   (SEE: IN A MONASTERY GARDEN, 1932)

MONDAY'S CHILD*   (1967, U.S., Arg.) 85m Andre Du Rona c

Arthur Kennedy, Geraldine Page, Deborah Reed, Gracilea Borges, Roberto Parilla, Jose De San.

Kennedy and wife Page move their family (including a dead son exhumed and reburied) to Puerto Rico, where Kennedy has taken a job. The subtle tensions in the family are exposed when Page gives away her daughter's doll to a disaster relief organization. When the girl learns what her mother has done, she flies into a tantrum and Page takes her to try to recover the toy. Gradually, in the face of the poverty they are exposed to, the family disintegrates. A good cast is wasted in this depressing drama. Argentine director Torre-Nilsson tried to break into the Hollywood mainstream with this picture.

p, Andre Du Rona; d, Leopoldo Torre-Nilsson; w, Beatriz Guido, Torre-Nilsson, Noelle Gillmour (based on a story by Du Rona); ph, Alex Phillips, Jr.; ed, Carl Workman.

Drama   **(PR:A-C MPAA:NR)**

MONDO TRASHO zero   (1970) 94m Dreamland/Film Makers c

Mary Vivian Pearce (Girl), John Leisenring (Shrimper), Sharon Sandrock, (Stepsister), Divine (Hit-and-Run Driver), Margie Skidmore (Madonna), Lizzy Temple Black (Madonna's Helper), Jack Walsh, Chris Atkinson (Attendants), Mink Stole (Tap Dancer), David Lochary (Dr. Coathanger), Berenica Cipcus (Nurse/Stepsister), Bob Skidmore (Cop), Mark P. Isherwood, Nancy P. Stoll.

A satirical look at sex and violence from John Waters, the ultimate trash director. It takes a day in the life of Pearce, a young woman who encounters a man with a foot fetish; meets her two evil stepsisters (a la Cinderella); is a hit-and-run victim of Divine; sees a miracle performed in a laundromat; and is finally killed in a knife fight, dying in a pig sty. A typically trashy one-man show from cult-figure Waters.

p&d, w,ph & ed, John Waters.

Comedy   **Cas.**   **(PR:O MPAA:NR)**

MONEY, THE**   (1975) 87m Calliope c

Laurence Luckinbill (Banks), Graham Beckel (Roland), Regina Baff (Lucy), Elizabeth Richards (Ellen), Sam Levene (Lou), Antonia Rey (Pearl).

Money's hold over people is the idea behind this independent picture which concerns a young con who visits his baby-sitting girl friend. She's working for an affluent businessman, giving the con an idea for a moneymaking scheme. He ties up his girl friend, kidnaps the child, and gets some ransom money from the businessman. Occasionally rises above typical standards, due mainly to Workman's sure-handed debut directorial effort.

d&w, Carl Workman; ph, Burleigh Wartes (Technicolor); ed, Paul Hirsch.

Crime   **(PR:O MPAA:R)**

MONEY AND THE WOMAN*   (1940) 80m WB-FN bw

Jeffrey Lynn (Dave Bennett), Brenda Marshall (Barbara Patterson), John Litel (Jerry Helm), Lee Patrick (Miss Church), Henry O'Neill (Mr. Nason), Roger Pryor (Charles Patterson), Guinn "Big Boy" Williams (Adler), Henry Kolker (Mr. Rollins), William Gould (Dyer), Ed Keane (Mr. Kaiser), William Marshall (Bank Clerk), Peter Ashley (Bank Teller), Mildred Coles (Secretary), Sandra Stephenson (Jeannie), Willie Best (George), Susan Peters, Stuart Holmes, Creighton Hale, Tom Wilson, Leo White, Dane Clark.

A weakly directed version of James M. Cain's story about a bank teller whose illegal financial dealings begin affecting his health. He ends up in a hospital, while his sneaky wife tries to patch things up by romancing the bank's vice president. When the teller finishes his hospital stay, however, he holds up the bank, but is caught in the ensuing chase.

d, William K. Howard; w, Robert Presnell (based on a story by James M. Cain); ph, L. William O'Connell; ed, Frank Magee.

Crime   **(PR:A MPAA:NR)**

MONEY FOR JAM   (SEE: IT AIN'T HAY, 1943)

MONEY FOR NOTHING**   (1932, Brit.) 72m BIP/Pathe bw

Seymour Hicks (Jeff Cheddar), Betty Stockfeld (Joan Blossom), Edmund Gwenn (Sir Henry Blossom), Donald Calthrop (Manager), Henry Wenman (Jay Cheddar), Philip Strange (Jackson), Amy Veness (Emma Bolt), Charles Farrell (Digger), Mike Johnson (Walter), Hal Gordon (Waiter), Renee Gadd (Maid), Billy Shine.

A fast-moving romantic comedy about a destitute gambler, Hicks, who falls in love with Stockfeld. She plays hard to get but things go Hicks' way when he is mistakenly identified as a financier. Even with luck on his side, he still cannot seem to connect with Stockfeld, so he drops her and goes off to the Riviera with Stockfeld's lovely maid, Gadd.

p, Seymour Hicks; d, Monty Banks; w, Victor Kendall, Walter C. Mycroft (based on a story by Hicks).

Romantic Comedy   **(PR:A MPAA:NR)**

MONEY FOR SPEED**

(1933, Brit.) 72m Hall Mark/UA bw

John Loder (Mitch), Ida Lupino (Jane), Cyril McLaglen (Bill), Moore Marriott (Shorty), Marie Ault (Ma), John Hoskins, Ginger Lees, "Cyclone" Davis, Lionel Van Praag.

Loder and McLaglen, rivals for the affection of Lupino, carry their feud into the motorcycle racing track, with the result that Loder is seriously injured. Because of this unsportsmanlike conduct, McLaglen is not allowed to continue racing. He turns to stunt riding instead, getting himself hurt in the process. Well-paced action film with Lupino, at the ripe age of 16 in only her second film, displaying talent that could easily be developed.

p&d, Bernard Vorhaus; w, Vera Allinson, Lionel Hale, Monica Ewer (based on the story by Vorhaus); ph, Eric Cross.

Adventure/Drama   (PR:A MPAA:NR)

MONEY FROM HOME**

(1953) 100m PAR c

Dean Martin (Honey Talk Nelson), Jerry Lewis (Virgil Yokum), Marjie Millar (Phyllis Leigh), Pat Crowley (Autumn Claypool), Richard Haydn (Bertie Searles), Robert Strauss (Seldom Seen Kid), Gerald Mohr (Marshall Preston), Sheldon Leonard (Jumbo Schneider), Romo Vincent (The Poojah), Jack Kruschen (Short Boy), Lou Lubin (Sam), Joe McTurk (Hard Top Harry), Frank F. Mitchell (Lead Pipe Louie), Sam Hogan (Society Kid Himself), Phil Arnold (Crossfire), Louis Nicoletti (Hot Horse Herbie), Charles Frank Horvath, Richard J. Reeves, Frank Richards, Harry Hayden, Henry McLemore, Mortie Dutra, Wendell Niles, Edward Clark, Grace Hayle, Bobby Barber, Al Hill, Drew Cahill, Buck Young, Jack Roberts, Ben Astar, Arthur Gould Porter, Robin Hughes, Elizabeth Slifer.

A lame Martin and Lewis effort which casts Martin as a horse racing gambler indebted to racketeer Leonard, who gives him the choice of paying up or fixing an upcoming race. With his cousin Lewis, Martin hides out from Leonard's gang of thugs. Lewis gets mixed up with an Arab sheik and, pretending to be one of his harem, ends up impersonating a famous British jockey. Lewis rides in the big race and it is up to Martin to straighten everything out. The film originally was made in 3-D, but had few 3-D thrills to offer and the plan fell as flat as the picture itself. Martin sings "Love is the Same" (Jack Brooks, Joseph J. Lilley) and "Moments Like This" (Burton Lane, Frank Loesser). Lewis sings "Be Careful Song" (Brooks, Lilley).

p, Hal B. Wallis; d, George Marshall; w, Hal Kanter, James Allardice (based on a story by Damon Runyon); ph, Daniel L. Fapp (Technicolor); m, Leigh Harline; ed, Warren Low.

Comedy/Musical   (PR:A MPAA:NR)

MONEY ISN'T EVERYTHING

(SEE: JEEPERS CREEPERS, 1939)

MONEY JUNGLE, THE**

(1968) 95m Commonwealth United Entertainment/United Pictures (AKA: THE SILKEN TRAP; THE BILLION DOLLAR CAPER)

John Ericson (Blake Heller), Lola Albright (Peggy Lido), Leslie Parrish (Treva Saint), Nehemiah Persoff (Lt. Dow Reeves), Charles Drake (Harvey Sheppard), Kent Smith (Paul Kimmel), Don Rickles (Harry Darkwater), Michael Forest, Mark Roberts, Edy Williams, Marilyn Devin, Jim Adams, Leslie McRae, Dale Monroe, Dodie Warren, Dub Taylor, Tex Armstrong, John Cliff, George De Normand, Byrd Holland, Richard Norris, Ed Parker.

Ericson is hired by a fearful oil company executive who wants the supposedly accidental deaths of four of his geologists investigated. Ericson's snooping leads him to cafe-singer Albright, who is also the ex-wife of an oil company head. She has recently got her hands on some of the company's stock and is determined to make life difficult for her ex and his lover, another stockholder. Ericson uncovers the tangled plot before any more blood is shed. Albright delivers a couple of tolerable nitery tunes: "Two Lovers" and "Help a Good Girl Go Bad."

p, Earle Lyon, Harold Goldman; d, Francis D. Lyon; w, Charles A. Wallace; ph, Alan Stensvold; m, Paul Dunlap; art d, Paul Sylos; set d, Raymond G. Boltz; cos, Frank Tauss; m/l, "Two Lovers," Paul Dunlap, "Help a Good Girl Go Bad," Bob Haymes, Alan Brandt; makeup, Gus Norin.

Crime/Mystery   (PR:A MPAA:NR)

MONEY MAD*

(1934, Brit.) 64m Champion/MGM bw

Virginia Cherrill (Linda), Garry Marsh (Rutherford), D. A. Clarke-Smith (Phillips), Peter Gawthorne (Sir John Leyland), Helen Haye (Lady Leyland), Lawrence Anderson (Chauffeur), Dennis Wyndham (Assistant).

A very dull picture in which Cherrill plays the heroine in avoiding a British financial disaster by acting as the reconciliatory factor in a feud between her fiance and her uncle, both giants in the business world. A sure remedy for those suffering from insomnia.

p, Basil Humphreys; d, Frank Richardson; w, Selwyn Jepson.

Drama   (PR:A MPAA:NR)

MONEY MADNESS*

(1948) 73m FC bw

Hugh Beaumont (Steve Clark), Frances Rafferty (Julie), Harlan Warde (Donald), Cecil Weston (Cora), Ida Moore (Mrs. Ferguson), Danny Morton (Rogers), Joel Friedkin (Dr. Wagner), Lane Chandler (Policeman).

Bank robber Beaumont is stricken with money madness when he must spend the $200,000 he netted in a heist. He marries Rafferty and then poisons her aunt, making it appear that the old woman died and left the newlyweds the money. It doesn't take Rafferty long to catch on to his scheme and she notifies the police, who deal Beaumont his just penalty.

p, Sigmund Neufeld; d, Peter Stewart; w, Al Martin; ph, Jack Greenhalgh; ed, Holbrook N. Todd; md, Leo Erdody; art d, Elias H. Reif; set d, Eugene C. Stone.

Crime   (PR:A MPAA:NR)

MONEY MEANS NOTHING*

(1932, Brit.) 70m British and Dominions/PAR bw

John Loder (Earl Egbert), Irene Richards (Livia Faringay), Gibb McLaughlin (Augustus Bethersyde), Dorothy Robinson (Daysie de Lille), Kay Hammond (Angel), Clive Currie (Sir Percival Puttock), A. Bromley Davenport (Earl of Massingham), Miles Malleson (Doorman).

Lifeless comedy in which McLaughlin plays the butler to Loder, an earl with a thing for a certain chorus girl. Using underhanded methods, though with only the noblest of intentions, McLaughlin turns Loder away from the conniving chorus girl and towards his own daughter. Laughs are few-and-far between despite a decent farcical premise.

p, Herbert Wilcox; d, Harcourt Templeman, Wilcox; w, Miles Malleson, Templeman (based on the story by Douglas Furber).

Comedy   (PR:A MPAA:NR)

MONEY MEANS NOTHING* 1/2

(1934) 64m MON bw

Wallace Ford (Kenneth), Gloria Shea (Julie), Edgar Kennedy (Green), Maidel Turner (Mrs. Green), Betty Blythe (Mrs. Ferris), Richard Tucker (George), Vivian Oakland (Helen), Tenen Holtz (Silverman), Edward Tamblyn (Robby), Ann Brody, Olaf Hytten.

Rich but clumsy Shea falls in love with Ford, but her family disapproves of the match to a mere tire clerk. All goes rockily for the pair until Ford gets mixed up in a tire hijacking, from which he emerges a hero, plus winning the nod from the "money means everything" family. Nice change from the time-worn booze hijacking story makes this one a bit plausible.

p, Ben Verschleiser; d, Christy Cabanne; w, Frances Hyland (based on the play "Cost of Living" by William Anthony McGuire); ph, Robert Planck.

Drama/Romance   (PR:A MPAA:NR)

MONEY, MONEY, MONEY

(SEE: COUNTERFEITERS OF PARIS, THE, 1962, Fr./Ital.)

MONEY MOVERS** 1/2

(1978, Aus.) 94m South Australia Film/Roadshow c

Terence Donovan (Eric Jackson), Ed Devereaux (Dick Martin), Tony Bonner (Leo Bassett), Lucky Grills (Robert Conway), Alan Cassell (Sammy Ross), Frank Wilson (Lionel Darcy), Candy Raymond (Mindel Seagers), Bryan Brown (Brian Jackson), Charles "Bud" Tingwell (Jack Henderson), Gary Files (Ernest Sainsbury), Hu Price (Griffiths), Ray Marshall (Ed Gallagher), Jeanie Drynan (Dawn Jackson), Terry Camilleri (Dino), Ted Hodgeman (Nacker), James Elliott (Bengal Lancer), Max Fairchild (Dim Sims), Rick Hart (Geronimo), Robert Essex (Tony Duggan), Alan Penney (Janitor), Tom Farley (Patterson), Stuart Littlemore (TV Reporter), Jo-Anne Moore (Brian's Girl Friend), Mimi Martin (Henderson's Mother), Brian Harrison (Managing Director), Kathy Dior (M.D.'s Secretary).

Thieves plan to rob a vault stuffed with over $20 million (Australian), but the plan goes awry. Well-done caper flick from Down Under manages to keep suspense, although almost all caper films have the same plot. Director Beresford used the good reviews this received in Australia and England to help finance his next film, BREAKER MORANT, which put Australian films on the map commercially.

p, Matt Carroll; d&w, Bruce Beresford (based on the novel by Devon Minchin); ph, Don McAlpine; ed, William Anderson; art d, David Copping; cos, Anna Senior; spec eff, Ian Jamieson; stunts, Alf Joint.

Crime   (PR:O MPAA:NR)

MONEY ON THE STREET**

(1930, Aust.) 78m Sascha bw (GELD AUF DER STRASSE).

Georg Alexander (Peter Paul Lutz), Leopold Kramer (Emil Reimbacher), Rosa Albach-Retty (Lona Reimbacher), Lydia Pollmann (Dodo), Hans Moser (Albin Jensch), Hugo Thimig (Mr. Kesselberg), Hans Thimig (Max Kesselberg), Franz Schafheitlin (Bornhausen), Karl Ziegler (Dallibor), Ernst Arnold (Lukas), Rose Mathe (Tschakowa), Alfred Neugebauer (Policeman), Wilhelm Heim (Bookkeeper), Hermann Wawra (Head Waiter), Franz Kammauf (Manager), Harry Payer (Singer in the Carlton Bar), Hedwig Kiesler [Hedy Lamarr] (Young Girl at Night Club Table).

Pollmann, the daughter of a banker, breaks off her engagement with H. Thimig, on the day she is supposed to marry him. She meets Alexander, a man whose philosophy is that there is money lying on the street and it simply needs to be picked up. She happens to fit the bill and the pair run off together. Notable only for the appearance of Hedwig Kiesler, who later changed her name to Lamarr. Only 17 years old at the time, she was spotted by director Jacoby among the observers on the set, where she was serving as a script girl. He thought she was attractive enough to don a black evening gown and sit at a table with the elegant comic Alexander as the camera turned on a nightclub scene. Afterward, she again took up the script but the experience was a turning point in her life—she wanted no other career than acting. (In German.)

p, Nikolaus Deutsch; d, Georg Jacoby; w, Rudolf Oesterreicher; ph, Nikolaus Farkas; m, Stephan Weiss; art d, Hans Jacoby; m/l, Peter Herz, Weiss.

Drama/Romance   (PR:A MPAA:NR)

MONEY ORDER, THE

(SEE: MANDABI, 1969, Senegal)

MONEY TALKS**¹/2

(1933, Brit.) 66m BIP bw

Julian Rose (*Abe Pilstein*), Kid Berg (*Kid Burke*), Gladdy Sewell (*Anna*), Judy Kelly(*Rosie Pilstein*), Gus McNaughton (*Solly Sax*), Griffith Jones (*Jimmy Dale*), Bernard Ansell (*Hymie Burkowitz*), Lena Maitland (*Mrs. Blumberg*), Hal Gordon (*Pug Wilson*), Mary Charles (*Nellie Kelly*), Jimmy Godden (*Joe Bell*), Rich & Galvin (*Dough & Wal Nut*).

A variation on the popular novel, *Brewster's Millions*, here given a Jewish background. Rose will inherit half a million dollars from his sister if he can get rid of all his money in 30 days. He squanders his sizable bank account backing prizefighters, racehorses, and even a suspender factory, but instead of losing his shirt he makes more than he spends. An average picture with a can't-miss premise.

d, Norman Lee; w, Lee, Frank Miller, Edwin Greenwood; ph, Walter Harvey; cos, Kathleen Kay, Maude Marsh, Andre-Ani.

Comedy   **(PR:A MPAA:NR)**

MONEY TO BURN*¹/2

(1940) 69m REP bw

James Gleason (*Joe Higgins*), Lucile Gleason (*Lil Higgins*), Russell Gleason (*Sidney Higgins*), Harry Davenport (*Grandpa*), Lois Ranson (*Betty Higgins*), Tommy Ryan (*Tommy Higgins*), Thurston Hall (*Mr. Ellis*), Winifred Harris (*Mrs. Davis*), Douglas Meins (*Bill*), Lucien Littlefield (*Irving*), Herbert Rawlinson (*Mr. Dover*), Jack Rice (*Thorne*), Andrew Tombes (*Brown*), Gladys Blake (*Miss Pitts*), Jean Fenwick (*Miss Murphy*).

A laughable entry in the Higgins Family series, which sees the Higgins household go into an uproar when Ma Higgins (Lucile Gleason) enters a dog biscuit contest that offers a $50,000 prize. Trouble is, Pop Higgins (James Gleason) works for the agency that handles the contest holder's account, thus disqualifying his wife's entry, even though she by now has bought up all the dog biscuits in town. (See HIGGINS FAMILY series, Index.)

p&d, Gus Meins; w, Jack Townley (based on a story by Townley, Taylor Caven); ph, Ernest Miller; ed, William Morgan; md, Cy Feuer.

Comedy   **(PR:A MPAA:NR)**

MONEY TRAP, THE*¹/2

(1966) 91m MGM bw

Glenn Ford (*Joe Baron*), Elke Sommer (*Lisa Baron*), Rita Hayworth (*Rosalie Kenny*), Joseph Cotten (*Dr. Horace Van Tilden*), Ricardo Montalban (*Pete Delanos*), Tom Reese (*Matthews*), James Mitchum (*Detective Wolski*), Argentina Brunetti (*Aunt*), Fred Essler (*Mr. Klein*), Eugene Iglesias (*Father*), Teri Lynn Sandoval (*Daughter*), Bill McLean (*Delivery Man*), Parley Baer (*Banker*), Robert S. Anderson (*Police Inspector*), Than Wyenn (*Phil Kenny*), Ted De Corsia (*Police Captain*), Marya Stevens, Carlita, Stacey King (*Women in Bar*), Fred Scheweiller (*Bartender*), Ward Wood (*Man in Bar*), William Campbell (*Jack Archer*), Walter Reed, Budd Landreth (*Detectives*), Paul Todd (*Intern*), Herman Boden (*Parking Lot Attendant*), George Sawaya (*Angelo*), Jo Summers (*Dead Mother*), Stacy Harris (*Drunk*), Cleo Tibbs, Sallie H. Dornan (*Nurses*).

An attempt at *film noir* that turns out to be little more than *film blah.* Hayworth, who was billed after Sommer, was 47 at the time of the film and her molars were getting a bit lengthy for that kind of femme fatale role. Ford is a 10 grand a year cop who lives high on the hog because his wife, Sommer, is the recipient of some stock and bonds left her by her late daddums. When the dividends fail to materialize one quarter, Ford is in bad financial trouble and Sommer's extravagant ways don't help. Ford's cop partner is Montalban and the picture starts as the two men are searching for an unemployed Mexican who killed his wife because she was working as a hooker in order to earn enough money for their child. That little saga has nothing to do with the main story which begins when Ford is investigating the shooting of a thief by Cotten, a wealthy physician who caters to the Park Avenue crowd. Ford discovers that Cotten is the leader of a huge narcotics ring and has lots of unmarked and untaxed cash in his safe. This is the loot that Ford hopes will get him out of his money woes. Montalban learns of the cache of cash and demands his cut of the proceeds. The dead thief, a junkie, had been married to Hayworth, now a blowsy waitress. When Ford runs into her, we learn that the two had been lovers a long time ago and they quickly resume their old-time affair. (They'd been in many films together in the past so that comes as no shock to anyone.) Hayworth is a lush and she knows about her late husband's business affiliation with Cotten who makes sure she won't talk by having her tossed out a window. Ford and Montalban sneak into Cotten's residence and are in the process of rifling his safe. Gunplay occurs and Ford and Montalban get away to Ford's house with some heroin which they hope to sell. Montalban is dying of his gunshot wounds and Cotten agrees to treat him if one of the two bags of narcotics is returned. Montalban dies and Cotten and Ford open fire on each other again. Cotten is dead and Ford is wounded. Sommer appeals to him to allow her to call in an ambulance and he reluctantly agrees, though knowing that there is no way he can explain this situation to his bosses and that he will eventually be incarcerated. This was one of a series of movies in which the cops were bad guys. Most of those were done in the 1950s with such films as ROGUE COP, THE BIG HEAT, and PUSHOVER, with Friedkin would do TO LIVE AND DIE IN L.A. and that suffered the same fate as THE MONEY TRAP in that there was no one to like in the picture, so there was no rooting interest. Making Montalban and Ford villains took away the opportunity to cheer and their major problem is that they were not interesting characters and hardly motivated into doing what they did. It wouldn't have even made a very good segment for the TV series "Police Story." Sommer spends most of her on-screen time parading about in a series of designer dresses that reveal her excellent figure but she has little else to do.

p, Max E. Youngstein, David Karr; d, Burt Kennedy; w, Walter Bernstein (based on the novel *The Money Trap* by Lionel White), ph, Paul C. Vogel (Panavision); m, Hal

Schaefer; ed, John McSweeney; art d, George W. Davis, Carl Anderson; set d, Henry Grace, Robert R. Benton; makeup, William Tuttle.

Crime Drama   **(PR:C MPAA:NR)**

MONEY, WOMEN AND GUNS**

(1958) 90m UNIV c

Jock Mahoney (*Hogan*), Kim Hunter (*Mary Kingman*), Tim Hovey (*Davey Kingman*), Gene Evans (*Sheriff Crowley*), Tom Drake (*Jess Ryerson*), Lon Chaney, Jr. (*Art Birdwell*), William Campbell (*Clint Gunston*), Jeffrey Stone (*Johnny Bee*), James Gleason (*Henry Devers*), Judy Meredith (*Sally Gunston*), Phillip Terry (*Damion Bard*), Richard Devon (*Setting Sun*), Ian MacDonald (*Nibbs*), Don Megowan (*John Briggs*), Nolan Leary (*Job Kingman*), Kelly Thordsen (*Joe*).

Frontier detective Mahoney takes on the search for four heirs to the fortune of an old prospector, who has been killed by three thugs. Along his travels he meets and falls in love with Hunter, and finally finds the heirs. He then discovers that Stone, one of the beneficiaries, was among the killer pack that did the prospector in, and Stone now asks forgiveness. Most of the excitement in this one is in the title, and that has little to do with the story.

p, Howie Horowitz; d, Richard Bartlett; w, Montgomery Pittman; ph, Philip Lathrop (CinemaScope, Eastmancolor); m, Joseph Gershenson; ed, Patrick McCormack; art d, Alexander Golitzen, Bob Smith.

Western   **(PR:A MPAA:NR)**

MONGOLS, THE**

(1966, Fr./Ital.) 105m Royal-France Cinema/Colorama c (LES MONGOLS: I MONGOLI)

Jack Palance (*Ogotai*), Anita Ekberg (*Huluna*), Antonella Lualdi (*Amina*), Franco Silva (*Stephen of Crakow*), Gianni Garko (*Henry de Valois*), Roldano Lupi (*Genghis Khan*), Gabriella Pallotta (*Lutezia*), Pierre Cressoy (*Igor*), Gabriele Antonini (*Temugin*), Tuen Wang (*Subodai*).

A 13th Century historical adventure with Palance playing the son of Genghis Khan, and Ekberg is his mistress. The lovers try to let the war between Khan's forces and the rebels continue, but finally peace is negotiated. Eventually, Ekberg kills Khan (Lupi), allowing Palance to become the new ruler. He leads his Mongol forces into battle but is severely beaten and kills himself. Originally released in 1961 at 115m.

p, Guido Giambartolomei; d, Andre De Toth, Leopoldo Savona, Riccardo Freda; w, Ugo Guerra, Luciano Martino, Ottavio Alessi, Alessandro Ferrau; ph, Aldo Giordani (CinemaScope, Eastmancolor); m, Mario Nascimbene; ed, Otello Colangeli, md, Franco Ferrara, Edrioni G. Campi; art d, Ottavio Scotti; cos, Enzo Bulgarelli.

Historical Adventure/War   **(PR:A MPAA:NR)**

MONGREL zero

(1982) 91m Rondo-Sutherland & Jenkins c

Terry Evans (*Jerry*), Aldo Ray, Catherine Molloy, Mitch Pileggi, J. M. Ingraffia.

Awful horror film about a young man plagued by violent nightmares that become reality when he is transformed into a dog-like creature and goes about ripping out the throats of the locals. Is he a monster? Is it all psychological? Does it matter? In the end it is just another bloodfest for the gore-hounds. Poor Aldo Ray makes another embarrassing cameo.

d&w, Robert A. Burns; ph, Richard Kooris; m, Ed Guinn; spec eff&makeup, Smith.

Horror   **Cas.**   **(PR:O MPAA:NR)**

MONITORS, THE**

(1969) 92m Bell and Howell-CUE-Wilding-Second City/Commonwealth United Entertainment c

Guy Stockwell (*Harry Jordan*), Susan Oliver (*Barbara Cole*), Avery Schreiber (*Max Jordan*), Sherry Jackson (*Mona*), Shepperd Strudwick (*Tersh*), Keenan Wynn (*General Blackwish*), Ed Begley (*The President*), Larry Storch (*Col. Stutz*), Alan Arkin, Adam Arkin, Xavier Cugat, Barbara Dana, Sen. Everett Dirksen, Stubby Kaye, Fred Kaz, Lynn Lipton, Jackie Vernon (*Cameos*), Mel Zellman, Thomas Erhart (*Narrators*).

Filmed in Chicago with the members of the legendary Second City troupe, this hippie-heavy 1960s trip failed to do much justice to the comic talents of those involved. Coproduced by film equipment manufacturer Bell and Howell, the film was an attempt to bring status to Chicago's filmmaking possibilities. The result is a spotty science-fiction comedy, with bizarre cameo appearances, about friendly alien invaders who attempt to control the world by ridding the nation of such nasty vices as sex, violence, and politics. Of course, a resistance movement forms and attempts to topple the "Monitor" (as the aliens are called) rule. The Monitors realize that Earthlings aren't prepared to live right, so they return home and let them be. Full of funny skits, and songs sung by Odetta and Sandy Holt are outstanding laugh provokers, but, as a whole, it is a disappointing film. Sadly also, the Bell and Howell plan to make Chicago a leading theatrical filmmaking center collapsed with THE MONITORS, and it would be years before studios ventured again to the Windy City.

p, Bernard Sahlins; d, Jack Shea; w, Myron J. Gold (based on a novel by Keith Laumer); ph, William [Vilmos] Zsigmond (Technicolor); m, Fred Kaz; ed, Patrick Kennedy; art d, Roy Henry; m/l, Kaz.

Comedy   **(PR:C MPAA:M)**

MONKEY BUSINESS***

(1931) 77m PAR bw

Groucho Marx (*Groucho*), Harpo Marx (*Harpo*), Chico Marx (*Chicago*), Zeppo Marx (*Zeppo*), Thelma Todd (*Lucille*), Tom Kennedy (*Gibson*), Ruth Hall (*Mary Helton*), Rockliffe Fellowes (*Joe Helton*), Harry Woods ("*Alky*" *Briggs*), Ben Taggart (*Capt. Corcoran*), Otto Fries (*2nd Mate*), Evelyn Pierce (*Manicurist*), Maxine Castle (*Opera Singer*).

The Marx Borthers are the MacDonald's of movies in that you always know that you're going to have consistency in one of their films just as you know, ahead of time, what a Big Mac is going to taste like. It was the first Marx Brothers picture written directly for the screen and it had all of the quips and situations for which they have become world famous. The boys have stowed away on an ocean liner and race from stateroom to stateroom in order to keep from being clapped in the brig. The most famous scene was the one which the Brothers, and what appear to be half the ship's staff, all cram into a tiny room. For sustained hysterical laughter, it's hard to beat that choreographed sequence. Harpo gets involved with a Punch and Judy Show and delights all of the kids on the vessel (as well as all the adults in the audience). Naturally, there are the heavies and the Marxes become embroiled with Fellowes and Woods, a pair of well-dressed and well-heeled gangsters. The Marx Brothers split up with two of them siding with each of the crooks. Hall, the daughter of a hoodlum, is kidnaped and winds up in a barn after being at a masquerade ball. In the finale, Zeppo, the "straight" brother, goes after the tough hoodlum, while Groucho leaps from one bale of hay to another, offering one-liners as punctuation to the punches. Sorely missing is Margaret Dumont, the best mature female foil in movies around that time. It slows down a bit when Chico tickles the ivories and Harpo plucks the harp. This is either a concession to their reputations or it might have been because of a plea from the Marx's mother, Minnie, who didn't want all that money she'd spent for piano and harp lessons to go to waste. Thelma Todd handles the female ingenue work well enough and dances the tango well with Groucho. All members of the supporting cast are as effective as they can be in the midst of the comedic cyclone known as the Marx Brothers. In later years, Zeppo would step out and leave the acting to the other three, but there was a fifth brother, Gummo (Milton), who left the act early and was replaced by Zeppo. Their career began with COCOANUTS in 1929 and ended, as a team, with LOVE HAPPY in 1950. They did work in THE STORY OF MANKIND but in unrelated episodes.

d, Norman McLeod; w, Arthur Sheekman (based on a story by S. J. Perelman, W. B. Johnstone, Roland Pertwee); ph, Arthur Todd.

Comedy **Cas.** **(PR:A MPAA:NR)**

MONKEY BUSINESS*** (1952) 97m FOX bw

Cary Grant *(Prof. Barnaby Fulton)*, Ginger Rogers *(Edwina Fulton)*, Charles Coburn *(Mr. Oliver Oxley)*, Marilyn Monroe *(Lois Laurel)*, Hugh Marlowe *(Harvey Entwhistle)*, Henri Letondal *(Dr. Siegfried Kitzel)*, Robert Cornthwaite *(Dr. Zoldeck)*, Larry Keating *(Mr. G. J. Culverly)*, Douglas Spencer *(Dr. Brunner)*, Esther Dale *(Mrs. Rhinelander)*, George "Foghorn" Winslow *(Little Indian)*, Emmett Lynn *(Jimmy)*, Joseph Mell *(Barber)*, George Eldredge *(Auto Salesman)*, Heinie Conklin *(Painter)*, Kathleen Freeman *(Nurse)*, Olan Soule *(Hotel Clerk)*, Harry Carey, Jr. *(Reporter)*, John McKee *(Photographer)*, Faire Binney *(Dowager)*, Billy McLean *(Bellboy)*, Paul Maxey, Mack Williams *(Dignitaries)*, Forbes Murray *(Man)*, Marjorie Halliday *(Bit Receptionist)*, Harry Seymour *(Clothing Store Salesman)*, Harry Bartell, Harry Carter, Jerry Paris *(Scientists)*, Roger Moore *(Man)*, Ruth Warren, Isabel Withers, Olive Carey *(Laundresses)*, Dabbs Greer *(Cab Driver)*, Russ Clark, Ray Montgomery *(Cops)*, Melinda Plowman *(Girl)*, Terry Goodman, Ronnie Clark, Rudy Lee, Mickey Little, Brad Mora, Jimmy Roebuck, Louis Lettieri *(Boys)*, Robert Nichols *(Garage Man)*, Mary Field *(Clerk)*, Jerry Sheldon *(Guard)*, Gil Stratton, Jr. *(Yale Man)*.

A 1950s version of a 1930s screwball comedy almost succeeds on its own but doesn't compare to the earlier work of anyone involved. Grant is a chemist engaged in some research on how to restore youth to tired cells and stop the aging process. He uses several chimps in his experiments and one of them escapes his cage and gets into playing with the various elements being used by Grant. He puts the chemicals together, mixes them in the manner he's seen humans do it, then pours the goop into the water cooler (the regular glass bottle is not there and awaiting replacement), and when the janitor puts another bottle on the open cooler, the H_2O mixes with the potion mixed by the monkey. Grant tries a bit of his own concoction the next day, just to see if it has any punch to it, then washes it down with some water from the cooler. In minutes, he is filled with fire and vigor and thinks that it is his formula that has done it. He gets younger and younger in attitude and is soon behaving like a freshman in college. Coburn, who is Grant's boss, sends his secretary, Monroe, to find Grant. Grant takes the pneumatic blonde, goes swimming, skating, and racing in a sports car, and Monroe just goes along with it. (Monroe is the cliched dumb blonde secretary in the movie, as witnessed by Coburn's famous line when he hands her a piece of paper and says: "Here, get someone to type this.") Grant's wife, Rogers, is mature enough to look the other way at Grant's shenanigans, especially when the formula's effects are not long-lasting. Rogers goes to Grant's lab and takes some water from the same cooler and, in no time at all, she is soon like a moon-eyed teenager. She wants to drag Grant off to a second honeymoon but Grant, who is not under the influence of the drug, is cool to the idea. When the formula ceases to have effect on Rogers, she returns to her mature senses. Later, Rogers and Grant make coffee by using the water from the lab's cooler and now the two of them are on the same youthful wavelength. But the fact that this is their second dose of the stuff takes them back far beyond teenage years and into a place just past infantilism. They begin acting like petulant and playful children, wreak havoc at an important meeting of their board of directors, and eventually make their way home. Once there, they team up with the local kids and Grant does something he's always wanted to do; he ties up Rogers' former boy friend, Marlowe, and snips off his hair as the local kids laugh along. Rogers goes to bed, wakes up normal, but finds a baby in bed next to her and panics. She thinks that Grant may have regressed all the way back but it's just a neighbor's child who has crawled into the room. Rogers doesn't know that and races to Coburn. Grant has gone back to the lab and fallen asleep, wakes up back to normal. Coburn and his board swallow the water cooler's laced contents and begin to cavort like kids. Coburn chases Monroe (who wouldn't?) and seltzer is squirted around the room with abandon. In the end, Grant is happy that the formula is only temporary and that it was discovered by accident. Seeing adults behave like children has not been a pretty sight. The point is made that maturity, rather than reckless youth, is the better state to live in. The man who wrote the original story departed from his usual celestial bailiwick for this one. Harry Segall had done the stories for HERE COMES MR. JORDAN, ANGEL ON MY SHOULDER, and FOR HEAVEN'S SAKE, among others. In small roles, note Roger Moore, TV director Jerry Paris, TV weatherman Gil Stratton, and veteran character actor Dabbs Greer. MONKEY BUSINESS was a slight film, made better by the actors than it really was. Even with such a venerable creative team, it barely manages to evoke memories of some earlier comedies of the same ilk.

p, Sol C. Siegel; d, Howard Hawks; w, Ben Hecht, Charles Lederer, I.A.L. Diamond (based on a story by Harry Segall); ph, Milton Krasner; m, Leigh Harline; ed, William B. Murphy; md, Lionel Newman; art d, Lyle Wheeler, George Patrick; set d, Thomas Little, Walter M. Scott; cos, Travilla; spec eff, Ray Kellogg; makeup, Ben Nye.

Comedy **(PR:A MPAA:NR)**

MONKEY GRIP ½** (1983, Aus.) 102m Pavilion-Cinecom-Mainline c

Noni Hazelhurst *(Nora)*, Colin Friels *(Javo)*, Alice Garner *(Gracie)*, Harold Hopkins *(Willie)*, Candy Raymond *(Lillian)*, Michael Caton *(Clive)*, Tim Burns *(Martin)*, Christina Amphlett *(Angela)*, Don Miller-Robinson *(Gerald)*, Lisa Peers *(Rita)*, Cathy Downes *(Eve)*, Justin Ridley, Pearl Christie, Vera Plevnik, Jamie Fonti, Esben Storm, Phil Motherwell, Dana Auzins, Gary Waddell, Bill Charlton, Carole Skinner, Vincent Lovegrove, Jeremy Paul, Mark McEntee, Dick Clappin, Laurel McGowan, Peter Cox, Kate Reid, Alister Jones, Rebecca Rigg.

Hazelhurst is a single mother involved with an unlikable drug addict in this beautifully shot attempt to examine a sincere relationship. It never quite succeeds, however. Hazelhurst's gripping performance is the film's saving grace.

p, Patricia Lovell; d, Ken Cameron; w, Cameron, Helen Garner (based on a novel by Garner); ph, David Gribble (Eastmancolor); m, Bruce Smeaton, Stephen McIntyre; ed, David Huggett; prod d, Clark Munro; art d, Ron Highfield.

Drama **(PR:A MPAA:NR)**

MONKEY HUSTLE, THE* ½ (1976) 90m AIP c

Yaphet Kotto *(Daddy Foxx)*, Rudy Ray Moore *(Goldie)*, Rosalind Cash *(Mama)*, Randy Brooks *(Win)*, Debbi Morgan *(Vi)*, Thomas Carter *(Player)*, Donn Harper *(Tiny)*, Lynn Caridine *(Jan-Jan)*, Patricia McCaskill *(Shirl)*, Lynn Harris *(Sweet Potato)*, Fuddle Bagley *(Mr. Molet)*, Frank Rice *(Black Night)*, Carl Crudup *(Joe)*, Duchyll Smith *(Beatrice)*, Kirk Calloway *(Baby D)*.

A waste of a fine cast, this film, shot in the ghettos of Chicago, is a poor comedy designed for black audiences. It stars Kotto as a black hustler who teaches youngsters his game. The film is held together by a razor-thin plot which has the ghetto neighborhood threatened to be torn down for the construction of a freeway, which actually serves as a stage for a sordid collection of characters.

p&d, Arthur Marks; w, Charles Johnson (based on a story by Odie Hawkins); ph, Jack L. Richards (Movielab Color); m, Jack Conrad; ed, Art Seid.

Drama **(PR:C-O MPAA:PG)**

MONKEY IN WINTER, A***

(1962, Fr.) 104m Cipra-Cite/MGM bw (UN SINGE EN HIVER; AKA: IT'S HOT IN HELL)

Jean Gabin *(Albert Quentin)*, Jean-Paul Belmondo *(Gabriel Fouquet)*, Suzanne Flon *(Suzanne Quentin)*, Noel Roquevert *(Landru)*, Paul Frankeur *(Esnault)*, Gabrielle Dorziat *(Victoria)*, Marcelle Arnold *(Nurse)*, Hella Petri *(Georgina)*, Lucien Raimbourg *(Gardiner)*, Genevieve Fontanel *(Marie-Jo)*, Sylvianne Margolle *(Marie)*, Charles Bouillaud *(Chauffeur)*, Camille Guerini *(Mayor)*, Andre Dalibert *(Chief of Police)*, Anne-Marie Coffinet *(Simone)*, Helene Dieudonne *(Josephine)*.

Gabin is a reformed alcoholic who is the proprietor of a small inn in Normandy. Belmondo visits the inn on the way to picking up his young daughter. Gabin spots Belmondo and senses that they are kindred spirits. Belmondo orders a drink, which Gabin, breaking his dry spell, decides also to do. They both get soused and fantasize of better things—Gabin of his adventurous days in China as a marine, Belmondo of his desire to lead an illustrious life in Spain. Soon their drunk wears off and they must face reality. Belmondo gets his daughter and Gabin relates a story to the pair. He tells them of a Chinese legend about hordes of monkeys which would descend from the mountains into the village. They would wander around without direction (a la Belmondo) until one of the more responsible townsfolk (a la Gabin) would send them back to the mountains. When the little girl asks if Gabin really helped any of the monkeys, Belmondo, acknowledging the allusion to himself, says yes. The second of Verneuil's Gabin trilogy which, as most of the director's work, was a commercial success in France. Teaming Gabin (THE GRAND ILLUSION, PEPE LE MOKO) with Belmondo (BREATHLESS) produced the same box-office buzzing as if John Wayne and Clint Eastwood appeared together in a film.

p, Jacques Bar; d, Henri Verneuil; w, Michel Audiard, Francois Boyer (based on the novel by Antoine Blondin); ph, Louis Page (Totalscope); m, Michel Magne; ed, Monique Bonnot, Francoise Bonnot; set d, Robert Clavel.

Comedy/Drama **(PR:A MPAA:NR)**

MONKEY ON MY BACK ½** (1957) 93m UA bw

Cameron Mitchell *(Barney Ross)*, Dianne Foster *(Cathy)*, Paul Richards *(Rico)*, Jack Albertson *(Sam Pian)*, Kathy Garver *(Noreen)*, Lisa Golm *(Barney's Mother)*, Barry Kelley *(Big Ralph)*, Dayton Lummis *(McAvoy)*, Lewis Charles *(Lew Surati)*, Raymond Greenleaf *(Latham)*, Richard Benedict *(Art Winch)*, Brad Harris *(Spike)*, Robert Holton *(Dr. Sullivan)*.

The monkey of the title is morphine addiction, and the back it's riding on is Mitchell's in his portrayal of former welter and lightweight boxing champ Barney Ross. A flamboyant high-living character, Mitchell takes off as a Marine for WW II and is awarded a medal for heroism at Guadalcanal. He soon contracts malaria and is given morphine to ease the pain. Upon his return home, and to the ring, his need for morphine increases, nearly ruining his career and his family life. The fighting sequences are especially well-staged, as is his four-and-a-half-month struggle in the U.S. Federal Hospital in Lexington, Kentucky, to shake the monkey.

p, Edward Small; d, Andre de Toth; w, Crane Wilbur, Anthony Veiller, Paul Dudley; ph, Maury Gertsman; m, Paul Sawtell, Bert Shefter; ed, Grant Whytock; art d, Frank Hotaling.

Biography **(PR:C MPAA:NR)**

MONKEYS, GO HOME!** (1967) 101m BV c

Maurice Chevalier *(Father Sylvain)*, Dean Jones *(Hank Dussard)*, Yvette Mimieux *(Maria Riserau)*, Bernard Woringer *(Marcel Cartucci)*, Clement Harari *(Emile Paraulis)*, Yvonne Constant *(Yolande Angelli)*, Marcel Hillaire *(Mayor Gaston Lou)*, Jules Munshin *(M. Piastillio)*, Alan Carney *(Grocer)*, Maurice Marsac *(Fontanino)*, Darleen Carr *(Sidoni Riserau)*, Peter Camlin *(Cabinet Maker)*.

After 68 years of show business the 79-year-old Chevalier starred in his final film role alongside a barrel of monkeys in this average Disney picture. Jones arrives in France from the States to farm an olive plantation willed to him by his late uncle. Chevalier, a local priest, warns Jones how expensive it can be to gather up all the olives, so Jones comes up with his own sure-fire plan. He hires four trained female monkeys to do the harvesting, an idea which meets considerable opposition from the neighbors. When a male chimp shows up, distracting the four females, things get out of hand. Eventually, Chevalier convinces Jones' neighbors to lend a hand. Great fun for the young ones who can never seem to get enough of monkeys. Though set in France, the picture was shot entirely on a Disney studio backlot, in a rehabbed ZORRO set.

p, Walt Disney, Ron Miller; d, Andrew V. McLaglen; w, Maurice Tombragel (based on "The Monkeys," by G.K. Wilkinson); ph, William Snyder (Technicolor); m, Robert F. Brunner; ed, Marsh Hendry; art d, Carroll Clark, John B. Mansbridge; set d, Emile Kuri, Frank R. McKelvy; cos, Bill Thomas, Chuck Keehne, Neva Rames; makeup, Pat McNalley; m/l, "Monkeys, Go Home!" Richard M., Robert B. Sherman (sung by Maurice Chevalier, Darleen Carr), "Joie de Vivre," Sherman and Sherman (sung by Chevalier, Children's Chorus).

Juvenile **(PR:AAA MPAA:NR)**

MONKEY'S PAW, THE½** (1933) 58m RKO bw

Ivan Simpson *(Mr. White)*, Louise Carter *(Mrs. White)*, C. Aubrey Smith *(Sgt.-Maj. Morris)*, Bramwell Fletcher *(Herbert)*, Betty Lawford *(Rose)*, Winter Hall *(Mr. Hartigan)*, Herbert Bunston *(Sampson, a Lawyer)*, Nena Quartero *(Nura)*, LeRoy Mason *(Afghan)*, Nick Shaid *(Hindu Fakir)*, Col. Gordon McGee *(Police Sergeant)*, Scott McKee *(Electrician)*, J. M. Kerrigan *(Cpl. O'Leary)*, Leo Britt *(Lance Corporal)*, Lal Chand Mehra *(Hindu Lover)*, Nigel DeBrulier *(Hindu Fakir in Prologue)*, George Edwards *(Juggler)*, Gordon Jones *(Soldier)*, James Bell *(Flute Player)*, Sidney Bracy *(Pensioner)*, Aggie Steele *(Barmaid)*, Harry Allen *(Commissioner)*, Will Stanton *(Bookmaker)*, Ed Miller *(Mule Driver)*, John George *(Hindu)*, Joey Ray *(Merchant)*, C. Monsoor *(Orchestra Leader)*, Harry Strang, Angus Darrock, Harold Hughes *(Sergeants)*.

A classic horror story retold many times, THE MONKEY'S PAW tells the story of an army sergeant, Smith, who brings a magical paw from India to England. A brief prolog was added to the film after principal photography was completed (this consisted of some scenes in India with Smith and a battle in the Khyber Pass). He drops in on a middle-aged couple (Simpson, Carter) he has not seen for many years. In telling of his adventures in India, he mentions the monkey's paw and how the three wishes it had granted had given him great sorrow. Next morning when the sergeant leaves, the husband surreptitiously takes the paw thinking to wish for a dowry for his son who wants to marry his sweetheart. However, the money comes in the form of compensation for the death of his son who had an accident at his place of work. He wishes for his son to be alive again but (remembering that the paw's wishes can cause misshapen results) cancels his request. He throws the paw in the fire. On the second day, he awakens to find that his son is alive and that he had dreamed the previous day's events. This story usually ended at the death sequence, but director Ruggles decided to go for the hackneyed dream ending. A decision that wrecked the movie for the discerning and did nothing for the blockheads who yapped it up on viewing all the morbidity involved. Remade in 1948 under the same title.

p, Merian C. Cooper; d, Wesley Ruggles, Ernest B. Schoedsack; w, Graham John (based on the story by W. W. Jacobs and stage play by Louis N. Parker); ph, Leo Tover, Jack McKenzie, Edward Cronjager, J. O. Taylor; m, Murray Spivack; ed, Charles L. Kimball; md, Max Steiner; art d, Carroll Clark; set d, Thomas Little, G. Rossi; spec eff, Lloyd Knechtel, Vernon L. Walker, Linwood Dunn; makeup, Sam Kaufman, Paul Stanhope, Mae Mark, J. Baker.

Horror **(PR:C MPAA:NR)**

MONKEY'S PAW, THE* (1948, Brit.) 64m Kay Films/BUT bw

Milton Rosmer *(Mr. Trelawne)*, Megs Jenkins *(Mrs. Trelawne)*, Joan Seton *(Dorothy Lang)*, Norman Shelley *(Monoghan)*, Michael Martin Harvey *(Kelly)*, Eric Micklewood *(Tom Trelawne)*, Brenda Hogan *(Beryl)*, Mackenzie Ward *(Noel Lang)*, Alfie Bass *(Speedway Track Manager)*, Hay Petrie *(Grimshaw)*, Rose Howlett *(Mrs. Gurney)*, Sydney Tafler *(The Dealer)*, Patrick Ward *(Sgt. Lawson)*, Vincent Lawson *(Morgan)*.

This common story was never treated with less finesse than in this hackneyed British version. Rosmer is the recipient of a magical monkey's paw which entitles the holder to three wishes. Hoping to be rid of gambling debts, he makes his first wish for enough cash to cover his debt load, only the money does not come to him directly but is a result of compensation for his son being killed in a motorcycle accident. Treated in a manner which hides the best content lurking in the story. Remake of the 1933 film.

p, Ernest G. Roy; d, Norman Lee; w, Lee, Barbara Toy (based on the play by W.W. Jacobs); ph, Bryan Langley; md, Stanley Black.

Thriller **(PR:A MPAA:NR)**

MONKEY'S UNCLE, THE** (1965) 90m BV c

Tommy Kirk *(Merlin Jones)*, Annette [Funicello] *(Jennifer)*, Leon Ames *(Judge Holmsby)*, Frank Faylen *(Mr. Dearborne)*, Arthur O'Connell *(Darius Green III)*, Leon Tyler *(Leon)*, Norman Grabowski *(Norman)*, Alan Hewitt *(Prof. Shattuck)*, Connie Gilchrist *(Housekeeper)*, Cheryl Miller *(Lisa)*, Gage Clarke *(College President)*, Mark Goddard *(Haywood)*, Harry Holcombe, Alexander Lockwood, Harry Antrim *(Board of Regents)*, Stanley the Chimp.

A dopey Disney picture which subscribes to the theory that if there's a monkey in a movie, kids will love it. Love it they may, but there's little here be thrilled with. A sequel to THE MISADVENTURES OF MERLIN JONES, this picture again casts Kirk as eccentric young inventor Jones. Kirk at first helps a pair of flunkies pass a test after performing some study-while-asleep tests on his pet chimp. The kids get A's, but are accused of cheating, a claim Kirk proves false. The school is then offered $10 million by O'Connell who will pay up if Jones can make man fly. A bicycle-powered winged machine is invented by Jones, who gets into the air, securing the big bucks. It turns out that O'Connell is really an escaped loon, who is recaptured by a pair of fellows in white coats. Ex-Mouseketeer Annette (as she was billed—leaving the Funicello off her name) costarred (actually she just held the chimp a lot).

p, Walt Disney, Ron Miller; d, Robert Stevenson; w, Tom and Helen August (based on a story by Bill Walsh); ph, Edward Colman (Technicolor); m, Buddy Baker; ed, Cotton Warburton; art d, Carroll Clark, William H. Tuntke; set d, Emile Kuri, Hal Gausman; spec eff, Robert A. Mattey, Eustace Lycett; cos, Chuck Keehne, Gertrude Casey; m/l, title song, Richard M., Robert B. Sherman (sung by Annette, The Beach Boys); makeup, Pat McNalley.

Juvenile **(PR:AAA MPAA:NR)**

MONOLITH MONSTERS, THE** (1957) 76m UNIV bw

Grant Williams *(Dave Miller)*, Lola Albright *(Cathy Barrett)*, Les Tremayne *(Martin Cochrane)*, Trevor Bardette *(Prof. Arthur Flanders)*, Phil Harvey *(Ben Gilbert)*, William Flaherty *(Police Chief Dan Corey)*, Harry Jackson *(Dr. Steve Hendricks)*, Richard Cutting *(Dr. Reynolds)*, Linda Scheley *(Ginny Simpson)*, Dean Cromer *(Highway Patrolman)*, Steve Darrell *(Joe Higgins)*, William Schallert *(Weatherman)*, Paul Frees *(Narrator)*.

A B horror film which, despite its simplicity, is yet a cornerstone in its genre. Based in realism, THE MONOLITH MONSTERS stars Williams as a geologist who, during a meteor shower, discovers that fragmented crystals have dropped into the Arizona desert. They grow larger by absorbing silicone from people's bodies, instantly turning them into stiffs (literally). A rainstorm nourishes the crystals and they grow to mammoth proportions. How can Williams prevent his own destruction? Will Albright get her schoolchildren safely out of town? Can world domination be stopped? Of course . . . it's easy, the monsters can be wiped out with common table salt.

p, Howard Christie; d, John Sherwood; w, Norman Jolley, Robert M. Fresco (based on a story by Jack Arnold, Fresco); ph, Ellis W. Carter; m, Joseph Gershenson; ed, Patrick McCormack; art d, Alexander Golitzen, Robert E. Smith; cos, Marilyn Sotto; spec eff, Clifford Stine; makeup, Bud Westmore.

Science Fiction **(PR:A MPAA:NR)**

MONSEIGNEUR** (1950, Fr.) 95m Roger Richebe bw

Bernard Blier *(Louis)*, Fernand Ledoux *(Professor)*, Nadia Gray *(Countess)*, Yves Deniaud *(Bellare)*, Marion Toures *(Maria)*.

An entertaining French film about a man who is thought to be a descendant of King Louis XVII, who had not been seen since his parents were beheaded during the French Revolution. Blier, an unassuming locksmith, is hired to open the eccentric Ledoux's door (he always loses his keys), and is discovered to possibly be of royal blood. With the help of a countess and some research, Ledoux proves that the humble locksmith indeed is the king's descendant and is heir to the throne. (In French.)

p,d&w, Roger Richebe, Pierre Lestringuez; ph, Philip Agostini; m, Henri Verdun; ed, Yvonne Martin.

Drama **(PR:A MPAA:NR)**

MONSIEUR** (1964, Fr.) 90m Copernie-Corona-Sanero/Comacico bw

Jean Gabin *(Monsieur)*, Liselotte Pulver *(Elizabeth)*, Philippe Noiret *(Husband)*, Mireille Darc *(Suzanne)*, Berthe Grandval *(Natalie)*, Gaby Morley *(Grandmother)*.

Gabin steals another film with his performance, this time as a despondent widower who nearly commits suicide when he learns his late wife was in love with someone else. He is given a new lease on life when he meets a prostitute, who at one time was his maid. He takes work as a valet, and the maid pretends to be his daughter. His employer's life is in disarray, but he gets the chance to put the household on the right track and discourages his boss' wife from having an affair. As usual, Gabin goes into a rage, blowing off the steam that has been building up throughout the picture—a trademark allowing him to show off his incredible talents.

d, Jean-Paul Le Chanois; w, Claude Sautet, Pascal Jardin (based on the play by Claude Gevel); ph, Louis Page (Franscope); ed, Emma Le Chanois.

Comedy **(PR:A MPAA:NR)**

MONSIEUR BEAUCAIRE*** (1946) 93m PAR bw

Bob Hope (Mons. Beaucaire), Joan Caulfield (Mimi), Patric Knowles (Duc de Chandre), Marjorie Reynolds (Princess Maria of Spain), Cecil Kellaway (Count D'Armand), Joseph Schildkraut (Don Francisco), Reginald Owen (King Louis XV of France), Constance Collier (The Queen), Hillary Brooke (Mme. Pompadour), Fortunio Bonanova (Don Carlos), Douglas Dumbrille (George Washington), Mary Nash (The Duenna), Leonid Kinskey (Rene), Howard Freeman (King Philip of Spain), Dorothy Vernon (Servant), Jack Mulhall, Philip Van Zandt (Guards), Eric Alden (Swordsman), Helen Freeman (Queen of Spain), Alan Hale, Jr., Hugh Prosser, John Maxwell (Couriers), Lane Chandler (Officer), George Sorel (Duke), Anthony Caruso (Masked Horseman), Jean De Briac (Minister of Finance), Jean Del Val (Minister of War), John Mylong (Minister of State), Nino Pipitone (Lackey), Lynne Lyons (Signora Gonzales), Mona Maris (Marquisa), Charles Coleman (Major Domo), Brandon Hurst (Marquis), Buddy Roosevelt, Manuel Paris (Spanish Guards), Catherine Craig (Duchess), Noreen Nash (Baroness), Nina Borget (Wife), Robert "Buddy" Shaw (Husband), Sherry Hall (Sentry), Tony Paton (Waiter).

A typical Bob Hope vehicle that casts him in his standard Casanova-type adventure role. This time he pretends to be a French nobleman pegged to wed a Spanish princess. The marriage will prevent a full-scale war; however, he wants to marry social-climber chambermaid Caulfield. The slapstick consequences of Hope's action are an assassination plot by a group who wants the war to break out, sending the pseudo-duke scurrying about in fear of his life. The patented finale has Hope marrying his chambermaid love and returning to life as a barber. Includes the songs "Warm as Wine," "A Coach and Four," and "We'll Drink Every Drop in the Shop" (Jay Livingston, Ray Evans).

p, Paul Jones; d, George Marshall; w, Melvin Frank, Norman Panama (based on the novel by Booth Tarkington); ph, Lionel Linden; m, Robert Emmett Dolan; ed, Arthur Schmidt; md, Dolan; art d, Hans Dreier, Earl Hedrick; cos, Mary Kay Dodson; ch, Billy Daniels, Josephine Earl; spec eff, Gordon Jennings, Farciot Edouart.

Comedy **(PR:A MPAA:NR)**

MONSIEUR COGNAC (SEE: WILD AND WONDERFUL, 1964)

MONSIEUR FABRE

(SEE: AMAZING MONSIEUR FABRE, THE, 1951, Fr./U.S.)

MONSIEUR HULOT'S HOLIDAY

(SEE: MR. HULOT'S HOLIDAY, 1951, Fr.)

MONSIEUR RIPOIS (SEE: LOVER'S HAPPY LOVER'S, 1954, Fr./Brit.)

MONSIEUR VERDOUX**1/2 (1947) 102m Chaplin/UA bw

Charles Chaplin (Henri Verdoux/Varney/Bonheur/Floray/Narrator), Mady Correll (Mona Verdoux, His Wife), Allison Roddan (Peter Verdoux, Their Son), Robert Lewis (Maurice Bottello), Audrey Betz (Martha Bottello), Martha Raye (Annabella Bonheur), Ada-May [Weeks] (Annette, Her Maid), Isobel Elsom (Marie Grosnay), Marjorie Bennett (Marie's Maid), Margaret Hoffman (Lydia Floray), Marilyn Nash (Girl), Helen Heigh (Yvonne), Irving Bacon (Pierre Couvais), Edwin Mills (Jean Couvais), Almira Sessions (Lena Couvais), Virginia Brissac (Carlotta Couvais), Bernard J. Nedell (Prefect of Police), Charles Evans (Detective Morrow), Arthur Hohl (Real Estate Agent), John Harmon (Joe Darwin), Vera Marshe (Mrs. Darwin), William Frawley (Jean La Salle, the Police Inspector), Fritz Leiber (Priest), Barbara Slater (Florist), Fred Karno (Mr. Karno), Barry Norton (Wedding Guest), Edna Purviance (Extra at Wedding Party), Pierre Watkin (Prison Official), Cyril Delevanti (Postman), Charles Wagenheim (Friend), Addison Richards (Bank Manager), James Craven (Annabella's Friend), Franklyn Farnum (Victim of the Crash), Herb Vigran (Reporter), Boyd Irwin (Prison Official), Paul Newlan (Wedding Guest), Joseph Crehan (Broker), Wheaton Chambers (Druggist), Frank Reicher (Doctor).

Chaplin, that master comedian, cannot seem to decide here which way to go, either into straight drama or farcical crime, but his black humor is in force and he has nevertheless produced a compelling film about the notorious Landru, better known as "Bluebeard." Instead of the time of WW I, when Landru was busy wooing scores of women and murdering them—mostly rich spinsters bereft of the males who had gone to fight at the front—Chaplin sets his tale during the end of the 1930s when France was at the brink of war with Germany. Though married and with a small son, Chaplin feels the need to murder for wealth to survive after losing his bank-clerk job. To support his family he advertises for rich widows in the lovelorn columns and is quickly supplied with a countless stream of victims. Raye is exceptional as the one woman who proves his nemesis and Chaplin is mesmerizing as the droll little methodical killer, putting on an eccentric and scary act when being tried for mass murder. Chaplin attempts to lift this depressing little film out of the pitch darkness of nightmare with little touches that fail to amuse. He falls into the Seine and is rescued by his intended drowning victim. His little boy pulls a cat's tail and he wonders where such cruelty has been learned. Little of it is funny, even though the great silent comedian subtitled this effort "A Comedy of Murders." Had Chaplin played the role straight rather than reaching too far for empathy and some bizarre black laughs, it might have been a minor masterpiece. As it is, MONSIEUR VERDOUX is a curiosity with flashes of brilliance but a film definitely not one of Chaplin's best. It is not recommended for children and to say that about any Chaplin film ought to indicate how frightening this sinister little picture really is. Later Chaplin stated that he made this film to protest the A-Bomb which is even more ridiculous than the premise of the story. The film was utterly rejected by audiences worldwide when released, although it has crawled into some cult status at this writing.

p,d&w, Charles Chaplin (based on an idea by Orson Welles); ph, Roland Totheroh, Curt Courant, Wallace Chewing; m, Chaplin; ed, Willard Nico; md, Rudolph Schrager, art d, John Beckman.

Crime Drama **Cas.** **(PR:O MPAA:NR)**

MONSIEUR VINCENT*** (1949, Fr.) 73m UGC-Edition Et Diffusion Cinematographiques/Lopert-Audio Brandon bw

Pierre Fresnay (Saint Vincent de Paul), Aime Clariond (Cardinal de Richelieu), Jean Debucourt (Count de Gondi), Lise Delamare (Countess de Gondi), Germaine Dermoz (Queen Anne of Austria), Gabrielle Dorziat (Mme. Groussault), Yvonne Godeau (Louise de Marillac), Jean Carmet (Abbe Portall), Pierre Dux (Chancellor Seguier), Georges Vitray (Mons. de Rougemont), Marcel Vallee (Hospital Supervisor), Michel Bouquet (Consumptive).

A visually stunning biography of St. Vincent de Paul, who humbly devoted himself to social work in France and was later canonized for his efforts. A stark, realistic film, MONSIEUR VINCENT follows the young peasant boy born in 1576 to his days of slavery in Algiers, and finally to his entry into the priesthood. Fresnay, one of France's most gifted actors, is perfect in his portrayal, assuming an aura of purity which brought him, and the film, numerous awards. Begun before the Occupation, this picture became Cloche's masterpiece, taking him years to complete because of the Nazi invasion. Instead of raising the necessary money through normal avenues, Cloche was forced, with the help of many parishes, to fund the picture by selling shares of the profits on a subscription basis. This spiritually moving, gorgeously photographed film won a special Oscar as the "most outstanding foreign language film released in the U.S. during 1948." (In French, English subtitles).

p, Viscount George de la Grandiere; d, Maurice Cloche; w, Jean Bernard Luc, Jean Anouilh, Cloche; ph, Claude Renoir; m, Jean-Jacques Grunenwald; ed, Jean Feyte; set d, Rene Renoux; English titles, Herman G. Weinberg.

Biography/Religious **Cas.** **(PR:A MPAA:NR)**

MONSIGNOR zero (1982) 122m FOX c

Christopher Reeve (Flaherty), Genevieve Bujold (Clara), Fernando Rey (Santoni), Jason Miller (Appolini), Joe Cortese (Varese), Adolfo Celi (Vinci), Leonard Cimino (Pope), Tomas Milian (Francisco), Robert J. Prosky (Bishop Walkman), Joe Pantoliano (Musso), Milena Vukotic (Sister Verna), Jan Danby (Lieutenant), Gregory Snegoff, Harrison Muller (Soldiers), David Mills (Major), Joe Spinell (Bride's Father), Ritza Brown (Maid of Honor), Lorendana Grappasonni (Bride), Ettore Mattia (Pietro), Carolyn Russoff, Yanti Somer, Paolo Scalondro (Secretaries), Domenico Poli (Priest), Elio Bonadonna, Giovanni Bonadonna, Remo DeAngelis (Killers), Pamela Prati, Annie Papa, Stefania D'Amario (Girls), Michele Messina (Guard), Agnes Nobencourt, Tracy Bonbrest (Postulants), Francesco Angrisano (Priest).

A wretched venture into melodrama played against the background of altars, papal blessings, and promiscuous priests—having all the content of an empty chalice. Superman Reeve does his quick change technique, switching from his clerical robe to street clothes, and preaching chastity while lusting after nun Bujold. In the same way that Michael Corleone rose to the top of the Mafia, Reeve starts at the bottom of the holy family and works his way into the financial end of the Vatican. He gets mixed up with Sicilian mobster Miller, choosing childhood friend Cortese as a go-between. Eventually, Reeve's ungodly behavior takes a turn for the worse when Cortese skips town with a hefty chunk of the Vatican bank account. MONSIGNOR is a horrible picture, mainly because of the catatonic performance by Reeve, but it, unfortunately, isn't nearly as trashy as Perry's previous picture MOMMIE DEAREST. The picture's only saving grace is the relentlessly adorable Bujold, who holds the film in the palm of her hand. Maybe they should have tried the same story with her in the lead; if anything, it would have kept Reeve out of sight for a while.

p, Frank Yablans, David Niven, Jr.; d, Frank Perry; w, Abraham Polonsky, Wendell Mayes (based on the novel by Jack Alain Leger); ph, Billy Williams (Technovision, DeLuxe Color); m, John Williams; prod d, John De Cuir; ed, Peter E. Berger; art d, Stefano Ortolani; set d, Joe Chevalier; cos, Theoni V. Aldredge.

Drama **Cas.** **(PR:O MPAA:R)**

MONSOON*1/2 (1953) 79m Film Group/UA c

Ursula Thiess (Jeanette), Diana Douglas (Julia), George Nader (Burton), Ellen Corby (Katie), Philip Stainton (Putsi), Myron Healey (Rault), Eric Pohlmann (Molac).

Filmed in India and set against the backdrop of the title weather conditions, the story concerns a betrothed couple, Douglas and Nader, who travel to an isolated village to meet Douglas' family. Nader falls for Thiess, Douglas' sister, prompting Douglas' attempted suicide. Nader returns to his fiancee and Thiess takes off to the hills, hoping to die, knowing she will never love again. When a film has to rely on bad weather, the viewer should sense trouble.

p, Forrest Judd; d, Rodney Amateau; w, Judd, David Robinson, Leonardo Bercovici (based on the play by Jean Anouilh); ph, Ernest Haller (Technicolor); m, Vasant Desai; ed, George Gale.

Drama **(PR:C MPAA:NR)**

MONSTER, 1980 (SEE: HUMANOIDS FROM THE DEEP, 1980)

MONSTER zero (1979) 98m Academy International c

John Carradine, Diane McBain, Roger Clark, Keenan Wynn, Stella Calle, John Lamont, Kelly Sill, Fernando Corredor, Jade Stuart, Glenn Ransom, Cesar Romero, Jim Mitchum, Anthony Eisley.

A good cast is gathered to do absolutely nothing in this rehash from 1950s horror combined with 1970s shock-'em. A giant monster is on the loose and terrorizing the unfortunate people who had to act in this thing.

p, Ken Hartford; d, Herbert L. Strock; w, Walter Robert Schmidt, Garland Scott, Herbert Strock.

Horror **(PR:O MPAA:NR)**

MONSTER A GO-GO zero
(1965) 70m B.I.& L. bw (AKA: TERROR AT HALFDAY)
Phil Morton, June Travis, George Perry, Lois Brooks, Henry Hite [Height].

Henry Hite, advertised as the tallest man in the world, plays a mutated giant astronaut who returns to Earth. A piece of garbage from director H. G. Lewis, who didn't even put it out under his own name. He bought up an old, unfinished science-fiction picture titled TERROR IN HALFDAY, added some new footage, and released it with his MOONSHINE MOUNTAIN. One of the worst.

p&d, Sheldon Seymour [Herschell Gordon Lewis], Bill Rebane; m/l, "Monster A Go-Go," Libby Quinn.

Science-Fiction **Cas.** **(PR:C MPAA:NR)**

MONSTER AND THE GIRL, THE** 1/2 (1941) 65m PAR bw
Ellen Drew (Susan Webster), Robert Paige (Larry Reed), Paul Lukas (W. S. Bruhl), Joseph Calleia (Deacon), Onslow Stevens (McMasters), George Zucco (Dr. Parry), Rod Cameron (Sam Daniels), Phillip Terry (Scott Webster), Marc Lawrence (Sleeper), Gerald Mohr (Munn), Tom Dugan (Capt. Alton), Willard Robertson (Lt. Strickland), Minor Watson (Judge Pulver), George F. Meader (Dr. Knight), Cliff Edwards (Leon Stokes), Frank M. Thomas (Jansen), Abner Biberman (Gregory), Corbet Morris (Claude Winters), Edward Van Sloan (Warden), Maynard Holmes (Tim Harper), Harry C. Bradley (Rev. Russell), Emma Dunn (Aunt Della), Sammy Blum (Popcorn Vendor), John H. Dilson (Employment Clerk), John Bleifer (Janitor), Jayne Hazard, Ethelreda Leopold (Party Girls), Florence Dudley (Madame), Matty Fain (Wade Stanton), Al Seymour, Bert Moorhouse (Henchmen), Bud Jamison (Tim The Doorman), Paul McVey (Monarch Hotel Clerk), Oscar Smith (Bootblack), Al M. Hill (Bruhl's Chauffeur), Emmett Vogan (Apartment Manager), Dave Willock (Charlie the Photographer), Anne O'Neal (Miss Julia), Eleanor Wesselhoeft (Elderly Housekeeper), Emory Parnell (Dumb Cop), Ruth Gillette (Woman), Fern Emmett (Woman Organizer), Charlie Gemora (The Ape), Skipper the Dog.

An unusually daring "horror" film which isn't that horrific at all, concentrating more on the characters than on a good scare. Church organist Terry is framed for murder when he ventures to the big city to get revenge on Paige, who faked a marriage to Terry's younger sister, Drew, in order to draw her into a life of prostitution. On the way to his execution, a scientist, Zucco, approaches him and asks for the use of his brain. Having little use for it, Terry agrees—his brain soon winding up in the skull of an ape. The ape-man goes on a rampage, destroying the gang responsible for the frame-up. Ultimately the ape is killed by the police after killing his last tormentor, and the shaken Drew is left in the care of reporter Cameron.

p, Jack Moss; d, Stuart Heisler; w, Stuart Anthony; ph, Victor Milner; m, Sigmund Krumgold; ed, Everett Douglas.

Horror **(PR:C MPAA:NR)**

MONSTER BARAN, THE (SEE: VARAN THE UNBELIEVABLE)

MONSTER CLUB, THE* 1/2 (1981, Brit.) 97m ITC c
Vincent Price (Erasmus), John Carradine (Ronald Chetwynd-Haynes), Roger Sloman (Club Secretary), Fran Fullenwider (Buxom Beauty), Anthony Steel (Lintom Busotsky), Suzanna Willis (The Stripper), The Viewers, B. A. Robertson, Night, Pretty Things (Bands); "The Shadmock Story": James Laurenson (Raven), Barbara Kellerman (Angela), Simon Ward (George), Geoffrey Bayldon (Psychiatrist); "The Vampire Story": Donald Pleasence (Pickering), Britt Ekland (Lintom's Mother), Richard Johnson (Lintom's Father), Warren Saire (Lintom), Neil McCarthy (Watson), Anthony Valentine (Mooney); "The Humgoo Story": Stuart Whitman (Sam), Lesley Dunlop (Luna), Patrick Magee (Innkeeper).

Vincent Price, who had not made a film in five years, made a poor choice in returning in this below-par horror anthology film. Price portrays a vampire who brings horror story writer Carradine to a wacky disco for Transylvanian freaks. The disco is used as a link between the three tales of supposed horror, and Price relates the three stories. In "The Vampire Story" Pleasence is a detective on Scotland Yard's "Vamp Squad," who finally catches up with and kills his nemesis but in the process is transformed into a vampire himself. At least there is some humor and a couple of shocks. The other two segments are devoid of both. In the disco, there are performances by rock groups—Pretty Things and UB40—and a female stripper who takes off everything but her bones. Songs include: "Sucker for Your Love" (performed by B. A. Robertson), "Monster Rule OK," "The Stripper" (performed by The Viewers), "The Monster Club" (performed by Pretty Things), "25 Per Cent" (performed by UB40), "Valentino Had Enough" (performed by The Expressions).

p, Milton Subotsky; d, Roy Ward Baker; w, Edward and Valerie Abraham (based on the novel by Ronald Chetwynd-Hayes); ed, Peter Tanner; art d, Tony Curtis.

Horror **Cas.** **(PR:C MPAA:NR)**

MONSTER FROM THE GREEN HELL* 1/2
(1958) 71m Grosse-Krasne/Distributors Corp. of America bw
Jim Davis (Quent Brady), Robert E. Griffin (Dan Morgan), Barbara Turner (Lorna Lorentz), Eduardo Ciannelli (Mahri), Vladimir Sokoloff (Dr. Lorentz), Joel Fluellen (Arobi), Tim Huntley (Territorial Agent), Frederic Potler (Radar Operator), LaVerne Jones (Kuana).

A cargo full of wasps crashes in the African jungle and is exposed to a dose of radiation. Davis leads an expedition in search of the cargo and discovers that the bugs have grown to gargantuan proportions. However, due to their size, they are unable to fly. They are killed when they fall to the bottom of a bubbling volcano. Silly but fun film which includes footage from 1939's STANLEY AND LIVINGSTON.

p, Al Zimbalist; d, Kenneth Crane; w, Louis Vittes, Endre Boehm; ph, Ray Flin; spec eff, Jess Davison, Jack Rabin, Louis DeWitt.

Science-Fiction **Cas.** **(PR:A MPAA:NR)**

MONSTER FROM THE OCEAN FLOOR, THE zero
(1954) 64m Palo Alto/Lippert bw (AKA: IT STALKED THE OCEAN FLOOR; MONSTER MAKER)
Stuart Wade (Steve Dunning), Anne Kimbell (Julie Blair), Dick Pinner (Dr. Baldwin), Jack Hayes (Joe), Wyott Ordung (Pablo), Inez Palang (Tula), David Garcia.

Completed in less than a week for under $12,000, this Roger Corman debut set the pace which would eventually make him "King of the Quickies." With a budget as cheap as this Corman simply couldn't go wrong, even with Ordung's non-direction. Kimbell is vacationing in Mexico when she takes a dip in the water and discovers that she isn't alone. Her visitor, a gigantic one-eyed octopus, sends her directly to marine biologist Wade. He, of course, doesn't believe her half-baked tale, so she takes to the water again. The tentacled-terror has had about enough and attacks her, but Wade comes to the rescue in his sporty mini-sub. He saves the day when he steers the sub into the monster's eye. As a budget-saver, Corman doesn't bother to show the monster until it is absolutely necessary. It may be a lousy movie but it was the beginning of something big . . . and cheap.

p, Roger Corman; d, Wyott Ordung; w, William Danch; ph, Floyd Crosby; m, Andre Brumer; prod d, Ben Hayne; ed, Ed Samson.

Horror/Science-Fiction **(PR:A MPAA:NR)**

MONSTER FROM THE SURF (SEE: BEACH GIRLS AND THE MONSTER, THE, 1965)

MONSTER ISLAND*
(1981, Span./U.S.) 100m Fort Films-Almena Films c (AKA: MYSTERY ON MONSTER ISLAND)
Terence Stamp (Taskinar), Peter Cushing (Kolderup), Gerard Tichy (Capt. Turkott), Paul Naschy (Flynt), Ian Serra (Jeff Morgan), David Hutton (Mr. Arttelet), Gasphar Ipua (Carefinatu), Blanca Estrada (Dominique), Frank Brana (Birling), Ana Obregon (Meg Hollaney).

Unsuspecting boaters are shipwrecked on a tiny island that is lorded over by the devious-minded Stamp and is inhabited by, among other things, prehistoric monsters. Based on a Jules Verne story, but lacking the ingenuity of the original tale, even though this is reportedly the most expensive film ever to be made in Spain. It's all done with a good dash of humor. The saurian critters look a bit like Macy's parade balloons, but why not? They turn out to be mechanized replicas planted on the island by young Serra's dad, who wants his pampered son to have a bit of adventure.

p&d, Juan Piquer Simon; w, Jorge Grau, Piquer Simon, R. Gantman (based on the story by Jules Verne); ph, Andres Beranguer (Eastmancolor); m, Alfonso Agullo; art d, Gumer Andres; spec eff, Emilio Ruiz; cos, Toni Puso.

Horror/Adventure/Comedy **(PR:C MPAA:NR)**

MONSTER MAKER, THE* (1944) 62m PRC bw
J. Carrol Naish (Dr. Igor Markoff), Ralph Morgan (Lawrence), Tala Birell (Maxine), Wanda McKay (Patricia Lawrence), Terry Frost (Blake), Glenn Strange (Giant), Alexander Pollard (Butler), Sam Flint (Dr. Adams), Ace (Himself).

Naish plays a mad scientist who experiments on humans—for commercial purposes only. He loves McKay, daughter of concert pianist Morgan, but she spurns his love. Naish injects Morgan with germs that turn him into a grotesque monster and hopes that by curing him he will win the heart of McKay, but things don't quite work out that way.

p, Sigmund Neufeld; d, Sam Newfield; w, Pierre Gendron, Martin Mooney (based on a story by Lawrence Williams); ph, Robert Cline; m, Albert Glasser; ed, Holbrook N. Todd; md, David Chudnow; art d, Paul Palmentola.

Horror **Cas.** **(PR:C MPAA:NR)**

MONSTER MAKER, 1954 (SEE: THE MONSTER FROM THE OCEAN FLOOR, 1954)

MONSTER MEETS THE GORILLA (SEE: BELA LUGOSI MEETS A BROOKLYN GORILLA, 1952)

MONSTER OF HIGHGATE PONDS, THE**
(1961, Brit.) 59m Halas and Batchelor/CFF bw
Roy Vincente (The Monster), Ronald Howard (Uncle Dick), Rachel Clay (Sophie), Michael Wade (David), Terry Raven (Chris), Frederick Piper (Sam), Michael Balfour (Bert), Beryl Cooke (Miss Haggerty).

Enjoyable tale about a gang of British kids who make friends with a mysterious monster that has hatched from an egg brought from Malaya. Struggling to keep itself out of the clutches of a profit-minded circus manager, the monster decides the best place for him is back home in Malaya. Bidding farewell to the helpful children, he sets off on the journey across the ocean. Well-executed combination of both live-action and animation. Director Cavalcanti is better known for the simplistic dramas he made in France during the early 1930s.

p, John Halas; d, Alberto Cavalcanti; w, Mary Cathcart Borer (based on the story by Joy Batchelor); ph, Frank North; m, Francis Chagrin; ed, Jack King, Robert Hilt; animation, Vic Hotchkiss.

Fantasy **(PR:AAA MPAA:NR)**

MONSTER OF LONDON CITY, THE*
(1967, Ger.) 87m CCC Filmkunst/PRC bw (DAS UNGEHEUER VON LONDON CITY)

Hansjorg Felmy (*Richard Sand*), Marianne Koch (*Ann Morlay*), Dietmar Schoenherr (*Dr. Morel Greely*), Hans Nielsen (*Dorne*), Charikila Baxevanos (*Betty Ball*), Fritz Tillman (*Sir George*), Walter Pfeil (*Horrlick*), Peer Schmidt (*Teddy Flynn*), Kurd Pieritz (*Maylor*), Elsa Wagner (*Housekeeper*), Adelheid Hinz (*Maid*), Gerda Blisse (*Assistant*), Manfred Grothe (*Detective*), Kai Fischer (*Helen Capstick*), Gudrun Schmidt (*Evelyn Nichols*).

A tame German horror film that takes place in modern day London during a stage production about Jack the Ripper. Lead actor Felmy, who is in love with the fiancee of his best friend, Schoenherr, gets shaken when a series of murders patterned after those in the play are committed. Felmy continues his role in the play until the night he discovers that his prop knife is now a real one. He runs from the stage and is led to a hotel room by a mysterious phone call; in the room he finds the body of a dead prostitute. The police are about to arrest him when a little girl clears his name. Felmy helps Scotland Yard track down the murderer, discovering that it is Schoenherr, who is jealous of Felmy's love for his fiancee. Having confessed to Felmy, Schoenherr commits suicide before the police arrive.

p, Artur Brauner; d, Edwin Zbonek; w, Robert A. Stemmle (based on a story by Bryan Edgar Wallace); ph, Siegfried Hold (Ultrascope); m, Martin Bottcher; ed, Walter Wischniewsky; prod d, Erwin Drager; art d, Hans Jurgen Kiebach, Ernst Schomer; cos, Trude Ulrich; makeup, Heinz Stamm, Ingrid Haas.

Horror/Mystery (PR:O MPAA:NR)

MONSTER OF PIEDRAS BLANCAS, THE* 1/2
(1959) 71m Vanwick/Film-Service bw

Les Tremayne (*Dr. Jorgenson*), Forrest Lewis (*Sheriff Matson*), John Harmon (*Sturges, the Lighthouse Keeper*), Don Sullivan (*The Biochemist*), Jeanne Carmen (*The Girl*), Frank Arvidson (*The Storekeeper*), Joseph La Cava (*Mike*), Peter Dunn (*Eddie*), Wayne Berwick (*Little Jimmy*), Jack Kevan (*The Monster*).

With thoughts of the popularity of CREATURE FROM THE BLACK LAGOON creeping about in the backs of the producers' minds, they came up with a similar monster, part man and part crustacean. Only this one is even better (played by producer Kevan) and much scarier; unfortunately after the initial exposure of this monster the plot goes right downhill. Lighthouse keeper Harmon leaves food out for the beast while none of the other inhabitants of the area believe actually exists. But a couple of fisherman turn up on the beach with their heads torn off their shoulders (the creature lives off blood), and everyone around is up in arms. Winner of the dubious Shock Award of the Year from *Monster Magazine*.

p, Jack Kevan; d, Irvin Berwick; w, Haile Chace; ph, Philip Lathrop; ed, George Gittens; art d, Walter Woodworth.

Horror Cas. (PR:C MPAA:NR)

MONSTER OF TERROR (SEE: DIE, MONSTER, DIE! 1965, U.S./Brit.)

MONSTER OF THE ISLAND* 1/2
(1953, Ital.) 87m Romana bw (IL MONSTRO DELL ISOLA)

Boris Karloff (*Don Gaetano*), Franco Marzi (*Andreani*), Renata Vicario (*Gloria*), Patrizia Remiddi, Iole Fierro, Carlo Duse, Germana Paolieri, Giuseppe Chinnici, Giulio Battifferi, Domenico De Ninno, Clara Gamberini, Salvatore Scibetta.

Karloff, an elderly fellow concerned with keeping his nursery open, gets involved in a kidnaping case. Narcotics investigator Marzi is tracking a gang of smugglers who are operating from a small island. In an attempt to get him off their trail, the gang abduct Marzi's daughter (Remiddi). Karloff offers to help, but is soon discovered to be the leader of the gang. It's not long, however, before the police drag them all into jail. Karloff and the kid are a joy to watch, but the film as a whole is full of holes. Its U.S. release saw the film, in its original Italian version, being shown only in Italian-language moviehouses. By the time it reached TV it had been dubbed.

p, Fortunato Misiano; d, Roberto B. Montero; w, Montero, Alberto Vechietti (based on a story by Vechietti); ph, Augusto Tiezzi; ed, Iolanda Benvenuti.

Crime Drama (PR:A MPAA:NR)

MONSTER OF THE WAX MUSEUM (SEE: NIGHTMARE IN WAX, 1969)

MONSTER ON THE CAMPUS* (1958) 76m UNIV bw

Arthur Franz (*Dr. Donald Blake*), Joanna Moore (*Madeline Howard*), Judson Pratt (*Lt. Mike Stevens*), Nancy Walters (*Sylvia Lockwood*), Troy Donahue (*Jimmy Flanders*), Phil Harvey (*Sgt. Powell*), Helen Westcott (*Molly Riordan*), Alexander Lockwood (*Gilbert Howard*), Whit Bissell (*Dr. Oliver Cole*), Ross Elliott (*Sgt. Eddie Daniels*), Eddie Parker (*The Monster*), Hank Patterson (*Mr. Townsend*).

A schlocky science-fiction tale about a college professor, Franz, who is involved in the study of a prehistoric fish that was discovered in Madagascar. A dragonfly bites the fish and becomes a "huge" menace; a dog comes in contact with the fish and is turned into a wolf. Then some of the fish slime makes its way into Franz's pipe; he smokes it and turns into a Neanderthal man. The prehistoric Franz goes on a rampage through the campus, swinging a murderous axe.

p, Joseph Gershenson; d, Jack Arnold; w, David Duncan; ph, Russell Metty; ed, Ted J. Kent; cos, Bill Thomas; spec eff, Clifford Stine.

Science-Fiction/Horror (PR:C MPAA:NR)

MONSTER THAT CHALLENGED THE WORLD, THE* 1/2
(1957) 83m UA bw

Tim Holt (*Lt. Comdr. John Twillinger*), Audrey Dalton (*Gail MacKenzie*), Hans Conried (*Dr. Jess Rogers*), Harlan Warde (*Lt. Bob Clemens*), Casey Adams [Max Showalter] (*Tad Johns*), Mimi Gibson (*Sandy MacKenzie*), Gordon Jones (*Josh Peters*), Marjorie Stapp (*Connie Blake*), Dennis McCarthy (*George Blake*), Barbara Darrow (*Jody Sims*), Bob Beneveds (*Mort Beatty*), Michael Dugan (*Clarke*), Mack Williams (*Capt. Masters*), Eileen Harley (*Sally*), Jody McCrea (*Seaman Fred Johnson*), William Swan (*Seaman Howard Sanders*), Charles Tannen (*Wyatt*), Byron Kane (*Coroner*), Hal Taggert (*Mr. Davis*), Gil Frye (*Deputy Scott*), Don Gachman (*Deputy Brewer*), Milton Parsons (*Lewis Clark Dobbs*), Ralph Moody (*Old Gatekeeper*).

Fine special effects help this film along by adding an atmosphere of impending danger. When the eggs of an ancient sea creature contaminate a lake in California, scientist Conried picks them up for study. They quickly hatch into oversized caterpillars and swarm around a nearby naval base in search of human food.

p, Arthur Gardner, Jules V. Levy; d, Arnold Laven; w, Pat Fielder (based on a story by David Duncan); ph, Lester White; m, Heinz Roemheld; ed, John Faure; md, Roemheld; art d, James Vance.

Science-Fiction (PR:A MPAA:NR)

MONSTER WALKED, THE (SEE: MONSTER WALKS, THE, 1932)

MONSTER WALKS, THE*
(1932) 63m Like/Action-Mayfair bw (GB: THE MONSTER WALKED)

Rex Lease (*Ted Clayton*), Vera Reynolds (*Ruth Earlton*), Sheldon Lewis (*Robert Earlton*), Mischa Auer (*Hanns Krug*), Martha Mattox (*Mrs. Krug*), Sidney Bracy (*Herbert Wilkes, Lawyer*), Sleep 'n' Eat [Willie Best] (*Exodus*).

An old dark house mystery made after the commercial successes of DRACULA (1931) and FRANKENSTEIN (1931), and whose plot is much indebted to THE CAT AND THE CANARY (1927). Reynolds inherits her father's estate (including the ape he kept for experiments), but her evil paralyzed uncle, Lewis, wants her killed so he can have the fortune for himself. He gets Auer, his moronic son, to kill Reynolds, but the confused boy kills his own mother instead. Auer, upset that Lewis' orders have caused him to kill his mother, turns upon the crippled man, and later goads the ape into attacking Reynolds, but Lease, her fiance, rescues her and the frenzied ape kills Auer.

p, Cliff Broughton; d, Frank B. Stayer; w, Robert Ellis; ph, Jules Cronjager; ed, Byron Robinson; md, Lee Zahler; art d, Ben Dore; set d, Ralph Black.

Horror Cas. (PR:A MPAA:NR)

MONSTER WANGMAGWI* (1967, S. K.) 80m Century c (WANG MA GWI)

Kungwon Nam, Haekyung Kim, Unjin Hahn, Hikap Kim.

A giant space monster stomps on Seoul, sending throngs of frightened Koreans running for safety. The aliens that sent it here had high hopes of dominating the planet, but, as usual, they were wrong. Rinky-dink special effects add nothing to this picture, the first all-Korean science-fiction film.

p, Hyukjin Kwon; w, Hayong Byun; ph, Changyong Ham (CinemaScope); spec eff, Soojai Byun.

Science-Fiction (PR:A MPAA:NR)

MONSTER YONGKARI
(SEE: YONGKARI MONSTER FROM THE DEEP, 1967, S.K.)

MONSTER ZERO*
(1970, Jap.) 92m Toho/Maron c (KAIJU DAISENSO; AKA: BATTLE OF THE ASTROS; INVASION OF THE ASTRO-MONSTERS; INVASION OF PLANET X)

Nick Adams (*Glenn*), Akira Takarada (*Fuji*), Kumi Mizuno (*Namikawa*), Keiko Sawai, Akira Kubo, Yoshio Tsuchiya, Jun Tazaki, Goro Naya.

Godzilla and Rodan are sent into space to help Planet X defeat the boisterous Ghidrah, here known as Monster Zero. When they get there, however, they are programmed by a computer to attack Earth. Adams has, in the meantime, fallen in love with Mizuno, who is really a spy from Planet X. An all-out war rages when the three giant invaders begin to attack, but Earth's laser beams overcome them. Top-flight science-fiction, which we've come to expect from Toho and Honda. Released in Japan in 1965. (English version.)

p, Tomoyuki Tanaka; d, Inoshiro Honda; w, Shinichi Sekizawa; ph, Hajime Koizumi (Tohoscope, Eastmancolor); m, Akira Ifukube; ed, Ryohei Fujii; art d, Takeo Kita; spec eff, Eiji Tsuburaya.

Science-Fiction (PR:A MPAA:G)

MONSTERS ARE LOOSE (SEE: THRILL KILLERS, THE, 1965)

MONSTERS FROM THE MOON (SEE: ROBOT MONSTER, 1953)

MONSTERS FROM THE UNKNOWN PLANET*
(1975, Jap.) 83m Toho-Eizo c (MEKAGOJIRA NO GYAKUSHU; AKA: TERROR OF MECHAGODZILLA; THE ESCAPE OF MEGAGODZILLA)

Katsuhiko Sasaki, Tomoko Ai, Akihiko Hirata, Tadao Nakamura, Katsumasu Uchida, Goro Mutsu, Kenji Sahara, Toru Kawane, Kazunari Mori, Tatsumi Fuyamoto.

An alien scientist has his daughter rebuilt after a fatal accident, turning her into somewhat of a robot. With the help of the monsters under her control they try, and try again, to seize the Earth.

p, Tomoyuki Tanaka; d, Inoshiro Honda; w, Yukiko Takayama; ph, Motoyoshi Tomioka; spec eff, Teruyoshi Nakano.

Science-Fiction (PR:A MPAA:NR)

MONSTROSITY (SEE: ATOMIC BRAIN, THE, 1964)

MONTANA**   (1950) 76m WB c

Errol Flynn (Morgan Lane), Alexis Smith (Maria Singleton), S. Z. "Cuddles" Sakall (Poppa Schultz), Douglas Kennedy (Rodney Ackroyd), James Brown (Tex Coyne), Ian MacDonald (Slim Reeves), Charles Irwin (MacKenzie), Paul E. Burns (Tecumseh Burke), Tudor Owen (Jock), Lester Matthews (George Forsythe), Nacho Galindo (Pedro), Lane Chandler (Jake Overby), Monte Blue (Charlie Penrose), Billy Vincent (Baker), Warren Jackson (Curley Bennett), Forrest Taylor (Clark), Almira Sessions (Gaunt Woman), Gertrude Astor, Nita Talbot (Women), Philo McCullough (Bystander), Dorothy Adams (Mrs. Maynard), Jack Mower, Creighton Hale (Ranchers), Maude Prickett, Jessie Adams (Rancher's Wives).

MONTANA is a blessedly short film. And yet, at 76 minutes, it feels like forever. Flynn was an Australian and this was only the second time he played a person from down under, the first film being DESPERATE JOURNEY. We also had the chance to hear his thin baritone warbling on a duet with Smith in "I Reckon I'm Falling In Love" (Mack David, Al Hoffman, Jerry Livingston), but that may be all there is to recommend this cliche "sheep man versus cattle folks" story. Filmed at the Calabasas Ranch owned by Warner Bros. in the far west region of the San Fernando Valley, it looks just fine, but there's far too much mushy stuff and not enough action for true fans of the genre. Flynn is an Australian sheepherder who comes to Montana to find some grazing space in Montana's predominantly cattle area. Smith is a rich cattle baroness who controls most of the territory, along with villain Kennedy, and she resents the intrusion of those smelly critters. Flynn doesn't reveal himself as a sheepman and pretends to be other than what he is in order to learn more about the situation. After another sheepman is knocked off, Flynn and Smith find each other attractive and that seems to be working out until she learns what his true vocation is. Once that's discovered, Flynn is whacked around and a range war is about to begin between the cowmen and the sheepmen. A stampede of cows is sent to trample the sheep, but Flynn diverts them, then takes his sheep to town and, in the end, he and Smith are reunited. One other song, "Cielito Lindo" (sung by Galindo), and some humor from Sakall but little else to separate this western from a thousand others. Flynn had starred in several huge westerns in the 1940s and this was an obvious attempt to recreate those vast films on a half vast budget.

p, William Jacobs; d, Ray Enright; w, James R. Webb, Borden Chase, Charles O'Neal (based on a story by Ernest Haycox); ph, Karl Freund (Technicolor); m, David Buttolph; ed, Frederick Richards; art d, Charles H. Clarke; set d, G. W. Berntsen; cos, Milo Anderson; makeup, Perc Westmore.

Western   (PR:A MPAA:NR)

MONTANA BELLE*   (1952) 81m Fidelity/RKO bw

Jane Russell (Belle Starr), George Brent (Tom Bradfield), Scott Brady (Bob Dalton), Forrest Tucker (Mac), Andy Devine (Pete Bivins), Jack Lambert (Ringo), John Litel (Matt Towner), Ray Teal (Emmett Dalton), Rory Mallinson (Grat Dalton), Roy Barcroft (Jim Clark), Holly Bane (Ben Dalton), Eugene [Gene] Roth (Marshal Ripple), Gregg Barton (Deputy Stewart), Glenn Strange, Pierce Lyden, George Chesebro (Deputies), Ned Davenport (Bank Clerk), Dennis Moore (Messenger), Kenneth MacDonald (Sheriff Irving), Rodney Bell (Hotel Clerk), Iron Eyes Cody (Cherokee), Rex Lease (Barfly), Charles Soldani (Indian), Hank Bell (Bartender), Franklyn Farnum (Man in Audience), Frank Ellis (Kibitzer), Paul Stader (Double for Scott Brady), Terry Wilson (Double for Forrest Tucker), Dave Sharpe (Rider for Iron Eyes Cody), Tom Steele (Rider for Stanley Andrews), Joe Yrigoyen (Double for Jack Lambert), Stanley Andrews (Marshal Combs), Dick Elliott (Banker Jeptha Rideout).

Although completed in 1948, the movie took nearly four years to be released. Howard Hughes had Russell under a personal contract and lent her to Fidelity Pictures which had been meaning to release it through Republic. After Hughes saw it, he decided he wanted the movie to go through RKO. He shouldn't have wasted his time or his money on this minor effort. Russell is Belle Starr, the fem bandit. She throws in her lot with the notorious Dalton gang, helmed by Brady and Teal, then has a falling out and takes off with Lambert and Tucker on a robbing spree. She meets Brent, a saloonkeeper, and plans to take him for his cash savings. They have a brief fling, despite herself, and she plans to double-cross the Daltons but winds up dead at their hands for her efforts. Mallinson and Bane are the other Daltons and Devine does cute comedy relief as a grizzled trader. Brent is yawnable as Russell's secondary love interest (she's already had a thing with Brady), and there is no outstanding acting on anyone's part. In between all the emptying of Winchesters and Colts, Russell takes some time to sing a bit and the best song is "The Gilded Lily." Made in Trucolor, a short-lived process, the film fails to satisfy on either visual or audio levels and should only be viewed to see how voluptuous Russell was at the time. Not the best work from legendary director Allan Dwan, who had already distinguished himself in the movie industry by lensing such comedies as BREWSTER'S MILLIONS, UP IN MABEL'S ROOM, and GETTING GERTIE'S GARTER, among what must be a hundred credits that began in 1911 and continued into the 1960s. This film has nothing to do with facts, which did not concern Dwan or writers McCoy and Hall. According to the bosomy Russell in her 1985 autobiography, "this epic was over so fast that I barely remember making it...." Her memory is way off the mark at present since she says "I played Calamity Jane," when her character was Belle Starr, but they could have called her by any name since her role is pure fiction.

p, Howard Welsch; d, Allan Dwan; w, Horace McCoy, Norman S. Hall (based on a story by Welsch, M. Coates Webster); ph, Jack Marta (Trucolor); m, Nathan Scott; ed, Arthur Roberts; art d, Frank Arrigo; set d, John McCarthy, Jr., George Milo; cos, Adele Palmer; spec eff, Howard and Theodore Lydecker; m/l, Portia Nelson, Margaret Martinez.

Western   (PR:A MPAA:NR)

MONTANA DESPERADO**   (1951) 51m Frontier/MON bw

Johnny Mack Brown (Dave Borden), Virginia Herrick (Sally Wilson), Myron Healey (Ron Logan), Marshall Reed (Hal Jackson), Steve Clark (The Sheriff), Edmund Cobb (Jim Berry), Lee Roberts (Jackson), Carl Mathews, Ben Corbett.

This Johnny Mack Brown oater deals with the familiar tale of a feud over a ranch which controls a valley's water flow. After four rancher deaths occur, Brown arrives on the scene to clear up the mess, pointing the guilty finger at a masked gunman. For some inexplicable reason the credits list Brown's character as Dave Borden, but everyone in the film calls him Johnny Mack Brown.

p, Vincent M. Fennelly; d, Wallace W. Fox; w, Dan Ullman; ph, Gilbert Warrenton; ed, Fred Maguire; md, Edward Kay; art d, David Milton.

Western   (PR:A MPAA:NR)

MONTANA JUSTICE   (SEE: MAN FROM MONTANA, 1941)

MONTANA KID, THE zero   (1931) 64m MON bw

Bill Cody (Bill Denton), Andy Shuford (Andy Burke), W. L. Thorne (Chuck Larson), G. D. Wood [Gordon DeMain] (Sheriff Barclay), Paul Panzer ("Gabby" Gable), John Elliott (John Burke), Doris Hill (Molly Moore).

Shuford is orphaned when his father is gunned down by the malevolent Thorne, who schemed a way to take over his ranch. Cody starts looking after the boy and arranges for the ranch to return to its rightful owner. He goes undercover, steals Thorne's money, and then buys back the property. One of a number of pictures that teamed Shuford and Cody.

p, Trem Carr; d, Harry Fraser; w, G. A. Durlam (based on a story by Fraser); ph, Archie Stout; ed, Lem Wheeler.

Western   (PR:A MPAA:NR)

MONTANA MIKE   (SEE: HEAVEN ONLY KNOWS, 1947)

MONTANA MOON**½   (1930) 91m MGM bw

Joan Crawford (Joan), Johnny Mack Brown (Larry), Dorothy Sebastian (Elizabeth), Ricardo Cortez (Jeff), Benny Rubin (The Doctor), Cliff Edwards (Froggy), Karl Dane (Hank), Lloyd Ingraham (Mr. Prescott).

This is a horse opera in the truest sense of the word, in that it combines a western story with some music by Arthur Freed, who would go on to be one of MGM's greatest musical producers, and Nacio Herb Brown (which means "born" Herb Brown in Spanish). Crawford is a spoiled young woman, the daughter of Ingraham, arguably the wealthiest rancher in all of Montana. She lives a hedonistic life and devotes herself to pleasure like a hayseed jazz baby. She's been in New York and is about to return to Montana; then she leaps off the train at a stop and recklessly decides to return to New York on the next train going east. Since she's on her dad's private train, that's not so easy, but she manages to get away unnoticed and finds herself in a whistle-stop where she meets Brown, a cowboy who has come north from Texas to settle in Montana. It's a few minutes and the two of them are in love, this causing Crawford to dispense with her plans to go back to the big city. Ingraham is thrilled with her choice, a far cry from the namby-pambies she's been associating with, and he gives his approval to the match. There's a huge party on their wedding night and Brown is outraged when Crawford does a hot dance with Cortez, a city-style cad. At the end of the dance, Brown decks Cortez with a haymaker and Crawford is humiliated by his behavior and leaps aboard the first train going to New York. The train is waylaid by a bunch of masked bandits and Crawford is forcibly taken. Then we learn that these criminals are hired cowpunchers engaged by Brown and that he is the leader of the brigands. The picture ends with Crawford and Brown reunited and the feeling that she will stray no more. In between the hootin' and hollerin', there's a bit of singin' as well, with the tunes being happily brief. The songs include: "The Moon Is Low," "Happy Cowboy" (Freed and Brown), "Montana Call," "Let Me Give You Love," and "Trailin' in Old Montana" (Herbert Stothart, Clifford Grey). It was not a hit at the box office, as there was some public apathy toward musicals at the time, especially musicals that didn't have good music. Still, it's worth a look and you'll have a few laughs at the antics of Benny Rubin and Cliff Edwards who provide the comic relief. Brown went on to make BILLY THE KID after this and that role was the one that sent him on a brief shooting star to the top of the cowboy heap. The sound recording in MONTANA MOON, although better than most of the musicals that preceded it, was still in an infant state and did nothing to enhance anyone's singing voice. It is presumed that writer Thalberg was related to the man who ran MGM in those years, Irving Thalberg. Nepotism ran as rampant as bathtub gin.

d, Malcolm St. Clair; w, Sylvia Thalberg, Frank Butler, Joe Farnham (based on a story by Thalberg, Butler); ph, William Daniels; ed, Carl L. Pierson, Leslie F. Wilder; art d, Cedric Gibbons; cos, Adrian.

Musical/Western   (PR:A MPAA:NR)

MONTANA TERRITORY*   (1952) 64m COL c

Lon McCallister (John Malvin), Wanda Hendrix (Clair Enoch), Preston Foster (Sheriff Plummer), Hugh Sanders (Jason Waterman), Jack Elam (Gimp), Clayton Moore (George Ives), Robert Griffin (Yeager), Myron Healey (Bill Landers), Eddy Waller (Possum), George Russell (Boone Helm), Ethan Laidlaw (Frank Parrish), Frank Matts (Jack Gallagher), Ruth Warren (Mrs. Nelson), Trevor Bardette (Lloyd Magruder), George Chesebro (Weasel).

This low-quality western takes place in Montana territory in its days before statehood. Foster is a crooked sheriff who uses his badge to commit crimes and misdeeds without interference from the populace. Young deputy McCallister idolizes Foster, until he falls in love with Hendrix, whose father is killed by the sheriff. Hendrix heads a vigilante committee to bring in the errant sheriff, opening

McCallister's eyes and inspiring him to help bring his former idol to justice. Somewhere in the footage, Montana is admitted to the Union.

p, Colbert Clark; d, Ray Nazarro; w, Barry Shipman; ph, Henry Freulich (Technicolor); ed, Paul Borofsky; md, Mischa Bakaleinikoff; art d, Charles Clague.

Western **(PR:A MPAA:NR)**

MONTE CARLO* 1/2** (1930) 90m PAR bw

Jack Buchanan *(Count Rudolph Falliere)*, Jeanette MacDonald *(Countess Vera von Conti)*, ZaSu Pitts *(Maria, Vera's Maid)*, Claude Allister *(Prince Otto von Seibenheim)*, Lionel Belmore *(Duke Gustave von Seibenheim, His Father)*, Tyler Brooke *(Armand, Rudolph's Friend)*, John Roche *(Paul, the "Real" Hairdresser)*, Albert Conti *(Prince Otto's Companion/M.C.)*, Helen Garden *("Lady Mary" in Stage Opera)*, Donald Novis *("Mons. Beaucaire" in Stage Opera)*, David Percy *(Herald)*, Erik Bey *(Lord Winterset)*, Billy Bevan *(Train Conductor)*, Sidney Bracey *(Hunchback at Casino)*, Frances Dee *(Receptionist)*, Rolfe Sedan *(Hairdresser)*, John Carroll *(Wedding Guest Officer)*, Geraldine Dvorak *(Extra in Casino)*, Edgar Norton.

MONTE CARLO did a lot for advancing the role of the talkie, something that was still not for certain when this picture was begun in 1929. But Lubitsch was able to so integrate the fluid cinematic techniques he'd used in silents with the new-found discovery of sound, that the outcome was delightful. MacDonald is Vera von Conti (a strange name when you come to think of it, because "Vera" is French, "Conti" is Italian, and "von" is German, so it can be assumed that she has a polyglot past), a countess who is about to marry Allister, a stuffy Teutonic twit who happens to be a Prince. She decides to toss over Allister and hops aboard the "Blue Express" train for Monte Carlo. While railroading for Monaco, she sings "Beyond the Blue Horizon" out the window and the peasants hear her and stop whatever they're doing to sing along on the second chorus. She hasn't much money left when she checks into one of the posh sleeperies but her heart is happy. She enters the casino and is immediately spotted by Buchanan (among many others), a wealthy count. He approaches her and says that if he touches her golden tresses, it may mean good luck at the tables. She allows him to stroke her hair and magically begins winning. MacDonald is so struck by her change of luck that she hires Buchanan to be her hairdresser, chauffeur, and valet. She doesn't know who he is and he bemusedly goes along with her mistake just to be close to her. At night, he calls her and never identifies himself, singing his love for her. She answers in kind. Time passes and she's running out of money again, reconsidering the marriage she ran out on in reel one. This anger causes her to vent her spleen on Buchanan, who takes it all. She attends the opera "Monsieur Beaucaire," which resembles her plight, in that Beaucaire pretends to be a commoner to be near the woman he loves. At the opera, she sees Buchanan in a box seat and realizes that he's not a servant at all. MacDonald confronts Buchanan, he admits that he is also the mysterious caller, and the two of them live happily and wealthily forever—just as in real life. Sure. It's a bit sugary and very dated but charming for most of the footage. Lubitsch shows his "touch" here and gets good comedy from everyone. MacDonald is ravishing to look at, lyrical to listen to, and just all-around swell. Buchanan was never able to show his legendary stage charisma on the screen and didn't do another U.S. feature until THE BAND WAGON in 1953. Tunes include: "Day of Days," "Give Me a Moment, Please," "This is Something New to Me," "Women, Just Women," "She'll Love Me and Like It," "Always in All Ways," "I'm a Simple-Hearted Man," "Whatever it is, it's Grand," and "Trimmin' the Women." Not a big hit at the box office, mainly due to the lack of popularity of Buchanan, who was excellent but never did cause American hearts to flutter.

p, Adolph Zukor; d, Ernst Lubitsch; w, Ernest Vajda, Vincent Lawrence (based on the play *The Blue Coast* by Hans Muller and the novelette *Monsieur Beaucaire* by Booth Tarkington, Evelyn Sutherland); ph, Victor Milner; m, Richard Whiting, Frank Harling; ed, Merrill White; set d, Hans Dreier; cos, Travis Banton; m/l, Whiting, Harling, Leo Robin.

Musical/Comedy **(PR:AA MPAA:NR)**

MONTE CARLO BABY*

(1953, Fr.) 79m GFD/Favorite Pictures bw (NOUS IRONS A MONTE CARLO)

Audrey Hepburn *(Linda Farrel)*, Jules Munshin *(Antoine)*, Michele Farmer *(Jacqueline)*, Cara Williams *(Marinette)*, Philippe Lemaire *(Philippe)*, Russell Collins *(Max)*, Ray Ventura and His Orchestra.

Poorly scripted and enacted farce about a lost baby who has a bunch of people up in arms, while all the while it is comfortably passing its time with the Ray Ventura Orchestra. Hepburn had a very small part in this film as an actress who pops up every once in awhile. Though MONTE CARLO BABY is a far cry from the brilliant films in which she would later star, it was during the filming of this picture that she made the acquaintance of author Colette. This meeting was probably the turning point in Hepburn's career, as the author recommended the rising star take the role of "Gigi" in the Broadway production of the popular play. It was only a little while before Hepburn would grace the screen in ROMAN HOLIDAY and SABRINA.

p, Ray Ventura; d, Jean Boyer, Lester Fuller; w, Boyer, Fuller, Alex Joffe; ph, Charles Suin; m, Paul Misraki; ed, Franchette Mazin; art d, Robert Giordani; m/l, Misraki, Geoffrey Parsons.

Musical/Comedy **(PR:A MPAA:NR)**

MONTE CARLO MADNESS

(SEE: BOMBARDMENT OF MONTE CARLO, THE, 1931, Ger.)

MONTE CARLO NIGHTS* (1934) 60m MON bw

Mary Brian, John Darrow, Kate Campbell, Robert Frazer, Yola D'Avril, Astrid Allwyn, George Hayes, Billie Van Every, Carl Stockdale, George Cleveland.

Having only the slimmest evidence with which to work, a convicted murderer proves his innocence. A unbelievable feat, made even harder to swallow because the police are after him to bring him back to jail.

p, Paul Malvern; d, William Nigh; w, Norman Houston (based on the story "Numbers of Death" by E. Phillips Oppenheim).

Crime **(PR:A MPAA:NR)**

MONTE CARLO OR BUST

(SEE: THOSE DARING YOUNG MEN IN THEIR JAUNTY JALOPIES, 1969, Fr./Brit./Ital.)

MONTE CARLO STORY, THE** (1957, Ital.) 99m Titanus/UA c

Marlene Dietrich *(Marquise Maria de Crevecoeur)*, Vittorio De Sica *(Count Dino della Fiaba)*, Arthur O'Connell *(Mr. Hinkley)*, Natalie Trundy *(Jane Hinkley)*, Jane Rose *(Mrs. Freeman)*, Clelia Matania *(Sophia)*, Alberto Rabagliati *(Albert the Portiere)*, Mischa Auer *(Hector the Maitre D')*, Renato Rascel *(Duval)*, Carlo Rizzo *(Henri, a Sailor)*, Truman Smith *(Mr. Freeman)*, Mimo Billi *(Roland the Barman)*, Marco Tulli *(Francoise the Chauffeur)*, Guido Martufi *(Paul the Elevator Boy)*, Jean Combal *(Hotel Managing Director)*, Vera Garretto *(Caroline the Hotel Maid)*, Yannick Geffroy *(Gabriel, Henri's Son)*, Betty Phillippsen *(Zizi the Cigarette Girl)*, Frank Colson *(Walter the 1st American)*, Serge Fliegers *(Harry the 2nd American)*, Frank Elliott *(Mr. Ewing)*, Betty Carter *(Mrs. Ewing)*, Gerlaine Fournier *(German Lady)*, Simonemarie Rose *(Lady in Magenta)*, Clara Beck *(American Oil Heiress)*, Ercole the Sporting Club Cashier, Jimmy the Pianist at Sporting Club, Hotel Assistant Director, Hotel Check-Room Attendant, Lartigau the Violinist *(Themselves)*.

This is Dietrich's only Italian-made movie and, unfortunately, the camera dwells too long on the Italian topography and not long enough on Dietrich. Cinematographer Rotunno was the man who lensed THE BIBLE and he was far better at that kind of grandeur then at filming a fabulous face. Dietrich and De Sica are the femme and "homme" fatale in director Taylor's script, which was based on a story by Risi and Girosi, and what might have been a frothy farce becomes somewhat leaden under his aegis. De Sica is an Italian count who has fallen on hard times by squandering his once-formidable fortune at the gaming tables. His loyal servants lend him a few francs so he can play a while at the casino nightly. They no longer work for him but are employed at the hotel and hate to see their former master broke. By this time, De Sica has racked up a considerable debt to them, but he thinks he has a way out and has devised an unbeatable system to win at roulette. (In Las Vegas, when the casino managers hear about someone who has a "system," they'll send a limo for him, pay all his expenses, and laugh as the wheel takes its toll.) De Sica's friends think that he may be able to repay them if he can only find some unsuspecting woman who will fall for his Neapolitan charm. They parade a series of prospective women past De Sica, but he is loath to give up his freedom until he sees Dietrich, a marquise. She interests him but he doesn't know that she is in the same boat. Her late husband left her a pile of money, but she's lost it all gambling and has arrived in Monte Carlo to find a wealthy man who will back her habit. The two of them meet, fall in love, and discover that they share the same penchant for risk. They decide to wed, but that's called off when they each learn that the other is masquerading as someone with money. This forces a split (and if you think it's permanent, then you haven't been watching enough movies) and they decide it's better that they seek other partners at that moment. O'Connell arrives on his huge yacht. He's a rich American widower and his ship bangs into De Sica's. O'Connell offers to pay for the damages and invites De Sica and Dietrich (now posing as De Sica's sister) aboard to stay until the repairs have been completed. O'Connell is taken by Dietrich instantly and it isn't long before he asks for her hand. Meanwhile, his young daughter, Trundy, is ga-ga over De Sica. Dietrich thinks she should come clean, so she confesses everything to O'Connell who shrugs, accepts her admission that she is a gambling junkie, and still wants to marry her. (This is not unlike the scene where Jack Lemmon is in drag and trying to talk Joe E. Brown out of his lust in SOME LIKE IT HOT. Even after Lemmon pulls off his wig and says, "We can't get married because I'm a man!" Brown smiles and replies, "Nobody's perfect!") Trundy realizes that De Sica is sad at losing his "sister", but she volunteers to take up the slack in his life and asks for his hand. De Sica argues that he is old enough to be her father, but she disputes that and thinks that they will become closer in age as the years go by. Now that she's 19, she is one-third his age, but in due time, she'll be half his age, etc. De Sica takes that as a message from on high and races to the roulette table to use the number "19" as the basis for his system. In a trice, he is raking in the chips. O'Connell now tells De Sica that Trudy isn't 19, she's 18, and that news, of course, wrecks De Sica's system and he begins to give it all back to the casino management. His former chauffeur, Tulli, whacks De Sica over the noggin before the count can lose everything. This happens while De Sica is at the tables, but it is done so surreptitiously that it seems as though the man has fainted, not been hit by a tiny metal tool. De Sica wakes up, pays off his creditors, and takes an oath never to gamble again. He is about to set sail for Naples, and Dietrich, who is living aboard O'Connell's yacht in preparation for their marriage, can't bear the thought of losing De Sica. She admits to O'Connell that she is not De Sica's sister but is, in fact, his lover. O'Connell allows his yacht to come alongside De Sica's and Dietrich climbs aboard the Italian ship. The two are united and will probably spend the rest of their lives gambling at Monte Carlo. This is about as contrived a plot as one can find and the result is generally disappointing. Dietrich plays the role as though she were sleepwalking and one wonders why she took it in the first place. De Sica reeks of continental charm but both of their underlying character traits never allow them to be lovable. It is not easy to sympathize with people who are so selfish and self-destructive and whose intentions, until the end of the movie, are so greed-oriented. Many of the actors in the movie were the real people who worked at the casino in Monte Carlo (see cast list) and play themselves very well. Trundy later married press agent-turned-producer Arthur Jacobs (DR. DOLITTLE, PLANET OF

THE APES, etc.) and paid less attention to her acting career. The story here might have made a cute half-hour episode for "Love, American Style."

p, Marcello Girosi; d&w, Samuel A. Taylor (based on a story by Girosi, Dino Risi); ph, Giuseppe Rotunno (Technirama, Technicolor); art d, Gastone Medin; cos, Jean Louis; m/l, "Les Jeux Sont Faits," Michael Emer, "Back Home in Indiana," James F. Hanley, Ballard MacDonald, "Rien ne va Plus."

Comedy/Drama **(PR:A MPAA:NR)**

MONTE CASSINO** (1948, Ital.) 93m Pastor/Superfilm bw

Alberto C. Lolli *(The Head Abbot)*, Gilberto Severi *(Don Martino)*, Ubaldo Lay *(Don Eusebio)*, Zora Piazza *(Maria)*, Pietro Bigerna *(Alberto)*, Silverio Blasi *(Marco)*, Vira Silenti *(Carmela)*, Rodolpho Neuhaus *(Capt. Richter)*, Livio Bussa *(Antonio)*, Giuseppe Forli *(Father of Antonio)*, a group of original survivors of Monte Cassino.

A fair docu-drama dealing with the siege and bombing of the abbey at Monte Cassino during WW II. Inside the walls of the 1,400-year-old abbey, the monks battled against the German troops holding the Cassino region. The abbey faces destruction as the American 5th Army presses forward and the Germans refuse to leave. The German high command's refusal to withdraw on time is held accountable for the abbey's bombing and destruction. Co-scripted by Paolucci, who is best known for his travelogs, an element that is clearly apparent in MONTE CASSINO. (In Italian; English subtitles.)

p&d, Arturo Gemmiti; w, Gemmiti, Virgilio Sabel, Giovanni Paolucci; ph, Piero Portalupi, Vittorio Dell a Balle, Angelo Jannarelli; m, Adriano Lualdi; English titles, Charles Clement.

War Drama **(PR:A MPAA:NR)**

MONTE CRISTO'S REVENGE

(SEE: RETURN OF MONTE CRISTO, THE, 1946)

MONTE WALSH*** (1970) 99m Palladian-Cinema Center/NG c

Lee Marvin *(Monte Walsh)*, Jeanne Moreau *(Martine Bernard)*, Jack Palance *(Chet Rollins)*, Mitch Ryan *(Shorty Austin)*, Jim Davis *(Cal Brennan)*, John "Bear" Hudkins *(Sonny Jacobs)*, Raymond Guth *(Sunfish Perkins)*, John McKee *(Petey Williams)*, Michael Conrad *(Dally Johnson)*, Tom Heaton *(Sugar Wyman)*, G. D. Spradlin *(Hat Henderson)*, Ted Gehring *(Skimpy Eagans)*, Bo Hopkins *(Jumpin' Joe Joslin)*, Matt Clark *(Rufus Brady)*, Billy "Green" Bush *(Powder Kent)*, Allyn Ann McLerie *(Mary Eagle)*, John McLiam *(Fightin' Joe Hooker)*, Leroy Johnson *(Marshal)*, Eric Christmas *(Col. Wilson)*, Charles Tyner *(Doctor)*, Dick [Richard] Farnsworth, Fred Waugh *(Cowboys)*, Jack Colvin *(Card Cheat)*, William Graeff, Jr. *(Bartender)*, John Carter *(Farmer)*, Guy Wilkerson *(Old Man)*, Roy Barcroft *(Saloon Proprietor)*, Blackie Escalante, Frank Green, Billy Fraker, Kurtis Roberts.

Cinematographer Fraker's directorial debut is a corker. After years of running the camera for several others, he finally got his chance to say "action" and made the most of it. MONTE WALSH is an interesting, atypical western romp that signals the end of the era. Fraker's eye for imagery is evident in every shot, although he didn't let that overtake the compelling characterizations of the actors. There is a similarity between this and LONELY ARE THE BRAVE (although that film is set quite a good deal later) in that both films are pessimistic in their heralding of the end and both leave the viewer with a sense of relative hopelessness. Marvin and Palance are two down-at-the-boot-heels cowboys who ride toward the ironically named town of Harmony and take jobs at a ranch run by Davis. They then encounter an old saddle-mate, Ryan, and go into the town where Marvin pays a call on his one-time mistress, Moreau, at the local saloon. When the ranch closes, Palance begins to woo McLerie, a new widow who now owns a thriving hardware store. Ryan loses his job and gets involved in a fracas which winds up when he kills the other man, Johnson, who just happens to be a minion of the law. Palance and McLerie tie the knot and he is immediately the soul of conservatism and family thinking, so he advises the grizzled Marvin to forget about his cowboy life and consider settling down. Moreau has left Harmony and Marvin trails her to her new town and asks if she will accompany him for the rest of his natural life. But she is reluctant, cites the fact that she's tubercular, and thinks it might be better if they avoided any long-term entanglements, for there is no way for Marvin to know how long she's going to be around. Marvin is distraught, has a few too many, and is leaving the town when he comes across a wild stallion and manages to "break" it. The steed is part of a Wild West show and the owner offers Marvin a job as a carnival attraction. Marvin, who is broke, has too much pride to accept the job of impersonating "Texas Jack Barrat" and says that there is no way he will compromise himself, starting "I ain't spittin' on my whole life." He rides the wild horse through the small town and destroys a good deal of the place as he does so, then returns to Harmony where he learns that Ryan was in the process of robbing the hardware store and murdered Palance. He rides out after Ryan, then hears that Moreau is very sick, so he travels to her new town and arrives after she's already died. Ryan is there, knowing full well that Marvin intends to exact revenge. The final scene is a stalk through the town until Walsh kills Ryan (who was making his film debut). After seeing Marvin in CAT BALLOU, the first tendency is to smile at his bust-out cowboy, but he soon puts a stop to that and we know he is a serious man this time. Palance grins his way through the picture with more charisma than he usually demonstrates. Fraker spends a tad too much time in re-creating Frederic Remington's style of painting on screen and there is more meandering than one might like at the start, but once the action begins and the relationships are established, the picture succeeds in satisfying on all levels. Filmed near Tucson, MONTE WALSH never made a lot of money but nearly everyone who saw it liked it. The ranch that the men work at is foreclosed on by Eastern financiers which, we suppose, is another plot point about the way the West was disintegrating because of absentee ownership. A barroom fight is shot entirely in closeups and doesn't work, although it was a bold attempt to make the picture lookdifferent from the thousands of westerns which preceded it. In small roles, note Fred Waugh (one of the best stunt men around) and Dick Farnsworth, who eventually came to the world's notice with his excellent role in THE GREY FOX. Note the great western and serial villain, Roy Barcroft, in one of his last bit roles in this film released after his death in 1969.

p, Hal Landers, Bobby Roberts; d, William A. Fraker; w, Lukas Heller, David Z. Goodman (based on the novel by Jack Warner Schaefer); ph, David M. Walsh (Panavision, Technicolor); m, John Barry; ed, Richard Brockway, Robert L. Wolfe, Raymond Daniels, Gene Fowler, Jr.; prod d, Albert Brenner; art d, Ward Preston; set d, Philip Abramson; cos, Brenner; spec eff, George Peckham, Roy Bolton; m/l, "Good Times are Comin'," Barry, Hal David; makeup, Emile La Vigne.

Western **Cas.** **(PR:C MPAA:GP)**

MONTENEGRO***

(1981, Brit./Swed.) 96m Viking-Europa-Smart Egg/New Realm-Atlantic c (AKA: MONTENEGRO—OR PIGS AND PEARLS)

Susan Anspach *(Marilyn Jordan)*, Erland Josephson *(Martin Jordan)*, Jamie Marsh *(Jimmy)*, Per Oscarsson *(Dr. Pazardjian)*, Bora Todorovic *(Alex)*, Marianne Jacobi *(Cookie)*, John Zacharias *(Grandpa)*, Svetozar Cvetkovic *(Montenegro)*, Patricia Gelin *(Tirke)*, Lisbeth Zachrisson *(Rita Rossignol)*, Marina Zindahl *(Secretary)*, Nikola Janic *(Moustapha)*, Lasse Aberg *(Customs Inspector)*, Dragan Ilic *(Hassan)*, Milo Petrovic *(Zanzibar Customer)*, John Parkinson *(Piano Player)*, Jan Nygren *(Police Officer)*, Kaarina Harvistola *(lst Policewoman)*, Ewa Gislen *(2nd Policewoman)*, Elsie Holm *(Tap-Dancing Lady)*, Paul Smith *(Cab Driver)*, Bo Ivan Peterson.

A comic and perverse social commentary on the animalistic nature of man from bizarre director Dusan Makavejev (WR: MYSTERIES OF THE ORGANISM). Anspach is a dejected American housewife living in Sweden with her wealthy business-trip-taking husband, their two children, and her grandfather (who thinks he's Buffalo Bill). After setting the bed on fire, her husband (Josephson) visits a psychiatrist who seems to be the looniest of them all, dressed in his oversized fur coat. When Anspach's husband announces he is leaving on another business trip (his 23rd that year) she hops a cab and meets him at the airport. She is detained by customs however, and causes him to miss his plane. While being searched, she meets a young girl from Yugoslavia who is smuggling alcohol and a dead pig into the country. The two become friendly and when Anspach can't locate her husband, she leaves with the girl and her ride. The trio travels along the expressway, drinking as they drive. On the way to their destination they pick up a man with a knife in his forehead (one of the oddest scenes in cinema, due to the characters' blase reactions). They continue on to a small village, where they visit a club called the Zanzibar. Anspach first witnesses a brawl in which two men hit each other with shovels. She comes to the aid of the loser, Montenegro (Cvetkovic), and gives him mouth-to-mouth resuscitation. During her visit to the Zanzibar, Anspach performs a torch song and watches an erotic dancer perform a routine with a radio-operated army tank (another of the oddest scenes in cinema). By the end of the evening she makes love to Cvetrovic and returns to her husband. Very few questions are asked as she explains to her family (which is politely seated at a dinner table) what happened, and adds that "they all lived happily ever after." Of course Makavejev doesn't let us off the hook that easily. An interesting and funny film that is by no means as unwatchable as some people have made Makavejev out to be. At times his animal symbolism gets heavy-handed, but it can be tolerated if taken lightly. Makavejev, like Luis Bunuel, is brilliant in his confrontation of the upper class, severely attacking the repression that festers underneath elegant facades. Marianne Faithfull sings the title tune among a list of songs that includes a pair by ABBA, "I Do, I Do, I Do" and "Why Did it Have to Be Me," Also: "The Ballad of Lucy Jordan," "The Rhythm," "Ramo, Ramo," "Gimme a Little Kiss."

p, Bo Jonsson; d, Dusan Makavejev; w, Makavejev (with Jonsson, Donald Arthur, Arnie Gelbert, Branko Vucicevic, Bojana Marijan); ph, Tomislav Pinter (Eastmancolor); m, Kornell Kovach; ed, Sylvia Ingermarsson; art d, Radu Borusescu; set d, Eric Johnson; ch, Boris van Dueren; cos, Inger Pehrsson.

Drama/Satire **Cas.** **(PR:O MPAA:NR)**

MONTENEGRO—OR PIGS AND PEARLS

(SEE: MONTENEGRO, 1981, Brit./Swed.)

MONTPARNASSE 19 (SEE: MODIGLIANI OF MONTPARNASSE, 1961, Fr.)

MONTREAL MAIN*½

(1974, Can.) 86m Videograph of Montreal-Canadian Film Development c

Frank Vitale.

Films with disturbing themes need a sensitive treatment supported by intelligent production qualities to gain acceptance by their intended audiences. However, this work, dealing with the relationship between an artist-photographer and a 14-year-old boy in the Bohemian section of Montreal, is a sort of shallow quasi-documentary. Using the actors' real names with improvised action encompassing the body of the work, it tells of the friendship between the boy and older man that is broken up by the boy's parents (played by the actual parents of the young actor) when they become suspicious of how far the relationship has gone. The film is a bundle of loose ends, spawned from a series of underdeveloped moments. It never goes anywhere, though it does scratch at some issues. Essentially, MONTREAL MAIN plays like someone wanted to make a filmed autobiography without the faintest idea of what he wanted to say or how to say it.

p, Frank Vitale, Allan Bozo Moyle; d, Vitale (based on a story by Vitale); ph, Eric Bloch; m, Beverly Glenn-Copelann; ed, Vitale.

Drama **(PR:O MPAA:NR)**

MONTY PYTHON AND THE HOLY GRAIL** 1/2**
(1975, Brit.) 89m Python (Monty)/Cinema 5 c

Graham Chapman *(King Arthur/Hiccoughing Guard/Three-Headed Knight)*, John Cleese *(Second Soldier with a Keen Interest in Birds/Large Man with Dead Body/Black Knight/Mr. Newt, a Village Blacksmith Interested in Burning Witches/A Quite Extraordinarily Rude Frenchman/Tim the Wizard/Sir Lancelot)*, Terry Gilliam *(Patsy/Arthur's Trusty Steed/The Green Knight/Soothsayer/Bridgekeeper/Sir Gawain, the First to be Killed by the Rabbit)*, Eric Idle *(The Dead Collector/Mr. Blint, a Village Ne'er-Do-Well Very Keen on Burning Witches/Sir Robin/The Guard Who Doesn't Hiccough but Tries to Get Things Straight/Concorde, Sir Lancelot's Trusty Steed/Roger the Shrubber, a shrubber/Brother Maynard)*, Neil Innes *(The First Self-Destructive Monk/Robin's Least Favourite Minstrel/The Page Crushed by a Rabbit/The Owner of a Duck)*, Terry Jones *(Dennis' Mother/Sir Bedevere/Three-Headed Knight/Prince Herbert)*, Michael Palin *(1st Soldier with a Keen Interest in Birds/Dennis/Mr. Duck, a Village Carpenter Who Is Almost Keener Than Anyone Else to Burn Witches/Three-Headed Knight/Sir Galahad/King of Swamp Castle/Brother Maynard's Roommate)*, Connie Booth *(The Witch)*, Carol Cleveland *(Zoot and Dingo)*, Bee Duffell *(Old Crone to Whom King Arthur Said "Ni!")*, John Young *(The Dead Body that Claims It Isn't/The Historian Who Isn't A.J.P. Taylor at All)*, Rita Davies *(The Historian Who Isn't A.J.P. Taylor, Honestly's, Wife)*, Sally Kinghorn *(Either Winston or Piglet)*, Avril Stewart *(Either Piglet or Winston)*.

A zany, bizarre, hysterically funny and sometimes brilliant but, often sophomoric send-up of every medieval movie ever made, brought to you by the wacky six-member cast of BBC-TV's "Monty Python's Flying Circus." Superior to their first film, AND NOW FOR SOMETHING COMPLETELY DIFFERENT (which was only a series of their televison vignettes released for the theaters), HOLY GRAIL is told in a straight (well all right, *fairly straight)* narrative structure that follows King Arthur (Chapman) and his knights in their search for the legendary Holy Grail. What transpires in the next 90 minutes is nearly impossible to describe to those unfamiliar with the lunacy of the Python bunch (the six male actors play nearly all the parts, including women's roles), but some of the highlights are well worth mentioning (this film must be *seen* to be understood). Due to the lack of horses in the kingdom (and a low budget), Chapman and his knights are followed throughout the movie by their servants, who smack two coconuts together to simulate the sound of hoofbeats. One of Chapman's first battles is against the Black Knight (Cleese), who refuses to let the king pass. A reluctant Chapman is then forced to cut the man limb from limb until all that is left of Cleese is a torso that yells at the King to come back and fight like a man. Meanwhile, Sir Lancelot (once again Cleese) rushes into a castle and hacks up several wedding guests in a bloody frenzy in an attempt to rescue an effeminate prince who really doesn't need to be rescued. After Cleese calms down and surveys the carnage, he manages a feeble, "I just get carried away" as an apology. Of course, every fan of this film has his favorite moment (the Trojan Rabbit, the Knights Who Say "Neeth", Robin and his Minstrels, the killer rabbit, the Holy Hand Grenade and the crazed bridgekeeper). But, all the insanity finally leads to a climactic battle scene populated with hundreds of costumed extras, which is stopped before it really gets started by a few carloads of policemen who interrupt the shooting and grab the camera. Not only is HOLY GRAIL a strange, occasionally funny film, but it paints a grubby, muddy, and vile portrait of life in the middle ages. The set design and visual style are detailed and rich, lending such credence to the film that at the end, when modern-day police arrive to break things up, it is a real shock.

p, Mark Forstater; d, Terry Gilliam, Terry Jones; w, Graham Chapman, John Cleese, Gilliam, Eric Idle, Jones, Michael Palin; ph, Terry Bedford; m, Neil Innes, DeWolfe; prod d, Roy Smith; ed, John Hackney.

Comedy **Cas.** **(PR:O MPAA:PG)**

MONTY PYTHON'S LIFE OF BRIAN**
(1979, Brit.) 93m WB-Orion c (AKA: LIFE OF BRIAN)

Terry Jones *(The Virgin Mandy/The Mother of Brian, a Ratbag/Colin/Simon the Holy Man/Saintly Passer-By)*, Graham Chapman *(1st Wise Man/Brian Called Brian/Biggus Dickus)*, Michael Palin *(2nd Wise Man/Mr. Big Nose/Francis a Revolutionary/Mrs. A. Who Casts the Second Stone/Ex-Leper/Ben, an Ancient Prisoner/Pontius Pilate, Roman Governor/A Boring Prophet/Eddie/Nisus Wettus)*, John Cleese *(3rd Wise Man/Reg, Leader of the Judean People's Front/Jewish Official at the Stoning/Centurion of the Yard/Deadly Dirk/Arthur)*, Ken Colley *(Jesus the Christ)*, Gwen Taylor *(Mrs. Big Nose/Woman with Sick Donkey/Young Girl)*, Eric Idle *(Mr. Cheeky/Stan Called Loretta, a Confused Revolutionary/Harry the Haggler, Beard and Stone Salesman/Culprit Woman, Who Casts the First Stone/Intensely Dull Youth/Otto, the Nazarene Jailer's Assistant/Mr. Frisbee III)*, Terence Bayler *(Gregory/Revolutionaries and Masked Commandos/Dennis)*, Carol Cleveland *(Mrs. Gregory/Elsie)*, Charles McKeown *(Man Further Forward/Revolutionaries and Masked Commandos/Roman Soldier Stig/Giggling Guard/A False Prophet/Blind Man)*, Terry Gilliam *(Another Person Further Forward/Revolutionaries and Masked Commandos/A Blood and Thunder Prophet/Geoffrey/Jailer)*, Sue Jones-Davis *(Judith, a Beautiful Revolutionary)*, John Young *(Matthias, a Stonee)*, Bernard McKenna *(Official Stone Helper/Revolutionaries and Masked Commandos/Giggling Guard/Parvus, a Centurion)*, Andrew MacLachlan *(Another Official Stoners Helper/Revolutionaries and Masked Commandos/Giggling Guard)*, Neil Innes *(A Weedy Samaritan at the Forum)*, Chris Langham *(Revolutionaries and Masked Commandos/Giggling Guard/Alfonso)*, John Case *(Pilate's Wife)*, Charles Knode *(Passer-By)*, Spike Milligan *(Spike)*, George Harrison *(Mr. Papadopoulis)*.

"Monty Python's" controversial follow-up to MONTY PYTHON AND THE HOLY GRAIL, MONTY PYTHON'S LIFE OF BRIAN, is intellectually amusing in spots, but mostly forced. The story begins as the three wise men travel to the manger where Chapman is born. Mistaking the child for the Messiah, the wise men give the baby gifts, only to take them back when they realize that the real Messiah is located in the next manger. This case of mistaken identity is one that plagues Chapman throughout his life. The film follows him from one strange adventure to another (including a ride in a spaceship!), until he is eventually brought before Pontius Pilate (played by Palin with a silly, but funny, speech impediment) and mistakenly sent to be crucified. This leads to the film's conclusion, also its funniest (and most distasteful) scene, in which Chapman and his fellow "crucifixees" happily sing "Always Look on the Bright Side of Life" while nailed to the cross.

p, John Goldstone; d, Terry Jones; w, Graham Chapman, John Cleese, Terry Gilliam, Eric Idle, Jones, Michael Palin; ph, Peter Biziou; m, Geoffrey Burgon, Andre Jacquemin, David Howman, Idle; ed, Julian Doyle; art d, Roger Christian; cos, Hazel Pethig, Charles Knode; animation d, Gilliam.

Comedy **Cas.** **(PR:O MPAA:R)**

MONTY PYTHON'S THE MEANING OF LIFE zero
(1983, Brit.) 107m Celandine-Monty Python Partnership/UNIV c

Graham Chapman, John Cleese, Terry Gilliam, Eric Idle, Terry Jones, Michael Palin, Carol Cleveland, Judy Loe, Simon Jones, Andrew MacLachlan, Valerie Whittington, Mark Holmes, Patricia Quinn, Jennifer Franks, Peter Lovstrom, Imogen Bickford-Smith, Victoria Plum, George Silver, Angela Mann, Anne Rosenfeld.

Unfortunately, for its fourth film, the "Monty Python" troupe inexplicably reverted to the vignette structure used in its first (and weakest) film, AND NOW FOR SOMETHING COMPLETELY DIFFERENT, and came up with another fairly weak effort. While the sketches are loosely connected in a structure that supposedly illustrates "The Meaning Of Life" (i.e. material regarding birth, education, sex, food, the military and, of course, death), the film is wildly uneven and badly structured. It gets off to a promising start, with a marvelous pre-credit sequence depicting a British financial building being raided by swashbuckling pirates and turned (literally) into a giant ship. Long before the end, the film begins to run out of gas, and the Python gang relies on a totally disgusting (this must be the grossest comedy bit ever committed to film) sketch in which an unbelievably fat man in a fancy restaurant eats everything in sight and then vomits large streams of yellow goo all over to make room for more food. Due to the homicidal cleverness of Cleese, the maitre d', the man eventually explodes, spewing the yellow muck all over. This is definitely not for anyone with taste, culture, intellectuality or humanity. Keep the children away.

p, John Goldstone; d, Terry Jones; w, Graham Chapman, John Cleese, Terry Gilliam, Eric Idle, Jones, Michael Palin; ph, Peter Hannan (Technicolor); m, Idle, John du Prez; ed, Julian Doyle; prod d, Harry Lange; art d, Richard Dawking; cos, Jim Acheson; ch, Arlene Phillips; animation d, Gilliam.

Comedy **Cas.** **(PR:O MPAA:R)**

MOON AND SIXPENCE, THE**** (1942) 89m UA bw-c

George Sanders *(Charles Strickland)*, Herbert Marshall *(Geoffrey Wolfe)*, Steve Geray *(Dirk Stroeve)*, Doris Dudley *(Blanche Stroeve)*, Eric Blore *(Capt. Nichols)*, Albert Basserman *(Doctor Coutras)*, Molly Lamont *(Mrs. Strickland)*, Elena Verdugo *(Ata)*, Florence Bates *(Tiara Johnson)*, Heather Thatcher *(Rose Waterford)*, Robert Grieg *(Maitland)*, Kenneth Hunter *(Col. MacAndrew)*, Irene Tedrow *(Mrs. MacAndrew)*.

Though Marshall is the svelte-voiced narrator of this riveting story, it is Sanders as the relentless cad and heartless artist who makes this film a standout. He is a stockbroker who decides he will take up his secret passion, painting, and discard his former life. To that end he convinces Geray, a successful but mediocre painter, to aid him in developing his art and, during the process, where Geray takes Sanders into his home as a protege, he seduces Geray's wife and ruins Geray himself. Marshall, who is Sanders' friend, narrates the rake's progress from broker to painter to homewrecker and exile in Tahiti where Sanders comes to grips with his own personality and discovers his great talent, producing one masterpiece after another until dying tragically. The Maugham story on which this film is based unabashedly profiles the profligate career of the brilliant Paul Gauguin and Sanders plays this introspective, brilliant, and cruel-streaked genius to the hilt. Lewin's direction is terse, swift, and often magnificent as he chronicles Sanders' meteoric career and love life, the best part of the film being that set in the tropical islands toward the end. Here a sepia tone is employed to capture some of the illustrative flavor of the paintings shown and, during the life-consuming fire of Sanders' Tahitian hut—one which destroys his masterpiece and himself—color is lavishly and correctly employed. Seitz's camerawork is terrific and the supporting cast, especially Geray, and Blore, as a drunken Englishman, is excellent.

p, David L. Loew; d, Albert Lewin; w, Lewin (based on a novel by W. Somerset Maugham); ph, John F. Seitz; m, Dmitri Tiomkin; ed, Richard L. Van Enger; prod d, Gordon Wills; art d, F. Paul Sylow.

Drama **(PR:A MPAA:NR)**

MOON IN THE GUTTER, THE***
(1983, Fr./Ital.) 126m GAU-TFI-Opera-SFPC/COL-Triumph c (LA LUNE DANS LE CANIVEAU)

Gerard Depardieu *(Gerard)*, Nastassia Kinski *(Loretta)*, Victoria Abril *(Bella)*, Vittorio Mezzogiorno *(Newton Channing)*, Dominique Pinon *(Frank)*, Bertice Reading *(Lola)*, Gabriel Monnet *(Tom)*, Milena Vukotic *(Frieda)*, Bernard Farcy *(Jesus)*, Anne-Marie Coffinet *(Dora)*, Katia Berger, Jacques Herlin, Rudo Alberti, Rosa Fumeto, Grasiano Giusti, Fred Ulysse, Victor Cavallo, Jean-Roger Milo, Jean-Pierre Laurent, Claudia Pola, Clarisse Deudon, Julien Arrichi, Jade Biarese, Jean-Pierre Airola.

A much-awaited follow-up to Beineix's DIVA, the enormously successful chic *policier*. Upon its release, however, THE MOON IN THE GUTTER was lambasted by the critics (it's been called the "film in the gutter"), audiences (unanimous booing from outraged viewers at Cannes) and the film's star, Depardieu (referring to the film as "The Moon in the Sewer"). A visually awesome production, MOON tells the story of a riverfront dock worker, Depardieu, who is tormented by the need to find out who raped his sister. The rape causes her to commit suicide while lying in the gutter, and as her blood drains into the flowing water along the street, the moon reflects from the night sky above. Stuck in a static relationship with Abril, a sexual powerhouse who lives in a shack, Depardieu becomes attracted to Kinski, a stunning mystery woman who cruises the waterfront in her blazing red convertible. As the billboard in front of his house reads—"Try Another World"—so he decides to live. The film is similar in some ways to Coppola's ONE FROM THE HEART, mainly in its near-exclusive use of sets (shot on Cinecitta's sound stage) and its use of Kinski. Far from an accomplished dramatic actress, Kinski is wonderfully directed by Beineix (perhaps better than she's ever been directed), who understands that her appeal is visual. Abril, who ultimately loses out to the other world of Depardieu, simply staggers about like a stunned lummox. The real fascination MOON holds is visual, creating a dingy but fluorescent world that is the antithesis of DIVA's cleansed chicness. Where DIVA overpowered with bright romanticism, MOON stuns with damp obsession. The script is often embarrassingly indulgent, not due to Beineix's ignorance but to his tunnel vision in creating a wholly personal poetic endeavor. For every failed line, action, and camera swirl, however, there is one that is astoundingly effective. An underrated wonder that will certainly find its due praise as Beineix's career explodes into full flower.

p, Lise Fayolle; d, Jean-Jacques Beineix; w, Beineix, Olivier Mergault (based on the novel by David Goodis); ph, Philippe Rousselot, Dominique Brenguier (Panavision, Eastmancolor); m, Gabriel Yared; ed, Monique Prim, Yves Deschamps; prod d, Hilton McConnico, Sandro dell'Orco, Angelo Santucci, Bernhard Vezat; cos, Claire Fraisse.

Drama **Cas.** **(PR:O MPAA:R)**

MOON IS BLUE, THE 1/2** (1953) 99m UA bw

William Holden *(Donald Gresham)*, David Niven *(David Slater)*, Maggie McNamara *(Patty O'Neill)*, Tom Tully *(Michael O'Neill)*, Dawn Addams *(Cynthia Slater)*, Fortunio Bonanova *(Television Announcer)*, Gregory Ratoff *(Taxi Driver)*, Hardy Kruger *(Sightseer)*, Johanna Matz *(His Wife)*.

This pleasant trifle received more publicity, and, therefore, more business than it deserved. It was a Broadway farce with what, for New York, was mild to spicy dialog. However, in the eyes of the movie censors who handed out the Production Code Seal of Approval, it was far too risque for movies because it dealt with the seduction of a virgin and used the word "virgin" in a cavalier fashion. (Evidently, the only time that word could be used is while singing "Silent Night.") The newspaper space accorded the brouhaha was truly a tempest in a teapot and the people who flocked to see this "hot" movie were disappointed by the tepidity. Niven's career had been in a downward spiral when Preminger, over the objections of the releasing company, hired the Englishman and his flagging business life went soaring after the movie hit the theaters. Niven won the Golden Globe for his work in THE MOON IS BLUE, which was Preminger's first independent movie for the company he started with playwright Herbert. Preminger had staged the Broadway version of Herbert's farce with a cast that included Barbara Bel Geddes, Barry Nelson, and Donald Cook, in the roles later played by McNamara, Holden, and Niven. At the same time he was directing this, Preminger was also making a version in German, DIE JUNGFRAU AUF DEM DACH (THE VIRGIN ON THE ROOF), with translated dialog by Carl Zuckmayer. That one starred Hardy Kruger in the Holden role, with Matz as the sweet young thing. This version begins atop the Empire State Building on Fifth Avenue at 34th Street in New York. Holden, an up-and-coming architect, meets McNamara, a young actress, and she accepts his invitation to have dinner. They stop at Holden's apartment for a moment on their way to a restaurant when she tells him that she is a wonderful cook, and if he has the fixings, she would be delighted to make them a meal right there. Holden tells her to relax and he will be back in a flash with enough food for them to dine upon. While he's gone, Addams arrives. She is Holden's one-time fiancee and more than a bit surprised to see McNamara. Now Niven arrives. He is Addams' roue father and he is instantly taken by McNamara's naiveté. She invites him to stay for dinner and he accepts. McNamara spills something on her dress and goes to Holden's bedroom where she dons his dressing gown. Holden is trying to calm down Addams somewhere else and Niven moves in on McNamara, who has already stated publicly that she's not against heavy necking but remains firm about her virginity, which must stay intact until she weds. Niven proposes marriage to McNamara and offers her a gift of $600, no strings attached. McNamara declines the marriage offer but happily accepts the $600, and she gives the old man a daughterly kiss as Holden enters and becomes enraged at the sight of this rakehell with the young girl in the dressing gown. Now Tully, McNamara's beefy father, enters and is angered when he finds her in a bachelor's pad in a state of semi-clothedness. He knocks Holden for a loop and despite Niven's attempts to reconcile matters, the romance goes out the window. The next day, Holden and McNamara are again both drawn to the top of the then-tallest building in New York. They meet Kruger and Matz, see each other on the observation deck and Holden promptly asks for her hand as the movie ends. McNamara and the title song received Oscar nominations. She only made three other films, THREE COINS IN THE FOUNTAIN, PRINCE OF PLAYERS, and THE CARDINAL, before committing suicide in February, 1978.

p, Otto Preminger, F. Hugh Herbert; d, Preminger; w, Herbert (based on his play); ph, Ernest Laszlo; m, Herschel Burke Gilbert; ed, Louis R. Loeffler, Otto Ludwig; prod d, Nicolai Remisoff; set d, Edward G. Boyle; cos, Don Loper; m/l, "The Moon Is Blue," Gilbert, Sylvia Fine.

Comedy **Cas.** **(PR:A-C MPAA:NR)**

MOON IS DOWN, THE* 1/2** (1943) 90m FOX bw

Sir Cedric Hardwicke *(Col. Lanser)*, Henry Travers *(Mayor Orden)*, Lee J. Cobb *(Dr. Winter)*, Dorris Bowdon *(Molly Morden)*, Margaret Wycherly *(Mme. Orden)*, Peter Van Eyck *(Lt. Tonder)*, William Post, Jr. *(Alex Morden)*, Henry Rowland *(Capt. Loft)*, E. J. Ballentine *(George Corell)*, Irving Pichel *(Inn Keeper)*, Violette Wilson *(Peder's Wife)*, Hans Schumm *(Capt. Bentick)*, Ernest Dorian *(Maj. Hunter)*, John Banner *(Lt. Prackle)*, Helene Thimig *(Annie)*, Ian Wolfe *(Joseph)*, Kurt Krueger *(Orderly)*, Jeff Corey *(Albert)*, Louis Arco *(Schumann)*, Ernst Hausman *(Moeller)*, Charles McGraw *(Ole)*, Trevor Bardette *(Foreman)*, John Mylong *(Staff Officer)*, Otto Reichow, Sven Hugo Borg *(Sergeants)*, Dorothy Peterson *(Mother)*.

This film version of John Steinbeck's novel (and play) about the Nazi occupation of a Norwegian village during WW II is superb, despite the lack of name stars. The film opens with the invasion of Norway by Nazis and the village being occupied by troops under the command of Hardwicke, an intelligent German officer of the old school who believes that Nazi cruelty and punishments only bring about acts of vengeful sabotage and needless killing. He is a man who believes that a live conquered enemy can produce more coal and raw materials than dead enemies. He at first tries to persuade the local authorities to cooperate but at every turn the villagers resist. His men are killed, his phone lines cut, his rail lines blown up with dynamite dropped by British planes. He appeals to town mayor Travers but the old man is a wily opponent. In the end, Ballentine, as a traitorous Quisling, lobbies for wholesale extermination of those who have resisted the Nazi rule. Town authorities are rounded up and sent to the gallows while citizens look on in horror. Travers, ever the gentleman, slips as he walks toward the hangman and then thanks a German soldier for helping him to his feet. Bowdon, a woman widowed by a Nazi firing squad, takes her revenge for the slaughter of the officials by inviting Nazi officer Van Eyck into her bedroom where she stabs him to death. In the end the Nazis are defeated but at a slaughterhouse cost to the village. This is a grim but moving propaganda film which, under Johnson's deft screenwriting hand, improves upon the original novel which was a well-written though hortatory piece of propaganda that sold more than a million copies and ran as a play only nine weeks on Broadway (but was a huge success on the road). Fox paid the author a whopping $300,000 for the book and lost a great deal of money at the box office, but produced an outstanding film, tautly directed by Pichel (who also plays a small part as an innkeeper). Travers and Hardwicke are superb and Cobb is wonderful as the humanitarian village doctor. Bowdon, who played the pregnant young woman in John Ford's THE GRAPES OF WRATH (1940) is also outstanding as the young widow (Nepotism worked well here; she was married to producer/screenwriter Johnson). Harsh and somber, the film dealt with the unsavory subject of slave labor to which Fox mogul Darryl Zanuck attributed its unpopular status. Said Zanuck later: "Any story about Germany or labor slaves appalls me. Every picture yet made dealing with occupied countries, including THE MOON IS DOWN, has laid a magnificent egg with the public. I can imagine no subject less inviting to an audience than the subject of slave labor." Newman's score is excellent, as are the village sets. The set from HOW GREEN WAS MY VALLEY was used for this film.

p, Nunnally Johnson; d, Irving Pichel; w, Johnson (based on the novel by John Steinbeck); ph, Arthur Miller; m, Alfred Newman; ed, Louis Loeffler; art d, James Basevi, Maurice Ransford; set d, Thomas Little, Walter M. Scott; spec eff, Fred Sersen.

War Drama **(PR:C MPAA:NR)**

MOON OVER BURMA** (1940) 74m A.M. Botsford/PAR bw

Dorothy Lamour *(Arla Dean)*, Robert Preston *(Chuck Lane)*, Preston Foster *(Bill Gordon)*, Doris Nolan *(Cynthia Harmon)*, Albert Bassermann *(Basil Renner)*, Frederick Worlock *(Stephen Harmon)*, Addison Richards *(Art Bryan)*, Harry Allen *(Sunshine)*, Frank Lackteen *(Khran)*, Stanley Price *(Khuda)*, Hans Schumm *(Baumgarten)*, Paul Porcasi *(Storekeeper)*, Henry Roquemore *(Jovial Plantation Owner)*, Catherine Wallace *(Plantation Owner's Wife)*, Ella Neal *(Girl on Rangoon Street)*, Ralph Sencuya *(Native Waiter)*, Nick Shaid, Ram Singh, Maro Cortez *(Natives)*.

Even an exotic setting can't breathe life into this routine adventure film. Preston and Foster operate a lumber camp in the woods near Rangoon, Burma, and run short of money for workers' pay and provisions. The real trouble starts when Preston meets stranded American showgirl Lamour, who becomes the subject of his and Foster's affections. She is put on hold, however, when the two men find themselves busy thwarting a scheme to ruin the lumber camp. After all is put right, she is able to choose the man she wants and sing a few tunes.

p, Anthony Veiller; d, Louis King; w, Frank Wead, W. P. Lipscomb, Harry Clork (based on a story by Wilson Collison); ph, William C. Mellor; ed, Stuart Gilmore; m/l, "Moon Over Burma," "Mexican Magic," Frederick Hollander, Harry Ravel, Frank Loesser (sung by Dorothy Lamour).

Adventure **(PR:A MPAA:NR)**

MOON OVER HER SHOULDER** (1941) 68m FOX bw

Lynn Bari *(Susan Rossiter)*, John Sutton *(Dr. Phillip Rossiter)*, Dan Dailey, Jr. *(Rex)*, Alan Mowbray *(Grover Sloan)*, Leonard Carey *(Dusty)*, Irving Bacon *(Taxi Driver)*, Joyce Compton *(Cecilia)*, Lillian Yarbo *(Juline)*, Eula Guy *(Mrs. Bates)*, Shirley Hill *(Baby)*, Sylvia Arslan *(Sister)*.

A harmless little comedy about a popular radio marriage counselor, Sutton, who ignores his wife, Bari. Dailey, on his boat one day, spots her and invites her to spend the day. He eventually falls in love with her, to Sutton's dismay. Sutton decides to fight for his wife, proving to the previously neglected Bari that he really does care for her.

p, Walter Morosco; d, Alfred Werker; w, Walter Bullock (based on a story by Helen Vreeland Smith and Eve Golden); ph, Lucien Andriot; ed, J. Watson Webb, Jr.; md, Emil Newman.

Comedy **(PR:A MPAA:NR)**

MOON OVER LAS VEGAS* 1/2 (1944) 65m UNIV bw

Anne Gwynne *(Marian Corbett)*, David Bruce *(Richard Corbett)*, Vera Vague [Barbara Jo Allen] *(Auntie)*, Vivian Austin *(Grace Towers)*, Alan Dinehart *(Hal Blake)*, Lee Patrick *(Mrs. Blake)*, Joe Sawyer *(Joe)*, Milburn Stone *(Jim Bradley)*, Addison Richards *(Judge)*, Mantan Moreland *(Porter)*, Eddie Dunn *(Conductor)*, Tom Dugan *(Herman)*, Pat West *(Taxi Driver)*, Muni Seroff *(Waiter)*, Ann Triola *(Accordion Girl)*, Claire Whitney *(Grace's Mother)*, Donald Kerr *(Sneak Player)*, Gene Austin, The Sherell Sisters, Connie Haines, Capella & Patricia, Lillian Cornell, Jimmy Dodd, The Sportsmen.

A listless musical romance about a young couple, Gwynne and Bruce, who find their relationship is on the rocks even though they still love each other. They seek a separation and journey to Las Vegas to get divorced. Meanwhile, Vague suggests to Gwynne that she make Bruce jealous in an effort to save the marriage. She succeeds and, after several madcap measures, the two get back together again, this time for good. Songs include "A Dream Ago" (Everett Carter, Milton Rosen, sung by Connie Haines), "Moon Over Las Vegas" (Carter, Rosen, sung by Lillian Cornell), "Faithful Flo," "So Goodnight" (Carter, Rosen), "A Touch of Texas" (Frank Loesser, Jimmy McHugh), "You Marvelous You" (Gene Austin), "Oklahoma's One With Me" (Jimmy Dodd), "My Blue Heaven" (George Whiting, Walter Donaldson).

p&d, Jean Yarbrough; w, George Jeske, Clyde Bruckman (based on a story by Jeske); ph, Jerome Ash; ed, Milton Carruth; art d, John B. Goodman, Abraham Grossman.

Musical/Romance **(PR:AA MPAA:NR)**

MOON OVER MIAMI 1/2** (1941) 91m FOX c

Don Ameche *(Phil O'Neil)*, Betty Grable *(Kay Latimer)*, Robert Cummings *(Jeff Bolton)*, Charlotte Greenwood *(Aunt Susie Latimer)*, Jack Haley *(Jack O'Hara)*, Carole Landis *(Barbara Latimer)*, Cobina Wright, Jr. *(Connie Fentress)*, George Lessey *(William Bolton)*, Robert Conway *(Lester)*, Condos Brothers *(Themselves)*, Robert Greig *(Brearley)*, Minor Watson *(Reynolds)*, Fortunio Bonanova *(Mr. Pretto)*, George Humbert *(Drive-in Boss)*, Spencer Charters *(Postman)*, Lynn Roberts *(Jennie May)*, Larry McGrath *(Bartender)*, Jack Cole & Co. *(Specialties)*, Mel Ruick *(Band Leader)*, Leyland Hodgson *(Victor the Waiter)*.

MOON OVER MIAMI was the second of three times around for this story. It was first done as THREE BLIND MICE in 1938, then remade in 1946 as THREE LITTLE GIRLS IN BLUE. A tuneful pastiche, it tells the tale of Grable and Landis, two Texas sisters who give up their lives in the Lone Star state (where Grable is working as a waitress in a hamburger stand) and take off for Florida with their high-kicking aunt, Greenwood, after a small legacy is bestowed on them. Their intention is to find a brace of wealthy husbands in the balmy Florida air. They take up residence in a swank hotel with Grable posing as a filthy-rich bachelorette, Greenwood as her aged retainer, and Landis playing the role of Grable's traveling companion-secretary. It isn't long before rich Cummings and once-rich Ameche arrive and start romancing Grable. She gets Cummings, but soon realizes that the object of her deep affections is really Ameche, although he's more than miffed when he learns that she is only out for money. Eventually, Cummings falls for Landis (phew! glad *that* complication is out of the way), thus clearing the path of Ameche and Grable. Along the road, there's a host of speciality numbers, including some good tap dancing from the Condos Brothers. Although the famous song, "Moon Over Miami," is played over the titles (Edgar Leslie, Joe Burke), the lyrics are never heard and the other tunes are all penned by Ralph Rainger and Leo Robin. They include: "I've Got You All to Myself," "What Can I Do For You?," "Kindergarten Conga," "You Started Something," "Oh Me Oh Mi-Am-Mi," "Solitary Seminole," "Is That Good?" and "Loveliness And Love." Nice location shots in Cypress Gardens and Silver Springs go along with the filming in Miami, which seems unbelievably tiny by comparison to what it looks like today. The comedy is provided by Greenwood and Haley as the slightly older folks. Excellent choreography by Hermes Pan and quick direction by Lang make this a pleasant way to spend 91 minutes.

p, Harry Joe Brown; d, Walter Lang; w, Vincent Lawrence, Brown Holmes, George Seaton, Lynn Starling (based on the play "Three Blind Mice" by Stephen Powys); ph, Peverell Marley, Leon Shamroy, Allen M. Davey (Technicolor); ed, Walter Thompson; md, Alfred Newman; art d, Richard Day, Wiard B. Inhen; ch, Hermes Pan.

Musical **(PR:A MPAA:NR)**

MOON OVER THE ALLEY zero (1980, Brit.) 107m British Film Institute bw

Doris Fishwick, Peter Farrell, Erna May, John Gay, Sean Caffrey, Sharon Forester, Patrick Murray, Lesley Roach, Basil Clarke, Bill Williams, Vari Sylvester, Joan Geary, Norman Mitchell, Leroy Hyde, Miguel Sergides, Debbie Evans.

An amateurish 16mm production financed in part by the British Film Institute in the hope of promoting new talent. Unfortunately there's not much talent here to promote. The film depicts onscreen the daily life of the boarders who populate London's Portobello Road. Every character in sight, however, is a blaring stereotype. The songs are no better, sounding like vicious retreads of old melodies that were big in the hippie heyday.

d, Joseph Despins; w, William Dumaresq; ph, Peter Hannan; m, Galt MacDermot; ed, Despins.

Musical **(PR:O MPAA:NR)**

MOON PILOT 1/2** (1962) 98m Disney/BV c

Tom Tryon *(Capt. Richmond Talbot)*, Brian Keith *(Maj. Gen. John Vanneman)*, Edmond O'Brien *(McClosky)*, Dany Saval *(Lyrae)*, Tommy Kirk *(Walter Talbot)*, Bob Sweeney *(Sen. McGuire)*, Kent Smith *(Secretary of the Air Force)*, Simon Scott *(Medical Officer)*, Bert Remsen *(Agent Brown)*, Sarah Selby *(Mrs. Celia Talbot)*, Bob Hastings *(Air Force Officer)*, Dick Whittinghill *(Col. Briggs)*, Nancy Kulp *(Nutritionist)*, Muriel Landers *(Fat Lady)*, Cheeta *(Charlie the Chimp)*, William Hudson, Robert Brubaker.

An uproarious satirical comedy from the Disney folks, who aren't especially known for their social criticism. It's primarily the space program that gets ribbed when Tryon is volunteered by a mischievous monkey to be the first man in orbit. He is given three days to say his goodbyes, and his first trip is to his mother's house. While in transit, he notices a mysterious girl, Saval, who seems to be following him. She shows up in his mother's town, and then again when the NASA officials lock him in a hotel. She reveals that she is an alien from planet Beta Lyrae and gives him a special rocket fuel formula. Soon afterward, Tryon is shot into space, and Saval reappears on board. The space officials demand an explanation, but are ignored by Tryon and Saval, who are busy making wedding plans. Disney had enough sense to throw in a monkey which, as always, guarantees the kids will love the heck out of the picture. Interestingly, Disney managed to poke fun not only at the space program, but made monkeys out of the FBI, the Secret Service, the Air Force, and the U.S. government as well.

p, Bill Anderson; d, James Neilson; w, Maurice Tombragel (based on a serialized story by Robert Buckner); ph, William Snyder (Technicolor); m, Paul Smith; ed, Cotton Warburton; art d, Carroll Clark, Marvin Aubrey Davis; set d, Emilie Kuri, William L. Stevens; cos, Bill Thomas, Chuck Keehne, Gertrude Casey; spec eff, Eustace Lycett; m/l, "True Love's an Apricot," "The Void," Richard M. Sherman, Robert B. Sherman, "Seven Moons of Beta Lyrae," Sherman, Sherman (sung by Tom Tryon, Dany Saval).

Juvenile/Science Fiction **(PR:AAA MPAA:NAR)**

MOON-SPINNERS, THE 1/2** (1964) 118m Disney/BV c

Hayley Mills *(Nikky Ferris)*, Eli Wallach *(Stratos)*, Pola Negri *(Mme. Habib)*, Peter McEnery *(Mark Camford)*, Joan Greenwood *(Aunt Frances Ferris)*, Irene Papas *(Sophia)*, Sheila Hancock *(Cynthia Gamble)*, Michael Davis *(Alexis)*, Paul Stassino *(Lambis)*, John Le Mesurier *(Anthony Gamble)*, Andre Morell *(Yacht Captain)*, George Pastell *(Police Lieutenant)*, Tutte Lemkow *(Orestes)*, Steve Plytas *(Hearse Driver)*, Harry Tardios *(Bus Driver)*, Pamela Barrie *(Ariadne)*.

Illogical, but still suspenseful enough to hold the audience's interest. Story focuses on the adventures of Mills and Greenwood. Mills stays at the Moon-Spinners Hotel and becomes involved with McEnery, a young Brit whom Mills finds in a deserted church. He has been shot by a friend of Wallach's. McEnery is at the hotel because he was fired after a jewel robbery and he thinks Wallach is the culprit. McEnery and Mills set off to gather evidence and run into Wallach's partner who plans to have the jewels bought by a wealthy woman. As McEnery chases Wallach, Mills works on the woman. After a fight, Wallach is captured by the police and McEnery is proven innocent. Now he and Mills can have more time together in Greece.

p, Bill Anderson, Hugh Attwooll; d, James Neilson; w, Michael Dyne (based on the novel by Mary Stewart); ph, Paul Beeson, John Wilcox, Michael Reed (Technicolor); m, Ron Grainer; ed, Gordon Stone; md, Grainer; art d, Tony Masters; cos, Anthony Mendleson; m/l, "The Moon-Spinners Song," Terry Gilkyson; makeup, Harry Frampton.

Juvenile/Mystery **Cas.** **(PR:AAA MPAA:NR)**

MOON WALK (SEE: TICKLISH AFFAIR, A, 1963)

MOON ZERO TWO* (1970, Brit.) 100m Hammer/WB c

James Olson *(Bill Kemp)*, Catherina von Schell *(Clementine Taplin)*, Warren Mitchell *(J. J. Hubbard)*, Adrienne Corri *(Liz Murphy)*, Ori Levy *(Karminski)*, Dudley Foster *(Whitsun)*, Bernard Bresslaw *(Harry)*, Neil McCallum *(Space Captain)*, Joby Blanshard *(Smith)*, Michael Ripper, Robert Tayman *(Card Players)*, Sam Kydd *(Bar Man)*, The Gojos *(Themselves)*, Keith Bonnard *(Junior Customs Officer)*, Leo Britt *(Senior Customs Officer)*, Carol Cleveland *(Hostess)*, Roy Evans *(Worker)*, Tom Kempinski *(2nd Officer)*, Lew Luton *(Immigration Officer)*, Claire Shenstone *(Female Hotel Clerk)*, Chrissie Shrimpton *(Boutique Attendant)*, Amber Dean Smith, Simone Silvera *(Hubbard's Girl Friends)*.

Some interesting ideas don't quite gel in this outer-space western, a predecessor to a flock of pictures ranging from mega-successes like STAR WARS (though keenly disguised) to mega-flops like OUTLAND (whose debt to HIGH NOON wasn't nearly repaid). It is the year 2021, and Olson is a samurai spaceman of sorts who hires himself out for various missions. He also has the honor of being the first man on Mars, which adds to his prestige. His services are employed by Mitchell, a lunar tycoon, who wants Olson to knock an asteroid out of orbit and crash it onto the moon's surface where, unknown to Olson, it will be used for Mitchell's get-richer-quick scheme. The crooked fellow intends to sell worthless land on the pretense that it is rich in precious sapphire, stones actually taken from the asteroid. Olson catches on to Mitchell's devious tactics and discovers he is guilty of murdering von Schell's brother. Geared mainly to the kids.

p, Michael Carreras; d, Roy Ward Baker; w, Carreras (based on a story by Gavin Lyall, Frank Hardman, Martin Davison); ph, Paul Beeson (Technicolor); m, Von Ellis; ed, Spencer Reeve; art d, Scott MacGregor; cos, Carl Toms; spec eff, Les Bowie, Kit West, Nick Allder; ch, Jo Cook.

Science Fiction **(PR:A MPAA:G)**

MOON'S OUR HOME, THE*** (1936) 80m PAR bw

Margaret Sullavan *(Sarah Brown/"Cherry Chester")*, Henry Fonda *(John Smith/"Anthony Amberton")*, Beulah Bondi *(Mrs. Boyce Medford)*, Henrietta Crosman *(Lucy Van Steedan)*, Lucien Littlefield *(Ogden Holbrook)*, Charles Butterworth *(Horace Van Steedan)*, Walter Brennan *(Lem)*, Brandon Hurst *(Babson)*, Spencer Charters *(Abner Simpson)*, Margaret Hamilton *(Mitty Simpson)*, Dorothy Stickney *(Hilda)*, Margaret Fielding *(Miss Manning)*, Grace Hayle *(Miss Hambridge)*, Monte Vandegrift *(Brakeman)*, Richard Powell *(Candy Butcher)*, Lorna Dunn, Eva

Dennison, Betty Farrington, Helen Dickson (*Women*), Harry Bowen, Harry Harvey (*Reporters*), John Graham Spacey (*Chauffeur*), Corbet Morris (*Secretary*), Georgie Cooper (*Maid*), Bobby Bolder (*Butler*), Thelma White, Andrea Leeds (*Salesgirls*), Gunnis Davis (*Footman*), Jack Norton (*Drunk*), Max Wagner (*Truck Driver*), Antrim Short (*Attendant*), Estelle Ettere (*Stewardess*), George Pearce (*Day Clerk*).

A bright romp that was better than the book on which it was based, THE MOON'S OUR HOME owes many of the best dialog lines to the husband-wife team of Parker and Campbell who came in to punch up the script. Fonda and Sullavan had been briefly married and retained their fascination with each other long enough to make this film after their divorce. She's a movie star and he's a big-time writer of high adventure. Both have assumed pseudonyms for their careers but use their real names when they opt out of the limelight. They meet, using their real names; fall in love and get married; and neither knows that the other is well known. The next few reels are a cavalcade of insults and even at their wedding, the justice of the peace, Brennan, has trouble keeping the peace between them. They honeymoon in a New England hotel and she uses a perfume that he is allergic to. She thinks that his attitude is due to his dislike of her and she soon exits. Fonda searches for her and they finally meet again and will spend the rest of their lives bickering. Hamilton is funny as the proprietor of the hotel where the honeymoon takes place, Butterworth is Sullavan's persistent suitor, and Bondi scores as Sullavan's secretary. Sullavan's character may have been patterned after Katharine Hepburn, and Fonda's, legend has it, was tailored from the life of writer Richard Halliburton. Sullavan also married director William Wyler and agent-turned-producer Leland Hayward. Her life and death by suicide at the age of 49 was chronicled by her actress-daughter, Brooke Hayward, in the book *Haywire*. The actual writing credit for Parker and Campbell was "additional dialog by" and you can just about recognize every quip they tossed into the script.

p, Walter Wanger; d, William A. Seiter; w, Isabel Dawn, Boyce DeGaw, Dorothy Parker, Alan Campbell (based on the novel by Faith Baldwin); ph, Joseph Valentine; md, Boris Morros.

Comedy   (PR:A MPAA:NR)

MOONBEAM MAN, THE
(SEE: MAN IN THE MOONLIGHT MASK, THE, 1958, Jap.)

MOONCHILD**   (1972) 90m Filmmakers Ltd. c (AKA: FULL MOON)
Victor Buono (*Maitre D'*), John Carradine (*The Walker*), Mike Travis (*The Student*), Pat Renella (*Manager of the Inn*), Frank Corsentino (*Hommunculus*), William Challee (*Alchemist*), Janet Landgard (*Girl*), Marie Denn (*Maid*).

Gadney made this strange little film as part of his master's thesis at USC. A reworking of the regular themes of reincarnation and eternal life has a person trapped into a cycle that makes him live the same 25 years over and over again. With such proven actors as Buono and Carradine to lend support, an air of professionalism is given to the bizarre atmosphere.

p, Dick Alexander; d&w, Alan Gadney; ph, Emmett Alston; m, Pat Williams, Bill Byers; ed, Jack H. Conrad; art d, Richard Tamburino; cos, Jane Alexander; makeup, Alexander.

Horror/Science Fiction   (PR:O MPAA:R)

MOONFIRE zero   (1970) 107m Hollywood Continental c
Richard Egan, Sonny Liston, Charles Napier, Dayton Lummis, Joaquin Martinez.

Awful crime drama has Napier as a trucker running up against an ex-Nazi hiding out in Mexico and directing criminal operations on both sides of the border. Worthless actioner has Egan barely making an appearance and Liston embarrassingly bad in his acting debut.

d, Michael Parkhurst.

Crime   (PR:O MPAA:NR)

MOONFLEET**1/2   (1955) 86m MGM c
Stewart Granger (*Jeremy Fox*), George Sanders (*Lord Ashwood*), Joan Greenwood (*Lady Ashwood*), Viveca Lindfors (*Mrs. Anna Minton*), Jon Whiteley (*John Mohune*), Liliane Montevecchi (*Gypsy Dancer*), Melville Cooper (*Felix Ratsey*), Sean McClory (*Elzevir Block*), Alan Napier (*Parson Glennie*), John Hoyt (*Magistrate Maskew*), Donna Corcoran (*Grace*), Jack Elam (*Damen*), Dan Seymour (*Hull*), Ian Wolfe (*Tewkesbury*), Lester Matthews (*Maj. Hennishaw*), Skelton Knaggs (*Jacobs*), Richard Hale (*Starkill*), John Alderson (*Greening*), Ashley Cowan (*Tomson*), Booth Colman (*Capt. Stanhope*), Frank Ferguson (*Coachman*), Lillian Kemble Cooper (*Mary Hicks*), Guy Kingsford (*Capt. Hawkins*), Ben Wright (*Officer*), Wilson Wood (*Soldier*), John O'Malley (*Lt. Upjohn*), Peggy Maley (*Tenant*).

In this film, set in the mid-1700s, Granger is given custody of the young Whiteley. However, instead of caring for the boy, he sends him off to school. Whiteley soon learns he should have inherited a famed diamond and, realizing he is being hoodwinked, returns to the village of Moonfleet. Granger gets his hands on the gem, long hidden in a well, but decides to return it to Whiteley, the rightful heir. Lang's first film for MGM since FURY (his first American film, in 1936) is also his first in CinemaScope, a process that, as he stated in Jean-Luc Godard's CONTEMPT (1936), is "only good for funerals and snakes." It is not an entirely successful picture (though definitely far from dismissible), and Lang can be faulted mainly for his growing need to please himself rather than the public—an attitude not subscribed to in most of his earlier works.

p, John Houseman, Jud Kinberg; d, Fritz Lang; w, Jan Lustig, Margaret Fitts (based on the novel by J. Meade Falkner); ph, Robert Planck (CinemaScope, Eastmancolor); m, Miklos Rozsa, Vicente Gomez; ed, Albert Akst; art d, Cedric Gibbons, Hans Peters; set d, Edwin B. Willis, Richard Pefferle; cos, Walter Plunkett.

Adventure   (PR:A MPAA:NR)

MOONLIGHT AND CACTUS**   (1944) 60m UNIV bw
The Andrews Sisters (*Patty, Maxine, Laverne*), Leo Carrillo (*Pasqualito*), Elyse Knox (*Louise Ferguson*), Tom Seidel (*Tom Garrison*), Shemp Howard (*Punchy*), Eddie Quillan (*Stubby*), Murray Alper (*Slugger*), Tom Kennedy (*Lucky*), Frank Lackteen (*Ogala*), Minerva Urecal (*Abigail*), Jacqueline de Wit (*Elsie*), Mary O'Brien (*Amanda*), Mitch Ayres Orchestra.

Patty, Maxine, and Laverne (the tuneful Andrews Sisters) shock cowhand Seidel on his return home from a stint with the Marines. Upset to find his ranch is now being run by the trio, he learns to accept it when tough female foreman Knox proves they can handle the job. Includes the tunes: "Send Me a Man, Amen" (Ray Gilbert, Sidney Miller), "Wa Hoo" (Cliff Friend), "C'Mere Baby" (Lanny Gray, Roy Jordan), "Heave Ho My Lads, Heave Ho" (Jack Lawrence), "Down in the Valley" (Frank Luther), "Sing" (Harold Mooney, Hughie Prince), "Home" (Harry and Jeff Clarkson).

p, Frank Gross; d, Edward F. Cline; w, Eugene Conrad, Paul Gerard Smith; ph, Jerome Ash; ed, Ray Snyder; art d, John B. Goodman, Martin Obzina; ch, Charles O'Curran.

Musical   (PR:A MPAA:NR)

MOONLIGHT AND MELODY (SEE: MOONLIGHT AND PRETZELS, 1933)

MOONLIGHT AND PRETZELS**1/2
(1933) 80m Rowland-Brice/UNIV bw (GB: MOONLIGHT AND MELODY)
Leo Carrillo (*Nick Pappacroplis*), Mary Brian (*Sally Upton*), Roger Pryor (*George Dwight*), Lillian Miles (*Elsie Warren*), Herbert Rawlinson (*Sport Powell*), Bobby Watson (*Bertie*), William Frawley (*Mack*), Jack Denny's Orchestra, Alexander Gray, Bernice Clair, Mary Lange, Max Stamm, James Carson, John Hundley, Richard Keene, Doris Carson, Four Eton Boys, Geraldine Dvorak, Frank and Milt Britton Band.

A tasty musical musical featuring Pryor as a song plugger stranded in an uneventful small town during the Depression. Glamor girl Brian lends a hand when Pryor tries to put on a Broadway show backed by wealthy gambler Carrillo. The highlight of the film is Miles' delivery of "Honey Are You Makin' Any Money?" (Herman Hupfeld, Sammy Fain, Al Siegel). Other songs include "Ah, But Is It Love?" "There's a Little Bit of You in Every Love Song" (Hupfeld, Fain, Siegel), "Moonlight and Pretzels," "Dusty Shoes," "Let's Make Love Like the Crocodiles" (E. Y. Harburg, Jay Gorney), "Gotta Get Up and Go to Work" (Hupfeld).

d, Karl Freund, Monte Brice; w, Brice, Sid Herzig (based on a story by Brice, Arthur Jarrett); ph, William Miller; cos, Brymer; ch, Bobby Connolly.

Musical   (PR:A MPAA:NR)

MOONLIGHT IN HAVANA**   (1942) 63m UNIV bw
Allan Jones (*Johnny Norton*), Jane Frazee (*Gloria Jackson*), Marjorie Lord (*Patsy Clark*), William Frawley (*Barney Crane*), Don Terry (*Eddie Daniels*), Sergio Orta (*Martinez*), Wade Boteler (*Joe Clark*), Hugh O'Connell (*Charlie*), Jack Norton (*George*), Dorothy Babb, Marilyn Kay (*Jivin' Jills*), Roland DuPree, Joe "Corky" Geil, Dick Humphreys (*Jivin' Jacks*), Love Jean Weber, Joyce Horne, Zedra de la Conde (*Dancers*), Grace and Nicco (*Dance Team*), Horton Dance Group (*Specialty Dancers*), Tom Dugan (*Doc*), Helen Lynd (*Daisy*), Robert E. Homans (*Mac*), Pat McVey (*Chuck*), Walter Tetley (*Newsboy*), Phil Warren (*Regan*), Eddie Coke (*Reporter*), Rico de Montez (*Hotel Clerk*), Alphonse Martell (*Hotel Manager*), David Clark (*2nd Player*), Lane Chandler (*Allison*), Clarence Straight (*1st Player*), Linda Brent (*Operator*), Joey Ray (*Band Leader*), Charles Sherlock (*Photographer*).

Western director Anthony Mann's second feature is a trite tale about Jones as a singing baseball player who can only sing when he has a cold. While Jones' old team is in spring training in Havana, Jones gets a job singing nights at a club, oscillating between sickness and health as he switches from the stage to the diamond. Songs include "Got Music," "Isn't It Lovely," sung by Allan Jones, Jane Frazee), "I Don't Need Money," "Rhythm of the Tropics," "Moonlight in Havana" (Franklin), "I Wonder Who's Kissing Her Now" (Will M. Hough, Frank R. Adams, Joseph E. Howard, Harold Orlob).

p, Bernard W. Burton; d, Anthony Mann; w, Oscar Brodney; ph, Charles Van Enger; ed, Russell Schoengarth; md, Charles Previn; art d, Jack Otterson; ch, Edward Prinz.

Musical   (PR:A MPAA:NR)

MOONLIGHT IN HAWAII*   (1941) 61m UNIV bw
Johnny Downs (*Pete*), Jane Frazee (*Toby*); The Merry Macs: Joe McMichael (*Beans Smith*), Ted McMichael (*Red Simpson*), Judd McMichael (*Ollie Barrett*), Mary Lou Cook (*Mary Lou*); Leon Errol (*Spencer*), Richard Carle (*Lawton*), Marjorie Gateson (*Mrs. Floto*), Mischa Auer (*Clipper*), Sunnie O'Dea (*Gloria*), Maria Montez (*Ilani*), Elaine Morey (*Doris*), Charles Coleman (*Butler*), Jean De Briac (*Headwaiter*), Ernie Stanton (*Truck Driver*), Eddie Lee (*Charlie*), Jim Spencer (*Chief Kikhanoui*).

Set in Hawaii, this sour musical casts Downs as an escort for the wealthy Gateson and her band of tourists. Errol and Carle are a pair of crooked Hawaiian pineapple juice manufacturers who want to reap the fruits of Gateson's fortune. The forgettable songs, performed by Downs, Frazee, The Merry Macs, Sunnie O'Dea, Elaine Morey and others, include "It's People Like You," "Poi," "We'll Have a Lot of Fun," "Moonlight in Hawaii," (Don Raye, Gene DePaul), and "Hawaiian War Chant" (Ralph Freed, Johnny Noble, Prince Leleiohaku of Hawaii).

p, Ken Goldsmith; d, Charles Lamont; w, Morton Grant, James Gow, Erna Lazarus (based on a story by Eve Greene); ph, Stanley Cortez; ed, Arthur Hilton; md, Charles Previn; art d, Jack Otterson.

Musical   (PR:A MPAA:NR)

MOONLIGHT IN VERMONT* ¹/₂　　　　　　　(1943) 62m UNIV bw

Gloria Jean (Gwen Harding), Ray Malone (Richard "Slick" Ellis), George Dolenz (Lionel Devereau), Fay Helm (Lucy Meadows), Betty McCabe (Joan), Sidney Miller (Cyril), Vivian Austin (Brenda Allenby), Patsy O'Connor (Alice), Mira McKinney (Elvira), Billy Benedict (Abel), Virginia Brissac (Aunt Bess), Russell Simpson (Uncle Rufus), Ruth Lee (Miss Evans), John Whitney (Larry Devine), Marilyn Day (Betty), Jean Davis (Ruth), Dolores Diane, Dariel Johnson, Irma Jeter, Elaine Campbell, Wanda Smith, Peggy Brant (The Jivin' Jills), Bill Henderson, Cal Rothenberg, Robert Coleman, John Truel, Jack Coffey, Pat Phelan, Joe "Corky" Geil, Bobby Scheerer (The Jivin' Jacks), Ralph Dunn (Taxi Driver), Barbara Brown (Miss Anderson), Dorothy Vaughan (Mrs. Costello), Alice Fleming (Mrs. Finchley), Harry Harvey, Jr. (Tommy), Joseph Bernard (Lavery), Francis Sayles (Dr. Stubbs), Alice Draper (Waitress).

Manufactured by the musical cookie cutter, this standard picture has a backwoods girl from the hills of Vermont (Jean) leaving her serene home to attend a lively New York drama school. Her cash flow soon comes to a halt and she is forced to return home to help on the farm. To lend a hand, her classmates head for the Vermont fields and put on a climactic barnyard show. Songs include "Something Tells Me," "Be a Good Girl," "Dobbin and a Wagon of Hay," "Pickin' the Beets" (Sidney Miller, Inez James, sung by Gloria Jean), "They've Got Me in the Middle of Things," "After the Beat" (Miller, James, sung by Ray Malone, Betty McCabe, Vivian Austin), "Lover" (Lorenz Hart, Richard Rodgers).

p, Bernard W. Burton; d, Edward Lilley; w, Eugene Conrad; ph, Jerome Ash; ed, Charles Maynard; md, Edward Ward; art d, John B. Goodman, Abraham Grossman; cos, Vera West; ch, Louis Da Pron.

Musical　　　　　　　　　　　　　　　　　(PR:A MPAA:NR)

MOONLIGHT MASQUERADE* ¹/₂　　　　　(1942) 67m REP bw

Dennis O'Keefe (John Bennett, Jr.), Jane Frazee (Vicki Forrester), Betty Kean (Mikki Marquette), Eddie Foy, Jr. (Lord Percy Ticklederry), Erno Verebes (Count Erie), Franklin Pangborn (Fairchild), Paul Harvey (John Bennett, Sr.), Jed Prouty (Robert Forrester), Tommye Adams (Miss Mink), The Three Chocolateers.

Oil company co-owners Harvey and Prouty agree to leave controlling interest in their company to their respective son and daughter, O'Keefe and Frazee, if the two marry by the time Frazee turns 21. The problem is that the kids have never met and have preconceived notions of what the other must be like. They both try to dissolve their fathers' agreement and still retain their inheritance, but finally meet and find that it's nearly love at first sight.

p&d, John H. Auer; w, Lawrence Kimble (based on a story by Auer); ph, John Alton; ed, Edward Mann; md, Cy Feuer; art d, Russell Kimball; ch, Nick Castle; m/l, "What Am I Doing Here In Your Arms?" Mort Greene, Harry Revel.

Drama　　　　　　　　　　　　　　　　　(PR:A MPAA:NR)

MOONLIGHT MURDER* ¹/₂　　　　　　　(1936) 65m MGM bw

Chester Morris (Steve Farrell), Madge Evans (Toni Adams), Leo Carrillo (Gino D'Acosta), Frank McHugh (William), Benita Hume (Diana), Grant Mitchell (Dr. Adams), Katharine Alexander (Louisa), J. Carrol Naish (Bejac), H. B. Warner (Godfred Chiltern), Duncan Renaldo (Pedro), Leonard Ceeley (Ivan Bosloff), Robert McWade (Quinlan), Pedro de Cordoba (Swami), Charles Trowbridge (Stage Manager).

Falling far below par is this murder mystery set against the background of a Hollywood Bowl opera performance. Carrillo is the lead tenor in the opera company who gets murdered during his performance. Morris is an amateur detective who cracks the case while sifting through a lunatic assortment of backstage characters. Wilhelm Von Wymetal arranged and directed the lengthy opera sequences.

p, Lucien Hubbard, Ned Marin; d, Edwin L. Marin; w, Florence Ryerson, Edgar Allen Woolf (based on a story by Albert J. Cohen, Robert T. Shannon); ph, Charles Clarke; m, Herbert Stothart, Edward Ward, Giuseppe Verdi; ed, Ben Lewis; art d, Cedric Gibbons.

Crime/Mystery　　　　　　　　　　　　　(PR:A MPAA:NR)

MOONLIGHT ON THE PRAIRIE**　　　　　(1936) 63m WB bw

Dick Foran (Ace Andrews), Sheila Mannors (Barbara Roberts), George E. Stone (Small Change), Joseph Sawyer (Luke Thomas), Gordon Elliott (Jeff), Joseph King (Sheriff), Robert Barrat (Buck), Dickie Jones (Dickie Roberts), Herbert Heywood (Pop), Raymond Brown (Lafe), Richard Carle (Col. Gowdy), Milton Kibbee, Bud Osborne, Ben Corbett, Gene Alsace [Rocky Camron], Glenn Strange, Vic Potel, Cactus Mack, Jack Kirk, Ronnie Cosby.

Foran's warbling cowboy debut has him as an out-of-work rodeo star who moonlights in a medicine show. He is accused of murdering a rancher and after meeting the widow and her son, decides to hunt the real culprit. Of course his search is an heroic success. Foran did many remakes of silent films for Warner Bros. Elliott, later billed as Wild Bill Elliott, went on to star in many B westerns.

p, Bryan Foy; d, D. Ross Lederman; w, William Jacobs (based on the story "Boss of the Bar B Ranch" by Jacobs); ph, Fred Jackman, Jr.; ed, Thomas Pratt; md, Leo F. Forbstein; art d, Esdras Hartley; m/l, "Covered Wagon Days," "Moonlight on the Prairie," M. K. Jerome, Joan Jasmyn, Vernon Spencer, Bob Nolan (sung by Dick Foran).

Western　　　　　　　　　　　　　　　　(PR:A MPAA:NR)

MOONLIGHT ON THE RANGE**　　　　　(1937) 62m Spectrum bw

Fred Scott, Al St. John, Lois January, Dick Curtis, Frank LaRue, Oscar Gahan, Jimmy Aubrey, Carl Mathews, Wade Walker, William McCall, Shorty Miller, Jack Evans, Rudy Sooter, Lew Meehan, Ed Cassidy, Tex Palmer, George Morrell, Sherry Tansey, Forrest Taylor.

This western musical stars Scott, who plays a dual role as the hero and his villainous identical half-brother. Scott, as the hero, is chased constantly by the law who believes that he is the evil half-brother. The good brother goes after his brother and, after a few good gun battles, Scott stops his brother's crime spree. Scott's dual role works well thanks to the special effects department and some clever camera angles. St. John is the good Scott's sidekick.

p, Jed Buell, George H. Callaghan; d, Sam Newfield; w, Fred Myton (based on a story by Whitney Williams); ph, Robert Cline; m, Don Swander, June Hershey; songs "Shindig," "Sundown Trail," "Albuquerque," "As Time Goes On" (sung by Fred Scott).

Western　　　　　　　　　　　　　　　　(PR:A MPAA:NR)

MOONLIGHT RAID　　　　　(SEE: CHALLENGE OF THE RANGE, 1949)

MOONLIGHT SONATA***　　　　　　　(1938, Brit.) 80m Malmar/UA bw

Ignace Jan Paderewski (Himself), Charles Farrell (Eric Molander), Marie Tempest (Baroness Lindenborg), Barbara Greene (Ingrid), Eric Portman (Mario de la costa), Graham Browne (Dr. Broman), Queenie Leonard (Margit, His Niece), Lawrence Hanray (Bishop), Binkie Stuart (Child), Fisher White, H. G. Stoker (Club Members), Bryan Powley (Nils the Butler), Sybil Brooke (Anna the Housekeeper).

Famed pianist Paderewski is the focal point of this tale of love and lies set in Sweden. Cutting from a scene of Paderewski playing, it goes to a large country estate and has Farrell professing his love for Greene, granddaughter of Tempest, who owns the place. But as Greene battles with her uncertainty, a plane carrying a handful of passengers, including Paderewski, is forced to land on the estate and Tempest is just overjoyed at having the famed pianist at her place. Portman starts flirting with Greene, who has led a very sheltered life at the estate. Portman is a boasting jerk, but Greene is still taken in by his charm. She wants to run off with him but Farrell begs her not to and comes up with a scheme to prevent it from happening. He runs to the grandmother and discloses that Portman is a fortune hunting hypnotist and is already married. Tempest buys Portman off and sends him on his way. But Greene spies the receipt and finds out what kind of man Portman really is, leaving the door open for Farrell to console her while Paderewski plays on the piano. Musical selections performed by Paderewski include: Frederic Chopin's "Polonaise," Franz Liszt's "Second Hungarian Rhapsody," Paderewski's "Minuet in G Major," and naturally the title number by Ludwig van Beethoven.

p&d, Lothar Mendes; w, Edward Knoblock, E. M. Delafield (based on a story by Hans Rameau); ph, Jan Stallich; ed, Philip Charlot.

Drama　　　　　　　　　　　　　　　　　(PR:A MPAA:NR)

MOONLIGHTER, THE*　　　　　　　　(1953) 77m WB bw/3-D

Barbara Stanwyck (Rela), Fred MacMurray (Wes Anderson), Ward Bond (Cole), William Ching (Tom Anderson), John Dierkes (Sheriff Daws), Morris Ankrum (Prince), Jack Elam (Strawboss), Charles Halton (Clem Usquebaugh), Norman Leavitt (Tidy), Sam Flint (Mr. Mott), Myra Marsh (Mrs. Anderson), Burt Mustin, Byron Foulger, Myron Healey, William Hunter, Robert Bice, Gregg Barton, Ron Kennedy, David Alpert, Steve Rowland, Joel Fluellen.

A strange western that squanders some fine talents and uses three-dimensional photography for no apparent reason. MacMurray is a bad guy incarcerated in a small town jail. He's been accused of "moonlighting," which means that he herds cows by day and rustles them at night. A lynch mob wants to string him up but he gets away from jail and the wrong guy, a saddletramp, is strung up. This causes MacMurray to exact revenge for the taking of the innocent man's life and to pay for a decent funeral for the unlucky prisoner. MacMurray's girl friend is Stanwyck, who is deputized as a one-woman posse when MacMurray goes on a bank-robbing spree. His brother, Ching, looks up to MacMurray and wants to be like him, but he is killed on the very first haul. In the end, MacMurray agrees to be captured by Stanwyck because he knows that she'll be waiting for him when he is released from jail somewhere down the line. There is some good supporting work by Bond as MacMurray's evil bank-robbing partner, and a few laughs are produced by just looking at Elam. The script is stronger than the direction and the result is that there are interesting people doing interesting things in a rather lethargic fashion. Stanwyck and MacMurray will always be recalled for their pairing in DOUBLE INDEMNITY, although they could have very well been forgotten for the results of this yawner. The 3-D black-and-white photography must have been used just as a gimmick, as they knew they didn't have much of a film to begin with and hoped that audiences of the 1950s would be willing to brave the dull headaches that came from those plastic 3-D glasses in order to watch this dull movie.

p, Joseph Bernhard; d, Roy Rowland; w, Niven Busch; ph, Bert Glennon (3-D, NaturalVison); m, Heinz Roemheld; ed, Terry Morse; md, Roemheld; art d, Dan Hall; set d, Fred MacLean; cos, Joe King, Ann Peck.

Western　　　　　　　　　　　　　　　　(PR:A MPAA:NR)

MOONLIGHTING****　　　　　　　　(1982, Brit.) 97m Miracle/UNIV c

Jeremy Irons (Nowak), Eugene Lipinski (Banaszak), Jiri Stanislav (Wolski), Eugeniusz Hackiewicz (Kudaj), Dorothy Zienciowska (Lot Airline Girl), Edward Arthur (Immigration Officer), Denis Holmes (Neighbor), Renu Setna (Junk Shop Owner), David Calder (Supermarket Manager), Judy Gridley (Supermarket Supervisor), Claire Toeman (Supermarket Cashier), Catherine Harding (Lady Shoplifter), Jill Johnson (Haughty Supermarket Customer), David Square (Supermarket Assistant), Mike Sarne (Builder's Merchant), Lucy Hornak, Robyn Mandell (Wrangler Shop Assistants), Ann Tirard (Lady In Telephone Box), Christopher Logue (Workman), Hugh Harper (Newspaper Boy), Julia Chambers (Chemist's Assistant), Fred Lee Own (Chinese Man), Kenny Ireland (Timber Man), Trevor Cooper, Ian Ormsby-Knox (Hire Shop Men), David Gant (Aquascutum Assistant), Jennifer

Landor *(Aquascutum Shoplifter)*, Jenny Seagrove *(Anna)*, Ian McCulloch *(Boss Lookalike)*, Laura Frances Hart *(His Woman)*.

One month after martial law was declared in Poland, Skolimowski began to work on this political allegory about a group of four Polish workers in England. Led by the only English-speaking one among them, Irons, the group is given one month to renovate a London flat so their Polish boss will have somewhere to stay in Britain. In return, they will be given more money than they could make in a year at home. Because of Irons' familiarity with the language (his British accent often leaking through his faked Polish) he takes charge of the other three. After a long week of work, dust, and uncomfortable living arrangements (they are staying in the flat where they are working), Irons purchases a television for relaxation and to pacify his comrades. They eagerly await Sunday, the day they are allowed to talk to their loved ones at home. During the following week, however, Soviet troops invade Poland and all communication is cut off. Instead of creating dissent among his workers, Irons chooses to remain silent, especially since the TV has broken down and the other three have no way of communicating with the neighbors. To keep on the strict budget they are given, Irons resorts to stealing, concocting a scheme to steal on a regular basis from the supermarket. He also takes newspapers out of his neighbors' mailbox to follow the events in Poland, making sure the others do not get to read (or more accurately see) the news. After a construction mishap, their schedule falls behind, taking a big chunk out of their remaining cash. The workers sometimes get only three hours of sleep, but Irons sets the clocks ahead so they will think they got more. His measures become more drastic, burning their letters from family members in Poland—anything to keep the workers working. The ban on airline flights in and out of Poland is eventually lifted and the four of them can return home. When Irons tells them about the Soviet invasion, all the anger which has built up in the workers comes out and they knock Irons to the street, beating and kicking him. As with Andrzej Wajda, Skolimowski has emerged from Poland with a keen sense of politics and of the rights of workers. As immersed in politics as MOONLIGHTING is, however, it rarely feels like a "political film." There are no manifestos, no slogans, and no political speeches. The situation in Poland is represented only by the forbidding presence of soldiers and tanks rolling down the deserted streets of Gdansk. It is political only in the allegorical sense—Irons represents the same threat to his three comrades as the Soviet troops represent to the Polish dock workers. He cuts their communication, news sources, and family ties in order to get the work done. The characters, instead of having a realistic presence so often associated with this sort of film, are nearly surreal, placed against the backdrop of a flat under construction (they almost never leave the building). The real politics are outside of the drama of the characters, rarely invading the story in a direct way. It is a political film which can be enjoyed even if one has no sense of world affairs.

p, Mark Shivas, Jerzy Skolimowski; d, Skolimowski; w, Skolimowski, Boleslaw Sulik, Barry Vince, Danuta Witold Stok; ph, Tony Pierce Roberts; m, Stanley Myers, Hans Zimmer; ed, Vince; prod d, Tony Woollard; cos, Jane Robinson.

Drama Cas. (PR:C MPAA:PG)

MOONLIGHTING WIVES zero (1966) 83m Morgan/Craddock c

Diane Vivienne *(Mrs. Joan Rand)*, Joan Nash *(Nancy Preston)*, John Aristedes *(Al Jordon)*, Fatima *(Belly Dancer)*, Chris Roberts, Tina Marie, Shariaya Lee, Joe Santos, Jackie Farrel, George Winship, Jody Lynn, Lisa Lillot, Bill Sullivan, Joe Jenckes, Sue Gibson.

A pure sexploitation film that allegedly is based on actual events. The story tells of an unhappy housewife, Vivienne, who figures out a scheme to come up with extra cash. She pulls in good looking housewives desperate for money and begins a prostitution ring. She quickly becomes a successful madam but the police shut her down.

p, Bob Moscow; d&w, Joe Sarno; ph, Jerry Kalogeratos (DeLuxe Color); m, Stan Free; ed, Pat Follner.

Drama (PR:O MPAA:NR)

MOONRAKER, THE $^{**1/2}$ (1958, Brit.) 82m ABF/ABF-Pathe c

George Baker ("The Moonraker", Earl Anthony of Dawlish), Sylvia Syms *(Anne Wyndham)*, Peter Arne *(Edmund Tyler)*, Marius Goring *(Col. Beaumont)*, Clive Morton *(Lord Harcourt)*, Gary Raymond *(Prince Charles Stuart)*, Richard Leech *(Henry Strangeways)*, Iris Russell *(Judith Strangeways)*, Michael Anderson, Jr. *(Martin Strangeways)*, Paul Whitsun-Jones *(Parfitt)*, Patrick Troughton *(Capt. Wilcox)*, John Le Mesurier *(Oliver Cromwell)*, Julian Somers *(Capt. Foster)*, Patrick Waddington *(Lord Dorset)*, Frances Rowe *(Lady Dorset)*, Jennifer Browne *(Henrietta Dorset)*, Richard Warner *(Trooper)*, George Woodbridge *(Capt. Lowry)*, Victor Brooks *(Blacksmith)*, Sylvia Bidmead, Frank Hawkins, Keith Banks, Victor Platt, Gillian Vaughan, Edward Dentith, Leslie Linder, John Crocker.

With the end of the English Civil War the Royalists and the Roundheads are still at odds. Baker, a Cavalier, has a bounty on his head and the Royalist must sneak the king, Raymond, from England to France. He sets up a ship to pick up Raymond, but Baker's scheme is discovered by one of Le Mesurier's agents. Cornered by Le Mesurier's Roundheads, Baker outsmarts and out-duels Le Mesurier's men and gets Raymond out of the country. The action scenes are compelling viewing. Syms is the lady with whom Baker falls in love and Arne is Baker's arch-rival.

p, Hamilton G. Inglis; d, David Macdonald; w, Robert Hall, Wilfrid Eades, Alistair Bell (based on a play by Arthur Watkyn); ph, Max Greene [Mutz Greenbaum]; m, Laurie Johnson; ed, Richard Best.

Adventure (PR:A MPAA:NR)

MOONRAKER*** (1979, Brit.) 126m UA c

Roger Moore *(James Bond)*, Lois Chiles *(Holly Goodhead)*, Michael [Michel] Lonsdale *(Drax)*, Richard Kiel *(Jaws)*, Corinne Clery *(Corinne Dufour)*, Bernard Lee *("M")*, Geoffrey Keen *(Frederick Gray)*, Desmond Llewelyn *("Q")*, Lois Maxwell *(Miss Moneypenny)*, Emily Bolton *(Manuela)*, Toshiro Suga *(Chang)*, Blanche Ravalec *(Dolly)*, Jean-Pierre Castaldi *(Pilot of Private Jet)*, Leila Shenna *(Hostess of Private Jet)*, Walter Gotell *(Gen. Gogol)*, Arthur Howard *(Cavendish)*, Irka Bochenko *(Blonde Beauty)*, Michael Marshall *(Col. Scott)*, Douglas Lambert *(Mission Control Director)*, Alfie Bass *(Consumptive Italian)*, Anne Lonnberg *(Museum Guide)*, Brian Keith *(U.S. Shuttle Captain)*, George Birt *(Boeing 747 Captain)*, Kim Fortune *(FRA Officer)*, Lizzie Warville *(Russian Girl)*, Chris Dillinger, Georges Beller, Johnny Traber, Chichinou Kaeppler, Francoise Gayat, Catherine Serre, Chrinstina Hui, Nicaise Jean-Louis, Beatrice Libert, Funambulists *(Johnny Traber's Troupe)*.

James Bond is back and more expensive than ever. This one goes after the space age theme and became the costliest of all the Bond films, costing nearly as much as the first eight films put together. This time Moore is assigned to search for a missing spaceship and along the way, discovers a plot by Lonsdale to take over the world. Lonsdale's plan is to destroy Earth, then breed a super race in outer space. He has built a huge space station, where the final battle takes place, and has stolen some space shuttles to get his people there. Kiel, a dentist's dream, returns again as the indestructible Jaws to foil Moore's attempts but turns good for the love of a woman and ends up helping Moore. Chiles is the mandatory Bond love interest, and the film is the last appearance of Lee as M. The gadgets live up to all Bond fans expectations but Bond is better back on Earth than floating around in space. (See JAMES BOND series, Index.)

p, Albert R. Broccoli; d, Lewis Gilbert; w, Christopher Wood (based on the novel by Ian Fleming); ph, Jean Tournier (Panavision); m, John Barry; ed, John Glen; prod d, Ken Adam; art d, Max Douy, Charles Bishop; set d, Peter Howitt; cos, Jacques Fonteray; spec eff, Dereck Meddings, John Evans, John Richardson; m/l, "Moonraker," Barry, Hal David (sung by Shirley Bassey); stunts, Bob Simmons.

Spy/Adventure Cas. (PR:A MPAA:PG)

MOONRISE $^{***1/2}$ (1948) 90m REP bw

Dane Clark *(Danny Hawkins)*, Gail Russell *(Gilly Johnson)*, Ethel Barrymore *(Grandma)*, Allyn Joslyn *(Clem Otis)*, Rex Ingram *(Mose)*, Henry [Harry] Morgan *(Billy Scripture)*, David Street *(Ken Williams)*, Selena Royle *(Aunt Jessie)*, Harry Carey, Jr. *(Jimmy Biff)*, Irving Bacon *(Judd Jenkins)*, Lloyd Bridges *(Jerry Sykes)*, Houseley Stevenson *(Uncle Joe Jingle)*, Phil Brown *(Elmer)*, Harry V. Cheshire *(J. B. Sykes)*, Lila Leeds *(Julie)*, Virginia Mullen *(Miss Simpkins)*, Oliver Blake *(Ed Conlon)*, Tom Fadden *(Homer Blackstone)*, Charles Lane *(Man in Black)*, Clem Bevans *(Jake)*, Helen Wallace *(Martha Otis)*, Michael Branden, Bill Borzage, Tiny Jimmie Kelly, Ed Rees, Casey MacGregor *(Barkers)*, John Harmon *(Baseball Attendant)*, Monte Lowell *(Man)*, Jimmie Hawkins, Gary Armstrong, Buzzy Henry, Jimmy Crane, Harry Lauter, Bob Hoffman, Joel McGinnis *(Boys)*, Timmie Hawkins *(Alfie)*, Doreen McCann, Candy Toxton *(Girls)*, Steven Peck *(Danny, Age 7)*, Johnny Calkins *(Danny, Age 13)*, *Tommy Ivo (Jerry, Age 7)*, Michael Dill *(Jerry, Age 13)*, Linda Lombard, Stelita Ravel *(Dancers)*, Renee Donatt *(Ticket Seller)*, George Backus, Monte Montague *(Hunters)*.

A grim but effective crime melodrama, MOONRISE stars the pensive, expansive Clark as the son of a murderer who was hanged for his crimes. Clark is haunted by his father's past and tormented by his peers in a small southern town where his only friend is Russell, a beautiful young girl in love with him. Carey, Jr., is the chief agitator and when the youth attacks Clark the latter kills his opponent is self-defense. He feels guilty of murder anyway and, despite pleas from Russell, flees to the swamps where he stays with former schoolteacher Barrymore. She sagely talks to Clark and helps him understand his motivations. When he no longer believes he is a product of "bad blood," Clark turns himself in to the law. In a somewhat lethargic film, Borzage nevertheless carefully develops his characters and makes them compelling. Russell's photography is exceptional and fine performances are rendered by all.

p, Charles Haas; d, Frank Borzage; w, Haas (based on the novel by Theodore Strauss); ph, John L. Russell; m, William Lava; ed, Harry Keller; prod d, Lionel Banks; set d, John McCarthy, Jr., George Sawley; cos, Adele Palmer; spec eff, Howard Lydecker, Theodore Lydecker; makeup, Bob Mark; m/l, "It Just Dawned on Me," Lava, Harry Tobias, sung by David Street, "Lonesome," Theodore Strauss, Lava, sung by Street.

Drama (PR:C MPAA:NR)

MOONRUNNERS $^{*1/2}$ (1975) 110m UA c

James Mitchum *(Grady)*, Kiel Martin *(Bobby Lee)*, Arthur Hunnicutt *(Uncle Jessie)*, Chris Forbes *(Beth)*, George Ellis *(Jake)*, Pete Munro *(Zeebo)*, Joan Blackman *(Reba)*, Waylon Jennings *(Balladeer)*, Spanky McFarland, Joey Giondello, Rick Hunter, Dick Steinborn, Happy Humphery.

A poor action comedy about an old moonshiner, Hunnicutt, and his two daredevil nephews, Mitchum and Martin. The story concerns the moonshiner's efforts to stay one step in front of the federal revenuers and a New York mob trying to take him over. There are a number of car chases and crashes in this overlong film. It was later adapted into the TV series "The Dukes of Hazzard." This is one of the last films Arthur Hunnicutt made. Kiel Martin is better known as one of the ensemble actors in TV's "Hill Street Blues". Actor James Mitchum is one of Robert Mitchum's sons.

p, Robert B. Clark; d&w, Gy Waldron; ph, Brian Roy; prod d, Peter Cornberg; ed, Avrum Fine; art d, Pat Mann; cos, Patty Shaw.

Action/Comedy (PR:A MPAA:PG)

MOONSHINE COUNTY EXPRESS**

(1977) 95m Universal Majestic-Sunshine/New World c

John Saxon *(J. B. Johnson)*, Susan Howard *(Dot Hammer)*, William Conrad *(Jack Starkey)*, Morgan Woodward *(Sweetwater)*, Claudia Jennings *(Betty Hammer)*, Jeff Corey *(Preacher Hagen)*, Dub Taylor *(Uncle Bill)*, Maureen McCormick *(Sissy*

Hammer), Albert Salmi *(Sheriff Larkin)*, Len Sesser *(Scoggins)*, Bruce Kimball *(Harley)*, Candice Rialson *(Mayella)*, E. J. Andre *(Lawyer Green)*, Fred Foresman *(Pap Hammer)*, Dick Esterly *(Hackberry)*, Tom Deaton *(Tiny)*, Rick Langston *(Gabe)*, William Luckey *(Hood)*, Lenka Novak *(Manicurist)*, Dean Christianson *(Leroy)*, Terry Pittsford, Stanley Creamer, Jim Springer, Mel Shahan *(Still Guards)*, Richard Wood, Stephen Dach, Roland Meyer, James Morales, John Young, Gene Livermore, Dave Brewer *(Starkey's Men)*.

Three daughters of a murdered moonshiner try to sell off their father's remaining stock of liquor. Conrad, the head of a local moonshine syndicate, is the one responsible for the death and tries to stop the girls from continuing the family business. The whiskey the girls own is from Prohibition and is worth lots of money. Conrad stops at nothing to get the shine and the girls get help from Saxon who works for Conrad. With blazing guns, the girls and Saxon take over Conrad's business.

p, Ed Carlin; d, Gus Trikonis; w, Hubert Smith, Daniel Ansley; ph, Gary Graver, R. Michael Stringer (Movielab Color); m, Fred Werner; ed, Gene Ruggiero; art d, Peter Jamison, Gerald Olson; set d, James Heggie; spec eff, Charles Spurgeon; m/l, "Fireman's Ball" (sung by the Tom and Dink Show); makeup, Gale Peterson; stunts, Bill Burton; stunt drivers, Frank Orsatti, Glen Wilder, Gary Combs.

Action/Crime   **Cas.**   **(PR:C MPAA:PG)**

MOONSHINE MOUNTAIN zero
(1964) 90m Creative Communications c (AKA: WHITE TRASH ON MOONSHINE MOUNTAIN)

Chuck Scott [Charles Glore] *(Doug Martin)*, Adam Sorg *(Asa Potter)*, Jeffrey Allen *(Jeb Carpenter)*, Bonnie Hinson *(Laura Carpenter)*, Carmen Sotir *(Angeline)*, Ben Moore *(Raf)*, Pat Patterson *(Hutto)*, Mark Douglas *(Ed Basham)*, Karin March *(Ma Basham)*, Gretchen Eisner *(Mary Lou)*, Harry Hoffman *(Luther)*, Bill Simpson *(Zero)*, William Harris *(Harley)*, Marilyn Walters *(Della Lawrence)*, Harry Kerr *(Wilson)*, Lee Collins *(Bentley)*, Claude Casey *(TV Announcer)*, James Preddy *(TV Singer)*, James Stokes, Jr. *(Electrician)*, The Catalinas, Gay Land and the Thunderbirds, The Sweet Gum Sisters and Brother.

Scott plays a popular country-western singer who returns to the Carolina hills with his girl friend, Walters. She is killed by Sorg when she refuses his advances. He goes on a killing spree and plots to dynamite the entire community. He is killed, however, by an ax-wielding retarded woman he once raped. Trash.

p&d, Herschell Gordon Lewis; w, Charles Glore; ed, Robert Sinise, Ron Closky.

Crime Drama   **(PR:A MPAA:NR)**

MOONSHINE WAR, THE**   (1970) 99m Filmways/MGM c

Patrick McGoohan *(Frank Long)*, Richard Widmark *(Dr. Taulbee)*, Alan Alda *(Son Martin)*, Lee Hazlewood *(Dual Meaders)*, Joe Williams *(Aaron)*, Will Geer *(Sheriff Baylor)*, Melodie Johnson *(Lizann Simpson)*, Suzanne Zenor *(Miley Mitchell)*, Max Showalter *(Mr. Worthman)*, Harry Carey, Jr. *(Stamper)*, Richard Peabody *(Boyd Caswell)*, Charles Tyner *(McClendon)*, Dick Crockett *(Carl)*, Claude Johnson *(Tourist)*, Terry Garr *(Tourist's Wife)*, Patty Sauers *(Waitress)*, John Schuck *(E. J. Royce)*, Tom Nolan *(Lowell)*, Bo Hopkins *(Bud Blackwell)*.

Top cast heroes are hurt by pathetic story that they cannot pull off. McGoohan is a U.S. revenue agent who wants to make a quick killing right before the repeal of Prohibition. An old Army buddy has plenty of whiskey and McGoohan wants it. But Alda backs down and McGoohan hires two ex-cons to scare him into completing the deal. The two thugs kill the local sheriff and his deputy and set their eyes on the whiskey. McGoohan now decides to help Alda with the out-of-control Widmark. Widmark murders McGoohan and takes four townspeople hostage. He wants the moonshine in exchange for the people. Alda relents and has Widmark start digging in a graveyard. Instead of moonshine, Widmark sets off some dynamite that Alda had buried there. To celebrate the end of Widmark, Alda tosses a party and he supplies the liquor.

p, Martin Ransohoff; d, Richard Quine; w, Elmore Leonard (based on the novel by Leonard); ph, Richard H. Kline (Panavision, Metrocolor); m, Fred Karger; ed, Allan Jacobs; art d, George W. Davis, Edward Carfagno; set d, Robert R. Benton, Hugh Hunt; cos, Edmund Kara; spec eff, Earl McCoy; m/l, "Ballad of the Moonshine," Hank Williams, Jr. (sung by Williams), "It Takes All Kinds of People," Roy Orbison (sung by Orbison), "Moonshine" (performed by The Five Man Electrical Band); makeup, William Tuttle, Allan Snyder.

Crime/Action   **(PR:C MPAA:GP)**

MOONSHINER'S WOMAN zero (1968) 79m Worldwide-Starline-Tasbem bw

Alan Davis, Linda Lee, Roy Huston, "Georgeanne", Bill Crisp.

The girl friend of a Tennessee moonshiner gets involved with the gangster who kills her boy friend, then promises her fame and fortune. She eventually gets hooked on LSD and makes love to one of the gangster's henchmen. She then informs the authorities of the gangster's operations.

p&d, D. E. Davison [Alan Davis].

Drama   **(PR:O MPAA:NR)**

MOONSHOT   (SEE: COUNTDOWN, 1968)

MOONSPINNERS, THE   (SEE: MOON SPINNERS, THE, 1964, Brit.)

MOONSTONE, THE**   (1934) 62m MON bw

David Manners *(Franklin Blake)*, Phyllis Barry *(Anne Verinder)*, Jameson Thomas *(Godfrey Ablewhite, Rare Book Dealer)*, Gustav von Seyffertitz *(Septimus Lucker, Money-Lender)*, Herbert Bunston *(Sir John Verinder)*, Evelyn Bostock *(Roseanna Spearman, Maid)*, John Davidson *(Yandoo, Blake's Hindu Servant)*, Elspeth

Dudgeon *(Betteredge, Housekeeper)*, Claude King *(Sir Basil Wynard)*, Olaf Hytten *(Dr. Ezra Jennings)*, Charles Irwin *(Inspector Cuff)*, Fred Walton *(Henry the Gardener)*.

Overly chatty adaptation of the Wilkie Collins adventure yarn detailing the theft of the moonstone from an Indian idol's forehead by British soldiers in 1799 and the havoc created by its possession when the priests of the temple travel to England to retrieve the gem.

p, Paul Malvern; d, Reginald Barker; w, Adele Buffington (based on the novel by Wilkie Collins); ph, Robert Planck; ed, Carl F. Pierson; md, Abe Meyer.

Drama   **(PR:A MPAA:NR)**

MOONTIDE**½   (1942) 94m FOX bw

Jean Gabin *(Bobo)*, Ida Lupino *(Anna)*, Thomas Mitchell *(Tiny)*, Claude Rains *(Nutsy)*, Jerome Cowan *(Dr. Brothers)*, Helene Reynolds *(Woman on Boat)*, Ralph Byrd *(Rev. Price)*, William Halligan *(Bartender)*, Sen Yung *(Takeo)*, Chester Gan *(Hirota)*, Robin Raymond *(Mildred)*, Arthur Aylesworth *(Pop Kelly)*, Arthur Hohl *(Jennings, Hotel Clerk)*, John Kelly *(Mac)*, Ralph Dunn *(Policeman)*, Tully Marshall *(Mr. Simpson)*, Tom Dugan *(lst Waiter)*, Vera Lewis *(Mrs. Simpson)*, Bruce Edwards *(Man)*, Gertrude Astor *(Woman)*, Marion Rosemund, Roseanne Murray *(Girls at Beach)*.

Despite this being French star Gabin's American film debut, MOONTIDE is a routine drama featuring him as a tough sailor who wakes up one morning after a long drunk to find that he has been accused of murder. Not being able to remember if he had done the deed, Gabin depends on his derelict friend Mitchell for support. But Mitchell blackmails Gabin into taking care of him in exchange for his silence. When Gabin saves lovely-but-distressed greasy-spoon waitress Lupino from suicide, he finds love has given him a new look on life. Lupino learns that Mitchell committed the murder about which Gabin feels guilt. When she threatens to tell Gabin, Mitchell nearly kills her. The ending has all the standard cliches including Mitchell meeting his doom in the sea. Fritz Lang worked as director for four days before Archie Mayo took over. Lang received no credit.

p, Mark Hellinger; d, Archie Mayo, Fritz Lang; w, John O'Hara (based on the novel by Willard Robertson); ph, Charles Clarke, Lucien Ballard; ed, William Reynolds; md, Cyril J. Mockridge, David Buttolph; art d, James Basevi, Richard Day; set d, Thomas Little.

Drama   **(PR:A MPAA:NR)**

MOONWOLF*½
(1966, Fin./Ger.) 74m Alfa-Suomen/AA bw (UND IMMER RUFT DAS HERZ)

Carl Mohner *(Dr. Holm)*, Ann Savo *(Ara)*, Helmut Schmid *(Woodsman)*, Paul Dahlke, Richard Haussler, Ingrid Lutz, Horst Janson, Ake Lindman, Wolf The Dog.

Swiss veterinarian Mohner allows his dog, Wolf, to be sent into orbit as part of a space project. The space capsule is launched and lands in the Artic region, near the home of one of Mohner's past loves. During the rescue mission, Mohner is reunited with the woman. First released in 1959.

p, Wolf Brauner, Martin Nosseck; d, Nosseck, George Freedland; w, Freedland, Johannes Hendrich; ph, Herbert Korner, Anton Markic, Esko Toyri; m, Henri Price, Albert Sendry, Peter Thomas; ed, Ralph Cushman; art d, Aarre Koivisto, Max A. Bienek.

Drama/Adventure   **(PR:A MPAA:NR)**

MORALIST, THE**
(1964, Ital.) 120m Avers-Napoleon/United bw (IL MORALISTA)

Alberto Sordi *(Agostino)*, Vittorio De Sica *(Il Presidente)*, Franca Valeri *(Virginia)*, Franco Fabrizi *(Giovanni)*, Maria Percy *(Monique)*, Sylvia Lopez, Mara Berni, Leopoldo Trieste, Christiane Nielsen.

An amusing farce centering on exploitive politicians in a corrupt government. Sordi is appointed by the president (De Sica) to head the censorship board, a job given to him only because De Sica wants to find a husband for his daughter. The well-meaning Sordi approaches his new positon with a moralistic attitude and quickly closes nightclubs that he sees as a menace. When Sordi falls in love with a striptease artist while away on a government function, he brings the woman back to his country, meeting with an indignant response from De Sica because he is now no longer an eligible husband for the president's daughter. Sordi loses his job and the slight efforts he made for change are quickly undone.

d, Giorgio Bianchi; w, Ettore M. Maragadonna, Luciana Corda, Rodolfo Sonego, Vincenzo Talarico, Oreste Biancoli (based on the story by Margadonna, Corda, Biancoli); ph, Alvaro Mancori; m, Carlo Savina.

Comedy   **(PR:A MPAA:NR)**

MORALS FOR WOMEN*½   (1931) 65m TIF bw

Bessie Love *(Helen Huston)*, Conway Tearle *(Van Dyne)*, John Holland *(Paul Cooper)*, Natalie Moorhead *(Flora)*, Emma Dunn *(Mrs. Huston)*, June Clyde *(Lorraine Huston)*, Edmund Bresse *(Mr. Huston)*, David Rollins *(Bill Huston)*, Lina Basquette *(Claudia)*, Virginia Lee Corbin *(Maybelle)*.

Maudlin soaper starring Love as a young secretary whose lecherous boss installs her in a luxurious apartment while he retains a set of keys. When Love runs into childhood sweetheart Holland, she blows town and returns to her hometown with him to start her life over. Unfortunately, pressures from home (destitute family, likable kid brother in trouble) force her to return to the big city to provide for the family. Holland, of course, eventually figures out what her living arrangement really means. There is much recrimination and sobbing until the predictable happy ending occurs.

p, Phil Goldstone; d, Mort Blumenstock; w, Frances Hyland; ph, Max Dupont; ed, Martin G. Cohn.

Drama **(PR:A MPAA:NR)**

MORALS OF MARCUS, THE** (1936, Brit.) 72m Real Art/GB bw

Lupe Velez *(Carlotta)*, Ian Hunter *(Sir Marcus Ordeyne)*, Adrianne Allen *(Judith Mainwaring)*, Noel Madison *(Tony Pasquale)*, J.H. Roberts, H.F. Maltby, Arnold Lucy, Frank Atkinson, D.J. Williams, James Raglan, Johnny Nit, Agnes Imlay.

A failed attempt at a racy comedy starring Velez as a Middle Eastern harem girl who escapes her servitude by stowing away on aristocratic archaeologist Hunter's boat which is returning to England so he may collect a large inheritance. Discovered en route, Velez pleads with Hunter not to turn her in and allow her to travel to England so she may track down some relatives to stay with. He agrees and lets her stay with him while searching for her family. Romance soon blossoms, and Velez is determined to marry Hunter. Allen, Hunter's friend, persuades Velez that Hunter cannot, and will not, marry her. The distraught Velez flees to Paris with sleazy gigolo Madison. Hunter travels to Paris to retrieve her and finds her singing in a cafe. When he learns that Velez and Madison parted company soon after their arrival in France, Hunter asks to marry her. Hunter's understated performance as the reluctant, introverted suitor saves this fairly routine film.

p, Julius Hagen; d, Miles Mander; w, Mander, Guy Bolton, H. Fowler Mear (based on the novel *The Morals of Marcus Ordeyne* by W.J. Locke); ph, Sidney Blythe; ed, Jack Harris; art d, James A. Carter; set d, Louis Brooks.

Comedy **(PR:A MPAA:NR)**

MORD UND TOTSCHLAG (SEE: DEGREE OF MURDER, A, 1969, Ger.)

MORDEI HA'OR (SEE: SANDS OF BEERSHEBA, 1966, U.S./Israel)

MORDER UNTER UNS (SEE: M, 1933, Ger.)

MORE** ½ (1969, Luxembourg) 110m Jet-Doric/Cinema V c

Mimsy Farmer *(Estelle)*, Klaus Grunberg *(Stefan)*, Heinz Engelmann *(Wolf)*, Michel Chanderli *(Charlie)*, Louise Wink *(Cathy)*, Henry Wolf *(Henry)*, Georges Montant *(Seller)*.

Increasingly archaic youth film of the late 1960s, which was the first directing effort by actor/producer Schroeder who was heavily involved in the post-New Wave cinema. MORE (presumably referring to what the 1960s youth wanted) stars Grunberg as a German college student who decides to drop out of society soon after completing his studies. He hitchhikes to Paris and meets Chanderli, a thief and gambler. Grunberg meet Farmer, an American expatriate, and despite Chanderli's warnings, falls in love. Farmer introduces Grunberg to drugs (marijuana at first) and he becomes obsessed with her free and easy manner. When she travels to Ibiza in the Mediterranean, Grunberg participates in a robbery with Chanderli to raise cash to follow her. Once on the island, Grunberg discovers Farmer living in an expensive villa with ex-Nazi-turned-drug-runner Engelmann. Soon after, Grunberg learns of Farmer's heavy drug use and a lesbian relationship with her friend, Wink. Farmer persudes Grunberg to make love to Wink and then sample some heroin. Soon Farmer and Grunberg are full-time addicts and their relationship rapidly deteriorates. After an attempt to cure themselves of their habit (by ingesting large amounts of LSD) fails, Farmer walks out leaving Grunberg to an eventual overdose that kills him. Grim and realistic, MORE was an insightful statement of concern from Schroeder as he saw his contemporaries wasted by the negative, aimless by-products of the youth counter-culture. Unfortunately, most of MORE's appeal for modern-day youth is that the popular rock band Pink Floyd performed the soundtrack music and it is often double-billed with Pink Floyd concert films at revival houses.

p, Dave Lewis, Charles Lachman; d, Barbet Schroeder; w, Paul Gegauff, Schroeder (based on a story by Schroeder); ph, Nestor Alemendros (Eastmancolor); m, Pink Floyd; ed, Denise de Casabianca; art d, Fran Lewis, Alemendros; m/l, Pink Floyd (performed by Pink Floyd).

Drama **(PR:O MPAA:NR)**

MORE AMERICAN GRAFFITI** (1979) 111m Lucasfilm/UNIV c

Candy Clark *(Debbie Dunham)*, Bo Hopkins *(Little Joe)*, Ron Howard *(Steve Bolander)*, Paul LeMat *(John Milner)*, Mackenzie Phillips *(Carol Rainbow)*, Charles Martin Smith *(Terry the Toad)*, Cindy Williams *(Laurie Bolander)*, Anna Bjorn *(Eva)*, Richard Bradford *(Maj. Creech)*, John Brent *(Ralph)*, Scott Glenn *(Newt)*, James Houghton *(Sinclair)*, John Lansing *(Lance)*, Manuel Padilla *(Carlos)*, Ken Place *(Beckwith)*, Mary Kay Place *(Teensa)*, Tom Ruben *(Eric)*, Doug Sahm *(Bobbie)*, Will Seltzer *(Andy Henderson)*, Monica Tenner *(Moonflower)*, Ralph Wilcox *(Felix)*, Carol-Ann Williams *(Vikki)*, Wolfman Jack *(Himself)*, Country Joe McDonald, Barry "the Fish" Melton, Robert Hogins, Robert Flurie, Peter Albin, Harold Aceves, Rosanna Arquette, Tom Baker, Eric Barnes, Becky Bedoy, Buzz Borelli, Ben Bottoms, Patrick Burns, Tim Burrus, George Cantero, Chet Carter, Dion Chesse, Gil Christner, Don Coughlin, Mark Courtney, Michael Courtney, Denny Delk, Frankie Di, Steve Evans, Nancy G. Fish, Rockey Flintermann, Michael Frost, Johnathan Gries, Paul Hensler, Julie Anna Hicks, Robert E. Hirschfeld, Erik Holland, Jay Jacobus, Naomi Judd, Leslie Gay Leace, Delroy Lindo, Dwight Reber, Sandra Rider, Kevin Sullivan, Morgan Upton, John Vella, Dan Woodworth, Clay Wright, Harrison Ford.

Pretty lame sequel to George Lucas' phenomenally successful AMERICAN GRAFFITI (but not directed by him) which traces most of the main characters' lives (with the Richard Dreyfuss character conspicuously absent) from the end of the first film well into the 1960s. Williams and Howard now are married and slowly being pulled into the protest movement. Le Mat is now trying to make a living drag-racing and tries to romance Bjorn, a gorgeous Swedish girl. Clark and Phillips have joined the San Francisco flower-power rock 'n' roll scene and are traveling with a band led by Glenn. This leaves Smith and Hopkins overseas and fighting in Vietnam. The idea here is to illustrate how the turbulent 1960s was able to pull a group of close-knit friends apart in so many different directions, but the film suffers from the splintered narrative. The most interesting aspect of MORE AMERICAN GRAFFITI is the visual realization. The different segments were shot in separate film processes. Split-screen, wide screen-anamorphic, 1:85 ratio and 16mm were all employed to emphasize the contrasting life-situations of the group. While this is an interesting concept, the reality is not as thrilling as the idea (the most successful is the 16mm Vietnam segments which lend a realistic air to the action, making it seem like news footage) which holds true for the film as a whole. Watch for Harrison Ford in an unbilled cameo as a motorcycle cop.

p, Howard Kazanjian; d, B.W.L. Norton; w, Norton (based on characters created by George Lucas, Gloria Katz, Willard Huyck); ph, Caleb Deschanel (Panavision, Technicolor); m, Gene Finley; ed, Tina Hirsch; art d, Ray Storey; set d, Doug Van Koss; cos, Agnes Rodgers; spec eff, Don Courtney; makeup, Don Le Page.

Drama **(PR:C MPAA:PG)**

MORE DEAD THAN ALIVE** ½ (1968) 99m UA c

Clint Walker *("Killer" Cain)*, Vincent Price *(Dan Ruffalo)*, Anne Francis *(Monica Alton)*, Paul Hampton *(Billy Eager)*, Mike Henry *(Luke Santee)*, Craig Littler *(Rafe Karma)*, Beverly Powers *(Sheree)*, Clarke Gordon *(Linus Carson)*, William Woodson *(Warden)*.

Walker stars in this fairly interesting Western about a former gunman who leaves prison after an 18-year stretch and vows to change his evil ways. Unfortunately the West has changed during his incarceration, and Walker must consider performing in a "Wild West" show run by Price (in a nice change-of-pace performance). Initially Walker refuses to degrade himself in the show and he drives a supply wagon. Once out on the trail however, Walker is ambushed and left for dead by the villainous Henry. He sought revenge against Walker after he had foiled Henry's younger brother's escape from prison. Nursed back to health by Francis, Walker agrees to join Price's company and is billed as "Killer" Cain. The younger sharpshooter, Hampton, is angered over Walker's arrival and constantly challenges the older man to shoot-outs. The fed up Walker leaves the show and settles down with Francis to run a small ranch. Meanwhile Hampton goes mad and kills Price, and then he is killed by Henry who has learned that Walker survived his ambush. Walker aids in Henry's capture and tries to begin a new life with Francis. But a man named Karma (bad, presumably) arrives at the ranch and kills Walker in revenge for a shooting Walker committed many years before.

p, Hal Klein; d, Robert Sparr; w, George Schenck; ph, Jack Marquette (DeLuxe Color); m, Philip Springer; ed, John Schreyer; art d, J. Arthur Loel; set d, William L. Kuehl; spec eff, Ralph Webb; makeup, Gary Liddiard.

Western **(PR:C MPAA:M)**

MORE DEADLY THAN THE MALE* (1961, Brit.) 60m U.N.A./Schoenfeld c

Jeremy White *(Saul Coe)*, John Mahoney *(Godfrey LeFol)*, Ann Davy *(Estelle LeFol)*, Edna Dore *(Ruth LeFol)*, Lorraine Peters *(Rita)*, Don Mason *(Narrator)*.

White is a half-crazed American traveling in London who meets Davy, who is unhappy with her marriage. White kills her husband but she ignores White. Before long, Davy kills White's girl friend then White kills Davy. In the end, he is locked in a blockhouse with the rest of his victims by Davy's dead husband's mother. White commits suicide.

p&d, Robert Bucknell; w, Paul Chevalier (based on the novel by Chevalier); ph, Bucknell (Eastmancolor); m, Louis Nordish, P. Gibbon; ed, Bucknell.

Crime/Drama **(PR:C MPAA:NR)**

MORE THAN A MIRACLE* ½

(1967, Ital./Fr.) 110m Champion-Les Films Concordia/MGM c (C'ERA UNA VOLTA; LA BELLE ET LE CAVALIER; AKA: CINDERELLA, ITALIAN STYLE, HAPPILY EVER AFTER; ONCE UPON A TIME)

Sophia Loren *(Isabella)*, Omar Sharif *(Prince Ramon)*, Dolores Del Rio *(Princess Mother)*, Georges Wilson *(Monzu)*, Leslie French *(Brother Joseph of Copertino)*, Marina Malfatti *(Devout Princess)*, Anna Nogara *(Impatient Princess)*, Rita Forzano *(Greedy Princess)*, Rosemary Martin *(Vain Princess)*, Carlotta Barilli *(Superstitious Princess)*, Fleur Mombelli *(Haughty Princess)*, Anna Liotti *(Infant Princess)*, Carla Pisacane *(Ist Witch)*, Chris Huerta *(Spanish Groom)*, Pietro Carloni *(Village Priest)*, Giovanni Tarallo *(Elderly Monk)*, Renato Pinciroli *(Prince's Chamberlain)*, Giacomo Furia *(Prior)*, Gladys Dawson, Kathleen St. John, Beatrice Greack *(Head Witches)*, Pasquale Di Napoli, Francesco Coppola, Salvatore Ruvo, Vincenzo Danaro, Luciano Di Mauro, Luigi Criscuolo, Francesco Lo Como *(Street Urchins)*, Valentino Macchi.

The picture had more name changes than Zsa Zsa Gabor but it didn't make much difference. A fairy tale in every sense of the word, it's a pleasant trifle and must have cost a fortune, but in the end, it is boring, even with Loren, at her most voluptuous, in the lead. Sharif is a prince in 17th-Century Spain and his mother, Del Rio, is after him to marry one of the septet of eligible misses they've lined up. He climbs aboard his horse and goes for a fast ride, gets tossed off the steed, and makes his way to a quiet monastery. There he meets French, a gentle friar who keeps all the local children laughing by his ability to levitate and fly around the area. Sharif asks French for help in finding the love of his life and French gives Sharif the gift of a dinky donkey and a bag of flour, plus the specific instructions that Sharif seek a woman who will make him seven dumplings. Once outside the monastery, Sharif finds his huge white stallion now being claimed by peasant girl Loren. Sharif finds her beauty breathtaking and hands her the sack of flour with the instructions that she make him seven dumplings. He eats six and she hungrily devours the seventh. Sharif pretends to be dead, then races away. Loren is terribly distressed, goes to meet with the local witches, and they give her a spell that will bring Sharif back to "life," but she forgets the words and juxtaposes them incorrectly and Sharif finds himself totally paralyzed in his castle. His men travel the area, find Loren, and bring her to the castle where she brings him back to normal with a kiss. Sharif thinks she's a witch, puts Loren into a barrel, nails it shut, and rolls it toward the sea. She is rescued by some street kids and winds up working happily in the kitchen of the castle. Sharif has been told he must choose his bride, so he gets Loren out of her rags and into some good clothes. Sharif says he will marry the woman who is the best dishwasher (thinking that Loren can't lose), but one of the other women breaks Loren's dishes with a trick. Loren is about to kill herself when the ghost of French appears and talks her out of drowning and sends her back to the castle. Loren and Sharif are united when she is able to expose the trickery of her rival. The picture swings between reality and fantasy and doesn't truly satisfy in either department. There's also just a bit too much of politics tossed into the script. Most of that will go over the heads of the tykes they hoped this film would appeal to but it did stick in the craws of adults. Loren's cleavage is so low that there's little left to the imagination, a blatant, tasteless bustline that fills the screen instead of story.

p, Carlo Ponti; d, Francesco Rosi; w, Tonino Guerra, Raffaele La Capria, Giuseppe Patroni Griffi, Rosi (based on a story by Guerra); ph, Pasquale De Santis (Franscope, Technicolor); m, Piero Piccioni; ed, Jolanda Benvenuti; art d, Piero Poletto; cos, Giulio Coltellacci; m/l, "More Than a Miracle," Piccioni, Larry Kusik, Eddie Synder (performed by Roger Williams Chorus and Orchestra); makeup, Giuseppe Annunziata, Ada Palombi, Mario Van Riel.

Fantasy (PR:O MPAA:NR)

MORE THAN A SECRETARY** (1936) 77m COL bw

Jean Arthur (*Carol Baldwin*), George Brent (*Fred Gilbert*), Lionel Stander (*Ernest*), Ruth Donnelly (*Helen Davis*), Reginald Denny (*Bill Houston*), Dorothea Kent (*Maizie West*), Charles Halton (*Mr. Crosby*), Geraldine Hall (*Enid*), Charles Irwin (*Mounted Policeman*), Myra Marsh (*Sour-Faced Woman*), Ann Meril (*Betty*), William Bartlett (*Contortionist*), Tom Ricketts (*Henry*), Josephine McKim (*Gladys*), Dorothy Short (*Ann*), Francis Sayles (*Waiter*), Nick Copeland, C.L. Sherwood (*Window Washers*), Frances Morris (*Clerk*), George Hickman (*Office Boy*), Joy Kendell (*Telephone Girl*), Cyril Ring, Ralph McCullough (*Department Heads*), Lily Stewart (*Woman*), William Wagner (*Man*).

Dumb comedy saved by the presence of Arthur who plays the plain-Jane secretary at a health magazine company who competes with dim-witted blonde Kent for the affections of their boss, Brent. Eventually Arthur lets her hair down and wows the boss. Routine stuff.

p, Everett Riskin; d, Alfred E. Green; w, Dale Van Every, Ethel Hill, Aben Kandel, Lyn Starling (based on the story "Safari in Manhattan" by Matt Taylor); ph, Henry Freulich; ed, Al Clark; md, Morris Stoloff; cos, Bernard Newman.

Comedy (PR:A MPAA:NR)

MORE THE MERRIER, THE ***½ (1943) 104m COL bw

Jean Arthur (*Connie Milligan*), Joel McCrea (*Joe Carter*), Charles Coburn (*Benjamin Dingle*), Richard Gaines (*Charles J. Pendergast*), Bruce Bennett (*Evans*), Frank Sully (*Pike*), Clyde Fillmore (*Sen. Noonan*), Stanley Clements (*Morton Rodakiewicz*), Don Douglas (*Harding*), Ann Savage (*Miss Dalton*), Grady Sutton (*Waiter*), Sugar Geise (*Dancer*), Don Barclay, Frank Sully (*Drunks*), Shirley Patterson (*Girl*), Ann Doran (*Miss Bilby*), Mary Treen (*Waitress*), Gladys Blake (*Barmaid*), Kay Linaker (*Miss Allen*), Nancy Gray (*Miss Chasen*), Byron Shores (*Air Corps Captain*), Betzi Beaton (*Miss Finch*), Harrison Greene (*Texan*), Robert McKenzie (*Southerner*), Vic Potel (*Cattleman*), Lon Poff (*Character*), Frank LaRue, Douglas Wood (*Senators*), Harry Bradley (*Minister*), Betty McMahan (*Miss Geeskin*), Helen Holmes (*Dumpy Woman*), Marshall Ruth (*Fat Statistician*), Hal Gerard (*2nd Statistician*), Henry Roquemore (*Reporter*), Jack Carr (*Taxi Driver*), Chester Clute (*Hotel Clerk*), Robert F. Hill (*Head Waiter*), Eddy Chandler (*Police Captain*), Peggy Carroll (*Dancer*), George Reed (*Caretaker*), Kitty McHugh (*Taxi Driver*).

A delightful and effervescent comedy marked with terrific performances. The film takes its cue from a simple (and true) premise: during WW II there is a significant housing shortage on the Washington, D.C. home front. Also in short supply is a substantial number of single young men, a fact that frustrates the city's female population. Arthur is a single woman who lives by herself in a tiny apartment. To do her part in alleviating housing problems, Arthur sublets half of the place to Coburn. The old gentleman is an affable roommate but is distressed to see Arthur without some male companionship of her own age. Coburn decides its his duty to fix her up with some nice young man, so he sets out on D.C.'s streets to find a suitable prospect. Eventually he meets McCrea, an Air Force mechanic in Washington to pick up some orders for a special assignment. Coburn rents McCrea half of *his* space and of course all sorts of slapstick complications ensue. Though there are plenty of fights over privacy and space in the quickly shrinking apartment, Coburn is able to rise above the mayhem. His Cupid role, albeit self-appointed, is successful. Before they realize what is going on Arthur and McCrea fall in love, uniting in marriage at the story's end. In lesser hands, this lighter-than-air farce could easily have gone flat, but under Stevens' skilled direction the three spirited leads pull it off and then some. Using the small confines of the set with precision, Stevens builds up the tension (and thus laughter) between the Coburn-crossed lovers with a marvelous series of perfectly timed scenes. Like the characters in their cramped confines, situations seem to stumble into one another, building up to a slapstick frenzied pitch. This was Stevens' last film before he entered the service himself, serving as a major in his position with the Army Signal Corps film unit. Arthur and McCrea play off each other in a fine display of comic acting. They shoot off the rapid-fire dialog well, never losing a punch line in the process. As the amiable and well-meaning Mr. Dingle, Coburn is nothing short of superb, stealing scene after scene with astonishing ease. Despite the constant pitfalls, he is able to work his matchmaking scheme with one of the most charming performances put on film. The Hollywood community

certainly agreed with that, awarding Coburn an Oscar in 1943 as Best Supporting Actor. Also receiving nominations were Arthur as Best Actress, Stevens for direction, Flournoy, Foster, Ross, and Russell for the screenplay, as well as a Best Picture nomination. Uncredited for his contribution to the screenplay was Garson Kanin, who came up with this script specifically to suit Arthur's comedic talents. Stevens was considerably impressed with Arthur, later remarking that she was "one of the greatest comediennes the screen has ever seen." THE MORE THE MERRIER often resembles a Frank Capra comedy in its situation and approach. Arthur, of course, had starred in several of Capra's social comedies in the late 1930s and there are a few references to those films here. However THE MORE THE MERRIER is certainly strong enough to stand on its own merits, a fine example of farce at its best. In 1966 this was remade as WALK, DON'T RUN.

p&d, George Stevens; w, Robert Russell, Frank Ross, Richard Flournoy, Lewis R. Foster (based on a story by Russell, Ross, Garson Kanin); ph, Ted Tetzlaff; m, Leigh Harline; ed, Otto Meyer; md, Morris W. Stoloff; art d, Lionel Banks, Rudolph Sternad; set d, Ray Babcock; m/l, "Damn the Torpedoes," Henry Myers, Edward Eliscu, Jay Gorney.

Comedy (PR:A MPAA:NR)

MORGAN!***

(1966, Brit.) 97m Quintra/Cinema V bw (GB: MORGAN: A SUITABLE CASE FOR TREATMENT; A SUITABLE CASE FOR TREATMENT)

Vanessa Redgrave (*Leonie Delt*), David Warner (*Morgan Delt*), Robert Stephens (*Charles Napier*), Irene Handl (*Mrs. Delt*), Newton Blick (*Mr. Henderson*), Nan Munro (*Mrs. Henderson*), Bernard Bresslaw (*Policeman*), Arthur Mullard (*Wally*), Graham Crowden (*Counsel*), Peter Cellier (*2nd Counsel*), John Rae (*Judge*), Angus MacKay (*Best Man*), Peter Collingwood, John Garrie, Marvis Edwards, Robert Bridges.

In the late 1950s and early 1960s, British films were densely populated with angry young men. In the case of MORGAN!, the young man is not only angry, he's crazier than a bedbug in BEDLAM, the British mental institution. By altering the nature of the role from the original TV play, they have attempted to say that anything is okay on screen if the leading character is whacked-out. Using that as a basis, all morality is tossed out the window and we are asked to accept the lead as he stands, or not. By 1980's standards, this picture is somewhat dated as the technique often overwhelms the story and we become tired of innumerable slow-motion shots, freeze frames, and surrealism for surrealism's sake. Warner (then only 24 and having only one film credit to speak of in TOM JONES) is a London artist married to Redgrave, a woman considerably above his working-class beginnings. He spends his time daydreaming about swinging through the jungle (and they use clips from KING KONG [1933] to make that point as well as a piece out of one of the TARZAN movies). His mother, Handl, is an ardent old Communist who spends lots of time at Karl Marx's grave. (Marx, in case you didn't know it, is buried in Highgate Cemetery in England.) Handl adores her son but feels he has betrayed his role in "The Great Revolution" by marrying Redgrave. Regrave secures a divorce and Warner, who was supposedly in Greece, shows up on the day it is to be granted and asks to be taken back by her. He doesn't want her to leave him and marry priggish Stephens, an art dealer who is closer to her in social status. Redgrave still adores Warner but she knows he's nuts and she is tired of being the Jane to his Tarzan. Warner will stop at nothing to get Redgrave to return to him and the middle of the picture concerns his tactics in that regard. He hides in her car, does some electronic work on their house so noise erupts when Redgrave and Stephens hug, he puts a real skeleton in her bed, and draws the hammer and sickle insignia on the furniture. He also puts a bomb under the bed to try and get Stephens out of Redgrave's life. None of it seems to help. He goes so far as to sleep with her one night when she wavers on her pledge to leave him. Eventually, with the help of Mullard, a wrestler, he kidnaps Redgrave, but she is saved by her parents, Munro and Blick. Warner is put in jail on Redgrave's testimony and released on the same day when she is to wed Stephens. Warner puts on a gorilla suit, crashes into the wedding reception, and winds up on fire. He is then pursued as he rides a motorcycle and winds up at the Thames. In his ravings, he thinks that he's being put up against a wall to face a firing squad which includes Redgrave, Stephens, and Handl. Finally, he is in an asylum and Redgrave, very pregnant, comes to visit him. He wonders if the child she's carrying is the result of their one brief liaison. She smiles enigmatically, gives the most subtle of nods, and walks away. Warner turns back to the garden he's been tending. It's all been reshaped into the form of a hammer and sickle. They attempted to blend reality and fantasy and it sometimes worked, but the truth was that Warner's character was certifiable and did deserve to be incarcerated before he did himself, or someone else, harm. It's bizarre, too heavy in places, and not light enough in others. The picture was released in England as MORGAN: A SUITABLE CASE FOR TREATMENT. Director Reisz, a Czech who was once married to actress Betsy Blair (who was once married to Gene Kelly, but that's another story), has made some fascinating pictures with SATURDAY NIGHT AND SUNDAY MORNING, THE GAMBLER, and WHO'LL STOP THE RAIN. This one tried so hard to be interesting that you can feel the effort in every frame.

p, Leon Clore; d, Karel Reisz; w, David Mercer (based on his television play *A Suitable Case for Treatment*); ph, Larry Pizer, Gerry Turpin; m, John Dankworth; ed, Victor Proctor, Tom Priestley; art d, Philip Harrison.

Comedy/Drama Cas. (PR:C MPAA:NR)

MORGAN THE PIRATE**

(1961, Fr./Ital.) 95m C.C.F. Lux-Lux Film-Adelphia Compagnia Cinematografica/MGM c (CAPITAINE MORGAN; MORGAN IL PIRATA)

Steve Reeves (*Sir Henry Morgan*), Valerie Lagrange (*Dona Inez*), Chelo Alonso (*Concepcion*), Lidia Alfonsi (*Dona Maria*), Armand Mestral (*L'Olannais*), Ivo Garrani (*The Governor*), Giulio Bosetti (*Sir Thomas Modyford*), Giorgio Ardisson

(Walter), Angelo Zanolli *(David)*, Dino Malacrida *(The Duke)*, Anita Todesco, Mimmo Poli.

Muscle-man Reeves stars as the title swashbuckler in this fairly well-made adventure film detailing the life of the famed pirate, beginning with his enslavement by the Spaniards in Panama. He is soon sold to Lagrange, who is the daughter of the governor, and he falls in love with her. As punishment for his insolence, Reeves is sent off to a life of hard labor on board a Spanish galleon. Eventually Reeves leads a mutiny and becomes a pirate raiding the Spanish for the British. Not satisfied, Reeves pushes on to Panama where he gets his revenge on the governor by capturing the capital city and the heart of his daughter. Fast-paced and nicely produced.

d, Primo Zeglio, Andre De Toth; w, Filippo Sanjust, Zeglio, De Toth; ph, Tonino Delli Colli (CinemaScope, Eastmancolor); m, Franco Mannireo; ed, Maurizio Lucidi, Cesare Cavagna; md, Mannireo; set d, Gianni Polidori, Renato Cardone; cos, Sanjust; spec eff, Eros Bacciucchi.

Adventure **(PR:A MPAA:NR)**

MORGAN'S MARAUDERS 1/2** (1929) 69m Distinctive bw

Margaret Livingston *(Capt. Lucy Morgan)*, Vivienne Osborne *(Patcheye)*, Dorothy Nolan *(Spunky)*, Ella Scott *(Gimp)*, Irene Dennis *(Howdy)*, Randall Bennett *(Ned)*, Don Ward *(Herman)*, Michele Hart *(Dolly)*.

Even back in the first creaky days of sound films, they were already doing spoofs of certain genres. In this case, it's a bounding main comedy but with a different twist: the pirates are all females and they prey on Caribbean vessels run by men. No sooner do they use their grappling hooks and overtake the ships, than they board, unscabbard their sabres and subdue the men who are either too stunned or too chivalrous to put up a fight. Once the men are captured, they are taken to the pirate's island, a small but comfortable atoll in the Dry Tortugas, where they are kept as prisoners to give the tired pirates balm and solace. Livingston is the daughter of the infamous Morgan, the pirate. But the scalawag had no sons to carry on the family's bad name so he trained his daughter in the lore of the skull and crossbones. She's assembled a motley crew of women who have been widowed or tossed aside by men and they are wreaking revenge by attacking ships and kidnaping the sailors. You won't believe any of it for a second but that's the way it's meant to be and the cliched old lines like 'avast there' and 'I'll keelhaul ye' become very funny in the lipsticked mouths of these salt-water daffies. There are all the usual pirate characters; Osborne wears a patch but can't remember which eye she's had it on before (it's just for effect), Nolan is the ship's cook and is always attempting new and bizarre recipes for the crew, Scott walks with a limp as the result of giving herself a bad pedicure, et al. Hart was 13 when she made the movie and does the distaff version of the boy played by Freddie Bartholomew many years later in CAPTAIN COURAGEOUS (1937). In the end, the men show the women the folly of their ways and when Ward and Bennett turn out to be the king's agents in disguise, they are almost burned at the stake until the two women, Livingston and Osborne, realize that they'd rather be knitting and tending a home than sailing the seven seas. It's all amiable nonsense and there are hardly any alterations from the standard pirate story. What makes it so funny is the role-switching, which goes to show that even the most hackneyed story can be made to look different if re-thought.

d, Fred Newmeyer; w, Mary C. McCall, Jr; ph, Fred S. Fitzgerald; ed, Joseph Seide; art d, Leib Rosenblum; set d, Judy Young; stunts, G.B. Biller.

Comedy **(PR:A MPAA:NR)**

MORITURI ***

(1965) 128m Arcola-Colony/FOX bw (AKA: THE SABOTEUR: CODE NAME MORITURI; THE SABOTEUR)

Marlon Brando *(Robert Crain)*, Yul Brynner *(Capt. Muller)*, Janet Margolin *(Esther)*, Trevor Howard *(Col. Statter)*, Martin Benrath *(Kruse)*, Hans Christian Blech *(Donkeyman)*, Wally Cox *(Dr. Ambach)*, Max Haufler *(Branner)*, Rainer Penkert *(Milkereit)*, William Redfield *(Baldwin)*, Oscar Beregi *(Admiral)*, Martin Brandt *(Nissen)*, Gary Crosby *(Ens. Sloan)*, Charles DeVries *(Kurz)*, Carl Esmond *(Busch)*, Martin Kosleck *(Wilke)*, Norbert Schiller *(Steward)*, Robert Sorrells *(German Crew Member)*, Rick Traeger *(Crew Member)*, Ivan Triesault *(Lt. Brandt)*, Robert Wilke *(Cdr. Kelling)*, Henry Hermann-Cattani *(Walzenredt)*, Robert Kino *(Capt. Hatsuma)*, Eric Braiden *(Radio Operator)*, Manfred Lating *(Lutz)*, Dr. Harold Dyrenforth *(Cornelson)*, Wilhelm Von Homburg, Paul Baxley, Henry Rowland, Roy Sickner, Gunter Weishoff, Norbert Siegfried, Heinz Brinkmann, Rick Weber *(Crew Members)*, Tommy Webb, Marvin Press, Sam Javis, Eugene Dynarski, John Logan, Harold Goodwin, David Manley, Gregg Barton, Hal Bokar, Frank London, James Goodwin, Buck Kartalian, Roy Jenson, Rusty Wescoatt *(Members of U.S. Merchant Marine)*, Rollin Moriyama *(Japanese Tug Pilot)*, George Takei *(Junior Officer)*, Gil Stuart, Keith McConnell *(Englishmen)*, John Regis *(Crewman)*, William White *(Williams)*, George Zaima *(Executive Officer)*.

Brynner is a German seaman assigned by the Nazis to deliver a cargo of much-needed rubber from Japan to occupied France. Though the politically neutral Brynner feels the assignment is foolish, he is overruled. The ship—partly crewed by political prisoners of the Nazi government—prepares for the voyage, a mission fervently supported by Brynner's first officer, Benrath. Brando plays a wealthy deserter from the German army, now living in India under the guise of a Swiss national. He is approached by Howard, a British Intelligence man, who threatens Brando with exposure unless he goes undercover for the British war effort. Brando is assigned to pose as an SS observer aboard Brynner's ship where he can be instrumental in helping the British capture the vessel. While aboard, he must disconnect the explosives the Germans have set up to destroy the craft in the event of its capture. Brando undertakes the mission, leaving Howard with the salutation "morituri te salutant," a phrase once used by Roman gladiators meaning "we who are about to die salute you." Brynner takes an immediate dislike to Brando once he is aboard ship, believing this new man to be a German officer sent to spy on him. Nazi fanatic Benrath, however, sees an ally in Brando, not knowing this would-be-SS officer is actually using him to help fulfil his secret mission. Brando tricks Benrath into revealing where the explosives have been hidden, then disarms all but one. When the ship emerges from a thick fog they discover a British fleet dangerously nearby. However a group of Japanese submarines intervenes, allowing the German vessel to get safely by. Later some American POWs and Margolin, a German Jew, are transferred to Brynner's ship. Brando confides in the woman and asks for her help to enlist the Americans for aid in a mutiny. She does so, but must offer herself in a gang rape in order to gain the Americans' cooperation. Soon afterwards a radio broadcast informs the ship of Brando's identity. The mutiny begins, but because the Nazi loyalists are better organized, Brando's plans are doomed. Margolin is killed in the onslaught by Benrath but Brando manages to escape, ending up in Brynner's cabin. He tries to convince the Germans to retake command rather than let Benrath hold control of the ship. Brynner refuses so Brando decides to blow the remaining explosives stowed in the ship's refrigeration hold. When the crew begins abandoning the crippled freighter, Brando once more confronts the captain, wondering why Brynner holds such loyalty to the Nazi cause he so clearly despises. Brando plugs the ship's ripped hold with lard, trying to give himself just a few more hours to successfully complete the mission. Once more he appeals to Brynner, asking him to radio a nearby allied vessel. Though Brynner is initially hesitant, the film's closing frames show the crippled ship against soundtrack revealing a radio key clicking. Brando and Brynner both give strong performances, complementing each other's role like two sides of the same coin. Though some critics felt the part was a bad career move for Brando, he comes off well with his driven character. MORITURI is a handsome looking film, photographed in black and white with often stunning effect by Hall. Unfortunately the work as a whole is not what it could have been, a victim (like so many other films) of various misunderstandings and indifferences. Brando and producer Rosenberg had previously worked together on MUTINY ON THE BOUNTY (1962) where the two had more than a few disagreements. That they would work again on a film involving mutiny surprised many in Hollywood. Despite Rosenberg's pleas that the project be allowed a three-month shooting schedule, studio executives insisted on a two month deadline. The production consequently ran over budget and well past the original schedule. Wicki, a German director working for the first time in Hollywood, found the situation to be nearly beyond his breaking point. Unlike the smaller-crewed filmmaking operations in his native country, Wicki found himself face-to-face with the conglomerate powers of the California movie business. Brando also proved to be a problem, though his issues involved the artistic ends rather than the monetary. Both he and Wicki believed in studied work, taking the proper amount of time needed to get the best each man could offer. However, even the meticulous star found Wicki's method of numerous takes (often as many as twenty) to be far beyond what was needed. For all the problems the studio raised with Wicki about money and budgets, Rosenberg did manage to get hold of an authentic merchant vessel circa 1938 to serve as Brynner's ship. A 540-foot Scottish vessel was found docked in Yokohama harbor and was subsequently chartered to California where the film was to be shot. Eighty thousand dollars were put into the creation of an authentic looking Japanese submarine, a remarkable replica built entirely of plywood. MORITURI was inspired by the fictionalized memoirs of a German part-Jew who was stationed as a naval attache in Tokyo during WW II until his heritage was discovered by authorities. He was returned to Germany on a freighter similar to the one portrayed here and was subsequently sent to the Russian front as part of his ethnic-transgression punishment. Appearing in a secondary role as a doctor is Cox, a friend of Brando's from childhood. Cox was having trouble with his career at the time so his close friend was able to get him cast in the film, a practice Brando was known for doing with friends down on their luck. Despite the various production problems, MORITURI is still a film of some interest. The psychological theme of divided loyalties is well-handled, with the everpresent spectre of unsettling things always hovering below. Its portrait of Germans was certainly a realistic one, going well beyond the Nazi stereotypes that were all too prevalent in Hollywood films.

p, Aaron Rosenberg; d, Bernhard Wicki; w, Daniel Taradash (based on the novel by Werne Joerg Luedecke); ph, Conrad Hall; m, Jerry Goldsmith; ed, Joseph Silver; art d, Jack Martin Smith, Herman A. Blumenthal; set d, Walter M. Scott, Jerry Wunderlich; cos, Moss Mabry; spec eff, L.B. Abbott, Emil Kosa, Jr.; makeup, Ben Nye.

Drama **(PR:C MPAA:NR)**

MORNING CALL

(SEE: STRANGE CASE OF DR. MANNING, THE, 1958, Brit.)

MORNING DEPARTURE (SEE: OPERATION DISASTER, 1951, Brit.)

MORNING GLORY*** (1933) 74m RKO bw

Katharine Hepburn *(Eva Lovelace)*, Douglas Fairbanks, Jr. *(Joseph Sheridan)*, Adolphe Menjou *(Louis Easton)*, Mary Duncan *(Rita Vernon)*, C. Aubrey Smith *(Robert Harley Hedges)*, Don Alvarado *(Pepe Velez, the Gigolo)*, Fred Santley *(Will Seymour)*, Richard Carle *(Henry Lawrence)*, Tyler Brooke *(Charles Van Dusen)*, Geneva Mitchell *(Gwendolyn Hall)*, Helen Ware *(Nellie Navarre)*, Theresa Harris *(Maid)*, Jed Prouty *(Seymour)*, Robert Greig *(Roberts)*.

Hepburn received her first Oscar nomination for this, her third film, and won the Oscar for her role, and she was three times as good as the picture itself. The story paralleled Hepburn's own real-life experiences so there was an undeniable streak of reality in her performance. Hepburn leaves a tiny burg in New England. She enters New York City as stagestruck as is humanly possible but she soon learns that there are a lot of worms in the Big Apple and it's not the most hospitable place to seek fame and fortune. She encounters veteran actor Smith, who has been around since stages were lit by candles, and he takes an interest in her, teaches her a few tricks about acting, and squires her to the right parties. He brings her to a cocktail bash tossed by Duncan, a successful actress and neurotic woman in the Margo Channing (Bette Davis' role in ALL ABOUT EVE) mold. Hepburn hasn't eaten anything so she gets very drunk on champagne and performs two Shakespearean soliloquies for the sake of the startled party-goers. Later, Hepburn takes up with slick Menjou, a manager, then tosses him aside in favor of young playwright Fairbanks, who has written a new show that Duncan is to star in. When the actress goes off the deep end and leaves the show on opening night, guess who steps in, does the role, and is an overnight sensation? By the story outline, it's easy to see where ALL ABOUT EVE got some of its characters and/or inspiration. The young actress, the older and temperamental star, the playwright, the manager . . . it should be evident. The picture was remade as STAGE STRUCK with Susan Strasberg as the aspiring hopeful and Henry Fonda and Christopher Plummer as the men in her life. That sequel was not as successful as this one, which was only raised in entertainment value by Hepburn's glowing performance. By 1933, the combination of backstage manipulations and overnight success was already a cliche that had been covered many times before. Merian C. Cooper served as the executive producer, and if that seems familiar, it's because he was also responsible for such films as THE FOUR FEATHERS, KING KONG, FORT APACHE, MIGHTY JOE YOUNG, THE QUIET MAN, and many more.

p, Pandro S. Berman; d, Lowell Sherman; w, Howard J. Green (based on a play by Zoe Akins); ph, Bert Glennon; m, Max Steiner; ed, George Nicholls, Jr.; art d, Van Nest Polglase, Charles Kirk cos, Walter Plunkett; makeup, Mel Burns.

Drama **Cas.** **(PR:C MPAA:NR)**

MORNING STAR**

(1962, USSR) 75m Lenfilm-Frunze/Artkino c (CHOLPON—UTRENNYAYA ZVEZDA)

Reina Chokoyeva *(Cholpon)*, Uran Sarbagishev *(Nurdfin)*, Nikolay Tugelov *(Temir Khan)*, Bibisara Beyshenaliyeva *(Ayday)*, S. Abduzhalilov *(Genie)*, Kirgiz State Opera Corps de Ballet, The Leningrad Philharmonic Orchestra.

A filmed ballet which tells the legend of a pair of lovers and their attempts to make romance work even though they are from different classes and are being harassed by an evil sorceress whose kiss can turn people to stone.

d, Roman Tikhomirov; w, I. Menaker, Nikolay Tugelov, Apollinariy Dudko, Tikhomirov (based on the story by I. Glickman from the ballet by Mikhail Rafailovich Raukhverger, L. Kramarevskiy, O. Sarbagishev); ph, Dudko; m, Raukhverger (performed by the Leningrad Philharmonic); ed, I. Glickman; art d, A. Blek; spec eff, A. Zavyalov, G. Senotov, M, Krotkin; makeup, V. Goryunov; ballet master, Tugelov.

Dance **(PR:A MPAA:NR)**

MORO WITCH DOCTOR*

(1964, U.S./Phil.) 61m Associated Producers-Hemisphere/FOX bw (AKA: AMOK)

Jock Mahoney *(Jefferson Stark)*, Margia Dean *(Paula Cameron)*, Pancho Magalona *(Martin Gonzaga)*, Reed Hadley *(Robert Collins)*, Paraluman *(Selisa Noble)*, Michael Parsons *(Ackerman)*, Dale Ishimoto *(Manuel Romblon)*, Vic Diaz *(Salek)*, Jay Ilagan *(Mahmud)*, Bruno Punzalan *(Datu Sumlang)*, Nemia Velasco *(Mulan)*, Jerry Uslander *(Tom Cameron)*, Paul Edwards, Jr. *(Arthur Kruger)*, Jess Montalban, Paquito Salcedo, Bill Kane.

Good-for-laughs B picture about the seedy world of drug smuggling, starring Mahoney as an Interpol agent sent to the Philippines to investigate an opium plantation where two Americans were murdered. Aided by Dean, the sister of one of the victims, Mahoney soon discovers a giant gun and drug-smuggling ring led by religious fanatic Punzalan, who turns the island into a living hell of death and destruction when he orders his followers to go on the rampage. It is finally revealed that Dean's brother's partner, Edwards, Jr. is behind the whole operation and when he is killed things get back to normal.

p, Eddie Romero; d, Romero, Gerardo de Leon; w, Romero; ph, Felipe Sacdalan; m, Ariston Avelino; ed, Joven Calub; art d, Vincente Bonus; spec eff, Santos Hilario; makeup, Remy Amazan.

Drama **(PR:C MPAA:NR)**

MOROCCO****

(1930) 90m PAR bw

Gary Cooper *(Tom Brown)*, Marlene Dietrich *(Amy Jolly)*, Adolphe Menjou *(Le Bessier)*, Ullrich Haupt *(Adjutant Caesar)*, Juliette Compton *(Anna Dolores)*, Francis McDonald *(Cpl. Tatoche)*, Albert Conti *(Col. Quinnevieres)*, Eve Southern *(Mme. Caesar)*, Michael Visaroff *(Barratire)*, Paul Porcasi *(Lo Tinto)*, Theresa Harris *(Camp Follower)*, Emile Chautard *(Officer)*, Harry Schultz *(German Sergeant)*.

One of the most stylistically perfect films every produced, MOROCCO is all magnificent detail and illusion, spun by that master of mystique, von Sternberg, and exemplified by Dietrich in her first American-made film, following her stupendous European success with THE BLUE ANGEL. Where Dietrich decimated Emil Jannings in THE BLUE ANGEL, she is humbled, if not humiliated, by Cooper in MOROCCO into blurting her undying love for him. Dietrich is a nighclub singer en route by ship to Morocco. On board is the suave and sophisticated Menjou, who offers Dietrich any kind of "assistance" she may require in a new and strange city. Dietrich no sooner arrives in Morocco than she lands a job as the headline singer in the best cafe where the elite gather and mix with officers and enlisted men of the French Foreign Legion. When Dietrich appears before the cafe crowd she is met with unruly revelers but the noise abates quickly as she begins to sing "What Am I Bid for My Apples?" (Karl Hajos, Leo Robin), selling an apple to the highest bidder as she sings. Menjou, who is obviously enthralled by Dietrich, motions her toward him, but she taunts him and shocks the audience by turning to a woman, stroking her hair, and then planting a kiss on her mouth. Snaking her way through the crowd, Dietrich encounters Cooper sitting at a table with a group of fellow legionnaires. Broke, he borrows enough francs to buy an apple from the singer, who makes change and also hands him a key to her apartment. Cooper shows up later in Dietrich's boudoir but seems almost indifferent to her torrid advances, then tells her laconically: "I met you ten years too late." He returns her key, shocking her, and leaves. Dietrich regains her composure, although this is obviously a new experience; she has never before been turned down, and she races after the man who has rejected her. Cooper makes his way back to his barracks but spots Southern standing in the shadows. She is the wife of the adjutant and has a deep passion for Cooper, having followed him to Dietrich's place. Dietrich appears and sees Southern and Cooper together but the married woman quickly vanishes into the shadows. Her husband, Haupt, suddenly appears looking for his wife and finds Cooper and Dietrich. He orders both of them to come to his office the next morning. When they arrive, Dietrich and Cooper find Menjou with Haupt. Cooper explains that he was with Dietrich, not Haupt's wife Southern, and Dietrich confirms this. Menjou intercedes for Dietrich and asks Haupt to let her off, which he does. Cooper, however, is sent on a perilous mission. He goes to Dietrich's dressing room at the cafe before leaving on patrol and talks about quitting the Legion, but when Dietrich returns to her dressing room she finds Cooper has gone, leaving a note scribbled on her mirror: "I changed my mind. Good luck." In Cooper's absence, and taking advantage of Dietrich's anger at once more being rejected by the Legionnaire, Menjou proposes to the cabaret singer and she quickly accepts. Menjou gives a posh party at his lavish estate to celebrate his engagement to Dietrich but his intended hears the marching feet of the Legion troops entering the city and runs outside to find one of Cooper's friends, McDonald, who tells her that her distant lover is probably dead. Dietrich frantically searches hospitals but cannot find Cooper, but when she goes into a cheap dive she finds him with Compton, a floozy. The recalcitrant lover tells Dietrich he's no longer interested in her and dismisses her but, as she is about to go, she notices that he's been carving her name on the top of the wooden table. She leaves and, at dawn, Dietrich sees the legionnaires preparing to leave the city. Dietrich notices a group of women huddled near the main gate and she asks Menjou what they are doing there. He tells her that these women are camp followers of the Legion, that they follow their men wherever they go on military campaigns. The soldiers march out of the city and into the desert. Dietrich walks to the main gate on high-heeled shoes. She stops and watches the troops and the camp followers go into the desert. Then, with winds whipping sand in her face, she removes her shoes and resolutely walks after them, determined to be with her man Cooper at any price. MOROCCO is splendidly acted and directed, with Dietrich enacting the ultimate *femme fatale*, unpredictable and utterly exotic, a mesmerizing performance that rocked American viewers seeing her for the first time. Cooper, on the other hand—who had already begun to establish himself as the American pie hero—does a huge back-step here as a manipulative lover who has scenes he would never again repeat, putting a rose behind his ear, using a fan to hide a kiss he gives Dietrich, smoking cigarettes with the limp wrist of a dilettante, an almost fey essay. Much of this turnabout posing had to do with Cooper's resentment of von Sternberg who lavished his attention on Dietrich, his German film star discovery, spending endless hours on her setup shots and lighting that would bathe her in soft light, increasing her image of mystery. Cooper was ignored by the director, who disliked Paramount's insistence that he be billed equally with Dietrich; he would later vainly demand to have Cooper's name dropped to the very bottom of the cast listing. Von Sternberg showed his indifference to Cooper by at first directing all of Dietrich's scenes in German, then using his native tongue when directing Cooper who, of course, did not understand a word. When von Sternberg was laboring over a particular delicate scene with his protege Dietrich, instructing her in German, he suddenly heard a purposely loud yawn from the male star. He turned on Cooper who was sitting nearby, appearing drowsy, and flashed an angry glare. "Iv you are schleepy you can go to ze home," snarled von Sternberg. Cooper gave him a jut-jawed look and snapped back: "Oh, no, it's just that this is America and we don't understand this kraut talk!" Von Sternberg seethed at the remark, clenching his fists and stomping about before he finally shouted: "Every von go home! Ve vill not vork anymore today. I haf been inzulted and I vant to dink dis ovah!" When the director once more called the cast together, he spoke English, forsaking his native tongue for the remainder of the film, at the behest of Paramount's front office. None of this affected Cooper's relationship with Dietrich, which was pleasant throughout the making of MOROCCO. This reportedly blossomed into an affair that continued on and off for some time. Following this film, Dietrich took up with fading silent film star John Gilbert and lobbied for his appearance as her co-star in her upcoming movie, DESIRE, another von Sternberg film. Dietrich moved in with Gilbert and coached him through his lines, persuading him to cut down on his alcoholic intake and even devising new lighting techniques that would shade the lines on his face which a decade of hard drinking had implanted. During Dietrich's nursing of the once-stellar male screen lover, Gilbert's one great love, Greta Garbo, suddenly drove up to his house. Gilbert, like a schoolboy, slavishly ran outside to excitedly greet the woman with whom he had shared screen glories during the silent era. Dietrich watched from a window, then, utterly humiliated, ran out of Gilbert's house, using the back door. Dietrich went back to Cooper; Gilbert, abandoned by both Garbo and Dietrich, went back to the bottle. According to Gilbert's daughter Leatrice, "Marlene was unable to resist Gary Cooper. The moment father found out, he went to pieces again, and didn't stop drinking until the day he died." That day came twenty-four hours after Cooper was announced as Dietrich's co-star in the upcoming film DESIRE. Reading the announcement in a local Hollywood paper, Gilbert took another stiff drink and dropped dead of a heart attack. Not since Garbo had Hollywood groomed an actress for superstardom as Paramount and von Sternberg did with Dietrich. She had finished THE BLUE ANGEL, which was the sensation of Europe, but the film was held up in release in the U.S. until Paramount could produce an American film and present their new star as an "American" product. Von Sternberg, meanwhile, set severe standards for Dietrich. He ordered her eyebrows shaved, with pencil-thin and widely arching eyebrows to replace the old, making her eyes even more expressive. She was placed on a strict diet and given hourly massages until her waist was trimmed, along with her famous legs. Von

Sternberg then ordered her legs wrapped tightly with surgical bandages, especially about the ankles, to redistribute small amounts of fat. It was during this period that Dietrich began wearing slacks to hide the bandages, even to special and important functions where she was widely photographed, and inadvertently created a fashion trend that swept the nation. Her intense diet caused her cheeks to hollow slightly which gave rise to the canard that she had had her back teeth pulled for appearance's sake, a gossipy untruth. Sternberg and Paramount then came up with Dietrich's first American vehicle, which was at first entitled AMY JOLLY, THE WOMAN OF MARRAKESH, but co-star Cooper fought against this, saying that such a title would put too much focus on Dietrich. Furthman was assigned to write a screenplay from the novel by Berlin newsman Vigny, which had reportedly been based on his personal experiences in the French Foreign Legion. It was retitled MOROCCO, and when it first went into production, von Sternberg gave master cinematographer Garmes instructions to light Dietrich only from one side, but the cameraman soon realized that all he was doing was creating an image in the likeness of Garbo and so, without telling the volatile von Sternberg, he created what he later termed "north light," which accented both sides of Dietrich's face, emphasizing the actress' cheekbones, her large heavy-lidded eyes, and the sweeping eyebrows penciled above them. Von Sternberg obviously knew what Garmes was doing and said nothing, but approved, since he was a master at lighting himself. He was a director who shaped Dietrich's entire world and created her as a superstar in one fabulous film after another, until he would later state to Peter Bogdanovich: "*I* am Miss Dietrich, Miss Dietrich is *me!*" This claim was supported by the actress herself years later. Sternberg shot endless takes of his star during the production, knowing that this was his as well as Dietrich's first American film and it had to be perfect to appease the scrutinizing eyes of Paramount mogul Adolph Zukor and his top-line producer, B.P. Schulberg, who watched the rushes daily. Von Sternberg worked hard with Dietrich so that her voice registered with the low tonality that would become her vocal trademark. The actress knew very little English and had difficulty with single words, let alone long sentences. Sternberg directed by rote, telling her in one scene to count to ten before delivering the terse line to Cooper: "Wait for me." She did, but Sternberg exploded, shouting: "If you're so stupid that you can't slowly, then count to twenty-five." She did it again and again, forty takes in all. Von Sternberg, a short man, complained that Cooper was too tall for his role and purposely posed Dietrich on the closed sets in such a way that for most of the film Cooper was looking up at *her*. This later gave rise to the speculation that the director was imposing his own image and will on actors who towered over him. Yet von Sternberg would later state that Cooper, whom he had already directed in CHILDREN OF DIVORCE, was "one of the nicest human beings I have ever met." Garmes, who would be nominated for an Oscar for his brilliant cinematography in MOROCCO (Sternberg, set designer Dreier, and Dietrich would also be nominated and also lose), later stated (in *Hollywood Cameramen* by Charles Higham), that von Sternberg directed every detail of lighting having to do with the sets and in this film "we had latticework in the streets; we shot at his [von Sternberg] suggestion at high noon for some interesting rippling shadows. Quite a lot of the picture was done in natural sunlight, rare at that time. The night scenes were shot at the Paramount ranch, and we did some of the best closeups of Marlene Dietrich against a white wall there; it was artificially lit to simulate daylight. . . . She had a great mechanical mind, and knew the camera. She would always stop in the exact position that was right for her." MOROCCO, when released, was an enormous success, reaping a fortune at the box office and securing a place and great future for Dietrich, Cooper, and the inventive von Sternberg.

p, Hector Turnbull; d, Joseph von Sternberg; w, Jules Furthman (based on the novel *Amy Jolly* by Benno Vigny); ph, Lee Garmes, Lucien Ballard; m, Karl Hajos; ed, Sam Winston; art d, Hans Dreier; cos, Travis Banton; m/l, Leo Robin, Hajos, Cremieux, "Give Me the Man," "What am I Bid for My Apples," Hajos, Leo Robin, "Quand l'Amour Meurt," Millandy and Cremieux.

Romance **(PR:C MPAA:NR)**

MOROZKO (SEE: JACK FROST, 1966, USSR)

MORTADELLA (SEE: LADY LIBERTY, 1972, Ital.)

MORTAL STORM, THE ***1/2 (1940) 100m MGM bw

Margaret Sullavan *(Freya Roth)*, James Stewart *(Martin Brietner)*, Robert Young *(Fritz Marlberg)*, Frank Morgan *(Prof. Roth)*, Robert Stack *(Otto von Rohn)*, Bonita Granville *(Elsa)*, Irene Rich *(Mrs. Roth)*, William T. Orr *(Erich von Rohn)*, Maria Ouspenskaya *(Mrs. Brietner)*, Gene Reynolds *(Rudi)*, Russell Hicks *(Rector)*, William Edmunds *(Lehman)*, Esther Dale *(Marta)*, Dan Dailey, Jr. *(Holl)*, Granville Bates *(Berg)*, Thomas Ross *(Prof. Werner)*, Ward Bond *(Franz)*, Sue Moore *(Theresa)*, Harry Depp *(2nd Colleague)*, Julius Tannen *(3rd Colleague)*, Gus Glassmire *(4th Colleague)*, Dick Rich, Ted Oliver *(Guards)*, Howard Lang *(Man)*, Bodil Rosing *(Woman)*, Lucien Prival, Dick Elliott *(Passport Officials)*, Henry Victor *(Gestapo Official)*, William Irving *(Waiter)*, Bert Roach *(Fat Man in Cafe)*, Bob Stevenson *(Gestapo Guard)*, Max Davidson *(Old Man)*, John Stark *(Gestapo Official)*, Fritz Leiber *(Oppenheim)*, Robert O. Davis [Rudolph Anders] *(Hartman)*.

Shortly before WW II, MGM, most powerful of all Hollywood film studios, openly declared its personal war on Hitler's Third Reich by producing the powerful film THE MORTAL STORM. Hitler took one look at the film and banned all MGM movies in Nazi Germany. Though the film deals with the rise of the Nazi regime in the early 1930s, it nevertheless scathingly profiles the hideous tyranny Hitler and his fellow thugs practiced over once-civilized Germany. Morgan is a professor with a large and happy family, celebrating his sixtieth birthday in 1933. Surrounding him is his wife Rich, his daughter Sullavan, his son Reynolds, and two stepsons, Stack and Orr, plus two young suitors for his daughter's hand, Young and Stewart. Sullavan later chooses pro-Nazi Young as her fiance, rejecting Stewart who returns to his farm in Austria, he being violently opposed to Hitler's regime, which comes into existence and immediately begins repressive measures. When Morgan's university students quiz him about Aryan supremacy, he ridicules the master-race notion and is quickly removed from his position and placed in a concentration camp where he ultimately dies. His sons Stack and Orr become members of the Nazi Youth Organization but young Reynolds, Rich, and Sullavan, who has broken her engagement with Young for his political views, now attempt to reach Stewart in Austria. They take a train out of the country but at the border, Nazi guards search their luggage and find a manuscript written by Morgan. Sullavan explains that it's a scientific treatise but the manuscript is seized and her passport is revoked. She convinces her mother and little brother to continue their journey to freedom. Later, Stewart comes to Germany and takes Sullavan on a perilous trip on skis, across the mountains, attempting to ski across the border. A patrol led by Bond and Young follows the fleeing pair and, just as they are about to cross the border, the Nazis fire at them and Sullavan is mortally wounded. Stewart, at her request, picks her up and skis into Austria so she can die in a free country. Young looks down upon the scene with sadness but believes he has done his duty for the Third Reich. Somber, even grim, this message film carried the theme of anti-Nazism in the words of Morgan the professor: "I've never prized safety either for myself or for my children. I've prized courage." The film appeared when America was on the brink of war with the Axis Powers and Americans had, by and large, mostly distrust, fear, and hatred for Hitler's awful regime, but THE MORTAL STORM was not a box-office success. It is propaganda, often crude in spots, and certainly sentimentally sloppy on occasions, but the leads play their roles with vigor. Sullavan—whom Borzage also directed two years earlier in THREE COMRADES, along with Young—is believable and sympathetic as the confused young woman who dies rather than yield to the Nazi philosophy. MGM executives thought long and hard about allowing her to live at film's end, then opted for death and a more dramatic if not maudlin finale. Sullavan's film career diminished after THE MORTAL STORM; she appeared sporadically in such movies as CRY HAVOC (1943) and NO SAID SONGS FOR ME (1950) preferring to act on Broadway. While preparing to go onstage during a Connecticut production, Sullavan suddenly took an overdose of sleeping pills and died on January 1, 1960. Stewart, who appears on and off in this film, was teamed with Sullavan earlier in NEXT TIME WE LOVE (1936) THE SHOPWORN ANGEL (1938) and THE SHOP AROUND THE CORNER (1940). Suprisingly good is Stack as the older stepbrother, one who realizes in the end that the Nazi path he has chosen is crooked. Orr, the younger brother, hears that he stepsister is dead and Stewart has escaped to freedom. "He's free to fight against everything we believe in," says Orr bitterly. "Yes," replies Stack, still dressed in his stormtrooper's uniform, "Thank God for that." Stack, with this remark, becomes one of the few sympathetic Germans portrayed in Hollywood just prior to, during, and after WW II. Borzage maintains a swift pace to this film and keeps his cameras fluid, employing many dolly shots, pans, and quick cuts. He often repeats his shots to emphasize the hopelessness of his characters' situations. The director ends where he began, outside Morgan's once happy home—now deserted, gutted of humanity by the Nazi storm—his camera at the final shot showing Stack's footsteps in the snow as he leaves the now empty home, the snow falling heavily and quickly obliterating his footprints, as if to say that the Nazi scourge will pass into history, a powerful ending. MGM still played it somewhat safe by stating at the beginning that the scene is set "somewhere in Europe," but no viewer can mistake it as being other than Germany. Warner Bros. production of CONFESSIONS OF A NAZI SPY a year earlier pulled no such punches.

p, Sidney Franklin, Victor Saville [uncredited]; d, Frank Borzage; w, Claudine West, Anderson Ellis, George Froeschel (based on the novel by Phyllis Bottome); ph, William Daniels; m, Edward Kane, Eugene Zador; ed, Elmo Vernon; art d, Cedric Gibbons, Wade Rubottom; set d, Edwin B. Willis; cos, Adrian, Gile Steele; makeup, Jack Dawn.

Drama **(PR:A MPAA:NR)**

MORTE A VENEZIA (SEE: DEATH IN VENICE, 1971, Ital./Fr.)

MORTON OF THE MOUNTED (SEE: TIMBER TERRORS, 1935)

MORTUARY zero (1983) 91m Artists Releasing/Film Ventures c

Mary McDonough *(Christie)*, David Wallace *(Greg Stevens)*, Lynda Day George *(Eve Parsons)*, Christopher George *(Dr. Hank Andrews)*, Bill Paxton *(Paul Andrews)*, Beth Schaffel, Curt Ayres, Alvy Moore.

Yet another in the series of bad splatter movies that infested the market in the late 1970s and early 1980s. This one stars Wallace and McDonough as a young couple who get entangled with creepy mortician C. George and his crazed son, Paxton (he has an affection for Mozart), leaders of a black magic sect. McDonough can't even trust her mom, Lynda Day George, because she has been seen sneaking off to the mortician's black masses herself. Not as gory as some of the other splatter films, MORTUARY's gimmick sees an embalming tool that extracts the bodily fluids and replaces them with formaldehyde put to good use for the sick ones out there.

p, Howard Avedis, Marlene Schmidt; d, Avedis; w, Avedis, Schmidt; ph, Gary Graver; m, John Cacavas; ed, Stanford C. Allen; art d, Randy Ser; makeup, Tim Gillespie, Diane Seletos.

Horror **Cas.** **(PR:O MPAA:R)**

MOSCOW—CASSIOPEIA1/2** (1974, USSR) 83m Gorki c (MOSKVA—KASSIOPEIA)

Innokenty Smoktunovsky, Volodya Basov, Ira Popova, Vasili Merkureyev, Natalya Fateyeva, Sasha Grigoriev.

A children's science-fiction adventure which has a teenage crew being sent toward a star in the constellation Cassiopeia. The intention is that they will be adults by the time they reach their destination, but comic problems, including teen romance, get in the way. An entertaining 2001—A SPACE ODYSSEY for the younger set.

d, Richard Viktorov; w, Avenir Zak, Isai Kuznetsov; ph, Andrei Kirillov.

Juvenile/Science Fiction (PR:A MPAA:NR)

MOSCOW DISTRUSTS TEARS
(SEE: MOSCOW DOES NOT BELIEVE IN TEARS, 1979, USSR)

MOSCOW DOES NOT BELIEVE IN TEARS**¹/₂
(1980, USSR) 145m Mosfilm c (MOSKWA SLJESAM NJE JERIT; GB: MOSCOW DISTRUSTS TEARS)

Vera Alentova (Katerina), Alexei Batalov (Goscha), Irina Murawjova (Ludmilla), Raissa Rjasanova (Antonia), Juri Wassiliev (Rudolf), Alexandr Fatiushin, Boris Smorchkov, Yuri Vasilyer, Natalya Vavilova, Oleg Tabakov, Yevgeniya Khanayeva, Valentina Ushakova, Viktor Uralsky, Zoya Fedorova, Lia Akhedzhakova, Tatyana Koniukhova, Innokenti Smoktunovsky.

Lightweight Russian comedy about three girls from the country who come to Moscow in 1958. Twenty years later we see them again and the various directions their lives have taken. An unusual film to come out of the Soviet Union, and though not especially good, the film won the Oscar for Best Foreign Language Film.

p, V. Kuchinsky; d, Vladimir Menshov; w, Valentin Tschernych; ph, Igor Slabnjewttsch (Sovcolor); m, Sergei Nikitin; ed, Jelene Mischajora; art d, Said Menyalshchikov.

Comedy Cas. (PR:A MPAA:NR)

MOSCOW NIGHTS (SEE: I STAND CONDEMNED, 1935, Brit.)

MOSCOW SHANGHAI**
(1936, Ger.) 90m Badal/Terra bw (MOSKAU SHANGHAI: DER WEG NACH SHANGHAI)

Pola Negri (Olga Petrowna), Wolfgang Keppler (Alexander Repin), Gustav Diesel (Serge Smirnow), Susi Lanner (Maria), Erich Ziegel (Gen. Martow), Karl Dannemann (Grischa), Hugo Werner Kahle (Commander), Paul Bildt (Gen. Nechludow), Karl Meixner (Pope), Rudolf Schindler (Galgenvogel), Heinz Wemper (Commander in Karewo), Franz Weilhammer (Railway Chief), Hans Waschatko (General in Shanghai), Edwin Juergensen (Director of Nitery), F. Grimmer (Train Rebel), Gustav Mahnke (Controller), Dorothea Thiess (Mrs. Iwanowna), Walter Gross (Manager in Shanghai), Serge Jaroff's Don Cossacks.

Melodramatic romantic tragedy directed by famed German Wegener (DER GOLEM) and starring Negri as a widowed Russian aristocrat whose life is turned upside down by the 1917 revolution. On the eve of a long trip to her estate, Negri attends a gala ball where she meets and falls in love with dashing young officer Keppler. The next day she leaves her 7-year-old daughter with a maid and departs for her estate accompanied by her close friend, Diesel, who has wanted to marry her for years. Midway through their journey, their train is captured by the Bolsheviks and Negri soon learns that both Keppler and Diesel have been captured by the revolutionaries. Diesel joins the Reds to aid his friends, and when Keppler is sentenced to die, Diesel commutes his sentence. Meanwhile, Negri has taken refuge with a priest and continues to search for her daughter, Keppler, and Diesel. In 1930, Negri is a nightclub singer in Shanghai where she runs into Diesel. He again proposes marriage but she declines because she is still carrying a torch for Keppler. At a party thrown for expatriate Russians at Easter time, Negri is shocked to discover Keppler is one of the singers hired for entertainment and she is further stunned when it is revealed that he is engaged to a young Russian girl who turns out to be her long-lost daughter. (In German.)

d, Paul Wegener; w, Kurt Heynicke, M. W. Kimmich; m, Hans Otto Borgmann; ph, Franz Weihmayr.

Drama (PR:A MPAA:NR)

MOSES**
(1976, Brit./Ital.) 140m ITC-RAI/AE c

Burt Lancaster (Moses), Anthony Quayle (Aaron), Ingrid Thulin (Miriam), Irene Papas (Zipporah), Mariangela Melato (Princess Bithia), William Lancaster (Young Moses), Laurent Terzieff (Mernefta), Aharon Ipale (Joshua), Marina Berti (Eliseba), Mario Ferrari (Pharaoh Ramses II), Yousef Shiloah (Dathan), Shumel Rodnesky (Jethro).

This was made as a television spectacular, then released in the U.S. as a long feature after having the fat trimmed. They did not trim enough. It is the story of the man who came down from the burning bush with a whole set of commandments, as played by Lancaster. Like most biblical films, it is filled with action, sex, gore, and all the things that the Bible-thumpers say are bad in films. The TV version, which aired on CBS as "Moses, The Lawgiver," was the basis for this movie but they added several scenes which would not have made it past CBS's Standards and Practices Department. Burt's son, Bill, plays the young Moses. He later grew up to be the screenwriter for THE BAD NEWS BEARS, among other credits. For once, Moses is not portrayed with such epic proportions that he becomes unbelievable. Lancaster shows him as a man touched by God and in awe of his being chosen. The Egyptian Pharaoh, Ferrari, and his son, Terzieff, are seen also as human beings rather than as total ogres. Cinematography is good and the sound is superior. The screenwriters have elected to slightly alter history or, at least, to interpret the Bible's Old Testament in a somewhat different light. This was an expensive picture and the special effects are superior. Bava's parting of the Red Sea is the best we have seen and far surpasses any of the others. There is truth to that section of the Bible in that others have crossed the Red Sea on foot at certain times when the water recedes enough for a quick traverse before it returns. It doesn't happen as dramatically as we are led to believe by movies, but the Red Sea does have an influence exerted on it by the moon and, if legend is correct, French troops did the same thing in the early 1800s.

p, Vincenzo Labella; d, Gianfranco de Bosio; w, Anthony Burgess, Victorio Bonicelli, de Bosio; ph, Marcello Gatti (Technicolor); m, Ennio Morricone; ed, Gerry Hambling, Peter Bolta, John Guthridge, Alberto Gallitti, Freddie Wilson; prod d, Pierluigi Basile; set d, Basile; cos, Enrico Sabbatini; spec eff, Mario Bava; ch, Dov Seltzer; m/l, Seltzer.

Biblical Epic Cas. (PR:A MPAA:PG)

MOSES AND AARON*** (1975, Ger./Fr./Ital.) 105m New Yorker c

Gunter Reich (Moses), Louis Devos (Aaron), Roger Lucas (Young Man), Eva Csapo (Young Woman), Richard Salter (Other Man), Werner Mann (Priest), Friedl Obrowsky (Sick Woman), Ladislav Illavsky (Ephraimite).

Straub and Huillet (Mr. & Mrs. Straub) followed up their short film INTRODUCTION TO ARNOLD SCHOENBERG'S ACCOMPANIMENT TO A CINEMATOGRAPHIC SCENE with this feature-length film adaptation of Schoenberg's Biblical opera. Though static, the film is a faithful adaptation and conveys both the philosophical aspects of the piece (the struggle between word and image), and the inherent drama (though Straub cuts Schoenberg somewhat). Technically marvelous and stunningly performed by singers Reich and Devos. (In German; English subtitles.)

d&w, Jean-Marie Straub, Daniele Huillet; ph, Ugo Piccone, Saverio Diamanti, Gianni Canfarelli, Renato Berta; m, Arnold Schoenberg; ed, Straub, Huillet; md, Michael Gielen; cos, Renata Morroni, Guerrino Todero.

Opera (PR:C MPAA:NR)

MOSQUITO SQUADRON** (1970, Brit.) 90m Oakmont/UA c

David McCallum (Quint Munroe), Suzanne Neve (Beth Scott), David Buck (Squadron Leader David Scott), David Dundas (Flt. Lt. Douglas Shelton), Dinsdale Landen (Wing Comdr. Penrose), Charles Gray (Air Commodore Hufford), Michael Anthony (Father Bellague), Vladek Sheybal (Lt. Schack), Gordon Sterne (Resistance Leader), Robert Urquhart (Maj. Kemble), Brian Grellis, George Layton (Pilot Officers), John Landry, Derek Steen (Flight Sergeants), Bryan Marshall (Neale), Michael Latimer (Clark), Nicky Henson (Wiley Bunce), Peggy Thorpe-Bates, Peter Copley, Michael McGovern.

Lackluster WW II film starring McCallum as an RAF pilot whose best friend, Buck, is killed in a bombing raid over France. McCallum informs Buck's wife, Neve, of her husband's death and soon their long-ago romance is rekindled (she was McCallum's girl before she married Buck). Meanwhile, McCallum learns that the Nazis are developing the V-3 rocket in France and his commanders order its destruction with a specially built bomb. Soon after, however, British intelligence informs the command that several British POW's are being held by the Nazis at the compound, including Buck. McCallum devises a plan wherein the first attack will free the prisoners so that they can escape harm, and then the bombers will return to destroy the V-3 shop. The raid is a success, but Buck is killed, leaving McCallum and Neve to each other.

p, Lewis J. Rachmil; d, Boris Sagal; w, Donald S. Sanford, Joyce Perry; ph, Paul Beeson (DeLuxe Color); m, Frank Cordell; ed, John S. Smith; art d, Bill Andrews; spec eff, Les Bowie; makeup, Benny Royston.

War (PR:A MPAA:G)

MOSS ROSE*** (1947) 82m FOX bw

Peggy Cummins (Belle Adair), Victor Mature (Sir Alexander Sterling), Ethel Barrymore (Lady Sterling), Vincent Price (Inspector Clinner), Margo Woode (Daisy Arrow), George Zucco (Craxton), Patricia Medina (Audrey Ashton), Rhys Williams (Deputy Inspector Evans), Felippa Rock (Liza), Carol Savage (Harriett), Victor Wood (Wilson), Patrick O'Moore (George Gilby), Billy Bevan (White Horse Cabby), Michael Dyne (Assistant Hotel Manager), John Rogers (Fothergill), Charles McNaughton (Alf), Alex Frazer (Mr. Bulke), Gilbert Wilson, Stanley Mann (Footmen), Alex Harford (Cassian), John Goldsworthy (Minister), Sally Sheppard (Maid), Paul England (Pub Owner), Al Ferguson, Russ Clark (Constables), Colin Campbell (Art Gallery Attendant), Leonard Carey (Coroner), Norman Ainslie (Deputy Coroner), Tom Moore (Foreman in Coroner's Court), Phil Sudano (Stevens), Basil Walker (Thompson), Wallace Scott, Colin Kenny (Cabdrivers), Frank Baker (Man Lodger), Doreen Munroe (Woman Lodger), Gerald Oliver Smith (Hotel Desk Clerk), Francis Pierlot (Train Conductor), Harry Allen (Threadbare Little Man), Clifford Brooke (Chemist), Stuart Holmes (Pompous English Colonel), Connie Leon (Seamstress), Norman Ainsley (Deputy Coroner), Maj. Sam Harris (Family Solicitor).

A tense turn-of-the-century mystery with several odd twists and turns, not the least of which is Vincent Price on the right side of the law, Victor Mature as what appears to be a deranged killer, and Ethel Barrymore, in one of her fine portrayals as a mother bent on saving her son. Everything about this film is visually correct and the mood of London is immediately evoked and remains, almost permeating the actors with fog, all through the picture. Cummins is a cockney singer-dancer whose roommate is killed by an unknown person. She is a beauty and is determined to get out of her poverty rut and use her charm and looks to snare a rich man. Cummins thinks that Mature, who was dating her dead pal, may be the killer so she uses blackmail to wangle an invitation from Mature to the family residence, a huge estate in Devonshire. Once there, Cummins learns that Mature is engaged to Medina, but that poor girl is soon dispatched as well. Price, a Scotland Yard detective, is sent to cover the case and manages to save the young Cummins before she, too, is slain by are you ready? Barrymore. Yep, it's the old lady who is doing in the young ladies as she will do anything to keep her boy at home. Why this was set in England is anybody's guess as there is not much of an attempt to maintain a British accent by the American players.

p, Gene Markey; d, Gregory Ratoff; w, Jules Furthman, Tom Reed, Niven Busch (based on the novel by Joseph Shearing); ph, Joe MacDonald; m, David Buttolph;

ed, James B. Clark; md, Alfred Newman; art d, Richard Day, Mark-Lee Kirk; set d, Edwin B. Willis, Paul S. Fox; spec eff, Fred Sersen.

Mystery   (PR:A   MPAA:NR)

MOST BEAUTIFUL AGE, THE**½

(1970, Czech.) 80m Barrandov-Ceskoslovensky/Grove bw (NEJKRASNEJSI VEK)

Jan Stockl (*Hanzlik*), Anna Pisarikova (*Kulharkova*), Hana Brejchova (*Vranova*), Josef Sebanek (*Vosta*), Ladislav Adam (*Ada*), Jiri Halek (*Franta*), Vladimir Smeral (*Professor*), Vera Kresadlova (*Susan*), Milada Jezkova (*Vosta's Wife*), Jiri Sykora (*Vranova's Husband*), M. Kriz, O. Marcin, B. Zemanek, Antonin Soukup, Josef Bartunek, J. Vosalik, S. Banzet, Josef Kolb, Helena Ruzickova, V. Cerny, M. Otava, J. Mrazek-Horicky, Bohuslav Kupsovsky, M. Vesely, Rudolf Rokl Quartet.

A charming little comedy essentially concerned with the problems of age. Set in an art school studio, the young art students use elderly pensioners as their models, but when a young mother is asked to pose in the nude tension arises between her and her husband, and she loses the assignment. High jinks and comedy antics with a sad, Chekhovian flavor.

p, Jaroslav Solnicka; d&w, Jaroslav Papousek; ph, Josef Ort-Snep; m, Karel Mares; ed, Jirina Lukesova; art d, Karel Cerny.

Comedy   (PR:C   MPAA:NR)

MOST DANGEROUS GAME, THE***

(1932) 63m RKO bw (GB: THE HOUNDS OF ZAROFF)

Joel McCrea (*Bob Rainsford*), Fay Wray (*Eve Trowbridge*), Leslie Banks (*Count Zaroff*), Robert Armstrong (*Martin Trowbridge*), Steve Clemento, Noble Johnson (*Tartar Servants*), Hale Hamilton.

This is a grim and morose film with strong undertones of sadism and, toward the end, brutality. It is also a genuinely frightening film involving Banks as a mad Russian count who lords it over a mist-enshrouded island and waits like a vicious spider for wayward ships to wreck themselves on the dangerous reefs surrounding his sinister domain. One of the sinking ships delivers up flotsam in the form of McCrea, Wray, and Armstrong, who are, at first, warmly welcomed to Banks' lavish estate. But slowly, as Banks describes his passion for hunting the wild beasts on the island, he begins to finger a livid scar on his forehead, one caused by a lion. Before they can realize their horrible situation, the shipwrecked survivors are compelled to flee into the thorny wilderness of the island with their host hunting them as he would animals, armed with bow and arrows, to give them a sporting chance. With Banks are his henchmen and a pack of the most vicious dogs ever unleashed in any film. Directors Schoedsack and Pichel dwell on the hunt, showing the victims fleeing madly through the brush and forests, narrowly missing death at the claws of wild animals or plunging into bottomless gorges. The hounds are shown in quick closeups that are terrifyingly abrupt and telescopic shots cutting from the hunter to the hunted heighten the tension. Banks is relentless in his pursuit, crazily blowing his hunting horn and drawing his bow with an accuracy that proves deadly. He finally meets the grim fate he has designed for others, plunging to his death while his own bloodthirsty hounds close in on him. There are wonderful atmospherics to this film—the count's looming, black castle, the primeval forests of the island—the same kind of environment producers Cooper and Schoedsack would create for their horror masterpiece, KING KONG, a year later. The studio thought that showing some decapitated heads, victims of Banks' unnatural hunts, might upset viewers, so these scenes were later cut. Wray, Armstrong, and Steiner, who composed the eerie score, would all be effectively used in KING KONG. The dark theme of this movie would be employed in countless films to come, as well as in radio and TV programs. RKO would remake this film as A GAME OF DEATH in 1946 and United Artists would explore the idea in RUN FOR THE SUN, 1956. Also that year, Rod Steiger would undergo the torment of being hunted by vicious Indians in RUN OF THE ARROW.

p, Merian C. Cooper, Ernest B. Schoedsack; d, Schoedsack, Irving Pichel; w, James A. Creelman (based on a story by Richard Connell); ph, Henry Gerrard; m, Max Steiner; ed, Archie Marshek.

Horror   **Cas.**   (PR:C-O   MPAA:NR)

MOST DANGEROUS MAN ALIVE, THE**½

(1961) 82m Trans-Global/COL c

Ron Randell (*Eddie Candell*), Debra Paget (*Linda Marlow*), Elaine Stewart (*Carla Angelo*), Anthony Caruso (*Andy Damon*), Gregg Palmer (*Lt. Fisher*), Morris Ankrum (*Capt. Davis*), Tudor Owen (*Dr. Meeker*), Steve Mitchell (*Devola*), Joel Donte (*Franscetti*).

Better-than-average sci-fi film which was the last picture directed by veteran helmsman Dwan. Randell stars as a framed convict who accidentally walks into a cobalt blast during his escape from prison. He survives the explosion only to discover that he is rapidly turning into a man of steel that makes him impervious to bullets. Seeking revenge on the men who framed him, Randell goes on the rampage and destroys everything in his path despite the best efforts of the police to stop him. Eventually he is killed by a member of the National Guard who burns him into dust with a flamethrower. Surprisingly compelling, THE MOST DANGEROUS MAN ALIVE was shot in Mexico in 1958 and was not released in the U.S. until 1961. German director Wim Wenders has his fictional film crew remaking THE MOST DANGEROUS MAN ALIVE as a backdrop to his indignant look at the politics of movie-making in THE STATE OF THINGS (1982).

p, Benedict Bogeaus; d, Allan Dwan; w, James Leicester, Phillip Rock (based on the story "The Steel Monster" by Rock, Michael Pate); ph, Carl Carvahal; m, Louis Forbes; ed, Carlo Lodato; cos, Gwen Wakeling.

Science Fiction   (PR:A   MPAA:NR)

MOST DANGEROUS MAN IN THE WORLD, THE

(SEE: CHAIRMAN, THE, 1969, Brit.)

MOST IMMORAL LADY, A*

(1929) 77m FN-WB bw

Leatrice Joy (*Laura Sargeant*), Walter Pidgeon (*Tony Williams*), Sydney Blackmer (*Humphrey Sargeant*), Montagu Love (*John Williams*), Josephine Dunn (*Joan Porter*), Robert Edeson (*Bradford-Fish*), Donald Reed (*Pedro, Gigolo*), Florence Oakley (*Natalie Davis*), Wilson Benge (*Hoskins, Butler*).

Tedious drama revolving around Joy who gives a shrill and unappealing performance as a wife who allows her husband, Blackmer, to use her as bait in a scheme to blackmail their wealthy friends. Joy, of course, is really in love with Pidgeon, but she inadvertently sets him up for extortion. However, it all ends happily in a Parisian night club.

d, John Griffith Wray; w, Forrest Halsey (based on the play by Townsend Martin); ph, John Seitz; ed, Peter Fritch; m/l, "Toujours," "That's How Much I Need You."

Drama   (PR:A   MPAA:NR)

MOST PRECIOUS THING IN LIFE**

(1934) 64m COL bw

Jean Arthur, Donald Cook, Richard Cromwell, Anita Louise, Mary Forbes, Jane Darwell, Ben Alexander, John Wray, Dutch Hendrian, Ward Bond, Paul Stanton.

Melodrama starring Arthur as a poor girl working as a waitress who falls in love and marries wealthy college student Cook and soon bears him a son. After the child's birth, Arthur is eased out of the family by Cook's parents, who never thought she was good enough for their son. Twenty years pass and Arthur is now scrubbing floors at the college her ex-husband attended. There she befriends a wealthy young college student (her long-lost son, of course) who is involved in a tragic romance with a poor girl against his father's wishes. Never revealing her identity, Arthur saves the youngster's relationship and convinces him to play football for the college. Only Arthur makes this soppy stuff worth sitting through.

d, Lambert Hillyer; w, Ethel Hill, Dore Schary (based on a magazine story by Travis Ingham); ph, John Stumar; ed, Robert Carlisle; cos, Robert Kalloch.

Drama   (PR:A   MPAA:NR)

MOST WANTED MAN, THE**

(1962, Fr./Ital.) 85m Cite Films-Fides-Cocinor-Peg Produzione/Astor bw (L'ENNEMI PUBLIC NO. 1; IL NEMICO PUBBLICO N. 1; AKA: THE MOST WANTED MAN IN THE WORLD)

Fernandel (*Joe Calvet*), Zsa-Zsa Gabor (*Lola*), Alfred Adam (*Sheriff*), Jean Marchat (*Attorney General*), Louis Seigner (*Prison Director*), Saturnin Fabre (*W. W. Stone*), David Opatoshu (*Slim*), Bob Ingarao (*Policeman*), Paolo Stoppa (*Tony Fallon*), Nicole Maurey, Cianfanelli, Arturo Bragaglia, Tino Buazzelli, Carlo Ninchi, Guglielmo Barnabo.

An entertaining crime comedy which cast French comedian Fernandel as a recently fired clerk who mistakenly takes the jacket of a gangster while leaving a movie theater. Later, as Fernandel is walking down the street, he pulls out a gun which was in the pocket and is arrested. The police believe him to be Public Enemy No. 1 and lock him up. He is rescued, however, by the real crook and eventually informs the police of the gang's hideout. Rota (LA DOLCE VITA, THE GODFATHER) co-wrote the score and Marcel Camus (BLACK ORPHEUS) acted as assistant director. originally released in 1953 at 105 minutes.

p, Jacques Bar; d, Henri Verneuil; w, Michel Audiard, Jean Manse (based on the story by Max Favalelli); ph, Armand Thirard; m, Nino Rota, Raymond Legrand; ed, Christian Gaudin; art d, Robert Giordani; set d, Andre Molles; cos, Rosine Delamare; makeup, Lina Gallet.

Crime Comedy   (PR:A   MPAA:NR)

MOST WONDERFUL EVENING OF MY LIFE, THE**½

(1972, Ital./Fr.) 106m Dino De Laurentiis-M.A.C.O.-S.P.A./COL c (LA PIU BELLA SERATA DELLA MIA VITA)

Alberto Sordi (*Alfredo Rossi*), Michel Simon (*Prosecuting Attorney*), Charles Vanel (*Judge*), Claude Dauphin (*Court Recorder*), Pierre Brasseur (*Defense Attorney*), Janet Agren (*Simonetta*), Giuseppe Maffioli (*Executioner*).

Italian comedy-drama starring Sordi as a successful businessman whose destiny leads him to a secluded Swiss chalet where his life is tried by a group of retired law professionals. Simon is the prosecuting attorney, Brasseur is the defense, Vanel is the judge, and Dauphin the court recorder. The men assemble to analyze and examine Sordi's rise to power and his increasingly immoral behavior as he attained success, and the warped perceptions of right and wrong he has adopted to remain successful. The film combines humor with compelling drama that sustains viewer interest until the verdict is delivered. Irony running throughout the film is typical of the oblique way the Swiss master of stagecraft, Duerrenmatt, looks at the world and the helplessness of the individual in that world in particular. The imposing French actor Brasseur, whose career began in the silent movie days, died near the end of photographing for the film, at 69 years of age.

d, Ettore Scola; w, Sergio Amidei, Scola (based on a story "La Panne" by Friedrich Duerrenmatt); ph, Claudio Cirillo (Eastmancolor); m, Armando Trovaioli; ed, Raimondo Crociani; art d, Luciano Ricceri.

Comedy/Drama   (PR:A   MPAA:NR)

MOSURA

(SEE: MOTHRA, 1962, Jap.)

MOTEL HELL zero

(1980) 106m Camp Hill/UA c

Rory Calhoun (*Vincent Smith*), Paul Linke (*Bruce Smith*), Nancy Parsons (*Ida Smith*), Nina Axelrod (*Terry*), Wolfman Jack (*Rev. Billy*), Elaine Joyce (*Edith Olsen*), Dick Curtis (*Guy Robaire*), Monique St. Pierre (*Debbie*), Rosanne Katon

(Suzi), E. Hampton Beagle (Bob Anderson), Michael Melvin (Ivan), Everett Creach (Bo), John Ratzenberger, Marc Silver, Victoria Hartman, Gwil Richards, Toni Gillman, Shaylin Hendrixson, Heather Hendrixson, Margot Hope, Barbara Goodson, Kim Fowler.

A film that should have been funnier. Horror-comedy starring Calhoun as "Farmer Vincent" who markets a famous brand of exclusive sausages from his lonely motel located far off the beaten path. Aided by his piggish sister, Parsons, Calhoun prepares his meats by capturing unsuspecting victims on the highway and then burying them up to their necks with their vocal cords cut (so they can't scream for help) until they are fat enough for his smokehouse, where he slaughters them and turns them into sausage. Enter the young and beautiful Axelrod who has a motorcycle accident nearby and seeks shelter in the motel. Calhoun's normal brother, Linke (there's a joke there somewhere), falls in love with Axelrod, but she is smitten with an old coot like Calhoun and wants nothing to do with his kid brother. Linke learns the real home-style recipe for his brother's sausages and there is a lengthy chainsaw fight between the siblings which leads to the film's best moment when Calhoun gives a long, hilarious speech while he lies dying with a chainsaw sticking out of his side. MOTEL HELL could have been a great black comedy, but the uneasy direction of Connor combined with the gore that comes with this territory fails to get most of the picture off the ground.

p, Steven-Charles Jaffe, Robert Jaffe; d, Kevin Connor; w, Jaffe and Jaffe; ph, Thomas Del Ruth (Technicolor); m, Lance Rubin; ed, Bernard Gribble; art d, Joseph M. Altadonna; set d, Jim Teegarden; spec eff, Adams R. Calvert.

Horror/Comedy   Cas.   **(PR:O MPAA:R)**

MOTEL, THE OPERATOR**
(1940) 88m Cinema Film bw

Chaim Tauber (Motel), Malvina Rappel (Motel's Wife), Joseph Schoengold (Motel's Son), Gertrude Krause (Fiancee of Motel's Son), Maurice Kroner (Blackmailer), Cantor Leible Waldman (Singer), Yetta Zwerling, Joseph Zanger.

Tauber is the leader in a clothing worker's strike. After he gets beat up by goons, his wife Rappel dies in childbirth. The baby is taken in by a rich couple, and Tauber cannot find him. Years go by and the baby has grown up and is about to marry Krause, but a blackmailer threatens to expose his real past. Of course, all works out well for everyone in this simple-minded Yiddish feature. Stock plot devices and characterizations quickly destroy the film's intent, despite its strong beginning. In Yiddish.

p&d, Joseph Seiden.

Drama   **(PR:C MPAA:NR)**

MOTH, THE*
(1934) 64m Showmen's Pictures/Marcy bw (GB: SEEING IT THROUGH)

Sally O'Neil (Diana Wyman), Paul Page (George Duncan), Wilfred Lucas (John Gale), Fred Kelsey (Detective Blake), Duncan Renaldo (Don Pedro), Rae Daggert (Marie), Nina Guilherd (Aunt Jane).

Maudlin drama starring O'Neil as a lame-brained and wild young heiress who overdraws on her inheritance and then runs out on the family after she causes a scandal. The executor sends Page off to locate the girl so that she doesn't get cut off entirely and he soon locates her in New Orleans and the Mardi Gras, where she nearly becomes involved in criminal activities with another woman. Page intercepts her, however, and soon the pair fall in love.

d, Fred Newmeyer, Jr.; w, Joe O'Donnell; ph, George Meehan; ed, S. Roy Luby.

Drama   **(PR:A MPAA:NR)**

MOTHER AND DAUGHTER**
(1965, USSR) 80m Dovzhenko/Artkino bw (SREDI DOBRYKH LYUDEY)

Vera Maretskaya (Mikhaylina), Soraya Pavlova (Olga Dmitriyevna), Ira Mitskik (Natasha), Yura Leontyev (Roman), Lyuda Zabrodskaya (Magda), B. Borisenok (Martsinyuk), Yu. Kritenko (Tikhonyuk), N. Antonova (Yaroshko), Oksana Sluzhenko (Tanya), Nina Borisova, N. Gnepovskaya, L. Danchishin, S. Karamash, O. Nozhkina, A. Nikolayeva, N. Naum, A. Poddubinskiy, N. Rushkovskiy, N. Talyura.

After WW II's end a woman evacuated from a Carpathian border village returns to her home town, but without the daughter she left with years before. She learns that a woman from a nearby village adopted a daughter at about the same time she was parted from hers, and finds that it is her daughter. The foster mother eventually finds the strength to give the girl up to her natural mother, even though they've grown quite close. Originally released in 1962, it stars one of the great actresses of the Russian theater, Maretskaya.

d, Yevgeniy Bryunchugin, Anatoliy Bukovskiy; w, Yuriy Zbanatskiy (based on a story by N. Orlova; ph, V. Tyshkovets; m, German Zhukovskiy; ed, I. Karpenko; art d, A. Mamontove, V. Migulko; set d, V. Tsirlina; cos, G. Nesterovskaya; spec eff, I. Tregubova, G. Lukashov; m/l, Zhukovskiy, A. Novitskiy; makeup, Ye. Shayner.

Drama   **(PR:A MPAA:NR)**

MOTHER AND SON*
(1931) 70m MON bw

Clara Kimball Young (Mother), Bruce Warren (Son), Gordon Wood (Joe Connors), Mildred Golden (Maurine Winfield), John Elliott (Mr. Winfield), Ernest Hilliard.

Melodrama starring Young as a wayward mother who runs a gambling den and keeps knowledge of it from her child, Warren, until he's grown up and learns the truth, which causes recriminations and tension until the final heart-tugging scene. This was the second film made by Young in an ill-fated comeback bid after the red-headed beauty retired from the screen in 1925 because her career had suddenly plummeted downward.

p, Trem Carr; d, John P. McCarthy; w, Wellyn Totman; ph, Archie Stout; ed, Lem Wheeler.

Drama   **(PR:A MPAA:NR)**

MOTHER AND THE WHORE, THE***
(1973, Fr.) 210m Films du Losange-Elite Films-Cine Qua Non-Simar Films-V.M. Productions/NPF-CECRT bw (LA MAMAN ET LA PUTAIN) bw (LA MAMAN ET LA PUTAIN)

Bernadette Lafont (Marie), Jean-Pierre Leaud (Alexandre), Francoise Lebrun (Veronika), Isabelle Weingarten (Gilberte), Jacques Renard (Friend), Jean-Noel Picq, Jessa Darrieux, Marinka Matuszewski, Genevieve Mnich, Berthe Grandval.

If any film signified that the French New Wave had come to an end, that film was THE MOTHER AND THE WHORE, a grueling three-and-a-half-hour dissertation that may be one of the most enlightening works the cinema has ever produced. Set against a background of Paris cafes and tiny one-room apartments, THE MOTHER AND THE WHORE traces the amorous adventures of Leaud, an irresponsible young man, pretending to be a leftist intellectual. He is really little more than a victim of the postwar existentialist thought that paved the way for the materialistic attitudes of the early 1970s and a generation filled with empty ideals. One morning Leaud finds an extraordinary need to marry; leaving the small flat he shares with Lafont, his lover and willing meal ticket, he sets out to pop the question to his old girl friend. Dragging her away from her university classes, Leaud brings the girl to a cafe where he engages in a long pseudo-intellectual monolog while asking for her hand. She flatly refuses, responding to Leaud with "What novel are you being a character in?" Which is a perfect example of how Leaud perceives himself, through novels or films. Later that same day he passes by a cafe where he spots the vampiristic looking Lebrun staring at him. He gets her phone number and agrees to meet her later. After several failed attempts to meet with Lebrun, the two eventually arrange to meet at a cafe. Lebrun works as a nurse, a job that allows her enough money to pay for her dingy room, to buy pretty clothes, and to keep herself numbed with alcohol. Other than this the only thing that interests her is sex, and she has no qualms about sleeping with any passing stranger. Leaud and Lebrun start a shaky affair that consists mainly of meeting in cafes and indulging in long monologs on Leaud's part. To Lebrun, Leaud has become much more than her usual casual fling; she latches on to him despite his situation with Lafont. She even calls Leaud while he is spending the evening with Lafont, then sleeps with both of them. But the three of them in bed together hardly create a scene of erotic lovemaking, with Lafont attempting suicide. The tension created by this triangle continually mounts until a gruesome finale in which Lebrun, who has remained aloof and unaffected up to this point, delivers a tear-filled soliloquy revealing her soul and spirit scarred through her self-perception of being little more than a sexual object. After this, Leaud follows her to her room and asks her to marry him. She accepts while throwing up into a bucket being held by Leaud. Prior to THE MOTHER AND THE WHORE, director Eustache had worked as an assistant director for New Wave directors, most notably Jean-Luc Godard (he even appeared briefly in WEEKEND). His first two solo efforts were medium-length features that were of some interest, but this picture proved he was a perceptive filmmaker. However Eustache's career was very short. After THE MOTHER AND THE WHORE won both the Grand Prix and the International Critics Award at Cannes he made only one more feature before his suicide in 1980. THE MOTHER AND THE WHORE, with its settings of dingy apartments and Paris cafes, its low key lighting which makes the viewer squint at any signs of brightness, takes us into the trying romance of three people. It captures a sense of realism rare in any type of film, for it brings us deep beneath the surface of the characters' exteriors. By doing so it allows us to see just what are the conditions of their existence. It's a pretty dismal one in which the characters are trapped beneath a social consciousness that really has little regard for human values. (In French; English subtitles.)

p, Pierre Cottrell; d&w, Jean Eustache; ph, Pierre l'Homme, Jacques Renard, Michel Cenet; ed, Eustache, Denise De Casabianca.

Drama   **(PR:C MPAA:NR)**

MOTHER CAREY'S CHICKENS**1/2
(1938) 82m RKO bw

Anne Shirley (Nancy Carey), Ruby Keeler (Kitty Carey), James Ellison (Ralph Thurston), Fay Bainter (Mrs. Carey), Walter Brennan (Mr. Popham), Frank Albertson (Tom Hamilton), Alma Kruger (Aunt Bertha), Virginia Weidler (Lally Joy), Donnie Dunagan (Peter Carey), Jackie Moran (Gilbert Carey), Margaret Hamilton (Mrs. Fuller), Ralph Morgan (Capt. Carey), Phyllis Kennedy (Annabelle), Harvey Clark (Mr. Fuller), Lucille Ward (Mrs. Popham), George Irving (Mr. Hamilton).

Heartwarming family film starring Bainter as the widowed wife (her husband never returned from the Spanish-American War) who is left alone to raise two daughters, Shirley and Keeler, and a son, Dunagan. The action centers on her efforts to keep ownership of her home, and the older girl's romances. Lots of homespun humor and character. Katharine Hepburn with her Bryn Mawr accent was originally slated to play the role that Keeler took, and her rejection of the script led RKO to tear up her contract. Remade in 1963 as SUMMER MAGIC with Hayley Mills.

p, Pandro S. Berman; d, Rowland V. Lee; w, S. K. Lauren, Gertrude Purcell (based on the novel by Kate Douglas Wiggin); ph, J. Roy Hunt; ed, George Hively; md, Frank Tours; cos, Edward Stevenson.

Drama   **(PR:A MPAA:NR)**

MOTHER DIDN'T TELL ME**1/2
(1950) 88m FOX bw

Dorothy McGuire (Jane), William Lundigan (Dr. William Wright), June Havoc (Katie), Gary Merrill (Dr. Mike Bell), Jessie Royce Landis (Mrs. Wright), Joyce McKenzie (Helen Porter), Leif Erickson (Dr. Bruce Gordon), Reiko Sato (Suki), Anthony Cobb (Johnny), Tracy Cobb (Sally), Georgia Backus (Mildred Tracy), Everett Glass (Minister), Michael Brandon (Dr. Tod Morgan), Mary Bear (Faith Morgan), Larry Keating (Dr. Tracy), Jean "Babe" London (Mrs. Hadley), Wilton Graff (Dr. Harold Jones), Ann Tyrrell (Mrs. Jones), Jessie Adams (Maid), Louise

Lorimer (*Nurse*), Frank Jenks (*Furniture Mover*), Caryl Lincoln (*Mrs. Raymond*), Ida Moore (*Old Lady*).

McGuire saves this otherwise routine comedy with her performance as a young woman who catches a terrible cold and must visit a doctor (Lundigan). They fall in love at first sight and soon after marry. McGuire finds that it is difficult being the neglected wife of a doctor and has trouble adjusting to his long hours and female patients. Though she tries hard, she makes many mistakes, much to the annoyance of Lundigan's doting mother, Landis. When Lundigan's new assistant tries to seduce him, McGuire goes on a rampage and saves the marriage.

p, Fred Kohlmar; d&w, Claude Binyon (based on the book *The Doctor Wears Three Faces* by Mary Bard); ph, Joseph La Shelle; m, Cyril Mockridge; ed, Harmon Jones; md, Lionel Newman; art d, Lyle Wheeler, Richard Irvine.

Comedy　　　　　　　　　　　　　　**(PR:A　MPAA:NR)**

MOTHER GOOSE A GO-GO*

(1966) 82m Tonylyn/VIP-Harris-U.S. Films c (AKA: THE UNKISSED BRIDE)

Tom Kirk (*Ted*), Anne Helm (*Margie*), Jacques Bergerac (*Jacques Phillipe*), Danica D'Hondt (*Dr. Marilyn Richards*), Robert Ball (*Ernest Sinclair*), Joe Pyne, Henny Youngman (*Themselves*), Melinda Fee, Margaret Teele.

Kirk and Helm star as a pair of lovebirds newly wed who are having trouble consummating the ultimate act. Comedy arises immediately when Helm picks up a copy of *Mother Goose* and begins to read in an effort to overcome her nervousness in bed, and her husband faints. Kirk then secretly visits a psychiatrist who persuades him that he has a "Mother Goose complex" that he can overcome by using an LSD spray, thus hallucinating and incorporating into reality the fairy tale characters from his fantasies. Another example of drug-confused cinema.

p, Jack H. Harris, Muriel G. Harris; d&w, Jack H. Harris; ph, Vilis Lapenieks (Panacolor); m, Douglas Lackey, Gene Kauer; ed, Hank Gotzenberg; prod d, Muriel G. Harris; art d, James E. Bechtold; cos, Maxwell Shieff; m/l, "Mother Goose a Go-Go," Tony Harris (sung by Tom Kirk), "Queen of Soul," T. Harris (sung by Barbara McNair).

Comedy　　　　　　　　　　　　　　**(PR:A　MPAA:NR)**

MOTHER IS A FRESHMAN** 1/2

(1949) 81m FOX c (GB: MOTHER KNOWS BEST)

Loretta Young (*Abigail "Abby" Fortitude Abbott*), Van Johnson (*Professor Richard Michaels*), Rudy Vallee (*John Heaslip*), Barbara Lawrence (*Louise Sharpe*), Robert Arthur (*Beaumont Jackson*), Betty Lynn (*Susan Abbott*), Griff Barnett (*Dean Gillingham*), Kathleen Hughes (*Rhoda Adams*), Eddie Dunn (*George*), Clair Meade (*Mrs. Gillingham*), Henri Letondal (*Professor Romaine*), Virginia Brissac (*Miss Grimes*), Charles Lane (*Mr. De Haven*), Kathryn Card (*Mrs. Grammerton*), Richard Taylor (*Butch*), Marietta Canty (*Beulah*), Debra Paget (*Linda*), Buster Phelps (*Jack*), Mickey Finn (*Joe Granite*), Ruth Tobey (*June Walker*), Bob Patten (*Young Man*), Gene Evans (*Man*), George Mathews, Pat Combs (*Cab Drivers*), Marion Colby, Geneva Gray (*Bit Girls*), John Miles, Roger McGee, Nelson King, Richard Clayton, Richard Dumas, Lee MacGregor (*College Students*).

Predictable comedy starring Young as a pretty widow who enrolls in college to validate a scholarship fund left by her grandmother. Unfortunately, her daughter, Lynn, is enrolled in the same college and has developed a crush on dashing teacher Johnson who has, in turn, fallen in love with Young. The romantic situation is worked out when Lynn falls for Arthur, who is closer to her own age. Funnier than it has any right to be. Filmed in its entirety at the beautiful campus of the University of Utah in the shadow of the Wasatch Mountain range.

p, Walter Morosco; d, Lloyd Bacon; w, Mary Loos, Richard Sale (based on a story by Raphael Blau); ph, Arthur E. Arling (Technicolor); m, Alfred Newman; ed, William Reynolds; art d, Lyle Wheeler, Maurice Ransford; set d, Thomas Little, Paul S. Fox; cos, Kay Nelson; spec eff, Fred Sersen; songs, "M-O-T-H-E-R," "Sweetheart of Sigma Chi," "Dream"; makeup, Ben Nye.

Comedy　　　　　　　　　　　　　　**(PR:A　MPAA:NR)**

MOTHER JOAN OF THE ANGELS?

(SEE: JOAN OF THE ANGELS?, 1962, Pol.)

MOTHER, JUGS & SPEEDzero

(1976) 95m FOX c

Raquel Welch (*Jugs*), Bill Cosby (*Mother*), Harvey Keitel (*Speed*), Allen Garfield [Goorwitz] (*Harry Fishbine*), Larry Hagman (*Murdoch*), L. Q. Jones (*Davey*), Bruce Davison (*LeRoy*), Dick Butkus (*Rodeo*), Milt Kamen (*Barney*), Barra Grant (*Miss Crocker*), Allan Warnick (*Bliss*), Valerie Curtin (*Naomi Fishbine*), Rick Carrott (*Harvey*), Severn Darden (*Moran*), Bill Henderson (*Charles Taylor*), Mike McManus (*Walker*), Toni Basil (*Addict*), Edwin Mills (*Addict's Doctor*), Erica Hagen (*Massage Girl*), Arnold Williams (*Albert*), Charles Knapp (*Man with Zipper*), Linda Geray (*Pregnant Woman*).

This disjointed, aimless film attempts to chronicle the experiences of three ambulance workers, Welch, a busty nurse who resents being called "Jugs," Cosby, and Keitel, all racing about the city in response to emergency calls. The idea here is to present many vignettes in which the principals encounter comic and tragic events while maintaining with great difficulty their composure and professional posture. Garfield plays the usual slob who runs the cheapie ambulance company and he isn't any better than the leading players who seem to want to finish this tasteless black comedy as soon as possible. Its dialog is crude, its direction sophomoric, and the whole thing is not worth a single viewing.

p, Peter Yates, Tom Mankiewicz; d, Yates; w, Mankiewicz (based on a story by Mankiewicz, Stephen Manes); ph, Ralph Woolsey (Panavision, DeLuxe Color); ed,

Frank P. Keller; prod d, Walter Scott Herndon; set d, Cheryl Kearney; m/l, "My Soul is a Witness," Bill Preston, Joe Greene.

Comedy　　　　　　　　　　　　　　**(PR:O　MPAA:PG)**

MOTHER KNOWS BEST**

(1928) 110m William Fox bw

Madge Bellamy (*Sally Quail*), Louise Dresser (*Ma Quail*), Barry Norton (*The Boy*), Albert Gran (*Sam Kingston*), Annette De Kirby (*Bessie as a Child*), Ivor De Kirby (*Ben as a Child*), Lucien Littlefield (*Pa Quail*), Dawn O'Day [Anne Shirley] (*Sally as a Child*), Stuart Erwin (*Ben*), Joy Auburn (*Bessie*).

Tedious mother-daughter picture redeemed only by Dresser's surprisingly nasty performance as the overbearing stage mother of budding actress Bellamy. While Bellamy was growing up, Dresser stole money out of her husband's drugstore till to ensure that the child would have everything she needed to succeed. When the old man died, Dresser hocked her wedding ring so that Bellamy would have cab fare back to Broadway. Eventually the pressure from her mother is too much (she even sent Bellamy's boy friend away) and Bellamy cracks. Luckily, a wise doctor advises Dresser to loosen her grip on the girl and the shamed woman tries her hardest to hasten the boy friend's return. He does and all goes well, including Bellamy's career, and Dresser lives to see a theater named after her daughter. This was Fox's first real dialog picture.

p, William Fox; d, John Blystone, Charles Judels, Dave Stamper; w, Marion Orth, Eugene Walter (based on the novel by Edna Ferber); ph, Gilbert Warrenton; m, Erno Rapee, S. L. "Roxy" Rothafel; ed, Margaret V. Clancy; m/l, "Sally of My Dreams," William Kernell.

Drama　　　　　　　　　　　　　　**(PR:A　MPAA:NR)**

MOTHER KNOWS BEST, 1949　(SEE: MOTHER IS A FRESHMAN, 1949)

MOTHER KUSTERS GOES TO HEAVEN** 1/2

(1976, Ger.) 108m Tango/New Yorker c (MUTTER KUSTERS FAHRT ZUM HIMMEL)

Brigitte Mira (*Mother Kusters*), Ingrid Caven (*Corinna Corinne*), Armin Meier (*Ernst Kusters*), Irm Hermann (*Helene Kusters*), Gottfried John (*Niemeyer*), Karlheinz Bohm (*Mr. Thalmann*), Margit Carstensen (*Mrs. Thalmann*), Gustav Holzapfel (*Company Representative*), Peter Kern, Peter Bollag, Kurt Raab, Peter Chattel, I Sa Lo.

Applying his keen wit and ironic sense of man's hopelessness to the 1929 film MOTHER KRAUSENS' JOURNEY TO HAPPINESS, Fassbinder created another emotionally distancing, disturbing, yet always funny and fascinating picture. Mira (best known for her role in FEAR EATS THE SOUL) is the middle-aged wife of a browbeaten factory worker who blows his lid one day, killing the owner's son and then himself. The quiet and reserved Mira suddenly finds herself the center of everyone's attentions; reporters hound her for details and her face appears on every TV news program. She makes a deal with one reporter (John) to give him an exclusive interview as long as he doesn't make her dead husband look like a fool. But this is exactly what he does. What's more, Mira's daughter (Caven) uses this same interview, and the unhappy incident as a whole, to boost her singing career. A prominent communist couple befriend Mira, and show an understanding of the husband's irrational act by applying their communist ideology to the plight of the helpless worker. Originally Mira hoped these two would shed light on the erroneous article written by John, but they only use the woman to further their own cause. In the end Mira is left alone, her family too immersed in their own selfish goals, and her fly-by-night friends having lost interest. In an upbeat, though subtly pessimistic ending (another version has her being killed), Mira agrees to have a simple meal with the building superintendent from the factory. This becomes the only non-selfish act she has encountered since her ordeal began. When MOTHER KUSTERS was first released it was praised by critics for being additional proof of Fassbinder's genius and ability to supply a starving audience with something new. In his own country, the film initially met with many political protests. Subsequently (though not necessarily as a result of the protests), MOTHER KUSTERS was barred from the Berlin Film Festival. Fassbinder was not being apolitical in this film, rather he was showing that politics was something that could not be trusted, along with family, friends, or anything else for that matter. A very dim view of life is revealed, but there's nothing like a cold slap in the face to help raise one's consciousness. (In German; English subtitles.)

p, Christian Hohoff; d, Rainer Werner Fassbinder; w, Fassbinder, Kurt Raab; (based on the script "Mutter Krausens Fahrt Ins Glueck" by Heinrich Zille); ph, Michael Ballhaus; m, Peer Raben; ed, Thea Eymes; art d, Raab; cos, Jo. Braun.

Drama　　　　　　　　　　　　　　**(PR:C-O　MPAA:NR)**

MOTHER LODE*

(1982) 101m Martin Shafter-Andrew Scheinman/Agamemnon c (AKA: SEARCH FOR THE MOTHER LODE; THE LAST GREAT TREASURE)

Charlton Heston (*Silas McGee/Ian McGee*), Nick Mancuso (*Jean Dupre*), Kim Basinger (*Andrea Spalding*), John Marley (*Elijah*), Dale Wilson (*Gerard Elliot*), Ricky Zantolas (*George Patterson*), Marie George (*Elijah's Wife*).

How does an untalented screenwriter-producer get Hollywood to finance a decent-sized budget turkey like this? By having a father by the name of Charlton Heston who has nothing better to do than lend his presence (not only acting, but *directing*) to the project so that funding will roll in. Charlton's son, Fraser, was the driving force behind this mediocre adventure film starring his dad in a dual role as Scottish twin brothers (Silas is the nasty one) who would rather kill than reveal the location of their gold mine in British Columbia (the scenery is about the only thing worth watching). Mancuso plays a bush pilot who takes off after fellow pilot Zantolas when the latter goes in search of gold. Accompanied by Basinger, Mancuso catches up with his buddy and finds that crazed miner Heston has killed him and threatens to do the same to them if they don't get lost. They don't leave fast enough because the Hestons capture Basinger, forcing Mancuso to kill Heston No. 2, and rescue Basinger from Heston No. 1 who is now swinging a double-bladed ax around. After half a dozen near fatal blows and falls, Manusco triumphs and the film is finally over. Less than thrilling.

p, Fraser Clarke Heston; d, Charlton Heston, Joe Canutt; w, Fraser Clarke Heston; ph, Richard Leiterman; m, Ken Wannberg; ed, Eric Boyd Perkins; md, Wannberg; prod d, Douglas Higgins; art d, Michael Bolton, James H. Crow; makeup, Jamie Brown, Phyllis Newman.

Adventure   **Cas.**   **(PR:C MPAA:PG)**

MOTHER OUGHT TO MARRY

(SEE: SECOND TIME AROUND, THE, 1961)

MOTHER RILEY MEETS THE VAMPIRE

(SEE: MY SON THE VAMPIRE, 1952, Brit.)

MOTHER SIR   (SEE: NAVY WIFE, 1956)

MOTHER SUPERIOR   (SEE: TROUBLE WITH ANGELS, THE, 1966)

MOTHER WORE TIGHTS***   (1947) 107m FOX c

Betty Grable (Myrtle McKinley Burt), Dan Dailey (Frank Burt), Mona Freeman (Iris Burt), Connie Marshall (Mikie Burt), Vanessa Brown (Bessie), Robert Arthur (Bob Clarkman), Sara Allgood (Grandmother McKinley), William Frawley (Mr. Schneider), Ruth Nelson (Miss Ridgeway), Anabel Shaw (Alice Flemmerhammer), Michael [Stephen] Dunne (Roy Bivens), George Cleveland (Grandfather McKinley), Veda Ann Borg (Rosemary Olcott), Sig Rumann (Papa), Lee Patrick (Lil), Senor Wences with Johnny (Specialty), Maude Eburne (Mrs. Muggins), William Forrest (Mr. Clarkman), Kathleen Lockhart (Mrs. Clarkman), Chick Chandler (Ed), Will Wright (Withers), Frank Orth (Stage Doorman), Harry Cheshire (Minister), Billy Greene (1st Policeman), David Thursby (2nd Policeman), Tom Stevenson (Hotel Clerk), Ann Gowland (Mikie at Age 3), Joan Gerians (Baby—One Month Old), Anne Baxter (Narrator), Kenny Williams (Dance Director), Eula Morgan (Opera Singer), Tom Moore, Harry Seymour (Men), Lee MacGregor (Boy), Stephen Kirchner (Myrtle's Dancing Partner), Alvin Hammer (Clarence), Brad Slaven, Ted Jordan (Sailors), George Davis (Waiter), Karolyn Grimes (Iris at Age 6), Lotte Stein (Mama), Antonio Filauri (Papa Capucci).

A bouncy domestic fluff that has little reason for existence except to entertain, and what is so bad about that? Grable is a turn-of-the century vaudevillian who takes time off from work to raise two daughters (Dailey is her husband). They grow up to be Freeman and Marshall and once they can take care of themselves, Grable decides to go back to work. The rest of the movie is a nostalgic look at the way it was, interspersed with a bit of domestic crisis when Freeman, who is attending an exclusive finishing school, is embarrassed to learn that her parents will do a one-night show at a theater near her exclusive educational institution. In the end, all of the snotty kids who come to the theater to hoot stay to cheer and Freeman learns a valuable lesson. A raft of songs from several writers include: "You Do," "Fare Thee Well Dear Alma Mater," "There's Nothing Like a Song," "Rolling Down to Bowling Green," "Kokomo, Indiana," "This is My Favorite City," (Mack Gordon, Joseph Myrow); "Burlington Bertie From Bow," (William Hargreaves); "Tra-La-La-La-La," (Harry Warren, Gordon); "Swingin' Down the Lane," (Gus Kahn, Isham Jones), "Lily of the Valley," (L. Wolfe Gilbert, Anatole Friedland), "Stumbling," (Zez Confrey), "Choo'n Gum," (Mann Curtis, Vic Mizzy), "Daddy, You've Been Like a Mother to Me," (Fred Fisher), "Put Your Arms Around Me Honey," (Junie McCree, Albert von Tilzer), "M-O-T-H-E-R," (Theodore F. Morse, Howard Johnson), "Ta-Ra-Ra-Boom-De-Ay," (Henry J. Sayers); "Silent Night" (Joseph Mohr, Franz Gruber). Grable and Dailey worked well together and made three more films. She always had a soft spot in her heart for MOTHER WORE TIGHTS and was quoted as having called it her favorite. The story is told through the eyes of Marshall and the voice of narrator Anne Baxter. Good specialty work by Ed Sullivan's ventriloquism star, Senor Wences, who was still saying "All right?" in early 1986. Newman and Henderson won an Oscar for musical direction and Jackson's cinematography and "You Do" took nominations.

p, Lamar Trotti; d, Walter Lang; w, Trotti (based on the novel by Miriam Young); ph, Harry Jackson (Technicolor); ed, J. Watson Webb, Jr.; md, Alfred Newman, Charles Henderson; art d, Richard Day, Joseph C. Wright; set d, Thomas Little; cos, Orry-Kelly; ch, Seymour Felix, Kenny Williams.

Musical/Comedy   **(PR:A MPAA:NR)**

MOTHER'S BOY*   (1929) 82m Pathe bw

John T. Doyle (Pa O'Day), Beryl Mercer (Ma O'Day), Morton Downey (Tommy O'Day), Brian Donlevy (Harry O'Day), Helen Chandler (Rose Lyndon), Osgood Perkins (Professor Jake Sturmberg), Lorin Raker (Joe Bush, Press Agent), Robert Gleckler (Gus Le Grand, Cafe Manager), Barbara Bennett (Beatrix Townleigh, Debutante), Jennie Moskowitz (Mrs. Apfelbaum), Jacob Frank (Mr. Apfelbaum), Tyrrell Davis (Duke of Pomplum), Allan Vincent (Dinslow), Leslie Stowe (Evangelist), Louis Sorin (Mr. Bumble).

Incredibly soppy melodrama starring Downey as an aspiring singer who is informed by his girl, Chandler, only moments before his Broadway debut that his mother, Mercer (who had sacrificed everything for his career), has taken ill. Downey walks out on the show and rushes to his mother's bedside to nurse her back to health. Luckily, the press gets hold of the story of his unselfish act and turns him into a star anyway. Unbelievably maudlin fare.

p, Robert T. Kane; d, Bradley Barker, James Semour; w, Gene Markey; ph, Phillip Tannura, Harry Stradling, Walter Strenge; ed, Edward Pfitzenmeier; set d, Clark

Robinson; m/l, "There'll Be You and Me," "Come to Me," "I'll Always Be Mother's Boy," "The World Is Yours and Mine," Sammy Stept, Bud Green.

Drama   **(PR:A MPAA:NR)**

MOTHERS CRY* ½   (1930) 75m FN-WB bw

Dorothy Peterson (Mary K. Williams), Helen Chandler (Beatty Williams), David Manners (Artie Williams), Sidney Blackmer (Gerald Hart), Edward Woods (Danny Williams), Evalyn Knapp (Jenny Williams), Jean Bary (Sadye), Pat O'Malley (Frank Williams), Claire McDowell (Mary's Mother), Charles Hill Mailes (Mary's Father), Reginald Pasch (Karl Muller), Boris Karloff, Marvin Jones, Meredyth Burel.

Yet another tear-jerking film dealing with the trials and tribulations of raising children alone. This one stars Peterson as the widowed mom who is left to raise four unruly children and she fails drearily. Over the course of nearly 30 years the children grow up and meet their fates. One daughter marries a man old enough to be her father and settles down to a bleak domestic life. A son, a gifted architect, flees town to avoid a scandal that would ruin his career. The other son becomes a small-time hood and murderer who even kills his own sister (the other daughter) when she tries to shield her lover from him. This cheerful family outing ends with the killer-son getting his in the electric chair. Karloff has a brief, unbilled part as one of the hoodlum son's murder victims.

p, Robert North; d, Hobart Henley; w, Lenore J. Coffee (based on the novel by Helen Grace Carlisle); ph, Gilbert Warrenton; ed, Frank Ware.

Drama   **(PR:A MPAA:NR)**

MOTHER'S DAY zero   (1980) 98m United Film Distribution c

Nancy Hendrickson (Abbey), Deborah Luce (Jackie), Tiana Pierce (Trina), Holden McGuire (Ike), Billy Rae McQuade (Addley), Rose Ross (Mother), Kevin Lowe (Ted), Karl Sandys (Brad), Ed Battle (Doorman), Stanley Knapp (Charlie), Marsella Davidson (Terry), Robert Carnegie (Tex), Scott Lucas (Storekeeper), Bobby Collins (Ernie).

Rancid horror film that suffers from pretentions of social significance. Two repulsive brothers, McGuire and McQuade, live in the woods of New Jersey with their equally pathetic mother, Ross. Their home is filled with sugary breakfast cereals, brand-name consumer products, and dozens of television sets (the media has driven them mad). Enter three young women who have the misfortune to wander near the geeks' home on their way to a class reunion. The brothers capture the gals and spend the next 80 minutes or so subjecting them to various tortures until two of the girls escape and get revenge by performing even grosser acts of violence on their tormentors. The film's got a lame "twist" ending guaranteed to irritate any sensible filmgoer with its obvious lack of thought. MOTHER'S DAY has some defenders who claim it is not your run-of-the-mill horror film, and they're right. It's worse.

p, Michael Kravitz, Charles Kaufman; d, Kaufman; w, Kaufman, Warren D. Leight; ph, Joe Mangine; m, Phil Gallo, Clem Vicari.

Horror   **Cas.**   **(PR:O MPAA:NR)**

MOTHER'S MILLIONS   (SEE: SHE-WOLF, THE, 1931)

MOTHERS OF TODAY**   (1939) 95m Apex bw

Esther Field, Max Rosenblatt, Gertie Krause, Simon Wolf, Leon Seidenberg, Paula Lubelsak, Vera Lubov, Arthur Winters, Louis Goldstein, Jack Shargel.

A lesser-quality Yiddish film about a Jewish mother (Field) who is neglected by her family. Lubelsak is her counterpart, a younger woman who neglects traditional roles much to her husband's dismay. The message here is about as subtle as a two-by-four to the skull. Older cast members do a pretty good job. (In Yiddish; English subtitles.)

d, Henry Lynn.

Drama   **(PR:C MPAA:NR)**

MOTHRA** ½   (1962, Jap.) 101m Toho/COL c (MOSURA)

Franky Sakai (Reporter), Hiroshi Koizumi (Photographer), Kyoko Kagawa (Showman), Emi Ito, Yumi Ito (Twins), Jerry Ito, Ken Uehara, Takashi Shimura, Seizaburo Kawazu, Kenji Sahara, Akihiko Hirata, Yoshio Kosugi, Yoshifumi Tajima, Yasushi Yamamoto, Haruya Kato, Ko Mishima, Tetsu Nakamura.

Good Japanese giant-monster epic dubbed into English starring Emi and Yumi Ito as tiny 6-inch twin princesses (who talk and sing in unison) who are taken from their island home and put on display by an unscrupulous nightclub owner in Japan. The girls pray to their god, Mothra, for rescue and back on the island a giant egg hatches and out crawls a big caterpillar. The caterpillar makes its way to Tokyo in search of its mistresses and inadvertently destroys much of the city. At one point it spins a cocoon and hatches as a monster-sized moth whose wings create tidal waves and windstorms that destroy the rest of Japan. Eventually, Mothra lands at the airport and picks up the tiny sisters and the happy trio heads for home, leaving the Japanese to reconstruct their country one more time. MOTHRA was a departure for Toho Studios because the monster was sympathetic and didn't really mean to cause death and destruction; it just was too big to gracefully fulfill its rescue mission. Mothra went on to become a "good" monster (as were Gammera and Godzilla) in subsequent movies and she-he-it went on to help defeat such "bad" monsters as Ghidorah.

p, Tomoyuki Tanaka, David D. Horne; d, Inoshiro Honda, Lee Kresel; w, Shinichi Sekizawa, Robert Myerson; (based on a story by Shinichiro Nakamura, Takehiko Fukunaga, Yoshie Hotta); ph, Hajime Koizumi (Tohoscope, Eastmancolor); m, Yuji Koseki; ed, Ichiji Taira; art d, Takeo Kita, Kimei Abe; spec eff, Eiji Tsuburaya, Hiroshi Mukouyama.

Science Fiction   **Cas.**   **(PR:A MPAA:NR)**

MOTIVE FOR REVENGE*   (1935) 62m Majestic bw

Donald Cook (*Barry Webster*), Irene Hervey (*Muriel Webster*), Doris Lloyd (*Mrs. Fleming*), Edwin Maxwell (*William King*), William Le Strange Millman (*Milroy*), Russell Simpson (*McAllister*), John Kelly (*Larkin*), Edwin Argus (*Red*), Billy West (*Ray*), Wheeler Oakman (*Doane*), Frank LaRue (*Warden*), Fern Emmett, Dorothy Wolbert.

Monotonous drama starring Cook as a henpecked bank teller who is caught embezzling the company funds so that he can buy his wife all the luxuries that his overbearing mother-in-law thinks her daughter should have. Lackluster central performances fail to spark any interest in the dull material.

p, Larry Darmour; d, Burt Lynwood; w, Stuart Anthony; ph, Herbert Kilpatrick; ed, Dwight Caldwell.

Drama   **(PR:A   MPAA:NR)**

MOTIVE WAS JEALOUSY, THE**

(1970 Ital./Span.) 105m Titanus-Dean Film-Juppiter Generale-Midega/WB c (PER MOTIVI DI GELOSIA)

Monica Vitti (*Adelaide*), Marcello Mastroianni (*Oreste*), Giancarlo Giannini (*Nello*), Marisa Merlini (*Adelaide's sister*).

Grim social satire starring Vitti as a flower vendor who first falls in love with bricklayer Mastroianni and then finds herself becoming involved with pizza baker Giannini. Instead of opting for one man or the other Vitti attempts to continue the triangle but Mastroianni eventually discovers the other man and goes insane, killing Vitti in a jealous rage. Structured as a flashback during Mastroianni's interrogation by police, THE MOTIVE WAS JEALOUSY parodies the neo-realist visual style and suffers somewhat from a fairly heavy-handed presentation.

p, Pio Angeletti, Adriano De Micheli; d, Ettore Scola; w, Age and Scarpelli, Scola; ph, Carlo Di Palma (Technicolor); m, Armando Trovajoli; ed, Alberto Gallitti; art d, Luciano Ricceri.

Drama/Satire   **(PR:C   MPAA:NR)**

MOTOR MADNESS*1/2   (1937) 61m COL bw

Rosalind Keith (*Peggy McNeil*), Allen Brook (*Joe Dunn*), Marc Lawrence (*Slater*), Richard Terry (*Givens*), J. M. Kerrigan (*Cap McNeil*), Arthur Loft (*Lucky Raymond*), Joseph Sawyer (*Steve Dolan*), George Ernest (*Pancho*), Al Hill (*Jeff*), John Tyrrell (*Pete Bailey*), Ralph Byrd (*Mike Burns*).

Brook stars as a small boat manufacturer who falls in with some crooked off-shore gamblers who assist transporting criminals past the 12-mile zone to freedom from the law in order to raise money to keep his company solvent. When he realizes his mistake, Brook tries to withdraw from the gang, but of course, life isn't that easy. Keith is his girl who helps him escape the crooks' grasp and prepares him for the big international race that he feels he must win to redeem himself.

d, D. Ross Lederman; w, Fred Niblo, Jr., Grace Neville; ph, Allen G. Siegler; ed, Byrd Robinson.

Crime/Drama   **(PR:A   MPAA:NR)**

MOTOR PATROL*   (1950) 67m Lippert bw

Don Castle (*Ken*), Jane Nigh (*Connie*), Reed Hadley (*Flynn*), Bill Henry (*Larry*), Gwen O'Connor (*Jean*), Sid Melton (*Omar*), Dick [Richard] Travis (*Bill*), Frank Jenks (*Mac*), Louis Fuller (*Tom Morgan*), Charles Victor (*Russ*), Onslow Stevens (*Lt. Dearborn*), Charles Wagenheim (*Bud Haynes*), Frank Jacquet (*Miller*).

Low-budget cop film starring Castle as a young police recruit. He joins the force to avenge the death of the motorcycle policeman brother of his fiancee who was killed by the Chicago gangsters behind an auto-theft ring. Castle proves his bravery when he smashes the gang in a shootout.

p, Barney Sarecky; d, Sam Newfield; w, Maurice Tombragel, Orville Hampton (based on a story by Tombragel); ph, Ernest W. Miller; ed, Stanley Frazen; md, Ozzie Caswell; art d, P. Frank Sylos.

Crime   **(PR:A   MPAA:NR)**

MOTOR PSYCHO   zero   (1965) 73m Eve Productions bw

Haji (*Ruby Bonner*), Alex Rocco (*Cory Maddox*), Stephen Oliver (*Brahmin*), Holle K. Winters (*Gail Maddox*), Joseph Cellini (*Dante*), Thomas Scott (*Slick*), Coleman Francis (*Harry Bonner*), Sharon Lee (*Jessica Fannin*), Steve Masters (*Frank*), Arshalouis Aivazian (*Wife*), E. E. Meyer (*Sheriff*), George Costello (*Doctor*), F. Rufus Owens (*Rufus*), Richard Brummer (*Ambulance Driver*).

Non-porno Russ Meyer film originally double-billed with his classic FASTER PUSSYCAT! KILL! KILL! which stars Rocco as a local veterinarian whose wife is beaten and raped by a crazed band of bloodthirsty (but incredibly clean-cut) psychopathic bikers. Joined by Haji (who also starred in FASTER PUSSYCAT! KILL! KILL!), whose husband was murdered by the gang, Rocco follows the depraved cyclists into the desert seeking revenge. Eventually Haji and Rocco get their vengeance by killing the gang in various brutal ways. Competent, inventive basement-budget filmmaking for the drive-in crowds.

p&d, Russ Meyer; w, William E. Sprague, Meyer (based on a story by Meyer, James Griffith, Hal Hopper); ph, Meyer; m, Igo Kantor; ed, Charles Schelling; spec eff, Orville Hallberg; m/l, Paul Sawtell, Bert Shefter.

Crime   **(PR:O   MPAA:NR)**

MOTORCYCLE GANG*1/2   (1957) 78m Golden State/AIP bw

Anne Neyland (*Terry*), Steven Terrell (*Randy*), John Ashley (*Nick*), Carl Switzer (*Speed*), Raymond Hatton (*Uncle Ed*), Russ Bender (*Joe*), Jean Moorhead (*Marilyn*), Scott Peters (*Hank*), Eddie Kafafian (*Jack*), Shirley Falls (*Darlene*), Aki Aleong (*Cyrus Wong*), Wayne Taylor (*Phil*), Hal Bogart (*Walt*), Phyllis Cole (*Mary*),

Suzanne Sydney (*Birdie*), Edmund Cobb (*Bill*), Paul Blaisdell (*Don*), Zon Murray (*Hal*), Felice Richmond (*Hal's Wife*).

Another in the seemingly never-ending "youth problem" films concerning the destructive and senseless teenage activity of street racing. This one stars Terrell as a good-guy gear-head who runs afoul of fellow biker bug Ashley when he gets out of the slammer after a 15-month term for a hit-and-run accident. Ashley and sexy troublemaker Neyland goad Terrell into participating in an illegal drag race, even though it will jeopardize his position in the police-sanctioned cycle club which is entering its national racing competition in a few days. Not being able to stand their teasing, Terrell agrees to race Ashley, but he learns his lesson when he crashes and winds up in the hospital. Though he made a mistake in judgment, the legal cycle club decides Terrell can participate in the race after all (what nice guys!). Terrell, however, quits halfway through the national competition when he learns that Ashley and three of his goons are terrorizing a nearby town, and leads an army of good-guy bikers to stop them.

p, Alex Gordon; d, Edward L. Cahn; w, Lou Rusoff; ph, Frederick E. West; m, Albert Glasser; ed, Richard C. Meyer; art d, Don Ament.

Drama   **(PR:C-O   MPAA:NR)**

MOTSART I SALVERI   (SEE: REQUIEM FOR MOZART, 1967, USSR)

MOUCHETTE***1/2   (1970, Fr.) 80m Argos-Parc/Cinema Ventures bw

Nadine Nortier (*Mouchette*), Marie Cardinal (*Mother*), Paul Hebert (*Father*), Jean Vimenet (*Mathieu*), J. C. Guilbert (*Arsene*), Marie Susini (*Mathieu's Wife*), Liliane Princet (*Teacher*), Raymonde Chabrun (*Grocer*), Suzanne Huguenin (*Layer Out Of The Dead*), Marie Trichet (*Louisa*), Robert Bresson.

Released in Paris in 1967, this was Bresson's second adaptation of a novel by Georges Bernanos (the first being DIARY OF A COUNTRY PRIEST). The story concerns Nortier, the title character, and the last 24 hours in her life of only 14 years. With her father an alcoholic bootlegger and her mother on her deathbed, Nortier lives a depressing life, without any friends at all. She meets a drunken poacher one day, who takes her back to his cabin and rapes her. She tries to tell her mother, but the sickly woman dies before she can. She grows increasingly hostile towards her surroundings and the people in them before she drowns herself. A dark and cruel film, strengthened by a powerful score, which features excerpts from Monteverdi's "Magnificat" sung by the Saint-Eustache Chorus.

p, Anatole Dauman; d&w, Robert Bresson (based on the novel Nouvelle Histoire De Mouchette by Georges Bernanos); ph, Ghislain Cloquet; m, Claudio Monteverdi, Jean Wiener; ed, Raymond Lamy; md, Emile Martin; art d, Pierre Guffroy; cos, Odette LeBarbenchon.

Drama   **(PR:C   MPAA:NR)**

MOULIN ROUGE**1/2   (1934) 69m FOX/UA bw

Constance Bennett (*Helen Hall/Racquel*), Franchot Tone (*Douglas Hall*), Tullio Carminati (*Victor Le Maire*), Helen Westley (*Mrs. Morris*), Andrew Tombes (*McBride*), Russ Brown (*Joe*), Hobart Cavanaugh (*Drunk*), Geoges Renevant (*Frenchman*), Fuzzy Knight (*Eddie*), Ivan Lebedeff (*Ramon*), Russ Columbo and The Boswell Sisters.

Well-done musical starring Bennett in two roles—Helen Hall, wife of songwriter Tone, and her sister, Racquel. The sisters were once a singing duo, but they split up and Racquel went to France where she became a singing star. As the film begins, Helen would like to resume her singing career, but Tone objects. When Racquel visits from France, the sisters meet and hatch a plan by which Helen will pose as her sister at various times. This allows Helen to re-enter show business and provides a cover for Racquel to use so that she can meet with her lover without arousing the suspicions of her husband. Eventually, the husband catches on and drags Racquel off while Helen goes on to become a star herself. Songs include: "The Boulevard of Broken Dreams," "Coffee In the Morning, and Kisses at Night," and "Song of Surrender" (Al Dubin, Harry Warren). This was the first film for Westley, who went on to appear in numerous musicals during the 1930s and early 1940s.

d, Sidney Lanfield; w, Nunnally Johnson, Henry Lehrman; ph, Charles Rosher; m, Harry Warren; ed, Lloyd Nesler; md, Alfred Newman; ch, Russell Markert.

Musical   **(PR:A   MPAA:NR)**

MOULIN ROUGE**   (1944, Fr.) 85m Andre Hugon bw

Lucien Baroux (*Losieau*), Rene Dary (*Lequerec*), Genevieve Callix (*Eva*), Pierre Larquey (*Director of Moulin Rouge*), Annie France (*Lulu*), Simone Berriau (*Simone*), Josephine Baker (*Princess Tam-Tam*).

French musical shot in Paris just before the Nazis took over starring Dary as an aspiring singer who is too poor to get into the Moulin Rouge and prove himself. Willing to work his way to the top, Dary takes a job as an undertaker's helper and then as a caretaker to make some money. When he and his pal Baroux land jobs as caretakers of a rich man's home, the duo borrows some of the man's best clothes and crash the Moulin Rouge where Dary is able to sneak onstage and show his stuff. Of course he is noticed by the show's producer (and his mistress) and before he knows what hit him, Dary is a star. Routine stuff with a fairly interesting appearance by Josephine Baker doing one of her famed dance routines. The film introduced Dary to U.S. audiences, with promotions billing him as "the sensational new French singing star." Though he didn't quite live up to the advanced billing, he did continue to make occasional film appearances up until 1960. (In French; English subtitles.)

p, Andre Hugon; d&w, Yves Mirande; m/l, Jean Lenoir, Van Parys, Rene Silviano, Raoul Moretti, Lucien Pipon, Roger Beernstein.

Musical   **(PR:Am   MPAA:NR)**

MOULIN ROUGE* 1/2** (1952) 123m Romulus/UA c

Jose Ferrer *(Henri de Toulouse-Lautrec/The Comte de Toulouse-Lautrec)*, Colette Marchand *(Marie Charlet)*, Suzanne Flon *(Myriamme Hayem)*, Zsa Zsa Gabor *(Jane Avril)*, Katherine Kath *(La Goulue)*, Claude Nollier *(Countess de Toulouse-Lautrec)*, Muriel Smith *(Aicha)*, Georges Lannes *(Patou)*, Walter Crisham *(Valentin Dessosse)*, Mary Clare *(Mme. Loubet)*, Harold Kasket *(Zidler)*, Lee Montague *(Maurice Joyant)*, Jill Bennett *(Sarah)*, Maureen Swanson *(Denise)*, Jim Gerald *(Pere Cotelle)*, Rupert John *(Chocolat)*, Tutte Lemkow *(Aicha's Partner)*, Eric Pohlmann *(Proprietor of 1st Bar)*, Christopher Lee *(Scurat)*, Jean Landlier *(Anquetin)*, Robert Le Fort *(Gauzi)*, Jean Claudio *(Drunken Reveller)*, Suzi Euzaine *(Lorette)*, Guy Motschen *(Delivery Boy)*, Mons. Tabourno *(Maitre D'Hotel Pre Catalan)*, Mons. Ledebur *(Maitre D'Hotel Maxim's)*, Fernard Fabre *(General)*, George Pastell *(Man at 1st Bar)*, M. Valerbe *(Sommelier)*, Jean Ozenne *(Felix)*, Francis de Wolff *(Victor)*, Michael Balfour *(Dodo)*, Theodore Bikel *(King)*, Peter Cushing *(Marcel de la Voisier)*, Terence O'Regan, Arissa Cooper, Jacques Cey, Charles Carson, Walter Cross, Rene Poirier, Margaret Maxwell, Hilary Allen, Maria Samina, Sari Luzita, Sheila Nelson, Aleta Morrison, Hugh Dempster, Charles Perry, Tim Turner, Michael Seavers, Bernard Rebel, Chrisopher Rhodes, Rene Laplat, Maria Britneva, Charles Reynolds, Ina de la Haye, Richard Molinas, Isobel George, Donovan Winter, Madge Brindley, Peter Haddon, Everley Gregg, Raymond Rollett, David Garth, Anthony Gray, Diane Cilento.

MOULIN ROUGE is a good movie but unless you've seen it recently, it remembers better than it really was. Nominated for Best Picture, Best Direction, Best Actor and Best Supporting Actor, it won none of those awards and only managed to take a statuette for Marcel Vertes' Best Costume Design (Color). The shame of it is that Oswald Morris' work was not even nominated and should have won an Oscar as it was, by far, the best color cinematography of 1952 and much better than the winning film, THE QUIET MAN. Ferrer was making his mark with portrayals of real or famous fictional characters (CYRANO DE BERGERAC, the Dauphin in JOAN OF ARC) and his role of the Artist Toulouse-Lautrec was a combination of the two as Huston's adaptation of the artist's life took many liberties with the truth. Ferrer, in a magnificent job that must have been painful as he played much of the film on his knees, is Toulouse-Lautrec, the son of wealthy Parisians. As a child, he had suffered an accident and his legs ceased to grow. The rest of his body continued growing. He becomes a painter and his works glorify the colorful Montmartre area of Paris, a neighborhood just slightly more liveable than the red-light district of Pigalle. Ferrer paints Gabor (Jane Avril, the redheaded dancer whom Huston chose to make a singer perhaps because Gabor dances like a bear with arthritis) and makes her famous. He falls hard for prostitute Marchand but that does not work. He then finds love with Flon, a model, but does not propose and she leaves him for someone else. Ferrer begins to drink to excess, his work suffers, and he is increasingly depressed. Eventually, he returns to the family chateau to be taken care of by his mother, a countess (Nollier) until the wine and high-living finally take his life at the age of 37. The drama is so relentlessly dreary (against the brilliant use of color) that one wonders if the fellow was really that unhappy all the time. Surely, his works do not reflect that dour attitude and so much of his art indicates the joie de vivre of the period and the area better than any photography (a medium that was just beginning). MOULIN ROUGE was filmed in France and England and had a few interesting people in small roles. Look hard for horrorists Christopher Lee and Peter Cushing as well as a young Tutte Lemkow (British choreographer/actor who was the Fiddler in FIDDLER ON THE ROOF. The first 25 minutes of the movie are outstanding as a can-can sequence sets the tone for what is to come. Unfortunately, everything that follows is pale and the picture begins to wallow in sentimentality and self-pity, something that Toulouse-Lautrec never betrayed in his art. The dance sequences, with the traditional can-can steps, eclipse Jean Renoir's FRENCH CANCAN and Walter Lang's CAN CAN.

p&d, John Huston; w, Anthony Veiller, Huston, (based on the novel by Pierre La Mure); ph, Oswald Morris (Technicolor); m, Georges Auric; ed, Ralph Kemplin; art d, Paul Sheriff, cos, Marcel Vertes, Jules Squire, Schiaparelli.

Biography **(PR:A-C MPAA:NR)**

MOUNTAIN, THE* (1935, Brit.) 82m Jackatoon/Equity British bw

Maurice Jones *(David Rodgers)*, Hope Sharpe *(Sylvia Goodhall)*, Alan F. Elliott *(Rev. Brian Goodhall)*, J. Vyne Clarke *(Old Sam)*, Rosemary Lee Booker *(Rose Harding)*, Sydney Dench *(John Rodgers)*.

Overly sentimental tearjerker with Elliott and wife on holiday in the lake district, a pleasant outing which ends in tragedy when the wife falls for mountain man Jones, and Elliott goes into a jealous rampage. The photographic beauty of the lake district adds nothing to the dismal proceedings.

p,d&w, Travis Jackson.

Drama **(PR:A MPAA:NR)**

MOUNTAIN, THE* 1/2 (1956) 104m PAR c

Spencer Tracy *(Zachary Teller)*, Robert Wagner *(Chris Teller)*, Claire Trevor *(Marie)*, William Demarest *(Father Belacchi)*, Barbara Darrow *(Simone)*, Richard Arlen *(Rivial)*, E. G. Marshall *(Solange)*, Anna Kashfi *(Hindu Girl)*, Richard Garrick *(Coloz)*, Harry Townes *(Joseph)*, Stacy Harris *(Servoz)*, Yves Brainville *(Andre)*, Mary Adams *(Mayor's Wife)*, Jim Hayward *(Mayor)*, Richard H. Cutting *(Doctor)*.

Tracy spent 20 years at MGM and this was his first film outside that studio's aegis. It was a mistake. Wagner is Tracy's younger brother (Tracy was 30 years older than Wagner when the picture was made and looked it) and a rotten kid. Tracy is a quiet, amiable mountaineer who has retired and is now devoting himself to raising Wagner. A Calcutta-to-Paris routed airplane crashes at the top of a nearby alp and Wagner wants to get up there right away and take money from the dead passengers. Tracy is against it, thinks the idea is grisly, but is eventually persuaded to accompany Wagner rather than let the young man go up that mountain alone. The scenes, as they climb the alp, are the most harrowing and interesting in the picture. Once at the top, they discover one survivor, Kashfi, still alive, but only barely. Wagner thinks she should be killed because her testimony can nail him as a thief. Tracy will not hear of such wanton slaughter. They have a battle and Tracy makes a sled for the injured girl as Wagner goes into the airliner and begins to pillage and plunder. Tracy goes down the hill with Kashfi and, after he has filled his pockets to overflowing with money and baubles, Wagner follows, hoping to cut them off. But it is Wagner who pays the price when he dies in a fall. Once Tracy and Kashfi reach bottom, Tracy tries to take the blame for the attempted robbery (to keep his brother's name clear) but the others at the mountain's base know that Tracy is a good man and that Wagner was a rotter so they do not buy that story. Neither did anyone else when this movie was released. Filmed in the French Alps and in the studio. The faked climbing scenes are awful, the real ones are terrific. They just do not match very well and the result of THE MOUNTAIN is a molehill.

p&d, Edward Dmytryk; w, Ranald MacDougall (based on a novel by Henri Troyat); ph, Franz F. Planer (VistaVision, Technicolor); m, Daniele Amfitheatrof; ed, Frank Bracht; art d, Hal Pereira, John Goodman; set d, Sam Comer, Grace Gregory; cos, Edith Head; spec eff, John Fulton; m/l, "The Mountain," Mack David, Amfitheatrof.

Drama **(PR:A MPAA:NR)**

MOUNTAIN DESPERADOES (SEE: LARAMIE MOUNTAINS, 1952)

MOUNTAIN FAMILY ROBINSON** (1979) 100m PI c

Robert Logan *(Skip)*, Susan Damante Shaw *(Pat)*, Heather Rattray *(Jenny)*, Ham Larsen *(Toby)*, William Bryant *(Forest Ranger)*, George "Buck" Flower *(Boomer)*, Calvin Bartlett *(Doctor)*, Jim Davidson *(Pilot)*.

Yet another "Wilderness Family" adventure which looks a lot like the last one. Once again kiddies are subjected to 100 minutes of blue skies, big mountains, wild animals, and maudlin sentiment. Big "plot" twist sees mom (Shaw) get fed up with the good life and want to return to civilization, but the rest of the family talks her out of it. Competently done, but really dull, even for the most indiscriminant children.

p, Arthur R. Dubs; d, John Cotter; w, Dubs; ph, James W. Roberson (Panavision/CFI); m, Robert O. Ragland; ed, Dan Greer, Clifford Katz; m/l, Carol Connors, Ragland.

Adventure **Cas.** **(PR:A MPAA:G)**

MOUNTAIN JUSTICE** (1930) 72m UNIV bw (AKA: KETTLE CREEK)

Ken Maynard *(Ken McTavish)*, Kathryn Crawford *(Coral Harland)*, Otis Harlan *(Jud McTavish)*, Paul Hurst *(Lem Harland)*, Richard Carlyle *(Judge Keets)*, Les Bates *(Abner Harland)*, Pee Wee Holmes *(Rusty)*, Blue Washington *(Sam)*, Fred Burns *(Sandy McTavish)*, Tarzan the Horse.

The first all-talkie Maynard oater (the previous films were only part sound) sees our hero as an Oklahoma rancher who goes further west in search of Bates, the murderer of his father. Routine stuff as usual, but this one contains some thrilling stunt work (done by Maynard) aboard a buckboard and moving train. Significant for its heavy emphasis on singing (predating the "singing cowboy" craze by quite a few years) and the fact that Maynard was allowed to contribute his own ideas to the script. Crawford sings "Seeing Nellie Home" and "Buffalo Gal."

p, Ken Maynard, Harry Joe Brown; d, Brown; w, Bennett Cohen, Lesley Mason; ph, Ted McCord; ed, Fred Allen.

Western **(PR:A MPAA:NR)**

MOUNTAIN JUSTICE 1/2** (1937) 82m WB bw

Josephine Hutchinson *(Ruth Harkins)*, George Brent *(Paul Cameron)*, Guy Kibbee *(Dr. Barnard)*, Robert Barrat *(Jeff Harkins)*, Mona Barrie *(Evelyn Wayne)*, Elisabeth Risdon *(Meg Harkins)*, Margaret Hamilton *(Phoebe)*, Edward Pawley *(Tod Miller)*, Marcia Mae Jones *(Bethy Harkins)*, Fuzzy Knight *(Clem Biggers)*, Robert McWade *(Horace Bamber)*, Granville Bates *(Judge Crawley)*, Russell Simpson *(Turnbull)*, Sibyl Harris *(Mrs. Turnbull)*, Guy Wilkerson *(Asaph Anderson)*, Claire DuBrey *(Young Woman)*, Gertrude Hoffman *(Granny Burnside)*, Alice Lyndon *(Charity Topping)*, Henry Hall *(Henniger)*, Harry Davenport *(Printer)*, Jim Toney *(Makeup Man)*, Earle Hodgins *(Vendor)*, Minerva Urecal *(Ella Crippen)*, Herbert Heywood *(Jury Foreman)*, Carl Stockdale *(Stout)*, Walter Soderling *(Sheriff Willis)*, Arthur Aylesworth *(Justice of the Peace)*, Virginia Brissac *(Miss Hughes)*, Heinie Conklin *(Jury Foreman)*, Dennis Moore *(Airplane Pilot)*.

Downbeat tale starring Hutchinson as the oldest daughter of cruel hillbilly Barrat who still believes in beating her even though she is an adult. Encouraged to escape the backwoods tyranny of her father by her mother and some family friends, Hutchinson flees to New York where she enrolls in nursing classes and meets up with charming young lawyer Brent who had helped convict her father on a shooting charge a few months earlier. Returning home to work for a doctor in a free clinic, Hutchinson is forbidden to enter the family house by her father. This suits her fine, but when her younger sister Jones flees the house rather than be sold off as a child bride, Barrat again whips Hutchinson for attempting to aid her sister. This time Hutchinson fights back and accidentally kills her father. Brent comes to her defense, but she is convicted of murder and sentenced to 25 years in prison. The sentence isn't enough to satisfy the vengeance-seeking locals, however, and they don hoods and surround the jail, threatening to lynch Hutchinson. Brent manages to save her in the nick of time and gets her on a plane to safety. Loosely based on an actual case in which a daughter killer her father under similar circumstances, the film's credibility is hampered by heavy-handed direction.

d, Michael Curtiz; w, Norman Reilly Raine, Luci Ward; ph, Ernest Haller; ed, George Amy; md, Leo F. Forbstein; art d, Max Parker; cos, Milo Anderson.

Drama **(PR:A MPAA:NR)**

MOUNTAIN MAN (SEE: GUARDIAN OF THE WILDERNESS, 1977)

MOUNTAIN MEN, THE* (1980) 102m COL c

Charlton Heston (*Bill Tyler*), Brian Keith (*Henry*), Victoria Racimo (*Running Moon*), Stephen Macht (*Heavy Eagle*), John Glover (*Nathan*), Seymour Cassel (*LaBont*), David Ackroyd (*Medicine Wolf*), Cal Bellini (*Cross Otter*), Bill Lucking (*Jim*), Ken Ruta (*Fontenelle*), Victor Jory (*Iron Belly*), Danny Zapien, Tim Haldeman, Buckley Norris, Daniel Knapp, Michael Greene, Steward East, Terry Leonard, Steve D. Chambers, Bennie Dobbins, Suzanna Trujillo, Melissa Sylvia, James Ecoffey.

A total mess which once again shows that the offspring of movie stars do not necessarily inherit the artistic talents of their parents. Written by Fraser Clarke Heston, son of star Charlton Heston, THE MOUNTAIN MEN is a mindless, bloody pseudo-western which purports to show the closing days of the fur-trapper era. The film opens as an Indian squaw, Racimo, deserts her brutal husband Macht and sets out on her own. Unfortunately, Macht doesn't take this lying down and he dispatches an army of warriors to bring her back. On the run, she meets two grizzled old trappers, Heston and Keith. The two veteran backwoodsmen commit themselves to several overly bloody battles against the marauding Indians with Keith spewing a litany of profanities on the pretext of being amusing. This tiresome act rambles along until both men are properly canonized as tragic-but-noble figures of a vanishing way of life. Though Heston and Keith seem to be having a bit of fun with their roles, one gets the feeling this is a home movie shot for some laughs while the family was on vacation at the National Parks. The inept script and direction (Lang's first effort) keep anything really interesting from happening. The portrayal of the mountain men and the Indians is cliched at best, exposing young Heston's and director Lang's total ignorance of what makes this genre work. One wonders if there was any point to this whole exercise other than to beef up Fraser Clarke Heston's resume. The film was shot on locations in the Bridger-Teton National Forest and the Shoshone National Forest, and looks properly gorgeous, but the aggravating screenplay and excess of gore distract from the beauty. This is a bad film, and another unfortunate nail in the coffin for the western genre. For a really good vanishing-breed movie, see LONELY ARE THE BRAVE (1962). The best thing about this film is the deft editing performed by Ruggiero.

p, Martin Shafer, Andrew Scheinman; d, Richard Lang; w, Fraser Clarke Heston; ph, Michael Hugo (Panavision, Metrocolor); m, Michael Legrand; ed, Eva Ruggiero; prod d, Bill Kenney; set d, Rick T. Gentz; cos, Thomas S. Dawson, Kathleen McGregor.

Western **Cas.** **(PR:O MPAA:R)**

MOUNTAIN MOONLIGHT* (1941) 68m REP bw (GB: MOVING IN SOCIETY)

Leon Weaver, June Weaver, Frank Weaver, Elviry Weaver, Betty Jane Rhodes, John Archer, Loretta Weaver, George Ernest, Andrew Tombes, George Chandler, Harry Hayden, Roscoe Ates, Leonard Carey, George Meeker, Edwin Stanley, Kane Richmond, Frank Sully, Johnny Arthur.

The Weaver Brothers discover that their ancestors loaned the government some cash way back in 1790. With interest, they stand to gain some sizeable returns, so they head off to Washington to see what's what. Cornpone comedy, but not much else. (See WEAVER FAMILY series, Index).

p, Armand Schaefer; d, Nick Grinde; w, John Krafft, Maurie Grashin, Dorrell McGowan, Stuart McGowan; ph, Jack Narta; ed, Charles Craft; md, Cy Feurer.

Comedy **(PR:A MPAA:NR)**

MOUNTAIN MUSIC* (1937) 76m PAR bw

Bob Burns (*Bob Burnside*), Martha Raye (*Mary Beamish*), John Howard (*Ardinger*), Terry Walker (*Lobelia*), Rufe Davis (*Ham*), George "Gabby" Hayes (*Grandpappy*), Spencer Charters (*Justice Sharody*), Charles Timblin (*Shep*), Jan Duggan (*Ma*), Olin Howland (*Pappy*), Fuzzy Knight (*Amos*), Wally Vernon (*Odette Potts*), Cliff Clark (*Medicine Show Doctor*), Goodee Montgomery (*Alice*), Rita LaRoy (*Mrs. Lovelace*), Red Donahue and Mule (*Themselves*), Arthur Hohl (*Prosecuting Attorney*), Charlie Arnt (*Hotel Manager*), Miranda Giles (*Aunt Effie*), Jimmy Conlin (*Medicine Show Shill*), Ward Bond, Wally Maher (*G-Men*), Eddie Tamblyn (*Bellboy*), Paul Kruger (*Attendant*), Lew Kelly (*Mailman*), Ellen Drew (*Helen*), Robert St. Angelo (*Chef*), Harvey Parry (*Bus Boy*), Charles Judela (*Orchestra Leader*), Louis Natheaux (*Mr. Lovelace*), Georgia Simmons (*Ma Shepardson*).

Hillbilly musical featuring Burns as a member of a feuding Arkansas family who wants him to marry the daughter of the rival family as a peace gesture. Knowing his brother really loves the girl he is to marry, Burns flees. Suffering from an odd malady that causes him to lose his memory when hit on the head, Burns meets and falls in love with Raye while suffering from this condition. When hit with some water, however, Burns reverts to his normal personality and has no memory of Raye or their romance. Eventually all the plot twists are straightened out and everything works out just fine. Songs include: "If I Put My Heart In A Song," "Can't You Hear That Mountain Music?" "Thar She Comes," "Hillbilly Wedding," "Good Morning," and "Mama Don't 'Low No Bull Fiddle Playin' In Heah" (Sam Coslow).

p, Benjamin Glazer; d, Robert Florey; w, John C. Moffitt, Duke Atteberry, Russell Crouse, Charles Lederer (based on a story by MacKinlay Kantor); ph, Karl Struss; m, Sam Coslow; ed, Eda Warren; md, Boris Morros; art d, Hans Dreier, John Goodman.

Musical/Comedy **(PR:Am MPAA:NR)**

MOUNTAIN RHYTHM* (1939) 61m REP bw

Gene Autry (*Gene*), Smiley Burnette (*Frog*), June Storey (*Alice*), Maude Eburne (*Ma*), Ferris Taylor (*Judge*), Walter Fenner (*Cavanaugh*), Jack Pennick (*Rocky*), Hooper Atchley (*Daniels*), Bernard Suss (*MacCauley*), Ed Cassidy (*Sheriff*), Jack Ingram (*Carney*), Tom London (*Deputy*), Roger Williams (*Kimball*), Frankie Marvin (*Burt*), Champion the Horse.

Really tedious Autry oater concerning the usual nonsense involving shady land deals that Gene must put an end to. Autry sings "It Makes No Difference Now."

p, Harry Grey; d, B. Reeves Eason; w, Gerald Geraghty (based on a story by Connie Lee); ph, Ernest Miller; ed, Lester Orlebeck.

Western **(PR:A MPAA:NR)**

MOUNTAIN RHYTHM** (1942) 70m REP bw (GB: Harvest Days)

Leon Weaver, Frank Weaver, June Weaver, Elviry Weaver, Lynn Merrick, Frank M. Thomas, Sally Payne, Dickie Jones, Joseph Allen, Jr., Billy Boy, Earle S. Sewey, Sam Flint, Ben Erway.

The Weavers (not to be confused with the classic folk group) were a discovery from the Grand Old Opry in Nashville, Tenn. They had enough popularity to warrant a film series in the late 1930s and early 1940s. In this support-the-war effort, the boys start a farm as their contribution. Problems stem from a local school which seems to be run by snobs for snobby children. Of course, the boys' cornpone charm is enough to handle these people, and all is well in a predictably happy ending. (See: THE WEAVER FAMILY series, Index)

p, Armand Schaeffer; d, Frank McDonald; w, Dorrell McGowan, Stuart McGowan (based on a story by Ray Harris); ph, Ernest Miller; ed, Richard Van Enger; md, Morton Scott; art d, Russell Kinball.

Comedy **(PR:AAA MPAA:NR)**

MOUNTAIN ROAD, THE**½** (1960) 102m COL bw

James Stewart (*Maj. Baldwin*), Lisa Lu (*Mme. Sue-Mei Hung*), Glenn Corbett (*Collins*), Henry [Harry] Morgan (*Michaelson*), Frank Silvera (*Gen. Kwan*), James Best (*Niergaard*), Rudy Bond (*Miller*), Mike Kellin (*Prince*), Frank Maxwell (*Ballo*), Eddie Firestone (*Lewis*), Alan Baxter (*Gen. Loomis*), Leo Chen (*Col. Li*), Bill Quinn (*Col. Magnusson*), Peter Chong (*Chinese Colonel*), P. C. Lee (*Chinese General*).

Uninspired Stewart vehicle set in China during WW II. Stewart is a U.S. Army major whose first command is to head an eight-man demolition team that is to destroy bridges and roads vital to the Japanese. Joined by two Chinese, Lu and Silvera, Stewart blows up a mountain bridge. Though the destruction of the pass is a strategic success, the military move leaves thousands of Chinese homeless. Lu is outraged at Stewart's apparent indifference to the situation he caused. Stewart's coldness toward the Chinese increases when one of his men is trampled to death by starving Chinese running to grab rations he had offered them. Things get worse when two more of Stewart's men are killed by Chinese military deserters. To avenge them, Stewart orders the destruction of a whole village, killing hundreds of innocent women and children. Having seen enough, Lu leaves Stewart to complete his assignment alone. He eventually realizes that his actions were misguided. Stewart's performance is interesting due to its fairly unsympathetic nature, but the film never really reaches his level of intensity.

p, William Goetz; d, Daniel Mann; w, Alfred Hayes (based on the novel by Theodore White); ph, Burnett Guffey; m, Jerome Moross; ed, Edward Curtiss; md, Morris Stoloff; art d, Cary Odell; set d, Bill Calvert, Sidney Clifford; makeup, Ben Lane.

War **(PR:A MPAA:NR)**

MOUNTAINS O'MOURNE**½** (1938, Brit.) 85m Rembrandt/BUT bw

Rene Ray (*Mary Macree*), Niall MacGinnis (*Paddy Kelly*), Jerry Verno (*Dip Evans*), Betty Ann Davies (*Violet Mayfair*), Charles Oliver (*Errol Finnegan*), Kaye Seely (*Peter O'Loughlin*), Maire O'Neill (*Maura Macree*), Eve Lynd (*Nikita Finchley*), Freda Jackson (*Biddy O'Hara*), Alexander Butler (*Tim Kelly*), Leonard Henry, Stanley Vilven, Johnnie Schofield, Wilfred Caithness, Vivienne Chatterton, Robert Irwin, Pat Noonan, Hamilton Keene, Langley Howard, Walter Tobias, Andre and Curtis, Cornelia and Eddie, Percival Mackey and His Band.

An amusing tale set among the green pastures of Ireland. MacGinnis and Ray are the romantically involved farmers who get kicked off their respective lands by an overbearing and pretentious landlord. MacGinnis takes off for the sweet life of London, where he hooks up with socialite Davies. Ray works as a hostess in a London restaurant where the inevitable meeting between her and MacGinnis occurs. The two continue where they left off and return to the farm where they discover that the overbearing landlord has left Ray an inheritance. Musical numbers are presented to add to the story's development, with the abundance of humorous situations making a generally entertaining film.

p&d, Harry Hughes; w, Gerald Brosnan (based on a story by Daisy L. Fielding).

Musical/Comedy **(PR:A MPAA:NR)**

MOUNTED FURY zero (1931) 63m SONO/World Wide bw

John Bowers, Blanche Mehaffey, Frank Rice, Lina Basquette, Robert Ellis, George Regas, John Ince.

Dull story of a drunk who finally agrees to go with his wife to the mountain retreat of a friend in order to get off the booze. His drying out is a failure however and he begins a fling with a local girl. He is eventually killed by the girl's lover, who is then killed by the girl, leaving the drunk's wife to marry his best friend. Ridiculous.

d, Stuart Paton; w, Betty Burbridge.

Drama **(PR:A MPAA:NR)**

MOUNTED STRANGER, THE* (1930) 65m UNIV bw

Hoot Gibson (*Pete Ainslee*), Louise Lorraine (*Bonita Coy*), Buddy Hunter (*Pete As a Boy*), Milton Brown ("Pop" Ainslee), Fred Burns (*Steve Gary*), James Corey ("White-Eye"), Francis Ford ("Spider" Coy), Walter Patterson (*His Lookout*), Francelia Billington (*Mrs. Coy*), Malcolm White.

Sleepy Gibson western which is a remake of his 1924 silent version. Plot sees Gibson out to avenge the murder of his father by Burns. Action also features a rescue when the villain kidnaps Lorraine. The silent version packed a better wallop.

p, Hoot Gibson; d&w, Arthur Rosson (based on the story "The Ridin' Kid from Powder River" by Henry H. Knibbs); ph, Harry Neumann; ed, Gilmore Walker.

Western **(PR:A MPAA:NR)**

MOURNING BECOMES ELECTRA** (1947) 173m RKO bw

Rosalind Russell *(Lavinia Mannon)*, Michael Redgrave *(Orin Mannon)*, Raymond Massey *(Ezra Mannon)*, Katina Paxinou *(Christine Mannon)*, Leo Genn *(Adam Brent)*, Kirk Douglas *(Peter Niles)*, Nancy Coleman *(Hazel Niles)*, Henry Hull *(Seth Beckwith)*, Thurston Hall *(Dr. Blake)*, Sara Allgood *(Landlady)*, Walter Baldwin *(Amos Ames)*, Elizabeth Risdon *(Mrs. Hills)*, Erskine Sanford *(Josiah Borden)*, Jimmy Conlin *(Abner Small)*, Tito Vuolo *(Joe Silva)*, Lee Baker *(Rev. Hills)*, Nora Cecil *(Louise Ames)*, Marie Blake *(Minnie Ames)*, Clem Bevans *(Ira Mackel)*, Jean Clarendon *(Eben Nobel)*, Colin Kenny *(Policeman)*, Emma Dunn *(Mrs. Borden)*.

The sheer audacity in attempting to boil down O'Neill's American version of a Greek tragedy from nearly six hours to just three rates a high mark for the effort. Not so for the result. It took nearly 16 years to get from the stage (where the leads were played by Alice Brady, Alla Nazimova, and Earle Larimore) to the screen where the same roles were done by Russell, Paxinou, and Redgrave. The picture lost almost $3 million when all quarters were heard from. Nichols attempted to compress the trilogy of "The Homecoming," "The Hunted," and "The Haunted" and remove the seams, but this is such a heavy story that it's hard to watch at any length. It takes place in 1865 in Massachusetts, and is a direct adaptation of "Oresteia" with the Electra character becoming Lavinia (Russell). The Civil War ends and Massey, the father of the house, returns. He is hated by his wife, Paxinou, who has been conducting an affair with Genn, a sea captain, while Massey was away. Russell hates her mother for having betrayed Massey and she is also jealous because she has a romantic yearning for her father that borders on mental derangement. Paxinou murders Massey, then Russell and her brother, Redgrave, murder Genn. This makes Paxinou go insane and she commits suicide. The rest of the film is gloomier from there. Douglas plays a suitor for Russell's evil hand but that doesn't work out (nothing much does in the story), and Coleman and Redgrave are also romantically entwined. This is a very static film and truly a photographed play although there is little power coming off that screen to compare with the stage version. Some good acting from Russell, Massey, and Genn but, in the end, it just proves that Greek tragedy doesn't play well west of Athens.

p,d,& w, Dudley Nichols (based on the play by Eugene O'Neill); ph, George Barnes; m, Richard Hageman; ed, Roland Gross, Chandler House; md, C. Bakaleinikoff; art d, Albert S. D'Agostino; set d, Darrell Silvera, Maurice Yates; cos, Travis Banton; spec eff, Vernon L. Walker, Russell Cully.

Drama **(PR:C MPAA:NR)**

MOURNING SUIT, THE** (1975, Can.) 90m March Films c

Allan Moyle *(Herschel)*, Norman Taviss *(Tailor)*, Marcia Diamond *(Mother)*, Brenda Donohue *(Girl)*, Helen Cooperstein *(Ruth)*.

Fairly tepid tale shot in 16mm and dealing with the contrasting values in the Jewish quarter of a Canadian city. Taviss plays an elderly tailor who befriends young-and-mixed-up Jewish kid Moyle after he returns home from abroad. Moyle's trendy values and attitudes cause much tension between him and his mother. When it is revealed he has fathered a child by a non-Jewish woman who will not marry him, his mother really flips, but the wise old tailor manages to salvage the situation.

d, Leonard Yakir; w, Joe Wiesenfeld; ph, Henry Fiks; m, Don Gillis; ed, Honor Griffith.

Drama **(PR:C MPAA:NR)**

MOUSE AND HIS CHILD, THE*
(1977) 83m deFaria-Lockhart-Murakami-Wolf/Sanrio c

Voices of: Peter Ustinov *(Manny)*, Cloris Leachman *(Euterpe)*, Sally Kellerman *(Seal)*, Andy Devine *(Frog)*, Alan Barzman *(Mouse)*, Marcy Swenson *(Mouse Child)*, Neville Brand *(Iggy)*, Regis Cordic *(Clock/Hawk)*, Joan Gerber *(Elephant)*, Bob Holt *(Muskrat)*, Maitzi Morgan *(Startling/Teller)*, Frank Nelson *(Crow)*, Cliff Norton *(Crow)*, Cliff Osmond *(Serpentina)*, Iris Rainer *(Paper People)*, Bob Ridgely *(Jack in the Box)*, Charles Woolf *(Bluejay/The Paper People)*, Mel Leven.

Pretty dull children's film based on the novel by Russell Hoban which tells the story of a mechanical mouse and his son whose wish is to be self-winding some day. The animation is very good, the voice talent fine, but most of the film is more talk than action. The material is preachy and pretentious and seems to have been written for 1960s adults, not children.

p, Walt deFaria; d, Fred Wolf, Chuck Swenson; w, Carol Mon Pere (based on the novel by Russell Hoban); ph, Wally Bulloch (DeLuxe Color); m, Roger Kellaway; ed, Rich Harrison; m/l, Kellaway, Gene Lees; animation, Murakami-Wolf Productions; animators, Wolf, Swenson, Dave Brain, Vince Davis, Gary Mooney, Mike Sanger, Lu Guarnier, Willie Lye, Bob Zamboni, Brad Case, Irv Anderson, Duane Crowther.

Animated **Cas.** **(PR:A MPAA:G)**

MOUSE AND THE WOMAN, THE 1/2** (1981, Brit.) 105m Alvicar/Facelift c

Dafydd Hywel, Karen Archer, Alan Devlin, Patricia Napier, Peter Sproule, Howard L. Lewis, Ionette Lloyd Davies, Beti Jones, Basil Painting, Dafydd Havard, John Pierce Jones, John Lehmann, Bob Mason, Huw Ceredig, Robert Blythe, Simon Coady, Brian Lee, John Cassady, Steve James, Glyn Davies, Ozi and Glesne, Joffre Swales Quartet.

This film is based on the short story by Dylan Thomas and set in Wales during the turbulent period during WW I. This probing and often insightful feature effectively weaves together the incidents which helped to forge a greater class consciousness, aiming at individual, as well as group, involvement. Demanding material was handled well by an unknown cast, with an atmospheric photography that captures a sense of the times.

p, Hayden Pearce, Karl Francis; d, Francis, w, Vincent Kane, Francis (based on the story by Dylan Thomas); ph, Nick Gifford; m, Alun Francis; ed, Neil Thomson; art d, Hayden Pearce.

Drama **(PR:O MPAA:NR)**

MOUSE ON THE MOON, THE 1/2** (1963, Brit.) 85m UA c

Margaret Rutherford *(The Grand Duchess Gloriana)*, Ron Moody *(Mountjoy)*, Bernard Cribbins *(Vincent)*, David Kossoff *(Kokintz)*, Terry-Thomas *(Spender)*, June Ritchie *(Cynthia)*, John Le Mesurier *(British Delegate)*, John Phillips *(Bracewell)*, Eric Barker *(M.I. 5 Man)*, Roddy McMillan *(Benter)*, Tom Aldredge *(Wendover)*, Michael Trubshawe *(British Aide)*, Peter Sallis *(Russian Delegate)*, Clive Dunn *(Bandleader)*, Hugh Lloyd *(Plumber)*, Graham Stark *(Standard Bearer)*, Mario Fabrizi *(Valet)*, Jan Conrad *(Russian Aide)*, John Bluthal *(Von Neidel)*, Archie Duncan *(American General)*, Guy Deghy *(German Scientist)*, Richard Marner *(Russian Air Force General)*, Allan Cuthbertson, Robin Bailey, Gerald Anderson *(Members of Whitehall Conference)*, Gordon Phillott *(Civil Servant)*, John Wood *(Countryman)*, George Chisholm *(Wine Waiter)*, Rosemary Scott *(Launching Lady)*, Vincent Ball *(Pilot)*, Frank Duncan *(News Announcer)*, Edward Bishop, Bill Edwards *(American Astronauts)*, Laurence Herder, Harvey Hall *(Russian Cosmonauts)*, Frankie Howerd *(Fenwickian)*, Coral Morphew *(Peasant Girl)*, Stuart Saunders *(Sergeant)*, Frank Lieberman *(American Civilian)*, Bruce Lacey *(Bandleader)*, Lucy Griffiths, Carol Dowell *(Ladies-in-Waiting)*, Stringer Davis *(1st Councillor)*, Carolyn Pertwee *(June)*, Sandra Hampton *(April)*, Kevin Scott *(American Journalist)*, Michael Caspi, Paul Cole, Murray Kash, Larry Cross, Robert Haynos, Beverly Bennett.

An inferior sequel to THE MOUSE THAT ROARED, this time the little Grand Duchy of Fenwick is in trouble again due to their wine output. The bottles explode upon opening and the Queen, Rutherford, doesn't know what to do. Moody, the Prime Minister, is handling all the complaints but his main concern is the problems with the castle's plumbing. He then devises the idea of asking the U.S. for funds so that Fenwick can join the space race and put one of their Fenwickians on the moon. It's all a ruse, of course, to get money and the U.S. falls for it, granting the tiny country some cash for their space program. The Russians, not to be outdone, donate one of their rockets to the country. Now the British step in and send their ace operative, Terry-Thomas, to see what's going on. Meanwhile Kossoff (who had made the Q-bomb in the first film) finds a use for the Fenwickian wine—it's perfect as rocket fuel. Moody's son, Cribbins, and Kossoff decide to launch the Russian rocket in order to get Cribbins' girl friend, Ritchie, back into Cribbins' arms. No one expects the rocket to work but it goes soaring heavenward with American and Russian space vehicles close behind. The flag of Grand Fenwick is placed on the moon and the American and Russian astronauts softly crash-land on the lunar surface where Cribbins offers them a free ride back to Earth. This doesn't come close to the original in wit, style, or farce although if the former had never been made, THE MOUSE ON THE MOON could weakly stand on its own as a mild comedy.

p, Walter Shenson; d, Richard Lester; w, Michael Pertwee (based on the novel by Leonard Wibberley); ph, Wilkie Cooper (Eastmancolor); m, Ron Grainer; ed, Bill Lenny; prod d, John Howell; cos, Anthony Mendleson; makeup, George Blackler; animator, Trevor Bond.

Comedy **(PR:AA MPAA:NR)**

MOUSE THAT ROARED, THE**** (1959, Brit.) 83m Open Road/COL c

Peter Sellers *(Tully Bascombe/Grand Duchess Gloriana XII/Prime Minister Count Mountjoy)*, Jean Seberg *(Helen)*, David Kossoff *(Prof. Kokintz)*, William Hartnell *(Will)*, Timothy Bateson *(Roger)*, MacDonald Parke *(Snippet)*, Monty Landis *(Cobbley)*, Leo McKern *(Benter)*, Harold Krasket *(Pedro)*, Colin Gordon *(BBC Announcer)*, George Margo *(O'Hara)*, Robin Gatehouse *(Mulligan)*, Jacques Cey *(Ticket Collector)*, Stuart Sanders *(Cunard Captain)*, Ken Stanely *(Cunard 2nd Officer)*, Bill Nagy *(U.S. Policeman)*, Mavis Villiers *(Telephone Operator)*, Charles Clay *(British Ambassador)*, Harry de Bray *(French Ambassador)*, Bill Edwards *(Army Captain)*, Austin Willis *(U.S. Secretary of Defense)*, Guy Deghy *(Soviet Ambassador)*, Robert O'Neill *(Reporter)*.

Connecticut-born Jack Arnold was tapped to direct this very British comedy by American producer Walter Shenson, who had been in England for many years and was to later produce the Beatles' films. Arnold is a much-overlooked director with an excellent flair for comedy to go along with his unerring eye for science fiction. (He also helmed THE CREATURE FROM THE BLACK LAGOON, TARANTULA, and THE INCREDIBLE SHRINKING MAN, and can be seen as the man in the elevator in 1985s INTO THE NIGHT.) Based on a serial in *The Saturday Evening Post* by Leonard Wibberley, THE MOUSE THAT ROARED is an outlandish and often hysterical story about a mythical country in the Alps that is on the verge of bankruptcy because their one export, a fine wine, has been duplicated and is being undercut by a California company. The prime minister, Sellers, tells the old queen, Sellers, that there is only one way to beat the U.S.: they must declare war on the opponent, lose immediately, and then settle back and enjoy all the aid that the U.S. traditionally lavishes upon beaten foes. In order to do that they send a small army of 20 men, clad in chain mail and armed with bows and arrows, led by Sellers again. (He did three roles in this picture, not as many as Guinness did in KIND HEARTS AND CORONETS, but with equal humorous results. Later, Sellers would play multiple roles again in DR. STRANGELOVE and UNDERCOVERS HERO.) They arrive in New York as the city is in the midst of an air-raid drill and the streets are empty. Kossoff is the inventor of the devastating Q-Bomb and Sellers and his men capture the scientist and his daughter, Seberg, and win the war! Now the U.S. has to sue for peace, as that bomb can destroy the entire country. All the other countries in the world want the Q-Bomb, so the U.S. decides to send an ambassador to the small country, withdraw the ersatz wine from the market, and make a loan to The Grand Duchy of Fenwick. In the end, the Q-Bomb is declared a dud, but by that time a deal has been cut between the two countries and what they'd attempted has been accomplished. There are several hysterical scenes that will have you reaching for tissues to keep your eyes from watering. George S. Kaufman once said that "Satire is what closes Saturday night." No so in this case. It's a deft blend of farce and satire with top-notch performances from all. Leo McKern is properly pompous as the leader of the "loyal oppostion" in Grand Fenwick, and all the roles are well cast. Seberg doesn't have much to do as the scientist's daughter but what she does, she does well. Monty Landis, a superior mime and comedian who spent many years in Paris, does a small role to perfection. When interviewed by THE MOTION PICTURE GUIDE in 1986, director Arnold stated that the invasion scenes in New York were done on a Sunday, hence the empty streets. The shooting was also hampered in England by bad weather and the fact that Sellers was in a London play, "Brouhaha," at the time, so he was rushed to the set every day by an ambulance in order to keep his breakneck schedule. The movie was made through the auspices of Carl Foreman's company, which had a deal with Columbia. Foreman was the screenwriter-producer who went to England after being blacklisted. He was forced to write under pseudonyms and without credit on such pictures as THE SLEEPING TIGER and THE BRIDGE ON THE RIVER KWAI until he came back into the industry's good graces. The sequel, MOUSE ON THE MOON, was directed by Richard Lester and was far less effective.

p, Jon Pennington, Walter Shenson; d, Jack Arnold; w, Roger MacDougall, Stanley Mann (based on the novel *The Wrath of the Grapes* by Leonard Wibberley); ph, John Wilcox (Eastman Color); m, Edwin Astley; ed, Raymond Poulton; md, Astley; art d, Geoffrey Drake; cos, Anthony Mendleson.

Comedy **Cas.** **(PR:AAA MPAA:NR)**

MOUTH TO MOUTH*** (1978, Aus.) 93m Vega c

Kim Krejus *(Carrie)*, Sonia Peat *(Jeannie)*, Ian Gilmour *(Tim)*, Sergio Frazzetto *(Serge)*, Walter Pym *(Fred)*, Michael Carman *(Tony)*.

Well-directed Australian film starring Krejus and Peat as two teen-agers who escape from a foster home and flee to the big city where they get jobs at a food bar and shoplift to supplement their meager incomes. Soon they meet fellow drifters Gilmour and Frazzetto and the four decide to set up house in an abandoned warehouse which the girls had previously found. When an old wino wanders in, the group adopts him and allows him to stay. When financial pressures move one of the guys to begin shoplifting, Krejus is outraged that he has sunk to her level and reprimands him. Later, she herself considers prostitution to make some extra money. A well made, insightful low-budget film.

p, Jon Sainken, John Duigan; d&w, Duigan; ph, Tom Cowan (Eastmancolor); m, Roy Ritchie; ed, Tony Paterson; art d, Tracy Watt.

Drama **(PR:C MPAA:NR)**

MOUTHPIECE, THE*** (1932) 90m WB bw

Warren William *(Vincent Day)*, Sidney Fox *(Celia)*, Aline McMahon *(Miss Hickey)*, William Janney *(John)*, John Wray *(Barton)*, Polly Walters *(Gladys)*, Ralph Ince *(J. B.)*, Mae Madison *(Elaine)*, Noel Francis *(Miss Da Vere)*, Morgan Wallace *(Smith)*, Guy Kibbee *(Bartender)*, Stanley Fields *(Pondapolis)*, J. Carrol Naish *(Tony)*, Walter Walker *(Forbes)*, Jack LaRue *(Garland)*, Murray Kinnell *(Jarvis)*, Emerson Treacy *(Wilson)*, Paulette Goddard *(Girl at Party)*, Selmer Jackson *(Prison Clerk)*, Charles Lane *(Desk Clerk)*, Willie Fung *(Waiter)*.

Hard-hitting crime drama starring William as an assistant D.A. who is horrified to discover that a man he sent to the chair was proven innocent only moments after the execution. Totally demoralized, William begins drinking heavily and accepting work from mobsters as their "mouthpiece." Bitter and cynical toward the legal system, William proves a great success at keeping swindlers and killers out of jail. With his new found success also comes expensive habits and lots of fast women. William begins to have doubts about his new lifestyle when he meets and falls hard for plain, wholesome stenographer Fox. Unfortunately, Fox has a steady boy friend, but when the kid gets in a legal jam, William rises to his rescue and saves the boy, even though it means double-crossing his mobster pals. Eventually the mob catches up to William and machine-gun him in the street while he reads a newspaper. Grim and powerful with few signs of aging. Remade unsuccessfully as THE MAN WHO TALKED TOO MUCH (1940) and ILLEGAL (1955). The story is partly based on the life of New York City attorney William J. Fallon. When the film opened in Syracuse, New York, Ruth Fallon, daughter of the late lawyer, filed a libel suit against the theater owner, who was fined $100. She later agreed to an out-of-court settlement with Warner Bros.

d, James Flood, Elliot Nugent; w, Earl Baldwin, Joseph Jackson (based on the play by Frank J. Collins); ph, Barney McGill; ed, George Amy; cos, Earl Luick.

Crime/Drama **(PR:A MPAA:NR)**

MOVE zero (1970) 90m FOX c

Elliot Gould *(Hiram Jaffe)*, Paula Prentiss *(Dolly Jaffe)*, Genevieve Waite *(Girl)*, John Larch *(Mounted Patrolman)*, Joe Silver *(Oscar)*, Graham Jarvis *(Dr. Picker)*, Ron O'Neal *(Peter)*, Garrie Beau *(Andrea)*, David Burns *(Doorman)*, Richard Bull *(Keith)*, Mae Questel *(Mrs. Katz)*, Aly Wassil *(Gupta)*, John Wheeler *(Brown Package)*, Rudy Bond *(Det. Sawyer)*, Yvonne D'Angers *(Jeanine)*, Amy Thomson *(Miss Landry)*, Roger Bowen *(Rabbi)*, Stanley Adams *(New Tenant)*.

Poor attempt at "hip" urban comedy starring Gould (who has made far too many of these stinkers) as a frustrated playwright who makes a living writing pornographic novels and walking rich people's dogs. When he and his wife Prentiss (whose own movie career has been marked by one blunder after another) decide to move into a larger apartment, the "comedy" begins as the nightmare of moving sends Gould into the fantasy world of his sleazy novels. Eventually the viewer has a hard time separating Gould's fantasies from reality (which may be the point), leading to a frustratingly long and unfunny movie-going experience. Stay away.

p, Pandro S. Berman; d, Stuart Rosenberg; w, Joel Lieber, Stanley Hart (based on the novel by Lieber); ph, William Daniels (Panavision, DeLuxe Color); m, Marvin Hamlisch; ed, Rita Roland; art d, Jack Martin Smith, Philip Jefferies; set d, Walter M. Scott, William Kiernan; spec eff, L. B. Abbott, Art Cruickshank; m/l, title song, Hamlisch, Alan Bergman, Marilyn Bergman (sung by Larry Marks).

Comedy **(PR:C MPAA:R)**

MOVE OVER, DARLING** (1963) 103m FOX c

Doris Day *(Ellen Wagstaff Arden)*, James Garner *(Nicholas Arden)*, Polly Bergen *(Bianca Steele Arden)*, Chuck Connors *(Stephen "Adam" Burkett)*, Thelma Ritter *(Grace Arden)*, Fred Clark *(Codd)*, Don Knotts *(Shoe Salesman)*, Elliott Reid *(Dr. Herman Schlick)*, Edgar Buchanan *(Judge Bryson)*, John Astin *(Clyde Prokey)*, Pat Harrington, Jr. *(District Attorney)*, Eddie Quillan *(Bellboy)*, Max Showalter *(Desk Clerk)*, Alvy Moore *(Waiter)*, Pami Lee *(Jenny Arden)*, Leslie Farrell *(Didi Arden)*, Rosa Turich *(Maria)*, Harold Goodwin *(Bailiff)*, Alan Sues *(Court Clerk)*, Pat Moran *(Drunk)*, Bess Flowers *(Woman)*, Rachel Romen *(Injured Man's Wife)*, Jack Orrison *(Bartender)*, Kelton Garwood, Joel Collins *(Ambulance Attendants)*, Sid Gould *(Waiter at Pool)*, Ed McNally *(Comdr.)*, James Patridge *(Skipper)*, Christopher Connelly *(Executive Seaman)*, Billy Halop, Med Flory *(Seamen)*, Emile Meyer, Brad Trumbull *(Process Servers)*, Michael Romanoff *(Floorwalker)*, John Harmon *(Cabdriver)*, Mary George *(Maid)*, Ted Jacques *(Pool Attendant)*, Bing Davidson *(Ens. J. G.)*, Jack Sahakian *(Exec. Officer, J. G)*, Stan Richards *(Officer)*, Joe Mell *(Stock Clerk)*, Sheila Rogers *(Secretary)*, Jimmy Bays *(Doorman)*.

A mildly amusing, sometimes funny remake of MY FAVORITE WIFE, this picture began as a vehicle for Marilyn Monroe called SOMETHING'S GOTTA GIVE, but that picture was never completed because of her still mysterious death. George Cukor was to have directed it with a cast that would have included Dean Martin, Cyd Charisse, Wally Cox, and Phil Silvers. After that tragedy, the script was refitted for Day and Garner (which meant, of course, that there had to be a crying scene for Doris as nobody sobs better without ruining her mascara than she does). It's the old "Enoch Arden" case of someone who disappears for a time, then comes back. They go so far as to name the characters "Arden" here so there is no mistaking where the idea was hatched. The original film had Irene Dunne, Cary Grant, Randolph Scott, and Gail Patrick in the roles played here by Day, Garner, Connors, and Bergen. Day is found on a remote island where her plane crash-landed five years before. She comes back to the U.S. on the very day that a judge, Buchanan, declares her officially dead, thus leaving Garner free to wed Bergen, an attractive but vacant woman who dotes on his every word. Garner and Bergen go off on their honeymoon as Day gets back from the island where she spent those years with the other survivor, Connors. Day returns to her house and is tearful when her own children, Lee and Farrell, do not recognize her. She is told the truth by her mother-in-law, Ritter (who steals every scene she is in and leaves the other actors looking like high-schoolers in a play with Olivier by comparison), and runs off to the resort hotel where Garner has taken Bergen. When she arrives there Garner spots her and is thrown for a loop, so he fakes a back injury and hurries back home with Bergen. Day takes a plane instead of a train or car and arrives there first, then masquerades as Garner's masseuse. It all seems to be working out when Garner learns that Day had been stranded with a man for all those years. He wants to know what the guy was like and Day describes him as a wimp. Garner visits Connors and sees that the guy is 6 feet 6 inches tall and has muscles in his toes. At the same time Day, seeking to get back her ex-husband, hires Knotts, who looks like the person she had described earlier, to pose as Connors. Later, Day and Knotts pretend to have had a platonic relationship on the island but Garner is hip to the truth and lets her know that. Embarrassed, Day goes back to her one-time residence and Garner follows shortly thereafter. Bergen is at the home and Garner comes clean, explaining who Day is and how this all came to pass. Now the police arrive, summoned by Ritter, and Garner is arrested for having two wives. In court Buchanan declares Day officially alive again when Connors speaks in her behalf. Then he declares the Bergen-Garner marriage void because of Day. Everything works out, the kids accept Day, the ex-spouses get together and Bergen winds up with her analyst, Reid. This version had little of the insouciance of the original and relied on obvious jokes that fell flatter than Nebraska. In one of his earliest roles, look for John Astin. Lots of good comedy people in the cast including: Sid Gould, Pat Harrington, Jr., Sues, Knotts, Clark, and silent screen veteran Quillan (a favorite of co-screenwriter Kanter who used him in a TV movie 15 years later, "For the Love of It.") Super saxophonist Med Flory does a bit and Hollywood legend Mike Romanoff plays a floorwalker. Romanoff owned the famous Rodeo Drive restaurant for many years where everyone ate. Songwirter Lubin wrote for several of Day's films and here collaborated with Kanter and Day's son, Terry Melcher.

p, Aaron Rosenberg, Martin Melcher; d, Michael Gordon; w, Hal Kanter, Jack Sher (based on the screenplay "My Favorite Wife" by Bella and Samuel Spewack, from a story by the Spewacks, Leo McCarey); ph, Daniel L. Fapp (CinemaScope, DeLuxe Color); m, Lionel Newman; ed, Robert Simpson; art d, Jack Martin Smith, Hilyard Brown; set d, Walter M. Scott, Paul S. Fox; cos, Moss Mabry; spec eff, L. B. Abbott, Emil Kosa, Jr.; m/l, "Move Over, Darling," Joe Lubin, Kanter, Terry Melcher, "Twinkle Lullaby," Lubin (sung by Doris Day); makeup, Ben Nye.

Comedy **(PR:A MPAA:NR)**

MOVIE CRAZY* 1/2** (1932) 81m PAR bw

Harold Lloyd *(Harold Hall)*, Constance Cummings *(Mary Sears)*, Kenneth Thomson *(Vance, A Gentleman Heavy)*, Sydney Jarvis *(The Director)*, Eddie

Fetherston (Bill, the Assistant Director), Robert McWade (Wesley Kitterman, The Producer), Louise Closser Hale (Mrs. Kitterman, His Wife), Spencer Charters (J. L. O'Brien), Harold Goodwin (Miller, a Director), Lucy Beaumont (Mrs. Hall, Harold's Mother), DeWitt Jennings (Mr. Hall, Harold's Father), Mary Doran (Margie, Screen-Test Actress), Noah Young (Traffic Cop), Constantine Romanoff (Duval, Sailor in Movie), Arthur Housman (Drunk), Grady Sutton (Man Afraid of Mice), Elinor Vanderveer (Mrs. Crumplin, a Guest), Harold "Hal" Varney (Kitterman's Chauffeur), Dick Rush (Studio Guard), Gus Leonard (Janitor), Fred Kohler, Jr. (Young Actor), Jack Perrin (Man in Screening Room), Sam McDaniel (Men's Room Valet), Edward Piel, Bill O'Brien (Waiters), Blackie Whiteford (Studio Cop), Wallace Howe, James Ford (Bits).

Silent comedian Harold Lloyd's best sound effort, and it's somewhat autobiographical. Lloyd plays a Kansas boy who lives with his parents and is enamored with the movies. Barely able to contain his excitement for the medium, he performs elaborate, dramatic scenes for the amusement of his mother and to the chagrin of his father. Lloyd sends a letter to Hollywood offering to appear in any film of their choosing. Through a mixup, a photograph of an extremely handsome lad is substituted for Lloyd's with the letter and soon Hollywood calls him for a screen test. Ecstatic, Lloyd hustles off to Hollywood to begin a career as a movie actor. Unfortunately, Hollywood gets more than it bargained for when it is discovered that Lloyd is no Lothario, but a bumbling Kansas clod who gets himself in all sorts of slapstick trouble on the set. While the studio heads decide just what to do with him, Lloyd begins a bizarre romance with actress Cummings, whom Lloyd had fallen for while she was made-up as a Mexican girl for a scene. When he meets her again, sans makeup, he doesn't realize that it's the same woman and falls in love with her again. Cummings allows the confusion to continue, just to have fun with Lloyd. Eventually the powers-that-be in the studio decide Lloyd would be perfect for comedy pictures and they sign him to a lucrative contract. Filled with creative gags and funny bits, MOVIE CRAZY is not only a successful comedy, but a fascinating behind-the-camera look at the studio system in the early days of talkies. Sadly, director Clyde Bruckman, who had worked with Lloyd and Buster Keaton several times, committed suicide in 1955 with a gun he had borrowed from Keaton.

p, Harold Lloyd; d, Clyde Bruckman; w, Vincent Lawrence (based on a story by Agnes Christine Johnson, John Grey, Felix Adler); ph, Walter Lundin; ed, Bernard Burton; art d, William MacDonald, Harry Oliver.

Comedy (PR:A MPAA:NR)

MOVIE MOVIE *** 1/2 (1978) 105m WB bw-c

"Dynamite Hands": George C. Scott (Gloves Malloy), Trish Van Devere (Betsy McGuire), Red Buttons (Peanuts), Eli Wallach (Vince Marlowe), Harry Hamlin (Joey Popchik), Ann Reinking (Troubles Moran), Jocelyn Brando (Mama Popchik), Michael Kidd (Pop Popchik), Kathleen Beller (Angie Popchik), Barry Bostwick (Johnny Danko), Art Carney (Dr. Blaine), Clay Hodges (Sailor Lawson), George P. Wilbur (Tony Norton), Peter T. Stader (Barney Keegle), George P. Wilbur (Tony Norton), Peter T. Stader (Barney Keegle), James Lennon, John Hudkins, Robert Herron, Denver R. Mattson, James Nickerson, Harvey G. Perry, Wally Rose, Fred Scheiwiller, James J. Casino, John R. McKee, Gary Stokes, Garth Thompson, Clifford Happy, Terry L. Nichols, Larry Hayden, Patrick Omeirs, Michael Rodgers, Thomas Morga, Clarence Beatty, Charlie Murray, Evelyn Moriarty, June McCall, Jack Slate, Michael Lansing, Chuck Hicks, George Fisher, James Winburn, Bud Ekins; "Baxter's Beauties of 1933": George C. Scott (Spats Baxter), Barbara Harris (Trixie Lane), Barry Bostwick (Dick Cummings), Trish Van Devere (Isobel Stuart), Red Buttons (Jinks Murphy), Eli Wallach (Pop), Rebecca York (Kitty), Art Carney (Dr. Bowers), Maidie Norman (Gussie), Jocelyn Brando (Mrs. Updike), Charles Lane (Pennington), Barney Martin (Motorcycle Cop), Dick Winslow (Tinkle Johnson), Sebastian Brook (Fritz), Jerry Von Hoeltke (Theater Workman), Paula Jones (Chorus Girl), John Henry (Chorus Boy), John Hudkins, Robert Herron (Movers).

An often funny sendup of movie cliches that was two movies in one (hence the double-gaited title) with many of the same actors appearing in both halves. It's a nostalgic look at a time when lawmen were "coppers" and people could say "swell" without smirking. Shot in both black-and-white and color, it's a whole evening at the movies with a trailer for next week's show, "Zero Hour," a war movie that obviously was never made. George Burns does a prologue to let you know that this is supposed to be funny and we are plunged into "Dynamite Hands," a movie that owes a great deal to BODY AND SOUL. Hamlin is the poor law student who needs to raise a bundle to save the eyesight of his sister, Beller. She must be sent to Vienna for an eye operation by an eminent Austrian surgeon. To do that, he has to put away his torts and take his chances in the boxing ring. It is not long before Hamlin is on his way to the championship, but a rabbit punch is thrown when Wallach, a crooked promoter, orders the young man to take a dive. He will not do it and that costs his trainer, Scott, his life. Hamlin is determined to bring Wallach to justice so he goes to law school and makes sure that Wallach is repaid by sending him to the electric chair. In "Baxter's Beauties of 1933," Scott is the Flo Ziegfeld-type who is trying to put on a big show. (This one owes its heritage to 42ND STREET.) You know the story: unknown girl gets the chance to star when the leading lady breaks her leg. Van Devere (Mrs. Scott) is the leading lady, York is the ingenue, and Bostwick is her beau. Michael Kidd does the choreography and manages to effect a passable imitation of Berkeley, despite the fact that he had nowhere near the budget for the chorines and the cameras. The satire gets a bit heavy at times and you will have to know a lot about the movies upon which this is based to glean the most out of the humor. Gelbart made his name in TV with his work on "M*A*S*H" and Keller is a longtime TV writer who also doubles as a bass player with the Dixieland Band once fronted by George Segal, The Beverly Hills Unlisted Jazz Band. The tunes by Burns, Gelbart, and Keller are exceptionally good, almost standing on their own as songs, rather than as satire. MOVIE MOVIE was more of a critical hit than it was a popular one although it did make some money for the studio that pioneered both

the boxing and the early musicals, Warner Bros. It's often a little too cute, forced, and more schmaltzy spoof than nostalgic, with embarrassing hamminess on the part of Scott and wife Van Devere.

p&d, Stanley Donen; w, Larry Gelbart, Sheldon Keller; ph, Charles Rosher, Jr. ("Dynamite Hands"), Bruce Surtees ("Baxter's Beauties"); m, Ralph Burns, Buster Davis; ed, George Hively; art d, Jack Fisk; set d, Chris Horner; cos, Patty Norris; ch, Michael Kidd; m/l, Gelbart, Keller.

Comedy Cas. (PR:A-C MPAA:PG)

MOVIE STAR, AMERICAN STYLE, OR, LSD I HATE YOU!

(1966) 99m Famous Players bw-c

Robert Strauss (Joe Horner, Producer), Del Moore (Dr. Horatio), T. C. Jones (Skippy Roper, Designer), Steve Drexel (Dr. Oscar Roscoe), Paula Lane (Honey Bunny, Great Screen Star), Steve Rogers (Barry James, Super-Star), Richard Clair (David Erickson, Writer), Jill Darling (Miranda Song, Nurse), Cara Garnett (Movie Queen), Sandra Lynn (Countess), Peter Van Boom (Harvey Homantash, Director), Ned York (Crash Dramm, All-American), Frank Delfino (Midget Photographer), Juliet Picaud (Miss Bee), Albert Zugsmith (Director).

Exploitation king Zugsmith's "LSD comedy" starring Lane as a dippy sex-bomb movie star who is sent by her sleazy producer, Strauss, to a rest home. The home is run by a crazed doctor who uses LSD to bring out the patient's own personal fantasies. Among the patient/victims are Jones, an effeminate dress designer; Rogers, a matinee idol; Clair, a writer; a fat lady, a midget, and Zugsmith himself. Funny only because Zugsmith thought it was funny. A sequence in which the patients act out LSD-induced fantasies was filmed in black-and-white and color-tinted.

p, Robert Caramico; d, Albert Zugsmith; w, Zugsmith, Graham Lee Mahin, Lulu Talmadge; ph, Caramico; m, Joe Greene; ed, Herman Freedman; m/l, title song, Greene (sung by T. C. Jones).

Comedy (PR:C MPAA:NR)

MOVIE STUNTMEN*

(1953) 56m Kosloff bw (AKA: HOLLYWOOD THRILLMAKERS; HOLLYWOOD STUNT MAN)

James Gleason (Risky Russell), Bill Henry (Dave Wilson), Thelia Darin (Marion Russell), Joan Holcombe (Joan Cummings), James Macklin (Bill Cummings).

Henry is a stunt man, retired because of his wife's fears, who takes a dangerous job that killed a friend so that the widow can receive the $5,000 stunt fee. Crudely made and rehashing Hollywood cliches, the thrilling stunts are mostly taken from old Richard Talmadge movies.

p, Maurice Kosloff; d, Bernard "B. B." Ray; w, Janet Clark (based on a story by Ray); ph, Elmer Dyer; m, Michael Terr; ed, Robert Jahns.

Drama (PR:A MPAA:NR)

MOVIE STRUCK (SEE: PICK A STAR, 1937)

MOVIETONE FOLLIES OF 1929 (SEE: FOX MOVIETONE FOLLIES, 1929)

MOVIETONE FOLLIES OF 1930

(SEE: FOX MOVIETONE FOLLIES OF 1930, 1930)

MOVING FINGER, THE*

(1963) 100m Moyer bw

Lionel Stander, Barbara London, Art Smith, Wendy Barrie, Alan Ansara, Monroe Arnold, Barry Newman, Carol Fleming, Gary Goodrow, Otto Mjaanes, Cornelius Jones, Michael Dana.

Low-budget independent feature shot in a "cinema verite" manner and set in Greenwich Village. The film opens with a bank robbery in which only one of the thieves survives, though wounded, and escapes with $90,000. He stumbles into the village where he is taken in by a group of beatniks who live in the basement of a coffee house. Despite the fact that the beatniks are supposed to shun wealth, they all plan to part the robber from his loot. The coffee house owner, a drunken doctor and his daughter, and the police also are plotting to get the money. London, one of the beatniks, convinces the thief to leave with her, and when he dies in the street, she gets the cash. Barrie, who had been a featured performer in films throughout the 1930s and early 1940s, makes a brief appearance as a wealthy woman who gets enjoyment out of hanging around with the village bohemians.

p&d, Larry Moyer; w, Moyer, Carlo Fiore; ph, Max Glenn; m, Teddy Vann; ed, Moyer.

Crime (PR:C MPAA:NR)

MOVING IN SOCIETY (SEE: MOUNTAIN MOONLIGHT, 1941)/

MOVING TARGET, THE (SEE: HARPER, 1966)

MOVING VIOLATION*

(1976) 91m Santa Fe/FOX c

Stephen McHattie (Eddie Moore), Kay Lenz (Cam Johnson), Eddie Albert (Alex Warren), Lonny Chapman (Sheriff Rankin), Will Geer (Rockfield), Jack Murdock (Bubba), John S. Ragin (Agent Shank), Dennis Redfield (Tylor), Michael Ross Verona (Harvey), Francis de Sales (Lawyer), Dick Miller (Mack).

Fast-moving car-chase epic starring McHattie and Lenz as a young couple who witness Sheriff Chapman murder his deputy on the orders of a small town's power broker, Geer. When Chapman realizes his crime has witnesses, he sends word out that the couple are underground terrorists who were sent by radicals to kill the deputy. This, of course, starts the chase and the rest of the film features some incredible stunt work as the couple strive to prove their innocence. Produced by Roger Corman's daughter Julie.

p, Julie Corman; d, Charles S. Dubin; w, David R. Osterhout, William Norton (based on a story by Osterhout); ph, Charles Correll (DeLuxe Color); m, Don Peake; ed, Richard Sprague, Howard Terrill; art d, Sherman Loudermilk.

Crime/Action　　　　　　　　　　**Cas.**　　　　　　**(PR:C MPAA:PG)**

MOZAMBIQUE*½
(1966, Brit.) 98m Towers of London-London & Overseas Film/Seven Arts c

Steven Cochran (*Brad Webster*), Hildegard Neff (*Ilona Valdez*), Vivi Bach (*Christina*), Paul Hubschmid (*Commarro*), Martin Benson (*Da Silva*), Dietmar Schonherr (*Henderson*), Gert Van den Bergh (*Arab*), George Leech (*Carl*), Vic Perry (*Himself*).

Cochran, who died before the picture's release, stars as an out-of-work American pilot who travels from Lisbon to Mozambique where he is to go to work for a mysterious colonel. Along the way, he meets Bach, who is going to be a singer in one of the colonel's nightclubs. Upon arrival, they find the colonel is dead and get caught up in intrigue involving the colonel's widow (Neff), narcotics smuggling and a murderous midget. The complicated plottings slow the film down, but the beautiful location shooting in Mozambique and at Victoria Falls helps to liven things up—though not enough to recommend the picture.

p, Harry Alan Towers, Oliver A. Anger; d, Robert Lynn; w, Peter Yeldham (based on a story by Peter Welbeck [Harry Alan Towers]); ph, Martin Curtis (Techniscope, Technicolor); m, Johnny Douglas; m/l, "Das Geht Beim Ersten Mal Vorbei" (Charley Niessen); "Hey You" (Gus Backus).

Drama　　　　　　　　　　　　　　　　　　　**(PR:A MPAA:NR)**

MOZART*½
(1940, Brit.) 76m ABF/Lopert bw (GB: WHOM THE GODS LOVE)

Stephen Haggard (*Wolfgang Amadeus Mozart*), Victoria Hopper (*Constanze Mozart*), John Loder (*Prince Lopkowitz*), Liane Haid (*Aloysia*), Jean Cadell (*Frau Mozart*), Hubert Harben (*Leopold Mozart*), Frederick Leister (*The Emperor*), Marie Lohr (*The Empress*), Lawrence Hanray (*Archbishop of Salzburg*), Diedre Gale (*Child Antoinette*), Pat Fitzpatrick (*Mozart as a Boy*), Norman Walker (*Schickaneder*), George Curzon (*Da Ponte*), Richard Goolden (*Weber*), Muriel George (*Frau Weber*), Leueen McGrath (*Josefa Weber*), Oda Slobodskaya, Percy Hemming, Tudor Davies, Enid James, Sylvia Nells, Rowena Sanders, Sir Thomas Beecham and the London Symphony Orchestra.

Yes, there was some cinematic interest in the life of Wolfgang Amadeus Mozart long before Milos Forman's Academy Award winning film AMADEUS. MOZART was one in a series of European 1930s and 1940s films based on the lives of great composers, and it is one of the weakest. Confused and weakly scripted, MOZART really doesn't seem to focus on any particular aspect of the brilliant composer's life, but instead hurriedly rushes through dozens of incidents without developing them. Haggard is miscast as Mozart and elicits little viewer sympathy (or interest for that matter), and Hopper as his wife is shrill and unappealing. The music however, is superb as performed by the London Philharmonic.

p&d, Basil Dean; w, Margaret Kennedy; ph, Jan Stalich; set d, Andre Andreiev; cos, Ernst Stern.

Biography/Musical　　　　　　　　　　　　**(PR:A MPAA:NR)**

MOZART　　　(SEE: LIFE AND LOVES OF MOZART, THE, 1959, Ger.)

MOZART STORY, THE**　　　(1948, Aust.) 91m Patrician/Screen Guild bw

Hans Holt (*Wolfgang Amadeus Mozart*), Winnie Markus (*Constance, His Wife*), Irene von Meyendorf (*Louise, Her Sister*), Rene Deltgen (*Ludwig von Beethoven*), Edward Vedder (*Joseph Haydn*), Wilton Graff (*Antonio Salieri*), Carol Forman (*Catherine Cavalleria*), Anthony Barr (*Ruffini*), Walther Jansson (*Leopold, Mozart's Father*), Rosa Albach-Retty (*Mozart's Mother*), Anita Rosar (*Mother Weber*), Thea Weiss (*Sophia Weber*), Curd Juergens [Curt Jurgens] (*Emperor Joseph II*), Paul Hoerbiger (*Strack, the Emperor's Chamberlain*), Jon Siebert (*Duke of Mannheim*), Richard Eybner (*Baron Gemmingen*), Eric Nocowitz (*Suessmeyer*), Theo Danagger (*Deinert*), Fred Imhoff (*Albrechtaberger*), Carl Bluhm (*Hofer*).

Another lackluster film biography of musical genius, Mozart, this time produced by Austrians. Holt does well as Mozart, and brings some energy to his portrayal of the brilliant young composer. Emphasis is not on the tragic aspects of Mozart's life, but his successes. The film is filled with musical excerpts from "The Magic Flute," "Requiem," "Don Giovanni," and "The Marriage of Figaro," performed by the Vienna Philharmonic and the Vienna State Opera. Originally filmed in Austria in 1939, additional scenes were added in Hollywood for its U.S. release in 1948. The songs are in German, but the dialog is dubbed in English.

d, Carl Hartl; w, Richard Billinger; additional dialog and sequences produced by Abrasha Haimson and directed by Frank Wisbar.

Biography/Musical　　　　　　　**Cas.**　　　　　**(PR:A MPAA:NR)**

MS. 45**　　(1981) 84m Navaron/Rochelle c (AKA: ANGEL OF VENGEANCE)

Zoe Tamerlis (*Thana*), Steve Singer (*Photographer*), Jack Thibeau (*Man in Bar*), Peter Yellen (*2nd Rapist*), Darlene Stuto (*Laurie*), Editta Sherman (*Landlady*), Albert Sinkys (*Boss*), Jimmy Laine [Abel Ferrara] (*1st Rapist*), Bogey (*Phil*).

Tamerlis is a mute girl working in New York City's garment district. On the way home, she's raped and once home she is raped again by a burglar. She kills her rapist and, to dispose of the body, she cuts it up, stores it in her refrigerator, and on a daily basis dumps parts in different sections of the city. One day while dumping a bag she is frightened by a man lounging on a street corner and drops her bag. The man picks it up thinking she forgot it, then corners her in an alley where she kills him with a .45 she had taken from the burglar. Tamerlis goes on a killing spree, slaying a photographer, a pimp, gang members, and a sheik. At a bar she meets a man whose wife has left him for another woman. The gun misfires when she tries to kill

him and the man takes the gun and kills himself. Dressed as a nun, Tamerlis goes to a Halloween party with her boss, Sinkys. Half-way through the party Sinkys takes Tamerlis upstairs and tries to seduce her until he finds the .45 strapped to her thigh. She kills him and then goes down to the party and begins to kill every male in sight until a female coworker, Stuto, kills Tamerlis with a knife. As she is dying, Tamerlis turns toward Stuto and utters her only line, "Sister." Ferrara's film is not an easy film to watch, not directly because of the violence, but because it is a calculated attack on the male-dominated audience of exploitation films. MS. 45 begins like any other exploitation film, unmotivated violence (the two consecutive rapes), but then throws ice water on every titillated viewer. One scene that exemplifies this attack on the audience is when Tamerlis begins to take off her shirt in front of a mirror. Anticipation grows with every button undone. Then the dead rapist appears from behind her and a hand grabs for her breast. It's a startling sequence, wonderfully set up and disturbingly effective. The film also explores the darker side of the revenge-vigilante films. Tamerlis has as much right as Charles Bronson to kill the bad guys, but Ferrara makes sure things aren't as black and white as in the DEATH WISH films. She's not just killing criminals and that can make it very uncomfortable for the man who identifies with the screen characters. It touches on an interesting and unexplored issue of vigilante characters—how stable is that person with the gun and can that person think clearly enough to be judge, jury and executioner? Ferrara doesn't fully develop Tamerlis' every action—why she has gone off the deep-end, killing any man in her sight is a mystery. MS. 45 would have been that much more powerful if the audience followed Tamerlis' progression from killing rapists, pimps, and thugs to killing every and any man. Ferrara has a gritty and powerful style which makes MS. 45 the standout that it is. His use of music (a spine-tingling saxophone), instinctive camera techniques (the overhead shots, the slow motion finale, and the powerful bathroom scene where the dead rapist suddenly materializes), and the colorful and humorous minor characters, make this low-budget picture an excellent noir film.

d, Abel Ferrara; w, Nicholas St. John; ph, James Momel (Cineffects Color); m, Joe Delia; ed, Christopher Andrews; spec eff, Matt Vogel, Sue Dalton; makeup, Lisa Monteleone.

Thriller　　　　　　　　　　**Cas.**　　　　　　**(PR:O MPAA:R)**

MUCEDNICI LASKY　　　　(SEE: MARTYRS OF LOVE, 1968, Czech.)

MUCH TOO SHY*½　　　　　(1942, Brit.) 92m Gainsborough/COL bw

George Formby (*George Andy*), Kathleen Harrison (*Amelia Peabody*), Hilda Bayley (*Lady Driscoll*), Eileen Bennett (*Jackie Somers*), Joss Ambler (*Sir George Driscoll*), Jimmy Clitheroe (*Jimmy*), Frederick Burtwell (*Mr. Harefield*), Brefni O'Rorke (*Mr. Somers*), Eric Clavering (*Robert Latimer*), Gibb McLaughlin (*Rev. Sheepshanks*), Gus McNaughton (*Manager*), Peter Gawthorne (*Counsel*), D. J. Williams, Valentine Dyall.

Formby plays a handyman with a knack for handling the paint brush, a talent he pursues by painting portraits of heads minus the body because he lacks the boldness to have his models pose nude for him. In a commercial art course fellow students add bodies to three of Formby's heads, forcing the painter into a mess with the models when the painting is used as a soap advertisement. A below par vehicle with which to take advantage of Formby's comic talents.

p, Ben Henry; d, Marcel Varnel; w, Ronald Frankau; ph, Arthur Crabtree.

Comedy　　　　　　　　　　　　　　　　**(PR:A MPAA:NR)**

MUD　　　　　　　　　　　(SEE: STICK UP, THE, 1978, Brit.)

MUD HONEY　　　　　　　　　(SEE: ROPE OF FLESH, 1965)

MUDDY RIVER***½
(1982, Jap.) 105m Kimura/Japan Film Center bw (DORO NO KAWA)

Nobutaka Asahara (*Nobuo*), Takahiro Tamura (*His Father, Shinpei*), Yumiko Fujita (*His Mother*), Minoru Sakurai (*Kiichi*), Makiko Shibata (*His Sister, Ginko*), Mariko Kaga (*Their Mother*), Gannosuke Ashiya (*Horse-car Man*), Reiko Hatsune (*Tobacco-shop Woman*), Keizo Kanie (*Policeman*), Yoshitaka Nishiyawa (*Guard*), Taiji Tonoyama (*Man on Boat*), Masako Yagi (*Shinpei's Former Wife*).

Oguri's moving, beautiful, and sensitive debut film which was nominated for an Academy Award as Best Foreign Film in 1982. Set in Japan in 1956, MUDDY RIVER details the lives of two young boys in a country still trying to recover from WW II. Asahara lives in a restaurant run by his parents. One day an old, weather-beaten houseboat docks nearby. Sakuari, a boy about Asahara's age, emerges from the boat where he lives with is older sister and mother. The boys become best friends. Asahara is confused, however, as to why he is never allowed onto the houseboat to meet Sakurai's mother. Eventually Asahara learns the truth when he spots Sakarai's mother earning her living as a prostitute. Sensing that the surrounding community has tolerated her presence long enough, Sakaria's mother gathers her children on the boat and sails off to another location with Asahara chasing the houseboat as it pulls away. Outstanding performances by the children, coupled with stunning black and white photography make this a film well worth watching. (In Japanese; English subtitles.)

p, Motoyasu Kimura; d, Kohei Oguri; w, Takako Shigemori (based on the novel by Teru Miyamoto); ph, Shohei Ando; m, Kuroudo Mori; ed, Nobuo Ogawa; art d, Akira Naito.

Drama　　　　　　　　　　　　　　　　**(PR:A MPAA:NR)**

MUDHONEY　　　　　　　　　(SEE: ROPE OF FLESH, 1965)

MUDLARK, THE**½　　　　　　　(1950, Brit.) 98m FOX bw

Irene Dunne (*Queen Victoria*), Alec Guinness (*Prime Minister Benjamin Disraeli*), Andrew Ray (*Wheeler, the Mudlark*), Beatrice Campbell (*Lady Emily Prior*), Finlay Currie (*John Brown, Queen's Ghillie*), Anthony Steel (*Lt. Charles McHatten*),

Raymond Lovell *(Sgt. Footman Naseby)*, Marjorie Fielding *(Lady Margaret Prior)*, Constance Smith *(Kate Noonan)*, Ronan O'Casey *(Slattery)*, Edward Rigby *(Watchman)*, Robin Stevens *(Herbert)*, William Strange *(Sparrow)*, Kynaston Reeves *(Gen. Sir Henry Ponsonby)*, Wilfrid Hyde-White *(Tucker)*, Ernest Clark *(Hammond)*, Eric Messiter *(Ahs, Lieutenant of Police)*, Pamela Arliss *(Princess Christian)*, Ian Selby *(Prince Christian)*, Maurice Warren *(Christian)*, Michael Brooke *(Albert)*, Jane Short *(Victoria)*, Howard Douglas *(Broom)*, Richard Nairne *(Didbit)*, George Dillon *(Jailer)*, Leonard Sharp *(Ben Fox)*, Vi Kaley *(Mrs. Feeney)*, Freddie Watts *(Iron George)*, Y. Yanai *(Al Hook)*, Paul Garrard *(Petey)*, Leonard Morris *(Hooker Morgan)*, Marjorie Gresley *(Meg Bownes)*, Bob Head *(Dandy Fitch)*, Vi Stevens *(Mrs. Dawkins)*, Alan Gordon *(Disraeli's Valet)*, Grace Denbeigh Russell *(Queen's Maid)*, Patricia Hitchcock.

Ray is a poor orphan who finds a medallion bearing the likeness of Queen Victoria and decides he wants to meet her Royal Highness. He's caught attempting to sneak into Windsor Castle and his intentions become the center of a raging controversy. He finally gets to mee the Queen, played by Dunne, who is charmed by the young urchin. She has been in seclusion, refusing to fulfill her royal obligations, but the boy renews her spirits and she returns to public life. This pleases Guinness, as Disraeli, who needs the Queen's assistance to gain Parliamentary approval of some new programs. Dunne is very good as the Queen, but Ray steals the show as the lovable youth. A warm and enjoyable movie that makes good use of famous sights such as Windsor Castle, the Tower of London, and the Parliament buildings. Superb makeup job by Aylot causes Dunne to look more like Victoria than one would imagine. Not surprisingly, THE MUDLARK was chosen as a command performance movie that was enjoyed by all the Royal Family. Dunne only made one more film, IT GROWS ON TREES, before retiring from the screen to devote herself to various posts within the Republican Party, eventually serving as an alternate delegate to the United Nations. Alfred Hitchcock's daughter Patricia appears briefly.

p, Nunnally Johnson; d, Jean Negulesco; w, Johnson (based on the novel by Theordore Bonnet); ph, Georges Perinal; m, William Alwyn; ed, Thelma Myers; md, Muir Mathieson; art d, C. P. Norman; cos, Edward Stevenson, Margaret Furse; spec. eff, W. Percy Day, makeup, Dave Aylot.

Drama **(PR:A MPAA:NR)**

MUERTO 4-3-2-1-0 (SEE: MISSION STARDUST, 1969, Ital.)

MUG TOWN* 1/2 (1943) 60m UNIV bw

Billy Halop *(Tommy Davis)*, Huntz Hall *(Pig)*, Gabriel Dell *(String)*, Bernard Punsley *(Ape)*, Grace McDonald *(Norene Seward)*, Edward Norris *(Clinker)*, Virgnia Brissac *(Alice Bell)*, Jed Prouty *(Mack Seward)*, Dick Hogan *(Don Bell)*, Murray Alper *(Shorty)*, Paul Fix *(Marco)*, Lee "Lasses" White *(Mr. Perkle)*, Tommy Kelly *(Steve Bell)*, Syd Saylor *(Drunk)*, Sidney Melton, Paul Dubov *(Waiters)*, June Bryde [Gittleson] *(Matilda, Fat Girl)*, Ralph Dunn *(Cop)*, Napoleon Simpson *(Singer)*, William Hall, Matt Willis *(Bouncers)*, Ernie Adams *(Thief)*, William Forrest *(District Attorney)*, Danny Beck *(Man in Flophouse)*, William Gould *(1st Detective)*, John Sheehan *(Manager)*, Danny Seymour *(Chef)*, John Bagni *(2nd Detective)*, Jack Marvin *(Detective)*, Joline Westbrook, Evelyn Cooke, Dorothy Cordray *(Girls)*, Clara Blore *(Hatchet-faced Woman)*, Eddie Parker *(Motorcycle Cop)*, Johnny Walsh *(Crap Shooter)*.

Halop's last DEAD END KIDS film sees the gang check into a rural flophouse where they meet a severely ill boy. The boy accompanies the gang while they perform their usual pastimes such as climbing around on boxcars, but he can't keep up with them and is killed while trying to escape a railroad detective. Feeling guilty, the boys locate the kid's mother to break the news, but her overwhelming kindness prevents them from making the announcement. Halop spins a yarn that moves the woman to allow the boys to stay in her home, and he earns his keep by getting a job pumping gas. Soon Halop finds himself involved with some shady trucking racketeers, and when he drives a wounded crook to a private doctor, rather than a hospital, he finds himself indicted. The dead boy's mother, however, comes to his rescue and clears his name by testifying as to his honesty. With that, and the news that the Japanese have bombed Pearl Harbor, the boys decide to join the Army. Halop, with his last line as a DEAD END KID, looks directly at the camera at film's end and says "And we're not kidding!," no doubt referring to the gang's enlistment. (See BOWERY BOYS series, Index.)

d, Ray Taylor; w, Brenda Weisberg, Lewis Amster, Harold Tarshis, Harry Sucher (based on a story by Charles Grayson); ph, Jack McKenzie; ed, Ed Curtis; md, Hans J. Salter; art d, Jack Otterson; cos, Vera West.

Comedy **(PR:A MPAA:NR)**

MUGGER, THE** (1958) 74m Barbizon/UA bw

Kent Smith *(Peter Graham)*, Nan Martin *(Claire Townsend)*, James Franciscus *(Eddie Baxter)*, Stefan Schnabel *(Fats Donner)*, Connie Vaness *(Katherine Elio)*, Sandra Church *(Jeannie)*, Dick O'Neil *(Policeman Cassidy)*, Leonard Stone *(Kelly)*, Arthur Storch *(Skippy Randolph)*, Albert Dennable *(Policeman Connelly)*, Boris Aplon *(Wilson)*, John Alexander.

Average programmer stars Smith as a police psychiatrist out to capture a crazed mugger who leaves small scars on the faces of his female victims when he takes off with their shoulder bags. During the investigation, a girl is murdered and it appears to be the work of the mugger. When the thief is apprehended and denies the killing, the cops set out to catch the real killer. As it turns out, the killer is the brother-in-law of the victim and a personal friend of Smith. Okay performances and a fast pace render this outing fairly entertaining.

p&d, William Berke; w, Henry Kane (based on the novel by Ed McBain); ph, J. Burgi Conter; m, Albert Glasser.

Crime **(PR:A MPAA:NR)**

MUHOMATSU NO ISSHO (SEE: RICKSHAW MAN, THE, 1960, Jap.)

MULE TRAIN** (1950) 69m COL bw

Gene Autry *(Himself)*, Pat Buttram *(Smokey Argyle)*, Sheila Ryan *(Carol Bannister)*, Robert Livingston *(Sam Brady)*, Frank Jacquet *(Clayton Hodges)*, Vince Barnett *(Barber Mulkey)*, Syd Saylor *(Skeeter)*, Sandy Sanders *(Bud)*, Gregg Barton *("Keg" Rollins)*, Kenne Duncan *(Latigo)*, Roy Gordon *(John MacKnight)*, Stanley Andrews *(Chalmers)*, Robert Hilton *(Bancroft)*, Bob Wilke *(Bradshaw)*, John Miljan *(Judd Holbrook)*, Robert Carson *(Bill Cummings)*, Pat O'Malley *(Charley Stewart)*, Eddie Parker, George Morrell, John R. McKee, George Slocum, Frank O'Connor, Norman Leavitt, Champion, Jr., the horse.

Loosely based on a million-selling song by Frankie Laine, this Autry oater sees Gene defending his friend's natural cement claim from evil freight shipper Livingston. A hefty cement contract is about to be let by a construction company that plans to build a dam, and Livingstone wants to cash in on it. For some reason this Autry vehicle was selected by New York's Museum of Modern Art to represent Autry's career in their collection. (See GENE AUTRY series, Index.)

p, Armand Schaefer; d, John English; w, Gerald Geraghty (based on a story by Alan James); ph, William Bradford (Sepiatone); ed, Richard Fantl; md, Mischa Bakaleinikoff; art d, Charles Clague; m/l, title song, Johnny Lange, Hy Heath, Fred Glickman.

Western **(PR:A MPAA:NR)**

MUMMY, THE**** (1932) 72m UNIV bw

Boris Karloff *(Im-Ho-Tep/Ardeth Bey)*, Zita Johann *(Helen Grosvenor/Princess Anck-es-en-Amon)*, David Manners *(Frank Whemple)*, Edward Van Sloan *(Professor Muller)*, Arthur Byron *(Sir Joseph Whemple)*, Bramwell Fletcher *(Norton)*, Noble Johnson *(The Nubian)*, Leonard Mudie *(Professor Pearson)*, Katherine Byron *(Frau Muller)*, Eddie Kane *(Doctor)*, Tony Marlow *(Inspector)*, Arnold Gray *(Knight)*, James Crane *(Pharaoh)*, Henry Victor *(Warrior)*.

Following his triumph as the monster in FRANKENSTEIN (1931), Karoloff created yet another unforgettable horror character with the help of makeup man Pierce and cinematographer-turned-director Freund. The film opens at an Egyptian archeological dig in 1921 as scientists Byron, Van Sloan, and a young student, Fletcher, examine their most recent findings. Having discovered a sarcophagus in an unmarked grave, Egyptologist Van Sloan surmises that the mummy had been buried alive. The coffin in which he rests had been stripped of all religious markings that would have ensured an afterlife for the deceased. The 3700-year-old corpse was obviously buried in disgrace after committing some horrible crime. Buried with the mummy is a large box upon which is written a warning to those who would dare open it. Van Sloan warns against violating the curse, but Byron and Fletcher have no such compunctions. To placate Van Sloan's fears, Byron takes him for a walk in the desert to discuss the matter. Now alone, Fletcher's curiosity gets the better of him and he opens the box. Fletcher finds an ancient scroll inside and begins reading and transcribing it. Behind him, in the open coffin, the mummy's eyes slowly flutter open. His arms begin to move. Engrossed in his work, Fletcher fails to notice the activity until the mummy reaches over and takes back the scroll. Fletcher sees the walking dead and immediately begins screaming and laughing hysterically. A trail of loose wrappings follows the mummy out the door. Hearing the screams, Byron and Van Sloan dash back to investigate. They find Fletcher already gripped in the throes of madness. When asked what has happened, Fletcher replies, "He went for a little walk! You should have seen his face!" Twelve years later, Byron's son, Manners, is on another archeological expedition in the area. One day an ancient-looking Egyptian archeologist, Karloff, arrives. His face is a mass of wrinkles. He walks with a slow, delicate gait, as if he could crumble at any second. Karloff tells the explorers where they should dig to find the tomb of Princess Anck-es-en-Amon. The tomb is unearthed exactly where Karloff indicated, and its treasures, including the princess' mummy, are transported to the Cairo museum. Late at night, alone in the museum, Karloff produces the missing scroll and begins an incantation to revive the long-dead mummy. His efforts fail. Interrupted by a museum guard, Karloff kills the man, but loses the scroll. Soon after, the ancient Egyptian meets Johann, Manners' fiancee. Her resemblance to the mummified princess startles Karloff, who becomes convinced that her soul has been reincarnated in the body of this young woman. Van Sloan, who has long suspected Karloff was up to no good, deduces that the weird-looking man is in fact the mummy that went missing in 1921. He confronts Karloff with his suspicions and the living mummy, confident of his ancient powers over these mortal men, admits the truth. Later, at Van Sloan's urging, Byron goes to burn the sacred scroll in his fireplace in the hope that Karloff will be destroyed. From his home several blocks away, Karloff uses his psychic powers to induce a heart attack in Byron, thus killing him and saving the scroll. Under Karloff's influence, Byron's Nubian servant, Johnson, retrieves the scroll and brings it to Karloff. Once again Karloff uses his powers to lure Johann to his home. In his swirling "pool of remembrance," Karloff shows Johann their former life together. In the days of ancient Egypt, Karloff was a high priest and Johann a princess; they were in love with each other. Distraught by her premature death, Karloff steals the sacred scroll of life and tries to revive his love. He is caught by the Pharaoh's guards and sentenced to be buried alive in an unmarked grave for his heresy. Now, 3,700 years later, Karloff intends to kill Johann so that their souls can be joined for all eternity. The ceremony takes place in the museum. Johann is dressed in the garments of the Princess Anck-es-en-Amon. Just as Karloff is about to plunge the ceremonial dagger into her heart, Johann snaps out of his spell and desperately pleads with the statue of the great god Isis to save her. At the same time, Van Sloan and Manners arrive. Karloff turns his attention to them and tries to kill them with his hypnotic powers, but the statue of Isis comes to life and destroys the sacred scroll. Before the amazed eyes of Van Sloan, Johann, and Manners, Karloff crumbles into a heap of bones. Whereas DRACULA and FRANKENSTEIN have had some basis in fact, legend, and literature, THE MUMMY is a fanciful creation sprung from the minds of

Universal screenwriters Putnam, Schayer, and Balderston. Obviously inspired by the recent discovery of King Tutankhamen's undisturbed tomb in 1922, the writers concocted this macabre love story and added ancient curses and life-giving scrolls. Though there were always rumors of curses against those who defiled the tombs of the pharaohs, there are few facts indicating that the ancient Egypitans themselves believed in such things (the curses were probably invented by modern-day Egyptians in an effort to scare off European archeologists). THE MUMMY marked the directorial debut of the brilliant German cinematographer, Karl Freund, who had photographed such classic German silents as THE LAST LAUGH, VARIETY, and METROPOLIS, and also DRACULA in the U.S. Though THE MUMMY is not an openly terrifying film (with the exception of the mummy's revival at the beginning), Freund creates an uneasy atmosphere of dread and foreboding. His camera is remarkably mobile, with impressive tracking and crane shots which seem to float through the action, creating an eerie mood (Freund's next and only other film as a director, MAD LOVE (1935), was more of a *Grand Guignol* horror show). The sparse muscial score works just as well, with Tchaikovsky's haunting "Swan Lake" used as the opening theme. Though the technical credits are excellent, it is Karloff who carries the film. Makeup genius Jack Pierce once again molded his magic to the actor, and the combination of linen, fuller's earth, and clay used to create the recently discovered mummy took over eight hours a day to apply. The effect is startling, though Karloff only appears as the mummy briefly. Perhaps more impressive is the more subtle makeup Pierce created for Karloff in his reincarnated state. The mass of delicate wrinkles on Karloff's face and hands, combined with the actor's deliberately gentle, flowing movements, creates a being who looks as if he may fall apart at any moment. In one scene Karloff tells an archeologist, "I don't like to be touched!," convincing the viewer that his arm would fall off if grabbed. Some of the most memorable footage comes in the form of a flashback to ancient Egypt. Entirely silent, the action is explained by Karloff in a voice-over. The recreation of the days of the pharaohs is quite effective, and the scene where Karloff is being wrapped alive, eyes going wider as his mouth is covered, is unforgettable. Other scenes showing Johann in her vairous reincarnations throughout history (as a martyred Christian, viking maiden, and noblewoman during the Crusades) were shot, but eventually scrapped and only some rare still photographs of these scenes remain. Strangely, actors Henry Victor and Arnold Gray (the first plays a Roman warrior, the second a medieval knight), who were featured in these scenes, remain billed in the onscreen credits though they do not appear in the final cut. While THE MUMMY does not have the manic energy and life of Karloff's future masterpiece, THE BRIDE OF FRANKENSTEIN, it has an effective, haunting quality wholly its own and is a classic of the horror genre. Four inferior sequels followed. The first, THE MUMMY'S HAND (1940), starred Tom Tyler as the mummy. The rest, THE MUMMY'S TOMB (1942), THE MUMMY'S GHOST (1944), and THE MUMMY'S CURSE (1944) all starred Lon Chaney, Jr. as the mummy. Hammer Films of England revived the series beginning in 1959 with THE MUMMY. (See MUMMY series, Index.)

p, Carl Laemmle, Jr.; d, Karl Freund; w, John L. Balderston (based on a story by Nina Wilcox Putnam, Richard Schayer); ph, Charles Stumar; ed, Milton Carruth; art d, Willy Pogany; spec eff, John P. Fulton; makeup, Jack P. Pierce.

Horror **Cas.** **(PR:C-O MPAA:NR)**

MUMMY, THE*** (1959, Brit.) 86m Hammer/UNIV c

Peter Cushing *(John Banning)*, Christopher Lee *(Kharis, the Mummy)*, Yvonne Furneaux *(Isobel Banning/Princess Ananka)*, Eddie Byrne *(Inspector Mulrooney)*, Felix Aylmer *(Stephen Banning)*, Raymond Huntley *(Joseph Whemple)*, George Pastell *(Mehemet, Priest)*, John Stuart *(Coroner)*, Harold Goodwin *(Pat)*, Dennis Shaw *(Mike)*, Michael Ripper *(Poacher)*, Willoughby Gray, Stanley Meadows, Frank Singuineau, Frank Sieman, Gerald Lawson, David Browning, John Harrison, James Clarke, Frederick Rawlings.

Pretty lively Hammer retelling of the classic mummy material starring Cushing as one of three British archaeologists who desecrate the tomb of an Egyptian princess despite the warnings of Pastell. What they manage to do is awaken Lee, the mummified ex-lover of the princess who was buried alive *(after* his tongue was cut out by the princess' angry father 3,000 years before) with the princess when she died. Lee and Pastell follow the archaeologists back to England where the mummy kills them off one by one. When Lee is about to kill Cushing, however, he is stopped when he sees his victim's beautiful wife, Furneaux, who happens to be the spitting image of the princess. Lee kidnaps Furneaux and after killing Pastell, he carries her to a nearby swamp where she is rescued by Cushing. The angry locals then literally blow the stuffings out of Lee with blast after blast of shotgun fire. What's left of Lee slowly sinks into the swamp (as have so many of the cinema's mummies). Stylishly directed by Fisher (the action scenes are breathtakingly choreographed), with a surprisingly energetic performance from Lee whose mummy moves swiftly and with strength, unlike the slow, shuffling mummies of the 1940s. By playing the Mummy, Lee completed something of a trinity of terror, having already starred as Frankenstein's monster and Dracula. This film, together with THE CURSE OF FRANKENSTEIN (1957) and THE HORROR OF DRACULA (1958), all directed by Fisher and starring Lee and Cushing, helped to revive the horror movie industry which had been slumbering since the mid-1940s.

p, Michael Carreras; d, Terence Fisher; w, Jimmy Sangster (based on the screenplays THE MUMMY by Nina Wilcox Putnam, and THE MUMMY'S TOMB by Griffin Jay); ph, Jack Asher (Technicolor); m, Franz Reizenstein; ed, James Needs, Alfred Cox; prod d, Bernard Robinson; md, John Hollingsworth; art d, Bernard Robinson.

Horror **Cas.** **(PR:C MPAA:NR)**

MUMMY'S BOYS* 1/2 (1936) 68m RKO bw

Bert Wheeler *(Stanley)*, Robert Woolsey *(Whittaker)*, Barbara Pepper *(Mary)*, Moroni Olsen *("Doc" Sterling)*, Frank M. Thomas *(Browning)*, Willie Best *(Catfish)*, Francis McDonald *(El Bey)*, Frank Lackteen *(2nd Oriental)*, Charles Coleman *(Butler)*, Mitchell Lewis *(Sheik)*, Frederick Burton *(Mr. Edwards)*.

Poor comedy from Wheeler and Woolsey who play ditch-diggers on an archaeological expedition where nine of the 10 archaeologists are killed. An old curse involving the desecration of the tomb is allegedly the cause of the deaths. As it turns out, digger No. 10, Olsen, has knocked off his associates himself so he can reap the rewards alone. Unfunny, with every obvious mummy joke told as if it were to be heard for the first time.

p, Lee Marcus; d, Fred Guiol; w, Jack Townley, Philip G. Epstein, Charles Roberts (based on a story by Townley, Lew Lipton); ph, Jack MacKenzie, Vernon Walker; m, Roy Webb; ed, John Lockert; cos, Edward Stevenson.

Comedy/Mystery **(PR:A MPAA:NR)**

MUMMY'S CURSE, THE* 1/2 (1944) 62m UNIV bw

Lon Chaney, Jr. *(Kharis, the Mummy)*, Peter Coe *(Dr. Ilzor Zardad)*, Virginia Christine *(Princess Ananka)*, Kay Harding *(Betty Walsh)*, Dennis Moore *(Dr. James Halsey)*, Martin Kosleck *(Raghab)*, Kurt Katch *(Cajun Joe)*, Addison Richards *(Maj. Pat Walsh)*, Holmes Herbert *(Dr. Cooper)*, Napoleon Simpson *(Goobie)*, Charles Stevens *(Skilles)*, William Farnum *(Michael the Caretaker)*, Ann Codee *(Tante Berthe)*, Claire Whitney.

Sequel to THE MUMMY'S GHOST and Lon Chaney, Jr.'s last appearance as the mummy. This one picks up where the last one left off and sees Kharis and Ananka dug out of the bog they sunk into and transported to Cajun country for study by archaeologists. Predictably, the duo revives and wreaks havoc on the locals. Eventually the hero, Moore, manages to render the pair inactive enough to be displayed in a museum. Padded with tons of footage from earlier mummy movies. Christine, who plays Ananka, would become a familiar sight to TV viewers years later as Mrs. Olsen on Folgers Coffee commercials.

p, Oliver Drake; d, Leslie Goodwins; w, Bernard Schubert (based on a story by Leon Abrams, Dwight V. Babcock); ph, Virgil Miller; ed, Fred R. Feitshans; md, Paul Sawtell; art d, John B. Goodman; m/l, "Hey You," Drake, Frank Orth; makeup, Jack Pierce.

Horror **(PR:A MPAA:NR)**

MUMMY'S GHOST, THE** (1944) 60m UNIV bw

Lon Chaney, Jr. *(Kharis, the Mummy)*, John Carradine *(Yousef Bey/Egyptian Priest)*, Ramsay Ames *(Amina Mansouri/Princess Ananka)*, Robert Lowery *(Tommy Hervey)*, Barton MacLane *(Inspector Walgreen)*, Claire Whitney *(Mrs. Ellen Norman)*, George Zucco *(High Priest)*, Frank Reicher *(Prof. Norman)*, Harry Shannon *(Sheriff Elwood)*, Emmett Vogan *(The Coroner)*, Lester Sharpe *(Dr. Ayab)*, Oscar O'Shea *(Night Watchman, Scripps Museum)*, Don Barclay *(Student, Tommy's Friend)*, Dorothy Vaughn *(Mrs. Ada Blake)*, Mira McKinney *(Mrs. Martha Evans)*, Bess Flowers *(Mapleton Woman)*, Eddy Waller *(Ben Evans)*, Anthony Warde *(Sheriff's Associate)*, Ivan Triesault *(Scripp's Museum Guide)*, Martha Vickers *(Norman's Girl Student)*, Peanuts, King *(Dogs)*.

Sequel to THE MUMMY'S TOMB starring Chaney, Jr. as the mummy. Since Turhan Bey failed in the previous movie, Egyptian priest Zucco sends Carradine to New England to help the mummy find his princess. This time a young college coed played by Ames is the Ananka look-alike and Chaney, Jr. spends most of the movie choking the life out of dozens of New Englanders while trying to reach his long-lost love. Complications arise when the mummy catches Carradine declaring his love for Ames, and the insanely jealous mummy kills him. The mummy grabs Ames and carries her to a nearby swamp and as the police and Ames' boy friend, Lowery, watch, the duo sink into the bog and Ames ages 3,000 years before their astonished eyes.

p, Ben Pivar; d, Reginald LeBorg; w, Griffith Jay, Henry Sucher, Brenda Weisberg (based on a story by Jay, Sucher); ph, William Sickner; ed, Saul Goodkind; md, Hans J. Salter; art d, John B. Goodman, Abraham Grossman; cos, Vera West; makeup, Jack Pierce.

Horror **(PR:A MPAA:NR)**

MUMMY'S HAND, THE*** (1940) 67m UNIV bw

Dick Foran *(Steve Banning)*, Peggy Moran *(Marta Solvani/Sullivan)*, Cecil Kellaway *(Solvani the Great/Tim Sullivan)*, Wallace Ford *(Babe Jenson)*, George Zucco *(Prof. Andoheb)*, Charles Trowbridge *(Dr. Petrie)*, Tom Tyler *(Kharis the Mummy)*, Siegfried [Sig] Arno *(Beggar)*, Eduardo Ciannelli *(High Priest)*, Leon Belasco *(Ali)*, Harry Stubbs *(Bartender)*, Michael Mark *(Bazaar Owner)*, Mara Tartar *(Girl Vendor)*, Frank Lackteen, Murdock McQuarrie *(Priests)*, Eddie Foster *(Egyptian)*.

First of the follow-ups to Boris Karloff's classic THE MUMMY, which has very little to do with the original. Zucco stars as the crazed high priest who revives the mummy (now named Kharis instead of Im-Ho-Tep) and sends him out to kill everyone who has defiled the tomb. Cowboy star Tyler plays the mummy who shuffles off to strangle the explorers until he meets the lovely Moran, whom he brings back to the temple and wants to make his bride. Zucco thinks it a fine idea and brews up a batch of tana leaves to make them all immortal, but Foran and Ford enter the tomb, shoot Zucco three times, and watch as he tumbles down a very long flight of Egyptian steps, spilling the tana juice all over. Tyler is taken care of when he is set on fire while trying to clean up the mess on the floor. Really low-budget with over 10 minutes of footage from the Karloff film, and the stunning tomb set was left over from GREEN HELL. The best of the mummy series of the 1940s.

p, Ben Pivar; d, Christy Cabanne; w, Griffith Jay, Maxwell Shane (based on a story by Jay); ph, Elwood Bredell; ed, Phil Cahn; md, H. J. Salter; cos, Vera West.

Horror **(PR:C MPAA:NR)**

MUMMY'S SHROUD, THE* (1967, Brit.) 90m Seven Arts-Hammer/FOX c

Andre Morell (*Sir Basil Walden*), John Phillips (*Stanley Preston*), David Buck (*Paul Preston*), Elizabeth Sellars (*Barbara Preston*), Maggie Kimberley (*Claire de Sangre, Linguist*), Michael Ripper (*Longbarrow*), Tim Barrett (*Harry Newton, Photographer*), Richard Warner (*Inspector Barrani*), Roger Delgado (*Hasmid Ali*), Catherine Lacey (*Haiti*), Dickie Owen (*Prem*), Bruno Barnabe (*Pharaoh*), Toni Gilpin (*Pharaoh's Wife*), Toolsie Persaud [Tulsi Prasad] (*Kah-to-Bey*), Eddie Powell (*Mummy*), Andreas Malandrinos (*Curator*).

Uninspired mummy epic set in 1920 and featuring Phillips as a rich industrialist who finances an Eygptian expedition. The object is to retrieve the mummy of an Egyptian pharaoh for display in a museum. The expedition succeeds and the pharaoh's slave, who had been removed from the tomb earlier, revives and sets out to murder all involved in the expedition. He dispatches several members of the group and is about to eliminate Buck and Kimberley, when he recites "The Words of Death" on the mummy's shroud, reducing him to dust. For this film, the mummy was designed to look more like the real thing, rather than the Hollywood version, but it's still a less than memorable outing.

p, Anthony Nelson Keys; d&w, John Gilling (based on a story by John Elder [Anthony Hinds]); ph, Arthur Grant (Technicolor); m, Don Banks, Franz Reizenstein; ed, James Needs; prod d, Bernard Robinson; art d, Don Mingaye; makeup, George Partleton; spec eff, Bowie Films.

Horror (PR:C MPAA:NR)

MUMMY'S TOMB, THE**1/2 (1942) 61m UNIV bw

Lon Chaney, Jr. (*Kharis, the Mummy*), Dick Foran (*Stephen A. Banning*), Elyse Knox (*Isobel Evans*), John Hubbard (*John Banning*), Mary Gordon (*Jane Banning*), Virginia Brissac (*Mrs. Evans*), Turhan Bey (*Mehemet Bey*), Wallace Ford (*Babe Hanson*), George Zucco (*Andoheb*), Cliff Clark (*Sheriff*), Paul E. Burns (*Pedro*), Frank Reicher (*Prof. Norman*), Emmett Vogan (*Coroner*), Janet Shaw (*Girl in Car*), Eddie Parker (*Stuntman*), Glenn Strange, Grace Cunard.

Sequel to THE MUMMY'S HAND sees Chaney, Jr. in wraps for the first time as crazed old high priest Zucco sends his aid Bey out with the mummy to America where they are to get revenge on Ford and Foran, who everyone thought killed Zucco and the mummy in the last movie. (The bullet only "crushed my arm," states Zucco, though it was actually three bullets and a nasty fall—never mind.) Hiding out in a cemetery, Bey and Chaney set up shop to get their revenge, but Chaney falls in love with Knox and has trouble taking orders anymore. When the angry villagers (shots from the original FRANKENSTEIN) attack the cemetery, Bey is killed and the mummy set on fire once again. The film also includes flashback footage of Peggy Moran and Charles Trowbridge from THE MUMMY'S HAND as well as the crowd footage from FRANKENSTEIN.

p, Ben Pivar; d, Harold Young; w, Griffith Jay, Henry Sucher (based on a story by Neil P. Varnick); ph, George Robinson; ed, Milton Carruth; md, H. J. Salter; art d, Jack Otterson.

Horror (PR:C MPAA:NR)

MUMSY, NANNY, SONNY, AND GIRLY zero (1970, Brit.) 101m Cinerama c (AKA: GIRLY)

Michael Bryant (*New Friend*), Ursula Howells (*Mumsy*), Pat Heywood (*Nanny*), Howard Trevor (*Sonny*), Vanessa Howard (*Girly*), Robert Swann (*Soldier*), Imogen Hassall (*Girl Friend*), Michael Ripper (*Zoo Attendant*), Hugh Armstrong (*Friend in No. 5*).

Distasteful crime film starring Howells, Heywood, Trevor, and Howard as the title looneys who live in a country estate and get their kicks from killing men who happen to wander by. The family likes to torture and play games with their victims like boiling their heads on a stove. When they pick up playboy Bryant, however, things change somewhat. The handsome victim melts the hearts of the three women and plays one off the other until they begin to kill each other off. Gruesome and too stupid to chill over.

p, Ronald J. Kahn; d, Freddie Francis; w, Brian Comport (based on the play "Happy Family" by Maisie Mosco); ph, David Muir (Eastmancolor); m, Bernard Ebbinghouse; ed, Tristam Cones; art d, Maggie Pinhorn; set d, Dimity Collins.

Crime/Horror (PR:O MPAA:R)

MUMU**1/2 (1961, USSR) 71m Mosfilm/Artkino bw

Afanasi Kochetkov (*Gerasim*), Nina Grebeshkova (*Tatyana*), Yelena Polevitskaya (*The Mistress*), Igor Bezyayev (*Kapiton*), Ivan Ryzhov (*Gavrila*), Yevgeniy Teterin (*Khariton*), Leonid Kmit (*Stepan*), V. Myasnikova (*Lyubimovna*), A. Denisova (*Housekeeper*), A. Fyodorova (*Ustinya*), G. Belov (*Potap*), A. Dobronravov (*Uncle Khvost*), L. Volskaya, A. Danilova, L. Korolyova, P. Lyubeshkin, A. Pavlova, A. Rumyanova, K. Rumyantseva, G. Sayfulin, V. Khmara.

An interesting tale about a deaf-mute who is led away from his country home by a wealthy woman who wants him to work at her estate in the city. He unwillingly obliges, but feels less depressed about his new environment when he meets and falls in love with a pretty, young laundress. She, however, is married off to a man chosen by the rich woman. The mute then finds a new companion, a sickly puppy which he names Mumu—one of the few sounds he can produce. He nurses the pup back to health, but it snaps at the lady and she orders him to get rid of it. He drowns it in a river and begins to walk back to his village.

d, Anatoli Bobrovsky, Yevgeniy Teterin; w, Chrisanf Kheronsky (based on the story by Ivan Sergeyevich Turgenev); ph, Konstantin Petrichenko; m, Aleksey Muravlev; ed, V. Chekan; art d, Arnold Vaysfeld, Aleksandr Borisov; cos, G. Ganevskaya; spec eff, V. Alekseyeva, S. Khizhnyak, B. Noskov; makeup, Yu Yemelyanov.

Drama (PR:A MPAA:NR)

MUNECOS INFERNALES (SEE: CURSE OF THE DOLL PEOPLE, 1968, Mex.)

MUNKBROGREVEN (SEE: COUNT OF THE MONK'S BRIDGE, THE, 1934, Swed.)

MUNSTER, GO HOME** (1966) 96m UNIV c

Fred Gwynne (*Herman Munster*), Yvonne De Carlo (*Lily Munster*), Al Lewis (*Grandpa Munster*), Butch Patrick (*Eddie Munster*), Debbie Watson (*Marilyn Munster*), Terry-Thomas (*Freddie Munster*), Hermione Gingold (*Lady Effigie Munster*), Robert Pine (*Roger Moresby*), John Carradine (*Cruikshank*), Bernard Fox (*Squire Moresby*), Richard Dawson (*Joey*), Jeanne Arnold (*Grace Munster*), Maria Lennard (*Millie*), Cliff Norton (*Herbert*), Diana Chesney (*Mrs. Moresby*), Arthur Malet (*Alfie*), Ben Wright (*Hennesy*), Jack Dodson (*Shipmate*).

Silly television shows inevitably make for silly feature films and MUNSTER, GO HOME is no exception. Story sees the Munsters inherit a British estate and they travel abroad to collect. Little do they know that the estate is being used as a front for a counterfeiting ring run by Gingold, Thomas, and Carradine, who try to scare the munster family back to the U.S. The highlight of the film sees Gwynne win a drag race in his custom Dragula coffin-car.

p, Joe Connelly, Bob Mosher; d, Earl Bellamy; w, George Tibbles, Connelly, Mosher (based on the TV series "The Munsters"); ph, Benjamin H. Kline (Technicolor); m, Jack Marshall; ed, Bud S. Isaacs; art d, Alexander Golitzen, John Lloyd; set d, John McCarthy, Julie Heron; cos, Grady Hunt; stunts Carey Loftin; makeup, Bud Westmore, Perc Westmore, Carl Silvera, Abe Haberman.

Comedy (PR:A MPAA:NR)

MUPPET MOVIE, THE*** (1979) 98m ITC Entertainment/Associated Film Distribution c

Muppet Performers: Jim Henson (*Kermit the Frog/Rowlf/Dr. Teeth/Waldorf*), Frank Oz (*Miss Piggy/Fozzie Bear/Animal/Sam the Eagle*), Jerry Nelson (*Floyd Pepper/Crazy Harry/Robin the Frog/Lew Zealand*), Richard Hunt (*Scooter/Statler/Janice/Sweetums/Beaker*), Dave Goelz (*The Great Gonzo/Zoot/Dr. Bunsen Honeydew*); Also Featuring: Charles Durning (*Doc Hopper*), Austin Pendleton (*Max*), Scott Walker (*Frog Killer*), Mel Brooks (*Prof. Krassman*), Edgar Bergen, Milton Berle, James Coburn, Dom DeLuise, Elliott Gould, Bob Hope, Madeline Kahn, Carol Kane, Cloris Leachman, Steve Martin, Richard Pryor, Telly Savalas, Orson Welles, Paul Williams, Carroll Spinney, Steve Whitmire, Kathryn Mullen, Bob Payne, Eren Ozker, Carolyn Wilcox, Olga Felgemacher, Bruce Schwartz, Michael Davis, Buz Suraci, Tony Basilicato, Adam Hunt.

Charming children's film starring the successful television puppets in their first feature film (two sequels followed). The loose plot sees Kermit the Frog and Fozzie Bear traveling across the country on their way to fame and fortune in Hollywood. On the road they pick up a variety of passengers (muppet and human) and sing a dozen songs (the musical numbers tend to bog down the film somewhat). The special effects are handled very well with the highlights featuring Kermit riding a bicycle and rowing a boat. Cute without being insipid, funny without being childish, THE MUPPET MOVIE contains enough magic to please even the most harsh movie goer. Songs include: "The Rainbow Connection," "Frog's Legs So Fine," "Movin Right Along," "Can You Picture That?," "Never Before," "Something Better," "This Looks Familiar," "I'm Going Back There Someday" (Paul Williams, Kenny Ascher).

p, Jim Henson; d, James Frawley; w, Jerry Juhl, Jack Burns; ph, Isidore Mankofsky (CFI color); m, Paul Williams; ed, Chris Greenbury; prod d, Joel Schiller; art d, Les Gobruegge; cos, Calista Hendrickson (Muppets), Gwen Capetanos.

Musical/Fantasy **Cas.** (PR:AA MPAA:G)

MURDER**** (1930, Brit.) 92m BIP bw

Herbert Marshall (*Sir John Menier*), Norah Baring (*Diana Baring*), Phyllis Konstam (*Dulcie Markham*), Edward Chapman (*Ted Markham*), Miles Mander (*Gordon Druce*), Esme Percy (*Handel Fane*), Donald Calthrop (*Ion Stewart*), Amy Brandon Thomas (*Defence*), Marie Wright (*Miss Mitcham*), Hannah Jones (*Mrs. Didsome*), Una O'Connor (*Mrs. Grogram*), R. E. Jeffrey (*Foreman*), Violet Farebrother (*Mrs. Ward*), Kenneth Kove (*Matthews*), Gus McNaughton (*Tom Trewitt*), Esme V. Chaplin, S. J. Warmington, William Fazan, Joynson Powell, Clare Greet.

This whodunit is not typically Hitchcock but he enjoyed the results of breaking his own credo in presenting surprise instead of suspense. In a story line that would be repeated many times, Baring, a young actress, is accused of killing one of her friends. As the jury deliberates Baring's fate during her trial, one of their number, producer-director-actor Marshall, who is also a gentleman knight, remains unconvinced of Baring's guilt. The other jurors are shown to swarm in on him chanting a sinister chorus of "guilty," and later the same refrain is heard through the open door of the jury room leading to the courtroom, along with Baring's death sentence. Marshall is so troubled by the flimsy circumstantial evidence used to convict the young woman that he decides to launch his own investigation into the murder, calling Konstam and Chapman to his lavish lodgings to help him reconstruct the murder and solve the case. Ever the patrician, Marshall is also considerate of the low-born status of his confederates. When they dine, Chapman has no idea of what spoon to use and employs the same for his soup as he does for his fruit cup. To avoid embarrassing him, Marshall also uses only one spoon. He then amusedly endures Konstam's air-laden postures of "gentility," as she awkwardly poses like a refined woman. (In this scene Hitchcock allowed the actors to improvise their lines, an early-day trait he soon corrected; he would increasingly demand that actors stick to the script in future films.) During the course of Marshall's investigation, where the entire crime is reenacted as a play within a play, he discovers that the real killer is a half-caste circus trapeze performer, Percy, who is also a transvestite and one who has acted on the boards in drag, a disguise the killer employed when slaying his victim. Baring is freed and winds up with her savior, Marshall. Among the many inventive shots created by Hitchcock, the director also offered for the first time in sound films the character's spoken thoughts as Marshall stood mute before a mirror shaving, a device that would be used myriad times afterward. This occurs while Marshall is looking at his own image while listening to the radio play classical music. In this early sound period it was next to impossible to create this effect until Hitchcock improvised brilliantly. He had Marshall prerecord his thought passage on a wire tape recorder, then played this back while shooting the scene where he stood tight-lipped. A live 35-piece orchestra was placed behind the bathroom wall playing the prelude to "Tristan and Isolde," to simulate the music supposedly coming from the radio. Marshall is superb as the gentlemen sleuth, his character based upon either Sir Gerald du Maurier or Sir Herbert Beerbohm Tree or both. He is austere and down-to-earth when the scene calls for humanity. In one sequence, Marshall takes a room in a shabby part of town and, when his busy landlady shows up with his morning tea, Marshall, still in bed, is overwhelmed by a horde of dirty little children who jump on his bed, one little girl with black greasy hands embracing him while he grimaces before a smile breaks through. The effect is charming and shows a gentleman capable of warmth as well as compassion. As was the custom of the time, Hitchcock also directed a German version of MURDER immediately after completing the British version. He later stated: "Although I spoke German, I didn't know the cadences of speech and I was lost on the set. The actors sounded colloquial to me, but I really couldn't understand what they were saying." He worked well with the German female lead, Olga Tchekowa, but the male star, the renowned Alfred Abel, gave him a hard time. Hitchcock told Abel that he was to wear a tweed suit when visiting the condemned woman in her cell but Abel snorted: "I don't visit a girl in these clothes!" He insisted upon wearing formal evening coat and striped trousers. Abel also refused to do the bedroom scene with the dirty children. Hitchcock vainly tried to reason with him, saying: "The whole point of comedy is to reduce dignity." Retorted Abel: "Not for the Germans!" The scene was not used in the German version. In the British version Hitchcock made a cameo appearance on the street, a lark that would blossom into a tradition with each new film. In trapping the killer, Hitchcock has Marshall direct the real killer in reading lines that will reveal his guilt, a device he would later expand upon when making STAGE FRIGHT.

p, John Maxwell; d, Alfred Hitchcock; w, Alma Reville, Walter C. Mycroft, Hitchcock (based on the novel and play *Enter Sir John* by Clemence Dane, Helen Simpson); ph, Jack Cox; m, John Reynders; ed, Emile de Ruelle, Rene Harrison, art d, J. F. Mead.

Mystery Cas. **(PR:A MPAA:NR)**

MURDER A LA MOD*

(1968) 80m Aries Documentaries bw

Margo Norton (*Karen*), Andra Akers (*Tracy*), Jared Martin (*Christopher*), William Finley (*Otto*), Ken Burrows (*Wiley*), Lorenzo Catlett (*Policeman*), Jennifer Salt, Melanie Mander, Laura Rubin, Laura Stevenson ("*Birds*").

Very early de Palma film wherein he first demonstrated his total obsession with visual style and his ignorance of characterization. A porno director pleads with his girl friend to help him against his wife because she is blackmailing him and he is broke. The girl friend then steals a friend's jewelry to raise some cash, but she is found murdered soon after. The film then delves into the lives of the three most likely suspects and observes their activities immediately after the murder. De Palma employs three elaborate visual styles throughout the film. The first is a standard, almost television-like style, comprised of close-ups and medium shots. The second style is Hitchcock influenced, and the third takes on the aspects of silent film chases. Unfortunately, de Palma pays more attention to the visuals than the characters, leaving the audience to wonder just who really cares about the people on screen.

p, Ken Burrows; d,w&ed, Brian de Palma; ph, Bruce Torbet; m, John Herbert McDowell; m/l, "Murder a la Mod," W. F. Finley.

Crime **(PR:C MPAA:NR)**

MURDER AHOY***

(1964, Brit.) 93m MGM bw

Margaret Rutherford (*Miss Marple*), Lionel Jeffries (*Capt. Sidney de Courcy Rhumstone*), Charles Tingwell (*Chief Inspector Craddock*), Stringer Davis (*Mr. Stringer*), William Mervyn (*Comdr. Breeze-Connington*), Francis Matthews (*Lt. Compton*), Terence Edmund (*Sgt. Bacon*), Tony Quinn (*Kelly, Tramp*), Joan Benham (*Matron Alice Fanbraid*), Gerald Cross (*Lt. Comdr. L. W. Brewer Dimchurch*), Roy Holder (*Petty Officer Lamb*), Bernard Adams (*Dusty Miller*), Derek Nimmo (*Sub-Lt. Humbert*), Miles Malleson (*Bishop Faulkner*), Norma Foster (*Assistant. Matron Shirley Boston*), Henry Longhurst (*Cecil Ffolly-Hardwicke*), Henry Oscar (*Lord Rudkin*), Nicholas Parsons (*Dr. Crump*), Lucy Griffiths (*Millie*), Edna Petrie (*Miss Pringle*).

This was the final "Miss Marple" film in the series that starred Margaret Rutherford. It was later rekindled with Angela Lansbury in the role but as good as Lansbury is, the picture of Rutherford as the tweedy sleuth is the one that remains in the viewer's mind. There's a huge meeting of an organization that oversees a boat used for the rehabilitation of wayward youth. One of the leading trustees, Longhurst, dies at the conclave before he can reveal some important information anent the boat. Rutherford is also a trustee and she suspects foul play surrounding Longhurst's death but the cops disregard her feelings (which is the usual case in mysteries of this sort; if the cops agreed, there would be no friction between the pros and the amateur, and therefore no story). Against the wishes of the captain, Jeffries, Rutherford goes aboard the ship and leaves her longtime aid, Davis, ashore to look after matters there. (Davis was Rutherford's husband in real life and often seen in small roles in the MARPLE series, as well as in many other films that starred the great lady.) Rutherford noses around and learns that Matthews is doing a Fagin-like job of teaching the unlikely lads how to break into houses. When Matthews and Foster,

a matron, are killed, Rutherford continues uncovering data until she discovers that Mervyn, another trustee, has been siphoning off funds from the charitable organization and has killed the other two in order to keep them mum. Rutherford gets the goods on Mervyn and he is arrested after a funny duel she and he have with swords. Funny, literate, and bouyant, it's a shame she didn't make more of these. (See MISS MARPLE series, Index.)

p, Lawrence P. Bachmann; d, George Pollock; w, David Pursall, Jack Seddon (based on the character created by Agatha Christie); ph, Desmond Dickinson, m, Ron Goodwin; ed, Ernest Walter; md, Goodwin; art d, Bill Andrews.

Comedy/Mystery **(PR:A MPAA:NR)**

MURDER AMONG FRIENDS**

(1941) 67m FOX bw

Marjorie Weaver (*Mary Lou*), John Hubbard (*Dr. Thomas Wilson*), Cobina Wright, Jr. (*Jessica Gerald*), Mona Barrie (*Clair Turk*), Douglas Dumbrille (*Carter Stevenson*), Sidney Blackmer (*Mr. Wheeler*), Truman Bradley (*McAndrews*), Lucien Littlefield (*Dr. Fred Turk*), Bill Halligan (*Dr. James Gerald*), Don Douglas (*Ellis*), Milton Parsons (*Douglass*), Eddie Conrad (*Proprietor*).

Standard murder mystery starring Weaver as an insurance clerk who notices that a number of elderly men are dying. They are all listed as beneficiaries of a lucrative policy they had agreed to when in college years ago. Weaver convinces her boy friend Hubbard to help locate the remaining men and warn them, though most of them are murdered before the killer is discovered.

p, Ralph Dietrich, Walter Morosco; d, Ray McCarey; w, John Larkin; ph, Charles Clarke; ed, Harry Reynolds; md, Emil Newman; cos, Herschel.

Crime **(PR:A MPAA:NR)**

MURDER AT COVENT GARDEN*1/2

(1932, Brit.) 68m Twickenham/Woolf and Freedman Film Service bw

Dennis Neilsen-Terry (*Jack Trencham*), Anne Grey (*Helen Osmond*), Walter Fitzgerald (*Donald Walpace*), Henri de Vries (*Van Blond*), George Curzon (*Belmont*), Fred Pease (*Snowball*), Binnie Barnes (*Girl*).

An indifferently treated crime drama in which Fitzgerald is the private detective hired to get to the bottom of a possible smuggling ring that may also be responsible for killing a nightclub owner. He performs this feat with what appears to be the greatest of ease, making for a pretty dull time.

p, Julius Hagen; d, Michael Barringer, Leslie Hiscott, w, Barringer, H. Fowler Mear (based on the novel by W. J. Makin).

Crime **(PR:A MPAA:NR)**

MURDER AT DAWN*

(1932) 55m Big Four bw

Jack Mulhall (*Danny*), Josephine Dunn (*Doris Farrington*), Marjorie Beebe (*Gertrude*), Eddie Boland (*Freddie, Gertrude's Husband*), Mischa Auer (*Henry, the Housekeeper's Son*), Martha Mattox (*Dr. Farrington's Housekeeper*), J. Crauford Kent (*Arnstein, the Stranger*), Phillips Smalley (*Judge Folger*), Al Cross (*Goddard*), Frank Ball (*Dr. Farrington*).

Badly done mystery-comedy involving a scientist who excitedly announces he has perfected a device to harness solar energy. When the inventor is visited by his daughter, Beebe, and her husband, Boland, the trouble begins. Crazed caretaker Auer duplicates the solar device, but hasn't been able to perfect it, so he kidnaps and tortures the scientist into revealing his secrets. Lots of trap doors, secret passages, and lousy jokes tell the tale for this unsuccessful farce.

p, John R. Freuler; d, Richard Thorpe; w, Barry Baringer; ph, Edward S. Kull; ed, Fred Bain; spec eff, Kenneth Strickfaden.

Mystery/Comedy **(PR:A MPAA:NR)**

MURDER AT 45 R.P.M.**

(1965, Fr.) 98m Cite/MGM bw (MEURTRE EN 45 TOURS)

Danielle Darrieux (*Eve Faugeres*), Michel Auclair (*Jean Le Prat*), Jean Servais (*Maurice Faugeres*), Henri Guisol (*Georges Meliot*), Jacqueline Danno (*Florence*), Bernard Lajarrige (*Moureu*), Raymond Gerome, Julien Verdier, Bernard Musson, Peggy Lonaty, Madeleine Barbulee, Hubert Deschamps, Mathilde Casadesus, Philippe Prince.

Average suspense film from France starring Darrieux as a famed singer and Auclair as her accompanist, who become lovers after her songwriter husband, Servais, leaves the marriage in a fit of jealousy. When Servais is killed in a mysterious car crash, the lovers begin to suspect each other of murder. Matters are further complicated when they receive a recorded message from Servais, and his friend and publisher, Guisol, receives a new song written by him. These revelations nearly destroy Darrieux and Auclair's relationship, for they fear that Servais has returned from the grave. Eventually they suspect that Guisol is perpetrating a hoax, but before he can confess his motives, he is killed in a fall down an elevator shaft, leaving the reunited lovers to wonder why.

p, Jacques Bar; d, Etienne Perier; w, Dominique Fabre, Perier, Albert Valentin; ph, Marcel Weiss; m, Yves Claoue; ed, Robert Isnardon; art d, Jean Mandaroux.

Mystery **(PR:A MPAA:NR)**

MURDER AT GLEN ATHOL*1/2

(1936) 64m CHES bw

John Miljan (*Bill Holt*), Irene Ware (*Jane Maxwell*), Noel Madison (*Gus Colleti*), Barry Norton (*Tom Randel*), Iris Adrian (*Muriel Randel*), Oscar Apfel (*Reuben Marshall*), Betty Blythe (*Ann Randel*), James P. Burtis (*Mike Jeffries*), Harry Holman (*Campbell Snowden*), James Eagles (*Harry Randel*), Wilson Benge (*Simpson*), Paul Ellis (*Cosmano*), Capt. E. H. Calvert (*District Attorney McDougal*), Henry Hull (*Dr. Burgher*), Frank O'Connor (*McGurn*), Robert Frazer (*Dr. Agnew*), Sidney Bracey (*Jenkins*), Lew Kelly.

Another in the series of films based on the "Crime Club" mystery novels. This one stars Miljan as the detective, Burtis as his buddy, Ware as the love interest, and Adrian as the married two-timer whom the mystery revolves around. Former silent screen star Betty Blythe appears in a character role as an elderly lady.

p, Maury M. Cohen; d, Frank R. Strayer; w, John W. Krafft (based on a "Crime Club" novel by Norman Lippincott); ph, M. A. Anderson; ed, Roland Reed.

Crime   **(PR:A MPAA:NR)**

MURDER AT MIDNIGHT* ¹/₂   (1931) 69m TIF bw

Aileen Pringle (Mrs. Kennedy), Alice White (Millie Scripps), Hale Hamilton (Montrose, Criminologist), Robert Elliott (Inspector Taylor), Clara Blandick (Aunt Mildred), Brandon Hurst (Lawrence the Butler), Leslie Fenton (Grayson, Mrs. Kennedy's Brother), William Humphrey (Colton), Tyrell Davis (Englishman), Aileen Carlisle (Maid), Kenneth Thomson (Mr. Kennedy), Robert Ellis (Channing).

Predictable murder mystery in which a roomfull of people are murdered one by one after Thomson accidentally kills his secretary with a gun during a game of charades (somebody slipped real bullets into the chamber). Thomson goes next, and then another and another, until it is revealed that Thomson's wife's lover, Hamilton, a noted criminologist, was the killer all along. He commits suicide (with a phone that sends a sharp spike into the brain through the ear—his own invention) which leaves the police nothing to do but clean up.

p, Phil Goldstone; d, Frank R. Strayer; w, Strayer, W. Scott Darling (based on a story by Strayer, Darling); ph, William Rees; ed, John Rawlins; md, Val Burton; art d, Ralph M. DeLacy; cos, Elizabeth Coleman.

Mystery   **Cas.**   **(PR:A MPAA:NR)**

MURDER AT MONTE CARLO*   (1935, Brit.) 70m WB-FN bw

Eve Gray (Gilian), Errol Flynn (Dyter, Newspaper Reporter), Paul Graetz (Dr. Heinrich Becker), Lawrence Hanray (Collum), Ellis Irving (Marc Orton), Henry Victor (Major), Brian Buchel (Yates), Peter Gawthorne (Duprez), Molly Lamont (Margaret Becker), Gabriel Toyne (Wesley), James Dale (Gustav), Henry Longhurst (editor), Ernest Sefton (Sankey).

A standard British crime film which would be completely forgotten had it not been for the appearance of Errol Flynn in his first starring role. The story concerns a crooked roulette scheme in Monte Carlo's casino, with Flynn leading the investigation. Upon his arrival Graetz, the inventor of the gambling system, mysteriously turns up dead. The film ends with the familiar reenactment of the crime, which proves successful in solving the case. The superstar-to-be had been working in England for about a year and a half before then-managing director of Frist National, Irving Asher, spotted young Flynn. A cable was wired to Burbank's Warner Bros. Studios announcing that Flynn was signed for a seven-year contract—without a screen test. The contract was soon amended to six-months at $150 per week. What followed for Flynn was almost unequalled fame—the sort that legends are made of. MURDER AT MONTE CARLO never saw a U.S. release, however. Flynn was originally to play only a small role in the picture, but Asher requested that he be given the lead, resulting in perhaps the most elaborate screen test in the history of film.

p, Irving Asher; d, Ralph Ince; w, John Hastings Turner, Michael Barringer (based on the novel by Tom Van Dyke); ph, Basil Emmott; art d, G. H. Ward.

Crime/Mystery   **(PR:A MPAA:NR)**

MURDER AT SITE THREE*   (1959, Brit.) 67m Francis Searle/Exclusive bw

Geoffrey Toone (Sexton Blake), Barbara Shelley (Susan), John Warwick (Comdr. Chambers), Jill Melford (Paula Dane), Richard Burrell (Tinker), Reed de Rouen (McGill), Harry Towb (Kenney), Theodore Wilhelm, Gordon Sterne.

An espionage theme treated in the most blatantly obvious manner has Toone and Burell as private detectives using a truth serum to uncover the spy operations at a RAF missile base. To no one's surprise the heavy turns out to be the man in charge of security operations.

p, Charles Leeds; d, Francis Searle; w, Manning O'Brine (based on the novel Crime Is My Business by W. Howard Baker); ph, Bert Mason.

Spy Drama   **(PR:A MPAA:NR)**

MURDER AT THE BASKERVILLES**¹/₂

(1941, Brit.) 66m Twickenham/ABF bw (GB: SILVER BLAZE)

Arthur Wontner (Sherlock Holmes), Ian Fleming (Dr. Watson), Lyn Harding (Prof. Moriarty), John Turnbull (Inspector Lestrade), Robert Horton (Col. Ross), Lawrence Grossmith (Sir Henry Baskerville), Judy Gunn (Diana Baskerville), Arthur Macrae (Jack Trevor), Arthur Goullet (Col. Sebastian Moran), Martin Walker (John Straker), Eve Gray (Mrs. Straker), Gilbert Davis (Miles Stamford), Minnie Rayner (Mrs. Hudson), D. J. Williams (Silas Brown), Ralph Truman (Bert Prince).

Twenty years after their mutual adventure with the Hound, Wontner, as the famed detective Sherlock Holmes (in his last Holmes film), is summoned by his old friend Baskerville (Grossmith) to the West Country. Silver Blaze, a prized race horse, has been stolen and its groom murdered. No. 1 suspect is Macrae, a young horseman involved with Grossmith's daughter, Gunn. Wontner discovers the steed on a nearby farm disguised with painted spots, and knows that his old nemesis Moriarty (Harding) is behind the crime, but chooses not to reveal this tidbit. Later Wontner and partner Dr. Watson (Fleming) are fired on by Goullet, Harding's evil partner in crime, who fortunately misses. The next day, at the Barchester Cup race, Horton, the owner of Silver Blaze, is surprised to see his horse in the line-up and stunned when Wontner announces that a kick from the beast killed the groomsman. The employee had tried to steal the horse for Harding and was killed for his efforts. Goullet shoots Silver Blaze's jockey with a gun concealed in a newsreel camera to keep the horse from winning the race. Fleming is kidnaped by Harding and taken

to his secret hideout above the London subways, with Wontner quick on the trail. He rescues his companion in the nick of time in an unspectacular finish as Harding gives himself up all too easily. MURDER AT THE BASKERVILLES suffers from too slight a plot stretched out to feature length. Wontner is good in his final portrayal of the great detective, and the film does have some interesting moments; but on the whole this is lackluster Holmes, an all too elementary case. Originally released in England in 1937, the American release was held back for a few years. Finally, with the success of Basil Rathbone in THE HOUNDS OF THE BASKERVILLES, American theaters were able to capitalize on the Rathbone film with this title. (See SHERLOCK HOLMES series, Index.)

p, Julius Hagen; d, Thomas Bentley; Arthur Mcrae, w, H. Fowler Mear (based on the story "Silver Blaze" by Sir Arthur Conan Doyle); ph, Sydney Blythe, William Luff; ed, Alan Smith.

Mystery   **Cas.**   **(PR:A MPAA:NR)**

MURDER AT THE BURLESQUE
(SEE: MYSTERY AT THE BURLESQUE, 1950, Brit.)

MURDER AT THE CABARET*   (1936, Brit.) 67m MB/PAR bw

Phyllis Robins (Jean), Freddie Forbes (Freddie), James Carew (Husband), Frederick Peisley (Jimmie), Kenneth Warrington (Toni), Peggy Crawford (Wife), Miska (Tash), Douglas Phillips (Inspector), Mark Daly, Chick Farr and Farland, Bernardi, Michael Ronni, Clifford Seagrave, Rosarita, Nina, Alvis and Capla, Holland's Magyar Band.

An actor is killed during the middle of a performance by a girl friend who is jealous because he is having affairs. In order to complete this crime, the girl places real bullets inside the stage prop which should have contained blanks. It is only a matter of time before the girl is tracked down, and the audience can wake from a pleasant slumber. Musical numbers are inserted in an awkward effort to add a touch of glamour.

p, Reginald Fogwell, Nell Emerald; d, Fogwell; w, Fogwell, Percy Robinson (based on the story by Fogwell); ph, Roy Fogwell.

Crime/Musical   **(PR:A MPAA:NR)**

MURDER AT THE GALLOP***¹/₂   (1963, Brit.) 81m MGM bw

Margaret Rutherford (Miss Marple), Robert Morley (Hector Enderby), Flora Robson (Miss Gilchrist), Charles Tingwell (Detective Inspector Craddock), Stringer Davis (Mr. Stringer), Duncan Lamont (Hillman), James Villiers (Michael Shane), Robert Urquhart (George Crossfield), Katya Douglas (Rosamund Shane), Gordon Harris (Sgt. Bacon), Noel Howlett (Mr. Trundell), Finlay Currie (Old Enderby), Kevin Stoney (Dr. Markwell).

Taken from Agatha Christie's After The Funeral, MURDER AT THE GALLOP is another mystery romp featuring Christie's distaff detective, Rutherford (as Miss Marple). This time, Rutherford's legendary scene-stealing abilities are matched by Morley as these two British character actors go at each other, but in a tongue-in-cheek manner. Rutherford and Davis are busily collecting alms for "The Reformed Criminals League," one of her favorite charities, when they witness the death of Currie. He is frightened by a cat and drops dead immediately. The police automatically ascribe this demise to a weak heart but Rutherford isn't so sure and she attends the reading of the dead man's will. It is there that she learns the old coot had a lot of money, which he has left to four members of his family. Currie's sister also suspects foul play and she is soon rewarded for her suspicions by a quick and painful exit. Robson had been Currie's sister's friend and she accuses Rutherford of having done the old man in, but the inspector, Tingwell, clears Rutherford so she is free to continue her snooping. Rutherford is now determined to get to the bottom of this so she moves into the riding club (The Gallop), owned by Currie's nephew, Morley. Once ensconced, she learns that the three remaining heirs are all interested in gleaning what is an apparently worthless painting owned by the late woman. The picture in question is, in fact, a French masterpiece worth a bundle of francs. Another relative, Urquhart, bites the dust and Rutherford has an idea of who the killer is but not enough evidence to prove her allegation. She goes into a wild dance and pretends to have a heart attack as she yells, "I know who the murderer is," then drops to the ground. She's placed in a room to recover and the killer slips in to dispatch the tweedy spinster. But the murderer, Robson, didn't count on Rutherford's pluck and she is soon nabbed by Tingwell, who was alerted by Rutherford of the attempt on her life. As she is about to leave the riding academy, Morley proposes marriage to Rutherford but she declines. It must have been Pollock's life's desire to direct such brilliant performers and he makes the most of it in one of the best of the "Miss Marple" films starring Rutherford. The same writers also wrote the screenplays for the pictures that preceded this and followed it. They had the formula down pat. (SEE MISS MARPLE series, Index.)

p, George H. Brown; d, George Pollock; w, James P. Cavanagh, David Pursall, Jack Seddon; ph, Arthur Ibbetson; m, Ron Goodwin; ed, Bert Rule; spec eff, Tom Howard; cos, Maude Churchill, Masada Wilmot, Charles Monet; makeup, Eddie Knight.

Comedy/Mystery   **(PR:A MPAA:NR)**

MURDER AT THE INN*   (1934, Brit.) 56m WB bw

Wendy Barrie (Angela Worthing), Harold French (Tony), Jane Carr (Fifi), Davy Burnaby (Col. Worthing), Nicholas Hannen (Dedreet), Minnie Rayner (Aunt), H. Saxon-Snell (Inspector).

Murder and blackmail interfere in Barrie and French's elopement. In an effort to heighten the suspense in this lifeless crime melodrama, French's ex-lover pops up at the inn in which the couple is staying.

p, Irving Asher; d, George King; w, Randall Faye.

Crime   **(PR:A MPAA:NR)**

MURDER AT THE VANITIES** 1/2   (1934) 95m PAR bw

Carl Brisson (Eric Lander), Victor McLaglen (Bill Murdock), Jack Oakie (Jack Ellery), Kitty Carlisle (Ann Ware), Dorothy Stickney (Norma Watson), Gertrude Michael (Rita Ross), Jessie Ralph (Mrs. Helen Smith), Charles B. Middleton (Homer Boothby), Gail Patrick (Sadie Evans), Donald Meek (Dr. Saunders), Otto Hoffman (Walsh), Charles McAvoy (Ben), Beryl Wallace (Beryl), Barbara Fritchie (Vivien), Toby Wing (Nancy), Lona Andre (Lona), Colin Tapley (Stage Manager), William Arnold (Treasurer), Cecil Weston (Miss Bernstein), Hal Greene (Call Boy), Stanley Blystone (Policeman), Betty Bethune (Fat Charwoman), Clara Lou [Ann] Sheridan (Lou), Gwenllian Gill (Gwen), Duke Ellington and His Orchestra (Themselves), Ernestine Anderson, Marion Callahan, Dorothy Dawes, Ruth Hilliard, Constance Jordan, Evelyn Kelly, Leda Necova, Wanda Perry, Laurie Shevlin, Anya Taranda (Earl Carroll Girls), Dave O'Brian (Chorus Boy), Teru Shimada.

A combination of musical and mystery starring McLaglen as a detective investigating killings perpetrated backstage during opening night of a new show. When the body of private eye Patrick is discovered on the catwalk, McLaglen must work fast (between musical numbers that is) to find the killer. Out-of-favor star Michael is the next to go (via a falling sandbag) and it soon becomes apparent that the leading lady, Carlisle, is marked for death. The eventual solution to the killings is contrived and weak. Ann Sheridan, who became the "Oomph Girl," appears in a bit part, billed under her real name, Clara Lou Sheridan. Songs include: "Marijuana" (now there's a popoular oldie!), "Lovely One," "Where Do They Come from Now," "Live and Love Tonight," "Cocktails for Two" (Arthur Johnson, Sam Coslow), "Ebony Rhapsody" (Johnson, Coslow, performed by Duke Ellington and His Orchestra).

p, E. Lloyd Sheldon; d, Mitchell Leisen; w, Carey Wilson, Joseph Gollomb, Sam Hellman (based on the play by Earl Carroll, Rufus King); ph, Leo Tover; m, Arthur Johnston; ed, Billy Shea.

Musical/Mystery   **(PR:A MPAA:NR)**

MURDER AT THE WINDMILL

        (SEE: MYSTERY AT THE BURLESQUE, 1950, Brit.)

MURDER AT 3 A.M.*   (1953, Brit.) 60m David Henley/REN bw

Dennis Price (Inspector Peter Lawton), Peggy Evans (Joan Lawton), Philip Saville (Edward/Jim King), Greta Mayaro (Lena), Rex Garner (Sgt. Bill Todd), Arnold Bell (McMann), Leonard Sharp (Old Skip), Nora Gordon (Nanna), Renee Goddard, Arthur Lovegrove, Daphne Maddox, Robert Weeden, John Davis.

Boring and uninteresting murder mystery in which Price plays a police detective with the hunch that his sister's boy friend (Saville) is guilty of murder. Price turns out to be wrong after jeopardizing his sister's relationship by using her as bait in trapping Saville. Technical, acting, and directorial facets are all far below par for even the "B" budget on which this was made.

p, John Ainsworth; d, Francis Searle; w, Ainsworth; ph, S. D. Onions.

Crime/Mystery   **(PR:A MPAA:NR)**

MURDER BY AGREEMENT (SEE: JOURNEY INTO NOWHERE, 1963, Brit.)

MURDER BY AN ARISTOCRAT* 1/2   (1936) 60m FN-WB bw

Lyle Talbot (Dr. Allen Carick), Marguerite Churchill (Sally Keating), Claire Dodd (Janice Thatcher), Virginia Brissac (Adela Thatcher), William B. Davidson (Bayard Thatcher), John Eldredge (John Tweed), Gordon Elliott (Dave Thatcher), Joseph Crehan (Hilary Thatcher), Florence Fair (Evelyn Thatcher), Stuart Holmes (Higby), Lottie Williams (Emeline), Mary Treen (Florrie), Milton Kibbee (Cab Driver), Henry Otho (Sheriff).

A dim murder mystery wherein blackmailer Davidson demands $25,000 dollars from his family and is murdered by one of his relatives before he can collect. Soon after, the other family members begin dropping like flies until things get sorted out.

p, Bryan Foy; d, Frank McDonald; w, Luci Ward, Roy Chanslor (based on a story by Mignon G. Eberhart); ph, Arthur Todd; ed, Louis Hasse; cos, Orry-Kelly.

Mystery   **(PR:A MPAA:NR)**

MURDER BY CONTRACT**   (1958) 81m COL bw

Vince Edwards (Claude), Phillip Pine (Marc), Herschel Bernardi (George), Michael Granger (Moon), Caprice Toriel (Billie Williams), Frances Osborne (Maid), Cathy Browne, Joseph Mell, Steven Ritch, Janet Brandt, Davis Roberts, Don Garrett, Gloria Victor.

Edwards stars as a cold-blooded hitman who travels from the East to Los Angeles to kill a woman about to testify against Edwards' employer. After two failed attempts to complete his mission (she is heavily guarded), Edwards finally enters the house and attempts to garrote her. He changes his mind at the last minute, deciding not to go through with it, but the cops gun him down anyway.

p, Leon Choeluck; d, Irving Lerner; w, Ben Simcoe; ph, Lucien Ballard; m, Perry Botkin; ed, Carlo Lodato; art d, Jack Poplin; spec eff, Jack Rubin, Louis DeWitt.

Crime/Suspense   **(PR:C MPAA:NR)**

MURDER BY DEATH****   (1976) 94m Rastar/COL c

Eileen Brennan (Tess Skeffington), Truman Capote (Lionel Twain), James Coco (Milo Perrier), Peter Falk (Sam Diamond), Alec Guinness (Butler Bensonmumum), Elsa Lanchester (Jessica Marbles), David Niven (Dick Charleston), Peter Sellers (Sidney Wang), Maggie Smith (Dora Charleston), Nancy Walker (Yetta the Maid), Estelle Winwood (Nurse Withers), James Cromwell (Marcel the Chauffeur), Richard Narita (Willie Wang), Myron the Dog.

For those who salivate over the absurd, this blatant spoof of the great fictional-film detectives offers consistently funny, often hysterical scenes sparked by Falk, Niven,

Sellers, and Guinness. Wealthy Lionel Twain (after the toy model, of course), portrayed by Capote in his film debut, invites the world's greatest detectives to his eerie castle-like home. These counterparts to Miss Marple, Nick and Nora Charles, Sam Spade, Hercule Poirot, and Charlie Chan, tumble and fumble into the dungeonlike fortress full tilt and off tilt. They soon discover that Capote is holding them prisoner in a home suddenly covered with bars and steel doors, rooms that lead nowhere and everywhere; the host attempts to kill off the mastermind sleuths while dispatching a blind butler, Guinness, and Walker, a deaf-mute temporary maid, or does he? The entire film is bizarre as it presents a game of (nit)wits to see who is the greatest gumshoe of them all. Falk is hysterical as the fiercely posturing Sam Spade prototype with the other leading players not far behind him in a race for the insane asylum. Snappy banter with double entendre loading all six cylinders is fired at a round per second in this zany, wholly confusing, and delightfully offbeat film. Capote is so bad an actor that he's funny which may or may not be the point. This one is also the film debut of director Moore and he does a fine job of presenting so many twists and turns that no viewer will be able to sort it all out, even at the finale.

p, Ray Stark; d, Robert Moore; w, Neil Simon; ph, David M. Walsh (Panavision); m, Dave Grusin; ed, Margaret Booth, John F. Burnett; prod d, Stephen Grimes; art d, Harry Kemm; set d, Marvin March; cos, Ann Roth; spec eff, Augie Lohman; makeup, Joseph De Bella.

Comedy   **Cas.**   **(PR:C MPAA:PG)**

MURDER BY DECREE***   (1979, Brit.) 121m Ambassador Films/AE c

Christopher Plummer (Sherlock Holmes), James Mason (Dr. Watson), David Hemmings (Inspector Foxborough), Anthony Quayle (Sir Charles Warren), Genevieve Bujold (Annie Crook), Frank Finlay (Inspector Lestrade), Sir John Gielgud (Prime Minister), Susan Oliver (Mary Kelly), Donald Sutherland (Robert Lees), Roy Lansford (Sir Thomas Smiley), Peter Fonfield (William Slade), Teddi Moore (Mrs. Lees), Catherine Kessler (Carrie), Ron Pember (Makins), Ken Jones (Dock Guard).

This is one of the most brilliant, well-acted, and chilling Sherlock Holmes films ever made, thanks to the wonderful and eccentric portrayal by Plummer as Holmes and the dowdy, phlegmatic essay of Watson by Mason. Not since the historic Basil Rathbone-Nigel Bruce combination has a Holmes mystery been so well conceived and produced—lavishly produced, in fact. The immortal detective is in search of London's most hideous human monster, Jack the Ripper. All of the quaint environment and atmosphere penned by Doyle comes effectively to the screen with swirling fog, rattling hansom cabs, and slippery-with-dew cobblestones as Plummer stalks the mass murderer of prostitutes in London's West End. Plummer even dons his Inverness Cape and deerstalker cap and smokes his famous pipe while delightedly shouting to faithful Mason, "the game's afoot!" Quayle, the new superintendent of Scotland Yard, purposely avoids having Plummer investigate the rash of brutal slashings attributed to Jack the Ripper but he becomes involved anyway, especially after Sutherland, playing a real-life psychic used by the Yard during the actual Ripper case, goads the great sleuth into action. Bujold, the discarded mistress of a high-born person who is also highly suspect, provides the key that unlocks a mystery baffling law enforcement officers for a century since Bloody Jack first used his surgical knives to vent his maniacal spleen on trollops and tarts. There is action aplenty, especially as the film nears its conclusion, one where Plummer reveals a conspiracy of Masons covering up the best-held secret in England, that a member of the royal household was the guilty party. A dockside battle where Plummer wields a lethal weight tied to his scarf against the mad killer is spectacular. Though the script is a bit dense and the film slightly overlong, it's exciting and engrossing on all levels. Hemmings, Gielgud, and Quayle are exceptional.

p, Rene Dupont, Bob Clark; d, Clark; w, John Hopkins (based on an original story by Clark and characters created by Sir Arthur Conan Doyle); ph, Reg Morris (Metrocolor); ed, Stan Cole; prod d, Harry Pottle; cos, Judy Moorcroft.

Mystery/Thriller   **Cas.**   **(PR:C-O MPAA:PG)**

MURDER BY INVITATION* 1/2   (1941) 67m MON bw

Wallace Ford (Bob White), Marian Marsh (Nora O'Brien), Sarah Padden (Aunt Cassie Denham), George Guhl (Sheriff Boggs), Wallis Clark (Judge Moore), Gavin Gordon (Garson Denham), Minerva Urecal (Maxine Denham), Arthur Young (Trowbridge), Herbert Vigran (Eddie, Photographer), Hazel Keener (Mary Denham), Lee Shumway, Dave O'Brien, John James, Philip Trent, Kay Deslys, Isabelle La Mal.

Run-of-the-mill whodunit starring Ford as a newspaperman invited to spend the weekend at the estate of eccentric old spinster Denham during a family reunion. At the stroke of midnight, the assembled family loses a member, and the bodies begin piling up soon after. Eventually the motive is revealed to be a stash of $3 million in cash hidden somewhere in the house by Denham. Fed up with the killings, Denham decides to end the mystery by burning the house down. The two killers reveal themselves, and Denham hands them the cash, which is worthless Confederate money.

p, A. W. Hackel; d, Phil Rosen; w, George Bricker; ph, Marcel Le Picard; ed, Martin G. Cohn.

Mystery   **(PR:A MPAA:NR)**

MURDER BY MAIL   (SEE: SCHIZOID, 1980)

MURDER BY PHONE   (SEE: BELLS, 1981, Can.)

MURDER BY PROXY   (SEE: BLACKOUT, 1954, Brit.)

MURDER BY ROPE* 　　　(1936, Brit.) 64m British and Dominions-PAR bw
Constance Godridge (*Daphne Farrow*), D. A. Clarke-Smith (*Hanson*), Sunday Wilshin (*Lucille Davine*), Wilfrid Hyde-White (*Alastair Dane*), Donald Read (*Peter Paxton*), Daphne Courtney (*Flora*), Dorothy Hamilton (*Mrs. Mulcaire*), Guy Belmore (*Simpson*), Philip Hewland (*Judge Paxton*), Alban Conway, William Collins, Charles Borrett.

A lame reworking of the old plot where a man comes back from the dead (he was supposed to have been hanged) to terrorize the good citizens who combined their efforts to have him convicted. For some reason this thing was pulled out and reissued again in 1948.

p, Anthony Havelock-Allan; d, George Pearson; w, Ralph Neale; ph, Ernest Palmer.
Crime　　　　　　　　　　　　　　**(PR:A　MPAA:NR)**

MURDER BY TELEVISION*
　　(1935) 60m Cameo/Imperial bw (AKA: THE HOUGHLAND MURDER CASE)
Bela Lugosi (*Arthur Perry, Professor Houghland's Assistant*), June Collyer (*June Houghland*), Huntley Gordon (*Dr. Scofield*), George Meeker (*Richard Grayson*), Henry Mowbray (*Nelson, Chief of Police*), Charles Hill Mailes, Charles K. French, Claire McDowell, Larry Francis, Hattie McDaniel, Henry Hall, Allan Jung, William Sullivan, William Tooker.

Not surprisingly, MURDER BY TELEVISION is an often overlooked film in the career of Bela Lugosi. Leaving his vampire character behind, he appears in a dual role as twin brothers, one evil and the other, as expected, good. During a television demonstration watched by a number of people, a professor is killed without any trace of the murderer. The evil Lugosi is killed soon afterwards, leaving the good one to solve the crime. Slow, talky, and not what the title implies. The most interesting aspect of this film is that television is implicated as the murder device and conceived of as a threat. Commercial TV was still more than a decade away and was considered futuristic. Perhaps, like other technological concepts designed for future use, there was a feeling among the public that television was dangerous or somehow harmful.

p, William M. Pizor; d, Clifford Sanforth; w, Joseph O'Donnell (based on an idea by Clarence Hennecke, Carl Coolidge); ph, James Brown, Arthur Reed; m, Oliver Wallace; ed, Lester Wilder; art d, Lewis Rachmil; m/l, Wallace; tech supv, Henry Spitz; television tech, Milton M. Stern.

Crime/Mystery　　　　**Cas.**　　　　**(PR:A　MPAA:NR)**

MURDER BY THE CLOCK** 1/2 　　　　　　　(1931) 75m PAR bw
William Boyd (*Lt. Valcour*), Irving Pichel (*Philip Endicott*), Lilyan Tashman (*Laura Endicott*), Regis Toomey (*Officer Cassidy*), Blanche Frederici (*Julia Endicott*), Walter McGrail (*Herbert Endicott*), Sally O'Neil (*Jane, a Maid*), Martha Mattox (*Miss Roberts*), Lester Vail (*Thomas Hollander*), Frank Sheridan (*Chief of Police*), Lenita Lane (*Nurse*), Charles D. Brown (*O'Brien*), Frederick Sullivan (*Medical Examiner*), Harry Burgess (*Coroner*), John Rogers (*Hollander's Valet*), Willard Robertson (*Police Captain*), Guy Oliver (*Watchman*).

A real thriller, one of the earliest talkie horror movies, which is recalled with many a fond shudder by anyone who saw it. There are several killings in and around the estate of a wealthy family that has a mausoleum on the premises. Inside the crypt, there is a horn that can be sounded eerily if anyone has been placed inside by mistake. Further, the mausoleum can be opened from the inside. An old lady is murdered, then the murderer is apparently killed himself, but he is actually revived just short of his demise. Suddenly, he meets his own killer and sees the old lady whom he thought he killed alive, and that causes his heart to stop, this time for keeps. Frederici is the mysterious woman who haunts the proceedings; Pichel is a huge half-wit who cackles and screams as a maniacal killer. Boyd is the police officer on the case, trying to uncover the truth and nail Tashman, who has been indirectly responsible for some of the deaths and is marked for her own death. She is excellent as she camps her way through a role that could have been a bore. Boyd falls for Tashman, then realizes that she is the femme fatale and that he has to turn her over to Toomey, another cop on the case. Lots of cobwebs, doors leading nowhere, sounds in the night, and ham acting by a number of the participants all contribute to make this film a terrifying experience with more goose bumps than a handful of HALLOWEENS.

d, Edward Sloman; w, Henry Myers (based on a play by Charles Beahan and a story by Rufus King); ph, Karl Struss.
Horror　　　　　　　　　　　　　　**(PR:C　MPAA:NR)**

MURDER CAN BE DEADLY* 1/2
(1963, Brit.) 60m Mancunian-Doverton/Colorama-Schoenfeld bw (GB: THE PAINTED SMILE)
Liz Fraser (*Jo Lake*), Kenneth Griffith (*Kleinie*), Peter Reynolds (*Mark Davies*), Anthony Wickert (*Tom*), Craig Douglas (*Nightclub Singer*), Nanette Newman (*Mary*), Ray Smith (*Glynn*), David Hemmings (*Roy*), Harold Berens (*Mikhala*), Grazina Frame (*Lucy*), Lionel Ngakane (*Barman*), Richard McNeff (*Police Inspector*), Gerald Sim (*Plainclothes Policeman*), Rosemary Chalmers (*Gloria*), Mia Karam (*Dawn*), Terence Maidment, Bill Stevens (*Henchmen*), Ann Wrigg (*Manageress*).

Fraser is a con lady whose partner is killed by Griffith, the vicious leader of a Soho gang. Unaware that he has been killed, Fraser brings Wickert, a drunken student, back to her house. They discover the body, and Wickert mistakenly touches the murder weapon. He is convinced by Fraser to dispose of the body, and in doing so he arouses the suspicions of the police. Wickert, with the help of his fiancee and a couple of friends, is able to track down Fraser, bring in the police, and clear his name. Fraser is killed in the process.

p, Tom Blakely; d, Lance Comfort; w, Pip Baker, Jane Baker (based on an idea by Brock Williams); ph, Basil Emmott; m, Martin Slavin; ed, John Trumper; art d,

George Provis; m/l, "Murder Can Be Deadly," Slavin, Abbe Gail, "Another You," Norrie Paramor, Bunny Lewis, Michael Carr.
Crime Drama　　　　　　　　　　　　**(PR:A　MPAA:NR)**

MURDER CLINIC, THE* 1/2
(1967, Ital./Fr.) 86m Leone-Orphee/Europix-Consolidated c (LA LAMA NEL CORPO; LES NUITS DE L'EPOUVANTE; AKA: THE MURDER SOCIETY; REVENGE OF THE LIVING DEAD; THE KNIFE IN THE BODY; THE NIGHT OF TERRORS)
William Berger (*Dr. Robert Vance*), Francoise Prevost (*Claudine*), Mary Young (*Lizabeth Vance*), Barbara Wilson (*Mary, a Nurse*), Delphi Maurin (*Laura, Lizabeth's Sister*), Max Dean (*Fred*), Harriet White (*Sheena*), Philippe Hersent, Anne Sherman, William Gold, Grant Laramy, Patricia Carr, Anne Field.

Gothic horror from the Italians set in England at the turn of the century. Berger stars as a crazed doctor who is suspected of murdering his female deaf-mute patients at his clinic. His purpose is to reconstruct the once-beautiful face of his sister-in-law who was disfigured when she fell into a vat of quicklime (some say she was pushed by the good doctor himself). Eventually it is revealed that it is the doctor's wife, Young, who is the depraved killer and when she and her sister are killed, Berger is able to start a new life.

p&d, Michael Hamilton [Elio Scardamaglia] (English version, Lewis E. Ciannelli); w, Julian Berry [Ernesto Gastaldi], Martin Hardy [Sergio Martino] (based on the novel *The Knife in the Body* by Robert Williams); ph, Marc Lane [Marcello Masciocchi] (Techniscope/Technicolor); m, Frank Mason [Franco DeMasi]; ed, Richard Hartley [Alberto Gallitti]; art d, Alberto Salvatori; makeup, Massimo Giustini.

Horror　　　　　　　　　　　　　　**(PR:C　MPAA:GP)**

MURDER CZECH STYLE***
(1968, Czech.) 90m Barrandov-Ceskoslovensky/Royal bw-c (VRAZDA PO CESKU, VRAZDA PO NASEM)
Rudolf Hrusinsky (*Frantisek Pokorny*), Kveta Fialova (*Alice Pokorny*), Vaclav Voska (*Assistant Manager*), Vladimir Mensik (*Emil*), Vera Uzelacova (*Bindrova*), Libuse Svormova (*Jindriska*), Vjaceslav Irmanov (*Dandy*), Frantisek Slegr, Jaroslav Solnicka, Jindrich Narenta.

This intelligent, witty comedy deals with the problems confronting a chubby office clerk when he marries an attractive woman from out of town. Hrusinsky, in a wonderfully clumsy manner, proposes to Fialova with encouragement from his assistant manager, Voska. However, because she lives a great distance away in Prague, they do not have much time together. She also complains of a childhood trauma that prevents them from ever consummating the marriage. To be closer to his wife, Hrusinksky asks Voska to transfer him to Prague. The request is denied, and before long it is discovered that Fialova and the assistant manager are having an affair. He entertains thoughts of a double murder and of suicide, but decides instead to blackmail Voska for a better-paying job. A fine example of Czech cinema from veteran director Weiss.

d, Jiri Weiss; w, Weiss, Jan Otcenasek; ph, Jan Nemecek; m, Zdenek Liska; ed, Miroslav Hajek; md, Ludek Hulan; art d, Karel Lier.
Comedy/Drama　　　　　　　　　　　**(PR:A　MPAA:NR)**

MURDER FOR SALE　　　(SEE: TEMPORARY WIDOW, 1930, Brit.)

MURDER GAME, THE**　　　　　(1966, Brit.) 72m Lippert/FOX bw
Ken Scott (*Steve Baldwin*), Marla Landi (*Marie Aldrich*), Trader Faulkner (*Chris Aldrich*), Conrad Phillips (*Peter Shanley*), Gerald Sim (*Larry Lindstrom*), Duncan Lamont (*Inspector Telford*), Rosamund Greenwood (*Mrs. Potter*), Victor Brooks (*Rev. Francis Hood*), Ballard Berkeley (*Sir Colin Chalmers*), Jimmy Gardner (*Arthur Gillett*), Peter Bathurst (*Dr. Knight*), Jennifer White (*Secretary*), Frank Thornton (*Radio Announcer*), Gretchen Franklin (*Landlady*), John Dunbar (*Parkhill*), Clement Freud (*Croupier*), Derek Partridge (*Police Sergeant*), John Richmond (*Prosecutor*).

Plodding British suspense drama stars Faulkner as a rich Englishman who slowly realizes his new bride, Landi, is plotting to kill him on their honeymoon. She and Scott, to whom she's still married, devised the scheme in order to inherit Faulkner's fortune. Deciding to strike back, he develops an elaborate plan in which he fakes his own death, and watches as Landi and Scott are accused of his murder.

p, Robert L. Lippert, Jack Parsons; d, Sidney Salkow; w, Harry Spalding (based on a story by Irving Yergin); ph, Geoffrey Faithfull; m, Carlo Martelli; ed, Robert Winter; art d, Harry White; makeup, Harold Fletcher.
Crime　　　　　　　　　　　　　　**(PR:A　MPAA:NR)**

MURDER GOES TO COLLEGE**　　　　　(1937) 77m PAR bw
Roscoe Karns (*Sim Perkins*), Marsha Hunt (*Nora Barry*), Lynne Overman (*Hank Hyer*), Astrid Allwyn (*Greta Barry*), Harvey Stephens (*Paul Broderick*), Larry [Buster] Crabbe (*Strike Belno*), Earle Foxe (*Tom Barry*), Anthony Nace (*Howard Sayforth*), John Indrisano (*Joe Torelli*), Barlow Borland (*Dean Olney*), Purnell Pratt (*President McShean*), Charles Wilson (*Inspector Simpson*), James Blain, Robert Perry (*Detectives*), James B. Carson (*Waiter*), Edward Emerson, Nick Lukats (*Drunks*), Terry Ray (*Ellen Drew*), Jack Chapin.

Comedy mystery starring Karns as a reporter and Overman as a private investigator who team up to solve a mysterious campus killing. The mystery and comedy elements are handled fairly well, and the killer's identity is kept hidden until the end.

d, Charles Riesner; w, Brian Marlow, Robert Wyler, Eddie Welch (based on the novel by Kurt Steel [Rudolph Kagey]); ph, Henry Sharp; ed, Edward Dmytryk.
Comedy/Mystery　　　　　　　　　　**(PR:A　MPAA:NR)**

MURDER, HE SAYS****

(1945) 91m PAR bw

Fred MacMurray (Pete Marshall), Helen Walker (Claire Mathews), Marjorie Main (Mamie Johnson), Jean Heather (Elany Fleagle), Porter Hall (Mr. Johnson), Peter Whitney (Mert Fleagle/Bert Fleagle), Mabel Paige (Grandma Fleagle), Barbara Pepper (Bonnie Fleagle), Walter Baldwin (Vic Hardy), James Flavin (Police Officer), Francis Ford (Lee), Si Jenks (80-Year-Old), Milton Parsons, Syd Saylor, Ralph Peters (Townsmen), Tom Fadden (Sheriff Murdock), George McKay (Storekeeper), Joel Friedkin (Little Man).

It's goodbye to logic and sanity in this one, a zany laugh riot where MacMurray shines as a statistics-gathering insurance salesman in the Ozarks, having to deal with hillbilly mentality and crazy twin killers, both played brilliantly by Whitney. MacMurray discovers, much to his hair-raising experiences, that the only sane person in the entire community is Walker, who is trying to vindicate her father, wrongly imprisoned for a robbery committed by female bandit Pepper. Meanwhile the Fleagle family members, who would just as soon kill a stranger as say hello, are frantically searching for Pepper's hidden $70,000 in stolen loot. "Ma" Main, doing something like her Ma Kettle routine but with sinister overtones, is splendid as she confuses MacMurray, already perplexed, in his quest for statistics. Further complicating matters is Pepper, who gets out of prison and is now looking to pick up her buried money. The chases—awkward, narrow escapes by MacMurray and Walker—are, granted, larded with slapstick, but the antics are so crazed and Marshall's clever direction so swift that the laughs are delivered rapid-fire. A truly hilarious, fun-filled movie in the then popular vein of the fatal farce exemplified in ARSENIC AND OLD LACE. MacMurray is in his element here and is nothing less than terrific.

p, E. D. Leshin; d, George Marshall; w, Lou Breslow (based on a story by Jack Moffitt); m, Robert Emmett Dolan; ph, Theodor Sparkuhl; ed, LeRoy Stone; art d, Hans Dreier, William Flannery; set d, George Sawley; spec eff, Gordon Jennings, Paul Lerpae; m/l, Lew Porter, Teepee Mitchell, F. J. Tablepoctor.

Comedy **(PR:A MPAA:NR)**

MURDER IN EDEN**

(1962, Brit.) 63m Luckwell/Colorama-Schoenfeld bw

Ray McAnally (Inspector Sharkey), Catherine Feller (Genevieve Beaujean), Yvonne Buckingham (Vicky Woolf), Norman Rodway (Michael Lucas), Mark Singleton (Arnold Woolf), Jack Aranson (Bill Robson), Robert Lepler (Max Aaronson, Art Critic), Angela Douglas (Beatnik), Francis O'Keefe (Sgt. Johnson), Noel Sheridan (Frenchman Jack), Ronald Walsh (Bodyguard), John Sterling (Art Expert), Frank O'Donovan (Manservant), Eithne Lydon (Receptionist).

When an art critic is murdered by a hit-and-run driver after learning a famous painting is a fake, McAnally, a Scotland Yard investigator, takes the case. Feller, a French magazine reporter, helps prove that an art restorer, the lover of the painting's original owner, pulled off the forgery and murder.

p, Bill Luckwell, Jock MacGregor; d, Max Varnel; w, H. E. Burden (based on the story by John Haggarty); ph, Walter J. Harvey, m, Wilfred Burns; ed, Robert Hill; art d, Tony Inglis.

Crime **(PR:A MPAA:NR)**

MURDER IN GREENWICH VILLAGE*

(1937) 68m COL bw

Richard Arlen (Steve Jackson, Photographer), Fay Wray (Kay Cabot), Raymond Walburn (The Senator), Wyn Cahoon (Flo Melville), Scott Colton (Larry Foster), Thurston Hall (Charles Cabot), Marc Lawrence (Rusty Morgan), Gene Morgan (Henderson), Mary Russell ("Angel Annie"), George McKay (Officer), Leon Ames (Rodney Hunter), Barry Macollum (Murphy), Marjorie Reynolds (Molly).

Arlen plays a defense lawyer who tries to clear Wray of a murder she didn't commit. The pair fall in love, eventually find the true culprit and look forward to domestic bliss.

d, Albert S. Rogell; w, Michael L. Simmons (based on a story by Robert T. Shannon); ph, Henry Freulich; ed, Dick Fantl; md, Morris Stoloff; cos, Robert Kalloch.

Mystery/Romance **(PR:A MPAA:NR)**

MURDER IN MISSISSIPPI zero

(1965) 85m Tiger/Supreme-Waldman bw (AKA: MURDER MISSISSIPPI)

Sheilla Britton (Carol Lee Byrd), Sam Stewart (Phil Loving), Derek Crane (Sheriff Engstrom), Lou Stone (Luther Barnes), Martin St. John (Tyrone Carver), John Steel (Deputy Sheriff Bob Engstrom), Wayne Foster (Andy Loving), Dick Stone (Dick Byrd), Otis Young (Paul Jackson), Irv Seldin (Bernie Samuelson), Frank Philadelphia (Assistant U.S. Attorney), Millie Moran (Guitar Player).

Tasteless exploitation film that attempts to capitalize on the controversy over the civil rights movement in the South. Taking place in Mississippi (though the film was shot in Philadelphia) the film focuses on a group of civil rights workers (three black, two white) who become victims of rapes, beatings, kidnapings and killings perpetrated by the less progressive members of the community, including the sheriff. It's obvious that the producers couldn't have cared less about the actual civil rights movement, but saw a chance to use the newspaper headlines as free advertising for this exploitative endeavor.

p, Herbert S. Altman; d, J. P. Mawra; w, Altman; ph, Warner Rose; m, Joe Lesko; ed, Mawra; spec eff, Technical Film Studios.

Drama **(PR:C MPAA:NR)**

MURDER IN MOROCCO

(SEE: SCREAM IN THE NIGHT, 1943)

MURDER IN REVERSE***

(1946, Brit.) 80m BN/Four Continents bw

William Hartnell (Tom Masterick), Jimmy Hanley (Peter Rogers), Chili Bouchier (Doris Masterick), John Slater (Fred Smith), Dinah Sheridan (Jill Masterick), Wylie

Watson (Tailor), Edward Rigby (Spike), Brefni O'Rorke (Sullivan), Maire O'Neill (Mrs. Moore), Ellis Irving (Sgt. Howell), Petula Clark (Jill as a Child), Kynaston Reeves (Crossley KC), John Salew (Blake KC), Aubrey Mallalieu (Judge), Scott Sanders (Landlord), Maudie Edwards (Customer), Ben Williams (Docker), Ethel Coleridge (Mrs. Green), Cyril Smith, K. Lung, Mary Norton, Henry White, Alfred Harris, Sonny Miller, Johnny Catcher, Ivor Barnard, Dick Francis, Peter Gawthorne, Geoffrey Dennis, Cyril Luckham.

Taut, grim crime film starring Hartnell as an ex-convict who, upon his release from a 15-year prison sentence for a murder that never happened, sets out to find his "victim" and clear his name. Obsessed with righting the wrong that was done to him, Hartnell lets nothing stand in his way. The crazed Hartnell eventually tracks down the man and kills him in front of a shocked courtroom. Having already been tried and served his sentence for the murder, Hartnell dares the courts to do it again. Powerful.

p, Louis H. Jackson; d&w, Montgomery Tully (based on the novel QUERY by "Seamark"); ph, Ernest Palmer; m, Hans May; ed, Eve Catchpole; art d, R. Holmes Paul.

Crime **(PR:A MPAA:NR)**

MURDER IN SOHO

(SEE: MURDER IN THE NIGHT, 1938, Brit.)

MURDER IN THE AIR**

(1940) 55m FN-WB bw

Ronald Reagan (Brass Bancroft), John Litel (Saxby), James Stephenson (Joe Garvey), Eddie Foy, Jr. (Gabby Watters), Lya Lys (Hilda Riker), Robert Warwick (Dr. Finchley), Victor Zimmerman (Rumford), William Gould (Adm. Winfield), Kenneth Harlan (Comdr. Wayne), Frank Wilcox (Jerry the Hotel Clerk), Owen King (George Hayden), Dick Rich (John Kramer), Charles Brokaw (Otto), Helen Lynd (Dolly), Jeffrey Sayre (Prescott the Radio Man), Carlyle Moore, Jr. (Sunnyvale Radio Operator), Cliff Clark (Police Chief), Ed Stanley (Congressman Courtney Rice), Selmer Jackson (Capt. Riddel), John Hamilton (Hargrave), Alexander Lockwood, Garland Smith (Navigation Officers), Alan Davis (Lt. Bell), Jack Mower (Chemist), Claude Wisberg (Bellboy), John "Skins" Miller (Taxi Driver), Julie Stevens (Nurse), Frank Mayo (Dr. Delby), Paul Panzer (Hans), John Deering (Radio Announcer), Paul Phillips, Richard Clayton (Sailors), Reid Kilpatrick (Radio Operator at Continental Airport), Lane Chandler (Flagship Radio Operator), David Newell (Man), Wedgwood Newell (Admiral), Charles Sherlock (Orderly), Mike Lally (Operative).

Reagan's last film in a series of FBI pictures casting him as heroic agent Brass Bancroft. Reagan takes on the identity of a known spy who was killed in a train wreck. The agency sees this as a perfect opportunity to expose suspected spy Stephenson, and Reagan goes into action. Upon meeting, Stephenson tells Reagan to board a Navy dirigible and obtain information on a new "inertia projector" being developed by the Americans, which will knock airplanes out of the sky. Reagan soon discovers one of the officials on the ship is working for Stephenson and intends to steal the blueprints for the new weapon. Reagan manages to save the machine from harm but, during a vicious storm, the spy escapes with the plans for the weapon. Reagan is forced to shoot down the crook's plane with the "inertia projector". Pretty silly stuff, but short and inoffensive.

p, Bryan Foy; d, Lewis Seiler; w, Raymond Schrock (based on his story "Uncle Sam Awakens"); ph, Ted McCord; ed, Frank Magee; art d, Stanley Fleisher; cos, Howard Shoup.

Spy Drama **(PR:A MPAA:NR)**

MURDER IN THE BIG HOUSE

(SEE: JAILBREAK, 1936)

MURDER IN THE BIG HOUSE* 1/2

(1942) 59m WB bw (GB: HUMAN SABOTAGE; AKA: BORN FOR TROUBLE)

Faye Emerson (Gladys Wayne), Van Johnson (Bert Bell), George Meeker ("Scoop" Conner), Frank Wilcox (Randall), Michael Ames ("Dapper Dan" Malloy), Roland Drew ("Mile-Away" Gordon), Ruth Ford (Mrs. Gordon), Joseph Crehan (Jim Ainslee), William Gould (Warden John Bevins), Douglas Wood (Bill Burgen), John Maxwell (Prison Doctor), Pat McVeigh [McVey] (Chief Electrician), Dick Rich (Guard), Fred Kelsey (Keeper), Bill Phillips (Mike), Jack Mower (Ramstead), Creighton Hale (Ritter), Henry Hall (Chaplain).

Fairly dull prison film starring Johnson (in his first big role) as a cub reporter who, along with veteran newshound Meeker, exposes a murder ring inside the state pen. Re-released in 1945 as BORN FOR TROUBLE after Johnson became a star and Emerson married a Roosevelt.

p, William Jacobs; d, B. Reeves Eason; w, Raymond L. Schrock (based on a story "Murder in the Death House" by Jerome Chodorov); ph, Ted McCord; ed, Terry Morse; art d, Hugh Reticker; cos, Orry-Kelly.

Crime **(PR:A MPAA:NR)**

MURDER IN THE BLUE ROOM* 1/2

(1944) 61m UNIV bw

Anne Gwynne (Nan Kirkland), Donald Cook (Steve Randall), John Litel (Frank Baldrich), Grace McDonald (Peggy), Betty Kean (Betty), June Preisser (Jerry), Regis Toomey (Inspector McDonald), Nella Walker (Linda Baldrich), Andrew Toombes (Dr. Carroll), Ian Wolfe (Edwards the Butler), Emmett Vogan (Hannagan), Bill MacWilliams [Williams] (Larry Dearden), Frank Marlowe (Curtin), Victoria Horne (Maid).

Third film version of a lame haunted house comedy (the first two were SECRET OF THE BLUE ROOM (1933) and THE MISSING GUEST (1938)) shows no improvement. Litel plays a theater manager recently married to Walker, his deceased best pal's widow. The couple decides to return and reopen the house her former husband was murdered in. The reluctant house guests arrive, and soon afterward secret panels, trap doors and corpses of other guests are discovered. In the end it is revealed that the family doctor bumped off the dead husband's father first, and polished off the son when he got too nosy. The laughs are few and far between. In this film, Gwynne sings "One Starry Night," and McDonald, Kean and Preisser, as "The Three Jazzybelles," do a novelty number and an Andrews Sisters-like rendition of "Boogie Woogie Boogie Man." The Jazzybelles also dance to "Dancing Away the Blues" and "I'm Always Chasing Rainbows."

p, Frank Gross; d, Leslie Goodwins; w, I. A. L. Diamond, Stanley Davis (based on a story by Erich Philippi; ph, George Robinson; ed, Charles Maynard; md, Sam Freed, Jr.; art d, John B. Goodman, Harold H. MacArthur; cos, Vera West; spec eff, John P. Fulton; ch, Carlos Romero.

Comedy/Mystery (PR:A MPAA:NR)

MURDER IN THE CATHEDRAL**

(1952, Brit.) 140m Film Traders/Classic bw

Father John Groser (Thomas a Becket), Alexander Gauge (King Henry II), David Ward (1st Tempter), George Woodbridge (2nd Tempter), Basil Burton (3rd Tempter), T. S. Eliot (4th Tempter [Voice]), Donald Bisset (1st Priest), Clement McCallin (2nd Priest), Michael Groser (3rd Priest), Mark Dignam (1st Knight), Michael Aldridge (2nd Knight), Leo McKern (3rd Knight), Paul Rogers (4th Knight), Alban Blakelock (Bishop Foliot), Niall MacGinnis (Herald).

Tedious adaptation of T. S. Eliot's play detailing the final days of Thomas a Becket. Groser plays the Archbishop of Canterbury, who returns to England after seven years of voluntary exile to avoid being used by the king to dominate the church. Nobly, Groser reinstates himself to defy the king, knowing that his death by assassination is inevitable. Well-written and acted, the film suffers from a ponderous, stagy realization, making it difficult to sit through.

p,d&w, George Hoellering (based on the play by T. S. Eliot); ph, David Kosky; m, Laszlo Lajtha; ed, Anne Alinatt.

Religious Drama (PR:A MPAA:NR)

MURDER IN THE CLOUDS**1/2

(1934) 61m FN-WB bw

Lyle Talbot (Three Star Bob Halsey), Ann Dvorak (Judy Wagner), Gordon Westcott (George Wexley), Robert Light (Tom Wagner), George Cooper (Wings Mahoney), Charles Wilson (Lackey), Henry O'Neill (John Brownell), Russell Hicks (Taggart), Arthur Pierson (Jason), Edward McWade, Clay Clement, Eddie Shubart, Wheeler Oakman, Nick Copeland.

Fast-paced, entertaining programmer starring Talbot as a crackerjack pilot hired to transport a brilliant scientist who has developed a new explosive to Washington. Unfortunately, the villainous Hicks and his cronies are out to snatch the plans at any cost. Dvorak is the air hostess love interest. Cooper, as an airplane mechanic, provides the comic relief, and the economical direction was provided by Lederman.

p, Sam Bischoff; d, D. Ross Lederman; w, Roy Chanslor, Dore Schary; ph, Warren Lynch; ed, Thomas Pratt; art d, Jack Holden.

Espionage (PR:A MPAA:NR)

MURDER IN THE FAMILY*1/2

(1938, Brit.) 75m FOX bw

Barry Jones (Stephen Osborne), Jessica Tandy (Ann Osborne), Evelyn Ankers (Dorothy Osborne), Donald Gray (Ted Fleming), Jessie Winter (Edith Osborne), David Markham (Michael Osborne), Glynis Johns (Marjorie Osborne), Roddy McDowall (Peter Osborne), Annie Esmond (Aunt Octavia), Rani Waller (Miss Mimms), Claire Arnold, A. Bromley Davenport, Stella Arbenina, W. Simpson Fraser, David Arnold, Edgar K. Bruce, Charles Childerstone.

Jones is accused of killing his rich aunt, Esmond, after she refuses to help him out of a monetary bind. The real culprit is the shiftless maid, who stabs the woman upon learning of her inclusion in the inheritance. Ponderous material makes the performers' hard work a waste.

p&d, Albert Parker; w, David Evans (based on the novel by James Ronald).

Mystery (PR:A MPAA:NR)

MURDER IN THE FLEET**1/2

(1935) 70m MGM bw

Robert Taylor (Lt. Tom Randolph), Jean Parker (Betty Lansing), Ted Healy (Mac O'Neill), Una Merkel ("Toots" Simmons), Nat Pendleton ("Spud" Burke), Jean Hersholt (Victor Hanson), Arthur Byron (Capt. Winslow), Frank Shields (Lt. Arnold), Raymond Hatton (Al Duval), Donald Cook (Lt. Cmdr. David Tucker), Mischa Auer (Manchukan Consul), Mary Doran (Jenny Lane), Tom Dugan ("Greasy"), Tony Hughes (Walter Drake), Ward Bond ("Heavy" Johnson), Richard Tucker (Harry Jeffries), John Hyams (Ambrose Justin), Leila McIntyre (Mrs. Justin).

Wildly uneven comedy/mystery film that starts out fairly funny and lighthearted, but then shifts to a rather grim and serious tone. Taylor stars as a navy lieutenant whose ship is being fitted with newly developed fire-control gear that will vastly improve its wartime potential. The only hitch is that the ship must be made fully operational in 24 hours, or the invention will be sold to rival countries. This, of course, leads to sabotage and murder, and it's up to Taylor to find out who's responsible. By the end of the film, Taylor must wrestle the crazed spy to stop him from blowing the entire ship out of the water. The mystery itself is confusing, with no clear handle on just who is sabotaging the ship and why (they could be Chinese, Japanese, Hindus). Good cast saves the floundering material.

p, Lucien Hubbard; d, Edward Sedgwick; w, Frank Wead, Leo Sherman (based on a story by Sedgwick); ph, Milton Krasner; ed, Conrad A. Nervig.

Mystery (PR:A MPAA:NR)

MURDER IN THE FOOTLIGHTS

(SEE: TROJAN BROTHERS, THE, 1946, Brit.)

MURDER IN THE MUSEUM*1/2

(1934) 60m Willis Kent/Progressive bw

Henry B. Walthall (Professor Mysto, Stage Magician), John Harron (Jerry Ross, Reporter), Phyllis Barrington (Lois, Brandon's Niece), Joseph Girard (Police Commissioner Brandon), John Elliott (Snell), Donald Kerr (Museum Barker), Symonia Boniface (Fortune Teller), Sam Flint (Councilman Newgate), Steve Clemente (Knife Thrower), Albert Knight (King Kiku), Lynton Brent (Museum Manager), Si Jenks (Rube), Al Hill (Detective).

This tale of love and revenge is played out with little imagination against the backdrop of a freak show. Walthall is a magician who is caught up in a mystery after Flint, an anti-alcohol crusading politician, is murdered. There's the usual myriad of suspects, and some trouble determining the caliber of the weapon. It ultimately proves that Walthall is the killer who had taken revenge on Brent by pointing all the evidence toward him. Brent had betrayed Walthall's late wife years before and the magician promised her he would get even. This is a confusing thriller without any thrills at all. The carnival-freak show atmosphere is never exploited for its wealth of creepy goings-on, and coupled with the laughably awful acting, the film quickly goes nowhere. Walthall had been one of D. W. Griffith's favorite actors in the silent era, but like this once great director, Walthall's career took a devastating plunge with the advent of sound.

d, Melville Shyer; w, E. B. Crosswhite; ph, James Diamond; ed, S. Roy Luby.

Crime/Suspense Cas. (PR:C MPAA:NR)

MURDER IN THE MUSIC HALL**1/2

(1946) 84m REP bw (AKA: MIDNIGHT MELODY)

Vera Hruba Ralston (Lila), William Marshall (Don), Helen Walker (Millicent), Nancy Kelly (Mrs. Morgan), William Gargan (Inspector Wilson), Ann Rutherford (Gracie), Julie Bishop (Diane), Jerome Cowan (George Morgan), Edward Norris (Carl), Paul Hurst (Hobarth), Frank Orth (Henderson, Stage Manager), Jack LaRue (Bruce Wilton), James Craven (Mr. Winters), Fay McKenzie (Singer in Mom's Cafe), Tom London (Ryan), Joe Yule (Doorman), Mary Field (Waitress), Anne Nagel (Mission Attendant), Ilka Gruning (Mom), Inez Palange (Mrs. Aldine), William Austin (Clerk), Spec O'Donnell, Billy Vernon (Ushers), Nolan Leary (Doctor), LeRoy Mason (Policeman), Brooks Benedict (Police Photographer), Lee Phelps (McCarthy), Virginia Carroll (Cashier), Lillian Bronson (Woman Cleaner), Wheaton Chambers (Evangelist Leader), John Wald (Radio Officer), James Farley (Police Sergeant), Conden and Bohland, Red McCarthy, Patti Phillippi, John Jolliffe, Henry Lie (Specialty Ice Stars).

Ice skating star Ralston is in love with the show's orchestra leader, played by Marshall. When a blackmailer who lives next door to the music hall where they perform is killed, Ralston and co-stars Walker, Kelly, Rutherford and Bishop are considered suspects. Marshall turns sleuth and, with the help of a police inspector (Gargan), solves the crime and the girls are exonerated. This is a better-than-average program mystery, with the suspense built nicely by the director. Unlike many films of this nature, the killer isn't obvious, and the investigation actually entails some thinking. In addition, there are some nice skating sequences featuring Ralston and some specialty acts. McKenzie sings some songs in the local cafe, with "My Wonderful One" and "Mess Me Up" among the numbers.

p, Herman Millakowsky; d, John English; w, Frances Hyland, Laszlo Gorog (based on a story by Arnold Phillips, Maria Matray); ph, Jack Marta, John Alton; ed, Arthur Roberts; md, Walter Scharf; art d, Russell Kimball; set d, John McCarthy, Jr., Earl Wooden; spec eff, Howard and Theodore Lydecker; m/l, Kim Gannon and Walter Kent, Phil Ohman and Ned Washington.

Mystery (PR:O MPAA:NR)

MURDER IN THE NIGHT zero

(1940, Brit.) 70m ABF/Film Alliance bw (GB: MURDER IN SOHO)

Jack La Rue (Steve Marco), Sandra Storme (Ruby Lane), Bernard Lee (Roy Barnes), Martin Walker (Inspector Hammond), James Hayter (Nick Green), Googie Withers (Lola Matthews), Drue Leyton (Myrtle), Arthur O'Connell (Lefty), Edmon Ryan (Spike), Francis Lister (Joe Lane), Alf Goddard (Mike), Diana Beaumont (Girl), Zillah Bateman, Renee Gadd, Diana Ward, Geoffrey Sumner, Robert Beatty, Joss Ambler.

La Rue, a Chicago gangster holed up in London, is operating a nightclub as a front for his underworld doings. Lister is a blackmailer who's quickly done away with after trying to frame the big guy. The dead man's wife, Storme, is the nightclub hostess who wants La Rue, along with henchmen Ryan and O'Connell, brought to justice. She pretends to fall for her boss, though she's really involved with Lee, a reporter. Storme and Lee trap the crooks, with the aid of police inspector Walker. The title implies mystery, but the only mystery here is how this film ever got released. The story has more holes in it than a Capone victim, and the acting is laughable. The direction and other production values aren't even up to the standards of most low-budget programmers.

p, Walter C. Mycroft; d, Norman Lee; w, F. McGrew Willis; ph, Claude Friese-Greene; ed, E. B. Jarvis.

Crime (PR:O MPAA:NR)

MURDER IN THE OLD RED BARN*

(1936, Brit.) 67m Sound City Studios/Olympic bw (GB: MARIA MARTEN)

Tod Slaughter (Squire William Corder), Sophie Stewart (Maria Marten), D. J. Williams (Farmer Marten), Clare Greet (Mrs. Marten), Eric Portman (Carlos), Gerrard Tyrell (Tim), Ann Trevor (Nan), Antonia Brough (Maud Sennett), Quentin McPhearson (Mr. Sennett), Dennis Hoey (Gambler), Stella Rho (Gypsy Crone), Herbert Leonard (Compere), Noel Dainton (Steel, Bow Street Runner), J. Leslie Frith (Lawyer).

A formula piece involving the adventures of a sweet young thing vs. the haughty naughty advances of an evil squire based on a real murder. The film, an update of an already dusty American stage melodrama, was played in full costume and with high drama. Unfortunately, the play is very stiff and the whole production dry, lacking any true drama or humor. The production qualities are below par for this sort of filler. MURDER IN THE OLD RED BARN was released in the U.S. by MGM as part of a quota deal with the English studio.

p, Gilbert Josephson; d, Milton Rosmer; w, Randall Faye; ed, Charles Saunders.

Drama   **Cas.**   **(PR:O MPAA:NR)**

MURDER IN THE PRIVATE CAR*¹/₂
                    (1934) 63m MGM bw (GB: MURDER ON THE RUNAWAY TRAIN)
Charlie Ruggles (Scott), Una Merkel (Georgia), Mary Carlisle (Ruth), Russell Hardie (Blake), Porter Hall (Murray), Willard Robertson (Hanks), Berton Churchill (Carson), Cliff Thompson (Allen), Snowflake (Titus, Porter).

Silly mystery starring Ruggles as a bumbling amateur detective out to help Merkel, a switchboard operator who is suddenly told she is the long-lost daughter of a rich old man. Traveling with her small entourage on a private railroad car, Merkel discovers on the way to meet her father that someone is trying to kidnap her. Enter a gorilla on the loose and a cache of explosives on the runaway train car, and the film launches into a Mack Sennett-like finale.

d, Harry Beaumont; w, Ralph Spence, Edgar Allan Woolf, Al Boasberg, Harvey Thew (based on the play "The Rear Car" by Edward E. Rose); ph, James Van Trees, Leonard Smith; ed, William S. Gray.

Mystery/Comedy   **(PR:A MPAA:NR)**

MURDER IN THORTON SQUARE   (SEE: GASLIGHT, 1944)

MURDER IN TIMES SQUARE**¹/₂   (1943) 65m COL bw
Edmund Lowe (Cory Williams), Marguerite Chapman (Melinda Matthews), John Litel (Dr. Blaine), William Wright (Detective Lt. Tabor), Bruce Bennett (Supal George), Esther Dale (Longacre Lil), Veda Ann Borg (Fiona Maclair), Gerald Mohr (O'Dell Gissing), Sidney Blackmer (George Nevins), Leslie Denison (Rob Slocumb), Douglas Leavitt (Henry Trigg), George McKay (Southcote).

Four people are murdered through the course of the story in one of the more original B-picture murder techniques: injection by rattlesnake venom. Lowe, a Broadway actor and egotist supreme, is one of the suspects. He's fingered by Dale, a local panhandler he continually has ignored. Chapman plays a press agent whom Lowe falls in love with, and Litel is the doctor ultimately found guilty of the crimes. Though the plot has a few holes, this is a fairly good little mystery that holds the suspense well throughout. The film has the audience guessing throughout who the culprit really is. Some good thespian jobs and better-than-average direction.

p, Colbert Clark; d, Lew Landers; w, Paul Gangelin (based on a story by Stuart Palmer); ph, W. O'Connell; ed, Richard Fantl; md, M. W. Stoloff; art d, Lionel Banks.

Mystery   **(PR:O MPAA:NR)**

MURDER IN TRINIDAD**   (1934) 74m FOX bw
Nigel Bruce (Bertram Lynch), Heather Angel (Joan Cassell), Victor Jory (Howard Sutter), Murray Kinnell (Maj. Bruce Cassell), Douglas Walton (Gregory Bronson), J. Carrol Naish (Duval), Claude King (Sir Ellery Bronson), Pat Somerset (Inspector Henley), Francis Ford (Davenant), John Davidson (Moah), Noble Johnson (Queochie).

Bruce is a standout in this otherwise mediocre offering. The mystery involves three knife-wielding murderers, stolen diamonds and a hideout protected by a quicksand-and-crocodile filled swamp. The film runs a bit longer than necessary, and the mystery is not very mysterious. However, Bruce's performance as a low-key Sherlock Holmes type is great fun. He carries the film well despite the inherent weaknesses.

p, Sol M. Wurtzel; d, Louis King; w, Seton I. Miller (based on the novel by John W. Vandercook); ph, Barney McGill; ed, Al DeGaetano; md, Samuel Kaylin.

Mystery   **(PR:O MPAA:NR)**

MURDER, INC.   (SEE: ENFORCER, THE, 1950)

MURDER, INC.***   (1960) 103m FOX bw
Stuart Whitman (Joey Collins), May Britt (Eadie Collins), Henry Morgan (Burton Turkus), Peter Falk (Abe Reles), David J. Stewart (Louis "Lepke" Buchalter), Simon Oakland (Detective Tobin), Warren Fennerty (Bug), Joseph Bernard (Mendy Weiss), Eli Mintz (Joe Rosen), Vince Gardenia (Lawyer Laslo), Josip Elic (Alpert), Helen Waters (Rose), Lou Polan (Louis), Howard I. Smith (Albert Anastasia), Joseph Campanella (Panto), Leon B. Stevens (Betty Shaw), Sylvia Miles (Sadie), Barbara Wilkens (Receptionist), Seymour Cassell, Paul Porter (Teenagers), David Kerman (1st Detective), Harold Gary (Sal), Bill Bassett (Eadie's Killer), Ed Simon (Johnny), Peter Gumeny (Policeman), Kent Montroy (Bailiff), Ricky Colletti (Victim), Ed Wagner (2nd Detective), Adrienne Mills (Lodge Dancer), Morey Amsterdam (Walter Sage), Sarah Vaughn (Herself).

Accurately based on the real and monstrous group of hired killers operating in New York during the 1930s, this film pulls no punches in depicting the animal brutality of MURDER, INC. Falk is shockingly effective as the thoroughly immoral hoodlum and hired murderer, Abe "Kid Twist" Reles, who, early on, graphically describes his evil philosophy by holding up his hands and telling friend Whitman: "What do you think these are for? To take—take! That's all!" Whitman and his sexy blonde wife, Britt, form a mindless subplot romance which serves, if nothing more, to soften a story that continually assails sensibilities. Morgan plays the crusading D.A., Turkus—who, in real life, doggedly investigated the killer-for-hire company and successfully

prosecuted its members, not the least of whom was Louis "Lepke" Buchalter, coolly played by Stewart. Whitman is sucked into gang activities until he is Falk's pawn, with Falk eventually raping his wife Britt and threatening both of them with death if they betray Murder, Inc. He compels them to take Stewart in when the crime czar is on the run. Then Stewart is betrayed by his own men into believing that they have "fixed" authorities and he will get a light sentence for his racketeering and murders. He turns himself in and gets 30 years, later convicted and executed with two henchmen, thanks to the efforts of Morgan-Turkus and dedicated cop Oakland. Falk, who turns state's witness, is shown being thrown out of a window of the Half Moon Hotel in Coney Island, where he was reportedly being protected by a half dozen cops who looked the other way. (Reles' unsolved death on November 12, 1941, is still being debated to this day, particularly how his bevy of police guards were all suddenly sleeping or out of the room when the mass killer went out the window to his death.) In the end the killers are rounded up but only Whitman—who also turns state's witness—survives to wreak vengeance on the mob, Britt being murdered and her body stuffed under a boardwalk. The direction here is brisk and grimly realistic but the script is rather routine. Falk, Stewart, and Oakland make all the difference. The story of this murder mob was profiled better in THE ENFORCER (1951) with Humphrey Bogart playing the role of the fighting district attorney and Everett Sloane profiling Lepke. Tony Curtis later essayed the mob czar in LEPKE, an inferior production.

p, Burt Balaban; d, Balaban, Stuart Rosenberg; w, Irv Tunick, Mel Barr (based on the book by Burton Turkus, Sid Feder); ph, Gayne Rescher (CinemaScope); m, Frank De Vol; ed, Ralph Rosenblum; art d, Dick Sylbert; set d, Charles Bailey; cos, Bill Walstrom; makeup, Bill Herman.

Crime   **(PR:O MPAA:NR)**

MURDER IS MY BEAT***   (1955) 77m AA bw
Paul Langton (Ray Patrick), Barbara Payton (Eden Lane), Robert Shayne (Bert Rawley), Selena Royle (Mrs. Abbott), Roy Gordon (Abbott), Tracey Roberts (Patsy Flint), Kate McKenna (Landlady), Henry A. Harvey, Sr. (Gas Station Attendant), Jay Adler (Bartender).

A body is found with its head in a fireplace completely burned so that identification is impossible. Payton, a nightclub singer, is arrested by cops Shayne and Langton as a suspect. She's convicted for the murder while maintaining her innocence. When Langton escorts her to prison via railroad, she sees the man she supposedly killed through the window. Langton believes her and the two leap off the train to find him. After a fruitless search, they find Roberts, Payton's former roommate, living at a hotel under an assumed name. Payton disappears and Shayne wants to arrest Langton, who pleads for 24 hours to solve the case. They find the supposed victim (Gordon), the owner of a local ceramics works. It is discovered that he had fallen in love with Payton and hired a private detective to follow her around. But when the detective threatened to blackmail Gordon by telling his wife (Royle), Gordon killed him and pinned the murder on Payton. After his arrest, Roberts is found dead at the hands of Royle following another blackmail attempt. Payton, meanwhile, turns herself over to the authorities but is freed to marry Langton. This quirky mystery rises above melodrama through intelligent and creative direction. Ulmer distorts the story with his use of flashback, jump-cutting (pre-dating Godard's classic gangster homage BREATHLESS) and few establishing shots. The viewer is given a world where reality is alienated from the darker forces of man's nature, well visualized within the mise-en-scene. Payton's performance leaves the viewer guessing: Is she really innocent or is she guilty? Her characterization is purposefully bland, making her role all the more ambiguous. Though by no means a great example of film noir, this film is definitely worth looking at. Its use of technique to improve an otherwise formula story should be studied by any aspiring filmmaker.

p, Aubrey Wisberg, Ilse Lahn; d, Edgar G. Ulmer; w, Wisberg (based on a story by Wisberg and Martin Field); ph, Harold E. Wellman; m, Al Glasser; ed, Fred R. Feitshans, Jr.; art d, James Sullivan; set d, Harry H. Reif; makeup, Jack Byron.

Mystery   **(PR:O MPAA:NR)**

MURDER IS MY BUSINESS**   (1946) 64m PRC bw
Hugh Beaumont (Michael Shayne), Cheryl Walker (Phyllis), Lyle Talbot (Duell Renslow), George Meeker (Carl Meldrum), Pierre Watkin (Mr. Ramsey), Richard Keene (Tim Rourke), David Reed (Ernst Ramsey), Carol Andrews (Mona Tabor), Julia McMillan (Dorothy Ramsey), Helene Heigh (Mrs. Ramsey), Ralph Dunn (Pete Rafferty), Parker Garvie (Joe Darnell), Virginia Christine (Dora Darnell), Donald Kerr.

An average although entertaining "Michael Shayne" mystery casts Beaumont as a detective chasing heavies Talbot and Meeker. Beaumont plays his part at a low-key level (not unlike his later role as Ward Cleaver on TV's "Leave It to Beaver"). The supporting cast is also strong, considering the B-picture elements. Subtle humor is contained within the murder/blackmail story line, making this a predictable yet entertaining detective yarn. (See MICHAEL SHAYNE Series, Index.)

p, Sigmund Neufeld; d, Sam Newfield; w, Fred Myton (based on original characters and story by Brett Halliday); ph, Jack Greenhalgh; ed, Holbrook N. Todd; md, Leo Erdody; art d, Edward C. Jewell; set d, Elias H. Reif.

Mystery   **(PR:O MPAA:NR)**

MURDER IS NEWS zero   (1939) 55m 1939 Warwick bw
John Gallaudet (Jerry Tracy), Iris Meredith (Ann Leslie), George McKay (Brains McGillicuddy), John Hamilton (David Corning), Frank C. Wilson (Tony Peyden), William McIntyre (Edgar Drake), Doris Lloyd (Pauline Drake), John G. Spacey (Fred Hammer), Colin Kenny (Inspector Fitzgerald), Fred Baes (R. A. Snyder).

Gallaudet is the only worthy item in this film about a Walter Winchell-type radio man who slowly uncovers a series of murders. When he breaks news of a society scandal, the son of one of the principals involved goes nuts and threatens revenge. Gallaudet is given a free rein by the cops to investigate after several murders are committed in connection with the scandal. It turns out that a man with dealings in the stock market has been killing people left and right, but neither his motivation nor motives for other murders are ever made clear. The production values are way below average, and the direction leaves many questions unanswered. This film was on the tail-end of a spate of radio newsman whodunits, a genre that had already worn out its welcome.

p, Kenneth J. Bishop; d, Leon Barsha; w, Edgar Edwards (based on a story by Theodore A. Tinsley); ph, George Meehan; ed, William Austin.

Mystery (PR:O MPAA:NR)

MURDER MAN*** (1935) 70m MGM bw

Spencer Tracy (*Steve Gray*), Virginia Bruce (*Mary Shannon*), Lionel Atwill (*Capt. Cole*), Harvey Stephens (*Henry Mander*), Robert Barrat (*Robbins*), James Stewart (*Shorty*), William Collier, Sr. (*Pop Gray*), Bobby Watson (*Carey Booth*), William Demarest (*Rod McGuire*), John Sheehan (*Maxie Sweeney, the Detective*), Lucien Littlefield (*Rafferty*), George Chandler (*Sol Hertzberger*), Fuzzy Knight (*Buck Hawkins, the Reporter*), Louise Henry (*Lillian Hopper*), Robert Warwick (*Coleville*), Joe Irving (*Tony*), Francis X. Bushman, Jr. (*Pendleton*), Ed Coppo (*Fingerprint Expert*), Heinie Conklin (*Warden's Secretary*), James Pierce (*Sing Sing Guard*), Ben Taggart (*Dave, the Sing Sing Guard*), Frank O'Connor (*Reporter*), Frank Mayo (*Bit*), John Dilson (*Meltzer, the City Editor*), William Norton Bailey (*Welch, the Police Photographer*), Harry Tyler (*Doc Warren*), Jennie Roberts (*Mabel*), George Guhl (*Miller—Cop at Apartment*), Stanley Andrews (*Police Commissioner*), Bob Murphy, Charles Delaney (*Cops*), Cyril Ring (*Court Officer*), Matty Roubert (*Newsboy*), Irving Bacon (*Merry-Go-Round Man*), Charles Trowbridge, Jack Cheatham, Larry Steers (*Investors*), Theodor Von Eltz (*James Spencer Halford*), Reginald Pash (*Third Mate*), Robert Warwick (*Defense Attorney*), Robert Frazer (*Doctor*).

This was Tracy's first film for MGM, where he would find a home for the next twenty years. (It was also the film debut of James Stewart, whose future career would place him in the same superstar status as Tracy.) Tracy is a rugged newspaperman whose specialty is homicide. He's always ten steps ahead of the police in solving sensational killings. Though his somewhat jealous peers consider Tracy to be one of the most tenacious, clever, and knowing reporters around, his editor calls him a "crazy, cynical, drunken bum!" He sleeps in elevators or may spend a night riding a merry-go-round, but he's indefatigable when it comes to his job, as fellow reporter Bruce knows; she's been in love with him for a long time and is always busy trying to reform him. Murder comes into Tracy's own life when crooked financier Stephens and his partner ruin Collier, Tracy's father, and cause the suicide of Tracy's estranged wife. He goes after the lethal con men with a vengeance, planning what he thinks is the perfect murder, killing Stephens' partner so that all the proof points to Stephens, who is quickly tried, convicted, and condemned for the crime. Tracy visits Stephens in his death cell and gloats about taking vengeance but his natural ideals and goodness overwhelm his bitter triumph; he cannot allow an innocent man to go to his death. Tracy confesses his guilt and accepts the inevitable punishment. Tracy is excellent in his role and Collier gives him good support in a brisk if predictable B melodrama. Stewart, playing a cub reporter sarcastically nicknamed "Shorty," because of his gangling stature, showed great promise in his brief role, his first on film, and became lifelong friends with Tracy. Stewart was nervous before his first scene and Tracy told him: "Forget the camera is there." Tracy later recalled how "that was all he needed; in his very first scene he showed he had all the good things."

p, Harry Rapf; d, Tim Whelan; w, Whelan, John C. Higgins (based on a story by Whelan, Guy Bolton); ph, Lester White; m, William Axt; ed, James E. Newcomb; art d, Cedric Gibbons, Eddie Imazu, Edwin B. Willis; set d, Willis.

Crime Drama (PR:C MPAA:NR)

MURDER MISSISSIPPI (SEE: MURDER IN MISSISSIPPI, 1965)

MURDER MOST FOUL*** (1964, Brit.) 91m MGM bw

Margaret Rutherford (*Miss Marple*), Ron Moody (*H. Driffold Cosgood*), Charles Tingwell (*Detective Inspector Craddock*), Andrew Cruickshank (*Justice Crosby*), Megs Jenkins (*Mrs. Thomas*), Dennis Price (*Theatrical Agent*), Ralph Michael (*Ralph Summers*), James Bolam (*Bill Hanson*), Stringer Davis (*Mr. Stringer*), Francesca Annis (*Sheila Upward*), Alison Seebohm (*Eva McGonigall*), Terry Scott (*Police Constable Wells*), Pauline Jameson (*Maureen Summers*), Maurice Good (*George Rowton*), Annette Kerr, Windsor Davies, Neil Stacey, Stella Tanner.

The third of three Miss Marple hits in a row, MURDER MOST FOUL again paired the mind of Christie with the acting ability of Rutherford to come up with an amusing and brainy mystery that never fails to please. Based on Christie's novel, *Mrs. McGinty's Dead*, the fast-moving script doesn't flag for more than a few seconds under Pollock's breezy direction. Rutherford is the only member of a British jury to cast a "not guilty" vote in a murder case and so the trial is declared a miss. She thinks she might have a better idea as to who committed the murder, so she sets out with Davis (her real-life husband) to solve the crime and winds up at the home of the victim. While there, a series of events occur which lead Rutherford to an acting repertory company chaired by Moody. She poses as an experienced actress with a few pounds in her purse and Moody thinks that her money might help the company out of the financial difficulty they are currently experiencing. Rutherford tries to get some help from Tingwell, the inspector she usually battles with in these cases, but he is certain that the accused is guilty as charged. When two members of the acting troupe are soon dispatched, Rutherford is positive she's on to something and that the alleged murderer is innocent. In the end, she discovers that the real killer is Bolam, another member of the acting fraternity. His mother, also a one-time actress, was executed for having murdered her husband and the earlier victim had been cadging money from Bolam to keep that news away from everyone. A good British mystery with enough humor in it to leaven the dead bodies, it was handled with the

same seamlessness director Pollock had demonstrated on both MURDER, SHE SAID and MURDER AT THE GALLOP. Moody is excellent as the company's director, Davis and Tingwell repeat their roles with aplomb, and Ron Goodman's score adds a great deal to the tingling of the spine.

p, Lawrence P. Bachmann, Ben Arbeid; d, George Pollock; w, David Pursall, Jack Seddon (based on the novel *Mrs. McGinty's Dead* by Agatha Christie); ph, Desmond Dickinson; m, Ron Goodwin; ed, Ernest Walter; md, Goodwin; art d, Frank White.

Comedy/Mystery (PR:A MPAA:NR)

MURDER, MY SWEET***** (1945) 95m RKO bw (GB: FAREWELL, MY LOVELY)

Dick Powell (*Philip Marlowe*), Claire Trevor (*Velma/Mrs. Grayle*), Anne Shirley (*Ann*), Otto Kruger (*Amthor*), Mike Mazurki (*Moose Malloy*), Miles Mander (*Mr. Grayle*), Douglas Walton (*Marriott*), Don Douglas (*Lt. Randall*), Ralf Harolde (*Dr. Sonderborg*), Esther Howard (*Mrs. Florian*), John Indrisano (*Chauffeur*), Jack Carr (*Short Guy*), Shimen Ruskin (*Elevator Operator*), Ernie Adams (*Bartender*), Dewey Robinson (*The Boss*), Larry Wheat (*Butler*), Sammy Finn (*Headwaiter*), Bernice Ahi (*Dancer*), Don Kerr (*Taxi Driver*), Paul Phillips (*Detective Nulty*), Ralph Dunn, George Anderson (*Detectives*), Paul Hilton (*Boy*).

This tough, sardonic, and unusually witty film brought one-time movie crooner Powell back from the brink of career catastrophe and made him a superstar, as well as establishing him as a man of immense acting ability. Next to Humphrey Bogart's essaying the classic *film noir* character Philip Marlowe in THE BIG SLEEP, no one could ever match Powell's personification of the down-and-out but highly principled gumshoe. He takes only $25 a day and expenses for wading through the worst kind of human mire and considers it honest labor. The film opens under a glaring light. Beneath it is Powell, being grilled by a bevy of anxious cops. After bantering with his interrogators, Powell, his eyes mysteriously bandaged, begins to relate in flashback his sinister experiences. Powell is in his shabby office when he is visited by giant, cretinous Mazurki, a thug who has just been released from prison and is searching for an old girl friend. He hires a leary Powell to find her and Powell accompanies Mazurki to a seedy dive where the goon's girl once worked as a singer. The neighborhood is in the worst part of Los Angeles, an area that had once seen better days. When Powell doesn't get any answers from the local owner, Mazurki breaks the place up and tosses owner Robinson about like a swizzle stick. As Mazurki and Powell walk out of the bar, Florian's by name, the goon tells the detective to keep looking for the girl, Velma by name, handing him some more money. Powell checks the background on the bar and finds that its owner has died but his widow is alive, who Powell visits and describes as a "charming middle-aged lady with a face like a bucket of mud. I gave her a drink. She was a gal who'd take a drink. She'd knock you down to get the bottle." Powell quizzes the drunken harridan, Howard, about Velma, but she can't recall her. She tells him to "hold on to your chair and don't step on no snakes," then goes into another room of her apartment. Powell follows her and sees her rummaging quickly through records, pulling photos out of a file and later she hands him the file and he goes back to her bedroom, drags out a photo of Velma, and asks Howard why she was hiding the photo. She tells him to "beat it," and collapses in a crying jag. Powell returns to his office building where the elevator operator tells him he has a visitor waiting in his office, that "he smells real nice." Well dressed, effeminate Walton, the new client, tells him he's meeting some men late that night, that he must deliver a large amount of money to them. Powell insults him, inferring he's a coward and Walton explodes, threatening to punch the detective in the nose. "I tremble at the thought of such violence," smirks Powell. Walton starts to go, then turns and offers Powell $100 for a few hours of his time. Powell learns that Walton has to meet these men on a remote canyon dead-end road and that Walton is buying back some priceless jewels taken in a holdup. Powell tells him that the odds of getting the jewels back are slim, that Walton will probably get beaten up, lose the money, and not get the jewels back at all, but Powell agrees to go along anyway, telling Walton he must hide in the back seat of the car. That night Powell drives to the deserted spot where the road comes to a dead-end, the rendezvous. He gets out of the car, looks about the secluded canyon, smelling double cross all the way. A gun in one hand, a flashlight in the other, Powell can see no one. He returns to the car. Suddenly, narrates Powell, "I caught the blackjack right behind my ear. A black pool opened up at my feet. I dived in. It had no bottom. I felt pretty good—like an amputated leg." He comes to with the glare of a flashlight on his face and a woman's voice asking him if he's all right. He stands up and she runs away. Powell looks into the car to see Walton, and he narrates: "He was doubled up on his face in that bag of old clothes position that always means the same thing. He had been killed by an amateur, or by somebody who wanted it to look like an amateur job. Nobody else would hit a man that many times with a sap." Powell is next shown being grilled by police lieutenant Douglas about Walton's death and then points out that it was he, Powell, who called police to the spot, getting angry at Douglas for inferring that he had something to do with Walton's death, telling him to either "book me or let me go home." Douglas sneers and tells him: "I'd rather be digging eggshells out of garbage cans than try to get information out of you . . . You're not a detective, you're a slot machine. You'd slit your own throat for six bits, plus tax." Douglas tells Powell to go home but to watch his step, and to stay away from Walton's associates, including Kruger. Powell hears this name for the first time. He returns to his office where Shirley is waiting for him, pretending to be a reporter. He tells her basically what happened with Walton. Shirley tells him that Walton was after the return of a jade object which piques Powell's interest; he immediately realizes that she is no reporter since she possesses information he does not have nor gave to the police. He dumps her purse out and discovers she's not a reporter and demands she tell him who the jade belongs to and she says that it belongs to her father, Mander, and makes a point of telling Powell that her father's wife is not her mother. Powell insists on talking "with your father . . . and your father's wife." Next Shirley drives Powell into a vast estate and he narrates: "It was a nice little front yard, cozy, okay for the average family, only you'd need a compass to go to the mail box. The house was all right, too, but it wasn't as big as Buckingham Palace." Powell waits in a huge foyer with large checkerboard tiles and, when summoned to see Mander and his wife, Trevor, in the enormous living room, he practices a little hopscotch on the tile floor before he enters. Mander quickly tells him that the missing jade necklace is worth about $125,000. Sexy Trevor explains that she wore the necklace to an affair and it was stolen from her in a holdup. Mander retires and Trevor tells Powell that Walton was carrying $8,000 of her money when he was killed and robbed. She flirts with Powell outlandishly as she informs Powell that the robbers acted peculiarly, giving her back one of her rings. Shirley looks in on the pair as they sit close on the couch and then slams the door in disgust. Trevor hires Powell and a moment later Kruger appears. Powell explains that "I was hired as a bodyguard and bungled the job. Now I'm investigating myself." He tells Kruger that the police mentioned his name, warning him against becoming involved with him. He tells Kruger he will call him later so they can talk about the case. Powell goes home to his dirty, cluttered apartment and, while shaving in his undershirt, Trevor walks in, commenting: "You've got a nice build for a detective." He gives her a scowl, saying: "It gets me around." She gives him some money, a retainer, which he quickly takes and then the two go to the Coconut Beach Club. While Trevor goes to powder her nose, Shirley hails Powell and tells him that she'll pay him twice what Trevor is paying him, $1,000, if he'll stay away from Trevor. He thinks it over, walks away, and bumps into Mazurki, who strong-arms him into meeting someone. They drive to Kruger's palatial penthouse apartment, taking the back elevator. Powell tells Kruger he doesn't understand what's going on. Kruger asks what the police want with him. Powell tells him he doesn't know, then asks what he does for a living. Kruger tells him he's called a quack by some but he is a "psychic physician." Powell tells him that Walton, Kruger's associate, was a shill for stickup men, that he took wealthy women out to dine, called the robbers, and set up the thefts as he accompanied the jewel-laden women, in this case Trevor, as they walked through dark parking lots. He goes on to accuse Kruger of engineering the theft of the jade necklace. Kruger tells him he wants the jade, doesn't have it, but will pay well for it. Powell tells him he won't work for him and then Mazurki comes back and Kruger tells the goon that Powell refuses to tell him where his old girl friend is. Mazurki loses control, shaking Powell, demanding to know where Velma is and Powell calls him a nitwit and hits the big man. Mazurki jumps up and begins strangling Powell while Kruger demands to know where he has hidden the jade necklace. Powell frees himself, strikes Kruger, and is sapped and dragged away. Powell now begins to live a nightmare with Kruger and Mazurki looming over him, demanding to know the whereabouts of the necklace. His world is full of cobwebs and hypodermic needles. He plunges downward into a whirlpool and awakes on a bed staring up at a light, thick stationary smoke surrounding him, and narrating: "The window was open but the smoke didn't move; it was a gray web woven by a thousand spiders. I wondered how they got them to work together." He screams but can only blubber to a heavyset male nurse who arrives. Later, he tries to come to, sitting up on the bed. He stands up and then collapses. "Okay, Marlowe," he tells himself. "You're a tough guy. You've been sapped twice, choked, beaten silly with a gun, shot in the arm until you're as crazy as a couple of waltzing mice. Now let's see you do something really tough—like puttin' your pants on!" He staggers up, struggles into his trousers. "Okay, you cuckoo, talk and walk." He forces himself to walk about the room on wobbly legs. "I walked," he narrates, "I don't know how long. I didn't have a watch. They don't make that kind of time in watches anyway." Then the smoke clears and Powell puts on his hat and coat. He takes a bar from the bed and hits the male nurse with it when he rushes in, escaping downstairs. There he confronts Harolde, the doctor in charge of the sleazy clinic where he has been held prisoner. Harolde tells him he's been "a very sick man" for three days and pulls a gun but Powell takes it away from him and holds it on him. The smoke reappears and Powell almost collapses. But he gets the key to the front door and makes good his escape. Mazurki runs into him on the street and puts Powell into a cab; the driver refuses to accept Powell, telling Mazurki that he's waiting for a fare. Mazurki rips his meter box out of its holdings and yells: "I'd like you to take my friend." The terrified driver agrees immediately and takes Powell to Shirley's place; Powell knows the police are watching his apartment and office. Shirley asks him if he's all right and Powell recognizes her voice, the same voice of the woman who asked him if he was all right before he was sapped and Walton killed. She denies having killed Walton. Then police lieutenant Douglas shows up and Powell offers to help him get Kruger. Douglas agrees. Powell and Shirley then go to Mander's estate and find Mander loading a gun. He tells them that he's frightened, that the police had been there and asked questions about his beach house. Mander is afraid of losing his young wife, Trevor, he tells Powell, and says he knows Walton was making a play for her. Powell believes the answers are at Mander's beach house. He drives there with Shirley and they find nothing. He tells her, after kissing her, that she probably tried to buy him off to keep him away from Trevor and protect her father's feelings. Angered, she insults him and he tells her he's probably wrong and then Trevor suddenly appears and Shirley calls her an "expensive blonde babe" and that inside she's made of "cold steel only not so clean." She leaves, telling Trevor that she'll tell her father Trevor is with Powell. Trevor tells Powell that Kruger has become a good friend and that she's attracted to him, that Kruger has helped her correct a "psychological impediment." Then she tells him that Kruger has been blackmailing her for her indiscretions, threatening to tell her husband. She planned to give Kruger the jade but it was stolen before he could turn it over. She asks Powell to help her kill Kruger. She tells him to lure Kruger to the beach house by telling him he's got the jade. Powell plays along with the scheme. He visits Kruger but finds his place torn up and Kruger dead. Comments Powell: "He wasn't hurt much; he was just snapped, the way a pretty girl would snap a stalk of celery." He believes that it would have taken Mazurki's strength to have killed Kruger. Mazurki shows up and Powell tells him that he'll take him to Velma. The next night he tells Mazurki to wait until he sees a light in Mander's beach house before coming up. In the beach house he meets with Trevor who hands him the necklace to entice Kruger. Powell doesn't tell her that Kruger is dead and then he asks her where she got it. Trevor tells him that it was never stolen at all, that she only lied about that so she wouldn't have to turn it over to blackmailer Kruger. Powell tells her that he believes she wanted to have him killed after he began unearthing her past for Mazurki, that she planned on killing him after Howard called her to warn her. She begs him to help her face Kruger. Powell tells her that she was probably being blackmailed because Kruger knew she had committed a crime with Mazurki and threatened to bring in the law. She pulls a gun, one stolen from Powell while she kissed him. Mander then arrives and pretends to help his wife. Trevor holds the gun on Powell and he begins to talk, letting it slip that Kruger is already dead. Before she can kill Powell, Mander shoots Trevor. Shirley arrives and then Mazurki, looking for his Velma. He finds Trevor dead, looks at her, and says: "She's hardly changed, only more fancy, cute as lace pants." Mazurki goes for Mander when he realizes that the old man killed the woman he loved. Powell leaps forward just as Mander fires and is blinded by the gunflash. Mazurki, after taking three bullets, falls dead. Powell collapses unconscious. It's the present and Powell is again at police headquarters, finishing his story, explaining that he had his eyeballs scorched. Douglas releases him after telling him that Mander was also killed by Mazurki. A cop named Nulty (Phillips) escorts Powell outside and puts him into a cab, while Shirley, her presence unknown to Powell, smilingly steps along with him. The blinded Powell sits back in the cab and Shirley, not detective Nulty, slips in beside him. Powell, getting a whiff of Shirley's perfume, prattles on, talking, then says: "Nulty . . . I haven't kissed anybody in a long time. Would it be all right if I kissed you, Nulty?" Shirley and Powell embrace. MURDER, MY SWEET is, beyond doubt, one of the great quintessential *film noir* productions. It is utterly faithful to author Chandler's perspective of the hard-bolled Marlowe and his netherworld, filling the screen with creatures motivated by dark, sinister motives. No one, not even Powell as the pummeled Marlowe with his own strange code of ethics, is a person of clean lifestyles, even Shirley who is streaked with bitterness and resentment. At every turn there is an element of the illegal, the immoral—murder, blackmail, fraud, drugs, robbery, sadism, masochism, violence, sexual misconduct. Dmytryk's direction is superb, inventive, and swift through every scene, and Powell is the whole tough-as-nails show, delivering Chandler's best witty lines with cool deftness. Trevor is the perfect rich lady tramp and Kruger is his usual calculating self. Mazurki is also the perfect goon as Moose Malloy. Shirley, Mander, and Walton do creditable jobs in their roles. All the technical ends come together tightly. This was the landmark film in the careers of both director Dmytryk and leading man Powell, vaulting both into stellar status in their respective professions. Dmytryk who had been helming a series of B-programmers since 1935, came into his own here and would go on to establish himself as an across-the-board superior director and one who did especially well in the netherworlds of *film noir*, following MURDER, MY SWEET with such crime classics as CORNERED (1945) and CROSSFIRE (1947). Producer Scott brought the MURDER, MY SWEET script to Dmytryk and, even though RKO had owned the property for some time and had used elements of the story in THE FALCON TAKES OVER (1942), the director decided to make something important. Charles Koerner, then RKO chief, allowed Dmytryk a considerable budget of $400,000. Koerner asked Dmytryk if he could think of using Powell in the role of Philip Marlowe. Said Dmytryk later: "The idea of the man who had sung 'Tiptoe Through the Tulips' playing a tough private eye was beyond our imaginations." Powell, Koerner explained, had appeared in dozens of musicals and his career as a crooner was in tatters. He was a middle-aged man typecast in the role of singing juvenile. In the 1930s Powell's star was high as a singing Warner Bros. talent in a string of successful musicals. He attempted to break out of the mold and had some success in Preston Sturges' CHRISTMAS IN JULY (1940), but had gone back to musicals in 1942 when signing on with Paramount to appear in such routine songfests as HAPPY GO LUCKY, RIDING HIGH, STAR SPANGLED RHYTHM, and TRUE TO LIFE. When Paramount decided to produce James M. Cain's hard-boiled story of marital deceit and murder, DOUBLE INDEMNITY (1944 screenplay by Chandler), Powell went to Paramount executives and begged for the role of the crafty insurance man but was turned down, with Fred MacMurray, an equally unlikely choice, having been typecast as a light comedian, getting the role. Powell longed to turn his image around from lightweight singer to two-fisted man of the world (which is what he really was in real life). He appeared in Rene Clair's comedy, IT HAPPENED TOMORROW (1944), but he kept missing out on the roles he really wanted. Koerner, not unmindful of the transition MacMurray had made from comedian to crime-glutted conspirator in DOUBLE INDEMNITY, thought Powell could do the same thing with MURDER, MY SWEET, and daringly proposed him for the role. The studio chief had ulterior motives. He wanted to star Powell in a string of RKO musicals but the actor would not sign a multi-film contract unless given the Marlowe part first. Dmytryk agreed to take on the singer and Powell was signed. Powell proved cooperative and eager to learn the role that would create his new image. He never complained, even when Dmytryk asked that he perform in unorthodox ways, pointing out that Mazurki, as Moose Malloy, was supposed to tower over him and that there was only two-and-a-half inches difference in their heights (Powell standing 6 feet 2 inches and Mazurki 6 foot 4 and a half). When the pair walked along the street, Powell walked in the gutter; when they faced each other during interior shots Powell was in his stocking feet and Mazurki stood on a box. Dmytryk's technical genius shows throughout the film, which is loaded with innovative visual effects. At the beginning, when Powell is in his office at night, with the only light coming from a neon light flashing on and off in the street, briefly illuminating the interior of the office, Powell looks out the window and sees, nervously, the reflection of Mazurki looming behind him. At first he only catches a glimpse of this monster and is unsure of his presence, but when the outside light again goes on he confirms that, indeed, he has an ugly, lumbering giant in the room with him. Dmytryk could not create enough of a menace by reflecting Mazurki in the window glass since he was too far from the camera, the closeup being on Powell. So Dmytryk removed the window glass and placed an 8 foot by 8 foot plate glass between the camera and the desk where Powell sits, placing Mazurki behind this on the camera side so that when the light from the street did flash his image, the reflection was shown in the plate glass close to the camera and the reflection showed Mazurki as immense and therefore much more menacing. Dmytryk would use the plate glass again at the end of the film where Powell dives for Mander's gun. To avoid really burning his eyes, since he appears to dive through the path of the gun, he is actually on the other side of the glass from Mander and dives toward it and when Mander's gun goes off, a mirror image is shown on camera which depicts Powell diving into the line of fire when he was several feet from the gun flash. So that this scene corresponded to earlier ones where Mander is holding the gun in his right hand, he held the gun in his left hand for the plate glass shot which reversed everything in a mirror image. To emphasize Powell's drugged state in the phony sanitarium, Dmytryk created a montage of looming faces, spiraling odd-shaped objects through which Powell falls. He increased the speed of the fall by using the traditional falling shot and reshooting the scene with a camera that moves away at an ever-increasing speed, thus accelerating the speed of Powell's fall (a technique used by Alfred Hitchcok in SABOTEUR, 1942, to show Norman Lloyd's spectacular fall from the arm of the Statue of Liberty). Also, to further emphasize Mazurki as a menace, Dmytryk, like Franz Murnau in SUNRISE and Orson Welles in THE MAGNIFICENT AMBERSONS, had slanted ceilings built so that, as Mazurki moved from the high side of the set to the low side, he became in the camera's eyes a great deal larger. This film was originally called FAREWELL, MY LOVELY, after the original Chandler book title, but when the film was released in New England and Minneapolis, hardly a soul came to the theater. RKO soon learned that the public thought the film, by virtue of its "soft" title, was another musical starring the 40-year-old Powell, and refused to attend; they had had enough of "Tiptoe Through the Tulips." The studio immediately changed the name to MURDER, MY SWEET and the public flocked to see Powell with his new image of glib tough guy. For many he was the consummate Philip Marlowe, quick-witted, sour on the world, wary of women but soft on females who dared to scrape the bark from his hide, and this could be done with one sweep of long fingernails. Powell was so effective in conveying the hardboiled image that RKO scrapped its plans to star him in a series of musicals and put him into such *film noir* pictures as CORNERED, 1945, and, for Columbia, he would do JOHNNY O'CLOCK, 1947, and TO THE ENDS OF THE EARTH. This film was Chandler's favorite version of FAREWELL, MY LOVELY and he wrote screenwriter Paxton a note of thanks for keeping his story intact and employing much of his smart talk. Though he received no money for this production, the rights having earlier been purchased by RKO, Chandler, in 1948, was proud that the film had a large budget and returned a great profit to RKO, writing to a friend (as quoted in *Raymond Chandler Speaking* by Dorothy Gardiner and Kathrine Sorley Walker): "THE MALTESE FALCON did not start the high budget mystery picture trend, although it ought to have. DOUBLE INDEMNITY and MURDER, MY SWEET did, and I was associated with both of them. The result is that everybody who used to be accused of writing like Hammett may now be accused of trying to write like Chandler." The remake of this film in 1975, which used Chandler's original book title, FAREWELL, MY LOVELY, and starred Robert Mitchum, came nowhere near the gritty and powerful original. Mitchum, though he projected a world-weary Marlowe in a by-then period film, sounds like he's reading his lines off cue cards held by skeletons and looks like a trenchcoat-wearing stand-in for the Robert Mitchum of 1947.

p, Adrian Scott; d, Edward Dmytryk; w, John Paxton (based on the novel *Farewell, My Lovely* by Raymond Chandler); ph, Harry J. Wild; m, Roy Webb; ed, Joseph Noreiga; md, Constantin Bakaleinikoff; art d, Albert S. D'Agostino, Carroll Clark; set d, Darrell Silvera, Michael Ohrenbach; cos, Edward Stevenson; spec eff, Vernon L. Walker.

Crime Drama **Cas.** **(PR:C-O MPAA:NR)**

MURDER OF DR. HARRIGAN, THE** (1936) 66m FN-WB bw

Kay Linaker *(Sally Keating)*, Ricardo Cortez *(Dr. George Lambert)*, Mary Astor *(Lillian Ash)*, John Eldredge *(Dr. Harrigan)*, Joseph Crehan *(Lt. Lamb)*, Frank Reicher *(Dr. Coate)*, Anita Kerry *(Agnes)*, Phillip Reed *(Simon)*, Robert Strange *(Peter Melady)*, Mary Treen *(Margaret Brody)*, Gordon Elliott *(Ladd)*, Don Barclay *(Jackson)*, Johnny Arthur *(Wentworth)*, Joan Blair *(Ina)*.

Routine murder-in-a-hospital story features Cortez as a doctor investigating the murder of a fellow medic known to use an experimental ether substitute. Doctors, nurses and orderlies are suspect, and the recipe also calls for a bit of blackmail and romance. An orderly is proved guilty at the end. The roles are well played (watch for an early appearance by Astor) but the formula story line is too straightforward to be of much interest.

p, Bryan Foy; d, Frank McDonald; w, Peter Milne, Sy Bartlett, Charles Belden (based on a story by Mignon G. Eberhart); ph, Arthur Todd; ed, William Clemens; md, Leo F. Forbstein; art d, Robert M. Haas.

Mystery **(PR:O MPAA:NR)**

MURDER ON A BRIDLE PATH** (1936) 63m RKO bw

James Gleason *(Inspector Piper)*, Helen Broderick *(Hildegarde Withers)*, Louise Latimer *(Barbara Foley)*, Owen Davis, Jr. *(Eddie Fry)*, John Arledge *(Joey)*, John Carroll *(Latigo Wells)*, Leslie Fenton *(Don Gregg)*, Christian Rub *(Thomas)*, Sheila Terry *(Violet)*, Willie Best [Sleep 'n' Eat] *(High Pockets)*, John Miltern *(Pat Gregg)*, Harry Jans *(Addie)*, James Donlan *(Kane)*, Gustav Von Seyffertitz *(Dr. Bloom)*, Frank Reicher *(Dr. Peters)*, Spencer Charters *(Mahoney)*.

In spite of a weak script, this Gleason-Broderick comedy/mystery has its moments. A wealthy society widow is found slain on Central Park's bridle path, and culprits abound. Gleason is the professional investigator and Broderick the amateur know-it-all who trail the killer. Routine motives including past affairs, unpaid alimony and a bit of forgery are all in their respective slots. The culprit is finally revealed and, wouldn't you know it, the butler did it! Gleason and Broderick, as the sleuthing comedy team, do an acceptable job. Broderick, who replaced Edna May Oliver as Hildegarde Withers, is a fine character actress who holds her own against the more stolid Gleason. But while the film gets off to a promising start, it quickly bogs down into typical formula stuff that moves too slowly for its own good. The fault clearly lies with the script (by four writers) and direction (two directors). This film is a good example of too many hands spoiling some otherwise fine efforts by the acting ensemble.

p, William Sistrom; d, William Hamilton, Edward Killy; w, Dorothy Yost, Thomas Lennon, Edmund North, James Gow (based on the novel by Stuart Palmer); ph, Nick Musuraca; ed, Jack Hively; md, Roy Webb.

Mystery/Comedy **(PR:O MPAA:NR)**

MURDER ON A HONEYMOON*** (1935) 74m RKO bw

Edna May Oliver *(Hildegarde Withers)*, James Gleason *(Oscar Piper)*, Lola Lane *(Phyllis La Font)*, Chick Chandler *(Pilot French)*, George Meeker *(Kelsey)*, Dorothy Libaire *(Kay Deving)*, Harry Ellerbee *(Marvin Deving)*, Spencer Charters *(Chief Britt)*, DeWitt Jennings *(Capt. Beegle)*, Leo G. Carroll *(Joseph B. Tate)*, Arthur Hoyt *(Dr. O'Rourke)*, Matt McHugh *(Pilot Madden)*, Sleep 'n' Eat [Willie Best] *(Porter)*, Morgan Wallace *(Arthur J. Mack)*, Brooks Benedict *(Forrest)*, Rollo Lloyd *(Hotel Clerk)*, Robert E. Homans, Irving Bacon.

Oliver (later replaced by Helen Broderick) plays amateur sleuth to Gleason's professional detective in this amusing mystery. She's a nosy school teacher who, while visiting Catalina, unwittingly becomes involved in a murder investigation. To Gleason's chagrin, she proves to be fairly competent. This was one of the best MURDER ON . . . films released by RKO in the 1930s, with some nice repartee between the two leads. Good use of location shooting lends the film an atmospheric quality, and the direction carries the story and suspense well. "Sleep 'n' Eat," who played a porter in this film, was also known as Willie Best. The witty screenplay was co-written by famed humorist Benchley.

p, Kenneth Macgowan; d, Lloyd Corrigan; w, Seton I. Miller, Robert Benchley (based on the novel *Puzzle of the Pepper Tree* by Stuart Palmer); ph, Nick Musuraca; ed, William Morgan; md, Albert Columbo; spec eff, Vernon Walker.

Mystery/Comedy **(PR:A MPAA:NR)**

MURDER ON APPROVAL*
(1956, Brit.) 70m Cipa/RKO bw (GB: BARBADOS QUEST)

Tom Conway *(Tom "Duke" Martin)*, Delphi Lawrence *(Jean Larsen)*, Brian Worth *(Geoffrey Blake)*, Michael Balfour *(Barney)*, Campbell Cotts *(Coburn, Stamp Dealer)*, John Horsley *(Inspector Taylor)*, Ronan O'Casey *(Stefan Gordoni, Engraver)*, Launce Maraschal *(Everleigh)*, Colin Tapley *(Lord Valchrist)*, Alan Gifford *(Henry Warburg)*, Grace Arnold *(Lady Hawksley)*, John Colicos *(1st Man)*, Mayura *(Yamina)*, John Watson *(Sgt. Grant)*, Reg Morris *(2nd Man)*, Marianne Stone *(Woman Cleaner)*, Derrick Whittingham *(Manager)*, Frank Pemberton *(Garage Attendant)*, Neil Wilson *(Fingerprinter)*, Olive Kirby *(Hawksley Maid)*, Rosamund Waring *(Receptionist)*, Margaret Rowe *(Air Stewardess)*, Maureen Connell *(Girl at Airport)*.

An inept mystery released in America through RKO features Conway as a British detective with skills similar to those of fictional countryman Sherlock Holmes. Brought in to confirm the authenticity of a rare stamp, he finds the sticky trail leads to murder. The direction is mediocre, and pacing is slow. The script contains weak dialog and an all-too-familiar unfolding plot. The ensemble does what it can with stereotyped characters. Conway played the super-sleuth once more in BREAKAWAY, a film never released in the U.S.

p, Robert S. Baker, Monty Berman; d, Bernard Knowles; w, Kenneth R. Hayles; ph, Berman; ed, Jack Slade; art d, Wilfred Arnold.

Mystery **(PR:C MPAA:NR)**

MURDER ON DIAMOND ROW**
(1937, Brit.) 77m LFP-Denham/UA bw (GB: THE SQUEAKER)

Edmund Lowe *(Inspector Barrabal)*, Sebastian Shaw *(Frank Sutton)*, Ann Todd *(Carol Stedman)*, Tamara Desni *(Tamara)*, Robert Newton *(Larry Graeme)*, Allan Jeayes *(Inspector Elford)*, Alastair Sim *(Joshua Collie, Reporter)*, Stewart Rome *(Superintendent Marshall)*, Mabel Terry-Lewis *(Mrs. Stedman)*, Gordon McLeod *(Mr. Field)*, Syd Crossley.

Lowe is a police inspector who has been discredited and, to redeem himself, goes undercover. Posing as an ex-convict, he captures Shaw, a killer who fences stolen goods. The main body of the story holds interest, but the film is hampered by an unnecessary romance between Newton and nightclub singer Desni, who sings the Kernell and Berkman penned tunes "He's Gone" and "I Can't Get Along Without You." Sims gives a commendable performance as a reporter. Todd, another superfluous character, provides a love interest for Lowe. This remake of a 1930 British film has its moments, but is bogged down by the unnecessary characterizations, some occasionally inept lensing and slowly-paced direction.

p, Alexander Korda; d, William K. Howard; w, Bryan Wallace, Edward O. Berkman (based on the novel *The Squeaker* by Edgar Wallace); ph, Georges Perinal; m, Miklos Rozsa; ed, Jack Dennis, Russell Lloyd; md, Muir Mathieson; prod d, Vincent Korda; m/l, William Kernell, Berkman.

Mystery **(PR:C MPAA:NR)**

MURDER ON MONDAY***
(1953, Brit.) 85m LFP/BL bw (GB: HOME AT SEVEN)

Ralph Richardson *(David Preston)*, Margaret Leighton *(Janet Preston)*, Jack Hawkins *(Dr. Sparling)*, Campbell Singer *(Inspector Hemingway)*, Frederick Piper *(Mr. Petherbridge)*, Diana Beaumont *(Ellen)*, Meriel Forbes *(Peggy Dobson)*, Michael Shepley *(Maj. Watson)*, Margaret Withers *(Mrs. Watson)*, Gerald Case *(Sgt. Evans)*.

Richardson made his directorial debut with this film, playing a bank clerk who suffers from amnesia for a day. Originally called HOME AT SEVEN in Britain because Richardson, for the first time in his life, does not return home at his normally prompt time of seven o'clock. He is horrified to discover that he can't remember the last 24 hours. His anxiety increases when he discovers that funds from his sports club have been stolen and the steward murdered. Afraid that he's somehow responsible, he gives the police a phony alibi for his time of the crime; but this backfires and he becomes a suspect. Convinced he is guilty, Richardson goes through severe mental anguish while trying to retrace his steps, until at last he proves his innocence. Taken from the British stage play, this movie relies heavily on suspense to carry the audience through, and is successful in this attempt. Richardson, with his usual subdued nature, gives just the right amount of emotional conviction necessary. This was the first and unfortunately last picture he directed, made with a low budget that proves that a good movie need not necessarily be expensive to work. The result is a fine feature for suspense fans.

p, Maurice Cowan; d, Ralph Richardson; w, Anatole de Grunwald (based on the play "Home at Seven" by R. C. Sherriff); ph, Jack Hildyard, Edward Scaife; m, Malcolm Arnold; ed, Bert Bates; prod d, Vincent Korda, Frederick Pusey; md, Muir Mathieson; cos, Ivy Baker.

Mystery/Suspense (PR:C MPAA:NR)

MURDER ON THE BLACKBOARD*** (1934) 71m RKO bw

Edna May Oliver (Hildegarde Withers), James Gleason (Inspector Piper), Bruce Cabot (Addison Stevens, Assistant Principal), Gertrude Michael (Miss Janey Davis), Regis Toomey (Smiley), Edgar Kennedy (Detective Donahue), Tully Marshall (MacFarland), Jackie Searl (Leland Jones), Fredrik Vogeding (Olaf, School Janitor), Barbara Fritchie (Louise Halloran), Gustav von Seyffertitz, Tom Herbert, Jed Prouty.

The second of RKO's MURDER ON . . . series features Oliver as the snoopy school teacher, who is a thorn in the side of Detective Gleason. Oliver has an ill-behaved student stay after school and discovers the corpse of the school's music teacher. But the body disappears and in comes the inspector, Kennedy, who appeared with almost every major comedian during the 1930s and 1940s, is a comedy cop assigned to the case as well. Eventually Oliver discovers that assistant principal Cabot is the killer through the clever device of deciphering seemingly meaningless music notes the late teacher scrawled on the blackboard before she died. Though the mystery is routine, the chemistry between Gleason and Oliver is what makes this film worth a look. They play well off of each other, with some clever dialog. Though this is a murder mystery, the laughs are natural and never uneasy. The good direction holds a nice balance between comedy and suspense.

p, Kenneth MacGowan; d, George Archainbaud; w, Willis Goldbeck (based on the story by Stuart Palmer); ph, Nick Musuraca; ed, Archie Marshek; md, Max Steiner.

Mystery/Comedy (PR:A MPAA:NR)

MURDER ON THE BRIDGE (SEE: END OF THE GAME, 1976)

MURDER ON THE CAMPUS***
(1934) 73m CHES/State Right bw (GB: ON THE STROKE OF NINE)

Shirley Grey (Lillian Voyne, Nightclub Singer), Charles Starrett (Bill Bartlett, Reporter), J. Farrell MacDonald (Capt. Ed Kyne), Ruth Hall (Ann Michaels), Edward Van Sloan (Professor Hawley, Chemist), Maurice Black (Blackie Atwater), Harry Bowen (Reporter), Dewey Robinson (Charlie Lorrimer), Jane Keckley (Hilda Lund), Harrison Greene (Brock).

Nice little mystery features Starrett as a reporter who is doing a piece on students who work their way through college. He meets Grey, a night club singer and student, one night and drives her back to campus. On the way, he accuses her of being in love with a star athlete whose job is to ring the chimes in the school's bell tower. After dropping her off, Starrett hears a gunshot coming from the tower. He becomes a suspect in the crime when police captain MacDonald finds him at the scene of the crime. He is not arrested, however; but Grey, also a suspect, is. Although a suspect in the murder, Starrett is placed on the story. After two more students are killed, he takes the bullets to Van Sloan, a respected professor and amateur sleuth. Van Sloan tells him that all three bullets came from the same gun. Story climaxes when Starrett figures out that the professor is responsible for the murders, confronts Van Sloan with the evidence, and the professor tries to kill him. Luckily the police have been secretly trailing Starrett and rush in to save him. Grey is released, and romance blossoms for her and Starrett. The plot of this tidy suspense mystery is developed neatly, with a believable solution to the murders. One curious development is that although a reporter, Starrett takes not one single note in the entire course of the picture, a technique reporters everywhere would probably find amazing. He later traded in his reporter's credentials and went on to make countless serial cowboy pictures.

p, George R. Batcheller; d, Richard Thorpe; w, Whitman Chambers, Andrew Moses (based on his novel The Campanile Murders); ph, M. A. Anderson; md, Abe Meyer; art d, Edward Jewell.

Mystery Cas. (PR:A MPAA:NR)

MURDER ON THE CAMPUS*½
(1963, Brit.) 61m Border/Colorama-Capitol bw (GB: OUT OF THE SHADOW)

Terence Longdon (Mark Kingston), Donald Gray (Inspector Wills), Diane Clare (Mary Johnson), Robertson Hare (Ronald Fortescue), Dermot Walsh (Research Prof. Taylor), Felicity Young (Waitress), Douglas Muir (Killer).

Hard-nosed reporter Kingston uncovers a gang of jewel thieves as those responsible for a series of murders at Cambridge. He started this investigation when trying to uncover the reason for his brother's death, not believing that he killed himself, as the records show. Some level of interest is maintained in the way that Kingston must

deal with uncooperative students, but once the plot starts up, picture becomes quite predictable.

p, Negus Fancey, Michael Winner; d&w, Winner; ph, Richard Bayley; m, Jackie Browne, Cy Payne; art d, Derek Barrington.

Mystery (PR:A MPAA:NR)

MURDER ON THE ORIENT EXPRESS***½ (1974, Brit.) 128m PAR c

Albert Finney (Hercule Poirot), Lauren Bacall (Mrs. Hubbard), Martin Balsam (Bianchi), Ingrid Bergman (Greta Ohlsson), Jacqueline Bisset (Countess Andrenyi), Jean-Pierre Cassel (Pierre Paul Michel), Sean Connery (Col. Arbuthnot), John Gielgud (Beddoes), Wendy Hiller (Princess Dragomiroff), Anthony Perkins (Hector McQueen), Vanessa Redgrave (Mary Debenham), Rachel Roberts (Hildegarde Schmidt), Richard Widmark (Ratchett), Michael York (Count Andrenyi), Colin Blakely (Hardman), George Coulouris (Dr. Constantine), Denis Quilley (Foscarelli), Vernon Dobtcheff (Concierge), Jeremy Lloyd (A.D.C.), John Moffatt (Chief Attendant), George Silver (Chef).

Elegant and stylish in the best Agatha Christie tradition, this film offers a host of stars who all contribute to a sparkling whodunit, but whose sheer numbers prevent any real character development other than that of detective Poirot. The Belgian sleuth is played by Finney with a great many quirks, oddball manners, and an accent that makes most of his lines mush. But the story line is fairly well established and discernible by the actors who contribute their pieces of the puzzle. It is 1934 and financier Widmark is traveling from Istanbul to Paris. He takes a stateroom on board the Orient Express. When he is later found dead, stabbed a dozen times, Finney is prevailed upon by Balsam, an executive of the railway, to solve the case. There is plenty of time since the train is stranded by a snowslide. Finney painstakingly interviews those in the same car, including Bergman, Connery, Perkins, Gielgud, Bisset, York, Hiller, Bacall, and Redgrave. Through an elaborate re-creation of the crime, Finney is able to determine exactly who the killer is at the surprise, sophisticated ending. Once the killing of Widmark has been managed, there's little action as Finney practices a game of wits with the culprit and/or culprits and Lumet's taut direction makes it fun to follow the detective as he puts the mystifying pieces together. Finney's histrionics are engrossing as are those of most of the cast, particularly that consummate actress Bergman, who won an Oscar as Supporting Actress, her third Academy Award. When Bergman stepped onto the set of the Christie-inspired film, she was dumfounded at the stellar talents surrounding her, later commenting: "I felt absolutely awed when we first gathered together for a cast and crew party. I hadn't felt this excited since my first days in Hollywood." Lumet, who had directed films of grim realism such as FAIL SAFE, 1964, THE PAWNBROKER, 1965, and SERPICO, 1973, wanted to provide pure escapist entertainment, and did. He later stated: "I want glamor, gaiety, and humor." He got it from everybody except Redgrave who gave him and viewers a poor imitation of Beulah Bondi with some Margaret Wycherly thrown in. For years author Christie refused to have this story filmed, but it was worth the wait as MURDER ON THE ORIENT EXPRESS is one of the best film versions of her terrific tales. The background upon which the tale is rooted, shown in sepia montage at the beginning of the film and later in color flashbacks as Finney reconstructs the facts, is almost wholly drawn from the Lindbergh kidnaping case. Sequel: DEATH ON THE NILE, 1978. Location shooting occurred in Turkey and France and in England at EMI-Elstree Studios.

p, John Brabourne, Richard Goodwin; d, Sidney Lumet; w, Paul Dehn (based on the novel by Agatha Christie); ph, Geoffrey Unsworth (Panavision, Technicolor); m, Richard Rodney Bennett; ed, Anne V. Coates; md, Marcus Dods; prod d, Tony Walton; art d, Jack Stephens; cos, Walton; montage, Richard Williams Studios.

Crime Drama Cas. (PR:C MPAA:PG)

MURDER ON THE ROOF** (1930) 60m COL bw

Dorothy Revier (Molly), Raymond Hatton (Drinkwater), Margaret Livingston (Marcia), David Newell (Ted Palmer), Paul Porcasi (Joe Carozzo), Virginia Brown Faire (Monica), William V. Mong (Anthony Sommers), Louis Natheaux (Victor), Fred Kelsey (Ryan), Richard Cramer (Joe Larkin), Pietro Sosso (Emile), Hazel Howell (Lucille), William Desmond.

Mong, a down and out attorney who had dealings with a diamond thief, is found guilty and jailed after the crook is found dead on the roof of Porcasi's night club. Revier is Mong's daughter who knows that despite his reputation, her father is innocent. She gets a job in the club as a singer and ends up becoming a celebrity in town. Eventually she proves that Porcasi is the real killer. In the end, Porcasi is killed and Hatton, who has played a drunk throughout the picture, reveals himself to be an undercover reporter investigating the case all along. The film, with a few minor exceptions, takes place on just two sets: the nightclub and Porcasi's penthouse suite. This was a reflection of the film's cheap production values, as well as the limited settings that numerous early talkies had to work with. Sound was still a new creature when this film was made and wiring entire studios for the new technique was an expensive venture, thus the two-set scene for MURDER ON THE ROOF. The acting and production values are okay. There is nothing special about this picture; just one of the many programmers put out to fill the double features of the day.

d, George B. Seitz; w, F. Hugh Herbert (based on a Liberty magazine story by Edward Doherty); ph, Joe Walker; ed, Robert Jahns.

Mystery (PR:A MPAA:NR)

MURDER ON THE RUNAWAY TRAIN
(SEE: MURDER IN THE PRIVATE CAR, 1934)

MURDER ON THE SECOND FLOOR* (1932, Brit.) 68m WB/FN-WB bw

John Longden (Hugh Bromilow), Pat Paterson (Sylvia Armitage), Sydney Fairbrother (Miss Snell), Ben Field (Mr. Armitage), Florence Desmond (Lucy),

Franklyn Bellamy *(Joseph Reynolds)*, John Turnbull *(Inspector)*, Amy Veness, Oswald Skilbeck.

Longden plays a struggling young writer whose imagination goes overboard in concocting a murder in his boarding house, with himself as the man who figures out the crime when all others are at a loss. Could have been an interesting idea, but not as it is revealed here.

p, Irving Asher; d, William McGann; w, Roland Pertwee, Challis Sanderson (based on the play by Frank Vosper).

Mystery   **(PR:A MPAA:NR)**

MURDER ON THE SET*

(1936, Brit.) 62m Twickenham/Globe Film bw (GB: DEATH ON THE SET)

Henry Kendall *(Cayley Morden/Charlie Marsh)*, Jeanne Stuart *(Lady Blanche)*, Eve Gray *(Laura Lane)*, Lewis Shaw *(Jimmy Frayle)*, Garry Marsh (Inspector Burford), Wally Patch *(Sgt. Crowther)*, Alfred Wellesley *(Studio Manager)*, Rita Helsham *(Constance Lyon)*, Ben Welden *(Freshman)*, Hal Walters *(Albert)*, Elizabeth Arkell *(Mrs. Hipkin)*, Robert Nainby *(Lord Umbridge)*.

Yankee gangster Kendall hides out in a British film studio posing as a director, whom he's a dead ringer for in looks. His double blackmails him, so Kendall establishes an alibi for his whereabouts one night and murders the director. Then he tries to blackmail Stuart, the actress with whom his alibi lies, but instead winds up strangling her. It takes the rest of this somewhat sloppily made picture for police inspector Marsh to figure it all out.

p, Julius Hagen; d, Leslie S. Hiscott; w, Michael Barringer (based on the novel by Victor MacClure); ph, Ernest Palmer, William Luff; ed, Ralph Kemlem.

Crime/Mystery   **(PR:A MPAA:NR)**

MURDER ON THE WATERFRONT zero

(1943) 49m WB bw

Warren Douglas *(Joe Davis)*, Joan Winfield *(Gloria)*, John Loder *(Lt. Comdr. Holbrook)*, Ruth Ford *(Lana Shane)*, Bill Crago *(Lt. Dawson)*, Bill Kennedy *(1st Officer Barnes)*, William B. Davidson *(Capt. David Towne)*, Don Costello *(Gordon Shane)*, James Flavin *(Comdr. George Kalin)*, Bill Edwards *(Guard)*, Ross Ford *(2nd Sentry)*, DeWolf [William] Hopper *(1st Sentry)*, John Maxwell *(Daniel Lewis)*, Philip Van Zandt *(Connors)*, Frank Mayo *(Petty Officer Thomas)*, Fred Kelsey *(Capt. Beal)*.

The inventor of a device to protect guns against high temperatures is mysteriously murdered. Unfortunately, there's no real motivation for the murder, nor the investigation. Eventually it's discovered that the culprit is a Nazi, but the situation is confusingly presented, with an unnecessary subplot involving entertainers and Nazi spies thrown in as well. This short film (a mere 49 minutes, which made it difficult to distribute) is a remake of the 1938 picture INVISIBLE MENACE.

p, William Jacobs; d, B. Reaves Eason; w, Robert E. Kent (based on the play "Without Warning" by Ralph Spencer Zink); ph, Harry Neumann; ed, James Gibbon; art d, Stanley Fleischer; cos, Leah Rhodes; ch, Matty King.

Wartime Mystery   **(PR:A MPAA:NR)**

MURDER ON THE YUKON**

(1940) 58m Criterion/MON bw

James Newill *(Renfrew)*, Polly Ann Young *(Jean)*, Dave O'Brien *(Kelly)*, Al St. John *(Bill)*, William Royle *(Weathers)*, Chief Thunder Cloud *(Monti)*, Karl Hackett *(Hawks)*, Snub Pollard *(Archie)*, Kenne Duncan *(Tom)*, Earl Douglas *(Steve)*, Budd Buster *(Jim)*, Jack Clifford.

An entry in the "Renfrew of the Royal Mounted" series finds our hero Newill, along with sidekick O'Brien, readying himself for a much needed vacation. Unfortunately, they have to put off their plans for awhile when the corpse of Buster with a bullet to his heart turns up in a canoe. The investigative trail leads the team to Royle, a crooked trading post operator. Young is the man's innocent partner. Plenty of action in this fairly routine serial entry, but the production was fairly rushed and shows it at times. Look for appearances by former Sennett clowns, St. John and Pollard.

p, Philip N. Krasne; d, Louis Gasnier; w, Milton Raison (based on "Renfrew Rides North" by Laurie York Erskine); ph, Elmer Dyer; m, Vick Knight, Johnny Lange, Lew Porter; ed, Guy V. Thayer, Jr.

Mystery   **(PR:A MPAA:NR)**

MURDER OVER NEW YORK** 1/2

(1940) 65m FOX bw

Sidney Toler *(Charlie Chan)*, Marjorie Weaver *(Patricia Shaw)*, Robert Lowery *(David Elliott)*, Ricardo Cortez *(George Kirby)*, Donald MacBride *(Inspector Vance)*, Melville Cooper *(Herbert Fenton)*, Joan Valerie *(June Preston)*, Kane Richmond *(Ralph Percy)*, Sen Yung *(Jimmy Chan)*, John Sutton *(Richard Jeffery)*, Leyland Hodgson *(Boggs)*, Clarence Muse *(Butler)*, Frederick Worlock *(Hugh Drake)*, Lal Chand Mehra *(Ramullah)*, Frank Coghlan, Jr. *(Gilroy)*.

An entry in the "Charlie Chan" mystery series (see Index) has the Oriental sleuth arriving in New York City to attend a police convention. On his arrival he is told about sabotage and murders against the airplane industry. Toler begins unraveling the mystery, with no thanks to his bumbling son, Yung. The junior sleuth is a humorous annoyance for his father, but eventually ends up helping to solve the crime. The culprit is revealed to be the leader of a spy ring, whom Toler exposes while all the culprits are airborne in a new bomber. There's plenty of pseudo-culprits along the way to keep the audience guessing and Worlock, as a British Intelligence man, gets killed in the proceedings. Standard production values and characterizations for the Chan series that fans undoubtedly will enjoy. This picture tied in with real-life sabotage activities of foreign agents during the 1940s. (See CHARLIE CHAN Series, Index.)

p, Sol M. Wurtzel; d, Harry Lachman; w, Lester Ziffren (based on a character

created by Earl Derr Biggers); ph, Virgil Miller; ed, Louis Loeffler; md, Emil Newman.

Mystery   **(PR:A MPAA:NR)**

MURDER REPORTED* 1/2

(1958, Brit.) 58m Fortress/COL bw

Paul Carpenter *(Jeff Holly, Reporter)*, Melissa Stribling *(Amanda North)*, John Laurie *(Mac North, Editor)*, Peter Swanwick *(Hatter)*, Patrick Holt *(Bill Stevens)*, Maurice Durant *(Carmady)*, Georgia Brown *(Myra)*, Yvonne Warren [Romain] *(Betty)*, Trevor Reid *(Inspector Palissy)*, Anne Blake *(Miss Jack)*, Edna Kove *(Mrs. Vince)*, Hal Osmonde *(Porter)*, David Coote *(Copy Boy)*, Gaylord Cavallaro *(Reporter)*, Robert Vossler *(Policeman)*, Joe Robinson *(Jim)*, Gladys Boot *(Dorothy)*, The Reg Wale Four, Gwen Solon, Reginald Hearne.

A murdered politician is found locked up in a trunk. Laurie is a newspaper editor who assigns ace reporter Carpenter to the story. There's just one little catch: Carpenter must take along his editor's daughter, Stribling. Of course Carpenter is displeased with this, but Stribling proves herself with some sharp reporting skills of her own. Naturally the pair comes to a mutual agreement and eventually a love relationship. The mystery is solved when the duo discovers that the dead man was disposed of by an opposing politician. Extremely formula, the film has a remarkably short running time considering the year of release. Characters and situations are all stereotypes, and while parts hold interest, this film is well below the standards of the formula B-newspaper flick.

p, Guido Coen; d, Charles Saunders; w, Doreen Montgomery (based on the novel *Murder for the Millions* by Robert Chapman); ph, Brendan Stafford; m, Reg Owen; ed, Jerry Levy; art d, Denyis Pavitt; m/l, Stanley Meyers.

Mystery   **(PR:O MPAA:NR)**

MURDER RING, THE

(SEE: ELLERY QUEEN AND THE MURDER RING, 1941)

MURDER SHE SAID** 1/2

(1961, Brit.) 87m MGM bw (AKA: MEET MISS MARPLE)

Margaret Rutherford *(Miss Jane Marple)*, Arthur Kennedy *(Dr. Quimper)*, Muriel Pavlow *(Emma Ackenthorpe)*, James Robertson Justice *(Ackenthorpe)*, Thorley Walters *(Cedric Ackenthorpe)*, Charles Tingwell *(Inspector Craddock)*, Conrad Phillips *(Harold)*, Ronald Howard *(Brian Eastley)*, Joan Hickson *(Mrs. Kidder)*, Stringer Davis *(Mr. Stringer)*, Ronnie Raymond *(Alexander Eastley)*, Gerald Cross *(Albert)*, Michael Golden *(Hillman)*, Barbara Hicks *(Mrs. Stainton)*, Gordon Harris *(Bacon)*, Peter Butterworth *(Conductor)*, Richard Briers *("Mrs. Binster")*, Lucy Griffiths *(Lucy)*.

The first, but not the best, of the "Miss Marple" stories that starred Margaret Rutherford was a bit talky and didn't have as much humor in it as the succeeding films. Nevertheless, it served as an excellent pilot for the remaining movies and Rutherford was just settling into the role as the redoubtable, jowled detective. Rutherford is the female version of Christie's Hercule Poirot, in that she always gets her man. She's on a train, reading a mystery novel, looks out the window and sees the shade of a train compartment fly up. Then she is shocked as the woman in the next train is being strangled. When she informs the railway cops and Tingwell, they think she's been imagining things, as there has been no report of a murder similar to her description. They believe it's the ravings of an old biddy and send her on her way. Annoyed at the short shrift, she thinks that the corpus delicti must have been hidden somewhere along the railroad tracks near the estate owned by Robertson-Justice, a wealthy member of the landed gentry. To keep the case alive, she goes to the mansion and offers to work as a maid in order to get inside the place. Her suspicions are confirmed when she finds the body secreted in a small building nearby. The person is believed to have been a French girl who was once married to a member of the family who had died years before in the war. Other children in the family are suspected, as they will all share in the estate and one wonders if they conspired to get rid of the woman who might have had a piece of the action. When two of the sons are killed, Rutherford gets to the bottom of things. The real killer is the family medico, Kennedy, who had throttled his wife on the train, then sought to make it look as though it was the aforementioned French woman. His plan was to kill everyone in the family except for the unmarried daughter, Pavlow, whom he would marry for all her money. With everyone else out of the way, all the money would go to her (and him) and it is presumed that he would eventually offer her the same fate as he did her brothers. Rutherford is delightful and her days as a comedienne stood her in good stead. Kennedy is a proper villain and Robertson-Justice, who did so well in the "Doctor In Love" series, is also just perfect as the father of the house. The success of this caused the sequels to be made, and it was the second one, MURDER AT THE GALLOP, that was the best. Scotland-born Robertson-Justice made his debut in 1944 at the age of 39 in FIDDLERS THREE and continued until his death in 1975. (See MISS MARPLE Series, Index)

p, George N. Brown; d, George Pollock; w, David Pursall, Jack Seddon, David Osborn (based on the novel *4:50 From Paddington* by Agatha Christie); ph, Geoffrey Faithfull; m, Ron Goodwin; ed, Ernest Walter; md, Goodwin; art d, Harry White; cos, Felix Evans; spec eff, Tom Howard; makeup, Eddie Knight.

Comedy/Mystery   **(PR:A MPAA:NR)**

MURDER SOCIETY, THE

(SEE: MURDER CLINIC, THE, 1969, Fr./Ital.)

MURDER TOMORROW* 1/2

(1938, Brit.) 69m Crusade/PAR bw

Gwenllian Gill *(Jean Andrews)*, Jack Livesey *(Peter Wilton)*, Molly Hamley-Clifford *(Miss Fitch)*, Rani Waller *(Miss Canning)*, Francis Roberts *(Sgt. Enfield)*, Raymond Lovell *(Inspector Travers)*, Jonathan Field *(PC Sanders)*, Charles Lincoln, Dempsey Stuart, Billy Bray.

Gill and Livesy are the lovers who try to hide the death of Gill's old husband, he having died accidentally during a heated argument with Gill. The two are kept on edge, almost finding themselves convicted of murder, until fate takes over and clears their path to a happy romance. Weak script hampers the efforts of the actors, but the picture is fairly good compared to the majority of British thrillers from this period.

p, Victor M. Greene; d&w, Donovan Pedelty (based on the play by Frank Harvey); ph, Ernest Palmer.

Crime/Drama   **(PR:A   MPAA:NR)**

MURDER WILL OUT*   (1930) 69m FN-WB bw

Lila Lee *(Jeanne Baldwin)*, Jack Mulhall *(Leonard Staunton)*, Noah Beery, Sr. *(Lt. Condon)*, Malcolm McGregor *(Jack Baldwin)*, Alec B. Francis *(Senator Baldwin)*, Tully Marshall *(Dr. Mansfield)*, Claude Allister *(Alan Fitzhugh)*, Hedda Hopper *(Aunt Pat)*.

Three blackmailers are out to ruin businessman Mulhall, collecting hush money from him for some underhanded dealings. When three murders occur aboard a New York Harbor docked submarine, the culprits are believed to be Chinese. Beery is the detective out to solve the crime and uncover the blackmailers, and Lee plays his love interest. In the end, when the blackmailers are unmasked, they turn out not to be Chinese at all. This film was made during a time when stereotypes were encouraged in films, and so did nothing to give the Chinese community a good reputation. Even at the end when the crooks turn out not to be Chinese, the feeling still prevails that as a people, they are sneaky and untrustworthy. Watch for an appearance by Hopper in her days before she became the notorious Hollywood gossip queen.

d, Clarence Badger; w, J. Grubb Alexander (based on a story by Murray Leinster, Will Jenkins); ph, John Seitz.

Mystery   **(PR:A   MPAA:NR)**

MURDER WILL OUT*   (1939, Brit.) 65m FN/WB bw

John Loder *(Dr. Paul Raymond)*, Jane Baxter *(Pamela Raymond)*, Jack Hawkins *(Stamp)*, Hartley Power *(Campbell)*, Peter Croft *(Nigel)*, Frederick Burtwell *(Morgan)*, Billy [William] Hartnell *(Dick)*, Ian Maclean *(Inspector)*, Richard George, Aubrey Mallalieu, Peter Miles, Roddy McDowall.

Unbelievably plotted drama has Loder and Baxter immersed in intrigue after receiving costly jade. Looking for assistance in averting any physical harm, all their leads disappear, including the man who gave them the jade in the first place. As it turns out, the three people they thought they could trust, and who have been disappearing, are actually the culprits responsible for the pair's sticky situation. Could have been a good film had more effort been placed in developing the plot, as is, it's almost impossible to figure out what is going on.

p, Sam Sax; d, Roy William Neill; w, Neill, Austin Melford, Brock Williams, Derek Twist; ph, Basil Emmott; cos, Edward Stevenson.

Mystery   **(PR:A   MPAA:NR)**

MURDER WILL OUT**   (1953, Brit.) 83m Tempean-Eros/Kramer-Hyams bw (GB: THE VOICE OF MERRILL)

Valerie Hobson *(Alycia Roach)*, Edward Underdown *(Hugh Allen)*, James Robertson Justice *(Jonathan Roach)*, Henry Kendall *(Ronald Parker)*, Garry Marsh *(Inspector Thornton)*, Daniel Wherry *(Pierce)*, Sam Kydd *(Sgt. Baker)*, Ian Fleming *(Dr. Forrest)*, Daphne Newton *(Miss Quinn)*, Johnnie Schofield *(Night Porter)*.

A murder of a blackmailer brings forth two main suspects: Justice, a renowned literary man with a mean disposition and an unpleasant personality as well as his unhappy wife, Hobson, who has taken an unsuccessful mystery writer, Underdown, as her lover. Underdown tells Hobson that he will confess to the murder and when she tries to stop him, she is hit by a truck and killed. Underdown is cleared by Marsh as the inspector brought in to investigate. This film has its moments, but they are few and far between in this overall confusing mess. The film is too long and overwritten, and the acting is either very good (Justice), or very bad (Hobson, Underwood, and Marsh). Direction by Gilling doesn't do much to unravel the complicated script or maintain suspense, but the photography by Berman is better than the film requires.

p, Robert S. Baker, Monty Berman; d&w, John Gilling (based on a story by Gerald Landeau, Terence Austin); ph, Berman; m, Frank Cordell.

Mystery   **(PR:A   MPAA:NR)**

MURDER WITH PICTURES**   (1936) 69m PAR bw

Lew Ayres *(Kent Murdock)*, Gail Patrick *(Meg Archer)*, Joyce Compton *(Hester Boone)*, Paul Kelly *(I. B. McGoogin)*, Onslow Stevens *(Nate Girard)*, Ernest Cossart *(Stanley Redfield)*, Anthony Nace *(Sam Cusick)*, Benny Baker *(Phil Doane)*, Joseph Sawyer *(Inspector Bacon)*, Frank Sheridan *(Police Chief)*, Irving Bacon *(Keogh)*, Purnell Pratt *(Eastern Editor)*, Christian Rub *(Olaf)*, Don Rowan *(Siki)*, Eddie Dunn *(Bailiff)*, Howard C. Hickman *(Judge)*, Mike Pat Donovan *(Foreman)*, DeWolf [William] Hopper *(Photographer)*, Earl M. Pingree *(Taxi Driver)*, Lee Shumway *(Cop)*, Rex Moore *(Newsboy)*, Davison Clark *(Overholt)*, Frank Marlowe *(Pipe Smoker)*, Art Rowland *(Assistant Editor)*, George Ovey *(Trunk Man)*, Harry C. Bradley *(Gas Station Attendant)*, Milburn Stone *(Operator)*, Pat West, Phil Tead, Robert Burkhardt, Edmund Burns, Paddy O'Flynn, Jerry Fletcher, Jack Chapin, Nick Lukats, Martin Lamont, Allen Saunders, Frank Losee, Jr., Paul Barrett *(Reporters)*, Robert Perry, Lee Phelps, Jack Mulhall, Harry Jordan, Harry Wallace *(Girard Henchmen)*, Margaret Harrison, Beatrice Coleman, Dorothy Stevens, Dorothy Thompson, Kay Gordon, Larry Steers, William Norton Bailey, Kai Schmidt, Patsy Bellamy, Jack Clark *(Guests)*.

Mobsters place one of their own as an undercover cameraman on a big city

newspaper. The pseudo-photo journalist (Nace) is equipped with a dummy camera that contains a gun with a silencer. Ayres is the go-getter youngster, investigating a suicide and double murder that has landed Patrick, his love interest, in jail. Though the dialog is crisp and natural, the script ultimately drags with its poorly constructed plot and a lack of emphasis when needed. The actors manage to get through the film fine though, with believable performances that almost cover the highly significant holes in the plot. MURDER WITH PICTURES is representative of what was both good and bad with studio crime programmers of the 1930s and 1940s.

p, A. M. Botsford; d, Charles Barton; w, John C. Moffitt, Sidney Salkow (based on a story by George Harmon Coxe); ph, Ted Tetzlaff; art d, Hans Dreier, John Goodman; cos, Edith Head.

Crime   **(PR:A   MPAA:NR)**

MURDER WITHOUT CRIME*   (1951, Brit.) 80m ABF/Stratford bw

Dennis Price *(Matthew, Stephen's Landlord)*, Derek Farr *(Stephen, Author)*, Patricia Plunkett *(Jan, His Wife)*, Joan Dowling *(Grena, Nightclub Hostess)*.

Farr and Plunkett are husband and wife. After a bitter argument, she walks out on him. Farr goes off to drown his sorrows at a local club and ends up returning home with the club's hostess, Dowling. They, too, fight and after she is knocked out, Farr believes he's killed her. Downstairs landlord Price sees a chance to blackmail Farr. Matters are further complicated when Plunkett telephones to announce she is coming home. Price ends up drinking a poisoned concoction that Farr had intended to take himself, in order to escape his contorted troubles. The film was an adaption of a play written by author-director Lee-Thompson. But MURDER WITHOUT CRIME suffers from a stagey presentation that never lets the celluloid medium take over. There is no attempt at drawing out suspense, instead presenting us with a visually simplistic recording of the play. The dialog doesn't work as well on screen, often drawing unintentional laughs. Despite the film's overriding weakness, it was an enormous hit in London's West End.

p, Victor Skutezky; d&w, J. Lee-Thompson (based on the play "Double Error" by Lee-Thompson); ph, Bill McLeod; m, Phillip Green; ed, E. B. Jarvis; md, Louis Levy; art d, Don Ashton.

Crime   **(PR:A   MPAA:NR)**

MURDER WITHOUT TEARS*   (1953) 64m AA bw

Craig Stevens *(Steve O'Malley)*, Joyce Holden *(Joyce Fitzgerald)*, Richard Benedict *(Candy Markwell)*, Eddie Norris *(Warren Richards)*, Clair Regis *(Lilly Richards)*, Tom Hubbard *(Pete Morgan)*, Murray Alper *(Bartender)*, Bob Carson *(District Attorney)*, Paul Murray *(Powers)*, Edith Angold *(Miss Watkins)*, Leonard Penn *(Parker)*, Hal Gerard *(Dr. Polito)*, Burt Wenland *(Taxi Driver)*, Fred Kelsey *(Court Attendant)*, Gregg Sanders *(Baliff)*, Charles Victor, Jack George.

Confusing and poorly written crime picture finds Norris arranging the murder of his wife, Regis, so that it looks like he did the killing during an alcoholic blackout. Bank clerk Holden provides the alibi and he gets off. However, policeman Stevens is suspicious and decides to follow Norris. He finds that Benedict was hired by Norris as the hitman. Stevens arranges things so that the two conspirators get into a fight, during which Benedict kills Norris. The hitman is then killed himself in a tangle with Stevens, who ends up in a romance with Holden. Overwritten with far too much dialog, this film presents a confusing and unclear "double jeopardy" angle, especially since the trial of Norris never reached a conclusion. Audiences, however, can conclude that this picture is poorly made and its solutions to the problems it presents, superficial.

p, William F. Broidy; d, William Beaudine, Sr.; w, Jo Pagano, Bill Raynor (based on the story "Double Jeopardy" by Pagano); ph, Virgil Miller; m, Edward J. Kay; ed, Ace Herman; art d, David Milton.

Crime   **(PR:A   MPAA:NR)**

MURDERER, THE   (SEE: ENOUGH ROPE, 1966, Fr./Ital./Ger.)

MURDERER AMONG US   (SEE: M, 1933, Ger.)

MURDERER DMITRI KARAMAZOV, THE
                                     (SEE: KARAMAZOV, 1931, Ger.)

MURDERER LIVES AT NUMBER 21, THE***
                        (1947, Fr.) 83m Liote/Mage Films bw (L'ASSASSIN HABITE AU 21)

Pierre Fresnay *(Wens)*, Suzy Delair *(Mila Malou)*, Jean Tissier *(Lalah-Poor)*, Pierre Larquey *(Colin)*, Odette Talazac *(Mme. Point)*, Noel Roquevert *(Dr. Linz)*, Maximillienne *(Melle Cuq)*, Jean Despeaux *(Kid Robert)*, Huguette Vivier *(Vania)*.

A killer is running amuck and Fresnay is the detective out to stop the crimes. The killer's trademark is to leave a calling card on each victim, enabling Fresnay to trace the murderer to a boarding house. He goes undercover as a minister in order to get closer to the residents, a collection of seedy characters, any of whom could easily be the killer. An arrest is made but the killings continue amid similar patterns recurring in each crime. Fresnay finally figures out that the killer is really a team of three men out on a homicidal lark. Some pretty funny situations and a nice sense of suspense are maintained throughout the film. Though Fresnay underplays a bit more than necessary, he's compensated by a lively supporting cast. Like so many foreign films, the American version was somewhat dampened by a semi-censored translation within the sub-titles. (In French, English subtitles)

d, Henri-Georges Clouzot; w, Clouzot, S. A. Steeman (based on the novel by Steeman); ph, Armand Thirard; m, Maurice Yvain; art d, Andre Andreieu; English titles, George Slocombe.

Mystery/Comedy   **(PR:A   MPAA:NR)**

MURDERERS AMONG US***

(1948, Ger.) 80m Defa/Artkino bw (DIE MOERDER SIND UNTER UNS; AKA: THE MURDERERS ARE AMONGST US)

Hildegard Knef [Neff] *(Susanna Wallner)*, Ernst Borchert *(Dr. Hans Mertens)*, Arno Paulsen *(Capt. Bruckner)*, Erna Sellner *(Frau Bruckner)*, Robert Forsch *(Herr Mondschein)*, Albert Johann *(Herr Timm)*.

This was one of the first films released from post-war Germany that dealt with the questions of responsibility and psychological guilt as a result of the Nazi atrocities. Borchert is a doctor driven to drink by the thought of his role in the concentration camps. He had witnessed several mass executions by his captain (Paulsen) while stationed in Poland. Paulsen is now retired, living a contented life as a family man. But Borchert believes the man must be punished for his crimes and attempts to have the man killed. Knef, Borchert's girlfriend, convinces him that the only way to achieve justice is through a proper trial and Paulsen is at last turned over to the authorities investigating Nazi crimes. The film is important for its subject matter and release date. The German people were still in the early recovery stages from the period of Hitler's reich and the issues of guilt were especially sensitive. MURDERERS AMONG US does not quite achieve everything it sets out to do, with too slow a pace and an over-emphasis on the romance between Borchert and Knef. On the other hand it raises some interesting questions, deliberately unanswered within the film, as well as employing an interesting use of technique. The final moments with Paulsen shouting "I am not guilty! I am not guilty!" imposed over a kaleidoscopic montage of war atrocities has a particularly haunting and unsettling feeling. The film was shot in the Russian sector of post-war Germany, just as the Cold War was beginning to heat up. (In German, English subtitles)

d&w, Wolfgang Staudtel; ph, Friedl Behn-Grund, Eugen Klagemann; m, Ernest Roters.

Drama **(PR:O MPAA:NR)**

MURDERERS ARE AMONGST US

(SEE: MURDERERS AMONG US, 1948, Ger.)

MURDERERS' ROW zero (1966) 108m COL c

Dean Martin *(Matt Helm)*, Ann-Margret *(Suzie Solaris)*, Karl Malden *(Julian Wall)*, Camilla Sparv *(Coco Duquette)*, James Gregory *(MacDonald)*, Beverly Adams *(Lovey Kravezit)*, Richard Eastham *(Dr. Norman Solaris)*, Tom Reese *(Ironhead)*, Duke Howard *(Billy Orcutt)*, Jacqueline Fontaine *(Singer at Wake)*, Ted Hartley *(Guard)*, Marcel Hillaire *(Capt. Devereaux)*, Corinne Cole *(Miss January)*, Robert Terry *(Dr. Rogas)*, Dino, Desi & Billy *(Themselves)*, Mary Jane Mangler, Amedee Chabot, Luci Ann Cook, Marilyn Tindall, Dee Duffy, Jan Watson, Dale Brown, Mary Hughes, Lynn Hartoch, Rena Horten, Barbara Burgess *(The Slaygirls)*.

One of Martin's more successful projects was the "Matt Helm" series, a sort of poor man's James Bond that at the very least kept Martin employed. It certainly didn't give him much to boast about, as MURDERER'S ROW proves. The plot involves Martin's adventures as he goes about rescuing Eastham, inventor of an ultra destructive "Helio Beam" capable of destroying Washington, D.C., who has been kidnapped by super bad guy Malden. Malden thinks he has destroyed every last agent of ICE (Intelligence and Counter-Espionage), one of those silly anagram spy units that exists wholly for the purpose of spy movies. Little does Malden realize that Martin lives and is actually posing as a hit man for Malden's organization. Margret is Eastham's daughter, constantly garbed in go-go outfits some studio executive must have mistaken as "with it and hip." Martin makes the obvious sexual wisecracks about her, but helps Margret from being killed by one of Malden's men. The film rambles on from adventure to adventure, culminating in a pseudo-exciting climax where Martin prevents Malden from destroying Washington D.C. with the Helio Beam. Dumb and overblown without a single redeeming quality, unless you count Martin's crooning "I'm Not the Marrying Kind" by Schifrin and Greenfield. There's also an appearance by Martin's son, Dino, appearing with his then semi-popular combo, "Dino, Desi, and Billy." Three other "Matt Helm" films were made: the original, THE SILENCERS (1965), and this movie's sequels, THE AMBUSHERS (1967) and THE WRECKING CREW (1968). (See MATT HELM series, Index)

p, Irving Allen; d, Henry Levin; w, Herbert Baker (based on the novel *Murderers' Row* by Donald Hamilton); ph, Sam Leavitt (Technicolor); m, Lalo Schifrin; ed, Walter Thompson; prod d, Ivan Wolkman; art d, Joe Wright; set d, George R. Nelson; cos, Moss Mabry; spec eff, Danny Lee, Howard Jensen; ch, Miriam Nelson; m/l, "If You're Thinking What I'm Thinking" (sung by Dean Martin) Tommy Boyce, Bobby Hart, "I'm Not the Marrying Kind" (sung by Dean Martin) Schifrin, Howard Greenfield; makeup, Joseph DiBella, Loren Cosand.

Thriller **Cas.** **(PR:C MPAA:NR)**

MURDERS IN THE RUE MORGUE 1/2** (1932) 75m UNIV bw

Bela Lugosi *(Dr. Mirakle)*, Sidney Fox *(Camille L'Espanaye)*, Leon Waycoff [Ames] *(Pierre Dupin)*, Bert Roach *(Paul)*, Brandon Hurst *(Prefect of Police)*, Noble Johnson *(Janos, the Black One)*, D'Arcy Corrigan *(Morgue Keeper)*, Betty Ross Clarke *(The Mother)*, Arlene Francis *(Monette, the Lady of the Streets)*, Charles Gemora *(Erik the Ape)*, Herman Bing.

Universal's third foray into the horror realm (DRACULA and FRANKENSTEIN came before it) and one of the first rip-offs of Edgar Allan Poe's name to sell a movie. Discarding everything but the gorilla and the title, MURDERS IN THE RUE MORGUE stars Lugosi as a crazed scientist obsessed with creating a bride for his pet ape. His experiments involve kidnaping young women, tying them up and injecting them with an ape-blood serum that few survive. Lugosi disposes of his failures in the river, where the bodies are found by the confused police. Lugosi also runs a sideshow with his ape to raise money for his experiments. It is there that the gorilla sees young medical student girlfriend Fox, with whom he immediately falls in love. When Fox will have nothing to do with either Lugosi or the ape, the mad doctor sends his simian friend off to kidnap her. When the ape sees that Lugosi is about to inject her with his serum, he breaks the doctor's neck and takes off with the girl (even the ape knows Lugosi's a failure as a scientist). Waycoff catches up with the ape, however, and after a harrowing roof-top chase, he shoots the ape and saves the girl. MURDERS IN THE RUE MORGUE doesn't hold up well at all, and is slow-moving and dull compared with DRACULA and FRANKENSTEIN, despite director Florey's fairly interesting visuals. After refusing to let him direct FRANKENSTEIN, Universal dropped George Melford and allowed Florey to direct. It wasn't an easy task, however; he had to fight to keep the film a period piece (it was set in 1840, but the studio wanted to update it). The studio gave in, but cut the budget by $40,000. Florey walked off the set, but was coaxed back when Universal waved an additional $10,000 in front of his face. Even then the problems continued, with the final version somewhat re-edited from Florey's original conception. Later filmed in 3-D as a PHANTOM OF THE RUE MORGUE, with Karl Malden in the lead role. Again, Gemora handled the task of sweating it out in the ape costume.

p, Carl Laemmle, Jr.; d, Robert Florey; w, Tom Reed, Dale Van Every, John Huston (based on the story by Edgar Allan Poe); ph, Karl Freund; ed, Milton Carruth.

Horror **(PR:C MPAA:NR)**

MURDERS IN THE RUE MORGUE** (1971) 87m AIP c

Jason Robards, Jr. *(Cesar Charron)*, Herbert Lom *(Marot)*, Christine Kaufmann *(Madeleine Charron)*, Adolfo Celi *(Inspector Vidocq)*, Lilli Palmer *(Madeleine's Mother)*, Maria Perschy *(Genevre)*, Michael Dunn *(Pierre)*, Jose Calvo *(Hunchback)*, Peter Arne *(Aubert)*, Werner Umburg *(Theatre Manager)*, Luis Rivera *(Actor)*, Virginia Stach *(Lucie)*, Dean Selmeir *(Jacques)*, Marshall Jones *(Luigi Orsini)*, Rosalind Elliot *(Gabrielle)*, Ruth Platt, Xan Das Bolas *(Orsini's Assistants)*, Maria Martin *(Mme. Adolphe)*, Sally Longley, Pamela McInnes, Rafael Hernandez *(Members of Repertory Company)*.

This was the fourth MURDERS IN THE RUE MORGUE brought to the screen, following the 1914 silent version, the first sound adaptation in 1932, and a 3-D version in 1954 (renamed PHANTOM OF THE RUE MORGUE). Based on Edgar Allan Poe's famous gory tale, Robards plays a Parisian theater owner producing a play entitled "Murders in the Rue Morgue." His daughter, Kaufmann, has recurring nightmares similar to the play, only these dreams always end with a man in an ape costume swinging towards her, and then falling to his death. After a series of murders among several of the theater company's actors, the evidence points to Lom, once Robards' partner who murdered Kaufmann's mother years ago because she spurned his love. It had been believed that Lom committed suicide following the murder, but his resurfacing proves that the suicide had just been an act. He talks Kaufmann into meeting him at a secluded estate where he confesses that he is in love with her because she so closely resembles her mother. Unbeknownst to Lom or Kaufmann, Robards has followed his daughter to the estate, where he attacks Lom and kills him. But once again Lom has faked his death, and he returns to the theater one night dressed in an ape costume to avoid detection, and corners Kaufmann. But as he swings toward her on a rope, she cuts it and he falls to his death. That night, as she is lying in bed, she hears footsteps coming towards the door. The picture ends with her sitting up in bed, screaming.

p, Louis M. Heyward; d, Gordon Hessler; w, Christopher Wicking, Henry Slesar (based on the story by Edgar Allan Poe); ph, Manuel Berenguer (Foto Film Color); m, Waldo de los Rios; ed, Max Benedict; prod d, Jose Luis Galicia; md, de los Rios; art d, Galicia; cos, Antonio Pueo; makeup, Jack Young.

Horror **(PR:O MPAA:GP)**

MURDERS IN THE ZOO** (1933) 66m PAR bw

Charles Ruggles *(Peter Yates, Zoo Press Agent)*, Lionel Atwill *(Eric Gorman, Zoologist)*, Gail Patrick *(Jerry Evans)*, Randolph Scott *(Dr. Woodford, Zoo Toxicologist)*, John Lodge *(Roger Hewitt)*, Kathleen Burke *(Evelyn Gorman)*, Harry Beresford *(Professor Evans, Zoo Curator)*, Edward McWade *(Dan)*.

Atwill is a noted zoologist and sportsman married to Burke (the Panther Woman of ISLAND OF THE LOST SOULS). His wife has been having a series of affairs and the insanely jealous Atwill uses the animals of his zoo to kill off her lovers. The picture opens with Atwill on a jungle safari, sewing up the lips of one of Burke's flings. Later when she tries to innocently ask if this friend has left any message for her before "leaving," Atwill replies that "he didn't say anything!" From there it's onto the reptile house at the zoo, where her various flames are killed by pythons, tossed into the crocodile pool, and then ending with a climatic stampede of a mixture of creatures let loose to wreak havoc. Ruggles plays the zoo's press agent, as the film's much needed comic relief. Scott, who plays the hero, later became famous as a B-Western cowboy star, while Lodge, one of Burke's lovers, left his thespian career and was elected Governor of Connecticut. Made during the height of horror films of the 1930s, the censors were appalled at what they saw, resulting in the film being often cut, with lopped out sequences varying from theater to theater.

d, Edward Sutherland; w, Phillip Wylie, Seton I. Miller; ph, Ernest Haller.

Horror **Cas.** **(PR:O MPAA:NR)**

MURIEL****

(1963, Fr./Ital.) 115m Argos-Alpha Productions-Eclair-Films de la Pleiade-Dear/Lopert c (MURIEL, OU LE TEMPS D'UN RETOUR; MURIEL, IL TEMPO DI UN RITORNO; AKA: THE TIME OF RETURN; MURIEL, OR THE TIME OF RETURN)

Delphine Seyrig *(Helene)*, Jean-Pierre Kerien *(Alphonse)*, Nita Klein *(Francoise)*, Jean-Baptiste Thierree *(Bernard)*, Claude Sainval *(de Smoke)*, Laurence Badie *(Claudie)*, Jean Champion *(Ernest)*, Jean Daste *(The Goat Man)*, Martine Vatel *(Marie-Dominique)*, Philippe Laudenbach *(Robert)*, Robert Bordenave *(The Crou-*

pier), Gaston Joly *(Antoine, the Tailor)*, Catherine de Seynes *(Angele)*, Julien Verdier *(The Stableman)*, Gerard Lorin, Francoise Bertin, Wanda Kerien, Jean-Jacques Lagarde, Yves Vincent.

Resnais' third and most complex film centers again on memory. Seyrig is a widow who sells antiques from her Boulogne-sur-mer apartment. She shares the place with her stepson, Thierree, a veteran of the Algerian conflict in which he took part in the torture and murder of a young Algerian named Muriel. He is haunted by the memory of Muriel, spending much of his time watching a grainy 8mm film of her. Seyrig, meanwhile, is reunited with a past lover, Kerien, but they cannot recapture what they once had. The remainder of the plot is extremely complicated, devoting time to seemingly minor characters who are brought into the film by the main characters. MURIEL marked the second time Resnais worked with screenwriter Jean Cayrol. Previously Cayrol had contributed the commentary for Resnais' short documentary NIGHT AND FOG. For Cayrol, Resnais' labyrinth of memory is a fascination which stems from his time as a concentration camp victim (the subject of NIGHT AND FOG), as well as victim of bouts of amnesia. Their collaboration has produced a technical masterpiece which makes brilliant use of montage, sound construction, and color photography.

p, Anatole Dauman; d, Alain Resnais; w, Jean Cayrol (based on the story by Cayrol); ph, Sacha Vierny (Eastmancolor); m, Hans Werner Henze; ed, Kenout Peltier, Eric Pluet, Claudine Merlin; art d, Jacques Saulnier; m/l, "Deja" Paul Colline, Paul Maye (sung by Jean Champion).

Drama **(PR:A MPAA:NR)**

MURIEL, OU LE TEMPS D'UN RETOUR (SEE: MURIEL, 1963, Fr./Ital.)

MURIETA*½

(1965, Span.) 107m Pro Artis Iberica/WB c (GB: VENDETTA; AKA: JOAQUIN MURRIETA)

Jeffrey Hunter *(Joaquin Murieta)*, Arthur Kennedy *(Capt. Love)*, Diana Lorys *(Kate)*, Sara Lezana *(Rosita Murieta)*, Roberto Camardiel *(Three Fingers)*, Pedro Osinaga *(Claudio)*, Mike Brendel, Gonzalo Esquiroz, Juan Cazalilla, Julio Perez Tabernero, David Thomson, Francisco Brana, Fernando Villena, Hector Quiroga, Maria Jesus Corella, Andy Anza, Pedro Barbero, Rufino Ingles.

Based on a true story, this is the tale of a Mexican immigrant turned bandit as a result of his wife's murder at the hands of some bigoted miners. Hunter plays the man in question, with Lezana as his wife. They immigrate to California in 1849 in hopes of cashing in on the Gold Rush. Their only friend is an army captain, played by Kennedy. After suffering from the taunts and racial slurs from a group of miners, Lezana is beaten, raped and murdered by three men. Hunter swears revenge and rounds a group together to help him. Along the way he finds success as a professional gambler and begins raiding mining camps in search of the murderers. In the end, Kennedy is forced to kill his friend when the raids get too out of hand. This could have been an interesting film about racial tensions and its results, but instead is reduced to violent and surprisingly dull melodrama. The script is too talky, without much character development. An earlier version of the story ROBIN HOOD OF EL DORADO was much better, while a later made-for-television version, featuring Ricardo Montalbon (made in 1970) equals the quality of this film.

p, Jose Sainz de Vicuna; d, George Sherman; w, James O'Hanlon (based on a story by O'Hanlon); ph, Miguel F. Mila (Eastmancolor); m, Antonio Perez Olea; ed, Alfonso Santacana; md, Olea; art d, Rafael Salazar; set d, Enrique Alarcon; cos, Catalina Moreno; spec eff, Manuel Baquero; m/l, ("Rosita," "Corrido of Joaquin Murieta") Paco Michel; makeup, Jose Maria Sanchez.

Western **(PR:O MPAA:NR)**

MURMUR OF THE HEART********

(1971, Fr./Ital./Ger.) 118m Nouvelles Editions-Marianne-Vides Cinematografica-Franz Seitz/Minerva-Walter Reade-CD c (LE SOUFFLE AU COEUR)

Lea Massari *(Clara Chevalier)*, Benoit Ferreux *(Laurent Chevalier)*, Daniel Gelin *(The Father)*, Marc Winocourt *(Marc)*, Fabien Ferreux *(Thomas)*, Michel Lonsdale *(Father Henri)*, Ave Ninchi *(Augusta)*, Gila Von Weitershausen *(Freda)*, Micheline Bona *(Aunt Claudine)*, Henri Poirier *(Uncle Leonce)*, Jacqueline Chauveau *(Helene)*, Corinne Kersten *(Daphne)*, Francois Werner *(Hubert)*, Liliane Sorval *(Fernande)*, Yvon Lec *(Father Superior)*, Nicole Carriere, Lia Wanjtal, Hughette Faget *(The Mothers)*, Michel Charrel *(Disquaire)*, Eric Burnelli *(Maitre D'Hotel)*, Annie Savarin *(Cook)*, Jean-Pierre Pessoz *(Soldier)*, Rene Bouloc *(Man at Bastille Day Party)*, Isabelle Kloucowsky *(Madeleine)*.

Among the French New Wave directors, Louis Malle is one of the most versatile and accessible. He isn't afraid to handle delicate issues, and he approaches his subjects with sensitivity and wit. Incest, perhaps the most unspeakable of all taboos, was the subject of MURMUR OF THE HEART. Malle's comic look at the subject makes for a wonderful, tender film which accurately portrays all the joys and agonies of adolescent sexuality. Ferreux is the 14-year-old son of a French gynecologist. His mother, who had married his father when she was 16, is perhaps his closest confidante. They are two kindred spirits because they both enjoy the lively things in life. It is easy to see how the surroundings of their bourgois life trap the pair, and force them to turn to one another for relief. Ferreux's two older brothers take him to a prostitute for his first sexual experience, but the drunken boys interrupt the tentative beginnings. When Ferreux contacts scarlet fever, which leaves him with a heart murmur, his mother takes him to a mountain health spa to recuperate. It is here that Massari sees a chance to break away from the suffocating atmosphere of her home life. While she flirts with another patient, Ferreux tries his own hand at love by attempting to pick up a pair of girls his own age. Mother and son are both rejected by their prospective lovers at a Bastille Day celebration. The pair return to their hotel room, get drunk, then fall into bed. Their mutual comforting leads to lovemaking. Massari is sensitive to her son's adolescent psyche, and explains that this will be their own special experience that will never be repeated or discussed. Ferreux later leaves the room and makes love with one of the teenage girls. Upon returning to his room, he's surprised to find his father and brothers waiting for him. The older boys realize where their brother has just come back from and they break out laughing. At first Massari feels a pang of rejection, but joins in the laughter. This is a film alive with energy. One never forgets those terrible moments of early adolescence, and this film recaptures the feelings with honesty and real sensitivity. Backed by a wonderful jazz score, the drama is made believable by its characters. Massari and Ferreux have a marvelous natural chemistry that makes their relationship honest and understandable. Their lovemaking is treated in a subtle manner. Malle never dwells upon it, nor does he make it seem like a moment of depraved abandon. Instead, this is a special moment for two people who cannot explain their actions to outsiders. Malle stated that this film, while not a biography, did have a certain basis in truth. At 14 he did have a heart murmur, and he did visit a prostitute. The mother-son relationship was taken from the lives of several friends for whom the experience was not painful, but as special a relationship as portrayed here. Rather than create a paean to incest, Malle has created a song of life. The film's comedy works because of the director's insight into adolescents and the pain they go through in discovering themselves. Ferreux's journey is the journey of us all, capturing the pain, passion, and utter brilliance that exists in life. (In French, English subtitles.)

p, Vincent Malle, Claude Nedjar; d&w, Louis Malle; ph, Ricardo Arnovich (Eastmancolor); m, Charlie Parker, Sidney Bechet, Gaston Freche, Henri Renaud; ed, Suzanne Baron; art d, Jean-Jacques Caziot, Philippe Turlure.

Drama/Comedy **(PR:O MPAA:NR)**

MURPH THE SURF***

(1974) 105m Caruth C. Byrd c (AKA: LIVE A LITTLE, STEAL A LOT; YOU CAN'T STEAL LOVE)

Robert Conrad *(Allan Kuhn)*, Don Stroud *(Jack Murphy)*, Donna Mills *(Ginny Eaton)*, Robyn Mills *(Sharon Kagel)*, Luther Adler *(Max "The Eye")*, Paul Stewart *(Avery)*, Morgan Paul *(Arnie Halcomb)*, Ben Frank *(Hopper Magee)*, Burt Young *(Sgt. Bernasconi)*, Pepper Martin *(Sgt. Terwilliger)*, Buffy Dee, Don Matheson, Lindsay Crosby, Mimi Saffian, Nancy Conrad, Jess Barker, Al Bordigi, Lloyd McLinn, Mel Stevens, Harvey Levine, Harriet Haindl, Kip King, Caruth C. Byrd, Joe Mell, Oak R. Gentry, Herb Vigran.

Based on a series of burglaries that fascinated the media in Miami, Florida, as well as capturing the imagination of the public, Conrad and Stroud play a pair of ne'er-do-well beach bums who turn to burglarizing posh Miami homes. Bored with their seemingly unchallenging booty, they decide to go after some real loot and head off to New York City to fetch the famed Star of India sapphire from the American Museum of Natural History. Though the actual events were toned down for the film, this is a quirky and entertaining little picture. Told partially in flashback, there's some interesting action sequences, including a motorboat race through Miami's inland waterways. Conrad and Stroud make for an unusual team. The film does have a problem in trying to decide whether it wants to be a comedy or drama, but it is entertaining. Allan Kuhn, one of the actual robbers (portrayed by Conrad), served as technical advisor after bringing the story to Conrad.

p, J. Skeet Wilson, Chuck Courtney; d, Marvin Chomsky; w, E. Arthur Kean (based on a story by Allan Dale Kuhn); ph, Michel Hugo (CFI Color); m, Phillip Lambro; ed, Howard Smith; prod d, James Vance.

Crime **Cas.** **(PR:C MPAA:PG)**

MURPHY'S WAR½**

(1971, Brit.) 106m Yates-Deeley-London Screenplays/PAR c

Peter O'Toole *(Murphy)*, Sian Phillips *(Dr. Hayden)*, Philippe Noiret *(Louis Brezan)*, Horst Janson *(Kapitan Lauchs)*, John Hallam *(Lt. Ellis)*, Ingo Mogendorf *(Lt. Voght)*.

O'Toole plays an Irish seaman who is traveling on an armed British merchant ship off the coast of Venezuela during the final days of WW II. Spotted by a German U-boat, the ship is sunk and its crew members, floundering helplessly in the water, are mercilessly machine-gunned under the orders of Janson, the U-boat's commander. O'Toole survives, however, and is rescued by Noiret, a Frenchman who lives at sea on his barge. O'Toole is taken to a remote mission along the banks of the Orinoco River, where he is nursed back to health by a woman doctor, Phillips (O'Toole's real-life wife). While recovering, O'Toole meets Hallam, a pilot whose plane crashed during an attack on the U-boat. Phillips radios a report that the U-boat is in hiding upriver. The message, however, is intercepted by Janson. The German raids the mission and kills Hallam, not realizing that O'Toole has also survived. Bent on revenge, O'Toole locates and repairs Hallam's plane and sets out to destroy the U-boat. He attacks the ship with Molotov cocktails and, thinking his raid a complete success, returns to the mission. The Germans retaliate and attack the mission, inciting O'Toole and Noiret to finish the battle. Although the Armistice has been signed, officially ending the war, O'Toole and Noiret continue on their path. By now O'Toole has been driven into a frenzied desire for revenge. He begins his assault on the U-boat with an armored barge, ignoring Janson's warning that the war is over. O'Toole's personal war has not ceased, and he refuses to give up. Janson fires a torpedo at the barge, but it is off course and lands, unexploded, on the beach. Janson is forced to take action and calls for the U-boat to dive. It gets grounded in the shallow waters of the Orinoco, however, and is a sitting duck for O'Toole. Realizing that O'Toole's war has become a personal vendetta, Noiret returns to shore. O'Toole retrieves the beached torpedo with a derrick on the barge and drops it onto the helpless U-boat, obliterating the Germans and himself in a tremendous splash of muddy water. While little more than a third-rate AFRICAN QUEEN, MURPHY'S WAR can boast some exciting action scenes and a picturesque South American locale. Unfortunately the script drags and the film limps across a number of lulls. What promises to be an effective relationship between O'Toole and Phillips, *a la* Bogart and Hepburn, is quickly extinguished in favor of O'Toole's mad vision.

There is also an uneasy question of morality in O'Toole's destroying a ship for personal reasons after the Armistice has been signed. After all, the attacks on O'Toole's mates *did* occur during wartime. Interestingly, after 12 years of film roles, which included playing Englishmen and Scotsmen, this was the first time O'Toole, an Irishman by birth, had actually played an Irishman.

p, Michael Deeley; d, Peter Yates; w, Stirling Silliphant (based on the novel by Max Catto); ph, Douglas Slocombe (Panavision, Eastmancolor); m, John Barry, Ken Thorne; ed, Frank P. Keller, John Glen; md, Barry; prod d, Disley Jones; spec eff, Ira Anderson, Roy Whybrow; makeup, Basil Newall; stunts, Bob Simmons.

War **(PR:C-O MPAA:GP)**

MURRI AFFAIR, THE (SEE: LA GRANDE BOURGEOISE, 1977, Ital.)

MUSCLE BEACH PARTY1/2** (1964) 94m Alta Vista/AIP c

Frankie Avalon *(Frankie)*, Annette Funicello *(Dee Dee)*, Luciana Paluzzi *(Julie)*, John Ashley *(Johnny)*, Don Rickles *(Jack Fanny)*, Peter Turgeon *(Theodore)*, Jody McCrea *(Deadhead)*, Dick Dale *(Dick)*, Candy Johnson *(Candy)*, Little Stevie Wonder [Stevie Wonder] *(Himself)*, Morey Amsterdam *(Cappy)*, Buddy Hackett *(S. Z. Matts)*, Rock Stevens [Peter Lupus] *(Flex Martian)*, Dolores Wells *(Sniffles)*, Donna Loren *(Donna)*, Valora Noland *(Animal)*, Alberta Nelson *(Lisa)*, Amedee Chabot *(Floe)*, Larry Scott *(Biff)*, Bob Seven *(Rock)*, Steve Merjanian *(Tug)*, Don Haggerty *(Riff)*, Chester Yorton *(Sulk)*, Gene Shuey *(Mash)*, Gordon Cohn *(Clod)*, Luree Holmes, Laura Nicholson, Lorie Summers, Darlene Lucht *(Beach Girls)*, Duane Ament, Gary Usher, Roger Christian, Guy Hemric *(Beach Boys)*, Mary Hughes, Kathy Kessler, Salli Sachse, Linda Opie, Linda Benson, Patricia Rane *(Surfer Girls)*, Butch Van Artsdalen, Mike Diffenderfer, Bill Graham, Charles Hasley, Larry Shaw, Duane King, Mike Nader, Ed Garner, John Fain, Mickey Dora *(Surfer Boys)*, Peter Lorre *(Mr. Strangdour)*, Peter Lupus Jr., The Del Tones.

Not only is this picture a bit of good campy fun, it's also a treasure trove for trivia fiends everywhere. In this sequel to BEACH PARTY (1963), Avalon and Funicello are distressed when a new gym, operated by Rickles, opens up next to their neat-o, keen-o strip of sun, sand, and surf. Egotist Stevens is the king of the musclemen down at Rickles' place. Paluzzi is a wealthy, young contessa who comes a chasin' after Stevens, then sets her sights on Avalon. Boy o' boy, does Funicello ever get sore! Some silly business involving a showdown between the beach gang and the muscle maniacs is broken up by a certain Mr. Strangdour, played in an unbilled appearance by Lorre. This was the great actor's final film and the studio kept his appearance a big secret. No mention of him was made in the opening credits, though the closing credits exclaim "The producers extend special thanks to Mr. Peter Lorre for his contribution to this film as 'Mr. Strangdour.' Soon to be seen in BIKINI BEACH." This next film in the Funicello-Avalon series was made, but without the contributions of Lorre, who died. He was substituted by another film veteran, Boris Karloff. MUSCLE BEACH PARTY marked the film debut of Rickles, as well as an appearance by "Little" Stevie Wonder, who would go on to great success with his music. Stevens ended up dropping his pseudonym and used his real name, Peter Lupus, for TV's "Mission Impossible." MUSCLE BEACH PARTY is typical of the silly beach movies of the late 1950s-early 1960s, with teenyboppers twisting to tunes like "Muscle Bustle," "My First Love," and "Surfin' Woodie" that are some of the songs co-written by Brian Wilson, a member of one of the great propagandizers of the lifestyle portrayed here (i.e. the rock group "The Beach Boys"). Of course it's dumb but what did you expect? The songs are performed by Avalon, Funicello, Dick Dale and the Del Tones, Wonder, and Donna Loren. Songs include: "Muscle Beach Party," "Runnin' Wild," "Muscle Bustle," "My First Love," "Surfin' Woodie," "Surfer's Holiday" (Roger Christian, Gary Usher, Wilson), "Happy Street," and "A Girl Needs a Boy" (Guy Hemric, Jerry Styner).

p, James H. Nicholson, Robert Dillon; d, William Asher; w, Dillon (based on a story by Dillon, Asher); ph, Harold Wellman (Panavision, Pathecolor); m, Les Baxter; ed, Eve Newman; art d, Lucius Croxton; set d, Harry Reif; cos, Marjorie Corso; makeup, Ted Coodley.

Teens/Musical **(PR:AA MPAA:NR)**

MUSEUM MYSTERY* (1937, Brit.) 69m British and Dominions/PAR bw

Jock McKay *(Jock)*, Elizabeth Inglis *(Ruth Carter)*, Gerald Case *(Peter Redding)*, Tony Wylde *(Mr. Varleigh)*, Charles Paton *(Clutters)*, Alfred Wellesley *(Mayor)*, Sebastian Smith *(Dr. Trapnell)*, Roy Byford *(Prof. Wickstead)*, J. Abercrombie, Geoffrey Clark.

A museum owner attempts to defraud his insurance company by stealing a priceless Burmese idol from himself, but he is tripped up by his own daughter and her boy friend. Badly written and played; instantly forgettable.

p, Anthony Havelock-Allan; d, Clifford Gulliver; w, Gerald Elliott; ph, Francis Carver.

Crime **(PR:A MPAA:NR)**

MUSHROOM EATER, THE*1/2** (1976, Mex.) 100m Conacine CCP c (EL HOMBRE DE LOS HONGOS)

Isela Vega *(Elvira)*, Ofelia Medin *(Lucila)*, Adolfo Marsellach *(Everardo)*, Fernando Allende *(Sebastian)*, Sandra Mozaro *(Emma)*, Philip-Michael Thomas *(Gaspar)*.

An elderly Mexican plantation owner finds a young black boy in the jungle and raises him as one of his own children. Though disliked by his two older children, the younger daughter grows close to the boy and as they mature, the two fall in love. They also take to a black panther chained in the courtyard that their mother hates. She tries to have an affair with her adopted son. But he repels her and she runs off, only to be killed by the panther which has mysteriously gotten loose. The father decides he wants no inter-racial love affairs in his household and relegates the boy to a position of mushroom taster. If the boy eats a poisoned mushroom, he will die and the pickers will know which batch to stay away from. But the boy escapes and makes love with the sister. She goes off by herself to the waterfall where the boy originally was found and sees the family panther. She tries to let it know she cares about it but the great cat kills her. The black boy, now a man returns back to the jungle he came from, knowing his civilized life is through. The film has a refreshing sense of innocence to it, with a good direction that faintly recalls a sense of the old Hollywood romanticism. Though the black panther is a little over-done for symbolism, this is an interesting, intriguing feature, well played throughout.

d, Roberto Gavaldon; w, Emilio Carbillido, Tito Davison, Gavaldon, Sergio Galindo; ph, Raul Perez Cubero, Miguel Arana (Eastmancolor); m, Raul Iavista.

Drama **(PR:O MPAA:NR)**

MUSIC AND MILLIONS (SEE: SUCH IS LIFE, 1936 Brit.)

MUSIC BOX KID, THE** (1960) 74m Premium/UA bw

Ronald Foster *(Larry Shaw)*, Luana Patten *(Margaret Shaw)*, Grant Richards *(Chesty Miller)*, Johnny Seven *(Tony Maldano)*, Carl Milletaire *(Pat Lamont)*, Dayton Lummis *(Father Gorman)*, Bernie Fein *(Biggie Gaines)*, Carleton Young *(George Gordon)*, Hugh Sanders *(Stanley Sandman)*, Phil Jackson *(Wally Federman)*, Stewart Conway *(Joe Burl)*, Michael Johnson *(Timmy Atkins)*, Gil Frye *(Steve Marino)*.

Foster is a 1920s gangster punk working his way up a bootlegging syndicate. He gets his nickname from his ruthless use of his tommy gun, which he dubs his "music box." Patten is his pregnant wife who eventually leads him to a downfall. This is a formula gangster flick, with cliched situations and stereotyped characters. The direction is efficient however, giving some workmanship to an otherwise standard piece. The cast gives the film a little soul as well with some spirited performances.

p, Robert E. Kent; d, Edward L. Cahn; w, Herbert Abbott Spiro; ph, Maury Gertsman; m, Paul Sawtell, Bert Shefter; ed, James Blakeley; art d, Bill Glasgow.

Crime **(PR:C MPAA:NR)**

MUSIC FOR MADAME* (1937) 77m RKO bw

Nino Martini *(Nino Maretti)*, Joan Fontaine *(Jean Clemens)*, Alan Mowbray *(Leon Rodowsky)*, Billy Gilbert *(Krause)*, Alan Hale *(Detective Flugelman)*, Grant Mitchell *(District Attorney Ernest Robinson)*, Erik Rhodes *(Spaghetti Nacio)*, Lee Patrick *(Nora Burns)*, Frank Conroy *(Morton Harding)*, Bradley Page *(Rollins)*, Ada Leonard *(Bride)*, Romo Vincent *(Truck Driver)*, Barbara Pepper *(Blonde on Bus)*, Edward H. Robbins *(William Goodwin)*, George Shelley *(Barret)*, Jack Carson *(Assistant Director)*, Alan Bruce *(Groom)*, Ralph Lewis, Mary Carr, Ben Hendricks, William Corson *(Bits)*, Ben Hall *(Bus Passenger)*, Jack Mulhall, Larry Steers, Harold Miller, Ralph Brooks *(Guests)*, Grace Hayle *(Fat Guest)*, Mira McKinney *(Admirer)*, George Meeker *(Orchestra Leader)*, Stanley Blystone, Pat O'Malley *(Cops)*, Robert E. Homans *(Desk Sergeant)*, Milburn Stone *(Detective)*, Harry Tenbrook *(Electrician)*, James Donlan *(Suspect with Cold)*, Russ Powell *("Asleep in the Deep" Singer)*, Ward Bond *(Violet, the Henchman)*, Sam Haynes *(KAFF Announcer)*, Jac George *(Violinist)*.

A fluff musical features Martini as a young opera star who wants to hit it big in Hollywood. Unfortunately he gets caught up with a group of thieves who use the naive Italian as their front man. The nonsense builds to Martini's eventual success at the Hollywood Bowl. This was Lasky's first attempt at producing for RKO and this third bid at making Martini a film star. Unfortunately, the film is a real dud except when Martini sings. Martini performs "Vesti La Guibba" from Leoncavallo's famed opera "Pagliacci." Best remembered as Fontaine's film debut, MUSIC FOR MADAME was box office poison, losing over $375,000.

p, Jesse L. Lasky; d, John Blystone; w, Gertrude Purcell, Robert Harari (based on a story by Harari); ph, Joseph H. August; ed, Desmond Marquette; md, Nathaniel Shilkret; art d, Van Nest Polglase; spec eff, Vernon L. Walker; m/l, "Music for Madame," Herb Magidson, Allie Wrubel, "My Sweet Bambino: I Want the World to Know," Rudolf Friml, Gus Kahn, "King of the Road," Shilkret, Eddie Cherkose (all sung by Nino Martini).

Musical **(PR:A MPAA:NR)**

MUSIC FOR MILLIONS** (1944) 120m MGM bw

Margaret O'Brien *("Mike")*, Jose Iturbi *(Himself)*, Jimmy Durante *(Andrews)*, June Allyson *(Barbara Ainsworth)*, Marsha Hunt *(Rosalind)*, Hugh Herbert *(Uncle Ferdinand)*, Harry Davenport *(Doctor)*, Marie Wilson *(Marie)*, Larry Adler *(Larry)*, Ben Lessy *(Kickebush)*, Connie Gilchrist *(Traveler's Aid Woman)*, Katharine Balfour *(Elsa)*, Helen Gilbert *(Helen)*, Mary Parker *(Anita)*, Madeleine LeBeau *(Jane)*, Ethel Griffies.

A classic example of the "something for everyone"-type feature popular with audiences during WW II. Allyson is a cellist in Iturbi's orchestra who is pregnant and worried about her soldier husband, who she hasn't heard from in months. Durante, seen in an uncharacteristic portrayal as Iturbi's manager, sings a few songs he composed with Irving Caesar. "Umbriago" is a funny number that became a Durante standard. Of course the husband turns up in the end and Allyson has a boy. O'Brien received a special Oscar that year for her work as a juvenile film star. MUSIC FOR MILLIONS is entertaining at best, clearly made with the mass market in mind. Production values are topnotch. Iturbi conducts the orchestra in selections from Dvorak, Grieg, Victor Herbert, Debussy, Tchaikovsky, Liszt, Handel and Chopin. Other songs include "Toscanini, Iturbi and Me" (Walter Bullock, Harold Spina; sung by Durante), "At Sundown" (Walter Donaldson), "Summer Holidays" (Helen Deutsch, Herbert Stothart).

p, Joe Pasternak; d, Henry Koster; w, Myles Connolly; ph, Robert Surtees; ed, Douglass Biggs; md, Georgie Stoll; art d, Cedric Gibbons, Hans Peters; cos, Irene.

Musical/Drama **(PR:AA MPAA:NR)**

MUSIC GOES 'ROUND, THE* 1/2   (1936) 80m COL bw

Harry Richman (*Harry Wallace*), Rochelle Hudson (*Susanna Courtney*), Walter Connolly (*Hector Courtney*), Douglas Dumbrille (*Bishop*), Lionel Stander (*O'Casey, Harry's Butler*), Henry Mollison (*Stephen*), Etienne Girardot (*Brewster*), Walter Kingsford (*Cobham*), Wyrley Birch (*Josh*), Victor Kilian (*Marshall*), Dora Early (*Eleanora*), Gene Morgan (*Nelson*), Herman Bing (*Singer*), Michael Bartlett (*Himself*), Eddie Farley, Mike Riley (*Themselves*), Onyx Club Band.

Richman is a Broadway star who is fed up with show biz. He goes AWOL from rehearsals and ends up down south on a showboat. Struck with a change of heart and amused by the innocent goodheartedness of the show business troupe, he brings his newfound players with him to New York and features them in his show. Of course, by New York standards, the showboat crew is amateursville, though they don't realize it. After being humiliated, Hudson walks off the stage and gives Richman a well-deserved sock in the jaw. This is about as interesting as it sounds. Aside from a few good musical numbers by Lew Brown, Harry Akst, Richman, and director Schertzinger, the bits by the show boat troupe are truly amateurish. It was no joke and the film was not funny. There's also a racist portrayal of a minstrel show, not uncommon in cheap Hollywood musicals. Musical numbers include "Life Begins When You're In Love" (Victor Schertzinger, Lew Brown, Harry Richman, sung by Richman), "There'll Be No South," "Susannah" (Brown, Harry Akst, sung by Richman), "Rolling Along," "This is Love" (Brown, Akst), "The Music Goes 'Round and Around" (Red Hodgson, Ed Farley, Mike Riley).

d, Victor Schertzinger; w, Jo Swerling (based on a story by Sidney Buchman); ph, Joseph Walker; ed, Gene Milford; md, Howard Jackson; ch, Larry Ceballos.

Musical   **(PR:A MPAA:NR)**

MUSIC HALL**   (1934, Brit.) 73m REA/RKO bw

George Carney, Ben Field, Mark Daly, Helena Pickard, Olive Sloane, Derrick de Marney, Wally Patch, Peggy Novak, Edgar Driver, C. Denier Warren, Walter Amner, Wilson Coleman, Freddie Watts, Roddy Hughes, Bertram Dench, Raymond Newell, G. H. Elliott, Eva Chapman, Macari's Dutch Serenaders, Gershom Parkington Quintet, Chester's Performing Dogs, Debroy Somers and His Band, The Sherman Fisher Girls.

Flimsy excuse for a plot has a retired showman coming back and using modern methods to help an old music hall stay open. Lots of good musical acts.

p, Julius Hagen, d&w, John Baxter.

Musical   **(PR:A MPAA:NR)**

MUSIC HALL PARADE**   (1939, Brit.) 80m But bw

Glen Raynham (*Jean Parker*), Richard Norris (*Dick Smart*), Charles Sewell (*Stage Manager*), Rita Grant (*Mrs. Whipsnade*), Frank E. Franks (*Tom Gamble*), Hughie Green (*Eve Becke*), Freddie Forbes (*Jack Stanford*), Sid Palmer, Bill Burley, Angela Barrie, Patricia Faye, The Australian Motor Air Aces, Macari and His Dutch Accordion Serenaders, The Arnaut Brothers, The Three Jokers, Billy Cotton and His Band.

Slightly above average revue has Raynham putting together a big show to save the small music hall she inherited when her father died. Publicity man Norris helps her scour the country for talent and the show is a great success. The plot is a thin excuse, but the acts are fun to watch.

p&d, Oswald Mitchell; w, Con West, Mitchell; ph, Geoffrey Faithfull.

Musical   **(PR:A MPAA:NR)**

MUSIC HATH CHARMS†††   (1935, Brit.) 70m BIP/Wardour bw

Henry Hall (*Himself*), W. H. Berry (*Basil Turner*), Carol Goodner (*Mrs. Norbray*), Arthur Margetson (*Alan Sterling*), Lorna Hubbard (*Marjorie Turner*), Antoinette Cellier (*Joan*), Billy Milton (*Jack Lawton*), Aubrey Mallalieu (*Judge*), Wallace Douglas (*George Sheridan*), Edith Sharpe (*Miss Wilkinson*), Gus McNaughton (*Goodwin*), Hugh Dempster (*Tony Blower*), Maidie Hope, Richard Grey, Marion [Howard] Crawford, Norma Varden, John Turnbull, Ivan Samson, Quintin McPherson, Charles Paton, Hildegarde, Dan Donovan, Len Berman, BBC Dance Orchestra.

Odd, funny musical shows British BBC bandleader Hall in the recording studio trying to keep his musicians in line, while outside the studio his music is having strange effects. It saves a party in the jungle from cannibals, helps mountain climbers find their way through the fog, starts romances, and breaks up marriages. Ahead of its time and well worth checking out, thanks in large measure to co-director Summers, who is famed for realism in his scripts, and Woods, who made some of the best moderate-budget British films of the 1930s.

p, Walter C. Mycroft; d, Thomas Bentley, Alexander Esway, Walter Summers, Arthur Woods; w, Jack Davies, Courtney Terrett (based on a story by L. DuGarde Peach); ph, Jack Cox, Claude Friese-Greene, Ronald Neame.

Musical   **(PR:A MPAA:NR)**

MUSIC IN MANHATTAN**   (1944) 81m RKO bw

Anne Shirley (*Frankie*), Dennis Day (*Stanley*), Phillip Terry (*Johnny*), Raymond Walburn (*Professor*), Jane Darwell (*Mrs. Pearson*), Patti Brill (*Gladys*), Minerva Urecal (*Landlady*), Don Dillaway (*Maj. Hargrove*), Edmund Glover, Carl Kent, Michael Road, Steve Winston, John Shaw (*Officers*), Mary Halsey (*Operator*), Margie Stewart (*Airplane Hostess*), Sherry Hall (*Chauffeur*), Chris Drake (*Bellboy*), John Hamilton (*Banker*), Gerald Pierce (*Elevator Boy*), Ralph Peters (*Truck Driver*), Jason Robards (*Desk Clerk*), David Thursby (*Clancy*), Harry Clay, Bert Moorhouse, Tom Bryson (*Photographers*), Frank Mayo (*Doorman*), Robert E. Homans (*Justice of the Peace*), Georgia Cooper (*Judge's Wife*), Chester Carlisle (*Businessman*), Bob Mascagno, Italia DeNubila (*Dance Specialty*), Byron Foulger (*Ticket Agent*), Bert

Roach (*Fat Man*), Joan Barclay (*Chorus Girl*), Charlie Barnet Orchestra, Nilo Menendez Rhumba Band.

Shirley and Day are a song-and-dance duo trying to crack big time show biz. They manage to win an amateur competition and clinch some important bookings, but they still can't find an audience. After Shirley flies to Washington to see if she can con her rich pop into helping them out, she is mistaken for the wife of famous flyer Terry. She is taken to Terry's suite, where she meets the pilot. The two fall in love, and Day is left out in the cold. The comedy is a cute little farce, played well by the principals. However, the songs by Herb Magidson and Lew Pollack, which include "When Romance Comes Along," "I Can See You Now" and "I Like a Man Who Makes Music," are well below the talents of Shirley and Day. The staging of the musical numbers is equally lackluster, thus bringing down the film's overall appeal significantly. Other songs include "Did You Happen to Find a Heart?," "One Night in Acapulco," "Mexico" (Magidson, Pollack).

p&d, John H. Auer; w, Lawrence Kimble (based on a story by Maurice Tombragel, Hal Smith, Jack Scholl); ph, Russell Metty; m, Leigh Harline; ed, Harry Marker; md, C. Bakaleinikoff; art d, Albert S. D'Agostino, Al Herman; cos, Renie; ch, Charles O'Curran.

Musical   **(PR:A MPAA:NR)**

MUSIC IN MY HEART*   (1940) 69m COL bw

Tony Martin (*Robert Gregory*), Rita Hayworth (*Patricia O'Malley*), Edith Fellows (*Mary O'Malley*), Alan Mowbray (*Charles Gardner*), Eric Blore (*Griggs, Butler*), George Tobias (*Sascha*), Joseph Crehan (*Mark C. Gilman*), George Humbert (*Luigi*), Joey Ray (*Miller*), Don Brodie (*Taxi Driver*), Julieta Novis (*Leading Lady*), Eddie Kane (*Blake*), Phil Tead (*Marshall*), Marten Lamont (*Barrett*), Andre Kostelanetz and His Orchestra.

This film opens with the most annoying of filmdom's conventions, the "cute meet." Two taxi cabs crash, thus allowing Martin and Hayworth to hook up. He's a talented crooner awaiting deportation; she's a singer engaged to marry newspaper publisher Mowbray. Ill-written, the film contains a series of musical numbers featuring the pair and Kostelanetz's orchestra. Kostelanetz was featured on a popular CBS radio show at the time and, in an unusual move, the program and network are mentioned in the film. Radio and films being in direct competiton, such a coupling was an unheard of thing in Hollywood filmmaking. This was Hayworth's last really low-budget film before she became a big star. Martin, who couldn't really act anyway, never made it big in motion pictures, and scores here only as a talented crooner. The Robert Wright/Chet Forrest songs are passable; "It's a Blue World" received an Oscar nomination that year. Songs also include "I've Got Music in My Heart," "Punchinello," "Oh, What a Lovely Dream," "No Other Love," "Hearts in the Sky," "Prelude to Love." Otherwise, this is a forgettable, insipid feature.

p, Irving Starr; d, Joseph Santley; w, James Edward Grant (based on the story "Passport to Happiness" by Grant); ph, John Stumar; ed, Otto Meyer; md, M. W. Stoloff; art d, Lionel Banks; cos, Kalloch.

Musical   **(PR:A MPAA:NR)**

MUSIC IN THE AIR** 1/2   (1934) 85m FOX bw

Gloria Swanson (*Frieda Hertefeld*), John Boles (*Bruno Mahler*), Douglass Montgomery (*Karl Roder*), June Lang (*Seiglinde Lessing*), Al Shean (*Dr. Walter Lessing*), Reginald Owen (*Ernst Weber, Music Publisher*), Joseph Cawthorn (*Hans Uppman, Orchestra Conductor*), Sara Haden (*Martha*), Hobart Bosworth (*Cornelius*), Jed Prouty (*Kirschner*), Roger Imhof (*Burgomeister*), George Chandler (*Assistant Stage Manager*), Marjorie Main (*Anna the Maid*), Ferdinand Munier (*Innkeeper*), Grace Hayle (*Innkeeper's Wife*), Otto Fries (*Butcher*), Torben Meyer (*Pharmacist*), Otis Harlan (*Baker*), Herbert Heywood (*Fire Captain*), Lee Kohlmar (*Priest*), Christian Rub (*Zipfelhuber*), Fuzzy Knight (*Nick*), Adolph Dorr (*Bearded Peasant*), Perry Ivins (*Radio Engineer*), Ann Howard (*Elsa*), Betty Jane Graham (*Marguerita*), James [Dave] O'Brien (*Montgomery's Voice Double*), Betty Heistand (*Lang's Voice Double*).

Despite her top billing, Swanson doesn't have all that much to do in this adaptation of Jerome Kern's and Oscar Hammerstein II's Broadway musical. The silent story, improved by co-writer Wilder (who went on to direct Swanson in the immortal SUNSET BOULEVARD) casts Swanson as a top-billed opera star and Boles as a librettist who are always fighting. Montgomery, a young schoolmaster, comes to the Bavarian Alps along with his fiance, Lang. They try to sell her father's music, and end up meeting Swanson and Boles. After the opera singer and lyricist fight, each tries to make the other jealous by pursuing Montgomery and Lang, respectively. There is a happy ending, with Lang's father's music being used by Swanson and Boles in their new opera. The cast does well in this film, though the transition from stage to film wasn't a smooth one. The dubbed voices are painfully obvious. But songs like "We Belong Together" and "The Song is You" come off well. Shean recreates his original Broadway role and is quite funny. This was Swanson's last film for the Fox studio. At the time it was made, she had been off screen for two years and was eager to do a new film. Though in negotiations with Irving Thalberg of MGM, she eventually was deemed a "loan-out" to Fox for this film once all the contracts had been signed. Songs also include "I've Told Every Little Star," "There's a Hill Beyond a Hill," "One More Dance," "I'm So Eager" (Oscar Hammerstein II, Jerome Kern).

p, Erich Pommer; d, Joe May; w, Billy Wilder, Howard I. Young (based on the stage operetta by Oscar Hammerstein II, Jerome Kern); ph, Ernest Palmer; md, Louis De Francesco; cos, Rene Hubert; ch, Jack Donohue.

Musical   **(PR:A MPA:NR)**

MUSIC IS MAGIC**   (1935) 66m FOX bw

Alice Faye (*Peggy Harper*), Ray Walker (*Jack Lambert*), Bebe Daniels (*Diane DeValle*), Frank Mitchell (*Peanuts Harper*), Jack Durant (*Eddie Harper*), Rosina

Lawrence (*Shirley DeValle*), Thomas Beck (*Tony Bennett*), Andrew Tombes (*Producer Ben Pomeroy*), Luis Alberni (*Senor Castellano*), Hattie McDaniel (*Amanda*), Hal K. Dawson (*Jim*), Charles C. Wilson (*Theater Manager*), Lynn Bari (*Theater Cashier*), Dorothy Dix (*Secretary*), Ernie Alexander (*Drunk*), Si Jenks (*Bus Passenger*), Arline Judge (*Girl at Theater*).

A simplistic stage door behind-the-scenes musical casts Daniels as a big star on her way down. She meets Faye, a youngster on her way up. Faye's stuck in the chorus and Daniels, finally realizing she's getting old, gives her part to the newcomer. This minor musical was made when the struggling Fox studio was starting its merger with 20th Century studios. Picture budgets were small, and there was no money for lavish musicals like those produced by rival MGM. Though short, the film is handily directed despite the relatively skimpy sets—Faye was fine in her shortest film ever, and this marked the last American production for Daniels. She went to England, where she made only a handful of films of virtually no significance. Oddly enough, the roles that Faye and Daniels had in MUSIC IS MAGIC were quite similar to the directions of their own careers—Faye as the up-and-coming starlet, with Daniels the fading star forced to realize her popularity was waning. Songs included "Honey Chile" and "Love Is Smiling at Me" (Oscar Levant, Sidney Clare), "Music Is Magic" (Arthur Johnston, Clare), "La Locumba" (Raul Roulien, Clare).

p, John Stone; d, George Marshall; w, Edward Eliscu, Lou Breslow (based on a play by Gladys Unger, Jesse Lasky, Jr.); ph, L. W. O'Connell; ed, Alexander Troffey; md, Samuel Kaylin; art d, Duncan Cramer; cos, Rega; ch, Jack Donohue.

Musical   (PR:A   MPAA:NR)

MUSIC LOVERS, THE zero   (1971, Brit.) 122m UA c

Richard Chamberlain (*Peter Tchaikovsky*), Glenda Jackson (*Nina Milyukova*), Max Adrian (*Nicholas Rubenstein*), Christopher Gable (*Count Anton Chiluvsky*), Kenneth Colley (*Modeste Tchaikovsky*), Izabella Telezynska (*Mme. Von Meck*), Maureen Pryor (*Mme. Milyukova, Nina's Mother*), Sabina Maydelle (*Sasha Tchaikovsky*), Andrew Faulds (*Davidov*), Bruce Robinson (*Alexei*), Ben Aris (*Young Lieutenant*), Xavier Russell (*Koyola*), Dennis Myers (*Vladimir Von Meck*), John Myers (*Anatole Von Meck*), Joanne Brown (*Olga Bredska*), Alex Jawdokinov (*Dimitri Shubelov*), Clive Gazes (*Doctor*), Georgina Parkinson (*Odile in "Swan Lake"*), Alain Dubreuil (*Prince Siegfried in "Swan Lake"*), Graham Armitage (*Prince Balukin*), Consuela Chapman (*Tchaikovsky's Mother*), James Russell (*Bobyek*), Ernest Bale (*Headwaiter*), Victoria Russell (*Tatiana*), Alex Brewer (*Young Tchaikovsky*), Alexander Russell (*Mme. Von Meck's Grandson*), Imogen Clair (*Lady in White*), Peter White (*Von Rothbart in "Swan Lake"*), Maggie Maxwell (*Queen in "Swan Lake"*).

Don't bother seeing this, just buy a few albums of music by Tchaikovsky and let it go at that. It's a spurious biography of a great composer that is so filled with wretched excesses that one hardly knows where to begin lambasting it. Russell enjoys debunking someone he can never be, a great man, and showed it in this film as well as MAHLER and several of his other sleazy attempts at stylishness. It is the supposed love story between a homosexual, Chamberlain, and a nymphomaniac, Jackson, and all the attendant surrealistic touches Russell has added to take this out of the realm of plausibility and into the depths of cheap gossip. He is coarse, vulgar, confounding and, because of that, he is also exciting at times. It's 1875 in Moscow and Chamberlain is waltzing through the snowy streets with his boy friend, Gable, until they crawl tiredly into bed together. On the following day, Chamberlain is taken to the concert hall to hear the first performance of his piano concerto. His brother, Colley, has dragged him from Gable's side so the composer can listen to his work. At the concert are Telezynska, a rich old lady who loves good music, and Jackson, a woman whose morals are as loose as a potato sack on an anorexic. Telezynska loves the concerto and decides to support the young Chamberlain on the condition that they never meet face to face. Chamberlain gives up his teaching job and concentrates on composing, all the while engaging in a lengthy letters relationship with his patroness. Colley is trying to keep Chamberlain and Gable apart because their homosexual affair is frowned upon by the Russian hierarchy, so Chamberlain decides to marry, in order to present a facade. He chooses Jackson and she, of course, wants that union to be consummated but Chamberlain cannot handle her sexual demands and she tries to kill herself. Chamberlain's mental state is edgy so he goes to the huge estate of Telezynska to recuperate while the old woman is off somewhere. Pryor, Jackson's mother, pushes the frustrated woman into working as a prostitute. That does not work out either and Jackson is soon in a psychiatric hospital where she is raped repeatedly by the inmates. Chamberlain gets his wits back but is soon depressed again when Gable jealously tells Telezynska that her charge is gay. She pulls out her patronage and Chamberlain has nowhere to turn. With the help of his brother, Colley, Chamberlain goes on to achieve great success until he finally chooses to infect himself with cholera (his mother died of the disease) and he perishes in a tub of boiling water, the same way his mother, Chapman, did. Russell's wife did the costumes and four of their children, Alexander, Victoria, James, and Xavier, appear in small roles. THE MUSIC LOVERS is lurid, exaggerated and should be missed by anyone who is a music lover. The music was played by the London Symphony Orchestra conducted by Andre Previn. Selections by Tchaikovsky include: "1812 Overture," "Romeo and Juliet," "Miniature March," "The Letter Song" (from "Eugene Onegin"), "Dance of the Clowns," "Scherzo Burlesque," "Swan Lake," "String Quartet No. 3," "Sixth Symphony," "Piano Concerto in B Flat Minor," and "Porgi Amor" by Wolfgang Amadeus Mozart. What is so rotten about Russell's work is that it *looks* so good: like putting swamp gas in a Lalique vase. Ken Russell should be tied to a chair and forced to watch films by John Ford and Howard Hawks while listening to compositions by John Cage.

p&d, Ken Russell; w, Melvyn Bragg (based on the novel *Beloved Friend* by Catherine Drinker Bowen, Barbara Von Meck); ph, Douglas Slocombe (Panavision, DeLuxe Color); m, Peter Ilyich Tchaikovsky; ed, Michael Bradsell; prod d, Natasha

Kroll; md, Andre Previn; art d, Michael Knight; set d, Ian Whittaker; cos, Shirley Russell; ch, Terry Gilbert; makeup, George Frost.

Musical Biography   (PR:O   MPAA:R)

MUSIC MACHINE, THE*   (1979, Brit.) 90m Norfolk International c

Gerry Sundquist (*Gerry*), Patti Boulaye (*Clare*), Clarke Peters (*Laurie*), David Easter (*Howard*), Mandy Perryment (*Candy*), Billy McColl (*Mark*), Chrissy Wickham (*Sue*), Ray Burdis (*Joe*), Frances Lowe (*Sharon*), Garry Shail (*Aldo*), Mickey Feast (*Nick*).

Here's England's answer to SATURDAY NIGHT FEVER, complete with a John Travolta look-alike dancing his heart away at the disco. Easter's the clone, a local disco king. Sundquist, along with dance partner Boulaye, unthrones the man at the local disco's super-exciting dance contest. SATURDAY NIGHT FEVER was an intelligent film that had something to say about the lifestyle of its characters, whereas this was made only with box-office bucks in mind. Not an ounce of originality is to be found here, though the direction takes the story through fairly competently. Boulaye also sang some of the disco tunes, backed by a band called The Music Machine.

p, Brian Smedley-Aston; d, Ian Sharp; w, Kenelm Clarke; ph, Phil Meheux; m, The Music Machine; ed, Smedley-Aston, Alan Patillo; art d, Roger King.

Teen Drama   (PR:O   MPAA:NR)

MUSIC MAKER, THE*   (1936, Brit.) 52m Inspiration/MGM bw

Arthur Young (*The Musician*), Violet Loxley (*His Wife*).

Tedious two-person picture has Young an aging violinist married to Loxley and finishing his one and only symphony just before he dies. Mercifully brief. Note the neat, self-effacing pseudonym under which composer and producer Shepherd directs this piece for Inspiration Films, of which he is producer-in-charge.

p, Horace Shepherd, Holt Turner; d, Hugh Kairs [Shepherd]; w, Shepherd.

Drama   (PR:A   MPAA:NR)

MUSIC MAN**   (1948) 66m MON bw

Phil Brito, Freddie Stewart, Jimmy Dorsey, Alan Hale, Jr., June Preisser, Noel Neill, Grazia Narciso, Chick Chandler, Norman Leavitt, Helen Woodford, Gertrude Astor, William Norton Bailey, Roy Aversa, Herman Cantor, Paul Bradley.

A pair of brothers who constantly bicker unknowingly end up working together on the same musical presentation. Simple story line serves as device on which to hang various swing musical numbers.

p&d, Will Jason; w, Sam Mintz (based on his story); ph, Jackson Rose; ed, William Austin; md, Edward Kay.

Musical   (PR:AA   MPAA:NR)

MUSIC MAN, THE***   (1962) 151m WB c

Robert Preston (*Harold Hill*), Shirley Jones (*Marian Paroo*), Buddy Hackett (*Marcellus Washburn*), Hermione Gingold (*Eulalie MacKechnie Shinn*), Paul Ford (*Mayor Shinn*), Ewart Dunlop, Oliver Hix, Jacey Squires, Olin Britt (*The Buffalo Bills*), Pert Kelton (*Mrs. Paroo*), Timmy Everett (*Tommy Djilas*), Susan Luckey (*Zaneeta Shinn*), Ronny [Ron] Howard (*Winthrop Paroo*), Harry Hickox (*Charlie Cowell*), Charles Lane (*Constable Locke*), Mary Wickes (*Mrs. Squires*), Monique Vermont (*Amaryllis*), Ronnie Dapo (*Norbert Smith*), Jesslyn Fax (*Avis Grubb*), Patty Lee Hilka (*Gracie Shinn*), Garry Potter (*Dewey*), J. Delos Jewkes (*Harley Mac-Cauley*), Ray Kellogg (*Harry Joseph*), William Fawcett (*Lester Lonnergan*), Rance Howard (*Oscar Jackson*), Roy Dean (*Gilbert Hawthorne*), David Swain (*Chet Glanville*), Arthur Mills (*Herbert Malthouse*), Rand Barker (*Duncan Shyball*), Jeannine Burnier (*Jessie Shyball*), Shirley Claire (*Amy Dakin*), Natalie Core (*Truthful Smith*), Therese Lyon (*Dolly Higgins*), Penelope Martin (*Lila O'Brink*), Barbara Pepper (*Feril Hawkes*), Anne Loos (*Stella Jackson*), Peggy Wynne (*Ada Nutting*), Hank Worden (*Undertaker*), Milton Parsons (*Farmer*), Natalie Masters (*Farmer's Wife*), Peggy Mondo, Sarah Seegar, Adnia Rice (*Townswomen*), Casey Adams, Charles Percheskly (*Salesmen*), Percy Helton (*Conductor*).

There have been many attempts to capture the heartland of America in Broadway musicals. There was "Oklahoma" and "Carousel" and "Shenandoah" and many more. Perhaps none did the job as well as THE MUSIC MAN, a nostalgic combination of corn, laughs, joy, and a wonderful score that resounds to this day whenever a big, brass band is heard. Jack Warner later made the mistake of wanting big names when he did MY FAIR LADY but this time he wisely stayed with Preston, the man who made Professor Harold Hill his very own. He also retained DaCosta, the same director, who had run the Broadway show and the result was perfection. DaCosta used many of the old silent film techniques and they fit right in with the nature of the story and the era depicted. Preston is a glib con man working his way across the country. He's first discovered on a train where all the other drummers (as traveling salesmen were once called) are talking about him. He gets off the train in the typical city of River City, Iowa. (Author Wilson had been born in Mason City, Iowa, so he knew of what he wrote.) It's 1912 and Hill gathers the townspeople around and persuades them that their village is on the way to degradation because of the installation of a pool room (never mind that it is owned by the mayor, Paul Ford). The only way to keep the kids away from the pocket billiards that will cause them to go to hell is to start a band. Preston says he will sell them all the instruments and teach the children how to play but his real plan is to take the money and flee before the instruments arrive because Preston could not tell a bass clef from a bass fish. He is surprised to find an old friend (and once a con man), Hackett, now working in the town. Preston tells the gullible folks that he is an expert music teacher with impeccable credentials but local librarian and music teacher, Jones, is soon on to his schemes. Nevertheless, he manages to make her believe that he has developed a new technique, known as the "Think System," with which he can teach anyone to play any instrument. All they have to do is think the tune (in this case it is Wolfgang Amadeus Mozart's "Minuet in G") and they can play it. Soon enough, Preston's charisma is turning the town upside down. He manages to make Howard, a lisping little lad, confident and able to speak sans the lisp. He unites the bickering school board and they are soon harmonizing (these are "The Buffalo Bills," an excellent barbershop quartet), he gathers the townswomen, a bunch of gossips, and assigns them the task of running a committee for the huge dance he has planned, and he changes Jones, nearing the age when she will be known as an old maid, into a radiant woman passionately in love with him. Hickox, another traveling salesman, arrives in town and is ready to tell everyone Preston is a fraud. Jones attempts to dissuade the anvil salesman but Hickox tells her that Preston has seduced many a music teacher around America and she will be just one more notch on the rogue's belt. The River Cityites plan to exact revenge on Preston for what he has done and he is about to leave but realizes that he loves Jones and that stops him from making his customary quick exit. The instruments have arrived and are being handed out at city hall as Preston is brought there by the angry burghers. Preston tells the kids to all think the "Minuet in G" and they manage to squeak it out. Next thing you know, they are a tight marching band and the last sequence is a huge parade with everyone blowing their horns perfectly, a stirring finish to a rousing piece of Americana. Preston was not even nominated for his work in the picture, a gross mistake on the part of the Academy. It was nominated as Best Picture and Heindorf put an Oscar under his arm for musical direction. Jones is excellent as the small-town lady and her singing voice is glorious. THE MUSIC MAN is just as colorful, exciting, and inspiring today as it was when first released, which just goes to prove that quality stands up. The songs by Willson include: "Seventy-six Trombones" (sung by Preston), "Trouble" (sung by Preston), "If You Don't Mind" (sung by Jones, Kelton), "Till There Was You" (sung by Preston, Jones), "The Wells Fargo Wagon" (sung by Howard), "Being in Love" (sung by Jones), "Goodnight, My Someone" (sung by the Buffalo Bills), "Rock Island" (sung by the chorus), "Iowa Stubborn" (sung by chorus), "Sincere" (sung by Buffalo Bills), "The Sadder but Wiser Girl" (sung by Preston, Hackett), "Gary, Indiana" (sung by Preston, Howard), "Marian, the Librarian" (sung by Preston), "Lida Rose/Will I Ever Tell You?" (sung by Jones, Buffalo Bills), "Shipoopi" (sung by Hackett, chorus), "Pick a Little" (sung by Gingold, women), "Goodnight Ladies" (sung by Buffalo Bills), "It's You," "My White Knight," and "The Piano Lesson." Ronny Howard grew up to star on TV in "The Andy Griffith Show" and "Happy Days," then became a successful director with SPLASH and COCOON. The screenwriter who adapted this musical wrote one of the 1940s favorite books, See Here, Private Hargrove. Gingold, Ford, Wickes, and all the rest contribute to the film but this is, and always will be, Preston's picture.

p&d, Morton DaCosta; w, Marion Hargrove (based on the musical by Meredith Willson, Franklin Lacey); ph, Robert Burks (Technirama, Technicolor); m, Willson; ed, William Ziegler; md, Ray Heindorf; art d, Paul Groesse; set d, George James Hopkins; ch, Onna White, Tom Panko; makeup, Gordon Bau.

Musical/Comedy　　　　　　　　　　　**(PR:AAA　MPAA:NR)**

MUSIC ROOM, THE***
(1963, India) 95m Edward Harrison bw (JALSAGHAR)

Chabi Biswas (Huzur Biswambhar Roy), Padma Devi (His Wife), Pinaki Sen Gupta (Khoka, His Son), Tulsi Lahari (Manager of Roy's Estate), Kali Sarkar (Roy's Servant), Ganga Pada Basu (Mahim Ganguly), Akhtari Bai, Salamat Khan (Singers), Roshan Kumari (Kathak Dancer), Begum Akhtar, Ustad Waheed Khan, Bismilla Khan (Musicians and Dancers), Pratap Mukhopdhya, Tarapada Nandy.

One of Satyajit Ray's finest works, THE MUSIC ROOM is also one of the most meditative and lyrical. Its basic concern is the demise of an aristocratic household led by Biswas. Feeling a growing resentment toward his neighbors' elaborate parties, Biswas decides to hold his own and sells his wife's jewels to finance it. Shortly afterward his wife and son die at sea during a thunderstorm, which sends him into seclusion. Four years later, when his neighbor plans a party in his newly built music room, Biswas decides to have his own party. He scrounges together all the money he has left and throws an elegant party. He loses his sanity, however, and takes off on his son's horse. He is thrown from the animal and dies in the arms of his servants. Beautifully photographed, THE MUSIC ROOM is a fine example of Ray's directorial mastery. Released in India in 1958, shortly before the completion of his Apu trilogy.

p,d&w, Satyajit Ray (based on a novel by Tarashankar Banerjee); ph, Subrata Mitra; m, Dakhin Mohan Takhur, Asis Kumar, Robin Majumder; ed, Dulal Dutta; md, Ustad Vilayat Khan; art d, Bansi Chandragupta; set d, R. R. Sinde.

Drama　　　　　　　　　　　　　　　**(PR:A　MPAA:NR)**

MUSICAL MUTINY zero
(1970) 74m Cinetron/Cineworld c

Iron Butterfly, Fantasy, New Society Band, Grit.

Caribbean pirate Don Williams the Great returns from the dead and goes to see his old hideout. A pirate-theme amusement park stands on the spot and he walks around it unnoticed. Iron Butterfly is playing a concert at the park and Williams decides to cause some trouble by passing himself off as a park official and turning the concert into a free show. The band walks off when the members find out they're playing for no money, and it is not until a rich hippie says he will pay the band's fee that they finish their set. The band does an interminable version of its album-long hit, "In-a-Gadda-Da-Vida," as well as "Soul Experience" and "In the Time of Our Lives." A stupid movie by one of the worst bands in rock 'n' roll history.

p, Barry Mahon.

Musical　　　　　　　　　　　　　　　**(PR:A　MPAA:G)**

MUSIK I MORKER
(SEE: NIGHT IS MY FUTURE, 1963, Swed.)

MUSUME TO WATASHI
(SEE: MY DAUGHTER AND I, 1963, Jap.)

MUSS 'EM UP***
(1936) 70m RKO bw (GB: THE HOUSE OF FATE)

Preston Foster (Tip O'Neil), Margaret Callahan (Amy Hutchins), Alan Mowbray (Paul Harding), Ralph Morgan (Jim Glenray), Guinn "Big Boy" Williams ("Red" Cable), Maxie Rosenbloom ("Snake"), Molly Lamont (Nancy Harding), John Carroll (Gene Leland), Florine McKinney (Corinne), Robert Middlemass (Inspector Brock), Noel Madison (Spivali), Maxine Jennings (Cleo), Harold Huber (Maratti), Clarence Muse (William), Paul Porcasi (Luigi), Ward Bond, John Adiar (Gangsters).

An entertaining "hard-boiled cop" adventure casts Foster as a private eye. The title reflects his manner in dealing with the bad guys, and actually was a well-known phrase used by New York Police Commissioner Lewis J. Valentine. Foster's stuck with finding the killer of a millionaire's mutt, but the case ends up leading to kidnaping, ransom, and murder. Funny and imaginative, though it does run a little longer than needed. Mowbray plays the millionaire in trouble . . . or is he? Real-life boxer Rosenbloom makes a few fancy moves in a brief cameo. The direction is fast-paced, striking the right balance between comedy and drama.

p, Pandro S. Berman; d, Charles Vidor; w, Erwin Gelsey (based on a story by James Edward Grant); ph, J. Roy Hunt, Joseph August; ed, Jack Hively; md, Roy Webb.

Crime　　　　　　　　　　　　　　　**(PR:A　MPAA:NR)**

MUSTANG zero
(1959) 73m UA bw

Jack Beutel (Gabe), Madalyn Trahey (Nancy), Steve Keyes (Lou), Milt Swift, Autumn Moon, Max M. Gilford, Paul Spahn.

Beutel is a rodeo star who is forced to become a lowly ranch hand after gambling away all of his prize money. Keyes hires him to work on an Oklahoma ranch he owns with sister Trahey. A beautiful wild stallion is seen running loose around the ranch, which upsets the mares. Keyes wants it killed, but Beutel captures the horse and breaks him. The story ends with Beutel and Trahey together and the horse now domesticated. The story is out of a 1940s western serial, but the production values are strictly amateur. Shots are mismatched because of confusing editing, and the sound recording is difficult to comprehend. The film is padded with numerous stock nature shots that have little to do with the plot. The grainy photography, and cropped shots suggest a 35mm blow-up from 16mm. At times this can be impeccably awful. Raccoons are identified as opossums, and one character tells how he spotted a moose, an animal not native to Oklahoma. Independently made, perhaps the studio executives at United Artists distributed this in a moment of supreme charity.

p, Robert Arnell; d, Peter Stephens; w, Tom Gries (based on the book Capture of the Golden Stallion by Rutherford Montgomery); ph, William C. Thompson; m, Raoul Kraushaar; ed, Mike Pozen; m/l, Lester Lee, Ned Washington.

Western　　　　　　　　　　　　　　**(PR:A　MPAA:NR)**

MUSTANG COUNTRY**
(1976) 79m UNIV c

Joel McCrea (Dan), Robert Fuller (Griff), Patrick Wayne (Tee Jay), Nika Mina (Nika).

McCrea is an ex-rancher-rodeo star who helps young Indian boy Mina pursue a wild mustang. That's the entire plot for this ambling little film. The story is padded with stock nature footage and scenes from earlier McCrea films to show his character's earlier life. Like his character, McCrea came out of retirement at age 70 to do this film, which was to be his last, and he does a nice job as the old cowman. The thin story unfortunately was overwritten with dialog, thereby flawing the overall production. A dog named Rote steals the whole show with his cute antics. A little boring at times, but the kids might enjoy it.

p,dw, John Champion; ph, J. Barry Herron (Technicolor); m, Lee Holdridge; ed, Douglas Robertson; set d, Peter Young; m/l, "Follow Your Restless Dreams," Joe Henry, Holdridge (sung by Denny Brooks).

Western/Family　　　　　　　　　　　**(PR:A　MPAA:G)**

MUTANT
(SEE: FORBIDDEN WORLD, 1982)

MUTATIONS, THE*
(1974, Brit.) 91m Getty/COL c (AKA: MUTATIONS; THE MUTATION)

Donald Pleasence (Dr. Nolter), Tom Baker (Lynch), Brad Harris (Brian), Julie Ege (Hedi), Michael Dunn (Burns), Scott Antony (Tony), Jill Haworth (Lauren), Olga Anthony (Bridget), Lisa Collings (Prostitute), Joan Scott (Landlady), Toby Lennon (Tramp), Richard Davies (Doctor), John Wreford (Policeman), Eithne Dunne (Nurse), Tony Mayne (Dwarf Tony), Molly Tweedlie (Dwarf Molly), Kathy Kitchen (Midget), Fran Fullenwider (Fat Lady), Lesley Roose (Skinny Lady), Fay Bura (Bearded Lady), Dee Bura (Fire-Eater), Madge Barnett (Monkey Woman), Willie Ingram (Popeye), Esther Blackmon (Alligator Girl), Hugh Baily (Pretzel Boy), Felix Duarte (Frog Boy).

Pleasence plays the stereotypical movie mad scientist, here trying to develop a cross between plant and animal. Baker is his creepy assistant who roams the countryside to kidnap people for his master's experiments. All the victims of experiments gone awry go to Dunn, a midget who runs a freak show. Eventually Pleasence creates the right combination, only to be destroyed by his own creation. Though at times the film is so bad it's unintentionally funny, it has a certain cruelty to it. The experimental creations were portrayed by actual sideshow people, including a lizard lady, a monkey woman, and a frog boy. Unlike Tod Browning's classic FREAKS (1932), which employed real-life sideshow performers with sympathy, the deformed men and women in THE MUTATIONS are portrayed as objects of attractive revulsion. Director Cardiff, the cinematographer on Michael Powell's The Red Shoes, does an adequate job with the story, but with little sense of humanity.

p, Robert D. Weinbach; d, Jack Cardiff; w, Weinbach, Edward Mann; ph, Paul

Beesen (Technicolor); m, Basil Kirchin; ed, Russell Weelnough, David Beesley; art d, Herbert Smith.

Horror   (PR:O   MPAA:R)

MUTINEERS, THE*   (1949) 60m COL bw (AKA: PIRATE SHIP)

Jon Hall (*Nick Shaw*), Adele Jergens (*Norma Harrison*), George Reeves (*Thomas Nagle*), Noel Cravat (*Dudley*), Don C. Harvey (*Joe Miles*), Matt Willis (*Toby Jarmin*), Tom Kennedy (*Butch*), Pat Gleason (*Rogers*), Frank Jaquet (*Capt. Stanton*), Lyle Talbot (*Capt. Duncan*), Smith Ballew (*Beasly*), Ted Adams (*Benson*), Allen Mathews (*Spencer*), Rusty Wescoatt (*Jenkins*), James Somers (*Kennedy*), Lee Roberts (*Andrews*).

Talbot, the captain of a freighter, is found by Hall murdered, with counterfeit money filling his pockets. The ship is then assigned to another man. Reeves, with girl friend Jergens, boards the ship and takes over. Reeves and his gang are the counterfeiters responsible for Talbot's death. They hold the real crew hostage, though Hall pretends to go along with the pirates. Just before the ship lands in Lisbon, where Reeves is to sell the phony money as well as some guns, Hall lets the crew loose and the evildoers are turned over to the authorities. Like a ship looming on the horizon, you'll be able to see what's going to happen long before it actually does. Unimaginative and slow moving, the cast is simply going through the motions, except for Jergens, who attempts to give her character some life.

p, Sam Katzman; d, Jean Yarbrough; w, Ben Bengal, Joseph Carole (based on a story by Dan Gordon); ph, Ira H. Morgan; m, Mischa Bakaleinikoff; ed, James Sweeney; art d, Paul Palmentola.

Adventure   (PR:A   MPAA:NR)

MUTINEERS, THE   (SEE: DAMN THE DEFIANT! 1962, Brit.)

MUTINY*½   (1952) 77m UA c

Mark Stevens (*James Marshall*), Angela Lansbury (*Leslie*), Patric Knowles (*Ben Waldridge*), Gene Evans (*Hook*), Rhys Williams (*Redlegs*), Robert Osterloh (*Faversham*), Peter Brocco (*Sykes*), Norman Leavitt (*Hackett*), Gene Roth (*Potter*), Walter Sande (*Stone*), Clayton Moore (*Peters*), Morris Ankrum (*Radford*), Todd Karnes (*Andrews*), Louis Jean Heydt (*Capt. Herwig*), Robin Hughes (*Lt. Vaughan*), Crane Whitley (*Col. Rogers*), Emerson Treacy (*Council Speaker*), Harry Antrim (*Chairman Parsons*).

Based on a true incident about a group of American soldiers sailing across the ocean from France. Their cargo is $10 million in gold bullion which will be used to fight the British in the War of 1812. Everyone aboard, however, gets gold fever and the war ends up on the ship. The performances are adequate, particularly by Knowles and his traitorous girl friend Lansbury; but the action is too predictable and, once the gold fever sets in, there's not much left to the film. Some nice Technicolor photography, which, unfortunately, doesn't cover the inherent weaknesses.

p, Maurice King, Frank King; d, Edward Dmytryk; w, Phillip Yordan, Sidney Harmon (based on a story by Hollister Noble); ph, Ernest Lazlo (Technicolor); m, Dimitri Tiomkin; ed, Frank Sullivan; md, Tiomkin; art d, Edward S. Haworth.

Adventure   (PR:A   MPAA:NR)

MUTINY AHEAD**   (1935) 65m Majestic bw

Neil Hamilton, Kathleen Burke, Leon Ames, Reginald Barlow, Noel Francis, Matthew Betz, Paul Fix, Maidel Turner, Edward Earle.

Adventure yarn from the Poverty Row filmmakers as a playboy gets himself involved in various intrigues. First he's mixed up with gamblers, and this leads to an underwater treasure.

p, Larry Darmour; d, Tommy Atkins; w, Stuart Anthony; ph, Herbert Kirkpatrick.

Adventure   (PR:A   MPAA:NR)

MUTINY IN OUTER SPACE, 1958   (SEE: SPACE MASTER X-7, 1958)

MUTINY IN OUTER SPACE**
(1965) 80m Woolner/AA bw (AKA: INVASION FROM THE MOON; SPACE STATION X-14; SPACE STATION X)

William Leslie (*Maj. Towers*), Dolores Faith (*Faith Montaine*), Pamela Curran (*Connie*), Richard Garland (*Col. Cromwell*), James Dobson (*Dr. Hoffman*), Carl Crow (*Capt. Webber*), Harold Lloyd, Jr. (*Enlisted Man*), Ron Stokes, Robert Palmer, Gabriel Curtis, Glenn Langan.

Leslie and Crow return to their space station after an exploration of lunar ice caves. Crow dies upon arrival of an unexplained fungus. Faith is the station's biochemist, who analyzes the material. After the ship's doctor, Dobson, contracts the infection, he unites with Leslie in telling commander Garland that Earth must be notified. But Garland doesn't want the mission to be disrupted and refuses their request. They go over his head and attempt contact with Earth but are foiled by Curran, the ship's communication officer, who's in love with Garland. The space station runs into a meteor shower which tears a hole in the station's side, causing the mysterious fungus to escape. Dobson concludes that the deadly fungus needs heat to survive and, after Leslie leads a mutiny against Garland, the station is put into a freeze and the fungus killed. By the time of the film's release, space travel was less mysterious than it had been in the genre's heyday 10 years before. Thus this routine fare, with standard production values and acting, was simply too late to stir up much interest.

p, Hugo Grimaldi, Arthur C. Pierce; d, Grimaldi; w, Pierce (based on a story by Grimaldi, Pierce); ph, Arch R. Dalzell; ed, George White; md, Gordon Zahler; art d, Paul Sylos; spec eff, Roger George; makeup, Ted Coodley; miniatures, Edwards Art Studios.

Science Fiction   (PR:A   MPAA:NR)

MUTINY IN THE ARCTIC**½   (1941) 61m UNIV bw

Richard Arlen (*Dick*), Andy Devine (*Andy*), Anne Nagel (*Gloria*), Addison Richards (*Ferguson*), Don Terry (*Cole*), Oscar O'Shea (*Capt. Morrissey*), Harry Cording (*Harmon*).

Fairly exciting programmer features Arlen and Devine looking for a radium deposit in the frozen North. Richards is a promoter who goes along, only to turn traitor. All turns out well in the end, thanks to some two-fisted action, surprisingly not as well staged as usual for a film like this. Nagel, ineffective in her minor role, plays Devine's sister and Arlen's sweetheart who accompanies them on the expedition. The production values are standard.

p, Ben Pivar; d, John Rawlins; w, Maurice Tombragel, Victor McLeod (based on a story by Paul Huston); ph, John W. Boyle; m, H. J. Salter.

Adventure   (PR:A   MPAA:NR)

MUTINY IN THE BIG HOUSE**   (1939) 83m MON bw

Charles Bickford (*Father Joe*), Barton MacLane (*Red Manson*), Pat Moriarity (*Warden*), Dennis Moore (*Johnny*), William Royle (*Cap Samson*), Charles Foy (*Bitsy*), George Cleveland (*Dad*), Nigel de Brulier (*Mike*), Ed Foster (*Duke*), Richard Austin (*Jim*), Russell Hopton (*Frankie*), Jeffrey Sayre (*Milo*), Jack Daley (*Evans*), Dave O'Brien (*Daniels*), Wheeler Oakman (*Benson*), Charles King, Merrill McCormick.

Moore is sent to prison for forging a $10 check. Once there, he's offered two possibilities: salvation with the prison chaplain (Bickford), or fighting it out along side tough convict MacLane. At first he sides with MacLane, but gradually sees the light and follows Bickford instead. Produced by one-time actor Withers, the film is fairly good and exhibits standard production values considering its small budget and programmer status. Bickford delivers a good performance in the stereotyped B-movie prison priest role. The character was supposedly based on the real-life events of Father Patrick O'Neil, who was honored for halting a prison break in Colorado in 1929. This minor programmer was also the basis for "Prison Break!" one of comedian Lenny Bruce's best known parodies.

p, Grant Withers; d, William Nigh; w, Robert D. Andrews (based on a story by Martin Mooney); ph, Harry Neumann; ed, Russell F. Schoengarth.

Prison   Cas.   (PR:A   MPAA:NR)

MUTINY OF THE ELSINORE, THE*   (1939, Brit.) 74m Argyle/Regal bw

Paul Lukas (*Jack Pathurst*), Lyn Harding (*Mr. Pike, !st Officer*), Kathleen Kelly (*Margaret West*), Clifford Evans (*Bert Rhyne*), Michael Martin-Harvey (*Charles Davis*), William Devlin (*O'Sullivan*), Ben Soutten (*Mr. Mellaire, 2nd Mate*), Conway Dixon (*Capt. West*), Pat Noonan (*Murphy*), Tony Sympson (*Shorty*), Hamilton Keene (*Twist*), Alec Fraser (*Benson*), Jiro Soneya (*Wada*).

Simplistic version of London's story features Lukas as a novelist on board a ship overrun by mutineers. After the captain is killed and the first mate incapacitated, Lukas fights back and wins control of the ship as well as the affections of the captain's daughter. Tedious and full of anachronisms, such as the star's modern day clothing and his cries of "Scram!"—a word not ordinarily used in London's novels or stories.

p, John Argyle; d, Roy Lockwood; w, Walter Summers, Beaufoy Milton (based on the novel by Jack London); ph, Bryan Langley; ed, F. H. Bickerton.

Adventure   (PR:A   MPAA:NR)

MUTINY ON THE BLACKHAWK**   (1939) 67m UNIV

Richard Arlen (*Capt. Robert Lawrence*), Andy Devine (*Slim Collins*), Constance Moore (*Helen*), Noah Beery, Sr. (*Captain*), Guinn "Big Boy" Williams (*Mate*), Mala (*Woni*), Thurston Hall (*Sam Bailey*), Sandra Kane (*Tania*), Paul Fix (*Jack*), Richard Lane (*Kit Carson*), Mabel Albertson (*Widow*), Charles Trowbridge (*Gen. Fremont*), Bill Moore (*Sailor*), Byron Foulger (*Coombs*), Francisco Maran (*Gen. Romero*), Eddy Waller (*Parson*), Mamo Clark (*Mamo*).

Starts off with a mutiny, ends up with the cavalry saving the day. This film, which combines two diverse story lines, featured the team of Arlen and Devine staving off mutineers and freed slaves aboard a naval ship, circa 1840. After the exciting opening, the ship lands at the California coastline and the pair wander the territory until they come across the Mexican army out to destroy a small California settlement. There's dangerous doings until the cavalry rescues the village from destruction. The weak script can never decide which direction to go. Is this a western or sea adventure; a comedy or drama? Whatever the case, the starring team manages to rise above the material because of the surprisingly strong direction that keeps the action moving. The laughs are natural and fight sequences expertly staged.

p, Ben Pivar; d, Christy Cabanne; w, Michael L. Simmons (based on a story by Pivar); ph, John Boyle; ed, Maurice Wright.

Adventure   (PR:A   MPAA:NR)

MUTINY ON THE BOUNTY*****   (1935) 132m MGM bw

Charles Laughton (*Capt. William Bligh*), Clark Gable (*1st Mate Fletcher Christian*), Franchot Tone (*Roger Byam*), Herbert Mundin (*Smith*), Eddie Quillan (*Ellison*), Dudley Digges (*Bacchus*), Donald Crisp (*Burkitt*), Henry Stephenson (*Sir Joseph Banks*), Francis Lister (*Capt. Nelson*), Spring Byington (*Mrs. Byam*), Movita Castaneda (*Tehani*), Mamo Clark (*Maimiti*), Ian Wolfe (*Maggs*), Ivan Simpson (*Morgan*), De Witt Jennings (*Fryer*), Stanley Fields (*Muspratt*), Wallis Clark (*Morrison*), Vernon Downing (*Hayward*), Dick Winslow (*Tinkler*), Byron Russell (*Quintal*), Percy Waram (*Coleman*), David Torrence (*Lord Hood*), John Harrington (*Mr. Purcell*), Robert Livingston (*Young*), Douglas Walton (*Stewart*), Alec Craig (*McCoy*), Doris Lloyd (*Cockney Moll*), Eric Wilton (*Captain of Board*), Lionel Belmore (*Innkeeper*), Nadine Beresford (*Ellison's Mother*), Marion Clayton (*Mary*

Ellison), Mary Gordon *(Peddler)*, Winter Hall *(Chaplain)*, James Cagney, David Niven *(Extras)*, Charles Nauu, Sam Wallace Driscoll *(Bits)*, Hal LeSueur *(Millard)*, William Bainbridge *(Hitihiti)*, David Thursby *(McIntosh)*, Crauford Kent *(Lt. Edwards)*, Pat Flaherty *(Churchill)*, Charles Irwin *(Byrne)*, John Powers *(Hilebrandt)*, King Mojave *(Richard Skinner)*, William Stack *(Judge Advocate)*, Harold Entwhistle *(Capt. Colpoys)*, Will Stanton *(Portsmouth Joe)*, Harry Cording *(Soldier)*.

Few adventure epics have ever approached MUTINY ON THE BOUNTY for excitement, drama, thrills, and the classic confrontation of good against evil. Truly a great film in every regard, this picture made box office history and Gable's name became synonymous with everything manly and noble. It also established Laughton as an insidious film menace, a heap of disgusting humanity who had no regard for life or liberty. He is simply the essence of hatefulness in a riveting role that would forever be linked to his normally likable self. Adding heartily to the high seas action tale was that the film was based upon hard fact, dealing with the astounding mutiny on board the British ship *Bounty* in the year 1788. The film opens in December, 1787, as the ship sails from Portsmouth, England, en route to Tahiti in the West Indies to transport breadfruit trees back to England. Just before it leaves native shores an exuberant Tone, playing idealistic midshipman Roger Byam, raises his glass in bon voyage to visitors and fellow ship's officers, toasting eloquently: "Here's to the voyage of the *Bounty*. Still waters and the great golden sea. Flying fish like streaks of silver. Mermaids who sing in the night. The Southern Cross and all the stars on the other side of the world." One of the visitors, Stephenson, as Sir Joseph Banks, is stirred by the young man's lyrical toast and responds with: "Bless my soul. To the voyage of the *Bounty*!" For Tone and the rest of the crew the future looks bright and beautiful, but it is full of desperate confrontations between a vicious, bullying captain and his courageous first mate, as the vessel heads across the Pacific to the tropical paradise of Tahiti and its ravishingly beautiful Polynesian girls. On the horizon is agony, torture, an historic mutiny, shipwrecks, a record survival in an open boat, and a manhunt that does not cease for decades. Right from the beginning, Laughton, as Captain Bligh, establishes his tradition of fear and punishment, ordering floggings, keelhaulings, and other torturous disciplines for the slightest infraction of the rules. He is not above cheating the men out of their rations, early on in the voyage ordering Gable to witness the disappearance of several large cheeses, inferring these have been stolen by his worthless crew. Gable objects, having learned that the food was taken off the ship before it sailed and delivered to Laughton's home. He confronts Laughton with this information and is soundly rebuffed and called a liar. When Gable protests against the inhuman treatment administered to the men, Laughton snorts: "They respect one law—fear." This echoes Laughton's earlier remark to a ship's visitor: "If you think there is no science in a cat-o'-nine-tails, you should see my bos'n." Laughton's reign of terror subsides when the *Bounty* reaches Tahiti. Here the crew leisurely gathers breadfruit trees and most of them find Polynesian sweethearts, including Gable and Tone. Laughton, jealous of Gable's popularity with the natives and his love affair with the chief's daughter, orders his first mate to stay aboard the ship but the chief, Bainbridge, insists that either Gable return to Tahitian shores to see his daughter and enjoy life while supervising the work crews or there will be no breadfruit trees for the *Bounty* to carry back to England. Laughton relents but seethes with an even deeper hatred for his first mate. Within six months the *Bounty* is loaded to the upper decks with breadfruit trees and Laughton orders his crew aboard and preparations are made for the return trip. Tone bids farewell to Castaneda, playing Tehani, and Gable says goodbye to Clark, playing Maimita. Gable promises that he will return to see Clark but they both know this is only wishful dreaming. As the ship sails homeward Laughton's actions become even more bestial. He orders sick men sent aloft into the masts, and others, for sneaking a drink of precious water, locked in chains in the ship's brig. Digges, the elderly, alcoholic ship's doctor, is gravely ill, yet Laughton orders him topside to witness a flogging. When Digges does manage to struggle to the deck, he dies from the effort. This is the last straw for Gable. He goes to the brig and there finds one of Laughton's men beating seaman Crisp, who is chained to the wall. He knocks down the henchman and then calls members of the crew he knows are bent on mutiny, telling them he has been in hell for weeks under Laughton's inhuman orders. He tells Crisp, Flaherty, Russell, Fields, and others that he's taking the ship and the mutiny ensues with the mutineers quickly overwhelming crew members loyal to Laughton. The captain is brought to the deck and tied to a mast. Quinlan and others wave knives and swords in his face, calling him "an old rogue," and Crisp points to his lacerated back, shouting: "Give me 20 lashes will you? I'll give you a hundred." He is about to lift his hand to strike the pugnacious Laughton when Gable stops him. He takes Laughton and those wishing to follow him to a longboat supplied with food, water, a sextant, and some tools, ordering the indignant captain to get in. "But you're taking my ship?" says Laughton. Roars Gable: "The king's ship, and you're not fit to command!" He tells him and his cohorts to take their chances with the sea and forces them into the longboat. Laughton and the others get into the longboat and fall astern of the *Bounty* from which crew members mockingly throw the breadfruit trees. A defiant Laughton stands up in the longboat and raises his fist at the jeering mutineers. He shouts: "Cast me adrift! You think you're sending me to my doom, eh? Well, you're wrong! . . . I'll live to see you, all of you, hang from the highest yardarm in the British fleet!" Crisp grabs a rifle and aims it at Laughton but Gable knocks the weapon skyward so it fires harmlessly. Now it's Laughton and his faithful minions against the open sea and Gable and his mutineers, who head back to Tahiti. Some of the passengers, including Tone, are unwilling passengers back to paradise. They had been below decks during the mutiny and had no choice but to remain on board in spite of wanting to go with Laughton. Gable tells them there is nothing that can be done about it now and that Tone and the others should make the best of their situation. When returning to Tahiti, Gable, Tone, and the others resume their wonderful idyll. Laughton, meanwhile, crosses 3,618 miles of open seas to reach Timor, safety, and the edifying feeling that he will be able to pursue his mutinous crew and see them hang for defying him. (Bligh's actual survival and voyage in an open boat, 49 days at sea until reaching the Dutch East Indies, is considered one of the greatest feats in seafaring history.) He is given another ship, the *Pandora*, and sets sail for Tahiti to track down Gable and the other mutineers. (In reality Bligh did not command this punitive expedition, which was led by a Capt. Edwards.) When the *Pandora* comes distantly into view, the mutineers scramble aboard the *Bounty*, taking with them their native sweethearts and Tahitian male recruits and sail away. Some of the men, including Tone, stay behind, wanting to be saved. But when the Pandora anchors offshore and Tone happily reports aboard, Laughton steps forward and orders him put in irons. Tone protests, explaining that he was taken against his will by the mutineers of the *Bounty*. "You can explain that to a court-martial," snaps the scowling Laughton. Tone is thrown into the brig with the other *Bounty* crew members found on the island, but Laughton is deprived of snaring the one man who serves as his terrible goad, Gable. The first mate of the *Bounty* sails the ship beyond the normal sea lanes and beyond any known landfalls. By accident Gable discovers desolate, tiny, Pitcairn Island which has been indicated on official British maps in the wrong spot, hundreds of miles from where it has been pinpointed on regular charts. In short, there is no way through regular navigation principles that a pursuing British ship can find Pitcairn. Gable orders the men to remove all supplies and equipment from the *Bounty*. Once all on board have left the ship, Gable orders the *Bounty* burned at anchorage so that even its masts disappear beneath the waves. He and his men and their native wives are now stranded for life on Pitcairn which has no natural harbors, and nothing but barren cliffs on all sides, making landings next to impossible. Meanwhile, the mutiny-haunted Laughton drives the *Pandora* relentlessly across wild seas in his wild hunt for Gable and in his blind desire to get his man he forces the *Pandora* upon a reef and wrecks her. Before Tone and the other prisoners can drown, Laughton makes sure they are brought up on deck and taken into the lifeboats. When Tone thanks Laughton, the smug captain tells him: "I wouldn't lose you for a flagship!" Laughton escorts the prisoners back to England where they are put on trial. Tone is convicted along with the rest of them but he makes an impassioned plea for his and their lives. Tone illustrates how Laughton starved, tortured, and killed his men and how Gable "would not endure" such inhuman treatment and rebelled against it. Tone describes in passionate terms how British seamen would serve willingly in ships not as the victims of press gangs but as free men if only the king's captains set an example, "not by flogging their backs but by lifting their hearts," and, in so doing, they would "sweep the seas for England." Though Tone is condemned with the others, the king, after hearing a plea from Stephenson, pardons the noble Tone and he is reassigned to a new ship. When boarding the vessel he is approached by fellow officers, one of whom repeats his now historic lines that they will "sweep the seas for England!" Laughton, though partly triumphant in badgering the admiralty court into an en masse conviction of the captured men enjoys only a pyrrhic victory. After the sentencing, the court departs, its admirals walking past Laughton without salutation. He abruptly steps forward to offer his hand to one of the admirals who tells him that he admires the spectacular open-boat voyage he made and then refuses to shake Laughton's hand, walking away, indicating the contempt all of the admirals have for his bestial conduct. The real Bligh, his own pompous memoirs to the contrary, was indeed the brutish, profane, and contemptible creature that Laughton portrayed him as being and his inhuman treatment of seamen brought about radical reforms in the British maritime laws. The film about this isolated but dramatic mutiny was so expertly crafted and brilliantly acted that it became one of the most durable and engrossing adventure films ever made. Gable, Laughton, and Tone are simply outstanding and, for the first and only time in history, all three were nominated for Oscars in the Best Actor division but all lost to Victor McLaglen for THE INFORMER. The film nevertheless walked off with the Best Picture Oscar and rightly so. Lloyd's direction is sure, quick with action, and visually gratifying. He captures the exotic South Seas island of Tahiti and the rigors of the hardscrabble voyage while developing wonderful characterizations in not only the leads but many of the supporting players. Lloyd had had a long-standing fascination with the *Bounty* incident and, with his agent Edward Small, quickly bought the rights to the Nordhoff-Hall novel (which was really a trilogy, *Mutiny on the Bounty, Men Against the Sea,* and *Pitcairn Island*, published in 1932), paying only $12,500 for the screen rights. The director had helmed the silent adventure film, THE SEA HAWK (1924), and had ample experience in handling the unwieldy problems normal to epic productions. Lloyd and Small then took the property to MGM, not to Irving Thalberg, the brilliant chief of studio production, but to the overall boss, Louis B. Mayer. Lloyd told Mayer that he would make a gift of the screen rights if he were allowed to direct the film. Mayer said he would think about it. While the mogul pondered, Walter Wanger later arrived and proposed that he produce the film and star Robert Montgomery in the role of first mate Fletcher Christian. Mayer finally decided that the entire project was out of the question, that nobody would be interested in a hero who was a mutineer, that there was a lack of romantic interest, and that the film would be excessively expensive. Besides, he said, Australian producer Charles Chauvel had already produced a film in 1932 dealing with the basic story, IN THE WAKE OF THE BOUNTY, starring, in his first film, a 23-year-old novice actor from Tasmania named Errol Flynn who played Fletcher Christian. No, no, no, said Louis B. Mayer, out of the question. But Lloyd and Small were persistent and when Thalberg returned from a European vacation they went to him and he became excited over doing the film. He argued with Mayer, telling him at one point: "People are fascinated by cruelty and that's why MUTINY will have appeal." These were the halcyon days of Thalberg who had produced one great film after another and Mayer bowed to his wishes, but waited patiently for MUTINY ON THE BOUNTY to eat up a fortune in costs and then dismally flop at the box office. Meanwhile, the rights for the Chauvel film, really a crude semi-documentary shot on a small budget, were bought to keep this film off the American market, although much of its footage was subsequently used piecemeal in short promotion films heralding the forthcoming major MGM production. (Chauvel had actually gone to Pitcairn Island and filmed its rough, forbidding crags and landscapes, also getting some underwater shots of the real *Bounty*, or its remains, at the bottom of the shallow waters off the island.) Thalberg, from the beginning, had only one actor in mind for the role of Fletcher Christian, and that was MGM's hottest male star, Gable. But Gable, when hearing about the role, wanted no part of it. He sank into black moods and argued with Thalberg. At one point he was quoted as telling the mogul: "Look, Irving. I'm a realistic kind of actor. I've never played in a costume picture in my life. Now you want me to wear a pigtail and velvet knee pants and shoes with silver buckles! The audience will laugh me off the screen. And I'll be damned if I'll shave off my mustache just because the British navy didn't allow them. This mustache has been damned lucky for me." Gable went on to point out that his bandied legs would appear ungainly in the knicker uniforms of a British navy officer and that his voice would sound flat in comparison to the accents of the British actors appearing in the film. He also hated the idea of appearing to be a dandy. His father, a rugged individualist, a wildcatting oil driller and rigger (a job Gable adopted for a while in his youth), had warned him that becoming an actor would probably mean that he would turn into a sissy, "a painted pretty boy," a homosexual maybe. Gable's worst fear was that he would appear in a role which might project the image, no matter how slight, of such a person, an image that would question what he prized most, his masculinity, his virility. Throughout the production he was always on guard to maintain his real man image. At one point, when a makeup man tried to powder his shiny nose with a puff, Gable exploded and shoved him away. Thalberg got his way as usual, asking Gable, according to Samuel Marx writing in *Mayer and Thalberg*: "Do this one for me. If it isn't one of your greatest successes I'll never ask you again to play a part you don't want to do." The King of Hollywood need not have worried about his manliness. His portrayal has not a trace of the fop, the weakling, or the dandy. He is full of integrity, strong decision, and courage, though he displays a tenderness in his brief romantic scenes with Clark that clutched the hearts of female viewers. Laughton was another matter. His role as Captain Bligh, which ranks as one of the all-time portrayals of complete villainy, almost went to Wallace Beery but he was too "American" for the role, Thalberg concluded, and Lloyd and company looked elsewhere, finally selecting Laughton because of his roles as insensitive, truculent, and mostly hateful creatures such as the tyrannical monarch of THE PRIVATE LIFE OF HENRY VIII (1935), and the equally harsh and unfeeling father in THE BARRETTS OF WIMPOLE STREET, 1934, the latter being a pet project of Thalbergs, a smash hit starring his wife and then MGM queen of the lot Norma Shearer. Laughton himself was not eager to portray the loathesome Bligh. He felt that taking the top billing as Thalberg insisted upon would immediately put him at odds with Gable. He also made some snide remarks about Lloyd's ability to handle actors, saying that the director knew only how to move about props and extras and that the real star of the film was the ship. The great character actor nevertheless threw himself into the role with such vigor, sometimes slipping on the ham, that he *became* the hateful Bligh and his oft-repeated line, full of venom—"Mr. Christian— come here!"—chilled the spines of generations of moviegoers and caused endless comics to mimic his role. The acid fairly dripped from Laughton's tongue and some of it burned Gable. In one scene where Laughton addresses Gable, he refused to look at his costar and Gable exploded, going to Lloyd immediately after the scene and shouting in front of the cast and crew: "Laughton's treating me like an extra! He didn't even look at me when he addressed me. The audience won't see me in the sequence! Laughton hogged it!" Lloyd took Gable aside and the director tried to calm him down while Laughton fumed. Neither actor would continue working with the other until Thalberg flew to Catalina Island where Lloyd was shooting on location, and talked to both stars, telling Gable that he must follow Lloyd's direction and ordering Laughton to look Gable straight in the eyes when talking to him. But battles continued in other quarters. Lloyd and MGM officials overseeing the production on location constantly battled about soaring costs and expensive scenes and Thalberg again had to fly to the island off the California coast to put things right. Tone, who had taken the part of the luckless Midshipman Byam after Robert Montgomery turned it down, spent much of his time off-camera trying to settle quarrels between warring stars and a director battling executives. The cost of the production, which was almost two years in the making, soared out of sight, until MGM discovered it had spent almost $2 million, then a whopping amount. (The film would prove, however, to be one of the studio's all-time money makers in the 1930s, returning a gross of $4,460,000 the first time out.) Much of the overhead went into Lloyd's insistence upon authentic locale shooting and the lifesize reproductions of the ships *Bounty* and *Pandora*. These ships were actually sailed 14,000 miles to Tahiti and back. In Tahiti, the second unit crew shot miles of film, using 2,500 native extras. The ships, which had to battle severe storms, were repaired at additional expense and, when they returned, it was discoverd that a negligent technician had failed to dehydrate the film in the tropical weather and the complete footage was underexposed and useless. The second unit set sail again for Tahiti and made the entire arduous voyage all over again to get the necessary background shots. Most of the principal shooting was done on Catalina Island but even in this normally tranquil area, hazards abounded. The camera barge sank in a mishap and with it went $50,000 in vital equipment. A technician drowned trying to save it. Two more technicians were almost drowned while operating an 18-foot model of the *Bounty* in a real storm. The replica was actually hurled out to sea in the storm and was lost for several days until found, the two men inside close to death. While the film was still in production it became chic for rising actors or even superstars to sneak themselves into crowd scenes as extras. David Niven was an extra aboard the *Bounty* and even James Cagney reportedly found a way to get into a crowd scene. The Warner Bros. tough guy was sailing off Catalina in his yacht *Martha* when he spotted the *Bounty*, according to one report, and was pressed into becoming a member of the crew for a few hours, although no one has ever pinpointed Cagney in any specific scene. The film was written by a host of scribes, the most colorful of the group being Wilson, who was Louis B. Mayer's handpicked writer. Wilson, who started the script alone, busied himself with plans for a lavish wedding, and, when he did settle down to work on the screenplay, MGM executives grew alarmed at the infrequency of his manuscript deliveries. So few pages were forthcoming from his residence—Wilson was allowed the privilege of working at home, being a Mayer pet—that Thalberg had detectives watch Wilson's house. They later reported to the mogul that Wilson had been working through the night, his typewriter going a mile a minute but the product churned off that machine was not going toward MGM. Messengers arrived at Wilson's residence every morning and received from the haggard writer large Manila envelopes. The detectives trailed the messengers always to the same spot, the studio of Samuel Goldwyn and to producer Walter Wanger who occupied offices there. It was learned that Wilson was working on a script completely different from MUTINY ON THE BOUNTY for which he was receiving a large stipend. He was moonlighting for Wanger, writing a sequel to GABRIEL OVER THE WHITE HOUSE, which Wilson had earlier written. The new film was entitled THE PRESIDENT VANISHES but it would have to wait, Wilson was told, when he was brought to Thalberg to explain his actions. Wilson admitted that he had been moonlighting for several weeks but Thalberg, who had every right to fire him, as studio executive Eddie Mannix suggested, merely warned him to stop and resume his duties on MUTINY ON THE BOUNTY. The MGM genius was wholly unpredictable. He had recently had a battle royal with the Screen Writers Guild and could have used this incident to retaliate against the Guild. He did send Wanger a bill for Wilson's services and cautioned all within earshot that he would tolerate no more looting of staff members. It was later said that MUTINY ON THE BOUNTY presented a distorted portrait of Capt. William Bligh, that Laughton's despicable characterization was unfair and inaccurate. On the contrary. Bligh was a pompous, cold-hearted, vindictive brute whose sadistic treatment of crew members was a matter of record. Certain British writers strove mightily to scrape the stain from his image but this whitewashing is wholly refuted by citations in British maritime laws that were changed for the better *because* of Bligh's inhuman behavior. He was a monster and Laughton authentically captured the real Bligh. Following the mutiny, Bligh returned to Tahiti and obtained a boatload of the precious breadfruit trees. He fought in naval battles and was cited for bravery but by 1805 he was back to ordering men's backs whipped to the bone as governor of New South Wales in Australia. So tyrannical was he that he caused another mutiny, this time among the land garrison, and was shipped back to England in disgrace. The mutineers were tracked down and punished and again Bligh was vindicated by the guardians of his profession. His peers even went so far as to elevate this wretch to the position of vice admiral before his death in 1817 at the age of 65. He went to his grave not really sure of the fate of the man he hated most on earth, Fletcher Christian. Three years earlier, in 1814, the British ship *Briton* located Pitcairn Island and found only one of the original mutineers, John Adams, still alive. He was allowed to live on the island, free of charges, until his death in 1829. Christian and the rest, according to Adams, had died violently a few years after the *Bounty* mutineers arrived at Pitcairn. Male natives that accompanied the white men from Tahiti objected to the mutineers stealing their wives, and all the whites except for Adams, who was hunting at the time, were murdered. Christian, however, remains enigmatic to this day. It is known that he had sailed twice earlier with Bligh before the fatal *Bounty* voyage and that he was well-educated but low born, realizing he had little chance to rise in the service beyond first mate status. He was never a fop but a manly, rough-and-tough character who could not be bullied and resented Bligh's inhumanity, finally, out of principle, rebelling openly against it. In the few rough woodcuts of Christian he is shown wearing a beard, contrary to British regulations, and had Gable seen these early-day engravings of the character he was to play in the splendid MUTINY ON THE BOUNTY, he most certainly would have never shaved off that famous mustache; he would have been able to point to the real Christian's facial hair with triumph. Remade as THE BOUNTY, 1984.

p, Irving Thalberg; d, Frank Lloyd; w, Talbot Jennings, Jules Furthman, Carey Wilson (based on the novels *Mutiny on the Bounty* and *Men Against the Sea* by Charles Nordhoff, James Norman Hall); ph, Arthur Edeson; m, Herbert Stothart; ed, Margaret Booth; art d, Cedric Gibbons, Arnold Gillespie; m/l, "Love Song of Tahiti," Gus Kahn, Bronislau Kaper, Walter Jurmann.

Adventure **Cas.** **(PR:A MPAA:NR)**

MUTINY ON THE BOUNTY ½** (1962) 179m Arcola/MGM c

Marlon Brando *(Fletcher Christian)*, Trevor Howard *(Capt. William Bligh)*, Richard Harris *(John Mills)*, Hugh Griffith *(Alexander Smith)*, Richard Haydn *(William Brown)*, Tarita *(Maimiti)*, Tim Seely *(Edward Young)*, Percy Herbert *(Mattew Quintal)*, Gordon Jackson *(Edward Birkett)*, Noel Purcell *(William McCoy)*, Duncan Lamont *(John Williams)*, Chips Rafferty *(Michael Byrne)*, Ashley Cowan *(Samuel Mack)*, Eddie Byrne *(John Fryer)*, Keith McConnell *(James Morrison)*, Frank Silvera *(Minarii)*, Ben Wright *(Graves)*, Henry Daniell *(Court Martial Judge)*, Torin Thatcher *(Staines)*, Matahiarii Tama *(Chief Hitihiti)*.

The old Hollywood credo of "if a film's a hit once it'll be a hit again" does not work here (and rarely does, but try to tell that to most road-rutted producers). Though the production values are excellent, the story, the acting, and the editing of this colossal and expensive remake all fall miserably short of Frank Lloyd's 1935 film classic. Again viewers can sail with the *Bounty* to Tahiti and watch Howard as Bligh beat and mistreat his crew members for 14,000 miles while Brando hides out in his cabin trying on new uniforms replete with frills, lace, and immaculate knee-high stockings. The ship docks at the island paradise and crew members gather breadfruit and sexually promiscuous native girls. Then it's back to civilization and more torture at the hands of Howard with a mutiny thrown in to break up the tedium. Howard is set adrift and Brando takes the stolen *Bounty* to Pitcairn Island where mutineer Harris burns the ship against Brando's wishes so that none can ever return to England again. Brando, in a clumsy attempt to put out the fire on the sinking ship, is fatally charred (to a black crisp), and dies with the flaming masts of the famous ship burning behind the final credits. Brando is simply awful as Fletcher Christian, playing this real-life knuckle-breaker as a light-footed fop with no more concern for crew members than he would have for a breadfruit-bearing Tahitian native. He lisps ludicrously, sways obscenely, and postures like a female ingenue at a garden party—he's dreadful, even repugnant, and wholly out of character. It's obvious that director Milestone could not control Brando for a moment and that the famous, sometimes brilliant actor directed himself. His is one of the most impossible performances in screen history, infecting Harris, who plays a sort of seagoing Iago and is equally hammy and unbelievable. Howard tries to bring some sanity and reason to the part of Bligh and makes a mistake in doing so; the real Bligh, as Charles Laughton so aptly played him in 1935, was psychopathic, a beast, who had no humanity whatsoever. This film version goes historically beyond the Lloyd version, ending at Pitcairn Island but wrongly showing the death of Christian, who lived for some time after the mutineers settled on the island. The second film did not portray Midshipman Roger Byam (enacted by Franchot Tone in 1935) and many more liberties, mostly nonsensical, were taken. Howard, for instance, does not confine Brando to the ship after the *Bounty* reaches Tahiti but actually orders him to go ashore and copiously copulate with the chief's daughter to establish good relationships with the natives. The mutiny in the 1962 version is almost a whim of Brando's. Howard kicks a water ladle out of his first mate's hand when Brando is about to give a sick crew member a drink. This so incenses Brando that he instantly mutinies with others. Though this version got seven Oscar nominations, it rightly received none. Movita Castenada, who had played Tone's native lover in the 1935 version, married Brando while he was doing the 1962 remake, but they were later divorced. Brando, who cost an estimated $6 million, later complained that "it was the worst experience of my acting career." Said director Milestone: "This picture should have been called "The Mutiny of Marlon Brando." And Harris chimed in: "The whole picture was just a large, dreadful nightmare to me." None of these gentlemen, however, had the good grace to quit the production and save MGM from near ruin which almost came about when the studio only recouped $9,800,000 in its initial release. Brando reportedly stuffed himself while making the film and ended with forty more pounds than he began. Little in this film is based on truth and even the *Bounty* itself was distorted, built to order 30 feet longer than the real ship to accommodate huge engines to drive it. The concept for the messy story and Brando's disgraceful posturing role was all Rosenberg, who should have turned in his producer's card and bought a used car lot—more in keeping with his perception of artistry—after seeing this expensive flop. Carol Reed was originally slated to direct, but he fell out with Rosenberg and was replaced by the once mighty Milestone, who here limply lent his name and no effort. Lederer's screenplay is only a cliche picked out of the Hollywood junkyard.

p, Aaron Rosenburg; d, Lewis Milestone; w, Charles Lederer, (uncredited, Eric Ambler, William L. Driscoll, Borden Chase, John Gay, Ben Hecht, based on the novel by Charles Nordhoff, James Norman Hall); ph, Robert L. Surtees (Ultra Panavision, Technicolor); m, Bronislau Kaper; ed, John McSweeney, Jr.; md, Robert Armbruster; art d, George W. Davis, J. McMillan Johnson; set d, Henry Grace, Hugh Hunt; cos, Moss Mabry; spec eff, A. Arnold Gillespie, Lee LeBlanc, Robert R. Hoag; ch, Hamil Petroff; makeup, William Tuttle.

Adventure **Cas.** **(PR:C-O MPAA:NR)**

MUTINY ON THE SEAS (SEE: OUTSIDE THE 3-MILE LIMIT, 1940)

MY AIN FOLK (1944, Brit.) 75m But bw

Mabel Constanduros *(Mrs. Mackenzie)*, Moira Lister *(Joan Mackenzie)*, Norman Prince *(Malcolm Keir)*, Herbert Cameron *(Mr. Keir)*, Nicolette Roeg *(Betty Stewart)*, John Turner *(Robertson)*, Ben Williams *(Jack McAllister)*, Charles Rolfe *(Alan Macgregor)*, Walter Midgeley, Lowry and Richardson, Lorna Martin, Herbert Thorpe, Gordon Begg, Desmond Roberts, Harry Angers, David Keir.

During World War II, beautiful blonde Lister is engaged to sailor Prince. She leaves her home in the highlands to take a factory job in Glasgow and later hears that her love is missing and presumed dead. She refuses to believe him dead and works to avert a strike at the factory. She organizes a radio show to raise worker morale and while she is on stage Prince returns for a tearful reunion. Stickily sentimental, laden with stiff-upper-lip wartime propaganda, and filled with an unbearable number of Scottish songs.

p, F. W. Baker; d, Germaine Burger; w, Kathleen Butler; ph, Ernest Palmer.

Musical Drama **(PR:A MPAA:NR)**

MY AIN FOLK** (1974, Brit.) 54m British Film Institute bw

Stephen Archibald, Hughie Restorick, Jean Taylor-Smith, Bernard McKenna.

A short piece which has some moments of delight but is ultimately unsatisfying. A nine-year-old boy lives with his maternal grandmother in England during the 1940s. When she dies he is passed to his paternal grandmother, who eventually sends him to an orphanage. The photography offers some nice compositions and an interesting use of black and white, but the film can't seem to follow through on the situations it builds up. This was the second film in a planned trilogy by the director; the first, MY CHILDHOOD, won the Golden Palm Award at the 1972 Chicago International Film Festival.

d&w, Bill Douglas; ph, Gale Tattersall; ed, Peter West.

Drama **(PR:A MPAA:NR)**

MY AMERICAN UNCLE (SEE: MON ONCLE D'AMERICAIN, 1980, Fr.)

MY AMERICAN WIFE** (1936) 65m PAR

Francis Lederer *(Count Ferdinand von und su Reidenach)*, Ann Sothern *(Mary Cantillon)*, Fred Stone *(Lafe Cantillon)*, Billie Burke *(Mrs. Robert Cantillon)*, Ernest Cossart *(Adolph)*, Grant Mitchell *(Robert Cantillon)*, Hal K. Dawson *(Vincent)*, Adrian Morris *(Stephen)*, Dora Clemant *(Agnes)*, Montague Shaw.

Stone plays a retired cowpuncher with an eccentric family. Burke is his sister-in-law who fixes up her daughter (Sothern) with Lederer, a handsome count. At first Stone doesn't care for the idea of a fancy foreigner in the family, but when he discovers that Lederer can ride wild horses and spit tobacco with the best of them, Stone quickly changes his mind much to the surprise of the whole family. A ridiculous comedy brightened by the clever performance of Lederer. The direction is sufficient, though the comedic pacing is off. A less than average programmer from the 1930s, based on a 1923 film.

p, Albert Lewis; d, Harold Young; w, Virginia Van Upp, Edith Fitzgerald (based on a story by Elmer Davis); ph, Harry Fischbeck; ed, Paul Weatherwax; md, Boris Morros; cos, Travis Banton.

Comedy **(PR:A MPAA:NR)**

MY APPLE (SEE: JUST ME, 1950, Fr.)

MY BABY IS BLACK!**

(1965, Fr.) 75m Lodice-General France-Groupement des Editeurs de Films-Athos/U.S. bw (LES LACHES VIVENT D'ESPOIR)

Gordon Heath *(Daniel)*, Francoise Giret *(Francoise)*, Aram Stephan *(The Professor)*, Mag-Avril *(The Concierge)*, Herve Watine *(The Guitarist)*, Fred Carault *(Francoise's Father)*, Viviane Mery *(Francoise's Mother)*, Claude Berri, Jacques Champreux, Arlette Didier, Philippe Prince.

A young French girl, Giret, gets involved with a Black student, Heath, against his better judgment. He is concerned with the prejudice the couple will have to face. They pursue their mutual attraction for each other, however, and she soon becomes pregnant. After an attack on another Black student upsets Heath, she decides not to tell him about the baby. They are separated when he is arrested for coming to the aid of a small Black boy who was being abused by a shop owner; meanwhile, Giret has the baby. He returns to her and they begin a life together. An average film with a horrible, exploitative title.

p&d, Claude Bernard-Aubert; w, Bernard-Aubert, Jean Rousselot; ph, Jean Collomb; m, Michel Magne; ed, Bernard-Aubert.

Drama **(PR:A MPAA:NR)**

MY BEST GAL* (1944) 67m REP bw

Jane Withers *(Kitty O'Hara)*, Jimmy Lydon *(Johnny McCloud)*, Frank Craven *(Danny O'Hara)*, Fortunio Bonanova *(Charlie)*, George Cleveland *(Ralph Hodges)*, Franklin Pangborn *(Mr. Porter)*, Mary Newton *(Miss Simpson)*, Jack Boyle *(Freddy)*.

Withers plays a drugstore assistant who comes from a show business family. They try to get her on the stage as well, providing her with music written by budding composer Lydon. Withers finally gives in and, of course, Lydon is a natural talent. She then attempts to find a backer for his show. The film was designed to fill out a double bill, and was undoubtedly made in haste on a small budget, which shows in the inadequate direction and poor production values. Withers manages to rise above the inept production with her singing and dancing. Songs include: "Where There's Love," "Upsy Downsy," "I've Got the Flyin'est Feelin'" (Kim Gannon, Walter Kent). MY BEST GAL represents an early directorial effort by Anthony Mann, best known for his well-crafted westerns of the 1950s, particularly those starring James Stewart.

p, Harry Grey; d, Anthony Mann; w, Olive Cooper, Earl Felton (based on a story by Richard Brooks); ph, Jack Marta; ed, Ralph Dixon; md, Morton Scott; art d, Russell Kimball, Gano Chittenden; ch, Dave Gould; cos, Adele Palmer.

Musical **(PR:A MPAA:NR)**

MY BILL** (1938) 60m FN-WB/WB bw

Kay Francis *(Mary Colbrook)*, Bonita Granville *(Gwen Colbrook)*, Anita Louise *(Muriel Colbrook)*, Bobby Jordan *(Reginald Colbrook)*, John Litel *(Mr. Rudlin)*, Dickie Moore *(Bill Colbrook)*, Bernice Pilot *(Beulah)*, Maurice Murphy *(Lynn Willard)*, Elisabeth Risdon *(Aunt Caroline)*, Helena Phillips Evans *(Mrs. Crosby)*, John Ridgely *(Florist)*, Jan Holm *(Secretary)*, Sidney Bracy *(Jenner)*.

Francis is the mother of four kids, three of whom are ungrateful to their widowed mom and move in with their wealthy aunt. Only Moore remains faithful to his mother, as well as endearing himself to a wealthy neighbor. When the neighbor passes away, it is discovered she has left her entire fortune to Moore. You can only guess who comes back all misty-eyed. Francis is miscast, looking far too young (and handsomely wardrobed) to be a struggling mother of four. A remake of the 1930 film COURAGE, a far superior film.

p, Bryan Foy; d, John Farrow; w, Vincent Sherman, Robertson White (based on the play "Courage" by Tom Barry); ph, Sid Hickox; ed, Frank Magee; art d, Max Parker; cos, Orry-Kelly.

Drama **(PR:A MPAA:NR)**

MY BLOOD RUNS COLD* 1/2 (1965) 103m WB bw

Troy Donahue *(Ben Gunther)*, Joey Heatherton *(Julie Merriday)*, Barry Sullivan *(Julian Merriday)*, Nicolas Coster *(Harry Lindsay, Attorney)*, Jeanette Nolan *(Aunt Sarah)*, Russell Thorson *(Sheriff)*, Ben Wright *(Lansbury)*, Shirley Mitchell *(Mrs. Courtland)*, Howard McNear *(Henry)*, Howard Wendell *(Mayor)*, John Holland *(Mr. Courtland)*, John McCook *(Owen)*.

Heatherton and her boy friend Coster are out for a drive when they crash into motorcyclist Donahue. She gives him a lift, though he insists on calling her "Barbara" rather than her real name. After arriving home, Heatherton tells her aunt (Nolan) about the stranger and Nolan explains that Heatherton's great-great grandmother was named Barbara and had an affair with a man named Benjamin Gunther (Donahue's name in the film). Donahue insists that they are reincarnations of the ancestral lovers and she elopes with him only to discover that Donahue is an escapee from the nut house. The film ends with him attempting to strangle would-be rescuer Sullivan and finally falling to his death from atop a tower. It starts off well but MY BLOOD RUNS COLD quickly dribbles off into boredom. Donahue is fair, if not a bit laughable, and Heatherton is wholly unbelievable. The direction is ineffectual, with no sense for suspense at all. Director Conrad wisely turned to acting, becoming television's "Cannon."

p&d, William Conrad; w, John Mantley (based on the story "The Girl Who Was Two" by John Meredyth Lucas); ph, Sam Leavitt (Panavision); m, George Duning; ed, William Ziegler; art d, LeRoy Deane; set d, Ralph S. Hurst; makeup, Gordon Bau.

Drama (PR:O MPAA:NR)

MY BLOODY VALENTINE zero (1981, Can.) 91m Secret/PAR c

Paul Kelman (T.J.), Lori Hallier (Sarah), Neil Affleck (Axel), Keith Knight (Hollis), Alf Humphreys (Howard), Cynthia Dale (Patty), Helene Udy (Sylvia), Rob Stein (John), Tom Kovacs (Mike), Terry Waterland (Harriet), Carl Marotte (Dave), Jim Murchison (Tommy), Gina Dick (Gretchen), Peter Cowper (Miner/Harry Warden), Don Francks (Newby), Patricia Hamilton (Mabel), Larry Reynolds (Mayor), Jack Van Evera (Happy), Jeff Danks (Young Axel), Pat Hemingway (Woman), Graham Whitehead (Mac), Fred Watters, Jeff Fulton (Supervisors), Pat Walsh (Harvey), Marguerite McNeil (Mrs. Raleigh), Sandy Leim (Ben), John MacDonald (Rescuer).

With the success of HALLOWEEN in 1978, a spate of low-budget horror films about mad slashers attacking teenagers filled the movie theaters across the land. One of these was MY BLOODY VALENTINE. It's similar to HALLOWEEN in plot: a mad slasher goes about preying on innocent victims with machine-like efficiency. This film, however, has none of the style or intelligence of its predecessor. Rather, a masked coal miner takes his pick-ax and sinks it into the chests of locals in the town of Valentine Bluffs. The hearts of his victims get delivered to the police, wrapped up in candy boxes. Absolutely disgusting, with the usual sick attitude towards women which these "mad slasher" films unfortunately espoused. The producers, Dunning and Link (MEATBALLS), cut some of the goriest footage to avoid an X-rating. Averaging a murder every 7 1/2 minutes, this undoubtedly will please the mindless audiences it was aimed for. Absolutely disgusting.

p, John Dunning, Andre Link, Stephen Miller; d, George Mihalka; w, John Beaird (based on a story concept by Miller); ph, Rodney Gibbons (Movielab Color); m, Paul Zaza; ed, Jean LaFleur, Kit Wallis, Gerald Vansier; art d, Penny Hadfield; cos, Susan Hall.

Horror **Cas.** (PR:O MPAA:R)

MY BLUE HEAVEN** 1/2 (1950) 96m FOX c

Betty Grable (Molly Moran), Dan Dailey (Jack Moran), David Wayne (Walter Pringle), Jane Wyatt (Janet Pringle), Mitzi Gaynor (Gloria Adams), Una Merkel (Miss Gilbert), Louise Beavers (Selma), Laura Pierpont (Mrs. Johnson), Don Hicks (Young Man), Beulah Parkington (Nurse), Ann Burr (Laura), Billy Daniels (Dance Director), Larry Keating (Doctor), Minerva Urecal (Miss Bates), Mae Marsh (Maid), Noel Reyburn (Studio Employee), Phyllis Coates (Woman), Barbara Pepper (Waitress), Myron Healey (Father), Lois Hall (Mother), Frank Remley (Orchestra Leader), Melinda Plowman, Vicki Lee Blunt (Pringle Girls), Gary Pagett, Bill McKenzie, Bobby Stevens (Pringle Boys), Buddy Pryor, Irving Fulton (Specialty Dancers), Fred Lewis, Conrad Binyon, Alex Gerry, Dorothy Neumann, Isabel Withers, William Baldwin, John Hedloe, Thomas Brown Henry, Eula Guy, Marion Marshall, Harry Carter.

A paper-thin plot that mostly served as a reason to reunite Grable and Dailey after their success in WHEN MY BABY SMILES AT ME. It also served to introduce a pert, energetic and brunette Mitzi Gaynor to the movies. Dailey and Grable are a successful radio team who are just about to jump into TV and are happily expecting a child. But they get into a car accident, she loses the child, and is told it will be impossible for her to bear another. Their best friends are Wayne and Wyatt, who have five children (Plowman, Blunt, Pagett, Stevens, and McKenzie) and the sight of the happy family causes Dailey and Grable to try adoption but they are stymied by the red tape and that the adoption agencies dislike theater people, no matter how successful they may be. They manage to get a baby but it is not for long. After the head of an orphanage gets them a different child, they then get the first one back so they now have two. Suddenly, Grable discovers she is pregnant, despite what all the doctors said, and they wind up with an instant family. Along the way, there are a few good satires of TV commercials for cosmetics and a number of songs, including the title tune, written by George Whiting and Walter Donaldson and sung by Grable and Dailey and several more by Ralph Blane and Harold Arlen: "Live Hard, Work Hard, Love Hard" (sung by Gaynor), "What A Man," "It's Deductible," "Don't Rock the Boat, Dear," "Friendly Islands," "I Love a New Yorker," and "Halloween." Other than the title song, none of the others rocked the charts.

p, Sol C. Siegel; d, Henry Koster; w, Lamar Trotti, Claude Binyon (based on the story "Storks Don't Bring Babies" by S. K. Lauren); ph, Arthur E. Arling (Technicolor); ed, James B. Clark; md, Alfred Newman; art d, Lyle Wheeler, Joseph C. Wright; cos, Charles Le Maire.

Musical Comedy (PR:A MPAA:NR)

MY BODY HUNGERS* (1967) 80m Amalfi Films No. 3/Iaven International bw

Gretchen Rudolph (Marcia Teel), John Aristedes (Detective Rod Loring), Tammy Latour (Joan Reynolds), Tony King (George Harvey), Liz Love (Mavis Harvey), Joe Santos (Truck Driver), Rose Marie Stadler, Rickey Bell, Carolyn Fawcett, Lola Adams (Olga and Her Oomphettes), Joy Durden (Pianist/Geri), George Winship (Detective Pete Forsythe), Bob Franklin (Newscaster), Laurene Claire (Lynn Phillips), Geraldine Baron (Janet Teel), Pat Powers (M.C.), Diane Moss (Waitress), Brandy Case (Woman Clerk).

In an effort to uncover the psychotic murderer of her sister, Rudolph takes over the dead woman's position at the striptease joint where she worked before her death. The killer turns out to be a rich mama's boy who fell in love with the sister. He also falls in love with Rudolph and attempts to murder her, but the fiery woman narrowly

escapes death several times before the maniac is killed in a car crash. Unoriginal concepts are handled in a manner which heightens exploitive elements.

p, Gerard Conti; d&w, Joe Sarno; ph, Anthony Lover; m, Stan Free; ed, Kemper Peacock.

Crime/Horror (PR:O MPAA:NR)

MY BODYGUARD*** 1/2 (1980) 96m FOX c

Chris Makepeace (Clifford), Adam Baldwin (Linderman), Matt Dillon (Moody), Paul Quandt (Carson), Joan Cusack (Shelley), Dean R. Miller (Hightower), Tim Reyna (Koontz), Richard Bradley (Dubrow), Denise Baske (Leilani), Hank Salas (Mike), Vicky Nelson (Freddy), Ruth Gordon (Gramma), Martin Mull (Mr. Peache), John Houseman (Dobbs), Craig Richard Nelson (Griffith), Kathryn Grody (Miss Jump), Richard Cusack (Principal Rath), Dorothy Scott (Librarian), Angelo Buscaglia (Basketball Coach), Kitt York (Stewardess), Marge Kotusky (Mrs. Linderman), Tom Reilly, Paul Charvonneau, Laura Salenger, Bert Hoddinott, Jonathan Turk, Cindy Russ, Laurie McEathron, Lori Mandell, Dean Devlin, Tim Kazurinsky Bill Koza, Vivian Smolen, Bruce Jarchow, Andrea Dillon, Leonard Mack, George Wendt, Jerome Myers, Freddy Moss, Joseph Cohn, Patrick Billingsley, Barbara Hoddinott, Eddie Gomez.

What a shame that MY BODYGUARD didn't get nearly the attention that it warranted. The executive producer, Melvin Simon, is an Indianapolis real estate mogul who came to California with lots of money and lots of big ideas. He oversaw this film and the excellent Richard Rush film, THE STUNT MAN, neither of which made much money. MY BODYGUARD is, essentially, a revenge picture, although not like one of the mindless Charles Bronson films. This is revenge with intelligence and sensitivity and, despite being populated by teenagers, it bears as much resemblance to a teenage exploitation film as BUGSY MALONE. Makepeace is a youngster who has moved to a new area with his father, Mull, and grandmother, Gordon. Mull manages a fancy hotel and Gordon does her wisecracking, horny grandma routine. They are in Chicago and Makepeace's high school is ruled by bully Dillon, who is running a protection racket and takes money from the smaller kids so they won't be pummeled by Baldwin, a huge giant who is reclusive and whom everyone fears is seething with violence because the gossip has it that he once killed someone. Nobody knows for sure if that's true because Baldwin doesn't talk at all. Makepeace gets tired of giving up his lunch money to Dillon, so he decides to go straight to the source of all the anxiety and offers Baldwin money to protect him from Dillon. Baldwin is shocked when he hears Makepeace's tale because he is not involved in Dillon's scheming, and he is ready to take Dillon apart, but Makepeace convinces him to get all the already-paid money back from Dillon and distribute it to the payers. The tide of terror turns as Baldwin and Makepeace become friends and Baldwin takes on the job of being the younger, weaker boy's bodyguard. It turns out that Baldwin is shy and ridden with guilt because he and his late brother had been handling their father's revolver when it fired, killing Baldwin's brother. The giant had never forgiven himself and decided to impose a silence on his life until now. Things go along too well for a while and Dillon isn't heard from. Then he surfaces with his own bodyguard, a behemoth with a shaved head who seems to have taken his coiffure from Mr. T. There is a battle and baldy whacks Baldwin for a loop. Later, revenge is exacted, with Dillon getting his at the hands of Makepeace, and the bald hunk also being taken care of. The movie ends as all of the kids are walking along Lake Michigan and Baldwin has been totally accepted. A heart-warming story, done well, with mostly no-name actors and superior direction by one-time actor Bill (COME BLOW YOUR HORN, etc.). Makepeace is excellent as the slight protagonist who takes on bully Dillon, who turns out to be a blowhard. Baldwin is a "find" as the brooding mammoth and his presence has the kids at the school (and the audience) believing that he just might have been capable of all the violence ascribed to him. As the picture unspools, we see that he is just bigger and shyer and more ungainly than the others. The adults in the picture are merely counterpoint, with Houseman doing a brief bit as one of Gordon's potential elderly lovers. The screenplay is honest, the kids talk the way kids do, and there is not one false note. Dave Grusin's score adds immeasurably to the tone of MY BODY-GUARD, although the totality of the movie is somewhat downgraded by poor looping and some muddied sound. That aside, this makes RUMBLEFISH and some of the other pretentious teenage films look like what they are, pretentious. MY BODYGUARD was a modest film with an important message that never got in the way of the story. Bill may have had a greater success by producing THE STING, but it's hard to believe he could be any prouder than of his work on MY BODYGUARD.

p, Don Devlin; d, Tony Bill; w, Alan Ormsby; ph, Michael D. Margulies (DeLuxe Color); m, Dave Grusin; ed, Stu Linder; prod d, Jackson DeGovia; set d, Jeannine Oppewall.

Drama **Cas.** (PR:A MPAA:NR)

MY BOYS ARE GOOD BOYS* (1978) 90m Peter Perry c

Ralph Meeker, Ida Lupino, Lloyd Nolan, Robert Cokjlat, Sean T. Roche, Kerry Lynn.

An interesting cast of veteran performers is the only reason to check out this silly tale of juvenile delinquents robbing an armored car. One of Lupino's infrequent screen appearances (and an unfortunate one at that), since she turned to writing and directing, and helming for a short time a producing company in the 1950s.

p, Collenn Meeker, Bethel Buckalew; d, Buckalew; w, Buckalew, Fred F. Finklehoffe.

Crime (PR:A MPAA:PG)

MY BREAKFAST WITH BLASSIE** (1983) 60m Artist Endeavours c

Andy Kaufman, Freddie Blassie, Lynne Elaine, Laura Burdick, Linda Burdick, Linda Hirsch, Bob Zmuda.

An offbeat parody of MY DINNER WITH ANDRE features pro wrestler Blassie dining with comedian Kaufman, the self-proclaimed "Inter-Gender Wrestling Champion of the World." The two try to outdo each other in ego stories; Blassie going on and on with his wrestling stories with Kaufman proudly retorting, "I'm a famous TV star!" in the midst of passers-by. There's a running gag about the two avoiding any contact with fans in order to stay germ-free. The humor in this film borders more on strange than funny and it's definitely not for everyone. Kaufman, who died of cancer in 1984, was either a nutty guy who got lucky or an unparalleled comic trend-setter way ahead of his time. Allowed to improvise freely, he and Blassie have a hit and miss comic style that is often crude, but always creative. The lower star rating is for the technique of the film. Shot in three days on video tape, the photography (blown up to 16mm) is not what it should be, and the sound recording could have been a lot better. The ending, with obnoxious fan Zmuda bringing some rubber vomit to Kaufman and Blassie, was unnecessary. Still, this is definitely worth a look.

p&d, Johnny Legend, Linda Lautrec; w, (based on an idea by Legend, Lautrec); m, Linda Mitchel; ed, Legend, Lautrec, Lynne Margulies.

Comedy   **Cas.**   **(PR:O MPAA:NR)**

MY BRILLIANT CAREER****

(1980, Aus.) 98m New South Wales-GUO-Analysis c

Judy Davis (Sybylla Melvyn), Sam Neill (Harry Beecham), Wendy Hughes (Aunt Helen), Robert Grubb (Frank Hawdon), Max Cullen (Mr. McSwat, Pat Kennedy (Aunt Gussie), Aileen Brittain (Grandma Bossier), Peter Whitford (Uncle Julius), Carole Skinner (Mrs. McSwat), Alan Hopgood (Father), Julia Blake (Mother), Tony Hughes (Peter McSwat), Tina Robinson (Lizer McSwat), Aaron Corrin (Jimmy McSwat), Sharon Crouch (Sarah McSwat), Simone Buchanan (Mary Anne McSwat), Haylely Anderson (Rosie Jane McSwat), David Franklin (Horace), Aaron Wood (Stanley), Marion Schad (Gertie), Max Meldrum (Mr. Harris), Suzanne Roylance (Biddy), Zelda Smyth (Ethel), Bobby Ward (Mrs. Butler), Amanda Pratt (Blanche Derrick).

It is late in the 19th Century in the Australian outback, and everyone in a small farming community knows his or her place and what is expected. All except Davis, that is, a headstrong young woman who wants a career—an idea which is fairly blasphemous to her family and friends. Resisting marriage offers and the rigidness of society, Davis plows ahead with pluck and charm, giving a lively and humanistic performance. The direction, by female filmmaker Armstrong, matches its heroine: strong, with a good sense of wanting to get something done and then doing it. The mise-en-scene is well-composed and the story is told well in this wonderful Australian work.

p, Margaret Fink; d, Gillian Armstrong; w, Eleanor Witcombe (based on the novel by Miles Franklin); ph, Don McAlpine (Panavision, Eastmancolor); m, Nathan Waks; ed, Nick Beauman; prod d, Luciana Arrighi; cos, Anna Senior.

Drama   **Cas.**   **(PR:O MPAA:NR)**

MY BROTHER HAS BAD DREAMS*

(1977) 91m AM c

Nick Kleinholtz.

Another one of the all too many mad slasher-on-the-loose pictures, boasting low art and cheap thrills. This variation on the genre's woman-being-stalked theme has a young man going crazy with jealousy when his sister starts up with a new fellow. Three guesses what happens next. Better than some of its type, which isn't saying a whole lot.

p&d, Robert Emery.

Horror   **(PR:O MPAA:NR)**

MY BROTHER JONATHAN**

(1949, Brit.) 102m ABF/AA bw

Michael Denison (Jonathan Dakers), Dulcie Gray (Rachel Hammond), Stephen Murray (Dr. Craig), Ronald Howard (Harold Dakers), Mary Clare (Mrs. Dakers), Finlay Currie (Dr. Hammond), Beatrice Campbell (Edie Martyn), Arthur Young (Sir Joseph Higgins), James Robertson Justice (Eugene Dakers), James Hayter (Tom Morse), Peter Murray (Tony Dakers), Jessica Spencer (Connie), Desmond Newling (Young Jonathan), Alan Goodwin (Young Harold), Felix Deebank (Alec Martyn), R. Stuart Lindsell (Mr. Martyn), Avice Landone (Mrs. Martyn), Hilda Bayley (Mrs. Perry), Wylie Watson (Bagley), Josephine Stuart (Lily), Fred Groves (Lisha Hodgkiss), Beatrice Varley (Mrs. Hodgkiss), Eric Messiter (Lloyd Moore, Surgeon), Paul Farrell (Dr. Lucas), Jack Melford (Dr. Martock), John Salew (Wilburn), David Ward (Dr. Frampton), Peter Hobbes (Dr. Monaghan), Kathleen Boutall (Mrs. Gaige), Wilfrid Hyde-White (Mr. Gaige), George Woodbridge (Stevens), Leslie Weston (Wheeler), Merle Tottenham (Alice Rudge), Grace Denbeigh-Russell (The Matron), Howard Douglas, Hilary Pritchard (Bailiffs), Derek Farge (Edward Willis), Eunice Gayson (A Young Girl), Nora Gordon (Mrs. Stevens), Cameron Hall (Hospital Porter, Joseph), Kathleen Harrison (A Barmaid), Paul Blake (Edward Smith Watson), Thora Hird (Ada), Maurice Jones (Foundry Foreman), Vi Kaley (Old Crone), Fred Kitchen (Tyldesley), Daniel King (The Rev. Perry), Ruth Lodge (Mrs. Craig), Johnny Schofield (Trade Union Man), Jane Shirley (Maid), Wendy Thompson (Nurse), Elsie Wagstaff (Factory Worker), Hazel Adair (Mary), Grace Arnold (Woman in Court), Ernest Borrow (Butler), Ernest Butcher (Porter), Raymond Cooney (Ralph Hingston), Basil Cunard (Police Sergeant), Andrea Malandrinos (French Postman), Beatrice Marsden (Mary, 1946), Elizabeth Maude (Mrs. Bagley), Janet Morrison (Sister Cronshaw), Sydney Monckton (Dancer at Martyn's Party), Paul Sheridan (French Guest at Hotel Cecil), Michael Caborne (Alec Martyn as a Boy).

In the early part of the 20th Century, Denison is an Englishman who dreams of becoming a great surgeon and marrying Campbell. But after finishing medical school, his father dies and he must return home to support his mother and send brother Howard to school. He is forced to take partnership in an impoverished practice for a small industrial town and watch in dismay as Campbell ends up with Howard. When Howard is killed during WW I, Campbell later gives birth to his illegitimate son. Denison marries Campbell, but she dies in childbirth and her son becomes his responsibility. He marries Gray, and together they raise the boy. The story is told in flashback by Murray, the grown boy from Campbell and Howard's union. Essentially a soaper, the story is well told and nicely acted, though it has an artificial look that clearly shows its studio production. This was common in British postwar films.

p, Warwick Ward; d, Harold French; w, Leslie Landau, Adrian Arlington (based on the novel by Frances Brett Young); ph, Derick Williams; m, Hans May; ed, Charles Hasse; md, May; art d, Douglas Daniels; cos, J. Gower Parks; makeup, Harry Hayward.

Drama   **(PR:A MPAA:NR)**

MY BROTHER TALKS TO HORSES***

(1946) 93m MGM bw

"Butch" Jenkins (Lewis Penrose), Peter Lawford (John S. Penrose), Beverly Tyler (Martha), Edward Arnold (Mr. Bledsoe), Charlie Ruggles (Richard Pennington Roeder), Spring Byington (Mrs. Penrose), O. Z. Whitehead (Mr. Puddy), Paul Langton (Mr. Gillespie), Ernest Whitman (Mr. Mordecai), Irving Bacon (Mr. Piper), Lillian Yarbo (Psyche), Howard Freeman (Hector Damson), Harry Hayden (Mr. Gibley).

An absolute charmer features 9-year-old Jenkins as a kid with psychic powers which enable him to talk with race horses. They let him know who will win the race causing, of course, gamblers to trail after him for their own evil purposes. Lawford is his slightly bewildered older brother and Tyler the love interest. Byington is wonderful as the mother of the two. This was Zinnemann's third film with Jenkins, and he directs well, playing the story believably without overdoing the sentimentality or comedy within. The film looks good, with nice art decoration and a fine job of photography. The kids will eat it up.

p, Samuel Marx; d, Fred Zinnemann; w, Morton Thompson; ph, Harold Rosson; m, Rudolph G. Kopp; ed, George White; art d, Cedric Gibbons, Leonid Vasian; set d, Edwin B. Willis, Alfred D. Spencer; cos, Walter Plunkett.

Comedy   **(PR:AAA MPAA:NR)**

MY BROTHER, THE OUTLAW*

(1951) 82m EL bw (AKA: MY OUTLAW BROTHER)

Mickey Rooney (Denny O'More), Wanda Hendrix (Senorita Carmel Alvarado), Robert Preston (Joe Warnder), Robert Stack (Patrick O'More), Carlos Muzquiz (El Captain), Jose Torvay (Ortiz), Fernando Waggner (Burger), Filipe Flores (Jose), Hilda Moreno (Senora), Guilderma Calles (Indio), Margarita Luna (Lorenzo), Jose Velasquez (Pablo), Enrique Cansino (Enrique), Chel Lopez (Pancho).

Rooney is completely miscast as a city slicker traveling West to visit his brother Stack. He teams up along the trail with ranger Preston and discovers that his brother is really an outlaw. Together Rooney and Preston put Stack behind bars. Trite story, adapted from a novel by western writer Brand, is far below the talents of its three stars. Rooney seems out of place while Preston and Stack give mechanical performances. Shot outside of Mexico City, this film is aimed at children, but they'll probably leave it for just about anything else.

p, Benedict Bogeaus; d, Elliott Nugent; w, Gene Fowler, Jr. (based on the story "South of the Border" by Max Brand); ph, Jose Ortiz Ramos; ed, George Crone; art d, Edward Fitzgerald.

Western   **(PR:A MPAA:NR)**

MY BROTHER'S KEEPER**1/2

(1949, Brit.) 96m Gainsborough-Rank/EL bw

Jack Warner (George Martin), Jane Hylton (Nora Lawrence), David Tomlinson (Ronnie Waring), Bill Owen (Syd Evans), George Cole (Willie Stannard), Yvonne Owen (Margaret "Meg" Waring), Raymond Lovell (Bill Wainwright), Beatrice Varley (Mrs. Martin), Amy Veness (Mrs. Gulley), Brenda Bruce (Winnie Foreman), Susan Shaw (Beryl), John Boxer (Bert Foreman), Fred Groves (Landlord), Garry Marsh (Brewster), Wilfrid Hyde-White (Harding), Frederick Piper (Gordon, Caretaker), Maurice Denham (Trent), Jack Raine (Chief Constable), Valentine Dyall (Inspector), Douglas Stewart (The Major), Arthur Hambling (Hodges), George Merritt, Ben Williams, Norman Pierce (Policemen), Daphne Scorer (Receptionist), John Warren (Motorist), Gerald Pring (Minister), Reginald Beckwith (lst Barber), Hedley Briggs (2nd Barber), Keith Shepherd (Warden), Edie Martin (Woman Handshaker), Dorothy Vernon (Woman Next Door), Cyril Chamberlain (Archer), Hamilton Keane (Inspector), Lyn Evans (Guard), Leslie Handford (Policeman, Country Road).

Warner, a hardened criminal, escapes from prison handcuffed to Cole, a frightened young kid in trouble for the first time in his life. They race across the countryside pursued by a never-ending manhunt for the pair. A fairly well made drama, it suffers from an unfortunately lengthy beginning and too much dialog. Once the story starts to move, however, it builds to a thrilling climax. Cole is particularly good as the younger of the pair, who finally cracks under pressure and turns the two in.

p, Sydney Box, Antony Darnborough; d, Alfred Roome, Roy Rich; w, Frank Harvey, Jr. (based on a story by Maurice Wiltshire); ph, Gordon Lang, Frank Bassill; m, Clifton Parker; ed, Esmond Seal; art d, George Provis; cos, Julie Harris.

Drama   **(PR:A MPAA:NR)**

MY BROTHER'S WEDDING***1/2

(1983) 116m Charles Burnett c

Everett Silas (Pierce Monday), Jessie Holmes (Mrs. Monday), Gaye Shannon-Burnett (Sonia), Ronnie Bell (Soldier Richards), Dennis Kemper (Wendell Monday), Sy Richardson (Sonia's Father), Frances Nealy (Sonia's Mother).

An excellent independent feature stars Silas as an angry resident of Watts, California who works in the family dry cleaning business. He has a love-hate relationship with the surrounding community, identifying with the people, yet resenting the disadvantages he must deal with every day. His feelings are tested when he is faced with the choice of attending the funeral of his best friend or going to the wedding of his brother, whom he resents for his upwardly mobile status. Unlike so many black-themed films made by white production teams, this is an excellent example of the black culture being presented for what it is. There is a good feel of authenticity and realism here, letting the audience know what the character feels about himself and his race without being overly dramatic or symbolic. The nonprofessional actors are natural, playing their roles well. These are people we are seeing, not someone else's idea of what people are like in Watts. Even in our enlightened era (as we so love to believe) Hollywood has only begun to deal with racial themes. Independent films like this are the real thing.

p, Charles Burnett, Gaye Shannon-Burnett; d,w&ph, Charles Burnett; ed, Tom Pennick.

Drama **(PR:A MPAA:NR)**

MY BUDDY 1/2** (1944) 67m REP bw

Donald Barry *(Eddie Ballinger)*, Ruth Terry *(Lola)*, Lynne Roberts *(Lucy Manners)*, Alexander Granach *(Tim Oberta)*, Emma Dunn *(Mary Ballinger)*, John Litel *(Father Jim Donnelly)*, George E. Stone *(Pete)*, Jonathan Hale *(Sen. Henry)*, Ray Walker *(Russ)*, Joe Devlin *(Nicky Piastro)*, Matt McHugh *(Happy)*, Jack Ingram *(Charlie)*, George Humbert *(Albert)*, Gayne Whitman *(Young Senator)*, Edward Earle *(Chairman)*, Emmett Vogan *(2nd Senator)*, Jimmy Zaner *(Messenger)*, Jack Baxley *(Jim)*, Connie Leon *(Housekeeper)*, Milton Kibbee *(Pa Manners)*, Almeda Fowler *(Ma Manners)*, Sam Bernard *(Salesman)*, Constance Purdy *(Woman)*, Blake Edwards *(Prison Kid)*, Sven-Hugo Borg *(German Sniper)*, George Lloyd *(Hendricks)*, Lee Shumway *(Jim, the Guard)*, Harry Strang *(lst Detective)*, Jack Gardner *(Mike)*, Russ Whiteman *(Tommy)*, Boots Brown *(Kid)*, Robert Middlemass *(Judge)*, Marshall Reed *(2nd Detective)*, Nolan Leary *(Lawyer)*, Ralph Linn *(Jury Foreman)*, Roy Darmour, Lynton Brent *(Detectives)*, Frank Marlowe *(Joe)*, Charlie Sullivan *(Loudmouth Mug)*, Larry Steers *(Prosecuting Attorney)*, Jack Rockwell *(Jail Attendent, in Shadows)*, Charles P. Sherlock *(Policeman)*, Kid Chissell *(2nd Mobster)*, John Bagni *(1st Mobster)*, Jay Norris *(Spats)*, Poison Gardner Trio *(Prison Singers)*, Arthur Loft *(Warden)*, Jack Mulhall *(Announcer at Convicts' Show)*, Larry Burke *(Singer at Convicts' Show)*.

Litel is a priest delivering testimony before the Washington Post-War Planning Committee. He talks about his friend Barry and the man's experiences after returning home from World War I, a story we see in flashback. Barry returns from the war, and unable to get a job, is forced to put off his marriage to Roberts. He gets involved in bootlegging and ends up taking a rap for his boss and going to prison where he forms a gang. Upon his release from prison, a gang war erupts and he ends up killing Granach and is then himself killed in a rooftop shootout. The film ends with Litel once more before the committee, explaining how a note from Barry was left to the priest, begging to tell the veteran's story so this might never happen to another. Classic in its B-movie cliches, this really isn't a bad little film. Like so many of the lower-case features of the times, this one had its roots in the vehicle of another star and his film: James Cagney and THE ROARING TWENTIES. The plot of the 1939 film is copied fairly well here, right down to the character names for Cagney *(Eddie Bartlett)* and Barry *(Eddie Ballinger)*. What's more, Barry's physical resemblance to Cagney was incredible. Being a short, red-haired man with similar facial features, Barry easily could have passed as a brother to the famous star, a similarity Republic studios undoubtedly must have hoped audiences would take to. Songs include: "My Buddy," "Whodunit?" "Waiting for the Evening Mail."

p, Eddy White; d, Steve Sekely; w, Arnold Manoff (based on a story by Prescott Chaplin); ph, Reggie Lanning; ed, Tony Martinelli; md, Morton Scott; art d, J. Frank Hotaling; m/l, "Whodunit?" (sung by Ruth Terry), "My Buddy," "Waiting for the Evening Mail," Walter Donaldson, Gus Kahn, Jack Elliott, Billy Baskett.

Crime/Drama **(PR:A MPAA:NR)**

MY CHILDHOOD 1/2** (1972, Brit.) 50m British Film Institute bw

Stephen Archibald, Hughie Restorick, Jean Taylor-Smith, Karl Fieseler.

A young boy and his grandmother living in war-torn England along with the boy's half brother develop an unusual friendship with a German POW who works in a nearby field project. Shot in 16mm black and white, this is an oft times beautiful-looking piece, with a fine eye for shot composition. Though some of the performances (which are mostly by non professionals) tend to be a little wooden, the film has some wonderful moments. Winner of the Golden Palm Award in the 1972 Chicago International Film Festival, this was the first of a three-part series, financed by the British Film Institute.

p, Geoffrey Evans; d&w, Bill Douglas; ph, Mick Campbell.

Drama **(PR:A MPAA:NR)**

MY COUSIN RACHEL*** (1952) 98m FOX bw

Olivia de Havilland *(Rachel Ashley)*, Richard Burton *(Philip Ashley)*, Audrey Dalton *(Louise)*, Ronald Squire *(Nick Kendall)*, George Dolenz *(Rainaldi, Rachel's Lawyer)*, John Sutton *(Ambrose Ashley)*, Tudor Owen *(Seecombe)*, J.M. Kerrigan *(Rev. Pascoe)*, Margaret Brewster *(Mrs. Pascoe)*, Alma Lawton *(Mary Pascoe)*, Ola Lorraine, Kathleen Mason *(Pascoe Children)*, Earl Robie *(Philip at Age 5)*, Argentina Brunetti *(Signora)*, Mario Siletti *(Caretaker)*, Lumsden Hare *(Tamblyn)*, Trevor Ward *(Lewin)*, Victor Wood *(Foreman)*, George Plues *(Coachman)*, Bruce Payne *(Groom)*, James Fairfax, Oreste Seragnoli *(Servants)*, Nicholas Koster *(Philip at Age 10)*, Robin Camp *(Philip at Age 15)*.

The versatile de Havilland had been away from pictures for about three years when she was lured back for this Gothic period piece that was adapted from du Maurier's best seller. It had originally been slated for George Cukor to direct and he wanted Garbo for the role but she, of course, chose to be alone, and Cukor eventually stepped aside because he and producer-writer Johnson couldn't agree on the script. Koster was tapped to direct de Havilland and a young Welshman, Burton, who had just galvanized Londoners in his version of "Hamlet," was selected as the male lead. If the picture was not a resounding success (the conclusion was unsatisfying), it did manage to get Burton a Fox contract and that became the reason for his long and exciting stay in the U.S. It's early 1800s in Cornwall, England. Burton lives in a huge stone house overlooking the thrashing sea. He learns that his cousin and best friend, Sutton, has died in Italy and the reasons for the man's demise have not been clearly explained. Sutton had been sending letters to Burton and the last few missives indicated that perhaps he was being subtly poisoned by his attractive young wife, de Havilland. The widow arrives at the estate and Burton is both fascinated and repelled by her. She is beautiful and sweet but Burton can't rid his mind of the suspicion that she killed Sutton. A relationship begins and Burton falls in love with her against his better judgment. Sutton's will is probated and Burton is the sole heir and executor. When he feels the time is right, Burton brings up the matter of the letters written by her late husband and she has a ready explanation for the allegations, saying that Sutton had a brain tumor and the pressure of it caused him to become paranoid and suspect everyone around him of some attempt on his life. Burton thinks that sounds right and accepts her contention that Sutton was at death's door from natural causes. Burton turns 25 (he was actually 27 at the time) and gives de Havilland everything he owns: the mansion, the land, and a horde of jewels which have been in the family since no one can recall. The two of them are enormously happy, but there is, as yet, no mention of a permanent alliance. Dolenz arrives. He is an Italian lawyer in the employ of de Havilland (in truth, Dolenz was born in Trieste, Italy, despite his Germanic name) and appear to be a wolf in attorney's clothing. When de Havilland brews up some of her "special" tea, Dolenz suggests Burton try it and the result is that Burton gets violently sick. His mind races, he fancies that he and de Havilland have been married, and he is almost on an LSD trip. She helps him recover his senses and when he is again healthy, he asks for her hand but she won't marry him. Burton explodes and physically attacks de Havilland, throttling her within an inch of her life. He stops just short of choking her to death, then apologizes profusely, but his fury is again flamed when he sees de Havilland and Dolenz in what he mistakes to be a romantic conversation. Burton's one-time amour, Dalton, arrives, and he is happy when de Havilland says that she is now going to leave the Cornwall estate. Burton is so sure that she did kill Sutton that he deliberately doesn't tell de Havilland that the rickety bridge she must cross is not fit for a human foot. The bridge crashes and de Havilland falls to the rocks below. Burton races to help her and she expires in his arms. Later, he reads a letter from Dolenz to de Havilland and sees that their relationship was strictly counselor and client, and the picture ends as Burton is riddled with guilt about de Havilland. He will go to his grave wondering if she was or she wasn't a murderess. It was this "lady or the tiger" ending that caused moviegoers to frown at the end of the film. 98 minutes is a long time to sit and not be satisfied by the denouement. Waxman did a good score that subtly played against the story. He also wrote the music for de Havilland's sister's picture, REBECCA, another story by du Maurier. And if you don't know who de Havilland's sister is, her first name is Joan and her last name is Fontaine. Those are all the clues we can offer.

p, Nunnally Johnson; d, Henry Koster; w, Johnson (based on the novel by Daphne du Maurier); ph, Joseph La Shelle; m, Franz Waxman; ed, Louis Loeffler; art d, Lyle Wheeler, John De Cuir; set d, Walter M. Scott; cos, Dorothy Jeakins; spec eff, Ray Kellogg.

Mystery/Romance **(PR:A MPAA:NR)**

MY DARLING CLEMENTINE ***** (1946) 97m FOX bw

Henry Fonda *(Wyatt Earp)*, Linda Darnell *(Chihauahua)*, Victor Mature *(Doc Holliday)*, Walter Brennan *(Old Man Clanton)*, Tim Holt *(Virgil Earp)*, Cathy Downs *(Clementine)*, Ward Bond *(Morgan Earp)*, Alan Mowbray *(Granville Thorndyke)*, John Ireland *(Billy Clanton)*, Roy Roberts *(Mayor)*, Jane Darwell *(Kate)*, Grant Withers *(Ike Clanton)*, J. Farrell MacDonald *(Mac the Bartender)*, Russell Simpson *(John Simpson)*, Don Garner *(James Earp)*, Francis Ford *(Town Drunk)*, Ben Hall *(Barber)*, Arthur Walsh *(Hotel Clerk)*, Louis Mercier *(Francois)*, Mickey Simpson *(Sam Clanton)*, Fred Libby *(Phin Clanton)*, William B. Davidson *(Owner of Oriental Saloon)*, Earle Foxe *(Gambler)*, Aleth "Speed" Hansen *(Guitar Player-Townsman)*, Dan Borzage *(Accordian Player-Townsman)*, Charles Anderson, Duke Lee *(Townsmen)*, Don Barclay *(Opera House Owner)*, Margaret Martin, Mae Marsh, Frances Rey *(Women)*, Robert Adler, Jack Pennick *(Stagecoach Drivers)*, Frank Conlan *(Piano Player)*, Charles Stevens *(Indian Charlie)*, Harry Woods *(Marshal)*.

No other western figure inspired more filmic lore and created more romantic legend in and out of print in his own time and beyond than the indomitable Wyatt Earp. He was the courageous champion of the law and defender of decency, if the Old West myths are to be believed, and they are, if for no other reasons than that they warm the heart and excite the imagination. Master filmmaker Ford, of course, knew this when he undertook to make one of the finest films of his great career. Fonda, recently returned from WW II and four years in the Navy, gives a wonderfully mature and restrained essay of the famous frontier lawman. He and his brothers, Bond, Holt, and Garner, have driven a small herd of cattle to the outskirts of rough-and-tumble Tombstone, Arizona, in the year 1882 (the events portrayed actually took place in 1881). Coming upon their campsite is Brennan, leader of the outlaw Clanton clan, and his oldest son, Withers. Brennan offers Fonda a cut-rate price for the cattle, which Fonda rejects, stating that they intend to get a better price in town, and mentions he'll be going into Tombstone that night with his brothers, Bond and Holt, leaving young Garner to mind the cattle. When Fonda arrives in Tombstone he sees it's a wide open hellhole with the saloons roaring. He goes to the barber shop with his brothers but just as he is about to have a shave the barber shop is riddled with bullets, narrowly missing Fonda and his brothers. He walks outside to see Stevens, a drunken Indian, recklessly firing his pistol from the now emptied

Oriental Saloon. Fonda, indignant, his face still lathered, marches up to the town mayor, Roberts, and sees the local marshal resigning on the spot. Incensed, Fonda goes to the building housing the saloon, enters at the second floor level, and is then seen dragging an unconscious Stevens out of the saloon. He drops him next to the mayor and says with disgust: "What kind of town is this, serving liquor to Indians?" Stevens comes to and Fonda tells him to get out of town, kicking him in the pants to get him started. Roberts offers Fonda the job of town marshal but he refuses, saying he's only come to town for a relaxing shave. When he and his brothers return to their camp they find Garner killed and their cattle stolen. Fonda rides back into town, wakes up Roberts, and takes the marshal's job, making his brothers deputies. As he is leaving the hotel where the mayor lives, Fonda sees Brennan and his four brutish, bearded sons enter. He tells Brennan that his herd was stolen and that he's taken the job of marshal. Brennan cackles: "Marshaling? In Tombstone?" Before he leaves Brennan asks his name and Fonda brings a shocked look to Brennan's face by telling him he is Wyatt Earp. As Fonda and his brothers work to gather evidence against the Clanton mob, Fonda becomes more involved in the raucous life of the community. While playing poker in a saloon, Fonda watches Mature, playing the notorious gunman Doc Holliday, enter and grab a gambler at his table and run him out of town. He joins Mature at the bar and the two have a drink together, but Mature pulls a gun on him, then learns Fonda is not wearing his pistol. He also turns to see Bond and Holt standing nearby and they are wearing their irons. Mature slips his pistol back into his holster and then invites all the Earp brothers to have a drink with him. They do. Mowbray, a Shakespearian actor, arrives and announces his new show at the local theater but, on opening night, he vanishes and a riot in the theater almost ensues. Fonda promises to find the actor and return him to the stage. He, with Mature at his side—the two are now fast friends—find Mowbray in a small saloon, being held by Brennan and his boys and forced to recite from the works of the Immortal Bard at their pleasure. The actor, under strain and half drunk, standing on a table, forgets his lines from *Hamlet*, but Mature steps forward to finish them: "The undiscovered country, from whose bourn/No traveller returns, puzzles the will/And makes us rather bear those ills we have/Than fly to others that we know not of?/Thus conscience does make cowards of us all." Mature is seized by uncontrollable coughing and one of the Clantons tries to pull a gun but Fonda knocks it out of his hand and takes the actor out of the saloon. With the drop on him, Brennan tells Fonda before he leaves that his boys have had too much to drink. After Fonda, Mature, and Mowbray leave, Brennan flies into a rage, whipping his sons mercilessly, shouting: "When you pull a gun, kill a man!" The next day Downs (Clementine) arrives on the stage and Fonda is immediately smitten, taking the new schoolteacher's bags from the top of the coach. Downs goes to the hotel where she asks for Mature. Fonda shows his fondness for Downs by quietly telling the hotel clerk to provide the new guest "with a couple buckets of hot water so she can take a bath." That night Downs goes looking for Mature and finds him dining in the back of the saloon with Fonda. Darnell, Mature's dancehall singer girlfriend, sees Downs and immediately resents her presence. When Downs meets Mature he tells her to "go back where you belong." He has another coughing seizure and she asks him if that's the reason why he left her. He denies it and she says: "You can't run away from me any more than you can run away from yourself." He tells her to take the morning stage and if she does not, he will move on. That night, alone in his room, with the noise from the saloons blaring, Mature stares at his diplomas hung on his wall, takes a drink, and says with derision: "Dr. John Holliday!" (Holliday was a dentist at one time.) He throws his drink at the diploma, smashing the glass frame, and later he goes on a bender. In the saloon Darnell sings to him and kisses him but he does not respond, telling her to sing "your stupid little songs" elsewhere and leave him alone. She goes to the end of the bar and throws an empty glass at him, smashing it. Mature later tries to force Fonda into having a drink. Fonda refuses and lectures Mature about how fine a girl Downs is, but Mature tells him it's none of his business. Mature begins to cough and swills down a drink. Fonda tells him: "Keep that up and you'll be out of business." Mature angrily pulls a gun and is about to shoot up the bar when Fonda knocks him out and drags him from the saloon. In the morning, Darnell storms into Downs' room to tell her to keep packing and get out of town because *she* is Mature's girlfriend. As Downs later waits for the stage to arrive she meets Fonda, who has just come from the barber, and she asks if he will accompany her to the services at the unfinished church. They hear town elder Simpson announce the opening of the church but because they have no preacher yet they have decided to have a dance. Fonda asks Downs to dance and stiffly moves her about on the open-air floor of the church. Bond and Holt arrive to see, amazed, their lawman brother dancing with Downs. Meanwhile, the stage comes roaring through Tombstone with Mature riding shotgun. He hurls a money pouch from a bank at Darnell who is standing near the street. Fonda later finds Darnell in Downs' room, trying to get Downs to leave town. He ousts her from Downs' room and a piece of jewelry falls from her hands, the same piece Garner, Fonda's younger brother, had stolen when he was killed. Fonda later learns that Mature quickly grabbed his guns and took his savings out of the local bank and left town in a hurry. Fonda rides wildly after the stage, using relay horses to catch up with it. Mature forces the stage driver to whip the horses to a frenzy but Fonda manages to catch up with the stage by cutting cross country, stopping the stage on a narrow road. Mature and Fonda face off against each other and both draw, Mature shooting the gun out of Fonda's hand. Next both Fonda and Mature are pounding on Darnell's door and, inside of her room, is Ireland, one of Brennan's sons. Mature and Fonda burst into Darnell's room just after Ireland goes out the window. Mature shows Darnell the trinket and asks her where she got it. She says Mature gave it to her. He denies it, but Fonda charges Mature with the murder of his brother. Darnell, fearful of getting Mature into more trouble, admits that she got the trinket from Ireland and just at that moment Ireland, hiding outside, shoots Darnell and escapes. As Ireland rides out of town, Fonda, from the rooftop of the hotel, calls down to his brother Holt that he should follow Ireland and the younger Earp brother rides after the outlaw. Meanwhile, Darnell is stretched out on some poker tables of the saloon and Mature attempts to operate on her. Holt rides after Ireland and they exchange gunfire. Ireland makes it to the Clanton ranch and drops dead. Brennan and the rest of his brood are waiting for Holt when he arrives and Holt is blasted with a shotgun after Brennan snorts: "My boy Billy, shot down in the streets of Tombstone, murdered!" Brennan orders his remaining three sons to mount their horses. They head toward Tombstone. Mature finishes his operation and Darnell briefly lives to thank him. Mature is toasted by Fonda as "Doctor Holliday," and Mature proudly grabs his doctor's bag and leaves the saloon. Brennan and his boys then ride into town and fire off several rounds into the saloon, which draws Fonda forward. Outside Brennan drops Holt's body into the street and shouts: "We'll be waiting for you at the O.K. Corral!" The civic leaders come to Fonda later and offer their services in battling the Clantons but Fonda tells Simpson and Roberts: "This is strictly a family affair." Mature then appears to tell Fonda that Darnell is dead. He grabs a shotgun and asks: "When do we start?" Replies Fonda: "Sunup." At dawn, Fonda, Bond, and Mature, accompanied by Roberts and Simpson, march down the street toward the O.K. Corral but Roberts and Simpson drop back and only Fonda, Bond, and Mature proceed toward the corral. The lawmen enter the corral from different directions. Then a shot rings out and Fonda dives for cover. Fonda bids Brennan good morning and says: "Let's talk awhile." Brennan tells him to go ahead. Fonda says that he has warrants charging Brennan and his sons for the murders of James and Virgil Earp and further warrants for cattle rustling and robbery. Brennan yells: "Come in here and serve your warrants!" Fonda asks him who killed his youngest brother. "I did," boasts Brennan, "and the other one, too." Then Withers, half drunk, kicks open the gate to the O.K. Corral and steps forward, shotgun in hand, saying to Fonda: "And I'm gonna kill you." Fonda shoots him down and then the gunfight is on. Mature coughs and is shot several times but he manages to kill one of the Clanton boys and Bond gets the other. Fonda tells Brennan to come out. He steps forward, calling out the names of his sons. Fonda steps up to him, holding a pistol on him, saying: "They're all dead . . . I'm not going to kill you. I hope you live a hundred years so you can feel just a little what my Pa's gonna feel. Now get out of town! Start wandering!" The old man goes to his horse and begins to ride away but he pulls a hidden gun. Before he shoots Fonda, Bond shoots Brennan out of his saddle. Bond then tells Fonda that Mature is dead and the lawman inspects the remains of his gunslinger friend. At the outskirts of Tombstone the next day, with a vast horizon of far buttes stretching beyond, Bond rides a buckboard past Downs, saying goodbye to her. Then Fonda stops to speak with her, telling her that he will be going to see his father and tell him what happened. He learns that she is staying in Tombstone to teach school and he tells her that he will be back and will stop by the school house. He then kisses her on the cheek, steps back, shakes her hand, mounts his horse, smiles, and says: "Mam, I sure like that name, Clementine." Fonda rides off down the long, long road stretching to the horizon while Downs watches him diminish to a moving speck in the camera's eye. Prosaic, yet dramatic and wonderfuly brooding with shadows at night and blinding bright at day with sky that never stops, MY DARLING CLEMENTINE is Ford's homage to legend and as such is magnificent. "I knew Wyatt Earp," Ford once said, "and he told me about the fight at the O.K. Corral. So in MY DARLING CLEMENTINE we did it exactly the way it had been." Not exactly, but close, with the exception that there was no Old Man Clanton at the O.K. Corral, Virgil Earp was not killed before the fight but was wounded in it, Doc Holliday was not killed in the gun battle, and no mention of the McLowery Brothers is made, among other pertinent facts of the most famous gunfight in the Old West. Fonda's wonderfully simple, direct lawman has a heart and more than a little humor as he embodies Ford's staunch theme of law and order. Mature is also outstanding, acting out his doomed gunslinger role with amazing restraint. Bond, Brennan, and Holt are true grit westerners while Darnell is a pretty little dancehall girl, hapless, but believing at death that Mature, who has tried to save her life, loves her. Downs is more of a refined and pretty statue than a flesh and blood girl and only during the delightful church dance does she become happily human. This is, of course, a man's film and one of Ford's best among his 54 westerns. Beyond the legendary leads, the most hateful character of this film or most any other is the vile Brennan, who prefers to raise his sons as beasts instead of men, beating them when they *don't* kill a man. Ford, who reportedly did not want to make this film, owed Fox one more film on his contract before beginning independent production with his own company, Argosy Pictures. He shot the entire film in 45 days in his favorite location site, Monument Valley, in northern Arizona, not in the south where the real Tombstone is located. When Fox mogul Darryl Zanuck viewed the film, he decided that it was too long and some of it lacked cohesion, so he arbitrarily cut 30 minutes from the original. Yet he did it with loving care since he believed Ford to be the greatest director who ever lived in the sound era. Almost every scene in this splendidly constructed film is a visual treat, even the small scene where Fonda, just come from the barber, does a little bicycle movement with his legs against a porch post while Darnell is lambasting him, a verbal barrage which bothers him not a tad. As with other films by Ford, there is no sustained and dynamic score, with Newman merely providing haunting little variations on the title song on a harmonica, and other western folk ballads played on fiddles, a guitar, and sung by a cowboy chorus. Engel and Miller cut a simple story but provide wry, ironic, and down-home dialog. At one point, while Fonda is thinking about Downs, he asks bartender MacDonald: "Mac—have you ever been in love?" MacDonald thinks for a long time, then replies: "No, I've been a bartender all my life." And throughout is the startlingly grand photography of Joseph MacDonald who followed the pointing finger of Ford, the consummate film artist, in providing graphics so broad and sweeping that the whole of the West seems to be captured in his frames. Although other films about Wyatt Earp and the fabulous gunfight at the O.K. Corral have been made, none capture the visual grimness, the impromptu nature of that bullet-ridden moment, with the possible exception of the superlative GUNFIGHT AT THE O.K. CORRAL. Other films depicting Earp in or out of Tombstone include LAW AND ORDER (1932), with Walter Huston, FRONTIER MARSHAL (1934), with George O'Brien, Randolph Scott in FRONTIER MARSHAL (1939), TOMBSTONE, THE TOWN TOO TOUGH TO DIE (1942), with Richard Dix, Joel McCrea in WICHITA (1955), Burt Lancaster in

GUNFIGHT AT THE O.K. CORRAL (1957), HOUR OF THE GUN (1967), and DOC (1971), the latter being nothing more than a psychodrama.

p, Samuel G. Engel; d, John Ford; w, Engel, Winston Miller (based on a story by Sam Hellman from the novel *Wyatt Earp, Frontier Marshall* by Stuart N. Lake); ph, Joseph P. MacDonald; m, Cyril J. Mockridge, David Buttolph; ed, Dorothy Spencer; art d, James Basevi, Lyle R. Wheeler; set d, Thomas Little, Fred J. Rode; cos, Rene Hubert; spec eff, Fred Sersen.

Western (PR:A MPAA:NR)

MY DAUGHTER JOY (SEE: OPERATION X, 1951, Brit.)

MY DAYS WITH JEAN MARC (SEE: ANATOMY OF A MARRIAGE, 1964, Fr.)

MY DEAR MISS ALDRICH*** (1937) 73m MGM bw

Edna May Oliver *(Mrs. Atherton)*, Maureen O'Sullivan *(Martha Aldrich)*, Walter Pidgeon *(Ken Morley)*, Rita Johnson *(Ellen Warfield)*, Janet Beecher *(Mrs. Sinclair)*, Paul Harvey *(Mr. Sinclair)*, Charles Waldron *(Ex-Governor Warfield)*, Walter Kingsford *(Mr. Talbot)*, Roger Converse *(Ted Martin)*, Guinn "Big Boy" Williams *(An Attendant)*, Leonid Kinskey *(Tony, A Waiter)*, Brent Sargent *(Gregory)*, J. Farrell MacDonald *("Doc" Howe)*, Robert Greig *(Major Domo)*, Lya Lys *(The Queen)*, Renie Riano *(Maid)*, Carl Stockdale *(Apartment House Manager)*, Gwen Lee *(Hat Saleswoman)*, Sonny Bupp *(Little Boy)*, Marie Blake *(Telephone Operator)*, Jack Baxley *(Customer)*, Bud Fine *(Doctor)*, Arthur Belasco *(Press Man)*, Jack Norton, Don Barclay *(Drunks)*.

Pidgeon is the editor of a newspaper that is taken over by the glamorous O'Sullivan. She's an independent woman and the sparks do fly. Not quite THE FRONT PAGE, but the dialog is witty and delivered well by the leads. The direction has a fine feel for comic timing, making this a nice little farce. This was Pidgeon's first lead role at MGM, even though, by 1937, he had already appeared on stage and screen for 20 years and had started out in the early talkies as a singing hero in operetta musicals.

p, Herman J. Mankiewicz; d, George B. Seitz; w, Mankiewicz; ph, Charles Lawton, Jr.; m, David Snell; ed, William S. Gray; art d, Cedric Gibbons.

Comedy (PR:A MPAA:NR)

MY DEAR SECRETARY½** (1948) 94m UA bw

Laraine Day *(Stephanie Gaylord)*, Kirk Douglas *(Owen Waterbury)*, Keenan Wynn *(Ronnie Hastings)*, Helen Walker *(Elsie)*, Rudy Vallee *(Charles Harris)*, Florence Bates *(Mrs. Reeves)*, Alan Mowbray *(Deveny)*, Grady Sutton *(Scott)*, Irene Ryan *(Mary)*, Gale Robbins *(Dawn O'Malley)*, Virginia Hewitt *(Felicia)*, Abe Reynolds *(Taxi Driver)*, Jody Gilbert *(Hilda Sneebacher)*, Helene Stanley *(Miss Pidgeon)*, Joe Kirk *(Process Server)*, Russell Hicks *(Publisher)*, Gertrude Astor *(Miss Gee)*, Martin Lamont *(Male Secretary)*, Charles Halton *(Teacher)*, Stanley Andrews.

Douglas had already established his dramatic acting potential in a few films and was eager to show that he could play comedy, so he chose to accept the role of a rakehell novelist in this trifling farce. Day is a secretary for book publisher Vallee who handles all of novelist Douglas' works. She gives up her steady but dull position to sign on as Douglas' secretary, but soon finds that it's not all beer and skittles. Douglas is a gambler, a womanizer, a horse bettor, and a man who thinks that a secretary is a toy who must also do double duty as a lover. Day can only take so much of Douglas' slovenly and caddish ways and she eventually gives him notice, but by this time, he's gaga over her and begins a chase that winds up in marriage. They move to a tranquil home in the quiet mountains and both begin writing novels. They finish their books simultaneously and Douglas is stung when his book is spurned and hers is sought after. No egotist worth his salt can handle that and the couple are quickly apart. Day would like to keep her husband and she deliberately won't allow her book to be printed, but it doesn't help as Douglas has been cut to the quick. Day resubmits the book and it's published to great critical reviews and monetary success, as well as a major award. With Bates and Ryan and Wynn behind matters, they manage to get the couple together and the picture ends happily. The comedy work from the supporting cast is far better than anything from Day and Douglas, and Wynn is excellent as Douglas' next door neighbor, a man who cooks, irons, bakes, and even helps his pal find women. A nice comedy turn from Mowbray and the usual chuckles from Grady Sutton, who was one of W.C. Fields's favorite straight men.

p, Leo G. Popkin; d&w, Charles Martin; ph, Joseph Biroc; m, Heinz Roemheld; ed, Arthur H. Nadel; art d, Rudi Feld.

Comedy Cas. (PR:A-C MPAA:NR)

MY DEATH IS A MOCKERY** (1952, Brit.) 75m Park Lane/Adelphi bw

Donald Houston *(John Bradley)*, Kathleen Byron *(Helen Bradley)*, Bill Kerr *(Hansen)*, Edward Leslie *(Le Cambre)*.

This routine crime drama features Welsh star Houston as a failure in the trawling business. With the encouragement of bad man Kerr, he goes into the smuggling business, little realizing that his new partner desires his wife (Byron). When the police catch up with the outlaws, Houston accidentally kills Leslie, a third partner in the ring. Kerr believes the death to be a murder, and breaks down under interrogation after helping get rid of the corpse. Houston is hanged for his crimes, once more proving that justice always triumphs in low-budget thrillers.

p, David Dent; d, Tony Young; w, Douglas Baber (based on his novel); ph, Phil Grindrod.

Crime (PR:C-O MPAA:NR)

MY DINNER WITH ANDRE* (1981) 110m Andre/New Yorker c

Wallace Shawn *(Wally)*, Andre Gregory *(Andre)*, Jean Lenauer *(Waiter)*, Roy Butler *(Bartender)*.

If nothing else, they tried to do something different here. Different it was, entertaining it wasn't. Still, the attempt was made and there were a few good observations to be listened to, but it has as much to do with movies as Joe DiMaggio had to do with pre-Columbian sculpture. With the possible exception of Andy Warhol's EmPIRE (a 15 hour single shot of the famed edifice on the corner of Fifth Avenue at 34th Street), MY DINNER WITH ANDRE is, perhaps, the least movie-like motion picture since Fred Ott sneezed, spreading the germs of cinema, nearly 100 years ago. MY DINNER WITH ANDRE is more like watching a play than a film and, perhaps, it never should have been a film. This is not to say that it doesn't at times, get interesting. But so does watching chickens scratch, for a while. What this movie brings is the assorted rantings, ravings, musings, and self-aggrandizement of one Andre Gregory, a man who wants you to know that he is the hippest person to ever schlepp to the four corners of the earth. The premise, if there is one, is simple. Wallace Shawn is going out to dinner with Gregory. They eat, they talk, they leave. And that's it. Shawn is the neurotic New Yorker, a plump, balder version of Woody Allen, without the one-liners. He is a man in search of comfort, a good cup of coffee, and the right electric blanket to warm his nights. He doesn't do much thinking about anything important and if he does, we are not privy to those thoughts. This is Gregory's night to talk and Shawn is little more than a sounding board. As Gregory prattles on, we learn that he is a man in search of himself, traveling the circumference of the Earth in an attempt to find reality and a meaning for his existence. He is an excellent storyteller and Shawn sits there enraptured as Gregory regales him with tales of his travels. He's meditated, he's eaten dirt, he's been buried alive, and done all of those things that the pop culture of the 1960s and 1970s demanded. He probably went through est, Actualization, rolfing and the Feldenkrais Method while he was at it. Gregory is the epitome of "Me-ism," whereas Shawn is the picture of "Mee Too-ism." Gregory has spent the last several years with his colleagues in a vain attempt to get answers to the ancient questions which have stumped minds far deeper than theirs. As the picture drones, we get the feeling that, despite his meanderings on faraway beaches and high mountains, there is lots more he has to learn (like how to make a decent picture, for one). We also have the notion that here is a man who truly enjoys feeling *angst*. The best, and perhaps the only, element of this film to reckon with is that it forces the audience to actively participate and to use our imaginations to be part of the movie. In that sense, the audience is the director and must find the sub-text in the monolog. In order to exact any enjoyment from the movie, we must visualize the people he's met and the places he's been. Malle's direction is virtually nonexistent other than a few push-ins and pull-outs as the two men dine. He had very little to do and the movie is proof positive that it's much easier to talk about a car chase than film one. There have been many films with just two major characters, like HELL IN THE PACIFIC or even ENEMY MINE, but they had two strong opponents. In this, Shawn is a wimp who has but one job to do and that's to listen. Both men wrote the screenplay and Shawn has since gone on to write a few plays that have received excellent notices, probably from the same pseudo-intellectual critics who thought that this film actually said something. MY DINNER WITH ANDRE is the cinematic equivalent of playing tennis against a wall. Later, comedian Andy Kaufman would do a satire of this by having breakfast with a one-time wrestler-turned-manager. He called it "My Breakfast With Blassie," and it made just a little more sense than this did. Still, with all of the above, there are about 20 minutes of MY DINNER WITH ANDRE that have some merit. The only trouble is that they are spread across 110 minutes.

p, George W. George, Beverly Karp; d, Louis Malle; w, Wallace Shawn, Andre Gregory; ph, Jeri Sopanen (Movielab Color); m, Allen Shawn; ed, Suzanne Baron; prod d, David Mitchell; art d, Stephen McCabe; cos, Jeffrey Ullman.

Drama Cas. (PR:A-C MPAA:PG)

MY DOG, BUDDY** (1960) 76m B.R. and Gordon McLendon/COL bw

London *(Buddy)*, Travis Lemmond *(Ted Dodd)*, Ken Curtis *(Dr. Lusk)*, Ken Knox *(Dr. White)*, James H. Foster *(Jim Foster)*, Jane Murchison *(Jane Foster)*, Bob Thompson *(Salizar)*, Jo Palmie *(Nurse Lewis)*, Judge Dupree *(Special Detective)*, Chuck Eisenmann *(Patrol Officer)*, Gerry Johnson *(Elizabeth Lynch)*, Don Keyes *(George Lynch)*, Bart McLendon *(Junior Lynch)*, Honest Joe *(Junkyard Owner)*, Bob Euler *(Artist Fuller)*, Desmond Dhooge *(Kolinzky)*, C.B. Lemmond *(Mr. Dodd)*, Lilla Lemmond *(Mrs. Dodd)*.

After his parents are both killed in an auto accident, young Lemmond is left with the family's German Shepherd, London (star of THE LITTLEST HOBO). The two go through the standard "boy and his dog" adventures, which the kids undoubtedly will love. The film itself is not so bad but is hampered by its low budget and poor use of flashback narration. The scene at the canine show where the dogs "talk" to each other is too hokey for words. Additionally, this film embarrassingly portrays several scenes with black actors in sterotyped roles more fitting for Stepin Fetchit. By 1960, one would think that filmmakers would be above that sort of thing for cheap laughs. Here it comes off as ugly and mean-spirited, and strongly detracts from the film. It may have you think twice before showing it to the kids.

p, Ken Curtis; d&w, Ray Kellogg; ph, Ralph Hammeras; m, Jack Marshall; ed, Aaron Stell; set d, Louise Caldwell.

Dog (PR:C MPAA:NR)

MY DOG RUSTY** (1948) 67m COL bw

Ted Donaldson *(Danny Mitchell)*, John Litel *(Hugh Mitchell)*, Ann Doran *(Mrs. Mitchell)*, Mona Barrie *(Dr. Toni Cordell)*, Whitford Kane *(Mr. Tucker)*, Jimmy Lloyd *(Rodney Pyle)*, Lewis L. Russell *(Mayor Fulderwilder)*, Harry Harvey *(Hebble)*, Olin Howlin *(Frank Foley)*, Ferris Taylor *(Bill Worden)*, Mickey McGuire *(Gerald Hebble)*, Dwayne Hickman *(Nip Worden)*, David Ackles *(Tuck Worden)*, Teddy Infuhr *(Squeaky Foley)*, Minta Durfee Arbuckle *(Mrs. Foley)*, Flame *(Rusty)*.

Donaldson is a young boy whose constant lying gets his father, the town mayor, into big trouble. But all is righted in the end, thanks to canine star Flame. Overly cute, with mediocre production values, this is a minor and forgettable "boy and his dog" film. Donaldson is completely inept. Don't miss a bit part by Hickman, who would become famous as TV's "Dobie Gillis".

p, Wallace MacDonald; d, Lew Landers; w, Brenda Weisberg (based on a story by William R. Sackheim, Weisberg, based upon characters created by Al Martin); ph, Vincent Farrar; ed, Jerome Thoms; md, Mischa Bakaleinikoff; art d, George Brooks.

Children **(PR:AAA MPAA:NR)**

MY DREAM IS YOURS1/2** (1949) 99m WB c

Jack Carson *(Doug Blake)*, Doris Day *(Martha Gibson)*, Lee Bowman *(Gary Mitchell)*, Adolphe Menjou *(Thomas Hutchins)*, Eve Arden *(Vivian Martin)*, S.Z. Sakall *(Felix Hofer)*, Selena Royle *(Freda Hofer)*, Edgar Kennedy *(Uncle Charlie)*, Sheldon Leonard *(Grimes)*, Franklin Pangborn *(Sourpuss Manager)*, John Berkes *(Character Actor)*, Ada Leonard *(Herself)*, Frankie Carle *(Himself)*, Ross Wesson *(Hilliard)*, Sandra Gould *(Mildred)*, Iris Adrian *(Peggy)*, Jan Kayne *(Polly)*, Bob Carson *(Jeff)*, Lennie Bremen *(Louis)*, Marion Martin *(Blonde)*, Frank Scannell *(Car Salesman)*, Chili Williams *(Fan Club President)*, Art Gilmore *(Radio Announcer)*, Kenneth Britton *(Richards the Butler)*, James Flavin *(Waiter)*, Rudy Friml *(Orchestra Leader)*, Duncan Richardson *(Freddie Manners)*, Jack Kenny *(Cab Driver)*, Paul Maxey *(Bald Man)*, Belle Daube *(Elderly Actress)*, Louise Sarayder *(Actress)*, Patricia Northrup *(Gary Mitchell Fan)*, Don Brodie *(Engineer)*, Tristram Coffin *(Head Waiter)*, Edward Colmans *(Radio Voice)*, Chester Clute, George Neise, Joan Vohs, Maynard Holmes, Eve Whitney *(Party Guests)*.

Carson plays a radio talent scout looking for the next big sensation. He takes girl-next-door type Day and transforms her into a major star. That's about it for plot in this Technicolor remake of the 1934 Dick Powell film TWENTY MILLION SWEETHEARTS. Though competently made and well-acted, the film was trite and well below the talents of all involved. The highlight is a dream sequence where Day cavorts with Bugs Bunny and Tweety Bird. Songs include: "My Dream Is Yours," "Some Like You," "Tic, Tic, Tic," "Love Finds a Way" (Ralph Freed, Harry Warren), "I'll String Along with You" (Al Dubin, Warren), "Canadian Capers" (Gus Chandler, Bert White, Henry Cohen, Earl Burtnett), "Freddie Get Ready" (to the tune of the "Hungarian Rhapsody II"), "You Must Have Been a Beautiful Baby," "Jeepers, Creepers" (Johnny Mercer, Warren), "Nagasaki" (Mort Dixon, Warren), "With Plenty of Money and You" (Dubin, Warren).

p&d, Michael Curtiz; w, Harry Kurnitz, Dane Lussier, Allen Rivkin, Laura Kerr (based on the story "Hot Air" by Jerry Wald, Paul Moss); ph, Ernest Haller, Wilfred M. Cline (Technicolor); m, Harry Warren; ed, Folmar Blangsted; md, Ray Heindorf; art d, Robert Haas; set d, Howard Winterbottom; cos, Milo Anderson; spec eff, Edwin DuPar; ch, LeRoy Prinz; cartoon sequence d, I. Freeling.

Musical **(PR:A MPAA:NR)**

MY ENEMY, THE SEA (SEE: ALONE ON THE PACIFIC, 1964, Jap.)

MY FAIR LADY**** (1964) 170m WB c

Audrey Hepburn *(Eliza Doolittle)*, Rex Harrison *(Prof. Henry Higgins)*, Stanley Holloway *(Alfred P. Doolittle)*, Wilfrid Hyde-White *(Col. Hugh Pickering)*, Gladys Cooper *(Mrs. Higgins)*, Jeremy Brett *(Freddy Eynsford-Hill)*, Theodore Bikel *(Zoltan Karpathy)*, Isobel Elsom *(Mrs. Eynsford-Hill)*, Mona Washbourne *(Mrs. Pearce)*, John Alderson *(Jamie)*, John McLiam *(Harry)*, Marni Nixon *(Singing Voice of Eliza)*, Bill Shirley *(Singing Voice of Freddie)*, Ben Wrigley, Clive Halliday, Richard Peel, Eric Heath, James O'Hara *(Costermongers)*, Kendrick Huxham, Frank Baker *(Elegant Bystanders)*, Walter Burke *(Main Bystander)*, Queenie Leonard *(Cockney Bystander)*, Laurie Main *(Hoxton Man)*, Maurice Dallimore *(Selsey Man)*, Owen McGiveney *(Man at Coffee Stand)*, Jack Raine *(Male Member)*, Marjorie Bennett *(Cockney with Pipe)*, Britannia Beatey *(Daughter of Elegant Bystander)*, Beatrice Greenough *(Grand Lady)*, Hilda Plowright *(Bystander)*, Dinah Anne Rogers, Lois Battle *(Maids)*, Jacqueline Squire *(Parlor Maid)*, Gwen Watts *(Cook)*, Eugene Hoffman, Kai Farrelli *(Jugglers)*, Raymond Foster, Joe Evans, Marie Busch, Mary Alexander, William Linkie, Henry Sweetman, Andrew Brown, Samuel Holmes, Thomas Dick, William Taylor, James Wood, Goldie Kleban, Elizabeth Aimers, Joy Tierney, Lenore Miller, Donna Day, Corinne Ross, Phyllis Kennedy, Davie Robel *(Cockneys)*, Iris Briston, Alma Lawton *(Flower Girls)*, Gigi Michel, Sandy Steffens, Sandy Edmundson, Marlene Marrow, Carol Merrill, Sue Bronson, Lea Genovese *(Toffs)*, Jack Greening *(George)*, Ron Whelan *(Algernon/Bartender)*, John Holland *(Butler)*, Roy Dean *(Footman)*, Charles Fredericks *(King)*, Lily Kemble-Cooper *(Lady Ambassador)*, Barbara Pepper *(Doolittle's Dance Partner)*, Ayllene Gibbons *(Fat Woman at Pub)*, Baroness Rothschild *(Queen of Transylvania)*, Ben Wright *(Footman at Ball)*, Oscar Beregi *(Greek Ambassador)*, Buddy Bryan *(Prince)*, Grady Sutton, Orville Sherman, Harvey Dunn, Barbara Morrison, Natalie Core, Helen Albrecht, Diana Bourbon *(Ascot Types)*, Moyna MacGill *(Lady Boxington)*, Colin Campbell *(Ascot Gavotte)*, Marjory Hawtrey, Paulle Clark, Allison Daniell *(Ad Libs at Ascot)*, Betty Blythe *(Ad Lib at Ball)*, Nick Navarro *(Dancer)*, Tom Cound, William Beckley *(Footmen)*, Alan Napier *(Ambassador)*, Geoffrey Steele *(Taxi Driver)*, Jennifer Crier *(Mrs. Higgins' Maid)*, Henry Daniell *(Prince Gregor of Transylvania)*, Pat O'Moore *(Man)*, Victor Rogers *(Policeman)*, Michael St. Clair *(Bartender)*, Brendon Dillon *(Leaning Man)*, Olive Reeves-Smith *(Mrs. Hopkins)*, Miriam Schiller *(Landlady)*, Elzada Wilson, Jeanne Carson, Buddy Shea, Jack Goldie, Sid Marion, Stanley Fraser, George Pelling, Colin Kenny, Phyllis Kennedy, LaWana Backer, Monika Henried, Anne Dore, Pauline Drake, Shirley Melline, Wendy Russell, Meg Brown, Clyde Howdy, Nicholas Wolcuff, Martin Eric, John Mitchum *(Ad Libs at Church)*, Maj. Sam Harris *(Guest at Ball)*.

Jack Warner may have been getting a little soft in the head when he made this picture because he originally wanted Cary Grant or Rock Hudson to play Higgins and Jimmy Cagney to be Doolittle. Grant said that if Warner chose anyone but Rex Harrison he would not even bother to see the film. But Warner was worried. He had put up more than $5 million for the rights to the musical and earmarked nearly $20 million as production cost. He also made a deal that promised the authors and producers of the stage show almost 50 percent of the net and he was attempting to bolster his position. As it turned out, the picture made a fortune and took Oscars in almost every category that year, with the one glaring exception being Best Actress, an award given to Julie Andrews for MARY POPPINS. It was especially ironic as Hepburn was not even nominated for the role that Andrews originated on the stage. MY FAIR LADY won as Best Picture, for Best Actor, Best Director, Best Color Cinematography, Best Costume Design, Best Musical Score, Best Sound, and Best Art Direction. Cukor and designer Beaton never saw eye to eye on the movie and battled from start to finish. Those disagreements did not hurt the film one bit and both men carted awards away from the Oscar ceremonies. Hepburn, who received a fee of $1 million, was a weak link because she could never truly persuade anyone that she was a guttersnipe in the first reels of the movie. The transition of waif to lady is not easy although Wendy Hiller accomplished it in PYGMALION. If you do not know the story, it goes like this: Harrison is coming out of the theater when he meets Hyde-White and it turns out that both men have admired each other's work in linguistics for years. Harrison hears Hepburn bawl and makes a bet with Hyde-White that he can turn this cockney into a lady with an accent so pure that no one will know her background. They make her an offer and she declines. Later, she arrives at Harrison's home, where Hyde-White is now staying, and she has money for diction lessons. Her goal in life is to acquire enough of an upper-class manner of speech so she can get a job in a shop and quit selling on the street. Harrison finds her delightfully tacky and agrees. The two men work hard with Hepburn until they feel she is ready to be seen, and heard, in public. They squire her to the races at Ascot where she meets Harrison's dowager mother, Cooper, and charms her. She also charms young Brett, a vapid man who, as Oscar Wilde said of Algernon "has nothing, but looks everything." Later, they take her to a huge social event where she is the belle of the ball and even fools Bikel, a notorious linguist who brags he can tell where anyone came from. Bikel once was a student of Harrison's and he declares that Hepburn is of a royal background. Once back at the house, Harrison and Hyde-White pat each other on the back and forget all about Hepburn. She is furious and leaves. Her father, Holloway, a man with a ready wit and voracious thirst, had been to the Harrison home and agreed to allow his daughter to stay there if the men crossed his palm with pounds. Hepburn discovers that her father is about to finally marry the woman he has lived with for years. The whole thing came to pass when Harrison had given Holloway's name to an American millionaire and Holloway has achieved respectability through the mogul, something he had been successfully avoiding for years. Hepburn goes to see Cooper who has some sage advice as to how to handle her bachelor son. Meanwhile, Brett moons about on the street waiting to catch a glance of Hepburn and she threatens to marry the man. Harrison realizes that he has fallen in love with Hepburn and when he walks into his now-quiet home, he sits down and listens to the early recordings Hepburn made when she was still speaking with her thick accent. She walks in behind him and starts talking (in place of the recordings) and he senses that she is there although he cannot bring himself to acknowledge it by saying anything other than "Eliza, bring me my slippers." But she knows that means he loves her. The picture ends and sniffles can be heard. Only Harrison, Hyde-White, and Reeves-Smith were in the play. This also marked the final film for Henry Daniell, who was so brilliant in so many films. He died just before the picture was released. The songs? Glorious. By Lerner and Loewe, they include: "Why Can't the English?" (sung by Harrison), "Wouldn't It Be Loverly?" (sung by Hepburn, Nixon and chorus), "I'm an Ordinary Man" (sung by Harrison), "With a Little Bit of Luck" (sung by Harrison, Holloway, Alderson, McLiam), "Just You Wait, 'Enry 'Iggins" (sung by Hepburn, Nixon), "The Servant's Chorus" (sung by chorus), "The Rain in Spain" (sung by Hepburn, Nixon, Harrison, Hyde-White), "I Could Have Danced all Night" (sung by Hepburn, Nixon and chorus), "Ascot Gavotte" (sung by chorus), "On the Street Where You Live" (sung by Brett, Shirley), "The Embassy Waltz," "You Did It" (sung by Hyde-White, Harrison and chorus), "Show Me" (sung by Hepburn, Nixon), "The Flower Market," "Get Me to the Church on Time" (sung by Holloway and chorus), "A Hymn to Him" (sung by Harrison), "Without You" (sung by Hepburn, Nixon), "I've Grown Accustomed to Her Face" (sung by Harrison). To see how this was conceived, watch PYGMALION (either the play or the Leslie Howard film) and you'll note the close resemblance between the dialog and the way it was musicalized by Lerner and Loewe. The Shaw estate insisted that much of the original be maintained and Lerner adhered to that, so much so that many of the songs spring directly from Shaw's script. Lerner, whose family owned the Lerner Shops chain of women's stores, worked on the lyrics for this in his uncle's "hunting lodge" which was a full floor in a building on the corner of Fifth Avenue and 57th Street that the uncle kept because his wife did not like his animal trophies. They also wrote in a rented house on the estate of Burgess Meredith in New York City, New York, and in Loewe's Palm Springs home. MY FAIR LADY, for all its kudos, is often bloodless and never revs up to the joy that they presented on the Mark Hellinger theater stage eight times each week from 1956 through 1962. The *Pygmalion* story was not an original by Shaw. Rather it was a legend, *Pygmalion and Galatea*, which was also used by W.S. Gilbert for a play that preceded Shaw's in London. At 10 minutes under three hours, the musical is a trifle long, although audiences did not seem to mind. One other oddity; this is one of the rare musicals that did not have a title song. It took its name from the old poem about London Bridge falling down. After the play opened, Billy Gray, a Los Angeles comic who owned a nighclub on Fairfax Avenue in the Jewish section of the city, commissioned a burlesque by veteran writer Sid Kuller. It was called "My Fairfax Lady" and told the story of a British woman who came to the area to work at CBS (which is across the street from Gray's club, The Bandbox (no longer there), and was fired. Then she discovered that she couldn't fit in the neighborhood unless she learned to talk with a Jewish accent. With the help of Gray (as Higgins) and Bert Gordon, the Mad Russian, as Colonel "DillPickling," they begin to teach her the "right way" to talk. Eventually, Gray attempts to show her how to speak the Yiddish word for horseradish which is chrane (pronounced with a growl on the "ch") and she must repeat after him "der chrane in Spain iss mainly red or plain." When Lerner came to see the show, he and the cast members (who were appearing in Los Angeles) were convulsed by the satire. Although the authors had every legal right to stop the show (there is a law about "Grand Rights" to material that states a parody cannot be done without permission, which is seldom given), they allowed Gray's version to continue with the agreement that the show could not be recorded or taken on the road. Gray also did parodies of GOLDFINGER ("Goldfinkel") and "The Cohen Mutiny" all written by Kuller. "My Fairfax Lady" was one of the funniest evenings ever devised and Lerner and Loewe are to be thanked for letting it go on.

p, Jack L. Warner; d, George Cukor; w, Alan Jay Lerner (based on a musical play by Lerner, Frederick Loewe and the play "Pygmalion" by George Bernard Shaw); ph, Harry Stading (Super Panavision, Technicolor); m, Loewe; ed, William Ziegler; prod d, Cecil Beaton; md, Andre Previn; art d, Gene Allen; set d, George James Hopkins; cos, Beaton; ch, Hermes Pan; makeup, Gordon Bau.

Musical Comedy   **Cas.**   **(PR:AA   MPAA:NR)**

MY FATHER'S HOUSE*   (1947, Palestine) 85m Kline-Levin/IN bw

Ronnie Cohen (David), Irene Broza (Miriam), Isaac Danziger (Avram), Herman Heuser (Abba), Joseph Pacovsky (Yehuda), Zalman Leiviush (Smulik), R. Klatchkin (Waiter), Miriam Laserson (Nahama), I. Finklestein (Zev), Israela Epstein (Shulamith), Michael Cohen (Maccabee), Naomi Salzberger (Dvora), P. Goldman (Welsbrod), Y. Adaki (Jamal), Josef Sandia (Mustafa).

Before being separated by Nazis, an 11-year-old boy is told by his father that they will meet in Palestine. A few years after the war, the young man goes to the Holy Land looking for his father, against the wishes of adults who know he is dead. This is an intriguing story, but is handled so poorly here it's a crime. The actors used were all amateurs and it shows. What's worse is the unbelievable portrait of Palestine (soon to become Israel) that we are shown. If this film is to be believed, Jews and Arabs live next door to one another in peace and harmony, and the problems they had with the British in 1947 are non-existent. Financed, in part, by the Jewish National Fund, which sponsored many of its screenings in this country.

p, Herbert Kline, Meyer Levin; d, Kline; w, Levin; ph, Floyd Crosby; m, Henry Brant; ed, Peter Elgar.

Drama   **(PR:A   MPAA:NR)**

MY FATHER'S MISTRESS*1/2
(1970, Swed.) 110m A-Produktion/Chevron c (AKA: BAMSE; THE TEDDY BEAR)

Grynet Molvig (Barbro "Bamse" Persson), Folke Sundquist (Christer Berg), Ulla Jacobsson (Vera Berg), Bjorn Thambert (Chris, the Son), Henning Sjostrom (The Lawyer), Gio Petre (The Blonde), Paul Hagen (Danish Porter), Gunilla Dahlmann (Brunette), Sune Mangs (Drunk), Pia Rydwall (Greta), Rune Lundstrom, Lasse Krantz.

Depressing love story from Sweden about a youth who falls in love with his dead father's mistress. The boy (Thambert) discovers the existence of mistress Molvig from the teddy bear that was in the father's car when it crashed. He then threatens to tell his mother about the affair unless Molvig agrees to pretend she is his fiancee. Somehow, something in the boy sparks her fancy and she falls in love with him. But their romance is short-lived: she finds out that she is pregnant by Thambert's father and decides to make her presence scarce.

p, Ewert Granholm; d, Arne Mattsson; w, Mattsson, Elsa Prawitz; ph, Lars Bjorne (Eastmancolor); m, Wolfgang Amadeus Mozart, Johann Strauss; ed, Wic Kjellin; art d, Harold Garmland; cos, Per LeKang, Bertha Sannell.

Drama   **(PR:C   MPAA:PG)**

MY FAVORITE BLONDE*   (1942) 78m PAR bw

Bob Hope (Larry Haines), Madeleine Carroll (Karen Bentley), Gale Sondergaard (Mme. Stephanie Runick), George Zucco (Dr. Hugo Streger), Lionel Royce (Karl), Walter Kingsford (Dr. Faber), Victor Varconi (Miller), Otto Reichow (Lanz), Charles Cane (Turk O'Flaherty), Crane Whitley (Ulrich), Erville Alderson (Sheriff), Esther Howard (Mrs. Topley), Ed Gargan (Mulrooney), James Burke (Union Secretary), Dooley Wilson (Porter), Bing Crosby (Man Giving Directions), Milton Parsons (Mortician), Tom Fadden (Tom Douglas), Fred Kelsey (Sam), Edgar Dearing (Joe), Leslie Denison (Elvan), Robert Emmett Keane (Burton), Addison Richards (Herbert Wilson), Matthew Boulton (Col. Ashmont), Wade Boteler (Conductor), William Forrest (Col. Raeburn), Carl "Alfalfa" Switzer (Frederick), Isabel Randolph (Frederick's Mother), Edward Hearn (Train Official), Leyland Hodgson (English Driver), Jack Luden, Mary Akin (Spectators), Monte Blue, Jack Clifford (Cops at Union Hall), Dick Elliott (Backstage Doorman), Arno Frey (Male Nurse), Lloyd Whitlock (Apartment Manager), Vernon Dent (Ole, Bartender), Sarah Edwards (Mrs. Weatherwax), Paul Scardon (Dr. Higby), Bill Lally (Telegraph Operator), Minerva Urecal (Frozen-Faced Woman), James Millican (Truck Driver), Edmund Cobb (Yard Man), Jimmy Dodd (Stuttering Boy), Eddie Dew, George Turner, Kirby Grant, William Cabanne (Pilots), Harry Hollingsworth (Irish Cop), Ed Peil, Sr., Dick Rush (Cops), Art Miles (Cop Outside Union Hall), Max Wagner (Man with Truck), William Irving (Waiter), Charles R. Moore (Pullman Porter), Dudley Dickerson (Red Cap), Charles McAvoy (Brakeman), George Hickman (Elevator Boy), Joe Recht, Rex Moore, Gerald A. Pierce, Allan Ramsey, Johnny Erickson, David McKim (Newsboys), Frank Mills (New York Taxi Driver), Frank Marlowe, Mike Lally (Chicago Taxi Drivers), Alice Keating, Betty Farrington, Nell Craig (Women), Rose Allen (Outraged Woman).

Carroll is a beautiful spy who posesses plans involving the shipment of war planes to England and is being chased by Nazis who want the plans for themselves. While in New York she escapes from them by ducking into a small dressing room at a theater. Coincidentally, this happens to be the dressing room of Hope, a wise-cracking ladies' man who's preparing his performing penguin for its Hollywood debut. Without much pleading, the lovely Carroll convinces Hope to aid her escape. From there it's a comic cross-country chase, with lots of disguises and silliness. Hope

is wonderful, with something smart to say no matter what the situation. His smug behavior is very funny (far and away superior to anything he ever did in the television work that made him rich) and the pacing is good, as it usually is in these Hope comedies. His old partner from the ROAD TO . . . films, the wonderfully laidback Crosby, makes a cameo (as he so often did in Hope's solo comedies) as a man giving the two travelers directions. "No, it can't be," mutters Hope after the benefactor leaves. Some good fun, but the poor penguin was treated like a toy rather than an animal, getting bounced around more than necessary. Penguins are inherently funny animals (as TV's "Monty Python's Flying Circus" proved time and again) and there was no need for the knockabout treatment of the bird.

p, Paul Jones; d, Sidney Lanfield; w, Don Hartman, Frank Butler (based on a story by Melvin Frank, Norman Panama); ph, William Mellor; m, David Buttolph; ed, William O'Shea; art d, Hans Dreier, Robert Usher.

Comedy   **(PR:A   MPAA:NR)**

MY FAVORITE BRUNETTE**   (1947) 87m PAR bw

Bob Hope (Ronnie Jackson), Dorothy Lamour (Carlotta Montay), Peter Lorre (Kismet), Lon Chaney, Jr. (Willie), Charles Dingle (Maj. Simon Montague), Reginald Denny (James Collins), Frank Puglia (Baron Montay), Ann Doran (Miss Rogers), Willard Robertson (Prison Warden), Jack LaRue (Tony), Charles Arnt (Crawford), John Hoyt (Dr. Lundau), Garry Owen, Richard Keane (Reporters), Tony [Anthony] Caruso ("George Raft" Type), Matt McHugh ("Jimmy Cagney" Type), George Lloyd (Prison Guard-Sergeant), Jack Clifford (Prison Guard-Captain), Ray Teal, Al Hill (State Troopers), Boyd Davis (Mr. Dawsen), Clarence Muse (Man in Condemned Row), Helena Evans (Mabel), Roland Soo Hoo (Baby Fong), Jean Wong (Mrs. Fong), Charley Cooley (Waiter), John Westley (Doctor), Ted Rand (Waiter Captain), Tom Dillon (Policeman), Harland Tucker (Room Clerk), Reginald Simpson (Assistant Manager), James Flavin (Mac the Detective), Jim Pierce, Budd Fine (Detectives), John Tyrrell (Bell Captain), Joe Recht (Newsboy), Bing Crosby (Executioner), Alan Ladd (Private Detective), Eddie Johnson (Caddy), Betty Farrington (Matron), Brandon Hurst (Butler), Jack Chefe (Henri the Waiter).

In what ranks as one of his best comedies, Hope plays a harried baby photographer who is asked by his private-eye pal to watch the business for a few days while the dick goes on vacation. Hope agrees and finds himself getting involved with a lot more than watching the dust settle. Lamour enters the office and believes Hope to be the real private eye. She hires him to search for her uncle, a wealthy baron who has vanished, and gives the dubious detective a map, warning him to guard it with his life. Hope goes off to the palatial estate of a former associate of the missing man, Dingle, who introduces Hope to a man in a wheelchair that is supposedly the missing man. Chaney enters the scene as a doctor who insists Lamour has a few screws loose. The twosome have Hope convinced until he is about to leave and spots the "disabled" baron walking about. He snaps a quick picture and Dingle gets one of his crazed henchmen (Lorre in a wonderful self-parody) to knock out Hope and recover the film. Hope and Lamour later pay a visit to the geologist who drew up the map, in an effort to find out its importance but Lorre has killed him using Hope's gun and Hope is framed for the murder. He is scheduled for execution and is saved only minutes before by evidence discovered by Lamour. The executioner, furious that his day has been ruined, takes off his hood and reveals himself to be none other than Hope's off-screen (and sometimes on-screen) pal Crosby. "Boy," says Hope as he turns to the camera, "he'll take any kind of a part!" This is a classic Hope film, with one gag following another in rapid succession. Particularly good is Lorre, who was known at this stage in his career for doing serious films of this genre. His characterization as a crazy man so tough he'll crack walnuts with his eyelids (to say nothing of what he does to good guys!) is great fun. Ladd is equally as amusing in his cameo role of the vacationing detective.

p, Daniel Dare; d, Elliott Nugent; w, Edmund Beloin; Jack Rose; ph, Lionel Lindon; m, Robert Emmett Dolan; ed, Ellsworth Hoagland; md, Dolan; art d, Hans Dreier, Earl Hedrick; cos, Edith Head; spec eff, Gordon Jennings; m/l, "Beside You," Jay Livingston, Ray Evans.

Comedy   **Cas.**   **(PR:A   MPAA:NR)**

MY FAVORITE SPY*   (1942) 86m RKO bw

Kay Kyser (Himself), Ellen Drew (Terry Kyser), Jane Wyman (Connie), Robert Armstrong (Harry Robinson), Helen Westley (Aunt Jessie), William Demarest (Flower Pot Cop), Una O'Connor (Cora the Maid), Lionel Royce (Winters), Moroni Olsen (Maj. Allen), George Cleveland (Gus), Vaughan Glaser (Col. Moffett), Hobart Cavanaugh (Jules), Chester Clute (Higgenbotham), Teddy Hart (Soldier), Ish Kabibble (Ish), Kay Kyser's Band featuring Harry Babbitt, Sully Mason, Dorothy Dunn, Trudy Irwin (Themselves), Edmund Glover (Selvin), Selmer Jackson (Minister), Dorothy Phillips (Bit at Wedding), Hal K. Dawson (Eberle the Hotel Manager), Matt Moore (Desk Sergeant), Charles Williams, Earle Hodgins, Henry Roquemore (Speakers), Sammy Stein, Larry Lawson, Bud Geary, Fred Graham (Marines), Bert Roach (Bit in Park), Barbara Pepper ("B" Girl), Frank Hagney (Bit in Kelly's), Sammy Finn (Dave), Murray Alper (Kay's Driver), Harold Daniels (Madman), Ralph Sanford (Theater Cop), Ed Deering (Cop, Tagwriting Sergeant), Al Hill (Cooper), Louis Adlon (Lefty), Tony Marrill (Bit in Allen's Office), Harold Kruger (Jail Inmate), Stanley Blystone (Turnkey), Vince Barnett (Kay's Driver No. 2), Carli Elinor (Phillips), Jack Norton (Drunk), Roy Gordon (Maj. Updyke), William Ruhl (Maj. Allen's Friend), William Forrest (Captain), Pat Flaherty (Recruit), Bobby Barber (Man in Park), Kit Guard (Henchman), Walter Reed (Nightclub Patron), John James (Recruit).

Famed bandleader Kyser turns spy in this nonsense. A spy ring hangs out in his club and the Army chooses him to be the man to infiltrate them. Wyman's a love interest, and at least you get to hear Kyser's band play "Just Plain Lonesome" and "I've Got the Moon in My Pocket" (Johnny Burke, Jimmy Van Heusen). The direction has no feel for comedy, nor does the excruciatingly unfunny Kyser. Produced by the great silent clown Lloyd, his last such effort for RKO.

p, Harold Lloyd; d, Tay Garnett; w, Sig Herzig, William Bowers (based on a story by M. Coates Webster); ph, Robert de Grasse; m, Roy Webb; ed, Desmond Marquette; md, C. Bakaleinikoff; art d, Albert S. D'Agostino, Carroll Clark; spec eff, Vernon L. Walker.

Musical/Comedy (PR:A MPAA:NR)

MY FAVORITE SPY*** (1951) 93m PAR bw

Bob Hope *(Peanuts White/Eric Augustine)*, Hedy Lamarr *(Lily Dalbray)*, Francis L. Sullivan *(Karl Brubaker)*, Arnold Moss *(Tasso)*, John Archer *(Henderson)*, Luis Van Rooten *(Hoenig)*, Stephen Chase *(Donald Bailey)*, Morris Ankrum *(Gen. Fraser)*, Angela Clarke *(Gypsy Fortune Teller)*, Iris Adrian *(Lola)*, Frank Faylen *(Newton)*, Mike Mazurki *(Monkara)*, Marc Lawrence *(Ben Ali)*, Ralph Smiley *(El Sarif)*, Joseph Vitale *(Fireman)*, Nestor Paiva *(Fire Chief)*, Tonio Selwart *(Harry Crock)*, Suzannae Dalbert *(Barefoot Maid)*, Laura Elliott *(Maria)*, Mary Murphy *(Manicurist)*, Torben Meyer *(Headwaiter)*, Charles Cooley *(Man)*, Jack Chefe, Rolfe Sedan, Michael A. Cirillo, Dario Piazza *(Waiters)*, Henry Hope, William C. Quealy *(Patrons)*, Jerry Lane, Marie Thomas *(Cafe Patrons)*, Michael Ansara, Don Dunning *(House Servants)*, Norbert Schiller *(Dr. Estrallo)*, Roy Roberts *(Johnson)*, William Johnstone *(Prentice)*, Jack Pepper, Herrick Herrick, Jimmie Dundee, Jerry James, Lee Bennett *(FBI Men)*, Roger Creed *(Photo Double)*, Peggy Gordon, Suzanne Ridgway, Charlotte Hunter, Sethma Williams, Patti McKaye *(Dancers)*, Ivan Triesault *(Gunman)*, Crane Whitley *(Willie)*, Geraldine Knapp *(Maid with Towels)*, Eugene Borden *(Manager)*, Sue Casey, Dorothy Abbott *(Pretty Girls)*, Monique Chantal *(Denise)*, Ralph Byrd, George Lynn *(Officials)*, Sayre Dearing *(Dealer in Gambling Room)*, Jean DeBriac, Steven Geray *(Croupiers)*, Nancy Duke, Mimi Berry, Mary Ellen Gleason, Edith Sheets, Leah Waggner, Carolyn Wolfson *(Girls in Gambling Room)*, Pepe Hern *(Bellboy)*, Alfredo Santos *(Servant)*, Vyola Vonn *(Tara)*, Lillian Molieri *(Girl)*, Henry Mirelez, Tony Mirelez *(Shine Boys)*, Ed Loredo, Myron Marks *(Doormen)*, Gay Gayle *(Flower Girl)*, Carlos Conde, Felipe Turich *(Porters)*, Alphonse Martell *(Assistant Manager of French Hotel)*, Alberto Morin *(Hotel Employee)*, Pat Moran *(Little Man)*, Duke York *(Man)*, Loyal Underwood, Delmar Costello *(Beggars)*, Rudy Rama *(Knife Man)*, Frank Hagney *(Camel Herdsman)*, Ralph Montgomery *(Grant)*, Mike Mahoney *(Murphy)*, Michael Ross, Paul "Tiny" Newlan, Edward Agresti *(Tangier Policemen)*, Alvina Temple *(Miss Murphy)*, Fritz Feld *(Dress Designer)*, Roy Butler *(Barber)*, Jon Tegner *(Judo Expert)*, Bobbie Hall *(Tailor)*, Charles D. Campbell *(Hatter)*, Helen Chapman *(Miss Dieckers)*, Joan Whitney *(Burlesque Blonde)*, Howard Negley, Stanley Blystone *(Guards)*, Billy Engle, Chester Conklin, Hank Mann *(Comics)*, Ralph Sanford *(Straight Man)*, Lyle L. Moraine *(Foster)*, Abdullah Abbas *(Fireman/Egyptian Porter)*.

Hope plays a dual role as a burlesque comic and international spy. The spy is all set to meet a scientist in Europe and pick up some important microfilm but is captured by other agents. The burlesque comic, picked up by the cops who mistake him for the spy, is induced into making the trip to fetch the microfilm. He goes to Tangier to make the contact and meets Lamarr, the real spy's girl. She is also an agent for a ring run by Sullivan. Sullivan wants the microfilm himself and is soon chasing the would-be agent. Meanwhile, the real agent has escaped and arrives in Tangier. But he is killed and the comic confesses all to a slightly confused Lamarr. She helps Hope escape Sullivan's clutches and the latter is finally arrested. Hope is given $10,000 for his efforts, which he uses to open up a little haberdashery for himself and Lamarr in the more quiet land of New Jersey. A nice rollicking comedy, this was a good vehicle for Hope's talents. He makes the two different characters believable, keeping the old "dual-identity" plot fresh. Lamarr is also good, though apparently she was a lot better than this film let on. It seems Hope was enraged because she had stolen the show from him in the final studio cut, so at his insistence, the film was further edited so he would be the funnier one. Lamarr was naturally furious and never forgave Hope. The direction was fine for comedy, taking the film along at a breakneck pace. Two songs are seemingly sung by Lamarr, but the numbers were actually a well-synched dubbing.

p, Paul Jones; d, Norman Z. McLeod; w, Edmund Hartmann, Jack Sher, Edmund Beloin, Lou Breslow, Hal Kanter (based on a story by Beloin, Breslow); ph, Victor Milner; m, Victor Young; ed, Frank Bracht; art d, Hal Pereira, Roland Anderson; cos, Edith Head; m/l, "I Wind Up Taking a Fall," Johnny Mercer, Robert Emmett Dolan, "Just a Moment More," Jay Livingston, Ray Evans.

Comedy (PR:A MPAA:NR)

MY FAVORITE WIFE*** (1940) 88m RKO bw

Irene Dunne *(Ellen Arden)*, Cary Grant *(Nick Arden)*, Randolph Scott *(Stephen Burkett)*, Gail Patrick *(Bianca)*, Ann Shoemaker *(Ma)*, Scotty Beckett *(Tim Arden)*, Mary Lou Harrington *(Chinch Arden)*, Donald MacBride *(Hotel Clerk)*, Hugh O'Connell *(Johnson)*, Granville Bates *(Judge)*, Pedro de Cordoba *(Dr. Kohlmar)*, Brandon Tynan *(Dr. Manning)*, Leon Belasco *(Henri)*, Harold Gerald *(Assistant Clerk)*, Murray Alper *(Bartender)*, Earle Hodgins *(Court Clerk)*, Cyril Ring *(Contestant)*, Clive Morgan, Bert Moorhouse *(Lawyers)*, Florence Dudley, Jean Acker *(Witnesses)*, Joe Cabrillas *(Phillip)*, Frank Marlowe *(Photographer)*, Thelma Joel *(Miss Rosenthal)*, Horace MacMahon *(Truck Driver)*, Chester Clute *(Little Man)*, Eli Schmudkler *(Janitor)*, Franco Corsaro *(Waiter)*, Cy Kendall *(Detective)*, Pat West *(Caretaker)*.

After Grant and Dunne came off such a success with THE AWFUL TRUTH, they were reteamed for this up-to-date version of the "Enoch Arden" story. Producer McCarey was supposed to direct, but he had a terrible auto accident just before shooting, so Kanin was handed the task and came through with a fast-moving, often amusing film. Dunne has supposedly been dead for seven years, the result of having been shipwrecked, when Grant, now able to remarry, takes Patrick as his lawful wedded wife. In a twinkling, Dunne shows up. She's been rescued after having spent all those years on an island with burly Scott, the other survivor. Grant takes Patrick on their honeymoon to Yosemite National Park and Dunne follows them there. When Grant spots her, he can't tell Patrick what's happened, so he avoids it and takes Patrick back to their home. Dunne had left two small children behind when she took the ill-fated South Seas voyage and they don't recognize her. At the Grant-Patrick house, Dunne is already in residence when the lovebirds return and she pretends to be a friend. When Grant learns that Dunne had been on the island with a man all that time, he becomes concerned that she may have been compromised. She circumvents that by hiring a shoe salesman, a much older man, to pretend to be her island companion. Grant buys that for a while, then learns it was handsome Scott all the while. Grant takes Dunne to lunch with Scott and there is the cliche scene where she falls into the swimming pool at Scott's hotel-apartment building. Meanwhile, Patrick is getting mentally disturbed, so she begins to consult psychiatrist de Cordoba. In the end, Grant realizes that he still loves Dunne and, after a riotous scene in a courtroom with Bates presiding, the second marriage is annulled and Grant and Dunne are free to resume their lives together. Lots of laughs for the first three-quarters of the film but then it peters out for the expected finale. Remade, not as well, as MOVE OVER, DARLING, which starred Doris Day and James Garner in the Dunne and Grant roles.

p, Leo McCarey; d, Garson Kanin; w, Sam and Bella Spewack (based on a story by McCarey, the Spewacks); ph, Rudolph Mate; m, Roy Webb; ed, Robert Wise; art d, Van Nest Polglase, Mark-Lee Kirk; set d, Darrell Silvera; cos, Howard Greer.

Comedy Cas. (PR:A MPAA:NR)

MY FAVORITE YEAR ****

(1982) 92m Brooksfilms/MGM-UA c (GB: MY FAVOURITE YEAR)

Peter O'Toole *(Alan Swann)*, Mark Linn-Baker *(Benjy Stone)*, Jessica Harper *(K.C. Downing)*, Joseph Bologna *(King Kaiser)*, Bill Macy *(Sy Benson)*, Lainie Kazan *(Belle Carroca)*, Anne DeSalvo *(Alice Miller)*, Basil Hoffman *(Herb Lee)*, Lou Jacobi *(Uncle Morty)*, Adolph Green *(Leo Silver)*, Tony DiBenedetto *(Alfie Bumbacelli)*, George Wyner *(Myron Fein)*, Selma Diamond *(Lil)*, Cameron Mitchell *(Karl Rojeck)*, Jenny Neumann, Corinne Bohrer, George Marshall Ruge, Barbra Horan, John Welsh.

A thoroughly delightful film with a deep and poignant portrait of TV life and life styles in the early 1950s. Linn-Baker is a fledgling writer for the popular live comedy TV show hosted by zany, tough, yet soft-hearted Bologna. He is assigned to chaperone the equally unpredictable, heavy-boozing one-time Hollywood swash-buckler O'Toole, who is to make his first appearance on TV in a Bologna skit. This mission is not a common or easy task. O'Toole arrives in Manhattan drunk but crafty and uncontrollable and he begins to lead Linn-Baker in a wild night of revelry. Over several days all who encounter O'Toole are close to nervous breakdowns. O'Toole steals a beautiful girl from The Stork Club while Linn-Baker creates a "diversion." Then they invade a penthouse party by dropping O'Toole by a firehose to the next level below. They carouse through Central Park and O'Toole steals a policeman's horse (while the cop is relieving himself in the bushes) and both men ride madly down the bridle path. The show itself is a disaster, or it seems to be, as O'Toole staggers about with the near-DTs, forgetting his lines and, just before going on, panics when he learns that the show is live. "I'm a film actor!" he rages, but he does go on, gets into a fight with a bunch of union goons invading the set over Bologna's past insults, and helps the host defeat the bad guys for a hilarious wow finish. O'Toole is superb as one-time matinee idol and Bologna is outstanding as the brusque and brawling comic. Linn-Baker, who would later go on to his own TV series in 1986, is excellent, playing out a real-life incident where novice comedy writer Mel Brooks was assigned to chaperone the colorful Errol Flynn before he appeared on Sid Caesar's "Your Show of Shows." Playing a union crime boss is Mitchell and he does it with lead-foot accuracy and deadpan deadliness. Benjamin's direction, which is usually as exciting as an empty olive jar, surprisingly provides a dizzy pace and inventive set-ups, aided greatly by cinematographer Hirschfeld and editor Chew.

p, Michael Gruskoff; d, Richard Benjamin; w, Norman Steinberg, Dennis Palumbo (based on a story by Palumbo); ph, Gerald Hirschfeld *(Metrocolor)*; m, Ralph Burns; ed, Richard Chew; prod d, Charles Rosen; set d, Kandy Remacle, Herb Mulligan; cos, May Routh.

Comedy Cas. (PR:C MPAA:PG)

MY FIRST LOVE**

(1978, Fr.) 100m 7 Films-GAU-FR3/GAU c (MON PREMIER AMOUR)

Anouk Aimee *(Mother)*, Richard Berry *(Son)*, Gabriele Ferzetti *(Father)*, Jacques Villeret *(Friend)*, Nathalie Baye *(Girl)*.

Aimee is the beautiful mother of 20-year-old Berry. He has never really known her and now she is dying of leukemia. Slowly they let the barriers break down and when she finally passes away, they have reached a fulfilling relationship. What could have been a fine drama is instead little more than a routine soaper. Emotions are only touched upon and there's a myriad of cliched scenes and dialog. The ending attempts to say something (Did Aimee die naturally or did she kill herself for fear of losing her looks?) but doesn't quite pull it off. The direction is competent, however. This was the first film done by the assistant of famed Nouvelle Vague figure Claude Lelouch. Though newcomer Chouraqui doesn't quite know what to do with emotional values, the director still shows a good feel for the medium.

p,d&w, Elie Chouraqui (based on the book by Jack Alain Leger); ph, Bernard Zitzermann (Eastmancolor); ed, Marie-Josephe Yoyotte.

Drama (PR:O MPAA:NR)

MY FOOLISH HEART 1/2** (1949) 98m RKO bw

Dana Andrews *(Walt Dreiser)*, Susan Hayward *(Eloise Winters)*, Kent Smith *(Lew Wengler)*, Lois Wheeler *(Mary Jane)*, Jessie Royce Landis *(Martha Winters)*, Robert

Keith *(Henry Winters)*, Gigi Perreau *(Ramona)*, Karin Booth *(Miriam Ball)*, Tod Karns *(Her Escort)*, Philip Pine *(Sgt. Lucey)*, Martha Mears *(Nightclub Singer)*, Edna Holland *(Dean Whiting)*, Marietta Canty *(Grace)*, Barbara Woodell *(Red Cross Receptionist)*, Regina Wallace *(Mrs. Crandall)*, Jerry Paris *(Usher)*, Phyllis Coates *(Girl on Phone)*, Bud Stark *(Elevator Operator)*, Ed Peil, Sr. *(Conductor)*, Marcel de la Brosse *(Waiter)*, Billy Lord, Tom Gibson, Bob Strong, Kay Marlowe, Sam Ash *(Spectators)*, Kerry O'Day.

They opened this in the latter part of 1949 in order to qualify for the Oscars but the picture didn't go into general release until 1950. It was Hayward's only movie for Goldwyn and the second one she did with Andrews, a longtime Goldwyn contract player. Based on a short story by J.D. Salinger which first appeared in *The New Yorker* magazine and later became part of Salinger's collection, *Nine Stories*, the movie managed a nomination for Hayward (she lost to De Havilland in THE HEIRESS) and the title song. (It became a huge hit and no doubt helped the movie. Nevertheless, the winning song that year was Frank Loesser's "Baby, It's Cold Outside" from NEPTUNE'S DAUGHTER.) Bring several fresh hankies when you see this one, as it aims straight for the tear ducts and doesn't stop jerking for a moment. Hayward is a drinker and unhappily married to Smith, a one-time army man. She had been pregnant by another man and fooled Smith into marrying her several years before, after stealing him from her college roommate, Wheeler. Smith wants a divorce and she is about to tell him that their daughter, Perreau, is not his when Wheeler convinces her that the secret is better left undiscovered. Smith wants to marry Wheeler now and Hayward is packing her gear to leave the house when she discovers an old evening dress and that sends her back in time to 1941. She's at a swank party in New York and the dress has occasioned some remarks from the snobs. Andrews has crashed the soiree, they meet, and she is attracted to him. After a date, he takes her to his place and tries to seduce her but she refuses, despite being drawn to his devilish character. She's attending a posh boarding school and begins seeing Andrews whenever they can get together. When he goes to her school and they are caught necking, she's tossed out. Her parents come to New York and her mother, Landis, fears that the young girl's virginity may have been breached. Her father, Keith (whose son Brian later made his mark in movies and TV), believes what Hayward tells him and has a heart-to-heart with Andrews, who swears up and down that the affair was never consummated. Hayward's folks want her to return home with them, but she prefers life in the Big City and they agree to let her stay. The Japanese attack Pearl Harbor and Andrews is about to leave for his stint in the Air Corps (which is what they called it in those days), so they spend one final passionate night together. Andrews writes a letter to Hayward asking for her hand in marriage, then takes off on the flight that costs him his life. She gets the letter after hearing of his death, then learns that she is pregnant by her late lover. Fearful of the consequences, she comes between Smith and Wheeler and gets him to marry her, and when Perreau is born, Smith thinks that the child is his. Wheeler disappears and a loveless marriage continues. Flash forward and Hayward now understands how many lives she has manipulated, so she tells Smith that she will grant him the divorce and hopes that he and Wheeler will have the happiness that they should have had all these years. She offers to leave without Perreau but Smith, ever the gentleman, won't hear of that. Wheeler and Smith exit happily and Hayward remains with Perreau and hopes that she can make some semblance of happiness for herself and her daughter in the years to come. Keith was smashing as Hayward's father, his first large role after playing some bits in only five films since 1924, including BOOMERANG and KISS OF DEATH. In a tiny role as an usher, note Jerry Paris, who also played Ernest Borgnine's bother-in-law in MARTY and a few other roles before becoming an enormously successful TV director. The song "My Foolish Heart" became a pop standard.

p, Samuel Goldwyn; d, Mark Robson; w, Julius J. and Philip G. Epstein (based on the short story "Uncle Wiggily in Connecticut" by J.D. Salinger); ph, Lee Garmes; m, Victor Young; ed, Daniel Mandell; md, Emil Newman; art d, Richard Day; set d, Julia Heron; cos, Mary Wills, Edith Head; spec eff, John Fulton; m/l, Young, Ned Washington; makeup, Blagoe Stephanoff.

Romance **(PR:A-C MPAA:NR)**

MY FORBIDDEN PAST ** 1/2 (1951) 81m RKO bw

Robert Mitchum *(Dr. Mark Lucas)*, Ava Gardner *(Barbara Beaurevel)*, Melvyn Douglas *(Paul Beaurevel)*, Lucile Watson *(Aunt Eula)*, Janis Carter *(Corinne)*, Gordon Oliver *(Clay Duchesne)*, Basil Ruysdael *(Dean Cazzley)*, Clarence Muse *(Pompey)*, Walter Kingsford *(Coroner)*, Jack Briggs *(Cousin Phillipe)*, Will Wright *(Luther Toplady)*, Watson Downs *(Hotel Clerk)*, Cliff Clark *(Horse Vendor)*, John B. Williams *(Fishmonger)*, Louis Payne *(Man)*, Johnny Lee *(Toy Vendor)*, George Douglas *(Deputy)*, Ken MacDonald *(Police Lieutenant)*, Everett Glass *(Elderly Doctor)*, Barry Brooks *(Policeman)*, Daniel DeLaurentis *(Candle Boy)*.

This murky period melodrama has some fair performances by Mitchum and Gardner but they are bogged down in an 1890s soap opera that is both tired and confusing. Gardner is a New Orleans beauty whose adventuress grandmother earned her fortune by less than reputable means and who leaves Gardner her great wealth upon her death. Gardner has anything and anyone at her command but all she can see is the bulky body of Mitchum, a married man. She tries to use her money to obtain his love but Mitchum manages to resist her. Then Mitchum's wife, Carter, who is being wooed by cad Douglas (at Gardner's request to break up Mitchum's marriage) is suddenly killed and Mitchum is blamed for Carter's death. He is tried and about to be convicted when Gardner comes forward at the last moment to save him, but at the expense of revealing the ugly skeletons in her family closet. The production values are high and the costuming and sets exceptional but the story is turgid and torpid and nothing director Stevenson can do can bring this one to life. Ann Sheridan was originally slated to play the lead role but Howard Hughes, then the RKO mogul, decided he didn't like her in the vixen part, and borrowed Gardner from MGM for the *femme fatale* role. Sheridan later sued RKO and Hughes for $350,000 but settled the matter out of court and was later given a part in RKO's APPOINTMENT IN HONDURAS, 1953, as a sop. MY FORBIDDEN PAST, though a curiosity today, is as hopelessly mired down in uninteresting detail today as it was when first released. Viewers didn't care for it then, either, and the film lost more than $700,000 at the box office.

p, Robert Sparks, Polan Banks; d, Robert Stevenson; w, Marion Parsonnet, Leopold Atlas (based on the novel *Carriage Entrance* by Banks); ph, Harry J. Wild; m, Frederick Hollander; ed, George Shrader; md, C. Bakaleinikoff; art d, Albert S. D'Agostino, Alfred Herman.

Drama **Cas.** **(PR:C MPAA:NR)**

MY FRIEND FLICKA**** (1943) 89m FOX c

Roddy McDowall *(Ken McLaughlin)*, Preston Foster *(Rob McLaughlin)*, Rita Johnson *(Nell)*, James Bell *(Gus)*, Jeff Corey *(Tim Murphy)*, Diana Hale *(Hildy)*, Arthur Loft *(Charley Sargent)*, Jimmy Aubrey.

A wonderful film, beautifully photographed and sensitively told. McDowall is a young boy who longs for a colt of his own. His rancher father finally gives in and is displeased when the boy chooses the foal from an unruly mare. But through painstaking work by McDowall, the colt is trained and nurtured, eventually growing to become a fine mare and a loyal companion. The performances and direction are as fine as they come. The humanistic qualities within the film come through well, without being the least bit overbearing or overly sentimental. The color photography is wonderful, capturing all the grandeur of the Rocky Mountains. Perfect for the whole family. A 1945 sequel was made with almost the same cast: THUNDERHEAD, SON OF FLICKA. Later a series on TV.

p, Ralph Dietrich; d, Harold Schuster; w, Lillie Hayward, Frances Edwards Faragoh (based on the novel by Mary O'Hara); ph, Dewey Wrigley (Technicolor); m, Alfred Newman; ed, Robert Fritch; art d, Richard Day, Chester Gore; cos, Herschel.

Family **(PR:AAA MPAA:NR)**

MY FRIEND IRMA** (1949) 102m PAR bw

John Lund *(Al)*, Diana Lynn *(Jane Stacey)*, Don DeFore *(Richard Rhinelander)*, Marie Wilson *(Irma Peterson)*, Dean Martin *(Steve Baird)*, Jerry Lewis *(Seymour)*, Hans Conried *(Prof. Kropotkin)*, Kathryn Givney *(Mrs. Rhinelander)*, Percy Helton *(Mr. Clyde)*, Erno Verebes *(Mr. Chang)*, Gloria Gordon *(Mrs. O'Reilly)*, Margaret Field *(Alice)*, Charles Coleman *(Butler)*, Douglas Spencer *(Interior Decorator)*, Ken Niles *(Announcer)*, Francis Pierlot *(Income Tax Man)*, Chief Yowlachie *(Indian)*, Jimmy Dundee *(Wallpaper Man)*, Tony Merrill *(Newspaper Man)*, Jack Mulhall *(Photographer)*, Nick Cravat *(Mushie)*, Leonard B. Ingoldest *(Orchestra Leader)*.

An adaptation of the popular radio series finds Wilson and Lynn as roommates. Wilson's having trouble with her cocksure boy friend, Lund, a would-be music promoter. This film probably would have been a forgotten programmer had it not marked the film debut of Martin and Lewis. Lewis mugs it up all over the place, while Martin croons three tunes. On the whole this is not terribly funny or original, but it is certainly competent for what it is. The direction does the job efficiently, with fairly good production values. A sequel, MY FRIEND IRMA GOES WEST, was released the following year.

p, Hal Wallis; d, George Marshall; w, Cy Howard, Parke Levy (based on the radio show "My Friend Irma" created by Howard); ph, Leo Tover; m, Roy Webb; ed, LeRoy Stone; art d, Henry Bumstead, Hans Dreier; cos, Edith Head; m/l, "Here's to Love," "Just for Fun," "My Own, My Only, My All" Ray Evans, Jay Livingston (sung by Dean Martin), "The Donkey Serenade" (sung by Martin, Jerry Lewis).

Comedy **(PR:A MPAA:NR)**

MY FRIEND IRMA GOES WEST 1/2** (1950) 90m PAR bw

John Lund *(Al)*, Marie Wilson *(Irma Peterson)*, Diana Lynn *(Jane Stacey)*, Dean Martin *(Steve Baird)*, Jerry Lewis *(Seymour)*, Corinne Calvet *(Yvonne Yvonne)*, Lloyd Corrigan *(Sharpie)*, Donald Porter *(Mr. Brent)*, Harold Huber *(Pete)*, Joseph Vitale *(Slim)*, Charles Evans *(Mr. C.Y. Sanford)*, Kenneth Tobey *(Pilot)*, James Flavin *(Sheriff)*, David Clark *(Deputy Sheriff)*, Wendell Niles *(M.C.)*, George Humbert *(Chef)*, Roy Gordon *(Jensen)*, Link Clayton *(Henry)*, Mike Mahoney *(Cigarette Gag Man)*, Bob Johnson *(Red Cap)*, Al Ferguson *(News Vendor)*, Napoleon Whiting *(Waiter)*, Paul Lees *(Unemployment Clerk)*, Stan Johnson, Charles Dayton *(Reporters)*, Jasper D. Weldon, Ivan H. Browning *(Reporters)*, Julia Montoya, Rose Higgins *(Indian Women)*, Maxie Thrower *(Bartender)*, Chief Yowlachie *(Indian Chief)*, Joe Hecht *(Vendor)*, Gil Herman, Gregg Palmer *(Attendants)*, Jimmie Dundee *(Deputy)*.

Better than the previous outing, this sequel to the film based on the popular radio show has pretty much the same cast all heading out West to try their luck in the movie business. Lewis just about carries the film with his zany antics, including an amusing bit with a plate of spaghetti and a scene where he apes a chimp (or is that the other way around?). The rest of the "Irma" cast is there but seems to take a back seat to the two clowns. Some good direction and production values make this a nice little comedy. The songs include: "Baby, Obey Me," "I'll Always Love You," "Querida Mia," "Fiddle and Gittar Band" (Jay Livingston, Ray Evans, sung by Dean Martin), "Love You" (Livingston, Evans, sung by Martin, Corinne Calvet).

p, Hal Wallis; d, Hal Walker; w, Cy Howard, Parke Levy (based on the radio show "My Friend Irma" created by Howard); ph, Lee Garmes; m, Leigh Harline; ed, Warren Low; art d, Hans Dreier, Henry Bumstead.

Comedy **(PR:A MPAA:NR)**

MY FRIEND THE KING** (1931, Brit.) 52m Film Engineering/FOX bw

Jerry Verno *(Jim)*, Robert Holmes *(Capt. Felz)*, Tracey Holmes *(Count Huelin)*, Eric Pavitt *(King Ludwig)*, Phyllis Loring *(Princess Helma)*, Luli Hohenberg *(Countess Zena)*, H. Saxon Snell *(Karl)*, Victor Fairley.

When a young Ruritanian prince's life is in danger because of revolutionaries, cabbie Verno unwittingly gets involved in saving the royal heir. Verno must go to outrageous lengths to save the man, as he must disguise himself as a fetching young countess to fool the revolutionaries. Short on humor, but with enough energy to get by on quirks alone. An early effort for the great British director Powell.

p, Jerome Jackson; d, Michael Powell; w, J. Jefferson Farjeon.

Comedy **(PR:A MPAA:NR)**

MY GAL LOVES MUSIC*** (1944) 60m UNIV bw

Bob Crosby *(Mel Murray)*, Alan Mowbray *(Rodney Spoonyer)*, Grace McDonald *(Judy Mason)*, Betty Kean *(Peggy Quinn)*, Walter Catlett *(Dr. Bilbo)*, Freddie Mercer *(Clarence)*, Paulina Carter *(Child Pianist)*, Tom Daly *(Montague Underdunk)*, Gayne Whitman *(Announcer)*, Chinita, Trixie, John Hamilton, Chester Clute *(Doctors)*, Clifford Holland, Carl Jones, Gen. White, James Shaw *(Quartet)*.

Catlett is a medicine show operator who decides to strike it rich by having his assistant McDonald pose as a 14-year-old and enter a singing contest. She wins and goes to the Big Apple to do a show sponsored by a vitamin pill company. Catlett goes along, pretending to be McDonald's uncle. Complications arise when Crosby, a band leader, falls for McDonald but tries to stop himself because he believes her to be underaged. Though only one hour and designed to fill out double bills, this is a well-made light comedy that never lets its genre limit what it can do. The principals are funny, with McDonald performing a wonderful tune by Carter and Rosen called "Over and Over." The direction keeps things going with just the right touch.

p&d, Edward Lilley; w, Eugene Conrad (based on a story "My Baby Loves Music" by Patricia Harper); ph, Hal Mohr; ed, Russell Schoengarth; art d, John B. Goodman, Abraham Grossman; m/l, "Over and Over," Milton Rosen, Everett Carter (sung by Grace McDonald), "Somebody's Rockin' My Rainbow," Rosen, Carter (sung by Bob Crosby), "Give Out, Pepita," Carter, Rosen, "I Need Vitamin U," Clarence Gaskill (sung by Betty Kean).

Comedy/Music **(PR:A MPAA:NR)**

MY GAL SAL*** (1942) 103m FOX c

Rita Hayworth *(Sally Elliott)*, Victor Mature *(Paul Dreiser)*, John Sutton *(Fred Haviland)*, Carole Landis *(Mae Collins)*, James Gleason *(Pat Hawley)*, Phil Silvers *(Wiley)*, Walter Catlett *(Col. Truckee)*, Mona Maris *(Countess Rossini)*, Frank Orth *(McGuinness)*, Stanley Andrews *(Mr. Dreiser)*, Margaret Moffat *(Mrs. Dreiser)*, Libby Taylor *(Ida)*, John Kelly *(John L. Sullivan)*, Curt Bois *(De Rochemont)*, Gregory Gaye *(Mons. Garnier)*, Andrew Tombes *(Corbin)*, Albert Conti *(Henri)*, Charles Arnt *(Tailor)*, Chief Thundercloud *(Murphy)*, Hermes Pan *(Specialty Dancer)*, Robert Lowery, Dorothy Dearing, Michael "Ted" North, Roseanne Murray *(Sally's Friends)*, Harry Strang *(Bartender)*, Milton Kibbee, Luke Cosgrave, Ernie Adams, Joe Bernard, John "Skins" Miller, Gus Glassmire, Tom O'Grady, Frank Ferguson, Cyril Ring *(Men)*, Billy Wayne *(Delivery Man)*, Edward McNamara, Ed Dearing *(Policemen)*, Rosina Galli *(Maid)*, Larry Wheat *(Stage Door Man)*, Eddy Waller *(Buggy Driver)*, Judy Ford [Terry Moore] *(Carrie)*, Barry Downing *(Theodore)*, Tommy Seidel *(Usher)*, Billy Curtis *(Midget Driver)*, Tommy Cotton *(Midget Footman)*, Paul Burns *(Ferris Wheel Operator)*, George Melford *(Conductor)*, Charles Tannen *(Hotel Clerk)*, Clarence Badger, Kenneth Rundquist, Delos Jewkes, Gene Ramey *(Quartet)*.

An entertaining, though fundamentally fictitious, story of songwriter Paul Dresser, the brother of novelist Theodore Dreiser, who wrote the story from whence this screenplay sprang. As in the case of many films, the backstage tale of how this came to pass is most interesting. Studio mogul Zanuck thought that Dreiser's story might be just the ticket for Alice Faye, who had starred in so many Gay Nineties films for Fox. She backed out because of a pregnancy so Zanuck had the script remolded for Irene Dunne but she was busy for the next year and a half so Mae West was offered the role but declined. Zanuck had offered Landis BLOOD AND SAND but she refused that so he wreaked revenge by giving her a throwaway role in this film instead of the lead. Zanuck thought he could talk Betty Grable into the part but after Hayworth did so well in BLOOD AND SAND and YOU'LL NEVER GET RICH, he contacted Columbia's chief, Harry Cohn, and nabbed Hayworth. Fritz Lang began pre-production on the film but was replaced by Cummings after a week and the picture began. Mature played the songwriter and was better than most people would have expected, although they did not realize that he had come from the Broadway musical stage where he made his first impact in LADY IN THE DARK. Although Dresser wrote several songs, only a few were used in the picture and a number of new ones were added by other writers. Mature is seen as Dreiser's brother (the young Theodore is played by Barry Downing), who was, in real life, a behemoth of a man, tipping the scales at more than 250 pounds. He leaves his Indiana home, changes his name to Dresser, and joins a medicine show (Landis works in the show and vanishes early) that pays off when he is tarred and feathered and ridden out of town on a rail. Mature goes to New York, takes up with musical star Hayworth, they have the usual number of disagreements and wind up together, with Mature as the rage of Tin Pan Alley. Mature writes "My Gal Sal" for his love although the truth was that it was the last song Dresser ever wrote and he died at the age of 46, about a year after penning that tune. Excellent choreography, gorgeous costumes, good comedy from Silvers, Gleason, and Catlett and a host of tunes that include: "Come Tell Me What's Your Answer (Yes Or No)," "On the Banks of the Wabash," "I'se Your Honey, if You Wants Me, Liza Jane," "The Convict and the Bird," "Mr. Volunteer," and, of course, "My Gal Sal" (by Dresser). The songs by Leo Robin and Ralph Rainger include: "On the Gay White Way," "Me and My Fella," "Here You Are," "Midnight at the Masquerade," and "Oh, the Pity of it All." Charles Graham wrote "Two Little Girls in Blue" and Harry Dacre penned "Daisy Bell" to round out the music. Co-choreographer Pan does a dance number with Hayworth and his feet twinkle. Hayworth's voice was dubbed by Nan Wynn and no one knew the difference. Although screenwriter Helen Richardson received no credit, she is reputed to have aided Dreiser in shaping the story for the film. In a small role, look for Terry Moore as "Carrie"—while she was still known as Judy Ford. Oscars went to Day, Wright, and Little for art direction and set decoration plus a nomination for Newman.

p, Robert Bassler; d, Irving Cummings; w, Seton I. Miller, Darrell Ware, Karl Tunberg (based on the book *My Brother Paul* by Theodore Dreiser); ph, Ernest Palmer (Technicolor); ed, Robert Simpson; md, Alfred Newman; art d, Richard Day, Joseph C. Wright; set d, Thomas Little; cos, Gwen Wakeling; ch, Hermes Pan, Val Raset; makeup, Guy Pearce.

Musical Biography **(PR:A MPAA:NR)**

MY GEISHA** (1962) 119m PAR c

Shirley MacLaine *(Lucy Dell/Yoko Mori)*, Yves Montand *(Paul Robaix)*, Edward G. Robinson *(Sam Lewis)*, Bob Cummings *(Bob Moore)*, Yoko Tani *(Kazumi Ito)*, Tatsuo Saito *(Kenichi Takata)*, Tamae Kyokawa *(Amatsu Hisako)*, Ichi Hayakawa *(Kaida)*, Alex Gerry *(Leonard Lewis)*, Taugendo Maki *(Shiga)*, Satoko Kuni *(Maid)*, Kazue Kaneko, Akemi Shimomura, Mayumi Momose, Kyoko Takeuchi, Junko Aoki *(Geishas)*, Nariko Muramatsu, Akiko Tsuda *(Head Waitresses)*, Marion Furness *(Bob's Girl Friend)*, George Furness *(Butler George)*, Nobuo Chiba *(Shig)*, Tamae Kiyokawa, Tsugundo Maki.

Sometimes amusing, more often flat comedy produced by MacLaine's husband, Steve Parker, who lived in Japan for many years. Montand plays a famed motion picture director who has made a career working on his wife MacLaine's pictures. He is tired of being known as her husband and wants to do a version of "Madame Butterfly" with a Japanese woman (yet to be discovered) in the lead. MacLaine is furious and goes to Japan (where the picture will be shot) with the film's producer, Robinson. Once there, she masquerades as a geisha at a party and Montand does not recognize her. This presents MacLaine with an idea; she will audition for the leading role in his movie. Tani, a real geisha, gives MacLaine lessons in how to serve men and MacLaine reads for and gets the title role in Montand's movie. He is thrilled to have a different leading lady and takes great pride in his Asian "discovery." Problems set in when the movie's leading man, Cummings, falls hard for MacLaine (in her Japanese attire and attitude) and now asks Montand to help him win her—a la Cyrano and Christian. While watching the day's filming rushes, Montand finally figures out why this Japanese girl seems so familiar to him (it certainly took him long enough to see through her rice makeup, wig, and obi) but he does not let on that he knows. Instead, he begins to make advances on her, thus improving her performance in the film as she gets angrier and angrier at what he is doing. The picture premieres in Tokyo and MacLaine, as herself, tells the crowd that the Japanese star has given up show business to enter the religious life; then she introduces Montand to the breathless crowd and gives him all the credit for the film. Montand has his moment in the Rising Sun although he knows, deep inside, that he still has not made a movie without his devoted wife. The song "You Are Sympathy to Me" and the glorious original score by Puccini and the wonderful cinematography are not enough to elevate this picture from a yawner. It was a one-joke premise and stretched far too long at a minute under two hours. MY GEISHA was a film-within-a-film and neither one was much.

p, Steve Parker; d, Jack Cardiff; w, Norman Krasna; ph, Shunichiro Nakao (Technirama, Technicolor); m, Franz Waxman; ed, Archie Marshek; art d, Hal Pereira, Arthur Lonegan, Makoto Kikuchi; cos, Edith Head; m/l, "You Are Sympathy to Me," Hal David, Waxman, selections from "Madame Butterfly," Giacomo Puccini; makeup, Frank Westmore.

Comedy/Drama **(PR:A MPAA:NR)**

MY GIRL TISA½** (1948) 95m United States Pictures/WB bw

Lilli Palmer *(Tisa Kepes)*, Sam Wanamaker *(Mark Denek)*, Akim Tamiroff *(Mr. Grumbach)*, Alan Hale *(Dugan)*, Hugo Haas *(Tescu)*, Gale Robbins *(Jenny Kepes)*, Stella Adler *(Mrs. Faludi)*, Benny Baker *(Herman)*, Sumner Getchell *(Georgie)*, Sid Tomack *(Binka)*, John Qualen *(Svenson)*, Tom Dillon *(Riley)*, Sidney Blackmer *(Theodore Roosevelt)*, Fritz Feld *(Prof. Tabor)*, John Banner *(Otto)*.

Immigrants arriving in America in 1902 go through a series of episodic adventures. Tamiroff is a cruel sweatshop owner; Haas is a travel agent taking advantage of greenhorns; and Wanamaker, in one of his first films, is a young would-be lawyer. He wants to help Palmer in her efforts to get her father to America. The film is refreshing in its look at the plight of the immigrant, but falls down at the end when Blackmer is awkwardly brought in as the famous president in an unneeded bit of historical namedropping.

p, Milton Sperling; d, Elliott Nugent; w, Allen Boretz (based on the play "Ever the Beginning" by Lucille S. Prumbs, Sara B. Smith); ph, Ernest Haller; m, Max Steiner; ed, Christian Nyby; md, Leo F. Forbstein; art d, Robert Haas; cos, Leah Rhodes.

Drama **(PR:A MPAA:NR)**

MY GUN IS QUICK*½ (1957) 88m Victor Saville/UA bw

Robert Bray *(Mike Hammer)*, Whitney Blake *(Nancy)*, Pat Donahue *(Dione)*, Donald Randolph *(Holloway)*, Pamela Duncan *(Velda)*, Booth Coleman *(Capt. Pat)*, Jan Chaney *(Red)*, Gina Core *(Maria)*, Richard Garland *(Lou)*, Charles Boaz *(Gangster)*, Peter Mamakos *(La Roche)*, Claire Carleton *(Proprietress)*, Phil Arnold *(Shorty)*, John Dennis *(Al)*, Terrence De Marney *(Jean)*, Jackie Paul *(Stripper)*, Leon Askin *(Teller)*, Jack Holland *(Hotel Clerk)*.

The third of UA's Mike Hammer films in the 1950s finds Bray slugging it out with the baddies in an effort to discover what happened to an important diamond ring. In the end, it's revealed that his girl is responsible, but not before the usual amount of fisticuffs, killings, and love scenes are presented. This is a lesser work in the series. Though well-crafted, the story is empty and not really worth the effort given here. The violence is often senseless and the sex seems to exist for its own sake. Well produced, but still a boring and tasteless piece. (See MIKE HAMMER series, Index.)

p&d, George White, Phil Victor; w, Richard Collins, Richard Powell (based on the novel by Mickey Spillane); ph, Harry Neumann; m, Marlin Skiles; ed, Frank Sullivan; art d, Boris Levin.

Action/Crime   **(PR:O MPAA:NR)**

MY HANDS ARE CLAY*   (1948, Irish) 60m Dublin/Monarch bw

Richard Aherne *(Shean Regan)*, Bernadette Leahy *(Mary)*, Robert Dawson *(Michael)*, Sheila Richards *(Lady Killane)*, Terry Wilson *(Father O'Brien)*, Cecil Brock *(Peter)*, Francis Riedy *(Singer)*, Isobel Conser, Cathleen Delany, Hamilton Humphries, Brian O'Shea.

Dawson is an Irish sculptor who is helped financially by Brock. He grows jealous after seeing his benefactor dancing with mutual friend Leahy. These feelings don't dissipate when Dawson marries Leahy, and he nearly destroys his best work when their friend calls with a gift for the couple's first child. Dawson gets a dose of religion, though, and through the power of prayer overcomes his jealous nature. This is an amateurish production through and through, with a religious message subtle as Scarlett O'Hara's love for Ashley Wilkes.

p, Patrick McCrossan; d, Lionel Tomlinson; w, Paul Trippe; ph, Stanley Clinton.

Drama   **(PR:A MPAA:NR)**

MY HEART BELONGS TO DADDY*   (1942) 75m PAR bw

Richard Carlson *(R.I.C. Kay)*, Martha O'Driscoll *(Joyce)*, Cecil Kellaway *(Alfred)*, Frances Gifford *(Grace)*, Florence Bates *(Mrs. Saunders "Mummy")*, Velma Berg *(Babs)*, Francis Pierlot *(Dr. Mitchell)*, Fern Emmett *(Josephine)*, Betty Farrington *(Cook)*, Milton Kibbee *(Chauffeur)*, Maurice Cass *(Dean Remington)*, Alfred Hall *(Minister)*, Mabel Paige *(Miss Eckles)*.

When a Nobel Prize-winning astrophysicist professor is forced to take in a widowed, pregnant ex-bubble dancer, his household gets turned on its ear. It's about as plausible as it sounds. The screenplay provides nothing extraordinary as the principals meander through their parts mouthing what's expected of them. Kellaway, as the butler who runs the house and then some, is the only believable character in the film, and that's stretching things. Production values were standard in this inane B programmer.

p, Sol C. Siegel; d, Robert Siodmak; w, F. Hugh Herbert; ph, Daniel Fapp; ed, Alma Macrorie; art d, Hans Dreier, Haldane Douglas.

Drama   **(PR:A MPAA:NR)**

MY HEART GOES CRAZY* ¹/₂
     (1953, Brit.) 70m UA c (GB: LONDON TOWN)

Sid Field *(Jerry Sanford)*, Greta Gynt *(Mrs. Barry)*, Tessie O'Shea *(Tessie)*, Claude Hulbert *(Belgrave)*, Sonnie Hale *(Charlie)*, Mary Clare *(Mrs. Gates)*, Petula Clark *(Peggy Sanford)*, Kay Kendall *(Patsy)*, Jerry Desmonde *(George)*, Beryl Davis *(Paula)*, Scotty McHarg *(Bill)*, Reginald Purdell *(Stage Manager)*, W.G. Fay *(Mike)*, Lucas Hovinga, Marion Saunders, Jack Parnell, Pamela Carroll, Alfie Dean, Charles Paton, James Kennedy, Susan Shaw.

Field is an old-time British music hall comic who returns to London believing he is going to be the star of a new revue. Upon arrival he's disappointed to learn that he's only an understudy. His daughter, Clark, manages to fool the headliner into missing the opening, ensuring Field a chance to strut his talents. He does and is a big hit. The film, however, was not. Overlong and overblown, this was to become one of the biggest commercial disasters of Britain's postwar film industry.

p&d, Wesley Ruggles; w, Elliot Paul, Sigfried Herzig, Val Guest (based on a story by Ruggles); ph, Erwin Hillier (Technicolor); m, Jimmy Van Heusen, Johnny Burke; ed, Sid Stone; art d, Ernst Fegte; cos, Orry-Kelly.

Musical   **(PR:A MPAA:NR)**

MY HEART IS CALLING* ¹/₂   (1935, Brit.) 86m CA/GAU bw

Jan Kiepura *(Mario Delmonte)*, Marta Eggerth *(Carla)*, Sonnie Hale *(Alphonse Rosee)*, Hugh Wakefield *(Arvelle, Director)*, Ernest Thesiger *(Fevrier)*, Marie Lohr *(Modiste, Manageress)*, Jeanne Stuart *(Margo)*, Johnny Singer *(Page Boy)*, Anthony Hankey *(Singer)*, Mickey Brantford *(Singer)*, Parry Jones, Hilde von Stolz, Frederick Peisley, Anton Imkamp.

A grand opera troupe is on its last legs as it tours. Aboard its booked ship are found Eggerth, a stowaway who ends up in a romance with tenor Kiepura. After they are canceled for a booking in Monte Carlo (thanks to the dirty work of a rival company) the troupe has its revenge, singing "Tosca" in the square outside the main opera house and stealing the audience. That's about the only audience that this film could steal. Despite the good performances, especially Hale's comic relief, the story is too improbable to be believed. Songs are added in an unnatural way which looks more silly than operatic. Some good spots, but they are few and far between. There are versions in three languages, including English.

p, Arnold Pressburger; d, Carmine Gallone; w, Sidney Gilliat, Robert Edmunds, Richard Benson (based on a story by Ernst Marischka); ph, Glen MacWilliams; m, Robert Stolz; ed, Ralph Kemplin; m/l, "My Heart is Calling," Harry S. Pepper, T. Connor (sung by Jan Kiepura).

Musical   **(PR:A MPAA:NR)**

MY HERO   (SEE: SOUTHERN YANKEE, A, 1948)

MY HOBO***

     (1963, Jap.) 98m Tokyo Eiga/Toho c (BURARI BURABURA MONOGATARI)

Keiju Kobayashi *(Jumpei)*, Hideko Takamine *(Komako)*, Norihei Miki *(Takeo)*, Reiko Dan *(Mariko)*.

Kobayashi is a semi-wealthy hobo who has saved his money over the years. He keeps it taped to his side wherever he goes. He is arrested after trying to get out of

paying a restaurant bill, and meets Takamine, a lady hobo who's decided to tell people she's an A-Bomb victim, thereby grabbing some fast sympathy—and cash. They take off together, but one morning Kobayashi awakens to discover that Takamine has stolen his money. He goes looking for her and meets two abandoned kids (Miki and Dan). He takes them to his home and finds a letter from Takamine. She has invested his money and made a nice profit, so why not get married? This is a cute little comedy with some good-natured laughs. The principals are funny and realistic, never needing to over-emote. Some excellent comedy sequences, as well as a semi-travelog of the Japanese countryside make this one a real treat. (In Japanese; English subtitles.)

d&w, Zenzo Matsuyama; ph, Hiroshi Murai (Eastmancolor); m, Hikaru Hayashi.

Comedy   **(PR:A MPAA:NR)**

MY IRISH MOLLY   (SEE: LITTLE MISS MOLLY, 1940, Brit.)

MY KINGDOM FOR A COOK****   (1943) 81m COL bw

Charles Coburn *(Rudyard Morley)*, Marguerite Chapman *(Pamela Morley)*, Bill Carter *(Mike Scott)*, Isobel Elsom *(Lucille Scott)*, Edward Gargan *(Duke)*, Mary Wickes *(Agnes Willoughby)*, Almira Sessions *(Hattie)*, Eddy Waller *(Sam Thornton)*, Ralph Peters *("Pretty Boy" Peterson)*, Ivan Simpson *(Prof. Harlow)*, Betty Brewer *(Jerry)*, Melville Cooper *(Angus Sheffield)*, Kathleen Howard *(Mrs. Carter)*, Charles Halton *(Oliver Bradbury)*, Andrew Tombes *(Abe Mason)*.

Coburn plays a George Bernard Shaw-type author who's on a tour of the U.S. When his regular cook is left behind, he is forced to replace the man. He steals away Sessions, the fine cook of Massachusetts socialite Elsom. She is naturally furious and does whatever she can to get back her favorite servant. Complications arise when Coburn's daughter Chapman falls for Elsom's son Carter, but all is set right in the end. A sort of poor man's version of THE MAN WHO CAME TO DINNER, this has its funny moments. It's directed with a jaunty feeling for comedy, and while nothing special, it's good for a few laughs. The ensemble plays well together, though Coburn's part is a bit underwritten.

p, P.J. Wolfson; d, Richard Wallace; w, Harold Goldman, Andrew Solt, Joseph Hoffman, Jack Henley (based on a story by Lilli Hatvany, Solt); ph, Franz E. Planer; m, John Leipold; ed, Otto Meyer; md, M.W. Stoloff; art d, Lionel Banks.

Comedy   **(PR:A MPAA:NR)**

MY LAST DUCHESS   (SEE: ARRIVEDERCI, BABY!, 1966, Brit.)

MY LEARNED FRIEND****   (1943, Brit.) 74m EAL bw

Will Hay *(William Fitch)*, Claude Hulbert *(Claude Babbington)*, Mervyn Johns *(Grimshaw)*, Laurence Hanray *(Sir Norman)*, Aubrey Mallalieu *(Magistrate)*, Charles Victor *("Safety" Wilson)*, Derna Hazell *(Gloria)*, Leslie Harcourt *(Barman)*, Eddie Phillips *("Basher" Blake)*, G.H. Mulcaster *(Dr. Scudamore)*, Ernest Thesiger *(Ferris)*, Lloyd Pearson *(Col. Chudleigh)*, Gibb McLaughlin *(Butler)*, Maudie Edwards *(Aladdin)*, Eddie Phillips, Valerie White.

In what was to be Hay's final film before his death, Johns is a forger released from prison who is determined to kill every and any one responsible for sending him there. Hay is the altogether unprofessional barrister who had defended the man, thus being last on the list. The film climaxes in an exciting chase as Hay and his fellow bumbling lawyer pal, Hulbert, are chased across the face of London's famed Big Ben by the vengeance-crazed Johns. This black-humored farce moves with great agility, though Hay's performance is overshadowed by Hulbert and Johns. The script, by John Dighton, is sort of a structural foreshadowing of his KIND HEARTS AND CORONETS (1949).

p, Robert Hamer; d, Will Hay, Basil Dearden; w, John Dighton, Angus Mcphail; ph, Wilkie Cooper; m, Ernest Irving; ed, Charles Hasse; art d, Michael Relph.

Comedy/Crime   **(PR:A MPAA:NR)**

MY LIFE IS YOURS   (SEE: PEOPLE VS. DR. KILDARE, THE, 1941)

MY LIFE TO LIVE*****
(1963, Fr.) 85m Films de la Pleiade/Union-Pathe Contemporary bw (VIVRE SA VIE; GB: IT'S MY LIFE)

Anna Karina *(Nana)*, Saddy Rebbot *(Raoul)*, Andre S. Labarthe *(Paul)*, Guylaine Schlumberger *(Yvette)*, Gerard Hoffman *(The Cook)*, Monique Messine *(Elizabeth)*, Paul Pavel *(A Journalist)*, Dimitri Dineff *(A Youth)*, Peter Kassowitz *(A Young Man)*, Eric Schlumberger *(Luigi)*, Brice Parain *(Himself)*, Henri Attal *(Arthur)*, Gilles Queant *(A Man)*, Odile Geoffroy *(Barmaid)*, Marcel Charton *(A Policeman)*, Jack Florency *(A Bystander)*, Gisele Hauchecorne *(Concierge)*, Jean-Luc Godard *(Voice)*.

Godard's fourth feature stars his wife, Anna Karina, as Nana, a Parisian sales clerk who, after separating from her husband Labarthe, tries to make it as an actress. After seeing Carl Dreyer's THE PASSION OF JOAN OF ARC (1928), this idea is short-lived and she decides to give prostitution a try. She is soon working for a pimp, Rebbot, who sells her to another pimp. An argument between the sellers ensues and gunfire is exchanged, resulting in Karina's death. Divided into 12 tableaux, Godard's film is a series of sequences strung together which are of a truly Godardian nature. He casts his wife, delves into the subject of prostitution (which he backs up with quoted facts and figures), experiments with narration (using his own voice), alludes to films and literature (Renoir's NANA (1926), Zola's *Nana*, Truffaut's JULES AND JIM (1961), Dreyer, and Edgar Allen Poe's "The Oval Portrait"), and includes discussions on life (with linguistic philosopher Brice Parain). For the first time Godard has successfully combined the facets which define him as a filmmaker—the genre elements of BREATHLESS (1960), the politics of LE PETIT SOLDAT (1963), and the narrative experimentation of A WOMAN IS A WOMAN (1961). Technically MY LIFE TO LIVE is far ahead of its time, knocking down the traditional walls of sound recording. Godard refused to mix the sound in the studio (except for

Legrand's barely used score), instead applying the same rules for sound as for picture—capturing life directly. He amended his style of editing (the "jump-cut" which he became identified with after BREATHLESS) by allowing shots to last six-eight minutes as the camera wandered through the set. He also devised a sort of machinegun style of editing, in which a camera pan was shortened by cutting, which in turn was dictated by machinegun sounds in the scene. A masterful acheivement which not only is one of his greatest works, but has since been assimilated into present day techniques of filmmaking. Portions of "Ou en Est La Prostitution?" by Judge Marcel Sacotte are read in the narrative.

p, Pierre Braunberger; d&w, Jean-Luc Godard; ph, Raoul Coutard; m, Michel Legrand; ed, Agnes Guillemot; m/l, "Ma Mome, Elle Joue Pas Les Starlettes," Jean Ferrat, Pierre Frachet; makeup, Jackie Reynal.

Drama **(PR:A MPAA:NR)**

MY LIFE WITH CAROLINE* ½ (1941) 78m United Producers/RKO bw

Ronald Colman *(Anthony Mason)*, Anna Lee *(Caroline Mason)*, Charles Winninger *(Bliss)*, Reginald Gardiner *(Paul Martindale)*, Gilbert Roland *(Paco Del Valle)*, Katherine Leslie *(Helen)*, Hugh O'Connell *(Muirhead)*, Matt Moore *(Walters the Butler)*, Murray Alper *(Jenkins the Chauffeur)*, Richard Carle *(Dr. Curtis)*, Clarence Straight *(Bill the Pilot)*, Dorothy Adams *(Rodwell)*, Nicholas Soussanin *(Pinnock)*, Jeanine Crispin *(Delta)*, James Farley *(Railroad Conductor)*, Billy Mitchell *(Railroad Porter)*, Gar Smith *(Radio Announcer)*, Jack Mulhall *(Man)*, Frances Kellogg *(Stunt Double)*.

Colman and William Hawks got together to start their own firm and made two failures, this and LUCKY PARTNERS, which should be proof that actors often don't know what's best for them. What might have been a frothy farce in another director's hands turns out to be flatter than last night's champagne under Milestone. Based on a hare-brained French play, the location of the story was switched from Venice, Italy to California and all the elan disappeared. Colman's co-star was pert Lee, who looked young enough to be his daughter (and could have been as she was 25 years his junior) and yet there was no mention of a May-December relationship. He's a successful publisher who is spending entirely too much time at his work so his wife, Lee, begins to chase around with several younger men. She first takes up with sculptor Gardiner and sends Colman a telegram to that effect. He leaves his office and goes traipsing after her to put a stop to her dizziness. On his way to her side, he flashes back (talking to the camera, saying things like "I'll explain this all to you later.") to the affair she had with Roland, a wealthy Argentine she'd once had a fling with in Palm Beach. He arrives in time to stop the latest romance and winds up with Lee once more, although, if patterns are to be believed, she'll be straying off with someone else in due time. The picture of urbane Colman having to woo his blithering wife back from the likes of Roland and Gardiner did not sit well with anyone and this picture vanished beneath the surface like the *Lusitania*. British born Lee began her career in 1932 with EBB TIDE and will best be remembered for HOW GREEN WAS MY VALLEY. She married playwright-novelist Robert Nathan in 1970 when she was 57-years-old after doing her last important role in STAR (1968).

p&d, Lewis Milestone; w, John Van Druten, Arnold Belgard (based on the play "Train to Venice" by Louis Verneuil, Georges Berr); ph, Victor Milner; m, Werner Heymann; ed, Edward Donahue; prod d, Nicolai Remisoff; cos, Edward Stevenson.

Comedy **(PR:A-C MPAA:NR)**

MY LIPS BETRAY* ½ (1933) 70m FOX bw

Lillian Harvey *(Lili)*, John Boles *(King Rupert)*, El Brendel *(Stigmat)*, Irene Browne *(Queen Mother)*, Maude Eburne *(Mamma Watcheck)*, Henry Stephenson *(De Conti)*, Herman Bing *(Weininger)*.

In the mythical kingdom of Ruthania, the great king, Boles disguises himself as a common song writer and mingles with his people. He meets a poverty stricken lass, Harvey, and it's true love for the unlikely pair. This film's plot smacks of operetta yet doesn't quite have the charm needed to pull it off successfully. The dialog is witless and overly cute. But the costumes are wondrous creations and the dance sequences nicely staged. Of course a film with a songster king would not be complete without music, thus ditties such as "His Majesty's Car," "The Band Is Gaily Playing," "To Romance," and "Why am I Happy?" (William Kernell) are included.

d, John Blystone; w, Hans Kraly, S.N. Behrman, Jane Storm (based on the play "Der Komet" by Attila Orbok); ph, Lee Garmes; ed, Alex Troffey; cos, Joe Stressner; ch, Sammy Lee.

Musical Comedy/Romance **(PR:A MPAA:NR)**

MY LITTLE CHICKADEE ½** (1940) 83m UNIV bw

W.C. Fields *(Cuthbert J. Twillie)*, Mae West *(Flower Belle Lee)*, Joseph Calleia *(Jeff Badger, The Masked Bandit)*, Dick Foran *(Wayne Carter, Editor)*, Margaret Hamilton *(Mrs. Gideon)*, George Moran *(Clarence)*, Si Jenks *(Deputy)*, Gene Austin *(Himself)*, Russell Hall *(Candy)*, Otto Heimel *(Coco)*, Fuzzy Knight *(Cousin Zeb)*, Anne Nagel *(Miss Ermingarde Foster)*, Ruth Donnelly *(Aunt Lou)*, Willard Robertson *(Uncle John)*, Donald Meek *(Amos Budget, Cardsharp)*, William B. Davidson *(Sheriff)*, Addison Richards *(Judge)*, Jackie Searle *(Boy)*, Fay Adler *(Mrs. "Pygmy" Allen)*, Jan Duggan *(Woman)*, Harlan Briggs *(Hotel Clerk)*, James Conlon *(Squawk Mulligan the Bartender)*, Eddie Butler, Bing Conley, John Kelly, Jack Roper *(Henchmen)*, Otto F. Hoffman *(Pete the Printer)*, Chester Gan *(Chinaman)*, George Melford *(Sheriff)*, Jackie Searle, Delmar Watson, Ben Hall *(Schoolboys)*, Billy Benedict *(Lem the Schoolboy)*, Buster Slaven, Danny Jackson, Charles Hart, George Billings *(Boys)*, Morgan Wallace *(Gambler)*, Vester Pegg *(Gambler, Townsman)*, Wade Boteler, Lloyd Ingraham *(Leading Citizens)*, Bud Harris *(Porter)*, Slim Gant *(Bowlegged Man)*, Alan Bridge, Edward Hearn, Bill Wolfe *(Barflies)*, Bob Burns, Bob Reeves *(Barfly-Dandies)*, Al Ferguson *(Train Passenger)*, Mark Anthony, Frank Ellis *(Townsmen)*, Dorothy Vernon *(Diner)*, Lita Chevret *(Indian Squaw)*, Lane Chandler *(Porter)*, Bob McKenzie, James C. Morton, Joe Whitehead, Charles McMurphy, Dick Rush, Hank Bell, Jeff Conlon, Walter McGrail.

MY LITTLE CHICKADEE should have been a lot funnier than it was. Although both West and Fields get credit for the script, it was essentially by her, with a few insertions by Fields, mostly after West had finished her work on the movie. She was a perfectionist who honed every punch line as though it were a multi-faceted diamond and he was a man to whom a script was a place to put his martini, much preferring to let the camera roll and have his ad-lib way with the scene. As a team, they were far less amusing than they were apart, and situations come one after another without the guffaws to go with them. It was shot on the western lot at Universal and the studio-bound sets show that. They didn't go on location because the stars were getting a lot of money; West received $300,000 for writing and acting, while Fields, who was under contract to the Valley lot, got $25,000 for writing and $125,000 for acting. That was very heavy money in those days and corners had to be cut somewhere. Directed by ex-Keystone Kop Cline, this was expected to be a wrestling match between the two volatile stars but the expected battles never came off and the shooting went smoothly, if not hilariously. West had been off the screen for two years and audiences eagerly flocked to see MY LITTLE CHICKADEE, which was a weird western satire punctuated with a few of Field's polished skits. West is a woman of medium-to-loose morals who has been romanced by a masked bandit. The women of her town find that unpalatable and she is dispatched aboard the train to Greasewood City. While on the train, she meets Fields, a con man, and thinks that his suitcase is filled with money (actually coupons) which impresses her. When the train is attacked by Indians, she shows a bit of marksmanship by knocking off a mess of the devils. West knows that she can't arrive in the new town as a single woman because her reputation is likely to have preceded her there, so she arranges to marry Fields aboard the train and the service is performed by professional card-cheater Meek. They arrive in the small town and check into a hotel but she won't consummate the marriage and switches places with a goat in the nuptial bed. Fields says, "Darling, have you changed your perfume?" as his famed proboscis sniffs the air. West goes out on the town and meets Calleia, owner of the local watering spot, and it isn't a few minutes before these two are madly in love. Now Fields is made sheriff of the town and shortly thereafter, while donning a cloak and mask to impress West, someone thinks that he may be the masked bandit, so he's hauled into his own jail and prepared for a necktie party. West asks that the real bandit make his presence known in order that the innocent Fields be released. It turns out to be Calleia, who returns all the money he's stolen. Foran is the crusading newspaper editor who wants to nail Calleia. He would also like to see the man out of the way because he loves West. The two men struggle for West and, near the film's conclusion, she tells Fields that their marriage is a sham. He gets ready to depart, with the question of who gets her, Calleia or Foran, not yet determined. Fields is going east to sell shares in hair-oil wells. He tells her to "come up and see me sometime" as she mounts the stairs at their hotel. She replies that she will, "my little chickadee." Fields and West never could connect in the movie. After the film was completed West told newsmen: "There's no one in the world like Bill [Fields] . . . Thank God!" She stipulated in her contract that he was not allowed to drink or smoke on the set and that was like taking milk and cookies from a baby. According to film lore, he only got drunk once during the shooting, but he did get some flak for encouraging some children who were near the soundstage door to go out and play in traffic, but that may be only hearsay. The poker scene in the bar is a classic if only for the moment when Fuzzy Knight asks, "Is this a game of chance?" and Fields replies, "Not the way I play it." One song: "Willie Of The Valley." (Ben Oakland, Milton Drake).

p, Lester Cowan; d, Edward Cline; w, Mae West, W.C. Fields; ph, Joseph Valentine; m, Frank Skinner; ed, Ed Curtiss; md, Charles Previn; art d, Jack Otterson; cos, Vera West.

Comedy/Western **Cas.** **(PR:A MPAA:NR)**

MY LOVE CAME BACK*** (1940) 81m WB bw

Olivia de Havilland *(Amelia Cullen)*, Jeffrey Lynn *(Tony Baldwin)*, Eddie Albert *(Dusty Rhodes)*, Jane Wyman *(Joy O'Keefe)*, Charles Winninger *(Julius Malette)*, Spring Byington *(Mrs. Malette)*, William Orr *(Paul Malette)*, Ann Gillis *(Valerie Malette)*, S. Z. Sakall *(Ludwig)*, Grant Mitchell *(Dr. Kobbe)*, Charles Trowbridge *(Dr. Downey)*, Mabel Taliaferro *(Dowager)*, Sidney Bracy *(Butler)*, Nanette Vallon *(Sophie)*, William B. Davidson *(Agent)*, Tommy Baker *(Boy)*, Creighton Hale *(Clerk)*, William Roberts *(Office Boy)*, Wedgwood Newell *(Treasurer)*, Jack Mower, Richard Kipling *(Executives)*, Richard Clayton *(Valerie's Escort)*.

A light comedy, this features de Havilland as a talented, though somewhat neurotic violin student at the Brissac Academy. When it's discovered she is giving lessons (which is grounds for expulsion) in order to make ends meet, Winninger tells the school's principal he will put de Havilland through school as long as his name is kept secret. He runs a music company and has a secret crush on de Havilland. His adult children, Orr and Gillis, discover their father is paying out money for a young girl and they suspect the worst. They also resent their father turning over the management of his company to Lynn. De Havilland discovers that her scholarship is really funds from an admirer and she tries to return the check. But fellow music students Albert and Wyman forge her name on the check so they can join the musicians union and start their own band. They persuade de Havilland to join up as they try to set the music world on fire by putting classical pieces to swing tempos. Of course their first engagement is for none other than Winninger, in a private party at his home. Complications are added as de Havilland has fallen in love with Lynn after meeting him at a ball. They see each other once more at the party and she faints from shock. Winninger's wife takes care of her and discovers the truth behind the whole matter while Albert explains to Lynn how he forged de Havilland's name on the check. Everything is cleared up and the orchestra is a big hit, prompting the formerly stuffy principal of Brissac to add swingmusic to the curriculum. This was a refreshing and amiable comedy, well scripted and with sharp and breezy direction.

The principal players are fine, handling the humorous complications with good comic timing. The only real problem with the film is de Havilland. It's not that she gives a bad performance, for she does a fine job in the lead. The problem is that this was her first film after her enormous success in GONE WITH THE WIND for MGM. After returning to Warner Bros.' lot, she was offered a rash of bad scripts, finally accepting this simply so she could work again. GWTW showed what she could do and this light comedy would have better suited an up-and-coming young starlet rather than the now-seasoned de Havilland.

p, Wolfgang Reinhardt; d, Curtis Bernhardt; w, Ivan Goff, Robert Buckner, Earl Baldwin (based on the story "Episode" by Walter Reisch); ph, Charles Rosher; m, Heinz Roemheld; ed, Rudi Fehr; md, Leo F. Forbstein; art d, Max Parker; cos, Orry-Kelly.

Comedy (PR:A MPAA:NR)

MY LOVE FOR YOURS (SEE: HONEYMOON IN BALI, 1939)

MY LOVE LETTERS (SEE: LOVE LETTERS, 1983)

MY LOVER, MY SON* (1970, Brit.) 96m Sagittarius/MGM c

Romy Schneider (Francesca Anderson), Donald Houston (Robert Anderson), Dennis Waterman (James Anderson), Patricia Brake (Julie), Peter Sallis (Sir Sidney Brent), William Dexter (Parks), Alexander Bastedo (Cicely Clarkson), Mark Hawkins (Macer), Maggie Wright (Prostitute), Janet Brown (Mrs. Woods), Tom Chatto (Mr. Woods), Michael Forest (Detective Inspector Chidley), Peter Gilmore (Barman), Rosalie Horner (Receptionist), Arthur Howard (Judge), Chrissie Shrimpton (Kenworthy's Girl Friend), David Warbeck (Kenworthy), Robert Wilde (Park's Assistant), Cleo Sylvestre (Dressmaker), Paul Dawkins (Foreman of the Jury).

Schneider is an unhappy woman married to Houston, a wealthy boor. After her lover drowns in an accident she turns to her son Waterman for comfort. Houston doesn't like what he thinks he sees happening and sends the boy off to college. There the boy meets Brake and loses his virginity. But he eventually goes home and gets to know his mom much better as she makes advances toward him. Houston returns from a trip one day to find the two in a clinch. A fight ensues and Schneider ends up killing Houston with a gold club. Waterman takes the rap for his mother, having been knocked unconcious during the fight and believing he had killed Houston. He's acquitted for defending his mother but learns that she was responsible for the crime and that her dead lover was his real father. Stunned, he leaves his mother and returns to Brake. Despite some good photography, this is a terrible film. It's hard to believe that Schneider and Waterman are far enough apart in age to be mother and son and their thespian talents don't help to keep the illusion going. Too much cheap psychology and a preponderance of nude scenes are present, without much sensitivity for the film's darker themes. Incest can be dealt with intelligently in films (Louis Malle's MURMER OF THE HEART (1978) being the best example) but this film lacks any real thought or feeling. The final sequence has Brake and Waterman reuniting in a slow motion shot showing the pair running towards one another. All that's missing is an announcer extolling the virtues of some product.

p, Wilbur Stark; d, John Newland; w, William Marchant, Jennie Hall (based on the story "Second Level" by Stark and the novel Reputation for a Song by Edward Grierson); ph, David Muir (Metrocolor); m, Norrie Paramor, Mike Vickers; ed, Peter Musgrave; md, Vickers, Paramor; art d, Bill Andrews; cos, Gail Ansell; m/l, "I Want the Good Things," "Summer's Here," and "What's On Your Mind" (Vickers, Paramor, Sue Vickers).

Drama (PR:O MPAA:R)

MY LUCKY STAR* (1933, Brit.) 63m Masquerader/W&F bw

Florence Desmond (Mlle. de Capo), Oscar Asche (President), Naughton & Gold (Housepainters), Harry Tate (Director), Harold Huth (Hero), Carol Coombe (Lucette), Reginald Purdell (Artist), Herman Darewski (Conductor), George Baker (Foreman), Henry Longhurst (Dudley Collins), Ernest Jay, Alfred Arthur, Della Rega.

Desmond is a shop clerk who meets Longhurst, an artist. To get him to fall for her, Desmond poses as a glamorous movie star, only to learn that Longhurst has also been putting up a ruse. The would-be artist is actually a railroad porter. Minor fluff that stifles the natural comic talents of Desmond. First film (co)directed by Harlow, who was to go on to make some fair British thrillers.

p, Louis Blattner; d, Blattner, John Harlow; w, Harlow.

Comedy (PR:A MPAA:NR)

MY LUCKY STAR** 1/2 (1938) 81m FOX bw

Sonja Henie (Kristina Nielson), Richard Greene (Larry Taylor), Joan Davis (Mary Boop), Cesar Romero (George Cabot, Jr.), Buddy Ebsen (Buddy), Arthur Treacher (Whipple), George Barbier (George Cabot, Sr.), Louise Hovick [Gypsy Rose Lee] (Marcelle), Billy Gilbert (Nick), Patricia Wilder (Dorothy), Paul Hurst (Louie), Elisha Cook, Jr. (Waldo), Robert Kellard (Pennell), Brewster Twins (June and Jean), Kay Griffith (Ethel), Charles Tannen (Saier), Paul Stanton (Dean Reed), Edward J. Le Saint (Executive), Frederick Burton (Pillsbury), Frank Jaquet (Burton), Arthur Jarrett, Jr. (Bill), Kay Griffith (Ethel), Sumner Getchell (Fat Freshman), Cully Richards (Photographer), John Dilson (Department Head), Matt McHugh (Cab Driver), Dora Clement, June Gale (Secretaries), Art Rankin, Harold Goodwin (Cameramen), Fred Kelsey (Detective), Eddy Conrad (Gypsy).

Henie is a clerk in a department store who catches the eye of Romero, son of the store's owner, as she is out skating one day. Her skating prowess prompts store officials to send her off to college where she'll be the center of attention and model clothes from the store's sports line. Her stunning wardrobe causes jealousy among her fellow students, and she falls in love with a teacher (Greene), but she succeeds in convincing school officials to stage their winter ice show at her bosses' store. The

plot was contrived only to provide opportunities for Henie to skate, and she does beautifully, especially in a performance of "Alice in Wonderland Ice Ballet," staged by Harry Losee. This was the last film in which Gypsy Rose Lee would be billed under her real name of Louise Hovick. In her next screen appearance, STAGE DOOR CANTEEN (1943), she would use her more famous moniker. Songs include "I've Got a Date With a Dream," "Could You Pass in Love," "This May Be the Night," "The All-American Swing," and "Plymouth University Song" (Mack Gordon, Harry Revel).

p, Darryl F. Zanuck; d, Roy Del Ruth; w, Harry Tugend, Jack Yellen (based on the story "They Met in Chicago" by Karl Tunberg, Don Ettlinger); ph, John Mescall; ed, Allen McNeil; md, Louis Silvers; cos, Royer.

Musical (PR:A MPAA:NR)

MY MAIN MAN FROM STONY ISLAND (SEE: STONY ISLAND, 1978)

MY MAN* 1/2 (1928) 99m WB bw

Fannie Brice (Fannie Brand), Guinn "Big Boy" Williams (Joe Halsey), Edna Murphy (Edna Brand), Andre de Segurola (Landau, Producer), Richard Tucker (Waldo), Billy Seay (Sammy), Arthur Hoyt (Thorne), Ann Brody (Mrs. Schultz), Clarissa Selwynne (Forelady).

More than one-third of this musical was silent and that jarred audiences who were expecting to see and hear the great Brice do her stuff. She runs a theatrical costume shop, but her biggest problem is her wild sister, Murphy, who gets involved with Broadway producer de Segurola, then gets tossed aside by him. Meanwhile, Brice is having a fling with Williams, a physical culture demonstrator who works in a store window, whom she saves from the police when he is found sleeping on a park bench. Murphy watches Brice and Williams prepare to get married, then she puts the vamp on the musclebound oaf and steals him away. While Brice, who has gotten to be a big star in a manner that only Hollywood screenwriters can concoct, is singing a big song, Williams is in the theater with Murphy and decides that his heart belongs to Brice, so he dumps the sister and marches backstage. The whole movie is little more than an excuse for Brice's clowning and singing and she gets a chance to show movie audiences why she was so popular with the Broadway crowd as she does several sketches and songs in the course of the film. The story was written by Darryl Zanuck (using his pen name) but the sketches were from Brice's act and include her famous "Mrs. Cohen at the Beach" routine. Songs include: "I'd Rather Be Blue" (Billy Rose, Fred Fisher), "I Was a Flora Dora Baby" (Harry Carroll, Ballard MacDonald). "Second Hand Rose" (James Hanley, Grant Clarke), "I'm an Indian" (Leo Edwards, Blanche Merrill), "If You Want to Have a Rainbow" (Rose, Oscar Levant, Mort Dixon), and, of course, "My Man" (adapted by Channing Pollock from Maurice Yvain's French tune "Mon Homme"). This is not to be confused with the all-silent picture of the same name that starred Patsy Ruth Miller for Vitagraph in 1924.

d, Archie Mayo; w, Joe Jackson, James Storr, Robert Lord (based on a story by Mark Canfield [Darryl F. Zanuck]); ph, Frank Kesson; ed, Owen Marks.

Musical Comedy (PR:A MPAA:NR)

MY MAN AND I* 1/2 (1952) 99m MGM bw

Shelley Winters (Nancy), Ricardo Montalban (Chu Chu Ramirez), Wendell Corey (Ansel Ames), Claire Trevor (Mrs. Ansel Ames), Robert Burton (Sheriff), Jose Torvay (Manuel Ramirez), Jack Elam (Celestino Garcia), Pasqual Garcia Pena (Willie Chung), George Chandler (Frankie), Juan Torena (Vincente Aguilar), Carlos Conde (Joe Mendacio).

Montalban plays a hard-working Mexican in California's San Joaquin Valley who's very proud of his recently acquired American citizenship. He shuns the carousing ways of his fellow workers and strives to better himself, but trouble begins when he does some work for Corey, who hates Mexicans. When Corey's check bounces, Montalban confronts him, a struggle ensues and Corey is wounded with his own rifle. With the aid of his wife Trevor, who is unhappy because Montalban ignored her advances, Corey concocts a story which lands Montalban in jail. Eventually, Montalban's friends get a confession out of Corey and Montalban is freed, returning to his love, Winters. Strong performances by Montalban, Trevor, and Winters and a good script make this a worthwhile film.

p, Stephen Ames; d, William A. Wellman; w, John Fante, Jack Leonard; ph, William Mellor; m, David Buttolph; ed, John Dunning; art d, Cedric Gibbons, James Baseui; set d, Edwin B. Willis, Fred MacClean.

Drama (PR:A MPAA:NR)

MY MAN GODFREY*** (1936) 94m UNIV bw

William Powell (Godfrey Parke), Carole Lombard (Irene Bullock), Alice Brady (Angelica Bullock), Eugene Pallette (Alexander Bullock), Gail Patrick (Cornelia Bullock), Alan Mowbray (Tommy Gray), Jean Dixon (Molly, Maid), Mischa Auer (Carlo), Robert Light (Faithful George), Pat Flaherty (Mike), Robert Perry (Bob, the Hobo), Franklin Pangborn (Scorekeeper), Selmer Jackson (Blake, a Guest), Ernie Adams (Forgotten Man), Phyllis Crane (Party Guest), Jean Rogers (Girl), Grady Sutton (Van Rumple), Jack Chefe (Headwaiter), Eddie Featherston (Process Server), Edward Gargan, James Flavin (Detectives), Art Singley (Chauffeur), Reginald Mason (Mayor), Jane Wyman (Girl at Party), Bess Flowers (Guest), Grace Field, Kathryn Perry, Harley Wood, Elaine Cochrane, David Horsley, Philip Merrick (Socialites), Chic Collins (Double for William Powell), Arthur Wanzer (Man).

It's hard to believe that this superb comedy was nominated for six Oscars and won none of them, but that was the year that another Powell film, THE GREAT ZIEGFELD, was entered and it was also the year of ANTHONY ADVERSE, MR. DEEDS GOES TO TOWN, DODSWORTH, and THE STORY OF LOUIS PASTEUR so the competition was stiffer than Jack Norton's patented drunk role. MY MAN GODFREY is a comedy with a social conscience although the message is very subtle and has to be searched for through all the humor. Lombard and Patrick are two Park Avenue spoiled brats who are in the midst of a scavenger hunt as part of a gala evening. They have a list of odd items that includes tennis rackets, goldfish, and the nabbing of a "forgotten man" from one of Manhattan's hobo jungles. Lombard is flakey—sweet as can be—but dancing to a different drummer, and Patrick is her calculating sister, dark and sensuous. They wind up at a location near the East River at the southern end of the city and locate Powell, who is living with the other survivors of the Depression in a village of knocked-together lean-to's. When Patrick approaches him to be her forgotten man, Powell is incensed at the callousness of this charade and forces the gowned young woman back into a heap of debris. Patrick is angered by Powell's response and leaves but Lombard, intrigued by Powell, remains and tells him that Patrick, who is accustomed to winning everything she's ever attempted, will probably find some other bum and take him back to the posh hotel where the hunt's winner will be decided. Rather than allow the snobby Patrick to take the banner, Powell agrees to go with Lombard and act as her forgotten man. He accompanies Lombard to the hotel and delivers a punchy speech to the bejeweled and tuxed crowd about the silliness of their quest and Lombard wins the hunt. She is thrilled at having beaten Patrick for a change and she is also attracted to Powell so she offers him the job of butler to the immensely wealthy family in their Park Avenue digs. The father is put-upon Pallette, whose voice always sounded as though it came from the bottom of the Holland Tunnel, and the mother is feather-brained Brady, doing a role that Billie Burke is usually associated with. Powell is immediately welcomed into the family and begins to set the household straight. Lombard is rapidly falling for Powell who does his best to keep her away and never betrays the fact that he is from a wealthy Boston family and was driven to his lowly station as the result of an abortive love affair. There is a huge party at the residence and Powell is spotted by an old pal, Mowbray, who can't believe that his one-time Harvard school chum has been reduced to being a butler. Mowbray senses that Powell wants to keep his background mum so he goes along with the story that Powell offers: that Mowbray had hired Powell to be his valet at school. Later, Powell and Mowbray meet, and Powell explains that he was terribly depressed by his circumstances but his faith in humanity was again flamed by the dauntless spirit of the other, less fortunate men, that he met in the shantytown. At the Park Avenue home, Powell continues his work, avoiding a frame-up that Patrick attempts in order to get to the bottom of Powell's history. She deliberately plants a valuable necklace in his room, then tells the police that he may have stolen it. But Powell is wise to her ways, finds the necklace and when the cops, led by Gargan, can't find the bauble, she is stunned. Powell also notes that Brady has a live-in gigolo, Auer (in a role not unlike that of the ballet teacher in YOU CAN'T TAKE IT WITH YOU), and he manages to toss the man out. When Pallette gets into financial trouble, Powell helps him by purchasing stock in the man's company (using the money gleaned from pawning Patrick's necklace; after the stock goes up, he uses some of his profits to get the necklace back). In the end, Powell enlists Mowbray's vast fortune, using some of his own, and the men build a fabulous nightclub on the site once occupied by the tarpaper shacks. He hires all of the hoboes and the place is soon a rip-roaring success. Lombard arrives with a preacher in tow and won't take no for an answer so she and Powell are married in Powell's office at the nightclub as the picture fades out. The rich are made to look very foolish and the poor appear very noble in the screenplay, something that Depression audiences must have appreciated. Two years later, a film inspired by this one, MERRILY WE LIVE, was released, but it and the 1957 remake of MY MAN GODFREY were inferior attempts at recreating the bubbling joy of this film. Powell did three other films in 1936 besides the aforementioned—LIBELED LADY, AFTER THE THIN MAN, and THE EX-MRS. BRADFORD. Did any actor ever have a better year! Powell and Lombard, married in 1931 and divorced in 1933, remained friendly enough to make this marvelous movie together. In a tiny part in the party scene, Jane Wyman makes her film debut. She had already done a bit in GOLD DIGGERS OF 1937 but that wasn't released until after this one. MY MAN GODFREY must be listed as one of the best of the screwball comedies and stands as an excellent example of witty scripting, direction, and editing.

p, Charles R. Rogers; d, Gregory La Cava; w, Morrie Ryskind, Eric Hatch, La Cava (based on the story "1101 Park Avenue" by Hatch); ph, Ted Tetzlaff; m, Charles Previn; ed, Ted Kent; md, Previn; art d, Charles D. Hall; cos, Brymer, Travis Banton.

Comedy   **Cas.**   **(PR:A   MPAA:NR)**

MY MAN GODFREY**   (1957) 92m UNIV c

June Allyson (*Irene Bullock*), David Niven (*Godfrey*), Jessie Royce Landis (*Angelica Bullock*), Robert Keith (*Mr. Bullock*), Eva Gabor (*Francesca*), Jay Robinson (*Vincent*), Martha Hyer (*Cordelia Bullock*), Jeff Donnell (*Molly, Maid*), Eric Sinclair (*Brent*), Herbert Anderson (*Hubert*), Dabbs Greer (*Lt. O'Connor*), Fred Essler (*Captain*), Jack Mather (*Second Detective*), Paul Levitt (*Young Man at Bar*), Harry Cheshire (*Elliott*), Robert Clarke (*George*), Robert Brubaker (*Man with Monkey*), Fred Coby (*Investigator*), Voltaire Perkins (*Man at Bar*), William Hudson (*Howard*), Robert Foulk (*Motor Cop*), Thomas B. Henry (*Henderson*), Richard Deacon (*Farnsworth*).

Not nearly as charming as the original, this film does have its moments. Niven is an Austrian diplomat illegally staying in the U.S., posing as a butler to avoid detection. Allyson plays the rich girl who learns a few things about life from him. She's cute in her role but once again, nothing much compared to the original character created by Lombard. The only standout is Landis as Allyson's crazy mother, who adds some comic flavor. This version lacks the screwball timing and madcap glee of the original. The direction by Koster is passable.

p, Ross Hunter; d, Henry Koster; w, Everett Freeman, Peter Berneis, William Bowers (based on the screenplay by Morrie Ryskind, Eric Hatch and the novel by Hatch); ph, William Daniels (CinemaScope, Eastmancolor); m, Frank Skinner; ed,

Milton Carruth; md, Joseph Gershenson; art d, Alexander Golitzen, Richard H. Riedel; cos, Bill Thomas; m/l, "My Man Godfrey," Peggy Lee, Sonny Burke (sung by Sarah Vaughn).

Comedy   **(PR:A   MPAA:NR)**

MY MARGO** ½
(1969, Israel) 90m Golan-Globous/Noah Films, Ltd. c (AKA: LOVE IN JERUSALEM)

Levana Finklstein (*Margo*), Avner Hizkyahu (*Her Father*), Oded Teomi (*Talmor*), Beracha Ne'eman (*His Wife*), Avraham Ronay (*Her Father*), Lia Dolitzkaya (*Her Mother*), Joseph Shilcach (*Hotel Manager*), Arik Lavi (*Zeev*), Tova Pardo (*Neighbor*), Ya'acoy Bodo (*Barber*).

Finklstein is a 24-year-old woman who must look after her brothers and sisters. Their mother is gone and her father (Hizkyahu) is a lazy drunkard. She falls in love with a professor and has her first affair. The film is written and directed by Golan, one of the world's most prolific film producers. Unfortunately, he didn't have much talent behind the typewriter, for the script is little more than soap opera. However, he has a good director's eye, showing some wonderful insights into everyday Jerusalem and its populace. Finklstein gives a fine performance and makes the slight plot believable with her sensitivity and mature handling of her role. After finishing this film she went back to her work as a member of the Women Units of the Israel Defence Army.

p, Yoram Globous; d&w, Menahem Golan; ph, Ya'acov Kalach; m, Dov Seltzer; ed, Dov Henig; m/l, title song, Uriel Ofek (sung by Yehoram Gaon).

Drama   **(PR:C   MPAA:NR)**

MY MARRIAGE**   (1936) 73m FOX bw

Claire Trevor (*Carol Barton*), Kent Taylor (*John DeWitt Tyler III*), Pauline Frederick (*Mrs. DeWitt Tyler II*), Paul Kelly (*Barney Dolan*), Helen Wood (*Elizabeth Tyler*), Thomas Beck (*Roger Tyler*), Beryl Mercer (*Mrs. Dolan*), Henry Kolker (*Maj. Vaile*), Colin Tapley (*Sir Phillip Burleigh*), Frank Dawson (*Saunders*), Barbara Blane (*Doris*), Lynn Bari (*Pat*), Paul McVey (*Detective*), Charles Richman, Ralf Harolde, Noel Madison.

Trevor's a girl whose father has been murdered by gangsters. She's about to marry Taylor but his mother (Frederick) doesn't want that sort of riffraff mixed up with her family of blue bloods. She consents to the marriage only because she wants the chance to break it up. However, when it is revealed that her other son (Beck) was inadvertently involved with the murder of Trevor's father, mom gives her blessing to the wedding. Pure soap opera with some nice photography of posh country estates, MY MARRIAGE suffers from weak dialog that definitely called for more spice than what was served up. Frederick is wonderfully bitchy as the mother-in-law who eats some humble pie.

p, Sol M. Wurtzel; d, George Archainbaud; w, Frances Hyland; ph, Barney McGill; ed, Alex Troffey; md, Samuel Kaylin; cos, Helen A. Myron.

Drama   **(PR:A   MPAA:NR)**

MY MOTHER**   (1933) 67m MON/FD bw

Pauline Frederick, Claire Windsor, Theodore Von Eltz, Robert Elliott, Barbara Kent, Henry B. Walthall, Jameson Thomas, George Hackathorne, Willie Fong, Lafe McKee, Si Jenks, George Hayes.

Frederick runs a gambling house though her daughter (Kent) believes it to be a hotel. After a pair of loaded dice cause some trouble, an angry gambler convinces Kent to join her mother's business, and the place does indeed become a hotel. Though well acted, the story is weak. In addition, the script doesn't ring true and the photography is below average for programmers such as this.

p, Trem Carr; d, Phil Rosen; w, Tristram Tupper (based on the story "The Just Judge" by Peter B. Kyne); ph, Archie Stout.

Drama   **(PR:A   MPAA:NR)**

MY NAME IS IVAN**
(1963, USSR) 97m Mosfilm/Sig Shore bw (IVANOVO DETSTVO; AKA: IVAN'S CHILDHOOD, THE YOUNGEST SPY)

Kolya Burlyayev (*Ivan*), Valentin Zubkov (*Capt. Kholin*), Ye. Zharikov (*Lt. Galtsev*), S. Krylov (*Cpl. Katasonych*), N. Grinko (*Col. Gryaznov*), D. Milyutenko (*Old Man*), V. Malyavina (*Masha*), I. Tarkovsky (*Ivan's Mother*), A. Konchalovsky, Ivan Savkin, V. Marenkov, Vera Miturich.

With his entire family killed by Nazis, the only thought on twelve-year-old Burlyayev's mind is revenge. He joins a Russian military intelligence unit and sneaks behind enemy lines to gather information about troop movements. Though high-ranking officers Zubkov and Grinko like the boy and are pleased with his efforts, they decide to send him to a safer area. Transferred to the rear of battle, Burlyayev rebels and runs away. He eventually returns and is allowed once more to go on dangerous assignments. He is given an order to cross the river to determine the enemy's strength; he steals into the dark forest, but is never seen again. Later the two officers sort out some captured Nazi documents and find the boy's picture with the word "executed" stamped across his face. Though the story line is interesting, the film may seem confusing because of the foreign sensibilities in terms of editing, and also the director's predilection for both visual and aural symbolism. The poor translation of the Russian dialog into English subtitles may add to the confusion. However, Burlyayev, in spite of his youth, carries the film with a maturity and a great sense of pathos. His determination never flagging, he stands out as a natural actor of great accomplishment.

d, Andrei Tarkovsky; w, Vladimir Osipovich Bogomolov, Mikhail Papava, E. Smirnov (based on the short story "Ivan" by Bogomolov); ph, Vadim Yusov; m,

Vyacheslav Ovchinnikov; ed, L. Feyginova; md, E. Kachaturyan; art d, Ye. Chernyayev; spec eff, V. Sevostyanov, S. Mukhin; makeup, L. Baskakova.

Drama   **(PR:O MPAA:NR)**

MY NAME IS JULIA ROSS*1/2   (1945) 64m COL bw

Nina Foch (Julia Ross), Dame May Whitty (Mrs. Hughes), George Macready (Ralph Hughes), Roland Varno (Dennis Bruce), Anita Bolster (Sparkes), Doris Lloyd (Mrs. Mackie), Leonard Mudie (Peters, Butler), Joy Harrington (Bertha), Queenie Leonard (Alice), Harry Hayes Morgan (Robinson), Ottola Nesmith (Mrs. Robinson), Olaf Hytten (Rev. Lewis), Evan Thomas (Dr. Keller), Marilyn Johnson (Nurse), Milton Owens, Leyland Hodgson (Policemen), Reginald Sheffield (McQuarrie), Charles McNaughton (Gatekeeper).

An excellent example of film noir, with a lean plot and atmospheric camera work. Foch stars as a woman caught up in a situation beyond her conceptions or control. After accepting employment as a secretary for wealthy matron Whitty, she meets her employer's son, Macready. He shows her around the mansion, takes Foch to her room, and brings her dinner. She awakens after a deep sleep in a different house wearing someone else's clothes. She was actually drugged by Macready who tells her that she is really his wife, just home from a mental institution. Trying to flee, Foch discovers she is in a mansion surrounded by a 10-foot wall with a heavily secured entrance. On a trip to town, Foch manages to slip a note in the mailbox to her boyfriend Varno in London. Eventually she overhears Whitty and Macready in conversation, and learns that they plan to kill her and make it look like suicide in order to cover the murder of Macready's real wife. Desperate, Foch pretends to take poison and pleads for a doctor. But she is fooled when they bring in butler Mudie posing as the doctor. She confesses the whole story, including the letter to her boy friend. Mudie attempts to intercept the letter in London, but when he is caught stealing it from the post office, he confesses all. Varno and the police rush to the Cornwall estate arriving just as Macready is about to kill Foch. Whitty is arrested but her son is killed trying to escape. Together once more, Foch and Varno return to London. "The next time I apply for a job I'll ask for *their* references!" exclaims Foch. This humorous bit of dialog aside, MY NAME IS JULIA ROSS is harrowing and suspenseful. Tension is created largely through a display of closeups, while such devices as a dizzying 360-degree pan encircling the room to represent Foch's drugged state when she awakens, indicate a cinematic sophistication. Unlike many 1940s mysteries, the love story doesn't get in the way of the suspense. The actors are very good: Macready, with his scarred cheek, is evil personified, at once threatening to Foch but utterly charming to the outside world; Whitty, the delightful old lady of Hitchcock's THE LADY VANISHES, is appropriate as the mother, though casting against her type doesn't work well here. This was Lewis' first directorial effort in the film noir genre, which is known for its simple, low-budgeted films that are examples of high quality cinema. Lewis considered this film to be the true beginning of his successful career.

p, Wallace MacDonald; d, Joseph H. Lewis; w, Muriel Roy Bolton (based on the novel *The Woman in Red* by Anthony Gilbert); ph, Burnett Guffey; m, Mischa Bakaleinikoff; ed, James Sweeney, Henry Batista; art d, Jerome Pycha, Jr.; set d, Milton Stumph.

Mystery   **(PR:A MPAA:NR)**

MY NAME IS NOBODY*   (1974, Ital./Fr./Ger.) 117m Rafran Cinematografica-Les Films Jaques Leitienne-La Societe Alcinter La Societe Imp. Ex. Ci.-Rialto-KG/UNIV c (IL MIO NOME E NESSUNO)

Terence Hill (Nobody), Henry Fonda (Jack Beauregard), Jean Martin (Sullivan), Piero Lulli (Sheriff), Leo Gordon (Red), R.G. Armstrong (Honest John), Neil Summers (Westerner), Steve Kanaly (Flase Barber), Geoffrey Lewis (Scape).

An offbeat Italian western that has a sense of cocky fun about it. Hill is a young man who relishes the days of the Wild West with its shooting, killing, and looting. He's hired to kill Fonda, a retired outlaw who really wants to settle down in Europe. Hill sets out to blow up Fonda with a bomb, but can't go through with it because he admires Fonda too much to kill him. Fonda leaves New Mexico for New Orleans with Hill tagging along. He's convinced the only way for the old gunfighter to retire is in a blaze of glory and is determined to see this happen. Fonda finally agrees, and faces a 150-man Wild Bunch. Like John Wayne's great scene in TRUE GRIT or many serial westerns of the 1940s, Fonda becomes a one-man dynamo, shooting outlaws left and right, setting off masses of explosives, and utilizing other forms of destruction. In the final scene, a bespectacled Fonda is seen, quietly writing at his desk. Though the directorial credit is given to Valerii, MY NAME IS NOBODY is clearly a product of its producer, Sergio Leone. Here Leone parodies his own westerns, as well as Sam Peckinpah's THE WILD BUNCH. Fonda made this his farewell western after 15 films in the genre. He plays the role with utmost believability, but nevertheless, Fonda seems to be having a good time with his character. Hill is not as good, though, resorting to wild gestures and overacting, atypical of Italian westerns. The film is too long, with an eclectic score that runs the gamut from ragtime to rock, both inappropriate styles for the genre. The Italian version runs 130 minutes.

p, Claudio Mancini, Sergio Leone; d, Tonino Valerii; w, Ernesto Gastaldi (based on a story by Fulvio Masella and Gastaldi); ph, Armando Nannuzzi, Giuseppe Ruzzolini (Panavision, Technicolor); m, Ennio Morricone; ed, Nino Baragli; art d, Cianni Polidori; cos, Vera Marzot.

Western   **(PR:O MPAA:PG)**

MY NAME IS PECOS*1/2   (1966, Ital.) 83m Italcine bw (MIO NOME E PECOS)

Robert Woods (Pecos), Lucia Modugno, Peter Carsten, Peter Kapp, Louis Cassel, Christina Josani.

Woods returns to his hometown, intent on avenging the murder of his parents. He tracks down Carsten and his gang, leaving a trail of bodies behind, which are collected by an overly enthusiastic grave-digger.

p, Franco Palombi; d&w, Maurizio Lucidi; ph, Franco Villa (CinemaScope)

Western   **(PR:C MPAA:NR)**

MY NAME IS ROCCO PAPALEO   (SEE: ROCCO PAPALEO, 1979)

MY NIGHT AT MAUD'S**

(1970, Fr.) 105m F.F.P.-Les Films du Losange-Films du Carrosse-Renn-Films des Deux Mondes-Productions de la Gueville-Simar-Films de la Pleiade/Pathe Contemporary-Corinth bw (MA NUIT CHEZ MAUD; AKA: MY NIGHT WITH MAUD)

Jean-Louis Trintignant (Jean-Louis), Francoise Fabian (Maud), Marie-Christine Barrault (Francoise), Antoine Vitez (Vidal), Leonide Kogan (Concert Violinist), Anne Dubot (Blonde Friend), Guy Leger (Preacher), Marie Becker (Marie, Maud's Daughter), Marie-Claude Rauzier (Student).

Third film in director Eric Rohmer's six-part "Moral Tales," moral in the sense that the characters question their motivations and feelings. The film stars Trintignant as a devout Catholic in love with a pretty blonde student (Barrault) he often sees at church but is too shy to approach. While at a bookstore he runs into an old friend, Vitez, who invites him to have dinner at Fabian's house. The threesome become involved in a lively conversation about the philosophy of Pascal and the freedom of choice. Because of a bad snowstorm and Trintignant's drunken state, Vitez suggests that Trintignant stay the night at Fabian's. Fabian teasingly attempts to seduce Trintignant, but the shy and morally upright man sleeps in a chair fully clothed. He eventually makes it to Fabian's bed, but still resists making love to her. Later, Trintignant finally has a chance to meet Barrault, which leads to their marriage. He discovers that Barrault once had an affair with a married man, who turns out to have been Fabian's ex-husband. As in all of Rohmer's films, there is little action. Rohmer instead is concerned with the thoughts of his characters, and the manner in which they explain themselves and their actions. Here, Trintignant prefers to remain true to his choice of chastity until marriage. Photographed in black and white, the film successfully captures the mood of the snowy Christmas season. A stickler for atmosphere, Rohmer put off shooting for an entire year when Trintignant could not make the first shooting date on Christmas Eve, preferring to wait in order to have the correct presence. MY NIGHT AT MAUD'S was nominated for two Oscars: Best Foreign Language Film, and Best Original Screenplay. It also won the New York Film Critics Award for Best Screenwriting (1970).

p, Pierre Cottrell, Barbet Schroeder; d&w, Eric Rohmer; ph, Nestor Almendros; ed, Cecile Decugis; art d, Nicole Rachline.

Drama   **(PR:A MPAA:GP)**

MY NIGHT WITH MAUD   (SEE: MY NIGHT AT MAUD'S, 1970, Fr.)

MY NIGHTS WITH FRANCOISE

(SEE: ANATOMY OF A MARRIAGE, 1964, Fr.)

MY OLD DUCHESS

(1933, Brit.) 65m BIP/Pathe bw (AKA: OH WHAT A DUCHESS!)

George Lacy (Irving), Betty Davies (Sally Martin), Dennis Hoey (Montagu Neilson), Fred Duprez (Jesse Martin), Renee Macready (Valerie), Florence Vie (Mrs. Neilson), Hugh E. Wright (Higgins), Pat Aherne (Gaston).

To win the attentions of an important film producer, a theatrical stage manager takes up the guise of a duchess. This film is an expanded version of one of Fred Karno's "Mumming Bird" sketches, and may be of historical interest to anyone interested in the history of the British music hall. It was the Karno troupe where both Charlie Chaplin and Stan Laurel (the latter serving as the former's understudy on the troupe's first American tour) learned many of the basics in comedy which they later transferred to their film work.

d, Lupino Lane; w, Con West, Herbert Sargent (based on a Fred Karno "Mumming Bird" sketch).

Comedy   **(PR:A MPAA:NR)**

MY OLD DUTCH   (1934, Brit.) 82m Gainsborough/GAU bw

Betty Balfour (Lil), Gordon Harker (Ernie), Michael Hogan (Bert), Florrie Forde (Aunt Bertha), Mickey Brantford (Jim), Glennis Lorimer (Valerie Paraday), Peter Gawthorne (Mr. Paraday), Frank Pettingell (Uncle Alf), Robert Nainby (Grandpa), Billy Shine (Cousin Arry), Finlay Currie (MO), Felix Aylmer (Judge), John Singer (Jim as a Child), Peggy Simpson, Ronald Shiner.

A simple, straighforward boy-meets-girl story. A couple from Cockney London meet and get married. They have a son and raise him to manhood. On the night before he goes into the army, the young man marries his sweetheart. He's killed in the war but she bears his son. This is a nice film, though it's simplicity eventually undermines it's sweetness. Ultimately it becomes boring, with a predictable sequence of events. Balfour, who handles the lead, is funny and effective. MY OLD DUTCH was actually based on a Cockney song, and was previously made in 1915 starring Albert Chevalier, who sang the song originally, and also co-scripted this version of the film.

p, Ivor Montagu; d, Sinclair Hill; w, Bryan Wallace, Marjorie Gaffney, Mary Murillo, Michael Hogan (based on a story by Wallace, Albert Chevalier, Arthur Shirley, Leslie Arliss); ph, Leslie Rowson.

Drama   **(PR:A MPAA:NR)**

MY OLD KENTUCKY HOME   (1938) 72m MON bw

Evelyn Venable, J. Farrell MacDonald, Grant Richards, Bernadene Hayes, Clara Blandick, Paul White, Mildred Gover, Margaret Marquis, Cornelius Keefe, Kitty McHugh, Raquel Davido, The Hall Johnson Choir.

Richards is a concert singer who goes blind after a jealous rival throws acid in his face. He leaves New York and girl friend Venable to return to his grandmother's plantation in Kentucky. It turns out that she has rigged a centennial celebration for the town designed specifically for Richards to regain his confidence. Using the plantation employees as back up (the Hall Johnson Choir, an all black chorus of some note), Richards sings some beloved Stephen Foster melodies and once more feels whole with himself. Since the Foster songs are the only real reason this film was made, Monogram Studios did an credible job of creating a highlight feature. The music blends in naturally. This film was shot almost entirely indoors, with little action to propel the story forward, thus making the songs its key feature.

p, E. B. Derr; d, Lambert Hillyer; w, John T. Neville; ph, Arthur Martinelli; ed, Finn Ulback.

Drama/Music **(PR:A MPAA:NR)**

MY OLD MAN'S PLACE (SEE: GLORY BOY, 1972)

MY OUTLAW BROTHER (SEE: MY BROTHER, THE OUTLAW, 1951)

MY OWN TRUE LOVE** (1948) 84m PAR bw

Phyllis Calvert *(Joan Clews)*, Melvyn Douglas *(Clive Heath)*, Wanda Hendrix *(Sheila Heath)*, Philip Friend *(Michael Heath)*, Binnie Barnes *(Geraldine)*, Alan Napier *(Kittredge)*, Arthur Shields *(Iverson)*, Phyllis Morris *(Mrs. Peach)*, Richard Webb *(Corporal)*, Norma Varden *(Red Cross Nurse)*, Peter Coe *(Rene)*, Clifford Brooke *(Coffee Stall Proprietor)*, Leyland Hodgson *(Taxi Driver)*, David Thursby *(Mechanic)*, Jean Fenwick *(Corporal)*, Betty Fairfax, Mary MacLaren *(Women-Nissen Hut)*, William Meader *(Room Clerk)*, George Douglas *(Cutter)*, Patrick Whyte *(Flight Lieutenant)*, Wilson Benge *(Waiter)*, Joseph Marr *(Proprietor)*, Erno Verebes *(Captain of Waiters)*, Paul Kreibich *(Maitre D')*, T. Arthur Hughes *(Doorman)*, Marie Osborne *(Woman Passenger)*, Leslie Denison *(Man)*, Queenie Leonard *(Woman)*, Robin Hughes *(English Officer)*, Miriam Jordan *(Miss Robinson)*.

Story features Douglas as a middle-aged man who's having a romance with Calvert. His son is supposed to be missing in a Japanese prison camp but the boy shows up. The son (Friend) has lost a leg in the war and has no interest in life. Though Douglas can't understand, his fiancee does. It seems she was a prisoner herself and knows what Friend is going through. When she learns that Friend also lost a Malayan wife and son in the war, her heart truly goes out to him. She leaves Douglas in an effort to reunite the father and son. Friend interprets her compassion as romantic interest, and when he finds out the truth, he tries to kill himself; but eventually, with Calvert's help, he decides to go back to school. Douglas and Calvert reunite and all ends happily. Despite the fine performances by the principals, this is not a very good movie. This was the second film for British leading lady Phyllis Calvert. Although speculation had it that she and the film's producer, Val Lewton, were anything but the best of friends, her skilled performance remains as the picture's highlight. Lewton, a master of the fantasy-horror film, was less adept when he ventured beyond the limits of that genre, and MY OWN TRUE LOVE is sadly lacking in the famed Lewton touches (moments of determined understatement, subtle visual shadings, pregnant silences). It also falls victim to the over-bookishness that marred some of his productions. Still, Lewton's passion for exotic drinks finds its way into the film—note the fuss Shields makes over a concoction called a Glowing Heart. The script, however, is weak, going for easy payoffs and is short on dramatic tension. Bennett's direction is similar, presenting the events without the slightest effort at insight. MY OWN TRUE LOVE is little more than a film to bring a box full of Kleenex.

p, Val Lewton; d, Compton Bennett; w, Theodore Strauss, Josef Mischel, Arthur Kober (based on the novel *Make You a Good Wife* by Yolanda Foldes); ph, Charles B. Lang, Jr.; m, Robert Emmett Dolan; ed, LeRoy Stone; art d, Hans Dreier, Henry Bumstead; set d, Sam Comer, Ross Dowd; cos, Edith Head; spec eff, Gordon Jennings.

Drama **(PR:A MPAA:NR)**

MY PAL GUS** (1952) 83m FOX bw

Richard Widmark *(Dave Jennings)*, Joanne Dru *(Lydia Marble)*, Audrey Totter *(Joyce)*, George Winslow *(Gus Jennings)*, Joan Banks *(Ivy Tolliver)*, Regis Toomey *(Farley Norris)*, Ludwig Donath *(Karl)*, Ann Morrison *(Polly Pahlman)*, Lisa Golm *(Anna)*, Christopher Olsen *(Tommy)*, Robert Foulk *(Mr. Evans)*, Mimi Gibson *(Judy)*, Sandy Descher *(Tot)*, Marie M. Brown *(Mrs. Lipton)*, Gordon Nelson *(Mr. Wilbur)*, William Cottrell *(Hotel Manager)*, Jay Adler *(Van Every)*, Frank Marlowe *(Delivery Man)*, Franklyn Farnum *(Attorney)*, William Dyer, Jr. *(Reporter)*, Otto Forrest *(Toy Store Clerk)*, James Flavin *(Bailiff)*, Jonathan Hale *(Judge)*, Frank Nelson *(McNary)*, Mabel Albertson, Jerrilyn Flannery.

Widmark plays a wealthy candy manufacturer. He's a workaholic, which has caused his wife to divorce him, leaving Widmark with their five-year-old son (Winslow). The kid is a real hell-raiser, so Widmark places the boy in a progressive school. Class is taught by Dru, who improves the boy's behavior and eventually becomes the romantic figure in Widmark's life. Along comes ex-wife Totter, claiming that their Mexican divorce is invalid. She claims he must pay her a large endowment or lose custody of Winslow. Though she loses the suit against her "ex," Totter gains custody of Winslow. Realizing what's important to him, Widmark pays Totter the money, regains custody of the boy and together they start a new life with Dru. A pleasant little comedy, though the leads seem to be thinking a little more about their next pictures rather than the one they were working on. Winslow naturally steals the show, playing a real child rather than a cute movie kid. The direction isn't bad, with good comic flair when appropriate.

p, Stanley Rubin; d, Robert Parrish; w, Fay and Michael Kanin; ph, Leo Tover; m, Leigh Harline; ed, Robert Fritch; md, Lionel Newman; art d, Lyle Wheeler, Albert Hogsett; set d, Thomas Little, Paul S. Fox; cos, Charles LeMaire.

Comedy/Drama **(PR:A MPAA:NR)**

MY PAL, THE KING*** (1932) 60m UNIV bw

Tom Mix *(Tom Reed)*, Mickey Rooney *(King Charles V)*, Paul Hurst *(Red)*, Noel Francis *(Princess Elsa)*, Finis Barton *(Gretchen)*, Stuart Holmes *(Kluckstein)*, James Kirkwood *(Schwartz, Count DeMar)*, Jim Thorpe *(Cloudy)*, Christian Frank *(Etzel)*, Clarissa Selwynne *(Dowager Queen)*, Ferdinand Schumann-Heink *(Gen. Wiedeman)*, Wallis Clark *(Dr. Lorenz)*, Tony the Wonder Horse.

This delightful little charmer features a very young Rooney as the pint-sized King of Ruritania. Bored with a high-level cabinet meeting, the youngster walks out and ends up with Mix, the proprietor of a wild west show. Rooney (as well as the audience) is then treated to a great display of ropin', ridin', and shootin'. Holmes plays an evil minister who wants the throne for himself. He kidnaps the boy ruler and tosses him into a pool that slowly fills up. Mix and his cohorts (including Olympic hero Thorpe) come riding to the castle just in the nick of time. Offbeat and as enjoyable as they come, MY PAL, THE KING has just the right mixture of whimsy and action, successfully pulled off on all levels. The direction keeps the melodramatic plot moving nicely. Mix's wild west show doesn't seem like it's grafted onto the story. It's all very natural and just a good old time at the movies. The kids will eat it up.

p, Carl Laemmle, Jr.; d, Kurt Neumann; w, Jack Natteford, Tom Crizer (based on a story by Richard Schayer); ph, Dan Clark.

Western/Action **(PR:A MPAA:NR)**

MY PAL TRIGGER*½** (1946) 79m REP bw

Roy Rogers *(Roy Rogers)*, George "Gabby" Hayes *(Gabby Kendrick)*, Dale Evans *(Susan)*, Jack Holt *(Brett Scoville)*, LeRoy Mason *(Carson)*, Roy Barcroft *(Hunter)*, Sam Flint *(Sheriff)*, Kenne Duncan *(Croupier)*, Ralph Sanford *(Auctioneer)*, Francis McDonald *(Storekeeper)*, Harlan Briggs *(Dr. Bentley)*, William Haade *(Davis)*, Alan Bridge *(Wallace)*, Paul E. Burns *(Walling)*, Frank Reicher *(Magistrate)*, Bob Nolan and the Sons of the Pioneers, Fred Graham, Ted Mapes, Trigger the Horse.

Rogers claims this to be the favorite of all his films and for good reason. It's well plotted, the direction is lively, and the camera work is far better than most of the "Singing Cowboy's" other films. He plays a horse trader, planning to mate a prize mare with a stallion belonging to good pal Hayes. But Holt (the real-life father of movie cowboy Tim Holt) is a gambler with similar plans for his own mare. He tries to steal Hayes' stallion but it escapes and mates with Rogers' mare. Holt catches up to the horse and shoots the beast. Rogers is blamed but he escapes from authorities, taking his now-pregnant mare with him. The mare's colt is born and, of course, grows up to be the famed horse Trigger. Meanwhile, Hayes has amounted some hefty gambling debts. Rogers returns and races his horse against Holt's. Of course, the white hat wins and Holt accidentally reveals himself to be the cause of the stallion's death years before. All is resolved as he is taken away by the sheriff. This is the quintessential Rogers film, with some fine acting (undoubtedly some of the best the genre would ever see) and, of course, musical numbers by the Sons of the Pioneers and duets by Rogers and Evans. In addition to being Rogers' favorite, this was also the most successful of all his films. Trigger had been obtained in 1938 at a cost of $2500. When one considers how much money the faithful steed made back for Rogers on the initial investment, he was one horse worth his weight in box-office receipts. After his loyal companion's death, Rogers had the horse stuffed and mounted for the Roy Rogers Museum.

p, Armand Schaefer; d, Frank McDonald; w, Jack Townley, John K. Butler (based on a story by Paul Gangelin); ph, William Bradford; ed, Harry Keller; md, Morton Scott; art d, Gano Chittenden; spec eff, Howard and Theodore Lydecker.

Western **Cas.** **(PR:AAA MPAA:NR)**

MY PAL, WOLF*** (1944) 75m RKO bw

Sharyn Moffett *(Gretchen Anstey)*, Jill Esmond *(Miss Munn, Governess)*, Una O'Connor *(Mrs. Blevins, the Housekeeper)*, George Cleveland *(Wilson, Handyman)*, Charles Arnt *(Papa Eisdaar)*, Claire Carleton *(Ruby, the Cook)*, Leona Maricle *(Mrs. Anstey)*, Bruce Edwards *(Mr. Anstey)*, Edward Fielding *(Secretary of War)*, Olga Fabian *(Mama Eisdaar)*, Larry Olsen *(Fred)*, Jerry Michelsen *(Alf)*, Bobby Larson *(Karl)*, Marc Cramer *(Sgt. Blake)*, Victor Cutler *(Wolf's trainer No. 1)*, Carl Kent *(Wolf's trainer No. 2)*, Bryant Washburn *(Commanding Officer)*, J. Louis Johnson *(Butler)*, Joan Barclay *(Willie)*, Chris Drake *(Bit)*, Tom Burton *(Reporter)*, Bert Moorhouse *(Cop)*, Alan Ward *(Truck Driver)*, Grey Shadow the Dog *(Wolf)*.

Rich Virginians Maricle and Edwards are much too busy to take care of their daughter, played by Moffett. They hire a strict British nanny (Esmond) to watch over their girl. Esmond's stern ways are the polar opposite of Moffett's unkempt, fun loving manner. Much to the chagrin of all the household help, "Miss Pruneface" takes over the house and promptly gets her little charge out of dirty jeans and into a dress and hair ribbons. One day Moffett sees a German shepherd running near the estate. She follows it and falls into a well. The dog (whom she dubs "Wolf") runs for help and Moffett adopts him. Of course, Esmond is angered by the new addition to the household. The dog and girl quickly become the best of friends, upsetting the rigidity that Esmond had instituted. But Esmond soon learns that the dog is a runaway Army canine and has Wolf sent back. Broken hearted, Moffett runs away and hitchhikes to Washington, D.C. There she wangles an audience with the secretary of war (Fielding). She pleads her case, hoping to regain the much beloved companion. However, Fielding explains that Wolf is needed to help win the war. Moffett understands and proudly returns home with a service star to hang in the window. Upon her return, Esmond is fired and Moffett's parents realize they must spend more time with their daughter. An added surprise comes from Fielding, who sends the patriotic young lady a German Shepherd pup. Though the plot sounds hackneyed, MY PAL, WOLF handles seemingly tired material with freshness and sensitivity. Moffett, RKO's answer to MGM's juvenile lead Margaret O'Brien, was absolutely natural in her role. Unaffected, the girl was a born actress with great warmth and appeal. She could have easily run away with the picture had it been produced by lesser hands. But RKO wisely gave this film some intelligent production credits. The direction, focusing on the humanistic qualities of the script, never indulges in sticky sentimentality. Though there are a few cliches within, for the most part, they are downplayed. The supporting cast is equally fine. O'Connor, who played the amiable and salty housemaid, was a veteran of Ireland's Abbey Theater. Her characterization is excellent and believable. As for Esmond, her mean-spirited nanny never stoops to stereotype. As for Grey Shadow ("Wolf"), he truly looked like he was enjoying himself in the picture. Unlike so many movie canines, his behavior is real and not a learned response. The film's biggest weakness is found during the scene with Fielding. Being a WW II era film, the patriotic "We've all got to do our part" speech is a little overdone, with unnecessary comments about children being set ablaze in Europe. That may be a little much for younger children, but otherwise, this is intelligent entertainment that's perfect for family viewing.

p, Adrian Scott; d, Alfred Werker; w, Lillie Hayward, Leonard Praskins, John Paxton (based on a story by Frederick Hazlitt Brennan); ph, Jack MacKenzie; m, Werner R. Heymann; ed, Harry Marker; md, Constantin Bakaleinikoff; art d, Albert S. D'Agostino, Carroll Clark; cos, Renie; spec eff, Vernon L. Walker.

Adventure   **(PR:A MPAA:NR)**

MY PARTNER MR. DAVIS

(SEE: MYSTERIOUS MR. DAVIS, THE, 1936, Brit.)

MY PAST***   (1931) 83m WB bw

Bebe Daniels (Dora Macy), Ben Lyon (Robert Byrne), Lewis Stone (John Thornley), Joan Blondell (Marion Moore), Natalie Moorhead (Consuelo Byrne), Albert Gran (Lionel Reich), Daisy Belmore (Mrs. Bennett), Virginia Sale.

Stone is the elderly bachelor business partner of Lyon. Both are interested in a young divorced actress, played by Lyon's real-life wife at the time, Daniels. But Lyon is a married man and complications arise with the situation. Though the script is fairly simple, the performances make up for it. Lyon and Stone are both very strong as the business partners confused by love. Daniels, though a good actress, just doesn't have quite the spark that her character needs. Mild by today's standards, this was quite a racy film for it's time despite some studio censoring.

d, Roy Del Ruth; w, Charles Kenyon (based on the novel Ex-Mistress by Dora Macy); ph, Chick McGill; ed, Ralph Dawson.

Drama   **(PR:A MPAA:NR)**

MY REPUTATION**   (1946) 94m WB bw

Barbara Stanwyck (Jessica Drummond), George Brent (Maj. Scott Landis), Warner Anderson (Frank Everett), Lucile Watson (Mrs. Kimball), John Ridgely (Cary Abbott), Eve Arden (Ginna Abbott), Jerome Cowan (George Van Orman), Esther Dale (Anna), Scotty Beckett (Kim Drummond), Bobby Cooper (Keith Drummond), Leona Maricle (Riette Van Orman), Mary Servoss (Mary), Cecil Cunningham (Mrs. Thompson), Janis Wilson (Penny Boardman), Ann Todd (Gretchen Van Orman), Nancy Evans (Baby Hawks), Oliver Blake (Dave), Charles Jordan (Butcher), Darwood Kaye (Bill "Droopy" Hawks), Fred Kelsey (Conductor), Marjorie Hoshelle (Phyllis), Bruce Warren (Man in Bar), Harry Seymour (Hotel Desk Clerk), Frank Darien (Elevator Operator), Leah Baird (Woman), Hugh Prosser (Les Hanson), Helen Eby Rock (Mrs. Hanson), Alan Ward, Dan Dowling, Tom Quinn, Elyse Browne, Rosalie Roy (Party Guests), Dickie Humphreys, Marilyn Kaye, Shirley Doble, Dale Cornell (Jitterbugs), Sam McDaniel (Johnson), Dick Winslow (Orchestra Leader), Dick Elliott (Tipsy Man), Robert Shayne ("Hank" Hawks), Ellsworth Blake.

Critics didn't much care for this picture, but the public, tired of war movies, flocked to see it and it was a large success. The studio finished the shooting at the beginning of March, 1944, but waited until after January 1, 1946 before releasing it. Stanwyck has just buried her husband in the wealthy area of Lake Forest, Illinois, and is now faced with the prospect of raising her two young sons, Cooper and Beckett, alone. If she lives frugally, she can stay in the large home and manage. With her husband gone, she throws herself into work for the war effort and devotes herself to the boys, while fending off the advances of the various men (all married) who think she is fair game for their romantic ploys. Her sons are going through puberty, and Stanwyck realizes that she has to let go of them and make her own way, so they are sent away to school. Totally alone, she is very unhappy and not made any happier by her mother, Watson, who is always attempting to fix her up with eligible men. Stanwyck's best friend is Arden, who is married to Ridgely, and the couple prevail upon Stanwyck to put a little fun in her life and join them in the mountains for a bit of shussing and slaloming. On holiday, she meets rakish Brent, a military man on leave, and he puts a move on her, but she resists him in a conservative fashion and will not have an affair without benefit of a gold ring. She returns to her home, where Anderson, a stodgy type, wants to marry her. Watson likes Anderson and tries to encourage Stanwyck to accept the ho-hummer's proposal. She goes to a local nightclub where she meets Brent again and although the attraction is evident, Brent is a confirmed bachelor and will offer her nothing more than a romp in the hay. Stanwyck feels she must decide between the good, gray Anderson and the exciting Brent. Meanwhile, there is some talk about her and Brent, and tongues wag with the speed of flags in a hurricane. Soon, her sons hear about her involvement (benign though it may be) with Brent, and are turning against her because they feel she is insulting the memory of their late father. Stanwyck takes Brent to a party tossed by Maricle, a neighbor for whom gossip has been raised to the state of the art, and she gives the woman what for. Later, Brent informs Stanwyck that he is being shipped from Illinois to New York and then going off to Europe. She'd like to go east with him but thinks that it might destroy her boys if she does. Then Brent says he is in

love with Stanwyck and plans to marry her when he returns, after the war has been won. Brent leaves on a train as Stanwyck waves goodbye and the picture ends. Lots of suds, a so-so score by Steiner, and a generally sappy performance by Brent are what mar this film, but the fault must be laid at Bernhardt's direction which was sluggish, despite the use of camera trickery that did little more than subtract from the story's soapy content.

p, Henry Blanke; d, Curtis Bernhardt; w, Catherine Turney (based on the novel Instruct My Sorrows by Clare Jaynes); ph, James Wong Howe; m, Max Steiner; ed, David Weisbart; md, Leo F. Forbstein; art d, Anton Grot; set d, George James Hopkins; cos, Edith Head, Leah Rhodes; spec eff, Roy Davidson; m/l, "While You're Away," Steiner, Stanley Adams; makeup, Perc Westmore.

Romance   **(PR:A-C MPAA:NR)**

MY SEVEN LITTLE SINS**¹/₂

(1956, Fr./Ital.) 98m Francinalp-Faro-Consortium Du Film/Kingsley International c
(J'AVAIS SEPT FILLES; AKA: I HAVE SEVEN DAUGHTERS)

Maurice Chevalier (Count Andre), Delia Scala (Luisella), Colette Ripert (Linda), Maria Frau (Lolita), Annick Tanguy (Nadine), Lucianna Paoluzzi [Paluzzi] (Pat), Mimi Medard (Daisy), Maria Luisa Da Silva (Blanchette), Gaby Basset (Maria), Paolo Stoppa (Antonio), Pasquali (Prof. Gorbiggi), Louis Velle (Edouard), Robert Destrain (Bertoul).

A charming piece of fluff which is entertaining solely because of Chevalier. He plays a graying count from the South of France who keeps an indexed system of all his past loves. One day a young lovely turns up at his doorstep claiming to be an offspring from a past affair. He accepts her with open arms, taking her into his chateau and offering the best treatment. But when a half-dozen more gals arrive with the same story, Chevalier becomes suspicious. His son returns home from a scientific expedition and falls in love with one of the girls and soon after Chevalier tells them all that he knows that something's up. The girls admit their deceit, identifying themselves as unemployed stage actresses who are just waiting for work. A pleasant return to the American screen for Chevalier, whose politicizing got a ban put on his visa in earlier days. Includes a pair of tunes sung by Chevalier, "C'est l'Amour" and "Demain J'ai Vingt Ans" (Fred Freed).

d, Jean Boyer; w, Serge Veber, Jean Des Vallieres, Boyer (based on a story by Aldo de Benedetti); ph, Charles Suin (Ferraniacolor); m, Fred Freed; ed, A. Laurent.

Musical   **(PR:A MPAA:NR)**

MY SIDE OF THE MOUNTAIN***   (1969) 100m PAR c

Teddy Eccles (Sam Gribley), Theodore Bikel (Bando), Tudi Wiggins (Miss Turner), Frank Perry (Mr. Gribley), Peggi Loder (Mrs. Gribley), Gina Dick (Daughter No. 1), Karen Pearson (Daughter No. 2), Danny McIlravey (Little Boy), Cosette Lee (Mrs. Fielder), Larry Reynolds (Hunter No. 1), Tom Harvey (Hunter No. 2), Paul Hebert (Hunter No. 3), Ralph Endersby (1st Boy), George Allan (2nd Boy), Patrick Pervion (Ranger), Ed Persons, Max Rosenbloom, Gus the Raccoon, Frightful the Falcon.

Charming little film features 13-year-old Eccles as a young man enamored of Thoreau. Emulating his hero, Eccles runs away to live in the Canadian woodlands, leaving a note telling his parents that he will be back in one year. Taking some camping equipment and his pet raccoon Gus, he builds himself a home in a hollow tree. Using the resources of a nearby library (as well as the help of Wiggins, an understanding librarian) Eccles learns various survival methods and teaches himself about falconry. He captures a baby falcon and trains it. He meets Bikel, delightfully portraying a wandering folk singer. Impressed by Eccles, Bikel stays awhile and teaches the boy some additional woodland knowledge. But setbacks occur when Eccles' falcon is killed by hunters and winter approaches. Alone and depressed on Christmas day, he is happily surprised by Wiggins and Bikel, who bring him a special dinner. They also show him some press clippings about his parents' hunt for their son. Eccles realizes that he has accomplished what he set out to do and finally agrees to return home. This film manages to be entertaining and educational all at once. Eccles' day to day life in the woods is nicely portrayed and completely believable. His inventiveness and pluck are completely natural, without any hint of movie contrivances. Bikel and Wiggins are good in support, though the raccoon definitely steals the show. Intelligently made, with respect for its pre-teen subject, MY SIDE OF THE MOUNTAIN is good family viewing that will delight the kids and probably hold a few of the grown-ups as well.

p, Robert B. Radnitz; d, James B. Clark; w, Ted Sherdeman, Jane Klove, Joanna Crawford (based on the novel by Jean Craighead George); ph, Denys Coop (Panavision, Technicolor); m, Wilfred Josephs; ed, Peter Thornton, Alastair McIntyre; md, Muir Mathieson; art d, George Lack; set d, Johnny Allett.

Adventure/Family   **Cas.**   **(PR:AAA MPAA:G)**

MY SIN*   (1931) 80m PAR bw

Tallulah Bankhead (Carlotta/"Ann Trevor"), Fredric March (Dick Grady), Harry Davenport (Roger Metcalf), Scott Kolk (Larry Gordon), Anne Sutherland (Mrs. Gordon), Margaret Adams (Paula Marsden), Jay Fassett (James Bradford), Lily Cahill (Helen Grace), Averell Harris, Charles Fang.

This was Bankhead's second talkie after the rotten debut in THE NIGHT ANGEL. Unfortunately, this entry was no better and the energy and charisma of Bankhead's stage performances was untranslatable to the screen. MY SIN opens in Panama where March, an attorney who has fallen upon drunken times, is imbibing his way to destruction. He encounters Bankhead, a nitery chirper, whose mate is hounding her for money. She gets into a battle with the man and shoots him dead. But her reputation is such in Panama that no one will undertake her defense until March decides to clean up his act and handle her case. He goes from besotted counselor to another Clarence Darrow in a few minutes and manages to get her acquitted. This case puts him back on his game and he is soon riding high again as a lawyer, so he lends her enough money to return to New York where she becomes a high-powered interior decorator and is on the verge of marrying a wealthy young man who comes from a socially-upstanding family. March goes to New York, gets in touch with Bankhead, and tells her that she would be wise to come clean about her history because those things have a nasty habit of coming up just when you think they've been buried. She chooses to keep mum about the matter in Panama until both she and March are spotted at a party by a former acquaintance from Panama and she decides to tell her new beau the truth. Although the fiance, Kolk, says that he loves Bankhead despite anything she may have done in the long ago, she gets the feeling that he is not quite telling the truth and leaves the 24 karat marriage proposal in favor of March, whom she has loved all along but didn't acknowledge until the last reel. Bankhead's voice was already husky but nowhere near as deep as it wound up to be. Her first name was so unusual that she successfully sued a shampoo company when they attempted to use the name, Tallulah, to represent a tube of their product. Her contention was that since her name was a one-of-a-kind, it indicated that she was lending her support to the shampoo.

d, George Abbott; w, Owen Davis, Adelaide Heilbron, Abbott (based on a story by Fred Jackson); ph, George Folsey; ed, Emma Hill.

Drama **(PR:A-C MPAA:NR)**

MY SISTER AND I* (1948, Brit.) 97m GFD bw

Sally Ann Howes *(Robina Adams)*, Dermot Walsh *(Graham Forbes)*, Martita Hunt *(Mrs. Camelot)*, Barbara Mullen *(Hypatia Foley)*, Patrick Holt *(Roger Crisp)*, Hazel Court *(Helena Forsythe)*, Joan Rees *(Ardath Bondage)*, Jane Hylton *(Elsie)*, Michael Medwin *(Charlie)*, Rory McDermott *(Michael Marsh)*, Hugh Miller *(Hubert Bondage)*, Ian Wilson *(Horsnell)*, Niall Lawlor *(Harry)*, Elizabeth Sydney *(Phyllis)*, Jack Vyvyan *(Pomfret)*, Helen Goss *(Mrs. Pomfret)*, Stewart Rome *(Col. Thursby)*, Olwen Brookes *(Mrs. Lippincott)*, Diana Dors *(Dreary Girl)*, James Knight *(Dustman)*, Wilfred Caithness *(Coroner)*, John Miller *(Bishop)*, Amy Dalby *(Female Cleaner)*, Barbara Leake *(Woman)*.

Howes is an innocent young woman who arrives in a small town. She is to become the scenic designer for the local theater company run by the very odd Hunt. Walsh is an actor vying for Howes' affections with Holt, a local attorney. When Hunt is found dead by gas poisoning, the search is on for a motive. Eventually, it is discovered that Hunt's late husband fathered her sister's daughter. Poorly made, with uninteresting development, this minor British feature is about as amateurish as they come. The acting is mediocre at best.

p, John Corfield, Harold Huth; d, Huth; w, A. R. Rawlinson, Joan Rees, Michael Medwin, Robert Westerby (based on the novel *High Pavement* by Emery Bonnet); ph, Harry Waxman; m, Bretton Byrd; ed, John Guthridge; md, Byrd; art d, J. Elder Willis; set d, Colleen Browning; makeup, Tony Sforzini.

Drama **(PR:C MPAA:NR)**

MY SISTER EILEEN*** (1942) 96m COL bw

Rosalind Russell *(Ruth Sherwood)*, Brian Aherne *(Robert Baker)*, Janet Blair *(Eileen Sherwood)*, George Tobias *(Appopolous, Landlord)*, Allyn Joslyn *(Chick Clark)*, Elizabeth Patterson *(Grandma Sherwood)*, Grant Mitchell *(Walter Sherwood)*, Richard Quine *(Frank Lippincott)*, June Havoc *(Effie Shelton)*, Donald MacBride *(Officer Lonigan)*, Gordon Jones *("The Wreck")*, Jeff Donnell *(Helen Loomis)*, Clyde Fillmore *(Ralph Craven)*, Minna Phillips *(Mrs. Wade)*, Frank Sully *(Jansen, Janitor)*, Charles La Torre *(Capt. Anadato)*, Danny Mummert *(Boy)*, Almira Sessions *(Prospective Tenant)*, Kirk Alyn, George Adrian, Tom Lincir *(Cadets)*, Ann Doran *(Receptionist)*, Bob Kellard *(Bus Driver)*, Forrest Tucker *(Sand Hog)*, The Three Stooges *(Bus Passengers)*, Walter Sande, Pat Lane, Ralph Dunn *(Policemen)*, Arnold Stang *(Jimmy)*.

When Ruth McKenney and her sister Eileen came to New York City from Columbus, Ohio, the older sister took many notes about their lives in Greenwich Village, wrote some stories, and sent them into the *New Yorker Magazine*. They were published and served as the basis for the hit Broadway comedy by Joseph Fields and Jerome Chodorov. This film version is much like the stage show, as it was written by the same authors. The sisters move into a basement apartment in a building owned by Greek Tobias. Their neighbors are the usual nutty group, including Jones (who is known as "the Wreck" because he went to Georgia Tech, and never lets you forget that he played football there and was one of the "Rambling Wrecks") and his wife, Donnell, who live with her mother, Phillips. In the course of the action, the apartment is as busy as the house in YOU CAN'T TAKE IT WITH YOU, with hot and cold running subplots. Joslyn is the journalist who has an eye for Blair, and Aherne is the magazine editor Russell wants to sell her stories to. Aherne's boss is unctuous, pompous Fillmore, and MacBride does his usual flatfoot role as the contentious cop on the Village beat. The play was a one-set show of the basement apartment, and they've opened it up a bit to include scenes back in Ohio and other sequences which were only referred to in the play script. The Three Stooges are seen briefly as workmen digging a new subway in the area and coming up through the basement floor. There is no real single plot to speak of, just a series of incidents and character sketches, all of which are funny and true to the life in Greenwich Village. Director-writer Richard Quine began as an actor on Broadway and also appeared in this film. He later directed such films as THE SOLID GOLD CADILLAC; BELL, BOOK AND CANDLE; THE NOTORIOUS LANDLADY; THE WORLD OF SUSIE WONG; and the 1955 musical version of MY SISTER EILEEN. Jeff Donnell was sometimes referred to as "Miss" Jeff Donnell so there would be no mistaking her sex. She achieved nationwide fame as George Gobel's TV wife in his 1956 series.

p, Max Gordon; d, Alexander Hall; w, Joseph Fields, Jerome Chodorov (based on the play by Fields, Chodorov, from the stories by Ruth McKenney); ph, Joseph Walker; ed, Viola Lawrence; md, Morris Stoloff; art d, Lionel Banks, set d, Ray Babcock.

Comedy **(PR:AA MPAA:NR)**

MY SISTER EILEEN* 1/2** (1955) 108m COL c

Janet Leigh *(Eileen Sherwood)*, Betty Garrett *(Ruth Sherwood)*, Jack Lemmon *(Bob Baker)*, Robert [Bob] Fosse *(Frank Lippencott)*, Kurt Kasznar *(Appopolous)*, Richard [Dick] York *("Wreck")*, Lucy Marlow *(Helen)*, Tommy Rall *(Chick Clark)*, Barbara Brown *(Helen's Mother)*, Horace McMahon *(Lonigan)*, Henry Slate, Hal March *(Drunks)*, Alberto Morin *(Brazilian Consul)*, Queenie Smith *(Alice)*, Richard Deacon *(George)*, Ken Christy *(Police Sergeant)*.

Richard Quine, who played a supporting role in the Broadway play and 1942 movie, returns to co-write the screenplay and direct this musical version. This is a unique story in that *two* musicals were drawn from it. The first was "Wonderful Town," a Broadway play with Roz Russell reprising her film role (that ran more than 550 performances and had a superb score by Leonard Bernstein and Comden and Green), and then this one, which had nothing at all to do with the stage musical. It's virtually the same story as the original play and film with different people playing the roles. Fosse acts as well as choreographs and dances (and gives us an inkling of what was to come in his career); Lemmon is charming in the first of several films he was to do with Quine (OPERATION MAD BALL; BELL, BOOK AND CANDLE; IT HAPPENED TO JANE; THE NOTORIOUS LANDLADY; and HOW TO MURDER YOUR WIFE). Co-screenwriter Edwards would later direct Lemmon in DAYS OF WINE AND ROSES and THE GREAT RACE. None of the songs made much noise, and, to the best of our knowledge, there was never a cast album recorded or distributed. The plot, as already indicated in the earlier film's review (MY SISTER EILEEN [1942]), is a series of incidents and complications which happen to a pair of sisters (Garrett and Leigh) who come to New York from Ohio and wind up in what must be the busiest apartment in the city since Polly Adler's place. It's a fast-moving and charming version of the play and the songs, although not notable, do add greatly to the overall fun. They include: "This is Greenwich Village," "Conga." Lemmon, who is a fair pianist and has made an album purporting that, is no singer, but his acting ability carries him through the song he has to sing. This is a small musical, not a lot of production values, but it has a great deal of energy, and the dialog crackles with sage observations about the publishing business in particular and New York in general. The real-life Eileen married author Nathanael West (DAY OF THE LOCUST, MISS LONELYHEARTS, etc.) Jule Styne, Leo Robin songs include: "Give Me a Band and My Baby" (sung by Betty Garrett, Janet Leigh, Robert Fosse, Tommy Rall), "It's Bigger Than You and Me" (sung by Jack Lemmon), "There's Nothing Like Love" (sung by Leigh, Garrett, reprised by Fosse), "As Soon As They See Eileen" (sung by Garrett), "I'm Great!" (sung by Kurt Kasznar, Richard York, Garrett, Leigh, reprised by Garrett, Leigh), "Conga" (danced by Betty Garrett, Leigh, reprised by the Entire Cast), "Atmosphere" (chorus).

p, Fred Kohlmar; d, Richard Quine; w, Blake Edwards, Quine (based on the play by Joseph Fields, Jerome Chodorov from the stories by Ruth McKenney); ph, Charles Lawton, Jr. (CinemaScope, Technicolor); m, George Duning; ed, Charles Nelson; md, Morris Stoloff; art d, Walter Holscher; set d, William Kiernan; cos, Jean Louis; ch, Bob Fosse.

Musical Comedy **(PR:AA MPAA:NR)**

MY SISTER, MY LOVE (SEE: MAFU CAGE, THE, 1978)

MY SIX CONVICTS*** (1952) 104m COL bw

Millard Mitchell *(James Connie)*, Gilbert Roland *(Punch Pinero)*, John Beal *(Doc)*, Marshall Thompson *(Blivens Scott)*, Alf Kjellin *(Clem Randall)*, Henry [Harry] Morgan *(Dawson)*, Jay Adler *(Steve Kopac)*, Regis Toomey *(Doctor Gordon)*, Fay Roope *(Warden Potter)*, Carlton Young *(Capt. Haggerty)*, John Marley *(Knotty Johnson)*, Russ Conway *(Dr. Hughes)*, Byron Foulger *(Doc Brint)*, Charles Buchinsky [Bronson] *(Jocko)*, Peter Virgo, George Eldredge, Paul Hoffman, Dick Cogan, Allen Mathews, H. George Stern *(Convicts)*, Jack Carr *(Higgins)*, Carol Savage *(Mrs. Randall)*, Danny Jackson *(Convict 1538)*, Joe Haworth *(Convict 9670)*, Chester Jones *(Convict 7546)*, Vincent Renno *(Convict 9919)*, Frank Mitchell *(Convict 3007)*, Joe McTurk *(Big Benny)*, Harry Stanton, *(Banker)*, Fred Kelsey *(Store Detective)*, Edwin Parker *(Guard on Dump Truck)*, Joe Palma *(Convict Driver)*, Barney Philips *(Baker Foreman)*, Dick Curtis, John Monaghan *(Guards)*.

A lightweight, but socially relevant prison drama which follows, in an episodic manner, the relationships between six convicts and the newly instated prison psychologist. Beal plays the mind-probing newcomer whose presence is met with some opposition by the prison population. Eventually one of the convicts, Mitchell—a safecracker—pays a visit to Beal. Before long five more convicts are frequenting Beal's office: Roland, a crook with more brains than the rest of the men; Morgan, a callous killer with a burning desire to escape; Kjellin, a diehard romantic who only wants to be with his wife; Thompson, a hard-drinking baseball player wrongly imprisoned after taking the rap for a girl; and Adler, an embezzler. Mitchell's respect for Beal and their growing friendship pays off for the safecracker when he is given a chance to prove himself. He is called on to help open an accidentally locked bank vault outside the prison walls. As payment for his services he is given a 24-hour respite from the prison. Morgan, on the other hand, has little concern for Beal and tries to make him a pawn in an escape attempt. Coming to Beal's aid, the other convicts suggest that the psychologist's role as a shield in the escape attempt be taken by a despised dentist. By the film's end Beal's mind has been tested and probed by the difficult but likable prisoners just as much as he has tested and probed theirs. The film's major fault is its lack of believable characters. The six convicts seem more like the Bowery Boys grown up than hardened criminals—most of them seem to be prime candidates for rehabilitation, hardly a realistic portrayal of prison life. If anything, MY SIX CONVICTS can boast a realistic setting. For 9 days, filming took place in the newly refurbished San Quentin (called "Harbor State Prison" in the film, which is based on actual studies for the U.S. Public Health Service at Leavenworth), using actual prisoners as extras. As a security measure, those involved with the film were carefully checked and searched upon their entrance and exit; had their hands stamped with invisible ink; and were required to wear identification tags which listed their roles on the production under the word "offense."

p, Stanley Kramer; d, Hugo Fregonese; w, Michael Blankfort (based on a book by Donald Powell Wilson); ph, Guy Roe; m, Dimitri Tiomkin; ed, Gene Havlick; art d, Edward Ilou.

Prison Drama   **(PR:A-C   MPAA:NR)**

MY SIX LOVES**   (1963) 105m PAR c

Debbie Reynolds (Janice Courtney), Cliff Robertson (Rev. Jim Larkin), David Janssen (Martin Bliss), Eileen Heckart (Ethel Swenson), Jim Backus (The Sheriff), Pippa Scott (Diane Soper), John McGiver (Judge Harris), Hans Conried (Kingsley Cross), Mary McCarty (Doreen Smith), Alice Ghostley (Selina), Alice Pearce (Bus Driver), Max Showalter (B. J. Smith), Claude Stroud (Dr. Miller), Darlene Tompkins (Ava), Leon Belasco (Mario), Billy Hughes (Leo), Colleen Peters (Amy), Sally Smith (Brenda), Barry Livingston (Sherman), Debbie Price (Dulcie), Teddy Eccles (Sonny), Pat Moran (Studio Executive), Leon Tyler (Columnist), Yvonne Peattie (Lady Columnist), Maurice Kelly (Man with Mike), Sterling Holloway (Oliver Dodds), William Wood (Judge's Clerk), Gary Getzman (Bus Driver's Son), Thomas Thomas (Stage Manager), Richard Fitzgerald (Actor), Mimi Dillard (Receptionist), Tommy Farrell (Studio Representative), Victor Buono (Fat Man), Georgine Cleveland, Molly Dodd (Women), Ted Bergen, Bill Hudson, Ted Quillin (Reporters), Larry Alderette, Paul Rees, Robert Cole, Robert Karl, Cass Jaeger, Frank Radcliff, Terry Terrill (Photographers).

Reynolds plays a Broadway star in need of rest. She heads for a Connecticut hideaway and 15 minutes into the film is confronted by six of the most adorably nauseating moppets ever to grace the silver screen. Naturally she falls for the tykes and gets temporary custody of them. She finally heads back to the Great White Way for a new show, but when word comes that one of the kids has run off, Reynolds knows what she must do. Quitting show biz for good, she heads back to the farm, the sextet, and the waiting arms of Robertson. Though the leads are suitable, the talent is clearly wasted in this overly cute froth. Sets are undeniably studio with no hint at realism. This was the first directorial effort for Champion, a real surprise considering the quality of his Broadway projects. This film is not recommended for diabetics.

p, Gant Gaither; d, Gower Champion; w, John Fante, Joseph Calvelli, William Wood (based on the story by Peter V. K. Funk); ph, Arthur E. Arling (Vistavision, Technicolor); m, Walter Scharf; ed, John Woodcock; art d, Hal Pereira, Roland Anderson; set d, Sam Comer, Grace Gregory; cos, Edith Head; spec eff, John P. Fulton; ch, Jack Regas; m/l, "It's A Darn Good Thing," Sammy Cahn, James Van Heusen (sung by Debbie Reynolds); makeup, Wally Westmore.

Comedy   **(PR:AA   MPAA:NR)**

MY SON ALONE   (SEE: AMERICAN EMPIRE, 1942)

MY SON IS A CRIMINAL**¹/₂   (1939) 59m COL bw

Alan Baxter (Tim Halloran, Jr.), Jacqueline Wells [Julie Bishop] (Myrna Kingsley), Gordon Oliver (Allen Coltrin), Willard Robertson (Tim Halloran, Sr.), Joseph King (Jerry Kingsley), Eddie Laughton (Walt Fraser), John Tyrell (Jersey).

After retiring from the police force, Robertson entertains the notion that his son (Baxter) might carry on the tradition. Baxter ends up in the cops and robbers business all right, but on the wrong side of the law. Robertson sadly comes out of retirement to capture his son, killing the boy in a shootout. Better than it sounds, the somewhat cliched characters are fleshed out with some well-written dialog and a fine ensemble performance. The direction is brisk, and sensitive to Robertson's confusions, keeping the commercial end of the project well-balanced with the more artistic qualities.

d, C. C. Coleman, Jr.; w, Arthur T. Horman; ph, Allen G. Siegler; ed, Gene Havlick.

Crime   **(PR:A   MPAA:NR)**

MY SON IS GUILTY**   (1940) 63m COL bw

Bruce Cabot (Ritzy Kerry), Jacqueline Wells [Julie Bishop] (Julia Allen), Harry Carey (Tim Kerry), Glenn Ford (Barney), Wynne Gibson (Claire Morelli), Don Beddoe (Duke Mason), John Tyrell (Whitey Morris), Bruce Bennett (Lefty), Dick Curtis (Monk), Edgar Buchanan (Dan), Al Bridge (Police Lieutenant), Robert Sterling (Clerk), Edmund Cobb (Detective), Howard Hickman (Police Commissioner), Ivan "Dusty" Miller (Capt. Hespelt), Hermine Sterler (Barney's Mother), Mary Gordon (Mrs. Monticelli), Stanley Brown (Police Announcer), Richard Fiske (Cop), Beatrice Blinn (Telephone Girl), Eddie Fetherston (Harry), Hal Price (Gateman), Josef Forte (First Aid Man), Forrest Taylor, Ed Peil, Sr. (Cops), Julian Madison (Taxi Driver), Joe Scully (Peddler), Roger Gray (Workman), Roger Haliday (Young Man), Hugh Chapman (Boy), Bessie Wade (Woman), Jack Gardner, James Coughlin (Men).

Carey is a veteran policeman in Hell's Kitchen. His son (Cabot) turned to crime but is now being released from prison. Carey tries to help the young man make a new start, but Cabot is soon back with his old cronies. He rejoins the mob and kills a police officer. Having no choice, Carey kills his son in a shootout. Though a formal picture through and through, the direction manages to inject some life into the stock situations. Carey is able to escape his stereotype as well, turning in a fairly good performance. However, the skimpy plot and weak dialog ultimately catch up with the film. The majority of the cast, all programmer veterans, just seem to be going through the motions and hoping for a big break. Still, be on the lookout for Glenn Ford in an early role.

d, Charles Barton; w, Harry Shumate, Joseph Carole (based on a story by Karl Brown); ph, Benjamin Kline; ed, William Lyon.

Crime   **(PR:C   MPAA:NR)**

**MY SON, JOHN ****¹/₂   (1952) 122m PAR bw

Helen Hayes (Lucille Jefferson), Van Heflin (Stedman of the FBI), Robert Walker (John Jefferson), Dean Jagger (Dan Jefferson), Minor Watson (Dr. Carver), Frank McHugh (Father O'Dowd), Richard Jaeckel (Chuck Jefferson), James Young (Ben Jefferson), Nancy Hale, Margaret Wells (Nurses), Todd Karns (Bedford), Frances Morris (Secretary), Douglas Evans (Government Employee), Gail Bonney (Jail Matron), Irene Winston (Ruth Carlin), David Newell (FBI Agent), Erskine Sanford (Professor), Mishka Egan (Man), David Bond, Eghiche Harout (College Professors), Jimmie Dundee (Taxi Driver).

This is one of the few films that blatantly supported the witchhunts of the McCarthy era, portraying the insidious enemy within as dwelling right in the heart of America— in the home. The alien occupant here is American born and bred Walker, a federal agency worker. He fails to appear at a send off party for his younger brothers Jaeckel and Young, who are about to embark with their unit to fight in the Korean War. Walker shows up later to sneer derision for his brothers' stupidity in fighting for America and make fun of his father in an alma mater speech, mimicking Jagger singing "Uncle Sammy." Walker, the strutting intellectual, so infuriates his Bible-quoting father that Jagger strikes him with the Good Book. Hayes, the ever-devoted mother, cannot believe Heflin, an FBI man who tells her that her son Walker is a traitor and a Communist spy. She goes through hell and then flies to Washington, D.C., where she has Walker swear his allegiance on the Bible, but of course, he's lying. Then Hayes learns that Winston, the girl her son is dating, is also under FBI surveillance and she then accepts the idea that Walker is a Quisling. In the end, however, Walker has a patriotic seizure and, instead of escaping with secrets to Lisbon and the waiting arms of the Communists, he confesses his guilt and is shot to death by Red agents for his candor. He breathes his last on the steps of the Lincoln Memorial and his confession is later played for students at his former high school where Walker's taped talk ends with him pleading for the young to "hold fast to honor." The story is impossible and could have been produced by the House Un-American Activities Committee to support its Spanish Inquisition-type hearings. The film is nevertheless a curiosity because of the stellar talents involved in it. Hayes ended a 17-year hiatus from the screen to make this film and McCarey, one of the brightest Hollywood writer-directors, inexplicably lent his full energies to this embarrassing propaganda. Walker, another brilliant actor, died while the film was still in production and some footage from Alfred Hitchcock's STRANGERS ON A TRAIN, in which Walker had earlier appeared, was used to patch up final scenes. Stradling's cinematography is exceptional.

p&d, Leo McCarey; w, Myles Connolly, McCarey, John Lee Mahin (based on a story by McCarey); ph, Henry Stradling; m, Robert Emmet Dolan; ed, Marvin Coil; art d, Hal Pereira, William Flannery.

Drama   **(PR:C   MPAA:NR)**

MY SON, MY SON!**   (1940) 115m UA bw

Madeleine Carroll (Livia Vaynol), Brian Aherne (William Essex), Louis Hayward (Oliver Essex), Laraine Day (Maeve O'Riorden), Henry Hull (Dermont O'Riorden), Josephine Hutchinson (Nellie Essex), Sophie Stewart (Shella O'Riorden), Bruce Lester (Rory O'Riorden), Scotty Beckett (Oliver as a Child), Brenda Henderson (Maeve as a Child), Teddy Moorwood (Rory as a Child), May Beatty (Annie), Stanley Logan (The Colonel), Lionel Belmore (Mr. Moscrop), Mary Gordon (Mrs. Mulvaney), David Clyde (Drayman), Vesey O'Davoran (Butler), Pat Flaherty (Joe Baxter), Victor Kendall (Pogson), Mary Field (1st Maid), Audrey Manners (2nd Maid), Sibyl Harris (1st Landlady), Connie Leon (2nd Landlady), Howard Davies, Montagu Shaw, Leland Hodgson.

A superb drama has Aherne in one of his best roles as a gentle and considerate writer of romantic novels, a man who sacrifices most of his life for others, chiefly an ungrateful, hurtful son, Hayward. Aherne is a product of the Manchester slums but he struggles heroically and becomes a famous novelist. He is devoted to his son, played first by Beckett, then, as an adult, by Hayward. The boy and then the young man prove, over 25 years, to be thoroughly rotten. Hayward makes fun of his father's writing, brings tragedy to his childhood girl friend Day, and even tries to seduce artist Carroll, the woman his widowed father loves and plans to marry. Yet Aherne cannot bring himself to condemn the boy he has given his heart to. Both wind up in the trenches during WW I, with Aherne covering the war as a correspondent and his son a young officer. Aherne meets his son for the last time and begs him to reform, telling him he still loves him and that he forgives him for breaking his heart. Hayward tells him that his father has loved him too much, but in the end, Hayward redeems himself by dying in a hero's death, leaving Aherne to cry out in agony: "My son, my son!" Carroll is beautiful and Day is pure springtime in this poignant and powerful film but it is cold-hearted Hayward and his merciless inhuman ways who steals this film which Vidor directs with great care and innovative style.

p, Edward Small; d, Charles Vidor; w, Lenore Coffee (based on the novel by Howard Spring); ph, Harry Stradling; ed, Grant Whytock, Fred R. Feitshans; md, Edward Ward; art d, John DuCasse Schultze; spec eff, Howard Anderson.

Drama   **(PR:A   MPAA:NR)**

MY SON NERO   (SEE: NERO'S MISTRESS, 1962, Ital.)

MY SON, THE HERO**   (1943) 66m PRC bw

Patsy Kelly (Gerty), Roscoe Karns (Big Time), Joan Blair (Cynthia), Carol Hughes (Linda), Maxie Rosenbloom (Kid Slug), Luis Alberni (Tony), Joseph Allen, Jr. (Michael), Lois Collier (Nancy), Jennie Le Gon (Lambie), Nick Stewart

(*Nicodemus*), Hal Price (*Manager*), Al St. John (*Night Clerk*), Elvira Curci (*Rositta*), Isobel La Mel (*Mrs. Olmstead*), Maxine Leslie (*Girl Reporter*).

After writing elaborate tales to his war correspondent son (Allen), Karns finds himself in hot water when he receives a telegram announcing Allen's coming visit. With the help of Rosenbloom, as well as ex-wife Kelly, Karns manages to pull off a successful war bond drive. Allen arrives thinking dad's a great local hero and all ends happily. Kelly, as usual, is very funny and Rosenbloom's mugging is good fun. But the film suffers from lackluster direction with no feel for comedy. Consequently this off-the-wall story just doesn't ring true. Weaknesses within the script aren't covered and the film ends up being a minor and disappointing programmer.

p, Peter R. Van Duinen; d, Edgar G. Ulmer; w, Doris Malloy, Ulmer; ph, Robert Cline, Jack Greenhalgh; ed, Charles Henkel, Jr.

Comedy (PR:A MPAA:NR)

MY SON, THE HERO**1/2

(1963, Ital./Fr.) 111m Vides-Ariane-Filmsonor/UA c (ARRIVANO I TITANI; I TITANI; LES TITANS)

Pedro Armendariz (*Cadmus, King of Thebes*), Jacqueline Sassard (*Antiope, Cadmus' Daughter*), Antonella Lualdi (*Hermione*), Giuliano Gemma (*Crios*), Gerard Sety (*Hippolytos*), Serge Nubret (*Rator*), Tanya Lopert (*Licina*), Ingrid Schoeller (*Emerate*), Franco Lantieri, Monika Berger, Isarco Ravaioli, Luisa Ruspoli.

An Italian action picture which had it's original meaning changed, a la Woody Allen's WHAT'S UP TIGER LILY? (1966), through the technique of creative dubbing. Gemma steals a helmet which makes him invisible, enabling him to prove that he is the titan with the most brain and brawn. The jokes wear thin, but this can't-miss approach produces a number of side-splitting laughs.

p, Alexander Mnouchkine; d, Duccio Tessari; w, Tom Rowe (English dialog), Ennio De Cocini, Tessari; ph, Alfio Contini (Technicolor); m, Carlo Rustichelli; ed, Renzo Lucidi; set d, Ottavio Scott; cos, Vittorio Rossi; spec eff, Joseph Natanson.

Comedy (PR:A MPAA:NR)

MY SON, THE VAMPIRE*1/2

(1963, Brit.) 72m Fernwood-REN-Blue Chip bw (AKA: THE VAMPIRE AND THE ROBOT; OLD MOTHER RILEY MEETS THE VAMPIRE; VAMPIRE OVER LONDON; MOTHER RILEY MEETS THE VAMPIRE)

Bela Lugosi (*Baron Von Housen*), Arthur Lucan (*Mrs. Riley*), Dora Bryan (*Tillie*), Richard Wattis (*Police Constable Freddie*), Judith Furse (*Freda*), Philip Leaver (*Anton*), Maria Mercedes (*Julia Loretti*), Roderick Lovell (*Douglas*), David Hurst (*Mugsy*), Hattie Jacques (*Mrs. Jenks*), Graham Moffatt (*Yokel*), Dandy Nichols, Arthur Brander, Ian Wilson, Cyril Smith, Charles Lloyd-Pack, Peter Bathurst, George Benson, David Hannaford, Bill Shine, John le Mesurier.

The last of the OLD MOTHER RILEY series (it began in 1937) sees Lucan again in drag as the Irish scullery maid who gets herself in all sorts of tough spots. In this one, Lucan gets involved with crazed scientist Lugosi, who is out to find the map of a uranium deposit in order to fuel his monster-robot, with which he seeks to control the world. The "vampire" tag was added by the producer in the hopes that an American distributor would decide to release the film in the states, and was explained in the film by Lugosi's penchant for sleeping in coffins and having a strong desire for human blood (the nutty doctor just *thought* he was a vampire). The British retitled the film VAMPIRE OVER LONDON, still seeking American distribution, but no one took. Desperate, the studio tried to create a new film by removing all the Lugosi footage and combining it with new scenes to make the never-to-be-seen epic KING ROBOT, but by this time Lugosi was too ill to participate and the idea was scrapped. Eventually, American exploitation distributor Jack H. Harris bought the rights to the film and attempted to release it as CARRY ON VAMPIRE, but he was sued by the producers of the popular British comedy series. Finally OLD MOTHER RILEY MEETS THE VAMPIRE was released as MY SON THE VAMPIRE in America in 1963, (seven years after Logosi's death) with an introduction by comedian Alan Sherman tacked on. (See OLD MOTHER RILEY series, Index.)

p&d, John Gilling; w, Val Valentine; ph, Stan Pavey, Dudley Lovell; m/l, "My Son the Vampire," Alan Sherman.

Horror/Comedy (PR:A MPAA:NR)

MY SONG FOR YOU***

(1935, Brit.) 75m GAU bw

Jan Kiepura (*Gatti*), Sonnie Hale (*Charlie*), Emlyn Williams (*Theodore*), Aileen Marson (*Mary Newberg*), Gina Malo (*Fifi*), Muriel George (*Mrs. Newberg*), George Merritt (*Mr. Newberg*), Reginald Smith (*Kleeberg*), Bruce Winston.

A hot shot young tenor (Kiepura) comes to Venice for a production of "Aida." Bored between rehearsals, he amuses himself by drawing cartoons. Marson is a young girl who sneaks into the opera house and captures the roving eye of Kiepura. He asks her to tea but she declines. It seems she has been set up by her pianist fiance to try to obtain a position in the opera's orchestra. Eventually she consents to tea and tells Kiepura the story, changing her fiance's position to her "brother." He discovers the deception, but gives a card that will get the man the job. Marson is filled with guilt and angrily tears up the card. She breaks off the engagement, and consents to marry her parents' choice, a wealthy society man. But right before the wedding, she changes her mind and marries Kiepura instead. Charming in parts, this is a nicely done musical with some good detailed direction.

p, Jerome Jackson; d, Maurice Elvey; w, Austin Melford, Robert Edmunds, Richard Benson (based on "Ein Leid fur Dich" by Ernst Marischka, Irma Von Cube); ph, Charles Van Enger; m, Mischa Spoliansky; md, Louis Levy; m/l, Spoliansky, F. Eyton.

Musical (PR:A MPAA:NR)

MY SONG GOES ROUND THE WORLD*1/2

(1934, Brit.) 68m BIP/Wardour bw

Joseph Schmidt (*Ricardo*), John Loder (*Rico*), Charlotte Ander (*Nina*), Jack Barty (*Simoni*), Jimmy Godden (*Manager*), Hal Gordon (*Stage Manager*).

Schmidt is a tenor for a singing trio. He has designs on Ander, the group's lady singer, but despite his recordings and stage successes, the short man loses her to the group's third (and taller) member, handsome Loder. Schmidt isn't the only short thing in this dumb comedy.

p&d, Richard Oswald; w, Clifford Grey, Frank Miller (based on "Ein Leid Geht Um Die Welt" by Ernst Neubach); ph, Reinhardt Kuntze.

Musical (PR:A MPAA:NR)

MY SOUL RUNS NAKED (SEE: RAT FINK, 1965)

MY TEENAGE DAUGHTER (SEE: TEENAGE BAD GIRL, 1956, Brit.)

MY THIRD WIFE BY GEORGE (SEE: MY THIRD WIFE GEORGE, 1968)

MY THIRD WIFE GEORGE**

(1968) 66m K&W/Monique-J.E.R. bw (AKA: MY THIRD WIFE BY GEORGE)

Thomas Wood (*Ralph Higbee*), Ingrid Kerr (*Gigi*), Duke Moberly (*Doc Holliday*), Joseph Sexhauer (*Charlie*), Douglas Blake (*Mother Higbee*), Regina Koo (*Maid*), Erika Von Zaros (*Josephine Higbee*), Bunny Ware (*Polly, 1st Hippy*), Barbara Walker (*Trixie, 2nd Hippy*), Sheila Howard (*Chloe, 3rd Hippy*), Dan Roper (*Swimming Instructor*), Olivar Farquat (*Fencing Instructor*), Chris Martell (*Gorilla*), Gene Burk (*Private Detective*), Bonnie Laurant (*Public Stenographer*), Claude Pounds (*Photographer*), Majesta (*Stripper*), Jeri Winters (*Georgie Higbee*), Cal Slade, Belle Teleone (*The Couple*).

Off-beat comedy stars Wood as a man severely dominated by his mother until her death, when he is 40 years old. Life after that is one mad rollercoaster ride after another. First he meets 3 hippies who introduce him to LSD and then invite him to participate in an all-night orgy, which he does. Soon after he marries Von Zaros, but she turns out to be too kinky for him and he promptly divorces her. His next wife marries him for his money, but when she demands a divorce, he refuses. Undaunted, she hires detectives to trail him, hoping to catch him in the act of being unfaithful. This fails, so they force him at gunpoint to rape a virgin. After he divorces his second wife, Wood marries for the third time. This marriage is reasonably successful, until Wood has an affair. Jealous, his wife decides to teach him a lesson he will never forget.

p&d, Harry E. Kerwin; w, Wayne Rafferty; ph, Tom Barnett; m, Sol Tosco; ed, Kerwin, Earl Wainwright; set d, Pierre Du Kane; makeup, Edith Johns.

Comedy (PR:A MPAA:NR)

MY TRUE STORY*1/2

(1951) 67m COL bw

Helen Walker (*Ann Martin*), Willard Parker (*Bill Phillips*), Elisabeth Risdon (*Mme. Rousseau*), Emory Parnell (*Ed Praskins*), Aldo DaRe [Ray] (*Mark Foster*), Wilton Graff (*George Trent*), Ivan Triesault (*Alexis Dellos*), Ben Welden (*Buzz Edwards*), Fred J. Sears (*Carlyle*), Mary Newton (*Miss Harrison*), Ann Tyrell (*Sophie*).

Produced in association with *True Story* magazine, this is a classic tabloid plot. Walker plays a convicted jewel thief who is paroled thanks to Graff, a mob boss. He wants her to help him steal some expensive perfume from wealthy widow Risdon. But Walker wants to go straight and with the help of policeman Parker, she foils the nefarious scheme. Everything here is routine and uninteresting, from the bland performances to the cliched script. Much of the film's trouble lies in the direction. Amateurish, with a poor sense of timing and suspense, this film has the dubious distinction of being the first directorial effort of none other than Mickey Rooney. Note early appearance by Aldo Ray under his real name.

p, Milton Feldman; d, Mickey Rooney; w, Howard J. Green, Brown Holmes (based on a story by Margit Mantical); ph, Henry Freulich; ed, Richard Fantl; md, Mischa Bakaleinikoff; art d, Cary Odell.

Crime (PR:A MPAA:NR)

MY TUTOR**

(1983) 97m Marimark/Crown International c

Caren Kaye (*Terry*), Matt Lattanzi (*Bobby Chrystal*), Kevin McCarthy (*Mr. Chrystal*), Clark Brandon (*Billy*), Bruce Bauer (*Don*), Arlene Golonka (*Mrs. Chrystal*), Crispin Glover (*Jack*), Amber Denyse Austin (*Bonnie*), John Vargas (*Manuel*), Maria Melendez (*Maria*), Graem McGavin (*Sylvia*), Rex Ryon (*Biker*), Kathleen Shea (*Mud Wrestler*), Brioni Farrel (*Mrs. Fontana*), Shelley Taylor Morgan (*Louisa*), Kitten Natividad (*Ana Maria*), Jewel Shepard (*Girl in Phone Booth*), Michael Yama (*Russell*), Robin Honeywell (*Sue-Ann*), Mora Gray (*Ramona*), Jim Kester (*Parking Attendant*), Derek Partridge (*Waiter*), Gene Patton (*Workman*), Eric Lantis (*Weight Lifter*), Lyle Kanouse (*Biker*), Marilyn Tokuda (*Aerobics Instructor*), Jacqueline Jacobs (*Bootsie*).

Another in a line of 1980s films is the older woman/teenage boy love affair. Catering to the ultimate in adolescent fantasies, this genre produced such forgettable pictures as HOMEWORK and PRIVATE LESSONS. MY TUTOR is more of the same. Lattanzi plays a teenage boy who does well in all of his subjects except two, French and sex. His father, McCarthy, hires a tutor, played by Kaye, to help teach his boy French. She helps him with the language and a whole lot more. McCarthy openly lusts after her, but she prefers the sensitive son. There's some amusing moments early in the film, as Lattanzi's friends try to teach him about sex as only teenaged boys can. Kaye is surprisingly intelligent in a role that only requires her to bare her flesh and speak some French. The real irony is that this picture's R rating means the adolescent audience it is aimed at can't even get into the theaters to see the film.

p, Marilyn J. Tenser; d, George Bowers; w, Joe Roberts (based on the story by Mark

Tenser); ph, Mac Ahlberg (Deluxe Color); m, Webster Lewis; ed, Sidney Wolinsky; art d, Linda Pearl; cos, Kristin Nelson.

Teenage Drama Cas. **(PR:O MPAA:R)**

MY TWO HUSBANDS (SEE: TOO MANY HUSBANDS, 1940)

MY UNCLE****
(1958, Fr.) 110m Specta-Gray-Alter-Cady Film del Centauro/Continental c (MON ONCLE)

Jacques Tati (*Mons. Hulot*), Jean-Pierre Zola (*Mons. Arpel*), Adrienne Servantie (*Mme. Arpel*), Alain Becourt (*Gerald Arpel*), Lucien Fregis (*Mons. Pichard*), Betty Schneider (*Betty, Landlord's Daughter*), Yvonne Arnaud (*Georgette, Arpel's Maid*), Dominique Marie (*Neighbor*), J. F. Martial (*Walter*), Andre Dino (*Sweep*), Claude Badolle (*Rag Picker*), Nicolas Bataille (*Worker*), Regis Fontenay (*Suspenders Seller*), Adelaide Danielli (*Mme. Pichard*), Denise Peronne (*Mlle. Fevier*), Michel Goyot (*Car Seller*), Dominique Derly (*Arpel's Secretary*), Max Martel, Francomme, Claire Rocca, Jean Remoleux, Rene Lord, Nicole Regnault, Loriot, Mancini, Jean Meyet, Suzanne Franck.

Tati, France's most loved director, follows MR. HULOT'S HOLIDAY (1953) with this impressive satire on technological gadgetry and the people who devote their lives to modern convenience. Tati himself is cast in the role of Hulot, the disheveled common man who seems as helpless as a lost puppy in the rain. Content with living in neglected quarters, Tati is contrasted with his brother-in-law Zola, who lives in stylized, modernized, desensitized suburbia. Zola's house is cluttered with gadgets that are meant to save time but instead do nothing but waste it, while filling the room with clanking noises. The simple life style proves attractive to Becourt, Zola's young son, who prefers his uncle Hulot's back-street environment. As much as he would like to, Tati cannot completely escape modernization. The film's most precious scenes are those in which he must battle the stubbornness of modern appliances—this lucid visual style perfectly countering his frustration. Life becomes more complex for Tati when he is employed by Zola and sent away on business. To this end Tati has learned something about modern living, while Zola and Becourt are once again able to communicate as real people. MY UNCLE is less a condemnation of technology than it is of those people who become enslaved to it. It is not until Tati's next film PLAYTIME (1967) that these ideas are fully developed. Tati, who completed only six films in nearly 30 years, has described his own comedy as a "laughter born of a certain fundamental absurdity. Some things are not funny of themselves but become so on being dissected." It is this quality that Tati's films share which such effective satires as Rene Clair's A NOUS LA LIBERTE (1931), Charles Chaplin's MODERN TIMES (1936), and even Albert Brooks' LOST IN AMERICA (1985).

p&d, Jacques Tati; w, Tati, Jacques Lagrange, Jean L'Hote; ph, Jean Bourgoin (Eastmancolor); m, Franck Barcellini, Alains Romans; ed, Suzanne Baron; art d, Henri Schmitt, Pierre Etaix.

Comedy Cas. **(PR:AAA MPAA:NR)**

MY UNCLE ANTOINE***1/2
(1971, Can.) 110m National Film Board of Canada/Gendon c (MON ONCLE ANTOINE)

Jean Duceppe (*Uncle Antoine*), Olivette Thibault (*Aunt Cecile*), Claude Jutra (*Fernand, Clerk*), Jacques Gagnon (*Benoit*), Lyne Champagne (*Carmen*), Lionel Villeneauve (*Joe Poulin*), Helene Loiselle (*Mme. Poulin*), Mario Dubuc, Lise Burnelle, Alain Legendre, Serge Evers, Robin Marcoux (*Poulin Children*), Monique Mercure (*Alexandrine*), Georges Alexander (*The Big Boss*), Rene Salvatore Catta (*The Priest*), Jean Dubost (*The Foreman*), Benoit Marcoux (*Carmen's Father*), Dominque Joly (*Maurice*), Lise Talbot, Michel Talbot (*The Engaged Couple*), Simeon Dallaire (*A Client*), Sydney Harris (*The Helper*), Roger Garland (*Euclide*).

Though a boy's coming of age has been given innumberable screen treatments, MY UNCLE ANTOINE must rank as one of the best of the genre. Gagnon is a 14-year-old orphan living in a small French Canadian mining town during the 1940s. Under the care of aunt and uncle Thibault and Duceppe, who run the local general store, Gagnon participates in the annual Christmas celebration by flirting with Champagne, his foster sister, but the adults put a stop to this. That evening the townspeople gather at the store for the annual holiday gathering. A phone call interrupts the festivities when Loiselle needs Duceppe's services. (In addition to running the store, he is also the local undertaker.) Loiselle's son has just died, and with her husband away at a logging camp, she needs the man to remove the body. Gagnon accompanies his uncle on the sleigh ride to the home. On the way back, the old man reflects on his life while slowly getting drunk. The sleigh goes out of control and the casket falls off. Since his uncle is too drunk to help recover it, Gagnon must rush back to the store for help. There he finds his aunt and a store clerk locked in a tight embrace. The clerk (Jutra) goes to help, but they discover the casket missing. Arriving at the deceased boy's home, Gagnon looks through the window and sees the family sadly standing over the body. Apparently his father had found the body and taken it back home. Gagnon is left alone with his thoughts, learning much about human nature and its foibles on this Christmas Eve. This sad heart-felt drama avoids cliches and shows genuine sensitivity for its subject. There isn't a false note in the story. Gagnon carries his load well, giving the kind of sincere performance that other actors take years to achieve. The story had some basis in truth. Screenwriter Perron had grown up in the French Canadian mining areas and used his childhood memories to fashion the screenplay. The direction, though for the most part strong, has an annoying predilection for the zoom lens, using it more often than needed. Occasionally the zooming defeats its own purpose, imposing false drama where it should simply have allowed characters and actions to speak for themselves. Overall though, this is a beautiful piece and took Grand Prize at the 1971 Chicago Film Festival. (In French; English subtitles.)

p, Marc Beaudet; d, Claude Jutra; w, Jutra, Clement Perron (based on a story by Perron); ph, Michel Brault (Eastmancolor); m, Jean Cousineau; ed, Jutra, Claire Boyer; art d, Denis Boucher, Lawrence O'Brien; makeup, Suzanne Garand, Rene Demers.

Drama **(PR:C MPAA:NR)**

MY UNCLE FROM AMERICA (SEE: MON ONCLE D'AMERIQUE, 1980, Fr.)

MY UNCLE, MR. HULOT (SEE: MY UNCLE, 1958, Fr.)

MY UNIVERSITY (SEE: UNIVERSITY OF LIFE, 1941, USSR)

MY WAY**
(1974, South Africa) 92m Joseph Brenner Associates c (AKA: THE WINNER)

Joe Stewardson (*Will Maddox*), Richard Loring (*Paul Maddox*), Marie Du Toit (*Fran Maddox*), Tony Jay (*Natie Kaplan*), Madeleine Usher (*Gillian Scott*), John Higgins (*Barry Maddox*), Ken Leach (*Tony Maddox*), Diane Ridler (*Gina*), Jenny Meyer (*Sandra Maddox*), Ian Yule (*Andy*), Gregorio Fiascanaro (*Mario*), Clive Scott (*Reporter*), Barbara Kinghorn (*Daisy*), John Hayter (*Doctor*), Norman Coombes (*Chairman*), Marcello Fianscanaro (*McAllister*), Kerry Jordan, Maria Bosworth, Sheilagh Holliday, Peter Tobin, Penny Jackson, Bart Ceccon, Edward Davies, Gillian Garlick, Richard Knibbs, Lorraine Lithgow, Julian Osieki, Kevin Basel.

A sports-filled drama follows the inner turmoil of a family ruled by a driven man. Stewardson is a former Olympic champion who wants his sons to be as successful as he is. He pushes them to compete, with victory being the only goal. When one son is killed and another severely injured in a big auto race, the family turns on Stewardson. The story climaxes with a marathon race between father and son, with Stewardson losing and learning something about competition. This old story is told reasonably well, but the film is padded with far too much footage of various competitions, including auto races, track competitions, and swim meets. Much of this has little to do with the story and severely limits what the actors can do with their parts. Another bothersome note is the total absence of blacks in any role. Though a minority, the whites rule South Africa, and without so much as a single black face (even in crowd scenes), MY WAY reflects the racist situation that exists there.

p, Emil Nofal; d, Nofal, Roy Sargent; w, Nofal; ph, Vincent G. Cox (Technicolor); ed, David De Beyer, Peter Henkel; md, Robin Netcher.

Sports/Family Drama **(PR:A MPAA:PG)**

MY WAY HOME zero (1978, Brit.) 78m British Film Institute bw
Confused presentation shows aimless life of bored Scottish lad named Jamie from a squalid youth home to his first friendship while in the armed forces. This last film of a trilogy might have been less muddled had one the benefit of the earlier parts.
d&w, Bill Douglas.

Drama **(PR:C MPAA:NR)**

MY WEAKNESS*** (1933) 72m FOX bw
Lillian Harvey (*Looloo Blake*), Lew Ayres (*Ronnie Gregory*), Charles Butterworth (*Gerald Gregory*), Harry Langdon (*Cupid*), Sid Silvers (*Maxie*), Irene Bentley (*Jane Holman*), Henry Travers (*Ellery Gregory*), Adrian Rosely (*Baptiste*), Mary Howard (*Diana Griffith*), Irene Ware (*Eve Millstead*), Barbara Weeks (*Lois Crowley*), Susan Fleming (*Jacqueline Wood*), Marcelle Edwards, Marjorie King, Jean Allen, Gladys Blake, Dixie Francis.

A "Cinderella" type story stars Harvey as a simple hotel clerk. She's mad for Ayres but can't match him in sophistication. Her girl friends take two weeks to transform Harvey from her common status into a classy socialite. Of course she ends up with Ayres, but not without some problems along the way. Butterworth is an "ardent philatelist" who almost wins Harvey's heart. Langdon, looking painfully old with his well-known baby face showing its lines, is Cupid guiding his charge to a successful romance. This was Harvey's American debut after a successful career with Ufa in Germany. She is an ethereal presence, making the fantasy work with her charm and grace. Some unusual production numbers are included. One imaginative sequence contains a chorus of singing toy animals and building gargoyles. Also included is a shot of four fan magazines with Will Rogers, Clara Bow, Warner Baxter, and Janet Gaynor on the respective covers. Like the toys, these famous faces also sang, using the voices of the real stars. Song include: "How Do I Look?" "Gather Lip Rouge While You May," "You Can Be Had So Be Careful."

p, B.G. De Sylva; d, David Butler; w, De Sylva, Butler, Ben Ryan, Bert Hanlon; ph, Arthur Miller; ed, Irene Morra; m/l, De Sylva, Leo Robin, Richard A. Whiting.

Musical Fantasy **(PR:AAA MPAA:NR)**

MY WIDOW AND I*** (1950, Ital.) 81m Fauno/Distinguished Films bw
Vittorio De Sica (*Adriano Lari*), Isa Miranda (*Maria Lari*), Gino Cervi (*Guglielmi*), Dina Galli (*Mme. Guglielmi*), Luigi Almiranti (*Caretaker*).

Neo-realist director De Sica makes a rare acting appearance in this off-beat Italian comedy. He plays a man who pretends he is dead so that he and his wife, Miranda, can cash in on his huge insurance policy. He pretends to be his brother-in-law, but trouble arises when his former employer, Cervi, makes a play for the bereaved "widow." He also has to endure Cervi insulting his memory. The story takes a twist towards pathos when the wealthy employer wins over Miranda. Having lost his wife and his job, De Sica becomes a grave digger at the cemetery he is supposedly buried in. Though the initial gag wears thin, there is some genuine wit within the occasionally over-talky screenplay. De Sica is not bad as an actor, giving a good black-comic performance. Miranda is equally as funny as his confused wife caught up in their web of lies. (In Italian; English subtitles.)

d, Carlo L. Bragaglia; w, Aldo de Benedetti; ph, Arturo Gallea; m, Nino Rota; English subtitles, William Mishkin.

Comedy (PR:C MPAA:NR)

MY WIFE'S BEST FRIEND**   (1952) 87m FOX bw

Anne Baxter (*Virginia Mason*), Macdonald Carey (*George Mason*), Cecil Kellaway (*Rev. Chamberlain*), Casey Adams [Max Showalter] (*Pete Bentham*), Catherine McLeod (*Jane Richards*), Leif Erickson (*Nicholas Reed*), Frances Bavier (*Mrs. Chamberlain*), Martin Milner (*Buddy Chamberlain*), Billie Bird (*Katie*), Wild Red Berry, Henry Kulky (*Pugs*), John Hedloe (*Pilot*), John McKee (*Co-Pilot*), Phil Hartman (*Cab Driver*), Michael Ross (*Mike*), Junius Matthews (*Dr. Smith*), Joe Hanworth (*Steward*), Ed Dearing (*Police Chief*), Morgan Farley (*Dr. McCarran*), Ann Staunton (*Hannah*), Emmett Vogan (*Walter Rogers*), May Winn (*Stewardess*).

A plane develops engine trouble and appears to be going down. Baxter and Carey, a couple en route to Hawaii for their eighth anniversary, bare all to each other in what they believe to be their last moments together. She begs forgiveness for being an overdemanding, selfish wife. He forgives her, and then makes the mistake of confessing about having had an affair three years ago with her best friend, McLeod. Baxter, it seems, is not quite as forgiving. She fantasizes all sorts of tortures for her husband, including imagining herself as both Joan of Arc and Cleopatra, each giving Carey historically appropriate punishments. After the plane has landed safely in their home base, Carey gets the silent treatment from Baxter until he has his wife's minister, Kellaway, talk to her about forgiving and forgetting. After that, Baxter goes through several stages in her attempt to deal with her husband's affair, including working like a slave to help his business and then making a big play for his boss, Erickson. But the couple is reconciled in the end when Carey admits that the affair was all basically in his mind. It seems that after he made his big move on McLeod, he passed out from one too many martinis. While the script is imaginative, this film pulls all the stops trying to be overly humorous when a more sedate, witty style would have been more appropriate. As it is, MY WIFE'S BEST FRIEND works in parts, but fails to work overall.

p, Robert Bassler; d, Richard Sale; w, Isobel Lennart (based on a story by John Briard Harding); ph, Leo Tover; m, Leigh Harline; ed, Robert Simpson; md, Lionel Newman; art d, Lyle Wheeler, Mark Lee Kirk; set d, Thomas Little, Stuart Reiss.

Comedy (PR:A MPAA:NR)

MY WIFE'S ENEMY**   (1967, Ital.) 90m DD/Magna Pictures bw (IL NEMICO DI MIA MOGLIE)

Marcello Mastroianni (*Marco*), Giovanna Ralli (*Luciana*), Memmo Carotenuto (*Nando*), Luciana Paluzzi (*Giulia*), Andrea Checchi, Giacomo Furia, Vittorio De Sica, Teddy Reno [Ricordi Ferruccio], Riccardo Garrone, Gisella Sofio, Salvo Libassi, Raimondo Vianello.

Italian melodrama about Mastroianni, a soccer referee, who loves soccer more than his wife, Ralli. His strained marriage is further weakened by Mastroianni's father, who dislikes Ralli and soccer. After each has resorted to several affairs, they attend a soccer match where they realize that they really do love each other. Also stars famous Italian neorealist director, De Sica.

d, Gianni Puccini; w, Bruno Baratti, Renato Castellani, Pipolo [Giuseppe Moccia], Puccini; ph, Gianni Di Venanzo.

Comedy (PR:A MPAA:NR)

MY WIFE'S FAMILY**   (1932, Brit.) 80m BIP bw

Gene Gerrard (*Jack Gay*), Muriel Angelus (*Peggy Gay*), Amy Veness (*Arabella Nagg*), Charles Paton (*Noah Nagg*), Dodo Watts (*Ima Nagg*), Tom Helmore (*Willie Nagg*), Molly Lamont (*Sally*), Ellen Pollock (*Dolly White*), Jimmy Godden (*Doc Knott*).

This mildly amusing British farce is hampered by dusty jokes about mothers-in-law, bad puns, and a variety of old gags. The premise has Angelus overhearing her husband, Gerrard, in conversation. She thinks he's talking with a doctor about his out-of-wedlock child. Actually, he's chatting with a piano tuner about a new instrument. Typically British in humor, MY WIFE'S FAMILY was remade in 1941 and again in 1956.

p, John Maxwell; d, Monty Banks; w, Fred Duprez, Val Valentine (based on the play by Duprez, Hal Stephens, Harry B. Linton); ph, Claude Friese-Greene; ed, A. C. Hammond.

Comedy (PR:A MPAA:NR)

MY WIFE'S FAMILY**   (1941, Brit.) 82m ABF/Pathe bw

Charlie Clapham (*Doc Knott*), John Warwick (*Jack Gay*), Patricia Roc (*Peggy Gay*), Wylie Watson (*Noah Bagshott*), Chili Bouchier (*Rosa Latour*), Peggy Bryan (*Sally*), Margaret Scudamore (*Arabella Bagshott*), Leslie Fuller (*Policeman*), David Tomlinson (*Willie Bagshott*), Joan Greenwood (*Irma Bagshott*).

Every old joke you never wanted to hear repeated is packed into this dusty, but still mildly amusing comedy. Warwick and beautiful Roc are a married couple who get some unwanted troubles from Wagnerian-voiced mother-in-law Scudamore, her husband Watson, traveling man Clapham, and actress Bouchier. Expected situations pop up right on schedule from Bouchier being caught in a clinch with Watson, to a hidden piano being mistaken for an illegitimate child. One-time box office great Fuller contributes in his role as a policeman. It was only the second film for 20-year-old petite seductress Greenwood, who would later take her distinctly velvety voice to Broadway and Hollywood.

p&d, Walter C. Mycroft; w, Norman Lee, Clifford Grey (based on the play by Fred Duprez); ph, Walter Harvey.

Comedy (PR:A MPAA:NR)

MY WIFE'S FAMILY* 1/2   (1962, Brit.) 76m Forth Films/ABF/Pathe c

Ronald Shiner (*Doc Knott*), Ted Ray (*Jack Gay*), Greta Gynt (*Gloria Marsh*), Robertson Hare (*Noah Parker*), Fabia Drake (*Arabella Parker*), Diane Hart (*Stella Gay*), Zena Marshall (*Hilda*), Benny Lee (*Arnold*), Jessica Cairns (*Irma Parker*), Jimmy Mageean (*Dobson*), Gilbert Harding (*Himself*), Virginia Clay, Martin Wyldeck, Patrick Westwood, Robert Dickens, Charles Wright, Peggyann Clifford, Laurie Main, Frank Hawkins, Ian Whittaker, Audrey Nicholson, Ian Wilson, Charles Doran, Frank Royde.

The third screen version of Fred Duprez's play proves once and for all there's no hope of reviving the dead. Ray is the newlywed with the overbearing mother-in-law who ends up being accused of fathering an illegitimate child when he tries to surprise his wife with a baby grand piano. The arrival of Ray's old sweetheart, blonde glamor girl Gynt, further complicates matters. The farce is overplayed without shame, but that doesn't help the ancient jokes any.

p, Hamilton Inglis; d, Gilbert Gunn; w, Talbot Rothwell, Gunn (based on the play by Fred Duprez); ph, Gilbert Taylor (Eastmancolor).

Comedy (PR:A MPAA:NR)

MY WIFE'S HUSBAND**

(1965, Fr./Ital.) 85m Corona-Dear/Lopert c (LA CUISINE AU BEURRE; CUCINA AL BURRO)

Fernandel (*Fernand Jouvin*), Bourvil (*Andre Colomber*), Claire Maurier (*Christiane Colomber*), Henri Vilbert (*Me Sarrazin, Lawyer*), Michel Galabru (*Maximin*), Andrex (*Pellatan*), Mag-Avril (*Mme. Rose*), Evelyne Selena (*Louise*), Laurence Ligneres (*Marinette*), Henri Arius (*The Mayor*), Gaston Rey (*Espinasse*), Ardisson (*Carlotti*), Andre Tomasi (*Gervasoni*), Anne Marie Carriere (*Gerda*), Roger Bernard (*Fernand's Nephew*).

Comedian Fernandel is a French prisoner of war in WWII who escapes and hides out at an inn run by Carriere. When the war ends, Fernandel decides to stay with her and help her run the inn, instead of returning home to his wife. Ten years later, Carriere's husband returns, so she sends Fernandel back to his wife, where he finds much has changed in the last decade. His little cafe has expanded and his wife is now married to Bourvil, Fernandel's former chef. Seeing that Fernandel is still alive, Maurier refuses to sleep with Bourvil until Fernandel gives her a divorce. Feeling he is out of the picture, Bourvil returns home to Normandy. Fernandel goes after Bourvil and tells him he will grant the divorce if Bourvil will come back and marry Maurier and take responsibility for the restaurant. Alone now, Fernandel becomes depressed until Carriere shows up and tells him that her husband has left for Siberia, and that they are now free to wed.

p, Robert Dorfman, Louis Manella; d, Gilles Grangier; w, Jean Levitte, Pierre Levy-Corti, Michel Galabru; ph, Roger Hubert; m, Jean Marion; ed, Madeleine Gug; art d, Rino Mondellini.

Comedy (PR:A MPAA:NR)

MY WIFE'S LODGER**   (1952, Brit.) 80m Advance/Adelphi bw

Dominic Roche (*Willie Higginbotham*), Olive Sloane (*Maggie Higginbotham*), Leslie Dwyer (*Roger the Lodger*), Diana Dors (*Eunice Higginbotham*), Alan Sedgwick (*Tex*), Vincent Downing (*Norman Higginbotham*), Vi Kaley (*Mother-in-Law*).

Upon returning home from six years of military service, Roche has an unpleasant surprise awaiting. His house now resembles a circus, with Dwyer a lodger who is loved by all. After getting drunk, Roche learns that he's inherited a Texas ranch. Dwyer is also revealed to be a crook, finally bringing some peace to the ex-soldier. It's not much of a farce, but the energy of the ensemble partly makes up for its lack of coherence and taste.

p, David Dent; d, Maurice Elvey; w, Dominic Roche, Stafford Dickens (based on the play by Roche); ph, Len Harris.

Comedy (PR:A MPAA:NR)

MY WIFE'S RELATIVES*   (1939) 65m REP bw

James Gleason (*Joe Higgins*), Lucille Gleason (*Lil Higgins*), Russell Gleason (*Sid Higgins*), Harry Davenport (*Grandpa Higgins*), Mary Hart (*Jean Higgins*), Purnell Pratt (*Mr. Ellis*), Maude Eburne (*Widow Jones*), Marjorie Gateson (*Mrs. Ellis*), Tommy Ryan (*Tommy Higgins*), Henry Arthur (*Bill Ellis*), Sally Payne (*Lizzie*), Edward Keane (*Jarvis*).

This entry in the Higgins family series offers little more than cliched gag lines and an overused plot. The conventional story-line is the old boy-meets-girl, with his wealthy parents unhappy that he wants to marry below his station. Hart is the poor man's daughter involved in romance with the candy baron's son, Arthur. Her father, Gleason, starts his own candy factory that takes off overnight when his wife loses her diamond ring, offers $5,000 for its recovery, and the misquoted ad states that it's in one of the candy bars. (See HIGGINS FAMILY series, Index.)

p, Sol C. Siegel; d, Gus Meins; w, Jack Townley (based on the story by Dorrell McGowan, Stuart McGowan); ph, Jack Marta; ed, Ernest Nims.

Family Comedy (PR:AAA MPAA:NR)

MY WILD IRISH ROSE** 1/2   (1947) 101m WB c

Dennis Morgan (*Chauncey Olcott/Jack Chancellor*), Arlene Dahl (*Rose Donovan*), Andrea King (*Lillian Russell*), Alan Hale (*John Donovan*), George Tobias (*Nick Popolis*), George O'Brien (*William "Duke" Muldoon*), Sara Allgood (*Mrs. Brennan*), Ben Blue (*Hopper*), William Frawley (*William Scanlan*), Don McGuire (*Terry O'Rourke*), Charles Irwin (*Foote*), Clifton Young (*Joe Brennan*), Paul Stanton (*Augustus Pitou*), George Cleveland (*Capt. Brennan*), Oscar O'Shea (*Pat Daly*), Ruby Dandridge (*Della*), William B. Davidson (*Brewster*), Douglas Wood (*Rawson*), Charles Marsh (*Stone*), Grady Sutton (*Brown*), Andrew Tombes (*Hermon*), Robert Lowell (*Tenor*), Philo McCullough (*Theater Manager*), Gino Corrado (*Maitre 'D*),

Eddie Parker (*Bruiser*), Ross Ford (*Office Boy*), Eddie Kane (*Joe Webb*), Tom Stevenson (*Lee*), Peggy Knudsen (*Eileen, Leading Lady*), Monte Blue (*Barman*), Wally Ruth (*Drummer*), Emmett Vogan (*Doctor*), Edward Clark (*Justice of the Peace*), William Gould (*Mr. O'Rourke*), Brandon Hurst (*Michael the Gardener*), Forbes Murray (*Stage Father*), Winifred Harris (*Stage Mother*), Billy Greene (*Riverboat Captain*), Penny Edwards (*Singer*), Rodney Bell (*Pat*), Igor Dega, Pierre Andre, The Three Dunhills, Lou Wills, Jr. (*Specialties*).

Hollywood went through a spate of musicals based on the lives of famous song composers. Warner Brothers had just about run out of musicals when along came the story of Chauncey Olcott, composer of "My Wild Irish Rose" and "Mother Machree." If the real Olcott led the life that this film depicts, then it's understandable why Irishmen drink so much. Morgan in the lead role has him getting involved with famed vaudevillian Lillian Russell (played by King). The only real standout is Dahl in one of her first roles, as the alderman's daughter that Morgan finally marries. Confusingly told, the story is dotted with dance numbers and Olcott's songs. Songs include: "Mother Machree" (Chauncey Olcott, Ernest R. Ball, Rida Johnson Young), "When Irish Eyes Are Smiling" (Olcott, Ball, George Graff, Jr.), "Wee Rose of Killarney," "Miss Lindy Lou," "There's Room in My Heart For Them All," "The Natchez and the Robert E. Lee" (M. K. Jerome, Ted Koehler), "One Little, Sweet Little Girl" (Dan Sullivan), "My Wild Irish Rose" (Olcott), "A Little Bit of Heaven" (J. Keirn Brennan, Ball), "My Nellie's Blue Eyes" (William J. Scanlan), "Come Down Ma' Evenin' Star" (Edgar Smith, John Stromberg).

p, William Jacobs; d, David Butler; w, Peter Milne, Edwin Gilbert, Sidney Fields (based on the story "Song in His Heart" by Rita Olcott); ph, Arthur Edeson, William V. Skall (Technicolor); m, Max Steiner; ed, Irene Morris; md, Leo F. Forbstein; art d, Ed Carrere, Harry Barndollar; ch, Le Roy Prinz.

Musical   **(PR:A MPAA:NR)**

MY WOMAN**   (1933) 73m COL bw

Helen Twelvetrees (*Connie Riley*), Victor Jory (*John Bradley, Radio Network President*), Wallace Ford (*Chick Rollins*), Claire Dodd (*Muriel Bennett*), Warren Hymer (*Al the Butler*), Raymond Brown (*Pop Riley*), Hobart Cavanaugh (*Mr. Miller*), Charles Levison (*Agent*), Ralph Freud (*Mr. McCluskey*), William Jeffrey (*Cargie*), Lester Crawford (*Treech*), Boothe Howard (*Webster*), Edwin Stanley (*Studio Manager*), Lorin Raker (*Assistant Manager*), Harry Holman (*2nd Agent*).

The old show business story of rags-to-riches-to-rags with a radio setting. Ford is a song and dance man who starts out small, but gets some lucky breaks and finds himself a success. With his new found fame comes an over-swelled ego which untimately leads to his downfall. Entertaining enough, with okay production. The ending, where Ford's wife reconciles with her caddish husband, is a little hard to swallow.

d, Victor Schertzinger; w, Brian Marlowe (based on a story by Marlowe); ph, Benjamin Kline; m, Schertzinger.

Drama   **(PR:A MPAA:NR)**

MY WORLD DIES SCREAMING**
                             (1958) 81m Howco International/States Rights bw

Gerald Mohr (*Philip Tierney*), Cathy O'Donnell (*Sheila Wayne*), William Ching (*Mark Snell*), John Qualen (*Jonah Snell*), Barry Bernard (*Dr. Victor Forel*).

Film opens with a dialog by Mohr explaining, "Not only will this picture communicate with you visually, but subconsciously through your brain." From there it's hardly a subconscious journey, as Mohr makes his wife confront her internal demons. He takes O'Donnell back to the mansion where as a child she witnessed a brutal axe murder. Of course this cures the poor woman of her horror complex, but not before the audience has been scared as well. Though short on action and long on dialog, this film does have some interesting moments of suspense as Mohr and O'Donnell lurk about the mansion. But the big pay off never really happens and the film comes full circle, using a strange and effective epilogue as Mohr returns to explain, "What's been getting to your subconscious mind." Images of fluttering hands and crawling snakes are superimposed, causing an interesting and mildly disturbing effect.

p, William S. Edwards; d, Harold Daniels; w, Robert C. Dennis; ph, Frederick West; m, Darrell Calker; ed, Tholen Gladden.

Psy/Horror   **(PR:C MPAA:NR)**

MYRT AND MARGE zero
                           (1934) 65m UNIV bw (GB: LAUGHTER IN THE AIR)

Myrtle Vail (*Myrt Minter*), Donna Damerel (*Marge Spear*), Trixie Friganza (*Mrs. Minter, Myrt's Mother*), Eddie Foy, Jr. (*Eddie Hanley, Comic*), J. Farrell MacDonald (*Grady the Producer*), Thomas E. Jackson (*Jackson the Angel*), Ted Healy (*Mullins*), Moe Howard, Larry Fine, Curly Howard [The Three Stooges] (*Mullin's Helpers*), Ray Hedge (*Clarence*), Grace Hayes (*Grace*), Bonnie Bonnell.

Real-life radio team Vail and Damerel (who were also real mother and daughter) play the parts of Myrt and Marge, major radio stars of the 1930s, in this slow-moving backstage musical. It's the old story of a struggling troupe making it big on Broadway. There's no real wit or imagination used, unfortunately, but Three Stooges fans may care to watch for an early film appearance of their favorite trio when they still were errand boys for Ted Healy. Songs include: "Draggin' My Heels Around," "Isle of Blues," "What is Sweeter?"

p, Bryan Foy; d&w, Al Boasberg (based on a story by Beatrice Banyard); ph, Joseph A. Valentine; ch, Jack Haskell; m/l, M. K. Jerome, Joan Jasmin.

Musical Comedy   **(PR:A MPAA:NR)**

MYSTERIANS, THE**
         (1959, Jap.) 87m Toho/MGM c (CHIKYU BOELGUN; AKA; EARTH DEFENSE
                                                               FORCES)

Kenji Sahara (*Joji Atsumi*), Yumi Shirakawa (*Etsuko Shiraishi*), Momoko Kochi (*Hiroko*), Akihiko Hirata (*Ryoichi Schiraishi*), Takashi Shirmura (*Dr. Adachi*), Susumu Fujita (*Comdr. Morita*), Hisaya Ito (*Capt. Seki*), Yoshio Kosugi (*Comdr. Sugimoto*), Fuyuki Murakami (*Dr. Kawanami*), Minosuke Yamada (*Gen. Hamamoto*), Harold S. Conway.

From the team that brought forth GODZILLA comes THE MYSTERIANS, creatures from the nuclear destroyed planet of Mysteroid. They've come to Earth in search of women, and their goals are to take over the Earth, procreate with Earth women, and start a new civilization. With a myriad of flying saucers, as well as a giant metallic bird with electronic fire rays beaming from its eyes, the unwelcome visitors nearly succeed in their mission. But with bombs, tanks, and explosions, they are finally destroyed. This picture can be great fun with those wonderful, cheap special effects that always get a good laugh, unless the audience is looking for realism. Originally this film was released in the U.S. by RKO studios. However, owner Howard Hughes closed down the works shortly after purchasing the distribution rights to THE MYSTERIANS, and sold it to MGM.

p, Tamoyuki Tanaka, Peter Riethof, Carlos Montalban; d, Inoshiro Honda; w, Takeshi Kimura, Shigeru Kayama (based on the story by Jojiro Okami); ph, Hajime Kolzumi (CinemaScope, Eastmancolor); m, Akaira Ifukube; ed, Hiroichi Iwashita; art d, Teruaki Aba; spec eff, Eiji Tsuburaya.

Science Fiction   **Cas.**   **(PR:A MPAA:NR)**

MYSTERIES zero*   (1979, Neth.) 100m Sigma Film/Cine-Vog c

Rutger Hauer (*Johan Nagel*), Sylvia Kristel (*Dany Kielland*), David Rappaport (*Minuut the Midget*), Rita Tushingham (*Martha Gude*), Andrea Ferreol (*Kamma*), Kees Brusse (*Dr. Stenerson*), Liesbeth List (*Mrs. Stenerson*), Fons Rademakers (*Commissioner*), Adrian Brine (*Innkeeper*), Peter Faber (*Karlsen*).

This is a film that from beginning to end is a complete mystery. Hauer is a stranger in a small coastal village. Who is he? Where did he come from? Was he involved with a murder? The film offers no insight into the human condition, let alone the characters here. Hauer would soon leave from America where he received better parts in such films as BLADE RUNNER. Kristel shows absolutely no acting ability in one of her few "legitimate" films. For comic relief, there is a midget.

p, Matthijs Van Heyningen, Yannick Bernard; d&w, Paul De Lussanet (based on the novel by Knut Hamsun); ph, Robby Muller; m, Laurens Van Rooyen; ed, Jane Sperr.

Drama   **(PR:C MPAA:NR)**

MYSTERIOUS AVENGER, THE***   (1936) 54m COL bw

Charles Starrett (*Ranny*), Joan Perry (*Alice*), Wheeler Oakman (*Brophy*), Edward Le Saint (*Lockhart*), Lafe McKee (*Maitland*), Hal Price (*Sheriff*), Charles Locher [Jon Hall] (*Lafe*), George Chesebro (*Foley*), Roy Rogers, Bob Nolan, Hugh Farr, Karl Farr, Tim Spencer (*The Sons of the Pioneers*), Jack Rockwell, Dick Botiller, Edmund Cobb.

The second of Starrett's western films in his long running Columbia series finds him checking out a strange story. It seems that McKee and Le Saint are two ranchers, each accusing the other of rustling cattle. Starrett has a job on his hands because one of the accused is his father. He uncovers the fact that neither party is guilty; that the real rustler is Oakman. Popular western writer Kyne provided the original story for this well done formula piece. Music is provided by the Sons of the Pioneers, led by none other than Roy Rogers. Rogers and the Pioneers soon parted company with Starrett, and went on to make their own successful series.

p, Harry Decker; d, David Selman; w, Ford Beebe (based on the story by Peter B. Kyne); ph, George Meehan; ed, Richard Cahoon.

Western   **(PR:A MPAA:NR)**

MYSTERIOUS CROSSING**   (1937) 56m UNIV bw

James Dunn (*Murphy*), Jean Rogers (*Yvonne Fontaine*), Andy Devine (*Carolina*), John Eldredge (*Briand*), Hobart Cavanaugh (*Stebbins*), Herbert Rawlinson (*District Attorney*), J. Farrell MacDonald (*Chief Bullock*), Clarence Muse (*Lincoln*), Jonathan Hale (*Garland*), Loren Baker (*Wilson*), Libby Taylor (*Hattie*), James Flavin (*Plainsclothesman*), Pat O'Malley (*Sergeant*).

Traveling around the country in a boxcar, reporter Dunn finds himself deep in trouble. He accidentally gets involved in an unusual murder case involving a rich man. The cops are incompetents (as they always seem to be whenever a reporter investigates a movie murder) and Dunn solves the crime. Devine is his guitar-plucking hillbilly sidekick who provides comic relief. Rogers is the young woman whose fiancee killed her future father-in-law. After the mystery is solved Rogers winds up with none other than Dunn.

p, Val Paul; d, Arthur Lubin; w, Jefferson Parker, John Grey (based on the story by Fred MacIsaacs); ph, Milton Krasner; ed, Bernard W. Burton; md, Charles Previn.

Crime   **(PR:AC MPAA:NR)**

MYSTERIOUS DESPERADO, THE***   (1949) 61m RKO bw

Tim Holt (*Tim*), Richard Martin (*Chito*), Edward Norris (*Ramon*), Movita Castaneda (*Luisa*), Robert Livingston (*Jordan*), Frank Wilcox (*Stevens*), William Tannen (*Barton*), Robert B. Williams (*Whittaker*), Kenneth MacDonald (*Sheriff*), Frank Lackteen (*Pedro*), Leander DeCordova (*Padre*).

When Holt's partner Martin receives notice that his uncle has died, the two ride off to see about the inheritance. Upon arrival they find the uncle was murdered and his son (Norris) accused of the crime. Investigation proves that a local official and two real estate promotors (Wilcox, Livingston, and Tannen) are the real culprits, out to steal the ranch from its rightful owners. Though the plot seems like just another Western, this is a fairly good entry in the Holt series. There's a nice air of suspense in the telling, mixed in with humor, action, and a little romance. The music is a nice touch, giving a suspenseful ambiance to the action.

p, Herman Schlom; d, Lesley Selander; w, Norman Houston; ph, Nicholas Musuraca; m Paul Sawtell; ed, Les Millbrook; md, C. Bakaleinikoff; art d, Albert S. D'Agostino, Feild Grey.

Western **Cas.** **(PR:A MPAA:NR)**

MYSTERIOUS DOCTOR, THE zero (1943) 57m WB bw

John Loder *(Sir Henry Leland)*, Eleanor Parker *(Letty Carstairs)*, Bruce Lester *(Lt. Christopher Hilton)*, Lester Matthews *(Dr. Frederick Holmes)*, Forrester Harvey *(Hugh Penhryn)*, Matt Willis *(Bart Raymond)*, Art Foster *(Saul Bevans)*, Clyde Cook *(Herbert)*, Creighton Hale *(Luke)*, Phyllis Barry *(Ruby)*, David Clyde *(Tom Andrews)*, Harold de Becker *(The Peddler)*, Frank Mayo *(Simon Tewksbury)*, Hank Mann *(Roger)*, DeWolf [William] Hopper *(Orderly)*, Jack Mower *(Watson)*, Crauford Kent *(The Commandant)*, Leo White *(Headless man)*.

Camp fan alert! Here's another feature in the "So Bad It's Good" genre that is known and loved. Though barely a year into the war, Warner Bros. apparently ran out of plots for WW II films. Somewhere they got the idea for this inane piece of junk: a small British mining village is being sabotaged by a mysterious stranger. The locals don't know who is responsible until at last the stranger is discovered: the headless ghost of a Nazi! The actors are more than a little embarrassed as they go through the motions, though Willis gives a surprisingly realistic portrayal of the village idiot. Makes you wonder. The direction is very serious, as though this were CASABLANCA quality. A classic in bad filmmaking.

p, William Jacobs; d, Ben Stoloff; w, Richard Weil; ph, Henry Sharp; ed, Clarence Kolster; art d, Charles Novi; set d, Casey Roberts; cos, Milo Anderson.

War/Horror **(PR:C MPAA:NR)**

MYSTERIOUS DR. FU MANCHU, THE*** (1929) 80m PAR bw

Warner Oland *(Dr. Fu Manchu)*, Jean Arthur *(Lia Eltham)*, Neil Hamilton *(Dr. Jack Petrie)*, O. P. Heggie *(Nayland Smith)*, William Austin *(Sylvester Wadsworth)*, Claude King *(Sir John Petrie)*, Charles Stevenson *(Gen. Petrie)*, Noble Johnson *(Li Po)*, Evelyn Selbie *(Fai Lu)*, Charles Giblyn *(Weymouth)*, Donald MacKenzie *(Trent)*, Lawrence Davidson *(Clarkson)*, Laska Winter *(Fu Mela)*, Charles Stevens *(Singh)*, Chappell Dossett *(Rev. Mr. Eltham)*, Tully Marshall *(Chinese Ambassador)*.

The first of the popular Sax Rohmer (Arthur Sarsfield Ward) mystery novels to be made into a talking feature is a fairly good job, reaching the same level of chilling suspense as the novels and later radio shows. Benevolent looking, overweight Oland (known for his renditions of Charlie Chan) is the evil green-eyed Chinese doctor bent on revenge against the British officer who commanded forces during the Boxer rebellion. It was during this time that Oland's wife and son were killed, warping the doctor's mind to the extent where all he can think about is vengeance. To assist him, he uses the daughter of an English official, killed during the rebellion. The girl is put into a trance and forced to do Oland's dirty work. After having killed several of the British officers he is after, Oland then attempts to gain vengeance against King and son Hamilton. But before this can happen, Scotland Yard is aware of Oland's pattern, and warns King before he meets with a disastrous end. Oland is quite convincing in the title role that would later be shared by such greats as Boris Karloff and Christopher Lee. The eerie atmosphere and steadily building suspense make this early entry in the series as frightening as those made in the 1960s. (See FU MANCHU series; Index)

d, Rowland V. Lee; w, Florence Ryerson, Lloyd Corrigan (based on the story by Sax Rohmer); ph, Harry Fischbeck; ed, George Nichols, Jr..

Mystery **(PR:A MPAA:NR)**

MYSTERIOUS HOUSE OF DR. C., THE*½** (1976) 88m Samuel Bronston c

Walter Slezak *(Dr. Coppelius)*, Claudia Corday *(Swanilda)*, Caj Selling *(Franz)*, Eileen Elliott *(Brigitta)*, Terry-Thomas *(Voice of the Bull)*.

The title sounds like a Corman horror flick, but this actually is a well-made version of the ballet "Coppelia." The simple story involves the adventures of a group of dolls locked up in Slezaks' laboratory. The macabre elements of the original have been pared out, leaving a nicely choreographed story that's perfect for both children and dance lovers. American dancer Corday is marvelous, as is her partner Selling, a veteran of the Royal Swedish Ballet. Also in the film are animated sequences involving the dreams of Slezak. He dreams of being a toreador, with British comic actor Thomas providing the bull's voice. This film was produced and choreographed by dance innovators, Ted and Jo Anna Kneeland.

p&d, Ted Kneeland; w, T. Kneeland, Jo Anna Kneeland (based on the "Coppelia" ballet by the Kneelands); ph, Cecillo Paniagua; m, Leo Delibes; md, Adrian Sardo; ch, J. Kneeland.

Dance **(PR:A MPAA:NR)**

MYSTERIOUS INTRUDER*** (1946) 61m COL bw

Richard Dix *(Don Gale)*, Barton MacLane *(Detective Taggart)*, Nina Vale *(Joan Hill)*, Regis Toomey *(James Summers)*, Helen Mowery *(Freda Hanson)*, Mike Mazurki *(Harry Pontos)*, Pamela Blake *(Elora Lund)*, Charles Lane *(Detective Burns)*, Paul Burns *(Edward Stillwell)*, Kathleen Howard *(Rose Denning)*, Harlan Briggs *(Brown)*.

The fifth film based on the popular "Whistler" radio series finds private eye Dix battling the cops in trying to solve a murder. It seems some homicides have taken place in a race for some rare recordings wanted by a Swedish millionaire. Though routine in plot, this is a well paced film with some good moments of suspense. At one point Dix feels his way through a dark, abandoned house searching for the killer. The direction keeps the audience on edge, with a good nervous laugh thrown in as well, while Dix gropes in the darkness. Though classically hardboiled, Dix's characterization has a soft spot, as well as providing some humor within the mystery. Some interesting camera work and a tightly plotted script make this a nifty programmer. (See THE WHISTLER series, Index.)

p, Rudolph C. Fothow; d, William Castle; w, Eric Taylor (based on a story by Taylor); ph, Philip Tannura; m, Wilbur Hatch; ed, Dwight Caldwell; md, Mischa Bakaleinikoff; art d, Hans Radon; set d, Robert Priestley.

Mystery **(PR:A MPAA:NR)**

MYSTERIOUS INVADER, THE

(SEE; ASTOUNDING SHE-MONSTER, THE, 1958)

MYSTERIOUS ISLAND*

(1929) 95m MGM c/bw (AKA: THE MYSTERIOUS ISLAND)

Lionel Barrymore *(Count Dakkar)*, Jane Daly *(Sonia)*, Lloyd Hughes *(Nikolai)*, Montagu Love *(Falon)*, Harry Gribbon *(Mikhail)*, Snitz Edwards *(Anton)*, Gibson Gowland *(Dmitry)*, Dolores Brinkman *(Teresa)*, Pauline Starke, Karl Dane.

An unfortunate, fascinating, uneven, and apparently accursed film with three directors which took that same number of years to complete. The cost of this interesting failure was well over a million dollars, a staggering sum at the time. Barring underwater sequences, the entire film was shot in the old two-color Technicolor process, an expensive system which required special projection equipment in the theaters. The entire second unit was destroyed while filming on location near the Bahamas. The original director, the celebrated Tourneur, suffered artistic differences with MGM *wunderkind* Irving Thalberg and departed when the film was half completed. He was replaced by writer Hubbard, assisted by Christenson. The narrative departs from author Verne's novel in almost every detail. A sequel to *Twenty Thousand Leagues Under the Sea*, the novel tells of the further adventures of its major protagonist, Captain Nemo. The celebrated captain does not even appear in this film. His place is taken by Count Dakkar—Barrymore—who constructs two submarines in the hope of confirming his theory (based on skeletal evidence) that a strange creature, half fish, half human, exists near the ocean bottom. Villain Love hopes to gain the throne of Russia with the help of Barrymore's inventions, which he attempts to commandeer. Capturing the count and his shore crew while one of the submersibles explores the surrounding sea, Love subjects Barrymore to torture. When the undersea craft returns to the island to successfully rescue Barrymore it is crippled by gunfire and sinks to the bottom, where its occupants discover the race of tiny mermen they sought. Wearing diving suits, Barrymore's men mingle with the merpersons, winning their regard by staving off the attack of a sea monster. Meanwhile, Barrymore's sister Daly, in the second of the two submarines, does battle with Love—who in a plot twist, loves her—and his men. Sensing defeat, she sinks the submarine sending it to the bottom alongside its crippled sister ship, where the battle continues. The merpersons—who seem to have a bit of shark in their makeup—are incited to frenzy by the blood of the combat mixing with the water, and attack the humans. Love is killed and his men defeated. Barrymore is fatally wounded by the embrace of a giant octopus which the seapeople sic on the surface-dwellers. One submarine is repaired and the survivors surface, but the fatally wounded Barrymore opts to make the submarine his coffin and goes to his watery grave. While this embattled film was in production and on the shelf, synchronized sound made its appearance in the world's moviehouses. Consequently, sound was added to the picture after the fact. The dialog sequences occur mostly in the opening scenes, with Barrymore pontificating about his remarkable inventions. Technically, the film is excellent. The seapeople were midgets, suspended from wires in a studio setting. The other effects are fine. Though well received by critics, this fascinating failure lost more than three-quarters of a million dollars for the studio. Remade in 1941, 1951, and 1961 under the same title.

d, Lucien Hubbard (uncredited, Maurice Tourneur, Benjamin Christensen); w, Hubbard, Carl L. Pierson (based on the novel *L'Isle Mysterieuse* by Jules Verne); ph, Percy Hilburn (two-color Technicolor); m, Martin Broones, Arthur Lange; ed, Pierson; art d, Cedric Gibbons; spec eff, James Basevi, Louis H. Tolhurst, Irving Ries.

Science Fiction **(PR:A MPAA:NR)**

MYSTERIOUS ISLAND***

(1941, USSR) 75m Gorki/Children's Film Studio bw (TAINSTVENNI OSTROV)

M. V. Kommisarov, A. S. Krasnapolski, P. I. Klansky, R. Ross, A. A. Andrienkov, Yura Grammapykaty, A. K. Sona, I. C. Koslov.

The first remake of MGM's 1929 silent fiasco, this version of the Verne story is more faithful to its source than its predecessor. Continuing the story of Captain Nemo after the departure of Captain Grant, the Soviets paid close attention to detail and technology. The special effects were nothing extraordinary but the design for the submarine *Nautilus* was very artistic.

d, E. A. Penzlin, B. M. Chelintsev; w, Chelintsev, M. P. Kalinin (based on the novel *L'Isle Mysterieuse* by Jules Verne); ph, M. B. Belskin; spec eff, Mikhail Karyukov.

Science Fiction **(PR:A MPAA:NR)**

MYSTERIOUS ISLAND*** (1961, U.S./Brit.) 100m Ameran/COL c

Michael Craig *(Capt. Cyrus Harding)*, Joan Greenwood *(Lady Mary Fairchild)*, Michael Callan *(Herbert Brown)*, Gary Merrill *(Gideon Spilettt)*, Herbert Lom *(Capt. Nemo)*, Beth Rogan *(Elena)*, Percy Herbert *(Sgt. Pencroft)*, Dan Jackson *(Neb)*, Nigel Green *(Tom)*.

Jules Verne's sequel to *20,000 Leagues Under the Sea* was the subject of several films by various production companies worldwide. There was MGM's two-color Technicolor disaster in 1929, the Soviet's 1941 version, a 1951 fifteen-part Columbia serial, and an international production made in 1972. Despite the common source, each version differed in its approach to the material. This 1961 version is probably the most popular. Craig is the leader of some Union soldiers (and one confederate deserter) escaping by balloon from a Confederate jail. They descend at sea and wash up on the shores of a strange island. There they encounter the marvelous creations of Harryhausen, including giant bees, giant crabs, and other oversized (and nicely created) monstrosities, plus a pair of pretty ladies. After being attacked by some pirates, Craig and company are saved by Nemo (Lom), who explains that the giant beasties are the results of his experiments. He's convinced that his mutations will solve the world food shortage. The crew ends up leaving the island just as a volcano is about to explode, but their farsighted host is buried under the rocks and lava. The direction gives the film a spirited feeling, but there are too many plot holes to pull this off as effectively as it could have been. The best things here are the inimitable Harryhausen effects. Harryhausen was a master in dealing with miniatures, making quite a name for himself in the late 1950s with films based on Greek and Roman myths. MYSTERIOUS ISLAND also benefits from a score by the great film composer Herrmann, energetically rendered by the London Symphony Orchestra.

p, Charles H. Schneer; d, Cy Endfield; w, John Prebble, Daniel Ullman, Crane Wilbur (based on the novel *L'Ile Mysterieuse* by Jules Verne); ph, Wilkie Cooper, Egil Woxholt (Eastmancolor); m, Bernard Herrmann; ed, Frederick Wilson; md, Herrmann; art d, Bill Andrews; spec eff, Ray Harryhausen.

Science Fiction   **Cas.**   **(PR:AA MPAA:NR)**

MYSTERIOUS ISLAND, THE 1973
(SEE: MYSTERIOUS ISLAND OF CAPTAIN NEMO, THE, 1973, Fr./Ital./Span./
Cameroon)

MYSTERIOUS ISLAND OF CAPTAIN NEMO, THE
(1973, Fr./Ital. 87m Span./Cameroon) Cite-Cameroons Development-Albina/Cinerama c (L'ISLE MYSTERIEUSE; L'ISOLA MISTERIOSA E IL CAPITANO NEMO; AKA: THE MYSTERIOUS ISLAND)

Omar Sharif *(Capt. Nemo)*, Philippe Nicaud *(Gideon Spilett, the Journalist)*, Ambroise M'Bia *(Nebuchadnezzar)*, Jess Hahn *(Bonaventure Pencroft)*, Gerard Tichy *(Cyrus Smith)*, Gabriel Tinti *(Ayrton, the Castaway)*, Rafael Bardem *(Herbert Brown)*, Vidal Molina *(Harvey)*, Rick Battaglia *(Finch)*.

This slapdash version of the famed story follows its plot line fairly closely, save for some updating involving radiation beams in order to work in the popular nuclear element (which has Sharif's submarine *Nautilus* crewmen inadvertently dying from radiation poisoning). Civil war survivors balloon to an uncharted island where they are assisted by the technically adept Captain Nemo, here essayed by Sharif, the only box-office draw in the credits. Sharif rescues the rest from a pirate attack, but remains behind when they leave the island, which is threatened by volcanic activity. The undersea creatures appear to have more life in them than the human characters in this strangely wooden production.

p, Jacques Bar; d, Juan Antonio Bardem, Henri Colpi; w, Bardem, Jacques Campreaux (based on the novel *L'Isle Mysterieuse* by Jules Verne); ph, Enzio Serafin, Guy Delecluse, Julio Ortaz (Eastmancolor); m, Gianni Ferrio; ed, Paul Cayatte, Aurore Camp, Frederique Michaud; prod d, Cubero y Galicia, Philippe Ancellin; cos, Leon Revuelta, Peris Hermanos.

Science Fiction   **(PR:AA MPAA:NR)**

MYSTERIOUS MISS X, THE**   (1939) 62m REP bw
Michael Whalen *(Keith Neville)*, Mary Hart *(Julie)*, Mabel Todd *(Miss Botts)*, Chick Chandler *(Dan Casey)*, Frank M. Thomas *(Ross)*, Regis Toomey *(Jack Webster)*, Don Douglas *(Fredericks)*, Wade Boteler *(Chief McDougal)*, Dorothy Tree *(Alma)*, Eddie Acuff *(Policeman)*, Pierre Watkin *(Winslow)*, Harlan Briggs *(Graham)*.

Two vaudevillians from England are stranded in America. Someone mistakes them for Scotland Yard detectives and before they know it, Whalen and Chandler are helping police solve a hotel murder. This is mildly amusing, though the dialog is poorly written and hampers some potentially funny performances and scenes. Whalen has a good moment as interrogator, though his partner overplays his lines. The mystery can hardly be considered as such. You'll have figured out who the killer is long before the dubious sleuths.

p, Herman Schlom; d, Gus Meins; w, Olive Copper (based on the original story by George W. Yates); ph, Ernest Miller; ed, Lester Orlebeck; md, Cy Feuer; cos, Irene Saltern.

Comedy   **(PR:A MPAA:NR)**

MYSTERIOUS MR. DAVIS, THE*
(1936, Brit.) 58m Oxford/RKO bw (GB: MY PARTNER, MR. DAVIS)

Henry Kendall *(Julian Roscoe)*, Kathleen Kelly *(Audrey Roscoe)*, Morris Harvey *(Cecil Goldenburg)*, A. Bromley Davenport *(Sir George Miller)*, Alastair Sim *(Theodore F. Wilcox)*, Guy Middleton *(Martin)*.

Kendall, beset by creditors, invents a fictitious partner. Entirely predictable complications ensue until Kendall is able to rid himself of his creation. Badly written and produced, though interesting as French director Autant-Lara's second feature and his only British film.

p&d, Claude Autant-Lara; w, Jacques Prevert (based on a novel by Jenaro Prieto).

Comedy   **(PR:A MPAA:NR)**

MYSTERIOUS MR. MOTO***
(1938) 62m FOX bw (AKA: THE MYSTERIOUS MR. MOTO)

Peter Lorre *(Mr. Moto)*, Mary MaGuire *(Ann Richman)*, Henry Wilcoxon *(Anton Darvak)*, Erik Rhodes *(David Scott-Frensham)*, Harold Huber *(Ernst Litmar)*, Leon Ames *(Paul Brissac)*, Forrester Harvey *(George Higgins)*, Fredrik Vogeding *(Gottfried Brujo)*, Lester Matthews *(Sir Charles Murchison)*, John Rogers *(Sniffy)*, Karen Sorrell *(Lotus Liu)*, Mitchell Lewis *(Nola)*, Frank S. Hagney *(Bouncer)*.

The second of the eight films comprising the MR. MOTO series. The League of Assassins is a group of vicious European killers. Lorre is out to break the gang by infiltrating it. He poses as a prisoner on Devil's Island and gets in good with gang member Ames. The pair escape from the infamous prison and Lorre becomes Ames' houseboy. This makes him privy to all the goings on, which he relays back to Scotland Yard. After witnessing a few murders, Lorre realizes that the gang leader always has a street musician play the tune "Madrid" whenever he wants to signal other members to commit murder. The League tries to blackmail rich tycoon Wilcoxon but he refuses to listen to their demands. Rhodes, the gang's secret ringleader, gets a position as Wilcoxon's assistant. He is to signal the gang at an art opening when the time is ripe for murder. But Lorre, disguised as a little German man (which, in fact, he was) sets off the tune "Madrid" prematurely and Rhodes is the murder victim. The gang members are arrested and the League destroyed. This was a clever entry in Lorre's very popular "Mr. Moto" series. The Japanese detective was one of those super sleuths in the mold of Sherlock Holmes or Charlie Chan. Moto could pull off any disguise, take any punch, and outwit the cleverest of criminals. Though little more than formula material, THE MYSTERIOUS MR. MOTO is loads of fun, with a sly performance by Lorre. Stock shots of London are well blended with the realistic studio settings, reflecting a budget higher than studios normally put into a film like this. The direction is efficient, though perhaps not as lively as possible (See MR. MOTO series, Index.)

p, Sol M. Wurtzel; d, Norman Foster; w, Foster, Philip MacDonald (based on the character created by J. P. Marquand); ph, Virgil Miller; m, Samuel Kaylin; ed, Norman Colbert; md, Kaylin; art d, Bernard Herzbrun, Lewis Creber.

Crime   **(PR:A MPAA:NR)**

MYSTERIOUS MR. NICHOLSON, THE* ½
(1947, Brit.) 78m Bushey/Ambassador bw

Anthony Hulme *(Mr. Nicholson/ Mr. Raeburn)*, Lesley Osmond *(Peggy Dundas)*, Frank Hawkins *(Inspector Morley)*, Andrew Laurence *(Waring)*, Douglas Stewart *(Seymour)*, George Bishop *(Mr. Browne)*, Josie Bradley *(Freda)*, Ivy Collins *(Mrs. Barnes)*.

When Osmond goes to deliver a will to a wealthy knight, she finds him murdered. Dapper burglar Hulme is identified as the killer, but Osmond manages to find the real killer, his double. Below-average British crime programmer.

p, Gilbert Church; d, Oswald Mitchell; w, Francis Miller, Mitchell (based on a story by Miller); ph, S. D. Onions.

Crime   **(PR:A MPAA:NR)**

MYSTERIOUS MR. MOTO OF DEVIL'S ISLAND
(SEE: MYSTERIOUS MR. MOTO, 1938)

MYSTERIOUS MR. REEDER, THE**
(1940, Brit.) 61m Jack Raymond/MON bw (GB: THE MIND OF MR. REEDER)

Will Fyffe *(J. G. Reeder)*, Kay Walsh *(Peggy Gillette)*, George Curzon *(Welford)*, Chili Bouchier *(Elsa Welford)*, John Warwick *(Ted Bracher)*, Lesley Wareing *(Mrs. Gaylor)*, Romilly Lunge *(Inspector Gaylor)*, Derek Gorst *(Langdon)*, Ronald Shiner *(Sam Hackett)*, Wally Patch *(Lomer)*, George Hayes *(Brady)*, Betty Astell *(Barmaid)*, Dorothy Dewhurst, Patricia Roc.

Kindly old gentleman Fyffe is really a detective. Poking his nose around, the private eye discovers the secret behind a nightclub owner's murder. He exposes a known counterfeiter and solves a homicide. Fyffe is quite humorous, carrying the role well. He is the best thing this film has to offer, unfortunately. The mystery is difficult to follow, with actors speaking in impossibly thick English accents. The dialog is further hampered by poor recording. The direction has no sense for suspense, taking the story along at much too slow a pace to be effective.

p, Charles Q. Steele; d, Jack Raymond; w, Byran Wallace, Marjorie Gaffney, Michael Hogan (based on the novel by Edgar Wallace); ph, George Stretton; ed, Peggy Hennessy.

Crime   **(PR:A-C MPAA:NR)**

MYSTERIOUS MR. VALENTINE, THE**   (1946) 56m REP bw
William Henry, Linda Stirling, Virginia Christine, Thomas Jackson, Barbara Wooddell, Kenne Duncan, Virginia Brissac, Lyle Latell, Ernie Adams, Tristram Coffin, Arthur Space, Robert Bice.

When a young woman's car has a blowout, it unexpectedly sets off a mystery that leads to blackmail and murder. A simple murder mystery from Republic Studios, the sort of film that might have inspired Jean-Luc Godard to dedicate his classic BREATHLESS to the studio.

p, Donald H. Brown; d, Philip Ford; w, Milton Raison; ph, Alfred Keller; m, Mort Glickman; ed, Richard L. Van Enger; art d, Hilyard Brown; set d, John McCarthy, Jr., George Milo; cos, Adele Palmer.

Crime   **(PR:A MPAA:NR)**

MYSTERIOUS MR. WONG***
(1935) 60m MON bw (AKA: THE MYSTERIOUS MR. WONG)

Bela Lugosi *(Mr. Wong, Mandarin)*, Wallace Ford *(Jason Barton, Feature Writer)*, Alrine Judge *(Peg, Jason's fiancee)*, Fred Warren *(Tsung)*, Lotus Long

(Moonflower, Wong's niece), Robert Emmett O'Connor *(McGillicuddy)*, Edward Piel *(Jen Yu)*, Luke Chan *(Chan Fu)*, Lee Shumway *(Brandon, Editor)*, Etta Lee, Ernest F. Young, Theodore Lorch, James B. Leong, Chester Gan.

Lugosi, despite his Slavic accent, plays an evil oriental madman. He's after "the twelve coins of Confucius" which, according to legend, will make him the ruler of a province of China. He outwits the cops, but not wisecracking reporter Ford who ends up solving Lugosi's mysterious murders. The scene in Lugosi's torture chamber is a classic in maddened camp. Well made, this was designed as a programmer to soothe Depression audiences eager for escape at the movies. Though produced by Monogram, this film has nothing to do with their "Mr. Wong" series starring Lugosi's monstrous rival Boris Karloff. Typical of its time, the film's snappy dialog is filled with ethnic slurs. This was one of the last films made by Monogram (which had no studio, this was shot on the rented RKO-Pathe lot in Culver City) before the poverty-row production company was integrated, with other independents, into Republic Studios. The company, Phoenix-like, was reborn the following year under the aegis of its originator, W. Ray Johnson.

p, George Yohalem; d, William Nigh; w, Nina Howatt, Lew Levinson, James Herbuveaux (based on the novel *The Twelve Coins of Confucius* by Harry Stephen Keeler); ph, Harry Neumann; ed, Jack Ogilvie; md, Abe Meyer; set d, E. R. Hickson.

Mystery　　　　　　　　　Cas.　　　　　　　　**(PR:C MPAA:NR)**

MYSTERIOUS RIDER, THE** 1/2

　　　　　　(1933) 59m PAR bw (AKA: THE FIGHTING PHANTOM)

Kent Taylor *(Wade Benton)*, Lona Andre *(Dorothy)*, Gail Patrick *(Mary Foster)*, Warren Hymer *(Jitney Smith)*, Berton Churchill *(Mark King)*, Irving Pichel *(Cliff Harkness)*, Cora Sue Collins *(Jo-Jo)*, E. H. Calvert *(Sheriff Matt Arnold)*, Sherwood Bailey *("Sheriff" Arnold, Jr.)*, Niles Welch *(John Foster)*, Clarence Wilson *(Gentry)*.

Pichel is the bad guy, cheating homesteaders out of the money they've put down for land. In rides cowboy hero Taylor to right the wrongs, and to win the heart of Patrick as well. Based on a Zane Grey novel, the dialog and story are typical for a western, though some of the camera work and lighting effects are such as are not normally found in a film like this. Otherwise it's all routine. The two lovely ladies, Andre and Patrick, were "discovered" by Paramount during a promotion for ISLAND OF LOST SOULS, with Charles Laughton and Bela Lugosi. The studio had announced a "Panther Woman" contest; it was seeking a catlike creature to play the role of Lota, the Panther Woman in that adaptation of H. G. Wells' *The Island of Doctor Moreau*. Both beauties bombed as felines; the part went to Kathleen Burke. The studio signed losers Andre and Patrick anyway (Patrick had appeared in one previous film).

p, Harold Hurley; d, Fred Allen; w, Harvey Gates, Robert N. Lee (based on the novel by Zane Grey); ph, Archie Stout.

Western　　　　　　　　　　　　　　　　**(PR:A MPAA:NR)**

MYSTERIOUS RIDER, THE** 1/2

　　　　　　(1938) 75m PAR bw (AKA: MARK OF THE AVENGER)

Douglas Dumbrille *(Pecos Bill/BenWade)*, Sidney Toler *(Frosty Kilburn)*, Russell Hayden *(Wils Moore)*, Charlotte Field *(Collie)*, Stanley Andrews *(William Bellounds, Foreman)*, Weldon Heyburn *(Jack Bellounds)*, Monte Blue *(Cap. Folsom)*, Glenn Strange *(Cramer)*, Earl Dwire *(Sheriff Burley)*, Jack Rockwell *(Lem)*, Leo McMahon *(Montana)*, Arch Hall *(Andrews)*, Bruce Mitchell *(Baker)*, Ed Brady *(Jake)*, Dick Alexander *(Hudson)*, Bob Kortman *(Morris)*, Mabel Colcord *(Woman)*, Price Mitchell.

A remake of the 1933 film has a somewhat different plot. Dumbrille, wrongly accused of murder, redeems himself after Hayden tries to cheat homesteaders out of their land. This time the bad guy fools the innocent farmers by having them sign their contracts in invisible ink. The story works well and there's some good photography, though this still is nothing more than a good Saturday afternoon western. Dumbrille was normally a bad guy but got to wear the white hat for this film when George Bancroft walked off the set in a salary dispute. Toler, best known for his work in the CHARLIE CHAN series, here plays an unusual role as the comic-cook sidekick. Actress Field played the ingenue well in a couple of Paramount westerns—PRIDE OF THE WEST was another— and then dropped out of the business forever.

p, Harry Sherman; d, Lesley Selander; w, Maurice Geraghty (based on the novel by Zane Grey); ph, Russell Harlan; ed, Sherman Rose; md, Boris Morros; art d, Lewis Rachmil.

Western　　　　　　　　　　　　　　　　**(PR:A MPAA:NR)**

MYSTERIOUS RIDER, THE**　　　　　　(1942) 56m PRC bw

Buster Crabbe *(Billy the Kid)*, Al "Fuzzy" St. John, Caroline Burke, John Merton, Kermit Maynard, Jack Ingram, Slim Whitaker, Ted Adams, Guy Wilkerson, Edwin Brien, Frank Ellis.

Crabbe and sidekick St. John help two children protect the mine they've inherited from villain Merton. Routine western by an experienced crew. One of the many highly successful Billy the Kid movies Crabbe made with comic sidekick St. John as he diligently tried to diversify into other hero action roles from the Tarzan that began his movie career. Released in 1947 as the 40 minute featurette PANHANDLE TRAIL. (See BILLY THE KID Series, Index.)

p, Sigmund Neufeld; d, Sherman Scott [Sam Newfield]; w, Steve Braxton [Sam Robins]; ph, Jack Greenhalgh; ed, Holbrook N. Todd.

Western　　　　　　　　　　　　　　　　**(PR:A MPAA:NR)**

MYSTERIOUS SATELLITE, THE** 1/2

(1956, Jap.) 87m Daiei c (UCHUJIN TOKYO NI ARAWARU; AKA: THE COSMIC MAN APPEARS IN TOKYO; SPACE MEN APPEAR IN TOKYO; WARNING

FROM SPACE; UNKNOWN SATELLITE OVER TOKYO)

Toyomi Karita, Keizo Kawasaki, Isao Yamagata, Shozo Nanbu, Buntaro Miake, Mieko Nagai, Kiyoko Hirai.

A departure from the usual aliens-are-here-to-conquer-Earth theme, this Japanese picture has a friendly group of invaders land on our planet. Led by Karita, the natives of Paira request our assistance in destroying a flaming planet that is heading for Earth. In order not to scare us off, the Pairans disguise their one-eyed starfish shape, appearing as normal people. As the collision draws near and tidal waves take their course, scientist Yamagata creates a device that the Pairans fire into the satellite, saving the Earth from doomsday. A well-scripted illustration of how atomic weapons can be used to save lives rather than obliterating them.

p, Masaichi Nagata; d, Koji Shima; w, Hideo Oguni (based on the novel *Uchujin Tokyo ni Arawaru* by Gentaro Nakajima); ph, Kimio Watanabe; spec eff, Kenmai Yuasa

Science Fiction　　　　　　　　　　　　　**(PR:A MPAA:NR)**

MYSTERIOUS STRANGER, THE 1937　　(SEE: WESTERN GOLD, 1937)

MYSTERIOUS STRANGER, THE 1945

　　　　　　　　　　　　(SEE: CODE OF THE LAWLESS, 1945)

MYSTERY AT MONTE CARLO

　　　　　　　　　　(SEE: REVENGE AT MONTE CARLO, 1933)

MYSTERY AT THE BURLESQUE**

(1950, Brit.) 59m MON bw (GB: MURDER AT THE WINDMILL; AKA: MURDER AT THE BURLESQUE)

Garry Marsh *(Detective Inspector)*, Jon Pertwee *(Sergeant)*, Jack Livesey *(Vivian Van Damm)*, Elliot Makeham *(Gimpy)*, Jimmy Edwards *(Jimmy)*, Diana Decker *(Frankie)*, Donald Clive *(Donald)*, Jill Anstey *(Patsy)*, Margot Johns *(Box Office Girl)*, Genine Graham *(Usherette)*, Peter Butterworth *(Police Constable)*, Robin Richmond, Christine Welsford, Johnnie Gale, Ron Perriam, Anita D'Ray, Johnnie McGregor, Pamela Deeming, Ivan Craig, John Powe, Mary Valange, Constance Smith, Barry O'Neil, Ron Perriam, Margo Johns, The Windmill Theatre Company and Staff.

A show is over and the curtain falls. The audience all flies out with one exception— a murdered man in the front row. Since the angle of his bullet wound proves the murderer was on stage, the cast must go through the entire second act of the play. In the end Makeham, a stage handyman, is proven guilty. The mystery is little more than an excuse to film a few song and dance numbers. These are nicely staged and come off a good deal better than the investigation. Hampered by trite dialog and an easy solution, Marsh and sidekick Pertwee do what they can in discovering the murderer's identity. Filmed at London's famed Windmill. Songs include "I'll Settle For You" (Val Guest) and "Mexico" (Ronald Bridges, Charles Rose).

p, Daniel N. Angel, Nat Cohen; d&w, Val Guest; ph, Bert Mason; m, Philip Martel; Douglas Myers; art d, Bernard Robinson; ch, Jack Billings; m/l, Guest, Ronald Bridges, Charles Rose, Bill Currie.

Mystery/Musical　　　　　　　　　　　　**(PR:A MPAA:NR)**

MYSTERY AT THE VILLA ROSE**

(1930, Brit.) 78m Twickenham/Harold Auten bw (GB: AT THE VILLA ROSE)

Norah Baring *(Celia Harland)*, Austin Trevor *(Inspector Hanaud)*, Richard Cooper *(Ricardo)*, Barbara Gott *(Madame d'Auray, Widow)*, Francis Lister *(Harry Wethermill)*, Amy Brandon Thomas *(Adele Starling)*, Violet Farebrother *(Helen)*, John Hamilton *(Starling)*.

Some valuable jewels are stolen from a wealthy widow. In order to cover the crime, she is murdered with an innocent phoney medium friend getting framed for the dastardly deeds. It's up to Trevor to solve the crime. Though a little slow to start, once it gets going this is a fairly interesting little mystery. It has pure British flavor, though set in France, with literate dialog and drawing-room-style investigation. The direction and sound recording were not quite as good as they could have been. A French verison of the film was shot simultaneously, directed by Louis Mercanton and Rene Herville. The case included Simone Vaudry, Baron, Jr. (son of the famed French mime Baron, Sr.), Leon Mathot, and George Peclet. A silent version of this story was made in 1920, with another remake filmed in 1939.

p, Julius Hagen, Henry Edwards; d, Leslie Hiscott; w, Cyril Twyford (based on the novel by A. E. W. Mason), ph, Sidney Blythe.

Mystery　　　　　　　　　　　　　　　**(PR:A MPAA:NR)**

MYSTERY BROADCAST**　　　　　　　(1943) 63m REP bw

Frank Albertson *(Michael Jerome)*, Ruth Terry *(Jan Cornell)*, Nils Asther *(Ricky Moreno)*, Wynne Gibson *(Eve Stanley)*, Paul Harvey *(A. J. Stanley)*, Mary Treen *(Smitty)*, Addison Richards *(Bill Burton)*, Joseph Crehan *(Chief Daniels)*, Alice Fleming *(Mida Kent)*, Francis Pierlot *(Crunch)*, Ken Carpenter *(Announcer)*, Emmett Vogan *(Don Fletcher)*.

When her popular mystery show has ratings trouble, radio writer Terry takes to solving real mysteries on the air. This leads to an unplanned murder investigation that gets her in a lot of trouble. Albertson, a rival radio show writer and love interest, helps his girl friend solve the case. Every necessary component is properly placed in this otherwise routine thriller. Despite its generic acting and script, the direction is fairly well paced and the film holds some suspense.

p&d, George Sherman; w, Dane Lussier, Gertrude Walker; ph, William Bradford; ed, Arthur Roberts; md, Morton Scott; art d, Russell Kimball; set d, Otto Siegel; cos, Adele.

Crime　　　　　　　　　　　　　　　　**(PR:A MPAA:NR)**

MYSTERY HOUSE* (1938) 56m FN/WB bw

Dick Purcell *(Lance O'Leary)*, Ann Sheridan *(Sarah Keate)*, Anne Nagel *(Gwen Kingery)*, William Hopper *(Lal Killian)*, Anthony Averill *(Julian Barre)*, Dennie Moore *(Annette)*, Hugh O'Connell *(Newell Morse)*, Ben Welden *(Gerald Frawley)*, Sheila Bromley *(Terice Von Elm)*, Elspeth Dudgeon *(Aunt Lucy Kingery)*, Anderson Lawlor *(Joe Paggi)*, Trevor Bardette *(Bruker)*, Eric Stanley *(Huber Kingery)*, Jean Benedict *(Helen Page)*, Jack Mower *(Coroner)*, Stuart Holmes *(Jury Foreman)*, Loia Cheaney *(Secretary)*, John Harron *(Director)*.

A banker invites some colleagues to his hunting lodge in order to discover who has been embezzling funds. When he's murdered, his daughter (Nagel) calls in private eye Purcell. It seems everyone's the killer as more bodies pile up until Purcell at last finds the murderer. In an unusual twist, he doesn't romance the daughter at all. She quietly fades out of the picture while he makes time with Sheridan, a nurse. Even so, this is an unimaginative film. The plot is confusing, with too many loose ends and unexplained motivations. The direction is as dead as one of the many corpses Purcell stumbles on.

p, Bryan Foy; d, Noel Smith; w, Sherman L. Lowe, Robertson White (based on the novel *Mystery of Hunting's End* by Mignon G. Eberhart); ph, L. William O'Connell; ed, Frank Magee.

Crime (PR:A MPAA:NR)

MYSTERY IN MEXICO 1/2** (1948) 66m RKO bw

William Lundigan *(Steve)*, Jacqueline White *(Victoria)*, Ricardo Cortez *(Norcross)*, Tony Barrett *(Carlos)*, Jacqueline Dalya *(Dolores)*, Walter Reed *(Glenn)*, Jose Torvay *(Swigart)*, Jaime Jiminez *(Pancho)*, Antonio Frausto *(Pancho's Father)*, Dolores Camerillo *(Pancho's Mother)*, Eduardo Casado *(Commandant Rodriguez)*, Thalia Draper *(Floracita)*.

An insurance agent is missing in Mexico City. Lundigan is dispatched by the insurance company to investigate his colleague's disappearance, accompanied by the man's sister (White). They have to face the rough tactics of Cortez and his cab-driving henchman Barrett, but at last the missing man is found and the bad guys are put away. Lundigan and White make an interesting team, with Cortez giving his stock characterization all it's worth. The actual Mexico City locations are well used, with some good performances by locals in the film's minor roles. This is nothing out of the ordinary but it's well handled, harmless fun.

p, Sid Rogell; d, Robert Wise; w, Lawrence Kimble (based on a story by Muriel Roy Bolton); ph, Jack Draper; m, Paul Sawtell; ed, Samuel E. Beetley; md, C. Bakaleinikoff; art d, Gunther Gerzso; cos, Renie.

Crime (PR:A MPAA:NR)

MYSTERY JUNCTION*

(1951, Brit.) 67m Merton Park/Anglo Amalgamated bw

Sydney Tafler *(Larry Gordon)*, Barbara Murray *(Pat Dawn)*, Pat Owens *(Mabel Dawn)*, Martin Benson *(Steve Harding)*, Christine Silver *(Miss Owens)*, Philip Dale *(Elliot Fisher)*, Pearl Cameron *(Helen Mason)*, John Salew *(John Martin)*, Denis Webb *(Inspector Clarke)*, David Davies *(Benson)*, Charles Irwin *(Hooker)*, Ewen Solon, Cyril Smith, Sidney Monckton, Stanley Rose.

Novelist Tafler proves that escaped convict Benson did not kill two people aboard a train at a snowbound station, though both the killer and Benson die before police can arrive. Boring crime drama, ameliorated by the fact that it was only the second feature directed by McCarthy, who would go on to make several passable crime thrillers.

p, William H. Williams; d&w, Michael McCarthy; ph, Bob Lapresle.

Crime (PR:A MPAA:NR)

MYSTERY LAKE 1/2** (1953) 64m Larry Lansburgh c

George Fenneman *(Bill Richards)*, Gloria McGough *(Lainie Thorne)*, Bogue Bell *(The Hermit)*, R. P. Alexander *(Uncle Tobe)*, Edgar Bergen *(Dr. Sorenson)*.

The success of Disney Studio's "True-Life Adventure" films inspired similar projects. This film, produced and directed by a Disney veteran, is a handsomely mounted, informative feature with some strange casting. Fenneman (Groucho Marx's long suffering announcer for the hit TV show "You Bet Your Life") plays a naturalist sent off to a wild-life sanctuary in order to find out about the animal inhabitants. He has no luck until local girl McGough shows the fumbling scientist where to look. The professor is played by ventriloquist Bergen (sans sidekick Charlie McCarthy). The roles are well played but the real stars of the film are the various creatures Fenneman is supposedly observing. In true psuedo-documentary fashion, Fenneman narrates the action as we see a variety of everyday woodland activity. Spadefoot toads are shown digging holes, a water moccasin eats a salamander, and there's even a swimming rabbit. For what this is, the film's not bad, though the story has a forced charm that doesn't quite work. The nature photography is excellent. Filmed at Reelfoot Lake, Tennessee.

p&d, Larry Lansburgh; w, Rosalie and John Bodrero (based on an original story by Janet Lansburgh); ph, Floyd Crosby, Karl Maslowski, W. W. Goodpaster (Ansco Color); m, William Lava; ed, William Morgan.

Drama (PR:A MPAA:NR)

MYSTERY LINER***

(1934) 62m MON bw (GB: GHOST OF JOHN HOLLING, THE)

Noah Beery, Sr. *(Capt. Holling)*, Astrid Allwyn *(Lila, Nurse)*, Cornelius Keefe *(Cliff Rogers, 2nd Officer)*, Gustav von Seyffertitz *(Von Kessling)*, Edwin Maxwell *(Maj. Pope)*, Ralph Lewis *(Grimson, Inventor)*, Boothe Howard *(Downey, 1st Mate)*, John Maurice Sullivan *(Watson)*, Gordon DeMain *(Cmdr. Bryson)*, Zeffie Tilbury *(Granny Plimpton)*, Howard Hickman *(Dr. Howard)*, Jerry Stewart *(Edgar, Granny's Nephew)*, George ["Gabby"] Hayes *(Watchman)*, George Cleveland *(Simms, Steward)*, Olaf Hytten *(Grimson's Assistant)*, Ray Brown *(His Excellency)*, George Nash *(Waiter)*.

This film is a rare example of a well-made thriller created on the programmer assembly line. Several different story threads are neatly woven together in an intriguing and tightly controlled mystery that takes place aboard a luxury liner. There's murder, mayhem, and a mad captain (well played by Beery). When a couple of murdered corpses are found, fingers point at suspects everywhere. There are a few obvious characters who just may have pulled off the crime, but the ending is a real surprise, as the role of detective and leading suspect are reversed. The mystery progresses nicely with mounting suspense and a little romance, as well. The direction and script are fine, letting things rise and fall naturally, with no loose ends at the film's close.

p, Paul Malvern; d, William Nigh; w, Wellyn Totman (based on the novel *The Ghost of John Holling* by Edgar Wallace); ph, Archie J. Stout; ed, Carl Pierson; md, Abe Meyer; set d, E. R. Hickson.

Mystery Cas. (PR:A MPAA:NR)

MYSTERY MAN, THE 1/2** (1935) 65m MON bw

Robert Armstrong *(Larry)*, Maxine Doyle *(Anne)*, Henry Kolker *(Jonas)*, LeRoy Mason *(Eel)*, James Burke *(Marvin)*, Guy Usher *(District Attorney)*, Jimmie Burtis *(Whalen)*, Monte Collins *(Dunn)*, Sam Lufkin *(Weeks)*, Del Henderson *(Hotel Manager)*, Otto Fries, Norman Houston.

Chicago reporter Armstrong solves a difficult mystery and gets a big bonus. He celebrates just a little too hard and the next morning wakes up in St. Louis. He meets Doyle and convinces her to help him get a hotel room by putting on a big front. The ruse is discovered when his editor refuses to send him money for fare back to Chicago. But his luck changes when he solves a St. Louis mystery. In the end, he marries Doyle since the papers have reported them to be married anyway. The film starts off slowly but the direction is good, with the comedy sparking an energy that makes the film work. Doyle and Armstrong make an interesting and funny team.

p, Trem Carr; d, Ray McCarey; w, John Krafft, Rollo Lloyd (based on a story by Kate Finn); ph, Harry Neumann; ed, Carl Pierson.

Comedy/Mystery Cas. (PR:A MPAA:NR)

MYSTERY MAN* 1/2 (1944) 58m UA bw

William Boyd *(Hopalong Cassidy)*, Andy Clyde *(California Carlson)*, Jimmy Rogers *(Himself)*, Don Costello *(Bud Trilling)*, Francis McDonald *(Bert Rogan)*, Forrest Taylor *(Sheriff Sam Newhall)*, Eleanor Stewart *(Diane Newhall)*, Jack Rockwell *(Marshal Ted Blane)*, Pierce Lyden *(Red)*, John Merton *(Bill)*, Bill Hunter *(Joe)*, Bob Burns *(Tom Hanlon)*, Ozie Waters *(Tex)*, Art Mix *(Bank Robber)*, George Morrell *(Townsman)*, Bob Baker *(Bar 20 Boy)*, Hank Bell *(Deputy Ed)*.

A lesser entry in the "Hopalong Cassidy" series. Boyd stars as Hopalong, here a rancher plagued by rustlers. Typically, the problem is solved through horse and gun play mixed with some two-fisted action. Clyde provides the humor in this below-par and poorly titled western. (See HOPALONG CASSIDY series, Index.)

p, Harry A. Sherman; d, George Archainbaud; w, J. Benton Cheney (based on characters created by Clarence E. Mulford); ph, Russell Harlan; ed, Frederick Berger; md, Irvin Talbot.

Western (PR:A MPAA:NR)

MYSTERY OF DIAMOND ISLAND, THE

(SEE: RIP ROARING RILEY, 1935)

MYSTERY OF EDWIN DROOD, THE*** (1935) 85m UNIV bw

Claude Rains *(John Jasper)*, Douglass Montgomery *(Neville Landless)*, Heather Angel *(Rosa Bud)*, David Manners *(Edwin Drood)*, Valerie Hobson *(Helena Landless)*, Francis L. Sullivan *(Mr. Crisparkle)*, Walter Kingsford *(Hiram Grewigious)*, E. E. Clive *(Thomas Sapsea)*, Vera Buckland *(Tope)*, Forrester Harvey *(Durdles)*, Louise Carter *(Mrs. Crisparkle)*, Ethel Griffies *(Miss Twinkleton)*, George Ernest *(Deputy)*, Zeffie Tilbury *(Opium Den Hag)*, Joseph M. Kerrigan.

Rains is a cathedral choirmaster and opium addict who falls in love with Angel, the fiancee of his nephew, Manners. During a raging storm on Christmas Eve he strangles Manners and dumps his body in a quicklime pit in the crypt under the cathedral. He tries to pin the murder on Montgomery, just back from Ceylon, but he is foiled and eventually the crypt is opened and in the lime pit can be seen the impression left by Manners' body, with his engagement ring plainly visible where his hand used to be. As accusing eyes fall on Rains, he climbs to the top of the church tower and jumps to his death. Charles Dickens died before completing the novel on which the film is based, and how he would have resolved this situations he set up has been a subject of debate among literature professors ever since. This variation on one of the suggested scenarios works reasonably well despite some tortuous twists in logic, but it is Rains—in his fourth feature—who carries the film as he smokes opium and is wracked with unholy lust for Angel and with guilt over his crime. The look of the film is shadowy gothic, perfectly complementing the Gothic horror story the Universal writers made of Dickens' unfinished work, and the crypt set was the one built for DRACULA (1931), one of many appearances that mossy basement was to make in Universal's films.

p, Edmund Grainger; d, Stuart Walker; w, John L. Balderston, Gladys Unger, Leopold Atlas, Bradley King (based on an unfinished novel by Charles Dickens); ph, George Robinson; m, Edward Ward; ed, Edward Curtis; art d, Albert S. D'Agostino; spec eff, John P. Fulton.

Horror (PR:C MPAA:NR)

MYSTERY OF KASPAR HAUSER, THE

(SEE: EVERY MAN FOR HIMSELF AND GOD AGAINST ALL, 1975, Ger.)

MYSTERY OF MARIE ROGET, THE**

(1942) 61m UNIV bw (AKA: PHANTOM OF PARIS)

Patric Knowles *(Dr. Paul Dupin)*, Maria Montez *(Marie Roget)*, Maria Ouspenskaya *(Mme. Cecile Roget)*, Lloyd Corrigan *(Gobelin, the Prefect of Police)*, John Litel *(Henri Beauvais)*, Nell O'Day *(Camille Roget)*, Edward Norris *(Marcel Vignon)*, Frank Reicher *(Magistrate)*, Clyde Fillmore *(Mons. De Luc)*, Norma Drury *(Mme. De Luc)*, John Maxwell, Bill Ruhl, Paul Bryar *(Detectives)*, Paul E. Burns *(Gardener)*, Charles Middleton *(Curator of the Zoo)*, Reed Hadley *(Naval Officer)*, Paul Dubov *(Pierre, the News Vendor)*, Joe Bernard, Frank O'Connor *(Men)*, Ray Bailey *(Gendarme)*, Charles Wagenheim, Lester Dorr *(Subordinates to Prefect)*. Alphonse

Martel *(Vegetable Cart Driver)*, Francis Sayles, Jimmie Lucas *(Parisians)*, Beatrice Roberts *(Wife on Street)*, Caroline Cooke *(Woman)*.

Montez stars as a Parisian music hall star who plots to kill her younger sister O'Day. Norris knows about her scheme, but things go awry when Montez herself is murdered. Another woman is found with her face horribly mutilated. Knowles attempts to discover "who is the phantom mangler of Paris?" The story unfolds at a good pace with some neat plot twists, but the film is severely hampered by a weak script and small budget. Loosely adapted from a story by Poe, which itself was based on a real murder in 1842.

p, Paul Malvern; d, Phil Rosen; w, Michael Jacoby (based on the story by Edgar Allen Poe); ph, Elwood "Woody" Bredell; m, H. J. Salter; ed, Milton Carruth; md, Salter; art d, Jack Otterson; m/l, "Maman Dites Moi," Everett Carter, Milton Rosen (sung by Montez, dubbed by Dorothy Triden).

Mystery **(PR:A MPAA:NR)**

MYSTERY OF MR. WONG, THE*** (1939) 67m MON bw

Boris Karloff *(James Lee Wong)*, Grant Withers *(Capt. Sam Street)*, Dorothy Tree *(Valerie Edwards)*, Craig Reynolds *(Peter Harrison)*, Lotus Long *(Drina, Maid)*, Morgan Wallace *(Brendan Edwards, Curio Collector)*, Holmes Herbert *(Prof. Ed Janney)*, Ivan Lebedeff *(Michael Strogonoff)*, Hooper Atchley *(Carslake)*, Bruce Wong *(Man)*, Lee Tong Foo *(Willie)*, Chester Gan *(Sing, Servant)*.

"Eye of the Daughter of the Moon" is the largest star sapphire in the world. Stolen from China, it comes into the possession of Wallace, a gem collector, who has obtained it through nefarious means and now his life is in danger. He receives a letter with a death threat and calls in Karloff, explaining that should he die, the letter will give important clues to the murderer's identity. Meanwhile Wallace discovers Reynolds, his wife's secretary, trying to talk her into divorcing Wallace. Later, during a game of charades, the lights go out and Wallace is shot. At first Reynolds is accused but is soon proven innocent. Next attention turns to a maid (Long), an Oriental woman who wants to return the diamond to the museum where it belonged. She too is murdered, and the mysterious letter disappears. Finally Karloff proves the murderer to be Herbert, a long-time friend of Karloff's whose sister was Wallace's first wife. The gem is returned to it's rightful owners and the killer turned over to the police. Though Karloff is primarily remembered for his monster movies, he also starred in the "Mr. Wong" films for Monogram studios. This, the second of the series, is an evenly paced mystery. Though occasionally it's drawing room manner is dull, Karloff is excellent. His careful diction, combined with that unforgettable voice, creates a marvelous characterization. Though not Oriental, Karloff is still believable as the Chinese detective. The supporting cast leaves something to be desired: Tree and Reynolds are unimpressive as the lovers, though Wallace and Herbert are adequate. (See MR. WONG series, Index.)

p, Scott R. Dunlap; d, William Nigh; w, W. Scott Darling (based on the short stories by Hugh Wiley); ph, Harry Neumann; ed, Russell Schoengarth; makeup, Gordon Bau.

Mystery **Cas.** **(PR:A MPAA:NR)**

MYSTERY OF MR. X, THE*** (1934) 84m MGM bw

Robert Montgomery *(Nicholas Revel)*, Elizabeth Allan *(Jane Frensham)*, Lewis Stone *(Inspector Connor)*, Ralph Forbes *(Sir Christopher Marche)*, Henry Stephenson *(Sir Herbert Frensham)*, Forrester Harvey *(Palmer)*, Ivan Simpson *(Hutchinson)*, Leonard Mudie *(Mr. X)*, Alec B. Francis *(Judge Malpas)*, Charles Irwin *(Willis)*, Colin Kenny *(Constable)*, Pearl Varvell *(Barmaid)*, Henry Mowbray *(Detective)*, Barlowe Borland *(Headwaiter)*, Alfred Cross, Olaf Hytten, Norman Ainslie, Terry Spencer, Victor Gammon, Captain Francis *(Reporters)*, Eric Wilton *(Butler)*, Richard Lancaster, Robert A'Dair, Pat Moriarity *(Policemen)*, Harrington Reynolds *(Motor Cop)*, Milton Royce *(London Bobby)*, William Stack *(Travers Gordon)*, Claude King *(Cummings)*, Douglas Gordon *(Court Clerk)*, Raymond Milland *(Forbes)*, Clive Morgan *(Blanchard)*, Pat Somerset *(Bit)*, Montague Shaw *(Doctor)*, John Power *(Bobbie)*, Raymond Lawrence *(Padgot)*.

Mudie plays a maniacal killer released from prison after serving 15 years. He begins killing one policeman for each year spent in prison, baffling Scotland Yard. Montgomery is a jewel thief who becomes the chief suspect. In order to save himself, Montgomery goes after the killer and stops Mudie. This is a well-crafted thriller, sparsely written and to the point. The direction makes the most of the London setting, creating suspense through the use of a foggy atmosphere. Well paced, with believable performances. The romance between Montgomery and Allan (the daughter of the head of Scotland Yard) is out of place, but it never detracts from the plot.

p, Lawrence Weingarten; d, Edgar Selwyn; w, Howard Emmett Rogers, Monckton Hoffe, Philip MacDonald (based on the novel *Mystery of the Dead Police* by MacDonald); ph, Oliver T. Marsh; ed, Hugh Wynn.

Crime **(PR:C MPAA:NR)**

MYSTERY OF ROOM 13**

(1941, Brit.) 71m BN/Alliance bw (GB: MR. REEDER IN ROOM 13)

Gibb McLaughlin *(J. G. Reeder)*, Sara Seegar *(Lila)*, Peter Murray Hill *(Johnnie Gray)*, Sally Gray *(Claire Kane)*, Malcolm Keen *(Peter Kane)*, Leslie Perrins *(Jeff Legge)*, D. J. Williams *(Emmanuel Legge)*, Robert Cochran *(Barker)*, George Merritt *(Stevens)*, Philip Ray, Rex Carvel, Florence Groves.

McLaughlin is a detective who catches on to a forgery ring. He gets Hill to go to prison in order to crack the gang. If that's not improbable enough for a plot twist, poor Hill finds upon his release three years later that his girl (Gray) has hitched up with the gang's ruler, Perrins. McLaughlin saves Hill from being hanged by the gang in this witless, utterly implausible story.

p, John Corfield; d, Norman Lee; w, Doreen Montgomery, Victor Kendall, Elizabeth Meehan (based on the novel *Room 13* by Edgar Wallace)

Crime **Cas.** **(PR:A MPAA:NR)**

MYSTERY OF THE BLACK JUNGLE*

(1955) 72m Cosmopolitan/REP bw (AKA: BLACK DEVILS OF KALI, THE)

Lex Barker, Jane Maxwell, Luigi Tosi, Paul Muller, Jack Rex, Pamela Palma.

Ethnocentric trash has ex-movie TARZAN Barker and his comrades going off to India, where they meet up with a tribe of idol worshippers. Film follows an expected course of events in the lowest form that failing Republic Studios was able to muster at the time. A sad warning of the impending doom that was finally to hit the studio once known for its near perfect B pictures.

p, Georges Venturini; d, Ralph Murphy; w, Murphy, Jean Paul Callegari (based on the novel *Misterio Nero Bosco* by Emillio Salgari); ph, Masimo Dallamano; m, Georges Tzipine, Giovanni Fusco; ed, Louris Bellero; cos, Maud Strudthoff; ch, Anna Gorilovich.

Adventure **(PR:A MPAA:NR)**

MYSTERY OF THE GOLDEN EYE, THE*

(1948) 69m MON bw (AKA: GOLDEN EYE, THE)

Roland Winters *(Charlie Chan)*, Mantan Moreland *(Birmingham Brown)*, Victor Sen Young *(Tommy Chan)*, Tim Ryan *(Lt. Ruark)*, Bruce Kellogg *(Bartlett)*, Wanda McKay *(Evelyn)*, Ralph Dunn *(Driscoll)*, Forrest Taylor *(Manning)*, Evelyn Brent *(Teresa)*, Lois Austin *(Mrs. Driscoll)*, Lee "Lasses" White *(Pete)*, Edmund Cobb *(1st Miner)*, Tom Tyler, George L. Spaulding, Barbara Jean Wong, Lee Tung Foo, Richard Loo, Bill Walker, Herman Cantor, John Merton.

Winters, in his first time as Chan, finds himself out West investigating what appears to be an empty mine that suddenly is producing gold. It turns out that gold is being smuggled out of Mexico and sold at exorbitant prices, the empty mine being used as a front. Standard production values for the fare. A forgettable addition to the "Chan" series. (See CHARLIE CHAN series, Index.)

p, James S. Burkett; d, William Beaudine; w, W. Scott Darling (based on characters created by Earl Derr Biggers); ph, William Sickner; ed, Ace Herman; md, Edward J. Kay; art d, Dave Milton; set d, Raymond Boltz, Jr.; makeup, Webb Overlander.

Mystery **(PR:A MPAA:NR)**

MYSTERY OF THE HOODED HORSEMEN, THE½**

(1937) 59m GN WB bw

Tex Ritter *(Tex Martin)*, Iris Meredith *(Nancy)*, Horace Murphy *(Stubby)*, Charles King *(Blackie)*, Earl Dwire *(Sheriff)*, Forrest Taylor *(Norton)*, Joseph Girard *(Dan Farley)*, Lafe McKee *(Tom Wilson)*, Oscar Gahan, Jack C. Smith, Chick Hannon, Tex Palmer, Lynton Brent, Heber Snow [Hank Worden], Ray Whitley and his Range Ramblers [Ken Card, the Phelps Brothers], White Flash the Horse.

Unlike other westerns which featured various masked riders in the role of hero, this Ritter film features hoods on the villains. Though any western fan worth his saddle soap will know it's King beneath the hood, the villain is still marvelously evil. As expected, Ritter unmasks King in the end. Energetic direction makes this film better than most serial westerns. Unfortunately it's marred by the overindulgence of Ritter's singing, which gets in the way of the action.

p, Edward Finney; d, Ray Taylor; w, Edmund Kelso; ph, Gus Peterson; m, Tex Ritter, Fred Rose, Michael David, Frank Sanucci; ed, Frederick Bain.

Western **Cas.** **(PR:A MPAA:NR)**

MYSTERY OF THE MARIE CELESTE (SEE: PHANTOM SHIP, 1935, Brit.)

MYSTERY OF THE PINK VILLA, THE

1930, Brit. (SEE: MYSTERY AT THE VILLA ROSE, 1930, Brit)

MYSTERY OF THE PINK VILLA, THE **½

(1930, Fr.) 100m Twickenham bw

Simone Vaudry, Baron, Jr., Leon Mathot, George Peclet.

Made in both a French and English version, this is an interesting film about a jewel robbery in France. Baron, Jr., (son of the famous French mime, Baron, Sr.) provides comic relief to Mathot's subtle performance as the detective. Counting less on physical action, this is one of the many early talkies that thrived on the medium, without overdoing the speeches. In the early sound cinema, before subtitles, making two or three versions of a film in various languages was a common practice.

d, Leslie Hiscott; w, Louis Mercanton, Renee Hervil (based on the story by A. E. W. Mason).

Crime **(PR:A MPAA:NR)**

MYSTERY OF THE 13TH GUEST, THE* (1943) 61m MON bw

Dick Purcell *(Johnny)*, Helen Parrish *(Marie)*, Tim Ryan *(Burke)*, Frank Faylen *(Speed)*, John Duncan *(Harold)*, Jon Dawson *(Jackson)*, Paul McVey *(Morgan)*, Jacqueline Dalya *(Marjory)*, Cyril Ring *(Barksdale)*, Addison Richards *(District Attorney)*, Lloyd Ingraham.

There's danger afoot as people are being killed because someone's trying to get rid of the beneficiary to a will. Purcell is the detective investigating the proceedings, and Parrish the girl in trouble. Poorly directed, the film drags on until the happy ending, which is no surprise. A remake of a 1932 Ginger Rogers film.

p, Lindsley Parsons; d, William Beaudine; w, Charles Marion, Arthur Hoerl, Tim Ryan (based on "The 13th Guest" by Armitage Trail); ph, Mack Stengler; ed, Dick Currier; art d, Dave Milton.

Crime **Cas.** **(PR:A MPAA:NR)**

MYSTERY OF THE WAX MUSEUM, THE**** (1933) 73m WB c

Lionel Atwill *(Ivan Igor)*, Fay Wray *(Charlotte Duncan)*, Glenda Farrell *(Florence Dempsey)*, Frank McHugh *(Jim)*, Gavin Gordon *(Harold Winton)*, Edwin Maxwell *(Joe Worth)*, Holmes Herbert *(Dr. Rasmussen)*, Arthur Edmund Carewe *(Sparrow)*, Allen Vincent *(Ralph Burton)*, Monica Bannister *(Joan Gale)*, Matthew Betz *(Hugo)*, DeWitt Jennings *(Captain of Police)*, Thomas E. Jackson *(Detective)*, Bull Anderson *(The Janitor)*, Pat O'Malley *(Plain clothesman)*.

The second outing with stars Atwill and Wray for director Curtiz in another two-strip Technicolor horror film (the first was Dr. X in 1932) produced by Warner Bros. The film opens in London, 1921. We see Atwill, a brilliant sculptor, hard at work on hislatest creation. He is surrounded by a beautiful series of wax figures based on historical characters such as Joan of Arc and Marie Antoinette. Having eschewed the more sensational—and therefore, more lucrative—figures of killers like Jack the Ripper in favor of his beautiful creations, Atwill finds his wax museum on the brink of bankruptcy. His sculpting is interrupted by a visit from a friend who has brought along a man interested in investing in the museum. The man is very impressed with Atwill's work and vows to finance the museum after he returns from a business trip abroad. After his guests leave, Atwill's partner, Maxwell, arrives and dismisses the investor's promises. Maxwell wants an immediate return on his investment, so he announces that he's going to burn the museum down and collect the insurance money. Enraged that his "children" will be destroyed by the flames, Atwill tries to stop Maxwell. A vicious fight ensues as the wax figures burn and melt around them. Atwill is knocked unconscious and left to die as the museum burns. New Year's Eve in New York City, 1933. Atwill, now with gray hair and confined to a wheelchair, his hands crippled from the fire, watches the festivities from a window. That night a wealthy socialite girl who lived life in the fast lane makes headlines by killing herself with an overdose of drugs. A tough-talking female reporter, Farrell, is assigned to investigate the case. Later that night a man with a horribly distorted face, dressed in a black cloak and hat, enters the morgue and steals the body of the dead socialite. The incident becomes a front-page scandal and Farrell is told to stay on the story. Meanwhile, the wheelchair-bound Atwill prepares to open a new wax museum in New York. Since his hands are crippled and he can no longer sculpt, Atwill has hired a strange mix of artists who create wax figures under his supervision. With the exception of Vincent, a young art student, the sculptors look as if they have escaped from prison. One of them, Carewe, is a junkie, the other, Betz, is a hulking deaf mute. That afternoon, Carewe delivers his latest sculpture—Joan of Arc. Almost as beautiful as the original figure lost in the fire, this display bears an uncanny resemblance to the socialite who killed herself. The fact is not lost on Farrell who sees the statue while accompanying her roommate, Wray, to the museum. Wray is Vincent's fiancee, and while Vincent introduces her to Atwill, Farrell wanders off to examine the wax figure. Atwill is quite taken with Wray and tells her that she greatly resembles the wax figure of Marie Antoinette that was destroyed in the fire. He asks if she will pose for his sculptors sometime and she agrees. In the meantime, Farrell has become convinced that the Joan of Arc figure is the wax-covered corpse of the dead socialite and sets out to expose Atwill (the figure of Voltaire, too, resembles a local judge who has been missing for weeks). On her urging, the police arrest Carewe the next day and brutally interrogate him. Suffering from painful withdrawal because he hasn't had a fix, Carewe confesses. At the same time, Wray has gone to the wax museum to meet Vincent. She finds Atwill instead and he begins to rave alarmingly about preserving her beauty forever. As she tries to back away from him, Atwill stands up out of his wheelchair and walks, unaided, toward her. The confused girl becomes hysterical and when Atwill tries to put his arms around her, she slaps his face. The slap, however, seems to splinter and crack Atwill's face. The terrified girl hits him again, harder this time. More of Atwill's face cracks and falls to the floor. Seized with panic, Wray pulls the rest of Atwill's face off to reveal the horrible twisted and scarred visage beneath the wax shell. Atwill had been hideously disfigured in the fire 12 years before. Wray screams and faints. Atwill takes the girl to his basement laboratory where he strips her naked and places her under a device that will drip hot wax over her body. As the wax begins to boil, Farrell and the police arrive. On the catwalk above the cauldron of boiling wax, Atwill fights the lawmen with insane strength. Eventually the police overpower him and Atwill falls into the hot wax. Wray is saved just before the wax would have covered her. Feared to be a lost film for many years, THE MYSTERY OF THE WAX MUSEUM gained a mighty reputation based on recollections of historians whose memories were jarred by the 1953 3-D remake, HOUSE OF WAX. When a print of the original film surfaced in the late 1960s (it was found in Jack Warner's private vault), many were disappointed with it and shrugged it off as a somewhat silly mystery picture. Interest in the film waned and all talk of expensive restoration ceased. Knowing that they could sell the film to television, the studio struck cheaply made prints from the original negative. While certainly better than nothing, the color quality of the prints is awful, with most of each film appearing to be tinted in an orange-green hue. It is a tragedy that a film known in 1933 for its remarkable use of color must now be seen impaired due to economic frugality. The initial reactions of malcontent historians and critics to the resurrection of the film were closed-minded and entirely unfounded. THE MYSTERY OF THE WAX MUSEUM is an amazing film filled with stunning sets, exceptional moments, and perhaps Atwill's greatest performance. It is an surprisingly adult picture that deals quite explicitly with drug addiction, necrophilia, and insanity. Notably, it was also one of the first horror films to be set in the everyday reality of modern-day New York and not in a detached, mystical foreign land like the Transylvania of DRACULA or the Bavarian township of FRANKENSTEIN. This must have made the horror all the more real to audiences used to being able to comfort themselves with the fact that the action was taking place in a faraway place wholly unrelated to their own existence. THE MYSTERY OF THE WAX MUSEUM is brimming with horrific moments. The opening fire that destroys Atwill's museum and drives him mad is a true show-stopper. The figures take on horrible expressions as the wax melts away, making their glass eyes appear to bulge wider and wider. The scenes of Atwill prowling about unmasked in his black garb are played in total silence, lending an air of quiet unease and terror. The climactic fight on the catwalk is also done with expert flair, but the scene where Wray cracks apart Atwill's wax face to reveal the scarred mass of black flesh underneath ranks as one of the truly great moments in horror film history. The 3-D remake in 1953, HOUSE OF WAX, starring Vincent Price, is a fine achievement in its own right and by far the best 3-D film ever made.

p, Henry Blanke; d, Michael Curtiz; w, Don Mullally, Carl Erickson (based on a play by Charles S. Belden); ph, Ray Rennahan (Technicolor); ed, George Amy; art d, Anton Grot.

Horror **(PR:C MPAA:NR)**

MYSTERY OF THE WENTWORTH CASTLE, THE
(SEE: DOOMED TO DIE, 1940)

MYSTERY OF THE WHITE ROOM zero (1939) 58m UNIV bw

Bruce Cabot *(Dr. Bob Clayton)*, Helen Mack *(Carole Dale, Nurse)*, Constance Worth *(Ann Stokes)*, Joan Woodbury *(Lila Haines, Nurse)*, Mabel Todd *(Dora Stanley)*, Tom Dugan *(Hank Manley)*, Roland Drew *(Dr. Norman Kennedy)*, Addison Richards *(Dr. Martin)*, Tommy Jackson *(Sgt. Mack Spencer)*, Frank Reicher *(Dr. Amos Thornton)*, Frank Puglia *(Tony, Janitor)*, Holmes Herbert *(Hospital Administrator)*.

There's murder in the operating room! Cabot and Mack are a romantically paired surgeon and nurse caught up in the search for the killer. They're also caught up in a bad movie. The script is impossible to follow and direction gives it no help at all. Motivations, logic, and plotting are all missing.

p, Irving Starr; d, Otis Garrett; w, Alex Gottlieb (based on the story "Murder in Surgery" by James G. Edwards [James William MacQueen]); ph, John Boyle; ed, Harry Keller.

Drama **(PR:A MPAA:NR)**

MYSTERY OF THUG ISLAND, THE*½

(1966, Ital./Ger.) 96m Liber-Eichberg/COL c (I MISTERI DELLA GIUNGLA NERA; DAS GEHEIMNIS DER LEDERSCHLINGE)

Guy Madison *(Souyadhana [Boujdhans])*, Ingeborg Schoner *(Edy [Ada])*, Giacomo Rossi Stuart *(Tremal-Naik)*, Ivan Desny *(Maciadi)*, Giulia Rubini *(Gundali)*, Nando Poggi *(Kammamuri)*, Peter Van Eyck *(MacPherson)*, Aldo Bufi-Landi, Aldo Cristiani, Romano Giomini.

Madison is the leader of a murderous island cult who kidnaps the daughter of British officer Van Eyck. Fifteen years later the officer organizes an expedition to recover his daughter, who is being prepared for a virginal sacrifice. A local snake hunter falls in love with the girl and is captured by the gang. He is ordered to kill Van Eyck or he'll never see the girl again. Instead he pairs up with the officer and together they defeat Madison and rescue the girl. Released in Italy in 1964, it was a remake of a similarly titled 1953 picture.

p, Nino Battieferri; d, Luigi Capuano; w, Arpad De Riso, Ottavio Poggi (based on the novel *I Misteri Della Jungla Nera* by Emilio Salgari); ph, Guglielmo Mancori (Eastmancolor); m, Carlo Rustichelli; ed, Antonietta Zita; art d, Ernesto Kromberg; set d, Camillo Del Signore; cos, Casa d'Arte Firenze; ch, Nando Poggi; makeup, Anacleto Giustini.

Adventure **(PR:A MPAA:NR)**

MYSTERY ON BIRD ISLAND***

(1954, Brit.) 57m Rayant-Children's Film Foundation/BL bw

Mavis Sage *(Marion)*, Jennifer Beach *(Jeanne)*, Nicky Emdett *(Victor)*, Alexander Gauge *(Bronson)*, Vernon Morris *(John)*, Peter Arne *(Henri)*, Roddy Hughes *(Grumpy)*, Howard Connell *(Gaston)*, Alan Mackay, John Drake

When two children take a vacation on an island, they meet two residents of their age. The four become friends and together discover that a smuggling operation is being run out of a local bird sanctuary. Gauge is the leader who tries to stop the youthful quartet, but his efforts are to no avail as the kids turn the gang over to authorities. This children's mystery is nicely told, with good pacing. Fine entertainment for younger viewers.

p, Anthony Gilkison; d, John Haggerty; w, Mary Cathcart Borer, Haggerty (based on a story by Mary Dunn); ph, William Pollard.

Children's Mystery **(PR:A MPAA:NR)**

MYSTERY ON MONSTER ISLAND
(SEE: MONSTER ISLAND, 1981, U.S./Span.)

MYSTERY PLANE** (1939) 60m MON bw

John Trent *(Tailspin Tommy)*, Milburn Stone *(Skeeter)*, Marjorie Reynolds *(Betty Lou)*, Jason Robards [Sr.] *(Paul)*, Peter George Lynn *(Brandy)*, Lucien Littlefield *(Winslow)*, Polly Ann Young *(Anita)*, Sayre Deering *(Fred)*, John Peters *(Carl)*, Tommy Bupp *(Tommy as a child)*, Betsy Gay *(Betty Lou as a child)*

Plucky teen-agers invent a device that improves the bombing ability of airplanes. They gladly will fork it over to the government but only if they can keep the new invention from falling into the hands of Littlefield and company. Based on the semi-popular "Tailspin Tommy" comic strip, this is a cute little film with some nice aerial footage.

p, Paul Malvern; d, George Waggner; w, Paul Schofield, Joseph West (based on the comic strip "Tailspin Tommy" by Hal Forrest); ph, Archie Stout; m, Frank Sanucci; ed, Carl Pierson; md, Sanucci; spec eff, Fred Jackman.

Drama **Cas.** **(PR:A MPAA:NR)**

MYSTERY RANCH*** (1932) 56m FOX bw (AKA: KILLER, THE)

George O'Brien *(Bob Sanborn)*, Cecilia Parker *(Jane Emory)*, Charles Middleton *(Henry Steele)*, Charles Stevens *(Tonto)*, Forrester Harvey *(Artie Drower)*, Noble Johnson *(Mudo)*, Roy Stewart *(Buck)*, Virginia Herdman *(Homesteader's Wife)*, Betty Francisco *(Mae)*, Russ Powell *(Sheriff)*.

Parker is a rancher in peril. Middleton is holding her hostage, trying to get her to marry him so he can control her vast land holdings. O'Brien rides in to save the day, courtesy of some hard fighting and shooting. O'Brien plays his role well and Middleton is appropriately sinister. Of special interest is the photography, which is more atmospheric than in most westerns. The cameraman was August, the regular cinematographer for the great western director John Ford.

p, Bernard B. Ray; d, David Howard; w, Al Cohn (based on the novel *The Killer* by Stewart Edward White); ph, Joseph August; ed, Paul Weatherwax.

Western **(PR:A MPAA:NR)**

MYSTERY RANGE** (1937) 56m Victory bw

Tom Tyler, Jerry Bergh, Milburn Morante, Lafe McKee, Roger Williams, Dick Alexander, Jim Corey, Slim Whitaker.

When rustlers turn to murder, it's up to Tyler to stop them. After lots of rip-roaring gunplay, the nefarious dudes are stopped by the law-abiding cowpokes and Tyler scores another notch on his popularity gun, which eventually would lead him to the Three Mesquiteer series.

p, Sam Katzman; d, Bob Hill; w, Basil Dickey.

Western **(PR:A MPAA:NR)**

MYSTERY SEA RAIDER** (1940) 75m PAR bw

Carole Landis *(June McCarthy)*, Henry Wilcoxon *(Capt. Jimmy Madden)*, Onslow Stevens *(Carl Cutler)*, Kathleen Howard *(Maggie Clancy)*, Wallace Rairden *(Blake, 3rd Mate)*, Sven-Hugo Borg *(Sven)*, Henry Victor *(Cmdr. Bulow)*, Roland Varno *(Lt. Schmidt)*, Louis Adlon *(Lerner)*, Will Kaufman *(Lt. Felder)*, Monte Blue *(Capt. Norberg)*, Matthew Boulton *(Capt. Howard)*, Gohr Van Vleck *(Capt. Van Wyck)*, Jean Del Val *(Capt. Benoit)*, Kay Linaker *(Flossie La Mare)*, Reed Howes *(Hughes, Carl's Chauffeur)*, Philip Warren *(Sparks, Radio Operator)*.

Standard melodrama-intrigue film about a freighter hijacked by Nazis in the Carribean. Landis happens to be aboard, thus causing some romantic interest with the danger. Much newsreel footage of German ships and submarines is incorporated into the film and it's all easily spotted. Eventually a British cruiser comes to save the day, with Landis doing her part as well. Stevens is fairly convincing as the Nazi captain. The direction and script are standard.

p, Eugene J. Zukor; d, Edward Dmytryk; w, Edward E. Paramore, Jr. (based on a story by Robert Grant); ph, Harry Fischbeck, Dewey Wrigley; ed, Archie Marshek; md, Andrea Setaro; art d, Hans Dreier, Robert Odell.

Drama **(PR:A MPAA:NR)**

MYSTERY SHIP** (1941) 65m COL bw

Paul Kelly *(Allan Harper)*, Lola Lane *(Patricia Marshall)*, Larry Parks *(Tommy Baker)*, Trevor Bardette *(Ernst Madek)*, Cy Kendall *(Condor)*, Roger Imhof *(Capt. Randall)*, Eddie Laughton *(Turillo)*, John Tyrell *(Sam)*, Byron Foulger *(Wasserman)*, Dick Curtis *(Van Brock)*, Dwight Frye *(Rader)*, Kenneth MacDonald *(Gorman)*.

Kelly is a G-Man selected to escort a group of assorted crooks, thugs, and other nasties who are being deported to an unnamed country. They're all locked up in the hold of a ship and when they break out there's plenty of two-fisted action. Lane's a reporter and Kelly's girl friend who comes along for a story. Short on plot but long on action, this is a film that doesn't pretend to be something it's not. Parks shows talent in his film debut, somehow rising above the material.

p, Jack Fier; d, Lew Landers; w, David Silverstein, Houston Branch (based on a story by Alex Gottlieb); ph, L. W. O'Connell; ed, James Sweeney.

Action/Drama **(PR:A MPAA:NR)**

MYSTERY STREET*½** (1950) 93m MGM bw

Ricardo Montalban *(Lt. Peter Moralas)*, Sally Forrest *(Grace Shanway)*, Bruce Bennett *(Dr. McAdoo)*, Elsa Lanchester *(Mrs. Smerrling)*, Marshall Thompson *(Henry Shanway)*, Jan Sterling *(Vivian Heldon)*, Edmon Ryan *(James Joshua Harkley)*, Betsy Blair *(Jackie Elcott)*, Wally Maher *(Tim Sharkey)*, Ralph Dumke *(Tattooist)*, Willard Waterman *(Mortician)*, Walter Burke *(Ornithologist)*, Don Shelton *(District Attorney)*, Brad Hatton *(Bartender)*, Douglas Carter *(Counterman)*, William F. Leicester *(Doctor)*, Arthur Lowe, Jr. *(Sailor)*, Sherry Hall *(Clerk)*, James Hayward *(Constable Fischer)*, Eula Guy *(Mrs. Fischer)*, Virginia Mullen *(Neighbor)*, King Donovan, George Cooper, Ralph Brooks, George Sherwood, John Crawford *(Reporters)*, Fred E. Sherman, Allen O'Locklin *(Photographers)*, Melvin H. Moore *(Oyster Shucker)*, Ned Glass *(Dr. Levy)*, Matt Moore *(Dr. Rockton)*, Maurice Samuels *(Tailor)*, John Maxwell *(Kilrain)*, Robert Foulk *(O'Hara)*, Louise Lorimer *(Mrs. Shanway)*, Napoleon Whiting *(Redcap)*, Jack Shea *(Policeman)*, Mary Jane Smith, Juanita Quigley *(Daughters)*, Lucille Curtis *(Mrs. Harkley)*, Charles Wagenheim *(Clerk)*, David McMahon *(Garrity)*, Michael Patrick Donovan *(Porter)*, Frank Overton *(Guard)*, Bert Davidson *(Dr. Thorpe)*, May McAvoy *(Nurse)*, Mack Chandler *(Doorman)*, Elsie Baker *(Elderly Lady)*, Ralph Montgomery *(Waiter)*, Jim Frasher *(High School Boy)*, Ernesto Morelli *(Portuguese Fisherman)*, Robert Strong *(Cop)*, George Brand *(Man in Bedroom)*, Fred Santley *(Pawnbroker)*, Perry Ivins *(Alienist)*, Peter Thompson *(Law Student)*.

Ryan is a married man, the descendent of a fine old Boston family. Sterling is a floozy he's having an affair with. Discovering she is pregnant, Sterling arranges to meet her lover on a remote beachfront but encounters Thompson, a sympathetic stranger. She tells him her story and he offers to drive her to meet Ryan. But she tricks him and takes his car. At her rendezvous with Ryan, the pregnancy is revealed. Horrified at the consequences, Ryan shoots her and removes the clothing from the corpse. After dumping the naked body into the ocean, he drives the car to a nearby bog and sinks it. Thompson meanwhile has reported his car stolen. Soon the remains of the body wash up on shore. Montalban, head of the investigative team, along with Harvard medical expert Bennett, determine the victim's identity and how she was killed. After the car is found Thompson is arrested for murder. But Montalban is not convinced of the man's guilt and probes further. Lanchester, the dead girl's landlady, has meanwhile discovered Ryan's phone number in Sterling's room. She blackmails the man and manages to steal the murder weapon. Ryan goes to the rooming house to confront Lanchester but is met by Montalban and Thompson's wife, Forrest. He escapes, but Montalban gets hold of a key to the bus station locker where Lanchester has hidden the gun. The next morning he catches the real killer in the bus station. Though MGM was not well known for *film noir*, under the direction of Dore Schary a number of these well-made, moody crime films were produced between 1948 and 1956. Though a standard police drama, MYSTERY STREET is a taut, well paced thriller. Filmed in a semi-documentary style with an atmospheric and moody photography job, the location shooting at Harvard and the Boston area is well employed. Montalban is fine in the lead role, playing well against Ryan. The ethnic detective versus the upper crust murderer not only makes for good mystery, but also provides an interesting social commentary. Though Ryan represents a class where everything fits into it's neat little place, he finds himself fighting for his lifestyle and his life against a man of more common means. One of a series of films in the 1950s which concentrated on the science of forensics in police work. Here, the Harvard Department of Legal Medicine reconstructed the murder of Sterling for Montalban and then found the guilty man out of 86 suspects, by the scientific treatment of Sterling's skeleton.

p, Frank E. Taylor; d, John Sturges; w, Sydney Boehm, Richard Brooks (based on an unpublished story by Leonard Spigelgass); ph, John Alton; m, Rudolph G. Kopp; ed, Ferris Webster; art d, Cedric Gibbons, Gabriel Scognamillo; set d, Edwin B. Willis, Ralph S. Hurst; makeup, Jack Dawn, Sam Palo.

Mystery/Crime **(PR:C MPAA:NR)**

MYSTERY SUBMARINE*½ (1950) 78m UNIV bw

Macdonald Carey *(Dr. Brett Young)*, Marta Toren *(Madeleine Brenner)*, Robert Douglas *(Comdr. von Molter)*, Carl Esmond *(Lt. Heldman)*, Ludwig Donath *(Dr. Adolph Guernitz)*, Jacqueline Dalya Hilliard *(Carla)*, Fred Nurney *(Bruno)*, Katherine Warren *(Mrs. Weber)*, Howard Negley *(Capt. Elliott)*, Bruce Morgan *(Kramer)*, Ralph Brooke *(Stefan)*, Paul Hoffman *(Hartwig)*, Peter Michael, Larry Winter, Frank Rawls, Peter Similuk *(Members of the Crew)*, Lester Sharpe *(Citadel Captain)*, Jimmy Best *(Navy Lieutenant)*.

Insipid plot features Douglas as the commander of a renegade submarine. He tricks Toren into believing her husband is alive (though he was killed in the war). This way he can use her to get famed German scientist Donath for an unnamed foreign power. Carey is the hero who rescues Donath and Toren, then destroys the sub. This was Sirk's first directorial effort for Universal but shows none of the director's talent. The script is simplistic, with stereotyped characters and stock situations, and the direction is flat and uninspired. This embarrassing feature was Sirk's first for Universal under a seven-year contract, and one of which he says, "I remember nothing about many of the early Universal pictures, and, anyway, they are best forgotten."

p, Ralph Dietrich; d, Douglas Sirk; w, George W. George, George F. Slavin (based on a story by Dietrich); ph, Clifford Stine; m, Joseph Gershenson; ed, Virgil Vogel; art d, Bernard Herzbrun, Robert Boyle; set d, Russell A. Gausman, Otto Siegel; cos, Bill Thomas; spec eff, David S. Horsley.

Drama **(PR:A MPAA:NR)**

MYSTERY SUBMARINE**
(1963, Brit.) 92m Bertram Ostrer Prod/UNIV bw (AKA: DECOY)

Edward Judd *(Lt. Comdr. Tarlton)*, James Robertson-Justice *(Rear-Adm. Rainbird)*, Laurence Payne *(Lt. Seaton)*, Joachim Fuchsberger *(Cmdr. Scheffler)*, Arthur O'Sullivan *(Mike Fitzgerald)*, Albert Lieven *(Capt. Neymarck)*, Robert Flemyng *(Vice-Adm. Sir James Carver)*, Richard Carpenter *(Lt. Haskins)*, Richard Thorp *(Lt. Chatterton)*, Jeremy Hawk *(Adm. Saintsbury)*, Robert Brown *(Coxswain Drage)*, Frederick Jaeger *(Lt. Henze)*, George Mikell *(Lt. Remer)*, Peter Myers *(Telegraphist Packshaw)*, Leslie Randall *(Leading Seaman Donnithorne)*, Ewen Solon *(Lt. Comdr. Kirklees)*, Roberta D'Esti *(3rd Officer Mather)*, Brian Peck *(Able Seaman Winner)*, Fulton Mackaw *(Leading Torpedoman McKerrow)*, Gerard Heinz *(German Admiral)*, Hamilton Deck *(Comdr. Sivewright)*, Peter Stanwick *(Lt. Lyncker)*, Peter Zander *(Lt. Jahn)*, Sean Kelly *(Lt. Heilborn)*, Dennis Edwards *(Lt. Neumann)*, Keigh Anderson *(German Radio Operator)*, Brandon Brady *(Pilot of Catalina)*, John Chappell *(Bomb Aimer)*, Desmond Davies *(Radar Operator)*, Nigel Green *(Chief ERA Lovejoy)*, Ray Smith *(Signalman Lewis)*, Anthony Wickert *(ERA Barnes)*, David Glover *(P.O. Tel. Hubbard)*, Hedger Wallace *(Stoker Thompson)*, Michael Ritterman *(Lt. Comdr. Torgau)*, Graeme Bruce *(Lt. Schliemann)*, Dixon Adams *(Lt. Anstey)*, Norman Johns *(German ASDIC Operator)*, Declan Mulholland *(Duty Chef)*, Frank Wilson Taylor *(1st Sailor)*, William Semour *(Leading Seaman Grant)*, Derek Smek *(Leading Seaman Boydell)*, Dusty Hood *(Leading Seaman Fuller)*, Henry Kaufman *(Stoker Mechanic Parham)*.

A potentially interesting film is severely hampered by routine handling. When a Nazi U-boat is abandoned by its crew, the British capture the sub. They find its codebook still on board, along with the complete ship's log. The sub is outfitted with British seamen who infiltrate a "wolfpack" of Nazi U-boats. But the ruse is discovered and they engage in battle. The damaged U-boat managed to escape but ends up destroyed on a reef. The seamen are attacked by a British frigate which rescues the sailors and finds that the crew consists of fellow Englishmen. Everything is standard, with a plodding direction that moves the story forward without providing much insight. There's a good integration of stock submarine footage. The ensemble cast is workmanlike, though Judd is a standout as the ship's captain, and O'Sullivan provides some comic relief as a civilian Irish engineer.

p, Bertram Ostrer; d, C. M. Pennington-Richards; w, Hugh Woodhouse, Jon Manchip White, Ostrer (based on the play by White); ph, Stanley Pavey; m, Clifton Parker; ed, Bill Lewthwaite; md, John Hollingsworth; art d, Charles Bishop; spec eff, Wally Veevers; makeup, Phil Leakey.

War **(PR:A MPAA:NR)**

MYSTERY TRAIN* (1931) 62m Standard/Continental bw

Hedda Hopper *(Mrs. Radcliffe)*, Bryant Washburn *(William Mortimer)*, Jack Stuart *(Ronald Stanhope)*, Marceline Day *(Joan)*, Jack Richardson *(A Crook)*, Al Cooke *(Bridegroom)*, Eddie Fetherston *(Archie Benson)*, Joe Girard *(Sheriff)*.

A train car gets loose and coasts down a mountain slope. While everyone aboard is frightened, the good guy and bad guy fight it out on the rear platform. Using a lot of leftover footage from a similarly themed silent film, MYSTERY TRAIN is somehow stretched out to an hour. That's the mystery. The photography is good and old-time movie goers may get a thrill seeing future gossip queen Hopper in this trash.

p, Larry J. Darmour; d, Phil Whitman; w, Hampton Del Ruth (based on a story by Del Ruth, Whitman); ph, J. S. Brown.

Drama **(PR:A MPAA:NR)**

MYSTERY WOMAN** (1935) 69m FOX bw

Mona Barrie *(Margaret Benoit)*, Gilbert Roland *(Juan Santanda)*, John Halliday *(Dr. Theodore Van Wyke)*, Rod LaRocque *(Jacques Benoit)*, Mischa Auer *(Dmitri)*, William Faversham *(Cambon)*, Billy Bevan *(Jepson)*, Howard Lang *(Bergstrom)*, George Barraud *(Stanton)*, Arno Frey *(Schultz)*.

LaRocque has been wrongly sent to Devil's Island. His freedom depends on a document that proves he is innocent of treason. The chase is on between enemies Roland, Halliday, and LaRocque's wife, Barrie, on who will get the important paper.

The usual intrigues and murders occur but, as expected, Barrie winds up freeing her husband. The cat-and-mouse game between the three principals is interesting at first but quickly wears down under the uninspired direction and weak dialog.

d, Eugene Forde; w, Phillip MacDonald (based on a story by Dudley Nichols, E. E. Paramore, Jr.); ph, Ernest Palmer; m, Samuel Kaylin; cos, Royer.

Drama   **(PR:A MPAA:NR)**

MYSTIC CIRCLE MURDER*

    (1939) 69m Merit bw (AKA: RELIGIOUS RACKETEERS)

Betty Compson (*Ada Barnard*), Robert Fiske (*Great La Gagge*), Helene Le Berthon (*Martha Morgan*), Arthur Gardner (*Elliot Cole, Reporter*), David Kerman (*Wilson*), Robert Fraza (*Inspector Burke*), Mme. Harry Houdini.

Gardner is a reporter who goes after fake mediums. Fiske is the ringleader with Compson and Le Berthon as his assistants. This is cheaply made with stock shots of the Pyramids providing supposed intrigue. But the flat dialog and bad acting can't do a thing for the film, which seems like it was slapped together quickly. There's a cameo appearance by famed magician Houdini's wife. The two often exposed fake mediums before his death on Halloween Day in 1926.

p, Fanchon Royer; d, Frank O'Connor; w, Charles Condon, Don Gallaher (based on a story by O'Connor); ph, Jack Greenhalgh; ed, George Halligan; art d, Paul Palmentola.

Drama   **(PR:A MPAA:NR)**

MYSTIC HOUR, THE**½   (1934) 63m Progressive/States' Rights bw

Montagu Love (*Capt. James*), Lucille Powers (*Mary Marshall*), Charles Middleton (*Roger Thurston, Mary's Guardian*), Edith Thornton (*Myra Marshall*), Eddie Phillips (*Bradley Thurston, Roger's Brother*), Charles Hutchison (*Robert Randall*), James Aubrey (*Blinkey*).

Hutchison is a wealthy young playboy who accidentally gets caught up in the chase for a crook (Love). He catches Love's flunky in Powers' bedroom, but the victim is eventually poisoned by the crafty Love. Next, the master criminal (who goes under the moniker "Fox") sets up a woman for a potential jewel robbery, posing as "Capt. James" in order to protect her. In a coincidence that could only be believed in the movies, the woman turns out to be Hutchison's aunt. Hutchison has started to date Powers, but her brother Middleton, (just as inept here as he is as Ming in the FLASH GORDON series), has been embezzling her money. He arranges to kidnap her guy, while Love has been sending out similar threats. After being kidnaped, Love volunteers to find the man. Eventually, Hutchison realizes that the "Fox" and James are one and the same. All the bad guys, including Middleton, are neatly handled in a climactic cliffside ending, as the two lovers end up together. Fairly competent production for a thriller from one of the Poverty Row studios. Hutchison had been an actor and director for silent serial thrillers in the 1920s, and performed his own hair-raising stunts in this film.

d, Melville DeLay; w, John Francis Nattiford (based on a story by Susan Embry); ph, Leon Shamroy, Bernard B. Ray.

Crime/Thriller   **(PR:A MPAA:NR)**

MYSTIFIERS, THE   (SEE: SYMPHONY FOR A MASSACRE, 1965, Fr./Ital.)

MYSTIQUE zero   (1981) 97m Mehlman c (AKA: CIRCLE OF POWER)

Yvette Mimieux (*Bianca Ray*), Christopher Allport (*Jack Nisson*), Cindy Pickett (*Lyn Nilsson*), John Considine (*Jordon Carelli*), Scott Marlowe (*Ted Bartel*), Walter Olkewitz (*Buddy Gordon*), Carmen Argenziano (*Tony Annese*), Mary McCusker (*Jane Annese*), Hugh Gillin (*Ben Davis*), Fran Ryan (*Marie Davis*), Leo Rossi (*Chris Morris*), Hanna Hertelendy (*Sylvia Arnold*), Danny Dayton (*David Arnold*), Denny Miller (*Uwe*), Wally Taylor (*Charlie Carter*), Tony Plana (*Reza Haddad*), Susan Lynch (*Clare Bartel*), Micol Mercuiro (*Mrs. Gordon*), Peggy Kaye (*Mrs. Morris*), Barbara Thorpe (*Mrs. Haddad*).

Everyone in this film has a problem. One man has become homosexual, a result of seeing his mother making love to a stranger when he was a child. Another is a drunkard and a third is a cross dresser. They all meet at an EDT session (Executive Development Training) run by the sadistic Mimieux. This is supposed to make the unhappy group better executives. If making a fat man eat garbage and a transvestite prance around the room causes someone to become a better executive, then Mimieux knows something that the people at Fortune Magazine haven't heard about. Poorly acted and directed without an iota of humanity.

p, Gary L. Mehlman, Jeffrey White; d, Bobby Roth; w, Beth Sullivan, Stephen Bello (based on the book by Gene Church, Conrad D. Carnes); ph. Alfonso Beato; m, Richard Markowitz; ed, Gail Yasunaga.

Drama   **(PR:O MPAA:R)**

MYTH, THE**

(1965, Ital.) 89m Jamir Cinematografica/Times Film bw (IL MITO; LA VIOLENZA E L'AMORE; AKA: PUSHOVER, THE)

"Violence": Lisa Gastoni (*Luisa*), Raoul Grassilli (*Marco*), Dino Mele (*Nando*), Nini Rosso (*Renzino*), Gino Barbacane, Aldo Berti, Bruno Cattanco, Peter Martell (*The Toughs*), Rossella D'Aquino, Erika Di Centa, Mauro Del Vecchio, Jacques Stany, Renato Terra; "Love": Norma Bengell (*Anna*), Umberto Orsini (*Roberto*), Lidia Alfonsi (*Lucia*), Vittorio Caprioli (*Poet*), Mario Pisu, Annie Gorassini, Stelvio Rosi, Evi Farinelli, Carlo Lima, Filippo Sallustri, Ermanno Adriani, Isabel Hurt.

The nature of love and marriage is studied in two episodes. The first, titled "Violence," follows a young married couple as the wife is gang-raped while the husband is forced to watch, unable to come to his wife's aid. After this horrid event occurs, the couple practically refuses to acknowledge that it ever took place. Instead of comforting one another, thus confirming their mutual embarrassment and fear, they remain aloof, denying their vulnerability to the common emotional responses. "Love," the second segment, has a woman being hospitalized after an attempted suicide. When a pretty young woman remains at her side during the hospital stay, the victim's husband innocently flirts with this friend, obviously strongly attracted to her. The wife dies, leaving the husband to wallow in his guilt because he felt unfaithful to her.

p, Umberto Ghignone; d, Adimaro Sala; w, Sala, Ugo Guerra; ph, Franco Villa; m, Armando Trovajoli.

Drama   **(PR:O MPAA:NR)**

Cottage Grove Public Library
700 E Gibbs Ave
Cottage Grove OR 97424